A

DICTIONARY

ENGLISH AND MARATHI,

COMPLIED FOR THE

GOVERNMENT OF BOMBAY

A DICTIONARY ENGLISH AND MARATHI,

COMPLIED FOR THE

GOVERNMENT OF BOMBAY

COMPILER

T. CANDY

GYAN

Published by

GYAN

Gyan Publishing House
5, Ansari Road
Daryaganj, New Delhi-110002
Phone: 011-47034999, 9811692060
E-mail: books@gyanbooks.com

Distribution Network
gyanbooks.com
India, USA, Canada, UK, Australia

ISBN: 978-93-6433-588-1 (PB)
First Published, 1873

2nd Impression 2024

Printed at: Gyan Press, Delhi.

A DICTIONARY ENGLISH AND MARATHI,
COMPLIED FOR THE GOVERNMENT OF BOMBAY

Compiler: T. CANDY

A

DICTIONARY

ENGLISH AND MARÁTHÍ

A

DICTIONARY

ENGLISH AND MARÁTHÍ,

COMPILED FOR THE

GOVERNMENT OF BOMBAY.

PLANNED AND COMMENCED BY

J. T. MOLESWORTH.

CONTINUED AND COMPLETED BY

T. CANDY.

Second Edition,

REVISED AND ENLARGED BY

T. CANDY.

Bombay:

PRINTED AT GANPAT KRISHNÁJÍ'S PRESS.

BY THE PROPRIETOR ATMARAM KANOBA.

1873.

PREFACE.

Twenty six years have elapsed since the first edition of this Dictionary was published.

The compiler acknowledges with feelings of great gratification the favor with which it was received by Maráṭhí scholars, and by the Public at large. The gentlemen whom the Government of Bombay requested to report on the work, made a very favorable report; and the learned Boden Professor of Sanskrit at the University of Oxford, in his preface to his English and Sanskrit Dictionary, mentioned it in terms of great commendation. The compiler trusts that this revised and enlarged edition will be received with the same favor.

As the Preface to the first edition, which explains the plan of the work, and the Essay on the English and Maráṭhí languages written by the late Dr. Stevenson, are both reprinted in this edition, very few words are here required.

It is a pity that the revision of the Dictionary was not commenced earlier, as then it might have been more leisurely carried on, and more satisfactorily completed. But from causes which it is not necessary here to detail, the revision was put off till no copies of the first edition remained in store, and till the compiler had been overtaken by old age and infirmities.

A good many leading words (English) have been added, as also new meanings and new renderings. The new meanings and renderings have been chiefly taken from the revised and enlarged edition of Molesworth's Maráṭhí and English Dictionary, which was carefully consulted.

In the preface to the first edition the following sentence occurs: "The names of fruits, flowers, animals, and substances, which are not known to Maráṭhás, and which, therefore, have no corresponding terms in Maráṭhí, have been omitted." But this class of words has been admitted into this edition, as it occurred to the compiler that the addition of these words would make the Dictionary more useful to Natives learning English than it otherwise would be.

An admission was made in the preface to the first edition that perfect uniformity would not be found in the work. That admission must be repeated here. The work is generally consistent; but instances of deviation will be found.

The compiler has not been surrounded by a circle of Pandits in this revision of his work. His personal Pandit, Mr. Parshurám Pant, has usually been at hand to solve doubts and answer questions. And the compiler has received some assistance from Mr. Shrí Krishna Shástrí Talekar, Deputy Educational Inspector, and from Mr. Ráwjí Shástrí Godbole, the Secretary and Reviser to the Dakshiná Prize Committee. The former was, through the kindness of the Director of Public Instruction and of Government, permitted to join him for three months in the Monsoon of 1871.

Valuable assistance in the correction of the Press has been rendered by Mr. Balwant Parshurám Godbole.

The compiler presents his grateful acknowledgments to the successive Directors of Public Instruction who have fostered his work, to the Government of Bombay for the liberal remuneration given for his labor of revision, and to the Native Chiefs who manifested their interest in the work by contributing to its expenses.

Lastly the compiler would express his thanks to God for giving him strength to complete the work.

THOMAS CANDY.

POONA, *November*, 1873.

PREFACE TO THE FIRST EDITION.

As the Dictionary here presented to the Public is not the work of a single compiler, and he who planned it had not the satisfaction of completing it, it seems suitable to begin the Preface with an account of the *authorship* of the work.

The work was commenced by Captain Molesworth, the chief compiler of the Maráṭhí* and English Dictionary, on the publication of that work in 1831. He took Todd's edition of Johnson, and transferred its columns to the pages of several blank folios, omitting only words altogether obsolete or unsuitable. With the English Dictionary thus arranged before him, he took up the Maráṭhí and English Dictionary, and went over its pages, transferring the words to the blank spaces opposite their corresponding terms in English.

It may be hastily supposed by some, that this was all that was necessary to compile the present Dictionary, and that it was a work which a short time would suffice to complete; but an examination of the renderings of Maráṭhí words on the pages of the Maráṭhí and English Dictionary, and a consideration of the nature of the subject, would soon shew such a supposition to be fallacious. The compilers of the Maráṭhí and English Dictionary generally gave explanatory and paraphrastic meanings, in preference to simple synonymes, as being more likely to convey to the mind of the student the general power and use of the words rendered. In reversing the Dictionary, these paraphrastic renderings had, of course, to be converted into simple terms; and the compilers had to seek out the English words which best answered as synonymes to the Maráṭhí, that the latter might be placed beside them.

The M. and E. Dictionary was most carefully examined, and the words of it transferred to the E. and M. Dictionary, so far as the compilers found their corresponding places; but by this process little more, probably, than a third of the words were rendered; but these ranged, of course, from the beginning of A to the end of Z.

While Captain Molesworth was engaged in reversing the Maráṭhí and English Dictionary, the Writer of this Preface rejoined him from England at the close of 1832, and assisted him in his labors till the middle of 1835; when the health of both was so impaired, that Captain Molesworth was under the necessity of proceeding to Europe, and the Writer to intermit lexicographical labor. The work was thus suspended; but Captain Molesworth took the MS. with him, in the hope that restored health would speedily enable him to resume it in Europe. This hope was not realized; and after some years had elapsed without power to labor having returned, he sent out the MS. to the Writer. By the desire of the Hon'ble the Governor in Council of Bom-

* Subsequently to the publication of the Maráṭhí and English Dictionary, Captain Molesworth's opinion of the relative merits of the systems of Sir W. Jones and Dr. Gilchrist for expressing oriental sounds by Roman characters changed. He adopted in the present work the Jonesian system, and it has been preserved to the end.

bay, the Writer took up the work towards the close of 1840, and has toiled at it unremittingly till the present time.

No one can regret more than the Writer, that He whose superior mind planned, and whose master-hand commenced, the work, was prevented by sickness from carrying it to completion. In taking up his work, the Writer has endeavoured to follow him, but he readily acknowledges that it has been *haud passibus æquis.* He will add that whatever be the merits of the work, they are mainly attributable to his friend, while its defects and blemishes must necessarily be chargeable chiefly to himself, from whose hands it has passed to the Press.

After this notice of its authorship, some account of the *plan* of the Dictionary will be deemed proper. Herein it differs from all Lexicons and Dictionaries with which the Writer is acquainted. In all works of the kind that he has seen, words are arranged and rendered without any reference to the relation in which they stand to one another, as words derived from a common origin, and as expressing the same quality or action under different aspects. Though every adjective must have its noun, and every verb its verbal nouns, participles, and participial adjectives, they are all, usually, rendered independently and irrespectively. *Sweetness* must be the quality or property of the adjective *sweet,* and as many meanings as belong to the adjective, so many should the noun possess. Again, if we take a verb, say *To Beat,* the participial nouns *beating* and *beater,* the participle *beaten,* and the participial adjective *beating,* must necessarily refer to the verb with which they are connected, and from which they are formed: and were languages framed and spoken by philosophical rules, the relation would be sustained and carried out in all the meanings of every relative word. The preservation and exhibition of the connection here spoken of, between the different parts of speech embracing the same word, is the first feature of the plan of this Dictionary. This plan, besides the benefit of showing the relation of the parts of speech to one another, possesses the advantage of saving space, as it obviates the necessity of repeating the explanations of the several meanings. If the different meanings of *an adjective* be explained and numbered, all that is required *under its noun* is a reference, by the numbers, to the several meanings of the adjective. For example, the adjective CONFORMABLE has three meanings given to it in this Dictionary, viz. 1. *resembling*; 2. *agreeable, congruous*; 3. *compliant, obsequious.* According to the plan of this work, the noun CONFORMABLENESS or CONFORMITY, is not explained as 1. *resemblance,* 2. *congruousness,* and 3. *obsequiousness;* but a reference is made to the adjective CONFORMABLE. Thus CONFORMABLENESS, v. A. 1. (vide the adjective in its first meaning) means, of course, *resemblance*: the next figure 2. refers to the second meaning of CONFORMABLE, and means *agreeableness, congruousness*; the last figure 3. refers to the third meaning of CONFORMABLE, and means *compliancy, obsequiousness.* In the same way, the adverb CONFORMABLY is referred by the figures 1. 2. 3. to the three meanings of the adjective CONFORMABLE, and is rendered in accordance with them. For another illustration, turn to the verb To APPOINT, in this work: it has three meanings, which are fully explained and numbered. It was not necessary, therefore, under the noun APPOINTMENT, to repeat these meanings, and say *the act of establishing, the act of ordering* or *the state of being ordered,* &c. but reference is made, by figures, to the several meanings of the verb; and the noun, *as corresponding with them,* is rendered. The word APPOINTMENT, however, has meanings which have no relation to the verb, To APPOINT; these are therefore distinguished by a different kind of figure, and are numbered I. II. III. The same rule has been applied to the other parts of speech, as will be seen by a reference to APPOINTED and APPOINTER. In short, all words which stand in relation to another primary or leading word, are referred to that word, and to its several meanings, by the figures which number those meanings; other meanings of subordinate words, which have no relation to the leading word, are numbered so as to point out that no relation exists. In cases where the relation between the different parts of speech is not carried out in practice, no attempt has been made to force it by giving renderings.

Another feature of the plan is the endeavour to combine *copiousness* with *compendiousness.* The attainment of this object has been sought by the use of a system of *classification* and *reference.* Instead of giving under every English word every Maráṭhí word that would answer to it, the most comprehensive and general word of a number of English synonymes has been selected, and *under it* have been given all the Maráṭhi words that express the comprehensive and general meaning; while under the other synonymes, only a few renderings have been given (viz. those which best express the shade of meaning of the particular word), and a reference has been made from each of these synonymes to the comprehensive word under which the general collection of renderings is given. Thus, under the verbs To ABANDON, To RENOUNCE, To RESIGN, To RELINQUISH, a reference is made to the verb To GIVE UP, which is the most comprehensive of its class. Under To GIVE UP, therefore, the student will find all the renderings of the general sense collected; while under the verbs from which a reference is made to it, he will see only a few of such renderings as were deemed most suitable for them. In the same way; under the verbs To ABET, To AID, To ASSIST, &c. reference is made to the verb To HELP; and under the verbs To DEMOLISH, To RAZE, To DEVASTATE, &c. &c. a reference is made to the verb To DESTROY. Again, under the adjective JUST, are collected the general renderings of UPRIGHT, EQUITABLE, HONEST, FAIR, &c.; and from these words, which all have their particular renderings, a reference is made to this comprehensive word. The same rule has been followed with nouns and adverbs.

There are many words and combinations in every language of lax phraseology and of licentious use, which, to be rightly rendered in another language, must be rendered by similarly free combinations and phrases. The Maráṭhí abounds with colloquialisms and licentious formations, which, though they would be out of place if put by the side of sober English words, and given as renderings of them, may be very advantageously collected and given to the student, with a notice of their quality, under the English words that best express their general meaning. Such words and phrases have been thus collected and given in this work. A knowledge of them, and power to use them, will greatly facilitate an idiomatic acquaintance with the language. If the Reader will turn to, and examine the verbs To DIE, To DEFEAT, To DECEIVE, To CONTEMN, To EAT, To HUMBLE, To PRATE, To SCOLD; the nouns BACHELOR, BLACK-GUARD, DISGRACE, DECEIT, CONTEMPT, HEIGHT, GLORY; the adjectives CLEVER, LARGE, MISCHIEVOUS, PASSIONATE, PITIFUL, PROUD, RICH; the adverbs IMPETUOUSLY, SMARTLY; and the participle EXHAUSTED, he will have a better apprehension of this part of the plan of the work than pages of explanation would give. The Reader may turn to and study also the words To BEAT, To CONFOUND, To KILL, To LABOR, as further illustrating the plan of the work with respect to *verbs;* to the words EFFORT, EXUBERANCE, FAMILY, FRIGHT, HYPOCRITE, INCENDIARY, INGRATE, MADCAP, MISER, NATURE, POT, POVERTY, VESSEL, WOMAN, WORLD, as illustrating it with respect to *nouns;* and to COWARDLY, IMPETUOUS, EXCESSIVE, FIERCE, FAT, INFINITE, as further illustrations of *adjectives.*

It has been also an object with the compilers of this Dictionary to communicate to the student *miscellaneous useful information* connected with the words rendered. The words ADDRESS, BRÁHMAN, BRIDE, COMPELLATION, HEAVEN, HELL, HOLYDAY, INTERJECTION, INTENSITIVE, LAND, LUNAR MANSION, MANES, MARRIAGE, MAXIM, MEAL, MEASURE, MENDICANT, MUSIC, NAME, NATURE, OBEISANCE, OBSERVANCE, OCEAN, OFFICER, RITE, SCRIPTURE, may, be referred to as examples.

The student may perhaps observe that the plan of the work has not been sustained and carried out in all its points with perfect uniformity through the book. To expect it, would be to expect too much, even under the most favorable circumstances; for in a work carried on through a course of years, inadvertence will overtake the most vigilant, and weariness will, at times, oppress the most energetic. This work, moreover, has laboured under its own peculiar disadvantages and difficulties. It has not been the work of one man, nor the product of the joint labor of two, but it has been partly one and partly the other. The plan originally drawn out was that of a complete Thesaurus; but he who drew it out, and commenced filling it up, soon found that it would require more years than he could hope to give to it. He therefore proceeded to contract his plan.

Ere long his health began to fail, and under the combined influence of sickness, and the fear that failure of health would involve failure of the work, he made still greater contractions, and deviated considerably from the course on which he had entered. Feeling that a work unequal in its parts was still better than no work at all, he expunged page after page of the folios he had drawn out, in the hope of getting to the end ere disabled by sickness; but in vain. A considerable part of the labor of the Writer of this Preface has been that of restoring the proportions of the work, by retracing the plan and re-entering what had been expunged. Under these circumstances, he hopes that the student's feeling will be that of contentment with what is presented to him, rather than of dissatisfaction that he has not all that he desires.

The Writer of this Preface made notes, during the progress of his labor at the Dictionary, of various points of resemblance and dissimilarity between the English and Maràṭhí languages; but as he foresaw that to connect and amplify them would occupy considerable time, and would delay the publication of the work, he requested his friend the Rev. Dr. Stevenson, whose philological researches are so well known, to favor him with a dissertation on this interesting subject. Dr. Stevenson has kindly complied with the request made to him, and the Writer has the great satisfaction of prefixing to the Dictionary the paper which his learned friend has prepared. As the student will doubtless give it a careful perusal, a reference to it will supply the place of many observations that would otherwise be required, and will obviate the necessity of extending this Preface, which may now be concluded with some *miscellaneous remarks.*

The inexperienced student is cautioned against supposing that this Dictionary will enable one who is ignorant of Maráṭhí to compose correctly in that language. The object of a work of this kind is not to supersede a diligent study of the language, but to facilitate it, and to assist him who has acquired the language, by presenting to him a number of words from which he may select the particular one that he wants, thus saving him time and trouble. Many words will be found clubbed together, because of their having the same general meaning, and every one rendering the English word under which they are collected in some aspect or other; but unless the student knows their particular implications and aspects, he will run the risk of using a word which conveys a different shade of meaning from that which he wishes to express. Where the student is ignorant of the power of a particular word, it will be wise for him to verify it before he uses it.

The compiler of this Dictionary had in view the Native student of English, as well as the European student of Maráṭhi. It has been specially for the former that the English leading words have been so generally explained. The utility of this explanation to Native students of English, was not so clearly apprehended when the early part of the work was sent to the Press as it afterwards became, which will account for the explanations being few at the beginning of the work. The names of fruits, flowers, animals, and substances, which are not known to the Maraṭhás and which, therefore, have no corresponding terms in Maráṭhí, have been omitted.

There are several points of Maráṭhí Orthography which have not yet been settled by grammarians and writers. And as in the course of the work, the mind of the compiler has sometimes inclined to one form, and at other times to another, variations will appear. One of the points yet unsettled is, whether the final long vowel of a word, whether adjective or noun, should be shortened in a word formed or derived from it, or framed by the combination of it with another word. As, for instance, whether कठीणपणा or कठिणपणा, रोगीपणा or रोगिपणा, माळीपणा or माळिपणा, जरूरी or जरुरी, जामीनकी or जामिनकी, फूलबाग or फुलबाग, दूमदार or दुमदार, जमीनझाडा or जमिनझाडा, जमीनदोस्त or जमिनदोस्त, जीवदार or जिवदार, &c. &c. are right. Both forms are in common use, and both will occasionally be found in this work. But the mode now approved of by the Writer, and which has been generally followed by him, is to shorten the vowel of words which end with a consonant, but to keep it long in others. He therefore prefers कठिणपणा, खणखणितपणा, कडकडितपणा, &c, to कठीणपणा, खणखणीतपणा, कडकडीतपणा, &c.

He also prefers जरुरी to जरूरी. In cases of compounds, he prefers the final vowel of the first word being shortened, and therefore would use फुलबाग, जामिनखत, जमिनझाडा, &c. rather than फूलबाग, जामीनखत, जमीनझाडा, &c.

Many words that are given as renderings of English nouns of agency are properly speaking adjectives, and require a noun to be understood though not expressed. The English nouns SINGER, EATER, GOER, OPPONENT, BEGGAR, &c. are rendered by गाणारा, खाणारा, जाणारा, विरोधी, याचक, &c. but these are all adjectives. गाणारा requires some such word as माणूस to be understood, and means a *singing man or person.* गाणारी means *a female singer,* and requires बायको, स्त्री, or some such word, to be understood. At first, the sign of the masculine gender was affixed to these forms; it was subsequently omitted on the ground of their being adjectives. The student will bear in mind, however, that where no sign of gender is given, the masculine form is that which is presented to him.

Feminine formations have not usually been given, but it has been left to the student to make them for himself. There is much greater regularity in the construction of feminine formations in Maráṭhí than in English. In English we have *shepherd-shepherdess, author-authoress, poet-poetess,* but we have not *singer singeress, gardener-gardeneress, carpenter-caprenteres, sawyer-sawyeress, tailor-tailoress, farmer-farmeress, &c.* Again, we have *workman-workwoman, shopman-shopwoman,* and a few more like them, but we cannot form them *ad libitum* as may be done in Maráṭhí. The Maráṭhás have गवई-गवईण, माळी-माळीण, सुतार-सुतारीण, शिंपी-शिंपीण, कासार-कासारीण, कामकरी-कामकरीण, शेतकरी-शेतकरीण, ब्राह्मण-ब्राह्मणीण, भट-भटीण, &c. Indeed, following their rule, the Maráṭhás have formed सोजरीण from *soldier,* and apply the word not only to a soldier's wife or a female soldier, but to European women-servants generally. The feminine forms usually express both *a female agent* and *the wife of the masculine agent;* as for example, माळीण is either a woman who does gardening work, or simply a gardener's wife, or a woman of the gardener-caste. An exception to this rule may be given in the word कुणबीण, which according to the rule should mean a female farmer or a Kunbì woman, but a Kunbí's wife or daughter would be very angry at being called a कुणबीण, which word is now restricted to a domestic female slave. There are some cases of nice distinction between the wife of a person and a woman of his caste, as in the case of the words शूद्र, आचार्य्य, उपाध्याय, &c. the form for *a Shudra's wife* being शूद्री, and for a *female Shudra* (a woman of the Shudra caste) being शूद्रा; also in the case of आचार्य्य or a spiritual teacher, for a woman who teaches is आचार्य्या, while *a teacher's wife* is आचार्य्यानी. This nice distinction, however, is not attended to in Maráṭhí. High Sanskrit words are often used in Maráṭhí by learned speakers, who, of course, generally employ the Sanskrit terminations for the feminine form when required; but with respect to Sanskrit words that are in general use in Maráṭhí, the common Maráṭhí feminine formations are usually affixed to them, though they who affect to be classical, may and do give the Sanskrit formations. For instance, the feminine formations of the words प्रतिवादी, प्रतिपक्षी, विरोधी, &c. will generally be प्रतिवादीण, प्रतिपक्षीण, विरोधीण, &c. though speakers will be found to say प्रतिवादिनी, प्रतिपक्षिणी, विरोधिनी, &c. Such Sanskrit words as प्रतिवादी, प्रतिपक्षी, विरोधी, याचक, &c. &c. will often be used without any change for the feminine form, as ती माझी प्रतिवादी आहे, ती कोण याचक आली ? &c.

Another point to be noticed is the use of the *Anuswár.* The number of words with which the use of it is optional, is very great. It may be mentioned as a general rule that Bráhmans more frequently use it than the other classes, and, again, that the Bráhmans of the Konkan make more use of it than those above the Ghauts. In the preparation of this work, it has sometimes been used and sometimes omitted, even in the case of the same words occurring in different places. Had the printing been delayed till the compilation of the work was completed, these minor variations might have been corrected as the sheets were sent to the Press. But the Public wanted the work, and it was thought a less evil to let a few inadvertent variations go without correction than to keep back the book. One or two variations indeed have been designedly made since the work entered the Press, because they seemed *improvements*, and the desire of improvement was stronger than the desire of uniformity.

Sanskrit words ending in ल that have come into general use, have also a Maráṭhí form; as चंचळ for चंचल, चपळ for चपल, कुशळ for कुशल, &c. In combination with Maráṭhí words the Maráṭhí form is of course to be used, as बुद्धीचा चंचळ (बुद्धि is so common that its Sanskrit origin is here lost sight of) हाताचाकुशळ, पायाचा चपळ, &c.; but in combination with Sanskrit words by Sanskrit rules, the Sanskrit form must always be used, as चंचलबुद्धि, बुद्धिचांचल्य, चपलहस्त, हस्तचापल्य, कर्मकुशल, &c. To Sanskrit words that have become common in Maráṭhí, the Maráṭhí affixes पण and पणा are generally attached to make abstract nouns. The abstract nouns formed by the affixes त्व and ता are usully above common colloquial speech. With respect to these affixes पण and पणा, त्व and ता, it may be here mentioned that usually only one is given, but the student must understand that the other may always be used with equal propriety.

It may be thought by some that this Dictionary is overstocked with high Sanskrit, and deficient in common Maráṭhí words; but it is hoped that a close examination of the work will show this to be a misapprehension. It is only with respect to words from which a reference is made to a leading word, that such a thought can suggest itself; but the intelligent student will observe that in their case *an &c. supplies the place of six or eight renderings.* Look, for an example, at the participle ACCOMPLISHED in its first meaning; there are only three common Maráṭhí words given, viz साधलेला, झेपलेला, and उरकलेला, but the v. V. 1. refers the Student to the verb, To ACCOMPLISH, and the &c. which follows the three common Maráṭhí renderings given, stands for संपादलेला, जोडलेला, झोकलेला, पेललेला, उलगडलेला, अटपलेला, निभावलेला, थडीसनेलेला, &c. &c. &c. which the student is left to form for himself from the common Maráṭhí verbs given under To ACCOMPLISH. These are all formed by a rule of Maráṭhí grammar, and may therefore be omitted to save space; but the Sanskrit participles which follow (समाप्त, समापित, साधित, सिद्ध, संपादित, &c. &c.) are not formed by a rule with which the student can be assumed to be acquainted, and they, therefore, must be given at length. In the same way, under a noun referred to an adjective, the &c. which follows a noun formed by affixing पणा, indicates that the student may affix पणा and पण to *all* the pure Maráṭhí adjectives which he finds under the leading word to which he is referred. The same rule holds in the case of verbal nouns; an &c. following a noun, intimates to the student that he can form others from the words under the leading verb to which he is referred.

Very many adjectives will be found, in this Dictionary, formed by affixing the possessive sign चा to nouns, as कामाचा, उपयोगाचा, प्रीतीचा, ममतेचा, आसक्तीचा, &c. i. e. *useful, affectionate, diligent, &c. &c.* They apply both to persons and to things, but especially to the latter; प्रीतीचें or ममतेचें बोलणें well renders *affectionate speech*, but प्रीतीचा or ममतेचा माणूस is not so good as ममताळू माणूस as a rendering for *an affectionate man.*

With respect to *the phrases* that are given in such abundance, the inexperienced student is cautioned against supposing that he may use them without a previous knowledge of their implication, or that they supersede the usual formations. Phrases are given, because they are very useful to him whose knowledge of the language enables him to use them correctly, and because if not inserted they might not otherwise be known.

If the student should look for some English word and cannot find it, let him turn to one of its synonymes. If it should be one of the numerous verbs in English that are formed with an adverb, as *To give forth, to give out, &c.* let him turn to its *simple* synonymous verb, as for instance, to the verb *To publish* for the abovementioned adverbial verbs. Some verbs that begin with *en*, but which are not common under it, will be found under their more common form without the *en*, as To Shield for Enshield, To Kindle for Enkindle, To Link for Enlink, &c. If a word be looked for in vain under some privative prefix, let it be sought under another; under *un*, for instance, if not found under *in*, and vice versá.

The participle ending in "ing," is given in this work in its adjectival, not in its verbal sense. *Singing,* for instance, is rendered as equivalent to *singer,* i. e. *a singing person,* not in its verbal sense, as "*he is singing.*" The participle is therefore marked *p. a.* or participial adjective.

The general style in which this work has been printed is excellent, but, owing to causes which it is not necessary to detail, there are several errata, for which indulgence is craved.*

This Preface is now brought to a conclusion with a repetition of the Writer's great regret that the Public has lost the benefit which it would have had, if his able friend who planned and commenced the Dictionary, had been able to carry it on to completion. He has done his best to supply his friend's place, and to produce a work that may be worthy of the approbation of the Public. He gratefully acknowledges the goodness of God, who has enabled him to persevere in his toil, notwithstanding many hinderances and much bodily weakness, and has permitted him to finish the work. He supplicates His blessing on it, that it may be instrumental in the diffusion of TRUTH, *scientific, historical, moral,* and *religious,* through the countries in which the Maráṭhí language is spoken.

THOMAS CANDY, Major,
Superintendent Poona College.

Poona; September, 1847.

* It has not been thought necessary to give a sheet of errata, which is seldom attended to, but the writer would here mention that the phrase "Death unprepared for or unexpected, काळ आला होता पण वेळ आली नव्हती," which is given in page 176 under DEATH, is wrong. It should be "Narrow escape from death." For the correction of this error he is indebted to the late Bal Gungadhur Shastree, who pointed it out in a note eulogistic of the work. The author is not aware of there being another such an error in the whole book.

AN ESSAY

ON THE

POINTS OF SIMILARITY AND DISSIMILARITY

BETWEEN

THE ENGLISH AND MARÁṬHÍ LANGUAGES.

---

1. To consult with advantage a dictionary, rendering the words of one language into another, it is requisite that the genius of the two languages should have been studied, and that their points of agreement and disagreement be present to the mind. Every language has words for which no exactly corresponding terms will be found in any other, and the idiom of a language must be understood, as well as its vocabulary learned. The English and Maráṭhì languages have some remarkable points of coincidence, and other as remarkable points of difference. On the former we need not dwell, as they will readily suggest themselves to the student as he advances in the knowledge of the language; of the latter we shall treat somewhat more diffusely.

2. In reference to points of similarity we may remark generally, that neither the English nor Maráṭhì has any claim to the character of an original language. The former can be traced back to the Anglo-Saxon and Norman French as its two fundamental elements, though it has also in modern times received copious additions from the Latin and Greek, as well as from other sources. The latter, in like manner, is a language formed from the ancient Mágadhì, the spoken tongue of the ruling powers in India for many centuries, with a copious admixture of an old Aboriginal tongue of the Tamil, or Indian Peninsular family. In modern times many additions from the Sanscrit and Hindustáni have also been made to it, so as to give the language a character for force and copiousness purchased at the expense of simplicity, exactly that which the English bears among the languages of modern Europe. The introduction through the Mágadhì of most of the Sanscrit vocables, that exist in a more or less modified form in the Maráṭhì, requires a passing remark, as it is a subject which has scarcely been noticed either by natives or Europeans. The word Prácrit, is a term employed by Bráhmans in Maháráshtra to designate, sometimes any Indian language which is not Sanscrit, sometimes any of the old formations from the Sanscrit, which are now only to be found in Books, but which were probably once the spoken languages of the country. One of these ancient languages is called Mágadhí from the region of Magadh or Behár.* The sovereign of Magadh was considered a *Samrát*, a Universal Monarch or Emperor, and hence the Mágadhì was the dialect spoken at the Imperial Court. The only compositions now to be found in this dialect of Prácrit, are portions of some plays in the Hindu Drama, but the Kalpa Sùtra, a Jain work, composed probably about the fifth century of our era, is written in a modified Mágadhí, which nevertheless contains most of the essential attributes of the dialect, as laid down by the Grammarian Vararuchi. It is from this language then, that the modern Maráṭhí through various changes has been derived. One of the peculiarities of the Ancient Mágadhì, which can still be traced in the Maráṭhì, is the change of ज into य in deriving words from the Sanscrit; thus, the Mágadhí for राजा, is राया. This very word is still retained in Maráṭhì, although in a modified and degraded sense, the dignified form being राय; it is also changed into राई, in the compound word शिवराई, the name of a copper coin struck by the great Siváji. On the same principle the word राई, *mustard*, is corrupted from राजिका. Notwithstanding it is more common in modern Maráṭhí to follow the common Prácrit law, and change य to ज; as in जू *a yoke* from युग, also जोगा from योग्य, &c.—Other peculiarities of the Mágadhí are the use of श for स, of ण for न, and

---

* I have changed "Berar" of the first edition into Behàr, the modern name of Magadh, and have cancelled a clause which the correction rendered unsuitable. T. C.

generally of the cerebral letters for the dental. Now these are all peculiarities also of the Maráṭhí. Before the Palatine vowels इ and ए, the स is almost always changed to श; thus, the Maráṭhás say शेवा for सेवा; and though in this word the substitution is reckoned vulgar, yet शेंदव, *saltness*, is the proper substitute for the Sanscrit सैंदव; also सीमा *a boundary* becomes शिव, and the Hindustání सेवती from the Sanscrit सेमंती, the name of the China rose, becomes in Maráṭhí शेंवती. Again पाणी *water*, is the corruption of the Sanscrit पानीय; गांठ *a knot*, of ग्रंथि; वाणी *a voice*, of ध्वनि; डंश *a bite* of दंश; डंभ *hypocrisy*, of दंभ. That rather puzzling form of the verb used in old Maráṭhí books as a present and future tense, and in the modern dialect as a past habitual, is derived from the Mágadhí; thus करी comes from करेइ, the Mágadhí for करोति *he makes*, and is thus properly a present tense. The use of the present for the future needs no explanation; but it may be asked, how can a present tense express a past habitual act ? In order to understand this we must bear in mind that such an act or rather series of acts, is partly present as well as past, and may even in English be expressed by the present tense. Thus, " he writes in the Collector's office, " expresses past as well as present agency; the meaning is not only that the person referred to , writes at the present time, but that he has done so for days or weeks, or even years past; and there is no essential difference in the sense of this phrase from what would have been conveyed by the words, " He has been for some time a writer in the Collector's office. " In the latter instance the verb, though in the past tense, implies also present time; and in the former, though in the present, it implies also past time. The tense in question is a great acquisition to the Maráṭhí language, enabling us to express by the addition of a single syllable to the root, all that is done in English by the periphrasis, " He was in the habit of, " " he used, " or " he was wont. " In the thirteenth century of our era, the language of Maháráshtra was no longer Mágadhí, but a dialect between that and the present spoken tongue, of which we have a good specimen in Dnánobá's Commentary on the Bhagavat Gita, and other works. In the works of Tuká Rám, who flourished about two hundred years ago, the language is still farther modified, approaching considerably nearer to the spoken Maráṭhí. At last we get, in the various Bakhars (Chronicles) of the transactions of the Maráṭhí kings and leaders, a language which differs from the modern dialect only by the introduction of a profusion of Arabic, Persian, and other foreign words, which the Mussulman rule and connection then rendered current in the Deccan.

3. There is a remarkable similarity also in the general structure of the English and Maráṭhì languages, the nouns being in both chiefly inflected by Particles of the nature of Prepositions, and the Verbs by means of Auxiliaries, though in the English these are generally placed before, and in the Maráṭhí after the principal word. In the principle of their inflections, they exhibit a striking contrast to the Latin and Sanscrit, the learned tongues to which respectively they are mainly indebted for their scientific terms.

4. In noticing the points of difference between the English and Maráṭhí, we must presuppose as known what has been pointed out in the Grammars of the language already published, and in the Preface to the Maráṭhí and English Dictionary, supplementing former publications rather than going again over the same ground. Neither can we descend into those minute difficulties, which relate to the use of some particular word, or peculiar unconnected idiom. A work on this subject, containing a collection and resolution of idiomatic phrases, is still a desideratum in Maráṭhí, though much of very great value on this topic will be found, under different articles, in this and the former Dictionary. See especially लागणें, पडणें, घेणें, तोंड, पाठ, of the former; and *able, account, ear, eye, hand*, of this. Our attention at present is to be directed to points of a general nature, to classes of words rather than to individual phrases and expressions. It is the Philology, and not the Grammar, of Maráṭhí, that claims our notice, and that especially in reference to the points in which it differs from the English.

5. One great and obvious point of difference between the two languages is the want of an Article in the Maráṭhí, while the English has no less than two. Neither the Latin nor Sanscrit has any article, and although the sacred tongue of the Bráhmans has the advantage of the Greek in several points, this single small member of the classic speech in which Homer wrote, gives it a grace and flexibility which more than compensate for all the greater variety and harmony of sound, which have justly been attributed to the language in which the Indian Epics of Válmíki and Vyása have been handed down to posterity. The student, therefore, accustomed to the use of articles in his own language, is apt to seek out some expedient for supplying their place in Maráṭhí. Against this he must be on his guard; पोथी आण means " bring a book, " and the Maráṭhás never say simply to express this idea, एक पोथी आण. The student will nevertheless in his intercourse with the natives occasionally hear एक used apparently for the Indefinite Article, but he must not attempt to imitate them in this till he has, by attentively studying and analyzing such sentences, learned the nice shade of idea intended to be expressed. वैद्याला बोलाव, may mean simply " call a physician," or it may mean " call the physician, " that is, the practitioner who usually attends the family. In case, however, of some sudden accident occurring to any member of the family, or great haste being required, the master of the house might probably call out, एका वैद्याला बोलाव, *call a physician*, that is some physician or other, any one you can find. एखादा is often used

much in the same way, and with an implication, which practice alone can explain. The general rule is to translate from English into Maráthí as if the Indefinite Article had no existence.

6. In reference to the Definite Article, it may safely be neglected in translating, when it marks that there is but one of a class, as the Sun, the Moon, the Ganges; that the noun following is the name of a species, as the lion, the horse, &c. when it points out that individual of a class, who bears special relation to the speaker or the person whom he is addressing, as the king, the colonel, the servant. Also when this Article is used to distinguish particular persons or objects in the eye of the speaker, no word is required to express it in Maráṭhí; thus, बापाला दे, पुत्राला देऊं नको, *give it to the father, dont give it to the son.* When, however, in a sentence of two clauses with a relative pronoun, there is a reference made by means of the Article from the one to the other, the co-relative must be used in Maráṭhí for the Article; thus, to translate the phrase, " the shepherd is here of whom I spoke yesterday, " we must say ज्या धनगरा विषयीं मी काल बोललों होतों तो हाजीर आहे; just as if it had been in English, " *that* shephered, &c. " only that the word *that* would give an emphasis to the sentence, which would require तोच instead of तो. To express fully the sense of the Article when prefixed to honorific titles as " Alexander *the* Great," will require circumlocution; thus सिकंदर थोर संज्ञी or म्हटलेला. Before a large collection of similar objects, as the stars, the planets, &c. the force of the Article will sometimes be expressed by a separate word, and sometimes not, as तारा गण, ग्रह. These and other nicer distinctions, however, must be left to the student's own discernment and taste.

7. Nouns being the names of objects and ideas, it might be thought that there would be an exact correspondence between those of any two given languages; the study of a foreign language however soon dispels this illusion, whenever it exists. The term घोडा in Maráṭhí suggests, as nearly as is necessary for any useful purpose, the same idea as the English word horse; but the noun गाई, though it may, and indeed generally must, be translated by the word cow, suggests to the Indian mind a different species, or at any rate sub-species of the genus *bos*, from that brought before the mind of an Englishman by the word cow. In an Indian description of the bull, the hump must occupy a prominent place, both from its own intrinsic importance, and from the favour it has obtained among the poets. In translating such a description into English, the want of correspondence between the two languages would force itself upon the notice of the translator, and induce him by the introduction of an epithet into the text, or by a noto appended, to provide a remedy. In the Maráṭhí translation of Esop's fables, the English student will find his old friend the fox metamorphosed into a jackal (कोल्हा); whether this be a just retribution on Esop and other European fabulists for changing the jackal into a fox, while pilfering the best of their Apologues from the Indian Panchatantra, we need not at present determine; but if in order to remedy this mishap we subtitute खोकड for कोल्हा, the naturalist will inform us that the animal so named by the Maráṭhás is not the English fox, but merely that species in the genus that comes the nearest to it. Turning from the material to the immaterial world, such difficulties multiply fast upon us. Neither ब्रह्म, nor परमेश्वर, nor ईश्वर, nor देव, suggests the same ideas to the mind that the English word God, and Θεος in Greek do. The first is a mere philosophical abstraction, and it is quite incorrect to say that " ब्रह्म made the world." He makes nothing, and does nothing but enjoy his own beatitude, till he is seized with a fit of माया, and then he is no longer ब्रह्म, but ब्रह्मा. The second of the above words, however, would answer very well in the sentence " God created the world, " but try by this word to translate the first Commandment, and you run into the absurdity or inaptitude of saying that there is no *Supreme* Lord but one, which no body ever denied, and which is not the meaning intended. The sense is, " Thou shalt have no other *object of worship* besides me. " In this case देव answers admirably; yet generally when a Maráṭhá uses that word, he thinks of some village god, some local idol, or red painted stone, and rarely of the Supreme Being; nor has the language as yet capitals, like our own, or an article like the Greek, to mark the distinction. After all, as capitals are now being introduced into Maráṭhí देव thus written will be the best term, by which to render the word God. As to ईश्वर and भगवान, they express, like परमेश्वर, the idea of the Supreme Active Intelligence, and can only answer when that idea will bring out the meaning of the writer without any allusion to, or comparison with, other objects of worship. Into such niceties of language, however, (absolutely requisite as they are to be understood), the lexicographer can but partially enter, and the student must acquire them from intercourse with the natives, and the study of their literature. It is only when by these means he has rendered himself capable of entering into their minds and seeing with their eyes, that familiarized to their modes of thinking, he will be able to use such words with correctness and propriety. With an abundance of metaphysical terms for which we have no equivalents, because our systems of mental philosophy differ widely from theirs, the Hindús have no names for many valuable words in our language, expressive of metaphysical ideas. Thus, for example, for the important word *conscience*, for *perception* as a mental faculty, neither the Maráṭhí nor its parent Sanscrit furnishes any tolerable equivalents. In such cases, the lexicographer has given some words which convey something near the idea, and which, till the natives agree in inventing suitable terms as they become better acquainted with our literature, may convey the general sense, or he has formed from existing

elements a new word suited to convey the meaning intended.

8. There is a large class of nouns in Maráṭhí derived from Imitative Adverbs, which requires a few remarks. We have indeed such nouns in English, as, *banging* derived from bang, *whizzing* from whiz, *dashing* from dash, *cawing* from caw, *cooing* from coo, &c. Besides these, there are many words of this class, which, though used by the vulgar, hardly find admission into polite discourse; as thumping, bumping, &c. Now the Maráṭhás, being more the children of nature than the English, above all things delight in the use of this class of words, which are even by the Bráhmans dignified with the name of अनुकरणशब्द. Many of the adverbs are reduplicated syllables, as कटकट, पटपट, झडझड, गुडगूड, थरथर; or to express greater force, the first syllable is lengthened, as पटापट, चटाचट; or the last syllable, as झडझडां, थरथरां. The latter syllable, instead of being a reduplication of the former, is often कन, कर, or पट; as झटकन, चटकर, चटपट. Now most of these imitative adverbs may have nouns formed from them, and generally also verbs; thus we have झटका, *a smart blow*, from झटकन; we have गुडगुडी, *the smoking instrument*, called by the English soldier a *hubble bubble* from गुडगूड, both names being intended to mark the rumbling or bubbling noise the smoke makes in passing through the water. Such words then being much more abundant, and of much more common use in the Maráṭhí than in the English language, the student must not look on them with contempt, but familiarize himself with their peculiar meanings and shades of distinction, as with other words. Cases innumerable occur where important ideas cannot be expressed without them, as for example, the word थरथराट *excessive trembling*, which requires two English words to render it, and is by no means synonymous with कांपरी, *a shaking or quivering*. The same remarks may be applied to the verbs derived from these Imitative Adverbs, though the Maráṭhás prefer joining the Adverb to a verb derived from another root, when the language permits; thus to render the phrase, "His whole body shook with terror," a Maráṭhá would say, सर्वांगांत थरथरां कांपला. How much more expressive is the word कटकट to indicate the jangling and squabbling of a street brawl, than the word भांडण, which may be any sober quarrel, carried on for years in courts of justice through every grade, from the village Amíns to the Sadar Adálat. On this and the allied subject of reduplicated nouns, the remarks made in the Preface to the former Dictionary, Paragraphs 4, 5, 12, 13, render any farther observations in this place unnecessary.

9. The formation of abstract nouns is an easier matter in Maráṭhí than it is in English. We have *head, hood, ship, dom, ness, th,* all of Saxon origin, affixed to nouns and adjectives to form abstract nouns, and it is difficult to lay down the rule that points out when one of these terminations is to be used and when the other. The terminations *ty* and *tude*, imply that the words to which they are affixed are derived from the Latin, but when the one and when the other should be used, can be understood only by those who are skilled in that learned language, or have acquired by practice the power of using them with propriety. We have also many abstracts of this class, the primitives of which have no place in the language, as verity, equity, gratitude, &c. In Maráṭhí again पणा *mas.* and पण *neut.* may at pleasure be affixed to all Maráṭhí nouns; and त्व *neut.* or ता *fem.* to nouns derived from the Sanscrit. The rule is so simple and easy of application that I think the compilers of the Maráṭhí and English Dictionary judged rightly in leaving the formation of such words to the judgment of the student. A few exceptions may indeed be pointed out, as अहंपणा *egotism,* derived from अहम्, which is a pure Sanscrit word; अहंता is used, but rarely compared with अहंपणा. The Hindustání words बढाई, घट्टाई, &c. may be considered as introduced, already formed into the language, rather than as Maráṭhí abstracts, formed after a different model, by the addition of the termination आई. All words of this class; and those which form exceptions to the general rule, will be found in their proper places in the Dictionary, and what is said on the subject of Abstract Nouns in the preface to the former work, should also be carefully studied.

10. In reference to the Inflection of Nouns, this in Maráṭhí as in English is a pretty simple affair; yet it may be interesting to dwell for a little on those Postpositive Particles, which serve the purpose of Prepositions among ourselves, and the terminations of cases in Sanscrit, and many other languages. The Objective case in modern Maráṭhí, as in our own language, is not distinguished by any particular termination from the Nominative, although the Dative is often used where we would prefer the Accusative. For the Dative case, the terminations ला and स are used indiscriminately, the former generally by the natives of the Deccan, and the latter by persons educated in the Concan. The termination ला is an abreviation of लागीं, frequently used to mark the Dative case in the old Maráṭhí; thus, we have तुजलागीं, for तुजला or तुला, meaning literally, "so as to come in contact with thee," from the verb लागणें *to affect, or come in contact with.* We can easily see how this termination will also readily convey the idea of objectiveness; thus, यानें त्याला मारिलें, *this man struck that man*; the meaning being that the one struck *so as to affect* the other. The Dative termination स is a contraction of पासीं, the Maráṭhí for the Sanscrit पार्श्वे. Even the word जवळ may occasionally be used in a Dative sense; thus, त्याजवळ दे, त्यापासीं दे, त्यास दे, and त्याला दे, have all the meaning of "give it to him;" the idea embodied is स, then, is not quite so strong as that embraced in ला, the former expressing that the object is brought *to the side* of him to whom it is given, and the latter that it is brought into *actual contact* with him. The second or

Proper Ablative in the form of पासून, is evidently the same word as पासीं, with the proper ablative termination ऊन, generally changed into हून, affixed. This again may perhaps be derived from the word ऊन, meaning "deficient," or it may be a mere corruption of the Mágadhí Ablative, whose sign is ऊं. The Locative or third Ablative, which terminates in ईं, is evidently from that language, in which this case is frequently marked with the affix इसि. The vocal and nasal elements of this compound termination are retained, and the sibilant rejected to form the sign of the case in Maráṭhí. The Páli ह्म and Sanscrit स्मिन्, are all different forms of the same original termination, which, in the classic language of the Bráhmans, generally becomes simply ए or इ. The other Locative ending in त,preceded by a nasal, is so evidently an abbreviation of आंत *in*, contracted from the Sanscrit अंतर, as scarcely to require even this brief notice.—The modern Genitive ends in चा, ची, चें, varying according to the gender of the noun that follows, exactly as if it were an Adjective. In the old Maráṭhí, we find occasionally चेनी, which I conceive to be the oldest form of the Genitive case. It is impossible I believe to derive this from any Sanscrit root, and it is probably one of the remains of that old aboriginal speech, which prevailed in India before the inhabitants came in contact with the Bráhmans. A syllable of which the consonantal element is न, is used in most of the Indian languages to mark this case. Thus we have in Gujaráthí नो,नी,नु,according to the gender, and in Tamil इन. In Telugu नि, and in Canarese इना, are also frequent signs of this case, which the student if he pleases may connect with the English Genitives, mine and thine; and the German mein, dein, gutten, &c. To distinguish the mark of the Genitive from the true adjective termination चा, it is generally enough to consider whether the last syllable of the word before receiving the affix, be lengthened or not. If it be, it is most probably the Genitive; if not, it is the Adjective. घराचा, is the Genitive case, and घरचा, an adjective formed by the affix चा. Thus घराचे वासे, are the rafters of the house, घरचे वासे, are household rafters, in or somewhere near the house, which may be used when required, but at present forming no part of the house; घराचा धनी, is the master or owner of the house, but घरचीं माणसें, are the householders, persons merely living in the house, exactly the same as घरांतलीं माणसें, where an adjective is formed by adding लीं to the locative case, instead of affixing it to the root, as in the former instance. In reference to that class of words, where sameness of substance in indicated by the addition of the termination चा, as far as the sense is concerned, they may either be esteemed Adjectives or the Genitive of the noun; thus लाकडाचा may be rendered *wooden* or *of wood*, तांब्याचा, *brazen* or *of brass*, &c. These words all take the long vowel before the termination, for which reason I am inclined to consider them still as Genitives, not as Adjectives. When any of these have another Adjective formed from the same root associated with them, the other form sometimes has a laxer meaning attributed to it. Thus, while सोन्याचा, can mean only *golden*, सोनेरी, may mean either *golden* or *gilt*. The words कामाचा *useful*, and उपयोगाचा, *advantageous*, are undoubted instances showing the need of the qualifying clause in our rule. Some words are doubtful, as हाताचा or हातचा, *manual*, and similar Adjectives formed from most parts of the body. But the vast majority of Adjectives make the penultimate vowel short; as, आंगचा, तोंडचा, मुळचा, पदरचा, स्थळचा, देशचा, गांवचा, देऊळचा, मावळचा, उत्तरचा, दक्षिणचा, &c. A number of Adjectives formed from adverbs by adding चा, also follow the same law; as, कालचा, आजचा, वरचा, खालचा, &c.

Not only do the Maráṭhás form an Instrumental case from the noun, prepared according to rules for inflection, by adding नें, (most probably a substitute for the Sanscrit नां,) but they add नें to the Genitive, and thus form a compound Instrumental, which they employ chiefly in the Potential Mode. Thus from त्याच्या, we have त्याच्यानें; as in such a phrase as, तो घोडा त्याच्यानें आटपवत नाहीं, literally "That horse is not to be controlled through the instrumentality of that man," that is "he cannot manage that horse." The other Instrumental or first Ablative, terminating in एं, is probably the Sanscrit एन, and the plural form in हीं, is the Mágadhí for the Sanscrit भिः. The other particles affixed to nouns to connect them with other words in the sentence, such as करून *making*, कडे *to the side of*, कडून *from the side of*, पावेतों *so as to reach*, &c. will admit of easy resolution, when the student has made some considerable progress in the language.

11. In the use of Adjectives in Maráṭhí, it is important to consider whether the Adjective belongs to the subject or predicate of a sentence, as its position is usually materially affected by this consideration, in the former case preceding, and in the latter coming after the noun. This rule is frequently transgressed by learners, and they render the phrase, "He is a good man," by the Maráṭhí words, तो चांगला माणूस आहे; whereas the proper rendering is, तो माणूस चांगला आहे. But if the sentence be such as the following, The black horse has run off, then the Maráṭhí will be काळा घोडा पळाला. Such a phrase as कालचा शिपायी आहे, means "the soldier who was here yesterday, is present." In the first instance, the subject is तो माणूस, and the predicate is चांगला. In the second instance, the subject is काळा घोडा, and the predicate is पळाला; and in the third, the subject is कालचा शिपायी, and the predicate आहे, the word *here* being understood; but in such a sentence आहे may also mean *"exists,"* that is, *he is still alive*; thus, तुमचा बाप आहे? may mean, "Is your father still alive?" or more briefly, "have you a father?" Yet the rule here laid down does not hold when you are answering a question that has been put to you, for in such a case the proper answer would be, तो चांगला माणूस आहे,

and not तो माणूस चांगला आहे. To explain the reason of this, observe that the sentence, "He is a good man," is in English equivalent to the words, "That man is a good man," where the subject is *that man*, and the predicate is *good man*, *is* being the *copula*, or connective link between the two. This sentence rendered literally into Maráṭhí, would be तो माणूस चांगला माणूस आहे, where तो माणूस is the subject, चांगला माणूस the predicate, and आहे the copula. When then the Maráṭhás say, as they usually do in beginning to speak on a subject, तो माणूस चांगला आहे, they omit the second माणूस, and consider that implied in चांगला. On the contrary, in English we omit the first *man*, and substitute for *that* the substantive pronoun *he*. If then a Maráṭhá be asked, तो माणूस कसा आहे? The answer, if favourable, will usually be, तो चांगला आहे; but he may also probably say, तो चांगला माणूस आहे. The full answer would have been, तो माणूस चांगला माणूस आहे, but it is the custom of the Maráṭhás in such a case to adopt the last words of the previous speaker as their own, and therefore the first माणूस is dropped as a matter of course, which being once removed out of the way, he feels no reluctance in using the word in the second clause. Every one feels the awkwardness of using the word *man* or माणूस twice in so short a sentence. We in English easily get over the difficulty by the substantive pronoun *he*, substituted for *that man*. The Maráṭhás do not feel themselves at liberty to drop the name of the subject of discourse माणूस, in the first instance, but having used it once, they do not need to repeat it after चांगला. I trust then the student will see that, though in strict propriety, the adjective always precedes the noun as in English, yet that, owing to the suppression of the word माणूस in the latter part of the Maráṭhí sentence, the natural order seems reversed in ordinary cases, and adhered to only in exceptional. I have, then, I hope succeeded in explaining the reason of the rule, as well as of the exception, and placed before the student an interesting example of the niceties of Maráṭhí Philology.

12. Beginners are apt to suppose that the words *more* and *most*, when signs of the degrees of comparison, must have some corresponding words in Maráṭhí; but this is a mistake. *More*, when it is an adjective, is indeed translated by अधिक; thus, "There are more fools than wise men in the world," will in Maráṭhí be, जगांत शाहण्यापेक्षां मुर्खांची कोटि अधिक आहे; but in such a sentence as, "She is more industrious than he," the Maráṭhí is, ती त्यापेक्षां उद्योगी आहे. There must be no अधिक before the adjective; the comparative degree is fully expressed by affixing हून or पेक्षां to the subject of comparison. In like manner, सर्वांहून or सर्वांपेक्षां, appended in the same way, expresses the superlative. In this, the Maràṭhi deserts entirely the Sanscrit, and all that great class of languages called Indo-Germanic, and harmonizes with the Hebrew, Arabic, and other allied tongues, furnishing one among the many proofs of its drawing from Aboriginal Indian sources, wholly unconnected with the Sanscrit. In this too, the Maráṭhí agrees not only with the Canarese and other languages of the south, but also with the Hindustání and other northern tongues, shewing that they all still retain some common ancient element not derived from the language of the Bráhmans. As to the idea of such an agreement being produced in modern times by Mahomedan influence, it could only be suggested by one entirely unacquainted with these languages, with their history, and the changes actually effected by the Mussulmans.

13. The Pronouns of the first and second persons correspond in their use very much with the same pronouns in English; perhaps the first person plural is somewhat more freely used by a single person, and the second person singular more commonly employed in speaking to young persons and inferiors than in our language. In speaking to superiors and equals, the plural is used for the singular as with us. In addressing the Deity or any other object of worship, there seems to be a variety of practice among the natives; yet there is no aversion to the adoption of the English custom of using always the singular. The want of a substantive pronoun of the third person is supplied by the adjective pronouns, हा, ही, हें, *this* and तो, ती, तें *that ;* most frequently by the latter however, when only one person is mentioned in a sentence. When two persons are mentioned, the nearer is pointed out by हा, and the farther distant by तो. Thus the English sentence, "Let him go, and let this man remain," would be, rendered, तो जावो, हा राहवो. In like manner "Let him go and that man stay" would be हा जावो, तो राहवो. Again the sentence, "It was not he, but the messenger who came in the morning that informed me," would become, ह्यानें मला सांगितलें नाहीं, जो जासूद सकाळीं आला होता, त्यानें सांगितलें. The pronoun हा also is used to take up proper names, especially those of foreign origin, and receive their proper inflection; thus we have दावीद याचा पुत्र for दावीदाचा पुत्र; as in English it was formerly customary to say, *John Mair his book.* It is also used to connect a number of nouns together before joining them to a verb, as explained in the Grammar; thus, हिरा, नील, लाल, हे पाषाण फार किमतीचे आहेत. "*The diamond, sapphire, and ruby, are very valuable stones.*

14. The powers of the Maráṭhí language appear to great advantage in these pronouns; त्याचा आहे, त्याची आहे, & त्याचें आहे are all Englished by "It is his," in which English word no hint is given of the gender of that which is said to belong to him; whereas the Maráṭhí points out the gender of that which is possessed. Again in French, they say *son fils*, intimating the gender of the word *fils*, but leaving you in the dark as to whether the possessor be a male or a female, whether in English the rendering should be *his son* or *her son*. The English tells the gender of the possessor only, the French only of that which is possessed, the Maráṭhí does both. The Latin is no better than the French, and even

the Sanscrit cannot by any single phrase do what the Maráṭhí does in the phrases त्याचा पुत्र and तीचा पुत्र. To bring out the gender of the possessor we must in that language say, एतस्य पुत्रः and एतस्याः पुत्रः and of the thing possessed एतदीयः पुत्रः Such is the nicety of a tongue, which has till lately been despised as a mere jargon.

15. There is no relative pronoun in Maráṭhí corresponding exactly to *who* and *which* in our language. The pronoun जो, जी, जें, is properly a compound relative, meaning *what* or *whatever.* Sometimes indeed it may be rendered by *who*; thus, " He who is but a student should not find fault with his teacher, " will in Máráṭhí be, जो विद्यार्थी मात्र आहे, त्यानें गुरुला दोष ठेवूं नये. The full force of the word, however, is brought out in such a sentence as the following, जो येईल त्याला दे, literally, *Whoever comes to him give it.*

16. The Maráṭhás not content with an ordinal form of numerals, as in other languages, have formed such words from कितका *how many* or *how much*, and इतका and तितका, *so many or so much.* Thus they would ask, तो रांगेत कितकावा मुलगा आहे ? *What is the number of the place that boy holds in the class?* केवढाला from केवढा is used in the same sense. The other corresponding words may also be employed; thus, तो एवढाला आहे, म्हणून पंतोजीनें सांगितलें. *The teacher said he held such a place.* This is another of the beauties of Maráṭhí Philology, which must strike every one who has a taste for such studies.

17. If, however, the Maráṭhí outstrips us in its analytical powers, we have the advantage in synthesis.For such words as *the mass, the majority, the minority, &c.* when used thus, " the mass of mankind, " " the majority of the meeting, " &c., they have no corresponding terms, and in translating, such words must be rendered by a periphrasis. Thus, such a sentence as, " There was a majority of the Council resolved on going to war, though all the most distinguished leaders were in the minority, " might be rendered in several ways in Maráṭhí, one of which might be the following, युद्ध करावें, असें फार करून सभेंतील लोकांचें मत होतें, तथापि सर्व मोठे शिष्ट सरदारांचें मन निराळें होतें. This however certainly is but a poor translation of the English.

18. The verb, as being the most important part of speech, may be supposed to afford the most fertile theme for Philological remark, though much of what might have been said in this place, has been anticipated in the Maráṭhí Grammar. As a general and important consideration under this head, it may be stated that the Maráṭhí has few verbs in general use, compared with the English and other European languages. The deficiency is most commonly supplied by nouns coupled with some one of the following verbs, करणें *to make,* घालणें *to throw,* धरणें *to lay hold of,* ठेवणें *to place,* देणें *to give,* टाकणें *to throw away,* मारणें *to beat,* पावणें *to reach,* वाटणें *to seem,* खाणें *to eat,* नेणें *to lead,* and occasionally a few others. Of this mode of supplying verbs the Maráṭhás are exceedingly fond, and use it even when there is not the least necessity for it; thus, instead of saying विश्वासणें *to trust,* they say विश्वास करणें-धरणें or ठेवणें; for धावणें *to run,* they prefer saying धाव मारणें or टाकणें. In other instances as प्रीति करणें, and उद्योग करणें, they have no other way of expressing the verbal act; the former is indeed nearly synonymous with अवडणें, and the latter with झटणें, but there is in both instances a shade of difference, which makes the latter applicable where the former are not. The compound verbs have a dignity in those instances that the simple want, while these again have a familiarity and force not possessed by the others. In all instances where such compound verbs are formed by the student, he must be especially careful to learn from the Dictionary what the particular verb is, which, joined to a noun, serves the purpose of a new verb, as it will not do to choose any one he pleases. Thus with the preposition वर coming after the object, *to love* may be expressed by प्रीति ठेवणें, or करणें, but if धरणें or बाळगणें be used, the genitive of the object must be joined with it. Nor can you take the verb घालणें, or any other than those here mentioned; thus, you say त्यावर प्रीति केली or ठेवली, and त्याची प्रीति बाळगली or धरली.—Sometimes an adverb may supply the place of a noun and be joined to a verb to change or define its meaning; thus मारणें means "to kill" or "beat;" to remove the ambiguity the adverb ठार is joined to it, and ठार मारणें means only "to kill," being synonymous with जीवें मारणें lit. *to strike in the life.* To form another class of verbs the Maráṭhí prefixes a pluperfect participle to some one of the verbs mentioned above, which gives often the force of a preposition coming after the verb in English: Thus धुऊन टाक means, "wash thoroughly," टाकून दे " cast away," and भरून दे " fill up. " It is true that the general meaning is the same as if धू, टाक, and भर only had been used; but these latter expressions want the emphasis and force of the former. Many verbs in this form can be rendered into English by one word, as घेऊन येणें often used for आणणें *to bring,* and घेऊन जाणें *to remove* or *take away.* In these latter examples the principal act is not in the participle, as in the former cases, but in the supplemental verb. Such is the case also in बांधून ठेवणें *to put away,* साधून घेणें *to acquire, &c.* Sometimes a new verb, or at least what answers to a simple verb in English, is formed by one of the class of verbs mentioned at the beginning of this paragraph, and a noun not in its simple but in an inflected form; thus, सिद्धीस नेणें *to complete, perfect,* पेचांत घालणें *to entangle.* These are the forms of expression in which the Maráṭhí language delights, and even when simple verbs are given in the Dictionary, the student will often find it more idiomatical to form a verb in some one or other of the abovementioned ways, or choose one so formed to express his ideas. On the other hand there are compound verbs in English, that require to be

expressed by simple verbs in Maráṭhí, as "To give away," "take down," "bring out," &c. Thus, "He gave away a hundred Rupees in charity," will in Maráṭhí be, त्यानें धर्मार्थ शंभर रुपये दिल्हे. "Take down that turban," will be तें पागोटें उतर—or उतरून दे; but this latter will imply that it is not only to be taken down, but also probably that it is to be given to the person from whom the order issues. "Bring out the jewels" will be expressed in Maráṭhí by दागिणे काढ. These hints then must suffice to put the student on his guard upon this subject, and to lead him in every particular instance to enquire how far the two languages conform to one another, and in what points they differ.

19. The present tense in all the Vernacular Indian tongues is merely the Present Participle with the verb *to be* after it, as in the Hindustáni and Gujaráthí, or with the signs of the persons, as in the Támil, Telugu, and Canarese. The Maráṭhi has two Presents, one constructed after each of these models. Thus in the verb करणें, we have करीत आहें, and करितों, करितोस, &c. The terminations of the persons seem derived from the Indo-Germanic stock; thus the first person is ओं, partly agreeing with the Latin termination *o* in *amo*, and the termination *em* in *amem* of the subjunctive mode; स, as the sign of the second person singular, is the same as the sign which we have almost uniformly in Latin, Greek, and Sanscrit, for that person. The English *s* for the third person is a corruption of the old termination *th*, and the type for the second person is *st*, being in conformity with the languages of its family marked especially by the *s*. The third person singular is an exception in Maráṭhí, having Adjective terminations agreeing in Gender with Nominative, a mode of construction of which the Maráṭhás are passionately fond. The first person plural is the same as the singular. The second person plural has आं, probably a corruption of आत, so we have in Maráṭhi occasionally तुम्ही आहांत, for तुम्ही आहां; the त seems to have been dropped to prevent its being confounded with the आत of the third person plural, the *ant* of the Latin, and the अत्ति or अति of the Sanscrit. The terminations of the past tense are essentially the same, except that the third person plural, as well as the third person singular, is drawn away into the Adjective terminations to agree with the Nominative. The marks of the first and second persons again in the future are न and स, of the persons of the plural ऊं, आ, and त respectively, the इल which there so often occurs, marking the tense.

20. If it should be asked whence comes this इल (or एल as it becomes generally in intransitive verbs), that marks future time, till a better solution be found, the following may be accepted:—The Maráṭhás are often in the habit of dropping an initial व, or supplying its place with a य; a familiar example of this is the name of the village at which the traveller first rests after leaving Puna, to go to Sattara by the way of Kátraj. The village is properly named वेळू, the name for a *Bamboo*. This is, however, generally corrupted to येळू or एळू. If then we suppose the first letter of वेळ time, or विळ or विळा as it is also written, dropped, we get the sign of the future required without much difficulty, by the easy change of ळ into ल in the first and second instance, and by dropping the final in the last. तो शिकेल *he will learn*, will on this supposition mean literally in Maráṭhí, *learning is to him only a matter of time*. Though, at the hazard of trespassing a little longer on the territory of speculation, I must state, that I think the sign of the Past Tense in Maráṭhi, may in like manner be traced to a word meaning what has *passed*. The signs of the past tense in the old Maráṭhí are धलें, as in दिधलें, for दिलें, तलें, as in सांगितलें, मागितलें, &c. yet in common use, and येलें, as in धरियेलें for धरिलें. The first of these terminations, rejecting the ल, is retained in the Southern Gujaráth Dialect, and accordingly we have दिधुं for दिधलें. In the Northern Gujaráthì, we have the य of येलें retained, still dropping the ल; that य itself is a common substitute in Mágadhí for त and द, and I suppose all the terminations originally the same. Whereas then in the south they say किधुं, in the north they use कयूं for the Maráṭhí केलें. In Hindí also the य is used as the sign of past tense, and we have किया, though even this is frequently dropped, and the terminations denoting the persons are affixed immediately to the root, as किआ. Again in all the languages of the Peninsula, the simple त, or that letter changed into द, marks the past tense, no traces of the ल appearing. But in the Bengáli, as in the modern Maráṭhí the ल alone remains to mark the Preterit. The root ढळ in Maráṭhí implies "a moving off," or "passing into oblivion," the allied root टळ means "to pass by as time;" डल is a Bengali root also meaning "movement." In Tamil too, the root तळु means "to dispatch with diligence;" and I think there is a strong probability that this is an old Indian vocable, which by various corruptions has formed the Preterit tense in all the modern Dialects of Hindustan. Let these speculations at least teach the learner to analyze not only sentences, but the words themselves of which they are composed, tracing them to their primitive elements, and he will find his labour more than repaid when he experiences how much such analyses tend to fix words in the memory.—The reduplicated form of the past tense ending in लेलें is rather a participle than a verb, at least it is always in modern Maráṭhí to be considered. Thus बांधलेली नौका पाहिजे, मोकळली नको, means "I want the tied boat, I don't want the loose one." The simple form is not commonly used as a participle, though Bráhmans say केलें and केलेलें are the same.

21. In the Potential and Conditional modes both the English and Maráṭhí are copious, but there is far from a correspondence between the two. The *miniature* of this subject will be found in the Maráṭhí Grammar; one or two

points however, may here be specially noticed. The young student must be on his guard against following the Hindustání, and clumsily using शकणें to express potentiality. There are proper idiomatical forms, as he will see in the Grammar, adapted to any case that can occur; and that unidiomatical construction, although adopted by some natives in Bombay, should be wholly exploded as both inelegant and useless. The only real difficulty under this head in translating from English into Maráṭhí is to render *may* or *might* signifying *permission* or *liberty.* You may indeed well enough translate the phrase "you may go," by तुम्ही जावें: but the sentence, "I may go wherever I please," meaning that I am *at liberty* or *have permission* to do so, is not so easily rendered into Maráṭhí. If the words be those of an inferior who has asked and obtained leave of his superior, the translation would probably run thus; जेथें इच्छेस येईल तेथें मला जाण्याची आज्ञा आहे; but there is an additional element introduced here by the word आज्ञा, which means properly not *permission* but *command.* The idea expressed by the word *permission* is foreign to the mode of thinking among the Hindus. There is implied in this word, that an inferior has laid down a plan of action for himself, and proposes this for the passive acquiescence of his superior. This is however a degree of presumption that upsets all Hindu notions of propriety, making the inferior active, and the superior passive. Even when a Bráhman comes to visit you at your house, he considers himself your servant for the time being, and when he wishes to take leave, he says आज्ञा आहे ? meaning have I your commands to depart ? Not to be behind him in politeness you give indeed a command, but it is not that he should go away, but that he should come again when he finds it convenient, which you express by the single term या.—Again if the words, "I may go wherever I please," be those of a superior or person independent of foreign control and expressive of inherent liberty, the Maráṭhí rendering would be जेथें इच्छेस येईल तेथें जाण्याची सत्ता (or अधिकार) आहे. This again implies something more than mere liberty. It speaks of some inherent *power* or *authority* possessed by the speaker over and above what the English phrase expresses. If we chose instead of सत्ता &c.मोकळीक, this may mean nothing more than freedom from external restraint. If to remedy this, and add moral fitness we say जावयास योग्य, the person may for any thing necessarily implied have his feet fast in the stocks. When the Arabic word रजा is used for permission in Maráṭhí, it always, at least in popular speech, means leave *of absence.* No Maráṭhá would ever say मला एथें राहण्याची रजा आहे, meaning I have *permission* to stay here; supposing it to be a case where there is no remission of any duty, but simply leave to reside in a particular place, he would use आज्ञा, or say रहावयाचा हुकूम or अधिकार. It is evident then, that every particular case of this use of *may* must be considered with its attendant circumstances, before a proper translation can be made, and that at the best all we can do, is to make a near approximation, since to give the exact idea is beyond the powers of the language. These remarks will apply to *might* when used in the sense of *liberty* and *permission,* the slight shade of difference that exists between the two words cannot be expressed in Maráṭhí, consisting as it does only in *might,* indicating a restricted liberty. *Should* and *would* do not present great difficulties. When conditional futurity is the idea they express, the simple future is used in Maráṭhì; when *should* means *propriety,* पाहिजे with the past tense of the verb will suffice, and *would.* when it means *willingness,* may be translated by the Genitive Gerund and पाहिजे, इच्छा, or मर्जी, all of which points are fully explained in the Grammar.

22. The passive voice in the old Maráṭhí is a modification of the Sanscrit, in which especially ज supplies the place of य, as its characteristic work; thus the Sanscrit क्रियते is changed in the old dialect into करिजेतें "*it is being done.*" In the modern Maráṭhí, particularly in translations from the Sanscrit and Persian, a passive somewhat similar to our own, has been formed of the past Participle, and the verb जाणें *to go*, for this has been adopted as the Auxiliary in the place of our verb *to be.* In the Southern Peninsular languages the root पड *to fall*, prevails instead of जा; the principle however is the same, and the Hindustání conforms in every respect in idioms to the Maráṭhí. The Passive, although it can scarcely yet be said to belong to the colloquial language of the Maráṭhás will likely, from the facilities it furnishes, in translation, keep its place in books, and there are in truth instances when an exact translation from English cannot be made without it. Thus, "He was saved from the sea," would require, fully to express it in Maráṭhí, तो समुद्रांतून तारिला गेला. No Maráṭhá indeed would in all probability so express himself; he would probably say, तो समुद्रांतून तरला, but then this conveys only the idea of the safety of the person spoken of, and leaves out altogether the notion of this safety being the point of foreign influence. It means no more in fact, than that he escaped from being swallowed up in the sea. The Maráṭhás, if the avoiding of this ambiguity were considered important, would probably express the agent to whom the deliverance was due, thus भावानें त्याला पाण्यांतून तारिलें, *His brother saved him from the water*; but then the writer may not wish to reveal the agent, and therefore if this were an object, a Maráṭhá might say एकानें &c. *a certain one, &c.*, but the writer may wish the causes of the deliverance to remain wrapt up in the clouds of his own obscurity, not even deigning to draw aside the curtain so far as to let us know whether it were a man, or angel, or other superior being, who was the agent of good on the present occasion, and in such an instance we should have to recur to the first mentioned rendering with the Past Participle of तारणें and the verb जाणें. The instances are however few

indeed where a Maráṭhá would find himself in this predicament, and they have a multitude of ingenious ways of avoiding the use of such Passive verbs. These the student should study and imitate, if he wishes to speak the language idiomatically and elegantly. The most common of these, as we have already indicated, is by the use of an Intransitive verb. Wherever this can be done, it should be the plan adopted. And indeed the Passives in English, which belong properly to what the Latins call the Deponent class of verbs, must be thus rendered; for example, *To be finished, to be wearied, to be fatigued,&c.* These are expressed in Maráṭhí correctly by संपणें, दमणें, थकणें. In some instances when a suitable verb in Maráṭhí is not to be found, the sentence can be thrown into a different form; thus, "I am acquainted with him," may be translated, माझी त्याची ओळख आहे, and "I was accompanied by twenty men," by, माझ्या संगतीं वीस माणसें होतीं. In the former of these cases, the Nominative of the noun from which the verb is derived, with the Substantive verb, is used; and in the other, a preposition, or better a noun in the locative case, takes the place of the English verb; the latter alternative takes place also in the following phrase, "I am disposed to learn the Maráṭhí language," which may be rendered thus, मराठी भाषा शिकावी हें माझ्या मनांत आहे. The difficulty, however, does not lie so much in these instances as in others. No one who knows the meaning of words, would ever think of saying मी दमला गेलों, when a moment's reflection would teach him that मी दमलों, the idiomatic phrase, expressed all the idea, which he wanted to convey. It is in the case of the Passive of Transitive verbs, where the real difficulty lies, of which I have given an instance above. Yet even in reference to this, the natives have the way of avoiding the use of the Passive; thus, for "He was beaten," instead of saying तो मारला गेला, they say त्यानें मार खाल्ला, *he ate a beating.* He was slain in battle would be, not तो लढाईंत मारिला गेला, but तो लढाईंत मेला. "It is said," will be rendered by ह्मणतात, "*they say,*" perhaps by ह्मटलें आहे, but never by ह्मटलें जातें; or ह्मटलें गेलें; though the simple word गेलें itself will sometimes nearly express the same idea; thus शास्त्रांत गेलें means, "It is said," or "to be met with" in the Shástra.

23. The student must not lose sight of the great advantage possessed by the Maráṭhí over the English, in having a causal form of the verb. Instead of having awkwardly to introduce a new verb, "to cause, to make," &c. as we do, they effect the same end by simply adding व, or वि, to the root, before affixing the terminations; thus from करणें *to do,* we have करविणें *to cause to do*; from पळणें *to flee,* we get पळविणें *to put to flight*; from शिकणें to learn, शिकविणें *to cause to learn,* or *to teach.* The Hebrew, Arabic, and other languages of that class, have what is called the Hiphil form of the Verb, corresponding to the Maráṭhí causal. The Sanscrit has also a similar form, and even we seem to have the remains of such a modification of the verb, in *fell* from *fall, lay* from *lie, seat* from *sit, &c.*

24. The great peculiarity of Adverbs in Maráṭhí is, that the large proportion of them that end in ए, may agree occasionally with the agent, and occasionally with the object of the verbs they qualify, exactly as if they were Adjectives. Indeed, most of these words are both Adjectives and Adverbs, and nothing but the sense indicates when they are the one, and when the other. This mode of construction is not uncommon in Greek, though by no means nearly so prevalent as in Maráṭhí, and is called by the Grammarians *Attraction,* implying that a word swerves from its own philosophical construction to agree with some word near it, to which it is drawn by proximity rather than by any natural relation. In sentences containing a Transitive verb, as often as the object is expressed, the rule is, that the adverb should agree with it; thus त्यानें शब्दांचा उच्चार चांगला केला, *he pronounced the words well.* In this sentence it is evident that चांगला, is not an attribute of उच्चार, but of केला, yet no one would use चांगलें, the proper adverbial form, in such an instance. So in like manner, we should say in Maráṭhí त्यानें गोष्ट असीच सांगितली, *he told the story exactly in this way,* the असीच agrees with गोष्ट, instead of keeping the true adverbial form of असेंच; though the meaning be most distinctly, that he told the story in that particular manner, and not that particular story, as it would be, were असीच an adjective. Again in Intransitive verbs, when the agent is expressed, the adverb generally agrees with it; thus we say ती तसीच गेली, *thereupon she went away*; सोटा आडवा पडला, *the beam lies crosswise.* In Transitive verbs, where the object is not expressed, and generally in all cases where the termination of the verb is unaffected by the gender of the nominative, or object, it is best to keep the adverb in its natural state, that is the same as the Nominative singular neuter of the Adjective; thus, त्यानें खरें सांगितलें; though if वार्त्ता or गोष्ट were supplied, the adverb and verb would both change, and become खरी सांगितली. Again we should say तो असें करणार नाहीं, hardly if at all तो असा करणार नाहीं. The best practical rule, then, is that which is given above, though it may not be universally binding.

25. Adverbs have frequently their place supplied in Maráṭhí, by a noun in the third or Instrumental case; thus तो आनंदानें गेला, *he went joyfully away*; एकनिष्ठेनें कोशाचें काम करितो, *he labours devotedly at the dictionary.* In such cases, we could generally also in English use *with* before the noun instead of the adverb; thus, *with joy, with devotedness.* Sometimes also we may use the pluperfect participle; thus, तो भिऊन येतो, *he comes fearingly,* or with fear, the same as if भीतीनें had been used. The words पूर्वक and आत्मक and परी, are of great use in the formatian of adverbs, in what may be considered the higher or Bráhminical dialect of Maráṭhí; thus, for *certainly* we may say निश्चयपूर्वक, or निश्चयात्मक. Almost any Sanscrit noun can in this way have given to it an adverbial form.—There is however one class of English

adverbs, which cannot be rendered by any one corresponding word in Maráṭhí, and which require a modification in the construction of the sentence to express their general idea. They are such as lamentably, deplorably, charmingly, beautifully, &c. especially when they qualify an adjective. Sometimes the adverb, may be put into an adjective form, and the adjective made a noun; as, "He is lamentably deficient in knowledge," which may be rendered त्याची विद्येविषयीं दुःख उत्पन्न करायाजोगी न्यूनता आहे; and "He is deplorably wicked," त्याची नेत्रास अश्रु आणायाजोगी दुष्टता आहे. Or both may be made adjective; thus, "Her singing is charmingly sweet," which may be rendered, तिचें गाणें अति मधुर मनोहर आहे. The student will not forget what under the head of nouns was said of the imitative Maráṭhí adverbs, त्यानें तें झटकन, पटकन, कडकडून, चकचक, झाडून, पाठ करावें.

26. The use of the conjunction *and*, is much less frequent in Maráṭhí than in English. Instead of coupling a number of verbs together as we do, the Maráṭhás put those that come first into the participial form, and reserve the verbal form for the last; thus, for the sentence, "He rose from dinner, put on his turban, and went out;" they would say, तो जेवून, उठून, पागोटें घालून, बाहेर गेला. As regards the respective places of व and आणि, I believe it to be mainly a matter of taste. Pandits from the Deccan generally avoid व, as vulgar, while Concaní Bráhmans use it freely. In all serious compositions आणि alone should be used. The proper place of व is to string a number of articles together; as, भात व तूप व गूड वगैरे. In translating *but*, when the meaning is, that the excepted point is directly opposed to the foregoing, परंतु or पण should not be used; तर should be employed or no word at all used, the opposition being marked simply by the tone of the voice. To express the idea contained in the sentence, "If a man take such a medicine, he will not recover, but die," the Maráṭhás say, असें औषध खाल्लें असतां माणूस वांचणार नाहीं, तर मरेल. They could not here use परंतु for तर, but they might without any word say मरेल, or with the emphatic particle मरेलच, with a pause before the word. In such a phrase as the following, we have a case in which परंतु or पण should be used, तो बोलला खरा, पण फार हळू बोलला. *He spoke indeed, but he did so in a very low tone of voice.* When *but* has the sense of *notwithstanding, nevertheless, &c.* it is best expressed in Maráṭhí by तरीं; thus, "I did not see him do it, but I have no doubt that he committed the theft," will in Maráṭhí be, म्या साक्षात् पाहिलें नाहीं, तरीं त्यानेंच चोरी केली याविषयीं मला संशय नाहीं.

27. Though the Interjection होय, corresponds to *yes*, it is not so liberally used as *yes* in English; thus, if questioning a Maráṭhá, you were to say काम झालें? he would probably repeat your words, changing the tone of the voice, or reply by झालें, or perhaps, though scarcely, by होय झालें, but never by होय alone. The interjection होय is a part of the verb होणें, and properly means *it is*, which most likely is also the original meaning of *yes*. If therefore the verb by which you ask the question is आहे, the word होय may suffice for an answer. Thus, in addressing a company of agriculturists, if you were to say तुम्ही कुणबी आहां? the reply might be simply होय, though most likely even here आहों would be added. The rule here then in replying to a question, is to do it by repeating the verb used by the questioner, prefixing होय or not, as you please, if the answer be in the affirmative, and subjoining or prefixing नाहीं, if in the negative; thus, the answer to भूक लागली? *are you hungry?* would be लागली नाहीं, or नाहीं लागली, *I am not*; but never नाहीं alone: If however, the question were भूक आहे? the answer would be नाहीं, as this is considered the negative form of the verb आहे, and the rule is that the verb used in a question must be repeated in the answer.

28. The construction of sentences in Maráṭhí is generally very simple, so that a few hints on this subject may suffice. Parentheses should be altogether avoided in Maráṭhí composition, and when they occur in a sentence which requires to be translated, they should be incorporated with, or subjoined to, the principal sentence. In ordinary cases when no peculiar emphasis leads to a diffierent arrangement, the words of a sentence in Maráṭhí should follow one another in the following order; first the agent, next the object, and last the verb. If there be an instrument, it comes preferably between the object and the verb; and if an adverb, its usual place is immediately before the verb, as in the following sentence, दुष्ट पारध्यानें आमची मैना तिरानें ठार मारली. The student who has paid proper attention to the Grammar of the language, will be aware that sentences, which have in them a relative pronoun in English, must be inverted when put into Maráṭhí; thus, "That is the man of whom I told you yesterday," becomes in Maráṭhí ज्या मनुष्याविषयीं मी तुम्हास काल सांगितलें तो हाच आहे. The word man, however, is transferred to the opposite member of the sentence from that in which it occurs in English, and therefore belongs to the first member also in Maráṭhí, as the genius of the language requires the subject of discourse to be introduced in the first member of a sentence.

29. The construction of the past tenses of Transitive verbs by the instrumental case of the agent, and the simple or unreduplicated form of the Past Participle, which agrees with the object, or if there is no object, is put in the neuter gender, is a curious part of Maráṭhí Syntax, and well deserving the attention of the Philologist. The former of the two modes of construction is called the कर्मणी, and the latter the भावे प्रयोग, by Maráṭhí Grammarians; त्यानें गोष्ट सांगितली is an instance of the former, and त्यानें सांगितलें of the latter mode of construction. This latter is indeed the more difficult of the two to resolve, yet I think if we compare it with the corresponding phrase in Sanscrit, we shall come to the conclu-

sion, that the theory laid down in the commencement of this paragraph is the true one. Thus, त्यानें केलें is exactly तेन कृतं, and answers to "it was done by him," in English. The substantive verb *was*, requires indeed to be expressed in English, but in the other two languages it is usually understood. If the verb in Maráṭhí be expressed, it answers to our English Perfect Tense, which is properly a Past-present, for past and present time are both united in it; thus, त्यानें तें केलें आहे will usually be rendered "he has done that," but it may also be tanslated in the very form and idiom of the Maráṭhí "that is done by him." "The letter *is* finished," in Maráṭhí will stand exactly as in English, पत्र संपलें आहे, though if there be no emphasis on the substantive verb it will be omitted in Maráṭhí. It does indeed seem strange that any language should tie itself down to such an inverse mode of construction, but the limitation is a fact, in whatever way it may be explained. In Sanscrit, they can say स अकरोत्, as well as तेन कृतं, as we in English can say "He did (it)," as well as ("It) was done by him," but in Maráṭhì they have only the latter alternative. That the नें in Maráṭhí really expresses the sense of the third case in Sanscrit is evident from this, that it is not only used for agency, but with equal propriety also for instrumentality. Thus to translate the following sentence, "He slew the enemy with a sword," it is necessary to employ the नें for the instrument as well as for the agent, no other affix suiting so well the idiom of the language: the translation then runs thus, त्यानें शत्रूला तरवारीनें मारिलें. The explanation of the भावे प्रयोग given by the natives is, that the भाव or substance of the verb is the Nominative; thus त्यानें मारिलें is त्यानें मारणें मारिलें, *A striking was struck by him.* As however the Maráṭhí delights in forming verbs from nouns with करणें, I should be inclined to think that the true resolution was त्याणें मारणें केलें, *a strinking was effected by him*, and that this is the true theory of the भावे प्रयोग. The other form of construction called the कर्मणी प्रयोग need not now detain us long; there the object is expressed, and the verb agrees with it, as would any other declinable participle. Thus, मुलानें पोथी आणिली आहे, means "a book has been brought by the boy," or more exactly in Latin, "*puero liber latus est.*' Again आईनें तीं फुलें दिल्हीं, is "*matre isti flores dati.*"

30. This peculiarity of the Maráṭhí language is not only puzzling to a European, it puzzles also the natives as soon as they begin to translate from other languages into their own. The Sanscrit, as we have seen, resembles the English. The Bráhmans then, when translating into Maráṭhí from that language, finding that though त्यानें केलें will translate exactly तेन कृतं *it was done by him*, it will not do the same for स अकरोत् "*he did*," have invented the new form तो करिता झाला, and this they term the कर्त्तरी प्रयोग, in which the agent as in Sanscrit and English, is the Nominative to the verb. करिता here is probably the same word originally as कर्त्ता, and the literal meaning is "he became the doer." धृतराष्ट्र उवाच is accordingly rendered धृतराष्ट्र बोलता झाला.

31. What is called by the Latin Grammarians the Ablative Absolute, which is in Greek a Genitive Absolute, is termed by Sanscrit Grammarians सति सप्तमि, as requiring in that language the seventh case, and is in English a Nominative Absolute, is also a Nominative Absolute in Maráṭhí, but it is of much more extensive use than in our language. Thus it is very frequently used to date one event of less consequence, but which is the immediate subject of discourse, by another of greater consequence; as, भोज राजा राज्य करीत असतां एका ब्राह्मणानें शेत साधिलें, *during the reign of king Bhoja a certain Bráhman procured a field.* It is employed also generally when one event is stated as occurring during the currency of another; as आह्मी जेवितांना तो आला, *he came while we were at dinner.* The Maráṭhás however do not admit this form of construction with a past participle; thus, "the work being finished (or when the work is finished) we will play," cannot be rendered काम झालें असतां खेळूं; this would mean if any thing "*should* the work be finished;" but we must say काम झाल्या नंतर, or वर, or काम झालें ह्मणजे, खेळूं.

32. As a general rule, the student, when translating from English into Maráṭhí, must be guided more by the sense than the particular words employed, and he will often in his own mind require to throw a sentence into a different form, before he commence rendering from the one language into the other. Thus we form a great many verbs with the substantive verb *to be*, and a preposition following; there will here generally be no exactly corresponding verbs in Maráṭhí, but by translating them first into other English, our end will be easily gained. *To be over*, for example, may mean *to have authority* अध्यक्ष होणें, or it may mean *to be a remaining surplus*, and so be rendered by उरणें. And so with *to be in*, *to be out*, *&c.* Sometimes the Maráṭhás will look at a subject from a different point from that from which it is viewed by the English. Thus, the Maráṭhás say त्या भांड्यांत दोन शेर येतील, the grain or liquid is looked on as the agent, and it is said "into that vessel two seers *may come.*" In English, the vessel is looked on as the agent, and we say "that vessel *will hold two seers.*"

33. In fine, the customs, manners, and religious ceremonies of the natives, must be studied in order to use the language properly. Thus, if the student is in doubt about the use of the word प्रायश्चित्त, and the meaning of the verbs देणें & घेणें when used in connection with it, how is he to resolve his doubts but by studying the subject of the native *Práyaschitta?* When he knows that the common cause rendering the rite necessary, is the transgression of the rules of caste or some ceremonial impurity, that the thing consists in some penance, or else in a vile compost administered

by a Bráhman, that it is supposed only to take away some one, or some series of transgressions, that the Bráhman administrator is the देणारा and the recipient the घेणारा; having thus ascertained the exact sense of the word as used by natives, he will be prepared to employ it, so as not to confirm them in false ideas, while wishing to impart to them important and heavenly truth.

I ought to add that Major Candy has carefully looked over this paper, and thereby enabled me to correct some of the mistakes into which I had fallen; what remain must be laid to my account. Many of the points discussed also were originally suggested by Major Candy. May the Divine blessing rest on this essay, and on the whole work.

J. S.

LIST AND EXPLANATION OF THE CONTRACTIONS USED.

g. of o. (genitive of object) means that the object must be in the genitive case; thus, To ABANDON त्याग *m.* करणें *g. of o.* Ex. मी त्या पुरुषाचा त्याग करीन, I will abandon that man. Here the object (पुरुष) is in the genitive case.

g. of s. (genitive of subject) means that the subject must be in the genitive case; thus, To ABATE उपशम *m.* होणें *g. of s.* Ex. त्याच्या रोगाचा उपशम झाला आहे, His disorder has abated. Here the subject (रोग) is in the genitive case.

in. (or inv.) con. (inverse construction) means that the idiom requires the inverse construction; thus, To be able येणें; Ex. मला लिहायास येतें, I am able to write.

neg. con. (negative construction) means that the word is in a negative construction or in a construction of negative import.

Act. after a verbal noun indicates that the renderings which follow *express action;* Ex. ABANDONMENT, *n.* v. V. 1.—*act.* Here the—*act.* indicates that the renderings टाकणें, त्याग, त्यजन, &c. &c. express *the act of abandoning;*—*state* indicates that the renderings which follow *express a state;* thus, under the above word ABANDONMENT, the renderings which follow—*state,* टाकलेपणा, त्याग, त्यक्तता, &c. &c. express *the state of being abandoned;* the renderings which follow —*a. or s.* express either *act or state.*

The hyphen (-) is used to connect two or more words with another which is common to them all. Thus, under the second meaning of To ABANDON, the student will find त्याग *m.*-परित्यजन *n.*- परित्याग *m.*-&c. करणें; here the hyphen obviates the necessity of repeating the verb करणें after each noun; also under the word ABANDONER, the hyphen between the words त्याग-वर्जन-उत्सर्जन-&c. कर्त्ता renders it unnecessary to say त्यागकर्त्ता, वर्जनकर्त्ता, उत्सर्जनकर्त्ता, &c. one कर्त्ता does for all that are thus connected with it.

The &c. after a rendering or renderings, indicates that more words of the same kind may be used. For instance, under ABAFT, the &c. after गलबताच्या indicates that *any word signifying ship or boat,* may be used in the possessive case with मागल्या भागास. Again, the &c. after टाकलेला under ABANDONED, intimates that the reader may take the participle of any of the verbs given under the verb To ABANDON.

In the *phrases* which are given under leading words, only the initial letter of the leading word is repeated.

The following abbreviations need no explanation:

a. for adjective.
n. for noun.
adv. for adverb.
prep. for preposition.
v. for verb.
p. for participle.
s. for singular.
pl. for plural.

m. for masculine.
f. for feminine.
n. for neuter.
v. a. for verb active.
v. n. for verb neuter.
v. for vide.
p. a. for participial adjective.

in. or *inv.* for inverse.
lit. for literal.
fig. for figurative.
pop. for popularly.
con. for construction.
neg. for negative.
intens. for intensitive.

enhanc. for enhanced.
gener. for generally.
compreh. for comprehensive.
decl. for declinable.
impers. for impersonal.
demon. for demonstrative.
interr. for interrogation.

There may be a few others but they will be easily understood.

T. C.

A

DICTIONARY

ENGLISH AND MARÁṬHÍ.

A.

A. This letter is represented by अ and आ, but by these can be conveyed only three of its numerous sounds, viz. by अ the obscure sound which it bears in *collar*, *jocular*, *Christmas*, *America*, (which is the sound of *u* in *sun*, *run*, *bun*); and the still obscurer sound which may be distinguished as medial between this and the sound of *A* in *sand*, *ran*, *band*:—and, by आ the sound, of *A* open, as in *father*, *chance*, *last*. Its long or slender sound, as in *place*, *face*, is represented by the letter ए.

The broad sound of *A*, as in *all*, *wall*,—the shortened sound of *A* open, as in *hand*, *hat*,—and the sound (of *E* short) as occurring in numberless English words,—have no existence in the *Maráṭhí* language.

A or *an* the article is rendered by एक *one*, or by एखादा *any one*; or it is conveyed by the noun simply. Thus एक पुस्तक, एखादें पुस्तक, *or* पुस्तक *a book*. There is however a delicacy in the use and omission of एक in its capacity of representative of the article *a*, of which, as it would, with difficulty, be conveyed by statements or examples, this brief notice must suffice.

A, as a noun, is still rendered by अ & आ or by अकार & आकार, bearing the masculine gender. *All* the letters are, in like manner, masculine nouns; and whether *simply* as, इ, ई, उ, ऊ, क, का, &c. or in combination with the particle कार, as इकार, उकार, ककार &c.

A, as a contraction of *at* or corruption of *on* (in the sense of *in*.) and as appearing before participles, is rendered by आयास or आयाला as attached to the root, as, *a*-begging, *a*-swimming, मागायास, पोहायास.

A, *particularly* or *pre-eminently*, is expressed by एक, as *a* hero, *a* liar, &c. (i. e. a hero, &c. *unrivalled*, standing *single* or *sole*,) एक वीर, एक लबाड, एक कारभारी.

A, in the sense of *each one*, *each* or *every one severally*, as *a* year, *a* tree, *a* man, is rendered by प्रत्येक, एकएक, दर, प्रति, and, in the objective case, by स as, *to each man*, *tree*, *&c.* माणसास, झाडास.

A, as in the adverbs *anight*, *abroad*, *aback*, *aland*, *alive*, *away*, *afoot*, *asleep*, &c., as it is corrupted from *on*, and is used in the sense of *on*, *in*, *at*, *&c.*, so it is expressed in *Maráṭhí* by various prepositions or by suitable inflections of the words. Adverbs of this class do, for the most part, appear in the Dictionary.

A, is often redundant, as in *arise*, *arouse*, *awake*; and so is its *Maráṭhí* representative आ as in आभास, आल्हाद, आघ्राण.

ABACK, *adv.*—in navig उलट्यावर, उलटून डोल्यासीं.

To be taken a. उलट्यावर येणें, उलटा राहणें.

To be taken a.-fig. थक्क-थकित होऊन जाणें, दचकणें, चरकणें, बुद्धि *f.*-अक्कल *f.* चरकहोणें *g of s.*

ABAFT, *adv. at the stern.* वरामीं, वरामास, वरामाच्या ठायीं, नौकेच्या-नावेच्या-तारवाच्या-गलबताच्या-&c. मागल्या भागास, नौकेच्या-&c. पश्चिमभागीं,

2 *towards the stern.* वरामाकडे. नावेच्या-&c. मागल्याभागाकडे.

ABAFT, *prep.* वरामाकडल्या बाजूस भागास-&c. *with g. of o.*

To ABANDON, *v. a. renounce, resign;* v. To GIVE UP. टाकणें, सोडून देणें, सांडणें, त्याग *m.* करणें *g of o.* वर्जणें, विसर्जणें, सांडणें.

2 *desert, forsake,* सोडणें, सोडून-टाकून-सांडून-&c जाणें, टाकणें, त्यागणें, त्याग *m.*-त्यजन *n.*-परित्याग *m.*-परित्यजन *n.*-&c. करणें *g. of o.* त्यजणें, अंतर *n.* देणें, अंतरणें.

3 (one's self) to. नाद *m.*-छंद *m.* घेणें-धरणें *g. of o.* नाद *m.*-छंद *m.* लागणें *in. con.*

ABANDONABLE, *a.* v. V. 1. टाकाया-सोडाया-वर्जाया-&c. जोगता-जोगा-&c. टाकाऊ, टाकवणा, त्याज्य, त्यजनीय, वर्ज्य, वर्जनीय, विसर्जनीय, विसृज्य. [त्यजनीय.

2 सोडाया-&c. जोगता-जोगा-&c. त्यक्तव्य, परित्याज्य, हेय, त्याज्य.

ABANDONED, *p. & a.* v. V. 1. टाकलेला-&c. त्यक्त, त्यागित, त्याजित, वर्जित, विसर्जित, उत्सृष्ट, विसृष्ट.

2 सोडलेला-&c. त्यागित, त्याजित, त्यक्त, परित्यक्त.

I. *reprobate, &c.* v. SHAMELESS. कोडगा, देवाधर्मांनें टाकलेला, निसवलेला, धर्मबाह्य, त्यक्तधर्म, त्यक्तलज्ज, निसत, निसूक.

II.—a town, village, house, v. DESOLATE. उजाड, ओस, ओसाड, उद्वस्त, उद्वस, बेचिराग.

To be or become a. काटी *f.* लागणें (नगरास-गांवास-घरास-&c.) ओस-उजाड-&c. पडणें. [&c. गयाळ.

III.—a tenement. गतकुळी, गतकूळ, कुळानेंटाकलेला-सोडलेला-

ABANDONER, *n.* v. V. 1. टाकणारा, त्यागणारा, वर्जणारा, &c. त्यागी, त्याग-वर्जन-विसर्जन-उत्सर्ग-उत्सर्जन-&c. कर्ता, वर्जक, विसर्जक

2 सोडणारा &c. त्यागी, परित्यागी, त्याग-त्यजन-परित्याग &c. कर्त्ता.

ABANDONMENT, *n.* v. V. 1.—*act.* टाकणें *n.* सोडणें *n.* &c. त्याग *m.* त्यजन *n.* वर्जन *n.* विसर्जन *n.* उत्सर्ग *m.* उत्सर्जन *n.*—*state.* टाकलेपणा *m.* &c. त्याग *m.* त्यक्तता *f.* वर्जितत्व *n.* विसर्जितत्व *n.* उत्सर्ग *m.* उत्सृष्टता *f.* विसृष्टता *f.* विसर्ग *m.*

2 –*act.* सोडणें *n.* सोडून जाणें *n.* &c. त्याग *m.* परित्याग *m.* त्यजन *n.* परित्यजन *n.*—*state.* सोडलेपणा *m.* &c. त्याग *m.* परित्याग *m.* त्यक्तता *f.* परित्यक्तता *f.*

To ABASE, *v.a. degrade, &c.* v. To HUMBLE. नमवणें, खालावणें, उतरणें, मोडणें, मान *f.* खालीं करणें *g.of o.* अभिमान खंडन *n.* करणें *g.of o.*

2 (one's self). कमीपणा *m.*-हलकेपणा *m.*-&c. घेणें, मस्तक *n.* टेंगणें करणें, नमणें, अभिमान *m.* टाकणें-सोडणें, लघुत्व *n.*-लघुता *f.*-हीनत्व *n.*-गरीबपणा *m.*-नम्रता *f.*-नीचपणा-&c. मानणें-अंगीकारणें-स्वीकारणें, लघुत्वस्वीकार *m.*-&c. करणें, लघुत्वांगीकार *m.*-&c. करणें, स्वमहत्वत्याग *m.*-अहंकारत्याग *m.*-अभिमानत्याग *m.* करणें, स्वमहत्व *n.*-अहंकार *m.*-&c. टाकणें-सोडणें.

ABASED, *p.* v. V. 1. नमवलेला &c.

2. नमलेला &c. हतगर्व, हताहंकार, हतदंभ, खंडिताभिमान, नष्टाभिमान, नम्र झालेला, त्यक्तस्वमहत्व, स्वीकृतलघुत्व, स्वीकृतहीनत्व, जिताहंकार, त्यक्ताहम्मति, अभिमानातीत, वीताहंकार, विगताभिमान, मानवर्जित, जातविनय.

ABASEMENT, *n.* v. V. 1. –*act.* नमवणें *n.* खालावणें *n.* &c. अभिमानखंडन *n.*—*state.* मानभंग *m.* मानभ्रष्टता *f.* मानहानि *f.* मानविध्वंस *m.* तेजोभंग *m.*

2.—*state.* नमलेपणा *m.* नम्रता *f.* लघुत्वस्वीकार *m.* हीनत्वस्वीकार *m.* लघुत्वांगीकार *m.* हीनत्वांगीकार *m.* जिताहंकारता *f.*

To ABASH, *v.a.* v. To SHAME. लाजवणें, चपापवणें, खालीं पहायास लावणें, संकोच *m.*-मुखसंकोच *m.*-&c. करणें *g.of o.* ओशाळा करणें.

ABASHED, *p.* v. V. *and* ASHAMED. लाजवलेला &c. लाजलेला, फजीत, लज्जित, लाजिरवाणा.

To be or become a. लाजणें, चपापणें, ओशाळणें, फजीत-ओशाळा होणें.

ABASHMENT, *n.* v. V. *state of confusion.* लाजवलेपणा *m.* लाजलेपणा *m.* लज्जितत्व *n.* संकोच *m.* मुखसंकोच *m.* ओशाळगत *f.* ओशाळी *f.* ओशाळीक *f.*

To ABATE, *v.a. make lower, less, weaker*, v. To LESSEN. उतरणें, कमी-मंद-हलका-न्यून- &c. करणें.

2 (force or intenseness of) *mitigate.* हलका &c. करणें, उतार *m.*-उपशम *m.*-उपशमन *n.*-उपशांति *f.*-&c. करणें. *g.of o.* निववणें.

3 (a demand, &c.) सूट *f.* घालणें-देणें, सूटसांड *f.*-सोडसांड *f.* करणें.

To ABATE, *v. n. grow lower, less, weaker*, v. To LESSEN. खालावणें, उणावणें, उतरणें, थोडकावणें.

2—as to force or intenseness; *decrease.* हलकावणें, मंदावणें, उणावणें, उतरणें, कमतावणें, ओसरणें, पडणें, कमरणें, नमणें, कानपणें, मंद पडणें *or* होणें, काढणें, उपशम *m.*-उपशमन *n.*-उपशांति *f.*-ओसारा *m.*-&c. होणें *g of s.*

ABATEMENT, *n.* v. V. A. 1.—*act.* उतरणें *n.* कमी करणें *n.* &c. न्यूनीकरण *n.*-*state.* कमी केलेलेपणा *m.* उतरलेलेपणा *m.*

2—*state.* उतार *m.* हलका केलेलेपणा *m.* &c.

v. V. N. 1.—*state.* खालावलेपणा *m.* उतरलेपणा *m.* &c.

2—*state.* हलकावलेपणा *m.* मंदावलेपणा *m.* &c. कमी झालेपणा *m.* उतार *m.* मंदी *f.* उपशम *m.* उपशांति *f.* उपशमन *n.* ओसार *m.* ओसारा *m.*

I. *sum abated* सूट *f.*

ABBESS *n.* मठाधिकारिणी *f.* मठस्वामिनी *f.*

ABBEY, *n.* मठ *m.* योगिगृह *n.* योग्यालय *n.*

ABBOT, *n.* महंत *m.* मठाधिपति *m.* मठाध्यक्ष *m.* मठगुरु *m.* नायक *m.*

To ABBREVIATE, *v. a.* v. To ABRIDGE. संक्षेपणें, संक्षेप *m.*-संक्षेपण *n.* करणें *g.of o.* संक्षिप्त करणें.

2—in grammar, लोपविशिष्ट करणें, लोपानें लहान करणें, नष्ट करणें.

3—in mathematics, अपवर्त्त *m.*-अपवर्त्तन *n.* करणें *g.of o.*

ABBREVIATED, *p.* v. V. 1. संक्षिप्त, सांक्षेपिक, संक्षेप केलेला, संक्षेपाचा.

2 लोपविशिष्ट, लोपयुक्त, लुप्ताक्षर, नष्ट *or* लुप्तपद *or* लुप्तांश *or* लुप्तावयव &c.

ABBREVIATION, *n.* v. V. 1.—*act* संक्षेपणें *n.* संक्षेप करणें *n.* संक्षेप *m* संक्षेपण *n.*—*state.* संक्षेप *m.* संक्षेपपणा *m.* संक्षिप्तता *f.* सांक्षेपिकत्व *n.*

2—*state.* लोपविशिष्टता *f.* लोपयुक्तता *f.* नष्टता *f.*

3—*act.* अपवर्त्त *m.* अपवर्त्तन *n.*

I. *mark of a.* संक्षेपचिन्ह *n.*

II. *thing abbreviated*, v. ABRIDGEMENT. संक्षेप *m.* समाहार *m.*

ABBREVIATOR, *n.* v. V. 1. संक्षेपणारा, संक्षेप करणारा, संक्षेपकर्त्ता.

3 अपवर्त्तक, अपवर्त्तकारी, अपवर्त्तकर्त्ता.

A. B. C. v. ALPHABET. अक्षरानुक्रम *m.* अक्षरमाला *f.* वर्णमाला *f.* क ख *m.* बाराखड्या *f. pl.*

2 v. RUDIMENTS. ओनामा *m.*

Beginning one's a.b. c. ओनामा घोकणें *n.* अक्षरारंभ *m.* वर्णाध्ययन *n.* प्रथमाभ्यास *m.* नूतनाभ्यास *m.* विद्योपक्रम *m.* पठनोपक्रम *m.* नवारोह *m.*

To ABDICATE, *v. n. yield a right.* हक्क *m.*-वारसा *m.*-दावा *m.* सोडणें, स्वत्वत्याग *m.*-स्वत्वनिवृत्ति *f.*-सत्तानिवृत्ति *f.*-सत्तात्याग *m.*-स्वामित्वविसर्जन *n.*-पतित्वोपसर्ग *m.*-&c. करणें.

To ABDICATE, *v.a. relinquish a rightful possession.* सोडणें, सोडून देणें, त्यागणें, टाकणें, टाकून जाणें, त्याग *m.*-उत्सर्ग *m.*-उत्सर्जन *n.*-विसर्जन *n.*-विसर्ग *m.*-वर्जन *n.*-&c. करणें, स्वत्वत्याग-करून सोडणें, सत्तानिवृत्तिपूर्वक विसर्जन *n.*-स्वामित्वविसर्जनपूर्वक-त्याग *m.*-सत्तात्यागपूर्वकोत्सर्ग *m.* करणें *g.of o.*

To a. the throne. सिंहासन *n.*-राज्य *n.*-राजपद *n.*-राजाधिकार *m.*-राजासन *n.*-छत्रचामर *n.*- &c. सोडणें-सोडून देणें-सोडून जाणें, सिंहासनत्याग *m.*-राजासनत्याग *m.*-राजपदोत्सर्ग *m.*-राजपदविसर्जन *n.*-राजपदत्याग *m.*-राजाधिकारत्याग *m.*-राज्यत्यजन *n.*-छत्रचामरोत्सर्जन *n.*-&c. करणें.

To a. an office or trust. अधिकारत्याग *m.*-अधिकारविसर्जन *n.*-अधिकारोत्सर्ग *m.*-पदत्याग *m.*-पदोत्सर्जन *n.*-पदत्यजन *n.*-&c. करणें.

ABDICATED, *p.* v. V. N. स्वत्वत्याग &c. केलेला, सोडलेला, त्यागी, त्याग केलेला, त्यक्त, कृतविसर्जन, कृतोत्सर्जन, कृतोत्सर्ग, कृतस्वत्वत्याग, कृतस्वत्वनिवृत्ति, कृतस्वामित्वविसर्जन, त्यक्तस्वत्व, त्यक्तस्वसत्त, त्यक्तस्वामित्व, त्यक्तपतित्व.

v. V. A. सोडलेला &c. त्याजित, त्यागित, त्यक्त, उत्सृष्ट, विसर्जित, विसृष्ट, वर्जित, उत्सर्ग &c. झालेला *g.of s.* गतस्वामिक, गतनायक.

Throne-a. सिंहासन-राजपद-&c. सोडलेला, त्यक्तसिंहासन, त्यक्तराजासन, त्यक्तराजपद, त्यक्तराज्य, त्यक्तराजाधिकार, छत्रचामरविसर्जित, छत्रसिंहासनोत्सर्जित, कृतसिंहासनत्याग &c.

Trust or office-a. अधिकार-पद-&c. सोडलेला, त्यक्ताधिकार, त्यक्तपद, कृताधिकारत्याग &c.

ABDICATION, *n.* v. V. A.—*act.* सोडणें *n.* सोडून जाणें *n.* सोडून देणें *n.*

त्याग *m.* उत्सर्जन *n.* विसर्जन *n.* उत्सर्ग *m.* विसर्ग *m.* सत्तात्यागपूर्वकोत्सर्ग *m.* सत्तानिवृत्तिपूर्वक त्याग *m.* स्वामित्वविसर्जनपूर्वक त्याग *m.*
Deed of a. वेदावापत्र *n.* वेदावासन *n* सत्तात्यागप्रदर्शक पत्र *n.* स्वत्वनिवृत्त्यर्थक लेख *m.*

ABDICATOR, *n.* ABDICANT, *a.* v. V. N. सोडणारा &c. स्वत्वत्यागी, सत्तात्यागी, स्वत्वत्याग-स्वत्वनिवृत्ति-सत्तानिवृत्ति-सत्तात्याग-स्वामित्वविसर्जन- &c. कर्त्ता.
v. V. A. सोडणारा &c. उत्सर्ग-उत्सर्जन-विसर्जन वर्जन-&c. कर्त्ता, स्वत्वत्याग-सत्तानिवृत्ति-&c करून सोडणारा.
Throne-a. सिंहासन-राजासन-राजपद-राजाधिकार-राज्य-&c. सोडणारा, सिंहासन-राजासन &c. त्यागी, सिंहासनत्याग-राजासनत्याग-&c. कर्त्ता, सिंहासनोत्सर्ग-&c. कर्त्ता, सिंहासनविसर्जन-&c. कर्त्ता.
Trust-or office-a. अधिकार-पद सोडणारा, अधिकारत्यागी, पदत्यागी, अधिकारत्याग-पदत्याग-&c. कर्त्ता.

ABDOMEN, *n.* v. BELLY. उदर *n.* पोट *n.* कुक्षि *m.* जठर *n.* बस्ति *f.* Lower portion of the a. ओटी *f.*

ABDOMINAL, *a.* v. N. उदरी, उदरचा, पोटचा, उदरसंबंधी, कुक्षिसंबंधी, कौक्ष, औदरिक, जाठर, बास्तेय.

ABDOMINOUS, *a.* v. POTBELLIED. ढोंदील, ढेऱ्या.

ABDUCTION *n* -in Law, (लेंकरूं *n.*-बायको *f.*-&c.) कपटानें-फुसलावून-जुल्मानें नेणें *n.*

ABECEDARIAN, *n.* *teacher of a. b. c. (or rudiments.)* ओनाम्या *m.* रूपावळ्या *m.* ओनामा-अक्षरमाला-वर्णमाला-&c. सांगणारा-शिकवणारा-&c. क-ख घोकव्या *m.* वर्णमातृकाध्यापक *m.*
2 *learner of a. b. c.* v. SMATTERER. ओनाम्या *m.* ओनामा घोकणारा *or* घोक्या *m.* बाराखड्या घोकणारा *or* घोक्या *m.* धुळीचा लिहणारा *m.* पंचअक्षरी *m.* आठवड्या *m.* खडे मांडणारा *m.* कखचापंडित *m.* अक्षरोळख साधलेला *m* अक्षरारंभकर्त्ता *m.* विद्योपक्रमकर्त्ता *m.* प्रथमाभ्यासी *m.* नूतनाभ्यासी *m.* वर्णाभ्यासी *m.*

ABED, *adv.* *on or in bed.* शेजेवर, बिछान्यावर, माच्यावर, खाटेवर, शय्यास्थ, शयोपरि, शय्यागत, शयंगत, खट्वारूढ, मंचकारूढ.

ABERRANCE, ABERRATION, *n.* v. DEVIATION विचलन *n.* विगति *f.* विषमचलन *n.* विषमगति *f.* विपथगमन *n.* सूत्रविक्षेप *m.*
A. of mind, intellect, &c. भ्रम *m.* भ्रमण *n.*

ABERRANT, *a.* *devious,* v. ERRING. विचलन-विगति-&c. कर्त्ता, अपथगामी, विपथगामी.

To ABET, *v. a.* *back,* v. TO HELP. गुड्घा *m.* देणें, फूस *f.* देणें, दुमाला *m.* पुरवणें *g. of o.* पाठपुरावा *m.*-पुरस्तपना *m.* करणें *g. of o.* हिमाईत *f.* देणें दाखवणें करणें. पाठिंबाहोणें.

ABETTOR, *n.* ABETTING. *p.* v. V. गुड्घा देणारा, दुमाला पुरवणारा, &c. मेढा *m.* पाठिंगा *m.* पाठिंबा *m.*

ABEYANCE ,That is in a. तहकूब, बिगर अम्मल, तटस्थ.

To ABHOR. *v. a.* *hate intensely; abominate, detest.* अत्यंत द्वेषणें, ओंगळ-ओलटा-&c. मानणें, विष मानणें, द्वेषणें, अतिद्वेष *m.*-अतिद्वेषण *n.* करणें *g. of o.* वीट *m.*-ओकारी *f.*-&c. येणें *g of o. in. con.* पाण्यांत (पितांना) पाहणें, *or, inversely,* दिसणें, नांवानें पाणी *n.* तावणें *g. of o.* नांवानें पिचणें-जळणें-तर्पण करणें-धोंडे *m. pl.* फोडणें-तिलांजलि *mf.* देणें-घेणें *g. of o.*

ABHORRED, *p.* v. V. ओंगळ-&c. मानलेला, अतिद्वेषित, अतिद्विष्ट.

ABHORRENCE, *n.* *extreme hatred.* अतिद्वेष *m.* परमद्वेष *m.* अत्यंतद्वेष *m.* बीभत्स *m.* विकृत *n.*

ABHORRENT, *a.* ABHORRER, *n.* v. V. ओंगळ &c. मानणारा. द्वेषणारा, अतिद्वेष-&c. कर्त्ता, अतिद्वेष्टा.
I. *irreconcilable with,* v. INCONSISTENT. विपरीत, विरुद्ध, विरोधी, असंबद्ध, असंगत, संदर्भविरुद्ध.

To ABIDE, *v. n.* *stay for a short time,* v. TO SOJOURN. उमरणें, डेरा *m.* देणें, मुकाम *m.* करणें, चारदिवस-स्वल्पकाल-&c. राहणें, बिऱ्हाड *n.* करणें. [खी *f.* करणें.
2 *dwell,* v. TO RESIDE. राहणें, नांदणें, वास *m.*-वसति *pop.* वसणें-&c.
3 *not cease or fail,* v. TO CONTINUE. ठरणें, टिकणें, थिरावणें, स्थिर राहणें, अक्षय राहणें.
4 *bear up against, stand out,* v. TO ENDURE. निभणें, निभावणें, टिकणें.
5 by ; *stick to.* चिकटून-अंवटाळून-घेऊन-धरून-&c. असणें-च-

To ABIDE, *v. a.* v. TO AWAIT. खोळंबणें, खोळंबून बसणें-राहणें-&c. तिष्ठणें *with* साठीं *of o.*
2 v. TO BEAR. सोसणें, सहन *n.* करणें *g. of o.*

ABIDING. See ENDURING.

ABILITY, *n.* v. POWER. शक्ति *f.* सामर्थ्य *n.* बल *pop.* बळ *n.* ताकत *or* द *f.* खुदरत *f.* (*neg. con.*)
2 -mental, v. UNDERSTANDING, CAPACITY. बुद्धिवैभव *n.* बुद्धिपाटव *n.* अवांका *m.*

ABJECT, *a.* *mean, base,* v. LOW, MEAN. नीच, पाजी, हलका, अधम, निकृष्ट, पामर.

ABJECTLY, *adv.* v. A. पाजीपणानें, हलकेपणानें *m.* अधमबुद्धीनें.

ABJECTNESS *n.* v. A. पाजीपणा *m.* हलकेपणा *m.* *&c.* अधमत्व *n.*

ABJURATION *n.* v. V. क्रिया घेऊन सोडणें *n.* *&c.* शपथपूर्वकत्याग *m.* सशपथत्याग *m.*

To ABJURE, *v. a.* *renounce, &c. on oath.* क्रिया घेऊन सोडणें-टाकणें त्याग *m.* करणें, आणभाक करून *or* वाहून सोडणें-टाकणें-परित्याग *m.* करणें, शपथपूर्वक त्याग *m.*-सशपथत्याग *m* करणें *g. of o.*

ABLATION, *n.* *act of taking away.* अपादान *n.* अपहार *m.* अपहरण *n.* हरण *n.* अपवाह *m.*

ABLATIVE, *a.* *that takes away* अपहारक, अपहारी, अपहर्त्ता, हारक, हर (esp. in comp.), हर्त्ता, अपवाहक, अपवाही, अपादान-अपहार-अपहरण-हरण-अपवाह-&c. कर्त्ता, नेणारा.
A. case. अपादान *n.*
A. case absolute. सतिसप्तमी *f.*

ABLE, *a.* v. POWERFUL. शक्तिमान, सामर्थ्यवान, शक्त, समर्थ, बलवान. [काबील.
2—mentally, v. CLEVER, SKILFUL. समर्थ, दक्ष, पटु, कुशल,
3 *of adequate ability or power,* v. COMPETENT. लायक, कार्यक्षम, क्षम.
4—in comp. *admitting of, susceptible of, having the power.* The form of the English verb thus constituted is rendered into *Maráthí* by attaching, to the gerundial form of the *Maráthí* verb, the particle चा, (ex. Eatable खायाचा, Drinkable प्यायाचा,):—also the adjective सारखा *like, equal, adequate,* (ex. खायासारखा): —also the adjective योग्य or, popularly, जोगता or जोगा *proper, fit, worthy,* (ex. खाया or खायास or खायाला योग्य-जोगता-जोगा,):also the adjective, शक्य *possible* after adding स or ला (ex. खायास or खायाला शक्य,):—and thus, with a liberty unknown in English, *throughout* the *Maráthí* verbs. It is further rendered, when it expresses the sense *proper, fit, worthy (to be),*

by compounding with *Sanskrit* nouns such words as योग्य, उपयुक्त, उचित, अर्ह,-&c. all expressing this sense; ex. दानयोग्य, भक्षणोपयुक्त, लेखनोचित, पूजनार्ह, &c.
This form is also, in very numerous instances, well rendered by *Sanskrit* gerunds or participles (e. g. *eatable* खाद्य, खादनीय, खादितव्य, or भक्ष्य, भक्षणीय, भक्षितव्य or भक्षयितव्य) and by such forms it will here be abundantly rendered; but for the rules of formation, as they are not quite simple, and as they belong not to *Maráṭhí*, the learner is referred to the grammar of the *Sanskrit*. Here it is necessary to state, 1st. That by the terminations "able" spoken of, are to be understood as well the terminations "ible, eble, uble," (e. g. *miscible, deleble, soluble,*) whether occurring euphonously in the constitution of *English* verbal adjectives, or appearing in adjectives, introduced from the *Latin;* and whether viewed as derived from Abal *Goth*, or Ablez *Norm.*, or from Habilis *Lat.* 2ndly. That, as this termination "able," though it, viewed as *English*, can mean and therefore can be interpreted only as above (viz. *having the power*); and though, accordingly, its incomparably most common implication is that of *susceptibility* or *practicableness*, is yet employed (perhaps from a power derived from Habilis), to express the sense *fit* or *suitable*, (e. g. *observable, edible,*) and the sense *subject* or *liable*, (e. g. *finable, punishable.*) so, in like manner, are employed the participle चा and the adjectives सारखा and योग्य, &c 3dly. That the *Sanskrit* formations given, and all similar formations, (with the affixes यत्, अनीयर्, and तव्य,) are, though they involve differences and admit delicate preferences, employed in *Maráṭhí* with equal amplitude. 4thly. That the *Maráṭhí* formations with the participle चा and the adjectives सारखा and योग्य, as well as the *Sanskrit* formations, bear, additionally to the senses given above as common both to them and to the English formations with "able", the senses *designed* or *intended, about* or *on the point, and demanding, requiring,* or *claiming*. Lastly. That the detailed explanation here presented is designed to stand in substitution of detail and of unexplained repetition throughout the class of the *ables*; and that, therefore, it is to be borne in mind and applied by the student according to his occasions.

To be ABLE. v. ABLE. शकणें, शक्तिमान्-सामर्थ्यवान्-&c होणें, येणें, होणें (these two require *inverse construction*, as, I can write, मला लिहुणें *or* लिहतां *or* लिहायास येतें. Can you do it? हें तुला होतें कीं ? *or* हें तुझ्यानें होइल कीं ?) Here it may be observed that the verb होणें, additionally to its requiring *inv. con.* admits of the use of the agent in the objective case,—as per example: also, that the idiomatic and far preferable mode of rendering the English verb *to be able* is this mode of *inverse construction*. The verb is further rendered by the use, with a construction *inverse* or *in which the agent is put objectively*, of the third person of the causal verb, and *throughout the verbs*; as, I can eat this mango, हा आंबा मला *or* माझ्यानें खाववतो, and हें मला *or* माझ्यानें करवनें-सांगवतें-मारवलें-घालवलें-धरवेल-सोडवेल-देवणार-घेवणार, &c.: though of this last form "वणार" it must be added, that it is restricted to the *negative construction* or to the *interrogative construction* with negative implication; as, हें मला or माझ्यानें करवणार-सांगवणार-&c. नाहीं, *or* हें मला *or* माझ्यानें करवणार काय? साधणें, घडणें, (these two with the construction noted under होणें) हातानें घडणें *g of o.* मणगटांत *or* मणगटास जोर *m.* असणें *g. of s.* हात *m.* चालणें *g.of s.*

ABLE-BODIED, *a.* आंगचा बलकट-बळी-खंबीर-भक्कम-&c. अंगपटु, अंगदृढ, शारीरबलवान्, शारीरबली, देहदृढ, शरीरशक्त, शरीरदृढ, दृढदेह, गाढगात्र, वपुर्गाढ.

ABLUENT, *a. washing clean.* स्वच्छ करणारा, मळकाढणारा, स्वच्छकारी.

ABLUTION *n.v.* WASHING. धुणें *n.* धावन *n.* प्रक्षालन *n.* क्षालन *n.*
2 *bathing.* आंघोळ *f.* आंगधुणें *n.* स्नान *n.* मलस्नान *n.* मलापकर्षस्नान *n.*
3—in relig. sense. स्नान *n.*
A. of the body. अंगस्नान.
A. of the feet. पाद्य *n.* पादप्रक्षालन.
A. of the head. शिरःस्नान.
A. of the waist to the feet. कटिस्नान.
A. from the throat to the feet. कंठस्नान.
A. of the mouth. आचमन *pop.* आंचवण *or* आंचवणें *n.* मुखमार्जन *n.* मुखप्रक्षालन *n.* मुखधावन *n.* मुखशुद्धि *f.*
A. in one's garments सचेलस्नान *n.*
A. in the morning. प्रातःस्नान.
A. at a sacred place. तीर्थस्नान, गंगास्नान.
A. in the sea. समुद्रस्नान.
A. after inunction. अभ्यंगस्नान, अभ्यंगपूर्वकस्नान.
A. and inunction: used esp. of women and children. नाहाण माखण *n.*
A. performed mentally. मानसस्नान.
A. performed by rubbing earth on the body. मृत्तिकास्नान.
A. performed by rubbing cowdung on the body. गोमयस्नान.
A. performed with certain incantations. मंत्रस्नान.
A. performed by rubbing ashes. भस्मस्नान.
A. performed in company with others. गणस्नान.
Assistant or attendant at a. स्नान घालणारा *m.* स्नापक.
Cloth worn at a. पडदणी *f.*
Cursory or hurried a. —with the power or implication of *going through the form, doing enough to swear by,* - भुडभुडगंगा *f.* दंडस्नान *n.* मुसळस्नान, शाखास स्नान, धोपटस्नान.
Laws and rules of a. शौचविधि *m. pl.* शौचाचार *m.*
Materials (water, ashes, powder, &c.) for a. स्नानीय *n.* स्नान *n.*
That performs a. स्नानकर्त्ता, स्नायी, स्नाता, स्नानशील.
That has performed a. स्नान केलेला, स्नात, कृतस्नान, जातस्नान.
Unpurified by the daily a. *yet unwashed,*—of persons, vessels, &c. पारोसा; and by reduplic. आरोसापारोसा, अस्नान, अकृतस्नान.

Yet wet (unwiped) after a. ओलटा *or* ओलेता.

ABLUTION-CLOTH, *n.* ओलाणें *n* ओलावणें *n.* स्नानवस्त्र *n.* पडदणी *f.*

ABLUTION-STONE, *n.* स्नानाची शीळ *f.* शिला *f.* पाथर *f.* स्नानशिला *or* स्नानशीळ *f.*

ABLUTIONARY, *a.* v. N. *relating, &c. to ablution.* आंघोळीचा, स्नानाचा, स्नानसंबंधी, स्नानीय, स्नानविषयक, स्नानांतर्गत, स्नानान्वित, स्नानाभिप्रायक, स्नानप्रकरणांतला.

ABLY, *adv.* v. N. 1. शक्तीनें &c. सशक्ति, ससामर्थ्य.

2 कुशलतेनें, कौशल्यानें, दक्षतेनें, सुगराईनें, कुशलतापूर्वक, कौशल्यपूर्वक, दक्षतापूर्वक.

To ABNEGATE, ABNEGATION. See To DENY, DENIAL.

ABNORMAL, *a.* v. IRREGULAR. विधिभंजक, विधिविरुद्ध, अयथाशास्त्र.

ABOARD, *adv.* and *prep.* वर, वरतीं, वरतें, आंत, मध्यें, used after any word signifying *ship or boat.*

ABODE, ABIDING, *n.*—*act.* v. STAY. राहणें *n.* नांदणें *n.* नांदणूक *f.*

2—*place.* v. RESIDENCE. ठिकाणा *m.* ठिकाण *n.* राहण्याची जागा *f.* [वास *m.* करणें.

To make one's a. To take up one's a. v. To RESIDE. राहणें,

To ABOLISH, *v. a. abrogate, annul.* मोडणें *or* मोडून टाकणें, नाहींसा-दूर-महकूब-मना-रद्द-&c. करणें, मार्जा पाडणें-करणें-घालणें, महकुबी *f.*-मनाई *f.*-उच्छेद *m.*- भंग *m.*- भंजन *n.*- दूरीकरण *n.*- खंडण *n.*-अवरोप *m.*-अवरोपण *n.*- निरुद्धरण *n.*-लोप *m.*-निवर्त्तन *n.*-प्रचारनिवर्त्तन *n.*-प्रचाररोध *m.*-प्रचारखडन *n.*-अवस्थितिभंजन *n.*-अवस्थितिभंग *m.*-अवस्थितिखंडन *n.* करणें.

To a. a rite, practice, rule, &c. नियमोच्छेद *m.*-नियमभंग *m.*-रीत्यवरोप *m.*-रीत्युच्छेद *m.*-आचारभंग *m.*-आचारापालन *n.*-नियमखंडन *n.*-संप्रदायखंडन *n.*-विधिखंडन *n.* करणें. [स्रा&c.

ABOLISHABLE, *a* v. V. मोडाया-रद्दकराया-&c. जोगता जोगा-सार-

ABOLISHED, *p.* v. V. मोडलेला &c. नाहींसा केलेला *or* झालेला, महकूब, मना, रद्द, उच्छिन्न, दूरीकृत, निरुद्धृत, निवृत्त, अवरोपित, लुप्त.

ABOLISHER, *n.* v. V. मोडणारा &c. नाहींसा दूर-&c. करणारा.

ABOLITION, *n.* v. V.—*act.* मोडणें *n.* मोडून टाकणें *n.* नाहींसा-&c. करणें *n.* &c. खंडन *n.*—*state.* मोडलेपणा *m.* &c. महकुबी *f.* मनाई *f.* उच्छेद *m* भंग *m.* लोप *m.* अवरोप *m* निवृत्ति *f.* निष्कृति *f.* दूरीकृति *f.* उच्छिन्नत्व *n* प्रचाररोध *m.* अवस्थितिभंग *m.*

ABOMINABLE, *a. detestable, execrable,* v. HATEFUL. अमंगल, अघोरी, ओंगळ, ओंगटा, विषतुल्य, विषप्राय, केवलविष, अतिद्वेष्य, अतिद्वेषयोग्य, अतिद्वेषार्ह, अत्यप्रिय, कुत्सनीय, कुत्सित.

A. person. मुरदाड *or* मुडदार *n.* चंडालमूर्ति *f.* चंडाल *m.* दुर्जन *m n.* पिंगळ *m.* बीभत्सविषय *m.* द्वेषपात्र *n.* द्वेषलक्ष्य *n.*

ABOMINABLENESS, *n.* v. A. अघोरपणा *m.* अमंगलपणा *m.* &c. विषतुल्यता *f.* अतिद्वेष्यता *f.* अत्यप्रियता *f.* अतिद्वेषार्हता *f.* कुत्सनीयता *f.*

To ABOMINATE, *v. a. hate utterly,* v. To ABHOR. अत्यंत द्वेषणें, विष मानणें, अतिद्वेष *m.*-अतिद्वेषण *n.* करणें. *g. of o.*

ABOMINATION, *n. object of a.* घाण *f.* विष *n.* ओंगटें *n.* अतिद्वेषपात्र *n.* बीभत्सविषय *m* विकृतविषय *m.* विकृतलक्ष्य *n.* द्वेषलक्ष्य *n.*

ABORIGINAL, *a.* v. ORIGINAL. मूळचा, पहिला, प्रथमस्थित.

ABORIGINES, *n. primitive inhabitants.* मूळचे राहणार *m. pl.* स्थायिलोक *m. pl.* स्थायी *m. pl.* भूमे *m. pl.* स्थायिकजन *m. pl.* प्रथमस्थितलोक *m. pl.* प्राचीनलोक *m. pl.* प्राचीनपुरुष *m. pl.* देशचे *m. pl.* अनादिसिद्ध *m. pl.*

ABORTION, *n.*—*act. miscarriage.* गर्भपात *m.* दुबेत *n.* गर्भपतन *n.* गर्भस्राव *m.* गर्भस्रव *m.* गर्भप्रस्रवण *n.* गर्भच्युति *f.* गर्भविस्रंसन *n.* गर्भस्यंदन *n.* पिंडपतन *n.* स्रव *m.* स्राव *m.*

Procurer of a. पिंडघातक, भ्रूणहत्यारा, पिंडघात &c. कर्त्ता.

To procure a. पोट *n.* पाडणें-झाडणें-सांडणें-जिरवणें-मारणें, पिंडघात *m.*-भ्रूणहत्या *f* करणें.

To suffer a. पोट *n.* पडणें-जिरणें *g. of s.*

2—*produce, castling.* गर्भ *m.* गर्भशेष *m.* मृतगर्भ *m.* गोळा *m.* अकालपिंड *m.* अपूर्णगर्भ *m.* गर्भपात *m.* गर्भस्राव *m.*

ABORTIVE, *a. brought forth untimely.* काळपूर्ण होण्यापूर्वी जन्मलेला, अकाल, अपूर्णकालजन्मा, अपक्वजन्मा, अपूर्णकालज, अकालज, अकालजात, अकालोत्पन्न, अनवसर, असमय, आमजन्मा.

2 *that fails, proves vain,* v. VAIN. व्यर्थ, निष्फल, निरर्थक, अनर्थक.

3—in medicine, *causing abortion.* गर्भपातकारक &c. गर्भश्रावी.

ABORTIVELY *adv.* v. A. 2. फुकट, वायां, व्यर्थ, वृथा.

To ABOUND, *v. n. have plentifully.* बहुत-पुष्कळ-विपुळ-प्रचुर-&c. असणें *or* होणें *inv. con.* पोहणें.

2 *be plentiful.* बहुत-पुष्कळ-विपुळ-प्रचुर-&c. असणें *or* होणें, महामुरी *f.*—ऊत *m.*-उत्कर्ष *m.*-प्रकर्ष *m.*-प्राचुर्य *n.*-वैपुल्य *n.*-&c. असणें *or* होणें *g. of s.* लोटणें, वाहणें.

ABOUT, *prep. over the outside of, around.* वरल्या आंगावरून, बाहेरल्या बाजूवरून, बाहेरून, वरून, भोंवतां, भोंवताला, भोंवतीं *or* तें, सभोंवर, सभोंवतां, परितः.

2 *in the vicinity of.* जवळपास, जवळसर, आसपास, आसींपासीं, लागींभागीं, लागीं, शिवशेजारीं, लगत, वाटला, आदिपश्चात्.

3 *concerning.* विषयीं, संबंधीं, प्रकरणीं, स *or* ला (*as* मी कांहीं कामाला आलों आहें).

4—in quantity, quality, &c. *near to.* सुमाराचा, उणापुरा, कमकसर, सुमारास, सुमारावर, सुमारें. [रावर, सुमारें.

5—in time; *near to.* जवळ, लगत, आदिपश्चात्, सुमारास, सुमा-

6 *appendantly to the person.* आंगावर, आंगासीं, वर, जवळ, पासीं. [चौगर्द or र्दां औरसचौरस.

7 *in compass or circumference of* घेरास, परिधीस, चौफेर,

8 *on the point of, in the act of.* उन्मुख (ex. a. to die. मरणोन्मुख; a. to go गमनोन्मुख, and प्रसवोन्मुख, दानोन्मुख, भक्षणोन्मुख, पठनोन्मुख &c.) अभिमुख (ex मरणाभिमुख &c.*v. supra*)

To be a. टेकणें, टेकावणें, लागास-सुमारास येणें-रंगास-&c. येणें *or* लागांत-सुमारांत-&c. असणें, गुडणें.

9 *at, in, in engagedness upon.* आंत, मध्यें.

ABOUT, *adv. circularly.* चक्रर-गिरकांडा-&c. मारून, चक्रवत्, मंडलवत्, गरगर *or* रां, गिरगिर or रां, मंडल घालून.

2 *in circuit, in compass.* घेऱ्यास, घेऱ्यानें, औरसचौरस, गर्भीस, परितः, परिधीस, परिधिव्यापून-धरून-मापडवून-&c.

3 *nearly, circiter.* आडनाड, आडनीट *or* ड्या आडनेड, सुमारास, सुमारानें, सुमारावर, एक (ex. about a mile कोस एक, and शेर एक, मण एक, घटका एक, प्रहर एक, महिना एक, वर्ष एक &c. about six, about seven, &c. साहा एक, सात एक, शंभर एक, हजार एक, &c.).

4 *here and there, circa.* आजूबाजूस, आजूबाजू, आसपास, अरसपरस, अरतां परतां, इकडे तिकडे, जिकडे तिकडे, जेथें तेथें.

5 *circuitously.* फेऱ्यानें, भोंवाड्यानें, फेरा खाऊन घेऊन &c. गरका मारून-घेऊन &c. गिरकांडा घेऊन *or inversely.* पडून वळून.

To bring a. *To bring to pass.* घडवणें, घडवून आणणें.

To come a. *To come to pass.* घडून येणें. घडणें.

To go a. *To enter upon, be engaged in.* प्रवर्त्तणें, प्रवृत्तहोणें.

Above, *prep. over.* वर, वरता-वरती-तें, वरतीं, उपरि.

From a. वरून, उंचून.

2 v. Upon. वर, वरतां.

3—in quantity, number, &c. वर, पेंलीकडे, उपर, शिवाई, अधिक-&c. *used with* पेक्षां.

Above, *adv. overhead, upwards.* वर, वरतीं, वरतें, ऊर्ध्व, डोईवर, समथ्याकडे, उंचीं.

2 *in the heavens.* वर,वरतीं, वरतें,ऊर्ध्व, आकाशांत, अंतरिक्षांत, अंतराळीं, अधांतरीं. [सर्वोपरि, मुख्यशः.

Above all, *adv.* v. Chiefly. पहिला प्रथम, पहिल्यानेंच, पहिलाच,

Above-board, *adv. not clandestinely.* v. Openly. बोलून चालून, उघडबाघड, उघडपणीं.

Above-cited, Above-mentioned, Above-named, &c. *a.* मजकूर, पूर्वोक्त, पूर्वोदित, पूर्वचोदित, सदरहू, मशारनिल्हे *or* ल्हे, (only in writings.) मिनहू, (only in writings.) वरतीं-पूर्वीं-&c.सांगितला.

To **Abrade**, *v. a rub or wear off* चोळवटणें, चोळटणें, चोळणें, घासटणें, घसवटणें, घसटणें, घासणें, खरडणें, झिजवणें, अवघर्षण *n.*-विघट्टन *n.* करणें *g. of o.*

Abraded, *p.* v. V. चोळवटलेला &c खरचटलेला,अवघर्षित,विघट्टित.

To be or become a. खरचटणें, खरडणें, खरंगटणें.

Abrasion, *n.* v. V.—*act.* चोळणें *n.* चोळवटणें *n.* घासटणें *n.* &c. अवघषण *n.* विघट्टन *n.*—*state.* चोळवटलेपणा *m.* &c. चोळ *f.* अवघर्षितत्व *n.*

Mark of a. अरखुडा or ओरखडा *m.*

Abreast, *adv. with the breasts in a line.* उरासीं ऊर असें,छातीस छाती,आंगास आंग,खांद्यास खांदा लावून,समपार्श्वतः,पार्श्वपंक्तितः.

To **Abridge**, *v. a. epitomize, digest, abstract.* थोडक्यांत आणणें, संक्षेपणें,संक्षेप*m* समाहार*m*-संहार*m*.-समास *m.*- संक्षेपीकरण*n.*-समाहरण *n.*- संकलन *n.*-प्रतिसंहार *m.* करणें *g.of o.* संक्षिप्त-सांक्षेपिक-&c- करणें.

2 *shorten, diminish.* v. To Lessen. कमी न्यून &c. करणें.

Abridged, *p.* v.V. 1. संक्षेप केलेला &c. संक्षिप्त, सांक्षेपिक, संक्षेपीरुन, सामासिक, संहित, समाहृत, संहृत, तांत्रिक.

Abridgedly. *adv.* v. N. संक्षेपानें,संक्षेपकरून, संक्षेपतः, ससंक्षेप, सार-सारांश सारार्थ-&c. घेऊन.

Abridgement, *n.* v. V. 1.—*act.* संक्षेपणें *n.* संक्षेप करणें *n.* —*state.* संक्षेप *m.* संक्षिप्तता *f.* संक्षेपणा *m* सांक्षेपिकत्व *n* संक्षिप्ति *f.* समाहृति *f.* संहृति *f.* संहितता *f.*

I. *book, &c. abridged; compendium, epitome, digest, summary, abstract.* संक्षेप*m.*सारांश*m.*सारार्थ*m.*सारसंग्रह*m.* सारग्रंथ *m.* समाहार *m.* तात्पर्यग्रंथ *m.* वेंचा *m.* संग्रह *m.*संहार *m.* संहिता*f.* निष्कर्ष *m.*

Abridger, *n.* v.V.1. संक्षेपणारा, संक्षेप करणारा, संक्षेप-समाहार-संहार-सारग्रंथ-&c. कर्त्ता. [मोकारा.

Abroad, *adv. at large.* मोकळा,मोकळेपणीं, मोकाट,मोकार, मोकळ,

2 *out of doors, without.* घराबाहेर, बाहेर.

3 *out of home, in foreign place.* गांवाबाहेर, ग्रामांतरीं, देशांतरीं, स्थलांतरीं, परदेशांत, विदेशीं, प्रवासीं, बाहेर.

To go a. देशांतरीं जाणें, देशांतर *n.*-विदेशगमन *n.*-देशांतराटन *n.*-परदेशाटन *n.* करणें, प्रवासास जाणें.

4 *over the region, far and wide.* देशावर, देशांत, मुलकावर, मुलकांत (ex. देवी देवळांत नायटे मुलकांत), गांवांत,चौघांत, ठ'व.

To get a. बाहेरपडणें, चट्कुणीं होणें-पडणें,स्फुटन *n.*-स्फोट *m.*-जघन्य *n.* होणें *g. of s.* पेंठ *f.* लागणें *g. of s.* चौघांत जाणें-येणें, लौकिक *m.*होणें *g. of s.*

5 *in the open air.* उघड वाऱ्यांत,उघडवासऱ्यांत,वारधाटीं.

To **Abrogate**, *v. a. repeal, annul,* v. To Abolish. मोडणें, मोडूनटाकणें, माजी करणें-पाडणें-घालणें, रद्द करणें, नाहींसा करणें.

Abrogation, *n.* v. V. मोडणें *n.* रद्दकरणें *n.* &c.

Abrupt, *a. precipitous.* कडा तुटलेला,कड्याचा,तुटलेल्या कड्याचा, तुटक्या कड्याचा, छिन्नतट, प्रपानमय.

2 *without proper notice,* v. Sudden. पूर्वसूचनारहित-शून्य &c. धसक्याचा,धडकावणीचा,एकाएकींचा,पूर्वपीठिकारहित,आकस्मिक.

3 *unconnected.* तुटक, तुटका.

Abruptly, *adv.* v. A. 2.न सांगतां, न बोलतां, सूचना केल्यावांचून, धड, धडक, बेधडक, बेचरक, एकाएकीं, अकस्मात्.

Abruptness, *n.* v. A. 1. कडा तुटलेलेपणा *m.* छिन्नतटत्व *n.*

2 पूर्वसूचनाराहित्य*n.* धसकेपणा*m.* &c.

Abscess, *n. impostume.* फोड*m.* पूभरलेलें क्षत*n.*सपूयक्षत*n.*विद्रधि*m.*

To **Abscond**, *v. n. withdraw or absent one's self clandestinely.* पळून दडणें, निघून छपणें, दडून छपून असणें, आड सरणें, दडी *f.* मारणें, दडी मारून बसणें, बुडी मारणें, दडून बसणें, लपून बसणें, निघून नाहींसा होणें, निघून जाणें, तोंड*n.*काळें करण, गासलापूर*n.* करणें.

Absconder, *n.* **Absconding** *p. a.* v. V. निघून छपणारा, दडून बसणारा, &c.

Abscondingly, *adv.* v. A. लपून छपून, दबून छपून, बुडी मारून, दडी मारून.

Absence, *n.* v. A. 1. गैरहाजिरी *f.* गैररुजूपणा *m.* अविद्यमानता *f.* असमक्षता *f.* अवर्त्तमानता *f.* परोक्षता *f.* असाक्षात्पणा *m.* अभाव *m.*विप्रकर्ष *m.* विप्रकृष्टता *f.* असंनिधि *f.* दूरी *or* दूरस्थिति *f.*

In the a. of.परोक्ष, बेहुजूर, नसतां, नसतांना, असमक्ष, अभावीं (also in comp. as एतदभावीं, तदभावीं, विवक्षिताभावीं) मागें, पाठीमागें.

2 असावधपणा *m.* अनवधान *n.* अनवधानता *f.* अनवधानत्व *n.* अप्रस्तुतलक्षता *f.*

Absent, *a not present.* गैरहाजीर,गैररुजू, असमक्ष, अविद्यमान, अवर्त्तमान, परोक्ष, असाक्षात्, दूर*or*दूरस्थ *or* दूरस्थित, असंनिहित, विप्रकृष्ट, असंगत.

2—*mentally,* v. Inattentive. अनवधान, असावध,अनवहित, अदत्तांतःकरण, अतन्मनस्क, अप्रस्तुतलक्ष, ध्यानस्थ.

Terms, phrases, sayings, &c. designative or descriptive of *an a. person,* and corresponding with *wool-gatherer, wanderer, cloud dweller, &c.* are भ्रमिष्ट, भ्रमी, झावळ, भांब्या, भांबळ *or* ळ्या, झांपऱ्या, भ्रांतिखोर, भ्रांतहृदय, कर्णेस्पृश्रेक टिंचाल्यनि.

To be a. देहादर नसणें, देहभान *n.* नसणें *inr. con.* भांबावणें.

To **Absent** *v.a.* (one's self) *forbear to appear.* गैरहाजीर असणें-राहणें, न येणें, हाजीर न होणें.

Absentee, *n. person absent from his place, post,* &c. गैरहाजीर गैररुजू-&c. माणस *n.*-&c. प्रोषित मनुष्य *n.*

Absolute, *a. sovereign, despotic, arbitrary.* मुखत्यार, स्वतंत्र, स्ववश, स्वाधीन, स्वेच्छ, स्वायत्त, यथाकामी, यथेच्छ, यथेष्ट, कामकर, अपराधीन, अनिर्बंध.

2 *unconditional, unqualified.* अप्रतिबंध, अप्रतिबंधक, असांकेतिक, संकेतहीन-रहित-शून्य&c. बिन अडीचा, बिनतरीचा.

ABSOLUTELY, *adv.* v. A. 1. आपले इच्छेप्रमाणें, स्वाधीनतापूर्वक, स्वातंत्र्यपूर्वक, मुखत्यारीनें, यथेच्छ, यथाकाम, अनन्याधीनतेनें, स्वेच्छानुसारें. [अडीवांचून, तरीवांचून.

2 प्रतिबंधावांचून, प्रतिबंधहीन-रहित-&c. संकेतहीन-शून्य &c.

I. *peremptorily*, v. POSITIVELY. परिछिन्न, निक्षूण, हडसून, खडसून, खामखा, निखालस.

II. *utterly*, v. WHOLLY. अगदीं, निस्तूक.

ABSOLUTENESS, *n.* v. A. 1. मुखत्यारी *f.* स्वतंत्रता *f.* स्वातंत्र्य *n.* स्वाधीनता *f.* अपराधीनता *f.* स्ववशता *f.* यथेष्टता *f.*

2 अप्रतिबंधत्व *n.* प्रतिबंधाभाव *m.* असांकेतिकत्व *n.* प्रकर्ष *m.* संकेताभाव *m.* संकेतराहित्य *n.* [*n.*

ABSOLUTION, *n.* v. V. 1.—*act.* सोडणें *n.* निरपराध-निर्दोष&c.ठरवणें दोषमोचन *n.* निर्दोषीकरण *n.* &c. —*state.* उघडामाथा *m.* उजळतामाथा *or* उजळमाथा *m.* उजळतोंड *n.* दोषमुक्तता *f.* दोषमुक्ति *f.*

2—*act.* सोडणें *n.* मोकळा करणें *n.* सोडवणूक *f.* सोडवण *f.*—*state.* सोडलेपणा *m.* सुटलेपणा *m.* मोकळेपणा *m.* मोकळीक *f.* सोडवणूक *f.* सोडवण *f.* सुटका *f.* मुक्ति *f.* मुक्तता *f.*

To ABSOLVE, *v. a. exonerate, excuse, exculpate, acquit* (*of criminality.*) निरपराध-निर्दोष-निष्पाप- &c. ठरवणें, सोडणें, निर्दूषण *n.*-अदूषण *n.*-दोषमोचन *n.*-निर्दोषीकरण *n.*-अदोषीकरण *n.* करणें *g. of o.* दोषमुक्त करणें, उघडामाथा *m.*-उजळतामाथा *or* उजळमाथा *m.*-उजळतोंड *n.* करणें *g. of o.* उजळ-साफ-निष्कलंक-&c. करणें.

2 *free from a promise or engagement.* सोडणें, मोकळा करणें, मोकळीक *f.*-मुक्ति *f.*-मुक्तता *f.*-मोचन *n.*-सोडवणी *f.*-सोडवणूक *f.*-सोडवण *f.*-सुटका *f.* करणें *g. of o.* मोकळा-मुक्त-&c. करणें, वचन *n.*-भाक *f.*-शपथ *f.*-&c. सोडणें-परत देणें.

ABSOLVED, *p.* v. V. 1. निरपराध &c. ठरावलेला, सोडलेला, उजळतामाथा &c. केलेला *or* झालेला, निर्दूषित, अदूषित, दोषमुक्त, निर्दोषीकृत.

2 सोडलेला&c. मोकळा, सुटा, मुक्त, वचनमुक्त, शपथमुक्त &c.

To ABSORB, *v. a. suck up.* शोषणें, शोषून घेणें, शोखणें, पिणें, खाणें, गिळणें, पिऊन घेणें, शोष *m.*-शोषण *n.*-शुष्कीकरण *n.*-प्राशन *n.* करणें *g. of o.*

2 *wholly engage, engross.* गुंग-गरक-मग्न-निमग्न-तत्पर-धुंद-&c. करणें *and, inv. con.* होणें, व्यापणें, वेढणें.

3 *swallow up, consume, devour, take.* खाणें, अटणें, अटवणें, जिरवणें, मुरवणें, गडप-गडद्-गडगप-*or* गडलगप *adv.* करणें, *and, inv. con.* होणें, लय *mn.* करणें *g. of o.*

ABSORBED, *p.* v. V. 1. शोषलेला, शोषून घेतलेला &c. शोषित, प्राशित.

2 गुंग, गरक, धुंद, चूर, ग्रस्त, मग्न *pop.* मगन, निमग्न, तत्पर, तल्लीन, एकतान (in comp. as गायनैकतान, शृंगारैकतान, भजनैकतान,), लीन (esp. in comp. as तल्लीन, विषयलीन, विद्यालीन,), पर (in comp. as तत्पर, ध्यानपर, अध्ययनपर,) , आविष्ट, (in comp. as मदनाविष्ट, मोहाविष्ट, अध्ययनाविष्ट,), तन्मय, तन्मना, तन्मनस्क, सन्निविष्ट.

To be a. निमग्नें, मुरणें, गडणें, गडून जाणें, थिजणें, निधावणें.

3 जिरवलेला *or* जिरलेला, अटलेला *or* अटवलेला, गडप &c.झालेला.

To be a. मुरणें, जिरणें, जिरणीं पडणें, लमणें.

I. (into the Deity) मोक्ष पावलेला, मुक्त, प्राप्तमुक्ति, प्राप्तमोक्ष, प्राप्तकैवल्य, प्राप्तसायुज्य, प्राप्तब्रह्मनिर्वाण *or* प्राप्तब्रह्म, प्राप्तापवर्ग.

ABSORBENCY, *n.* v. A. शोष *m.* शोषणशक्ति *f.* शोषकत्व *n.*

ABSORBENT, *n.*—medicine. शोषक-शोषकर-&c. औषध *n.*-द्रव्य *n.*

2—vessel. रसाद्नी *f.*

ABSORBER, *n.* ABSORBENT, *a.* v. V. 1. शोषणारा &c. शोषक, शोष *or* शोषकर्त्ता-कारी-कर &c.

ABSORPTION, *n.* v. V. 1.—*act.* शोषणें *n.* पिणें *n.* पिऊन घेणें *n.* &c. शोषण *n.* प्राशन *n.* शुष्कीकरण *n.*—*state.* शोषलेपणा *m.* &c. शोष *m.* शोषितत्व *n.*

2—*state.* गुंगपणा *m.* &c. निमग्नता *f.* तत्परत्व *n.* तल्लीनता *f.* गुंगी *f.* धुंदी *f.* लय *mn.* ग्रस्तता *f.* आवेश *m.* (esp. in comp. as अध्ययनावेश, मदनावेश,), सन्निवेश *m.* तन्मयता *f.*

3—*state.* जिरवलेपणा *or* जिरलेपणा *m.* &c. लय *mn.*

I. (into the Deity.) मुक्ति *f.* मोक्ष *m.* ब्रह्मसायुज्य *n.* ब्रह्मप्राप्ति *f.* ब्रह्मनिर्वाण *n.* भगवत्प्राप्ति *f.* कैवल्य *n.*

Rapture or bliss of a. अद्वैतसुख *n.* ब्रह्मानंद *m.* ब्रह्मसुख *n.*

To ABSTAIN, *v. n. refrain, forbear.* वांचून-शिवाय &c. राहणें used with the verb expressing the object (ex. अन्न जवळ असतांना भूक लागल्यावर खाल्यावांचून राहणें कठीण), नांव *n.* न घेणें *g. of o.* वर्जन *n.*-भोगवर्जन *n.*-भोगत्याग *m.*-अभोग *m.* करणें, धिरणें, खळणें, वर्ज्य करणें, भोगव्यतिरिक्त-अभुक्त राहणें.

ABSTEMIOUS, ABSTINENT, *a.* (in diet,) v. TEMPERATE. बेतानें आहार करणारा, अल्पाहार, अल्पाहारी, अल्पभोजी, अल्पाशी, अल्पभक्षी, लघ्वाहारी, लघ्वाहार.

2 (in enjoyments, gener.) *temperate.* बेतानें विहार करणारा, अल्पभोगी, अल्पविहारी, आहारविहारनियमवान्, संयमी, यमवान्, नियमी, नियतभोक्ता, नियतेंद्रिय, नियतवर्ती, नियतवृत्ति, नियमकृत्, किंचित्सेवी, ईषद्ग्राही, ईषद्भुक्, नियंता.

3—diet, regimen, life, *sparing*, *&c.* अल्पाहाराचा, लघ्वाहाराचा, नियमितविहाराचा, परिमित भोगाचा.

ABSTEMIOUSLY, *adv.* v. A. 1. 2. अल्पभोगानें, अल्पभोगपूर्वक, अल्पाहारपूर्वक, अर्धपोट, अर्धपोटीं, इंद्रियनिग्रह करून, किंचित्सेवनपूर्वक, इंद्रियसंयमपूर्वक.

ABSTEMIOUSNESS, *n.* v. A. 1. अल्पाहारत्व *n.* अल्पाहारित्व *n.* &c.

2 नियतभोक्तृत्व *n.* नियंतत्व *n.* अल्पविहारित्व *n.* नियतवृत्ति *f.* किंचित्सेवित्व *n.* &c.

3. अल्पाहारत्व *n.* &c. [त्याग *m.*

ABSTINENCE, *n.* v. V.—*act.* भोगवर्जन *n.* भोगत्याग *m.* भोगपरि-

v. A. 1. अल्पाहार *m.* अल्पभक्षण *n.* अल्पाशन *n.* अल्पभोजन *n.* नियताहार *m.* &c. यताहार *m.* आहारनियम *m.* लघ्वाहार *m.* &c.

2 अल्पभोग *m.* अल्पविहार *m.* संयम *m.* संयमन *n.* संयाम *m.* नियम *m.* नियतवर्त्तन *n.* नियतवृत्ति *f.* संयतवर्त्तन *n.* संयतवृत्ति *f.* संयताचार *m.* विहारनियम *m.* किंचित्सेवन *n.* आहारविहारनियम *m.*

I. v. FASTING उपास *m.* निराहार *m.* अनाहार *m.* उपोषण *n.* अनशन *n.*

To ABSTRACT *v. a. separate from.* काढणें *or* काढून घेणें, निष्कासन *n.* करणें.

2 *epitomize*, v. TO ABRIDGE सारांश *m.* काढणें, संक्षेपणें, संक्षेप *m.*-सारग्रंथ *m.* करणें *g. of o.*

ABSTRACT, *n.* v. ABRIDGMENT. सार *m.* सारग्रंथ *m.* सारांश *m.* सारार्थ *m.* [रजुमा *m.*

2 (esp. of rolls, lists, accounts.) गोश्वारा *or* गोशेरा *m.* त-

3 *essence extracted*, v. EXTRACT. निष्कर्ष m. निर्यास m.

In the a. *without reference to particular persons or things.* पृथग्भाव धरून, संबंधभावरहित, &c.

ABSTRACT, *a.* पृथक्,पृथक्रून, पृथग्भावाचा.—in grammar.साधित.

ABSTRACTION, *n.*—of mind, v. ABSENCE. अनवधान *n.* अनवधानत्व *n.* [माधि m.

2 (from the world) वैराग्य *m.* विरक्ति *f.* प्रपंचविरक्ति*f.* कर्मस-

ABSTRACTLY, *adv.* v. A. *unconnected with any thing else.* संबंध भावरहित, पृथग्भाव धरून.

ABSTRUSE, *a. hidden, secret, recondite, occult.* गूढ, गहन, गुप्तार्थ, निगूढ, गहनार्थ, खोल, सखोल, गूढार्थ, गुह्यार्थ, दुर्गम्य, अगम्य, दुर्ज्ञेय, गुरुगम्य, दुर्बोध, दुरवबोध.

ABSTRUSELY, *adv.* v. A. गूढपणानें, गूढपणीं, सखोल, अस्पष्ट.

ABSTRUSENESS, *n.* v. A. खोलपणा *m.* &c. गूढता *f.* निगूढता *f.* गहनत्व *n.* गुप्तार्थकत्व *n.* गहनार्थकत्व*n.* गूढार्थकत्व *n.* दुर्गम्यता *f.* अगम्यता *f.* दुर्ज्ञेयता *f.* गुरुगम्यता *f.*

ABSURD, *a.* v. UNREASONABLE,—of persons. विवेकशून्य, असमंजस, असमंजीक.

—of acts, judgments, &c.असमंजस, अयुक्तिक, अयथोचित, अयथायुक्त, युक्तिविरुद्ध, बुद्धिविपर्यासाचा, असमर्पक, अनर्थक, अयुक्त, असंबद्ध.

ABSURDITY,ABSURDNESS, *n.* v.A. 1.—of persons. विवेकशून्यत्व *n.* विवेकाभाव *m.* असमंजसपणा *m.* वेडेपणा *m.*

—of acts, &c. बुद्धिविपर्यास *m.* असमंजसपणा *m.* अयुक्तिकत्व *n.* युक्तिविरुद्धता *f.* अनर्थकता *f.*

I.—*that which is absurd.* अयुक्तिकगोष्ट *f.*- विषय *m.* &c.

ABUNDANCE, *n. great plenty.* पुष्कळपणा *m.* &c. विपुलता *f.* प्रचुरता *f.* बाहुल्य*n.* वैपुल्य*n.* बहुत्व *n.* महामुरी *f.*महामूर *f.* ऊत *m.* बाहुतबारा *m.*प्राचुर्य *n.* उत्कर्ष*m.* प्रकर्ष*m.* प्राशस्त्य*n.* मात *f.*

—intensely; *superabundance, &c.* v. EXUBERANCE.ऊरपूर *f.* पुरपुराट*m.* समृद्धि *f.* अतिशय *m.* चळचळाट *m.* चेहळ *f.* चेळ *f.* रेल *f.* रेल *f. m.*

ABUNDANT, *a.* ABOUNDING, *p. a.* v. V. 1. पोहणारा &c. आढ्य (esp.in comp. as, धनाढ्य, धान्याढ्य, गुणाढ्य, विद्याढ्य, ज्ञानाढ्य, पुण्याढ्य, बलाढ्य,) प्रचुर (in comp. as, पुष्पप्रचुर, फलप्रचुर, पर्णप्रचुर, वृक्षप्रचुर,) मय (in comp. as, जलमय, वृक्षमय &c.)

2 पुष्कळ, बहुत, फार, विपुल, प्रचुर,उदंड, सुबलक, *or*स, प्रशस्त. —intensely; *superabundant, overflowing, &c.*v. EXUBERANT. महामुर, मनस्वी, मनमुराद, अतिरिक्त, समृद्ध, अतिशय, अतिशयित, चळचळीत, ठेल, घरांघरचा, वाटेवर पडलेला, रानोमाळ पडलेला, झाडोझाड लागलेला.

ABUNDANTLY, ABOUNDINGLY, *adv.* v. A. बहुत, पुष्कळ, फार, पुष्कळपणीं, विपुळपणीं.

To ABUSE, *v. a. vituperate, revile.* शिवी *f. or* शिव्या *f. pl.*देणें, गाळी *f.* देणें, निंदणें, हेटाळणें, कंडणें,निर्भर्त्सणें,झाडणें, हेटाळी *f.*-गालिप्रदान *n.*-छीथू *f.*-निंदा *f.*-&c. करणें *g. of o.* नांवें *n. pl.* ठेवणें,—intensely, vehemently, &c.v. To SCOLD. खरड *or* खरडपट्टी*f.* काढणें *g.of o.* झाज-झाडणें, मंत्रपुष्पांजलि*f.* टाकणें, ताव*m.* देणें, तोंडाचा पट्टा सोडून शिवी देणें, शिव्या *f.pl.* सडकणें *or* सडकून-कचकावून-रगडून-रपाटून-&c. देणें, सोनताव *m.* देणें, उधळपट्टी *f.* काढणें *g.of o.* दांतकिसाळी *f.* करणें, शिव्याची तान *f.* घेणें-झाडणें, लाखोली *f.* उधळणें-उडवणें &c.

—coarsely or filthily. Expressive of this sense there are some scores of filthy formations; but we omit them.

To begin to a. लौकिकावर येणें.

2 *ill use, misuse.* भलत्याकामास लावणें, खुदळणें, घुसडणें, घुसडणी *f.*-घुसडा*m.* करणें *g.of o.*असदूव्यापार*m.*-असाधूपभोग *m.* -असदूव्यवहार*m.*-असत्प्रयोग *m.*-असत्विनियोग *m.*-कुव्यवहार*m.*-&c. करणें *g. of o.*

3 *trick*, v. To DECEIVE. ठकवणें, भोळसावणें, भोळावणें, फसवणें, फशी देणें-पाडणें.

4 *violate,defile.*बलात्कार*m.*-बळजोरी *f.*-जुलूम*m.*-जबरदस्ती-&c. करणें *with* वर *of o.* बाटवणें, भ्रष्ट करणें, असन्मैथुन *n.*-कुव्यवाय *m.* करणें.

ABUSE, ABUSING, *n.* v.V. 1. —*act.* हेटाळणें *n.* &c. हेटाळणी *f.* हेटाळी *f.* गालीप्रदान *n.* छीथू *f.* निंदा *f.* निंदन *n.* निर्भर्त्सना *f.* निर्भर्त्सन *n.* भर्त्सना *f.* कुत्सा *f.* जुगुप्सा *f.* कुत्सन *n.* विकथन *n.* तर्जन *n.* घृणा *f.* गर्हा *f.* गर्हणा *f.* वाचिकहिंसा *f.*

—intensely, vehemently, &c. दांतकसाळ *or* ळी *or* दांतकिसाळी *f.* खरवड *or* खरड *f.* खरडपट्टी *f.* खरडी *f.* उधळपट्टी *f.* मुंडन *pop.* मुंडण *n.*

2-*act.* खुदळणें *n.* &c. घुसडणी *f.* असदूव्यापार *m.* असदूव्यवहार *m.* असदूप्रयोग*m.*असदूविनियोग *m.* कुव्यवहार *m.*असाधूपभोग *m.*

3—*act.* ठकवणें *n.* &c. ठकवणूक *f.* ठकवणी *f.* वंचना *f.*

4—*act.* भ्रष्ट करणें *n.* बाटवणें *n.* &c. बलात्कार *m.* जुलूम *m.* कुव्यवाय *m.* असन्मैथुन *n.* असदुपभोग *m.*

I. *abusive language.* शिवी*f. or* शिव्या *f. pl.* गाळी *f.* गाली *f.* शिवीगाळ *or* ळी *f.* दुर्भाषण *n.*दुरुक्ति *f.* दुरुक्त*n.*दुर्वचन *n.*दुर्वाच्य *n.* दुरुत्तर *n.* अपभाषण *n.* अपशब्द *m.* गालीगलोची *f.* दांताचें विष *n.* वाक्पारुष्य *n.*

Strain of a. Torrent, shower, volley, &c. of a. शिव्याची तान *f.* लाखोली *f.* [गर्हित,

ABUSED, *p.* v. V. 1. निंदलेला, &c. निंदित, निर्भर्त्सित, कुत्सित,

To be a. शिवी *f.* खाणें.

ABUSINGLY, ABUSIVELY, *adv.* v. A. 1. शिवी-गाळी &c.-देऊन, हेटाळणी-&c. करून, निंदापूर्वक, निर्भर्त्सना -&c. पूर्वक, हेडस फेडस.

ABUSIVE, *a.* v.V.1. *vituperative, scurrilous, &c.* शिवरा, तोंडाळ, गाळ्यारा, अर्वाच्य, निंदक, निंदाखोर, दांतकसाळ्या, तोंडाचा फटकळ, निंदापरायण, निंदापर, मुखर, वाग्दुष्ट, कुटाळ, कुटाळखोर.

To grow or become a. तोंड*n.* सुटणें-माजणें-फिरणें *g. of s.* तोंडाचापट्टा *m.* सुटणें *g. of s.*

Terms for *an busive person*, corresponding with *scurrilous dog, black-mouthed, foul spoken, loose-tongued, &c. fellow, are* कुत्र्याचें तोंड, तोंडास कुत्रें बांधलेला, कुत्र्याचें मूत, तोंडाचा पट्टा सुटलेला, ज्याचे जिभेस हाड नाहीं, तोंड-सुटलेला-माजलेला &c. पिंगूळ *m.*

I.—words, language.&c.शिवीचा, गाळीचा, निंदापर, निंदारूप.

To ABUT, *v. n. border upon.* भिडणें, सीमासंयोग*m.* असणें *g.of s.* with शीं *of o.* लागून असणें, लगत *f.*-लगता*m.* असणें *g. of o.*

ABUTMENT, ABUTTING, *n.* v. V. *state.* लगत *f.* लगता *m.* सीमासंयोग*m.* मर्यादैक्य*n.* क्षेत्रांतर-देशांतर-स्थलांतर-&c. सन्निधि*f.*

ABUTTAL, ABUTMENT,*n. headland.* सीमासंधि *m.*

ABYSM, ABYSS, *n.bottomless gulf.* अगाध-अतलस्पर्श-&c. आखात *n.* विवर *n.*-&c.

2 *deep water*. अगाधजल *n*. न्हद *m*.

ABYSSINIAN, *n*. हबशी *m*. सिद्दी *or* सिद्धी *m*.

ACACIA, *n*. *gum-arabic-tree*. बाभूळ *or* बाभळ *f*. Some *species* or *varieties* are देवबाभूळ *f*. *or* किंकर *f*., पुळाटी *f*. *or* रामकांटी *f*.

2—the gum. बाभळीचा डिंक *or* डीक*m*.-गोंद*m*.

ACADEMIAL, ACADEMIC, ACADEMICAL, *a*. *belonging to an academy*. विद्यालयसंबंधी, पाठशालासंबंधी, मठसंबंधी, शालासंबंधी.

ACADEMIAN, ACADEMICIAN, *n*. *member of an a*. विद्यार्थी *m*. गणाभ्यंतर *m*. विद्यालयाभ्यासी *m*. पाठशालाभ्यासी *m*.

ACADEMY, *n*. *association of learned men*. पंडितसमूह*m*. पंडितगण*m*. पंडितसंघात*m*. विद्वन्मंडली*f*. विद्वज्जनमंडली*f*. विद्वत्समाज*m*. विज्ञव्रज*m* विद्वद्वृंद *n*.

2 *place of education*. शाला *f*. पाठशाला *f*. विद्याभ्यासस्थान*n*. विद्यालय *m*. मठ *m*.

To ACCEDE, *v*. *n*. *assent to*, v. To AGREE. मान्य-कबूल-अनुमत, &c. होणें, अनुमोदन *n*.-अनुमति *f*.-सम्मति *f*. देणें.

To ACCELERATE, *v*. *a*. *expedite*, v.To HASTEN.गति*f*. वाढविणें *g.of o*.गतिवर्द्धन*n*.-गतिवृद्धि *f*.-गतित्वरा*f*.-त्वरावर्द्धन *n*.-वेगवर्द्धन *n*. -वेगवृद्धि *f*.- त्वरोत्तेजन *n*. करणें.

ACCELERATED, *p*. v. V. वेगवर्द्धित, त्वरावर्द्धित, &c.

ACCELERATION, *n*. v. V.—*act*. वेगवर्द्धन *n*. त्वरावर्द्धन *n*. गतिवर्द्धन *n*.—*act* or *state*. वेगवृद्धि *f*.गतिवृद्धि*f*.

ACCELERATIVE, *a*. v. V. *adding to velocity*. त्वरा *f*.-वेग *m*.-गति *f*.-&c. वाढवणारा, त्वरावर्द्धक, वेगवर्द्धक, गतिवर्द्धक, त्वरोत्तेजक, वेगवृद्धिकर्ता-कारी-कारक-जनक-&c.

ACCENT, *n*. *modulation of the voice*. स्वरविकृति *f*. स्वरभेद *m*.

2 *stress or force of voice*. स्वर *m*. जोर*m*. आघात *m*.

Acute a. उदात्त *m*.

Circumflex a. स्वरित *m*.

Grave a. अनुदात्त *m*. प्लुत *mn*.

Attention to a. गुरुलघुविचार *m*.

3 *mark directing the voice*. स्वरचिन्ह *n*. स्वरज्ञापक चिन्ह *n*. स्वरांक *m*. स्वरोद्बोधकांक *m*. स्वरप्रदर्शकांक *m*.

4 *or* accents; *tone, speech*. स्वर *m*. ध्वनि *m*. वाणी *f*.

Pleasing a. सुस्वर *m*.

Soft, gentle, &c. a. कलध्वनि *m*. कलस्वर *m*. कलरव *m*.

Tremulous or broken a. भग्नस्वर *m*.

5 *peculiar tone*. स्वर *pop*. सूर *m*. गळा *m*.

To ACCENT, *To* ACCENTUATE, *v.a*.—in speaking or reading. स्वर *m*. देऊन बोलणें-उच्चारणें-म्हणणें-वाचणें-&c. सस्वर बोलणें-उच्चारणें-&c. स्वरयुक्त बोलणें-उच्चारणें-&c.

2 *mark with an accent or with accents*. स्वराची खूण *f*.-स्वराच्याखुणा *f*. *pl*.-स्वरचिन्ह *n*.-स्वरचिन्हें*n*. *pl*.-&c.देणें-करणें.

To ACCENTUATE, *v*. *n*. *observe the accent*;—in speaking or reading. स्वर*m*. देऊन बोलणें-उच्चारणें-वाचणें-&c. सस्वर बोलणें-उच्चारणें-&c. स्वरयुक्त बोलणें- &c. सस्वरोच्चार *m*.-सस्वरोच्चारण *n*. करणें, स्वरदान*n*. करणें, प्लुतोच्चारण*n*. करणें.

ACCENTED, ACCENTUATED, *p*. v. V. A. 1. सस्वर, स्वरित, स्वरानें उच्चारलेला-म्हटलेला-वाचलेला-&c. सस्वरोच्चारित, सस्वरोक्त, सस्वरोदित, सस्वरपठित, सस्वरकथित, स्वरयुक्त-उच्चारित-उक्त-उदित-कथित-&c. स्वरगत, स्वरप्राप्त, स्वरयुक्त, जातस्वर, स्वरविशिष्ट, स्वरान्वित.

2 स्वराचीखूण-स्वराच्याखुणा- &c.दिलेला-केलेला.

ACCENTER, ACCENTUATER, *n*. v. V. स्वर*m*. देऊन बोलणारा -उच्चारणारा- &c. सस्वर बोलणारा-&c. स्वरयुक्त बोलणारा-&c. सस्वरोच्चार कर्त्ता, स्वरदानकर्त्ता.

ACCENTUATION, ACCENTING, *n*. v. V. A. 1.—*act*. सस्वरोच्चारण*n*. स्वरयुक्तोच्चारण*n*.—*state*. स्वरप्राप्ति *f*. स्वरितता *f*. स्वरयुक्तता *f*. —*a*. *or s*. स्वरयुक्तोच्चार*m*.

v. V. N.—*act*. स्वर देऊन-स्वरानें-सस्वर-स्वरयुक्त बोलणें*n*.-उच्चारणें*n*.-&c. सस्वरोच्चार *m*. सस्वरोच्चारण *n*.स्वरदान *n*.स्वरपालन *n*. प्लुतोच्चारण*n*. सस्वरोक्ति *f*. सस्वरकथन*n*. सस्वरपठण*n*. स्वरयुक्तोच्चारण *n*. स्वरयुक्तोक्ति *f*.

To ACCEPT, *v*. *a*. *receive kindly*. घेणें, कृपाकरून घेणें, ग्रहण *n*. करणें *g*. *of o*. मान्य-गोड करून घेणें, मानून घेणें, स्वीकारणें, प्रतिग्रह *m*.-स्वीकार *m*.-स्वीकरण *n*.-ग्रह *m*.-आदान *n*.-उपादान *n*. करणें *g*. *of o*.

2 (a bill of exchange.) सकारणें, सचकारणें, आदर*m*. करणें *g*. *of o*. पतकरणें.

ACCEPTABLE, *a*. v. V. 1. घ्याया-चा-सारखा-योग्य-जोगता-जोगा, ग्रहणीय, ग्राह्य, ग्रहणार्ह, ग्रहणोपयुक्त, प्रतिग्राह्य, प्रतिगृह्य, स्वीकरणीय, आदेय, उपादेय, समादेय.

I. v. AGREEABLE. आवडता, मान्य, प्रिय, काम्य, मनोरम.

ACCEPTABLENESS, *n*. v. A. 1. घ्यायाची योग्यता *f*.-अर्हता *f*.&c. ग्राह्यता *f*. ग्रहणार्हता *f*. ग्रहणोपयुक्तता *f*.

I. आवडतेपणा *m*. काम्यता *f*.

ACCEPTABLY, *adv*. v. A. 1. ग्रहण होई असें, पसंत होण्यासारखा, मर्जीस उतरायासारखा, मर्जीमाफक-सारखा-जोगा *a*. *dec*. पसंतीनें, यथायोग्य, योग्य.

ACCEPTANCE, ACCEPTATION, ACCEPTING,*n*.v.V.1.—*act*.घेणें *n*. ग्रहण *n*. उपादान *n*. स्वीकरण *n*. आदान *n*.—*a*. *or s*. ग्रह*m*. स्वीकार*m*. प्रतिग्रह*m*.

2—*act*. सकारणें*n*. पतकरणें *n*. आदरण *n*.—*a*. *or s*. सकार *m*. आदर*m*. सचकार*m*. सकराई *f*.

Charge for a. सकराई *f*.

ACCEPTATION, *n*. (as of a word.) v. MEANING. शक्तिग्रह *m*. अर्थबोध *m*.

The common or popular a. रूढि *f*. प्रवृत्ति *f*. बहुमत *n*.

ACCEPTED, *p*. v. V. 1. घेतलेला, ग्रहण केलेला, स्वीकार-&c. केलेला, गृहीत, स्वीकृत, प्रतिगृहीत, उपात्त.

2—सकारलेला, आदर केलेला, पतरलेला, आदृत.

To be a. पटणें, सकारणें.

I. *received by grace, favored*. अनुगृहीत.

ACCEPTER, *n*. v. V. 1. घेणारा, ग्रहण करणारा, ग्राहक, स्वीकार-प्रतिग्रह-&c. करणारा, ग्रहण-स्वीकार-&c. कर्त्ता, प्रतिग्राहक, प्रतिग्राही.

2 सकारणारा, &c.सकार-सचकार-आदर-&c.-करणारा.

ACCESS, *n*. *coming to*,v. APPROACH. येणें*n*. पावणें*n*. आगम*m*. आगमन*n*. आगति*f*. आयान*n*. उपागम*m*.

2 *way of coming to*. वाट *f*. मार्ग *m*. आगमनमार्ग *m*. आयानपथ *m*. आगतिपथ *m*.

3 *liberty of coming to*. गति *f*. येण्याची मोकळीक *f*.-परवानगी *f*.-आज्ञा *f*.-&c. प्रवेश *m*. चलती *f*. मुक्तद्वार *n*. आगमाज्ञा *f*. आगत्यनुज्ञा *f*. आगममुक्तता *f*. आगमाप्रतिबंध *m*.

4 (of a fever, fit, &c.) चढ *m*. भरती *f*.भरतें *n*. भरून येणें*n*.

आवेश *m.* (esp. in comp. as ज्वरावेश, कामावेश, क्रोधावेश, &c.) प्राप्ति *f. or* संप्राप्ति *f.* (esp. in comp. as ज्वरप्राप्ति, ज्वर-संप्राप्ति, &c.).

5 See INCREASE. [फी, कुसहायकारी, कुसहाय.

ACCESSARY, *a. assistant to a crime.* मिळणीचा, सामील, मिला-

2 *helpful, contributive,* v. CONDUCIVE. सहाय, सहकारी, उपकारक, उपकारी, उपयोगी, उपयुक्त, उपकर्त्ता.

ACCESSARY, *n. helper in a crime.* साग्या *m.* कुसहाय *c.* अशुभ-सहायकर्त्ता *m.* कुकर्मसहकर्त्ता *m.*

2 *thing a. or helpful.* उपस्कर *m.*

ACCESSIBLE, *a.* v. N. 1. याया *or* पावाया-चा-योग्य-जोगता-जोगा, आगम-&c. व्हाया जोगता, यायास सोपा, आगम्य, गम्य, गमनीय, सुगम, सुगम्य, आयानयोग्य, आयानार्ह, अभिगम्य, अभिगमनीय, अभिगंतव्य, उपसार्य, सवघड.

1—of persons. सहज भेटणारा, सुलभ, दर्शनसुलभ.

ACCESSIBLENESS, *n.* v. A. 1. याया *or* पावायाची योग्यता *f.*-शक्यता *f.*-अर्हता *f.*-&c. यायाची सोई *f.* आगम्यता *f.* गमनीयता *f.* सुगमता *f.* आयानयोग्यता *f.* आयानार्हता *f.* आगमनार्हता *f.* सौगम्य *n.* सवघडपणा *m.*

ACCESSION, *n. increment,* v. INCREASE. वाढ *f.* वृद्धि *f.*

2 (to the throne.) गादीवर बसणें *n.* गादीचा अधिकार *m.* येणें-प्राप्त होणें *n.*-&c. *inv. con.* सिंहासनप्राप्ति *f.* राजासनप्राप्ति *f.* राजाधिकारापत्ति *f.* राजपदावाप्ति*f.* राजत्वसंप्राप्ति*f.* राज्यधूराप्ति*f.* छत्रचामरोपलब्धि *f.*

3—to an office, gener. अधिकारागम *m.* अधिकारसंप्राप्ति *f.* अधिकारप्राप्ति *f.* अधिकारोपलब्धि *f.*

4 *or* ACCEDING TO, v. V.1.—*act.* मान्य होणें *n.* कबूल होणें*n.* अनुमोदन *n.*-अनुमति *f.* देणें *n.*

5 (of a fever, &c.) See ACCESS.

ACCESSORY, See ACCESSARY.

ACCIDENCE, *n. rudiments of grammar.* व्याकरणमूलतत्वें *n. pl.* व्याकरणपूर्वांश *m.* व्याकरणप्रथमांश *m.* व्याकरणादि *m.* अष्टाध्यायी *f.* चतुर्दशसूत्री *f.*

ACCIDENT, *n. non-essential quality or mode; circumstance, adjunct.* आगंतुकधर्म *m.* आहार्यधर्म *m.* असहजधर्म *m.* अमूलधर्म *m.* कृत्रिमधर्म *m.* आगंतुक-&c. गुण *m.* अस्वाभाविकगुण *m.*

2 *chance, casualty, contingency, fortuitousness.* योग *m.* संयोग *m.* मध्येयोग *m.* दैवयोग *m.* यदृच्छा *f.* अकारणत्व *n.*

By a. v. ACCIDENTALLY. दैवानें, दैवयोगेंकरून.

By rare a. कर्मधर्मसंयोगानें.

3 an a. *a casual occurrence,an incident.* दैवानें घडून आलेली गोष्ट *f.* दैवघटितगोष्ट *f.* दैवसिद्धगोष्ट *f.* दैवकृत्य *n.*

4 an evil a. *a disaster,* v. CALAMITY. अवचट *n.* अनिष्टापात *m.* अरिष्ट *n.* आदान *n.* आदावत *f.*

Accidents,—compreh. जडजोखीम *n.*

Fatal a. अपघात *m.*

In case of a. जडजोखीम पडल्यास.

ACCIDENTAL, *a.* v. N. 1. *non-essential.* आगंतुक, आहार्य, असहज, असहजसिद्ध, आरोपित, अस्वाभाविक, असमवायी.

2 *chance, casual, contingent, fortuitous, incidental.* आगंतुक, असांकेतिक, असंकेतित, दैवजात, दैवयोगिक, दैवनिर्मित, दैवहेतुक, दैवोपस्थित, दैवागत, दैवघटित, यदृच्छाजात, यदृच्छाभूत, अकारणोद्भव, निर्हेतुकोत्पन्न, अनिमित्तोत्पन्न, यायी, आपतिक, अकल्पित, अनिश्चित, काकतालीयन्यायवत्.

ACCIDENTALLY, *adv.* v. A. 1. आगंतुकधर्मानें, आहार्यधर्मेंकरून, आगंतुकत्वपूर्वक.

2 दैवयोगेंकरून, दैवानें, दैववशात्, दैववशें, दैवानें *or* दैवें, यदृच्छेकरून, दैवात्, अदृष्टवशात्, अकस्मात्, काकतालीयन्यायानें.

ACCIDENTALNESS, *n.*v.A.1. आगंतुकत्व *n.* आहार्यता *f.* आरोपितत्व *n.* अस्वाभाविकत्व *n.*

2 दैवयोग *m.* यदृच्छा *f.* दैवघटितत्व *n.*

ACCLAIM, ACCLAMATION, *n.* v. SHOUT. जयजयकार *m.* जयजय *m.* जयघोष *m.* जयशब्द *m.* गजर *or* एकगजर*m.* प्रशंसोद्गार *m.*

To ACCLIMATE, ACCLIMATIZE, *v. a. habituate or inure to a climate not native.* परदेशच्या हवेच्या सवयींचा-सात्म्याचा-&c. करणें. [सवयींचा केलेला &c.

ACCLIMATED, ACCLIMATIZED, *p. & a.* v. V. परदेशच्या हवेच्या

To be a. परदेशच्या हवेचें सात्म्य होणें, हवेचा राबता *m.*-राब *m.* पडणें. हवा *f.* &c. शरीरास-प्रकृतीस-&c.मानून जाणें, *all with* स *or* ला *of s.*

ACCLIVITY, *n. acclivousness of ground.* चढण *f.* चढ *m.*

2 an a. *a rising ground.* चढण *f.* चढाव *m.* घाटी *f.* डाग *m.f.*

ACCLIVOUS, *a. rising.* चढता, चढणीचा, चढाचा, चढावाचा.

To ACCOMMODATE, *v. a. supply with a convenience.* सोई *f.* करणें, बेगमी *or* बेजमी *f.* करणें, गरज *f.* चालविणें.

2 *adapt,* v. To FIT. जम *m.*-जवा *m.*-जुगल *f.*-जुळणी *f.*-&c. बसविणें-पाडणें-घालणें-करणें, जमवणें.

3 *reconcile, make consistent.* जमवणें,जुळणी *f.*-जम*m.*-मेळ*m.* -समेट *m.*-मिलाफ*m.* घालणें-करणें करून देणें.

ACCOMMODATE, *a. suitable,* v. FIT. योग्य, लायक.

ACCOMMODATING, *a. obliging,* v.KIND. परोपकारशील, परोपकारी.

ACCOMMODATION, *n. conveniences as respects lodgings.* राहण्याची सोई *f.* जाग्याची-बिऱ्हाडाची सोई *f.*

ACCOMPANIER, *n.*ACCOMPANYING, *p.a.* v. V. 1. *and* COMPANION. संगें-&c. जाणारा-येणारा-चालणारा, सहगति-सहगमन-&c. कर्त्ता, सहगामी, सहचर, सहचारी, संसर्गी, सहचरित, संयायी, अनुषंगी, आनुषंगिक.

2 संगें-&c. असणारा-राहणारा, संगति-संग-समागम-सहवास-&c. करणारा, सहवासी, संगी (esp. in comp. as सत्संगी, साधुसंगी, दुष्टसंगी,) सोबती, साथी, सहस्थित, सोबत धरणारा, अनुषंगी, आनुषंगिक, समवेत, समेत.

ACCOMPANIMENT, ACCOMPANYING, *n.* v. V. 1.—*act.* संगें-&c. जाणें *n.*-येणें *n.* सहगति *f.* सहगमन *n.* &c.

2—*state.* संगें-&c. असणें-राहणें*n.* संगति *f.* संग*m.* सहस्थिति *f.* अनुषंग *m.* समवस्थान *n.* सहवर्त्तमानत्व *n.*

I.—*thing accompanying.* संगें असणारा-आनुषंगिक वस्तु *n.*-विषय *m.* पदार्थ *m.*-कर्म *n.*-&c.

To ACCOMPANY,*v.a. go or come with.* संगें-संगतीं *or* तें-समागमें-सहित-बराबर-&c. जाणें-येणें-चालणें &c. सहगति *f.*-सहगमन*n.*-संयान *n.*-संसर्ग *m.*-साहचर्य *n.*-सहचरत्व *n.* करणें.

2 *be with, associate,&c.* संगें-संगतीं *or* तें समागमें-&c. असणें, राहणें, संगति *f.* करणें, संग *m.*-समागम *m.*-सहवास *m.*-सोबत *f.* करणें, संघट्टणें, सहस्थिति *f.*-समवस्थान*n.*-सहवर्त्तमानत्व*n.* करणें.

ACCOMPLICE, *n. associate in crime.* साग्या*m.* मिलाफी *m.*दुष्कर्मीचा सोबती *m.* मिळणीचा मनुष्य*m.* कुसहाय *c.* कुकर्मसहचारी *m.*

Accomplices.—gener. सागेलागे *m. pl.*

To Accomplish, *v. a. complete, consummate, achieve, effect, execute fully.* साधणें, संपादणें, क्षेपणें, जोडणें, झोकणें, पेलणें, उरकणें, उलगडणें, अटपणें, निभावणें, निर्वाहणें, तारणें, अनुष्ठणें, साध्यकरणें, तडीस *or* थडीस लावणें-नेणें-आणणें-घालणें-पोहोंचवणें-&c. पार *adv.* पाडणें, तरीपार करणें, शेवटास नेणें, बजावणें, पूर्ण-स.पूर्ण-सिद्ध-&c. करणें, सिद्धीस नेणें, परिणामास आणणें, सर करणें, आराधन *n.*-आराधना *f.*-संपादन *n.*-संपादणी *f.*-संपादणूक *f.*-&c. करणें *g. of o.* [&c. करणें.

2 (a period or term) *complete, fill.* भरणें, पूर्ण-पुरा- पुरता-

3 (a prophecy, &c.) v. To Fulfil. पूर्ण-पुरा-&c. करणें, पुरवणें, सत्य करणें. [करणें.

4 *attain, obtain,* v. To Get. संपादणें, साधणें, मिळवणें, प्राप्त

Accomplishable, *a.* v. V. 1. *and* Attainable. साधाया-चा-जोगता-जोगा- &c. साध्य, (used abundantly in comp. as *easily a.* अल्पसाध्य, अनायाससाध्य, *hardly a.* श्रमसाध्य, कष्टसाध्य, and धनसाध्य, ज्ञानसाध्य, बलसाध्य, शौर्यसाध्य, पराक्रमसाध्य, धैर्यसाध्य, अनेकसाध्य, बहुसाध्य, हस्तसाध्य, &c.) संपादनीय.

2 भराया-चा-&c. पूर्ण कराया-चा-&c.

3 पुरवाया-चा-&c. पूर्ण कराया-चा-&c.

4 साधाया-चा-&c. संपादनीय, साध्य, प्राप्य, प्राप्तव्य, संप्राप्य.

Accomplished, *p.* v.V.1. साधलेला, क्षेपलेला, उरकलेला, तडीसनेलेला, &c. समाप्त, साध्य, साधित, सिद्ध, संपादित, संपन्न, समापित, समापन्न, आराधित, निष्पादित, निष्पन्न, संस्थित, प्रतिष्ठित.

To be a. तडीस *or* थडीस लागणें येणें-जाणें-पोहोंचणें, पार *adv.* पडणें, तरीपार *adv.* होणें, शेवटास येणें.

2 पुरा-पुरता केलेला- झालेला, पूर्ण, संपूर्ण, भरलेला &c.

3 पूर्ण, पूर्ण केलेला-झालेला.

4 संपादित, साध्य, मिळवलेला, प्राप्त, आराधित.

I. *complete in acquirements, finished, proficient.* v. Clever. गुणी, गुणाढ्य, गुणिजन, बहुगुणी, गुणसंपन्न, सकलगुणसंपन्न, कलाकुशल, अभ्यासप्रवीण, सर्वसिद्ध, दीक्षित, सिद्ध, तरबेत *or* द.

Some terms for *An a. person* are सभादीप, सभादीपक, सभारत्न, तेजः पुंज, अपरसूर्य. *See further under* Clever.

Accomplisher, *n.* v. V. 1. साधणारा, संपादणारा, &c. साध्य करणारा, तडीस लावणारा-नेणारा &c. साधक, संपादक, समापक.

2 भरणारा, पूर्ण करणारा.

3 पूर्ण-सत्य-पुरा- &c. करणारा.

4 संपादणारा &c. संपादनकर्ता, संपादक.

Accomplishment, *n.* v. V. 1.—*act.* साधणें *n.* तडीस नेणें *n.*&c. साधन *n.* साधणूक *f.* संपादणी *f.* संपादणूक *f.* संपादन *n.* निष्पादन *n.* समापन *n.* आसाधन *n.* आसादन *n.*

—*state.* संपादणूक *f.* समाप्ति *f.* सिद्धि *f.* सिद्धता *f.* निष्पत्ति *f.* इतिश्री *f.* संस्थिति *f.*

A means of a. साधनसूत्र *n.*

A. of an undertaking. साध्यसिद्धि *f.*

2—*act.* भरणें *n.* पूर्ण-&c. करणें *n.* पूरण *n.*

—*state.* भरती *f.* भरलेपणा *m.* पूर्णता *f.* पूर्णत्व *n.*

I. *an a. an attainment, a grace.* शोभा *f.* अलंकार *m.* भूषण *n.* गुण *m.* कसब *n.*

Accomplishments—compreh. कळाकुसरी *f. pl.*

To Accord, *v.n.* v. To Agree. मिळणें, जमणें, बसणें, बनणें, संभवणें.

To Accord, *v. a.* See To Settle, To Give.

Accord, *n. just correspondence,* v. Agreement. मेळ *m.* जम *m.* जमाव *m.* बनाव *m.*

2 *union of heart,* v. Agreement. एकचित्त *n.* मिलाफ *m.* एकोपा *m.* ऐक्य *n.* सम्मति *f.*

With one a. एकचित्तानें, एकमतानें *or* एका चित्तानें- एका मतानें, एक बुद्धीनें, एकजुटीनें.

3 own a. ; *spontaneous agreement with.* स्वसंतोष *m.* आपखुशी *f.*

Of one's own a. आपले आपण, आप, आपजांत, आपोआप, आपआप, आपशांच *or* आपशेंच, स्वतः *pop.* स्वतां, सुखासंतोषानें, सुखासमाधानानें, सुखासुखीं, आत्मसंतोषानें, स्वभावीक.

Accordance, *n.*v. V.N.*and* Agreement.—*state.* मेळ *m.* जम *m.* जमाव *m.* बनाव *m.*

In a. with. अन्वयें, अन्वयानें, बेतानें, बरहुकूम.

Accordant, *a.* According, *p. a.*v. V.N. मिळणारा &c. मिलाफाचा, बेताचा, अनुकूल, माफक.

2 *and* Accordantly, Accordingly, *conformable, conformably.* N. B. The word, being never a *preposition,* is not here treated as such. प्रमाणें (in comp. as ह्याप्रमाणें, त्याप्रमाणें, मोलाप्रमाणें,&c.), सारखा (in comp. as मालासारखा, केल्यासारखा, &c.), बरहुकूम, बमुजीब, माफक, अनुरूप(in comp. as आज्ञानुरूप, कालानुरूप, देशानुरूप, एतदनुरूप, तदनुरूप, &c.), अनुसार (in comp. as श्रमानुसार, सामर्थ्यानुसार, गुणानुसार &c.), यथा (in comp. as यथान्याय, यथाविधि, यथाशक्ति, &c.), परत्वें *or* परत्वेंकरून (in comp. as ज्ञानपरत्वें *or* परत्वेंकरून, वयोपरत्वें, गुणपरत्वें, योग्यतापरत्वें, &c.), परी (in comp. as वडिलांपरी, लेंकरांपरी, &c.), अनुलक्षून (lit. regardingly, observingly, advertently; as योग्यता अनुलक्षून काम सांगावें), वारीं (in comp. as तृणावारीं मोजणें, पाण्यावारीं खरचणें, &c.), गत (in comp. as वेड्याचेगत), यथावत्.

Accordion, *n.* एक वाद्याचें नांव आहे.

To Accost, *v. a. speak to first.* हटकणें, पहिल्यानें बोलणें, संबोधणें, प्राक्भाषण *n.*-आदिभाषण *n.* करणें.

Accouchement, *n.* v. Delivery. प्रसव क्रिया *f.*

Accoucheur. *n.* प्रसवकारविद्य *m.* सूतिवैद्य *m.*

Account, *n.* (of debts, expenses, costs.) हिशेब *or* हिशोब *m.* जमाखर्च *m.* मोसबा *m.* आयव्यय *m.*

There are certain *Lines* drawn in *Papers of accounts:* and these have particular significancies and particular names. Some are अज, अडांक, एकुणात, दुकारी, बीत, वासलात, हिशेब हिशोब *or* हिशेब कितेब. [डणी *f.*

Abstract, or General a. अडावा *m.*-Framing of it. सदरघ-

Budget or bag of accounts. रुमाल *m.* हातरुमाल *m.*

Current a. चालता हिशेब *m.*-जमाखर्च *m.*

Payment-side of an a. खर्च *m.* To enter (an item)upon it. खर्चांत लिहणें-मांडणें.

Receipt-side of an a. जमा *f.* To commit or enter upon it. जमा धरणें-करणें, जमेस धरणें.

Rough a. कच्चा आकार *m.* कच्चा हिशेब *m.* कच्चा खरडा *m.*

Rough entry into an a. एकबेरजी *f.*

Running a अलाल हिशेब *m.* अलालनामा *m.*

Belonging or relating to accounts. जमाखर्ची, जमाखर्चा-

बा, हिशेबी or हिशोबी, हिशेबाचा or हिशोबाचा.

Remaining over of an a. उचार.

That has an a. with खातेवाईक.

To balance an a. शिल्लक झाडा m. काढणें-उतरणें, खातेबाकी or बाकी f. काढणें, जमाखर्च m. करणें.

To call to a. fig. हिशोबm.-झाडा m.-झडती f.-झाडाझडती f.-&c. घेणें, पाहून घेणें, पुसून घेणें, पुसणें.

To clear accounts. झाडा m.- झडती f.-&c. काढणें, फडशाm. करणें, फारीख f.-दुफेरफे or. रफेदफे f. करणें, बाकी f. पूज करणें.

To have an a. with. खातें n. असणें g.of s. recipr.

To make up and settle accounts or an a. बजावाट f.-फडशा m.-&c. करणें.

To put to the a. of. नांवावर-नांवें &c. लिहणें-मांडणें g.of s. खातीं लिहणें-मांडणें-धरणें g.of s.

To turn to a. कारणीं-कार्यास-&c.लावणें, फळास-लाभास-&c. आणणें, and v. n. कामावर पडणें, कामास येणें, फळास-लाभास-&c. येणें.

2 regard, estimation, v. VALUE. हिशेब m. लेखा m. गणती f. किंमत f. मजकूर m. खिसगणती f. (neg. con.) केवा m. (neg. con.).

3 narrative, statement, relation, story. इतिहासm. मजकूर m. कैफियत f. गोष्ट f. कथा f. अहवाल m. वाका m. हकिकत f. बयाणा or नाम. खबर f. वृत्तांतm. वृत्तकथनn. वृत्तनिरूपणn. वृत्तवर्णन n. वृत्तांतवर्णन n. इतिहासाख्यापन n. इतिहासव्याख्यान n. वार्त्ताकीर्त्तन n.

Accounts, tidings, v.NEWS. बातमीf. खबरf. वृत्तांतm.वृत्तn.

Accounts of emissaries, v. INTELLIGENCE. अखबार or अखबर f.

Circumstantial a. तपशील m.

Detailed a. वाचन f. [पण n.

True and exact a. कर्मकथा f. इत्थंभूतकथन n. इत्थंभूतनिरू-

Written a. हकिकतनामा m.

4 explanation, assignment of causes. निर्वचनn. हेतुकथन n. निदानकीर्त्तनn. बीजनिर्देश m.n. कारणाख्यापन n. प्रयोजनवर्णन n. इतिकृत्योपदेशm. एवंविधा f. इतिक्रियानिरूपण n.

5 ground, v. REASON. निमित्त n. कारण n. सबब f.

On a. of. मुळें, (ex. ह्यामुळें, पावसामुळें &c.) साठीं, करितां, वाचन, बाबें, पायीं, निमित्त, (ex. लबाडीनिमित्त मारलें,) अर्थी, अर्थ (in comp. with Sanskrit words, as एतदर्थ, तदर्थ &c.) प्रीत्यर्थ.

On that a. त्यामुळें-स्तव-साठीं &c.

On this a. ह्यामुळें-स्तव-कारणें, अतएव, अतःकारणात्, अतः.

6 invoice, inventory, catalogue, v. LIST. याद f. मोजदादीची याद f. झडती f.

To take an a. झडती f.-टीप f. घेणें, मोजदास्त f.-गणना f.-याद f.-संख्या f. करणें.

ACCOUNT-BOOK, n. खातेवही f. वही f. चोपडी f. हिशेबाची वही f.

To ACCOUNT, v. a. reckon, regard, v. To VALUE. गणणें, लेखणें, मानणें, मोजणें.

To ACCOUNT, v. n. for; assign causes. कारणn. सांगणें, प्रयोजनवर्णनn.-कारणाख्यापन n.-इतिकृत्योपदेश m. इतिक्रियानिरूपण n.-बीजनिर्देश m.-&c. करणें.

2 for; answer for. हिशेबm.-जाबm.-मोसबाm.-झाडाm.-&c.देणें,

ACCOUNTABLE, a. v. V. N. 1. वाच्य, निर्वाच्य, निर्वचनीय, निरूप्य कारण, निर्वाच्यबीज, निर्देश्य, व्याख्येय, आख्यापनीय.

2 v. ANSWERABLE. हिशेब-जाब-मोसबा &c. देणारा, जबाबदार, मोसबेदार, उत्तर देण्याचा अधिकारी.

To be a. for. मोसबा m. माथ्यावर असणें g. of s.

ACCOUNTABLENESS, ACCOUNTABILITY, n. v.A. 2 मोसबेदारी f. जबाबदारी f. उत्तर देण्याचा अधिकार m.

ACCOUNTANT, n. one skilled in a. हिशेबी or हिशोबीm. गणकm.

Accurate and exact a. संख्यावित्m.कोरड्या टांकानें हिशोब करणार-देणारा-&c.

2 keeper of accounts. मोसबेदार m. हिशेबदार m. मुतसद्दी m.

To ACCOUTRE, v.a. equip with arms, arm. हत्यारबंद or हतेरबंद-शिलेपोस्त or पोस-शिल्याभाल्यानिशीं सिद्ध or सज्ज-आयुधसज्ज-आयुध सिद्ध-सायुध-सशस्त्र-&c. करणें, सायुधीकरण n.-सशस्त्रीकरणn.-&c. करणें g. of o.

2 (with dress, trappings, gener.) equip. सजवणें, सजणें, सज्जनn.-सज्जना f.-&c. करणें g. of o. संजोगणें.

ACCOUTRED, p. v. V. 1. हत्यारबंद or हतेरबंद, सज्ज, सज्जित, सायुध, सशस्त्र, शस्त्रपाणि, शस्त्री, शस्त्रसज्ज, शस्त्रधर, शिलेपोस्त or पोस, उपात्तशस्त्र, सन्नद्ध.

2 सजलेला, &c. सज्ज, सज्जित, सज्जीरून, सज्य, कडीकोट.

ACCOUTREDNESS, n.v.P.1. हत्यारबंदी or हतेरबंदी f.शस्त्रसज्जता f. सशस्त्रता f. सज्जता f.

2 सजलेलेपणा m. सज्जता f. सज्जितत्व n.

ACCOUTREMENTS, n. trappings of war.लढाईचा सरंजामm. युद्धोपकरणें n. pl. युद्धोपसाहित्यें n. pl.

2 trappings, gener. साजसरंजाम m. संचसरंजाम m.

ACCOUTRING, n.v.V.1.—act. हतेरबंद करणें n.&c. सायुधीकरण n. सशस्त्रीकरण n. सन्नद्धीकरण n. सप्रहरणीकरण n.

2—act. सजवणें n.&c. सजणी f. सज्जीकरणn. सज्जनn. सज्जना f. ससामग्रीकरण n. सोपकरणीकरण n. सोपस्करीकरण n.

To ACCREDIT, v. a. give authority or credit to. साचपणा m. -खरेपणा m.-&c. आणणें-करणें-देणें-प्राप्त करणें &c. सत्यापन n.-सत्यप्रापणn.-सत्यताज्ञापनn.-प्रामाण्योद्भावनn.-श्रद्धेयतोद्भावनn.-श्रद्धेयतानयन n. करणें.

ACCRETION, n. growing to so as to cause increase. वृद्धिजनक अभिसंयोग m. अन्यसंयोगवर्धन n. समुत्थान n.

To ACCRUE, v. n. arise to, proceed, come from. चढणें, उपजणें, मिळणें, लाभणें, लाधणें, लाहणें, पदरीं येणें-पडणें, प्राप्त होणें, राशी पुंजीस येणें.

ACCUMULABLE, a.v. V. A. सांचाया-चा-जोगता-जोगा &c. संग्राह्य, संग्रहणीय, संचेय.

To ACCUMULATE, v. a. amass, v. To HEAP. सांचवणें, सांठवणें, गोळा करणें, गोळावणें, राशिm.-ढीगm.-&c. करणें-पाडणें, जोडणें, सांठवणn. -संचयm.-संचयनn.-चयनn.-चयm.-&c. करणें g. of o.

To ACCUMULATE, v. n. collect, form in mass or quantity. सांचणें, सांठणें, गोळा होणें.

2—as waters, &c. swell, rise. तुंबणें, चढणें, फुगणें, फुगा m. धरणें. [जमणें.

3—business, matters, &c. increase upon, thicken around.

ACCUMULATED, p. v. V. A. सांचवलेला, सांठवलेला, गोळा केलेला, &c. संचित, संग्रहीत.

v. V. N. 1. सांचलेला, सांठलेला, सांचीव.

ACCUMULATION, *n.* v.V. A. 1.—*act.* सांचवणें *n.* सांठवणें *n.*&c. सांठवण *n.* संचय *m.* चय *m.* संचयन *n.* संचयीकरण *n.*संग्रहण *n.* —*state.* सांचवलेपणा *m.* संग्रह *m.* संचय *m.* चय *m.* संचितत्व *n.*

v. V.N. 1. —*a. or s.* सांचणें *n.* सांठणें *n.* गोळा *m.*

I. *matter accumulated, collection,* v. HEAP. सांठ*m.* सांठा*m.* संग्रह *m.* संचय *m.*

ACCUMULATOR, *n.* ACCUMULATIVE, *a.* v. V. A. सांचवणारा, सांठवणारा, &c. संचयकर्त्ता-कारी- &c. संग्रहकर्त्ता-कारी- &c.

ACCUMULATIVE, *a.* v. V. N. *that is accumulated.* गोळा झालेला, राशीभूत, राशीकृत, पुंजीभूत.

ACCURACY, *n.* v. A. 1. सुत्रेपणा *m.* सुतीपणा *m.* सूत्रकारित्व *n.* अचूकसंधानत्व *n.* सुयंत्रता *f.*

2 खराई *f.* तबताकपणा*m.* रेखलेपणा*m.* सुतीपणा*m.* &c.टापटीप *f.*

ACCURATE, *a. careful in execution; exact, precise, nice.* सुतरा *or* सूत्रा, सूत्रक, सूत्री, सुती, सुतानें काम करणारा, बेतानें काम करणारा, बेत बात्या, बेताबाताचा, टापटिप्या, साचा, खरा, अचूक, अचूकसंधानी, कडकडीत, सुयंत्र.

2 *carefully executed; exact, correct.* तबताक,रेखलेला,रेखला, रेखितसा, मेजलेला, मेजला,बरोबर, बेताचा,बेताबाताचा,बंदिस्त, बंदिस्तीचा, रजपजचा, सुती, सुतानें केलेला,टापटिपेचा,जंजीरबंद, स्पष्ट, सुयंत्र, ठीक, दुरुस्त, शुद्ध.

ACCURATELY, *adv.*v.A. सुतानें, दोरीसूत, बराबर, अचूक, बिनचूक.

ACCURSED, *a.*See CURSED. [शापास्पद.

2 *worthy of being cursed,* v. VILE. दुष्ट, अतिदुष्ट, शापपात्र,

ACCUSABLE, *a.* v. V. 1. दोषलावावयाजोगा, &c. निंदापात्र, दूषणीय, दूषणार्ह, दोषारोपणीय, दूष्य.

ACCUSATION, *n.* v. V. 1.—*act.*दूषणें *n.*&c. अपराधारोप *m.* अपराधारोपण *n.* दोषारोप *m.* दोषारोपण *n.* दोषाधान *n.* दोषाभियोग *m.* अभियोग *m.*

2—*act.* आळ घेणें *n.* बालंट घेणें *n.* &c. अभिशाप *m.* अपवाद *m.* अपजाळ *f.* मिथ्याभिशाप *m.* मिथ्यापवाद *m.*

ACCUSATIVE CASE. *n.* कर्मपद *n.* कर्मणिद्वितीया *f.* कर्म *n.*

To ACCUSE, *v. a. charge, impeach, arraign.* दोषणें, दोष *m.* आणणें-लावणें, दूषण*n.*-अपराधारोप*m.*-अपराधारोपण*n.*-दोषारोप *m.*-दोषारोपण*n.*-दोषाभियोग *m.*-दोषाक्षेप *m.*-आरोप *m.*-अभियोग *m.* करणें, वळवणें.

2—falsely, v. To ASPERSE. आळ *fm.*-तुफान *n.*-बालंट or बलांट*n.* घेणें, कैवाड*n.* रचणें-घेणें *with* वर *of o.* मिथ्यारोप*m.*-मिथ्यापवाद *m.*-मिथ्याभिशाप *m.*-अपवाद*m.* करणें, डोक्यावर खापर*n.* फोडणें, गळां बांधणें, गळीं पडणें.

ACCUSED, *p.* v. V. 1. दोषलावलेला, &c. अभियुक्त, दोषारोपित, अपराधारोपित, दोषाभियुक्त, अपराधाभियुक्त.

2 आळघेतलेला, &c. अभिशप्त, अभिशस्त.

ACCUSER, *n.* v. V. 1. दोष लावणारा, &c. फिर्यादी *m.* वादी *m.* मुद्दई *m.* मुदाईम *m.* दोषारोपक, अपराधारोपक, दूषक, अभियोगी *m.* दोषाभियोगी *m.*

2 v. SLANDERER. आळ-&c. घेणारा, कैवाड रचणारा, अपवादक, अपवादकर्त्ता, अपवादी.

To ACCUSTOM, *v. a. habituate, inure, use.* सवई *f.*-सराव *m.*-अभ्यास*m.*-राबता*m.*-राब *m.*-खांद *m.* पाडणें-लावणें-घालणें, सरावांत आणणें, चोप *f.* लावणें, अभ्यास*m.* करवणें, वहिवाटीखालीं-घसबटीखालीं-अभ्यासाखालीं-&c.or वहिवाटींत-घसबटींत-अभ्यासांत-&c. आणणें-पाडणें, अभ्यासविधान *n.*-अभ्यस्तीकरण *n.* करणें, अभ्यस्त करणें, वहिवाटणें, रांबवणें.

ACCUSTOMED, *p. & a.* v. V. राबता पाडलेला, घसबटींतआणलेला, &c. रांबलेला, रुळलेला, सराव लागलेला, अभ्यस्त.

To be or become a. सबई *f.* पडणें-लागणें, सराव*m.* पडणें, खांद*m.* पडणें, चोप *f.* लागणें, रांबणें, रुळणें, मुरणें—esp. in an ill sense. संवकणें, पडकणें, बळसावणें.

I. *customary,* v. USUAL.नित्यांतला,नित्याभ्यासाचा, परिपाठींतला,नित्यपाठांतला.

ACE, *n.*—at cards. एका *or* एक्का *or* एकया *m.*

2—on a die. पै *or* पव *m.* [रती *f.*

3 *particle, whit,* v. BIT. लेश *m.* काडी *f.* कण *m.* कणिका *f.*

ACERB, *a. roughly sour,* v. SOUR. आंबटतुरट, तुरटांबट, तुरट.

2 fig. (of temper) कडवा, कडू, खाष्टी, कठीण, कठोर.

ACERBITY, *n.*v.A. 1. अंबटाई तुरटाई *f.* तुरटाई अंबटाई *f.* तुरटाई *f.*

2 कडवेपणा *m.* खाष्टपणा *m.* खाष्टीपणा *m.* कठोरपणा *m.*

ACESCENCY, *n.* v. A. अंबूसपणा *m.* अंबसरपणा *m.*

ACESCENT, *a. turning sour, moderately sour.* अंबू लागलेला, अंबटसा, अंबूस, अंबसर, अपूर्णाम्ल, आसन्नाम्ल.

ACETOSE, ACETOUS, *a.* v. SOUR. अंबट, अंबटसा, शुक्त.

ACETOSENESS, *n.* v.A. अंबटपणा *m.* शुक्तता *f.*

To ACHE, *v .n. be in pain.* दुखणें, दुखून येणें.-the head, उठणें.

There are numerous verbs bearing, together with the general sense of *To Ache,* particular aspects or implications. These it is advantageous to set down separately.

To a. and feel broken, laxated, relaxed, &c.—as before fever. कसकसणें, कसणें, फुटणें, मोडून येणें-मोडणें-आंग *n.* कणकणणें, बळणें *n.* घळघळणें, आंगाचा चकनाचूर *m.* वाटणें-होणें.

To a. with soreness and shootings, —as from rheumatism, &c. तिडकणें, शिणकणें, निडीक *f.*-शिणक *f.*-कण *f.* -करक *f.*-कचक *f.*-उसण *f.*-हूक *f.*-शिळक *f.* भरणें-लागणें.

To feel sore, tender, stiff,—as from bruises, a beating, &c. अंबणें, कुस्न होणें.

*To a. with a dull,diffused, and continuing pain.*कसकसणें.

To a. with a sense of stiffness and tenseness,—as from cold. तडतडणें, तडाडणें.

2 (the heart) *be distressed.* दुःख *n.* वाटणें *in con.* दुखारणें, हृद्रोग *m.*-मनोव्यथा *f.* होणें.

ACHE, ACHING, *n.*v.V. *and* PAIN. दुःख *n.*शूल *pop.*शूळ *m.* रग*f.*

ACHIEVABLE, *a.* v. V. साधाया-चा-जोगता-जोगा-सारखा, संपादायाचा-जोगता-&c. साध्य.

To ACHIEVE, *v. a. perform, &c.* v. To ACCOMPLISH. साधणें, सर करणें, संपादणें, साधन *n.*-संपादन*n.*-संपादणी *f.*-संपादणूक *f.*-&c. करणें *g. of o.*

ACHIEVED, *p.* v. V. साधलेला, &c. साधित, संपादित.

ACHIEVEMENT, *n.* v. V.—*act.* साधणें *n.* संपादणें *n.* सर करणें *n.* साधणूक *f.* संपादणी *f.* संपादणूक *f.* साधन *n.* संपादन *n.*

I. *exploit, feat,* v. DEED. मोठें काम *n.* महत्कृत्य*n.* कृतकृत्य*n.* मर्दुमीचें काम *n.* बशर्तीचें काम *n.*

ACID, *a.* v. SOUR. आंबट, अम्ल.

ACIDITY, *n.* v. A. आंबटपणा *m.* अम्लता *f.* अम्लभाव *m.*

I. (on the stomach, &c.) अम्लपित्त *m.*

To ACIDULATE, *v. a. make somewhat acid.* आंबटसा-आंबटसर-ईषदम्ल-आंबूस-किंचिदम्ल-&c. करणें.

ACIDULATED, *p.* v. V. आंबसर-&c. केलेला.

ACIDULOUS, *a. somewhat acid.* आंबटसर, आंबूस, आंबसर, ईषदम्ल, किंचिदम्ल.

ACIDULOUSNESS, *n.* v. A. आंबूसपणा *m.* आंबसरपणा *m* ईषदम्लता *f.*

To ACKNOWLEDGE, *v. a. own knowledge of.* जाणणें, ओळखणें, मानणें.

2 *own, confess, allow, admit.* स्वीकारणें, अंगीकारणें, मानणें, मान्य करणें, कबूल करणें, वदणें, घेणें, हो-होय-हुं-हां-&c. म्हणणें, होय कार *m.*-हुंकार *m.*-होकार *m.* करणें, पदरीं घेणें, आंगावर-शिरावर-माथ्यावर-&c. घेणें, होकारणें, आंगीं लावून घेणें, अंगीकरण *n.*-अंगीकार *m.*-स्वीकरण *n.*-स्वीकार *m.*-प्रतिज्ञा *f.* करणें.

3 (a favor, benefit, &c.) *own, admit.* जाणणें, आदरणें, घेणें, मानणें, उपकार *m.*-कृपा *f.*-सत्कृति *f.* मानणें, जाण *f.* जाणणें, मान्यता *f.* करणें *g. of o.*

4 (virtue, merit, &c.) *recognize, allow and honor.* जाण *f.* जाणणें, आदरणें, जाणणें, ग्रहण *n.* करणें, घेणें, बूज *f.* करणें-राखणें.

5 (a letter, &c.) पैवस्ती *f.*-पहोंच *f.* कळवणें.

ACKNOWLEDGED, *p.* v. V. 1. जाणलेला, ओळखलेला, &c.
2 स्वीकारलेला, अंगीकारलेला, &c. स्वीकृत, अंगीकृत, प्रतिज्ञात.
3 जाणलेला, आदरलेला, &c. [मानणें *n.*

ACKNOWLEDGEMENT, *n.* v. V. 1.—*act.* जाणणें *n.* ओळखणें *n.*
2—*act.* मानणें *n.* स्वीकारणें *n.* &c. स्वीकरण *n.* अंगीकरण *n.* मानणें *n.*—*a. or s.* स्वीकार *m.* अंगीकार *m.* मान्यता *f.* वदणूक *f.* इकरार *m.*
3.—*act.* जाणणें *n.* आदरणें *n.* मानणें *n.* &c. आदरण *n.*
I. *note of hand*, v. RECEIPT, NOTE. दस्तऐवज *m.* खत *n.* रोखा *m.*

ACME, *n.* v. HEIGHT. शिखर *m.* कळस *m.* पराकाष्ठा *f.* भर *m.*

ACNE, *n. pimple on the face*, v. PIMPLE. यौवनकंटक *m.* यौवनपिटका *f.*

ACONITE, *n.* —ferox. वत्सनाभ *m.*
2 v. POISON प्राणहारक *n.*

ACORN, *n.* ओकनामक वृक्षाचें फळ किंवा बीज *n.*

ACOUSTIC, *a. pertaining to hearing.* श्रवणसंबंधी, श्रवणविषयक, श्रुतिसंबंधी, श्रुतिविषयक, श्रौत.

ACOUSTICS, *n. science of sounds.* श्रवणविषयकविद्या *f.* श्रावणविद्या *f.* ध्वनिशास्त्र *n.*
2 *medicines to help hearing.* श्रवणोपकारी औषध *n.*

To ACQUAINT, *v. a. make acquainted with.* v. To INFORM. कळवणें, जाणवणें, बोधणें, बोधवणें, विज्ञापणें, माहितगार-विदित-बोधित-ज्ञात-&c. करणें, बातमी *f.* देणें.

2 (one's self, with) ओळख *f.*-माहितगारी *f.*-माहिती *f.*-वाकबगारी *f.* करणें-करून घेणें *g. of o.* आपणास वाकब-वाकबदार-&c. करणें.

ACQUAINTANCE, ACQUAINTANCESHIP, *n.* (with matters), v. KNOWLEDGE. ओळख *f.* माहितगारी *f.* माहीत *f.* जाणसाळ *f.* परिचय *m.* वाकबगारी *f.* विज्ञान *n.* परीक्षा *f.* वेत्तृत्व *n.*

2 (with persons), ओळख *f.* जानपछान *f.* परिचय *m.* जानसाळ *f.* दंडक *m.*

A.—loosely, indef. gener. &c. ओळखपाळख *f.* ओळखदेख *or* देखओळख *f.* जानपछान *f.*

A. by sight. तोंडओळख *f.*

Bowing a. रामरामी *f.* सलामालकी *f.* सलामी *f.*

Mere a. Slight a. स्नान ओळख *f.* [*g. of o.*

To drop the a. of. हात *m.* सोडणें *g. of o.* ओळख *f.* सांडणें

To have a slight a. with. पोंहची *f.* ओळखणें *g. of o.*

3 *an a. a person known.* ओळखीचा मनुष्य-माणूस-गृहस्थ-गडी-&c. ओळखी *c.* परिचित *c.* जानपछान *m.* यार *m.*

Acquaintances and connections. सुहृत्संबंधी *m. pl.*

A mere a. स्नानओळखी *c.* उदासीन *m.*

Of one's friends or acquaintances. ओळखीदेखी, ओळखीदेखीचा, ओळखीपाळखी, ओळख्यादेख्या, ओळख्यापाळख्या.

ACQUAINTED, *p. a.* v. V. *informed, having knowledge.* माहितगार, माहितदार, वाकबदार, वाकबगार, जातज्ञान, प्राप्तज्ञान, लब्धज्ञान.

To be a. with (a person). ओळख *f.*-परिचय *m.*-जानपछान *f.*-&c. असणें *g. of s. recip.*

I. *known to.* माहीत, परिचित.

ACQUEST. *See* ACQUISITION.

To ACQUIESCE, *v. n. rest satisfied with or in*, v. To AGREE. मान्य-कबूल-राजी-अनुमत-सम्मत-&c. होणें-असणें, होय-बरें-&c. म्हणणें, अनुमोदन *n.* करणें-देणें.

ACQUIESCENCE, ACQUIESCING, *n.* v. V.—*state.* मान्यता *f.* अनुमत *n.* अनुमति *f.* सम्मति *f.* खुशरजावंती *f.*

With ready a. प्रसन्न अंतःकरणें करून. [जावंत.

ACQUIESCENT, *a.* v. V. मान्य, राजी, कबूल, पसंत *or* द, खुशर-

ACQUIRABLE, *a.* v. V. संपादाया-चा-जोगता-जोगा-&c. मिळवाया-चा-जोगा-&c. प्राप्य, प्राप्तव्य, प्रापणीय, लभ्य, उपलभ्य, आप्य, उपार्जनीय, अधिगम्य.

To ACQUIRE, *v. a.* v. To GET. संपादणें, प्राप्त करणें, मिळवणें, जोडणें, अर्जणें, प्राप्ति *f.*-उपार्जन *n.*-उपार्जना *f.*-उपलब्धि *f.*-लब्धि *f.*-&c. करणें *g. of o.*

ACQUIRED, *p.* v. V. मिळवलेला, संपादलेला, &c. प्राप्त, उपार्जित, अर्जित, उपलब्ध, लब्ध, संपादित, आसादित.

ACQUIREMENT, ACQUIRING, ACQUISITION, *n.* v. V.—*act.* मिळवणें *n.* संपादणें *n.* &c. संपादणी *f.* संपादणूक *f.* संपादन *n.* उपार्जन *n.* उपार्जना *f.* अर्जन *n.* अर्जना *f.* आसादन *n.*—*state.* लाभ *m.* प्राप्ति *f.* संप्राप्ति *f.* आपत्ति *f.* (in comp. as इष्टापत्ति, हितापत्ति, दुःखापत्ति, सुखापत्ति, फलापत्ति, स्तुत्यापत्ति, निंदापत्ति, दोषापत्ति,), अवाप्ति *f.* (in comp. as धनावाप्ति, यशोवाप्ति &c.), आप्ति *f.* (in comp. as धनाप्ति &c.), संपत्ति *f.* लब्धि *f.* उपलब्धि *f.*
I. *thing acquired.* संपादलेली गोष्ट *f.*-वस्तू *f.*-&c. लाभ *m.* प्राप्ति *f.* लब्धद्रव्य *n.* उपार्जितद्रव्य *n.*

Acquirements, v. ATTAINMENTS. साधितगुण *m. pl.* उपार्जितगुण *m. pl.*

To ACQUIT, *v. a.* (of criminality), v. To ABSOLVE. निरपराध-निर्दोष-&c. ठरवणें, उघडा माथा *m.*-उजळता माथा *or* उजळ माथा *m.*-उजळ तोंड *n.* करणें *g. of o.* दोषमुक्त करणें.

2 (from obligation or claim), v. To FREE. सोडवणें, मोकळा-मुक्त-&c. करणें, मोकळीक *f.*- सोडवणूक *f.*-सोडवणी *f.*-सोडवण *f.* करणें *g. of o.*

3 (one's self), *act one's part.* आपल्याकडून करायाचें करणें, आपला निर्वाह *m.*-आपला बचाव *m.* करणें, आपल्याकडून करणें-झटणें-उद्योग *m.* करणें.

ACQUITTAL, *n.* v. V. 1.—*act.* निरपराध ठरवणें *n.*&c. अपराधमोचन *n.* दोषमोचन *n.* निर्दोषीकरण *n.* अदोषीकरण*n.*—*state.* दोषमुक्ति *f.* दोषमुक्तता *f.* उघडा माथा *m.* उजळता माथा *m.* उजळ माथा *m.* उजळ तोंड *n.*

ACQUITTANCE, *n. discharge from a debt; discharge, release.* रदकर्ज *n.* ऋणशोधन *n.* ऋणापनयन *n.* ऋणमोचन *n.*
2 *deed of a.* फारखत *n.* फारखती *f.* सोडचिठ्ठी *f.* बेदावापत्र*n. or* बेदावा *m.* निदावापत्र *n. or* निदावा *m.*

ACQUITTED, *p.v.*V.1. उजळमाथ्याचा, उजळतोंडाचा, निरपराध&c. ठरवलेला, अपराधमुक्त, दोषमुक्त, निर्दोषीकृत.

ACRE, *n.* As the land-measures of the Maráthás differ from those of the English they have of course no word answering to acre. For their various measures see under MEASURE.

ACRID, *a. hot and biting,* v. PUNGENT. तिखट *intens.* तिखटडोंब, खवरा *remiss.* खवरट, खंविरडा, खवट, तीक्ष्ण, तिक्त, तीव्र, कटु, प्रखर, खरमरीत, तलख, जहाल *or* झाल, कडक, झणझणीत, जळजळीत, भगभगीत. [कटु, तीक्ष्ण.

ACRIMONIOUS, *a. acrid.* खवरा, खंविरडा, खवट, जहाल *or* झाल,
2 fig. *bitter, malignant, &c.* खवचट, खवट *or* खऊट, कटु *pop.* कडू, दंशी, दंशीक, झोंबायाचा, लागट, लागीर, दंशाचा *or* डंशाचा, डंशी, डंशीक.

ACRIMONIOUSLY, *adv.* v. A. 2. खवचटपणानें, डंखानें, कटुतापूर्वक, तैक्ष्ण्यपूर्वक.

ACRIMONY, ACRIMONIOUSNESS, *n.* v. A. 1. खवरेपणा *m.* खवटपणा *m.* जहाली *f.*
2 डंख*m.* डंश *or* दंश*m.*खवटपणा*m.*खवचटपणा*m.*कटुता*f.*जहाली*f.*

ACRITUDE, ACRIDNESS, *n.* v. A. खवखव *f.* तिखटाई *f.* तिखटपणा *m.* खवरेपणा *m.* झणझणीतपणा *m.* तिक्तता *f.* तीक्ष्णता *f.* कटुता *f.* जहाली *or* झाली *f.* कटुस्वाद *m.*

ACROAMATIC, ACROATIC. See ABSTRUSE.

ACROSPIRE, *n. sprout,* v. SHOOT मोड *m.* कोम *m.*

ACROSPIRED, *a. having sprouted.* मोड आलेला, मोड फुटलेला, मोडाचा.

ACROSS, *prep. from side to side;*—noting state. वरून.
2 —*from side to side;* —noting passage. पार, आरपार.
3—*intersecting.* आडवा.

ACROSS, *adv.* आडवा.

ACROSTIC, *n.* आद्याक्षरबंद *m.* प्रथमाक्षरबंध *m.*

To ACT, *v. a.*—in the Drama; (a part, a character). सोंग*n.* आणणें, सोंगाची संपादणी *f.*-बतावणी *f.* करणें, सोंगसंपादणी *f.* करणें, सोंगाचे हावभाव*m.pl.*-आविर्भाव*m.*-अभिनय*m.* करणें.
2 (one's part). आपल्याकडून करायाचें करणें, आपल्याकडून करणें *n.*-उद्योग *m.*-&c. करणें.
3 See To ACTUATE.

To ACT, *v. n. be in action.* चालणें, चालता-चालू- &c. असणें-होणें, खेळणें, चलनवलन *n.*-चेष्टा *f.*-खेळ *m.*- &c. होणें *g. of s.* प्रवर्त्तणें, प्रवृत्तहोणें.
2 *perform duties, &c.* v. To BEHAVE. काम *n.* करणें, चालणें, वर्त्तणें,वागणें,आचरणें,वर्त्तणूक *f.*-वागणूक *f.*-करणी*f.*-कृति *f.*करणें.
3 *perform functions, work.* चालणें, वर्त्तणें, खेळणें, चलनवलन *n.*-चेष्टा *f.*-व्यापार*m.*-कृति *f.*-खेळ*m.*करणें—*and*होणें *with g. of s.*
4 *discharge the duty of an office temporarily.* चारदिवसकांहींदिवस-&c. काम*n.*- &c. पाहणें-चालवणें, अमानी असणें.
5 upon; *exert power, work causatively.* कर्तृत्व *n.*-कृति *f.*-गुण*m.*-कार्य*n.*-स्वकर्म *n.*करणें, चालणें, चालता *or* चालू-लागू होणें *with* वर.
6—in the Drama; *perform a part.*सोंग*n.*घेणें-संपादणें-आणणें &c. नटणें, नर्त्तन*n.*-नटन*n.*-नाटन *n.*-नृत्य *n.*-नाट्य *n.*-&c. करणें.

ACT, *n. deed,* v. ACTION. काम *n.* कर्म *n.* कृत्य *n.* क्रिया *f.*
One's own a. आत्मकर्म *n.* स्वकर्म *n.* निजकर्म *n.*
2 *existing state,* v. ACTUALITY. विद्यमानता *f.* वर्त्तमानता *f.* वास्तविकता *f.*
3 (of a play). अंक *m.* [फैसलनामा *m.*
4 (of a court of justice, &c.) v. DECREE. हुकूमनामा *m.*
5 (of a legislature, &c.) v. LAW. सूत्र *n.* शासन *n.* आईन *m.* दस्तूर *m.* कायदा *m.* आक्त *m.* (from the English.)

ACTING, ACTION, *n.* v. V. A. 1.—*act.* संपादणी *f.* बतावणी *f.* सोंगसंपादणी *f.*
v. V. N. 1.—*act.*चालणें *n.* खेळणें *n.* &c. खेळ *m.* चलनवलन *n.* चेष्टा *f.* प्रवर्त्तन *n.* [गति *f.*
2—*act.* चालणें *n.* वर्त्तणें *n.* &c. चाल *f.* वर्त्तणूक *f.* वर्त्तन *n.*
3—*act.* चालणें *n.* &c. हालचाल *f.* कृति *f.*
5—*act, agency, operation, working.* करणी *f.* कर्तृत्व *n.* कृति *f.*कर्तेपणा *m.*करण *n.*कारकत्व *n.*करत्व *n.*कारिका *f.*कारिता *f.*
The sense of this word is often best rendered by words expressing, *combination, connection, &c.*as योग *m.* संयोग *m.* संबंध *m.*
6—*act.* सोंगघेणें *n.* &c. अभिनय *m.*
I. *gesture, gesticulation.* हावभाव *m.pl.* इंगित *n.* आंगिकचेष्टा *f.* अंगविक्षेप *m.* अभिनय *m.* अदा *m.* सूची *f.*
Manual a. हातवारे *m. pl.*
Represented by a. आंगिक.
II. *series of events represented,* v. PLOT. वस्तु *n.*
III. in law. व्यवहार *m.* व्यवहारविषय *m.* अर्थ *m.* मुकद्दमा *m.* खटला *m.* दावा *m.*
IV. in grammar. कारक *n.*
V. *an a. an act, a deed, a doing.* काम *n.* कर्म *n.* कृत्य *n.* क्रिया *f.* कृति *f.* कार्य *n.* करणें *n.* करणी *f.* कर्त्तव्य *n.* कर्तृत्व *n.*
VI. *battle, engagement.* v. FIGHT. लढाई *f.* युद्ध *n.* संग्राम *m.*

ACTING, *p.* v. V. N. 1. 3. 5. चालता, चालू, चेष्टमान.
4 चारदिवस काम पाहणारा, आमानी, आक्टिंग (from the English.)

ACTIONABLE, *a. admitting of an a. at law.*व्यवहार्य, व्यवहारार्ह, व्यवहारयोग्य, अदालती, खटल्याचा, तकरारी, तकरारीचा.
An a. matter or business. व्यवहारविषय *m.* व्यवहारपद *n.* व्यवहारस्थान *n.*

ACTIVE, *a. having the power to act, not inert.* करणशक्त, क्रियाशक्त, क्रियाकारक, जिता, कर्मात्मा. [कारक, कारक.
2 *that acts, not passive or patient.* कर्त्ता, क्रियाकार, क्रिया-
3 *nimble, agile.* चपल *or* ळ, जलद, चलाक *or* ख, चपळा, अंगचपल, चपलांग, आंगाचा चपळ, आंगसूट,सुटसुटीत, सुडसुडीत, हलक्या आंगाचा.
4 *not idle or sedentary, ever in action,* v.BUSTLING. कामसू, कामी,कर्मी, उद्योगी, उद्योगशील, उद्योगवान्, उद्योगतत्पर, निरलस, निरालस्य.
5 *requiring action,* opposed to speculative. व्यापारमय,

व्यापाररूप, व्यापारात्मक, व्यापारप्रचुर, कर्मरूप, कर्मात्मक, कार्यरूप, कार्यमय, व्यवहारमय-रूप-&c.

A. life. प्रवृत्ति *f.* प्रवृत्तिमार्ग. *m.* [प्रगुणावह.

6— a medicine, &c. जलद, जलाल, जाज्वल्य, आशुकारी, शी-

7—quicksilver. जिना, जीवंत.

8—in gram. कर्त्तरि, सकर्मक. [चापल्यपूर्वक.

ACTIVELY, *adv.* v. A. 3. *nimbly.* चपलाईनें, चलाकीनें, जलदीनें,

4 *busily.* निरालस्यपूर्वक, उद्योगपूर्वक. [मंशक्ति *f.*

ACTIVENESS, ACTIVITY, *n.* v. A.1. क्रियाशक्ति *f.* करणशक्ति *f.* क-

2. चपलाई *f.* चलाकी or खी *f.* जलदी *f.* आंगचपलाई *f.* आंगसफाई *f.* अंगचापल्य *n.* चापल्य *n.* [निरलसता *f.*

3 कामसूपणा *m.* उद्योगीपणा *m.* उद्योगित्व *n.* उद्योगशीलता *f.*

ACTOR, *n.* v. V. A. 1. & V. N. 6. *performer, player.* सोंग आणणारा, सोंगाची संपादणी-बनावणी-&c. करणारा, सोंगाडी or सोंगाड्या *m.* सोंगी or सोंग्या *m.* सोंगाल्या *m.* बहुरूपी *pop.* भोरपी *m.* खेळकरी *m.* नट *m.* नटवा *m.* नटभांड *m.* नाटकी *m.* दासरी *m.* नर्त्तन-नटन-&c. कर्त्ता.

2 v. AGENT. करणारा, कर्त्ता.

ACTRESS, *n.* सोंगाडीण *f.* खेळकरीण *f.* नाटकी *f.* नटी *f.* नर्त्तकी *f.* बहुरूपिणी *pop.* भोरपीण *f.* नाटकशाळा or नाटकसाळ *f.*

ACTUAL, *a. belonging to or comprising action.* क्रियासंबंधी, क्रियान्वयी, क्रियाश्रयी, क्रियामय, चेष्टारूप, चेष्टामय, चेष्टात्मक.

2 *in act, not potential.* क्रियेचा, क्रियारूप, क्रियात्मक, कर्मपरिणामभूत, सिद्ध.

3 *not speculative or imaginary,* v. REAL. खरेंचा, खरा, सत्य, तथ्य, वास्तविक, वास्तव, विद्यमान, वर्त्तमान.

ACTUALLY, *ad.* v. A. 1. कर्मतः, कार्यतः.

2 क्रियेनें, क्रियापूर्वक.

3 खरेपणीं, खरेंच, तत्वतः, तथ्य, वस्तुतः, वस्तुगत्या.

As it actually happened. इत्थंभूत.

ACTUALNESS, ACTUALITY. *n.* v. A. 1. क्रियासंबधिता *f.* क्रियाश्रयिता *f.* क्रियान्वयिता *f.*

2 क्रियारूपता *f.* क्रियात्मकता *f.*

3 आहेपण *n.* आहेपणा *m.* वास्तविकपणा *m.* अस्तित्व *n.* तथ्यत्व *n.* वास्तवत्व *n.* वास्तविकत्व *n.* विद्यमानता *f.* वर्त्तमानता *f.*

ACTUARY. See REGISTRAR.

To ACTUATE, *v. a. put into action.* चालवणें, चालता-चालू-&c. करणें, वर्तवणें, प्रवर्त्तवणें, खेळवणें, करवणें.

2 *influence, move, induce.* वर्त्तवणें, प्रवर्त्तवणें, वळवणें, वागवणें, प्रवर्त्तन *n.*-प्रवृत्ति *f.* करणें *g. of o.* प्रवृत्त करणें.

ACTUATED, *p.* v. V. 1. चालवलेला, &c. चालित, प्रवर्त्तित.

2 वर्त्तवलेला, प्रवर्त्तवलेला, &c. प्रवर्त्तित, प्रवृत्त केलेला. [चालक.

ACTUATER, *n.* v. V. 1. 2. चालवणारा, वर्त्तवणारा, &c. प्रवर्त्तक,

ACTUATION, *n.* v. V. 1.—*act.* चालवणें *n.* &c. प्रवर्त्तन *n.* चालन *n.*—*state.* चालवलेलेपणा *m.* वर्त्तवलेलेपणा *m.* &c. प्रवृत्ति *f.*

2—*act.* वर्त्तवणें *n.* प्रवृत्त करणें *n.* &c. प्रवर्त्तन *n.*—*state.* प्रवर्त्तवलेलेपणा *m.* प्रवृत्ति *f.*

ACUMEN *n.* See POINT. 2. *sharpness of wits* or *sharpwittedness.* तीक्ष्णबुद्धि *f.* कुशाग्रबुद्धि *f.* कुशाग्रमति *f.* शीघ्रबुद्धि *f.* शीघ्रमति *f.* बुद्धिकौशल *n.* प्रज्ञा *f.* मेधा *f.* तार्किक्य *n.* सुधी *f.*

ACUMINATE, ACUMINATED, *a.* See POINTED.

ACUPUNCTURE, *n.* सुईनें टोंचणें *n.*

ACUTE, *a. that has a sharp end,* v. POINTED. बोचेरा, अणीदार, अणीचा, कांचीचा, तीक्ष्णाग्र.

2 *sharp-witted,* v. SHARP. कुशाग्रबुद्धि, कुशाग्रमति, प्रज्ञात, सुधी, तीक्ष्णबुद्धि, तीव्रबुद्धि, प्रखरबुद्धि, सूक्ष्मबुद्धि.

3 *vigorous, quick,*—a sense. तिखट, तीक्ष्ण, तीव्र, जलद, सूक्ष्म, सुग्राही, आशुग्राही, शीघ्रग्राही.

4 —a disease. आशुपरिणामी, शीघ्रपरिणामी, शीघ्रविपाकी, शीघ्रपरिपाकी, जोराचा. [तिखट-&c.

5—as pain. तिखट, तीक्ष्ण, तीव्र, भेदक, सुईच्या टोंकाप्रमाणें

6—an accent, a sound. उदात्त.

ACUTELY, *adv.* v. A. 1. बोचेरेपणानें, तीक्ष्णाग्रतापूर्वक, &c.

2 कुशाग्रबुद्धीनें, बुद्धितैक्ष्ण्यपूर्वक, तीक्ष्णबुद्धिपूर्वक, &c.

3 तिखटाईनें, तैक्ष्ण्यपूर्वक, तीक्ष्णतापूर्वक.

ACUTENESS, *n.* v. A. 1. बोचेरेपण *n.* बोचेरेपणा *m.* तीक्ष्णाग्रता *f.*

2 कुशाग्रबुद्धि *f.* कुशाग्रमति *f.* बुद्धितीक्ष्णता *f.* बुद्धितैक्ष्ण्य *n.*

3 तिखटपणा *m.* तिखटाई *f.* तीक्ष्णता *f.* तैक्ष्ण्य *n.* जलदी *f.* शीघ्रग्राहित्व *n.* सूक्ष्मता *f.*

4 शीघ्रपरिणामित्व *n.* शीघ्रविपाकित्व *n.*

ADAGE, *n. saying.* v. PROVERB. म्हण *f.* न्याय *m.* आहणा *m.*

ADAGIO, *n. slow time.* विलंबित *n.*

ADAMANT, *n.* v. DIAMOND. हिरा *m.* हीरक *m.* वज्र *mn.*

2 v. LOADSTONE. लोहचुंबक *m.*

3 *hard metal, stone, &c.* वज्र *mn.*

ADAMANTEAN, ADAMANTINE, *a.* वज्रसा, वज्रासारखा, वज्रसदृश, वज्रवत्, वज्रप्राय, वज्रमय, वज्र.

A. frame. वज्रदेह *m.* वज्रशरीर *n.* –

ADAM'S APPLE, *n. the prominent part of the throat.* घांटी *f.* घांटूं *n.* घंटिका *f.* कंठमणि *m.* कंठ *m.* ढाल *f.* मानेचा खाखोटा *m.*

ADAM'S BRIDGE, *n.* रामसेतु *m.* सेतुबंध *m.*

To ADAPT, *v. a. make suitable.* मिळवणें, लावणें, योग्य-बराबरमाफक-तदुपयोगी-तदुपयुक्त-&c. करणें, जमवणें, बसवणें, जम *m.*-जवा *m.*-जुळणी *f.*-जोडी *f.*-जुगल *f.*-&c. पाडणें-बसवणें-करणें *g. of o. recip.*

ADAPTATION, *n.* v. V.—*act.* मिळवणें *n.* लावणें *n.* &c. योग्य करणें *n.* जम &c. पाडणें *n.* मिळवणी *f.*—*state.* लाग *m.* योग्यता *f.* उपयुक्तता *f.* जम *m.* जवा *m.* जुगल *f.* जुळणी *f.*

ADAPTED, *p. & a.* v. V. मिळवलेला, योग्य केलेला, &c.

I. *fit.* v. SUITABLE. जोगता-जोगा (in comp.), कार्यक्षम, योग्य, उपयुक्त.

To ADD, *v. a. put to, affix, annex, attach, subjoin.* मिळवणें, जोडणें, घालणें, देणें, मारणें, लावणें, सांधणें, जडणें, दुमाल्यास लावणें, संयोग *m.*-संयोजन *n.*-&c. करणें *g. of o.*

2 up; *sum.* मिळवणें, जोडणें, मिळवणी *f.*-बेरीज *f.*-संकलन *n.* करणें *g. of o.* गोळा करणें.

ADDED, *p.* v. V. 1. जोडलेला, मिळवलेला, &c. संयुत, संयुक्त, संयोजित, विलग्न, सलग्न.

2 मिळवलेला, बेरीज केलेला, संकलित, पिंडित, मिश्रित, एकीकृत, समीकृत, राशिगत.

ADDENDUM, *n.*—in arithmetic. धन *n.* (as opposed to ऋण *n.* Subtrahend.) मिळवणी *f.* क्षेप *m.*

2 See APPENDIX.

ADDER, *n.* See SNAKE.

ADDICE, *n.* v. ADZ. वांकस *mn.* तासणी *f.*

To ADDICT, *v. a.* (one's self to). *To be or become addicted.*

छंदास-नादास *or* नादांत-नादीं लागणें-भरणें *g. of o.* भरीं भरणें *g. of o.* नादावणें, नादांत *or* नादीं पडणें-होणें *g. of o.* सवई *f.*-चट *f.*-चटक *f.*-खोड *f.*-व्यसन *n.*-छंद *m.* लागणें-पडणें *g. of o.* संवकणें *or* सोकणें, सोकावणें, पडकणें, लांचावणें.

ADDICTED, *p.* v. V. नादीं लागलेला, भरीं भरलेला, &c. नादखोर, सोंकील *or* सोकील, पडकलेला, चटावलेला, लागट, तलबी, लंपट, गरक, शोखी *or* शौकी, लाहडी, लब्द, उपसेवी (in comp. as मद्योपसेवी, द्यूतोपसेवी, &c.), परायण *or* पर (in comp. as. विषयपरायण *or* विषयपर), निरत, अनुषंगी, लांफाळ, आसक्त.

ADDICTEDNESS, *n.* v. P. चट *f.* चटक *f.* लंपटपणा *m.* सवई *f.* व्यसन *n.* खोड *f.* तलब *f.* छंद *m.* नाद *m.* आसक्ति *f.* शोक *or* शौक *m.*

ADDICTION, *n.* v. V.—*state.* See ADDICTEDNESS.

ADDITAMENT, *n. thing added.* जोड *m.* जोडलेला-मिळवलेला पदार्थ *m.*-विषय *m.*-भाग *m.*-अंग *n.* आवापद्रव्य *n.* प्रक्षेपद्रव्य *n.* उपस्करद्रव्य *n.*

ADDITION, *n.*v.V. 1.—*act.* जोडणें *n.* मिळवणें *n.* &c. जोडणी *f.* संयोग *m.* संयोजन *n.* लावालाव *f.*—*state.* संयोग *m.* योग *m.*
2—*act.* बेरीज करणें *n.* मिळवणी *f.* मिळवणें *n.*&c. मिश्रण *n.* संकलन *n.* एकीकरण *n.* समीकरण *n.*
Cross proof in a. आड आंखताळा *m.*
Successive substraction-proof in a. सारोळा *m.v.* कर, उतर.
I. *thing added,* v. ADDITAMENT. जोड *m.* जोडलेला भाग *m.*-अंग *n.* &c. [लेला, &c.

ADDITIONAL, *a.* शिवाई, खेरीज, वाढीचा, अधिक, अधिक घात-

ADDITIONALLY, *adv.* अणखी, अणीक, ही.

ADDLE, ADDLED, *a.* —of eggs. उमळलेला, उगळलेला, उबळलेला.
2—of the brains. पोकळ, कल्पनाशून्य, कल्पनारहित, कल्पनाशक्त्यक्षम.

ADDLE-HEADED, ADDLE-PATED, *a.* v. STUPID. बुद्धिशून्य, ठणठणपाळ, माठ्या, गयाळ, गयाळी.

To ADDRESS, *v. a. direct to, apply,* (esp. a speech). लावणें, योजणें, योजन *n.*-योजना *f.*-योजणूक *f.*- योग *m.* करणें *g. of o.*
2 (a charm, a spell, &c.) *set against.* योजणें, प्रयोग *m.*-योजन *n.*-योजना *f.*-योजणूक *f.*-योग *m.* करणें *g. of o.*
3 (one's self *for* or *unto.*) कमर *f.* बांधणें, जुडणें, प्रवृत्त-उद्युक्त होणें, लागणें.
4 *accost, speak to.* हटकणें, बोलणें, संबोधणें, संबोधून बोलणें, भाषणप्रयोग *m.*-वाक्यप्रयोग *m.* करणें, भाषणाची योजना *f.*-योजणूक *f.*-&c. करणें, आभाषण *n.*-आलाप *m.* करणें.
To a. a superior. विनंती *f.*-निवेदन *n.*-अर्ज *m.* &c. करणें, अभिवाद *m.*-अभिवादन *n.* करणें.
To a. respectfully. अहो जाहो म्हणणें-बोलणें.
5 (a letter) नांवाचा-नांवें-नांवानें लिहणें-पाठवणें, पत्ता *m.* लिहणें, नामस्थानांकित करणें.
6 *consign to the care of*—ship. दिम्मतीस पाठवणें.

ADDRESS, ADDRESSING, *n.*v.V. 1.—*act.* योजणें *n.* लावणें *n.* &c. योग *m.* योजना *f.* योजन *n.* योजणूक *f.* [*f.* करणी *f.*
2—*act.* योजणें *n.* &c. प्रयोग *m.* योग *m.* योजना *f.* योजणूक
3—*act.* हटकणें *n.* संबोधणें *n.* संबोधन *n.* अभिवादन *n.* अभिमंत्रण *n.* आभाषण *n.* आलाप *m.* आपृच्छा *f.*
I. *manner of a.* बोलण्याची ढब *f.*-धज *f.*-चाल *f.*-रीत *f.*-&c.
II. *skill, management, conduct.* ओज *f.* आबर *m.* आबरकशि *f.* आवरण *n.* अटोप *m.* कर्तृत्व *n.* नेतृत्व *n.* नियंतृत्व *n.* व्यवहर्तृत्व *n.* युक्ति *pop.* जुगूत *f.* युगुत *f.* धज *f.* सौकर्य *n.*
III. (of a letter, &c.) पत्ता *m.* नामस्थानबोधनलेख *m.*
IV. *complimentary introduction of letters.* अलकाब *m.* मायना *or* माना *m.* प्रशस्ती *f.* पूर्वी *f.* इजत *f.* आदाबअलकाब *m.* मंगलाचार *m.*
There are particular *Forms of address*—particular designations and titles or appropriate and allusive terms or phrases.
The a. to a father is तीर्थरूप.
—to a mother मातृश्री *pop.* मातोश्री *or* मातुश्री, तीर्थरूप.
—to a son, younger brother, young protegee, &c. चिरंजीव.
—to a daughter, &c. चिरंजीवी. [तीर्थस्वरूप.
—to an elderly person (male or female) तीर्थसरूप *pop.*
—to a superior or an elder, शिरसाष्टांगनमस्कार.
—to an unwidowed woman, वज्रचूडेमंडित.
—to a widow. गंगाभागीरथी, गंगाजलनिर्मल, अयाळ, कोम.
—to Bráhmans, esp. as learned, devout, &c. वेदमूर्त्ति, वेदोनारायण, वेदशास्त्रसंपन्न, विद्याविनयसंपन्न, पंडितशिरोमणि, अपरसूर्य.
—to a *Shudra*, पाटील, गोसावी.
—to a *Shudra, &c.* from a *Bráhman.* पुराणोक्त आशीर्वाद.
—to Europeans, Muhammadans, &c.of dignity, अजम, आलीशां.
—to powerful or affluent *Maráthás.* अखंडितलक्ष्म्यलंकृत *pop.* अखंडितलक्ष्मी अलंकृत.
—to a *Gosáwi* or ascetic, तपोधन, तपोनिधि, तपोराशि, तपोमूर्त्ति, &c.
—of honor, gener. राजश्री, राजश्रि *pop.* राजश्रियाविराजित-राजमान्यराजश्री, सर्वगुणसंपन्न.
V. *addresses,* See COURTSHIP. [सत्कारपत्र *n.*
VI. *complimentary &c. letter.* मानपत्र *n.* सन्मानपत्र *n.*

ADDRESSED *p.* v. V. 1. योजलेला, लावलेला, &c. योजित.
2 योजलेला, योजित.
4 हटकलेला, संबोधित, अभिवादित, अभिमंत्रित.
5 नांवानें लिहिलेला, &c.
6 दिम्मतीस पाठवलेला.

ADDRESSER, *n.* ADDRESSING, *p. a.*v. V.1. योजणारा, लावणारा, &c. योजक, योजन-&c. कर्त्ता.
2 योजणारा, &c. योजक, प्रयोग-&c. कर्त्ता.
4 हटकणारा, संबोधन-आभाषण-&c. कर्त्ता, आलापी, अभिवादक.

To ADDUCE, *v. a.* (an argument, a reason, &c.) *allege, assign, advance.* पुढें करणें, उभा करणें, लावणें, दाखवणें, प्रदर्शन *n.* करणें, बोलणें, सांगणें, बोलण्यांत &c. आणणें, उपन्यास *m.* करणें *g. of o.* [उपन्यस्त.

ADDUCED, *p.* v. V. पुढें केलेला, दाखवलेला, सांगितलेला, &c.

ADDUCIBLE, *n.* v. V. पुढें कराया-चा-जोगता-जोगा-&c. उपन्यसनीय, उपन्यास्य. [उपन्यास *m.*

ADDUCTION, *a.* v. V.—*act.* पुढें करणें *n.* दाखवणें *n.* सांगणें *n.*&c.

ADEPT, *a. well skilled or versed.* v. CLEVER. पुरा, पक्का, पूर्ण, पुरा माहीत, निपुण, संपन्न, पारंगत, प्रवीण, निष्णात, अभिज्ञ, धुरीण, अभ्यासप्रवीण, दीक्षित, सराईत, गाढा, तरबेत *or* द.
2—in alchemy, magic, &c. सिद्ध.

3—in villainy or knavery, v. ARRANT. पक्का, पोक्त or पोक्ता, महा(in comp. as महासोदा, महालुच्चा, महाहरामी), बस्ताद.
To be or become a. चौपार्यी (viz. in चोरी, शिनळकी, चाहडी, लबाडी, &c.) उगवणें or उजवणें.

ADEPT, n. one fully skilled in, v. CLEVER. पट्टाईत or पटाईतm. बस्ताद m. पक्का-पोक्ता निपुण &c. मनुष्य m.-माणूस-&c.

ADEQUATE, a. proportionate to, equal to. सारखा, बराबर, योग्य, समान, सम, तुल्य, पुरा, पुरता, esp. in comp. as कामापुरता, कार्यापुरता, &c. पुरायाजोगा-सारखा, &c. उपयुक्त, पर्याप्त, क्षम, समर्थ.
That is barely a. चुटपुटता, चुटपुरता, चुटपूट, चुटपुटीत, जिनक्यास तिनका, तावन्मात्र.

ADEQUATELY, adv. v. A. पुरता, पुरा, बराबर, यथायोग्य, कामा पुरतें.

ADEQUATENESS, ADEQUACY, n. v. A. बराबरी f. पुरतेपणा m. पर्याप्ति f. योग्यता f. सामर्थ्य n. क्षमता f. [बिलगणें.

To ADHERE, v. n. stick to, v. To STICK. चिकटणें, लगटणें, डकणें,
2 stick to, fig. be attached, faithful, &c. लिगटणें, चिकटणें, बिलगणें, बिलगून-चिकटून-लगटून-जडून-धरून-&c. राहणें-असणें -&c. सुस्थिरावलंबन n.-सुस्थिरावलंब m. करणें.

ADHERENCE, ADHERING, ADHESION, n. v. V. 1.—act. चिकटणेंn. लगटणें n. चिकटून असणें n. &c.
2—act. बिलगून राहणें n. &c. सुस्थिरावलंबनn. सुस्थिरावलंबm. —state or quality. सक्ति f. आसक्ति f. निष्ठा f. एकनिष्ठता f. सुस्थिरावलंबता f.

ADHERENT, a. ADHERER, n. ADHERING, p. a. v. V. 1. चिकटणारा, लगटणारा, &c. चिकटून-&c. राहिलेला.
2 बिलगून राहणारा-राहिलेला &c. सुस्थिरावलंबी, परायण(in comp. as नानकपरायण, कबीरपरायण).

ADHERENT, n. follower, partizan. v. FOLLOWER. आश्रयी, अनुयायी, अनुगामी, आश्रित, सपक्ष, पक्षी, अनुषंगी, अवलंबी.

ADHESIVE, a. v. STICKY. चिकट, चिकण, चिकटाऊ.

ADHESIVENESS, n. v. A. चिकटाई f. चिकटपणाm. चिकटण f. धरm.

To ADHIBIT, v. a. use, v. To APPLY. कामांत आणणें, प्रयोग m. करणें g. of o. योजणें, योजना f. योजणूक f.-&c. करणें g. of o.
2 (in one's own person). सेवणें, सेवन n.-&c. करणें g. of o.

ADHIBITED, p. v. V. 1. योजलेला, योजित, प्रयुक्त.
2 सेवलेला, सेवित.

ADHIBITER, n. v. V. 1. योजणारा &c. प्रयोगकर्त्ता.
2 सेवणारा, सेवी, सेवक. [योजणूक f.

ADHIBITION, n. v. V. 1.—act. योजणें n. प्रयोग m. योजना f.
2—act. सेवणें n. सेवन n. सेवा f. उपसेवन n.

ADIEU, n. जातेवेळचा आशीर्वाद m. चरममंगल n. गतिकालिकात्य भाषण n. Some of the common modes of expression are कल्याण असो, ऊर्जित असो, देवतुमचें बरें करो, क्षेम असो, स्वस्ति, ईश्वर आहे.

ADIPOSE, ADIPOUS, a. See FAT.

ADJACENCY, n. v. A. जवळपणा m. लगत f. लगता m. समीपता f. निकटवर्त्तित्व n.

ADJACENT, a. contiguous. v. NEAR. जवळचा, पासचा, जवळपासचा, लगत्याचा, शेजारचा, निकटवर्त्ती, समीपस्थ.

To ADJECT, ADJECTION. See To ADD. ADDING.

ADJECTIVE, n.—in grammar. गुणवाचक m. गुणवचन n. विशेषण n. विशेष्यनिघ्न n.

Relation between an a. and its noun. विशेषणविशेष्यभावm.

To ADJOIN, v. a. See To JOIN.

To ADJOIN, v. n. be contiguous. लगत adv. असणें, शेजारीं असणें, लगत f.-लगता m. असणें in con. & g. of s.

ADJOINING, p. a. v. V. N. लगतीचा, लगत्याचा, जवळचा, पासचा or ला, शेजारचा, संसर्गी, संसक्त, अव्यवहित, अव्यवहितवर्त्ती, उपश्लिष्ट. [उपश्लेष m.

ADJOINING, ADJUNCTION, n. v. V. N.—state. लगत f. लगताm.

To ADJOURN, v. a. put off. दुसऱ्यादिवसापर्यंत-दुसऱ्यादिवसास-&c. ठेवणें, ठेवणें, महकूब or तकूब करणें or ठेवणें, कालांतरावधिक स्थापणें करणें.

ADJOURNMENT, n. v. V.—act. ठेवणें n. दुसऱ्यादिवसाला ठेवणेंn. महकूब ठेवणें n.&c. कालांतरपर्यंत स्थापन n.

To ADJUDGE v. a. doom to. v. To CONDEMN. दंडनास नेमणें, शिक्षा f. सांगणें, शिक्षेची आज्ञा f.-हुकूम m.-&c. करणें.
2 v. To AWARD. मनसुबी f.-चौकसी f.-पंचाईत f.-तपासणीf.-&c. करून देववणें, निवाडा-फैसला-&c. करून देवविणें, दापित करणें.

To ADJUDICATE, v. a. See To ADJUDGE.

ADJUDICATION, ADJUDGMENT, n. v. V. 2—act. निवाडा करून देवविणें n. फैसला करून देवविणें n. &c. वादशुद्धिपूर्वक दापन n.
I. award, v. SENTENCE. निवाडा m. फैसला m.

ADJUNCT, a. united with, immediately consequent. अनुषंगी, आनुषंगिक, अनुयोगी, अनुबंधी.

ADJUNCT, n. v. APPENDAGE. अनुषंगानें असणारा-आनुषंगिक-अनुयोगी-अनुबंधी-&c. पदार्थm.-विषयm.-गुण m.-&c. अनुबंधm.
2—in grammar. अनुबंध m. कार्य n.

ADJURATION, n. v. V.—act. शपथ f.-&c. घालणें n. शपन n.
I. oath put or taken. शपथ f. आण f.

To ADJURE, v. a. impose an oath on, charge on oath. शपथf. -आण f.-द्वाही f.-&c. घालणें or घालून बोलणें-बजावणें-ताकीद f. करणें-&c.

ADJURED, p. v. V. शपथ घातलेला, आण घातलेला, शापित.

To ADJUST v. a. fix or set rightly, put in order. निटावणें, सुधारणें, सुधारणें, सजवणें or सजणें, नीट-बराबर-दुरुस्त-&c. करणें ठेवणें, बंदोबस्तm.-बंदोबस्ती f.-व्यवस्था f.-&c. करणेंg. of o. सोईवर आणणें.
2 (a dispute, debt, &c.) v. To SETTLE. तोडणें, चुकवणें, तोडीवर घेणें, न्याय m. तोडणें-निवडणें g. of o. तोडजोड f. करणें g. of o. तोड f. पाडणें g. of o.

ADJUSTED, p. v. V. 1. निटावलेला, सुधारलेला, बंदोबस्त केलेला-झालेला, व्यवस्था केलेला-झालेला, व्यवस्थित, व्यवस्थापित.
2 चुकवलेला, तोडलेला, तोडजोड केलेला, चुकता, तोडीवर घेतलेला-आणलेला.

ADJUSTMENT, n. v. V. 1.—act. निटावणें n. सुधारणें n. &c. व्यवस्थापन n.—state. बंदोबस्त m. बंदोबस्ती f. ठाकठिकी f. व्यवस्था f.
2—act. चुकवणें n. तोडीवर घेणें n. &c.—state. चुकवती f घटवटना f. तोड f. तोडजोड f.

ADJUTANT, n. लशकरांतला एक कारभारी आहे.

ADJUTOR, ADJUVANT, n. See HELPER.

AD LIBITUM, adv. without restriction. मनसोक्त, मनास येईल तसें.

To ADMEASURE, ADMEASUREMENT, See To MEASURE, &c.

To ADMINISTER v. a. serve, supply, afford, v. To GIVE. देणें, दान n. करणें, अर्पणें, अर्पण n. करणें g. of o.

2 (a government, a business, an estate, &c.) v. To CONDUCT. चालवणें, वहिवाटणें, निर्वाहणें, निर्वाह m.-वहिवाट f. करणें-चालवणें g. of o.
3 (justice). न्याय m. पाहणें-तोडणें-करणें, न्यायदर्शन n. करणें.
4 (an oath). घालणें, देणें.
5 (physic, &c.) देणें, चारणें.
6 (alms, &c.) घालणें, देणें, वांटणें, वाढणें.

To ADMINISTER, *v. n. contribute*, v. To HELP. सहाय-सहकारी-&c. असणें.

ADMINISTRATION, *n.* v. V. 1.—*act.* देणें n. अर्पणें n. &c.
2—*act.* वहिवाटणें n. चालवणें n.&c. वहिवाट f. निर्वाह m.कार्य-निर्वाह m.
Letters of a. to an estate. वहिवाटचालविण्याची सनद f.
I. *executive part of a Government.* राजकारभारमंडळी f.
Change of a. हालीमाजी f. नवेंजुनें n.
II. *reign, rule,* अमल m. राज्य n. कारकीर्द f.
Rigorous or severe a. करडा अमल n.

ADMINISTRATOR, *n.* (of a government). राज्यकाभारचालवणारा m. वहिवाटदार c. [वकील m.
2(to an estate, &c.) वहिवाट चालविणारा m. वहिवाटदार m.
3 (in divine rites)v. OFFICIATER. आचार्य m.

ADMIRABLE, *a.* v. V. *and* GOOD. सानंदाश्चर्यकारक-कारी-&c. साल्हादाश्चर्यकारी- &c. मौज वाटाया-चा-जोगा-सारखा- &c. उत्तम, खासा, उत्कृष्ट, नामी.

ADMIRABLY, *adv.* v. A. मौज वाटाया जोगा-सारखा-&c. *a. decl.* उत्तमरीतीनें, उत्तम, फार चांगलें, खूब, खासा, उत्कृष्ट.

ADMIRAL, *n.* अरमाराचा पति m.-अधीश m.-अध्यक्ष m.-मुख्य m.- &c.

ADMIRATION, *n.* —the sentiment. आश्चर्य n. अचंबा m.चमत्कार m. मौज f. सानंदाश्चर्य n. साल्हादाश्चर्य n.

To ADMIRE, *v. a. regard with wonder and pleasure.* सानंदाश्चर्य n.-साल्हादाश्चर्य n.-&c. करणें *and, in. con.* वाटणें g. of o. कौतुक n.-मौज f.-चमत्कार m.- &c. वाटणें *in. con. g. of o.* आवडणें *in. con.*

ADMIRER, *n.* See LOVER. [शदानाई.

ADMISSIBLE, *a.* v. V. 1. येऊं द्याया-चा-जोगता-जोगा-&c. प्रवे-
2 घ्याया-चा-जोगता-जोगा- &c. मानाया &c.- चा-जोगा- &c. उपादेय, प्रतिग्राह्य.
3 स्वीकारायाजोगा- &c. पदरींघ्यायाजोगा-&c. स्वीकरणीय.

ADMISSION, ADMITTANCE, *n.* v. V. 1—*act.* येऊं देणें n. आंत येऊं देणें n. प्रवेशदान n.
2—*act.* घेणें n. मानणें n. पतकरणें n. &c. आदरण n. उपादान n.—*state.* मान्यता f.—*a. or s.* पतकर *or* पतकार m. प्रामाण्यग्रह m. प्रतिग्रह m.
3 *a. or s.* स्वीकार m. अंगीकार m.

To ADMIT, *v. a. suffer to enter.* येऊं देणें *or* आंत येऊं देणें.
2 *suffer to pass; allow, grant, concede.* घेणें, मानणें, मान्य करणें, बार देणें-करणें, पतकरणें *or* पतकारण, कबूल करणें-होणें, झेलणें, आदरणें, भजणें, ग्रहण n.-प्रतिग्रह m.-उपादान n.करणें g. of o.
3 v. To ACKNOWLEDGE. स्वीकारणें, अंगीकारणें, पदरीं घेणें, कबूल करण.
4 *take in, receive amongst.* घेणें, आंतघेणें, कवळणें, कवंटाळणें.

ADMITTED, *p.* v. V. 1. येऊं दिल्हेला, आंत येऊं दिल्हेला.
2 घेतलेला, मानलेला, &c. मान्य, कबूल, रुजू, अनुमत, उपात्त, अभिमत, प्रतिगृहीत, परिगृहीत, प्रतिज्ञात, मत.
3 स्वीकारलेला, अंगीकारलेला, &c. स्वीकृत, अंगीकृत.

To ADMIX, ADMIXTURE, &c. See To MIX, &c.

To ADMONISH, *v. a. warn of, counsel against,* v. To WARN. ताकीद f.-सूचना f.-सूचन n.-&c. करणें, पूर्वबोध m.-उद्बोध m.-उद्बोधन n.-उपदेश m.- &c. करणें g. of o. सुचवणें, उद्बुद्ध-उपदिष्ट-&c. करणें.
2 *reprove gently.* कान m. pl. उघडणें g. of o. कानास खडा m. लावणें g. of o. तोंडची शिक्षा f.-शब्दाचा मार m.-वाक्‌शिक्षा f.-वागूदंड n. करणें.

ADMONISHER, *n.* ADMONISHING, *p.a.* ADMONITOR, *n.*v.V. 1. ताकीद करणारा, &c. सूचक, सूचनकर्त्ता, उपदेशक, उद्बोधक, पूर्वबोधकर्त्ता.
2 तोंडचीशिक्षा करणारा &c.

ADMONISHING, ADMONISHMENT, ADMONITION, *n.*v.V. 1.—*act.* ताकीद करणें n. सूचना करणें n. &c. सूचन n. सूचना f. पूर्वबोधन n. उद्बोधन n.
2 कान उघडणें n. &c. कान उघडणी f.
I. *the warning given.* ताकीद f.सूचना f.उपदेश m. बुद्धिवाद m. पूर्वबोध m. उद्बोध m.
II. *the reproof given.* तोंडची शिक्षा f. वाक्‌शिक्षा f. वागूदंड शब्दाचा मार m.

ADO, *n. labour, difficulty, pains,* v. TROUBLE. झटे पटे *or* झट्टे पट्टे m. pl. v. खा, घे, खस्ता f. pl. v. खा, काढ, खटपट f. खवदव f. दगदग f. उपदूव्याप m.
With much a. मारून कुटून, मारून धुमकून, मारून मुटकून, झटून झोंबून, बलेंबलें, लोंबी झोंबीनें.
2 *confused hurry, pother, stir,* v. BUSTLE. गोंधळ m. घोळ m. घप्पाघोळ m. हुलहूल f.
To make much a. about nothing. डोंगर खणून उंदीर काढणें, अबाबा m.-अबांव n.-तांडव n.-&c. करणें, निधाई f. लावणें-पाडणें, हुलहूल f. लावणें.

ADOLESCENCE, *n.* v. YOUTH. वाढती पराई f. जवानी f. चढती पराई f. वाढतीदशा f. पोगंड n. पौगंडावस्था f.

ADOLESCENT, *a.* v. STRIPLING. चढते पराईचा, चढत्या वयाचा, पौगंडावस्थेचा.

To ADONIZE, *v. n. deck out the person.* पोशाक m.-चट्टीपट्टी f.-चाकचोपी *or* चापचोपी f.-चापीचोपी f.-शानशुकी f.-शोकी f.-टाकमटिला m.-टाकमटिका m.-टिलेपट्टे m.pl.-टिलाटोपी f.-&c.करणें.

ADONIZING, *n.* v. V.—*act.* चट्टीपट्टी f. चाकचोपी *or* चापचोपी f. चापीचापी f. टिलाटोपी f. टेब *or* टेवरेव m. pl. शानशुकी *or* शोकी f. डामडौल m.

To ADOPT, *v. a.* (a son). दत्तक-दत्तपुत्र-दत्त-पोसणा-&c. घेणें, मांडीवर घेणें, ओटींत-ओट्यांत घेणें, आपंगणें, पुत्र m. करून घेणें.
2 (a measure, custom, &c.) आदरणें, घेणें, धरणें, पाळणें, सेवणें, आश्रयणें, स्वीकारण, अंगीकारणें, स्वीकार m.-अंगीकार m.-सेवन n.-ग्रहण n.-&c. करणें.

ADOPTED, *p.* ADOPTIVE, *a.* v. V. 1. दत्त-दत्तक-&c. घेतलेला, पासगा *or* का, पोसणा, पोष्णा, पोष्या, मांडीवर घेतलेला, ओटींत घेतलेला, मांडीवरचा, ओटींतला.
An a. child. धर्मसंतति f. धर्मसंतान n.
2 आदरलेला, &c. सेवित, आदृत, गृहीत.

ADOPTER, *n.* ADOPTING, *p. a.* ADOPTIVE, *a.* v.V.1. दत्त-दत्तक-

घेतला-&c. घेणारा, मांडीवर घेणारा, ओंटींत घेणारा, दत्तक-दत्त-&c. ग्राहक, ग्राही.

2 आदरणारा, &c. सेवी &c. सेवक(esp. in comp.)

ADOPTION, *n.*v.V.I.—*act.* मांडीवर घेणें *n.* ओंटींत घेणें *n.* दत्त *or* दत्तक घेणें *n.* दत्तकग्रहण *n.* दत्तकस्वीकार *m.*—*state.* दत्त घेतलेपणा *m.* ओंटींत घेतलेपणा *m.* &c. दत्तकत्व *n.* दत्तकगृहीतत्व *n.* दत्तकस्वीकृतत्व *n.* [कृत्रिमपुत्र.

Boy given into a. दत्त *m.* दत्तपुत्र *m.* दत्तक *m.* पालकपुत्र*m.*—revilingly. दत्तया *or* दत्तूया—familiarly. दत्तोपंत, दत्तोबा.

Boy given (after investiture with the thread) into a. in a family not related to him. He is heir both to his natural and to his adoptive parent. द्व्यामुष्यायण *m.*

Boy self-given into a. स्वयंदत्त *m.*

Ceremonies or rites of a. दत्तविधान *n.* दत्तविधि *m.*

Deed of a. मांडपत्र *n.* दत्तपत्र *n.* [णें-ठेवणें.

To give into a.दत्त करणें, मांडीवर-ओंटींत-ओट्यांत देणें-घाल-

2—*act.* आदरणें *n.* सेवणें *n.* &c. ग्रहण *n.* धारण *n.* पालन *n.* सेवन *n.* उपसेवन *n.*

ADORABLE, *a.* v. V. पुजाया-चा-योग्य-&c. पूजनीय, पूज्य, पूजनार्ह, पूजायोग्य, पूजार्ह, भजनीय, भजनार्ह, अर्चनीय, अर्च्य, वंदनीय, वंद्य, नमस्य, आराधनीय, आराध्य, उपास्य, सेव्य, अर्घ्य, पूजापात्र, पूजाविषय, भजनपात्र, &c.

ADORABLENESS, *n.* v. A. पुजायाची-भजायाची-&c. योग्यता *f.*-अर्हता *f.*- &c.पूजनीयता *f.*पूज्यता *f.*पूजनार्हता *f.*&c.अर्घ्यता *f.*

ADORATION, *n.* v. V.—*act.* पुजणें *n.* भजणें *n.* &c. पूजन *n.* भजन *n.* पूजा *f.* अर्चन *n.* अर्चा *f.* वंदन*n.* भक्ति *f.* आराधना *f.* आराधन *n.* उपासना *f.*

To ADORE, *v. a.* v. To WORSHIP. पुजणें, भजणें, अर्चणें, आराधणें, उपासणें, वंदणें, पूजन *n.*-भजन*n.*-&c. करणें *g. of o.*

ADORED, *p.* v. V. पुजलेला, भजलेला, &c. पूजित, अर्चित, आराधित, उपासित, वंदित.

ADORER, *n.* ADORING, *p. a.* v. V. पुजणारा, &c. पूजक, आराधक, उपासक, वंदक, भक्त, भजक, पूजन-भजन-अर्चन-&c. कर्त्ता.

ADORINGLY, *adv.* v. V. पूजाबुद्धीनें, भक्तिपूर्वक.

To ADORN, *v. a. decorate, embellish, ornament.* अलंकारणें, श्रृंगारणें, भूषवणें, शोभवणें, शोभेसा करणें, शोभित-सुशोभित-&c. करणें, शोभा *f.*-रंग *m.*-&c. देणें-आणणें, शोभन *n.*-भूषण *n.*-भूषा *f.*-मंडन *n.*-&c. करणें *g. of o.*

2 *beseem, grace,* v. To BECOME. शोभणें, साजणें, सजणें.

ADORNED. *p.* v. V. I. अलंकारलेला, &c. अलंकारयुक्त, शोभायुक्त, &c.अलंकारान्वित &c. अलंकृत, शोभित, भूषित, मंडित, विभूषित, श्रृंगारित, सुशोभित, साजरा.

ADORNER, *n.* ADORNING, *p. a.* v.V. 1. अलंकार करणारा, &c. अलंकारकर्त्ता, अलंकर्त्ता, अलंकारावह, शोभाप्रद, भूषादायक.

ADORNMENT, ADORNING, *n.* v. V. 1.—*act.* अलंकारणें *n.* &c. अलंकरण *n.* अलंक्रिया *f.* अलंकृति *f.* शोभन*n.* भूषण *n.* मंडन*n.* विभूषण *n.*—*state.* श्रृंगार *m.* साजरेपणा*m.* शोभा *f.* अलंकृति *f.* भूषा *f.* शोभितत्व*n.* &c.

ADOWN, *prep. along, downwards.* आंगावरून, सरसून, सरपटून, अधः, अधोग्र, वरून.

ADRIFT, *adv. floating at random.* वाहतां, मोकळपणीं तरतां, सुटून तरंगत असतां,वहावतां, मोकळ, मोकाट, मोकार,ओघाधीन, प्रवाहाधीन.

To be a. -lit-fig. तरंगणें, वहावणें.

To cast a.-lit. ओघावर-प्रवाहावर टाकणें.-fig.वाऱ्यावर टाकणें.

To get a.-lit. ओघांत-प्रवाहांत-&c. पडणें,-fig.वाऱ्यावर सरणें.

ADROIT, *a. dexterous,* v. EXPERT. कुशल, सुगर, सुघड, पट्टाईत, सराईत, दक्ष, पटु, अटोकाट.

ADROITLY, *adv.* v. A. सुगरपणानें, &c. सुगराईनें, कुशलतेनें, कुशळपणानें, दक्षतेनें, दक्षता-&c. पूर्वक.

ADROITNESS, *n.* v. A, कुशळपणा *m.* सुगरपणा *m.* &c. कुशलता *f.* सुगराई *f.* सुगरावा *m.* दक्षता *f.* दाक्ष्य *n.* कौशल*n.* सौकर्य *n.*

ADRY. *a.* See THIRSTY.

ADSCITITIOUS, *a. taken up, called in,* v. ASSUMED. मानलेला, कल्पित, आहार्य, आणलेला, आहृत. [TER, &c.

ADULATION, To ADULATE, &c. See FLATTERING. To FLAT-

ADULT, *a. arrived at mature age.* वयांत आलेला, पणांत आलेला, उमेदींत आलेला, उमरींत आलेला, मोठा, जाणता, प्रौढ, पोक्त, पोका, सरसोंदा, प्राप्तयौवन, अंकुरितयौवन, ज्ञातयौवन, तारुण्यावस्थापन्न, वयस्थ *or* वयःस्थ.

To become a. वयांत-पणांत-&c. येणें.

ADULT, *n.*v. A. वयांत-&c. आलेला माणूस *m.*-स्त्री *f.*-&c. पुरुष*m.* बाप्या *m.* गोखमा *m.*

To ADULTERATE, *v. a. corrupt by mixture.* भेल *f.*-मिसळ *f.*-&c. घालून वाईट करणें - बिघडणें, हीनद्रव्यमिश्रणदूषित करणें, हीनसंसर्गदूषित करणें.

ADULTERATE, *a.* ADULTERATED, *p.*v.V. भेल घालून बिघडलेला, हीनसंसर्गदूषित *or* दुष्ट, हीनमिश्रणदूषित-दुष्ट, हीनसंपर्कदूषित-दुष्ट.

ADULTERATION, *n.* v. V. *act.* भिसळ-&c. घालून वाईट करणें *n.* हीन मिश्रणद्वारा दूषित करण *n.*हीनसंसर्गद्वारा दूषित करण *n.*—*state.* हीनमिश्रणदूषितत्व *n.* हीनसंसर्गदूषितत्व *n.*

ADULTERER, *n. man guilty of adultery.* परद्वारी, परद्वारकर्त्ता, व्यभिचारकर्त्ता, व्यभिचारी, परदारगामी, जारकर्मकर्त्ता, जारकर्मी, अन्यागामी, पारदारिक, परदारोपसेवी, परदाराभिमर्शी, परतल्पग, बाहेरख्याली, बहिर्व्यसनी.

ADULTERESS, *n. woman guilty of adultery.*अपतिव्रता, जारिणी, व्यभिचारिणी, जारकर्मकर्त्री, परगामिनी, परद्वारकर्त्री,व्यभिचारकर्त्री, अन्यगामिनी.

ADULTERINE, *n.* v. BASTARD. जारज, जारजात.

ADULTEROUS, *a. guilty of adultery,* See ADULTERER & ADULTERESS.

2 *pertaining to adultery.*जारकर्माचा,व्यभिचाराचा, जारकर्मसंबंधी, जारकर्मविषयक, व्यभिचारसंबंधी,परशय्यासंबंधी-विषयक.

ADULTERY, *n. conjugal infidelity,*—of the male or female. जारकर्म *n.* व्यभिचार*m.* परशय्या *f.* बदकर्म *n.* बदअमल *m.* जारी *f.*—of the male. परदारगमन *n.* परद्वार *n.* परस्त्री *f.* अन्यागमन *n.* परस्त्रीगमन*n.* परकलत्राभिगमन *n.* पारदार्य *n.* परभार्यागमन *n.* परतल्पगमन *n.*—of the female. परगमन *n.* परगृह *pop.* परघर *n.* v.पाह-रिघ-शिर. परपुरुषगमन *n.* अन्यगमन *n.*—in cant or covert phrase, and of male & female. बाहेरख्याल *m.* बहिर्द्वार *n.* बहिर्व्यसन *n.*

ADULTNESS, *n.* v. A. & N. उमेद *f.* जाणतेपणा *m.* प्रौढपणा *m.* प्रौढदशा *f.* पुरुषत्व *n.*

To ADUMBRATE,*v. a. shadow out, exhibit a faint resemblance of.* ईषत्सदृशरूप *n.* काढणें-करून दाखवणें, छाया *f.* काढ-

णें-काढून दाखवणें-उतरणें, छायाप्रदर्शन *n.* करणें, छायाभास *m.* उतरणें-काढणें.

ADUMBRATION, *n.* v. V.*matter shadowed out.* छाया *f.*

ADUST,*a. burnt up.*जळून गेलेला,दग्ध, खरखरीत, रुखा, रुक्ष.

To ADVANCE. *v. a. bring to the front or fore-ground.* पुढें-पुढले कडे करणें-आणणें-काढणें-चालवणें-घालणें, समोर *adv.* करणें -काढणें-&c. अघाडीस आणणें.

2 *promote, prefer.* चढवणें, वाढवणें, पदवी *f.* चढवणें-वाढवणें *g. of o.* थोरवी *f.*-थोरपणा *m.*-&c. देणें, सरफराजी *f.* करणें, न्यहाल करणें,·पदवृद्धि *f.* करणें *g. of o.*

3 *make better,* &c. v. To IMPROVE. संवर्द्धन *n.*-संवृद्धि *f.*-&c. करणें *g. of o.* रंगास आणणें. [*g. of o.*

4 *forward, bring on.* चालवणें, वाढवणें, वाढ *f.*- वृद्धि *f.* करणें

5 v. To PROPOSE. उहू *m.* काढणें-करणें *g. of o.* पूर्वरंग *m.*-उपोद्घात *m.*-प्रस्तावना *f.*- प्रस्ताव *m.*- उपक्रम *m.* करणें *g. of o.*

6 (money &c.) अगाऊ *adv.*-आगप *adv.* देणें, तगाई *f.* देणें.

To ADVANCE, *v. n. come forward.* पुढें *adv.* येणें-निघणें-चालणें-होणें-सरणें-वाढणें, पुढारणें, समोर &c. येणें &c. वाढणें, पाऊल*n.* पुढें टाकणें, पाऊल *n.* पुढें पडणें-पडत चालणें *g. of s.*

To a. boldly, readily,&c.सरकणें,सरकावणें,धजणें,धजावणें, सरसावणें, सरळणें, सरणें, पुढाकार *m.* करणें.

To a. against, upon. चढून जाणें-येणें, चढाई *f.*-चढ *m.*-चढाव *m.* करणें *with* वर.

2 *grow better, &c.*v. To IMPROVE. चांगला होत जाणें, वर्धणें, रंगास-रूपास-तेजास-&c. चढणें.

3 *move apace.* बरें *adv.* चालणें.

4 *progress, proceed,* v. To RISE. वाढणें,चालणें, चढणें, वाढत-चढत-&c. चालणें, वृद्धिंगत होणें.

ADVANCE, ADVANCEMENT, *n.* v. V. A. 1.—*act.* पुढें करणें *n.* अघाडीस आणणें *n.* &c.

2—*act.* चढवणें *n.* वाढवणें *n.* &c. पुरस्कार *m.* पदवर्द्धन *n.* —*state.* वाढवलेपणा *m.* &c. सरफराजी *f.* पदवृद्धि *f.*

3—*act.* संवर्द्धन *n.*—*state.* संवृद्धि *f.* वर्द्धितत्व *n.*

4—*act.* चालवणें *n.* &c.

I. *money advanced.* अगाऊ दिलेला पैका *m.*—esp. to cultivators, तगाई *f.*

v. V. N. 1.—*a. or s.* पुढें येणें*n.* &c. क्रमण*n.* क्रम*m.* क्रांति *f.*

2—*state.* वर्द्धणें *n.* &c. चढती *f.* संवर्द्धन *n.* वर्द्धन *n.* संवृद्धि *f.* चढती कळा *f.* चढतीपायरी *f.* चढतापाया *m.* चढती कमान *f.* संपत्ति *f.*

3—*state.* वाढणें*n.* चालणें *n.* &c. वाढ *f.* चढती *f.* चढ *m.*

In a. *in front.* पुढें, मोहरे.

2 *before-hand.* अगाऊ, आगप.

ADVANCE-GURAD, ADVANCED-GUARD, *n.* बिनी *f.*

ADVANCED, *p.* v. V. A. 1. पुढें केलेला-आणलेला, &c.

2 चढवलेला, वाढवलेला, &c. सरफराज, न्यहाल.

3 रंगास आणलेला, वर्द्धित, संवर्द्धित.

4 चालवलेला, &c.

v. V. N. 1. पुढें आलेला, पुढारलेला, सरसावलेला, &c. पुरोगत, पुरोयात, अग्रगत, अग्रयात, क्रांत.

2 रंगास-रूपास-तेजास- &c. चढलेला.

4 वाढलेला, चढलेला, &c. वृद्ध (esp. in comp. as वयोवृद्ध, ज्ञानवृद्ध, विद्यावृद्ध, धनवृद्ध, यशोवृद्ध, तपोवृद्ध).

ADVANCER, *n.* ADVANCING, *p. a.* v. V. A. 1. पुढें करणारा-आणणारा, &c. [वृद्धिकारक.

2 वाढवणारा, चढवणारा, &c. पुरस्कर्त्ता, पुरस्कारी, पदवर्द्धक, पद-

3 वर्द्धक, संवर्द्धक, संवर्द्धनकर्त्ता.

4 चालवणारा, वाढवणारा, &c.

5 काढणारा, उहू करणारा, &c. [खागामी.

v. V. N. 1. पुढें येणारा &c. पुरोयायी, अभिमुखागंता, अभिमु-

2 चढता, रंगास-रूपास- &c. चढणारा, &c. वृद्धिंगत, वर्धमान.

3 वाढणारा &c. वाढता.

ADVANTAGE, *n. superiority over,* v. SUPERIORITY. वर्चस *n.* वर्चस्व *n.* वरिष्ठता *f.* उपराळा *m.* उपरदवडा *m.* उपर *m.*

To have the a. of. आगळा-अधिक होणें, थाप *f.* असणें*g. of s. with* वर *of o.*

To obtain an a. over. आपला दशक *m.* चढवणें, शेर होणें, जिंकणें, पाणी *n.* पाजणें.

2 *benefit, profit, good, avail, use.* फायदा *m.* फळ *n.* फळश्रुति *or* फळश्रुत *f.* हित*n.* बरें*n.* उपयोग *m.* उपकार*m.* किफायत *f.* सरफा *or* सरिफा *m.* मयना *or* माना*m.* फलितार्थ*m.* फलोत्पत्ति *f.* फळादेश *m.* फलोदय *m.* गुण *m.* लाभ *m.* (*and,* loosely लाभागोभा *m.*) स्वार्थ *m.*

A. and disadvantage. हिताहित *n.* लाभालाभ *m.*

To appear to a. शोभणें, खुलणें, विराजणें, विलसणें, राजणें.

To show, set, &c. to a. छत *n.* भरणें *g. of o.*शोभवणें.

3 *emolument, profit,* v.GAIN. नफा *m.* लाभ *m.* प्राप्ति *f.*

4 *preponderation on one side.* वर्चस *n.* वर्चस्व *n.*

To ADVANTAGE, *v. a. avail, boot, benefit, profit,serve.* लाभणें, लाधणें, लाहणें, उपयोगी होणें-पडणें, उपयोग *m.* होणें *in. con. with g. of o.*

ADVANTAGEOUS, *a.* v. N. 2 *beneficial, profitable, availing.* हितदायक, हितावह, हितप्रद, हितकारक, हितकर,हितजनक, हित, किफायती, किफायतवार, उपयोगी,उपकारी, उपकारक, लाभदायक, लाभप्रद, फलावह, गुणकारी, गुणावह, फलोपधायक, फलप्रद.

3 v. GAINFUL. नफ्याचा, नफेवार, किफायतवार, किफाइती, किफायतीचा, मिळकतीचा, सरफेवार, कसरीचा.

ADVANTAGEOUSLY, *adv.* v.N.2 सोईवार,सोईसार, सोईचा, *a. decl.* 3 किफायतवार, नफेवार, सरफेवार.

ADVANTAGEOUSNESS *n.* v. A. 1. उपयोगीपणा *m.* उपयोगिता *f.* साफल्य *n.* फलवैशिष्ट्य *n.* लाभ-&c. दायकत्व *n.* उपकारिता *f.* औपकार्य *n.*

ADVENIENT, ADVENTITIOUS, *a.* v. ACCIDENTAL. आगंतुक, आणलेला, असहज, आहार्य.

ADVENT, *n.* v. COMING. येणें *n.* आगमन *n.* आगम *m.*

ADVENTURE, *n. accident, chance.* दैवयोग *m.* दैवघटना *f.* दैवगत *f.* दैवगति *f.*

2 *hazardous deed,* v. ENTERPRISE. जोखीम *n f.* जोखमाचें काम *n.* धोक्याचें काम *n.* कचाट *n.* दुर्गकर्म *n.* [चरित *n.*

Adventures, *remarkable events in the life of.* चरित्र *pop.*

To ADVENTURE, *v. n. try the chance, dare,* v. To VENTURE. जोखीम *n.*-&c. आंगावर आणणें-घेणें-स्वीकारणें-पदरीं बांधणें, जोखीम *n.* खाणें, तवकल *n f.* करणें.

To ADVENTURE, *v. a. put into the power of chance.* v. To VENTURE. जोखमांत ठेवणें-घालणें, अदृष्टाधीन-दैवाधीन ठेवणें-घालणें-करणें, दैवावर हवालणें.

ADVENTURER, n. v. V. *one who seeks occasions of chance.* दैवावर हवाला घालून उद्योग पाहणारा, जोखीम *or* जोखम पाहणारा, जोखीम आंगावर घेणारा, &c.

ADVENTUROUS, *a. inclined to adventures.* कचाटी *or* कचाट्या, जोखीम खाण्याच्या स्वभावाचा, खटपट्या, रुटलेखोर, हरदमख्याली, उलेढाल्या, उत्पाती, अचाटबुद्धि खेळवणारा, अचाट उद्योगी, साहसी, साहसिक, अचाट करणारा, लागूभागूदिवाळ्या, यद् भावी यद् भविष्यति म्हणणारा, प्रौढ, देहंवापातयंत् अथवा साधयेत् म्हणणारा. [धर्मक.

2 v. HAZARDOUS. जोखमी, जोखमाचा, तवकलीचा, भयप्रदता-

ADVENTUROUSLY, *adv.* v. A. 1. आंगावर जोखीम घेऊन, जोखीम सोसून-खाऊन-&c. साहसपूर्वक, साहसबुद्ध्या.

ADVENTUROUSNESS, n. v. A. जोखीम खाण्याचा स्वभाव*m.* हांव*f.* कचाटेपणा *m.* प्रौढी *f.*

ADVERB, *n.*—gener. अव्यय *n.* अव्ययपद *n.*

2—to a verb, क्रियाविशेषण अव्यय *n.* विधिविशेषण अव्यय *n.* क्रियाविशेषण *n.* विधिविशेषण *n.*

ADVERBIAL, *a. pertaining to an a.* अव्ययसंबंधी, अव्ययाचा, अव्ययरूप, अव्ययात्मक, अव्ययभूत, अव्ययान्वित, &c. साव्यय, क्रियाविशेषणरूप-आत्मक-पूर्वक-मूलक-प्रधान-&c.

ADVERBIALLY, *adv.* v. A. अव्ययरूपें, क्रियाविशेषणरूपें, अव्ययपूर्वक, साव्यय, अव्यययोगानें, क्रियाविशेषणाचे योगें करून.

ADVERSARIA, *n. common-place book.* कोडपत्र *n.* कोड *n.* बाड*n.* गाबाळग्रंथ *m.* बेचे *m.pl.* [गी *m.*

ADVERSARY, *n. foe.* v. ENEMY. वैरी *c.* शत्रु *c.* विपक्ष *m.*प्रतियो-

2—as in litigation, &c. v. OPPONENT. प्रतिपक्षी *m.* विपक्ष*m.* प्रतिपक्ष *m.* प्रतियोगी *m.* प्रतिस्पर्धी *m.*

ADVERSE, *a. turned against; opposite,* v. CONTRARY. उलटा, आडवा, विरुद्ध, विपरीत.

2 *inimical, hostile, repugnant, unfriendly.* आडवा, विपरीत, विरोधी, द्वेषी, वैरी, प्रतिकूल *or* ळ, अननुकूल, विषम, विमना, विमनस्क, अमित्र, असुहृत्, असख, विमत, विपक्ष, विगुण, शत्रु (in com. as बुद्धिशत्रु, ज्ञानशत्रु, आत्मशत्रु, &c.) पर, पराङ्मुख, विमुख *pop.* विन्मुख, अहित, अहितमना, अहितमनस्क, विप्रिय.

3 *calamitous.* अभद्र, अमंगल, अनिष्ट, अनभीष्ट.

ADVERSELY, *adv.* v. A. 1. आडवा, उलटा, &c. उलट्यानें, विपक्षतः,

2 आडवा, &c. विरोधानें, शत्रुबुद्ध्या, शत्रुदृष्ट्या, शत्रुभावानें, विपक्षतः, विरोधपूर्वक, वैषम्यपूर्वक, &c.

ADVERSENESS, *n.* v. A. 1. उलटेपणा *m.* आडवेपणा *m.* विरोध *m.* विरुद्धता *f.* विरोधित्व *n.* विरुद्धभाव *m.*

2 आडवेपणा *m.* प्रातिकूल्य *n* विरोध *m.* विरोधित्व*n.* शत्रुभाव*m.* द्वेषभाव *m.* विषमत्व *n.* विमति *f.* विपरीतता *f.* वैपरीत्य *n.* वैषम्य *n.* पराङ्मुखता *f.* विमुखता *f.*

3 अमंगळपणा *m.* अभद्रता *f.* अनिष्टता *f.*

ADVERSITY, *n. state of affliction, distress, misery, &c.* विपत्ति *f.* आपत्ति *f.* अनुपपत्ति *f.* आपदवस्था *f.* संकटावस्था *f.* विपदवस्था *f.* अकल्याण *n.* विषमावस्था *f.* अभाग्यदशा *f.* अवदशा *f.* कष्टदशा *f.* संकटदशा *f.* आपत्, विपत् (in comp as आपदान्वित, विपद्ग्रस्त, आपन्निवृत्ति, विपदुद्धार) हाल *m. pl.* दुर्गति *f.* उतरतीदशा *f.* उतरतीपायरी *f.* उतरतीकमाण *f.* आकाबाईची दया *f.*

Delivering or extricating from a. विपदुद्धार*m.* विपदुद्धरण*n.*

Religion of a. आपद्धर्म *m.* विपद्धर्म *m.*

Season of a. *adverse times,* आपत्काल *m.* विपत्काल*m.* आपत्तिकाल *m.* विपत्तिकाल *m.* अभाग्यकाल *m.* विषमकाल *m.* विमुखकाल *m.* कडूकाळ *m.* उतरतीवेळ *f.* उतरताकाळ *m.*

Suffering, overwhelmed by, &c. a. आपद्ग्रस्त, आपन्न, विपन्न, आपत्प्राप्त, आपदान्वित, आपद्युक्त, विपद्ग्रस्त, विपद्युक्त, विषमस्थ.

To ADVERT, *v.n. turn to, attend to, animadvert.* मन*n.*-लक्ष्य*n.* -ध्यान *n.* देणें-लावणें, डोळा *m.*-दृष्टि *f.* घालणें-देणें, आठवणें, नजर *f.*-दृष्टि *f.*-लक्ष्य *n.*-डोळा *m.*-अनुसंधान *n.*-अवधान *n.* असणें *g. of s.*

ADVERTENCE, ADVERTING, *n.* v. V.—*act.* लक्ष्य लावणें *n.* मन देणें *n.* &c. अनुसंधान *n.* अवधान *n.* ध्यान *n.*

With a. to अनुलक्षून.

To ADVERTISE, *v. a.* v. To INFORM. जाणवणें, कळवणें, बोधवणें, माहितगार-माहीत-जाणता-सावध-बोधित-सूचित-&c.करणें.

2 *give notice of publicly.* जाहीर-प्रगट-प्रसिद्ध- &c. करणें, जाहिरनामा *m.* फिरवणें-लावणें *g.of o.* दवंडी *f.*-दांडोरा *m.*-&c. पिटवणें *g. of o.* प्रकटीकरण *n.*- &c. करणें.

ADVERTISED, *p.* v. V. 1. जाणवलेला, बोधवलेला, &c. माहितगार-&c. केलेला, बोधित, प्रबोधित, विज्ञापित.

2 जाहीर-प्रगट-प्रसिद्ध-&c. केलेला, प्रकटीकृत, प्रसिद्धीकृत.

ADVERTISEMENT, *n.* v. V. 1.—*act.* जाणवणें *n.* &c. माहितगार -&c. करणें *n.* विज्ञापन *n.* बोधन *n.* प्रबोधन *n.*

2 जाहीर करणें *n.* प्रकटीकरण *n.* प्रसिद्धीकरण *n.*

I. *notice published.* जाहिरनामा*m.* जाहिरात *f.* जाहिरखबर *f.*

ADVERTISER, *n.* ADVERTISING, *p. a.* v. V. 1. जाणवणारा, &c. माहितगार-&c. करणारा, बोधक, प्रबोधक, विज्ञापक. [कर्त्ता.

2 जाहीर- &c. करणारा, दवंडी पिटवणारा, &c.प्रकटकर्त्ता, प्रसिद्ध-

To ADVESPERATE, *v. n. draw towards evening.* सांजवणें, सांजळणें *or* सांझळणें, रातावणें.

ADVICE, *n. counsel.* उपदेश *m.* मसलत *f.* बोध *m.* आदेश *m.* सल्ला *m. f.* बुद्धिवाद *m. v.* सांग.

Bad a. कुमंत्र *m.* कुबोध *m.* [सुमंत्र *m.*

Good a. or instruction. हितोपदेश *m.* सुबोध *m.* हितबोध*m.*

2 *information,* v. INTELLIGENCE. खबर *f.* बातमी *f.* सूचना *f.* समाचार *m.* [चार *f.*

A. from emissaries at foreign courts. अखबार *or* अक-

Commercial a. पेंठ *f.*

ADVISABLE, *a. proper to be advised or practised,* v. PROPER. योग्य, उचित, लायक, बुद्धिवादाचा, उपदेशनीय, उपदेश्य, उपदेष्टव्य, उपदेशार्ह, उपदेशोचित, उपदेशकरणीय, उपदेशास्पद.

ADVISABILITY, ADVISABLENESS, *n.* v. A. योग्यता *f.* औचित्य *n.* लायकी *f.* उपदेश्यता *f.* उपदेशार्हता *f.*

To ADVISE, *v. a. give counsel to.* मसलत *f.*-सल्ला*m. f.*-उपदेश*m.* -&c. देणें, उपदेशणें, चार गोष्टी *f. pl.*-अक्कल *f.*-&c. सांगणें-देणें, बुद्धिवाद *m.* सांगणें-देणें, बोधन *n.*-प्रबोधन*n.*-मंत्रण*n.*-अभिमंत्रण *n.*-&c. करणें.

2 *recommend by counsel.* उपदेश *m.*-मसलत *f.*-सल्ला *m. f.*-&c. करणें *g. of o.* बुद्धिवाद *m.* सांगणें-देणें *g.of o.*

3 *make acquainted.* v. To INFORM. कळवणें, जाणवणें, माहितगार-माहीत-बोधित-सूचित-&c. करणें.

ADVISED, *p.* v. V. 1. 2. उपदेश-&c. केलेला, उपदिष्ट, आदिष्ट, बोधित, प्रबोधित, अभिमंत्रित, मंत्रित.

3 माहितगार केलेला, सूचित, बोधित, विज्ञापित.

ADVISEDLY, *adv. deliberately, purposely, heedfully.* विचारानें, विचारपूर्वक, विचार पाहून, बुद्धिपुरःसर, बुद्धिपूर्वक, बुद्ध्या, मनन करून, सावधपणीं, मंत्रतः.

ADVISEDNESS, *n. deliberateness.* सविचारता *f.* सविवेकता *f.* विचारसाहित्य *n.* विमृश्यकारिता *f.* समीक्ष्यकारिता *f.*

ADVISER, *n.* ADVISING, *p. a.* v. V. 1. 2. उपदेशणारा, &c. बुद्धिसहाय, उपदेशक, मसलतदार, अभिमंत्री, मंत्री, अभिमंता, आदेशी, उपदेष्टा, उपदेशकर्त्ता, बोधनकर्त्ता, बोधक, प्रबोधक, चार गोष्टी-अक्कल- &c. सांगणारा.

Evil a. कुमंत्री.

3 See INFORMANT.

ADVISING, *n.* v. V. 1.—*act.* उपदेशणें *n.* &c. बुद्धिवाद *m.* *v.* सांग, बोध *m.* बोधन *n.* प्रबोध *m.* प्रबोधन *n.* आदेश *m.* अभिमंत्रण *n.* मंत्रण *n.* उपदेशन. *n.*

2—*act.* जाणवणें *n.* बोधवणें *n.* &c. विज्ञापन *n.* बोधन *n.* प्रबोधन *n.* सूचन *n.*

ADVOCACY, ADVOCATION, *n.* v.V.1.—*act.* वकिली *f.* वकालत *f.* परार्थ विवदन *n.* परार्थप्रार्थन *n.* पक्षधारण *n.*

To ADVOCATE, *v. a. plead for.* पक्ष *m.* धरून बोलणें-प्रार्थना *f.* करणें, वकिली *f.*-वकालत *f.* करणें *g. of o.* परार्थविवदन *n*- परार्थवाद *m.*-परार्थविवाद *m.*-परार्थप्रार्थन *n*- परार्थप्रार्थना *f.* करणें.

ADVOCATE, ADVOCATER, *n.* v. V. पक्ष धरून बोलणारा &c. परार्थविवादी, परपक्षविवादी.

I. *pleader in a Court.* वकील *m.*

ADYTUM, *n. inner division of a temple.* गाभार *or* राम.गर्भगृह *n.*

ADZ, ADDICE, *n.* तासणी *f.* बांकस *or* बाकस *m.* बसुला *m.* बसुली *f.* तक्षणी *f.*

To cut with an a. (to pare, chip, plane, &c.) तासणें.

Cut with an a. तासींव.

Work done with an a. तासकाम *n.* तास *m.*

Worker with an a. तासकामी or ऱ्या.

ÆGILOPS, *n.* नासूर *m. n.*

AERIAL, *a. belonging to the air.* वायुसंबंधी, पवनसंबंधी, वातसंबंधी, वायुविषयक, वातविषयक, वायूचा, &c. आकाशीय, आकाशी, वायव्य.

2 *consisting of air.* वायूचा, वायुरूप, वातरूप, वातमय, वायुमय, वातात्मक, वाय्वात्मक.

3 *inhabiting the air.* आकाशांत- &c. राहणारा, आकाशवासी, आकाशस्थायी, आकाशगामी, अंतरिक्षगामी, अंतरिक्षस्थायी, अंतरिक्षवासी, खचर *or* खेचर, आकाशचारी, आकाशचर.

4 *placed, being, &c. in the air.* आकाशस्थ, अंतरिक्षस्थ, अंतरालस्थ, खस्थ, नभोनिष्ठ, नभःस्थित.

AERIFIED, *p.* v. V. वायु घातलेला-&c. वायुभरित, वायुमिश्रित.

AERIFORM, *a. having the form, &c. of air.* वायुरूप, वातरूप, वातमय, वातात्मक, वाय्वाकार.

To AERIFY, *v. a. fill with air, combine with air.* वायु *m.* आंतघालणें-भरणें.

AEROGRAPHY, AEROLOGY. *n. description of the air.* वायुशास्त्र *n.* वायुविद्या *f.* वायुवर्णन *n.* [ला दगड *m.*

AEROLITE, *n. stone fallen from the air.* आकाशांतून-&c. पडले-

AEROMETER, *n.* वायुयंत्र *n.* वायुमापकयंत्र *n.*

AEROMETRY, *n.* वायुमिति *f.* वायुमापनविद्या *f.*

AERONAUT, *n.* विमानांत बसून आकाशांत फिरणारा, आकाशचारी *m.* आकाशगामी *m.* खचर *m.*

AEROSTATION, *n. aerial navigation.* आकाशगमन *n.* आकाशयान *n.* आकाशसंचार *m.* आकाशोड्डीन *n.*

2 *science of weighing air.* वायुमिति *f.* वायुमापनविद्या *f.*

AEROSTATICS, *n. science of weighing air.* वायुप्रमाणविद्या *f.*

ÆSTHETICS, *n. the science of the beautiful,* &c. सौंदर्य तत्वानुशासनविद्या *f.* कृत्रिमाकृत्रिमपदार्थसौंदर्यविज्ञान *n.*

ÆTHIOPS MINERAL, *n. sulphuret of mercury.* कज्जली *f.*

AFAR, *adv.* दूर, लांब, लांबीवर, दूरवर, दूरतः.

From a. दुरून, लांबून.

That is a. off. दूरचा, दूरस्थ.

AFFABILITY, AFFABLENESS, *n.* v. A. तोंडचीगोडी *f.*-भलाई *f.* &c. भलमाणसाई *f.* सुजनता *f.* सुजनत्व *n.* सौजन्य *n.* हळबळीतपणा *m.* हळबळेपणा *m.* घळघळीतपणा *m.*

AFFABLE, *a. courteous, &c.* बोलून चांगला-भला-गोड, तोंडचाभला, तोंडचागोड, तोंडचानीट, चालकाबोलका *or* बोलकाचालका, जाचसाली, हळबळा, हळबळीत, घळघळीत, गोडबोल्या.

AFFABLY, *adv.* v. A. भलमाणसाईनें, हळबळीतपणानें, घळघळीतपणानें, सौजन्यपूर्वक.

AFFAIR, *n matter to be done, or done.* काम *n.* कार्य *n.* कर्त्तव्य *n.* काज *n.* मुकद्दमा *m.* प्रयोज्य *n.*

2 *matter, business, concern,—freely.* काम *n.* कार्य *n.* गोष्ट *f.* व्यवहार *m.* बाका *m.* खटलें *n.* खटला *m.* वस्तु *f.* गाणें *n.* प्रकरण *n.* विषय *m.* मात *f.* बाबत *f.* बाब *f.*

A confused and perplexed a. भानगड *f.* घोंटाळा *m.*

A delicate a. नाजूक काम. *n.*

A pressing, urgent, &c. a. निकडीची गोष्ट *f.* [हार *m.*

A private, obscure, &c. a. सांदींतली गोष्ट *f.* सांदींतला व्यव-

A vexatious or troublesome a. सुकालफडा *m.*

Settlement of an a. कार्यनिर्णय *m.*

A. of honor. See DUEL.

3 affairs: *public concerns.* सरकारचीं कामें *n. pl.*-प्रकरणें *n.pl.*

To AFFECT, *v. a. act upon.* कार्य *n.*-कर्तृत्व *n.*-कृती *f.*-गुण *m.*-&c. करणें, लागणें, लागू होणें-चालणें-चालू *or* चालता होणें *with* वर *of o.* आंगीं *or* आंगास येणें.—injuriously, बाधणें, विकार *m.*-विकृति *f.* होणें *with* पासून.

2 (the passions) *touch, move.* वेधणें, गळा *m. or* कंठ *m.* भरून आणणें-दाटून आणणें *g. of o.* सद्गद-सद्गदित करणें, पघळवणें, द्रवणें, पाझरवणें, पाझर *m.*-कलवळ *f.*-कलवळा *m.*-गहिंवर *m.*-&c. आणणें, लागणें.

3 *aim at, aspire after.* इच्छा धरून डोळा *m.* ठेवणें, इच्छापूर्वक उद्देश *m.* करणें-लक्षिणें, अभिलाषपूर्वकदृष्टि *f.* ठेवणें.

4 *assume and display.* v. To PRETEND. दंभ *m.*-ढोंग *n.*-आडंबर *n.*-पोम *n.*-स्तोम *n.* करणें-माजवणें-वाढवणें *g. of o.* डौल *m.* करणें-दाखवणें-मांडणें *g. of o.* घेणें, नस्ता *a.* (used with a noun) आणणें-दाखवणें.

AFFECTATION, *n.* v. AIRS. अकड *f.* अकडबाजी *f.* कुर्रा *m.* तोरा *m.* नाजकाई *f.* नाजूकपणा *m.* नटणें *n.*

—esp. of females. नखरा *m.* गमजे *m. pl.* ठमका *m.* ठमकणें *n.*

2 v. PRETENCE. दंभ *or* डंभ *m.* पोम *n.* डौल *or* नस्ता डौल *m.* ढोंग *m.* स्तोम *n.* दाखवणूक *f.* *v.* दाखव.

AFFECTED, *p.* v. V. 1. गुण आलेला-लागलेला, प्राप्तगुण, बाधलेला.

2 *moved, touched.* कंठ भरून आलेला, गळा भरून आलेला, सद्गद, सद्गदित, रसाभिनिविष्ट.

To be a. तडतड तोडणें (पोटांत) *v. imp.* कंठ *m.*-गळा *m.* भरून येणें, गळा *m.*-कंठ *m.* दाटून येणें, सद्गदित होणें.

4 v. PRETENDED. आणलेला, कृत्रिम, सोंगाचा, ढोंगाचा, डौलाचा, बरकरणी, बरकर्मी.

I. *having affectation.* अकडबाज, अकडखोर, कुरेंदार, कुरेंबाज, तोरेदार, मिजाजी, नाजूक, मुरडुगा.

—esp. of females. नखरेबाज, नखरेदार, गमजेखोर, मुरडुगी.

II. *labored, strained,* v. FORCED. ओढून आणलेला, क्लिष्ट.

AFFECTEDLY, *adv. with affectation.* अकड करून, अकडीनें, नाजकाईनें, नाजूकपणें, तोऱ्यानें, नटून थटून, थटून, डौलानें.

—esp. of females. नखऱ्यानें, गमजा करून-लावून.

AFFECTING, *p. a.* v. V. 2. *moving, touching,* v. PATHETIC. वेधक, अंतर्यामी, हृदयवेधक, हृदयंगम, करुण, करुणापर, रसिक.

AFFECTION, *n. fondness,* v. LOVE. ममता *f.* माया *f.* मोह *m.* आवड *f.* लोभ *m.* चाड *f.* प्रेम *n.* प्रेमा *m.* स्नेह *m.* स्नेहभाव *m.*

Disengagedness of the affections. मनसुटका *f.*

Empty, hollow, barren, &c. a.कोरडी ममता*f.*सुकी ममता*f.*

True, active, &c. a. ओली ममता *f.*

Maternal a. पोटची आग *f.* पोटाग *f.*

Object of a. प्रीतिपात्र*n.*मोहपात्र *n.*ममतास्पद*n.*ममतायतन*n.*

Overflowing (rising and swelling) of a. प्रेमपान्हा *m.* प्रेमा *m.* प्रेम *n.* गहिंवर *m.*

Paternal a. सुतस्नेह *m.* पुत्रस्नेह *m.* पुत्रलोभ *m.*

Platonic a. पाकदोस्ती *f.*

Single or undivided a. अनन्यभाव *m.*

To pretend great a. for. तोंडांत तोंड *n.* घालणें.

2 (of the mind), *a passion, a mental feeling.* मनोधर्म*m.* मनोविकार *m.* मनोविकृति *f.* मनोवृत्ति *f.* वृत्ति *f.* विकार*m.* &c. विकृति *f.* (esp. in comp. as कामविकार, क्रोधविकार, लोभविकार, मोहविकार, and कामविकृति &c.) भाव *m.* राग *m.* रस *m.*

3 (of the body), *state arising from, and indicative of the working of a passion or sentiment.* आकार *m.* अनुभाव *m.* विकार *m.* भाव *m.* वृत्ति *f.*

4 (of the mind or body), *emotion, mood, or condition of it.* भाव *m.* These are distinguished into स्थायीभाव and व्यभिचारिभाव or संचारिभाव (*regular, fixed, essential, &c.* and *irregular, advenient, &c.* passions or conditions.) The first are eight—रति, हास, शोक, क्रोध, उत्साह, भय, जुगुप्सा, विस्मय; the second are thirty-two—निर्वेद, ग्लानि, शंका, असूया, मद, श्रम, आलस्य, दैन्य, चिंता, मोह, स्मृति, धृति, व्रीडा, चपलता, हर्ष, आवेग, जडता, गर्व, विषाद, औत्सुक्य, निद्रा, अपस्मार, शय, विबोध, अमर्ष, अवहित्था, उग्रता, मति, उपालंभ, व्याधि, उन्माद, मरण, to which are sometimes added two others—त्रास, वितर्क. There is, further, a middle class named सात्विकभाव. They consist of eight—स्तंभ, प्रलय, रोमांच, स्वेद, वैवर्ण्य, वेपथु, अश्रु, वैस्वर्य.

5 *affectedness from external action.* विकार*m.*विकृति*f.*as of the eyes नेत्रविकार—of the ear कर्णविकार &c. and—of milk, blood, water, air, &c.दुग्धविकार, रक्तविकार, जलविकार, वातविकार.

AFFECTIONATE, *a.* v. N. and LOVING. ममतेचा, प्रेमाचा, &c. ममतालु *or* ळू, प्रेमाळू, मायाळू, प्रेमवान्, प्रेमवंत, प्रेमल *or* ळ, स्नेहाळू, मायावान्, मायावंत, मायाशील, ममताशील, वत्सल.

AFFECTIONATELY, *adv.* v. A. ममतेनें, मायेनें, प्रेमानें, प्रीतीनें, ममता-प्रीति-&c. पूर्वक, आवडीनें.

AFFECTIONATENESS, *n.* v. A. प्रेमळपणा *m.* ममताळूपणा *m.*&c. ममतालुत्व *n.* वात्सल्य *n.* वत्सलता *f.* प्रेमलता *f.* प्रीतिमत्व *n.* मायाशीलता *f.*

AFFECTIONED, *a. disposed, inclined.* भावाचा, बुद्धीचा, (as kindly a. स्नेहभावाचा).

AFFIANCE, *n. marriage-contract.* वाङ्निश्चय *or* वाग्निश्चय*m.*

2 *faith reposed,* v. TRUST. भरवसा *m.* विश्वास *m.* प्रत्यय *m.* श्रद्धा *f.*

To AFFIANCE, See To BETROTH.

AFFIDAVIT, *n.* v. OATH. शपथ *f,* v. बाह, सत्योत्तर *n.*

Upon one's a. सत्योत्तर, सत्योत्तरें.

Written a. शपथेवर जबानी *f.* क्रियापत्र *n.* सशपथलेख *m.* शपथपूर्वकपत्र *n.*

To AFFILIATE, *v. a.* See To ADOPT. 2 *receive into a society* &c. सख्यसंबंधानें जोडणें, मंडळींत घेणें, स्वसंबंधी करणें.

AFFILIATED, *p.*v.V.2 सख्यसंबंधानें जोडलेला, स्वसंबंधी केलेला, &c.

AFFINITY, *n. relation by marriage.* सोयरीक *f.* सोयरगत *f.* नातें *n.* लगत *f.* आप्तभाव *m.* आप्तपणा *m.* पदर *m.* पालव *m.* पल्लव *m.* अन्वय *m.* शरीरसंबंध *m.* योनिसंबंध *m.* यौनसंबंध *m.* विवाहसंबंध *m.* साक्षात्संबंध *m.* विवाहभूतसंबंध *m.* विवाहकृतसंबंध *m.* विवाहद्वारासंबंध *m.*

2 *relation, resemblance, &c.* v. LIKENESS. संबंध *m.* सादृश्य *n.* आभास *m.* आनुगुण्य *n.* अभ्युपगम *m.*

3—in chemistry. प्रीति *f.* जम *m.*

To AFFIRM, *v. n. assert, aver, asseverate, protest; allege.* स्वचीतपणें *adv.*—खंबीरपणें *adv.*-निखालस-प्रतिज्ञापूर्वक-निश्चयपूर्वक*adv.*—बोलणें-म्हणणें &c.

To AFFIRM, *v. a. declare positively.* प्रतिज्ञेनें-प्रतिज्ञापूर्वक-निश्चयात्मक-स्वचीतपणें-खंबीरपणें-निश्चयपूर्वक-&c. सांगणें-म्हणणें, &c.

2 *confirm,* v. To RATIFY. खरा-रुजू-बहाल-काईम-&c. करणें, खरावणें.

AFFIRMATION, *n.* v. V. A.—*act.* स्वचीतपणें-&c. सांगणें *n.* निश्चयात्मक कथन *n.* निश्चितकथन *n.* दृढकथन *n.*

2—*act.* खरा-काईम-&c. करणें *n.*

I. *matter affirmed.* वचन *n.* निश्चितवाक्य *n.* निश्चितोक्ति *f.* निर्वाद *m.* प्रतिज्ञा *f.*

AFFIRMATIVE, *a.*—opp. to negative. आहेपणाचा, होयपक्षाचा, होयपक्षी, अस्तिपक्षाचा, अस्तिपक्षस्थापक, अस्त्यर्थक.

AFFIRMATIVE, *n.* अस्तिपक्ष *m.* होयपक्ष *m.*

AFFIRMATIVELY, *adv.* v.A. होयपक्ष धरून, होकार*or* हुकार देऊन, होय म्हणून, अस्तिपक्षस्थापनपूर्वक.

AFFIRMED, *p.* v. V. A. 1. स्वचीतपणें सांगितलेला, &c. निश्चयात्मककथित, दृढकथित, प्रतिज्ञात.

To AFFIX, *v. a, join or add to,* v. To ADD. जोडणें, जडणें, दुमाल्यास लावणें, बसविणें.

2 *attach to*—freely. लावणें, आरोपणें, आरोप*m.*-आरोपण *n.* करणें *g. of o.* आरोपित करणें.

AFFIX, *n.* in gram. अनुबंध *m.* प्रत्यय *m.* आप्तोक्ति *f.*

AFFLATUS, *n. blast of wind*, वाऱ्याचा झटका *m.*- झटकारा *m.*
2 *inspiration*, वारें *n.* घुमारा *m.* अवसर *m.*
Subject of a. (देवाचें) झाड *n. or* झाड्या *m.*

To AFFLICT, *v. a. pain, distress.* दुःख *n.*-पीडा *f.*-क्लेश *m.*-&c. देणें, दुखवणें *or* दुखावणें, पिडणें, पिडवणें, क्लेशणें, श्रमवणें, कष्टवणें, रडवणें, दुःखी-श्रमी-कष्टी-पीडित-क्लेशी-क्लेशित-&c. करणें.

AFFLICTED, *p.* v. V. दुखवलेला, पिडलेला, &c. दुःखित, दुःखी, दुःखयुक्त, दुःखान्वित, पीडित, पीडाकुल, श्रमी, कष्टी, व्यथित, आर्त्त, खिन्न, खेदित, खेदान्वित, क्लेशी, क्लेशित, क्लेशापन्न, शोकान्वित, संतापित, मनस्तापित.—in high degree. दुःखाक्रांत, दुःखग्रस्त, दुःखव्याप्त, दुःखदग्ध, दुःखाप्लुत, दुःखछिन्न, शोकाक्रांत, शोकाकुल, शोकग्रस्त, शोकातुर, शोकाविष्ट, शोकदग्ध, शोकाभिसंतप्त, शोकार्त्त, शोकाप्लुत, शोकविह्वल, कृच्छ्रगत, हतोत्साह, भग्नोत्साह, समुत्सुक.
An a. person. दुःखाचा प्राणी *m.*
To be a. दुखारणें, दुःख *n.* पावणें, क्लेश *m.* भोगणें.
To comfort the a. रडत्याचें आंसू *n.* पुसणें.

AFFLICTER, *n.* AFFLICTING, *p.a.* AFFLICTIVE, *a.*v.V. दुःख देणारा, दुखवणारा, &c. दुःखकर, दुःखकारक, दुःखदायक, दुःखजनक, दुःखप्रद, दुःखद, दुःखावह, पीडाकर, पीडाकर्त्ता, व्यथक, श्रमकर, श्रमकारक, श्रमजनक, श्रमावह, कष्टकर, कष्टकारक-कारी-&c. क्लेशक, क्लेशदायक, क्लेशप्रद, शोकद, शोकप्रद, शोकावह.

AFFLICTION, *n.* v. V. —*act.* दुखवणें *n.* पिडणें *n.* &c. दुखवणूक *f.* दुःखप्रदान *n.* पीडन *n.* पीडाकरण *n.* पीडा *f.*
—*state;* or, *grief, sorrow, &c.* दुःख *n.* खेद *m.* शोक *m.* दुःखीपणा *m.* श्रमीपणा *m.* &c. श्रम *m.* कष्ट *m.* क्लेश *m.* खिन्नत्व *n.* दुःखिता *f.* आर्त्ति *f.* व्यथा *f.* संताप *m.* मनस्ताप *m.* दुःखावस्था *f.*
Partner in a. समदुःखी *m.* दुःखाचा सोबती *m.*
I. *cause of a.* v. CALAMITY, TROUBLE. दुःख *n.* अनिष्ट *n.* आकांत *m.* अनर्थ *m.* गंडांत *n.* गंडांतर *n.* [हन *n.*

AFFLUENCE, *n. flowing into.* वाहून येणें *n.* आवहन *n.* अभिव-
2 *abundance of riches*, v. RICHES. संपत्ति *f.* संपदा *f.* धनबाहुल्य *n.* श्री *f.* धनसमृद्धि *f.* धनविपुलता *f.* धनवैपुल्य *n.*

AFFLUENT, *a.* v. N. अभिवाही, वहमान.
2 v. RICH. द्रव्यवान्, पैकेवान्, श्रीमान्, श्रीमंत, संपन्न, धनसंपन्न, धनसमृद्ध, धनविपुल, धनबहुल.

AFFLUX, *n. flowing unto.* अभिवहन *n.* आवहन *n.*
2 *matter flowing unto.* वाहवण *f.* वाहणी *or* वहाणी *f.*

To AFFORD, *v. a. yield unto*, v. To PRODUCE. उपजणें, निपजणें, प्रापण *n.* करणें, प्राप्ति *f.*-पैदास्त *f.*-उपज *m.*-उत्पन्न *n.*-&c. होणें *s. governed by* पासून, पदरीं येणें *or* हातास लागणें *or* प्राप्त होणें *s. with* पासून, पावणें *or* पोंहचणें *s. with* पासून.
2 *grant, confer*, v. To GIVE. देणें, दान *n.* करणें *g. of o.* उपधान *n.*-प्रापण *n.* करणें *g. of o.*
3 (some expense, cost, loss, &c.) In every construction in this sense To AFFORD is resolvable into *To be able to give*. This verb therefore is ever to be so resolved. Thus, *I can a. to bear, to yield, to lose, to pay for, to sell for, to part with for the getting of*, (which applications comprehend the whole power of the verb) signifying simply *I am able to give* —away or up, —in purchase of,—in sale for,—in exchange with,—is to be rendered, (See Able, and To be Able) मला देववतें-देतां येतें &c. or through some verb expressing a variation of the sense *Giving*, as, मला सोडवतें-टाकवतें-खरचवतें-विकवतें-बदलवतें-&c.

AFFRAY, *n.* See FIGHT, QUARREL.

AFFREIGHT, &c. See FREIGHT, &c.

AFFRIGHT, See FRIGHT. &c.

To AFFRONT, *v.a. insult openly.* तोंडावर मारणें, तोंडावर अप्रतिष्ठा *f.*-अपमान *m.*-&c. करणें *g. of o.* तोंडावर आब्रू *f.* घेणें, तोंडाची *or* डोळ्याची भीड *f.*-मुरवत *f.* मोडणें.
2 *make slightly angry*, v. To OFFEND. खिजवणें, चिडवणें, चीढ *f.* आणणें, रुसवणें, रुष्ट-खपा-&c. करणें. [अप्रतिष्ठा *f.*

AFFRONT, *n. an insult to the face.* तोंडावर अपमान *m.* तोंडावर
2—gener. See INSULT.
To take a. खिजणें, चिडणें, रुसणें, रुसवा *m.* धरणें, खपा होणें, वाईट मानणें.

AFFRONTED, *p.* v. V. 2. खपा, रुष्ट, रुसलेला, रुसवा धरलेला.

To AFFUSE, *v. a. pour to or upon.* ओतणें-घालणें *with* वर, धार *f.* सोडणें-धरणें *with* वर.

AFFUSION, *n.* v. V. *act.* ओतणें *n.* धार सोडणें *n.* धारोपपातन *n.* धाराभ्युपपातन *n.*
I. *matter poured.* सोडलेलीधार *f.* उपपातितधारा *f.*

AFIRE, *adv.* जळतां, जळत असतां, जळत.

AFIELD, *adv.* शेतांत, शेताला.

AFLOAT, *adv. or a. floating.* तरतां, तरत असतां, तरंगत असतां, वाहतां, पोवतां, पोवत असतां, पाण्यावर.
2—a rumour, &c. उडतउडत, तोंडातोंडीं, कर्णोपकर्णीं.
3 *unfixed, in disorder.* अव्यवस्थित, अस्ताव्यस्त.

AFOOT, *adv.* पायीं, पायानें, पाय उतारां, पादचालीनें *or* पादचालीं, चरण चालीनें *or* चरणचालीं.
2 *in action.* चालू, सुरू, उगा, प्रवृत्त.
To set a. v. To SET UP. उठवणें, उडवणें, मांडणें, चालू करणें.

AFORE, AFOREGOING, AFOREHAND. For AFORE and its compounds, See BEFORE, & ABOVE.

AFORTIORI, विशेषेंकरून, अधिकतर, दृढतर.

AFRAID, *a.* v. FRIGHTENED. भयभीत, भययुक्त, भीत, सभय, भयान्वित, सशंक, साशंक, शंकामय, आशंकित.
To be a. v. To FEAR. भय *n.* वाटणें *in. con.*

AFRESH, *adv.* v. AGAIN. नव्यानें, दुसऱ्यानें, उलटून, उलट (in comp. as उलटतपासणी), मागल्यानें, फिरून, अणखी, पुनः *pop.* पुन्हा, दुसऱ्या आवृत्तीनें.
To do a. उलटणें.

AFRONT, *adv. in front.* पुढें, समोर, मोहरें, तोंडापुढें, पुरः (in comp. as पुरोगामी, पुरोवर्त्ती).

AFT, *adv. towards the stern.* वरामाकडे, मागल्या भागाकडे.

AFTER, *a. later, posterior, subsequent.* To this word, appearing only in composition, correspond मागचा, पाठीमागचा, मागला, उत्तर, पश्चात्, पश्चिम, पृष्ठ, अगामी, अनंतर.
For exemplification See *After-life, Afternoon*, and other compounds amongst these following in order.

AFTER, *prep. following in place or order.* मागें, पाठीमागें, पाठीवर, पाठीं, पश्चात्, पलीकडे, मागल्याबाजूस, पृष्ठभागीं, न (in comp. as झाडानझाड, घरानघर, पैशानपैसा, रुपयानरुपया, Tree *after* tree, penny *after* penny, &c .).

Immediately a. मागोमाग, पाठोपाठ, लगोलग.

2 *following in line.* मागें, पाठीमागें, पाठीवर, पाठीं, पाठीहून, पाठोस, मागून or मागाहून, वर, वरून, पश्चात् (esp. in comp. as पश्चादागामी, पश्चात्ताप), उत्तर (in comp. as फाल्गुनोत्तर, एतदुत्तर, तदुत्तर,), उपरांत, उपरांतीक, उपरी, उपर, अर्वाक, अंती (as अनुभवअंतीं, केल्याअंतीं, घेतल्याअंती). [*g. of o.*

To follow a. v. To PURSUE मागें-पाठीमागें-&c. जाणें, *with*

3 *according to,* v. ACCORDING. प्रमाणें, सारखा, अनुरूप.

4 *in imitation of,* v. LIKE. अनुलक्षून, पाहून, सारखा, वर, वाणीं (as वेड्यावाणीं), परी (as लेंकरापरी, मूर्खापरी), गत, चाल, तऱ्हा, डौल *m.*-&c. उतरून.

5 *respecting, concerning.* विषयीं.

AFTER, *adv.* v. AFTERWARDS. मग, मागें, पश्चात्.

For direction on the rendering of this adverb as it occurs in composition, see the *adjective,* and, for exemplification, see amongst the compounds below.

AFTER-ACCOUNT, *n.* मागचा हिशेब *m.* पश्चात्गणना *f.* पश्चात्संख्याकलन *n.* पश्चात्यायव्ययदर्शन *n.* पश्चात्संख्यान *n.*

AFTER-ACT, *n.* मागचें काम *n.* पश्चात्कर्म *n.* पश्चात्-क्रिया *f.*-कृति *f.*-करण *n.*

AFTER-AGES, *n. succeeding ages.* मागचे लोक *m. pl.* पश्चात्परंपरा *f.* पश्चादन्वय *m.*

2 *future ages.* पुढचे लोक *m.pl.* पुढें येणारे *m.pl.* पुढील काळ *m.* उत्तरकाल *m.* आजपासून पुढल्या पिढ्या *f. pl.* पुत्रपौत्रादिवंशपरंपरा *f.* आगामिपरंपरा *f.* आगमिष्यमाणवंश *m.*

AFTER-ALL, *adv.* v. AT LAST. शेवटीं, निदानीं, सर्वोपरांतीक.

AFTER-BIRTH, *n. secundines.* वार *f.* गर्भवेष्टन *n.* गर्भाशय *m.* जरायु *m. pop.* जार *mn.* खोळ *f.* कूस *f.*

AFTER-COMER, *n.* मागचा or पाठीमागें येणारा, पृष्ठग, पृष्ठानुयायी, अनंतरागामी, पश्चादागामी, अनुगामी, &c.

AFTER-COST, *n.* मागचा खर्च *m.* पश्चाद्व्यय *m.*

AFTER-CROP, *n. subsequent or later crop.* गिमवस *f.* or गिमवसचें पीक *n.* बांत्रगणें *n.* or बांत्रगण्याचें पीक *n.* बांत्रगणेंपीक *n.* (esp. of the pulses) दुसोटा *m.* दुसोट्याचें पीक *n.* पश्चिम धान्य *n.* पश्चाद्धान्य *n.*

AFTER-GAME, *n.* पश्चात्चेष्टा *f.* अतीतकालव्यापार *m.*

AFTER-HOURS, *n.* अवेळ *f.* अतिक्रांतसमय *m.*

AFTER-LIFE, *n. latter part of life.* उत्तरपराई *f.* उत्तरवय *n.* उतरतीपराई *f.* परिणतवय *n.* अस्तंगामिवय *n.* परार्ध *n.*

AFTERMATH, *n. second crop of grass.* गवताची दुसरी फूट *f.* दुसरा फुटवा *m.*

AFTERMOST, *a.* सर्वांचे पाठीमागचा, सर्वानंतरचा, सर्वचरम, सर्वांत्य, सर्वपृष्ठग, सर्वांतिक, पश्चात्तम.

AFTER-NOON, *n.* दोनप्रहरानंतरचाकाळ *m.* दोनप्रहरानंतरचीवेळ *f* तिसराप्रहर *m.* परतवेळ *f.* परान्ह *m.* अपरान्ह *f. m.* [वेळ *f.*

A. and evening, *the declining half.* उतरतीवेळ *f.* उतार-

AFTER-PAINS, *n.* जारवेण *f.* जरायुवेदना *f.* पश्चादावी *f.*

AFTER-PART, *n.* पश्चादंग *m.* पश्चाद्भाग *m.* पश्चाद्विभाग *m.* उत्तरार्ध *n.* उत्तरभाग *m.* उत्तरांश *m.*

AFTER-STING, *n.* परिणामदुःख *n.* परिणतिक्लेश *m.*

AFTER-THOUGHT, *n.* पश्चिमबुद्धि *f* पश्चाद्बुद्धि *f.* पश्चात्कल्पना *f.* पश्चान्मति *f.* पश्चिमज्ञान *n.* पश्चात्ज्ञान *n.* पश्चात्कलना *f.* पश्चात्भावना *f.* पश्चाद्विचार *m.* पश्चात्कल्प *m.* पश्चाद्वेदन *n.* पृष्ठबुद्धि *f.*

AFTER-TIME, *n.* पश्चात्-काल *m.*-समय *m.*-अवसर *m.*-दिवस *m.*-दिन *nm.*-&c.

AFTER-WARDS, *adv. in subsequent time.* मागून or मागाहून, मागें, मग, अनंतर *pop.* नंतर, उपर, उपरांतिक, तदुपरांतिक, तदुपरि, उत्तरतः, उत्तरत्र, तदुत्तर, तदनंतर, नंतर (with झाल्या &c. as हें झाल्यानंतर), तेव्हां, पृष्ठतः, परतः.

AFTER-WISE, *a.* पश्चाज्ज्ञानी, पश्चाज्ज्ञानवान्, पश्चाद्वित्, पश्चाज्ज्ञ, पश्चाद्विज, पश्चान्निपुण, पश्चाद्विचारी.

AFTER-WIT, *n.* v. AFTER-THOUGHT. पश्चात्ज्ञान *n.* पश्चिमबुद्धि *f.* पश्चाद्वेदन *n.*

AFTER-WRATH, *n.* पश्चादमर्ष *m.* पश्चाद्रोष *m.*

AFTERINGS, *n. strokings.* चिटणें *n.* चिटलेलें दूध *n.*

AGAIN, *adv. another time.* अणखी, अणीक, दुसऱ्यान् or नें, फिरून, परतून, पुनः *pop.* पुन्हा, मागुत्यान् or नी or नें, or माकुत्यान् &c. मागतीं, उजू or जूं, अन्यदा, फेर, अणखी एकदां, पुढतीं, दुसारणी, भूयः.

A. and a. पुनःपुनः, पुनःपुनरपि, वारंवार, फिरून फिरून.

A. and yet a. पुनरपि, पुनश्च, फिर फिरून.

As much a. अणखी इतका or एवढा, दुपट, द्विगुण.

2 *back in restitution,* v. BACK. पुनः, परत, परतून, फिरून, माघारां, or रीं.

3 *in return for, in recompense of.* बद्दल or ला, ठिकाणीं, पायीं, उलटून, उलट, बदलखातर. [अन्यच्च.

4 *on the other hand.* अन्यपक्षीं, पुनः, परंतु, प्रत्युत, अन्यत् or

AGAINST, *prep. in opposition to.* विरुद्ध, वर, प्रति, वि, &c.

Note. The genius of the *Maráthí* language does not permit exact rendering of this word. Sentences therefore constructed with it should be broken down, and rendered with single eye to the *sense.* For this mode will be wanted prepositions and particles and nouns and adjectives of varying meanings and powers and bearings; and, of such words there will be found abundance. Thus—to render *I am or I act against him,* may be employed—विरुद्ध, विपरीत, प्रतिकूल, शत्रु, वैरी, विषम, अमित्र, अडवा, उलटा, *(opposed, opposite,)* as, मी त्यास विरुद्ध-विपरीत-&c. आहें:—विरोध, विपर्यास, विपर्यय, प्रातिकूल्य, द्वेष, वैषम्य, विरोधभाव, अडवेपणा, उलटेपणा, *(opposition)* as, माझा त्यासीं विरोध-विरोधभाव-द्वेष-अडवेपणा-&c. आहे, or मी त्यासीं विरोध करितों त्याचा द्वेष करितों:—तोंडावर *(in the face or teeth of;)* as त्याचे तोंडावर करितों:—सीं *(with ;)* as, त्यासीं लढून-झुंजून-भांडून-&c. करितों:—and such phrases as विरोध करून, वैर बाळगून, कमर बांधून, वर चढून, तोंडावर मारून, मरजी मोडून, &c.&c. The *Sanskrit* prepositions प्रति and वि well express the sense of *against*; but they are *inseparable* prepositions; ex. प्रत्युद्गम or प्रत्युद्गमन *going against,* प्रत्युद्गत *gone against,* प्रतिकार or प्रतिक्रिया *acting against,* and विपक्ष, विमत, विमुख, &c. In *Sanskrit* प्रति as well as some other *inseparable* prepositions, appear separately, as प्रतिसूर्य *against the sun,* प्रतिवात *against the wind.*

2—in place, v. OPPOSITE. समोर, सम्मुख *pop.* सन्मुख.

3 *in provision for or expectation of.* लक्षून, लक्ष्य *n.*-धो-

रण *n*.-संधान*n*.-&c. धरून-ठेवून *g. of s.* सधीस-संधीवर *with g. of o.* वर.

4 *bearing upon.* शीं.

Agallochum *n. aloe wood.* अगर *m. n.* अगरू *m.*

Agape, *adv.* तोंड वासून, तोंड पसरून, तोंड विचकून, आ पसरून.

Agate, *n.* गोमेद*m.* गोमेदक*m.* [दांय *m.*

Age, *n. whole duration or term of.* आयुष्य *n.* आयु *m.* आयु-

2 v. Generation. पिढी. *f.*

3 (of the world) युग *n.* The four *ages* of the *Hindus*, corresponding somewhat with the *golden, silver, &c.*, *ages*, are कृत, त्रेता, द्वापर, कलि. [आहे.

Ages rolled away. युगयुगांतरें लोटलीं आहेत, कैककाळ गेला

Beginning of an a. युगादि*m.*

End of an a. युगांत *m.*

Golden a. सत्ययुग *n.* सत्य *n.*

Interval between two ages. संधि*m.* संध्या *f.*

Lapse of ages. कालगति *f.*

4 *division of life.* वयोवस्था *f.* दशा *f.* पराई *f.*

The three ages. अवस्थात्रय *n.* These are *childhood* (i. e. infancy and adolescence.)बाल्यावस्था *f.* बालत्व*n.* *youth* (i. e. puberty and manhood,) तारुण्यावस्था *f.* तरुणत्व*n.* *age* (i. e. declining years and senility,) वार्धक्यावस्था *f.* वृद्धत्व*n.* वार्धक्य*n.* Another account makes four ages. अवस्थाचतुष्टय*n.*

The two ages. अवस्थाद्वय*n.* दोन्हीपराया *f.* These are *advance to maturity*, चढती पराई *f.* पूर्ववय*n.* पूर्वार्द्ध*n.* and *decline into aje*, उतरती पराई *f.* उत्तरपराई *f.* उत्तरवय*n.* उत्तरार्द्ध*n.* उतारवय*n.*

5 *time of life.* वय*n.* उमर *f.* शीण *mf.*

A. of twenty, विसी or विशी *f.*—of twenty-five, पंचविसी or शी—of thirty, तिसी or शी—of forty, चाळसी or शी—of fifty, पन्नासी or शी—of sixty, साठी.

Disparity of a. लाहनवीथोरवी *f.* लहानीथोरी *f.*

6 old age. म्हातारपणा *m.* म्हातारपण*n.* बुड्ढेपणा*m.* वृद्धत्व*n.* वृद्धावस्था *f* वृद्धापकाल*m* वार्धक्य*n.* वार्धवयावस्था *f.* जरा *f.* पांढरे केश *m. pl.* काळ्याचे पांढरे *m. pl.*

Imbecility of old a. म्हातारचळ*mn.*

Reverence, &c. for a. वृद्धसेवा *f.* वृद्धसत्कार *m.*

Bent, &c. under the infirmities of a. जरापरिणत.

7 *ripe age, maturity*, v. Puberty. वय *n.* तारुण्यावस्था *f.* तरुणत्व *n.* भरजवानी *or* ज्वानी *f.* यौवन*n.*प्रौढदशा *f.*मोठेपणा*m.* वयस्कता *f.*

That is of mature a. भरवयाचा, वयस्क, वयस्थ, वयस्कर.

That is of a. v. Major. जातव्यवहार, प्राप्तव्यवहार *or* व्यवहारप्राप्त, लब्धव्यवहार, योग्यव्यहार, व्यवहारज्ञ.

That is under a. v. Minor. अप्राप्तव्यवहार, अप्राप्तकाल, अजातव्यवहार, किशोर *m.*

To come of a. वयांत येणें.

8 v. Century. शतक*n.*

Aged, *a. elderly, old*, v. Old. म्हातारा, वृद्ध, वयःस्थ *or* वयस्थ, वयोवृद्ध, वयातीत, वयस्क, वयोगत.

Middle-a. मध्यमवयस्क, वयःस्थ *or* वयस्थ.

2 *having a certain age*, वयाचा, उमरीचा.

Agency, *n. action.* करणी *f.* कर्तृत्व*n.* कृति *f.* कर्त्तेपणा*m.* कारकत्व*n.* करण*n.* करणत्व*n.*

2 See Agentship.

Agent, *n. doer, actuater.* कर्त्ता, करणारा, कारक, चालवणारा, प्रवर्त्तवणारा, कर *in comp.*

2 *factor, deputy.* गुमास्ता*m.* कारभारी*m.* मुनीम*m.* वकील*m.* मुतालीक*m.* जाबसाल करणारा*m.* [लकुल्ला*m.*

A. with full powers. कुलकारभारी*m.* कुलअखत्यार*m.* कु-

3—in commerce, &c. अडत्या*m.*

Agentship, *n.* v. N. 2. गुमास्तेगिरी *f.* गुमास्तेपणा*m.* कारभारीपणा*m.* वकिलात *f.* वकिली *f.* वकीलपणा*m.* वकीलगिरी *f.*

3 अडत *f.*

To **Agglomerate**, *v. c. gather into a ball or mass.* गोळा*m.*-गोल*m.*- गोलक*m.*-पिंड*m.*-गोलाकृति *f.*- पिंडाकृति *f.*-&c. करणें *g. of o. or* होणें *g. of s.*

To **Agglutinate** *v. a. unite as by glue.* सरस *m.*-&c. लावणें, सरसानें-&c. चिकटविणें.

To **Aggrandize**, *v. a.* v. To Exalt. मोठाई *f.*- मोठेपणा*m.*- थोरपणा*m.*- &c. देणें, मोठा करणें, उंच करणें, वाढवणें, महत्व *n.*-&c. वाढवणें *g. of o.*

To **Aggravate**, *v. a. make more grievous.* अधिक जड-अधिक भारी-अधिक कठिन *pop.* कठीण-&c. करणें, अधिक करणें, दुःसहतर करणें. [जाणें.

To be or become aggravated. जडावणें,जडकावणें, विकोपास

2 *make more enormous or heinous.* अधिक वाईट- अधिक दुष्ट-दुष्टतर-&c. करणें, दोष*m.* वाढवणें, दोषाधिक्य*n.* करणें.

3 v. To Provoke. खोड *f.*- खोडी *f.*-कुरापत *f.* करणें-काढणें *g. of o.* चिढेस देणें.

4 See To Exaggerate.

Aggravation, *n.* v. V. 1.—*act.* अधिक जड करणें*n.* &c.

2—*act.* अधिक वाईट करणें*n.* &c.

3—*act.* खोड काढणें*n.* &c. खवंडाळी *f.*

I. *ajjravatinj cause.* वृद्धिकारण*n.* जड होण्यास कारण*n.*

Aggregate, *a. collected into a sum or mass*, एकंदर केलेला,&c. सामवायिक, समवायी, सामुदायिक, सामाजिक, सामासिक, समुदित, समाजीकृत, पिंडीकृत, समाजीभूत, पिंडित.

Aggregate, *n. collected sum or quantity.* समुदाय*m.* समवाय*m.* समाज*m.* समूह*m.* एकुणजमा *f.* एकुणतेरीज *f.* जमा *f.* समुच्चय *m.* गण*m.* (as अहर्गण, मासगण, वर्षगण, भगण &c.), जात*n.*

To **Aggregate**, *v. a. collect*, v. To Gather. एकवट *adv.*- एकंदर *adv.*-एकत्र *adv.* करणें, एकवटणें, गोळा करणें, मिळवणें, समाहार*m.*-समाहरण*n.*-&c. करणें *g. of o.*

Aggregately, *adv.* v. A. एकंदर, एकवट, संघशः, समुदायरूप, समवायरूप.

Aggregation, *n.* v. V.—*act.* एकवट-&c. करणें *n.* गोळा करणें *n.* एकवटणें *n.* &c. समाहार *m.* समाहरण *n.* पिंडीकरण*n.*

—*state.* एकवटलेपणा *m.* एकंदरपणा *m.* एकत्रपणा*m.* समुदायत्व *n.* गोळा *m.* एकपुठा *m.* पिंडित्व *n.* समाहार *m.* समाहृति *f.*

Aggregator, *n.* v. V. एकवट-&c. करणारा, एकवटणारा, &c. समाहरण *n.*-समाहार *m.*-&c. कर्त्ता, पिंडीकर्त्ता.

To **Aggress**, *v. n. commit the first act of offence.* पहिली चढाई *f.*-पहिला चढाव *or* चढ*m.*-पहिली चाल*f.*-अगळी*f.*-अगळीक *f.*-अगळीत *f.*-उपराळा *m.*-विरोधोपक्रम *m.*-वादोपक्रम *m.*-&c.

करणें, कुरापत *f.* काढणें-करणें, (कज्जास &c.) मूळ *n.*-प्रारंभ *m.* करणें.

AGGRESSION, *n.* v. V.—*act.* अगळी *f.* अगळीक *f.* अगळीन *f.* विरोधोपक्रम *m.* वादोपक्रम *m.* उपराळा *m.* प्रथमातिक्रम*m.* प्रथमातिक्रमण *n.*

AGGRESSOR, *n.* v. V. अगळीक करणारा, उपराळाकरणारा, &c. प्रथम अन्यायी *m.* अग्रवादी *m.* (कज्जास &c.) मूळ करणारा-काढणारा-प्रारंभ करणारा, उचलून येणारा-जाणारा, (कज्जा &c.) उपस्थित करणारा.

To AGGRIEVE, *v.a. bear heavy upon,* v. To AFFLICT. पिडणें, कुंथणें, जड-अवघड-&c. जाणें-वाटणें *in. con.* दुःख *n.*-&c. देणें.
2 *wrong, injure,* v. To OPPRESS. अन्याय *m.*-अपराध *m.*-अपकार *m.*-&c. करणें *g. of o.*

AGHAST, *a.* v. FRIGHTENED. तारका वारका, बावरा, घाबरा, छक्कून गेलेला, मृतप्राय, गतप्राण, काष्ठवत्, चरख.
To be struck a. कांटा *m.*-कांटे *m. pl.* उभा-उभेराहणें.

AGILE, *a.* v. ACTIVE. चपळा, आंगचूट, सुटसुटीत, चपल *or* ळ, अंगचपल, आंगाचा चपळ, चपलांग.

AGILENESS, AGILITY, *n.* v. A. चपळाई *f.* आंगचपळाई *f.* आंगसफाई *f.* चापल्य *n.* चपलांगता *f.*

To AGIST, *v. a. take in cattle to feed.* चारणीस *or* चारणीवर घेणें, चरणावळ घेऊन चारणें. [भवणें.

To AGITATE, *v. a.* v. To SHAKE. हालवणें, घोळणें, खुदळणें, क्षो-
2 *discuss,* v. To ARGUE. घोळणें, घासणें, घाटणें, वाटाघाट *f.*-घाटाघाट *f.*-घालघोळ *m.*-&c. करणें *g. of o.*
3 (the mind or passions) *disturb, disorder, flurry.* गढूळणें, खडुळणें, गदळणें, घाबरवणें, तळमळवणें, खळबळणें, क्षोभवणें, घाबरा-हैराण-क्षुब्ध-व्यग्र-व्याकुल-&c. करणें, क्षोभ*m.*-व्याक्षोभ*m.*-&c. करणें *g. of o.*

AGITATED, *p.* v. V.1. हालवलेला, घोळलेला, क्षोभवलेला, &c. घोळीव, क्षुब्ध, क्षोभित.
2 घोळलेला, घाटाघाट-वाटाघाट-&c. झालेला, आलोडित.
3 गढुळलेला, क्षोभवलेला, &c. गढूळ, गदळ, विव्हल *or* ळ, डामडूळ, क्षुब्ध, शोभित, व्यग्र, व्याकुल, कासावीस, हैराण, संतप्त, संतापित, आतुर & आकुळ (in comp. as क्षुधातुर, तृषातुर, कामातुर, लोभातुर, भयातुर, शोकातुर, चिंतातुर, रोगातुर, &c.क्षुधाकुल,&c.) संविग्न, संविग्नमानस, उन्मना, उन्मनस्क, गतधृति, उपहतात्मा.

AGITATION, *n.* v. V. 1.—*act.* हालवणें *n.* घोळणें *n.* क्षोभवणें *n.* आलोडन *n.*—*state.* हालवलेलेपणा *m.* क्षोभवलेलेपणा *m.* क्षुब्धता *f.* क्षोभितत्व *n.* आलोडितत्व *n.*
2—*act.* घोळणें*n.* घाटणें *n.*&c. वाटाघाट *f.* घाटाघाट *f.* घालघोळ *m.* आलोडन *n.*—*state.* घोळलेलेपणा *f.* वाटाघाट झालेलेपणा *m.* &c. आलोडितत्व *n.*
3—*act.* गढुळणें *n.* खडुळणें *n.*&c.—*state.* तळमळ *f.* तळतळ *f.* तलखली *f.* हळहळ *f.* डामाडूळ *f.* संताप *m* क्षोभ *m.* व्याक्षोभ *m.* उद्वेग*m.* आवेग *m.* क्षुब्धता *f.* व्याकुलता *f.* कासाविसी *f.* व्यग्रता *f.* हैराणी *f.* हैराणगत *f.*
—*a. or s.* ताणाताण *f.* ओढाताण *f.*

AGNAIL, *n.* v. WHITLOW. नखरूड *n.* नखुरडें *n.* नखुरडा *m.*

AGNATE, *a. akin by the father's side.* गोत्रज, गोत्रसबंधी, पितृकुळाचा, पितृकुलीन.

AGNATION, *n. relation by the father's side only.* गोत्रसंबंध*m.*

AGO, *adv. gone.* v. PAST. झाला, गेला, गत, विगत, अतीत.
A month a. एक महिना झाला.
Three years a. तीन वर्षें झालीं.
A while a. आतां, मगां, थोडीवेळ झाली, घटका दोनघटका झाल्या, नुकता.
Long a. फार दिवस झाले, चिरकाल झाला, कधींच, कधींचा, कैक काळाचा, केव्हांच, केव्हांचा.

AGOG, *adv. in a state of excitement.* उत्कंठित दशेंत, हुरहुरलेला
To be all a. भुऱ्यावणें, भुऱ्यो भुऱ्यो *adv.* करणें, फुरफुरणें, हुरळणें, भरारणें, हुरहुरणें, उमळणें *or* उबळणें.
To set a. हुरशी *f.*-हुरूप *f. m.* देणें-आणणें, भर *f.* देणें-घालणें, चढीं देणें.

AGOING, *a.* चालता, चालू.
To set a. चालू करणें.

To AGONIZE, *v. n. strive hard,* v. To STRIVE. कुंथणें, कटणें, नेटणें, झटणें, आयास *m.*-श्रम *m.*-प्रयत्न *m.*-&c. करणें.
2 *writhe, &c. in pain.* कळवळणें, वळवळणें, रोमरोम वेदना *f.* होणें *in. con.* तळमळणें, तळतळणें, केशागणीत-केशागणीक वेदना *f.* होणें *in. con.*

To AGONIZE, *v. a. distress with extreme pain.* फार दुःख*n.*-अतिवेदना *f.*-&c.देणें.

AGONIZER, *n.* AGONIZING, *p. a.* v. V. N. 1. कुंथणारा &c. आयासकर्त्ता, कष्टकर्त्ता. [संतापित.
2 कळवळणारा, तळमळलेला, तळतळलेला, &c. कासावीस, संतप्त, v. V. A. फार दुःख देणारा, &c.

AGONIZING, *n.* v. V. N. 1.—*act.* कुंथणें *n.*&c. अटाघाट *m. f.* उरस्फोड *or* ऊरफोड *m. f.* आयासकरण *n.* अट्टाहास *m.*
2—*act.* कळवळणें *n.* &c. वळवळ *f.* वळापिळा *m.* अळुकेपिळुके *m. pl. v.* दे,—intens. तळतळाट *m.* वळावळ *f.*

AGONY, *n. intense pain.* अतिव्यथा *f.* प्राणांतव्यथा *f.* प्राणांतयातना *f.*-दुःख*n.*-&c. यातना *f.* व्यथा *f.* &c. संताप *m.* रोमरोमवेदना *f.* रोमागणीत वेदना *f.* केशागणगणीं वेदना *f.*
The mortal a. v. PAINS OF DEATH. प्राणांतव्यथा *f.*-यातना *f.*- दुःख *n.* &c.

AGRARIAN, *a. relating to fields and lands.* काळीसंबंधी, जिरायती, जिरायताविषयींचा, शेतगण्याचा, क्षेत्रसंबंधी, क्षेत्रिक, शेतजमिनीच्या प्रकरणांतला, शेतजमीनसंबंधी, क्षेत्रभूमिसंबंधी, कृषिभूमिविषयक, क्षेत्रविषयक.

To AGREE, *v. n. be in concord.* मिळणें, मिळून राहणें, जमणें, जुगणें, जुळणें, मिलाफ *m.* असणें-होणें *g. of s. recipr.* बनणें-पडणें *g. of s. recipr.* जम *m.*-जवा *m.*-सांधा *m.*-&c. बसणें *g. of s. recipr.* गोत *n.* मिळणें *g. of s. recipr.* एकोपा *m.*-ऐक्य *n.*-ऐक्यभाव *m.*-सौरस्य *n.* असणें, मिळणींत असणें, तिळागुणी *n.* असणें-होणें.
2 to,with, in, on; *accede, assent, consent,comply,acquiesce.* अनुमत-सम्मत-&c. होणें, अनुमत *n.*-सम्मत *n.*-अनुमोदन *n.*-अनुमति *f.*- सम्मति*f.* देणें, मान्य *a.or* मान्यता *f.* करणें, रुकार *m.*-होयकार *m.* देणें, मान्य-राजी-&c. होणें, कबूल *a.* होणें-करणें, होय-बरें-&c. म्हणणें.
3 *settle terms, stipulate.* खडणें, सई करणें-म्हणणें, बोली *f.*-करार *m.*-ठराव *m.*-&c. करणें, देऊं करणें, मोल *n.* करणें, निश्चय *m.* करणें, टाळी *f.* मारणें.
4 *be consistent, accord, concur, coincide:* also *unite or suit well with.* मिळणें, जमणें, बसणें,बनणें, जुळणें, उतरणें, लागणें,

पडणें, घटाव *m.* बनणें, घडी *f.*-जवा *m.*-जम *m.*-जमा *m.*-जुगल *f.*-सांधा *m.*-&c. बसणें *g.of s. recipr.* संभवणें, मिळणींत असणें, मेळ *m.* मिळणें-पडणें-बसणें *g. of s. recipr.* जुगणें, दुंडणें.

5 with; *be wholesome to or for.* मानणें, मानवणें, जिरणें, सोसणें, भावणें, पचणीस-पचनीं-जिरमाणीं-जिरमाणीस-ठायीं पडणें, मिलाफ *m.* होणें, पाळणें, रुचणें, पथ्य *or* पथ्यकर होणें, पुरवणें, दुंडणें.

6 *answer*, v. To TALLY. मिळणें, उतरणें, जमणें, जुळणें, जुडणें, बसणें, जम *m.*-ताळा*m.*-जडप*n.* बसणें *g. of s. recipr.*

AGREEABLE, *a.congruous*, v. CONSISTENT. मिलाफाचा, बेताचा, मेळाचा, संभावित, यथायोग्य, अनुकूल, माफक.

2 *pleasant, pleasing, delightful, charming.* आवडता, गोड, मान्य, प्रिय, मनःप्रिय, सुप्रिय, मनासारखा, मनमुराद, मधुर, मंजूर, रुचिकर, रुचिर, रुच्य, रिझाऊ, चवदार, दिलपसंद, अभिमत, यथासुख, सुखद, सुखप्रद, सुखदायक, प्रशस्त, काम्य, चाटु, अभिराम, राम, रम्य, कमनीय, रमणीय, मनोरम, मनोभिराम, मनोज्ञ, हृदयंगम, हृद्य, सुरभि, रंजन, रंजक, मनोरंजक.

AGREEABLENESS, *n.* v.A. 1. मेळ*m.* मिलाफ*m.* लाग*m.* संभव*m.* आनुकूल्य*n.* अनुकूलता*f.*

2. आवडतेपणा*m.* गोडी*f.* चव*f.* चवदारी*f.* रुचिरपणा*m.* रुच्यता *f.* रुचित्व *n.* काम्यता *f.* कमनीयता *f.* चाटुत्व *n.* माधुर्य *n.* प्राशस्त्य *n.* मधुरपणा *m.* सौरभ्य *n.*

AGREEABLY, *adv.* v. A. 1. *and* ACCORDING. मिलाफानें, बेतानें, प्रमाणें, यथायोग्य, अनुसार (in comp.), अनुरूप (in comp.).

2 *pleasantly.* सुखानें, सुखरूपें, यथासुख, सहल, मनोरंजनपूर्वक.

AGREED, *p.* v. V.1. *See* AGREEING.

2. v. AGREEING. अनुमत, सम्मत.

3. सई केलेला- म्हटलेला, पणित, प्रतिज्ञात, संकेतित, निश्चित, सांकेतिक, संविदित, सामयिक.

4—6. See AGREEING.

AGREEING, *p. a.* v.V. 1. मिळणारा &c. मिलाफी, मिलाफाचा, मेळाचा, मिलाफ *m.*-&c. करणारा, एकमताचा, एकदिलाचा, एकचित्ताचा, एकचित्त, एकमत, एकमूठ, एकमुठी, एकाविचाराचा, एकारथावर आलेला.

2. मान्य, राजी, कबूल, खुशरजावंत, अनुमत, सम्मत, अभिमत, होयकार-रुकार*m.* देणारा-भरणारा, होय-बरें म्हणणारा, अनुमोदक, अभ्युपगत.

3. खंडणारा, सई करणारा-म्हणणारा, निश्चयकर्त्ता.

4. मिळणारा, &c. अनुकूल.

5. मानणारा, &c. पथ्य, पथ्यकर, पथ्याचा.

6. मिळणारा, &c.

I.—in gram. समानाधिकरण.

AGREEMENT, *n.* v. V. 1.—*state.* मिळणें *n.* &c. मिलाफ *m.* मेळ *m.* एकोपा *m.* ऐक्य *n.* ऐक्यभाव *m.* ऐक्यमत्य *n.* एकी *f.* एक्का *m.* बनाव *m.* जम *m.* जमाव *m.* जुगल *f.* जवा *m.* तह *m.* सौलत *or* सोहलत *f.* चक *m.* सौरस्य *n.* तिळागुणी *n.*

2—*state.* अनुमत *n.* सम्मत *n.* अनुमति *f.* सम्मति *f.* अनुमत्य *n.* मान्यता *f.* राजीपणा *m.* कबूलपणा *m.* दिलखुशी *f.* खुशरजावंती *f.* अभ्युपगम *m.*

3—*act.* खंडणूक *f.* सई करणें *n.* &c. बोली *f.* वदणूक *f.* पैज *f.* *v.* मार, कर, पाड, प्रतिज्ञा *f.* पण *n.* संकेत *m.* निश्चय *m.* समयकार *m.*

4—*state.* मिळणें *n.* &c. अनुमत *n.* अनुमति *f.* सम्मति *f.* सम्मत *n.* मिलाफ *m.* मेळ *m.* जम *m.* जमाव *m.* बनाव *m.* जवा *m.* जुगल *f.* जुळणी *f.* संगम *m.* संक्रम *m.* संक्रमण *n.* उतारा *m.* घटाव *m.* घड *m.* *v.* बन, जम, लाग *m.* जोडी *f.* संभव *m.* संभावना *f.* संभूति *f.*

5—*state.* मानणें *n.* &c. पथ्यपणा *m.* मिलाफ *m.*

6—*state.* मिळणें *n.* &c. जम *m.* लाग *m.* जडप *n.* ताळ *m.* ताळा *m.*

I. *contract, compact, covenant, bargain.* खंडणूक *f.* खंड *m.* होड *f.* बोली *f.* भाक *f.* भाष *f.* करार *m.* प्रतिज्ञा *f.* संकेत *m.* समय *m.* वायदा *m.* नियम *m.* संवित् *f.*

Agreements and engagements,—compreh. करारमदार *m. pl.* कौल करार *m. pl.*

A. for a year सालबोली *f.*

Breaking an a. समयभेद *m.* समयव्यभिचार *m.*

Written a. करारनामा *m.* इकरारनामा *m.* कौलनामा *m.* राजीनामा *m.* कबुलात *or* कबुलायत *f.* लेख *m.* लेखपत्र *n.*

II. (of opinion, views, &c.) ऐकमत्य *n.* आनुमत्य *n.* सम्मति *f.* अनुमति *f.* अनुमत *n.* सम्मत *n.* ऐक्य *n.*

III.—in grammar. अन्वय *m.* सामानाधिकरण्य *n.*

IV. (of different books, statements, &c.) एकवाक्यता *f.* ताळा *m.* उतारा *m.* जडप *n.* *v.* बस.

AGRESTIC, *a.* v. RURAL, RUSTIC. गांवरानी, शेतपोतचा, शेतसंबंधी, क्षेत्रिक.

AGRICULTURAL, *a.* v. N. शेतचा, शेतकामाचा, शेतीचा, शेतीविषयींचा, शेतपोतचा *or* शेतापोताचा, शेतसंबंधी, शेताभाताचा *or* शेतभातचा, खेतीचा, कुणबाव्याचा, कृषीचा, कृषिसंबंधी, कृषिकर्मसंबंधी, कृषिविषयक, कृषिकर्मविषयक, कृष्यंतर्गत, कृषिकर्मांतर्गत.

AGRICULTURE, *n. husbandry.* शेती *f.* शेतकी *f.* शेतीक *f.* शेतकाम *n.* कृषि *f.* कृषिकर्म *n.* कर्षण *n.* खेती *f.* कुणबावा *m.* कुणबीक *f.* कुळवाडकी *f.*

2—gener. *or* compreh. *field-business-operations, work.* शेतपोत *n.* शेतभात *n.* शेतीभाती *f.* शेतकाम *n.* शेतखटपट *f.* शेतीक *f.* शेतकी *f.* वाहील *or* वाहेल *f.* लावणी दुपणी *f.* कृष्यंतर्गतव्यापार *m.*

Hire of a beast upon a.-employment. वाफ *f.* उडी *f.* खांद *m.* खांदवडा *m.*

Implements of a.—compreh. अऊतकाठी *f.* The common ones are नांगर, पाभर, कुळव, कोळपें, गुठा *or* गुठें, रासनी, तिफण, मोघण, डिफळा.

Reciprocal service in a. इरजिक *or* विरजीक *f.* हांदा *m.* पडकय *f.* Man or beast rendering it इरज्या *or* विरज्या, हांदेकरी *or* हांदलेकरी, पडकेल, पळटेल.

AGRICULTURIST, *n. cultivator.* शेतकरी *m.* शेतकाम्या *m.* शेतखप्या *m.* शेतक्या *m.* कृषिकरणारा *m.* कृषिकर्मकर्त्ता *m.* कृषिक, कृषीवल, कर्षक, क्षेत्रजीवी, क्षेत्रोपजीवी, क्षेत्राजिवि, क्षेत्री, कृषिजीवी, कुणबी, खेती, शेतीभाती, कुलवाडी *m.* हली *m.*

AGROSTIS, *n. bent grass.* दूर्वा *pop.* दुरवा *f.* हरळी *f.*

AGROUND, *adv.* तळास लागून असा, तळावर, भुईस, कोरड्यावर.

To be a. लागणें, लागून असणें.

AGUE, *n. intermittent fever.* v. FEVER. हिंवताप *m.* अंतऱ्याताप *m.* शीतज्वर *m.*

2. *cold fit.* हिंव *or* हींव *n.* थंडी *f.* *v.* भर, ये, कुडकुडी *f.* हुड-

कुडी *f.* कुडकुड *f.* काटे *m. pl. v.* ये, रेंपा *f. pl.* शिरशिरी *f.* [ज्वरातीत.

Ague-cake, *n.* कौलू *f.*

Ague-proof, *a.* जितशीतज्वर, जितशीत, शीतज्वराबाध्य, शीत-

Ague-spell, *n.* हिंवाचा *or* हिंवतापाचा मंत्र *m.* शीतज्वरबाधक मंत्र *m.*-जप *m.*-तप *m.*-उपचार *m.*-&c.

Ague-struck, Agued, *a.* शीतज्वरताडित-क्षत-पीडित-आर्त्त-क्षिप्त-क्लिष्ट-ग्रस्त-बाधित-अवलंबित-आश्रित-व्याप्त-आपन्न-प्राप्त- विशिष्ट-आविष्ट- &c.

Aguish, *a. chilly.* थंडीभरलेला, कुडकुडी भरलेला.

Aguishness *n.* v. A. कुडकुडी *f.* कुडकुडा *m.* हींव *n.*

Ah, Aha, *interj.*—noting censure. हा, हांहां, अहा, छी.

2—noting complaint, compassion, &c. हा, हाय हाय, हाहा, अहा, अहाहा, अरेरे, अल्लल, रेरेरेरे.

3—noting exultation, हां, अहाहा.

Ah! oh!—as under great pain. हाय हूय, हाया हूया, हुंहुं.

Ahead, *adv. on in front.* पुढें, समोर, मोहरें, तोंडावरून पुढें, पलीकडे, अघाडी.

To get or go a. पुढावणें, मोहरणें.

To **Aid,** *v. a.* v. To Help. साह्य *n.* करणें *g. of o.* साहाय्य *n.*-सहकार *m.*-मदद *f.*-मददगारी *f.*-बाहीदारी *f.*-कुमक *f.* करणें *g. of o.* हात *m.* देणें.

Aid, *n.* v. Help. साह्य *n.* कुमक *f.* मदद *f.* मददगारी *f.*

Aid de camp, *n.* नकीब *m.* निरोप्या *m.* पारिधस्थ *m.*

To **Ail,** *v. n.* दुखणें, दुखणें *n.*-दुःख *n.*-दरद *f.*-विकार *m.*-बाधा *f.* &c. होणें *in. con.*

I ail, I am ailing. मला *or* माझ्या जिवाला बरें वाटत नाहीं-स्वस्थ नाहीं-समाधान नाहीं-सुख नाहीं-बाईट वाटतें.

What ails thee? तुला काय लागलें-झालें?

Ailing, *a.* v. Sick. दुखणाईत, दुखणेकरी, अस्वस्थ, असमाधानी.

Ever a. v. Sickly. दुखाळू.

Ailment, Ailing, *n.* v. Sickness, Disorder. दुःख *n.* दुखणें *n.* दरद *f.m.* विकार *m.* विकृति *f.* असमाधान *n.* असुख *n.* अस्वास्थ्य *n.*

2 *a slight disorder.* चालतें बोलतें दुखणें *n.* खातें पितें दुखणें *n.* हिंडतें फिरतें दुखणें *n.* हिंडफिरें दुखणें *n.* क्षुद्ररोग *m.* अल्परोग *m.*

To **Aim,** *v. a. direct or point.* नेमणें, रोखणें, योजणें, लावणें, धरणें.

To **Aim,** *v. n.*—with a weapon, &c. शिस्त *f.* धरणें-बांधणें, नेम *m.*-लक्ष *n.*-संधान *n.*-&c. धरणें लावणें.

2 fig. *point one's view or attention at.* लक्ष्य *n.*- लक्ष *n.*-संधान *n.*-धोरण *n.*-&c. धरणें-लावणें-ठेवणें.

Aim, *n. direction given.* शिस्त *f. v.* धर, बांध, नेम *m.* संधान *n.*

2 *view directed,* नेम *m.* संधान *n.* अनुसंधान *n.* लक्ष *n.* लक्ष्य *n.* संधि *m. v.* ठेव, अभिसंधि *m.* अवधान *n.* लाग *m.* मुजरा *m. v.* धर.

Unerring a. अचूकसंधान *n.*

Of unerring a. अचूकसंधानी. [पण *n.*

3 *point aimed at.* v. Butt. निशाण *n.* लक्ष्य *n.* लक्ष *n.* टि-

4 *object of a design,* v. Design. निमित्त *n.* तात्पर्य *n.* आशय *m.* अभिप्राय *m.* मतलब *m.* इंगित *n.* विषय *m.* कटाक्ष *m.*

Of single a. (or purpose). अनन्यवृत्ति.

Aimed, *p.* v. V. A. योजलेला, नेमलेला, &c. योजित.

Aimer, *n.* v. V. A. योजणारा, नेमणारा, लावणारा, &c. योजक.

Aiming, *n.* v. V. A—*act.* नेमणें *n.* योजणें *n.* अनुसंधान *n.* योजना *f.*

Air, *n.* v. Wind. वायु *m.* वारा *m.* हवा *f.* वात *m.* प्राण *m.* आत्मा *m.* जगत्प्राण *m.* हवा *f.* श्वसन *m.* स्पर्श *m.* स्पर्शन *m.*

N.B. But little difference is perceived by the *Hindús* between *air* and *wind.*

In the open a. *exposed to the air.* वाऱ्यांत, उघड वाऱ्यांत, उघडवसाऱ्यांत *or* वासऱ्यांत, उघड पसाऱ्यांत, उघड्यांत, वारघाटीवर, वाऱ्याबावधानांत.

In the a. *in mid-space.* अधांतरीं, अंतरिक्ष, अंतराळ.

To snuff up the a.—colts, &c. वारा *m.* घेणें-पिणें.

To take the a. हवा *f.*-वारा *m.* खाणें, वारा पाणी *n.* खाणें, सहल *f.* करणें, बाहेर *adv.* फिरणें, सैर *f.* करणें, तलाव्यास जाणें.

To beat the a. जलताडन *n.* करणें.

2 (with respect to temperature-&c.) हवा *f.*

3—as a humour of the body. वात *m.* वायु *m* अनिल *m.*

4 *vital air.* प्राण *m.* वायु *m.* मारुत *m.* Five are enumerated—प्राण, अपान, व्यान, उदान, समान, and five inferior or secondary (उपप्राण)—नाग, कूर्म, कृकल, देवदत्त, धनंजय. [रें *n.*

5 *an* a. *a gentle wind,* v. Breeze. झुळूक *f.* मंदवायु *m.* वा-

6 *mien, look.* मुद्रा *f.* चर्या *f.* चेहरा *m.* स्वरूप *n.* ढब *f.* आकार *m.* वारें *n.*

7 *affected or particular manner.* झोक *m.* छटा *f.* ठेव *f.* ठेवण *f.* नोक *f.* नोकझोक *f.*

8 *general aspect,* v. Appearance. डौल *m.* घटाव *m.* ढब *f.* ठेव *f.* ठेवण *f.* घाट *m.* रंग *m.* आकार *m.*

9 airs; *haughty pretensions, notions, manners.* अकड *f.* अकडबाजी *f.* कुर्रा *m.* तोरा *m.* पत्रास *f.* मिजाज *f.* आढ्यता *f. v.* ओढ, बाळग, मिरव, उड्या *f. pl. v.* मार, प्रतिष्ठा *f. v.* मिरव, बाळग, ओढूनआण, कर, जंगमशेठाई *f.* फुशारकी *f.* बढाई *f.* बढाइकी *f. v.* कर, शेखी *f. v.* मिरव, तेगार *m. v.* कर, मगरुरी *f.* नखरा *m.* इसीम *f.* ऊतमात *m.*

To give one's self airs. ओढून प्रतिष्ठा *f.* आणणें, ओढून चंद्रबळ *n.* आणणें, ऊतमात *m.* करणें-मांडणें.

10 See Tune, Song.

11 *publicity.* उघड *f.* उघडीक *f.* फूट *f.*

To **Air,** *v. a. expose to the a. dry in the a.* सुकत-वाळत-सुकूं-वाळूं-&c. घालणें, वाऱ्यांत- वारेवासीं घालणें-ठेवणें, वारा *m.* देणें-दाखवणें, वायु पुट *n.*-वाऱ्याचें पुट *n.* देणें.

2 *dry by exposure to a fire.* विस्तवाच्यायोगानें वाळविणें-सुकविणें. विस्तवापुढें वाळत घालणें.

Air-gun, *n.* वातनलिका *f.*

Air-hole, *n. opening for air.* गवाक्ष *n.* झरोका *m.* धारें *n.* खिडकी *f.* आकाशजननी *f.* वाताघ्व *m.* वातायन *n.*

A. of a water conduit. उच्छ्वास *pop.* उस्वास *m.*

Air-pump, *n.* वाताकर्षकयंत्र *n.* वाय्वाकर्षकयंत्र *n.* वातशोषक-वायुरेचक-&c. यंत्र.

Air-tight, *a.* वायु *or* वातनिरोधक-प्रतिबंधक, वातागम्य, वाताभेद्य, वाय्वभेद्य.

Airiness, *n.* v. A. 3. हवेदारी *f.* हवाशीरपणा *m.*

4 पोकळपणा *m.* रिकामेपणा *m.*

5 हलकेपणा *m.* छिछोरी *f.* छिछोरपणा *m.* अलबेलेपणा *m.*

Airing, *n. ramble for the air.* सहल *f.* सैर *f.* फिरणें *n.* तलावा

m. वायुसेवनार्थ भ्रमण *n.*

AIRY, *a. composed of air.* वायूचा, &c. वायुमय, वातमय, वायुरूप, वातरूप, वातनिर्मित.

2 *belonging or relating to air.* वायूचा, &c. वायुसंबंधी, वातविषयक, वायुविषयक, वातसंबंधी, पवनसंबंधी.

3 *windy, breezy,*—of places. हवाशीर, हवेदार, हवेचा, वारेवासीचा, वारधाटीचा, वाऱ्याचा.

4 *light, hollow,* v. EMPTY. पोकळ, रिकामा, वावकळ *or* वायकळ, वायफट, वायकरणी *or* वायकरणीचा.

5 *frivolous, trifling, &c.* v. LIGHT. हलका, छिछोर *or* चिचोर, वावकळ *or* वायकळ, कमतोल, अलबेला.

AIT, EYGHT, *n. island in a river.* जू *n.* जुवा *m.* जुवें *n.* दिवें *n.*

AJAR, *adv.* अर्ध उघडा *a. decl.* किलकिला *a. decl.* अर्धोद्घाटित, ईषदुद्घाटित.

AKIN, *a.* v. RELATED. आप्त, आप्तविषय, आंगलग, नातलग, नातेवाईक.

2 *partaking of the same properties.* एकेजातीचा, समधर्मक, समानधर्मक, समगुण, एकधर्मक, समानजातीय, समानजाति, एकजातीय, हमजात.

ALACK, ALACKADAY, *interj.* v. ALAS. हाय, हायहाय.

ALACRITY, *n. cheerful readiness.* उत्साह *m.* उल्लास *m.* हर्ष *m.* उत्साव *m.* औत्सुक्य *n.* उत्सुकता *f.* धमक *f.* प्रोत्साह *m.* हवस *or* हौस *f.*

ALAMODE, *adv.* मोळ्या-चाली-परिपाठा-प्रचारा-प्रघाता-रीती-&c. प्रमाणें, परिपाठानुसार &c. परिपाठानुरूप &c. परिपाठानुयायी &c.

ALARM, *n. cry or call to await some danger.* हाक *f.* ओरड *f.* कुई *f.* भयाची-&c. सूचना *f.* आसन्नभयसूचना *f.* आसन्नभयघोषणा *f.*- ज्ञापना *f.* &c. आसन्नभयनिमित्ताव्हान *n.* सज्जताकरणसूचना *f.*

2 *hubbub,* v. TUMULT. हुलड *f.* हूल *f.* हाकहूल *f.* हूलचाल *f.* गलबल *f.* गलबा *m.* गडबड *f. intens.* गडबडाट *m.* हंगामा *m.*

3 v. FRIGHT. हैबत *f.* दहशत *f.* धास्ती *f.* भेदरा *m.* वित्रास *m.*

To take a. at. हाय *f.* खाणें-घेणें, हैबत *f.* घेणें, बाचकणें, बाचटणें.

To ALARM, *v. a.* v. N. 1. भयाची खबर *f.*-बातमी *f.*-&c. देणें, नगारा *m.* करणें, तैयारीची नौबत *f.* वाजवणें, तैयारीचानगारा-हुलीचानगारा *m.*-&c. वाजवणें, भयाविषयीं सावध-हुशार-&c. करणें, आसन्नभयसूचित-बोधित-ज्ञापित-&c. करणें.

3 v. To FRIGHTEN. भिवविणें, भेडावणें, भेडसावणें, भेदरावणें, भयभीत *pop.* भयाभीत-वित्रस्त-&c. करणें.

ALARM-BELL, *n.* हुलीचानगारा *m.* हुलीचें जंगट *n.* घोषघंटा *f.* आसन्नभयज्ञापकघंटा *f.*

ALARM-CLOCK, ALARM-WATCH, *n.* विवक्षित वेळेस वाजून सावध करणारें घड्याळ. *n.*

ALARMED, *p.* v. V. 1. भयाविषयीं सावध केलेला &c. आसन्नभयसूचित- बोधित-ज्ञापित- &c.

2 v. FRIGHTENED. भयभीत *pop.* भयाभीत, हौलदिल, वित्रस्त.

ALARMING, *p.a. terrifying.* भयंकर, भयानक, भयजनक, भयप्रद, भयावह.

ALARMIST, *n. one given to raise alarm.* भय भाकणारा, भयभाक्या, भयभाषी, भयाशंसी, भयमात्राशंसी.

ALAS, *interj.* हाय, हायहाय, अरेरे, हाहा, अहह, अहाय अहाय, कटकटा.

ALBATROSS, *n.* एक मोठें पांखरूं आहे.

ALBEIT, *adv.* v. ALTHOUGH. जरीं, यद्यपि.

ALBINO, *n.* काळ्यावर्णाच्या आईबापांपासून झालेलें गोरें मूल *n.*

ALBUGO, *n. white speck in the eye.* फूल *n.* पुष्प *n.* पुष्पक *n.* शुक्र *n.* [पुस्तक *n.*

ALBUM, *n.* चित्रें-मित्रांचे हस्तलेख इत्यादि ठेवावयाचें कोरे कागदाचें

ALBUMEN, *n. white of an egg.* पांढरा बील-बलक *m.*

ALCHEMICAL, *a.* v. N. किमयेचा, रसायनाचा, रससिद्धिसंबंधी-विषयक, रसायनसंबंधी-विषयक.

ALCHEMIST, *n.* किमया करणारा, किमयागार, रसायनी, रसज्ञपुरुष, रससिद्ध, सिद्ध *or* सिद्धपुरुष *m.*

ALCHEMY, *n.* किमया *f.* रसायन *n.* रससिद्धि *f.* धातुपरिवर्तन विद्या *f.*

ALCOHOL, *n.* मद्याचा अर्क *m.* मद्यार्क *m.* मद्यसार *m.*

ALCOHOLIC, *a.* मद्याच्या अर्काचा, मद्यार्क धर्मक.

ALCOVE, *n. large recess.* मोठी कमाण *f.* मोठा कोनाडा *m.*

2 (in a garden.) बंगला *m.* मंडप *m.*

ALDERMAN *n.* सनदी गांवाचा एक अधिकारी आहे.

ALE, *n.* सातूची केलेली एक प्रकारची दारू आहे, बोजा *m.*

ALEMBIC, *n. still.* मद्य काढायाचें यंत्र *n.* भबकारा *m.* आसुतिपात्र *n.* शुंडायंत्र *n.*

ALERT, *a. vigilant, ready.* बांधल्या कमरेचा, कमरबंद, सावध, हुशार, जागा, जागता, सावधान, जागरूक.

2 *brisk, nimble,* v. ACTIVE. चपळ, आंगसूट. [हुशारी *f.*

ALERTNESS, *n.* v. A. सावधपणा *m.* सावधगिरी *f.* जागेपणा *m.*

2 आंगचपळाई *f.* चपळाई *f.*

ALEXIPHARMIC, *a. expelling poison.* विषाचा मारणारा, विषहर, विषहारी, विषहारक, विषघ्न, विषनाशन, विषशत्रु, विषभंजन, विषारि, विषापह, विषघाती.

ALGEBRA, *n.* बीजगणित *n.* बीज *n.* अव्यक्तगणित *n.*

Addition, subtraction, multiplication, division, in a. अव्यक्तसंकलन *n.*-व्यवकलन *n.*-गुणन *n.*-भाजन *n.*

Known quantity in a. रूप *n.*

Operation or working in a. अव्यक्तक्रिया *f.*

Unknown quantity or number in a. अव्यक्त *n.*

An unknown quantity, &c. अव्यक्तराशि *m.*

Equation of unknown quantity, &c. अव्यक्तसाम्य *n.*

Relation of unknown quantity to its co-efficient. यावत्तावत् *n.*

ALGEBRAIC, *a.* बीजगणितसंबंधी, बीजगणिताचा, बीजगणितांतला, बीजसंबंधी, बीजगणितविषयक, वर्णगत.

ALGEBRAIST, *n.* बीजगणिती *m.* बीजगणित्या *m.* बीजगणितज्ञ, बीजगणितवेत्ता.

ALIAS, *adv. otherwise*—as to a name. उर्फ. [स्थलीं

ALIBI, *adv.* दुसऱ्या जागीं, दुसऱ्या ठिकाणीं, अन्य ठिकाणीं, अन्य

ALIEN, *a.* v. FOREIGN. परदेशी, विदेशी, परदेशचा, बाहेरच्या देशचा, बाहेरचा.

2 v. STRANGE, STRANGER. परका *or* खा, पारखा, परकी, परपुरुष, परगोत्री, बाहेरचा, पराया, पर.

ALIEN, *n.* v. A. परदेशचा मनुष्य *m.* परदेशी *m.* विदेशी *m.* बाहेरच्या देशचा मनुष्य *m.* &c. [विक्रेयता *f.*

ALIENABILITY, *n.* v. A. दुसऱ्याचे हातीं द्यायाजोगेपणा &c. देयता *f.*

ALIENABLE, *a.* v. V. 1, दुसऱ्याच्या हातीं द्याया-कराया-&c. चाजोगा-&c. देय, विक्रेय, परहस्तदेय.

To ALIENATE, *v. a.* (a property), *estrange.* दुसऱ्याचे हातीं देणें

-करणें-विकणें, देणें, विकणें, बाहेर घालणें-देणें, परहस्तगत करणें, परसत्तान्वित करणें, सत्तानिवृत्त करणें.

2 (the affections, or a person), *estrange*. प्रीति *f*.-मन*n*. -&c. उठवणें-फिरवणें-विटवणें-विटवून नेणें-उठेसें *or* तुटेसें करणें *g. of o*. पाय *m*. वळवणें, सोडणें, स्नेह *m*.-मैत्रकी *f*.-&c. तोडणें, विमुख-विरुन-&c. करणें, स्नेहभेद *m*. करणें.

ALIENATED, *p*. v. V. 1. दुसऱ्याचे हातीं दिलेला-&c. दिलेला, विकलेला, परहस्तगत केलेला, परहस्तगत.

2 विमना, विमनस्क, विरुत, विमुख, विरक्त, निराळा, पाठमोरा, वेगळा, उडाळ.

ALIENATION, *n*. v.V. 1.—*act*. दुसऱ्याचे हातीं देणें *n*. परहस्तगत करणें *n*. &c. परहस्तदान *n*.-विधान*n*.-विक्रय *m*. देणें *n*. विकणें*n*. परस्वत्वापादन*n*.—*state*.स्वत्वनिवृत्ति *f*. सत्तानिवृत्ति *f*.परायत्तता*f*. पराधीनता *f*. परहस्तगतता *f*.

2—*act*. मन उठवणें *n*.मन फिरवणें *n*.तोडणें *n*. —*state*. विकृति *f*. निराळेपणा *m*. वेगळेपणा *m*. द्वैत *n*. द्वैतभाव *m*. विषाद *m*. विरक्ति *f*. विमुखता *f*. वैमनस्य *n*. स्नेहभेद *m*. [*n*. करणें.

To ALIGHT, *v. n*.v. To DISMOUNT.उतरणें, अवरोह *m*.-अवरोहण-

2 *fall and lodge*. उतरून पडणें-राहणें-बसणें-येणें, उतरणें, पडणें, पडून राहणें-असणें-ठरणें-थारणें-थिरावणें.

3 at; *stop at, &c*. उतरणें, डेरा *m*. देणें, प्रस्थान*n*. ठेवणें, मुकाम *m*. करणें, बिऱ्हाड *n*. करणें-लावणें.

ALIGHTED, *p*. v. V. 1. उतरलेला, अवरूढ, कृतावरोह.

2 उतरून पडलेला-बसलेला-&c. उतरलेला, पडलेला.

ALIGHTING, *n*. v. V. 1.—*act*. उतरणें *n*. अवरोह *m*. अवरोहण *n*. अवतरण *n*.

2—*act*. उतरणें *n*. उतरून पडणें *n*.-बसणें *n*.-&c.

3—*act*. उतरणें *n*. मुकाम *m*.-बिऱ्हाड *n*. करणें.

Place of a. मुकाम *m*. ठेवण *n*. बिऱ्हाड *n*.

ALIKE, *a*.v. LIKE. एकसारखा, एकाकार, एकमुखी, सारखा, बराबर, तुल्यरूप, एकरूप, समसमान, सरूप, समवर्ण, प्रातिभासिक.

2 *of one kind or quality*. एकराशि, एकरास, एकसारखा, एकजातीय, एकप्रतीचा, समवर्ण, समभाव, एकेमाळेचे मणी, समानजातीय, समानजाती, हमजात. [बराबर.

ALIKE, *adv*. एकसारखा, एकचप्रकारें, एकचरीतीनें, एकचमार्गानें,

ALIKE-MINDED, *a*. एकचित्त, एकदिल, एकमत, एकमताचे, एक.

ALIMENT, *n*. *nutriment*, v. FOOD. खाणें *n*. आहार *m*. अन्न *n*. भक्ष *m*. भक्ष्य *n*. जीवन *n*, प्राणन *n*.

ALIMENTAL, ALIMENTARY, *a*. *belonging to a*.खाण्याचा, भक्ष्यसंबंधी, खाद्यसंबंधी. [पोषक.

2 *nourishing*, v. NUTRITIOUS. पुष्टिकर-कारक-प्रद, पौष्टिक,

ALIMONY, *n*. *allowance to a separated wife*. विभक्त झालेल्या बायकोस अन्नवस्त्राची नेमणूक *f*. विभक्तदारोपजीवकधन *n*. जितरोटी *f*.

ALIQUANT, *a*. सशेषभाजक, साग्रभाजक.

ALIQUOT, *a*. निःशेषभाजक, निरग्रभाजक. [सप्राण.

ALIVE,*a*. v. LIVING. जिता, जीवंत *pop*. जिवंत, जिवा, सजीव,

2 *active, in full being, vigour, virtue, &c*. जिता, जागता, चालता, जागृत, जागरूक, सतेज.

All a. Alive and hearty. जिता जागता, जिताजीव, जिताजिवंत, धडधडीतजिवंत.

3 *lively, swarming*. गजबजीत.

ALKAHEST, *n*. सर्वद्रावक *n*.

ALKALI, *n*. v. POTASH, SODA, AMMONIA. खार *m*. क्षार *m*. योगवाही *f*. *m*.

ALKALINE, *a*. क्षाराच्या गुणाचा, क्षारधर्मक, क्षारगुणी, क्षारगुणक.

A. ashes. काच *m*.

To ALKALIZE, *v. a*. क्षारण *n*. करणें, क्षारीभूत करणें.

ALKALIZED, *p*. v. V. क्षारित, क्षारीभूत.

ALL, *n*. सर्व-सकल-सगळा-अवघा-&c. समुदाय *m*.-संग्रह *m*.-संचय *m*.-राशि *f*.-मंडळी *f*.-&c. कात्स्नर्य *n*.

A. along. *See under* BEGINNING. अवल अखेर, आद्यंत, पहिल्यापासून, मुळापासून, आदिपासून.

A. at once, v.SUDDENLY. एकाएकीं.

A. alone. एकटा एकसुरा, एकला एकट, केवळ एकटा.

A. through. भर (as दिवसभर, रात्रभर, वर्षभर &c.)

At a. कांहींच, अगदी, निस्तूक, निश्शंक, सुतराम्, नितराम्, बालाग्र, यत्किंचित्, अणुमात्र, किमपि. All these words demand, like the English word, the negative construction. See therefore NOT, NONE.

One's a. सर्वस्व*n*.

ALL, *adv*. *completely, quite*, v. WHOLLY. अगदीं.

A. one. एकूनेक.

ALL, *a*. *the whole (mass or multitude), total*. सगळा, सकल, सर्व, समस्त, सारा, अवघा, दरोबस्त, आखा, आघा, अखिल, निखिल, सकळीक, अस्का, समग्र, संपूर्ण, एकूनएक, कृत्स्न, विश्व.

A. without exception, a. whatsoever or whosoever. झाडून सगळा, अटोकाट, दरोबस्त, यावत्, यच्चयावत्.

ALL, in comp. is rendered by सर्व, सकल, समस्त, विश्व, संपूर्ण, जगत्, अखिल, as the following examples will shew.

A.—accomplished, सकल गुणसंपन्न, सर्वसिद्ध, सर्वगुणी, अखिलगुण संपन्न.

A.–adorable. विश्ववंद्य, सर्ववंद्य, सकलवंद्य, जगद्वंद्य, जगत्पूज्य, अखिलपूज्य, &c.

A.–conquering. A.–subduing. सर्वजित्, सकल-अखिल-&c. जित्, विश्वजित्.

A.–creating. सर्व-सकल-अखिल- &c. निर्माता, विश्वकृत्, विश्वकर, विश्वसृक्.

A.–destroying. सर्वनाशी, सकलविनाशी, अखिलध्वंसी, &c.

A.–eating, A.–devouring. सर्वभक्ष, सर्वभक्षक, सर्वभक्षी,&c.

A.–enduring. सर्वसह, विश्वसह.

A.–fours. To go on a. घोडुला*m*. करणें.

A.–knowing. सर्वज्ञ, सर्वज्ञाता, सकल-अखिल-&c. वेत्ता.

A.-pervading. सर्वव्यापी, विश्वव्यापी, विश्वव्यापक, सर्वभूतांतर, जलींस्थलीं काष्ठींपाषाणीं असणारा, पूर्णघन, सर्वभूतमय, सर्वभूतस्थ, सर्वग, विभु.

A.–powerful. सर्वकार्यशक्त, सर्वकार्यसमर्थ, सर्वशक्तिक, सर्वशक्तिमान्, सर्वसमर्थ, अनंतशक्तिक.

A.–searching. सर्वशोधी, सर्वशोधक.

A.–seeing सर्वदर्शी, सर्वद्रष्टा, विश्वदर्शी, सर्वसाक्षी, सर्वदृक्, विश्वद्रष्टा, सकल दृष्टि, सहस्राक्ष.

A.–surpassing. सर्वजित्.

A.–sustaining, A.—upholding. विश्वधारी, विश्वाधार.

A.–wise. अनंतबुद्धि, अपारबुद्धि.

To ALLAY, *v. a. pacify*. v. To COMPOSE. शांतवणें, शमवणें, विझवणें, थंड करणें, उपशम*m*.-उपशमन*n*.-उपशांति *f*.करणें *g. of o*.

2 *mitigate*, See To Ease.

Allegation, *n.* v. V. 1.—*act.* सूचीतपणें-&c.-सांगणेंn. &c. निश्चित कथनn. दृढकथन *n.*

2—*act.* निमित्त सांगणेंn. &c. उपन्यासm.

I. *excuse*, v. Plea. निमित्त *n.* बहाणाm. बाबf. बाबतf.

To Allege, *v. a.* v. To Affirm. निश्चयपूर्वक-सूचीतपणें-सूचीत– &c. बोलणें-सांगणें-म्हणणें.

2 *produce as an argument, &c.* v. To Plead. निमित्तn.-सबबf.-कारणn.- &c. सांगणें, उपन्यासm. करणें *g. of o.* उपन्यस्त करणें. [ज्ञार्भक्ति *f.*

Allegiance, *n.* प्रजाधर्मm. राजसेवाधर्मm. राजाज्ञासेविताf. राजा-

Allegorical, *a.* दृष्टांताचा, दाखल्याचा, दृष्टांतरूप, दृष्टांतात्मक, समासोक्तिरूप,परोक्षकथेचा.

To Allegorize, *v. a. turn into allegory.* रूपकानें-दृष्टांतानें-अन्योक्तीनें-&c. दर्शिवणें, कथणें.

2 *understand figuratively.* दृष्टांतदृष्टीनें-दृष्टांतबुद्धीनें-&c.घेणें-समजणें- अर्थm.करणें.

Allegory, *n.*दृष्टांतरूपकथा *f.* परोक्षकथा *f.* समासोक्तिरूपकथा *f.* दृष्टांत *m.*अप्रस्तुतप्रशंसा *f.* अन्योक्ति.

To Alleviate, *v. a. make light, mitigate*, v.To Ease. हलका-&c. करणें,शमवणें, शांतवणें,उपशमm.-प्रशमm.-शमm.-उपशमनn.-प्रशमनn.-शमनn.-&c. करणें *g.of o.*

Alleviation, *n.* v. V.—*act.* शमवणेंn. शांतवणेंn. शमm. शमनn. उपशमm. उपशमनn. प्रशमm. प्रशमनn.—*state.* शमm. उपशमm. प्रशमm. शांति *f.* उपशांति*f.*

Alley, *n. walk in a garden.* बागांतील रस्ता *m.*-वाट *f.* उपवनमार्ग *m.* आराममार्ग *m.*

2 (of towns, &c.) v. Lane. अळी *f.* आळ *f.* गल्ली *f.*

Alliance, *n.* v. Affinity. सोयरीक *f.* लगत *f.* नातें *n.* शरीरसंबंध *m.* विवाहसंबंध *m.*

2 *league*, v. Combination. एकवळा *m.* मिळण *f.* संगनमतn.

3 v. Connection. संबंध *m.* संयोग *m.*

Alligation, *n.*—in arithmetic—medial. मिश्रगणित *n.* सुवर्णगणित *n.*

Alligator, *n.* मकर *m. pop.* मगर *m.* सुसर *f.* सुस्वर *f.* मगरमच्छ *m.* कुंभीर *m.* नक्र *m.* गोधा *f. dim.* गोधिका *f.*

Grasp or seizure of an a. मगरमिठी *f.*

Alliteration, यमक *mn.* प्रास *m.* अनुप्रास *m.* श्रुत्यनुप्रास *m.*

Alliterative, *a. pertaining to, or consisting in a.* अनुप्राससंबंधी, आनुप्रासिक, अनुप्रासरूप, अनुप्रासमय, अनुप्रासबद्ध.

Allodial, *a.* स्वाधिपत्याचा, अनन्याधिपत्याचा, स्वसत्ताक, स्वस्वामिक.

Allodium, *n. freehold estate.* स्वसत्ताक-स्वाधिपत्याचा-&c. क्षेत्र *n.*-वतन *n.*-&c.

Allopathy, *n.* रोगविकृतीहून भिन्न विकृति उत्पन्न करून रोग दूर-करण्याचा मार्ग *m.*-विद्या *f.*

To Allot, *v. a. give by lot.* चिठ्ठ्या टाकून-घालून-&c. विभागणें-वांटून देणें.

2 *apportion, assign.* वांटा करून *or* वांटून देणें, विभागून देणें, विभाग करून देणें, विभागास-विभागीं देणें-लावणें, वांट्यास देणें, नेमून देणें.

Allotment, *n.* v. V. 2—*act.* वांटून देणें *n.* विभागून-नेमून-&c. देणें *n.* वांटप *n.* वांटणी *f.*

I. *thing allotted*, v. Share. वांटणी *f.* वांटा *m.* भाग *m.*

II. (*of the things of life.*) अन्नोदककरणानुबंध *m.* भोग *m.* भोक्तृत्व *n.*

To Allow, *v. a. grant, concede*, v. To Admit. मानणें, मान्य करणें, बार देणें-करणें, कबूल करणें-होणें, घेणें, प्रतिग्रह *m.*-उपादान *n.* करणें *g. of o.*

2 *let, suffer*, v. To Permit. देणें, परवानगी *f.*- हुकूम *m.*-मोकळीक *f.*-&c. देणें.

3 *give as pay, wages, stipend, &c.* नेमणें, नेमणूक *f.* करणें-करून देणें, नेमणुकीनें देणें.

4 *give as rations, provisions, &c.* मोताद *f.*-नेमणूक *f.* करणें-देणें, मोतादीनें देणें, मोतादीचा देणें, नेमणुकीनें देणें.

5 for; *make abatement for.* मुजरा *m.* करणें, वजपा *m.* काढणें-घेणें.—fig. सांड *f.*-सोड *f.*-सोडसांड *f.*-सांडसोड *f.* करणें-देणें.

6 for; *give in consideration of*मुजरा *m.*देणें,वजपा *m.*घालणें.

Allowable, *a.* v. V. 1. मानाया-जोगा- जोगता-&c. मान्य करायास योग्य, प्रतिग्राह्य, उपादेय. [वाजवी.

2 *and* Lawful. अनिषिद्ध, अवर्जित, मान्य, उचित, योग्य,

Allowableness, *n.* v. A. 2. *and* Lawfulness. अवर्जितत्व *n.* योग्यता *f.* औचित्य *n.*

Allowably, *adv* v. A. 2. *and.* Lawfully. दोषावांचून, प्रत्यवाया वांचून, विनादोष, विनाप्रत्यवाय, यथायोग्य, अनिषेधानुसार, अप्रतिषेधानुरूप.

Allowance, *n. pay, wages, stipend, salary.* दरमाहा *m.* रोजमुरा *m.* मुशारा *or* मुशाहरा *m.* वेतन *n.* नेमणूक *f.* तलब *f.* कर *m.* रकम *f.*

Annual a. वर्षासन *n.*

Extra allowances. खेरीजमुशारा *m.* भत्ता *m.* भातें *n.*

Monthly a. दरमाहा *m.* मासिक *n.*

2 *rations, &c. food allowed.* शेर *m.* शेरपीठ *n.* शेरसिधा *m.* मोताद *f.* चंदी *f.* टोकळा *m.*

Monthly a. (as to a servant). अडशेरी *f.*

3 *matter allowed*, gener. *sum* or *quantity.* मोताद *f.* रतीब *or* रातब *m.* नेमणूक *f.* नेमून दिलेला पैका *m.*-रकम *f.*-चंदी *f.*-&c.

Daily a. रोजी *f.* रोजिनदारी *f.*

Person receiving a daily a. रोजिनदार *c.*

4 See Permission.

5 *abatement, deduction.* मुजरा *m.* वजपा *m.* सूट *f.* सांड *f.* सांड *f.* सांडसोड *f.* सोडसांड *f.* [उपात्त.

Allowed, *p.* v. V. 1. मान्य केलेला, मानलेला, &c. प्रतिगृहीत,

2 परवानगीचा, अप्रतिबंधाचा, अप्रतिषेधाचा, अनुमोदनाचा,अनुमोदित.

I.—used of articles of food, of offerings, &c. हलाल.

To Alloy, *v. a. mix baser metal with.* हीण *n.* घालणें, हिणकट-हिणवट-हिणकस- &c. करणें.

2—fig. हीन-न्यून-&c. करणें, न्यूनता *f.* आणणें, कलंक *m.* लावणें, अनिष्टमिश्र-सकलंक करणें.

Alloy, *n. baser metal mixed with.* हीण *n.* कलंक *m.*

2 fig. कसर *f.* हीनता *f.* उणीव *f.* दुखाची भेळ *f.* भिसळ *f.*

Alloyed, *p.* v. V. 1. हिणकट केलेला, &c. हिणवट, हिणकट, हिणकस, खोटा, खोटसाळ, हिणाचा, गैरसाळ, मिसळीचा.

2 अनिष्टमिश्र, सकलंक, डागिल.

ALLSPICE, *n. myrtus pimenta.* शीतत्वचिनी *f.* कापुरचिनी *f.* कंकोळ *m. n.*

To ALLUDE, *v. n. refer to indirectly, hint at.* सूचना करून दर्शवणें, सूचना *f.* करणें *g.of o.* लक्ष्यानें-लक्षानें-धोरणानें-लक्ष धरून-धोरण धरून-&c. बोलणें *with g. of o.* लक्ष्य *n.*-धोरण *n.* ठेवून-लावून बोलणें *with* वर *of o.* बोलण्याचें लक्ष्य *n.*-धोरण *n.*-रोक *m.*-&c. असणें *with* वर *or* कडे *in. con.*

ALLUDER, *n.* ALLUDING, *p. a.* v. V. सूचना करून दर्शवणारा, &c. सूचक, सूचनाकारक, सूचनात्मक.

To ALLURE, *v. a. entice, lure, decoy, tempt.* मोहणें, मंथणें *or* मथणें, लांचावणें, लोभवणें, गूळ खोबरें *n.* देणें, लालूच *f.*-लोभ*m.*-खाऊ *m.*-&c. दाखवणें, साखर *f.* पसरणें, मधाचें बोट *n.* लावून ठेवणें, मोह *m.*-मोहन *n.* घालणें, मोहन *n.*-विमोहन *n*- प्रलोभन *n*-&c. करणें *g. of o.*

ALLURED, *p.* v. V. मोह घातलेला, लांचावलेला, मोहित, प्रलोभित.

ALLUREMENT, ALLURING, *n.* v. V.—*act.* मोहणें *n.* मथणें *n.* &c. मोहन *n.* विमोहन *n.* प्रलोभन *n.*—*a. or s.* मोह *m.*

I. *alluring object or cause.* प्रलोभन *n.* आमिष *n.* खाऊ*m.* लालूच *f.*

ALLURER, *n.* ALLURING, *p. a.* v. V. मोहणारा, मोह घालणारा, मोहक, प्रलोभक, प्रलोभनकर्त्ता, मोहनकर्त्ता.

ALLUSION, *n.* v. V.—*act.* सूचना करून दर्शिवणें*n.*सूचनापूर्वकदर्शन *n.* सूचन *n.* सूचना *f.*

I. *a. made,* v. HINT. सूचना *f.*

ALLUSIVE, *a. having reference to something not fully expressed.* सूचनेचा, व्यंग्योक्तीचा, संकेताचा, सूचनात्मक, संज्ञिक.

ALLUSIVELY, *adv.* v. A. सूचनारूपें *or* रूपानें, संकेतानें, व्यंग्योक्तीनें.

ALLUVIAL, *a.* मळीचा, मळईचा, मळईच्या जमिनीचा.

A. soil गट्टीजमीन *f.* गट्टी *f.*

ALLUVION, ALLUVIUM, *n.* मळी *f.* सळमळ *m.* होर *f.* साय *f.* मळकी *f.* गजेरी *f.* साका *m.*

To ALLY, *v. a. connect by marriage.* सोइरीक *f.*-सोइरगत *f.*-शरीरसंबंध *m.*-योनिसंबंध *m.*-विवाहसंबंध *m.*-&c. करणें, घर *n.* जोडणें.

2 (by treaty or league.) सख्यसंकेतसंबंध *m.*- सख्यसंबंध *m.*-मित्रत्वसंबंध *m.*-एकोपा *m.*-&c. करणें.

3 *form relation between,* v. To CONNECT. संबंध*m.* करणें.

ALLY, *n. confederate, &c.* पक्षी *m.* संकेतानें साह्यकरणारा, परस्परोपकारी, सख्यसंकेतसंबंधी *m.* संकेतसहकारी, सख्यसंबंधी *m.* सखा *m.* साहाय्यसंकेती *m.*

ALMANAC, *n.* पंचांग *n.* पातडें *n.*

ALMANAC-MAKER, *n.* पंचांग्या *m.* पंचांगकर्त्ता *m.* गणक *m.*

ALMIGHTINESS, *n.* v. A. सर्वशक्ति *f.* अनंतशक्ति*f.* सर्वशक्तिता*f.* सर्वशक्तित्व *n.*

ALMIGHTY, *a.* सर्वशक्ति, सर्वशक्तिक, अनंतशक्ति, सर्वकार्यशक्त, सर्वकार्यसमर्थ, अमितौजा, सर्वशक्तिमान्.

ALMIGHTY, *n.* v. GOD. परमेश्वर *m.* भगवान् *m.* अनंतशक्तीचा-प्रभु *m.*

ALMOND *a.* बादामी *or* बदामी.

ALMOND, *n.*—tree. बादाम *or* बदाम *f.* बादामी *f.*—fruit बादाम *or* बदाम *n. m.* बादामगोळा *m.*

ALMONER, *n. official distributer of alms.* दानाध्यक्ष*m.* दानाधिकारी *m.* धर्माध्यक्ष *m.* धर्माधिकारी *m.*

ALMONRY, ALMRY, *n. place for distribution of alms.* दानशाला *f.* दानगृह *n.* दानमंदिर *n.* धर्मपोई *f.* अन्नसत्र *n.* सत्रशाला *f.* सत्र *n.*

ALMOST, *adv. nearly, well nigh, for the most part.* बहुत करून, प्रायः, जवळ, आसन्न, उपकंठ, ईषदून, सावशेष, आसमाप्त्यवधि. This adverb, however, is best rendered by other constructions, as in the following examples, *My work is almost done,* माझें काम संपत आलें आहे, *It is almost ten o'clock,* दाहा वाजायास आले *or* थोडक्यांत दाहा वाजतील, *He had almost reached the village,* तो गांवाजवळ पोहोंचला होता, &c. &c.

ALMS, *n.* भिक्षा *pop.* भीक *f.* भिकणें *n.* धर्म *m.* धर्मादाय *or* धर्मादाव *m.* खैरात *f.*

A. asked by worshippers of *Dewi,* जोगवा*m.*—of *Khandobá,* वारी *f.*

Daily a. नित्यदान *n.*

Liver upon a. भिक्षोपजीवी.

Victuals given as a. माधुकरी *f.* one who lives on them माधुकरी *m.*

To live on a. भीक दूक *f.* मागून असणें, भीक मागून पोट *n.* भरणें, भिक्षोपजीविका *f.*-भैक्षजीविका *f.*- भिक्षोपजीवन *n.*-&c. करणें.

To live on unsolicited a. अयाचितवृत्ति *f.* करणें.

It is easier to take poison than a. विख घेववतें पण भीक घेववत नाहीं.

ALMS-BASKET, ALMS-BOX, ALMS-BAG, &c. *n.* झोळी *f.* चौपद्री *f.* अन्नपूर्णा *f.* कामधेनु *f.* भिक्षापात्र *n.*

A.-vessel of worshippers of *Khandobá,* कोटंबा*m.*—of *Dewi,* परडी *f.*

ALMS-BEGGING *n.* भिक्षुकी *f.* भिक्षाटन *n.*

Luck in a. भिक्षाभाग्य *n.*

ALMS-DEED, *n.* धर्मकार्य *n.* धर्मकृत्य *n.* धर्मादाय *m.* धर्मादाव *m.*

ALMS-GIVING, *n.* धर्म *m.* दानधर्म *m.*

ALMS-HOUSE, *n.* धर्मशाला *pop.* धर्मसाळ *f.* धर्मवासगृह *n.*

ALMS-MAN, *n.* भीक खाणारा *m.* भिक्षोपजीवी *m.* भिक्षुक *m.* भिक्षाजीवी *m.*

ALOE, *n.*-plant, *aloe perfoliata.*कोरफड *f.n.* कोरकांडें*n.* कुंवारकांडें *n.* कुंवारफोड *n.* घृतकुमारी *pop.* कुमारी *f.* तरुणी *f.*

2—inspissated juice. काळाबोळ *m.* एळियाबोळ *m.* कोरकांडें *n.* कोरफड *n.* कुंवारकांडें *n* कुंवारफोड *n.*

ALOE-WOOD, *aquilaria agalocha.* अगर *mn.* अगरू *m.*

ALOFT, *adv. on high,* v. ABOVE. उंच, उंचीं, वर, वरतें.

ALONE, *a.* v. SINGLE. एकटा, एकला, एकएकटा, एकएकला, एकाकी.

To leave or let a. सोडणें, सोडून देणें, जाऊं-राहूं-असूं-देणें.

2 *without company.* एकटा, परका-बाहेरचा- &c. कोणी नाहीं असा.

ALONG, *adv. and prep. at length, lengthwise.* उभा-निजता-पासला *adv. decl.* [सूत्रानें.

2 *in the direction of the length.* लांबीच्या धोरणानें-

3 *onward, on,* v. FORWARD. पुढें.

Get a. Go a. चलजा, जाजा, चलनिघ, तोंड काळें कर

4 *through the length of, all along*, v. THROUGHOUT. दोन्ही शेवट-दोन्ही टोकें-दोन्ही अवधि-उभयसीमा-&c. धरून-व्यापून -मिळवून-सांपडवून-&c. अवल आखेर, पहिल्यापासून, आरंभापासून शेवटपर्यंत, अह्दतहद, साद्यंत, वरून, जवळून, सरसून.

5 along with. v. WITH. बरोबर, सहित, सहवर्तमान, समेत.

ALOOF, *adv. at a distance, distinct from.* दूर, अलग, वेगळा *decl.* निराळा *decl.* फटकून, सटकून, निसटून, तुटून.

ALOPECY, *n. falling off of the hair.* उंदरी *f.* चाई *f.* कातर *f.* कातरी *f.* इंद्रलुप्त *n.*

ALOUD, *adv.* मोठ्यानें, मोठ्यास्वरानें, शब्द मोठा करून, स्वर उंच करून, उच्चस्वरानें.

ALPACA, *n.* उंटा सारखें पेरू देशांतील एक जनावर आहे.

2 त्याच जनावराचे केशांचें केलेलें कापड *n.*

ALPHABET, *n.* अक्षरमाला *f.* वर्णमाला *f.* मूलवर्ण *m. pl.* वर्णक्रम *m.* अक्षरानुक्रम *m.* वर्णमातृका *f.* अक्षरविन्यास *m.* अक्षरसमाहार *m.* बारासड्या *or* बत्तीस बारासड्या *f. pl.* क ख *m.* फळवले *m. pl.*

Acquaintance with the a. अक्षर ओळख *f.*

Class of letters in the a. फळवला *or* फळोला *m.* बिल्हे *f.*

Letter of the a. with its several combinations with the vowels and *anuswára and wisarga.* बारसकडी *or* खडी *f. or* बाराखडी *f.*

Series of the vowels and *anuswára and wisarga.* बारसकडी *or* खडी *f. or* बाराखडी *f.* [घोक्या *m.*

ALPHABETARIAN, *n.* v. ABECEDARIAN. ओनाम्या *m.* क ख

ALPHABETICAL, *a.* अक्षरानुक्रमाचा, वर्णक्रमाचा, अक्षरानुक्रमानुयायी, अक्षरानुक्रमविशिष्ट. [सार.

ALPHABETICALLY, *adv.* अक्षरानुक्रमानें, बिल्हेवार, अक्षरानुक्रमानु-

ALREADY, *adv. in time past or present.* आधीं, आदीं, पहिलेंच, पूर्वी, मागें. The sense of the word is often best rendered by चुकणें, as मी सांगून चुकलों-करून चुकलों-देऊन चुकलों-I have told-done-given already.

ALSO, *adv.* ही, पण, देखील *or* देखीत, तसाच *decl.*

ALTAR, *n.* वेदि *or* वेदी *m.* स्थंडिल *n.* यज्ञवेदी *m.*

To ALTER, *v. a.* v. To CHANGE. बदलणें, पालटणें, फिरवणें.

To ALTER, *v. n.* v. To CHANGE. बदलणें, पालटणें, फिरणें.

ALTERABLE, *a.* v. V. A. बदलाया-चा-जोगा-&c. फिरवाया-चा-जोगा-&c. फेरफार कराया-चा-जोगा-&c. रूपांतरकरणीय, रूपभेदकरणीय.

ALTERANT, ALTERATIVE, *a.* बदलणारा &c. फेरफार करणारा, रूपांतरकारक, रूपभेदकारक.

ALTERANT, ALTERATIVE, *n.*—in medicine. प्रकृति-तबियत-&c. बदलणारें औषध *n.* फिरवणारें ओषध *n.*

ALTERATION, *n.* v. V.—*act.* बदलणें *n.* पालटणें *n.* फिरवणें *n.* *(neuter* फिरणें *n.)*—*state.* v. CHANGE. भेद *m.* फेर *m.* फेरफार *m.* पालट *m.* रूपांतर *n.* रूपभेद *m.*

To ALTERCATE, See To WRANGLE.

ALTERCATION, *n. wrangling.* झटपट *f.* झटापट *f.* झटापटी *f.* लटपट *f.* हटतट *m.* तोंडासतोंड *n.* धसकस *f.* धसाफसी *f.* धुसफूस *f.* धुसमूस *f.* रसकस *f.* रसघस *f.* होराबारी *f.* हुंवेतुंबे *f.* हमरीतुमरी *f.* वाग्युद्ध *n.* हर्षामर्षा *m.* हर्षामर्ष *m.*

ALTERN, ALTERNATE, *a. being in reciprocal succession.* परस्पर अदलाबदलीचा-फेरीफेरीचा-बारीबारीचा, &c. एक आड एक, आळीपाळीचा, परस्परानुगामी, परस्परानुवर्त्ती, अन्योन्यानुगामी, अन्योन्यानुवर्त्ती, अन्योन्यानुसेवी, अन्योन्यपृष्ठानुगामी, अन्योन्यपृष्ठानुपृष्ठ, पृष्ठानुपृष्ठगामी. [त्राड.

On a. days or periods. एकांतरा *or* त्रा, एकांत्रा आड, एकां-

To ALTERNATE, *v. a. perform by turns.* अदलाबदलीनें-आळींपाळीनें-फेरपाळीनें-पारगीवारगीनें-अरगीपारगीनें-&c. करणें.

2 *change reciprocally.* परस्पर पालट *m.*-पालटापालट *f.*-अदलाबदल *f.*-फेरमुबादला *m.*-फिरवाफिरव *f.*- &c. करणें *g. of o.*

To ALTERNATE, *v. n. happen, act, &c. by turns.* अदलूनबदलून-आलटूनपालटून-आळीपाळीनें-फेरपाळीनें-पारगीवारगीनें-&c. येणें-घडणें-घडून येणें-काम करणें.

2 *follow reciprocally.* एक आड एक येणें-होणें &c. परस्परानुगमन *n.* परस्परानुवर्त्तन *n.*-अन्योन्यानुगमन *n.*-&c. होणें *g. of o.*

ALTERNATELY, *adv.* v. A. *in reciprocal succession.* परस्पर अदलाबदलीनें, &c. अदलून बदलून, आलटून पालटून, चाळूनपाळून, एक आड एक, पृष्ठानुपृष्ठ, अन्योन्यपृष्ठानुपृष्ठ, अन्योन्यानुगमन -&c. पूर्वक.

ALTERNATENESS, *n.* v. A. एकआडएकपणा *m.* एकांत्राडपणा *m.* परस्परानुगामित्व *n.* परस्परानुवर्त्तित्व *n.* अन्योन्यानुगामित्व *n.* पृष्ठानुपृष्ठगामिता *f.* &c.

ALTERNATION, *n. reciprocal succession.* परस्पर पालट *fm.* परस्परअदलाबदल *f.* परस्परानुगमन *n.* परस्परानुवर्त्तन *n.* अन्योन्यपृष्ठानुगमन *n.* अन्योन्यानुगमन *n.* अन्योन्यानुवर्त्तन *n.*

ALTERNATIVE, *n. a choice of two things.* विकल्प *m.* कल्प *m.* गौणकल्प *m.* अनुकल्प *m.* पक्ष *m.* विभाषा *f.*

ALTERNATIVE, *a.* वैकल्पिक, विकल्पाचा.

ALTERNATIVENESS, *n.* v. A. वैकल्प्य *n.*

ALTHOUGH, *adv.* जरीं, जरींही, यद्यपि, यद्यपिचेत्.

ALTILOQUENCE, *n. pompous speech.* शब्दप्रौढीचें भाषण *n.* शब्दप्रागल्भ्याचें भाषण *n.* शब्दप्रौढी *f.* शब्दप्रागल्भ्य *n.*

ALTILOQUENT, *a.* v. N. अति प्रौढभाषी, अति प्रगल्भवक्ता.

ALTIMETRY, *n. art of measuring heights.* उच्चत्व मापनविद्या *f.* उंची काढण्याची-मोजण्याचीविद्या *f.*

ALTISONANT, *a.* v. POMPOUS. अतिप्रौढ, अतिप्रगल्भ, उंचउंच.

ALTITUDE, *n.* v. HEIGHT. उंची *f.* उच्चत्व *n.*

2 (of a heavenly body). उंची *f.* लंबोन्नति *f.* उन्नति *f.* उन्नत *n.* उन्नतांश *m.*

To take the a. उंची *f.*-&c. गणणें-काढणें-मोजणें.

ALTOGETHER, *adv. in a body.* मिळून, सर्व मिळून, संघशः, समुदायशः, एकामेळीं, एकजुटीनें, एकमेळणी.

2 *utterly, quite*, v. WHOLLY. अगदीं, निपट, केवळ *or* ळ, निताम्, निस्तूक, एकजात.

3 *on the whole.* एकूण *or* न, मिळून.

ALUM, *n.* फटकी *f.* फटकडी *f.* तुरटी *f.* स्फटी *f.*

ALUMINOUS, *a.* फटकीचा, फटकडीचा, तुरटीचा, स्फटीमय.

ALVINE, *a. belonging to the belly.* पोटाचा, उदरसंबंधी, औदरिक, कोष्ठ (in comp.).

ALWAYS, *adv.* v. EVER. सर्वदा *pop.* सर्वदां, सदा *pop.* सदां, सदासर्वदां, सदाकदा, सदैव, सदोदित, हमेश *or* हमेशा, हरहमेश *or* शा, नित्य, नित्यशः, नित्यदा, उठतां बसतां, उठल्या बसल्या.

AMAIN, *adv. vehemently, violently.* मोठ्या बळानें, मोठ्या जोरानें, मोठ्या तडाक्यानें, सत्राण, अनर्थाचा *decl.* शर्त्तीचा *decl.*

AMALGAM, *n. mixture of some metal with quicksilver.* पारदमिश्रधातु *m.*

2 *mixture*, gener. See MIXTURE.

To AMALGAMATE, *v. a. mix quicksilver with another metal.* पारदमिश्रितधातु *m.* करणें.

2 See To MIX.

To AMALGAMATE, *v. n. blend, &c.* v. To MIX. मिळणें, मिळून जाणें, मिसळणें, जमून जाणें, गोत *n.* मिळणें *g. of s. recip.*

AMALGAMATION, *n.* v. V. A. 1—*act.* पारदान्यधातुमेलन *n.* पारदान्यधातुमिश्रीकरण *n.*

v. V. N.—*state.* जमून-मिळून-गेलेपणा *m.* मिसळ *f.* मिश्रीभाव *m.* सायुज्य *n.* सायुज्यता *f.* मेल्नैकरूपता *f.*

AMANUENSIS, *n.* दुसऱ्यानें सांगितलेला मजकूर लिहणारा *m.* अन्यकथितलेखक *m.* लेखक *m.* अन्योक्त लेखनकारी *m.*

Error of a. लेखक दोष *m.* लेखकप्रमाद *m.*

Written by an a. लेखकी.

AMARANTH, *n.*—yellow, the plant. आचोल *f.* आबोली *f.*—flower. आचोल *or* ल्रें *n.*—globe, the plant or flower. गुल मखमल *m.*

To AMASS, *v. a.* v. To HEAP. गोळा करणें, गोळावणें, जोडणें, जथणें, जथाजथ *f.*-जथापथ *f.*-संग्रह *m.*-संचय *m.*-राशि *m.*-ढीग *m.* करणें *g. of o.*

AMASSABLE, *a.* v. V. गोळाकराया- चा-जोगा- &c. संग्राह्य, संचेय, संचितव्य, संग्रहणीय.

AMASSING, AMASSMENT, *n.* v. V.—*act.* गोळा करणें *n.* &c. जथाजथ *f.* जथापथ *f.* संचय *m.* संग्रह *m.* चय *m.* चयन *n.*

I. *the collection made.* संग्रह *m.* संचय *m.*

AMATEUR, *n.* शौकी *c.* हौशी *c.* इष्की *c.* व्यसनी *c.* (as तो गाण्याचा शौकी). [रता *f.*

AMATIVENESS, *n. propensity to love.* शृंगार प्रवणता *f.* शृंगारप-

AMATORY, AMATORIAL, *a. relating to love.* शृंगाराचा, शृंगारीक, शृंगारी, शृंगाररससंबंधी, शृंगाररसान्वित, शृंगारात्मक, शृंगारविषयक.

2 *causing love.* मोहक, वशक्रियाकारक, रतिजनक, रत्युत्पादक.

AMAUROSIS, *n.* तिमिर *n.*

To AMAZE, *v. a.* v. To FRIGHTEN. चरकवणें, घाबरवणें, घाबरा करणें, गांगरवणें, धांदरवणें, बाकचूक-माटमूट करायास लावणें, पांचावर धारण *f.* बसवणें *g. of o.* त्रेधा *f.*-तिरपीट *f.* उडवणें-करणें *g. of o.*

2 v. To ASTONISH. चकवणें, चक्र-चकभूल-&c. करणें, चकभूल *f.* करणें-उडवणें *g. of o.* [दिल, घाबरा.

AMAZED, *p.* v. V. 1. घाबरवलेला, &c. चरख, तारकाबारका, हौल-

2 चक्र, चकभूल, विस्मयापन्न.

To be a. तोंडांत बोट *n.* घालणें, चकणें.

AMAZEMENT, AMAZEDNESS, *n.* v. A. 1. *and* FRIGHT. घाबरलेपणा *m.* गडघड *f.* त्रेधा *f.* तिरपीट *f.*

2 *and* WONDER. विस्मय *m.* चकभूल *f.*

AMAZER, *n.* AMAZING, *p. a.* v. V. 1. *and* FRIGHTFUL. घाबरवणारा &c. भयंकर, भयप्रद, त्रेधा करणारा- उडवणारा, अद्भुत, अक्टोविकट, अकराळ विकराळ.

2 *and* WONDERFUL. चकवणारा &c. विस्मयकारक-जनक, आश्चर्यकारक-जनक, अद्भुत, अद्भुतरसोत्पादक.

AMAZINGLY, *adv.* v. WONDERFULLY. विस्मय वाटायाजोगा-सारखा-&c. *decl.* विस्मयजनकरूपानें, अद्भुत, पराकाष्ठेचा.

AMAZON, *n.* स्त्रीमल्याळची पद्मीण *f.* शूरांवक्रमा *f.*

AMBAGES, *n.* v. CIRCUMLOCUTION. गिरकांडा *m.* द्राविडप्राणायाम *m.* चरपटपंजरी *f.*

AMBASSADOR, *n.* वकील *m* दूत *m.* राजदूत *m.* राजप्रेषितपुरुष *m.*

Credentials of a. वकीलनामा *m.*

AMBASSADORSHIP, *n.* वकिली *f.* वकालत *f.* दूतत्व *n.*

AMBER, *n.* तृणमणि *m.* तृणग्राही *m.* तैलस्फटिक *m.*

AMBERGRIS, *n.* अंबर *m.*

AMBIDEXTER, AMBIDEXTROUS, *a. able to use both hands alike.* दोन्ही हातांनीं सारखा, समसंधानी, सव्यसाची, हस्तद्वयसमानकुशल, हस्तद्वयसमानदक्ष.

2 *double dealing*, v. DECEITFUL, उभयपक्षसिमान, उभयसाधारण. [शल्य *n.*

AMBIDEXTERITY, *n.* v. A. 1. सव्यसाचित्व *n.* हस्तद्वयसमानकौ-

2 उभयसाधारणत्व *n.* [ता.

AMBIENT, *a.* v. SURROUNDING. परिवेष्टक, परिवेष्टनकर्त्ता, वलयि-

AMBIGUITY, AMBIGUOUSNESS, *n.* v. A. दुटप्पीपणा *m.* दुग्धा *f.* *m.* द्व्यामुष्य *or* द्व्यामुष्य *n.* द्व्यर्थता *f.* द्व्यर्थकत्व *n.*

AMBIGUOUS, *a. equivocal.* दुटप्पी, दुतर्फा, दुधड, द्व्यर्थ, द्व्यर्थक, मुग्ध, मुग्धा, दुग्ध्याचा, द्व्यामुष्याचा, भ्रांतिकर, भ्रांतिवट, भ्रांतिकट, नरोबा कुंजरोबा.

AMBIGUOUSLY, *adv.* v. A. दुटप्प्या, दुटप्यानें, दुग्धा, मुग्धा, द्व्यामुष्य, उभारत, अळमटळम, द्व्यर्थरूपानें.

AMBITION, *n. desire of greatness, power, &c.* मोठेपणा मिळविण्याची इच्छा *f.*-हौस *f.*-&c. हवस *or* हौस *f.* दम *m.* धांव *f.* महत्वाकांक्षा *f.* महत्वतृष्णा *f.* जिगीषा *f.* राज्यलोभ *m.* प्रभुत्वलिप्सा *f.* प्रभावाकांक्षा *f.* यशोलिप्सा *f.* यशस्तृष्णा *f.*

AMBITIOUS, *a.* v. N. हवसदार *or* हौसदार, हवळा, महत्वाकांक्षी, महत्वेच्छु, प्रभुत्वलिप्सु, प्रभावलिप्सु, जिगीषु, यशस्काम, सतृष, ऊर्ध्वदृष्टि, दीर्घसंधानी.

To AMBLE, *v. n.* सात्रक चालीनें चालणें, सात्रकचालणें-जाणें.

AMBLE, *n.* सात्रकचाल *f.* रहिवाळचाल *f.* डुलतचाल *f.* टांकणचाल *f.* चवडचाल *f.*

AMBLINGLY, *adv.* डुडुकडुडुक *or* डुडुकडुडुक, सात्रकचालीनें &c. तुरतुर *or* रां.

AMBROSIA, *n. sustenance of the gods.* अमृत *n.* सुधा *f.*

AMBROSIAL, *a.* अमृताचा, अमृतमय, अमृततुल्य.

AMBULANCE, *n. movable hospital.* फिरतें इस्पिताल *n.*

AMBULATION, &c. See WALKING, &c.

AMBUSCADE, AMBUSH, *n. the place.* दबा धरण्याची- दडून राहण्याची- &c. जागा *f.* दडण *f.* लिकण *f.*

2—the state. दबा *m.* दडी *f.* दडा *m.* *v.* धर, मार.

3—the men posted. दबा धरलेलीं-दडून राहिलेलीं-&c. माणसें *n. pl.* दडा *m.*

To AMELIORATE, AMELIORATION, See To IMPROVE, &c.

AMEN, *adv.* असो, तथास्तु, अस्तु, स्वस्ति.

AMENABILITY, AMENABLENESS, *n.* v. A. मोसबेदारी *f.* जबाबदारी *f.* उत्तर देण्याचाअधिकार *m.*

AMENABLE, *a. responsible*, v. ANSWERABLE. जाब—हिशोब-मोसबा-&c. देणारा, मोसबेदार, उत्तर-जाब-&c. देण्याचा अधिकारी.

To AMEND, *v. a.* v. To RECTIFY. सुधारणें, नीठ-दुरूस्त-शुद्ध- चांगला-&c. करणें, चूक *f.* काढणें *g. of o.*

2 v. To REFORM. सुधारणें, वाटेवर मार्गावर-ताळ्यावर-सुतावर-रीतीवर-&c. आणणें.

To AMEND, *v. n.* v. To REFORM. निटावणें, उजरणें, सुधारणें,

बाटेवर-मार्गावर- ताळ्यावर-&c. येणें.

2 *become better*, v. To RECOVER. सावरणें, सावर *m.* घेणें, नीट होणें-होऊं लागणें, उजरणें, जीव *m.* धरणें.

AMENDMENT, *n.* v. V. A. 1.—*act.* सुधारणें *n.* नीट करणें*n.* &c. शोधन *n.* शोध *m.*—*state.* सुधारलेलेपणा *m.* &c. दुरुस्ती *f.* शुद्धि *f.* विशुद्धि *f.*

v. V. N. 2. *act or state.* सावर *m.* उतार *m.*

AMENDS, *n. recompense.* प्रतिफल*n.* दुःख-अनिष्ट-&c. परिमार्जक*n.*

To make a. निरपणें, निस्तरणें, निष्कृति *f.*- प्रतिक्रिया *f.*-प्रतिकार *m.*-&c. करणें *g. of o.* [सौरम्य *n.*

AMENITY, *n.* v. AGREEABLENESS. रम्यता *f.* रम्यत्व *n.* रंजकत्व *n.*

To AMERCE, AMERCEMENT. See To FINE, &c.

AMETHYST, *n.* याकूत *m.*

AMIABLE, *a. worthy of love.* v. AGREEABLE. प्रियकर, प्रीतिपात्र, सात्विक, भला, आवडत्या गुणाचा, प्रियगुण, प्रियगुणक, प्रीत्युत्पादकगुणयुक्त.

AMIABLENESS, AMIABILITY. *n.* v. A. भलेपणा *m.* भलाई *f.* भलाइकी *f.* प्रियकरत्व *n.* प्रियगुणत्व *n.* प्रियगुणकत्व *n.* प्रीत्युत्पादकगुणकत्व *n.*

AMIABLY, *adv.* v. A. आवडतेपणानें, भलाईनें, भलेपणानें.

AMICABLE, *a.* v. FRIENDLY. मित्रत्वाचा, इष्टत्वाचा, सख्याचा, स्नेहभावाचा, भाऊबंदकीचा, मित्रभावाचा.

AMICABLY, *adv.* v. A. स्नेहभावानें, भाऊबंदीनें, भाईचाऱ्यानें.

AMIDST, *prep.* v. AMONGST. मध्यें. मधीं, माजीं, माझारीं.

AMISS, *adv. improperly*, v. WRONG. अन्यथा, वाईट, वांकडें, अयथान्याय, अयथायुक्त, अयथायोग्य.

AMISS, *a. improper*, v. WRONG. गैरवाजवी, सदाचरणास-&c. वांकडा, अयोग्य, अनुचित. [भाव *m.*

AMITY, *n.* v. FRIENDSHIP. सख्य *n.* मित्रत्व*n.* स्नेहभाव *m.* सुहृद्-

AMMONIAC, *n.* sal. नवसागर *m.*

AMMUNITION, *n.* दारूगोळा *m.* दारूगोळी *f.* जिनसीसामान *n.* जंगीसामान *n.* युद्धसामग्री *f.* युद्धसाहित्य *n.*

AMNESTY, *n. general pardon.* सरमाफी *f.* सकलदंड्यमुक्ति *f.* सकलदंड्यमोचन *n.* सकलापराधमोचन *n.* सकलदंडमोचन *n.*

2 *act or edict of pardon.* सरमाफीचा जाहीरनामा, माफीनामा *m.* क्षमापत्र *n.*

AMONG, AMONGST, *prep.* मध्यें, मधीं, माजीं, माझारीं, आंत-ईत, *used with the noun inflected.*

From a. मधून, पैकीं.

AMORIST, AMOROSO, See LOVER.

AMOROUS, *a. disposed to love, loving.*कामी, कामुक, सकाम, कामेच्छु, शृंगारी, शृंगारीक, इष्की, कामप्रवण, शृंगारप्रवण, स्त्रीलंपट, स्त्रैण, विलासी,

2 *belonging or relating to love*, v. AMATORY. शृंगाराचा, शृंगारी, शृंगारीक, शृंगाररसाचा.

AMOROUSLY, *adv.*v. A.1. कामुकपणानें, कामभावानें, सकाम, कामपूर्वक, कामभावपूर्वक, कामेच्छापूर्वक, विलासपूर्वक.

AMOROUSNESS, *n.* v. A. 1. कामीपणा, *m.* कामुकपणा *m.* इष्कबाजी *f.* कामभाव *m.* कामुकता *f.* सकामता *f.* कामप्रवणता *f.* शृंगारप्रवणता *f.*

AMORPHOUS, *a. having no determinate shape.* बेडौल, बेढब.

To AMOUNT, *v. n.* येणें, होणें *or* एकंदर होणें, मिळून होणें, भरणें.

2 *result in.* एकंदरी *f.*-हाशील *n.*-तात्पर्य *n.*-सारांश *m.* असणें.

AMOUNT, *n.* v. SUM. जमा *f.* एकुणजमा *f.* सुमार *m.* जुमला *m.* मान *n.*

Gross a. गोळाबेरीज *f.* एकंदर आकार *m.*

2 *effect, substance, &c.* हाशील *n.* तात्पर्य *n.* सारांश *m.*

AMOUR, *n. affair of love.* इष्कबाजीचें लटलें *n.* इष्कबाजीचा फंद *m.* जारकर्माचाविषय *m.* दोस्ती *f.* कामचरित्र *n.*

AMPHIBIOUS, *a. living in two elements.* जमिनीवर आणि पाण्यांत राहणारा, उभयचर, जलस्थलचारी, द्विधागति.

AMPHIBOLOGICAL, AMPHIBOLOGOUS, *a.* v. N. *ambiguous.* दुटप्पी, श्लिष्ट, द्व्यर्थक.

AMPHIBOLOGY,*n. language of a double or uncertain meaning.* श्लेष *m.* दुटप्पी बोलणें *n.* द्व्यर्थकभाषण *n.*

AMPHISBENA, *n.* (kind of snake) दुतोंडें *n.* महांडूळ *n.* मांडूळ *n.* मालुड *n.* द्विमुखाहि *m.*

AMPHITHEATRE, *n.* दीर्घवर्तुलाकार-अर्धचंद्राकार रंगशाळा *f.* वदामी डोलाचा तालीमखाना *m.*

AMPLE, *a. of large dimensions*, v. SPACIOUS. लांबरुंद, प्रशस्त, विस्तीर्ण, विशद, विशाल *or* ळ.

2 *diffusive, not contracted or brief, &c.* प्रशस्त, सविस्तर, असंक्षिप्त, विस्ताराचा, पाल्हाळाचा.

3 *lavish, copious, profuse*, v. EXUBERANT. उदार, पुरून उरायाचा-जोगा-&c. गडगंज, प्रशस्त, चळचळीत, घळघळीत, अघळपघळ.

4 *magnificent, munificent*, v. LIBERAL. उदार, प्रशस्त, धौताल.

AMPLIFICATION, *n.* v. V. 1.—*act.* विस्तारणें *n.* वाढवणें *n.* &c. —*state.* विस्तार *m.* विस्तारितत्व *n.*

2—*act.* फुगवणें *n.* फुगवून &c. सांगणें *n.*—*state.* तांडव *n.* टीका *f.* पाल्हाळ *m.* शब्दपाल्हाळ *m.* अर्थवाद *m.*

To AMPLIFY, *v. a. enlarge, expand.* विस्तारणें, वाढवणें, प्रशस्त-विस्तीर्ण-&c. करणें, विस्तार *m.* करणें *g. of o.*

2 *enlarge in discussion or representation.* फुगवणें, फुगवून-वाढवून-लांबवून-&c. सांगणें, पाल्हाळ *m.* करणें-लावणें, पाल्हाळ करून सांगणें, तांडव *n.*-टीका *f.*- विस्तार *m.* करणें.

To AMPLIFY *v. n.* पाल्हाळ *m.* करणें-लावणें, तांडव *n.*-&c. करणें, विस्तार *m.* करणें.

AMPLITUDE, AMPLENESS, *n.* v. A. 1. प्राशस्त्य *n.* प्रशस्तता *f.* प्रशस्तपणा *m.* विस्तीर्णता *f.* विशाळपणा *m.* वैशद्य *n.*

2 प्राशस्त्य *n.* विस्तार *m.* प्रशस्तपणा *m.* सविस्तरता *f.* असंक्षिप्तता *f.*

3 चळचळीतपणा *m.* अघळपघळपणा *m.* प्राशस्त्य *n.* औदार्य *n.*

4 धौताली *f.* प्राशस्त्य *n.* औदार्य *n.* उदारत्व *n.*

I. (of the sun). अग्र *n.*

AMPLY, *adv.* v. A. 1. प्रशस्तपणीं, प्रशस्तपणानें.

2 विस्तारानें, विस्तारपूर्वक, प्रशस्तपणें, सविस्तर.

3 प्रशस्तपणें, घळघळीत, चळचळीत, उदारपणानें, रेलचेलीनें.

4 प्रशस्तपणें, उदारपणानें, औदार्यपूर्वक, सढळपणानें, धौतालीनें.

To AMPUTATE, *v. a. cut off.* तोडणें, सोडवणें, कापून काढणें, उतरणें, कलम करणें.

AMPUTATION, *n.* v. V.—*act.* तोडणें *n.* कापणें *n.* सोडवणें *n.* &c. अंगछेद *m.* अंगछेदन *n.* [कवच *nm.*

AMULET, *n. a charm as worn.* ताईत *m.* तोटका *or* तोडगा *m.*

To AMUSE, *v. a. divert, entertain.* रमवणें, रंजवणें, खेळवणें, करमणूक *f.*-रमणूक *f.*-अनुरंजन *n.*-रंजन *n.*-मनोरंजन *n.*-&c. करणें *g. of o.*

2 (one's self) v. To PLAY. रमणें, विरंगुळणें, रतणें, विहरणें.
3 *delude, deceive.* भुलविणें, भुलथाप-थाप *f.* देणें.

AMUSED, *p.* v. V. 1. रमवलेला, रंजवलेला, &c. अनुरंजित, रंजित.
To be a. मौज *f.* वाटणें *in. con.*

AMUSEMENT, AMUSING, *n.* v. V. 1.—*act.* रमवणें *n.* रंजवणें *n.* अनुरंजन *n.* रंजन *n.* मनोरंजन *n.*
2—*act.* रमणूक *f.* रमण *n.* विरंगुळा *m.* गमत *f.* करमणूक *f.* विहार *m.* विहरण *n.* विनोद *m.* इच्छाविलास *m.* विलास *m.*
1. *object or cause of a.* v. PLAY. गमत *f.* विरंगुळा *m.* करमणूक *f.* तमाशा *m.* कौतुक *n.*

AMUSER, *n.* AMUSING, *p. a.* v. V. 1. रमवणारा &c. मौजेचा, कौतुकाचा, तमाशाचा, गमती, अनुरंजक, रंजक, अभिराम, मनोरंजक, मनमोहन, रुचीक, रुचिकर.

An.—the article, See A.

ANACARDIUM, *n. marking nut.* बिबा *m.* बिबवा *m.* भिलावा *m.* —covertly, काळा *m.*

ANACHRONISM, *n. error in chronology.* कालगणनाव्यत्यय *m.* कालसंख्याविपर्यय *m.* मितिव्यत्यास *m.*

ANAGRAM, *n.* नामाक्षरविपर्यास सिद्धनाम *n.*

ANALECTIC, *a. made up of selections.* वेंच्यांचा, वेंच्यांचा केलेला, अनेकग्रंथांश विशिष्ट.

ANALECTS, *n. collection of extracts.* वेंचे *m. pl.* अनेकग्रंथांशसंग्रह *m.* गाबाल्ग्रंथ *m.*

ANALEPTIC, *a. strengthening.* पुष्टिकर, पुष्टिकारक, पौष्टिक.

ANALOGICAL, ANALOGUS, *a.* उपमितीचा, अभ्युपगत, आनुषंगिक, सारखा, तुल्य, सदृश.

ANALOGY, *n. likeness in some respects.* उपमान *n.* उपमिती *f.* अभ्युपगम *m.* औपम्य *n.* सारखेपणा *m.* तुल्यभाव *m.* तुलना *f.* सादृश्य *n.*

ANALYSIS, *n.* मूलतत्वशोधन. *n.* मूलतत्वशोधनार्थपृथक्करण *n.* उपोद्घात *m.* पृथक्कृति *f.*

ANALYST, *n.* मूलतत्वशोधनकर्त्ता, मूलतत्वपृथक्कर्त्ता, पृथक्कृतिकर्त्ता.

ANALYTIC, ANALYTICAL, *a.* मूलतत्वशोधनसंबंधी, मूलपदार्थपृथक्करणसंबंधी-विषयक, पृथक्कृतिसंबंधी.

To ANALYZE, *v. a. resolve into its elements.* मुळाचीं तत्वें निराळीं करणें, मूलतत्वशोधन *n.*-मूलतत्वविवेचन *n.*-मूलतत्वशोधनार्थपृथक्करण *n.* करणें, पृथक्कृति *f.*-पृथक्करण *n.* करणें *g. of. o.*

ANARCHIC, ANARCHICAL, *a.* v. N. अनायक, निर्नायक, अराजक, बेबंद, निर्नायकीचा, अंधाधुंद, अंधाधुंदीचा, अशासन, शासनरहित, अव्यवस्थराजक.

ANARCHIST, ANARCH, *n.* अशासनकर्त्ता, बंडाळ्या *m.* बंड्या *m.* बंडी *m.* राज्याव्यवस्थाकर्त्ता.

ANARCHY, *n. want or confusion of government.* निर्नायकी *f.* अनायकी *f.* अनायक *n.* अराजक *n.* झोटिंगपादशाही *f.* अंधाधुंदी *f.* अशासन *n.* राज्याव्यवस्था *f.*

ANASARCA, *n.* नाळगूत or द *n.* जलत्वक् *f.* जलनिदानशोथ *m.*

ANATHEMA, *n. ecclesiastical curse.* बहिष्काराभिशाप *m.*

To ANATHEMATIZE, *v. a.* बहिष्काराभिशाप *m.* करणें-देणें.

ANATOMICAL, *a.* v. N. *belonging to anatomy.* शरीरव्यवच्छेदनविद्यासंबंधी, शारीरसंबंधी, शारीरविषयक.

ANATOMIST, *n.* शरीरव्यवच्छेदनकर्त्ता, शरीरव्यवच्छेदनवेत्ता.

To ANATOMIZE, *v. a. dissect.* शरीरव्यवच्छेदन *n.* -शरीरव्यवच्छेद *m.*- अंगव्यवच्छेद *m.* करणें.

ANATOMY, *n. science of the structure of the body.* शारीर *n.* शारीरक *n.*
2 *art of dissection.* शरीरव्यवच्छेदनविद्या *f.*

ANCESTOR, *n.* वडील *c.* पितर *m.* पूर्वज *c.* कुलपुरुष *m.* मागलापिढीदार *m.* मागलेपिढीचें मनुष्य *n.* डोई *f.*
Ancestors, v. ANCESTRY. बापदादे *m. pl.* बापजादे *m. pl.* आजेपणजे *m. pl.* वडील *m. pl.* वाडवडील *m. pl.* पूर्वज *m. pl.* पितरें *n. pl.*
The three ancestors (paternal or maternal) त्रयी *f.*
The three male ancestors. त्रिपुरुष *m. pl.* [*n.* मूलपीठ *n.*
Seat or place of one's ancestors. आद्यपीठ *n.* आद्यस्थान
Acquired by one's ancestors. वडिलोपार्जित.
Through one's ancestors. वडिलोवडिलीं.
To abuse one's ancestors. त्रयी *f.*-पित्रें *n. pl.*-तीनपिढ्या *f. pl.*-सातपिढ्या *f. pl.*-बेचाळीसपिढ्या *f. pl.* उद्धरणें-खबर *f.* घेणें *g. of o.*

ANCESTRAL, ANCESTORIAL, *a. belonging or relating to ancestors.* पूर्वजांचा, वडिलांचा, वडिलांसंबंधी, पैत्र, पैतृक, कौलिक, पूर्वजसंबंधी, पूर्वजविषयक. [पित्र्यायात.
2 *descending from a.* वडीलपरंपरागत, परंपरागत, परंपरायात,

ANCESTRY, *n.* v. ANCESTORS, *series of ancestors.* वडील or वाडवडील *m. pl.* वडीलपरंपरा *f.* कुलपरंपरा *f.* वृद्धपरंपरा *f.* कुलावली *f.* पितृसामान्य *n.*

ANCHOR, *n.* नांगर *m.* लंगर *m.*
Flook of an a or grapnel, पावडा *m.*
Small a. See GRAPNEL.
To cast a. v. To ANCHOR. नांगर *m.* टाकणें.
To lie at a. नांगरणीवर असणें, नांगर *m.* सोडून-टाकून असणें.

To ANCHOR, *v. n.* नांगर or लंगर *m.* टाकणें, नांगरणें, नांगरणी *f.*-नांगरण *f.* करणें or होणें *g. of o.* [करणें.
2 (for some short occasion). ओरवा *m.* करणें, बंदर *n.*

ANCHORAGE, *n. duty levied on anchoring.* खुटवा *m.*
2 *place of a.* नांगरवाडा *m.* ओरवा *m.* ठेवण *n.*

ANCHORET, ANCHORITE. *n. hermit,* v. RECLUSE. वनवासी *m.* अरण्यवासी *m.* (among Bràhmans) वानप्रस्थ *m.*

ANCHORING, *n.* v. V. 1.—*act.* नांगरणें *n.* नांगरणी *f.* नांगरण *f.*
2—*act.* ओरवा *m.*

ANCIENT, *a. belonging to old times.* जुना, जुनाट, प्राचीन, प्राचीनकाळचा, पूर्वकालीन, पूर्वकालिक, प्राक्कालिक, प्राक्कालीन, प्राक्तन, पुरातन, कदीम.

ANCIENT, *n.* प्राचीनमनुष्य *n.* पुरातनपुरुष *m.*
Ancients. वाडवडील *m. pl.* प्राचीन-प्राचीनकाळचीं मनुष्यें *n. pl.* पूर्वसिद्ध *m. pl.* पुरातनकालचीं-प्राक्कालचीं-&c. मनुष्यें *n. pl.* वृद्धपरंपरा *f.*
Practice of the a. वृद्धाचार *m.*
Track or path of the a. वडिलांची फरपट *f.*

ANCIENTLY, *adv.* जुन्या काळीं, पूर्वकाळीं, प्राचीनकाळीं, प्राक्कालीं, प्राचीनसमयीं, पूर्वी.

ANCIENTNESS, *n.* v. A. जुनेपणा *m.* जुनाटपणा *m.* प्राचीनत्व *n.* पुरातनत्व *n.* प्राक्कालिकत्व *n.* &c.

AND, *conj.* आणि, आण, अणखी, अणखीन, अणीख, नी, व.
A. so forth. इत्यादि, इत्यादिक, वगैरे, प्रभृति.

ANDROGYNE, ANDROGYNAL, See HERMAPHROLITE.

ANECDOTE, *n. family or personal story.* कुळकट *f.* कुळकथा *f.* खणकन *f.* [चरडक *n.*
2—gener. उपाख्यान *n.* फरडूक *n.* फरडुकें *n.* गनक *n. v.* घाल,
ANES, AWNS, *n. beard of corn.* कुसळ *n.* शूक *mn.*
ANEURISM, *n.* धमनीशोथ *m.* [पुन्हा, फिरून.
ANEW, *adv. over again,* v. AGAIN. नव्यानें, उलटून, पुनः *pop.*
ANGEL, *n.* दूत *m.* देवदूत *m.* ईश्वरदूत *m.* [फुलणें *n.*
A.'s visit. *fig.* उंबराचें फूल *n.* चांदसलामी *f.* साठावर्षी सुंठ
A. of death. यमदूत.
Recording a. चित्रगुप्त. [देवदूतवत्.
ANGELIC, ANGELICAL, *a.* देवदूताचा, देवदूतसंबंधी, देवदूतधर्मक,
ANGER, *n. ire, wrath, indignation, resentment.* राग *m.* क्रोध *m.* कोप *m.* रोष *m.* जळ *or* जाळ *m.* घुसा *m.* तवक *m.* क्रोधभाव *m.* रौद्र *n.* अमर्ष *m.* संताप *m.* तैष *m.*
Assumed a. A. in sport. क्रीडाकोप *m.*
To be excited into a. *See under* ANGRY. रागास येणें-भरणें-पेटणें-चढणें, चेतळणें *or* चेताळणें.
To calm, cool, remove, &c. the a. of. रागाचेंपाणी *n.*-बारापाणी *n.* करणें *g. of o.*
To draw down (upon self) the a. of. कढ *m.* ओढून घेणें, रागें भरून घेणें.
To vent a. upon. To be angry with. रागें भरणें *with* वर *or* ला, क्रोधाग्निशिखा *f. pl.* टाकणें.
To ANGER, *v. a. provoke, enrage, excite, irritate, &c.* तापवणें, संतापवणें, क्षोभवणें, कोपवणें, पेटवणें, राग *m.*-कोप *m.*-&c. आणणें, रागास आणणें, कातावणें, चितावणें, चेतवणें, चेतळवणें, खिजवणें, खाजवणें, उसळवणें, पित्त *n.* तापवणें-खवळवणें-उसळवणें -&c. *g. of o.* तापन *n.*-संतापन *n.*-क्षोभन *n.*-क्रोधोद्दीपन *n.*-क्रोधोद्बोध *m.*-&c. करणें *g. of o.* संतप्त-क्रुद्ध-कुपित-&c. करणें.
2 *inflame, cause to smart.* दाह *m.* करणें *g. of o.* संतप्त करणें.
ANGERED, *p.* v. V. 1. *and* ANGRY. रागास आणलेला, &c. तप्त, संतप्त, रुष्ट.
To ANGLE, *v. n. fish with a rod and hook.* गळ *m.* टाकणें, गळानें धरणें, छडीगळानें मासे *m. pl.* धरणें.
ANGLE, *n.* कोण *or* कोन *m.* कोपरा *m.* अस्र *n.*
Acute a. लघुकोण, न्यूनकोण.
A. of elevation. उन्नतांश *m.*
A. of depression. अधः कोण *m.*
Obtuse a. अधिककोण, विशालकोण.
Right a. समकोण, काटकोन.
ANGLED, *a.* कोणाचा, सकोण.
Right a. समकोण.
ANGLER, *n.* गळकरी *m.*
ANGLICAN, *a.* इंग्लंद देशचा, इंग्लंद देशसंबंधी, &c.
ANGLICISM, *n. an English idiom.* इंग्लिश भाषेचा संप्रदाय *m.* इंग्रेजी भाषेच्या रीतीचा शब्द *m.*-वाक्य *n.*-रचना *f.*
To ANGLICIZE, *v. a. make conformable to English.* इंग्रेजी भाषेच्या रीती प्रमाणें करणें-रूपदेणें.
ANGRILY, *adv.* रागानें &c. रागें भरून-येऊन, क्रोधभावानें, क्रोधबुद्ध्या, क्रोधदृष्ट्या, क्रोध-&c. पूर्वक, डोळे चढवून.
ANGRY, *a.* रागावलेला, रागें भरलेला, रागास आलेला, क्रोधयमान, कोपायमान, कुपित, क्रुद्ध, क्रोधारूढ, क्रोधान्वित, क्रोधयुक्त, कोपयुक्त, जात क्रोध, सक्रोध, तप्त, संतप्त, रुष्ट.
—in high degree; as expressed by such words as *incensed, inflamed, infuriated, enraged, exasperated.* क्रोधातुर, क्रोधक्षुब्द, क्रोधवश, क्रोधाक्रांत, क्रोधाकुल, क्रोधग्रस्त, क्रोधमय, क्रोधाविष्ट, क्रोधार्त्त, क्रोधपीडित, क्रोधविव्हल, कोपाविष्ट, कोपज्वलित, कोपदीप्त, रोषाविष्ट, क्रोधानलदग्ध, क्रोधमूर्च्छित.
A. feelings. क्रोधभाव *m.*
A. words, *sharp speeches,* v. ALTERCATION. धसफस *or* धुसफूस *f.* धुसमूस *f.*
To be a. रागें भरणें, रागवणें *or* रागावणें.
To become a. रागावणें, कोपणें, पेटणें, चेतणें, क्रोधावणें, क्रोधणें, तापणें, संतापणें, क्षोभणें, खिजणें, रागास येणें-चढणें-भरणें-पेटणें, चेतळणें *or* चेताळणें, आंगाची लाही *f.* होणें, उभा जळणें.
2—as used of speech, &c. क्रोधाचा, रागाचा, &c. कडक, क्रोधमय, क्रोधयुक्त.
ANGUISH, *n.* v. PAIN. पीडा *f.* यातना *f.*
A. of mind. मनस्ताप *m.* संताप *m.*
To ANGUISH, &c. See To PAIN, &c.
ANGULAR, *a. having angles or corner.* कोणाचा, सकोण, कोणविशिष्ट, कोणात्मक.
ANGULARITY, ANGULARNESS, *n.* v. A. सकोणता *f.* कोणवैशिष्ट्य *n.* कोणविशिष्टता *f.*
ANHELATION, See PANTING.
ANIGHT, *adv.* रात्रीं, रात्रौ, रात्रीस.
ANIL, *indigo plant.* नीली *pop.* नीळ *f.*
ANILITY. See DOTAGE.
ANIMADVERSION, *n.* v. BLAME. बोल *m.* दोषारोप *m.* दोषारोपण *n.* दोषारोपकभाषण *n.*
To ANIMADVERT, *v. n.* See To ADVERT.
2 *remark upon censuringly,* v. To BLAME. बोल *m.* लावणें, दोष देऊन-काढून- आणून- लावून-ठेवून-&c. बोलणें-म्हणणें.
ANIMAL, *n. living creature.* जीव *m.* प्राणी *m.* जंतु *m.* जनावर *nm.* हयवान *or* हैवान *nm.* पशु *m.* सत्त्व *nm.*
The four classes (चार खाणी) into which all *Animals* are collected, are अंडज, जरायुज, स्वेदज, उद्भिज्ज.
ANIMAL, *a. of or belonging to animals.* प्राण्याचा, प्राणिविषयक, प्राणिसंबंधी, जीवसंबंधी, सजीवसंबंधी, सजीवसंभव, पशुसंभव.
A. food, v. FLESHMEAT. मांसाचें भक्ष्य *n.*
A. functions, प्राणिक्रिया.
A. kingdom. प्राणिकोटि *f.* प्राणिजाति *f.*
A. substance. प्राणिज. प्राण्युत्पन्न पदार्थ *m.*-वस्तु *n.*
2 not intellectual; *relating to the a. functions.* प्राणिक्रियेचा, प्राणिक्रियासंबंधी-विषयक.
ANIMALCULAR, *a.* लहान जिवांविषयींचा, क्षुद्रजतुसंबंधी-विषयक, अल्पजंतुसंबधी-विषयक.
ANIMALCULE, *n.* लहानजीव *m.* क्षुद्रजंतु *m.* अल्पजंतु *m.* अतिसूक्ष्म जंतु *m.* परमाणुतुल्यजंतु *m.* केशवमाधव *m. pl.*
ANIMALISM, *n. state of mere animals.* पशुधर्म *m.* पशुवृत्ति *f.*
ANIMALITY, ANIMALNESS, *n.* प्राणित्व *n.* पशुत्व *n.*
To ANIMATE, *v. a. quicken, make alive.* जीव *m.*-जीवनकळा *f.*-जीवनशक्ति *f.*-जीवित्व *n.*-चैतन्य-&c. देणें-घालणें, सजीव-सप्राण-सचेतन-&c. करणें, जीवन *n.* घालणें, जीवदान *n.*-प्राणदान *n.* करणें.
2 *inspirit, inspire, enliven, cheer, exhilarate.* जीव *m.*-धैर्य *n.*-दम *m.*-धमक *f.*- हिम्मत *f.*- उत्साह *m.*-चेव *m.*-&c. आणणें-देणें-घा-

ळणें, उठावणी *f.*- उचल *f.*- उत्तेजन *n.*- प्रोत्साहन *n.*-&c. करणें.

Animate, *a.* v. Living. सजीव, जीवदार, सप्राण, सचेतन, सचेष्ट, जीव विशिष्ट.

A. & Inanimate. सजीवनिर्जीव, चेतनाचेतन, चराचर.

Animated, *p.* & *a.* v. V. 1. *and* Living. सजीव केलेला, &c. प्राप्तचैतन्य, जातचैतन्य, जीवित.

2 उत्तेजित, प्रोत्साहित, प्राप्तोत्साह, जातोत्साह.

I. v. Lively. जिवट, जीवदार, दणक्याचा, कडकडीत, कडाख्याचा, धडाक्याचा, सतेज.

Animation, *n.* v. V. 1.—*act.* जीव घालणें *n.* सजीव करणें *n.* सचेतन करणें *n.*

2—*act.* उत्तेजन *n.* उठावणी *f.* उचल *f.* प्रोत्साहन *n.* उद्दीपन *n.*
I. *life, vivacity, spirit*, v. Liveliness. जीव *m.* तेज *n.* पाणी *n.* रंग *m.*

Animosity, *n.* v. Hatred. वैरभाव *m.* द्वेषभाव *m.* अंतर्दाह *m.* अतिशत्रुत्व *n.* बद्धकटाक्ष *m.*

Anise, *n.* *Anethum pimpinella*—plant. शेपु *f.* बडीशेप *or* शोप *f.* अतिच्छत्रा *f.*—seed. शेप *f.* शोप *f.* बडीशेप *or* शोप *f.* अतिच्छत्रा *f.*

Anise-scented, Anise-smelling, *a.*—of mangoes and other fruits. शेपा *or* शेप्या, शोपा *or* शोप्या *dim.* शेपट *or* शोपट.

Ankle, *n.* मणगट *n.* गोफा *m.* गुल्फा *f.* गुल्फ *m.* घुटिका *f.*

Region of the a. इंद्रगेळ *n.*

Ankle-bone, *n.* घोटा *m.* पायाचा डोळा *m*-खुबा *m.*

Ankle-joint, *n.* मणगटाची खीळ *f.*

Anklet, *n.* *ornament for the ankle.* वाळा *m.*

Silver a. for a child. काडवाळा *m.* कांडोळें *n.*

Annals, *n.* v. History. सालवार बखर *f.* दरवर्षाचा-प्रतिवार्षिक [वृत्तांत *m.*

Annats, *n.* v. First fruits. नवाळी *f.* नवीनवाळ *f.* नवान्न *n.* नवधान्य *n.*

To **Anneal**, *v.a.* तापवून नरम करणें.

To **Annex**, *v. a. subjoin,* v. To Add. जोडणें, लावणें, दुमाल्यास लावणें-घालणें, योग *m.*-संयोग *m.* करणें *g. of o.*

2 (province, country.) खालशांत घेणें-मिळवणें, खालसा करणें.

Annexation, *n.* v. V. 1.—*act.* जोडणें *n.* लावणें *n.*, &c.

2 खालसा करणें *n.*

Annexed, *p.* v. V. 1. जोडलेला, लावलेला, &c.

2 खालसा केलेला &c.

Annihilable, *a.* v. V. नाहींसा कराया-चा-जोगता-जोगा-सारखा [-&c. नाशवंत.

To **Annihilate**, *v. a.* v. To Destroy. नाहींसा करणें, नाबूद *adv.* करणें, पस्त *adv.* करणें, उच्छेदणें, निपातणें, ठाव ठिकाणा *m.* नाहींसा करणें *g. of o.* सत्यनाश *m.*-विनाश *m.*-तळमूस *n.*-तळपूस *f.*-&c.-करणें *g. of o.* मागमूस *m.* मोडणें *g. of o.*

Annihilated, *p.* v. V. नाहींसा केलेला-झालेला, उच्छिन्न, विनष्ट, [विनाशित.

Annihilater, *n.* v. V. नाहींसा करणारा, &c. विनाशक, विनाशी, उच्छेदक, विनाश &c. कर्त्ता.

Annihilation, *n.* v. V.—*act.* नाहींसा करणें *n.* &c. उच्छेद *m.* उच्छेदन *n.*—*state.* नाश *m.* सत्यनाश *pop.* सत्यानास *m.* विनाश *m.* फन्ना *m.* बींचूड *n. f.* उच्छेद *m.* क्षय *m.* विलय *m.* लय *m.* प्रलय *m.* निःपात *m.* निधन *n.*

Anniversary, *a.* *annual,* v. Yearly. प्रतिवर्षाचा, प्रतिवार्षिक, प्रतिसांवत्सरिक.

Anniversary, *n.* वर्षाचा दिवस *m.* प्रतिवार्षिकदिवस *m.*

A. of a brith. वाढदिवस *m.* वाढदीस *m.* वर्षगांठ *f.* वर्धापनदिवस *m.*

A. of a death. मृततिथि *f.* मृतदिवस *m.* प्रतिसांवत्सरिक *n.* क्षयदिवस *m.*

To **Annotate**. *v. n.* v. To Comment. टीका *f.*-भाष्य *n.*-&c. [करणें.

Annotation, *n.* v. Comment. टीका *f.* भाष्य *n.* व्याख्या *f.*

Annotator, *n.* v. Commentator. टीकाकार *m.* भाष्यकार *m.*

To **Announce**, *v. a. give notice, proclaim.* v. To Publish. खबर *f.*-&c. देणें *g. of o.* जाहीर-विदित-&c. करणें, घोषणा *f.* करणें *g. of o.*

Announcement, Annunciation, *n.* v. V.—*act.* खबर देणें *n.* जाहीर करणें *n.* घोषणा *f.*

To **Annoy**, *v. a. molest,* v. To Tease. छडणें, छळणें, घोळणें, उपद्रव *m.*-त्रास *m.*-इजा *f.*-दुःख *n.*-तसदी *f.*-&c. देणें-करणें, उपसर्ग *m.* लावणें, त्रासणें, त्रासविणें.

Annoyance, Annoying, *n.* v. V.—*act.* छडणें *n.* &c. छडणूक *f.* छळणूक *f.* जाचणूक *f.* नड *f.* नडाव *m.* छल *or* ळ *m.* उपद्रव *m.* त्रास *m.* उपसर्ग *m.* छलना *f.* इजा *f.* तसदी *f.* [नडाव *m.*

I. *annoying matter or cause,* v. Plague. उपद्रव *m.* नड *f.*

Annoyed, *p.* v. V. उपद्रव &c. केलेला-पावलेला, छडलेला, &c. छलित, क्लेशित, क्लेशयुक्त, त्रस्त, त्रासित.

Annoyer, *n.* Annoying, *p. a.* v. V. छडणारा, उपद्रव-इजा-तसदी-दुःख-&c. देणारा-करणारा, क्लेशकारक, क्लेशद, क्लेशक, त्रासक.

Annual, *a.* v. Yearly. वर्षाचा, वार्षिक, प्रतिवार्षिक, सालाबाद, सांवत्सरिक, सांवत्सर, प्रतिसांवत्सरिक.

Annual, *n.* *an a. plant.* वर्षाचें झाड *n.*-भाजी *f.* बरशिकीभाजी *f.* बरशिकें झाड *n.* ओषधी *f.*

2 *book published yearly.* वार्षिक पुस्तक *n.*

Annually, *adv.* v. Yearly. प्रतिवर्षी, दरवर्षास, दरसाल, सालदरसाल, सालबसाल, सालीना, सालोसाल.

Annuitant, *n.* वर्षासनी *m.* वर्षासनदार *c.* वर्षासनवाला, वर्षासन्या *m.* वर्षाशनभोक्ता *m.*

Annuity, *n.* *annual allowance.* वर्षाशन *pop.* वर्षासन *n.* साल *n.* वार्षिक *n.* वार्षिक नेमणूक *f.* वार्षिक देणगी *f.*

To **Annul**, *v. a.* v. To Abolish. मोडणें, मोडून टाकणें, नाहींसा-रद्द-रहित-&c. करणें, लोपवणें, पूज *n.* घालणें *with* वर *of o.*

Annular, Annulary, *a.* वळ्याचे आकाराचा, वलयाकार, मंडलाकार, वृत्ताकार, कंकणाकार.

Annulment, *n.* v. V.—*act.* मोडणें *n.* &c. लोप *m.*

Annulled, *p.* v. V. मोडलेला, &c. लुप्त, रद्द.

To **Annunciate**, See To Announce.

Anodyne, *n.* शमन *n.* उपशमन *n.* प्रशमन *n.* दुःखहर-हारक-हर्त्ता-&c. औषध *n.*

To **Anoint**, *v. a. rub over with unctuous substance.* माखणें, उटणें, उटणें *n.* लावणें, चोपडणें, मर्दणें, चर्चिणें, अभ्यंग *m.*-अभ्यंजन *n.*-&c. करणें *g. of o.*

To a. with oil. तेल *n.* लावणें, तेलावणें, गजणें, तैलाभ्यंग *m.* करणें *g. of o.*

2 *consecrate by unction, sprinkling, &c.* अभिषेकणें, अभिषेचणें, अभिषेक *m.*-अभिषेचन *n.* करणें *g. of o.* अभिषिक्त करणें.

Anointed, *p.* v. V. 1. माखलेला &c. चर्चित, अभ्यक्त, अनुलिप्त.

2 अभिषेक केलेला-झालेला, अभिषिक्त, कृताभिषेक, जाताभिषेक, मूर्धाभिषिक्त. [लेपी.

Anointer, *n.* v. V. 1. माखणारा, &c. अभ्यंगकर्त्ता, अनुलेपक, अनु-

2 अभिषेकणारा, अभिषेक्या, अभिषेककर्त्ता, अभिषेक्ता.

ANOINTING, ANOINTMENT, *n.v.* V. 1.—*act.* माखणें *n.* &c. माखण *n.* उटणें *n.* मर्दणें *n.* उटी *f.* अनुलेप *m.* अनुलेपन *n.* मर्दन *n.* अभ्यंग *m.* अभ्यंजन *n.* चर्चन *n.* चर्चा *f.* स्नेहन *n.*—*state.* See INUNCTION.

A. with oil. तैलाभ्यंग *m.*

2—*act.* अभिषेकणें *n.* अभिषेचणें *n.* अभिषेक *m.* अभिषेचन *n.* मूर्धाभिषेक *m.*

ANOMALOUS, ANOMALISTIC, *a. irregular.* संप्रदायास-नियमास-&c. विरुद्ध, विधिभंजक, अयथामार्ग, अयथाविधि, अयथासंप्रदाय, विलक्षण, नियमविरुद्ध.

The a. equation of a planet. मंदफल *n.*

ANOMALOUSLY, *adv.* v. A. मार्ग-विधि-&c. सोडून, अविधि, अविधीनें, अयथाविधि, रूढि सोडून. [ण्य *n.*

ANOMALOUSNESS, *n.* v. A. व्यभिचार *m.* विधिभंजकत्व *n.* वैलक्ष-

ANOMALY, *n. irregularity.* व्यभिचार *m.*

2 *an a.* विधिभंजकगोष्ट *f.*-विषय *m.*-&c.

Argument of a. मंदकेंद्र *n.*

ANON, *adv.* v. SOON. लवकर.

Ever and a. *now and then.* कधींकधीं, मध्येंमध्यें, वरचेवर.

ANONYMOUS, *a.* निनांव्या, निनांवाचा, बिननांवाचा, अनामक, अनामिक, निर्नामक, गुप्तनामक, नामहीन-रहित-&c.

ANONYMOUSLY, *adv.* v. A. नांवावांचून, निनांव, विनानाम.

ANOREXY, *n. want of appetite.* अरुचि *f.* अग्निमांद्य *n.* क्षुधाभाव *m.*

ANOTHER, *a. one more.* दुसरा, अणखीएक, दुजा, द्वितीय.

2 *not the same,* दुसरा, अन्य, इतर, निराळा, वेगळा, अपर, अंतर (in comp. as भाषांतर, देहांतर, स्थलांतर, वृक्षांतर, पुष्पांतर, गृहांतर, &c.) दुजा, अणीक, भिन्न. [अणीक.

3 *any other, any one else.* दुसरा, दुसराकोणी, इतर, अन्य,

4 *not self.* दुसरा, परावा, परका, परकीय.

One another एकमेक.

To ANSWER, *v. a. reply to.* उत्तर *n.*-प्रत्युत्तर *n.*-जबाब *or* जाब *m.*-&c. देणें-करणें.

Unable to a. अनुत्तर, निरुत्तर.

To a. again, *reply to saucily.* उलटून बोलणें, उलटून गोष्ट *f.* सांगणें, उलटजबाब *m.* देणें, उत्तरास प्रत्युत्तर करणें, बेजबाब बोलणें, परत गोष्ट सांगणें, तोंडासींतोंड *n.* देणें, तोंडीं लागणें *g.of o.*

To a. petulantly, snappishly, &c. बचकर जाब देणें-बोलणें.

To a. promptly or smartly, (*flatly, smart, outright,* &c.) तोंडावर-तोंडच्यातोंडीं बोलणें- उत्तर *n.* करणें, तटका *m.* तोडून टाकणें, तुकडा *m.* तोडून देणें, फडका *m.* फाडून देणें, कांडें *n.* मोडून देणें-पाडणें.

2 (a matter stated) *refute, confute.* खंडणें, खंडन *n.* करणें *g. of o.* उत्तर *n.* देणें.

3 *satisfy, supply.* पुरवणें, पूर्ण करणें, पर्याप्ति *f.* करणें *g. of o.* निर्वाह *m.* करणें *g. of o.*

4 *act in return or opposition.* उलटून-परतून *with the verb required.* प्रतिकर्म *n.*-प्रतिक्रिया *f.*-प्रतिकार *m.*-क्रियोत्तर *n* करणें, परत (in comp.) देणें-करणें. [देणें-करणें.

To ANSWER, *v. n. make answer, reply.* उत्तर *n.*-प्रत्युत्तर *n.*-जाब *m.*

To a. to a call. ओ *f.*-साद *m.*-हाक *f.* देणें, सादवणें.

To a. back saucily, &c. उलट गोष्ट *or* फेर गोष्ट *f.* सांगणें, उलट जबाब *m.* सांगणें-करणें- देणें, फेर घोडी *f.*-फेरपगडी *f.* करणें, जापारणें *or* जोपरणें.

2 *succeed, serve, do.* उतरणें, लागणें, चालणें, बसणें, जमणें, पडणें, जम *m.*-जुवा *m.*-जुगल *f.*-उतारा *m.* पडणें-बसणें, चरितार्थ-कृतार्थ-कृतकृतार्थ होणें. [करणें.

3 *give account of.* जाब *m.*-हिशोब *m.*-मोसबा *m.*-उत्तर *n.*-&c. देणें-

4 *be correspondent with, suit with,* v. To SUIT. मिळणें, जुळणें, जुगणें, जुडणें, जमणें, गांठ *f.* पडणें *g. of o.*

ANSWER, *n. reply, &c.* v. V. 1. उत्तर *n.* प्रत्युत्तर *n.* जबाब *or* जाब *m.* प्रतिवचन *n.* प्रतिवाद *m.* प्रतिवाक्य *n.* प्रतिवाणी *f.* उलथा *m.*

Decided a. नेमोत्तर *n.*

Devious or irrelevant answers. बावांचे *m. pl.* बावट्या *f. pl.* भावांखे *m. pl.*

Disrespectful a. तोंडपिटी *f.* गैरजबाब *m.*

Evasive, inapplicable, &c a. अनुत्तर *n.*

Ready a. हाजीरजबाब *m.* [जबेतराश *or* स.

Ready of or at a. हाजीरजबाबी *or* हाजीरजबाब, जबाबी,

Requiring a.—order &c. जबाबी.

Soft a. सांत्ववाद *m.* [डा *m.*

I. *key, solution.* उत्तर *n.* किल्ली *f.* उतारा *m.* उलटा *m.* उलग-

ANSWERABLE, *a.* v. V. N. 3. *responsible, accountable, amenable, &c.* जाब-हिशोब- मोसबा-&c. देणारा, मोसबेदार, धनी, निसबतदार, उत्तर-जाब-मोसबा-हिशोब-&c. देण्याचा अधिकारी-धनी-&c.

ANT, *n.* मुंगी *f.* पिपीलिका *f.*

Black or red a. मुंगळा. *m. dim.* मुंगळी *f.*

Red a. चांचण *or* चांचड *n.* उंबला *or* ओंबील *m.* वाळंबा *m.*

White a. *termes.* वाळवी *f.* वाळंबा *m.* उदई *or* उधई *f.*

Certain other kinds of *Ant* are काडमुंगी, गांडमोडी मुंगी, घाणेरी मुंगी, डोंगळा *m.* ढुंगणमोडें *n.* दांन्या *m.* धांवरी मुंगी, बळचिच *or* जन. हुरण *n.* हुळहुळी मुंगी, पिसोळी मुंगी.

Hillock cast up by white ants. वारूळ *n.* भोम *n. enhanc.* भोमाड *n.* वल्मीक *n.* वामलूर *m.*

Swarm of ants. हुरण *n.*

Train or line in progress of ants. साईर *f.* वन्हाड *n.*

ANT-HILL, *n.* भोम *n. enhanc.* भोमाड *n.* क्रिमिशैल *m.*

ANT-LION, *n.* एड्का *m.* मोर *m.*

ANTAGONIST, *n.* v. OPPONENT. प्रतिपक्षी *m.* विरोधी *m.* विपक्ष, विपक्षी *m.* प्रतियोगी *m.*

ANTAGONIST, *a.* See OPPOSING.

ANTAPHRODISIAC, ANTAPHRODITIC, *a. abating sexual desire.* कामघ्न, कामहारक, कामनाशक, कामशमक, कामाग्निशमक.

2 v. ANTIVENEREAL. उपदंशघ्न, उपदंशशमक, उपदंशहारक.

ANTAPOPLECTIC. *a. good against apoplexy.* अंगविभ्रंशघ्न, सन्न्यासघ्न, सन्न्यासनाशक, सन्निपातमूर्च्छापरिहारक.

ANTARCTIC, *a. relating to the southern pole.* दक्षिणध्रुवसंबंधी, दक्षिणध्रुवाकडचा-कडील.

ANTARTHRITIC, *a. counteracting gout.* क्षुद्रग्रंथिस्थवातरोगघ्न, पादांगुष्ठरोगनाशक.

ANTASTHMATIC, *a. counteracting asthma.* श्वासरोगघ्न, श्वासरोगनाशक-शमक.

ANTE. This particle in its signification of *before* may be rendered by पूर्व and अग्र. For its significations of *against* See ANTI.

ANTECEDENCE, *n. act or state of going before in time.* पूर्वसिद्धि *f.* पूर्वसिद्धता *f.* पूर्वभवन*n.* पूर्वास्तित्व*n.* पूर्वसत्ता *f.*

ANTECEDENT, *a. preceding in time.* मागला, अगोदरचा, अगोदरील, अधींचा, अधील, पूर्व, पूर्वभूत, पूर्वजात, पूर्वगत, प्रागागत, पूर्वसिद्ध, पूर्वसत्ताक, भूतपूर्व, जातपूर्व.

ANTECEDENT, *n.* पूर्वींची गोष्ट *f.*-विषय*m.*- &c. [परामृष्ट.
2—in gram. तत्पदवाच्य, तत्‌शब्दवाच्य, तत्‌शब्दसंबंधी, तत्पद-
3—in logic. प्रतिज्ञावाक्य*n*
4— in math. प्रमाणांतलें पहिलें पद *n.*
Antecedents. पूर्वाचरण *n.* पूर्वचरित्र*n.* पूर्ववृत्त *n.* पूर्ववृत्तांत *m.*

ANTECEDENTLY, *adv.* अगोदर, पूर्वी.

ANTECHAMBER, *n.* सदरेची-दिवाणखान्याची-&c.पुढची खोली *f.*बाहेरची खोली *f.* सभोपगृह*n.* सभासीमगृह*n.* [रीस *f.*

ANTEDATE, *n. prior date.* पूर्वमिती *f.* मागली मिती *f.* मागली ता-

To ANTEDATE, *v. a. date before the true time.* पूर्वीची मिती *f*-मागली मिती *f.*- मागली तारीख *f.*-&c. घालणें.
2 See To ANTICIPATE.

ANTEDILUVIAN. *a. before the deluge.* प्रलयापूर्वींचा, प्रलयप्राक्कालिक, प्रलयपूर्वकालिक.

ANTELOPE, *n.* v. DEER. हरण*mn.* हरिण*m.* मृग*m.* कुरंग*m.*
Black a. काळवीट *m.* कृष्णमृग*m.* कृष्णसार*m.* कृष्णसारंग*m.*
Spotted a. चित्तळ or चितळ *m. n.* चित्रमृग *m.*
Dagger of a.-horn. माडू*m.* [लिक.

ANTEMERIDIAN, *a. beforenoon.* दोन प्रहरच्या पूर्वींचा, पूर्वाह्णका-

ANTEMETIC,*a. checking vomiting.* ढलटी बसवणारा, वांतिशमक-नाशक-&c. वांतिघ्न.

ANTEMUNDANE, *a. before the world.* पृथ्वीच्या पूर्वींचा, पृथ्वीच्या अगोदरचा, पृथ्व्युत्पत्तिपूर्वकालिक, जगत्सृष्टिपूर्वकालिक.

ANTENNÆ *n.*—of insects, &c. मिशी *f.* [पूर्वींचा.

ANTENUPTIAL, *a. being before marriage.* विवाहापूर्वींचा, लग्नाच्या

ANTEPAST. *n.* v. FORETASTE. पूर्वभोग*m.* आदिभोग*m.* पूर्वानुभव*m.* कालापकर्षभोग*m.* [स्थित.

ANTEPENULT, ANTEPENULTIMATE, *a.* उपांत्यपूर्ववर्त्ती, उपांत्यपूर्व-

ANTEPILEPTIC, *a. counteracting epilepsy.* फेंपरें-मिरगी-&c दूरकरणारा, अपस्मारनाशक- हारक-शमक, अपस्मारघ्न.

ANTERIOR, *a.—in time.* v. FORMER. अगला, पूर्वींचा, अगोदरचा, पूर्वकालीन, पूर्वकालिक, भूतपूर्व.
2—*in space,* v. FORE. अग्रवर्त्ती, पूर्ववर्त्ती, प्राग्वर्त्ती,

ANTEROOM, *n.* See ANTECHAMBER.

ANTHELMINTIC,*n.* *n. medicine against worms.* कृमिघ्न-कृमिहर-कृमिनाशक-औषध.

ANTHEM, *n.* See HYMN.

ANTHER, *n. top of stamen.* केसराग्र *n.* परागकोश *m.*

ANTHOLOGY, *n. discourse on flowers.* पुष्पवर्णन *n.*पुष्पाख्यान *n.*
2 See GARLAND.

ANTHRAX, *n. tumor on the spine,*v. CARBUNCLE. देंटपुळी *f.*

ANTHROPOPHAGIST, ANTHROPOPHAGY, See CANNIBAL, CANNIBALISM.

ANTI, *prep.* This preposition may be rendered by such words as शत्रु, (ex. antibilious पित्तशत्रु, कफशत्रु, वातशत्रु, ज्वरशत्रु, विषशत्रु &c.), नाशक or नाशन or नाशी, (ex. कफनाशक, पित्तनाशक), घ्न (ex. पित्तघ्न, ज्वरघ्न), हर, हर्त्ता, हारक, हारी, (ex. विषहर, शूलहर, दुःखहर), भंजन, मारक.

ANTIARTHRITIC, *a.* See ANTARTHRITIC.

ANTIBILIOUS, *a.* पित्तशत्रु, पित्तघ्न, पित्तनाशक-हारक-शमक-&c.

ANTIC, *a. odd, grotesque.* मस्करीचा, माकडचेष्टेचा, विलक्षण.

ANTIC, *n.* v. BUFFOON. मस्कऱ्या *m.* भांड*m.* हंडीबाग *m.*
2 *trick.* खेळकुडी *f.* माकडचेष्टा *f.* टिबल्या बाव्हल्या *f. pl.* माकडचाळे *m. pl.*

ANTICHRIST, *n.* ख्रीस्तविपक्षी *m.* ख्रीस्तविरोधी *m.*

ANTICHRISTIAN, *a.* ख्रीस्तविरुद्ध.

To ANTICIPATE, *v. a. take before the time.* अगाऊ घेणें, अपकर्षणें, अपकर्ष *m.*-अपकर्षण *n.* करणें *g. of o.* अप्राप्तकालग्रहण *n.*-नियमितकालपूर्वग्रहण करणें *g. of o.*
2 *take before another, forestall.* अवली*f.*—आघाडी *f.* साधणें-मारणें *g. of o.* आगपाई *f.* करणें-साधणें *g. of o.*
3 *foretaste.* अप्राप्तकालभोग *m.* -पूर्वभोग *m.* -कालापकर्षभोग *m.* करणें *g. of o.*
4 *have an impression of as probable,* v. To EXPECT. होऱ्यांत - धोरणांत - ध्यानांत - लक्ष्यांत - दिलांत - अटकळींत -&c. येणें - असणें *in. con.* घांग *f.*-अगा *fm.* येणें-असणें.

ANTICIPATED, *p.* v. V. 1. अपकर्ष झालेला-केलेला, अगाऊ घेतलेला, अपकर्षलेला, अपकृष्ट, अप्राप्तकालगृहीत.

ANTICIPATION, *n.* v.V.1.—*act.* अपकर्षणें*n.* अपकर्ष करणें*n.* अपकर्ष*m.* अपकर्षण *n.* अप्राप्तकालग्रहण*n.* कालापकर्षग्रहण*n.*
2—*act.* अवली साधणें*n.* &c. आगपाई *f.* अवली *f.*
3 अप्राप्तकाल भोग*m.* कालापकर्ष भोग*m.* उदर्कपूर्वभोग*m.*
4 अगा*m. f.* होरा*m.* घांग *f.*

ANTICLIMAX, *n.* सारालंकारविपक्ष*m.* सारप्रतिलोम*m.*

ANTIDOTAL, *a.* v.N. विषापहारक, विषहर, विषनाशक, गरघ्न, नाशक, भंजक, मारक, भंजन, नाशन.

ANTIDOTE, *n. remedy against poison.* विषावरचें औषध*n* विषभंजन*n.* विषापहारक औषध*n.*
2—*gener.* भंजन*n.* नाशन*n.* गोहो*m.* धगड*m.* बस्ताद*m.*

ANTIDYSENTERIC, *a.* अतिसारघ्न, अतिसारनाशक-शमक-&c.

ANTIFEBRILE, *a.* ज्वरघ्न, ज्वरनाशक-हारक-शमक-&c.

ANTIHYSTERIC, *a.* वायुगोळा बसवणारा.

ANTIMONARCHICAL, *a.* एकस्वामिक विरोधी, एकराजशासनविपक्ष.

ANTIMONIAL, *a.* सुरम्याचा.

ANTIMONY, *n.* सुरम्याचा धातु*m.*
A collyriun of a. सुरमा*m.* कापोत*m.* कापोतांजन*n.*
Sulphuret of a. सुरमा*m.* मेचक*n.* सौवीर*n.*

ANTINOMIAN *a.* कर्मत्यागी, कर्मविरागी.

ANTIPARALYTIC, *a.* पक्षवातघ्न, पक्षवातनाशक-हारक- शमक-&c.

ANTIPATHETICAL, *a. having a natural aversion to.* स्वभावविरुद्ध, सहजविरुद्ध, निसर्गविरुद्ध, नैसर्गिक विरोधी.

ANTIPATHY, *n. natural aversion or contrariety.* स्वभाववैरुद्ध्य*n.* सहजविरोध*m.* सहजद्वेष*m.* सहजवैर*n.* नैसर्गिक शत्रुत्व*n.* नैसर्गिकद्वेष*m.*

ANTIPHLEGMATIC, *a.* कफशत्रु, कफघ्न, कफनाशक, कफनाशन.

ANTIPHRASIS, *n. use of words in a sense opposite to their meaning.* विपरीत लक्षणा *f.*

ANTIPODES, *n. persons who live on the opposite side of the globe.* परस्परसम्मुखपाद जन*m.* परस्पराभिमुखपाद लोक*m.*

ANTIPSORIC, *a. counteracting itch.* पामाघ्न, पामानाशक-हारक-

हर-&c.

ANTIQUARIAN, *a. pertaining to antiquaries or antiquity.* प्राक्कालिकद्रव्यसंग्रहिसंबंधी- विषयक, प्राचीनकालसंबंधी.

ANTIQUARY, *n.* प्राचीनकालचे वस्तूंचा शोध करणारा-जाणता, प्राचीनकालमार्गणकर्त्ता, प्राक्कालिकान्वेषी, प्राक्कालिकद्रव्यसंग्रही.

To ANTIQUATE, *v. a. make old or obsolete.* जुना-माजी-&c. करणें, मागें पाडणें, पडीं पाडणें. [कालांतरित.

ANTIQUATED, *a.* v.V. *and* OBSOLETE. माजी, गतकालिक, लुप्त,
To be or become a. लांचणें, पडीं पडणें.

ANTIQUE, ANTIQUENESS. See ANCIENT, &c.

ANTIQUITY, *n.* See ANCIENTNESS.
2 *old times.* प्राचीनकालm. पुरातनकालm. प्राक्कालm. पूर्वकालm.
3 v. ANCIENTS. पुरातनकालचीं-प्राचीनकालचींमनुष्यें *n.pl.* पूर्वसिद्धm. *pl.* वाडवडील *m.pl.*
4 *a work of old times.* प्राचीनकालचीवस्तू *f.*-कृत्य*n.* पूर्वकालसिद्धद्रव्य *n.* प्राचीनकालिकवस्तु *n.* प्राचीनवस्तु *n.* प्राक्कालिक कृत्य *n.*

ANTIRHEUMATIC, *a.* वातरोगहारक-नाशक-&c.

ANTISCORBUTIC, *a. counteracting scurvy.* नाविकरक्तपित्तनाशक-हारक-शमक.

ANTISEPTIC, *a. counteracting putescency.* पूतिनाशक- भंजक-निवारक-स्तंभक, अतिपाकनिवारक.

ANTISPASMODIC, *a. counteracting spasm or convulsions.* पेटके बसवणारा, अंगग्रहनाशक.

ANTISPLENETIC, *a. good against the spleen.* प्लीहशत्रु, प्लीहाशत्रु, प्लीहारोगशमक.

ANTITHESIS, *n. opposition of words or sentiments.* अर्थांतरन्यास *m.* अर्थांतर *n.* शब्दार्थविपर्यास *m.* विरोध *m.* भावविरोध*m.* अर्थ-शब्द-वाक्य-&c. विरोध *m.*

ANTITHETICAL, *a.* v. N. अर्थांतरन्याससंबंधी, अर्थांतरन्यासविषयक, अर्थांतरन्यासरूप, अर्थांतरमय.

ANTITYPE, *n.* प्रतिबिंबमूल *n.* बिंब *n.* दृश्यविषय *m.*

ANTITYPICAL, *a.* बिंबरूप, बिंबभूत, प्रतिबिंबमूलक, प्रतिबिंबसंबंधी.

ANTIVENEREAL, *a.* उपदंशनाशक, उपदंशघ्न.

ANTLER, *n.* भारशिंग *n.* शृंगशाखा *f.*

ANTONOMASIA, *n.*—the figure. गुणगुण्यभिधान *n.* [द्वार *n.*

ANUS, *n.* गांड *f.* गुद *n.* अपानद्वार *n.* अपान *n.* मलद्वार *n.* पश्चिम-
Fistula in ano. गुदव्रण *m.* [आंग *n.*
Prolapsus ani. गुदभ्रंश *m.* The prolapsed gut. आगेरू*n.*

ANVIL, *n.* ऐरण *f.* हरण *f.* शिंगाडा *m.* खुसा *m.* संदान *n.f.* These words express varieties.
2 (of a farrier) उभारा *m.* उभाळा *m.*

ANXIETY, ANXIOUSNESS, *n.* v. A. *and* CARE. काळजी *f.* चिंता *f.* हूरहूर *f.* कळकळ *f.* घोर *m.* चुरचूर *f.* आंच *f.* आंचणी *f.* परवा *f.* भेंदरा *m.* सत्ता *f.* धास्त *f.* धास्ती *f.* क्लेश *m.* ताप *m.* उद्वेग *m.* कोजळी *f.* हृद्रोग *m.* दमदग *f.*—intens. चुरचुराट *m.* हरणकाळजी *f.*
2—in medicine. असमाधान *n.* अस्वास्थ्य *n.* अस्वस्थता *f.* अशांति *f.*

ANXIOUS, *a. solicitous,* v. CAREFUL. काळजीचा, चिंतेचा, चिंतागत, चिंतायुक्त, चिंतान्वित, सचिंत, उद्वेगी, दगदगी.
—intens. चिंतातुर, चिंताक्रांत, चिंताग्रस्त, चिंताकुल, चिंतार्त्त.
To be a. चिंतावणें, काळीज *n.*-हृदय *n.*-छाती *f.* फाटणें-फुटणें-तरकणें.

ANXIOUSLY, *adv.* v. A. काळजीनें, चिंता धरून, काळजी धरून, चिंतापूर्वक, सचिंत, चिंतापुरस्सर.

ANY, *a.* कोणी *or* कोण्ही, कांहीं, अन्यतम.
A. how, A. wise. भलतसा, कसेंही, कसेंपण, कसेंतरी, जसेंतसें, सरासरी, सरासरीस, यथाकथंचित्, यथातथा.
A. like. भलतसा.
A. one. भलता कोणी, हरकोण्ही, कोणताही, अन्यतम.
A. soever,—of persons or things. भलता, भलतासलता.
A. thing. भलता.
A. where. कोठें *or* कुठें, कोठेंही *or* कुठेंही, कुत्रापि, बाहेरभितर.

AORIST, *n. indefinite tense.* अनियमितकाल *m.*
A. past. अद्यतनभूतकाल *m.*

AORTA, *n.* रक्ताशयाची मोठी धमनी *f.* [यींचा.

AORTAL, AORTIC, *a.* v. N. रक्ताशयाचे मोठी धमनीचा-च्याविषयींचा.

APACE, *adv.* v. QUICKLY. वेगीं, वेगून, जलदपायीं, जलदीच्या पावलानें-पायानें-पगानें, शीघ्रगतीनें.

APART, *adv. asunder,* v. SEPARATELY. अलग, अलगत, अलाहिदा, फटकून, निसटून, पृथक्.
2 *aside.* एकीकडे *or* एकीकडेस, एकेबाजूस, कडेकाठास.
3 from. एकीकडे-&c. ठेवून.

APARTMENT, *n. chamber.* v. ROOM. कोठडी *f.* खोली *f.* वठाण *n.*
Cooking a. v. KITCHEN. ओयरा *m.* ओवरा *m.*
2 *division of a building.* खण *m.* गस्त *n.* भद्र *n.* कक्षा *f.*
The largest a. चापेखण *m.*
Having two apartments. दुखणी, दुघई. Having three, तिखणी, तिघई. Having four, चौखणी, चौघई.

APATHETIC, *a.* v. COLD. जड, मंद, विराग, अरति.

APATHY, *n. want of feeling,* v. COLDNESS. जडपणा *m.* जाड्य*n.* जडत्व *n.* जडिमा *m.* मांद्य *n.* विराग *m.* रागाभाव *m.* अरति *f.*

APE, *n.* माकड *mn.* वानर *m.* मर्कट *m.* कपि *m.*

To APE, *v. a. copy.* v. To IMITATE. नकल *f.* करणें-उतरणें *g. of o.* टाक *f.* टाकणें, ठेव *f.*-ठेवण *f.*-धाटी *f.*-धाटणी *f.*- ठी *f.*-टीप*f.*-&c. उतरणें-साधणें-आणणें *g. of o.*

APERIENT, *a. gently purgative.* सुखढाळ, सौम्यरेचक, सुखरेचनकारक, सुखरेचक.

APERIENT, *n.* सुखाचा ढाळ *m.* सुखाचें ढाळक *n.*

APERTURE, *n. gap, cleft, &c.* v. OPENING. भोंक *n.* रंध्र *n.* खिड *f. dim.* खिडकुली *f.* खिडकुलें *n. or* खिडुकली *f.* खिडुकलें *n.*

APETALOUS, *a.* बिनपाकोळी, दलहीन. [मस्तक *n.*

APEX, *n. point or summit.* कळस *m.* शिखर *n.* अग्र *n.* अग्रभाग*m.*

APHELION, *n.* मंदोच्च *n. m.* उच्च *n.* उच्चस्थान *n.* मृदूच्च *n.*

APHONY, *n. loss of voice.* वाण्यभाव *m.* वाक्स्तंभ *m.* वाग्विहीनत्व*n.* वाग्बंध *m.*

APHORISM, *n.* v. MAXIM. वाक्य *n.* वचन *n.* सूत्र *n.*

APHRODISIAC, *n.* वाजीकरण *n.* बंदेज *n.*

APHRODISIAC, *a. exciting sexual desire.* वाजीकर, कामोत्पादक, कामोद्दीपक, कामोत्तेजक.

APIARY, *n.* मधमाशा राखून ठेवण्याचें स्थळ *n.* मधुमक्षिकालय *n.* मधुमक्षिकापालनस्थल *n.*

APIECE, *adv.* एकेकास, हरेकास, प्रत्येकास, शिरगणती.

APISH, *a. inclined to ape, imitative.* माकडचेष्टया, नकल्या, मर्कटस्वभावाचा, अनुसरणशील, अनुकरणशील.

APITPAT, *adv. with palpitation.* धडधड.

Apocope, *n. omission of the last letter.* शेवटल्या अक्षराचालोप *m.* अंत्याक्षरलोपालंकार *m.* अंत्याक्षरलोप *m.*

Apocrypha, *n.* ईश्वर प्रेरणेनें लिहिलेलीं नाहींत म्हणून यहुदीलोकांच्या धर्म पुस्तकांबरोबर जीं पुस्तकें मानली जात नाहींत तीं.

Apocryphal, *a. of uncertain authority.* अनिश्चित आधाराचा.

Apogee, Apogeum, *n.* उच्च *n.*

Apologetic, Apologetical, *a.* v. N. दोषनिवारक, अपराध-&c. न्यूनतादर्शक, स्वीकारपूर्वकक्षमायाचक.

Apologist, *n.* दोषन्यूनता दर्शक-कथक-&c. क्षमायाचक.

To **Apologize**, *v. n. make apology.* गुन्हा-अपराध-&c.पदरीं घेऊन माफी *f.* मागणें, अन्यायक्षमाप्रार्थन *n.*-क्षमायाचना *f.*-&c. करणें, अन्यायस्वीकारपूर्वक क्षमा *f.* मागणें, चुकलों म्हणणें.

Apologue, *n.* v. Story. कहाणी *f.* उपाख्यान *n.* आख्यान*n.* आख्यायिका *f.*

Apology, *n. something said or written in defence or extenuation.* गुन्हा पदरीं घेऊन माफीची विनंती *f.* दोषनिवारक भाषण*n.* अपराधस्वीकार पूर्वकक्षमाविनति *f.* क्षमायाचना *f.*

Apophthegm, *n. saying.* वाक्य *n.* वचन *n.* अभियुक्तोक्ति *f.*

Apoplectic, Apoplectical, *a.* v. N. *relating to apoplexy.* सन्न्यासाचा, सन्न्याससंबंधी-विषयक.

Apoplexy, *n. abolition of sense and voluntary motion.* सन्न्यास *m.* शरीरविभ्रंश *m.* अंगविभ्रंश *m.* अंगविकृति *f.*

Apostasy, *n. abandonment of one's religion, party, &c.* स्वधर्मत्याग *m.* स्वधर्मविसर्जन *n.* स्वधर्मत्यजन *n.* स्वधर्मभ्रंश *m.* स्वमतत्याग *m.* स्वपक्षत्याग *m.*

Apostate, *n.* स्वधर्मत्यागी, स्वमतत्यागी, स्वपक्षत्यागी.

To **Apostatize**, *v. n. abandon one's faith, party, &c.* स्वधर्मत्याग*m.*-स्वधर्मविसर्जन*n.*-&c.करणें,स्वधर्मभ्रष्ट-स्वधर्मच्युत-&c.होणें, स्वधर्मभ्रंश *m.*-स्वधर्मच्युति *f.* होणें *g. of s.*

Aposteriori, a. reasoning. कार्यानुमेय कारणानुमान पद्धति *f.*

Apostle, *n.* प्रेषितमनुष्य *m.* [पित-&c.

Apostolical, *a.* प्रेषितांचा, प्रेषितसंबंधी,प्रेषितोक्त,प्रेषितसिद्ध-स्था-

Apostrophe, *n. address to an absent person.* परोक्षसंबोधन *n.* परोक्षजन संबोधनोक्ति *f.* संबोधितान्यसंबोधन *n,* [बोधणें,

To **Apostrophize**, *v. a. address as present.* हाजीर समजून सं-

Apothecary, *n.* औषधतयारकरणारा-करूनविकणारा *m.* औषधसिद्ध करणारा *m.* औषधविक्रयकर्त्ता *m.*

Apothegm. See **Apophthegm.**

Apozem, *n.* v. Decoction. काढा *m.* कषाय *m.* क्काथ *m.*

To **Appal**, *v.a. dismay, alarm.*v. To Frighten.भय*n.*-दहशत*f.*-भेदरा*m.*-धाक*m.*-&c.घालणें-बसवणें, त्रेधा *f.* करणें *g.of o.*पांचाबर धारण *f.* बसवणें *g. of o.* [हौलदिल

Appalled, *p.*v.V.धाक बसलेला&c.दरारलेला,पांचांबर धारण बसलेला,

Appaller, *n.* **Appalling**, *p. a.* v.V. धाक घालणारा, &c. धाकपडायाचा-जोगता-&c. धाक घालाया-चा-जोगा-&c. भयजनक,भीतिजनक, उग्र, अकटोविकट, अकराळविकराळ.

Apparatus, *n.* सज*m.* संच*m.*साज*m.*सरंजाम*m.* साहित्य*n.* सामग्री*f.* सामान *n.* यंत्र *n.* उपचार *m. pl.* उपकरणीं *n. pl.*

A. and necessaries—compreh. or gener. साजसरंजाम*m.* साजसामान *n.* साजबीज *m.* आयतें सुयतें*n.* संभार *m.*

Apparel, *n.*v. Clothes. पांघरुणें *n.pl.* पोशाक *or* सल*m.*परिधान*n.* वेष*m.*

Article of a. पांघरूण *n.* कांबरूण *n.*

Articles of a. presented in honor from off one's own person, उतारपोशाक *m.* उतारतसरीफ *f.*

Old article of a. जुनेर *n.* जुनेरें *n.*

Splendid a. प्रतिष्ठावस्त्र *n.*

To **Apparel**, See To Clothe. [आविर्भवन *n.*

Apparency, *n.* v. A. 1. प्रादुर्भाव *m.* आविर्भाव *m.* प्रकटीभाव *m.*

Apparent, *a. manifest, evident,* v. Plain. उघड, उघडा, स्पष्ट, व्यक्त, प्रकट *pop.* प्रगट, आविर्भूत, विशद.

2 *seeming;*—in distinction from true or real. दिसण्याचा, दिसणारा, भासणारा, आभासाचा, दिसण्यांतमात्रखरा, दर्शनीय, दर्शनमात्रसत्य, वरकरणी, वरकर्मी, वरवंचाइचा, प्रातिभासिक, स्फुट. [गोचर.

3 *not secret, not hidden,* v. Visible. उघडा, दृश्य, दृष्ट, दृ-

Apparently, *adv.* v. A. 1. उघड, उघडपणीं, स्पष्ट, स्पष्टपणीं.

2 दिसण्यांत, दिसण्यांत मात्र, दिसायास, पहायास.

Apparition, *n. spectre,* v. Ghost. भूत *n.* छाया *f.* समंध *m.*

To **Appeal**, *v. n. remove a cause to a higher court.* वरच्या न्यायाधीशाकडे खटलें*n.* नेणें, उपरिस्थन्यायाधीशसमीपव्यवहारनयन *n.* करणें.

The English word is commonly used, as अपील *n.* करणें.

2 *refer to another as judge.* पंच करणें, तिन्हाईत करणें.

3 *refer to another as witness.* साक्षी-पडसाक्षी ठेवणें.

Appeal, Appealing, *n.* v. V. 1.—*act.* अपील from the English is commonly used. उपरिस्थन्यायाधीशसमीपव्यवहारनयन *n.* परावर्त्यव्यवहार *m.*

Appealer, *n.* **Appellant**. *n.* v. V. 1. अपीलकरणारा, उपरिस्थन्यायाधीशसमीप व्यवहारनेता.

To **Appear**, *v. n. be in sight, be visible.* दिसणें, दृष्टींत येणें, दृष्टीं पडणें, दृष्टीस-नजरेस येणें, दृश्य-दृग्विषय-दृग्गोचर-&c. असणें.

2 *become visible.* दिसणें, दृष्टावा *m.*-दृष्टांत *m.*-देखावा *m.*दाखवणें, दृष्टीस पडणें, दर्शन *n.* देणें, दर्शन *n.* होणें *g. of s.*

3 *be clear from evidence.* दिसणें, दिसून येणें, कळणें, उघडा-उघड-स्पष्ट-सिद्ध-&c. होणें.

4 *look, seem, be in appearance.* वाटणें, दिसणें, दिसायास-पहायास-पाहण्यांत-दिसण्यांत असणें, भासणें.

5 *be revealed, become manifest.*आविर्भवणें, उद्भवणें, प्रकट*pop.* प्रगट-स्पष्ट-व्यक्त-&c. होणें.

6 *come to light, come forth clearly.* उमगणें *or* उमंगणें, उमटणें *or* उमढणें, उमग *m.*-उमट *m.* पडणें *g. of. s.* कळणें.

7 to, unto; *stand or come into the judgment of.* भावणें, दिसणें, वाटणें, गमणें, भासणें. N. B. All these verbs are impersonal. नजरेस-दृष्टीस येणें.

8 *be in attendance.* हाजीर-रुजू होणें.

Appearance, *n.*v. V. 1. 2. *act of coming into sight, act of becoming visible.* दिसणें *n.* दृश्य होणें *n.*दृष्टींपडणें *n.* दृष्टावा*m.* दृष्टांत *m. v.* दाखव, दर्शन *n.* सन्निधान *n.* सन्निधि*m.*

5 प्रगट होणें *n.*&c. आविर्भवन *n.* आविर्भाव *m.* प्रादुर्भाव *m.* आविष्कृति *f.* उद्भव *m.* प्राकट्य *n.*

6 उगवणें *n.* उमटणें *n.* उमग *m.* उमट *m.*

8 हाजीर होणें *n.* हाजिरी *f.*

I. *semblance, look, apparent likeness.* रूप *n.*आकार *m.*स्वरूप *n.* डौल *m.* आभास *m.* भास *m.* रंग *m.*

In a. दिसण्यांत, दिसायास, बाहेरून, बाह्यात्कारीं.

Of pleasing a. देखणा.
Slight or faint a. आसभास *m.*
II. *mere external show, assumed semblance.* सोंग *n.* पोकळ-डौल *m.* बाह्यभाव *m.* पोम *n.*
III. See PHENOMENON.

APPEASABLE, *a.* v. V. सांत्वनीय, क्षमापनीय, सांत्वनयोग्य, सांत्व-[नशक्य.
APPEASABLENESS, *n.* v. A. सांत्वनयोग्यता *f.* सांत्वनीयता *f.* क्षमापनीयता *f.*
To APPEASE, *v.a. pacify, calm,* v. To COMPOSE. शांतवणें *or* सांतवणें, संतावणें *or* संधावणें, सांत्वन *n.*-क्षमापन *n.*-शांति *f.*-&c. करणें *g. of o.* शांत-थंड-थंडा-&c. करणें.
APPEASEMENT, *n.* v. V.—*act.* शांतवणें *n.* &c. मनसमजावणी *f.* मनसमजावशी *f.* सांत्वन *n.* क्षमापन *n.* शमन *n.*—*state.* शांति *f.* शम *m.* शांतता *f.*
APPELLATE, *a. pertaining to appeals.* अपिलाविषयींचा, अपिलाचा, अपिलाच्यासंबंधाचा.
2 *having cognizance of appeals.* अपीलघेण्याच्या अधिकाराचा.
APPELLATION, *n.* v. NAME. संज्ञा *f.* आख्या *f.* अभिधान *n.* संकेतशब्द *m.* संकेतवाचक *m.*
APPELLATIVE, *n. common name.* जातिवाचकनाम *n.* सामान्यनाम *n.*
APPELLATIVE, *a. pertaining to a common name.* अभिधायिक, अभिधायी, जातिवाचक, संज्ञावाचक.
To APPEND, *v. a. hang or attach to.* लावणें, टांगून देणें.
2 v. To ADD. जोडणें, लावणें, दुमाल्यास लावणें.
APPENDAGE, APPENDANT, *n. something added to a greater thing.* अवयव *m.* प्रत्यंग *n.* उपांग *n.* आनुषंगिक-अनुबंधी-अनुयोगी-&c. पदार्थ *m.*-विषय *m.*-&c. अंगभूतपदार्थ *m.*-विषय *m.*-वस्तु *n.* अप्रधानभूतांग *n.* गौणांग *n.* अनुबंध *m.*
APPENDANT, *a.* APPENDING, *a. hanging to.* v. V. टांगलेला.
I. *annexed, concomitant,* v. BELONGING. संबंधी, अंगभूत, आनुषंगिक, अनुबंधी.
APPENDED, *p.* v. V. 1. टांगून दिल्हेला, टांगलेला, जोडलेला, लावलेला.
2 जोडलेला, लावलेला, जडींब, अनुगत.
APPENDIX, *n.* See APPENDAGE.
2—to a book, &c. v. SUPPLEMENT. पुरवणी *f.* ग्रंथशेष *m.* परिशिष्ट *n.* शेषसंग्रह *m.*
To APPERTAIN, See To BELONG.
APPETENCE, APPETENCY. *carnal desire,* v. LUST. काम *m.* विषयसुखाभिलाष *m.* विषयवासना *f.*
2 *natural propensity.* सहजप्रावण्य *n.* स्वभाव *m.* स्वभावसिद्धि *f.*
APPETITE, *n.* v. DESIRE. इच्छा *f.* वासना *f.* आशा *f.* तृष्णा *f.* तृषा *f.* कामना *f.* स्पृहा *f.*
Restraint or regulation of a. इंद्रियसंयमन *n.*
Carnal a. काम *m.* विषयवासना *f.*
2 *keenness of stomach,* v. HUNGER. भूक *f.* अन्नावर मनशा *f.* अन्नाची इच्छा *f.* अन्नेच्छा *f.* अन्नाकांक्षा *f.* क्षुद्बोध *m.*
Destruction of a. (through waiting, &c.) भूकमोड, *f.* बुभुक्षाभंग *m.*
3 *wonted power of eating, stomach.* आहार *m.* खाणें *n.* जेवण *n.* भोजन *n.* भोजनप्रमाण *n.*
Delicateness of a. नाजूकजेवण *n.*
Improving the a. अग्निवर्द्धन *n.* अग्निवृद्धि *f.*
Loss or want of a. अन्नद्वेष *m.* अग्न्यभाव *m.*
Of ravenous a. भुकेचा अळका-अळकुंबा.
Of tender a. भुकेचाहळवट-हलका.
To bridle one's a. तोंड *n.* बंदावर राखणें-ठेवणें-आटोपणें.
To indulge one's a. तोंड *n.* सोडणें.
To lose one's a. अन्न *n.* राहणें *g. of s.* भूक *f.* मरणें. *g. of s.*
To APPLAUD, *v. a. praise by clapping the hands, &c.* टाळी *f.* देणें-वाजविणें-पिटणें, वाहवा *f.* करणें, शाबासकी *f.* देणें, धन्य-धन्य-भले भले-&c. म्हणणें, साधुवाद *m.* करणें.
2 *commend,* v. To PRAISE. वाखाणणें, अनुमोदणें, अभिनंदणें, नावाजणें, प्रशंसा *f.*-अनुमोदन *n.*-अभिनंदन *n.* करणें.
APPLAUDED, *p.* v. V. वाहवा केलेला-झालेला, &c. नावाजलेला, अनुमोदित, अभिनंदित.
APPLAUDER, *n.* v. V. टाळीदेणारा, वाहवा करणारा, &c. अनुमोदक, अभिनंदक, अनुमोदनकर्त्ता, अभिनंदनकर्त्ता.
APPLAUSE, *n.* v. PRAISE. शाबासकी *f.* वाहवा *f.* वाखाण *f.* नावाजस *f.* स्फीति *f.*
APPLE, *n.* एकाफळाचें नांव आहे.
2 (of the eye) v. PUPIL. पुतळी *f.* बाहुली *f.* तारा *m.*
A. of one's eye-*fig.* v. DARLING. कंठमणी *m.* जिवाचाकलिजा *m.*
To prize as the a. of one's eye. साता काळजांचे पलिकडे ठेवणें.
APPLICABILITY, APPLICABLENESS, *n.* v. A. लावायाची-योजायाची-घालायाची-&c. योग्यता *f.* योग्यता *f.* लायकी *f.* प्रयोक्तव्यता *f.*
2 लागूपणा *m.* लाग *m.*
APPLICABLE, *a. fit or suitable to be applied,* v. V. A. 1. 2. लावाया-चा-जोगता-जोगा-&c. योजाया-घालाया-&c. चा-जोगता-&c. योग्य, लायक, प्रयोक्तव्य, व्यवहार्य.
2 *that may have relation to.* v. V. 1. लागाया-चा-जोगता-जोगा-सारखा-&c.
APPLICANT, *n. petitioner.* अर्जदार *c.* अर्ज करणारा, दरखास्त करणारा, याचक *c.* अर्थी *in comp.*
APPLICATION, *n.* v. V. A. 1.—*act.* लावणें *n.* योजणें *n.* घालणें *n.* &c. आरोपण *n.* योजन *n.* योजना *f.* विधान *n.*—*a. or s.* आरोप *m.* प्रयोग *m.* विनियोग *m.* नियोग *m.* योग *m.* योजणूक *f.*
2—*act.* कार्यास-कारणीं लावणें *n.*-घालणें *n.* &c. प्रयोग *m.* योग *m.* विनियोग *m.*
3—*act.* v. STUDY. मन-लक्ष्य-&c. घालणें *n.*-लावणें *n.* व्यासंग *m.* अभिनिवेश *m.*—*state.* लाग *m.* आभिमुख्य *n.* अभिमुखता *f.*
4—*act.* योग *m.* प्रयोग *m.*
Of particular a. योगरूढ.
v. V. N. 1.—*state.* लागूपणा *m.* लाग *m.* प्रसक्ति *f.* व्यपेक्षा *f.*
2—*act.* अर्जकरणें *n.* &c. दरखास्त *f.* अर्ज *m.* विनंती *f.*
I. *thing applied.* लावलेला उपाय *m.*-उपचार *m.*- &c.
A. of hot leaves. लेप *m.* पेंड *m.*
APPLIED, *p.* v. V. A. 1. लावलेला, घातलेला, योजलेला, &c. योजित, युक्त, विनियोजित, विनियुक्त, प्रयुक्त, आरोपित, व्यपेक्षित, प्रसक्त.
APPLIER, *n.* v. V. A. 1. लावणारा, घालणारा, योजणारा, &c. योजक, प्रयोजक, प्रयोगी, विनियोजक, प्रयोक्ता, विधाता, विधायक, विधायी, आरोपक, आरोपणकर्त्ता.
To APPLY, *v. a. put or lay to.* लावणें, जोडणें, घालणें, योजणें, जुंपणें, जुळणें, धरणें, आरोपणें.
2 (to its end or purpose.) *employ,* v. To USE. कार्यास

लावणें, कारणीं-कामीं-काजीं-&c. लावणें, प्रयोग *m.*-योग *m.*-विनियोग *m.* करणें *g. of o.* सार्थकीं लावणें.

3 (the mind, &c.) मन *n.*-लक्ष्य &c. लावणें-घालणें, लाग *m.* करणें, मनोनिवेश *m.* करणें.

4—in gram. योग *m.*-प्रयोग *m.* करणें.

To APPLY, *v. n. have some connection, agreement, or analogy, suit.* v. To AGREE. लागणें, लागू पडणें, मिळणें, जुळणें, बसणें, येणें, *with* वर *or* कडे, बनणें.

2 *have recourse to as a solicitor.* दरखास्त *f.*-अर्ज *m.*- विनंती *f.*-&c. करणें, जाणें, *with* कडे *of o.*

To APPOINT, *v.a. establish, settle, fix by agreement.* नेमणें, संकेत *m.*-नियम *pop.* नेम*m.*-&c. करणें *g. of o.*

2 *order, prescribe, ordain.* नेमणें, स्थापणें, नेमून देणें, नियम *pop.* नेम *m.*-स्थापन *n.*-स्थापना *f.*-आदेश *m.*-संकेत *m.*-नियोग-*m.*-नियोजन *n.*-चोदन *n.*-चोदना *f.*-विधान *n.*-विधि *m.*-&c. करणें *g. of o.*

3 *nominate, designate, constitute.* नेमणें, योजणें, वरणें, योजन *n.*-योजना *f.*-नेमणूक *f.*-नियोजन *n.*-विनियोजन *n.*-नियोग *m.*-&c. करणें *g. of o.*

4 *accoutre, furnish, &c.* v. To EQUIP. सजवणें, सजणें, संजोगणें, सज्जित-&c. करणें.

APPOINTED, *p.* v. V. 1. नेमलेला, संकेतकेलेला, &c. नियमित.

2 नेमलेला, स्थापलेला, नेमून दिल्हेला-&c. नियमित, नियत, स्थापित, संकेतित, सांकेतिक, आदिष्ट, चोदित, विहित, वैध, नियुक्त, नियोजित.

3 नेमलेला, योजलेला, &c. नामजाद, नियुक्त, प्रयुक्त, विनियुक्त, विनियोजित, नियोजित, आदिष्ट.

4 सजवलेला &c. सज्जित, सज्ज.

APPOINTER, *n.* v. V. 1. 2. नेमणारा, स्थापणारा, स्थापक, स्थापन-नियोजन-&c. कर्त्ता, नियामक, विधाता, विधायक, विधायी, आदेशी, नियोगी.

3 नेमणारा, योजणारा, नियोगी, प्रयोजक, विनियोजक, योजना-नियोजन-विनियोजन-&c. कर्त्ता.

4 सजवणारा &c. सज्जना-&c. कर्त्ता.

APPOINTMENT, *n.* v. V. 1.—*act.* नेमणें *n.* संकेत करणें*n.* संकेत*m.*

2—*act.* नेमणें *n.* स्थापणें *n.* &c. नियमन *n.*स्थापन *n.*स्थापना *f.* विधान*n.*चोदना*f.*—*a. or s.*आदेश *m.*संकेत *m.*नियम *pop.*नेम *m.*

3—*act.* नेमणें *n.* योजणें *n.* &c. योजन *n.* योजना *f.* नियोजन-*n.* विनियोजन *n.*—*a. or s.* नेमणूक *f.* नियोग *m.* विनियोग *m.*

4—*act.* सजवणें *n.* सज्जकरणें *n.*

I. *an article of equipment,* v. ACCOUTREMENT. सरंजामाचा डागिना *m.* वस्तू *f.*

II. *public post or employment.* असामी *f.* सरकारी जागा *f.* अमल *m.* पद *n.*

Hereditary a. दर्क *m.* वतन *n.*

To get an a. वस्त्र *n.* होणें *inv. con.*

III. *engagement, assignation.* संकेत *m.* समय*m.* ठेवस*m.*

To APPORTION, *v. a. divide and assign in just proportion.* यथायोग्य विभागून देणें, योग्यतेप्रमाणें वांटूनदेणें, हिसेरशीनें वांटून देणें-वांटणी *f.*-वांटप *n.*-&c. करणें, यथार्थविभाजन *n.* करणें *g. of o.* यथाविभागें वांटून देणें.

APPOSITE, *a. suitable to time or circumstances.* योग्य, समर्पक, संगत, यथायोग्य, यथायुक्त, यथोचित, प्रसंगोचित, प्रसंगानुसार, प्रासंगिक, समयोचित, लायक, अवसरपठित.

APPOSITELY, *adv.* v. A. यथायोग्य, यथोचित, लायक, प्रसंगानुसार, समर्पकपणानें, प्रसंगोपात, समयानुसार, यथाप्रसंग, यथावसर.

APPOSITENESS, *n.*v.A. समर्पकपणा*m.* योग्यता *f.*लाग*m.*यथायोग *m.* यथायोग्यता *f.* समयोचित्य *n.*

APPOSITION, *n.*—in grammar. अभेदसंबंध *m.*

To APPRAISE, *v. a. appreciate, estimate, rate.* मोल *n.*-किम्मत *f.*-दर *m.*-दरदाम *m.*-अर्घ *m.*-&c. करणें-ठरविणें *g. of o.*

APPRAISEMENT, *n.* v.V.—*act.* मोल-दर-&c. करणें*n.*-ठरविणें*n.*&c.

APPRAISER, *n.*v.V.मोल-दर-&c. करणारा-ठरविणारा-&c. दरलाव्या.

APPRECIABLE, *a.that may be estimated.*परिमाण समजण्या जोगा, परिमेय, परिमाणशक्य.

To APPRECIATE, *v. a.* v. To APPRAISE. मोल *n.*-दर *m.* करणें-ठरविणें *g. of o.*

2 *admit the value of, acknowledge.* जाणणें, जाण *f.* जाणणें-*g. of o.* बूज *f.* राखणें-करणें *g. of o.* गुण *m.*-योग्यता *f.*-&c. जाणणें, आदरणें, ग्रहण *n.* करणें *g. of o.*

APPRECIATOR, *n.* v. V. 2. जाण जाणता, बूज राखणारा, ग्राहक.

To APPREHEND, *v. a. seize, lay hold of.* धरणें, पकडणें.

2 *conceive in the mind,* v. To UNDERSTAND. घेणें, आकळणें, धरणें, समजणें, उमजणें, उमज *m.*-समज *m. f.*-बोध *m.* होणें-पडणें *in. con. and g. of o.* बोध *m.* घेणें-आणणें, मनांत येणें-*in. con.* समजणें-उमजणें *used inversely.*

3 *dread,* v. To FEAR. आशंकणें, अंदेशा *m.*-वहमा *m.*-शंका *f.*-आशंका *f.*-संशय *m.*-खत्रा *m.*-&c. धरणें-बाळगणें, अंदेशा *m.*-शंका *f.*-&c. येणें-होणें *in. con.*

4 *be of opinion, think.* वाटणें-भावणें *in. con.* वसवसा*m.*-वचक *m.* होणें-जाणें *in. con.*

APPREHENDED, *p.* V. 1. धरलेला, पकडलेला.

2 घेतलेला, आकळलेला, धरलेला, बोध झालेला, &c. आकलित.

3 आशंकित, शंकित.

APPREHENSIBLE, *a.* v. V. 2. मनांत येण्या जोगता-जोगा-सारखा-&c. समजाया जोगता-जोगा-&c.बोधगम्य.

APPREHENSION, *n.* v. V. 1—*act.* धरणें *n.* पकडणें*n.*ग्रहण *n.* ग्रह*m.*

2—*act.* घेणें *n.* धरणें *n.* &c. ग्रह *m.* उमज *m.* समज *m.*बोज *m.* आकलन *n.*

I. *imperfect idea, an intellection.* उमज *m.* ग्रह *m.* बोध *m.* प्रबोध *m.* ज्ञान *n.* अधिगम *m.* भावना *f.*

II. *misgiving.* शंका *f.* संशय *m.* अंदेशा *m.* खत्रा *m.* वसवसा *m.* वहमा *m.* वहीम *m.* कल्पना *f.* घोर *m.* धोका *m.* धासरा *or* धोसरा *m.* v. धर. खरका *m.*

III. *faculty of apprehension.* v. UNDERSTANDING. ज्ञान *n.* बुद्धि *f.* उमज *m.* समज *m. f.* मेधा *f.*

Of quick or ready a. सरूद ग्राही.

Slowness of a. घृतबुद्धि *f.*

APPREHENSIVE, *a. dreading evil,* v. V. 3. शंकित, आशंकित, शंकान्वित, शंकायुक्त, संशययुक्त, संशयापन्न, सशंक.

APPRENTICE, *n.* करारनाम्याचाविद्यार्थी *m.*-शागिर्द *m.*-शिष्या *m.*-चेला *m.*-छात्र *m.* अंतेवासी *m.* संकेतबद्धविद्यार्थी *m.*-छात्र *m.*-शिष्य *m.*-&c. [रानें ठेवणें.

To APPRENTICE, *v. a.* धंदा *m.*-कसब *n.*-&c. शिकण्या करितां करा-

APPRENTICESHIP, *n.* v. N. शागिर्दी *f.* शिष्येपणा *m.* चेलेपणा *m.*

To APPRISE, APPRISING, See To INFORM, &c.

To APPRIZE,&c. See To APPRAISE, &c.

To APPROACH, *v. n. come near, approximate, appropinquate, advance.* जवळ येणें-जाणें, येणें, पावणें, आगम *m.*-आगमन *n.*-अभिगम *m.*-अभिगमन *n.*-&c. करणें.

APPROACH, APPROACHING, *n.* v. V.—*act.* येणें *n.* पावणें *n.* आगमन *n.* आगम *m.* आगति *f.* उपागम *m.* आयान *n.* समीपायान *n.* अभ्युपगम *m.* अभिगमन *n.* अभिगम *m.* उपसर्पण *n.* उपसर्जन *n.* सन्निध्यागति *f.* सन्निकृष्टागम *m.* सन्निकर्षण *n.*

I. *way of coming to, access.* वाट *f.* मार्ग *m.* आगमनमार्ग *m.*

APPROACHABLE,*a.* v. V. *and* ACCESSIBLE. जवळ जाया-चा-जोगता &c. आगम्य, अभिगम्य, अभिगमनीय, अभिगंतव्य, उपसार्य.

APPROACHED, *p.* v. V. अभिगत, अभ्युपगत, समीपागत, उपस्थित, कृतसन्निधान, कृतसंसर्ग.

APPROACHER, *n.* APPROACHING,*p.a.* v.V. जवळ येणारा-पावणारा &c. अभिगामी, अभ्युपगामी, आगमन-&c. कर्त्ता.

I. *that is at hand, near,*—time. &c. जवळचा, जवळ आलेला.

To APPROBATE, See To APPROVE.

APPROBATION, APPROVAL,*n.*v.V.—*act.* मान्य करणें*n.* पसंद करणें*n.* &c. अनुमोदन*n.* प्रतिग्रह*m.*

I. *the sentiment.* खुशमर्जी *f.* पसंती *f.* खातर *f.* खातरी *f.* मान्यता *f.* अनुमत *n.* अनुमति *f.* आनुमत्य *n.* अभिमत *n.*

To meet the a. of. मनास येणें-उतरणें, मर्जीस उतरणें, पसंतीस पडणें, खातरेस येणें-फटणें.

APPROBATORY, *a. containing or expressing a.* अनुमोदन-अनुमति-&c. ज्ञापक-कथक-सूचक &c. अनुमोदक.

To APPROPINQUATE, &c. See To APPROACH, &c.

APPROPRIABLE, *a.* v. V. 1. विनियोग कराया जोगा-&c. विनियोज्य.

To APPROPRIATE, *v. a. assign to particularly.* नांवाचा-नांवरशीनें-नांवानें-&c. ठेवणें-काढून ठेवणें-लावणें-संकल्पून ठेवणें, योजणें, योजना *f.*-विनियोग*m.*-विनियोजन*n.*-&c. करणें *g. of o.*

2 *take to self.* आत्मसात् करणें, आपलासा करणें, कंवटाळणें, खासगीकडे ठेवणें-घेणें, स्वत्वाक्रांत-स्वत्वोपात्त-&c. करणें.

3 *take fraudulently,* v. To EMBEZZLE. खाणें, डल्ला*m.* मारणें-देणें *g. of o.* ग्रासणें, गट्ट करणें, गिळंकृत करणें, धडांत-धड्यांत टाकणें-सोडवणें.

APPROPRIATE, APPROPRIATENESS. See PROPER, &c.

APPROPRIATED, *p.* v. V. 1. नांवानें-नांवाचा-&c. ठेवलेला, &c.विनियोजित, विनियुक्त.

2 खासगीकडे ठेवलेला, आपलासा केलेला, &c. आत्मसात्कृत, स्वत्वाक्रांत केलेला.

3 खाल्लेला &c. ग्रस्त, ग्रसित.

APPROPRIATION,*n.*v.V.1.—*act.*नांवानें-&c. ठेवणें *n.*&c.विनियोजन *n.* विनियोग*m.*

2—*act.*खासगीकडे ठेवणें*n.* आपलासा करणें*n.*

3—*act.*खाणें*n.* ग्रासणें*n.*

I. *matter appropriated fraudulently,* v. EMBEZZLEMENT. ननाखोरी *f.* हरामखोरी *f.*

APPROVABLE, *a.* v. V. पसंद-कबूल-&c.कराया-चा-जोगता-जोगा&c. अनुमोदनीय, अनुमोदनार्ह, प्रतिग्राह्य.

To APPROVE, *v. a. like, be pleased with, admit as proper.* प्रतिग्रह*m.*-मान्यता*f.*-अनुमोदन *n.*-&c.करणें *g. of o.* अनुमति *f.* देणें, मान्य-पसंत *or* द-कबूल-रुजू-मंजूर-&c. करणें *and with in. con.* होणें, उचितास-मर्जीस-पसंतीस-खातरेस-&c. येणें-पडणें-&c. *g. of s. and in. con.* अनुमोदणें.

APPROVED, *p.* v. V. पसंद-मान्य-&c.केलेला-झालेला,मान्य, पसंत *or* द, खातरीचा, प्रतिगृहीत, परिगृहीत, कबूल, रुजू, अभिमत, सम्मत, अनुमत, अनुमोदित, इष्ट, मंजूर.

APPROVER, *n.* APPROVING, *p. a.* v. V. पसंद-मान्य-&c. करणारा, मान्य, अनुमत, अनुमोदक, प्रतिग्राहक, प्रतिग्राही, पसंत *or* द. अनुमोदन कर्त्ता, अनुमति-&c. देणारा.

APPROVINGLY, *adv.* पसंत-&c. करून, अनुमोदन पूर्वक.

To APPROXIMATE, &c. See To APPROACH, &c.

APPROXIMATE. See PROXIMATE.

APPULSE, *n. act of striking against.* लागणें*n.* धडक*f.* आघात*m.* अभिस्पर्श*m.* व्याघात*m.*

APPURTENANCE,*n.*v.APPENDAGE. प्रत्यंग*n.* उपांग*n.* अंगभूतपदार्थ*m.* —विषय*m.*-वस्तु*n.*-स्थान*n.* &c.

APRICOT,*n.* एक फळ आहे.

APRIL, *n.* इंग्रेजी वर्षाचा चौथा महिना*m.* चैत्रवैशाख*m.*

A. shower. श्रावणसरी *f.* श्रावण पाहळी *f.*

APRIORI, a. reasoning. सिद्ध किंवा सिद्धवत् ग्रहीत कारणापासून कार्याचें अनुमान करण्याची पद्धति *f.*

APRON, *n.* समोर बांधण्याचें मलवस्त्र*n.* [वस्त्रसदृश.

APROPOS, *adv.* नेमका, प्रसंगोपात्त, घडत्यास पडता,प्रास्ताविक, प्रस्ता-

To come a. प्रसंगास येणें.

APSIS, *plural* APSIDES, *n.* in astronomy. उच्चनीच *n.*

The line of the apsides. शीघ्रोच्चमंदोच्च सूत्र *n.*

APT, *a. qualified, suitable,* v. FIT. योग्य, उपयोगी, उपयुक्त.

2 *disposed, propense,* v. INCLINED. प्रवण, तयार, सिद्ध, सादर, स्वभावाचा-झोकाचा *conjoined with the object.* (as फुटण्याचे स्वभावाचा a. to break, &c.) शील in comp. स्वभाव.

N.B. The meaning of the word will often be most idiomatically rendered by adopting another construction, as, This cloth is apt to tear हें कापड लवकर फाटतें, That man is apt to quarrel तो माणूस लवकर भांडतो, My horse is apt to kick माझ्या घोड्यास लात मारण्याची सवई आहे or माझा घोडा लातमारीत असतो, &c. &c.

3 *ready, quick,*v. SHARP. सुजाण, चणचणीत, कडकडीत, तरतरा, हुशार, चरचीक, पटु, सकृद्ग्राही, तीक्ष्ण, मेधावी.

APTITUDE, APTNESS, *n.* v. A. 1. योग्यता *f.* उपयोगीपणा *m.* उपयुक्तता *f.* [*f.*

2 कल *m.* प्रावण्य *n.* ओढ *f.* प्रवाह *m.* स्वभाव *m.* झोंक*m.* प्रवृत्ति-

3 सुजाणपणा *m.* चणचणीतपणा *m.* हुशारी *f.* पाटव *n.* पटुत्व *n.* तिखटाई *f.* तैक्ष्ण्य *n.*

APTLY, *adv.* v. A. 1. यथायोग्य, यथायुक्त, ठीक, यथास्थित, यथार्ह, समर्पक. [पूर्वक.

3 हुशारीनें, चणचणीतपणानें, &c. तीक्ष्णतापूर्वक, सकृद्ग्राहित्व-

AQUA FORTIS, *n.* आगपाणी *n.*

AQUARIUM, *n. artificial pond for plants or fishes* वनस्पती-अगर मासे ठेवण्याकरितां केलेलें तळें *n.*

AQUARIUS, *n.*—sign in the Zodiac. कुंभ *m.*

AQUATIC, *a. living or growing in the water*—of animals and plants. जलजन्य, जलज, जलोद्भव, जलजात, जलस्थ, औदक, —of animals. जलचर, जलचारी, अंबुचर, अंबुचारी, जलजीवी, जलभव.—of plants. उदकशाक.

A. and terrestrial.जलास्थलाचा.

AQUATIC, *n.*—*animal*. पाण्यांतला जीव *m.* जलजंतु*m.* जलप्राणी*m.* जलचर-जलोद्भव-&c. प्राणी*m.*

—plant &c. जलज-जलोद्भव-&c. वनस्पति *f.*-विषय*m.*-&c.

AQUEDUCT, *n.* नळ*m.* नहर *m.* सारणी *f.* [दक.

AQUEOUS, *a.* v. WATERY. जलरूप, जलमय, जलप्राय, आप्य, ओ-

AQUILINE NOSE, *n.* गरुडनाक *n.* शुकनासिका *f.* [सिक.

That has an a. nose. गरुडनाशिक *pop.* गरुडनाक्या, शुकना-

ARABIAN, *a.* अरबी, अरबस्थानचा, अरबस्थानी.

ARABIAN, *n.* अरब *or* आरब *m.*

ARABIC, *n.* अरबीभाषा *f.*-बोली *f.*-&c.

ARABLE, *a. fit for ploughing, or that is tilled.* लागवडीचा, लागवडीच्या उपयोगाचा, लावणीचा, जिराइती, कीर्दसार, कृषियोग्य, किर्दीलायक.

A. land, *See under* LAND. जिराईत*n.* काळी *f.*

ARANEOUS, *a. resembling a cobweb.* सुतेऱ्याच्या जाळ्यासारखा, कोशेट्यासारखा, ऊर्णनाभिजालवत्. [हल्य,सैरिक.

ARATORY, *a. contributing to tillage.* कृषिकर्मोपयोगी, हालिक,

ARBITER, ARBITRATOR, *n. umpire.* पंचाईतदार *m.* अमीन *m.* पंच *m.*लवाद*m.* तिऱ्हाईत *c.* मध्यस्थ *c.*

Arbitrators.—*collect.* पंच *m. pl.* मेळा *m.*

Meeting of private a. शेळसभा *f.* [च्छावश.

ARBITRABLE, *a. depending on the will.* ऐच्छिक, इच्छाधीन, इ-

ARBITRAMENT, ARBITREMENT, *n.* See WILL.

2 *award of arbitrators.* पंचाईतमत *n.* पंचमत *n.* पंचाईत *f.* लवादीचानिवाडा *m.*

ARBITRARILY, *adv. by will only.* v. ABSOLUTELY. इच्छेप्रमाणें, मनःपूत, यथेच्छ, मनास येईल तसें, मनास मानेल तसें, मनस्तोक.

ARBITRARINESS,*n.* v. A. 1. मुखत्यारी *f.* स्वाधीनता *f.* स्वातंत्र्य*n.* अनन्याधीनता *f.* यथाकामशासनता *f.*

2 ऐच्छिकता *f.* इच्छाधीनता *f.*

ARBITRARY, *a.*v. ABSOLUTE. स्वाधीन, स्वतंत्र, यथाकामी, यथेच्छ, स्वैर, मुखत्यार, यथाकामशासन.

2 *depending on mere will.* ऐच्छिक, इच्छाधीन, इच्छावश, मनास येईल तसा.

To ARBITRATE, *v. n. hear and decide as arbitrator.* पंचाईत *f.* -तिऱ्हाइती *f.*-मध्यस्थी *f.*-अमिनी *f.*- मनसुबी *f.* -मेळा *m.* करणें.

ARBITRATION, *n.* v. V.—*act.* पंचाईत *f.* तिऱ्हाईती *f.* अमिनी *f.* मुनसिफी *f.* लवादी *f.* मनसुबी *f.* मेळा *m.*

Assembly of a. पंच *m. pl.* मेळा *m.*

Paper of agreement given in by the parties before an assembly of a. कबूलकतबा *m.* कतबा.

Paper of acquiescence in the award of an assembly of a. समजूतपत्र *n.* [तिऱ्हाइतीचा.

ARBITRATORY, *a. of or belonging to an arbitrator.* तिऱ्हाइती,

ARBORARY, ARBOREOUS, *a. belonging to trees.* वृक्षाचा, वृक्षसंबंधी, वार्क्ष, वृक्षात्मक, वृक्षमय, वृक्षरूप, वृक्षविषयक.

ARBORIST, *n. one versed in trees.* वृक्षज्ञ, वृक्षवेत्ता. [ह *n.*

ARBOUR, *n. bower.* कुंज *mn.* निकुंज *mn.* गुंफा *f.* मंडप *mn.* लतागृ-

ARC, *n. segment of circle.* धनुष्य *n.* धनु *m.* चाप *m.*

Chord of an a. ज्या *f.* एकज्या *f.*जीवा *f.*चापकर्ण *n.* गुण*m.*

Complement of an a. to 90°. कोटि *f.*

Measurement of an a. धनुःफल *n.* ज्याफल *n.*

Versed sine of an a. उत्तरज्या *f.*

ARCADE, *n. walk arched above.* लदावाचा रस्ता *m.*-वाट *f.* लादनीचा रस्ता *m.*-वाट *f.* मंडप *m.* मांडव *m.*

ARCH, *n.* कमाण *or* न *f.* मेहराब *f.*

To ARCH, *v. a.* कमाणेची-कमाणदार-मेहराबदार-&c. करणें, कमाण *f.* करणें-लावणें.

ARCH, *a.* v. CHIEF. मुख्य, अग्र, श्रेष्ठ, प्रधान, वर in comp. अग्र्य, —as used of *knaves and rogues*, and with the power of, *atrocious, monstrous, thoroughsped, thoroughbred, &c.* v. ARRANT. महा, चिलंद, चिलंदी, इरसाल, अट्टल.

2 *waggish, shrewd, sly.* धूर्त्त, गुंडा, गुंड, बाट, विनोदी, मस्कऱ्या, हंडीबाग, ठट्टेखोर, ठट्टेबाज.

ARCHÆOLOGICAL, *a.* v. N. प्राचीनकालिक ज्ञानसंबंधी-विषयक.

ARCHÆOLOGIST, *n.* प्राचीनकालिकज्ञान-विद्या-इत्यादिकवेत्ता.

ARCHÆOLOGY, *n. learning pertaining to antiquity.* प्राचीनकाल विषयकज्ञान *n.*-विद्या *f.*

ARCH-ANGEL, *n.* मुख्यवर्गाचा देवदूत. [पाद्री.

ARCH-BISHOP, *n.* मुख्य वर्गाचा धर्माध्यक्ष, बिशप ह्यांच्या वरचा

ARCH-DEACON, *n.* बिशपाच्या खालचा अधिकारी.

ARCHED, *p.* v. V. कमाणेचा केलेला, &c. कमाणदार, कमाणेचा, मेहराबदार, मेहराबेचा.

ARCHER, *n. bowman.* तिरंदाज, तिराईत, तीरकमठ्या *m.* तीरकमान्या *m.* तीरकमठेवाला, धनुर्धर, धनुर्धारी, शरोपजीवी, धनुष्मान्, धनुष्क, धन्वी.

ARCHERY, *n. use of the bow and arrow.* तिरंदाजी *f.* धनुर्विद्या *f.*

Skilled in a. तिराईत.

2 *arrow shooting.* शरासन *n.* बाणविसर्जन *n.* शराभ्यास *m.*

Fence for the arm in a. practice. गोंधा *f.*

Glove for the fingers in a. practice. अंगुलित्राण *n.*

ARCHETYPE, *n.* v. ORIGINAL. मूळ *n.* प्रत *f.* असल used with the noun required.

ARCHIPELAGO, *n. group of islands.* द्वीपसमूह *m.*

ARCHITECT, *one who designs or plans buildings.* घरबेत्या *m.* शिल्पशास्त्री *m.* गृहशिल्पी *m.* गृहांकनकर्त्ता, गृहनिर्मितिवेत्ता.

ARCHITECTURAL, *a.* शिल्पशास्त्रसंबंधी-अनुसार-अनुरूप &c. शिल्पशास्त्री, गृहादिनिर्माणविद्यासंबंधी-विषयक.

ARCHITECTURE,*n.*—the science. घरवगैरे इमारत बांधण्याची विद्या *f.* गृहादिनिर्माणविद्या *f.* शिल्पशास्त्र *n.* गृहशिल्पविद्या *f.* वास्तु *n.*

ARCHIVES, *n. place for records.* दफ्तरखाना *m.* दफ्तर *n.* राजकार्य-लेखरक्षणस्थान *n.*

2 *records and papers.* दफ्तर *n.* सरकारी जुनेलेख *m. pl.*

ARCHLY, *adv.* v. A. 2. ठट्टेनें, विनोदानें, विनोदपूर्वक.

ARCHNESS, *n.* v. A. 2. धूर्त्तपणा *m.* बाटपणा *m.* &c. ठट्टेखोरी *f.* ठट्टेबाजी *f.*

ARCHWISE, *adv.* कमाणीसारखा *decl.* कमाणीप्रमाणें.

ARCTIC, *a.* उत्तरध्रुवाचा, उत्तरध्रुवाकडील, उत्तरध्रुवसंबंधी, उत्तरकेंद्रीय.

A. circle. उत्तरध्रुववृत्त *m.*

ARCTURUS, *n.* स्वाती *f.*

ARDENCY, ARDENTNESS, ARDOR, *n.* v. A. 1. *heat, glow.* आंच *f.* दाह *m.* तलखाई *f.* संताप *m.* प्रखर्य *n.*

2 आग *f.* तलखी *f.* जहाली *f.* गरमी *f.* गुरमी *f.* आवेश *m.* हांव *f.* तीव्रता *f.* तीक्ष्णता *f.*

3 उत्साह *m.* उत्साव *m.* हांव *f.* हौस *or* हवस *f.*उत्कंठा *f.* औत्सु-

क्य *n.* उत्सुकता *f.* प्रोत्साह *m.* हर्ष *m.* उल्लास *m.*

Sudden impulse of a. झुरूप *m.* झुरशी *f. v.* ये, चढ, सुट, धर.

ARDENT, *a. hot, glowing.* v. GLOWING. कडक, जलाल, चणचणीत. 2 *fierce, fiery, vehement.* उष्ण, कडक, तलख, तलखल्या, जलाल, जहाल *or* झाल, चंड, प्रचंड, तीव्र, तीक्ष्ण, खंदा, खमशा. 3 *impassionate, eager, warm, zealous.* v. EARNEST. उष्ण, उत्साहाचा, उत्साही, सोत्साह, हवसदार *or* हौसदार, उत्सुक, उत्कंठित, उत्साहवान्, धजदार. [तैक्ष्ण्यपूर्वक.

ARDENTLY, *adv.* v. A. 2. कडकडून, कडकावून, जहालीनें, तलखीनें, 3 उत्साहानें, उत्साहपूर्वक, उत्कंठेनें, हौशीनें.

ARDUOUS. *a. attended with great labor.* v. DIFFICULT. कठीण, दुर्घट, दुष्कर, दुःसाध्य, जबर, श्रमसाध्य. [नः.

ARDUOUSLY, *adv.* v. A. श्रमघेऊन, कष्टकरून, आयासपूर्वक, प्रयत्न-

ARDUOUSNESS, *n.* v. V. 1. कठीणपणा *m.* दुर्घटता *f.* दुःसाध्यता *f.* दौष्कर्य *n.*

AREA, *n.*—in geom. गर्भ *m.* गर्भी *f.* गर्भा *m.* गाभा *m.* मधगर्भ *m.* मधगर्भी *f.* अभ्यंतर *n.* फल *n.* क्षेत्रफल *n.*

2 *any open surface.* अंगण *n.* क्षेत्र *n.* मैदान *n.*

ARECA NUT, See BETEL.

ARENA, *n. place of public contest, &c.* तालीमखाना *m.* मल्लभू *f.* रंगांगण *n.* रंगभूमि *f.* रंग *m.*

ARENACIOUS, ARENARIOUS, ARENOSE, *a.* v. SANDY. रेतीचा, रेंवट, रेंवसाळ, रेंवाळ. [तंडी *f.*

ARENATION, *n. sand bath.* वाळूची ऊब घेणें *n.*-देणें *n.* वाळूची पो-

ARGENT, ARGENTAL, ARGENTINE, See SILVER, &c.

ARGIL, *n. potter's clay,* v. CLAY. कुंभारमाती *f.* कुंभारीमाती *f.*

ARGILLACEOUS, *a.* कुंभारमातीचा.

ARGOSY, *n. trading vessel.* जिन्नसी गलबत *n.* बारकस *n.* महागिरी *f.*

ARGUABLE, ARGUMENTABLE, *a.* v. V. A. 1. आलोड्य, आलोडनीय, आलोडनार्ह, आलोडनयोग्य, आलोडनशक्य, मथनीय, घाटाया-वाटाघाटकराया-जोगा-&c.

To ARGUE, *v. n. dispute, debate.* विवादणें, वाग्युद्ध *n.* करणें, वाद *m.*-विवाद *m.*-वादविवाद *m.*-बोलाचाली *f.*-तकरार *f.*-&c. करणें, भवति नभवति *f.* करणें.

To a. deviously, wildly. आडरानांत शिरणें.

To a. idly, fruitlessly, vainly. काथा *m.*-ताग *m.*-कथील *n.* कुटणें, काथाकूट *f.*-कथिलकूट *f.*-तागकूट *f.*-कडाकूट *f.*-&c. करणें.

To ARGUE. *v. a. discuss, debate, agitate.* घाटणें, घोळणें, मंथणें *or* मथणें, घासणें, कुटणें, खल *m.*-काटकूट *or* काटकुटी *f.* करणें-*g. of o.* वाटणें, घोटणें, वाटाघाट *f.*-वाटावाट *f.*-घोळ *m.*-घालघोळ *m.*-&c. करणें *g. of o.* आलोडन *n.*-मंथन *n.* करणें *g. of o.*

2 *prove, evince, shew.* दर्शवणें, दाखवणें, सुचवणें, प्रमाणभूतअसणें, लक्षण *n.*-चिन्ह *n.* असणें *g. of o. with in. con.* भावदर्शक असणें.

ARGUED, *p.* v. V. A. 1. घाटलेला, घोळलेला, &c. आलोडित, मथित.

ARGUER, *n.* v. V. N. वाद-विवाद-&c. करणारा, वादी, वाद्या, वादकर्त्ता, विवादकर्त्ता, विवदमान.

ARGUING *n.* v. V. A. 1.—*act.* घाटणें *n.* घोळणें *n.* &c. घाटाघाट *f.* घालघोळ *m.* घोळ *m.* वाटाघाट *f.* वाटावाट *or* टी *f.* काटकूट *f.* काटकुटी *f.* कुटाकूट *f.* कुटाकुटी *f.* घसघस *f.* घर्षण *n.* आलोडन *n.* मंथन *or* मथन *n.* मंथित *or* मथित *n.* वाटींव *f.* खाराखिरी *or* खारासीर *f.* प्रघट्टक *n.*

v. V. N.—*act. argumentation.* वादविवाद *m.* वाद *m.* विवाद *m.* वाग्युद्ध *n.* बोलाचाली *f.* बोलाबोली *f.* कडाकूट *f.* तकरार *f.* विप्रतिपत्ति *f.*

Empty or idle a. काथाकूट *f.* कथीलकूट *f.* तागकूट *f.*

Inconclusive a. अनुपपत्ति *f.*

Line of a. लाघाळ *f. v.* लाव, लाग.

Noisy, &c. a. नादवाद *m.* झंगड *f.* लाताळें *n.*

To warm or get animated in a. मटेखुंटीस येणें.

ARGUMENT, *n. reason alleged.* कारण *n.* हेतु *m.* सबब *f.* प्रमाण *n.* मुद्दा *m.* गमक *n.* साधक *n.* साधन *n.* उपोद्घात *m.* उदाहार *m.* कोटि *f.*

To adduce an a. अर्थांतरोपन्यास *m.* करणें.

To make the most of a bad a. आपत्पुरवणी *f.* करणें.

2 (of a reasoning or discourse) v. SUBJECT. विषय *m.* पक्ष *m.* प्रमेय *n.* वादहेतु *m.* हेतु *m.* वादास्पद *n.* [मणिका *f.*

3 *contents, heads.* पूर्वपीठिका *f.* उपोद्घात *m.* ग्रंथस्थविषयानुक्र-

4 *argumentation,* See ARGUING.—*act of* V. N.

ARGUMENTAL, *a. belonging or relating to a.* वादविवादाचा, वादविवादसंबंधी, विवादविषयक.

ARGUMENTATION, *n.* See ARGUING,—*act of* V. N.

ARGUMENTATIVE, *a. consisting of a.* वादाचा, विवादाचा, वादविवादविषयक, विवादरूप, विवादात्मक, उपपत्तीचा, उपपत्तिसंबद्ध, उपपत्तिविशिष्ट, वादार्थक. [तकरारी.

2 *fond of a.* v. DISPUTATIOUS. वादी, विवादी, वादेली, वादरत,

ARID, *a. adust, parched and dry:*—of a country, &c. रखरखीत, रुखा, रुक्ष, भुकिस्त, जलशून्य, जलरहित.

2 *dry and meagre:*—of soil. उखर, धापड, निखरड, निपराळ, निपळवट, जलशून्य, जलरहित.

ARIDITY, *n.* v. A. 1. रखरखीतपणा *m.* रखरखाट *m.* रुखेपणा *m.* रौक्ष्य *n.* रुक्षता *f.*

2 उखरपणा *m.* निखरडपणा *m.* &c. जलराहित्य *n.*

ARIES, *n.*—the sign. मेष *m.*

ARIGHT, *adv.* v. RIGHTLY. नीट, बरोबर. [होणें *g. of s.*

To ARISE, *v. n.* v. To RISE. उठणें, येणें, उदय *m.* पावणें, उदय *m.*

2 *proceed, issue, spring, flow, emanate.* उत्पन्न होणें, येणें, सुटणें, निघणें, लागणें, उद्भवणें.

ARISTARCHY, *n. government by excellent men.* शिष्टाधिपत्य *n.* शिष्टप्रभुत्व *n.* शिष्टशासन *n.*

2 *body of excellent men.* शिष्टजनसमूह *m.* शिष्टसमुदाय *m.*

ARISTOCRACY. *n. government by nobles.* बडेलोकांचें प्रभुत्व *n.* &c. महाकुलीनाधिपत्य *n.* महाकुलीनप्रभुत्व *n.* महाकुलप्रभुत्व *n.*

2 *body of nobles.* बडेलोक *m. pl.* अमीरउमराव *m. pl.* महाकुलीनसमूह *m.*

ARISTOCRATIC, ARISTOCRATICAL, *a.* v. N. बडेलोकांचा, अमीरउमरावांचा, महाकुलीनाधिपत्यसंबंधी-विषयक.

ARITHMETIC, *n.* गणित *n.* अंकगणित *n.* संख्याविद्या *f.* अंकविद्या *f.* गणनविद्या *f.* हिशेब *or* हिशोब *m.* गुणांक भागोत्री *f.* पाटीगणित *n.*

A.—gener. *or* loosely. गुणांक भागोत्री *f.* हिशेब कितेब *m.* हिशेब ठिशेब *m.* सांजण्या भाजण्या *f. pl.*

A. of fractions. अपूर्णांक गणित *n.*

A. of integers. पूर्णांक गणित *n.*

A. of known quantities. व्यक्त गणित *n.*

A. of unknown quantities. अव्यक्त गणित *n.*

A book of a. *book of sums and questions.* मेस्तक *n.*

Operation in a. with an assumed number. इष्टकर्म *n.*

The eight rules of a. परिकर्माष्टक *n.* These are *addition, subtraction, multiplication, division, raising to the square, extracting the square-root, raising to the cube, extracting the cube-root.* संकलनn. व्यवकलनn. गुणनn. भजनn. वर्गm. वर्गपदn. घनm. घनपदn. or, *pop.* मिळवणी *f.* वजाबाकी *f.* गुणाकारm. भागाकारm. वर्गm. वर्गपदn. घनm. घनपदn.

ARITHMETIC, ARITHMETICAL, *a. belonging to or according to a.* गणिताचा, गणिती, हिशेबाचा, हिशेबी or हिशोबी, गणितानुगत, गणितानुसार, गणितानुरूप.

ARITHMETICALLY, *adv.* गणिताच्या रीतीनें, हिशेबकरून.

ARITHMETICIAN, *n.* गणितीm. गणित्याm. गणकm. हिशेबी or हिशोबीm. अंकविद्यावेत्ता, गणितज्ञ.

ARK, *n. small chest.* पेटी *f.*

2 (of Noah) नौका *f.* गलबतn.

ARM, *n.*—from the shoulder-joint to the wrist. बाही *f.* बाहुm. भुजm. हातm.

—from the shoulder-joint to the elbow. दंडm. बाहुm. बाहुटाm. बाहुदंडm. भुजदंडm.

—from the elbow to the wrist or finger-ends. हातm.

A. to a.—fighting, &c. बाहुबाहवि *adv.*

Arms as pinioned. मुसक्या *f. pl. v.* बांध, पिचुंड्या or पिचोंड्या *f. pl.* पिचुंडे or पिचोंडे *m. pl.*

Interlocking of arms and striving. हात झोंबी *f.*

Locking within the arms. आंगकवळी *f.*

Ornament of the a. बाहुभूषणn.

Root of the a. बगोटाm. बगोटेंn. बाहुमूलn.

Snatching or seizing by force of the a. मूठमर्दाई *f.*

Strength of a. बाहुबलn. भुजबलn.

Of outstretched a. उद्यतबाहु, उद्यतदंड.

Upper and outer part of the a. near the shoulder. बाव्हळा or बावळा or बाहुळाm. बाबखंडn.

To know the weight of the a. of. पोंची *f.* ओळखणें *g. of o.*

To slap the arms (in token of readiness to fight). बाह्या *f. pl.*-भुजm. *pl.* पिटणें-थापटणें.

To whip up under the a. बगलेंत मारणें, काखाटणें.

2 (of a tree) v. BRANCH. खांदाm. फांदडाm. फांटाm. *dim.* फांटी *f.* स्कंध. *m.*

3 (of the sea). खाडी *f.* फाटाm.

Arm of an a. of the sea; *a branch of.* ओहर m. खोंची *f.* फांसून. पोहडी *f.* पोई *f.* पोईडn.

Navigable a. तरती खाडी *f.*

4 (of a garment). बाही *f.* हातपाm.

5 (of a mathematical figure). भूज *f.*

ARM-CHAIR, *n.* हाताची कुरशी or खुरशी *f.*

ARMFUL, *n. (of grass, sticks, &c.)* कवळn. कवळाm. *dim.* कवळी *f.* आडव *f.* बेंग *f.*

ARM-HOLE, ARM-PIT, *n.* काख *f.* बगल *f.* कक्षm.

Tumor in the a. काखमांजरी *f.* मांजरी *f.* काखबळm. बळm.

ARM-STALL, *n.* (of a पट्टा &c.) खोबळाm.

ARMS-REACH, *n.* हातटप्पा or हाताचा टप्पाm.

To ARM, *v. n. take arms.* सजणें, हत्यारबंदी or हतेरबंदी *f.* करणें, कमरबंदी *f.*-कमरबस्ताm. करणें, सशस्त्र होणें.

To ARM, *v. a.* v. TO ACCOUTRE. हत्यारबंद or हतेरबंद-सशस्त्र-सज्ज-सज्जित-&c. करणें, सज्जनn.-सज्जना *f.*-सज्जीकरणn. करणें.

ARMAMENT, *n.* v. FORCE. सेनाभारm. दलभारm. सैन्यभारm. सलतन *f.* सलतनत *f.*

Light a. सडीफौज *f.*

ARMED, *p.* v. V. A. हतेरबंद or हत्यारबंद, शस्त्री, शस्त्रपाणि, सायुध, उपात्तशस्त्र, धृतशस्त्र, धृतायुध, सज्ज, सज्जित, सज्जीकृत.

ARMENIAN BOLE, *n.* मुलतानी or मुलतान माती *f.* हुरमूज *f.*

ARMILLARY, *a. resembling a bracelet.* कंकणाकार.

A. sphere. खगोलm.

ARMISTICE, *n.* संकेतानें केलेली लढाईची तहकुबी *f.* सांकेतिकयुद्धविरामm. सल्लाm. संकेतपूर्वकयुद्धविश्रांति *f.* युद्धोपरामm.

ARMLET, See BRACELET.

ARMORER, *n. maker of arms.* हत्यार करणारा, शस्त्रकार, शस्त्रकारक, अस्त्रकारक, शस्त्रनिर्माणकर्त्ता, करचकर.

2 *furbisher of arms.* शिकलकर or गारm. करचकर or करजकर शस्त्रमार्ज, असिधावक. [कावचिक.

ARMORIAL, *a. of or belonging to armour.* कवचाचा, कवचसंबंधी, 2 *belonging to the arms of a family.* कुलमान द्योतक ध्वजादि चित्रित चिन्हांचा.

ARMORY, *n. place for keeping arms.* शिलेखानाm. शस्त्रागारn. अस्त्रागारn. आयुधागारn.

ARMOUR, *n.* चिलखतn. कवचmn. वर्मn. कंचुकm. शिलाm. पेटी *f.* अंगत्राणn. सन्नाहm.

A. of iron netting or little rings. बकतर or बक्तरn.

A. for a war-horse. पाखर *f.*

A. for the breast, &c. *cuirass.* उदरत्राणn. उरस्त्राणn. उरश्छदm.

A. for the head. शिलेटोपm.

A. for thigh, *cuish.* जंघात्राण *n.*

Piece of a. शिलाm.

Clad &c. in a. कवची, सन्नद्ध.

ARMOUR-BEARER. *n.* ढाल वगैरे वाहणारा-नेणारा.

ARMS, *n.* v. WEAPONS. हत्यारें or हतेरें *n.pl.* शस्त्रें *n. pl.* शिलेभालेm. *pl.* ढालतलवार *f.*

Lustration of a. नीराजनn. लोहाभिसारm.

Practice or exercise with a. शस्त्राभ्यासm. शस्त्रव्यवहारm. शस्त्रपरिशीलनn.

Under a. शिल्या भाल्या निशीं, शिल्याभाल्यासुद्धां.

To take up a. against. शस्त्रn. धरणें *with* वर, उठावणें, उठावणी *f.*-उठावाm. करणें.

2 coat of arms. *escutcheon, &c.* कुलमान द्योतक ध्वजादि चित्रित चिन्हें *n. pl.*

ARMY, *a.* लशकरचा, लशकरी, सैनिक, सेनासंबंधी.

ARMY, *n.* लशकर or लषकरn. फौज *f.* सैन्यn. सेना *f.* सेनाभारm. चक्रn. दल or दळn. दलभारm. कटकn. पृतना *f.* चमू *f.* अनीकm.n. बलn.

—compreh. फौजफांटाm.

Baggage and followers of an a. बहीरबुणगेंn. बुणगेंn. बाजारबुणगेंn. कतवारn.

Command of an a. सैनापत्यn. [फौजदारm.

Commander of an a. सेनापतिm. सेनाधिपतिm. सेनाधीशm.

Complete a. चतुरंगसैन्यn. चतुरंगबलn. अक्षौहिणी *f.*

Component part of an a. सेनांगn. (These are हस्ती, अश्व, रथ, पदाति).

Division or corps of an a. सेनाभागm. दस्ताm. सेनामुखn.
Follower of an a. (suttlers. &c). सेनाचर, सैनिक.
Foreign and invading a. परचक्रn.
Having a standing a. फौजबंद.

AROMA, *n.* v. FRAGRANCE. सुगंधm. सौगंध्यn. आमोदm.

AROMATIC, *a.* v. FRAGRANT. सुगंधक, सुगंधिक, सुगंधि.
2 See SPICY.

AROUND, *adv. in a circle.* गरगर or रां, गरागर, गरारां, गिरगिर or रां, मंडलवत्, चक्रवत्.
2 *on every side.* आजूबाजूस, आजूबाजू, चहुंकडे, आसपास, आशींपाशीं, अरसपरस, चौतर्फा, चौगर्द or दां, चौफेर, चौरस्तां, भोवतीं or तें, भोवतां, भोवताला, सभोंवतां, सभोंवताली, सभोंवती, सभोंवर, सभोंवार, औरस चौरस, प्रतिदिश, परितः, आसमंतात्, समंततः.

AROUND, *prep. about, encircling.* आसपास, भोवता, भोवताला, भोवतीं or तें, सभोंवता, सभोंवताला, सभोंवती, सभोंवर, सभोंवार.

To AROUSE, *v. a. stir up, stir,* v. To EXCITE. चेष्टवणें, ठोठावणें, उचल *f.*-उठावणी *f.* करणें, बोध *m.*-प्रबोध *m.*-&c. करणें *g. of o.* जागता-जागा-जागृत-&c. करणें.

AROUSING, *n.* v. V.—*act.* चेष्टवणें *n.* ठोठावणें *n.* &c. बोध *m.* बोधन *n.* उद्बोध *m.* उद्बोधन *n.* प्रबोध *m.* प्रबोधन *n.*

ARRACK, *n.*—the spirituous liquor. ताडी *f.* (from the fan-palm), माडी *f.* (from the cocoanut tree), शिंदी *m. f.* (from the wild date tree).

To ARRAIGN, *v. a.* चौकशी होण्याकरितां न्यायसभेपुढें आणणें, आरोपितदोषाबद्दल जाब देण्यासाठीं कोर्तां पुढें उभा करणें.
2 v. To ACCUSE. दोषारोप *m.*-अपराधारोप *m.*-दोषाभियोगm.-आरोपm.-अभियोग *m.* करणें *g. of o.*

To ARRANGE, *v. a. put in proper order.* v. To DISPOSE. व्यवस्थेनें-बंदोबस्तानें-&c. ठेवणें- मांडणें-&c. योजणें, रचणें, रचना *f*-योजना *f.*-&c करणें *g. of o.*
2 *adjust, settle, put in order.* व्यवस्था *f.*-बंदोबस्त *m.*-तजवीज-&c. करणें *g. of o.*

ARRANGEMENT, *n.* v. V. 1.—*act.* व्यवस्थेनें ठेवणें *n.* &c. रचणें *n.* योजणें *n.* &c. रचना *f.* रचायी *f.* आसादन *n.* बिन्यास *m.* बस्तन- or बस्तान *n.* योजणूक *f.* रचणूक *f.* अनुसंधान *n.* प्रतिविधान *n.*
2 बंदोबस्त *m.* बंदोबस्ती *f.* व्यवस्था *f.* [अनुसंधानn.
I. *preparatory measure.* तजवीज *f.* तरतूद *f.* तोड *f.* युक्ति *f.*

ARRANT, *a.*—as used of rogues and villains, and as agreeing with *arch, thoroughbred, thoroughsped, thoroughpaced, genuine, prime, proper, rank, regular, gallows* (vulg. *gallous*), &c. अट्टल or अट्टुल (as अट्टल सोदा, अट्टल लबाड, अट्टल चोर-शिनळ-हरामी-&c. or अट्टुल सोदा &c.), अलेल (as अलेल सोदा &c.), बिलंद, एकनिष्ठ, झळझळीत, निस्तूक, निपट, महा (as महालुच्चा, महाहरामी, महामात्रागमनी), बिनीचा, नितुंला, बियांचा or ब्यांचा, (*of the true breed,*) अगदीं, पक्का, पुक्का or पोक्का, काढींव or काढाऊ, ऐन (as ऐनसोदा, ऐन लबाड, ऐनलुच्चा), गाळींव, सोलींव, एक (as एकलबाड, एकलुच्चा, एक काशीकर), इरसाल. *See numerous others under Blackguard.*

ARRAY, *n. display.* v. SHOW. थाट *m.* थाटमाट *m.* घटाव *m.* कटाव *m.* बनाव *m.* आराष or स *f.*
2 (of troops) सैन्याचीरचना *f.*-व्यवस्था *f.* व्यूह *pop.* बिहू or बिभू *m.* सेनारचना *f.*—in a circle. मंडलव्यूह *m.* चक्रव्यूह *pop.* चक्रबिहू or चक्रबिभू *m.* सर्वतोभद्र *m. n.*—in square, सर्वतोभद्र*m.* कोट *m.*—in line, दंडव्यूह *m.* कोरबंदी *f.*—in column, भोग व्यूह *m.* कट *m.*—in mixed order. असंहत व्यूह *m.*—in dense order, gener. घटाव *m.* कटाव *m.* थट or थाट *m.* Some other forms of *Array* are बुरूज, शकटव्यूह, मकरव्यूह, पताकाव्यूह, स्कंध.

To ARRAY, *v. a. put or set orderly,* v. To DISPOSE. थाटणें, थटकारणें, रचणें, योजणें, प्रतिविधान *n.* करणें.
2 v. To DECK. सज्जणें, सज्जना *f.*-सज्जीकरण *n.* करणें *g. of o.* थाटमाट *m.* करणें *g. of o.*
3 (a jury) *call man by man.* असामीवार योजणें.

ARRAYED, *p.* v. V. 1. रचलेला, योजलेला, &c. प्रतिविहित.
2 सज्जलेला, सज्ज, सज्जीकृत.

ARREAR, ARREARAGE, *n. that which is behind in payment.* चढलेला-तुंबलेला-जमलेला-राहिलेला-&c. पगार *m.*-वेतन *n.*-मुशारा or मुशाहिरा *m.*-&c.
2 *balance unpaid.* बाकी *f.* शिलक *f.*
In Arrears, See BEHIND HAND.

ARREST, ARRESTING, *n.* v. V.—*act.* धरून थांबवणें *n.* &c. गतिभंग *m.* स्तंभन *n.* स्तंभ *m.* निग्रह *m.* गतिस्तंभन *n.* गतिस्तंभ *m.* गतिरोध *m.*
2—*act.* धरणें *n.* आसेध *m.*—*state.* आसिद्धता. *f.*
Open a. *arrest with liberty to move about.* खुलीकैद *f.*

To ARREST, *v. a. catch in progress and fix,* v. To STOP. धरून थांबवणें-खोळंबवणें, गतिभंग *m.*-गतिस्तंभन *n.*—गतिस्तंभ *m.*-गतिरोध *m.*-अटकाव *m.* करणें *g. of o.* कुंठित करणें.
2 *seize by a writ or warrant.* सर्कारहुकुमानें-राजाज्ञेनें-&c. धरणें-पकडणें, आसेध *m.*-आसिद्धता *f.* करणें *g. of o.* आसिद्ध-करणें. [आगमन *n.*

ARRIVAL, ARRIVING, *n.*v. V.—*act.* येणें *n.* पोहोंचणें *n.* आगमm.
I. *person or thing arrived, or to arrive.* दाखलझालेलें मनुष्य *n.*-वस्तु *n.* दाखलहोणारें मनुष्य *n.*-वस्तु *n.*

To ARRIVE, *v. n. come to, reach,* v. To COME. पावणें, पोहोंचणें, दाखल होणें, लगटणें, प्रविष्ट-प्राप्त होणें.
To be arrived and pausing. येऊन ठेपणें.

ARROGANCE, *n.* v. PRIDE. गर्व *m.* अहंकार *m.* अभिमान *m.* आढ्यता *f.* मान *m.* मगरुरी *f.* दिमाख *m.* दिमाखदारी *f.* तोरा *m.* तोरेदारी *f.* उन्माद *m.*

ARROGANT, *a.* v. PROUD. गर्वी, गर्विष्ट, गर्वित, अहंकारी, अभिमानी, मगरूर, ओढून चंद्रबळ आणणारा, दिमाखदार, दिमाखी, तोरेदार.
2(of things.) गर्वाचा, दिमाखाचा, अभिमानाचा, आढ्यतेचा, &c.

ARROGANTLY, *adv.* v. A. गर्वानें, मगरूरीनें, दिमाखानें &c. गर्वपूर्वक, अहंकारपूर्वक, अभिमानपूर्वक, &c.

To ARROGATE, *v. a. lay claim to, make pretension to.* अभिमान *m.* धरणें-बाळगणें *g. of o.* पोम *n.* दाखवणें-मिरवणें-वाढवणें *g. of o.* स्तोम *n.* करणें *g. of o.* आढ्यता *f.* ओढणें-बाळगणें-मिरवणें *g. of o.*

ARROGATION, *n.* v. V.—*act.* अभिमान धरणें *n.* आढ्यता बाळगणें *n.* &c. स्तोम *n.* पोम *n.*

ARROW, *n.* तीर *m.* बाण *m.* शर *m.* पत्री *m.* विशिख *m.* सायक *m.*
Blunt a. तुक्का *m.* बुठणा तीर *m.*
Bow and arrows. तीरकमठा *m.* तीरकमाण or न *f.*
Feather of an a.पिसारा *m.*पीस *n.* पक्ष *m.* पुंख *m.* शरपुंखा *f.*
Flight or shower of arrows. शरजाल *n.* शरवर्ष *m.* शरवृष्टि

f. बाणजाल *n.*

Shooting arrows. शरासन *n.* बाणविसर्जन *n.* शराभ्यास *m.*

Struck by an a. शरहत.

Strung,—an a. कृतपुंख. [भल्ल *m.*

Arrow-head, Arrow-barb, *n.* तिराचें फळ *n.* शरफल *n.* भाल *f.*

Arrow-root, *n.* एका वनस्पतीच्या कंदापासून काढलेलें तवकील*n.*

Arse, See Backside.

Arsenal, *n.* तोफखाना *m.* युद्धद्रव्यागार *n.* युद्धसाहित्यगृह *n.*

Arsenic, *n.* सोमल *m.* सोमलखार *m.* शिला *m.*

Sulphuret of a. हरिताल *n. pop.* हरताळ *m. f.*

Red sulphuret of a. मनःशिला *pop.* मनशीळ *or* सीळ *f.* आग्यासोमल *m.*

White oxyde of a. शंख्यासोमल *m.* फटक्यासोमल *m.*

Arsenical, Arsenious, *a.* सोमली, सोमलाचा, सोमलसंबंधी.

Arson, *n. malicious burning of a house, &c.* आग लावणें *n.* गृहदाह *m.* आगारदाह *m.*

Art, *n.*—as disting. from Nature; *human skill.* मनुष्यकला *f.* कला *f.* युक्ति *f.* शिल्पविद्या *f.* करणी*f.*

2 *subtlety, craft.* v. Cunning. कावा *m.* कावादावा *m.* कावित्र *n.* धूर्तता *f.* [*m. pl.*

Arts, v. Artifices. छक्केपंजे *m. pl.* डावपेंच *m. pl.* घावडाव

3—as disting. from Science; *system of rules and steps and acts, a craft.* कला *or* कळा *f.* कसब *n.* हुनर *m. f.* शिल्प *n.* शिल्पकर्म *n.*

Arts,—collect. or compreh. कळाकुसरी *f. pl.*

Fine a. Liberal a. Polite a. बुद्धिसाध्य कला *f. pl.*

Mechanical a. श्रमसाध्य कला *f. pl.*

Bachelor of a. विद्यालयसंबंधीं एक पदवी आहे.

Master of a. विद्यालयसंबंधीं एक पदवी आहे.

Skilled in the arts. कलाकुशल, कलाप्रवीण, कलानिपुण.

4 *trick, secret, device, contrivance of.* युक्ति *f.* युगूत *f.* कृति *f.* हिकमत *f.* कुलंगडें *n.* कलागूत *f.* मर्म *n.* सूत्र *n.* घडमोड *or* घडामोड *f.* मखी *f.* किल्ली *or* गुरुकिल्ली *f.* कला *f.* कळ *f.* कल्पना *f.* कुसि *f.*

Arts, *contrivances, devices, ingenious schemes or plans or modes.* युक्तिप्रयुक्ति *f.*

Finding out the a. of. मर्मभेद *m.*

5 *dexterity, expertness,* v. Skill. युक्ति *f.* जुगूत *f.* कला *or* कळा *f.* कसब *n.* कळाकुशळता *f.*

6 v. Ingenuity. हिकमत *f.*

Arterial, *a.* धमनीचा, नाडीचा,

A. system. नाडीचक्र *n.*

Arteriotomy, *n.* धमनीछेदन *n.* धमनीमोचन *n.*

Artery, *n.* धमनी *f.* शीर *f.* नाड *f.* नाडी *f.* शिरा *f.*

Artful, *a. crafty.* v. Cunning. काबेखोर, कावेदार, कावेबाज, छच्ची, कसबाती, कारस्थानी.

2 *proceeding from craft.* काव्याचा, काव्यादाव्याचा, छक्क्यापंज्याचा, कावेदारीचा, काटाचा.

Artfully, *adv.* v. A. काव्यानें, काव्यादाव्यानें, डावपेंच करून, छक्केपंजे &c. करून.

I. *skilfully.* युक्तीनें, हिकमतीनें, कसबानें, युक्तिवता, युक्त्या.

Artfulness, *n.* v. A. *and* Cunning. कावेदारी *f.* कावेबाजी *f.* धूर्तता *f.*

Arthritic, Arthritis, See Gouty, Gout.

Arthropuosis, *n. swelling at the joints.* पूयालस *m.*

Article, *n.* v. Thing. जिन्नस *f.* पदार्थ *m.* चीज *f.* वस्तु *f.*

A. of merchandise. जिन्नस *m.* केणें *n.* बाना *m.*

Article by a. जिन्नसवार.

2 (as of implements, pieces of apparel, &c. in numbering them); *item, piece.* नग *m.* डाग *m.* डागिणा *or* ना *m.* वस्तु *f.*

3 *clause, item, point.* कलम *n.* रकम *f.* बाब *f.* बाबत *f.* प्रकरण *n.*

Article by a. कलमवार.

4 *condition, term.* कलम *n.* संकेत *m.* शरत *f.* मुद्दा *m.*

5—in botany. कांडें *n.* पेर *n.* ग्रंथि *m.* पर्व *n.*

To be in the article of death. कंठीं प्राण *m.* येणें-उरणें, तंतीं प्राण *m.* उरणें-लागणें.

Articles of war. लष्करी कायदे *m. pl.*

To **Article,** *v. a. draw up in articles.* कलमबंदी *f.* करणें.

2 *bind by articles.* करारनाम्यानें बांधून-गुंतवून-&c. कसब-शिकण्याकरितां ठेवणें.

Articular, *a. belonging, &c. to the joints.* पर्वाचा, पर्वसंबंधी, पर्वनिष्ठ, संधिसंबंधी, संधिगत, संधिस्थ.

Articulate, *a.* **Articulated,** *p.* v. V. 1. *jointed, &c.* सांधलेला, सांधीव, संधियुक्त, संधिविशिष्ट.

2 *distinct;*—speech. स्पष्ट, साफ, व्यक्त, स्वरित, स्फुट, प्रांजल *or* ळ, निर्मल *or* ळ.

3—of speaker. साफ जिभेचा, स्वच्छवाणीचा, स्पष्टवक्ता, स्पष्टोच्चारक, अस्खलज्जिव्ह.

To **Articulate,** *v. a. join bones or parts.* संधि *m.*-संध *f.*-सांध *f.*-सांधा *m.* जोडणें-बसवणें-मिळवणें, सांधणें, सांधपणें.

2 *utter words,* v. To Pronounce. बोलणें, उच्चारणें, स्पष्टोच्चारण *n.*-स्पष्टोच्चार *m.* करणें. [वचनेंकरून.

Articulately, *adv.* v. A. 3. स्पष्ट, व्यक्त, स्पष्टोच्चारपूर्वक, स्फुट-

Articulateness, *n.* v. A. 1. संधिवैशिष्टय *n.* संधिविशिष्टता *f.* सांधलेलेपणा *m.*

2 साफी *f.* स्पष्टता *f.* व्यक्तता *f.* स्फुटत्व *n.*

Articulation, *n.*—in anatomy. v. Joint. खीळ *f.* सांध *f.* सांधा *m.* संधि *m.* ग्रंथि *m.* चाळा *m.* खुबा *m.*

2—in botany, *knot.* कांडें *n.* पेर *n.* पेरें *n.* पर्व *n.*

Portion included between two a.s पेर *n.* पेरें *n.* कांडें *n.*

3 v. Pronunciation. उच्चार *m.*

Artifice, *n. trick, stratagem.* शकल *f.* फट *f.* फटवण *f.* डाव *m.* छक्कड *f.* कसब *n.* पेंच *m.* कृति *f.* हिल्ला *m.*

Artifices, *arts, tricks, stratagems, wiles, finesse, chicanery,* छक्केपंजे *m. pl.* छकडभेद *m. pl.* पेचपाच *or* पाचपेच *m. pl.* कतरभेद *m. pl.* शकटभेद *m. pl.* घावडाव *m. pl.* डावपेच *m. pl.* चकरमकर *f.* चक्रफक्र *m. pl.* कवाईद *f.* कुडें *n.* कुडेपावडें *n.* गड्डेपड्डे *m. pl.* गद्यपद्य *n.* गारूड *n.* भानुमती *f. pop.* भानामती *f.* गौडबंगाल *n.* चेटक *n.*

Artificer, *n. artisan, artist.* कारिगर *m.* कारु *m.* शिल्पी *m.* शिल्पकार *m.* शिल्पोपजीवी, शिल्पकर्मकारी,

Artificial, *a. made by art, not natural.* कृत्रिम, कृत्रिमी, केलेला, कृतीचा, करणीचा, कृतिजन्य, कृतिसिद्ध, क्रियानिर्वृत्त, कृतक, यौक्तिक, काल्पनिक,

2 *fictitious,* v. False. खोटा, कपटाचा, कृत्रिम, अवास्तव,

अवास्तविक.

3 *not of spontaneous growth.* लावणीचा. [कलेनें.

ARTIFICIALLY, *adv.* v. A. 1. करणीनें, कृतीनें, युक्तीनें, मनुष्य-

ARTILLERY, *n. ordnance.* तोफखाना *m.* तोफा *f. pl.*

2 *weapons*—gener. शस्त्रें *n. pl.* हत्यारें *n. pl.*

3 *body of artillery men.* तोफखान्याकडील लोक *m. pl.* तोफखाना *m.*

ARTILLERY-MAN, *n.* खलासी *m.* गोलंदाज *m.*

ARTISAN, See ARTIFICER.

ARTIST, *n. skilful workman.* कारिगर *m.* कसबी *m.* कारु *m.*

2 *professor of the fine arts.* शिल्पी *m.* शिल्पशास्त्री *m.* शिल्पकर्मपंडित *m.* शिल्पज्ञ.

ARTISTIC, ARTISTICAL. *a.* कारागिरीचा, शिल्पचातुर्याचा, खुबीदार, बस्तादाच्याहातचा. [तुर्यपूर्वक.

ARTISTICALLY, *adv.* v. A. कारागिरीनें, शिल्पचातुर्यानें, शिल्पचा-

ARTLESS, *a. guileless.* v. SIMPLE. निष्कपट, अकपट, निष्कृत्रिम, अकृत्रिम, निष्प्रपंच, अमायी, अमायिक, अमाय, भोळा, मनाचा भोळा, मनाचा उथळा, भावडा.

2 *framed without art.* साधा, साधारण, सरल *or* ळ, भावडा.

ARTLESSLY, *adv.* v. A. 1. निष्कपटपणानें, निष्कृत्रिमपणानें, भोळेपणानें, भोळेभावानें.

ARTLESSNESS, *n.* v. A. 1. अकृत्रिम *n.* निष्कपटपणा *m.* निष्कृत्रिमपणा *m.* निष्कापट्य *n.* अमाया *f.* भोळाभाव *m.* भोळेपणा *m.* भोळाभावार्थ *m.* सरलभाव *m.*

2 साधेपणा *m.* सरळपणा *m.* भावडेपणा *m.* &c.

As, *conj.* जसा (correl. with तसा), यथा (correl. with तथा), जेवीं (correl. with तेवीं). जो-जी-जें (correl. with तो-ती-तें).

As if. जणू.

As it were. जणू.

As, all one as. दाखल.

2 *in the instant that.* जो (जो, जी, जें *mfn.*), तसा (तसा, तसी, तसें *mfn.*).

3 *like as.* सारखा, वत् (in comp. as वृक्षवत्, पाषाणवत्, एतद्वत्, तद्वत्), प्रमाणें.

4 *while, during.* जेव्हां (correl. with तेव्हां), ज्याबेळेस (correl. with त्याबेळेस). The sense is best rendered by the use of the present participle, as, He trembled as he spoke तो बोलतांना *or* बोलत असतां कांपला.

As for, as to. विषयीं.

As yet. अजून, अद्याप.

As well. ही, सुद्धां, देखील.

ASAFŒTIDA, See ASSAFŒTIDA.

To ASCEND, *v. n.* v. To RISE. चढणें, उठणें, उद्गम *m.*-उद्गमन *n.*-आरोह *m.*-आरोहण *n.* करणें *and with in. con.* होणें.

2—a heavenly body, v. To RISE. उगवणें, उदय *m.* पावणें, उदय *m.* होणें *g. of o.* उदित-उद्यत-&c. होणें. [करणें.

To ASCEND, *v. a. climb.* चढणें *with* वर, आरोह *m.*-आरोहण *n.*

ASCENDABLE, *a.* v. V. A. चढाया-चा-जोगा- जोगता-&c. आरोहणीय, आरोहणयोग्य.

ASCENDANT, *n.*—in astrology. उच्च *n.*

2 *ascendancy,* v. SUPERIORITY. उपराळा *m.* उपरदबडा *m.* बर्चस *n.* बर्चस्व *n.* ऊपर *m.*

ASCENDANT, *a.*—in astrology. उदित, उदयंगत.

2 *predominant.* v. SUPERIOR. वर्चस्वी, बरचढ, जबरदस्त.

ASCENDANCY, *n. predominance.* v. SUPERIORITY. उपर *m.* दसक *m. v.* चढ, मात्रा *f.* चढ *m.* शह *m.* प्राबल्य *n.* प्राधान्य *n.*

ASCENSION, ASCENDING, ASCENT, *n.* v. V. N. 1.—*act.* चढणें *n.* चढ *m.* उद्गम *m.* उद्गमन *n.* आरोह *m.* आरोहण *n.* उत्क्रमण *n.*

2—*act.* उगवणें *n.* &c, उदय *m.*

Ascensional difference चर *n.* चरखंड *n.* चरदल *n.* चरार्ध *n.*

The sine of a. d. चरज्या *f.*

ASCENT, *n.* See ASCENSION.

2 *acclivity, rise of ground.* चढ *m.* चढण *f.*

A. and descent. चढउतार *m.* चढणउतरण *f.* [ग *f.*

3 *an* a. *an acclivity,* चढण *f.* घाटी *f.* चढाव *m.* चढणी *f.* ढा-

Steep a. उभासूळ *m.*

To ASCERTAIN, *v. a. make sure or certain.* दर्याफ्त *f.*-दर्याफ्ती *f.* करणें *g. of o.* निश्चय *m.*-निर्णय *m.*-निर्णयन *n.*-निर्धार *m.*-निर्धारण *n.*-अवधारण *n.*-निरूहण *n.*- निरूपण *n.*-खचिती *f.* करणें-करून घेणें, शोध *m.* करणें, अवधारणें, तहकीक-खचीत-निश्चित-&c. करणें, निर्धारणें.

ASCERTAINABLE, *a.* v. V. निर्धार-&c. कराया-चा-जोगता-जोगा-&c. निर्धार्य, निर्धारणीय, निर्धारणयोग्य, अवधार्य, आवधारणीय.

ASCERTAINED, *p.* v. V. निर्धार केलेला-झालेला, निर्णीत, खचीत, निश्चित, निर्धारित, अवधारित, तहकीक, निरूपित.

ASCERTAINMENT, *n.* v. V.—*act.* निर्धार-&c. करणें *n.* दर्याफ्त *f.* शोध *m.* निर्णय *m.* निर्णयन *n.* निश्चय *m.* निर्धार *m.* निर्धारण *n.* आवधारण *n.* निरूहण *n.* निरूह *m.* निरूपण *n.* ध्रुव *m.* अध्यवसाय *m.*

ASCETIC, *n. one who practices austerity,* बैरागी *m.* संन्यासी *m.* योगी *pop.* जोगी *m.* गोस्वामी *pop.* गोसावी *m.* (of this class some orders are आनंद, उदासी, कानफाटा *or* ट्या *or* टी, गिरी, नाथपंथी, पुरी, बन, भराडी, भारती, हंस,) तपी *m.* तपस्वी *m.* तापस *m.* तापसी *m.* बैरंगिक *m.* मुनि *m.* अजगर *m.* कर्मसंन्यासी *m.* कर्मसंन्यासिक *m.* सर्वसंगपरित्यागी *m.* (*Note. Female* a. बैरागीण, गोसावीण, जोगीण, &c.)

A marrying a. संजोगी *m.* संयोगी *m.* [समाधि *mf.*

Self-immolation of an a. by drowning or burning.

Smoke-fire of an a. धुणी *or* धुनी *f.* धुमी *f.*

ASCETIC, *a.* विरक्त, तपोनिष्ठ, तपस्यासक्त.

ASCETICISM, *n.* v. AUSTERITY. तपश्चर्या *f.* तपस्या *f.* बैराग्य *n.*

ASCITES, *n.* v. DROPSY. उदर *n.* जलोदर *n. m.*

ASCITITIOUS, *a. not inherent.* मागून जडलेला, जडणीचा, आगंतुक, असहज.

A. name. जडेंनांव *n.* [आरोप्य.

ASCRIBABLE, *a.* v. V. लावाया-चा-जोगता-जोगा-&c. आरोपणीय,

To ASCRIBE, *v. a. attribute, impute, assign.* ठेवणें, लावणें, घालणें, आरोपणें, आंगावर घालणें, आरोप *m.*-आरोपण *n.*-&c. करणें *g. of o.* Note. The sense of this word (to refer as to a cause) is best rendered thus.—I ascribe his poverty to his laziness: त्याच्या गरीबीचें कारण त्याचा आळस आहे असें मी मानतों-म्हणतों-&c. [रोपित.

ASCRIBED, *p.* v. V. ठेवलेला, आरोपलेला, आरोप केलेला &c. आ-

ASCRIPTION, *n.* v. V.—*act.* आरोपणें *n.* लावणें *n.* &c. आरोप *m.* आरोपण *n.*

ASH *n.* एक झाडआहे.

2 आश झाडाचें लांकूड *n.*

Ashamed, *a.* लाजलेला, लज्जित, लज्जमान *pop.* लज्जायमान, शरमिंदा *or* धा, ओशाळा, लाजिंद्रा, लाजिमदार, घायाळ, मिंधा, दबेल, पांगातला, लाजिरवाणा, सजील, सपीप, लज्जान्वित, त्रपान्वित, अवाङ्मुख, अधोमुख.

To be a. लाजणें, शरमणें, ओशाळणें, लाज *f.* वाटणें *in. con.*

Ashamedly, *adv. bashfully.* लाजिरवाणीं *or* णें, तोंडाला पदर लावून, तोंड खालीं करून, मुठींत नाक धरून, खालीं पाहून, मानखालीं घालून, खालचेमानेनें.

Ashes, *n.* रास *f.* रखा *f.* रक्षा *f.* राखाडी *f.* भस्म *n.* भुरी *f* क्षार *m.*

A. as heaped or strewed. राखाडी *f.* राखुंडा *m.* राखवडा *m.*

A. of a body burnt on a pyre. चिताभस्म *n.*

A. for smearing the body. विभूति *pop.* विभूत *f.*

Hot a. मुमर *or* मुमीर *nm.* फुपेटा *or* फुपाटा *m.*

Of the color of a. भस्मरंग *pop.* भस्मरंगी, भस्मवर्ण, भस्मी.

Place bestrewed with a. राखमंडळ *n.* राखाडमंडळ *n.*

Reducing to a. भस्मीकरण *n.*

Rubbing a. by way of ablution. भस्मस्नान *n.*

Reduced to a. भस्मीकृत, भस्मीभूत.

To a. (reduced, burned,) खाक, भस्मसात् (करून टाकला &c.), ज़र (जळला &c.), फस्त, हुत.

To become a. भस्मणें.

Ashore, *adv.* किनाऱ्यास, किनाऱ्यावर, तडीस, तडीवर, कडेस.

Ashy, *a. made of a.* राखेचा, भस्मी, भस्माचा, भास्मन.

2 *like a. pale.* भस्मरंगी, भस्मवर्णी, भस्मवर्णक.

3 *dry and loose like a.*—soil, &c. राखोंडा *or* राखोडा.

Asian, Asiatic, *a.* आशियाखंडाचा, आशियाखंडांतला, &c.

Aside, *adv. apart.* एकीकडे *or* कडेस, एकेबाजूस, कडेकांठास, फरक, आडमोरा, आडबाजूस, आडकुशीस, आड.

To move a. खिसणें.

To set a. रद्दकरणें, नामंजूरकरणें.

To turn a. *deviate.* बिचलणें, बिथरणें, पाऊल *n.* वांकडें पडणें *g. of o.*

2—in the drama. आत्मगत.

Asinine, *a.* गाढवाचा, गर्दभसंबंधी, रासभसंबंधी.

To **Ask**, *v. a. inquire, question, interrogate.* पुसणें, विचारणें, हटकणें, प्रश्न *n.*-पृच्छा *f.*-सवाल *m.*-&c. करणें.

2 *beg, request.* मागणें, याचणें, अर्थणें, विनंती *f.*-याचन *n.*-याचना *f.*-अर्थना *f.*-&c. करणें *g. of o.* [*n.* सांगणें.

3 *ask for, claim, demand, require.* मागणें, सांगणें, *or* मोल

4 about, for. पुसणें, विचारणें, वास्तपुस्त *f.*-विचारपूस *f.* करणें, नांव *n.*-स्मरण *n.*-याद *f.*-आठवण *f.*-सई *f.*-उल्लेख *m.*-&c. काढणें-करणें *g. of o.*

5 v. To Invite. बोलावणें *or* बोलवणें, बाहणें, अंबतणें.

Asked, *p.* v. V. 1. पुसलेला &c. पृष्ट.

2 मागितलेला &c. याचित, प्रार्थित, अर्थित.

5 बोलावलेला &c. आमंत्रित, निमंत्रित.

Asker, *n.* v. V. 1. पुसणारा, &c. पुस्ता, पृच्छक, प्रष्टा.

Askew, Askaunt, Askance, Aslant, *adv. obliquely.* झांजरता, ओझरता, कापता, कातरता, कसरता, कहाता, काकरता, कातरा, तिर्यक्, तिरकस, आडवा, बांकडा.

To look at a. काण्या डोळयानें पाहणें, बांकड्या डोळयानें पाहणें, अपांगवीक्षण *n.* करणें.

Asleep, *a.* or *adv.* झोंपेंत, निद्रेंत, झोंपीं, झोंप लागलेला, निद्रित, निद्रिस्त, शयित, सुप्त, जातनिद्र, प्राप्तनिद्र, निद्रागत, लब्धनिद्र.

Fast a. Sound a. सुषुप्त, प्रसुप्त.

Half a. निजसुरा.

To fall a. झोंप *f.* लागणें *in. con.*

Aslope, *adv. with declivity.* v. Obliquely. कसरता, कातरता, उतरता, ढाळता *or* ढळता, कलता.

Asp, *n.* एक लहान जातीचा विखारी सर्प आहे.

Asparagus, *n. a. racemosus.* शतावरी *pop.* शतावली *f.* शितागोंड *f.* शिताचंवरी *f.* दिसमावळी *f.*

Aspect, *n. look, semblance, seeming.* आकार *m.* रूप *n.* डौल *m.* शकल *f.* कटाक्ष *m.* घटाव *m.*

2 *look, air,* v. Countenance. चेहरा *m.* सुरत *f.* मुख *n.* वदन *n.*

3 *view facing, position.* रोंख *m.* लक्ष्य *n.* मुख *n.* तोंड *n.* अभिमुखता *f.* आभिमुख्य *n.*

4 (of a planet.) दृष्टि *f.* दशा *f.*

Asperity, Asperous. See Roughness, Harshness, Rough.

To **Asperse**, *v. a. defame, traduce, slander, calumniate.* काजळी *f.* लावणें, कोरडी किटाळ *f.* घालणें-उठवणें, कुभांड *n.*-कुफरांड *or* कुफराण *n.*-बलांट *or* बालांट *n.* घेणें-घालणें-रचणें, निमित्त *n.* ठेवणें -घेणें, चहाडी *f.*-चुगली *f.* खाणें-सांगणें-करणें *g. of o.* तुफान *n.*-तोहमत *f.* घेणें-घालणें, कफारत *or* कफालत *f.* घेणें-आणणें, लिंपण *n.* लावणें, कलंक *m.* लावणें, आळ *f. m.* घालणें-घेणें, कैवाड *n.* रचणें-घेणें *with* वर *of o.* कुचविंधी *f.*-कुचिंदी *f.*-कुचनिंदा *f.* करणें *g. of o.* कुटाळकी *f.*-कुटाळी *f.* करणें, कूट *f.* खाणें *g. of o.* अदावत *f.* घालणें-घेणें-करणें, अभिशंसन *n.*-अभिशाप *m.*-अपवाद *m.* करणें *g. of o.*

Aspersed, *p.* v. V. आळ आलेला-घातलेला &c. &c. कलंकित, कलंकी, कलंकमय, क्षिप्त, अभिशप्त, अभिशस्त.

Asperser, *n.* v. V. काजळी लावणारा, आळ घेणारा-&c. आळघाल्या, चुगलखोर *or* चुगलीखोर, चुगल *or* ल्या, चहाडखोर, चहाडबुचका, चहाड, कुभांडी *or* ड्या, कुभांडखोर, कुफरांडी *or* ड्या, कुफराणी, कुदांडी *or* ड्या, बलांटखोर *or* बालांटखोर, बालंटी *or* ट्या, गळेपडू, तुफानखोर, तुफानी, धोतांडी, बगलांटी *or* टी, कुटाळखोर, कुटाळ *or* कुचाळ, कुचाळखोर, कुचिंद, कुचिंदा, कंबटाल्या *or* ळ्या *or* ळी, अभिशंसी, अपवादक.

Aspersion, *n.* v. V.—*act.* तुफान घेणें *n.* चुगली खाणें *n.* आळ घालणें *n.* &c. कुटाळकी *f.* कुटाळी *f.* अपवाद *m.* अभिशंसन *n.* विकथन *n.* धूलिप्रक्षेप *m.* [मित्त *n.*

I. *an* a. v. Slander. तोहमत *f.* तुफान *n.* बलांट *n.* आळ *f.* नि-

Aspirant, *n. one who desires eagerly.* इच्छु (in comp. as धनेच्छु, कीर्त्तीच्छु,) अर्थी (in comp. धनार्थी, विद्यार्थी &c.) उमेदवार.

To **Aspirate**, *v. a.* महाप्राणानें उच्चारणें, महाप्राणाचा उच्चार *m.* करणें, महाप्राणोच्चारण *n.* करणें.

Aspirate, *a.* **Aspirated**, *p.* v. V. महाप्राण, महाप्राणाचा, महाप्राणोच्चारणीय, महाप्राणोच्चारित.

Aspiration, *n.* v. V. (To Aspirate,)—*act.* महाप्राणाचा उच्चार करणें *n.* महाप्राणोच्चारण *n.* महाप्राणोच्चार *m.* [लसा *f.*

v. V. (To Aspire,) *and* Desire,—*act.* आशा *f.* आस *f.* ला-

2—*act.* दम *m.* हांव *f.* v. धर, महत्वाकांक्षा *f.* महत्त्वापेक्षा *f.*

To **Aspire**, *v. n. pant or breathe after,* v. To Desire. आशा *f.*-आस *f.*-उमेद *f.*-हांव *f.*-लालसा *f.*-&c. धरणें, आशावणें.

2 *aim at something elevated.* थोरदृष्टि *f.*-मोठीदृष्टि *f.* धरणें, म-

हृत्त्वाकांक्षा *f.*-महत्वलिप्सा *f.*-&c. धरणें-करणें.

ASPIRER, *n.* ASPIRING, *p. a.* v. V. 1. *and* DESIROUS. इच्छा धरणारा, आशा धरणारा.

2 *and* AMBITIOUS. ऊर्ध्वदृष्टि, हवसदार *or* हौसदार, महत्वाकांक्षी, महत्त्वलिप्सु, महत्त्वापेक्षी.

ASQUAT, *adv. in a squatting posture.* उकड, उकडवा.

ASQUINT, *adv. to the corner of the eye.* काणें, तिरकें, तिरळें, तिरवें, काण्या डोळ्यानें, वांकड्या डोळ्यानें.

ASS, *n.*—neuter. गाढव,—male. गाढव, रासभ, गर्दभ *pop.* गधंव, खर, लंबकर्ण,—female, गाढव, गाढवी, गाढवीण, गर्दभी, रासभी. —in contempt, गधडा *m.*

Wild a. गोरखर *m.*

2 *dolt, &c.* v. FOOL. गाढव *m.* गद्धा *m.* गाढवाचा लेंक *m.* गाढवाचा खरारा *m.*

ASSAFŒTIDA, *n.*—plant, हिंगाचें झाड *n.* हिंगु *m.*—gum or ooze, हिंग *m.* हिंगु *m.* हिंगुनिर्यास *m.*—in contempt, हिंगडा *m.*—in cant, covert, &c. phraseology, वास *m.*

A. water. हिंगवणी *n.*

Bump supervening (upon a wound or sore) through the eating of a. हिंगुरडें *n.* हिंगरूड *n.*

Fine, bright a. हिराहिंग *m.*

To ASSAIL, ASSAULT, &c. See To ATTACK, &c.

ASSASSIN, *n.* v. V. मारेकरी, दग्यानें मारणारा, कपटहिंसक, गुप्तघाल्या.

To ASSASSINATE, *v. a. murder by treachery or sudden violence.* दग्यानें मारणें-जीव *m.* घेणें-प्राण *m.* घेणें, गुप्तमान्यानें-चोरमान्यानें-चोरून-नकळवितां-&c. मारणें-जीव *m.* घेणें-&c.

ASSASSINATION, v. V.—*act.* दग्यानें मारणें *n.* &c.

ASSAULT, *n.* v. ATTACK. घाला *m.* *v.* घाल, पड, चढ *m.* चढाई *f.* हल्ला *m.* चाल *f.* उचल *f.*

A. and battery. दंडपारुष्य *n.*

To ASSAULT, See To ATTACK.

ASSAY, ASSAYING, *n.* v. V. A. 1.—*act.* परीक्षणें *n.* &c. परीक्षा *f.* पारख *f.* परीक्षण *n.*

2—*act.* कसणें *n.* कस पाहणें *n.* नाणकपरीक्षा *f.* पारख *f.*

To ASSAY, *v. a. make experiment of.* v. To TRY. परीक्षणें, परीक्षा *f.*-परीक्षण *n.*-पारख *f.*-&c. करणें-घेणें-पाहणें *g. of o.*

2 (metals, &c.) कसणें, कसून पाहणें, कस *m.* पाहणें *g. of o.*

To ASSAY, *v. n. endeavor,* v. To TRY. यत्न *m.*-प्रयत्न *m.* करणें.

ASSAYER, *n.* v. V. A. 1. परीक्षणारा, परीक्षक, पारख-परीक्षा करणारा-पाहणारा.

2 कसणारा, परीक्षक, नाणकपरीक्षक, धातुवादी.

ASSEMBLAGE, *n. collection,* v. HEAP. गोळा *m.* जमाव *m.* मेळावा *m.* समुच्चय *m.* संचय *m.* चय *m.* समाहार *m.* कदंब *n.* गुच्छ *m.* जुटी *f.* समवाय *m.* संघात *m.* मंडल *n.*

2 *assembled state.* जमलेपणा *m.* एकवटपणा *m.* समुदितत्व *n.* समुच्चयता *f.* समाहारता *f.*

To ASSEMBLE, *v. a.* v. To GATHER. जमा करणें, गोळा करणें.

2 *convoke, convene.* मिळवणें, जमविणें, एकत्र-एकवट करणें, एकवटणें, जमावणें.

To ASSEMBLE *v. n.* v. To GATHER. मिळणें, जमणें, एकवटणें, जमा होणें, जुटणें, जुडणें.

ASSEMBLED, *p.* v. V. A. 1. जमा केलेला, गोळा केलेला, समुदित, संहत.

2 मिळवलेला, जमावलेला, &c.

v. V. N. मिळालेला, जमलेला, &c.

ASSEMBLING, ASSEMBLY, *n.* v. V. A. 1.—*act.* जमा करणें *n.* गोळा करणें *n.* संग्रह *m.* समाहार *m.* संचयन *n.*

2 मिळवणें *n.* जमविणें *n.*

v. V. N. 1.—*act.* मिळणें *n.* जमणें *n.* जमा होणें *n.* &c.

I. *body assembled; meeting, company, congregation, congress, convention, synod, convocation.* सभा *f.* मंडली *or* ळी *f.* बैठक *f.* जमाव *m.* जमात *f.* मेळा *m.* मजलस *f* मजालस *f.* अखाडा *m.* अड्डा *m.* संघ *m.* संघान *m.* समाज *m.* समुच्चय *m.* समुदाय *m.*

A line or row of (learned Brâhmans) in an a. पट्टी *f.*

Dismissal of an a. सभाविसर्जन *n.*

Full a. *full meeting, session, &c.* भरमजालस *f.*

Member of an. a. or council. सभासद् *m.* सभ्य *m.* सदस्य *m.* सामाजिक *m.*

Person present in an a. हाजीरमजालस.

ASSEMBLY-ROOM, *n.* सभामंदिर *n.* सभा *f.* आखाडा *m.* सभागृह *n.* सभास्थान *n.* सभामंडप *n.*

ASSENT, ASSENTING, *n.* v. V.—*act.* मान्य करणें *n.* &c. होयकार *m.* होकार *m.* रुकार *m.* अनुमत *n.* अनुमति *f* सम्मत *n.* सम्मति *f.* तह *m.*

To ASSENT, *v. n. acquiesce in,* v. To AGREE. मान्य करणें, कबूल करणें-होणें, अनुमत-सम्मत-&c. होणें, रुकार *m.*-होयकार *m.*-सम्मत *n.*-सम्मति *f.*-&c. देणें.

To ASSERT, *v. a.* v. To AFFIRM. खचीतपणीं-खंबीरपणीं-निश्चितपणीं-निश्चयपूर्वक-प्रतिज्ञापूर्वक-&c. बोलणें-म्हणणें-&c.

2 *maintain, vindicate.* प्रपादणें, पुरवणें, संभाळणें, राखणें, रक्षण *n.* करणें *g. of o.* स्थापणें, स्थापन *n.*-स्थापना *f* करणें *g. of o.* निर्वाह *m.* करणें *g. of o.* संभार *m.* करणें *g. of o.*

3 (a system of doctrines, &c.) उपपादन *n.*-उपपत्ति *f.*-प्रतिपादन *n.*-स्थापन *n.*-&c. करणें *g. of o.* कैवार *m.*-पक्ष *m.* धरणें-करणें-घेणें *g. of o.*

ASSERTION, *n. positive declaration.* वचन *n.* प्रतिज्ञा *f.* प्रतिज्ञावचन *n.* निश्चितवाक्य *n.* निश्चयात्मकवाक्य *n.* निर्वाद *m.*

2 *position advanced.* प्रतिज्ञा *f.* पक्ष *m.* मत *n.*

To ASSESS, *v. a. set a tax,* v. To TAX. पट्टी *f.*-कर *m.*-सरकारदेणें *n.*-ठोका *m.*-&c. फाळणें, बसवणें, ठोक्याची-&c. फाळणी *f.*- वर्गणी *f.*-वर्गत *f. n.* घालणें. [नेमणें-&c.

2 *set a value in order to tax.* जमाबंदी *f.*-&c. करणें-ठरवणें-

3 *fix, settle* (damages) ठरविणें, ठराव *m.*-इयत्ता *f.*-नियम *m.*- &c. करणें *g. of o.*

ASSESS, ASSESSMENT, *n.* v. V. 1.—*act.* पट्टी बसवणें *n.*

2 जमाबंदी *f.*

I. *sum assessed,* v. TAX. पट्टी *f.*

Reduced or low a. कमदस्त *m.* कमदर *m.*

ASSESSOR, *n.* v. V. I. पट्टी-&c. बसवणारा-घालणारा.

2 जमाबंदी करणारा-बसवणारा.

I. *assistant judge, counsellor, &c.* सभासद *m.* सहकारी *m.* सदस्य *m.* [विषय *m.*

ASSETS, *n. effects.* पुंजी *f.* जायदाद *f.* बुटी *f.* केवा *m.* ऐवज *m.*

To ASSEVERATE, *v. a. affirm solemnly.* सत्योत्तर *n.* करणें, सत्योत्तरें *or* सत्योत्तरकरून बोलणें, सत्यस्मरूनबोलणें.

2—gener. See To AFFIRM.

Asseveration, *n. solemn affirmation.* सत्योत्तर *n.* सत्यवचन *n.*

Assiduity, Assiduousness, *n.* v. A. आसक्ति *f.* संसक्ति *f.* अभ्यास *m.* व्यवसाय *m.* अध्यवसाय *m.* ताण *m.* खणती *f.* उद्यम *m.* उद्योग *m.* व्यासंग *m.*

Assiduous, *a.* v. Diligent. आसक्त, संसक्त, उद्यमी, उद्योगी, खपाठ्या, व्यासंगी, व्यवसायी, अध्यवसायी, साक्षेपी.

Assiduously, *adv.* v. A. आसक्तीनें, व्यासंगानें, &c. व्यासंगपूर्वक, व्यवसायपूर्वक, साक्षेपें.

Assign, *n.* मुखत्यार *m.*

To **Assign**, *v. a. appoint, apportion,* v. To Allot. वांट्यास देणें, विभागास-विभागीं देणें-लावणें, नेमणें, नेमून देणें, लावूनदेणें.

2 *designate, appropriate* v. To Appoint. योजणें, योजना *f.*-विनियोग *m.*-विनियोजन *n.* करणें *g. of o.* नांवरशीनें लावणें-ठेवणें, निर्देश *m.* करणें *g. of o.*

3 *allege, show,* v. To Adduce. लावणें, सांगणें, दाखवणें, प्रदर्शन *n.* करणें *g. of o.* उपन्यास *m.* करणें *g. of o.*

4 *make over*, v. To Transfer. स्वाधीन करणें, सोंपणें, सोंपून देणें.

Assignable, *a.* v. V. 1. वांट्यास-विभागास-&c. द्याया-चा-जोगा-सारखा-&c. नेमून द्याया-चा-जोगा-सारखा-&c. [शार्ह.

2 योजाया-चा-जोगा-&c. विनियोज्य, नियोज्य, निर्देश्य, निर्दे-

3 सांगाया-चा-जोगा-सारखा-&c.

4 (दुसऱ्यास) स्वाधीन कराया-जोगा-&c. सोंपायाजोगा-&c.

Assignation, *n. appointment between lovers.* संकेत *m.* ठवस *m.*

Female making a. अभिसारिका.

Place of a. संकेतस्थान *n.* संकेत *m.* [दिमतीचा.

Assigned, *p.* v. V. 1. वांट्यास दिल्हेला, नेमून दिल्हेला, &c. तैनाती,

2 योजलेला, विनियोग केलेला, &c. निर्दिष्ट, विनियुक्त, नियुक्त.

3 सांगितलेला, लावलेला, &c.

4 (दुसऱ्यास) सोंपलेला- स्वाधीन केलेला, &c. [ऱ्मतदार *c.*

Assignee, *n.* तैनाती *m.* अखत्यारी *m.* मुखत्यार *m.* वकील *m.* दि-

Assignment, *n.* v. V. 1.—*act.* वांट्यास देणें *n.* नेमून देणें *n.* &c.

An a. or order on the revenues. बरात *f.* तनखा *m.*

Person who has an a. बरातदार *c.* [निर्देश *m.*

2—*act.* योजणें *n.* &c. योजना *f.* विनियोग *m.* विनियोजन *n.*

3—*act.* लावणें *n.* सांगणें *n.* &c.

4—*act.* सोंपणें *n.* सोंपून देणें *n.*

To **Assimilate**, *v. a. bring to a likeness.* सारखा-सदृश-सम-समधर्मक-अनुगुण- &c. करणें, सादृश्य *n.*-आनुगुण्य *n.*- &c. करणें *g. of o. recip.*

2 *convert into a like substance.* आंगीं लावणें-लावून घेणें, रूप *n.* करणें, विपाक *m.* करणें, जिरवणें, जिरेसा करणें.

To **Assimilate**, *v. n. come to a likeness.* सारखा-सदृश-अनुगुण-&c. होणें-होऊन जाणें.

2 *be converted into a like substance.* आंगीं *or* आंगास लागणें, लागणें, जिरणीस पडणें, पचनीं पडणें. [झालेला.

Assimilated, *p.* v. V. 1. सारखा-सदृश-अनुगुण- &c. केलेला *or*

2 आंगीं लावलेला *or* लागलेला, &c.

Assimilation, *n.* v. V. A. 1—*act.* सारखा-&c. करणें *n.*

2 आंगीं लावणें *n.* &c.

v. V. N. 1.—*act.* सारखा-&c. होणें *n.*

2 आंगीं लागणें *n.* &c. विपाक *m.*

To **Assist**, *v. a.* v. To Help. मदद *f.*-कुमक *f.*-मददगारी *f.*-पुस्ती *f.*- सहकार *m.*-&c. करणें-देणें, हात *m.* देणें.

To **Assist** *v. n. lend aid.* कुमक *f.*-&c. करणें-देणें, हात *m.* देणें, सहाय-सहकारी-&c. होणें-असणें.

Assistance, *n.* v. Help. मदद *f.* कुमक *f.* सहाय *n.* साह्य *n.* पुस्ती *f.* सहकार *m.*

Assistant, *n. helper, auxiliary.* मददगार *c.* मदतनीस *c.* मदत्या *m.* सहाय *m.* सहकारी.

2 v. Mate. बगल्या *m.* हस्तक्या *m.* हस्तक *m.*

Assize, *n. court of justice.* न्यायसभा *f.* न्यायाची कचेरी *f.* अदालत *f.* [धारण *f.*

2 *measure of price, weight, &c.* निरख *m.* भाव *m.* दर *m.*

To **Assize**, *v. a. fix price, rate, &c.* निरख *m.*-भाव *m.*-दर *m.*-धारण *f.*-&c. ठरावणें-नेमणें.

To **Associate**, *v. a.* v. To Unite, To Join. संयोग *m* -संबंध *m.*-&c. करणें g. *of o.* जोड *f.*-जूट *f.*-सांगड *f.*-लांकण *or* लांखण *f.*-लांख *f.* घालणें-घालून देणें.

To **Associate**, *v. n. keep company.* संग *m.*-संगत *f.*-समागम *m.*-सोबत *f.*-सहवास *m.*-साहचर्य *n.*-&c. करणें, संघट्टणें.

Associate, *a.* **Associated**, *p.* v. V. A. संयोग केलेला-&c. सांगड-&c. घातलेला, सांगडीचा, जोडीचा, संबद्ध, सहित, प्रयुक्त, संयुक्त, संसर्गी, संसृष्ट, सामलाती.

Associate, *n. companion, mate,* v. Fellow. साथी *m.* सोबती *m.* संगती *m.* बंधु *m.* (Note. *female* a. सोबतीण, संगतीण, &c.) [पी *m.*

2—in business, &c. v. Partner. अंशी *m.* भागी *m.* जोड-

3—in crime, &c. v. Accomplice. साग्या *m.* मिळणीचा मनुष्य *m.*

Associater, *n.* **Associating**, *p. a.* v. V. A. संयोग-संबंध-&c. करणारा, जोड जुट-सांगड-&c. घालणारा.

v. V. N. संग &c. करणारा, सोबती, साथी, सोबतीचा, साथीचा, संगी (esp. in comp. as साधुसंगी, स्त्रीसंगी, खलसंगी,) सामील.

Association, *n.* v. V. A.—*act.* संयोग करणें *n.* &c. संयोग *m.* संयोजन *n.* संबंधन *n.* संबंध *m.*

2 *state.* सांगड *f.* जूट *f.* जोड *m.* संबंध *m.*

v. V. N.—*state.* संग *m.* संगम *m.* प्रसंग *m.* अनुषंग *m.* समायोग *m.* समागम *m.* साह्य *n.* साहित्य *n.* संसृष्टत्व *n.*

I. *an* a. v. Company, Combination. मंडळी *f.* मुठाण *n.* गट्ट *m.* एकवळा *m.* जूट *f. m.* जूग *n.*

Member of an a. गणाभ्यंतर *m.*

To **Assort**, *v. a. sort, separate into classes,* v. To Classify. प्रत *f.*-प्रती *f. pl.*-&c. लावणें, छाटणें, छाट, *m.* करणें *g. of o.* उत्तम मध्यम कनिष्ठ पर्याय *m. pl.* करणें *g. of o.*

To **Assort**, *v. n. agree, suit.* मिळणें, जमणें, जुळणें, बनणें.

Assorted, *p.* v. V. A. छाटलेला, छाटकेलेला.

Assortment, *n.* v. V. A. प्रत *f.* लावणें *n.* छाटणें *n.* छाट *n.* विल्हेवाटी *f.*

I. *a number of things assorted.* एक जातीच्या जिन्नसांचा-वस्तूचा वगैबारसंच *m.*-संचय *m.* जातवार जिन्नसांचा-पदार्थांचा-&c. संग्रह *m.*- संचय *m.*

To **Assuage**, *v. a. allay, alleviate,* v. To Ease. हलका करणें, समाधान *n.*-उपशम *m.*-उपशमन *n.*-उपशांति *f.*-&c. करणें *g. of o.*

2 *appease, pacify, calm,* v. To Compose. शमवणें, शांतवणें, *or* सांतवणें, धंड-धंडा करणें, संतावणें *or* संथावणें, स्वस्थावणें.

To **Assuage**, *v. n.* v. To Abate. हलकावणें, मंदावणें.

ASSUAGEMENT, *n.* v. V. A. 1.—*act.* हलका करणें *n.* उपशम *m.* उपशमन *n.*—*state.* उतार *m.* समाधान *n.* उपशम *m.* उपशांति *f.*
2—*act.* शमवणें *n.* शांतवणें *n.* थंड करणें *n.* &c. शमन *n.* प्रशमन *n.* —*state.* शांति *f.* शम *m.* प्रशम *m.*

ASSUMABLE, *a.* v. V. A. 1. आपणाकडे घ्याया-चा-जोगता-&c. उचलाया-चा-जोगता-&c. धार्य, धारणीय.
2 प्रमाणावांचून घ्याया-चा-जोगा-&c.

To ASSUME, *v. a. take upon one's self.* आपल्याकडे घेणें, अंगीकारणें, स्वीकारणें, आदरणें, उचलणें, घेणें.
2 *take for granted,* v. TO SUPPOSE. प्रमाणावांचून घेणें-ग्रहण करणें, प्रमाण न पाहतां मानणें, कल्पिणें, सिद्धवत् मानणें.

To ASSUME, *v. n. be arrogant,* v. TO PRESUME. ओढून प्रतिष्ठा *f.* आणणें, ऊतमात *m.* करणें-मांडणें.

ASSUMED, *p.* v. V. A. 1. आपल्याकडे घेतलेला, अंगीकारलेला, &c. अंगीकृत, स्वीकृत.
2 प्रमाणावांचून घेतलेला, आहार्य, कल्पित, प्रमाणविचारव्यतिरे- [कगृहीत, इष्ट.

ASSUMING, *a. arrogant,* v. PROUD. मगरूर, अभिमानी, आढ्यतेचा, दिमाखाचा.

ASSUMPTION, *n.* v. V. A. 1.—*act.* आपल्याकडे घेणें *n.* अंगीकारणें *n.* &c. स्वीकरण *n.* अंगीकरण *n.*—*a. or s.* अंगीकार *m.* स्वीकार *m.*
2—*act.* प्रमाणावांचून घेणें *n.* &c. आहार्यारोप *m.* प्रमाणविचारव्यतिरिक्त ग्रहण *n.* प्रमाणविचारव्यतिरिक्तस्वीकार *m.* प्रमाणविचारव्यतिरिक्तादरण *n.* विनाधारग्रहण *n.*
I. *point assumed,* v. SUPPOSITION. प्रमाणावांचून मानलेली गोष्ट *f.* कल्पना *f.* इष्टपक्ष *m.* इष्टमत *n.* &c. प्रमाणविचारव्यतिरेकगृहीतपक्ष *m.*

ASSURANCE, ASSURING, *n.* v. V. 1.—*act.* खातर करणें *n.* भरवसा देणें *n.* &c. अभयदान *n.*
Hand as stretched forth in a. अभयहस्त *m.*
Proclamation of a. अभयडंका *m.* अभयडिंडिम *m.*
Writ of a. अभयपत्र *n.* अभयलेख *m.*
I. v. PROMISE, वचन *n.* प्रतिज्ञा *f.* भाक *or* भाष *f.*
II. *trust in self,* v. CONFIDENCE. ऊब *f.* उमेद *f.* उमेदवारी *f.* धीर *m.* दम *m.*
III. *firm persuasion,* v. CONFIDENCE. धडा *m.* निधडा *m.* खातरजमा *f.* खातर *or* री *f.* निशा *f.* निश्चय *m.*
Perfect a. बालबालखातरी *f.*
IV. *effrontery,* v. IMPUDENCE. अभयमुद्रा *f.* तोंड *n.*
V. *testimony of credit.* निशा *f.* खातरी *f.*

To ASSURE, *v. a. make sure or confident.* खातर *f.*-खातरी *f.*-खातरजमा *f.* करणें-करून देणें *g. of o.* भरवसा *m.*-दिलभरवसा *m.*-दिलासा *m.*-दिल दिलासा *m.*-धैर्य *n.*-धीर *m.*-&c. देणें, अभयवचन *n.*-अभय *n.*-अभयपत्र *n.*-होवासा *m.* देणें, अभयदान *n.* करणें.
2 *make firm or secure to.* खचीत-निश्चित-सत्यापित-&c. करणें.
3 See TO INSURE.

ASSURED, *p.* v. V. 1. खातरी झालेला-केलेला, भरवसा झालेला-केलेला, &c. गतशंक, विगतशंक, नष्टशंक, गतसंदेह, गतसंशय, जातनिश्चय, दृढनिश्चय, निर्भ्रांत.

ASSUREDLY, *adv.* v. CERTAINLY. खचीत, निश्चय, निश्चयपूर्वक, निश्चयात्मक.

ASSUREDNESS, See CERTAINTY, CONFIDENCE.

ASTERISK, *n.* फुली *f.* चौफुली *f.*

ASTERISM, *n. constellation.* नक्षत्र *n.*
Table of asterisms in the moon's path. नक्षत्रमाला *f.*
2 *cluster of stars.* नक्षत्रांचा घड *m.* नक्षत्रगण *m.*

ASTERN, *adv. at or towards the hinder part*—of a ship &c. पिछाडीस, पिछाडीकडे *or* गलबताचे-&c. पिछाडीस-मागल्याबाजूस.

ASTEROID, *n. minor planet.* उपग्रह *m.* लघुग्रह *m.*

ASTHMA. धाप *f.* दमा *m.* श्वास *m.* श्वासावरोध *m.* कासश्वास *or* श्वासकास *m.*

ASTHMATIC, *a.* धापाळू, धाप्या, धापकरी, दमेकरी, कासश्वासग्रस्त.
2 *pertaining to asthma.* दम्याचा, &c. दम्याविषयींचा.

To ASTONISH, *To* ASTOUND, *v. a. amaze, surprise,* &c. चकवणें, चोजवणें, चकित-दंग-चकभूल-सचकित-चक्क-विस्मित-विस्मयापन्न-साश्चर्य-&c. करणें, चकभूल *f.* उडवणें-करणें *g. of o.* चौकडी *f.* भुलवणें *or* गुंग करणें *g. of o.* विस्मापन *n.* करणें *g. of o.* आश्चर्यांत-&c. निमग्न-गर्क-&c. करणें.

ASTONISHED, ASTOUNDED. *p.* v. V. चकवललो, &c. थक्क, थक्कित *or* थक्कीत, थकित, चकित, चक्क, चकभूल, चरख, दंग, सचकित, विस्मित, चमत्कृत, विस्मयान्वित, सविस्मय, विस्मयापन्न, आश्चर्ययुक्त, साश्चर्य, विस्मापित.

ASTONISHING, *p. a.* v. V. *and* WONDERFUL. विस्मयकारक, विस्मयजनक, आश्चर्यकारक, चमत्कारिक, चमत्कारी, विस्मापक.

ASTONISHING, *n.* v. V.—*act.* चकवणें *n.* चोजवणें *n.* &c. विस्मापन *n.*

ASTONISHMENT, *n.* v. V. *and* WONDER.—*state.* विस्मय *m.* चकभूल *f.* अचंबा *m.* आश्चर्य *n.*

ASTRADDLE, ASTRIDE, *adv. with the legs across.* घोडेबसणीं, दोहोबाजूस पाय ठेवून, दोनीकडे पाय टाकून, यथोभयपार्श्वपाद.

ASTRAL, *a.* v. STARRY. तारांचा, तारासंबंधी.

ASTRAY, *adv.* वाटचुकून, वाटभुलून, गलत, गप्प, रानांत, आडरानांत, गैरबिल्हेस.
To go a. बहकणें, पाऊल *n.* वांकडें पडणें *g. of s.*
To lead a. बहकावणें.

To ASTRICT, *To* ASTRINGE, *v. a. constrict, cause parts to draw together.* आवळणें, संकुचित करणें.

ASTRINGENCY, *n.* v. A. तुरटाई *f.* तुरटपणा *m.* राप *or* रांप *m.* कषाय *mn.* तुवर *mn.*

ASTRINGENT, *a.* तुरट, ग्राही, कषाय, कषायान्वित, तुवर.

ASTROLOGER, *n. astronomer.* ज्योतिषी *pop.* जोशी *m.* गणक.
2 *or* ASTROMANCER. प्रश्नज्योतिषी *pop.* जोशी *m.* मुहूर्त्या *m.* मौहूर्त्त *m.* फलग्रंथ्या जोशी *m.* नक्षत्रसूचक, नक्षत्रसूची, भसूचक, भसूची, दैवज्ञ.

ASTROLOGICAL, *a.* v. N. प्रश्नज्योतिषाचा, मुहूर्त्तज्योतिषाचा, ज्योतिष, ज्योतिषसंबंधी, नक्षत्रफलगणनविद्यासंबंधी-विषयक.

ASTROLOGICALLY, *adv.* प्रश्नज्योतिषाच्यारीतीनें, &c. मुहूर्त्तज्योतिषानुसार.

ASTROLOGY, *n.* प्रश्नज्योतिष *n.* मुहूर्त्तज्योतिष *n.* फलज्योतिष *n.* उपश्रुति *f.* नक्षत्रफलगणनविद्या *f.*

ASTRONOMER, *n.* ज्योतिषी *pop.* जोशी *m.* खगोलवेत्ता, खगोलवि- [द्यावेत्ता.

ASTRONOMICAL, *a.* ज्योतिषाचा, ज्योतिषसंबंधी-विषयक, ज्योतिष, गणितानुगत.

ASTRONOMICALLY, *adv.* ज्योतिःशास्त्राप्रमाणें.

ASTRONOMY, ज्योतिष *n.* ज्योतिर्विद्या *f.* ज्योतिःशास्त्र *n.* खगोल *m.* खगोलविद्या *f.* नक्षत्रविद्या *f.* केरली *f.*

The *astronomical periods* called *Karana* are, बव, बालव, कौलव, तैतिल, गर, वणिज, भद्रा, शकुनि, चतुरंघ्रि, नाग, किंस्तुघ्न.
The *astronomical divisions* called *Yoga* are, विष्कंभ, प्रीति, आयुष्मान्, सौभाग्य, शोभन, अतिगंड, सुकर्मा, धृति, शूल, गंड, वृद्धि, ध्रुव, व्याघात, हर्षण, वज्र, सिद्धि, व्यतीपात, वरीयान्, परिघ, शिव, सिद्ध, साध्य, शुभ, शुक्र, ब्रह्मा, ऐंद्र, वैधृति.

ASTUTE, *a. shrewd.* शाहणा, अक्कलवंत,अक्कलवान्, अकलबाज, धूर्त.

ASTUTELY, *adv.* v. A. शाहणपणानें, धूर्त्ताईनें.

ASTUTENESS, *n.* v. A. शाहणपण *n.* धूर्त्ताई *f.* धूर्त्तावा *m.*

ASUNDER, *adv. apart*, v. SEPARATELY. अलग, अलगत, वेगळा, पृथक्.
To fall a. सुटून पडणें, सुटणें.

ASYLUM, *n. refuge, shelter, retreat.* आश्रय *pop.* आसरा*m.* थार*m.* थारा *m.* ठाव*m.* मायपोट *n.* माहेर*n.* महालय *n.* शरणस्थान*n.*
2 (for the poor and helpless) धर्मशाळ *f.* धर्मशाळा, अनाथाश्रय *m.*

AT, *prep.* स *or* शीं *or* ला *or* ई (*added to the noun*). पाशीं, जवळ, प्रत, लागीं, कडे.
For phrases of which it forms a part (at first, at last, at least, &c. &c.) see the word to which it is prefixed.

ATABAL, *n. kind of kettle drum.* तबला*m.*

ATARAXIA, *n.* v. QUIETISM. अक्षोभ *m.* शम *m.* शांति *f.*

ATHEISM, *n. denial of the existence of god.* नास्तिकमत *n.* नास्तिक्य *n.* नास्तिकत्व *n.* नास्तिकता *f.* अनीश्वरवाद *m.* अनीश्वरमत *n.* अनीश्वरभाव *m.*

ATHEIST, *n.* नास्तिक *m.* अनीश्वरवादी, नास्तिकमतानुयायी.

ATHEISTICAL, *a.* नास्तिकमताचा, नास्तिकमतानुयायी, नास्तिकमतानुसारी.

ATHIRST, *a.* v. THIRSTY. तान्हेला.

ATHLETE, *n. agonist, prize-contender, wrestler, &c.* पहिलवान *m.* मल्ल *m.* जेठी *m.* तालिमबाज, मल्लयोद्धा *m.* मल्लक्रीडक *m.*
Business or skill of the pahilwàn. पहिलवानकी *f.*
Contests or feats of athletæ. मल्लयुद्ध *n.* मल्लक्रीडा *f.* व्यायाम *m.*
Training of athletæ. तालीम *f.*

ATHLETIC, *a.* v. GYMNASTIC. पहिलवानाचा, मल्लक्रीडाविषयक, मल्लक्रीडासंबंधी. [जोमदार.
2 *robust, lusty*, v. STRONG. जोधा, जोरकस, कट्टा, धट्टाकट्टा,

ATHWART, *prep.* v. ACROSS. आड, आडवा *a. decl.*

A-TILT, *adv. inclining forward.* पुढें कलता-झोंकता *a. decl.*

ATLAS, *n. collection of maps.* नकाशांचीवही *f.* देशालेख्यमाला *f.*

ATMOSPHERE, *n. the air which encompasses the earth.* आकाश *n.* वायुचक्र *n.* घनाश्रय *m.* मेघमंडल *or* ळ *n.* वातावरण *n.* वाय्वावरण *n.* वाय्वास्पद *n.*

ATMOSPHERIC, ATMOSPHERICAL, *a.* v. N. वायुचक्राचा, आकाशाचा, आकाशीय, आकाशी, वायुचक्रसंबंधी, वातावरणसंबंधी.

ATOM, *n. indivisible particle.* अणु *m.* परमाणु *m.* सूक्ष्म *m.* कण *m.*
2 *fig. minute thing.* कणिका *f.* अतिसूक्ष्मपदार्थ *m.*-विषय *m.* लव *m.* लेश *n.*

ATOMIC, ATOMICAL, *a. consisting of atoms.* परमाणुनिर्मित, परमाणुरूप, परमाणुमय, परमाणूचा, अतिसूक्ष्म, सूक्ष्म.

ATOMISM, *n. doctrine of atoms.* परमाणुवाद *m.* सूक्ष्मवाद *m.*

ATOMIST, *n. holder of the atomical philosophy.* परमाणुवादी *m.* सूक्ष्मवादी *m.*

To **ATONE**, *v. n. make amends or satisfaction for a crime.* प्रायश्चित्त *n.* करणें-घेणें, प्रायश्चित्त-&c. करून-घेऊन घालवणें-निरपणें-निपटणें-निस्तारणें, पापनिष्कृति *f.*-निरसन *n.*-&c. करणें.

ATONEMENT, *n.* v.V.—*act.* प्रायश्चित्त करून घालवणें *n.* निरपणें *n.* &c. प्रायश्चित्त *n.* पापनिष्कृति *f.* पापनिरसन *n.*
I. See RECONCILIATION.

ATONIC, *a. debilitated.* धातुक्षीण.

ATONY, *n. debility.* धातुक्षीणता *f.*

ATOP, *adv. on the top.* वर, वरतीं.

ATRABILARIAN, ATRABILARIOUS, *a.* v. MELANCHOLY. रुग्णपित्ती, उदास, विषण्ण. [कज्जलवर्ण.

ATRAMENTAL, ATRAMENTOUS, *a.* v. BLACK. शाईसारखाकाळा,

ATROCIOUS, *a. heinous, horrible, enormous*, v. WICKED. अकटोविकट, उग्र, घोर, महापातकाचा, महापातकी, अतिदुष्ट, महापापरूप, महापापात्मक, राक्षसी, आसुर, तामस, भीमकर्मा, घोरकर्मा.

ATROCIOUSLY, *adv.* v. A. उग्रपणानें, घोरपणानें, महापापपूर्वक, अतिदुराचरणपूर्वक.

ATROCIOUSNESS, ATROCITY, *n.* v. A. घोरपणा *m.* उग्रता *f.* अतिदुष्टता *f.* दुष्कर्मता *f.* [पातक*n.*
I. *an atrocity, an enormity*, &c. महापाप, *n.* घोरकर्म *n.* महा-

ATROPHY, *n.* v. CONSUMPTION. किरी *f.* झिजणी *f.* झिरकणी *f.* सुसवशी *f.* सुकारोग *m.* क्षरण *n.*

To **ATTACH**, *v. a. seize by writ, &c.*—goods, &c. जप्त करणें, टांच *f.* मारणें-लावणें.
2 *fix one's affections to.* मन *n*-प्रीति *f.*-स्नेह *m.*-&c. जडवणें -जोडणें-लावणें-बळवणें, आसक्त-सक्त-अनुरक्त-&c. करणें.
3 *put to, annex, &c.* v. To ADD. जोडणें, लावणें, संयोग *m.*-संबंध *m.* करणें.
4 *fig. affix, apply.* लावणें, आरोपणें,आरोप*m.*-आरोपण*n.*करणें.

ATTACHED, *p.* v. V. 1. जप्त केलेला, टांच मारलेला-लावलेला, जप्त.
2 *fond of*, v. LOVING, स्नेही, अनुरत, निरत, अनुरक्त, अनुरागी, रक्त, रत, लग्न, अनुगत, परायण, पर, आसक्त, सक्त, संसक्त.
3 जोडलेला, जडींव, युक्त, संयुक्त, संयुत, संबद्ध, लग्न, संलग्न, संहित, अनुषंगी.
4 आरोपलेला, आरोपित.

ATTACHMENT, *n.* v. V. A. 1. जप्ती *f.* टांच *f.*
2 *fondness, affection*, v. LOVE. स्नेह *m.* निष्ठा *f.* अनुराग *m.* अनुरक्ति *f.* अनुरति *f.* अनुशीलन *n.* आसक्ति *f.* संसक्ति *f.*
Affected a. भावाभास *m.*

To **ATTACK**, *v. a. assail, assault.* चढ *m.*-चढाई *f.* करणें *or* चढून-जाणें, चाल *f.* करणें *or* चालून जाणें *with* वर *of o.* घाला *m.* घालणें, हल्ला *m.* करणें, उचल *f.* करणें, आंगावर येणें-जाणें-पडणें-तुटून पडणें *g. of o.* मारणें, घसरणें *with* वर *of o.* गळीं पडणें, उडणें *with* वर, उपटणें, तोंडीं *or* तोंडास लागणें.
To a. in front. अघाडी *f.* मारणें.
To a. insidiously, darkly, &c. गुप्तघाला *m.*-गुप्तमारा *or* गुप्तमार *m.*-मुकामारा *m.*-&c. करणें.
To make an a. upon. स्वारी *f.* करणें.
To a. suddenly. छप्पा *m.* छापा *m.* घालणें, झपाटा*m.* मारणें.
2 fig. *apply one's self to vehemently.* In this sense, and in the variations of it as conveyed by *To set to or upon*,

To fall to, upon, on, To rush or dash at, to, upon; some imitative or expressive formations are झुरावणें, झुरळणें, घेगावणें, मार *m.* मारणें-देणें, घेगा *m.*-घेमार *or* घेघेमार *m.*-घेघे *f.*-हल्ला *m.*-एलगार *m.*-&c. करणें, पडणें, लागणें, जुडणें, घसरणें, घसरा *m.* करणें, झोड *f.*-मार*m.* पडणें *with* वर *of o. & g. of s.* झटणें, लगट *mf.* करणें, उठावणें, उठावणी *f.* करणें, झडझडणें.

ATTACK, ATTACKING, *n.* v. V.1.—*act.* चाल करणें *n.* घाला घालणें *n.* &c. चढ *m.* चढाई *f.* चढाव *m* चाल *f.* घाला *m.* हल्ला *m.* धाड *f.* घाल *f.* मार *m.* उचल *f.* आक्रम *m.* आक्रमण *n.* अधिक्रम *m.* अधिक्रमण *n.* कहात *f.*

A. of a band of robbers. दरवडा *m.*

Sudden a. a coup de main. छप्पा *m.*छाप *m.* छापा *m.*

To ATTAIN, *v. a. obtain, gain, acquire,* v. To GET. संपादणें, मिळवणें, प्राप्त-लब्ध-&c. करणें- करून घेणें, संपादन *n.*-&c. करणें *g. of o.*

2 *arrive at, come to,* v. To REACH. पावणें, पोहोंचणें,प्राप्त होणें.

3 *achieve,* v. To ACCOMPLISH. संपादणें, साधणें.

ATTAINABLE, *a.* v. V. 1. मिळावया-चा-जोगा-सारखा-&c. प्राप्य, प्राप्तव्य, प्रापणीय, लभ्य.

2 *and* ACCESSIBLE. गम्य,गमनीय, आगम्य.

3 साध्य, संपादनीय, गम्य, गमनीय, अधिगम्य, अधिगमनीय, अधिगंतव्य, आक्रमणीय.

ATTAINDER, *n.* v. V. दूषित करणें *n.* दूषण *n.*

Act of a. दूषित करण्याचा आक्त *m.*-कायदा *m.*

ATTAINMENT, *n.* v. V. 1.—*act.* संपादणें *n.* &c. संपादन *n.* संपादणी *f.* संपादणूक *f.*—*state.* प्राप्ति *f.* संप्राप्ति *f.* आपत्ति *f* संपत्ति *f.* लब्धि *f.* उपलब्धि *f.*

Difficult of a. दुर्लभ, दुष्प्राप *or* दुःप्राप.

Easy of a. सुलभ, सुप्राप, सुखप्राप.

3—*act.* संपादणें *n.* साधणें *n.* संपादन *n.* संपादणी *f.* संपादणूक *f.* साधन *n.* अधिगम *m.*

I. *that which is attained.*लाभ *m.* लब्ध द्रव्य *n.*-विषय *m.*-&c.

Attainments. संपादितगुण *m. pl.*

To ATTAINT, *v.a. corrupt, taint.* दूषणें, दूषण *n.* करणें *g. of o.* दूषित-कलंकित-&c. करणें.

To ATTEMPER, ATTEMPERATE, *v. a. moderate, reduce unto,* v. To TEMPER. नरम-हलका-सुमाराचा-माफक-बेताचा-परिमित-&c. करणें.

To ATTEMPT, *v. n. try, endeavour to do.* लाग *m.*-प्रयत्न *m.*-यत्न *m.*-उद्योग *m.*-उपाय *m.*-उपचार *m.* करणें-चालवणें *or* करून-चालवून पाहणें, अजमावणें, परीक्षा *f.* करून पाहणें.

ATTEMPT, ATTEMPTING, *n.* v. V.—*act. essay, trial, endeavour.* लाग *m.* यत्न *m.* प्रयत्न *m.* उपचार *m.* उद्योग *m.*

To ATTEND, *v. n. & v. a. yield attention, hearken, listen, mind, heed.* मन *n.*-चित्त *n.*-अवधान *n.*-ध्यान *n.*-लक्ष्य *n.*-दृष्टि *f.* घालणें-देणें-पुरविणें-ठेवणें-राखणें, जपणें, जागणें, ऐकणें, कान *m.* देणें, विचारणें.

To a. vigilantly, warily, &c. डोळ्यांत तेल घालून जपणें.

2 at; *be present.* हाजीर राहणें, जवळ-समीप असणें.

3 on *or* upon; *wait on; serve,* v. To SERVE. सेवणें, सेवा *f.*-चाकरी *f.*-खिदमत *f.*-शुश्रूषा *f.*-अनुगमन *n.*-&c. करणें *g. of o.*

N. B. Such sentences as "He has a cold attended with fever," "A measure attended with ill effects," &c. are best rendered in some such way as the following. त्याला पडसें आलें आणि पडशामुळें तापही आला. ह्या गोष्टीपासून अनेक वाईट परिणाम झाले.

ATTENDANCE, ATTENDING, *n.* v. V. 1. *and* ATTENTION. लक्ष्य-देणें *n.* &c. अवधान *n.* ध्यान *n.*

2 हाजीर राहणें *n.* जवळ असणें *n.* हाजिरी *f.*

3 *and* SERVICE. चाकरी *f.* खिदमत *f.* सेवा *f.* सेवन *n.* परिचर्या *f.* शुश्रूषा *f.* अनुवर्त्तन *n.* अनुवृत्ति *f.*

Close a. खडीचाकरी *f.*

ATTENDANT, *a.* See ACCOMPANYING.

ATTENDANT, *n. follower, retainer, &c.* v. SERVANT. हुजऱ्या *m.* सैरिंध्र *m.* (सैरिंध्री *f.*) अनुगामी, जिलीबदार *m.* अनुचर, अनुचारी, अनुवर्त्ती, अनुग, परिचारक *m.* (परिचारिका *f.*) परिचर *m.* पार्श्वक *m.*

Armed a. शिपायी *m.*

Body of mounted attendants. सवारी *f.*

ATTENT, ATTENTIVE, *a.* v. V. 1. एकचित्त, सावध, सावधान, सावचित्त, सुचित्त, जागा, जागृत, तत्पर, सादर, एकाग्र, एकाग्रचित्त, एकतान, एकाकार, दत्तावधान, दत्तलक्ष्य, दत्तचित्त, अवहित.

ATTENTION, *n.* v. V. 1.—*act.* लक्ष्य देणें *n.* चित्त देणें *n.* लक्ष्य घालणें *n.* &c. अवधान *n.* लक्ष्य *n.* लक्ष *n.* संधान *n.* ध्यान *n.* दृष्टि *f.* एकचित्त *n.* भान *n.* लय *n.* मनोयोग *m.* अवेक्षण *n.* अवेक्षा *f.*

I. Attentions, v. CIVILITIES. आदरमान *m.* आदरसत्कार *m.* आदरउपचार *mpl.* तवाजू *f.* उजूतवाजू *f.* तारतीम*n.* समाचार*m.*

ATTENTIVELY, *adv.* v. A. एकचित्तानें, लक्ष्य-मन-ध्यान-&c. लावून-घालून-देऊन, कान देऊन, एकटक.

ATTENTIVENESS, *n.* v.A. सावधपणा *m.* सावधगिरी *f.* सावचित्तपणा *m.*अवधान *n.* सावधानता *f.* एकचित्तता *f.* एकाग्रता *f.*

ATTENUANT, *a.*—in medicine. कर्शन, कृशकारक.

To ATTENUATE *v. a. to make thin.* बारीक करणें, कृशकरणें, पातळ करणें. [कृशीकृत.

ATTENUATE, *a.* ATTENUATED, *p.* v. V. बारीक-कृश-पातळ केलेला,

ATTENUATION, *n.* v. V.—*act.* पातळ-&c. करणें *n.* कृशीकरण *n.*

To ATTERATE, See To WEAR AWAY.

To ATTEST, *v. a. bear witness of.* साक्ष *f.*-साक्षी *f.*-साक्ष्य *n.*-शाहिदी *f.* देणें-घालणें *g. of o.* साक्षी-शाहिदीदार-&c. होणें *with* विषयीं *of o.*

2 *call to witness, attest.* साक्षी ठेवणें, साक्षीस ठेवणें.

3 (a writing &c.) खरेपणाविषयीं सही *f.* घालणें-करणें.

An attested copy. सही निशीची नकल *f.*-प्रत *f.*

ATTESTATION, *n.* v. V. 1. *and* EVIDENCE,—*act.* साक्षी&c.देणें*n.* साक्षी *f.* साक्ष *f.*

ATTIC, ATTICSTORY, *n.* अगदीं वरचा मजला *m.* सातवा मजला *m.*

ATTIRE, *n.* v. DRESS, CLOTHES. वेष *m.* पोशाक *or* ग *m.* लिभास *m.*

To ATTIRE, *v. a.* v. To DRESS. वस्त्र *n.*-वस्त्रें *n. pl.* नेसवणें, पोशाक *m.* घालणें, सजवणें, वेषान्वित-वेषयुक्त करणें, लेणें, सज्ज-सज्जित-&c. करणें, सज्जना *f.* करणें *g. of o.*

ATTITUDE, *n.* v. POSTURE. आसन *n.* अंगस्थिति *f.* ठाण *n.* ठाणमाण *n.*मुद्रा *f.*

ATTORNEY, *n. person empowered to act for another.* वकील *m.* प्रतिनिधि *m.* मुखत्यार *m.*

Letter of a. वकीलनामा *m.* मुखत्यारपत्र *n.*

To ATTRACT, *v. a. draw towards.* आकर्षणें, आपल्याकडे ओढणें-

ओढून घेणें, आक्षेपणें, आकर्षण *n.*-आक्षेप *m.* करणें *g. of o.*

2 *allure, invite,engage.* आकर्षणें, लोभवणें, मोहणें, आक्षेपणें, प्रलोभन *n.*-मोहन *n.*-&c. करणें *g. of o.* मोह *m.* घालणें, प्रलोभित-&c.करणें.

ATTRACTED, *p.* v. V. 1. आकर्षलेला, ओढून घेतलेला, &c. आकर्षित, आकृष्ट.

2 लोभवलेला, &c. प्रलोभित, मोहित.

ATTRACTER, *n.* ATTRACTIVE, *a.* v. V. 1. आकर्षणारा, आकर्षक, आकर्षिक, आकर्षी, आकर्षणकर्त्ता.

2 *and* CHARMING. मोहणारा, मोह घालणारा, &c. प्रलोभक, लोभजनक, मोहक, प्रलोभन कर्त्ता-&c.

ATTRACTION, *n.* v. V. 1.—*act.* आकर्षणें *n.* &c. आकर्षण *n.* आक्षेप *m.* अनुकर्ष *m.*

2—*act.* लोभवणें *n.* &c. प्रलोभन *n.* मोहन *n.*

The attractions and allurements (of the world, &c.) ओढ *f.* ओढा *m.*

I.—the power or quality. आकर्षणशक्ति *f.* आकर्षण *n.*

A. of gravitation. गुरुत्वाकर्षण *n.*

Capillary a. केशाकर्षण *n.* [णm. *pl.*

Attractions, *charms.* मोहक-प्रलोभक-आकर्षक-&c. गु-

ATTRIBUTABLE, *a.* v. V. आरोप्य, अरोपणीय.

To ATTRIBUTE, *v. a. assign; impute,* v. To ASCRIBE. ठेवणें, लावणें, घालणें, आरोपणें.

ATTRIBUTE, गुण *m.* धर्म *m.*

The *Divine attributes,* (i. e. the *attributes* of *Shiwa* as the Deity) are अणिमा, महिमा, गरिमा, लघिमा, प्राप्ति, ईशता, वशिता, प्राकाम्य. They are called अष्टसिद्धि.

ATTRIBUTION, *n.* v. V.—*act.* लावणें *n.* आरोपणें *n.* &c. आरोपण *n.* आरोप *m.*

ATTRIBUTIVE, *a.* विशेषण, वाच्य.

ATTRIBUTIVE, *n.* विशेषण *n.*

ATTRITE, *a. worn by friction.* झिजलेला, संघर्षित.

ATTRITION, *n. abrasion,* v. RUBBING, WEAR. झिजणें *n.* घासणें *n.* संहर्ष *m.* संघर्ष *m.* संघर्षण *n.*

Waste by a. झीज *f.* झिजणावळ *f.* घस *f.*

To waste from a. झिजणें.

To ATTUNE, *v. a. make musical, tune.* लावणें, सूर *m.* लावणें-बांधणें-मिळवणें, स्वरबंधन *n.* करणें.

2 *fig. make accordant.* मेळ *m.*-जम *m.*-&c. बसवणें, जमवणें.

AUBURN, *a. reddish brown,* सोनसळा, पिंगट, पिंगळा, पिंगा.

Bright a. गोराभुरका.

AUCTION, *n.* निलाम *n.* लिलाम *or* लिलांव *n.* पावणी *f.*

AUCTIONEER, *n.* लिलामवाला *m.* लिलांवकरणारा *m.* [नू.

AUDACIOUS, *a. daring,* v. BOLD. निधड, निधडा, धीट, धारिष्टवा-

2 v. IMPUDENT. धीट, उद्धत *pop.* उद्धट, धृष्ट.

3 *proceeding from effrontery.* धिटाईचा, उद्धटपणाचा.

AUDACIOUSNESS, AUDACITY, *n.* v. V. 1. धिटाई *f.* धारिष्ट *n.*

2 धिटाई *f.* धार्ष्ट्य *n.* औद्धत्य *n.* उद्धटपण *n.*

AUDIBLE, *a. perceivable by the ear.* ऐकूं याया-जाया-चा-जोगता-जोगा-&c. श्रोतव्य, श्राव्य, श्रवणगोचर, कर्णगोचर.

2 *loud enough to be heard.* ऐकूं येण्या-जाण्याजोगा-जोगता-सारखा-&c. ऐकूंयेईसा, ऐकूंजाईसा.

AUDIBLENESS, *n.* v. A. 2. ऐकू येण्या-जाण्याजोगेपणा *m.* &c.

AUDIBLY, *adv.* v. A. ऐकेसा *adv. decl.* ऐकूं येईसा *adv. decl.* ऐकूं जाईसा *adv. decl.* कानीं पडेसा *adv. decl.*

AUDIENCE, *n. hearing or attending to.* ऐकणें *n.* ऐकून घेणें *n.* श्रवण *n.* आकर्णन *n.*

2 *admittance to a hearing.* सुनावणीची भेट *f.* कानावर घालण्यासाठीं भेट *f.*-मुलाखत *f.* श्रवणार्थकदर्शन *n.*

3 *assembly of hearers, auditory.* श्रोते *m.pl.* श्रोतृमंडलn.श्रोतेमंडळी *f.* श्रोतृसमूह *m.* श्रोतृसमाज *m.* श्रोतृजन *m.pl.*श्रोतृगण *m.*

AUDIENCE-CHAMBER, *n.* सुनावणीची जागा *f.* श्रवणमंदिर *n.* दिवाणखाना *m.*

AUDIT, *n. final account.* शेवटचा तपास *m.* शेवटची तपासणी *f.*

To AUDIT, *v. a. examine and pass.* तपास *or* तपासणी करून-रुजूपाहून-&c. बार करणें.

AUDITED, *p.* v. V. तपासणी होऊन बार झालेला, रुजू, बार, रुकार.

AUDITOR, *n.* v. V. हिशोब तपासून बार करणारा *m.* हिशोबाचा तपासनीस *m.* तजकरनीस *m.*

I. v. HEARER. ऐकणारा, ऐकता, श्रोता, श्रवणकर्त्ता.

AUDITORY, *a. belonging to hearing.* श्रवणाचा, श्रवणसंबंधी, श्रावण, श्रवणेंद्रियाचा, श्रुतिविषयक, श्रुतिसंबंधी.

Outer a. passage. कर्णछिद्र *n.* [तृसमूह *m.*

AUDITORY, *n.* v. AUDIENCE. श्रोतृमंडल *n. pop.* श्रोतेमंडळी *f.* श्रो-

2 v. LECTURE-ROOM. पाठ सांगण्याची जागा *f.* पाठशाला *f.* व्याख्यानशाला *f.*

AUFAIT, That is a. वस्ताद.

AUGER, AUGRE, *n.* सामता *m.* वेधन *n.* बरमा *m.* खोलबत *n.* सळई *f.*

AUGHT, *pro.* कांहीं, किंचित्.

AUGMENT, *n.*—*in grammar.* आगम *m.* आप्तोक्ति *f.*

To AUGMENT, AUGMENTATION. See To INCREASE, &c.

AUGUR, *n.* शकुन्या *or* शकुन्याजोशी *m.* शकुनवक्ता, प्रश्नवक्ता, शकुनप्रश्न सांगणारा-पाहणारा.

To AUGUR, *v. a. presage, betoken.* सुचवणें, दर्शिवणें, सूचन *n.*-प्रदर्शन *n.*-&c. करणें *g. of o.* लक्षण *n.*-चिन्ह *n.* असणें *g. of o. with in. con.*

To AUGUR, *v. n. gather or infer from omens, &c.* शकुनावरून समजणें-तर्क *m.* करणें-अनुमान *n.* करणें, शकुनगांठ *f.* बांधणें.

AUGURAL, AUGURIAL, *a.* शकुनाचा, प्रश्नाचा, शाकुनिक, प्राश्निक, शकुनसंबंधी-विषयक.

AUGURATION, AUGURY, *n.* v. V. N. शकुनावरून समजणें *n.*-तर्क करणें *n.*-अनुमान करणें *n.* &c. शाकुनिक *n.* शकुनविद्या *f.* प्रश्नविद्या *f.*

2 See OMEN.

AUGUST, *a.* v. GRAND. प्रतापान्वित, प्रतापशाली, प्रभावविशिष्ट-युक्त, प्रभावशाली.

AUGUST, *n.* इंग्रेजी सालाचा आठवा महिना *m.* श्रावण—भाद्रपद *m.*

AUGUSTNESS, *n.* v.A. प्रताप *m.*प्रभाव *m.*प्रतापवत्ता *f.* प्रतापशालिता *f.*

AUNT, *n. father's sister.* आत *f.* मावळण *f.* फुई *f.* फुइजी *f.* पितृभगिनी *f.*

Daughter of paternal a. मेहुणी *f.*

Son of husband's paternal a. आतेदीर *m.*

2 *mother's sister.* मावसी *f.* मातृभगिनी *f.*

3 *wife of paternal uncle.* चुलती *f.* काकी *f.* काकू *f.* पितृव्यपत्नी *f.*

4 *wife of maternal uncle.* मामी *f.* मावळण *f.* मातुलानी *f.*

Husband of mat. a. मावसा *m.*

Aureola, *n. circle of rays.* तेजोमंडल *n.*

Auricle, *n. external ear.* बाहेरचा कान *m.* बाहेरील कान *m.* कर्णशष्कुली *f.*

2 रक्ताशयाचा एक अवयव आहे.

Auricular, *a. relating, &c. to the ear.* कानाचा, कर्णसंबंधी, कर्णविषयक, कर्णगोचर, कार्ण, श्रवणेंद्रियाचा.

2 *told in the ear.* कानीं सांगितलेला, कर्णजप्त, कर्णोपदिष्ट.

3 v. Traditional. कानोकानीं आलेला, कर्णपरंपरागत, कर्णोपकर्णीचा.

Auriculate, Auriform, *a. ear-shaped.* कानाच्या आकाराचा, कर्णरूप, कर्णरूपी.

Auriferous, *a. gold producing.* सुवर्णप्रसव (*f.* वा).

Aurist, *n.* कर्णवैद्य *m.* कर्णरोगवैद्य *m.*

Aurora, *n.* v. Morning. अरुण *m.*

Auspice, *n. presage. augury,* v. Omen. शकुन *m n.*

Of evil a. अभद्र.

2 auspices; *protection, &c.* v. Favor. कृपादृष्टि *f.* नेक नजर *f.* हिमाईत *f.* प्रसाद *m.* आश्रयबल *n.*

Auspicious, *a. of prospering influence, propitious, benign, favorable,* शुभ, मंगल, शुभंकर, श्रेयस्कर, जयावह, शुभावह, भद्रकर, भद्रक, यशस्वी, सभाग्य, यशस्कर, मंगलदायक, मांगलिक, शंकर, अनुकूल, कल्याणी, इष्ट.

A. season or period. सुबत्ताकाळ *m.*

To be a. (for). लाभणें, लाधणें.

2 *having omens of success.* सुशकुनाचा, शुभप्रश्नाचा, सुलक्षणाचा, शुभ, मंगल, सुलक्षणविशिष्ट-युक्त, सुलक्षणसंपन्न.

Auspiciously, *adv.* v. A. 2. सुशकुनपूर्वक, सुचिन्हपूर्वक, सुलक्षणपूर्वक.

Auspiciousness, *n.* v. A. 1. शुभता *f.* मंगलता *f.* श्रेय *n.* कल्याण *n.* सद्दी *f.* सभाग्यता *f.* भाग्यशालित्व *n.* सलाबतपणा *m.*

2 शुभ *n.* सुलक्षणविशिष्टता *f.*

Austere, *a. harsh, &c. of taste,* v. Sour. रूक्ष *pop.* रुखा, खट्टा *or* खट्ट्या, परुष.

2 *rigid, rigorous, severe, stern.* खरमरा, खरमऱ्या, करडा, कडवा, कठीण, कठोर, सख्त, निष्ठुर, कर्कश, परुष.

Austerity, *n.* v. A. 1. रुखेपणा *m.* रौक्ष्य *n.* रूक्षता *f.* नैस्नेह्य *n.* पारुष्य *n.*

2 करडेपणा *m.* खरमरेपणा *m.* पारुष्य *n.*

I.—in Religion. तप *n.* तपश्चर्या *f.* तपस्या *f.* तपश्चरण *pop.* तपाचरण *n.*

Austerities and penances,—compreh. उपासतापास *m.* तपबीप *or* तपगीप *n.*

Some of the numerous *austerities* of the Hindus are उंच्छवृत्ति *or* शिलोंच्छवृत्ति, ऊर्ध्वबाहु, एकान्न (& एकधान्य, एकभक्त *or* एकभुक्त *or* कि, एकव्रत) करतलभिक्षा, कुंभक, कृच्छ्र, चांद्रायण, धूम्रपान, पंचाग्नि, प्राजापत्य, बगाड, लोटांगण, सांतपन, सौम्यकृच्छ्र.

Emaciated by a. तपःकृश.

Power acquired through a. तपःसामर्थ्य *n.* तपोबल *n.*

Practice of a. योगाभ्यास *m.* तपस्समाधि *m.*

Austral, Austrine, *a.* v. Southern. दक्षिणेचा, दक्षिणेकडचा.

Authentic, Authentical, *a. genuine, true.* खरा, सत्य, बित्तीम, तहकीक, असल, सप्रमाण, ठिकाणचा, कलमी, आप्त, मुळींचा, मुळचा, स्थलींचा, थेट, थेटचा.

Authenticalness, Authenticity, *n.* v. A. खरेपणा *m.* सत्यता *f.* असलपणा *m.* बित्तीमपणा *m.* सप्रमाणता *f.* आप्तता *f.* आप्तत्व *n.*

To **Authenticate**, *v. a. render authentic.* खरा-सत्य-तहकीक-साबीत-&c. करणें-करूनदेणें, प्रमाण करून देणें.

Author, *n. first mover, beginner, &c.* कर्ता *m.* मूळकर्ता *m.* जनक *m.* जनिता *m.* उत्पादक *m.* स्रष्टा *m.*

2 *composer of a book, &c.* ग्रंथकार *m.* ग्रंथकर्ता *m.* कर्ता *m.*

Authoress, *n.* ग्रंथकारिणी *f.* ग्रंथकर्त्री *f.*

Authoritative, *a. having due authority.* प्रमाणाचा, सप्रमाण, प्रमाणविशिष्ट-युक्त, आप्त, आर्ष, प्रामाणिक.

2 *imperative, commanding, &c.* दबदब्याचा, दाबाचा, दरदऱ्याचा, धनीपणाचे डौलाचा, स्वामीपणाचे डौलाचा, स्वामित्वसूचक.

Authoritatively, *adv.* v. A. 1. प्रमाणेंकरून, सप्रमाण, प्रमाणतः.

2 धनीपणाच्या डौलानें, दबदब्यानें, खरमरीत, दाबाचा *a. decl.*

Authoritativeness, *n.* v. A. 1. सप्रमाणता *f.* प्रामाणिकता *f.* आप्तता *f.* आप्तत्व *n.*

2 दाब *m.* दबदबा *m.* दबाव *m.* सलाबत *f.* सलाबतपणा *m.* प्रताप *m.* धनीपणाचा डौल *m.*

Authority, *n. warranted power,* v. Rule. अखत्यार *m.* सत्ता *f.* अधिकार *m.* हवाला *m.* जोरा *m.* दस्त *m.* ऐश्वर्य *n.*

Full a. मुखत्यारी *f.*

One invested with a. अधिकारी, अखत्यारी.

To be in a. over. डोईवर-उरावर असणें.

2 *grounds for credence, &c. warrant, sanction, support.* आधार *m.* आश्रय *m.* प्रमाण *n.* गमक *n.* मान *n.* प्रामाण्य *n.*

Of little a. अल्पप्रमाण, अल्पप्रमाणक.

3 *influence, credit, power,* v. Weight. चाल *f.* चलती *f.* चलचल *f.* गौरव *n.* कदर *f.* भारदारी *f.* भारदस्ती *f.* अनुभाव *m.*

4 *authoritative opinion or saying.* आप्तवचन *n.* आप्तवाक्य *n.* आप्तोक्ति *f.* अभियुक्तोक्ति *f.* अभियुक्तप्रयोग *m.* अभियुक्तवचन *n.*

That has a.— a writing, a writer, &c. आप्त, अभियुक्त.

5 *order, &c.* v. Warrant. सनद *f.* हुकूमनामा *m.* हुकूम *m.* अधिकार पत्र *n.*

6 *ruling person or body.* v. Government. सर्कार *n.* अधिकारी *m.*

Authorization, *n.* v. V. 1.—*act.* अधिकार-&c. देणें *n.*

2—*act.* विहित-&c.करणें *n.*

To **Authorize**, *v. a. give authority or right to.* मुखत्यारी *f.*-अखत्यार *m.*-अधिकार *m.*-सत्ता *f.*-हुकूम *m.*-&c. देणें, अखत्यारी-मुखत्यार-&c. करणें.

2 *establish by authority, make lawful.* हुकूम *m.*-आज्ञा *f.*-मोकळीक *f.*- &c. करणें-देणें *g. of o.* सत्तेचा-साधिकार-ससत्ताक-विहित-विधेय-प्रामाणिक-आचारिक-&c.करणें.

Authorized, *p.* v. V. 1. अखत्यार दिलेला, &c. मुखत्यार, अखत्यारी, प्राप्ताधिकार.

2 See Lawful.

Authorless, *a.* अकर्तृक, कर्तृहीन-विरहित-&c.

Autobiography, *n.* आत्मचरित्र *n.*

Autocrasy, *n. independent power.* स्वायत्ताधिपत्य *n.* स्वाधिपत्य *n.* मुखत्यारी *f.* अनन्याधीनाधिकार *m.* अपराधीनाधिकार *m.*

Autocrat, *n. an absolute ruler.* स्वायत्ताधिपति *m.* मुखत्यार राजा *m.* अनन्याधीनाधिकारी *m.*

Autocratic, Autocratical, *a.* स्वायत्ताधिपत्याचा, &c. स्वाय

स्वाधिपत्यसंबंधी, स्वायत्ताधिपत्यविषयक, स्वायत्त, स्वतंत्र.

AUTOGRAPH, *n. a person's own hand writing.* स्वदस्तूर कागद *m.*-स्तन *n.*-पत्र *n.*-लेख *m.*-&c.स्वहस्ताक्षर *n.*

AUTOGRAPHIC, AUTOGRAPHICAL, *a.* v. N. स्वदस्तूरचा, स्वहस्ताक्षरचा, &c.

AUTOMATICAL, AUTOMATOUS, *a. having the power of moving itself.* स्वयंवह, आत्मचालक, स्वचेष्ट, आत्मचेष्ट.

AUTOMATON, *n. a self moving machine.* आपोआप चालणारें यंत्र *n.* स्वयंवह-आत्मचालक-स्वचेष्ट-&c. यन्त्र *n.*

AUTONOMY, *n. self government.* आत्मशासन *n.*

AUTUMN, *n.* शरत् *or* शरद *f.* शरत्काल *m.* शरदृतु, खरीफाची वेळ *f.*

AUTUMNAL, *a.* शरत्कालाचा, शरदृतूचा, शारद, शारदी, शारदीय, शरत्कालीन, शरत्कालिक, खरीफाचे वेळेचा.

The a. harvest खरीफ *or* खरीप *m.*

AUXILIAR, AUXILIARY, *a.* v. HELPING. कुमकेचा, सहाय, साहाय्यकारी-कर्त्ता-कारक, उपकर्त्ता, उपकारक.

A. verb—in grammar. सहायधातु *m.*

AUXILIARY, *n.* v. HELPER. मददगार *c.* सहकारी *m.* सहाय करणारा.

Auxiliaries. कुमकेस आलेली फौज *f.*

To AVAIL, *v. n. answer the purpose, be of use.* कामास-कामीं-उपयोगास-उपयोगीं पडणें-येणें, यश *n.* येणें *inv. con.* फळणें, साधणें, फलद्रूप- फलित-&c. होणें

To a. nothing. पोकळीखालीं *or* पोकळीस जाणें.

2 *be of use or advantage unto,* v. To ADVANTAGE. लाभणें, लाधणें, लाहणें, लाभ *m.* होणें.

AVAIL, *n. profit,* v. ADVANTAGE. फल *or* ळ *n.* फायदा *m.* उपयोग *m.*

AVAILABLE, AVAILING, *p. a.* v. V. 1. *efficacious, serviceable.* कामाचा, उपयोगाचा, उपयोगी, उपयोगीं-कामीं पडण्याजोगा-सारखा-&c. उपयुक्त, अमोघ, फलद्रूप, कार्योपकारक-कर्त्ता-कारी, कार्यसाधक.

2 *profitable, beneficial,* v. ADVANTAGEOUS. उपयोगाचा, लाभदायक-जनक, फलद, फलप्रद.

I. *in force,* v, VALID. चालू, चालता.

AVAILABLENESS, *n.* v. A. 1. उपयोग *m.* उपयोगीपणा *m.* उपयोगित्व *n.* उपयुक्तता *f.* कार्योपकारित्व *n.* कार्यसाधकत्व *n.*

AVALANCHE, *n. mass of snow or ice sliding.* डोंगरावरून घसरत येणारा बर्फाचा खडप *m.*-धोंड *f.*

AVANT COURIER, *n.*-पुढें पाठवलेला जासूद *m.* अग्रदूत *m.* पुरोदूत *m.*

AVANT GUARD, *n. vanguard.* बिनी *f.* आघाडीची फौज *f.*

AVARICE, *n.* v. COVETOUSNESS. धनलोभ *m.* द्रव्यलोभ *m.* धनाशा *f.* धनतृष्णा *f.* लालूच *f.* अर्थकाम *m.*

AVARICIOUS, *a.* v. N. *and* COVETOUS. लोभी, धनलोभी, द्रव्यलोभी, कृपण, कदर्य, कद्रू. [द्रव्या.

AVARICIOUSLY, *adv.* v. N. धनलोभानें, धनलोभपूर्वक, धनलोभबु-

AVARICIOUSNESS, *n.* v. A. धनलोभीपणा *m.* कृपणपणा *m.*

AVAST, *interj.* पुरे, पुरेकरा, हांहां.

AVAUNT, *interj.* दूरहो, चलजा, तोंड काळेंकर, हत्त.

To AVENGE, *v. a.* v. To REVENGE. सूड *m.*- द्वेष *m.*- वैर *n.*-उसणें *n.*- &c. उगवणें, सूड *m.* घेणें, प्रतिफल *n.* देणें.

AVENGEMENT, AVENGING, *n.* v. V.—*act.* सूडघेणें *n.* &c. अपराध प्रतीकार *m.* अपराधप्रतिक्रिया *f.*

AVENGER, *n.* v. V. सूड घेणारा-उगवणारा-&c. कैवारी.

A. of his people. भक्तकाजकैवारी.

AVENUE, *n. way of approach,* v. ENTRANCE. प्रवेशपथ *m.* प्रवेशमार्ग *m.* द्वार *pop.* दार *n.* दरवाजा *m.* [रस्ता *m.*

2 *road lined with trees.* दुरस्तां झाडीची वाट *f.* दुतर्फा झाडीचा

To AVER, AVERMENT, See To AFFIRM, &c.

AVERAGE, *n. mean proportion.* शेरा *m.* बसतन *or* बसतान *n.* मध्यप्रमाण *n.* सरासरी *f.* सरदाबरदी *f.*

In the a. On an a. सरासरी.

Average price or rate. एकंदर भाव *m.*

AVERAGE, *a.* v. MIDDLING. मध्यम.

To AVERAGE, *v. n.* सरासरीनें भरणें-निघणें-होणें.

AVERSE, *a. unpropitious to, turned from.* पाठमोरा, पराङ्मुख, विमुख, अप्रसन्न, प्रतिकूल.

2 *reluctant, backward, loath,* v. UNWILLING. माघार घेणाऱ्या मनाचा, विमुख, पराङ्मुख, पश्चान्मनस्क, विमनस्क, विमना, निवृत्तमनस्क, विमत, विमेधस.

AVERSENESS, AVERSION, *n.* v. A.1. पाठमोरेपणा *m.* पराङ्मुखता *f.* विमुखता *f.* प्रातिकूल्य *n.* प्रतिकूलता *f.*

2 *reluctance, dislike, loathing, &c.* नावड *f.* अनावड *f.* चिकारा *m.* चिणका *m.* चिणकारा *m.* चिळस *f.* रीस *f.* विरक्ति *f.* विमुखता *f.* विमति *f.* विमनस्कता *f.* विमेधा *f.*

I. *cause of dislike.* त्रास *m.*

To AVERT, *v. a. keep off, divert.* चुकवणें, निवारणें, वारणें, टाळणें, टळवणें, वहिवाटणें, टाळा *m.* देणें, निवारण *n.*-वारण *n.*-&c. करणें *g. of o.*

2 *turn from or away.* फिरवणें, काढणें, परतविणें, परावर्त्तन *n.* करणें *g. of o.*

AVERTED, *p.* v. V. 1. चुकवलेला, &c. निवारित, वारित, आवृत्त, परिहृत, परास्त.

2 फिरवलेला, काढलेला, परावृत्त.

AVERTER, *n.* v. V. 1. चुकवणारा, वारणारा, &c. निवारक, निवारणकर्त्ता.

AVERTIBLE, *a.* v. V. 1. चुकवाया-चा-जोगा-सारखा-&c.निवारणीय, निवार्य, परिहार्य.

AVIARY, *n.* पांखरांचा शिकारखाना *m.* पांखरखाना *m.* पक्षिशाला *f.* कुलायिका *f.*

AVIDITY, *n* v. GREEDINESS. अधाशीपणा *m.* खवखव *f* हवस *f.* नितांतलेपणा *m.* हांव *f.* सोस *m.*

2 v. EAGERNESS. हव्यास *m.* हावरेपणा *m.*

AVOCATION, *n. calling, employment,* v. BUSINESS. धंदा *m.* काम *n.* पेशा *m.*

To AVOID, *v. a. eschew, shun.* वर्जणें, वर्जकरणें, बगळणें *or* वेगळणें, टाकणें, निवडून टाकणें, फिरणें *with* पासून *of o.* अलग राहणें, दूर टाकणें, असेवन *n.*-अनाचरण *n.*-अस्वीकार *m.*-&c. करणें *g. of o.*

2 *shift off, escape, &c.* चुकविणें, टाळणें, झुकविणें, ढुकविणें.

AVOIDABLE, *a.* v. V. 1. वर्जकराया-चा-जोगा-&c. टाकाया-चा- जोगा-&c.

2. टाळाया-चा-जोगा-जोगता-सारखा-&c.

AVOIDANCE, AVOIDING, v. V. 1. *act.* बगळणें *n.* वर्जणें *n.* वर्ज करणें *n.* वर्जन *n.* असेवन *n.* अनाचरण *n.* अस्वीकार *m.*

2—*act.* टाळणें *n.* चुकवणें *n.* &c.

To AVOUCH, *v. a. assert, aver,* v. To AFFIRM. खचीतपणें-नि-

श्रयपूर्वक-प्रतिज्ञेनें-प्रतिज्ञापूर्वक-&c. बोलणें-म्हणणें.

To AVOW, *v. a. own, declare openly*, v. To ACKNOWLEDGE. अभिमानणें, कबूल करणें, अंगीकारणें, स्वीकारणें, आंगावर घेणें, अंगीकारपूर्वक सांगणें.

AVOWAL, AVOWING, *n.* v. V.—*act.* कबूल करणें *n.* &c. अंगीकार *m.* स्वीकार *m.*

AVOWED, *p.* v. V. कबूल केलेला, &c. अंगीकृत, स्वीकृत.

AVOWEDLY, *adv. with frank acknowledgement.* सांगून सवरून, हटकून.

AVOWER, *n.* v. V. अंगीकारणारा, स्वीकारणारा, &c. अंगीकारकर्त्ता, स्वीकारकर्त्ता.

To AWAIT, *v. a. wait for, look for, abide, expect.* वाट *f.* पाहणें *g. of o.* मार्ग *m.* लक्षिणें *g. of o.* प्रतीक्षणें, खोळंबणें, तिष्ठणें *with* साठीं &c. *of o.*

AWAITING, *n.* v. V.—*act.* वाट पाहणें *n.* &c. प्रतीक्षणें *n.* प्रतीक्षा *f.* मार्गप्रतीक्षा *f.*

To AWAKE, *To* AWAKEN, *v. a.* जागा-जागृत-&c. करणें, उठवणें, जागविणें, झोंपमोड *f.*-नीजमोड *f.* करणें *g. of o.* निद्राभंग*m.*-बोध *m.*-प्रबोध *m.*-बोधन *n.*-प्रबोधन *n.*-&c. करणें.

To AWAKE, *v. n.* जागा-जागृत-सावध-&c. होणें, हुशारणें, उठणें.

AWAKE, *a.* जागा, जागृत, सावध, हुशार, अनिद्रित, अनिद्र, विनिद्र, गतनिद्र, त्यक्तनिद्र, मुक्तनिद्र.

To be a. जागणें.

To be a. to. जागणें.

AWAKED, AWAKENED, *p.* v. V. जागा केलेला *or* झालेला, भग्ननिद्र, प्रबुद्ध, प्रबोधित.

AWAKENING, *a. rousing, exciting.* जागा-प्रबुद्ध-प्रबोधित-&c. करणारा, प्रबोधक.

AWAKING, AWAKENING, *n.* v. V.A.—*act.* जागा करणें*n.* निद्राभंग *m.* बोधन *n.* बोध *m.* प्रबोधन *n.* प्रबोध *m.*

To AWARD, *v. a. give by judicial determination.* फैसला करून-निवाडा करून-निर्णय करून-&c. देवविणें, चौकसी-मनसुबी-तपासणी-पंचाईत-&c. करून देवविणें.

AWARD, *n.* v. SENTENCE. निवाडा *m.* फैसल *m. f.* फैसला *m.* नीर *m.* निर्णय *m.*

Written a. निवाडपत्र *n.* निर्णयपत्र *n.* हुकूमनामा *m.* फैसलनामा *m.* महजर *m.*

AWARDED *p.* v. V. निवाडा करून देवविलेला, &c.

AWARE, *a. vigilant, attentive.* सावध, सावचित्त, सुचित्त, हुशार.

2 *apprized, made acquainted.* माहितगार-हुशार-वाकबदार-&c. झालेला, बोधित, प्राप्तबोध, जातबोध, प्रबुद्ध, प्रबोधित, विज्ञापित.

AWAY, *adv. in absence from.* गैरहजीर, परोक्ष, अप्रत्यक्ष, अन्यस्थानीं.

2 *from, on its way from.* The sense of this word as used with a verb is best expressed in Maráthí by the use of another verb, as निघून जाणें To go a. देऊन टाकणें To give a. टाकून देणें To throw a. पळून जाणें To run a.

To make a. with. वाट *f.* लावणें-करणें *g. of o.* गरक करणें, लांबविणें.

AWAY! AWAY WITH! *interj.* चल, चलनिघ, दूरहो.

AWE, *n. dread, reverence,* v. FEAR. दबदबा *m.* दाब *m.* दरदरा *m.* दरारा *m.* धास्त *or* स्ती *f.* दगदगा *m.* धाक *m.* वचक *m. v.* खा, बाळग, बाज *m.* चक *m.* हैबत *f.* जरब *f. v.* बस, दर्प *m.*

To lose one's a. of. भीड*f.* चेपणें-मरणें *g.of o.* जरब *f.* पिणें.

To stand in a. of, v. To FEAR. भिडावणें, वचकणें, जरब *f.* खाणें, जुमान *m.n.* खाणें, जुमानणें.

To AWE, *v. a.* दाब *m.*-दबदबा *m.*-दरारा *m.*-&c. बसवणें, धाक *m.* दाखवणें, भयप्रदर्शन *n.* करणें, जरब *f.* देणें-दाखविणें.

AWE-STRUCK, *a.* धाक &c. बसलेला, दरारलेला.

AWFUL, *a. that strikes with a.* धाकाचा, दराऱ्याचा, दरदऱ्याचा, जरबेचा, वचकाचा, वचक्याचा, इब्रतीचा, धाक घालायाचा, धाकबसवायाजोगा-सारखा, जरबी, अघोर.

AWFULNESS, *n.* v. A. दबदबा *m.* दबाव *m.* दाब *m.* इब्रत *or* इभ्रत *f.* दरदरा *m.* दरारा *m.* दगदगा *m.* जरब *f.* सलाबत *f.*

AWHILE, *adv.* कांहीं वेळपर्यंत, कांहीं काळपर्यंत, कांहींवेळ, अमळ, अमळसा.

AWKWARD, *a. clumsy, unskilful, unhandy.* अडाणी, अनाडी, आडमूठ, आडमुठ्या, आडकसबी, नाकसबी, घसक्या, घसट्या, अवसुती, अवसुत्या, गवत्या, कबाडी *or* ड्या, कबाडकामी, हेंगाडा, दुघड, गंवार, झोडकाम्या, बेहिकमती, बेहुनरी, अकुशल, अपटु, अदक्ष.

The a. and rude,—compreh. अडाणी कबाडी *m. pl.* गवतेगोमाजी *m. pl.*

2—of things, v. CLUMSY. धोबड, ओबडधोबड *or* आबडधोबड, बेडौल, बेढब, बेडौली, गैरबेताचा, ढोबळ, अवसुती.

3 *unpleasant, disagreeable, untoward, &c.* अवघड, कठीण, अडचणीचा, नडीचा, गैरसोईचा.

AWKWARDLY, *adv.* v. A. 1. अडाण्यासारखा, अडाण्यापरीं, अनाड्यावाणी, अडाणीपणानें, अकुशलतेनें.

AWKWARDNESS, *n.* v. A. 1. अडाणीपणा *or* अडाणपणा *m.* अनाडपणा *m.* आडमुठेपणा *m.* &c. अकौशल्य*n.* अकुशलता *f.* अपटुता *f.*

2 धोबडपणा *m.* ढोबळपणा *m.* बेडौलपणा *m.* बेडौली *f.*

3 अवघडपणा *m.* कठीणपणा *m.*

AWL, *n.* अरी *f.* आर *f.* टोपण *n.* टोपणें *n.*

To bore with an a. (टोपण) टोपणें, टोपसणें.

AWLESS, *a.* v. FEARLESS. निर्भय, निर्धास्त.

AWN, *n.* कुसळ *n.* कूस *n.* कुसूं *n.*

AWNING, *n.* छत *n. v.* बांध, चांदणी *f.* आस्मानगिरी *f.* चांदवा *m* सायबान *n.* शमिना *or* समिना *m.* शामाणा *or* ना *m.* वितान *n.*

To cover with an a. छतावणें.

AWRY, *a.* v. OBLIQUE. बांकडा, तिरकस, तिरका, तिरपा.

AXE, *n.* कुऱ्हाड *f.* कुठार *m.* परशु *pop.* परश *m.* तबल *m.*

AXILLA, *n. arm pit.* काख *f.* बगल *f.* कक्ष *m.*

AXILLAR, *a.* काखेचा, कक्षसंबंधी.

AXIOM, *n. self-evident truth.* प्रत्यक्षसिद्धवाक्य *n.*-वचन *n.*-&c.

AXIOMATIC, AXIOMATICAL, *a.* v. N. प्रत्यक्षसिद्ध, स्वतःसिद्ध.

AXIS, AXLE, AXLE-TREE, *n.* आंस *m.* आंख *m.* अक्ष *m.* कणा *m.* गुणा *m.*

Axle-box of a cart. खोबळा *m.*

Grease for a. ओंगण *n.*

Transverse beam of a. चाकपाटी *f.*

AY, AYE, *adv.* v. YES. हो, होय, सई, बरें.

AYE, *adv. continually,* v. EVER. सतत, निरंतर.

For a. सर्वकाल.

AZIMUTH, *n.* (of a heavenly body.) समांश *m.*

The co-azimuth. दिगंश *m.* दिग्लव *m.*

AZURE, *a.* आस्मानी, आकाशवर्णी.

B.

B. This letter is represented by ब, and, when aspirated, by भ.

To BAA, *v. n.*—as a sheep. चेंबावणें, बेंबें *n.* करणें, बेंबटणें.

To BABBLE, *v. n.*—as a child, v. To PRATTLE. बोबडें बोलणें.
2 *talk idly*, v. To PRATE.बकणें, बकबकणें, बटवटणें, बडबडणें.
3 *tell secrets*, v. To BLAB. फोडणें, बटणें, तोंडाळणें, तोंड *n.*-मुतरस *m.*-जीभ *f.*-&c. पाघळणें *g. of s.*
4—as a stream,&c. सळकन-सळसळ-&c. वाजणें-वाहणें.

BABBLE, BABBLEMENT, BABBLING, *n.* v. V. 1.—*act.* बोबडें बोलणें *n.*
2 बकणें *n.* &c. बकबक *f.* बडबड *f.* बटवट *f.* बकणी *f.* बकवा *m.* बकवाद *m.*गचाळकी *f.* गचाळी *f.*
3 फोडणें *n.* &c. सांगासांगी *f.* सांगाबांगी *f.* लभाशाई *f.*
4 सळसळ *f.* सळखळी *f.*

BABBLER, *n.* BABBLING, *p. a.* v. V. 1. बोबडें बोलणारा, बोबडा.
2 बडबडणारा, &c. बडबड्या, बटवट्या, बकबक्या, गचाळी *or* ळ्या, चाभरा.
3 फोडणारा, तोंडाळणारा, &c. लुतरा, लभेचाटू, लाहबर, जिभेचा हलका, कानाचा हलका, घांट *f.*
4 सळसळ वाजणारा, &c.

BABE, BABY, *n.* v. INFANT. तान्हेंमूल *n.* आंगावरचेंमूल *n.* कडेबरचेंमूल *n.* [मराज्य *n.*

BABEL, *n. hubbub*, v. UPROAR. बलबल *f.* बलबलपुरी *f.* टमट-

BABOON, *n.* एकाजातीचा माकड आहे.

BABYHOOD, *n.* तान्हेपणा *m.*

BABYISH, See CHILDISH.

BACCHANAL, BACCHANALIAN, *n. one who indulges in reveling.* झिंग्या *m.* छाकटा, दारूबाज, पानोत्सुक, पानासक्त, पानरत.

BACCHANAL, BACCHANALIAN, *a. pertaining to reveling.* पानोत्सवाचा, पानसमारंभाचा, पानोत्सवसंबंधी, पानोत्सवविषयक.

BACCHANALS, *n. drinking feasts, revels.* पानोत्सव *m.* पानसमारंभ *m.* पानकोत्सव *m.*

BACHELOR, *n. unmarried man.* अविवाहित-अनूढ-&c. पुरुष *m.* ब्रम्हचारी *m.* अपत्नीक, निंबा, अवरठा, निस्संग.
For the exact expression of the sense of this word there is perhaps no word in *Maráṭhí*; for the *Maráṭhás* and the Hindus generally hold celibacy, excepting in the instance of saints and ascetics, as unnatural and abominable. From the same reason however, there are very numerous and very significant terms and phrases of reproach and contumely. To the man studying the *mind and spirit* of the *Maráṭhá* people the study of these terms (which are here collected) in their particular aspects and allusions, will afford instruction. मसणखुंट, बणव्यांतलाखुंट, खुंटारा, सोठ, सडेसोट, सडाशिंग, सोटशिंग, सडाफटिंग, सडेहुपट *or* सडेहुप्या, सडाधस, खुंटावरचाकाबळा, थोंटापिंपळ, पारोसापिंपळ, वडपिंपळ, फटिंग *or* फटिंगभाई, बांडफरीद, उपडसुंभा, पिंपळावरचामुंज्या, जन्मसन्यासी, जन्ममुंज्या *or* जन्माचामुंज्या, जन्मवट्, एकटा टिकोजी, एकटा एकसुरा, फकीर, सोटभैरव, लोटाश्रम.
And for the expression of the sense as *enlarged*—as including together with the idea of *lack of spouse and seed*, the ideas of *homelessness, unsettledness, uncomfortableness, disconnectedness* and *disregardedness*, some terms and phrases are, घरनादार आणि देवळीं बिऱ्हाड, त्याचें बिऱ्हाड वाजलें संगातीच आहे, त्याचा सोटा दुपटा बरोबरच आहे, नदीवर न्हाण गांवांत भीक आणि देवळीं निद्रा, आगेलंड पिच्छेगंड.

BACHELOR'S BUTTON, *n.*—the flower. गुलटोप *n.*

BACHELORSHIP, *n.* अवरेठपणा *m.* अविवाहितत्व *m.* अनूढत्व *n.* अविवाहितावस्था *f.* ब्रह्मचर्य *n.*

BACK, *n.* पाठ *f.* पृष्ठ *n.* पृष्ठभाग *m.*
—in contempt, &c. पाठाड *or* पाटाण *or* पाठण *n.* पठार *f.*
Behind the b. of. पाठीमागें, पाठीं, असमक्ष, अप्रत्यक्ष, पश्चात्, परोक्ष, बेहुजूर, पृष्ठतः. [मधुपुळी *f.*
Carbuncle on the b. काळपुळी *f.* काळफोड *m.* देंठपुळी *f.*
Hump on the b. कुबड *n.* पोंक *n.* कोंक *n.* पृष्ठग्रंथि *m.*
Having the b. towards. पाठमोरा *or* मोहरा, मागमोरा *or* मोहरा, पराङ्मुख.
Of a broad or large b.—a centipede. पठारा.
On the b. of, *pick back.* पाठकुळी *or* पाठकुळीस *or* पाठगुळीस.
To be on one's b. *be helpless from sickness, &c.* जमिनीस *or* भुईस पाठ लागणें *or* असणें, जमीन धरून असणें, निजणें *or* निजून असणें, उताणा असणें *or* पडणें, दांतवांसून पडणें.
To break one's b. मान *f.* कापणें, मान *f.* मुरगाळणें, मुंढी *f.* मुरगाळणें.
To turn one's b. on. पाठ *f.* देणें, पाठ *f.* बळणें, पाठ *f.* दाखवणें, पाठमोरा-पाठसामोरा होणें.
2 *hinder part*—gener. पाठ *f.* पिच्छाडा *m.* पिच्छाडी *f.* पिच्छवाडा *or* पिच्छोडा *m.* पाठवसा *or* पाठोसा *m.* पृष्ठ *n.* पृष्ठभाग *m.* पृष्ठदेश *m.* दुमाला *m.* [पृष्ठतः.
At the b. of. *lit. fig.* पाठीवर, पाठीमागें, पाठीं, मागें, पश्चात्,
Blank or unwritten at the b. पाठकोरा.
From the b. of. पाठीमागून, मागून, पाठून, पिच्छवाड्याकडून.
To append or add to the b. of. दुमाल्यावर लावणें.
To be at the b. of. पाठीवर-दुमाल्यावर-पल्ल्यावर-&c. असणें *g. of o.* [फिरून, मागें, उलट.

BACK, *adv. in return,*—of place. माघारां*orरीं or* रें, परत, परतून,
2 *behind, in the hinder place, &c.* मागें, पाठीमागें, पाठलेकडे, पाठेशीं, पाठवशास, पाठसरीं, पृष्ठतः, पृष्ठभागीं, पृष्ठदेशीं.
3 *again, in return.* परत, परतून, माघारां *or* रीं *or* रें, फिरून, पुनः *pop.* पुन्हा, उलट & उलटा (esp. in comp. as उलट उत्तर, उलटपत्र, उलटमान, &c.), फेर (esp. in comp. as फेरजाब, फेरचिट्टी, &c.), प्रति (in comp. as प्रतिदान, प्रतिध्वनि).
4 *with the b. forward.* पाठमोरा *or* पाठसामोरा.

To BACK, *v. a. mount on the b. of.* पाठीवर चढणें, पाठीवर बसणें, सवार होणें, पृष्ठारोहण *n.* करणें *g. of o.*
2 *aid, support*, v. To HELP. पाठ *f.* देणें, पाठ *f.* राखणें *g. of o.* पाठीवर असणें *g. of o.* पाठिंबा असणें, पाठबळ *n.* देणें-करणें, बाहीदारी *f.* करणें *g. of o.* उपराळ्यास येणें, उपराळा *m.* करणें,
3 *put backward, cause to recede.* मागें घेणें-सारणें-करणें-काढणें, मागल्यापायीं घेणें-सारणें, हटविणें.

4—in wrestling; *throw on the b.* चीत-जमीनदोस्त-उलथा-&c. करणें, उताणा पाडणें-घालणें.

5 (a boat, with an oar). वल्हें फांट *m.* धरणें *or* करणें (नावेस, होडीस, गलबतास, &c.).

To BACK, *v. n. go backwards.* मागें *or* पाठीमागें हटणें-सरणें-होणें, गांडमोरा-पाठमोरा-&c. चालणें. [&c. घेणें.

2 out; v. To DRAW BACK. माघार *f.* घेणें, काढतें *n.*-निघतें-

To BACK-BITE. *v. a. slander one absent,* v. To ASPERSE. पाठीमागें चहाडी *f.*-चुगली *f.*-&c.करणें-खाणें-सांगणें *g. of o.* परोक्षनिंदा *f.* परोक्षपैशुन्य *n.*-परोक्षापवाद *m.* करणें *g. of o.* कूट *f.* खाणें *g. of o.*

BACK-BITER, *n.* BACK-BITING, *p. a.* v. V. पाठीमागें चहाडी सांगणारा, &c. चहाड, चहाडबुचका, चहाडखोर, चहाडलुतरा, परोक्षपिशुन, परोक्षनिंदक, परोक्षापवादक, कर्णेजप.

BACK-BITING, *n.* v. V.—*act.* चहाडी सांगणें *n.* चहाडी *f.* चुगली *f.* कूट *f.* परोक्षनिंदा *f.* परोक्षापवाद *m.* परोक्षपैशुन्य *n.* चर्चा *f.*

BACK-BONE, *n.* कणा *m.* कांटा *m.* दांडा *m.* दांडारा *m.* वासा *m.* पृष्ठवंश *m.*

Fore end of the b. of beasts. मोऱ्हांटा *m.*

BACK-DOOR, *n.* परूसदार *or* परसदार *n.* मागीलदार *n.* मागलेंदार *n.* चोरदार *n.* खिडकी *f.*

BACK-GROUND, *n.*—fig. *state of neglect or loss of notice.* मागलट *f.* मागसणी *f.*

To throw into the b. उणें *n.*-उणीव *f.* आणणें *with* स *or* ला, मागलटीस-मागसणीस टाकणें.

BACK-PAY, *n.* मागल्याकाळाचा पगार *m.*-वेतन *n.*-&c.

BACK-ROOM, *n.* मागल्या आंगाची खोली *f.*-कोठडी *f.*

BACK-SIDE, *n. posteriors.* गांड *f.* गुद *n.* बृहती *f.*

2 *hinder side,* v. BACK. पाठ *f.* पृष्ठ *n.* पृष्ठभाग *m.* पृष्ठदेश *m.* पिछाडी *f.* मागलें आंग *n.*

To BACK-SLIDE, *v. n. fall off from a religious course.* बिथरणें, बिचलणें, बिचळणें, पतित-भ्रष्ट-&c. होणें, सन्मार्ग *m.*-मार्ग *m.* सोडणें.

BACK-SLIDER, *n.* BACK-SLIDING, *p. a.* v. V. बिथरणारा, &c. सन्मार्गत्यागी, सन्मार्गच्युत, भ्रष्ट, पतित.

BACK-STAIRS, *n.* चोरजिना *m.* आडजिना *m.*

BACK-SWORD, *n.* एकधारी तरवार *f.* [पाठांगण *n.*

BACK-YARD, *n.* परस *or* परूस *n.* परसूं *n.* परडें *n.* मागलें अंगण *n.*

BACKER, *n.* v. V. A. 2. पाठदेणारा, पाठराखणारा, &c. पाठराख्या, पाठराखणा, पठंगा *or* पठिंगा *or* पठिंबा *or* पाठिंगा *or* पाठिंया, मेढा *m.* बाजू *f.* बाहीदार, कौंशा.

BACKING, v. V. A. 2—*act.* पाठ देणें *n.* पाठ राखणें *n.* &c. पाठपुरावा *m.* पाठ *f.* पुस्तपना *or* पन्हा *m.* पुस्ती *f.* पुस्तगारी *f.* पुस्तवानी *or* णी *f.* गुडघा *m.* दुमाला *m.* उपराळा *m.*

v. V. N. 1.—*act.* मागें हटणें *n.* मागें सरणें *n.*

2 माघार घेणें *n.* काढतें घेणें *n.* &c. [कडे.

BACKWARD, *adv. towards one's back.* पाठीमागें, मागें, पृष्ठभागा-

2 *with the b. forward.* पाठमोरा, पाठसामोरा, पाठीनेंसरकत, पाठीनें, मागल्यापायीं, मागल्यापावलीं, मागच्यापायांनीं.

3 *from the wrong end.* उलट, उलटा, उलट्यानें, व्युत्क्रमानें, उफराटा, उफराट्यानें, विलोम.

B. and forward. उलटासुलटा, उलटापालटा, उफराटसुफराट, उफराटासुफराटा, अनुलोमविलोम, क्रमोत्क्रम.

BACKWARD, *a. unwilling,* v. AVERSE. माघारघेणाऱ्यामनाचा, विमुख, विमनस्क, विमत.

2 v. DILATORY. ढिला, ढिल्या, ढील, चेंगट, चेंगटी, सुस्त, मंद.

3 *not proficient,* मागस, मागसलेला, मागसावलेला, मागें पडलेला.

4 *late in season, not early.* मागस, मागाहून पिकणारा.

BACKWARDNESS, v. A. 1. विमुखता *f.* विमनस्कता *f.* विमति *f.*

2 ढिलेपणा *m.* ढिली *f.* चेंगटपणा *m.* चेंगटाई *f.* सुस्ती *f.*

BACON, *n.* डुकराचें मास *n.* [णें-संभाळणें.

To save one's b. आंगसुटका *f.* करून घेणें, पागोटें *n.* बचाव-

BAD, *a. ill, evil,*—gener. वाईट, खराब, नाकारा, ओंगळ, ओखटा, नठारा, कुत्सित, खटनट, खकान.

—freely *or* compreh. वाईटसाईट, वाईटबिट्टूळ, वाईटबांकडा, वाईटओखटा, खटनट, खोटानाटा, नासकाकुजका, ओंगळसोंगळ, खुदरा पादरा.

Badish. वाईटवाणा *or* णी.

To make b. worse. काट्याचा नायटा *m.* करणें, गळ्यांतगोणी *f.* आणणें, हालवून खुंटा बळकट करणें.

2 *vicious, sinful,* v. WICKED. दुष्ट, पापी, पापिष्ठ, असत्, कुशील, दुश्शील, दुर् (in comp. as दुराचारी, दुर्जन, &c.), कु (in comp. as कुजन, कुपुत्र, &c.).

3 v. UNWHOLESOME. दुष्ट, बाधक, बावडा, अहितकारक, जाचक.

BAD-HEARTED, *a.* दुर्हृदय, दुर्हृद, दुष्टहृदय, दुष्टमानस, दुष्टांतःकरण.

BADGE, *n. mark of distinction.* चिन्ह *n.* खूण *f.* निशानी *f.* लक्षण *n.* बिरीद *or* बिरुद *n.* कंकण *n.* चंग *m.*

BADGER, *n.* एक जनावर आहे.

To BADGER, *v. a. persecute, worry, &c.* v. To TEASE. जाचणें, घोळणें, तोडणें, जाचणूक *f.*-तोडातोड *f.*-&c. करणें *g. of o.* जीव *m.* खाणें-जिवाचा घोंट *m.* घेणें *g. of o.* पाठीस लागणें-पाठलाग *m.* करणें *g. of o.*

BADINAGE, *n. light talk.* ठट्ठेचें-चिचोरीचें बोलणें *n.*-भाषण *n.*

BADLY, *adv.* v. A. 1. वाईट, खराब, वाईट रीतीनें, नापसंत.

BADNESS, *n.* v. A. 1. वाईटपणा *m.* खराबपणा *m.* नाकारेपणा *m.* &c. कौत्सित्य *n.*

2 दुष्टपणा *m.* दौष्ट्य *n.* पापिष्ठता *f.*

3 दुष्टाई *f.* बावडेपणा *m.* बाधकता *f.*

To BAFFLE, *v. a. foil,* v. To DEFEAT. लटपटविणें, मोडणें, घालवणें, व्यर्थ-भ्रष्ट-निष्फल-&c. करणें, वाहवणें, चालेनासा करणें, प्रतिहत-भ्रष्टसंकल्प-खंडिताशस-&c. करणें.

BAFFLED, *p.* v. V. लटपटविलेला, चालेनासाकेलेला, व्यर्थकेलेला, &c.

BAG, *n. sack, &c.* थैला *m. dim.* थैली *f.* ठेला *m. dim.* ठेली *f.* पोतें *n.*

B. to hold paper and traps. गबाळें *n.* जुगदान *or* जुजदान *n.*

B. with pockets or divisions. चंची *f.* बटवा *m. dim.* बटवी *f.* बाटवा *m.* पुरवटा *m.*

Bag and baggage. बाडबिछात *or* बिशात *f.* पालपइद्ळ *n.* गबाळें चबाळें *n.* गबाळगुबाळ *n.* बाडबिछाना *m.*

Four mouthed b. झोळणा *m.* झोळी *f.*

String to draw the mouth of a b. उघडदोरा *m.* ओढदोरा *m.* मणदोरा *m.* कसा *m.*

Two-mouthed b. धोंगटी *f.* हडपी *f.* पडशी *f.*

2 (for holding money). v. PURSE. पिशवी *f.* खलिता *m.* कसा *m.* हमिणी *f.* हमीचा *m.*

Money, &c. b. of shroffs and goldsmiths. कटुळतें *n.* बाटवा

m. पोतडी *f.* पोतडें *n.* बोरी *f.*
3 (of animals). कोश *or* कोष *m.*

To BAG, *v. a.* fig. *pocket, appropriate, &c.* पिशवींत-गवसणींत घालणें, गवाळ्यांत-पोत्यांत घालणें-टाकणें, राशी पुंजीस घालणें-आणणें.

To BAG, *v. n.* *swell like a bag, belly, swag.* झोलणें, झोल *m.*-झोलका *m.* येणें, भोंगळणें.
2 about; *hang or sit loosely.* घळघळणें, घळघळ *or* ळां *adv.* लोंबणें-बसणें-असणें. [*n.*
Clothes, ornaments, &c. that hang bagging. घळघळ पोतें

BAG-PIPE, *n.* एका प्रकारचें वाद्य आहे.
B. for charming snakes. नागसर *or* नागसूर *n.*

BAGATELLE, *n.* v. TRIFLE. हलकीगोष्ट *f.*
2 एका प्रकारचा खेळ आहे.

BAGGAGE, *n.* (of an army). खेलखाना *m.* लशकरीलबैदा *m.* बुणगें *n.* बहिर्बुणगें *n.* बाजारबुणगें *n.* कतवार *n.* खालीखटला *m.*
2 (of an individual). सामान *n.* सामानसुमान *n.* खटला *m.* खटलें *n.* खाट खटलें *n.* खाटखडबड *f.* बाडबिशात *or* द *f.* वस्त्रपात्र *n.* पडतल *or* पडदळ *n.* लटंबर *or* लटंबळ *n.*लाहुंबर *n.* सारसुर *f.* मुस्तायकी *f.*
Bag and b. v. BAG. बाडबिछात *f.*
3 *worthless woman.* बायरू *n.* बायाबलू *n.* बायलें *n.* बाळें *n.* बटकरूं *n.* बटकुली *f.*

BAGGER, *n.* BAGGING, *p. a.* v. V. N. भोंगळ, घळघळीत, नेभळा, झोलर *or* झोलार, झोलकट, डगळ *or* डघळ.

BAGNIO, *n.* v. BATH-ROOM. नहाणघर *n.* हमामखाना *m.*
2 v. BROTHEL. वेश्यालय *n.* वेश्याशाला *f.*

BAIL, *n.* the security given. जामिनी *f.* जामीनकी *f.*
To give leg b. गच्च *or* गच्छंतीचें *n.* म्हणणें.
2—the person. जामीन *c.* जामीनदार, प्रतिभू *m.*
B. for appearance. हाजीरजामीन, दर्शनप्रतिभू *m.*
B. for good conduct. फैलजामीन, खातरजामीन, विश्वासजामीन.
B. for pecuniary liability. मालजामीन.
To admit to b. जामीन घेऊन सोडणें.

To BAIL, *v. a.* *free on bail.* जामीन *m.*-जामीनकी *f.*-जामीनी *f.* -जामीनगत *f.* घेऊन सोडणें.
2 *stand bail for.* जामीन होणें, जामीनकी *f.*-जामिनी *f.* देणें.

BAILABLE, *a.*—a person. जामीनी घेऊन सोडण्यास योग्य.
2—an offence. जामीन घेण्यास योग्य, जामीन घेण्या सारखा.

BAILIFF, *n.* नाजराच्या हाताखालचा एक कामदार आहे.
2 *subordinate officer.* वर्त्तक *m.* (his office, वर्त्तकी *f.*).

To BAIT, *v. a.* (a hook, &c.). कुंडी *f.*-घास *m.*-आमिष *n.*-&c. लावणें, आमिषयुक्त-आमिषविशिष्ट-&c. करणें.
2 *give refreshment, &c. upon the road.* चरिंदा *or* चरिंदा*m.*-चाचाचबिना *m.* देणें-करणें, घास बैरण देऊन असुदा करणें.
3 *worry, harass,* v. To TEASE. जाचणें, तोडणें, घोळणें, तोडातोड *f.* करणें *g. of o.*

BAIT, *n.* (for a hook, &c.). कुंडी *f.* घास *m.* आमिष *n.*
2 *lure, enticement.* आमिष *n.* लांच *f.* पेंडीचाखडा *m.* प्रलोभन*n.*
To hold out some b. मधाचेंबोट *n.* लावून ठेवणें, सास्वर *f.* पसरणें, लाल्लूच *f.*-खाऊ *m.*-खाजें *n.*-गूळखोबरें *n.*-अंबोण *f.* दाखवणें देणें.

BAIZE, *n.* पट्टू *n.*

To BAKE, *v. a.* भाजणें, भर्जन *n.*-&c. करणें *g. of o.*
2—in chemistry, &c. (by fire). अग्निपुट *n.* देणें-करणें, (by the sun), सूर्यपुट *or* सूर्यकिरणपुट *n.* देणें-करणें, (in a pit), गजपुट *or* ठ *n.* देणें-करणें.

BAKED, *p.* v. V. 1. भाजलेला, भार्जीव.

BAKER, *n.* v. V. 1. भाजणारा, भर्जनकर्त्ता.
I. *person who makes and sells bread.* रोटीवाला *m.*

BAKER-LEGGED, *a.* संहतजानु, संहतजानुक, संज्ञु.

BAKERY, *n.* रोटीवाल्याचें काम *n.*
2 रोटीवाल्याची काम करण्याची जागा *f.*

BAKING, *n.* v. V. 1.—*act.* भाजणें *n.* भर्जन.

BAKING-PLATE, *n.*—iron or earthen, तवा*m.*—earthen,रान्हें*n.*

BALANCE, *n.* *pair of scales.* तागडी *f.* तराजू *f.* तुला *f.* उन्मान *n.*—large, धट *m.* तग*m.*—small, esp. of jewellers, &c. कांटा *m.* ताजवा *m.* फिरकी *f.*
B. having a tongue. कांटा *m.*
B. for nice weighing कंपणकांटा *m.*
Beam of a b. दांडी *f.*
Dish of a b. परडें *n.*
False b. दीड दांडी *f.*
Fraudulent turn of a b. in weighing. झोका *m. v.* दे.
Inclination of an unequal b. पासंग *m.*
Inequality (untrueness) of a b. तट *m.*
Strings of a b. शिकें *n.* तुलासूत्र *n.* शिक्य *n.*
Tongue of a b. कांटा *m.*
2 (of an account). बाकी *f.* शिलक *f.* शिलक बाकी *f.* बाकीसाकी *f.* उबार *f.* वर्त्तांळा *m.*
B. brought forward. ओढण *f.* ओढणबाकी *f.*
B. (for or against) on a tradesman's books. खातेबाकी *f.*
B. as drawn or set down. शिलक झाडा *m.*
B. sheet. शिलकबंद *m.*
Chain of balances. शिलकसांखळी *f.*
Dead balances. *b.s given up as not forthcoming.* जळीतबाकी *f.* बुडीत बाकी *f.*
Outstanding b. जेरबाकी *f.*
To leave a b. राहता-उरता करणें.
To leave no b. निबाकी *f.*-बेबाक *f.* करणें *g. of o.* चुकती बाकी *f.* देणें.
To settle or discharge a b. बाकी *f.* पूज करणें, बाकी *f.* चुकविणें, बाकी *f.* फडशा करणें.
3 See EQUIPOISE. 4—the sign. तुला *f.* तूळ *f.*

To BALANCE, *v. a.* *counterpoise, &c.* v. To WEIGH. तोलणें, पेलणें, तुलना *f.* करणें, समतोल राखणें-करणें.
2 (an account). शिलकझाडा *m.* काढणें-उतरणें, खातेबाकी *or* बाकी *f.* काढणें, जमाखर्च *m.* करणें-पाहणें.

To BALANCE, *v. n.* *be on a poise.* समतोल असणें.
2 See To HESITATE.

BALCONY, *n.* सज्जा *m.*

BALD, *a.* *wanting hair.* टकल्या, तरट्या, केशहीन, केशविरहित, गलितकेश, खल्बाट, अकच, लुंडामुंडा.
A b. spot. टक्कल *n.*

2 *naked, unadorned &c.* v. BARE. बोडका, सुना, बुचा, ओंका, मुंढा.

3 *inelegant, mean,*—composition, &c. रुक्ष, नीरस, भाकड, अप्रौढ, रसहीन.

BALDERDASH, *n.* v. PRATE. बकबक *f.*

BALDNESS, *n.* v. A. 1. टक्कल *n.* तरटें *n.* खल्वाट *n.* केशहीनत्व *n.* केशराहित्य *n.*

2 बोडकेपणा *m.* सुनेपणा *m.* बुचेपणा *m.* &c.

3 भाकडपणा *m.* &c. रुक्षता *f.* रसहीनता *f.*

BALDPATE, *n.* टकलीडोई *f.* टक्कलमाथा *m.*

BALDPATED, *a.* टक्कलमाथ्या, तरटया, खल्वाट्या.

BALDRICK, *n. ornamented belt.* नकशीदार पट्टा *m.*

BALE, *n.* v. BUNDLE. गठ्ठा *m.* बस्ता *m.* दिंड *n.* तक्का *m.* बिंडा *m.* *dim.* बिंदडी *or* बिंदली *f.*

Strap of a b. दाटणी *f.*

Wrapper of a b. बारदान *n.* बासन *n.*

To BALE, *v. a. lade out water, &c.* उसपणें *or* उपसणें, शेलणें, उसपा *m.*-उसपणी *or* उपसणी *f.*- उसपण *or* उपसण *n.* करणें *g. of o.*

2 *make into a bale.* गठ्ठा *m.* बांधणें.

BALEFUL, *a. evil,* v. CALAMITOUS. दुष्ट, वाईट, अनर्थकारक, अपायकारक, दुःखकारक.

BALEFULNESS, *n.* v. A. दुष्टपणा *m.* &c. अनर्थकारकत्व *n.* &c.

BALING, *n.* v. V. 1.—*act.* उसपणें *n.* &c. उसपा *m.* उसपणी *f.* उसपण *n. or* उपसा-उपसणी-उपसण.

BALK, *n. ridge unploughed.* खावडें *n.* वरळ *f.* भांगणी *f.*

2 *beam.* बहाल *n.*

3 v. DISAPPOITMENT. आशाभंग *m.* ढोला *m.*

To BALK, *v.a. disappoint, deceive.* आशा *f.* मोडणें, आशाभंग *m.* करणें *g. of o.* ठकवणें, फटवणें, बंचणें, ढोला *m.*-झोका *m.* देणें, फजीत करणें, हताश- निराश-आशाभंग- &c. करणें.

2 *to plow leaving balks.* खावडें *n.*-वरळ *f.* ठेवून नांगरणें.

BALL, *n.*—gener. गोल *m. pop.* गोळा *m. dim.* गोळी *f.* गोलक *m.* पिंड *m.* गोटा *m. dim.* गोटी *f.* उंडा *m.*

2—to play with. चेंडू *m.* कंदुक *m.*

Pile placed to be thrown down by a b. लगोऱ्या *f.pl.*

3 (of medicines). *pill, &c.* गोळी *f.* गुटी *f.* गुटिका *pop.* गुटका *f.* गुलिका *f.* गोलिका *f.*

4 (of the eye). बुबूळ *n.* नेत्रगोल *m.* नेत्रगोलक *m.* अक्षिगोल *m.* अक्षिगोलक *m.*

5 (of thread, &c.). गुंडी *f.* गुंजडी *f.* गुंजडें *n.* गुंडळी *f. or* ळें *n.* गुंडाळी *f. or* ळें *n.* गुंडाळा *m.* गुंडा *m.* पिंडा *m.* पिलंडा *m.* मुठ्ठा *m.*

6 *entertainment of dancing.* नाच *m.* नृत्योत्सव *m.* नृत्यसमारंभ *m.* नृत्य *n.*

BALL-FIRING, BALL-PRACTICE, *n.* गोळीबार *m.*

BALL-ROOM, *n.* नृत्यशाला *f.* नृत्यमंदिर *n.* नाचण्याचा अड्डा *m.*

BALLAD, *n. trifling song,* v. SONG. लावणी *f.* ठुंबरी *f.* ग्राम्यगीत *n.*

BALLAD-SINGER, *n.* लावणीबाज *c.* लावणीवाला *m.* शाहीर *m.*

BALLAST, *n.* (for a ship, &c.). निलीम *or* निरीम *n. m.*

2 fig. स्थिरताकारक गुण *m.*

To BALLAST, *v. a.* निलीम *or* निरीम *n. m.* भरणें.

BALLET, *n.* हावभावपूर्वक नृत्य *n.* लास्य *n.*

BALLOON, *n. vehicle which proceeds through the air.* आकाशयान *n.* आकाशवहन *n.* व्योमयान *n.* विमान *n.*

BALLOT, *n. ball or ticket,* (in voting). गुप्तानुमतिसूचकगुलिका *f.*-लेख *m.*-चिन्ह *n.*

2 *voting by ballot.* v. V. गुलिकाद्वारा *or* लेखद्वारा गुप्त सम्मतिदान-करण *n.*

To BALLOT, *v. n. vote by ballot or ticket.* गुलिकाद्वारा *or* लेखद्वारा *or* चिन्हद्वारा गुप्तसम्मति *f.* देणें-करणें.

BALM, *n.* झाडाचा सुगंधित रस *m.*-चीक *m.*-डीक *m.*

2 *fragrant ointment.* सुगंधित उटणें *n.*

3 *any thing that heals or soothes.* उपशमन *n.* उपशामक औषध *n.*-&c. [जनक.

BALMY, *a.*—of slumbers. गोड, सुखाचा, सुखकर, स्वास्थ्यकारक-

2 v. FRAGRANT. सुवासिक.

BALNEARY, *n.* v. BATH-ROOM. नहाणघर *n.* स्नानागार *n.*

BALNEATORY, BALNEAL, *a.* नहाणघरचा, स्नानागारसंबंधी.

BALSAM, *n.*—common b. तरेडा *m.* 2 See OINTMENT.

BALSAMIC, *a. soothing, softening.* उपशमकारक, स्वास्थ्यजनक-कारक, मृदुकारक.

BALUSTER, *n.* फिरकी *f.* कठड्याचा गज *m.* गरादा *m.* कठड्याची गराद *f.* गराज *f.*

BALUSTERADE, *n. row of balusters.* कठडा *m.* कठरडा *m.* कठारा *or* डा *m.* कठंजन *n.*

BAMBOO, *a. belonging to or made of bamboo.* बांबूचा, वेळूचा *or* वेळवाचा, वेळवी, वंशय, वंशी, वांश, वैणव.

BAMBOO, *n.*—the plant. बांबू *m.* वंश *m.* कीचक *m.*

Some of the kinds or varieties are, कळक *or* कळंक, कागदीवेळू, कोंडा *or* कोंढा, चिवा, रानचिवा, चिवार, टोंकर, डवगा, भालेकाठी, माणगा *or* माणगारा, माणा *or* ण्या, मेस.

B. shoot or sprout. वंशांकुर *m.*

Clump or cluster of bamboos. बेट *n.* कळंक *f.*

The efflorescence of the b. मेळ *m.*

Manna of the b. त्वक्क्षीरा *f. pop.* तवकीर *or* खीर *or* कील *or* खील *n.* वंशक्षीर *n.* वंशक्षीरी *f.* वंशलोचन *n.* वंशलोचना *f.* वंशरोचना *f.*

Seeding of a b. काटे *m. pl.* मळ *m.*

2—a stick; *single cane.* बांबू *m.* वेळू *m.* कळंक *m.* वंश *m.* बांस *m. or* बास *m.* कार्मुक *n.* वेणु *m.* कीचक *m.*

B. basket or vessel. वंशपात्र *n.* [दुरडी *f.*

B.-basket or sieve (for washing rice, vegetables, &c.).

B.-crook. डांग *f.* डांग काठी *f.*

B.-flute or pipe. वेणु *m.*

Frame work of light slips of b. भाळी *f.*

Outer strip from a b. पाठकांब *f.* पाठवील *n.*

Piece or bit of a b. कळकूट *or* कळंकूट *n.* वेळकट *or* कूट *n.*

Pin or spike of b.—to tack leaves, &c. together. चुई *or* चोई *f.* चुइटी *or* चोइटी *f.* शिलक *f.* शिगर *n.* शिरळक *f.*

Shaving or thin slice of a b. (for basket-work &c.) बीळ *or* बेळ *n.*

Strip or slip of a b. कांब *f.* कांबीट *n.* सरी *f.* सारण *f.* चिंब *n.* चिंबट *n.*

To BAMBOOZLE, *v. a. cozen, gull,* v. TO DECEIVE. फसवणें, धंदरणें, धाब्यावर बसवणें, तोंडीं पान *n.* पुसणें, धतुरा *m.* दाखवणें,

धूर *m.* देणें.

BAN, *n. proclamation or edict of proscription, interdiction, &c.* बहिष्कारपत्र *n.* निषेधपत्र *n.* वाळीतपत्र *n.* बहिष्कारोद्घोष *m.* निषेधोद्घोष *m.*

2 v. CURSE. शाप *m.*

3 bans; *notice of marriage.* लग्नाची-विवाहाची-&c. जाहिरात *f.*

To BAN, See TO CURSE.

BANANA, *n.*—the tree, *musa sapientum*, v. PLANTAIN. सुवर्ण कदली *f. pop.* सोनकेळ *or* सोनेळ *f.*

2—the fruit. सोनकेळें *n.* सोनकेळ *n.* सोनेळें *n.* सोनेळ *n.*

BAND, *n. binding, bandage.* बंधन *n.* पट्टी *f.* बंद *m.* बंध *m.* बांध *m.* आत्रा *m.* बंधाटी *or* बांधाटी *f.* [डें *n.* कट *m.*

2 *encompassing binder, a hoop, &c.* आटा *m.* आळा *m.* क-

3 *means of union*, v. CONNECTION. लगा *m.* लगाबांधा *m.* संबंध *m.* शृंखला *f.*

4 *company, troop, body, multitude assembled.* मंडली *or* ळी *f.* जमात *f.* जथा *m.* थवा *m.* तांडा *m.* थाट *m. dim.* थाटी *f.* चुंग *f.* चुंगी *f.* तुंग *m.* टोळी *f.* मुठाण *n.* जूट *f.* जूग *n.* झुंड *f.* गण *m.* मेळा *m.* मंडल *n.* गट *or* गट्ट *m.* गट्टा *m.* गट्टी *f.* पेंडें *n.* भिड *n.* पोवा *or* पोहा *m.* घोळका *m.* चळक *f.* पंक्ति *f.* स्तोम *n.*

5 (of insurgents or robbers). बंड *n.* खूळ *n.* गट *or* गट्ट *m.* गट्टा *m.* धडा *m.*

6 (of dancing girls, musicians, &c.). ताफा *m.* फड *m.* चक्री *f.* मेळ *m.*

Man belonging to a b. फडकरी *m.*

7 (of music). नगारखाना *m.* वाद्यभांड *n.* चौघडा *m.* बाजा *m.*

Flourish or closing beat upon a b. आखेर नौबत *f.*

8 (of knaves, libertines, idlers, &c. gener.) The word here has the power of *pack, crew, gang, knot, &c.* and is answered by चांडाळचौकडी *f.* चौकट *f.* चौक *m.* चांडाळ *m.* नवग्रह *m.* अठराबाबू *m. pl.* प्रकरण *n.* भुताबळ *f.* सोदेमंडळ *n.* शकुनिचतुष्टय *n.* मुठाण *n.*

To BAND, *v. n. unite together*, v. To COMBINE. जुटणें, जुडणें, जडणें, एकमुसणें, एकमूस *f.* करणें.

BAND-BOX, *n.* जाडकागदाची पेटी *f.*

BAND-ROOM, *n.* नगारखाना *m.* वादनशाला *f.* वाद्यशाला *f.*

BANDAGE, *n. binding*, v. BAND. पट्टी *f.* (large, पट्टा *m.*) बंद *m.* बंधन *n.* [चक्री *f.*

BANDALOUR, *n.*—the play thing. चक्र *pop.* चकीर *or* चक्कर *n.*

BANDICOTE, *n. mus malabaricus.* घूस *f.*

BANDIT, *n.* v. OUTLAW. देशबहिष्कृतमनुष्य *m.* देशनिकाला *m.* हद्दपारकेलेला माणूस *m.*

2 v. ROBBER. वाटमाऱ्या *m.* वाटपाड्या *m.* लुटारू *c.*

BANDITTI, *n. body of bandits.* बंड *n.* लुटाऱ्यांचा गट्ट *m.* खूळ *n.* दरवडा *or* दरोडा *m.*

One of the body. दरवडेकरी *or* दरोडेकरी *m.*

Depredations and ravages of b. बंडावा *m.* बंडावें *n.* चोरावें *n.* चौरटावें *n.* चोरवण *n.* चोरयें *n.* चोरक्रांत *f.* चोरक्रांति *f.* जाळपोळ *f.* पुंडाई *f.* पुंडावें *n.* भिल्लावें *n.* कोळावें *n.*

BANDROL, *n. streamer, &c.* पताका *pop.* पताक *f.*

BANDY, *n.* अंकडीदार दांडू *m.*

To BANDY, *beat to and fro*; lit. fig. परस्पर उलट सुलट मारणें, इकडून तिकडे तिकडून इकडे मारणें-फेंकणें, घोळणें, टोलवाटोलव *f.*-कोलवा कोलव *f.*-परतवापरतव *f.* करणें *g. of o.* अन्योन्यदिक्प्रक्षेप *m.*-अन्योन्यदिक्प्रेरणा *f.* करणें.

To b. blows. हातापळीस *or* हातोफळीस-हातापिटीस-हातघाईस-हातचिरडीस-&c. येणें.

To b. sharp speeches, v. To WRANGLE. धुसफुसणें, धुसफूस *f.*- धुसमूस *f.*-फटकाफटकी *f.*-झटापटी *f.* करणें.

BANDY-LEG, *n.* फेंगडा पाय *m.* [नुक.

BANDY-LEGGED, *a.* फेंगड्या, फेंगड्या पायाचा, प्रगतजानु, प्रगतजा-

BANE, *n.* lit. *poison*, fig. *cause of evil or ruin.* विष *n.* विख *n.* विषाचा प्याला *m.* विषाची पुडी *f.*-वाटी *f.* विषाचें घर *n.* मरण *n.* मृत्यु *m.* काळ *m.*

BANEFUL, *a. poisonous, pernicious.* विखारी, विखारा, अपकारक, अपायकारक, अहितकारक, घातक, मारक, नाशक.

To BANG, *v. a. beat violently and soundingly*, v. To BEAT. दणकावणें, दणगारणें, रपाटणें, सडकणें, धमकणें, कडकावणें.

2 *strike against forcibly.* आदळणें, अपटणें, आफळणें, धडकणें, धडकणें,

BANG, *n.* v. BLOW. दणका *m.* दणकारा *m.* खणका *m.* धडका *m.*

BANG, *adv.* धाड-कन-कर-&c. धड-कन-कर-&c.

BANGING, *a.* See LARGE.

BANGLE, *native bracelet*, See BRACELET.

BANIAN, *n. merchant.* वाणी *m.* वणिक् *m.* वैश्य *m.*

—in contempt, &c. वाणगट *mn.* वाणगंड *mn.* वाणकूट *mn.*

2 banian tree, *ficus indica.* वड *m.* वट. *m.*

To BANISH, *v, a. expatriate, exile.* देश *or* मुलूख पार करणें, देशनिकाला-देशपारखा-देशहद्द-&c. करणें, देशपार-राज्यपार-तरपार-&c. करणें, देशांतरास-द्वीपांतरास-&c. घालवून देणें, देशनिष्कासन *n.*-देशनिर्वासन *n.*-देशबहिष्कार *m.*-देशबहिष्कृति *f.* करणें.

2 fig. *drive away.* घालविणें, घालवून देणें, दूरकरणें, दवडणें.

BANISHED, *p.* v. V. 1. देशपार केलेला, &c. देशनिकाला, देशपारखा *or* पारका, मुलूख पारखा *or* पारका, देशबहिष्कृत, निर्वासित, देशनिर्वासित, देशनिष्कासित.

BANISHMENT, *n.* v. V. 1.—*act.* देशपार करणें *n.* &c. देशनिष्कासन *n.* देशबहिष्कार *m.* निर्वासन *n.*—*state.* देशनिकाली *f.* देशबहिष्कृति *f.* देशबहिष्कृतत्व *n.* देशनिष्कासितत्व *n.*

BANISTER, See BALUSTER.

BANK, *n.* (of a river, &c.). तड *or* थड *f.* तीर *n.* तट *m.* तटाक *m.* बांधरा *m.* [*n.*

Farther or other b. पैलथड *f.* पैलथडी *f.* पैलतीर *n.* परतीर परपार *m.* पैलपार *m.* पलतड *f.*

Hither or near b. ऐलथड *f.* ऐलथडी *f.* ऐलतीर *n.*

Hither and further banks. पारावार *m.*

On both banks. दुथडी.

2 *high or steep bank.* डगर *f.* दरड *f.* धस *m.* धसरड *f.*

Full of banks or ridges. दरडवट.

3 *dike, mound, mole*, v. DAM. बांध *m. dim.* बांधोळी *f.* बंधारा *m.* पेंडवळ *m.* पेंडवळा *m.*

Little b. to stop water. ताल *f.* पाळ *f.*

4 *shelf, shallow, flat*, v. SHOAL. भाट *n.* भाटी *f.* लाग *m.*

5 (for money). कोठी *f.* पेढी *f.* ठेवपेढी *f.* ब्यांक *f.* (from the English). [घालणें.

To BANK, *v. a. confine with banks.* बांधणें, बांधारणें, बांध *m.*

BANKER, *n.* सावकार *m.* साव *m.* हुंडीवाला *m.* पेढीवाला *m.*

Bankers and Banking,—compreh. सावसावकारा *m.*

Fraternity or body (in a town, &c.) of bankers. सावकारा *m.*

Sitting carpet of a b. सावकाराची गादी *f.*

Banking, *a.* सावकारी, सावकारांचा, सावका-याचा.

Banking, *n. banker's business.* सावकारी *f.* सावकारकी *f.* सावकारा *m.* पेढीचा व्यापार *m.* धनव्यवहार *m.*

B. upon a poor or petty scale. सांदींतली सावकारी *f.* बाथावापड्यांची सावकारी *f.*

Bank-note, *n.* ब्यांकनोट *f.* (from the English.)

Bankrupt, *a.* दिवाळें निघालेला, नादार, शेणाचा दिवा लावलेला, दारफळणीचा.

Bankrupt, *n. an insolvent.* दिवाळया, दिवाळनिघ्या, सूर्यभक्त.

Division of the money of a b. दामाशाई *f.*

To become b. दिवाळें *n.* निघणें *g. of s.* तुटणें, थकणें, वाजणें *g. of s.* वासणें *g. of s.* बसणें *g. of s.* भदें *n.* वाजणें *g. of s.*

Bankruptcy, *n.* नादारी *f.* दिवाळें *n.* दिवाळूं *n.* दारफळणी *f.* भांगोरें *n.*

To declare b. दिवाळें *n.* काढणें, शेणाचा दिवा *m.* लावणें, कास्रा *f. pl.* वर करणें, बगला *f. pl.* वरत्या करणें. [केतु *m.*

Banner, *n.* (of a chieftain), v. Flag. ढाल *f.* झेंडा *m.* पताका *f.*

Banquet, To **Banquet**, See Feast, &c.

Banqueting-house, *n.* भोजनोत्सवमंदिर *n.* उत्सवमंदिर *n.* उत्सवशाला *f.* रंगमहाल *m.*

To **Banter**, *v. a. rally, play upon,* v. To Ridicule. थट्टा *or* ठट्टा *f.*-मस्करी *f.*-चेष्टा *f.*-विनोद *m.*-&c. करणें *g. of o.* उपहासणें.

Banter, **Bantering**, *n.* v. V.—*act.* ठट्टा करणें *n.* थट्टा *or* ठट्टा *f.* मस्करी *f.* चेष्टा *f.* उपहास *m.* परिहास *m.* विनोद *m.*

Bantling, *n. brat,* v. Child. पोरटें *n.* कारटें *n.*

Baptism, *n.* The word बाप्तिस्मा from the Greek is commonly used. The word may be rendered by धर्मनिवेशार्थकावगाहन *n.* धर्मनिवेशार्थक मज्जन *n.* धर्मनिवेशार्थक जलसंस्कार *m.*

Baptismal, *a.* v. N. बाप्तिस्म्याचा, बाप्तिस्म्याविषयींचा, धर्मनिवेशार्थकावगाहनसंबंधी *or* विषयक, धर्मनिवेशार्थक जलसंस्कारसंबंधी *or* विषयक.

Baptist, *n.* बाप्तिस्मा करणारा-देणारा.

2 मुलांचा बाप्तिस्मा करूंनये, वयांत आलेल्यांचा मात्र करावा असें ज्याचें मत आहे तो.

Baptistery, *n.* बाप्तिस्मा करण्याची जागा *f.*

To **Baptize**, *v. a.* v. N. बाप्तिस्मा *m.* करणें-देणें, धर्मनिवेशार्थावगाहित करणें, जलसंस्कारद्वारा धर्मनिविष्ट करणें, मज्जनद्वारा धर्मांतःपाती करणें.

Bar, *n. piece of wood &c. laid across.* गज *m.* गजी *f.* अडवट *m.* अडवण *n.* गातडी *or* गाताडी *f.* अडू *m.* अट *f.* लाट *f.* गव्हाण *or* णी *f.*

Pinning with a b. one's arms and legs. कोलदांडा *m.*

2 (of a door). अडसर *m.* अर्गला *f. pop.* अर्गळ *or* अगळ *f. m.* आडगळ *f.* आडखिळी *f.* अडणा *m.* अडणी *f.* अडणें *n.* खीळ *f.* अडू *m.* आडिंबा *m.*

3 *obstacle, let,* v. Hinderance. अट *f.* अडती *f.* आड *f.* अटक *f.* आडकाठी *f.* अडथळा *m.*

4 (of a harbour). दांडा *m.* नस्त *n.* तिबंध *m.*

5 *preventative, exception,* v. Objection. बाध *m.* अड *f.* प्र-

6 (of metal). लगड *f.* कांब *f.* [खळी *f.*

B. of iron set round with rings. गोरखचाळा *m.* गोरखसां-

B. of iron,—to punch rocks, &c. पारई *or* य *f.* पहार *f.*

7 (of a window, railing, &c.). गज *m.* गराज *f.* गराद *f.* गरादा *m.*

8 (of a capstan). अढें *n.*

9 *railed off place for the prisoner in a court of justice.* कोर्तांत-न्यायसभेंत कैदी उभा राहण्याची कठड्याची जागा *f.*

10 *railed off place for barristers in a court of justice.* कोर्तांत सनदी वकिलांची बसण्याची कठड्याची जागा *f.*

11 *the whole body of barristers.* सनदी वकिलांची मंडळी *f.*

To **Bar**, *v. a. close and secure with a bar.* अडसर *m.*-अर्गळ *f.*-अगळ *f. m.*-आडगळ *f.*-आडिंबा *m.*-&c. घालणें-लावणें-सारणें *or* घालून-&c. बंद करणें.

2 *oppose, obstruct,* v. To Hinder. अटकावणें, अडविणें, अवरोधणें, अटकाव *m.* घालणें-करणें, अट *f.*-आड *f.* घालणें, आड येणें.

Barb, *n.* (of an arrow, &c.). कांटा *m. or* उलटकांटा *m.* उलटाकांटा *m.* आंकडा *m.*

2 (of grain, grasses, &c.). भुसी *f.* कुसूं *or* कूस *m.*

3 *armour for a horse or elephant.* पाखर *f.*

To **Barb**, *v. a.* आंकडा *m.*-उलटकांटा *m.* लावणें-घालणें.

2 (a horse, &c.). पाखर *f.* घालणें.

Barbarian, *n. savage.* रानटी-रानवट-जंगली-&c. माणूस *c.* रानमनुष्य *c.* म्लेच्छ *c.* बरबर *c.* पुलिंद *c.* यवन *m.* अडाणजात *f.* अरबूजजात *f.*

2 *fig. cruel person.* मांग हृदयाचा माणूस *m.* राक्षस *m.* यम *m.* महार *m.* मांग *m.* खाटीक *m.*

Barbarian, **Barbarous**, *a. belonging to barbarians, uncivilized, savage.* रानटी, रानवट, जंगली, म्लेच्छसंबंधी, वनचरसंबंधी, असभ्य, अशिक्षित, आचारशून्य, विद्याचारहीन, विद्याचाररहित.

2 *inhuman, &c.* v. Cruel. क्रूर, निर्दय, दयाहीन, मांगहृदयी.

3—of speech. हेंगाडा *or* हेंगडा, रानटी, अपशब्दाचा, अपप्रयोगाचा, अपशब्दयुक्त, अपप्रयोगविशिष्ट, तारवटी, कानडा, अबद्धप्रयोगविशिष्ट, गैरढ, सैरढ *or* सैराट, गव्हार, आडाणी.

4—of the speaker. हेंगाडा *or* हेंगडा, कानडा, आडाणी, वाग्दुष्ट, वाग्दोषी.

Barbarism, *n. uncivilizedness,* See Barbarity.

2 *a b. a solecism, &c.* अपशब्द *m.* अपप्रयोग *m.* अशुद्धप्रयोग *m.* अबद्धप्रयोग *m.* कानडें *n.*

Barbarity, **Barbarousness**, *n.* v. A. 1. रानवटपणा *m.* रानटीपणा *m.* &c. शिक्षाराहित्य *f.* आचारशून्यता *f.* अनाचारता *f.* अनक्षरता *f.* विद्याचारहीनता *f.* विद्याचारराहित्य *n.*

2 क्रूरता *f.* क्रौर्य *n.* निर्दयता *f.* निर्दयपणा *m.* दयाराहित्य *n.*

3 हेंगाडेपणा *m.* रानटीपणा *m.* अपशब्दता *f.* अपप्रयोगवैशिष्ट्य *n.* अबद्धप्रयोगवैशिष्ट्य *n.*

Barbarously, *adv.* v. A. 2 क्रूरतेनें, निर्दयतेनें, क्रौर्यपूर्वक.

3 हेंगाडेरीतीनें, हेंगाडेबोलीनें, अपप्रयोगपूर्वक.

Barbed, *a. jagged with hooks or points.* आंकडेदार, आंकड्याचा.

2—an arrow. कर्णाचा, कर्णी, सकर्ण, गलाचा.

3 *furnished with armour.*—horse. पाखरेचा.

Barber, *n.* न्हावी *or* नाह्वी *m.* नापित *m.* हजाम *m.* वारीक *m.* दिवाकीर्ति *pop.* दिवाकीर्त्त *m.*

—in contempt, &c. डोईचा *m.* नाहवगंड *nm.* तृणशत्रु *m.*

Business of a b. हजामत *f.* नापित्य *n.*

Razor case of a b. धोकटी *or* धोंकटी *f.*

Shop of a b. वारीकवाडा *m.* नापितशाला *f.*

Strap of a b. थापटणें *n.*

Terms of courtesy prefixed to the name of a b. महाला *or* महालापा *or* महाल्या *or* महाली *or* माली.

Vessel of a b. (holding shaving-water). तांबोटी *f.*

BARD, *n. poet and singer.* भाट *m.* बंदी *m.* बंदिजन *m.* मागध *m.* स्तुतिपाठक *m.* चारण *m.*

2 See POET.

BARE, *a. uncovered*, v. NAKED. नागवा, खुला, बोडखा *or* का, उघडा, अवस्त्र, वस्त्रहीन, अनावृत, आच्छादनरहित-हीन-शून्य-&c.

2—a tree or plant. निपानी, सडसडीत, निष्पर्ण, निष्पत्र, खरांटलेला, खरांट.

3 *plain, unadorned, bald.* भुंडा *or* भुंढा, बुचा, बोडका, ओंका, साधा, शून्य *pop.* सुना, सुनका, लकलकीत, लक्क, लकीलक्क, रंडका *or* रांडका, मुंढा, अभूषित, भूषणरहित-हीन-&c.

4 *mere*, v. SIMPLE. नुस्ता *or* नुस्था, निस्ता, केवल *or* ळ, शुद्ध.

5 See BAREHEADED.

To **BARE**, *v. a. make bare or naked.* बोडकावणें, नागवा-बोडका-उघडा-बुचा-सुना-&c. करणें.

BAREBACK, *adv. without saddle.* उपलाणीं, मोकळ्या पाठीवर.

To ride (upon a horse, &c.) b. उपलाणीं बसणें.

BAREBONED, *a.* v. LEAN. हाडगळ, हाडळ, हाडक्या.

BAREBONES, *n. lean person.* जरत्कारू *c.* सुदामदेव *m.* शुकस्वामी *m.* षाप्यांचापितर *m.* सांपळा *m.*

To become or be a mere b. सांपळा *m.* वळणें-राहणें *g. of s.*

BAREFACED, *a. with the face bare.* उघड्या तोंडाचा, बिनमुखवट्याचा, अनावृतमुख, अपिहितमुख, अनाच्छादितमुख.

2 v. SHAMELESS. निर्लज्ज, निलाजरा, निश्शंक, उघड्यामाथ्याचा, उजागीर.

BAREFACEDLY, *adv.* v. A. 2. *and* OPENLY. उघड्यातोंडानें, निलाजरेपणानें, उघडपणानें, उघड्यामाथ्यानें, उजागरीनें.

BAREFOOT, **BAREFOOTED**, *a.* अणवाणी, अणव्यापायांचा, पादत्राणरहित-शून्य-&c.

BAREFOOT, *adv.* अणवाणी *or* अणव्यापायानें, उघड्यापायांनीं, नागव्यापायानें, मोकळ्यापायानें.

BAREHEADED, *a.* बोडखा *or* का, उघड्या डोईचा, नग्नशिरस्क, शिरोवेष्टन रहित-हीन-&c. शिरस्त्राणरहित- हीन-&c.

BARELY, *adv.* v. A. 1. *merely, simply*, v. ONLY. फक्त, मात्र, केवल *or* ळ, निखळ.

BARENESS, *n.* v. A. 1. नागवेपणा *m.* खुलेपणा *m.* बोडकेपणा *m.* &c. आच्छादनराहित्य *n.* अनावृतता *f.*

2 निपानीपणा *m.* निष्पर्णत्व *n.* निष्पत्रता *f.*

3 बुचेपणा *m.* बोडकेपणा *m.* ओकेपणा *m.* साधेपणा *m.* &c. भूषणराहित्य *n.*

BARGAIN, *n. contract, compact,* v. AGREEMENT. बोली *f.* पैज *f.* होड *f.* करार *m.*

Into the b. वर, शिवाइ, वर्त्तोळयास, काढ्यास.

To strike a b. टाळी *f.* मारणें-देणें, हातावरहात *m.* मारणें-देणें होणें. [घोबें *n.*

2 *a gainful purchase.* किफायतीचा-किफायतवारघेतलेला सौदा *m.*

To **BARGAIN**, *v. n. make contract or agreement for.* खंडणें, खंडणूक *f.*-खंड *m.* करणें-ठरवणें, बोली *f.* करणें-ठरवणें, पैज *f.* मारणें-करणें-पाडणें.

2 *chaffer in settling a price.* घासाघास *f.*-घासाघीस *f.*-घासघीस *f.*-घिसघीस *f.*-खारास्वीर *f.*-&c. करणें.

BARGE, *n. boat for pleasure,* v. VESSEL. बरकीण *f.* क्रीडानौका *f.*

2 *flat bottomed boat.* पडाव *m.* [त्वचा *f.*

BARK, *n.* (of plants). साल *f.* सालपट *n.* चामडें *n.* चर्म *n.*

Inner b. अंतरसाल *f.* वल्कल *n.*

Outer b. उपरसाल *f.*

2 Peruvian bark. औषधाच्या उपयोगाची एका झाडाची साल *f.*

3 *cry of the dog.* भोंक *f.* भोंकणी *f.* श्वनाद *m.*

To **BARK**, *v. a.* (trees or plants). साल *f.* काढणें, सोलणें *or* साळणें, ओंसणें, छिलणें.

To **BARK**, *v. n.*—a dog. भुंकणें, भोंकणें, श्वनाद *m.* करणें.

BARK, **BARQUE**, *n.* v. VESSEL. बारकस *n.*

BARKING, *n.* v. V. N.—*act.* भोंकणें *n.* भुंकणें *n.* भोंकणी *f.*

BARLEY, *n.* यव *pop.* जव *m.* सातू *m.* सक्तु *m.*

BARLEY-CORN, *n.* जवाचा-सातूचा एकदाणा *m.*

Golden b. (as used in bracelets, &c.) जवा *m.*

2—the measure यव *pop.* जव *m.*

Measure of eight barley-corns laid side by side. अंगुल *pop.* अंगूळ *n.*

Exceeding by a b. जवा आगळा.

BARLEY-WATER, *n.* जवाचा *or* चें काट *mn.* सातूचा *or* चें काट *mn.* यवोदक *n.*

BARM, *n.* v. YEAST. सातूच्या दारूवरची साय *f.* सुरामंड *m.* कारोत्तम *m.* कारोत्तर *m.* यवमंड *m.*

BARN, *n. house for storing grain, &c.* कोठार *n.* गुरांचें कोठार *n.* धान्याची दांडसाळ *f.*

2 fig. *long, low, &c. house.*—contemptuously. घोडवळ *f.* मागर घर *n.* दांडसाळ *f.* दांडळ *f.*

BARNACLE, *n.*—the fish. खुबा *m. dim.* खुबी *f.* खुबडी *f.*

2—of farriers. काजगी *f.* काजा *m.*

BAROMETER, *n.* हवेचें वजन मोजण्याचें यंत्र *n.* वातोन्मान *n.* वायुमापकयंत्र *n.* वायुगुरुत्वज्ञापकयंत्र *n.*

BAROMETRICAL, *a.* वायुमापक यंत्राचा, वायुमापक यंत्रसंबंधी-विषयक, वायुमापकयंत्रानें केलेला.

BARON, *n.* विलायतेंत बडेलोकांची एक पदवी आहे.

BARONET, *n.* एक पदवी आहे.

BARRACK, *n.* अलंग *f.* शिपाइ राहण्याची चाळ *f.*

The word बराक from the English is becoming common.

BARREL, *n.* पीप *or* पिंप *n.*

2 (of a gun, &c.) v. TUBE. नळी *f.* नलिका *f.*

BARREN, *a.*—of woman. वंध्य *pop.* वांझ.

A b. woman. वंध्या *f.* अजातापत्या *f.* अप्रसूता *f.*

—in contempt. वांझटोळी *f.* वांझोटी *f.* वांझोळी *f.* वांझोडी *f.* ओंडा *m.* खुंटाळी *f.*

N. B. *Pandits* designate three classes of women as barren, viz. वंध्या she who has no offspring, काकवंध्या she who bears only one child, मृतवंध्या she whose offspring die.

2—of cow or female animal. वांझ, वंडा *or* ओंडा *a. ind.*

3—of trees. वांझा.

Rather or somewhat b. वांझट.

4—of soil or country, *unproductive, bad.* नापीक, नापिकी, भुकड, भुकिस्त, निखरड, बरड *or* भरड, मानटी, रखरखीत, रुक्ष,

नाकीर्देसार, खरांट, रानट, खंगार, खचरट, अफल, अफलवान्.
5 *scanty, not copious,* v. EMPTY. बांझा, भाकड, सुना, सुनका.
6 *dull, uninventive,*—the mind. कल्पनाशक्तिशून्य, अकल्पक, बोथा, बोथट. [फलता *f.*

BARRENNESS, *n.* v. A. 1. वांझपणा *m.* वंध्यत्व *n.* अफलत्व *n.* अ-
4 नापीकपणा *m.* भुकडपणा *m.* &c.

BARRICADE, BARRICADO, *n. hasty fortification of trees, earth, &c.* मेढेबंदी *f.* मेढेकोट *m.* मेढा *m.* अडकूट *n.* मार्गावरोधकरचना *f.* मार्गप्रतिबंधकरचना *f.*

To BARRICADE, *v. a.* मेढेबंदीनें कोंडणें, मेढेबंदी *f.* करणें.

BARRIER, *n.* See BARRICADE.
2 *bar, stop, obstruction,* v. HINDERANCE. आडकाठी *f.* अट *f.* अटक *f.* अडकूट *n.* अवरोधक *n.* प्रतिबंधक *n.*
3 *boundary,* v. BOUND. हद्द *f.* सरहद्द *f.*
4 *town, fort, &c. on the confines.* हद्दबंदीचा-हद्दीचा-कडमहालचा गांव *m.*-किल्ला *m.*-&c.

BARRISTER, *n.* कोर्तातला वकील *m.* बारिस्तर *vulgo.* बालिस्टर *m.*

BARROW, *n.*—hand b. मंज्या *m.*
2—wheel b. एक चाकीगाडी *f.* हातगाडी *f.*
3 *mound covering corpses.* प्रेतें पुरून रचलेलें टेंकाड *n.*-ढिगारा *m.*

To BARTER, *v. a.* मोबदला देणें, बदलाबदल *f.*-अदलाबदल *f.* करणें *g. of o.* केजें *n.* करणें *g. of o.* केज्यानें देणें-घेणें.

To BARTER, *v. n.* मालासमाल *m.*-ऐवजासऐवज *m.*-नगासनग *m.*-&c. देणें-घेणें, जिन्नसानें जिन्नस *m.* घेणें, ऐवजमोबादला *m.* करणें, फेरमोबादल्याचा व्यवहार *m.* करणें, भांडप्रतिभांडक व्यापार *m.* करणें, विनिमय *m.* करणें.

BARTER, *n.* साटेंलोटें *n.* साटलोट *f.* फेरमोबादला *m.* मोबादला *m.* फेरमोबादल्याचाव्यवहार *m.* विनिमय *m.* परिदान *n.*

BASALT, *n.* एका जातीचा खडक आहे.

BASE, *a. mean, vile;*—of things, v. WORTHLESS. हलका, नीच, उणा, एर, सेर, गैरी, अल्प, निरस, उणास, निपटारा.
2 *disreputable, dishonorable,*—of persons, v. VILE. हलका, नीच, पाजी, पामर, हीन, लुच्चा, लुचा, निपटारा, रिजाला.
3 *of low station or rank, of little account,* v. LOW. हलका, हीन, नीच, लहान, अधम, कनिष्ठ, पामर, हीनकुल, अकुलीन, क्षुल्लक, हीनयेाग्यतेचा.
4 See BASE-BORN. 5—of metals. हिणाचा, हिणकस, हिणकट, हिणवट, खोटसाळ, गैरसाळ.
6 *deep, grave;* —of sounds. नीचा, खरजांतला, गंभीर.

BASE, *n. foot, pedestal, stand,* v. BOTTOM. पडगी *or* पडघी *f.* पेंदी *or* पेंधी *f.* तल *n. pop.* तळ *m.* बुड *n.*
2—the chord or sound. घोर *m.* धूम *m.* खरज *m.*
3—in music or singing. नीचसवन *f. n.* नीच *n.* खरजसूर *m.* खरज *m.*
4—in reading. तृतीयसवन *n. f.*
5 (of a tabor, &c.) *bass end.* धूम *m.* धुमा *m.* धुमाचापुरा *m.* धुमाडा *m.*
6—in geom. भूमि *f.* मूर्धा *f.*

BASE-BORN, *a. born out of wedlock,* v. BASTARD. बटकीचा, रांडेचा, हरामजादा, बांदीचा.
2 *born of low parentage.* कमजात, हीनजात, अकुलीन, हीनकुल, कमअसल, विजात.

BASELESS, *a. unfounded,* fig. निराधार, निर्मूल, आधारशून्य.

BASELY, *adv.* v. A. 2. *dishonorably.* पाजीपणानें, हलकेपणानें, दौर्जन्यानें, दुर्जनतेनें, दौर्जन्यपूर्वक, पामरवृत्तीनें.

BASEMENT, *n. ground floor.* खालचामजला *m.* पहिला मजला *m.*
2 *story below the level of the ground.* तळघर *n.*

BASE-MINDED, *a.* v. MEAN. हलक्यामनाचा, मनाचा हलका, पाजी, पामर. [त्तीनें.

BASE-MINDEDLY, *adv.* v. A. पाजीपणानें, हलक्यामनानें, पामरवृ-

BASE-MINDEDNESS, *n.* v. A. पाजीपणा *m.* &c. पामरवृत्ति *f.*

BASENESS, *n.* v. A. 1. हलकेपणा *m.* नीचपणा *m.* &c. उणवाई *f.* उणाखी *f.*
2 पाजीपणा *m.* उणेपणा *m.* हीण *n.* हीनता *f.* हीनत्व *n.* पामरत्व *n.* पामरवृत्ति *f.*
3 हलकेपणा *m.* नीचपणा *m.* &c. उणवाई *f.* अधमत्व *n.* हीनयेाग्यता *f.* हीनकुलत्व *n.* अकुलीनता *f.*
4 See BASTARDY.

BASE- SOULED, BASE-SPIRITED, See MEAN.

BASE-STRING, *n.* खरजाची तार *f.*

BASE-VIOL, *n.* खरजसुराचें एक तंतुवाद्य आहे.

BASHFUL, *a. modest to excess; sheepish.* लाजाळू, लाजरा, लाजखोर, लाजवट, लाजट, लज्जाशील, भिडस्त, भिडसारू *or* रू भिडसर, भिडसूळ, भेजूड, संकोची, संकोचशील, संकोचस्वभाव, दिवाभीत, सभाभीत, जनभीत, दृष्टिभीत, नजरभीड.
Some significant terms for *A bashful person* corresp. with *shycock, sheepface, mealymouth,* &c. are लाजकोंबडा, गायतोंड्या, गोमुख्या, मुंगसतोंड्या, मेलतोंड्या, मेमलतोंडा, मेमुळगाडा, मेशपात्र, मेषा, मेंगा *or* ग्या, मेंगें, तोंडझांक्या, मुलदुबेल.

BASHFULLY, *adv.* v. A. लज्जेनें, लाजिरवाणी *or* णें, लाजरेपणानें, &c. लाजून, लाज धरून, लाजवटपणें, संकोचानें, संकोच धरून.

BASHFULNESS, *n.* v. A. लाजरेपणा *m.* &c. लाज *f.* लज्जा *f.* संकोच *m.* भीड *f.* डोळयांत पाणी *n.* अपत्रपा *f.* सभाभीति *f.* सभाकंप *m.* जनभीति *f.*

BASIL, *n. ocymum sanctum.* तुळस *f.* तुलसी *f.*
Some kinds are, Black b. काळीतुळस, कृष्णतुळस *or* तुलसी, वैजयंती *f.* White b. पांढरीतुळस, रामतुळस *or* तुलसी. Wild b. रानतुळस, मालेतुळस. Sweet b. सबजा *m.*
The little erection in which it is planted. तुलसीवृंदावन *n.* वृंदावन *n.*

BASILISK, *n.* विखारी कल्पित सर्प आहे.

BASIN, BASON, *n.* भांडें *n.* पातेलें *n.* तस्त *n.* बहुगुणें *n.* वाडगा *m.* वाटगा *m.*
2 *pool, &c.* v. POND. हौद *m.* कुंड *n.*
3 *hollow between hills.* पाठेन. ओंडण *f. n.* ओंडवण *n.* घोळ *f.*

BASIS, *n. foundation, groundwork.* मूल *n.* पाया *m.* आधार *m.* अधिकरण *n.* उपष्टंभ *m.*

To BASK, *v. n.* उनास-उनांत बसणें, ऊन *n.*-निबर *n.*-ओप *f.*-ओपळी *f.*-तिरीप *or* तिरीम *f.* खाणें-घेणें-घेत बसणें, तिरपेस बसणें, उनास पाठ *f.* देणें.

To BASK, *v. a.* ऊन *n.* देणें, उनांत ठेवणें.

BASKET, *n.* There are *Baskets* of endless diversifications of shape, size, &c. and of various uses. They are distinguished accordingly by peculiar names, of which the most common are, करंड *m.* करंडा *m.* करंडी *f.* करंडूल *n.* कुरकुला *m.* कुरकू *f.* कुरकूल *m. n.* केरी *f.* कोठी *f.* छबडी *f.* झाल *f.*

टोपला m. dim. टोपली f. or लें n. डाली f. डालें n. दुरडी f. परडी f. पांटी f. पांटें n. पेटारा m. dim. पेटारी f. रुमाली पांटी f. रोवळा m. dim. रोवळी f. शिपतर n. शिबुटलें n. संबळी f. सांगसी or साकरी f. हुणगें or हिणगें n. हुरा or हारा m.

Little covered b. संबळी f.

Round leathern b. टोकर m. टोकरा m. dim. टोकरी f.

Slung b. *basket of a shoulder-sling*. डाली f.

Wickerwork b. for a cart. कुरकुला m. or लें n. कुरकूल m. dim. कुरकुली f.

BASKET-HILT, n. (of a पट्टा), खोबळा m.

BASKET-MAKER, n. बुरूड m.

BASKET-WOMAN, n. पांटीवाली f. हेलकरीण f.

BASKET-WORK, n. बुरूडकाम n. बुरडींबकाम n.

BASS, n.—in music. See BASE.

BASS-RELIEF, n. थोडेंच बाहेर आलेलें कोरींव काम n.

BASSOON, n. भोंबारा m.

BASTARD, n. *illegitimate child*. रांडलेक m. f. दासीपुत्र m. असतीसुत m. (ता f.) असतूसंतान n. कन्यापुत्र m. कन्यकापुत्र m. अनूढासुत m. (ता f.) कन्यकासुत m. (ता f.) जारजसंतान n. कौलटेय m. अकरमाशा m. अठराधान्याचें कोडबुळें n.

2 *son of a concubine*. लेंकवळा m. राखेचा.

BASTARD, a. *born out of wedlock, illegitimate*. रांडेचा, दासीचा, बटकीचा, लवंडेचा, बांदीचा, पोटकरणीचा, जारज, दासीज, व्यभिचारज, अनौरस, कडवा, कडू, अदंपतिजात, अदंपत्युत्पन्न, अदंपत्युद्भव, अपत्नीजात, अधर्मजात, अविधिजात, कन्याजात, कन्यकाजात, अनूढाजात, अकरमाशा, दोहोबापांचा.

Note. The Hindu Law specifies several classes of *Bastards*; the words here given (both under the *noun* and under the *adjective*) refer some to one class, some to another.

2 *spurious*, v. FALSE. खोटा, खोटसाळ, मिथ्या.

To BASTARDIZE, v. a. जारज कोटींत आणणें-आहे असें ठरविणें.

BASTARDY, n. v. A. जारजता f. जारजावस्था f. दासीपुत्रत्व n. दासीजत्व n. अनौरसता f. कौलटेयत्व n. जारोत्पत्ति f. व्यभिचारोत्पत्ति f.

To BASTE, v. a. *cudgel*. v. To BEAT. दांडकणें, दांडाळणें, सोटाळणें, टोणपणें, चेचरणें, कुंदी f. काढणें g. of o.

2 *sew slightly*. टांचणें, टांके or टांचे m.pl.-धागे m. pl.मारणें.

3 (meat) मासभाजतांना त्याजवर लोणी n. घालणें.

BASTINADE, BASTINADO, n. *beating with a cudjel, &c.* बांसमार m. सोटेमार m. टोणपेमार m. दांडकेमार m. मारझोड f. दंडप्रहार m.

BASTION, n. बुरूज m. हुडा m.

Fortress of four bastions. चौबुरजी f.

Having four bastions. चौबुरजी.

To BASTINADE, v. a. *cudjel*, v. To BEAT. दांडकणें, सोटाळणें, मारझोड f. करणें g. of o. चेचरणें.

BAT, n. *stick, club*. दांडू m. दांडूक n. दांडकें or दांडगें n. सोटा m.

2—the animal. वागूळ or वाघूळ n. पाकोळी f. बदुरी f. अजिनपत्रा f.—Wild b.–flying fox. वडवागूळ n.

BATCH, n. *quantity made or done at once*. भट्टी f. सांचा m. घाणा m. घाणी f.

Of one b. v. ALIKE. एकेघाणीचा, एकेभट्टीचा, एकरास.

To BATE. See To ABATE.

BAT-FOWLING, n. रात्रीं पांखरें धरण्याचा एक प्रकार आहे.

BATH, n. *bathing place*. नहाणी f. मोरी or मोहरी f. हमामखाना m. स्नानकुंड n.

2 v. ABLUTION, आंघोळ f. स्नान n.

Cold b. थंडपाण्याची or थंडपाण्यानें आंघोळ f.-स्नान n.

Dry b. पोतंडीचा शेक m.

Hot b. ऊनपाण्याची or ऊनपाण्यानें आंघोळ f.-स्नान n.

Tepid b. कोंबटपाण्याची or कोंबटपाण्यानें आंघोळ f.-स्नान. n.

Vapour b. बाफारा m.

BATH-ROOM, BATHING-HOUSE, n. *balneary*. नहाणघर n. स्नानागार n. हमामखाना m.

To BATHE, v. a. *wash*. नाह्वणें, नाहणणें, नाहणें, आंघूळ or आंघोळ f.-स्नान n. घालणें.

To b. with inunction. नाहूं घालणें, नहाण n. घालणें.

2 *wash or moisten*. धुणें.

To BATHE, v. n. नाहणें, आंघोळ or आंघूळ f. करणें, स्नान n. करणें, आंग n. धुणें.

To b. with or in holy water. गंगानाहणें.

To b. in a river. नदीस्नान n. करणें.

To b. in the sea. समुद्रस्नान n. करणें. [आप्लुत.

BATHED, p. v. V. N. नाहलेला, आंघोळ केलेला or झालेला, स्नात,

To be b. in blood or sweat. रक्तानें-घामानें नाहणणें.

BATHER, n. v. V. N. आंघोळ करणारा, &c. स्नानकर्त्ता, स्नाता & स्नायी (esp. in comp. as जलस्नाता, गंगास्नाता, तीर्थस्नाता, तिलस्नाता, भस्मस्नाता, and जलस्नायी &c.).

BATHING, n. v. V. N. *and* ABLUTION. आंघोळ or आंघूळ f. स्नान n. आंगधुणें n.

Chunamed, &c. spot for b. नाहणी f. मोरी or मोहरी f.

Room or house for b. नाहणघर n. पाणघर n. Fire place in it. पाणचूल f.

BATING, p. v. EXCEPT. सोडून, वजाकरून.

BATLET, n. *small bat for beating linen*. कुंदी करायाची मोगरी f.

BATON, BATOON, n. v. STAFF. दंड *pop*. दांडा m. काठी f. राजदंड m.

BATTA, n. भत्ता m.

BATTALIA, n. *battle array*. रणरचना f. रणव्यूह m. सेनारचना f.

2 *army in array*. व्यूहितसेना f.-सैन्य n.

BATTALION, n. पलटण or न f. n. बटालण or पटालन f. Note. All these words are corruptions of the English.

BATTEN, n.—of wood. कडी f. चिरखांब m.

To BATTEN, v. a. v. To FATTEN. पुष्ट करणें, माजवणें.

To BATTEN, v. n. v. To FATTEN. पुष्ट होणें, माजणें, पोसणें.

To BATTER, v. a. *beat with successive blows to throw down*. ठोकणें, ठोकाठोकी f. करणें, मार m.-मारा m.-मारगिरी f. करणें-लावणें, भडमार m. करणें, खोमलणें, घनमार m.-घनाघात m. करणें.

2 *attack with artillery*. तोफांचा भडमार m. करणें.

3 *wear with service*. कावल करणें, खोमलणें, भुसडा m.-भुसाडा m.-भुसा m.-भूस n. पाडणें g. of o. खोचे m. pl.-खोमे m. pl. पाडणें, घुमा m. घालणें.

BATTERED, p. v. V. 1. खोमललेला, &c.

3 खोमललेला &c. चेचका, खोचे पाडलेला or पडलेला, &c.

BATTERING, BATTERY, n. v. V. 1.—*act*. खोमलणें n. मारा लावणें n. &c. मारा m. मार m. मारगिरी f.

BATTERING RAM, *n.* आघातांनीं भिंत पाडण्याचें यंत्र *n.*
BATTERY, *n. line of cannon.* मोरचा *m.*
The raised site for a b. दमदमा *or* धमधमा *m.* धमामा *m.*
Disposition or range of batteries. मोरचेबंदी *f.*
Erecting of batteries. मोरचेबंदी *f.*
2—in law. दंडपारुष्य *n.*
BATTLE, *n. fight.* लढाई *f.* युद्ध *n.* रण *mn.* संग्राम *m.* विग्रह *m.*
Brave in b. रणशूर, रणधीर, रणगंभीर, रणसिंह, झुंजार.
Close and furious b. सफेजंगी *f.*
Cowardice in b. रणभीति *f.*
Cowardly in b. रणभीत, रणभीरु.
Field of b. रणभूमि *f.* रणांगण *n.* युद्धांगण *n.* समरांगण *n.* मल्लभू *f.*
Mixed or tumultuary b. रणसंकुल *n.* तुमुल *mn.*
Mortal or furious b. रणतुंबळ *n.* रणकंदन *n.* धनचक्र *n.* रणधुमाळी *f.*
Pillar erected on the field of b. रणस्तंभ *m.* रणखांब *m.* यूप *m.*
To give b. लढाई *f.* घेणें-देणें.
BATTLE-ARRAY, *n.* रणरचना *f.* रणव्यूह *m.* फरेबंदी *f.*
BATTLE-AXE, *n.* परशु *pop.* फरश *or* स *m.* फरशी *f.*
BATTLE-FIELD, *n.* रणभूमि *f.* रणांगण *n.* समरांगण *n.* रणक्षेत्र *n.* मल्लभू *f.*
BATTLE-DOOR, *n.* खेळण्याचें एक साधन आहे.
BATTLEMENT, *n.* जंग्यांची भिंत *f.*
2 *embrasure.* जंगी *f.*
BAVIN, *n. stick of a faggot.* कोंडका *m.* कोंडकें *n.* फाटें *or* फाटें *n.*
2 See FAGGOT.
BAWBLE, BAUBLE, *n. thing gay or showy, without real value or use.* मुलामीवस्तु *f.* मुलाम्याचा-ओपेचा-पुराणाचा डागिणा *m.*-&c. भूसकेलड्डू *m. pl.* बेगडेचा जोडा *m.*
BAWD, *n. procuress.* कुट्टनी *pop.* कुंटण *or* कुंटीण *f.* भाडखाऊ *c.* दूती *f.* दूतिका *f.* शंभली *f.*
BAWDRY, *n. practice of a bawd.* कुंटणकी *f.* कुंटणपणा *m.* कुंटणगिरी *f.* दूतीकर्म *n.*
2 v. OBSCENITY. बीभत्सभाषण *n.* अचकटविचकट *or* विचकटबोलणें *n.*
BAWDY, *a.* v. OBSCENE. बीभत्स, अचकटविचकट, विचकट, अवाच्य.
BAWDY-HOUSE, *n.* v. BROTHEL. छिनालखाना *m.* रांडवाडा *m.* वेश्यागृह *n.*
To BAWL, *v. n.* (from pain, &c.) *bellow, roar.* अरडणें *or* ओरडणें, बोंबलणें, आकांतणें, आक्रंदणें, उक्शा बुक्शीं *adv.* रडणें, रडून जीव *m.* टाकणें, हेल काढून रडणें-ओरडणें-&c. गळा काढून रडणें &c. रडून अक्राळ *m.*-आक्रांत *m.*-&c. करणें, घसा *m.*-टाहो *m.* फोडणें *or* फोडून रडणें, भोकाड *n.* वासणें *or* वासून रडणें, तोंड *n.* घेणें, आकांत *m.*-आक्रोश *m.*-आक्रंदन *n.*-अरड *or* ओरड *f.*-अरडाओरड *f.*-&c. करणें.
2 *cry out, call loudly, vociferate.* गागणें, अरडणें *or* ओरडणें, पुकारणें, गरजणें, गळीं लागणें, ओरड *f.*-ओरडा *m.*-अरडाओरड *f.*-पुकार *or* रा *m.*-ललकारी *or* ललकारणी *f.*-कल्लोळ *m.*-कोल्हाळ *m.*-घोंघाट *m.*-&c. करणें, अरोळी *f.* मारणें, घुमरी *f.* घालणें.
3 *speak loudly.* घाटी *f.*-खाऊन-गळा *m.* फोडून-तंगाडून-गळा काढून-शिरा *f. pl.* ताणून-&c. बोलणें, कडकून बोलणें, जीव टाकून-ओढून-खाऊन-देऊन-तोडून-खरडून-&c. बोलणें, मोठ्या गळ्यानें बोलणें, गळेफोड *m.* करणें.
4 at; *bellow at, roar at,* v. To SCOLD. खणकावणें, दणकावणें, दणगारणें, उद्धारणें, डरकणें, कडकणें, ताव *m.* देणें, खांकरवसा *m.* घालणें.
BAWLER, *n.* BAWLING, *p. a.* v. V. ओरडणारा, बोंबलणारा, &c. बोंबल्या, बोंब मान्या-ठोक्या, अरड्या *or* ओरड्या, तोंडघेण्या.
BAWLING, *n.* v. V. ओरडणें *n.* बोंबलणें *n.* &c. आक्रांत *m.* आक्रोश *m.* &c. See the nouns under the verb.
2 गागणें *n.* ओरडणें *n.* पुकारणें *n.* &c. ओरड *f.* पुकारा *m.* गांगरडा *m.* ललकारी *f.* &c. See the nouns under the verb.
BAY, *n. laurus cassia.* तज *f.*
The bark of b. तज *n.* दालचिनी *f.* त्वक् *f.*
2 (of the Sea). कोळ *n.* बांकण *n.*—large. आखात *n.* उपसागर *m.*
BAY, *a.*—the color. कुमेत *or* कुमाईत, —chestnut b. तेल्याचोर, —dark b. सारंगा.
To BAY, See To BARK.
BAY. at b. शत्रूकडे तोंडकरून.
To keep at b. शत्रूकडे तोंड करून आंगावर येऊं न देणें.
BAY WINDOW, *n.* भिंतीचे बाहेर गेलेली खिडकी *f.*
To BAYONET, v. *a.* संगिनीनें मारणें-भोसकणें.
BAYONET, *n.* संगीन *f.*
BAZAR, *n. market.* बाजार *m.* हट्ट *pop.* हट *m.*
BDELLIUM, *n.* गुग्गुल *pop.* गुगूळ *m.* देवधूप *m.*
To BE, *v. n. exist, subsist.* होणें, असणें, वर्त्तणें.
It may be. न जाणो.
It never has been and it never will be. नभूतो नभविष्यति.
Let be, Be it so. असो, अस्तु, असूंद्या.
Not to be. नसणें.
BEACH, *n. sea shore.* समुद्रकांठ *m.* समुद्रकिनारा *m.* समुद्रतीर *n.* वेला *pop.* वेळा *f.* ढकशी *f.*
Sandy b. वाळवंट *n.* पुलिन *n. pop.* पुळण *f. n.*
BEACON, *n. light erected to give notice of danger.* आकाशदिवा *m.* आकाशदीप *m.* आगतशत्रुज्ञापकदीप *m.*
BEAD, *n.* मणि *or* मणी *m.* पोत *m. f.* मणका *m.*
Glass b. गळसर *m.* (String of such beads. गळसर *m.* गळसरी *f.*) करमरा मणी *m.*
Gold b. (rice-form). तांदळी पोत *f.* तांदूळ *m.*
Gold b. (round). करमरा मणी *m.* String of such beads. जव *m.*
Red glass b. गोविंद *or* गोविंद मणी *m.*
String of beads. माला *pop.* माळ *f.*
To be at one's beads. जप करीत असणें.
2—in architecture. गोलची *f.*—the implement with which it is made. गोलची *f.*
3 *sight of a gun.* माशी *f.*
4 *bubble on spirit.* मद्यावरचा फुगा *m.*
BEAD-PLANE, *n.* रंधागोल *m.*
BEADLE, *n.* छडीदार *m.* पाईक *or* पायक *m.* (His office, पायकी *f.*) भालदार *m.*
BEADS-MAN, *n.* जप्या *m.* जपाचा ब्राह्मण *m.* संध्याभट *m.*
BEAGLE, *n.* लहान जातीचा शिकारी कुत्रा *m.*
BEAK, *n. bill.* चोंच *f.* टोंच *f.* टोंक *f.* बोंच *f.* चंचु *f.* चंचुपुट *n.*
BEAM, *n. piece of timber.* तुळई *f.* तुळवट *n.* बहाल *n.* दांडी *f.* सर *m.* सरी *f.* बार *n.*
B. over two posts. *piece-b.* खांडतुळई *f.* खांड *n.*

Longitudinal division of a b. चिरसाब *m.*
Small and squared b. कडी *f.*
2 (of a balance). दांडी *f.*
3 (of a car, &c.). दांडी *f.*
4 (of the weaver). तुरी *f.*
5 (of the sun &c.). किरण *m.* रश्मि *m.* कर *m.*
Shorn of his beams. क्षततेजा, क्षततेजस्क.
6 (of a draw-well)—transverse, with stone. ओकती *f.*

To BEAM, *v. n. emit beams,* v. To SHINE. किरण *m.* पाडणें, तपणें, प्रकाशणें.
2—the countenance, &c. *glow with health, delight, &c.* टवटवणें, टकटकणें, लुसलुसणें, लिंबू *n.* फुटणें (तोंडावर &c.).

BEAMER, *n.* BEAMING, *p. a.* v. V. 1. तपणारा, &c. किरणमय, प्रकाशमान.
2 टवटवणारा, &c. टवटवीत, टकटकीत *or* टुकटुकीत, सुप्रसन्न.

BEAN, *n.* घेवडा *m.* घेवडी *f.* बारवा *m.* Some kinds are, बोटघेवडी, श्रावणघेवडा, फटाराघेवडा, मुगाघेवडा, पांढराघेवडा, काळाघेवडा, बालपापडी, मेहेंदळ.

To BEAR, *v. a. sustain, support, uphold.* साहणें, सोसणें, संभाळणें, वाहणें, वहन *n.*-सहन *n.*-संभाळ *m.* करणें *g. of o.*
2 (in the mind or affections), *entertain.* बाळगणें, धरणें, ठेवणें, राखणें, वागवणें, पाळणें.
3 *carry, convey, transport.* वाहणें, नेणें, घेऊन जाणें, चालवणें, वहन *n.* करणें *g. of o.*
4 *endure, undergo,* v. To SUFFER. सोसणें, साहणें, कंठणें, पुरवणें *inv.con.* काढणें, वाहणें, सहन *n.*-सोसणूक *f.* करणें *g. of o.*
As it can be borne. साहतसाहत.
To be borne. उपभोग्य.
5 *be capable of, admit.* घेणें.
6 (a child) *bring forth.* जन्मविणें, जन्म *m.* देणें, प्रसवणें, उद्भावणें, प्रसव *m.*-प्रसूति *f.*-सूत्या *f.*-उद्भावन *n.*-&c. करणें.
7 (a young animal, gener.) विणें (with exception of the *mare* and *ass*), गाभास जाणें, पोटचें *n.* पडणें, घालणें, उद्भावणें, पोट *n.* पिकणें.
That has borne twice. दुजाईत.
That has borne thrice. तिजाईत.
8 (fruit.) देणें, बार *m.*-बाज *m.* देणें.
9—as a mark of authority, &c. *wear, carry, hold.* बाळगणें, धरणें, धारण *n.* करणें.
10 *brook, endure, put up with.* सोसणें *or* सोसून घेणें, साहणें *or* साहून घेणें, पोटांत घालणें-ठेवणें, मुलाजा *m.*-सबुरी *f.* करणें, मूग *m. pl.* खाणें-गिळणें *or* मुगाचें *n.* करणें.
To be bearable or supportable. पुरवणें.
11 *exercise* (sway) चालविणें. [सोसणें.
12 *sustain* (expense, charge. &c.) आंगावरघेणें, पदरचा करणें,
13 (witness, testimony) देणें.
14 (blame) शिरावर-डोक्यावर-आंगावर-&c. घेणें.
15 (date) अमक्यातारखेचा-तिथीचा-मितीचा असणें.
16 up; *support.* संभाळणें, धीर *m.*-धैर्य *n.* देणें.
17 off; *carry away.* नेणें, हरणें, हरण *n.* करणें *g. of o.*
19 upon, or down, back, &c. See To PRESS, To URGE, To DRIVE.

To BEAR, *v. n. be fruitful.* फळ *n.* देणें, फळणें, बार *m.* धरणें, लागणें, ऋतु *m.* होणें *inv. con.* बाजणें.
To begin to b. लागास येणें, लागणें, बारास येणें.
That bears abundantly. बाजवट.
That bears once, annually. एकबारी—twice दुबारी.
2 against, towards, upon, &c; *tend, have direction.* कलणें, लागणें, मोड *f.*-मोडणी *f.*-झोंक *m.*-कल *m.*-रोंख *m.*-गम *m.*-कटाक्ष *m.*-धोरण *n.*-संधान *n.*-&c. असणें, गुलकावणी *f.* दाखवणें.
3 on; *refer to.* लागणें, अन्वय *m.*-संबंध *m.* ठेवणें-धरून असणें.
4 upon; *press and gall, pinch, &c.* लागणें, घासणें, रुपणें, रुतणें.
5 with; *deal considerately with.* वागवणें *or* वागवून घेणें, संभाळणें *or* संभाळून घेणें, चालढकलीवर घेणें, चालढकल *f.* करणें.

BEAR, *n.* अस्वल *m. f. n.* ऋक्ष *pop.* रीस *m.* भल्लूक *pop.* भालू *or* भालूक *m.* नडघ *n. m.* नडघा *m.* (घी *f.* घें *n.*) [लें *n.*
2 Ursa major. सप्तर्षि *pop.* सप्तऋषि *mpl.* खाटलें *n.* खाटलें बाज-
3 Lesser bear. ध्रुवपुच्छ *n.* [डा *m.*

BEAR-GARDEN, *n.place of uproar, tumult.* बाजार *m.* बाजारवा-
To become a b. g. or Babel. वेड्यांचाबाजार पिकणें.

BEAR'S GREASE, *n.* अस्वलाची चरबी *f.*

BEAR-SKIN, *n.* अस्वलाची कातडी *f.*

BEARD, *n.* दाढी *f.*—in contempt. &c. खाड *n.*
B., whiskers, and mustaches. श्मश्रु *n.* That has bushy b. w. and m. श्मश्रुल.
Tonsure of the b. and head. दाढीडोई *f. v.* कर.
Woman having a b. मिशाळी *f.* पोटा *f.* पुंसलक्ष्णा *f.*
To shave the b. दाढी *f.*-खाड *n.* करणें.
2 (of corn). कुसळ *n.* कुसूं *or* कूस *n.* शूक *n.* सस्यशूक *n.*
3 See BARB.

To BEARD, *v. a. oppose to the face.* दाढी *f.*-मिशा *f. pl.* उपटणें *g. of o.* नाकावर पाय *m.* देणें, नाक *n.* ठेचणें, पायावर पाय *m.* देणें, नाकास चुना *m.* लावणें, तोंडासतोंड *n.* देणें.

BEARDED, *a. having a b.* दाढीकरी, दाढीवाला, दाढीवाईक.
Large b. दाढ्या, दाढेल.
2—as corn. कुसळा, कुसळाचा, शूकवान्, शूकी.
3 See BARBED.

BEARDLESS, *a.* निखाडा *or* निखाड्या, निदाढ्या, खाडू, तूवर.
B. youth, v. STRIPLING. बारवर्षा, सोळवर्षा.

BEARER, *n.v.V.A.1. 3. carrier, conveyer, porter.* वाहणारा, &c. वाहक &c. वाही (esp. in comp.) बरदार (in comp. as इटेबरदार, बेलेबरदार, शिक्केबरदार).
Bearer (in a cheque or order) नेऊन दाखविणारा.
4 *and* SUFFERER. सोसणारा, सहणारा, &c. सोसीक, सह (in comp.) [नरसू.)
6 प्रसवणारा, &c. सू and प्रसू (in comp. as वीरसू, विश्वसू,
9 *wearer, holder.* बाळगणारा, &c. धर (in comp.) धारक & धारी (in comp.).
I. (of a palanquin, &c.) हमाल *or* हम्माल *m.* भोई *m.* कहार *m.*
II. (of a bier or corpse) खांदकरी.

BEARING, *n. leaning,* v. TENDENCY. रोंख *m.* कल *m.* झोंक *m.* मोड *f.* मोडणी *f.* संधान *n.*
2 See BEHAVIOUR.

BEARING, *a. on which postage is due.* हाशील न दिलेला, हाशील देण्याचा.

BEARISH, *a.* v. RUDE. धट्ट, गैरसाल, अशिष्ट.

BEAST, *n.* पशु *m.* हैवान *mfn.* चतुष्पाद *mfn.*

B. of burden. पाठीचा (बैल, घोडा, &c.), ओझेल *or* ओझेली (बैल, घोडा &c.), पाठाळ *or* पाठवळ *n.* पृष्ठवाह्य *m.* पृष्ठवाह.

B. of draught. वाहीम *m.*

B. broken in to carry a rider. पाठवळ *n.* पाठाळ *n.*

B. of pasture, *neat.* गुरूं *n.* ढोर *n.*

B. of prey, wild b. श्वापद *mn.* नखी *m.* सावज *n.* हिंस्रपशु *m.*

Horned b. शिंगोटी *f.*

Horned beasts,—gener. शिंगोटी *f.*

2 fig. *dirty or lubberly fellow.* म्हशा *or* म्हैशा *m.* म्हशागुग्गुळ *m.* रीस *m. n.* ऐदी *c.* [शीलता *f.*

BEASTLINESS, *n.* v. A. पशुवृत्ति *f.* पशुस्वभाव *m.* पशुधर्म *m.* पशु-

BEASTLY, *a. like a beast, filthy,* &c. पशूसारखा, पशुसदृश, &c. जनावराचा, पशूचा, पशुवृत्तीचा, पशुस्वभावाचा, पशुधर्मीचा, पशुशील.

To BEAT, *v. a. strike, knock.* मारणें, पिटणें, ठोकणें, ताडणें, मार *m.* देणें, ताडन *n.*-मर्दन *n.*-प्रहार *m.* करणें.

—mutually or generally. मारामार *f.*-मारामारी *f.*-हाणमार *or* हाणामार *or* री *f.* करणें.

2—with the power of such words as *to thump, pommel, bang, baste, belabour, cudgel, drub, thrash, leather, belt, lick, lace, &c.* बुकलणें, बडवणें, झोडणें, पिटणें, ठोकणें, कुटणें, कुचलणें, कुबलणें, कुदकणें, कुदवणें, कुमकणें, कुमलणें, झोडपणें, दांडकणें, दांडगणें, दांडाळणें, दुबकणें *or* बुदकणें, सोटाळणें, टोणपणें, खुंदलणें *or* खुंदळणें, खुबलणें, धोपटणें, चेचणें, चेचरणें *or* ठेंचणें, धमकणें *or* धुमकणें, बखलणें, सडकणें, घोळसणें, घोळसावणें, चोपटणें, चोपणें, सोतरणें *or* सोतारणें *or* सोताडणें, अंबविणें, कांडात काढणें *g. of o.* पिकवणें, लाता बुक्यानीं तुडवणें, बळकट *adv.* मारणें, हात *m.* टाकणें, आंगाचे धुडके *m. pl.* उडवणें *g. of o.* कुंदी *f.* काढणें-गाजवणें *g. of o.* गुण *m. pl.* काढणें *g. of o.* टांके *m. pl.* ढील करणें *g. of o.* कात्यायन *n.* करणें *g. of o.* बरडेल *n.* काढणें, कुच्या *m.* काढणें, पूजा *f.* करणें-घालणें *g. of o.* तेल *n.* काढणें *or* तेलवण *n.* काढणें-घालणें *g. of o.* मारून भूस *n.* भरणें, बुक्या *f. pl.*-लाता *f. pl.* सडकणें *or* सडकून-कचकून-कचकावून-रगडून-रपाटून-&c. देणें, त्राटणाचें *n.* घालणें, मारून भोत *m.* करणें *or* मारतां भोत भरणें, डोळे *m. pl.* पांढरे करणें *g. of o.* चामडी *f.* लोंबवणें *g. of o.* कुटण *or* कुट्टण *n.*-कुट्टा *m.*-कुटचेल *n.* काढणें *g. of o.* मारकूट *f.*-मारझोड *f.*-मारपीट *f.*-माराकुटी *f.* करणें, फरमाशी मार *m.*-पलाखतीचा मार *m.*-तंबीमार *m.* देणें, मारून उरता न ठेवणें, मारून भूस *n.* पाडणें, मारून पीठ *n.*-पिठार *n.* करणें, हाडें मोकळीं करणें *g. of o.* कणीक *f.* मऊ करणें-तिंबणें *g. of o.* कणकीसारखा तिंबणें.

A sound or good beating. फरमाशीमार *m.* हग्यामार *m.*

3—soundingly; *whack, &c.* कडकावणें, तडकावणें, फडफडवणें, दणकावणें, दणगारणें, धपकावणें *or* धबकावणें, थडाडां*or* थडाथड *adv.*-फडाफड *adv.* मारणें, रपाटणें.

4 (a musical instrument). ठोकणें, पिटणें, वाजवणें.

5 v. To DEFEAT, To CONQUER. जिंकणें, जेर करणें, जेरीस आणणें, आपटणें, अदळणें.

6 (a floor, &c.). चोपणें, चोपटणें, दाबादाबी *f.* करणें.

7 (a proclamation, &c.). पिटणें, वाजवणें.

8 down, (price, terms). पाडून देणें-घेणें.

9 off, back. v. To REPEL. हटवणें, माघारां लावून देणें.

10 (time)—in music. ताल *m.* धरणें.

11 up; *work up.* कमावणें, कमाई *f.*-मशागत *f.* करणें *g. of o.*

To BEAT, *v. n. pulsate,* v. To THROB. उडणें, ठणकणें, टचटचणें, टचटच *adv.* वाजणें, टणटण *or* टुणटुण *adv.* उडणें, टणटणणें, ठणका *m.* लागणें.

2 against; *dash against.* अपटणें, धडकणें, धडक *f.*-धडका *m.*-धडक *f.*-धडका *m.*-&c. लागणें-बसणें. [*f.* भरणें.

3—the heart, v. To PALPITATE. धडधडणें, धडकी *f.*-धडधडी

BEAT, *n.* See STROKE. 2 See PULSATION. [आहत.

BEATEN, *p.* v. V. A. 1. मारलेला, ठोकलेला, &c. ताडित, प्रहारित,

To be b. मार *m.* खाणें, तोंडांत खाणें.

I.—a road. राबत्याचा, वहिवाटीचा, मळलेला, दळवटयाचा.

To be b. रांबणें, मळगावणें, मळणें, चोळ *f.* पडणें *inv. con.*

BEATER, *n.* v. V. A. 1. मारणारा, ठोकणारा, &c.

I. (of bushes, for game). रानकाढ्या *m.* [बडवणी *f.*

II. (any instrument for beating or bruising) बडवणें *n.*

BEATIFIC, BEATIFICAL, *a.* सुखकर, सुखद, सुखप्रद.

BEATITUDE, *n. heavenly felicity,* v. HEAVEN. मुक्ति *f.* मोक्ष *m.* सिद्धि *f.* अपवर्ग *m.* निर्वाण *n.* निःश्रेय *n.* श्रेय *n.* निश्श्रेयस *m.*

The Hindus distinguish final beatitude into four kinds, viz. सायुज्य absorption into the essence of the deity, सलोकता residence with him, समीपता nearness to him or being in his presence, and सरूपता conformedness to his image.

BEAU, *n.* v. BUCK. छानछूक *or* छोक *c.* कुर्रेदार *c.* कुर्रेबाज *c.* अकडबाज *c.* छेला *m.*

BEAU IDEAL, मनांत मानलेली प्रतिमा *f.*-मूर्त्ति *f.*

BEAUISH, *a.* v. BUCKISH. छानीचा, छानदार, नोकदार, छानछुकीचा, चट्टीपट्टीचा, अकडेचा, नोकीझोकीचा.

BEAUISHNESS, *n.* v. A. चट्टीपट्टी *f.* छानदारी *f.* नोकझोक *f.* छानछुकी *or* छोकी *f.* अकड *f.* अकडबाजी *f.*

BEAU MONDE, *n.* छानछोकेलोक *m. pl.*

BEAUTEOUS, BEAUTIFUL, *a.* सुंदर, रूपवंत, रूपवान्, स्वरूपवान्, सुरूप, स्वरूप, खुबसुरत, सुदर्शन, दर्शनीय, दर्शनसंतोष, सुशोभित, शोभिवंत, सुरेख, सुभावणा, देखणा, साजरा, गोजरा, गोजिरवाणा, कांत, कांतिमान्, कामरूपी, कमनीय, मंजु, मंजुल, चारु, मनोज्ञ, मनोहर, मनोरम, खुबीदार.

BEAUTEOUSLY, BEAUTIFULLY, *adv.* सुंदर, सुशोभित, मनोहर, मनोरम, मंजुळ.

BEAUTEOUSNESS, BEAUTIFULNESS, *n.* v.A. *and* BEAUTY. सौंदर्य *n.* सुंदरपणा *m.* खुबसुरती *f.* सुरूपता *f.* स्वरूपता *f.* सौरूप्य *n.*

To BEAUTIFY, *v. a.* शोभविणें, सुशोभित-सुरेख-रंगदार-शोभाविशिष्ट-&c. करणें, शोभा *f.* आणणें-देणें, शोभन *n.* करणें *g. of o.*

BEAUTY, *n.* सौंदर्य *n.* सुंदरता *f.* सुंदरपणा *m.* लावण्य *n.* शोभा *f.* कांति *f.* छब *f.* छबी *f.* रूपसंपत्ति *f.* रूपलावण्य *n.*

Adventitious or artificial b. आहार्यशोभा *f.*

2 *particular excellence, grace, &c.* खुबी *f.* खोंच *f.* नोक *f.* रस *m.* तेज *n.* टूम *f.*

3 *a b. beautiful woman.* सुंदरी, सुंदरा, रूपवती, स्वरूपवती, चटकचांदणी, शालिनी, महताब, रामा, छबकडी, छबडी, परी, कुरंगनयना, मृगनयना, मृगलोचनी, नागकन्या, नागिनी, गजगामिनी, गजगति, मंदोदरी, ठिकडें *n.* चित्ररेखा *f.* स्त्रीरत्न *n.* अप्सरा, पद्मिनी *pop.* पद्मीण, गोमटी, नागीण, बिजली, चित्रींचालेख *m.*

BEAUTY-SPOT, *n.* सौंदर्य अधिक दिसण्या करितां केलेला तिलक *m.*

Beaver, *n.* एक जलस्थलचर प्राणी आहे.

To **Becalm**, &c. See To Calm, &c.

Because, *conj.* कांकीं, कांतर, कारण, सबब, ज्याअर्थी.
B. that. ज्यापेक्षां, जेव्हां, ज्याअर्थीं, ज्यासाठीं.

To **Bechance**. See To Happen.

Bechicks, *n. cough medicine.* कासघ्न-कासहारक औषध *n.*

Bechoba, *n. tent without a pole.* बेचोबा *or* बिचवा *m.*

Beck, *n. significant nod*, v. Sign. संकेत *m.* संज्ञा *f.* इंगित *n.* इशारा *m.* इशारत *f.* शिरःसंकेत *m.* शिरःसूचन *n.* शिरःसूचना *f.*
To be at the b. of. कह्यांत असणें, तिळीं असणें, अर्ध्यावचनांत-अर्ध्याशकुनांत असणें.

To **Beckon**, *To* **Beck**, *v. c. make a sign to.* खूण *f.* करणें, संकेत *m.*-इशारा *m.*-इशारत *f.*- सूचना *f.*करणें-देणें, खुणावणें, पालवणें, पालवण *f.* करणें.
2 (with the hand). हातखूण *f.*-हातपालवी *f.*-हस्तसंकेत *m.*-करसंकेत *m.*-करपल्लव *m.*-हस्तपल्लव *m.*-हस्तपाचारण *m.* करणें.
3 (with the eye or head). डोळा *m.* करणें-घालणें, डोईखूण *f.* करणें, नेत्रपल्लव *m.*-नेत्रसंकेत *m.*-कटाक्षसंकेत *m.*-भ्रूसंकेत *m.* करणें, डोईनें खुणावणें. [सूचना *f.*

Beckon, *n.* v. Sign. संकेत *m.* संज्ञा *f.* इशारत *f.* इशारा *m.* खूण *f.*

To **Becloud**, See To Cloud.

To **Become**, *v. n.* होणें, बनणें, पडणें, येणें.
2 of; *to be the final condition of.* वाट *f.*-परिणाम *m.*-गति *f.*-शेवट *m.*-&c. होणें *g. of s.*

To **Become**, *v. a. beseem, suit, grace, fit.* शोभणें, सजणें, साजणें, घटणें, बसणें, मिळणें, बाणणें.
2 *befit, behove, be meet unto.* शोभणें, सरणें, चांगला-उचित-लायक-योग्य-&c. असणें-होणें, ठीक-नीट पडणें.

Become, *p.* v. V. N. झालेला, भूत, संप्राप्त.

Becoming, *p. a.* v. V. A. 1. *beseeming, graceful.* शोभणारा, सुभावणा, शोभाप्रद, शोभादायक, योग्य.
2 *befitting, behooving, comely.* v. Fit. योग्य, लायक, उचित, शिस्त, शिस्तवार, लाजीम.

Becomingly, *adv.* v. A. शिस्तरीतीनें, शिस्तवार, शोभेसा *a. decl.* साजेसा *a. decl.*

Becomingness, *n.* v. A. 1. शोभादायकत्व *n.* योग्यता *f.*
2 लायकी *f.* शिस्तपणा *m.* औचित्य *n.*

Bed, *n.* बिछाना *m.* शेज *f.* शय्या *f.* शयन *n.* तल्प *n.*
B. and baggage—compreh. खाटखटलें *n.* खाटखडबड *n.*
Foot of a b. पायतें *n.* पायतर *or* रा *or* पायथर *or* रा *m.* पायथा *m. or* थें *n.* पायींत *n.* पायगत *n.* पायबंस *n.* पायांस *n.*
Head of a b. उसें *n.* उशागत *n.* उसेंगत *n.*
To be brought to b. बाळंत होणें, प्रसूत होणें, कोनीं निघणें.
To get up from b. निजून उठणें, अंथरूणचा उठणें.
To go to b. निजणें, पाठ *f.* टाकणें-लावणें, आंग *n.* टाकणें, अंथरुणास आंग *n.* लावणें.
To keep one's b. from sickness. निजणें, पडणें, खाट *f.*-अंथरूण *n.*-माचा-&c. *m.* धरणें, खाट *f.*-खाटलें *n.* कुजविणें-वशिवणें, खाटेस खिळणें,—to do so feigning sickness. खाटवाकळ *f.* घेणें.
To leave one's b. *get up after sickness.* उठूं बसूं लागणें, उठता बसता होणें, अंथरूण *n.*-जमीन *f.* सोडणें.
To make (a bed) घालणें, पसरणें.
2 (as of straw, for ripening fruits). अढी *or* अडी *f.*
3 (of a garden). तक्ता *m.* क्यारी *f.* पाटगा *m.* वाफा *m.* चिरा *m.*
Banked up b. कोंडकें *n.* कुणगा *m.* चौंढा *m.* खोंचा *m.*
4 (of a river). पात्र *n.* भांडें *n.* तास *m.* नरांडी *f.* पोट *n.*
5 *stratum, layer.* थर *m.* तह *m.* स्तर *m.*
6 *hold, seat, &c.* v. Socket. घर *n.* पात्र *n.* खुरशी *f.*

To **Bed**, *v. n.* v. To Cohabit. एकशय्या *f.*-एकतल्प *n.*-&c. करणें.

Bed-clothes, See Bedding.

Bed-fellow, **Bed-mate**, *n.* अंथरुणाचा सोबती *m.*-सोबतीण *f.* एकशय्यी, एकशयनी, शयनबंधु *m.* शयनसख *m.*-सखी *f.*

Bed-post, *n.* पलंगाचा-खाटल्याचा-&c. खूर *m.*

Bed-rid, **Bed-ridden**, *a. confined to bed.* खाटखिळ्या, खाटधन्या, सदाखाटलें कुजवणारा, खटवशव्या, उठवणकर, खाटलेंकरी, खाटलेवाईक.
To be b. उठवण *f.* घेणें *or* उठवणीस येणें, उताणा पडणें, नळावर असणें-राहणें.
Bed-ridden state. उठवण *f.* उठवणूक *f.* खिळण *f.*

Bed-room, **Bed-chamber**. निजायाची खोली *f.* शेजघर *n.* शयनगृह *n.* शयनागार *n.* निद्रागृह *n.*

Bedside, *n.* बिछान्याचीकड *f.*-बाजू *f.*-&c.

Bed-stead, *n. cot, couch.* खट्वा *f. pop.* खाट *f.* & *dim.* खाटलें *n.* खाटवा *m.* बाज *f. dim.* बाजट & बाजलें *n.* पलंग *m.* मंच *or* मंचक *pop.* माचवा *or* माचा *m.* पर्यंक *m.* तल्प *m.* शय्या *f.* शयन *n.*
B. with a canopy or top. छप्परपलंग *m.*
Death upon the b. खट्वामरण *n.* It is inauspicious.
Piece of the frame of a b. गात *n.*

Bed-time, *n.* निजायाचीवेळ *f.* निद्रासमय *m.*

To **Bedaub**, *v. a.* v. To Smear. लेथडणें, लिडबिडवणें, भरणें.

To **Bedazzle**, See To Dazzle.

Bedder, **Bedetter**, *n. nether stone of a mill.* तळी *or* खालची तळी *f.* खालचीपेड *f.*

Bedding, *n.* शेज *f.* बिछाना *or* बिछोना *m.* सुपेती *f.* शयनवस्त्र *n.*
The covering portion of b. पांघरूण *n.*
The spread portion of b. अंथरूण *n.*

To **Bedeck**, *v. a.* v. To Deck. सजवणें, साजरा करणें.
To be bedecked. सजणें, ठाकणें.

To **Bedew**, *v. a. moisten as with dew*, v. To Moisten. दंवसारणें, ओलविणें, तुसारणें.
To be bedewed. दंवारणें, दहिंवरणें, दंवसरणें, तुसारणें.

Bedlam, *n. mad house.* दिवानेलोकांचें इस्पिताल *n.* वेड्यांचा बंदीखाना *m.*

Bedlamite, *n. madman.* दिवानें मनुष्य *n.*

Bedunged, *a.* हगेरा, हगिरडा, हगुरडा.

Bee, *n.*—honey b. मधुमक्षिका *pop.* मधमाशी *f.* मोहोळमाशी *f.* मधुकर *m.* मधुप *m.* मधुकारी *m.* मधुलेह *m.* मधुलिट *m.* मुरकुटीमाशी *f.*
B.-nest v. Honey-comb. मोहळ *n.* मोहो *n.* आग्ये *n.*
To circle & buzz around,—a b. रुंजी *f.* घालणें.
2—burrowing b. भोवरा *m.* [अलि *m.*
3 humble b. भृंग *pop.* भुंगा *m.* भोंवर *m.* भोंबूल *m.* भ्रमर *m*

Bee-bread, *n.* हळद्या *m.*

Bees-nest, *n.* nest & honey comb. मोहळ *n.*

Bee-hive, *n.* मधमाशांचें कृत्रिमघर *n.* मक्षिकागृह *n.*

2 fig. *swarming town or house.* नंदाचें गोकूळ *n.* कुटुंबाळें घर *n.*

BEES-WAX, *n.* मेण *n.* शिक्थ *or* शिक्थक *n.* मदन *m.*

BEECH, *n.* एकवृक्ष आहे.

BEEF, *n. animal of the bovine kind* गुरूं *n.* ढोर *n.*

2 *flesh of the cow &c.* गाईचें-बैलाचें-&c. मास *n.* गोमांस *n.*

BEEF-WITTED. See STUPID.

BEEN, *p.* v. V. झालेला, भूत, जात.

BEER, *n.* सातूची केलेली एका प्रकारची दारू आहे, बोजा *m.* बीर *n.*

BEERBARREL, *n.* बीरचें पिंप.

BEER-HOUSE, *n.* बीर विकण्याचा पिठा *m.*

BEET, *n. Beta Bengalensis.* पालक *or* ख *f. m.*

BEETLE, *n.* किड्याची जात आहे.

2 *mallet, rammer.* मोगर *m.* मोगरा *m.*

To BEETLE, *v. n. jut.* पुढें येणें.

BEETLE-BROW, *n.* भृंग भ्रुकुटि *f.* उन्नत भ्रुकुटि *f.*

BEETLE-BROWED, *a.* भृंग भ्रुकुटि, उन्नत भ्रुकुटि.

BEETLE-HEADED, *a.* v. STUPID. मठ्या. [रूंढोर *n.*

BEEVES, *n. black cattle.* गुरें *n. pl.* गुरें ढोरें *n. pl.* ढोरगुरूं *or* गु-

To BEFALL, *v. n. happen to, betide,* v. To HAPPEN. वितणें, भिडणें, येणें, पडणें, भोवणें, गुजरणें *or* गुदरणें, लगटणें, बनणें, प्राप्त होणें, प्राप्ति *f.* होणें *g. of s.* [ठीकहोणें.

To BEFIT, *v. a. beseem,* v. To BECOME. घटणें, साजणें, शोभणें,

To BEFOOL, *v. a.* v. To DECEIVE. छकवणें *or* छकावणें, झकवणें, भोळसावणें, भोंदणें, धंदरणें, झकवण *f.*-झकवणी *f.*-झकवणूक *f.* करणें.

BEFORE, *prep. in the front or advance of.* पुढें, मोहरें, सामोरा, पुढतीं, पुढां, पुढारां.

B. and behind. मागेंपुढें, आगेमागें, आघाडीपिछाडी, पुढेंपाठीं.

From b. पुढून, मोहरून, समोरून.

2 *in the presence of.* पुढें, समक्ष, समक्षासमक्ष, समोर, सन्मुख, सवडें *or* सवड्या, देखतां, साक्षात्, अपरोक्ष, रूबरू *or* उरुबूरू, विद्यमान.

Immediately b. पुढच्यापुढें.

3 *preceding in time.* अगोदर, पूर्वी, आदीं, मागें.

4 *in preference to.* पेक्षां, हून.

BEFORE, *adv. in time preceding,* v. FORMERLY. आधीं, पूर्वी, अगोदर, पहिल्यानू, आदीं, प्रथम, आदौ, प्राक्, मागें.

A little before or after. आदि पश्चात्.

As b. पूर्ववत्, यथापूर्व.

2 *in front or in advance.* पुढें, मोहरें, पुढल्याकडे, पुढल्याआंगीं, अग्रतः, अग्रभागीं, पुढां, पुढारां, पुढतीं.

BEFOREHAND, *adv. in anticipation.* आगप, आगाऊ, पुढच्यापुढें, अगोदर, पहिल्यानेंच, आदींच.

To be b. with. आघाडी *f.* साधणें.

2 *before due, in advance.* आगप, आगाऊ.

To BEFOUL, *v. a.* v. To DIRTY. हिडसावणें, घाण *f.* करणें *g. of o.* हिडीस-हेंदरा- ओंगळ-&c. करणें.

To BEFRIEND, *v. a.* v. To HELP. बाजू *f.*-थापे *f.* राखणें-सभाळणें, पुस्तपना *m.* करणें, धावण्यास धावणें, उपकार *m.*- कृपा *f.*-मेहरबानी *f.* करणें, पाखर *f.* घालणें, हात *m.* देणें.

To BEG, *v. n. practise begging.* भीक *f.*-भिक्षा *f.*-&c. मागणें, भिक्षाटन *n.*-याचना *f.*-यात्र्यावृत्ति *f.* करणें, झोळीवर पोट *n.* भरणें, उलट्या अंबारींत बसणें, उलट्या अंबारीनें राज्य *n.* करणें.

—as used of Bráhmans. भिक्षुकी *f.* करणें.—as used of Bráhmans begging only of Bráhmans. शुक्लवृत्ति *f.* करणें.

To b. about in great wretchedness. अन्न ! अन्न ! करीत फिरणें, दयांदयां *or* भयांभयां करीत फिरणें-जाणें, दोमदोम करीत फिरणें-जाणें, अन्नानगत *f.* होणें *g. of s.* हडहड *f.* करणें, कण्या कण्या करणें.

To BEG, *v. a. ask earnestly, beseech, entreat, implore, supplicate, &c.* विनवणें, प्रार्थणें, याचणें, अर्थणें, विनवणी *f.*-विनंती *f.*- प्रार्थना *f.*-याचना *f.*-अर्ज *m.*-मिन्नत *f.*-मिन्नती *f.*-मिन्नतवारी *f.*-मिन्नतमाना *m.*-&c. करणें *g. of o.* पायां पडणें, हातांपायां पडणें, पाय *m.* धरणें, दाढी *f.* धरणें, पायधरणी *f.* करणें, दाढीसहनुवटीस हात *m.* लावणें, हात *m. pl.* जोडणें, पदर *m.* पसरणें, पायां पडून-हातांपायां पडून-&c. प्रार्थणें-अर्ज *m.* करणें-&c. नाक *n.* घासणें, नाकदुरई *f.* काढणें.

2 *ask in alms.* मागणें, याचणें, भिक्षणें, अर्थणें, भीक *f.*-भिक्षा *f.* मागणें *g. of o.* मागणी *f.*-याचना *f.*- प्रार्थना *f.*-विनंती *f.*-&c. करणें *g. of o.*

3 *assume without proof, take for granted.* प्रमाणावांचून-प्रमाण न पाहतां धरणें-मानणें.

To BEGET, *v. a. procreate, generate.* जन्मविणें, जन्म *m.* देणें, जनन *n.*-प्रजनन *n.* करणें *g. of o.* उत्पन्न करणें, जन्मास आणणें, उद्भावणें, काढणें.

2 v. To PRODUCE. To CAUSE. उत्पन्न करणें, पैदा करणें, उद्भावणें, उत्पादणें.

BEGGAR, *n.* मागतेकरी, मागणेंकरी, भिकारी, भिक्षेकरी, भीकमाग्या, भिक्षुक, भिक्षार्थी, याचक, भणंग *m.* मागणें *n.* अर्थी.—in contempt, anger, &c. agreeing with *a poor b. a wretch of a b. a dog of a b. &c.* भिकारडा *m.* भडंगभिकार *n.* भडंगभिकारी *m.* भिकारगंड *n.*

B. by profession. झोळीबंद *m.*

B. (of victuals) from door to door. माधुकरी *m.* The victuals given, माधुकरी *f.*

B's bowl or dish. भिक्षापात्र *n.* तुंबडी *f.* पत्तर *n.*

Beggars must not be choosers, (dainty, &c.). दरिद्र्यांस खोड असूं नये, अन्नसत्रीं जेवणें आणि मिरपूड मागणें (हें असूं नये).

Crowd or multitude of beggars. भिकार *n.* भडंगभिकार *n.*

Obstinate and troublesome b. खळभट *m.* तेलंगभट *m.* खळ्या, गळग्रह, गळफांशा, जीव घेणा *or* घेण्या, प्राणघेणा *or* घेण्या, डोईफोड्या, कपाळफोड्या, कपाळसुळ्या, डोकेउठव्या, धरणेकरी, खणपट्या, खांताड्या, मेंडजोगी.

B.-like trick, way, habit, &c. भिकारचाळा *m.* भिकारखोड *f.* भिकारलक्षण *n.* भिकारचट *f.* भिकारछंद *m* भिकेचा डोहळा *m.*

To turn b. चौपदरी *f.* घेणें, झोळी कोंपर गांवचा सुभा घेणें, हातीं नारळाची आई *f.* येणें *g. of s.* हातीं भोपळा *m.* घेणें, भीक *f.* लागणें *inv. con.* हातीं तपेली *f.*-नरोटी *f.*-तिडोळी *f.*- डवली *f.*-कामधेनु *f.* घेणें, उलट्या अंबारींत बसणें, उलट्या अंबारीनें राज्य करणें.

2 *craving person.* मागरा, माग्या.

To BEGGAR, *v. a. reduce to beggary.* भिकेस लावणें, भिकारी-कंगाल-कोल-&c. करणें, देसधडीस लावणें, धूळफुंकायास लावणें, धुळीचे दिवे खायास लावणें, देसधूळ *f.* करणें.

It beggars description. वर्णन करितां पुरवत नाहीं, सांगतां

पुरवत नाहीं.

BEGGARED, *p.* v. V. भिकेस लावलेला, &c. हतश्री, विगतश्री, नष्टश्री, हतधन, गतसंपत्ति.

BEGGARLINESS, *n.* v. A. भिकारपणा *m.* भिकारीपणा *m.*

BEGGARLY, *a. mean, poor, &c.* भिकार, भिकारी, कंगाल, भिकारवाणा *or* णी, भिकारपणाचा, कृपण, दरिद्री, भिकारलक्षणाचा, भिकारचाल्याचा.

BEGGARLY, *adv.* v. A. भिकारपणानें, भिकारवाणी.

BEGGARY, *n.* v. POVERTY. भिक्षुकी *f.* कंगाली *f.* याचकवृत्ति *f.* भिक्षुकवृत्ति *f.*

To be reduced to b. v. To turn beggar, under BEGGAR. भीक *f.* लागणें *inv. con.* भिकारणें.

BEGGED, *p.* v. V. A. 1. प्रार्थलेला, &c. याचित.

2 मागितलेला, &c. भिक्षित, याचित.

3 प्रमाणावांचून मानलेला, &c.

BEGGING, *n.* v. V. A. 1.—*act.* विनवणें *n.* प्रार्थणें *n.* &c. याचन *n.* याचना *f.* अभ्यर्थना *f.* यात्रूचा *f.*

v. V. N.—*act.* भीक मागणें *n.* &c. भिक्षाटन *n.* भिक्षुकी *f.* भिक्षार्थन *n.* भैक्ष्य *n.* भैक्षचर्या *f.* भैक्षजीविका *f.* यात्रूचा *f.*

B. is a better trade than working. घुसळतीपेक्षां उकळतीचे घरीं फार.

To BEGIN, *v. n. enter upon.* लागणें, आरंभणें, प्रारंभणें, उपक्रमणें, प्रवृत्त होणें, प्रवर्त्तणें, आरंभ *m.*-प्रारंभ *m.*-उपक्रम *m.*-मुहूर्त्त*m.*-&c. करणें, गण *m.* नमणें *or* नेमणें, पाऊल *n.* पुढें ठेवणें, पाय *m.* घालणें-शिरवणें, शिलान्यास *m.* करणें. [घालणें.

To b. in good earnest. मांडव मेड *f.* रोवणें, मुहूर्त्तमेड *f.*

2 *take existence, being, form,* v. To RISE. आरंभणें, प्रारंभणें, आरंभ *m.*-प्रारंभ *m.*-उपक्रम *m.*-&c. होणें *g. of s.* लागणें, प्रवृत्त होणें, चालू-सुरू होणें, टांका चालता होणें *g. of s.* तोंड *n.* लागणें *g. of s.* चालीस लागणें.

To BEGIN, *v. a.* आरंभणें, प्रारंभणें, आरंभ *m.*-प्रारंभ *m.*-&c. करणें *g. of o.* लावणें, उपक्रमणें, उपक्रम *m.* काढणें-करणें *g. of o.* टांका *m.* चालता करणें *g. of o.* सुरू करणें, सुरुवात *f.* करणें *g. of o.*

To be begun. आरभ्य, उपक्रम्य.

BEGINNER, *n. tyro, novice, &c.* नवा, नवशिक्या, नूतनअभ्यासी, नवीन, आरंभक.

BEGINNING, *n.* v. V. N. 1. & V. A. आरंभ *m.* प्रारंभ *m.* शुरवात *or* सुरवात *f.* उपक्रम *m.* मुहूर्त्त *m.* मंगलाचरण *n.* गणपतिपूजन *n.* श्रीकार *m.* श्री *f.*

Gradual and gentle b. अल्पारंभ *m.*

Very b. *the outset.* प्रथमारंभ *m.* प्रथमचरण *m.*

2 v. V. N. 2. *and* RISE. आगम *m.* उपक्रम *m.* मूल *m.*

At the very b. प्रथमारंभीं, मुळारंभीं, मुळींमुहूर्त्तीं *or* मुळामुहूर्त्तानें, मुळीं.

B. and end. *rise and close of a matter,* gener. आगमनिर्गम *m.* आदिअंत *or* आद्यंत *m.* उपजनिपज *m.* पूर्वापर *n.* शेंडाबुडखा *m.* शेंडाबुंधा *m.* आगापिच्छा *m.*

From the b. पहिल्यापासून, पूर्वीपासून, मुळाहून, मुळापासून, मूळ धरून, मुळींपासून, प्रथमपासून.

In the b. पूर्वीं, पहिला, पहिल्यानें, आदीं, आदौ, प्रारंभीं.

Very b. *the outset.* प्रथमारंभ *m.* मुळारंभ *m.* आद्यारंभ *m.* प्रथमचरण *m.*

I. *incipient portion or period.* प्रथमांश *m.* पहिलेंतोंड *n.* तोंड *n.* आदि *m.* अवल *f.* मुख *n.* चरण *or* प्रथमचरण *m.* पूर्वावधि*m.*

B. and end. आद्यंत *m.*

From b. to end, v. THROUGHOUT. आद्यंत, साद्यंत, अथपासूनइतिपर्यंत, अथेति, अवल आखर, आमूलचूड, आमूलाग्र.

Without b. middle, or end. आदिमध्यांतरहित.

II. *elements,* v. RUDIMENTS. मूळपीठिका *f.*

To BEGIRD. See To SURROUND.

BEGONE, *interj.* निघ ! काळें कर *or* काळेंकरून जा, तोंड घेऊन जा, आपला देश धे. [त, प्रजनित.

BEGOTTEN, *p.* v.V. 1. उत्पन्न केलेला, जन्मास आणलेला, &c. जनि-

2 पैदाकेलेला, उद्भावलेला, &c.

To BEGRIME, *v. a. soil deeply.* कटविणें *or* किटविणें, बिटविणें.

To be begrimed. कटणें, काटणें, किटणें, कट *m.* बसणें, मळानें रांपणें.

To BEGRUDGE, See To GRUDGE.

To BEGUILE, *v. a. trick, delude,* v. To DECEIVE. मोह *m.*-भुरळ *f.*-भुरळें *n.*-भोळें *n.*-भुलवण *f.* घालणें, गोफाटणें, भुलथाप *f.* देणें, मोहणें, झोका *m.*-ढोला *m.*-झोला *m.* देणें.

2 (time). झुलवणें, टाळणें, लोटणें, घालवणें, करमणें, करमणूक *f.* करणें, कालवंचन *n.*-कालवंचना *f.* करणें.

BEGUN, *p.* v. V. N. 1. & V. A. आरंभलेला, चालू केलेला-झालेला, &c. आरब्ध, प्रारब्ध, उपक्रांत, सुरू *or* शुरू, प्रवृत्त.

It has not yet been b. अझून हिंगला नाहीं वाफला नाहीं.

BEHALF, *n. part, side.* पक्ष *n.* तरफ *f.*

On the b. of. साठीं, करितां, बदल, बदलखातर, पक्ष धरून, वतीं *or* वतीनें, तर्फे, अंगत्वानें, अंगत्वें.

To BEHAVE, *v. n. act, conduct.* चालणें, वागणें, वर्त्तणें, आचरणें, आचरण *n.*-आचार *m.* करणें, बहिवाटणें, चेष्टा *f.* करणें.

To b. circumspectly, carefully, &c. जपून वर्त्तणें-चालणें-वागणें, मागेंपुढें पाहून चालणें, &c. उंच टांचकरून वागणें.

To BEHAVE. *v. a.* (one's self) v. V. N. चालणें, वर्त्तणें.

BEHAVIOUR, *n.* v. V. *and* CONDUCT. चाल *f.* चालचर्या *f.* चालचलणूक *f.* आचरण *n.* आचरित *n.* आचार *m.* वर्तन *n.* वर्तणूक *f.*

To BEHEAD, *v. a.* डोस्कें *n.*-डोकें *n.*- डोई *f.*-&c. मारणें-उडवणें *g. of o.* गर्दन *f.* मारणें *g. of o.* गळा *m.* सोडवणें *g. of o.* शिरश्छेद *m.*-शीर्षछेद *m.*-मस्तकछेदन *n.* करणें *g. of o.*

—in covert or cant phraseology. मुंडीमोचन *n.*करणें *g. of o.* शिरकमल *n.* उडविणें.

BEHEADED, *p.* v. V. डोस्कें उडवलेला, &c. छिन्नमस्तक, छिन्नशिरस्क.

BEHEADING, *n.* v.V. डोस्कें उडवणें *n.* &c. शिरच्छेद *m.* शीर्षछेद *m.* मस्तक छेदन *n.*

BEHELD, *p.* v. V. पाहिलेला, प्रेक्षित, लक्षित, अवलोकित, विलोकित, आलोचित, आलोकित, ईक्षित, वीक्षित, दृष्ट.

BEHEST, *n.* v. ORDER. आज्ञा *f.* आदेश *m.*

BEHIND, *adv. in the hinder place.* मागें, पाठीमागें, पिच्छाडीस, पाठीं, पृष्ठभागीं, पश्चात्, पश्चात्भागीं, पश्चिमभागीं, पृष्ठतः, परतः, उत्तरतः.

2 See BEHIND-HAND.

BEHIND, *prep. at the back of.* मागें, पाठीवर, पाठीमागें, पाठीं, पाठीशीं, पाठशीं, पश्चात्, पलिकडे *or* पैलिकडे.

Close b. मागोमाग, पाठोपाठ, लगोलग.

To look b. पाठमोरा पाहणें *or* वळणें, सिंहावलोकन *n.* करणें

2 *under the shelter or cover of.* आड, आडऊड.

From b. पाठीमागून, पाठून, मागून, पाठीकडून, पाठलेकडून, मागलेकडून, पलिकडून or पैलिकडून, आडून.

BEHIND-HAND, *adv. in a state of backwardness.* मागलटीस or मागलटीवर.

To fall b. मागें-पाठीमागें-मागलटीस or मागलटीवर पडणें, मागें पडणें, मागलटणें, मागसावणें, मागसणें, माघारणें.

To throw b. मागें-पाठीमागें-मागलटीस or मागलटीवर टाकणें, मागसांडणें, माघारणें.

To BEHOLD, *v. a. observe, contemplate, regard, view,* v. To SEE. पाहणें, लक्षिणें, निरिक्षणें, अवलोकणें, विलोकणें, प्रेक्षणें, वीक्षणें, अवलोकन *n.*-विलोकन *n.*-प्रेक्षण *n.*-&c. करणें.

BEHOLD, *interj.* पहा.

BEHOLDEN, *a. obliged,* v. BOUND. लागला, आभारी, उपकारी, उपकारबद्ध, उपकृत.

BEHOLDER, *n.* v. V. पाहणारा, द्रष्टा, प्रेक्षक, वीक्षक, निरीक्षक, लक्षक, आलोचक, अवलोकन-&c. कर्त्ता.

BEHOLDING, *n.* v. V.—*act.* पाहणें *n.* अवलोकणें *n.* अवलोकन *n.* विलोकन *n.* दर्शन *n* वीक्षण *n.* संदर्शन *n.*

BEHOOF. See ADVANTAGE.

To BEHOOVE. See To BECOME.

BEING, *p.* v. V. होतां, असतां, होत असतां (contracted into होत्सातां,), विद्यमान, भावुक, जन्मस्थ.

BEING, *n. existence.* आहेपण *n.* आहेपणा *m.* अस्तित्व *n.* भाव *m.* भव *m.* भवन *n.* असन *n.* स्थिति *f.* उपस्थिति *f.* सत्ता *f.* सत्व or सत्त्व *n.* सद्भाव *m.* वर्त्तन *n.*

To bring into b. जन्मास घालणें-आणणें, जन्म *mn.* देणें, उत्पन्न करणें.

2 *a* b. *an existing thing.* भूत *n.* वस्तु *n.* व्यक्ति *f.* घट *m.* सत्व or सत्त्व *mn.*

The Supreme Being, v. GOD. परमेश्वर *m.*

To BELABOUR, BELABOURING, &c. See To BEAT, &c.

To BELAY, *v. a. block up,* v. To OBSTRUCT. रोधणें, अवरोध *m.* करणें *g. of. o.*

2 *make fast.* बांधणें, आळपणें, आळपून-&c. बांधणें.

To BELCH, *v. a.* forth; *eject violently from within.* बाहेर टाकणें-काढणें, ओकणें.

To BELCH, *v. n.* ढेंकर *m. f.* देणें.

BELCH, *n.* ढेंकर or ढेंकूर *m. f.* उद्गार *m.*

Low or soft b. गुटकळी or गुटकुळी *f.* डचफळी *f.*

Sour b. करपट ढेंकर *m.* सारढेंकर *m.*

BELDAM, *n.* v. HAG. म्हातारडी *f.* थेरडी *f.* जरठीण *f.* डंखीण *f.*

To BELEAGUER *v. a.* v. To BESIEGE. वेढणें, वेढून घेणें, कोंडमारा *m.* करणें.

BELFRY, *n.* घांट *f.* or घांटा *f. pl.* बांधण्याची जागा *f.* घंटागार *n.* [घंटालय *n.*

To BELIE, *v. a. give the lie to.* खोटा-लटका-मिथ्या-लबाड-&c. करणें, खोटेपणा *m.*-लबाडी *f.*-लटीकवाद *m.*-असत्यता *f.*-&c.आणणें.

2 *misrepresent, misreport.* उलटा भासविणें, असन्निवेदन *n.*-अयथातथ्यकथन *n.* करणें, विपर्यस्त करणें.

3 *calumniate,* v. To ASPERSE. तुफान *n.*-&c. घेणें *with* वर *of o.* कंडी *f.* उठवणें *with* वर *of o.*

4 *counterfeit, mimic,* v.To IMITATE.नकल *f.*करणें-उतरणें *g.of o.*

BELIEF, *n. credit, credence, trust.* मान्यता *f.* विश्वास *m.* भरवसा *m.* इतबार *m.* प्रत्यय *m.* श्रद्धा *f.* आस्तिक्यबुद्धि *f.*

2 *religious belief,* v. FAITH. भाव *m.* विश्वास *m.* श्रद्धा *f.*

3 *a belief, a faith,* v. RELIGION. मत *n.* धर्म *m.* मार्ग *m.*

4 *persuasion, opinion.* भाव *m.* भावना *f.* मत *n.* बुद्धि *f.*

5 *object of belief.* श्रद्धाविषय *m.* विश्वासविषय *m.* श्रद्धा-&c. स्थान *n.*

6 *creed.* श्रद्धेयविषयमाला *f.*

7 (of a God)—opp. to Infidelity. आस्तिकता *f.* आस्तिक्य *n.* अस्तिभाव *m.*

To BELIEVE, *v. a. credit, trust.* मानणें, खरा मानणें, विश्वासणें, मान्यता *f.* करणें *g. of o.* विश्वास *m.*-भरवसा *m.*-भाव *m.*-इतबार *m.*-&c. ठेवणें-धरणें, खरा-सत्य-&c. वाटणें *in. con.*

A make believe. झुलकावणी *f. v.* दाखव, हूल *f. v.* दाखव.

BELIEVED, *p.* v. V. मानलेला, &c. विश्वसित, विश्वस्त, श्रद्धित, प्रत्ययित.

BELIEVER, *n.* BELIEVING, *p. a.* v. V. विश्वासठेवणारा, विश्वासणारा &c. विश्वासकर्त्ता, श्रद्धाकर्त्ता, मानणारा, श्रद्धावान्, श्रद्धालु, श्रद्धान्वित, श्रद्धासमन्वित, श्रद्धायुक्त, श्रद्धामय, विश्वासी, भावीक, भावुक.

I.—in theology (of a God). आस्तिक.

II. (of a divine revelation). शास्त्रमानी, शास्त्रमंता.

BELIEVINGLY, *adv.* v. A. विश्वास ठेवून, &c. भावपूर्वक.

BELIKE, *adv.* v. PERHAPS. कदाचित्, नकळे, नजाणो.

BELL, *n.* घंटा *f. pop.* घांट *f. & dim.* घांटी *f.* घन *n.*

Clanking or tinkling b. घणघणघंटा *f.* घागरी *f.*

Neck b. गळघांटी *f.*

String of litttle bells (as around a bullock's neck). घांटसर *m.* घुंगूरमाळ *f.* घागरमाळ *f.*

To bear the b. *be a leader.* पुढारी-&c. असणें.

2 *plate of bell-metal (used to strike on).* जंगट or झेंगट *n.* घड्याळ *n.* घंटा *f.* घन *n.*

3 (of a flower, &c.) v. CUP. वाटी *f.*

BELL-CLAPPER, *n.* घांटेची-घंटेची लोळी *f.* लोळा *m.*

BELL-FOUNDER, *n.* घांटकरणारा *m.* घंटाकार *m.*

BELL-MAN, *n.* घांटवाजविणारा *m.* घड्याळची or जी *m.* घंटाताड *m.*

2 *public crier.* दवंडीवाला *m.*

BELL-METAL, *n.* कांस्य *pop.* कांसें *n.*

BELL-SHAPED, *a.* घांटेच्या आकाराचा, घंटाकार.

BELLE, *n. smart young woman.* चांदणी or चटकचांदणी *f.* छानछूक or छोक *f.* शानशूक or शोक *f.* स्त्रीरत्न *n.*

BELLES-LETTRES, *n.* अलंकारशास्त्र *n.*

BELLIGERENT, *a. waging war.* युद्ध चालवणारा, युद्धमान.

To BELLOW, *v. n.*—the bull. ढेंकणें, ढेंक *f.* फोडणें-देणें, गरजणें, डरकणें, डरकण *n.*-डरकणी *f.*-डरका *m.*-डरकी *f.*-डरकाळी *f.* फोडणें-मारणें.

2 *call loudly, vociferate,* v. To BAWL. गागणें, अरडणें or ओरडणें, ओरडून बोलावणें-पुकारणें-बोलणें-&c. जीव खरडून बोलणें.

3 (from pain, &c.) v. To BAWL. आरडणें or ओरडणें, तोंड *n.* घेणें, आकांतणें, आकांत *m.*-आक्रोश *m.*-आक्रांत *m.*-आक्रंदन *n.*-अबांब *mn.*-&c. करणें, गळा काढून रडणें-ओरडणें, हेल काढून रडणें-ओरडणें.

To b. suddenly—a child. भोंक *n.* फोडणें.

To b. and beat the mouth. बोंबलणें, बोंबा *f. pl.* मारणें-

टाकणें, शंखध्वनि *m. f.*-पांचजन्य *n.*-महाशब्द *m.*-&c. करणें.

4—the sea, wind, &c. v. To Roar. गरजणें, गाजणें, घोषणें, सोसावणें, घोगावणें, खळाळ *m.*-कल्लोल *m.*-गर्जना *f.*-गर्जन *n.*-घोषण *n.*-घोष *m.*-घोंगाट *m.* करणें.

Bellow, Bellowing, *n.* v. V. 1. इरकणें *n.* डेंकणें *n.* &c. इरकन *n.* See the nouns under the verb.

2 गागणें *n.* पुकारणें *n.* &c. ओरड *f.* ओरडा *m.* पुकारा *m.* ललकारी *f.*

3 ओरडणें *n.* आकांतणें *n.* &c. आकांत *m.* आक्रोश *m.* &c. See under the verb.

4 गरजणें *n.* &c. गर्जना *f.* गर्जन *n.* खळाळ *m.* कल्लोल *m.*

Bellower, *n.* v. V. 3. *one given to bellowing.* बोंब्या, बोंबल्या, बोंबमाऱ्या, बोंबठोक्या.

Bellows, *n.* भाता *m. dim.* भातडी *f.* भातोटा *m.* भस्त्रा *m. dim.* भस्त्री *f.*

To blow with the b. To work the b. भाता *m.* फुंकणें, [धमकणें.

Belly. पोट *n.* उदर *n.* कुक्षि *m.* जठर *m. n.* तुंद *n.* [दरी *f.*

B.—allusively. दरा *m.* गार *f.* खळी *f.* खांच *f.* कोठा *m.*उदर-

B.—in contempt, endearment, &c. पोटकूळ *m.* पोटकली *or* कुली *f.* पोटनळी *f.*

B.—expenses. पोटखर्च *m.*

Distended b. रेंप *f.*

Empty b. अनोशें *or* अनशेंपोट *n.* रिक्तकोष्ठ *n.* रिक्तोदर *n.*

—with or upon an empty b. उपासीं, उपाशी पोटीं, निराळें पोटीं, अनशेपोटीं *or* अनशेपोटीं *or* अनशिळें पोटीं, उपवासीं.

—with or upon a full b. भरल्या पोटीं, जेवल्या पोटीं.

Shooting in the b. वेण *f. v.* दे, कर.

Stinting or pinching of the b. पोटमारा *m.* पोटमार *f.* पोटकोंडा *m.* पोटतंगचाई *f.*

Swelling or swollenness of the b. पोट फुगी *f.* आध्मात *m.* आध्मान *n.*

Certain combinations and phrases expressing this sense are, पोट डांबारलें *or* डांभारलें *or* डांबरलें, पोटानें *or* पोटांत डंबारा or डंभारा धरला, पोटामध्यें गुबारा धरला, पोटांत तडस भरले *or* पोटांत तडस लागले, पोटांत दब्ब झालें, पोट दब्ब भरलें, पोट तट्ट फुगलें-टमटमीत *or* टुमटुमीत भरलें *or* झालें-दबदबीत-दुमदुमीत—डेबरें-डुबरें-&c. झालें.

Shrunkenness and flattenedness of the b. is expressed with equal liveliness. पोटाची पत्रावळ झाली, पोट पाताळास गेलें, पोटाची बखळ पडली, पोट रसातळास गेलें, पोटाचीं भकाटें *n. pl.* बसलीं-पडलीं, *or* खपाटें *n. pl.* बसलीं &c. पोट भकाटीस *or* भकाळीस गेलें, पोट भकाटलें *or* भकाळलें, भकाळ्या *f. pl.* बसल्या *or* पडल्या, पाखली *or* बासली *f. pl.* बसल्या *or* पडल्या.

The three folds across the b. (from obesity or age). [त्रिवली *f.*

To be engrossed in providing for the b. पोटाचे पाठीस लागणें, पाठीस पोट *n.* लागणें *in. con.*

To go to the b. पोटीं पडणें, भक्ष्यस्थानीं पडणें.

To have a b. to fill. पोट *n.* पाठीस लागणें.

To pinch one's b. पोट बांधणें, पोटांत पोट करणें, पोटास बिब्बे *m. pl.* घालणें, पोटाला पाटा *m.* बांधणें, पोटकोंडा *m.* करणें, पोटतंगचाई *f.* करणें.

To pinch the b. to clothe the back. कण्या खाऊन मिशांस [तूप लावणें.

To touch one's b. पोटावर मारणें, नळीं नख देणें.

Whip my back, dont cut my b. पाठीवर मार पोटावर मारूं नको.

2 *belly fig. hold.* पोट *n.*

3 *bulging part.* पोट *n.* फुगा *m.* फुगारा *m.* फुगोटी *f.*

To Belly, *v. n. swell out, jut out, bulge.* फुगणें, फुगारणें, फुगा *m.*-फुगारा *m*-&c. येणें, फुगीर होणें.

2 *sway*, v. To Bag. भोंगळणें, झोल *m.*-झोलका *m.* येणें.

Belly-ache, *n.* पोटशूळ *or* सूळ *m.* पोट दुखणें *n.* पोटदुखी *f.* उदरशूल *m.* जठरव्यथा *f.* जठरज्वाला *f.* जठरशूल *m.*

Constitutional or constant b. पोटदुखा *m.* पोटदुखी *f.*

Belly-band, *n.* v. Girth. पेटी *f.*

2—gener. पोटबांधणें *n.* उदरत्राण *n.*

Belly-bound. *a.* v. Costive. बद्धकोष्ठ *pop.* बद्धकोष्ट्या.

Belly-fretting, *n. gripes in a horse's belly.* कुरकुरी *f.*

Belly-full, *n.* पोटभरती *f.* पोटभर *f.* पोटभर अन्न *n.*-जेवण *n.*

With half a b. अर्धपोटीं, अधपोटीं, निमेपोटीं.

To eat a b. पोटभर जेवणें-खाणें, रगडून-कचकावून-उपटून--&c. जेवणें.

Belly-god, *n.* v. Glutton. पोटभरू *m.* पोटभऱ्या *m.* पोटार्थी *m.* पोट्या *m.* पोटबाबू *m.* पुखानंद *c.* खादू *c.* खादुनंदन *m.* खाचू *c.* घमंड *c.* घमंडानंद *c.* घमंडनाथ *m.*

Belly-timber, Belly-cheer, *n.* पोटगी *f.*

Belly-worm, *n.* पोटकिडा *m.*

To Belong, *v. n. be the property of.* असणें *with* चा-कडे-&c. (as हें घर त्याचें आहे this house belongs to him). लागणें, माल *m.*-&c. असणें *in. con.*

2 *be the province or business of.* असणें *with* चा-कडे-&c. (as हें काम त्याचें आहे this work belongs to him). लागणें, इलाख्यांत-&c. असणें *g. of o.* काम *n.*-प्रकरण *n.*- &c. असणें *in. con.*

3 *have relation to.* लागणें, संबंध *m.*-&c' असणें, संबंधी-निसबतीचा-&c. असणें.

Belonging, *p.* v. V. 1. सत्तेचा.

2 अनुगत, हातचा.

3 अंगीभूत, अंगभूत, अंगसंबंधी, संबंधी, संबंधीक, आंगिक, अनुगत, निसबतीचा, पोटचा, विषयींचा, लागी, पर & परायण (in comp.).

Beloved, *a. loved, dear.* v. Darling. आवडता, प्रिय, प्राणसा, जीवसा, जिवलग, प्यारा, वाल्ही, बल्लभ, प्रीन, प्रेमास्पद, अभीष्ट, अभीप्सित, दयित.

B. by all. सर्वप्रिय.

Best b. इष्टतम.

Beloved, *n. beloved female, wife or mistress.* कामिनी *f.* कांता *f.* दयिता *f.* प्रिया *f.* प्रियतमा *f.* प्रीतिपात्र *n.* मनोरमा *f.* माशूक *f.* रमणी *f.* रामा *f.* बल्लभा *f.* वेल्हाळी *f.* प्यारी *f.* सजणी *f.* साजणी *f.*

2 *lover or husband.* प्राणनाथ *m.* प्राणपति *m.* प्राणसखा *m.* प्राणेश्वर *m.* प्राणेश *m.* प्राणप्रिय *m.* प्राणविसांवा *m.*

Below, *prep.* v. Under. खालतीं *or* खालतें, खालीं *or* खालें.

From b. खालून.

Below, *adv. in the lower place.* खालीं, खालता *a. decl.* खालतीं *or* खालतें, हेट, तळवटीं, अधः, अधरतः, अधरात्, अधस्तात्.

From b. खालून.

Here below, *on earth.* इहलोकीं.

The realms or regions below. पाताल *pop.* पाताळ *n.* अधोलोक *m.* अधोभुवन *n.*

BELT, *girdle, cincture, &c.* पट्टा *m.*

A leathern b. दाल *f.*

Plate of a b. चपरास *f.*

Sword b. दाली *f.* पडदाळें *n.* पट्टा *m.*

Waist b. कमरपट्टा *m.* कमरबंद *m.* कमरबस्ता *m.*

BELWETHER, *n.* मोहरक्यामेंढा *m.*

To BEMOAN, *v. a. bewail,* v. To LAMENT. शोक *m.*-खेद *m.*-विलाप *m.* करणें *g. of o.*

BENCH, *n. long seat of plank.* बांक *m.* मंच *m.*

2 *seat of a judge.* न्यायाधीशाची गादी *f.* धर्मासन *n.* न्यायासन *n.*

3 *the presiding judges; the Court.* बसलेले न्यायाधीश. *m.pl.* कोर्त *n.*

To BEND, *v. a. inflect, curve.* बांकवणें, बांकवणें, बागवणें, लववणें, नमवणें, बळवणें, मोडणें, बांक *m.*-बाग *m.*-वळण *n.*-मोड *f.*-मुरड *f.*-&c. देणें-आणणें, बांकडा-वक्र-&c. करणें.

To bend the brow. कपाळासआठी *f.*-आठ्या *f. pl.* घालणें.

2 *direct to a certain point.* लावणें, रोंखणें, रोंख *m.* लावणें-करणें.

3 down; (a bough, &c.) ओळंबणें, ओथंबणें.

4 See To SUBDUE.

To BEND, *v. n.* बाकणें, बागणें, बांकणें, लवणें, ममणें, झोकणें, वांक *m.*-बांक *m.*-बाग *m.*-मुरड *f.*-मोड *f.*-वळण *n.*-तीड *f.*-&c. खाणें-घेणें *and with in. con.* येणें.

BEND, *n. flexure, incurvation, curvature.* वळण *n.* वांकण *n.* बाक *or* बाक *m.* मुरड *f.* मोड *f.* मरोड *f.* तीट *f.n.* नति *f.*

2 (of a stick, &c. of a road, river, the ocean, &c.). वांक *m. f. n.* वांकण *n.* बांकाड *n.* वळण *n.* वळसा *m.* मुरड *f.*

BENDED, BENT, *p.*v.V.A.1. *and* CROOKED. बांकवलेला,&c. बांकडा, वक्र, तिडा, तिडका, तिडतिडा, भंगुर, नत, विनत, नम्र, ओणवा.

B. about, *bent in various directions.* वांकडकोंका, वांकडातिकडा, बांकडमुसका.

2 *and* INTENT. प्रणत, प्रवण, अभिनिविष्ट, अभिनिवेशी.

BENEATH, *prep. & adv.* See BELOW.

BENEDICTION, *n. blessing, or invocation of blessing.* आशीर्वाद *m.* आशीर्वचन *n.* श्रेयोवाद *m.* कल्याणवचन *n.* कल्याणवाद *m.* स्वस्तिवाचन *n.* दुवा *m. v.* माग.

BENEDICTORY, *a. expressive of blessing.* आशीर्वादाचा, आशीर्वादार्थ, आशीर्वादार्थक.

BENEFACTION, *n. benefit conferred.* उपकार *m.* दान *n.* कल्याणकर्म *n.* श्रेयस्कर्म *n.* एहसान *n.*

BENEFACTOR, *n.* उपकारकरणारा *m.* उपकारकर्त्ता *m.* कल्याणकर्त्ता *m.* दानकर्त्ता *m.* श्रेयस्कर *m.* श्रेयोर्थी *m.*

BENEFACTRESS, *n.* उपकार करणारी *f.* उपकारकर्त्री *f.* &c.

BENEFICE, *n. an ecclesiastical living.* धर्मादाय *m.* धर्मादाव *m.* उपाध्याची-धर्मशिक्षकाची-&c. वृत्ति *f.*

BENEFICENCE, *n.* v. A. परोपकार *m.* परोपकारता *f.* अन्योपकार *m.* जनोपकार *m.* लोकोपकार *m.*

BENEFICENT, *a. kind, charitable, &c.* परोपकारक, परोपकारी, जनोपकारक, लोकोपकारक, उपकारपर, परोपकारशूर, उपकारक, उपकारी.

BENEFICENTLY, *adv.* v. A. परोपकारबुद्धीनें, उपकारबुद्धीनें, परोपकारपूर्वक.

BENEFICIAL, *a. profitable, serviceable, useful,* v. ADVANTAGEOUS. उपकारी, उपकारक, हितकारक, हितकर, उपयोगी, श्रेयस्कर, श्रेयस्कारी, श्रेयोवह.

BENEFICIALLY, *adv.* v. A. उपयोग *m.*-हित *n.*-उपकार *m.*-&c. होईसा.

BENEFICIALNESS, *n.* v. A. उपयोगीपणा *m.* उपकारित्व *n.*

BENEFICIARY, *n. receiver of benefits.* उपकारपात्र *n.* उपकारास्पद *n.* उपकारभोगी, उपकारजीवी, कृपापात्र *n.* दानास्पद *n.* दानपात्र *n.*

BENEFIT, *n. kindness conferred.* उपकार *m.* उपकृति *f.* एहसान *n.*

A public b. लोकोपकार *m.* सर्वोपकार *m.* जनोपकार *m.*

2 *profit, avail, use, good,* v. ADVANTAGE. हित *n.* लाभ *m.* उपयोग *m.* गुण *m.* फायदा *m.*

To BENEFIT, *v. a. promote the good of.* हित *n.*-चांगलें *n.*-बरें *n.*-श्रेय *n.*-कल्याण *n.*-&c. करणें *g. of o.*

2 *profit, avail, serve,* v. To ADVANTAGE. उपयोग *m.*-गुण *m.*-उपकार *m.*-&c. होणें *g. of o. with inv. con.* गुणास येणें-पडणें, उपयोगीं पडणें.

To BENEFIT, *v. n. receive advantage.* कल्याण *n.*-बरें *n.*-चांगलें *n.*-हित *n.*-&c. होणें *g. of s.*

BENEFITED, *p.* v. V. A. उपकृत, कृतोपकार.

BENEVOLENCE, *n. disposition to do good.* उपकारबुद्धि *f.* परोपकारबुद्धि *f.* उपकारशीलता *f.* उपकारस्वभाव *m.* परहितबुद्धि *f.* धर्मबुद्धि *f.* जनहितेच्छा *f.* जनसौहृद *n.* जनकृपा *f.* जनदया *f.* भलाई *f.* भलाइकी *f.*

Universal b. भूतदया *f.*

BENEVOLENT, *a. disposed to do good.* परोपकारी, परोपकारबुद्धि, परोपकारशील, परोपकारपरायण, परोपकाररत, परकल्याण *or* अन्यकल्याण निष्ठ-पर-आसक्त-तत्पर-चिंतक-उत्सुक-&c. जनहितेच्छु, परकल्याणशील, धर्मबुद्धि, सात्विक, भला.

BENEVOLENTLY, *adv.* v. A. उपकारबुद्धीनें, परोपकारबुद्धीनें, धर्मबुद्धीनें, भलाईनें.

BENIGHTED, *a. overtaken by the night.* रात्रीनें घेरलेला-अटोपलेला-गांठलेला-&c. निशाक्रांत.

2 *involved in ignorance.* अज्ञानानें-&c. गांठलेला, अज्ञानग्रस्त, अज्ञानव्याप्त, अज्ञाननिमग्न.

BENIGN, BENIGNANT, *a. gracious, beneficent,* v. KIND. परोपकारी, परोकारक, उपकारशील, उपकारपर, परोपकारशूर.

2 *bland, mild, salutary,* v. WHOLESOME. सात्विक, सौम्य, हितकारक, हितावह.

3—of planets, aspects, &c. v. AUSPICIOUS. शुभ, मंगल, सु in comp. सत् in comp. श्रेयस्कर.

BENIGNLY, *adv.* v. N. कृपेनें, दयेनें, दयाबुद्धीनें, कृपादृष्टीनें, कृपापूर्वक, दयापूर्वक.

BENIGNNESS, BENIGNITY, *n.* v. A. 1. कृपा *f.* दया *f.* कृपाशीलता *f.* उपकारशीलता *f.* उपकारित्व *n.* उपकारकता *f.* कृपालुता *f.*

2 सात्विकता *f.* हितकारकता *f.*

3 शुभ *n.* शुभत्व *n.* मंगलत्व *n.* मांगल्य *n.*

BENISON. See BENEDICTION.

BENJAMIN. See BENZOIN.

BENT, *n. bended state, flexure, curvity.* वांक *or* वाक *mn.* बाग *f.* बाक *m.* बांकडेपणा *m.* वक्रता *f.* वक्रभाव *m.*

2 *disposition towards,* v. INCLINATION. मोड *f.* मोडणी *f.*

कल *m.* झोक *m.* रोंख *m.* तोल *m.*

3 v. TENDENCY. कल *m.* झोक *m.* तोल *m.*

BENT, *p.* See BENDED.

To BENUMB, *v. a.* v. To NUMB. बहिरा-सुना-&c. करणें.

2 (the senses) *stupefy.* भूल *f.* आणणें, इंद्रियस्तंभ *m.*-इंद्रियस्तंभन *n.* करणें.

BENUMBED, *p.* v. V. 1. बहिरा-सुना-&c. केलेला.

To be b. by cold. गारठणें.

BENZOIN, *n.*—of superior quality. लोहबंदी *or* लोभानीऊद *m.* लोभान *m.* देवधूप *m.* जनार्दनीऊद *m.* शिलारस *m.*

—of inferior quality. ऊद *m.* कवड्याऊद *m.* कपिश *m.*

To BEQUEATH, *v. a. leave by will.* मृतपत्रांत मृतलेखांत लिहून देणें-ठेवणें, मृतलेखदत्त-मृतलेखांकित-मृतपत्रदत्त-&c. करणें.

BEQUEST, *m. legacy.* मृतलेखदान *n.* मृतपत्रांकितदान *n.* मृतपत्रार्पितदान *n.*

To BEREAVE, *v. a. strip of, deprive of.* नागवणें, नाडणें, नागवा-उघडा-रांडका-&c. करणें-पाडणें, नागवणें *with* अंशीं-विषयीं-अर्थीं *of o.* निराळा-बेगळा-रहित-विरहित-हीन-&c. करणें (as जरीमरीनें मला पुत्रावेगळें केलें), नष्ट करणें.

BEREAVED, BEREFT, *p.* v. V. नागवलेला, नाडलेला, उघडा-नागवा-&c. केलेला *with* विषयीं *of o.* नष्ट in comp. (as नष्टधन).

BEREAVEMENT, *n.* v. V.—*act.* नागवणूक *f.* नागवण *f.* नागवा करणें *n.* &c. बेगळा करणें *n.* &c.—*state.* नागवण *f.* नागवणूक *f.* नागवलेलेपणा *m.* &c. हानि *f.*-नाश *m.*-हीनता *f.* &c. (in comp. with o. as पुत्रहानि *f.* धननाश, &c.).

BERRY, *n.* लहानफळ *n.* क्षुद्रफल *n.*

Jeweller's b. (seed of abrus precatorius). गुंज *f.* गुंजा *f.*

Ball of wax studded with this b. गुंजवडा *or* ला *m.* गुंजाडा *m.*

BERTH, *n. station or range of a ship at anchor.* नांगरलेल्यागलबताची जागा *f.* नांगरलेल्या गलबताची फिरण्याची जागा *f.*

2 *place for sleeping in a ship.* गलबतांत निजायाची जागा *f.*-सोई *f.*

3 *place or employment.* जागा *f.* आसामी *f.*

To give a wide b. to. दूर राहणें, लांब राहणें.

BERYL, *n.* पिरोजा *m.*?

To BESEECH, *v. a.* (a person) *supplicate, implore,* v. To BEG. मिन्नत *f.*-मिन्नती *f.*-मिन्नतमाना *m.*-मिन्नतवारी *f.*-&c. करणें *g. of o.* हातांपायां पडणें, पायां पडणें, पाय *m.* धरणें, पायधरणी *f.* करणें, दाढी *f.* धरणें, दाढीस-हनुवटीस हात *m.* लावणें, हात *m.pl.* जोडणें, नाक *n.* घासणें, नाकदुरई *f.* काढणें, उरासी धरणें, पदर *m.* पसरणें.

2 (a thing or matter), v. To BEG. मागणें, विनंती करून मागणें, प्रार्थणें, याचणें.

To BESEEM, BESEEMING. See To BECOME, &c.

To BESET, *v. a. environ, hem in,* v. To SURROUND. घेरणें, वेढणें, घेरा *m.*-वेढा *m.*-&c. घालणें.

2 *set at and press, throng around and worry;* &c. घेरणें, भोवणें, वेढणें, वेष्टणें, घेरा *m.*- वेढा *m.*- गराडा *m.*-&c. घालणें, कुत्तरनोड *f.*- कुत्तरओढ *f.*-लांडगेतोड *or* लांडकतोड *f.*-ओढाताण *f.*-&c. करणें *g. of o.*

BESET, *p.* v. V. घेरलेला, वेढलेला, घेराघातलेला, &c.

BESETTING, *a. habitually pressing*—a sin. पाठपुरविणारा, राशीसलागलेला, बोकांडीसबसलेला.

BESIDE, *prep. at the side of,* v. NEAR. बाजूस, बाजूकडेस, पाशीं, कुशीस, पार्श्वतः, पार्श्वभागीं, पार्श्वगत.

2 *on one side, out of, not of the course.* सोडून, टाकून, आड, आडबाजूस, आडवळणीस, एकीकडे, आडकुशीस, गैरलगामी, गैरसुतीं.

B. one's self. ठिकाणावर-भानावर-शुद्धीवर-देहावर-वृत्तीवर-स्थितीवर-&c. नाहीं.

3 *over and above, distinct from.* उपर, बेगळा, निराळा, बाजन *or* बाजद, इतर (as मनुष्येतर), वांचून, शिवाय, खेरीज, व्यतिरिक्त, बगर.

BESIDES, *prep.* See BESIDE 3.

BESIDE, BESIDES, *adv. additionally, moreover.* अणखी, अणीक, दिगर, दुसरा, अधिक.

To BESIEGE, *v. a. lay siege to.* घेरणें, वेढणें, वेष्टणें *or* घेरून-वेढून-वेष्टून घेणें, घेरा *m.*-वेढा *m.*- गराडा *m.*-वेष्टन *n.*-कडें *n.*-&c. घालणें-देणें, कोंडमारा *m.*-कोंडमार *m.* करणें *g. of o.*

To BESLAVER, *v. a. defile with slaver.* लाळीनें-मुखरसानें मळविणें-मळीण करणें, लाळ *f.* टाकणें-गाळणें.

To BESLUBBER, *To* BESLOBBER, *v. a. soil with spittle, &c.* लाळेनें-शेंबुडानें लेपटणें-लेथडणें-न्हाणें, भरणें, लेथडणें, बरबटिवणें, लाळ *f.* गाळणें.

To BESMEAR, *v. a. bedaub,* v. To SMEAR. भरणें, लेथडणें, लिडबिडवणें, लेपटणें.

BESOM, *n.* v. BROOM. केरसुणी *f.* झाडणी *f.*

To BESOM, *v. a.* केरसुणीनें झाडणें.

To BESORT. See To BECOME.

To BESOT, *v. a. make sottish, stupefy.* गुंग-धुंद-सुस्त-&c. करणें, गुंगी *f.*-धुंदी *f.* आणणें, गुंगविणें.

BESOTTED, *p.* v. V. गुंग, धुंद, गुंगवलेला, मूढमति.

To BESPANGLE, *v. a. adorn with spangles.* टिकल्यांनीं-चकमकीत द्रव्यांनें-&c. भूषित-सुशोभित-&c. करणें.

To BESPATTER, *v. a.* शिंतोडे *m.pl.*-छांटे *m.pl.* उडवणें *with* वर *of o.* शिंतोड्यांनीं भरणें, सिंचणें, शिंपणें, शिडकावणें, शिडकाव *m.* देणें, सडासारवण *n.* करणें *g. of o.*

To BESPAWL. See To BESLUBBER.

To BESPEAK, *v. a. order beforehand.* करूं सांगणें, करण्याविषयीं आगोदर सांगून ठेवणें, सांगून-बोलून ठेवणें, फर्मास *f.* करणें *g. of o.*

2 *betoken, indicate,* v. To SHOW. दर्शविणें, सांगणें, जाणवणें, सुचवणें.

3 *accost,* v. To ADDRESS. हटकणें, हटकून- संबोधून बोलणें.

To BESPREAD, *v. a. cover over.* विस्तरणें, विसरून भरणें.

To BESPRINKLE. See To SPRINKLE.

BEST, *a.* सर्वांहून-सर्वांपेक्षां चांगला-&c. उत्तम, अवल, श्रेष्ठ, ज्येष्ठ, सत्तम, उत्कृष्ट, वरीयान, परम, श्रेयान्, पर, वरिष्ठ, वर्य, अनुत्तर, वर (in comp. as नरवर, पशुवर, &c.).

At b. पराकाष्ठाझालीतरी.

B. of all. सर्वोत्तम, सर्वोत्कृष्ट, सर्वश्रेष्ठ, अत्युत्तम.

B. middling, worst. उत्तम, मध्यम, कनिष्ठ.

To make the best of hardships. गोडकरून खावें मऊकरून [निजावें.

Do your best. तुमच्यानें होईल तें करा, पराकाष्ठा होईल ती करा.

BESTIAL. See BEASTLY, BRUTAL.

To BESTIR, *v. a.* v. To ROUSE. सावध-हुशार-&c. करणें.

To Bestow, *v. a. confer, impart.* v. To Give. देणें, दान *n.* करणें, अर्पणें, समर्पणें, प्रतिपादणें, अर्पित-&c. करणें, अर्पण *n.*-समर्पण *n.*-&c. करणें *g. of o.*

2 *lay up*, v. To Store. सांठविणें, सांठवण *n.*-संचय *m.*-संग्रह *m.* करणें *g. of o.*

Bestowable, *a.* v.V. 1. दान कराया-चा-जोगा-&c. देय, दानीय, दानार्ह, अर्पणीय, अर्घ्य, समर्प्य.

Bestowal, Bestowing, Bestowment, *n.* v. V. 1.—*act.* दान करणें *n.* &c. दान *n.* अर्पण *n.* समर्पण *n.* प्रतिपादन *n.*उपधान*n.* I. See Gift.

To Bestraddle, *To* Bestride, *v. a. have between the legs.* ढेंगांत-दुपायांत धरणें, पायांचे बेचकांत-बेचांगळ्यांत धरणें *or* धरून बसणें.

To Bestrew. See To Strew.

Bet, *n.* v. Wager. पैज *f.* पण *m.* होड *f.* प्रतिज्ञा *f.*

To Bet, *v. c.* v. To Wager. पैज *f.* मारणें-करणें-बांधणें, पण *m.*-प्रतिज्ञा *f.* करणें, होड *f.* बांधणें-घालणें.

To Betake, *v. a.* (one's self.) v. To Resort. आश्रय *m.* करणें-धरणें *with g. of o.* आश्रयणें, आश्रयण *n.* करणें, सेवणें, सेवन *n.*-सेवा *f.* करणें *g.of o.*

Betel-nut, *n. areca catechu or faufel,*—the tree. सुपारी *f.* पोफळ *f.* पोफळी *f.* पूग *m.*

—the fruit or nut. सुपारी *f.* पोफळ *n.* पूग *n.* पूगफल *n.* पूगीफल *n.*

B. nut, which has ripened and hardened on the tree. घोंट *n.* दगडी सुपारी *f.*

B. nut gathered after it has fully ripened. बेडा *m.* रोंठा *m.* रोंठी सुपारी *f.*

B. nut decaying without ripening. कुंभारी सुपारी *f.*

B. nut—as on the tree or before shelling, &c. पोफळ *n.*

Branch of a b. nut tree. सांवळी *f.*

Base portion of a branch of a b. nut tree. पोवा *m.* पोवली *f.* विरी *f.* (a piece of do. विरखंड *n.*).

B. nut box. पूगपात्र *n.*

Core or heart of a b. nut. खोबरें *n.*

Dunging around the roots of a b. nut tree. शेण साऊळ *f.*

Fine cuttings of a b. nut. फूल *n.* [शिरटी *f.*

Fruit stalk of a b. nut. शिंपट *n.* शिंपटी *f.* शिंपटें *n.* शिंपूट *n.*

Implement for stripping off integuments of a b. nut. रांपा *m. dim.* रांपी *f.*

Scissors for cutting a b. nut. सरोता *m.* अडकिता *m.*

Spathe of a b. nut. गिरमी *f.* पागोटा *m.* गर्भी *f.*

Young b. nut plant. कावती *f.*

Young b. nut plantation. सरगड *n.*

Young and tender b. nut. पोंकाटी *or* पोंकोटी *or* पोंकटी *f.*

For *Betel-nut* prepared in particular ways, some of the terms are कापकडी सुपारी *f. or* खापकडी *f.* चिकणी सुपारी *or* चिकणी *f.* चवारी *f.* बरडा *m. or* बरडी सुपारी *f.* फूल बरडा *m. or* फूलबरडी सुपारी *f.* लवंगचुरी सुपारी *f. or* लवंगचूर *f.* वरखी सुपारी.

2—the Piper Betel tree. नागवेल *f.* पानवेल *f.* वेल *f.* नागवल्ली *f.* Some kinds or varieties are कापुरवेल *f.* काळी पानवेल *f.* जनी *f.* देंटी *f.* मागघी पान *pop.* मघई पान *n.*

B. leaf of the middling quality. बादखासा पान *n.*

Bundle of b. leaves (containing 550). कवळी *f.* (Aggregate of 36 कवळी is कुडतन *n.*).

Case (of bamboo, palm leaves, &c.) to hold b. leaf. पानपूड *n.* [पानसडें *n.*

Case to hold b. leaf with its accompaniments. पानदान *n.*

Leaf of b. पान *n.*

Leaf of b. of an elongated or bud form. कळीचें पान *or* कळीदारपान *n.* कळी *f.*

Lime placed to be eaten with b. leaf. चुनपट्टी *f.*

Pile of b. leaves. खाप *f.* कवळी *f.* काट *n.*

Plantation of b. पानमळा *m.*

Roll of b. leaf, of areca nut, &c. विडा *m.* वीटिका *f.* तांबूल *m.* पान *n.* पानपट्टी *f.* Some kinds or forms are. कातरविडा, कापूरविडा, कुलपीविडा, गोंदविडा, गोविंदविडा, मोडविडा, मोदक विडा.

Roll of b. leaf, areca nut, &c.—compreh. पानसुपारी *f.* Some significant terms for this roll are मुखभूषण *n.* मुखवास *m.* मुखशुद्धि *f.*

Roll of b. leaf, &c. given from one's own mouth (to children or women). तांबूल *m. n.*

Vender of b. leaf, b. nut, &c. तांबोळी *m.*

To Bethink, *v. a.* (one's self) *recall to mind.* आठवण *f.*-आठवणूक *f.* करणें.

To Bethink, *v. n. recollect.* आठवण *f.*-स्मरण *n.* होणें-असणें.

To Betide, *v. n. befall*, v. To Happen. बितणें, भिडणें, येणें, गुदरणें, पडणें, प्राप्त होणें.

Betimes, *adv. early, in good time*, v. Early. लवकर, वेळवारीं-*or* वेळेवारीं, सकळ *or* सकळवेळीं, सकाळवाणीं, आदींबिदीं.

To Betoken, *v. a. indicate*, v. To Show. दर्शविणें, सुचविणें, भासविणें, जाणवणें.

Betokener, *n.* Betokening *p. a.* v. V. दर्शविणारा, सुचविणारा, &c. सूची & सूचक (in comp. as हर्षसूची, खेदसूची, रोगसूची *or* हर्षसूचक &c. शुभसूची, अशुभसूची, कल्याणसूची, अकल्याणसूची, इष्टसूची, शिवसूची, यशःसूची, भविष्यसूची, *or* शुभसूचक &c.).

To Betray, *v. a. deliver by treachery.* दग्यानें-विश्वासघातानें-विश्वासघातपूर्वक-&c. स्वाधीन करणें-हवालें करणें-सोंपणें-देणें, विश्वासघात *m.* करणें, विश्वासानें गळा *m.* कापणें.

2 *disclose* (a secret). दग्यानें-विश्वासघातानें फोडणें-बाहेर पाडणें-षट्कर्णी करणें, मंत्रभेद *m.* करणें.

3 *discover, make manifest*, v. To Expose. प्रगट-उघड-&c. करणें, उघडा टाकणें-पाडणें. [घात *m.*

Betrayal, Betrayment, *n.*v.V.1.दग्यानें सोंपणें *n.*&c. विश्वास-

2 दग्यानें फोडणें *n.* &c.

To Betroth, *v. a. pledge in marriage, affiance.* वाग्दान *n.*-वाङ्निश्चय *pop.* वाग्निश्चय *m.*-वाग्नियम *m.* करणें *g.of o.* वाग्दत्त-वाचादत्त-वाग्विवाहित-प्रतिज्ञाविवाहित-&c.करणें, मागणी *f.* घालणें.

2 *take in affiance.* वाणीनें वरणें, वाक्प्रतिग्रह *m.*-वाक्स्वीकार *m.* करणें, *g. of o.* वाग्वरण *n.*-वागादान *n.* करणें *g. of o.*

Betrothed, *p.* v. V. 1. वाग्दत्त, वाचादत्त, मागणीची (used of a female), प्रतिज्ञाविवाहित, वाग्विवाहित, विवाहप्रतिज्ञात.

2 वाणीनें वरलेला, वाक्प्रतिगृहीत, वाक्स्वीकृत.

Betrothment, *n.* v. V. 1.—*act.* वाग्दान करणें *n.* &c. वाग्दान *n.* वाचादान *n.* मागणी *f.*

2—*act.* वाणीनें वरणें *n.* &c. वाग्वरण *n.* वागादान *n.*

Better, *a.* The most idiomatical way of expressing this comparative is by the use of the words for good with हून-पेक्षां-&c. उंचा, उंची, सरस, अधिक, अगळा, वरिष्ठ.

To get the b. of. To have the b. of. *See under* Advantage.

Better, *adv.* बरें. *Vide remark under the adjective.*

Better, *n. a superior, an elder.* वडील *c.* वरिष्ठ *c.* श्रेष्ठ *c.* ज्येष्ठ *c.*

To vie with one's betters. टाक *f.* टाकणें, बराबरी *f.*-सर *m. f.* करणें.

To Better, &c. See To Improve, &c.

Between, Betwixt, *prep. in the intermediate space.* मध्यें, मधीं, दर्म्यान, आड.

Betwixt and between. अधींमधीं *or* अध्येंमध्यें *or* अधेंमधें *or* अधींनामधीं. [दर्म्यान.

2 *from one to another*;—noting intercourse. मध्यें, आंत, The sense of this word is commonly expressed by the use of the genitive case reciprocally, as त्याचा इचा कांहीं वाद नाहीं. There is no dispute between him and her. त्याचें माझें देणें घेणें नाहीं, &c. &c.

3—noting difference. मध्यें.

Betwixt and between. अधींमधीं*or*अध्येंमध्यें*or*अधींनामधीं.

Beverage, *n.* v. Drink. पिण्याचा पदार्थ *m.* पेय *n.*

Bevy, *n. flock of birds.* साईर *f.* झांक *f.* झुंड *f.* पल्ला *m.* यूथ *n.*

2 (of girls, &c.) झुंड *f.* झुंडी *f.*

To Bewail, *v. a. bemoan, deplore,* v. To Lament. हायहाय *f.* करणें *g. of o.* रडणें, शोचणें, शोक *m.*-खेद *m.*-दुःख *n.*-&c. करणें-मानणें *g. of o.* विलाप *m.*-शोचन *n.*-रुदन *n.* करणें *g. of o.*

Bewailable. See Lamentable.

Bewailer, *n.* v. V. रडणारा, शोककर्त्ता, खेदकर्त्ता, शोचक, शोचिता, शोचनकर्त्ता. [संभाळणें.

To Beware, *v. n.* सावध-सावधान-हुशार-&c. असणें-राहणें, जपणें,

Beware! संभाळ.

To Bewilder, *v. a. lose in mazes.* गुरपटणें *or* गुरफाटणें, गळफटणें, घोंटाळवणें, बहकावणें *or* भकवणें.

2 *perplex, &c.* v. To Confound. घाबरविणें, भ्रमविणें, भांबवणें *or* भांबावणें, चौकडी *f.* भुलवणें *or* गुंगवणें *g. of o.* भूल *or* चकभूल *f.* घालणें-पाडणें- करणें.

Bewildered, *p.* v V. 1. *and* Erring. गुरपटलेला, गळफटलेला, &c. चुकार, भ्रांत.

2 घाबरवलेला, घाबरा केलेला-झालेला, चकभूल, चक्क, चकित, चरक, हैराण, बावरा, तारकाबारका, भ्रमिष्ट, भ्रमी, भ्रांत, संभ्रांत, विभ्रांत, गूढचेता, व्याकुल *or* व्याकुलमना.

To be b. घाबरणें, गलबलणें, घोंटाळणें, गोंधरणें, गोंधळणें, गोंधळणें, बावरणें, चकणें, बावचळणें, चौकडी *f.* भुलणें *or with g. of s.* गुंग होणें,भांबवणें *or* भांबावणें. [टाळा *m.*

Bewilderment, *n.* v. V. 1.—*state.* गळफटा *or* गळफाटा *m.* घोंं-

2—*state.* चकभूल *f.* भूल *f.* गडबड *f.* गोंधळ *m.* घोळ *m.* घोंटाळा *m.* हैराणी *f.* हैराणगत *f.* धांदल *f.* बावरणी *f.* भ्रांति *f.* भ्रम *m.* संभ्रम *m.* भ्रांतता *f.* मोह *m.* चित्तवैकल्य *n.*

To Bewitch, *v. a. affect by witchcraft,* v. To Charm. भारणें, मोहणें *or* मोहविणें, भारणी *f.* घालणें, चेटक *n.*-कंबंटाळ *n.*-करणी *f.* करणें, दृष्ट *f.*-दृष्टि *f.* लागणें -पडणें. *in. con.*

To be bewitched. भुरळणें, भुरळें *n.* पडणें.

2 fig. *enchant, fascinate,* v. To Charm. भारणें, मंत्रणें *or* मंतरणें, मोहणें *or* मोहविणें, मोह *m.* घालणें, भुरळ *f.*-भुलवण *f.*-&c. घालणें, मोहित- चकित-चक्क-चकभूल-&c. करणें.

Bewitching, Bewitchment, *n.* v. V. 1.—*act.* मोहणें *n.* भारणें *n.* &c. भारणी *f.* मोह *m.* मोहन *n.* मोहिनी *pop.* मोहनी *f.*—*state.* भुरळ *f.* भुरळें *n.* भुलवण *f.* भूल *f.* मोह *m.*

2—*act.* भारणें *n.* भारणी *f.*—*state.* चित्तभ्रम *m.* नजरबंदी *f.* भुरळ *f.* भुरळें *n.* भुलवण *f.* भूल *f.* मुंडवण *f.*

Bewitching, *a. engaging, captivating,* v. Charming. मोहक, मारू, चित्तहारी, चित्तापहारी, मनोहर, मनोहारी.

To Bewray. See To Betray.

Beyond, *prep. farther onward than.* पुढें, मोहरें, पुढां, पुढारां, पुढतीं, वर, वरता, वरतीं *or* वरतें.

2 *on the farther side of.* पलिकडे *or* पैलिकडे, पल्याड, बाहेर, पर, परतां.

From b. पलिकडून.

That is b. अतीत.

3 (in excellence, degree, &c.) *above.* वर, वरता, वरती *or* वरतें, अधिक, अगळा, उपर.

That is b. अतीत. [कापणें.

To go b.v. To Excel. मागें टाकणें, मागसांडणें, कान *m.pl.*

Bezel, Bezil, *n.* of a gem, &c. कोंदण *n.* घर *n.*

Bezoar, *n. anti-poison.* विषाचा मोहरा *m.* जहरी मोहरा*m.*

2—bovine. गोरोचना *f.* गोरोचन *n.* गोवर्धन *n.*

Biangulous, *a.* द्विकोण.

Bias, *n. leaning of the mind, prepossession, inclination.* बांक *m. n.* झोक *m.* कल *m.* तोल *m.* ओढ *f.* ओढा *m.* वळण *n.*

To Bias, *v. a. incline, warp, prepossess.* झोकविणें, वळविणें, तोलविणें, बांक *m. n.*-झोक *m.*-तोल *m.*-कल*m.*-वळण *n.*-&c. देणें.

Bib, *n.* मुलाच्या उरावरचें मळवस्त्र *n.*

Bibacious, *a. addicted to drinking.* पानप्रिय, पानव्यसनी, पेपीयक, पानशील, पानासक्त.

Bibacity, *n.* v. A. पानासक्ति *f.* पानव्यसन *n.*

Bibber, *n. drinker.* पी (in comp. as मद्यपी wine bibber.).

Bible, *n.* v. Scriptures. खिस्तीशास्त्र *n.* धर्मपुस्तक *n.*

Biblical, *a.* धर्मपुस्तकाचा, धर्मपुस्तकसंबंधी-विषयक. [धर्मक.

Bibulous, *a. that has the quality of imbibing.* शोषक, शोषण-

Bicapsular, *a.* द्विबीजकोश.

Bicephalous, Bicipital, Bicipitous, *a. that has two heads.*दोनडोक्यांचा, द्विमस्तक. [&c.

To Bicker, Bickering, See To Wrangle, To Squabble,

Bickern, *n.* पहार *f.* पारई *f.* संबळ *or* सबळ *f. m.*

Bicorn, Bicornous, *a. that has two horns.* दुशिंग्या, दुशिंग, द्विशृंग.

Bicorporal, *a. that has two bodies.* द्विदेही, देहद्वयी.

To Bid, *v. a.* v. To Command. आज्ञा *f.* करणें-देणें, सांगणें, सांगी *f.*-सांगणी *f.* सांगणें-करणें.

2 *call to,* v. To Invite. सांगणें, बोलावणें, पाचारणें, बाहणें.

3 *declare, pronounce,* v. To Say. सांगणें.

To bid adieu, *take leave.* निरोप *m.*-&c. घेणें.

To bid welcome. स्वागत *n.* करणें.

4 *propose a price.* मोल *n.*-किमत *f.*-&c. सांगणें-करणें-लावणें, गिऱ्हायकी *f.* करणें.

To b. high. मोल *n.*-किंमत *f.*-&c. हाकणें-चढवणें.

To b. up. *vie at auctions.* घोड्यावरघोडा *m.* घालणें, उडीव-रउडी *f.* घालणें. [*g. of s.*

To b. fair. *offer a good prospect.* रंग *m.* दिसणें-असणें

BIDDER, *n.* v. V. 4. मोल-किंमत-&c. सांगणारा-&c. गिऱ्हाईक.

BID, BIDDING, *n.* v. V. 1. *and* ORDER. सांगणें *n.* सांगणी *f.* सांगी *f.* सांग *m. v.* सांग.

2 सांगणें *n.* बोलावणें *n.* आमंत्रण *n.* निमंत्रण *n.* आकारण *n.*

4 मोल सांगणें *n.* गिऱ्हायकी *f.*

To BIDE. See To ABIDE. [द्विदंतक.

BIDENTAL, *a. having two teeth.* दोनदांतांचा, दुदांत्या, द्विदंत,

BIDUAL, *a. of or belonging to two days.* दोन दिवसांचा, द्व्याहिक, द्व्यहीन.

BIENNIAL, *a. that is for two years.* दोन वर्षांचा, दुवर्षी, दुवरसा, दुसाला *or* ली *a. ind.* द्व्यब्दिक.

BIER, *n.* तिरडी *f.* किरडी *f.* ताटी *f.* शवयान *n.*—in jocose phrase. शेवटची पालखी *f.*

BIER-BEARER, *n.* खांद्या *m.* खांदकरी *m.* खांदेली *n.* शववाहक *c.*

BIESTINGS, *n. first milk after calving.* चीक *m.* पीयूष *n.*

B. conglobated by boiling. खरोस *or* खरवस *or* खरस *or* खरूस *m.*

BIFEROUS, *a. bearing twice a year.* दुपिकी, दुबारी.

BIFID, BIFIDATE, *a. divided into two.* दुभाग, द्विभक्त.

BIFORM, *a. of two forms.* द्विविध, द्विरूप.

BIFRONTED, *a. of two fronts.* दुतोंडा, द्विमुख, उभयतोमुख.

BIFURCATE, BIFURCATED, *a. shooting into two branches.* दुखांद्यांचा, दुफांट्यांचा, दुखांदी, बेळक्याचा, &c.

A b. stick. डेळकी *f.* डेळकें *n.* डेळी *f.*

BIFURCATION, *n.* दुखांदा *m.* दुफांटा *m.* दुबाळकें *or* दुबेळकें *n.* दुभाळकें *n.* बेळकें *n.* बेंचक *n. f.* बेचकूल *n.* बेचकें *n.* बेचांगळें *n.* डेळकी *f.* डेळकें *n.*

BIG, *a.* v. LARGE. मोठा, महान्, स्थूल, बृहत् (mostly in comp.).

2 v. PREGNANT. पोटासी, गर्भार, गर्भिणी, गरोदर, दोनजिवांची, गाभीण *or* गाभण *or* गाभणा (confined in use to cattle and certain reptiles), सवर *or* सभर (confined to the mare and ass).

To become or be growing b. पिकणें, गाभणें (gener. conjoined with विणें and confined in use to cattle and certain reptiles), पोटळणें *or* पोटाळणें.

3 *haughty, puffed up,* v. PROUD. चढेल, दिमाखदार, दिमाखाचा, दिमाख्या, माजलेला, फुगलेला, शेफारलेला, मगरूर.

To grow b. शिरावणें.

BIGBELLIED, *a.* मोठ्या पोटाचा, ढेऱ्या, ढेरपोट्या, ढमढेरा, बृहदुदर, स्थूलोदर.

BIGBODIED, BIGHEADED, and similar compounds, *See under* LARGE.

BIGAMIST, *n. man of two wives,* दोहों बायकांचा नवरा *m.* द्विभार्य, द्विभार्यक, द्विपत्नीक, दुबायल्या, भार्याद्वयसंसर्गी.

2 *man twice married.* बिजवर, पुनर्विवाही, द्व्युद्वाही.

3 *a wife of two husbands.* दोननवऱ्यांची बायको *f.* द्विपतिका *f.*

BIGAMY, *n. the having two wives or two husbands at once.* एक बायको असतां दुसरी करणें *n.* एक नवरा असतां दुसरा करणें *n.* विवाहद्वय *m.*

BIGGER, *a.* अधिकमोठा-&c.

BIGGIN, *n. child's cap.* टोपडें *or* टोपरें *n.*

BIGHT, *n.* (of a rope, &c.). अढी *f.* मुदन *f.* वेंटाळें *n.*

BIGNESS, *n.* v. A. 1. मोठेपणा *m.* मोठाइ *f.* महत्त्व *pop.* महत्व *n.*

BIGNONIA, *n. trumpet flower.* पाडळ *or* ळी *f.* पाटला *f.* अमोघा *f.*

BIGOT, *n.* v. A. स्वमताभिमानी-स्वमताग्रही-&c. मनुष्य *m.* एकमार्गी पुरुष *m.*-मनुष्य-&c.

BIGOT, BIGOTED, *a. obstinately attached to one's own opinion, &c.* मतवादी, मताभिमानी, स्वमताभिमानी, स्वमताग्रही, हट्टवादी, एककल्ली, एकमोडी, एकमार्गी, एकचाली.

BIGOTRY, *n.* v. A. मताभिमान *m.* स्वमताभिमान *m.* स्वमताग्रह *m.* श्रद्धाजाड्य *n.* हट्टवाद *m.* एकमार्गबुद्धि *f.* एकमार्गभाव *m.* एकमार्गदृष्टि *f.*

BILATERAL *a.* द्विपार्श्व.

BILE, *n.* पित्त *n.*

BILE-DUCT, *n.* पित्तवाहिनी *f.*

BILGE, *n.* (of a ship, cask, &c.). पोट *n.* फुगारा *m.* फुगा *m.*

2 *hollow for b-water.* गमतड *or* गमतडी *or* गमताड *f.* (*or* घ *for* ग).

To BILGE, *v. n.* गमत *n.* करणें, गाबडें *n.* पडणें *in. con.*

BILGE-WATER, *n.* गमत *or* घमत *n.*

Hollow in which b. collects. गमतड *or* गमतडी *or* गमताड *f.* (*or* घ *for* ग).

BILIARY, *a. belonging to bile.* पित्ताचा, पित्तसंबंधी, पैत्त, पैत्तिक.

BILINGUAL, BILINGUAR, *a. that is in two languages.* दोनभाषांचा, द्विभाषिक. [जिव्ह.

BILINGUOUS, *a. having two tongues.* दुजिभी *or* दुजिभ्या, द्वि-

2 *speaking two languages.* दुभाषी, दुभाष्या.

BILIOUS, *a.* See BILIARY. 2 *having excessive, &c. bile.* पित्ताळू, पित्तप्रकोपी, पित्तप्रधान, पित्तग्रस्त, पित्ताभिभूत, पित्तक्षोभी, पित्तक्षुब्ध.

B. fever. पित्तज्वर *m.*

To feel b. पित्ताची जोत *f.* मारणें-भरणें (उरांत, घशांत), पित्तानें जळजळणें-उचमळणें *impers.*

BILIOUSNESS, *n. excess or vitiation of bile.* पित्तप्रकोप *m.* पित्तप्राधान्य *n.* पित्तक्षोभ *m.* पित्ताधिक्य *n.*

BILITERAL, *a. consisting of two letters.* दोन वर्णांचा, दोन अक्षरांचा, द्विवर्णात्मक.

To BILK. See To DISAPPOINT.

BILL, *n. hook of wood-men, &c.* कोयता *m. dim.* कोयती *f.* पायळा *or* पाळा *m.* पाईळ *m.* बोडसा *m.* बोडसें *n.* सराळ *m.* कुरंदी *or* कुरंधी *f.* लवित्र *n.*

Catch or lodge of a b. (fastened on the hip). अंकडी *f.* अंकडा *m.*

2 (of the *Bhandàri* caste employed upon the cocoanut). आऊत *n. m.*

3 v. BEAK. चोंच *f.* चंचु *f.* चंचुपुट *m. n.*

4 *account of thing sold, money due, &c.* विकल्या जिन्नसांचीयाद *f.* ग्रहीतव्यद्रव्यलेख *m.*

5—in law; *account of a crime.* अपराधलेख *m.* अपराधपत्र *n.* दोषाख्यापनपत्र *n.* [चिठ्ठी *f.*

6 *written statement,*—gener. पत्र *n.* लेख *m.* तपसील *m.*

7 (of exchange). हुंडी *f.* हुंडीचिठ्ठी *f.* हुंडीपत्र *n.*

Bills of exchange, Orders for payment, &c.—compreh. हुंडी पांडी *f.*

Acceptance of a b. सकार *m.*

B. as yet unaccepted. खडीहुंडी *f.*

B. at sight. रोकडी हुंडी *f.* दर्शनी हुंडी *f.*

B. given in lieu of a b. lost. पेंठ *f.*

B. payable to bearer. शाहजोग हुंडी *f.*

B. payable only to purchaser. धनीजोग हुंडी *f.*

B. receipted and remaining with the person cashing it. खोका *or* खोखा *m.*

B. upon one to whom cash or a good b. is sent to ensure his honoring of it. लहणीहुंडी *f.* Good b. or cash so sent. लहणें *n.*

Charge made on acceptance of a b. सकाराई *or* सकराई *f.*

Endorsement of a b. सकार *m.*

Forfeit upon the dishonoring of a b. नकाराई *or* नकराई *f.*

Letter of advice of a b. passed. पेंठ *f.*

Letter of advice pasted to a b. लगतहुंडी *f.* लगतलाखोटा *m.* लगताजाब *m.*

Price paid upon a b. हुंडणावळ *f.* हुंडावण *f.*

Rejection of a b. नकार *m.*

To accept a b. सकारणें.

To dishonor a b. नकारणें, फिरवणें.

To present a b. हुंडी *f.* लावणें.

8 (of lading). भरताडीचीयाद *f.* भरवणपत्र *n.* भरितपत्र *n.*

9 (of divorce). सांडसत *n.* सूटपत्र *n.* सोडचिट्ठी *f.*

10 (draft of a law) कायद्याचा-आकाचा खरडा *m.*-मसुदा *m.*

To BILL, *v. n.*—of birds. चोंचीची लाबालाबी *f.*-लाबालाब *f.* करणें, चोंचाचोंची *f.* करणें, चंचुचुंबन *n.* करणें.

BILLET, *n.* v. NOTE. चिट्ठी *f.* चकती *f* रुक्का *m.*

2 v. TICKET. चकती *f.*

3 (of wood) v. LOG. ओंडा *m. dim.* ओंडी *f.* ओंडकी *f.* ओंडकूर *n.* ओंडकें *n.* उसळषा *m.* फांटें *n.* टोणका *m. dim.* टोणी *f.* टोणकें *n.* टोटकें *n.* भितळा *m.*

To BILLET, *v. a.* चिठ्ठ्या *fpl.*-चकत्या *fpl.* देऊन रहायास नेमणें-योजणें.

BILLET-DOUX, *n. love letter,* कामलेख *m.* मदनलेख *m.* प्रीतिपत्र *n.*

BILLIARD, *a.* गोट्यांच्या खेळाचा.

BILLIARDS, *n.* गोट्यांचा खेळ *m.*

BILLION, *n.* महापद्म *m. n.*

Ten billions. शंकु *m.* शंख *m.* (This term is taken both for 10 and for 100 billions).

Hundred billions. जलधि *m.* शंख *m.*

Thousand billions. अंत्य *n.*

Ten thousand billions. मध्य *m.*

Hundred thousand billions. परार्ध *n.*

BILLOW, *n.* v. WAVE. दांडी *f.* कल्लोल *m.* गह्या *m.* लवलाट *m.*

Swelling and dashing of billows. खळबळी *f. intens.* खळबळाट *m.*

BIN, *n.* (for corn). कणगा *m.* कणंग *or* कणिंग *f. dim.* कणगुली *f.* &. कणगूल *n.* ठिकी *f.* भोत *m.* कोथळा *m. dim.* कोथळी *f.* पालटं *n.* पालें *n.*

BINARY, *a. composed of two.* दुहेरी, द्विगुण.

To BIND, *v. a. confine with bonds,* gener. v. To TIE. बांधणें, बांधून टाकणें-ठेवणें, कसणें, तांगडणें, बंधन *n.*-निबंधन *n*-&c. करणें *g. of o.*

2 *confine, cohibit,* v. To RESTRAIN. आकळणें, निबंधन *n.*-आकलन *n.* करणें, गांठणें, आळा *m.*- आळाबांधा *m.*-&c. घालणें.

3 *enwrap,* v. To WRAP. वेष्टणें, लपेटणें, आवरणें, गुंडाळणें.

4 *oblige by oath, promise, duty, law, &c.* बांधणें, बांधून घेणें, गोवणें, गोवून घेणें, गुंतवणें, गळा *m.* बांधणें-गोवणें, बंदावर बसवणें-आणणें, पाय *m. pl.* बांधून घेणें-गुंतवणें, पायांत खोडा *m.* देणें, अटकेंत घालणें, पिचुंड्या *f. pl.* बांधून घेणें.

5 (by kindness or favors), *oblige, make beholden.* बांधणें *or* बांधून घेणें, विकत घेणें, विकीत घेणें, उपकारबद्ध-उपकृत-मिंधा-ओशाळा-&c. करून ठेवणें, गुलाम करून घेणें.

6 *make costive, constipate.* पोट *n.* बंद करणें *g. of o.* बद्ध *or* बद्धकोष्ट करणें, मलावष्टंभ *m.* करणें *g. of. o.*

7—as sheaves, &c. वेंटणें, वेंटाळणें, वेंटाळणी *f.* करणें.

8 (a book). बांधणें, बांधणी *f.* करणें.

9 around. v. To GIRD. बांधणें, वेंटाळणें, वेष्टणें, गुंडाळणें, लपेटून बांधणें.

10—magically. बांधणें. लावणें.

11 *fasten with a band or border.* गोटी *f.*-गोटा *m.*-मगजी *f.* लावणें.

12—tightly, forcibly. v. To TIE. कसणें, करकचणें, कचकावणें *or* करकचून-कचकावून-&c. बांधणें-ओढणें-अवळणें-&c. करकटून अवळणें-ओढणें &c.

13 to, unto, at; v. To TIE. जखडणें *or* जखडून बांधणें, जवकणें *or* जवकून बांधणें, तांगडणें.

14 (over). हजीर होण्याविषयीं मुचलका *m.* घेणें.

BINDWEED, *n. convolvulus turpethum.* तडतडी *f.* तेड *n.*

BINDER, *n. bandage.* पट्टी *f.*

BINDING, *a.* v. OBLIGATORY. बांधणारा, अवश्यमाननीय.

BINDING, *n.* v. V. 1.—*act.* बांधणें *n.* कसणें *n.* &c. बांध *m.* बंधन *n.* निबंधन *n.*

2—*act.* आकळणें. *n.* &c. निबंधन *n.* आकलन *n.* निग्रह *m.*

3—*act.* वेष्टणें *n.* गुंडाळणें *n.* &c.

4—*act.* बांधणें *n.* गोवणें *n.* गोवून घेणें *n.* &c.

5—*act.* बांधणें *n.* विकत घेणें *n.* &c.

6—*act.* बद्धकोष्ट करणें *n.* मलावरोध *m.* मलावष्टंभ *m.*

7—*act.* वेंटणें *n.* वेंटाळणें *n.* वेंटाळणी *f.*

8—*act.* बांधणें *n.* बांधणी *f.*

Cost of b. बांधणावळ *f.*

9—*act.* बांधणें *n.* वेष्टणें *n.* गुंडाळणें *n.* &c.

10—*act.* बांधणें *n.*

11—*act.* गोटी *f.* मगजी लावणें *n.*

12—*act.* कसणें *n.* करकचणें *n.* &c.

13—*act.* जखडणें *n.* जवकणें *n.* &c.

I. *band, &c.* v. BANDAGE. पट्टी *f.*

II. *tie, fastening,* v. TIE. बंद *m.* बंध *m.* बंधन *n.* आळा *m.*

III. for edge of cloth. मगजी *f.* गोट *m.* गोटा *m.*

BINNACLE, *n.* गलबताच्या होकायंत्राची पेटी *f.*

BINOCULAR, *a. that has two eyes.* दुडोळ्या, द्विनेत्र, द्व्यक्ष.

2 (telescope, &c.) दोहो डोळ्यांच्या कामाचा, नेत्रद्वयोपयोगी.

BINOMIAL, *n. that has two members.* द्विपद, द्वियुक्पद.

BIOGRAPHER, *n.* चरित्रवर्णक, चरित्रवर्णनकर्त्ता, चरित्रकवि *m.*

BIOGRAPHICAL, *a.* v. N. चरित्रवर्णनाचा, चरित्रवर्णनसंबंधी, चरित्रवर्णक-निरूपक-&c.

BIOGRAPHY, *n. history of a particular person.* चरित्रवर्णन *n.*

चरित्रलेखन *n.* चरित्रनिरूपण *n.* चरित्राख्यान *n.*

BIPAROUS, *a. that brings forth two at a birth.* यमलप्रसू, द्विप्रसू.

BIPARTITE, *a. that is divided into two parts.* दुभाग, दुखंड, द्विभाग.

BIPED, *n.* दुपायांचा प्राणी- जीव *m.* [द्विचरण.

BIPED, BIPEDAL, *a. that has two feet.* दुपायी, दुपायांचा, द्विपद,

BIPENNATE, *a.* दोनपंखांचा, द्विपक्ष.

BIPETALOUS, *a.* द्विदल.

BIRCH, *n.* भूर्ज *m.*

BIRD, *n.* पांखरूं *n.* पक्षी *m.* खग *m.* खेचर *m.* पतंग *m.* शकुनि *m.*

—in contempt, &c. पांखुरडें *n.*

Certain of the common *birds* are कवडा, होला, सोनार, गोपिपी, करकोची *or* भारडी *or* खरपुडी, करडुवा, कुक्कडकोंभा *or* कुंभारकुक्कडा, कुंजर, कुंभा, कुवाकर, कोंका, कोंकाटी, कोंकेरी, कोळसा, परटीण, गवळण, गाय, चंडोल, जकात्या, डोळाफोडी, धनचिडी, सुतार, टांकारी, चारगा, दयर, सोनचिडी, टिटवी, लावा, हुम्मा, गण्या, न्हावी, कोकीळ, पातरकुरळी, पाथरवट, अडय, भिल्हा लांडोर.

A b. in the hand is worth two in the bush. गांठींचा एक बाहेरच्या शंभराबरोबर, अर्धी टाकून सगळीला धांवूं नये, गांठचें सोडून पळत्याचे पाठीस लागूं नये.

That has been pecked by birds. पाखरखाद, पक्षिचंचुछिन्न, पक्षिदष्ट.

Birds of a feather. एकेपासोडीचीं पाटगीं, एकातागडीचीं पारडीं, एकेमाळेचेमणी.

BIRD-CAGE, *n.* पिंजरा *m.* पांजरा *m.*

BIRD-CATCHER, *n.* पाखरपारधी *m.* वाघरी *m.* फांसेपारधी *m.* शाकुनिक *c.*

BIRD-LIME, *n.* चिकटा *m.* चिकोटा *m.* चिकोटी *f.*

Stick covered with b. चिकाटी *f.*

BIRD'S EYE, *a.*—view. वरून पाहण्याचा, एकंदरीनें पाहण्याचा, साधारण दृष्टीनें पाहण्याचा.

BIRDS-NEST, *n.* v. NEST. कोटें *n.* पाखराचा घरटा *m.* घरकुंडा *m.*

BIRTH, *n. coming into life.* जन्म *mn.* उत्पत्ति *f.* उपज *m.* उद्भव *m.* जनन *n.* पैदास्त *f.* जाति *f.* भव *m.* भाव *m.* भूति *f.* प्रभव *m.* उत्था *f.*

A former b. पूर्वजन्म *mn.* मागला जन्म *m.* प्राग्जन्म *mn.*

A genius from b. बालसरस्वती.

Another (past or future) b. जन्मांतर *n.* अन्यजन्म *mn.*

B. life, and death. उत्पत्ति-स्थिति-लय, सर्ग-पालन-नाश.

B. Being (or Life), Decline, and Destruction. (the four stages of a creature). जनन, असन, अपक्षयण, नशन.

B. again. B. after death. पुनर्जन्म *m. n.* पुढलाजन्म *m.* असकृद्गर्भवास *m.*

By b. जन्मतः.

From b. जन्मापासून, आजन्म, आजन्मपर्यंत, आजन्मप्रभृति, आजन्मांत, जन्मतः, जन्मारभ्य, जन्मप्रभृति.

In b. *in and from the natal hour.* उपजत (as, blind from birth, उपजतअंधळा; poet from birth उपजतकवि; *and* उपजतबहिरा, उपजतमुका, उपजतलंगडा, उपजतमूर्ख, उपजतशाहणा, &c.), जन्म in comp. (as जन्मरोगी, &c.)

In the present b. इहजन्मीं *or* इहजन्मांत.

In, through, during, &c. all one's births. जन्मजन्मांतरीं, जन्मजन्मीं *or* जन्मोजन्मीं.

New b. *regeneration.* नवाजन्म *m.* पुनर्जन्म *m.*

Seat or place of b. जन्मस्थान *n.* जन्मस्थल *n.* प्रभव *m.* योनि *f.*

Star of one's b. जन्मनक्षत्र *n.* जन्मभ *n.*

Untimely b. अकालजन्म *n. m.*

Acquired in some preceding b. पूर्वजन्मार्जित, पूर्वजन्मार्जित. [अंधळा.

Blind from b. जन्मांध, गर्भांध, जन्माचा अंधळा, जातीचा

Luckless or wretched from b. जन्मकरंटा.

Poor from b. जन्मदरिद्री, जन्मभिकारी *or* जन्माचा दरिद्री-भिकारी-कंगाल-रंक-&c.

Rich, fortunate, &c. from b. गर्भश्रीमंत.

Sickly from b. जन्मरोगी *or* जन्माचा रोगी, जातीचा रोगी, उपजत रोगी.

That is from b. जन्माचा.

To blame the author of one's b. जन्मास घालणारास रडणें, जन्म देणारास रडणें.

To give b. to. जन्म *m.* देणें.

2 *extraction, descent,* v. FAMILY. कुळी *f.* खाण *f.* उत्पत्ति *f.* विल्हय *f.* विल्हा *m.*

Noble or high b. वर्णश्रेष्ठता *f.* आभिजात्य *n.*

Of pure b. बियाचा, कुलीन, सद्वंश, वंशविशुद्ध, सद्वंशीय.

3 *thing born.* वेत *n.*

4 *bringing forth.* जनन *n.* जनि *f.* प्रसव *m.* प्रसूति *f.* सूति *f.* वीण *f.* [वर्षगांठ *f.*

BIRTH-DAY, *n.* जन्मदिवस *m.* जन्मदिन *m.* वाढदिवस *m.* वाढवीस *m.*

B. ceremonies. वर्धापन *n.* वर्षगांठ *f.* वाढवीस *m.*

BIRTH-PLACE, *n.* जन्मभूमि *f.* जन्मस्थान *n.* जन्मभूमिका *f.*

BIRTH-RIGHT, *n.* जन्ममूलकाधिकार *m.* जन्महेतुकाधिकार *m.*

BISCUIT, *n.* बिसकूट *n.* (corruption of the English word.)

To BISECT, *v. a. cut into two parts.* दुभागणें, दुखंड करणें, दुभेदणें, दुफोड *f.*-द्विधाकरण *n.*- द्वैधीकरण *n.* करणें *g. of o.*

BISECTED, *p.* v. V. दुभागलेला, दुभाग, दुखंड, द्विधाकृत, द्वैधीकृत.

BISECTION, *n.* v. V.—*act.* दुभागणें *n.* दुफोड *f.* द्विधाकरण *n.* द्वैधीकरण *n.*

BISHOP, *n.* धर्माध्यक्ष *m.* बिशप *m.*

BISHOPRIC, *n.* बिशपाची जागा *f.*-हुद्दा *m.*

2 *diocese.* बिशपाच्या अधिकाराखालचा प्रांत *m.*

BISON, *n.* गवा *m.* गवय *m.*

BISULCOUS, *a. cloven footed.* द्विशफ.

BIT, *n. morsel, mouthful.* ग्रास *pop.* घास *m.* कवल *m.*

A tid b. सुग्रास *m.*

2 *piece,* gener. तुकडा *m. dim.* तुकडी *f.* कुटका *m.* खंड *n.* खांड *n. dim.* खांडोळें *n.* खाप *f.* कोरका *m.* शकल *n.* कण *m.* कणिका *f.*

—in the sense of *the smallest particle,* or *the least quantity,* and of the grade and with the power of such words as *jot, iota, whit, grain, tittle, scruple, ace, particle, pin's head.* कांहींच, कांहींएक, तीळभर, तिलतुल्य, तिलप्राय, लवलेश, लेश, नखभर, काडीभर, काडीमात्र, अणुमात्र, बालाग्र, सुताचा तोडा, यत्किंचित्, रजभर, अभाविक, स्पर्श, मानसिक, जात, कण, कला.

A b. Not a b. *in (or not in) the smallest degree.* ल-

क्लेश नाहीं, कांहीं एक नाहीं, &c. As these phrases, like *At all*, demand the negative construction, See NOT, NONE.

B. by b. तीळतीळ, खंडशः. [लन.

3 (of a thing broken) v. FRAGMENT. तुकडाm. खंडn. शक-

4 (of a bridle). लगामf.m. मुखयंत्रणn.

B. shaped like an axe. कुऱ्हाड्यालगामm.

B. with four rings. कडोळी *or* कडोळ्यालगामm.

Rough b. B. with spikes and points. कांटेलगामm.

Under chain or strap of a b. जेरकडी *f.*

To BIT, *v.a.* तोंडांत लगाम *m.* घालणें.

BITCH, *n* कुतरी *f.* शुनी *f.* श्वानी *f.*

To BITE, *v. a.* चावणें, डसणें, चावm.-डांसm.-डांसाm. घेणें, दंशm.-दंशनn. करणें.

To b. the lips. दांत ओंठm. खाणें-चावणें.

2—as cold. खाणें, झोंबणें, लागणें *inv. con.*

3—as pungent substances. खवखवणें, खवणें, खाजणें.

4 *trick, gull,* v. To DECEIVE. फसवणें, मुंडणें,फटवणें, ढोलाm.-देणें, फसगत *f.*-फसगयबत *f.*-फसवणूक *f.*-फटवण *f.* करणें, मुंडवणf. घालणें.

5—as speech, &c. *sting, cut.* झोंबणें, खाणें, टोंचणें, बेधणें, डाचणें. चुरचुरणें, तोडणें, लागणें *in. con.*

6—snake. चावणें, डसणें, डंसणें, झोंबणें, खाणें.

7—ants, fleas, bugs, &c. झोंबणें.

—fiercely or eagerly. तोडणें, तडतड *or* डां *adv.* तोडणें, चणचण *or* णां-चटचट *or* टां-चणाचण-चणाणां-चटाचट-चटाटां-तडातड-तडाडां-&c. तोडणें.

8—esp. of a horse. डसणें, चावणें, तोंडn. टाकणें.

BITE, *n.* See BITING. 2 *part bitten, wound made, &c.* चावा *m.* डांस *m.* डांसा *m.* दंश *m.* लचका *m.* लवका *m.* लोळा *m.* चावलेली जागा *f.*

3 *piece bitten out,* (esp. of flesh). लवकाm. लचकाm. लंबकाm. लोळाm. लोधाm. *v.* घे, तोड, काढ, चावाm. *v.* घे, टैंकाm. *dim.* टैंकीf. टवराm. *v.* घे.

4 *cheat, take in.* ढोलाm. झोकाm.

5 *cheater.* See CHEAT.

BITING, *n.* v. V. 1.—*act.* चावणेंn. डसणेंn. &c. चावाm. *v.* घे, दंशm. *pop.* डांस *or* डांसा *m.* दंशनn.

2 खाणेंn. झोंबणेंn.

3 खवणेंn. &c. खवखव *f.* विरविरी *f.* विरवीरf. रवरवf. रवरवीf.

4 फसवणेंn. &c. फसवणूक *f.* फसवणी *f.*

5 झोंबणेंn. टोचणेंn. डाचणेंn. &c.

6 चावणेंn. डसणेंn. &c. दंश *pop.* डंशm. डंखm. दंशनn.

BITER, *n.* BITING, *p. a.* v. V. 1. चावणारा, डसणारा, &c.

2 झोंबणारा, &c. कडक, कडक्याचा, कडाख्याचा, हाडफोडा, प्रखर.

3 *and* PUNGENT. खवणारा, &c. खंवरा *remiss.* खंवरट, खाजरा, खरमरीत, चरचरीत, खविरडा, खडक, तिखट, तीक्ष्ण, तीव्र.

5 तिखट, तीक्ष्ण, तीव्र, अणखर, खंवट, खंवरा, कटु, मर्मी, बेधक, कठोर, कठिन *pop.* कठीण, धोंडेफोड.

6 चावणारा, डसणारा, &c. दंशक.

7 झोंबडा.

8 *addicted to biting.* चावरा, डसरा, डसकर, डसका.

BITLOBEN, BITNOBEN, *n.* गंधबीडn. पादेलोणn. बिडलवणn. बीडn. काललवणn. सोवर्चल *pop.* संचळn.

BITTEN, *p.* v. V. 1. चावलेला, डसलेला, &c. दंशित, दष्ट. [तिक्त.

BITTER, *a.* कटु *pop.* कडू and *remiss.* कडसर & कडपट bitterish.

Intensely b. Keenly b. B. as wormwood, gall, &c. कडूकडू विखूख, कडूकडू जहर. [चेचा.

2 fig. v. ACRIMONIOUS. कडू, खंवट, खंवचट, कटु, दंशीक, खों-

3 fig. *sharp, severe, painful.* कठिन *pop.* कठीण, विकट, कटु, प्रखर, जालीम.

The b. and the sweet (of life, &c.). इष्टानिष्ट.

4—as opp. to sweet, &c. and used of *varieties* among vegetables. कडवा.

BITTER GOURD, *n.* कडवाभोपळाm.

BITTERLY, *adv. severely, sharply reproachful.* फारच, निकरानें, निकरावर येऊन.

2 *with poignant grief.* मोठ्या दुःखानें-खेदानें-श्रमानें--&c. श्रमी-कष्टी-क्लेशी-&c. होऊन.

BITTERN, *n.* बगळ्याच्या जातीचा एक पक्षी आहे.

BITTERNESS, *n.* v. A. 1. कडूपणाm. कटुत्वn. कटुता *f.* तिक्तm. तिक्तता *f.* कटुस्वादm.

I. *rancour, malice.* चुरस *f.* बरकशी *f.* बरकस *f.* कुडेंn. कुडाभाव *m.* वितुष्ट *n.* [ष्टी पणा *m.*

II. *keenness of sorrow.* क्लेशm. श्रमm. दुःख *n.* श्रमीपणाm. क-

BITUMEN, *n.* शिलाजितm. शिलाजतुn.

BITUMINOUS, *a.* शिलाजितमय, शिलाजित धर्मक.

To BIVOUAC, *v. n. encamp without tents or covering.* उघड्यावर तळm. देणें.

BIVALVULAR, *a.* द्विदल.

To BLAB, *v. a. tell secrets.* फोडणें, वदणें, तोंडाळणें, उगळणें, ओकणें, ओकून टाकणें.

There are numerous lively colloquialisms expressive of this sense, तोंड *n.*-मुखरसm.-जीभ *f.*-&c. पाघळणें *g. of s.* जिभली *f.* हालणें *g. of s.* जीभf. चावळणें-बळबळणें *g. of s.* पुडी *f.*-पूड *f.* फोडणें *g. of o.* पेंठ *f.* देणें *g. of o.* बेंडn. फोडणें *or* बाहेर पाडणें *g. of o.* बोलण्याची मूस *f.* फोडणें, बभराm.-बोभाट *or* बोभाटाm.-बाजारm.-&c. करणें *g. of o.* षट्कर्णीं सांगणें-करणें.

And for *To be blabbed.* पुडी *f.*-पूड *f.*-बोलण्याची मूसf.-बेंडn.-&c. फुटणें *g. of s.* बभराm.-&c. होणें *g. of s.* षट्कर्णीं पडणें, नादावणें,बोभाटणें.

BLAB, BLABBER, *n.* BLABBING, *p. a.* v. V. फोडणारा, तोंडाळणारा, &c. बोंबल्यागणेश, गजघंटा *or* गजघांट, घांट, गजरघांट, अल्पकर्ण *or* अल्पकर्णी, कानाचा हलका, जिभेचा हलका, जिभेचा अधीर, जिभेचाढिला, जीभचोंढाळ, लुतरा, लभेचाटू, लाहंबर, चुरचोंबडा, चोंबडा, ज्याच्या तोंडीं तीळ भिजत नाहीं, अस्वाधीनजिव्ह.

BLABBING, *n.* v. V. तोंडाळणेंn. वदणेंn. फोडणेंn. &c. फोड *f.* लभाशाई *or* लभुशाई *f.* गवगवाm. परिस्फोटm. सांगासांगी *f.* सांगावांगी *f.*

BLACK, *n. blackamoor.* हबशीm. शिद्दी *or* शिद्दीm.

2 See MOURNING. 3 *black color.* काळारंगm. कृष्णवर्णm.

4 *soot, crock, &c.* मषी *pop.* मशी *f.* मसm. *f.*

BLACK, *a.* काळा, कृष्ण, कृष्णवर्ण, मेचक, असित.

B. and blue. हिरवानिळा, हिरवापिवळा.

B. as coal, soot, &c. *intensely b.* काळाकुळकुळीत, काळाकिट्ट *or* कीट, काळाकूट *or* कोट, काळामसकूट, काळुंद्रा, काळाडु-

स्स *or* धुश्श, काळाभोर, काळाढोण, काळाठिक्कर, काळाघूस, काळामोदळा, काळामिचकूट, काळाकभिन्न, काळाजहर, काळाकरजत, काळाकरंद, शेळोंद्रा.

Some terms for an extremely black person, are कोळशांतील माणीक, कोळशांतली अंतरसाल, काळामांग, काळाकोळसा, काळाभोल.

Blackish. काळसर, काळवट, काळेरा, काळानिळा.

Blackish,—complexion. काळगेला, काळेला, काळसावळा.

Spotted with b. and white,—cattle. पारा.

To say b. is white. तिळांत तेल नाहीं म्हणणें.

To put down in b. and white. पांढऱ्यावर काळें करणें.

2 *sullen, scowling, &c.* v. SULLEN. दुर्मुखला, ओंठरलेला, घुणा.

To look b. दुर्मुखणें.

3 *atrocious, wicked.* घोर, अकटोविकट, अतिदुष्ट.

To BLACK. See To BLACKEN.

BLACK-ART, *n.* v. MAGIC. कुविद्या *f.* असद्विद्या *f.*

BLACK-BALL, *n.* असम्मतिसूचक काळीगोळी *f.*

To BLACK-BALL, *v. a.* काळ्यागोळ्या टाकून वर्ज करणें.

BLACK-BERRY, *n.* एका फळझाडाचें फळ *n.*

BLACK-BIRD, *n.* काळ्यारंगाचा एक गाणारा पक्षी आहे.

BLACK BOARD, *n.* शाळेंतील काळा फळा *m.*

BLACK-CATTLE, *n.* ढोर *n.* गुरें *n. pl.* गुरेंढोरें *n. pl.*

BLACK-EARTH, *n.* काळी *f.* काळीमाती *f.* काळवटजमीन *f.* नील मृत्तिका *f.*

BLACK-EYED, *a.* काळ्या डोळ्यांचा, कृष्णनयन.

BLACK-GUARD, *n.* With words correspondent to this word, and to words of this class, the *Maráṭhí* language abounds. It teems and revels in names and epithets for persons, things, actions, &c. distinguished for evil. With this word, in both its senses, its correspondent words are numberless. They have all diversities of allusion and implication; they are extensively current; and they are in constant use. For *blackguard* in the sense *a low, mean, shabby, dirty, disreputable person,* as expressed by such words, as *scrub, scab, stinkard, vagabond, dog, hound, dunghill wretch, pot-house fellow, lowlived fellow, &c.* are खेटरखाऊ, खांसडेखाऊ, पायपोसखाऊ, पैजारखाऊ, सुडका *or* सुडकें, फजीतखोर, फटलंडी, टुच्चभाई, टुच्चामाणूस, कथलीव्याध *or* धी, घाण, घाणेरा, घाणेरडा, निपटारा, लिदबळ, दासरी, शिनळीचा, पाजी, कहीबाला, कुंजडा, चंडालमूर्त्ति, चंडाल, दम्र्या, गांवादेशानें ओवाळलेला, गांवाची खरवड, पांटींतलें मास, हगतें रान झाडणारा, गाढवाचा सदका, शाहण्याचा सदका, बाजार भरणा, बाजारी, ज्याची आबरू गाड्यावरून चालली.

—and in the sense of *a dishonest person,* as expressed by such words as *rogue, rascal, scoundrel, scamp, sharper, blackleg, black sheep, caitiff,* &c. are सोदा, लुच्चा, गुलाम, गुलामजादा, हरामी, पक्काहरामी, हरामजादा, बजात, काशीकर, दिल्लीकर, औरंगाबादी, पंजाबी, मारवाडी, त्रेपन्नमंगळीचा, सिकंदर, दिल्लीचा, दिल्लीवाला, गाळींववस्तु, देशठक, पांढरा परीस, सोदाशिरोमणी, साडेहरामी, साडेमात्रागमनी, गमनी, गुलामजादा, मात्रागमनी, काबुयार, काबू, काफर, खट, नट, खटनट, थोट *or* ठ, लकारबिल्हा *or* लकार बिल्ह्यांतला, त्रयीमध्यें उगवलेला, चौपायीं उगवलेला (*i. e.*—in चोरी, चाहडी, शिनळकी, लबाडी), अठरागुणांचा खंडोबा, छत्तिशा, छप्पनी, व्यक्ति, पंचाळ, वाटोळागोळा, फंदी, दीक्षित, कालभेल्या, झोट *or* ड, गुणांचें गुणपात्र, स *or* सकार *or* सकारबिल्हा (covertly from सोदा), भंगीचंगी *or* चंगीभंगी.

For others such as ऐनसोदा, ऐनलुच्चा, अट्टल-अद्दल-अव्वल-झळझळीत-&c. सोदा-लुच्चा-हरामी-&c. एकनिष्ठ सोदा-काशीकर-&c. See ARRANT, *and form ad libitum.*

Pack or crew of blackguards. चांडाळचौकडी *f.* होळीचेहोळकर *m. pl.* चौकट *f.* भुतावळ *f.* नवग्रह *m. pl.*

BLACK-GUARDISM, BLACK-GUARDRY, *n.* v. N. 1. *low and mean life or practices.* टुच्चेपणा *m.* पाजीपणा *m.* जघन्यवृत्ति *f.* नीचवृत्ति *f.* अपकृष्टवृत्ति *f.* अधमवृत्ति *f.* सोरटाई *f.*

2 *roguery, rascality, &c.* लुच्चारी *f.* सकारी *f.* काबुयारी *f.* लबाडी-लताडी *f.* गुलामगिरी *f.* थोटाई *f.* लुच्चेगिरी *f.* लुच्चेशाई *f.* लुच्चाई *f.* सोदेगिरी *f.* सोदेशाई *f.* सोदावें *n.*

BLACK-GUARD-LIKE, BLACK-GUARDLY, *a.* v. N. 1. टुच्चा, लुच्चा, पाजी, जघन्यवृत्तीचा.

2 सोदेगिरीचा, लुच्चेगिरीचा, काबुयारीचा, &c.

BLACK-HOLE, *n.* अंधारखोली *f.* अंधारकोंडी *f.* अंधारखण *m. f.* अंधारखणी *f.* आंधारी *f.* अंधारखेंड *f.*

BLACK-LEAD, *n.* मुरदाडशिसें *n.* मृतसीसक *n.*

BLACK-LEG, *n.* See BLACK-GUARD.

BLACK-MAIL, *n.* कोंबडीपट्टी *f.*

BLACK-WOOD-TREE, *n. dalberjia sisu.* शिंशपा *m. pop.* शिसव *or* शिसवा *m.* अग्नूस *m.*

Belonging to the b. शिसवी.

Oil obtained from the b. शिसवेल *n.*

BLACKAMOOR, *n. person of a very black complexion.* हबशी *m.* शिद्दी *or* शिद्दी *m.* कोळशांतली *or* कोळशाची अंतरसाल *f.* कोळशांतील माणिक *n.* धुतलेला विस्तू *m.* काळाभील *m.* काळामांग *m.* बाबरांत टाकला तर दिसायाचा नाहीं असा माणूस *m.*

To BLACKEN, *v. a. make black.* काळा-काळ्यारंगाचा-कृष्णवर्ण-&c. करणें, काळारंग *m.* देणें.

2 *defame;* v. To ASPERSE. काळें *n.*-काळोखी *f.*-कालिमा *f.*-कलंक *m.*-&c. लावणें-आणणें.

To BLACKEN, *v. n.* काळा-&c. होणें-पडणें, काळवटणें, काळवंडणें.

BLACKNESS, *n.* v. A. 1. काळेपणा *m.* कालिमा *m. f.* काळारंग *m.* कृष्णवर्ण *m.*

I. v. DARKNESS. काळोख *m. dim.* काळोखी *f.* काळोखें *n.*

BLACKSMITH, *n.* लोहकार *pop.* लोहार *m.* घिसाडी *m.*

Business of a b. लोहारकी *f.* लोहारकाम *n.* लोखंडकाम *n.*

BLADDER, *n.* मूत्राचा कोठा *m.* मूत्राशय *m.* तिलक *m.* बस्ति *m. f.*

Obstruction of the b. मूत्रग्रंथि *m.*

2 *blister, pustule.* फोड *m.* फुगारा *m.* फुगा *m.* स्फोट *m.*

Large water b. काचफोड *m.*

BLADE, *n.* (of grass, &c.). काडी *f.* तणसरी *f.* पान. *n.*

2 (of a weapon or tool). पान *n.* पाती *f.* पान *n.* पातें *n.*

Two-headed b. दुकटें *n.*

Two bladed. दुपानी.

3 *hot, swelling fellow, a blood, a swell,* v. BUCK. बांकाm. बांकडा *m.* फांकडा *m.* फंदी *m.* जुर्राबावरा *m.* ढेंगोजी *m.*

BLADE-BONE, *n.* खवाटयाचें हाड *n.* भुजवटयाचें हाड *n.*

BLAIN, *n. botch, blister.* फोड *m.*

Blamable, Blameworthy, *a.* v. V. दोषी, दूषणीय, दूष्य, दोषवान्, सदोष, दोषपात्र, दोषभाजन, दूषणार्ह, निंद्य, निंदनीय, निंदापात्र, निंदाभाजन, गर्हणीय, गर्ह्य.

Blamableness, Blameworthiness, *n.* v. A. दोष *m.* दूषणीयता *f.* दूषणार्हता *f.* सदोषता *f.* दूष्यत्व *n.*

Blamably, *adv.* दोषयायाजोगा *a. decl.* दोष येईल असा *a. decl.*

To **Blame,** *v. a. find fault with, censure.* दूषणें, निंदणें, खोडणें, दोष *m.* देणें-आणणें-ठेवणें-लावणें-काढणें, खोड *f.*-बट्टा *m.*-ऐब *m.*-ठपका *m.* ठेवणें, शब्द *m.*-बोल *m.*-इलजाम *m.* लावणें-ठेवणें, लिंपण *n.* लावणें *with* स *or* ला, निंब *m.* लावणें, ठूं *n.* ठेवणें, ठपकाविणें.

Blame, Blaming, *n.* v. V.—*act.* दूषणें *n.* निंदणें *n.*&c. दूषण*n.* दोष *m.* दोषारोप *m.* दोषकल्पन *n.* निंदा *f.* निंदन *n.* बोल *m.* शब्द *m.* ठपका *m.* अपवाद *m.* गर्हा *f.* विगर्हा *f.* इलजाम *m.*

A bear-b. अपयशाचा धनी *m.*

To bear the b. डोईवर घेणें.

To Blame, *culpable.* See Blamable.

I. v. Fault. दोष *m.* अपराध *m.*

Blamed, *p.* v. V. दूषलेला, दोष दिल्हेला-ठेवलेला, &c. दूषित, निंदित, अपवादित, गर्हित, विगर्हित.

Blameless, *a. not meriting censure, without fault.* निर्दोष, निर्दोषी, निरपराध, अनपराध, अनपराधी, अबाट, निर्बाध, निरपवाद, अनिंद्य, अनिंदनीय, अदूष्य, अदूषणीय, दूषणायोग्य, दूषणानर्ह, निष्कलंक, अकलंक, बिनअपराध, बिनठपका, बिनठपक्याचा.

Blamelessly, *adv.* v. A. निर्दोषपणानें &c. बिनअपराध, बिनठपका.

Blamelessness, *n.* v. A. निर्दोषपण *n.* निर्दोषपणा *m.* &c. अदूष्यता *f.* अनिंद्यत्व *n.* दूषण राहित्य *n.*

Blamer, *n.* v. V. दूषणारा, दोष देणारा-ठेवणारा, &c. दोषदाता, दोषारोपी, दूषक, निंदक, निंदाखोर, अपवादक, अपवादी.

Blamingly, *adv. censoriously.* दोषदृष्ट्या, दोषबुद्ध्या.

To **Blanch.** See To Whiten. 2 See To Peel.

Bland, *a.* v. Mild. मृदु, कोमल, सात्विक, सौम्य, शांत.

Blandishing, *a. soft, wheedling.* लाडीगोडीचा, गोडीगुलाबीचा, अलोलीक, अलोलीकबाणा, सांत्ववादाचा, प्रियवादी, प्रियंवद.

Blandishing, Blandishment, *n. soft airs, winning words, &c.* अदा *m.* हाव *m. pl.* नखरा *m.* ललित *m.* लालित्य *n.* बिलास *m.* लाडीगोडी *f.* सांत्ववाद *m.* गोडीगुलाबी *f.* खुबालीमबाली *f.* गुळपापडी *f.* गुळगुळथापडी *f.* गोडगोडगोष्टी *f.* गुळगुळगोष्टी *f. pl.* पुष्पितवाणी *f.* मधुरभाषण *n.* बसंताचें बोलणें *n.*

Blandly, *adv.* v. A. कोमळपणानें, लाडीगोडीनें. [शांति *f.*

Blandness, *n.* v. A. कोमळपणा *m.* कोमलता *f.* मृदुत्व *n.* सत्व *n.*

Blank, *a.* See Pale. 2 *unwritten.* कोरा, साफ, रिता, अलिखित.

B. at the back. पाठकोरा. A paper b. at the back. पाठकोरें *n.*

3 *without rhyme.* प्रासहीन-रहित-&c. मुक्तप्रास, यमकहीन.

4 *without ball or bullet,*—cartridge. बायबाराचा, बिनगोळीचा. B. firing. खालीबार *m.* बायबार *m.*

5 *void, empty.* खाली, रिता, शून्य, फाका *or* फांका.

Blank, *n.* कोराकागद *m.*

2 (of a lottery). कोरीचिट्ठी *f.*

3 *void spot.* खांडवा *m.* खाडा *m.* खांवडें *n.* खिंड *f.*

Blank-cartridge, *n.* बायबाराचा तोटा *m.*

Blanket, *n.* The woollen textures resembling this article are घोंगडी *f.* (It is coarse, loosely woven, and usually black). कांबळा *m.* (It is composed of two घोंगडी joined breadthwise). घोंगडें *n.* (The same as घोंगडी but a less particular and less definite word). कांबळें *n.* (An indefinite and a disparaging form of कांबळा; it is applied also to a woollen cloak-like texture gener.) धाबळ *or* धाबळी *f.* (A finer texture, usually white). चबाळें *n.* (A very coarse घोंगडी).

A worn and torn, old and worthless b. (*i. e.* कांबळा *or* घोंगडी). फटकुरी *f.* फटकूर *or* पटकूर *n.* रकटें *or* रगटें *n.*

Aggregate of four blankets (*i. e.* कांबळा). बोद *f.*

Blankness, *n.* v. A. कोरेपणा *m.* रितेपणा *m.*

Blarney. See Flattery.

To **Blaspheme,** *v. n. speak irreverently of God.* ईश्वरापवाद *m.*-ईश्वरनिंदा *f.*-ईश्वरगर्हा *f.*-ईश्वरपरिभाषण *n.*-ईश्वराक्षेप *m.* करणें, देवनिंदा *f.* करणें. [*g. of o.*

To **Blaspheme,** *v. a.* निंदा *f.*-भर्त्सना *f.*-अपवाद *m.*-&c. करणें

Blasphemer, *n.* v. V. N. ईश्वरनिंदक-भर्त्सक-गर्हक-परिभाषकक्षेपक, देवनिंदक.

Blasphemous, *a.* v. N. ईश्वरनिंदेचा, देवनिंदेचा, ईश्वरनिंदक, ईश्वरापवादक, ईश्वरनिंदात्मक.

Blasphemously, *adv.* v. A. ईश्वरनिंदेनें, ईश्वरनिंदाकरून, &c.

Blasphemy, *n.* ईश्वरनिंदा *f.* ईश्वरापवाद *m.* ईश्वराक्षेप *m.* ईश्वरपरिभाषण *n.* ईश्वरगर्हा *f.* देवनिंदा *f.* &c.

Blast, *n.* (of wind) *gust, puff.* झटका *m.* झटकारा *m.* चपेटा *m.* झपाटा *m.* सनाटा *m.* वारें *n.*

Hot b. झळ *f.* झळई *f.* हळ *f.* झ्याक *f.* भबका *m. dim.* भबकी *f.* भबकारा *m.* अही *f.* अहळी *f.*

2 (of a planet, &c.). संक्रांतीचें *n.* [दृष्टिबाधा *f.*

3 (of an evil eye). दृष्टिपात *m.* दृष्टि *f.* दृष्ट *f.* दृष्टिविकार*m.*

4 (of a devil). झपेट *f.* झटका *m.* झटकारा *m.* झपाटा *m.* झडपण *f.* झडप *f.* फटकारा *m.* भूतबाधा *f.* पिशाचबाधा *f.*

Blights, diseases, and diseased, damaged, or corrupt state (of trees, fruits, cattle, men, &c.), are lavishly ascribed to *devils, goblins, evil eyes, and malign planets;* and they receive indicative or allusive names. Not aiming at closeness and particularity in this matter, we throw together below the nouns and verbs expressing generally the sense of *To Blast* or *To be blasted.* लांवसटणें *or* लांवसरणें *or* लांवारणें, सठवणें *or* सठळणें, लागोरणें, बिंबशी *f.* लागणें *in. con.* दृष्टि *f.* पडणें-लागणें-होणें *in. con.* दृष्टावणें, दृष्टलणें *or* दृष्टाळणें, संक्रांतीचें बसणें *in. con.* पांचवीचें *or* सठवीचें *n.* होणें-लागणें.

5 (of lightning). वीज *f.* विद्युत्पात *m.*

6 (of the wind or weather). झपेट *f.* वारा *m.*

7 (with the mouth on a wind instrument). फुंक *m. f.* फुंकर *m.* फुंका *m.* फुंकारा *m.* फुंकारी *f.* फुंकार *m.* धमन नाद *m.*

To **Blast,** *v. a.*—an evil eye. दृष्टि *f.* बाधणें-पडणें-लागणें-होणें *in. con.* दृष्टिपात *m.*-दृष्टिदोष *m.*-दृष्टिविकार *m.*-दृष्टिबाधा *f.* होणें *in. con.*

2—a devil, v. N.4. झडपणें, बाधणें, बाधा *f.* होणें-लागणें, लागणें, पडणें, झडपण *f.*-&c. पाळणें, झपाटा *m.*-&c. लागणें *in. con.*

3—wind, weather, heat, cold. करपविणें, कोमबिणें, जाळणें

or जाळून टाकणें.

To be blasted. करपणें, करपून दग्ध होणें, जळणें.

4 *foil, ruin, &c.* v. To DEFEAT. मारणें, नासणें, हिसकणें, लटपटिवणें, लथडणें *or* लथाडणें, भंग *m.*-भंजन *n.*-नाश *m.*-मातेरा *m.*-मात्रा *f.*-विघात *m.* करणें *g. of o.* नष्ट-&c. करणें.

5 (rocks, &c. by an explosion of gunpowder). सुरुंगानें फोडणें-उडवणें-&c.

BLAZE, *n. glowing flame.* धग *or* धक *f. m.* भडका *or* भडाका *m.* भडाड *m.* आगीचा डोंब *or* डोंम *m.* धोत *m.* गलूल *m.* लोळ *m.* होळा *m.*

To set in a b. भडभडावणें.

2 *mark upon a horse.* मुखपट्टा *m.* नाम *m.*

That has the b. नाम्या.

3 *glowing light.* भणभणीत उजेड *m.*-प्रकाश *m.*

To BLAZE, *v. a. noise abroad,* v. To PUBLISH. गाजवणें, वाजवणें, गांवभर करणें, गाजावाजा *m.*-बभरा *m.*-बोभाटा *m.*-लौकिक *m.*-बाजार *m.*-पेंठ *f.*-बहुवस *f.*-&c. करणें *g. of o.* उघडा पाडणें, प्रगटणें, डांगोरा *m.*-दवंडी *f.*-&c. पिटणें *g. of o.* वेशीस बांधणें.

To BLAZE, *v. n. flame glowingly,* v. To GLOW. धडकणें, धगधगणें, धडधडणें.

2 up; *flash up suddenly.* भडकणें, भडभडणें *intens.* भडाडणें, भवकणें, कडकणें. [रणरणीत.

BLAZING, *p. a.* v. V. N. 1. धगधगीत, ढणढणीत, फणफणीत, Blazing noon. भणभणीत दुपार *f.*

To BLAZON, *v. a.* See To BLAZE. [ढणें.

2 (a coat of arms) कुलमान द्योतक चित्रित चिन्हें *n. pl.* का-

3 See To DECK.

BLEA, *n. inner bark.* अंतरसाल *f.* वल्कल *n.*

To BLEACH, *v. n. grow white.* ओपणें.

Cloth exposed to b. ओपतें *n.*

To put out to b. ओपत घालणें.

To BLEACH, *v. a. whiten.* ओपविणें, ओप *f.* देणें. ओपवणी *f.* करणें *g. of o.*

BLEACHED, *p.* v. V. A. ओपवलेला, ओपींव, ओप दिल्हेला.

BLEAK, *a. open, exposed to the winds.* उघडओसान्याचा, उघडवान्याचा, वारधाटीचा, बिन आसन्याचा, वाताप्रतिबंधक.

2 *cold, chilling.* सर्द, सर्दीचा.

BLEAKNESS, *n.* v. A. 1. उघड ओसारेपणा *m.* बिन आसरेपणा *m.*

2 सर्दपणा *m.* सर्दी *f.*

BLEAR, *a.* पिचका *remiss.* पिचकट-पिचकुडा, बरबरीत, चिपडा.

BLEAR-EYED, *a.* पिचक्या डोळ्यांचा, पिचका *remiss.* पिचकट-पिचकुडा, अंसुढाळ, आचोंढ्या, जाचंद *or* जाचोंढ्या, क्लिन्नाक्ष.

To BLEAT, *v. n.*—sheep. बेंबावणें, बेंबटणें, बेंबें *n.* करणें.

BLEAT, BLEATING, *n.* v. V. बें *n.* बेंबावणें *n.* बेंबटणें *n.*

To BLEED, *v. a. let blood.* रक्त *n.* काढणें, शीर *f.*-शिरा *f. pl.* काढणें-तोडणें-सोडवणें, नस *m.* तोडणें-घेणें, रक्तमोक्ष *m.*-रक्तमोक्षण *n.*-रक्तसांड *f.*-रक्तमोचन *n.*-&c. करणें.

To BLEED, *v. n. run with blood.* रक्त *n.* वाहणें-सुटणें-पाझरणें-ओघळणें, रक्ताचा ओघळ, *m.*-पाझर *m.*-&c. सुटणें, रक्तप्रवाह *m.* होणें, रक्तावणें, रक्ताळणें.

To b. at every pore. उपळणें, उमळणें, उवळणें.

To b. at the nose. घोणा *m.*- घुणघुणा *m.* फुटणें-वाहणें-स्रवणें.

2 (the heart) *feel extreme pain from pity.* दया येऊन हृदय *n.* फुटणें-ऊर *m.* उलणें.

BLEEDING, *p. a.* v. V. N. रक्तश्रावी *or* रक्तस्रावी, रक्तप्रवाही.

BLEEDING, *n.* v. V. A.—*act.* रक्त काढणें *n.* शीर काढणें *n.* शीर तोडणें *n.* रक्तमोक्ष *m.* रक्तमोक्षण *n.* रक्तमोचन *n.* रक्तसांड *f.*

v. V. N. रक्त वाहणें *n.* रक्तश्राव *or* रक्तस्राव *m.*

To BLEMISH, *v. a. deform, impair,* v. To INJURE. खोड *f.* करणें, व्यंग-विकल-&c. करणें, ऐब *m.* करणें-लावणें, ऐबदार-&c. करणें.

2 *tarnish, soil,* v. To STAIN. बट्टा *m.* लावणें, कलंक *m.*-लांच्छन *n.*-काळें *n.*-कालिमा *f.*-&c. लावणें-आणणें.

BLEMISH, *n. mark of deformity*; lit; or, *soil, sully,* fig. v. FLAW, STAIN. खोड *f.* दोष *m.* हीण *n.* ऐब *m.* बट्टा *m.* बाट *m.* v. ठेव, पड, गोम *f.* छिद्र *n.*

BLEMISHED, *p. & a.* v. V. 1. ऐब लावलेला, व्यंग-&c. केलेला.

I. *faulty.* दोषी, सदोष, ऐबदार, लागरा.

To BLEND, *v. a. mingle and confound,* v. To MIX, To CONFOUND. मिळवणें, मिसळणें, एकवटणें, एकत्र करणें, संकर *m.*-एकाकार *n.*-संपर्क *m.*-सायुज्य *n.*-एकरूपता *f.* करणें *g. of o. recipr.*

To BLEND, *v. n.* मिळून जाणें, गोत *n.* मिळणें *g. of s. recipr.* समावणें.

BLENDED, *p.* v. V. मिळवलेला, &c. मिश्र, मिश्रित, एकाकार, संकीर्ण.

To BLESS, *v. a. make prosperous or happy.* कल्याण *n.*-कुशल *n.*-क्षेम *n.*-ऊर्जित *n.*-बरें *n.*-चांगलें *n.*-मंगल *n.*-अभीष्ट *n.*-इष्टसिद्धि *f.*-&c. करणें *g. of o.* बरकत *f.* देणें, सुखी-स्वस्थ-संपन्न-&c. करणें, सुदशेस-ऊर्जितदशेस-&c. आणणें, सुखपदीं-सुखासनीं-सुखस्थानीं-&c. बसवणें, सुखपदारूढ करणें, सुखसंपन्न-कल्याणसंपन्न-&c. करणें.

To b. greatly. कोटकल्याण करणें *g. of o.*

2 *pronounce a blessing upon.* आशीर्वाद *m.*-आशीर्वचन *n.*-श्रेयोवाद *m.*-कल्याणवचन *n.*-आशी *f.*-&c. देणें, स्वस्तिवाचन *n.* करणें, मस्तकीं -डोईवर-&c. हात *m.* ठेवणें.

Bless (thee)! स्वस्ति.

3 *glorify for benefits,* v. To PRAISE. उपकार आठवून-मानून-स्तवणें, स्तवणें, वंदणें, स्तुति *f.*-स्तवन *n.*-&c. करणें *g. of o.*

4 *invoke a blessing on.* दुवा *m.* देणें-मागणें, बरें *n.* मागणें *g. of o.* अभीष्टचिंतन *n.*-कल्याणचिंतन *n.*-शुभचिंतन *n.*-&c. करणें *g. of o.*

BLESSED, *p. & a.* v. V. 1. सुखी केलेला, कल्याण केलेला, सुखासनीं बसवलेला, &c. कृतकल्याण, कृतक्षेम, कृतकुशल, बरदी, प्राप्तवर, प्राप्तानुग्रह, अनुगृहीत.

2 आशीर्वाद दिल्हेला, &c. प्राप्ताशीर्वाद, प्राप्ताशीः, लब्धाशीः, आशीःसंपन्न, साशीर्वाद.

3 स्तवलेला, वंदलेला, वंदित, सुवंदित.

4 दुवा दिल्हेला, दुवा मागितलेला, चिंतिताभीष्ट, &c.

I. *happy, prosperous, &c.* सुखी, धन्य, सुखसंपन्न, सुखप्राप्त, प्राप्तसुख, कुशली, प्राप्तार्थ, प्राप्तेष्ट, प्राप्तयश, प्राप्तकल्याण, प्राप्तक्षेम, जातकल्याण-क्षेम-कुशल-&c. कल्याण-क्षेम-&c. संपन्न, कृतकृत्य, कृतार्थ, सुखपदीं-सुखासनीं-&c. बसलेला.

BLESSEDNESS, *n.* v. A. *and* BLISS. धन्य *f.* धन्यता *f.* सिद्धि *f.* कृतार्थता *f.* कृतकृत्यता *f.*

BLESSER, *n.* BLESSING, *p. a.* v. V. 1. कल्याण करणारा, &c. कल्याण कर्त्ता-कारक-कारी, मंगलकर्त्ता-&c. क्षेमकर्त्ता-&c. श्रेयस्कर.

2 आशीर्वाद देणारा, &c. आशी, आशीर्वाद कर्त्ता-दाता, वरद.

BLESSING, *n.* v. V. 1.—*act.* कल्याण करणें *n.* &c. सुखी करणें *n.* &c. आढ्यंकरण *n.*

2 *and* BENEDICTION. आशीर्वाद देणें *n.* आशीर्वाद *m.* आशीर्वचन *n.* वरदान *n.* स्वस्त्ययन *n.*

3 स्तवणेंn. स्तुति करणेंn. &c. वंदनn. वंदना f.
4 दुवाm. दुवा देणेंn. दुवा मागणेंn. [ग्रहm.
I. *divine favour*. ईश्वरकृपा f. ईश्वरीकृपा f. भगवत्कृपा f. अनु-
II. *a* b. *a benefit, a good*. सुखn. श्रेयn. प्रसादm. गनिमात f. अनुग्रहफलn. प्रसादफलn. प्रासादिकपदार्थm.-विषयm. अनुग्रहलब्धपदार्थm.-विषयm.
III. *a* b.—as in the gift of a saint, god, &c. वर *m. v.* दे.
Granting of a b. वरदान *n.*
Granter of a b. वरद.

BLIGHT, *n. mildew, &c.* lit. बीट *m.* चिकटा *m.* मेकाड *n.* मेकाडा *m.* टाका *m.* ताका *m.* लासा *m.* मोवा *or* मवा *m.*
B. as attacking fields of wheat, &c. तांबरा *or* तांबाराm. तांब *f.* गेरवा *m.*
B. attacking the grain *dzondhalà*. अंगारा *m.* काजळी *f.* कोळशी *f.* सैरा *m.* मकळी *f.*
B. attacking rice crops. पीस *f.*
B. attacking the mango, &c. भिरड *or* भेरूड *nm.* (To be affected by it, भिरडणें *or* भेरुडणें).
B. as indicated by curling up. मुरटी *f.* (To be affected by it, मुरटणें).

To BLIGHT, *v. a.* टाका *m.*-ताका *m.*-मोवा *m.*-रोग *m.*-&c. पाडणें.
To be blighted. ताकाळणें, ताका *m.*-रोग *m.*-&c. पडणें *in. con.*
2 fig. See To BLAST.

BLIND, *a.* अंध *pop.* अंधळा, नेत्रहीन-रहित-विरहित-&c. हीनचक्षु, दृष्टीवेगळा *or* निराळा, व्यक्ष, प्रज्ञाचक्षु, डोळेफुटका.
—in covert phras. धृतराष्ट्र.
B. by night. रातांधळ्या, रातांधळा, रात्र्यंध, निशांध.
B. by day. दिवसांधळ्या, दिनांध, दिवांध.
B. from birth. जन्मांध.
Blindish. दीडडोळ्या, दीड डोळ्याचा, अर्धेडोळ्या, अंधकल्प.
Stone b. निपट अंधळा.
String of b. men under a blind leader. आंधळ्यांचीमाळ *f.* अंधपरंपरा *f.*
To become b. डोळे *m. pl.* जाणें-फुटणें *g. of s.* डोळे गांवचीं कवाडें *n. pl.* लागणें, डोळ्यांची भिंत *f.* होणें, डोळ्यांचीं खोगरें *n. pl.* होणें, (through riches, honors, &c.) डोळ्यांवर धूर *m.* येणें. [नेत्री.
2 (of one eye). एकडोळ्या, काणा, एकाक्ष, एकनेत्र *pop.* एक-
—in covert phras. शुक्राचार्य.
3—boils, tumors, &c. मुका.
4 *undiscerning, undiscriminating*,—of persons. अंध *pop.* अंधळा, अज्ञान, ज्ञानहीन, विवेकशून्य, विवेकहीन, असमंजस.
5 *inconsiderate*—of actions, &c. अविचाराचा, अविवेकाचा, असमंजसपणाचा.

BLIND, *n.* v. SCREEN. पडदा *m.* आडपडदा *m.* अंतर्धान *n.* अंतर्धायक *n.* अंतःपट *pop.* अंतरपट *m.*
2 (for a bullock, &c.). झांकणी *f.* झांपणी *f.* झांपडी *f.* ढांकणी *f.* ढांपणी *f.* (*or* डोळेढांपणें *n.* डोळेझांकणें *n.* &c.) झोपणें *n.*
3 (esp. for a horse.) अंधारी *f.*
4 *something to mislead*. झुलकावणी *f.* भुलकावणी *f.* फटकण *f.* फसवणी *f.*
As a b. निमित्तास.

To BLIND, *v. a. deprive of sight*. अंधळा करणें, डोळे *m. pl.* फोडणें-काढणें *g. of o.* सळई *f.* फिरवणें.
3 fig. *darken the understanding*. डोळे *m.pl.* बांधणें, दृष्टि *f.*-बंद करणें, डोळ्यांला पाटा *m.*बांधणें, डोळ्यांवर पडळ *n.*-झांपण *f.*-&c. घालणें, डोळ्यांतमाती *f.* घालणें, छकावणें.

BLINDED, *p.* v. V. 1. अंधळा केलेला, डोळे फोडलेला, अंधीकृत.

BLINDFOLD, *a.* BLINDFOLDED, *p.* v. V. डोळे बांधलेला, बांधडोळ्या, आच्छादित नेत्र-चक्षु, आवृतनेत्र.

To BLINDFOLD, *v. a. cover the eyes of*. डोळे *m.pl.* बांधणें *g. of o.* पडदा *m.*-अंधेरी *f.*-झांकणी *f.*-&c. बांधणें-घालणें-देणें, गणेशटोपी *f.* घालणें.

BLINDLY, *adv. implicitly, &c.* डोळे झांकून, डोळे मिटून, डोळे न-उघडतां, मागेंपुढें न पाहतां.

BLINDMAN'S BUFF, *n.* अंधळी कोशिंबीर *f.*

BLINDNESS, *n.* v. A. 1. अंधळेपणा *m.* अंधत्व *n.* आंध्य *n.* अंधावस्था *f.* नेत्राभाव *m.*
Night b. रातांधळें *n.*
4 अंधळेपणा *m.* अंधत्व *n.* विवेकराहित्य *n.* विचारराहित्य *n.* अविचार *m.* अविवेक *m.*
5 असमंजसपणा *m.*

BLIND-SIDE, *n. weakness, infirmity*. मर्मस्थान *n.* गुह्यस्थान *n.* लंगडें *n.* उघडें नागवें *n.*

BLIND-WORM, *n.* महांडूळ *n.*

To BLINK, *v. n. wink*. डोळे *m. pl.* मिचकावणें *or* पिचकावणें, पिचपिचणें, पिटपिटणें, मिटकावणें, डोळे *m. pl.* पिटपिट हालणें, मिटमिट पाहणें.

To BLINK, *v. a. evade, shut out of sight*. टाळणें, डोळे *m. pl.* झांकणें, डोळे झांक *f.* करणें, टाळणी *f.* करणें *g. of o.*

BLINK, *n.* See GLIMPSE.

BLINKARD, *n.* मिचकडोळ्या, डोळेमिचक्या, डोळेपिचक्या, मिचक्याडोळ्यांचा माणूस *m.*

BLINKING, *n.* v. V. N.—*act*. डोळेमिचकावणें *n.* &c. उघडमीट *f.* उघडझांक *f.* मिचमिच *f.* निमेषोन्मेष *m.*

BLISS, *n. felicity, blessedness, happiness*. सुख *n.* सुखीपणा *m.* आनंद *m.* सुखावस्था *f.* सौख्य *n.* सौख्यदशा *f.* सुखिता *f.* धन्य *f.* धन्यता *f.* कृतकृत्यता *f.* कृतार्थता *f.*
Highest b. परमसुख *n.*
2 *beatified state, heavenly joys*, v. HEAVEN. परमपद *n.* सुखपद *n.* परमगति *f.*

BLISSFUL, *a. full of bliss*. सुखाचा, आनंदाचा, परमसुखाचा, परमानंदाचा, आनंदमय, सुखमय.

BLISTER, *n. bladder*. फोड *m.* फुगारा *m.* फुगा *m.* पोपडा *m.* स्फोट *m.*
2 *application to raise a blister*. प्रस्फोटक *m.* प्रस्फोटकारी औषध *n.* प्लास्तर *n.* from the English is common.

To BLISTER, *v. n. rise in a blister*. फुगा *m.*-&c. येणें-उठणें, फोपेणें, फोपसणें, उफणणें *or* उफाणणें.

To BLISTER, *v. a. raise a blister*. फोड *m.*-स्फोट *m.*-&c. आणणें.

BLITHE, BLITHEFUL, BLITHESOME, *a. gay, airy*, v. MERRY. आनंदी, उल्लासी, हास्यमुख.

BLITHELY, *adv.* v. A. आनंदीपणानें, आनंदवृत्तीनें, उल्लासवृत्तीनें.

BLITHENESS, BLITHESOMENESS, v. A. आनंदीपणा *m.* उल्लासीपणा *m.* आनंदवृत्ति *f.*

To BLOAT, *v. n. grow turgid*. फोपसणें, कापुसणें, फोपसा-&c.

होणें, धोदरा *m.* चढणें, वातपुष्ट होणें.

To BLOAT, *v. a.* v. TO SWELL, TO PUFF. फुगवणें.

BLOATED, *p.* v. V. N. फोपशा *or* फोपसा, कापशा, पेजट, गुरगुरीत, धोदऱ्या, गदेल्या, वातपुष्ट.

BLOATEDNESS, *n.* v. P. फोपशी *f.* कापशी *f.* फुगवटी *f.* फुगवशी *f.* फूग *f.* शोफ *m.* शोफा *f.*

BLOBBER-LIP, *n. thick lip.* बाबर ओंठ *or* होंट *m.* जाड ओंठ *or* [होंठ *m.*

BLOBBER-LIPPED, *a.* बाबर ओंट्या *or* होंट्या, जाड ओंट्या *or* होंट्या.

BLOCK, *n. mass of wood, chump, chunk, clump.* करंडा *or* करांडा *m.* ठोकळा *m.* कांडका *m.* कोंडका *m.* ढोणका *m.* ढोण *n.* ढोणपा *m.* ढोणप *n.* ढोणकूर *n.* ठोंगळ *m.* ठिकीं *f.* फाटें *n.* ओंडा *m.* बाघी *f.* फोड *f. n.* खोड *n.* तोड *n.*

2 (of stone, &c.). गुंडा *m.* चिरा *m.*

3 *pulley block.* कप्पा *m. dim.* कप्पी *or* कपी *f.* Rope confining it, चावी *f.*

4 *chopping block, (of carpenters, &c.).* घोडी *f.* बाघी *f.* सांकटा *m.* सकोटण *or* न *n.* सांकटन *or* णें *n.* नेहा *m.*

Chips of the same b. एकेमाळेचे मणी *m. pl.* एके आईचीं लेंकरें *n. pl.* एके झाडाचीं फळें *n. pl.*

5 (of buildings) चाळ *f.*

6 *frame on which to make any thing.* कलबूत *or* द *m.*

7 शिरश्छेदाचा ठोकळा *m.*-सांकटा *m.*-&c.

8 See OBSTACLE.

To BLOCK, *v. a. stop up. &c.* v. TO OBSTRUCT. बुजवणें, बुजणें, कोंडणें, मुंदणें *or* मुंधणें, रोधणें, रोध *m.*-अवरोध *m.*-&c. करणें *g. of o.*

BLOCK-HEAD, *n.* v. FOOL. मूर्ख, धोंडा *m.* टोणपा, ठोंबा *or* ठोंब्या, [गावदी, ढ.

BLOCK-HEADED, *a.* v. STUPID. ठोंब्या.

BLOCKADE, *n.* कोंडमारा *m.* कोंडमार *m.* कोंडी *f.* कोंडणी *f.* वाटकोंडी *f.* वाटबंदी *f.* नाकेबंदी *f.* अवरोधजनकवेष्टन *n.*

To BLOCKADE, *v. a.* v. N. कोंडमारा *m.*-कोंडी *f.*-वाटकोंडी *f.*-नाकेबंदी *f.*-&c. करणें *g. of o.*

BLOCKED, *p.* v. V. कोंडलेला, बुजलेला, &c. बंद, रुद्ध, अवरुद्ध, प्रतिरुद्ध, प्रतिबद्ध.

To be b. बुजणें, कोंदणें, कोंदाटणें, मुंदणें *or* मुंधणें, रोधणें, रुधणें.

BLOCKING, *n.* v. V.—*act.* कोंडणें *n.* &c. कोंडी *f.* कोंडणी *f.* रोध *m.* अवरोध *m.* रोधन *n.* अवरोधन *n.*

BLOCKISH, BLOCKLIKE. See STUPID.

BLOOD, *n.* रक्त *n.* रुधिर *n.* शोणित *n.* लालपाणी *n.*

B. vomited upon the bite of certain serpents. झेंडू *m.*

Stoppage or congestion of b. रक्तावरोध *m.*

Extravasated b. मुडदाररक्त *n.*

In cold b. थंडापोटानें, थंडाईखालीं.

Vitiation or disorder of b. रक्तविकार *m.* रक्तदोष *m.*

To run with b.—a sore, &c. रक्तावणें *or* रक्ताळणें.

2 *high birth.* कुलीनता *f.* आभिजात्य *n.* वर्णश्रेष्ठता *f.* सद्वंशता *f.*

3 See KINDRED. 4 *blade, swell,* v. BUCK. फांकडा *m.* फंदी *m.* बांका *m.* बांकडा *m.* रगेल *c.* रग्या *m.*

Brother, &c. of whole b. सहोदर, समानोदर.—of half b. भिन्नोदर.

To BLOOD. See To BLEED.

BLOOD-COLORED, BLOOD-RED, *a.* रक्ताच्या रंगाचा, रक्तवर्ण, शोणित, शोण. [त, शोण.

BLOOD-HORSE, *n.* असल घोडा *m.* उत्तम जातीचा घोडा *m.*

BLOOD-LESS, *a.* रक्तशून्य-रहित-हीन-&c.

BLOOD-SHEDDING, BLOOD-SHED, *n.* रक्तपात *m.* रक्तवृष्टि *m.* रक्तस्राव *m.* रक्ताचासडा *m.*

To be great b. रक्ताचा पाऊस पडणें, कबंध *m. n.* नाचणें.

BLOOD-SHOT, BLOOD-SHOTTEN, *a.* राता *remiss.* रातड, आरक्त, गढूळ, तांबट.

To become b. खरावणें, खडुळणें, तळावणें.

BLOOD-SHOTTENNESS, *n.* रात *m.* नेत्रराग *m.*

BLOODTHIRSTINESS, *n.* v. A. घातुकपणा *m.* हिंस्रता *f.* जिघांसा *f.*

BBOOD-THIRSTY, *a.* v. CRUEL. हिंसक, हिंसालु, हिंस्र, जिघांसु, रक्तप्रिय.

BLOOD-VESSEL, *n.* रक्तवाहिनी *f.*

BLOODED, *a.* रक्ताचा.

Cold-b. शीतरक्ताचा, गूढबर्चा.

Hot-b. उष्णरक्ताचा.

BLOODINESS, *n.* v. A. 1. रक्ताचा डागीलपणा *m.* रक्तांकितत्व *n.* &c.

2 रक्तानें भरलेलेपणा *m.* रक्तबोंबाळपणा *m.* &c. रक्ताक्तता *f.*

3 खुनीपणा *m.* घातुकपणा *m.* &c. हिंस्रता *f.* जिघांसा *f.*

BLOODY, *a. stained with blood.* रक्ताचे डागाचा, रक्तानें डागलेला, रक्तदूषित, रक्तांकित, रक्तलांछित, रक्तचिन्हित.

2 *covered with blood.* रक्तानें भरलेला-माखलेला-न्हालेला, रक्तबोंबाळ *or* रक्तानें बोंबाळ, रक्तावलेला, रक्तांबर *or* रक्तांबील *or* ळ, रक्तारक्त, रक्ताक्त, रक्तमय.

3 *bloody-minded, sanguinary,* v. CRUEL. खुनी, रक्तप्रिय, हिंसक, हिंसालु, हिंस्र, घातुक, घातकी, जिघांसु, हत्यारा.

4 *attended with blood shed.* रक्तपाताचा, रक्तस्रावाचा, कत्तलीचा, रक्ताचा पूर वाहलेला.

BLOODY-FLUX, *n.* रक्त ओढ *f.* रक्ताचीहगवण *f.* रक्तातिसार *m.*

BLOOM, *n. opening and ripening state.* विकास *m.* स्फोट *m.* विकसनावस्था *f.* विकसनदशा *f.*

2 (of youth) नवती *f.* बहर *f. m.* यौवनावस्था *f.* तारुण्यावस्था [*f.*

3 *freshness or clearness of look.* टवटवी *f.* टकटकी *f.* टकमकी *f.* नळनळी *f.* लुसलुसी *f.* तजला *m.* तजेला *m.* तजेली *f.* उजळा *m.*

4 See BLOSSOM.

To BLOOM, *v. n.*—plants, v. TO BLOW. फुलणें, विकसणें.

2 *look fresh, clear, glowing.* टवटवणें, टकटकणें, लुसलुसणें, नळनळणें, टवटवीत-&c. दिसणें.

BLOOMING, *p. a.* v. V. 1. फुलता, विकसता, नवतीचा, नवनवतीचा.

2 टवटवीत, टकटकीत, टकमकीत, लुसलुसीत, नळनळीत, टवटवीचा, टकटकीचा, नळनळीचा, &c.

BLOSSOM, *n.* फूल *n.* पुष्प *n.*—of the mango and some other trees. मोहर *m.* केसर *n. m.*

Barren b. blind b. वायफूल *n.*

To BLOSSOM, *v. n.* फुलणें, फुलास येणें, फुलें *n. pl.* येणें *in. con.* पुष्पयुक्त होणें.—the mango and some other trees. मोहरणें, केसरणें.

BLOSSOMY, *a.* टवटवीचा, टकटकीचा, नवतीचा, नवनवतीचा, नळनळीचा. [नळीचा.

To BLOT, *v. a.* (as with ink). भरणें, भरविणें, ठिपकाळणें, बोळा *m.* पाडणें-घालणें, डाग *m.* देणें, डागील करणें, मसरडणें, बोळवणें.

2 *sully, soil, blur,* v. TO STAIN. डागणें *or* दागणें, डाग *m.* देणें-लावणें, कलंक *m.* लावणें, डागील करणें.

3 out; *obliterate,* v. TO EFFACE. पुसणें *or* पुसून टाकणें, बो-

ळा *m.*-पोतेरें *n.*-&c. घालणें-फिरवणें, काळा करणें, काळें *n.*-शाई *f.* घालणें.

To be blotted out of mind. बोळणें.

BLOT, *n.* (as of ink). बोळा *m.* ठिपका *m.* डाग *m.*

2 *slur, stigma,* v. STAIN. डाग *or* दाग *m.* ठपका *m.* काळें *n.* कलंक *m.* सोड *f.* कालिमा *m. f.* [बला *m.*

BLOTCH, *n.* चकंदळ *n.* चकदा *m. or* चफदें *n.* स्फोट *m.* ढाण *n.* ख-

BLOTTINGPAPER, *n.* टिपावयाचा कागद *m.*

BLOW, *n.* (with a stick, sword, &c.), *stroke.* काठी *f.* टोला *m.* आघात *m.* घात *m.* प्रहार *m.* चटकणी *f.* झटका *m.* झटकारा *m.* फटका *m.* फटकारा *m.* घसका *m.*

2 (with the fist, &c.), *thump.* बुकी *f.* ठोसरा *m.* ठोसा *m.* ठोंबरा *m.* ठोमणा *m.* ढुस्सा *m.* भतका *m.* भदका *m.* मुटका *m.* गुद्दा *m.* घुसा *or* घुस्सा *m.* ढोसरा *or.* ढोसा *m.* मुष्टिप्रहार *m.* मुष्टिमोदक *m.*

—in the sense and with the power of such words as, *whack, whap, bang, swinging blow, &c.* रपाटा *m.* धपाटा *or* धमाटा *m.* रबेद *or* त *m.* रबेदा *or* ता *m.* रबका *m.*धब्बल *f.*धब्ब *f.n.* रामटोला *m.* रामरट्टा *m.* रट्टा *or* रट्या *m.* तडाखा *m.* कडाखा *m.* दणका *m.* ढांका *m.*

3—gener. *box, buffet, cuff, hit, knock, polt, punch, dig, &c.* टोला *m.* बतका *or* भदका *m.* थाप *f.* धमाटा *m.* आघात *m.* घात *m.* ठोका *m.* ठोक *m.* चटकाणी *f.*

B. with the bottom of the fist. बुकी *f.* बतका *or* बदका *or* बुतका *m.* ढुबका *m.* &c. धुमका *m.* बुकांदा *or* बुकाडा *m. dim.* बुकांदी *f.*

Dead or flat b. ठसका *m.*

Heavy b. निर्घात *m.*

To come to blows. शरीर संबंधावर येणें, हाताफळीस-हातघाईस-हात घाईवर-हातपिटीस-हस्तव्यापारावर-&c. येणें.

4 (of calamity), v. STROKE. धका *or* धक्का *m.* गचका *m.* गजब *m.* चट्टा *m.* घाला *m.* घसरा *m.*

5 (in trade, &c.), v. LOSS. झोका *m. v.* बस, गोता *m. v.* खा, वस, छक्कड *f.* चट्टा *n.* घसरा *m.* खोंच *f.* धोका *f.* खरका *m.*

6 (of a fly). असडी *or* आसडी *f.* आसडा *m.* सडी *f.*

To BLOW, *v. n.*—the wind. वाहणें, चालणें.

2—softly, in gentle puffs, &c. v. To BREATHE. झुळकणें, झुळझुळ *adv.* वाहणें, थंड-मंद वाहणें.

3 *puff,* v. To PANT. धापणें, धापलणें, धापा *f. pl.* टाकणें-देणें, फुंकरणें, कांसळणें.

4 *sound on being blown.* वाजणें, नाद *m.* देणें-घेणें.

5 *bloom, blossom, open, expand.* फुलणें, विकसणें, विकासणें, पुष्पणें, उफलणें, उमलणें, उकलणें.

6 over; *pass away without effect.* वाहवणें, जिरणें, उडणें, विनुळणें, वाऱ्यावारीं-फुकटावारीं जाणें, वायबार *m.* होणें *g. of s.*

7 up;—from gunpowder. भडकणें, उडून जाणें.

8 out;—a light,&c. वाऱ्यानें जाणें-विझणें-मालवणें. [वून नेणें.

To BLOW, *v. a.*—the wind, &c. वाहविणें, चालवणें, उडवणें, उड-

2 *puff out,* v. To INFLATE. फुगवणें, फुगीर करणें.

3 (an instrument of wind-musick). फुंकणें, फुंकून वाजवणें, फुंक *f.*-फुंकर *m.*-फुंकारा *m.* मारणें-घालणें.

4 (with the breath). फुंकणें, फुंकरणें, फुंक *f.*-फुंकर *m.*-फुंका *m.*-फुंकार *m.*-फुंकारा *m.* मारणें-घालणें.

5 (the nose). शिंकरणें *or* नाक *n.* शिंकरणें, नाक *n.* फेडणें-फेकडणें-झाडणें.

6 (the fire) with a bellows. धमकणें.

7 See To PUBLISH.

8 *deposit eggs*—flies, &c. सडी *f.*-असडी *f.* घालणें. [वर्णे.

9 *put out of breath.* धापा टाकी असाकरणें,धापा टाकावयास ला-

10 up; *kindle,* v.To EXCITE. फुंकून देणें, फुंकणें, चेतवणें, पेटवणें.

11 up; (by gunpowder). दारूनें-सुरूंगानें उडवणें-उडवून देणें-फुंकून देणें.

12 up; *rate vehemently,* v. To SCOLD. खणकावणें, धडकावणें, दपटणें, तावणें, ताव *m.* देणें.

13 away. उडवणें, उडवून नेणें.

14 out, v. To EXTINGUISH. फुंकून विझवणें.

BLOW-PIPE, *n.* फुंकणी *f.* धमनी *f.*

BLOWING, *n.* v. V. N. 1.—*act.* वाहणें *n.* चालणें *n.*

3 धापणें *n.* धापा देणें *n.* &c. दम *m.* दमा *m.* हवाबी *f. v.* लाग.

4 बाजणें *n.* &c.

5 फुलणें *n.* &c. विकास *m.* विकासन *n.* विकसन *n.* स्फोट *m.* स्फोटन *n.* परिस्फोट *m.* स्फुटन *n.* प्रकाश *m.*

v. V. A. 1.—*act.* उडवणें *n.* &c.

2 फुगवणें *n.* &c.

3 फुंकणें *n.* फुंकून वाजवणें *n.* फुक-&c. मारणें *n.*-घालणें *n.*

4 फुंकणें *n.* फुंकरणें *n.* फुंक &c. मारणें *n.*-घालणें *n.*

BLOWN, *p.* v. V. N. 5. फुललेला, &c. विकसित, विकासित, उन्मीलित, प्रफुल्लित, प्रफुल्ल, उत्फुल्ल, स्फुट, स्फुटित, प्रस्फुट, प्रस्फुटित, हसित, स्मित.

v. V. A. 1. उडवलेला, उडवून नेलेला.

2 फुगवलेला, &c. फुगीर, *remiss.* फुगट, गुरगुरीत, ध्मात.

BLUBBER, *n. fat of the whale, &c.* देवमाशाची चरबी *f.*

2 *fat-like substance cast up by the sea.* जार *m. f.* गलगल*m.*

To BLUBBER, *v. n.* v. To CRY. गाल फुगवून-भरून रडणें.

BLUBBERER, *n. one ever blubbering.* अंसुढाळ्या, अंसुढाळ.

BLUDGEON, *n.* लोहांगीकाठी *f.* परिघ *m.* काष्ठलौही *m.* गदा *f.*

BLUE, *a.*—dark b. नील *pop.*निळा, नीलवर्ण, श्याम, श्यामल, श्यामवर्ण, कृष्ण, मेचक.—light b. sky b. आस्मानी, आस्मानी रंगाचा, मेघवर्ण.

True b. नील राग.

The Blues, *low spirits,* v. MELANCHOLY. विषाद *m.*

To look b. *be confused or terrified.* काळबंडणें.

BLUE-EYED, *a.* नीलनयन, नीलाक्ष.

BLUENESS, *n.* v. A. निळेपणा *m.* नीलिमा *m.* नैल्य *n.* नीलत्व *n.*

BLUFF, BLUFFNESS. See BOLD, &c.

BLUISH, *a.* निळसर, कांहींसा निळा.

To BLUNDER, *v. n.* v. To ERR. चुकणें, बहकणें *or* भकणें, भ्रमणें, घसरणें, भुलणें, चूक *f.* करणें, स्खलन *n.* पावणें, प्रमाद *m.* करणें.

BLUNDER, *n.* v. ERROR. चूक *dim.* चुकी *f.* भूल *f.* घसरण *f.* प्रमाद *m.*

2—in writing or speaking. अवाक्षर *n.* अशुद्ध *n.* अबद्ध *n.*

That isfull of blunders. अशुद्धाळ, सर्वाशुद्ध, प्रामादिक,सर्वाबद्ध.

BLUNDER-BUS, *n.* दमामा *m.* बकमार *or* बकमाल *f.*

BLUNDER-HEAD, *n.* BLUNDERER, *n.* BLUNDERING, *p. a.* v. V. *one given to blundering.* चुकणारा, भकणारा, चुकरा, गफलती *or* त्या, गलत्या, अशुद्ध्या, अशुद्धाळ, भांब्या, भांबळ *or* ळ्या, भु-

ल्या, झांबऱ्या, धंदऱ्या, गोंधळ्या, गह्याळ, झावळ, भ्रमिष्ट, भ्रमी.

BLUNDERINGLY, *adv.* चुकतचुकत, चुकतमाकत, चुकतवाकत, चुकतमुकत, चुकतभुलत, घसरत घसरत, प्रमादानें.

BLUNT, *a. not sharp.* बोंथा *remiss.* बोंथट, बुठणा, बोटका, बुंठा *or* बोंठा, नरम, मऊ, मुंढा, अतीक्ष्ण, अतीव्र, जड, बोध, ठोसर, मोठा, लोणकाप्या, धारबसलेला, बोंथलेला, &c.

To become b. बोंथणें, बोंथटणें, माठणें, बुठणें *or* बोठणें, बोळणें, मुंढणें, बसणें, बोधणें.

2 *dull &c.*—wit, intellect. मंद, जड, बोथट, अतीक्ष्ण, अतीव्र.

3 *roughly plain and open, free-spoken.* निखालस, सडीक, धोपट मार्ग्या, धोपट मार्गी, कडकडीत *or* खडखडीत, खडखडीतस्वभावाचा, खरमरीत, खसखसीत, खणखणीत, ठसठसीत, सणसणीत, झणझणीत, धडकफडक *or* धडकभडक, खरपूस, पडखर, उज्झड, निर्भिड.

To BLUNT, *v. a.* बोधवणें, बोळवणें, बसवणें, धार *f.* मोडणें-बुझविणें *g. of o.* धार *f.*-पाणी *n.* उतरणें *g. of o.* निपाणी करणें.

2 fig. तीक्ष्णता *f.*-तीव्रता *f.*-प्रखरता *f.*-&c. घालविणें-कमीकरणें.

BLUNTLY, *adv.* v. A. 1. बोंथेपणानें, &c. मंद, जड.

3 *plainly, roundly, downright, outright, plump, smack, flat, slap.* धड, धडधडीत, निक्षाडून, निक्षूण, निखालस, हडसूनखडसून, रोखठोक, रोख, चरचरीत, खसखसीत, धडकफडक, धडकभडक, परिछिन्न, धादांत, साफ, खरपूस.

BLUNTNESS, *n.* v.A.1. बोंथेपणा *m.* &c. मंदाई *f.* मंदत्व *n.*मऊपणा *m.* नरमाई *f.* अतीक्ष्णता *f.* अतीव्रता *f.*

2 मंदपणा *m.* जडपणा *m.* मंदत्व *n.* अतीक्ष्णता *f.* अतीव्रता *f.*

3 खरपूसपणा *m.* खरमरीतपणा *m.* खणखणीतपणा *m.* खसखसीतपणा *m.* सणसणीतपणा *m.* धोपटमार्गीपणा *m.* &c. धोपटमार्ग*m.* उघडीमराठी *f.*

BLUR, To BLUR. See STAIN, To STAIN.

To BLURT, *v. a. utter suddenly and inadvertently.* कडकावणें, धडकावणें, तडकावणें, धसकावणें *or* धसकाबून बोलणें, मडभडावणें, भडकावणें, बुरकणें.

BLURTER, *n.* BLURTING, *p. a.* v. V. कडकावणारा, धसकावून बोलणारा, &c. फटसूल, फटसाळ, फट्या *or* फट्या, फडसूळ, फट्याबाबरा, फटकळ *or* तोंडाचा फटकळ, तोंडचाहलका, भडभड्या, उज्झड.

To BLUSH, *v. n. betray shame or confusion by the face.* लाजेनें-&c. काळवटणें-काळवंडणें, काळोखी *f.*-काळी *f.*-कालिमा *f.* येणें, मुखचर्या *f.*-मुखश्री *f.*-नूर *m.*-&c. फिरणें-बदलणें, तोंडाचें पाणी *n.* पळणें, मुखवैवर्ण्य *n.* होणें *g. of s.* Note. The sense of shame is evinced in the countenances of Maráṭhás by a dark, not by a red color.

2 See To BLOOM.

BLUSH, *n. color in the cheeks raised by shame, confusion, &c.* v. V. लाजेची काळोखी *f.*-काळी *f.*-कालिमा *f.*-काळवंडी *f.* मुखवैवर्ण्य *n.* [दर्शनीं.

At the first b.*at the first appearance.* सकृद्दर्शनीं, प्रथम-

To BLUSTER, *v. n.*—the wind, v. To ROAR. घोघावणें, घोघेणें, सोसावणें, सोसो-घोघो-झोझो-धोधो-&c. वाहणें-येणें.

2 *puff, swagger, rant, vapor, gasconade, bellow at, roar at.* दणगारणें, दणदणणें, दणकावणें, डरडरणें, तमतमणें, तमणें, तम*m.* गाणें, ताल *m.* तोडणें, नाकपुड्या *f. pl.* पिंजारणें-फुगवणें-फुरफुरवणें, ताव *m.* झाडणें, शिरा *f. pl.* ताणणें, मोठाल्या गोष्टी *f. pl.*-तीनतेरा गोष्टी *f. pl.* सांगणें, बारा बत्तिशा *f. pl.* लावणें, गुरकावणी *f.* करणें.

BLUSTER, *n.* BLUSTERING, *n.* v. V. 1.—घोघावणें *n.* &c. घोघाट *m.* झोझाट *m.* सोसाट *or* सुसाट *m.* सोसाटा *or* सुसाटा *m.* सणाटा *m.*

2 अरेरावकी *f.* अरेरावी *f.* पादरधिट्टाई *f.* चढाईच्या गोष्टी *f. pl.* घटपटं *or* गटपटं *n.* गट्टापट्टा *m.* रगडमल्ली *f.* छांदूं *n. f.* खलेली *f.* मेघडंबर *or* मेघाडंबर *m.* तराठा *m.* वल्गना *f.* वल्ग *m. pl.* गुरकावणी *f.* गुरकी *f.* गुरकाई *f.* तम *m.* तमतमाशा *m.* तापतोबारा *m.*

BLUSTERER, *n.* BLUSTERING, *p. a.* BLUSTEROUS, *a.* v. V. 1. घोघावणारा, &c. घोघ्या, झोझ्या, सोसाट्या*or* सुसाट्या, सणाट्या.

2 *and* BULLY. HECTOR. दणगारणारा, &c. अरेराव *m.* रगडमल्ल, तालतोड्या, खलेल, गुरका *or* क्या, मोठाल्या गोष्टी बोलणारा, धटांगण, धटिंगण. [शत्रु *m.*

BOA-CONSTRICTOR, *n.* आर *or* आहार *m.* अजगर *m.* घणस *m.*

To lie torpidly like a b. आहारणें.

BOAR, *n.* डुकर *m.* वराह *m.*

Wild b. रानडुकर *m.*

BOARD, *n. plank, &c.* फळी *f.* (intens. फळा *m.*) फळें*n.* तख्ता *m.*

Writing b. पाटी *f.*

2 *table.* जेवायाचें मेज *n.* N. B. the Maráṭhás do not use a board or table: their food is placed on the ground.

Fellowship of board. पंक्तिव्यवहार *m.* पंक्तिसंसर्ग *m.* अन्नव्यवहार *m.*

Fault that excludes from the common b. पंक्तिदोष *m.*

3 *entertainment.* जेवण *n.* जेवणावळ *f.* जेवणखाण *n.* खाणें*n.* खाणें पिणें *n.*

Service in which b. is provided. सपोटीचाकरी *f.*

Service in which b. is not provided. निपोटी चाकरी *f.*

One that serves for his b. पोटार्थी, पोटचाकर, पोटावारीं राहणारा-राबणारा.

To serve for one's b. पोटावारीं राहणें.

4 *cost of eating.* खाणावळ *f.* जेवणावळ *f.*

5 *body of counsellors, &c.* सभासदसमुदाय *m.* सभासद *m.pl.* सामाजिक *m. pl.* सामाजिकसमूह *m.* पंच *m. pl.*

6—at chess, draughts, &c. (*or* chequered cloth). चौपट *f. n.* पट *m. f.*

7 *side of a ship.* गलबताची-&c. बाजू *f.* बोडद *n.*

Larboard. डावें बोडद.

Starboard. उजवें बोडद.

Aboard. गलबता-जहाजा-&c. वर.

Over board. गलबताच्या-&c. बाजूवरून.

To BOARD, *v. a.* See To PLANK. 2 *place as boarder.* जेवायास-जेवणावळीस-&c. ठेवणें-घालवणें

3 *receive as boarder.* जेवणावळीस घेणें. [ढून जाणें.

4 *enter (a ship) by force.* हल्ला करून जोरानें-&c. शिरणें-च-

To BOARD, *v. n. mess with.* जेवायास-जेवणावळीस असणें-राहणें, जेवणखाण *n.*-खाणेंपिणें *n.*-&c. करणें.

BOARD-WAGES, *n.* पोटगी *f.* पोटखर्च *m.*

B. as paid in grain. अडशेरी *f.*

BOARDER, *n.* v. V. N. जेवणावळीचा माणूस *m.* &c.

BOARDING-HOUSE, *n.* खाणावळीचें-जेवणावळीचें घर *n.*

BOARDING-SCHOOL, *n.* ज्या शाळेंत मुलांच्या खाण्यापिण्याची सोय होत असते ती शाळ *f.*

To BOAST, *v. a. brag of, display vauntingly.* बढाई *or* बढाइकी- *f.*-बडिवार *m.*-फुशारकी *or* फुशारी *f.* सांगणें *g. of o.* पडप *n.*-बुटटकी *f.*-प्रतिष्ठा *f.*-मोठाई *f.*-&c. सांगणें-मिरवणें *g. of o.* मिरवणें, महत्व *n.* वाढवणें *g. of o.*

2 (one's self of) v. To PLUME. बाणा *m.*-&c. बाळगणें.

To BOAST, *v. n. brag, vaunt, glory.* फुशारणें, जल्पणें, फुशारी *f.*-फुशारकी *f.* करणें-सांगणें, शेखी *f.* मिरवणें, बुटटकी *f.* मिरवणें-सांगणें-दासवणें, फुशारकीच्या-शेखीच्या-&c. गोष्टी *f. pl.* सांगणें, तोरा *m.* दासवणें, मोठाल्या गोष्टी *f. pl.* सांगणें, बल्गना *f.* करणें.

BOAST, BOASTING, *n.* v. V. N. फुशारकी *or* फुशारी *f.* शेखी *f.* लप्पंछप्पं *n. v.* लाव, मांड, गट्टं पट्टं *or* घटं पटं *n.* बुटटकी *f.* लटपटपंची *f.* बल्गना *f.* शूरमान *n.* आत्मश्लाघा *f.* शब्दपांडित्य *n.* स्तोम *n.* कोल्हांट्याचें शूरत्व *n.* चटक्याचे मांडव *m.pl.* ठेपराई *f.* फुगराई *f.*

I. *cause of boasting.* बाणा-अभिमान-&c. बाळगण्याचें कारण *n.*

BOASTER, *n.* BOASTING, *p. a.* BOASTFUL, *a.* v. V. N. फुशारकी सांगणारा, शेखीमिरवणारा, &c. बढाईखोर, फुशारखोर, सांगसुगरण, थाक्या सांगणारा, चटक्याचे मांडव घालणारा, तिसमारखान, तीसमारका, आत्मश्लाघी, शूरमानी, शूरम्मन्य.

BOASTINGLY, *adv.* शेखीनें, पडपानें, बडिवारानें, फुशारकीनें.

BOAT, *n.* v. VESSEL. नाव *f.* नौका *f.* नौ *f.* जलयान *n.* तरण *n.* तरणी *f.*

Master of a b. or small vessel. तांडेल *m.*

To be in the same b with. एके नावेंत असणें.

To BOAT. *v. a. convey in a b.* नावेंतून-&c. नेणें.

BOAT-MAN, *n.* नावाडी *or* नावाड्या *m.* नावबाला *m.* नावकरी *or* नावेकरी *m.* नाविक *m.*

Song of a b. whilst rowing. चकवा *m.*

BOATSWAIN, *n.* गलबतावरील एक अधिकारी आहे.

To BOB, *v. n. play backwards and forwards.* लटलटणें, लटलटहालणें, झोके *m. pl.* घेणें-खाणें.

2 up and down, (in drowning). गचकळणें, गचावणें, बुचकळ्या *f. pl.*-बुटकुळ्या *f. pl.* खाणें.

To BOB, *v. a.* v. To JERK, हिसकणें, हिसडणें, आसडणें.

BOB, *n.* v. PENDENT. झुबका *m.* झुमका *m.* लोळी *f.* झिलमिली *f.*

2 (of a song), v. BURDEN. अंकणकडवें *n.* पालवपद *or* पालुपद *n.* अकडकडवें *n.*

BOB-TAIL, *n.* तुटकी शेपटी *f.* लांडी शेपटी *f.* लांडें शेंपूट *n.*

BOB-TAILED, *a.* लांडा, छिन्नपुच्छ.

BOBBIN, *n.* (of the weaver). कांडी *f.*

BOBBING, *n.* v. V. N 1. लटलटणें *n.* &c.

2 गचकळणें *n.* &c. गचकळ्या *f. pl.* गटकळ्या *f. pl.* गटंगळ्या *f. pl.* गचंगळ्या *f. pl.* गुटकुळ्या *f. pl.* निमज्जनोन्मज्जन *n.*

To BODE, *v. a. foreshow, forebode, presage, portend.* सुचवणें, दर्शवणें, पुढला (used with the required noun) दाखवणें, सूचन *n.*-सूचना *f.*-दर्शन *n.*-प्रदर्शन *n.*-पूर्वसूचन *n.*-पूर्वसूचना *f.*-&c. करणें *g. of o.* लक्षण *n.*-चिन्ह *n.*-पूर्वलक्षण *n.*-पूर्वचिन्ह *n.*-&c. असणें *in. con. & g. of o.* [दर्शक.

BODER, *n.* BODING, *p. a.* v. V. सुचवणारा, दर्शवणारा, &c. सूचक, Ill-b. अनिष्ट-अभद्र-अमंगल-&c. सूचक-दर्शक-प्रदर्शक-&c.

Ill-b. sign or mark. करंटें लक्षण *n.* कुलक्षण *n.* दुर्लक्षण *n.* दुश्चिन्ह *n.*

BODEMENT, BODING, *n.* v. V.—*act.* सुचवणें *n.* दर्शवणें *n.* &c. सूचन *n.* सूचना *f.* दर्शन *n.* प्रदर्शन *n.* पूर्वसूचन *n.* पूर्वसूचना *f.*

B. of ill. अनिष्ट-अमंगल-अकल्याण-अभद्र-&c. सूचन *n.*-प्रदर्शन *n.*-&c.

B. of good. इष्ट-मंगल-भद्र-&c. सूचन *n.*-प्रदर्शन *n.*-&c.

BODICE, *n.* चोळी *f.* कांचोळी *f.* कंचुकी *f.*

BODIED, *a.* देही, सदेह, देहस्थ, अंगी, शरीरी, शरीरभाक्.

BODILESS, *a. incorporeal.* अदेही, विदेही, निर्देह, अमूर्त्तिमान्.

BODILY, *a. of or belonging to the body.* शरीराचा, देहाचा, शरीरी, आंग, आंगिक, कायिक, शारीर, शारीरिक, शारीरक, दैहिक, शरीरसंबंधी, देहसंबंधी, देहभव.

B. deformity or defect. अंगवैकल्य *n.* व्यंग *n.*

B. ease and comfort. शरीरसुख *n.* शरीरस्वास्थ्य *n.*

B. labor. आंगमेहनत *f.* शरीरकष्ट *m.* शरीरश्रम *m.*

B. strength. आंगजोर *m.* आंगबळ *n.* आंगवण *f.* कमरेचा-जोर *m.* शरीरशक्ति *f.* शरीरबल *n.*

B. suffering. शरीरव्यथा *f.* कायक्लेश *m.* अंगव्यथा *f.* देहयातना *f.*

B. vigour or health. शरीरसंपत्ति *f.*

B. violence or effort. आंगधटाई *or* आंगधिटाई *f.* आंगमर्दाई *or* आंगमर्दी *f.*

BODILY, *adv. united with a body.* सकुडी, देहासहित, कुडीसहित, देहासकट, सदेह, सतनु.

2 See WHOLLY.

BODKIN, *n. instrument for drawing tape, &c.* नाडी ओढायाची सळई *f.* सुवा *m.* मुंढें दाभण *n.*

BODY, *n.* अंग *pop.* आंग *n.* देह *m.* शरीर *n.* काय *m. n. pop.* काया *f.* कूड *f.* कुडी *f.* तनु *f.* तन *f. m.* कलेवर *n.* पिंड *m.* वपु *n.* मूर्ति *f.*

Some descriptive, allusive, or significant terms for the *body* are, भूतात्मा *m.* धाम *n.* क्षेत्र *n.* पंजर *or* पिंजर *m.* विग्रह *m.* झाड *n.* भोगायतन *n.* रोगभू *f.* प्राणसद्म *n.* इंद्रियायतन *n.* इंद्रियग्राम *m.* भूतग्राम *m.* कायापूर *n.* अहंकाराशय *m.* अहंकारास्पद *n.* जायजणेंघर *n.* जायजणी वस्तू *f.*—and with implication of *loggishness, lumpishness, inert heaviness or huddledness, &c.* मुरकुंडी *f.* गोळा *or* मोधागोळा *m.* मोट *f.* गठडी *f.* लोथ *f.*

According to the Hindu philosophy there are three bodies, viz. (1) the gross or material external body, स्थूलदेह *m.* स्थूलशरीर *n.* अन्नमयकोश *or* ष *m.* (2) the tenuous or etherial b. the inner envelopment, लिंगदेह, लिंगशरीर, सूक्ष्मदेह, सूक्ष्मशरीर. (3) the inner rudiment and causative frame or principle of the above two, कारणदेह, कारणशरीर, आनंदमयकोष or श. See these words, and also पंचकोष or श in MOLESWORTH's Maráthí and English Dictionary.

B. and soul. तनमन *n.*

Celestial or glorified b. दिव्यदेह *m.* [*m.*

Contortions or writhing of the b. आंगवळा *m.* आंगपिळा-

Daily operations or business of the b.—compreh. अश्याधिकार *m.*

Destinies or lot of the b. देहप्रारब्ध *n.*

Every b. *tout le monde.* जनलोक *m.* सर्वलोक *m. pl.*

Hair or down of the b. रोम *n.* लोम *n.* तनुरुह *or* तनूरुह.

In the b. *without dying or dropping the b.* सकुडी, सदेह.

Lightness and nimbleness of b. आंगचपळाई *f.* आंगसफाई *f.* शरीरचापल्य *n.* अंगचापल्य *n.*

Lower extremities of the b. अधःकाय *m.* अधोदेह *m.*

Mortal spot of the b. मर्मस्थान *n.* आडसंधि *f.* मर्मस्थल*n.* मर्मदेश *m.* In a by or mortal spot of the b. आडांतरीं, अवांगीं *v.* लाग, पड, मार &c. [विदेही.

One, though in the b., living as out of it. देहीं असून

Plump and roundish b. गोटी *f.*

Relation of the b. and its members. अंगांगिभाव *m.* अवयवावयविभाव *m.* [स्थ्य *n.*

Soundness or healthiness of b. शरीरपाटव *n.* शरीरस्वा-

Symmetry and beauty of b. अंगसौष्ठव *n.*

Unguents for the b. उटणें *n.* माखण *n.* अंगराग *m* अनुलेप *m.* [प्रत्यंग *n.*

Whole b. *b. and its limbs and members.* सर्वांग *n.* अंग-

To anoint the b. अंगराग *m.*-आंगमाखण *n.* करणें.

To cast or put off the b. देह *m.* टाकणें-ठेवणें-सोडणें, देहत्याग*m.*-देहविसर्जन *n.*-&c. करणें.

To macerate the b. शरीरकर्षण*n.*-शरीरशोषण*n.*-&c. करणें.

To mortify the b. देहदंड*m.*-देहदंडन*n.*-शरीरदंड*m.*-शरीरदमन*n.*-&c. करणें.

To purify the b. अंगशुद्धि *f.*-देहशुद्धि *f.*-&c. करणें.

2 a b. v. PERSON. जण *c.* माणूस*n.* मनुष्य *n.* गृहस्थ *m.*

Any b. some b. कोणी, कोणीतरी.

Any b.—any whoever. भलता, भलतासलता.

3 *troop, company,* v. BAND. गण *m.* मंडली *or* ळी *f.* थवा *m.* टोळी *f.* गट *or* गट्ट *m* गट्टा *m.* [घशः.

In a b. मिळून, एकमेळणीं, एकमेळीं, एकामीं *or* एकामें, सं-

4 *corporation, community.* मंडळी *f.* पंक्ति *pop.* पंगत *f.*

5 (as of a house, coach, tree, vessel, &c.) *main part.* पोट *n.* मुख्यभाग *m.*

6 (of a garment). चोला *or* चोळा *m.* [द्रव्य *n.*

7 *a substance, a material thing.* पदार्थ *m.* बिंब *n.* सत्व *n.*

8 *strength, good quality,* v. GOODNESS. ऐवज *m.* जीव *m.* सत्व*n.* तेज *n.* कस *m.*

9 *firm texture* (of cloth, &c.). बाणाताणा *m.* पोत *n. m.* सूतपोत *n. m.* जलराशी).

10 (as of fire, &c.) *volume, mass.* गोल *m.* राशी *m.* (*as*

11 *code.* संग्रह*m.* संहिता *f.*

12 See MATTER.

To BODY. See To EMBODY.

BODY-CLOTH, *n.* (of horses, elephants, &c.) झूल*f.* पृष्ठास्तरण*n.*

BODY-GUARD, *n.* हुजरात *f.* हुजूरहशम *m.*

BODY-SERVANT, *n.* हुजऱ्या *m.*

BOG, *n.* रुतण *f.* रुपण *f.* रेवण *f.* दलदल *f.* बांबर *n.* गलगली *f.* फसण *f.* फसाव *m.*

BOGLE, BOGGLE, *n.* v. BUGBEAR. बागूल *or* बागूलबावा *m.* बाऊ *m.* बू *m.*

To BOGGLE, *v. n.* v. To HESITATE. अडखळणें *or* अडखुळणें, अडणें, कांकरणें, कांकूं *f.* करणें, धरसोड *f.* करणें.

BOGGY, *a. swampy, &c.* दलदलीत, थलथलीत, बरबरीत, गलगलीत, दलदलीचा, &c.

To become b. गलगलणें.

To BOIL, *v. n.*—a liquor. खतखतणें *or* खुतखुतणें *or* खदखदणें, खितखितणें *or* खिदखिदणें, गदगदणें *or* गुदगुदणें, उकळणें, उबळणें, उबाळणें, उसळणें, उफाळणें, रटरटणें, रटमटणें, अधण *n.*-कढ*m.*-उबाळा *m.*-उमाळा *m.* येणें *in. con.* उकळी *f.* येणें-फुटणें *in. con.* उसळवटीं येणें, उतवणें, गदक *m.* येणें.

Water set to b. अधवणी *n.* अधण *n.*

2 *be in seething.* शिजणें, उकडणें.

3 over. उतणें, उतू जाणें *or* येणें *or* चालणें, ऊत*m.*येणें, उतास येणें.

4 (with passion, &c.) *or,*—passion, &c. v. To FUME. जळणें, खवळणें, खवंदळणें, रागाचा कढ *m.*-उचाळा *m.*-उमाळा*m.*-ऊत *m.*-&c. येणें.

To BOIL, *v. a.* (liquor, &c.). उकळणें, तापवणें, कढविणें, खतखतावणें, कढ *m.* देणें, उकळी *f.* आणणें.

2 *dress, &c. in boiling water, seeth.* शिजवणें, रांधणें, उकडणें, क्कथन *n.* करणें *g. of o.*

BOIL, *n.* गळू *n.* केसतूड *or* केसतोड *m.* फोड *m.* उठाणूं *n.* फिसकें *n.* बेंड *n.* गंड *n.* स्फोट *m.* विस्फोट *m.* करट *n. dim.* करटी *f.* खांडूक *n.*

A renewed b. or tumor. ढावर *m.* ढावर *m. v.* भर.

B. arising on the palm. कुरलें *n. dim.* कुरली *f.*

Heat and aching of a b. or tumor. कडमड *f.* कडमोड *f.*

Heart or core of a b. मोख *m.* गाईर *f.* आंठी *f.*

Prickly itching or burning of a b. गुदगुदी *f.*

To beat and throb—a boil टचटणें intens. टचाचणें.

BOILED, *p.* v. V. A. 1. उकळलेला, &c. शृत.

2 शिजवलेला, रांधलेला, &c. उकडीव, क्कथित, उत्कथित, स्थालीपक्क, शृत.

B. food. रांधप *n.* शिजवण *f. n.*

BOILER, *n. boiling vessel.* v. KETTLE. कढई *f.* कटाह *m.*स्थाली *f.*

A fixed b. ओतल *m.*

BOILING, *p. a.* v. V. N. 1. अधणाचा, कढाचा, &c. कडकडीत, कढत, उकळी आलेला, कढ आलेला, अधण आलेला, &c.

B. water. उतवणें *n.* उतवणी *n.*

BOILING, *n.* v. V. N. I.—*act or state.* खतखत *or* खुतखुत *or* खदखद *f.* कढ *m.* अधण *n.* उकळी *f.* गतका *or* गदका *m.v.* येउफाळ *or* ळा *m.* उबाळा *m.*

2 शिजणें *n.* &c.

3 उतणें *n.* ऊत *m.* उतू जाणें *n.*

4 *and* EBULLITION. रागाचा कढ *m.*-उबाळा*m.*-उमाळा*m*'-ऊत *m.* तळतळ *f.*

A b. (or a burning) to do, v. ITCH. कढ *m.* खतखत *m.* उताट *f.* उताटकी *f.* उत्कलिका *f.*

v. V. A. 1.—*act.* उकळणें*n.* कढवणें*n.* कढदेणें*n.* कढआणणें*n.*

2 शिजवणें*n.* रांधणें*n.* रांधा*m.* रांधप*n.* रंधन*n.* क्कथन*n.* श्रपण*n.*

That is easily cooked by b. शिजाळू.

BOISTEROUS, *a.*—of wind. सोसाट्याचा *or* सुसाट्याचा, घोघाट्याचा, सनाट्याचा, झपाट्याचा, सपाट्याचा, तडाख्याचा.

2 *noisy, turbulent, &c.*—of persons. धांगडधिंग्या, धामधुम्या, धुमाळ्या, धुमश्चक्र्या, गलबल्या, गडबड्या, गोंगाट्या, धांदल्या.

3—of proceedings, &c. धांगडधिंग्याचा, धुमाळीचा, धुडकुसाचा.

BOISTEROUSNESS, *n.* v. A. 1. सुसाटपणा*m.* सुसाटी *f.* तडाखा*m.* सुसाटा *or* सोसाटा*m.* सनाटा*m.* सत्तम *f.m.*

2 धामधुमेपणाm. गलबलेपणाm. &c. धुमाळी f. धुमाफळी f धांगडधिंगाई f. धिंगामस्ती f. सत्तम f.n.

Bold, *a. brave, courageous, fearless, intrepid, dauntless, daring, &c.*—of persons. शूर, छातीदार, छातीपूर, दिलदार, हिय्येदार, हिम्मतदार, हिम्मती, धाडसी, छातीचा, धाडसाचा, हिम्मतीचा, धमकेचा, शौर्याचा, &c. निधड, निधडा, निर्भय, भयहीन, धीट, धट्ट, साहसी, उद्दट, मर्दा, मर्दाना, जवानमर्द, बहादर *or* बहादूर, बांकडा, उद्दाम, धारिष्टवान्, अडुमाडू, गाढा, दाढा, द्राहट, मोठ्या काळिजाचा, जुरतदार, जुरती, अकुतोभय, अज्ञातभय, शौर्यशाली, शौर्यसंपन्न, शौर्यवान्.

2—of measures, *requiring &c. courage.* धैर्याचा, शौर्याचा, छातीचा, धाडसाचा, हिम्मतीचा, मर्दाईचा.

3 *standing out to view, prominent, bluff.* उदार, उद्दाम, उभार, उभट, मुस्तार.

4 *free, spirited, liberal.* उदार, शूर, प्रशस्त, प्रशस्तपणाचा.

5 See **Impudent**.

To make b. *to take liberty.* धीर m. करणें.

Boldly, *adv.* v. A. 1. छातीनें, छातीकरून, धाडस करून, मर्दाईनें, शौर्यानें, शौर्यपूर्वक, &c. निर्भयपणानें, &c. निधड, बेधडक, निश्शंक.

Boldness, *n.* v. A. 1. शूरपणाm. निर्भयपणाm. धाडसn. धाडीजn. शौर्यn. शूरत्वn. छाती f. काळीजn. दिलदारी f. धमक f. हिम्मत f. हिय्या f. जवानमर्दी f. मर्दाई f. मर्दुमकी f. मर्दुमी f. बहादुरी f. धिटाई f. धट्टाई f. शहामत f. जुरत f. दर्पm. साहसबुद्धि f. क्षत्रधर्मm.

3 उदारपणाm. उद्दामपणाm. उभारपणाm. &c.

4 उदारपणाm. प्रशस्तपणाm.

5 See **Impudence**.

Bole, *n.* मातीची एक जात आहे.

Bolster, *n.* (of a bed, &c.). उशी f. तक्याm.

2 (as for back of people sitting). लोडn.m.

3 (of a sadle). मांडगादी f. फराकी f. [करणें.

To **Bolster up**, *v.a.* v. To **Support**. संपादणी f.-संपादणूक f.

Bolt, *n.* (of a door, &c.) *metal pin*, v. **Bar**. खीळ f. खिळी f. कीलm. अगळ f.

2 See **Arrow**. 3. v. **Thunderbolt** वीज f. वज्र n.

Bolt-upright, *a.* तरतरीतउभा, सडकउभा, सरळउभा, सळनळीतउभा, उभासोट. [घालणें.

To **Bolt**, *v. a. fasten with a b.* v. To **Bar**. खीळ f.-&c. लावणें-

2 See To **Blurt**. 3 *swallow at once, gulp.* गोळाm.-गपकाm. मारणें, गटगोळाm-गटाणाm.-मटगोळाm.-गटंगोळाm.-गपाणा m. करून टाकणें, गटगट-गटागट-&c. गिळणें-खाणें, गट करणें, गप करणें.

4 *sift*—grain, &c. बैंचणें, आसुडणें, छाणणें, चाळणें.

To **Bolt**, *v.n. spring out or off suddenly.* निष्टणें, निसूटून जाणें, निसटणें, झटकणें, सटकणें, सडकणें, फटकणें, सटकपावली f. करणें.

Bolus, *n.* गुटिका f. *pop.* गुटका f. गोळी f.

Bomb, *n. shell, &c.* कुलपीगोळाm. छऱ्यांचा गोळाm.गर्भछाटगोळाm.

To **Bombard**, *v. a.* कुलपीगोळ्यांचा भडमारm. करणें-लावणें.

Bombardment, *n.* कुलपीगोळ्यांचा भडमार m.

Bombast, *n. high-sounding words, fustian.* ढबदारीचें-ढबीचें बोलणेंn. डौलाचें-डौलीबोलणेंn. शब्दमात्र प्रौढभाषणn. शब्दमात्र प्रगल्भभाषणn. पोकळ मोठमोठे शब्द m.pl. ठोसराई f.

Bombast, **Bombastic**, *a.* ढबदार, ढबदारीचा, डौली, डौलाचा, शब्दमात्र प्रागल्भ्यविशिष्ट.

Bombax, *n. silk cotton tree.* शेवरी f.

Bommelo, *n. a particular fish.* बोंबीलm.

Bona-fide, *in good faith, without fraud.* सद्भावानें, सुबुद्धीनें, कपटावांचून.

Bond, *n. fetter*, v. **Chain**. सांखळी f. शृंखला f. बेडी f. बंदm.

2 *ligament*, v. **Tie**. बंदm. बंधm. बंधनn.

3 *cement of union*, v. **Connection**. लग f. लगाm. लगाचांधाm. धागादोराm. दोराm. सूतn.

4 *writing of obligation*, v. **Deed**. खतn. रुका m. रोखा m. लेखm. मुचलकाm. कतबाm. कर्जखतn. दस्तऐवजm. प्रतिज्ञापत्रकn.

Dead or bad b. बुडीतखतn. जळीतखत n. [n.

Discharged and thus cancelled b.जळीतखत n.चांडाळखत

To pass a b. आपला हात कापून देणें, पांढऱ्यावर काळें करणें, टांकm.-लेखm.-हातm. गुंतणें g.of s. सरस्वतीदानn. करणें-देणें.

5 *obligation.* बंदm. बंधm. बंधनn.

Bond, *a. that is in bondage.* See **Slave**.

Bond-maid, *n.* v. **Slave**. दासी f. बटीक f. बांदी f. कुणबीण f.

Bond-man, **Bond-servant**, *n.*v. **Slave**. बंदा *or* बांदाm. दासm. गुलामm.

Bondage, *n. captivity*, v. **Imprisonment**. बंदी f. कैद f. सबद्धता f. सबंधता f. बंधनावस्था f.

2 v. **Slavery**. दासपणा m. दासत्व n.

Bone, *n.* हाड n. *dim.* हाडकी *or* हडकी f. हडूक *or* हाडूकn. अस्थिn.

A sin in the b. जन्मखोड f.

B. of contention, *ground of quarrel.* वादाचाविषयm.

Dryness and decay of the bones. अस्थिशोषm.

Ulcer in the b. हाड्यावर्णm. अस्थिव्रणm.

Uniting of a broken b. अस्थिसंधिm.

False or bad to the b. हाडाचा *or* हाडींचा खोटा-वाईट-&c.

Fever seated in the bones. हाडजरm. हाडकुरकुटी f. अस्थिज्वरm.

Seated in the bones—fever, rheumatism, &c. अस्थिगत.

True or good to the b.हाडाचा*or*हाडींचा खरा-चांगला-भला-&c.

To have one's bones standing out. हाडें n.pl. निघणें-पडणें-दिसणें g.of o.

To lay the knife to the b. हाडीं घावm. घालणें.

To make no bones. अंदेशाm.-संशयm.-शंका f. न धरणें,

Boneless, *a.* अस्थिहीन, अनस्थि.

Bonesetter, *n.* मोडलेलें हाड जोडणारा.

Bonfire, *n.* जय-आनंद-&c. सूचक-प्रदर्शक-ज्ञापक-&c. अग्निm.

Bonmot, *n.* चुटकाm. नुक्ताm.

Bonne-bouche, *n.* गोडघासm. सुग्रासm.

Bonnet, *n.* टोपी f.

Bonny. See **Beautiful**.

Bonny-clabber, *n.* v. **Buttermilk**. अंबटढाणताकn.

Bonus, *n. premium for a loan.* मनोती f.

Bony, *a. belonging &c. to bone.* हाडाचा, अस्थीचा, अस्थिसंबंधी, अस्थिमय.

2 *having large bones.* मोठ्या हाडांचा, हडस *or* हाडस.

3 *having many bones.* हाडकाळ *or* हाडकळ, अस्थिप्रचुर-विपुल-बहुल.

Booby, *n. blockhead, &c.* v. **Fool**. ढम. धोंडाm. टोणपा, (fem. टोणपी). टोणगाm. (fem. टोणगी), शुंभm. शिबापुढचा, बांठीचा

पिताm. गायीचा गोहोरा m. देवानांप्रिय m.
2 एकपक्षी विशेष आहे.

Book, *n.* पोथी *f.* पुस्तक *n.* ग्रंथ *m.* किताब *f.* निबंध *m.*
Books—compreh. or indef. पोथीपुस्तक *n.*
Books and papers,—compreh. पुस्तकपानरट *or* पुस्तकपानट *n.*
Board-cover of a b. पाटी *f.* फळी *f.*
Cover of a b. पुष्टिपत्र *n.*
Stitched b. वही *f.* चोपडी *f.* जुज *n.* Leathern cover of. पुठा *or* पुट्ठा *m.*
Torn or worm-eaten b. गाबाळग्रंथ *m.* गाबाळ *m.*
One b. explains another. ग्रंथाची ग्रंथांतर टीका *f.*
To get into the good books of. पोटांतशिरणें, रूपा *f.*-मर्जी *f.*-&c. संपादणें.
Without b. पुस्तक पाहिल्या बांचून, तोंडानें.
2 *division of a book.* पर्व *n.* स्कंध *m.* खंड *n.*

Book, *a. belonging to a book.* ग्रंथी, ग्रंथीय, ग्रांथिक, ग्रंथस्थ, ग्रंथसंबंधी.

To **Book**, *v. a. enter in a b.* चोपडीवर-वहीस-चोपडीस-&c. लावणें -लिहणें-मांडणें, लिहून ठेवणें, मांडून ठेवणें.

Book-binder, *m.* पुष्टिपत्र बांधणारा, वही बांधणारा, जिलद्गार.

Book-case, *n.* पुस्तक ठेवण्याचें कपाट *n.*

Book-hater, *n.* अक्षरशत्रु *c.*

Book-keeper, *n.* जमाखर्चाचा हिशोब ठेवणारा-राखणारा.

Book-keeping, *n.* वहीचें लिहणें *n.* जमाखर्ची लिहणें *n.*

Book-seller, *n.* पोथीविक्या, पुस्तकविक्रेता, पुस्तकविक्रयी, पुस्तकविक्रयोपजीवी.

Bookish, *a.* v. Studious. पोथीचा आवडता, पुस्तकप्रिय, पुस्तकव्यसनी.

Book-worm, *n.* कसर *f.* कस्तर *f.*
2 fig. *one addicted to study.* पोथींतला किडा *n.* पुस्तकांत खेळणारा *m.*

To **Boom**, *v. n. sound at a distance.* घुमघुमणें, घुमणें.

Boom, *n. chain across a river.* आडसांसळी *f.*

Boon, *n. grant, benefaction,* v. Gift. दान *n.* वर *m.*
Conferring a b. वरदान *n.* वरप्रदान *n.*
Conferrer of a b. वरद, वरदाता.
2 v. Petition. अर्ज *m.* विनंती *f.*

Boon, *a. gay, blithe,* v. Merry. आनंदी, उल्लासी, रंगी, हौशी.

Boor, *n. rustic, lout,* v. Countryman. खेडेमाणूस *c.* खेडेगांवचा माणूस *m.* खेड्या, खेडू *c.* गांवढी *c.* गांवढ्या.

Boorish, *a.* v. Clownish. गांवढळ, गंवार, खेडवाळ, खेडुला, खेडाळू, आडगळचा, जंगलट.
An unlettered b. fellow. ठोंबा, ठोल्या.

Boorishly, *adv.* v. A. गवारपणानें, गांवढळकीनें, &c.

Boorishness, *n.* v. A. गंवारपण *n.* गंवारकी *f.* गांवढळकी *f.* खेडवाळकी *f.*

To **Boose**, *To* **Booze**. *v. n. drink hard.* शोषणें *or* सोसणें, झोकणें.

To **Boot**, *v. a. profit, avail,* v. To Advantage. लाभणें, लाधणें, लाहणें.

Boot, *n. avail, profit,* v. Advantage. लाभ *m.* फळ *n.* सरका *m.*
To b. *over and above.* लाभावारी, नफेवारी, काढेवारी *or* काढ्यावारी, वर, काढ्यास.
2 *leather covering for leg.* उंचजोडा *m.* पोटरीजोडा *m.* चर्मी पायमोजा *m.* बूट *m.*
High b. Top b. गुडघे जोडा *m.*
Seven league boots. दिव्यपादुका *f.*

Boot-jack, *n.* बूट काढण्याचें साधन.

Booth, *n. hut of boughs, &c.* कावण *n.* टाहाळ्यांचें छप्पर *n.*-छपरी *f.* उन्हाळसावली *f.* आवसा *m.* पाल *n.* पर्णकुटी *f.* पर्णशाला *f.*

Bootless, *a.* v. Fruitless. निष्फल, निरर्थक, पोकळ, व्यर्थ.

Bootlessly, *adv.* v. A. व्यर्थ, वृथा, निरर्थक.

Bootlessness, *n.* v. A. निष्फलता *f.* निरर्थकता *f.* पोकळपणा *m.* फलराहित्य *n.*

Booty, *n. spoil, prey, pillage,* v. Plunder. लूट *f.*

Bo-peep, *n.* कुकडेकू *n.* कुकू *n.* कुक्कुटक्रीडा *f.*

Borax, *n.* टांकणखार *m.* टंकण *n.* कड्यासार *m.* सवागी *f.* सुहागी *f.* पाचनक *n.* धातुमारिणी *f.* धातुवल्लभ *m.* क्षार *m.*

Borborygm, *n.* कुरकुरी *f.* गुरगूर *f.* *intens.* गुरगुराट *m.*

Border, *n. brink, margin,* v. Edge. कांठ *m.* किनारा *m.* कड *f.*
Circular b. कडें *n.*
2 (esp. of a field). मेर *f.* मेंड *m.* कुपट *f.* शेव *m.*
3 (of a country, a village, &c.) *confine.* सीमा *pop.* शींव *f. or* शीम *f. or* शेव *m.* हद्द *f.* सरहद *pop.* सरद *f.*
Passage of the b. सीमोल्लंघन *n.*
Unto the borders. आसीमांत.
4 (of a garment or cloth). कांठ *m.* हशा *or* हाशा *m.* काठाळी *or* काठळी *f.* धडी *f.* कांठरें *n.* अचळ *f. m.*
B. esp. as narrow or fine. धारी *f.* किनारी *f.* काडी *f.* नखी *f.* धडी *f.* सगर *n.*
B. as woven separately or as appended. कोरपट्टी *f.* कोर *f.* गोट *m.*
Hemmed or raised b. गोट *m.* लोड *n.m.*
Ornamental b. संजाफ *or* संजाब *m.* पदर *m.* पल्ला *m.* कांठ *m.* मगजी *f.*
5 (as of wells and tanks) *raised edge.* गज *m.* पाळ *f.* धड *f.* बरवंडी *f.*

To **Border**, *v. n. confine upon.* लगटून-लागून-भिडून-चिकटून असणें, भिडणें, शिमेसशीम लागून असणें, लगत *f.*-लगता *m.* असणें *g. of s.*

To **Border**, *v. a.* गोट *m.*-&c. लावणें.

Bordered, *a.* v. N.4. घेरदार, कांठाचा, पदराचा, पदरी.
B. with working of gold or silver, &c. जरीकांठी, लफ्फेदार, जरीपदरी, संजाफी, संजाफदार, पल्लेदार, मगजीदार.
B. with trees and flowers. झाडपदरी.
Double b. दुपदरी, दुधारी, दुमजला *or* ली.
Narrow b. दाभणकांठी.
Silk b. रेशिमकांठी.
Single b. एकपदरी, एकमजला *or* ली.
Three b. तिपदरी, तिधारी, तिमजला *or* ली.

Borderer, *n.* **Bordering**, *p. a.* v. V. N. भिडणारा, लगतीचा, लगतचा, लगत्याचा, कडचा, शिंवेचा, शिवधड्या, सामंत.
I. *close neighbour.* शिवशेजारी, शिवधडी, शिवसोयरा, सामंतवासी.
II. *person dwelling on the border.* कड महालांतला राहणारा, कड महालचा मनुष्य *m.*

To **Bore**, *v. a. perforate,* v. To Pierce. बेधणें, विंधणें, भोकणें, छेदणें, वेधन *n*-रंध्रण *n.*-&c. करणें *g of o.* भोंक *n.*-&c. पाडणें.
2 v. To Weary. कंटाळा *m.*-त्रास *m.* आणणें-देणें.

Bore, *n. perforation,* v. Hole. भोंक *n.* छिद्र *n.* वेध *m.* विंध *n.* रंध्र *n.* भोंकू *m.* बुरास *m.* घरका *m.* घरा *m.*
2 (of the ear). कान *m.*

3 (of a gem, bead,&c.). बेजn.
To be enlarged in its b. बेजीं उतरणें.
4 *swelling tide*. घोडाm.
5 *a pest, trouble,* v. PLAGUE. उपाध *f*. व्याध *f*. पीडा *f*. झटn. काटाm. गळेपडू *c*.
6 v. AUGER. सामता *m*. वेधनn.
7 See CALIBER.
BOREAS, *n. north wind*. उत्तराण *f*.
BORED, *p*.v.V. वेधलेला, &c. वेधित, छेदित, वेध-&c. पाडलेला.
BORER, *n*. v.V. वेधणारा, भोंक पाडणारा, &c. छेदक, वेधक, वेधनकर्ता. I. v. AUGER. सामताm. वेधनn.
BORING, *n*. v.V.—*act*. वेधणेंn. बिंधणेंn. &c. वेधनn. रंध्रणn.
BORN, *p*. उत्पन्न, पैदा, जनित, जन्य, जात, प्रसूत, सूत, संभूत, उद्भूत, भव (in comp. as देहभव, मनोभव, समुद्रभव), भू (in comp.as देवीभू).
First b. ज्येष्ठ, अग्रज, वडील. Next b. पाठचा, पाठीमागचा *or* पाठीमागील, एकपाठी *or* ट्या, पाठीवर पाय देऊन आलेला. Middle b. मधला, मधिबला, मधबला. Last b. कनिष्ठ, शेवटचा, चर्मज, कुसधुवणा, शेंडेफळ.
Ill-b. Low-b. हीनजात, कमजात, बदजात, अकुलीन.
That is to be b. जनिष्यमाण.
That is being b. जायमान.
Untimely b. अकालज, अकालजन्मा.
Well-b. High b. कुलीन, कुलवंत, पिढीजाद, पिढीजादा, जानिवंत, जातीचा, अभिजात.
To be b. with face downwards. पालथायेणें.
To be b. जन्मणें, उपजणें, निपजणें, प्रसवणें, उद्भवणें, जन्मm. होणें *g.of s*.जन्मास येणें, जन्मm. घेणें.
To be b. again. *be regenerated*. नवाजन्मm. होणें *g. of s*.
BOROUGH, *n*. ज्या गांवास पार्लमेंत सभेस प्रतिनिधि पाठविण्याचा अधिकार असतो तो गांव.
To BORROW, *v.a.*—opposed to lend. उसना घेणें-आणणें, जाया *or* जायजणा आणणें-घेणें-मागणें, मागून आणणें-घेणें.
2(money, at interest). कर्जn.-ऋणn. काढणें-घेणें-करणें-आणणें, कर्जी काढणें, व्याजीं-व्याजावर काढणें-घेणें.
BORROWED, *p*. v.V.1. उसना घेतलेला, &c. उसना, उसनवारीचा, मागींव, मागून आणलेला.
B. for an occasion,—trinkets, furniture, utensils,&c. जायाचा, जायजण, जायजणा, याचितक.
2 कर्जी काढलेला, कर्जाऊ, कर्जाचा, व्याजी, व्याजाऊ, ऋणवयी.
BORROWER, *n*. v. V. 2 *and* DEBTOR. कर्ज काढणारा, &c. ऋणग्रह, ऋणग्राही, रिणको & रिणकोनाम *c*.
BORROWING, *n*. v. V. 1.—*act*. उसना घेणें *n*.-आणणें *n*. मागणें *n*. मागूनआणणें *n*. &c.
2 कर्जकाढणें *n*. काढणें *n*. व्याजावर घेणें *n*. ऋणग्रहण *n*.
B. from every quarter. काढाओढ *f*. काढाओढाm. ओढाओढ *f*. उचका *m*.
B. and lending, *money dealing*. घेवदेव *f*. घेणेंदेणेंn. घेवाणदेवाण *n*. घेवादेवा *m*. [स्थल *n*.
BOSOM, *n*. v. BREAST. उर *m*. छाती *f*. वक्ष *n*. वक्षोदेश *m*. वक्ष-
To press to the b. पोटाशीं धरणें.
B.-foe. अस्तनींतली आग *f*.
B.-friend. जिवींचा मित्र, सुख दुःखाचा सोबती, जिवींचा जिव्हाळा *m*. प्राणसखा, प्राणमित्र *m*.
B. of the earth. भूगर्भ *m*.
B.-secret. पोटची गोष्ट *f*. कुपींतली गोष्ट, बेंबीकडची गोष्ट *f*.
2 *heart, mind, &c.* मन *n*. अंतःकरण *n*. हृदय *n*. पोट *n*.
3 *clothing over the breast*. पडदा *m*. छाती *f*.
To BOSOM, *v. a*. मनांत-अंतःकरणांत-पोटांत-&c. ठेवणें.
2 See To HIDE.
BOSS, *n. knob, &c.* गेंद *f*. गोंडा *m*. बोंड *n*. [षयक.
BOTANICAL, *a*. उद्भिज्जविद्येचा, उद्भिज्जविद्यासंबंधी, उद्भिज्जविद्यावि-
BOTANIST, *n*. उद्भिज्जविद्याज्ञाता, वनस्पतिज्ञ, वनस्पतिवेत्ता.
BOTANY, *n*. उद्भिज्जविद्या *f*. वनस्पतिविद्या *f*.
BOTCH, *n*.—on the skin. खवंद *n*. खांडूक *n*.
2 *clumsy patch*. ओबडधोबड ठिगळ *n*.
3 *clumsy work*. गोदडशाईकाम *n*.
To BOTCH, *v. a. patch or mend clumsily*. ओबडधोबड तांगडणें.
BOTCHER, *n*. v. V. धोबड तांगडणारा, धोबडकाम्या.
BOTH, *pron*. दोन्ही, दोघे (घी *or* घ्या *f*. घें *or* घीं *n*.), उभय, उभयतां. The sense of *Both* is often expressed by ही (also) as मीं त्याला पाहिलें आणि त्याचा स्पर्शही केला I both saw and touched him.
B. hands हस्तद्वय *n*.
In both ways. उभयथा.
BOTHER, BOTHERATION, *n. fuss, ado, vexatious stir or toil*. खटपट *f*. खवदव *f*. दगदग *f*. खस्ता *f*. *pl*. झटेपटे *m*. *pl*. उपद्व्याप *m*. बोंबाळ *m*.
2 *bothered, (distracted, &c.) state*. तारंबळ *f*. घोळ *m*. घोळंकार *m*. घोंटाळा *m*. आटापीट *f*. घोळाणा *m*. घप्पाघोळ *m*. तारातीर *f*. गोंधळ *m*. कुतरओढ *f*. कुतरलोड *f*. धांदल *f*.
To BOTHER, *v. a. perplex, bewilder*, v. To CONFOUND. घोळणें, त्रेधा *f*.-घोळ *m*. करणें *g.ofo*. घोळांत-घोंटाळ्यांत-&c. घालणें-पाडणें.
To be bothered. बोंबाळणें.
BOTTLE, *n*. शिसा *m*. *dim*. शिसी *f*. कुपा *m*. *dim*. कुपी *f*. The word बाटली from the English has become very common.
2 (for oil, ghee, &c. made of skins) v. DUBBER. बुधला *m*. *or* बुधलें *n*. *dim*. बुधली *f*. दबडा *m*. *dim*. दबडें *or* डबडें *n*.
To BOTTLE, *v. a*. बाटलींत *or* बाटल्यांत-&c. भरणें. [ळा*m*.
BOTTLE-GOURD, *n*.—the plant. दूधभोपळी *f*.-the fruit.—दूधभोप-
BOTTOM, *n. lowest part, base, foot*. बूड *n*. तल *n*. *pop*. तळ *m*. बुंध *n*. बुंधा *m*. बुंधारा *m*. बुडखा *m*. बुडूस *n*. बसक *f*. बैठक *f*. अधोभाग *m*.
2 (of water, as of the sea, &c.). तळ *n*. *pop* तळ *m*. ठाव*m*.
That is without a b. or a shore. अनंतपार.
3 *foundation, ground work*. आधार *m*. पाया *m*. मूल *n*.
4 *bum*, v. BREECH. गांड *f*. गुद *n*. [दबका *m*.
5 *low ground*, v. HOLLOW. बदखल *n*. लवण *n*. सोलवा *m*.
6 *lowest end*. खालचाशेवट *m*. शेवट *m*. पाय *m*. पायगत *n*. पायतें *n*. [*n*. ठिकाणा *m*.
7 *foundation, beginning*. मूल *n*. आधार *m*. बीज *n*. ठिकाण
Sifting to the b. तळझाडा *m*.
That has gone to the b. of. पारंगत.
To get to the b. of. आधारास लागणें.
8 *utmost profundity or bound of*. ठाव *m*. ठिकाणा *m*. ठिकाण *n*. थांग *m*. थाक *m*. पार *m*. पारावार *m*. था *f*.

9 (of thread) v. BALL. गुंडा *m.* गुंडी *f.* गुंजडी *f.*
10 *power of endurance, stamina, pluck, &c.* v. SPIRIT. जीव *m.* दम *m.* ईर *f.* वीर्य *n.* जीवनपाणी *n.* त्राण *n.* जोर *m.*
Of sound b. हाडाचा खरा-चांगला-भला.
That has b. and pluck,—horse, &c. जिवट, जिवस, मगरमस्त, जीवदार, जोरदार.
11 See SHIP. 12 See DREGS. [शेवटील.

BOTTOM, *a.* बुडचा *or* बुडला, बुडील, खालचा, खालील, शेवटचा,

To BOTTOM, *v. a.*-च्या आधारावर बांधणें-रचणें.
To be bottomed on.-च्या आधारावर असणें.
2 *to furnish with a seat or bottom.* बैथक *f.* घालणें.

BOTTOMLESS, *a.* अतल, अथाक *or* अथाग, बेठाव, अगाध, अतलस्पर्श, तलहीन.

BOUGH, *n.* v. BRANCH. खांदा *m. dim.* खांदी *f. & intens.* खांदाड *n.* फांदी *f. dim.* फांदोरी *f. and intens.* फांदडा *or* फांदाडा *m.*

BOUGHT, *p.* v. V. विकत घेतलेला, खरीद केलेला, &c. खरीद, क्रीत.
B. of a private hand. आडगिराईक *or* इकी.

BOUGHT. See KNOT.

BOUGIE, *n.* सळई *f.* बत्ती *f.* वर्ति *f.* चिपनळी *f.* चिपळी *f.*

To BOUNCE, *v. n. spring or start suddenly.* सटकन-झटकन-पटकन-तटकन-&c. उडणें, सटकणें, झटकणें, उडणें, उसळणें, उसळी *f.* खाणें.—a fish from the water. उल्लाळणें *or* उल्हाळणें, उसळणें, उसळी *f.* खाणें-मारणें, उल्लाळा *or* उल्हाळा *m.* घेणें-मारणें खाणें-देणें.
2 *thump.* दणकन-दणकर-दणदण-&c. ठोकणें, मारणें.
3 See To BOAST. [लबाडी *f.*

BOUNCE, *n. a bold, downright lie.* धडधडीत-ठळठळीत-धादांत-&c.

BOUNCE, *interj.* सट-कन-कर-&c. *or* सुट-&c. तटकन-&c.

BOUNCING, *a. strapping,* v. STOUT. लठ्ठ, लोठा, धिपाड.
A. b. lie. See BOUNCE.

BOUND, *a. limit, boundary.* मर्यादा *f.* सीमा *pop.* सींव *or* शींव *f.* हद्द *f.* पार *m.* अवधि *m.* धुरा *m.* पेंडवळा *m.* पर्यंत *m.* अवच्छेद *m.* काष्ठा *f.*
B. and border. दांडपेंडोळा *m.* दांडपेंडोळें *n.* दांडमेंड *m.*
Bounds. अंतपार *m.* पारावार *m.* धारेपेंडवळे *m. pl.* दांडिपेंडवळे *m. pl.*
Overstepping of bounds. अमर्यादा *f.* सीमोल्लंघन *n.* सीमातिक्रमण *n.*
The bounds. चतुस्सीमा *f.*
To observe no bounds. बाकी *f.* न ठेवणें, इयत्ता *f.* न ठेवणें.
2 *spring, leap.* टिपण *n. v.* टाक, मार, किलाण *n.* किराण *n. v.* मार, साध, टाक, फलंग *f. v.* मार, झेंप *f.* झाप *f.*
3 (of a ball, &c.) *rebound.* टप्पा *m.* उसी *f.*

To BOUND, *v. a. limit, circumscribe, confine, define.* सीमा *f.*-मर्यादा *f.*-अवधि *m.*-हद्द *f.*-&c. करणें-घालणें-बांधणें, अवच्छेद *m.* करणें *g. of o.* ससीम-समर्याद-सावधिक-सावधि-वलयांकित-मर्यादाबद्ध-सीमाबद्ध-&c. करणें, आरेखणें, आरेखा *m.* करणें *g. of o.*

To BOUND, *v. n. rebound, hop, &c.* उडणें, टप्पा *m.* खाणें, उसीं येणें, उसी *f.* खाणें, टणटणणें.
2 *spring, skip, jump, leap.* उडणें, ठिकणें, उडी *f.* घालणें-मारणें, फांदणें, झेंप *f.*-झाप *f.* टाकणें-मारणें, झडप *f.* घालणें.
3—a horse. फटकडी *f.* मारणें. [शीरुत.

BOUND, *p.* v. V. 1. बांधलेला, &c. बद्ध, संबद्ध, सबंध, पाशित, पाशीरुत.
Firmly or fast b. निबद्ध, सन्निबद्ध, निबंधित,
2 आकळलेला, आकलित, निग्रहीत.
3 वेष्टलेला, गुंडाळलेला, &c.
4 बांधलेला, गोवलेला, &c.
5 बांधलेला, &c. बंदा *or* बांदा, बांधील, विकलेला, आभारी, उपकारी, लागला, उपकारबद्ध, उपरुत, मिंधा, ओशाळा, लिप्सा‌ळा.
To be b. लागला जाणें.
6 बंद केलेला, बद्ध.
I. *going or intending to go.* जाणार, जाणारा, जायाचा, गंतुकाम, गामी. [धारा *m.*

BOUNDARY, *n.* See BOUND. 2 (raised b. of a field). बांध *m.* बांधारा *m.*
Way or passage along a raised b. बांधवाट *f.* बांधाटी *f.*

BOUNDED, *p.* v. V. A. सावधि, सावधिक, रुतावधि, समर्याद, अवछिन्न, परिछिन्न, नियत, साकार, आयंतवान्.

BOUNDLESS, *a. unbounded, unlimited,* v. INFINITE. अपार, अपरंपार, अनंतपार, बेहद्द, निरवधि, निस्सीम, दुरंत.

BOUNDLESSNESS, *n.* v. A. बेहद्दपणा *m.* अपारता *f.* अनंतपारता *f.* अमर्यादता *f.* मर्यादाराहित्य *n.* &c.

BOUNTEOUS, BOUNTIFUL, *a.* v. GENEROUS. उदार, दाता, दानी, दानशील, वदान्य, सढळ, दानशूर.

BOUNTEOUSLY, BOUNTIFULLY, *adv.* v. A. औदार्यानें, औदार्यपूर्वक, उदार हस्तानें, मोकळया हातानें, सढळ हातानें.

BOUNTEOUSNESS, BOUNTIFULNESS, *n.* v. A. उदारपणा *m.* सढळपणा *m.* दानशीलता *f.* दातृत्व *n.* औदार्य *n.* दानशौर्य *n.* वदान्यता *f.*

BOUNTY, *n. liberality,* See BOUNTEOUSNESS.
2 *aliberal donation.* महादान *n.* बहुदान *n.* संभावना *f.*
3 चाकरी पतकरण्या बद्दल सरकारांतून जें बक्षीस मिळतें तें.

BOUQUET, *n. nosegay.* फुलांचा झेला *m.* झुबका *m.*
2 v. FRAGRANCE. आमोद *m.*

BOURN. See BOUND. [सणें.

To BOUSE, *v. n. drink hard, tope.* शोषणें *or* सोखणें, झोकणें, ढोसणें.

BOUSY, *a.* v. DRUNK. झिंगलेला.

BOUT, *n. as much of an action as is performed at once.* खेप *f.* दम *m.* अवसान *n.* पारुठ *f.* पर्याय *m.*

BOVINE, *a. pertaining to oxen and cows.* गुरांचा, गुरांविषयींचा, गव्य, गोसंबंधी, गोविषयक.

To BOW, *v. a.* v. To BEND. बांकविणें, लवविणें, नमविणें.
To b. the ear कान *m.* देणें.

To BOW, *v. n.* v. To BEND. बांकणें, लवणें.
2 *make obeisance.* नमणें, शिरसा *adv.* नमणें-वंदणें, नमन *n.*-नमस्कार *m.*-नमस्या *f.*-शिरोवंदन *n.*-शिरोनमन *n.*-&c. करणें.
To b. and scrape. लवणभंजन *n.*-नमोनमो *adv.* करणें.
3 to; *obey, &c. reverentially.* शिरसा *adv.* मानणें-घेणें-स्वीकारणें, शिरसा *or* शिरीं वाहणें.
4 (through age and infirmity). कमरेवर-गुडघ्यांवर हात *m. pl.* येणें *or* देणें, गुडघे *m. pl.* टेंकणें, गुडघे *m. pl.* मेटीं येणें, कमर *f.* वांकणें *g. of s.* कोंक *n.*-पोंग *n.* येणें, कुबड *n.* निघणें.

BOW, *n. reverence,* v. OBEISANCE. शिरोनमन *n.* शिरोवनति *f.*

BOW, *n.*—the weapon. कमाण *or* न *f.* कमटा *or* ठा *m.* धनुष्य *n.* धनु *n.* धन *n.* चाप *n. m.* गांडीव *n. m.* कोदंड *n.* कार्मुक *n.* शरासन *n.*
Armed with a b. धनुष्यपाणि.
B. and arrow. तीरकमाण *or* न *f.* तीरकमठा *m.*
B. and arrow maker. कमाणगर *or* गार *m.*
B. of Ulysses. गांडीव *m. n.*
End of a b. गोशा *m.* कोटि *f.*

Twang of a b. ज्याघोष *m.*
2 *thing bow-form*, gener. कमाण *or* न *f.* धनुष्य *n.*
3 (of a slipknot, &c.). अढी *f.* फांस *m.* दुमड *f.*
4 (of a saddle). खोड *n.*
5 (for cleaning cotton) धनुकली *f.* धनु *m.*
6 (of a ship) नाळेचीबाजू *f.*

Bow-LEG, *n.* फेंगड पाय *m.*

Bow-LEGGED, *a.* फेंगडा, फेंगड्या पायाचा.

Bow-MAN, *n.* v. ARCHER. तिरंदाज *m.* धनुर्धर *m.* धनुर्धारी *m.*

Bow-SHOT, *n.* तिराचा-बाणाचा टप्पा *m.*-मारा *m.*-मारका *m.* शरपात *m.* शरपातस्थान *n.*

Bow-SPRIT, *n.* नाळ्दांडा *m.*

Bow-STRING, *n.* धनुष्याची दोरी *f.* शीत *n.* चिल्ला *m.* ज्या *f.* धनुर्गुण *m.* प्रत्यंचा *f.* मौर्वी *f.* गुण *m.*

Bow-WINDOW. See BAY-WINDOW.

BOWED, *p.* v. V. A. वांकवलेला, नमवलेला, &c.
v. V. N. 1. वांकलेला, नमलेला, &c. नमित.
2 नमलेला, नमित, नम्रमूर्त्ति, नम्रांग, अवनत.
4 गुडघे टेंकलेला, कमरवांकलेला, कुबड निघालेला, &c. हातांपायांचा चौरंग झालेला, गोळंकारी, नम्रमूर्त्ति, नम्रांग.

BOWELS, *n. intestines, entrails.* अंतडीं *or* अंताडीं *n. pl.* आंतें*n. pl.* अंत्रें *n. pl.*
—in poetic, cant, &c. phraseol. अंतरमाळा *f. pl.*
Blocked up state of the b. सांखळा *m.*
Discharge of the b. v. EVACUATION. झाडा *m.* मलोत्सर्ग *m.* मलविसर्ग *m.* मलविसर्जन *n.* मलशुद्धि *f.*
Disorder of the b. through crudities. आमविकार *m.* आम*m.*
Irregular state of the b. संग्रहणी *f.*
Mucus of the b. voided. आंव *f.* आम *m.* शेंब *or* शेम *f.*
Part of the b. hanging out through a gash. पोटळा *or* पोटाळा *m.*
Sharp pain in the b. कळ*f.* शूल*m.* तिडीक *f.*
Wind in the b. उंड*m.* मुठा*m.* वायगोळा*m.* गुबार *or* गुबारा*m.*
B. of mercy, v. PITY. दया *f.* करुणा *f.*
2 *interior part.* पोट*m.* गर्भ*m.*

To BOWEL, *v. a.* अंतडीं*n. pl.*-&c. काढणें *g. of o.*

BOWER, *n. arbour.* गुंफा *f.* कुंज*m.n.* लतागृह*n.* मंडप*m.* लतामंडप*m.*
A natural & close b. जाळी *f.*

BOWL, *n. cup,* &c. कटोरा *m. dim.* कटोरी*f.* शराव *m.* प्याला *or* पेला *m.* वाटगा *m. dim.* वाटी*f.* तरसाळें *n.*
2(as of a ladle, spoon, &c.). हरडा *or* हिरडा*m.* टवळें*n.* माठलें*n.* माथळा*m.* परडें *n.* बोंड*n.*
3 (as of a Winâ, &c.). डेरा*m.* भोपळा*m.*
4 (of wood). काठवट *f.* पाळें*n.* पडगा *or* घाम. पडगें*n.*
Bowls & basins compreh. पडगें पाळें *n.* पाळें पडगें *n.*
5 (of earth). खर्पर *pop.* खापर *n.*
6 (of a gourd). तुंबा*m.* तुंबी *f.*
7 *ball to bowl.* गोल*m.* गोटा*m.* काष्ठगोलक*n.*

To BOWL, *v. a. roll as a bowl.* लोटणें, लोटून देणें, घुळवणें, घुळत जाईसा करणें, घरळवणें.

To BOWL, *v. n. move smoothly & swiftly.* घुळणें, घुळतजाणें.

BOWLDER, BOWLDER-STONE, *n.* गोटा*m. dim.* गोटी *f.* गडगडा-धोंडा *m.*

BOWYER, *n. maker of bows.* कमाणकरणेवाला, धनुष्कर.
2 v. ARCHER. तिरंदाज*c.* धनुर्धर, धनुर्धारी.

BOX, *n. chest, trunk.* पेटी *f. dim.* पेटूल*n.* संदूक *f.*—large हडपा *m.* मांदूस *f.*
2—as a snuff box, &c. *little box.* डबा*m.dim.* डबी *f.* पेटूल*n.*
3 *cuff*, v. BLOW.—with the fist. बुकी *f.* बुकांदा*m. dim.* बुकांदी *f.* ठोसा*m.*—with the open hand. चापट *f.* चापटी *f.* चपराक *f.*
4 एकवृक्ष आहे.
5 (in a theatre) नाटकगृहांत बसायाची केलेली खोली *f.*
6 coach box. गाडी हांकणाऱ्याची बसायाची जागा *f.*

To BOX, *v. n. fight with the fist.* ठोसाठोसी *f.*-बुकाबुकी *f.*-&c. करणें, मुष्टियुद्ध*n.*-मुष्टिप्रहार *m.* करणें.

To BOX, *v. a. strike with the fist.* बुकलणें, बुकणें, धबकणें, बुकी *f.*-ठोसा*m.*-&c. मारणें-देणें, मुष्टिमोदक*m.*-मुष्टिप्रहार*m.*देणें-करणें.
To b. the ears. कानशिलांत मारणें.
2 *shut up in a box.* पेटींत-&c.घालणें-बंदकरणें.

BOXER, *n.*v.V. N. मुष्टियोद्धा. [*f.* मुष्टिमुष्टि *f.*

BOXING-MATCH, *n.* ठोसाठोसी*f.* बुकाबुकी *f.* धप्पाधप्पी *or* धबाधबी

BOY, *n.* मुलगा*m.* पोर*m.* पोरगा*m.* मूल*m.* बाल*m.*बालक*m.* चेडा*m.* झिलगा*m.* झील*m.* बोड्या*m.* पोंगडा*m.* कुमार *pop.* कुंवर*m.* शिशु*m.*
Big, overgrown, lubberly b. घोडगा*m.* घोड्मुंज्या*m.*
Little, lively, & intelligent b. चिटलिंग*m.* चिटू*m.* चिंगाटी*or* चिंगोटी *f.*

BOYHOOD, *n.* पोरपण*n.* बाळपण*n.* पौगंड*n.* बालावस्था *f.* शिशुत्व*n.*

BOYISH, *a.* v. CHILDISH. पोरकट, पोरका, पोरकट,पोरगळ*or* पोरकळ, पोरासारखा.

BOYISHLY, *adv.* v. A. पोरासारखा *a. decl.* पोरपणानें.

BOYISHNESS, *n.* v. A. & CHILDISHNESS. पोरपणा*m.* पोरखेळ*m.* पोरस्वभाव*m.*

To BRACE, *v. a. strain up, make tense,*v. To TIGHTEN. ताणणें, ओढणें, ओढून घेणें, ओढ *f.*-ताण*m.* देणें, चढवणें.
2—as a medicine. दृढ करणें, पुष्टि *f.* देणें-करणें, आवळणें, आवळून घेणें, बळकटी *f.* आणणें. [दाटणी *f.*

BRACE, *n. straining strap or cord.* कसणी *f.* ओढण *f.* ओढणी*f.*
2 (of a drum). कांकर *or* कंकर*m.* ओढण *f.* माळूम.
3 *pair*, v. COUPLE. जुंवळी *or* जुळी *f.* जुळें*n.* जोडी *f.*
4 (in printing) कंस *m.* कुंडली *f.*
5 braces. इजार वगैरे अडकविण्याचे खांदेबंद*m.pl.*

BRACED, *p.* v. V. 1. ताणलेला, &c. ओढ दिल्हेला, ताण दिल्हेला.

BRACELET, *n.* चुडा*m.* कडें*n.* कटक*n.* करभूषण *n.* Certain *Bracelets* are बाळा, गोट, कंकण, कांकण, कंगणी, कडगुलें, पाटली, खिसमती, गजरा, तोडीची पाटली, चटईची वांक, छंद, जवा, जुळी *or* जुळें, ठोसला, लगदा, पहुंची, दोरा, हातसर, तोडा, मेढसर.
B. set with gems. मणगटी *f.*
2(of glass). बांगडी *f.* कडगुलें*n.*
Bracelets bound with (gold or silver) wire. लपेटा*m.*
B. given to boot (in purchases). वाढती बांगडी *f.*
Seller of bracelets. काजारी *m.* [कांसार.

BRACELET-MAKER, *n.* बांगडेकरी, लकिरी, मणेर *or* मणेरी *or* मण्यार,

BRACHIAL, *a. belonging to the arm.* बाहूचा, बाहुसंबंधी, भुजसंबंधी. [टी आणणारा.

BRACING, *p.* v. V. 2 *giving tension or tone.* पुष्टिकरणारा, बळक-

Bracken, *n. fern.* नेच्या *m.*

Bracket, *n.*—in printing. कुंडली *f.* बेलें *n.* कंस *m.*

To **Bracket**, *v. a.* कंसांत-&c. घालणें. [सऊळ.

Brackish, *a. somewhat salt,* v. Salt. खारट, मचूळ, सौळ *or*

Brackishness, *n.* v. A. मचुळाई *f.* मचूळपणा *m.* सौळपणा *m.*

Brad, *n.*—kind of nail. सुरसा*m* तुरई *f* गुलमेख *f.* मकुड्याचासिळा *m.*

To **Brag**, **Brag**. See To Boast, &c.

Braggart, **Braggadocio**. *n.* v. Boaster. बढाईखोर *c.* फुशारखोर *c.* तिसमारखान *m.* शेंदाडशिपाई *m.*

Brahmá, *n.* ब्रह्मा *m.*

Bráhman, *n.* ब्राह्मण *m.* भट *m.* विप्र *m.* There are numerous tribes, of which some are आपस्तंब, कण्व *or* काण्णव, कनोजा, करवंत, कऱ्हाडा, कुडाळदेसकर, कोकणस्थ *or* चित्तपावन *or* चिपोळणा *or* चिपुळणा *or* चिपुळा, गौड, चौबा, जवळ, तिरगूळ *or* त्रिगूळ, तुळवा, तेलंग, देवरुखा, देशस्थ, गुर्जर, मध्यंदिन *pop.* माध्यंजन *or* यजुर्वेदी *or* यजुःशाखी *or* यजू, मध्व *or* माधव, मिश्र, मैत्रायणी *pop.* मैत्राणी, मैथिल, मोताळा, सवाशा, सारस्वत. Some titles or distinctive appellations are भूदेव, द्विज, द्विजन्मा, जानव्याचाधनी, यज्ञोपवीताचा धनी, यज्ञोपवीतधारी, अठरावर्णांचा गुरु, वर्णोत्तम, उत्तमजाति, प्रथमवर्ण. To the above grand and exalting titles and epithets it seems just to append some of the current designations of the opposite character. कढी भुरक्या, कार्त्तिकस्वामीचे भिडेचा, गयावळ, बांभुरडा *or* बामुरडा, धोतरबडव्या, धोत्र्या, पोकळ भोत्र्या, पोकळ भट, भटोरा, भट्ट, शूद्रमुखी. Numerous *gifts* are demanded by *Bráhmans,* and upon endlessly diversified pretexts or pleas. Some are अष्टफली, उत्क्रांतधेनु, तिलधेनु, धान्यधेनु, धोंडवाण *or* धोंडवायण *or* धोंडा, नागाबिंब, पददान, पयस्विनी, प्राजापत्य, भूयसी, मोक्षधेनु, मृतशय्या, वैतरणी, सुखशय्या, सोळवंड, सौभाग्यबायन *pop.* वाण, हस्तगौरी, हिरेदिवे.

Bráhmans are by the *sháстras* divided into four religious orders (वर्णाश्रम *or* आश्रम *m.*) referable to the periods of life. They are, 1. ब्रह्मचर्य Order of the Student; 2. गार्हस्थ्य *or* गृहस्थाश्रम *m.* Order of the Householder; 3. वानप्रस्थाश्रम Order of the Anchorite; 4. सन्न्यासाश्रम Order of the Religious mendicant. A Bráhman of the first order is ब्रह्मचारी;—of the second order, गृहस्थ; —of the third order, वानप्रस्थ *or* वानप्रस्थाश्रमी;—of the fourth order, सन्न्यासी, सन्न्यासाश्रमी, सन्न्यस्त. A *popular* division of *Bráhmans* is made into two classes viz. भिक्षुक *or* भट Clerical B. and गृहस्थ Lay B.

B. from thread-investiture to marriage. ब्रह्मचारी *m.* वर्णी.

B. from thread-investiture to maturity. बटु *m.* बटुक *m.* बटुवामन *m.*

B. devoted to celibacy, study, and religion. नैष्ठिक ब्रह्मचारी *m.* (*and* the life of such नैष्ठिक ब्रह्मचर्य *n.*) भट गोसावी *m.* बालब्रह्मचारी *m.*

B. upon his begging rounds. देशावरकरी *m.*

Begging rounds of a b. देशावर *m.n.* Alms. &c. thus obtained, देशावर *m.n.* [करी *m.*

B. who begs dressed food from door to door. माधु-

Dressed food thus begged. माधुकरी *f.*

B.— cloths or apparel. ब्राह्मणधर *m.*

B.— mulcts. ब्रह्मदंड *m.*

B.—offspring. ब्राह्मणबीज *n.*

B.—property. ब्रह्मस्व *n.*

B.—town. ब्रह्मपुरी *f.*

B.—tribe or caste. ब्राह्मणजाति *f.*

Company or assembly of Bràhmans. ब्रह्मवृंद *m.*—in contempt भटोरखाना *m.*

Curse of a b. ब्रह्माख *n.*

Endowments (of villages or lands) to a b. अग्रहार *m.*

Feasting of Bráhmans. ब्राह्मणभोजन *n.* ब्राह्मणसंतर्पण *n.* प्रस्थ *n.* समाराधना *f.*

Feasting of 1000 Bràhmans. सहस्त्रभोजन *n.*-of 100,000. लक्षभोजन *n.*

Female b. ब्राह्मणी *f.*

Fit or suitable for a b. ब्राह्मणाऊ.

Glory or lustre around a b. ब्रह्मतेज *n.* ब्रह्मवर्चस *n.*

Hate to Bràhmans. ब्रह्मद्वेष *m.*

Hater of Bràhmans. ब्रह्मद्वेषी.

Learned b. पंडित *m.*

Menial b. ब्राह्मणजन *m.*

Money, &c. given to Bràhmans. दक्षिणा *f.* देकार *m.* पांतु *f. or* पांतूचें *n.*

Outcast b. ब्राह्मण चांडाल *m.*

Religious duties of a b. ब्रह्मकर्म *n.*

The Six acts or duties of a b. षट्कर्मे *n pl.*

Slovenly and dirty b. नेभळ भट *m.* भोंगळ भट *m.* पोकळ भट *m.* गयावळ *m.*

Give a b. an inch and he'll take an ell. भटास दिल्ही ओसरी भट पाय पसरी. [ब्राह्मण्य.

Bráhmanical, *a.* ब्राह्मणजातीचा, ब्राह्मणजातीय, ब्राह्म, ब्राह्मणी,

Bráhmanicide, *n.*—*act.* ब्रह्महत्या *f.* ब्रह्मवध *m.* ब्रह्मघात *m.*—agent ब्रह्मघ्न, ब्रह्मघातक.

Bráhmanism, *n.* ब्राह्मणपणा *m.* ब्राह्मण्य *n.*

Insignia of b. शिखासूत्र *n.*

To **Braid**, *v. a.* v. To Weave. गुंफणें, विणणें, वळणें.

Braid, *n.* वेणी *f.*

Triple b. त्रिवेणी *f.*

Braided, *p.* v. V. विणलेला, &c. विणींव, गुंफींव.

Brain, *n.* मगज *m.* गोर्द्दु *n.* मेंदू *m.* मस्तिष्क *n.* मस्तकस्नेह *m.* मस्तुलुंग *m.*

Creation of one's b. कल्पितकादंबरी *f.*

To rake or weary one's b. कपाळकूट *f.*-कपाळफोड *f.*-कपाळकष्टी *f.*-कपाळखटखट *f.*-डोईफोड *f.*-कडाकूट *f.*-&c. करणें.

2 Brains, v. Understanding. बुद्धि *f.* मति *f.*

To **Brain**, *v. a.* कपाळमोक्ष *m.* करणें *g. of o.* डोकें *n.*-&c फोडणें *g. of o.* [तिहीन.

Brainless, *a.* v. Stupid. निर्बुद्धि, बुद्धिहीन-रहित-शून्य-&c. म-

Brain-pan, *n.* v. Skull. मस्तक *m.n.* कपाल *pop.* कपाळ *m.* गोर्द्दुभाजन *n.*

Brain-sick, *a.* मूढ, मूढमति.

Brain sickness, *n.* v. A. मूढता *f.*

Brait, *n. rough diamond.* हिऱ्याचा धोंडा *m.* असंस्कृत हीरक *m.*

Brake, *n. thicket of thorns.* कांटवन *n.* कांटेरान *n.* कांटकील *n.*

काटेझाडी *f.* कांटेराई *f.*

2 *handle of a pump.* यंत्राचा दांडा *m.*-मूठ *f.*

3 (for wheels). ढकली *f.* घोरपड *f.*

4 *drag.* See HARROW.

5 *carriage for training horses.* खडखडा *m.* तक्का *m.*

BRAMBLE, *n. rubus indicus.* गौरी *f.*

B. berry. गौरीफळ *n.*

2 *thorny or prickly bush,*—gener. कांटेझाड *n.*

BRAN, *n.* कोंडा *m.* भुसा *m.*

2 (of sprinkled wheat). तरडा *or* तराडा *m.*तडरक*n.* तरडें *n.*

3—as remaining in fine flour. तांब *f.*

BRAN-NEW, BRAND-NEW, *a. new from the fire or forge,* v. NEW. घणकोरा, कोराकरकरीत, करकरीत, घणाखालचा.

BRANCH, *n.* (of a tree) *bough.* खांदा *m. dim.* खांदी *f.* & *intens.* खांदाड *n.* फांद *f.* फांदा *m. dim.* फांदी *f.* & फांदोरी *f.* & *intens.* फांदडा *or* फांदाडा *m.* फांटा *m. dim.* फांटी *f.* फणगाडा *m.* शाखा *f.* स्कंध *m.* माय *dim.* मायटी *f.*

Dead b. सल *n.* [डघळा *m.*

Small leafy b. टाहळा *or* डाहळा *m. dim.* टाहळी *or* डाहळी *f.*

To shoot out branches, फांदडणें.

2 (of a river). फांटा *m. dim.* फांटी *f.* पागोरा *n.* फांसू *n.*

3 (of a subject or discourse), v. DIVISION. शाखा *f.* अंग *n.* प्रकरण *n.* कथाभाग *m.*

Minor b. उपांग *n.*

4 (of a family,). शाखा *f.*

To BRANCH, *v. n. shoot in branches.* फुटणें, फांट्या *f. pl.*-फांटे*m. pl.* फुटणें, फांदळणें.

2 out; *ramify, spread diversely,* lit. fig. फुटणें, फांकणें, फांकटणें, फणगडे *m. pl.* फुटणें *g. of s.* फैलावणें. [करणें.

3 *amplify, speak or write diffusely.* पाल्हाळ *m.*-विस्तार *m.*

To BRANCH, *v. a. make subordinate divisions.* विभाग *m.pl.*-पोटविभाग *m. pl.* करणें *g. of o.*

2 *adorn with figured work.* बुटी *f.*-बुटे *m. pl.* काढणें, फुलाफांद्यांचा कशीदा काढणें.

BRANCH CANDLESTICK, *n.*दिव्याचें झाड *n.* झाड *n.* दीपवृक्ष *m.*

BRANCHING, BRANCHY, *a. furnished with branches, having many branches.* पुष्कळ फांद्यांचा-फांदड्यांचा-फणगाड्यांचा-&c. फांदळलेला, बहुशाख, बहुस्कंध, शाखी, शाखाबहुल.

B. and bushy. झांपाळ, झांपाळलेला, झांकराचा.

2 *striking or spreading out*—horns, &c. फांकट, फटांगा, फांकटीचा. [शाखाबहुत्व *n.*

BRANCHINESS, *n.* v. A. 1. फांदळलेलेपणा *m.* शाखाबाहुल्य *n.* शा-

2 फांकटपणा *m.* फांकटी *f.*

BRANCHLESS, *a.* शाखाहीन, स्कंधहीन.

BRANCHLET, *n.* लहान फांदी *f.*-&c. शिपटी *f.*

BRAND, *n.* v. FIREBRAND. कोलीत *n.* कोलती *f.*

2 *mark burned.* डाग *m.* डाव *m.* लास *m.* चुटका *m.* चरका *m.*

B. burned (upon hand or arm) with dung. धामा *m.* धमाटा *m.*

Circular b. गूल *m.*

3 *mark of infamy,* v. STIGMA. डाग *m.* कलंक *m.* लांछन *n.*

To BRAND, *v. a. burn with a hot iron.* दागणें *or* डागणें, डाबणें, लासणें, डाग *m.*-लास *m.*-डाव *m.*-गूल *m.*-&c. देणें.

2 fig. डागणें, डाग *m.*-कलंक *m.*-लांछन *n.*-&c. लावणें. [दाहन*n.*

BRAND-IRON, BRANDING-IRON, *n.* दागणी *or* डागणी *f.* डाहणी *f.*

BRANDED, *p.* v. V. 1. डागलेला, डाग दिल्हेला, &c. लाशा, डागील.

2 डागलेला, डागील, लांछित, कलंकित, कलंकयुक्त.

To BRANDISH, *v.a. flourish, wave.* फेळवणें, परजणें, भोवंडणें, फिरवणें,चमकवणें,पेलणें, खेळवणें, हात*m.*दाखवणें-फिरवणें*with g.of o.*

BRANDY, *n.* एकेप्रकारची दारू आहे, ब्रांडी *f.*

BRANGLE, To BRANGLE. See WRANGLE, &c.

BRANNY, *a.* v. N. कोंड्यासारखा, कोंड्याचा.

BRASIER, *n.* कांस्यकार *pop.* कांसार *m.*—in contempt कांसारडा*m.* करचकर *or* करजकर *m.*

2 *pan for holding coals.* शेगडी *f.*

BRASS, *n.* पित्तल *n. pop.* पितळ *f. n.*

Calx of b. पुष्पक *n.* पुष्पकेतु *m.* रीति *f.* रीतिपुष्प *n.* रीतिका *f.*

Circular and high edged b. dish. पितळी *f.*

Sounding b. fig. घणघणघंटा *f.*

2 *assurance,* v. IMPUDENCE. तिखें *n. (lit. steel.)* नाक *n.*

BRASS-FOIL, *n.* पितळेचा वर्ख *m.* पितळपान *n.*

BRASS-WIRE, *n.* पेचक *f. n.*

BRASSINESS, *n.* पितळपणा *m.* पित्तलत्व *n.*

BRASS, BRASSY, *a.* पितळेचा, पितळी, पितळेच्या रंगाचा, पित्तलसंबंधी, पित्तलमय.

BRAT, *n.* v. CHILD. कारटा *m.* (टी *f.* टें *n.*),पोरटा *m.* (टी *f.* टें *n.*).

BRAVADO, *n.* v. BOAST. फुशारकी *or* फुशारी *f.* गट्टंपट्टं *n.* लप्पंछप्पं *n.* ठेंगराई *f.*

BRAVE, *a. courageous, spirited, valiant, gallant, &c.* v. BOLD. शूर, दिलदार, धाडसी, धाडसाचा, छातीदार, छातीचा, बहादर *or*बहादूर, जवानमर्द, मर्दी, मर्दाना, हिम्मती, हिम्मतीचा, हिम्मतदार, शौर्यसंपन्न, शौर्यशाली.

2 *magnificent, noble, grand, &c.*—freely, v. FINE. खासा, नामी, शानदार, उमदा, उत्कृष्ट, सुंदर, उदार, नमूद *or* नमोद, चोखट, चखोट.

To BRAVE, *v. a. defy, challenge,* v. To DARE. हमतम *m.* दाखवणें, हमतमानें बोलावणें, नाकावर निंबू *n.* घासणें.

2 *encounter with fortitude.* धैर्यानें-&c. गांठणें, शिंगावर घेणें, छातीवर घेणें, छातीकरून उभा *a. decl.* राहणें.

BRAVE, *n. man of daring courage,* v. HERO. धारकरी *m.*

2 See HECTOR. [&c. शौर्यपूर्वक.

BRAVELY, *adv.* v. A. 1. दिलदारीनें, मर्दीनें, हिंमतीनें, शहामतीनें,

BRAVERY, *n.* v. A. 1. धाडस *n.* धाडीज *n.* शौर्य *n.* शूरत्व*n.* दिलदारी *f.* जवानमर्दी *f.* छाती *f.* मर्दी *f.* मर्दुमकी *f.* शहामत *f.* हिम्मत *f.* हिय्या *m.* दर्प *m.* क्षत्रधर्म *m.*

2 शान *f.* शानदारी *f.* उमदेपणा *m.*

BRAVO, *n. murderer for hire.* मारेकरी *m.* पैक्यानें जीवघेण्या *m.*

BRAVO, *interj.* भले, शाबाश *or* स, वाहवा, धन्य, जयजय, जयजया, लगे, लाट, ऐशी, खाशी.

Acclamations of bravo ! bravo ! शाबासकी *f.*

BRAWL, *n. clamorous contention,* v. SQUABBLE. कटकट *f.* कलागत *f.* खणकादणका *m.* खणाजंगी *f.* धडकाधडकी *f.* खडका *m.* खडकाधडका *m.* हर्षामर्ष *m.* हर्षामर्षा *m.*

To BRAWL, *v. n.* v. To SQUABBLE, To WRANGLE. खटपटणें, खडका *m.*- खडकाधडका *m.*-तडकाफडकी *f.* उडणें-झडणें-होणें- चालणें, कचक *f.*-रंजक *f.* उडणें- झडणें.

2 *speak loudly and indecently.* कळकळणें, गोंगाट*m.*-गलबल*f.*-गलबला *m.*- कळकळ *f.* करणें-करून बोलणें, खडखडून बोलणें.
3—as a brook or a stream. खळखळणें.

BRAWLER, *n.* BRAWLING, *p. a.* v. V. 1. कटकट करणारा, कलागती, कलागत्या, कटकट्या.
2 कळकळ्या, गोंगाट्या, गलबल्या, ओरड्या, खडखडून बोलणारा.

BRAWLING, *n.* v. V. 1.—*act.* खटपटणें *n.* &c. कटकट–कलागत-&c.-करणें *n.* कळकळ *f.*
2—*act.* कळकळणें *n.* गोंगाट-&c. करणें *n.*

BRAWN, *n. flesh of a boar.* डुकराचें मांस *n.*
2 *fleshy or musculous part.* मांसलप्रदेश *m.*
B. of the arm or leg, as full and prominent through exercise. बेडकी *f.* गांठ *f. or* गांठी *f. pl.* मेंडकी *f.* पेंडकी *f.*
3 एका प्रकारानें तयार करून ठेवलेलें डुकराचें मांस *n.* [त्व *n.*

BRAWNINESS, *n.* v. A. मासाळपणा*m.* गांठाळपणा *m.* &c. मांसल-

BRAWNY, *a. musculous,* v. FLESHY. मांसल *pop.* मासाळ, गांठळ *or* गांठाळ, गड्ड, गोंडस, गोलदार. [*of o.*

To BRAY, *v. a.* v. To POUND. खलणें, कुटणें, खल *m.* करणें *g.*

To BRAY, *v. n.*— an ass. The Marâthî has no rendering for this word. ओरडणें is commonly used, but it expresses the cry of an animal generally.

BRAY, *n.* खरशब्द *m.* गर्दभध्वनि *m.* रासभध्वनि *m.*

BRAZEN, *a. made, &c. of brass.* पितळी, पितळेचा *or* पितळाचा, पित्तलमय, पित्तलनिर्मित. [सळपांघरलेला.
2 v. SHAMELESS. निलाजरा, मुसळ नेसलेला, सुंभनेसलेला, मु-

BRAZEN-BROWED, BRAZEN-FACED, *a.* v. SHAMELESS. निलाजरा, मुसळ नेसलेला.

BRAZIER, See BRASIER.

BREACH, *n.* See BREAKING. 2 *break, gap, rupture, opening made.* भगदड *or* भगदाड *n.* भगदळ *n.* भगाड *n.* भगास *n.* भोंकसा *m.* भोसकू *m.* भोंसकट *n. or* भोसकटें *n.* भंगसाळ *f.* खिंड *f.* खिंडार *n.* खिंडारें *n.* संधि *m. f. pop.* सांध *f.*
3 *violation, infraction, infringement.* मोडणें *n.* तोडणें *n.* खंडन *n.* भंग *m.* (much used in comp.) भेद *m.* (in comp.) उल्लंघन *n.*
4 *rupture among friends,* v. QUARREL. फूट *f.* तूट *f.* तुटलीक *f.* भेद *m.* बिघाड *m.* अंतर *n.* नाचक्की *f.*
To heal a b. डांगपट्टी *f.* घालणें, निर्तुटक *n.* करणें.

To BREACH, *v. a. make a breach.* खिंडारें *n.*-&c. पाडणें.

BREAD, *n.* भाकर *f.* (This word means a *cake,* and of the flour of *bádzrí, dzondhalá,* and other inferior grains. It is not *commonly* applied to a *wheaten cake,*) पोळी *f.* (This means a *cake,* and of *wheaten* flour : also of the flour of *rice, dzondhalá,* &c. boiled.) रोट *m. dim.* रोटगा *m.* रोटी *f.* These words mean *cake, roll,* or *loaf,* and usually *wheaten,* but they belong, though they are current enough, to the *Hindustání.*) पांव *n.* (This is *fermented* bread or a *loaf* of it. It is from the *Portuguese.*) *See also* CAKE.
—in covert or jocose, &c. phraseol. भकारी *f.* भास्करी *f.* सूर्यकन्या *f.* सूर्यसंतान *n.*
B.—generally, *daily bread.* v. FOOD. अन्न *n.* अन्नपाणी *n.* दाणापाणी *n.* तुकडा *m.*
B.—compreh. *b. and cake, b. or cake.* पोळीतुकडा *m.* भाकरतुकडा *m.* तुकडा *m.*
B. made of flour of various grains parched and ground together. धपाटें *n.* भाजणीचीभाकर *f.*
B. baked in a leaf. पानगा *m. dim.* पानगी *f.*
B. and cheese, *humble fare.* भाजीभाकर *f.* मीठ भाकर *f.* मीठभात *m.* दूधभात *m.*
B. and water. अन्नपाणी *n.* अन्नोदक *n.*
That has eaten the b. of. अन्नाचा.
To beg for one's b. अन्नानगत *f.* होणें *g. of s.* अन्नार्थी *a.* होणें, अन्न अन्न *adv.* करीत फिरणें.
To begin to get one's b. तोंडीं घास *m.* येणें *g. of s.*
To be reduced to b. and water, (to a crust of b. &c.). चणवणी मिठवणी *n.* पिऊन असणें.
To deal out b. अन्नसत्र *n.* करणें.
To destroy, or injure one's b. पोटावर पाय *m.* देणें, पोटावर उठणें *or* येणें, पोटा आड *or* अन्नाआड येणें, पोटावर मारणें, अन्नांत माती *f.* घालणें *or* कालवणें, संसाराचीमात्रा *f.* करणें.
To give the b. out of one's mouth. तोंडचाघास *m.* देणें.
To lose one's b. अन्न *n.* जाणें *g. of s.* तपेलें *n.* बुडणें *g. of s.* क्षतवृत्ति होणें.
To put in the way of getting one's b. अन्नास लावणें.
To quarrel with one's b. and butter. पुढें वाढलेल्या पानास लात *f.* मारणें, आपल्या अन्नांत माती *f.* पाडून घेणें, उपजीव्यविरोध *m.* करणें.
To stand in the way of one's b. अन्ना आड येणें.
To take the b. out of one's mouth. तोंडचा घास*m.* काढणें-हिरून घेणें-&c.
To work for one's b. हातावर संसार*m.* करणें, हातावर पोट*n.* करणें.
Him laud whose b. you eat. ज्याची खावी पोळी त्याची वाजवावी टाळी.

BREADTH, *n.* v. A. रुंदी *f.* रुंदावा*m.* रुंदपणा*m.* विस्तार*m.* व्यास*m.*
To increase in b. रुंदावणें.
2 (of cloth). पन्हा*m.*
A single b. पाट*m.* पट्टें*m.* पाटगें *or* पाडगें*n.* अटपळें*n.*
Of a single b. एकवरी.

To BREAK, *v. a. part, sever, sunder, &c.* तोडणें, मोडणें, फाडणें, खंडणें, खांडणें, भंगणें, छेदणें, भेदणें, त्रोटणें, बिघडणें, भंग*m.*-विघात *m.*-&c. करणें *g. of o.*
2 v. To BURST. फोडणें.
3 *make bankrupt.* मोडणें, दिवाळें*n.* काढणें *g.of o.*बसविणें, निजविणें, नादार करणें, तळावर बसविणें, नापत *f.* करणें *g. of o.*
4 *violate, infringe, infract.* मोडणें, तोडणें, भंगणें, खंडणें, भंग*m.* करणें *g. of o.*
5 *interrupt, &c.* v. To STOP. मोडणें, मोडती *f.*-मोडा*m.* घालणें, खंड*m.*-खळ*m.* करणें *g. of o.*
6 in; *tame, train,* v. To DISCIPLINE. पेटवणें, काढणें, रांचणें, कमावणें, वठणीस- वळणीस-चालीवर-&c. आणणें, पाडगा *or* पाटगा करणें, खडविणें, पेटवणी *f.* करणें.
To be broken in. पेटणें.
7 up; *dissolve, &c.* v. To DISBAND. तोडणें, मोडणें.
8 up; *burst or force open.* उचकटणें *or* उसकटणें, फोडणें, विच-

करणें, तोडताड f.-फोडफाड f. करणें g. of o.

9 up; *take to pieces*. उखळणें, विसवळणें, निसळणें, विसळ f.- उखळा उखळ f. करणें, उलगडणें, उलकटणें, विशकलन n. करणें.

10 (wind) *crepitate*. पादणें, पादm. करणें-मोकलणें, पर्दनn. करणें, टरका m.- टारादुरी f. करणें.

11 *disclose*. फोडणें, काढणें, उद्गm. काढणें-करणें g. of o.

To BREAK, *v. n. part, come asunder*. मोडणें, तुटणें, फुटणें.

2 v. To BURST. फुटणें.

3 *become bankrupt*. मोडणें, मोडावणें, तुटणें, बसणें, थकणें, निजणें, दिवाळेंn. निघणें g. of s.

4 (in health, strength, spirits, &c.). तुटणें, थकणें, दमणें, मोडकळणें, मोडकळीस-मोडीसयेणें, मोडावणें, भागणें, घसरणें, पडणीस येणें, तुटारीस येणें.

5—the voice, *become hoarse or cracked*. गळाm.फुटणें-पडणें-पिंजणें-बसणें, घांटी f. फुटणें-बसणें.

6 *fall out*, v. To QUARREL. फुटणें, तुटणें, बिघडणें, बिघाडm.- फूट f.-तूट f. होणें g. of s.

7 down; *yield, fail, &c.* मोडणें, मोडावणें, मोडकळणें, भागणें.

8 loose; सुटणें, मोकळा होणें.

9 out, forth; *appear in eruptions*. उतणें, उगवणें, उफणणें, फुटणें, सुटणें, आंगफुटणी f. होणें, दरदरणें, दरदर or रां फोडm.pl. येणें.

10 out; *become dissolute, &c.* v. To RUN WILD. सुटणें, निसवणें, निसत होणें, बंधनांतून जाणें, आरवण्यांतून जाणें.

11up; *dissolve*,—as firms, associations,companies. भंगणें, तुटणें, सुटणें, फुटणें, फांटणें, फांकणें, संडलें तुटलेंn.-तुटातुटी or तुटातूट f.-भंगm.-भंजनn.-विघडm.-निर्तुटक n.-&c. होणें g. of s. —with implication of *completeness and ruinousness*. भया भंगास जाणें.

12 up; *come to pieces*. उखळणें, विसळणें, विखळ f.-उखळाउखळ f. होणें, सुटणें, फाटफूट f. होणें.

13 with; *fall out with*, v. To QUARREL. बिघडणें,फुटणें,तुटणें.

BREAK, *n. opening, gap*. खिंड f. *dim.* खिंडकुली f. or लेंn. or खिंडुकली f. & लेंn. खांड f. *dim.* खांडोरेंn. *and, enhanc.* खिंडार n. or रेंn. खांडारn.

2 *opening, interruption, stoppage*. खंडm. तूट f. फूट f. फट f. मोडाm. अंतरn. व्यवधानn.

3 (in the weather). उघाड f. or उघाडी f.उघडीक f. v. पड,हो.

4 *intermission of a time*. खाडाm. नागाm. अतरn.

5 (of day). See DAWN.

BREAKAGE, *n.* See BREAKING. 2 *allowance for things broken*. फुटीतुटीबदल सूट f.-नुकसानी f.

BREAKER, *n.* v.V. A. 1. तोडणारा, मोडणारा, &c. छेदक, भंजक, विघातक, विघाती, भंग-&c.कर्त्ता. [f.खावाडn.

I. *wave breaking against a rock*. खडकावर अपटणारी लाट

To BREAKFAST, *v. n*, न्याहारी f.-&c. करणें.

BREAKFAST, *n.* न्याहारी f. प्रातरन्न n. प्रातर्भोजन n. प्रातराश m.

BREAKING, *n.* v. V. A. I.—*act*. तोडणेंn. मोडणेंn. &c. भंगm. भंजनn. खंडनn. मोटनn. स्फोटm. स्फोटनn.

BREAK-WATER, *n.* पाणी थोपविण्याकरितां-अडविण्याकरितां-&c. केलेलाबांधm.-भिंत f.-बंधाराm.-&c. ढकशी f. थाप f. थोप f.

BREAST, *n.* उरn. *pop.* ऊरm. छाती f. उरस्स्थल n. वक्षn. वक्षस्स्थल n. वक्षःप्रदेशm. हृदयn. कोड n.—in contempt, anger, &c. उराडn. छाताडn.

Hollow of the b. उराचीशिंप f.

Pigeon b. *projecting b.* उराड n.

To beat or clap the b. ऊर m.-&c. बडवणें, उरोघात m.करणें.

To clasp to the b. उरासीं-पोटासीं-&c. धरणें, पोटाळणें.

2 (of woman, &c.) स्तन n. थान n. कुच m. छाती f. धना m. जोबन n. मिमी f. उरोज m. वक्षोज m. पयोधर m.—in covert, &c. phraseol. वरशीं or वरलाशीं n. pl.

A hard b. दगडी f.

Mothers b. अमा or आमा m माम n. अमू m.

To suck the b. स्तनपान n.- स्तनप्राशन n. करणें.

3 *heart, conscience, mind, &c.* हृदयn.हृदयमंदिरn. (answering to *temple of the breast*.) हृदयकमल n. अंतःकरण n. पोट n. मन n.

Weight upon one's b. उरावरचा गोहो-धगड-दडपण n.-&c.

To get a weight upon one's b. ऊर m. दडपणें g. of s.

To make a clean b. चोरून न ठेवितां सांगणें, मन मोकळें करून सांगणें.

BREAST-BONE, *n.* उरहाड or उराचेंहाड n. उरोस्थि n.

BREAST DEEP, BREAST-HIGH, *a.* छाती इतका उंच, छातीभर.

BREAST-PLATE, *n.*चपरास f. उरस्त्राण n.

BREAST-WORK, *n. parapet*. छातीएवढी उंचभिंत f. बरंडी f. वरंड f.

BREATH, *n.* श्वास m. उच्छ्वास *pop.* उसास m. दम m. प्राण m.

In a b. एकदम.

Sweetening the b. (as after a meal). मुखशुद्धि f.

Thing (betel leaf, &c.) to sweeten the b. मुखवास m. मुखवासन n.

That can retain his b. a long time. जितप्राण.

That is out of b. बेदम.

To draw b. श्वास m. ओढणें.

To hold one's b. दम m. छाटणें-धरणें.

To labor for b. धापलणें, धापणें.

To stop one's b. दम m. कोंडणें. [करणें.

To suspend or restrain the b. प्राणसंयम m.-प्राणायाम m.

To suffer to take b. दम m. देणें.

To take b. दम m. खाणें-घेणें-धरणें.

To waste (or lose) one's b तोंडाचीवाफ f.गमावणें, वाग्व्यय m. करणें.

2 (of air), v. BREEZE. झुळूक f. वाऱ्याची लहर f.

BREATH-LESS, *a. out of breath*. बेदम, दमलेला.

2 See DEAD.

To BREATHE, *v. n. respire*. श्वासोच्छ्वास *pop.* श्वासोश्वास m. करणें-टाकणें, श्वास m. सोडणें टाकणें, श्वास m. वाहणें-चालणें g. of s. श्वास m. असणें *in. con.*

2 *take breath, have an interval of rest*. v. To REST. दम m.खाणें-घेणें-टाकणें, उमास or उमासा m. टाकणें, उमस or उमास m. खाणें or *inv. con.* पडणें, उस्मरा m. घेणें.

3—the air, *blow softly*. झुळझुळणें, झुळझुळ *adv.* वाहणें, झुळकणें, झुणझुणणें, संत-थंड-मंद वाहणें.

4—hard, laboriously, &c. दम m.-श्वास m. लागणें *in. con.* दम m. चढणें, सुसकार m.- सुसकारा m. टाकणें,उश्मम or मा m. घेणें-टाकणें, धापणें.

5 out; *expire forcibly*. सुसकारणें, ढुसकारणें, सुसकार m.-सु-

सकारा m.- हुसकारा m. टाकणें. [त्यागm.करणें.
To b. one's last, expire, v. To DIE. प्राण m. सोडणें, प्राण-
To BREATHE, *v. a.* v. To INHALE. श्वासाबरोबर घेणें, खाणें, पिणें.
2 *utter softly*. हळू-उपांशु-&c. बोलणें.
3 *disclose*, v. To TELL. बदणें, उहू m. करणें g. of o.
Not to b. a syllable of. चकारशब्द m.-ब्र-&c. न सांगणें.
4 into; *inject by breathing*. श्वासाबरोबर घालणें.
5 out; *eject by breathing*. श्वासाबरोबर सोडणें.
6 *express, show*, v. To MANIFEST. दाखविणें.
BREATHER, *n.* BREATHING, *p. a.* v. V. N. 1. *and* LIVING. श्वासी, श्वासोच्छ्वासी *pop.* श्वासोश्वासी, प्राणमय, प्राणधारी, सप्राण.
BREATHING, *n.* v.V. N. 1.—*act.* श्वासोच्छ्वास *pop.* श्वासोश्वास m. श्वास m. उच्छ्वास m. श्वसन n. उच्छ्वसन n.
5 सुसकारणें n. &c. सुसकार *or* सुसकारा *or* हुसकारा m. v. टाक, सोड.
I. (through the nostrils, as practised by followers of the *Wedas* or *Tantras*) पूरक m. कुंभक m. रेचक m. प्राणायाम m. (These words express differences in the manner).
BREATHING-PLACE, *n. spiracle, vent, air-hole*. उच्छ्वास *pop.* उश्वास m. झरोका m.
BREATHLESS, *a.* बेदम, दमगेलेला.
BRED, *p.* v. V. 1. उत्पन्नकेलेला, &c. उत्पन्न.
3 पाळलेला, &c. लहानाचा मोठा केलेला.
BREECH, *n. bum, bottom*. गांड f. गुदप्रदेश m. ढुंग n. ढुंगण n.
2 *hinder part*, v. BACK. पाठीमागला भाग m. पृष्ठभाग m.
3 breeches. The varieties are *knee-b.* गुडघी f. चोळणा m. *B. just covering the posteriors*. गांडचोळणा m. *B. just covering the thighs*. मांडचोळणा *or* मांडीचोळणा m.
Woman that wears the b. स्वाधीनभर्तृका f. स्वाधीनपतिका f.
To wear the b. पगडी f. घालणें.
To BREECH, *v. a.* ईझार f.-&c. घालणें.
2 ढुंगणावर-&c. मारणें.
To BREED, *v. a. generate, engender*. उत्पन्न करणें, उत्पादणें, उद्भावणें, उत्पादन n.-उद्भावन n.-उत्पत्ति f. करणें g. of o.
2 *occasion, produce*, v. To CAUSE. उत्पन्न करणें, उत्पादणें, उद्भावणें, उपस्थित करणें, उपस्थापन n.-&c. करणें.
3 *bring up*, v. To REAR. पाळणें, पोसणें, पालन n. पोषण n.-&c. करणें g. of o. लहानाचा मोठा करणें.
4 See To EDUCATE.
5 (cattle) *raise, rear*. उपजवणें, निपजवणें, संतति f.-&c. वाढवणें g. of o. [वाढा m.
BREED, *n. progeny, race*, v. FAMILY, OFFSPRING. बिजवट n.
2 (of cattle) v. STOCK. ताणा m. बिजवट n. थळ n. थळी f. खाण f. जात f.
Of a good b. थळीचा, थळाचा.
BREED-BATE, *n.* v. INCENDIARY. कळलाव्या, आगलाव्या, कळीचा नारद m. नारदमुनि m.
BREEDER, *n.* BREEDING, *p. a.*—of female animals, *not barren*. वितीगाभती, वितीफळती, भादी.
BREEDING, *n. manners, &c.* माणुसकी f. सुजनता f. सुजनत्व n. सभाचातुर्य n.
BREEZE, *n.* वारें n. झुळूक f. वाऱ्याचीलहर f. मंदवायु m. मृदुवात m. मंदानिल m.
Balmy b. मंदसुगंध वायु m.
Cool and balmy b. शीतसुगंध वायु m.
Land-b. (i. e. from the E. or N. E.) मतलई f.
Sea-b. समुद्राकडला वारा m.
BREEZY, *a.* हवाशीर, हवेदार, हवेचा.
BRETHREN, *n.* भाऊ m. *pl.* बंधुजन m. *pl.* बंधुवर्ग m. *pl.*
2 gener. *b. and near relatives*. भाऊबंद m. *pl.*
BREVET, *n.* सन्मानाची-बहुमानाची-&c. पदवी f.
BREVIARY. See ABRIDGMENT.
BREVITY, *n.* v. A. 2. अल्पता f. विस्ताराभाव m. अविस्तार m. विस्तार राहित्य n. संक्षेप m. संक्षेपता f.
To BREW, *v. a.* (beer, ale &c.) काढणें, करणें.
2 *devise, &c.* v. To SCHEME. बांधणें, बनावणें, रचणें.
To BREW, *v. n.* fig. *be hatching*,—mischief or evil. पिकणें, धुमसणें, सिजणें.
BRIBE, *n.* लांच f. अंतस्थ n. शेलापागोटें n. पानसुपारी f. पान्हवण n. खाऊ m. मिठाई f. तोंडदाबणें n. रुशवत f. खुलबर f. n.
To stop the mouth with a. b. तोंड n. दाबणें.
To take bribes or a b. लांच f. खाणें, अबदान n.-हात m.-गपका m. मारणें, गळ्याखालीं उतरणें, चावणें, चरणें.
BRIBE-EATER, BRIBE-TAKER, *n.* लांच खाणारा, लांचखोर c. लांचखाऊ c. लिद्वळ, पेंडीचेंगुरूं n. [मृद f.
To BRIBE, *v. a.* लांच f. देणें, लांचावणें, अबदान n. देणें, हात m.-दाबणें-चेपणें-शेकणें, तोंड n. दावणें, पैसा चारणें, आडव्या हातानें देणें, हातीं घालणें.
To b. extensively. रान n. भारणें.
BRIBED, *p.* v. V. लांचावलेला, लांच खाल्लेला, अंतस्थ घेतलेला.
To be b. *be won over by bribery*. लांचावणें.
BRIBER, *n.* v. V. लांचदेणारा, लांचावणारा, खाऊ-मिठाई-&c. देणारा, मूठचेप्या-दाब्या, तोंडदाब्या, चाटू. [व्यापार m.
BRIBERY, *n.* लांचदेणें n.-घेणें n. लांचखोरी f. लांचेचें n. लांचेचा-
B.—compreh; *b. and corruption, venal practices*. लांचलुचपत f. लांचलूच f. चापसाचापसी f.
BRICK, *n.* ईट *or* वीट f. इष्टिका f.
Kiln-burned b. Baked b. पक्कीईट f. पक्केष्टका f.
Row of bricks (in a building) laid upright or on edge. खडंजा m.
Sun-dried b. कच्चीईट f. मोप n. मोपें n. भेंडा m. (this is a large and squared mass of kneaded earth).
Vitrified b. खंगर m. दग्धेष्टका f.
Vitrified excrescence upon a b. किटण n.
BRICK-BAT, *n.* इटकर *or* इटकूर f. n. ढोला m. रोडा m. वडा m.
BRICK-BUILT, *a.* इटांचा, इटांनीं बांधलेला.
BRICK-CLAY, *n.* इटेची माती f.
BRICK-DUST, *n.* गेरू f. इटकर f. n.
BRICK-DUST, *a. of the colour of b.* विटकरी *or* इटकरी.
BRICK-KILN, *n.* इटांचीभट्टी f.
BRICK-LAYER, *n.* v. MASON. गवंडी *or* गवंड्या *or* गौंडी m.
BRICK-MAKER, *n.* इटाकरणारा, कुंभार m. ईटवाला, इष्टिकाकार.
Frame of a b. for carrying earth. मंची f.
BRICK-MOULD, *n.* इटाळें n. मोपाळें n.
BRICK-WORK, *n.* ईटकाम n. ईटबंदी f.
To BRICK, *v. a.* ईटबंदी f. करणें, ईटबंदीचा करणें, इटांनीं बांधणें.

BRIDAL, *a.* लग्नाचा, विवाहाचा, वैवाहिक, औद्वाहिक, विवाहसंबंधी, विवाह विषयक. [लग्नप्रयोजन *n.*

BRIDAL, *n. nuptial feast.* लग्नोत्सव*m.* विवाहोत्सव *m.* लग्नकार्य *n.*

BRIDE, *n.* नवरी *f.* वधू *f.* नववधू *f.* नवोढा *f.*

An adult b. जाणती नवरी *f.* जाणती वधू *f.*

B. and bridegroom. वहूवर *or* ओहर*n.* वधूवरें*n.*

Cloth interposed (at weddings) between the b. and bridegroom. अंतःपट*n.*—Figures or lines drawn on it. नंद*m.* नंदी *f.*

Full grown or big girl standing as a b. घोडेनवरी *or* घोडनवरी *f.* घोडकुदळनवरी *f.*

Mother of the b. वधूमाय *or* वहूमाय *f.* ओहमाय *f.*

Party or company of the b. वधूपक्ष*m.*—Member of it. वधूपक्षीय.

To dance, holding the b. and bridegroom upon the hips. झेंडा नाचवणें.

To fix upon a b (for one's son). वधू नेमस्त करणें.

Some of the numerous terms expressive of rites and ceremonies observed by or towards a *bride,* of presents made to,and of persons and things pertaining or relating to a *bride,* are inserted here. Particular information can, whenever desired,be obtained upon consulting the M. and E. Dict. आगती, कन्याशुल्क, जाणवसा, जाणवसघर, देज, द्विरागमन, परतवण, पाटपासोडा, पाठरासणा *or* पाठराख्या, पावण, पावता, भांगसळई *or* भांगसळ, मंगळसूत्र, माघारपण, माघारी, माघारीण, मुहूर्त्तमणी, मुळारी *or* मुऱ्हाळी, मुऱ्हाळीपान, मूळ, लग्नचुडा, लाह्याचामान, वधूप्रवेश, वधूवस्त्र, वीध, मुनमुख, हातपाणी, शुल्क.

BRIDE-GROOM, *n.* नवरा*m.* वर*m.* नवरदेव*m.*

An adult b. जाणता नवरा *m.* जाणता वर *m.*

Alighting of the b. at the village of his intended. जाणवसा*m. v.* दे, कर.—House appointed for it. जाणवसघर *n.* जाणवसा *m.*

B. inferior (in age or size) to his bride. हिणवर.

Departure of the b. for the marriage. वरप्रस्थान*n.*

Father of the b. वरबाप*m.* वरपिता*m.*

Flowers, &c. bound around the brow of the b. मंडोळी *or* मंडवळी *f.* मुंडावळ *or* मुंडावळी *f.*

Full grown or big boy standing as a b. घोडजावाई*m.* घोडकुदळ नवरा*m.*

Man sent to bring the b. वरधावा*m.*

Mother of the b. वरमाय *f.* वरमाता *f.*

Offerings and honors paid to a b. मधुपर्क*m.* सीमांतपूजन*n.* [वरपक्षीय.

Party or company of the b. वरपक्ष*m.*—Member of it.

Presents to the b. वरदक्षिणा *f.* लाडाचा तांब्या*m.*

Presents to the mother of the b. भेटवकरा *m.* मांडचेपणें*n.* &c.

Procession of the b. वरघोडा*m.*

Pole carried before the b. in p. पालछत्र*n.*

Procession of the b. and bride towards home. वरात *f.* घरभरणी *f.*

To fix upon a b. (for one's daughter). वर नेमस्त करणें, वरानिश्चित करणें.

BRIDE-MAID, *n.* करवली *f.*

BRIDE-MAN, *n.* करवला *m.* वरसखा *m.*

BRIDGE, *n.* पूल *m.* सेतु *m.* दादर *m.* [सांकू *m.*

B. or float hastily constructed of rude materials.

A disposition of bridges. पूलबंदी *f.*

Wooden b. लकडपूल *or* लकडापूल *or* लकडीपूल *m.* [शम.

2 (of the nose). नाकाचा दांडा *or* वांसा *m.* नाकाड *n.* नासावं-

3 (of a music instrument). घोडी *f.* चौकी *f.* तारदानी *f.* अट *f.* अडती *f.* अटक *f.*

To BRIDGE, *v. a.* पूल *m.* बांधणें *with* वर *of o.*

BRIDGE-BUILDING, BRIDGE-LAYING, *n.* पूलबंदी *f.*

BRIDLE, *n.* lit. and fig. लगाम *m. f.* अनीन *f.*

Grooming b. काजगी *f.* काजा *m.* [णें *g. of o.*

To put one's b. in the jaws of. नाकीं वेसन *f.* घाल-

BRIDLE-HAND, *n.* लगामाचा हात *m.*

BRIDLE-ROAD, *n.* घोडेवाट *f.* [विणें.

To BRIDLE, *v. a. put a bridle on.* लगाम *m. f.* देणें-घालणें-चढ-

2 *restrain or guide by a bridle,* lit. fig. v. To RESTRAIN. लगामांत धरणें, आकळणें, आवरणें, लगामीं लावणें. [*f.*

To BRIDLE, *v. n. hold up the head and draw in the chin.* मान आखडणें, मानेचा आंकडा *m.* वळवणें.

To b. up (under huff, &c.) फुगणें. [बंद.

BRIDLED, *p.* v. V. 1. लगामदिल्हेला-घातलेला-चढविलेला, लगाम-

2 लगामांत धरलेला, &c. आवरलेला, अटोपलेला, आवृत्त.

BRIEF, *n. epitome,* v. ABRIDGMENT. संक्षेप *m.* [ण *n.*

2 *pleader's case.* वकिलाचें टांचण *n.*-टिपण *n.* मुकदम्याचें टांच-

3 See WRIT.

BRIEF, *a.* See SHORT. 2 *concise,*—writings, speech, &c. संक्षेपाचा, संक्षिप्त, संकोचाचा, संकोचित, अल्पविस्ताराचा, अल्पशब्दक, परिमितशब्दक.

3—speaker, &c. संक्षेपी, संक्षिप्तवक्ता, संक्षेपभाषी, मितभाषी.

In b. एकूण *or* न, एवंच.

BRIEFLY, *adv.* v. A. 2. थोडक्यांत, संक्षेपेंकरून, संक्षेपानें, संक्षेपतः, संकोचतः, अल्पविस्तारानें.

BRIEFNESS, *n.* v. A. 2. सक्षेप*m.* संक्षेपता *f.* संक्षेपभाव *m.* अल्पता *f.* विस्ताराभाव*m.*

BRIER, *n. wild rose.* रानगुलाब*m.* सदागुलाब*m.* खोटागुलाब*m.*

2—gener. v. THORN. कांटेझाड*n.*

BRIG, *n.* दुकाठी गलबत *n.*

BRIGADE, *n.* सैन्यभाग*m.* सैन्यदल*n.*

BRIGADIER, *n.* सैन्यदलाधिपति*m.*

BRIGAND, *n.* बंडकरी, बंडवाला, पुंड.

BRIGANDAGE, *n.* पुंडाई *f.* पुंडावें *n.* बंडाई *f* बंडावें *n.*

BRIGHT, *a. shining, lucid, luminous, lustrous, radiant, resplendent, refuljent, &c.* उजळ, सोज्वल *or* ळ, चकचकीत, तेजस्वी, तेजवान्, तेजवंत, तेजस्कर, तैजस, तेजोमय, सतेज, तेजाचा, तेजगीचा, &c. तेजाळ, तेजःशाली, जोतीवंत, जोतदार, प्रकाशमान, प्रभावान्, उज्वल, दीप्तिमान्, कांतिमान्, ओजस्वी, लक्क, नितळ, भास्कर, उजळपाजळ, उल्लसित.

—intens. *flaming, blazing, &c.* v. GLARING. जरकबरक, देदीप्यमान, जाज्वल्यमान, जाज्वल्य, सुप्रभ. *See also* BRILLIANT.

2—not dull, v. SHARP. चणचणीत, तीक्ष्ण, प्रखर, सतेज, प्रज्वलित, प्रदीप्त, उजळबुद्धीचा, चाणाख्य.
3—a colour, *clear and full.* गहिरा *or* गैहरा. [टीत.
4—the moon-beams. पिठूर, पिठासारखा, टिपरासारखा, फटफ-
5—the eyes. पाणीदार, चकचकीत, सतेज.
6 (prospects, &c.) बरें होण्याच्या रंगाचा, शुभसूचक.

To BRIGHTEN, *v. a. make bright.* उजळ-सोज्वळ-तेजस्वी-तेजवंत- &c. करणें, प्रकाशविणें, उजळणें, उजळपण्यास आणणें, रंगास आणणें.
2up; *make clever, sharp, &c.* उजरणें, चणचणीत-तीक्ष्ण-तीव्र-प्रखर-&c. करणें.

To BRIGHTEN, *v. n. become bright.* उजळणें, रंगास चढणें, खुलणें, चढणें, निवळणें.
2up ; *become clever, &c.* उजरणें, तीक्ष्ण-तीव्र-&c. होणें.

BRIGHTENING, *n.* v. V. A. 1.—*act.* उजळ करणें *n.* उजळणें *n.* उज्ज्वलन *n.*

BRIGHT-EYED, *a.* चकचकीत डोळ्यांचा.

BRIGHTLY, *adv.* v.A. 1. तेजानें, तेजेंकरून, तकतक, झकझक,चकचक, झ्याक, प्रकाशपूर्वक, तेजःपूर्वक.
4 टिपूर.

BRIGHTNESS, *n.* v. A. 1. उजळपणा*m.* &c. लकेरी *f.* तेज*n.* तेजगी *f.* तेजी *f.* झिलाई *f.* झील *f.* सफाई *f.* चाकचक्य*n.* कांति *pop.* कांत *f.* छवि *f.* उज्ज्वलत्व*n.* औज्वल्य*n.* उजळा*m.* तजला*m.* तजेला*m.* तजेली *f.*
2 *and* SHARPNESS. तीक्ष्णता *f.* बुद्धितीक्ष्णता *f.*

BRILLIANCE, BRILLIANCY, *n.* v. A. 1. लकलकी *f.* तकतकी *f.* चकचकी *f.* झगझगी *or* झिगझिगी *f.* झकझकी *f.* झगमग *or* गी *f.* झळझळ *f.* झळक *f.* झळकी *f.* चाकचक्य *n.*—intens. लकलकाट *m.* लकाकी *f.* चकाकी *f.* तकाकी *f.* चकचकाट*m.* झकझकाट *m.* झकाकी *f.* झळाळ *f. m.* झळझळाट*m.*झळाळी *f.*
2 v. LUSTRE. पाणी*n.* तेज*n.*

BRILLIANT, *a. sparkling, glittering.* लकलकीत, तकतकीत, चकचकीत, तकतकीचा, चकचकीचा, &c. झगझगीत *or* झिगझिगीत, झगमगीत, झकझकीत, झळझळीत, टळटळीत, झळकफळक, जरकबरक, उजळपाजळ. *See also* BRIGHT.
2—a gem, v.LUSTROUS. पाण्याचा, पाणीदार, ढाळदार.
3 *splendid, &c.* v. FINE. छानदार, छानदारीचा.
4—an exploit.&c. शर्तीचा, शर्तमर्दीचा, प्रभावाचा.

BRILLIANT, *n. diamond cut with facets.* तरतरा*m.*

BRILLIANTLY, *adv.* v. A. 1. लकलकीनें, तकतकीनें, &c. तकतक, झकझक, चकचक, लकलक.

BRIM, *n.* v. EDGE. कांठ *f.* कड *f.* किनारा*m.* तोंड*n.*
Up to the b. तंतोतंत, बंब. See BRIMFUL.

BRIMFUL, *a. & adv.* कांठासर, तोंडासर, भरपूर, बरसर, कांठोकांठ, टंकोटंक, तंतोतंत, तारोतार, तोंडोतोंड, तोंडवर, धारबोळ, बोळंबोळ, धारोधार, डळमळीत, डबडबीत *or* डुबडुबीत, गळगळीत *or* गिळगिळीत, जळमळीत, बरसांड, डुबूक, तुडुंब *or* तुडूम, तुरुंब, तुंद, तुडुंबंब, सबट.
To be b. डबडबणें, डब्ब असणें-भरणें.

To BRIM, *v. a.* डब्ब भरणें, कांठोकांठ-&c. भरणें.

BRIMMER, *n. glass, &c. full to the brim.* डबडबीत-भरपूर-&c. पेला*m.* परिपूर्णपात्र*n.*

BRIMMING, *a.* v. BRIMFUL. डबडबीत *or* डुबडुबीत, बरसांड.

BRIMSTONE, *n.* गंधक*m.*

BRIMSTONY, *a.* v. N. गंधकाचा, गंधकासारखा, गंधकधर्मक.

BRINDED, BRINDLED, *a. streaked.* बहाळा *or* बाहळा, चांडाळकमरा.

BRINE, *n.* पाणखार*m.* खार*m.* मिठवणी*n.*
Prepared with b. उदलावणिक.
2 See OCEAN. 3 See TEARS.

To BRINE, *v.a. steep in b.* मिठवण्यांत घालणें.
2 *mix salt with.* मीठ*n.* घालणें.

To BRING, *v. a.* आणणें, घेऊन येणें, आनयन *n.* करणें *g. of o.*
2 *produce unto* देणें, पावविणें, प्राप्ति *f.*-मिळकत *f.*-&c. असणें-होणें *in. con. & g. of o.* कारण*n.* होणें *in con. & g. of o.*
3 (to a certain condition) आणणें, लावणें, अवस्थेस-दशेस-&c. आणणें.
4 about; v. To EFFECT. घडवून-बनवून-जमवून-&c.आणणें, घडविणें, बधविणें.
5 down. See To HUMBLE.
6 forth; v. To BEAR. जन्मवणें, प्रसविणें.
7 forth-or to light; v. To PUBLISH. प्रसिद्धीस-उघडिकेस-उघडदशेस-उजेडास-उमाळ्यास-&c. आणणें, प्रसिद्ध करणें.
8 forward; v. To ADDUCE. पुढें करणें, उभा करणें, उपन्यास *m.* करणें *g. of o.* [*with* पासून.
9 in; *produce as income.* उत्पन्न *n.*-प्राप्ति *f.*- आय*m.*-&c.होणें
10 on; *occasion unto.* आणणें, करणें.
11 on one's self; (a trouble or evil). आपल्या पायावर धोंडा ओढून घेणें *or* पाडून घेणें *or* मारून घेणें, खाजवून खरूज *f.* काढणें, खाजवून अवधणा*m.* आणणें, खोकला*m.* विकत घेणें.
12 on one's way. बोळविणें.
13 over; v. To PERSUADE. मन *n.* मनावणें, मिळवून घेणें, समजावणें, समजाविशी *f.*-समजावीस *f.*- समजूत *f.*- समजी *f.*-&c. करणें. *g. of. o.* [णणें.
14 to; *restore to consciousness.* शुद्धीवर-देहभानावर-&c.आ-
15 under; v. To SUBDUE. हाताखालीं-हुकुमांत-ताब्यांत-लगामांत- &c. आणणें, वश करणें.
16 up; v. To REAR, To EDUCATE. बाळगणें, आपंगणें, पाळणें, पोसणें, पालनपोषण *n.* करणें.
17 up; *pull in, curb,* v. To RESTRAIN. आटोपून-ओढून-&c. धरणें, आकळणें, लगामीं धरणें. [ठेपलणें.
To be brought up by, *stopped in progress by.* ठेपणें,

BRINJAL *n.* eggplant,—the plant. वांगी *f.* वृंताकी *f.* वृंताक *m.*—the fruit. वांगें *n.* वृंताक *n.*
Summer b.—the plant. उन्हाळ वांगी *f.*
—the fruit. उन्हाळ वांगें *n.*

BRINJARRIE, *n. carrier of grain, &c.* वणजारा *or* वणजारी.
Camp or company of Brinjarries. वणजार *n.*

BRINK, *n.* v. EDGE. कड *f.* तड *or* थड *f.* किनारा *m.*

BRINY, BRINISH, *a. salt.* खारा, खारट, क्षारयुक्त.

BRISK, *a. sprightly, gay,* v. LIVELY. आनंदी, उल्हासी, आनंदवृत्ति, खुशमौजा, खुशमौजी.
2 *active, quick, &c.* v. SMART. चपल, चपळा, हुशार, जलद, झपाट्या, चलाक *or* चलाख.
3 *busy, &c.* v. BUSTLING. चटपट्या,गडबड्या, झटपट्या,झटपटी.
4—of towns, &c.*lively,* v. SWARMING. गजगजीत, गजबजीत.
5—trade, sale, &c. जिवट, तेजीचा, तेजगीचा, चढचढीचा,

भरभरीचा, भरभराटाचा.
6 (of fire) धगधगीत, धगधगीचा.
7 *effervescing*, उतणारा, ऊतयेण्याजोगा-सारखा.
BRISKET, *n.* ऊर *m.*
BRISKLY, *adv* v. A. 1. उल्लासानें, आनंदवृत्तीनें.
2 चलाकीनें, चटपटीनें, &c. चपचप *or* पां, तडक *or* का, कडक *or* का, झपकन-कर-&c. झपझप, धडक *or* का, झरझर, झराझर, हातोहात, भरभर, भरभरां.
—intens. चपाचप, चपापां, झरारां, झपाझप, झपापां.
5 तेजीनें, भरभरीनें, झरझर, झपाझप, &c. [सवृत्ति *f.*
BRISKNESS, *n.* v. V. 1. उल्लासीपणा *m.* &c. आनंदवृत्ति *f.* उल्ला-
2 चपळपणा *m.* हुशारी *f.* चटपट *f.* चकपक *f.* झटपट *f.* त्वरा *f.* चलाकी *or* चलाखी *f.* चपलता *f.* चापल्य *n.*
5 तेजगी *f.* तेजी *f.* जीव *m.* भरभर *f.* जिवटपणा *m.*
B. and dulness (of trade, sale, &c.). तेजीमंदी *f.*
BRISTLE, *n.* सड *m.* कांटा *m.* शूक *m. n.*
Bristles. दृढलोम *m. pl.*
To BRISTLE, *v. n.*—the hair. भुरभुरणें, थुरथुरणें *or* थरथरणें, धरारणें, उभारणें, उभारणी *f.* होणें *g. of. s.*
2 *set up its feathers*—a bird. पिसारणें.
To BRISTLE, *v. a.* थुरथुरविणें *or* थरथरावणें, उभारणें.
BRISTLY, *a. set with bristles.* सडांचा, शूकयुक्त, शूकविशिष्ट.
BRITISH, *a.* ब्रितनदेशाचा, ब्रितनदेशसंबंधी, इंग्रजी, साहेबी, ब्रितिश.
BRITON, *n.* ब्रितनदेशस्थ मनुष्य *c.* इंग्रेज.
BRITTLE, *a. of soft fibre.* ठिसूळ, ढिसळ, ढिसूळ, ठुसकर.—*that breaks easily.* कडक, चिरका, भंजनशील.
2—esp. of thread or cord. तुटरा, तुटीर, फुसका, फुसकुला.
BRITTLENESS, *n.* v. A. 1. ठिसूळपणा *m.* ढिसळपणा *m.* कडकी *f.*
To BROACH, *v. a. spit.* सुळ्यास-सुळावर टोंचणें.
2 *pierce in order to draw.* भोंक *n.*-तोंड *n.* पाडणें.
3 (a store). सोडणें, फोडणें, उघडणें.
4 *give out, disclose,* v. To TELL. फोडणें, काढणें, प्रसिद्ध-प्रगट-&c. करणें, चौघांत आणणें, लौकिक *n.* करणें *g. of o.*
BROACH. See SPIT. 2 See BROOCH.
BROAD, *a. wide.* रुंद, रुंदेला, रुंदीचा, विस्ताराचा, विस्तीर्ण, विस्तृत.
—of cloth. मोठ्यापन्ह्याचा.
B. as long. *fig.* एकूनएकच, एकून क्षेत्रफलसारखें, एकूनतेंच, एकून हिशेबएकच.
Broadish. रुंदट, रुंदड.
Very b. रुंदाळ, रुंदाट *or* रुंदाड.
2 *gross, coarse, rudely plain, blunt, &c.* धसक्याचा, बेमुरवतीचा, बेमुलाज्याचा, धडकभडक, धडकफडक, उद्धट, निर्भीड, मुखदाक्षिण्यरहित शून्य-&c. संकोचरहित-शून्य-&c.
3—day light. भणभणीत, फटफटीत, धडधडीत.
It is b. day light. भणभणीत उजेडलें.
4—views, sentiments, v. COMPREHENSIVE. प्रशस्तपणाचा, प्रशस्त, व्यापक, बहुग्रह.
BROAD-AWAKE, *a.* पुरता जागाझालेला.
BROAD-BREASTED, BROAD-CHESTED, *a.* गरछातीचा, छातीपूर, कपाटवक्षा, विशालवक्षा, उरस्वान्, अश्वोरस.
BROAD-BRIMMED, *a.* रुंद कांठाचा, रुंद किनाऱ्याचा.
BROAD-CAST, *a.* मुठीनें पेरलेला-टाकलेला, मुठीचे पेऱ्याचा.
BROAD-CAST, *adv.* मूठ.
Corn (esp. rice) sown b. मूठ *f.*
To sow b. मूठ *f.* पेरणें *or* टाकणें *g. of o.*
BROADCLOTH, *n.* बनात *or* बानात *f.* सकलात *or* द *f.* [दीचा.
Of or belonging to b. सकलातीं *or* दी, बनातीचा, सकला-
BROAD-SHOULDERED, *a.* विशालस्कंध, अंसल.
BROAD-SIDE, *n.* गलबताच्या एकेबाजूकडील सर्व तोफांचा भडमार *m.*
2 गलबताच्या-&c. बाजूचा मधला भाग *m.*
BROAD-SWORD, *n.* रुंद पानाची तरवार *f.* रुंदी तरवार *f.*
To BROADEN, *v. n. grow broad.* रुंदावणें, पसरट होणें.
To BROADEN, *v.a.* रुंद-&c. करणें, रुंदाविणें.
BROADISH, *a.* रुंदट *or* रुंदड.
BROADLY, *adv.* v. A. 1. रुंद.
2 बेमुरवत, बेमुरवतपणानें, बेमुलाज्यानें, मुखदाक्षिण्य-संकोच रहित-शून्य-&c.
BROADNESS, *n.* v. A. 1. रुंदी *f.* रुंदावा *m.* रुंदपणा *m.*
2 बेमुरवतपणा *m.* धसकेपणा *m.* धडकपणा *m.* संकोचराहित्य *n.*
BROADWISE, *adv.* आडवा, कडेकडून, पार्श्वभाग पुढें करून.
BROCADE, *n.* जर *m. f.* जरबाच *or* जरबाफ्त *f.* जरीकापड *n.* तमामी *f.* लफ्फा *m.* किनखाब *m.*
False b. or lace लोखंडीजर *m f.*
Old b. fringe, &c. जरीजरतार *f.* जरीबुटी *f.*
Old b. lace, &c.-merchant. जोहरी *m.*
BROCADED, *a. woven with gold or silver thread.* जरतारी, जरी, जरीचा, बादली.
Full or richly b. भरजरी, भरबादली.
2 *that has a border of brocade or gold thread.* लफ्फेदार, गोलदार, गोलाचा, पल्लेदार, जरीपदरी.
BROCAGE or BROKAGE, *n.* v. BROKERAGE. दलाली *f.* दस्तुरी *f.*
BROCOLI, *n.* एक शाक विशेष आहे.
BROGUE, *n.* v. SHOE. जोडा *m.*
2 *corrupt dialect.* अडाणीबोली *f.* हेंगाडीबोली *f.*
To BROIDER, BROIDERY, &c. See To EMBROIDER, &c.
BROIL or BRAWL, *n. noisy quarrel,* v. SQUABBLE. कटकट *f.* कलागत *f.* खणाजंगी *f.* बाचाबाच *f.* कचाकच *f.* कडाकडी *f.* तडकाफडकी *f.*
To BROIL, *v. a.* भाजणें *or* भुजणें, भाजणी *f.*-भाजण *n.*-भाजप *n.*-भर्जन *n.* करणें *g. of o.*
To BROIL, *v. n.* भाजणें.
2 fig. *suffer from the sun,* &c. तळतळणें, पोळणें, तळपणें, तळतळ *f.* होणें *g. of s.*
BROILED, *p.* v. V. A. भाजलेला, भाजका, भाजींव, भर्जित, भृष्ट.
To BROKE, *v. n. act as a broker.* दलाली *f.* करणें.
BROKEN, *p. & a.* v. V. A. 1. मोडलेला, &c. तुटका, मोडका, फुटका, खंडित, भग्न, भंगुर, छिन्न, छेदित, विच्छिन्न, भिन्न, विघटित.
B. and battered. लुळाखुडा *or* लुडाखुडा.
I. *discontinuous, interrupted.* तुटक, तुटका, फुटक, फुटका, सांतर.
II.—a discourse, utterance, &c. तुटक, तुटका.
III. *not entire, incomplete, odd.* फुटक, फुटकर.
BROKEN-HEARTED, *a.* भग्नहृदय, भिन्नहृदय, दलद्धृदय, भग्नाश.
BROKEN-KNEED, *a.* तुटलेल्या गुडघ्यांचा.
BROKEN-MEAT, *n.* उरलेलें अन्न *n.* तुकडेमाकडे *m.pl* तुकडेताकडे *m.pl.* उरलें सुरलें *n.* शिळेंपाकें *n.* शेषान्न *n.* [श्वास.
BROKEN-WINDED, *a.* फुटल्या दमाचा, दमफुटलेला, दमगेलला, भग्न-

BROKENNESS, *n. feeling of luxation & relaxation*, v. EXHAUSTION. चुराm. चूरm. मोडकळा f. खुरदा m. खुरदमा m. खुंदला or ळाm. घुमाm. आंगाचा चकनाचूरorचकाचूरm. अवयव वैशकल्यn.

To have the feeling of b. घळघळणें.

2 (as of a floor or pavement). उखळण f.

BROKER *n. one who buys or sells for another*. दलाल.

2 *seller of old apparel, &c.* जुनेरेंविक्या, जुन्याचा बाजारी, मोडतोडविक्या, मोडतोड्या, बोहारी.

3 v. PIMP. भडवा.

BROKERAGE, *n.* v. N. 1. *business of a broker*. दलाली f. दलालाचें काम n.

I. *hire or pay of a broker*. दलाली f. दस्तुरी f.

BRONCHIAL, *a. belonging to the throat*. गळ्याचा, कंठ्य, कंठगत, कंठस्थ, कंठसंबंधी, श्वासमार्गसंबंधी.

BRONCHOCELE, *n.* गलगंडm. गडुm. मन्यास्तंभ m.

BRONCHOTOMY, *n.* श्वासमार्गछेदनn. श्वासमार्गमोचन n.

BRONZE, *n.* तांब्याचा आणि कथिलाचा मिश्रधातुm. पंचरसधातुm.

BROOCH, *n.* वस्त्र अडकवायाचें भूषण n. वक्षस्थल भूषण n.

2 See JEWEL.

To BROOD, *v. n. incubate*. पाखर f. घालणें, खुरकूत f. करणें, अंडींn. pl. उबविणें, आंडउबाराm. करणें, रोवण f. घेणें, कुलायनिलाय m. करणें.

2 over; *ponder over*. ध्यासm.-चिंतनn.-&c. धरून बसणें, चिंता करीत बसणें, सचिंत बसणें.

BROOD, *n. hatch, the whole hatch*. बीण f. बेत n. [वट.n.

2 *breed, progeny, hatch, &c.* v. OFFSPRING. वाढाm. बिज-

BROOK, BROOKLET, *n.* v. RIVULET. ओढाm. नालाm. ओहळ m. पऱ्हा m.

A clattering b. खळाळी f.

Dry bed of a b. ओढवण n.

To BROOK, *v. a. put up with*, v. To BEAR. सोसणें, साहणें, पोटांत घालणें-ठेवणें.

BROOM, *n. besom*. केरसुणी or केरसोणी f. झाडू m. झाडण f. झाडणी f. बुताराm. *dim.* बुतारी f. सळाथी f. बाढवण f. बाढणी f. मार्जनी f. सम्मार्जनी f.

B. of strong and stiff stalks. खरांटाm.

B. of twigs or cuttings. शिरांटा.

B. with handle. दांड or दांडेकेरसुणी f.

B. worn to the stump. खुंटारा m. खरांटा m.

Stock or hinderpart of a b. बुंधm. बुंधाm. बुंधाराm. मुडगा or मुगडाm.

To beat with a b. बुंधारणें.

2 एक झाड आहे.

BROOMSTAFF, BROOMSTICK, *n.* केरसुणीचा दांडाm.

BROTH, *n. decoction of meat*. मासाचें कढण n. कढवण n. रसा m. शृतमांसपेयn.

B. of some pulse. कढण n. कढवण n.

BROTHEL, *n.* बटीकवाडाm. छिनालवाडाm. छिनालखाना m. शिंदळवाडाm.वेश्यालयn वेश्याश्रयm. वेश्यागृहn. वेश्याशालाf.वेश्यागारn.

BROTHER, *n.* भाऊm. बंधुm. भ्राता m. बंधुजन m. बांधवm.

Brothers, Brethren. बंधुजन m. pl. बंधुवर्ग m.pl.

Brothers and sisters—collect. भावंडn.pl. बहीणभावंडेंn. pl. भाऊबहिणी f. pl.

B. of whole blood. सख्खाभाऊm. सहोदर, सोदर, एकोदर, सगर्भ, सगर्भ्य.

B.'s wife भावजई f. भ्रातृजाया f.

Elder b. वडील भाऊ, पुढलाभाऊ, अग्रज, ज्येष्ठबंधु.

Half-b. *b. on the father's side*. सापत्नभाऊ, सावत्रभाऊ, सापत्नबंधु.

Husband's b.'s wife. जावू or जाऊ f.

Husband's b.'s daughter. ध्वाडी f.

Twin b. जुळाभाऊ, जावळा भाऊ.

Uterine b. समानमातृक-एकमातृक-&c. बंधुm. सनाभि.

Younger b. धाकटा भाऊ, मागलाभाऊ, पाठचाभाऊ, अनुज, अवरज.

2 *one closely allied by some tie*. भाऊ m. बंधु m.

BROTHER IN-LAW,*n.wife's brother*. मेहुणा m. श्यालकm.श्यालm.

2 *sister's husband*.मेहुणाm. श्यालक m.श्याल m. भगिनीपतिm. भामm.भावोजीm.(used only of an elder sister's husband).

3 *husband's brother*. देवर *pop.* दीरm. भावाm. भावोजीm.

BROTHERHOOD, *n.* भाऊबंदकी or भाईबंदकी f. भाऊपणा or भाईपणाm. भाईबंदी f. बंधुत्वn. भ्रातृत्वn. [अखाडा m.

2 *fraternity, association*, v. COMPANY. पंक्ति *pop.* पंगत f.

BROTHER-LIKE, BROTHERLY, *a.* भाऊपणाचा, भाऊबंदीचा, बंधुत्वाचा, भाईचाऱ्याचा, बंधुभावाचा, भाऊसा, भ्रात्रीय, बंधुवत्.

BROTHERLINESS, *n.* v. A. भाऊबंदकी or भाईबंदकी f. भाऊबंदी f. भाऊपणा or भाईपणा m. भाईदारी f. भाईचारा m. भाईचार m. बंधुभाव m. बंधुत्व n.

BROTHERLY, *adv.* भाऊपणानें, भाईचारानें, भाईबंदीनें, बंधुभावानें, बंधुवृत्तीनें.

BROUGHT, *p.* v. V. 1. आणलेला, &c. आनीत, आहृत.

2 प्रापित, प्राप्त. [भ्रू f.

BROW, *n. arch over the eye*. भोवई or भंवई or भिवई f. भ्रुकुटी f.

To knit the b.s भवयांस गांठी f. pl.-अढी f. घालणें, भंवया f. pl. चढविणें.

2 *the arch of hair over the brow*. भोवई or भवई or भिवई f. भ्रू f. भ्रुकुटी f. भवईचे केश m. pl.

3 v. FOREHEAD. कपाळ n. निढळ or निढाळ n. भाळ n.

By the sweat of the b. निढळच्या घामानें.

4 (of a hill, &c.). माथ्याची कड f. गळा m. गळवटा m.

To BROWBEAT, *v. a.* भंवया-डोळेचढवूनबोलणें, डोळे m. pl. चढवणें-उगारणें-गुरकावणें-वटारणें-फाडणें-पिंजारणें, डोळे m. pl. उगारून-गुरकावून-बटारून-फाडून-पिंजारून-&c. बोलणें-दाबणें-दपटणें &c. गुरकी f.-गुरकावणी f. दाखवणें, घसरा m. देणें-करणें.

BROWBEATING, *n.* v. V.—*act.* डोळे चढवून बोलणें n. &c. घसराm. गुरकी f. गुरकावणी f.

BROWN, *a.* उदी, उदीरंगाचा, बदामी, तपकिरी, मुगदुमी. N. B. These words express different shades of brown.

Brownish. उदीसर.

Dark b. घनसावळा, कपिश.

Light or reddish b. भुरा or भोरा, मळ्या.

To BROWN, *v. a.* उदीरंग m.-&c. देणें, उदीरंगाचा-&c. करणें.

BROWNNESS, *n.* v. A. उदीपणा m. उदीरंग m.

BROWN-STUDY, *n.* पोकळध्यान n. निरर्थकध्यान n.

To BROWSE, *v. n. feed on branches, leaves, &c.* झाडपाला m.-आलापाला m.-&c. खाणें, पल्लवभक्षण n.-पर्णभक्षण n. करणें.

2 *graze.* चरणें. [लें *n.*

Browse, *n.* झाडपाला *m.* आलापाला *m.* पानपागोरा *m.* पाला *m.* पा-

Bruin. See Bear.

To Bruise, *v. a.* ठेंचणें *remiss.* ठेंचळणें, चेंचणें, चेंचरणें, चेंदरणें, ब-डवणें, कुचलणें, जखमकरणें, काळानिळा करणें, मर्दणें.

2 (peppers, fruits, seeds, &c.) *pound lightly. break coarsely.* खरडणें, सरगटणें, दुखवणें *or* दुखावणें, चुरणें, घावटणें *dim.* घावटळणें.

Bruise, *n. contusion.* आघातानें झालेली दुखापत *f.* चेंचलेला हात *m.*-&c.

2 See Dint. [दिन, क्षुण्ण.

Bruised, *p.* v. V. 1. चेंचलेला, चेंचरलेला, &c. चेंचका, जखमी, म-

2 खरंगटलेला, खरडलेला, &c. [बदंता *f.*

Bruit, *n.* v. Report. अवई *f.* अफवा *f.* आख्या *f.* गाजावाजा *m.*

To Bruit, *v. a. noise abroad,* v. To Noise. गाजावणें, प्रसिद्ध-&c. करणें.

Brumal, *a. belonging to the winter.* हिंवाळ्याचा, हैम, हैमन.

Brunette, *n. woman of a dark complexion.* काळसांवळी *or* का-ळी सांवळी बायको *f.*

Brunt, *n. heat or violence of.* झपाटा *m.* नडाका *or* तडाखा *m.* धडाका *m.* कडाखा *m.* जोर *m.*

2 (of a blow). v. Shock. धडका *m.* धक्का *m.*

Brush, *n.* कुंची *f.* कुंचणी *f.* कुंचला *m.* कुंचली *f.* मार्जनी *f.*

2 (of painter). कुंची *f.* बोंथ *dim.* बोंथी *f.* कलम *n.* ईषिका *f.* तूलिका *f.* तूली *f.*

3 (of weaver). कुंची *f.* कुंचणी *f.*

4 (of peacock's feathers, palm leaves, &c.). कुंचा *m.*

5 *rub, rude collision.* घसरा *m.* घसका *m.* घष्टा *m.* खेव *f.*

6 *skirmish, slight encounter.* चकमक *f.* v. झड, झटापटी *f.*

To Brush, *v. a.* कुंचीनें &c. झाडणें-साफकरणें, झाडणें, कुंचलणें, कुंचणें.

2 away off; *whisk, flap, &c.* झाडणें, झटकणें, झटकावणें, झ-टकारणें, झटका *m.*- झटकारा *m.* मारणें देणें.

3 up; *retouch, polish, &c.* v. To Finish. ओजवणें, घास-णें, घासपूस *f.* करणें, नेपाळणें.

4 up; (learning, &c.). घासणें, उजरणें, उजळणें, उजळणी *f.* करणें *g. of o.* घर्षण *n.* करणें, जागृत-उपस्थित-तयार-&c. करणें.

To Brush, *v. n.* (by, along, against). ओझरता जाणें-प-डणें-लागणें, खेटणें, झगटणें, झटणें, झटकणें, खरकणें *or* खुरकणें, घसरा-घसका-घष्टा-&c. देऊनजाणें.

Brushwood, *n.* झाडी *f.* झुडप *or* झुडुप *n.* झुडपांची झाडी *f.*

2 *branches lopped.* कवळ *n.* काटकवळ *n.*

To Brustle, *v. n.* v. To Crackle. चरचरणें *intens.* चराडणें, भरभरणें *intens.* भरारणें, सरसरणें *intens.* सरारणें, कडकणें.

2 v. To Rustle. फडफडणें, फडफड वाजणें, कडकणें.

Brustlingly, *adv.* चरचर *or* रां *intens.* चरारां *or* चराचर, सर-सर *or* रां *intens.* सरारां *or* सरासर. [वधी.

Brutal, *a. belonging, &c. to a brute.* पशूचा, जनावराचा, पशुसं-

B. force. आंगबळ *n.* आंगजोर *m.* आंगरेटाई *f.*

2 *savage, inhuman,* v. Cruel. क्रूर, निर्दय, मांगहृदय, निष्ठुर.

Brutality, *n.* v. A. 1. पशूपणा *m.* पशुत्व *n.* पशुता *f.* पशुधर्म *m.*

2 क्रूरता *f.* क्रूरत्व *n.* निर्दयता *f.* निष्ठुरता *f.*

To Brutalize, *v. a.* पशूसारखा-पशुवत्-&c. करणें.

Brutally, *adv.* See Cruelly.

Brute, *a. senseless, irrational.* अज्ञान, ज्ञानहीन-बुद्धि-रहित-&c.

2 See Brutal, 1.

Brute, *n.* v. Beast. पशु *m.* जनावर *n.* हैवान *m.*

2 *cruel person; ruffian, monster.* कातक, फजाल, क्रूरकर्मा, अघोरकर्मा, खवीस *m.* सोरठ, इमामदांडगा, कर्मचंडाल, मांग *m.* दैत्य *m.* कंटक. [टोणपी).

3 *stupid person,* v. Fool. हैवान *m.* धोंडा *m.* टोणपा *m.* (*f.*

Brutish, *n. resmbling, &c. a beast.* पशूचा, पशुसंबंधी, पशूसार-खा, पशुवत्, पशुतुल्य, पशुसदृश. [त, असभ्य.

2 *rude, uncivilized.* पशूसारखा, पशुवत्, पशुसमान, अशिक्षि-

Brutishly, *adv.* v. A. पशूसारखा *a. decl.* पशूवाणी, पशुवत्, ज-नावरा-परी-वाणी.

Brutishness, *n.* v. A. 1. *qualities of a brute.* पशुता *f.* पशुत्व *n.* पशुस्वभाव *m.* पशुधर्म *m.* पशुवृत्ति *f.*

2 असभ्यता *f.* अशिक्षितत्व *n.* शिक्षाराहित्य *n.*

Bubble, *n.*—of water. बुडबुडा *m.* फुगा *m.* फुगारा *m.* बोंबडा *m.* तरंग *m.* बुद्बुद *m.* [माव्या.

2 *person gulled,* v. Gull. फसलेलें माणूस *n.* फशा, पागोटेंग-

3 *cheat, false show,* v. Deceit. माया *f.* माव *f.*

To Bubble, *v.n. rise in bubbles.* बुडबुडणें, बुडबुडे *m. pl.* येणें.

2 up; *be under ebullition.* खतखतणें *or* खदखदणें, खुतखुतणें, गदगदणें *or* गुदगुदणें, बुडबुडणें, सळसळणें (intens. सळाळणें), उ-फाळणें, उफळणें, उसळणें, रटरटणें, रटमटणें.

To Bubble, *v. a. gull, befool,* v. To Deceive. फसवणें, झो-का *m.*-ढोला *m.* देणें, छकावणें, झुकविणें.

Bubbling, *n.* v. V. N. 1.—*act.* बुडबुडणें *n.*

2—*act.* खतखतणें *n.* &c. खतखत *or* खुतखुत *m.* खदखद *m.* उबाळा *m.* उफाळा *m.* उफाळ *m.* कढ *m.*

Bubblingly, *adv.* खतखत *or* तां खदखद *or* दां, गदगद *or* दां, गुदगुद *or* दां, बुडबुड *or* डां, सळसळ *or* ळां.

Bubby, *n.* v. Breast. स्तन *m.* आमा *m.* मिमी *f.* वक्षोज *m.*

Bubo, *n.*—venereal. बद *m.* बळ *m.*

2—sympathetic. अवधणा *m.* अवधान *n.*

Buck, *n. beau, blade, blood, spark, swell.* छानछूक *or* छोक, शानशूक *or* शोक, फंदीफांकडा, फंदी, फांकडा, कुर्रेदार, कुर्रेबाज, अक्कडबाज, जुर्राबावरा, टेवखोर, ढेंगोजी, नटवा, छेला, नटबाज, नटवाजिंदा, नटवा, नखरेदार, नखरेबाज.

2 *male of deer.* काळवीट *m.* हरिण *m.*

3 *male of goat.* बोकड *m.* बकरा *m.* छाग *m.*

4 *male of sheep.* मेंढा *m.* एडका *m.*

5 *male of hare.* ससा *m.* [लांबणें *n.*

Bucket, *n.* डोल *m. dim.* डोलची *f.* काढणें *n.* शेंदणें *n.* शेनणें *n.* Some particular kinds are पोहरा *m.* (of metal or wood), डोल *m. dim.* डोलची *f.* (of leather or wood), बालदी *f.* (of leather or wood and used esp. on board ship), मोट *f.* (of a draw-well), ओकती *f.* (b. of the transverse beam and stone).

Buckish, *a.* छानदार, शानदार, छानीचा, छालछबीला *or* छबेला, फांकडा, छानछुकीचा, अलबेला. [करून.

Buckishly, *adv.* v. A. छानछुकीनें, &c. नटूनथटून, टाकमटिका

Buckishness, *n.* v. A. छानछुकी *or* छोकी *f.* शानशुकी *or* शोकी *f.* छान *f.* टाकमटिका *m.* टाकमटिकला *m.* टाकमटिला *m.* चट्टीप-ट्टी *f.* टूम *f.* डौल *m.* डामडौल *m.* धजाव *m.*

Buckle, *n.* एके प्रकारचें अडकवण *n.* बकल *f.* कांब्यानीकडी *f.*

To Buckle, *v. a.* कचकीनें अडकविणें, कचकींत अडकविणें.
2 *make ready*, v. To Prepare. सिद्ध-सज्ज करणें, सज्जणें, कमर *f.* बाधणें, कास *f.* घालणें. [लगट *m. f.* करणें.
To Buckle to, *v. n. apply with vigor.* v. To Set to. झटणें,
Buckler. See Shield.
Buckram, *n.* सरसानें कडकडीत केलेलें कापड *n.*
Buckram, *a.* v. Stiff. ताठ्याचा, आदराचे आढ्यतेचा.
Buckskin, *n.* हरिणाचें कातडें *n.* अजिन *n.*
Buckthorn, *n.* एक ओषधी आहे.
Buckwheat, *n.* एक वनस्पति आहे.
Bud, *n.* कली *pop.* कळी *f.* कलिका *f.* उत्कलिका *f.* पानाचाअंकूर *m.* मुकुल *m. n.* कोश *m.*
Large b. कळा *m.*
Nipper in the b. *fig.* मानमोडें *n.*
To Bud, *v. n.* v. N. फुटणें, कळ्या *f. pl.* फुटणें-येणें *in. con.*
To Bud, *v. a. inoculate.* पिवंदी *f.* करणें.
Budded, v. V. N. फुटलेला, कळ्या आलेला, अंकुरित.
Buddha, *n.* बुद्ध *m.* बौद्ध *m.*
Buddhism, *n.* बौद्धधर्म *m.*
Buddhist, *n.* बौद्ध *m.* बौद्धधर्मानुसारी.
To Budge, *v. n. move, stir.* सरकणें, सरणें, हलणें, हटणें, हिचमिचणें *neg. con.* ढिम *f.* करणें-खाणें *neg. con.*
2 for; (i. e. by implic. *care for, mind, heed*). जुमास *m.* खाणें, जुमान *m.* खाणें-पावणें, जुमानणें, *all with neg. con. and* स *or* ला *of o.*
Budgerow, *n. a particular boat.* बजरा *m.*
Budget, *n.* v. Bag. पिशवी *f.* थैली *f.*
2 *store*, v. Stock. पिशवी *f.* गठडें *n.* गांठोडें *n.* पोतें *n.* पुंजी *f.* भरणा *m.* (esp. in comp. as कथाभरणा b. of stories or tales. गत भरणा b. of tunes. गीत भरणा b. of songs, &c.).
3 (of business papers, of accounts, &c.). हातरुमाल *m.* रुमाल *m.*
Buff, *n. skin of the buffalo.* म्हसडें *n.* महिषचर्म *n.*
2 *skin of the deer.* हरणाचेंकातडें *n.* अजिन *n.* मृगचर्म *n.*
To go in b. नागमोडीचा पितांबर *m.* नेसणें, नागवापाटाव *m.* नेसणें.
Buffalo, *n.*—male. खुळगा, खुळा, खुळ्या, रेडा *or* रेडका, टोणगा, म्हैसा, हेलगा, हेला, हल्या, बांगर, महिष,—in endearment or contempt. टोणगट *n.* खुळगट *n.* म्हशा *m.* हेलगट *n.* होळगट *n.* —female. म्हैस *or* महीस, बगर, डोबड *or* दोबड, महिषी,—in endearment, disparagement, or contempt. म्हैसरूं *or* म्हसरूं *n.* म्हसरूड *n.* म्हैसरट *n.* रेडूक *n.*
B. carrying eleven months. अकरमाशीम्हैस.
Young female b. रेडी *f.* वांठ *f.*
Buffalo-calf. See Calf.
Buffet, *n.* v. Blow. ठोसरा *m.* ठोसा *m.* मुठीची चोट *f.* मुष्टिमोदक *m.* मुष्टिप्रहार *m.*
To Buffet, *v. a.* v. To Box. बुकलणें, धबकणें, बुक्या *f.* मारणें.
2 *contend against.* झोंबणें, तोडणें.
Buffoon, *n. jack pudding, zany, merry Andrew, Tom fool, clown, harlequin, macaroni.* नटवा *m.* नट *m.* भांड *m.* हुंडीबाग *m.* नकल्या *m.* मस्करा *or* मस्कऱ्या *m.* विदूषक *m.* तमासगीर *m.* माधवी *m.*
2 *jester, droll, wag, fool, &c.* खुशमस्कऱ्या *m.* मस्कऱ्या *m.* ठट्ठेबाज *c.* ठट्ठेखोर *c.* [मस्करी *f.*
Buffoonery, *n. business of a b.* माधवीपणा *m.* मस्करेपणा *m.*
2 *low jests, drollery, waggery.* मस्करी *f.* ठट्ठामस्करी *f.*
Bug, *n.* ढेंकूण *m.* भिकूण *m.* मत्कुण *m.* रक्तबीज *m.* रक्तप *m.*
—in covert or cant phras. भीष्म *m.*
Large and fat b. टेणा *or* टेण्या *m.* टोणा *or* टोण्या *m.* ढेण्या *m.*
Bug-trap, *n. little box drilled.* भिकणी *f.*
Bugbear, *n.* बौ *or* बाऊ *m.* बागूल *or* बागूलबावा *m.* घोंगडबाऊ *m.* भोंबा *m.* घोंगा *m.* These words correspond with Blackman, Bagman, Beggar man, Bull beggar, &c.
To make a b. of. बाऊ *or* भोंबा करणें *or* करून सांगणें *or* दासवणें.
Buggy, *a. abounding with bugs.* ढेंकूण भरलेला, ढेंकणांनीं दाटलेला-भरलेला, बुचबुचलेला.
Buggy, *n. gig.* एक घोड्याची गाडी *f.* बगी *f.*
Bugle, *n.* v. Horn. तुतारी *f.* मोरशिंग *n.* रणशिंग *n.* बांका *m.* *dim.* बांकी *f.* [मणि *m.*
2 *bead of black glass.* काचेचाकाळामणी *m.* काळीपोत *f.* कृष्ण-
Build. See Built.
To Build, *v. a. construct.* बांधणें, रचणें, उभारणें, उभाकरणें, बांधणी *f.*-इमारत *f.*-बंदिस्त *f.*-बंदिस्ती *f.* करणें *g. of o.*
To b. castles in the air. आधांतरीं घर बांधणें, मनःसृष्टि *f.* करणें, मनोराज्य *n.* करणें, कोरडे मनोरथ *m. pl.* करणें, मनीं मांडेखाणें आणिस्वप्नीं पुऱ्या खाणें.
2 up (doorway, &c.) चिणणें, चिणून टाकणें.
To Build, *v. n. depend on, rest on.* भरवसा *m.*-विश्वास *m.*-अधण *n.*-&c. ठेवणें, जाणें *with* वर.
Builder, *n.* v. Mason. गंवडी, राज *m.* घरबांधणारा.
Master b. मेस्तरी.
Building, *n.* v. V.—*act.* बांधणें *n.* रचणें *n.* &c. बांधणी *f.* इमारत *f.* बंदिस्त *f.* बंदिस्ती *f.*
Cost of b. बांधणावळ *f.*
I. *a b. edifice, structure, fabric.* बंदिस्त *f.* इमारत *f.* इमला *m.*
A long b. सोपा *m.*
A long narrow b. दांडळ *f.* दांडिसाळ *f.*
B. composed of four slips. चौसोपी *f.*
B. having a roof of two slopes. दुपाखी *f.* दुमोळी *f.*—of four slopes. चौपाखी *f.* चौमोळी *f.*
B. of two rooms lengthwise. दुघई *f.* दुवडी *f.*—of three तिघई *f.* तिवडी *f.*—of four चौघई *f.* चौवडी *f.*
Buildings of some other forms or constructions are designated by the epithets सावंत्राई, शृंगारी, हजारी, &c.
Division of a b. खण *m.* गस्त *n.* भद्र *n.*
Public or large b.—gener. वाडा *m.*
The wood work of a b. काजाणू *n.*
Built, *n. build, &c. make, structure, form, construction.* बांधणावळ *f.* बांधावळ *f.* बंदिस्त *f.* बंदिस्ती *f.* बांधा *m.* बांधणी *f.* बांधप *n.* बनावट *f.*
Built, *p.* v. V. A. बांधलेला, रचलेला, &c. बंदिस्त.
B. up. बंदिस्त.
Bulb, *n. round root.* कांदा *m.* गड्डा *m.* कंद *m.*
To Bulb out. See To Belly.

Bulbous, *a.v.N.* कांद्याचा, कंदाचा, कंदमय, कंदरूप, कंदयुक्त, कंदी.
Bulbul, *n. Indian nightingale.* बुलबुल or बुलडुलबोचा *m.*
Bulge, *n. protuberant part.* पोट *n.* फुगा *n.* फुगारा *m.*
To **Bulge**, *v. n. jut out, swell out.* कोस *m.*-पोंक *n.*-कोंक *n.*-फुगा *m.*-फुगारा *m.* येणें *in. con.* उराड *n.* वाढणें *g. of s.* बेंडाळणें.
2 See To Bilge.
Bulimy, *n.* भस्मरोग *m.*
Afflicted with b. भस्मरोगी.
Bulk, *n. size, magnitude.* v. Size. आकारमान*n.* आकृतिमान*n.* महत्त्वमान*n.*
2 *main mass or body.* मुख्यभाग*m.* मुख्यअंश*m.*
4 *main fabric, the body.* मुख्यभाग *m.* प्रधानभाग *m.*
Bulkiness, *n.* v. A. 1. स्थूलता *f.* स्थूलत्व *n.* स्थौल्य *n.* बृहत्त्व*n.* आकारमहत्त्व *n.*
Bulky, *a.* v. Large. स्थूल, बोजड, अबजड, झांबड, आकारमहत्त्वाचा, बृहत् (in comp.).
2—as used esp. of man or animal. धडेल, धडेलमोला, धडल्याव, मस्त, मातबर, मोधळा, अगडबंब, ढमाल, ढमाल्या, रट, रटेल. [ष *m.*
Bull, *n.* बैल *m.* वृषभ *m.* चांगर *m.* आंडीलबैल *m.* बलिवर्द *m.* वृ-
Bulls and b.— calves,—compreh. बैलपाडा *m.*
B.'s eye. गवाक्ष *n.*
Castrated b. See Bullock.
Dedicating of a b. to the manes, &c. and setting him at large. वृषोत्सर्ग *pop.* वखुसर्ग *m.*
B. so dedicated and enlarged. पोळ *m.* वसू *m.* षंड *pop.* सांड *m.* लगिन्या बैल *m.* धुळी *m.*
Gross, overfed b. गलेलठ्ठबैल *m.*
Learned b. नंदीबैल *m.* नांद्या or नांद्याबैल *m.* पांगूळ or पांगळ्याबैल *m.*
The class of mendicants who go about with it are called पांगूळ *m.*
2 See Blunder.
3 पोपाकडील पत्र *n.*
Bull-baiting, *n.* बैलाचीकुत्तर ओढ *f.*
Bull-beggar. See Bugbear.
Bull-dog, *n.* कुत्र्यांची एकजात आहे.
Bull-head, *n. blockhead*, v. Fool. बैल *m.* टोणपा *m.*
Bullet, *n.* गोळी *f.*
B.—pouch or case. गोलदानी *f.*
Bulletin, *n.* प्रकृतिमानपत्र *n.* प्रकृतिवर्तमानपत्र *n.*
Bullion, *n.* लोटीचें सोनें रुपें *n.* लगडीचें सोनें *n.*
Silver b. चांदी *f.*
Bullock, *n. castrated bull.* बैल *m.* चेंच्या-चेंचलेला-बडव्या- कुंव्या काढलेला-&c. बैल*m.*—in contempt. बैलट *n.*
Bell-band (piece of sackcloth, &c.) of a b.'s neck. घांटपान *n.*
Hump of a b. ओसंड or हें *n.*
Nose-rein of a b. नाथ *f.* वेसण or न *f.* नास्य *n.*
Rein or guiding string of a b. कासरा *m.* पाग *f.*
Single side or half of a b.-load. अटकें *n.* अर्खेन*n.*—esp. of the leaves of the Piper Betel. कुडतन or तान *n.*
String of bells around the neck of a b. घुंगुरमाळ *f.* घांटसर *m.* घागरमाळ *f.* [घालणें.
To tie the fore legs of a b.(or buffalo, &c.). डुबक *f.*
The horn-rope of a b. सर *m.*
2 *young bull.* खोंड *m.* गोऱ्हा *m.*
Bullock-driver, **Bullock-grazier**, *n.* बैलका or बैलक्या*m.*
Bullock's heart,*n. Annona reticulata.*—the tree. रामफळ *f.* अनवल or अनोल *f.*—the fruit. रामफळ *n.* अनवलें or अनोलें *f.*
Bullock-pass, *n.* बैल घाट *m.*
Bullock-road, *n.* बैलवाट *f.* बैलरस्ता *m.* बैलमार्ग *m.*
Bully, *n.* v. Hector. गरिबांचाकाळ *m.* इमामदांडगा *m.* बीरपीर *m.* रगडमल्ल *m.* धोट or धोठ, शिंगाळ, खणक्या, खलेल, लंड, लठ्ठनिरंजन *m.* लट्टभारती *m.* झोंट *m.* टोंग *m.*
To **Bully**, *v. a.* डरकावणें, डरावणें, खणकावणें, दणकावणें, दणगारणें, गुरकावणें, धमकावणें, दटावणें, दाडदपट *f.*-दांडगाई *f.*-टोंगाई *f.*-&c. करणें.
Bullying, *n.* v. V.—*act.* डरकावणें *n.* &c. डरकावणी *f.* डरावणी*f.* दटावणी *f.* दाडदपट *f.* मलई *f.* दांडगाई *f.* टोंगाई *f.* झोंटाई *f.* तापतोबारा *m.* रगडमल्ली *f.*
B. of bodily might. आंगरेंटाई *f.* आंगमस्ती *f.* आंगधटाई *f.* आंगमदाई or आंगमर्दी *f.* लट्ठाई *f.*
Bulrush, *n.* मोठ्या जातीचा लव्हाळा *m.*
Bulwark, *n. bastion.* बुरूज *m.*
2 *defence*—gener. रक्षणोपाय *m.* रक्षणसाधन *n.* रक्षण *n.*
Bum, *n. breech*, v. Buttocks. गांड *f.* कुले *m. pl.* ढुंग *n.* ढुंगण*n.*
Bumbailiff, *n.* दुताडा *m.*
Bumblebee. See Humble-bee.
Bumboat, *n.* बांबोट *f.*
Bump, *adv.* धब-कन-कर-&c. धाड-कन-कर-&c.भुद or भद-कन-कर-&c. फाड-कन-कर-&c.
Bump, *n.* (on the body, &c.) *swelling, blind tumor.* गांठ *f.* गांध *f. enhance.* गांधाड *n.* गांधट *n.* गरस *f.* गुल्म *n. pop.* गुळूम or गुळुंब *m.* गलंड*n.*गलांड *n.* गलांडा *m.* टुंग *n.* टुंगर *n.*टुंगळ *n.* टुंगूळ *n.* टेंगूळ *n.* टुंबर *n.* उटंगळ *n.* उटिंबरा *m.* गुठळी or गुठोळी or गोठुळी *f.* उबाळू *n.* वाठा *m.* गंडसगोळा *m.* खुबा *m.*फुगा*m.* फुगारा *m.*
B. as from a blow or pinch. बेडकी *f.* मेंडकी *f.* केळ *n.*
To have a b. टेंगुळणें, टेंगूळ *n.*-&c. येणें-उठणें.
2 v. Thump. धडक *f.* धडका *m.* धडक *f.* धडका *m.*
To **Bump**, *v. a.* v. To Thump. धडक *f.*-धडका *m.*-धडक *f.*-धडका *m.* मारणें.
To **Bump**, *v.n. thump against*, v. To Thump. धाड-कन-कर-&c. -फाड-कन-कर-&c.-धब-कन-कर-&c. लागणें, धडक *f.*-धडका *m.*-धडक *f.*-धडका *m.* लागणें-बसणें *in. con.* धडकणें.
Bumping, *n.* v. V. A.—*act.* धडक *f.* धडका *m.* धडक *f.* धडका*m.* v. V. N.—*act.* धडक *f.* धडका *m.* धडक *f.* धडका *m.*
B. (of a calf, kid, &c.) whilst sucking. ढुमणी *f.* ढुसकी *f.* ढुशी *f.* ढोंचा *m.* ढुंडका *m.* ढुंदडा *m.* ढुंदडी *f.* ढुंडकी *f.* ढुमणी *f.* हेमटी *f. v.* मार.
Bumper, *n. brimmer.* भरलेला पेला *m.* भरपूरपेला *m.*
Bumpkin, *n. clown*, v. Countryman. खेडेमाणूस *c.* खेडेगांवचामाणूस *m.* खेड्या *m.* गांवढ्या *m.*
Bun. See Cake.

Bunch, *n. hunch, protuberance*, v. **Hump**. टेंगळ *or* टेंगूळ *n.* टुंग *n.* टुंगर *n.* खुबा *m.*
B. of a camel's back. मदार *f.*
2 v. **Cluster**. घड *m.* झुबका *m.* झुमका *m.* गुच्छ *m.* घूड *m.* घोस *m.* स्तबक *m.* पुंजका *m.*
3 *number tied together*, v. **Bundle**. पेंढी *f.* जुडगा *m.* जुडगें *n.* जुडका *m.* जुडकें *n.* जुडा *m. dim.* जुडी *f.* गड्डी *f.*
4 *tuft, knot, clump.* झुबका *m.* झुमका *m.* चुबका *m.* गोंडा *m.* गुच्छ *m.* बुचडा *m.*
5 (esp. of flowers). झेला *m.*
To **Bunch**, *v. n.* टेंगळणें *or* टेंगुळणें, गांठळणें, टेंगळ *n.*-&c. येणें.
To **Bunch**, *v. a.* घोस *m.*-झुबका *m.*-&c. बांधणें *g. of o.*
Bunchiness, *n.* v. A. झुबकेदारी *f.* गोंडाळपणा *m.*
Bunchy, *a. growing &c. in bunches.* झुबकेदार, झुमकेदार, गोंडाळ, गोंड्यांचा, गोंडेदार.
Bundle, *n.* (as of clothes, &c.). गांठोडें *n. dim.* गांठोडी *f.* गठडें *n.* गांठोळें *n.* बासन *n.*
Disorderly or loose b. बोचका *m.* बोचकें *n.* मोटला *m. dim.* मोटली *or* ळी *f.* मोटकुळें *n.*
2 *things bundled together*,—gener. मोट *f. enhanc.* मोटला*m.* and *dim.* मोटली *or* मोटळी *f.* & मोटकुळें *n.* गुंडाळा *m.* *dim.* गुंडाळी *or* गुंडळी *f.* गुंडाळें *or* गुंडळें *n.* बिंडा *m.*
3 (as of hay, thatch-leaves, &c.) *load.* गठ्ठा *m.* बिंडा *m.* *dim.* बिंडकें *n.* बिंदडी *f.* बिंदली *f.* भारा *m.* बरंड *f.* ओझें *n.*
4 (of *kadbà* or grass). पेंढी *f. dim.* पेंढकी *f.* & पेंडकें *n.* & पेंढूक *n.* पुला *m. dim.* पुली *f.* चुंगी *f.*
Aggregate of five bundles. पाचुंदा *m.*
5 (esp. of rice-straw). गुंडी *f.*
6—long or spheroidal; *straw case.* मुडा *m.* वांठी *or* वांटचें *n.*
7 (as of matches, greens, sticks. &c.). *bunch.* जुळी *f.* जुडा *m. dim.* जुडी *f.* जुडगा *m.* जुडगें *n. or* जुडका *m.*& जुडकें *n.* गडी *or* गड्डी *f.* पुंजका *m.* जुंबाडें *or* जुंबाड *n.* जुंबाडा *m.* गुच्छ *m.* चुंगडा *m.* चुंगडें *n.*
8 (as of papers) *packet.* तबलक *f.* पुडका *m. or* पुडकें *n.* पुडा *m. dim.* पुडी *f.*
Tape or tie of a b. दाटणी *f.* तबलक *f.* दफ्तरणी *f.*
To **Bundle**, *v. a. tie or bind in a b.* गांठोडें *n.*-गठडें *n.*-गांठोळें *n.* -मोट *f.*-&c. बांधणें-करणें, एके ठिकाणीं बांधणें.
To b. neck and crop. मोठ *f.* बांधणें *g. of o.*
To b. off, *send off angrily.* धिसपिटाविणें.
Bung, *n.* दट्टा *m.* गट्टा *m.* बूज *m.* गुडदी *f.*
2 (esp. of *dubbers*, &c). डुंडी *f.*
To **Bung**, *v. a.* दट्टा *m.*-&c. बसविणें.
Bung-hole, *n.* दट्टा-&c. बसविण्याचें भोंक *n.*
Bungalow, *n. house.* बंगला *m.*
To **Bungle**, *v. n. perform clumsily.* अडाणकाम *n.*-आवडधोवड काम *n.*-धावडी काम *n.*- अडबंगकाम *n.*-अडमुठेंकाम *n.*-&c. करणें, अडाण्यावाणी करणें.
To **Bungle**, *v. a. cobble, botch.* आवडधोवड रीतीनें करणें, आवडधोवड तांगडणें-शिवणें-&c.
Bungle, *n. clumsy work.* See To **Bungle** V. N.
Bungler, *n.* v. V.N. *and* **Awkward**. नाकसबी, गवत काप्या, गवत्या गोमाजी, गवत्या, दगडघाशा, कबाडी, कबाड्या, अडाणी, आडमुठ्या, कुरणकाप्या.
Bunglers and cobblers,—compreh. अडाणीकबाडी *m.pl.*
Bungling, *a. clumsily or confusedly done*, v. **Clumsy**. नाकसब्याचा, नाकसबाचा, झोंडीव, ओवडधोवड, धावडी, भोंपळमुती.
2 *immethodical, blundering.* डावखुरा *or* डावखोरा, गडबडगुंड्याचा, गोंधळाचा.
Bunglingly, *adv.* आडाणेपणाच्यारीतीनें, ओवडधोवडरीतीनें, आडाण्यावाणी.
Bunion, *n. corn on the foot.* घट्टा *m.*
Buoy, *n.* तरतें *n.* बोयरा *m.*
To **Buoy**, *v. a. keep afloat.* तरता तरंगत-&c. ठेवणें-राखणें, तरंगविणें, तरविणें.
2 *mark out by buoys.* बोयरे *m. pl.* लावणें.
3 *keep from despondency*, v. To **Support**. धैर्य *n.*-धीर *m.*-अवसान *n.*- &c. देणें.
Buoyancy, *n.* v. A. तरतेपणा *m.* तरणशीलता *f.* तरणशक्ति *f.* तरणधर्म *m.* तरणगुण *m.*
B. of spirits सदानंदवृत्ति *f.* [धर्मक.
Buoyant, *a. that will not sink.* तरायासारखा, तरणशील, तरण-
Of b. spirits. सदानंदी, सदानंदवृत्ति.
Burden, *n.* v. **Load**. ओझें *n.* भार *m.* हेल *m. f.* बारदान *n.*
Beast of b. पाठवळ *or* पाठाळ *n.* पृष्ठवाह *m.*
Ship of b. बारकस *n.* जिन्नसी तारूं *n.*-गलबत *n.*-जहाज *n.*-&c. नोरी तारूं-गलबत &c.
Fit for b. वाहीक, धौरेय.
Of b. ओझेल, ओझेली.
2 fig. *a grief, an anxiety, a trouble.* ओझें *n.* भार *m.* उरावर *or* गळ्यावर धोंड *f.* धोंड *f.* दडपण *n.* बेध *m.* लकडा *m.* घोरपड *f.*
3 (of a favor received). आभार *m.* ओझें *n.* टापरण *n.* टेपरण *n.* टेपर *n.*
4 (of a business, as imposed; or as reposed or rested). ओझें *n.* भार *m.* अधण *n.* गडदू *m.*
5 (of a song). अंकण कडवें *or* अकडकडवें *n.* पेडाबंद *m.* पालवपद *or* पालुपद *n.* ध्रुपद *n.* [जप *m.*
6 *that which is often repeated*, v. To **Dwell** upon. गाणें *n.*
To **Burden**, *v. a.* v. To **Load** लादणें, ओझें *n.* घालणें-टाकणें -लादणें-देणें.
2 fig. *oppress, encumber, &c.* ओझें *n.*-भार *m.* &c. घालणें-लादणें, भारग्रस्त-भाराक्रांत &c. करणें.
Burdened, *p.* v. V. 1. लादलेला, ओझें घातलेला-&c.
2 भारग्रस्त, भाराक्रांत, भारपीडित.
Burdensome, *a. grievous, &c.* v. **Afflictive**. जड, भारी, दुर्भर, दुःसह, कष्टकर, श्रमकर.
2 v. **Cumbersome**. दुर्वह, दुर्वाह्य, अवघड, अवजड.
Bureau, *n.* खणांचीपटी *f.*
2 *department.* खातें *n.*
Burg. See **Borough**.
Burglar, *n.* घरफोड्या *c.* भिंतफोड्या, संधिभेत्ता, संधिचोर. [र्य *n.*
Burglary, *n. house-breaking.* घरफोडणें *n.* भिंतफोडणें *n.* संधिचौ-
Burial. See **Burying**.
Buried, *p.* v. V. पुरलेला, गाडलेला *or* गडलेला.
To be b. (in) lit. fig. पुरणें, गडणें.
Burlesque, *a. tending to raise laughter.* हास्यरसाचा, हास्यर-

सोत्पादक, हास्यरसास्पद, हास्यरसप्रधान.

To BURLESQUE, *v. a.* हासूं येण्याची नकल *f.* करणें, नकल *f.*- बनावणी *f.* करणें, हास्यजनकविडंबन *n.* करणें. [ता *f.*

BURLINESS, *n.* v. A. गवदुलपणा *m.* गलेलठ्ठपणा *m.* &c. देहस्थूल-

BURLY, *a. big, bulky.* v. LARGE. गवदूल, गलेलठ्ठ, लडदू *or* लडधू, धडेल, धडऱ्याव, धटिंगण, लठ्ठा *or* लठ्ठ्या, बोंगा, बोंगाडा, डाचर.

To BURN, *v. a. affect by heat*, जाळणें, भाजणें, पोळणें, दाहणें, दाह *m.*-दाहन *n.* करणें *g. of o.* दग्ध करणें.

To b. one's fingers. To be burned. *sustain loss, &c.* पोळणें, आंच *f.* बसणें *in. con.* चट्टा *m.* बसणें *in. con.* शेकणें, शेकावणें.

2 (bricks, &c.) भाजणें.

3 (the throat, &c.)—rancid, &c. substances. खवणें, खवखवणें, डाचणें, जाळणें.

4 (food in cookery). करपवणें, जाळणें.

5 *corrode, gnaw.* खणणें, डाचणें, जाळणें.

6 up; *consume by fire.* जाळूनटाकणें, जाळूनराख *f.*-&c. करणें, जाळूनपस्त करणें.

7 (ground before sowing seed). भाजणी *f.*-भाजावळ *f.*-भाजवट *n.*-&c. करणें, दाढ *f.* भाजणें.

8 See To CAUTERIZE.

To BURN, *v. n. be on fire.* जळणें, दहन *n.* होणें *g. of o.*

—fiercely, &c. v. To GLOW. धगधगणें, फणफणणें.

To b. with a crackling noise—dry grass, &c. भरभरणें, भुरभुरणें.

B. it! v. Curse it! जळो *n.*

2 a lamp or light. जळणें, तेवणें.

3 (with anger or lust). जळणें, तापणें, संतापणें, जळफळणें, धडकणें, फणफणणें *intens.* फणाणणें, संतप्त होणें, दाह *m.* होणें *g. of s.*

4 (with emulation, eagerness, desire). खवखवणें, खुरखुरणें, सळसळणें, सुरसुरणें, फुटफुटणें, फुटफुट *f.*-फुटफुटी *f.*-&c. भरणें-येणें.

5 (in being cooked);—food. करपणें, जळणें, आंच *f.* लागणें *in. con.* डागणें, डागळणें, वाळगणें.

6—corn fields, country, &c. *be burnt up, parched.* करपणें, जळणें, जळगणें, भाजणें, करपून दग्ध होणें, हुरपळणें *or* होरपळणें.

7—the mouth, &c. under acrid tastes. पोळणें, तिखटावणें, तिखावणें, झणझणणें, फणफणणें, धगधगणें, खवखवणें, भगभगणें, मिरमिरणें.

8 (in the throat, stomach, &c.). जळजळणें *v. impers.* (as पोटांत-उरांत-घशांत-&c. जळजळतें), डाचणें, डचडचणें (as घशांत-&c. डाचतें *or* डचडचतें).

9—the body in fever, &c. तापणें, तपणें, रसरसणें, आंगाची होळी-आंगाचादाह *m.* होणें, धगधगणें, फणफणणें, जळफळणें, धडकणें, रणरण *adv.* करणें.

10 *tingle &c. with heat*, v. To SMART. चुरचुरणें, चुणचुणणें, फणफणणें.

11 out. जळून राख होणें, जळूनखाक होणें, जळूनराहणें.

BURN, *n.* चरका *m.* चटका *m.* चट्टा *m.* लास *m.* दाहक्षत *n.*

Scar or mark of a b. चटका *m.*

Skin peeling off from a b. पळका *m.* भाता *m.* कळपा *m.* भोत *m.*

Smart of a b. चटका *m.* चरका *m.*

2 See BROOK.

BURNABLE, *a.* v. V. A. 1. जाळाया-चा जोगा-&c. जाळाऊ, जाळींव, दहनीय, दाह्य, दग्धव्य.

BURNED, BURNT, *p.* v. V. A. 1. जाळलेला, &c. जाळींव, भाजींव, दाहित, दग्ध, विदग्ध, ज्वलित, जळका *dim.* जळकट *rather* b.

To be b. पोळणें, भाजणें, आंच *f.* बसणें-लागणें *in. con.*

v. V. N. 5. करपलेला, जाळलेला, &c. करपट.

Victuals b. in the dressing. करप *f.* करपी *f.*

BURNER, *n.* BURNING, *p. a.* v. V. A. 1. जाळणारा, &c. दाहक, दाहकर्त्ता, दहनकर्त्ता.

v. V. N. 1. जळणारा, जळता, जळत, ज्वलित, दह्यमान, दाहवान्.

3 v. ANGRY. LUSTFUL. तापलेला &c. फणफणीत, संतप्त, तप्त.

4 See IMPATIENT, ARDENT.

7 झणझणीत, फणफणीत, रणरणीत, धगधगीत.

I.—as poisons, medicines, &c. जलाल, जहाल *or* झाल.

BURNING, *n.* v. V. A. 1. जाळणें *n.* &c. दाह *m.* दाहन *n.* दहन *n.*

v. V. N. 1.—*state.* जळणें *n.* दहन *n.* ज्वलन *n.*

2 जळणें *n.* तेवणें *n.*

3 जळणें *n.* &c. दाह *m.* संताप *m.*

4 खवखवणें *n.* &c. खवखव *f.* खुरखुर *f.* धक *or* धग *f.* हवस *or* हौस *f.* सळका *m.* v. सुट, चुळचूळ *f.* फुटफुट *f.* फुटफुटी *f. intens.* फुटाट *or* टा *m.*

7 धगधग *f. intens.* धगधगाट *m.* खवखव *f.* जळजळ *f. intens.* जळजळाट *m.* दाह *or* डाह *m.* झणक्या *f. pl.* झणझण्या *f. pl.* झणझणी *f. intens.* झणझणाट *m.* मिरमीर *f. intens.* मिरमिराट *m.* भगभग *f. intens.* भगभगाट *m.*

9 दाह *or* डाह *m.* डोंब *or* आंगाचा डोंब *m.* धगधग *f. intens.* धगधगाट *m.* फणका *m. intens.* फणफणाट *m.* फणाण *m.*

Internal b. अंतर्दाह *m.* जळजळ *f. intens.* जळजळाट *m.*

10 चुणचूण *f.* चुणफूण *f.* फुणफूण *f.* दाह *or* डाह *m.* फणका *m.* धणकारा *m. intens.* फणफणाट *m.* [ग *n.*

BURNING-GLASS, *n.* सूर्यकांत *n.* सूर्यकांताचें भिंग *n.* सूर्यकांती भिं-

The focus of a b. तेजःसंकर्षदेश *m.*

To BURNISH, *v. a. polish.* सिकल करणें, उजळणें, उजळणी *f.* करणें, निसळणें, उजळा *m.*-ओप *f.*-जिल्हे *f.* - जिल्हई *f.*-झील *f.*-झिगी *f.*- &c. देणें-आणणें. [&c. देणारा.

BURNISHER, *n.* v. V. सिकलगर *or* सिकलगार, उजळेकरी, ओप-

I. *dog's tooth, stone, &c. used to burnish.* मोहरा *m.* ओपणी *f.* ओपसळई *f.* घोटा *m.*

BURNT-OFFERING, *n.* होम *m.* हवन *n.*

BURROW, *n. hole of an animal.* बिल *pop.* बीळ *n.* पोखर *n.* पोखारा *m.* धावरें *n.* धाव *f.* बिबर *n.* [रून राहणें.

To BURROW, *v. n.* बीळ *n.*-पोखर *n.*-पोखारा *m.*-बिबर *n.* करणें-क-

BURSAR, *n.* विद्यालयाचा खजीनदार, धनाधिकारी *m.*

BURSARY, *n.* विद्यालयाचा खजीना *m.*

2 विद्यार्थी ह्यास नेमणूक *f.*

BURSE, *n.* व्यापाऱ्यांचा अड्डा *m.*-फड *m.*

To BURST, *v. n.* फुटणें, फाटणें, उतटणें, उताटणें.

To b. in pieces, कोसळणें, ढासळणें.

To b. into tears. रडें *n.* कोसळणें *in. con.*

To b. with laughter. हांसतां हांसतां आंतडीं *n. pl.* गळ्यास येणें, हांसतां हांसतां पोट फुगून गळयास लागणें.

2 forth, out, away, &c. उधळणें, उसळणें, सुटणें, फुटून बाहेर

येणें-पडणें, उसळ *f*.- उसळी *or* उसाळी *f*. खाणें.

3 through. फोडून जाणें, फळी फोडून जाणें, दपटून शिरणें, धसकणें, धसणें.

To BURST, *v. a*. फोडणें, फाडणें, स्फोट *m*.-स्फोटन *n*. करणें *g. of o*.

BURST, *n. sudden explosion*—of anger, &c. झटका *m*. झटकारा *m*. सर *f*. उकळी *f*. [स्फुटित.

BURST, *p*. v. V. N. 1. फुटलेला, &c. फुटका, फुटकर, फुटक, स्फुट, v. V. A. फोडलेला, फाडलेला, स्फुट, स्फुटित, विघटित, विघाटित, विदीर्ण, विदारित.

BURSTING, *n*. v. V. N. 1.—*act*. फुटणें *n*. फाटणें *n*. स्फुटन *n*. विघटन *n*. विघाटन *n*.

v. V. A.—*act* फोडणें *n*. &c. स्फोट *m*. स्फोटन *n*.

BURTHEN. See BURDEN.

To BURY, *v. a. inter, inhumate*. पुरणें, गाडणें, गडदणें, माती *or* मूठ माती *f*. देणें, माती आड-भुई आड करणें, भूमिगत करणें, खनन *n*. करणें *g. of o*.

2 (one's self)—as in a *Math*. पुरून घेणें, गाडून घेणें.

3 (seed, &c.) मातींत-&c. घालणें.

4 *overwhelm and cover*. गडप करणें,

To be buried. गडप होणें.

5 (in oblivion) माती *f*. घालणें-लोटणें *with* वर *of o*. विस्मृति *f*.-&c. पाडणें *with g. of o*.

BURYING, BURIAL. *n*. v. V.—*act*. पुरणें *n*. गाडणें *n*. मातीदेणें *n*. &c. खनन *n*. मूठमाती *f*.

B. and burning (of the dead). खनन दहन *n*.

Self b. (of a Sanyási). समाधि *f. m. pop*. समाध *f*. v. घे.

BURYING-GROUND, BURYING-PLACE, *n*.v. CEMETERY. गाडायाची जागा*f*. मसणवटी *f*. मसण*n*. प्रेतभूमि *f*. प्रेतवन*n*. प्रेतस्थान*n*.

BUSH, *n*. झुडप *or* झुडूप*n*. झाड*n*.

Close and dense b. झांकर*n*. जुंबाड*n*. जुंगाड*n*. झुडपी *f*. जाळी *f*. जाळ *f*.

Place overrun with bushes. बुरंट *or* बुरांट *or* बुरुंट*n*.

To beat the bushes (to raise game). रान*n*. काढणें, रान*n*. हांकणें.

2 *leafy branch broken off (to be set &c.)*. झांकर*n*. झांप*m*.

BUSHEL, *n*. (of the nave of a wheel). बसूं*n*. विडी *f*.

2 एक कैलीमाप आहे.

BUSHINESS, *n*. v. A.1. झांकर*n*. जुंबाड*n*.जुंगाड*n*.झुडपी *f*. झांपाळ*n*.

2 झाडी *f*. झाडोरा*m*.

BUSHY, *a. thick,&c. like a b*. झांपाळ,झांकराचा,जुंबाडाचा,निबिड.

To grow b. झांपाळणें, झांकरणें.

2 *full of bushes*. झुडपांचा, झुडपाळ, झाड्या झुडपांचा.

3 (tail, &c.) झुपक्याचा, झुपकेदार.

BUSILY, *adv*. उद्योगपूर्वक, निरालस्यपूर्वक.

BUSINESS, *n. employment, occupation*. काम*n*. धंदा*m*. उद्योग*m*. कसब *n*. खटला *m*. खटलें*n*. व्यापार*m*. उद्यम*m*. व्यवहार*m*.

2 *work to be done*. काम*n*. कामगत *f*. कामगिरी *f*. कारभार*m*. कामकाज*n*. कामकारभार*m*. कामधंदा*m*.

Daily or settled b. नित्यकर्म*n*.

Load of b. कामाचा पर्वत*m*. कामाचा गाडा*m*.-डोंगर*m*.

Mind your own b. Expressing the sense of this phrase, and of the similar phrases, *What's that to you, That's no concern of your's, You go to Bath—be hanged, &c.*— as used in repressing interference viewed as impertinent, there are some striking colloquialisms in *Maráthi*. जाय गड्या, आपला देश घे, तुला काय पडलें, तुझें काय नासलें, तुझ्या बापाचें काय जातें,यांत तुझी काय बाभळ बुडाली, जिकडे पांढरे कावळे असतील तिकडेजा, तूं आपलें घर संभाळ,महाराची आई चांभार घेऊ तुला काय, आपलें घोडें गेलें आतां महार बसो कीं चांभार बसो तुला काय, कोणाच्या म्हशी आणि कोणास उठाबशी.

To be sent about one's b. लटपटणें.

To do one's b. v. NATURE. परसाकडेस जाणें.

To do one's b. (i. e.the b. of) v. To RUIN. काम*n*. काढणें *g. of o*. खुरच्या*f. pl*. पाडणें*or* चटणी *f*.-छिंद् *f*. करणें*g.of o*.

3 *a* b. *a job, a matter to be done*. काम*n*. कार्य*n*. काज*n*. कर्तव्य*n*. प्रयोज्य*n*.

Light or easy b. हलकेंफूल*n*.

Losing b. बुडस्थळ*n*. गोता*m*. घालण *f*.

Troublesome b. बखेडा*m*. लचांड*n*.

To manage the secular b. of. खटला*m*. ओढणें *g. of o*.

4 *a matter* gener. v. AFFAIR. गोष्ट *f*. मुकद्दमा*m*. खटला*m*. *or* खटलें*n*. प्रकरण*n*. गाणें*n*.

5 *province, office*. काम*n*. स्वकर्म*n*. स्वधर्म*m*. प्रकरण*n*. हक्क*m*. टप्पा*m*. मान*m*. अरुता *f*. अरू *f*.

6 *traffic*, v. TRADE. उदीम*m*. घेणेंदेणें*n*. घडमोड *or* घडामोड *f*.

Extensive or vast b. मोठा कारखाना*m*. अलायी-लंगर-झझांड-&c. कारखाना*m*. फापटपसारा*m*. फाकडपसारा*m*. कामाचा परगणा*m*.

Departments of an extensive b. अठरा कारखाने*m.pl*.

Man of b. व्यवहारी *pop*. वेव्हारी*m*. साटोप*m*.

Skilled in b.व्यवहारदक्ष, व्यवहारपटु.

To thrive in b. दुकान*n*. वाढणें *g. of s*.

7 *bustle and stir of buyers and sellers*. गिऱ्हाइकी *f*.

8 *profession, art, vocation, occupation*, v. LIVELIHOOD. रोजगार*m*. कसब*n*. वृत्ति *f*. वृत्त*n*. व्यवहार*m*. उद्योग*m*. कर्म*n*. खटला*m*. *or* खटलें*n*.

BUSKIN, *n*. प्राचीन काळांतील नटाचीपादुका.

BUSS, *n. kiss*. मुका*m*. चुंबन*n*.

To BUSS, *v. a*. v. To KISS. चुंबणें.

BUST, *n*. कमरेपासून वरच्या शरीराचा पुतळा. *m*. मुखवटा *or* मुखोटा. *m*.शिरोभाग *m*.

BUSTARD, *n*. माळढोंक *m*.

To BUSTLE (about), *v. n*. नाच नाचणें, उपद्व्याप *m*.-व्याप *m*.-धांवाधांव *f*.-धांवधूप *f*.-&c. करणें.

BUSTLE, *n. stir, hurry, lively motion*. घाई *f*. धांवधांव *f*. धांवाधांवी *f*. धांवधूप *f*. गडबड *f*. गडबडी *f*. धामधूम *f*.

To be in a b. गडबडणें.

2 (as of business, &c.) *brisk and noisy stir*. खटपट *f* खबदब *f*. तडाका *or* खा *m*. वावर *m*.

3 *confused hurry, din, &c. pother, pudder, row, clutter, coil, ado*. गोंधळ *m*. घोळ *m*. घप्पाघोळ *m*. घालमेल *f*. आडंबर *n*. गडबड*f*. गडबडी *f*. हुलहूल *f*.

BUSTLER, BUSTLING, *a. busy, stirring, active*. कामसू, कामी, कामठ, कर्मी, खटपट्या, खबदब्या, उलेढाल्या, चटपटी *or* ट्या, झटपटी *or* ट्या, कचाट्या, उपद्व्यापी, घालमेल्या , गडबड्या, च-

बडब्या, चगढग्या, खटलेखोर, उद्योगी, उद्योगशील, उद्योगवान्, उद्योगतत्पर, चंचल.

BUSY, *a. engaged in business.* उद्योगांत लागलेला, कामांत गुंतलेला, उद्योगी, अनवकाश, गाड्याला जुंपलेला, कामांत गढलेला, कामांत चूर, उद्यमी, उद्योगनिमग्न, कार्यव्यापृत, कार्यस्थ, कार्यस्थित, उद्योगस्थ.

The sense of the word is often best rendered by कामांत, उद्योगांत, &c. as तो कामांत आहे He is busy.

2 *stirring, lively.* See BUSTLER.

3 *full of stir and life,*—a town, a house, &c. गजबजीत, गजगजीत, दणदणीत, उपद्व्यापी, उल्याढाल्याचा.

4 (day, &c.) कामाच्या गर्दीचा-तडाक्याचा.

5 *meddling,* v. OFFICIOUS. लुडबुड्या, लुबरा.

To BUSY. See To EMPLOY.

BUSY-BODY, *n.* बुचा कारभारी *m.* लांडा कारभारी *m.* लुडबुड्या *m.* (—female b. बुची कारभारीण- &c.).

BUT, *conj.* v. EXCEPT. शिवाई, खेरीज, वांचून, सोडून.

2 *yet, nevertheless, however, howbeit.* पण, पर, परंतु, तर, तरीं, तथापि, अथापि, किंतु.

There is a "but" in the case. मध्यें तर आहे *or* मध्यें तर दिसती.

3 *no more than,* v. ONLY. मात्र, केवल *or* केवळ, फक्त.

BUT-END, *n.* बूड *n.* बुडखा *m.* बुंधारा *m.*—esp. of a musket, &c. दस्ता *m.*

BUTCHER, *n.* कसाई*m.* कसाब *m.* खाटक *m.* खाटकी *m.*

To BUTCHER, *v. a. kill savagely, &c.* v. To KILL. जीव *m.*-प्राण *m.* घेणें *g. of o.* खून *m.*-कत्तल *f.*-सूदन *n.*-सूना *f.*-&c. करणें *g. of o.* हिंसणें.

BUTCHERY, *n. business of a butcher.* कसाबकाम *n.* कसाबकरणी *f.* खाटकपणा *m.*

2 *slaughter-house.* कसाईखाना *m.* बधशाला *f.* सूना *f.*

3 fig. *slaughter, massacre,* v. KILLING. कत्तल *f. v.* उड, उडिव, सूना *f.* सूदन *n.* कदन *n.*

BUTLER, *n.* बाकनीस *m.* कोठवळा *m.*The English word is common under the corrupt form of बुटलेर *m.*

BUTT, *n. object of aim.* निशान *or* ण *n.* हिंदण *or* न *n.* लक्ष्य *n.* लक्ष *n.* वेध्य *n.* दृष्टिगुण *m.*

A b. for archers. तोदा *m.*

2 *jesting-stock, laughing-stock.* पाठवळ *n.* पाठाळ *n.* खेळवणा *m.* विनोदास्पद *n.* उपहासास्पद *n.*

3 (of a horned animal). टक्कर *f.* ढुस्सी *f.* ढुमणी *or* ढेमणी *f.* टापशी *f.* टेप *f.* ढुसकी *f.* ढुसणी *f.* ढुंडका *m.*

4 मोठें पिंप *n.*

To BUTT, *v. a.* ढुसकणें, ढुसणें, ढुंदडणें *or* ढुंदाडणें, ढुंडारणें, टक्कर *f.*-ढुस्सी *f.*- &c. देणें. [मारकट.

That is given to butting. शिंगाळ, शिंगाळू, मारका *dim.*

BUTTER, *n.* लोणी *n.* मस्का *m.* नवनीत *n.* घुसळा *m.*

B. imperfectly separated. ताकट *f. n.*

Vessel for beating (and clarifying) b. तुपकढणी *f.*

Clarified b. तूप *n.* घी*n.* आज्य*n.* घृत *n.* सर्पि *n.*—in cant or covert phras. घट्टें *n.*

Clarified b. fresh and hot. लोणकढें तूप *n.*

Clarified b. washed (a hundred times). शतघृत *n.* (a thousand times) सहस्रघृत *n.*

Dregs of clarified b. बेरी *f.* [रकटतूप *n.*

Dreggy or badly clarified b. बेरकट*or* बेरकूट*n.*बेरट *n.*बे-

That smells or tastes of clarified b. तुपट.

2 *soap, palaver, blarney, &c.* v. FLATTERY. गुळपापडी *f.* घमटगुळवणी *n.*

To BUTTER, *v. a.* लोणी *n.* लावणें-घालणें.

2 v. To FLATTER. दुधातुपानें *or* दुधातुपांत माखणें.

BUTTER-BOAT, *n.* द्रोण *m.* डोणा *m. dim.* डोणी *f.* खोरा *m.* These words signify *a vessel made of leaves tacked together to hold clarified butter or oil.*

BUTTER-CUP, *n.* एक फूल आहे.

BUTTERFLY, *n.* पाकोळी *f.* फुलपाखरूं *n.* पिंगाणें *n.* बेबा *m.* पतंग*m.* काशीचा कापड्या *m.*

2—as applied to *A spruce and glittering but empty fellow,* and as synonymous with *Jay, Popinjay, Gossamer, Fluttering Spark, Airling, Fop, Cock's comb, Bawcock,* &c. some correspondent terms are गालिच्याचा बूट, फुलबिसनी, तिवाशीचाबूट, छेला, छेलछबीला.

BUTTERIS, *n.* खुंबतरास *m.*

BUTTER-MILK, *n.* ताक *n.* तक्र *n.* Some terms of abuse for *Buttermilk* considered as weak and wishy washy are ताकवणी *n.* शंखवणी *n.* पांढरें पाणी *n.* फळकवणी *n.* धोंडवणी *n.* काळयाचा डोळा *m.*

——compreh. *or* loosely, i. e. *b., curdled milk, whey,&c.* ताकपाणी *n.*

B. mixed with rice-gruel. पेजबुडें *n.* [*or* ब *f.*

B. warmed with spices, &c. ताकतई *or* ताकतब *f.* तिक्रय

That sells b. ताक्या.

To scald b. ताक *n.* फोडप्णें.

BUTTER-TOOTH, *n.* चौकीचा दांत *m.*

BUTTERY, *n.* v. PANTRY. सोंवळ्याचीखोली *f.* फराळाचीखोली *f.* खाद्यसंभारगृह *n.*

BUTTERY, *a.* लोण्याचा, लोणट, लोणचट.

BUTTOCK, *n.* ढुंग *n.* ढुंगण *n.* ढुंगाड *n.* ढुंगाण *or* ढोंग *n.* ढोंगण *&c.* कुला *or* कुल्ला *m.* टीर *f.* तिडें *n.* गांड *f.* पुठ्ठा *m.* (used esp. of beasts), नितंब *m.* श्रोणी *f.*

Ulcer on the b. गांडबोला *m.* [पिटणें.

To clap the buttocks in exultation. टिरी *f. pl.* बडविणें-

To move along upon the buttocks. खुरडणें *or* खरडणें, खुरगटणें, फरपटणें, फरकटणें, फरकडणें, फरकंदणें, रखडणें, गांडसरपट्या-गांड्यां फरपट्या *adv.* जाणें-चालणें.

BUTTON, *n.* गुंडी *f.* भुतावें *n.*

Holding by the b. मगरमिठी *f.*

2 (of wood, to fasten doors, &c.). चिमणी *f.*

3—gener. अडकण *n.* अडकवण *n.*

4 *knob or boss fitting a loop.* गुळसी *f.* गुळसें *n.* बिरडें *or* ढेंन.

Note. These words also mean the knob & loop together.

To BUTTON, *v. a.* गुंडीनें अडकविणें, गुंड्या *f.pl.* घालणें, अडकविणें.

BUTTON-HOLE, BUTTON-LOOP, *n.* गुंडीचेंघर *n.* बिरडें *n.* तुकमा *m.* मुदन *f.* मुदनी *f.* काज *m.* फांसा.

BUTTRESS, *n.* v. PROP. टेंका *m.* टेंकवा *m.* पुस्ती *f.* धिरा *m.* धिरासा *m.* पुस्तवान *n. m.*

To BUTTRESS, *v. a.* टेंका *m.*-&c. देणें. [तात्मक.

BUTYRACEOUS, BUTYROUS, *a.* लोण्याचा, लोणट, लोणचट, नवनी-

2—of milk; *rich, fat.* लोगस, चिकण, तुपाळ.

BUXOM, *a. gay, blythe,* &c. v. LIVELY. उल्लासी, रंगदार, रंगी, रंगेला, रंगेली, आनंदी, खुशमौजा.

BUXOMLY, *adv.* v. A. उल्लासवृत्तीनें, आनंदीपणानें, मौजामारून.

BUXOMNESS, *n.* v. A. आनंदीपणा*m.* उल्लासवृत्ति *f.* सदानंदवृत्ति *f.*

To BUY, *v. a.* विकत घेणें, खरीद करणें, खरीदी *f.*-क्रय *m.*-क्रीणन *n.* करणें *g. of o.* मोलदेऊन घेणें.

BUYER, *n.* v. V. विकतघेणारा, खरीदकरणारा, &c. खरीददार, गिऱ्हाईक, क्रयी, क्रेता. [क्रीणन *n.*

BUYING, *n.* v. V.—*act.* विकतघेणें *n.* &c. खरीदी *f.* क्रय *m.* B. and selling, v. TRADE. घेणेंदेणें *n.* घेवदेव *m.* क्रयविक्रय *m.* घडमोड *or* घडामोड *f.*

To BUZZ, *v. n.*—as flies, &c. गुंगणें *or* गोंगणें, गोगावणें *or* घोंगावणें, भणभणणें *intens.* भाणाणणें.

2 v. To WHISPER. फुसफुसणें, कुचकुचणें, गुणगुण *f.* करणें.

BUZZ, BUZZING, *n.* v. V. 1. गुणगुण *or* गिणगीण *f. intens.* गणगणाट *or* गिणगिणाट *or* घुणघुणाट *m.* घोंघों *n. intens.* घोंगाट *m.* घोंगाण *n.* भणभण *or* भिणभीण *f. intens.* भणभणाट *m.* भणाण *m.* गजबज *f.* रुंजी *f.* गुंजारव *m.* अलिविराव*m.*

2 गुणगुण *f.* फुसफुस *f.* कुचकुच *f.* कुजबुज *f.*

BY, *prep.*—noting agent. कडून, हातून, जवळून, पासून, वरून.

2 *with,*—noting insturment. करून, कडून, नें, वारीं.

3 *at, as soon as,*—noting time. करणें (ex. आज प्रारंभ केला तर उद्यां दोन प्रहरां करणें संपेल), पावेतों, पर्यंत, तों, वेरीं, कडे. By this time. By now. एव्हां करणें, एव्हांवेरीं.

4 *through,*—noting means or medium. करून, करवीं *or* करवें, द्वारा, योगेंकरून, परत्वें *or* परत्वेंकरून.

5 noting passage along. वरून, जवळून, पासून, सरसून.

BY, *adv. at hand, in presence,* v. NEAR. जवळ, समीप, निकट.

By, in composition, implying *indirectness, inferiority, irregularity, subordinacy,* &c. is expressed by आड, गैर, गौण, चोर, as आडकाम, आडखर्च, आडगांव, आडकथा, आडघोडा, आडदाळ, आडनांव, आडपेंठ, आडवेळ, आडसोंग, आडगडी, &c. गैररीत, गौणकल्प, &c. Other examples see in order.

BY AND BY, *in a short time.* काहींशा वेळानें, काहींवेळानें, मग, क्षणभरानें, अमळशानें, पुढें.

BY THE BY, सहज आठवण झाल्यावरून, बरेंच स्मरण झालें.

BY-AFFAIR, BY-BUSINESS, BY-JOB, BY-WORK, *n.* आडकाम *n.* शिवायकाम *n.* खेरीजकाम *n.* फिरकोळ काम *n.* अडपझडप काम *n.* अरतेंपरतें काम *n.* उपकर्म *n.* गौणकार्य *n.*

BY-CORNER, *n.* चोर कोनाडा *m.*

BY-DAY, *n.* आडदिवस *m.*

BY-DESIGN, BY-END, BY-OBJECT, *n.* गौणकल्प *m.* गौणाभिप्राय*m.* आनुषंगिककार्य *n.* [*m.* &c.

BY-EXPENSES, *n.* वरखर्च *m.* आडखर्च *m.* गैरखर्च *m.* शिवायखर्च

BY-GAIN, *n. pickings,* &c. आड मिळकत *f.* खेरीज मिळकत *f.* शिवाय मिळकत *f.* अरतीपरती मेळकत *f.* किरकोळ प्राप्ति *f.* आडप्राप्ति *f.* अवांतर प्राप्ति *f.* कसर *f.* गुंजाबीस *f.* कूस *f.* आगंतुक लाभ *m.* पोटस्त *or* पोटस्थ *n.* [गोंडी *f.*

BY-LANE, BY-STREET, *n.* आडगल्ली *f.* चोरगल्ली *f.* आडरस्ता *m.*

BY-LAW, *n.* आडकायदा *m.* शिवाय कायदा *m.* खेरीज कायदा *m.* पोटचा कायदा *m.* अवांतर कायदा *m.*

BY-MATTER, *n.* आडगोष्ट *f.* खेरीजगोष्ट *f.* शिवायकलम*n.* गौणविषय *m.* गौणकार्य *n.*

BY-NAME, *n.* टोंगमती नांव *or* टेंगमती नांव *n.* टोंगमताचें-&c. नांव *n.* पडलेलें नांव *n.* जडलेलें नांव *n.*

BY-PATH, BY-ROAD, BY-WAY, *n.* आडवाट *f.* आडमार्ग *m.* आडरस्ता *m.* चोरवाट *f.* गूढमार्ग *m.*

2 fig. *by-manner, by-method, &c.* गैररीत *f.* अपरीति *f.* गैरमार्ग *m.* [मौजपाहणारा.

BY-STANDER, *n.* जवळचा उभा राहिलेला माणूस *m.* तमासगीर *c.* Idle by-standers. आलेभाऊ कोल्हेभाऊ *m. pl.*

BY-STOCK, BY-STORE, *n.* आडसांठा *m.*

BY-STORY, BY-TALE, *n.* आडकथा *f.* [गैरवेळ *f.*

BY-TIME, BY-SEASON, *n.* आडवेळ *f.* आडसंधि *f.* भलतीवेळ *f.*

BY-VILLAGE, BY-TOWN, *n.* काणी पेंठ *f.*

BY-WORD, *n.* म्हण *f.* न्याय *m.* दृष्टांतास्पद *n.*

BY-WORK, *n.* आडकाम *n.*

C.

C. For the account of the two sounds of this letter as represented respectively by K and S, see under those letters. The combination Ch. is represented by च, and when aspirated by छ.

CAB, *n.* एक घोड्याची गाडी आहे. [वग्रह *m.*

CABAL, *n.* v. COMBINATION. जाळी *f.* कट *m.* जट *m.* कूट *n.* न-

2 v. INTRIGUE, फंद *m.* कचाट *m.* कंत्राण *n.*

To CABAL, *v. n.* v. To PLOT. फंद *m.*-मसलत *f.*-&c. करणें.

CABALISTIC, *a.* v. OCCULT. गुप्त, गुह्य, गूढार्थक.

C. letter. बीजाक्षर *n.* बीज *n.*

CABBAGE, *n.* कोबी *f. or* कोई *f.* from *Couve* Port. करम *n.* करमाची भाजी *f.*

Bulb or belly of a c. कोबीचा कांदा *m.*-गड्डा *m.* करमकांदा *m.* करमगड्डा *m.*

2 (of wick). कोजळी *f.* काजळी *f.* चिंचोळा *m.*

To CABBAGE, *v. n. form a head.* गड्डा *m.* होणें-येणें *in. con.*

2—a wick. कोजळणें, कोजळी *f.* येणें *in. con.*

To CABBAGE, *v. a. pick, &c.* v. To EMBEZZLE. खाणें, चापसणें, खादगी *f.* खाणें, ताव *m.* देणें *with* वर *of o.*

CABBAGE TREE *n.* गायदड *f.*

CABIN, *n.* (of a ship). पयाल *n.* वरांचल *n.* खोली *f.* खण *m.*

2 *cottage, cot,* v. HUT. खोपट *n. dim.* खोपटी *f.* झोंपडी *f.*

CABINET, *n.* v. CLOSET. लाहान खोली *f.*

2 *private council room.* खलबतखाना *m.* खास दिवाणखाना*m.* मंत्रणस्थान *n.* मंत्रगृह *n.*

3 *select body of ministers.* मंत्र्यांची-प्रधानांची खलबतकरणारी मंडळी *f.* मुख्यमंत्री *m. pl.* मुख्यप्रधान *m. pl.*

4 *box of drawers, cells, &c.* खणांची पेटी *f.* खानेदार पेटी *f.*

CABINET-COUNCIL *n.* मुख्यमंत्र्यांची-&c. सभा *f.*

CABINET-MAKER, *n.* v. CARPENTER. खणांच्यापेट्या वगैरे सामान करणारा सुतार.

CABLE, *n.* लंगरदोर *m.* दोरखंड *n.* दोरडें *n.* राजू *m.* कुरूम *n.*

Caboose, *n.* गलबतावरचा ओवरा *m.*

Cabriolet, *n.* एक घोड्याची एका प्रकारची गाडी आहे.

Cachectical, *a.* v. N. दुःस्थितभावनेचा, दुःस्थितभावन.

Cachexy, *n. ill habit of body.* दुःस्थितभावना *f.* प्रकृतीची दुःस्थिति *f.*

Cachinnation, *n.* अट्टहास *m.*

Cack, *n.* हगी *f.* [करणें.

To Cackle, *v. n.*—a goose. कलकल *m.*-हंसनाद *m.*-हंसध्वनि *m.*

2—a hen. कुकणें *or* कोकणें.

3 v. To Giggle. हिहिहि *f.* करणें.

4 v. To Prate. बडबडणें, जल्पणें. [हंसशब्द *m.*

Cackle, Cackling, *n.* v. V. 1.—cry made. कलकल*m.* हंसनाद*m.*

2 कुकणें *or* कोकणें *n.*

3—*act, &c.* हिहिहि *f.* हिहि *f.*

4—*act, &c.* बडबड *f.* जल्पना *f.*

Cacochymical, *n.* v. N. त्रिदोषविकाराचा, त्रिदोषी, दोषविकारी, धातुत्रयविकाराचा.

Cacochymy, *n. vicious state of the humors.* त्रिदोष *m.* त्रिदोषविकार *m.* धातुत्रयविकार *m.* दोषविकार *m.*

Cacophony, *n.* रुक्षोच्चार *m.* कर्कश उच्चार *m.*

Cad, *n.* पोऱ्या *m.* पोरगा *m.*

Cadaverous, *a, relating, &c. to a corpse.* प्रेतसंबंधी, शवसंबंधी, प्रेतसदृश, शववत्, मढ्यासारखा, शाव, शावक.

2 *ghastly, pale,* v. Wan. प्रेतकळेचा, प्रेतकलायुक्त, उफट *or* ओफट, मुडद्यासारखा, प्रेतवत्, शववत्, मृतप्राय, मृत्युरूपी.

Cadaverousness, *n.* v. A. 1. प्रेतसादृश्य *n.* प्रेतसदृशता *f.* प्रेतपणा *m.* शवपणा *m.*

2 प्रेतकला *pop.* प्रेतकळा *f.* मडेकळा *f.*

Cade, *a.* See Tame.

Cade, *n.* See Cask.

Cadence, *n.* (of the voice). उतरतास्वर *m.* उतार *m.*

2 *tone in reading, &c.* वाणी *f.* स्वर *m.*

Cadet, *n.* लशकरीखात्यांतील हुद्याचा पगारीउमेदवार.

Cadi, *n.* काजी *m.*

Cadjan, *n. branch of the cocoanut tree, &c.* झांप *m.* झावळी *f.* सावळी *f.* चुडवत *n.*

A matted c. झांप *m.*

Caffre, *n.* काफरी.

Cage, *n.* पिंजरा *m.* पांजरा *m.* पिंजर *n.* पंजर *n.*

To Cage, *v. a.* पिंजऱ्यांत-&c. घालणें-कोंडणें.

Cairn, *n. heap of stones.* खिळा *m.* वरंडा *m.* खिळपट*n.*

Caitiff, *n. knave,* v. Blackguard. गुलाम *m.* गुलामजादा *m.* हरामी, लुच्चा, धोट *or* ठ.

To Cajole, *v. a wheedle, &c.* फुसलावणें, गुळावणें *or* घोळावणें, चाळवणें, थापटून थोपटून वश करणें, भोंदणें, गुळ्गुळथापडी *f.* करणें *g. of o.* लुलुपुतू *n.* करणें, मुलकें *n.* बांधणें-घालणें, पागोट्यास *or* शेंडीस फुलें *n. pl.* बांधणें *g. of o.* हातावर चंद्र *m.* आणून देणें.

Cajoled, *p.* v. V. फुसलावलेला &c.

Cajoler, *n.* Cajoling, *p. a.* v. V. फुसलावणारा &c. फुसलाव्या, घुलाव्या, भोंदू, लुलुपुतू करणारा.

Cajolery, Cajoling, *n.* v. V.—*act.* फुसलावणें *n.* &c. चाळवण *f.* चाळवणूक *f.* गुळगुळथापडी *f.* लुलुपुतू *n.* मुखमार्जन *n.*

Cake, *n.* (of bread, gener.) v. Bread. रोटी *f.* चपाती *f.* चपटी *or* चापटी *f.* चकदळी *f.* चांदकी *f.* दामटी *f.* चांदुकली *f.* पोपी *f.* पोपली *f.* अपूप *m.*

2 (of wheaten or rice flour). पोळी *f.* रोटी *f.*

3 (of flour of बाजरी, जोंधळा, &c.). भाकर *f.* Some of the common *Cakes, Puffs, Puddings, &c.* are पुरणपोळी, खापरपोळी, गवसणीची पोळी, घडीची पोळी, करंजी, खाजी करंजी, कानवला, गुळपापडी, कडबू, कोंडेकड, गणा, घावन *or* ना, गुरोळी, कोंडोळें, पापडी, पाटवडी, मलीदा, पुरी, पुवा, अपूप *or* पूप, बडा, धावलवडा, विवर, मांडा, सांदण*n.* चिरोटा, तिळवडा, तेलची, सडदाळीचा वडा, अनरसा. [ती *f.*

A c. flattened with the hand without a roller. चपाटी *f.* चकती *f.*

Eighth of a c. नितकोर *m. f.*

Fourth of a c. चतकोर *or* चतकर *m. f.* चौस *f.* कोर *f.*

Pile of cakes. चवड *f.*

Small c. or flat loaf. चांदकी *f.* चांदुकली *f.*

Stool, &c. for rolling cakes पोळपाट *m.*

Thick or large c. रोट *m.* रोटगा *m.* रट्ट *m.* रट्टा *or* रट्या*m.* रेंट *n.* रेंटूक *n.* नंदाळें *n.*

4 *flat and circular mass,* gener. चाकी *f.* चाती *f.* चपटी *or* चापटी *f.* चकती *f.*

5. v. Pat. वडी *f.* वटी *f.* वटिका *f.* पापडी *f.*

6 *concreted matter.* गड्डा *m.* ढेप *f.* डिखळ *or* डिखूळ *n.* डिखळी *f.* डिखोळी *f.*

7 (as of dried mud, &c. &c.). खपला *m.* पापुदरा *or* पापोदरा *m.* पापोडा *or* पापोटा *m.* पोपडा *m.* खरपुडी *f.* कवंद *f.*

To Cake, *v. n. gather into a cake, concrete.* जमणें, गोठणें, डिखळ *n.*-&c. होणें *g. of s.* [शेंद *f.*

Calabash, *n. gourd-vessel.* तुंबडी *f.* तुंबी *f.* तुंबा *m.* भोपळा *m.*

Calamine, *n. impure carbonate of zinc.* कलखापरी *f.*

Calamitous, *a.* v. N. *distressful, miserable,*—of circumstances, &c. अनिष्टाचा, दुःखाचा, विपत्तीचा, अकल्याणाचा, हालांचा, हालअपेष्टेचा, आफतीचा, नष्टचर्याचा &c. अनिष्ट, अभद्र, अरिष्ट, अनिष्टरूप, अभद्ररूप, अनिष्टात्मक, अभद्रात्मक, अनिष्टान्वित, विपद्युक्त.

2 *producing distress and misery.* दुःखावह, दुःखप्रद, दुःखद, अनिष्टावह, अकल्याण कारक-जनक-&c. अनिष्ट कारक-जनक-दायक &c. अपाय कारक-जनक-&c.

3 *involved in distress, miserable,* v. Wretched. दुःखी, दुखापन्न, आपत्प्राप्त, विपत्प्राप्त, दुःखग्रस्त, विपद्ग्रस्त, आपन्न, विपन्न.

Calamity, *n. misfortune, disaster, evil.* अनिष्ट*n.* अनिष्टापात*m.* अरिष्ट*n.* अभद्र*n.* अशुभ*n.* विपत्ति *f.* अपाय*m.* आपदा *f.* संकट*n.* समय*m. v.* ये, पड *with* बर, अवचट*n.* काल *or* ळ*m.* गजब*m.* अवात*n.* आफत *f.* आपत्ति *f.* विपदा *f.* विनिपात*m.* गंडांत*n.* गंडांतर*n.* व्यसन*n.* लाग*m.* घाल *f.* कालकंटक*m.*—intens. *an overwhelming or extreme c.* अनर्थ*m.* अनर्थापात*m.* आकांत*m.* गजब*m.* कहर*m.* उल्कापात*m.* उल्बण*n.* अवधंडा*m.*

Unexpected c. or mishap. अवचट *n.*

C. from Heaven,—as drought, deluge, lightning, &c. आस्मानी आफत *f.* आस्मानी *f.* देवकीप्रलय*m.* देवकीउपद्रव*m.* दैविक प्रलय*m.*-उपद्रव*m.*

C. from Kings or Governments,—as oppression, marauding, invasion, &c. सुलतानी आफत *f.* सुलतानी *f.* राजकीय *pop.* राजकी प्रलय*m.* राजकीय *pop.* राजकी उपद्रव*m.*

C. of season. ईति *f.* Seven are reckoned, viz. Drought,

deluge, rats, locusts, parrots, ravages of the State or of Banditti, foreign invasion. These two last, consisting mainly in the devastations of marching troops, are equally with the others, *calamities of season.*

C. from wet (inundations, heavy rains, &c.) ओली-आगf.

Some terms for a calamity from Heaven, Nature or chance (as distinguished from evils inflicted by man) are आकाशाची कुऱ्हाड *f.* आकाशाची धाड *f.*

CALASH, *n.* एकाप्रकारची गाडी आहे.

CALCAREOUS, *a. having the properties of lime.* चुन्याचे गुणाचा, चूर्णमय, चूर्णात्मक, चूर्णगुणात्मक, चूर्णधर्मक. [करणाई.

CALCINABLE, *a.* v. V. भस्मकरायाजोगा, भस्मीकरणयोग्य, भस्मी-

CALCINATION, *n.* v. V.—*act.*मारणेंn. भस्मीकरणn. जारणn.—*a. or s.* भस्मीकृति *f.* प्रतीवाप *m.*

To CALCINE, *v. a. reduce to a calx.* भस्मn.-भस्मीकरणn.-जारणn. करणें *g. of o.* मारणें.

CALCINED, *p.* v. V. भस्म केलेला-झालेला, भस्मीभूत, भस्मीकृत, मारलेला, मृत. [णारा.

CALCINER, *n.* v. V. भस्म करणारा, भस्मकर्त्ता, जारणकर्त्ता, मार-

CALCULABLE, *a.* v. V. गणनीय, गण्य, गणेय, गणितव्य, परिगणनीय, संख्येय.

CALCULARY, *a. relating to the stone in the bladder.* मुतखड्याचा, मुतखड्याविषयींचा.

To CALCULATE, *v. a. compute, reckon.* गणणें, मोजणें, गणन n.-संख्यानn.-&c. करणें, हिशेबm. करणें. [आकारणें.

2—roughly, conjecturally. v. To ESTIMATE. अजमासणें,

3—in astronomy *or* astrology. गणणें, वर्त्तवणें, पाहणें.

CALCULATED, *p.* & *a.*v.V. 1. गणलेला, गणित, संख्यात, गणीभूत.

2 अजमासलेला, अजमासी.

3 गणलेला, गणित, वर्त्तवलेला.

I. *adapted, fit,* v. SUITABLE. योग्य, उपयुक्त, कार्यक्षम, जोगता-जोगा (in comp).

CALCULATION, *n.* v. V. 1.—*act.* गणणेंn. गणनn. गणना *f.* संख्यानn. हिशेब *or* हिशोबm.—*a. or s.* गणती *f.* बराबरद *or* बर्दाबर्दी *f.*

C.—by or in years, months, &c.—by or in *candies, maunds,* &c. वर्षोगणती *f.* सालोगणती, महिनोगणती, &c. खंडोगणती, मणोगणती, शेरोगणती, लक्षोगणती, सहस्रोगणती, &c. *v.* लाग, (ex. या गोष्टीला वर्षोगणती लागती).

Rustic or rude c. कुणबी हिशेबm.

2—*act.* अजमासणें *n.* अजमास *m.* आटंका *m.*

3—*act.* गणणें *n.* &c.

I. *result of a c.* गणित *m.*

CALCULATOR, *n.* v. V. 1. गणणारा, गणन करणारा, गणती करणारा, गणनकर्त्ता, गणक, संख्यानकरणारा, संख्यानकर्त्ता, संख्याता, हिशेब करणारा.

2 अजमासणारा, आकारणारा, अजमासकरणारा.

3 गणक, वर्त्तवणारा, पाहणारा.

CALCULOUS. See STONY.

CALCULUS, *n.* v. STONE. मुतखडा *m.* खडा *m.*

CALDRON, *n.* v. KETTLE. देग *f.* हांडा *m.* उदकस्थाली *f.* कटाह *m.*

To CALEFY. See To HEAT.

CALENDAR, *n. almanac.* पंचांग *n.* पातडें *n.*

2 v. LIST. फेरिस्त *n.* याद *f.*

C. month. सौरमास *m.*

To CALENDAR, *v. a. smooth, &c.* (linen). कुंदी *f.* करणें, घोटणें.

CALENDERING, *n.* v. V.—*act.* कुंदी *f* घोटणें *n.* घोटणी *f.*

CALENDRER, *n.* v. V. कुंदी करणारा, कुंदीगर *or* गार, कापड घोटणारा.

CALENDS, *n. first day of the month.* प्रतिपदा *f.* पाडवा *m.*

Ad Græcas Calendas, at latter Lammas. कडच्या आदितवारीं,शेवटच्यावारीं, कालच्या आदितवारीं, उद्यांच्या आदितवारीं.

CALF, *n.* (of a cow). वांसरूं *n.* पाडें *n.* वत्स *n.* पाडूक *n.*

Bull or male c. गोहरा *or* गोऱ्हा, पाडा, सोंड, वत्स.

Female c. गोजी *or* गुजी, पाडी, कालवड, वत्सा.

Bull c. (or bull) branded and set at large. वसू.

Female c. (or heifer) do. वस्तीण.

2 (of a buffalo). रेडूक *n.* रेडकूं *n.* पारडूं *n.* वत्स *n.*

Bull or male c. ताठ्या *or* टाठ्या, वत्स.

Female c. वांठ, रेडी,पारडी,—in endearment, disparagement, contempt, &c. वांटरूं *n.* मांगुली *f.* रेडूक *n.*

3 (of a cow or buffalo). जावपेंn. जोपें *n.* जायपेंn. जोपn.m.

Muzzle for a c. (to prevent its sucking). मोहळा *or* मोळा *m.* मोहळें *or* मोळें *n.* मोवाळें *n.*

Pen for calves. खुडी *f.*

That produces fine calves. जावपे शुद्ध. [*f.*

4 (of the leg). पायाची पोटरी *f.* पोटरी *or* पोठरी *f.* जंघा

5 *dolt, blockhead,* v. FOOL. वांठीचा पिता *m.* बैल *m.* नरपशु *m.*

CALF-SKIN, *n.* वांसराचें-&c. कातडें *n.*

CALIBER, *n.* तोफेच्या-बंदुकेच्या-&c.तोंडचा व्यास *m.*-रुंदी *f.*-&c.

2 *bore or cavity.* तोफेचा-&c.खजिना *m.*-पोट *n.*-पोकळी *f.*-&c.

3 *diameter.* व्यास *m.*

4 *capacity,* v. UNDERSTANDING. अवांका *m.* अटोका *m.* पोहोंच *f. m.* [सवख *n.*

CALICO, *n. cotton cloth,* v. COTTON. कापसाचें कापड *n.* कार्पा-

2 *printed cotton cloth,* v. CHINTZ. छीट *n.*

CALID, CALIDITY. See HOT, HEAT.

CALIGRAPHY, *n.* कलमसफाई *f.* सुंदरलिपि *f.* खुशखत *n.*

CALIPH, *n.* खलिफा *or* पा *m.*

CALISTHENICS, *n.* तालीम *f.* कसरत *f.*

CALIX, *n. cup of flowers, &c.* कचोळें *n.* गोंड *n.* कंचुकी *f.* गोंडण *n.* तुरमणें *n.*

To CALK, *v. a. stop the seams* (of a ship, &c.). दरजबंदी *f.*-दरजगिरी *f.* करणें, सांधे *m. pl.* भरणें *g. of o.* सणडामर *n.* करणें. [देणें.

To CALL, *v. a.* v. To NAME. म्हणणें, बोलणें, आव्हानणें, नांव *n.*

To c. one's self. म्हणवणें.

2 v. To SUMMON. बोलावणें *or* बोलवणें, आव्हानणें.

3 *summon by crying out to.* बोलावणें *or* बोलवणें, हेाकारणें, हांकारणें, सादवणें *or* सादावणें, बोहणें *or* वाहणें, पुकारणें, कुकारणें, ललकारणें, हाक *f.* मारणें, हटकणें, साद *m. f.* घालणें, आवाहणें, आव्हानणें, पाचारणें, आकारणें, आकारणn.-आव्हानn.-आवाहनn.-पाचारणn. &c. करणें. —with implication of loudness and vehemence, and of multitudes, whether *by* or

to, हाकाटणें. [पाचारणें.

4 v. To Invite. आमंत्रणें, आमंत्रण *n.* करणें, बोलावणें,

5 v. To Invoke. धांवा *m.* मारणें-करणें, आवाहणें.

6 *convoke, convene,* v. To Assemble. जमवणें, मिळवणें, जमावणें.

7 for; See To Demand. To Require.

To Call, *v. n. come into visit.* भेटीस-दर्शनास-&c. येणें-जाणें.

2 out; *cry out,* v. To Bawl. ओरडून बोलणें, ओरडणें.

3 out; *speak loudly, exclaim.* ओरडणें, ओरडून बोलणें, मोठ्यानें बोलणें, गागणें, पुकारणें.

4 out to; v. To Halloo. हाक *f.* मारणें, साद *m. f.* घालणें-देणें, कुकारणें, अरोळी *f.* मारणें.

Call, Calling, *n.* v. V. A. 1.—*act.* म्हणणें *n.* &c. आव्हान *n.*

2—*act.* बोलवणें *or* बोलावणें *n.* &c. निमंत्रण *n.* आव्हान *n.*

3—*act.* बोलावणें *n.* &c. होकार *m.* हाक *f.* साद *m. f.* पुकार *or* रा *m.* कुकार *or* रा *m.* ललकारा *m.* हक्कार *m.* हाक *f.* आवाहन *n.* आव्हान *n.* आकारण *n.*—with implication, &c. हाकाटणें *n.* हाकाटा *m. dim.* हाकाटी *f.* हाकारा *m.* हाकाहाक *f.* हाकहूल *f.*

4—*act.* बोलावणें *n.* पाचारणें *n* आमंत्रणें*n.*&c. आमंत्रण*n.*&c.

5—*act.* धांवा करणें *n.* आवाहन *n.* &c.

6—*act.* जमावणें *n.* निमंत्रण *n.* &c.

v. V. N. 1.—*act.* भेटीस-येणें *n.*-जाणें-*n.* दर्शनास आगम *m.*

2 ओरड *f.* आरड *f.* [*f.*

4 ललकारणी *f.* ललकारी *f.* कुकारा *m.* साद *m f.* अरोळी *f.* हाक

To answer to a c. ओ *f.*-हाक *f.*-साद *m. f.* देणें.

Distance or reach of a c. हाक *f.*

I. *vocation,* v. Business. धंदा *m.* काम *n.* उद्योग *m.*

Called, *p.* v. V. A. 1. म्हटलेला &c. नांवाचा, नामाचा, नामक.

2 बोलावलेला, &c. आकारित, निमंत्रित, आहूत.

3 बोलावलेला, होकारलेला &c. आकारित, आहूत.

4 बोलावलेला, पाचारलेला, आमंत्रित, निमंत्रित.

5 आवाहित, आहूत, आवाहलेला.

6 मिळवलेला, &c. निमंत्रित.

Callosity, Callousness, *n.* v. A. 1. बहिरेपणा *m.* बधिरत्व *n.* सुनेपणा *m.* &c. स्पर्शानभिज्ञता *f.*

2 कोडगेपणा *m.* निलाजरेपणा *m.* बेदरदीपणा *m.* &c.

I. *a callous part, callus.* घटा *or* घट्टा *m.* टरू *n.* किन्ह *n.* किणें *n.* किणा *m.* किण *n.*

Callous, *a. hard, insensible.* बहिरा, बधिर, सुना, सून, निर्जीव, कठीण, सख्त, मुरदाड, कडवा, स्पर्शानभिज्ञ, अवेद्यस्पर्श.

To become c. lit. fig. बहिरावणें, मरणें.

2 fig. *hardened in mind,* v. Shameless. कोडगा, निगर्गटा, घायकटर *or* घायकटार, घायसेंटर, निसूक *or* निसूग, निदरदी, बेपरवा, बेदरदी. Some terms or phrases for *A callous, incorrigible person,* answering *to hardened dog, shameless brute, &c.* are लतगाढव, लतकोडगा, लतकुठा, लातबुक्या, खेटरखाऊ, लातखाऊ, कोडगेखाऊ, लाजटाकलेला, निलाजरा, मेलेंमढें आधीला भीत नाहीं, लातबुकी सदासुखी.

Callously, *adv.* v. A. 2. कोडगेपणानें, &c. बेपरवा-&c. होऊन, लाजटाकून-सोडून.

Callow, *a. unfledged.* पर फुटलेला नाहीं, कोंवळा, मुंढा, बेपर, अजातपक्ष, अनागतपक्ष. [निर्वेग.

Calm, *a. not windy.* निर्वात, निवात, अवात, संत *or* संथ, शांत,

2 *not rough, ruffled, &c.* संत *or* संथ, शांत, अक्षुब्ध, थंड, निवळ, स्थिर, निश्चल.

3 fig. *serene, tranquil, quiet, still.* शांत, थंड, स्थिर, स्वस्थ, शांतात्मा, शांतचेता, शांतचित्त, स्वस्थचित्त, सुमना, सुमनस्क.

To become c. स्वस्थावणें.

Calm, *n. stillness,* lit. निर्वात *n.* निवात *n.* शम *m.*

2 fig. *serenity, tranquillity, quiet, stillness,* v. Composure. शांति *f.* शांतावस्था *f.* थंडपणा *m.* शम *m.* शांतचित्त *n.* सौमनस्य *n.*

To Calm, *v. a.* lit. *still, quiet.* संतावणें *or* संथावणें, शांत-थंड-स्थिर-&c. करणें, शमविणें, निवविणें.

2 fig. *serenize, tranquilize, quiet,* &c.v.To Compose. शांतवणें *or* सांतवणें, संतावणें *or* संथावणें, स्वस्थावणें, शांत-स्वस्थ-स्थिर-थंड-&c. करणें. [रावणें.

To Calm, *v. n. become still,* &c. शमणें, निवणें, निवळणें, स्थि-

Calmed, *p.* v. V. A. 1. संतावलेला, शमवलेला, &c. शमित, शांत, उपशांत, प्रशांत. [त्वित.

2 शांतवलेला, &c. शमित, शांत, उपशांत, प्रशांत, प्रशांतात्मा, सां-

Calmer, *n.* Calming, *p. a.* v. V. 1. संतावणारा, शमवणारा, &c. शांत-&c. करणारा.

2 शांत-थंड-&c. करणारा, शांतिकर, शांतिकर्त्ता, शांतिक, शमक.

Calming, *n.* v. V. 1.—*act.* संतावणें *n.* शमविणें *n.* &c. शम *m.* शमन *n.* प्रशमन *n.*

2—*act.* शांतवणें *n.* &c. सांत्वन *n.* सांत्वना *f.* शम *m.* शमन *n.* सांतवीण *f.* साम *n.* प्रशम *m.* प्रशमन *n.*

v. V. N.—*state.* शमणें *n.* निवणें *n.* &c. शमन *n.*

Calmly, *adv.* v. A. 1. संथ, संथपणानें, स्थिरतेनें, निःशब्द, अक्षोभपूर्वक.

3 शांतीनें, शांतिपूर्वक, शांतपणानें, थंडाईनें, स्वस्थमनानें, स्वस्थांतःकरणानें, समाधानानें. [त्य *n.*

Calmness, *n.* v. A. 1. निर्वात *n.* निवात *n.* वाताभाव *m.* वातराहि-

2 संथपणा *m.* &c. स्थिरता *f.* अक्षोभ *m.* क्षोभाभाव *m.* अक्षुब्धता *f.*

3 *and* Composure, शांति *f.* थंडाई *f.* थंडावा *m.* शांतता *f.* शम *m.* धीर *m.* शांतबुद्धि *f.* क्रोधाभाव *m.*

Calomel, *n.* पाऱ्याची मात्रा *f.* रसभस्म *n.* ? पारदभस्म *n.* ?

Caloric, *n.* तेजस्तत्व *n.* ? उष्णता *f.* उष्णताबीज *n.*

Caloric, *a.* उष्णतेचा.

Calorific, *a.* तापजनक, उष्णताजनक-कारक, दाहकारक.

Caltrops, *n.*—the plant. गोखरू*m.* गोखरूचें झाड*n.*—the fruit. गोखरू *m.*

Calumba, *n.*—the drug. कलम काचरी *f.*

To Calumniate, *v. a.* v. To Asperse. बालंट *n.*-तुफान *n.*-आळ *f. m.*-&c. घेणें-घालणें *with* वर *of o.* अभिशंसन *n.*-अभिशाप *m.* करणें *g. of o.*

Calumniation, *n.* v. V.—*act.* तुफान घेणें *n.* &c. अभिशंसन *n.* अपवाद *m.* विकथन *n.*

Calumniator, *n.* v. V. *and* Asperser. तुफान घेणारा, &c. बालंटखोर, बालंटी, बालंट्या, कुभांडी, कुभांडखोर, कुधांडी, तुफानखोर, कैवाडी, चहाडखोर, चहाडबुचका, अभिशापक, अपवादक, मिथ्याभिशंसी.

Calumniatory, Calumnious, *a.* v. Slanderous. तुफानाचा, बालंटाचा, कुभांडाचा, चुगलीचा, &c. तुफानी, बालंटी, कुभांडी, अभिशंसी, अभिशापक, अपवादक, मिथ्याभिशंसी,

CALUMNIOUSLY, *adv.* v. N. तुफानघेऊन, आळघेऊन, चहाडीकरून.

CALUMNY, *n.* v. SLANDER. तोहमत *f.* चुगली *f.* चहाडी *f.* आळ *f.* असूया *f.* तुफान *n.* कैवाड *n.* अभिशाप *m.* अपवाद *m.*

Covert or whispered c. फुसकी *f.* फुसकुली *f.*

To scatter calumnies. आग *f.* पाखडणें.

To CALVE, *v. n.* विणें, पसवणें, वांसरूं *n.*-वत्स *m.*-जावपें *or* जोपें *n.*-जोप *n.*-&c. देणें-घालणें.

That calves yearly. वर्षवीण, समस्की, सामाशी, सामास्की.

That has twice calved. दुजाईत, दुवेती, दोहोंविताची.

CALX, *n.* भस्म *n.* Some of the *calces* are ताम्रभस्म, पारदभस्म *or* रसभस्म, प्रवालभस्म, मौक्तिकभस्म, लोहभस्म, वंगभस्म, सुवर्ण भस्म, माक्षिक भस्म, अभ्रक भस्म, गंधक भस्म, हीरक भस्म, रत्नभस्म.

CALYX, *n.* *outer covering of a flower.* पुष्पकोश *m.* पुष्पवेष्टन *n.*

CAMBRIC, *n.* एक तलमसुती कापड आहे.

CAMEL, *n.*—male. उंट *or* ऊंट, उष्ट्र—female, उंटीण, सांड, सांडीण (—in contempt सांडरूं *n.*), उष्ट्री *or* उष्ट्रिका.—in jocose speech. आकाशमुनि *m.*

Bridle or nose-string of a c. नुकता *m.* नथणी *f.* Pin of it fixed in the nose. नकील *n.*

Bunch or hump of a c. मदार *f.* डुबर *n.*

C.–ground, C.–yard, &c. उष्टरखाना *m.*

Gun carried upon a c. शुतुरनाल *or* सुतरनाल *f.*

Line or string of camels. कतार *f.* कतारा *m.*

Rider upon a c. शुतरस्वार *c.*

Rider upon a female c. सांडणीस्वार *c.*

Rubbing c. *c. that rubs.* बगली उंट,—Soreness arising from rubbing. बगली *f.*

Sacking for the burden of a c. शलिता *or* सलिता *m.*

Saddle for a c. पलाण *n. f.*

Young c. करभ *m.*

Belonging or relating to a c. उंटाचा, औष्ट्र.

CAMEL-DRIVER, *n.* सारवान, दभाशी *or* सी.

CAMEL-NECKED *a.* उंटमान्या, उंटाचे मानेचा.

CAMLET, *n.* एकाप्रकारचें कापड आहे.

CAMELOPARD, *n.* एकाजातीचें जनावर आहे.

CAMEO, *n.* ज्याजवर वर आलेलें खोदकाम आहे असें रत्न किंवा शिंप.

CAMP, *n. ground.* तळ *m* गोट *m.* सेनानिवेश *m.* निवेश *m.* शिबिर *n.*

Appointed spot for a tent in a c. मिसल *f.*

Following a c. (for subsistence &c.). लशकरगिरी *f.*

Quarter or division of a c. गोट *m.* शिबिर *n.*

To CAMP, *v. n.* *encamp.* डेरे *m.pl.*-तळ *m.* देणें.

CAMP-FOLLOWER, *n.* लशकरीमाणूस *c.* लशकरगिरीकरणारा, सेनाचर.

CAMPAIGN, *n.* *level tract,* v. PLAIN. मैदान *n.* पटांगण *n.* सपाटी *f.* समस्थल *pop.* समथळ *n.*

2 (of an army). स्वारी *f.* सफर *f.* मोहीम *f.* मुलुकगिरी *f.*

CAMPAIGNER, *n.* *veteran.* बापरलेला-वहिवाटलेला शिपाई.

CAMPANIFORM, *a.* घांटेच्या आकाराचा, घंटाकार.

CAMPHOR, *n.* कापूर *m.* कर्पूर *m.* Some kinds or varieties are चंद्रसेनी कापूर, भीमसेनीकापूर, रंभाकर्पूर.

CAMPHOR-LINIMENT, *n.* कापरेल *n.* कर्पूरतैल *pop.* कापूरतेल *n.*

CAMPHOR-OIL, *n.* कापरेल *n.* कर्पूरतैल *n.*

CAMPHOR-TREE, *n.* कापराचें झाड *n.*

CAMPHOR-WATER, *n.* कापरवणी *n.*

CAMPHORATE, CAMPHORATED, *a.* कापुराचा, कर्पूराक्त, कर्पूरयुक्त, कर्पूरमिश्रित, कर्पूरान्वित.

To CAN, *v. n.* v. ABLE. सकणें *or* शकणें, समर्थ-&c. असणें.

CAN, *n.* आंकड्याचें पंचपात्र *n.*

CANAILLE, *n.* *dregs of the people,* v. PEOPLE. लोकांचा गाळ *m.* -गदळ *n.* लुलें *n.* लोकांची खरवड *f.* महारपोर *n.* गाबाळ लोक *m.pl.*

CANAL, *n.* कालवा *m.* मोठीप्रणाली *f.* सारणी *f.* कुल्या *f.* कृत्रिमनदी *f.* कृत्रिमासरित् *f.*

2 *duct or passage in the body.* नळ *m.* नळी *f.*

CANARY, *n.* एकाजातीचा गाणारापक्षी *m.*

To CANCEL, *v. a.* *cross out, obliterate, annul,* v. To EFFACE. छकणें, खोडणें, फांटा *m.* देणें-मारणें-घालणें, छेका *m.* मारणें, रद्द करणें, पूज *n.* घालणें, रेघ *f.* मारणें.

Line drawn in cancelling. छेका *m.*

CANCELLED, *p.* v.V. छकलेला, खोडलेला, छेकामारलेला, रद्दकेलेला, &c. रद्द.

CANCELLATION, CANCELLING, *n.* v. V. छकणें *n.* खोडणें *n.* छेकामारणें *n.*

CANCER, *n.* *crab fish.* खेकडा *m.*

2 (of the zodiac). कर्क *m.*

3—the tumor. पुळी *f.* चाळ *or* चाळणपुळी *f.* विद्रधि *m.*

C. of the breast. स्तनविद्रधि *m.* थानखांडूक *n.*

CANCHORIE ROOT-PLANT, *n.* कळलावी *f.* खड्यानाग *m.*

CANDID, *a.* *fair, open, ingenuous, sincere,* v. FRANK. निष्कपट, अकपट, मनाचा मोकळा, अकृत्रिम, निष्प्रांजल, प्रांजल *pop.* प्रांजळ, शुद्धमति, साळढाळ, मनाचा पाक, दिलपाक.

2 *fair &c.*—applied to things. निष्कपट, प्रांजळ, प्रांजळपणाचा, सरलबुद्धीचा, सरलभावाचा.

CANDIDATE, *n.* उमेदवार *c.* पदाभिलाषी, पदयाचक, पदकामुक.

CANDIDLY, *adv.* v. A. निष्कपट, कपटसोडून, मोकळ्यामनानें, मन मोकळें करून, निवळ, सालसाईनें, सरलबुद्धीनें, सरलभावानें.

CANDIDNESS, *n.* See CANDOUR.

CANDIED, *p.* v. V. पांकलेला, पांकविलेला.

CANDLE, *n.*—tallow. चरबत्ती *f.*—wax. मेणबत्ती *f.* मेणवात *f.*

C. of whitest wax. कपुरीमेणबत्ती *f.*

CANDLE-STICK, *n.* v. LAMP-STAND. बत्तीचेंघर *n.*

Branch c. दिव्याचें झाड *n.* दीपवृक्ष *m.* शिखातरु *m.*

CANDOUR, CANDIDNESS, *n.* v. A. 1.निष्कपटपणा *m.* निष्कपटता *f.* निष्कापट्य *n.* मनाचा मोकळेपणा *m.* सरलभाव *m.* सरलबुद्धि *f.* सालसाई *f.* दिलपाकी *f.* मनःप्राशस्त्य *n.*

To CANDY, *v. a.* *conserve with sugar, &c.* पांकणें, पांकविणें.

CANDY, *n.*—sugar c. खडीसाखर *f.* मिसरी *f.*

2—the Indian weight. खंडी *f.*

CANE, *n.* *calamus rotang.* वेत *m.* वेत्र *n.*

2 *switch, &c.* वेताची छडी *f.* छडी *f.* वेताटी *f.* वेताची काठी *f.* वेतकाठी *f.* कमची *f.* चमकी *f.*

3 See SUGAR-CANE.

To CANE, *v. a.* वेताखालीं-छड्या खालीं-&c. मारणें, वेतानें-छडीनें &c. पाठ *f.* फोडणें, छडी *f.* चमकावणें, चमकावणें, फडफडवणें, फडत्कार *m.*-दंडपारुष्य *n.* करणें.

To c. smartly. धडाधडी *f.* करणें *g. of o.* चमकाविणें.

CANE, *a.* *made, &c. of c.* वेताचा.

CANINE, *a.* कुत्र्याचा, श्वसंबंधी, श्वविषयक, शौन.

C. race. श्वजन m.
CANISTER, n. डबा m. dim. डबी f.
CANKER, n. v. WORM. कीड f. किडा m. कीट m.
2 See CANCER.
To CANKER. See To CORRODE.
CANNIBAL, n. मनुष्याचें मांस खाणारा, मनुष्याद, नरभक्षक, नरभोजी, नराशी, पुरुषाद, मानवाद.
CANNIBALISM, n. मनुष्यादन n. पुरुषाशन n. नरभक्षण n.
CANNON, n. तोफ f. नाळ f. भांडें n. जंबुरा m. उल्हाटयंत्र n.
Blank-discharge of c. बायबार m.
CANNON-BALL, CANNON-SHOT, n. गोळा m. गोळी f.
Range of a c. गोळ्याचा टप्पा m. गोळ्याची मारणी f. (or गोळीचा टप्पा-&c.).
To CANNONADE, v. a. तोफा f. pl. सोडणें-मारणें *with* वर *of* o. तोफेचा मार m.-मारा m.-मारगिरी f. करणें.
CANNONADE, n. तोफांचा मार m.-मारा m.-भडमार m.
CANNONEER, n. गोलंदाज m. तोफेचें काम करणारा m.
CANOE, n. डोणी f. डोंगा m. पगार m. पाग m. होडी f. dim. होडकी f. & होडकें or गें n. प्लुव m.
Outrigger of a c. उलंडी f.—Arm of it. बावखंड n.
CANON, n. *statute, institute,* v. LAW. कानू f. कायदा m. जाबता m. शेरा m. सूत्र n. विधिm. विधान n.
Sacred c. genuine books of the Holy Scriptures. बैबलाचीं-ख्रिस्तीशास्त्राचीं असल पुस्तकें n. pl.
2—the dignitary. ख्रिस्ती मंडळींतला एक धर्माधिकारी आहे.
3 *catalogue of saints.* संतावळी f.
CANON-LAW, n. *body of ecclesiastical law.* धर्मशास्त्रसंहिता f.
CANONICAL, a. *according to the canon.* कायद्याशीर, कायद्याचा, कायद्यासरुजू-बरोबर, विध्युक्त, विध्यनुयायी, विध्यनुसारी, विधिप्रोक्त, धर्मशास्त्रसम्मत, सौत्र, स्मार्त. [ध्यनुसार.
CANONICALLY, adv. v. A. यथाविधि, यथाशास्त्र, विध्यनुरूप, वि-
CANONIST, n. धर्मशास्त्री m. पाठक m. धर्मशास्त्रज्ञ, विधिज्ञ.
CANOPUS, n.—the star. अगस्ति m.
CANOPY, n.—of a bedstead, couch, &c. चांदवा m. छत n. v. भर, छप्पर n. घटाटोप m. [बरडोलm.
2 of a carriage, native palanquin, &c. पिंजरी f. घटाटोप m. चं-
C. of light frame work over an idol. मंडपी f. चंवरडोली f.
To CANOPY, v. a. छत n. लावणें-बांधणें, चांदवा m. बांधणें.
CANT, n. *particular phraseology.* श्रेणीभाषा f. विशेषभाषा f. सांकेतिक भाषा f. संज्ञेची भाषा f.
The cant language of tradesmen. नंदभाषा f. [बोली f.
2—religious. वाग्वेदांत m. वाग्वेदांताचें बोलणें n. मानभावी
To CANT, v. n. v. To WHINE. कन्हेरी f.-रड f. गाणें-सांगणें.
To CANT, v. a. *pitch forward, incline* (a cask, &c.) कानवडा करणें.
2 *give a sudden impulse to.* आचका m.-हिसका m.-&c. देणें.
CANTER, n.—the pace. चौकचाल f. सात्रकचाल f. प्लुतगति f.
2 v. HYPOCRITE. वाग्वेदांती, वागूब्रह्मज्ञानी, तोंडचा ब्रह्मज्ञानी.
To CANTER, v. n. चौकणें, चौकचालीनें चालणें.
To CANTER, v. a. चौकचालीवर चालविणें.
CANTERBURY-TALE, n. *fiction.* कल्पित कादंबरी f. भंडपुराण n.
CANTHUS, n. *angle of the eye.* डोळ्याचाकोपरा m. नेत्रकोण m.
Outer c. नेत्रप्रांत m. नयनोपांत m.

CANTICLE, See SONG.
CANTO, n. (of a poem). सर्ग m.
CANTON. See DISTRICT.
CANTONMENT, n. छावणी f.
CANVAS, n. *sailcloth.* चिवटा m. किंतान n. टाट n.
CANVAS, a. चिवट्याचा, टाटाचा, किंतानाचा, चिवटी.
To CANVAS, v. a. *sift,* v. To EXAMINE. छाननें, छान f. करणें, छडा m.-झाडा m.-शोध m. लावणें-काढणें-करणें.
2 *debate,* v. To ARGUE. घोळणें, घाटणें, घोळ m. घालणें.
To CANVAS, v. n. *solicit votes.* सम्मत n. मागणें-विचारणें.
CANY, a. वेताचा, वेतसमय, वेतसप्रचुर.
CANZONET. See SONG.
CAP, n. *covering for the head.* टोपी f. शिरोवेष्टन n. शिरस्त्राण n.
C. worn by women and children. टकोचें n. टोपडें or टोपरें n. कुंचडें n.
C. that covers the ears. कानटोपी f.
Military c. टोपी f.
"The cap of fools". मूर्खशिरोमणि. [पण n.
2 *knot of brass, &c.* शेंब f. or शेंबी f. शेंबलें or शेंबली f. टो-
To CAP, v. a. *cover with a c. or top.* शेंबी f.-शेंब f. लावणें-घालणें-बसवणें.
To c. verses. The exercises amongst scholars corresponding with *Capping of verses* are आद्याक्षरी f. अंत्याक्षरी f. प्रतिमाला f.
To win at capping verses. भंडी f. लावणें-चढवणें.
CAP A PIE, *adv. from head to foot.* आपादमस्तक, आनखशिख, नखशिखांत.
CAPABILITY, n. v. A. 1. मावूनघेण्याची योग्यता f. अवकाशपर्याप्ति f. धारणसामर्थ्य n.
2 शक्ति f. योग्यता f. कर्त्तृत्व n. क्षमता f. कार्यक्षमता f.
3 दक्षता f. दाक्षिण्य n. दाक्ष्य n. काबिली f. काबिलपणा m.
CAPABLE, a. *sufficiently capacious.* मावून घ्याया-जोगा-जोगता-&c. सांठव्याचा, अवकाशपर्याप्त, अवकाशपर्याप्तिविशिष्ट, निवासपर्याप्त, धारणसमर्थ.
2 *of adequate ability,* v. COMPETENT. योग्य, लायक, कार्यक्षम, क्षम, शक्त. [बील, प्रभु.
3—mentally; *able, talented,* &c. v. CLEVER. कर्त्ता, दक्ष, का-
4 See SUSCEPTIBLE.
CAPACIOUS, a. *wide, spacious,* v. ROOMY. ऐसपैसाचा, ऐसपैस, प्रशस्त, सावकाश, पोटारा, विशाल, बहुग्रह.
2 (of mind) v. COMPREHENSIVE. आटोपाचा, मोठ्या सांठव्याचा, मोठ्या आटंक्याचा, बहुग्रह.
CAPACIOUSNESS, n. v. A. 1. पैसपणा m. ऐसपैसपणा m. प्रशस्तपणा m. प्राशस्त्य n.
2 See CAPACITY. [करणें.
To CAPACITATE, v. a. *make fit.* योग्य-लायक-क्षम-कार्यक्षम-&c.
CAPACITY, n. v. A. 1. *power of containing, room.* सांच m. सांठ m. सांठपा m. धर m. पोट n. समाई f. समावा m. कोठी f.
Of c.—a measure. कैली, मापी, (ex. कैली खंडी-मण-शेर, &c. मापी खंडी-मण-&c.).
2 *reach or power of the mind,* v. UNDERSTANDING. आकलन शक्ति f. आक्रमशक्ति f. कक्ष f. कवळ n. अवांका m. अटोंका or आटंका m. आव m. जिव्हाळा m. बुद्धीची धांव f. पोहंच m. f.

Suitable or suitably with one's c. यथाबुद्धि, यथामति.

To be within one's c. आहारीं-अवसानांत-&c. असणें *g. of s.*

I. *condition, character.* नातें *n.* पेशा *m.* अधिकार *m.* पदवी *f.* हुद्दा *m.*

CAPARISON, *n.*—of a horse. गाशा*m.* चारजमा *or* चारजामा*m.*—of a horse or elephant. पाखर *f.*

To CAPARISON, *v. a.*—a horse. गाशा *m.*-चारजमा *m.* टाकणें-घालणें-करणें, सज्ज करणें.

2 *dress pompously.* वस्त्र भूषणानें सजविणें-नटविणें-शृंगारणें.

CAPE, *n. promontory.* भूमीचें टोंक *n.* भूशलाका *f.* भूशिर *n.*

2 (of a garment), *neck-piece.* खोळ *f.*

To CAPER, *v. n.* v. To FRISK. खिदडणें, खिदळणें, खिदडे *m. pl.* घालणें, उडणें, उड्या *f. pl.* मारणें, नाचणें.

To bound or c.—a horse. चौकणें.

To jump & caper about—a child, &c. टिणटिण-टणटण उड्या *f. pl.* मारणें.

CAPERS, CAPERING, *n.* v.V.—*act.* खिदडणें *n.* &c. खिदडा *m.* नाच *m.* उड्या *f. pl.*

Wild capering. बोकंदळ *or* बोकांदळ *n.*

CAPILLAMENT, *n.* केसर *m. pop.* केंसर *n.* तांनू *m.* तंतु *m.*

CAPILLARY, *a small like a hair.* केशासारखा बारीक, केशतुल्य, केशमात्र, अतिसूक्ष्म.

C. attraction. केशाकर्षण *n.*

CAPITAL, *a. relating to the head or top.* शिराचा, शिरोभागसंबंधी, मस्तकसंबंधी, वरचा, वरला, वरील, शीर्षण्य, मूर्धन्य.

2 *principal,* v. CHIEF. मुख्य, श्रेष्ठ, अग्रणी, अग्रगण्य, वर्य, वरेण्य.

3—punishment. प्राणांतिक, प्राणांत, देहांत, मरणांत.

4—crime. प्राणांतदंडाचा, मृत्युदंडाई, देहांतदंडाई, मृत्युद.

5 *noble, excellent, &c.* v. FINE. भला *or* भल्ला, खासा, नामी, उमदा, शेलका, उत्कृष्ट.

6—a letter. मोठा.

CAPITAL, *n. chief city.* राजधानी*f.* राजनगर*n.* मुख्यनगर*n.* तखताची जागा *f.*

2 *trader's stock,* v. STOCK. मुद्दल*n.* पुंजी *f.* भांडवल *or* भांडोल*n.* मूलद्रव्य *n.* मूलधन *n.*

3 *large letter.* मोठावर्ण *m.* मोठें अक्षर *n.*

4 *upper part of a pillar.* स्तंभशीर्ष *n.*

CAPITALIST, *n.* पुंजीवाला, भरण्याचा, भरणेवाईक, भरणेदार, भरणेकरी, भरणेवाला.

CAPITALLY, *adv.* v.A. 5 उत्कृष्टरीतीनें, उत्तमप्रकारानें.

CAPITATION, *n. numeration by the head.* शिरगणती *f.* शिरोगणना *f.*

C.—tax. डोईपट्टी *f.* माणूस पट्टी *f.*

To CAPITULATE, *v. n. draw up in articles.* कलमबंदी *f.* करणें, कलमवार लिहणें-करणें.

2 *surrender upon terms.* कौलानें-कौल मागून-कौल घेऊन-&c. सोडणें-हवाला*m.* देणें-वश होणें-शरण जाणें-&c. कौलास येणें.

To wave a flag or cloth in indication of capitulating. रुमाल*m.* फिरवणें-उडवणें.

CAPON, *n.* खची केलेला कोंबडा *m.*

To CAPON, CAPONIZE. *v. a.* खची करणें.

CAPRICE, *n.* v. WHIM. लहर *f.* तरंग *m.* छंद*m.* असद्रूह *m.*

CAPRICIOUS, *a.* v. CHANGEABLE. उचलचावडा, लहरी, लहरीदार, ऐच्छिक, चंचल, चंचलबुद्धीचा, क्षणिकबुद्धि, छंदखोर.

2—temper, &c. चंचलपणाचा, चंचलबुद्धीचा, क्षणिकबुद्धीचा, छंदिष्टपणाचा.

CAPRICIOUSLY, *adv.* v. A. लहरीनें *or* लहरलहरीनें, लहर येऊन, तालताल, छंदिष्टपणानें.

CAPRICIOUSNESS, *n.* v. A. 1. उचलचावडेपणा*m.* लहरीपणा*m.* छंदखोरी *f.* चांचल्य *n.* चंचलता *f.* चंचलबुद्धि *f.* मनोलौल्य *n.*

CAPRICORN, *n.*—sign of the zodiac. मकर*m.*

Entrance of the sun into c. मकरसंक्रांति *f.* मकरसंक्रमण*n.* This holiday is *especially* observed by women. Some of the numberless rites or acts upon the occasion are अवा लुटविणें, खेळणें रांगणें, सुगडें बसणें, and some of their offerings made to Bráhmans, or gifts interchanged amongst themselves, are अचळवीवाण, घासग्रास, चिरचोळी, तिळगूळ, तिळवण, पाठपोट, भोगविडा, रसरंग, हिरेंदिवे.

CAPRIOLE, *n.* बकरकुदाई *f.* बकरकुदी *f.*

CAPSICUM, *n.* v. PEPPER. मोगली मिरची *f.*

To CAPSIZE, *v. a. overturn.* उलथा-उपडा-&c. करणें, उलथणें.

CAPSTAN, *n.* नांगर उठविण्याचें यंत्र*n.*

CAPSULAR, CAPSULARY. See HOLLOW.

CAPSULE, *seed-vessel.* बोंड*n.* बीजकोश *m.* कर्णिका *f.*

CAPTAIN, *n. chief commander.* अधिपति*m.* धनी*m.*स्वामी*m.* सरदार*n.*

2 (of a ship). नाखोदा *or* नाखवा*m.* तांडेल*m.* नौकाध्यक्ष*m.* नौकाधिपति*m.* [नायकवडा*m.*

3 (of a band, gang, &c.). नायक *pop.* नाईक*m.* नायकडा*m.*

4 (of a body;—as of spearmen, couriers, peons, public laborers &c.). नायक, हवालदार, जमादार, तांडेल, मिरधा, मुकद्दम (his office &c. मुकद्दमी *f.*).

5 For the commander of a company in a Regiment the English word is familiarly known as कपतान.

6 *one skilled in war.* v. WARRIOR. युद्धकुशल.

CAPTAINCY, CAPTAINSHIP, *n. office, &c. of a captain.* सरदारी *f.* सरदारकी *f.*आधिपत्य *n.* स्वामित्व *n.*

2 (in a Regt.). कपतानाची जागा *f.*-पदवी *f.*-&c.

CAPTIOUS, *a. given to cavil.* तकरारी, तकरारखोर, दिकती, दिकतखोर, बोलभांड, अधांट्या, आडफांट्या, चिकित्सखोर, हुजतखोर, हुजती, कांक्षी, कांक्षाखोर, अढे वेढे घेणारा, आडफांटे फोढणारा, फांटे फोडणारा *f.* [चाचा.

2 *fitted to catch, insidious.* पकडीचा, धरपकडीचा, पेंचपा-

3 *proceeding from a cavilling disposition.* दिकतखोरीचा, हुज्जतखोरीचा, आडफांट्याचा.

CAPTIOUSLY, *adv.* v. A. दिकतखोरीनें,&c. तकरारीनें, अढेवेढे घेऊन, आडफांटे फोडून, &c.

CAPTIOUSNESS, *n.* v. A. 1. दिकतखोरी *f.* हुजतखोरी *f.* तकरारखोरी *f.*&c.

To CAPTIVATE, *v. a. take prisoner.* युद्धांत धरणें, धरणें, पाडावकरणें *or* करून घेणें.

2 *fascinate, enchant,* v. To CHARM. मोहून वश करणें, मोहणें, भारणें, मोह*m.*-मोहनी *f.* घालणें, मोहित करणें.

CAPTIVATING, *a.* v. CHARMING. मोहून वशकरणारा, मोहित करणारा, मनमोहक.

CAPTIVE, *n.* v. PRISONER. कैदी, पाडाव केलेला, युद्धदास.

CAPTIVE, *a.* युद्धांत धरलेला, पाडाव केलेला, युद्धधृत, युद्धगृहीत.

CAPTIVITY, *n. bondage.* बंदी *f.* कैद *f.* सबंधता *f.* संबद्धता *f.* संबद्धावस्था *f.* दासत्व *n.* वशीभूतता *f.*

CAPTOR, CAPTURER, *n.* v. V. युद्धांत धरणारा, पाडाव करणारा, धरणारा, जितद्रव्य. [निग्रह *m.*

CAPTURE, CAPTURING, *n.* v. V.—*act.* धरणें *n.* &c. पाडाव *m.* I. *thing taken,* v. PRIZE. पाडावजिन्नस *m.* जितद्रव्य *n.* लूट *f.*

To CAPTURE, *v. a.* युद्धांत धरणें, पाडाव करणें, धरणें, हस्तगत करून घेणें.

CAPTURED, *p.* v. V. युद्धांत धरलेला, पाडाव, धरलेला.

CAPUT MORTUUM, *n. worthless remains.* चोंथा *m.* गाळ *m.*

CAR, *n. chariot of war or splendor.* रथ *m.* स्यंदन *m.*

C.—warrior, *n.* रथी, रथिक.

Celestial c. विमान *n.*

Festival of cars. रथोत्सव *m.* रथोत्साह *m.*

Uncarred warrior. विरथवीर.

2 See CARRIAGE.

CARABINE, *n.* कराबीन *f.* करवलीबंदूक *f.* दामा *m.*

CARABINEER, *n.* करवल *m.*

CARAT, *n.* सोनाराचें एक वजन आहे.

CARAVAN, *n.* काफला *m.* पथिकसंतति *f.* सार्थ *m.*

C. of horse dealers. कारवान *m.*

CARAVANSARY, *n.* सराई *f.* धर्मशाळ *f.* पथिकशाला *f.*

CARAWAY, *n.* ओंवा *m.* अजमोदा *m.* अजवान *m.* [माणकी *f.*

CARBUNCLE, *n. ruby.* लाल *m.* माणिक्य *pop.* माणीक *m. dim.*

2 *red pimple, anthrax.* गरमीचा फोड *m.* गरमीची पुळी *f.*

3 (on the back). काळपुळी *f.* काळफोड *m.* देटपुळी *f.*

CARCANET, *n.* रत्नमाला *f.*

CARCASS, *n. dead body.* मढें *n.* मुडदा *m.* शव *n.* प्रेत *n.* लोथ *or* लोध *f.* लोधा *m.*—of a beast. पडें *n.*

2 *body,* —in contempt. कुडी *f.* कूड *f.* कलेवर *n.* लोधा *m.* लोथ *f.* मुरकुंडी *f.* [टा *m.*

3 *skeleton,* v. FRAME, SKELETON. सांगाडा *m.* खटारा *m.* सां-

CARD, *n. playing c.* गंजिफांतलें पान *n.* गंजीफ *f.* पान *n.*

Back of a c. पुस्त *f.*

Face of a c. रू *n.*

Picture c. चित्र *n.*

Pack of cards. गंजिफा *m.* गंजिफा *f.pl.* There are three packs of cards, viz. चंग कांचन गंजिफा, दशावतारी गंजिफा, and बाराराशीगंजिफा. The first has 8 suits, the second has 10 suits, and the third has 12 suits. Suit at cards रंग *m.* रुपें *n.* बाजू *or* बाजी *f.* The suits of the first pack are चंग, कांचन, बरात, खुमाश *or* स, ताज, गुलाम, रूप, समशेर. The suits of the second correspond with the 10 incarnations of Vishnu; and the suits of the third with the 12 signs of the zodiac. A few of the numerous terms used by *Card-players* are thrown together here. काट, काटणी, काटणी वाटणी, काडी, केंतेपान, घेणी, चंगचिह्नी *or* चंगचिह्नत, चंगाराणी, देणी, चढतीबाजू, चव्वा *or* चौवा, चाळणी, चोर, छक्का, छक्कापंजा, जबर, तावनदस्त, तिह्मल, तिक्का, तिगस्त, नहलू *or* ल्या, नादर, पानबाजी, बुळी, बूज, रंगडाव *or* रंगबाजी, रंगलूट, जेरजबर डाव, रंगघानी, सत्या, सेत्याचा डाव, दाबदुबीचा डाव, वहल्या, अहया, सुरक्या, राजतलफ, सर, हरडू.

To have a run of ill luck at cards. पड *f.* लागणें.

2 *note, ticket, &c.* चकती *f.* टिकिट *n.* from the English is common.

To CARD, *v. a. comb.* पिंजणें, पिंजारणें, धुणकणें, धनुकणें, तोडणें.

CARDAMON, *n.*—the plant. एलचीचेंझाड *n.* एला *f.*—the seed. इलाची *f.* एलदोडा *m.* एलची *f.* एला *f.* एलाची *f.*

CARDER, *n.* v. V. पिंजणारा, पिंजारणारा, पिंजारी.

Bow of c. धनुकली *f.* धनु *m.*

CARDIAC, *a. cordial.* हृद्रोगनिवारक. [हार्द.

CARDIAC, *a. belonging &c. to the heart.* हृदयाचा, हृदयसंबंधी,

CARDING, *n.* v. V.—*act.* पिंजणें *n.* पिंजारणें *n.* पिंजणी *f.*

Price or cost of c. पिंजणावळ *f.* पिंजारणावळ *f.*

CARDINAL, *a.* v. CHIEF. मुख्य, श्रेष्ठ.

CARDINAL, *n.* रोमनक्याथलिकपंथांतला एक धर्माधिकारी आहे.

CARE, *n. solicitude, anxiety, concern.* काळजी *f.* चिंता *f.* परवा *f.* आस्था *f.* आंच *f.* आंचणी *f.* फिकीर *f.* चुरचूर *f.* जिव्हाळा *m.* तिडीक *f.* दरद *f.m.* घोर *m.* कळकळ *f.* हळहळ *f.* कोजळ *f.* हृद्रोग *m.* उद्वेग *m.* ताप *m.* वेध *m.* क्षति *f.* क्षीत *f.*

2 *regard, heed, attention to.* जतन *n.* खबरदारी *f.* ओज *f.* ऊर्जा *pop.* उर्जा *f.* निगा *or* निघा *f.* निघादास्त *f.* माजबत *f.* केळवण *n.*

Take c.! Have a c.! खबरदार, जप, जपून ऐस, संभाळ.

With c. जपून, संभाळून, जतन करून.

3 *careful treatment or usage.* ओज *f.* उर्जा *f.* निगा *or* निघा *f.* निघादास्त *f.* बरदास्त *f.* तवाजू *f.* जोपासणी *f.* जोपासना *f.* जोपाशीर *or* जोपाशील *f.* माजबत *f.* निमूत *f.* निगुताई *f.*

To take c. of. जतन *n.* करणें-ठेवणें-राखणें *g. of o.* जतनेस ठेवणें, जपून ठेवणें, ओज *f.*-उर्जा *f.*-&c. राखणें *g. of o.* खबर *f.*-शोध *m.* ठेवणें *g. of o.* निघादास्त *f.* ठेवणें-करणें-पाहणें *g. of. o.* पाहणें, संभाळणें, जतनावणें, जोंबाळणें, जोगावणें, जोपासणें, संगोपन *n.* करणें, माजबत *f.* करणें *g. of o.* माजबतीनें-माजबतींत ठेवणें. [ताबा *m.*

3 *keeping, oversight, &c.* v. CHARGE. हवाला *m.* दिम्मत *f.*

To commit to the c. of. हवालीं देणें, हवालणें, दिम्मतीस -&c. ठेवणें.

To CARE, *v. n. have solicitude, anxiety, concern.* चिंता *f.* वाहणें *g. of o.* काळजी. *f.* वाहणें-करणें-धरणें *g. of o.* फिकीर *f.* करणें *g. of o.* चिंता *f.*- घोर *m.*-&c. लागणें *g. of o. in. con.*

2 *be inclined, disposed, desirous,* v. To DESIRE. चाहणें, चहा *f.*-आवड *f.*-चाड *f.* लागणें *in. con.* गरज *f.* ठेवणें *g. of o. or* शीं.

3 for; *mind, heed.* जुमानणें, गुमानणें, जुमास *m.*-जुमान *m.*-गुमान *m.* बाळगणें-खाणें.

CARE-CRAZED, *a.* चिंताविक्षिप्त, चिंतामूढ.

To CAREEN, *v. a. make to lie on one side,*—ship. कानवडा करणें, कुशीस करणें-आणणें.

CAREER, *n. race, course.* दौड *f.* धांव *f.* धांवड *f.* [&c.

2 *height of speed.* धांवण्याचाझपाठा *m.*-सपाटा *m.*-तडाखा *m.*-

3 *course of action,* v. COURSE. ओळ *f.* ओळा *m.* वर्तनक्रम *m.*

To CAREER, *v. n. move rapidly and smoothly.* सुरळीत-सुसाट-&c. चालणें.

CAREFUL, *a.* v. N. 1. *anxious, solicitous.* काळजीचा, चिंतायुक्त,

चिंताग्रस्त, चितान्वित, सचिंत, चिंतागत, उद्वेगी, आस्थेकरी, आस्थेवाईक, आस्थिक, दरदी, दरदवंत. [बधान.

2 *heedful, cautious, &c.* v. ATTENTIVE. सावध, हुशार, सा-

To be c. जपणें, संभाळणें.

CAREFULLY, *adv.* v. A. काळजीनें, सचिंत, चिंतापूर्वक.

2 खबरदारीनें, सावधगिरीनें, सावधपणानें, जपून, संभाळून.

CAREFULNESS, *n.* v. A. 1. *and* CARE. काळजी *f.* चिंता *f.* सचिंतता *f.*

2 सावधगिरी *f.* सावधपणा *m.* सावधानता *f.* खबरदारी *f.*

CARELESS, *a. unsolicitous, unanxious, unconcerned.* निश्चिंत *pop.* निचिंत, निकाळजी, निष्काळजी, बेपरवा, बेदरदी, बेफिकीर, निर्धास्त, अनास्थ, आस्थाहीन-रहित-&c. अजुरदा, निरपेक्ष, अनुत्सुक, अनिचाड, निघोरी, अघोर, निसूर.

2 *neglectful, unmindful, inattentive, &c.* गफलती *or* त्या, गाफल *or* गाफील, गाफली, बेफाम, गबाळी *or* ळ्या, गलत्या, निकाळजी, गैदी, गैबी, गैबती *or* त्या, विसराळू, असावध, असावधान, अनवधान, गैरसावध, बेफाम, गहाळ, गैरात, घळ्या, प्रमादी, अव्यवसायी, अव्यवसायवान्.

3 *arising through want of care.* अविचाराचा, अविचारी, बेफामीचा, अनवधानाचा, प्रमादाचा, प्रामादिक.

CARELESSLY, *adv.* v. A. 2. गफलतीनें, गाफीलपणानें, &c. हयगय करून, अनवधानपूर्वक, प्रमादपूर्वक.

CARELESSNESS, *n.* v. A. 1. निकाळजी *f.* निचिंतपणा *m.* बेदरदीपणा *m.* बेफिकिरी *f.* बेपरवाई *f.* अनास्था *f.* आस्थाराहित्य *n.* हयगई *f.* निघोरपणा *m.* निसूरपणा *m.* चिंताराहित्य *n.* निरपेक्षता *f.* अपेक्षाराहित्य *n.* अनुत्साह *m.* निश्चिंतता *f.*

2 गाफीलपणा *m.* हयगई *or* हयगय *f.* गफलत *f.* आनाकानी *f.* प्रमाद *m.* अनवधानता *f.* अनवधान *n.* असावधता *f.* गैरसावधगिरी *f.* विसराळूपणा *m.* गैदीपणा *m.* गबाळेपणा *m.* &c. अव्यवसाय *m.*

To CARESS, *v. a.* v. To FONDLE, &c. लाडकणें, पोटाळणें, जोंबाळणें, लाड *m.*-लडिवाळ *m.*-ळळा *m.*-लालन *n.*-&c. करणें *g. of o.*

CARESS, CARESSING, *n.* v. V.—*act.* लाडकणें *n.* &c. लाड *m.* लडिवाळ *m.* लाडकी *f.* लाडुकपणा *m.* लाडीगोडी *f.* कोड *n.* कोडकौतुक *n.* लालन *n.* See also EMBRACE. [णानें.

CARESSINGLY, *adv.* v. V. लाड-&c. करून, लाडीगोडीनें, लाडुकप-

CARET, *n. mark of omission.* काकपद *n.* हंसपद *n.*

CARGO, *n.* v. FREIGHT. भरगत *n.* भरीत *n.* भरत *f.* बारदान *n.* भरताड *f.*

CARICATURE, *n. ludicrous likeness or description.* सोंग *n.* नकल *f.* हास्यजनक चित्र *n.*-प्रतिमा *f.*-प्रतिकृति *f.*-वर्णन *n.*-&c.

To CARICATURE, *v. a.* हास्यजनक चित्र *n.*-&c. काढणें *g. of o.* हास्यजनक वर्णन *n.* करणें *g. of o.* सोंग *n.* करणें *g. of o.* नकल करून दाखविणें.

CARIES, CARIOSITY, *n. rottenness*—of a bone. कुजलेपणा *m.* कुजकेपणा *m.* कुजटपणा *m.* अस्थिगलितभाव *m.*

CARIOUS, *a.* v. N. कुजका, सडका, गलितभावविशिष्ट.

CARMAN, *n.* गाडेकरी *m.* गाडेवाला *m.* गाडेहाक्या *m.*

CARMINATIVE, *a. that expels wind.* वातहर, वातघ्न, वातनाशक, वायुनिस्सारक.

CARNAGE, *n. havoc, slaughter.* कत्तल *f.* v. उड, काटाकाट *f.* काटाकाटी *f.* कापाकापी *f.* रक्ताचा पूर *m.*-चिखल *m.*-नदी *f.*

There was great c. कबंध नाचलें.

CARNAL, CARNAL-MINDED, *a. not spiritual, fleshly,* v. SENSUAL. विषयाचा, विषयी, विषयासक्त, विषयाभिमुख, विषयग्रस्त, विषयपरायण, विषयतल्लीन, सकाम, इंद्रियवश, रजोगुणी, राजस, बहिर्मुख, आशाबद्ध.

C. knowledge, *sexual intercourse.* संभोग *m.* अंगसंग *m.*

CARNAL-MINDEDNESS, CARNALITY, *n.* v. A. विषयबुद्धि *f.* विषयवासना *f.* विषयासक्ति *f.* विषयाभिमुख्य *n.* विषयतल्लीनता *f.* सकामता *f.* रजोगुण *m.*

CARNATION, *n.*—flower. गुलनार *or* गुलअनार *m.*

CARNELIAN, *n.* अकीक *m.*

CARNEOUS, CARNOUS, *a. fleshy.* मांसाचा, मांसमय.

CARNIVOROUS, *a.* मांसखाणारा, मांसभक्षक, मांसाशी, मांसजीवी, मांसाहारी, क्रव्याद, क्रव्याशी, आमिषाशी.

CAROL. See SONG. HYMN. [समारंभ *m.*

CAROUSAL, *n. drinking feast.* पानोत्सव *m.* पानकोत्सव *m.* पान-

To CAROUSE, *v. n.* पानोत्सव *m.* करणें, दारू *f.*-&c. ढोसणें-झोकणें-शोषणें *or* सोखणें.

CARP, *n. Cyprinus denticulatus.* रोही *m.* रोहित *m.*

To CARP, *v. n. cavil.* अढेवेढे *m. pl.* घेणें, आडफांटा *m.*-आडफांटे *m. pl.*-फांटे *m. pl.* घेणें-फोडणें-काढणें, दिक्कत *f.* करणें-धरणें, आडवें *n.* घेणें, तकरार *f.* घेणें-करणें, फगरूड *n.*-फरगडे *or* फरगटे *m. pl.* फोडणें-घेणें-काढणें, फणगडे *m. pl.* फोडणें, हेंगल *f.* घालणें, कांक्षा *f.* घेणें-काढणें. [पर्यांचा.

CARPAL, *a. belonging, &c. to the wrist.* मणगटाचा, मणगटावि-

CARPENTER, *n.* सुतार, बढई, तक्षक, तक्षा, सूत्रधार, सूत्रधारी, सूत्रधर, सूत, काष्ठतक्षक.—in contempt. सुतारडा, तासकाम्या, खरडघाशा, खरड्या.

Business of a c. सुतारकाम *n.* सुतारकी *f.*

Work executed by a c. सुतारकाम *n.*

CARPENTRY, *n.* सुतारकी *f.* सुतारकाम *n.*

CARPER, *n.* v. V. *and* CAPTIOUS. आडफांटे घेणारा, &c. आडफांट्या, तकरारी, दिक्कती, दिक्कतखोर, चिकित्सखोर, कांक्षी.

CARPET, *n.* बिछायत *f.* बसक *f.* बैठक *f.* बसकर *or* बसकार *m. n.* आस्तरण *n.*

Carpets & Floor-cloths for ornament and for sitting are of various compositions and fashions. The names of some are गालिचा *m.* गाशा *m.* गेटम *n.* जमखाना *m.* जाजम *n.* बाजू *f.* रुजामा *m.* सतरंजी *f.*

A c. knight. गेहेशूर *m.*

That is on the c. *that is under discussion.* प्रस्तुत, प्रकृत.

To CARPET, *v. a.* बिछायत *f.*-&c. घालणें-पसरणें.

CARPING, *n.* v. V.—*act.* आडफांटा घेणें *n.* आडफांटा *m.* अढेवेढे *m. pl.* हेंगल *f.* पंचाईत *f.* v. मांड.

CARPUS, *n. the wrist.* मणगट *n.*

CARRIAGE, CARRYING, *n.* v. V. 1.—*act.* वाहणें *n.* वाहन *n.* हेल *m.*

Price of c. वाहणावळ *f.* हेल *m.* नेणावळ *f.* आणणावळ *f.* हमाली *f.* भाडें *n.*

Of c. *of burden.* ओझेल, ओझेली.

3 काढणें *n.* काढणी *f.*

I. *vehicle.* गाडी *f.* यान *n.* वहन *n.*

Certain sorts of *carriages* are करांती *f.* छकडा *m.* छकडी *f.* रथ *m.* रेंकला *m.* शकट *m.* कर्णीरथ *m.*

Pleasure-c. क्रीडारथ *m.* पुष्परथ *m.*

Wheel-c. चक्रयान *n.*

II. (as of cannon, &c. &c.). गाडा *m.* छकडा *m.*

III. deportment, v. CONDUCT. चाल *f.* गति *f.*
CARRIAGE-HORSE, *n.* गाडीचा घोडा *m.*
CARRIAGE-MAKER, *n.* गाडीकरणारा, रथकार.
CARRIED, v. V. 1. वाहलेला, नेलेला, &c.
CARRIER, *n.* v.V. 1. वाहणारा, नेणारा, वाहक, ओझ्याचा-ओझील-ओझेली (-माणूस-बैल-तट्टू-&c.) वाही, भारवाहक, भारवाही, भारवाह.
I. *one that conveys goods for hire in a cart.* भाडें घेऊन सामान गाडींत नेणारा.
CARRION, *n.* मुरदाड *or* मुडदार*n.* मुरदाडमास*n.* लोथ *or* लोथ *f.* असाद्यमांस*n.*
CARRION, *a.* मुरदाडमासाचा.
CARROT, *n.* गाजर *n.*
Core of a c. मांजर*n.*
CARROTY, *a.* गाजराच्या रंगाचा.
To CARRY, *v. a. convey, transport, bear.* वाहणें, नेणें, घेऊन-जाणें, वहन*n.* करणें.
2 See To IMPLY. 3 *remove the crop.* काढणें, काढणी *f.* करणें *g.of o.*
4—in arithm. हातचा घेणें-धरणें.
The number that comes to hand *to be carried* is called हातचा.
5 *effect, accomplish.* संपादणें, साधणें, सिद्धकरून घेणें, सरकरणें.
6 *get possession of by force.* घेणें, हस्तगत करणें-करून घेणें, सरकरणें, जिंकून घेणें.
7 across, *convey over.* उतरणें, पार करणें-पाडणें.
8 off *or* away. v. To ROB. हरणें *or* हिरणें, नेणें, हरण *n.* करणें *g. of o.*
9 off; *kill.* नेणें, परिणाम *m.*-शेवट *n.* करणें *g. of o.*
10 into effect, *execute.* बजावणें, अमलांत आणणें.
11 on, (business, &c.) v. To CONDUCT. चालविणें, हाकणें, वहिवाटणें, निर्वाहणें, निर्वाह*m.* करणें *g. of o.*
12 out; *bring to a successful end,* v. To ACCOMPLISH. सिद्धीस-शेवटास-&c. नेणें.
13 through, v. To ACCOMPLISH. निस्तरणें *or* निस्तारणें, तरीपार करणें, निर्वाह*m.* करणें *g. of o.* निभावणी *f.* पाडणें-करणें *g. of o.*
14 (one's self) v. To BEHAVE. चालणें, वागणें, वर्त्तणें.
CART, *n.* गाडा*m.* गाडी *dim.* गाडली *f.* & गाडलें *n.* छकडा *m.* शकट *m.* रेंकला*m.* रेड़ू*n.m.* रेड़का*m.*
Bottom of a c. साटी *or* साठी *f.*
Child's go-c. पांगुळ गाडा*m.* पांगुळ गाडी *f.*
To CART, *v. a.* गाड्यात-गाडींत नेणें·वाहून नेणें.
CART-GREASE, *n.* ओंगण *or* वंगण*n.*
CART-LOAD, *n.* गाडा*m.* गाडाभर (with the noun).
CART-ROAD, CART-WAY, *n.* गाडेवाट*f.* गाडेरस्ता *m.*
CART-ROPE, *n.* नाडा*m.* मणदोरा*m.* बीड*n.* भारकस*n.m.*
CART-RUT, *n.* चाकारी *f.*
CARTE-BLANCHE, *n.* पूर्णअधिकार सुचविणारा कोराकागद*m.* कुलअखत्यार *m.*
CARTEL, *n.* लढाईंत पाडाव केलेल्या शिपायांची अदला बदल करण्याचा करारनामा *m.*
CARTER, *n.* गाडेकरी, गाडेवाला, गाडीवान.
CARTILAGE, *n.* कूर्चा *m.* तरुणास्थि *n.* मृद्वस्थि*n.*
CARTILAGINOUS, *a.* तरुणास्थिमय, तरुणास्थिरूप.
CARTOUCH, *n. cartridge box.* तोसदान*n.* साज*m.* बोलशी *f.*
CARTRIDGE, *n.* तोटा*m.*
Ball c. गोळीचा तोटा*m.*
Blank c. सुकातोटा*m.* कोरडी दारू *f.* वायबाराचा तोटा*m.*
Firing of ball c. गोळीबार *m.*
Firing of blank c. वायबार *m.*
CARTRIDGE-BOX, *n.* तोसदान *n.*
CARUCATE, *n.* अऊत *or* औत*n.*
CARUNCLE, *n. protuberance of flesh.* मांसवृद्धि *f.*
To CARVE, *v. a. cut wood, stone, &c.* or *form by carving.* कोरणें, खोदणें, नकसणें *or* नकासणें, किरवणें, कोरून-खोदून काढणें.
2 (meat) कापणें, फांका *f. pl.* करणें-कापणें.
CARVED, *p.*v.V.1. कोरलेला, खोदलेला, &c. कोरींव, खोदींव, नकशीदार, नकशी, नकसींव.
CARVER, *n.* v. V. 1. कोरणारा, खोदणारा, &c. नकासकामी *or* न्या, नकसगीर, खोदकामी *or* न्या.
CARVING, *n.* v. V.1.—*act.* कोरणें *n.* खोदणें*n.* &c. कोरणी *f.* खोदणी *f.*
Price or cost of c. खोदणावळ *f.* खोदाई *f.*
I. *carved work.* खोदकाम *n.* नकासकाम *n.* नकशा *m.* नकशी *f.* नकसगिरी *f.*
CARVING-TOOL, *n.* कोरणी *f.* कोरणें *n.*
CASCADE, *n.* v. WATER-FALL. धबधबा *m.* धबधबी *f.* धोत *m.* धोदा *or* धोधा *m.* चादर *f.*
CASE, *n. covering, sheath.* आवरण *n.* वेष्टन *n.* टोपण *n.* घर *n.* म्यान *n.* मेण *n.* कोश *m.* खोळ *f.*
Needle-c. चंची *f.*
Pen-c. कलमदान *n.* कलमदानी *f.*
Razor-c. धोकटी *or* धोंगटी *f.*
2 (as of a pillow, couch, &c.) *cover.* गलेफ *m.* गवसणी *f.* ठेला *m.* पिशवी *f.* अभ्रा *m.*
3 (as of a mattress, quilt, &c.) *case to be stuffed.* खोळ*f.m.*
4 *state, condition, circumstances.* दशा *f.* अवस्था *f.* स्थिति *f.* गति *pop.* गत *f.* गोष्ट *f.* हवाल *f. m.*
In that c. तशांत, तसें असतांना, मग.
5 *case adduced or occurring, instance.* अढळ *m.* प्रतीक *n.* उदाहरण *n.* स्थल *n.*
6—in medicine; *state of the body,* v. HEALTH. देहस्थिति *f.* भावना *f.* देहभावना *f.*
To be in good c. खाऊन पिऊन पुष्ट असणें.
7 *history of a disease.* दुखण्याचा मजकूर *m.* रोगकथन *n.* रोगव्याख्यान *n.*
8—in law. *state of facts, the question.* मजकूर *m.* हकिकत *f.* कैफियत *f.* वाका *m.* तकरीर *m.* भूत *n.* प्रकरण *n.*
Written statement of a c. तकरीर नामा *m.*
9 *suit at law,* v. CAUSE. मुकदमा *m.* प्रकरण *n.* खटला *m.* खटलें *n.* दावा *m.*
10—in grammar, *variation of nouns.* विभक्ति *f.* कारक *n.* व्यक्ति *f.*
The six *Cases* are कर्त्ता, कर्म, करण, संप्रदान, अपादान, अधिकरण, *or* प्रथमा, द्वितीया, तृतीया, चतुर्थी, पंचमी, षष्ठी, सप्तमी.
11 (of instruments). गंज *m.*
12 See BOX.
CASE-WORM, *n.* न्हावी *m.* कोशकिडा *m.*

CASEMENT. See WINDOW.

CASH, *n.* रोकड *f.* नगद *n.* नगदी *f.* दाम *m.* सोनें नाणें *n.* रोस *or* रोकडापैसा *m.* [करणें.

To CASH, *v. a.* (note, bill, &c.) बटाविणें, मोडणें, टक्के *m.*-&c.

CASH-KEEPER, CASHIER, *n.* खजीनदार *c.* जामदार *c.* पोतनीस *m.* किल्लीदार *c.*

Private c. खासगीवाला *m.*

CASHEW, *n.*—tree, or apple, or nut. काजू *f. m.*

2 apple, *pulpous portion.* बोंडू *m.* बोंड *n.* बेंड *n.* काजूगोळा *m.*

To CASHIER, *v. a.* v. To DISMISS. बरतरफ करणें, स्थानभ्रष्ट-स्थानच्युत-पदच्युत-पदभ्रष्ट-&c. करणें.

CASK, *n.* पीप *n.* पिंप *n.* काष्ठतुंग *n.*

CASKET, *n.* डब्बा *m. dim.* डब्बी *f.* करंड *m.* करंडा *m.* बगवें *n.*

CASQUE, *n.* v. HELMET. शिरस्त्राण *n.*

CASSIA, *n.*—fistula. बाहवा *m.* शम्याक *m.* सुवर्ण *or* सुवर्णक *m.*

2—woody c. तज *f.* त्वक्पत्र *n.* त्वक्सार *m.*

To CAST, *v. a. throw, hurl, toss, fling.* झोकणें, टाकणें, फेंकणें, झुगारणें, घालणें, भिरकावणें, फिगारणें, उगारणें, होपटणें, होडंगणें, क्षेपणें, प्रक्षेपणें, प्रक्षेपण *n.*-प्रक्षेप *m.*-&c. करणें *g. of o.*

2 —as a fruit-tree, a bird, &c. v. To SHED. गाळणें, टाकणें, सांडणें.

3 *send forth, give out, &c.* v. To EMIT. सोडणें, टाकणें.

4 in law, *non-suit.* हतपक्ष-नष्टपक्ष-छिन्नपक्ष-हीनपक्ष-हतवाद-&c. करणें.

5 *throw in wrestling.* चीत करणें, पाडणें, जमीनदोस्त करणें.

6 *found.* ओतणें, ढाळणें.

7 *plot, strike out,* v. To CONTRIVE. योजणें, कल्पना *f.* करणें *g. of o.* काढणें.

8 away; *give to the winds, &c.* v. To THROW AWAY. गमावणें, घालवणें, हरवणें *or* हारवणें. [सांडणें.

9 away, off; v. To ABANDON. सोडणें, सोडून देणें, टाकून देणें,

10 off; (clothes, &c.). टाकणें, टाकाऊ करणें, उतारणें.

11 out; v. To EJECT. घालवणें, काढणें, काढून टाकणें.

12 up; v. To ADD. हिशोब *m.* करणें, बेरीज *f.* करणें.

13 upon. माथां *adv.* मारणें *g. of s.* टाकणें *with* वर *of s.*

CAST, *n. throw,* v. CASTING, 1. प्रक्षेप *m.* क्षेप *m.*

2 *throw of dice.* डाव *m. v.* टाक.

Turn to c. डाव *m.* [*f.* ढाळ *m.*

3 *mould, make, fashion,* v. FORM. घडण *f.* घडणी *f.* घडवण

4 *air, turn, manner.* नोक *f.* झोक *m.* ढब *f.* डौल *m.*

Having an affected c. —turban, &c. झोकदार.

5 *smack, smatch, savour,* v. TASTE. स्वाद *m. v.* मार, छटा *f.* धुनक *or* धुनूक *f.* लकेरी *f.* लकीर *f.* वास *m.* [छाया *f.*

6 *tint, touch, shade, tincture, &c.* छटा *f.* लकेरी *f.* छब *f.*

7 See SQUINT.

CAST, CASTE, *n. division of the Hindù body.* जात *f.* यात *f.* याती *f.* जाति *f.* ज्ञात *f.* वर्ण *m.* The four origiual *Castes* are ब्राह्मण, क्षत्रिय, वैश्य, शूद्र; and to this are added अतिशूद्र, अंत्यज, अनामिक, &c. all terms expressing collectively the low and impure classes, severally designated by महार, मांग, परीट, चांभार, नट, बुरूड, &c. &c. Certain of the *Castes, Classes, or Tribes are* कटई, कडबा *or* कडू, कंजारी, काछी, काजारी, कातकरी *or* कातोडी *or* काथकरी &c. कामत, कामाठी, कायत, कायस्थ, कांसार, काळण, कुंजरा, कुणबी, कैकाडी, कोंगा, कोमटी, कोष्टी, खतरी, खाटक, खारवी, खारीक, गवळी, गावडा, गिराशी *or* सी, गुरव, गोंधळी, गोप, गोलक (distinguished into कुंडगोलक and रंडगोलक), गोंडी, घडशी *or* सी, घिसाडी, चाटी *or* ट्या, चांभार *or* चाम्हार, चारण, चौकळशा, जाट, टंकारी, डाकोचा *or* ता, डोंब, डोंबारी, डोहार, ढोर, तांबट, तांबोळी, तिरमळी, धनगर, धवड *or* धावड, धीवर, धुरु, नट, निषाद, commonly कोळी, परभू, परीट, पळशा, पाटारा, पाथरवट, पूर्भय्या, बुरूड, बेदडा, बेरड, ब्राह्मणजाई, भय्या, भंगी, भंडारी, भोई, मातग, मणिकीर, (*pop.* मणेर *or* मणेरी), मण्यार, महार, (*or* बेसकर), मांग, मिठागरी, राउळ, रथकार, रथकारक, रामोशी *or* सी, लकेरी, लंबाण *or* लमाण, लोणारी, लोहार *or* लोहकार, बणजारा *or* री, बाघरी, वाघ्या, वाणी, शिंपी *or* सिंपी, शीक, सणगर, सुतार, सूत, सोनार.

C. and lineage,—compreh. जातकुळी *f.* जातकूळ *n.* जातपात *f.* कुळगोत *n.*

The C. collectively,—as assembled in investigation of offences, &c. काशीगोत *n.* गंगागोत *n.* गोत *n.* गोतगंगा *f.* गोतपात *n.f.* जातपात *f.* गोतवळा *or* गोतोळा *m.* गोतावळ *f.* जातगंगा *f.* जातगोत *n. f.* जातजमात *f.* दैव *n.*

A mixed c. or race. वर्णसंकर *m.* संकर जाति *f.* संकर *m.* अठरा धान्यांचें कोडबुळें *n.*

A low c. person. बाहेरचा *or* ला, गांवाबाहेरचा, दिवाकीर्त्ति *pop.* दिवाकीर्त्त *m.*

Brother or fellow by c. जातभाऊ *m.*

Ceremonies of receiving back into c. गोताई *f.* गोत *f.* पत *f.* जात पात *f.* जात *f.*

Circular notifying an ejection from c. बाळीतपत्र *n.* बहिष्कारपत्र *n.* अपांक्तपत्र *n.*

Confusion of c's. वर्णसंकर *m.*

Distinction of c. जातिभेद *m.*

Ejected from c. बाळ, बाळीत, बहिष्कृत, कृतघटस्फोट.

Ejection from c. बाळ *f. v.* घाल, पड, बाळीत. *n.* बहिष्कार *m.* घटस्फोट *m.*

Extinction of c. जातिलोप *m.* वर्णलोप *m.*

Falling from c. जातिभ्रंश *m.*

Fallen from c. जातिभ्रष्ट, बाटगा.

Feud in a c. तट *m.*

Of *or* as to c. जातीचा.

Of mixed c. or blood. संकीर्ण, मिश्र.

Pride of c. जात्यभिमान *m.*

The peculiar duty, virtues, &c. of a c. जातिधर्म *m.*

CAST, *p.* v. V. 1. झोकलेला, टाकलेला &c. क्षिप्त, प्रक्षिप्त, विक्षिप्त.

2 गाळलेला, सांडलेला, गलित, विगलित.

I. down; v. DISPIRITED. उदास, उदासी, गतोत्साह.

CASTANET, *n.* करताल *n.m.* झंझरी *f.* मंजरी *f.*

CASTAWAY, *a.* v. REPROBATE. देवाधर्मानें टाकलेला, देवत्यक्त, दैवत्यक्त, निक्षिप्त.

CASTELLAN, *n.* किल्लेदार *m.* दुर्गाधिकारी *m.* दुर्गाध्यक्ष *m.*

CASTER, *n.* v. V. 1. झोकणारा, टाकणारा, क्षेपक, क्षिपक, क्षेप्ता.

2 ओतणारा, ओतारी.

To CASTIGATE, CASTIGATION. See To PUNISH, &c.

CASTING, *n.* v. V. 1.—*act.* झोकणें *n.* टाकणें *n.* क्षेप *m.* प्रक्षेप *m.* वि-

क्षेपm. प्रक्षेपणn. क्षिपणn. [वाडा m.

Castle, *n. fort.* कोटm. कोठm. किल्लाm. गढी f. दुर्ग m. n. लढाऊ.
2 *house or mansion of a prince or nobleman.* वाडाm. हवेली f. महालm.
Castle in the air. मनोरथसृष्टि f. मानससृष्टि f.
To build c. in the air. आधांतरीं घरn. बांधणें, मनीं मांडेm. pl. खाणें, मनोरथसृष्टि f.-मानससृष्टि f.- मनोराज्यn. करणें.
3 (at chess). हत्ती m.

Castling, *n.* v. Abortion. गर्भपातm. गर्भस्रावm.

Castor-oil, *n.*—plant. एरंडm.—the oil एरंडेलn.—the seed एरंडी f. एरंडबीजn.—the root एरंडमूलn. Some varieties or species are एरंडी, सुरती एरंड, मोगली एरंड, गोडा एरंड, कडवा एरंड, जेपाळm. श्वेत एरंड.

To **Castrate**, *v. a.* अंडm. *pl.* काढणें *g. of o.* खसी करणें, अंडछेदm. -अंडछेदनn. करणें *g. of o.*
2 (by pounding the testicle). बडविणें, चेचणें.

Castrated, *p.* v. V. 1. खसीकेलेला, खसी, छिन्नांड.
2 बडविलेला, &c. भादा or भाद्या. [अंडछेदन n.

Castration, *n.* v. V. 1.—*act.* अंडकाढणेंn. खसी f. अंडछेदm.
2 बडविणेंn. चेचणेंn.

Casual, *a. fortuitous,* v. Accidental. असंकेतित, असांकेतिक, आगंतुक, दैवागत, दैवघटित, यदृच्छाजात. [स्थित.
2 *incidental,* v. Occasional. नैमित्तिक. प्रासंगिक, प्रसंगोप-

Casually, *adv.* v. Accidentally. दैवयोगानें, दैवानें, यदृच्छेकरून.

Casualness, *n.* v. A. 1. दैवयोगm. यदृच्छा f. दैवघटितत्वn. आगंतुकत्व n.

Casualty, *n.* See Casualness, 2. *a* c. v. Accident. दैवकृत्यn. दैव घटित गोष्ट f. काकतालीयn.
3 *a chance producing death.* अपघातm. आदानn. अपमृत्युm.
4 *a vacancy through death, &c.* मरण वगैरे कारणानें खाली झालेली जागा f.

Casuist, *n. one skilled in casuistry.* दोषादोषविवेकी, दोषादोषवेत्ता, सदसत्संशयनिवर्त्तक. [षयक, &c.

Casuistic, Casuistical. *a.* v. N. दोषादोषविवेचनसंबंधी-वि-

Casuistry, *n. science of determining the lawfulness or unlawfulness of acts.* दोषादोषविवेचनविद्या f. सदसत्संशयनिवर्त्तनविद्या f. धर्माधर्मविचारणविद्या.

Cat, *n.* मांजर or माजर m. f. n. मार्जार m. बिडाल or बिडालकm. —male, *he-c.* बोका, माजर,—female, *she-c.* माजर, भाटी, बिल्ली f.—in endearment; corresponding to *puss, pussy.* मंगी f. मंगोडें n. मांजरूं n.—in endearment, disparagement, or contempt. मांजरूं n.—in cant phraseol. वाघाची मावशी f. Tom c. बिठूबोका m.
Wild c. रानमाजर m. f. n. कांडेचोर m.
To let the c. out of the bag. घडा m. फोडणें, ढोलकें n. फोडणें, पुडी f. फोडणें.

Cat a mountain, *n.* रानमाजर m. f. n.

Cat-eyed, *a.* मांजरडोळ्या, घारडोळ्या, घारा, घाऱ्या.
Rather c. घारेला or घारोळा.

Cat-gut, *n.* सांव f. अंतड्यांची तार f.-तांत f.-तांध f. रोदा m.

Cat-hammed, *a.* टाळघाशा, टाळकुट्या.

Cat's-paw, *n. dupe,* v. Fool. क्रीडामृग m. हातखोरणें n.

Catachrestical, *a.* v. Forged. क्लिष्ट.

Catacombs, *n.* शववापिका f.

Catacoustic, *a.* प्रतिध्वनिविषयक, प्रतिध्वनिसंबंधी.

Catalepsy, *n.* ताटस्थवायु m. स्तब्धवायु m.

Catalogue, *n.* v. List. फेरिस्त n. अनुक्रमानें याद f.

Catamenia, *n.* v. Menses. पुष्प n. ऋतु m. रज n. m.

Catamenial, *a.* रजोविषयक.

Catamite, *n.* गांडू m. गांडमराउ m. गांडसुकाळ or गांडसुकाळ्या m.

Cataplasm. See Poultice. [धाणी f.

Cataract, *n.* v. Waterfall. धोत m. धोदा or धोधा m. धो-
2 (of the eye). मोतीं n. मोतींबिंदु m. मोतींबिंब n. पटल n.

Catarrh, *n.* पडसें n. शैत्य n. कास m.

Catarrhal, *a.* पडशाचा, पडशाविषयींचा, पडशानें झालेला.

Catastrophe, *n.* (of the drama, &c.). उद्यापन n. निष्ठा f.- निर्वहन or निर्वाहन n. उपसंहार m.
2 *ruinous issue,* &c. लबीत n. दुरंत m. दुष्परिणाम m. दुःखपरिणाम m.

To **Catch**, *v. a. lay hold, apprehend,* v. To Seize. धरणें, हातांत धरणें, पकडणें, पछाडणें.
2 *receive in its passage.* झेलणें, झेलूनघेणें, झिकणें.
3 *get hold of, get into one's power.* धरणें, डावाखालीं-डावांत-&c. आणणें, सांपडवणें, अवाक्यांत येणें *in. con.* घावाडावांत सांपडणें *in. con.*
4 (contagion or disease). घेणें, जडणें *in. con.* लागणें *in. con.* येणें *in. con.*
5 (a song or tune), *take up and follow.* झेलणें.
6 (as in speech or conduct), *lay hold of.* गोंवणें, कबजीं धरणें or पाडणें, पकडणें, पटकावणें, पछाडणें, कडसणींत धरणें.
7 v. To Overtake. अटपून घेणें, मिळवून घेणें.
8 v. To Snatch. हिसकावणें, हिसकावून घेणें.
9 up; v. To Snatch up. पटकावणें, मटकावणें, हात m. मारणें.

To **Catch**, *v. n. be contagious.* लागणें.
2 *hitch, fasten on, &c.* लागणें, गुंतणें, अडकणें.
To c. and tear, *to be scrieved.* आंसटणें or आंसडणें.
3 *take fire, ignite,* v. To Kindle. चेतणें or चेतवणें, पेटणें, लागणें, शिलगणें.
4 *sustain some morbid affection.* धरणें. [&c. घालणें.
5 at; *endeavor to seize,* v. To Snatch. झोंबाडा m.-झेप f.-

Catch, *n. seizure, &c.* See Catching, 1.
To lie upon the c. धरायास-निमित्तास टेकणें, धरूं पाहणें.
2 *clasp, hook, hold, chape.* अडकण n. अडकवण n. अंकडा m. कचक f.
3 *advantage,* v. Gain. लाभ m.
4 See Snatch.

Catching, *n.* v. V. 1.—*act.* धरणें n. पकडणें n. &c.

Catching, *p. a.* v. V. 4, *and* Contagious. सांसर्गिक, स्पर्शानुगामी, स्पर्शोपक्रामक.

Catechetical, *a.* प्रश्नोत्तराचा, प्रश्नोत्तररूप, पृच्छाप्रतिवाक्यात्मक, प्रश्नोत्तरमय-विशिष्ट.

Catechetically, *adv.* सवालकरून व जवाब घेऊन, प्रश्नोत्तरांनीं, प्रश्नोत्तरपूर्वक.

To **Catechise**, *v. a. instruct by questions.* सवाल पुसून-करून-शिकवणें, प्रश्नोत्तरपूर्वकशिक्षा f.-बोध m.-&c. करणें. [रणें.
2 *interrogate,* v. To Examine. पुसणें, पुरशीस f. घालणें-क-

CATECHISM, *n.* प्रश्नोत्तरावलि *f.* प्रश्नोत्तरमाला *f.* प्रश्नोत्तरपुस्तक *n.*

CATECHIST, *n.* v. V. 1. सवालकरून शिकवणारा, प्रश्नोत्तरपूर्वकशिक्षक.
2 पुसणारा, पुसता.

CATECHU, *n. terra japonica.* खैरसार *m.* कात *m.* (The tree is called खैर *m.* खदिर *m.*)—in cant or covert phraseol. चतुर्थ *m.* कडू *m.*

CATECHUMEN, *n.* बाप्तिस्मा घेण्याच्या पूर्वी ख्रिस्तीधर्माचीं तत्वें शिकणारा.

CATEGORICAL, *a. absolute, express,* v. POSITIVE. साफ, स्पष्ट, निश्चयाचा, निश्चयात्मक. [स्पष्ट.

CATEGORICALLY, *adv.* v. A. *and* POSITIVELY. निक्षूण, साफ,

CATEGORY, *n.* —in logic. *predicament.* पदार्थ *m.*
2 v. CLASS. वर्ग *m.* बिल्हा *m.* बिल्हे *f.*

To CATER, *v. n. provide food.* खाण्याच्या सामग्रीची योजना *f.* करणें, आहारयोजना *f.*-आहारनिर्वाह *m.*-&c. करणें, वाकनिशी *f.* करणें.

CATERER, *n.* v. V. खाण्याची योजना करणारा, मोदी *m.* वाकनीस *m.* आहारयोजक.

CATERPILLAR, *n.* कुसरूड *m.* कुसरीण *m.* घुलें *n.* शूककीट *m.* शूककीटक *m.* सुरट *or* सुरवंट *m.*

To CATERWAUL, *v. n.* गुरम्यांव *n.* करणें, मांजरासारखा ओरडणें.

CATERWAULING, *n.* v. V. गुरम्यांव *n.* बोकेजुंज *f.*

CATES, *n.* v. DAINTY. पक्वान्नें *n. pl.* मिष्टान्न *n.* भातुकें *n.*

CATHARIST, *n. pretender to great purity.* अतिसोवळा, लाकडें धुऊनघेणारा, मीठ धुऊनघेणारा.

CATHARTIC, *a.* v. PURGATIVE. ढाळक, रेचक.

CATHARTIC, *n.* v. PURGE. ढाळ *m.* रेच *m.* जुलाब *m.*

CATHEDRAL, *n.* बिशपाची गादी ज्या देवळांत आहे तें देऊळ.

CATHETER, *n.* मुतसळई *f.* मूत्रस्त्रावियंत्र *n.* मूत्रशलाका *f.*

CATHOLIC, *a.* v. UNIVERSAL. सर्वांचा, सर्वसंबंधी.
2 *not narrow minded.* प्रशस्तमनाचा, उदारमनाचा, प्रशस्त.
3 See ROMAN CATHOLIC.

CATHOLICISM, *n.* v. A. 1. सर्वसंबंधिता *f.*
2 मनाचा प्रशस्तपणा *m.* &c. मनाचें प्राशस्त्य *n.*-औदार्य *n.*

CATHOLICON, *n.* त्रैलोक्यचिंतामणि *m.*

CATOPTRICAL, *a.* v. N. परावृत्तकिरणसंबंधी, परावृत्तकिरणजन्य.

CATOPTRICS, *n. science of reflected light.* परावृत्तकिरणविषयकदर्शनानुशासन *n.*

CATTLE, *n.—horned.* गुरें *n. pl.* ढोरें *n. pl.*—compreh. *great and small.* गुरेंढोरें *n. pl.* गुरूं वासरूं *n.* Some of the diseases incidental to *Cattle* are कांसेफोड *m. pl.* कुकडें *n.* कुंद *m.* कोणें *n.* घांटरोग *m.* झेंडू *m.* सडी *f.* पायलाग *m.* पांसी *or* फांसी *f.* पेय *n.* फोडाळणें*n.* बरग *m.* लाळ *f.* नरड *m.* तोंडलाग*m.* खुरखूत *n.*
A cattle-pasture. गुरचरण *f.*
Cost of the use of it. गुरचराई *f.*
C.-lice. C.-ticks. खिरड *f.* दूड *f.*
C. track. गुरदंड *m.*
Hire for the use of draught c. शेक *n.*
Picketing line of c. दावण *f.*
Rope by which c. are tied to it. दावें *n. dim.* दावली *f.*
Loop of this rope, (it consists of two). कानी *f.* पडकें *n.* पेंडें *n.*
Spot on which the c. are assembled daily, to be driven out to pasture. गोंड *m.*
Tending or keeping of c. राखील *f.* राखणावळ *f.* राखूळ *f. v.* घाल, पशुरक्षण *n.* पशुपालन *n.* Hire of tending c. राखणावळ *f.* राखील *f.* राखूळ *f.*
Wealth, or property in c. गोधन *n.* चर्मधन *n.* [मय.

CAUDAL, *a. pertaining, &c. to a tail.* पुच्छसंबंधी-विषयक, पुच्छ-

CAUDLE, *n.* बाळंतकाढा *m.* सुंठवडा *m.* शिरें *n.* सोनवणी *n.*

CAUGHT, *p.* v. V. 1. धरलेला, गृहीत, धृत.
2 झेललेला &c.
3 सांपडवलेला, डावाखालीं आणलेला, &c.
To be c. सांपडणें *or* सांपटणें.

CAUL, *n.* v. OMENTUM. पोटाचा पडदा*m.* अंत्रवेष्टन*n.*
2 बायकोच्या मस्तकावर घालायाचें जाळें*n.*

CAULIFLOWER, *n.* फुलकोबी *f.* [मित्तभव्य.

CAUSABLE, *a.* v. V. उत्पादनीय, करणोत्पाद्य, निमित्तोत्पाद्य, नि-

CAUSAL, CAUSATIVE, *a. relating to or implying cause.* कारणसंबंधी, कारणविषयक, उत्पादक, कारणिक, हैतुक, साधक, कारणहेतु-साधन-&c. भूत.
2—in grammar. प्रयोज्य, वांत *or* व्यंत (*i. e.* व *or* वि & अंत, having व *or* वि added at the end of the root).
C. verb. प्रयोज्यधातु*m.*

CAUSALITY, CAUSATIVENESS, *n.* v.A.1. कारणत्व*n.* निमित्तत्व*n.* हेतुता *f.* साधकत्व *n.*

CAUSATION, *n.* V.—*act.* उत्पादणें*n.* &c. उत्पादन*n.* उद्भावन*n.*

CAUSE, *n. efficient, producer, author.* कारण*n.* कर्त्ता*m.* कारक*m.* प्रयोजक*m.* उपाधि*m.* आदि*m.*
Efficient c. कारकहेतु*m.*
Generative or originating c. प्रभव*m.*
Instrumental c. निमित्तकारण*n.* निमित्त*n.*
Primary or remote c. आदिकारण*n.* बीजभूतकारण*n.* निदान *n.* मूल*n.* आद्यबीज*n.* परंपराकारण*n.* कारणकारण*n.*
Proximate or immediate c. उपादान*n.* उपादानकारण*n.* निमित्तकारण*n.* साक्षात्कारण*n.* प्रत्यक्षकारण*n.*
Relation of c. and effect. कार्यकारणभाव*m.* जन्यजनकभाव*m.* हेतुहेतुमद्भाव*m.* प्रयोज्य प्रयोजकभाव*m.* साध्यसाधकभाव*m.*
2 *reason, ground, motive.* कारण*n.* हेतु *m.* प्रयोजन*n.* सबब *f.* निमित्त*n.*
Without c. कारणावांचून, निष्कारण, उगीच, सहज.
3—in law; *suit, action.* व्यवहारविषय*m.* खटला*m.* खटलें*n.* मुकदमा*m.* वाद*m.* प्रकरण*n.*
To lose one's c. हरणें.
4 *side, party.* पक्ष*m.* कड *f.* बाजू *f.* तरफ *f.*
Espousing a c. कैवार *m. v.* घे, धर, कर.
Espouser of a c. कैवारी.

To CAUSE, *v. a. produce, occasion, effect.* करणें, करवणें, उत्पादणें, उद्भावणें, उत्पन्न-&c. करणें, उत्पत्ति *f.*-उद्भव*m.* करणें *g. of o.* कारणभूत-निमित्तभूत-हेतुभूत-&c. होणें-असणें *in. con.*

CAUSED, *p.* v. V. केलेला, करवलेला, &c. उत्पादित, जनित, जन्य, निमित्ती (in comp.) हेतुमान्.

CAUSELESS, *a.* v. N. 1. अकारण, अकारणी, निःकारण, अहेतुक, अकर्त्तृक, कर्त्तृहीन.
2 अकारण, अकारणी, निःकारण, निष्कारण, विनाकारण, अहेतुक, निर्हेतुक, निर्निमित्त, निष्प्रयोजन.

Causelessly, *adv.* v. A. कारणावांचून, विनाकारण, निष्कारण.

Causelessness, *n.*v.A. अकारणत्व*n.* अहेतुकत्व*n.* अकर्तृकत्व*n.*&c.

Causer, *n.* v. V. करणारा, &c. कर्त्ता, जनक, जनिता, प्रयोजक, प्रवर्त्तक, कारणभूत.

Causey, Causeway, *n.* बांध*m.* बांधाचा रस्ता*m.*

Caustic, *a.* मासजाळणारा, मांसदाहक, मांस नाशक.
2 fig. *sharp, cutting*, v. Biting. तिखट, खंवट, कटु.

Caustic, *n.* मासजाळणारें औषध*n.* मांसदाहक *or* नाशक पदार्थ*m.* अरुष्कर*m.*
Stick c. काडीखार *or* खाड्याखार*m.*

Causticity, *n.* मांसदाहकत्व*n.* मांसदाहनशक्ति *f.*

Cautelous. See Cautious, Cunning.

Cauter, *n.* *searing iron.* डागणी *f.* दाहन*n.* डाहणी *f.*

To **Cauterize**, *v. a. fire.* डागणें*or* दागणें, लासणें, डावणें, डाग*m.*-डाव*m.*- गूल*m.* देणें, दाहन*n.* करणें.

Cauterizing, Cauterization, *n.* v. V.—*act* दागणें *or* डागणें *n.* डागदेणें*n.*&c. दाहन*n.*

Cautery, *n.*— actual. डाग*m.* दाह*m.*
Circular c. गूल*m.* गोदा*m.*
2—Potential. दाह*m.*

Caution, *n. prudence, providence, care, circumspection, wariness.* दुरंदेशा *m.* सावधगिरी *f.* सावधपणा *m.* हुशारी *f.* पगदस्तपणा *m.* सावधानता *f.* पूर्वापरविचार *m.* मागलापुढलाविचार *m.* आदिपश्चात्विचार *m.* आगचामागचा विचार *m.*
2 *monition*, v. Warning. ताकीद *f.* सांगी *f.* जतावणें *n.*
3 *provision against.* करून ठेवलेला उपाय *m.*-बंदोबस्त *m.* पूर्वोपाय *m.*
4 See Security.

To **Caution**, *v. a. admonish, &c.* v. To Warn. ताकीद *f.* करणें-देणें, जतावणें, जगावणें, सांगी *f.* करणें.

Cautionary, *a. given in pledge or security.* तारणाचा, बंधकीकृत, बंधकीभूत, तारण in comp.
2 *conveying warning.* ताकिदीचा, जतावणीचा, अवधानसूचक.

Cautious, *a. prudent, provident, careful, wary.* सावध, हुशार, पगदस्त, पगदस्ती, दुरंदेश, सावधान, सावचित्त, पूर्वापरविचारी, पूर्वदर्शी, मागें पुढें-चहोंकडें-पदोपदीं-&c. पाहणारा, अगापिच्छापाहणारा.

Cautiously, *adv.* v. A. सावधपणानें, मागें पुढें पाहून, पूर्वापरविचार करून, &c.

Cautiousness, *n.* v. A. *and* Caution. सावधपणा *m.* सावधगिरी *f.* हुशारी *f.* पगदस्ती *f.*

Cavalcade, *n.* सवारी *or* स्वारी *f.* अश्वस्वार यात्रा *f.*

Cavalier, *n.* v. Horseman. घोडेस्वार *m.* शिलेदार *m.* तुरंगी *m.* सादी *m.* अश्ववार *m.* अश्वसादी *m.*

Cavalier, *a. haughty, &c. like a c.* शिलेदारी, शिलेदारीढबेचा, शिलेदारीडौलाचा, राऊतचालीचा, रावकीचेचालीचा, पत्राजी, मगरूर, अभिमानी.

Cavalierly, *adv.* v. A. शिलेदारावारीं, राऊतचालीनें, शिलेदारी डौलानें, &c. पत्राजीनें, मगरुरीनें.

Cavalry, *n.* घोडदळ *n.* तुरुकस्वार *m. pl.* अश्वभार *m.* अश्वसेना *f.*

Cave, *n. hollow in a hill or rock.* गुहा *f.* गुंफा *f.* गव्हर *n. dim.* गव्हरी *f.* ढोल *f.* भुयार *n.* खबदड *n. f.* खबदडी *f.* विवर *n.* कणगार *f.* कंदरा *f.* कपार *n.* कंदर *mn.* कुहर *n.*

In caves and hollows and dens and chasms, &c. कडेकपारीं, दरींकंदरीं.

Cavern, *n. hollow in a hill, &c.* v. Cave. गुहा *f.* कपार *n. f.*
2 *deep mountainous recess or hollow.* खोरें *n.* खोंडा *m.* घोल *n.* दरा *m. dim.* दरी *f.*

Cavernous, *a. abounding with caverns.* गुहाप्रचुर, गुहामय, गुहाबहुल, गहीय.

To **Cavil, Cavilling**. See To Carp, &c.

Cavity, *n.* v. Hollow. खळगा *m. dim.* खळगी *f.* खळी *f.* खांच *f.* खोलगा *m.* खोलवा *m.*

To **Caw**, *v. n.* कावकाव *f.* करणें, करकरणें, काकशब्द *m.* करणें.

Cawing, *n.* v. V.—*act.* करकरणें *n.* कावकाव *f.* करकर *f. intens.* करकराट *m.*

To **Cease**, *v. n. stop, desist, leave off, give over.* राहणें, पुरें *adv.*-बस *adv.* करणें, स्थिरावणें, स्थिर होणें, खळणें, थांबणें, स्तब्धणें, स्तब्ध होणें, निवृत्तहोणें, विसावणें, विरमणें, उपरमणें, विराम *m.* पावणें, फिरणें, निवर्त्तणें, सोडणें (ex. बोलायास-जेवायास-भांडायास-&c. सोडणें), मोडती घेणें, हात *m.* काढणें-काढून घेणें-अटोपणें.
2 *become extinct, be no more.* उडणें, सरणें, जाणें, गळणें, संपणें, उलगणें, उरकणें, नाहींसा होणें.
3 *come to an end, stop*, v. To End. राहणें, संपणें, समाप्त होणें, उलगडणें.

Ceaseless, *a. incessant*, v. Perpetual. अखंड, निरंतर, संतत *or* सतत, अविश्रांत.

Ceaselessly, *adv.* v. Continually, Ever. निरंतर, सतत, एकसारखा.

Ceasing. See Cessation.

Cecity. See Blindness.

Cedar, *n.* देवदारूच्या जातीचें एकझाड आहे. The *Cedrus devadára* is called on the Himálayas, केलू.

To **Cede**, *v. a. surrender, yield*, v. To Give up. सोडणें, सोडून देणें, परित्यागपूर्वक देणें. स्वाधीन करणें.

Ceded, *p.* v. V. सोडलेला, &c.

To **Ceil**, *v. a.* छतावणें, छत *n.* भरणें-लावणें-देणें-बांधणें.

Ceiling, *n* छत *n.* वितान *n. m.*
To lay a c. छत *n.* भरणें.
2—of cloth. चांदवा *m.* आस्मानगिरी *f.*
3—of planks. तक्तपोशी *f.*

To **Celebrate**, *v. a. laud, extol*, v. To Praise. स्तवणें, कीर्त्तणें, गाणें, स्तवन *n.*-कीर्त्तन *n.*-संकीर्त्तन *n.* करणें *g. of o.*
2 *perform solemnly, solemnize.* समारंभानें करणें-आचरणें-पाळणें, समारंभ *m.*-उत्साह *m.*-&c. करणें *g. of o.* विधीप्रमाणें करणें-आचरणें-पाळणें.
To c. humbly उदकापाण्यानें करून टाकणें, फूलपाकळीनें करून टाकणें.
To c. with pomp and style. गाजवणें.

Celebrated, *p. & a.* v. V. 1. स्तवलेला, &c. कीर्त्तित, संकीर्त्तित,
2 समारंभानें केलेला, &c.
I. v. Famous. कीर्त्तिमान्, ख्यात, विख्यात, प्रख्यात, सुप्रसिद्ध, प्रतिष्ठित, नामी, नामांकित.

Celebration, *n.* v. V. 1.—*act.* स्तवणें *n.* कीर्त्तणें *n.* &c. कीर्त्तन *n.* संकीर्त्तन *n.*
2 समारंभानें करणें *n.* &c. समारंभ *m.*

Celebrity, *n.* v. Fame. नाम *pop.* नांव *n.* नांवलौकिक *m.* की-

तिं f. प्रतिष्ठा f. ख्याति f. विख्याति f.

I. a c. *person of distinction* प्रस्थान n. धेंड n.

CELERITY, *n.* v. SWIFTNESS. त्वरा *f.* वेग *m.* शीघ्रगति *f.* वेगगति *f.*

CELERY, *n.* एकभाजी आहे.

CELESTIAL, *a.* v. HEAVENLY. देवलोकाचा, देवलोकसंबंधी.

2 *belonging to the visible heavens or sky*, v. HEAVENLY. आकाशाचा, आकाशमंडल संबंधी.

C. Globe. खगोल *m.*

CELESTIAL, *n. inhabitant of heaven.* देवलोकवासी, देवलोकस्थ, स्वर्गवासी, स्वर्गी.

CELIBACY, CELIBATE, *n. unmarried state.* अवरठेपणा *m.* निबेपणा *m.* अविवाह *m.* अपरिणयन *n.* अनुद्वाह *m.* अविवाहितावस्था *f.* अनूढावस्था *f.*—of Bráhmans, ब्रह्मचर्य *n.* ब्रह्मचारिता *f.* ब्रह्मचारीपणा *m.*

Life of c., study, and devotion. नैष्ठिकब्रह्मचर्य *n.* (*and* Leader of it), नैष्ठिकब्रह्मचारी *m.* नैष्ठिकब्रह्मचारिणी *f.*

CELIBATE, *n.* v. BACHELOR. अविवाहित पुरुष *m.* [गर्त्ता *f.*

CELL, *n. small cavity*, v. HOLLOW. खळी *f.* खळगी *f.* घर *n.* सूक्ष्म-

2 *small apartment.* खण *m.* खाना *m.* पूड *m.*

C. with bars. पिंजरा *m.*

3—as in tables of calculation, &c. कोष्टक *m. n.* घर *n.*

4 *little bag or bladder (of animals).* कोश *m.* पिशवी *f.*

CELLAR, *n.* तळघर *n.* भुयार *n.* जिन्नसखाना *m.* बोखार *or* बोखारें *n.* बोगदा *m.*

C. for grain. पेंव *n.*

CELLULAR, *a. consisting of cells.* खळ्यांचा, खळग्यांचा, बारीकघरांचा, सूक्ष्मगर्त्ता प्रचुर, सूक्ष्मगर्त्तामय.

CEMENT, *n.* सांधणें *n.* जोडणें *n.* संधानसाधन *n.* संधानवस्तु *n.*-द्रव्य *n.*—of glue, paste, &c. चिकटवण *n.* डकवण *n.* लुकण *n.*—of mortar, गारा *m.* गिलावा *m.*—of tin, कस्तर *or* कस्तूर *m.n.*

2 fig. *bond of union.* लगा *m.* लगाबांधा *m.* [*g. of o.*

To CEMENT, *v. a.* सांधणें, जोडणें, सांधपणें, सांधप *n.*-&c. करणें

To CEMENT, *v. n. unite and cohere.* सांधणें.

CEMETERY, *n. repository for the dead.* श्मशान *pop.* मसण *n.* मसणवटी *f.* मसणवटा *m.* मसणखाई *f.* स्मशानभूमि *f.* प्रेतस्थान *n.* प्रेतभूमि *f.* प्रेतवन *n.* पितृवन *n.* मृतस्थान *n.* रुद्रभूमि *f.* शवालय *n.* शिवालय *n.* [छत्री *f.*

CENOTAPH, *n. empty monument.* अन्यस्थलीं पुरलेल्या मनुष्याची

To CENSE, *v. a.* v. *To* INCENSE. धूप *m.* देणें.

CENSER, *n.* धुपटणें *or* धुपाटणें *n.* धुपारती *f.*

CENSOR, *n. corrector of public morals.* कर्माध्यक्ष *c.* धर्माधिकारी, धर्माध्यक्ष *c.* [अधिकारी.

2 लेख पुस्तकें छापण्यास योग्य आहेत कीं नाहींत हें पाहण्याचा

CENSORIAL, *a. belonging to a censor.* धर्माधिकारिसंबंधी, धर्माध्यक्षसंबंधी.

CENSORIOUS, *a. addicted to censure.* खुसपट्या, दोषदृष्टि, दोषदर्शी, दोषग्राही, दोषारोपी, दोषान्वेषी, छिद्रदर्शी, छिद्रान्वेषी, छिद्रानुसारी, रंध्रान्वेषी, अवगुणदर्शी, क्षतदर्शी, दोषवादी, अगुणवादी, गुणघाती, निंदाखोर, निंदक, निमित्तखोर, दांतकसाळी, उणें पाहणारा.

2 *implying or expressing censure.* दोषदृष्टीचा, दोषबुद्धीचा.

CENSORIOUSLY, *adv.* v. A. दोषदृष्टीनें, छिद्रदृष्टीनें, दोषबुद्धीनें.

CENSORIOUSNESS, *n.* v. A. दोषदृष्टि *f.* दोषबुद्धि *f.* छिद्रदृष्टि *f.* छिद्रान्वेषण *n.* रंध्रान्वेषण *n.* दोषवादन *n.* दांतकसाळ *f.* In reprehension of *Censoriousness* there are some phrases and proverbs. These sufficiently agree with "*Physician heal thyself; First pluck the beam out of thine own eye, then the mote out of thy neighbour's eye; Look first at home; Keep your own house; Dress your own garden, &c.*" दुसऱ्याचे डोळ्यांतलें कुसळ आपले डोळ्यांतलें मुसळ, आपल्या पायांखालीं जळतें आणि डोंगरचें विझवायाला धावावें, अगोदर आपल्या पागोट्यासीं भांडावें मग दुसऱ्याचे पागोट्यासीं भांडावें.

CENSORSHIP, *n.* धर्माधिकार *m.* धर्माधिकरण *n.*

CENSURABLE. See BLAMABLE.

To CENSURE, CENSURE. See *To* BLAME, BLAME.

CENSUS, *n. enumeration of inhabitants.* लोकगणती *f.* खानेसुमारी *f.* प्रजागणन *n.*

CENT, *n.* शेंकडा *m.* शतक *n.*

Per c. शेंकडां, दरशेंकडा, दरसद्दे.

CENTAGE, *n.* शेंकड्याचा भाव *m.*

CENTAUR, *n.* नराश्व *m.* हयग्रीव *m.* हयांग *m.* धनूराशि *m.*

CENTENARIAN, *n. person a hundred years old.* शतायु, शतवयस्क, शतवार्षिक.

CENTENARY, *n.* शेंकडा *m.* शतक *n.*

CENTENNIAL, *a. consisting of* 100 *years.* शंभरवर्षांचा, शतवार्षिक, शताब्दिक.

2 *pertaining to* 100 *years.* शंभरवर्षांचा, शतवर्षीय, शंभरवर्षांच्या संबंधाचा, शतवार्षिक.

3 *happening every* 100 *years.* शंभरशंभर वर्षांनीं घडून येणारा, प्रतिशताब्दिक.

CENTESIMAL, *a.* शंभरावा.

CENTESIMAL, *n.* शतांश *m.*

CENTIFOLIOUS, *a.* शतपत्र, शतपत्रक.

CENTINODY, *n.* शतपर्वा *f.*

CENTIPEDE, *n.* गोम *f.* घोण *f.* शतपदी *f.*

CENTO, *n.* शेंकडा *m.* शतक *n.*

CENTRAL, CENTRICAL, *a. belonging to the centre*, v. MIDDLE. मधचा, मधला, मधील, मध्य. [स्थित.

2 *placed in centre*, v. MIDDLE. मध्यवर्त्ती, मध्यस्थ, मध्य-

CENTRALITY, *n.* v. A. मध्यत्व *n.* मध्यस्थता *f.* मध्यस्थितता *f.*

CENTRE, *n.* v. MIDDLE. मध्य *m.* गर्भ *f.*

2 (of a circle, &c.). केंद्र *n.* नाभि *m. f.* बिंदु *or* मध्यबिंदु *m.* मध्य (in comp. as वृत्तमध्य, &c). [करणें.

To CENTRE, *v. a. collect to a point.* एकलक्ष्यस्थित-स्थगित-&c.

To CENTRE, *v. n. be collected to a point.* एकलक्ष्यस्थित होणें-असणें, एकाच आधारावर होणें-असणें.

CENTRICALLY, *adv.* v. A. मध्यें, मध्यभागीं. [मध्यत्यागी.

CENTRIFUGAL, *a. that recedes from the centre.* मध्योत्सारी,

CENTRIPETAL, *a. that has a tendency to the centre.* मध्याभिगामी, मध्याभिसारी, मध्याभिसरणशील.

CENTUPLE, *a.* शंभरपट, शतगुण.

CENTURION, *n.* शतपति *m* शताधीश *m.*

CENTURY, *n. a hundred.* शेंकडा *m.* शतक *n.* सद्दी *f.*

2 *a hundred years.* शतक *n.* अब्दशत *n.* वर्षशत *n.*

CEPHALIC, *n. medicine for the headache.* नस *m.* नस्य *n.* नध *f. f.* मस्तकशूलहारि औषध *n.*

CEPHALIC, *a. belonging to the head.* मस्तकाचा, मस्तकसंबंधी,

शिरस्य, मूर्धन्य.

CEREAL, *n. edible grain.* खाण्या जोगें धान्य *n.* खाद्यधान्य *n.*

CEREAL, *a.* खाद्य धान्य संबंधी-विषयक.

CEREBELLUM, *n.* मस्तकांतील मगजाचा खालचा व मागला भाग *m.*

CEREBRAL, *a.* मस्तकांतील मगजाचा, मस्तकांतील मेंदूचा.

C. letter. मूर्धन्य.

CEREBRUM, *n.* मस्तकांतील मगजाचा वरचा व मोठा भाग *m.*

CERECLOTH, CEREMENT, *n. waxed cloth.* मेणकापड *n.*

CEREMONIAL, *a. belonging to ceremony, consisting in ceremony, ritual, &c.* कर्माचा, क्रियेचा, उपचाराचा, क्रियासंबंधी-विषयक, कर्मसंबंधी-विषयक, कर्मात्मक, क्रियात्मक, कर्मरूप, क्रियारूप, आचरणसंबंधी-विषयक. See also RITUAL.

CEREMONIAL, *n. outward form or rite.* क्रिया *f.* कर्म*n.* रीति*f.* संस्कार*m.* उपचार *m.pl.* आचरण*n.* आचार*m.*

CEREMONIALIST. See CEREMONIOUS, 1.

CEREMONIOUS, *a. observant of forms and rites.* कर्मनिष्ठ, क्रियानिष्ठ, आचारनिष्ठ, कर्मतत्पर, क्रियातत्पर, आचारतत्पर, कर्मठ, कर्मशील, आचारपूत, आचारसंपन्न, आचारशुद्ध, कर्मसंगी.

2 *observant of ceremony, formal.* आदरोपचारी, आदरोपचारशील, आदरसत्कारी, आदरोपचारनिष्ठ, आदरलक्षी, आदरमानी.

3 *consisting of ceremonies and rites.* See CEREMONIAL.

CEREMONIOUSLY, *adv.* v. A. 2. आदरोपचारानें, आदरसत्कारानें, आदरोपचारबुद्धीनें.

CEREMONIOUSNESS, *n.* v. A. 2. आदरोपचारनिष्ठा *f.* आदरोपचारभक्ति *f.* आदरोपचारबुद्धि *f.*

CEREMONY, *n.* v. RITE. क्रिया *f.* कर्म*n.* संस्कार*m.* रीति *f.*

—gener. or loosely. अनुष्ठानप्रसंग*m.*

Closing c.—gener. उद्यापन *n.*

Conductor of a c. याज्ञिक*m.*

2 *forms of civility,* v. CIVILITIES. आदरोपचार*m.* आदरसत्कार*m.* उठबस *f.* उठाबैस *f.*

3 *forms of state.* दर्बारीडौल*m.*-शिरस्ता*m.*-रीत *f.*-&c.

Master of the ceremonies, v. CONDUCTOR. समानायक*m.* सभापति*m.* संपादक *m.*

CERTAIN, *a. sure, confident, undoubting.* निस्सशय, निस्संदेह, निर्भ्रांत, निभ्रांत, निश्चयी, दृढनिश्चय, जातनिश्चय, कृतनिश्चय, बद्धनिश्चय, निश्चितमनस्क, निभ्रांतमनस्क, निभ्रांतचित्त, जातनिर्धार, निर्धारयुक्त, हीनसंशय, हीनसंदेह, संशय-&c. हीन-रहित-शून्य, बिनदिक्कत.

"I am certain." माझी खातरी आहे.

2 *indubitable, undeniable.* निश्चयाचा, निश्चयात्मक, असंदिग्ध, निस्संदिग्ध, निःसशय, निर्धाराचा, खचीत, निखालस, निश्चित, तहकीक, निभ्रांत, बिनदिक्कतीचा, बिनतकरारीचा, ससूस, निर्विवाद.

3 *of sure occurrence or action, unfailing.* खचीत, निश्चयाचा, निस्संदिग्ध, निस्संदेह, निस्संशय, आवश्यक, अवश्यंभावी, अचूक, भाव्य, ससूस.

4 *settled, stated, fixed.* नेमाचा, निश्चित, नियमित *pop.* नेमित, निर्धारित, खचीत, ठाम.

5 v. SOME. कोण्ही एक, कितीएक.

A c. person. अमुक, अमका, फलाणा *or* ना.

CERTAINLY, *adv.* v. A. 1. निर्भ्रांत, निभ्रांत, निभ्रांतपणीं, संशयावांचून, &c. निखालस, खचीत, निश्चयपूर्वक, निश्चयपुरस्सर, निश्चितबुद्धीनें, निश्चितमनानें.

3 *without fail.* खचीत, अगत्य, अगत्यानें, अगत्यपूर्वक, अगत्यरूप, अगत्यपुरस्सर, अवश्य,अवश्यक अवश्यमेव, निश्चय, निश्चयपूर्वक, निश्चयात्मक, निस्संदिग्ध, निस्संदेह, निस्संशय, असंशय, अलबत्त*or* त्तां, खामखा, ससूस, खास, खरोखर *or* रीं *or* रें, आहस्त्य, नियत, निरुतां *or* तें, मुक्रर, कीर, निखालस, परिछिन्न.

CERTAINNESS, CERTAINTY, *n.* v. A. 1. निर्भ्रांत *f.* निभ्रांतपणा*m.* निर्धार *m.* निश्चय *m.* निधडा *m.* खातर *f.* खातरजमा *f.* निस्संशयत्व *n.* निस्संदेहत्व *n.* संदेह-&c. राहित्य *n.* संदेहाभाव *m.* संशयाभाव *m.*

2 निभ्रांत *f.* निखालसपणा *m.* निखालसता *f.* खचीतपणा *m.* खचिती *f.* निस्संदिग्धता *f.* तहकीकपणा *m.*

3 निश्चय *m.* नैश्चित्य *n.* आवश्यकता *f.* अवश्यंभाविता *f.* निश्चयघटमानता *f.*

I. *a c. a real and fixed thing.* खचीत-निश्चित-निर्धारित-&c. गोष्ट *f.*-विषय *m.*-&c. निश्चितार्थ *m.*

CERTIFICATE, *n.* चिठ्ठी *f.* लेख *m.* दाखला *m.* सड *f.* दस्तऐवज *m.* प्रमाणलेख*m.* आगम*m.* पत्र *n.* (in comp. with the indicating noun, as शुद्धिपत्र c. of purification; अर्जितपत्र c. of pre-eminence; आब्रूपत्र c. of good character, &c.) The word सरटिफिकेत from the English is common.

To CERTIFY, *v. n. testify to a thing in writing.* दाखला *m.*-दस्तऐवज *m.*-प्रमाणलेख *m.*-खातरीचालेख *m.*-निशेचा कागद *m.*-&c. देणें-लिहून देणें, निश्चयपूर्वक लिहून देणें.

To CERTIFY, *v. a. assure of, apprize,* v. To INFORM. माहितगार-ज्ञात-ज्ञापित-&c. करणें.

CERTITUDE, See CERTAINTY.

CERULEAN, *a. sky-colored.* आस्मानी, आकाशवर्ण.

CERUMEN, *n. wax of the ear.* कानांतलामळ *m.* कर्णमल *m.*

CERUSE, *n. white-lead.* सफेता *or* दा *m.*

CERVICAL, *a. belonging to the neck.* मानेचा, ग्रैव, ग्रैवेय, ग्रीवासंबंधी.

CESSATION, *n. ceasing, stopping.* राहणें *n.* &c. उपरम *m.* उपराम *m.* उपरति *f.* विराम *m.* विरति *f.* निवृत्ति *f.* निवर्त्तन *n.* याम *m.*

2 v. INTERMISSION. महकुबी *f.* अवसान *n.* अवसाय *m.*

CESSION, v. V.—*act.* सोडणें *n.* सोडून देणें *n.* स्वीयत्याग करण *n.* त्यागपूर्वकदान *n.*

CEYLON, *n.* लंका *f.* सिंहलद्वीप *m. n.* सिंहल *n.* सिंहला *f.*

To CHAFE, *v. a. excite by rubbing.* चोळून-&c. चेतना *f.*-जीव*m.*-उबारा *m.*-चेतव *m.*-&c. आणणें, चेतनासंपादकमर्दन *n.* करणें.

2 *wear by rubbing, fret, abrade,* v. To RUB. चोळणें, चोळवटणें.

3 v. To ANGER. चेतवणें, चिडवणें, खिजावणें.

To CHAFE, *v. n. rave, boil,* v. To FUME. चडफडणें, तडफडणें, उबगणें, खलखलणें, तडफड *f. intens.* तडफडाट *m.*-चडफड *f. intens.* चडफडाट *m.* करणें.

CHAFE, *n. heat excited by friction.* घर्षणानें झालेली उष्णता *f.*

2 *mental commotion,* v. HEAT. संताप *m.* मनस्ताप *m.*

CHAFF, *n.* v. HUSKS. भुसा *m.* भूस *n.* भुसकट *n.* भुशी *f.* फोल *n.* तुष *m. pop.* तूस *n. m.* बोघगें *n.*

To CHAFFER. See To HAGGLE.

CHAFFINCH, *n.* पांखराची एक जात आहे.

CHAFFY, *a. having much chaff.* भुसकट.

2 v. LIGHT भुसासारखा हलका, भुसकट, तृणवत्.

CHAFING-DISH, *n.* शेगडी *f.* हसती *f.* शकटी *f.*

CHAGRIN, *n.* रुसवा *m.* खफामर्जी *f.* रुष्टभाव *m.* रुष्टता *f.* खट्टूपणा*m.*
To CHAGRIN, *v. a. vex.* खपाकरणें, रुसवणें, रुष्टकरणें, खट्टूकरणें.
CHAIN, *n.* सांखळ *dim.* सांखळी *f.* शृंखला *f.*
Fine c. (as of a watch, &c.). जंजिरी *f.* जंजीर *f.*
Large iron c. लंगर *m.*
Large and thick c. सांखळदंड *m.*
Little c. C. of two or three links. कडी *f.*
2 *fetter, bond, shackle,* lit. fig. बंद *m.* बंधन *n.* बंध *m.* चिडी *or* बेडी *f.* शृंखलाबंध *m.* शृंखलाबंधन *n.*
To rivet one's chains. *fig.* गळ्यांत गोणी *f.* आणणें.
3 *series, concatenation, &c.* सांखळी *f.* शृंखला *f.* माला *pop.* माळ *f.* ओळ *f.* सिलसिला *m.* शेज *n. f.* श्रेणि *f.* अन्वय *m.* आनुपूर्वी *f.* आनुपूर्व्य *n.*
To CHAIN, *v. a.* सांखळणें, सांखळीनें बंदकरणें, शृंखलाबद्ध करणें.
CHAIN SHOT *n.* जंजिरी गोळी *f.* जोडगोळी *f.*
CHAINED, *p.* v. V. सांखळीनें बांधलेला, शृंखलाबद्ध.
CHAINING, *n.* v. V.—*act.* सांखळणें *n.* शृंखलाबंध *m.* शृंखलाबंधन*n.*
CHAIR, *n.* खुरसी *f.*
Easy c. or seat. सुखासन *n.* [क्षासन *n.*
2 *seat of authority.* गादी *f.* अग्रासन *n.* मुख्यासन *n.* अध्य-
3 (Professor's) गुरुपीठ *n.* गुरुचीजागा *f.*
4 sedan c. नालकी *f.*
5 *or* chair-days. बसण्याचे दिवस *m. pl.* वृद्धापकाळ *m.*
CHAIRMAN, *n.* v. PRESIDENT. सभानायक *m.* सभापति *m.* सभाध्यक्ष *m.* सारथी *m.*
2 See BEARER.
CHAISE. See CARRIAGE.
CHALCEDONY, *n.* शिवधातु *m.*
CHALDRON, *n.* एक माप आहे.
CHALICE, *n.* प्याला *or* पेला *m.* अर्घ्या *f.*
CHALK, *n.* कठिनी *f.* सितधातु *m.* ओक *f.* दुधीमाती *f.* The English word under the form of चाक*m.* is commonly used.
Red c. रक्तधातु *m.* सुरंगधातु *m.*
To CHALK, *v. a.* चाकानें रेखाटणें-अंकणें-&c.
2 out. v. To DESCRIBE. रेखाटणें, काढणें, बेतणें.
To CHALLENGE, *v.a. call to contest.* लढाई *f.* मागणें *with* जवळ *of o.* युद्धाह्वान *n.*-युद्धामंत्रण-युद्धनिमंत्रण*n.*-&c. करणें, दाली *f.* बांधणें *with* सीं *of o.* हटकणें.
2 See To CLAIM. 3—as a sentry. हटकणें, ललकारणें.
4 (in a trial) आपल्या खटल्याची चौकशी करण्यांत अमूक पंच नसावा असें म्हणणें.
CHALLENGE, CHALLENGING, *n.* v. V. I.—*act.* लढाई मागणें*n.* युद्धाह्वान*n.* युद्धामंत्रण*n.* युद्धनिमंत्रण*n.*
To accept a c. विडा*m.* उचलणें.
I. written c. युद्धाह्वानपत्र*n.*
CHALYBEATE, *a. impregnated with iron.* लोहगुण मिश्रित, लोहगुणान्वित, लोहगुणात्मक.
CHAMADE. *n.* रुमालफिरवणें*n.*
CHAMBER, *n. apartment,* v. ROOM. कोठडी *f.* खोली *f.*
2 (of a gun). खजीना*m.* कोठा*m.* कोठी *f.* पेट*m.*
3 See ASSEMBLY, BOARD.
CHAMBERLAIN, *n.* खासगीकडचा कारभारी.
CHAMELEON, *n.* सरड*m.* सरडा*m.* सरट *or* शरट*m.*

CHAMFER, CHAMFRET, *n.* v. GROOVE. खांचणी *f.*
CHAMOIS. See GOAT.
CHAMOMILE, *n. anthemis nobilis,* बाबुना*m.*
To CHAMP, *v. a.* चावणें, चघळणें.
CHAMPAIGN, *flat, open country,* v. PLAIN. पटंगण *or* पटांगण*n.* पाटा*m.* मैदान*n.*
CHAMPION, *n. one who combats in the place or cause of another.* वारचा योद्धा*m.* कैवारी*m.*
2 *warrior, &c.* v. HERO. वीर*m.* एकांगवीर*m.* एकांड्या*m.* योद्धा*m.* [वगति *f.*
CHANCE, *n.*—as the *cause* of events, v. FORTUNE. दैव*n.* दै-
By c. दैवानें, दैवयोगानें, दैववशें, दैववशात्, दैवात्, प्रारब्धगत्या, यदृच्छेकरून.
2 *fortune, fate, turn up, luck,* v. FORTUNE, DESTINY. दैवदशा *f.* दैवगत *f.* दैवरेषा *f.* कपाळरेखा *f.* दैवयोग*m.* दैवघटित*n.* विधियोग*m.* प्राक्तनयोग*m.* अदृष्टयोग*m.* दैव*n.* प्रारब्ध*n.*
3 *causal or fortuitous occurrence,* v. ACCIDENT. दैवकृत्य*n.* दैवघटित*n.* काकतालीय*n.* यदृच्छा *f.*
4 *possibility of occurrence.* संभव*m.* संभावना *f. or* होण्याची-घडण्याची-&c. संभावना *f.*-संभव*m.*-संभूति *f.* घटनायोग*m.* घटनशक्यता *f.*
CHANCE, *a. casual,* v. ACCIDENTAL. दैवागत, दैवघटित, दैवप्राप्त, आगंतुक, विधिप्राप्त.
To CHANCE, *v. n.* v. To HAPPEN. घडणें, घडून येणें.
CHANCEL, *n.* देवळांत कठड्याच्या पलीकडील भाग.
CHANCELLOR, *n.*—one of the ministers. पंडितराव*m.*
CHANCERY, *n.* सदर अदालत *f.*
Suit in c. *fig.* साहा महिन्यांची जांभई *f.* तोंड धरून बुक्यांचा मार*m.* खटकर्म*n.*
CHANCRE, *n.* चट्टा*m.*
CHANDELIER, *n.* झुंबर*m.* झाड*n.* or दिव्यांचें झाड*n.* झुगर*n.* दीपवृक्ष*m.*
CHANDLER, *n.* विक्या. See CORN-CHANDLER, &c.
To CHANGE, *v. a. put or quit for, shift.* बदलणें, पालटणें, बदली *f.* करणें.
2 *interchange.* v. To EXCHANGE. अदलाबदल *f.*-बदलाबदल *f.* -&c. करणें *g. of o.*
3 *alter, vary.* बदलणें, पालटणें, फिरवणें, परतणें, नवाजुना करणें, फेर*m.*-फेरफार*m.*-भेद*m.*-रूपांतर*n.*-रूपभेद*m.*-&c. करणें *g. of o.*
4 (money). मोडणें, वटाविणें.
To c. a rupee. खुर्दा *m.* करणें.
5 *make acid.* See To TURN.
To CHANGE, *v. n. suffer change.* बदलणें, फिरणें, परतणें, पालटणें, फेर*m.*-भेद*m.*-अंतर*n.*-&c. पडणें *in. con. or* होणें *g. of o.* अवस्थांतर*n.*-स्थित्यंतर*n.*-अन्यथाभाव*m.*-&c. पावणें.
To c. for worse.—esp. of persons. बदल*m.* खाणें, बिचल *f.* खाणें, बिचलणें, बिथरणें, पगडी *f.* फिरणें *or* फेरपगडी करणें.
CHANGE, CHANGING, *n.* v. V. A. 1.—*act.* पालटणें*n.* बदलणें*n.*
2 अदलाबदल *f.* बदलाबदल *f.* विनिमय*m.*
3 फिरवणें*n.* पालटणें*n.*&c. भेद*m.* पालट*m.* पालटणी *f.* पालटवाणी *f.*
4 मोडणें*n.*
v. V. N.—*state.* फेर *m.* भेद *m.* पालट *m.* विकार *m.* विकृति *f.* अवस्थांतर *n.* स्थित्यंतर *n.* रूपांतर *n.* रूपभेद *m.* अन्यथाभाव*m.* परिणाम *m.* विपरिणमन *n.*

I. *small money.* खुर्दा *m.* (copper change). मोड *f.*
Keeper of c. for traffic. खुर्देकरी.

CHANGEABLE, *a.* v. V. A. 1. *possible to be changed.* फिरवाया-परताया-&c. चा-जोगा-जोगता-&c. फेरफार कराचा जोगा-&c. विपरिणमनीय.
I. *changeful, mutable, variable, inconstant, fickle, versatile, &c.* चंचल, चपल, चंचलचित्त, चंचलवृत्ति, तरल *or* प्रकृति तरल, बावसा, लहरी, लहरीदार, लहरीबहरी, उडलटप्पू, उडाणटप्पू, उचलचावडा, अस्थायी, अस्थिर, अस्थिरबुद्धि, क्षणिकबुद्धि, क्षणिकचित्त, अस्थिरचित्त, क्षणिकवृत्ति, तिरतिरा *or* -र्या, हरिद्वाराग, छंदसोर, छंदिष्ट, इतलतितल.

CHANGEABLENESS, *n.* v. A. 1. फिरावया &c. जोगेपणा *m.*
1. चांचल्य *n.* चापल्य *n.* चंचलता *f.* चपलता *f.* चंचलवृत्ति *f.* चंचलबुद्धि *f.* पाउलबुद्धि *f.* क्षणिकबुद्धि *f.*-विचार*m.* -निश्चय *m.*-कल्पना *f.*

CHANGED, *p.* v. V. N. बदललेला, फिरलेला, फेर पडलेला-झालेला, &c. विकारित, विरुत, वैरुत, परिणत.

CHANGEFUL. See CHANGEABLE.

CHANGELESS, *a.* v. CONSTANT. अचंचल, स्थिर.

CHANGELING, *n. changed child.* बदलेंमूल *n.* परिवर्तित संतान *n.*
2 *fickle person,* v. CHANGEABLE. उडाणटप्पू *c.* उडलटप्पू *c.*

CHANNEL, *n.* (of a river, &c.) v. BED. पात्र *n.* तास *m.*
2 (for water, for irrigation, &c.). पाट *m.* टरळी *f.* सारणी *f.* कुल्या *f. pop.* कालवा *m.*
Ever running c. ओला दंड *m.*
Raised c. or course. दांडा *m.*
3 (to carry off water) *gutter.* मोहरी *or* मोरी *f.* नहर *m.* प्रणालिका *f.* प्रणाली *f.* सारणी *f.*
4 (as of a pillar, &c.). खांचणी *f.* बलकी *f.*
5 *strait.* महासामुद्रधुनी *f.* रुंदसामुद्रधुनी *f.*
6 *medium.* द्वार *pop.* दार *n.* मार्ग *m.* वाट *f.*

To CHANNEL, *v. a.* खांचणी *f.*-&c. पाडणें.

To CHANT, CHANT, &c. See To SING, SONG, &c.

CHANTICLEER. See COCK.

CHAOS, *n. primeval confusion.* अपंचीकृत भूतस्थिति *f.* भूतसंकर *m.* भूताव्यवस्था *f.*
Reduction of c. पंचीकरण *n.*
2 v. JUMBLE. घोटाळा *m.* घालमेल *f.* संकर *m.*

CHAOTIC, *a.* v. N. 1. अपंचीकृत, अपंचीकृतात्मक, अपंचीकृतरूप.
2 v. CONFUSED. घोटाळ्याचा, अव्यवस्थित, अस्ताव्यस्त, अक्रम.

To CHAP, *v. n.* v. To CRACK. फुटणें, उलणें, तडतडणें, भेगळणें.
Ready to c. फुटरा.

To CHAP, *v. a.* भेगा *f. pl.*-चिरा *f. pl.*-&c. पाडणें *g. of o.*

CHAP, *n.* v. CRACK. भेग *f.* तीड *f.* चीर *f.*
2 v. JAW. बेचाळी *f. or* ळें *n.* हनु *f.*
Chaps. जबडा *or* जावडा *m.* चावडा *m.* जांभाड *n.* टाळीं *n. pl.* मुसकुरी *f.* मुसकें *n.* [*m. pl.* पाजवणें.
To lick the c. जिभल्या *f. pl.* चाटणें, लाळ *f.* घोटणें. दांत
3 (of a channel, river, &c.). तोंड *n.*

CHAP, *n.* v. FELLOW. गडी *m.* बच्चाजी *m.* बच्चाराम *m.*

CHAP-FALLEN, *a.* तोंड उतरलेला, हिमटतोंड्या, हिरमूसतोंड्या, हिंपुटी, हिंपूट *or* हिमट.
To be c. तोंड *n.* फुटणें-उतरणें-खरकणें *g. of s.* दांत *m. pl.* पडणें *g. of s.*

CHAPE, *n. hold, hook.* v. CATCH. अडकण *n.* अडकवण *n.*
2 (of a scabbard, &c.). तैनाल *or* तहनाल *m. n.*

CHAPEL. See CHURCH.

CHAPERON, *n.* संभाळण्याकरितां बरोबर जाणारा.

CHAPITER, *n. upper part of a pillar.* स्तंभशीर्ष *n.*

CHAPLAIN, *n.* पाद्री *m.*

CHAPLET, *n. garland for the head,* v. GARLAND. पुष्पमाला *f.* शेखर *m.* घोंसा *m.*
C. used at marriages. मुंडावळ *f.* मुंडावळी *f.* शेघळ *or* शिघळ *m. f.* बाशिंग *n.*
Reticulated c. जाळी *f.* जाळिदांडा *m.* [ला *f.*
2 *string of beads,* v. ROSARY. जपमाला *f.* स्मरणी *f.* अक्षमा-

CHAPTER, *n. division of a book.* अध्याय *m.* कांड *n. m.* स्कंध *m.* वर्ग *m.* पर्व *n.* प्रकरण *n.* परिच्छेद *m.* उल्लास *m.* स्तबक *m.* अंक *m.* खंड *m. n.*
2 मोठ्या देवळांतील धर्मोपदेशकांची मंडळी.

To CHAR, *v. a.* कोळसा *m.* करणें *g. of o.*

To CHAR, *v. n.* आडकाम *n.*-रोजकाम *n.*-&c. करणें.

CHAR, CHAR-WORK, *n. odd or day work.* रोजकाम *n.* मोलकाम *n.* आडकाम *n.* दळाकांडा *m.* केरकोंडा *m.* दळणभरडण *n.*

CHAR-WOMAN, *n.* आडकामी *f.* कामकरीण *f.* रोजकरीण *f.* मोलकामी *f.* मोलकरीण *f.* मोलारीण *f.*

CHARACTER, *n.* v. MARK. चिन्ह *n.* अंक *m.* मुद्रा *f.*
2 *letter used in writing or printing.* अक्षर *n.* वर्ण *m.*
3 *manner of writing,* v. HAND. लिपि *pop.* लीप *f.* बळण *n.*
Arabic or Persian c. यवनलिपि *f.* यवनानी *f.*
Common business-c. of the Maráṭhás. मोड *f.* मराठी लिपि *f.* पिशाच लिपि *f.* हेमाडपंती *f.*
The book c. बाळबद *or* बालबोध *n.* देवनागरी *f.*
4 (of a person) *distinguishing qualities.* धर्म *m.* स्वधर्म *m.* स्वभाव *m.* विशेषगुण *m. pl.* विशेषधर्म *m.* गुणलक्षण *n.* स्वभावाचीं लक्षणें *n. pl* स्वरूप *n.* शील *n.*
5 (of a thing, place, &c.). मुद्रा *f.* स्वधर्म *m.* गुणागुण *m. pl.* गुणावगुण *m. pl.* गुणदोष *m. pl.*
6 v. PERSON, PERSONAGE. व्यक्ति *f.* शिष्टजन *m.*
7 (in a play) *part.* सोंग *n.* रूप *n.* वेष *m.*
Costume of a c. भूमिका *f.*
Of an assumed c. कपटरूपी.
To act in c. *act like one's self.* आपलीसी *adv.* करणें.
We must act in c. बेडीचें सोंग घेतलें तर पाटांव फाडला पाहिजे.
8 *certificate of the c. of.* आब्रूपत्र *n.* गुणावगुणपत्र *n.* गुणवर्णनपत्र *n.* वर्त्तनपत्र *n.*
9 *credit, reputation.* आब्रू *f.* आब *m.* नांव *n.* पत *f.*
To lose one's c. तोंड *n.* फुटणें *g. of s.*

CHARACTERISTIC, *n.* लक्षण *n.* विशेष *m.* उपाधि *m.* खुबी *f.*

CHARACTERISTIC, CHARACTERISTICAL, *a.* लाक्षणिक, असाधारण, विशेषक, स्वभावदर्शक-सूचक, स्वधर्म-लक्षण सूचक-दर्शक, विशेषगुणबोधक.

To CHARACTERIZE, *v. a. designate by some stamp or mark.* अंकित-मुद्रित-&c. करणें.
2 *describe the c. of.* लक्षण *n.* करणें-करून सांगणें *g. of o.*

लक्षण कथन *n.*-लक्षणवर्णन *n.*-गुणवर्णन *n.* करणें *g. of o.*

CHARACTERIZED, *p.* v. V. 1. अंकित, लक्षित, लक्षणलक्षित, लक्षणयुक्त, विशेषित, विशिष्ट.

CHARCOAL, *n.* कोळसा *m.*

Red hot c. जितकोळसा *or* जिताकोळसा.

CHARCOAL-BURNER, *n.* लोणारी, कोळसेकरी.

To CHARGE, *v. a.* See To FILL. To LOAD. 2 (with some business, matter or thing,) *commission, entrust,* v. To COMMIT. दिम्मतीस-तैनातीस-तसलमातीस-पागेस-दुमाल्यास-विल्हेस-&c. लावणें-घालणें-देणें, माथां *or* माथीं मारणें, गळयांत घालणें, ओझें *n.*-भार *m.*-माळ *f.*-माळखंड *n.* गळयांत घालणें, स्वाधीन करणें. Note. In all these renderings *the business charged* is the object of the verb, and the *person charged with* it is in the genitive case. सांगणें, घालणें, आरोपणें *with* वर.

3 (with a crime) *accuse.* आरोपणें, आरोप *m.*-अभियोग *m.* करणें *with* वर, माथां *or* माथीं मारणें, आणणें *with* वर, चार्ज *m.* ठेवणें.

4 *enjoin, exhort, &c.* v. To COMMAND. खरावणें, बजावणें, हुडसणें, तटकारणें *or* खरावून-बजावून-हुडसून-&c. सांगणें.

5 *rush upon, assail,* v. To ATTACK. हल्ला*m.*-चाल *f.*-चढ*m.* करणें, चालून जाणें *with* वर *of o.* तुटून आंगावर येणें-जाणें-पडणें.

6 *lay against or set to as a debt.* नांवीं-नांवावर लिहणें-मांडणें, *g. of s.* खात्यास मांडणें- लावणें.

7 *ask as price, payment, &c.* मोल*n.*-किम्मत *f.*-हेल *m.f.*-भाडें *n.*-&c. मागणें सांगणें.

CHARGE, CHARGING, *n.* v. V. 2—*act.* आरोपणें*n.* दुमाल्यास लावणें*n.* &c. निरवणूक *f.* निरवणी *f.* [mon.

3 आरोप*m.* अभियोग*m.* चार्ज*m.* from the English is com-

A malicious or false c. तकरीर *m.* [वाट *or* टी *f.*

4 बजावणें*n.* खरावणें*n.* &c. ताकीद *f.* सांगणी *f.* आज्ञा *f.* वाटा-

5 चाल *f.* चढ *m.* चढाई *f.*

C. by a body of horse. मांड *f.*

I. *powder, &c. filled in a gun.* बार*m.* भर*m.* पेट*m.*

C. of nails, stones, balls, &c. छर्रा *m.*

II. *responsible custody, control, care, &c.* हवाला*m.* जिम्मा *m.f.* दिम्मत *f.* तसलमात *f* निसबत *f.* रखवाली *f* राखण *f.*

—gener. or freely. हवालाटवाला *m.* हवालाकपाला *m.*

Released from a c. जिम्मा पारक.

That holds a c. or trust. जिम्मेदार.

That is under the c. of. दिम्मतवार, दिम्मती.

Under the c. or care of. स्वाधीन, हवालां *or* लीं *or* लें.

III. *command or conduct of.* दिम्मत *f.* तैनात *f.* तसलमात *f.*

IV. *object committed to the c. of.* अनामत *f.* आपई *f.* दिम्मत *f.* दिम्मतीचा.

V. *body (as troops) under the c. of.* दिम्मत *f.*

VI. *business, &c. charged, trust conferred, commission, &c.* काम*n.* सोंपलेलें काम*n* अधिकार*m.*

VII. *expense,* v. COST. खर्च*m.* [करणें.

To CHARGE, *v. n. make an onset.* चाल *f.*-चढ*m.*-हल्ला*m.*-&c.

CHARGÉ D' AFFAIRES, *n.* v. CONDUCTOR, बहिवाटदार*m.*

CHARGER, *n.* v. DISH. थाळा *m.* तबक*n.*

2 *war horse.* लढाऊ घोडा*m.* रणघोडा*m.* रणाश्व*m.*

CHARILY, *adv.* v. A. काटकसरीनें, हात राखून.

CHARIOT, *n.* v. CARRIAGE. रथ *m.*

CHARIOTEER, *n.* सारथि *or* सारथी, सूत, रथसादी.

CHARIOTEERING, *n.* सारथ्य *n.* अश्वसारथ्य *n.*

CHARITABLE, *a. kind in judging, &c.* दयाळू, कृपादृष्टि, कृपादर्शी, गुणदृष्टि, अदोषदृष्टि, अदोषदर्शी, दोषादर्शी, दोष-छिद्र-&c. छादक गोप्ता.

2 *alms-giving.* दानधर्मी, दानधर्म करणारा, धर्मबुद्धि, धार्मिक, धर्मिष्ट, दीनदयाळ, दाता, दीनदयालु, दीनपोषक, दीनदाता, अन्नवस्त्रप्रदाता, धर्माचेपारी बसलेला, धर्मपरायण.

3 *pertaining, &c. to charity.* धर्माचा, दान धर्माचा, धर्मकृत्याचा, लोकोपकाराचा.

CHARITABLENESS, *n.* v. A.1. दयाळूपणा*m.* कृपादृष्टि *f.* दयालुता *f.* गरीब लोकांवर दया *f.* दातेपणा*m.* धार्मिकपणा *m.* धर्मबुद्धि *f.* धर्मस्वभाव*m.*

CHARITABLY, *adv.* v. A. 1. दयाळूपणानें, कृपादृष्टीनें, &c.

2 धार्मिकपणानें, धर्मबुद्धीनें.

CHARITY, *n. love, kindness, benevolence.* दया *f.* कृपा *f.* अनुकंपा *f.* परोपकारबुद्धि *f.* परहितबुद्धि *f.* परहितेच्छा *f.*

2 *liberality to the poor.* दीनदयाळूपणा*m.* दीनदया *f.* दीनदातृत्व*n.* दीनवात्सल्य*n.*—compreh. *charitable acts and works.* दानधर्म*m.* धर्मकृत्यें*n. pl.*

A charitable impulse. धर्मवासना *f.*

C. begins at home. घरांत दिवा तर देउळांत दिवा.

C. is always on the morrow. धर्मावर सोमवार.

Object of c. दानपात्र *n.*

Work or act of public c. लोकोपकार*m.* इष्टापूर्त*n.* पूर्त*n.*

To devote to c. (to charitable purposes). धर्मादाय *adv.* टाकणें *or* सोडणें.

3 *alms.* भिक्षा *pop.* भीक *f.* धर्म *m.* खैरात *f.* अन्नवस्त्र प्रदान *n.*

C.—paper. धर्मादाय पट्टी *f.* धर्मदाव पट्टी *f.*

By or on c. धर्मधर्मी, धर्मधर्मीनें.

In c. For c. &c. धर्मार्थ, धर्मादाय, धर्मपरायण.

Dine upon c. and call out for sauce! अन्नसत्रीं जेवणें आणि मिरपूड मागणें!

CHARLATAN, &c. See QUACK, &c.

CHARLES'S WAIN, *n.* v. BEAR. खाटलें बाजलें *n.* खाटलें *n.*

CHARM, *n. magic words, spell, &c.* मंत्र *m.* तंत्र *n.* कुबेडें *n.* तोडगा *or* तोटगा *m.* भारणी *f.* चेटक *n.*

Charms and spells,—compreh. जंतरमंतर *n.*टाणाटोणा *or* टोणाटाणा *m.* आसुरीमाया *f.* माव *f.* जादूटोणा *m.* ताडातोडा *m.*

Charms and incantations to produce death or evil. जारण *n.* जारणमारण *n.* There are amongst the Hindus *charms* and *charmed things* addressed against all the afflictions and afflictive apprehensions of life. Some are ओलांडा, केसारी, गंडा, गालबोट, चिरीपान, तापाचा देरा, धरण, धारबंद, तीट, दृश्मिणी, पाचुंदाचे मणी, निंबलोण, पंचाक्षरी *or* पंचाक्षरी मंत्र, भालदोरी, मंत्राक्षत *or* मंत्राक्षता, मिठकणी, मुष्टि *pop.* मूठ *f.* मृतसंजीविनी, यंत्र, रक्षा, राखांदुळी, राखी, रामरक्षा, वज्राबळ *or* वज्रावें, सलकडें.

Command of charms and spells. मंत्रसिद्धि *f.*

Idiocy produced through the misapplication of a c. (मंत्र) मंत्रचळ *m.* (*and* the person so affected, मंत्रचळया).

To acquire command over charms, &c. मंत्रसाधन *n.* करणें.
To apply, set, or cast a c. मंत्रप्रयोग *m.*-करणें, मंत्र *m.* मारणें-घालणें-टाकणें, भार *m.*-मारणी *f.* घालणें-टाकणें, करणी *f.* करणें.
2 charms; v. BEAUTY. रंजक गुण *m. pl.* मोहकगुण *m. pl.*

To CHARM, *v. a. subdue or affect by charms, bewitch, &c.* मारणें, मंत्रणें *or* मंतरणें, मोहणें, भारणी *f.* घालणें-टाकणें, भार *m.* घालणें-टाकणें, अभिमंत्रणें, मोह *m.*-मोहनी *f.* भुरळ *f.*-भुरळें *n.*-भूल *f.*-भुलवण *f.*-&c. घालणें-करणें, चेटक *n.*-कुबेडें *n.*-कुसळ *n.*-&c. करणें, मंत्रित-&c. करणें.
2 fig. *enchant, captivate, fascinate.* मोहणें, मोह *m.*-मोहनी *f.* -भूल *f.* &c. घालणें, भारणें, वशकरणें, भुलवणें, रंजन *n.*-मनोरंजन *n.*-&c. करणें *g. of o.* मोहित-रंजित-&c. करणें.
3 off; (scorpion-sting, &c.). मंत्रानें-मंत्र टाकून-मंत्र घालून -&c. उतरणें. [त, मोहित.

CHARMED, *p.* v. V. 1. भारलेला, मंतरलेला, &c. मंत्रित, अभिमंत्रि-
2 मोहलेला, भारलेला, भुललेला, मोहित, रंजित, गुणवेल्हाळ, वश.

CHARMER, *n.* CHARMING, *p. a.* v. V. 1. भारणारा, मंतरणारा, &c. मंत्री, मंत्रवादी, मोहक.
2 *and* AGREEABLE. मोहक, मारू, चित्तहारी, चित्तापहारी, मनोहर, मनोहारी, मनोरम, मनोभिराम, मनोज्ञ, मनोरंजक, रंजक, हृदयग्राही, हारी, हारक, दिव्य, कामरूप, कामरूपी, खुबीदार.
3 मंत्रफुंकून उतरणारा, उतारी.

CHARMING, *n.* v. V. 1. भारणें *n.* मोहणें *n.* &c. मोहन *n.* मोह *m.* मोहिनी *pop.* मोहनी *f.* मंत्रण *n.* अभिमंत्रण *n.* वशीकरण *n.* वशक्रिया *f.*
2 मारणें *n.* मोह घालणें *n.* मोहिन करणें *n.* &c. मोहन *n.* मोह *m.* मनोहरण *n.* चित्तहरण *n.* मनोरंजन *n.* रंजन *n.*

CHARMINGLY, *adv.* v. A. 2. मनोरंजन होण्याजोगा, मनोरंजनपूर्वक.

CHARMINGNESS, *n.* v. A. 2. मोहकत्व *n.* रंजकत्व *n.*

CHARNEL-HOUSE, *n.* अस्थिसंचय गृह *n.*

CHARON, *n.* यमदूत *m.*

CHART, *n. marine map.* समुद्राचा नकाशा *m.* समुद्रालेख्यपत्रक *n.* तीरस्थलालेख्य पत्रक *n.*

CHARTER, *n. deed of grant.* सनद *f.* शासन *n.* शासनपत्र *n.*
2 *license, liberty.* राजरोशी *f.* मुबा.

To CHARTER, *v. a. hire or let by charter* (a ship). करार नामा करून भाड्यानें घेणें-देणें.

CHARTER-PARTY, *n.* गलबताविषयींचा करारनामा *m.*

CHARY, *a. frugal, sparing,* v. ECONOMICAL. हात राखून खर्च करणारा, काटकसरी, कतरबेती.

To CHASE, CHASE. See To HUNT, HUNT.

CHASM, *n. cleft, fissure, breach.* चीर *f.* भेग *f.* चील *f.* त्रिलण *f.* भगाड *n.* भगदाड *n.* भगदळ *n.* भगस्थल *n.* घोल *m.*

CHASTE, *a.*—of females. सती, पतिव्रता, साध्वी, परपुरुषविमुखी, अव्यभिचारिणी, पवित्र, कासोट्याची बळकट-खबरदार, बद्धनीवी. N. B. These words apply chiefly to married women; for words applicable to unmarried, See CONTINENT, and VIRGIN. For words for chaste—of men, See also CONTINENT.
2 *not obscene; decent, pure.* अबीभत्स, बीभत्स भाव रहित-शून्य-&c. सलज्ज, पवित्र, निर्मल, निष्कलंक, समर्याद, पाक.
3—language or style. साधु, शुद्ध, निर्दोष.

To CHASTEN, *To* CHASTISE. See To PUNISH.

CHASTELY, *adv.* v. A. पवित्रपणानें, उपस्थनिग्रहानें, उपस्थनिग्रहपूर्वक.

CHASTENESS, CHASTITY, *n.* v. A. 1. सतीपणा *m.* साध्वीपणा *m.* पवित्रपणा *m.* पातिव्रत्य *n.* सतीत्व *n.* साध्वीत्व *n.* अव्यभिचार *m.*
2 बीभत्सभावराहित्य *n.* सलज्जता *f.* पवित्रता *f.* निर्मलता *f.*
3 शुद्धि *f.* साधुत्व *n.* शुद्धता *f.*

CHASTE-TREE, *n. vitex.* निरगुडी *f.* निगडी *f.*

CHASTISEMENT. See PUNISHMENT.

To CHAT, *v. n. talk familiarly or easily.* गोष्टी *f. pl.* सांगणें-करणें, गोष्टि बाता *f. pl.*-गोष्टिमाता *f. pl.*-गोष्टिश्राद्ध *n.* -गप्पाष्टक *n.*-&c. करणें, गप्पा *f. pl.* छाटणें, बाता *f. pl.* खबालणें-मारणें-ठोकणें-छाटणें, चकाट्या *f. pl.* पिटणें-मारणें. [कुटणें.
2 *talk idly,* v. To PRATE. बकणें, बाता *f. pl* कुटणें, काथा *m.*

CHAT, CHATTING, *n.* v. V. 1. गोष्टि बाता *or* माता *f. pl.* बात *f.* गप्पाष्टक *n.* गप *or* गप्प *f.* चकाट्या *or* चटक्या *f. pl.* गोष्टिश्राद्ध *n.* गजलगोष्टी *f. pl.* गजाल *f.*
2 *and* PRATE. बका *f. pl.* बकबक *f.* बकवा *m.* बकवाद *m.* गाथा *f.* कोरड्यागाथा *f. pl.* अकडं तिकडं *n.* काथाकूट *or* काथेकूट *f.*

CHATEAU, *n. mansion,* v. CASTLE. वाडा *m.* महाल *m.*

CHATTEL, *n. moveable possession.* घरजिंदगी *f.* चरद्रव्य *n.* जंगमद्रव्य *n.*
Chattels. जिंदगी *f.* चिजवस्त *f.* मालमत्ता *f.* चरद्रव्य *n.* इस्ताद *m. f.* इस्त्रिवेळा *m.*

To CHATTER, *v. n.*—as a pie, &c. किलकिलणें, किलबिलणें, चिवचिवणें, कचकचणें, *intens.* कचाचणें, चिवचीव *f.* तोडणें, किजबिजणें.
2—as a monkey. किचकिचणें *or* कचकचणें *intens.* कचाचणें, चकचकावणें, खेसणें. [कडणें.
3—the teeth. करकरां *adv.*- खुडखुड *adv.* वाजणें, बाजणें, कड-
4 *talk idly,* v. To PRATE. बकणें, बकबकणें, बडबडणें, बाता *f. pl.* कुटणें-खबाळणें-छाटणें-मारणें हाणणें- तासणें, फाल्या *f. pl.* करणें-मारणें-पाडणें.

CHATTER, CHATTERING, *n.* v. V. 1. चिवचीव *f.* कलकल *m.* किलकील *f. m.* किलबील *f. m.* किजबिज *f.* टकटक *f.* कचकच *f.*—*intens.* कलकलाट *or* किलकिलाट *m.* किलबिलाट *m.* कचाच *m.* किल्लाण *m.* चिलचिलाट *m.* चिलबिलाट *m.* चिवचिवाट *m.*
2 किचकिचणें *n.* चकचकावणें *n.* खेसणें *n.* &c.
3 वाजणें *n.* कडकडणें *n.*
4 *and* PRATE, बकबक *f.* बकवा *m.* बकवाद *m.* बकणी *f.* गप *or* गप्प *f.* गप्पाष्टक *n.* फाल्या *f. pl.* चरबट *f.*

CHATTER-BOX, *n.* v. PRATER. गप्पाष्टक्या, गप्पी *or* गप्या, गप्पीदास, बकवादी *or* द्या, बडबड्या, बोलघेवडा, बोलगाडा.

CHATTERER, *n.* CHATTERING, *p. a.* v. V. 4. *and* PRATER. बकबककरणारा, घाताकुटणारा, गप्पाष्टक्या, बकबक्या. [बोलका.

CHATTY, *a.* v. N. 1. *and* TALKATIVE. गोष्टिप्रिय, गोष्टिवेल्हाळ,

CHAT-WOOD, *n. little sticks,* v. FUEL. लाकूड फांटे *m. pl.* फाटीं *n. pl.* काबळ काट्या *f. pl* काटक्या कुटक्या *f. pl.*

To CHAW. See To CHEW.

CHEAP, *a.* सस्ता, सवंग, स्वस्त, स्वस्ता, स्वस्थ, हलक्या मोलाचा, थोडक्या मोलाचा-किम्मतीचा-&c. अल्प मोली, समर्घ, मंदा.
Dirt-c. पैशापायली, पैशाशेराचा, मातीच्या मोलाचा, टकेशेर.
To become c. v. To CHEAPEN. सस्तावणें, सवंगणें.

To be dirt-c. वाटेवर पडणें, मातीचे मोलानें विकणें-देणें-जाणें, स्वस m. होणें g. of s. डू m. गाजणें g. of s.

To CHEAPEN, *v. a.* सस्ता करणें, सस्तावणें, स्वस्तावणें, किमत *f.*-मोल *n.* पाडणें-कमी करवणें, पाडून-देणें-घेणें, &c.

To CHEAPEN, *v. n.* सस्ता होणें, सस्तावणें, सवंगणें, सवंगावणें, स्वस्तावणें, मोल *n.*-किमत *f.*-भाव *m.*-धारण *f.*-&c. पडणें-उतरणें-कमी होणें-हलकावणें-मंदावणें, &c.

CHEAPLY, *adv.* v. A. सस्तेबार, सस्ताईनें, सवंगाईनें, थोडक्या मोलांत-मोलानें-मोलावर-दरानें-&c.

CHEAPNESS, *n.* v. A. सस्ताई *f.* सबंगाई *f.* स्वस्ताई *f.* मंदाई *f.* समर्घता *f.* अल्पमूल्यता *f.*

To CHEAT, *v. a. defraud, trick,* v. To DECEIVE. ठकवणें, फसवणें, धुतारणें, बंचणें, प्रतारणें, मुंडवण *f.* घालणें, धतुरा *m.* दाखवणें. [हाकणें.

To c. and give the slip. बाला *m.*-बाल्या *m.* देणें-मारणें-

CHEAT, *n. fraud, trick, imposture.* फटवण *f.* ठकवण *f.* फसवण *f.*

2 *cheater,* v. ROGUE. फसव्या, ठकव्या, धतुऱ्या, धुतारा, ठक *c.* ठकबाज *c.* ठग *c.* वंचक, प्रतारक.

CHEATED, *p.* v. V. ठकवलेला, फसवलेला, &c. वंचित, प्रतारित.

CHEATING, *n.* v. V.—*act.* ठकवणें *n.* फसवणें *n.* ठकवणी *f.* ठकवणूक *f.* धतुरा *m.* ठकबाजी *f.* वंचन *n.* वंचना *f.* प्रतारण *n.* प्रतारणा *f.*

To CHECK, *v. a. repress, curb,* v. To RESTRAIN. दडपणें, दाबणें, दाब *m.* देणें, आवरणें, अटोपणें, आकळणें, आकलन *n.*-निग्रह *m.* करणें *g. of o.*

2 (an account, paper, &c.) v. To COMPARE. ताडून-मिळवून-&c. पाहणें.

CHECK, CHECKING, *n.* v. V. 1.—*act.* दडपणें *n.* आवरणें *n.*&c. दाब *m.* अडपदडप *f.* आवर *m.* आकलन *n.* निग्रह *m.*

To be under the c. of. अडकित्यांत-कातरींत-कैंचींत असणें.

I. *person, &c. checking.* दडपण *n.* दाबता, दडपता, उरावर कोणी.

II. *term at chess.* शह *m.* v. दे.

III. *order for money.* सावकारावर चिठ्ठी *f.*

CHECK-MATE, *n.* मात *f.*

C. with a pawn. प्यादेमात *f.* प्यादी *f.* पकारी *f.*

To CHECKER, *v. a. variegate, diversify.* खिडकीदार करणें, दुरंगी-चित्रविचित्र-&c. करणें.

CHECKER-WORK, *n.* विचित्र-चित्रविचित्र-&c. काम *n.*

CHECKERED, *p.* v. V. खिडकीदार, पोफळी, चित्रविचित्र.

CHEEK, *n.* गाल *m.* गालफट *or* ड *or* र *n.* कानशील *or* कानसल *n.* कपोल *m.* गंड *m.* गंडप्रदेश *m.* गल्ल *m.*—in abusive or angry style. थोबाड *n.* थोबाडी *f.* थोतरी *or* थोंदरी *f.*

The cheeks,—revilingly. गालठें *n. pl.*

Dimple on the c. गालकुचा *m.*

Flush or color in the c. कपोलराग *m.*

Flushed cheeks. पिकलेले रातंबे *m. pl.* To get one's cheeks flushed. रातंबे *m. pl.* पिकणें *g. of s.*

Hollow or concavity of the c. puffed out. गालफट *or* ड *n.* गालदोडी *f.* गालोडी *f.*

Slap over the c. गालगुंडा *m.*

To pinch and pull the cheeks of. गालडी *or* गालोडी *f.* पिसुडणें, गालगुचा *m.*-गालबिंधा *m.*-गालोरा *m.* घेणें *g. of o.*

To smack or slap the cheeks, v. FACE. थोबाडणें, चकचकाविणें. [सम.

CHEEK-BONE, *n.* गालाचें हाड *n.* गालाचाढोपर *m.* गल्लास्थि *n.* ग-

CHEER, *n. provisions for a feast or meal,* v. FOOD. अन्नें *n. pl.* स्वयंपाक *pop.* सैंपाक *m.* भोज्योपचार *m. pl.* [*f.*

2 *state of gladness,* v. JOY. उल्लास *m.* आनंद *m.* आनंदावस्था

Be of good cheer! धैर्यधरा, धीरधरा.

3 *acclamation,* v. SHOUT. गजर *m.* आनंदघोष *m.* जयशब्द *m.*

To CHEER, *v. a. gladden,* v. To REJOICE. संतोष *m.* करणें *g. of o.* संतोषविणें, संतुष्ट-हृष्ट-हर्षित-खुश-&c. करणें.

2 *comfort,* v. To CONSOLE. सांतवणें, स्वस्थावणें, आश्वासणें.

3 *incite, inspirit,* v. To ANIMATE. धैर्य *n.*-धीर *m.* देणें, उत्साह *m.* आणणें-देणें, आश्वासणें, आश्वासन *n.*-प्रोत्साहन *n.*-उत्तेजन *n.*-&c. करणें. *g. of o.*

4 *salute with cheers.* जयजयकार *m.*-वाहवा *f.* करणें *g. of o.*

To CHEER UP, *v. n. become cheerful.* धैर्य *n.*-धीर *m.* धरणें.

CHEERED, *p.* v. V. 1. संतोषवलेला, संतोषित, संतुष्ट.

2 सांतवलेला, &c.

3 आश्वासलेला, आश्वासित, प्रोत्साहित.

CHEERER, *n.* CHEERING, *p. a.* v. V. 1. संतोषवणारा, &c. संतोषकारक-कारी, आनंदकारक-दायक-&c. संतोषवणा.

2 उत्साह देणारा-आणणारा, &c. प्रोत्साहक, उत्तेजक, आश्वासक, आश्वासन-प्रोत्साहन-&c. कर्त्ता-कारी.

CHEERFUL, *a. gay, lively,* v. MERRY. उल्लासी, खुश, हास्यमुख, हास्यवदन, प्रसन्नमुख, प्रसन्नवदन, हृष्टचित्त, खुशवख्त.

2 (of disposition) *habitually cheerful.* आनंदी, उल्लासी, संतोषी, सदानंद *or* सदानंदी, आनंदवृत्ति, संतोषवृत्ति, खुशमौज्या, खुशमौजी.

CHEERFULLY, *adv.* v. A. 1. 2. *with gaiety, willingness, &c.* आनंदानें, खुशीनें, सुखासंतोषानें *or* सुखासंतोषें, सुखासमाधानानें, खुशरजावंतीनें, प्रसन्न अंतःकरणें करून.

CHEERFULNESS, *n.* v. A. 1. आनद *m.* उल्लास *m.* उल्लासवृत्ति *f.* उल्लासित्व *n.* आनंदभाव *m.* हृष्टचित्त *n.*

2 आनंदस्वभाव *m.* आनंदभाव *m.* सुखप्रकृति *f.* आनंदवृत्ति *f.* सदानंदित्व *n.*

CHEERLESS, CHEERLESSNESS, See COMFORTLESS. &c.

CHEERLY. See CHEERFUL, CHEERFULLY.

CHEESE, *n.* पनीर *m.* चक्का *m.* चक्कादहीं *n.* खवा *m.* मठ्ठा *m.*

CHEESECAKE, *n.* एका प्रकारची पोळी आहे.

CHEMICAL, *a.* v. N. रसायनविद्येचा, रसायनविद्यासंबंधी-विषयक-अनुयायी-&c.

CHEMISE, *n.* बायकोचें कमीज.

CHEMIST, *n.* रसायनवेत्ता, रसायनविद्यावेत्ता, रसायनशास्त्रज्ञ, रसायनीवैद्य *m.* रसायनी.

CHEMISTRY, CHIMISTRY, *n.* रसायन *pop.* रसायण *n.* रसायनविद्या *f.* रसायनशास्त्र *n.* पदार्थतत्वविवेचकविद्या *f.*

To CHERISH, *v. a. foster, &c.* v. To NOURISH. पाळणें, पोसणें, पाळण *n.*-पाळग्रहण *n.*-पालनपोषण *n.*-&c. करणें *g. of o.*

2 *harbor, indulge.* बाळगणें, राखणें, धरणें.

CHERISHER, *n.* CHERISHING, *p. a.* v. V. 1. पाळणारा, पालक, प्रतिपालक, पालन-&c. कर्त्ता-कारक.

CHERISHING, v. V. 1.—*act.* पाळणें *n.* &c. पालन *pop.* पाळण *n.* पाळग्रहण *n.* प्रतिपाल *m.* प्रतिपालन *n.*

CHEROOT, *n.* चुट्टा *m.* विडी *f.*

Cherry, *n.* एक फळ आहे.

Cherrymerry, *n. present.* चेरीमेरी *f.* पोस्त *n.* पानसुपारी *f.*

Chess, *n.* बुद्धिबळ *pop.* बुदबळ *n. or* बुदबळांचाखेळ *m.* सतरंग *or* सतरंज *m.*

To play at c. बुदबळें *or* बुदबळानें खेळणें. Some of the terms used at *Chess* are उपरप्यादी, काढशाहा, घोडगाठ, घोडमात, घोडशहा, जोरी, तिजोर *or* री, दुजोर *or* रा, प्यादी, प्यादेमात, फरजी, बळाचा, बळी,बुरजी, भरडाव, शैली, शैलीबाजी, सबळी, हस्त, हस्तपगदस्त *or* स्ती, हुचमस्ती.

Chess-board, *n.* चौपट *m.* पट *m. f.*

Chess-man, *n.* बुदबळ *n.* मोहरें *n.* The pieces are King राजा, Queen वजीर *or* फर्जी, Bishop उंट, Knight घोडा, Castle हत्ती, Pawn प्यादें *n.*

Chest, *n.* v. Box. संदूक *f.* हडपा *m.* मांदूस *f.* बारदान *n.* सलद *m.*

C. of drawers. खणांची पेटी *f.*

2 (of the body). छाती *f.* पंजर *m.* उरस्थल *n.* वक्षस्स्थल *n.* कडणी *f. pl.* कडसण्या *f. pl.*

Pain of the c. उरोग्रह *m.* उरोघात *m.*

Broad-chested. अश्वोरस, उरस्वान्, उरसिल.

Chest-foundered, *a.* उरींभरलेला-फुटलेला.

To be c. उरींभरणें, उरींफुटणें, उरबणें *or* उरपणें.

Chestnut, *n.* एक फळ आहे.

Chestnut, *a.*—of horses. तांबडा बोर, तेल्याकुमाईत.

Chevaux de frise, *n.* a kind of. शतघ्नी *f.* कारलें *n.*

To **Chew**, *v. a. masticate.* चावणें, चर्वणें, चर्वण *n.* करणें *g. of o.*

2 *roll in the mouth, champ.* चावणें, चघळणें.

3 fig. *ruminate, &c.* जप *m.* करणें, घोळणें, जपमाळ *f.*-स्मरणी *f.* घेणें *g. of o.*

To c. the cud. रवंथ *n. m.* करणें.

To **Chew**, *v. n. ruminate upon.* ध्यान *n.* करणें-लावणें.

2 *eat tobacco, opium, bhang, &c.* गोळी *f.* चढवणें.

Chewing, *n.* v. V. A. 1.—*act.* चावणें *n.* &c. चर्वण *n.*

Chicane, Chicanery, *n.* v. **Artifices**. घावडाव *m. pl.* छक्केपंजे *m. pl.* पेंचपांच *or* पांचपेंच *m. pl.* मारपेंच *m.* गारूड *n.* गोडबंगाल *n.*

Chick, Chicken, *n.* कोंबडीचें पिलूं *n.* कुक्कुटसंतान *n.*

Chicken-hearted, *a. timid,* v. **Cowardly**. भितरा.

Chick-pea, *n. cicer arictinum.* v. **Gram**. चणा *m.*

Chicken-pox, *n.* कांजण्या *f. pl.* A pock of it. कांजणी *f.*

To **Chide**, See To **Reprove**, To **Scold**.

Chief, *a. principal, capital, head, first.* मुख्य, प्रथम, पहिला प्रथम, मुसरण *or* णी, मुसरीण, मुखंड, आदि, आद्य, आदिम, अग्रगण्य, अग्रणी, अग्र्य, अग्र, अग्रगामी, अग्रसर *or* अग्रेसर, श्रेष्ठ, उत्तम, परम, प्रधान, प्रमुख, प्रवर, बिनीचा, खासा, वृंदारक, ग्रामणी, राजा (in comp. as राजगुरू, राजोपाध्याय, राजपुरोहित chief priest, &c.), वर & वर्य (in comp. as द्विजवर्य, गुरुवर्य, नरवर्य), सिंह (in comp. as पंडित सिंह, पुरुष सिंह, नरसिंह, वीरसिंह), अनुत्तर.

Chief, Chieftain, *n. commander, leader,* v. A. *and* **Conductor**. सरदार *m.* सरसेल *m.* नायक *pop.* नाईक *m.*

Chief, Chiefly, *adv.* v. A. मुख्यत्वेंकरून, प्राधान्येंकरून, विशेषेंकरून, बहुतकरून, मुख्यशः, प्राधान्यतः, विशेषतः, आधिक्येंकरून, सर्वोपरि.

Chiefship, Chieftainry, *n.* v. N. सरदारी *f.* सरदारकी *f.* नायकी *f.* नाइकपणा *m.*

Chilblain, *n.* थंडीचीभेग *f.*-फूट *f.*-कातरा *m.*-चीर *f.*-तडा *m.* जाळवात *m.* विपादिका *f.*

To be affected with c.—a limb. थंडीनें फुटणें.

Child, *n.* लेंकरूं *n.* पोर *m. f. n.* पोरगा *m.* (गी *f.* गें *n.*) मूल *m. f. n.* मुलगा *m.* (गी *f.* गें *n.*) पोंगडें *n.* संतान *n.* बाल *n.* बालक *m. n.* अपत्य *n.* शिशु *m.* अर्भक *m. n.* (अर्भकी *f.*) केलाडूं *n.* बचडा *m.* (डी *f.* डें *n.*) पोरसोदा *c.*—carelessly, generally, &c. लेंकपूत *m.* लेंकबाळ *n. m.* मूलबाळ *n.* पोरसोर *n.* पोरबाळ *n.* पोरसोदा *m.* पोरजिनस *m. f.*—in endearment. बावा *m.* बा *m.* बाबा *or* बाब्या *m.* छाबडें *n.* छावडा *m.* (डी *f.* डें *n.*) छकडें *n.* बचडा *m. or* डें *n.* बाचला *or* ल्या *n.* लबाड (like *rogue*) वत्स *m. n.* सोनकुला *m.* सोनक्या *m.* सोनटका *m.* सोना *or* न्या *m.* बेटा *m.*—to a female c. बया *f.* बचडी *f.*—in anger or contempt, as *brat, imp, &c.* पोरटा *m.* (टी *f.* टें *n.*) कारटा पोरटा *or* कारटा *m.* (टी *f.* टें *n.*).

C. of one's old age. शेंडफळ *n.* शेंडेफळ *n.* सरत्या पालवाचें मुलगें *n.*

C.'s play. बालक्रीडा *f.* बाललीला *f.* बालचरित्र *n.* बालचरित *n.*

C.'s speech. बालभाषा *f.*

Dotingly fond of children. पोरपिसा.

Extravagant fondness for children. पोरपिसें *n.*

Tonsure of the head of a c.(to form शेंडी). चूडाकर्म *n.* चौल *n.* मुंडन *n.*

Spoiled c. दुधखुळा, गोंबळा.

Better no c. than a bad c. कुसंतानापेक्षां निसंतान बरें.

To be with c. v. **Pregnant**. पोटासी-गर्भार-&c. होणें-राहणें.

Children. मुलेंबाळें *n.pl.* पोरेंबाळें *n.pl.* मुलेंलेकरें *n.pl.* लेंकरूं बाळ *n.* चिलीं पिलीं *n.pl.* कच्चे बच्चे *m.pl.* चेंढळ मेंढळ *n.* पोरें सोरें *n.pl.* बालापत्य *n.* बालखिल्यें *n.pl.*

Amongst, by, with, &c. c. पोरापोरीं, लेंकरालेंकरीं.

Fondness for c. लेंकुरछंद *m.*

Trinkets, &c. worn by c. बाळलेणें *or* ल्याणें.

Fitting c.—articles of clothing, &c. बचकणा *or* णी.

Readily intelligible to c. बालबोध.

Child-bearing, Child-birth, Child-bed, *n. the state of being in labor; also, the act of bringing forth.* बाळंतपणा *m.* बाळंतदशा *f.* प्रसूतिदशा *f.* प्रसवावस्था *f.* प्रसव *m.* प्रसूती *f.* गर्भविमोचन *n.*

Easy c. सुखप्रसव *m.*

Pains of c. गर्भवेदना *f.* प्रसववेदना *f.* प्रसूती वेदना *f.*

Woman after c. (just delivered). बाळंत *f.* बाळंतीण *f.* प्रसूतिका *f.* सूतिका *f.*

Woman in c. कोनी निघालेली स्त्री *f.* दोनजिवांचें माणूस *n.*

Attendance upon a w. in c. बाळंतपणा *m.* कुमारभृत्या *f.*

Betel-roll. baby-clothes, &c. presented to a w. after c. बाळंतविडा *m.*

Bracelets given to a w. recovered from impurity of c. बाळंतचुडा *m.*

Caudle to a w. in c. बाळंतकाढा *m.* मेथोडा *m.*

Chamber for or of a w. in c. बाळंत खोली *f.* बाळंत घर *n.*

Disease incidental to a w. in c. बाळंतरोग *m.* स्त्रीरोग *m.*

Foul clothes of a w. in c. बाळंतें *n.* बाळबलें *n.*

House in which is a w. in c. बाळंत घर *n.*

Necessaries for her infant given to a poor w. after c. बाळशिरें *n.* [णें *n.*

Rice, &c. sent to a w. on the tenth day after c. तिम-

String cast (after consecration) around the neck of the w. and her infant. रक्षा *f.*

Worship of deities on the fifth day after c. पांचवी *f.*—on the sixth. सठ *or* सठी *f.* षष्ठीपूजन *n.* साव्वी *f.*—on the tenth. दाह्यावी *f.*

Belonging to c. बाळंतप्रकरणाचा, प्रासूतिक.

CHILD-HOOD, *n.* बाळपण *n.* लेंकुरपणा *m.* पोरपण *n.* पोरपणा *m.* लहानपण *n.* धाकुटपण *n.* बाल्य *n.* बाल्यावस्था *f.* कौमार *n.* शैशव *n.* शिशुत्व *n.* शिशुदशा *f.*

Second c. बाळें *n.* [बालाभ्यस्त.

Practised or versed in from c. बाळस्वार, बालाभ्यासी,

CHILDISH, *a.* पोरका, पोरकट, पोरगळ, पोरवट, लेंकुरवा, लेंकुरवट, बालबुद्धि, पोरबुद्धि, लेंकुरबुद्धि, पोरस्वभावाचा.

To be c. बाळसणें, बाळेणें. [रपणाचा.

2—of things. पोरबुद्धीचा, पोरसमजुतीचा, पोरस्वभावाचा, पो-

CHILDISHNESS, *n.* v. A. लेंकुरपणा *m.* लेंकुरस्वभाव *m.* लेंकुरछंद *m.* लेंकुरसमजूत *f.* लेंकुरबुद्धि *f.* पोरपण *n.* पोरसमजूत *f.* पोरखेळ *m.* पोरबुद्धि *f.* पोरस्वभाव *m.* बालबुद्धि *f.*

CHILDLESS, *a.* असंतान, असंतति, असुत, अनपत्य, अप्रज, अपत्यहीन, संतानशून्य, &c.

C. woman. अप्रसूत.

CHILDLESSNESS, *n.* v. A. निसंतान *n.* बेचिराग *m.*

CHILD-LIKE, *a. resembling or becoming a c.* बाळासारखा, बालाई, बालसदृश, बालोचित, अपत्य धर्मक.

CHILI, *n. capsicum frutescens.* मिरची *f.* मिरशंग *or* शेंग *f.*

Chilis pounded into a mass. तिखट *n.* चाबूक *m.*

Red chilis pounded. भगवती *f.* भसकापुरी *f.* भुरका *m.*

CHILIAD, *n.* सहस्रक *n.* साहस्र *m.*

CHILL, CHILLY, *a.*—of the air or things, v. COLD. सरद, शीतल, हिम.

2—of the feeling, v. COLD. थंडावलेला, कडकुडलेला, हींव *or* हिंव-कुडकुडी-&c. भरलेला.

3 *without warmth or cordiality*, v. COLD. थंडाईचा.

CHILL, CHILLINESS, *n.* v. A. 1. सरदी *f.* शिळट *f.* शिळटी *f.*

Of which the c. is taken off. शिळबुडा, शिळमोडा.

To take off the c. of, *or* to lose its c. (—water). पाण्याचा काटा *m.* मोडणें.

2 *chilly feeling.* हिंव *n.* हिंवडी *or* हिंवाडी *f.* हिम *n.* कुडकुडा *m.* कुडकुडी *f.* रेपा *f. pl.* शैत्य *n.*

Chills and flushings. सरद गरमी *f.*

To **CHILL**, *v. n. be affected with cold.* हिंवणें, हिंवडणें.

2 *be chill-struck,*—plants. शिळटणें.

To **CHILL**, *v. a. make chilly.* सरद थंड-&c. करणें.

2 *dispirit*, v. To DISCOURAGE. मोडणें, पाणी *n.* घालणें-ओतणें, हीरमोड *f. m.*-हीरसांड *f.* करणें. [समसूर *m.*

CHIME, *n.* (of musical instruments). ताळमेळ *m.* समस्वर *pop.*

C. beaten at the end of a watch. गजर *m.* *v.* वाज, हो.

Closing c. *or* peal (as of a चौघडा &c). उतार *m.* उतारबाजी *f.*

To **CHIME**. See To CORRESPOND.

CHIMERA, *n. fabulous or unreal thing.* असत् पदार्थ *m.* असत्वस्तु *n.* Some particular *Chimeras* or some significant terms for an *unreality* are खपुष्प *or* आकाशपुष्प *n.* (sky-flower), कर्पूरभस्म *n.* (camphor calx), वालुकातैल *or* सिकता तैल *n.* (sand-oil), शशविषाण *or* शशशृंग *n.* (hare horn), वंध्यापुत्र *m.* (son of a barren woman).

2 *vain fancy or thought*, v. FANCY. असत्कल्पना *f.* असंभवत्कल्पना *f.*

CHIMERICAL, *a.* v. N. *merely imaginary*, v. IMAGINARY. असंभवत्कल्पनेचा, असत्कल्पनेचा, असत्कल्पनासिद्ध-जात-&c. असंभूत, मानसिक, अप्रसिद्ध. [का *f.*

CHIMNEY, *n. vent for smoke.* धुराडें *n.* धुराळें *n.* धारें *n.* धूमनलि-

2 *glass for the flame of a lamp.* दिव्याच्या वातीवर जी कांचेची नळी ठेवितात ती.

CHIN, *n.* हनवटी *or* हनुवटी *or* हणवटी *f.* हणु *f.* अनवठी *f.* हनु *f.*

The hollow above the c. बेचाळी *f.* बेचाळें *n.*

CHIN-ACHE, *n.* हनुग्रहवात *m.*

CHIN-COUGH, *n.* डांग्याखोकला *m.*

CHINA, CHINESE, *a.* चिनी, चीनदेशचा.

CHINA-ROOT, *n. smilax china.* चोबचिनी *f.*

CHINE, *n.* कणा *m.* कण्याचा भाग *m.* कण्याचा प्रदेश *m.*

CHINK, *n.* v. CRACK. सापट *f.* फट *f.* चिरण *f.* चिलण *f.* संधि *m. pop.* सांध *f. or* सांधा *m.* चीर *f.* चील *f.*

CHINK, *adv.* छण-कर-कण-&c. छम-कन-कर-&c. छण छण *or* णां (intens. छणाछण, छणाणां).

To **CHINK**, *v. n. make a sharp sound.* छण-कर-कण-&c.-छणछण *or* णां वाजणें, छणछणणें (intens. छणाणणें).

To **CHINK**, *v. a.* छणछणावणें, छण छण वाजविणें, खळखळविणें.

CHINTZ, *n.* छीट *n.* रंगीकापड *n.* Some of the *chintzes* or fashions of chintz are जाजमी छीट, कळसपाक, डाळिंबी छीट, फुटाणी छीट.

Belonging to c. छिंटी, छिटवी. [तष्ट करणें.

To **CHIP**, *v. a.* तासणें, धलपे *m. pl.*-&c. काढणें, तुकडे *m.pl.* करणें,

To **CHIP**, *v. n. break off in small pieces.* कवची *f.*-&c. निघणें.

CHIP, *n.* (of wood). धपला *or* ढपला *m. dim.* धपली *or* ढपली *f.* ढलपट *n.* धलपा & ढलपा *m. dim.* धलपी *f.* & ढलपी *f.* & धलपट *n.* चैली *f.* कपळा *m.* कुळपटा *or* कुळपुटा *m.* कुटकी *f.* काटकी *f.* काटूक *n.* काटकुटी *f.* काडूक *n.* कुडी *f.* भितळा *or* भेतळा *m. dim.* भेत *f. n.* & भेतूक *n.*

2 (of stone, &c.) *piece chipped or sliced off.* कपचा *m. dim.* कपची *f.* कवची *f.* कपरा *m. dim.* कपरी *f.* टोंचा *or* टोंका *m. dim.* टोंची *or* टोंकी *f.* धपला *or* ढपला *m. dim.* धपली *or* ढपली *f. or* धलपा & ढलपा *m. dim.* धलपी & ढलपी *f.* & धलपट *or* ढलपट *n.* किपळी *f.* करप *n.* टिवळी *or* टवळी *f.* काचोळा *m.* काचळ *f.* ठिकरी *f.* [लपा *m.*

Chips, Chippings. काटकूट *f.* काटक्या कुटक्या *f. pl.* सा-

CHIPPED, *p.* v. V.A. तासलेला, तासीव, तष्ट. [*n.* तक्षण *n.*

CHIPPING, *n.*v.V.A.—*act.* तासणें *n.* तास *m.* तासणी *f.* तासकाम

CHIROLOGIST, *n.* v. N. करपल्लव्या.

CHIROLOGY, *n. art of talking with the fingers.* करपल्लवीभाषा *f.* करपल्लवी *f.*

CHIROMANCER, CHIROGRAPHIST, *n.* v. N. हातपाहणारा, सामुद्रि-

क, हस्तलक्षणवादी, हस्तरेषापरीक्षक.

CHIROMANCY, *n. divination by the hand.* सामुद्रिक *n.* हस्तसामुद्रिक *n.* हस्तलक्षण विद्या *f.*

To CHIRP, *v. n.*—of birds. चिवचिवणें, चिवचीव *f.*-चूंचूं *n.* करणें —noisily, &c. किलकिलणें.

2—of insects. किर्र-किण्ण *adv.* करणें, चिणचीण *or* चिनीचिनी *adv.* करणें.

CHIRP, CHIRPING, *n.* v. V. 1.—*act.* चिवचिवणें *n.* चिवचीव *f.* चूंचूं *n.* चिची *f.*—noisily, &c. कुलकुलाट *m.* किल्लाण *m.*

2 चिणचीण *or* चिनीचिनी *n.* किण्ण *n.* किर्र *n.*

CHIRURGEON. See SURGEON.

CHISEL, *n.*—of a carpenter. किंकरें *n.* विंधणें *n.* चिरणें *n.* आंसें *n.*

Smith's c. घातली *f.*

Stone cutter's c. टांकी *f.* टंक *m.* पाषाणदारक *m.* Incision made with it. टांकी *f.* One who works with it. टांकेकरी *m.*

To CHISEL, *v. a.* किंकऱ्यानें-विंधण्यानें-&c. कापणें-तोडणें, कोरणें.

2 (stone) *roughen with incisions.* टांकणें, टांक्या *f.pl.* पाडणें.

CHIT, *n. note or small epistle.* चिट्टी *or* चिठ्ठी *f.*

CHIT, *n.* v. SPROUT. कोंब *m.*

2 v. CHILD, चिटलिंग *m.* चिटू *m.*

CHITCHAT, See CHAT.

CHITTERLINGS. See BOWELS.

CHIVALRIC, CHIVALROUS, *a. pertaining, &c. to chivalry.* सरदार बाहदरीचा, सरदार बाहदरीच्या विषयींचा.

2 *gallant,* &c. v. BRAVE. दिलदार, दिलदारीचा, शौर्यशाली, प्रतापशाली.

CHIVALROUSLY, *adv.* v.A. सरदार बहादराच्या रीतीनें, दिलदारीनें.

CHIVALRY, *n.* सरदार बहादरी *f.*

2 *gallantry,* &c. v. BRAVERY. दिलदारी *f.* शौर्यशालिता *f.* प्रतापशालिता *f.* वीर्य *n.*

CHIVES, *n.*—in botany. केशर *n.*

CHOICE, *n.* See CHOOSING. 2 *power of choosing, option.* निवडण्याची मुखत्यारी *f.*-सत्ता *f.*-अधिकार *m.*-&c. पसंती *f.* खुशी *f.* दिलखुशी *f.* खातर *f.* मरजी *f.* (ex. खातरेस वाटेल तें करूं, हें खातरेस येत नाहीं).

3 *object of choice.* निवड *f.* निवडकवस्तू *f.*

To make c. of, v. To CHOOSE. निवडून घेणें, पसंत करणें.

4 *best part.* निवड *f.* उत्तमांश *m.* उत्तमभाग *m.*

5 *skill in discriminating.* तरतम *n.* तारतम्य *n.* तरतम भाव *m.*

CHOICE, *a. select, excellent, precious, &c.* निवड, निवडक, निवडींव, वेंचला, शेलका, असल, पसंत, खातरीचा, नगदानगदी, सांट्याचा, आटछाटीचा, उत्कृष्ट, उत्तम, उंचा, सरस, मनोनीत.

2 *careful, &c. in choosing.* निवड करणारा, निवडण्याविषयीं खबरदार, शोधक, परीक्षक, सूक्ष्मदर्शी, सूक्ष्मपरीक्षक.

3 *using with care.* जपून खर्च करणारा, जोगवून खर्च करणारा.

CHOICENESS, *n. valuableness, excellence.* उत्कृष्टता *f.* उत्कर्ष *m.* श्रेष्ठत्व *n.* चोखपणा *m.*

CHOIR, *n. band of singers.* गाणारांची मंडळी *f.*-चुंग *f.*- फड *m.*-ताफा *m.* गायकगण *m.*

2 गाणारांची मंडळी बसण्याची जागा *f.*

To CHOKE, *v. n. be under suffocation.* गुदमरणें *or* गुदमुरणें, घुसमटणें, घुटवळणें, घुटमळणें *or* घुटमुळणें, अडमुसणें, उदान *n.* लागणें.

That is choking. अडमुशी, अडमुसा.

2—esp. through violent emotion. ऊर *m.* दाटणें *g. of s.* गळा *m.* दाटणें *or* भरून येणें *g. of s.* गहिंवरणें, गहिंवर *m.* येणें *in. con.* घुसमटणें, सद्गदित होणें.

To CHOKE, *v. a.* गुदमारून-घुसमाटून मारणें, नाकतोंड दाबून-कोंडून-&c. मारणें, नरडा *m.*-नरडें *n.*-नरडी *f.*-गळा *m.*-&c. दाबणें *or* दाबून मारणें, दम-श्वास-&c. कोंडून मारणें. [करणें.

2 *hinder or check growth.* वाढ *f.*-&c. खुंटविणें, खुजट-&c.

3 *block up.* v. To OBSTRUCT. रोधणें, कोंडणें, बुजविणें.

CHOKEFULL, *a.*v. BRIMFULL. तुडुंब,तुडूम *or* तुंब, आकंठ भरलेला.

CHOLAGOGUES, *n. medicine to evacuate bile.* पित्तघ्न-पित्तनाशक-पित्तशमक-&c. औषध *n.*

CHOLER, *n.* v. BILE. पित्त *n.*

2 *irascibility.* पित्त *n.* तमोगुण *m.* पित्तप्रकृति *f.* पित्तस्वभाव *m.*

3 v. ANGER. क्रोध *m.*

CHOLERA, *n.* मोडसी *f.* तरळ *f.* तरळमोडशी *f.* तरळमेंढी *f.* हगवोक *f.* कुळीक *f.* विषूचिका *or* विशूचिका *f.*

Inveterate or long standing c. मेणीमोडसी *f.*

Spasmodic or epidemic c. जरीमरी *f.* महामारी *f.* पटकी *f.*

To be affected with तरळ or c. तरळणें.

CHOLERIC, *a. irascible,* v. PASSIONATE. तापट, तापड, पित्तवेगी, पितळा, तामस, तामसी, तमोगुणी, पित्तप्रकृति, चंड.

2 *indicating or proceeding from anger.* रागाचा, क्रोधाचा, क्रोधमूलक.

To CHOOSE, *v. a. elect, prefer.* निवडणें, निवडून घेणें-काढणें, वरणें, पसंत करणें, निवडून कूम करणें.

2 *select, pick, cull.* निवडणें, वेंचणें, छानणें, परिगणणें, परिगणन *n.*-परिगणना *f.* करणें *g. of o.*

To CHOOSE, *v. n. please.* खुशीस मनास-चित्तास-पसंतीस-&c. येणें *in. con.* [&c. निवड *f.*

CHOOSING, CHOICE, *n.* v. V. A. 1.—*act.* निवडणें *n.* वरणें *n.*

The c. of a husband by a woman. स्वयंवर *m.*

The woman that chooses a husband. स्वयंवरा *f.*

2 निवडणें *n.* वेचणें *n.* &c. परिगणन *n.* परिगणना *f.*

To CHOP, *v. a. cut off.* तोडणें, खांडणें, कलम *n.* करणें, छिंदणें.

2 up; *c. into pieces.* तोडणें, सांकटणें, तोडा *m.* करणें *g. of o.* अडकसणें.

Price of chopping up. तोडणावळ *f.* सांकटणावळ *f.*

To CHOP, *v. n. c. and change, c. about,*—the wind. घोटाळणें, कोंडाळणें.

To CHOP. *v. a. exchange.* See To BARTER.

CHOP, *n. piece chopped off.* खंड *n.* खांड *n.* खांडोळें *n.* तोडा *m.*

2 (esp. of timber). तोड *f.* तोडा *m.* फोड *f.*

CHOPPED, *p.* v. V. A. 1. तोडलेला, कलमकेलेला, &c. तोडींव.

2 सांकटलेला, &c.

CHOPPING, *n.* v. V. A. 1.—*act.* तोडणें *n.* &c. कलम *n.*

2 सांकटणें *n.* तोडा *m.*

v. V. N. घोटाळणें *n.* घोटाळा *m.*

CHOPPING-BLOCK, *n.* सांकटणें *n.* सकोटण *or* न *n.* नेट *m. n.* घोडा *m.* घोडी *f.*

CHOPPING-KNIFE, *n.* सुरा *m.*

CHORAL, *a. belonging to a choir.* गाणाऱ्यामंडळीचा, गायकगण-संबंधी-विषयक.

Chord, *n. string of a musical instrument.* तंतुm. *pop.* तंत *or* तांत *f.* तार *f.*
2—in geometry. ज्या *f.* पूर्णज्या *f.* चापकर्ण *n.*
Chorister, *n. one of a choir.* फडांतलागाणारा, गायकगणांतला एक गाणारा, सहगायक.
Celestial c. किन्नर *m.*
Chorus, *n. band of singers*, v. Choir. गायकगण*m.*
2 (in the drama) पार्श्वस्थ *m.* पारिपार्श्विक *m.*
3 *recurring stanza of a song.* ध्रुपद*n.* ध्रुव*m.* आंकणकडवें *n.* आंकडकडवें*n.* अस्ताई *f.* आंत्रा*m.* पेडाबंद*m.*
Chosen, *p. & a.* v.V.1. निवडलेला, वरलेला,&c.निवडींव, मनोनीत.
2 निवडलेला, वेंचलेला, &c. परिगणित.
I. *select*, v. Choice. निवडींव, निवडक, मनोनीत.
To **Chouse**, *v. a. gull, &c.* v. To Deceive. धुतारणें, मुंडणें, भोंदणें.
Chowrie, *n. tail of the Bos grunniens used to whisk off flies &c.* चौंरी *or* चवरी *f.*चंवर *n.* चामर*n.* Holder or bearer of it. चौंरी बरदार.
To **Christen**, *v. a.* v. To Baptize. बाप्तिस्मा*m.* देणें, जलसंस्काराद्वारा ख्रिस्ती करणें-ख्रिस्ती धर्मांत आणणें &c.
2 *name.* नाम*n.*-नांव*n.* ठेवणें-देणें, बारसें*n.* करणें.
Christendom, *n.* ख्रिस्तीस्थान *n.* यावत्ख्रिस्ती देश *m.pl.*
Christening, *n.* v. V. 1.—*act.* जलसंस्कारद्वारा ख्रिस्ती करणें *n.*
2 नांव ठेवणें *n.* नामकरण *n.* बारसें *n.*
I was present at your c. तुझ्या बारशास मी जेवलों आहें.
Christian, *n.* v. A. ख्रिस्ती, ख्रिस्तभक्त.
Christian, *a.* ख्रिस्ती धर्माचा, ख्रिस्ती धर्मानुयायी, ख्रिस्ती मतानुसारी, ख्रिस्ती धर्मसंबंधी, ख्रिस्ती धर्मविषयक.
Christianity, *n.* ख्रिस्तीधर्म *m.* ख्रिस्तीमत *n.*
Christmas, *n.* नाताळ *or* ळें *n.*
Christmas-box, *n.* नाताळास दिलेलें बक्षीस *n.*
Chromatic, *a. relating to color.* वर्णसंबंधी, वर्णविषयक.
2 (in music) ग्रामिक, ग्रामीण.
Chronic, **Chronical**, *a. of long standing.* जुनाट, बहुकालिक, दीर्घकालिक, चिरकालिक, बद्धमूल.
Chronicle, *n.* v. History. कालक्रमकवृत्तांत*m.* क्रालानुपूर्वकोपाख्यान *n.* पट *m.*
Chronological, *a.* v. N. कालगणनविषेचा, कालमानविषेचा, कालानुपूर्वीदर्शक-बोधक-&c.
Chronologically, *adv.* कालानुक्रमाप्रमाणें, कालानुपूर्वीनें.
Chronologist, *n.* कालगणनवेत्ता, कालमानवेत्ता,कालक्रमनिर्णायक.
Chronology, *n.* कालगणनविद्या *f.* कालमानविद्या *f.* कालक्रमनिर्णयनविद्या *f.* कालानुपूर्वीदर्शनविद्या *f.*
Chronometer, *n. time measurer*,—gener. कालसाधन *n.* कालमान *n.* घटीयंत्र *n.* कालप्रमापकयंत्र *n.*
Chrysalis, *n.* कोशवासी *m.* कोशस्थ *m.*
Chrysolite, *n.* लसणा *or* लसण्या *m.*
Chrystal, *n.* काच *f.* बिलोर *n.*
Chrystal, *a.* काचेचा, बिलोराचा, काचमय.
Chub, *n.* नदींतला एक मासा आहे.
Chubbed, **Chubby**, *a. short& thick.* गबदू, गबदुला, गबदूल.
Chubby-cheeked, **Chubby-faced**, *a. having a fat face.* फुललेगालांचा, गुरोळी गालांचा, फुगीरगाल्या, गालफुग्या.

To get c. and plump. गालावर गाल *m.* चढणें *g. of s.*
To **Chuck**, *To* **Chuckle**, *v. n. call as a hen.* खुटखुटणें, खुटखुट *f.* करणें.
To **Chuck**, *v. a. throw, pitch.* फेकणें, टाकणें, चकणें, फकदिशी-फकशिरी *adv.* टाकणें.
2 (grain or powders or dry food, into the mouth). फांकणें *or* फाकणें.
Matter (parched corn, meal, &c.) chucked into the mouth. फक्का *m.* फांका *or* फाका *m. v.* मार, फकाणा *m.* फकी *or* फक्की *f. v.* मार. बकणी *f.* बकणा *m. v.* मार.
3 (under the chin) हृणवटी *f* उचलणें *g. of o.*
Chuck, *interj.* फक-फन-कर-&c.
To **Chuckle**, *v. n. laugh inwardly.* गालच्या गालांत-तोंडच्या तोंडांत हासणें.
Chuff, **Chuffy**. See Churl, Churlish.
Chum, *n.* v. Companion. बिऱ्हाडसोबती.
Chump, *n.* (of wood) v. Block. ठोकळा *m.* ठिकी *f.* ओंडा *m.*
Chunam, *n.* चुना *m.* चूर्ण *n.* सुधा *f.*
Terrace or floor of c. *or* C. work. चुनेगच्ची *f.* गच्ची *f.* गच्चगिरी *f.* आगाशी *f.* अटाली *or* ळी *f.*
Making of a c.-floor, &c. गच्चगिरी *f.*
Of c.-work,—a floor, a wall, &c. चुनेगच्ची.
Church, *n. place of worship*, v. Temple. देऊळ *n.* देवालय *n.* भजनालय *n.* भजनगृह *n.* भजनमंदिर *n.*
2 *body of believers.* भक्तांची मंडळी *f.* भक्तसमूह *m.* यावत्भक्तगण *m.* भक्तवृंद *n.*
C.-property. देवस्व *n.*
Churl, *n. surly or rude fellow.* कुरठा-तुसडा-द्राष्ट-&c. मनुष्य*m.* धसमुसळ्या *m.* दुर्जन *m.*
2 See Miser. 3 See Countryman.
Churlish, *a. rude, surly, sour.* v. Cross. कुरठा, तुसडा, तुसड, द्राष्ट *or* दाष्ट, द्रुष्ट, खाष्ट, दाष्टीक, दुष्ट, दुःशील, दुःस्वभाव.
Churlishly, *adv.* v. A. कुरठेपणानें, तुसडेपणानें, &c. दाष्ट-&c. होऊन.
Churlishness, *n.* v. A. कुरठेपणा *m.* तुसडेपणा *m.* द्रुष्टपणा *m.* दुःशीलता *f.* दुःस्वभाव *m.*
Churn, *n.* माथण *f.* माथणी *f.* मंथनघटी *f.*
Loop of the fixed part of a c. मांजरी *f.*
Churn-rope, *n.* रवीदोर *m.* मंथरी *f.* आंसणी *f.* पारडें *n.* बारडी *f.*
Churn-staff, *n.* रवी *f.* मंथान *m.*
Knob or head of a c. माथा *or* थ्या *m.* मंथा *m.* माठलें *n.*
Hand c. हातरवी *f.*
Post, pillar, stake, &c. with which the c. is connected. घुसळखांब *m.* ताकमेढ *f.*
To **Churn**, *v. a.* घुसळणें, मथणें *or* मंथणें, घुसळण *n.*-मंथन *n.* करणें *g. of o.*
Matter (curds, &c.) to be churned. घुसळण *n.*
Matter obtained by churning. घुसळा *m.*
Churned, *p.* v. V. घुसळलेला, &c. घुसळींव, मंथित, मथित.
Churning, *n.* घुसळणें *n.* मंथणें *n.* घुसळण *n.* मंथन *n.* मथन *n.*
Chylaceous, **Chylous**, *a. belonging to chyle.* अन्नरससंबंधी, अन्नरसाचा.
2 *consisting of chyle.* अन्नरसमय.
Chyle, *n. the fluid prepared from chyme.* अन्नरस *m.* रस *m.*

धातुप m. अन्नमातृका f. आहारसंभव m. आहारसार m. [क.
CHYLIFACTIVE, CHYLOPOETIC, a. अन्नरसकारक, अन्नरसोत्पाद-
CHYME, n. *the modification which food assumes in the stomach.* पचलेल्याअन्नाचा-जीर्णअन्नाचा परिणाम m. आमरस m.
CHYMIST. See CHEMIST. [स्वाद्.
CIBARIOUS, a. *pertaining to or fit for food.* अन्नाचा, अन्नमय,
CICATRICE, CICATRIX, n. v. SCAR. माव f. वण n. चट्टा m. क्षतचिन्ह n. किण n. [सा-&c. करणें.
To CICATRIZE, v. a. *make to heal.* माठेसा-भरेसा-खपली f. धरे-
To CICATRIZE, v. n. *heal.* माठणें, माठळणें, भरणें *or* भरून येणें, खपली f. धरणें.
CI-DEVANT, a. *former, late.* माजी, मागला, मागचा.
C. minister, officer, &c. गलितपत्र n.
CIELING. See CEILING.
CIGAR, n. चुट्टा m. विडी f. [पक्ष्मसंबंधी.
CILIARY, a. *belonging to the eye lids.* पापणीचा, पापणीसंबंधीचा,
CILICIOUS, a. *made of hair.* लोकरीचा, केशांचा, केशनिर्मित, लोमनिर्मित.
CINCTURE. See GIRDLE.
CINDER, n. कोळपलेला-कोळंजलेला कोळसा m. [हार m.
Hot cinders. फुंपाटा m. फोपेटा m. मुमीर *or* मुमूर nm. आ-
CINERATION, n. v. ASHES. भस्मीकरण n. [वर्ण.
CINEREOUS, CINERITIOUS, v. ASHY. भस्मवत्, भस्मतुल्य, भस्म-
CINNABAR, n. *vermilion.* रक्तपारद m. रसस्थान n.
Factitious c. हिंगुल *pop.* हिंगूळ & हिंगुळूक m. रससिंदूर mn.
CINNAMON, n. दालचिनी f. कलमीदालचिनी f.
CION, n. *graft.* कलम n.
2 *shoot,* v. SPROUT. कोम m. अंकुर m.
CIPHER, n. *arithmetical character.* अंकडा m. अंक m. आंख m.
2 *mark for nothing.* पूज n. शून्य n.
3 *occult writing.* गूढलिपि f. गुप्तलिपी f. सांकेतिकलिपि f. Some particular *ciphers* are अंकलिपि *or* अंकभाषा f. चिकारी f. *or* चिकारीबोली *or* भाषा f. फुलकारी *or* फुलारी f. *or* फुलकारी बोली *or* भाषा, फुलारी-&c. छत्रबंध m. मिताक्षरा f.
4 *mere nominal person.* टिकोजी m. टिकोबा m. टिक्याचा धनी m. दिपाचा कवडा m.
To CIPHER, v. n. हिशोबm. करणें.
CIPHERING, n. See ARITHMETIC. [फेरी f.
CIRCLE, n. मंडलn. वर्तुलn. वृत्तn. कुंडली f. वेढाm. गरकाm. फेराm.
Area of a c. फलn.
C. of illumination. प्रकाशवृत्तn.
Forth of a c. *quadrant.* पदn.
Great c. महद्वृत्तn. बृहद्वृत्त n.
Small c. लघुवृत्तn.
Segment of a c. खंडमंडलn. वृत्तखंड. n.
The eccentric c. प्रतिवृत्तn. प्रतिमंडलn.
2 *compass, circuit, district, region.* मंडलn. चक्रn. मंडलभूमि f. वृत्तभूमि f.
3 *band, body, ring,* v. COMPANY. मंडली *or* ळी f. चाकोळें *or* चाखोळेंn. कचोळेंn. कोंडाळेंn. पंक्ति f. ओळ f. पेंढेंn.
Reasoning in a circle. अन्योन्याश्रयदोषm. आत्माश्रयदोषm.
To CIRCLE, v. n. *move circularly.* फेराm.-फेरी f.-गरकाm.-गिरकी f.-&c. खाणें-घेणें-मारणें, गिरटी *or* घिरटी f. घालणें, गिरगिर *or* रां-गरगर *or* रां (and *intens.* गरागर & गरारां) फिरणें-जाणें.
To CIRCLE, v. a. *enclose.* See To SURROUND. 2 *revolve round.* फेराm.-फेरी f.-गरकाm.-&c. मारणें-घेणें-&c. *with* भोवताला *of o.*
CIRCUIT, n. *passage around or about, compass.* फेराm. फेरी f. भोवाडाm. गिरकांडाm. *dim.* गिरकांडी f. v. दे, मार, घे, गिरटी *or* घिरटी f. v. घाल, गरकाm. v. घे, मार, बस, बळसाm.
To fetch a c. फेराm.-फेरी f. खाणें-घेणें, गरकाm. मारणें-घेणें, गिरटी *or* घिरटी f. घालणें.
2 *circular, circle, region.* मंडलn. चक्रn. मंडलभूमि f. वृत्तभूमि f.
CIRCUITOUS, a. *not direct.* फेऱ्याचा, घेऱ्याचा, गरक्याचा, गिरकांड्याचा, भोवाड्याचा, &c.
CIRCUITOUSLY, adv. *in a circuit.* फेऱ्यानें, फेराघेऊन-&c.
CIRCULAR, a. v. ROUND. चक्राकार, चक्रवान्, मंडलाकार, चक्रवत्, वृत्त, वृत्ताकार.
CIRCULAR, n. *letter or notice to a circle.* जाहिरात f. प्रसिद्धिपत्रn. सरचिठ्ठी f. अनेकज्ञापक पत्रकn.
C. order. बट्टहुकूमm.
CIRCULARITY, n. v. A. गोलm. गोळपणाm. गोलत्वn. गोलाकारm. गोलाकृति f. चक्राकारm. वृत्ताकारm. [वृत्तवत्.
CIRCULARLY, adv. v. A. *in a circular form.* चक्रवत्, मंडलवत्,
I. *with a circular motion.* चक्रगतीनें, वर्तुलगतीनें.
To CIRCULATE, v. a. *cause to pass about.* फिरवणें, चालवणें, चालू करणें, हातोहात-हातोहातीं-हातोपात-हाजिराहाजिरीं फिरवणें-चालवणें, परिभ्रमणn.-परिक्रमणn. करवणें *g. of o.*
To CIRCULATE, v. n. फिरणें, भ्रमणें, चालणें, हातोहात-&c. फिरणें, परिभ्रमणn.- परिक्रमणn. करणें.
CIRCULATION, n. v.V. A.—*act.* फिरवणेंn. चालवणेंn. &c.
v. V. N. फिरणेंn. भ्रमणेंn. भ्रमm. भ्रमणn.
I. (of coins) *currency.* चाल f. चलनn.
CIRCUMAMBIENT, a. v. SURROUNDING. वेष्टक, आवरक.
To CIRCUMAMBULATE, v. n. सभोवता फिरणें, गरकाm.-बळसाm.-फेराm.-&c. घालणें-मारणें.
To c. an object keeping it on the right. प्रदक्षिणा f. *or* प्रादक्षिण्यn. घालणें-करणें, परिक्रमm.-परिक्रमणn. करणें.
To CIRCUMCISE, v. a. सुनत f.-सुंता f.-शेफाग्रचर्मच्छेदm. करणें, *g. of o.* [परिकर्त्तनn.
CIRCUMCISION, v. V.—*act.* सुनत f. सुंता f. शेफाग्रचर्मच्छेदm.
CIRCUMFERENCE, n.. घेराm. घेरm. फेराm. फेरm. वेढm. परिधिm. मंडलn. वृत्ति f. गरकाm. लपेट f.
CIRCUMFLEX, n.—the accent. स्वरितm. [दिङ्कुस्थ.
CIRCUMJACENT, a. *bordering.* भोवरपासचा, आसपासचा, चतु-
CIRCUMLOCUTION, n. *circuit of words.* गिरकांडा m. गिरकांड्याचें-फेऱ्याचें-वळश्याचें बोलणें n. द्राविडप्राणायाम m. चरपट f. चरपटपंजरी f. चर्पटिका f.
CIRCUMLOCUTORY, a. v. N. फेऱ्याचा, गिरकांड्याचा, भोवाड्याचा, द्राविडप्राणायामाचा, &c.
To CIRCUMNAVIGATE, v. a. गलबतांत बसून प्रदक्षिणा f. घालणें.
To CIRCUMSCRIBE, v. a. *limit,* v. To BOUND. हद्द f. करणें-बांधणें, समर्याद-सावधि-सावधिक-वलयांकित-&c. करणें, आरेखणें, आरेखा m. करणें.
CIRCUMSCRIBED, p. & a. v. V. समर्याद-सावधिक केलेला, &c.

परिछिन्न.

I. *confined*, v. NARROW. अप्रशस्त.

CIRCUMSPECT, CIRCUMSPECTIVE, *a.* v. CAUTIOUS. पगदस्त, पगदस्ती, चहोंकडे-मागेंपुढें-पदोपदीं-&c. पाहणारा, संप्रेक्ष्यकारी, समीक्ष्यकारी.

CIRCUMSPECTON, CIRCUMSPECTNESS, *n.* v. A. *and* CAUTION. पगदस्ती *f.* सावधानता *f.*

CIRCUMSPECTLY, CIRCUMSPECTIVELY, *adv.* v. A. मागें पुढें-चहूंकडे-&c. पाहून, सावधपणानें, &c.

CIRCUMSTANCE, *n. appendage, adjunct, accident.* आगंतुकधर्म *m.* असहजधर्म *m.* अस्वाभाविकगुण *m.* आनुषंगिक-अनुपयोगी-अनुबंधी-&c. पदार्थ *m.*-विषय *m.*-&c.

2 *incident, matter, point.* गोष्ट *f.* प्रकरण *n.* प्रकार *m.* गाणें *n.*

By the force of circumstances. प्रसंगवशात्, प्रसंगवशें, प्रसंगोपात.

Under such circumstances. तशांत.

3 circumstances; *state of affairs.* गोष्ट *f.* हवाल *m.f.* अवस्था *f.* दशा *f.* वर्त्तमान *n.*

Easiness of c. *or* Easy c. v. COMPETENCE. द्रव्यानुकूल्य *n.* ताजीरोटी *f.* सुगति *f.*

Straitness of c. धरणें पारणें *n.* धूळफुंकण्याची दशा *f.*-गति *f.* ओढगस्ती *f.* ओढ *f.* गिरिबदारी *f.* चणचण *f.* चडचड *f.*चडफड *f.* द्रव्यप्रातिकूल्य *n.*

Of easy c.v. COMPETENCE. खाऊन पिऊन खुशाल *or* सुखी, खाऊन जेवून खुशाल-&. खातापिता, खाताजेवता, घरचा सुखी.

CIRCUMSTANCED, *a.* दशेंतला, अवस्थेंतला, दशापन्न, अवस्थापन्न.

CIRCUMSTANTIAL, *a. appendant, adventitious,* v. ACCIDENTAL. आगंतुक, आहार्य्य.

2 *particular, in detail,* v. DETAIL. तपसिलाचा, बयादीचा, सविस्तर, विस्तृत.

3 (evidence) अनुमानसिद्ध, आनुमानिक.

C. evidence. अनुमानप्रमाण *n.* प्रत्यंतरीपुरावा *m.*

CIRCUMSTANTIALITY, *n.* v. A. 1. आगंतुकत्व *n.* आहार्य्यत्व *n.* 2 विस्तार *m.* विस्तृतता *f.*

CIRCUMSTANTIALLY, *adv.* v. A. 1. See ACCIDENTALLY. 2 तपसीलवार, बितपसील, बयादवार, सविस्तर.

To CIRCUMVALLATE, *v. a.* चहोंकडें कोटबंदी *f.*-तटबंदी *f.* करणें.

CIRCUMVALLATION, *n.* चहोंकडें केलेली कोटबंदी *f.*-तटबंदी *f.*-मोरचेबंदी *f.*

To CIRCUMVENT, CIRCUMVENTION, &c. See To DECEIVE, DECEPTION, &c.

To CIRCUMVOLVE, &c. See To REVOLVE, &c.

CIRCUS, *n. area for shows and games.* रंगभूमि *f.* रंगांगण *n.* रंग *m.* तालीमखाना *m.*

CIS,—as used in comp. इकडचा *or* ला, इकडील.

CISTERN, *n.* टाकी *f.* टाकें *n.* धमधमा *m.* खजिना *m.* हौद *m.* कुंड *n.*

CITADEL, *n.*आंतला कोट *m.*आंतला किल्ला *m.*बालेकिल्ला *m.*अंतर्दुर्ग *n.*

CITATION. See SUMMONS.

To CITE. See To SUMMON, To QUOTE.

CITIZEN, *n. resident of a city.* नगरकरी, नगरवासी, शहरवाला, नगरवाला, नगरस्थ, पौरजन.

CITIZENSHIP, *n.* v. N. नगरकरीपणा *m.* नगरवासिता *f.* नगरस्थता *f.* पौरजनत्व *n.*

Fellow c. पौरसख्य *n.*

CITRON, *n.* the tree. मातुलुंग *m. pop.* मातुलिंग *n. and* महाळुंग *f.* ईड *f.* तोरंजन *n.* महाफल *n.*—the fruit. मातुलुंग *n.pop.* मातुलिंग *n.* महाळुंग *n.* ईड *n.* इडनिंबू *n.* तोरंजन *n.* महाफल *n.*

CITY, *n.* शहर *n.* नगर *n. dim.* नगरी *f.* पत्तन *n.* पुर *pop.* पूर *n.*

Holy c. धर्मपुरी *f.*

Walls of a c. or town. शहरपन्हा *m.*

CITY, *a. urban, oppidan.* शहरी, शहरचा, नगरचा, नगरसंबंधी, नागर, नागरिक, पौर.

CIVET, *n.* जवादी मांजराची कस्तूरी *f.* मार्जार कस्तूरिका *f.*

CIVET-CAT, *n.* जवादी मांजर *n.* गंधमार्जार *m.*

Perfume bag of the c. जवादी *f.* जवादें *n.*

CIVIC, *a. of or belonging to a city.* शहराचा, नगराचा, शहरी, नगरसंबंधी, नगरविषयक, नागरिक.

CIVIL, *a.relating to the community, to civil affairs, usage, &c.* जनव्यवहाराचा, लोकव्यवहाराचा, जनव्यवहारविषयक, जनव्यवहारसंबंधी, लोकव्यवहारविषयक-संबंधी, लोक यात्रेचा, नीतीचा, नीतिविषयक.

2 *relating to a man as a member of a community.* जानपदांतःपातित्वाचा, जानपदांतःपातित्व संबंधी-विषयक-मूलक-&c. जानपदत्व विषयक, जानपदत्वसंबंधी, जानपदीय.

3 *not ecclesiastical or military.* मुलकी, मुलकी कामाचा, मुलकीप्रकरणाचा, गांवखात्याचा, गांवखात्याकडील, गांवखात्याकडचा.

4 *complaisant, polite, courteous, &c.* बोलूनचालून चांगला-गोड-&c. माणुसकीचा, मिळाऊ, मिळताऊ, गोडबोल्या, माणुसपणाचा, गृहस्थपणाचा, &c. गृहस्थी, सुशील, आदरशील, आदरमानी, सत्कारी, सज्जनशिष्ट, शिष्टसंप्रदायी, सभ्य, आदरनिष्ठ, सानुनय, अनुनयी, अनुरोधी, अनुवर्त्ती, युक्तव्यवहारी.

5 (court,&c.) दिवाणी.

C. case दिवाणीखटला *m.*-विषय *m.*

C. court दिवाणी अदालत *f.*

CIVIL-ENGINEER, *n.* पूल-तळीं-बाडे वगैरे बांधणारा.

CIVILIAN, *n. one employed on civil duties.* मुलकी काम करणारा-पाहणारा-&c. गांव खात्याचें काम पाहणारा, &c.

CIVILITY, *n.* v. A. 4 *complaisance, politeness, courteousness.* शिष्टता *f.* माणुसकी *f.* मनुष्यपणा *m.* माणुसपणा *m.* गृहस्थगिरी *f.* गृहस्थपणा *m.* तवाजू *f.* भलमाणसाई *f.* सभ्यता *f.* सुजनता *f.* सुजनत्व *n.* सौजन्य *n.* अनुनय *m.* अनुवृत्ति *f.* अनुरोध *m.*

Civilities and courtesies. आदरसत्कार *m.* आदरमान *m.* आदरउपचार *m.pl.* मानसन्मान *m* ताजीमतवाजू *f.* उजूतवाजू *f.* आगतस्वागत *n.* मुजारत *f.* पाटपाणी *n.* उपचार *m. pl.* तारतम्य *pop.* तारतीम *n.* आदरतारतम्य *n.* उठबैस *f.* उठाबस *f. v.* कर, ठेव.

Empty c. शुष्कोपचार *m. pl.*

For the civil civility, for the saucy sauce. अरे तर कारे अहोतरकायहो, तूं लंड तर मी भंड.

CIVILIZATION, *n.* v. V.—*act.* मनुष्यांत आणणें *n.* &c.—*state.* माणुसकी *f.* माणुसपणा *m.* सुशिक्षितता *f.* सुशिक्षितावस्था *f.*

To CIVILIZE, *v. a.* मनुष्यांत-माणुसकींत आणणें, माणुसकी *f.*-माणुसकळा *f.* आणणें *with* स *of o.* मनुष्यसा करणें, सुधारणें, शिक्षित करणें, विद्याचार संपन्न करणें.

CIVILIZED, v. V. मनुष्यांत आणलेला, &c. विद्याचार संपन्न.

CIVILLY, *adv.* v. A. 4. माणुसकीनें, गृहस्थपणानें, गृहस्थरीतीनें, भलेपणानें.

I. *in law, not naturally*. कायद्याचे दृष्टीनें, कायद्यानें.

CLACK, *n. unceasing & wearying speech*. बटबट *f.* टक *f.* टकटक *f.* टकळी *f.* ठकठक *f.* खटखट *f.* खटकखटक *f.*

2 *vociferous woman*. बटबटीबाई *f.* बटबट करणारी *f.* गजघंटा *f.* कर्कशा *f.* [&c. वाजणें.

To CLACK, *v. n. make a sharp noise*. खटखटणें, खटखट-ठकठक-

2 v. To PRATE. लबलब बोलणें, बटबटणें, बकबकणें.

CLACKER, *n. clacking instrument* (*to frighten birds, &c.*). खटखटें *n.* ठकठकें *or* ठुकठुकें *n.* फटफटें *n.*

CLAD, *a.* v. CLOTHED. परिधानयुक्त, धारितवस्त्र, सचैल.

C. with space, i. e. *naked*. दिगंबर.

To CLAIM, *v. a. demand of right*. हक्काचा-हक्कानें-दाव्यानें-दाव्याचा-वारशानें-&c. मागणें,दावा *m.*करणें-सांगणें, सत्ता *f.* करणें *with* ला *or* स *of o.* स्वीकारणें, अंगीकारणें, सत्तापूर्वक याचना *f.* करणें, मागणें. [&c. बांधणें.

2 *assert, profess*, v. To PRETEND. बिरीद *n.* बाळगणें, चंग *m.*-

CLAIM, *n. demand*. मागणें *n.* तलब *f.* सत्तापूर्वक याचन *n.*

2 *title, right*. इलाखा *m.* दावा *m.* वारसा *m.* अधिकार *m.* हक्क *m.*

CLAIMANT, CLAIMER, *n.* v.V. हक्कानें मागणारा, &c. दावेदार, दावेकरी, वारसा-दावा-हक्क-&c. सांगणारा.

CLAIMED, *p.* v. V. हक्काचा मागितलेला, &c. स्वीकृत, अंगीकृत.

CLAIMING, *n.* v. V.—*act*. हक्काचें मागणें *n.* दाव्याचें मागणें *n.* &c. स्वीकार *m.* अंगीकार *m.* स्वीकरण *n.* अंगीकरण *n.*

CLAIRVOYANCE, *n.* अप्रत्यक्षविषयदर्शन *n.*

CLAIRVOYANT, *n.* अप्रत्यक्ष विषयद्रष्टा *m.* पाहण्या *m.*

To CLAMBER, *v. n. climb with difficulty*. धरून धरून-वेंघत वेंघत-हातापायांनीं-हातपाय टेकून-&c. चढणें.

CLAMMINESS, *n.* v. A. चिकटण *f.* चिकटाई *f.* चिकटी *f.* चिकचीक *f. intens.* चिकचिकाट *m.* किचकीच *f. intens.* किचकिचाट *m.*

CLAMMY, *a.* v. STICKY. चिकचिकीत, गिचगिचीत *or* गिजगिजीत, चिडचिडीत, पिठाळ, पिठा *or* पिठ्या.

C. ooze or adhering matter. चिकटा *m.* चिकटी *f.*

To be c. चिकचिकणें, चिडचिडणें.

CLAMOROUS, *a.* v. N. गलगल्या, गलबल्या, गोंगाट्या, बोभाट्या, ओरड्या, गलबलाचा, गलक्याचा &c. कळकळ्या, गलगल-गलबल-&c. करणारा.

CLAMOROUSLY, *adv.* v. N. गलबलीनें, गलबल-गलगल-&c. करून.

CLAMOUR *n. vociferation, noise, outcry*, v. UPROAR. गलग्रा *m.* गलका *m.* गलबल *f.* गलबला *m.* गलगल *f.* गवगव *f.* गवगवा *m.* कलकल *or* कळकळ *f.* घोळका *m.* कोलाहल *m.* रोराण *n.*

—intens. गलबलाट *m.* गलगलाट *m.* गोंगाट *m.* कोकाट *m.*

To CLAMOUR, *v. n.* पुकारा *m.*-गोंगाट *m.*-गलका *m.*-गलबला *m*-&c. करणें-मांडणें, कळाकळा *adv.* करणें, कळकळणें.

2 against; *exclaim against*. नावें बोंब *f.*-हाका *f. pl.* मारणें *g. of o.* नावें शंख *m.*-बोंबलपट्टी *f.*-शंखाचें *n.*-हाकाटा *m.*-हाकाटी *f.* करणें *g. of o.*

CLAMP, *n.* पट्टी *f.* जोरपट्टी *f.* अडू *m.*

To CLAMP, *v. a.* पट्टी *f.*-जोरपट्टी *f.* देणें-मारणें.

CLAN, *n.* v. FAMILY. कुल *n.* वंश *m.* घराणें *n.* गोत्र *n.* खूम *m.*

CLANCULAR. See CLANDESTINE.

CLANDESTINE, *a. secret, sly, &c.* चोरीचा, चोरटा, लिकाचोरीचा, गुपचुपीचा, लपंडाईचा, लपंडावाचा, लपनछपनीचा, छपावणीचा, कांदीकोंदीचा.

C. doings. लपंडाव *m.* लपंडाई *f. v.* कर, खेळ.

CLANDESTINELY, *adv.* v. A. चोरून, लिकून चोरून, लिकाचोरीनें, चोरगत्तीनें, लपतछपत *or* लपूनछपून.

To give c. अडव्या हातानें देणें.

CLANDESTINENESS, *n.* v. A. चोरटेपणा *m.* गुपचुपपणा *m.*

CLANG, CLANK, CLANGOUR, *n. sharp, shrill sound*. खणका *m.* दणका *m.* ठणत्कार *m.* झणकार *or* रा *m.* झणत्कार *m.* ठांका *m.* ठांडू *n. f.*— intens. खणखणाट *m.* खणाण *m.* दणदणाट *m.* दणाणा *m.* ठणठणाट *m.* ठणाण *m.* झणझणाट *m.* झणाण *m.* ठणाका *m.* घणघणाट *m.*

To CLANG, *To* CLANK, *v. n.* खणखणणें, ठणठणणें, झणझणणें, झणत्कारणें, ढणढणणें, घणघणणें,—intens. खणाणणें,ठणाणणें, झणाणणें, घणाणणें.

CLANGER, *n.* CLANKER, *n.* CLANGING, *p. a.* v. V. खणखणणारा, ठणठणणारा, &c. खणखण-झणझण-&c. वाजणारा.

CLANGINGLY, CLANKINGLY, *adv.* खण-कन-कर-&c. खणखण *or* णा, झणझण *or* णां, ढणढण, घणघण *or* णां,—intens. खणाखण, खणाणां, झणाझण, झणाणां, ढणाढण, घणाणां.

To CLAP, *v. a. strike loudly or smartly*. तडकून-झडकन-झटकन-&c. मारणें-लावणें-थोकणें, थोपटणें, झडपडावणें.

2 to, on, at, in, &c. *apply smartly*. मारणें, फटकन-झटकन-सटकन-&c. लावणें-मारणें-घालणें-टाकणें.

3 (the hands). टाळी *f.* पिटणें-वाजविणें-मारणें.

4 (the sides, exultingly). कुले *m.pl.* थोपटणें-बडवणें,काखा *f. pl.* वाजवणें, टिरी *f.pl.* वाजवणें-बडवणें-थोपटणें.

CLAP, *n. loud noise,&c.* दणका *m.* तडाखा *n.m.* कडाखा *m.* धडाका *m.* झडाका *m.*

2 (of the hands). टाळी *f.*

3 (of thunder). कडाड *m.* गडगडाट *m.*

CLAPPER, *n.* (of a bell, &c.) लोळा *m. dim* लोळी *f.*

CLARET, *n.* एक मद्य आहे, लालशराब *m.*

CLARIFICATION, *n.* v. V. A.—*act*. शोधणें *n.* मळ काढणें *n.* &c. शोध *m.* शोधन *n.*—*state*. शुद्धि *f.* शोधितत्व *n.* निर्गलितत्व *n.*

CLARIFIED, *p.* v. V. A. शोधलेला, मळ छाटलेला, &c. शोधित, शोधींव, निर्गलित.

CLARIFIER, *n.* v. V. A. शोधणारा, &c. शोधक.

To CLARIFY, *v. a. defecate, fine, clear*, शोधणें, मळ *m.*-मळी *f.* काढणें-छाटणें *g.of o.*निवळवणें,साफ-शुद्ध-स्वच्छ-निर्मल-&c. करणें.

To CLARIFY, *v. n. become clear from feculence*. निवळणें, मळ *m.*-मळी *f.* बसणें *g. of s.*

CLARION, *n.* v. TRUMPET. तुतारी *f.* सनई *f.* रणशिंग *n.*

CLARIONET, *n.* एक वाद्य आहे.

To CLASH, *v. n. strike or drive against with force*. एकमेकाशीं लागणें, धडक *f.*-धक्का *m.*-घसरा *m.* बसणें, परस्परांचा झपाटा *m.*-सपाटा *m.*-तडाका *m.*-धडाका *m.*-&c. बसणें.

2 fig. *meet opposingly, interfere, collide, &c.* घासणें, घासणी *f.*-&c. होणें *g. of s.* लढणें, एकमेकास आडवा-वांकडा-&c. येणें, एकमेकास नडणें, कचक *f.* झडणें-उडणें *g. of s.* परस्पर विरोध *m.*-विपर्यास *m.* पडणें-होणें *g. of s.*

CLASH, CLASHING, *n.* v. V. 1.—*act*. एकमेकाशीं लागणें *n.* धक्का-&c. बसणें *n.*

2 घासणी *f.* घासाघास *or* घीस *f.* कच *or* कचक *f.* कचाकची *f.* तडवड *f.* नकमक *f.* तलतल *f.* संघर्ष *m.* संघर्षण *n.* द्वंद्व *n.*—intens.

कचकचाट *m.* कचाकच *f.* कचाचm. खळाळ *m.*

I. *clashing sound.* तडाका or खाm. धडाकाm. कडाका or खाm. —intens. घडाडm. घडघडाटm. [कडाखाm.

II. (as of musical instruments). गजरm. झंगड *f.* कडका *m.*

III. (of swords). तरवारींचा झपाटाm. झमाझमी *f.* चकमक *f.* चकाचकी *f.* कचाकची *f.*

Clashing, *p.* v. V. 2. परस्पर विरोधी, अन्योन्य विरोधी.

Clasp, *n. hook, hold,* v. Catch. फासाm. अडकणn. अडकवणn.

That has a c. सफांशी.

2 See Clasping.

To Clasp, *v. a. hug,* v. To Embrace. आलिंगणें, कवळणें, कंवटाळणें, वेंगाटणें, कवळून-&c. धरणें, कव *f.*-गव *f.* घालणें or कवेंत-गवेंत धरणें.

To c. to one's bosom. पोटाळणें.

2 *catch and hold, grasp, &c.* अवळणें, अवळून धरणें, मुठींत-चौड्यांत धरणें.

Clasped, *p.* v. V. 1. कवळलेला, कंवटाळलेला, &c. आलिंगित.

2 अवळलेला, अवळून धरलेला, आलिंगित.

Clasping, *n.* v. V. 1.—*act.* कवळणें *n.* कंवटाळणें *n.* कवळून धरणें *n.*&c. आलिंगन *n.* खेम *f.* आंगकवळी *f.*

2 अवळणें *n.* अवळून धरणें*n.* &c.

Clasp-knife, *n.* मोडसुरा *m. dim.* मोडसुरी *f.*

Class, *n. rank, order: set, number, body.* जाति *f.* जात *f.* गण *m.* वर्ग *m.* वर्ण *m.* पक्षm. विल्हे or विल्हय *f.* विल्हाm. प्रत *f.* खातेंn. प्रकरणn. प्रकारm.

2 (of scholars). वर्गm.

3 (of people or men). जाति *f.* जात *f.* मंडळी *f.* लोक (in comp. as ब्राह्मणलोक, शूद्रलोक, &c.).

The higher classes,—compreh. पांढरपेशा *m.* गृहस्थलोक *m. pl.* मोठेलोक *m. pl.*

The lower classes,—compreh. आडजात *f.* आडाणजात *f.* तेलीतांबोळी *m. pl.* कुणबीमाळी *m. pl.* हलके लोक *m. pl.*

To Class, *To* Classify, *v. a.* जात *f.*-जाति *f.*-प्रत *f.*-विल्हा *m.*- विल्हे *f.* लावणें, प्रतवार-जातवार-विल्हेवार-&c. लावणें, वर्ग *m.* करणें-बांधणें.

Classed, Classified, *p.* v. V. जातवार-&c. लावलेला, गणीभूत, आंतर्गणिक, वर्गीय, वर्गीभूत.

Classic, Classical, *a. belonging, &c. to ancient or superior authors.* अभियुक्तकवीचा, आदिकवीचा, अभियुक्तकवितेचा, आद्यकविता संबंधी, आदिकविकृत, प्राचीनकवीचा, &c.

2 *pure, chaste,*—style, &c. प्रशस्त, शुद्ध, संस्कृत.

Classically, *adv. by classes or sets.* प्रतवार, विल्हेवार, जातवार.

Classification, Classing, *n.* v. V.—*act.* जातवार लावणें *n.* प्रतवार लावणें *n.* &c. विल्हेवारी *f.* पृथक्करण *n.* गणीकरण *n.* वर्गीकरण *n.*

C. of soils. प्रत बंदी *f.*

Roll of the classes of soils. प्रतवारी *f.*

To Clatter, *v. n.* v. To Rattle. खटखटणें, खटखटवाजणें, घडघडणें or गडगडणें, कडकडणें, कडकणें, खळखळणें, खळखळ वाजणें. —intens. घडाडणें, कडाडणें, खळाळणें.

2 *chatter, rattle away, run on,* v. To Prate. बडबडणें, बकबकणें, बटबटणें, पचापचा बोलणें-करणें.

Clatter, Clattering, *n.* v. V. 1.—*act.* खटखटणें *n.* घडघडणें *n.* &c. तडाका or खा *m.* धडाखा *m.* कडाकडी *f.* धडाधडी *f.* डमडम *f.* —intens. खडखडाट *m.* खडाड *m.* घडघडाट or गडगडाट *m.* कडकडाट *m.* कडाड *m.* घडाड *m.* खळखळाट *m.* खळाळ *m.* फडफडाट *m.* फडाड *m.*

2 बडबडणें *n.* &c. टकळी *f.* बडबड *f.* बकबक *f.* टकटक *f.*

I. *hubbub,* v. Uproar. कडाकडी *f.* धडाधडी *f.* गोंगाट *m.* गलगल *f.* गूल *f.* गलबल *f.*

Clatteringly, *adv.* v. Rattlingly. घडघड or डां, गडगड or डां, खळखळ.—intens. खडाखड, घडाडां, फडाफड, फडाडां.

Clause, *n.* (of a sentence). वाक्यांग *n.* वाक्यावयव *m.* वाक्यखंड *n.* वाक्यैकदेश *m.*

Annexing of a c. अर्थांतरोपन्यास *m.* [करण *n.*

2 *item of a stipulation, article.* कलम *n.* पोटचें कलम *n.* प्र-

Clavicle, *n. collar-bone.* सरी *f.* जत्रु *n.*

Clavicular, *a.* सरीचा, जत्रुसंबंधी, जत्रुविषयक.

Claw, *n.* नख *n. m.* नखी *f.* नखुट *n.* पंजा *m.*

2 (of a lobster, crawfish, &c.). नांगा *m.* नांगी *f.* नांगडा or नांगाडा or नांगोडा *m.* आंकडा *m.*

3 *nail*—in contempt. नखरूड *n.*

To Claw, *v. a.* नखानें तोडणें-धरणें, विचकुरणें, बुचकरणें or बुचकुरणें or बोचकडणें or बोचकरणें, विचकुरा *m.*-बोचकरा or बोचकडा *m.* घेणें *g. of o.* बोचकरणें or बोचकडणें or बोचकुरणें.

Clawed, *p. & a.* v. V. नखानें तोडलेला, विचकुरलेला-&c.

I. *having claws.* नखी, नखाचा.

Clawing, *n.* v. V.—*act.* विचकुरणें *n.* विचकुरा *m.* बुचकरा or बुचकुरा *m.* बोचकडा or रा *m.* कुरचा *m.* [माण *f.*

Clay, *n.* चिकणमाती *f.* शेडमाती *f.* शेडी *f.* शाडू or शेडू *f.* शेड *f.*

Potter's c. कुंभारमाती *f.* कृष्णमृत्तिका *f.*

White c. गोपीचंदन *pop.* गोपचंदन *n.*

Clay-ground, Clay-land, Clay-soil, *n.* शाडवट जमीन *f.* माणजमीन *f.* मान or माण *f.* शाडूची जमीन *f.*

Clay-pit. *n.* शाडूचीखाण *f.* शेडखाण *f.* मातखण or मातखाण *f.*

Clayey, *a.* शाडूचा, शेडीचा, शाडवट.

Clean, *a.* lit. fig. साफ, निर्मल, स्वच्छ, शुद्ध, पवित्र, पाक, चोख, चोखट, प्रांजल, शुचि, शुचिष्मंत, विमल, मलहीन-रहित-&c.

2 See Bright, Clear. 3 *naked, void, &c.* v. Bare. लकलकीत, लक्ख, लकीलक्ख, शुद्धबुद्ध. [ष्मंत.

4—ceremonially. सोवळा, पवित्र, शुचि, शुचिष्मान् *pop.* शुचि-

5 *uncontaminate, &c.* v. Pure. पवित्र, निरपराध, निष्पाप, अलिप्त.

6—shirt, &c. *washed & ready for use.* धुवट, धुवटघडीचा.

Clean, *adv. quite, utterly,* v. Wholly. साफ, शुद्ध, चट, चपाट, झाडून, सफई, ठार, बिलकूल, निका *a. decl.*

2 *in a clear, dextrous, happy &c. manner.* अचानक, अलग, अलगत, अलागत, अलाद.

To Clean, *To* Cleanse, *v. a.* साफ-शुद्ध-स्वच्छ-निर्मल-&c. करणें, मळ *m.*-मळी *f.* काढणें *g. of o.* शोधणें, चोखाळणें, शोध *m.* शोधन *n.*-शुद्धि *f.*-शौच *n.*- मलापकर्षण *n.*-परिमार्जन *n.*-मार्जन *n.*-&c. करणें *g. of o.*

2 (with perfumes or unguents). उटणें, उद्वर्त्तन *n.*-मार्जना *f.* करणें, *g. of o.*

3 out; (a well, pond, ditch, &c.). गाळणें, गाळ *m.* काढणें *g. of o.* उसपणें, उसपा or उपसा *m.* करणें *g. of o.*

CLEANED, CLEANSED, *p.* v. V. 1. *and* CLEAN. साफ-&c.केलेला, शोधलेला, शुद्ध, शोधित, विशुद्ध, परिशुद्ध, शुचिर्भूत, धावित, परिमार्जित, अपकृष्टमल. [*m.*

CLEANEDNESS, CLEANSEDNESS, *n.* v. P. शुद्धि *f.* विशुद्धि *f.* शौच

CLEANER, CLEANSER, *n.* CLEANSING, *p. a.* v. V. 1. साफ-&c. करणारा, शोधणारा, मलापकर्षक, शोधक, धावक, परिमार्जक, परिमार्जन-&c. कर्त्ता.

CLEANING, CLEANSING, *n.* v.V. 1.—*act.* साफ-&c. करणें *n.* शोधन *n.* शोध *m.* शौच *n.* मलापकर्षण *n.* मार्जन *n.* सम्मार्जन *n.* परिमार्जन *n.* धावन *n.*

2 उटणें *n.* उटी *f.* उद्वर्तन *n.*

CLEANLINESS, *n.* v. A. सोंगळपणा *m.* चोखाळपणा *m.* चाकपाकी *f.* चकपकी *f.* चाकचोपी *f.* मलद्वेष *m.*

CLEANLY, *a. careful to be clean.* चाकपाक, चकपक, चकपकीत, चाकचोप, चोखाळ, सोंगळ, मलद्वेषी.

CLEANNESS, *n.* v. A. 1. साफी *f.* साफपणा *m.* निर्मळपणा *m.* निर्मलता *f.* स्वच्छपणा *m.* स्वच्छता *f.* शुद्धि *f.* विशुद्धि *f.* पवित्रता *f* शौच *n.* नैर्मल्य *n.* मलाभाव *m.* मलराहित्य *n.* मलहीनता *f.*

CLEAR, *a. pellucid, transpicuous.* निवळ, साफ, नितळ, स्वच्छ, निर्मल *or* ळ, प्रांजल, प्रसन्न, शुद्ध, काचेसारखा, भिंगासारखा.

Very c. water. मोराचें असूं *n.* [सन्न.

2 *free from clouds or haze.* निवळ, स्वच्छ, निरभ्र, प्रांजल, प्र-

3 *manifest, evident, apparent,* v. PLAIN. स्पष्ट, व्यक्त, उघड, उघडा, साफ, प्रकट *pop.* प्रगट, प्रत्यक्ष, अभिव्यक्त, प्रसिद्ध, झळझळीत, टळटळीत.

4 *perspicuous, free from ambiguity or obscurity.* उघड, उघडा, स्पष्ट, सुबोध, बालबोध, व्यक्त, अभिव्यक्त, प्रकट *pop.* प्रगट, उत्तानार्थ, अगूढ, अगूढार्थक, विशद, झळझळीत, टळटळीत.

5 *guiltless, blameless,* v. INNOCENT, ABSOLVED. निरपराध, निर्दोष, निर्बाध, निष्प्रांजल, अलिप्त, शुद्ध.

6 *unobstructed, unencumbered,*—of places, v. OPEN. मोकळा, खुलास, खुलाशाचा, खुला, प्रशस्त, निर्विघ्न.

7 *not entangled, that is free of.* मोकळा, सुटा, मुक्त.

Clear of debt. अनृण *pop.* अनृणी.

8—of sounds, the voice, &c. *clear-sounding.* खणखणीत, घणघणीत, स्पष्ट, क्षार, ठास, प्रांजल, व्यक्त, निकोप.

9—of stamps, marks, letters, &c. *clear-looking, conspicuous, distinct, bright.* झळझळीत, टळटळीत *or* ठळठळीत, ढळढळीत, ठळक.

10 (profits, &c.) v. NET. निका, निवळ.

11 (sight) निवळ, तीक्ष्ण, तीव्र.

To CLEAR, *v. a. make fine,* v. To CLARIFY. शोधणें, मळ *m.*-मळी *f.* छाटणें *g. of o.*

2 *free from obstructions.* मोकळा-साफ-खुलास-खुलाशाचा-रिकामा-&c. करणें, अडगळ *f.* काढणें.

3 *free from bushes, grass, rubbish,* &c. चोखलणें, केरकचरा *m.* काढणें, साफ करणें, उजेरणें, झाडें झुडपें काढून साफकरणें.

4 off; (debts, &c.) *liquidate, discharge.* झाडणें, फेडणें, वारणें, बाकी पूज करणें, बेवारा *m.* करणें *g. of o.* निरानिपटा *m.*-निरानिपटारा *m.* करणें *g. of o.* फडशा *m.* करणें-करून टाकणें *g. of o.* दफेरफे-फारीक *or* ख-फिटं फाट-बेबाक-&c. करणें, उरता न ठेवणें

5 away; *remove.* काढणें, काढून घेणें, नेणें, घेऊन जाणें, वारावार *f.*-वारासार *f.* करणें *g. of o.*

6 up; *free from ambiguity, &c.* v. To EXPLAIN. उलगडणें, उलगडा *m.* करणें *g. of o.* उघडा-स्पष्ट-&c. करणें.

7 *free from guilt.* निर्दोष-निरपराध-निष्कलंक-दोषमुक्त-उजळमाथ्याचा करणें, उजळतामाथा *m.* करणें *g. of o.*

8 *gain without deduction.* नफ्यांत-घरीं पाडणें, उरणें-मिळणें-नफ्यांत पडणें *in. con.*

9 (the bowels) v. To PURGE. साफ करणें, मलशुद्धि *f.*-कोष्ठशुद्धि *f.* करणें.

10 (hedge, ditch, &c.) *pass over without touching.* अलगत-अचानक-&c. जाणें-पारजाणें.

To CLEAR, *v. n.*—as the sky or weather. उघडणें, निवळणें, खुलणें, नितळणें, उभणें, उघड *f.*-उघाड *f.*-उघाडी *f.* पडणें-होणें *g. of s.*

2 See To CLARIFY.

CLEAR, *adv.* v. CLEAN. अचानक, अलगत.

CLEAR-SIGHTED, *a.* v. WISE. प्राज्ञ, प्रज्ञावान्, दीर्घदर्शी, तार्किक.

CLEARANCE, *n.* गलबताची-&c. दाखलेचिट्ठी *f.*

CLEARED, *p.* v. V. A. 1. मळ छाटलेला, शोधित.

2 मोकळा केलेला, &c.

3 चोखललेला, &c. [फिटंफाट.

4 फेडलेला, वारलेला, &c. बेबाक, दफेरफे *or* रफेदफे, फारीक *or* ख,

To be c. फिटणें.

CLEARLY, *adv.* v. A. 3, *and* PLAINLY. उघड, प्रत्यक्ष, प्रत्यक्षतः, साफ, स्पष्ट, निवळ, साक्षात्, सव्यगत, धड, धडधडीत.

4 उघड, साफ, स्पष्ट, धडधडीत.

CLEARNESS, *n.* v. A. 1. निवळपणा *m.* नितळपणा *m.* नितळाई *f.* निवळाई *f.* निर्मळपणा *m.* साफी *f.* स्वच्छता *f.* निर्मलता *f.*

2 निवळपणा *m.* स्वच्छता *f.* निरभ्रता *f.* प्रसाद *m.*

3 उघडेपणा *m.* &c. साफी *f.* स्पष्टता *f.* व्यक्ति *f.* प्राकट्य *n.* अभिव्यक्ति *f.* वैशद्य *n.*

4 उघडेपणा *m.* &c. स्पष्टता *f.* व्यक्ति *f.* व्यक्तता *f.* प्राकट्य *n.* वैशद्य *n.* उत्तानार्थ *m.*

6 मोकळेपणा *m.* खुलासा *m.* प्रशस्तता *f.* प्राशस्त्य *n.*

CLEAT, *n.* लाकडाचीपट्टी *f.* जोरपट्टी *f.*

CLEAVABLE, *a.* v. V. फोडाया-तोडायाजोगा-सारखा-&c.

To CLEAVE, *v. a.* v. To SPLIT. फोडणें, तोडणें, खांडणें, खापलणें, बळानें भेद *m.* करणें *g. of o.*

To CLEAVE, *v. n.* v. To STICK. चिकटणें, चिकटून राहणें.

2 *open, part, split, &c.* तडकणें, तडणें, उलणें.

CLEAVER, *n. chopper.* सुरा *m.* मांसछेदनी *f.* स्वधिति *m.*

CLEFT, *n. fissure, opening,* v. CRACK. भेग *f.* संधि *m. f. pop.* सांध *f.* & सांधा *m.* भेर *f.* छेद *m.*

C. between hills, &c. खिंड *f. intens.* खिंडार *or* रेंन. गोंड *f.n.* घोळ *m.*

2 *piece made by splitting.* खाप *f.* फांक *f.*

CLEMENT, CLEMENCY. See MERCIFUL, MERCY.

CLENCH. See CLINCH. [*f.*

CLERGY, *n.* धर्मोपदेशकगण *m.* पाद्रीलोकांची पांढर *f.* धर्मपदस्थजनता

CLERGYMAN, *n.* धर्मोपदेशक, धर्मपदस्थ, पाद्री from the Portuguese is universally applied to a Christian minister.

CLERICAL, *a.* धर्मोपदेशकगणसंबंधी- विषयक, धर्मपदस्थजनताविषयक-संबंधी, पाद्रीलोकांचा.

CLERK, *n.* v. WRITER. कारकून, लेखक, परभू. N. B. This is the name of a particular tribe which usually follows the trade of writing.

2 See CLERGYMAN. 3 *man of letters,* See SCHOLAR.

4 पाद्रीच्या हातांखालचा एक मनुष्य आहे.

CLERKSHIP, *n.* कारकुनी *f.* कारकुनीपेशा *m.*

CLEVER, *a. capable, able, adroit, &c.* कुशल, शाहणा, चतुर, चातुर्यवान्, पटु, दक्ष, विचक्षण, सुगर, सुघड, खबरदार, कलावंत, काबील, सुबुद्धि, कुशलबुद्धि, चंच, चंचिबाग *or* ज *or* चंचुबाग, बाट, खंदा, अट्ठल, कौशल्यशाली, प्रभु. Of this word the sense, viewed as combined, and as expressible by the combination *talented and expert,* and as usually expressed accordingly by combinations or consecutive utterance of two or more of such words as, *able, capable, acute, apt, sharp, skilful, shrewd, smart, quick, prompt, long-headed, quick-witted, clear-sighted, &c. &c.* is conveyed in Maráthí by numerous expressions of a particular construction, and of strong significance. They are mostly *imitatives* and *onomatopoias* and *compounds* and *phrases*: they are in the commonest use and most extensive currency; and they would, as the most cursory inspection of them will evince, have been imperfectly and very injuriously exhibited, had they been scattered abroad in the Dictionary, or had they been gathered together without a notice of their power: करामती, हुनरी, अटोकाट, अटोपी, जाहंबाज, पटाईत, सराईत, बहादुर, *or* बहाद्दर, बाजिंदा (-लिहणार-बोलणार-धावणार-कारकून-&c.) खबरदार, पक्का, पुरा, कट्टा, जोतदार, धुरंधर, धुरीण, धनुर्धारी, धनुर्धर, अवधानी, संधानी, अष्टावधानी, अष्टसावध, अष्टपैलू, चतुरस्र *pop.* चौरस, लौकिकी, पुढच्याजोताचा, मेरव्या, कट्टा, खडाण, दलदपट, कागडा, खावराडिवरा, कर्त्ता, कर्त्तुमकर्त्ता, जेथें लात मारील तेथें पाणी काढील. And as viewed more particularly under the form of a *noun* as in "*A clever (a talented, gifted, highly,* and *variously endowed) person,*" it is well conveyed by गुणी, गुणनिधान, गुणग्राम, गुणनिधि, गुणिजन, गुणपात्र, गुणराशि, गुणसागर, गुणाकर, गुणाचीरास, गुणाचीखाण, बहुगुणी, गुणसंपन्न *or* सकलगुणसंपन्न, बत्तीसगुणी, सहस्रगुणी, गुणाढ्य, बत्तीसलक्षणी, बावनबीर, हरभास, हरहुनरी, हरकामी *or* म्या, कसबी, हरकसबी, सररास, महारथ *or* महारथी, मोहरा, बिरबल, दीक्षित, फरडा, फांकडा, सोमाजीसकलकळ्या.

2 *executed with skill, &c.* शाहणपणाचा, चतुराईचा, कौशल्याचा, कुशलबुद्धीचा.

CLEVERLY, *adv.* v. A. युक्तीनें, चतुराईनें, कसबानें, कौशल्यानें, कौशल्यपूर्वक, चातुर्यपूर्वक, हिकमतीनें, दक्षतेनें, युक्त्या.

CLEVERNESS, *n.* v. A. शहाणपणा *m.* चतुराई *f.* युक्ति *f.* चातुर्य *n.* कौशल्य *n.* कौशल *n.* सुगराई *f.* सुगरावा *m.* कला *f.* कसब *n.* कुसरी *f.* जुगूत *f.* जुगताई *f.* दक्षता *f.* दाक्षिण्य *n.* दाक्ष्य *n.* वैचक्षण्य *n.* प्रावीण्य *n.* मतिप्रकर्ष *m.*

CLEW, *n. ball of thread,* v. BALL. सुताची गुंडी *f.*-गुंडाळी *f.*-&c.

2 *guide, direction.* थांगदोरा *m.* पत्तादोरा *m.* पत्ता *m.* थांगपत्ता *m.* मुद्दा *m.*

C. to the bottom of. आधारास पंथ *m.* *v.*लाग, मिळ, अस.

To CLICK, *v. n. make a small, sharp noise.* चुकचुकणें, चुकचूक *f.* करणें, टिकटिक करणें-वाजणें, खुटकन-किटकिट-कटकट-टिचकण-&c. वाजणें.

CLIENT, *n.*—of a lawyer, &c. असामी *f.* कूळ *n.*

CLIFF, *n.* कडा *m.* खडपा *m.* पहाड *m.* भृगु *m.*

CLIMATE, *n. air of a country with reference to salubrity.* हवा *f.* हवापाणी *n.* देशप्रकृति *f.*

2 See COUNTRY.

CLIMAX, *n.*—in rhetoric. सार *m.* उत्तरोत्तरोत्कर्ष *m.*

To reach its c.—a pain or trouble. गळ्यापर्यंत येणें.

To CLIMB, *v. a.* चढणें *with* वर *of o.* वेंघणें *or* वेंगणें, वेंघूनचढणें, आरोहण *n.*-अधिरोहण *n.* करणें.

CLIMBER, *n.* v. V. चढणारा, वेंघणारा, आरोहण कर्त्ता.

An expert c.चढाईत,—*esp. on trees.*रुखाडी, रुखाड्या, रुख्या.

I. *climbing plant.* वेल *f.* लता *f.*

CLIMBING, *n.* v. V.—*act.* वेंघणें *n.* वेंघून चढणें *n.* &c.

CLIME. See CLIMATE.

To CLINCH, *v. a.* (the hand) *double in the fingers.* मूठ *f.* अवळणें-चेपणें-वळणें-बांधणें.

2 (a nail) वोळवणें, वाळणें, उमळणें, वळविणें.

To c. the nail for one's self. ओढून बळकट करणें.

3 v. To CLASP. मुठींत धरणें.

4 (an argument, &c.) बळकट-दृढ-सुदृढ-&c. करणें.

CLINCH, *n. pun.* श्लेष *m.*

To CLING, *v. n.*—as for protection. कासेस लागणें-कास *f.* धरणें *g. of o.* दुमाला *m.* धरणें-धरून असणें-&c. *g. of o.* पाठ *f.* घेणें, अवलंबणें, आश्रयणें, आश्रय *m.* धरणें *g. of o.* अवलंब *m.*-अवलंबन *n.*-आश्रयण *n.* करणें *g. of o.*

2 *hold fast upon.* कवळणें, कवटाळणें, झगटणें, बिलगणें.

3 *adhere to,* v. To STICK. चिकटणे, बिलगणें, लगटून-चिकटून असणें.

CLINIC, *n. bed ridden person.* खाटले वाईक.

CLINIC, CLINICAL, *a. pertaining &c. to a bed.* अंथरुणाचा, बिछान्याचा, अंथरुणाजवळचा.

To CLINK, *v. n. make a sharp sound.* छणछणणें *intens.* छणाणणें, खणखणणें *intens.* खणाणणें, खिणखिणणें, खणखण-खिणखिण-छणछण-छुमछुम-&c. *adv.* वाजणें.

CLINK, CLINKING, *n.*v.V. छणछणणें *n.* खणखणणें *n.* &c.—intens. छणछणाट *m.* खणखणाट *m.*

To CLIP, *v. a. cut with shears.* कातरणें, कापणें, छाटणें, भादरणें, निकृंतणें, कर्त्तन *n.*-निकृंतन *n.*-निकंदन *n.* करणें *g. of o.*

2 *curtail, cut short.* कमी-न्यून-लांडा-बुंठा-थोटा-अखूड-तोकडा -&c. करणें.

3 (allowances, expenses, &c.). कापणें, छाटणें.

4 (coin) किसून काढणें, खरवडून काढणें.

CLIPPER, *n.* CLIPPING, *p. a.* v. V. 1. कातरणारा, छाटणारा, &c.

I. एका प्रकारचें जलद चालणारें गलबत *n.*

CLIPPING, *n.* v. V. 1.—*act.* कातरणें *n.* छाटणें *n.* &c. छाटणी *f.* छाटछूट *f.* कर्त्तन *n.* निकृंतन *n.* निकंदन *n.*

Clippings. काटकसर *f.* काटकूट *f. m.* छाट *m.* छाटछूट *f. m.* छाटींव *n.* कातरा *m.*

3 कापणें *n.* छाटणें *n.* &c. [छाट *f. m.*

C. and cutting. काटाकाट *f.* काटाकाटी *f.* काटकसर *f.*छाटा-

CLIQUE, *n. circle of persons,* v. PARTY. जूट *m.*पक्षाचीं मनुष्यें *n.*

pl. चाकोलें *n.*

CLOAK. See CLOKE.

CLOCK, *n.* मोठें घड्याळ *n.*

What's o'clock ? किती वाजले ? दिवस किती आला?

CLOCK-MAKER, *n.* घड्याळची *or* जी *m.*

CLOCK-WORK, *n. machinery of a clock.* घड्याळांतले कीलकांटे *m. pl.* घड्याळांतलें काम *n.*

CLOD, *n.* ढेप *n.* ढेपूळ *or* ढेपळ *n.* ढेकळ *or* ढेकूळ *n.* डिफळ *n.* ढेपसा *m.* लोष्ठ *n.*

Implement for breaking clods. थापा *m.* डिफळा *m.*

Spade for turning up clods. खणपटें *n.*

To smooth or break the clods of a field. ढाळणें, ढाळणी *f.* करणें.

CLOD-HOPPER, *n.* v. COUNTRYMAN. शेतखण्या, नांगऱ्या, जोत्या.

CLOD-PATE, CLOD-POLL, *n. block-head,* v. FOOL. धोंडा *m.* टोणपा *m.* ठोंब्या *m.*

CLODDY, *a.* ढेपळांचा, लोष्ठमय, लोष्ठप्रचुर.

To CLOG, *v. a. encumber, embarrass, &c.* lit. fig. लोढणें *n.*-अडकण *n.*-खोडा *m.*-&c. बांधणें-घालणें-ठेवणें, अडखळवणें, अडकवणें, अडकवून-अडखळवून वेणें, अट *f.*-अड *f.*-&c. लावणें-घालणें -&c. बांधून घेणें, पाय *m. pl.* गुंतवणें, पायगुंता *m.* करणें *g. of o.* पायमोडा *m.*-पायमोडें *n.* घालणें.

CLOG, *n.*—for cattle, &c. लोढणें *or* लोंढणें *n.* लोडणा *m.* लोडणें *n.* खोडा *m.* पायखुंट *n.* पायखुंटी *f.* मानखुंट *n.* मानखोडा *m.* अडकण *n.* अडकवण *n.*

2—fig. *or* gener. लोढणें *or* लोंढणें *n.* गळ्यांत घोंगडें *n.* गळग्रह *m.* पायबंद *m* खोडा *m.* बिडी *f.* फास *m.* लकडा *m.* शकट *m.* जंजाळ *m.* हडदा *m. or* दें *n.* अडकण *n.* अडकवण *n.* सेंकटें *n.* सुदर्शन *n.* वेध *m.* अनुबंध *m.*

3 *wooden shoe.* खडव *f.* (*pl.* खडवा *or* खडावा) पादुका *f.*

Clogs, *clumsy shoes.* जासुदी जोडा *m.* कोल्हापुरी माप *n.*

CLOGGINESS, *n.* v. A. चिकटण *f.*

CLOGGY, *a.*—mud, &c. चिकचिकीत, चिडचिडीत.

CLOISTER, *n.* मठ *m.*

To CLOISTER, *v. a.* मठांत ठेवणें-कोंडणें.

CLOKE, *n.* घोंगडी *f.* घोंगडें *n.* पासोडी *f.* लेप *mn.* कफणी *f.* ओढणी *f.*

Cloth thrown over the head and body as a c. बुंथ *f.* बुंधी *f.* बोंध *f.* बोंथी *f.* बोंथारा *m.* बोंथारी *f.* *v.* घे, मार—To be muffled or covered with it. बोंथारणें.

Hooded c. (against rain, &c.). खोळ *f.* टापशी *f.* टापर *or* टाफर *f.* खोंडा*m.* घोंगता *m.* बुचडी *f.* टोपी *f.* घुगी *or* घोगी *f.* घुंगट *m.* घुंगूट *n.*

Hooded c. (for children). कुंची *f.* खोळ *f.* घोंगता *m.*

2 fig. *mask, blind, veil.* पडदा *m.* आडपडदा *m.* व्याज *n.*

To CLOKE, *v. a. conceal,* v. To HIDE. झांकणें, लपवणें, चोरणें, दावणें, पांघरूण*n.* घालणें.

To CLOSE, *v. a. lay together or to,* v.To SHUT. लावणें, झांकणें, ढांपणें, मिटणें, चिपणें (as डोळेचिपणें, नाकचिपणें, तोंडचिपणें,&c.).

2 *conclude, shut up,* v. To END. बंद करणें, संपविणें, समाप्त करणें, गुंडाळणें, अटोपता घेणें, अटोपणें, उपसंहार*m.* करणें *g.of o.*

3 *unite, make whole,* v. To JOIN. जोडणें, मिळवणें, मिळवून घेणें, मिटणें.

4 (a quarrel, &c.) v. To SETTLE. मिटणें, तोडणें, मोडणें, फैसल *f.* फैसला*m.* करणें *g.of o.*

To CLOSE, *v. n. fall together or to,* v. To SHUT. लागणें, झांकणें, ढांपणें, मिटणें,—esp. of flowers. पाकुळणें, मिटणें, (and, at decline of day) मावळणें, संकोच*m.* होणें *g.of s.* [णें.

2 *conclude,* v. To END.संपणें, बंद होणें, अटपणें—the day बुडणें.

3 *coalesce, unite, come to.* मिळणें, मिटणें, मिळूनजाणें.

4 *grow compact and firm.* घटणें, दाटणें, जमणें.

5—with; See To AGREE. 6—in wrestling. भिडणें, लगटणें.

CLOSE, *n. conclusion, cessation,* v. END. अंत*m.* समाप्ति *f.* असेरी *f.* अवसान *n.* [*f.* वाडगें *n.*

2 *enclosed piece of meadow, field, &c.*v. ENCLOSURE—वाडी

CLOSE, *a. shut fast, fallen to.* घट्ट-गच्च बसलेला-लागलेला-मिटलेला-&c. *or* लावलेला-बांधलेला-&c. [सांद्र.

2 *dense, solid,* v. COMPACT. घट *or* घट्ट, घटमूट, घन *or* घण,

3 *compressed, condensed.* घन *or* घण, दाट, घणदाट, सघन, संकुल, अनंतर.

4 *contiguous,* v. NEAR. जवळचा, समीप, निकटवर्ती. [तर.

5 *of close texture.* सणसर, सणसणीत, घण, घनवट, सांद्र, अनं-

6 *reserved, incommunicatite.* आंतल्या गांठीचा, मनाचाखोल, खोलमनाचा, खोल, संकोची, लिकीर, मखुस.

7 *hot and calm, sultry.* उबाळ्याचा, उकाड्याचा, उबाऱ्याचा, गदमदण्याचा, उबट.

To be c. उबावणें, उबणें, उकडणें, उबटणें, खतखतणें, डगडगणें, (All *impersonal*).

To feel it to be c. उबगणें, डगडगणें.

8 *without ventilation.* उबट, उबटलेला, कोंड माऱ्याचा, कोंड मारलेला, उबावलेला.

C. and hot place. उबवलें *n.*

9 *private, concealed,* v. HID. गुप्त, झांकलेला, दाबलेला.

10 *penurious,* v. MISERLY. चिकण, चिकट, चिंबट, बद्धमुष्टि.

11 *strictly adhering to the original.* थेटमुळासारखा, मूलानुसारी, मूल प्रतिम, यथामूल, यथाप्रत, हुबहूचा.

12 (of translation, &c.). मूलशब्दानुसारी, मूलपदानुसारी, मूलार्थानुसारी, मूलार्थमात्रग्राही.

13 (friendship, acquaintance, &c.) *intimate.* सलमीचा, घसणीचा, अंतर्यामी.

CLOSE, *adv.* See CLOSELY.

CLOSE-COMPACTED, CLOSE SET, *a.* v. COMPACT. दृढसंधि.

CLOSE-FISTED, CLOSE-HANDED, *a.* v. MISERLY. दृढमुष्टि, बद्धमुष्टि, चिकण, चिकट, चिकू, चिंबट.

CLOSE-TEXTURED, *a.* घनवट, सणसर, सणसणीत.

CLOSELY, *adv. compressedly, crowdedly.* गच्च, खच्च, गडगच्च, दाट, लगत, दाटणीवाटणीनें, दाटीवाटीनें.

2 *tightly.* अडच, अटस, गच्च, दाट.

3 *immediately after.* पाठोपाठ, मागोमाग, लागोपाठ.

4 v. ATTENTIVELY. एकचित्तानें, मनलावून, लक्ष्यदेऊन.

CLOSENESS, *n.* v. A. 2. घट्टाई *f.* घटपणा *m.* घनता *f.* दार्ढ्य *n.* द्रढिमा *m.*

3 दाटी *f.* घणदाटपणा *m.* घनत्व *n.*

4 जवळपणा *m.* जवळीक *f.* समीपता *f.*

5 घनवटपणा *m.* सणसणीतपणा *m.* सांद्रता *f.*

6 खोलपणा *m.* मनाचा खोलपणा *m.* संकोच *m.* मखसपणा *m.*

7 उबारा *m.* उधाण *n.* उबाळा *m.* उकाडा *m.* धमका *m.*

8 उबटपणा *m.* कोंडमारलेलेपणा *m.* &c. कोंडलेली हवा *f.*

10 चिकटेपणा *m.* किरटेपणा *m.* बारीकदृष्टि *f.* बारीकनजर *f.*

CLOSET, *n.* एकांताची खोली *f.* खलबतखाना *m.* एकांतस्थल *n.*

To be closeted. *to have private consultation.* खलबत *n.* करणें. [ठेवण्याचा.

CLOSING, *a. final,* v. LAST. समाप्तीचा, असेरीचा, अटोपण्याचा,

CLOT, *n. concretion.* गुठळी *or* गुठोळी *or* गोठुळी *f.* डल्ला *m.* डिखळ *or* डिखूळ *n. dim.* डिखळी *f.*

2 v. CLOD. गोळा *m.* ढेप *n.* ढेकळ *n.*

3 *clotted mass.* लाखोटा *m.*

To CLOT, *v. n. form into clots, concrete.* गोठणें, बोळणें, लगटणें, सांखळणें, सांखणें, जमणें, अटणें.

Clotted and matted hair. जटा *pop.* जट *f.*

CLOTH, *n.* कापड *n.* वस्त्र *n.* चिरगूट *n.* चीर *n.* चैल *n.* अंशुक *n.* वासन *n.* वसन *n.* वास *n.m.* पट *m.* Some kinds of *Cloth* are अनरस, अलिता, किंतान, खंडकी *or* खणकी, खादी, खारवा, खारांऊ *or* व, खुतणी *or* नी *or* कुतनी, खेंडा, खेंस, गंगाजमनी, गजनी, गर्भसुतीकापड, गुजरी, गेटम, घनवेल, चकला, चंद्रकळा, जामदानी, जोट *or* ठ, झोन्या, दोरवा, नाव, परकाळा *or* ळें, मशरू, मादरपाट, रांबेरी, शालू, सुजनी, सुताडा, सुसी, हमरू.

A c. with figures painted on it. चित्रपट *m.*

C. worn threadbare. माशांचें जाळें *n.* चाळण *f.*

Coarse and stout c. धोंगडा *m.* धोबला *m.*

End of a c. पदर *m.* पल्लव *m.* अंचल *m.*

Piece of c. फडका *m.* फडकें *n.*

Rising of c. (through washing). फुलणें *n.*

Roll of c. (as for a wick). काकडा *m.*

Shred or slip of c. धांत *or* धांद *f.* धांतळी *f.* धांदोटी *f.*

Threads (unwoven) at the end of c. दशा *f. pl.* अंचळ्या *f. pl.*

Upper or outer fold of a c. वरघडी *f.* दर्शनीपदर *m.*

Web or whole piece of c. ताका *or* तागा *m.* थान *n.*

A wet c. ओलें *n.* ओलेटें *or* तें *n.*

To overlay with c. कापडणें.

CLOTH-DEALER, CLOTH-MERCHANT, *n.* कापडकरी, कापडविक्या, बजाज, चाटी *or* टया.

Itinerant c. मरेकरी.

To CLOTHE, *v. a.* वस्त्र *n.* नेसवणें, पांघरविणें, पांघरूण *n.* घालणें, वस्त्रवेष्टित-वस्त्राछादित-&c. करणें.

To feed and c. अन्नवस्त्र *n.* देणें-पुरवणें. [विणें.

To c. (thoughts) with words. शब्दरूपानें व्यक्तकरणें-दर्शविणें.

CLOTHED, *p.* v. V. वस्त्रनेसलेला-नेसवलेला, सचैल, वासित, वस्त्रधारित, धारितवस्त्र, वस्त्रवेष्टित, अंबर (in comp. as नीलांबर, पीतांबर, व्याघ्रचर्मांबर, गजचर्मांबर, दिगंबर).

I. fig. *invested.* युक्त, संपन्न, विशिष्ट.

CLOTHES, CLOTHING, *n. apparel, raiment, dress, &c.* पांघरूण *n. or* पांघरुणें *n. pl.* वस्त्र *n. or* वस्त्रें *n. pl.* अंबर *n.* वसन *n.* वासन *n.* परिधान *n.* देहावरण *n.* परिधेय *n.*—compreh. *or* gener. चिरगूटपांघरूण *n.* वस्त्रप्रावरण *n.* कपडालत्ता *m.* The ordinary articles of *Clothing* are—of males अंगरखा, धोतर, आडधोतर, पंचा, आडपंचा, पंचेजोडी, कांचचा, लुंगी, बंडी, दुपट्टा, निमा, अलखालक;—and of females चोळी, काचोळी, कंचुकी, लुगडें, तपशिला. And the names of some of the parts of them are कच्छ, कास, कासोटा, काष्टा, ओंचा, खोंचा, काच्या, कडोसरी, कणवट, कुणगा, पंखा.

Article of c. for daily wear. धडवत *or* धडोत *n.* धडोनीचीवस्तू *or* वस्त *f.*

C. for daily wear, working c. धडवती *or* धडोती *f.* धडवतें *n. pl.*

C. to cast loosely around. पांघरूण*n.* प्रावरण*n.*

C. for the loins or waist. नेसण*n.* नेसणें*n.*

C. and ornaments presented to visitors,&c.पेहरावणी*f.*

C.-line. *line for wet c.* ओलाणी *f.* ओळण *f.*

Coarse c. (or *a* coarse garment). धोंगडा*m.* धबला*m.*

Fine c. *splendid apparel.* पोशाक *or* ख*m.* पोशाखी वस्त्रें*n. pl.* प्रतिष्ठावस्त्र*n.* महावस्त्र*n.* [वणी*f.*

Presenting c. and ornaments to visitors, &c. पेहरा-

Wet article of c. ओलें*n.* ओलेटें *or* तें—that has it on. ओलेटा *or* ओलेता.

With one's c. on. सचैल *or* सचेल.

To change one's c. वस्त्रांतर होणें *g. of s.*

To hang out c. to dry. वस्त्रांचा ताणा लावणें.

To punch and thump c. (in washing). चुचकणें,पोंचारणें.

To put on c. वस्त्रपरिधान*n.* करणें.

To strike (clothes in washing them) against a stone or board सोबकणें.

To tear one's c. off his back. फेरधोंगडें*n.* करणें *g. of o.*

CLOTHIER, *n,* कापडकरी.

CLOTTED, *a.*—the hair. जटेचा, जटबळलेला.

CLOTTEDNESS, *n.* v. A. चिकटी *f.*

CLOTPOLL, *n.* v. FOOL. टोणपा*m.* ठोंब्या*m.*

CLOTTY, *a.* गुठळयांचा, गोठलेला.

CLOUD, *n.* ढक *or* ढग *m.n. intens.* ढकार *or* ढगार *n. or* ढगारा*m. or* ढगाड *n.* मेघ*m.* अभ्र*n.* घन*m.*नभ*n.*पयोधर*m.*मेहुडा*m.*मलश्री*f.*

The clouds,—collect. The cloudy sphere. घनचक्र*n.* मेघमंडल*n.* घनमंडल*n.* मेघमाला *f.*

Canopy of clouds. अभ्रपटल *pop.* अभ्रपडल*n.* मेघमंडप*m.* मांड्व*m.* मेघपटल*n.*

Dense array or mass of clouds. घनघटा *f.* मेघघटा *f.* घटा *f.* जौळ *or* जवळ*n.* घनचय*m.*

Empty c. बांझेंढक *n.*

Gathering of clouds. घोंगाड *n.* घनजाल*n.* मेघजाल*n.* अभ्रजाल*n.* घनचय*m.*

Light, fleecy clouds. कसर *f.* सार *f.* खर *f.*

Reddish streak of c.—as indicative of rain. कोंचडें*n.*

Threatening or lowering of the clouds. मेघडंबर *or* मेघाडंबर*n.*

The clouds have gathered, are lowering, &c. मेघांनीं छत्र धरलें, मेघांनीं *or* पावसानें झांपड घातली-ओंधघातली-अंधारी घातली-मांड घातला, अभाळ*n. or* पाऊस*m.* डवरला, पाऊस भरून आला, पाऊस मांडतो.

To be covered with clouds. डवरणें *or* डोरणें.

To be clear of clouds—the sky. निखरणें.

To gather thickly—clouds. घोंगाडणें.

2 (of dust) धुरला—ळा *m.*

3 (of smoke) धुराचा लोट *m.*

To be under a cloud (of trouble, affliction &c.) अ-

भाळn. येणें *with* वर *of s.*

To CLOUD, *v. a. cover with clouds.* अभाळn.-&c. आणणें, मेघाच्छादित-मेघाछन्न-&c. करणें.

2 *make sullen and gloomy.* दुर्मुखवणें, काळोखीf.-दौर्मुख्यn. आणणें, काळा करणें.

CLOUD-CAPT, CLOUD-TOPT, *a.* मेघाच्छादित, मेघावृत.

CLOUD-COMPELLING, *a.* मेघावह.

CLOUD-COVERED, CLOUD-SPREAD, *a.* v. CLOUDY. मेघाकीर्ण.

CLOUDINESS, *n.* v. A. अभाळn. *v.* ये, आभn. अभ्रn. *v.* ये, धोंगाटn. *v.* घाल, ओंध *f.* अंधारी *f.* जबळ *or* जौळn. मळभn. जलदजालn. मेघतिमिर *n.*

CLOUD-KISSING, *a.* मेघचुंबित, गगनचुंबित.

CLOUDLESS, *a.* निवळ, निरभ्र, निर्मल, मेघरहित-शून्य-&c.

CLOUDLESSNESS, *n.* v. A. निरभ्रn. निरभ्रता *f.* अभ्राभावm. मेघराहित्यn.

CLOUDY, *a.* अभाळ आलेला, डबरलेला, मेघाकीर्ण, मेघव्याप्त, मेघाच्छादित, घनाभ्र, मेघभरित, मेघबहुल, ढगाळ.

To become c. ढगm.-&c. येणें, ढगाळणें.

CLOUT, *n. mean cloth.* फडकाm. फडकेंn. चिरगूटn. पोतेरेंn. चिथडाm. चिथडी *f.* पुसणेंn. सुडकाm. सुडकें *n.* [कुली *f.*

2 *garment,*—in contempt. सुडकाm. सुडकेंn. बोळा *m.* चिंध-

3 See PATCH. 4 See BLOW.

To CLOUT, *v. a.* See To PATCH. 2 See To BEAT.

CLOVE, *n.* —the plant or flower. लवंग *f.* देवकुसुम *n.*

Oil of c. लवंगेल *n.*

2 (of garlic, ginger, turmeric, &c.). कांडी *f.* कुडें *n.* पाकळी *f.* बी *f.* बोय *f.*

CLOVEN, *p.* v. V. फोडलेला, &c. फोडींव.

CLOVEN-FOOTED, *a.* द्विशफ.

CLOVER, *n.* गवताची एक जात आहे.

To live in c. चंगळींत असणें, चंगळ *f.*-चेहळ *f.*-बहार *f.*-&c. चालणें *g. of o.*

CLOWN, *n. rustic, peasant,* v. COUNTRYMAN. शेतखव्या, शेतकाव्या, नांगरहाक्या, खेडेगांवचामाणूस, रानमाणूस, रान्या, रानकरी.

Clowns and boors,—compreh. आडाणी कबाडी *m. pl.*

2 *zany, &c.* v. BUFFOON. भांड *m.* हुंडीबाग *m.* मस्कऱ्या *m.*

CLOWNISH, *a.* v. RUSTIC & COUNTRYMAN. गंवार, गांवढळ, खेडवाळ, खेडुळा, खेडाळू, खेडवळ, खेडे गांवचा, कुणबाऊ, आडगळचा, आडमुठ्या, रानट, जंगलट, बणजारदांड, अरबटदांड, अरबट.

CLOWNISHNESS, *n.* v. A. गंवारपण *n.* गांवढळपण *n.* राणटपण *n.* &c. गंवारी *f.* गंवारकी *f.* गांवढळकी *f.*

To CLOY, *v. a. satiate, sate, glut.* बिटवणें, वीट *m.*-ओकारी *f.* आणणें, अतितृप्ति *f.* करणें, ओयेईतों खाऊं घालणें-वाढणें, मिठी *f.* बसविणें, पुरेपुरेसें करणें, नकोनकोसें करणें.

CLOYED, *p.* v. V. मिठी बसलेला.

To be c. तोंडाला मिठी *f.* बसणें, खातांखातां तोंड *n.* फिरणें *g. of s.* खातां खातां घसरा *m.* धरणें, पुरेपुरेसें होणें.

CLOYING, *p. a.* v. V. मिठी बसवणारा, मिठीबसवायाचा *or* बसायाचा, शीघ्रतर्पक.

CLUB, *n.* v. CUDGEL. सोंटा *or* सोटा *m.* सोटगें *n.* सोडगा *m.* गदा *f.*

2 *knot, gang,* v. BAND. चाकोळें *or* चाखोळें *n.* अखाडा *m.* गट्ट *m.* गट्टा *m.* गट्टी *f.* जुट *m. f.* जुग *n.*

To CLUB, *v. n. contribute together.* वर्गणी *f.*- पट्टी *f.* करणें.

2 *join together to one end.* मिळणें, जुटणें, जुडणें, मथणें, मिळून-जुटून-जुडून-&c. काम *n.* करणें.

To CLUB, *v. a. unite for a common end.* मिळवणें.

2 वर्गणी *f.*- पट्टी *f.* करणें.

CLUB-FOOT, *n.* खुरंट पाय *or* खुरटापाय *m.*

CLUB-FOOTED, *a.* खुरंट पायाचा, खुरट्या पायाचा.

CLUB-LAW, *n.* बळी तो कान पिळी अशी अवस्था *f.* सोटे शाई *f.*

To CLUCK, *v. n.*—a hen. खुटखुटणें, खुटखुट *f.* करणें.

CLUE. See CLEW. [ठिकी *f.*

CLUMP, *n.* (of wood) v. BLOCK. करडा *or* करांडा *m.* ठोकळाm.

2 *plump, cluster, tuft.* झुंड *f.* गुच्छ *m.* बेट *n.* स्तबक *m.*

CLUMSILY, *adv.* v. A. 1. अडाणीपणानें, आडमुठेपणानें, अनाडीपणानें, अडाण्या सारखा, अडाण्या परी, अकुशलतेनें.

2 बेडौलानें, बेढब.

CLUMSINESS, *n.* v. A. 1. अडाणीपण *n.*-पणा *m.* अनाडीपण *n.*-पणा *m.* अकौशल्य *n.* अपटुता *f.*

2 धोबडपणा *m.* ओबडधोबडपणा *m.* ढोबळेपणा *m.* बोजडपणा *m.* &c. बेडौली *f.* ढबळशाई *f.*

CLUMSY, *a.*—of persons, v. AWKWARD. आडमुठ्या, अडाणी, अनाडी, नाकसबी, अकुशल, अपटु.

2—of things. धोबड *or* ओबडधोबड *or* आबडधोबड, बेडौल, बेडौली, बेढब, ढोबळ *or* ळा, रटाला, रटेल, धोंगड, नाकसबाचा, नाकसब्याचा, गेरबेताचा, भसाडा, भोंपळसुती, ऐवट, बोजड, ढवळ, ढबळशाई.

CLUSTER, *n. bunch.* घड *m.* घूड *m.* गुच्छ *m.* घोस *m.* झुमका *m.* झुबका *m.* पुंजका *m.* स्तबक *m.*

2 (of persons) v. GROUP. गट्टा *m.* थवा *m.* पुट्टा *m.*

3 (of bees, &c.) पुंजका *m.* चुबका *m.*

To CLUSTER, *v. n.*—*blossoms, fruits, &c.* झोंबणें, घोसानें लागणें, घडानें लागणें, घोस *m.*- &c. येणें-लागणें.

2 *produce fruit in clusters.* घडारणें, घड *m.*-घडांचे घड *m. pl.*-घोस *m.* येणें *in. con.*

3 *collect into a close body*—people. गट्टा *m.*-थवा *m.*-पुट्टा-*m.* जमणें *g. of s.*

To CLUTCH, *v. a. gripe, grasp,* v. To SEIZE. मुठींत-हातांत-पंजांत-&c. धरणें, धरणें, झोंबणें, मटकावणें, मट्टा *m.* मारणें *with* वर *of o.* [बांधणें.

2 (the hand or fingers) *clinch.* मूठ *f.* अवळणें-चेपणें-बळणें-

CLUTCH, CLUTCHING, *n.* v. V.—*act.* मुठींत धरणेंn. धरणेंn.&c.

I. clutches; *talons, hands, power.* डाबm. आबडाबm. घावडाबm. आवांकाm. चपेटf.

In the c. of. ताबडीस, तावडींत, आवाडाबांत, पंजांत, कबजांत.

Out of the c. of. ताबडींतून.

To be caught in the c. of. सांपडणें *or* सांपटणें, गावणें, तावडीस-कबजांत-पंजांत-दाढेंत सांपडणें, शेंडी *f.* सांपडणें *or* गुंतणें (कोण्हा एकाचे हातीं), खेमेंबेंगेस येणें, संपुष्टांत येणें, हकाटकांत येणें, चपेटेखालीं येणें- पडणें.

CLUTTER. See CLATTER.

CLYSTER, *n.* पिचकारी *f. v.* मार, बस्तिm. *f.*

Oily or unctuous c. अन्वासन बस्ति.

Ununctuous c. निरूहण बस्ति.

CLYSTER-BAG *or* BLADDER, CLYSTER-PIPE, *n.* पिचकारी *f.* बस्तिm. *f.* बस्तियंत्रn. *f.* बस्तिनलिका *f.* बस्तीचीनळी *f.*

COACH, *n.* v. CARRIAGE. गाडी *f.* रथ *m.*

COACH-BOX, *n.* गाडीहाकणाऱ्याची बसायाची जागा *f.*

COACH-MAKER, *n.* गाडी करणारा, रथकार.

COACH-MAN, *n.* गाडीवान *m.* सारथी *m.*

COACH-MANSHIP, *n.* अश्वसारथ्य *n.* अश्वनियंतृत्व *n.*

COACTION, COACTIVE. See COMPULSION, COMPULSORY.

COADJUTANT, *a.* v. HELPING. सहकारी.

COADJUTOR, *n. assistant.* सहकारी, संभूयकारी.

To COAGULATE, *v.a.* विरजणें, जमविणें, गोठविणें, घट्ट करणें. [*n.* Vessel for coagulating (milk, &c.). विरजणी *f.* विरजणें.

To COAGULATE, *v. n.* जमणें, विरजणें, गोठणें, दाटणें, सांसणें, सांखळणें, सांखळा *m.* धरणें, घट्ट होणें.

COAGULATION, *n.* v. V. N.—*act.* विरजणें *n.* जमणें *n.* &c.—*state.* जमलेलेपणा *m.* विरजलेपणा *m.* &c. सांखळा *m.* घनीभाव *m.*

COAL, *n.* दगडी कोळसा *m.* खाणींतला कोळसा *m.* विलायती कोळसा *m.*

Live c. निखारा *m.* इंगळ *or* इंगळा *m.* अंगार *m.*

Mass of hot and glowing coals. झगरें *n.* आहार *m.* रसाण *n.*

To call over the coals. फुपाट्यावरून ओढणें, फुपाट्यांत घालणें, धसावरून ओढणें, उलटी सुलटी हजामत *f.* करणें, भाजणें, धसरा *m.* देणें.

To carry coals to Newcastle. समुद्रांत पाणी *n.* आणून सोडणें, तृप्तास भोजन *n.* घालणें.

COAL-BLACK, *a.* v. BLACK काळाकूट, काळाढुस्स.

COAL-MINE, COAL-PIT, *n.* कोळशांची खाण *f.*

To COALESCE, *v. n.* v. TO JOIN, TO COMBINE. मिळणें, जमणें, जुडणें, गोत *n.* मिळणें, मेथकूट *n.* मिळणें-जमणें *g. of s.* एकाराथावर बसणें-असणें, एकगोत *n.*-एक सूत *n.*-एकतंत्र *n.*-&c. होणें *g. of s.*

COALESCENCE, COALITION, *n.*v.V.—*act.* मिळणें *n.* जमणें *n.* &c. —*state.* समागम *m.* संसृष्टि *f.* संयोग *m.*

Coalition of letters. संधि *m.*

I. *confederacy.* See COMBINATION.

COAPTATION, *n. adaptation, &c.* तानमान *n.* तालामाला *m.* जम *m.* जुगल *f.* समन्वय *m.* सभव *m.* लाग *m.*

COARSE, *a.*—of cloth, paper, &c. जाडसुती, मोटसुती, जाड, जाडा, जाडगा, धनकट *or* गट, दणगट, धसकट, धसाडा, घन *pop.* घण, घण घाव, भरभरीत, भरड, भसाडा, खसखसीत, ठोसर, धोंगड, धांगड, घस्मर, दडस, दडदडीत.—indef. *or* carelessly. जाडा धोंगडा, मोटाधोटा *or* धाटामोटा *or* मोटाधाटा, जाडाभरडा.

2—of things, gener. *rude, rough,* v. CLUMSY. धोबड, ढोबळ *or* ळा, रटाला, रटेल, भोंपळसुती.

3 *not delicate, fine, &c. gross.* मोटा, मोटाधोटा, भोंपळसुती, भसाडा, रटाला, रटेल, स्थूल.

4—as a workman, v. ROUGH, AWKWARD. झोडकामी *or* म्या, दगडघाशा, भसाडा, घसक्या, घसट्या.

5—as a work done, v. ROUGH. भसाडा, भरड, भोंपळसुती, भसाळ, रांठ, वेठीचा, धांगड धिंगड, धोंगड.

6 as the hair; *dry, stiff, &c.* करडा, भरभरीत, रांठ *or* रंठ.

7 *unpolished, inelegant, low, &c.* v. RUDE. असभ्य, अशिष्ट, रानट, रानवट, जंगलट, गंवार, अशिक्षित, गैरसाळ, गैरशिस्त, अचकट विचकट.

8—of diet, &c. अरबट, अरबट चरबट, ताककण्याचा.

C. fare, v. FARE. कुभोजन *n.* कदन्न *n.*

COARSELY, *adv.* v. A. 1.—*not finely, &c.* जाड, भरड, मोटा *a. decl.* जाडा *a. decl.* &c.

COARSENESS, *n.* v. A. 1. जाडपणा *m.* जाडेपणा *m.* मोटेपणा *m.* धोंगडपणा *m.* भरडपणा *m.* &c. जाडी *f.*

2 धोबडपणा *m.* ढोबळेपणा *m.* रटेलपणा *m.* &c.

3 रटेलपणा *m.* मोठेपणा *m.*

4 स्थूलता *f.* स्थूलत्व *n.* स्थौल्य *n.*

5 भसाडेपणा *m.* &c.

COAST, *n. shore.* कांठ *m.* कांठा *m.* तीर *n.* समुद्रकांठ *or* कांठा *m.* समुद्रकिनारा *m.* बंदरकांठ *or* कांठा *m.* बंदरकिनारा *m.*

Down the c. हेट.

The coast is clear. भयनाहींसें झालें, रस्तामोकळाआहे.

To COAST, *v. n.* कांठ *m.*-किनारा *m.*-&c. धरून जाणें, कांठानें-किनाऱ्यानें-तडीनें-&c. जाणें.

COAT, *n.* डगलें *n.* डगला *m.* कुडती *f.* कुडतें *n.* कंचुक *m.*

C. of mail, v. ARMOUR. बक्तर *n.* चिलखत *n.*

Great c. or cloak. झबा *or* झुबा *m.* [पाय पसरावे.

Cut your c. according to your cloth. आंथरूण पाहून

2 *or* coating; *tegument or covering,* gener. कवच *n.* आवरण *n.* आच्छादन *n.* कंचुक *m.*

3 (of the eye). पडदा *m.* पटल *n.* [पुदरा *m.*

4 *layer, fold, crust.* थर *m.* पदर *m.* पडदा *m.* पापदरा *or* पा-

5 (of paint, mud, cowdung-wash, &c.). लेप *m.* लेवा *m.* लिंपण *n.* लपेटा *m.* हात *m.*

6 c. of arms. See ARMS.

To COAX, *v. a. persuade by soothing &c. words.* आळवणें, मठारणें, थापटणें *or* थोपटणें, फुसलावणें, आर्जवणें, बरधावणें, घुलावणें *or* घोलावणें, गोंजारणें, उरींपोटीं धरणें, आर्जव *n.*-लाडीगोडी *f.*-लुलुपुतू *n.*-&c. करणें *g. of o.*

To c. a female. आई बाई करणें.

To c. a male. दादा बाबा करणें, बाबा पुता करणें.

COAXED, *p.* v. V. आळवलेला, &c. लालित.

COAXER, *n.* COAXING, *p. a.* v. V. आळवणारा, &c. लडिवाळ, लाडिका, आर्जवी, आर्जवू.

COAXING, *n.* v. V.—*act.* आळवणें *n.* &c. लाडीगोडी *f.* लाडूकपणा *m.* रळी *f.* लुलुपुतू *n.* आर्जव *n.* गुळगुळथापडी *f.* लालन *n.*

COAXINGLY, *adv.* लाडीगोडीनें, लाडुकपणानें, लाडेंकोडें, दादाबाबाआईबाई-&c. करून.

COB, *n.* v. PONY. तट्टू *m.*

2 cob-wall. कूड *m.*

To COBBLE, *v. a. mend* (*shoes*). (जोडा *m.* &c.) तांगडणें-जसातसा सांधणें.

2 *make or do clumsily, bungle.* ओबड धोबड करणें, अनाडीपणानें-&c. करणें, झोडणें.

COBBLER, *n.* v.V. 1. जोडे तांगडणारा-सांधणारा, चांभार *or* चाह्मार, कटई, पारादोज.

2 झोडणारा, अनाडीपणानें करणारा, दगडघाशा, नाकसबी.

COBBLERY, *n.* पारादोजी *f.* चांभारकी *f.* चांभारकाम *n.*

COBRA DE CAPELLO, *n.* नाग *m.* भुजंग *m.*—in covert, &c. phraseol. मोठाब्बा *m.* नागोबा *m.* [फण *m. n.*

Expanded hood of c. फडा *m. dim.* फडी *f.* फणी *f.* फणा. *f.*

Figure of ten fancied in the form of the hood of a c. दशांकचिन्ह पद्म *n.*

Gem found in head of a c. मोहरा *m.*

To expand its hood—the c. फडी *f.* फिंदारणें.

Cobweb, *n.* जाळें *n.* कोरडक *n.* कोळिष्क *n.*

Cobwebs and pendulous filaments,—gener. घेरोसा *or* घरोसा *m.* जळमटें *n. pl.* घरू *or* घरंब *m.*

Filament of a c. सुतेरा *m.* शिळमिळया *f. pl.*

Stretched line of a c. तणावा *m.*

Coccyx, *n.* माकडहाड *n.*

Cochin leg, *n.* हत्तीरोग *m.* पादवल्मीक *n.*

Cochineal, *n.* किरमीज *n.* कृमि *m.*

Ball or lump of c. किरमिजीदाणा *m.*

Cochineal, *a.* किरमिजी.

Cochleary, Cochleate, *a.* शंखाकार, मळसूत्राकार.

Cock, *n.* कोंबडा *m.* कुक्कुट *m.* चरणायुध *m.*

C. of the walk. धारराव *m.* बुटटनाईक *m.* महंत *m.* बडेम्या *m.* टिकोजी *m.* टिकोबा *m.*

C. of one's own walk. आपल्या घरचा थोर, आपल्या घरचा राजा.

Wild c. रानकोंबडा *m.* वनकुक्कुट *m.*

2 *male of birds.* नर *m.* पुरुष *m.*

3 (of a gun). घोडा *m.*

4 (of hay, &c.). गंज *m.* ढिगार *m.*

5 (of a balance) *needle.* कांटा *m.*

6 (as of a hat, turban, &c.). झोक *m.*

To put on with a c. लटकाविणें.

Having a c. *cocked.* झोकदार.

7 *spout.* कुलपी तोट्री *f.* मळसूत्री तोटी *f.*

To be cock-a hoop. कासा *f. pl.* वाजविणें.

Cock and bull story. कुत्र्यामांजराची गोष्ट *f.* एरंडाचें गुऱ्हाळ *n.*

To **Cock**, *v. a.* (the ears). कान *m. pl.* टवकारणें (*or* टवकारून पाहणें)-उभारणें-उभेकरणें *or* तरतरीत *adv.* उभेकरणें.

2 (the nose). नाक *n.* वर करणें-मुरडणें.

3 (a gun). घोडा *m.* चढवणें.

Cockatoo, *n.* काकातू *m.* काकाकव्वा *m.*

Cock-boat, *n.* लहान नाव *f.*

Cock-chafer, *n.* एक सपक्ष किडा आहे.

Cock-crow, Cock-crowing, *n.—act.* आरवणी *or* ओरवणी *f.* कोंबडे आरवणी *f.* ओरडणें *n.* कोंबड्याची बांग *or* क *f.* कोंबडसाद *f.*

2 *early morn,* v. **Dawn.** कोंबडेपहाट *f.* कोंबडेकुई *f.* कोंबडेरात *or* रात्र *f.* कोल्हेभूंक *f.* कोल्हेहूक *f.*

At c. कोंबडे आरणें, कोंबडसादीं.

Cock-fight, *n.* कोंबड्यांचें झुंज *n.* कौलीन *n.*

Cock-pit, *n.* कोंबड्यांचें झुंज करण्याचा अखाडा *m.*

To **Cocker.** See To **Indulge.**

Cock-horse, *a.* घोड्यावर बसलेला.

2 *exultant, triumphant.* कासावाजविणारा, टिरीपिटणारा.

Cockle, *n. testaceous shell.* शिंप *f.* शिंपी *f.* दीर्घकोषी *or* दीर्घकोशी *f.* पंकशुक्ति *f.* जलशुक्ति *f.*

Cockroach, *n.* झुरळ *n.* झुरळें *n.* बागुरडा *m.*

Cock's comb, *n. comb of a cock.* कोंबड्याची शेंडी *f.* कुक्कुटचूडा *f.*

2—the flower. गुलकेश *m.* मोराची शेंडी *f.* मयूरशिखा *f.* कलगी *f.* मयूर *m.*

3 *fop,* v. **Buck.** अक्कडबाज, कुर्रेदार, नटबाज.

Cock sure, To be c. पण भोगणें, मनांत स्थापून असणें, मनांत ठसून असणें.

Cock swain, *n.* गलबतावर एक खालचा अधिकारी आहे.

Cocoa, *n.—the tree.* माड *m.* नारळ *f.* नारळी *f.* नारिकेल *m.*

Branch or frond of a c. nut-tree. झांप *m.* झावळी *f.*—a half of it कडण *n.*

C. nut-tree kept for fruit. नारळमाड, (*as opp. to* मंडार माड *one kept for toddy*). [स *n.*

Fruit stalk of the c. nut tree. शिंपा *m.* शिंपटी *f.* कणी-

Matted branch of c. nuttree for roofing. झांप *m.* झावळी *f.*

Spathe of c. nut tree. *f.* पोगी *f.* पोई *f.*

Young c. nut tree, *plantlet.* कोंभा *m.* पात *f.*

2—*the nut.* नारळ *m.* नारिकेल *n.* श्रीफल *n.* महाफल *n.*—contemptuously बोंडफळ *n.* बेलटें *n.*

A couple of c. nuts. जोडें *n.*

C. nut of which the kernel is thin and scanty. खापऱ्या नारळ.

Cluster or bunch of young c. nuts. पेंड *f.* [डें *n.*

Dry and rattling c. nut. गोटा *m.* गुडगुडा नारळ *m.* गुडगु-

Empty c. nut. वाहील *or* वाहेल *n.*

End piece of a c. nut. टेंची *f.*

Fibrous integuments of the shell of a c. nut. काथा *m.* चोड *n.* चवड *n.* सोडण *n.*—a single fibre of them. काथकडी *f.* खरडी *f.* [मरांदा *m.*

Fungous mass in the middle of the c. nut. मारंदा *m.*

Greenish c. nut; *nut of which the milk is not dried.* आडसर *m.* कांकडें *n.* आंधळा नारळ *m.*

Half of a c. nut. कवड *f.*

Half of a c. nut shell used as a vessel. नारळी *f.* नारळी पात्र *n.* बेली *f.* वाटी *f.*

Hollowed c. nut, used to dish out water, for keeping things in, &c. ओळग *or* ओळक *m.* ओळकी *f.* शेंद *f.* डऊ *or* डव *or* डौ *m.* डवला *m.* डहू *m.* बेला *m.* बेलका *m.* बेलें *n.* कवंडल *n.*

Integuments of the shell of a c. nut drawn into strings. काबाळ *m.*—twisted into cords. सुंभ *or* सुंब *n.*—A piece or bit of it. सुंभखंड *n.* सुंभखंडी *f.* (*or* सुंबखंड&c.)

Kernel of a c. nut. खोबरें *n.*

Oil from the kernel of the c. nut. खोबरेल *n.* नारळेल *n.*

Oil obtained from c. nut shells by burning them. नरटेल *n.* [आवेल *n.*

Oil obtained from heated scrapings of young c. nuts.

Oil obtained from the kernel of the c. nut by squeezing with the hand. मुठेल *n.* [shell. खुरडी *f.*

Piece of the kernel of a c. nut cut out from the

Ripe and dry c. nut. सुखड *or* सुकड *f.*

Ripe c. nut fallen from the tree. गळींव *or* गळी सुखड *f.*

Scrapings of c. nut. चव *m.* चोव *m.* चून *n.*

Shell of a c. nut. नरोटी *f.* नरटी *f.* करोटी *f.* करंटी *f.* तरटें *n.* नारळाची आई *f.*

Young c. nut. खांखोटा *m.* पोंकटा *m.* शहाळें *n.* मुका नारळ *m.* कांकडा *m.*

Cocoon, *n.* कोशम. कोसला *m.*

Cod, *n. pod.* शेंग *f.*

2 एक मासा आहे.

CODE, *n. collection.* संग्रहm. संहिता *f.*

2 (of regulations &c.). कानूजाबताm. कलमबंदी *f.* ठरावबंदm.

CODICIL, *n.* मृतपत्राची पुरवणी *f.* मृत्युलेखशेषm.

To CODDLE, *v. a. parboil.* अर्धशिजा करणें, अर्धकच्चा *pop.* अदकाचा करणें.

2 *cocker,* v. To INDULGE. लाड *n.* करणें, लाडकावणें.

CO EFFICACY, *n.* समगुणकारिता *f.*

CO-EFFICIENT. See COOPERATING.

CO-EFFICIENT, *n.*—in arithmetic. वर्णm.

CO-EQUAL, *a.* v. EQUAL. समसमान, समतोल, तोलाचा, तोडीचा, एकपदवीचा.

CO-EQUALITY, *n.* v. A. समसमानता *f.* समतोलता *f.* पदवीची समता *f.* बरोबरी *f.*

CO-EQUALLY, *adv.* v. A. बरोबरीनें.

To COERCE, *v. a.* v. To COMPEL. बलात्कारm.-बळजोरी *f.*-&c. करणें-चालवणें.

2 See To RESTRAIN.

COERCION, *n.* See COMPULSION, RESTRAINT.

COERCIVE. See COMPULSORY.

CO-ESSENTIAL, *a. partaking of the same essence.* समभाव, सहज सिद्ध, समतत्व, समवस्तु.

CO-ESSENTIALITY, *n.* समभावता *f.* भावसमता *f.* भावसमानता *f.* तत्वसमानता *f.*

CO-ETANEOUS, *a. of the same age.* समवयस्क, समवय, समानवयस्क, समानवयी, एकवयस्क, एकवयी.

CO-ETERNAL, *a.* समनित्य भावी, समनित्यस्थायी.

CO-EVAL, *a. of the same age.* समानकाली, एककालिक, समकालिक, समवयस्क, समकालज.

CO-EXISTENCE, *n.* सहजीवित्वn. संसर्गm. एककालिकत्वn.

CO EXISTENT, *a.* एका कालाचा, एका समयाचा, एक कालिक, सहजीवी, सहज.

CO-EXTENSIVE, *a.* समव्यापक, समाक्रमक, समावधिक, समसीम.

COFFEE, *n.*—the berry. बुंदm.

2—the infusion. कवाm. काफी *f.* is common.

COFFEE-HOUSE, *n.* कवाखाना *m.*

COFFEE-POT, *n.* कवादानी *f.*

COFFER, *n.* v. BOX. संदूक *f.* हडपाm. मांदूस *f.*

2 v. TREASURE. भांडारn.

COFFIN, *n.* प्रेताची संदूक *f.*-पेटी *f.* शवपेटिका *f.*

2 *grocer's paper-case.* पुडाm. *dim.* पुडी *f.* खोलपाm. *dim.* खोलपी *f.*

To COG, *v. a.* (a wheel &c.). दांतावणें, दांतळणें.

2 *wheedle,* v. To COAX. मठारणें.

COG, *n. tooth of a wheel.* दांताm. दांतm.

Interstice between cogs. अंधारी *f.*

COGENCY, *n.* v. A. बळकटी *f.* दृढता *f.* प्रबलता *f.* प्राबल्य *n.* जोर *m.* जोरावाm. जीवm. ऐवजम.

COGENT, *a. forcible.* बळकट, दृढ, प्रबल, जोराचा, जोरदार, वजप्राय.

To COGITATE, COGITATION. See To THINK, THOUGHT.

COGNATE, *a. born together.* सहजात, सहज, एकजात.

2 v. RELATED. सजातीय, सवर्ण, एकजातीय.

COGNATION, *n.* v. RELATION. आत्मीयसंबंधm. स्वीयसंबंधm. एकशरीरान्वयm.

COGNITION, *n. certain knowledge.* अनुभवसिद्ध ज्ञानn. विज्ञानn. परिज्ञान *n.*

COGNIZABLE, *a. that falls under judicial notice.* चौकशी करण्याजोगा-सारखा-&c.

2 *that may be known.* जाणण्याजोगा-&c. ज्ञेय, गोचर (in comp. as इंद्रियगोचर c. by the senses).

COGNIZANCE, *n. judicial notice.* बाजपुशी *f.* बाजपूस *f.* चौकशी *f.*

2 *jurisdiction.* चौकशीकरण्याचा अधिकारm.-अमलm.

3 See PERCEPTION.

4 *badge.* निशाणी *f.*

COGNIZANT, *a. having knowledge of.* माहितगार, वाकबदार.

COGNOMINAL, *a. having the same name.* एकचनांवाचा, स्वनामी, सनाम, एकनामी.

To COHABIT, *v. n. dwell with.* सहवासm.-एकस्थान वास *m.*-एकत्रवासm.-&c. करणें, एकेठिकाणीं राहणें.

2 *live together as husband and wife.* दादल्या बायकोच्या नात्यानें राहणें-वागणें, दंपतिभाव धरून-दंपतिभावानें राहणें- असणें -वागणें-&c. स्त्रीपुरुषधर्मकसंसर्गm. करणें, एकशय्या *f.*-एकतल्पn. -&c. करणें.

COHABITATION, *n.* v. V. 1.—*act or state.* सहवासm. एकस्थान वासm. एकत्रवासm.

2 दांपत्य सहवासm. स्त्रीपुरुष धर्मकसंसर्गm. एकशय्या *f.* एकतल्पn.

COHEIR, *n.* वतनभाऊm. वतनबंधुm. घरभाऊm. विभागी, भागी, भागहर, भागधेय, अंशी, अंशक.

CO-HEIRESS, *n.* वतनबहीण *f.* विभागिनी *pop.* विभागीण *f.* &c.

To COHERE, *v. n. stick together.* एकमेकासीं लगटून-चिकटून असणें, परस्पर सलग्न-संयुक्त-&c. असणें.

2 *be well connected.* जुळणें, जमणें, संदर्भाचा-जुळणीचा-संगतवार-संदर्भशुद्ध-&c. असणें.

COHERENCE, COHESION, *n.* v. V. 1.—*state.* संयोगm. सलग्नता-*f.* संयुक्तता *f.* संसक्ति *f.*

2 संदर्भm. संगति *f.* संबंधm. संदर्भशुद्धि *f.* पूर्वापराविरोधm.

COHERENT, *a.* v. V. 1.—सलग्न, संयुक्त, संसक्त.

2 *and* CONSISTENT. संदर्भाचा, सुसंगत, संगतवार, संदर्भशुद्ध, समर्थ.

COHERENTLY, *adv.* v. A. 2 संगतवार, संदर्भपूर्वक.

COHESIVE, *a.* v. STICKY. चिकट, चिकण, स्निग्ध.

COHESIVENESS, *n.* v.A. चिकटपणाm. &c. धरm.स्नेहm. स्निग्धता *f.*

To COHIBIT, COHIBITION. See To RESTRAIN, RESTRAINT.

COIF. *n.* एकाप्रकारची टोपी आहे.

To COIL, *v. a. gather into a ring.* वेंटाळणें, वेंटाळेm.*pl.*-वेंटाळ्या-*f. pl.*-वेटाळींn. *pl.* करणें-घालणें, मंडलीकरणn.-कुंडलीकरणn. करणें.

COIL, *n.* (as of a rope). वेंटाळाm. वेंटाळी *f.* वेंटाळेंn. कुंडलेंn. [वळी *f.* मुदनn.

2 *coiled mass.* गुंडी *f.* पेंडोळेंn. गुंडाळी *f.* गुंडाळेंn.

3 *noise, tumult,* v. BUSTLE. गडबड *f.* गोंधळm. घोळm.

COIN, *n.* नाणेंn. मुद्रा *f.* मुद्रिका *f.* नाणकn.

Some of the *Coins* are. पैसा, बुळापैसा,ढब्बू, दिडकी *f.* आणी *f.* चौली, पावली, अधेली, रुपया, होन, पुतळी, बोळीहोन, पांची, मोहर, फलम, वरयी, सोनटका, एकेरी होन. See RUPEE, MONEY.

Bored c. सुलाखी (रुपया &c.).

Consisting of various coins. नाणेवारी.

Cracked c. फुटकर, फुटक,फाटफूट, बालफुटका, कची (रुपया-&c.).

Payment in various coins. नाणेवार देणेंn.
Stamped or marked c. छापी(रुपया, पैसा &c.) नरमछापी.
Cracked and rubbed,—coins. कचीडेली.

To COIN, *v. a. stamp metals for money.* पाडणें, शिक्का *m.* मारणें -पाडणें, अंकन *n.*-मुद्रांकन *n.* करणें.
Coining die. शिक्का *m.*
2 *fabricate, forge,* v. To INVENT. रचणें, योजणें, रचना *f.*-योजना *f.*-&c. करणें, नवा करणें, बनावणें.

COINAGE, COINING, *n.* v. V. 1.—*act.* पाडणें *m.* शिक्कामारणें *n.* मुद्रांकन *n.*
2—*act.* रचणें *n.* &c. रचना *f.* योजना *f.*
I. *matter coined.* See COIN.

To COINCIDE, *v. n. fall together, meet in the same point.* संपात *m* होणें *g. of s.*
2 v. To AGREE. मिळणें, जुळणें, जुगणें, मेळ *m.*-जम *m.*-, जवा *m.* बसणें *g. of s.*

COINCIDENCE, *n.* v. V. 1. संपात *m.*
2 *and* AGREEMENT. मेळ *m.* जम *m.* जवा *m.* मिलाफ *m.*

COINCIDENT, *a.* v. V. 2. *and* AGREEING. मिळणारा, &c. मिलाफाचा.

COINER, *n.* v. V. 1. नाणें पाडणारा, टांकसाळ्या.

COIR, *n.* काथा *m.*

COITION, COITUS, *n.* v. COPULATION. संग *m.* संयोग *m.* सुरत*n.*

CO-JUROR, *n. one who swears to another's credibility.* पडसाक्षी, प्रतिसाक्षी.

COKE, *n.* माजलेला दगडी कोळसा *m.*

COLANDER, *n. strainer.* रोवळा *or* वरळा *m. dim.* रोवळी *or* वरळी *f.* जाळी *f.* बेळणी *f.* हजारी *f.* चाळण *f.* चाळणी *f.*

COLD, *n.*—as a principle or cause. हिम *pop.* हिंव *or* हींव *n.* थंडाई *f.* थंडी *f.* शीत *n.*
2—the sensation, v. COLDNESS. थंडी *f.* हिंव *or* हींव *n.* हिंवडी *or* हिंवाडी *f.* शीत *n.*
Cramp from c. काकड *n.* काकडी *f. v.* भर.
Stiff from c. काकडकुडा.
To be stiff & cramped from c. काकडणें, गारठणें.
3 *catarrh.* पडसें *n.* सरदी *f.* प्रतिश्याय *m.* धेटेंपडसें*n.* बरसन*n.*
4 (in the system). सरदी *f.* थंडी *f.* शितलाई *f.* शैत्य*n.*
C. in the eyes. वावशी *f. v.* धर.

COLD, *a.*—of substances, gener. थंड, शीतल *pop.* शितळ, हिंवसा, शीत, गार, शीतस्पर्श.
Very c. *cold as clay.* काल्यासारखा थंड.
To become or be c. गारसणें.
2—esp. weather or wind. गार, थंड, शीत, सरद, हिम, हिमवान्, हिमवंत, हैम, हैमन.
Bitter, biting, piercing, icy, &c. c. (*also*—of water). गार, थंडगार, गारगार करवंद *or* गारगार करवत, गारगारथंड, गारगारठणक.
To be sharply c.—weather, water, &c. करवंदणें, गारठणें.
3 *having the sense of cold.* थंडी बाजलेला, हिंवभरलेला, &c. थंडावलेला, कुडकुडलेला, हिंवालेला *or* हिंवलेला, हिंवडलेला, शीतग्रस्त, शीतपीडित, शीतार्त्त, शीतव्यथित, &c. [हिंवडणें.
To feel or be c.थंडी *f.*-हिंव *n.*-&c. बाजणें *inv. con.* हिंवणें,
4 *having c. or cooling qualities.* थंड, शीतल *pop.* शितळ, सरद, शीतगुण, शीतवीर्य.
5 *frigid, apathetic, phlegmatic.* थंड, थंडा, शिळा, शीत, जड, मंद, थंड प्रकृतीचा, थंडस्वभावाचा, उदास, उदासीन, विराग, अरति, शीतप्रकृतिक, शीतस्वभाव, उदासीन, निस्पृह. Some terms for *a cold, phlegmatic, apathetic person,* are शिळाबिब्बा*m.* शनि *m.*
6 *not affectionate, not cordial.* थंड, थंडा, थंडाईचा, अनमानीक, निस्नेह, निर्मम, स्नेहाभावाचा, अस्नेहाचा, अस्नेहात्मक.
To be c. मनांत सरद होणें, थंडाई *f.* धरणें.
In cold blood. थंड्यापोटानें, रागनसतां.
7 *not having sexual desire.* थंड, थंडा, कामवासना रहित, शीतप्रकृतीचा.

COLD-BLOODED, COLD-HEARTED, *a. unfeeling.* निदर्दी, निर्दय, करुणारहित. [गीवांचून, &c.

COLDLY, *adv.* v. A. 5. उदासपणानें, थंडाईनें, कळकळीवांचून, पोटा-
6 थंडाईनें, स्नेहावांचून, स्नेहाभावपूर्वक, अस्नेहपूर्वक.

COLDNESS, *n.* v. A. 1. थंडी *f.* थंडपणा *m.* शितळाई *f.* शीत *n.* शैत्य *n.* थंडाई *f.*
2 थंडी *f.* हिव *pop.* हिंव *or* हींव *n.* शीत *n.* शैत्य *n.* सरदी *f.*
Rigors of c., extreme, intense, bitter, biting, &c. c. थंडीचाताठा-गारठा *or* गारोठा-गारोंडा-गारिवठा-गारिवडा-गारवा*m.*
3 हिंव *or* हींव*n.* थंडी *f.* शैत्य*n.* शीत *n.* हिंवाडी *or* हिंवडी *f.* कुडकुडी *f.*
4 थंडपणा *m.* शीतळपणा*m.* सरदी *f.* शीतगुणित्व *n.*
5 थंडपणा*m.* उदासी *f.* मांद्य*n.* जाड्य*n.* जडत्व*n.* जडिमा *m.* विराग*m.* रागाभाव*m.* अरति *f.* उदासीनत्व*n.* शीतप्रकृति *f.*
6 थंडपणा*m.* थंडाई *f.* अस्नेह *m.* नैस्नेह्य*n.* निस्नेहता *f.* निर्ममत्व *n.* स्नेहाभाव*m.*
7 थंडपणा *m.* कामवासना राहित्य *n.* शीतप्रकृति *f.*

COLD SHOULDER, To give the c. to. स्नेहाचा डोळा न दाखविणें, न पाहिल्या सारखा *a. decl.* करणें.

COLIC, *n.* पोटशूल *or* पोटसूळ *m.* शूल *pop.* सूळ *m.* पक्तिशूल *m.* परिणामशूल *m.* आमशूल *m.* वातशूल *m.*
That has c. पोटसुळ्या, शूली.

To COLLAPSE, *v. n. fall together.* बसणें *or* बसून जाणें, चोपणें, दबणें *or* दबूनजाणें, मिळून जाणें. [चोप *f.*

COLLAPSE, COLLAPSION, *n.* v. V.—*state.* बसणें *n.* &c. चेपटी*f.*

COLLAPSED, *p.* v. V. बसूनगलेला, दबूनगलेला, &c.

COLLAR, *n.* (for the neck). गळेबंद *m.* गळेपट्टी *f.* कंठवस्त्र *n.* कंठवेष्टन *n.*
C. of silver worn by the worshippers of Khandobá. गांठा *or* गांठ्या *m.*
Ornamental c. of gold or silver. हसळी *f.*
2 (as of dogs, &c.). तोक *or* तोख *or* तौक *m.*
3 (of horses, &c.). गळपेंडें *n.* सरी *f.* हसळी *f.*
To slip the c. आंग *n.* काढून घेणें.

To COLLAR, *v. a. seize. by the throat.* गळचिपी *f.*-गरगोटी *f.*-नरडी *f.*-&c. धरणें *g.of o.*

COLLAR-BONE, *n.* सरी *f.* जत्रु *n.*

To COLLATE, *v. a.* v. To COMPARE. जोडणें *or* जोडून पाहणें, पडतळणें *or* पडताळणें, पडताळून पाहणें, पडोसा *m.* पाहणें, रुजुवात *f.*-रुजुमुकाबला *m*-एक वाक्यता *f.* घेणें-करणें *g. of o.*
2 *gather & place in order.* जुळणें, लावणें.

COLLATED, *p.* v. V. 1. पडताळून पाहिलेला, &c.

COLLATERAL, *a. being side to side.* अन्योन्य पार्श्वस्थित, अन्योन्यपार्श्वसलग्न.
2 (of relationship). शाखासंबंधाचा, शाखासंबंधी, बाजूच्या नात्याचा, कूटस्थसमान्वयी.
3 *not direct,*—of testimony, &c. पेंठचा, पडोशाचा.
4 See PARALLEL.

COLLATION, *n.* v. V. 1.—*act.* पडताळणें *n.* &c. पडोसापाहणें *n.* पडताळा *m.* पडोसा *m.* रुजूमुकाबला *m.*
I. *repast.* फराळ *m.* उपाहार *m.*

COLLATOR, *n.* v. V. 1. पडताळून पाहणारा, &c.

COLLEAGUE, *n.* कामाचा सोबती *m.* सोबती *m.* कार्यबंधु *m.* सहाधिकारी *m.* सहकारी *m.* संभूयकारी *m.*

To COLLECT, *v. a.* v. To GATHER. मिळवणें, जमावणें, जमाकरणें, गोळा करणें, संग्रह *m.*-संचय *m.* करणें *g.of o.*
2 (monies). वसूल करणें, उकळणें, उगवणें, उगवणी *f.*-उग्राणी *f.*-उगावा *m.*-&c. करणें *g.of o.*
3 *infer.* अनुमान *n.*-तर्क *m.*-&c. करणें, घेणें, सिद्ध करणें.
4 (one's self) शुद्धीवर-भानावर-&c. येणें, चित्त *n.* धावरणें थाऱ्यावर आणणें.

To COLLECT, *v. n. accumulate.* गोळा होणें, जमणें, साचणें, सांठणें, संग्रह *m.*-संचय *m.* होणें *g.of s.*
2 *assemble,* v. To GATHER. मिळणें, एकवटणें, जमणें.

COLLECT, *n. short comprehensive prayer.* सारप्रार्थना *f.*

COLLECTED, *a. self-possessed.* स्थिरचित्त, स्वस्थचित्त, अक्षुब्धचित्त, सावध, सावधान, समाहितमनस्क-मना.

COLLECTION, *n.* v. V. A. 1.—*act.* मिळवणें *n.* जमावणें *n.* &c. जमाव*m.* संग्रह *m.* संहार *m.* चय *m.*
2—*act.* उकळणें *n.* उगवणें *n.* &c. उगावा *m.* उगवण *f.* उगवणी *f.* उगवील *f.* उग्राणी *f.* उगवणूक *f.* उकळणी *f.* उकळणूक *f.* उकळीत *f.* उकळ *f.* उकळाउकळ *f.*
C. of the revenue of a district. मामला *m.* मामलत *f.* कमाविशी *f.* कमावीस *f.* तहशील *or* सील *f.*
v. V. N. 1.—*act.* जमणें *n.* सांचणें *n.* सांठणें *n.*
2 मिळणें *n.* एकवटणें *n.* जमणें *n.*
I. *collected body,* v. HEAP. सांठ *m.* सांठा *m.* संग्रह *m.* संचय *m.* राशि *m. pop.* रास *f.* मेळावा *m.* संघात *m.* संघ *m.* कलाप *m.* (used esp. in comp. as केश कलाप, क्रिया कलाप).
Collections (as of sums, monies, &c.). उगवण *f.* उगवणी *f.* उग्राणी *f.* उगवील *f.* उगावा *m.* उकळीत *f.* उकळीतजमा *f.* वसूल *m.* उकाळा *m.*
Contingent collections (or levies). सादिलवार जमा *f.*
Extra collections. शिवाई जमा *f.* खेरीज जमा *f.*
General c. or levy (of monies). पट्टी *f.* पट्टीपासोडी *f.*
Miscellaneous c. सर्वसंग्रह *m.*

COLLECTIVE, *a.* v. AGGREGATE. सामवायिक, सामाजिक, सामुदायिक, समुदित.
2—in grammar. समुदायवाचक.

COLLECTIVELY, *adv.* v. A. 1. एकवट, संघशः, समुदायरूप, समवायरूप.

COLLECTOR, *n.* v. A. 1. जमविणारा, मिळवणारा, &c. संग्रही, संग्राहक, संग्रहकर्त्ता-कारक-कारी-&c.
2 उगवणारा, उकळणारा, &c. उकळ्या, उगळ्या.
I. (of revenue). मामलेदार, मामलतदार, (his office मामलतदारी *f.*) कमावीसदार, (his office कमावीसदारी *f.*), वसूलदार, तहशीलदार, (his office तहशीलदारी *f.*) The European Collector is called कलेकतर *or*-टर.

COLLEGE, *n. society of learned men.* शाला *f.* विद्वज्जनसमूह *m.* विद्वज्जनवृंद *n.*
2 *edifice for students.* पाठशाला *f.* विद्यालय *n.* मठ *m.* छात्रनिलय *m.*
3 *associated body*—gener. v. ASSEMBLY. मंडळी *f.* सभा *f.* शाला *f.*

COLLEGIAL, COLLEGIATE, *a.* v. N. 2. पाठशालेचा, पाठशालासंबंधी, विद्यालयसंबंधी, विद्यालयविषयक.

COLLEGIAN, COLLEGIATE, *n.* विद्यार्थी *m.* छात्र *m.* विद्यालयनिवासी.

COLLET, *n.* See COLLAR. 2 *the part of a ring in which the stone is set.* घर *n.* कोंदण *n.*

To COLLIDE, *v. n. strike against each other.* एकमेकाची धडक *f.*-धक्का *m.*-&c. लागणें-बसणें, एकमेकासीं लागणें, संघट्टणें, झटणें, झगटणें, खेटणें, घसटणें, धडकणें, टेपलणें.
2 fig. *interfere with, &c.* v. To CLASH. घासणें, घासणी *f.* होणें, लढणें, चकमक *f.* झडणें *g. of s.*

COLLIER, *n.* दगडी कोळशांचे खाणींत काम करणारा.
2 दगडी कोळशांचा व्यापारी.
3 दगडी कोळशांचें बारकस *m.*

COLLIERY, *n.* खाणींतून दगडी कोळसे खणून काढण्याचा कारखाना
2 दगडी कोळशांचा व्यापार *m.*

To COLLIQUATE, &c. See To MELT, &c.

COLLISION, v. V.1.—*act.* संघट्टणें *n.* झगटणें *n.* &c. एकमेकांचा धक्का *m.*-धडका *m.*-&c. संघट्टन *n.* परस्पर आघात *m.*
2—*act.* घासणें *n.* घासणी *f.* चकमक *f.*

To COLLOCATE. See To PLACE.

COLLOCUTION. See CONVERSATION.

COLLOP, *n.* सागुतीचा रवा *m.*-तुकडा *m.* मांसखंड *n.*

COLLOQUIAL, *a. relating, &c. to common conversation.* बोलाचालीचा, बोलाबोलीचा, जाबसाली, जाबसालाचा, संभाषणसंबंधी.

COLLOQUIALISM, *n.* जाबसाली बोलण्यांत येण्या जोगा भाषणाचा प्रकार *m.*

COLLOQUY, *n.* v. CONVERSATION. बोलाबोली *f.* बोलाचाली *f.* संभाषण *n.* संवाद *m.*

To COLLUDE, *v. n. conspire in a fraud.* फसवणीचा-&c. कट *m.*-कूट *n.*-गट्टी *f.*-&c. करणें, संगनमत *n.*-संगमत *n.*-प्रतारणसंकेत *m.*-कपटमंत्र *m.*-&c. करणें.

COLLUDER, *n.* COLLUDING, *p. a.* v. V. संगनमत करणारा, &c. संगनमत्या, संगमत्या, संगनमती.

COLLUSION, *n.* v. V. फसवणीचा कट *m.*-कूट *n.*-कट्टा *m.*-गट्टी *f.*-&c. संगनमत *n.* संगमत *n.* प्रतारणसंकेत *m.* कपटमंत्र *m.*
Share or concern in a collusive agreement. अंग *n.* मिलाफ *m.*

COLLUSIVE, COLLUSORY, *a.* संगनमताचा, संगमताचा.

COLLUSIVELY, *adv.* संगनमतानें, संगमतानें, प्रतारणसंकेतानें, प्रतारणसंकेतपूर्वक.

COLLY, *n.* कोळशाची मशी *f.*-मस *m. f.*-मळ *n.*

COLLYRIUM, *n. application for the eyes.* अंजन *n.* नेत्ररंजन *n.* नेत्रौषध *n.* अक्षिभेषज *n.*
C. of antimony. सुरमा *m.*
Wire for applying c. सळई *f.*

COLOCYNTH, *n.*—the plant. इंद्रवारुणी *pop.* इंद्रावण *f.* कडूवृंदावन *n.* कंवडल *f.* विशाली *f.*—the *fruit.* इंद्रवारुणी *f. pop.* इंद्रावण *n.* कंवडल *n.*

COLON, *n.* नळ *m.* नस *m.*

Wind in the c. नळवायु *m.* धुमक *f.*

2 एक विराम चिन्ह आहे, तें असें (:).

COLONEL, *n.* पलटणींतला मुख्य अमलदार *m.* कर्नेल *m.*

COLONIAL, *a.* v. N. नवे वसविलेले देशशाखेचा, देशांतरस्थदेशशाखासंबंधी, नवे वसविलेलेराज्यशाखेचा, देशांतरस्थराज्यशाखासंबंधी.

COLONIST, *n.* देशशाखेच्याठाईं राहणारा.

To COLONIZE, *v. a. establish a colony in.* आपल्या देशाचा-आपल्या राज्याचा फांटा *m.*-&c. वसविणें.

2 *migrate and settle in.* वसविणें, दिवेलावणी *f.*-नवीवसात *f.*-नवीवस्ती *f.* करणें *g. of o.* [वलि *f.*

COLONNADE, *n. row of pillars.* खांबांची रांग *f.* स्तंभ पंक्ति *f.* स्तंभा-

COLONY, *n. body of people migrated to another country and remaining under the mother state.* आपल्या देशाचा *or* आपल्याराज्याचा फांटा वसविणारी मडंळी *f.*-वसविणारे लोक *m. pl.* &c. देशशाखाधिष्ठित जन *m. pl.* देशशाखास्थजन *m. pl.*

2 *the country colonized.* आपला देश सोडलेल्यालोकांनीं वसविलेलादेशफांटा *m.* देशशाखा *f.* राज्यशाखा *f.* देशांतरस्थराज्यशाखा *f.* देशांतरस्थ देशशाखा *f.*

COLOQUINTIDA. See COLOCYNTH.

COLOR, *n.* रंग *m.* वर्ण *m. pop.* वाण *or* वान *m. n.* राग *m.*

To change c. v. To BLUSH. तोंडाचें पाणी *n.* पळणें, मुखवैवर्ण्य *n.* होणें *g. of s.*

2 *coloring substance or composition.* रंग *m.* रंगद्रव्य *n.*

3 v. PRETENCE. बहाणा *m.* निमित्त *n.*

4 *sort,* v. KIND. जात *f.* प्रकार *m.*

5 colors; *standard, ensign,* v. FLAG. निशाण *or* न *n.*

Hanging out false c. हूल *f.*-हुलकावणी *f. v.* दाखव.

To haul down one's c. *fig.* कान *m. pl.* पाडणें.

To COLOR, *v. a.* रंगणें, रंगवणें, रंग *m.* देणें, रंगदार-रंगी-रंगीत करणें.

2 *varnish, gloss, &c.* v. To EMBELLISH. बनावणें, बनावून सांगणें, तिखटमीठ *n.*-मीठमिरची *f.* लावून सांगणें.

3 *palliate,* v. To EXCUSE. निमित्त *n.*-बहाणा *m.* सांगणें.

To COLOR, *v. n.* See To BLUSH.

COLORABLE, *a. specious,* v. PLAUSIBLE. सत्यसदृश, सत्यसन्निभ.

COLORED, *p. & a.* v. V. A. & N. रंगलेला, रंगदिल्हेला, रंगदार, रंगी, रंगीत, रंगीन, वर्णगत.

2 तिखटमीठ लावून सांगितलेला, &c. [रंजन *n.*

COLORING, *n.* v. V. A. 1.—*act.* रंगणें *n.* रंगदेणें *n.* &c. वर्णन *n.*

I. *cost or price of c.* रंगणावळ *f.* रंगाई *f.*

II. *specious appearance.* सत्याभास *m.* सत्यसादृश्य *n.*

COLORLESS, *a.* नीरक्त, विवर्ण, रंगहीन-रहित-विरहित-विहीन-शून्य-&c. वर्णहीन-रहित-&c.

COLOSSAL. See LARGE.

COLOSSUS, *n. gigantic statue.* मोठा पुतळा *m.*

COLT, *n.* शिंगा *m.* शिंगरूं *n.* लुंगा *m.* अश्वशाव *m.*—in contempt, endearment, &c. शिंगरट *n.*

2 *big and giddy boy.* घोडा *m.* घोडगा *m.* घोंडकुदळ मुलगा *m.*

COLTER, *n.*—of a plough. फाळ *m.*

COLTISH, *a.* शिंगरवट, नाचरा, ठिकरा.

COLUMBARY, *n.* v. DOVE-COTE. खुबडी *f.* [comp.

COLUMBINE, *a.* v. DOVE-COLORED. पारव्याच्या रंगाचा, पारवा in.

COLUMN, *n.* v. PILLAR. खांब *m.* गोलस्तंभ *m.* स्तंभ *m.*

2 (of troops). गोल *m.* भोगव्यूह *m.*

Close c. कट *m.*

3 (of a page). आसन *n.* रकाना *m.* मोड *f.* कालम *m.* from the English is in use.

COLUMNAR, *a.* खांबाच्या आकाराचा, स्तंभाकार.

COLURES, *n.*—in geography. याम्योत्तरवृत्त *n.*

COMA, *n.* v. LETHARGY. झांप *f.* झांपड *f.*

COMATOSE, COMATOUS, *a.* v. LETHARGIC. झांपड पडलेला, अतिनिद्रालु. [फणकूट *n.*

COMB, *n.* विंचरणी *or* विंचुरणी *f.* फणी *f.* कंगवा *m.*—in contempt.

Small toothed c. लिखी *f.* [लणें-करणें.

To draw the c. forcibly through the hair. ओरप *f.* घा-

2 (of a cock). कोंबड्याची शेंडी *f.* शिरगीर *f.* चूडा *f.*

3 *honey-comb.* पोळी *f.* पोळें *n.*

4 *hollow between hills,* v. VALLEY. खोरें *n.* दरी *f.*

To COMB, *v. a.* विंचरणें *or* विंचुरणें.

2 (wool, &c.) v. To CARD. पिंजणें, पिंजारणें.

COMB-BAG, *n.* फणेरें *n.*

To COMBAT, COMBAT, COMBATANT. See To FIGHT, &c.

COMBATIVE, *a.* युद्धशील, युद्धप्रवण, युद्धतत्पर.

COMBATIVENESS, *n.* v. A. युद्धप्रावण्य *n.* युद्धप्रवणता *f.*

COMBED, *p.* v. V. 1. विंचरलेला.

2 पिंजलेला, पिंजारलेला.

COMBINATION, *n.* v. V. A.—*act.* मिळवणें *n.* जोडणें *n.* जडण *f.* एकी करण *n.* समाहार *m.* समाहरण *n.* संयोजन *n.* संयोग *m.* संधान *n.* संधानकरण *n.* संमेलन *n.*—*state.* and UNION. संयोम *m.* संयुक्तता *f.* संधि *m.* संसृष्टि *f.* संगम *m.* समागम *m.*

I. *combined body; band, confederacy, cabal, &c.* कट *m.* जट *m.* जाळी *f.* जूट *m. f.* जूग *n.* जुटी *f.* गट *or* गट्ट *m.*

II. *confederation, league, conspiracy, &c.* एकवळा *m.* जूट *m.* जुटी *f.* जट *m.* कट *m.* कटाव *m.* कट्टा *m.* गट्टी *f.* मिळण *f.* एकोपा *or* बा *m.* कूट *n.* जूग *n.* संगनमत *n.* संगमत *n.* जत *f.* जतीमती *f.* संप *m.* समा *m.* एकतंत्र *n.* एकसूत *n.* एकगोत *n.*

III.—in mathematics. एकीकरण *n.*

To COMBINE, *v. a. unite,* v. To JOIN. मिळवणें, जोडणें, जडणें, एक करणें, संयोग *m.*-समाहरण *n.*-&c. करणें *g. of o.*

To COMBINE, *v. n. coalesce, mingle, mix,* v. To JOIN. मिळणें, एकहोणें, जमणें.

2 *confederate, conspire, league together.* मिळणें, जुटणें, जुडणें, जटणें, वेंट *m.* वळणें, गोत *m.* मिळणें, मेथकूट *n.* मिळणें-जमणें *g. of s.* एकवटणें, मिथणें *or* मथणें, कट *m.* बांधणें-करणें, जुगल *f.*-संगनमत *n.*-एकोपा *m.*-मिळणी *f.*-कट *n.*-&c. करणें, एकतंत्र *n.*-एकसूत *n.*- एकगोत *n.* होणें *g. of s.*

COMBINER, *n.* COMBINING, *p. a.* v. V. A. मिळवणारा, &c. संयोग-संयोजन-&c. कर्त्ता.

v. V. N. मिळणारा, जमणारा, &c.

2 मिळणारा, जुटणारा, &c. संगनमती, संगमती.

COMBING, *n.* v. V. 1.—*act.* विंचरणें *m.* विंचरणी *f.*

2 पिंजणें *n.* &c. पिंजणी *f.* पिंजारणी *f.*

I. Combings (of hair, of the शेंडी, &c.) गुंता *m.* गुताड *n. f.*

गुंफ *f.* गूथ *f.*

COMBUSTIBILITY, *n.* v. A. 1. जळाया सारखेपणा *m.* &c. दहनीयत्व *n.* दाह्यत्व *n.*

2 शीघ्रदहनीयत्व *n.* शीघ्रज्वालाग्राहित्व *n.*

COMBUSTIBLE, *a. that will burn.* जळायाचा, जळायासारखा-जोगा-&c. दहनीय, दाह्य, ज्वलनीय, दहनाई.

2 *that easily takes fire.* लौकरपेट घेणारा-घ्यायाचा-&c. शीघ्रज्वलनीय, सहजज्वलनीय, शीघ्रज्वालाग्राही, दारूसारखा.

COMBUSTION. See BURNING, TUMULT.

To COME, *v. n. arrive, approach, advance, &c.* येणें, जवळ-समीप-&c. येणें, प्राप्त होणें, आगम *m.*-आगमन *n.*-आयान *n.*-&c. करणें.

Come! Come along! चल, चलये, चल निघून ये लवकर.

To c. and go. येणेंजाणें *n.*-येवाजावा *m.*-गमनागमन *n.*-&c. करणें.

2 *draw being,* v. To RISE, To PROCEED. होणें, उपजणें, लागणें, उत्पन्न होणें, उपस्थित होणें. [लागणें.

3 *attain to, reach.* पावणें, पहोंचणें, प्राप्त होणें, येणें, मिळणें,

4 about; to pass, v. To HAPPEN. घडून-बनून-होऊन-&c. येणें, घडणें, होणें.

5 closely upon; *press hard upon, be at hand.* नेहटणें *or* नेटणें, खेटणें, भिडणें, चितणें, टेकणें, टेकावणें, लगटणें, हातावर येणें, हाताबोटावर येणें, आंगावर येणें.

6 off; *be detached.* निघणें, सुटणें.

7 off; *escape.* सुटणें, निभणें, निभावणें, पार पडणें, बटावणें.

8 off; clearly or prominently;—an impression. ओठणें, उटाळणें, निघणें, उठणें, उमटणें.

9 off; *take place.* होणें, चालू होणें.

10 out, forth; *c. to light, appear clearly.* उमग्रणें *or* उमठणें, उमगणें *or* उमंगणें, फुटणें, उघाडीस-उजाडीस-प्रसिद्धीस-&c. येणें, प्रगट होणें.

11 to; *recover as from a swoon, &c.* शुद्धीवर-ध्यानावर-स्मृती वर-देहभानावर-&c. येणें, सावध होणें.

12 under; *be included.* मोडणें, ओढणें, पोटांत असणें.

13 up, out;—a tree, a peg, stake, &c. उपटणें, उपडणें.

14 *up with,* v. To OVERTAKE. अटपून घेणें.

To c. to. See To AMOUNT. To c. short See To FAIL.

To c. upon. See To HAPPEN, To ATTACK.

To come, *to happen hereafter,* v. FUTURE. यायाचा, व्हायाचा, येणार.

COME, *p.* v. V. 1. आलेला, &c. आयात, आगत, समागत, दाखल, उपस्थित, लागू, प्रविष्ट (used esp. of epistles.).

COMEDIAN, *n. player,* v. ACTOR. नट *m.*

2 *a writer of comedy.* हास्यरसप्रधाननाटक कर्त्ता. [नn.

COMEDY, *n.* हास्यरसप्रधान नाटक *n.* सुखपरिणामक नाटक *n.* प्रहस-

COMELINESS, *n.* v. A. 2. सुरेखपणा *m.* सुरेखाई *f.* साजरेपणा *m.* सुबकपणा *m.* &c. लवलक्षण *n.* कला *f.* खुबी *f.* खुमास *f.*

COMELY, *a. decent, becoming,* v. FIT. योग्य, उचित, लायक, शिस्त.

2 *graceful, handsome,* v. BEAUTIFUL. सुरेख, साजरा, गोजरा, गोजिरवाणा, सुबक, छबदार, छबडा, सुदर्शन, सुभावणा, सुरूप.

COMER, *n.* v. V. 1. येणारा, &c. आगम-आगमन-&c. कर्त्ता, आगामी.

COMET, *n.* धूमकेतु *m.* शेंडेनक्षत्र *n.*

Tail of a c. शेंडी *f.*

COMETARY, COMETIC, *a.* धूमकेतुसंबंधी-विषयक. [ठाई *f.*

COMFIT, COMFITURE, *n. dry sweetmeat.* कोरडा मोरब्बा *m.* मि-

To COMFORT, *v. a. cheer, enliven, &c.* v. To ENCOURAGE. आश्वासणें, आश्वासन *n.*-प्रोत्साहन *n.*- &c. करणें *g. of o.* धीर *m.*-धैर्य *n.* देणें.

2 *cheer under trouble.* v. To CONSOLE. सांतवणें, आश्वासणें, सांत्वन *n.*-समाधान *n.*-&c. करणें *g. of o.*

COMFORT, *n. relief or rest from pain, distress, &c.* v. EASE. सुख *n.* चैन *n.* समाधान *n.* स्वस्थपणा *m.* आराम *m.*

2 *solace under affliction,* See CONSOLATION. 3 *enjoyment, comfortableness.* सुख *n.* कुशल *n.* सुखापा *m.* सुखापा *m.* सुखावा *m.* सुखवा *m.* खुशाली *f.* सुगति *f.* संस्था *f.* सुखरूपता *f.* सुखीपणा *m.* स्वस्थता *f.* स्वास्थ्य *n.*

4 *ground or cause of c.* सुखहेतु *m.* सुखासकारण *n.* समाधानासकारण *n.* सुखसाधन *n.* सुखस्थान *n.* सुखास्पद *n.*

COMFORTABLE, *a.* v. N. 1. *relieved, easy.* स्वस्थ, समाधानी, आराम, आराम पावलेला, समाधान पावलेला, हायसा, प्राप्तसमाधान, जातसमाधान, गतदुःख, गतपीड.

2 *consoled, composed, &c.* शांत, स्वस्थ, समाधानी, सुमना *or* सुमनस्क, समाधान पावलेला, प्राप्तसमाधान, जातसमाधान, गतखेद, गतशोक.

3 *having enjoyment, c. or ease.* खुशाल, स्वस्थ, कुशल *or* ल, सुखी, सुखरूप, सुखाचा, स्वस्तिक्षेम, सुगति, सुगतिक, सुखापन्न, सुखसंपन्न, सुचित्त, संस्थित, सुस्थ.

To feel c. सुखास पडणें-येणें-वाटणें-*inverse & impers.*

I. *convenient, &c.* v. COMMODIOUS. सुखाचा, सोईचा, सोईवार, सोईसार, सुखद, सुखप्रद, सुखावह, यथासुख.

II. *affording c. or consolation,* v. CONSOLATORY. शांतिकारक, शांतिदायक, शोकापह, क्लेशापह, दुःखहारक, शोकहारक.

COMFORTABLENESS, *n.* v. A. 1. स्वस्थपणा *m.* आरामी *f.* स्वस्थता *f.* स्वास्थ्य *n.*

3 सुखीपणा *m.* सुखरूपपणा *m.* सुखरूपता *f.* सुखिता *f.* सुखावस्था *f.* संस्था *f.* संस्थिति *f.* स्वास्थ्य *n.*

I. सोई *f.* सोईवारपणा *m.* सोईसारपणा *m.*

II. शांतिदायकत्व *n.* शांतिकारकत्व *n.* &c.

COMFORTABLY, *adv.* v. A. 3. सुखानें, सुखसमाधानानें, सुखरूप, सुखेनैव, खुशाल, सुदामत, सुचित्त, सहल, यथासुख.

II. समाधान-सुख-&c. वाटेसा-होईसा, *a. decl.*

COMFORTED, *p.* v. V. 2. सांतवलेला, &c. आश्वासित, प्राप्तसमाधान, जातसमाधान.

COMFORTER, *n.* COMFORTING, *p. a.* v. V. 2. सांतवणारा, समाधानकरणारा, &c. आश्वासक, आश्वासनकर्त्ता, सांत्वनकर्त्ता-कारक-कारी, दुखहारक, शोकहारक.

I.—woolen c. गळ्यास गुंडाळण्याकरितां लोकरीची पट्टी *f.*

COMFORTING, *n.* v. V. 2.—*act.* सांतवणें *n.* आश्वासन *n.* सांत्वन *n.* दुःखापहरण *n.* क्लेशापहरण *n.* दुःखहरण *n.* शोकहरण *n.*

COMFORTLESS, *a.* v. N. 1. 2. 3. असुखी, असमाधानी, अस्वस्थ, सुखहीन, दुःखाचा, शांतिहीन-रहित-&c.

I. गैरसोईचा, गैरलागींचा, सुखसाधनरहित.

COMIC, COMICAL, *a. relating to comedy.* हास्यरस प्रधान नाटक संबंधी-विषयक.

2 *droll, queer, odd.* कौतुकी, हास्यकारक-जनक-&c. हसवायाजोगा, तऱ्हेचा, तऱ्हेदार, तऱ्हेवाईक.

COMICALNESS, *n.* v. A. 2. कौतुक *n.* कौतुकपणा *m.* तऱ्हेवाईकपणा*m.*

COMING, *n.* v. V. 1.—*and* APPROACH. येणें *n.* पावणें *n.* आगम *m.* आगमन *n.* [मन *n.*

C. and going. येणें जाणें *n.* येवा जावा *m.* येजा *f.* गमनाग-

COMITY, *n. suavity of manners,* v. COURTEOUSNESS. सुजनता *f.* सौजन्य *n.* अनुनय *m.*

COMMA, *n.* एक बिरामचिन्ह आहे, तें असें (,).

To COMMAND, *v. a. order, direct, bid.* आज्ञा *f.*-हुकूम*m.*-&c. करणें-देणें, आज्ञापणें, सांगणें, सांगणी *f.*-सांगी *f.* करणें,—strictly, positively, &c. *enjoin, charge, &c.* सरावणें, बजावणें, तटकारणें, खडसावणें, खडसणें, जतावणें, सरावून-बजावून-खडसून-हडसून-हटकून-&c. सांगणें-बोलणें-&c.—as used of the *intimation of their pleasure,* of kings, &c. फरमावणें.

2 *bear rule over.* हुकुमत *f.*-शासन*n.*-स्वामित्व*n.*-आधिपत्य*n.*-सत्ता *f.*-सरदारी *f.*-सरदारकी *f.*-अमल *m.*-धनीपणा *m.*-&c. करणें -चालवणें *with* वर *of o.*

3 *overlook, &c.* रोंखणें, लक्षणें, गजणें, अटोक्यांत-अटोण्यांत-माऱ्यांत-रोखांत-&c. ठेवणें and *with in. con.* असणें (as हा गांव त्या डोंगराच्या माऱ्यांत आहे).

COMMAND, COMMANDMENT, *n. mandate, order, precept, &c.* आज्ञा *f.* आदेश *m.* शासन *n.* हुकूम *m.* विधि *m.* विधान *n.* अनुज्ञा *f.* चोदना *f.* कह्या *m.* निदेश *m.* निर्देश *m.* नियोग *m.*—as used *of the intimation of their pleasure,* of kings, &c. परमाश *or* स *f.* अनुज्ञा *f.* [ज्ञांकित.

That is under the c. of. हुकमती, हुकमी, हुकुमबंदा, आ-

2 v. RULE. हुकमत *f.* शासन *n.* नायकी *f.*-स्वामित्व *n.* आधिपत्य *n.* सरदारी *f.* [दारी *f.*

3 *military charge.* तैनात *f.* तसलमात *f.* जमातदारी *or* जमा-

COMMANDANT, *n.* COMMANDER, *n.* COMMANDING, *p. a.* v. V. 1. आज्ञा-हुकूम-&c. करणारा-देणारा, आज्ञापक.

2 हुकमत-शासन-स्वामित्व धनीपणा-&c. करणारा, चालविणारा, अधिपति, नायक, सरदार, सरखेल, जमातदार *or* जमादार.

C. in chief. सेनापति, सेनाधिपति, बख्शी *or* षी *or* बक्षी, सेनानायक, सैन्याध्यक्ष.

COMMANDED, *p.* v. V. 1. आज्ञापलेला, &c. आज्ञापित, आज्ञप्त, आज्ञात, आनुज्ञात, आदिष्ट, विध्युक्त. [क.

COMMATERIAL, *a.* v. CONSUBSTANTIAL. समद्रव्यक, समानद्रव्य-

COMMATERIALITY, *n.* v. A. द्रव्यसमता *f.* द्रव्यसाम्य *n.*

To COMMEMORATE, *v. a. call to remembrance by a solemn act.* उत्सव*m.*-स्मरणोत्सव*m.*-स्मृत्युत्सव*m.*-सोत्सवस्मरण*n.*-व्रतोत्सव *m.* करणें *g. of o.* उत्सवानें आठवण *f.* करणें *g. of o.*

COMMEMORATION, *n.* v. V.—*act.* उत्सव *m.* स्मृतिपूर्वकोत्सव *m.* स्मृत्युत्सव *m.* स्मरणोत्सव *m.*

COMMEMORATIVE, COMMEMORATORY, *a.* v. V. आठवणुकीचा, स्मारक, स्मरणाधायक.

To COMMENCE, COMMENCEMENT, &c. See To BEGIN, &c.

To COMMEND, *v. a.* v. To RECOMMEND. शिफारस *f.* करणें *g. of o.*

2 *intrust,* v. To COMMIT. सोपणें, समर्पणें, निरवणें.

3 v. To PRAISE. स्तुति *f.*-स्तव *m.* करणें *g. of o.*

COMMENDABLE, *a. laudable,* v. PRAISEWORTHY, स्तवायाजोगा, &c. स्तवनीय, स्तवनार्ह, स्तुत्य.

COMMENDABLENESS, *n.* v. A. स्तवनीयता *f.* स्तवनार्हता *f.*

COMMENDABLY, *adv.* v. A. स्तवायाजोगा *a. decl.* &c.

COMMENDATION, *n.* v. V. 1. शिफारस *f.*

3 v. PRAISE. स्तुति *f.* स्तव *m.* प्रशंसा *f.*

COMMENSAL, *a.* v. N. पंक्तिव्यवहाराचा, &c. समपंक्तीचा, एकपंक्तीचा, एकभक्त.

COMMENSALITY, COMMENSATION, *n. eating together.* एकताटीजेवणें *n.* पंक्तिव्यवहार*m.* अन्नव्यवहार *m.* पंक्तिभोजन*n.* सहभोजन*n.* एकपंक्तिभोजन*n.* पंक्तिसंसर्ग*m.*

COMMENSURABILITY, COMMENSURABLENESS, *n.* v. A. समपरिमाणता *f.* समपरिमाणभाव*m.* सममानता *f.*

COMMENSURABLE, COMMENSURATE, *a. having equal extent, &c.* सारख्यापरिमाणाचा, समपरिमाण, सममान, समान, सममात्र, समप्रमाणक.

To COMMENT, *v. n. make notes, annotations, &c.* टीका *f.*-भाष्य *n.*-विवरण*n.*-व्याख्या *f.*-व्याख्यान*n.*-टिप्पण*n.*-टिप्पणी *f.*-&c. करणें. [करणें.

2 *remark censoriously.* टीका *f.*-व्याख्या *f.*-परिभाषण *n.*-&c.

COMMENT, *n.* टीका *f.* भाष्य*n.* आदर्श*m.* विवरण*n.* व्याख्या *f.* अवतरण*n.* अवतरणिका *f.*

COMMENTARY, *n. book of annotations, &c.* टीका *f.* टीकाग्रंथ*m.* भाष्य*n.* आदर्श*m.*

2 *historical narrative.* बखर *f.*

To COMMENTATE, See To COMMENT.

COMMENTATOR, COMMENTER, *n.* v. V. 1. टीका-&c. करणारा, टीकाकार, टीकाकर्त्ता, भाष्यकार, भाष्यकर्त्ता, व्याख्याकार, व्याख्याकर्त्ता.

COMMERCE, *n.* v. TRADE. देणें घेणें*n.* दे घे *f.* उदीम *m.* व्यापार*m.* व्यवहार*m.* व्यवसाय*m.* सट्टा*m.* क्रयविक्रय*m.*

2 v. INTERCOURSE. दळणवळण*n.* दळवटा*m.* वहिवाट *f.*

C. of the sexes. स्त्रीपुरुषसंग*m.*

COMMERCIAL. *a.* v. N. 1. उदिमाचा, व्यवहाराचा, व्यापाराचा, &c. उदीमसंबंधी, व्यवहारसंबंधी, व्यावहारिक *pop.* व्यवहारीक, सौदागरी.

The c. interest. सावसावकारा*m.*

COMMINATION, COMMINATORY. See THREAT, THREATENING.

To COMMINGLE, *v. a.* v. To MIX. मिसळणें, एकमेळ*m.*-सम्मीलन *n.* करणें *g. of o.*

To COMMINGLE, *v. n.* v. To MIX. मिसळणें, एकमेळ*m.* होणें.

To COMMINUTE, *v. a.* v. To PULVERIZE. चूर्ण*n.*-पूड *f.*-&c. करणें *g. of o.* चूर्णिकरण*n.* करणें *g. of o.*

To COMMISERATE, COMMISERATION. See To PITY, PITY.

COMMISSARIAT, *n.* मोदीखाना*m.*

C.-supplies. कोठी *f.*

COMMISSARY, *n.* (of an army). कोठीवाला*m.* मोदी*m.*

2 See COMMISSIONER.

COMMISSION, *n.* v. V. (To COMMISSION.)—*act.* अखत्यार देणें*n.* नियोग करणें*n.* &c. नियोजन*n.* नियोग*m.*

2—*act.* फरमास करणें*n.*

I. See COMMITTING. 2. 3. II. *authority given, charge, trust.* हवाला*m.* अखत्यार*m.* शेरा*m.* नियोग*m.*

III. *paper conveying authority.* सनद *f.* मुखत्यारनामा*m.* अखत्यारनामा*m.* हुकूमनामा*m.* पत्रक*n.* आज्ञापत्र *n.* शासनपत्रक*n.*

IV.—in commerce; *order.* फरमाश *or* स *f.*

V. *allowance made to a factor, &c.* दस्तुरी *f.* अडत *f.* दलाली *f.*

To Commission, *v. a. authorize, empower, warrant.* अखत्यारm.-मुखत्यारी f.-अधिकारm.-हुकूमm.-सनद f.-&c. देणें, नियोगm.-&c. करणें g. of o. नियुक्त-अधिकृत-&c. करणें.
 2—in commerce; *order.* फरमास or फरमाश f. करणें-देणें.

Commissioned, *p.* v. V. 1. मुखत्यारी पावलेला-दिल्हेला, अखत्यार दिल्हेला-पावलेला, अधिकृत, नियुक्त, नियोजित.
 2 फरमाशी or सो, काढींव, काढाऊ.

Commissioner, *n. person commissioned.* अमीनm. अखत्यारी, मुनीमm. करोडाm.

To Commit, *v. a. consign, intrust, deliver to.* सोपणें, हवालणें, गुजरणें, निरवणें, ओपणें, हवालां-हवालीं-हातीं-स्वाधीन-&c. करणें-ठेवणें-देणें, पदरीं घालणें, अर्पणें, समर्पणें, निरवणी f.-निरवणूक f.-समर्पणn-&c. करणें g. of o.
 To c. with confidence. विश्वासणें, पात्यवणें.
 To c. to memory. पाठ-तोंडपाठ-मुखपाठ- कंठ-मुखोद्गत-कंठगत-&c. करणें.
 2 (a work or business,unto). गुजरणें, ओपणें, घालणें, टाकणें, आरोपणें, संकल्पिणें, हवालणें, सांगणें, दिम्मतीस-तैनातीस-तसलमातीस-दुमाल्यास-पागेस-विल्हेस-&c. लावणें-घालणें-देणें g. of s. माथां or माथीं मारणें, गळयांत घालणें, ओझें n.-भार m.-माळ f.-माळखंडn.-&c. गळयांत घालणें, स्वाधीन-हातीं-&c. करणें-ठेवणें-देणें, पदरीं घालणें.
 3 *perpetrate,* v. To Do. करणें.
 4 *send to for imprisonment.* तुरुंगांत-&c. पाठवणें, कैद होण्यासाठीं पाठवणें, कारागृह प्रेषण n.-काराप्रेषण n. करणें.

Committee, *n.* पंचाईत f. पंच m. pl. नियुक्तसभा f. कामिटी f. from the English word is common.

Committing, Commitment, *n.* v. V. 1.—*act.* सोपणें n. निरवणें n. हवालणें n. &c. निरवणी f. निरवणूक f. अर्पण n. समर्पण n. विधाम n.
 2—*act.* गुजरणें n. आरोपणें n. &c. आरोपण n. आरोप m.
 4 तुरुंगांत पाठवणें n. &c. कारागृहप्रेषण n. काराप्रेषण n.

To Commix. See To Mix.

Commode, *n.* मलविसर्जनाच्या सोईची पेटी f.

Commodious, *a. convenient, accommodate, comfortable.* सोईचा, सुखाचा, सोईवार, सोईसार, उपयुक्त, उपयोगी, अनुकूल, यथानुकूल, यथासुख, यथापेक्ष.

Commodiously, *adv.* v. A. सोईवार, सोईसार, आनुकूल्यपूर्वक.

Commodiousness, *n.* v. A. सोई f. सोईवारपणा m. सोईसारपणा m. उपयुक्तता f. उपयोग m. आनुकूल्य n. अनुकूलता f. लाग m. यथानुकूल्य n. यथापेक्षत्व n.

Commodity, *n. item of wares or goods.* जिन्नस m. केणें n. सौदा m. माल m.
 Commodities,—compreh. *wares, goods, merchandise.* जिन्नस m. pl. जिन्नसपानस m. pl. हरजिन्नस m. pl. माल m. सौदा m.

Commodore, *n.* अरमाराच्या तुकडीचा अधिकारी.

Common, *a. belonging to more than one.* सामान्या,साधारण, सामायिक pop. समाईक, अनेकसामान्य, अनेकसाधारण, बहुसाधारण, बहुसामान्य, अनेकसत्ताक, सामान्यसत्ताक, साधारणसत्ताक, अनेकस्वामिक, सामान्यस्वामिक, अन्यसाधारण, औत्सर्गिक.
 In common. समाईकपणानें, साधारणपणें.
 2 *belonging to the public, having no separate owner.* सर्वांचा, सर्वांच्या सत्तेंतला, सर्वसाधारण, साधारणसत्ताक, सामान्यसत्ताक, सर्वसत्ताक, साधारणस्वामिक, सर्वस्वामिक, अविशेषस्वामिक, अविशिष्टस्वामिक, अपरिछिन्नस्वामिक, सर्वजनोपयोगी, सर्वोपभोग्य, सर्वोपयुक्त.
 A c. woman, *prostitute, &c.* सामान्या f. साधारणस्त्री f.
 3 *belonging to all, universal, general.* सर्वांचा, सर्वांच्या संबंधाचा, &c. सर्वसाधारण, सर्वसंबंधी, सर्वविषयक, आपामरसाधारण, सार्वजनिक, सार्वजनीन, सर्वमय, सार्ववर्णिक, सरीसर्वत्राचा.
 4 *public, popular, general.* लोकांचा, लोकांतला, लोकांच्यातोंडांतला, लोकांच्या व्यवहारांतला, लौकिक, प्रसिद्ध, लोकप्रसिद्ध, लोकसिद्ध, लोकरूढींतला, लोकरूढीचा, जनपरिपाटींतला, &c.
 5 *not rare or scarce,* v. Abundant. बहुत, पुष्कळ, विपुल, प्रचुर, मुबलक, प्रायिक, अविरल,वाटेवर पडलेला, रानोमाळ पडलेला.
 6 *ordinary, customary, usual, frequent.* परिपाठाचा, परिपाठांतला, परिपाटीचा, व्याबहारिक pop. व्यवहारिक or रीक, व्यवहाराचा, व्यवहारांतला, प्रायिक, अविरल, रोजचा, नित्यांतला, बहिवाटींतला, राबत्यांतला.
 7—of persons, *not noble.* सामान्य, सामान्य प्रतीचा, सामान्य पदवीचा, साधारण प्रतीचा, साधारण पदवीचा, प्राकृत, हीनकुल, हीनजात.
 8—of things, *ordinary, not excellent, for daily use, &c.* हलका, खरची, वागायाचा, वापरण्याचा, खैराती, चालीचा, नित्यघालायाचा, नित्याचा, नित्यबहिवाटीचा, राशी, रासवट, साधारण, सामान्य, बाजारी, बाजारू, उणाख, छोटेखानी, प्राकृत.
 That is above c. असाधारण, अधिकोत्तर.
 9—in grammar,—verb. उभयविध.
 C. gender. सामान्यलिंग n.
 C. noun सामान्य नाम n.
 10—ceremonially, *neither defiled nor quite pure.* ओवळा.

Common, *n. common ground.* समाईकशेतn.-जमीन f.-&c.गायरान n. गोपचारm. गोचारm.

Common-law, *n.* देशाचारm. जनाचार m. लोकाचारm. रिवाजm.

Common-place, *a. trite, &c.* सामान्य, उष्टा, उच्छिष्ट, लोकोच्छिष्ट, रांडापोरांच्या तोंडचा.

Common-place-book, *n.* कोडपत्रेंn. pl. कोडn. गबाळग्रंथm. बहाड or बाडn. वेचे m.pl.

Common-sense, *n.* व्यवहारिकज्ञान n. लौकिकज्ञानn. अक्कल f.

Commonalty, *n. commons, common people,*v. People. सामान्यलोक m. pl. साधारण लोक m. pl. कुणबीमाळी m. pl. वाणी बकाल m.pl.

Commoner, *n. common person.* साधारणमनुष्यc. सामान्यमनुष्यc. साधारण पदवीचें मनुष्यn. छोटेखानी माणूसm. सामान्य पदवीचा गृहस्थm.

Commonly, *adv.* v. A. 4. 6. सामान्यतः, बहुतकरून, बहुधा, बहुशः, प्रायः, प्रायशः.

Commonness, *n.* v. A.1. सामान्यn. सामान्यता f. सामान्यभावm. साधारणत्वn. साधारण्यn. अनेकसाधारण्यn. बहुसाधारण्यn. चौघाचारm. अनेकसत्ताकत्वn. अनेकस्वामिकत्वn.
 2 सर्वसाधारणता f. सर्वसाधारण्यn. साधारणस्वामिकत्वn. सामान्यस्वामिकत्व n. &c.
 3 सर्वसंबंधिता f. आपामरसाधारणता f.आपामरसाधारण्यn. &c.
 4 लौकिकपणाm. प्रसिद्धपणाm. रूढि f. प्रसिद्धि f. लोकप्रसिद्धि f. लौकिकत्वn. लोकसिद्धता f. प्रचारm.

5 पुष्कळपणाm. मात f. प्राचुर्यn. बाहुल्यn. बैपुल्यn. प्रायिकताf. प्रायिकत्वn. अविरलता f.
6 प्रायिकता f. प्रायिकत्वn. अविरलता f.
8 रासवटपणाm. बाजारीपणाm. हलकेपणाm. &c. सामान्यता f.
10 ओंवळेपणाm.

COMMONS, n. See COMMONALTY. 2. House of c. लोकप्रतिनिधी ह्यांची सभा. [n. गणान्न n.
3 *food provided at a common table*, v. FOOD. बिशीचें अन्न

COMMONWEAL, COMMONWEALTH, n, v. REPUBLIC. लोकसत्ताक राज्य n.
2 *the public*, v. COMMUNITY. लोक mpl. समाकुल मंडळी f.

COMMOTION, n, *perturbation*, v. AGITATION. क्षोभm. व्याक्षोभm. संतापm. व्यग्रता f.
2 *combustion, &c.* v. TUMULT. गडबड f. हडबड or डी f. हुलड or हुल्लड f. हूल f. बंडाळ or ळी f. खूळn.

To COMMOVE. See To AGITATE.

To COMMUNE, *To* COMMUNICATE, *v. n. hold intercourse.* संघट्टणें, बोलणेंn.-बोलणेंचालणेंn.-डळणn.-दळणवळणn.-वळणदळण n.-वळणn.-वलवटाm.-संघट्टनn.-संघट्टना f.-संसर्गm.-&c. ठेवणें-करणें-राखणें *and with in. con.* असणें.
2 *confer together or with*, v. To CONVERSE. संभाषणn.-संलापm.-&c. करणें, परस्पर गोष्टी f.pl. सांगणें-करणें.
3 *partake of the Lord's supper.* प्रभुभोजनn. घेणें.

COMMUNICABLE, a. v. V. A. 1. देण्याजोगा-&c. देय, अन्यदेय.
2 कळविण्याजोगा-&c. निवेद्य, निवेदनीय.

COMMUNICANT, n. प्रभुभोजन घेणारा.

To COMMUNICATE, *v. a. impart*, v. To GIVE. देणें, दानn.-उपधानn.-&c. करणें g. of o. सहभोगm.-संभोगm. करविणें g.of o.
2 *reveal, disclose*, v. To TELL. कळवणें, जाणविणें, बोधविणें, निवेदणें, निवेदनn. करणें g.of o. जाहीर-माहीत-विदित-&c.करणें.

To COMMUNICATE, *v. n. have a passage from one to the other.* जाण्यायेण्याचा रस्ताm.-मार्गm.-संबंधm. असणें in. con.

COMMUNICATION, n. v. V. A. 1.—*act.* देणेंn. दानn. प्रदानn. उपधानn. निवेदन n.
2—*act.* कळवणेंn. सांगणेंn. निवेदनn.
I. *communion*, v. INTERCOURSE. वळणn. दळणवळणn. वळणदळणn. डळणn. संसर्गm. [बोलाचाली.
II. *conference, colloquy*, v. CONVERSATION. बोलाबोली f.
III. *line, means, &c. of c.* लगा m. v. लाव,जाण्यायेण्याचा संबंध m.-रस्ता m.-मार्ग m.
IV. *matter communicated*, v. MESSAGE. निरोप m. संदेश m.

COMMUNICATIVE, a. *not reserved.* सांगण्याचाआवडता, बोलका, मोकळ्या मनाचा, कथनोत्सुक, कथनप्रवण, कथनपरायण.

COMMUNION, n. v. INTERCOURSE. वळण n. वळणदळण n. दळणवळण n. संसर्ग m. [व्यवहार m.
2 *intercourse or union in worship, &c.* धर्मसंबंध m. भजन-
3 *celebration of the Lord's supper.* प्रभुभोजनोत्सव m.

COMMUNITY, n. *common possession or enjoyment.* समाईक मालकी f. समाईक धनीपणा m. साधारण प्रभुत्व n. साधारण स्वामित्व n. साधारणसत्ता f.
2 *commonwealth, public body, public.* पांढर f. शाई f. लोकm. pl. मंडळी f. रयासत f. जमात f. खलकत f. The sense of the word is often expressed by the words. देश m. राष्ट्र n. गांव m. &c.

To COMMUTE, &c. See To EXCHANGE, &c.

COMPACT, a. *close, dense, solid*, v. FIRM. घट or घट्ट, घटमूट, दृढ, सदृढ, सुदृढ, दाट, दाट धमकट, कुब्बल, खंबीर, घन, घनीकृत, जंजीरबंद, सांद्र.
2 *close-set, thick-set, strong-knit, well-knit.* अटस, अटींव, अटकर, बांधेशुद्ध, गट्ट, गटू or ठू, घटींव, दृढसंधि, बळींव, ताठर, अटोपसार, अटोपशुद्ध, अटपता, सुटसुटीत, सुटखुटीत, सणसर, सणसणीत, काकट or काकड, बंदिस्त, बंदिस्ती,जंजीरबंद, सुप्रयुक्त, संहत.
3 *not diffuse or verbose.* अटोपसार, अटपता, सुसंबद्ध, सुप्रयुक्त, पुष्टार्थ, पुष्टार्थक.

COMPACT, n. *contract*, v. AGREEMENT. बोली f. होड f. प्रतिज्ञा f. संकेत m. समय m.

To COMPACT, v. a. v. A. 1. घट-दृढ-दाट-घन-&c. करणें.
2 See To COMPOSE, To MAKE.

COMPACTNESS, n. v. A. 1. खंबिरी f. घटमूटपणा m. घट्टपणा m. &c. घट्टाई f. दृढता f. सुदृढता f. दाढर्य n. द्रढिमा m. नैरंतर्य n. नैबिड्य n. घनीभाव m. घनता f.
2 अटसपणा m. गट्टपणा m. अटोपशुद्धपणा m. &c. कटाव m. अंगदार्ढ्य n. दृढसंधिता f. सुप्रयुक्तता f. संहति f.
3 अटोपसारपणा m. &c. सुसंबद्धता f. सुप्रयुक्तता f.

COMPAGES, COMPACTURE, n. *naked structure.* सांगाडा m. मांडणूक f. मांडावळ f. मांडणावळ f.

COMPANION, n. *one who accompanies another.* बराबरचा, संगति pop. संगती or संगाती, सोबती, सहचर, सहचारी, सहयायी, सहगामी, संयाची, सहाय, पक्षचर, पार्श्विक, संगत.
Companions and associates,—compreh. *or* gener. संगती सोबती *or* सोबती संगती m. pl.
2 *associate, comrade, partner*, v. FELLOW. साथी, सोबती, संगति pop. संगती or संगाती, गडी, गडा, सहाय, संगबई or यी.
3 *intimate associate*, v. FRIEND. सखा, खेळीमेळीचा, अनुषंगी, सहवासी.
Female c. or friend. सखी f. सहेली f. सय f. साजणी f. परिचारिका f.

COMPANIONSHIP, n. v. N. 1. संग m. संगत f. सोबत f. सहगमनn. सहगति f. समागम m. साहचर्य n. सहचरण n.
2 संग m. संगती pop. संगत f. साथ f. सोबत f. साथीपणा m. गडी f. साह्य n. साहित्य n. साहाय्य n. साहचर्य n.
C. or fellowship,—compreh. *or* indef. सोबतसंगत f. संगतसोबत f.
Closeness of c. जवळीक f.
In constant or close c. संगेमंगे.
3 सख्य n. सहवास m. सखित्व n. साख्य n. पंक्ति pop. पंगत f. अनुषंग m. साहाय्य n.

COMPANY, n. *body, troop, multitude*, v. BAND. मंडली or ळी f. मंडल n. टोळी f. जमात f. जथा m. झुंड f.
2 *assembly for conversation, &c. party.* मंडळी f. बैठक f. सभा f. चक्री f. चाकोळें or चाखोळें n. कचोळें n. चारमंडळी f.
Address in c. सभाचातुर्य n.
Bold or confident in c. सभाधीट, सभाशूर.
Boldness or confidence in c. सभाधैर्य n. [सभारत्न n.
The grace or ornament of a c. सभादीप m. सभादीपक m.
Self-possession in c. सभास्फूर्ति f.

Suitable to good c. सभोचित, सभ्य.
Sweetmeats served to c. at breaking up. खिरापत *f.*
Timid or diffident in c. सभाभीरु.
Timidity or diffidence in c. सभाकंप *m.*
3 *companionship, society, consociation, consorting.* संगति *pop.* संगत *f.* संग *m.* संगम *m.* समागम *m.* सोबत *f.* गडी *f.* पंक्ति *pop.* पंगत *f.* अनुषंग *m.* सहचरण *n.* सहाचर्य *n.* साथ *f.* साहित्य *n.* साह्य *n.* संसृष्टत्व *n.* [कुसंगति.
Bad c. दुष्टसंग, दुर्जनसंग, असत्संग, खलसंग, दुःसंग, कुसंग,
Good c. सत्संग, साधुसंग, सुसंग, सत्संगति, सुसंगति, सत्समागम.
In the c. of (or in connection with). संगतीं *or* तें, संगीं *or* गें *g. of o.*
The keeping bad c. हीनसख्य *n.* हीनसमागम *m.* खलसंसर्ग *m.* असत्संसर्ग *m.*
The keeping good c. सत्संग *m.* सत्संसर्ग *m.* सत्सन्निधान *n.*
Virtue of c. संगतगुण *m.*
Bad c. leads to ruin. असंगासीं संग प्राणासीं गांठ.
Man is according to his c. कसीगेसुमे? घरासारखी. There is also a Hindustání proverb of the same import. पाणी तेरा रंग कैसा ? जिसमें मिलूंगा वैसा.
To bear c. To keep c. with. v. To Accompany. संग *m.*-सहवास *m.*- समागम *m.*-सोबत *f.*-&c. करणें *g. of o.*
4 *body corporate, association, society, corporation.* घर *n.* फड *m.* अखाडा *m.* अड्डा *m.* मंडळी *f.* जथा *m.* पंक्ति *pop.* पंगत *f.* श्रेणि *m.f.*
5 (of a regiment). The English word under the form of कंपनी *f.* is commonly used.

To Company, *v. n. associate with,* v. To Accompany. संग *m.*-सहवास *m.*-सोबत *f.*-&c. धरणें.

Comparable, *a.* v. V. 1. पडताळाया-चा-जोगा-&c. मिळवून पाह्या-या-जोगा-जोगता-&c. तुळायाजोगा-&c. बरोबरीचा, तोलाचा, समतोल, समतुल्य.
2 उपमा करण्याचे योग्यतेचा, तुळायाजोगा-&c. उपमेय.

Comparates, *n.*—in logic. उपमानोपमेय *n.*

Comparative, *a. estimated by comparison.* अवधिसाकांक्ष, अवधिसापेक्ष, अन्यसापेक्ष, अन्यापेक्ष, सापेक्ष, सावधिक.
2—in grammar. See Comparison.

Comparatively, *adv.* v. A. तरतमभाव *m.*-तारतम्य *n.* पाहिलें असतां, बरोबरी केली असतां, मिळवून पाहिलें असतां, सापेक्ष.

To Compare, *v. a. examine by setting or bringing together.* जोडणें, जोडून पाहणें, तुळणें, पडताळणें, पडताळून पाहणें, पडताळा *m.*-ताळा *m.*-पडोसा *m.*-&c. पाहणें *g. of o.* मिळवून-लावून-ताडून-&c. पाहणें, रुजू घेणें, उमाणणें, उमापणें, तुलना *f.*-मुकाबला *m.*-रुजुमुकाबला *m.*-रुजुवात *f.*-&c. करणें-पाहणें *g. of o.*
2—in rhetoric, *illustrate, liken.* उपमा *f.*-तुलना *f.*-बरोबरी *f.* -&c. देणें-करणें, उपमणें, तुळणें, तोलणें. [&c. तुलित.

Compared, *p.* v. V. 1. जोडून-ताडून-पडताळून-&c. पाहिलेला,
2 तुळलेला, &c. उपमित, तुलित.

Comparison, Comparing, *n.* v. V. 1.—*act.* पडताळणें *n.* पडताळून पाहणें *n.* &c. पडताळा *m.* पडोसा *m.* मुकाबला *m.* रुजुमुकाबला *m.* रुजुवात *f.* तुलना *f.* उपमान *n.*
Standard or measure of c. अवधि *m.*
To stand a c. with. पडोशास उतरणें.
2 तुलना *f.* उपमान *n.*
I. In grammar the degrees of c. are expressed, 1st simply by the power of the particles हून, पेक्षां, परीस (answering to *than*) attached to the words, as याहून-त्या घोड्यापेक्षां-मजपरीस-हा चांगला &c.—there being no variation whatever of the adjective expressing the quality: 2dly, though less idiomatically, by the use, for the expression of the *comparative* degree, of अधिक *(more)* before the adjective, as अधिक चांगला *more good,* and, for the expression of the *superlative* degree of अति, परम, फार, *(extremely, utterly, &c.)* before the adjective, as अति चांगला *extremely good,* or of सर्वांहून, अवघ्यांहून &c. as सर्वांहून चांगला: 3dly, by the attachment, to *Sanskrit* adjectives, of the particles तर & तम for the *comparative* & *superlative* degrees respectively; as उच्चतर, इष्टतर-उच्चतम, इष्टतम, *higher, dearer, highest, dearest.*
II. *illustration,* v. Simile. उपमा *f.* दृष्टांत *m.*
Subject of c. उपमेय *n.*
III. *possibility of being compared, proportion &c.* बरोबरी *f.* तुलना *f.* तुल्यभाव *m.* सादृश्य *n.* उपमा *f.* साम्य *n.*

Compartment, *n. cell, partition,* v. Division. घर *n.* पड *m.n.* पूड *m. n.* खिसा *m.*

To Compass, *v. a. encircle, environ,* v. To Surround. घेरणें, वेढणें, वेष्टणें, घेरा *m.*-वेढा *m.*-&c. घालणें.
2 *attain,* v. To Accomplish. साधणें, सर करणें, प्राप्त करणें, सिद्ध करणें.
3 See To Circumambulate. 4 *purpose, devise,* v. To Intend. मनांत योजणें, बेत *m.* करणें *g. of o.*

Compass, *n.* v. Circumference. घेरा *m.* घेर *m.* परिधि *m.*
2 *circuitous route,* v. Circuit. फेरा *m.* गिरकांडा *m. dim.* गिरकांडी *f.* गरका *m.* वळसा *m.*
To fetch a c. गिरकांडा *m.*-फेरा *m.*-वळसा *m.*-गरका *m.*-&c. घेणें-मारणें, घिरटी *f.* घालणें.
3 *comprehension, inclusion, embrace, sphere, capacity.* पोट *n.* कव *f.* कवळ *n.* खातें *n.* हक्काटक्का *m.*
To come into a small c. संपुष्टांत येणें.
To contract into a small c. संपुष्टांत आणणें.
4 *range, extent,* v. Reach. अटोका *m.* अवांका *m.* पोहोंच *f. m.* धांव *f.* टप्पा *m.*
5 (of the voice). फेर *m.* घर *n.*
6 (of mariners). होका *m.* होकायंत्र *n.* मच्छयंत्र *n.*
Point of the c. दिशा *f.* दिग्विभाग *m.* The eight points are अष्टदिशा *f. pl.* and with inclusion of the *zenith and nadir* दशदिशा *f. pl.* The minor or remaining points are उपदिशा *f. pl.* विदिशा *f. pl.* The points collectively are. दिग्चक्र *n.*
Building open to all the points of the c. सर्वतोभद्र *n.*
Determining the points of the c. दिक्साधन *n.*
Elephant of one of the eight points. दिग्गज *m.*
To box the c. दिक्कथन *n.* करणें.
7 compasses. कर्कट *m.* कैवार *m.* कर्काटक *m.* [घृणा *f.*

Compassion, *n.* v. Pity. दया *f.* करुणा *f.* कारुण्य *n.* माया *f.*

Compassionate, *a.* v. **Pitiful.** दयाळू, दयावानू, दयाशील, करुण, कारुणिक, घृणी, कन्हवाळू, करुणार्द्र.

To **Compassionate.** See To **Pity.**

Compassionately, *adv.* v. A. दयेनें, दयाकरून, दयापूर्वक.

Compatibility, *n.* v. A. संभावना *f.* संभूति *f.* संभव *m.* संभाव्यता *f.* अविरोध *m.* विरोधाभाव *m.* सामानाधिकरण्य *n.*

Compatible, *a.* v. **Consistent.** जुळाया-चा-जोगा-जोगता-&c. जमाया-चा-जोगा-&c.संभावनीय,संभाव्य,अविरुद्ध,समानाधिकरण.

Compatibly, *adv.* v. A. जुळायाजोगा *a. decl.* संभवपूर्वक, विरोधाभावपूर्वक.

Compatriot, *n.* स्वदेशी, एकदेशीय, एकदेशी, सदेश.

Compeer, *n.* v. **Equal.** बरोबरीचा, समतोल, समकक्ष.

To **Compel**, *v. a. constrain, force, oblige, necessitate, make.* बळ *n* -बळजोरी *f.*-बळात्कार *m.*-जोर*m.*-जोरा *m.*-जोरावरी *f.*-&c. करणें-चालवणें *with* वर *of o.* बळें-बळजोरीनें-&c. करवणें-करवून घेणें-&c. बळेंच लावणें-योजणें-प्रवर्त्तवणें-&c. गळ *m.* घालणें, नाकीं वेसण घालून (*or* टोंचून) करवणें, भागपाडणें, भागासआणणें.

Compellation, *n.style of address, word of salutation.* टोपणनांव *n.* उपचारिकनाम *n.* पोषाकी-प्रतिष्ठित-&c. नांव *n.* बाहर्तेबोलावतें-&c. नांव *n.* The terms of *Compellation* are very numerous, and they are in constant use. As we have but few corresponding terms in English, they cannot be inserted in order, yet, as they are valuable, they must not be rejected. Here, accordingly, they are set down. Some are *respectful*, some *tender* or *affectionate*, some *familiar*, and some *contemptuous.* अजी, अजीबाई, अजोबा, अका, अण्णा, अपा, अबा, आत्या, आतू, काका, काकी, काकू, जी, जिजी, ताई, तात्या, तातोबा, दाजी, दादा, दादी, नाना, नानी, फुईजी *or* फुई, ब, बंधुराज, बया, बाई, बापू, बाबा, बावा, बाबू, भाईराज *or* भाइराय,भाओ *or* भाओजी,भावो *or* भावोजी, महाराज, मामजी *or* मामाजी, मामा, माई, रावजी, रावसाहेब, वनसें, वहिनी, साहेब. It may be here noted that names have commonly three forms, viz. the simple, the respectful, and the contemptuous; ex. महादू *or* माहदू, नबलू, येडू simple form; महादबा, महादजी, नवलूजी, येडनाक respectful form; महाद्या, नब्ऱ्या, येड्या contemptuous form.

Compendious, *a.*v. **Abridged.** थोडक्यांत आणलेला, संक्षेपाचा, संक्षिप्त, सांक्षेपिक, संक्षेपरूप, सामासिक, संहृत.

Compendiously, *adv.* v. A. संक्षेपानें, संक्षेपेंकरून, थोडक्यांत.

Compendiousness, *n.* v. A. संक्षेप *m.* संक्षिप्तता *f.*

Compendium, *n.* v. **Abridgment.** सारग्रंथ *m.* सारसंग्रह *m.* संक्षिप्तग्रंथ *m.*

To **Compensate**, *To* **Compense**, *v. a. recompense, make amends to for.* भरणें, भरून देणें, क्षतिपूरण *n.*-हानिपूरण *n.*-क्षतिनिष्कृति *f.*-हानिनिष्कृति *f.*-&c. करणें.

2 *be equivalent to.* बरोबर-समतोल-&c. होणें, बरोबरी *f.*करणें, पासंगास पुरणें *with neg. con.*

Compensater, *n.* **Compensating**, *p. a.* **Compensative**, *a.* v. V. तोटा भरून देणारा, क्षतिपूरक, हानिपूरक, हानिनिष्कारक.

Compensation, *n. equivalent given for loss, sufferings, &c.* नुकसानी-&c. बदल दिल्हेला पैसा *m.*-ऐवज *m.*-देणें *n.*-&c. हानिमूल्य *n.* तुष्टिकर *n.*

To **Compete**, *v. n. cope or vie with,* v. To **Rival.** बराबरी *f.* करणें *g. of o.* स्पर्धणें, प्रतिस्पर्धणें, तुळणें, डाली *f.*बांधणें, मांडीस मांडी *f.* टेकून बसणें, मणगटासीं मणगट *n.* घासणें.

Competence, **Competency**, *n.* v. A. पुरतेपणा *m.* सामर्थ्य *n.* लायकी *f.* योग्यता *f.* उपयुक्तता *f.* क्षमता *f.* कार्यक्षमता *f.* कर्मक्षमता *f.*

I. *easy fortune, good circumstances.* निर्वाहापुरतें धन *n.* द्रव्यानुकूल्य *n.* खागा भोगा पुरता (पैका *m.*संपत्ति *f.*द्रव्य *n.* &c.) योगक्षेमपर्याप्तधन *n.* ताजीरोटी *f.*

That enjoys a c. *that is in easy circumstances, comfortably provided, well off in the world, comfortable, happy, &c.* खातापिता, खाताजेवता, खाऊनजेवून खुशाल *or* सुखी, घरचासुखी, निर्दंदात *or* निर्दधात, सुखी, अलंजीविक, पर्याप्तभोग.

Competent, *a. qualified for, equal unto, adequate.* पुरता,पुरेसा, समर्थ, लायक, योग्य, उपयुक्त, पर्याप्त, कार्यक्षम, क्षम, कर्मक्षम, अलंकर्मीण, शक्त, कल्प, योग्यतासंपन्न.

To be competent to. अखत्यार*m.*-हक्क*m.*-&c. असणें.

Competently, *adv.* v. A. पुरता *a. decl.* कार्यापुरता *a. decl.* कार्याकारण.

Competition, *n.* v. V. *and* **Rivalry.** स्पर्धा *f.* प्रतिस्पर्धा *f.* बरकशी *or* बरकस *f.* हेवा*m.* चढाचढी *f.* एकार्थाभिलाष *f.* एकार्थाकांक्षा *f.* एकार्थ शत्रुत्व*n.*

Competitor, *n.* **Competing**, *p. a.* v.V. *and* **Rival.** प्रतिस्पर्धी, एकार्थाभिलाषी, एकार्थेच्छु, एकार्थप्रवृत्त,एकार्थदृष्टि, प्रतियोगी.

Compilation, **Compilement**, *n.* v.V.1.—*act.* संग्रहकरणें*n.* संग्रह*m.* संग्रहण*n.* संग्रहीकरण*n.* समाहरण*n.* समाहृति *f.*

I. *thing compiled.* संहिता *f.* संग्रह*m.* संग्रहग्रंथ*m.*

To **Compile**, *v. a. collect together.* संग्रह*m.*-संग्रहण*n.*-संग्रहीकरण*n.*-संहिता *f.*-&c. करणें *g. of o.*

2 *write.* See To **Compose.**

Compiler, *n.* v. V. 1. संग्रह कर्त्ता-कारी, संहिता कर्त्ता.

Complacence, **Complacency**, *n. pleasure, satisfaction of mind.* संतोष*m.* खुशी *f.* खुशाली *f.* प्रसन्नता *f.* चित्तप्रसन्नता *f.* चित्तप्रसाद*m.* चित्तस्वास्थ्य*n.* चित्तसंतोष*m.* चित्तसमाधान*n.*

2 See **Civility.**

Complacent, *a.* v. N. 1. खुशदिल, प्रसन्नचित्त, चित्तप्रसन्न, प्रीतात्मा, संतुष्ट, संतुष्टात्मा.

2 See **Civil.**

Complacently, *adv.* v. A. 1. संतोषानें, चित्तसंतोषानें, चित्तसमाधानानें, चित्तसंतोषपूर्वक.

To **Complain**, *v. n. lament, repine, mourn, &c.* रडणें, कळकळ्या *or* किळकिळ्या *f. pl.* देणें, हुरहुरणें, विल्हळणें, हळहळणें, हायहाय *f.*-खेद*m.*-विलाप*m.*-विपळाप*m.*-दुःखोद्गार*m.*-&c. करणें, दुःख *n.* करणें-धरणें-मानणें-भाकणें, रड *f.*-रडगाणें *n.* गाणेंसांगणें, विल्हळ*m.* लावणें.

To c. peevishly. किरकीर *f.*-पिरपीर *f.*-&c. करणें,किरकिरणें.

2 *represent injury or crime.* फिर्याद *f.* करणें-ठोकणें, नालिस्त *f.*-नालिस्ती *f.* करणें-सांगणें, गऱ्हाणें *n.*-गिल्ला *m.* सांगणें, दाद *f.* लावणें, अभियोग*m.* करणें.

3 (of pain, thirst, &c.). आहे असें म्हणणें.

Complainant, *n.* v. V. 2 फिर्यादकरणारा, &c. फिर्यादी, पूर्ववादी, भाषावादी, पूर्वपक्षी.

Complainer, *n.* **Complaining**, *p. a.* v. V. 1. दुःखकरणारा, रडणारा, विल्हळणारा, &c. किरकिरा *or* ऱ्या, पिरपिरा *or* ऱ्या,

बिल्हळ्या. Some terms for *a person ever complaining, (ever whining, moaning, &c.)* are रडका, रडवा, रड्या, रडतोंड्या, रडतलक्ष्मी, रडिवाल, रडताराऊत, दुखाळू;—and for a *female* esp. बिल्हळगौर, रडतलक्ष्मी, रडतगौरी, रडतपार्वती, रडवी.

COMPLAINT, COMPLAINING, *n.* v. N. 1.—*act.* रडणें*n.* बिल्हळणें*n.* &c. हुरहूर *f.* बिल्हाळ *or* बिल्हळ *m.* जिवाचा बिल्हाळ *m.* काकळूत *f.*

Peevish c. किरकीर *f.* पिरपीर *f.* टुरटूर *f.*

Piteous c. रड *f. v.* सांग, गा, रडगाणें*n.*

A string of piteous complaints. रडकथा *f.* रडकहाणी *f.*

2 फिर्याद *f.* नालीश *or* नालिस्त *or* स्ती *f.* दाद *f.* गिल्ला*m.* गऱ्हाणें*n.* कागाळी *or* गागाळी *f.*

To go or come to lodge a c. फिर्याद जाणें *or* येणें.

I.—in law; *charge*, v. ACCUSATION. वाद*m.* पूर्वपक्ष*m.* आक्षेप*m.*

II. *cause or ground of c.* दुःख*n.* रड *f.* गऱ्हाणें*n.* दुःखासकारण*n.* दुःखहेतु*m.* [*m.n.*

III. *malady, disease*, v. DISORDER. रोग *m.* दुखणें *n.* दरद *f.*-

COMPLAISANCE, *n.* v. A. 1. माणुसकी *f.* गृहस्थपणा*m.* गृहस्थगिरी*f.* अनुवृत्ति *f.* अनुरोध *m.*

COMPLAISANT, *a.* v. CIVIL. बोलूनचालून गोड, आदरमानी, सत्कारी, गोडबोल्या, अनुरोधी, अनुवर्त्ती.

2—deportment, &c. माणुसकीचा, गृहस्थपणाचा, सभ्यरीतीचा.

COMPLAISANTLY, *adv.* v. A. माणुसकीनें, गृहस्थपणानें, &c.

COMPLEMENT, *n. full quantity or number.* भरती *f.* भरगत *f.* भरतें *n.* भरणा *m.* भर *f.* भरताड *f.* भरतक *n.* पुरवणी *f.*

2 *quantity, &c. completing, supplement.* पुरवणी *f.* पूरण *n.* भर *f.* भरती *f.* भरण *f.*

C. of an arc to 90°. कोटि *f.*

C. of a segment. पीठ *f.*

COMPLEMENTAL, *a. completive, supplementary.* भरीचा, भरतीचा, पुरवणीचा, पूरक.

To COMPLETE, *v. a. make full or whole.* भरती *f.*-भरणा *m.*-पूर्त्ति *f.*-पूर्णता *f.*-&c. करणें *g. of o.* पुरा- पुरता-पूर्ण-&c. करणें.

2 *execute fully*, v. To ACCOMPLISH. पूर्ण-पुरा-पुरता-समाप्त-&c. करणें, सिद्धीस-शेवटास-तडीस-&c.-नेणें-आणणें.

3 (a period or term). भरणें, पूर्ण-पुरा-&c. करणें.

COMPLETE, *a.* COMPLETED, *p.* v. V. 1. पूर्ण &c. केलेला, पुरा, पुरता, पूर्ण, परिपूर्ण, संपूर्ण, पूरित, पूर्त्त, पर्याप्त, सुपर्याप्त, सांग, सोपस्कर, निःशेष, अन्यून.

2 पूर्ण केलेला, &c. पुरा, पुरता, तमाम, समाप्त, संपूर्ण, निष्पन्न, समापन्न, समापित, संसिद्ध, निर्वृत्त.

3 भरलेला, पूर्णकेलेला.

To be c. भरणें.

COMPLETELY, *adv. entirely*, v. WHOLLY. अगदी, तमाम, पूर्णपणें.

COMPLETENESS, COMPLETEDNESS, *n.* v. A. 1. पुरेपणा *m.* &c. पूर्णता *f.* परिपूर्णता *f.* संपूर्णता *f.* पूर्त्ति *f.* परिपूर्त्ति *f.*

2 पुरेपणा *m.* &c. संपूर्णता *f.* &c. समाप्ति *f.* निष्पत्ति *f.* संसिद्धि *f.* निर्वृत्ति *f.* इतिश्री *f.*

COMPLETION, *n.* v. V. 1.—*act.* पूर्णकरणें *n.* &c. पुरवणी *f.* पुरवणूक *f.* भरती *f.* भरणा *m.* पूरण *n.* परिपूरण *n.*—*state.* पुरेपणा *m.* पूर्णता *f.* परिपूर्णता *f.* संपूर्णता *f.* पूर्त्ति *f.* पर्याप्ति *f.* परिपूर्त्ति *f.*

2—*act.* पूर्णकरणें *n.* सिद्धीस नेणें *n.* &c. समापन *n.*—*state.* पुरेपणा *m.* &c. संपूर्णता *f.* &c. समाप्ति *f.* निष्पत्ति *f.* संसिद्धि *f.* निर्वृत्ति *f.*

To draw to c. आकारास येणें.

COMPLETIVE, *a.* v. V. 1. भरीचा, भरतीचा, पूरक.

COMPLEX, *a. not simple, composed of two or more parts.* अनेकवस्तुघटित, अनेकवस्तुमय, मिश्र, असरळ.

2 v. COMPLICATED. गुंतागुंतीचा, घोटाळ्याचा.

COMPLEXION, *n. color of the skin or external parts.* अंगवर्ण *m.* अंगकांति *f.* रंग *m.* वर्ण *m.* वाण *m.*

2 *temperament*, v. CONSTITUTION. प्रकृति *f.* स्वभाव *m.*

COMPLEXITY, COMPLEXNESS, v. A. 1. अनेकवस्तुघटितत्व *n.*

2 गुंतागूत *f.* घोटाळा *m.*

COMPLIANCE, *n.* v. V.—*act.* मान्य करणें *n.* कबूल करणें *n.* &c. स्वीकार *m.* रुकार *m.* मान्यता *f.* अनुवर्त्तन *n.* अनुरोध *m.* वचनग्रहण *n.*

To yield c. बधणें.

v. A. 2. *and* CIVILITY. अनुवृत्ति *f.* अनुलक्ष्य *n.*

COMPLIANT, *a. yielding, tractable*, v. OBEDIENT. विनयी, विनयस्थ, विनीत, विनयग्राही, वचनग्राही, वचनेंस्थित, विधेय, अनुविधायी.

To make c. बधविणें.

2 *obliging, conceding*, v. CIVIL. अनुरोधी, अनुवर्त्ती, विनयी, सत्कारी, सभ्य, सानुनय.

To COMPLICATE, *v. a. involve*, v. To ENTANGLE. गुंतवणें, गुरफटणें *or* गुरफटणें *or* गुरफाटणें, गळफटणें, गुतागूत *f.* करणें *g. of o.*

COMPLICATE, *a.* COMPLICATED, *p.* v. V. गुंतवलेला, &c. गुंतागुंतीचा, गुंफागुंफीचा, गळफट्याचा, गुरफाट्याचा, घोटाळ्याचा, गुंताडीचा, गुतवळीचा, गुंताड्याचा.

COMPLICATION, *n.* v. V.—*act.* गुंतवणें *n.* गुरफटणें*n.* &c.—*state.* गुंताड *f.* गुंताडा *m.* गुतवळ *f.* गळफटा *m* गुरपटा *or* फटा *or* फाटा *n.* गुतागूत *f.* जाळें *n.* गोंधळ *m.*

COMPLIMENT, *n. expression of approbation, civility, &c.* स्तुतिवाद*m.* स्तुतिवचन*n.* स्तुतिवाक्य*n.* स्तवोक्ति *f.* आदरवचन*n.*

Hollow compliments. पैटणी आदर *m.* शुष्कोपचार *m.*

2 compliments;—as sent or conveyed. रामराम *m.* सलाम *m. pl.*—amongst Brâhmans. नमस्कार *m.*

Interchange of c. सलामी *f.*

To COMPLIMENT. See To PRAISE.

COMPLIMENTAL, COMPLIMENTARY, *a.* v. N. 1. स्तुतीचा, स्तुतिवाचक, स्तुति ज्ञापक-बोधक-&c. आदराचा, आदरदर्शक-सूचक-&c. उपचाराचा, औपचारिक.

COMPLOT, &c. See PLOT, &c.

To COMPLY, *v. n. yield to, accede to*, v. To AGREE. मान्य-कबूल-&c. करणें, रुकार *m.* देणें, स्वीकारणें, स्वीकार *m.* करणें, वचनग्रहण *n.*-अनुवर्त्तन *n.*-&c. करणें. [अंगभूत.

COMPONENT, *a. that constitutes, forms, &c.* अंशभूत, अवयवभूत,

COMPONENT, *n. constituent part.* अंशभूत-अवयवभूत-अंगभूत पदार्थ *m.*-विषय *m.*-&c.

To COMPORT. See To AGREE. 2 (one's self) See To BEHAVE.

COMPORT, COMPORTMENT. See BEHAVIOUR.

COMPOS MENTIS, *a. sane.* शुद्धीवर-स्थितीवर असणारा, अविक्षिप्त.

To COMPOSE, *v. a. constitute, form.* अंगभूत-अवयवभूत-अंशभूत असणें *in. con.* करणें, बनवणें, *or* बनावणें.

2 *lay, calm, still, tranquilize, quiet, &c.* शांतवणें *or* सांतवणें,

संतावणें *or* संथावणें, स्वस्थावणें, बसवणें, शमविणें, निवविणें, शांत-स्वस्थ-स्थिर-थंड-&c. करणें, शम *m*.-शमन *n*.-शांति *f*.-प्रशमन *n*.-उपशमन *n*.-&c. करणें *g. of o.* संतापहरण *n*. करणें *g. of o.*
3 (a discourse, &c.). करणें, रचणें, बांधणें, जुळणें, कवणें.
4 *adjust*, v. To SETTLE. तोडणें, समेटणें, समेट *m*.-तोड *f*.-&c. करणें *g. of o.*
5 *place in proper state, &c.* See To DISPOSE.

COMPOSED, *p. & a.* v. V. 1. केलेला, बनाबलेला, चा used with the noun (*as* मातीचा, सोन्याचा &c.), मय (*in comp. as* सुवर्णमय &c.), आत्मक (in comp. as सुवर्णात्मक, रौप्यात्मक), घटित (in comp. as प्रीतिघटित भाषण, सुशब्दघटितवाक्य, तत्वघटितदेह). [मनस्क.
2 *and* CALM. सांतवलेला, &c. स्वस्थ, शांत, उपशांत, सुमना, सु-
3 रचलेला, &c. रचित, घटित (in comp. as सुशब्द घटित, &c.), ग्रथित, प्रणीत (in comp. as व्यासप्रणीत, गौतमप्रणीत, &c.).
I. *staid, sedate, steady.* स्थिर, भरकुंब *or* भरखुम, गंभीर.

COMPOSEDLY, *adv.* v. A. 2. *and* CALMLY. स्वस्थपणानें, स्वस्थमनानें.

COMPOSEDNESS, *n.* See COMPOSURE. 2 *sedateness, staidness.* भरखुमी *f*. गंभीरपणा *m*. गांभीर्य *n*. स्थिरता *f*.

COMPOSER, *n.* COMPOSING, *p. a.* v. V. 2. सांतवणारा, &c. शांत-स्वस्थ-&c. करणारा, शमन-प्रशमन-शांति-&c. कर्त्ता-कारी, संतापहर-हर्त्ता-हारक-हारी.
3 करणारा, रचणारा, &c. कर्त्ता, रचक, ग्रंथकार, ग्रंथकर्त्ता.

COMPOSITE, *a. made up of parts.* अनेकावयवघटित. [बणी *f*.

COMPOSITION, COMPOSING, *n.* v. V. 1.—*act.* बनावणें *n*. बना-
2—*act.* सांतवणें *n*. स्वस्थावणें *n*. शमविणें *n*. &c. शमन *n*. प्रशमन *n*. उपशमन *n*. शम *m*. क्षमापन *n*. संतापहरण *n*.—*state.* शांति (esp. in comp. as रोगशांति, ज्वरशांति, क्रोधशांति, लोभशांति, &c.), शम *m*. उपशम *m*. उपशांति *f*.
3—*act.* करणें *n*. रचणें *n*. &c. कवन *n*. ग्रंथन *n*. रचना *f*. पदरचना *f*. पद्योजना *f*.—*a. or s.* बांधणावळ *or* बांधावळ *f*. जडाब *m*. संदर्भ *m*. ग्रंथ *m*. प्रबंध *m*.
4—*act.* तोडणें *n*. समेटणें *n*. घटवटना *f*.—*a. or s.* तोड *f*. *v.* पाड, तोडजोड *f*. तोडमोड *or* मोडतोड *f*. समेट *m*.
I. *discourse, &c. composed,* v. BOOK. ग्रंथ *m*. कवन *n*. काव्य *n*. कविता *f*.
II. See COMPOUNDING, COMPOUND. III.—in grammar. समास *m*. समाहार *m*.
The chief forms of c. are अव्ययीभाव, तत्पुरुष, बहुव्रीहि, द्वंद्व; but of these there are many subdivisions.
IV.—in mathematics. भावन *n*.

COMPOSITOR, *n.* छापाचे ठसे-खिळे जुळणारा.

COMPOST. See MANURE.

COMPOSURE, *n. adjustment*, v. SETTLEMENT. तोड *f*. तोडमोड *f*. मोडतोड *f*. तोडजोड *f*.
2 *calmness, quietness, tranquility.* चित्ताची स्वस्थता *f*. शांति *f*. उपशांति *f*. उपशम *m*. शम *m*. शांतावस्था *f*. थंडपणा *m*. थंडावा *m*. थमन *n*. स्थैर्य *n*. शांतचित्त *n*. स्वस्थचित्त *n*. चित्तस्वास्थ्य *n*. सौमनस्य *n*. स्वस्थता *f*. स्वास्थ्य *n*. क्षोभाभाव *m*.

COMPOTATION, *n. drinking together.* संपीति *f*. सपीति *f*. सहपान *n*.

COMPOTATOR, *n.* सहपान कर्त्ता-कारी-कारक-&c. सहपानी.

To COMPOUND, *v. a. mingle, combine,* v. To MIX. मिळवणें, मिसळणें, एकवट करणें, सम्मिश्रण *n*.-सम्मेलन *n*. करणें *g. of o.*
2 *constitute, form.* See To COMPOSE. 3 *adjust*, v. To SETTLE. तोडणें, तोड *f*. पाडणें-काढणें-करणें, तोडजोड *f*.-तोडमोड *f*.-मोडतोड *f*. करणें *g. of o.*
4—in grammar. समास *m*.-समाहार *m*.-&c. करणें.

To COMPOUND, *v. n. come to terms of agreement.* तोडजोड *f*.-कावडताबड *f*.-सांजणी भांजणी *f*.- तोडमोड *f*.-&c. करणें, तोडीवर येणें.

COMPOUND, *a. not simple.* मिसळीचा, भेळीचा, मिसळ, मिश्र, मिश्रित, सामासिक.
2—in grammar. समासाचा, सामासिक, समासबानू, समस्त.

COMPOUND, *n. mass compounded*, v. MIXTURE. मिसळ *f*. मिसळा *m*.
2—in medicine. रसायन *n*. संधा *m*. पाक *m*. Certain medicinal or chemical *Compounds* are अग्निकुमार, अग्निमुख, अश्विनीकुमार *or* पुत्र, आनंदभैरव, उन्मत्त भैरव, कुडेपाक, जिरेपाक, ज्वरांकुश, डाळिंबपाक, त्रैलोक्य चिंतामणि, दशमूल, द्राक्षापाक, द्राक्षासव, नवरत्न राजमृगांक, प्रतापलंकेश्वर, मंडूर, मधपिंपळी, मालिनी वसंत, योगराज गुग्गुल, रतनजोत, लक्ष्मी विलास, लोकनाथ, लोहकांत, वातविध्वंस, वैश्वानर, श्वासकुठार, शंखवटिका, सुवर्ण मालिनी वसंत, सूतशेखर, सौभाग्य शुंठी *or* सुंठ, हेमगर्भ.
3—in grammar. समास *m*.
Explication of a c. विग्रह *m*.
4 *yard around house.* परस *or* परसूं *or* परूस *n*. वाडा *m*. वखबाडा *m*. वाडगें *n*. वाडकुलें *n*. अवाड *n*. परडें *n*. वाडी *f*. घरवाडी *f*.

COMPOUNDED, *p.* v. V. A. 1. मिसळलेला, &c. मिश्र, मिश्रित, मेलित, सम्मिश्रित, सम्मेलित.
3 तोडपाडलेला, तोडजोड केलेला-झालेला.
4 समासाचा, समस्त, सामासिक, यौगिक. [कारी-&c.

COMPOUNDER, *n.* v. V. A. 1. मिसळणारा-&c. सम्मिश्रण कर्त्ता-
v. V. N. तोडजोड करणारा, तोडमोडकरणारा, &c. तोडीवरयेणारा, तोडमोड्या.

COMPOUNDING, *n.* v. V. A. 1.—*act.* मिसळणें *n*. मिळवणें *n*. &c. मिश्रण *n*. सम्मिश्रण *n*. सम्मेलन *n*.—*state.* मिसळ *f*. मिसळा *m*.
3 तोडणें *n*. तोडजोड करणें *n*. तोडमोड करणें *n*. &c.
4 See COMPOSITION.

To COMPREHEND, *v. a. comprise, contain, include, embrace.* आकळणें, कवळणें, कंवटाळणें, अवटाळणें, धरणें, आंत घेणें, व्यापणें, आकलन *n*.-समावेश *m*.-&c. करणें *g. of o.* घेऊन बसणें,
2 *conceive*, v. To UNDERSTAND. आकळणें, घेणें, धरणें, समजणें, उमजणें, ग्रह *m*. करणें *g. of o.* बोध *m*.-समज *m*.-उमज *m*. होणें-पडणें *g. of o. with in. con.* ध्यानांत येणें *in. con.*
3 *involve*, v. To IMPLY. गर्भितकरणें.

COMPREHENDED, *p.* v. V. 1. आकळलेला, धरलेला, &c. आकलित, समाविष्ट, अंतर्भूत, अंतर्गत, प्रतिसंहृत, संगृहीत,
2 घेतलेला, बोधझालेला, &c. आकलित, ज्ञानस्पृक्, बुद्ध्यारूढ, बुद्धिप्रविष्ट.
3 गर्भित.

COMPREHENSIBLE, *a.* v. V. 1. आकळाया-चा-जोगा-&c. आकलनीय, आकलनयोग्य, व्याप्य.

2 समजाया-चा-जोगा-जोगता-सारखा-&c. बुद्धिगम्य, बोधगम्य, ज्ञानगम्य, ग्राह्य, बुद्धिग्राह्य, ज्ञानग्राह्य.

COMPREHENSION, *n.* v. V. 1.—*act.* आकळणें *n.* &c. आकलन *n.* प्रतिसंहार *m.* क्रोडीकरण *n.*—*state.* जमा *f.* गणती *f.* गणना *f.* संख्या *f.* अंतर्भाव *m.* समावेश *m.* प्रतिसंहार *m.*

2—*act.* समजणें *n.* समज *m.f.* बोध *m.* अवगम *m.* अनुगम *m.*

I. *inclusion, sphere, embrace,* v. COMPASS. कव *f.* कवळ *n.*

II. *capacity of knowing,* v. UNDERSTANDING. समज *m.f.* समजूत *f.* बुद्धि *f.* आकलनशक्ति *f.*

COMPREHENSIVE, *a.* v. V. 1. व्यापक, व्यापी, बहुसमावेशक, बहुग्रह, बहुग्राही. [लक्ष्यसमन्वयी.

2 बहुग्रह, बहुग्राही, बहुविषय ग्राही-ग्राहक, व्यापक, व्यापी, बहु-

COMPREHENSIVENESS, *n.* v. A. 1. व्यापकता *f.* बहुसमावेशकत्व *n.*

To COMPRESS, *v. a. condense, concentrate.* थोडक्यांत आणणें, संकलित *pop.* संकळीत करणें-सांगणें-लिहणें, आकलन *n.*-उपसंहार *m.*-प्रतिसंहार *m.*-संहार *m.*-संहृति *f.*-&c. करणें *g. of o.* संकीर्ण-संहृत-&c. करणें, संपुष्टांत-अनुष्टुपांत आणणें. [णें, दडपणें.

2 *force together,* v. To PRESS. दाबणें, चापणें, चेपटणें, चेंबट-

COMPRESS, *n.* दाबण्याची बरघडी *f.*-पट्टी *f.*

COMPRESSED, *p.* v. V. 1. थोडक्यांत आणलेला, &c. संकलित, संकीर्ण, सामासिक, प्रतिसंहृत.

2 चेपटलेला, &c. चेपट, चिंबका, चिंबा, चिबळ.

COMPRESSIBLE, *a.* v. V. 1. थोडक्यांत आणाया-जोगा-जोगता-&c. संकलनीय, प्रतिसंहार योग्य, &c.

2 चापायाचा-जोगा-जोगता-&c.

COMPRESSION, *n.* v. V. 1.—*act.* थोडक्यांत आणणें *n.* &c. संकलन *n.* आकलन *n.* प्रतिसंहार *m.* उपसंहार *m.*—*state.* प्रतिसंहृति *f.* समाहृति *f.*

2—*act.* चापणें *n.* चेपटणें *n.* &c.

COMPRESSURE. See PRESSURE.

COMPRISAL, *n.* v. V.—*act.* आकलन *n.* क्रोडीकरण *n.*—*state.* समावेश *m.* अंतर्भाव *m.*

To COMPRISE. See To COMPREHEND.

COMPROMISE, *n. compact upon concessions.* तोड *f.* *v.* पाड, तोड जोड *f.* तोडमोड *or* मोडतोड *f.*

2—in law. कबूलकतबा *m.* कतबा *m.*

To COMPROMISE, *v. a.* v. N. 1. *and* To SETTLE. तोडणें, तोड *f.* पाडणें-काढणें, तोडजोड *f.*-तोडमोड *f.* करणें, तोडीवर येणें.

2 *put to hazard.* धोक्यांत-भयांत-संकटांत-अडचणींत-&c. घालणें-आणणें.

COMPULSATORY, COMPULSIVE, COMPULSORY, *a.* v. V. To COMPEL. बळाचा, बळजोरीचा, जबरीचा, बळात्काराचा, जुलुमाचा, जुलमा जुलमीचा, बलप्रधान, बलकर्तृक.

COMPULSION, COMPULSIVENESS, *n.* v. V. *force applied,* v. VIOLENCE. बलात्कार *pop.* बळात्कार *m.* जुलूम *m.* जुलूमदस्ती *f.* जुलूमजास्ती *f.* जबरी *f.*

COMPULSIVELY, COMPULSORILY, *adv.* v. A. बळें, जुलमानें, जुलमावर, जुलमाजुलमी, जुलमाजुलमीनें, जबरीनें, जबरदस्तीनें, जुलूमदस्तीनें, अळेंबळें, दाटून, दाटबळें, हटात्.

COMPUNCTION, *n.* v. REPENTANCE. पस्तावा *m.* दुःख *n.* चुणचूण *f.* चुरचूर *f.* रुखरूख *f.* खरखर *f.* हुरहूर *f.* मनस्ताप *m.*

COMPUNCTIONLESS, *a.* पश्चात्तापहीन-शून्य-रहित, अननुतापी.

COMPUNCTIOUS, *a.* v. REPENTANT. पश्चात्तापी, अनुतापी, चुणचुणीचा, चुरचुरीचा.

COMPUNCTIVE, *a. causing remorse.* पश्चात्ताप कारक-जनक-&c. मनस्ताप कारक-&c.

COMPURGATION, *n.* पडसाक्ष *f.*

COMPURGATOR, *n.* पडसाक्षी.

To COMPUTE. COMPUTATION. See To CALCULATE, CALCULATION. [*m.* बंधु *m.*

COMRADE, *n.* v. FELLOW. सलगी, सोबती, संगवयी, संवगडी, भाऊ

CON. To this inseparable preposition correspond सम् and सह or as substituted for them, स.

To CON, *v. a. fix in the mind.* घोकणें, घट्ट करणें, गुणणें, संथा *f.* देणें-घेणें-म्हणणें, घोष *m.*-उद्घोष *m.*-गुण्णिका *f.* करणें, घासणें.

To CONCATENATE. See To LINK.

CONCATENATION, *n.* v. SERIES. सांखळी *f.* शृंखला *f.* शिलशिल्ला *m.*

CONCAVE, *a. hollow and arched.* अंडकटाहाकृति, कटाहाकाशाकृति, गगनाकृति, गोलांतर.

CONCAVITY, *n.* v. A. अंडकटाहाकृति *f.* अंडकटाहाकार *m.* कटाहाकाश *m. n.* कटाहाकृत्याकाश *m. n.* गोलपोकळी *f.*

I. a c. पुट *n.*

CONCAVO-CONCAVE, *a. concave on both sides.* उर्ध्वाधःकटाहाकृति, उभयतःकटाहाकृति.

CONCAVO-CONVEX, *a.* अंतर्बाह्य कटाहाकृति.

To CONCEAL, *v. a.* v. To HIDE. झांकणें, ढांकणें, लपवणें, दाबणें, दडविणें, दाबा धरणें-देणें, चोरणें, गुप्त ठेवणें, छपवणी *f.*-गोपन *n.*-&c. करणें *g. of o.*

CONCEALABLE, *a.* v. V. झांकाया-चा-जोगा-जोगता-&c. गोपनीय, गोप्य, आच्छादनीय, गुह्य, आच्छाद्य.

CONCEALED, *p.* v. V. झांकलेला, &c. गुप्त, गोपित, आच्छादित, प्रच्छादित, प्रच्छन्न, तिरोहित.

CONCEALER, *n.* CONCEALING, *p. a.* v. V. झांकणारा, लपवणारा, &c. गोपक, आच्छादक.

CONCEALMENT, *n.* v. V.—*act.* झांकणें *n.* दाबणें *n.* चोरणें *n.* &c. छपवणूक *f.* छपवणी *f.* दाबादाबी *f.* गोपन *n.* प्रच्छादन *n.* तिरोधान *n.*—*state.* झांकलेले पणा *m.* &c. गुप्तता *f.* आच्छादितत्व *n.* अप्रकाश *m.* अप्रसिद्धि *f.*

I. *hiding place.* लिकण *f.* दडण *f. n.*

To CONCEDE, *v. a. allow, grant, yield,* v. To ADMIT. सोडणें, देणें, मान्य-कबूल-&c. करणें, रुकारणें. [भावना *f.*

CONCEIT, *n. image or idea formed,* v. CONCEPTION. कल्पना *f.*

2 *high estimate of self or own.* मीपणा *m.* अभिमान *m.* अहंकार *m.* दम *m.* गुमान *m.* दिमाख *m.* पतरास *f.* रग *f.* सै *or* सयी *f. v.* मोड, जिरव, फुंद *m. v.* चढ, भर, सैरी *f.* ऊब *f.* माज *m.* बदमस्ती *f.* खरमस्ती *f.* मिजाज *f.* मान *m.* आढ्यता *f. v.* ओढ, बाळग, मिरव, अहम्मान *m.* अहम्मति *f.* आत्माभिमान *m.* स्वाभिमान *m.* अंतर्हास *m.*

C. of, *pluming one's self on.* बाणा *m.*

To lose one's c. माज *m.* मोडणें-जिरणें *g. of s.*

To be out of c. with. अभिमान *m.* सुटणें *g. of o.* ग्रह *m.* जाणें, मन *n.* उठणें *with* वरून.

To take the c. out of. खोड *f.*-माज *m.*-&c. मोडणें *g. of o.* नाक काटणी *f.* करणें, कढ *m.*-ऊब *f.*-&c. जिरवणें.

3 See FANCY.

CONCEITED, *a.* v. N. 2. रगदार, रंगेल, रग्या, माजोरा, माजुरी *or*

माजोरी, मस्त, मस्तवाला, सरमस्त, दिमाखदार, दिमाखी, गुमानी, पतरासी, फुंद, बदमस्त, मिजाजी, मिजाज खोर, अहंकारी, अभिमानी, साभिमान, अहम्मानी, साहंकार, आत्माभिमानी, स्वाभिमान. [दार.

C. of or respecting. बाणाईत, बाण्याचा, बाणीचा, बाणी-

CONCEITEDLY, *adv.* v. N. 2. अभिमानानें, दिमाखानें, अभिमानपूर्वक.

CONCEITEDNESS. See CONCEIT 2.

CONCEIVABLE, *a.* v. V. A. 2. कल्पाया-जोगा-सारखा-&c. कल्पनीय, भावनीय.

3 समजाया-चा-जोगा-जोगता &c. बुद्धिगम्य, बोधगम्य, मनोगम्य.

CONCEIVABLENESS, *n.* v. A. 1. कल्पायाजोगेपणा *m.*-&c. कल्पनीयता *f.* भावनीयता *f.*

2 समजायाजोगेपणा*m.* &c. बुद्धिगम्यता *f.* बोधगम्यता *f.* &c.

To CONCEIVE, *v. a. form in the womb.* धरणें, पोटांत धरणें, गर्भांत धरणें.

2 *imagine*, v. To FANCY. कल्पिणें, धरणें, बांधणें.

3 *apprehend*, v. To UNDERSTAND. धरणें, घेणें, आकळणें, समजणें, बोध*m.*-समज*m.*-उमज*m.*-&c. होणें *g.of o. with in con.*

To CONCEIVE, *v. n. become pregnant.* पोटांत धरणें, गर्भधारण *n.* करणें, पोटासी-गर्भार-गर्भवती-&c. होणें-राहणें, गर्भ *m.* संभवणें-समावणें-राहणें *in. con.*

2—of beasts. गाभास जाणें, गाभणी होणें, फळणें,—esp. of mares. सभर *or* सबर होणें.

3 *have opinion or idea of*, v.To THINK. मनांत-ध्यानांत-चित्तांत-दिलांत-&c. येणें *in. con.*

CONCEIVED, *p.* v. V. A. 1. पोटांत धरलेला.

2 मनांत धरलेला-रचलेला-&c. कल्पित, भावित.

3 धरलेला, &c. आकलित, ज्ञानस्पृक्, बुद्ध्यारूढ, बौद्ध, हृद्गत.

CONCENT. See CONCORD.

To CONCENTRATE, *To* CONCENTRE, *v. a. bring to a common centre, bring to one point.* समकेंद्र-एककेंद्र-एकाग्र-एकतान-एकायन-एकस्थ-&c. करणें, एकेठिकाण्यावर-एकेलक्षावर-&c. आणणें-मिळवणें-बसवणें, संश्लेष*m.*-संसक्ति *f.*-संहति *f.*-&c. करणें *g. of o.* संश्लिष्ट-संहत-&c. करणें.

To CONCENTRATE, *To* CONCENTRE, *v. n.* समकेंद्रस्थित-एककेंद्रस्थित-एकाग्रस्थित-&c. होणें.

CONCENTRICAL, *a.* समकेंद्र, एककेंद्र.

CONCEPTION, *n.* v. V. A. 1. & V. N. 1.—*act.* पोटांत धरणें*n.* गर्भधारण*n.* गर्भग्रहण*n.* गर्भसंभव *m.*

Indication or sign of c. गर्भछाया *f.*

2—*act*. कल्पिणें*n.* मनांत रचणें*n.* &c. कल्पना *f.* भावना *f.*

3—*act*. समजणें*n.* &c. समज*m.* उमज*m.* अनुगम*m.* आकलन*n.*

Clear c. of. स्पष्ट प्रतिपत्ति *f.*

I. *image formed, idea.* कल्पना *f.* भावना *f.* बुद्धिविषय*m.* ग्रह*m.* आकार*m.*

To CONCERN, *v. a. relate to, belong to.* संबंध*m.*-इलाखा*m.*-&c. असणें *in. con.* संबंधीं-विषयीं-&c. लागणें, जवळ असणें, असणें *g. of o.* कडचा-लगेचा-संबंधाचा-संसर्गाचा-&c. असणें *in. con.*

2 (one's self) *feel an interest in.* काळजी *f.*-चिंता *f.*-कळकळ*f.*-पोटाग *f.*-&c. असणें *in. con. with* विषयीं *of o.* काळजी*f.* -चिंता *f.*-&c. धरणें-वागवणें-वाळगणें *g. of o.*

3 (one's self) *intermeddle, be busy.* हात*m.* घालणें, मध्यें पडणें, धजणें, उद्युक्त होणें.

CONCERN, CONCERNMENT, *n. matter concerning or belonging to,* v. AFFAIR. काम*n.* कडचें काम*n.* (*as* आमच्या कडचें काम) खटला*m.* खटलें*n.* प्रकरण*n.* विषय*m.*

To prove a losing c. दांतावर येणें, आंगावर येणें.

2 *passion, interest, engagedness, feeling, emotion.* काळजी *f.* चिंता *f.* आस्था *f.* पोटाग *f.* कळकळ *f.* होष*m.* उद्वेग*m.* जिव्हाळा*m.* अगत्य*n.* तिडीक *f.* गरळ *f.* ईषणा *f.* उदमेख*m.* दरद *f. m.* फिकीर *f.* परवा *f.* क्षीत *f.* क्षति *f.*

To cease to take any care or c. about. कथा *f.*-कथावार्त्ता *f.*-वास्तपुस्त *f.*-नांव*n.*-&c. सोडणें *g. of o.*

3 *importance, moment,* v. WEIGHT. वजनदारी*f.* भारीपणा*m.*

4 *connection, interest in.* अंग*n.* संबंध*m.* इलाखा*m.* इतल्ला*m.* लगा*m.* सामलात *f.* तनखा *m.*

CONCERNED, *a.* v. N. 2. आस्थेकरी, आस्थिक, काळजीचा, जिव्हाळ्याचा, कळकळीचा, कळकळ्या, दरदी, उदमेखी, चिंतातुर, चिंतायुक्त.

4 *having an interest in or connexion with.* संबंधी, संबंधाचा, संबंधविशिष्ट, भागीदार, बिभागी, अंशी, वांटेदार.

CONCERNEDLY, *adv.* v. N. 2. काळजीनें, उदमेखून, पोटागीनें, आस्थापूर्वक, &c.

CONCERNING, *p.* (or vulgo, *prep.*). विषयीं, संबंधीं, विषयक *in comp.* संबंधी *in comp.*

To CONCERT, *v. a. contrive together.* एकोप्यानें-एकवट्यानें-मिळून-सम्मतीनें-संगनमतानें-सहविचारानें-&c. योजणें-रचणें-बांधणें-युक्ति *f.* काढणें-तजवीज *f.* करणें, &c. जथणें, संयोजन*n.* करणें.

CONCERT, CONCERTING, *n.* v. V.—*act.* एकोप्यानें योजणें *n.*&c. संयोजन*n.* सहयोजन*n.* संभूययोजना *f.* संभूयरचना *f.*

I.—of music, &c. फडाचा बाजा*m.* संभूयवादनसमारंभ*m.* संहत्यवादनोत्सव*m.*

C. of singing, playing, and dancing. संगीत*n.* तौर्य्य*n.* तौर्य्यत्रिक*n.*

C.-room. गाण्याचा अड्डा*m.*-फड*m.* संगीतशाळा *f.*

II. v. AGREEMENT. एकोपा *or* बा*m.* समा*m.* जुगल *f.* ऐकमत्य*n.* एकविचार*m.*

CONCESSION, *n.* v. V.—*act.* देणें*n.* कबूल करणें*n.* सोडणें*n.* &c.

I. *point conceded.* सोडलेली गोष्ट *f.*-विषय*m.*-&c. सूट *f.*

CONCH, *n.* शंख*m.* कंबु*m.* सिंधुपुष्प*n.*

C.—menstruum. शंखद्राव*m.*

CONCHOLOGY, *n.* शंखशास्त्र*n.* शंखविद्या *f.*

CONCILIAR, *a. pertaining to a council.* सभेचा, सभेसंबंधी, सभ्य, सामाजिक, सामवायिक.

To CONCILIATE, *v. a. win, gain over.* मनावणें, मिळवणें, मिळवून घेणें, वळवणें, आळवणें, आराधणें, आपलासा-अनुकूल-प्रसन्न-&c. करणें-करून घेणें, मनधरणी *f.*-आराधना *f.*-&c. करणें *g.of o.*

CONCILIATED, *p.* v. V. मनावलेला, वळवलेला, &c. आराधित.

CONCILIATION, *n.* v. V.—*act.* मनावणें*n.* वळवणें*n.* आराधणें*n.* &c. मनधरणी *f.* मनमनावणी *f.* मनावणी *f.* आराधणी *f.* मनवळणी *f.* आराधना *f.* साम*n.*

CONCILIATOR, *n.* CONCILIATING, *p. a.* CONCILIATORY, *a.* v. V. मनधरणीचा, समेटाचा, सामाचा, मनमिळाऊ, मनमेळ, मिळाऊ, मिळताऊ, आराधक, चित्ताकर्षक, द्वेषहारक, द्वेषापहारक.

C. measure सामोपचार*m.*

CONCINNITY, CONCINNOUS. See FITNESS, FIT.

CONCISE, *a.* v. BRIEF. संक्षेपाचा, अल्पविस्ताराचा, अल्पशब्दक.
CONCISELY, *adv.* v. A. थोडक्यांत, संक्षेपेंकरून, अल्पविस्तारानें.
CONCISENESS, *n.* v. A. संक्षेप*m.* संक्षिप्तता *f.* विस्ताराभाव*m.* अल्पविस्तार *m.*
To CONCLUDE, *v. a. finish, close,* v. To END. समाप्त-तमाम-बंद-पुरा-&c. करणें, संपवणें, सारणें, अटोपणें, उलगणें.
2 *determine,* v. To DECIDE. ठरावणें, निश्चय*m.*-निर्णय*m.*-निर्धार*m.*-&c. करणें. [णें-समजणें.
3 *collect logically,* v. To INFER. तर्कानें-अनुमानानें काढणें-घे-
4 *include.* See To COMPREHEND.
To CONCLUDE, *v. n. finish, close,* v. To END. संपणें, अटोपणें, अखेर-समाप्त-तमाम-&c. होणें, उरकणें.
2—in logic. अनुमान*n.*-तर्क*m.* करणें, अनुमानणें, ताडणें.
CONCLUDED, *p.* v. V. A. 1. समाप्त केलेला, &c. समापित, समाप्त, तमाम, उपसंहृत, अखेर, खलास.
CONCLUDING, *p. a.* v. V. N. 1. *and* LAST. शेवटला *or* चा, शेवटील, शेवटींचा, अंतींचा, समाप्तीचा, अखेरीचा, सरता.
CONCLUDING, CONCLUSION, *n.* v. V. A. 1.—*act.* समाप्त करणें*n.* अटोपणें*n.* &c. समापन *n.* उपसंहार*m.*
v. V. N. 1. *and* END. अखेरी *f.* समाप्ति *f.* अंत*m.* अवसान*n.* अवसाय*m.* मखलासी *f.*
2 अनुमान करणें*n.* अनुमान*n.*
I. *c. drawn, consequence, deduction.* सिद्धांत *m.* निश्चितार्थ*m.* घटितार्थ*m.* खचितार्थ*m.* मथितार्थ*m.* निर्णीतार्थ*m.* कृतांत*m.* आनुपूर्व्य *n.* उपपत्ति *f.* शोध *m.*
Grounds or warrant of a c. साधन *n.*
Illogical c. अपसिद्धांत*m.* अविनिगम*m.*
CONCLUSIVE, *a. determinative* v. DECISIVE. निर्णायक, निश्चायक, सिद्धांतस्थापक. [तिपादित.
2—in logic; *regularly consequential.* सैद्धांतिक, सिद्धांत प्र-
CONCLUSIVENESS, *n.* v. A. निर्णायकत्व *n.*
To CONCOCT, *v. a.* v. To DIGEST. पचवणें, पाक *m.* करणें.
2 *prepare in the mind,* v. To PLAN. कल्पना *f.* करणें, काढणें, योजणें.
CONCOCTION, *n.* v. V. 1. पचवणें *n.* पाक*m.* परिपाक *m.*
2 कल्पना *f.*
CONCOMITANCE, CONCOMITANT. See ACCOMPANIMENT, ACCOMPANYING.
CONCORD, CONCORDANCE, CONCORDANCY, *n.* (of sound) *harmony.* स्वरांचा *pop.* सुरांचा जम*m.*-जबा*m.*-मेळ*m.*-समा*m.*-जुळणी *f.*-&c. स्वरसाम्य*n.* स्वरैक्य*n.* सामस्वर्य*n.* समस्वरता *f.*
A c. सुस्वर *m.* [करण्य *n.*
2—in grammar. अन्वय *m.* विशेष्यनिघ्नता *f.* सामानाधिक-
3 (of intercourse, &c.) v. AGREEMENT. मिलाफ*m.* मेळ*m.* एकोपा*m.* एकी *f.* ऐक्य*n.* ऐक्यभाव*m.* ऐक्यमत*n.*
4 *compact.* See AGREEMENT. [मेळाचा.
CONCORDANT, *a.* v. AGREEING. मिलाफी, मिलाफाचा, जमाचा,
CONCORDAT, *n.* धर्माच्यागोष्टींविषयीं पोपाशीं कोणाराजानें केलेला करार. [कत्र होणें *n.*
CONCOURSE, *n. confluence to one place.* जमाव*m.* मिळणें *n.* ए-
2 v. CROWD. जमाव*m.* मेळा*m.* संपर्क*m.* राष्ट्र *n.*
3 See JUNCTION.
CONCREMATION, *n.*—of a widow. सहमरण *n.* सहगमन *n.*

To CONCRETE, *v. n.* v. To CLOT. गोठणें, अटणें, जमणें.
To CONCRETE, *v. a.* जमवणें, गोठवणें, अटवणें.
CONCRETE, *a.* v. THICK. घट्ट, घण, दाट.
2—in logic. अधिष्ठानविषयक ! अधिकरणसंबंधी ! धर्मिवाचक.
3—in grammar. सिद्ध.
CONCRETION, *n.* v. V. N.—*act.* गोठणें*n.* अटणें*n.* जमणें*n.*
I. *mass concreted.* गोळा*m.* गुठळी *f.* डिखळ *or* डिखूळ*n.* *dim.* डिखळी *f.* ढेप *n.*
CONCUBINAGE, *n.* संभोगसंबंध*m.* मानितपतिपत्नीभाव*m.*
CONCUBINE, *n. inferior wife, &c.* उपपत्नी *f.* उपस्त्री *f.* भोगस्त्री *f.* भोगपत्नी *f.* भोगिनी *f.* पाटाची-मुहूर्ताची *pop.* मोहोतराची-&c. बायको *f.* (among Shúdras);—one of many वारांगना *f.* वारस्त्री *f.* वारवधू *f.* वारयुवती *f.*
2 *kept woman.* v. MISTRESS. रास *f.* रक्षा *f.* दासी *f.*
CONCUPISCENCE, *n.* v. LUST. पापवासना *f.* विषयवासना *f.* दुर्वासना *f.* मद *m.*
CONCUPISCENT, *a.* v. LUSTFUL. कामी, सकाम, कामबुद्धि.
To CONCUR, *v. n.* v. To AGREE. मिळणें, मान्य-कबूल-सम्मत-एक-&c. होणें, सम्मत*n.*-सम्मति *f.*-अनुमत*n.*-अनुगति *f.*-अनुमोदन*n.* देणें and *in. con.* होणें *g. of s.*
2 *unite or be conjoined.* जुळणें, जमणें, जुळणी *f.*-&c. होणें, *g. of s. recip.*
CONCURRENCE, *n.* v. V. 1. *and* AGREEMENT. अनुमत*n.* सम्मत*n.* अनुमति *f.* सम्मति *f.* ऐक्य *n.* मेळ*m.*
CONCURRENT, *a.* v. V. 1. *and* AGREEING. मिळणारा, &c. एकदिल, एकचित्त, अनुमत, सम्मत.
CONCUSSION, *n.* v. SHOCK. धक्का*m.* गचका*m.* हबका*m.*
To CONDEMN, *v. a. find guilty and doom.* अन्याय-&c. आंगीं लावून शिक्षा *f.* सांगणें, अपराधी-सापराध-सदोष-&c. असा निश्चय करून दंडनास नेमणें, अपराध लागू करून शिक्षेची आज्ञा *f.* करणें, अपराधी म्हणून शिक्षेस सांगणें, अन्याय-&c. साबूत करून दंडनास देणें, अपराधकथनपूर्वकदंडाभिदान*n.*-अपराधमूलक दंडाभिदान *n.* करणें.
2 *disapprove.* दोष*m.* ठेवणें-लावणें, नापसंत-सदोष-दूषित-&c. करणें-ठरावणें.
3 *find to be unfit for service.* निकामी-निरुपयोगी-अनुपयोगी-&c. ठरवणें, रद्द करणें.
CONDEMNATION, *n.* v. V. 1.—*act.* अन्याय आंगीं लावून शिक्षा सांगणें *n.* दंडनास नेमणें *n.* &c. दंडनियोजन *n.* सापराधदंडाभिदान *n.*—*state.* नियोजितदंडत्व *n.* नियोजितदंडपात्रता *f.* स्थापितदंडपात्रत्व-*n.* कथितदंडत्व *n.*
I. *ground or reason of c.* दंडनियोजनहेतु *m.* दंडनियोजनाधार *m.* दंडनियोजनकारण *n.*
CONDENSABLE, *a.* v. V. 1. घट्ट-घण-&c. करावयाजोगा-सारखा-&c. घनकरणीय.
CONDENSATION, CONDENSING, *n.* v. V. A. 1.—*act.* घट्ट करणें *n.* &c. घनीकरण *n.*
2—*act.* संकलन *n.* संकलीत करणें *n.*
To CONDENSE, *To* CONDENSATE, *v. a.* v. To THICKEN. घन *pop.* घण-घट्ट-दाट-घनावयव-&c. करणें. [&c. करणें.
2 v. To COMPRESS. संकलन *n.* करणें *g. of o.* संकलित-संकीर्ण-
To CONDENSE, *v. n.* v. To THICKEN. घन *pop.* घण-घट्ट-&c. होणें.
CONDENSE, *a.* See DENSE.

To CONDESCEND, *v. n. deign, stoop, &c.* अभिमान सोडून वागणें, मोठेपणा *m.* एकीकडे ठेवणें, अभिमानत्यागपूर्वक आचरण *n.*-त्यक्ताभिमानाचरण *n.* करणें, मेहरबानी *f.*-&c. करणें.

CONDESCENDING, *p. a.* v. V. नम्र, विनयी, सविनय, विनयशील, निरभिमानी, त्यक्ताभिमानाचरणी, मेहरबान.

CONDESCENDINGLY, *adv.* v. V. मोठेपणा-&c. एकीकडे ठेवून, नम्रतेनें, मेहरबानीनें, अभिमानत्यागपूर्वक.

CONDESCENSION, *n.* v. V. नम्रता *f.* निरभिमान *m.* अभिमानत्याग *m.* विनय *m.* त्यक्ताभिमानाचरण *n.* त्यक्ताभिमानाचार *m.* मेहरबानी *or* मेहरबानगी *f.* मेहर *f.*

CONDIGN, *a.* v. SUITABLE. योग्य, यथायोग्य, यथायुक्त, वाजबी.

CONDIMENT, *n.* v. SEASONING, SAUCE. मसाला *m.* तोंडीं लावणें *n.* व्यंजन *n.*

CONDISCIPLE, *n.* गुरुबंधु *m.* गुरुभाऊ *m.* बंधु *m.* सहाध्यायी, सतीर्थ्य, सतीर्थ.

CONDITION, *n. state, present circumstances.* अवस्था *f.* दशा *f.* स्थिति *pop.* स्थीत *f.* गति *f.* गत *f.* अहवाल *or* हवाल *m. f.* वर्त्तमान *n* कैफियत *f.*

To get into a good c. रंगास-रूपास येणें.

2 *state of body.* भावना *f.* प्रकृति *f.* देहभावना *f.* शरीरस्थिति *f.* शरीरावस्था *f.*

That is in good c. ताजा, ताजातवना, टमटमीत, टुमटुमीत, तुंद.

To come into c. आंग *n.* धरणें-घेणें, रंगास येणें.

To get out of c. आंग *n.* टाकणें-सोडणें.

3 v. RANK. स्थिति *pop.* स्थीत *f.* पदवी *f.*

4 *term, stipulation.* संकेत *m.* प्रतिज्ञा *f.* अड *f.* अट *f.* अडती *f.* मुद्दा *m.* शरत *f.* तर *f.*

To CONDITION. See To STIPULATE.

CONDITIONAL, *a. implying terms, dependinj on conditions.* अटीचा, अडतीचा, अटकावाचा, सांकेतिक, सप्रतिबंध, तरीचा, सापेक्ष, सप्रतिज्ञ, यद्यर्थगर्भित.

2—in grammar. संकेतार्थक.

CONDITIONALITY, *n.* v. A. सांकेतिकत्व *n.* सप्रतिबंधत्व *n.* सापेक्षता *f.*

CONDITIONALLY, *adv.* v. A. अट-अडती-तर-&c. घालून-घेऊन-करून, सप्रतिज्ञ.

To CONDOLE, *v. n. grieve with another.* दुसऱ्याचे दुःखाला रडणें, परदुःख दुःखित-समदुःखी-&c. होणें, दुःखाचा वांटा *m.* घेणें, सहदुःख *n.*-सहशोक *m.*-&c. करणें, डोळेपूस *f.* करणें—on account of a death, दुखवटा *m.* करणें-काढणें.

CONDOLEMENT, CONDOLENCE, *n.* v. V. दुसऱ्याचे दुःखाला रडणें *n.* समदुःखीहोणें *n.* परदुःखदुःख *n.* सहदुःख *n.* सहशोक *m.*

CONDOLER, *n.* CONDOLING, *p. a.* v. V. दुसऱ्याच्या दुःखाला रडणारा, समदुःखी, परदुःख दुःखी.

To CONDONE. See To PARDON, To PASS by.

To CONDUCE, *v. n. contribute, help, tend towards.* उपयोगास येणें-पडणें, उपयोगी-सहाय-सहकारी-साधक-प्रयोजक-&c. होणें, मदद *f.* करणें-देणें.

CONDUCENT, CONDUCIVE, *a.* v. V. उपयोगाचा, साधक, उपयोगी, उपयुक्त, कारणी, उपकारक, उपकारी, प्रयोजक, सहाय, सहकारी, आवह *in comp.*

CONDUCIVENESS, *n.* v. A. उपयोगीपणा *m.* उपयोगिता *f.* उपकारित्व *n.* उपकारकता *f.*

CONDUCT, CONDUCTING, *n.* v. V. 1.—*act.* वाट दाखवून नेणें *n.* वाटेनें नेणें *n.* &c. सहनयन *n.* सहप्रापण *n.*

2—*act.* निर्वाहणें *n.* वहिवाटणें *n.* &c. निर्वाह *m.* वहिवाट *f.* चालवणूक *f.* वलावणी *f.* आचरण *n.* निभावणी *f.* निभावणूक *f.* वागवणूक *f.*

3 *behaviour, deportment, carriage.* वर्त्तणूक *f.* वर्त्तन *n.* आचरण *n.* आचरित *n.* आचार *m.* वागणूक *f.* वाग *f.* वागवागणूक *f.* चाल *f.* गति *f.* चर्या *f.* चालचर्या *f.* चालचलाव *m.* चळणवळण *n.* वहिवाट *f.* व्यवहार *m.* स्थितिरीति *f.* स्थीतरीत *f.* स्थीत *f.* वृत्त *n.* पाऊल *n.* पदन्यास *m.*

Bad c. दुराचरण *n.* दुराचार *m.* दुर्वृत्त *n.*

Good c. सदाचरण *n.* सदाचार *m.* सद्वृत्त *n.* शिष्टाइकी *f.* शिष्टाई *f.*

General c. आचारपद्धति *f.*

4 पुढाकार *m.* पुरस्कार *m.* पुढार *m.*

I. *management, skill,* v. ADDRESS. आवरकशक्ति *f.* आवर *m.* कर्तृत्व *n.* नेतृत्व *n.* नियंतृत्व *n.* व्यवहर्तृत्व *n.*

II. safe c. अभयपत्र *n.*

To CONDUCT, *v. a. lead, accompany, to guide, &c.* वाट दाखवून नेणें-पहोंचविणें-&c. वाटेनें नेणें, पावणें, पहोंचविणें, सहनयन *n.*-सहप्रापण *n.* करणें *g. of o.*

2 *carry on, transact, manage.* निर्वाहणें, वहिवाटणें, चालवणें, वागवणें, वलवणें *or* वलावणें, हाकणें, आचरणें, निर्वाह *m.*-वहिवाट *f.*- &c. करणें *g. of o.*

3 one's self; v. To BEHAVE. चालणें, आचरणें, वागणें, वर्त्तणें.

4 v. To LEAD. पुढाकार *m.*-पुरस्कार *m.*-पुढार *m.*-&c. करणें *g. of o.*

CONDUCTOR, *n.* v. V. 1. वाट दाखवून नेणारा, &c. सहनयनकर्त्ता, सहनेता, सहनायक.

2 *and* 4. *person presiding and managing.* As this is the sense of the terms and phrases *Manager, Foreman, Headman, Leader, Leadingman, Captain, Coryphœus, Charge d' Affaires, that holds the reins, that sits at the helm, that mounts the box, that plays the first fiddle, &c. &c.* and as many of the *Maráthi* terms which are employed to convey this sense, bear also a latent sense agreeing well with the latent sense borne by one or other of these terms, here we have collected the terms of both tongues. वहिवाटणारा, वलवणारा, &c. निर्वाहक, कारभारी, व्यवहर्त्ता, वहिवाटदार, पुढाईत, पुढाकारी, पुरस्कर्त्ता, पुरस्कारी, पुढारी, मोहरकाढ्या, मोहरक्या, मोहरपी, चालक, नायक, घटक, नेता, वाहक, मुखरण, मुखरणी, मुखरीण, सरचष्मा, सुकाण्या, सुकाणदार, नांगऱ्या, पुढच्या जोताचा, सूत्रधार, सूत्रधारी, बिनीचा, सारथि *or* सारथी, मुकुटमणी, अध्वर्यु, धनुर्धर, कारणी, धनी, नरसिंह, नाक, प्रमुख (in comp.), पुरस्सर (in comp.).

I. (of ceremonies, esp. *religious*). आचार्य, याज्ञिक.

C. of heat. उष्णता वाहक.

CONDUIT, *n. aqueduct.* नळ *m.* नहर *m.* सारणी *f.*

CONE, *n.* सुळका *m. dim.* सुळकी *f.* सूचि *f.* गोपुच्छाकृति *f.* शंकु *m.*

2 (in botany) देवदारू वगैरे झाडाचें फळ *n.*

CONFABULATION, &c. See CONVERSATION, &c.

CONFECTION, *n.* v. SWEETMEAT. मिठाई *f.* मुरब्बा *or* मुरंबा *m.* हलवा *m.*

CONFECTIONER, *n.* हलवई *or* वाई, मिठाईवाला.

CONFEDERACY, *n. federal compact, league,* v. COMBINATION.

एकवळा *m.* कट *m.* जट *m.* कूट *n.* जत *f.* मिळण *f.* जूग *n.* संगनमत *n.* कट्टा *m.*

2 *confederate body*, v. COMBINATION. जट *m.* कट *m.* जूट *m. f.* जूग *n.* जथा *m.*

To CONFEDERATE, *v. n.* v. To COMBINE. जटणें, जुटणें, मिळणें.

CONFEDERATE, *a.* मिलाफी, मिळणीचा, संगनमती *or* त्या.

CONFEDERATE, *n. ally, associate, accomplice.* मिलाफी, मिळणीचा, कुटांतला, साथी, सोबती, संगनमती, संगनमत्या.

CONFEDERATION. See CONFEDERACY.

To CONFER, *v. n. speak with*, v. To CONVERSE. बोलणें *n.*-भाषण *n.*-जाबसाल *m.*-बोलीचाली *f.*-बोलाचाली *f.*-संभाषण *n.*-संवाद *m.*-&c. करणें *with* सीं.

To c. in private. खलबत *n.*-एकांत *m.* करणें.

To CONFER, *v. a.* v. To GIVE. देणें, दान *n.* करणें, बहाल करणें, प्रापण *n.*-उपधान *n.*-&c. करणें.

CONFERENCE, *n.* v. V. N. *and* CONVERSATION. संभाषण *n.* बोलाचाली *f.* बोलीचाली *f.* बोलीभाष *f.*

I. *meeting for discourse.* मसलत-मनसुबा-खलबत-विचार-&c. करण्याराठीं बैठक *f.*-भेट *f.*

CONFERRIBLE, *a.* v. V. A. द्यावाजोगता-जोगा-&c. द्यायास योग्य, देय, दानीच, दानार्ह.

To CONFESS, *v. a. own*, v. To ACKNOWLEDGE. मानणें, स्वीकारणें, अंगीकारणें, कबूलकरणें, पदरीं घेणें.

2 *grant, concede*, v. To ADMIT. मान्य करणें, कबूल करणें.

3 *own and acknowledge*, v. To OWN. अंगीकारणें, स्वीकारणें, जाणणें, ओळखणें.

4 (sins to a priest) पाद्रीजवळ कबूल करणें.

To CONFESS, *v. n.* पाद्री जवळ पापें कबूल करणें.

CONFESSEDLY, *adv. avowedly, undeniably.* निभ्रांत, निसालस, निस्संशय, उघड, प्रत्यक्ष, खचीत, धडधडीत, निर्विवाद.

2 *with avowed purpose.* दाटून, हटकून, बुद्ध्या. [कारम.

CONFESSION, *n.* v. V. A.1.—*act.* मानणें *n.* &c. अंगीकार *m.* स्वी-

Full c. पोटउकल *f.* पोटफोड *f.* [&c.कर्त्ता.

CONFESSOR, *n.* v. V. A.1. स्वीकारणारा, कबूल करणारा, स्वीकार-

I. *one who hears confessions.* ज्या पाद्रीजवळ पापें कबूल करायाचीं तो, दोषश्रोतृगुरु *m.* दोषश्रवणगुरु *m.*

II. *one who suffers for his faith.* स्वधर्मार्थदुःखभोगी.

CONFIDANT, *n. bosom friend.* सखा *m.* एकांतसखा *m.* एकांतमित्र *m.* रहस्यमित्र *m.* रहस्यास्पद *n.* रहस्यपात्र *n.*

CONFIDANTE, *n.* सखी *f.* सजणी *f.* सखीजन *n.* एकांतमैत्रीण *f.*

To CONFIDE, *v. a. intrust*, v. To COMMIT. सोपणें, ओपणें, पात्यवणें, विश्वासणें.

To CONFIDE, *v. n. rely on, trust in.* विश्वासणें, ओठंगणें, पात्यवणें, पातणें, पातेजणें, विश्वास *m.*-भरवसा *m.*-इतबार *m.*-&c. ठेवणें *with* वर *of o.* कपाळ *n.* टेकणें, विश्वासावर-भरवशावर असणें *in. con. with g. of o.* and धरणें *with g. of o.*

CONFIDED, *p.* v. V. N. विश्वासलेला, &c. विश्वस्त, प्रत्ययित.

v. V. A. ओपलेला, विश्वासलेला, &c.

CONFIDENCE, CONFIDING, *n.* v. V. N. विश्वास *m.* भरोसा *or* भरवसा *m.* भाव *m.* भावना *f.* धडा *m.* निधड़ा *m.* निष्ठा *f.* इतबार *m.* प्रत्यय *m.* पात्सर *or* पात्सार *m.* अधण *n.* कपाळटेक *or* कपाळटेकणी *f.*

C. (or assurance) given. होबासा *m.*

In c. फोडणार नाहीं-फुटणार नाहीं-&c. अशा विश्वासानें, विश्वासानें.

Violation or abuse of c. विश्वासघात *m.* विश्वासभंग *m.* विश्वस्तवंचन *n.* [स्तवंचक.

Violator or abuser of c. विश्वासघातक *or* घातकी, विश्व-

Inspired with c. जातप्रत्यय, जातविश्वास.

I. *firm conviction or belief.* खातरजमा *f.* खातर *f.* खातरी *f.* धडा *m.* निधडा *m.* निभ्रांत *f.* निशा *f.* निश्चय *m.* निर्धार *m.* ठसा *m.* विश्वास *m.* भरवसा *or* भरोसा *m.* भाव *m.* भावार्थ *m.* भावना *f.*

Perfect c. बालबालखातरी *f.* बालोबालखातरी *f.*

II. *trust in self, assurance.* धमक *f.* उब *f.* आव *m.* उमेद *f.* उमेदवारी *f.* दम *m.* अवसान *n.* जुरत *f.* स्वास्थ्य *n.* प्रागल्भ्य *n.* छुंबाडी *f.* हमतम *m. f.* हिय्या *m.* हांव *f.* हिम्मत *f.*

III. *cause or ground of c.* खातरीला-&c. आधार *m.*-आश्रय *m.*-कारण *n.*

CONFIDENT, *a.* CONFIDING, *p. a.* v. V. N. विश्वासणारा, पात्यवणारा, विश्वास ठेवणारा, &c. भावडा, भावीक, भावुक, विश्वासवान्, श्रद्धालु, श्रद्धावान्, विश्वासी, श्राद्ध, विश्वस्त.

I. *convinced, assured, sure*, v. CERTAIN. निभ्रांत, निश्चयी, निश्शंक, निस्संदेह, दृढनिश्चय, कृतनिश्चय, बद्धनिश्चय.

To be or feel c. खातर*or* खातरी *f.*-&c. असणें *in. con.*

II. *secure, &c. assured and bold.* अवसानी, अवसानाचा, दमदार, दमाचा, निश्शंक, निर्भय, बिनधोक, उमेदवार, निधड, निधडा, निधड्याचा, छातीदार, हिंमतदार, हिय्येदार, स्वस्थ, प्रगल्भ.

CONFIDENTIAL, *a. trusty, trustworthy.* विश्वासी, विश्वासू, विश्वासूक, भरवशाचा, विश्वासाचा, खातरीचा, खातरजमेचा, विश्वास-&c. ठेवायाजोगा-&c. इतबारी, विश्वासनीय, विश्वास्य, विश्वासपात्र, विश्वासास्पद, श्रद्धेय, श्रद्धार्ह, माननीय, आप्त.

2 *that is to be kept in confidence; private.* नफोडायाचा, गुप्तठेवायाचा. [अशाविश्वासानें.

CONFIDENTIALLY, *adv.* v. A. 2 फोडणारनाहीं-फुटणारनाहीं-&c.

CONFIDENTLY, *adv.* v. A. विश्वासानें, भावानें, &c. विश्वास-भरवसा-&c. ठेवून-धरून, विश्वासपूर्वक, श्रद्धापूर्वक.

I. खातरीनें, निश्चयानें, निश्शंक, निश्शंकपणानें, निभ्रांत *or* निभ्रांत.

II. निधड, निश्शंक, निश्शंकपणानें, आव धरून, उमेदीनें, दमानें, अवसानानें, धमक धरून, &c.

CONFIDENTNESS. See CONFIDENCE.

CONFIGURATION. See FORM.

CONFINE, *pl.* CONFINES, *n. frontier, border.* हद्दीचादेश*m.* शिवेलगतेचादेश*m.* प्रांतदेश *m.* पालव*m.* लत्ता*m.* लगता*m.* सरद *f.*

To CONFINE, *v. n.* v. To BORDER. लागून-लगटून-भिडून-&c. असणें.

To CONFINE, *v. a. limit.* आकळणें, बांधणें, गांठणें, ठेवणें-धरणें-चसवणें-&c. with वर (ex. म्यां आपलें जेवण दोन भाकरींवर ठेविलें आहे), आकलन*n.*-आळाबांधा*m.*-आळा*m.*-मर्यादा *f.*-सीमा*f.*-नेम*m.*-बंधारण*n.*-&c. करणें-करून देणें.

2 v. To IMPRISON. कोंडणें, कैद करणें, कोंडी *f.*-कोंडणी *f.* करणें *g. of o.* कैदेंत- बंदींत घालणें-टाकणें, अटकेंत घालणें.

3 v. To RESTRAIN. आकळणें, आकलन*n.*-निबंध*m.*-निबंधन*n.*-निग्रह*m.*-निग्रहण*n.*-निरोध*m.*-निरोधन*n.*-प्रतिबंध*m.*-&c. करणें.

CONFINED, *p. & a.* v. V. A.1. आकळलेला, आळाबांधा घातलेला, &c. आकलित.

2 कोंडलेला, बंदींत घातलेला, &c. कैद, कैदी.

3 आकळलेला, &c. निबंधित, निबद्ध, निरुद्ध, निगृहीत.

I. *not roomy*, v. NARROW. अवघड, सांकड, कुंचड, अडचणीचा, दाटीबाटीचा, संकोचाचा, अप्रशस्त.

II. *delivered*. बाळंत झालेली, प्रसूतझालेली.

To be c. बाळंत-प्रसूत-&c. होणें.

III.—the bowels. बद्ध. See COSTIVE.

To be c. परसाकडे साफ होत नाहीं.

CONFINEDNESS, *n.* v.A. 1. *want of room*. अडचण *f.* संकोच*m.*

To suffer or feel c. अडचणणें, अवघडणें.

CONFINEMENT, *n.* v. V. A. 1.—*act*. आकळणें*n.* बांधणें*n.* &c. आकलन*n.*—*state*. आळाबांधा*m.* आळा*m.* बंधारण*n.* बंध*m.* बंद*m.* धरबंद*m.* बंधन*n.*

2—*state*. बंद*m.* बंदी *f.* कैद *f.* अटक *f.* कोंडी *f.* कोंडणी *f.*

C. to a place. स्थानासेध*m.*

Place of c. बंदखाना *or* बंदीखाना*m.* बंदीशाळा *f.* अंधारकोंडी *f.* अंधारखण*m.* *or* णी *f.*

Release from c. बंदखलास*m.*

Released from c. बंदखलास.

Solitary c. एकांत कैद *f.* अंधारी कोठडी *f.*

3—*state*. निग्रह *m.* निबंध*m.* निरोध*m.*

I. *delivery*, v. CHILDBED. प्रसव*m.* प्रसूति *f.*

To CONFIRM, *v. a. corroborate, establish, make sure, &c.* खरा-सत्य-बळकट-साबीत*or* साबूत-पक्का-दृढ-सुदृढ-खचीत-निश्चित-&c. करणें, खरावणें, दुणावणें *or* दुणारणें, पडसाक्ष *f.* देणें-देऊन साबीत-&c. करणें, स्थापणें, बळकटी *f.*-बळ*n.*-जोर*m.*-पक्केपणा*m.*-&c. आणणें, सत्यकार*m.* करणें *g.of o.* पुष्टि *f.* देणें, पुष्टीकरण*n.* करणें.

2 *ratify, &c.* बहाल-काईम-मुकरर-मंजूर-&c. करणें, सई *f.* करणें.

3 *strengthen, fix*,—a disease, &c. घट-बळकट-बद्धमूल-&c. करणें.

To be confirmed, जडावणें, जडकावणें, बळावणें, जुनावणें.

CONFIRMATION, *n.* v. V. 1.—*act*. खरावणें*n.* बळकट करणें*n.* &c. सत्यापन*n.* सत्यंकार*m.* सत्यकरण *n.* दृढीकरण*n.* निश्चितकरण*n.* स्थापन*n.* स्थापना *f.* पुष्टीकरण*n.*—*state*. खरावलेलेपणा*m.* &c, बळकटी *f.* मजबुती *f.* मुकररी *f.* दार्ढ्य*n.* पुष्टि *f.*

2 बहाल करणें *n.* &c. सई *f.* बहाली *f.* मंजूरी *f.*

I. *corroborative evidence*. पडसाक्ष *f.* प्रतिप्रमाण *n.*

CONFIRMATORY, *a.* CONFIRMER, *n.* v. V. 1. खरावणारा, बळकट करणारा, साबीत करणारा, &c. सत्यापनकर्त्ता, पुष्टिकर्त्ता, स्थापक, स्थापनकर्त्ता.

CONFIRMED, *p.* v. V. 1. खरा-बळकट-&c. केलेला.

2 बहाल केलेला, मुकरर केलेला, मंजूर.

To CONFISCATE, *v. a. take in penalty*. दंडासाठीं घेणें-जप्तकरणें, सरकारांत घेणें, दंडार्थहरण *n.*-दंडमूलकहरण *n.*-&c. करणें.

CONFISCATE, *a.* CONFISCATED, *p.* v. V. सरकारांत घेतलेला, &c. दंडार्थापहृत.

CONFISCATION, *n.* v. V.—*act*. सरकारांत घेणें *n.* दंडार्थहरण *n.* दंडमूलकहरण *n.* दंडरूपहरण *n.* दंडार्थापहार *m.*

Total c. सर्वस्वदंड *m.* सर्वस्वहरण *n.* सर्वहार *m.*

CONFLAGRATION, *n.* *general or great fire*. आगीचा डोंब *m.* आगधाड *f.* डोंबाळा *m.* डोंबाळी *f.* प्रलयाग्नि *m.*

C. of a forest. वणवा *m.* दावाग्नि *m.* दावानल *m.*

To CONFLICT, *v. n.* v. To FIGHT. लढणें, झुंजणें, झुंज *n.*-झोंबट *n.*-द्वंद्व *n.*-&c. करणें, *or in. con. with g.of s.* लागणें, झोंबी *f.* घेणें.

CONFLICT, *n. combat, contest*, v. FIGHT. युद्ध *n.* झुंज *n.* झोंबट *n.* झोंबी *f.* द्वंद्व *n.* संप्रहार *m.* संग्राम *m.*

2 See COLLISION.

CONFLICTING, *a. contrary, opposite*. प्रतिकूल, विरुद्ध, विरोधाचा, विरोधी, परस्परविरोधी. [*m.* संभेद *m.*

CONFLUENCE, CONFLUX, *n.* (of streams, &c.). संगम *m.* संग

C. from opposite directions. प्रीतिसंगम *m.*

2 *crowding together*. जमाव *m.* संघीभवन *n.*

3 *people crowded*, v. CROWD. जमाव *m.* मेळा *m.*

CONFLUENT, *a.* एके ठिकाणाकडे वाहणारा-संगमहोणारा, मिळणारा.

C. small pox. मसुऱ्यादेवी *f. pl.*

To CONFORM, *v. a. make like*. सारखा-बेताचा-सदृश-अनुरूप-अनुसार-&c. करणें-वागवणें-चालवणें.

To CONFORM, *v. n. comply with, act according to*. सारखें-प्रमाणें-पाहून-&c. वागणें-वर्त्तणें-आचरणें-चालणें-करणें-&c. अनुसरणें, अनुवर्त्तणें, अनुसरण *n.* करणें.

CONFORMABLE, *a. resembling*, v. LIKE. सारखा, बेताचा, सदृश, अनुरूप, समरूप.

2 *agreeable, congruous*, v. CONSISTENT, मिलाफाचा, बेताचा, माफक, अनुकूल, अनुसार (in comp.), अनुसारी (in comp.), समर्पक, संभावित, संभूत.

3 *compliant, obsequious*, v. OBEDIENT. मिलाफी, मिळताऊ, अनुरोधी, अनुलक्षी, विनीत, अनुविधायी.

CONFORMABLENESS, CONFORMITY, *n.* v. A. 1. सारखेपणा *m.* सदृशता *f.* सादृश्य *n.* सामरूप्य *n.* समरूपता *f.* सरूपता *f.* सारूप्य *n.* आनुरूप्य *n.*

2 मिलाफ *m.* जम *m.* लाग *m.* संभावना *f.* संभूति *f.* संभव *m.* आनुरूप्य *n.* अनुरूपता *f.*

3 अनुलक्ष्य *n.* अनुरोध *m.* अनुवर्त्तन *n.* अनुवृत्ति *f.*

CONFORMABLY, *adv.* v. A. 1. सारखा.

2 *and* ACCORDINGLY, सारखा, अन्वयें, अनुरूप, अनुसार (in comp.), यथा (in comp.), बरहुकूम, यथावत्.

3 अनुरोधानें, अनुलक्षून.

CONFORMATION. See FORM.

CONFORMER, COMFORMIST, *n.* v. V. N. अनुसरणारा, अनुवर्त्तणारा, अनुसरण-&c. कर्त्ता-कारी, अनुसारी (in comp.).

I. कायद्यानें स्थापलेल्या धर्मास अनुसरून वागणारा.

To CONFOUND, To CONFUSE, *v. a. mingle confusedly, disorder, jumble, derange*. ढवळणें, गळहाटणें, गफलतणें, गोंधळणें, गळफटणें, गाबाळणें, भानगडणें, गदळणें, गोबडणें, गडबडवणें, गोंधळवणें, विसकटणें, उसकटणें, उलकटणें, एका काठीनें हाकणें, घालमेल *f.*-गोंधळ *m.*-धांदल *f.*-गडबड *f.*-भानगड *f.*-गलत *f.*-उलटापालट *f.*-उलथापालथ *f.*-संकर *m.*-संकरीकरण *n.*-&c. करणें *g. ofo.*

2 *perplex, puzzle, bother, bewilder, &c.* घाबरविणें, भ्रमविणें, बहकावणें *or* भकावणें, गळफटणें, गळफटवणें, गोफाटणें, गांगरविणें, भांबवणें *or* भांबावणें, चकवणें, तजावजा *adv.* करणें, भ्रमांत पाडणें-घालणें, भ्रम *m.* घालणें-पाडणें, घोळांत-गळफट्यांत-गोफाट्यांत-&c. पाडणें-घालणें, गडबड *f.*-हडबड *or* डी *f.*-धांदल *f.*-घोंटाळा *m.*-घोळ *m.*-गोंधळ *m.*-&c. करणें *g. of o.* भूल *f.*-चकभूल *f.* घालणें-करणें *g. of o.* चक्री *f.*-चौकडी *f.*-चंद्री *f.* भुलवणें-गुंगवणें-गुंग करणें *g. of o.*

3 *blast, disconcert*, v. To DEFEAT. उडवणें, हरवणें, लथडणें *or* लथाडणें, उपमर्द *m.*-उपमर्दन *n.*-भंग *m.*-भंजन *n.*-विघात *m.*-

&c. करणें, *g. of o.* [यास लावणें,मिधा-&c. करणें.

4 *abash, put to shame,* v. To SHAME. लाजवणें, खालीं पहा-

CONFOUNDED, CONFUSED, *p.* v.V. 1. गोंधळलेला,गाबाळलेला,&c. अस्तव्यस्त, गदळ, बिसकळीत, शबल, संकीर्ण, संकुल, संकरीकृत.

To be or become c. गोंधळणें, गोंधवणें, गोंधरणें, गडबडणें, गळफटणें, गलबलणें.

2 घाबरा, चकित, चकभूल, चक्क, थक्क, थक्कीत, चरक, बावरा, भ्रमिष्ट, भ्रमित, भ्रांत, संभ्रांत, जातभ्रम, हतज्ञान, विक्षिप्त, व्याकुल, व्याकुलमना, व्यस्त.

To be or become c. घाबरणें, घोंटाळणें, गडबडणें, गलबलणें, गोंधळणें, हडबडणें, धांदलणें, चकणें, भांबवणें *or* भांबावणें, बहकणें *or* भकणें, बावरणें, छकणें, गांगरणें *or* गेंगरणें, गांगावणें, गणबणणें *or* गणमणणें, गोंधरणें, गोंधवणें, गुपटणें, रानभरी होणें, हांवभरी होणें.

CONFOUNDER, *n.* CONFOUNDING, *p. a.* CONFUSER, *n.* v. V. 1. गोंधळणारा, &c. गोंधळ-&c. करणारा, घालमेल्या, गलबल्या, गोंधळ्या, भानगड्या, भानगडखोर, गळफट्या, गदळ्या, घोंटाळ्या, गुरपट्या. [रा, &c. भ्रामक.

2 घाबरविणारा, &c.भ्रम-&c. पाडणारा-घालणारा, भ्रमांत पाडणा-

CONFOUNDING, CONFUSION, *n.* v. V. 1.—*act.* ढवळणें *n.* गोंधळणें *n.* &c. &c. संकरी करण *n.*—*state.* अव्यवस्था *f.* घालमेल *f.* गोंधळ *m.* घोळ *m.* घप्पाघोळ *m.* घोळंकार *m.* घोळाणा *m.* गदळ *m.* गाबाळ *m. n.* गळ्हाटा *or* ठा *m.* गफलत *f.* गडबड *f.* गलबल *f.* गलफटा *m.* घोंटाळा *m.* गुरपटा *or* फटा *m.* गोबळगाथा *m.* गाबाळगाथा *m.* संकर *m.* ब्रह्मघोळ *m.* बिसकळ *f.* अफरातफर *f.* गलत *f.* गलतान *f.* शबल *n.* एकबाट *m. f.* एकमंगळ *n.* गाळण *f.* एकाकार *m.* ढपलंशायी *f.* बचमंगळ *n.* भिसमिल्ला *m.* झंगड *f.* भानगड *f.* बचबच *f.* चवचव *f.* चवढव *f.* ढवढव *f.* ढवळा *m.* ढवळाढवळ *f.* बचढव *f.* धांदल *f.* धांदलपट्टी *f.* धांदलाधांदल *f.* गोहोत *n.* गडबडगुंडा *m.* घाण *f.* गुघाण *f.*

Every thing there is in c. and disorder. तेथें बेड्याचा बाजार पिकला आहे.

2—*act.* घाबरविणें *n.* बहकावणें *n.* &c.—*state.* गडबड *f.* हडबड *or* डी *f.* धांदल *f.* गोंधळ *m.* गळफटा *m.* घोंटाळा *m.* घोळ *m.* घोळंकार *m.* घोळाणा *m.* घप्पाघोळ *m.* गलबल *f.* हैराणी *f.* हैराणगत *f.* चकभूल *f.* भूल *f.* त्रेधा *f.* तारातीर *f.* तारातिरपीट *f.* भ्रम *m.* संभ्रम *m.* विक्षेप *m.* वैचित्य *n.* चित्तवैकल्य *n.*

I. v. SHAME. कालिमा *f.*

CONFRATERNITY, *n. a brotherhood.* भाउमंडळी *f.* भाउबळ *f.* बंधुमंडल *n.* बंधुवर्ग *m.*

To CONFRONT, *v. a.* See To FACE. 2 *bring face to face.* मुकाबला *m.*-रुजुमुकाबला *m.*- रुजुवात *f.*-उरुबुरू *f.* करणें-घेणें *g.ofo.* समक्षासमक्ष *f. n.*-प्रत्यक्षाप्रत्यक्ष *f. n.*-तोंडातोंड *n.* करणें *g. of o.* रुबरू-समक्ष-&c. करणें *with* सीं.

CONFRONTATION, *n.* v. V. 2.—*act or state.* रुजुमुकाबला *m.* मुकाबला *m.* रुजुवात *f.* प्रत्यक्षता *f.*

To CONFUSE, &c. See To CONFOUND, &c.

CONFUTABLE, *a.* v. V. खंडाया-चा-जोगता-जोगा-&c.मोडाया-जोगा-&c. खंडनीय, खंडनार्ह, खंडन योग्य, खंडनशक्य.

CONFUTATION, *n.* v. V.—*act.* खंडणें *n.* मोडणें *n.* &c. खंडन *n.* मोड *m.* वितंडा *f.*

To CONFUTE, *v. a. prove to be wrong*—person or statement. कोंडणें, खंडणें, काईल-कुंठित-निरुत्तर-&c. करणें, खुंटवणें, मोड *m.*-खंडन *n.*-वितंडा *f.* करणें *g. of o.* मोडून काढणें, खोटा करून दाखवणें.

CONFUTED, *p.* v. V. खंडलेला, &c. खंडित, प्रतिहत, कुंठित, काईल.

CONGÉ. See OBEISANCE.

To CONGEAL, *v. a. change to a solid state.* जमवणें, थिजवणें, गोठवणें, सांखवणें, सांखळवणें, घण-घट्ट-&c. करणें.

To CONGEAL, *v. n.* जमणें, थिजणें, गोठणें, सांखणें, सांखळणें, घण-&c. होणें.

CONGEALED *p.* v. V. A. जमवलेला, &c. घनीकृत.

2 v. V. N. जमलेला, &c. घनीभूत.

CONGEALMENT, CONGELATION, *n.* v. V. A.—*act.* जमवणें *n.* थिजवणें *n.* &c. थिजवणूक *f.* थिजवणी *f.* गोठवणी *f.*—*state.* जमवलेलेपणा *m.* &c. घनीकृतता *f.*

v. V. N.—*act.* जमणें *n.* थिजणें *n.* &c. गोठणी *f.*—*state.* थिजलेपणा *m.* घनीभाव *m.* घनीभूतत्व *n.*

CONGENERACY, CONGENEROUSNESS, *n.* v. A. एकजातपणा *m.* हमजातपणा *m.* एकजातीयता *f.* सजातीयता *f.* समानजातीयता *f.* &c.

CONGENER, CONGENERIC, CONGENEROUS, *a. of the same kind or nature, allied in origin,&c.* हमजात, सजातीय, समजातीय, एकजातीय, समानजातीय, एककारणक, समबीजक.

CONGENIAL, *a.* See CONGENERIC. 2 *agreeable to the nature of.* सात्म्याचा, अनुगुण, अनुकूल, आनुगुण्याचा, आनुकूल्याचा, स्वभावानुगुण, स्वभावानुसार, स्वभावानुरूप, प्रकृत्यनुगुण-अनुसार-अनुसारी-अनुरूप-अनुकूल-&c.

3 *of the same nature or disposition.* समशील, समानशील, समस्वभाव, समभाव, समानभाव, एकभाव, समधर्मक, समानप्रकृतिक, समप्रकृतिक.

CONGENIALITY, *n.* See CONGENERACY. 2 v. A. 2. सात्म्य *n.* आनुगुण्य *n.* आनुकूल्य *n.* अनुकूलता *f.*

3 समानशीलता *f.* समशीलता *f.* समानप्रकृति *f.* समभाव *m.* साधर्म्य *n.* समधर्मता *f.* स्वभावसाम्य *n.* प्रकृतिसाम्य *n.*

CONGENITAL. See CONNATE.

CONGER. CONGER EEL, *n.* समुद्रांतली बाम *f.*

CONGERIES, *n. collection, mass.* पुंज *m.* राशि *m.* जाल *n.* (in comp as नक्षत्रजाल, शब्दजाल, अंकजाल, वृक्षजाल, &c.).

CONGESTION, *n.* (of humors into a tumor). गांठ *f.* ग्रंथि *m.*

2 (of blood). रक्तसांकळ *f.* रक्तावरोध *m.* रक्तावष्टंभ *m.* रक्तस्तंभन *n.*

CONGESTIVE, *a.* रक्तावरोधसूचक-दर्शक.

To CONGLOBATE, *v. a. collect into a ball.* गोठवणें, घट्टगोळा *m.*-घट्टभेंडा *m.* करणें *g. of o.* पिंडी करण *n.* करणें *g. of o.*

CONGLOBATE, *a.* CONGLOBATED, *p.*v. V. गोठवलेला, गोळा केलेला, पिंडीकृत.

CONGLOBATION, *n.* v. V.—*act.* गोठवणें *n.* &c. पिंडीकरण *n.*

I. *round mass.* गोळा *m.*

To CONGLOMERATE, *v. a.* गोळा *m.*-गुंडा *m.*-गुंडाळें *n.* करणें *g.ofo.* गुंडाळ्याच्या आकाराचा करणें, गुंडासा करणें.

CONGLOMERATE, *a.* CONGLOMERATED, *p.*v.V. गोळा केलेला-झालेला, गुंडाळ्याच्या आकाराचा.

To CONGRATULATE, *v. a.* सहानंदोक्ति *f.*-सहानंदकथन *n.*-सहानंद प्रकाश *m.*-&c. करणें, मुबारकी *f.*-मुबारकबादी *f.* करणें, अभिनंदन *n.*-अनुमोदन *n.* करणें.

CONGRATULATED, *p.* v. V. अभिनंदित, अनुमोदित.

CONGRATULATION, *n.* v. V. सहानंदोक्ति *f.* सहानंदकथन *n.* &c. अभिनंदन *n.* मुबारकी *f.* मुबारकबादी *f.* अनुमोदन *n.*

CONGRATULATORY, *a.* सहानंददर्शक-सूचक-प्रकाशक-&c. मुबारकीचा, मुबारकबादीचा. [णें, जमावणें.

To CONGREGATE, *v. a.* v. To ASSEMBLE. जमा करणें, गोळा कर-

To CONGREGATE, *v. n.* v. To GATHER. मिळणें, जमा होणें.

CONGREGATION, *n. congregated body*, v. ASSEMBLY. सभा *f.* मंडळी *f.* जमाव *m.* समाज *m.* [सामाजिक.

CONGREGATIONAL, *a.* मंडळीच्या संबंधाचा, समाजाच्या संबंधाचा,

CONGRESS, *n. meeting*, v. ASSEMBLY, सभा *f.* मंडळी *f.*

Sexual c. स्त्रीपुरुषसंग *m.* मिथुन *n.* मैथुन *n.*

To be joined in sexual c. जुगणें, लागणें.

CONGRUENCE, CONGRUITY, CONGRUOUSNESS, *n.* v. A. मेळ *m.* मिलाफ *m.* जम *m.* अनुसंधान *n.* आनुगुण्य *n.* आनुकूल्य *n.* अनुकूलता *f.* समन्वय *m.* गांठ *f.* योग *m.* लाग *m.* सोईसुमार *m.* संविधान *n.*

CONGRUENT, CONGRUOUS, *a. agreeable, suitable, &c.* v. CONSISTENT. बेताचा, मिलाफाचा, मिलाफी, माफक, जमाचा, जमावाचा, जुगलीचा, योग्य, यथायोग्य, सुयुक्त, उपयुक्त, समर्पक, समन्वित.

CONGRUOUSLY, *adv.* v. A. *and* SUITABLY. योग्य, यथायोग्य.

CONIC, CONICAL, *a.* निमुळता *or* निमोळता, गायदूम, गोपुच्छाकृति, गोपुच्छाकार, शंकाकार, सूच्यग्र.

CONIC SECTIONS, *n.* शंकुच्छेद *m.* शंकुछिन्न *n.*

CONJECTURABLE, *a.* v. V. अनुमेय, अनुमानगम्य, अनुमानसाध्य.

CONJECTURAL, *a. done or said by guess.* अनुमानाचा, अनुमानप्रमाणक, अनुमानिक, अनुमानमूलक, तर्काचा, कल्पनेचा.

CONJECTURALLY, *adv.* v. A. अनुमानानें, अनुमानें करून, तर्कानें, अनुमानतः, कल्पनेनें.

CONJECTURE, *n.* अनुमान *n.* अटकळ *f.* तर्क *m.* अजमास *m.* कल्पना *f.* अनुमिति *f.*

2 *conjectural statement.* अटकळपंचविसीचें-तगदमपट्टीचें-तगदम्याचें-&c. बोलणें *n.*-भाषण *n.*-&c. अनुमानोक्ति *f.*

To CONJECTURE, *v. a.* v. To GUESS. अटकळणें *in. con.* अटकळून-अटकळ करून-&c. सांगणें-बोलणें-&c. अजमासणें, अनुमान *n.*-&c. करणें *g. of o.* [*g. of o.*

To CONJOIN, *v. a.* v. To JOIN. जोडणें, मिळवणें, संयोग *m.* करणें

CONJOINED, *p.* CONJOINT, *a.* CONJUNCT, *a.* v. V. जोडलेला, &c. संबद्ध, संयुक्त, संयोजित, संयुत, संयोगित, अनुयुक्त, समेत, सामलाती.

CONJOINTLY, CONJUNCTLY, *adv. jointly, together.* मिळून, संगतीनें, सोबतीनें, योगतः, संयोगतः, युगपत्, यौगपद्यानें.

CONJUGAL, *a. belonging to marriage.* विवाहाचा, विवाहविषयक, विवाहसंबंधी, वैवाहिक, औद्वाहिक.

2 *belonging to the relation between husband and wife.* दंपति धर्माचा, दांपत्याचा, दंपति भावाचा, स्त्री पुरुष भावाचा.

To CONJUGATE, *v. a. inflect verbs.* रूपें *n. pl.* चालवणें, रूपाख्यापन *n.*-वाच्यता *f.*-आख्यान *n.* करणें.

CONJUGATION, *n.* v. V.—*act.* रूपें चालवणें *n.* रूपाख्यापन *n.* वाच्यता *f.* आख्यान *n.*

I. *a c. a class of roots.* गण *m.* [न *n.*

CONJUNCTION, *n.* v. V.—*act.* जोडणें *n.* &c. संबंधन *n.* संयोज—*state*, v. UNION. संयोग *m.* समायोग *m.* संबंध *m.* संधि *m.* *f.* संपर्क *m.*

I.—in astronomy (of stars). योग *m.* संयोग *m.* संगम *m.*

Auspicious c. सुयोग *m.* शकुनगांठ *f.* अमृतसिद्धि योग. This term is especially applied to seven conjunctions, viz. to the occurrence upon Sunday and thence in order through the week, of the *nakshatra* हस्त and thence in order respectively of श्रवण, अश्विनी, अनुराधा, पुष्य, रेवती, रोहिणी.

Inauspicious c. कुयोग *m.* दुर्योग *m.* पापग्रह *m.*

C. of sun and moon. सूर्येंदुसंगम *m.* अर्केंदुसंगम *m.* युति *f.*

Day of c. of sun and moon. अमावास्या *pop.* अंवस *f.* अमा *f.* दर्श *m.*

II.—in grammar; *connecting word.* उभयान्वयि अव्यय *m.*

CONJUNCTIVE, *a.* जोडणारा, संयोग करणारा.

CONJUNCTURE, *n. juncture, crisis.* प्रसंग *m.* योग *m.* संधि *m. f.* बाणी *f.* अणी *f.* अणीबाणी *f.* गडसंद *or* ध *f.* लग्नघटिका *f.* टिपण *m.* [पुसणें *n.* &c.

CONJURATION, CONJURING, *n.* v. V. A. 1.—*act.* शपथ घालून 2—*act.* भारणें *n.* &c. भारणी *f.*

v. V. N. इलम *m.* जादूटोणा *m.* बाजीगरी *or* गारी *f.* सिद्धसाधन *n.* चाक्षुषी विद्या *f.*

I *conjuring tricks.* फांफूं*n.* छांछूं*n.* ठांठूं*n.* तंतरमंतर*n.* धंतरमंतर*n.* गौडबंगाल*n.* गारूड*n.* माव *f.* कुसृति *f.* भूतसृष्टि *f.*

To CONJURE, *v. a. charge &c. by oath.* शपथ-सत्य-आण-&c. घालून सांगणें-बोलणें-पुसणें, ताकीद *f.* करणें, विनंती *f.* करणें, शपथ *f.*-आण *f.*-सत्य*n.*-&c. घालणें, सशपथ विनंति *f.*-&c. करणें.

2 *enchant, &c.* v. To CHARM. भारणें, मंतरणें, भारणी *f.*-&c. करणें, मंत्रप्रयोग*m.* करणें, इलम*m.* चालवणें *with* वर *of o.*

To CONJURE, *v. n. practise conjuring.* फांफूं*n.*—छांछूं*n.*-तंतरमंतर*n.*-गौडबंगाल*n.*-गारूड*n.*-नजरबंदी *f.*-दृष्टिबंध*m.*-इलम*m.*-&c. करणें.

CONJURER, *n.* v. V. A. 2 *and* V. N. मंत्र घालणारा-मारणारा-करणारा, मंत्रवादी, मंत्री, गारुडी *or* गारोडी, गौडबंगाली, गौडबंगाल्या, भानामत्या, पंचाक्षरी, इलमबाज, इलमी, इलमवाला, बाजीगर *or* गार, नजरबंद, नजरबंद्या, मायावी, मायाकार, मायाजीवी, मदारी, ऐंद्रजालिक.

CONNASCENCE, *n.* v. A. 1. एकजन्म*n. m.* सहजन्म*n. m.* सहजसिद्धि *f.* एकोत्पत्ति *f.*

2 सहजन्म*n. m.* सहोत्पत्ति *f.*

CONNATE, *a. born with, connatural.* जन्माचा, स्वाभाविक, निसर्गज, नैसर्गिक, सांसिद्धिक, सहज, सहजसिद्ध.

2 *born with another.* सहज, सहजसिद्ध, सहजात, सहोत्पन्न, सहजन्म, सहभव, समकालज.

CONNATURAL, *a. born with.* See CONNATE. 2 *having the same nature with.* हमजात, एकजातीय, सजातीय, समजातीय, समानजातीय, समभाव, समानभाव, एकभाव, समधर्मक.

CONNATURALITY, CONNATURALNESS, *n.* v. A. 2. एकजातपणा*m.* समभाव*m.* समभावता *f.* जातिसाम्य*n.* जातिसमता *f.* एकजातीयता *f.* &c.

To CONNECT, *v.a.* v. To JOIN. जोडणें, संबंध*m.*-योग*m.*-संयोग*m.*-&c. करणें *g. of o.* संबद्ध-संयुक्त-सलग्न-&c. करणें.

2 *join coherently.* अनुसंधान*n.*-संदर्भ*m.*-पूर्वापर संबंध*m.*-संगति *f.*-मागलें पुढलें धोरण *n.*-&c. बांधणें-ठेवणें-राखणें-धरणें.

CONNECTED, *p.* v. V. 1. जोडलेला, &c. संबद्ध, संयुक्त, संयोगित,

संयोजित, संयुत, समन्वित, संसृष्ट, सलग्न, संसक्त.
2 संगत, संगतवार, सुसंबद्ध, सुसंगत, संदर्भशुद्ध.
I. v. RELATED. संबंधी, आप्त, आप्तविषय, नातलग.
II.—gener. *or* freely, as by blood, marriage, business, &c. आंगलग, लागू, लागू भागू, लागी.

CONNECTEDLY, *adv. coherently.* संगतवार, मागलें पुढलें धोरण ठेवून, संदर्भपूर्वक.

CONNECTION, CONNEXION, *n.* v. V. 1.—*act.* जोडणें*n.* &c. संबंधन*n.* संयोजन*n.*—*state.* संयोग*m.* संबंध*m.* लगत*f.* संधि*m.f.* संपर्क*m.* संसक्ति*f.* संसृष्टत्व*n.* सलग्नता*f.*
Intimate & constant c. समवाय*m.*
2 अनुसंधान*n.* संदर्भ*m.* धोरण*n.*
I. *coherence,* v. CONSISTECY. संगति *pop.* संगत*f.* अन्वय*m.* संबंध*m.* लाग*m.* संदर्भ*m.*
II. *a.* c. *person connected,* v. RELATION. सोयरा, संबंधी, नातेदार, नातेवाईक, शरीर संबंधी.—gener. or indef. सोयराधायरा *m.*
C.s and acquaintances—compreh. सोयरे धायरे*m. pl.*
III. gener. *or* freely, as by blood, marriage, business, &c. *bond, band, link, tie, thread.* संबंध*m.* लगाबांधा*m.* लगा*m.* लग*m.f.* नातें*n.* सूतगोत*n.* धागा दोरा*m.* दोरा*m.* सूत*m.*
Indissoluble c. जन्मगांठ*f.*
Nearness or closeness of c. जवळीक*f.*
IV.—esp. of matters; *relation, link, &c.* दोरा*m.* धागादोरा *m.* लग*m. f.* लगा*m.* तंतु*m.* इलाखा*m.* तालुका*m.* पागोरा*m.*
In c. with. संबंधीं, निसबत.
V. *carnal* c. v. COPULATION. संग*m.* संयोग*m.*

CONNECTOR, *n.* CONNECTING, *p. a.* CONNECTIVE, *a.* v. V. 1. जोडणारा, &c. संयोजक, संयोजन-&c. कर्त्ता-कारी-कारक, संबंधकर्त्ता-कारी.

CONNED, *p.* v. V. घोकलेला &c. घोकींव.

CONNING, *n.*v.V.—*act.* घोकणें*n.*घोष*m.* उद्घोष*m.*गुणिका*f.* संथा*f.* *v.* दे, घे, हो, म्हण.

CONNIVANCE, CONNIVING, *n.* v. V.—*act.* डोळे झांकणें*n.* कान डोळा *or* कानाडोळा*m.* डोळेझांक*f.* आनाकानी*f.*

To CONNIVE, *v. n. wink at, let pass unnoticed.* डोळे*m. pl.* झांकणें, कानाडोळा*m.*-आनाकानी*f.*-डोळेझांक*f.*-&c. करणें, पाहिलें नपाहिलें-ऐकिलें नऐकिलें-&c. करणें, डोळ्यावर पापणी*f.*-कातडें*n.* ओढणें.

CONNOISSEUR, *n. critical judge.* जाणता, पारखी, परीक्षक, परीक्षावंत, ग्राहक, दर्शक, रसज्ञ, रसिक, मार्मिक, मर्मज्ञ, गुणज्ञ, गुणग्राही, चिकित्सक.
—ironically, v. WISEACRE. गाजरपारखी *or* ख्या.

CONNUBIAL, *a. belonging to mariage.* विवाहाचा, विवाहसंबंधी-विषयक, वैवाहिक, विवाहमूलक.
2 *belonging to the relation between husband and wife,* v. CONJUGAL. दंपतिभावाचा, स्त्रीपुरुषभावाचा.

To CONQUER, *v. a. vanquish, overcome, subdue.* जिंकणें, पराजय*m.*-पराभव*m.*-जय*m.* करणें *g. of o.* शिकस्त-पराजित-जित-विजित-परभूत-&c. करणें.
That has conquered his passions. जितेंद्रिय.
2 *acquire by conquest.* जिंकणें, जिंकून-जयकरून-युद्धकरून-&c. घेणें-मिळवणें, हस्तगत करून घेणें.

To CONQUER, *v. n.* जय*m.* पावणें-मिळवणें. [पराभव्य.

CONQUERABLE, *a.* v. V. A. 1. जेतव्य, जय, जय्य, पराभवनीय,

CONQUERED, *p.* v. V. A. 1. जिंकलेला, &c. पराजित, पराभूत, जित, विजित, निर्जित.
2 जिंकून घेतलेला, &c. जित.

CONQUERING, CONQUEST, *n.* v. V. A. 1.—*act.* जिंकणें*n.* &c. जय*m.* विजय*m.* पराजय *m.*
Universal c. दिग्विजय*m.*
2—*act.* जिंकून घेणें*n.* जिंकणें*n.*
I. *thing conquered.* जयलब्धवस्तु*n.* जितद्रव्य*n.* जितवस्तु*n.*

CONQUEROR, *n.* v. V. A. 1. जिंकणारा, &c. पराजय-पराभव-&c. कर्त्ता.
2 जिंकणारा, जिंकून घेणारा.
v. V. N. जयी, विजयी, जयकर्त्ता, जययुक्त, जयमान.
A mighty c. दिग्विजयी.

CONSANGUINEOUS, *a.* v. RELATED. एकारक्ताचा, एकारक्तामांसाचा, एका हाडामासाचा, एकरक्त, एकशरीर, सगोत्रज, एकशरीरावयव.

CONSANGUINITY, *n.* v. A. एकरक्तसंबंध*m.* समरक्तसंबंध*m.* एकशरीरसंबंध*m.* एकशरीरान्वय*m.*

CONSCIENCE, *n.* There seems to be no word in *Maráthi* exactly answering to this word. The following words convey, under suitable connections, the general sense of it. मन*n.* बुद्धि*f.* अंतरदीप*m.* अंतःकरण*n.* अंतर्यामी*m.* अभिमंता*m.* इमान*n.* खंत*f.*
Clearness of c. चित्तशुद्धि*f.* अंतःकरण शुद्धि*f.*
No witness is so strong as one's c. मना एवढा गाही त्रिभुवनांत नाहीं.
To resist or fight against c. बुद्धीसीं वैर*n.* करणें.
To make a c. of. इमानाची गोष्ट*f.* असणें *in.con.*

CONSCIENTIOUS, *a. influenced by conscience*—person, v. JUST. नेकीचा, नेतीचा, नेकराखणारा, न्यायनिष्ठ, परनिष्ठ, सत्यनिष्ठ, मनःपूताचारी, इमानी, इमानाचा.
2 *regulated by conscience.* नेकीचा, नेतीचा, इमानाचा.

CONSCIENTIOUSLY, *adv.* इमानानें, इमानराखून, सत्यबुद्धीनें.

CONSCIENTIOUSNESS, *n.* v. A. इमानीपणा *m.* न्यायनिष्ठा*f.* सत्यनिष्ठा*f.*

CONSCIONABLE, &c. See JUST &c.

CONSCIOUS, *a. possessing one's senses,* v. SENSIBLE. सावध, सुचित्त, देहभानी, सचेतन, सचेता, चेतन, संज्ञावान्.
2 *knowing internally.* स्वबोधित, स्वसूचित, स्वज्ञात, आत्मबुद्ध, आत्मबोधित, मनोबोधित, मनःसाक्षी.
To be c. of. जाणणें, जाणून-समजून असणें, मनसाक्ष असणें.
3 *knowing, perceiving, aware.* वाकबदार, माहितगार, *or* वाकबदार-माहितगार-&c. झालेला, प्राप्तज्ञान, जातज्ञान, लब्धज्ञान, जातबोध, प्राप्तबोध.

CONSCIOUSLY, *adv.* v. A. 1. देहभानानें, देहभानावर असून, शुद्धीनें, शुद्धीवर असून, &c. सदेहभान, सचेतन.

CONSCIOUSNESS, *n.* v. A. 1. शुद्धि*f.* देहशुद्धि*f.* भान *n.* देहभान*n.* सावधगिरी*f.* सावधपणा *m.* चैतन्य *n.* होष *m.* फाम *f.* प्रबोध *m.* संज्ञा*f.*
Bereft of c. v. INSENSIBLE. बेशुद्ध, बेहोष, निचेष्टित, निश्चेतन, निचेतन, बेसावध.
To return to c. देहावर-देहभानावर-शुद्धीवर-स्थितीवर-ध्या-

नावर- स्मृतीवर-&c. येणें, संज्ञा *f.* होणें *g. of. s.*

2 आत्मबोध *m.* अंतर्बोध *m.* अनुव्यवसाय *m.*

3 समज *m.* माहिती *f.* उमट *m. v.* पड, प्रमा *f.* संवेद *m.*

I. *conscious feeling, sense of self.* अहंकार *m.* अहंमति *f.* अहंभाव *m.*

CONSCRIPT, *a. enrolled.* पट्टावर लिहिलेला, पट्टावर मांडलेला.

CONSCRIPT, *n.* पट्टावरलिहिलेल्यांपैकीं ज्यावर लशकरांत नौकरी करण्याची पाळी आली तो.

CONSCRIPTION, *n.* लशकरांत पाठविण्याच्या उद्देशानें अमुक वयाच्या मनुष्यांचीं नांवें पट्टावर मांडणें *n.*-मांडण्याची चाल *f.*

To CONSECRATE, *v. a. dedicate.* उत्सर्ग *m.* करणें *g. of o.* प्रतिष्ठणें, प्रतिष्ठा *f.* करणें *g. of o.* देणें-लावणें-वाहणें-अर्पण *n.* करणें *with* कडे.

2 (by distillation, streaming, or sprinkling). अभिषेकणें, अभिषेक *m.*-अभिषेचन *n.* करणें *g. of o.*

CONSECRATE, *a.* CONSECRATED, *p.* v. V. 1. प्रतिष्ठित, अभिमंत्रित, उत्सृष्ट, संस्कृत,(देवाकडे &c.) लावलेला-वाहिलेला-&c.

2 अभिषेकलेला, अभिषिक्त, अभिषेचित.

CONSECRATION, *n.* v. V. 1.—*act.* प्रतिष्ठणें *n.* प्रतिष्ठापन *n.* उत्सर्ग *m.* अभिमंत्रण *n.*—*a. or s.* प्रतिष्ठा *f.* संस्कार *m.*

2—*act.* अभिषेकणें *n.* अभिषेक *m.* अभिषेचन *n.*

CONSECTARY, See CONSEQUENT.

CONSECUTION, *n.* v. SUCCESSION. परंपरा *f.* अनुक्रम *m.* अन्वय *m.* आनुपूर्वी *f.* आनुपूर्व्य *n.* अनुषंग *m.* अनुवृत्ति *f.* अनुबंध *m.*

In close c. बराबर, हारोहार, तारोतार, लागोपाठ, पाठोपाठ, लगोलग, मागोमाग, लगत.

2—in logic, *train of consequences.* सिद्धांतमाला *f.* सिद्धांतानुक्रम *m.* अनुमानपरंपरा *f.*

CONSECUTIVE, *a.* v SUCCESSIVE. अनुक्रमाचा, लागोपाठचा, पाठोपाठचा, मागोमागचा, &c. पारंपरिक, आनुक्रमिक, आन्वयिक, अविछिन्न क्रमिक.

CONSECUTIVELY, *adv.* v. A. एकापाठीमागें एक, अनुक्रमानें, अनुक्रमशः, अनुक्रमतः, बराबर, लगत, अनुपूर्वशः, तारोतार, हारोहार.

CONSENT, *n. assent, concurrence, &c.* v. AGREEMENT. रुकार *m.* होयकार *or* होकार *m.* अनुमत *n.* अनुमति *f.* सम्मत *n.* सम्मति *f.* खुशरजावंती *f.*

Tacit or implied c. मानस *n.*

With free c. (or choice). सुखसंतोषानें, सुखासमाधानानें, राजीरजावंतीनें, खुशरजावंतीनें, राजीखुशीनें.

To express c. (or concurrence). रुकारणें, रुकार *m.*-हां *f.* देणें, होय *n.* म्हणणें.

2 *accord of minds,* v. AGREEMENT. एकचित्त *n.* एकमत *n.*

With one c. एकचित्तानें, एकमतानें.

To CONSENT, *v. n. assent, concur, &c* v. To AGREE. रुकार *m.* -होकार *m.* देणें-भरणें, कबूल-अनुमत-सम्मत-&c. होणें, अनुमत *n.* देणें.

CONSENTANEOUS, *a. agreeable.* See CONSISTENT.

CONSENTER, *n.* CONSENTIENT, *a.* CONSENTING, *p. a.* v. V. रुकारदेणारा, &c. अनुमत, सम्मत, कबूल, राजी, खुशरजावंत, एकचित्त.

CONSEQUENCE, *n. result, issue, end, product, effect, fruit.* फल *or* फळ *n.* फलोत्पत्ति *f.* फलोदय *m.* फलश्रुति *pop.* फळश्रुत *f.* फळादेश *m.* फलितार्थ *m.* परिणाम *m.* परिपाक *m.* अर्थ *m.* कार्य *n.* निष्पन्न *n.* गुण *m.* योग *m.* प्रयोग *m.* प्रयुक्ति *f.*

In c. v. CONSEQUENTIALLY. त्यामुळें, त्यावरून, म्हणून.

2 *connection of cause and effect.* कार्यकारणसंबंध *m.* कार्यकारणान्वय *m.* हेतुहेतु मदन्वय *m.* कार्य हेतुसंबंध *m.* [*m.*

3 *result, deduction,* v. CONCLUSION. सिद्धांत *m.* निश्चितार्थ.

4 *moment, importance,* v. WEIGHT. मुजारवा *m.* (*neg. con.*) भार *m.* वजनदारी *f.* भारीपणा *m.*

5 *dignity, respectability,* v. WEIGHT. मोठेपणा *m.* गौरव *n. m.* भारदस्ती *f.*

CONSEQUENT, *a. resulting, following.* आनुषंगिक, अनुयायी, अनुयोगी, अनुवृत्त, अनुसारी, आन्वयिक, कार्यकारण संबंधी, औपाधिक, उपाधिजन्य, प्रयुक्त (in comp.).

CONSEQUENTIAL, *a.* See CONSEQUENT. 2 *big, lofty,* v. CONCEITED. दिमाखदार, दिमाखाचा, पत्रासी *or* जी, तोरेदार, तोऱ्याचा, मिजाजी.

CONSEQUENTIALLY, *adv.* v.A. 1. त्यामुळें, तस्मात्, म्हणून, अर्थात्, कार्यकारणान्वयेंकरून, कार्यकारणभावानें, अतएव, फलतः, अतःकारणात्, तदर्थ.

2 दिमाखानें, तोऱ्यानें, &c.

CONSEQUENTIALNESS, *n.* v. A. 2 *and* AIRS. दिमाख *m.* तोरा *m.* पत्रास *f.* मिजाज *f.* शेखी *f.* बढाई *f.* बढाइकी *f.*

CONSEQUENTLY. See CONSEQUENTIALLY.

CONSERVATORY, *n.* जनावरें-वनस्पति-वगैरे सुरक्षित ठेवण्याचें स्थळ *m.* रक्षणशाला *f.* रक्षणस्थान *n.*

To CONSERVE, &c. See To PRESERVE, &c.2 See To CANDY.

To CONSIDER, *v. a. ponder, study, weigh.* मनास आणणें, चित्तास आणणें, घोळणें, कुटणें, मंथणें *or* मथणें, विचारणें, तोलणें, तुकणें, मनन *n.*-विचार *m.*-विचारण *n.*-विचारणा *f.*-&c. करणें *g. of o.*

2 *view, regard, hold.* पाहणें, मानणें, भावणें, मोजणें, गणणें, लेखणें, धरणें.

3 *take into view, respect.* पाहणें, लक्षिणें, मनांत-ध्यानांत-लक्ष्यांत-&c. आणणें, लक्ष्य *n.*-&c. देणें *with* कडे *of o.* जमेस धरणें.

To CONSIDER, *v. n. deliberate,* v. To THINK. चिंतणें, पाहणें, चिंतन *n.* करणें, विचारांत असणें.

CONSIDERABLE, *a. worthy of consideration.* विचारकरायाजोगा-&c. विचारणीय, विचार्य, मननीय, मंतव्य. [न्यतेचा.

2 v. RESPECTABLE. संभावनीय, संभावित, मान्य, योग्य, मा-

3 *moderately large, &c.* बरा, बरासा, बराच, सुमाराचा, सांगायाजोगा, जमेस धरायाजोगा-&c. गण्य, अनुपेक्षणीय, अनुपेक्ष्य.

CONSIDERABLY, *adv.* v. A. 3. बराच, सुमाराचा, &c. *all decl.*

CONSIDERATE, *a. deliberate, reflecting, pondering.* विचारी, विचारशील, विचारवान् *pop.* विचारवंत, विचारदर्शी, विचारदृष्टि, विचारसंपन्न, विचारानुयायी, विचारानुसारी, जाण, गंभीर, प्रेक्षावान्, प्रेक्षावंत, विमृश्यकारी.

2—of measures or acts. विचारपूर्वक, विचारपुरस्सर, सविचार, विचारपुरस्कृत, बुद्धिपूर्वक, बुद्धिपुरस्सर, बुद्धिपुरस्कृत.

CONSIDERATELY, *adv.* v. A. 1. विचारानें, विचारेंकरून, विचारपूर्वक, विचारपुरस्सर, बुद्ध्या.

CONSIDERATENESS, *n.* v. A. 1. विचारीपणा *m.* विचारशीलता *f.* विचारदृष्टि *f.* विचारस्वभाव *m.* विचारिता *f.* विमृश्यकारिता *f.*

CONSIDERATION, *n.* v. V. A. 1. घोळणें *n.* &c. विचार *m.* विचारण *n.* विचारणा *f.* विभावन *n.* विभावना *f.* संभावना *f.* ऊहापो-

ह m. मंथन or मथन n. मंथित or मथित n. मनन n. छान f. आलोडन n. विमर्श m. पेक्षा f. चर्चा f. तजवीज f.

C. of pros and cons. कार्याकार्यविचार, फलाफलविचार, सदसद्विचार, कर्तव्याकर्तव्यविचार.

Mature c. खरपूसविचार.

Minute c. सूक्ष्मविचार, गुरुलघुविचार.

Upon c. If we consider, &c. पाहिलें असतां, पाहिल्यार्थी, पाहतार्थी, विचार केला असतां.

v. V. N. विचार m. चिंतन n. मनन n. चिंतणूक f.

I. *worthiness of regard*, v. WEIGHT. मान्यता f. योग्यता f. वजन n. भारदस्ती f. वजनदारी f.

II. for; *deference, &c.* भीड f. मुलाजा m. मुरवत f. चाड f.

To treat with allowance and c. संभाळून घेणें-वागविणें-&c.

III. for; *care or concern about*, v. CONCERN. विचार m. परवा f. खातर or री f. चिंता f. आंच f. गुमान m.

IV. *motive, reason.* हेतु m. कारण n. निमित्त n. सबब f.

V. *equivalent, recompense.* मोबदला or मोबादला m.

CONSIDERED, *p.* v. V. A. 1. घोळलेला, &c. विचारित, चिंतित, विभावित, मंथित or मथित, आलोडित.

To CONSIGN, *v. a. intrust, &c.* v. To COMMIT. सोपणें, हवालणें, निरवणें, निरवणी f.-निरवणूक f.-अर्पण n.-समर्पण n.-&c. करणें g. of o.

2—goods to an agent (अडत्याकडे) पाठविणें.

CONSIGNABLE, *a.* v. V. सोपायाचा, &c. अर्पणीय, अर्प्य, समर्प्य.

CONSIGNEE, *n.* अडत्या m.

CONSIGNED, *p.* v. V. सोपलेला, हवाललेला, न्यस्त, अर्पित, समर्पित.

2 अडत्याकडे पाठविलेला.

CONSIGNMENT, *n.* v. V.—*act.* सोपणें n. हवालणें n. निरवणें n. &c. निरवणूक f. निरवणी f. न्यास m. निक्षेप m. निक्षेपण n. अर्पण n. समर्पण n.

I. *goods consigned.* अडत्याकडे पाठविलेला माल m.

To CONSIST, *v. n. subsist,* v. To BE. असणें, होणें.

2 *be constituted or composed.* असणें *with g. of s.* घटितमय-रूप-आत्मक-&c.असणें (in comp.).

3 with; *accord with,* v To AGREE. संभवणें, जुगणें, जुळणें, जमणें, मिळणें, बनणें, घटाव m. बनणें, जम m.-जबा m.-&c. बसणें g. of s. recip. [BEING.

CONSISTENCE, CONSISTENCY, CONSISTING, *n.* v. V. 1. See 3. *and* AGREEMENT. मिलाफ m. मेळ m. जम m. जमाव m. संभव m. संभावना f. संभूति f. सुमार m. लाग m.

I. *agreement with self; coherence.* ताळ m. ताळतंत m. तालामाला m. धरनेम m. धरबंध or द m. धारबंद m. धारबोळ m. धारमेर f. धर m. ठिकाण n. ठिकाणा m. अनुसंधान n. धोरण n. or मागचेंपुढचें धोरण n. सुमार m. संदर्भ m. संदर्भशुद्धि f. गांठ f. पूर्वापराविरोध m. धार m.

II. *degree of denseness.* घटपणा m. घणपणा m. दाटपणा m. घनता f सांद्रता f.

CONSISTENT, *a* CONSISTING, *p. a.* v. V. 1. असणारा, &c.

2 मय (in comp. as सुवर्णमय &c.), रूप (in comp. as सुवर्णरूप, &c.), आत्मक (in comp. as सुवर्णात्मक &c.), भूत (lit. *been* or *being*; much and elegant use is made of this word in comp. as आश्रयभूत, आधारभूत, अवयवभूत, being, standing, &c. in the capacity, quality, nature. &c. of), घटित (in comp.).

3 *congruous, consonant, accordant, with,* &c. मिळाफाचा, मिलाफी, जुळणीचा, बेताचा, जमाचा, जमावाचा, मेळाचा, संभावित, संभूत, यथायोग्य, अनुकूल, उपयुक्त, सुयुक्त, माफक, समर्पक, समन्वित, अनुसार (in comp.), अनुसारी (in comp.), अनुरूप (in comp.).

I. *agreeing with itself, coherent.* संगतीचा, संगतवार, सुसंगत, संदर्भाचा, जुळणीचा, संदर्भशुद्ध, पूर्वापराविरुद्ध, संबद्ध, संगत, अन्वयशुद्ध, संयुक्तिक, समन्वित, समर्थ.

II. *firm, not fluid.* घन pop. घण, घट्ट, जाड, दाट, सांद्र.

CONSISTENTLY, *adv.* v.A. 3. *and* ACCORDANTLY. बेतानें, अन्वयानें, अन्वयधरून, अनुरोधानें, संधानानें, सुमारानें, अनुसंधानानें, अनुरूप (in comp.), अनुसार (in comp.).

I. *in a consistent manner.* संगतवार, मागलें पुढलें धोरण धरून-राखून-&c. एकरीतीनें, एकमार्गानें, &c. पूर्वापराविरोधानें, पूर्वापराविरोधपूर्वक, &c.

CONSOCIATE. See ASSOCIATE, CONFEDERATE.

To CONSOCIATE. See To JOIN, To COMBINE.

CONSOLABLE, *a.* v. V. सांतवाया-चा-जोगा-&c. शमनीय, सांत्वनीय, सांत्वनाई, सांत्वनशक्य.

CONSOLATION, CONSOLING, *n.*v.V.—*act.* डोळेपुसणेंn. सांतवणेंn. &c.सांत्वनn. सांत्वनाf. आश्वासनn. मनसमजावणीf. मनसमजावशीf. दुःखापहरणn. क्लेशापहरणn. संतापहरणn. दुःखपरिमार्जनn. दुःखपरिहार m.—*state.* समाधान n. चित्तसमाधान n. चित्तस्वास्थ्य n. चित्तस्वस्थता f. दुःखशांति f. श्रमशांति f.

I. *cause of c. comfort.* समाधानहेतु m. समाधानास कारण n. समाधानस्थल n. समाधानसाधन n. दुःखाच्यापरिहाराचीगोष्ट f.-विषय m.-&c.

To CONSOLE, *v. a. solace, comfort.* आसवें or आंसूं n. pl.-डोळे m. pl. पुसणें g. of o. सांतवणें, स्वस्थावणें, आश्वासणें, दुःखाची शांति f. करणें, दुःख n. घालवणें g. of o. समाधान n.-चित्तसमाधान n.-सांत्वन n.-सांत्वना f.-आश्वासन n.-दुःखापहरण n.-संतापहरण n.-&c. करणें g. of o. जीव m.-चित्त n. थंड करणें g. of o.

CONSOLED, *p.* v. V. सांतवलेला, &c. आश्वासित, जातसांत्वन, जातसमाधान, प्राप्तसांत्वन, लब्धसमाधान, शांतदुःख, शांतश्रम, शांतक्लेश.

CONSOLER, *n.* CONSOLING, *p. a.* CONSOLATORY, *a.* v. V. सांतवणारा, &c. सांत्वन कर्त्ता-कारक-जनक-&c. आश्वासक, आश्वासन कर्त्ता-कारक, दुःखहर-हारक-&c. शोकहर-हर्त्ता-हारक-हारी, शोकापह, तापहर-हर्त्ता-&c. क्लेशापह, क्लेशहर-हर्त्ता-&c. संतापहर-हारी-&c. दुःखशमक.

To CONSOLIDATE, *v. a. make solid, dense,* &c. दृढ-कठिन pop. कठीण-घट्ट-घन pop. घण-&c. करणें, घटविणें, अटविणें, गोठवणें.

2 See To JOIN.

To CONSOLIDATE, *v. n. become solid, &c.* गोठणें, घटणें, अटणें, दृढावणें, दृढ-घट्ट-&c. होणें.

CONSOLIDATE, *a.* CONSOLIDATED, *p.* v. V. A. 1. दृढ-घट्ट-&c. केलेला, घनीकृत, दृढीकृत, सांद्रीकृत.

2 See JOINED.

v. V. N. घटलेला &c. घटींव, अटींव, घनीभूत, दृढीभूत, सांद्रीभूत.

CONSOLIDATION, *n.* v. V. A. 1.—*act.* दृढकरणें n. घट्टकरणें n. &c. घनीकरण n. दृढीकरण n. सांद्रीकरण n.

v. V. N. घटणें n. अटणें n. &c.

CONSONANCY, CONSONOUSNESS, *n.* v. A. 1. *and* CONCORD. स्वरैक्य *n.* स्वरसाम्य *n.* समस्वरता *f.* सामस्वर्य *n.*
2 मिलाफ *m.* जम *m.* जवा *m.* जमाव *m.* मेळ *m.*

CONSONANT, CONSONOUS, *a. agreeing in sound.* समस्वर, एकस्वर, समनाद, एकनाद.
2 *congruous*, v. CONSISTENT. मिलाफाचा, मिलाफी, जमाचा, बेनाचा, &c. उपयुक्त.

CONSONANT, *n.* व्यंजन *n.* हलूवर्ण *m.*
Conjunct or double c. संयोग *m.*

To CONSORT, *v. n. associate with*, v. To ACCOMPANY. संग *m.*-संगति *f.*-समागम *m.*-सहवास *m.*-साहचर्य *n.*-&c. करणें *g. of o.*

CONSORT, *n. husband or wife*, q. v. लग्नाचा झालेला सोबती-साथी-संगती-जोडपी (*and fem.* सोबतीण &c.) दादला *m.* बायको *f.*

CONSPICUOUS, *a. easy to be seen.* पाहण्यांत सहज यायाजोगा-&c. सुदर्श, सुदृश्य, सुदर्शनीय, सहजदृश्य, सुव्यक्त, प्रसिद्ध. [सिद्धीचा.
2—of marks, &c. See CLEAR. 3. v. EMINENT. प्रसिद्ध, प्र-
To become c. निवटणें, निसवणें.

CONSPICUOUSLY, *adv.* v. A. 1. पाहण्यांत सहज यायाजोगा *a. decl.* प्रसिद्धपणें, उघडपणें, सुव्यक्त.

CONSPICUOUSNESS, *n.* v. A. 1. सुदृश्यता *f.* सहजदृश्यता *f.* सुव्यक्ति *f.* सुव्यक्तता *f.*
3 प्रसिद्धपणा *m.* प्रसिद्धि *f.* [कूट *n.*

CONSPIRACY, *n.* v. COMBINATION. संगनमत *n.* कट *m.* एककट *m.*

CONSPIRATOR *n.* संगनमती, संगनमत्या, कुटांतला.

To CONSPIRE, *v. n.* v. To COMBINE. मिळणें, कट *m.*-जूट *m. f.*-&c. बांधणें-करणें, कूट *n.*-एकोपा *m.*-संगनमत *n.*-&c. करणें.
2 *concur.* See To AGREE.

CONSPISSATION. See THICKENING.

CONSTABLE, *n.* पोलीस खात्यांत एक अधिकारी आहे.

CONSTANCY, *n.* v. A. 1. सततपणा *m.* नित्यता *f.* सातत्य *n.* नैरंतर्य *n.* सततभाव *m.*
2 धर *m.* स्थैर्य *n.* स्थिरता *f.* स्थिति *pop.* स्थीत *f.* अव्यभिचार *m.* निश्चंचलता *f.* अचांचल्य *n.*

CONSTANT, *a. continuing*, v. CONTINUAL. नित्य, निरंतर, सतत.
2 *persistent, steady, firmly adherent.* स्थिर, स्थिरात्मा, स्थिरचेता, स्थिरचित्त, स्थायी, निश्चंचल, अचंचल, अचल, अव्यभिचारी, सत्वधीर, नीलराग.

CONSTANTLY, *adv.* v. A. 1. *and* EVER. नित्य, नित्यानें, नित्यें, नेमी *or* नेहमीं, नेमानें, नित्यशः, नित्यउठून, रोजउठून, सतत, संतत, सदोदित, येऊनजाऊन, येरयेरां, रात्रंदिवस, अहोरात्र, निशिदिनि.
2 स्थिरतेनें, स्थिरचित्तानें, स्थैर्यपूर्वक. [नक्षत्रगण *n.*

CONSTELLATION, *n. cluster of stars.* नक्षत्र *n.* नक्षत्रांचा घड *m.*
2 fig. *genius, star, &c.* v. PRODIGY. तारा *m.* तेजःपुंज *m.* अपरसूर्य *m.*

CONSTERNATION, *n.* v. FRIGHT. तिरपीट *f.* त्रेधा *f.* गात्रभंग *m.* चळकांप *m.* पांचावरधारण *f. v.* बस, लटपट *f.*

To CONSTIPATE, *v. a. make costive.* कोठा *m.* बंद करणें *g. of o.* बद्धकोष्ठ करणें, मलावरोध *m.*-&c. करणें.

CONSTIPATED, *p.* v. V. बद्धकोष्ठ.

CONSTIPATION, *n.* v. COSTIVENESS. सांसळा *m.* बद्धकोष्ठ *n.* मलावरोध *m.* मलावष्टंभ *m.*

CONSTITUENCY, *n. body of constituents.* नेमणारे *m. pl.* योजणारे *m. pl.* नियोजकसमूह *m.*

CONSTITUENT, *a. elemental, essential.* कारणभूत, अधिकरणभूत, मूलभूत, बीजभूत, हेतुभूत, मूलरूप, मूलात्मक, अवयवभूत, अंशभूत, अंगभूत.

CONSTITUENT, *n.* v. A. *essential part.* कारणभूत-&c. पदार्थ *m.*-विषय *m.*-&c. अवयवभूत-अंशभूत-अंगभूतपदार्थ *m.*-विषय *m.*
2 See CONSTITUTER.

To CONSTITUTE, *v. a.* See To COMPOSE. To MAKE.
2 *nominate, elect*, v. To APPOINT. नेमणें, योजणें, नेमणूक *f.*-योजना *f.*-योजणूक *f.*-&c. करणें *g. of o.* नियुक्तकरणें.

CONSTITUTER, *n.* v. V. 2. नेमणारा, योजणारा, &c. नियोजक, नियोगकर्त्ता.

CONSTITUTION. *n. native state or character*, v. NATURE. प्रकृति *f.* प्रकृतिभाव *m.* निसर्ग *m.* निसर्गभाव *m.* स्वभाव *m.*
2 (of mind or body). *particular temperament or temper.* प्रकृति *f.* स्वभाव *m.* तबियत *f.* अंगस्वभाव *m.* देहस्वभाव *m.*
To lose its tone, soundness &c.—the constitution. प्रकृतीचा ताळ बिघडणें-नासणें-जाणें, प्रकृतीनें ताल *m.* सोडणें-टाकणें.
To recover healthy tone—the constitution. प्रकृति ताळ्यावर येणें.
3 *form of government.* राज्यव्यवस्थास्वरूप *n.* राज्यनीतिस्वरूप *n.* राज्यरीति *f.* राज्यकरणनियम *m. pl.* राज्यप्रवृत्तिनियम *m. pl.*

CONSTITUTIONAL, *a.* v. N. 1. *and* NATURAL. जातीचा, स्वाभाविक *pop.* स्वभाविक *or* वीक, स्वभावसिद्ध, नैसर्गिक, निसर्गज, स्वभावज, प्रकृत्यनुरूप, प्रकृत्यनुसार, प्राकृत.
2 प्रकृतीचा, तबियतीचा, अंगस्वभावाचा. [मानुसार.
3 *legal &c.* राज्यव्यवस्थानुरूप, राज्यव्यवस्थानुसार, राज्यनिय-

CONSTITUTIONALLY, *adv.* v. A. 1. प्रकृतीनें, स्वभावानें, जातीनें, स्वभावतः, निसर्गतः, प्रकृतितः, प्रकृत्या, जात्या.
3 राज्यनियमानुसार, राज्यव्यवस्थानुरूप, &c.

To CONSTRAIN, *v. a. force, oblige*, v. To COMPELL. बळ *n.*-बळात्कार *m.*-&c. करणें-चालवणें *with* वर *of o.* गळ *m.* घालणें.
2 *confine, bind*, v. To RESTRAIN. आवळणें, आवरणें, निग्रह *m.*-&c. करणें *g. of o.* बंद-बद्ध-&c. करणें. [रीस्तव.

CONSTRAINEDLY, *adv. by compulsion.* बळानें, बळात्कारामुळें, जब-

CONSTRAINT, *n.* v. V. 1.—*state.* परबलवशता *f.* परबलाधीनता *f.* जातबलात्कारता *f.*
2—*state.* निग्रह *m.* निबंध *m.* निरोध *m.* आवर *m.* आटणी *f.* आळा *m.* आळाबांधा *m.*
I. *constraining power*, v. COMPULSION. जोर *m.* बळजोरी *f.* जबरी *f.* बळात्कार *m.*
By c. जबरीनें, जबरीस्तव, जबरीमुळें, बळात्कारावर, &c.

To CONSTRICT, *To* CONSTRINGE, &c. See To CONTRACT, &c.

To CONSTRUCT. See To BUILD, To COMPOSE.

CONSTRUCTION, *n.*—*in grammar*, v. SYNTAX. अन्वय *m.* पदान्वय *m.* वाक्यपद्धति *f.* वाक्यरचना *f.* पदयोजना *f.* अन्वयरचना *f.* अन्वययोजना *f.* प्रयोग *m.* [शय *m.*
2 v. INTERPRETATION, MEANING. अर्थ *m.* अभिप्राय *m.* आ-

CONSTRUCTIVE, *a. inferred, implied.* अनुमानसिद्ध, आनुमानिक, अर्थसिद्ध, अर्थापत्तिसिद्ध, आर्थिक.

To CONSTRUE, *v. a. arrange in natural order.* अन्वय *m.* लावणें-जुळणें-करणें *g. of o.* लावणें, अन्वययोजना *f.*-अन्वयलापन *n.*-अन्वयलापनिका *f.*-लापन *n.*-लापनिका *f.* करणें *g. of o.*
2 v. To INTERPRET. अर्थ *m.* लावणें-करणें.

CONSTRUING, *n.* v. V. 1.—*act.* अन्वयलावणें*n.*&c. अन्वययोजना *f.* अन्वयलापन*n.* अन्वयलापनिका *f.* लापन*n.* लापनिका *f.*

To CONSTRUPATE. See To RAVISH.

CONSUBSISTENCE, *n.* v. A. सहस्थिति *f.* सहभवन*n.*

CONSUBSISTENT, *a. existing together.* सहस्थित, सहस्थितिक, आनुषंगिक, सहजसिद्ध.

CONSUBSTANTIAL, *a. of the same substance.* समतत्व, समानतत्व, एकतत्व, समवस्तुक, समद्रव्यक, समानद्रव्यक, एकद्रव्यक, समजातीय, एकजातीय, सजातीय.

CONSUBSTANTIALITY, *n.* v. A. समतत्वता *f.* समानतत्वता *f.* तत्वसाम्य*n.* वस्तुसाम्य*n.* द्रव्यसाम्य*n.* सजातीयता *f.* तादात्म्य*n.*

CONSUETUDE, CONSUETUDINAL. See CUSTOM, CUSTOMARY.

CONSUL, *n. commercial agent of a state.* व्यापाराच्या संबंधाचा कोणस्या सरकारानें परराष्ट्रांत राहण्यास पाठविलेला वकील.

To CONSULT, *v. a. ask counsel of.* पुसणें, विचारणें, विचार *m.*-सल्ला *f.*-मसलत *f.*-अभिप्राय*m.*-मत*n.*-&c. घेणें *g. of o.*

2 *regard, consider the interests of.* पाहणें, विचार*m.* करणें *g. of o.* लक्ष्य*n.*-दृष्टि *f.*-नजर *f.*-&c. देणें-ठेवणें *with* कडे *or*वर*of o.*

3 (books &c.) पाहणें, अभिप्राय*m.*-अनुमत *n.*-&c.घेणें *g. of o.*

To CONSULT, *v. n. take counsel together.* मसलत *f.*-विचार*m.*-मनसुबा*m.*-&c. करणें.

CONSULTATION, *n.* v. V. N. मसलत *f.* विचार*m.* मनसुबा*m.*

Secret c. खलबत*n.* एकांत*m.* मंत्र*m.* हितगूज*n.*

To CONSUME, *v. a. devour, swallow up, burn, &c.* खाणें, खाऊन टाकणें, खाक करणें, जाळून टाकणें, स्वाहा *adv.* करणें, गिळणें, ग्रासणें, सग्रास*m.* करणें *g. of o.* फस्त *adv.* खाणें-करून टाकणें, खाऊन कडाचूर*m.* करून टाकणें.

2 *expend, use wholly,* v. To EXHAUST. खर्चणें, सारणें, फन्ना *m.*-फडशा*m.* करणें-उडवणें *g. of o.* अटवणें.

3 *annihilate, ruin, &c.* v. To DESTROY. लय*m.*-नाश*m.*-सत्यानाश*m.*-क्षय*m.*-&c. करणें *g. of o.* खाक करणें.

To CONSUME, *v. n. waste, be exhausted.* लय*m.*-क्षय*m.*-&c. होणें *g. of s.* क्षप*m.* पावणें, खिपणें.

CONSUMED, *p.* v. V. A.1. खाऊन टाकलेला, खाक केलेला, &c.

2 खर्चलेला, &c. खलास, फारीक, समाप्त, फडशा केलेला-झालेला, निश्शेष.

3 नाशकेलेला, नष्ट.

CONSUMER, *n. user, &c.*—as opposed to *producer, productive.* घेणेकरी, घेणेदार, ऋणकरी, ऋणस्वरूपी.

CONSUMMATE, *a.* See PERFECT.

To CONSUMMATE, *v. a. complete,* v. To PERFECT. पूर्ण-पुरता-पुरा-संपन्न-पक्का-&c. करणें, पूर्णता *f.*-संसिद्धि *f.*-&c. करणें *g.ofo.*

CONSUMMATED, *p.* v. V. पूर्णकलेला,&c.

CONSUMMATION, *n.* v. V.—*act.* पूर्णकरणें*n.* &c. पूर्णकरण*n.* —*state.* पूर्णता *f.* पूर्ति *f.* संसिद्धि *f.* निष्पत्ति *f.* संपूर्णता *f.*

CONSUMPTION, *n.* v. V. A.—*act.* खाणें*n.* खाऊन टाकणें*n.* खाक करणें*n.*—*state.* फन्ना*m.* फडशा*m.* सप्पा*m.* सग्रास*m.* क्षय*m.*

2 *act.* खर्चणें*n.* फडशा करणें*n.* &c. खर्च*m.*—*state.* बेबारा*m.*फडशा*m.* खर्च*m.* व्यय*m.* फन्ना*m.*

3 See DESTRUCTION. [राज*m.*

I. v. PHTHISIS. क्षयरोग*m.* कफक्षय*m.* यक्ष्मा *or* यक्ष्मरोग*m.*रोगII.—gener. *wasting disease, tabies.* झड *or* झडी *f.* सडी *f.* क्षयरोग*m.* भेरूड*n.* क्षरण*n.* किरी *f.* झिजणी *f.* झिरकणी *f.* झुरणी *f.* झुरवशी *f.* सुसवशी *f.* [गग्रस्त.

CONSUMPTIVE, *a. affected with c.* झडया, क्षयी, क्षयरोगी,क्षयरो-

2 *inclined to c.* क्षयभावनेचा, आसन्नक्षयी, क्षयोन्मुख.

CONTABULATION, *n.* तक्तपोशी.

CONTACT, *n. touch, close union.* स्पर्श *m.* संस्पर्श *m.* लगत *f.* लगता *m.* संयोग *m.* संयोजन *n.* नैरंतर्य *n.* आनंतर्य *n.* संपर्क *m.* संघट्टन *n.* संघट्टना *f.* सक्ति *f.* संसक्ति *f.* संसर्ग *m.* सन्निपात *m.* प्रत्यासत्ति *f.* साक्षात्संबंध *m.*

Ascertainment by c. त्वाचप्रत्यक्ष *m.*

In c. लगत.

Mediate c. or connection. अंतरास्पर्श *m.* परंपरास्पर्श *m.* सांतरस्पर्श *m.* परंपरासंबंध *m.* संयुक्तसंयोग*m.* [*s. recip.*

To come into c. संघट्टणें, संघट्टन *n.* होणें *in. con. or g. of*

CONTAGION, *n. communication by contact.* स्पर्शसंचार *m.* स्पर्शसंक्रमण *n.* स्पर्शानुप्राप्ति *f.*

2 *fig.* दुष्टसंसर्ग *m.*

CONTAGIOUS, *a. infectious, &c.* स्पर्शानें-संसर्गानें लागणारा-लागायाजोगा-&c. स्पर्शसंचारी, स्पर्शसंक्रमी,त्वाच, सांसर्गिक, सांक्रामिक, स्पर्शाक्रामक.

CONTAGIOUSNESS, *n.* v. A. स्पर्शसंचारित्व *n.* स्पर्शसंक्रमिता *f.* &c.

To CONTAIN, *v. a. hold, comprehend, comprise.* धरणें, ठेवणें, सांठवणें, सांठवून-मावून घेणें, समावेश *m.*-&c. होणें-असणें *g. of. o. with in. con.* The word is most idiomatically rendered reversely *To be contained* (*q. v.*) as, This vessel will contain two seers, ह्या पात्रांत दोन शेर मावतील.

2 See To RESTRAIN.

To CONTAIN, *v. n. live in continence.* इंद्रियनिग्रह *m.*-उपस्थनिग्रह *m.*-कामजय *m.*-&c. करणें.

CONTAINABLE, *a.* v. V. *that may be contained.* मावाया-समावाया-रहाया-&c. जोगा-जोगता-&c.

CONTAINED, *p.* v.V.A. 1. धरलेला, समावेश झालेला, &c. समाविष्ट, अंतर्भूत, गर्भित, धृत, अंतःपाती (in comp.).

To be c. मावणें, समावणें, माणें, सांठणें, राहणें, जाणें.

CONTAINER, *n.* CONTAINING, *p. a.* v. V. A.1. भरणारा, मावून घेणारा, &c. धारक, धारी.

To CONTAMINATE, CONTAMINATION, &c. See To DEFILE, &c.

To CONTEMN, *v. a. despise, scorn, disdain, disesteem, &c.* हेटणें, तिटकारणें, तिरस्कारणें, हेलसांडणें, अवगणणें, अपमानणें, अवमानणें, अनमानणें, अनादरणें, तुच्छ-हलका कःपदार्थ-&c. मानणें-समजणें-जाणणें, अमान्य करणें, अपमान *m.*-अवमान *m.*-तिटकारा *m.*-तिरस्कार *m.*-हेटाळणी *f.*-हेलसांड *f.*-हेलसांडणी *f.*-हेळा *f.*-&c. करणें *g. of o.* In this general sense *To hold lightly* or *To reject scornfully,* but as better agreeing with the more expressive and emphatic words *To Scout, To Flout, To Fleer, &c.* are कसपटाप्रमाणें मोजणें-मानणें-लेखणें-गणणें-&c. शेंटळणें *or* शेंटाळणें, झिडकावणें, झिडकारणें, हिडसणें *or* हिडसावणें, वारापाणी*n.*-केरवारा*m.*करून टाकणें *g.of o.*उडवणें, हडबडावणें, हडहडावणें, हडहड *adv.* करणें, धिस *interj.* पिटावणें, हेडसावणें, लथडणें *or* लथाडणें, छुन्योछुन्यो *adv.* करणें, थेर*n.* करणें, केंडणें, नाखुश करणें, गुमान*m.* नसणें *g. of o.* जुमास *or* जुमान*m.* नसणें *with* स *or* ला *of o.* (*with neg. con.*) जुमानणें, छिथु *f.*- थुथु *f.*-गाळण *f.*-उडवाउडव *f.*-उडवणी *f.*-पायमल्ली *f.*-&c. करणें *g. of o.* And some phrases and idiomatic expressions are पासंगीं आणीत नाहीं (त्याला, तुला, &c.) मग बजनाला कोठें आणणार ? भीक देखील घालणार नाहीं (तुला &c. *i. e.* I hold thee unworthy of notice even as a beggar). मी &c. परवा बाळगीत नाहीं *g. of o. or* काय परवा-काय कथा-काय पाड-काय किमत- काय बिशात—काय पदार्थ—काय मजकूर—&c. *g. of s.* कोणत्याझाडाचा पाला (हा, तूं &c.) ?

CONTEMNED, *p.v.*V. अवगणलेला, अवमानलेला, हेळसांडलेला,तुच्छमानलेला, अवगणित, अगणित, अवमानित, अवमत, अपमानित, अनादृत, तुच्छीकृत, तिरस्कृत, अवज्ञात, अवहेलित, लघूकृत, निराकृत.

CONTEMNER, *n.* v. V. तिरस्कारणारा, हेळणारा, &c. अवमान-अपमान-अनादर-&c. कर्त्ता-कारी-&c. तिरस्कर्त्ता, तिरस्कारी.

To CONTEMPER, *To* CONTEMPERATE. See To TEMPER.

CONTEMPLABLE, *a.* v. V. 1. ध्यानलावून पहायाजोगा-&c. बिलोकनीय. [नीय, मंतव्य.

2 ध्यानकरायाजोगा-&c. ध्यातव्य, ध्येय, चिंत्य, चिंतनीय, मन-

To CONTEMPLATE, *v. a. regard or consider fixedly.* लक्षिणें, ध्यानलावून-लक्ष्यलावून-टक लावून-&c. पाहणें.

2 (abstractedly). ध्यान *n.*-ध्यास *m.*-चिंतन *n.*-चिंतना *f.*-&c. करणें *g. of o.* ध्याणें.

3 *have in view with reference to a future event.* ध्यानांत-लक्ष्यांत-मनांत-धोरणांत-डो॰यांत-&c. असणें *in. con.*

To CONTEMPLATE, *v. n. muse, meditate.* ध्यान *n.*-चिंतन *n.*-मनन *n.*-&c. करणें, ध्यानांत-चिंतेंत-&c. असणें.

CONTEMPLATED, *p.* v. V. A. 1. ध्यान लावून पाहिलेला, &c. लक्षित, विलोकित.

2 ध्यान केलेला, ध्यात, चिंतित.

CONTEMPLATION, *n.* v. V. A. 1.—*act.* ध्यानलावून पाहणें *n.* &c.

2 ध्यान करणें *n.* ध्यान *n.* ध्यास *m.* निदिध्यास *pop.* निजध्यास *m.* निदिध्यासन *n.* अनुध्यास *m.* अध्यास *m.* प्रेक्षा *f.*

—esp. of the deity, or one's own soul. ध्यान *n.* समाधान *n.* समाधि *m.*

Absorbed in c. of the deity. ध्यानस्थ, समाधिस्थ, समाहित, ब्रह्मभूत, समाधिमान्.

Air or look of c. ध्यानमुद्रा *f.*

v. V.N. मनन *n.* चिंतन *n.* मानसपूजा *f.*

CONTEMPLATIVE, *a.* CONTEMPLATOR, *n.* v. V. A. 2 *and* V. N. *meditative, thoughtful.* ध्यानशील, मननशील, ध्यानी, चिंतनशील, चिंताशील, ध्याता, ध्यानस्थ.

—esp. on the deity, &c. ध्याता, ध्याननिष्ठ, ध्यानी, ब्रह्मनिष्ठ, समाधिमान्, आत्माराम, अंतर्मुख, अंतर्निष्ठ, ज्ञानाभ्यासी.

CONTEMPORANEOUS, CONTEMPORARY, *a. living or being at the same time.* एकाकाळचा, एकेवेळचा, समकाली, समकालिक, समानकाली, एककालिक, बराबरचा, समानकालिक.

CONTEMPORARY, *n.* एके काळीं असणारा-राहणारा.

CONTEMPT, CONTEMNING, *n.* v. V.—*act.* तिरस्कारणें *n.* हेळणें *n.* अवमानणें *n.* अवगणणें *n.* &c. हेटाळणी *f.* हेळसांड *f.* हेळसांडणी *f.* तिटकारा *m.* तिरस्कार *m.* अवहेलन *n.* अवज्ञा *f.* हेला *f.* अपमानन *n.* अवमानन *n.* अवगणन *n.* अवगणना *f.* लघूकरण *n.* तुच्छकरण *n.* तिरस्कृति *f.* तिरस्करण *n.* निराकरण *n.* धिक्कार *m.* धिक्करण *n.* न्यक्करण *n.* न्यक्कार *m.* अवक्रिया *f.*—as better agreeing with *scouting, flouting,* &c. गाळण *f.* उडवणी *f.* उडवाउडव *f.* पायमल्ली *f.* पायमाली *f.* कडीलोट *or* कडेलोट *m.*

—*state.* अपमान *m.* अवमान *m.* अवगणना *f.* हेळसांड *f.* हेलना *f.* अवहेलना (*pop.* णा) *f.* हेटाळणी *f.* नाचक्की *f.*परिभव *m.* अपमानितत्व *n.* अवमानितत्व *n.* See also under DISGRACE. I.—the sentiment or passion. तिरस्कार *m.* तिटकारा, अवमति *f.* अवमानता *f.* अनादरबुद्धि *f.* तुच्छभाव *m.* तिरस्कारभाव *m.*

CONTEMPTIBLE, *a.* v. V. *and* MEAN. हेळणे जोगा, हेळसांड करायाजोगा, &c. तुच्छमानाया जोगा, &c. तिरस्कार्य, अवगणनीय, अवगणनार्ह, हेलनीय, अवमान्य, अवमाननीय, अवज्ञेय, निर्भर्त्स्य, धिक्कारकार्य, गर्हणीय, गर्ह्य, अपमानार्ह, अवमानार्ह, &c.

CONTEMPTIBLENESS, *n.* v. A. तुच्छपणा *m.* हलकेपणा *m.* तिरस्कार्यता *f.* अवमाननीयता *f.* &c. अवमानार्हता *f.* अवगणनार्हता *f.* &c.

CONTEMPTUOUS, *a. scornful, disdainful.*—person. तिरस्कारी, बरडोळ्या, दिमाखदार, दिमाखी, दिमाखाचा, ताठल्याडोळ्यांचा, ताठ्याचा, अवमानी, अवमंता, तिरस्कारकर्त्ता, मानी, ऊर्ध्वदृष्टि, उन्नतशिरस्क.

2 *expressing scorn.*—language, &c. अपमानाचा, तिरस्काराचा, धिक्काराचा, दिमाखाचा, &c. अनादरयुक्त, तिरस्कारयुक्त, अवहेलनात्मक, निंदात्मक, तिरस्कारबोधक-सूचक.

CONTEMPTUOUSLY, *adv.* v. A. अनादरानें, अपमानानें, तिरस्कारानें, &c. तुच्छ करून-मानून, अनादर-अपमान-तिरस्कार-&c. पूर्वक-पुरस्सर, नाक वर करून, नाक मुरडून, टाकून, कवडीचा माल करून, उडवाउडव. *f.* करून, हेळसांड करून, &c.

To CONTEND, *To* CONTEST, *v. n. dispute, strive, fight,* v. To QUARREL. लढणें, झगटणें *or* झगडणें, झोंबी *f.* घेणें, जुंजणें *or* झुंजणें, भांडणें, घासणें, तंडणें, लढाई *f.*-वाद *m.*-कज्जा *m.*-भांडण *n.*-झगडा *m.*-विरोध *m.*-शत्रुत्व *n.*-&c. करणें.

CONTENDER, *n.* CONTENTIOUS, *a.* CONTESTER, *n.* v. V. *and* QUARRELSOME. कटकट्या, कज्जेखोर, भांडखोर, बोलभांड, घसघशा *or* घिसघिशा, खळवादी, तकरारी, तकरारखोर, विवादी.

CONTENT, CONTENTED, *a. satisfied, not wishing more.* समाधानी, खुश, संतुष्ट, संतोषी, तृप्त, तृप्तात्मा, निष्पृह *or* निस्पृह, प्रीतात्मा, खुशवखत, तृप्तांतःकरण, प्राप्तसमाधान, जातसमाधान, गततृष्ण, निवृत्ततर्ष, गतेच्छ, निवृत्तेच्छ, शांतेच्छ.

Easily c. अल्पसंतोषी, अल्पसंतुष्ट.

2 See WILLING.

CONTENT, CONTENTMENT, *n. satisfaction, acquiescence, &c.* समाधान *n.* संतोष *m.* चित्तसमाधान *n.* चित्तसंतोष *m.* मनशामोड *f.* इच्छातृप्ति *f.* तृप्ति *f.* पूर्त्ति *f.* इच्छानिवृत्ति *f.* चित्तनिवृत्ति *f.* इच्छाशांति *f.* तृष्णाक्षय *m.* अशोच *m.* अलंबुद्धि *f.*

2 contents; (of a receptacle) . भरलेला जिन्नस *m.* आंतला जिन्नस *m.* भरगत *f. n.* भरीत *n.* भरवण *n.* भरकत *n.* समाविष्ट-अंतर्गत-अंतरस्थ-&c. वस्तु *n.*

3 (of a book or writing). मजकूर *m.* लिखितार्थ *m.*

" C.s. received." भरपाई.

Table of c. अनुक्रमणिका *f.* सूचीपत्र *n.*

4—in geometry. क्षेत्रफळ *n.*

Superficial contents. पृष्ठफल *n.*

To CONTENT, *v. a.* v. To SATISFY. पुरवणें, समाधान *n.*-संतोष *m.*-तृप्ति *f.*-इच्छातृप्ति *f.*-इच्छापूर्त्ति *f.*-मनशामोड *f.*-&c. करणें *g. of o.* संतुष्ट-तृप्त-संतृप्त-&c. करणें.

CONTENTEDLY, *adv.* v. A. 1. समाधानानें, चित्तसमाधानानें, &c. समाधानपूर्वक.

CONTENTION, CONTENDING, CONTESTING, CONTEST, *n.* v. V.—*act.* भांडण *n.* झटापटी *or* झटापट *f.* घासाघास *or* घीस *f.* घसघस *or* घिसघीस *f.* घासणी *f.* झोंबी *f.* जुंज *or* झुंज *n.* लटपट *f.* तकरार *f.* संघर्षण *n.* संघर्ष *m.* घर्षण *n.* द्वंद्व *pop.* दंद *n.* कलि *m. pop.* कळ *f.* कलह *m.* हर्षामर्ष *m.* हडवंग *m.* दुसग *or* दुसगोयी *f.* खडबड *f.* बादविवाद *m.*

CONTERMINOUS, *a. bordering.* लगत्याचा, शिवधड्याचा, एकेशिवेचा, एकसीम, समसीम.

To CONTEST, *v. a. controvert.* See To DISPUTE.

To CONTEST, *v. n.* See To CONTEND.

CONTESTABLE, *a. controvertible, &c.* बादासयोग्य, बादकरायाजोगा-&c. बादाचा, तकरारीचा, विप्रतिपद्य, विप्रतिपत्तियोग्य, विवादार्ह, विवादयोग्य, विवादास्पद, विवादस्थान.

CONTEXT, *n.* वाक्यसंबंध *m.* वाक्यानुसंधान *n.* कथासंदर्भ *m.* ग्रंथसंदर्भ *m.* अर्थान्वय *m.* वाक्यान्वय *m.* पूर्वापरसंबंध *m.* पूर्वापरसंदर्भ *m.*

Rule or law of c. प्रत्यासत्ति न्याय *m.*

CONTEXTURE. See TEXTURE.

CONTIGUITY, CONTIGUOUSNESS, *n.* v. A. *and* CONTACT. लगत *f.* लगता *m.* निकटानिकटी *f.* नैकट्य *n.* आनंतर्य *n.* प्रत्यासत्ति *f.* संसक्ति *f.* सीमैक्य *n.*

CONTIGUOUS, *a. touching.* लगतीचा, लगत्याचा, अनंतर, संसक्त, एकसीम, समसीम, प्रत्यासन्न, अव्यवहित.

2 See NEAR.

CONTINENCE, *n.* v. A. 1. संयमन*n.* नियतवर्त्तन*n.* नियतवृत्ति *f.* संयतवर्त्तन*n.* संयतवृत्ति *f.*

2 स्त्रीसंगनियम*m.* कामनिग्रह*m.* उपस्थनिग्रह*m.* उपस्थनियम*m.* व्यवायनियम*m.* एकपत्नीव्रत *n.*

3 नाडबंदपणा*m.* &c. नाडबंदी *f.* ब्रह्मचारिता *f.* ब्रह्मचर्य*n.* स्त्रीविरक्ति*f.* स्त्रीनिस्पृहता *f.*

4 ब्रह्मचारिता *f.* ब्रह्मचर्य*n.* पुरुषनिस्पृहता *f.*

CONTINENT, *a. self-restraining,* v. ABSTINENT. संयमी, नियमी, नियतवर्त्ती, नियतेंद्रिय.

2 *moderate or pure in the indulgence of sexual passion.*—of men. एकपत्नी, एकपत्नीव्रती, अव्यभिचारी, परनारीसोदर, नियतकाम, मितकाम, नियतव्यवाय, उपस्थनिग्रही, ऋतुगामी.

—in covert phraseol. कासोट्याचा बळकट-खबरदार-धड, काछ्याचा बळकट-&c. कटिबंद.

3 *refraining from woman.* बंदिस्त, बंदेज, ऊर्ध्वरेता *or* ऊर्ध्वरेतस्क, स्त्रीपराङ्मुख, स्त्रीविमुख-विरक्त-निस्पृह, अज्ञातव्यवाय, त्यक्तकाम, त्यक्तव्यवाय.

A c. man. ब्रह्मचारी, ब्रह्मचर्याश्रमी, सत्कुमार, नाडबंद, लंगोटबंद, भीष्म, कार्तिकस्वामी.

4 *refraining from man.* पुरुषपराङ्मुखी-विमुखी-निस्पृहा, अज्ञातव्यवाया, अज्ञातकामा, त्यक्तकामा, त्यक्तव्यवाया, कटिबंद.

A c. female. ब्रह्मचारिणी, परिव्राजिका.

CONTINENT, *n.*—in geography. खुशकी *or* खुषकी *f.* महाद्वीप *m. n.* स्थल *n.* समुद्रापरिछिन्नभूमि *f.*

CONTINENTAL, *a.* महाद्वीपाचा, महाद्वीपाच्यासंबंधाचा, महाद्वीपविषयक.

CONTINENTLY, *adv.* v. A. इंद्रियनिग्रहपूर्वक, कामनिग्रहपूर्वक.

CONTINGENCY, *n.* v. A. 1. *possibility of occurrence.* दिष्टसंभावना *f.* दैवसाध्यता *f.* दैवघटनीयता *f.* यदृच्छासाध्यता *f.*

2 *accidentalness.* यदृच्छा *f.* दैवयोग *m.* देवघटितत्व *n.*

I. *a* c. v. ACCIDENT, दैवकृत्य *n.* दैवघटितगोष्ट *f.*

CONTINGENT, *a. possible of occurrence.* दिष्टसंभाव्य, दैवसाध्य, दैवघटनीय, यदृच्छाघटनीय.

2 *fortuitous,* v. ACCIDENTAL. दैवयोगाचा, आगंतुक, दैवजात, दैवघटित, दैवयोगिक, यदृच्छाजात.

C. expenses. सादिलवार खर्च *m.*

CONTINGENT, *n. fortuitous event.* दैवकृत्य *n.* दैवघटित गोष्ट *f.* दैवयोगाची गोष्ट *f.*

2 *proportion,* v. SHARE. वर्गणी *f.* वर्गत *f.* वांटा *m.*

CONTINGENTLY, *adv.* v. A. 2. *and* ACCIDENTALLY. दैवयोगानें, यदृच्छेकरून.

CONTINGENTNESS. See CONTINGENCY.

CONTINUAL, *a. continuing, constant.* निरंतर, नित्य, सतत, संतत, अखंड, अविरत, अनवरत, अनारत, अश्रांत, अव्यवहित, नित्याचा, नेहमींचा.

CONTINUALLY, *adv.* v. A. *and* EVER. निरंतर, नित्य, नित्यानें, नित्यें, नित्यांत, नित्यानित्य, नेहमीं, हरघडी, हरवखत, घडीघडी, घडोघडी, अष्टौप्रहर, सतत, संतत, अनुधार, प्रतिपद, पदोपदी, पदेपदे, अजस्र.

CONTINUALNESS, *n.* v. A. नैरंतर्य *n.* निरंतरता *f.* सातत्य *n.* सांतत्य *n.* सततभाव *m.*

CONTINUANCE, CONTINUATION, *n.* v. V. A. 1.—*act.* चालवणें *n.* &c. चालवणूक *f.* चालवणी *f.*

2—*act.* वाढवणें *n.* &c.

v. V. N. 1.—*state.* टिकणें *n.* &c. टिकाव *or* टिकावा *m.* स्थिति *pop.* स्थीत *f.*

2 राहणें *n.* नांदणें *n.* &c. नांदणूक *f.* स्थिति *pop.* स्थीत *f.*

3 स्थिति *pop.* स्थीत *f.*

To CONTINUE, *v. a. carry on longer, not to cease from.* चालवणें *or* पुढें चालवणें, चालू-चालता राखणें-ठेवणें, चालवीत-करीत-&c. जाणें.

2 *extend, carry on in length.* वाढवणें, लांबवणें.

To CONTINUE, *v. n. remain, last,* v. To ENDURE. टिकणें, राहणें, धारणें, थारावणें, थिरावणें, ठरणें.

2 *stay, abide, dwell,* v. To RESIDE. राहणें, नांदणें, असणें, स्थिरावणें, थावरणें.

3 *persist.* v. To PERSEVERE. राहणें-चालणें used with the present participle of another verb.

CONTINUITY, CONTINUOUSNESS, *n.* v. A. 1. नैरंतर्य *n.* आनंतर्य*n.* निरंतरता *f.* सातत्य *n.* सांतत्य *n.* आविरत्य *n.*

2 नैरंतर्य *n.* निरंतरता *f.* अखंडता *f.* अव्यवधान *n.* अव्यवधानता *f.* अविच्छेद *m.* अविच्छिन्नता *f.*

CONTINUOUS, *a.*— in time, v. CONTINUAL. निरंतर, अनंतर, सतत, अनवरत, अविरत.

2—of space. निरंतर, अव्यवधान, अखंड, अखंडित, अव्यवहित, अविच्छिन्न, लगत in comp. (as लगतमजकूर).

CONTINUOUSLY, *adv.* v. A. निरंतर, अखंड.

To CONTORT, *v. a.* v. To TWIST. मुरंगळणें *or* गाळणें, पिळवटणें, मोडणें.

CONTORTION, *n. twist.* पिरंगाळा *m.* मुरंगळा *m.* पीळ *m.* पिळा *m.*

—as used pl. contortions. अळेपिळे *m. pl.* वक्रेपिळे *m.pl.* अळोके पिळोके *m. pl.* अळ्यापिळ्या *f. pl.v.* दे, ये. अळंगेविळंगें*n.*

CONTOUR, *n. outlines of the figure.* रूपरेषा *f.* रूपरेखा *f.* आंगलट *f. m.* आंगबठा *m.*

CONTRABAND, *a.* वाणिज्यनिषेधाचा, मनाईचा, बर्जित, निषिद्ध.

To CONTRACT, *v. a. draw up, in, together.* अखडणें or अखुडणें, आवरणें, आकर्षणें, आवटरणें, अटपणें, अटपता घणें- धरणें, आकुसणें, संकोच *m.*-उपसंहार *m.* करणें *g. of o.* संकोचित or संकुचित-उपसंहृत–&c.करणें.

To c. the brow. कपाळास अठी *f.*-अठ्या *f. pl.* घालणें.

2 *draw upon self, incur, &c.* घेणें, लागणें *in. con.* जोडणें, मिळवणें, संपादणें.

3 *epitomize, &c.* v. To ABRIDGE. संक्षेपणें, संक्षेप *m.*-संकोच *m.*-संकलन *n.*-&c.करणें *g. of o.*

4 See To BETROTH.

To CONTRACT, *v. n. be drawn up, in, &c.* अखडणें or अखुडणें, आठरणें, आवटरणें, ओढणें, आक्रसणें or आकुसणें, अवळणें, अटणें, दाटणें, घटणें, संकोचणें, काकडणें, ठांठुरणें, संकोच*m.*-&c. होणें *g. of s.*

2 *bargain.* खंडणें, खंड *m.*-मक्ता *m.*-&c. करणें.

CONTRACT, *n. agreement for work,&c.* v. AGREEMENT, MONOPOLY. खंड *m.* खंडणूक *f.* मक्ता *m.* गुतका *m.* गुत्ता *m.* कुंडवा *or* हुंडा *m.*

By c. उक्ता, उधडा *or* उधड.

C. or agreement on binding conditions. अटीचा करार *m.* अटीची बोली *f.*-बोलणें *n.*

Contracts and monopolies,—compreh. खंडमक्ता *m.*

Work to be done by c. खंडकाम *n.* खंडितकाम *n.* उक्केकाम *n.*

To give by c. खंडून देणें, तोडून देणें.

To take by c. खंडून घेणें, तोडून घेणें.

2 *paper of agreement.* करारनामा *m.*

CONTRACTED, *p.* v. V. A. 1. अखुडलेला, आवरलेला,&c. संकुचित, संकोचित, संकीर्ण, आकर्षित.

2 घेतलेला, जोडलेला, &c.

3 संक्षेपकेलेला, संक्षिप्त.

4 See BETROTHED.

v. V. N. 2. खंडलेला, खंडित, संविदित.

I. *a.* v. NARROW. अप्रशस्त.

CONTRACTILE, *a. having the power of contracting itself.* संकोची, संकोचशील, संकोचधर्मक.

CONTRACTILITY, *n.* v. A. संकोचशीलता *f.* संकोचधर्म *m.*

CONTRACTING, CONTRACTION, *n.* v. V. A. 1.—*act.* अखडणें *n.* आवटरणें *n.* आवरणें *n.* &c. आकर्षण *n.* आकुंचन *n.* संकोचन *n.* संकोचकरण *n.*—*act or state.* अखडणी *f.* अखडणूक *f.* आवटरणी *f.* आवटरणूक *f.* संकोच *m.* आवरण *n.*आबर *m.* अटोप *m.*

2 घेणें *n.* &c.

3 संक्षेपणें *n.* संक्षेपण *n.* उपसंहार *m.* उपसंहृति *f.*

v. V. N. 1. अखडणें *n.* &c. संकोच *m.* आवटरणी *f.* आवटरणूक *f.* अखडणी *f.* अखडणूक *f.*

2 खंडणें *n.* खंड करणें *n.* खंडणूक *f.*

CONTRACTOR, *n.* v. V. N. 2. *and* MONOPOLIST. मक्तेकरी, मक्तेदार, मक्तेवाला, खोत, खंडकरी, खंडवाला, गुत्तेकरी, गुत्तेवाला.

To CONTRADICT, *v. a. oppose verbally, deny.* उलटा-&c. बोलणें, खोडणें, खंडणें, रद्दकरणें, उडवणें, उलटणें, नाहीं पक्षानें मोडणें, नाहीं पक्षांत आणणें, प्रतिषेध *m.*-प्रतिवाद *m.*-प्रत्याख्यान *n.*-विसंवाद *m.*-&c. करणें.

2 See To OPPOSE. [पन्न.

CONTRADICTED, *p.* v. V. 1.—*act.* प्रतिषिध, प्रत्याख्यात, विप्रति-

CONTRADICTION, *n.* v. V. 1.—*act.* उलटें बोलणें *n.* प्रतिषेध *m.* प्रत्याख्यान *n.* प्रत्याख्यापन *n.* प्रतीपवचन *n.* वचनविरोध *m.* प्रतिवाद *m.* विसंवाद *m.* विकत्था *f.*

I. *a c. a contrariety, an inconsistency, &c.* फेर *m.* विपर्यय *m.* विपर्यास *m.* विप्रतिपत्ति *f.* अपसव्य *n.*

To make a statement with contradictions or inconsistencies. सातपांच करणें, तीनतेरा गोष्टी *f. pl.* सांगणें.

CONTRADICTIOUS. See CAPTIOUS. 2 See INCONSISTENT.

CONTRADICTORY, *a. opposite,* v. CONTRARY. आडवा, उलटा, विरोधी, विरुद्ध, विपरीत, विप्रतिपन्न.

2 *inconsistent with itself,* v. INCONSISTENT. असंगत, विसंगत, संदर्भविरुद्ध, पूर्वापरविरुद्ध.

CONTRADISTINCTION, *n.* विरुद्धगुणजन्यभेद *m.*

To CONTRADISTINGUISH, *v. a. distinguish by opposite qualities.* विरुद्धगुणांनीं-विरुद्धगुणांवरून भेद *m.* पाहणें-करणें.

CONTRARIETY, CONTRARINESS, *n.* v. A. 1. उलटेपणा *m.* व्यत्यय *m.* व्यत्यास *pop.* बेत्यास *m.* विपर्यय *m.* विपर्यास *m.* वैपरीत्य *n.* विपरीतता *f.* वैलोम्य *n.* विपरीत भाव *m.* विरुद्धता *f.*

2 आडवेपणा *m.* विरोध *m.* विपक्षता *f.* प्रातिकूल्य *n.* प्रतिकूलता *f.* प्रतिकूलभाव *m.*

3 करनकरेपणा *m.* अकरताळेपणा *m.* अगस्ताळेपणा *m.* करन्नकर *f.* विपरीतकारिता *m.*

4 उलटेपणा *m.* &c.

CONTRARILY, CONTRARIWISE, *adv.* v. A. 1. उलटून, उलट, उलटा, उफराट, उफराटा, उलटयानें, प्रत्युत.

2 आडवेपणानें, विरुद्धभावानें, विरुद्ध, प्रतिकूलभावानें, विपक्षतः, प्रतिकूलतः.

CONTRARIOUS, CONTRARY, *a. opposite, opposed to, adverse,* v. REVERSE. उलटा, आडवा, विपरीत, विरुद्ध, विपर्यस्त, विपर्यासाचा, व्यत्यासाचा, विपर्ययाचा, विलोम.

2 *cross, repugnant, hostile, &c.* v. ADVERSE. आडवा, प्रतिकूल, विरुद्ध, विपरीत, विपक्ष, पराङ्मुख, विगुण, अपर.

3 *contrary willed, cross,* v. PERVERSE. करनकर, अकरनकर, करनकऱ्या or करनकरा, अकरताळा, अगस्ताळा, विपरीतकारी, विपरीतकर्त्ता.

4—wind, tide, &c. उलटा, तोंडचा, समोरचा, तोंडावरचा.

CONTRARY, *n. an opposite.* विपक्ष *m.* प्रतिपक्ष *m.* प्रतिपक्षी *m.* प्रतियोगी *m.*

On the c. See CONTRARIWISE.

CONTRAST, *n. opposition of things or qualities.* गुणागुणसामीप्य *n.* गुणागुणसान्निध्य *n.* गुणागुणाभिमुख्य *n.* विरोध *m.* वैलक्षण्य *n.* समभिव्याहार *m.*

To CONTRAST, *v. a.* परस्परांचें वैलक्षण्य *n.*-विरोध *n.*-&c. दाखविणें, परस्परगुणागुणप्रदर्शन *n.*-परस्परगुणागुणप्रकाश *m.* करणें, समभिव्याहार *m.* करणें *g. of o.*

To CONTRAVENE, *v. a.* v. To OPPOSE. आडवा येणें-होणें.

CONTRAVENTION. See OPPOSITION.

To CONTRIBUTE, *v.a. give to a common purpose,* v. To GIVE. वर्गणीचा-पट्टीचा-टिपेचा-&c. देणें, भर *f.* घालणें, वर्गणी *f.* देणें, अंश *m.*-वांटा *m.*-&c. देणें. [*f.* करणें-देणें.

To CONTRIBUTE, *v. n.* v. To HELP. सहाय-सहकारी होणें, मदत

CONTRIBUTIVE, *a.* CONTRIBUTOR, *n.* CONTRIBUTORY, *a.* v. V. A. वर्गणी देणारा, भरघालणारा, अंशदेणारा, &c. भरीचा, सहाय.

v.V.N. *and* CONDUCIVE. सहाय,सहकारी, सहाय्य कर्त्ता-कारी.

CONTRIBUTION, *n.* v. V. A. *thing contributed.* वर्गणी *f.* वर्गंत *f.* भर *f.* अनेकसाध्यकार्यसहाय्यार्थदान *n.*

Military c. खंडम. खंडणी *f.*

CONTRITE, *a. penitent,* v. REPENTANT. पश्चात्तापी, अनुतापी, अनुतप्त, पापस्मृतिपीडित-दुःखित-&c.

CONTRITELY, *adv.* v.A. पश्चात्तापानें, पश्चात्तापबुद्धीनें,पश्चात्तापपूर्वक.

CONTRITION, CONTRITENESS, *n.* v. A. *and* REPENTANCE. पश्चात्ताप*m.* अनुताप*m.*

CONTRIVABLE, *a.* v. A. योजाया-चा-जोगता-&c. कल्पनीय, कल्प्य, योजनीय, योज्य.

CONTRIVANCE, CONTRIVING, *n.* v. V.A.1.—*act.* योजणें*n.* रचणें *n.* &c. योजना*f.* योजणूक*f.* रचना*f.* रचणी*f.* रचणूक*f.* चिंतन*n.*

I. *inventiveness,* v. INGENUITY. युक्ति *f.* युगूत *f.* हिकमत *f.* हुनर*m. f.* इलम *m.*

II. *scheme, device, plan.* युक्ति *f.* तोड *f.* कल्पना *f.* बुद्धि *f.* उपाय*m.* जुगूत *f.* तजबीज *f.* इलाज*m.* शकल *f.* अनुसंधान*n.* ग्रंथ*m.* कृप्ति *f.*

III. *engine, piece of mechanism.* यंत्र*n.* कुलंगडें*n.* करामत *f.*

To CONTRIVE, *v. a. plan, devise, invent.* बांधणें, योजणें, रचणें, कल्पिणें, चिंतणें, काढणें, करणें, योजना *f.*-योजणूक *f.*-&c. करणें *g. of o.*

To CONTRIVE, *v. n.* युक्ति *f.*-तजबीज *f.*-उपाय*m.*-&c.करणें.

CONTRIVED, *p.* v. V. A. योजलेला, रचलेला, &c. योजित, रचित, घटित, काल्पनिक, कृप्त.

CONTRIVER, *n.* CONTRIVING, *p. a.* v. V. A. योजणारा, काढणारा, रचणारा, &c. योजक, रचक, योजना कर्त्ता, रचनाकर्त्ता.

I. *inventive,* v. INGENIOUS. कल्पक, योजक, युक्त्या, उपाणी, हिकमती *or* त्या, हुनरी, करामती, लागलाव्या, लाग्या, अनुसंधानी, संधानी, साधनी.

CONTROL, CONTROLMENT, *n.* v. V.—*act.* आवरणें*n.* आटोपणें*n.* &c. निबंधन*n.* नियमन*n.*आवरण *n.*—*a. or s.* आवर*m.*निग्रह*m.* कद *f.* आटोप*m.* आळा *m.* आळाबांधा*m.* आटणी *f.*

At the c. or command of. स्वाधीन, लगामीं, हुकमांत, ताब्यांत, कह्यांत.

I. *power or authority to control.* जोरा*m.* हुकूम*m.*सत्ता *f.* तैनात *f.* तसलमात *f.* अधिकार*m.* कैद *f.* नियंतृत्व*n.*

To CONTROL, *v. a.* v. To RESTRAIN, To RULE. आवरणें, अटोपणें, आकळणें, आवरण*n.*-आवर*m.*-आकलन*n.*-आटोप*m.*-&c. करणें *g. of o.* लगामीं धरणें, ताब्यांत-कह्यांत-हुकमांत-&c. ठेवणें, आळा*m.*-आळा बांधा*m.* घालणें-बांधणें.

CONTROLLABLE, *a.* v. V. आवराया-चा-जोगता-सारखा-&c. लगामीं धरायाजोगा- &c. नियम्य, आकलनीय, शासनीय.

CONTROLLER, *n.* CONTROLLING, *p. a.* v. V. आवरणारा, आटोपणारा, आवरण करणारा, &c. आवरक, नियंता, शास्ता.

CONTROVERSIAL, *n.* विवादाचा, विवाद संबंधी-विषयक, विप्रतिपत्तीचा, विप्रतिपत्तिसंबंधी-विषयक, खंडन मंडन विषयक-संबंधी, खंडन मंडनाचा.

CONTROVERSIALIST, *n.* विवादी, विवादकर्त्ता, वादकर्त्ता.

CONTROVERSY, *n. dispute, discussion of contrary opinions.* विवाद*m.* वादानुवाद*m.* वादविवाद*m.* वाद*m.* विप्रतिपत्ति *f.* वाग्युद्ध *n.* तोंडासतोंड*n.* शंकासमाधानें*n. pl.* पूर्वपक्षसमाधान*n.* आक्षेपसमाधान*n.*

To CONTROVERT, *v. a. contest,* v. To DISPUTE. वाद *m.*-विवाद *m.*-विप्रतिपत्ति *f.*-विप्रतिपादन*n.*-प्रत्याख्यान*n.*-अस्वीकार*m.*-निरसन*n.*-निराकरण*n.*-निराकृति *f.*-&c. करणें *g. of o.*

CONTROVERTED, *p.* v. V. विप्रतिपन्न, वादग्रस्त, विवादास्पदीभूत, प्रत्याख्यात, निराकृत, निरस्त, अस्वीकृत.

CONTROVERTIBLE, *a.* v.V. वादासयोग्य, वादकरायाजोगा-&c. विप्रतिपद्य, प्रत्याख्येय, निरसनीय, प्रत्याख्यानार्ह, प्रत्याख्यानशक्य.

CONTUMACIOUS, *a. stubborn,* v. OBSTINATE. जिद्दखोर, जिद्दी, शिरजोर, हट्टखोर, आग्रही, दुराग्रही, आपगंड, आपलबुद्धि.

CONTUMACIOUSLY, *adv.* v. A. जिद्दखोरीनें, दुराग्रहानें, दुराग्रहपूर्वक.

CONTUMACY, CONTUMACIOUSNESS, *n.* v. A. जिद्द *f.* जिद्दखोरी *f.* जळ*m.* दुराग्रह*m.* हटतट*n.* दुर्मद*m.*

CONTUMELIOUS, *a. rude, insolent, &c.*—of persons. v. CONTEMPTUOUS. निंदक, अपवादक, निर्भर्त्सक.

2—language, &c. निंदेचा, निर्भर्त्सनेचा, निंदात्मक, निंदासूचक.

CONTUMELIOUSLY, *adv.* v. A. निंदाकरून, निंदेनें, निर्भर्त्सनापूर्वक.

CONTUMELIOUSNESS, CONTUMELY, *n.* v. A. *and* CONTEMPT. निंदा *f.* अवहेलना *f.* निर्भर्त्सना *f.* खिंचना *f.*

To CONTUSE. CONTUSION. See BRUISE, &c.

CONUNDRUM, *n.* प्रहेलिका *f.* प्रवह्लिका *f.*

CONVALESCENCE, *n.* v. A. सांवरतीदशा *f.* पालवी *f.* हिंडतेफिरतेपणा *m.* वांचतीभावना *f.* रोगमुक्तता *f.* आरोग्यपूर्वावस्था *f.*

CONVALESCENT, *a. recovering.* दुखण्यांतून उतरलेला-उठलेला, ताकोला बरा, हिंडता फिरता, हिंडफिऱ्या, दांडि स्वार, हिंडायाजोगा, चिट्ठी फिरवलेला.

To be c. बागायाला निघणें, साकर *f.* घेणें.

To CONVENE. See To ASSEMBLE.

CONVENIENCE, CONVENIENCY, *n.* v. A. उपयोग *m.* सोई *f.* सोईसारपणा *m.* लाग *m.* आनुकूल्य *n.* अनुकूलता *f.* उपयुक्तता *f.*

At one's c. यथासुख.

CONVENIENT, *a. adapted, accommodate,* v. COMMODIOUS. उपयोगी, सोईचा, सोईवार, सोईसार, उपयुक्त, अनुकूल, यथासुख.

CONVENIENTLY, *adv.* v. A. सोईनें, सोईवार, सोईसार.

CONVENT, *n. religious house for men.* मठ *m.* आश्रम *m.*

2 *for women.* अविवाहव्रतस्थ स्त्रीगणालय *n.* स्त्रीमठ *m.*

CONVENTICLE. See ASSEMBLY.

CONVENTION. See ASSEMBLY. 2 See AGREEMENT.

CONVENTIONAL, *a. formed by agreement.* संकेताचा, सामयिक, सांकेतिक, संकेतगर्भित, संकेतसिद्ध, समयसिद्ध.

2 *arising out of custom or tacit agreement.* लोकांच्या समजुतीचा, लोकव्यवहारास अनुसरणारा, संकेताचा.

CONVENTUAL, *a.* मठसंबंधी, मठविषयक, मठवासी.

To CONVERGE, *v. n. tend to one point.* एककेंद्राकडे वळणें, एककेंद्रप्रवण-एकप्रवण-एककेंद्राभिसारी-एककेंद्राभिमुख-&c. होणें.

CONVERGENCE, *n.* v. A. एककेंद्रप्रावण्य *n.* एककेंद्राभिसारित्व *n.* एककेंद्राभिसरण *n.* एककेंद्राभिमुखता *f.*

CONVERGENT, *a.* CONVERGING, *p. a.*v. V. केंद्राभिमुख, एककेंद्राभिमुख, एककेंद्रप्रवण, एककेंद्राभिसारी, एकप्रवण.

CONVERSABLE. See AFFABLE.

CONVERSANCE, CONVERSANCY, *n.* v. A. 1. अभ्यास *m.* वहिवाट *f.* घसवट *f.* घसण *f.* घटण *f.* वाकबगारी *f.* वाकबदारी *f.* माहितगारी *f.* परिचय *m.* परिज्ञान *n.* प्रावीण्य *n.* नैपुण्य *n.* आलोड्य *n. pop.* अलोड्य *or* अलोड *n.* गम्य *n.* गति *f.* बासना *f.* कसरत *f.* दसलगिरी *f.* इस्तमाली *f.*

2 *and* INTERCOURSE. वहिवाट *f.* वळण *n.* वळवटा *m.* घसण *f.* वाग *f.* वागणूक *f.* संघट्टन *n.* परिचय *m.* रहवास *m.*

CONVERSANT, *a. versed, well acquainted.* अभ्यासी, माहित्या, जाणता, वाकबगार, वाकबदार, माहितगार, वहिवाटलेला, घसवटलेला, रहाटलेला, वापरलेला, &c. प्रवीण, निपुण, अभ्यस्त, शिक्षित, निष्णात, परिज्ञाता, कसरती.

To be c. with. वहिवाटणें, वापरणें, रहाटणें, रहाळणें, घसवटणें, मळगावणें.

2 *having intercourse.* वागीचा, वागणुकीचा, वहिवाटीचा, घसणीचा, घसवटीचा, परिचयाचा, वागलेला, रुळलेला, परिचित.

3 about: *having relation to.* संबंधाचा, विषयींचा, संबंधीविषयक *in. comp.*

CONVERSATION, CONVERSE, *n.* v. V. 1.—*and* INTERCOURSE. वळण *n.* वळवटा *m.* वळवट *f.* वाग *f.* वागणूक *f.* रहवास *m.* रुळणी *f.* सोबत *f.*

2 बोलाबोली *f.* बोलाचाली *f.* गोष्टी बाता *or* माता *f. pl.* जाबसाल *m.* संभाषण *n.* संवाद *m.* गप्पाष्टक *n.* कथोपकथन *n.* संकथन *n.* आलाप *m.* संलाप *m.* कथावार्त्ता *or* वार्त्ता *f. v.* कर.

3 संग *m.* समागम *m.* एकशय्या *f.* एकतल्प *n.*

Criminal c. अयोनिसंग *m.*

I. See BEHAVIOUR.

CONVERSATIONAL, *a.* जाबसाली, जाबसालाचा, संभाषण संबंधीविषयक.

CONVERSAZIONE, *n.* विद्यादिविषयांवर संभाषण करण्याची सभा *f.*- बैठक *f.*

To CONVERSE, *v. n. hold intercourse with.* वहिवाट *f.*-रहवास *m.*-वाग *f.*-वळवटा *m.*-वळण *n.*-सोबत *f.*-संगत *f.*-&c. करणें-राखणें-ठेवणें *with* सीं *of o. or* असणें *with g. of s.*

2 *confer or talk with.* बोलाबोली *f.*-संभाषण *n.*-संलाप *m.*-&c. करणें, गोष्टी *f. pl.* सांगणें, कथावार्त्ता *or* वार्त्ता *f.* करणें-सांगणें.

3 *have sexual intercourse.* संग *m.*-समागम*m.*-संयोग *m.*-एकशय्या *f.*-&c. करणें.

CONVERSE, *a. contrary,* v. REVERSE. उलटा, व्यस्त, व्युत्क्रमाचा.

CONVERSE, *n. opposite proposition.* उलट *f.* उलट पक्ष *m.* व्युत्क्रम *m.*

CONVERSELY, *adv.* v. A. उलट क्रमानें, उलट पक्षानें, व्युत्क्रमानें, तुल्यवित्तिवेद्यतेनें.

CONVERSION, *n.* v. V. 1.—*act.* रूपांतर करणें *n.* रूपभेद करणें *n.* परिणमन *n.*—*state.* रूपांतर *n.* रूपभेद *m.*स्थित्यंतर *n.*स्थितिभेद *m.* अवस्थांतर *n.* परिणाम *m.*

2—*act.* दुसऱ्या धर्मांत आणणें *n.* धर्मांतर प्रापण *n.*—*state.* धर्मभेद *m.* मतभेद *m.* मतांतर *n.*

3—*act.* सन्मार्गप्रापण *n.* मन पालटवणें *n.* मनः परिवर्त्तन *n.* चित्तपरिवर्त्तन *n.*

To CONVERT, *v. a. change into another substance or form,* v. To CHANGE. रूप *n.* पालटवणें *g. of o.* करणें *with* चा *of o.* (as थंडी पाण्याचें बर्फ करिते), रूपांतर *n.*-रूपभेद *m.*-स्थित्यंतर *n.*-स्थितिभेद *m.*-&c. करणें *g. of o.* परिणाम *m.* करणें *with* रूप (as गर्दभाचा अश्वरूप परिणाम केला), भिन्नरूपक-&c.करणें.

2 *change from one faith to another.* दुसऱ्या धर्मांत आणणें, धर्म *m.*-मत *n.*-&c. पालटवणें-फिरवणें *g. of o.* धर्मांतरप्रापण *n.*-मतपरिवर्त्तन *n.*-&c. करणें *g. of o.* धर्मभेद *m.*-मतभेद *m.* -मतांतर *m.*-&c. करविणें *g. of o.*

3 *change from sin to holiness.* मन *n.* पालटवणें-फिरवणें, सन्मार्गाकडे मन *n.* फिरवणें, सन्मार्ग प्रापण *n.* करणें, मनः परिवर्त्तन *n.*-चित्त परिवर्त्तन *n.*-&c. करणें *g. of o.*

4 See To APPROPRIATE.

CONVERT, *n.* v. V. 2. दुसऱ्या धर्मांत आलेला मनुष्य-&c. धर्मांतरयात-धर्मांतरप्राप्त-&c. मनुष्य, अन्यधर्मावलंबी.

CONVERTIBLE, *a.* v. V. 1. रूपांतर-&c. करायाजोगा-&c. रूपांतरकरणीय.

I. v. INTERCHANGEABLE. पर्यायाचा.

CONVEX, *a. rising on the outside into a round form.* गोल बाह्य, अधोमुख दुंदुभ्याकार, कूर्मपृष्ठाकार, बिंबाकार.

CONVEXITY, *n.* v. A. गोल बाह्य आकृति *f.* अधोमुख दुंदुभ्याकृति *f.* कूर्मपृष्ठाकृति *f.* बिंबाकृति *f.*

CONVEXO-CONCAVE, *a.* बाह्यांतर्दुंदुभ्याकार.

To CONVEY, *v. a. carry, transport.* घेऊन जाणें, नेणें, वाहणें, पावणें, पोहोंचविणें *or* पोहंचविणें.

2 *transmit, impart, &c.* v. To SEND, To GIVE. प्रापण *n.* करणें, पावता-पोहोंचता-&c.करणें, प्राप्त-हस्तगत-सादर-&c. करणें.

3 See To TRANSFER.

CONVEYANCE, CONVEYING, *n.* v. V. 1.—*act.* नेणें *n.* घेऊन जाणें *n.* &c. नयन *n.*

2—*act.* सादरकरणें *n.* &c. प्रापण *n.*

I. *means of c.* v. CARRIAGE. यान *n.* वाहन *n.*

Human c. नरयान *n.* नरवाहन *n.*

Water c. जलयान *n.*

To CONVICT, *v. a. prove guilty.* अपराध *m.*-&c. ठरवणें-लागू करणें-साबीत करणें *with* वर *of o.* अन्यायी-अपराधी-सापराध-&c. ठरवणें, आंगीं लावणें, पदरीं घालणें, पदरीं माप *n.* घालणें, मणगट *m.* धरणें, अपराध स्थापन *n.* करणें *g. of o.* सापराधी करण *n.* करणें *g. of o.*

CONVICT, *n.* अपराधी-&c. ठरवलेला मनुष्य-&c. स्थापितापराध.

CONVICTION, *n.* v. V.—*act.* अपराध ठरवणें *n.* &c. सापराधी करण *n.* दोषी करण *n.* अपराधस्थापन *n.* अपराधस्थापना *f.*

I. *convincedness.* खातरजमा *f.* खातर *f.* खातरी *f.* भरोसा *or* भरवसा *m.* निशा *f.* प्रबोध *m.* व्यवसाय *m.*

To CONVINCE, *v. a. satisfy respecting.* समजावणें, समजाविशी *f.*-समजावीस *f.*-समजी *f.*-समजूत *f.*-खातर *f.*-खातरी *f.*-खातरजमा *f.*-निशा *f.*-&c. करणें *g. of o.* मनांत आणून देणें-भरून देणें *g. of o.* अनुभवास-हिशोबास-प्रत्ययास-ताळ्यास-&c. आणून देणें *g. of o.* संदेह भंजन *n.*-शंकानिवृत्ति *f.*-&c. करणें. *g. of o.*

CONVINCER,*n.* CONVINCING,*p.a. conclusive, compelling assent.* खातरीचा, निश्चायक, निश्चयकारक, संदेहभंजक, संशय निवर्त्तक, संशय छेदक, विनिगमक, सबल.

CONVINCINGLY, *adv.* v. A. खातरी होईल असें, संशय फिटे असें, शंकानिवृत्ति पूर्वक.

CONVIVIAL, *a. relating to entertainments, &c.* मेजवानीचा, जेवणावळीचा, भोजनसमारंभाचा, आहारविहारसंबंधी, आहारविहार विषयक.

2 *jovial, &c.* मेजमानीचा आवडता, आहारविहारपर, थमंड्या.

CONVIVIALITY, *n.* v.A. 1. ख्यालतमाशा *m* .आहारविहार *m*.

2 आहारविहार निष्ठा *f*.

CONVOCATION. See ASSEMBLY.

To CONVOKE, *v. a. call together*, v. To ASSEMBLE. बोलवणें, जमवणें, आव्हानपूर्वक एकत्र करणें.

To CONVOLVE, *v. a. twist*. वळणें.

CONVOLVULUS, *n.—turpethum*. तडतडी *f*. तेड *n*.

CONVOLUTION, *n*. v. TWIST. वळ *m*. पीळ *m*.

To CONVOY, *v. a, escort*. वाटेस राखण करून पोहोंचविणें, बरोबर जाऊन सुखरूप पोहोंचता करणें, मार्गरक्षण करून नेणें.

CONVOY, *n*. v. ESCORT. वलावा *m*. पावणी *f*.

To CONVULSE, *v. a. affect by spasms*. पिळणें, पिळवटणें, पिळावळा *m*. करणें *g. of o*.

2 v. To AGITATE. क्षोभ *m*.-व्याक्षोभ *m*.-&c. करणें *g. of o*.

CONVULSED, *p*. v. A. 1. पिळलेला, पिळवटलेला. [घुटवळणें.

To be c. ओढी *f. pl*. येणें, पेटके *m. pl*. घेणें, वळणें, वळवळणें,

2 क्षुब्ध, क्षुभित.

CONVULSION, *n*. v. V.1.—*act*. पिळणें *n*. &c.—*state*. पिळावळा *m*. वळवळ *f*. पेटका *m*.

2 क्षोभ *m*. व्याक्षोभ *m*.

Political c. राज्याची-&c. उलटापालट *f*.

CONY, *n*. ससा सारखें एक जनावर आहे.

To COO, *v. n*.—as doves. घुमणें, घुघू करणें.

COO, COOING, *n*.v. V. घुमणें *n*. घुघू *n*. घुंबरडा *m*.

COOK, *n*. स्वयंपाकी *pop*. स्वैंपाकी *m*. (and स्वयंपाकीण *pop*. स्वैंपाकीण female c.), आचारी, रांधपी *m*. (रांधपीण *f*.), पाचक *m*. (पाचकी *f*.), मुनबसी *m*. पाककर्त्ता *m*.—in contempt. भाकर बडव्या.

C.'s mate. खटपट्या.

Skilful c. (female). सुगरण *f*. कोंड्याचा मांडा करणारी.

To COOK, *v. a*.—gener. स्वयंपाक *pop*. स्वैंपाक *m*.-पाक *m*.-पाकसिद्धि *f*. करणें, सिद्ध-तयार करणें.

2—by boiling. शिजवणें, उकडणें, रांधणें.

3—by roasting, broiling, &c. भाजणें.

Swept and smeared square to c. in. चौका *m*.

COOKED, *p*. v. V.—gener. स्वैंपाक केलेला, पक्व *pop*. पक्का, पाचित (in comp. as तैल पाचित, घृत पाचित, *or* ब्राह्मण पाचित, स्त्रीपाचित), भक्त, सिद्ध.

Under c. हिरवा, हिरवस.

COOKERY, COOKING, *n*. v. V.—gener. स्वयंपाक *pop*. स्वैंपाक *m*. पाक *m*. पाकसिद्धि *f*. पाकनिष्पत्ति *f*. पाकक्रिया *f*. पचन *n*. पचा *f*. चरुस्थाली *f*. [विद्या *f*.

I. *skill in c*. पाकनिष्पत्ति *f*. पाककौशल्य *n*. पाकचातुर्य *n*. पाक-

COOK-ROOM, *n*. स्वैंपाक घर *n*. ओंवरा *m*. पाकशाला *f*. पाकस्थान *n*. रांधतें घर *n*. पाकगृह *n*.

COOL, *a. coldish*. थंड, अमळ थंड, थंडसा, मंदशीत, नातिशीत.

2 fig. *not zealous, not ardent, &c*. थड, थंडा, थंडाईचा, उदास, उदासीन, अनुत्साही, अनुत्सुक, अनास्थ, अनुत्कंठित, अनासक्त, शीत.

3 *not affectionate*, v. COLD. थंड, थंडाईचा, निस्स्नेह.

4 *not angry, not perturbed*, v. CALM. शांत, थंड, अव्यग्र, क्षोभरहित-&c. अक्षुब्ध. [गारव्याचा.

5 *not retaining heat*,—dress. थंड, ऊब न वाटण्यासारखा,

COOL, *n*. थंडावा *m*. थंडोसा *m*. थंडी *f*.

C. of the day, *hours of morning and evening*. शिळावेळ *m. f*. शिळोपा *m*. शिरोळ *m. f*.

To COOL, *v. a. make coldish*. थंड-&c. करणें, उष्णता *f*. मोडणें-घालवणें *g. of o*. निववणें.

2 fig. (one's ardor, affection, &c.). थंड-मंद-&c. करणें, विरजण *n*.-बिबवा *m*.-विझण *n*. घालणें, पातळ करणें.

3 (anger). थंड-शीतल-&c.-करणें, निबवणें, शांत करणें.

To COOL, *v. n*. lit. थंडावणें, निवणें, थंड होणें, उष्णता *f*.-&c. जाणें-मोडणें *g. of s*.

2 fig.—zeal, ardor, affection. थंडावणें, निवणें, थंड होणें, अळसणें, अळसावणें, विरजण *n*.-विझण *n*. पडणें *in. con*.

3—anger. निवणें, थंडावणें, निवळणें, शांत-थंड-&c. होणें.

COOLED, *p*. v. V. A. 1. थंड केलेला, निववलेला, मोडलेल्या उष्णतेचा, शीतीकृत, कृतशीत, हतताप, हतोष्ण.

v. V. N. थंडावलेला, निवालेला, &c. [प्रीति.

2 थंडावलेला, &c. हतताप, वीतराग, वीतानुराग, गतानुराग, गत-

3 निवालेला, शांत झालेला, &c. क्रोधातीत, वीतराग, गतकोप, गतक्रोध.

COOLING, *a*.—an article of diet, a medicine &c. थंड, थंडा, शीतल *pop*. शितळ, सरद, शीतवीर्य, दाहशामक, तापहर-हारक, &c.

COOLLY, *adv. without passion, ardor, &c*. थंडाईनें, थंडपणानें, शांतपणानें, सावकाशीनें, दमाखालीं, थिराईखालीं, थिरेंथिरें.

COOLNESS, *n*. v. A. 1. थंडपणा *m*. थंडी *f*. थंडाई *f*. शितळाई *f*. मंदशैत्य *n*.

2 थंडपणा *m*. &c. थंडाई *f*. अनुत्साह *m*. अनुत्सुकता *f*. सावकाशी *f*.

3 स्नेहाची-&c. मंदी *f*.-पातळाई *f*. थंडाई *f*. न्यूनमित्रत्व *n*. न्यूनमित्रभाव *m*.

I. (after heat). थंडावा *m*. थंडोसा *m*.

COOLY, *n*. हेलकरी *m*. (fem. हेलकरीण) पांटीवाला *m*. (fem. पांटीवाली).

Business of a c. हेलपांटी *f*.

COOM, *n*. किटण *n*. कीटन *n*. मळ *m*.

COOP, *n*.—for fowls. खुराड *n*. खुराडें *n*.

2 See PEN. 3 See BARREL.

To COOP, *v. a. shut up, &c*. कोंडणें, कोंडून ठेवणें, कोंडींत घालणें, कोंडी *f*. करणें *g. of o*.

COOPER, *n*. पिंपें करणारा.

COOPERAGE, *n*. पिंपें करण्याचा कारखाना *m*.

To CO-OPERATE, *v. n. act jointly with*. मिळून-सोबतीनें-&c. काम *n*.-उद्योग *m*.-&c. करणें, सहकार *m*.-सहकरण *n*.-सहकारिता *f*.-साहाय्य *n*.-&c. करणें, सहाय-सहकारी-समान क्रियाकारी-&c. होणें.

CO-OPERATION, *n*. v. V.—*act*. सहकार *m*. सहकरण *n*. सहक्रिया *f*. सहकारिता *f*. सहकारित्व *n*. साहाय्य *n*.

CO-OPERATOR, *n*. CO-OPERATING, *p. a*. CO-OPERATIVE, *a*. v. V. मिळून कामकरणारा, सहकारी, सहकार-सहकरण-&c. कर्त्ता, समानक्रिय, एककार्यान्वित, एककार्योन्मुख.

CO-ORDINATE, *a. of the same rank, &c*. एकपदवीचा, बरोबरीचा, समानपदवीचा, समपर्याय, समपदस्थ, समतोल.

COOT, *n*. पाणबुडी *or* ड्याम. ?

COPAL, *n*.—the gum. चंद्रस *m*.

COPARCENARY, *n. joint heirship*. समभागित्व *n*. समभागिभाव *m*. समांशित्व *n*. भागसाम्य *n*. अंशसाम्य *n*.

COPARCENER, *n. co-heir*. घर भाऊ *m*. विभागी, समभाग, समभा-

गी, समांशी, तक्सीमदार.

COPARCENY, *n. equal share.* वारिसाचा *or* बारसाचा सारखा वांटाm. रिक्थसमांशm. रिक्थ समभागm. तक्सीम *f.*

COPARTNER, *n.* v. PARTNER. सरकतदार, पातीदार, समभागी, समांशी, संभूयकारी.

COPARTNERSHIP, *n.* v. PARTNERSHIP. सरकत*f.* भागी*f.* संभूयकारित्व*n.* संभूयसमुत्थान*n.*

To COPE, *v. n. contend or vie with, emulate,* v. To RIVAL. लढणें, झुंजणें, बरोबरी *f.*-सरोबरी *f.*-&c. करणें, पोटरीस पोटरी *f.* घासणें, पायास पाय*m.* देणें, भुजेस भूज*f.* देणें *or* देऊन असणें, टक्कर *f.* मारणें-देणें, खांद*m.* बांधणें-करणें *with* शीं *of o.* स्पर्धणें.

COPIED, *p.* v. V. 1. उतरलेला, उतरून घेतलेला, लेखकी, नकलेचा लिहिलेला.

2 उतरलेला, &c. नकली.

COPIER, COPYIST, *n.* v. V. 1. उतरणारा, उतरून घेणारा, नकलप्रत-&c. लिहणारा, लेखक.

Error of the c. (amanuensis). लेखकदोष*m.* लेखकप्रमाद*m.* हस्तदोष*m.*

2 कित्ता घेणारा, थाकी उतरणारा, &c. अनुसारी, अनुसरणकर्त्ता.

COPING, *n.* (of a wall). मुंढरी *or* मुंढेरी *or* मुंडेरी *f.* मुंडलावा *m.* वरवंडी *or* वरंडी *f.*

COPIOUS, *a.* v. ABUNDANT. बहुत, प्रचुर, पुष्कळ, विपुल, मनस्वी.

COPIOUSLY, *adv.* v.A. बहुत, पुष्कळ, पुष्कळपणीं, विपुळपणीं.

COPIOUSNESS, *n.* v. A. पुष्कळपणा *m.* बाहुल्य *n.* प्राचुर्य *n.* वैपुल्य *n.*

COPPER, *n.* तांबें *n.* ताम्र *n.*

Brick (solid and flat mass) of c. तांबोटी *f.*

Calx of c. ताम्रभस्म *n.* ताम्र *n.*

Copperchange. खुर्दा *m.* [ण *m.*

C.-piece. ताम्रमुद्रा *f.*—in cant phraseol. धाकटा नारायण *m.*

Coppery decoction,—as a vomit. उकाळा *m.*

Sulphate of c. मोरचूत *or* द *n.* ताम्रगर्भ *m.* [मिश्रित.

COPPER, COPPERY, *a.* तांब्याचा, ताम्र, ताम्रिक, ताम्रमय, ताम्रमिश्रित.

COPPER-COLORED, *a.* तांब्याच्या रंगाचा, ताम्रवर्ण, ताम्रमुख.

COPPER-PLATE, *n.* तांब्याची पाटी *f.* ताम्रपत्र *n.* ताम्रफलक *n.*

A c. on which grants &c. are inscribed. ताम्रपट *m.*

COPPER- SMITH, *n.* तांबट, ताम्रकार, ताम्रिक.

COPPERAS, *n. sulphate of iron,* v. VITRIOL. हिराकस *m.*

COPPICE, COPSE, *n. a wood of low trees, &c.* झाडी *f.* झुडप *or* झुडूप *n.* झुडपाळरान *n.* वृक्षवाटिका *f.* कृत्रिमवन *n.*

To COPULATE, *v. n. unite in sexual intercourse.* जुगणें, लागणें, रतणें, अंगसंग *m.*-संग *m.*-मैथुन *n.*-&c.करणें.

COPULATION, *n.* v. V. जुगणें *n.* &c. मिथुन *n.* मैथुन *n.* अंगसंग *m.* रति *f.* रत *f.* रतिक्रिया *f.* संग *m.* संयोग *m.* समागम *m.* सुरत *n.* रमण *n.* संभोग *m.* शयन *n.* संयोजन *n.* शृंगार *m.* व्यवाय *m.* ग्राम्यधर्म *m.*

I.—in grammar. समाहार*m.* समुच्चय*m.*

COPULATIVE, *n.*—in grammar,v. CONJUNCTION. उभयान्वयी.

COPY, *n. transcript.* नकल *f.* उतारा *m.* प्रत *f.* प्रत्यतर *n* उलटा*m.* नमुना *or* नमोना *m.*—esp. of an official paper. तालीक *f.*

Foul c. खरडा *m.* खरडें *n.* मसुदा *m.*

2 *one book of many.* प्रत *f.* [क *n.*

3 *archetype,* v. ORIGINAL. प्रत *f.* मूलप्रत *f.* मूल *n.* मूलपुस्तक *n.*

4 *model, exemplar,* v. PATTERN. कित्ता *m.*

5 *piece of writing for scholars.* कित्ता *m.*

6 *paper written by scholars.* पुस्ती *f.*

To COPY, *v. a. transcribe.* उतरणें, उतरून घेणें, नकल *f.*-प्रत *f.*-प्रत्यंतर *n.*-उतारा *m.*-&c. करणें *g. of o.*

2 v. To IMITATE. उतरणें, कित्ता *m.*- वळण *n.* घेणें *g. of. o.* थाकी *f.* उतरणें-साधणें-आणणें *g. of o.* अनुसरण *n.*-&c.करणें, धरणें, घेणें.

COPY-BOOK, *n.* कित्यांची वही *f.*

COPY-HOLD, *n.* पट्टा *m.*

COPYING, *n.* v. V. 1.—*act.* उतरणें, *n.* नक्कल करणें *n.* &c.

2—*act. and* IMITATION. उतरणें *n.* &c. अनुसरण *n.* अनुकरण *n.* [नीस.

COPY-IST, *n.* नकल करणारा, प्रतकरणारा, लेखक, नकलनवीस *or* नकलनीस.

COPY-RIGHT, *n.* ग्रंथाची मालकी *f.* ग्रंथावरचा हक्क *m.*

To COQUET, *v. n.* नखरा *m.*-हाव *m. pl.*-हाव भाव *m. pl.*-अदा *m.* -&c. करणें.

COQUETRY, COQUETTING, *n.* नखरा *m.* हाव *m.* हावभाव *m.pl.* अदा *m.* टेव *or* टेवरेव *m.pl.* नखरेबाजी *f.* गमजे*m.pl.* विलास*m.*

COQUETTE, *n.* नखरेदार-नखरेबाज-&c. बायको *f.* टेवखोर, चाळक, चाळकभवानी *f.* नाचण *f.*

CORACLE, *n. boat composed of leather over a frame.* टोकरा *or* टोंकरा *m.* टोकर *or* टोंकर *m.*

CORAL, *n.* प्रवाल *n. pop.* पोवळी *f. or* पोवळें *n.* विद्रुम *n.*

Bracelet formed of c. पोवळसर *m.*

Calx of c. प्रवालभस्म *n.*

Child's c. चुंफणी *f.* चोपण *or* णी *f.* चोपणें *n.* चोखणें *n.*

Imitation c. कापूर पोवळें *n.*

CORAL, CORALINE, *a.* v. N. पोवळ्याचा, प्रवालमय.

CORAL-TREE, *n.* पारिजात *m.* पारिजातक *m.*

CORD, *n.* v. STRING. दोरी *f.* चऱ्हाट *n.* गुण *m.* दोरक *m.*

2 v. ROPE. नाडा *m.* सडक *f.* सडा *m.* गुण *m.* दोरक *m.* सोल*m.*

A fastening c. कस्तान *n.*

To CORD, *v. a.* दोरी *f.* बांधणें, दोरीनें बांधणें.

CORDAGE, *n.* दोरखंडें *n. pl.* दोरडीं *n. pl.*

CORDIAL, *a. hearty,* v. SINCERE. मनापासूनचा, बेंबीच्या देंठापासूनचा, मनः पुरस्सर, अंतःकरणपूर्वक, हृद्य, मनोभावाचा, जिव्हाळ्याचा, पोटागीचा.

2 *strengthening.* पुष्टिकारक, पौष्टिक, तेजोवर्द्धक.

CORDIAL, *n. strengthening medicine.* तेजोवर्द्धक-पुष्टिकारक-&c. औषध*n.*

CORDIALITY, *n.* v. A. 1. निष्कपटपणा*m.* खरेपणा*m.* निष्कापट्य*n.* मनः पूर्वकता *f.* सौहृद*n.* सौमनस्य *n.*

CORDIALLY, *adv.* v.A.1. मनापासून,बेंबीच्या देंठापासून,मनःपूर्वक, अंतःकरणपूर्वक.

CORDON, *n.*—in architecture. कंगोरा*m.* कंगणी *f.*

CORE, *n.*v. HEART. गर्भ *pop.* गाभा*m.*

Rotten, &c. at the c. हाडाचा खोटा-कुजका-वाईट-&c.

2 (of a boil) मोख*m.* गाईर *f.* आंठी *f.*

CORIANDER,*n.*—the plant. कोथिंबरी *or* कोथिंबीर *f.* धणा*m.*

—the seed. धणा*m.* भोवी *f.* धान्यक*n.* [गुडदी *f.*

CORK, *n. bung, stopple, plug.* बूज *m.* दट्टा *m.* बुचटणें*n.* बुटणें *n.*

To CORK, *v. a.* बूज*m.*-दट्टा*m.*- &c. मारणें- बसवणें.

CORK-SCREW, *n.* बूजम.-दट्टाम.-&c. काढायाचें साधनn.

CORMORANT, *n.* करढोंकm.

2 v. GLUTTON. अधासा, स्वाद, कुक्षिंभरि.

CORN, *n.* धान्यn. *pop.* धानn. दाणाm. गल्लाm. कणm. अन्नn.सस्यn.

Beard of c. कुसळn. कूसn. कोशीf. [घाटा m.

C. (esp. *Bádzri* or *Dzondhalà*) husked and boiled.

C. as trodden out. *c. and straws mixed.* मदनn.

C. (rice, wheat, *Dzondhalà*, &c.) soaked and puffed by parching. लाह्याf. *pl.* भुरंगुल्याf. *pl. or* भुरंगुलींn. *pl.*

C. which ripens before the close of the rains. पाणपिकलेंn. पाणपीकn.

Grown c. Sprouted c. रोहm. रोवm.

Head or full ear of c. तटोरी *or* टटोरीf. पोटरा *or* पोठराm. गाभोळीf. (*and* To come to a head पोटऱ्यास येणें).

New c. (of the year). नवधान्यn. नवान्नn.

Undressed c. (as given in charity). कोरान्नn. आमान्नn.

Whilst you've c. to give out, you'll have friends round about. असतील शितें तर मिळतील भुतें.

2 *a single c.* दाणाm. कण m. लुंगाm.

3 *growing or reaped c.* शेतn. शेतीकn. शेतीf. शेतकीf. शेतसरीf. जिनजितरबn.

Bare or blank in c. दळाm. दल्हेंn. ओंसाm.

Breaking off the ears of (reaped) c. मोडणीf.

Bundles of unthreshed c. गूड *or* ढन.

Carrying off(to threshing floor)of sheaves of c.वाहणीf.

C. blasted whilst young and tender. मुराणn.

C. (or a stalk) blasted before coming to head. (or of which the heads have been eaten off). बांड m. n.

C. just sprung up. वापf. रुजवण *or* रुझवणn.

Ears lying on a reaped field of c. सरवाm. निसरवाm.

Erection (as of sheaves) over a heap of c. अढीf.

Erection amidst c. for the watcher. माळोंचाm. माळाm. अटोलाm.

Grass and weeds amidst c. निदणn.

Heads of c. tied together. बुचडाm.

Heap of c. the produce of the first treading of the ears. राशि *pop.* रासf.—worship of it. रासपुजाf.

Patch of green c. amidst withered c. जिताडf.

Rich or fine patch amidst c. डांभाn. डांभा डचकाm.

Shooting of (reaped) c.—through rain. कराm.

Weeding instrument of c. कोळपें (the blade or iron-member of it is लांडगी, a cheek of it is जानवळेंn.).

To tread out c. मळणें.

To tread out c. with stalks undetached. सगडमळf.करणें.

To weed and clear c. निदणें, कोळपणें, भांगलणें.

4 (on the foot). जोड्याचा घट्टा m.-किणा m.

To CORN, *v. a. salt.* मिठांत-मिठानें मळणें, मीठ n. घालणें, खारवणें.

CORN-BIN, *n.* v. BIN. कोथळाm.*dim.*कोथळीf. पालेंn.पालेंn.ठिकीf.

CORN-CHANDLER, *n.* भुसारी, गल्लेकरी, मोदी, वाणी.

Corn-chandlers,—gener. or collect. भुसार n.

CORN-COUNTRY, *n.* धान्य देश m.

CORN-FIELD, *n.* शेत n. उभें शेत n. भरलेलें शेत n.

CORN-FLOOR, *n.* खळें n.

CORN-LAND, *n.* जिराईतf. शेत जमीनf.

CORN-MARKET, *n.* भुसारपेठf.

CORNEA, *n.* बाहुलीचें ढांपण n.-पडदा m. तारकापिधान n.

CORNELIAN, *n.* अकीक m.

CORNEOUS, *a. horny.* शिंगाचा, शृंगरूप, शृंगमय, शृंगात्मक, शार्ङ्ग,

CORNER, *n.* कोन m. कोण m. कोपरा m. कोना m. कोनपडा m. कोनपा m. अस्र n.

Changing the c.(as of a cat with kittens).कोनपालटm.

Holes and corners, *nooks and recesses.* कोनकोपरे m.*pl.* सांधी कोंडी f. *pl.*

In every hole and c. कोणेकाणीं, सांधीं कोंदीं.

To drive up into a c. *stop one's mouth, pose, &c.* कोलणें, कोंडमारा m.-कोंडमार m. करणें g. *of o.*

2 *secret or remote place.* कोनपडा m. एकवसा *or* एकोसा m.

In a c. एकोशास, एकोशीं.

Thing done in a c. सांदींतली गोष्ट.

To do great things (mighty feats, &c.) in a c. सुन्याघरीं वाण n. देणें.

CORNER-STONE, *n.* कोपऱ्याचा-कोन्याचा-&c. दगड m. कोन्यादगडm.

CORNER-WISE, *adv. diagonally.* तिरकस, तिर्यक्.

CORNERED, *a.* कोणाचा, कोनी (in comp. as चौकोनी &c.), कोन (in comp. as त्रिकोन).

CORNET, *n.*—instrument. शृंग *pop.* शिंग m.

2 तुरूकस्वारांचा एक अमलदार आहे.

CORNETER, *n.* शिंगवाजविणारा, शिंगकरी.

CORNICE, *n.* कंगोरा m. कंगणी f.

C. under a cieling. गोठ m. छतपट्टी f.

CORNICLE, *n.* लहानशिंग n.

COROLLARY, *n.* v. CONCLUSION. सिद्धांतm.आनुषंगिक सिद्ध गोष्टf.

CORONAL, *a. belonging to the top of the head.* टाळूचा, टाळूच्या संबंधाचा.

CORONAL, *n.* See CROWN.

CORONATION. See CROWNING.

CORONER, *n.* अपघाताचा चौकसनीस.

C.'s. inquest. मैयतकयास m. मैयतचौकशी f.

CORONET, *n.* बडेलोकांचा मुकुट m. टोप m.

CORPORAL, *a. relating to the body,* v. BODILY. शरीराचा, शरीरी, शारीर, शारीरिक, शारीरक, कायिक, दैहिक.

2 See CORPOREAL.

CORPORAL, *n.* The word नाईक corresponds.

CORPORATE, *a. united in a body authorized to act as one.* मिळणीचे सनदेचा, जमातीचे सनदेचा, एकव्यक्तीभूत, संभूयकारित्वाधिकार विशिष्ट, संभूयकार्यकारक.

2 See COLLECTIVE.

CORPORATION, *n.* एक होऊन काम करण्याचे सनदेची मंडळी f. सनदी जमात f.-पुड्डा m.-&c. पुड्डा m. जमात f. मंडळी f. संभूयकार्यकारक समुदाय m.

CORPOREAL, *a. embodied,* v. BODIED. देही, अंगी, शरीरी, आंगिक.

2 See MATERIAL.

CORPOREITY, CORPOREALNESS, *n.* v.A.1. देहित्वn. अंगित्व n. शरीरिताf. सदेहताf. देहिभाव m.

CORPS, *n.* v. ARMY. सैन्यदलn. चक्रn. सेनाभागm. Some of the *Corps* or *Bodies of Troops* named in Hindu writings are गुल्म, गण, सेनामुख, वाहिनी, पृतना, चमू, अनीकिनी, अक्षौहिणी.

CORPSE, *n. dead body.* मडें *n.* प्रेत *n.* मुरडा or मुडदा *m.* मरतीक *n.* शव *n.* लोथ *f.* लोघ *f.m.* कुणप *m.*

Collecting the bones after burning a c. अस्थिसंचय *m.* अस्थिसंचयन *n.*

Ground for burning or burying a c. श्मशान *pop.* मसण or मसाण *n.* मसणवटी *f.*

CORPSE-BEARER, *n.* खांद्या, शववाहक, प्रेतवाहक, वाहक.

CORPULENCE, CORPULENCY, *n.* v. A. ढमालेपणा *m.* दुलदुलीतपणा *m.* मेद *n.* मेदोवृद्धि *f.* मेदोवात *m.* रेप *f.* भोपळयारोग *m.* स्थौल्य *n.* स्थूलता *f.* मेदोबाहुल्य *n.*

CORPULENT, *a. fleshy, bulky,* v. FAT. ढमाल or ढमाल्या, कापशा, धोनशा, मेदोवृद्धीचा, स्थूल, स्थूलकाय, वृद्धनाभि.

C. and weak. पोंदी or पोंधी, पोया.

CORPUSCLE, *a.* v. ATOM. अणु *m.* सूक्ष्म *m.*

CORPUSCULAR, *a.* v. ATOMICAL. अणुरूप, अणुमय.

CORPUSCULARIAN, *n. atomist.* सूक्ष्मवादी.

To CORRECT, *v. a. chastise, chasten,* v. To PUNISH. शिक्षा *f.*-शिक्षण *n.*-नसीहत *f.*-पारपत्य *n.*-&c. करणें-देणें-लावणें, शिक्षणें.

2 v. To RECTIFY. सुधारणें, निटावणें, नीट-शुद्ध-&c. करणें.

3 (a literary work). चुकी *f. pl.* काढणें, शोधणें, शोध *m.*-शोधन *n.* करणें *g. of o.* शुद्ध करणें, शेणगोळे *m. pl.* घालणें.

4—in medicine. साम्याचा-समधात-&c. करणें, दोषनिरास *m.*-दोषापहरण *n.* करणें *g. of o.* निर्बाधता *f.* आणणें.

CORRECT, *a. just, proper,* v. RIGHT. बराबर, नीट, टीक, दुरूस्त, यथायोग्य, शिष्ट, शिस्तवार, नीत, नीतीचा.

2—esp. of conduct, or of language. नीट, ठीक, शुद्ध, विशुद्ध, निर्दोष, दोषहीन-शून्य-&c.

CORRECTED, *p.* v. V. 1. शिक्षा केलेला, &c. शिक्षित, शासित, दंडित.

2 सुधारलेला, निटावलेला, नीट केलेला, &c.

3 शोधलेला, &c. शुद्ध केलेला, शोधित, शुद्धीकृत.

CORRECTION, *n.* v. V. 1.—*act.* शिक्षा करणें *n.* शिक्षा देणें *n.* &c. शिक्षण*n.*शिक्षा *f.*शासन *n.* नसीहत or नश्यत *f.* पारपत्य *n.*तंबी *f.*

House of c. See JAIL.

2—*act.* निटावणें *n.* नीट करणें *n.* &c. सुधारणी *f.* सुधारणूक *f.*

3—*act.* शोधणें *n.* &c. शोध *m.* शोधन *n.* शुद्धि *f.* विशुद्धि *f.*

I. a. c. *an error corrected.* शोध *m.*

Sheet or paper of corrections. शोधपत्र *n.* शुद्धिपत्र *n.*

CORRECTLY, *adv.* v. A. बराबर, ठीक, नीट, यथायोग्य, यथायुक्त, चुकीवांचून, बिनचूक.

CORRECTNESS, *n.* v.A. 1. ठीकपणा*m.* दुरुस्तपणा*m.* यथायोग्यता *f.* शिष्टाइकी *f.* शिष्टाई *f.* नीति *f.*

2 शुद्धपणा*m.* शुद्धि *f.* विशुद्धि *f.* शुद्धता *f.* निर्दोषता *f.* दोषराहित्य*n.* दोषहीनता*f.*

CORRECTOR, *n.* CORRECTIVE, *a.* v. V. 1. शिक्षा-&c. करणारा-देणारा-लावणारा, शिक्षा-शासन कर्त्ता-कारी-&c. शिक्षक.

2 सुधारणारा, नीट करणारा, &c.

3 शोधणारा, चुकी काढणारा, &c. शोधक.

4 भंजक, समधात करणारा, &c. दोषापहारक.

CORRELATIVE, *a. having a reciprocal relation.* परस्पर संबंधाचा, अन्योन्यसंबंधाचा, अन्योन्याश्रयाचा, अन्योन्य-परस्पर संबंधी, अन्योन्यान्वयी, अन्यांन्याश्रित, परस्पराश्रित.

CORRELATIVENESS, *n.* v. A. परस्पर संबंध*m.* अन्योन्यसंबंध*m.* परस्पराश्रय*m.* अन्योन्यान्वय*m.*

To CORRESPOND, *v. n. be adapted, adequate, &c.*v. To TALLY. मिळणें, जुगणें, जुडणें, जुळणें, जमणें, उतरणें, संभवणें,जम*m.*-जबा*m.*- &c. बसणें *g. of s. recip.* जोडी *f.* बनणें *g. of o. recip.*

2 (by epistles, &c.). कागद पत्राची वहिवाट *f.*-&c. ठेवणें,पत्रें *n. pl.* येणें जाणें *g. of s. recip.* पत्रव्यवहार *m.* ठेवणें.

CORRESPONDENCE, *n.* CORRESPONDING, *n.* v. V. 1. ताळा *m.* v. घे, पाह, पड, तालामाला *m.* मेळ *m.* जम *m.* जवा *m* उतारा *m.* जुळणी *f.*जुगल *f.*लाग*m.*संभावना *f.* संभूति *f.*संभव *m.*समन्वय *m.*

2 कागद पत्राची वहिवाट *f.*-भेट *f.*-संबंध *m.*-&c.

I. (as of an event with a prediction). ताळा *m.* गांठ *f.*

Event corresponding with a prediction. ठोका *m.*

II.—in commerce. अडत *f.*

III. *mass of letters.* कागदपत्रें *n. pl.* जाबसाली कागद *m. pl.* जाबसाली पत्रें *n. pl.*

CORRESPONDENT, *a.* CORRESPONDER, *n.* CORRESPONDING, *p.a.* CORRESPONSIVE, *a.* v. V. 1. मिळणारा, मिलाफाचा, जमाचा, एकसारखा, बेताचा, समन्वित, अनुरूप, संभावित, अनुगुण.

CORRESPONDENT, *n.* v. V. 2. कागदपत्राची वहिवाट ठेवणारा.

I.—in commerce. अडत्या *m.* गुमास्ता *m.* वार्त्तिक *m.* [बाट *f.*

CORRIDOR, *n. gallery or passage in a house.* घरांतील बोळाची

CORRIGIBLE, *a.* v. V. 1. शिक्षणीय, शिक्षार्ह, दंडनीय, दंड्य.

2 सुधारायाजोगा-जोगता-&c.

To CORROBORATE, *v. a. invigorate,* v. To STRENGTHEN. शक्ति *f.*-बळकटी *f.*-बळ *n.*-जोर *m.*-&c. देणें-आणणें, पुष्टि *f.*-पुष्टीकरण *n.* करणें.

2 *establish, &c.* v. To CONFIRM. बळकटी *f.*-बळ *n.*-&c. देणें-करणें-आणणें,खराकरणें, सबलकरण *n.*-पुष्टीकरण *n.*करणें*g.of o.*

CORROBORATION, *n.* v. V. 1.—*act.* बळकटी आणणें *n.* &c. पुष्टीकरण *n.* बलवर्द्धन *n.*

2—*act.* बळकटी देणें*n.*&c.पुष्टीकरण*n.* सबलकरण *n.* दृढीकरण*n.*

—*state.* बळकटी *f.* बळ *n.*

CORROBORATIVE, CORROBORANT, *a.* v. V. 1. धातुपुष्ट, पौष्टिक, पुष्टिकर-कारक-&c. बलवर्द्धक.

2 बळकटी देणारा-आणणारा, &c.

To CORRODE, *v. a. eat away.* खातांखातां खाणें, खाणें, खणणें, खांडणें, चरणें.

CORROSION, *n.* v. V.—*act.* खाणें *n.* खणणें *n.* खणती *f.*

CORROSIVE, *a.* v. A. खाणारा, खणणारा, &c. अरुष्कर, खादक.

CORROSIVENESS, *n.* v. A. अरुष्करता *f.* खादकत्व *n.*

To CORRUGATE, &c. See To WRINKLE, &c.

To CORRUPT, *v. a. make putrid, rotten, &c.* कुजवणें, सडवणें, बिघडणें, बिघडवणें, बिनासणें or बिनसणें, नासवणें,खराब करणें, बिरसुडणें.

2 fig. *deprave, vitiate, spoil.* बिघडणें, बिघडवणें, नासणें, भ्रष्ट-आचार भ्रष्ट-गुणभ्रष्ट-&c. करणें, बिथरवणें, बिथरणें, सत्वनाश *m.*-&c. करणें *g. of o.*

To CORRUPT, *v. n. become putrid, &c.* कुजणें, सडणें, बिघडणें, बिनासणें or बिनसणें, नासणें, बिरसुडणें.

2 fig. *become depraved, &c.* बिघडणें, बिथरणें, बिचलणें, बिनसणें or बिनासणें,नासणें,खराब-भ्रष्ट-गुणभ्रष्ट-आचारभ्रष्ट-&c. होणें.

3—fruit, article of food, &c. बाचकुडणें.

Corrupt, *a.* **Corrupted**, *p.* v. V. N. 1. *putrid, rotten, &c.* नासका, कुजका, सडका, नासलेला, कुजलेला, &c. दूषित, शीर्ण.
2 *vitious, depraved, &c.* v. Wicked. दुष्ट, नासलेला, बिघडलेला, &c. आचारभ्रष्ट, गुणभ्रष्ट, विगुण.

Corruptible, *a.* v. V. N. 1. नाशवंत, विनाशी, नश्वर, क्षयिष्णु.

Corruptibility, *n.* v. A. विनाशित्व *n.* नश्वरता *f.*

Corrupting, Corruption, *n.* v. V. A. 1.—*act.* कुजवणें, बिघडवणें *n.* नासवणें *n.* &c. बिघडणूक *f.* दूषण *n.*—*state.* बिघड *or* बिघाड *m.*
2—*act.* नासणें *n.* खराब करणें *n.* भ्रष्ट करणें *n.* &c. बिघडणूक *f.* भ्रष्टकरण *n.* दूषण *n.*—*state.* v. Wickedness. दुष्टत्व *n.* आचार भ्रष्टता *f.*
I. *purulent matter*, v. Pus. पू *m.*
II.—in grammar. अपभ्रंश *m.* अपशब्द *m.*
III. See Bribery.

Corruptness, *n.* v. A. 1. कुजकेपणा *m.* &c. शीर्णता *f.* शीर्णभाव *m.*
2 v. Wickedness. दुष्टपणा *m.* दुष्टाई *f.* आचारभ्रष्टता *f.*

Corsair, *n. pirate.* चांचा *m.*
2 चांच्यांचें गलबत *n.*

Corse. See Corpse.

Corselet, *n.* v. Armour. उरस्त्राण *n.* उरश्छद *m.*

Corset. See Bodice.

Cortege, *n.* v. Train. स्वारी *f.* जिलीब *f.*

Cortical, *a. belonging, &c. to bark, &c.* सालीचा, त्वाच, त्वक्संबंधी, वल्कलसंबंधी.

Coruscation. See Flash.

Cos, Coss, *n.*—the measure of distance. कोस *m.* कोश *m.*

Cosey, *a. snug, comfortable,*—persons. सुखी, सुखरूप.
2—places. सुखाचा, अटोपसार.

Cosmetic, *n. wash, &c. for the skin.* उटणें *n.* अंगराग *m.*

Cosmic, Cosmical, *a.* जगत्संबंधी, जगद्विषयक, सृष्टिसंबंधी.

Cosmogony, *n.* जगदुत्पत्ति *f.* जगत्सृष्टि *f.*

Cosmography, *n.* भूसृष्टिविद्या *f.* भूसृष्टि वर्णन *n.* जगद्वर्णन *n.*

Cosmopolite, *n.* देशसमदृष्टि, जगद्देशी, जगन्मित्र.

Cost, *n.* v. Price. मोल *n.* किमत *f.* दाम *m.*
Prime c. अवलकिमत *f.* ऐनकिमत *f.* असलकिमत *f.*
2 *expense, charge.* खर्च *m.* व्यय *m.* वेच *m.*
Free of c. फुकटशाई, फुकटचा, फुकटा *or* ट्या, फुकटाईचा, मुफतचा.
The costs exceed the profits. घोडें खाई भाडें.
To live at one's own c. पदर *m.* खर्चणें-खाणें-मोडणें.
3 costs:—in law. खर्च *m.*

To **Cost**, *v. a.* मोल *n.*-किमत *f.*-खर्च *m.*-रुपये *m. pl.*-पैसे *m. pl.*-&c. पडणें-बसणें-लागणें-येणें-होणें *in. con.* लागणें-पडणें *in. con.*

Costal, *a. pertaining to the sides or the ribs.* कुशीचा, बरगड्यांचा, फासोळ्यांचा, पार्श्वीय.

Coster-monger, *n.* मेवा विकणारा फेरीवाला.

Costive, *a. constipated.* जडकोठ्याचा, बंद, बद्धकोष्ठ, क्रूरकोष्ठ, अवरुद्धमल, मलावष्टब्ध.
To become c. सांखळणें.

Costiveness, *n.* v. A. कबज *n.* सांखळा *m.* v. घर, बद्धकोष्ठ *m.* क्रूरकोष्ठ *m.* बद्धक *n.* मलस्तब्धि *f.* मलावरोध *m.* मलावष्टंभ *m.*
C. with flatulence. आमवात *m.*

Costliness, *n.* v. A. उंची *f.* मोठेंमोल *n.* बहुमूल्यता *f.* महामूल्यता *f.*

Costly, *a. sumptuous, high-priced*, v. Dear. मोठ्या मोलाचा, मोठे किमतीचा, बहुमोली, बहुमूल्य, महामूल्य, जड.

Costume, *n.* v. Dress. वेष *pop.* भेष *or* भेश *or* भेस *m.* पेहराव *or* पैराव *m.* पेहरावा *or* पैरावा *m.* बाणा *m.* लिबास *m.*

Co-sufferer, *n.* समदुःखी.

Cot, *n.* v. Hut. खोपट *n.* खोपटी *f.* कुटि *or* कुटी *f.* पर्णकुटी *f.* पर्णशाला *f.*
2 v. Bedstead. खाट *n. dim.* खाटलें *n.* माचा *m.* पलंग *m.*
A swinging c. झोंपाळा *m.*

Cot-quean, *n. man who busies himself in women's affairs, &c.* बायक्या, बायल्या, बटक्या, बटकुऱ्या, रांड्या रांघांबा, चुल्भानवशा.

Cotemporary. See Contemporary.

Coterie, *n. club.* कचोळें *n.* चाकोळें *or* चाखोळें *n.*

Cottage, *n.* v. Hut. झोंपडी *f.* झोंपडें *n.* खोप *f.* खोपटी *f.* खोपडी *f.* खोपट *n.* कुटि *or* कुटी *f.*
2 *a small but tasteful dwelling.* सुबकबंगला *m.*

Cottager, Cotter, *n.* झोंपड्या, खोपट्या, कुटिनिवासी, कुटिस्थ.

Cotton, *n.*—the plant. कापशी *f.* कार्पास *m.* कार्पासी *f.* Some species of the *cotton-plant* are देवकापशी, देवपल्ही, रानकापशी, शेतकापशी, इंद्रकापशी.—the produce. कापूस *m.* कर्पास *m. n.* तूल *m.*
Bow used in carding c. धनुकली *or* धुनकुली *f.* धनु *n.*
Carded c. गाळा *m.* रुई *f.* रू *m.*
C.-seed. सरकी *f.* बरकी *f.*
C.-thread. सूत *n.*
Cushion or case stuffed with c. रुजामा *m.*
Dry culm remaining of c.-plant. पळ्हांटी *f.*
Flock of c. इंद्रतूल *m.*
Flocks of c. (floating in the air). वाततूल *m.*
Pat of c. (as steeped in a dye, &c.). कापसाची वडी *f.*
Plantation of the c.-plant. पळ्हें *n.*
Silk c.-tree. सावरी *or* सावर *f.*—Gum of it. मोचरस *m.*—Pole of it (used as rafter, &c.). सावऱ्या *m.*
Stuffed with c. Quilted with c. रूदार, रूगरद्दा.
To card c. धनुकणें.
To seed (extract the seeds of) c. बटणें, लोढणें.—Instrument of extracting the seeds. बटणें *n.*
2 *cotton cloth.* सुताचें कापड *n.* सुती कापड *n.* Some sorts are पडम *n.* सुताडा *m.* खादी *f.*

Cotton, *a. belonging to c.* सुती, सुताचा, कार्पास, कार्पासिक.

Cotton cleaner, *n.* पिंजारी.—the instrument of. मुसता *m.* कुंकंड *n.*

Cotton-gin, *n.* बटणें *n*

Cotton-press, *n.* चाप *m.* गिरणी *f.*

Cotyledon, *n. seed-lobe.* डाळिंबी *f.*

To **Couch**, *v. n. lower, cower.* दबणें, दबून बसणें-असणें, दबा *m.* धरणें-मारणें *or* धरून-मारून बसणें-असणें.

To **Couch**, *v. a. lay down as on a couch.* निजवणें, बसवणें, ठेवणें, टाकणें.
2 *involve, include*, v. To Imply. ध्वनन *n.* करणें *g. of o.* ध्वनित-गार्भित-&c. करणें.
3 (spear, &c.) लागावर-&c. धरणें-ठेवणें-रोवणें.
4 (a cataract.) सुईनें दाबणें.

COUCH, *n.* v. BEDSTEAD. पलंग *m.* खट्वा *f. pop.* खाट *f. and dim.* खाटलें *n.* मंच *or* मंचक *pop.* माचवा *or* माचा *m.* तल्प *n.*
2 *sofa, &c. seat for rest,*—gener. शय्या *f.* शयन *n.* सुखशयन *n.* सुखशय्या *f.* सुखशेज *f.* सुखासन *n.* कोच *or* कोंच *m.n.* from the English.

COUCHANT, *a.* दबा धरलेला, दबा धरून बसलेला.

COUGH, *n.* खोकला *or* खोखला *m.* खांसी *f.* कास *m.*
Consumptive c. क्षयकास *m.*
Dry wheezing c. खेंस *f.*
Whooping c. डांग्या खोकला *m.*
Lingering and moist c. खैन *n. m.* One affected with it. खैन्या, खैनी, खैनकरी.
Obstinate dry c. esp-of horses & cattle ढांस *f.* ढांसणी *f.* Affected with it. ढांसरा. [ढांसणें.

To COUGH, *v. n.* खोकणें *or* खोखणें, खोकाळणें, खासणें, खसणें,
To c. wheezingly. खेंसणें.
A fit of coughing. उबळ *or* उभळ *f. v.* ये. खोकल्याचीसर *f.*

To COUGH, *v.a.with* up. *expectorate.* खाकरणें,खोकून बाहेर टाकणें.

COUNCIL, *n.* मसलतकरणारांची मंडळी *f.* मंत्रणसभा *f.* सभा *f.* मंत्रिसमाज *m.*
Award or decision of a c. समुच्चय *m.*
Member of c. v. COUNSELLOR. सभासद, सभ्य.
Member (or other person) present at a c. हाजीर मजालस. [मंत्रशाला *f.*

COUNCIL-CHAMBER, COUNCIL-HALL, *n.* सभा *f.* दिवाणखाना *m.*

COUNCILLOR, *n. member of a c.* v. COUNSELLOR. सभासद, कौंसिलदार (a formation from the English with दार).

COUNSEL, *n. advice.* मसलत *f.* उपदेश *m.* सल्ला *m.* मंत्र *m.* बुद्धिवाद *m. v.* सांग, सल्लामसलत *f.*
2 *scheme, measure, device, &c. counselled out.* विचार *m.* मसलत *f.* तजवीज *f.* तोड *f.* कारस्थान *n.* काट *m.* कूट *n.*
Band holding c. कचोळें *n.*
Betraying or divulging c. मंत्रभेद *m.*
Deep or complex c. चक्रव्यूह *m.*
Of deep c. मसलती, मनसुबी, मनसुबदार.
Nice or delicate c. नाजूक मसलत *f.*
Well digested c. सरपूस विचार *m.*
"All whose c. cometh to pass." सत्यसंकल्प.
To keep one's own c. आपली मसलत-आपली गोष्ट-आपला भेद-&c. आपल्या मनांतच ठेवणें.
3 See CONSULTATION.

To COUNSEL, *v. a.* v. To ADVISE. बुद्धिवाद *m.*-बुद्धि *f.*-विचार *m.*-अक्कल *f.*-&c. सांगणें, मसलत *f* -सल्ला *m f.* देणें.

COUNSELLED, *p.* v. V. उपदिष्ट, मंत्रित, अभिमंत्रित.

COUNSELLING, *n.* v.V.—*act.* बुद्धिवाद सांगणें *n.* &c. मंत्रण *n.* अभिमंत्रण *n.* बोधन *n.* प्रबोधन *n.* बोध *m.* प्रबोध *m.*
Secret c. मंत्रगुप्ति *f.*

COUNSELLOR, *n.* v. V. बुद्धिवाद सांगणारा, &c. मंत्री, अभिमंता, मसलतदार, उपदेशक.
I. *member of a council.* सभासद, सभ्य,सामवायिक, सामाजिक.
II. (as of a king or ruler). मंत्री, अमात्य, सचिव, धीसख, धीसचिव, ग्रंथिहर, बुद्धिसहाय.
III. See LAWYER.

To COUNT, *v. a. number, reckon.* गणणें, मोजणें, मेजणें, गणती *f.*-मोजणी *f.*-मोजदाद *f.*-गणन *n.*-गणना *f.*-संख्या *f.* -&c. करणें *g. of o.* [लिखणें.
2 *account, regard,* v. To VALUE. मोजणें, मानणें, गणणें,

To COUNT, *v. n.* मोजण्यांत येणें, भरीस उपयोगी पडणें.
2 on; *reckon on, rely.* भरवसा *m.*-अधण *n.*-&c. ठेवणें, जाणें with वर.

COUNT, *n.* बडेलोकांत एक पदवी आहे.

COUNTABLE, *a.*v.V.1. गणायाजोगा-&c. गणितव्य, गणेय, गणनीय.

COUNTED, *p.* v.V. A. 1. गणलेला, &c. गणित, परिगणित, संख्यात, मोजींव, मेजींव.
2 मोजलेला, &c.

COUNTENANCE, *n. visage, features,* v. FACE. मुख *n.* तोंडवळण *n.* तोंडवळा *m.* चेहरा *m.* चेहरामोरा *m.*
Change of c.(through shame, alarm, &c.) मुखवैवर्ण्य *n.*
Freshness and liveliness of c. टवटवी *f.* टकटकी *f.* तजला *m.* तेजगी *f.* मुखश्री *f.* मुखराग *m* मुखचर्या *f.*
Of a fine or handsome c. चेहरेदार, सुरूप.
Of a laughing or smiling c. हास्यमुख, हास्यवदन.
A weeping c. रडतें तोंड *n.* रडती सुरत *f.*
Of a weeping c. रडतोंड्या.
Putting out of c. मुखभंजन *n.*
To let the c. fall. तोंड *n.*-मुद्रा *f.* उतरणें *g. of s.*
To keep in c. पाठ *f.* राखणें *g. of o.*
To put out of c. खालीं पहायास लावणें.
It was as much as I could do to keep my countenance. हसें आवरतां मला पुरेसें झालें.
I could not keep my c. हासल्यावांचून राहवेना. [ढब *f.*
2 *air, look, aspect.* चेहरा *m.* मुद्रा *f.* चर्या *f.* सुरत *f.* आकार *m.*
3 *favorable regard,* v. FAVOR, PATRONAGE. कृपादृष्टि *f.* कृपावलोकन *n.* दृष्टि *f.* नजर *f.* हिमाईत *f.* सिफारस *f.* आश्रय *m.*

To COUNTENANCE, *v. a.* v. To PATRONIZE, To FAVOR. कृपादृष्टि *f.*-नजर *f.*-डोळा *m.*-&c. करणें-ठेवणें-देणें, पाठ *f.* राखणें *g. of o.* पाठीसीं घालणें, मेहरबानी *f.* करणें.

COUNTER. See CONTRARY,CONTRARYWISE.

COUNTER, *n. piece used in counting.* नरद *f.* चकती *f.* बोंद *n.*
2 *board or table of a shop.* चौकी *f.* चौरंग *m.*

To COUNTERACT, *v. a.* उलटउपाय *m.*-उलटव्यापार *m.*-&c. करणें-चालवणें *or* करून-&c. मोडणें-खंडणें-&c. प्रतिकार *m.*-प्रतिक्रिया *f.*-प्रतियोग *m.*-प्रत्युपाय *m.*-&c. करणें *or* करून मोडणें-नष्ट करणें -&c. उलटविणें, उलटणें, मोडणें, खंडणें, पाडणें.

COUNTERACTER, *n.* COUNTERACTING, *p. a.* v. V. उलट उपाय करणारा-करून मोडणारा,&c.प्रतिकारक, प्रतिकार-&c. कर्त्ता-कारी-&c. प्रतियोगी, कार्यहंता.

COUNTERACTION, *n.* v. V. उलट उपाय चालवणें *n.* उलट व्यापार *m.* प्रतिकार *m.* प्रतिक्रिया *f.* कार्यहनन *n.*

COUNTERBALANCE, *n. equivalent weight, &c.* तुला *or* तुळा *f.* धडा *m.* आभंड *or* आभांड *n.* समभाराचा-भारंभारचा विषय *m.*-गोष्ट *f.*-&c.
2 *state of equipoise.* समतोल *m.* भारसाम्य *n.* भारसमता *f.*

To COUNTERBALANCE, *v. a. act against with equal weight, be equivalent to.* तोलणें, तोलून धरणें, तुळणेस येणें, बराबर-समभार-समतोल-समान-&c. असणें.

COUNTERCHARM, *n.* उलटमंत्र *m.* प्रतिकारकमंत्र *m.* प्रतिप्रयोग *m.*

COUNTER-EVIDENCE, *n.* उलटसाक्ष *f.* प्रतिकारक साक्ष्य *n.*

To COUNTERFEIT, *v. a. copy fraudulently,* v. To FORGE. कपटानें नकल *f.*-सोंग *n* -मिष *pop.* मीस *n.*-वेष *m.*-&c. धरणें-घेणें *g. of o.* कपटानुकरण*n.*-कपटानुकार*m.*-कपटानुकृति*f.* करणें *g.of o.*
2 See To IMITATE.

COUNTERFEIT, *a.* v. FALSE. नकली, बनाऊ, बनावलेला, खोटा, खोटसाळ, सोंगाचा, कपटाचा, कपटी, कृत्रिम, छद्माचा, मिथ्या.

COUNTERFEIT, *n. thing made in fraudulent imitation.* मिष *pop.* मीस *n.* सोंग *n.* छल *m. n.*
2 See DECEIVER, HYPOCRITE.

To COUNTERMAND, *v. a.* उलटहुकूम-परत हुकूम*m.*-&c. देणें-करणें, फिरवणें, परतवणें, रद्द करणें.

COUNTERMAND, *n.* उलट हुकूम*m.* परत हुकूम*m.* मनाईचा हुकूम*m.* प्रतिविधि*m.*

COUNTERMARCH, *n.march back.* उलटकूच*n.m.* फेरकूच*n.m.* परतकूच*n. m.* प्रत्यागमन*n.*

COUNTER-MURE, *n. outer wall.* पडभिंत *f.* पडकोट*m.*

COUNTER-PANE, *n.* (of a bed). पलंगपोश*m.*

COUNTER-PART, *n.* उतारा*m.* उलटा*m.* प्रतियोगी*m.* जोडा*m.* जोडीचा, प्रतिरूप*n.*

To COUNTER-POISE. See To COUNTER-BALANCE.

COUNTER-SCARP, *n.* रेवणी *f.*

To COUNTER-SIGN, *v. a.* मखलासी *f.* करणें, रुजू *f.* घालणें-करणें.

COUNTER-SIGNATURE. मखलासी *f.* रुजू *f.*

To COUNTER-VAIL. See To COUNTER-BALANCE.

COUNTER-WEIGHT, *n. weight to counter-balance a vessel.* अमंड*or* अभांड *or* आमंड*n.* धडा*m.*

To COUNTER-WORK, *v. a.*v. To COUNTERACT. प्रतिकार*m.*-प्रतिक्रिया *f.* करणें.

COUNTING, *n.* v. V. A. 1.– *act..* गणणें*n.* &c. गणन*n.* परिगणन*n.* संख्यान*n.* गणती *f.* गणना *f.* परिगणना *f.* मोजदाद *f.* मोजदास्त *f.* मोजप*n.*

COUNTING-HOUSE. *n.* व्यापाऱ्याच्या कारभाराचें घर *n.*

COUNTLESS, *a.* असंख्य, अगणनीय, अगण्य, असंख्यात, अगणित, बेसुमार, कोट्यवधि.

COUNTRIFIED. See RUSTIC, RURAL.

COUNTRY, *n. region, land, territory.* देश*m.* मुलूक *or* मुलूख*m.* प्रांत*m.* राष्ट्र*n.* चक्र*n.* भूमि *f.*
At, in, to, &c. every c. देशोदेश.
Centre or heart of a c. मध्यदेश*m.*
Customs and manners of a c. देशचाल *f.* देशाचार*m.* देशरीति *f.* देशसंप्रदाय*m.*
Foreign c. परदेश*m.* विदेश*m.* देशांतर*n.* परमुलूख*m.*परभूमि *f.*
Inhabited or peopled c. बसात *or* वसाहत *f.* जनपद*m.*
Native c. स्वदेश *m.* स्वभूमि *f.* जन्मभूमि *f.* उत्पत्तिस्थान *n. m.* बिलायत *f.*
Of a far c. दुरादूरचा, दूरदेशचा.
Residing in a foreign c. परदेशी, प्रवासी, दूरवासी, परमुलखी.
The low c. हेटप्रांत*m.*
Inhabitant of low c. हेटकरी.
To return to one's native c. देशीं जाणें.
2 *rural parts.* खेडें पाडें*n.* बाहेर गांव*m.* नगराबाहेरचा प्रदेश*m.* शहराबेगळा देश*m.*
3 *villages and hamlets,*—as distinguished from towns. गांवखेडीं*n. pl.* गांवगांवढें*n.* आडगळ*f.* खेडेंपाडें*n.*

COUNTRY, *a.* v. RUSTIC. खेडे गांवचा, खेड्या पाड्याचा, खेड्या पाड्यांतला, खेडे गांवांतील, बाहेर गांवचा, ग्राम्य. [वगिरी.
2 *produced in the c.* गांवरानी, मुलकी, गांवठी, गांवढ, गां-

COUNTRYMAN, *n. one of the same c.* देशभाऊ*m.* देशबंधु*m.* एकदेशी, एकदेशीय, एकदेशिक, समानदेशिक, सदेश, स्वदेशीय, सदेशीय, सांस्थानिक.
2 *rustic, peasant, swain,hind.* खेडे गांवचा माणूस, शेतखाऊ्या, शेतकाऱ्या, गांवढळ, गंवार, गुरेराख्या, नांगऱ्या, नांगरहाक्या, जोत्या, क्षेत्राजीव, क्षेत्री.—as used contemptuously, and as corresponding with *Clown, clodhopper, boor, lout.* आडगळचा, आडमुठ्या, कांबळ्या, घोंगड्या, रान्या, रानकरी, रानमाणूस, रानट, जंगलट, जंगली जट, वणजारदांड.

COUNTY, *n.* प्रांत*m.* देशविभाग*m.*
The common words expressing certain *Divisions of a country,* and thus, somewhat answering to *County, Shire, Circuit, District, Province, Hundred, &c.* are चकला, पेटा, जिल्हा, टप्पा *or* तप्पा, तरफ, तालुका, परगणा, प्रांत, महाल, सुभा.

COUNTY-TOWN, *n.* कसबा *m.* somewhat answers.

COUP DE MAIN, *n.* छापा *n.* छप्पा *m. v.* घाल.

COUP DE SOLEIL, *n.* उन्हाचा चटका *m.* झळ *f.* झळई *f.* लपेट *f.* उन्हाची झाक *f.* तिरमी *f.*

COUPLE, *n. brace, two, pair.* जोडी *f.* जुंवळी *or* जुळी *f.* जुळें *n.* द्वंद्व *n.* द्वय *n.* (in comp. as पुस्तकद्वय, हस्तद्वय, फलद्वय *n.*) युग *n.* युगुल *n.* युग्म *n.* यमल *n.*
2 *male & female.* जोडा *m.* जोडपें *n.* जोडें *n.* द्वंद्व *n.* मिथुन *n.*
A married c. स्त्रीपुरुषें *n.* दंपती *n. m.* दंपत्य *n.* मेहूण *n.*
A newly married c. ओवर *or* ओहर *n.* ओवरें *n. pl. or* वहूवर*n.*—Entertainment given to them, ओवर जेवण *n.* —Their first visit to the family god (*going to church*). ओवर जत्रा *f.*
3 *frame of transverse rafters, &c.* कैंची *f.* कातर *f.* चवा *m.* घिगी *f.* मोरवा *or* मोरावा*m.*

To COUPLE, *v. a. join two together.* जोडी *f.* करणें-बांधणें-घालणें, जूळ *f.* घालणें, जोडणें.
2 See To MARRY.

To COUPLE, *v. n.* See To COPULATE.

COUPLET, *n.* दोहरा *m.* बैत *f.*

COURAGE, COURAGEOUSNESS, *n.* v. BOLDNESS. हिम्मत *f.* हिय्या *f.* छाती *f.* दिलदारी *f.* मर्दाई *f.* मर्दुमकी *f.* मर्दी *f.* अवसान *n.* आव *m.*
To lose c. धीर *m.*-अवसान *n.*-&c. टाकणें-सोडणें, धीर *m.* फुटणें, दम *m.* सुटणें-हात पाय *m. pl.* गळणें-पाय *m. pl.* मोडणें-मटें *n. pl.* बसणें *g. of s.* कान *m. pl.* पाडणें, कमर *f.* बसणें-मोडणें-खचणें *g. of s.* टिरी *or* टिऱ्या *f. pl.* कांपणें *g. of s.*
To take c. To pluck up c. दम *m.*-अवसान *n.*-धैर्य *n.*-&c. धरणें, धैर्यावलंबन *n.* करणें.

COURAGEOUS, *a.* v. BOLD. शूर, हिम्मतदार, हिम्मती, हिम्मताचा, हिय्येदार, छातीदार, छातीचा.

Courageously, *adv.* v. A. *and* Boldly. धैर्य-अवसान-&c. धरून, छातीनें, छातीकरून.

Courier, *n.* v. Messenger. जासूद, कासीद, हलकारा *or* हरकारा, कागदी. [धांवणी *f.*

Course, *n. career, race, run.* दवड *f.* धांव *f.* धांवण *f.* धांवणें *n.*
2 (as of a river, road, &c.). सरणि *or* सरणी *f.* मार्ग *m.* गति *f.* ओघ *m.* प्रवाह*m.*
3 *race-ground.* शरयतीची *or* शर्तीची जागा *f.* पैजेची जागा *f.* घोडदवडीची जागा *f.*
4 *progress, proceeding, process.* गति*f.* चाल*f.* गमन *n.* चार *m.* प्रवृत्ति *f.* प्रवाह *m.*
Course of time. कालगति *f.* [ति *f.*
Hobbling and halting c. (of a work, &c.). अगतिकग-
5 *method of life, train of actions, procedure.* ओळ *f.* ओळा *m.* वळण *n.* मोळा *m.* नित्यनियम *m.* निष्ठा *f.* चालचलणूक*f.* वृत्ति*f* वृत्त *n.* प्रवृत्ति *f.* रहा *f.* रहणी *f.* रहाटी *f.* रीति *f.* आचार *m.* आचरण *n.* रवेस *f.* रीतरवेस *f.* तंत्र*n.* दीक्षा *f.* प्रस्थान*n.*
Devious or evil c. गैरमार्ग, गैररहा, असन्मार्ग. [णें.
To turn to an evil c. पगडी *f.* फिरवणें *or* फेरपगडी *f.* कर-
To enter on a right c. रहणीस लागणें, (*and* To set upon &c.—लावणें,) मार्गास लागणें, वाटेवर येणें.
6 *train, tenor, line or order of proceeding.* ओळ *f.* ओळा*m.* वळण *n.* बळवटा *m.* रीति *pop.* रीत *f.* मार्ग *m.* वाट *f.* धारा *m.* धारापेंडोळा *m.* धारेंपेंडोळें *n.* परिपाठ *m.* पाठ *m.* ओघ *m.* संप्रदाय *m.* ओढण *n. f.* सरणि *or* सरणी *f.* मोड *f.* प्रवाह *m.* बळी *f.* रहाटी *f.* दंडक *m.* सड *f.* पद्धति *f.* चक *m.* पर्याय *m.* आनुपूर्वी *f.* आनुपूर्व्य *n.*
C. through ages without beginning. अनादिपरंपरा *f.*
C. of events or Nature. गति *f.*
Of c. As a matter of c. *as a natural consequence.* सहज, साहजिक, सहजगतीनें, सहजगत्या, सहजरीतीनें, सहजरीत्या, अर्थात, अर्थतः, कैमुतिकन्यायेंकरून.
Of c. *as a matter of rule.* नियमानें *or* नेमानें, नेमी.
Of due c. संप्रदाय शुद्ध, रीतीचा, रुईचा.
Of c. *to be sure, certainly.* अलबत, खचीत.
That is of c. *of natural consequence.* सहजाचा, सहजगतीचा, सहजरीतीचा, साहजिक.
That is of c. *of rule.* नियमाचा *or* नेमाचा.
To chalk or mark out a c. for. रेघ *or* रेषा *f.* ओढून देणें *or* काढून देणें.
To come in the c. of (conversation, &c.). ओळीस येणें.
To fall into or along with the c. (or custom) of. रुईस येणें.
To take another c. रान *n.* बदलणें-सोडणें.
7 *regular succession,* v. Order. अनुक्रम *m.* क्रम *m.* परिपाटी *f.* पर्याय *m.*
8 (as of ceremonies or works). अनुष्ठान *n.*
Conductor of a c. अनुष्ठानी, अनुष्ठाता.
9 courses, v. Menses. पुष्प *n.* रज *n.*

To **Course**, *v. a. chase,* v. To Hunt. पारध *f.*-शिकार *f.*-मृगया *f.* -अनुधावन *n.*-&c. करणें *g. of o.*

To **Course**, *v. n. run, &c.* जलद धावणें, त्वरितगतीनें चालणें.

Courser, *n.* शिकारीचा-&c. घोडा *m.*

Court, *n.* (of a king, &c.), *palace.* राजवाडा*m.* सरकारवाडा *m.* राजमंदिर *n.* राजगृह *n.* राजालय *m.*
2 *retinue, &c. of a king, body of courtiers.* राजमंडल *n.* राजपुरुष *m. pl.* राजसभा *f.* राजभृत्य *m. pl.* दरबारीमनुष्य *m. pl.*
3 *royal audience, levee, &c.* राजदरबार*m.* दरबार*m.* राजकचेरी *f.* कचेरी *f.* दिवाणदरबार *m.* राजसभा *f.* राजमजलस *f.* मजलस *or* मजालस *f.*
Familiar with courts and levees. दरबारमहशूर, दरबारप्रसिद्ध, सरकारमहशूर.
Friend at c. मुरब्बी *m.*
Full c. भरदरबार *m.* भरमजलस *or* मजालस *f.* भरकचेरी *f.*
Holding a c. or levee. दरबार *m.*
In, at, to, before the c. हुजूर.
In open c. हाजीरमजालस.
4 (of justice). अदालत *f.* न्यायसभा *f.* सरकार*n.* दिवाणखाना *m.* राजद्वार *n.* धर्मशाला *f.* धर्मसभा *f.* धर्माधिकरण *n.* कोर्त *or* कोडट*n.* is now used.
Civil c. दिवाणी अदालत *f.*
Criminal c. फौजदारी अदालत *f.*
Highest c. *the Sadar Adálut.* सदर *f.* सदरअदालत *f.*
5 (of public business), *hall, &c.* कचेरी *f.* सरकारवाडा *m.* राजद्वार *n.* [*f.* सभा *f.*
6 *meeting for the administration of public business.* कचेरी
7 *body of judges.* न्यायाधीश *m. pl.* न्यायसभा *f.* न्यायाधीशसमूह *m.*
8 v. Yard. अंगन *or* अंगण *n.* खळ *or* खळें *n.* [जांगण *n.*
C. before the mansions of the Great. माणीकचौक*m.* रा-
Square or oblong c. चौक *m.* चौदिवाली *f.*
9 See Flattery.

To **Court**, *v. a. seek in marriage, woo.* मागणी *f.* करणें-घालणें, विवाहहेतुकस्नेह *m.* करणें *g. of o.* लमासाठीं भजनीं लागणें *g. of o.* विवाहार्थचित्ताराधन *n.* करणें.
2 *woo by praising, fawning upon, &c.* v. To Flatter. आर्जवणें, आराधणें, भजनीं *or* भजनास लागणें, जी *or* जीजीहांजी *interj.* करणें-म्हणणें.

Court-day, *n.* कोर्त भरण्याचा दिवस *m.*

Court-dress, *n.* दरबारीपोषाक*m.*

Court-house, *n.* कोर्ताची जागा *f.*

Court-martial, *n.* लशकरीअदालत *f.* सैनिकन्यायसभा *f.* कोर्त्तमार्शल *n.* is in common use from the English.

Court-yard, *n.* अंगण *or* आंगण *n.*

Courted, *p.* v. V. 2. आराधलेला, &c. आराधित, उपार्जित.

Courteous, *a. polite,*—persons, v. Civil. बोलूनचालून चांगला, सभ्य, शिष्ट, आदरसत्कारी, अनुनयी, सानुनय.
2—manners, &c. माणुसकीचा, गृहस्थगिरीचा, सभ्यपणाचा.

Courteously, *adv.* v. A. माणुसकीनें, गृहस्थपणानें, &c. सौजन्यपूर्वक.

Courteousness, **Courtesy**, *n.* v. A. माणुसकी *f.* गृहस्थगिरी *f.* गृहस्थपणा *m.* भलमाणसाई *f.* सभ्यता *f.* सभ्यपणा *m.* शिष्टता *f.* तवाजू *f.* सुजनता *f.* सुजनत्व *n.* अनुनय *m.*
By c. मानास्तव, मानासाठीं, मानावरून.
Courtesies and civilities,—compreh. आदरउपचार *m. pl.* आदरसत्कार *m. pl.* आदरमान *m. pl.*

COURTER, *n.* v. V. 1. लग्नासाठीं भजनीं-नादीं-&c. लागणारा, विवाहार्थस्नेही.
2 आर्जव करणारा, &c. आर्जवी *or* बृ, मनधरणीचा, जी *or* जी-जी-ह्रांजी-करणारा-म्हणणारा, आराधक, उपार्जक. [श्या *f.*
COURTESAN, *n.* v. HARLOT. कळवंतीण *f.* कसबीण *f.* कंचनी *f.* वे-
COURTESY, *n.* स्त्रीचें नमन *n.*-वंदन *n.*
To COURTESY, *v. n.* नमन *n.*-वंदन *n.* करणें.
COURTIER, *n.* दरबारीमनुष्य *m.* राजपुरुष *m.* राजभृत्य *m.*
Courtiers—collectively, राजमंडल *n.* मंडलदेवता *f. pl.*
2 See FLATTERER.
COURTING, *n.* v. V. 2.—*act.* आर्जवणें *n.* आराधणें *n.* &c. आर्जव *m.* मनधरणी *f.* आराधना *f.* उपार्जना *f.*
COURTLINESS, *n.* v. A. सभ्यता *f.* प्रौढी *f.* सुजनता *f.*
COURTLY, *a. belonging, suitable, &c. to a court.* दरबारी, दरबाराचा, दरबारी डौलाचा, श्रीमंती, सभ्य, शिष्ट, प्रौढ.
COURTSHIP, *n. act of wooing in love.* लग्नासाठीं स्त्रीचें आर्जव करणें *n.* विवाहार्थस्त्र्युपासना *f.*
COUSIN, *n.*—gener. भावंड *n.* भाऊ *m.* बहीण *f.* बंधु *m.* बंधुजन *m.* बंधुजनी *f.* सहजमित्र *m. f.*—paternal uncle's child (male or female), चुलतभावंड *n.* —pat. uncle's son, चुलतभाऊ, चुलतबंधु.—pat. uncle's daughter. चुलतबहीण. —pat. aunt's child, आतेभावंड *n.*—pat. aunt's son, आतेभाऊ, आतेबंधु.—pat. aunt's daughter. आतेबहीण.—maternal uncle's child, मामेभावंड *n.*—maternal uncle's son, मामेभाऊ, मामेबंधु.—maternal uncle's daughter, मामेबहीण.—mat. aunt's child, माऊसभावंड *n.*—mat. aunt's son. माऊसभाऊ, माऊसबंधु.—mat. aunt's daughter, माऊसबहीण.
CO-UTERINE, *a.* एकोदर, समानोदर.
COVE, *n.* v. CREEK. खाडी *f.* [ज्ञा *f.*
COVENANT, *n.* v. AGREEMENT. करार *m.* समय *m.* संकेत *m.* प्रति-
2 *paper of agreement.* करारनामा *m.*
To COVENANT, *v. n.* v. To AGREE. करार *m.*-ठराव *m.*-&c.करणें.
COVENANT-KEEPING, *a.* करारी, सत्यप्रतिज्ञ, सत्यवचन, सत्यसंकल्प.
To COVER, *v. a. overspread and hide.* आच्छादणें, आवरणें, प्रच्छादणें, व्यापणें, झांकणें, आच्छादन, *n.*-आवरण *n.*-व्यापन *n.*-&c. करणें *g. of o.*
2 *conceal,* v. To HIDE. झांकणें, ढांकणें, ढांपणें, दाबा देणें-धरणें, पांघरूण *n.*-प्रावरण *n.*-झांकण *n.*-आच्छादन *n.*-&c. घालणें.
3 *close with a lid or top.* झांकणें, झांपणें, ढांकणें, ढांपणें, झांकण *n.*-&c. घालणें.
4 *be joined with the female in sexual congress.* लागणें, उडणें.
To be covered—female beast. फळणें.
5 (expenses, &c.) खर्च भागाया पुरता असणें.
COVER, *n.*—gener. *covering thing or cause.* आच्छादन *n.* आवरण *n.* पिधान *n.*
Under the c. of. आड.
From under the c. of. आडून. [मुळें.
Under the c. of night. रात्रीचा पडदा पडल्यानें-पडल्या-
That is under the c. of. आडचा, आडील.
2 *concealing cause; screen, blind.* आडपडदा *m.* पडदा *m.* अंतर्धान *n.* तिरोधान *n.* [लपण *f.*
3 *sheltering cause; shelter.* आश्रय *m.* आसरा *m.* दडण *f.*
4 (as of a pillow, couch, cushion, &c.) गलेफ *m.* गवसणी *f.* अभ्रा *m.* तह *m.* थैला *m.* पिशवी *f.* मलवस्त्र *n.* मुखवस्त्र *n.*
5 (as over a carriage, palanquin, &c.). बुरका *or* बुरखा *m.* भुरकी *f.* अभ्रा *m.* गवसणी *f.* मलवस्त्र *n.* गर्दपोस *m.* सरपोस *m.*
6 *lid, top.* झांकण *n.* झांपण *n.* ढांकण *n.* ढांपण *n.* ढांपा *m.* झांकणी *f.* झांकणें *n.* सरपोस *m.* टोपण *n.* झडपा *m.* पिधान *n.*
7 *under brush, &c.* झाडी *f.*
8 (at a meal) ठाव *m.* पान *n.*
9 *pretext,* v. PRETENCE. मिष *pop.* मीस *n.* व्याज *n.*
10 (of a letter) *envelope.* लखोटा *m.*
COVERED, *p.* v. V. 1. आच्छादलेला, &c. आच्छादित, आच्छन्न, प्रच्छादित, प्रच्छन्न, आस्तीर्ण, आस्तृत, प्रावृत, आकीर्ण (in comp. as मेघाकीर्ण, नक्षत्राकीर्ण, वृक्षाकीर्ण, सैन्याकीर्ण, जलाकीर्ण, पुष्पाकीर्ण).
2 झांकलेला, &c. छन्न, अंतर्हित, तिरोहित, आच्छादित.
COVERER, *n.* COVERING, *p. a.* v. V. 1. आच्छादणारा, &c. आच्छादक, प्रच्छादक, आच्छादन-&c. कर्त्ता-कारी-&c.
2 झांकणारा, &c. झांक्या, ढांक्या, ढांप्या, आच्छादक, अंतर्धायक.
COVERING, *n.* v. V. 1.—*act.* आच्छादणें *n.* आवरणें *n.* &c. आच्छादन *n.* आवरण *n.* प्रच्छादन *n.*
2—*act.* झांकणें *n.* दाबा देणें *n.* &c. ढांपणी *f.*
I. *thing covering; thing concealing,* See COVER. II. *clothing,* v. CLOTHES. पांघरूण *n.* प्रावरण *n.* वेष्टन *n.*
COVERLET, *n.* पलंगपोश *m.*
COVERT, *a. sheltered, not exposed.* सावटीचा, सावटी, आश्रयाचा *pop.* आरुयाचा, साश्रय, वसव्याचा.
2 *hidden,* v. SECRET. चोरटा, गुप्त.
3 *disguised, sarcastic, &c.* उपरोधाचा, उपरोधी, उपरोधीक, औपरोधिक.
C. speech. व्याजोक्ति *f.* [र्तृवश.
4—a married woman. नवऱ्याचे स्वाधीन-&c. भर्तृधीन, भ-
COVERT, *n. shelter, hiding place.* लपण *f.* दडण *f.* सावट *f.* आश्रय *m. pop.* आस्रा *m.* आडोसा *m.*
Under c. आडमोहरीं.
COVERTLY. See SECRETLY. [शता *f.*
COVERTURE, *n. state of a married woman.* भर्तृधीनता *f.* भर्तृव-
To COVET, *v. n. be affected with strong desire.* लोभणें, लुब्धणें, लोभ *m.*-हांव *f.*-&c. सुटणें *in.con.* लुब्ध-लोभयुक्त-लोभिष्ट-&c.होणें.
To COVET, *v. a. desire earnestly,* v. To DESIRE. लोभ *m.*-लालूच *f.*-लालची *f.* धरणें *g.of o.* अभिलाषणें, अभिलाष *m.* करणें *g. of o.* लाहो *m.* घेणें *g. of o.*
COVETING, *n.* v. V. A.—*act.* लोभ धरणें *n.* अभिलाषणें *n.* &c. लाहो *m.* v. घे, लोभ *m.* अभिलाष *m.*
COVETOUS, *a. cupidinous, avaricious, greedy.* लोभी, लालची, हावरा, लालुचखोर, अहोपी, लोभिष्ट, लोभान्वित, लोभयुक्त, सोसी, सोसघेवडा, लाभाळू, हव्यासी, बराडी, अभिलाषी, स्पृहयालु, सतृष्ण, लुब्ध, लोलुप, रजोगुणी, राजस—in high degree. लोभाधीन, लोभग्रस्त, लोभमय, लोभात्मक, लोभाविष्ट, लोभाक्रांत, लोभाकुल, लोभातुर, सर्वार्थी. Some terms for *a covetous person* are आशाभूत *or* आशाळभूत, आपलपोट्या *or* आपलपोटाऱ्या, पुढलेंपान ओढणारा, आत्मंभरि. [लुब्ध.
2 (of wealth or riches). धनलोभी, धनार्थी, द्रव्यलोभी, धन-
COVETOUSLY, *adv.* v. A. लोभानें, लोभेंकरून, लोभबुद्ध्या, लोभदृष्ट्या, लोभभावानें, लोभपूर्वक, लोभपुरस्सर.

COVETOUSNESS, *n.* v.A. 1. लोभ*m.* लालूच *f.* हांव *f.* सोस*m.* हेवा*m.* अभिलाष*m.* हांवरेपणा*m.* लाहो*m.* लिप्सा *f.* लालसा *f.*

Free from c. लोभावेगळा *or* निराळा, लोभहीन-&c. निर्लोभ.

2 धनलोभ*m.* धनतृष्णा *f.* धनाशा *f.* अर्थकाम*m.*

COVEY, *n.* v. FLOCK. पल्ला*m.* झांक*f.* झुंड *f.*

COW, *n.* गाय *f.* धेनु *f.* गौ *f.* गो *f.* (in comp. as गोमुख, गोदान, गोपाल), कपिला *f.*—in contempt. गायरट*n.* गायरूं*n.*—in endearment. गायरूं*n.* गावली*f.* मावली (*or* गाउली & माउली), गोजरूं *n.*

C. conceiving whilst suckling. तानगाभी *f.*

C. produce, (milk, butter, &c.). गोरस*m.* गव्य*n.*

C. that bears annually. बर्षवीण *f.*

C. that reconceives in six months. समस्की *or* सामासकी *f.* सामाशी *f.*

C.-track. गुरदंड *m.* गोंड *f. n.* गोष्पद *n.* गोपद *n.* गोक्षुर *n.*

C. wholly of one color. कपिला *f.*(as black c. काळीकपिला, red c. तांबडी कपिला, &c.).

Frame work to confine a c. during milking. आडी *or* आडी *f.*

Hair from the tail of a c. गोवाल *m.* गंगावन *n.*

Milch c. दुपती *or* दुभतीगाय *f.*दुभतीधेनु *f.* पयस्विनी *f.*

Reach of a c.'s lowing. गौकोश *m.* [*v.* घाल.

Tie of legs of a c. during milking. भाला *m.or* बाहला *m.*

Twitching and quivering of a c.'s. hide. गोस्फुरण *n.*

Wild c. बनगाय *f.* बनगौ *f.*

To COW, *v. a.* v. To INTIMIDATE. दबावणें, दबकाविणें, धमकावणें, भेडसावणें, भेडावणें, हिम्मत *f.*-&c. मोडणें *g. of o.* धैर्यभंग *m.*-धैर्यनाश *m.*-उत्साहभंग *m.*-&c. करणें *g. of o.*

COW-DUNG, *n.* शेण *n.* गोमय *n.*

Basket for c. शेणपाटी *f.* शेणसूप *n.*

Basket for dry (or jungle) c. तिरडें *n.*

Cake of c. गोवरी *f.* थापटी *f.* थापा *m.* बळशिणी *or* बळशेणी *f.* बळशिणीगोरी *f.* वडी *f.* शुभा *f.*

Cake of c. as dabbed upon the roof or wall. गायगोळा*m.* थापा *m.*

C. as found in the fields. रानशेण *n.* रानगोंवरी *f.* राणशिणी *f.*

C.-wash,—to be used in smearing floors, &c. शेणवणी *n.* शेणप *n.* शेणपाणी *n.* शेणखळा *m.* सारवण*n.* शेणकाला *m.*

Crumbly or crumbled c. गोवर *m.* शेणकूट *n.* शेणपुडी *f.* किटण *n.*

Kindled heap of bits of c. झगरें *n.* फूलझगरें *n.* फोरप *n.*

Lump or dab of c. शेणगोळा *m.*

Lump of c.—as voided at one time. शेणपोहो *or* पोव *m.* शेणपा *m.* शेण्या *m.* पोहो *m.* [पेंडा*m.*

Lump of moist c. in which fire is preserved under ashes.

Pelting with c.-clots. शेणमार *m.* शेणपूजा *f.*

Piece of c. (cake, lump, or bit). शेण *n.* शेणखंड *n.* शेणखुड *n.* शेणकूट *n.* [*f.*

Pile of cakes of c. arranged for kindling. थाळ *f.* थाळण

Pile of pieces of c. plastered over. कलोड *or* कलवड *m.*

Pit for the daily c. शेणकी *f.* शेणकई *or* काई *f.* शेणखळी *f.* शेणखाई *f.* शेणगाईर *f.*

The business of cow-dung smearing. शेणगोटा *m.* शेणगोंकूर *n.* शेणपोतेरें *n.* शेणसडा *m.* सडासारवण *n.* सडासंमार्जन *n.*

To sprinkle with c.-wash. शेणसडा *or* सडा *m.* घालणें-देणें.

To smear with c.-wash. सारवणें, सारवण *n.* घालणें.

To sprinkle and smear with c.-wash. सडा सारवण *n.*-सडासंमार्जन *n.* करणें.

COW-HAGE, COW-ITCH, *n.* कवचकुइरी *or* ली *f.* कवसकुइरी *or* ली *f.* कुइरी *or* ली *f.* कपिकच्छु *f.* आत्मगुप्ता *f.*

The pod of c. कुहरें *n.*

COW-HERD, COW-KEEPER, *n.* गुराखी *or* गुराख्या, गवळी, गोवळा, गायक्या, गोवरी, गोपाल, गोरक्षक, जांगली, अहीर, अभीर, भीर.

Female c. गवळीण *f.* गोवारीण *f.* गुराखीण *f.* अहिरण *or* अहिरणी *f.*&c. गोपिका *f.* गोपी *f.*

Quarter or station of cow-herds. गवळवाडा*m.* गवळहाट *m.* घोष *m.* व्रज *m.*

COW-HIDE, *n.* गायीचें कातडें *n.*

2 *leather whip.* कोरडा *m.*

COW-HOUSE, COW-SHED, *n.* गोंवळ *m.* गोंवळगोठा *m.* खुडी *f.* बेडें *n.* गोशाला *f.*

Litter of c. गोंदरड *f.* गोवरी *f.*

COW-LEECH, *n.* गायीचा पारखी, गायपारखी, गोवैद्य.

COW-PEN, *n.* गोठा *m.* गोष्ठ *n. m.*

COW-POX, *n.* गोस्तन शीतला *f.*

Note. The Maráthás do not distinguish between the cow-pox and the small pox, but use the word देवी for both.

COWS-LIP, *n.* एक फूल आहे.

COWARD, COWARDLY, *a. timid, wanting in courage.* भितरा, भिकूट, भिकुड, भ्याड, नामर्द, कातर, निर्वीर्य, अधीर, अवीर, न्यूनधैर्य, पळपटा *or* ट्या, हीनधैर्य, हीनशौर्य, हीनपराक्रम *or* शौर्यहीन, धैर्यहीन, &c.रणभीरु.Some phrases, proverbs, sayings, and various formations conveying the sense of *a cowardly person*, and answering to *Dastard, Poltroon, Nidget, Craven, Pusillanimous wretch, Faint-heart, Lack-pluck, White-liver, Cream-face, Pigeon-heart, Chicken, Woman,* are रांड *f.* रांडमाणूस *c.* लंडी *c.* फटलंडी *c.* झुंझारराव *m.* धारराव *m.* मागूबाई *f.* पादरा, हगरा, तरस गांड्या, हुरडफुंक्या, मारल्याचे मागें आणि पळल्याचे पुढें असणारा, कचलपट *m.*

2—actions, &c. भितरेपणाचा, नामर्दीचा, &c.भीतिसूचक-दर्शक.

COWARDICE, COWARDLINESS, *n.* v. V. भितरेपणा *m.* &c. नामर्दी *f.* कातर्य *n.* अधीरता *f.* हीनशौर्य *n.* हीनधैर्य *n.* अविक्रम *m.* अपराक्रम *m.* रणभीति *f.* रणभीरुता *f.*

COWARDLY, *adv.*v.A. भित्र्यासारखा-बाणी-परी-&c. भितरेपणानें.

COWED, *p.* v. V. दबावलेला, दबकावलेला, &c.

To be c. दबकणें, दबणें.

To COWER, *v. n. sink in at the knees, &c. give way.* दबणें, दबकणें, मेटें *n. pl.* बसणें-मोडणें *g. of s.* डगणें.

COWL-STAFF, *n.* नवघण *f. n.*

COWRIE, *n. particular shell.* कवडा *m. dim.* कवडी *f.* वराटक *m.* वराटिका *f.* कपर्दक *m.* काकिणी *f.*

Some kinds are. पोपटी, भवानीकवडी, वाघीकवडी, दहीकवडी, सगुणीकवडी.

COXCOMB, *n.* v. FOP. अकडबाज, नखरेबाज, कुर्रेबाज.

2—the flower tree & flower. मोरशिखा *m.* [कुर्रा*m.*

COXCOMBRY, *n.* v. FOPPISHNESS. अकडबाजी *f.* नखरेबाजी *f.*

COXCOMICAL, *a.* v. FOPPISH. अकडबाजीचा, नखरेबाजीचा.

To COY, *v. n. affect reserve, &c.* मुरकणें, तोंड *n.* मुरकणें, मुरकें *m. pl.* मारणें, ओढामाणक्या *f. pl.* धरणें-लावणें-करणें.

COY, *a.*—a female. मुरकेखोर, मुरके मारणारी, तोंड मुरडी, सलज्ज, लज्जाशील.

COYLY, *adv.* v. A. तोंडमुरकोन, मुरके मारून.

COYNESS, *n.* v. A. मुरका *m.* नखरा *m.* लाज *f.* सलज्जता *f.*

To COZEN, &c. See To DECEIVE, &c.

CRAB, *n.* सेंकडा *m. or* डें *n.* खेंकड *n.* किरबें *n.* बेलकडें *n.* कुरलें *n.* कुरली *f.* चिमोरी *f.* चामठा *m.* मुट्या *m.* कर्क *m.* कर्कट *m.* कर्कटक *m.* तिर्यक् *m.*

Claw of a c. अंकडा *m.*

2—the sign cancer. कर्क *m.*

3 एक रानफळ आहे.

CRABBED, *a. morose, &c.* v. CROSS. खट्याळ, हिरवा, हिरवट, तुटक, खाष्टी *or* खास्ती, तिरसट, तिडका, करडी मरजीचा, दाष्ट.

2 *perplexing, hard,* v. DIFFICULT. खडतर, खचरट, खष्ट, किचर, किचरट.

CRABBEDLY, *adv.* v. A. 1. खाष्टीपणानें, तिरसटपणानें, &c.

CRABBEDNESS, *n.* v. A. 1. खाष्टीपणा *m.* दाष्टपणा *m.* &c. करडी मरजी *f.*

2 खचरटपणा *m.* &c.

CRACK, *n. chink, fissure, cranny, cleft, crevice.* फट *f.* संधि *m. f. pop.* सांध *f.* सांधा *m.* भेग *f.* भेर *f.* खांड *f.* भडोळ *or* भडवळ *f.* भळ *f.* चिरण *f.* रेम *f.* तडा *m.* बिंच *f.* चीर *f.* चील *f.* चीण *f.* सापट *f.* छेद *m.* फाटफूट *f.*

Cracks and crannies,—compreh. *nooks, crevices, and corners.* सांधीकोंदी *f. pl.*

2 (as of some vessel or thing). चीर *f.* फूट *f.* दोरा *m.* दोरवा *m.* तडक *f.* तडा *m.* तीड *f.* छेद *m.* फाटफूट *f.*

3 *sudden and sharp sound.* तडक *f.* तडका *m.* तडाखा *m.* कडाखा *m.* तडतडाट *m.*

With a c. चड-कन-कर-&c. चडचड, तट *or* तट्कन-कर-&c. तटतट & टां—intens. तटातट, तटाटां.

4 *sounding stroke.* फटकारा *m.* चटकारा *m.* चटकणी *f.* चडक *f.* चडकण *f.* चडकणी *f.* तटकारा *m.*

With a c. ताड *or* थाड-कन-कर-&c.

5 See LIE.

To CRACK, *v. n. break into cracks or chinks.* भेगलणें, तडकणें, उलणें, तडतडणें, *intens.* तडाडणें, भेतलणें, फाटणें, तडक *f.* जाणें *in. con.*

2 *open, split, part.* उलणें, फुटणें, तडकणें, तडणें, तडावणें, पिचणें.

To c. from intense dryness. कडकणें.

3 *burst with a sound.* तटतटणें *or* तडतडणें *intens.* तटाटणें *or* तडाडणें, तुडतुडणें, तटतट-तटकन-&c. फुटणें. [खराणें.

4 *make a loud sound.* कडकणें, *intens.* कडाडणें, खडाडणें *or*

5 *emit a cracked sound,*—a rupee, &c. नादावणें.

6—the voice. (गळा) फुटणें, चिरकणें, चिरचिरणें.

To CRACK, *v. a.* v. To BREAK, To SPLIT. फोडणें, मोडणें.

2 (a whip, &c.) *make to sound loudly.* कडकावणें, वाजवणें, तडतडवणें, कडकडवणें. [ला.

CRACK-BRAINED, *a. crazy,* v. MAD. बेडगळ, वेडसर, वायकळले-

CRACKED, *p.* v. V. N. 1. भेगलेला, तडकलेला, &c.

2 फुटका, फुटकर, फुटीर, फुटक, पिचका, पिंजका, *remiss.* पिंजट *or* पिंजकट.

5—esp. of coins. बालफूट *or* बालफुटका, फुटका, कची, फाटफूट.

C. and rubbed, &c. कचीढेली.

6 फुटका.

I. *crazy,* v. MAD. वेडसर, विक्षिप्त.

CRACKER, *n.* (of gun-powder). फटाकडा *or* फटाका *m.* (*dim.* फटाकडी *or* फटकडी *f.*)

Cluster of crackers closed up. पेटी *f.*

C. that makes seven reports. सातबारी फटाका *m.*

C. made of paper only. फटाका *m.* कोरडा फटाका *m.*

2 *cracking whirligig.* किंकरें *n.* किरकिरें *n.*

CRACKINGLY, *adv. with noise of cracking.* कडाडां *or* खडाडां, कडाकड *or* खडाखड, कडडड.

2 *briskly, swimmingly, &c.* तडक *or* तडका, धडक *or* धडका, धडकून, कडक, कडकावून, तडाक्यानें.

To CRACKLE, *v. n.*—substances in the flame. चटचटणें, चरचरणें, फुरफुरणें, तडतडणें *or* तुडतुडणें *or* तिडतिडणें.—intens. चरारणें, फुरारणें.

2—as stiff paper, cloth, &c. फडफडणें, खडखडणें, कडकणें.

3 *burn rapidly and cracklingly.* भरभरणें *or* भुरभुरणें *intens.* भरारणें, कडकणें. [डणें.

4—substances under eating, &c. कुडकुडणें, कडकणें, कडक-

CRACKLER, *n.* CRACKLING, *p. a.* v. V. 1. तडतडीत, तुडतुडीत, तिडतिडा.

2 कडकडीत, कडबडीत, करकरीत, तडतडीत, सणसणीत.

3 कडकडीत, कडबडीत.

4 कुडकुडीत, कडकडीत, करकरीत, कुरकुरीत, तुडतुडीत,

CRACKLING, *n.* v. V. 1.—the sound emitted. फुरफुराट *m.* तडतडाट *m.* स्फूत्कार *m.*

2 फडफडाट *m.* खडखडाट *m.* खडाड *m.*

3 कडकडाट *m.* खडखडाट *m.*

CRACKLINGLY, *adv.* v. V. 1. चटचट *or* टां, चरचर *or* रां, *intens.* चटाचट, चटाटां, चराचर, चरारां.

2 फडफड *or* डां, *intens.* फडाफड &c. फडाडां, खडखड *or* डां

3 भुरभुर *or* रां, भुरुभुरु.

4 कुडकुड *or* डां.

CRADLE, *n.* पाळणा *m.* पालक *or* पालख *n.* टारलें *n.*

C. suspended from a stand. घोडपाळणा *or* घोडेपाळणा *m.*

Cord, bar, &c. supporting a c. बारती *f.* बरात *f.*

From one's c. पाळण्यापासून, पाळण्यांतल्यापासून, बाळपणापासून.

Leg of a c. भोई *f.*

Rope to swing a c. झेंपसा *m.* झिपुटा *m.*

2—as for a broken bone, &c. भाळी *f.*

3 *frame, bed, &c.* घोडी *f.*

To CRADLE, *v. a.* पाळण्यांत-&c. निजविणें.

CRAFT, *n. manual art,* v. ART. कला *or* कळा *f.* शिल्प *n.* हुनर *m. f.* कसब *n.*

2 *artifice, guile,* v. CUNNING. कावा *m.* कावा दावा *m.* काबित्र *n.* कपट *n.*

3 *ship, &c.* See VESSEL.

CRAFTILY. See ARTFULLY.

CRAFTINESS, *n.* v. A. *and* CUNNING. कावा *m.* कपट *n.* कावित्र *n.* शाठ्य *n.*

CRAFTSMAN, *n.* v. ARTIFICER. कारिगर *or* कारागीर. *m.* शिल्पी*m.*

CRAFTY, *a.* v. CUNNING. कावेबाज, कावेदार, कपटी, धूर्त्त, शठ, मतलबी.

CRAG, *n. protuberance of a rock, &c.* खडपा *m.* खरपट *n.* खरपड *n.* सुळका *m.* शृंग *n.*

A perpendicular c. उभाखडपा *m.*

2 *fore end of the back bone.* मोन्हांटा *m.*

The c. or neck piece of mutton. यिव *or* यीव *f.*

The c. and the rump. यिवकुकडी *f.*

CRAGGED, CRAGGY, *a.* खडप्यांचा, सुळक्यांचा, उंचसखल.

To CRAM, *v. a. over fill,* v. To STUFF. चिकार *adv.* भरणें, ठासून-ठेचून-तकटून-दपटून-दडपून-चेपून-&c. भरणें.

2 *force in, drive in,* v. To STUFF. चिणणें, खचणें, ठासणें, चोंदणें, चोंदडणें, चोंदाटणें, ठेंचणें, ठोंबरणें, ढसणें, तकटणें, चिळणें, ठासणी *f.*-&c. करणें.

To CRAM, *v. n. eat gluttonously,* v. To GLUTTONIZE. दपटून-तकटून-उपटून-रपाटून-रगडून-कचकावून-&c. जेवणें-खाणें.

CRAMMING, *n.*—in study. ताजी तयारी करणें *n.* कल्हईची तयारी करणें *n.*

CRAMP, *n. spasm.* वळ *m. f.* वरवंट *m.* वरवंटा *m.* अकडवांब *f.* पेटका *m.* पेटकी *f.* पेडगा *m.* मेंडका *m.* मेंडकी *f.* वात *m. v.* ये. वायु *m. v.* होणें, कराळी *f. or* कराळ्या *f. pl. v.* चढ.

C. from cold. काकड *n. v.* भर.

C. in the neck, back, or loins. कण *f. v.* भर. [m.

2 *fig.* v. RESTRAINT. अवरोधक-प्रतिबंधक- &c. गोष्ट *f.*- विषय

3 *or* cramp-iron. पट्टी *f.* आंकड्यांची कांब *f.*

To CRAMP, *v. a. affect with c.* आखडवणें, अंकडा *m.*-खोडा *m.*-खोडामोडा *m.*-&c. करणें *g. of o.* धरणें. [धक होणें.

2 *fig.* v. To RESTRICT. अवरोध *m.*-प्रतिबंध*m.*-&c. करणें, बा-

CRAMPED, *p. & a.* v. V. 1.—*affected with cramp.* आखडवलेला, ओढलेला, धरलेला.

C. state (of the limbs, &c.). खोडा *m.* खोडामोडा *m.* खोडाविडी *f.* अंकडा *m.* हातापायांची गठडी *f.*

To be c. खोडावणें. [संकीर्ण.

I.—of language, &c. *stiff, constrained.* अप्रशस्त, असरल,

CRANBERRY, *n.* एक फळ आहे.

CRANE, *n.* करकोचा *m.* करकोची *f.* सारस *m.*(सारसी *f.*) पिंगळा*m.* क्रौंच *m.* (क्रौंचा *f.*).

Descent of a flock of cranes. करकोच धाड *f.*

Screaming of a c.कचकच *f*—*intens.* कचकचाट*m.*कचाच*m.*

2 *machine for raising weights.* यारी *f.* गाडी *f.*

CRANIOLOGY, *n.* कपालसामुद्रिक *n.* कपालविद्या *f.* कपालशास्त्र *n.*

CRANIUM, *n.* v. SKULL. करोटी *f.* करटी *f.* कपाल *n.*

CRANK, CRANKY, *a.*—a boat, &c. उलंडा,कलथा, कलंडा.

CRANNIED, *a. full of chinks.* बहूतफटींचा, बहूतसापटींचा, बहुरंध्र, बहुछिद्र.

CRANNY, *n.* v. CRACK. चिरण *f.* चीर *f.* सापट *f.* फट *f.* सांध *f.*

CRAPE, *n.* एक कापड आहे, वाल *n.*

To CRAPE. See To CURL.

CRAPULENCE. See CROP-SICKNESS.

CRAPULENT, CRAPULOUS. See DRUNKEN, CROP-SICK.

To CRASH, *v. n.* v. N. कडाडणें *or* खडाडणें *or* खरारणें, घडाडणें,

2—esp. as a tree, branch, &c. breaking. धसकणें.

CRASH,*n. loud mingled sound of things falling.* धडाका*m.* कडाखा *m.* कडाड *or* खडाड *or* खराड *m.* कडकडाट *or* खडखडाट *or* खरखराट*m.* घडाड *m.* घडघडाट *m.* धडाड *m.* कडाकडी *f.*

With a c. v. CRASHINGLY. खाड-कन-कर- &c. [धडाखा*m.*

2 (as of many musical instruments).कडाका*m.* कडाखा*m.*

CRASHINGLY, *adv.* कडडड, फडाकड, कडाडां, खडाखड, खडाडां, खरारां, घडाडां, धडाडां.

CRASSAMENTUM, *n.* सार *n.* सारांश *m.* घनांश *m.* [*f.*

CRATCH, *n. frame in which hay is put.* गव्हाण *or* णी *f.* गाताडी

CRATE, *n. texture of sticks, &c.* सांकाटा *m.* सांपडा *m.* सांकाटी *f.* साट *m.* ताटी *f.*

2 See BASKET.

CRATER, *n.* ज्वलत्पर्वताचें-ज्वालामुखीचें तोंड *n.* ज्वालामुखीमुख *n.*

To CRAUNCH, *v.a. crush with the teeth.* कडकड *or* डां *or* कडकडून-कडाकड-कडाडां-कराकर *or* रां-*adv.* चावणें-खाणें.

CRAVAT, *n. neckcloth, &c.* गळेबंद *m.* कंठवस्त्र *n.* गलबंधन *n.*

To CRAVE, *v. a. supplicate,* v. To BEG. प्रार्थणें, विनवणें, मिन्नतवार-मिन्नतीनें-पायधरणी करून-&c. मागणें, मिन्नत *f.* करणें.

2 *long for, hanker,* v. To DESIRE. खवखवणें, खवखव *f.* सुटणें *in. con. with g. of o.* आशावणें, आशा *f.* लागणें *in. con. g. of o.*

3 *be ravenously hungry,* v. To HUNGER. खाखावणें, धादावणें, वखवखणें, चणचणणें, चणाणणें, खाखा *f.* सुटणें.

CRAVEN. See COWARD.

CRAVING, CRAVINGNESS, *n.* v. V. 2. 3. खवखव *f.* वखवख *f.*

CRAW. See CROP. [चिमोरें*n.*

CRAW-FISH,*n.* v. CRAB. नदींतला खेकडा*m.* चिमोरा*m.* चिमोरी *f.*

To CRAWL, *v. n. creep.* रांगणें, रेंगणें, सरपटणें, सरपटत चालणें-जाणें, सरपट्यां *or* भुईसरपट्यां *adv.* चालणें-जाणें, रेंगत चालणें-जाणें, भुईस लागून चालणें-जाणें, खुरडणें, उरानें चालणें-जाणें, उरोगमन*n.* करणें.

2—a child. घोडा *or* घोडुला*m.* करणें, रांगणें &c.

3 fig. *move slowly, feebly, heavily, &c.* रडतरडत-रडतखडत-झरतमरत-झुरूमुरू-फेंदत-लंघत लंघत-अटकत अटकत-&c. जाणें-चालणें-फिरणें-करणें, फेंदीखालीं जाणें, रखडणें.

4 *move secretly and slily.* लपून-दडून-छपून-चोरून-चोरगस्तीनें-मुंगीच्या पायानें-&c. चालणें-जाणें-येणें-&c.

CRAWLER, *n.* CRAWLING, *p. a.* v. V. 1. रांगणारा, सरपटणारा, सरपटत चालणारा, &c. उरोगामी.

CRAWLING, *n.* v. V. 1.—*act.* रेंगणें*n.* रांगणें*n.* सरपटत चालणें*n.* उरानें चालणें*n.* रिंगण*n.* उरोगमन*n.*

CRAWLINGLY, *adv.* v. V. 1. रेंगत रेंगत, सरपटत, &c. &c. भुईसरपटत *or* टां, सरपट्यां.

3 See the adverbs under the Verb.

CRAY-FISH. See CRAW-FISH.

To CRAZE, *v. a. impair the energy of.*v. To WEAKEN.जर्जर-जर्जरीत-&c. करणें.

2 *impair the intellect.* वेड*n.* भरविणें, वेडगळ-&c. करणें.

CRAZED, CRAZY, *a. crack-brained, distraught,*v. MAD. वेडगळ, वेडसर, वेडका, वेडपा, बायचळलेला *or* बायकळलेला *or* बावकळलेला, बावसा, मंत्रचळ्या, विक्षिप्त, पिसाटीक, फांटाफुटलेला.

To turn or become c. चळणें, बायचळणें, बायकळणें *or* बावकळणें, बावचळणें, फांटा*m.* फुटणें-भरणें *in. con.* खुळावणें, विकळणें.—esp. from demoniac influence, passion, &c. पिसळणें, पिसटणें, पिसाटणें.

2 v. WEAK. लुळाखुडा, जर्जर, जर्जरीत, जीर्ण.

CRAZEDNESS, CRAZINESS, *n.* v. A.1. वेडगळपणा*m.* &c. चळ*m.*-बायचळ*m.* बावचळ*m.* खूळ*n.* विक्षेप*m.*

2 जर्जरपणा*m.* &c. जीर्णता *f.*

To CREAK, *v. n. make a sharp noise, &c.* करकरणें, किरकिरणें, खिरखिरणें, घिरघिरणें, करकरशब्द*m.* करणें, करकर वाजणें.

CREAKER, *n.* CREAKING, *p.a.* v. V. करकरणारा, करकर वाजणारा, करकरा *or* करकऱ्या. [कराट*m.*

CREAKING, *n.* v. V.—*act.* करकरणें*n.* &c. करकर *f. intens.* कर-

CREAM, *n.*—of milk.साई *or* साय *f.*सहा *f.*मलई *or* मळई *f.* सार*n.*

Thin and poor c. सायटें*n.* सायटी *f.*

2 fig. *pith, marrow, &c.* v. ESSENCE. सार*n. m.* सारांश*m.* तत्व*n.* तत्वार्थ*m.* सत्व*n.* तत्तामाल*m.* गर्भ*m.*

To CREAM, *v. a.* साई *f.*-मळई *f.*-&c. काढणें.

CREAM-FACED, *a.* फिक्का, निस्तेज, फिक्क्यातोंडाचा.

CREAMY, *a.* साईचा, साईसारखा.

CREASE, *n. mark made by doubling.* मोड *f.* दूण *f.* दुमड *f.*सळ*m.*

To CREASE, *v. a.* v. N. मोड *f.*-सळ*m.*-&c. पाडणें.

CREASED, *p.* v. V. मोड पाडलेला, &c.

To CREATE, *v. a. bring into being, make, &c.* निर्माण-उत्पन्न-पैदा-&c. करणें, निर्मिणें, उत्पादणें, उद्भावणें, सृजणें, उत्पादन*n.*-सर्जन*n.*-निर्मिति *f.*&c. करणें *g. of o.* करणें.

2 *produce, occassion,* v. To CAUSE. उत्पन्न-&c. करणें, उत्पत्ति *f.*-उद्भव*m.*-&c. करणें *g. of o.* आणणें.

3 *make, by investing with a new character.* करणें.

CREATED, *p.* v. V. 1. केलेला, &c. उत्पन्न, निर्माण, निर्मित, उत्पादित, पैदा, सृष्ट, जन्य.

CREATION, *p.* v. V.1.—*act.* उत्पन्न करणें*n.* &c. उत्पादन*n.*उत्पत्ति *f.* निर्मिति *f.* सर्जन.—*state.* सृष्टि *f.* उत्पत्ति *f.* उद्भव*m.*

I. v. UNIVERSE. सृष्टि *f.* भूतसृष्टि *f.* प्रत्यक्षसृष्टि *f.* सर्ग*m.*

CREATOR, *n.* CREATIVE, *a.* v. V. 1. करणारा, उत्पन्न करणारा, उत्पन्न-निर्माण-&c. कर्त्ता, जनिता, जनक, उत्पादक.

C. of the world. जगत्कर्त्ता, जगत्स्रष्टा, स्रष्टा, जगदुत्पादक.

CREATT, *n. gentiana cherayta.* किराईत *or* चिराईत*n.* Some varieties are किराईत फुलकी, कांटे किराईत, गांठी किराईत *or* चिराईत.

CREATURE, *n. thing created,*—gener. भूत*n.* घट*n.* ईश्वरीयंत्र*n.* सृष्ट वस्तु*n.*-अर्थ*m.*-पदार्थ*m.* [राचर *n.*

The creatures—compreh. *or* collect. चेतनाचेतन *n.* च-

Crawling or creeping c.—gener. किडूक (*dim.* किडकलें) *n.* कीडमुंगी *f.*

Dumb c. *brute, &c.* मुकें जनावर *n.* मोनजात *f.*

Living c. जीव *m.* प्राणी *m.* जंतु *m.* जिताजीव *m.* ईश्वराचा प्राणी *m.* जन्मी *m.* [*m. pl.*

Living creatures—compreh. जीवजंतु *m. pl.* जीवजिवडे

Small living c.—gener. जीवजंतु*m.*जिवडा*m.*जीवजिवडा*m.*

2 *dependent.* See FOLLOWER. 3 See MAN, PERSON.

CREDENCE, *n.* v. BELIEF. विश्वास *m.* मान्यता *f.*

Letter of c. विश्वासपत्र *n.*

CREDENDA, *n. articles of faith.* विश्वासविषय *m. pl.* श्रद्धाविषय *m. pl.* श्रद्धेयमाला *f.*

CREDENTIAL, *n. warrant for claiming belief.* विश्वास्यपत्र *n.* विश्वासाधार पत्रक *n.* सनद *f.* कागद *m.* हूकूमनामा *m.* मुखत्यारनामा *m.*

CREDIBILITY, CREDIBLENESS, *n.* v. A. विश्वासयोग्यता *f.* विश्वासार्हता *f* विश्वासौचित्य *n.* विश्वासनीयता *f.* विश्वास्यता *f.* श्रद्धेयता *f.* प्रामाण्य *n.* सत्यता *f.*

CREDIBLE, *a. worthy of credit or belief.* खरा मानाया जोगा-&c. विश्वासयोग्य, विश्वासार्ह, विश्वासोचित, विश्वास्य, विश्वसनीय, श्रद्धेय.

CREDIBLY, *adv.* v. A. सुप्रमाणावरून, विश्वासयोग्य प्रमाणावरून, विश्वासठेवण्याजोगा *decl.*

CREDIT, *n. credence, faith yielded,* v. BELIEF. मान्यता *f.* विश्वास *m.* श्रद्धा *f.*

2 *honor, lustre, eclat. &c,* v. GLORY. यश *n.* नाबरूप *n.* प्रतिष्ठा *f.* तेज *n.* भूषण *n.*

3 *character, name,* v. REPUTATION. नांव *n.* आब्रू *f.* आब *m.* आबदाब *m.* हुरमत *f.* इजत *f.* नाबरूप *n.* भरम *m.* साबका *m.* साख *f.* साखी *f.* वकर *n. f.* नामोश *m.*

With c. and honor. आबादाबानें.

To destroy one's c. नाद *m.* दवडणें-घालवणें.

To preserve one's c. पागोटें *n. or* पागोट्याचे पेच *m. pl.* संभाळणें.

4 *mercantile c.* पत *f* साख *f.* साखी *f.* गव *f.* आब *m.*— freely *or* compreh. *c. and character.* पतपासोडी *f.* पतपात *f.* पतपातेरा *m.* आबदाब *m.*

Bad or low c. नापत *f.*

That is of bad or low c. नापत.

Testimony of c. खातरी *f.* निशा *f.*

That has c. साखबाज.

To grow in c. पतीस चढणें.

To lose one's c. पतीवर पाणी *n.* पडणें *g. of s.* पत *f.* बुडणें *g. of s.* नाद *m.* जाणें *g. of s.*

5 *estimation, consideration, influence,* v. WEIGHT. आब *or* आबदाब *m.* मानमान्यता *f.* भारदस्ती *f.*

6—*as opposed to* debt *or* debit. येणें *n.* जमा *f.*

7—as given or taken. *tick, trust.* उचापत *f.* उधार *m.*

On c. उधार.

Letter of c. भलावण *f.* [घेणें.

To CREDIT, *v. a.* v. To BELIEVE. मानणें, खरा-सत्य &c. मानणें,

2 *opposed to* debit. जमेस *or* जमा धरणें, जमेकडे मांडणें.

CREDITABLE, *a. bearing or bringing credit,* v. HONORABLE. आब्रूचा, प्रतिष्ठेचा, यशस्कर, इजतदेणा, यशःप्रद.

2 *worthy of credit or trust,* v. REPUTABLE. शहाजोग, साख, हुरमतदार, हुरमतीचा, हुरमती, आब्रूदार, आब्रूचा, संभावित, माननीय, भला.

CREDITABLY, *adv.* v. A. 1. आब्रूनें, आब्रू-नांव-लौकिक-&c. राखून-संभाळून-&c. आबादाबानें.

CREDITED, *p.* v. V. 1. खरामानलेला, &c. विश्वस्त, प्रत्ययित.

2 जमेकडे मांडलेला.

CREDITOR, *n. person to whom a debt is owed.* ऋणकरी, ऋणाईत, घेणेकरी, घेणेदार, कर्जदार, उत्तमर्ण, उत्तमर्णी.—in bonds and notes or in free phraseol. धनको & धनकोनाम (from धन Money, &c. and *as opposed to* Debtor रिणको &रिणको नाम from ऋण Debt).

C. of. सावकार.

CREDULITY, CREDULOUSNESS, *n.* v. A. भोळेपणा *m.* श्रद्धा *f.* श्रद्धालुता *f.* अल्पप्रमाणकत्व *n.* कानपिसें *n.*

CREDULOUS, *a. that believes readily or without grounds.* कानाचा हलका, हलक्या कानाचा, कानपिसा, भावीक, भोळा, भावीकभोळा, भजनी, विश्वासी, श्रद्धालु, अल्पकर्णी, अल्पप्रमाणक, शीघ्रप्रमाणक, शीघ्रविश्वासी, यथाश्रुतग्राही.

CREDULOUSLY, *adv.* v. A. भोळेपणानें, कानाच्या हलकेपणानें, अतिश्रद्धापूर्वक.

CREED, *n. summary of articles of faith.* विश्वासनीयविषय सूत्रसंग्रह *m.* विश्वासनीयविषयमालिका *f.*

2 v. RELIGION. मार्ग *m.* मत *n.*

CREEK, *n. cove, inlet, small bay.* खाडी *f.* बांकण *n.* बांक *m.*

Branch off from a c. पोहडी *f.* कोळ *n.*

CREEL, *n.* v. BASKET. कुरकुली *f.* कुरकुलें *n.*

To CREEP. See To CRAWL.

CREEPER, *n. creeping or climbing plant.* लता *f.* वल्ली *pop.* बेल *f.* ताणा *m.*

Stick planted to aid c. ढांक *n.* ठोंबा *m.* ओथंबा *m.*

2 *creeping creature, reptile.* किडूक *n.* किडें *n.* किडूं *n.*

C. creatures,—gener. कीडमुंगी *f.*

CREEP-HOLE, *n. subterfuge, excuse.* खिडकी *f.* छिद्र *n.* जागा *f.* खिड *f.* फट *f.* सवड *f.*

To keep a c. निसर गांठ *f.* देऊन ठेवणें.

CREMATION, *n. burning of a corpse.* प्रेत जाळणें *n.* प्रेतदहन *n.*

To CREPITATE, *v. n.* See To CRACKLE. 2 *break wind.* पादणें, पाद *m.* सोडणें, पर्दन *n.* करणें.

CREPITATION, *n.* See CRACKLING.—v. V. 2.—*act.* पादणें *n.* पाद *m.* पर्दन *n.*

Soft c. फुसकी *f.* फुसकुली *f.*

CREPUSCLE, *n. glimmerings of dawn,* v. DAWN. चांचपड चांचपड *n.* चिपडचिपड *n.* उस्तें *n.*

CREPUSCULOUS, CREPUSCULAR, *a.* चिपड चिपडाचा, चांचपड चांचपडाचा, झुंजुक मुंजुकाचा.

CRESCENT, *n.* वाढता चांद *m.* वृद्धिचंद्र *m.* कलावृद्धिक चंद्र *m.* अर्धचंद्र *m.* अर्धचंद्राकृति *f.*

CRESCENT, CRESCIVE, *a.* वाढता, वाढणारा, वर्द्धमान, वर्द्धिष्णु.

CRESS, *n. lepidium sativum.* अहाळींब *or* आहळींव *or* हाळींव *n.*

CRESSET, *n. beacon light.* आकाशदिवा *m.* आकाशदीप *m.*

CREST, *n.* (of a cock). शेंडी *f.* शिखा *f.* कुक्कुट चूडा *f.*

2 *plume, tuft.* तुरा *m.*कलगी *f.*शिखा *f.*शिखर *n.*शेखर *m.*चूडा *f.* मुकुट *pop.* मुगूट *m.* किरीट *m. n.* अवतंस *m.*

Jewel worn in a c. चूडामणि *m.* शिखामणि *m.* शिरोमणि *m.* शिखरमणि *m.*

3 (of a mountain, &c.). माथा *m.* शिखर *n.* टेंबा *m.*

4 *lofty mien,* v. PRIDE. दिमाख *m. f.* मान *f.* अभिमान *m.* नाक *n.* छान *f.*

To let fall or lower one's c. मान *f.* खालीं घालणें, कान *m. pl.* पाडणें.

To lower the c. of. See To HUMBLE.

5 (of a wave) (लाटेचा) माथा *m.*

CREST-FALLEN. See HUMBLED.

CRESTED, *a.* v. N. 2. तुरेवाला &c. चूडावान्, चूडाधर, शिखाधर, शिखरी, शिखी, शृंगी.

CRETACEOUS, CRETOSE, *a. chalky.* कठिनीमय, कठिनीप्रचुर.

CREVICE, *n. chink, cranny,* v. CRACK. फट *f.* भेग *f.* चीर *f.* सांध *f.*

CREW, *n. company, body,* v. BAND. मंडळी *f.* जमात *f.* तांडा *m.* समाज *m.*

2–in a bad sense; *pack, gang, &c.*v. BAND. चौक *m.* मुठाण *n.*

3 (of a ship). एकागलबताबरील नाबाडी लोकांची मंडळी *f.* नाबाडीलोक *m. pl.* नाविकगण *m.*

CRIB, *n. manger for corn. &c.* v. TROUGH. कोटंबा *m.*

2 *stall.* ठाण *n.* मेढें *n.* गोथवड *f.*

3 *cot, cabin,* v. HUT. खोपट *n. dim.* खोपटी *f.*

4 *small bedstead.* पलंगडी *f.*

To CRIB, *v. a. pilfer,* v. To STEAL. भुटे चोरी *f.* करणें.

2 *confine in a lock up house, &c.* कोंड बाडयांत-कोंडींत-&c. ठेवणें-घालणें, कोंडून ठेवणें.

CRIBBLE. To CRIBBLE. See SIEVE. To SIFT.

CRICK, *n.* (in the neck or back). अंबटळा *or* अंबटाळा *m.* ताठा *m.* अवघडा *m.* कण *f.* *v.* भर.

To have a c.—the neck. तिरपणें, तिरपावणें, अंबटळणें *or* अंबटाळणें, ताठणें, अवघडणें, अवटरणें.

CRICKET, *n.* राळ *f.* रात *f.* रातकिडा *m.* झिल्ली *f.* भिंगरूट *f.*

The mole c. घोंगेरा *m.* घुरघुरा *m.* [झिल्लीरव *m.*

Chirping of crickets. चिनीचिनी *or* चिणचीण *n.* किरं *n.*

2 चेंडूफळीचा खेळ *m.* [रुदित.

CRIER, *n.* CRYING, *p. a.* v. V. N. 3. रडणारा, &c. रोदनकर्त्ता, v. V. A. 1. *proclaimer.* दवंडी पिटणारा, &c. डांगोऱ्या, दवंडी पिट्या, थाळीपिट्या, &c. थाळ्या, धांडोऱ्या.

CRIM. CON. v. ADULTERY. *unlawful intercourse with a married woman.* अयोनिसंग *m.* [त *n.*

CRIME, *n. transgression,* v. SIN. पाप *n.* पातक *n.* दुरित *n.* दुष्कृ-

2 *a c.an offence, trespass, fault, misdeed, misdemeanour,&c.* अपराध *m.* अन्याय *m.* अन्याव *m.* अकर्म *n.* कुकर्म *n.* दुष्कर्म *n.* बदकर्म *n.* कुक्रिया *f.* पातक *n.* पाप *n.* गुन्हा *m.* तकसीर *f.* दुष्कृत *n.* दुष्कृति *f.*

Capital c. मरणदंडक अपराध *m.* वधोपयुक्त अपराध *m.*

C. of high degree. महापातक *n.* महापाप *n.* These are ब्रह्महत्या *f.*सुरापान *n.* सुवर्णस्तेय *n.* गुरुतल्पगमन *n.* तत्संसर्ग *m.*—That has committed any one of them. महापातकी, महापापी.

CRIMINAL, *a.* v. N. 1. 2. *guilty, faulty.* अन्यायी, अपराधी, कुकर्मी, अकर्मी, पातकी, गुन्हेगार, सापराध, दोषी, सदोष, दोषयुक्त, दोषवान्, कृतापराध, कृतान्याय.

I. *contrary to right,* v. WRONG. अन्यायाचा, अनीतीचा, अधर्माचा, सदोष, अन्याय्य, प्रत्यवायी, पापदायक, पापप्रद.

II.—*as opposed to* civil. फौजदारी, फौजदारीचा.

CRIMINAL, *n.* See the ADJECTIVE.

CRIMINALITY, *n.* v. A. अन्यायीपणा *m.* अपराधीपणा *m.* गुन्हेगारी *f.* दोष *m.* अपराधिता *f.* अनयित्व *n.* &c. कृतापराधता *f.* &c.

I. अन्याय *m.* दोष *m.* वाईटपणा *m.* पाप *n.* अधर्म *m.* प्रत्यवाय *m.* नीतिविपर्यास *m.* नीतिव्यत्यय *m.*

To CRIMINATE, *v. a. involve in a charge of crime.* दोष *m.* आ-

णणें *with* वर *of o.* दोषारोप *m.* करणें, अन्यायांत-&c. सांपडवणें-गांठवणें- गोवणें-&c. माळकेंत आणणें.

CRIMINATION, *n.* v.V. अन्यायांत सांपडवणें *n.* &c. दोषारोप *m.* दोषारोपण *n.*

CRIMP. See CRISP. To CRIMP. See To CRIMPLE.

To CRIMPLE, *v. a.* (puffs, frills, &c.). कातणें, मुरुडणें *or* मुरडणें, चुणी *f.*-चूण *f.*-निरी *f.* घालणें.

2 See To CURL.

CRIMPLED, *p.* v. V. 1. कातलेला, मुरुडलेला, &c. मुरडींव.

CRIMPLER, *n. crimpling instrument.* कातणें *n.* (and the cuttings made by it. कातण *n.*). चिरणी *f.* चिरणें *n.*

2 *instrument of tailors to crimple cloth.* चुणकस *f.*

CRIMPLING, *n.* v. V. 1.—*act.* कातणें*n.* मुरुडणें*n.* चूणघालणें*n.* &c.

CRIMSON, *n.* किरमिजी रंग *m.* गुलाली रंग *m.* गुलबासी रंग *m.* अब्बाशाई *or* अब्बाशी रंग *m.*

CRIMSON, *a.* किरमिजी रंगाचा, गुलाली, गुलाली रंगाचा, गुलबासी रंगाचा, अब्बाशी रंगाचा. [रंगविणें.

To CRIMSON, *v. a* किरमिजी रंग *m.*-&c. देणें, किरमिजी रंगानें &c.

To CRIMSON, *v. n.* किरमिजी रंग *m.*-&c. येणें.

To CRINGE, *v. n. bow and scrape, make court, crouch,* v. To FAWN. लवण भंजन *n.*-नमोनमो *adv.* करणें, पुढच्या पुढें नाचणें, थुंकी *f.*-थुंका *m.* झेलणें, थुंकीला ओणवणें, नाक *n.* घासणें, जीजी *f.* करणें, हांजी *f.* करणें-म्हणणें.

CRINGE, CRINGING, *n.* v. V. लवण भंजन *n.* &c. आर्जव *m.*

CRINGER, *n.* CRINGING, *p. a.* v. V. *and* OBSEQUIOUS. लवण भंजन करणारा, थुंकी झेलणारा, &c. आर्जवी, आर्जवू.

To CRINKLE. See To WIND.

To CRIPPLE, *v. a.* लंगडा-पांगळा-पांगा-लुला-&c. करणें.

2 *fig. make helpless.* पंगू-बळहीन-&c. करणें.

CRIPPLE, *a.* CRIPPLED, *p. a.* v. V. 1. लंगडा, पांगळा, पांगा, पांगूळ, पंगु, *pop.* पंगू, हातापायांनीं अधू, लुला, खंज, व्यंग, अपांग.

2 पंगू, बळहीन केलेला-झालेला.

CRIPPLE, *n.* लंगडशाई *or* लंगडशादी *c.* लंगडदीन *c.* See also the words under the adjective.

To be or become a c. पांगुळणें.

CRISIS, *n.*—of a disease. परिणाम सुचविणारा रोगाचा भेद*m.* परिणामदर्शक *or* सूचकभेद *m.*-रूपभेद *m.*-अवस्थांतर *n.*-स्थित्यंतर*n.*-भावांतर *n.*

2 *critical time or juncture,* gener. बन्यावाइटाचा-हारजिताचा-सोक्षमोक्षाचा-&c. समय *m.*-वेळ *f.*-संधि *f. m.*-&c. टिपण *n.* गव *f.* बाणी *f.* आणी *f.* आणीबाणीची वेळ *f.* ढांसण *n.* प्रसंग*m.*

CRISP, *a.*—an article of food, &c. कडंग, कडक, कुडकुडीत *or* कुरकुरीत, कडकडीत, चुरचुरीत, तुडतुडीत, खरपूस.

2 See CURLED.

To CRISP, *v. a.* (as by frying, roasting, &c.). खरंगणें, कडंग-खरपूस-कुडकूड *adv.* भाजणें.

2 See To CURL.

CRISPNESS, *n.* v. A. कडंगाई *f.* कडंगपणा *m.* कुडकुडी *f.* कडकडीतपणा *m.* &c.

CRITERION, *n. mark, standard.* लक्षण *n.* चिन्ह *n.* गुणागुणलक्षण *n.* गुणागुणनिर्णायकचिन्ह *n.* गुणागुणमान *n.*

CRITIC, *n.* रसज्ञ, रसिक, परीक्षक, जाणता, गुणदोषवेत्ता, शोधक, दोषादोषविवेचक, गुणागुणज्ञ.

CRITICAL, *a. belonging &c. to criticism.* दोषादोषविवेचनाचा, दोषादोषविवेचन संबंधी-विषयक.

2 *judicious, discerning,* रसज्ञ, रसिक, परीक्षक, गुणागुणविवेचक, गुणदोषवेत्ता, गुणागुणोद्बोधक, सूक्ष्मद्रष्टा. [न्वेषी.

3 *inclined to find fault.* दोषदृष्टि, दोषदर्शी, छिद्रदर्शी, छिद्रा-

4—in medicine. रोगाच्यापरिणामसूचकभेदाविषयींचा, परिणामदर्शकभेदसंबंधी-विषयक, परिणामज्ञानावसराचा.

C. discharge. रोगवणी *n.*

5 *relating to a crisis.* बऱ्यावाइटाच्या समयाचा, हारजिताचे वेळेचा, आणीबाणीचे वेळेचा.

To CRITICISE, *v. a. notice beauties and faults.* गुणदोष *m. pl.* काढणें, दोषादोषविवेचन *n.*-गुणदोषोद्घाटन *n.*-&c. करणें.

2 *animadvert on as faulty.* दोष *m.* ठेवणें, दोष *m.* काढणें *g. of o.* दूषणें, व्याख्या *f.*-टीका *f.*-&c. करणें *g. of o.*

CRITICISING, CRITICISM, *n.* v. V. 1.—*act.* गुणदोष काढणें *n.* &c. गुणागुणविवेचन *n.* गुणदोषोद्घाटन *n.* गुणदोषप्रकाशन *n.* शुद्धाशुद्धविचार *m.* गुणदोषव्याख्या *f.*

2—*act.* दोष ठेवणें *n.* दूषणें *n.* &c. व्याख्या *f.* टीका *f.*

CRITIQUE, *n.* गुणदोषचंद्रिका *f.* दोषादोषप्रकाशिका *f.*

To CROAK, *v. n.*—the frog. डरकणें *or* डुरकणें, डुरडुरणें, डरांव डरांव *m.*-&c. करणें.

2—the raven or crow. करकरणें, करांव करांव *adv.* करणें.

3 fig. *prognosticate evil.* बाचा *f.* फोडणें, अभद्रवाचा *f.* फोडणें, नास्ति *f.* भाकणें, अभद्र बोलणें-भाकणें.

CROAK, CROAKING, *n.* v. V. 1.—*act.* डरकणें *n.* &c. डरावणी *f.* डुरडूर *f.* डरांव डरांव *adv.* टरॉवटरॉव *adv.* टुरुटुरू *f.* टरंटरं *n.* ट्रोत्रट्रोत्र *n.*

2—*act.* करकरणें *n.* करकर *f.* करांवकरांव *m.*

3 वाचाफोडणें *n.* अभद्रबोलणें *n.*-&c. अशुभसूचन *n.*

CROAKER, *n.* CROAKING, *p.a.*v.V. 3. अभद्र बोलणारा, &c. अभद्रभाक्या, अभद्रभाषी. Terms or phrases for a *person ever croaking* (i. e. *foreboding ill*) and answering to *Croaker, Screech-owl, Raven, Damper,* are नास्ति भाक्या, अवसान घातकी, काळजिभ्या, हीरमोड्या, मोड्या.

CROCEOUS, *a. of or like saffron.* कुंकुमाचा, केशराचा, केशरमय, केशरी, केशरीरंगाचा.

CROCK, *n. earthen vessel.* मातीचें भांडें *n.* मृन्मयपात्र *n.*

2 *soot on pots, kettles &c.* मस *m. f.* मशी *or* मषी *f.* खरप *f.* खरपी *f.* जळ *f.*

CROCKERY, *n. earthen ware.* गाडगीं मडकीं *n. pl.* मातीचीं भांडीं *n. pl.* कुंभारी सामान *n.* कुंभारी भांडीं *n. pl.* मृन्मयपात्रें *n.pl.*

CROCODILE, सुसर *f.* मगर *m.* नक्र *m.*

C.'s tears. वरवर रडणें *n.* आणलेलेंरडें *n.* कोरडेंरडें *n.*

CROCUS. See SAFFRON.

CRŒSUS, *n.* v. RICH. कुबेर *m.* जगत्शेट *m.* नवकोटिनारायण *m.*

CROFT, *n. close.* वाडी *f. dim.* वाडगें *n.* वाडकुलें *n.*

CRONE, *n. old woman.* थेरडी म्हातारी *f.* डोकरी *or* डोकरीण *f.*

CRONY, *n.* v. INTIMATE. सलगी, जिवींचा मित्र, खेळमेळ्या, गडा, नाकचा बाल *m.*

CRONYSHIP, *n.* गडी *f.* गडीपणा*m.* गट्टी *f.* रहस्य*n.* स्नेहवाद*m.* रहश्श*n.* अकरावा*m.* अकरावें*n.*

CROOK, *n. curved end.* आंकडा*m* मेढा*m.* फेल*n.*

2 *curved stick, &c.* आंकडी *f.* अंकुश*m.* डांग *f.*

By hook or by c. करेंहीकरून, जसेंतसेंकरून, जसातसा, जेमतेमकरून.

C. used to pull down pods, flowers, &c. शेकाटी *f.*

3 (of a shepherd.) मेंढक्याचा बाकदार दांडा*m.*

4 *curvature.* See BEND.

To CROOK. See To BEND.

CROOK-BACK, *n.* कुबड*n.*

CROOK-BACKED, *a.* कुबडा, खुबडमोड्या, कुब्ज.

CROOKED, *a. curved, bent.* वांकडा, तेडा *or* तेढा, वक्र, तिडा, तिडका, कुटिल, अनृजु, नत, विनत, नम्र.

That is very crooked & unshapely—a person. अष्टावक्र*n.* अष्टवक्र.

C. and curved,—compreh. *bent and bowed and turned and warped, &c.* वांकड कोंका, वांकड मुसका, वांकडा तिकडा, वेडा वांकडा, वेडा बागडा.

2 fig. See PERVERSE.

CROOKEDLY, *adv.* v. A. वांकडा *a. decl.*

CROOKEDNESS, *n.* v. A. वांकडेपणा*m.* तेडेपणा*m.* &c. वांक*m.n.* तीड *f.* तेढाई *f.* वक्रता *f.* कुटिलता *f.* कौटिल्य*n.* नति *f.* वक्रभाव *or* वक्रीभाव*m.*

CROP, *n. craw.* गचूर*m.* चुनाळ*m.* पांखराचे गळयांतली पिशवी *f.*

2 *head, top.* बोंखा*m.* शेंडा*m.* तिटाळी *f.*

3 (of a field, &c.). पीक*n.* पिकदाव*m.* पिकराड *or* पिकलाड*n.* पिकलें*n.* फसल *f.* उपज*m.*—freely or indif. पीक पाणी*n.*

Crops, *growing corn.* शेतें*n.pl.* शेतीक*f.n.* शेतकी *f.* शेती*f.* शेतसरी *f.* जिनजित्रब*n.*

Crops still standing (yet unreaped) उभा माल*m.*

Blasted or parched c. सुकवें*n.* मयत *or* मैयत*n.*

Brownness of ripening c. काळवटी *f.* काळवंडी *f.*

C. cut and stacked (yet unshared, unascertained, &c.). उभीरास *f.* भररास *f.* समरास *f.* [येणें *n.*

Declining of ripening crops. अंकड्यास येणें*n.* पडणीस

Failure of c. नापीक*n.* नापिकलें*n.* बांड*n.*

Failure *utterly* of c. बींबूड*n.*

Inspection of blasted crops. मैयतपाहणी *f.*

Plentiful or good c. सुपीक*n.*

Ripeness or maturity of a c. पीक *n.*

Share in a c. of the land-holder. धनीवांटा*m.* शेतवांटा*m.* मालकवांटा*m.*—of the bullock-owner. बैलवांटा*m.*—of cultivator. आंगवांटा*m.*

Share of the lessor or lessee of a c. धल*n.* Half share. अर्धेल *or* अर्धल *f.* निमधल*n.* निमखाई *f.* निमाई *f.* Third share. तिरधल *or* तिरधेल *f.*

That bears but one annual c. एकपिकी, एकबारी.—two. दुपिकी, दुबारी.—three. तिपिकी, तिंबारी.—four. चौपिकी, चोबारी.

The Autumnal c. (or harvest) खरीप *or* फ *m.*

The Vernal c. (or harvest). रबी *or* रब्बी *f.*

To cut the c. सनंगणें, कापणें, सनंगणी *f.* करणें.

4 (esp. of fruits or flowers). लाग *m.* बाज *m.* बार *m.* उफर *or* उफरा *m.*

Of fruit-trees, &c. which yield two crops, the first c. is called मिठाबार, the second, खट्टाबार.

To estimate and purchase the coming c. पूट *or* पूठ *n.* करणें-घेणें.

To sell the coming c. पूठ *n.* देणें.

To CROP, *v. a. pluck or nip off the c.* बोंखडणें *or* बोंखाडणें, खुटणें, खुडणें, तोडणें, बोडकावणें.

CROP-EAR, CROP-EARED, *a.* मुंडेकानाचा, लांड्याकानाचा, छिन्नकर्ण, रुत्तकर्ण.

CROP-FULL, *a.* भरलेल्या पोटाचा, पूर्णोदर.

CROP-TAILED, *a.* लांडा, लंडपुच्छ, छिन्नपुच्छ.

CROPPED, *p.* v. V. बोंखडलेला, &c. बोडखा.

I.—the tail, &c. मुंढा, लांडा, थोंटा.

CROP-SICK, *a.* अतिजेवल्याचा अथवा प्याल्याचा असमाधानी.

CROP-SICKNESS, *n.* अतिजेवल्याचें अथवा प्याल्याचें असमाधान*n.*

CRORE, *n. ten millions.* क्रोड*m.f.* कोटि *f.*

Crores or by crores. क्रोडों, कोटिशः.

CROSS, *n.* क्रूस*m.* [चवा*m.*

St. Andrew's c. *an oblique, a couple.* कैंची *f.* धिंगी *f.*

2 *line drawn through.* छेका*m.* फांटा*m.* रेघ *f.*

3fig. *obstruction, thwarting accident,&c.* आडमेळें*n.* मानमोडें*n.* प्रतिकूल*n.* शल्य*n.* विघ्न*n.* नड *f.* नडाव*m.*

4 *ornament in the shape of a c.* क्रूसाच्या आकाराचें भूषण*n.*

5 *mark of a c. instead of signature.* क्रूसाचीनिशाणी *f.*

CROSS, *a. transverse, falling athwart.* आडवा.

2 *opposite, hostile,* v. ADVERSE. आडवा, प्रतिकूल, विपरीत.

3 *peevish, fretful, ill humoured, testy, crusty.* खिसखिशा, खाष्टी, खाष्टीखोर, खंक, खंकाल *or* ल्या, खट्याळ, खाट,कटकट्या, जिद्खोर, जितखोर, खेकड, खडतर, खलेल, खैन्या, खडंगूळ, काबिरडा, जिकिरी, तिरसट, तिसकूड, तिडका, तिडतिडा, तडतड्या, सदावक्र, हिरवा, हिरवट, तुडस, तुसडा, तुटक, तुटसाळ, कैंदी, कर्कश, द्वाष्ट, दाष्ट, दाष्टीक, असंतोषी.

Some terms for *a cross, crabbed, testy, crusty person; a cross-patch &c.* are, तिरशिंगराव, तिरमळ्या, आडजात.

4 *crooked, froward, awkward, cross-grained,* v.PERVERSE. आडगात्या, आडफांट्या, आडजात, अडिवाळ, तिडतिडा, खेकड, खेंकटेखोर.

5—marriage, &c. साट्यालोट्याचा, अदलाबदलीचा, बदलाचा.

6—breed, &c. संकराचा, संकरजात.

To CROSS, *v. a. lay athwart.* आडवा ठेवणें-लावणें.

2 *pass over.* ओलंडणें *or* ओलांडणें,उतरणें, तरणें, उलंघणें,लंघणें, खेटणें, पार जाणें.

3 *thwart, counterwork,* v. To HINDER, To OBSTRUCT. अबरोधणें, अडथळणें, आडवा-बांकडा येणें, मोडा*m.* घालणें,हरकत *f.* करणें, अवरोध*m.*-प्रतिरोध*m.*-&c. करणें *g. of o.*

4 *cancel, strike out.* छकणें *or* छेकणें, खोडणें, छेका*m.*- फांटा*m.* देणें-मारणें- घालणें, फुली फांटा*m.* देणें.

5 *make the sign of the cross.* क्रूसाचीखूण *f.*-चिन्ह-&c.करणें *with.* वर *of o.*

CROSS-BIRTH. To have a c. आडवें येणें in. con. (Ex. या बाईला आडवें आलें).

CROSS-BITE, *n.* उलटफसवण *f.*

To CROSS-BITE, *v. a.* उलटफसवण *f.* करणें.

CROSS-BOW, *n.* दस्त्याचा-कुंद्याचा कमठा*m.*-धनुष्य*n.*

CROSS-BREED, *n.* भिसळीचीजात *f.* संकर*m.* संकरजाति *f.*

To Cross-examine, *v. a.* उलट सवालm. घालणें, प्रतिप्रश्नm.-प्रतिपक्षप्रश्नm. करणें. [नाडीक.

Cross-grained, *a. lit.* आडव्याशिरांचा, आडव्यादोराचा, तिर्यङ्-
2 fig. *cross, crooked,* v. Perverse. आडगात्या, आडफांट्या, अडिवाळ.

Cross-legged, *a.* अढी घालून बसलेला, प्रौढपाद.
Sitting c. आसनमांडी *f.* अलखटपालखटor अलखंडपालखंड*f.* अढी *f. v.* घालून बसणें. N.B. The postures are not all the same.

Cross-patch, *n.* v. Cross. 3. आडजात.

To Cross-plough, *v. a.* बेरणें, बेरणी *f.* करणें.

Cross-purpose. To be at cross purposes. एकानें म्हणावें एक दुसऱ्यानें समजावें बेक.

To Cross-question, *v. a. question closely, searchingly, &c.* छडणें, घोळणें, कसणें, आसूडपाखुड *f.*-उलटापालट *f.*-छडणूक *f.* -&c. करणें *g. of o.*

Cross-road, *n.* आडवा रस्ताm. आडवी वाट *f.*

Cross-way, *n. place where roads cross.* चवाठाm. तिवाठा *m.*

Crossed, *p.* v.V. 2. ओलंडलेला, उतरलेला, &c. उल्लंघित, अतिक्रांत, उत्तीर्ण, तीर्ण.
3 अडथळलेला, &c. अवरोधित, प्रतिरोधित, अवरुद्ध, प्रतिरुद्ध.
4 छकलेला, खोडलेला, फांटा मारलेला, &c.

Crossing, *n.* v. V. 1.—*act.* आडवा ठेवणेंn.
2—*act.* ओलंडणें *n.* उतरणें *n.* &c. ओलांडणी *f.* उल्लंघन *n.* उल्लंघ *m.* लंघन *n.* उतरण *n.* अतिक्रमण *n.*
3—*act.* अडथळणें *n.* &c. अवरोध *m.* प्रतिरोध *m.*
4—*act.* छेकणें *n.* खोडणें *n.* &c. छेकणी *f.* छेकणूक *f.*

Crossly, *adv.* v. A. 3. खाष्टपणानें, तिरसटपणानें.

Crossness, *n.* v. A. 1. आडवेपणा *m.* &c.
2 आडवेपणा *m.* प्रतिकूलपणा *m.* &c. प्रातिकूल्य *n.* वैपरीत्य *n.* प्रतिकूलभाव *m.* विपरीतभाव *m.*
3 संकाळपणा *m.* खाष्टपणा *m.* &c. तिडतीड *f.* करडीमरजी *f.* खलेली *f.*
4 आडगातेपणा *m.* आडजातपणा *m.*

Crosswise, *adv. athwart.* आडवा *a. decl.* आड.

Crotch, *n. furcation.* बेळकें or दुबेळकें *n.* नांगें *n.* वेचक *f.*
2 *furcated stick, &c.* See Crotchet. [चर्फे *n.*

Crotchet, *n. furcated stick, &c.* बेळें *n.* दुबेळकें *n.* कुडघई *f.* बे-
2—in printing. बेळें *n.*
3 *conceit,* v. Fancy. लहर *f.* तरंग *m.*

Crotchety, *a.* v. Fanciful. लहरी, लहरीदार.

Croton oil, *n.* जेपाळाचे बियाचें तेल *n.*

To Crouch, *v. n. lie low and close.* दबणें, दबकणें, दबा *m.* धरणें-मारणें, दबून-दबकून-दबा धरून-&c.बसणें-असणें, मुडी *f.* मारणें-मारून बसणें, मुरमुशी *f.* मारणें, मुरमुसणें or मुरमुसून बसणें-निजणें.
2 *cringe,* v. To Fawn. पायां-हातां पायां-हातीं पायीं-&c. पडणें, पदर *m.* पसरणें, लवण भंजन *n.* करणें.

Croup, (of animals) v. Rump. ढिमोरा *m.* ढुंगण *n.* चौक *n.*
2 मुलांचा एक रोग आहे.

Crow, *n.* कावळा *m.* काक *m.* वायस *m.* Some species are रुष्णकावळा, डोंबकावळा or द्रोणकाक, महारकावळा, दग्धकाक.
Carrion c. महारकावळा *m.* दग्धकाक *m.*
Offerings (rice, &c. thrown out) to crows. काकबलि *pop.* काकबळ & काकबळी *f.* आघारी *f.*
2 (of iron). संबळ *m.* तोमर *m. n.*
3 (of the cock). आरवणी *f.* आरव *f.* कोकणी or कुकणी *f.* कुक *f.* बांगणी *f.* बांग *f.* साद *f.*
Second c. (in the morning). दुसारणी *f.*—Third c. तिसारणी *f.*

To Crow, *v. n.*—the cock. आरवणें, आरणें, कोकणें or कुकणें, आरवणी *f.*-&c. करणें, बांग *f.*-साद *f.* देणें.—the second time दुसारणें.—the third time तिसारणें.
2 fig. *exult,* v. To Triumph. कुले *m.pl.* थोपटणें, टिरी *f.pl.* थोपटणें-थापटणें-पिटणें-बडवणें-वाजवणें, काखा *f.pl.* वाजवणें.

Crow-bar, *n.* संबळ *m.* तोमर *m. n.* छेळणें *n.*

Crows-feet, *n.* म्हातारपणीं डोळ्याखालीं ज्या वळ्या *f. pl.*-सुरकुत्या *f. pl.* पडतात त्या.

Crowd, *n. multitude assembled, concourse, throng, press.* चेप *m.* चेपारा *m.* थट or थाट *m. f.* रामरगडा *m.* रगडा *m.* रट्ट *m.* गट *m.* or गट्ट *m.* गट्टा *m.* हाजिमा *m.* दाटीचा-रगड्याचा-&c. समुदाय *m.* गळागोठा *m.* पुठा or पुह्वा *m.* घोळका *m.* मंडण *n.*
In crowds. थाटाचे थाट, गट्टाचे गट्ट, &c.संघशः, घवघव orवां.
To open out—a c. पैसावणें.
To reduce or thin a c. पैसाविणें.
N. B. The words under Crowdedness are used idiomatically to express a throng, as देवळांत लोकांची मोठी दाटी झाली होती.
2 *promiscuous mass,* v. Jumble. घालमेल *f.* गोंधळ *m.* एकबाट *m.* एकाकार *m.* [*mpl.*
3 *the common people, the vulgar,* v. People. तेलीतांबोळी

To Crowd, *v. a. fill to excess, fill by pressing together.* भरून काटणें, खेटून काटणें, अडचणविणें, दाटवणें, दाटी *f.*—रगडा *m.*—गर्दी *f.*-&c. करणें *with* आंत *of o.*
2 *press confusedly together.* खेटवणें, दाटवणें, दाटी *f.*-दाटण *f.*-दाटणी *f.*-चेपाचेप *f.*-&c. करणें-करवणें *g. of o.*
3 *incommode by pressing on.* दाटी *f.*-&c. करणें,अडचणविणें.

To Crowd, *v. n.* दाटणें, खेटणें, भिडणें, दाटी *f.*-दाटणीवाटणी *f.* करणें, घणबटणें, ठेलणें, लोटणें, ढेसणें, बेट *m.* बळणें *g. of s.* चेपm.-चेपाचेप *f.*-चेपाराm.-खेटाखेट *f.*-ठेल *f.*-ठेलाठेल or ली *f.*-ठेच *f.*-धिचडी *f.*-&c. करणें or होणें *g. of s.* मुंडपघसणी *f.*-रेंटाई *f.*-रेंटारेंट *f.*-&c. करणें, मिठण *n.* घालणें or *with g. of s.* पडणें.

Crowded, *p.*v.V.N.घणदाट,घण,गडगच्च, संकुल, संकीर्ण, अनवकाश.
To be c. अडचणणें, दाटणें, गच्चभरून निघणें, पायांपैस *m.* नसणें.

Crowdedness, *n.* v. P. गच्ची *f.* दाटी *f.* अडचण *f.* ऐचण *f.* भीड *f.* गचाड or गिचाड *n.* किचाटी *f.* चेपाचेप *f.* गर्दी *f.* खच or कच *f.* चिडचोड *f.* चिडमोड or चिडिमिडी or चिडिकामिडी *f.* दाटण *f.* दाटणी *f.* खेट *f.* खेटा *m.* चिलचिलाट *m.* चिरंगट or चेंगरट *f.* थट or थाट *m.* ठेल *f.* ठेच *f.* चेपारा *m.* चेंद *f.* चेंदाड *f.* रगडा or रगाडा *m.* रट्ट or ठ *m.* दवडगा *m.*

Crown, *n. diadem,* v. Crest. मुकुट *pop.* मुगूट *m.* किरीट *m. n.* राजमुकुट *m.*
Assuming the c. किरीटधारण *n.*
Gem or jewel of a c. मुकुटमणिm.
2 (of the head, of a mountain, &c.). माथा *m.* टाळू *f.*

C. of the human head. ब्रह्मांड *n.* खाकोळें *n.*
Lock of hair on the c. मौलि *or* मौली *m.*
3 *completion, &c.* सिद्धि *f.* संसिद्धि *f.* सार्थक्य *pop.* सार्थक *n.* कळस *m.* शिरोभाग *m.*
4 (of a hat, &c.) माथा *m.*
5—the coin. अडीच रुपयांच्या किमतीचें इंग्लंदांत एक नाणें आहे.
6 See GOVERNMENT.

To CROWN, *v. a. invest with the c.* मुगूट *m.*-&c. घालणें, मस्तकावर मुगूट ठेवून अभिषेक *m.* करणें, पट्टाभिषेक *m.* करणें, मुकुटसंस्कार *m.* करणें, पट्टबंधन *n.* करणें, किरीटी-&c. करणें.
2 (with success). सार्थक्य *pop.* सार्थक *n.*-साफल्य *n.*-सिद्धि *f.*-संसिद्धि *f.*-&c. करणें *g. of o.*

CROWNED, *p.* v.V.1. मुकुटधारी, किरीटधारी, किरीटी, किरीटमौली, जात-प्राप्त मुकुटसंस्कार.
To be c. with success. सार्थक्य *pop.* सार्थक *n.*-साफल्य *n.*-&c. होणें *g. of s.*कृतकृत्य होणें. [पट्टबंधन *n.*

CROWNING, CORONATION, *n.*v. V.1. पट्टाभिषेक *m.*मुकुटसंस्कार *m.*

CRUCIAL, *a.* क्रुसाच्या आकाराचा.
2 *severe, trying.* जिवावरचा, जिवापरता, प्रखर.

CRUCIBLE, *n.melting pot.* मूस *f.*आवर्त्तनी *f.* तैजसावर्त्तनी *f.*पुट*n.*
Dipping rod of a c. ईषीका *f.* तूलिका *f.*

CRUCIFIX, *n.* क्रुसावरील ख्रिस्ताचीमूर्त्ति *f.*

CRUCIFIXION, *n.* v. V. क्रुसावर देणें *n.*

CRUCIFORM, *a.* क्रुसाच्या आकाराचा.

To CRUCIFY, *v. a.* क्रुसावर चढवणें-देणें.
2 fig. See To MORTIFY.

CRUDE, *a.* v. RAW. कच्चा, आम, अपक्व, कोवळा.
2 *undigested.* आम, कच्चा, विदग्ध, अजीर्ण.
3 *not matured, &c.* कच्चा, अपक्व, अप्रौढ.

CRUDITY, CRUDENESS, *n.* v. A. 1. कच्चेपणा *m.*कच्चाई *f.*अपक्वत्व *n.*
2 कच्चेपणा *m.* विदग्धता *f.*
3 कच्चेपणा *m.* अप्रौढता *f.*
I. *a* c.—in medicine. आम*m. pop.*आंव *f.*आमांश*m.*कुपित्थ*n.*

CRUEL, *a pitiless, merciless, savage, barbarous, brutal, inhuman.* निर्दय, क्रूर, उग्र, निष्ठुर, दयाहीन, दयाशून्य, दुःखदेण्या, दुःख देण्याच स्वभावाचा, परदुःखसंतोषी, परपीडनसंतोषी, पाषाणहृदयी, मांगहृदयी, कर्कश, कठोर, परुष, निर्घृण, कठिन *pop.* कठीण, कजाख, खुनी, खाटकी, घातकी, हिंसालु, हिंसक, हिंस्र, आसुर, राक्षसी, दैत्यांशी, राक्षसधर्मा, असुरधर्मा, मनुष्यविधर्मा. Some terms for a cruel, savage, hard-hearted person are. कर्मचांडाळ, यम, यमाचा अवतार, यमदूत.

CRUELLY, *adv.* v. A. निर्दयपणानें, क्रूरतेनें, निष्ठुरतेनें, क्रौर्यपूर्वक.

CRUELTY, *n.* v. A. निर्दयपणा *m.* निष्ठुरपणा *m.* क्रूरता *f.* निर्दयता *f.* निष्ठुरता *f.* निर्घृणता *f.* परपीडनसंतोष *m.* परदुःखसंतोष *m.* क्रौर्य *n.*
I. cruel deed. क्रूरकर्म *n.*

CRUET, *n. bottle for vinegar.* सिरकादानी *f.*

CRUET-STAND, *n.* घड *m.*

CRUISE, *n.* See CUP. 2 v. V. दर्या फिरणें *n.* समुद्रपर्यटन *n.*

To CRUISE, *v. n. sail about.* दर्या फिरणें, समुद्रांत फिरणें, समुद्र पर्यटन *n.* करणें.

CRUISER, *n.* शत्रूचीं गलबतें धरण्या करितां व आपले देशच्या गलबतांचें रक्षण करण्या करितां समुद्रांत फिरणारें गलबत *n.*

CRUMB, *n.*—as opposed to crust. गर *m.*गीर *m.* गर्भ *m.* मगज *m.*
2 (of bread, &c.) *bit.* तुकडा *m.* नितकोर *m.* निमूकोर *m.*
Crumbs,*bits,fragments.* कुसकुरा *or* कुसकूर *m.*चूर *m.*चुरा*m.*

To CRUMBLE, *v. a. break into small pieces.* कुसकुरणें *or* खुसकुरणें, चुरणें, चुरडणें, चूर *m.*-चुरा *m.*-चुराडा *m.*-भगरा *m.*-&c. करणें *g. of o.*
To c. by squeezing in the hand. खुसखुरणें.

To CRUMBLE, *v. n.* चुरणें, चुराडा *m.*-&c. होणें *g. of s.* विरणें.
2 down; *fall to pieces*—a wall of sand. &c. रेलणें, ढ्ढरणें.

CRUMBLING, CRUMBLY, *a. soft, friable, &c.* खुसखुसीत, फुसफुसीत, भुसभुसीत, खुटखुटीत, फुसका, फुसकुला, विरणा, विरका, पिठा *or* ठ्या, पिठूळ.

CRUMP-BACKED. See CROOK-BACKED.

CRUMPET, *n.* भाकरीचा एक प्रकार आहे.

To CRUMPLE, *v. a. rumple, &c.* चुरणें, चुरडणें, कुसमडणें *or* कुसमाडणें, गुधडणें *or* गुडधावणें, चुरंगटणें, चुरगळणें, घुसडणें, घुरदळणें, खुरंदळणें, चोळामोळा *m.* करणें, गुरधळ *or* ळी *f.* घालणें-मांडणें,उपमर्द*m.*-अबमर्द*m.*-उपमर्दन*n.*-अबमर्दन*n.*-&c.करणें*g.ofo.*

CRUMPLED, *p.* & *a.* v. V. चुरलेला, कुसमडलेला, चोळामोळा केलेला, &c.
I.—a horn. मुंढा, मुंढरा.
Of which the horns are c.—a beast. मुंडा,
A cow with c. horns. मुंडीगाय *f.*

CRUNK, CRUNKLING, *n.* v. V. कचकच *f.* (*intens.* कचाच *m.* कचाकच *f.* कचकचाट *or* किचकिचाट *m.*).

To CRUNK, *To* CRUNKLE, *v. n. cry*—the crane. कचकचणें *or* किचकिचणें, *intens.* कचाचणें.

CRUPPER, *n.* लेंडी *f.* दुमची *f.*
Boss (of silk, silver, &c.) on a c. गेंद *m.*
2 *croup,* v. RUMP. ढिमोरा *m.* चौक *m.*

CRURAL, *a. belonging to the leg.* पायाचा, पायसंबंधी, जांघिक.

CRUSADE, *n.* यरूशालेमशहर मुसलमानलोकांपासून घेण्याकरितां ख्रिस्ती लोकांनीं मागें अनेकवेळ स्वारीकेली होती ती.

CRUSE, *n.* लहान पेला *m.*

CRUSET, *n.* See CRUCIBLE.

To CRUSH, *v. a. break or bruise by squeezing or pressing.* ठेचणें, चुरणें, चुरडणें,चेचणें, चेचरणें, कुसकुरणें, चेंदा*m.*करणें *g.ofo.*
2 *mash, jam, &c. by squeezing.* v. To SQUEEZE. चिवडणें, चिरंगटणें, चिरडणें, चेंबटणें, चेंगरणें, चेंदणें, चेंदरणें, मर्दणें, चेंदामेंदा *m.*-चेंदूमेंदू *m.*-चेंदू *m.*-&c. करणें *g. of o.*
3 *overwhelm, &c.* v. To SUBDUE. जमीनदोस्त-चीत-पादाक्रांत -जर्जर-&c.करणें, लोळवणें, लोळसावणें, मारून चुना *m.* करणें, मारून-पीठ *n.* पाडणें *g.ofo.* धूळ *f.* करणें *g.of o.* धुळीस मिळवणें.

CRUSHED, *p.* v. V. 1. ठेचलेला, चुरलेला, चेचलेला, &c.
2 चिवडलेला, चेंगरलेला,&c. क्षुण्ण, विशीर्ण.
3 जमीनदोस्त केलेला, लोळवलेला, &c. [चणी *f.*

CRUSHING, *n,* v. V. 1.—*act.* ठेचणें *n.* चेचणें *n.*&c. ठेचणी *f.* चे-
2—*act.* चिवडणें*n.*चेंगरणें *n.*चेंबटणें *n.* &c. उपमर्द *m.* उपमर्दन *n.*

CRUST, *n. external coat, case, incrustation, &c.* कवच *n.* कंचुंकी *f.* पूट *n.* तरंग *m.*
C. of dirt. किटण *n.* कीट *n.*
2 (over a sore, &c.). खवल *or* ळ *n.* खपला *dim.* खपली *f.* खवंद *n.* कवंद *f.*

3—as peeling off, v. PEELING. पोपडा *m.* पापोडा *or* टा *m.* पातोडा *or* पातवडा *m.* पापुद्रा *m.* चकदळ *n.* चकदा *m.* कळपा *m.*

4 *outer hard part,*—of bread. तळकाm. बाहेरला कठीणभागm.

C. of the earth. भूगोलाचा घनभाग *m.*

5 *piece of bread.* कोर *f. m.* कोरका *m.* नितकोर *m.* चतकोर *m.* निमकोर *m.* भाकरीचा तुकडा *m.*

To CRUST, *v. n. gather into a hard covering.* खवळ *n.*-खपला *m.*-&c. धरणें.

CRUSTACEOUS, *a.* कवचाचा, कंवचीचा, कवचमय.

CRUSTILY, *adv.* v. A. 2. खट्याळपणानें, तिरसटपणानें.

CRUSTINESS, *n.* v. A. 2. खट्याळपणा *m.* खाष्टीपणा *m.*

CRUSTY, *a.* कवचाचा, कंवचीचा.

2 *crabbed,* v. CROSS. खट्याळ, खाष्टी, दाष्ट.

CRUTCH, *n.* कुबडी *f.* पांगूळकाठी *f.* पांगूळघोडा *m.* पांगूळधिरा *m.*

To CRY, *v. n. speak loudly, vehemently, &c;* v. To BAWL. मोठ्यानें बोलणें, ओरडणें, ओरडून बोलणें, पुकारणें, पुकाराm. करणें.

2 unto, to; *call upon in prayer, &c.* धांवा *m.*-धावणें *n.* करणें, हाका *f. pl.* मारणें.

3 *weep.* रडणें, रडें *or* रडूं *n.* येणें *in. con.* र *f.*-रचें *n.*-रुदंती *f.*-रुदंतीचें *n.*-रुदन *or* रोदन *n.*-&c. करणें, मुसमुस *f.* करणें, मुसमुसणें, डोळे *m. pl.* पुसणें.—out, aloud; v. To BAWL. अरडणें *or* ओरडणें, अकांतणें, आकांत *m.*-आक्रोश *m.*-आक्रंदन *n.*-&c. करणें—with plentiful tears. ढळढळ-ढळढळां-ढळाढळ-ढळाळां-भळभळ-भळभळां-खळखळ-खळखळां -घळघळ-घळघळां-टचटचून-टचाचून-&c. रडणें, टचाचून-&c. पाणीn. डोळ्यांत येणें *in. con.* र र *f.* करणें, पागोळ्या *f. pl.* सोडणें, गाया *f. pl.* पाण्यावर आणणें.—ungovernably, unceasingly, &c. उकशाबुकशीं *adv.* रडणें, चळ *m. f.* घेणें, चळणें, चेतवणें, चेकळणें, रडण्याची टकf. लावणें, रडण्याचा टाहोm.-लाहोm. घेणें, रडून आकांतm.-अनर्थm.-दंगाm.-&c. करणें, रडf.-रडेंn. घेणें-मांडणें-लावणें.—sobbingly, &c. हुमसणें, फुंदणें, हुंदके येऊन *or* काढून-उमासे येऊन *or* काढून-उमाडे येऊन-काढून-&c. रडणें.

4—esp. of children; agreeing with *whine, whimper, wawl, pipe, snivel, &c.* केंकणें, केंकटणें, केंकावणें, टेंटावणें, खेंकाटणें, ठिणकणें, भेकणें, टाहो *or* टहाm. फोडणें-घेणें, ट्याहां ट्याहां-टेंटें-रडूंरडूं *adv.* करणें, कोंकलणें, किरकणें, पिरंगणें, कुसमुसणें, मुसमुसणें, धुसमुसणें, फुसफूस *f.*-&c. करणें-लावणें, किरकिरणें, पिरपिरणें, मिणमिणणें, पिटपिटणें, कन्हेरी *f.* गाणें, ताहीं *or* टाहीं भरणें.

5—an animal, gener. ओरडणें *or* अरडणें, पुकारणें, बोलणें, शब्दm. करणें.—a bird. आरवणें.—the elephant. किंकळणें *or* किंकाळणें, किरकणें, किंकाटणें, किराळणें, किंकळी *f.*-&c. फोडणें.—the crane. किचकिचणें *or* कचकचणें, टाहोm. फोडणें-घेणें.—the bandikote. रारेणें, राराणn. करणें.

6 out upon; on; against. नांवानें बोंबलणें, बोंब *f.* ठोकणें-मारणें, शंखm. करणें-&c. *all with g. of o.* नांवाचा हाकाटाm.-पुकाराm.-बोभाटाm.-&c. करणें *g. of o.*

To CRY, *v. a.* See To PROCLAIM. 2 up; *laud,* v. To PRAISE. वडिवारm.-बढाई *f.*-बढाईकी *f.*-तारीफ *f.*-थोरवी *f.*-प्रतिष्ठा *f.*-&c. सांगणें *g. of o.*

3 down; v. To DEPRECIATE. उणेपणाm.-उणावकी *f.*-उणीव *f.*- लहानवी *f.*-अप्रतिष्ठा *f.*-&c. करणें-सांगणें.

CRY, CRYING, *n.* v. V. N. 1.—*act.* ओरडणेंn.-&c. अरड *or* आरड *f.* पुकारm. पुकाराm. अरोळी *f.*

2 धांवाm. धावणेंn. हाक *f.*

3 रडणेंn. र *f.* रर *f.* रचेंn. रुदंती *f.* रुदंतीचेंn. रुदन *or* रोदनn.—aloud, &c. ओरडणेंn. अरड *or* आरड *f.* ओरडाm. अरडाओरड *f.* आकांतm. आक्रोशm. आक्रंदनn.

Given to crying. रडवा, रड्या.

A long or continued c. रड *f.*

To seem ready to cry. रडकुंडीस येणें, रडकुंडी होणें.

5 ओरडणेंn. ओरडणी *f.* ओरड *f.* शब्दm.—of a bird. आरवणी *f.* आरवणेंn.—of the elephant. किंकळी *or* किंकाळी *f.* चीत्कारm.—of the crane. टाहोm.—of the bandikote. रराणn.—of the hare, squirrel, &c. कुई *f.*

CRYING, *a.*—sin, abuse, &c. मोठा, भारी, जबर.

CRYPT, *n.* देवळाखालील भुयारn.

CRYPTIC, CRYPTICAL, *a.* v. OCCULT. गूढ, गूढार्थ.

CRYSTAL, *n* स्फटिकm. स्फाटिकn. काचमणिm. बिलोरn. स्फटिकाश्माm. शीताश्माm.

CRYSTAL, CRYSTALLINE, *a.* स्फटिकाचा, स्फटिकमय, स्फाटिक, स्फटिकप्रभ, स्फटिकनिभ, बिलोरी.

To CRYSTALIZE, *v.n.* कांड्या *f. pl.*-खडे *m.pl.* बनणें-होणें *g. of s.*

To CRYSTALIZE, *v.a.* कांड्या *f. pl.*-खडेm. *pl.* करणें *g. of o.*

CUB, *n.* पिलूं*n.* बच्चाm. पशुशावकm.—of a tiger or lion, पेटाm.

CUBE, *n.*—in geometry. घनm.

Cubical contents. घनफलn.

2—in arithmetic. घनm.

Square of c. घनवर्गm. वर्गघनm.

CUBE-ROOT, *n.* घनमूलn. घनपदn. मूलn. पदn.

CUBEBS, *n.* कबाबचिनी *f.* सुगंधमरीचn.

CUBIC, CUBICAL, *a.* घन.

CUBIT, *n. measure from the elbow to the tip of the middle finger.* हातm. हस्तm. काकिणी *f.*

2—to the tip of the little finger. अरत्निm.

3—to the hand clenched. मुंढाहातm. मुंढाm.

CUCKOLD, *n. husband of an adulteress.* छिनालबायकोचाभ्रतारm. ढवा *m.* जारिणीपति *m.* कुलटापति *m.*

CUCKOO, *n.*—the Indian. कोकिल *m.* (कोकिला *f. and, pop.* कोकीळ *or* कोयीळ *f.*) कासर *m.* पिक *pop.* पीक *m.* रोडकी *f.*

Cry of the c. कुहू *n.* पिहू *n.*

CUCUMBER, *n.* काकडी *f.* खिरा *m.* शेतवाळूक *n.* Some of the common species are टरकाकडी, बालमखिरा, तुरई, पावसळी काकडी, सातपानी काकडी.

CUCURBITE, *n.*—the chemical apparatus. डमरुयंत्र *n.*

CUD, *n.* रोंथ *m.* रवंथ *m.*

Chewing the c. रोमंथ *pop.* रोंथ *m.* रवंथ *n. m.* रोवंथ *m.* रोहंथ *f.* रोहमत *f.*

To chew the c. रोंथणें *or* रवंथणें *or* रोवंथणें, रोंथ *m.*-रवंथ *m.* करणें.

2 (of tobacco, &c.) गोळी *f.*

To CUDDLE, *v. n. lie close.* लगटून-चिकटून-घुसून-&c. निजणें, कुशींत शिरणें.

To CUDDLE, *v. a.* पोटाशींधरून-जवळकरून-कुशींतघुसून-&c. निजवणें.

CUDGEL, *n.* सोंटा *or* सोटा *m. dim.* सोटगें *n.* टोणपा *or* टोणका *or* टोणा *m. dim.* टोणपें *or* टोणकें *n.* टोंबा *m.* दांड *or* दंड *m.*

दांडका *m. dim.* दांडकें *or* दांडगें *or* दांडूक *n.* दंडुका *or* दडोका *m.* लट्ठ *m.* लरिंगा *m.* लटोरा *m.* डेंगरणें *n.* बडघा*m.*

Conflict with cudgels. लट्ठालट्ठी *f.*

Cudgel-coaxing. दांडेपान्हवण *n.* सोटेपान्हवण *n.*

Cudgel-playing. सोटेबाजी *f.* लट्ठालट्ठी *f.* चोपाचोप *f.*

To CUDGEL, *v. a.* दांडावणें, दांडकणें *or* दांडगणें, टोणकणें, टोणपणें, टोणकावणें, चोपणें, चोपटणें, बडवणें, झोड *f.*-झोडपट्टी *f.* काढणें *g. of o.*

Given to cudgeling. दंडुक्या.

CUE, *n.* v. TAIL. शेपूट *n.* पुच्छ *n.* लांगूल *n.*

2 *hint, &c.* सूचना *f.* इंगित *n.*

To give one his c. बार *m.* भरणें-देणें-ठासणें.

3 *humour, temper.* वृत्ति *f.* मन *n.* चित्त *n.*

To be in the c. for. स्वर *m. pl.* भजणें *or* वाहणें *g. of o.*

CUFF, *n. blow with the fist,* v. BLOW. मुटका *m.* बुकी *f.* मुष्टिप्रहार *m.* मुष्टिमोदक *m.*

2 (of a sleeve). मुहळी *f.*

To CUFF, *v. a.* v. To BEAT. धपकावणें *or* धबकावणें, मुटका *m.*-&c. मारणें. मुष्टिप्रयोग *m.* करणें, चपराकणें.

CUI BONO? किमर्थं.

CUIRASS, *n.* v. ARMOUR. उरस्त्राण *n.* उदरत्राण *n.* उरश्छद *m.*

CUISH, *n.* v. ARMOUR. ताराचा चोळणा *m.* जंघात्राण *n.*

CULINARY, *a. relating to cooking, &c.* स्वैंपाकाचा, पाकसंबंधी, पाकक्रिया विषयक-संबंधी, पाकशालासंबंधी.

To CULL, *v. a.* v. To CHOOSE. निवडणें, वेचणें, छानणें.

CULLY. See GULL.

CULM, *n.* v. STALK. तांट *n.*

To CULMINATE, *v. n. be vertical.* खम्वस्तिकीं-डोक्यावर-&c. येणें.

To attain its acme or culminating point. कळस *m.* होणें *g. of s.*

CULMINATION, *n.* डोक्यावर येणें. *n.*

2 *culminating point; highest point.* कळस *m.* पराकाष्ठा *f.*

CULPABLE, CULPABILITY. See BLAMABLE, &c.

CULPRIT, *n.* अपराधी, अन्यायी, गुन्हेगार, दोषपात्र *n.* दोषास्पद *n.*

CULTIVABLE, *a.* v.V.1. राबायाजोगा,लागवडीस आणायाजोगा,&c.

To CULTIVATE, *v. a. till.* राबणें, नांगरणें दुणणें, कीर्द *f.*-राबणी *f.*-राबणूक *f.*-कृषि *f.*-कर्षण *n.*-&c. करणें *g. of o.* किर्दीस-राबणुकीस-लागवडीस-&c. आणणें.

2 *raise by tillage.* पीक *n.* करणें *g. of o.* कीर्द *f.*-राबणूक *f.* करणें *g. of o.* राबणुकीनें-&c. पिकवणें-उत्पन्न करणें.

3 (the faculties, a taste, &c.). मशागत *f.*-कमाई *f.*-&c. करणें,कमावणें, बळवणें, गिरवणें, अभ्यासानें-मेहनत करून वाढविणें.

CULTIVATED, *p.* v. V. 1. राबलेला, &c. वहीत, किर्दसार, राबणुकीचा, राबणीचा, लागवडीचा, कर्षित, हल्य.

CULTIVATION, CULTURE, *n.* v. V. 1. *and* AGRICULTURE. राबणें *n.* &c. शेती *f.* शेतकाम *n.* कृषि *f.* कृषिकर्म *n.* राबणी *f.* राबणूक *f.* लावणी *f.* लागवड *f.* किर्द *f.* कर्षण *n.* वाहील *or* वाहेल *f.*

That is under c. *not fallow.* वाहीत, वाहोळ.

2 पीक करणें *n.* &c.

3 कमावणें *n.* कमाई *f.* मशागत *f.*

CULTIVATOR, *n.* v. AGRICULTURIST. शेतकरी, शेतखध्या, कुणबी, क्षेत्री, कर्षक, कृषिक, कृषीवल, क्षेत्राजीवी, कृषिजीवी.

Actual c. of a farm. करदा *m.*

Non-resident c. ओवंडेकरी, केवी.

CULVER. See PIGEON.

To CUMBER. See To ENCUMBER.

CUMBERSOME, CUMBROUS, *a. burdensome, embarrassing, unwieldy, &c.* दुर्भर, दुर्वाह्य, अवघड,अवजड, लचरट, लडतर, क्लिष्ट, क्लेशवाह्य.

CUMBERSOMENESS, CUMBROUSNESS, *n.* v. A. अवजडपणा *m.* अवघडपणा *m.* &c. दुर्वाह्यत्व *n.* दुर्भरत्व. *n.* क्लेशवाह्यता *f.*

CUMIN-SEED, *n.* जीरक *pop.* जिरें *n.* कणा *f.* अजाजी *f.*

Single seed of c. जिरूं *n.*

To CUMULATE, CUMULATION. See To ACCUMULATE, &c.

CUMULATIVE, *a.* जमतजमत गेलेला, सांचलेला.

CUNEIFORM, *a.* पाचरीच्या आकाराचा.

CUNNING, *a knowing,* v SKILFUL. शाहणा, चतुर, कुशल, हिकमती, हिकमत्या, जाणता.

2 *wrought with skill.* चतुराईचा, चातुर्याचा, हिकमतीचा, &c.

3 *sly, subtle, crafty, wily, artful.*—person. कावेदार, कावेखोर, कावेबाज, काबू, मकरी, कपटी, कसबाती, धूर्त, शठ, बाट, बाटगा, छद्मी, कारस्थानी, मतलबी, लागलाव्या, लाग्या, हुनरी, हिकमती, हिलेबाज, गुंड, गुंडा, मतलबदार, कवाइती *or* दी, कवाईतदार, छक्यापंज्याचा.

4—acts, &c. काव्यादाव्याचा, कपटाचा, काटाचा, डावपेंचाचा, छक्यापंज्याचा.

CUNNING, *n. art,* v. SKILL. शहाणपण *n.* चतुराई *f.* युक्ति *f.* युगूत *f.* हिकमत *f.* चातुर्य *n.* कुशलता *f.* कौशल्य *n.* सूक्ष्म *n.*

2 *artfulness, craftiness, craft, subtleness, wiliness, &c.* कावेदारी *f.* कावेबाजी *f.* कावा *m.* कावादावा *m.* कालेंबेलें *n.* कपट *n.* बाटपणा *m.* कावित्र *n.* कापट्य *n.* चेटक *n.* शाठ्य *n.* शठता *f.* धौर्त्य *n.* धूर्तता *f.*

CUNNINGLY, *adv.* v. A. 3 *and* ARTFULLY. काव्यानें, काव्यादाव्यानें, डावपेंच-&c. करून.

CUNNING-MAN, *n. one who tells fortunes, discovers lost goods, &c.* जाणता, पाहण्या, इलमबाज, इलमी.

CUNNING-WOMAN, *n.* कुसळण *or* कुसळीण *f.*

CUP, *n.* कटोरा *m.* वाटी *f.* प्याला *or* पेला *m.* पात्र *n.* जांब *or* जाम *m.*

To have one's c. full (of joy, desire, &c.) तुंबडी *f.*-टोवणें *n.* भरणें *g. of s.*

2 (of a flower, &c.) वाटी *f.* गोंड *n.*

3 See CUPPING-GLASS. 4 cups. See CAROUSAL.

To CUP, *v. a.* तुंबडी *f.*-रोंबी *f.*-रोंबें *n.*-&c. लावणें-काढणें *or* लावून रक्त *n.* काढणें, शिंगानें रक्त *n.* काढणें.

2—by scarification. फासण्या *f. pl.* मारणें-टाकणें-घालणें.

CUP-BEARER, *n.* प्यालेबरदार, जांबबरदार.

CUP-BOARD, *n.* फडताळ *or* फडताळ *or* फडतार *n.* दुलाब *f.* भंडारी *f.* हडपा *m.* बोखारा *m.*

CUPID, *n.* काम *m.* कामदेव *m.* दीपक *m.* अनंग *m.*

CUPIDINOUS, CUPIDITY. See COVETOUS, COVETOUSNESS.

CUPOLA, *n.* घुमट *m. dim.* घुमटी *f.* घटाटोप *m.* कळस *m.* डेरा *m.*

CUPPER, *n.* CUPPING. *p. a.* v. V. 1. तुंबडी लावणारा.

CUPPING, *n.* v. V.1. तुंबडी लावणें *n.* तुंबडी काढणें *n.* &c.

Blisters raised by c. मधा *f. pl.*

Incisions previously to c. फासण्या *f. pl.* v. मार, टाक.

CUPPING GLASS, *n. cupping instrument.* रोंमें *or* रोंबें *n.* तुंबडी *f.*

बेंतस *or* बेंतूस*n*. शिंग*n*.

CUPREOUS. See COPPERY.

CUR, *n. worthless dog.* कुतरडें*n*.

2 fig. *a snarling fellow.* कडूवृंदावन*n*.

CURABLE, *a.* v. V. 1. 2. बराकरण्या-होण्या सारखा, उपायसाध्य, साध्य, चिकित्साधीन, चिकित्सावश, चिकित्सनीय, चिकित्स्य, उपायाधीन, उपायवश.

CURATE, *n.* पाद्रीचा हस्तक*m*.

CURATIVE, *a.* v. V. 1. 2. रोग बरा करणारा, रोगनिवारक-&c.

CURATOR. See KEEPER, GUARDIAN.

CURB, *n.* (of a bridle). कडी *f.* जेरकडी *f.*

2 fig. *check, control,* v. RESTRAINT. आवर*m*. आवरण*n*.दाब*m*. आळा*m*. बंधन*n*. आडकाठी *f.* आटणी *f.*

3 (round a well,) वरंडी *or* बरांडी *f.*

To CURB, *v. a. check,* v. To RESTRAIN. आवरणें, दाबणें, लगामीं धरणें-ठेवणें,दाबांत-आळयांत-आळयाबांध्यांत-&c.ठेवणें-राखणें.

CURB-CHAIN, *n.* जेरकडी *f.*

CURB-STONE, *n.* अटीचादगड *m.* ? पाटधरा *m.* [आटोप*m*.

CURBING, *n.* v. V.—*act.* आवरणें *n.* &c. आवर *m.* आवरण *n.*

CURBY, *n. dried stalks of holcus sorghum.* कडबा *m.*

Chewed and trampled c. stalks. चोंथा *m.*

CURD, CURDS, *n. coagulated part of milk.* दहीं *n.* दधि *n.*

C. conglobated by churning. मठा *or* मठ्ठा *m.*

Nodule of c. कवडी *or* दह्याचीकवडी *f.* डिखळ *or* डिखूळ *n.* डिखळी *f.* डिखोळी *f.*

Rivers of c. and whey. दधिकुल्या *f. pl.*

Vessel to hold c. and whey. दहीहंडी *or* दहेंडी *or* दह्यांडी *f.* दधिभांड *n.*

To CURD, *To* CURDLE, *v. n.* जमणें, गोठणें, विरजणें, घट होणें, दहीं *n.* होणें *g. of s.*

To CURDLE, *v. a.* जमवणें, विरजणें, घट करणें.

CURE, CURING, *n.* v. V. 1.—*act.* बरा करणें*n.* आरोग्य देणें*n.*&c. रोगमोचन*n.*रोगनिरसन*n.*रोगनिरास*m.*रोगनिवारण*n.*&c.—*state* निरोगीपणा *m.* रोगमुक्तता *f.* रोगमुक्ति *f.*

2 बराकरणें *n.* &c. निवारण *n.* &c. See the Verb. उपाय *m.*

I. *remedy, restorative.* उपाय *m.*

To CURE, *v. a. heal.*—a patient. बरा-निरोगी-चांगला-स्वस्थ-निरामय-शांतरोग-रोगमुक्त-&c. करणें, आरोग्य *n.*-शरीरसंपत्ति *f.*देणें.

2 *remove, heal*—a disease. बरा करणें, दूर करणें, घालवणें, निवारण *n.*-परिहार *m.*-निरसन *n.*-निरास *m.*-शांति *f.*-&c. करणें *g. of o.* उपाय *m.* करणें *g. of o.*

3 See To REMEDY.

4 *preserve with salt, &c.* साराबणें, मिठांत-मिठानें मळणें, मीठ *n.* घालणें, संधित करणें.

CURED, *p.* v. V. 1. 2. बरा केलेला, &c. मुक्तरोग, निवृत्तरोग, नष्टरोग, गतरोग, विगतरोग.

To be c. बरा होणें.

CURELESS, *a.* असाध्य, अचिकित्सनीय, उपायहीन, उपायशून्य.

CURER, *n.* CURATIVE, *a.* v. V. 1. 2. बरा करणारा, रोग हर-हर्त्ता-हारक-हारी, रोगापह, रोगांतक, रोगघ्न, आरोग्य कारक-कारी-दायक-&c.

CURIOSITY, CURIOUSNESS, *n.* v. A. 1. शोधकपणा *m.* चौकसपणा *m.* शोधकबुद्धि *f.* शोधकत्व *n.* जिज्ञासा *f.* बुभुत्सा *f.* हवस *or* हौस *f.* अपूर्वदर्शनोत्सुकता *f.* श्रवणदर्शनोत्सुकता *f.* अन्वेषणासक्ति *f.* गवेषणतत्परता*f.*

Idle c. उठाठेव *f.*

I. *a c. curious thing.* चमत्कारिक वस्तु *f.*करामत *f.* बूट *m.* कौतुक *n.* टूम *f.*

CURIOUS, *a. inquisitive, prying.* शोधक, सर्वशोधी, बहुशोधी, मार्मिक, जिज्ञासु, बुभुत्सु, अपूर्वदर्शनोत्सुक, श्रवणदर्शनोत्सुक, गवेषणासक्त, अन्वेषणासक्त, चौकस, चौकसदार, हवसदार *or* हौसदार, हवसी, तलाशी, हुंग्या, कानवशा.

2 *novel, &c.* v. STRANGE. विलक्षण, कौतुकाचा, नवलाचा.

3 *wrought with art.* कलाकुसरीचा, कलाचातुर्याचा, करामतीचा, कलाकौशल्याचा, कारागिरीचा, हुनराचा, हुनरबाजीचा.

CURIOUSLY, *adv. with nice inspection,* v. A. 1. बारीकदृष्टीनें, चाकसपणानें, शोधकबुद्धीनें.

2 चमत्कारिक रीतीनें, तऱ्हे वाईक रीतीनें.

3 करामतीनें, कलाकुसरीनें.

CURL, *n.* (of hair). केसांचें वेंटाळें *n.* कुरळ केशांचा झुबका *m.* झुलूप *n.* कुरळ *f.* कुरल *or* कुरुल *m.* अलक *m.*

To CURL, *v. a.* (the hair). वेंटाळें *n.* घालणें, पेंच *m.* देणें.

2 *twist, bend over, crisp.* कुरळ करणें, पेंचदार करणें, मुरडणें, मुरटा करणें, वळवणें, मुरड *f.* घालणें, वेंट *or* वेंठ *m.* देणें.

To CURL, *v. n. bend into ringlets.* वेंटाळणें, कुरळ होणें.

2 *rise in a winding current.*लहरी *f.pl.*-लाटा *f.pl.* घेतचालणें.

CURLED, *p.* CURLY,*a.* v. V. कुरल *or* कुरुल *pop.* कुरळ *or* कुरूळ. मुधाळ *or* मुध्याळ *or* मुद्याळ.

CURLEW, *n.* एक पक्षी आहे.

CURMUDGEON. See MISER.

CURRANT, *n.* एक लहान फळ आहे.

2 एक लहान जातीचें वाळववलेलें द्राक्ष आहे.

CURRENCY, *n.* v. A. 1. चाल *f.* चलन *n.*

Cessation or depreciation of c. वाळ *f.* गैरचलन *n.*

2 परिपाठ *m.* पाठ *m.* प्रघात *m.* प्रचार *m.*प्रवृत्ति *f.* प्रसिद्धि *f.* रूढि *f.* वृत्ति *f.*लोकप्रसिद्धि *f.*लोकप्रख्याति *f.*लोकविश्रुति *f.* रिवाज *or* रेवाज*m*.

To bring into c. or vogue. जारींत आणणें.

4 रूढि *f.*

I. *a c. particular coin.* नाणें *n.*

CURRENT, *a.*—as money. चलनी, चालता.

Not c. गैरचलनी.

2 *prevailing popularly, flowing.* चालता, चालू, प्रसिद्ध, लौकिक, लोकप्रसिद्ध, लोकप्रख्यात, जारी, लोकप्रचारांतला, लोकव्यवहारांतला, लोकपरिपाठांतला, लोकरूढींतला, वर्त्तमान, व्यावहारिक, लोकविश्रुत. [वर्त्तमान.

3—as the year, month, &c. *running.* चालता, मजकूर,

4—a word, &c. रूढ, रूढींतला.

CURRENT, *n. flow, course,* lit. fig. v. STREAM. ओघ *m.* प्रवाह *m.* धार *f.* ओत *m.*

2 *rivulet, &c.* v. STREAM. ओढ *m.*

CURRENTLY, *adv.* v. A. 2. लोकांत, चौघांत, चौघांच्या तोंडांत.

CURRICLE, *n.* गाडीचा एक भेद आहे.

CURRICULUM, *n.* अध्ययनक्रम *m.* शिक्षणक्रम *m.*

CURRIER, *n.* v. V. चांभार *or* चाम्हार, चर्मक, चर्मकार.

Rubber of a c. इंगा *m.* रांपा *m.* रांपी *f.*

CURRISH, *a. like a cur, &c.* कुतऱ्यासारखा, कुत्रें तोंडीं बांधलेला.

To CURRY, *v. a. dress leather.* कमावणें *or* कामावणें, रांपवणें, ओजवणें.

2 (a horse). खरारा *m.*-चाकरी *f.* करणें *g. of o.* खाजवणें.

3 (favor). See To FLATTER, To FAWN.

CURRY, *n.*—the dish. कढी *f.* But कढी is different from the "curry" Europeans make. That is better rendered by अंबटी *or* आमटी *f.* A kind of meat curry is बरबट *n.*

CURRY-COMB, *n.* खरारा *m.*

CURRYING, *n.* v. V. 1.—*act.* कमावणें *n.* &c. कमावणी *f.*

To CURSE, *v. a. execrate.* शापणें, शाप *m.*-अभिशाप *m.* देणें, अभिशापणें, अभिशापन *n.*-शपन *n.* करणें, अनिष्टचिंतन *n.*-अकल्याणचिंतन *n.* करणें, बोटें *n. pl.* मोडणें, तळतळाट *m.*-हृपाप *m.* देणें.

C. it ! burn it ! blast it ! foul befal it ! ruin seize it ! &c. जळो, बत्ती लागली, आग लागली *with* ला *or* स, मटपडो, बत्तीलागो, नांवजळो, नांवासहूळदलागो *g. of o.* जरजाऊ *with* वरून, निग्राहूस्ते भूयान्.

2 See To PLAGUE.

CURSE, *n.* शाप *m.* दातांचेंविष *n.* अभिशाप *m.* तळतळाट *m.* हृपाप *m.*

Delivered from a c. शापमुक्त, विशाप.

Effect of a c. शापगुण *m.* द्रोह *m.*

To deliver or free from a c. शापोद्धार *m.*-शापमुक्ति *f.* करणें, उच्छाप *m. pop.* उःशाप *or* उश्राप *or* उश्शाप *m.* देणें.

To take effect,—a c. दांत *m. pl.* बठणें *with* वर *of o.* बत्तिशी *f.* बठणें *with* वर *of o.*

2 See PLAGUE.

CURSED, CURST, *p.* v. V. शापलेला, &c. शपित, शप्त, अभिशप्त, शापित, शापग्रस्त, शापदग्ध.

I. *execrable, detestable,* v. HATEFUL. शापार्ह, शाप्य, अतिद्वेष्य, अतिद्वेषयोग्य, अतिद्वेषार्ह, अतिनिंद्य, कुत्सनीय.

CURSING, *n.* v. V.—*act.* शाप देणें *n.* &c. शपन *n.* अभिशापन *n.* अनिष्टचिंतन *n.* गालिप्रदान *n.* दांतकसळ *or*-कसाळ *or*-किसाळी *f.* वाचिकहिंसा *f.*

CURSORILY, *adv.* v. A. सरासरी, वरचेवर, वरवर, उपराउपर, जलदीनें, यथाकथंचित्.

CURSORINESS, *n.* v. A. सरासरीपणा *m.* वरवरपणा *m.* उपराउपरपणा *m.*

CURSORY, *a. hasty, superficial.* सरासरीचा, वरवरचा, उपराउपरचा, जलदीचा, उपेक्षाबुद्धीचा.

CURT. See SHORT.

To CURTAIL, *v. a. cut, abridge, shorten.* उणा-कमी-न्यून-&c. करणें, छाटणें, कापणें, संक्षेप *m.* करणें *g. of o.*

CURTAIL-DOG, *n.* लांडाकुत्रा *m.* [रस्करिणी *f.*

CURTAIN, *n.* पडदा *m.* प्रच्छादनपट *m.* जवनिका *f.* प्रतिसीरा *f.* ति-

Behind the c. पडद्या आड, पडद्याच्या पलीकडे, पडद्याचे आंत.

Mosquito c. मच्छरदानी *f.*

String passing through the rings of a c. कडसणी *f.*

CURTAIN-LECTURE, *n.* रात्रीचे एकांतीं असलां भ्रताराला बायकोनें केलेली कानझाडणी *f.* कांतेचा उपदेश *m.*

CURTSY, *n. courtesy.* स्त्रीचें नमन *n.*

CURVATURE. *n.* v. BEND. बांक *or* बाक *n. m.* बांकणें *n.* वळण *n.*

CURVE, *n.*—in geometry &c. वक्ररेषा *f.* वक्ररेषाकृति *f.* धनुर्मार्ग *m.* भुज *m.*

To CURVE. See To BEND.

CURVE, CURVED, *a.* v. CROOKED. बांकडा, तेढा, वक्र, बांकाचा, बांकाचा, बांकदार.

To CURVET, *v. n.*—a horse. ठिकणें, फांदणें, नाचणें, कुदणें, उडणें.

CURVET, *n.* v. V. ठिकणें *n.* उडी *f.* लंघन *n.* उड्डान *n.*

CURVILINEAR, *a. consisting of curved lines.* वक्ररेषांचा, वक्ररेखाघटित-निर्मित, वक्ररेखारूप. [गाशा *m.*

CUSHION, *n. stuffed case to sit on.* गादी *f.* गदेला *m.* लेपडी *f.*

Small circular c. or pad. गिरदा *m.* गिरदी *f.*

Stuffed with cotton—a c. रुगरदा *or* रुगर्दा.

2—to lean against. तिवाशा *m. dim.* तिवाशी *f.* तक्या *m.* लोड *m. n.*

CUSP, *n. horn*—of the moon, &c. शृंग *n.* विषाण *n.* [सूच्यग्र.

CUSPIDATE, CUSPIDATED, *a. having a sharp end.* अणकुचीचा,

CUSTARD, *n.* राबडी *f.* बासुंदी *or* बासोंदी *f.*

CUSTARD-APPLE, *n. the tree.* सीताफल *n. pop.* शिताफळ *or* शिताफळी *f.* लवनी *f.*

2—the *fruit.* सीताफल *pop.* शिताफळ *n.* आंत *n.* मुक्ताफल *n.*

A square or division of a c. खवल *n.*

CUSTODIAL, *a.* रखवालीचा, रखवालीविषयींचा.

CUSTODIAN, *n.* v. GUARDIAN. रखवालदार, राखणदार.

CUSTODY, *n. care, keeping,* v. CHARGE. रखवाली *f.* राखण *f.* दिम्मत *f.* निसबत *f.*

2 *imprisonment.* कैद *f.* बंदी *f.* बंद *m.*

CUSTOM, *n. fashion, manner, practice, usage.* चाल *f.* दस्तूर *m.* रीति *pop.* रीत *f.* मार्ग *m.* पंथ *or* पथ *m.* शिरिस्ता *or* शिरस्ता *m.* संप्रदाय *m.* पद्धति *pop.* पद्धत *f.* परिपाठ *m.* पाठ *m.* धारा *m.* धारापेंडोळा *m.* धारापेंडोळें *n.* वहिवाट *f.* भांत *f.* रिवाज *or* रेवाज *m.* मामूल *m.* शेरा *m.* बळवटा *m.* रहाटी *f.* रहा *f.* रहाळी *f.* रवेस *f.* प्रघात *m.* प्रचार *m.* प्रथा *f.* दंडक *m.* मोळा *m.* आचार *m.* आचरण *n.* व्यवहार *m.* चर्या *f.* अनुसरण *n.* अनुसार *m.*

According to c. चालीप्रमाणें, यथापद्धति-संप्रदाय-रीति-&c.

Ancient. c. वृद्धाचार *m.* पूर्वपाठ *m.* वृद्धपरंपरा *f.*

Customs and manners,—compreh. *or* collect. रीतभात *f. or* रितीभाती *f. pl.* आचार विचार *m.*

C. and course of the high and honorable. शिष्टाचार *m.*

Family c. कुलाचार *m.* कुलधर्म *m.*

General c. शाईशिरस्ता *m.* पांढरशिरस्ता *m.* जनसंप्रदाय *m.* जनशिरिस्ता *m.* लोकरीति *f.*

National or local c. देशाचार *m.* देशरीति *f.*

Popular c. लोकाचार *m.*

Right or good c. सदाचार *m.* शिष्टसंप्रदाय *m.* [रीत *f.*

2 *a c. a practice, an usage.* संप्रदाय *m.* चाल *f.* रीति *pop.*

A fixed and firm c. दगडावरची रेघ *f.*

Accordiug to the c. चालीबजा.

3 *habit, wont.* चाल *f.* सराव *m.* अभ्यास *m.* रहाटी *f.* रीति *pop.* रीत *f.* वहिवाट *f.* परिपाठ *m.* बळवटा *m.* रफूत *m.* राबता *m.* राब *m.*

4 *practice of dealing with.* गिऱ्हाइकी *f.*

To have increasing c. दुकान *n.* वाढणें *g. of s.*

5 *perquisite upon purchases.* दस्तुरी *f.*

6 *tax on goods.* जकात *f.* शुल्क *n.*

Farmer of customs. जकातदार. [*n.* सायर *n.*

CUSTOM-BOX, C.-BOOTH, C.-STAND; &c. *n.* जकातनाकें, *n.* नाकें

CUSTOM-HOUSE, *n.* मांडवी *f.*

Custom-officer, *n.* जकात्या. Some particular *officers of the customs* are पतक्या, डांगी *or* डांग्या, धुरू, पांड्या, पाणसरा.

Customable. See Customary.

Customarily, *adv.* v. Commonly. बहुतकरून, प्रायः, प्रायशः, सामान्यतः.

Customariness, *n.* v. A. 1. रूढि *f.* प्रसिद्धि *f.* लोकप्रसिद्धि *f.* परिपाठ *m.* प्रघात *m.* प्रचार *m.* लौकिकपणा *m.* प्रायिकता *f.*
2 परिपाठ *m.* वहिवाट *f.* राब *m.*
I. See Frequency. [*usage.*

Customary, *a. that is according to custom or established* चालीचा, रीतीचा, मार्गाचा, रुईचा, &c. लोकसिद्ध, लौकिक, लोकाचाराचा, जनाचाराचा, लोकप्रचारांतला, लोकपद्धतीचा, लोकरूढींतला, &c. शिरस्तेबाईक, शिरस्तेमाफक, दस्तुरमाफक, &c. मामूल, यथापद्धति, यथासंप्रदाय, संप्रदायारूढ, संप्रदायसिद्ध, संप्रदायानुसार, सांप्रदायिक, व्यावहारिक *pop.* व्यवहारिक, प्रायिक, यौगिक.
2 *habitual.* नित्यपाठांतला, पाठांतला, परिपाठाचा *or* परिपाठांतला, सरावाचा, सवईचा, सवईंतला, अभ्यासांतला, राबत्यांतला, राबत्याचा, वहिवाटीचा, &c.

Customer, *n. constant dealer with.* घेतादेता *or* देताघेता, गिऱ्हाईक, ग्राहक, खरीददार, यजमान.

To **Cut**, *v. a.* कापणें, कातरणें, छेदणें, त्रोटणें.
2 (pay, wages), *clip, reduce.* कापणें, छाटणें, तोडणें.
3 *hew, cut off, &c.* तोडणें, खांडणें, छाटणें, काटणें.
4—as speech, &c. *bite, sting.* वेधणें, झोंबणें, लागणें.
To c. to the quick. जिव्हाळीं लागणें.
5 (cards) काटणें, तरासणें, तरास *m.*-तरासणी *f.* करणें.
Turn to c. काटणी *f.* तरास *m.* तरासणी *f.*
Cutting and dealing. काटणी वाटणी *f.*
6 *intersect.* छेदणें.
7 off; away from. कापून काढणें-घेणें, काटणें, अवच्छेद *m.*-उच्छेद *m.*-उत्कर्त्तन *n.*-निकृंतन *n.*-निकृति *f.* करणें, अवकर्त्तन *n.* करणें.
8 off; *render extinct.* उच्छेदणें *or* उच्छेद *m.* करणें (esp. in comp. as कुलोच्छेद-वंशोच्छेद-धर्मोच्छेद-वृत्त्युच्छेद करणें), निपात *pop.* निःपात*m.*-निर्वंश *m.*-निर्मूलन *n.*-निर्दलन *n.*-वंशक्षय *m.*-&c. करणें *g. of o.*
9 out; *shape, form.* बेतणें, बेतून कापणें-काढणें, आंकून कापणें, बेतणी *f.* करणें.
10 short; *break off,* (a matter). तुकडा *m.*-तनखा *m.*-तटका *m.* तोडणें *or* तोडून टाकणें, खुटवणें, कांडका *m.* पाडणें, मध्येंच बंद करणें.
11 up; to pieces; v. To Kill. काटणें (*and* कटणें To be cut up), कत्तल *f.*-कट्टा *m.*-काटाकाटी *f.*-निकंदन *n.*-निकृंतन *n.* करणें, खस्त मारून टाकणें, (*and* मारून खस्त होणें *To be* cut up), सांकटणें. [करणें.
12 (an acquaintance) डावलणें, डावलूनजाणें, नपाहिलेंसें
13 interfere as a horse. नेबर *m. n.* लागणें *g. of s.*

To **Cut**, *v. n.*—teeth or a tooth. फुटणें.

Cut, *p.* v. V. A. 1. कापलेला, &c. कापींव, छेदित, छिन्न, अवछिन्न, त्रुटित, त्रोटित, कर्त्तित.
I. out; *suited,* v. Fit. लायक.

Cut, *n.* घाव *m.* घाय *m.* वार *m.* चोट *f.* [डौल *m.*
2 *shape, make, cast,* v. Form. बेत *m.* तोड *f.* मोड *f.* घाट *m.*
Of the c. of. बेताचा, तोडीचा.
3 *stripe,* v. Lash. फटका *m.*
4 *picture.* छापीलचित्र *n.* छापीलतस्वीर *f.*
5 *short road.* जवळची वाट *f.*-रस्ता *m.*-&c.

Cut-purse, Cut-pocket, *n.* कातऱ्या चोर, उचक्या, उचल्या, भामट्या.

Cut-throat, *n.* v. Brute. मान-गळा कापणारा.

Cutaneous, *a. relating to the skin.* कातडीचा, त्वचेचा, त्वाच, त्वक्संबंधी, चर्मसंबंधी, चार्मिक.
C. disorder. त्वग्रोग *m.* चर्मदूषिका *f.* [त्वक् *f.*

Cuticle, *n. scarf-skin,* v. Skin. बाहेरील पातळ कातडी *f.* बाह्य-
2 (of plants) बाहेरील पातळ साल *f.*
3 *pellicle,* v. Film. तरंग *m.* तवंग *m.*

Cuticular, *a.* v. N. बाहेरील कातडीचा-सालीचा.

Cutis, *n.* अंतर्साल *f.* आंतरसाल *f.*

Cutlas, *n.* v. Sword. नेगा *m.*

Cutler, *n.* कारजकर, लोहार, छुरिकाकार.

Cutlery, *n.* तरवारी सुऱ्या वगैरे सामान *n.*

Cutter, *n.* v. V. 1. कापणारा.
I. होडीचा एक भेद आहे.

Cutting, *p. a.* v. V. A. 4. अणखर, मर्मी, वेधक, तिखट, जिव्हाळीं लागणारा, धोंडेफोड.

Cutting, *n.* v. V. A. 1.—*act.* कापणें *n.* &c. छेद *m.* छेदन *n.* कर्त्तन *n.* कृंतन *n.* अवछेद *m.* त्रोटन *n.*
C. and clipping. lit. & fig. छाटाछाट *f. m.*
Cost of c. कापणावळ *f.*
I. cuttings; *chips, shreds, clippings.* काटकूट *f.* छाट *m.* छाटछूट *m. f.* छाटींव *n.* कातरा *m.*
II. डोंगर पोखरून केलेला रस्ता *m.*

Cuttle-fish, *n.* म्हाकूल *m. n.*

Cuttle-fish-bone, *n.* समुद्रमाणकी *f.* समुद्रकफ *m.* समुद्रफेन *m.* समुद्रफेस *m.* सिंधुकफ *m.* सुफेन *m.* These words are used also for the fish.

Cycle, *n. round of time.* कालचक्र *n.* चक्र *n.* संवत्सरचक्र *n.* संवत्सराची रहाटी *f.*
Year of the c. of sixty. संवत्सर *m.* These are १ प्रभव, २ विभव, ३ शुक्ल, ४ प्रमोद, ५ प्रजापति, ६ अंगिरा, ७ श्रीमुख, ८ भाव, ९ युवा, १० धाता, ११ ईश्वर, १२ बहुधान्य, १३ प्रमाथी, १४ विक्रम, १५ वृष, १६ चित्रभानु, १७ सुभानु, १८ तारण, १९ पार्थिव, २० व्यय, २१ सर्वजित्, २२ सर्वधारी, २३ विरोधी, २४ विकृति, २५ खर, २६ नंदन, २७ विजय, २८ जय, २९ मन्मथ, ३० दुर्मुखी, ३१ हेमलंबी, ३२ विलंबी, ३३ विकारी, ३४ शार्वरी, ३५ प्लव, ३६ शुभकृत्, ३७ शोभकृत्, ३८ क्रोधी, ३९ विश्वावसु, ४० पराभव, ४१ प्लवंग, ४२ कीलक, ४३ सौम्य, ४४ साधारण, ४५ विरोधकृत्, ४६ परिधावी, ४७ प्रमाथी, ४८ आनंद, ४९ राक्षस, ५० नल, ५१ पिंगल, ५२ कालयुक्त, ५३ सिद्धार्थी, ५४ रौद्र, ५५ दुर्मति, ५६ दुंदुभि, ५७ रुधिरोद्गारी, ५८ रक्ताक्षी, ५९ क्रोधन, ६० क्षय.

Cyclops, *n.* भाललोचन, भालदृक्.

Cyclopœdia, *n. circle of the sciences.* विद्यामाला *f.* विद्यावलि *f.* यावत् विद्यासंग्रह *m.*
2 सर्व विद्यांच्या संग्रहाचें पुस्तक *n.*

Cygnet, *n.* हंसशावक *m.* बालहंस *m.*

CYLINDER, *n.* लंबवर्तुल *n.* गोल *m.*

CYLINDRIC, CYLINDRICAL, *a.* लंबवर्तुलाकार, वर्तुलस्तंभाकार, दीर्घवर्तुलाकार, गोलदार, गोल, वरवंट्याचे आकाराचा.

CYMBAL, *n.* झांज *or* झ *f. dim.* झांझरी *f.* ताल *pop.* ताळ *or* टाळ *m.* कांसाळ *f.* झल्लरी *f.* झंपा *m. f.* [टाळघाई *f.*

Hurried or animated clashing of cymbals. टाळघोळ *m.*

Tinkling c. *empty professions.* घणघणघंटा *f.*

CYMBAL-PLAYER, *n.* टाळधरी *or* ऱ्या, टाळकरी, झांजकरी, झांज्या, —in contempt. टाळकुट्या, झांजकुट्या, टाळघाशा.

CYNIC, CYNICAL, *a. sour, misanthropic.* तुसडा, तिरसट, खवना, नसनसखवडा, माणुसघाण्या.

CYNIC, *n.* कडूवृंदावन *n.* कडूकंबडळ *n.* टेंभुरणीचा कोळसा *m.*

CYPHER. See CIPHER.

CYPRESS-TREE, *n.* सरू *or* सुरू *m.*

One ready alike to bear c. or myrtle. आंब्याचें डाहळें*n.* आम्रपल्लव *m.* [रूदार.

Tall or straight as a c. सरूचा, सरूदार *or* सुरूचा, सु-

D.

D softly sounded is represented by द, and when aspirated by ध ; as harshly sounded it is represented by ड, and when aspirated by ढ.

To DAB, *v. a. strike gently with the hand.* थापटणें, थापणें, थोपटणें.

2 *cast (something soft) against.* थापणें.

3 up ; on ; &c. टिपणें.

DAB, *n. soft blow.* थाप *f.* बदका *or* भदका *m.* कोमलाघात *m.*

2 *soft lump.* ढबक *n.* ढबका *m.* लादा *m.* लगदा *m.* लपका *m.*

3 *mass dabbed.* बदका *or* भदका *m.* रपका *m.* लपका *or* लबका *m.*

4 *expert fellow.* See DABSTER.

To DABBLE, *v. n. play in water or mud.* डुबणें *or* डुंबणें, डुबकणें, बुडकणें, पंकक्रीडा *f.* करणें, राड *f.* खेळणें, ताबडणें.

2 fig. *dip into lightly, &c.* डुबणें, डुबकणें, बुचकळणें *or* बुचकुळणें, ओरखडणें.

DABBLER, *n.* v. V. 2. डुबणारा, तडीचा-कडेचा पोहणारा, टाणाटोण्या, ओरखडलेला.

DABSTER, *n.* v. CLEVER. फरडा, वस्ताद, पट्टाईत, जाहंबाज*or* द.

DACE, *n.* मत्स्याचा भेद आहे.

DACTYL, *n.* तीन अक्षरांचा एक गण आहे.

DACTYLOLOGY, *n. art of talking with the fingers.* करपल्लवी भाषा *f.* करपल्लवी *f.*

DAD, DADDY, *n.* v. FATHER. बा *m.* बाबा *m.* तात *m.*

DAFFODIL, *n.* एक फूल आहे.

DAFT, v. MAD. वेडगळ, वेडसर.

DAGGER, *n.* Some of the common kinds are कटार *f.* जंबा *or* जंब्या*m.* संजीर*m.* पालकोयती*f.* पेशकबज*n.* बाक*f.* बिचवा*m.* माडू *m.* सुरा*m.* [रीवर-&c. येणें.

To be at dagger's drawing. कटारीवर-हातघाईवर-मारामा-

To plunge a. d. *fig. to reproach.* कटार *f* लावणें.

To DAGGLE, *v. n.* लिडबिडणें, लडबडणें.

To DAGGLE, *v. a. trail in mud, &c.* लिडबिडविणें, लडबडविणें.

DAILY, *a.* रोजचा, दिवसाचा, दिवसादिवसाचा, प्रतिदिवसाचा, नित्य, नित्याचा, नित्यांतला, दैनंदिन, आन्हिक, प्रात्यहिक, दिवातन.

D. allowance. रोजी *f.*

D. bread. नित्यान्न*n.*

D. duties, business, or work. नित्यकर्म*n.* नित्यकृत्य*n.* आन्हिकाचार*m.* आन्हिक*n.*

D. expenses (as of a family). रोजखर्च*m.* रोजी *f.*

DAILY, *a. adv.* रोज, रोजचेरोज, रोजरोज, दिसोड *or* दिसबड, दिवसानदिवस, प्रतिदिवशीं, रोजिना, रोज उठून, दररोज, नित्य, आला दिवस, अनुदिन, प्रत्यहीं.

DAINTILY, *adv.* v. A. 1. *deliciously.* गोड.

To fare d. रोजपक्वान्नें *n. pl.* खाणें, *and, with in.con.* खायालामिळणें.

2 *fastidiously.* चोखनळपणानें, &c. चारा चारांनीं *or* चारेंचारें, चाखत माखत, ओलें कोरडें पाहून, नाकाओंठावर.

DAINTINESS, *n.* v. A. 1. गोडी *f.* रुचिकपणा*m.* रुचि *f.* मिष्टता *f.* मजेदारी *f.*

2 चोखनळपणा*m.* चोखाळेपणा*m.* सोंगळपणा*m.* &c. मिजाज *f.* नाजूक जेवण*n.* नाजकाई *f.* खंत *f.* खोड *f.*

DAINTY, *n.* गोडघास*m.* सुग्रास*m.* मिष्टान्न*n.* स्वादून्न*n.* पक्वान्न*n.* भोजनविशेष*m.* पंचामृत*n.*

DAINTY, *a. nice, of exquisite taste,* v. DELICIOUS. गोड, रुचीक, रुचिकर, स्वादिष्ट, मिष्ट.

2 *dainty-mouthed, squeamish, fastidious, nice, delicate.* गोडघांशा, गोडखाउ, गोडखाया, गोडजिभ्या, चवनट, चोखनळ, चोखारी, चोकांदळ्या, चोखाळा, खोराकी, खोराक्या, कंटाळखोर, मिजाजखोर, खंतखोर, किळखोर, मिजाजी, खोडकर, चिकित्सखोर, जीभशिंदळ, जिभेचाशिंदळ, सोंगळ, खोड्याळ, नाजूक, स्वादुकार, तिटकारी, तिरस्कारी.

To be d. ओलेंकोरडें पाहणें, चव *f.* काढणें, चाखतमाखत *adv.* खाणें-जेवणें, नाका ओंठावर जेवणें.

To become d. तोंड*n.* माजणें *g. of s.*

3 See DELICATE.

DAIRY, *n.*—the business. दुपतें *or* दुभतें*n.*

2—the place. दुभत्याची खोली *f.*-घर*n.* गव्यगृह*n.*

DAIRY-MAID, *n.* दुभतेकरीण *f.*

DAIS, *n. raised floor, &c.* बडेलोकांचीगादी-कुरसी-&c. ठेवायाला उंचकेलेली जागा *f.* ओटा, *m.* मंच *m.*

DAISY, *n.* एक फूल आहे. [ण*n.* आड *f.*

DALE, *n.* v. VALLEY. दरा *m. dim.* दरी *f.* खोंडा*m.* खोरा*m.* लव-

Valleys & dales—compreh. दराखोरा*m.*

DALLIANCE, DALLYING, *n.* v. V. 1.—*act.* रमणें*n.* &c. कामचेष्टा *f.* इष्कबाजी *f.* विषयक्रीडा *f.* विषयविलास*m.* विलास*m.* कामकेलि *f.* रमणूक *f.* रमण*n.* हाव*m.pl.* हेला *f.*

2 गमणें*n.* &c. जोगवण *f.* जोगवणी *f.* अळमटळम*n. f.* घालघसर *f.* चेंगटाई *f.* हयगई *or* हैगई *f.* उपेक्षा *f.*

DALLIER, *n.* DALLYING, *p. a.* v. V. 1. रमणारा, &c. कामचेष्टा-&c. कर्ता.

2 गमणारा, &c. गमदसडा *or* दासडा *or* दासरा, घालघसऱ्या, चेंगट, उपेक्षक, भिणभिण्या.

To DALLY, *v. n. toy and wanton.* कामचेष्टा *f.*-इष्कबाजी *f.*-विषयक्रीडा *f.*-&c. करणें, रमणें.

2 *delay, idle, lose time*, v. To DAWDLE. ताणणें, गमणें, जोगावणें, खेळणें, गुरमळणें, गुटमळणें, गोंधळणें, वेळ *f.* लावणें, उपेक्षा *f.*-अळमटळम*n.*-घालघसर *f.*-&c. करणें.

DAM, *n.* v. MOTHER. आई *f.*

2 *mole, bank, embankment.* बांध *m. dim.* बांधोळी *f.* धरण*n.* बांधण*n.* बंधारा*m.* बंधारण*n.* ताल *f.* थोप *f.* पेंडबळ *or* पेंडवळा*m.* जलबंधक*m.* तुंग*m.* तुंब*n.* सेतु*m.* [धबंधारा *m.*

Dams, embankments, &c.—compreh. बांधबांधोळी *f.* बां-

D. to turn off. वळण *n.*

Field (for rice, &c.) formed by a d. बांधण *n.*

3 (as in a field, across a road, &c.) शेतबांधण *n.* मूळबांध *m.* ताल *f.*

To DAM, *v. a. confine by a dam.* बंधारा *m.*-बांध *m.*-&c. घालणें, बांधणें, बांध *m.*-&c. घालून तुंबवणें-थोपवणें.

DAMAGE, *n. damnum*, v. LOSS. नुकसान *n. f.* नुकसानी *f.* नह्राब *m.* नह्राबी *or* नाह्बी *f.* नाश *m.* अपाय *m.*

2 *harm, detriment, injury*, v. HURT. खराबी *f.* नुकसान *n. f.* नुकसानी *f.* ढक्का *or* धक्का *m.* हानि *f.* क्षति *f.*

3 damages; *reparation for injury.* नुकसान*n. f.* नुकसानी *f.* नुकसानीचा पैसा *m.*-ऐवज *m.*-&c. [बिघडणें.

To DAMAGE, *v. a.* v. To HURT. नासणें, बिनासणें *or* बिनसणें,

DAMAGEABLE, *a.* v. V. नासायाजोगा-&c. बिघडायाजोगा-&c. नाशवंत, विनाशी, नश्वर.

DAMAGED, *p.* v. V. नासलेला, &c. खराब केलेला-झालेला, नासका, जायबंदा, जायबंदी, नाशित, विनष्ट.

The d. and spoiled (goods, &c.)—compreh. *or* collect. खोटानाटा-नासका कुचका-वाईटसाईट(जिन्नस*m.*-माल*m.*&c.)

DAMASK, *n.* धुमास *n.*

DAME, *n. lady, mistress of a family.* बाई *f.* बाईसाहेब *f.* माईसाहेब *f.* ताई *f.* (Ex. ताई रास्तीचें घर.) [बाजी *f.*

2 *elderly woman.* बया *f.* बाई *f.* आई *f.* आऊ *or* अवा *or* अ-

DAMMER, *n. particular resinous exudation.* डामर*n.* यक्षधूप*m.*

To DAMN, *v. a. doom to hell.* नरकांत टाकणें-घालणें-बुडवणें, नरकदंडाह ठरवणें.

2 *cause the eternal punishment of.* नरकास-अधोगतीस-&c. नेणें-पाववणें, अधोगति *f.*-नरक *m.* करणें-देणें.

3 *censure, blame.* दोष *m.* ठेवणें- लावणें, नापसंत-सदोष-&c. करणें-ठरवणें. [कपात्र.

DAMNABLE, *a.* v. V. 1. 2. नरकांत टाकायाजोगा, नरकदंडार्ह, नर-

I. See DETESTABLE.

DAMNATION, *n.* v. V. 1. 2—*act.* नरकांत टाकणें *n.* &c.—*state.* दुर्गति *f.* अधोगति *f.* नरक *m.* नरकवास *m.* अध:पात *m.*

To DAMNIFY, &c. See To HURT, &c.

DAMP, *a.*—of things. ओलसर, ओलट, दमट, दमसर, दामट, दमकट, अंबटओला, चेंबट *or* चिंबटढाण, अर्धसुका, आंबसुका.

To get d. सादळणें, बादळणें, सरदणें, सरदावणें, थंडावणें, दमटणें, दमसरणें. [ओलीचा.

2—of the air, places, &c. सरद, दमसर, दमट, ओलाचा *or*

DAMP, *n. moist air.* सरदी *f.* सरदहवा *f.*

To cast a d. *to depress.* See To DAMP.

To DAMP, *v. a. moisten.* ओलवणें *or* ओलावणें, ओला-ओलसर-आर्द्र-&c. करणें.

2 *depress, chill, dullen, &c.* हिरमोड *m. f.*-उत्साहभंग *m.*-आशाभंग *m.*-निराशा *f.*-भंग*m.*-&c. करणें *g. of o.* पाय *m. pl.*-कमर *f.* मोडणें *g. of o.* बिरजण *n.*-पाणी *n.* घालणें *with* वर *of o.* मोडणें, खचवणें.

DAMPED, *p.* v. V. 1. ओलवलेला, ओला केलेला, &c.

2 हिरमोड केलेला, &c. हिरमुस, हीरमुशी, हिंवसलेला, भग्नोत्साह, भग्नाश.

To be d. हिरमुसणें,

DAMPER, *n.* DAMPING, *p. a.* v. V. 1. ओलावणारा, ओला करणारा, &c. [शाभंजक.

2 हिरमोड करणारा, मोडणारा, &c. मोड्या, उत्साहभंजक, आ-

I. *damping occurrence, &c.* मानमोडें *n.*

DAMPING, *n.* v. V. 1.—*act.* ओलवणें *n.* ओला करणें *n.* &c.

2—*act.* मोडणें *n.* पाणी घालणें *n.* &c. हिरमोड *f. m.* उत्साहभंजन *n.* आशाभंजन *n.* उत्साहभंग *m.* आशाभंग *m.*

DAMPISH, *a.* आंबटओला.

DAMPNESS, *n.* v. A. 1. ओलेपणा *m.* ओलसरपणा *m.* दमटपणा *m.* आंबसुकेपणा *m.* &c. ओल *f. n.* ओलसर *f.* ओलावा *m.* आर्द्रता *f.*

2 सरदी *f.* दमसरपणा *m.* &c.

To be affected by d. दमटणें. [*f.* मुग्धा *f.*

DAMSEL, *n. young woman.* तरुणीस्त्री *f.* तरुणी *f.* बाला *f.* युवती

Bevy of damsels. तरुणीगण *m.*

DAMSON, *n.* एक फळ आहे. [करणें.

To DANCE, *v. n.* नाचणें, नाच *m.*-नृत्य *n.*-नर्त्तन *n.*-नटन *n.*-&c.

To d. and skip about, v. To FRISK. नाचूंउडूं लागणें.

To d. attendance on. नादीं-भजनीं-भजनास-कच्छपीं-&c. लागणें *g. of o.* कासोटा *m.* धरणें *g. of o.*

To d. for joy. नागवा नाचणें, धोतर सोडून-टाकून-फेडून-&c. नाचणें, थैयथैय नाचणें.

To DANCE, *v. a.* नाचवणें. [नाट्य *n.*

DANCE, DANCING, *n.* v. V. N. नाच *m.* नृत्य *n.* नटन *n.* नर्त्तन*n.*

D. in a ring. मंडलनृत्य *n.* रासनृत्य *n.*

D. with gesticulation. तांडव *n.*

Lively and merry d. थैथैं थैथैय्या नाचणें *n.* तातकथय्या *m.* ताथय्या *m.* थैथैय्या *m.* थैथैय्याट *m.* झमझमाट *m.* छमछमाट *m.* छमाछमी *f.* [बडणें.

To lead a d. *make to tramp about.* नाच *m.* नाचवणें, भां-

DANCER, *n.* DANCING, *p. a.* v. V. N. नाचणारा, नर्त्तन-नृत्य-&c. कर्त्ता, नाचा, नटवा, नाटकी, नटनर्त्तक.

I. *disposed to dancing.* नाचरा.

DANCING-GIRL, *n.* कलावंतीण *or* कळवंतीण *f.* कंचनी *f.* नटी *f.* नर्त्तकी *f.* पात्रा *f.* वेश्या *f.* नायकीण *f.*

Attendant on a d. भडवा *m.* [*m.* चाळ *f.*

Bell on the toes of a d. घागरी *f.* घुंगरू *m. or* रूं *n.* घुंगूर

Gallant kept by a d. सोयरा *m.*

Girl bought and bred up as a d. (or actress). नाटकशाळा *or* नाटकसाळ *f.*

Male dressed and dancing as a female. नाचा पोऱ्या *m.* नाचा *m.* नारा *m.* पोऱ्या *m.* पोरगा *m.* राधा *f.* कोळीण *f.* घेरीण *f.*

Master or keeper of dancing girls. वेश्याचार्य *m.*

Musician attendant upon a d. साजिंदा *m.*—reproachfully. ढवा *m.*

Present made to a d. while dancing. मुजरा *m.*

Robe worn by a d. पेशवाज *m.* पिस्वाद *m.*

Dancing-master, *n.* नाचण्याचीतालीम देणारा, नाचण्याचावस्ताद, नृत्यशिक्षक.

Dancing-room, *n.* नाचण्याचा अड्डा *m.* नृत्यशाला *f.* नृत्यमंदिर*n.* नृत्यालय *m. n.*

Dandelion, *n.* एक फूल आहे.

Dandi-prat, *n. urchin.* चिटलिंग *m.* चिमखडा *m.* चिंपाटी *f.*

To **Dandle**, *v. a.* मांडीवर-हातावर नाचवणें, लालन *n.* करणें *g. of o.*
2 See To Fondle.

Dandruff, *n.* दारुणा *or* दारणा *m.*

Dandy, *n.* v. Fop. अकडबाज *c.* अयटबाज *c.* नटबाज *c.*

Dandyism, *n.* अकडबाजी *f.* अयटबाजी *f.* अयट *f.* नटबाजी *f.*

Danger, Dangerousness, *n. peril.* भय *n.* भयहेतु *m.* धोका *m.* जोखीम *f. n.* सत्रा *m.* मरण *n.* काल *m.*
2 (of life) v. Jeopardy. प्राणसंकट *n.* जिवासीं *or* प्राणासीं सापका *m. v.* पड, प्राणसंदेह *m.* प्राणांत *m.*

Dangerous, *a.* v. N. 1. भयाचा, धोक्याचा, जोखमाचा, सभय, जोखमी, सकंटक, दुस्तर, भयहेतुक.
2 प्राणसंकटाचा, प्राणसंदेहाचा, जिवावरचा, जिवावरला, प्राणघातक, प्राणघातकी, जिवासांड, प्राणांत (in comp. as प्राणांतबुद्धि d. counsel. प्राणांतव्यवहार a d. business).

To **Dangle**, *v. n. hang loosely.* ओळंबणें, ओळकंबणें *or* कुंबणें, लोंबकळणें, ओळंगणें, लटकणें, लटलटणें, झळंबणें *or* झोळंबणें, झोळकंबणें, झुलकणें, अलगणें, हिलगणें, हिलगडणें, ओळकंबा *m.*-ओंबकळा *m.*-झोळकंबा *m.*-&c. घेणें-खाणें.
2 fig. *hang about or after.* कासोटा*m.*-&c.धरणें *g.of o.* पाठ*f.* -दूम *f.* पुरवणें *g. of o.* नादीं-कच्छपीं-पाठीं लागणें *g. of o.*

Dangler, *n.* **Dangling**, *p. a.* v. V. 1. ओळंबणारा, ओळंबता, &c. झळम, अवलंबित, लुलित.
2 कासोटा धरणारा, दूमपुरव्या, नादीं लागणारा, &c. नादी, नाद्या, नादखोर.

Dangling, *n.* v. V.1.—*act.* ओळकंबणें*n.* &c. ओळकंबा *or* कुंबा*m.* झोळकंबा *or* कुंबा*m.*
2—*act.* कासोटा धरणें *n.* दूमपुरवणें*n.* नादीं लागणें*n.* &c.

Dank. See Damp.

Dapper, *a. short and brisk.* टसका, ठेंगणाटुसका, ठेंगणारेंगणा, अल्पता, सुबक, लुटलुटीत, सुटसुटीत,* खुडखुडीत *or* खुटखुटीत, अटकर, लहानखुरा.
A d. man. फटकडा*m.*

Dapperling, *n. dandiprat.* चिटलिंग*m.* चिमखडा*m.* चिंगाटी *f.*

Dapple, *a. variegated.* अबलक *or* ख, चित्रवर्णी, दुरंगी, पंचरंगी.

To **Dapple**, *v. a.* अबलक-&c. करणें.

To **Dare**, *v. a. defy, brave, challenge.* इरेस-ईर्षेस-इरश्रीस-अभिमानास-&c. घालणें, हटकून बोलावणें, हमातमानें बोलावणें, हमतम*m.* दाखवणें, नाकावर निंबू*n.* घासणें, नाकावर पाय*m.* देणें, नाकासचुना*m.* लावणें, तुच्छ करणें-मानणें.

To **Dare**, *v. n.* धमक *f.*-धैर्य*n.*-हिय्या*m.*-हिम्मत *f.*-&c. असणें *in. con. with g. of s.* अंगीं साहस*n.* असणें *g. of s.* धजणें, छाती *f.* करणें.

Dareful, Daring, *p. a.* v. V. N. *and* Bold. धीट, धडछातीचा, उद्दाम, उद्धट, उत्पाती, खंदा, बांका, बांकडा, साहसी, साहसिक, साहसबुद्धि, साहसबुद्धीचा, निर्वाणी, आगींत उडी घालणारा, हातावर शीर घेऊन असणारा, उरफाट्या काळजाचा, पाठीच्या काळजाचा.

Daring, *n. daringness, darefulness,* v. Boldness. धिटाई *f.* धारिष्ट*n.* धार्ष्ट्य*n.* साहस*n.*
2 *bold act.* साहसकर्म*n.* साहस*n.*

Daringly, *adv.* v. A. धिटाईनें, धीटपणानें, साहसबुद्धीनें.

Dark, *a.* अंधाराचा, अंधकारमय, अंधकारयुक्त, ओंधट, तामस, तमस्वी, निःप्रभ.
A d. night (i. e. without the moon). काळोखी रात्र *f.*
Pitch d. गुरूप *or* ब.
2 *not of vivid or showy color.* काळसर, काळवट, गेह्रा *or* गहिरा, मेचक.
3—the complexion. काळगेला, काळेला, काळासावळा, काळसर.
4 v. Ignorant. अज्ञानाचा, तामस, तमस्वी, अंधळा.
5 *not easily understood,* v. Obscure. दुर्बोध, दुर्ज्ञेय.
6 v. Gloomy. उदास, उदासपणाचा.

Dark, *n.* v. Darkness. अंधार*m.* काळोख*m.* मेचक*m. n.*
To go in the d. काळोखांतून-अंधारांतून-&c. जाणें-फिरणें.
2 v. Ignorance, अंधार*m.* अज्ञान*n.*

To **Darken**, *v. a. make dark.* अंधार*m.*-काळोख*m.* करणें-आणणें-पाडणें, अंधकारमय-युक्त-&c. करणें.
2 See To Obscure.
3 (the complexion) v. To Tan. काळवंडणें, काळेपणा आणणें.
4 *render ignorant.* अंधार *m.*-आंध्य *n.*-अज्ञान*n.*-&c. पाडणें, अंधकार युक्त करणें.

Darkly. See Obscurely.

Darkness, *n.* v. A. 1. अंधकार *pop.* अंधःकार*m.* अंधार*m.* काळोक*or* काळोख *m.* काळोखी *f.* काळोखें *n.* आंध्य*n.* तम *n.* तिमिर*n.*
Pitch d. Thick d. काळोखमेट*m.* गडद*n.* अंधारगडत*n.* घनांधकार*m.* अंधतमस*n.* भिन्नकाळोख*m.* भिन्नअंधकार*m.*
The quality or property of d. तमगुण*m.* तम*m. n.*
2 काळसरपणा*m.* &c.
3 काळेसावळेपणा *or* काळसावळेपणा*m.* काळगेलेपणा*m.*&c.
4 अंधार*m.* अंधकार*m.* आंध्य*n.* अज्ञान*n.*

Darksome, *a.* उण्या उजेडाचा, न्यूनप्रकाश, न्यूनप्रभ, अल्पप्रकाश.

Darling, *a. dear, beloved, favorite.* आवडीचा, आवडता, लाडका, लाडांतला, ममतेचा, प्रीतीचा, प्रीतींतला, लडिवाळ, प्रिय, प्यारा, जिवलग, जीवसा, प्राणसा, वल्लभ, बाल्ही, प्रीत, प्रेमास्पद, अभीष्ट, अभीप्सित, हृदयंगम, हृद्य, हृदिस्पृक्, दयित, अंतरंग.

Darling, *n. dear, jewel, pet, love.* जीवप्राण*m.* प्राण*m.* जिवींचा जिव्हाळा*m.* जिवडा*m.* कलिजा *or* जिवाचा ताईत*m.* गळ्याचा ताईत *m.* काळजाचाघड*m.* कंठमणि*m.* छावडें*n.* पुतळा*m.*आत्मलिंग*n.* प्रीतिपात्र*n.* देव्हारें*n.* दैवत*n.*
2—esp. as used in amatory phraseology by Lovers and Mistresses. खेळवणी *f.* पांखरूं *n.* पुतळी *f.* पियो *or* पिहू *m.* प्यारा *m.* पंछी *m.* पुतळा *m.*

To **Darn**, *v. a.* रफू *m. f.* करणें, तुणणें.

Darn, *n. the part darned.* रफू *f.m.*

Darned, *p.* v. V. रफू केलेला, तुणलेला, तुर्णीव.

Darnel, *n.* गवताचा एकभेद आहे.

Darner, *n.* v. V. रफू करणारा, &c. रफूकरी, रफूगर.

Darning, *n.* v. V.—*act.* तुणणें *n.* रफू *m.*
Price or cost of d. तुणणावळ *f.* तुणवाई *or* तुणाई *f.*

Dart, *n.* v. Spear. बरची *f.* भल्ल *m.dim.* भल्ली *f.* सांग *f.* शक्ति *f.*
Bearded d. प्रास *m.*

D. or javelin with a string attached. सैती *f.*

To DART, *v. a.* v. To THROW. फेंकणें, टाकणें, मारणें.

2 v. To EMIT. सोडणें, पाडणें.

To DART, *v. n.* See To BOLT, To SPRING.

To DASH, *v. a. strike against.* अदळणें, अपटणें, आफळणें, टाकणें, फेंकून टाकणें, सोबकणें.

2 *throw water in flashes.* सिंतोडणें, सिंतोडे *m. pl.* उडवणें, उडवणें, हुंडारणें.

3 in or to pieces. फोडणें, तुकडे तुकडे *m.pl.* करणें-उडवणें *g.ofo.*

4 out; *cancel &c.* v. To EFFACE. फांटा *m.* मारणें-देणें, खोडणें, रेघ *f.* मारणें.

5 *confound, disconcert,* v. To DEFEAT. लथडणें *or* लथाडणें, भंग *m.*-विघात *m.*-&c. करणें *g. of o.*

6 See To DISPIRIT, To SHAME. [बिघडवणें.

7 *mix with, adulterate.* भेळ *f.*-मिसळ *f.*-&c. घालणें-घालून

To DASH, *v. n. strike against.* अदळणें, अपटणें, धडकणें, धडकणें, धडक *f.* लागणें-बसणें *g. of s.*

2 *splash up, fly off, &c.*;—of water. उसळणें, हिसळणें *or* हेसळणें, हेलकावून सांडणें, डचडच-डचकन-&c. उडणें.

3 at, amongst, through, away, &c. उसळणें, उसळी *f.* मारणें-खाणें, अदळून पडणें, धसणें, धडकेसरसा-धडकून-झपाट्यानें-&c. जाणें-शिरणें.

To d. through thick and thin. धसून-उसळून जाणें, उसळी *f.* मारून जाणें.

4 down;—rain, fruits, &c. *fall violently.* कोसळणें, ढासळणें *or* धासळणें, सडसडणें.

DASH, DASHING, *n.* v. V. A.—*act.* अदळणें *n.* अपटणें *n.*

D. and banging about. अदळ अपट *f.*

Smart d. (of water, &c.) with the hand. आपका *m.v.* दे, टाक, मार.

v. V. N. 1.—*act.* अदळणें *n.* अपटणें *n.* धडक *f.* धडका *m.*

3 *and* RUSH. उसळणें *n.* उसळी *f.* मुसांडी *f.* सुरकांडी *f.*

I. *display, flash,* v. SHOW. टामटूम *or* टुमटाम *f.* टिमटीम *f.*

To cut a d. फड *m.* मारणें-संपादणें. *See under* FIGURE.

II.—*cast, smack.* छटा *m.* लकेरी *f.* झुणूक *f.* धुनक *f.* छब *f.*

To have a d. of. मारणें as हा रंग तांबडा मारतो *also* ह्या रंगांत तांबडेपणा *m.* मारतो.

III.(—)ह्या प्रकारची खुण *f.*

DASHING, *p. a.* v. V. N. 3. *precipitate, tearing, &c.* v. IMPETUOUS. धसक्या, धसकधक्या, धसकट्या, धसकनंदन, रगड्या, रगडमल्ल.

I. *cutting a dash,* v. FINE. टुमीचा, टुमदार, छानीचा, छानदार, अयटबाज, विलसित, बिराजमान, विराजित.

DASTARD, DASTARDLY, &c. See COWARD, &c.

DATA, *n.* v. GROUND. मुद्दा *m.* आश्रय *m.* गमक *n.*

DATE, *n.*—the tree. खजुरी *f.* खजूर *m.* खर्जूर *n.* खर्जूरी *f.*—the fruit. खजूर *m.* खर्जूर *m.*—the stone or seed. आंठोळ *f.* आंठोळी *f.*—wild d. tree. शिंद *f.* शिंदी *or* शिंधी *f.*

Dates plucked and dried whilst immature. खारीक *f.*

Lumped dates. पेंडखजूर *m.* Not lumped d. जावदी खजूर *m.*

Spirituous exudation from the wild date tree. शिंदी *f.*

2 (of letter, &c.). तारीख *f. day of the moon, considered as a* d. मिती *f.* चंद्र *m.*

Actual or true d. वाजबमिती *f.*

3 *time or period of.* काळ *m.* समय *m.* दिवस *m.* [ठेपणें.

To fix or appoint for a certain d. ठेपावणें—To be fixed

To go out of d. माजी -पडीं *adv.* पडणें, जुनावणें, लांबचाशिळा होणें.

4 v. DURATION कालमर्यादा *f.*

To DATE, *v. a* तारीख *f.*-मिती *f.* मांडणें-लिहणें-धरणें-मोजणें.

To DATE, *v. n.* See To BEGIN.

DATIVE, *n.* चतुर्थी *f.* संप्रदान *n.*

DATURA, *n. thorn apple.* धत्तूर *m.*

To DAUB, *v. a.* v. To SMEAR. लपणें, लिंपणें, लथडणें, लपटणें *or* लेपडणें, भरवणें.

DAUB, *n. bad picture.* वाईट चित्र *n.* कुचित्र *n.*

DAUGHTER, *n.* लेंक *or* लेंक *f.* मुलगी *f.* पुत्री *f.* पुत्रिका *f.* कन्या *f* चिरंजीवी *f.* अंगजा *f.* तनुजा *f.* आत्मजा *f.* तनया *f.* दुहिता *f.* नंदिनी *f.* धूव *f.* सूना *f.* सुता *f.*—allusively. धर्मसंतति *f.* धर्मसंतान *n.* जातीवस्त *f.* जायजणी *f.*—in endearment कन्यारत्न *n.*

D. in law. सून *f.* पुत्रजाया *f.* स्नुषा *f.* वहू *f.*

Son of d. दौहित्र *m.* कन्यापुत्र *m.*

DAUGHTERLINESS, *n.* कन्याधर्म *m.*

DAUGHTERLY, *a.* कन्याधर्मासक्त, कन्याधर्मतत्पर.

To DAUNT, *v. a.* v. To INTIMIDATE. भय *n.*-धाक *m.* दाखवणें-घालणें, भेडावणें, भेडसावणें, डरावणें, डरकावणें.

DAUNTLESS, *a.* v. BOLD. धीट, निर्भय, अकुतोभय.

DAUNTLESSLY, *adv.* v. A. निर्भयपणानें, छातीकरून.

DAUNTLESSNESS, *n* v. A. धिटाई *f* निर्भयपणा *m.* छाती *f.*

To DAWDLE, *v. n. trifle, idle, play, dally, work lazily or languidly.* गमणें, खेळणें, जोगवणें, बिरंगुळणें, रेंगणें, रेंगळणें, गुटमळणें, गुपटणें, गुरमळणें, टेंगाळणें, गोंधळणें, घोंटाळणें, वेळ *f.* लावणें, अळमटळम *f. n.* करणें-मांडणें, विरंगुळा *m.*-जोगवण *f.*-जोगवणी *f.*-चेंगटाई *f.*-हैगई *f.*-उपेक्षा *f.*-कंगुमंगु *n. f.*-कंगमंग *f.*-&c. करणें, माशा *f. pl.* मारीत बसणें.

To DAWDLE AWAY, *v. a.* (time, &c.). झुलवणें, खेळाखालीं दवडणें, गमावणें, घालवणें.

DAWDLE, *n.* DAWDLER, *n.* v. V. N. गमणारा, रेंगणारा, &c. गमरा, गम्या, गमदसडा *or* दासडा *or* दासरा, रिकामटवळा, चेंगट, मिणमिण्या, मळमळीत, रोंगा, उपेक्षक, दीर्घसूत्री—and as agreeing with *Snail, Slow coach, Poke, &c.* some terms are रेंग्या, दिरिंग्या, सावकाश्या, उशिऱ्या, वेळलाव्या, गोयाबा, चघळ, रेमेडोक्या, रड्या, अगट चिगट.

DAWDLING, *n.* v. V. N. गमणें *n.* खेळणें *n.* &c. जोगवण *f.* जोगवणी *f.* जोगवणूक *f.* अळमटळम *f n.* अळमटाळ *or* ळी *f.* आळाटाळी *f.* विरंगुळा *m.* चेंगटाई *f.* गमटम *f.* हैगई *f.* उपेक्षा *f.* आनाकानी *f.* [झडत.

DAWDLINGLY, *adv.* रेंगत, गमतरमत, रडतरडत *or* रडतखडत, रडत

DAWK, *n. post.* डांक *f.* टप्पाल *n.*

To DAWN, *v. n.*—the day. उजेडणें, फटफटणें, फटफटीत होणें, तांबडें *n.* फुटणें, तांबेसांज *f.* होणें, पहाट *f.*-&c. होणें.—brightly, glowingly, &c. दिशा *f. pl.* भणभणणें-भडकणें-फुलणें-फांकणें-उजळणें, धुनकणें *or* धुनुकणें.

2 fig. *begin to open &c.* उदय *m.* होणें *g. of s.* उदय *m.* पावणें.

DAWN, DAWNING, *n.* v. V. 1. पहाट *f.* अरुण *m.* अरुणोदय *m.* पूर्व-

सध्या *f.* दिनादि *m.* दिनमुख *n.* प्रत्यूष *m.* प्रभात *n.*
At the peep of d. उजेडतां,उजेडतांक्षणीं, दमसूट, पहांटपटीं.
Early d. पहानपट *f.* सुप्रभात *n.* उर्त्ते *n.* चिमणचिटकें *n.*
First glimmerings of d. चांचपड चांचपड *n.* चिपड चिपड *n.* झुंजरूक मुंजरूक *n.* झुंजूक मुंजूक *n.* झुंजूमुंजू *n.* धुंदूक *n.* धुंदूकधुंदूक *n.* धुंदूकमुंदूक *n.* झांजड झांजड *or* झांझर मांजर *n.* झावळझावळ *or* झावळमावळ *n.* भिबिरिटें *or* डें *n.* भिभिरकटें *n.*
Time of d. उजेडताकाळ *m.* प्रातःकाल *or* ळ *m.* प्रभात *n.* कोल्हेभूक *f.* कोल्हेहूक *f.* चिमणचिटकें *n.* कोंबडेरान *or* रात्र *f.* कोंबडे पहाट *f.* प्रातःसमय *m.* उषःकाल *m.*
2 fig. *rise, beginning.* उदय *m.*

DAY, *n.*—artificial, दिवस *m.* दिन *m.*
Advancing d. चढती बेळ *f.*
All the d. long दिवसभर, सारासुदीस, दिसोड *or* दिसबड.
Blind by d. दिवांध.
By d. and night. निशिदिनि, अहोरात्र *pop.* अहोरात्रीं.
Close of the d. दिनांत*m.* दिनमर्यादा *f.*
D. and night. रात्रंदिवस, अहोरात्र, अहर्निश *pop.* अहर्निशीं, अष्टोप्रहर *pop.* आठोपहार.
Declining d. उतरतीवेळ *f.* उतारदिवस*m.*
Half of the d. वेळ*m.f.* During or through one half of the d. वेळभर.
Fine (clear, sunny) d. सुदिन*m.n.*
Fine (clear and cloudless) days. निवरणीचे दिवस*m.pl.*
Foul (dull, hazy) d. दुर्दिन *m.n.* [ळ्या.
In open d. *in broad daylight.* दिवसा ढवळ्या, दाहाढव-
Of a full or whole d. दिवसा भऱ्याचा.
Pay of a d. रोजी *f.* रोज*m.* दिवसावडा*m.*
Whilst it is d. *before night closes.* दिशींच, सूर्यउजेडीं, दिसाउजेडीं, दिवा, दिवस घेऊन.
To go down—the d. धारेबर जाणें—दिवस.
2—natural. दिवस*m.* दिन*m.n.* रोज*m.* वासर *m.* एकाह*m.* एकरात्र*n.* अद्यतन*n.* अहोरात्र*m.n.* Some of the terms for the periods into which the day is divided are अरुण, उषःकाल, गर्गाचार्याचा मुहूर्त्त, गोधूल *or* गोरज, ब्राह्ममुहूर्त्त, अभिजिन्मुहूर्त्त *or* अभिजित्, रामपाहरा, कुतप, शिवमुहूर्त्त, राक्षसीवेळ *and* अमृतवेळ, उद्वेगवेळ, रोगवेळ, लाभवेळ, शुभवेळ, &c.
Auspicious d. सुदिन*m.n.* सुदिवस*m.*
Auspiciousness of the d. दिनशुद्धि *f.*
Biduum. द्विरात्र *n.*
D. of the week. वार *m.* वासर *m.*
D. after d. दिवसानदिवस, दिवसेंदिवस, दिवसोंदिवस.
D. by d. v. DAILY. रोज, दररोज, रोजउठून.
Declining days (of life or fortune). उतार दिवस*m. pl.*
Eating d.—*as opposed to* Fast day. जेवणवार *m.*
Every d. रोजचेरोज, दररोज, रोज उठून, आला दिवस.
Every other d. एक दिवस आड.
Evil days, dark, blind, &c. days. असत्काल *f.*
From to d. आजपासून, अद्यप्रभृति, अद्यावधि.
Happy d. a faustus dies. सोन्याचा दिवस *m.* सुदिन*m. n.* सुदिवस *m.*
Hire or wages for a d. रोजी *f*
Inauspicious d. कुदिन *m.n.* वर्जदिवस *m.* वर्जवार *m.*काळवार *m.* कर *f.*
Now a days. आजकाल.
Odd (by, extra, blank, &c.) d. आड दिवस *m.* आडवार*m.*
Of one d. ऐकाहिक. [शीं.
On the d. after. दुसऱ्या दिवसीं, पुढल्या दिवशीं, उत्तर दिव-
On the d. before. अदल्या दिवसीं. [d. नेरवां.
On the third d. (past or future). तेरवां.On the fourth
Person employed by the d. रोजकरी.
Roster or rotation d. पाळीचा दिवस *m.* वार *m.*
Through the d. All the d. एकरात्र, अठोपहार, अष्टोप्रहर.
Triduum. त्रिदिन *m.* त्रिरात्र *n.* त्रिरात्रि *f.*
To d. आज, आजचादिवस *m.* अद्य; to-morrow, उद्यां, उदयीक; the next day, *also* the day before yesterday, परवां; the third day, future or past, तेरवां; the fourth day, नेरवां. These words are also *adverbial.*
Unlucky d. कर *f.*
Unseasonable or wrong d. आड दिवस *m.* [द्यावधि.
Up to to d. आजपर्यंत, आजवर, आजपावेतों, अद्ययावत्, अ-
To win the d. शेर होणें, जय *m.*-यश *n.*-&c. पावणें.
Thy days are numbered. तुझी घटका घातली आहे.
3 *time specified, time with reference to a person or thing.* दिवस *m.* काळ *m.* वेळ *f.*

DAY-BOOK, *n.* रोज खरडा *m.* खरडा *m.* *or* खरडें *n.* रोजकीर्द *f.* कच्चा खरडा *m.* कीर्द *f.* रोजनामा *m.* खडेबंद *m.*

DAY-BREAK, *n.* v. DAWN. प्रातःकाल *or* ळ *m.* प्रातःसमय *m.* प्रभात *n.* अरुणोदय *m.* सुप्रभात *n.* उषःकाल *m.*
At d. उजेडतां, सुप्रभात *or* सुप्रभातें, झुंजुरकां *or* कीं.

DAY-LABOR, *n.* दिवसमजुरी *f.* रोजमजुरी *f.*

DAY-LABORER, *n.* रोजकरी, रोजदार, रोजिनदार, रोजमजुऱ्या, पैरा, पैरें *n.* (woman or child).

DAY-LIGHT, *n.* दिवसाचा उजेड *m.* सूर्यप्रकाश *m.* सूर्याचा उजेड *m.* दिवसबळ *n.*
At d. उजेडतां.
By or with d. *before night falls.* दिवसा उजेडीं, दिवस घेऊन, सूर्यउजेडीं.
In broad d. धडधडीत दिवसास, दिवसाढवळ्या.
It is broad d. भणभणीत उजेडलें,फटफटीत उजेडलें, फटफटलें, फटाटलें.

DAYSMAN. See MEDIATOR.

DAY-SPRING, See DAWN.

DAY-STAR, *n.* पहांटचा तारा *m.* दिवसागमनसूचक तारा *m.*

DAY-TIME, *n.* दिवसाचीवेळ *f.* दिवस *m.* दिवस उजेडाचीवेळ *f.* दिवसबळ *n.*
In the d. दिवसां, दिवसास, दिवस घेऊन.

To DAZE, *To* DAZZLE, *v. a.* दिपवणें, झकमकावणें, चकवणें, झकवणें, दृष्टिमोषण *n.*-नेत्रमोषण *n.* करणें, चकित-&c. करणें.

To DAZZLE, *v. n.* दिपणें, चकणें.

DAZZLED, *p.* v. V. A. दिपवलेला, &c. चकित, चक्र, उपहतदृष्टि.
To be d. दिपणें *or* दिपावणें, चकणें, झकणें, झांकुळणें *or* झांकोळणें.

DAZZLER, *n.* DAZZLING, *p. a.* v. V. A. दिपवणारा, &c. दृष्टिमोषक, नेत्रमोषक.

DEACON, *n.* पाद्रीत्री एक पदवी आहे.

DEAD, *a. exanimate.* मेलेला *or* मेला, मृत, गेलेला *or* गेला, गमावलेला, गत, गतप्राण, विगतप्राण, गतासु, गतजीव, विगतजीव, निचेष्ट, निःप्राण, *or* निचेष्ट-निःप्राण-&c. झालेला, निर्वाण, अतीत, मयत *or* मैयत, प्राणवियुक्त, प्राणविरहित-विहीन-&c.

Some covert or softening terms used in mentioning *a dead person* are वैकुंठवासी (if he had been a worshipper of *Wishnu*), कैलासवासी (if a worshipper of *Shiwa*), स्वर्गवासी, स्वर्यात, लोकांतरगत, लोकांतर प्राप्त, परलोकगत, परलोकप्राप्त.

D. body, v. CORPSE. मुडदा *m.*

2 *inanimate.* निर्जीव, अजीव, अप्राण, अचेतन, अचेष्ट.

3 *without feeling, insensible,* v. CALLOUS. बधिर *pop.* बहिरा, मेलेला, मृत.

4—a limb or member. लटका, अधू, असम.

5 *tasteless, vapid,* v. FLAT. फिका *or* फिक्का, हिमळ, निस्सार, निस्सत्व, गतसार, गतरस, गतसत्व, नीरस.

6—of sound, *flat.* तरळ.

7—of sleep, &c. v. DEEP. घोर, गाढ, कुंभकर्णी.

8 *without spirit, &c.* See DULL.

9 (a language) प्रचारांतून-व्यवहारांतून गेलेला.

DEAD, *n. midst,* v. HEIGHT. ऐन in. comp. as a prefix, as ऐनरात्रीं in the d. of night. ऐनहिंवाळ्यांत in the d. of winter, &c. भर as a prefix, as भररात्रीं in the d. of night.

DEAD, *adv.* See WHOLLY.

To DEADEN, *v. a.* हलका-मंद-न्यून-&c. करणें, बलऱ्हास *m.*-तेजोऱ्हास *m.*-&c. करणें *g. of o.*

2 See To BLUNT.

DEAD LETTER, *n.* ज्याचाधनी अगर वारीसदार सांपडत नाहीं तें पत्र, बिन वारीस पत्र *n.*

2 काळ अगर चाल बदलल्या मुळें ज्याची सत्ता-वजन नष्ट झालें आहे असा कायदा वगैरे.

DEADLINESS, *n.* v. A. घातकपणा *m.* घातकीपणा *m.* घातुकत्व *n.*

DEADLY, *a. mortal, killing, deleterious.* जीवघेणा, प्राणघेणा, घातक, घात्की, घातुक, प्राणहर-हर्त्ता-हारक-हारी, प्राणांतिक, प्राणापहारी, प्राणघातक, प्राणनाशक, मारक, मृत्युप्रद-दायक-&c. निधनकारक-कारी-कर्त्ता-कर, अंतकर-कारक-&c. अंतक, द्वेषी.

D. hatred. बद्धवैर *n.*

DEADLY, *adv.* See MORTALLY.

DEADNESS, *n.* v. A. 1. मेलेलेपणा *m.* प्राणराहित्य *n.* जीवराहित्य *n.* गतप्राणता *f.* &c.

3 मेलेलेपणा *m.* बहिरेपणा *m.* बधिरत्व *n.*

5 फिक्केपणा *m.* हिमळपणा *m.* &c. गतसारता *f.*

DEAD-STOCK, *n.* ज्या पासून मिळकत नाहीं असें सामान, शिलकी-सामान *n.*

DEAF, *a.* बहिरा *remiss.* बहिरट, कर्णशून्य, श्रवणेंद्रियरहित, दीडकानाचा, फुटक्याकानाचा, कानफुटका, भेरा *remiss.* भेरकट, बधिर, मंदश्रवण, मंदकर्ण.—as used of the ear. फुटका.

A d. person. भैरी, भैरोबा *or* ज्याला भैरोबाची *or* भैरवाची सेवाआहे, ज्याचें कानपूर ओस झालें.

To become d. बहिरावणें.

To DEAFEN, *v. n.* बहिरावणें, कानठळीं *or* ठेंक *n. pl. or* क्या *f. pl. or* टाळीं *or* ठेंक *n.pl.* बसणें, कान *m. pl.* जाणें-फुटणें *g. of s.*

To DEAFEN, *v. a.* बहिरा-बधिर-&c. करणें, कान *m. pl.* फोडणें-बंद-करणें *g. of o.* कानठळीं *n. pl. or* टाळीं *n. pl.* बसविणें *g. of o.*

DEAFNESS, *n.* v. A. बहिरेपणा *m.* बधिरत्व *n.* बाधिर्य *n.* श्रवणाभाव *m.* श्रवणेंद्रियराहित्य *n.*

DEAL, *n.* See QUANTITY. 2 *fir-wood.* देवदारु *m.n. pop.* देवदार *m.*

Of or belonging to d. देवदारी.

3—in card playing. वांटणी *f.*

To DEAL, *v. a. distribute, dole,* v. To DIVIDE. वांटणें, विभागणें, वाढणें, वांटून देणें, वांटणी *f.*-&c. करणें *g. of o.*

2 (cards) वांटणें, वांटणी *f.* करणें *g. of o.*

3 out:—blows. मारणें, देणें.

To DEAL, *v. n. traffic in,* v. To TRADE. व्यापार *m.*-उदीम *m.*-व्यवहार *m.*-&c. करणें *g. of o.*

2 with; *trade with, have business with.* वहिवाटणें, देवघेव *f. m.*-देणेंघेणें *n.*- देवाघेवा *m.*-&c. करणें *with* सीं *of s.* वहिवाट *f.*-दळणवळण *n.*-दळवटा *m.*-&c. ठेवणें-राखणें *with* सीं *of s.*

To have to d. with. गांठ *f.*-प्रसंग *m.* असणें *in. con.*

3 with, by; v. To BEHAVE. वागणें, वर्त्तणें, वर्त्तणूक *f.*-वर्त्तन *n.* करणें.

DEALER, *n.* v. V. N. 1. व्यापार करणारा, &c. उदमी, व्यापारी, [व्यवसायी.

2 देवघेव करणारा, &c. संसर्गी.

DEALING, *n.* v. V. N. 1. उदीम *m.* बकाली *f.* व्यापार *m.*

2 *and* INTERCOURSE. घेणें देणें *n.* घेवदेव *f. m.* घेवादेवा *m.* घेवादेवी *f.* लेवादेवा *m.* खातें पोतें *n.* परवत *m.* वहिवाट *f.* संसर्ग *m.* गांठ *f.*

3 *and* CONDUCT. वर्त्तणूक *f.* वर्त्तन *n.*

Plain d. Double d. See in their places.

DEAR, *n. pet, love, &c.* v. DARLING. जीवप्राण *m.* जिवाचाकलिजा *m.*

DEAR, *a. beloved,* v. DARLING. लाडका, लडिवाळ, प्रिय, प्यारा.

2 *high-priced, costly.* महाग, उंचमोलाचा, मोठ्यामोलाचा, मोठेकिमतीचा, महर्घ, जड, भारी, महागमोलाचा, महामूल्य, बहुमूल्य, बहुमोली.—in high degree; *exorbitantly, enormously, &c. d.* मोला आगळा, भारी मोलाचा, भारी-जबर-जरब-वज्र-&c. महाग, मोला महागाचा.

To be or become d. महागणें, महागाई *f.* माजणें *g. of s.* चडचडणें, चणचणणें, चणाणणें, बहकणें, तुकडे *m. pl.* पडणें *g. of s.* भीक *f.* लागणें *g. of s.* काटविकरा *m.* येणें *with* ला *or* स.

Dear me! oh dear! (in the female vocab.) अगई.

DEAR-BOUGHT, *a.* महाग घेतलेला, मोठ्या मोलानें घेतलेला, अक्रीत घेतलेला-आलेला.

DEAR-SELLER, *n.* महागरा, महाग्या, वज्रमहाग्या, अक्रीतविक्या, ओढून विकणारा.

DEAREST, *n.* See DARLING.

DEARLY, *adv.* v. A. 1. लडिवाळपणानें, लाडकेपणानें, प्रीतिपूर्वक, अ-[तिस्नेहपूर्वक.

2 महागाईनें, महर्घतापूर्वक, मोठ्यामोलानें.

DEARNESS, *n.* v. A. 1. लाडकेपणा *m.* प्रेम *n.* प्रेमा *m.* प्रेमळपणा *m.*

2 महागाई *f.* महर्घता *f.* मोठें मोल *n.* मोठी किम्मत *f.* बहुमूल्यता *f.*

DEARTH, *n. famine,* v. SCARCITY. महागाई *f.* दुष्काल *pop.* दुकळ *or* दुकाळ *m.* अटंकाळ *m.* असरी *f.* चणचण *f. intens.* चणचणाट *m.* हाक *f.* दुर्भिक्ष *n.* काटविकरा *m. v.* ये, महर्घता *f.*

DEATH, *n.* मरण *n.* मृत्यु *m.* मृति *f.*

Of the following significant terms, the greater part are extensively current. अंत *m.* अवसान *n.* देवाज्ञा *f.* निधन *n.* काल *m.* निर्वाण *n.* प्राणवियोग *m.* प्राणोत्क्रमण *n.* प्राणव्यय *m.* प्राणांत *m.* प्राणावसान *n.* देहावसान *n.* देहत्याग *m.* देहयात्रा *f.* देहांत

m. देहविसर्जन n. दीर्घनिद्रा f. महानिद्रा f. कालधर्म m. कालनिद्रा f. महाप्रस्थान n. कूच m. n. महापथगमन n. शांति f. निवृत्ति f. निपात m. निस्सरण n. परलोकगम m. परलोकगमन n. पंचत्व n. पंचता f. [यम m.

D.—as personified. काल or काळ m. काळसर्प m. कृतांत m.

Accidental d. अपघात m.

A lingering d. खितपणीचें मरण n.

Anniversary, &c. of a d. क्षयतिथि f. क्षयदिवस m. मृततिथि f. मृतदिवस m. मृताह m.

Bands of d. Snare of d. कालपाश m. यमपाश m. मृत्युपाश m.

Continuing till d. आमरणांतिक.

D. abroad. प्रोषितमरण n.

D. at will. इच्छामरण n.

D.—struggle. The mortal agony. The pains of d. प्राणांतव्यथा f. प्राणांत यातना f. प्राणांत दुःख n. खुडखुड f. घुटमुळणें n.

D. upon the bedstead. खट्वामरण n.

Exempt from d. and decay. अजरामर.

Fear of d. जीवितसंशय m.

Feigned d. मरणसोंग n.

Hour of d. अंतकाल m. चरमकाल m. प्राणांतीक n.

Impurity contracted through a d. मृताशौच m.

Labored breathing at time of d. ऊर्ध्व m. ऊर्ध्व वायु m.

Like d. D.-like. कालसदृश, कालकल्प.

Livor of d. मडेकळा f. मरणकळा f. मरतीकळा f.

Narrow escape from d. काळ आला होता पण मरण आलें नव्हतें or वेळ अली नव्हती.

Natural d. आपमौती or मौती f. आपमरण n.

One lean as d. मरतमडें n.

One on the point of d. कठीण, अंत्यावस्थ, अत्यवस्थ, आसन्नमरण, आसन्नमृत्यु, मरणोन्मुख, मरणानें जिंकलेला, मरणाभिमुख, गंतुकाम, गतीवर घातलेला or पडलेला, नाकीं or नाकासीं सूत धरलेला, उत्तरपंथ धरलेला or उत्तरपंथास लागलेला, घटका घातलेली ज्याची, मुमूर्षित, मुमूर्षु, अद्यश्वीन, कंठगतप्राण.

Sleep of d. काळनिद्रा f. काळझोंप f. महानिद्रा f. दीर्घनिद्रा f.

Tidings of a d. from abroad. गुढी f. प्रोषितमरणवार्त्ता f.

Until d. आमरणांत.

Violent or unnatural d. दुर्मरण n. अपघात m. आदान n.

Voluntary d. काम्यमरण n. देहत्याग m.

Worse than d. प्राणापेक्षां कठीण.

To await or wish the d. of. तिलांजलि घेऊन उभा राहणें, नावानें पाणी तावणें g. of o.

To cheat or elude d. कालवंचना f. करणें.

To die a natural d. अपल्या मरणानें मरणें.

To draw up in d. हातपाय m. pl. गुंडाळणें.

To worry to d. जिवाचाघोट घेणें, जीव खाणें or घेणें, प्राण खाणें, मरो मरोसें करणें.

To be on the point of d. मरायास टेकणें or गुडणें, यमलोकाची वाट धरणें, पंथास or मरणाचे पंथास लागणें, कंठीं प्राण उरणें, डफघायीस येणें, नाडी f. अटपणें g. of s. काठी शिरवरास लागणें, तंतीं प्राण उरणें, पाणी देखील घोटूं नये असें होणें, हातपाय गुंडाळणें, कंठासीं प्राण येणें, जीव खळबटणें, गुडणें, उत्तरपंथास लागणें or टेकणें, घुटमळणें or घुटमुळणें, घुटवळणें, नाकासीं सूत n. धरणें.

To be quivering or flickering in d. एक जीव येणें एक जीव जाणें g. of s. मरूं मरूं adv.-सिरूं मिरूं adv. करणें, टिकटिक adv. करून असणें.

To draw towards d. मरीस येणें-जाणें, मरीं जाणें.

To have one's eyes fixed in d. डोळे m. pl. थिजणें g. of s.

DEATH-BED, n. मरणशय्या f. मृत्युशय्या f.

DEATHLESS, a. v. IMMORTAL. अमर.

DEATH-RATTLE, n. घरघर f. घरघरा m. घरघरी f.

DEATH'S DOOR, n. यमद्वार n.

To be at d. मरणाचे दारीं बसणें.

To DEBAR, v. a. *preclude, exclude,* v. To HINDER. वारणें, निवारणें, आड-आडवा येणें *with* स or ला, अडवणें.

To DEBARK, v. c. नावेंतून-नौकेंतून-&c. उतरणें.

To DEBASE, v. a. *reduce, lower,* v. To DEGRADE. पायरी f. उतरणें g. of o. खालच्यापायरीवर-नीचपदवींत-कनिष्ठप्रतीत-&c. आणणें, कमीदराचा करणें, हलका-नीच-हीन-&c. करणें.

2 (coins or metals). हीण n. मिळवणें-घालणें, हिणकस-हिणकट-हिणवट-निरस-&c. करणें. [मान.

DEBASED, p. v. V. 1. हलका केलेला, &c. अपकृष्ट, नष्टमान, भ्रष्ट-

2 हिणकसकेलेला, हीणमिळवलेला, हिणकस, हिणवट.

DEBASEMENT, DEBASING, n. v. V. 1.—*act.* पायरी उतरणें n. हलका करणें n. &c. अपकर्ष m.—*state.* मानहानि f. तेजोहानि f. मानन्यूनता f.

2—*act.* हीणमिळवणें n. हिणकस करणें n. &c.

To DEBATE, v. a. *discuss,* v. To ARGUE. घाटणें, घोळणें, भवति-न भवति f.-वाटाघाट f.-काटकूट f.-काटाकुटी f.-&c. करणें g. of o.

To DEBATE, v. n. *dispute,* v. To ARGUE. वाद m.-विवाद m.-वाद् विवाद m.-&c. करणें.

2 v. To DELIBERATE. विचार m. करणें, विचारांत असणें

DEBATE, DEBATING, n. v. V. A.—*and* ARGUING. काटकूट f. काटाकुटी f. घाटाघाट f. वाटाघाट f. भवतिनभवति f.

2 v. V. N. वाद m. विवाद m. वादानुवाद m.

To DEBAUCH, v. a. *seduce, corrupt.* बिचलविणें, बिथरवणें, बिघडवणें, दुर्व्यसनांत-बदफैलींत-बदकर्मांत घालणें-शिरवणें-आणणें.

2 (a female.) फितविणें, भ्रष्टकरणें, दूषण n. करणें g. of o.

3 *seduce from allegiance.* फितविणें, फितवणी f. करणें g. of o.

DEBAUCHED, a. *corrupt in morals,* v. LOOSE. दुराचारी, दुराचरणी, भ्रष्टाचारी.

DEBAUCHEE, n. *loose, licentious person.* बिसनी, फंदी, भंगीचंगी or चंगीभंगी, बदफैल, बाहेरख्याली, बहिर्व्यसनी, सोदा.

DEBAUCHERY, n. *practice of lewdness.* बदफैली f. बदकर्म n. दुर्व्यसन n. बाहेरख्याल m. बहिर्व्यसन n. सोदेशाई f. सोदावें n.

DEBENTURE. See BOND. DEED.

To DEBILITATE, v. a. v. To WEAKEN. निजोर-कमजोर-निशक्त-&c. करणें, शक्ति f.-बळ n.-जोर m.-&c. कमी करणें g. of o.

DEBILITATING, a. v. WEAKENING. कमजोर करणारा, शक्तिक्षयकारी.

DEBILITY, n. v. WEAKNESS. कमजोरी f. कमकुवत f. शक्तिहीनता f. बलन्यूनता f.

DEBIT; debit side. खर्चाची बाजू f.

To DEBIT, v. a. खर्ची घालणें-मांडणें-लिहणें. [of o.

2 *charge to.* नावें-नांवानें लिहणें g. of o. खात्याबर मांडणें g.

Debonair, *a. complaisant*, v. Civil. सुशील, सभ्य.

To **Debouch**, *v. n.* कोंडलेल्या जाग्यांतून बाहेर पडणें.

Debris, *n.* मलमा *n.* खिंडार *or* रें *n.*

Debt, *n. monies due from.* देणें *n.* ऋण *n.* कर्ज *n.* ब्रह्मस्व *n.*

Debts or debt—compreh. indef. &c. कर्जधाम *n.* कर्जपाणी *n.* ऋणपाणी *n.*

Bad d. बुडीत *n.* जळीतबाकी *f.*—Account or register of bad debts. बुडीतखातें *n.*

Bondage of d. ऋणबंध *m.* ऋणबंधन *n.*

Bound by d. ऋणबद्ध

Closing payment in discharge of a d. झाडबाकी *f.*

D. upon easy terms. मुसरीण *n.*

Discharge or liquidation of a d. रदकर्ज *n.* ऋणशोधन *n.* ऋणदान *n.* ऋणापनयन *n.* ऋणमोक्ष *m.* ऋणमुक्ति *f.* ऋणापकरण *n.* रीणफेड *f.*

Disputed or disputable d. बांध्याचें-लडथडीचें-लढ्याचें-&c. कर्ज *n.*-ऋण *n.*-&c.

Free from d. अऋणी, अनृण, अनृणी.

Freedom from d. आनृण्य *n.*

Load of d. कर्जाचापर्वत *m.* ब्रह्मांडकर्ज *n.*

One over head and ears in d. कर्जबाजारी, कर्जभरी, काढ्या ओढ्याचा धनी, ऋणग्रस्त, ऋणबोड *or* बूड, ऋणबुड्या.

To be over head & ears in d. डोईवरून पाणी जाई इतकें कर्ज *n.* असणें.

Principal of a d. ऐनकर्ज *n.*

Recovery of a d. ऋणदान *n.* ऋणोद्ग्रहण *n.*

Released from d. ऋणमुक्त, ऋणमोचित.

That is in d. ऋणवान्.

The d. of nature. मरण *n.*

Written acknowledgement of a d. कर्जखत *n.* कर्जरोखा *m.*

Written release from d. फारखत *n.* फारखती *f.*

To settle or adjust a d. चुकवती *or* चुकोती *f.*-चुकती *f.* करणें.

2 *monies due to, outstanding d.* येणें *n.* खरकटें *n.*

Debtor, *n.* ऋणकरी, ऋणी, ऋणाईत, ऋणवान्, देणेकरी, देणेदार, कर्जदार, कर्जकरी, अधमर्ण, ऋणिक, कूळ.—in bonds and notes. रिणको *or* रिणकोनाम (from ऋण debt: and, as opposed to creditor धनको *or* धनकोनाम, from धन money).

Allowance made to a d. in durance. भत्ता *m. or* भातें *n.*

Bad (bankrupt, &c.) d. बुडीतकूळ *n.* थकलेंकूळ *n.*

Good (substantial, thriving, &c.) d. तरतेंकूळ *n.* ताजेंकूळ *n.*

Hard (tough-fisted, &c.) d. खटकूळ *n.*

Shutting up (by a creditor) of a d. in his own house. दारकोंड *f.*

Debtorship, *n.* v. N. ऋणीपणा *m.* &c. आधमर्ण्य *n.*

Decade, *n. aggregate of ten.* दशक *pop.* दसक *m.*

D. of soldiers. दाहिजा *m.*

Decadence. Decadency, See Decay.

Decagon, *n.* दशकोन *m.* दशकोनाकृति *f.*

Decalogue, *n.* दशाज्ञावलि *f.* आज्ञादशक *m.*

To **Decamp**, *v. n. march from a camp.* तळ *m.* उठवणें-उठवून जाणें-सोडणें, तळ *m.* उठणें *in. con. g. of s.* कूच *m. n.* करणें.

2 *run away, make off.* पळणें, तोंड *n.* काळें करणें, घोडा *m.* हाकणें, गबाळें *n.* अटोपणें, गाशा *m.* गुंडाळणें, गासलापूर *n.* करणें, झांझांचें *n.* करणें, झां *f.* म्हणणें, झ्या *f.* म्हणणें *or* करणें, झुकणें, झुकाटणें, झटकणें, झुकाटी *f.*-झुकांडी *f.*-झुकापुरी *f.*-झुगारा *m.* देणें, पबबारा *m.* करणें *or* म्हणणें, चलसू *f.* करणें, गच्छ *n.*-गच्छंती *f.*-गच्छंतीचें *n.* करणें-म्हणणें,—esp. with implication of previous cheating or fraud. बाळ्या *f. pl.* हाकणें, गुंगारा *m.* देणें-मारणें.

Decamping, Decampment, *n.* v. V. 1.—*act.* तळ उठवणें *n.* तळ उठणें *n.* उठावणी *f.* उठावा *m.* कूच *m. n.*

To **Decant**, *v. a. pour off.* कलंडवून-उलंडवून ओतणें.

Decanter, *n.* ओतलेल्या दारूचें सुरईचे आकाराचें कांचेचें भांडें *n.*

To **Decapitate**. See To Behead.

To **Decay**, *v. n. fail, sink, become impaired*, v. To Decline. उतरणें, मोडणें, झरणें, गळणें, क्षय *m.*-ऱ्हास *m.*-&c. पावणें *or in. con.* होणें *g. of s.*

Decay, *n.* v. Decline. उतरता पाया *m.* उतार *m.* उतारी *f.* उतरण *f.* क्षय *m.*-ऱ्हास *m.* क्षीणावस्था *f.* ऱ्हासावस्था *f.*

Decayable, *a.* v. V. नाशवंत, विनाशी, नश्वर.

Decayed, *p.* v. V. झरलेला, गळलेला, गलित, बिगलित, जीर्ण, खंगार, खोंकड *or* र *or* खांकर, खलड, क्षित, अपक्षीण, विशीर्ण, अपचित.

Decaying, *p.a.* v.V. उतरणारा, झरणारा, &c. उतरता, क्षयी, क्षयिष्णु.

Decease, *n.* v. Death. मरणें *n.* मरण *n.* देहावसान *n.* निवृत्ति *f.* निस्सरण *n.* परलोकगमन *n.*

To **Decease**, *v. n.* v. To Die. मरणें, प्राण *m.* सोडणें. [-&c.

Deceased, *a.* v. Dead. मयत, परलोकगत, परलोकप्राप्त, स्वर्गवासी.

Deceit, *n. fraud, guile, knavery.* कपट *n.* कृत्रिम *n.* माया *f.* माव *f.* कापट्य *n.* छद्म *n.* कैतव *n.* प्रपंच *m.* छल *m.* मिष *pop.* मीस *n.* दगल *f.* दगलबाजी *f.* दगा *m.* दगाबाजी *f.* ठकबाजी *f.* मगल *f.* चेटक *n.* मकर *n.* चकरमकर *f.* छल *m. n.* व्याज *m.* कूट *n. m.* धौर्त्य *n.* कपटविद्या *f.* ठकविद्या *f.* In expression of *Deceit* as understood in the words and phrases, *a cheat, illusion, trickery, false show, a make believe, an empty flourish, &c.* some words and phrases are, माया *f.* माव *f.* मावेचें मंथन आण धुक्याचें काजळ, मावेचा मृग *m.* धंदरा धंदरं (प्रवर्तते), धंदरा धंदरीचा (व्यवहार-व्यापार-विषय-वस्तू-&c.), भूतसृष्टि *f.* ऐंद्रजाल *n.* ठकवण *f.* फसवण *f.* फटवण *f.* दासवणूक *f.* झुलकावणी *f.* थकवणूक *f.* फसवणूक *f.* छद्मव्यवहार *m.* माकडशेंडा *m.*

D. and knavery,—compreh. दगा फटका *m.* दगलफसल *f.* ढोंग धत्तुरा *m.* कपटप्रबंध *m.*

A master piece of treachery or d. दगेमात *f.*

Deceitful, Deceptive, *a.*—person. ठकाऊ *or* बू *or* रू, ठकू, ठकडा, ठकवरा, ठकव्या, कपटी, सकपट, कृत्रिमी, दगाबाज, दगलबाज, लटकुरा, मकरी, छलनापर, कपटबुद्धि, इंद्रजालिक, मायावी, छद्मरूपी, छद्मवेषी, छद्मी, धूर्त्त, छट, शठ.

2—thing, &c. कपटाचा, कृत्रिमाचा, दगलबाजीचा, दग्याचा, मकराचा, कपटविद्येचा, कपटबुद्धीचा, मावेचा, बर बंचाईचा, कपटी, सकपट.

Deceitfully, *adv.* v. A. कपटानें, कृत्रिमानें, दग्यानें, दगलबाजीनें, &c. सकपट, कापट्यपूर्वक, &c. कपटबुद्धीनें.

Deceitfulness. *n.* v. A. दगलबाजी *f.* दगाबाजी *f.* कापट्य *n.*

Deceivable, *a.* v. V. ठकवाया-चा-जोगा-सारखा-&c. फसवाया-जोगा-&c. प्रतारणीय, व्यंस्य, व्यंसनीय, व्यंसितव्य.

To DECEIVE, *v. a. delude, defraud, impose upon.* ठकवणें, फसवणें, भोंदणें, बंचणें, प्रतारणें, भोळसावणें, भोळावणें, घुलकावणें, दगा *m.* देणें, ठकवणूक *f.*-फसवणूक *f.*-बंचना *f.*-प्रतारणा *f.*-&c. करणें *g. of o.*—freely, with the power of such words as, *to gull, bubble, befool, bamboozle, bob, bite, cozen, cully, chouse, diddle, do, &c.* मुंडणें *or* मुंडवण *f.* घालणें, छकवणें *or* छकावणें, झकवणें, भोंदणें, ठेंगाळणें, दांडळणें, धुतारणें, फटवणें, धंदरणें, झाजरणें, शिंगाटणें, शेंटाळणें, हिसडणें, हिसकणें, गळा *m.* कापणें *g. of o.* गुंगारा *m.*- झोळा*m.*-ढोला *m.*-पटकी *f.*-चट्टी*f.*-गोता *m.*-झोका*m.*-धुरी *f.*-धूर *m.*-चाला *m.*-&c. देणें, गुंगारा *m.* मारणें, डोईवर हात ठेवणें *or* फिरवणें, तोंडावरून हात फिरवणें, तोंडास पानें पुसणें, धाब्यावर बसवणें, धूप*m.*-धत्तुरा *m.* दाखवणें, पागोटें *n.* गुंडाळणें *g. of o.* हातावर तुरी *f.* देणें *or* देऊन पळणें.

DECEIVED, *p.* v. V. ठकवलेला, फसवलेला, &c. फशाळा, वंचित, प्रतारित, व्यंसित.

To be d. *be taken in.* फसणें. ठकणें.

DECEIVER, *n.* v. V. *and* DECEITFUL. ठकवणारा, फसवणारा, &c. फसव्या, ठक, ठग, ठकबाज, भोंदू, काबूयार, वंचक, प्रतारक, व्यंसक.

A gay d. कितव, धूर्त.

DECEIVING, DECEPTION, *n.* v. V.—*act.* ठकवणें *n.* फसवणें *n.* &c. ठकवणूक *f.* फसवणूक *f.* फसवणी *f.* वंचन *n.* वंचना *f.* प्रतारण *n.* प्रतारणा *f.* व्यंसन *n.*—*state.* फसगत *f.* फसगपत *or* फसगैवत *f.* फटवण *f.* फसाव *m.* फसण *f.* फशाळी *f.*

I. *artifice practised, cheat.* फटवण *f.* ठकवण *f.* फसवण *f.* झोला *m.* झोका *m.*

DECEMBER, *n.* इंग्रेजी वर्षाचा बारावा महिना *m.* मार्गशीर्षाचा उत्तरार्ध आणि पौषाचा पूर्वार्ध *m.*

DECENCY, *n.* v. A. 1. शिस्तपणा *m.* शिष्टाइकी *f.* शिष्टाई *f.* योग्यता *f.* औचित्य *n.* लायकी *f.*

2 लज्जा *f.* मर्यादा *f.* सलज्जता *f.*

To keep up d. पडदा *m.* राखणें.

DECENNIAL, *a. consisting of ten years.* दहावर्षांचा, दशाब्दिक.

2 *continuing for ten years.* दहा वर्षें चालणारा, दशवर्षावधि.

3 *happening every ten years.* दहादहा वर्षांनीं होणारा-येणारा-घडणारा, दशवर्षांतरित.

DECENT, *a. becoming, beseeming, befitting,* v. FIT. शिस्त, शिस्तवार, योग्य, उचित, लायक.

2 *not obscene; modest, &c.* लज्जेचा, मर्यादेचा, सलज्ज, सुलज्ज, समर्याद, निर्मल, विमलार्थक, बीभत्सभावशून्य.

DECENTLY, *adv.* v. A. 1. शिस्तपणानें, शिस्तवार, यथायोग्य, यथोचित, शिष्टाईनें, लज्जेनें, सलज्ज, लज्जापूर्वक, पडदा राखून.

DECEPTIBLE. See DECEIVABLE.

DECEPTIOUS, See DECEITFUL.

DECIDABLE, *a.* v.V. A. ठरावयाजोगा-&c.निर्णयकरावयाजोगा,&c.

To DECIDE, *v. a. determine, settle.* ठरावणें, ठराव*m.*-निर्णय*m.*-निश्चय *m.*-&c. करणें *g. of o.* निवाडा *m.*-फैसल *m. f.*-फैसला *m.*-&c. करणें *g. of o.* निश्चित-निर्णीत-सचीत-&c. करणें.

To DECIDE, *v. n. come to a conclusion.* निश्चय*m.*-ठराव *m.*-&c. करणें.

DECIDED, *p. and a.* v. V. A. ठरावलेला, फैसला केलेला-झालेला, &c. निर्णीत, निश्चित, सिद्ध.

I. *unequivocal, energetic, prompt, &c.*—of measures, &c. खरमरीत, ससरसीत, खरपूस, खमशा, निसालस, खणखणीत, कडकडीत, धडधडीत. [धिराचा.

II. *resolute, determined,*—of persons, v. FIRM.धीर, सुधीर,

DECIDEDLY, *adv.* v. A.I. II. निखालसपणें, कडकडीतपणानें, स्पष्ट, सचीत, निक्षूण.

DECIDER, *n.* v. V. A. ठरावणारा, फैसला करणारा,&c. निर्णय-&c. कर्त्ता, निर्णायक.

DECIDUOUS, *a. not perennial.* वर्षांत गळणारा-पडणारा, वर्षांतर्गलत्पर्ण, वर्षांतःपतत्पर्ण.

DECIMAL, *a.* दशांशाचा, दशांश.

D. arithmetic. दशांशगणित *n.*

D. figure or point. दशांशचिन्ह *n.*

D. fraction, दशांश अपूर्णांक *m.*

2 *numbered by ten.* दशगुणक, दशगुणोत्तर, दशघ्नोत्तर.

DECIMAL, *n.* दशांश *m.*

To DECIMATE, *v. a. take the tenth.* दहावा दहावा घेणें, नवमातृपरग्रहण *n.* करणें.

To DECIPHER, *v. a.* सांकेतिक लिपीचा-गूढलिपीचा-&c. अर्थ *m.* काढणें-लावणें, उलगडा *m.* करणें.

DECISION, *n.* v. V. ठराव *m.* निवाडा *m.* निर्णय *m.* निश्चय *m.* विचार *m.* फैसल *m. f.* फैसला *m.*

I. *determinedness,* v. FIRMNESS. धैर्य *n.* धीर *m.* सुधीरता *f.*

DECISIVE, *a. conclusive, determinative.* निर्णय-&c. करणारा, निर्णायक, निश्चायक, वादभंजक-निवर्त्तक-समापक, संदेहभंजक-&c.

DECISIVENESS, *n.* v. A. निर्णायकत्व *n.* निश्चायकत्व *n.*

DECK, *a.* (of a ship). मजला *m.*

To clear the decks, fig. v. To EAT UP. तळझाडा *m.*-निरानिपटा *m.* करणें.

To DECK, *v. a. array, adorn.* सजवणें, सजणें, साजरा-सुशोभित-&c. करणें, नटवणें, शृंगारणें, मंडन *n.* करणें *g. of o.*

DECKED, *p. v.* V. सजवलेला, साजराकेलेला, &c. सज्ज, सज्जित.

DECKER, *a. having decks.* मजला & मजली (in comp. as one-d. एकमजला *or* ली, two-d. दुमजला *or* ली, three-d. तिमजला *or* ली).

To DECLAIM, *v. n. speak rhetorically, harangue.* आलंकारिक-सालंकार-सुवचनपूर्वक-सुप्रलापात्मक-&c. भाषण *n.* करणें, पांडित्य *n.* करणें.

DECLAMATORY, *a.* आलंकारिक, सालंकार, &c. पांडित्याचा.

DECLAMATION, *n.* v. V. आलंकारिक-सुवचनात्मक-सुप्रलापात्मक-सालंकार-&c. भाषण *n.*

Empty d. पोकळपांडित्य *n.*

DECLARABLE, *a.* v.V.1. स्पष्टसांगाया-चा-जोगा-&c. बोलून कळवायाचा-&c. कथनीय, कथ्य, वाच्य, वचनीय, वक्तव्य, वेदितव्य, ज्ञाप्य.

2 जाहीर-&c. कराया-चा-जोगा-&c.

DECLARATION, *n.* v. V. A. 1.—*act.* स्पष्टसांगणें *n.* वदणूक *f.* ज्ञापन *n.* निवेदन *n.*

2 जाहीर करणें*n.*-&c. आविष्करण *n.* प्रकटीकरण *n.*

I. *matter declared.* वचन *n.*

II. See AFFIRMATION.

To DECLARE, *v. a. tell plainly, make known.* स्पष्टपणें-स्पष्ट-सचीत-साफ-&c. सांगणें, वदणें, निवेदणें, ज्ञापणें, बोलून कळवणें.

2 *show, make known.* v.To MANIFEST. ठाऊक-विदित-जाहीर-प्रगट-&c. करणें, प्रकाश *m.* करणें *g. of o.*

3 (one's self). आपलें स्वरूप प्रगट करणें-दर्शविणें.—in a bad sense स्वरूपावर-गुणावर येणें.

To DECLARE, *v. n.* See To AFFIRM. 2 for or against.अमुकपक्ष स्वीकारणार असें उघड पणें सांगणें-वदणें.

DECLARER *n.* DECLARATIVE, *a.* DECLARATORY, *a.* v. V.A. 1. बोलून कळवणारा, वदणारा, &c. ज्ञापक, वाचक.

2 जाहीर करणारा &c. उद्बोधक, प्रकाशक.

DECLENSION, *n.*—in grammar. विभक्ति *f.* रूप *n.*विभक्तिपद्धति *f.*

DECLINABLE, *a.* v. V. A. 2. वाच्य, विभक्तिसाध्य, सविभक्तिक.

DECLINATION, DECLINING, DECLINE, *n.* v. V. N. 1. कल *m.* झोंक *m.* लवणूक *f.* वांक *m. n.* वांकण *n.* प्रावण्य *n.*

2 उतार *m.* उतारी *f.* उतरण *f.* क्षय *m.* अपक्षय *m.* अपचय *m.* अपक्षयण *n.* अपकर्ष *m.* ऱ्हास *m.* क्षिति *f.* जातापाया*m.* उतरतापाया *m.* खचतापाया *m.* अटतापाया *m.* बुडतापाया *m.* पडतापाया *m.* उतरतीकमाण *or* न *f.* उतरती कळा *f.* उतरतीपायरी *f.* उतरतीबाजू *f.* उत्तरावस्था *f.* अवकल *f.* अवकळा *f.* सरतापालव *m.* तेजोऱ्हास *m.* ऱ्हासावस्था *f.* गुणऱ्हास *m.* गुणक्षिति *f.*

Time or season of d. उतरतीवेळ *f.* उतारदिवस *m.* अटताकाळ *m.* बुडताकाळ *m.* ऱ्हासकाल *m.*

I. (of a star). क्रांति *f.* अपम *m.* स्पष्टक्रांति *f.* स्पष्टापम *m.*

Sine of a planet's d. क्रमज्या *f.* क्रांतिज्या *f.*

Sine of the sun's greatest d. परमापम *m.*

The radius of a parallel of it. द्युजीवा *f.* द्युज्या *f.*

II. v. CONSUMPTION. क्षयरोग *m.* झडी *f.*

III. *declining years.* उत्तरवय *n.* उत्तरपराई *f.* उतरतीपराई *f.* उतारवय *n.* उतराई *f.* अपक्षयण *n.*

To DECLINE, *v. a. avoid, shun, not to accept, &c.*, v. To REFUSE. नकारणें, नको म्हणणें, वर्जणें, टाकणें, फिरणें *with* पासून *of o.* अस्वीकार *m.*-अनंगीकार *m.*- असेवन*n.*-नकार *m.*-&c. करणें, पड *f.* घेणें.

2—in grammar. रूप *n.* चालवणें, विभक्ति *f. pl.* सांगणें *g. of o.* विभक्ति *f. pl.* लावणें *with* स *or* ला. विभक्तिनिर्देश *m.*-लिंगनिर्देश *m.* करणें.

To DECLINE, *v. n. lean downward, incline.* उतरणें, कलणें, तोलणें, झोकणें *or* झुकणें, वाकणें.

2 *deteriorate, decrease, decay.* उतरणें, खालावणें, उणावणें, मोडणें, घसरणें, ओसरणें, गळणें, क्षीण होणें, क्षय *m.*-ऱ्हास *m.*-&c. पावणें, क्षय *m.*-ऱ्हास *m.*-&c. होणें *g. of s.* अवकलणें.

3 (in years.). उत्तरवयांत येणें, पडणीस-पडघाईस येणें.

4 (in the world). बसणें, घर *n.* बसणें *g. of s.* पडघाईस-पडणीस येणें, घसरणें, ऊट *f.* उतरणें *g. of s.*

5—the day; *pass noon.* कलणें, उतरणें, कसरणें.

DECLINER, *n.* DECLINING, *p. a.* v. V. N. 1. झुकणारा, कलणारा, &c. उतरता, प्रवण.

2 उतरणारा, &c. उतरता, उतरत्या पायाचा, उतरते कमाणीचा, उतरते पायरीचा, क्षयगामी, क्षयिष्णु, अपक्षीण.

3 उतार, उत्तरवयस्क, उत्तरवयाचा, उतारवयाचा, उतरतेपराईचा.

DECLIVITY, *n.* v. DESCENT. उतार *m.* उतरण *f.* उतरड *f.* उतरडी *f.* उतरवण *f.* बरंगळ *f.*

DECLIVOUS, *a.* उतरता, उतरणीचा, उतरवट, उतरट, बरंगळीचा.

To DECOCT, *v. a.*—medicinally. उकळणें, काढा *m.*-कषाय *m.*-पाक *m.*-&c. करणें *g. of o.*

DECOCTION, *n. thing decocted, decocture.* काढा *m.* कषाय *m.*उकाळा *m.* क्काथ *m.* निर्यास *m.* कट *m.* पाक *m.* रस *m.*

D. (of acids, &c.) for scouring metals. उकाडा *m.*

Second d. निकाढा *m.*

To DECOLLATE, &c. See To BEHEAD, &c.

To DECOMPOSE, *v. a. resolve into its simple parts.* मूलतत्वें *n. pl.* भिन्नकरणें *g. of o.* तत्वपृथक्करण *n.* करणें.

To DECOMPOSE, *v. n.* मूलतत्वें *n. pl.*-पंचतत्वें *n. pl.* भिन्न होणें, तत्वांस तत्वें *n. pl.* मिळणें *g. of s.*

DECOMPOSITION, *n.* v. V. N. तत्वांस तत्वें मिळण्याची अवस्था *f.* तत्वांस तत्वें मिळणें *n.* पंचताप्राप्ति *f.* पंचत्वापत्ति *f.*

To DECORATE, *v. a.* v. To ADORN. श्रृंगारणें, सजणें, सजवणें, मंडन *n.* करणें *g. of o.*

DECORATED, *p.* v. V. श्रृंगारलेला, &c. मंडित, विभूषित.

DECORATING, *p. a.* DECORATOR, *n.* v. V. श्रृंगारणारा, &c. मंडनकर्त्ता-कारी-&c.

DECORATION, *n.* See ORNAMENT.

DECOROUS, *a.* v. N. शिष्ट, शिस्तवार, शिष्टाचाराचा, सुलज्ज, सलज्ज, समर्याद, सविनय, योग्य, उचित.

DECOROUSLY, *adv.* मर्यादेनें, शिष्टाईनें, सभ्यरीतिनें, &c. विनयपूर्वक.

DECORTICATION, *n.* v. PEELING. खरपुडी *f.*

DECORUM, DECOROUSNESS, *n. decency, propriety of behaviour.* मर्यादा *f.* शिष्टाचार*m.* शिष्टाई *f.* शिष्टाइकी*f.* सभ्यरीति *f.* विनय*m.*

To DECOY, *v. a. lure, entrap, draw into a snare.* लोभ *m.*-आमिष *n.*-आशा *f.*-&c. दाखवून फसवणें-फसगत *f.*-&c. करणें *g. of o.*-फाशांत पाडणें *or* आणणें-पाशबद्ध करणें, मोहणें, मोह *m.* घालून पाशांत पाडणें, &c.

DECOY. See LURE.

To DECREASE, *v. a.* v. To LESSEN. कमी-उणा-न्यून-&c. करणें.

To DECREASE, *v. n.* v. To LESSEN. घटणें, थोडकावणें, तुटणें, कमी-उणा-न्यून-&c. होणें, क्षय *m.*-ऱ्हास *m.*-&c. होणें *g. of s.*

2 as to force or intenseness; *remit, slacken, abate.* उतरणें, उणावणें, हलकावणें, कमतावणें, हलका-मंद-&c. पडणें-होणें, मंदावणें, खालावणें, थोडकावणें, कानपणें, वरमणें, कसरणें, बसणें, पडणें, नमणें, नरमणें, निवणें, निमणें, उतार *m.*-मंदाई *f.*-मंदी *f.*-उपशम *m.*-उपशमन *n.*-ओसारा *m.*-&c. होणें *g. of s.*

DECREASE, DECREASING, *n.* v. V. N. 1. उतार *m.* घट *f.* घटती *f.* घडती *f.* तूट *f.* क्षय *m.* अपक्षय *m.* अपचय *m.* ऱ्हास *m.* क्षिति *f.*

2 उतार *m.* मंदाई *f.* मंदी *f.* उपशम *m.* उपशमन *n.* उपशांति *f.* ओसार *or* ओसारा *m.*

DECREASED, *p.* v. V. 1. कमी केलेला-झालेला, &c. अपचित, प्राप्तक्षय, जातक्षय, अपक्षीण.

DECREE, *n. judicial decision.* फैसलनामा *m.* हुकूमनामा *m.* निर्णयपत्र *n.* व्यवस्था *f.*

2 *edict,* v. LAW. आज्ञा *f.* हुकूम *m.* सूत्र *n.* शासन *n.* निर्देश *m.* उक्तवाक्य *n.*

3 (of God) ईश्वरी संकल्प.

To DECREE, *v. a. determine judicially.* फैसला *m.*-निवाडा *m.*-&c. करणें. [नेमणें.

2 *appoint, order, &c.* हुकूम *m.*-आज्ञा *f.*-शासन *n.*-&c. करणें,

DECREPIT, *a. old and infirm,* v. OLD. लुळाखुडा *or* लुडाखुडा, जर्जर, जर्जरीत, जरठ, जराग्रस्त, खेंकड, खेंकडा, खोंकड *or* खोंकर, खंगार, खप्पड, खल्लड, जख्खड.

To DECREPITATE, *v. n.* v. To CRACKLE. तडतडणें.

Decrepitude, *n.* v. A. तुटारी *f.* जरा *f.* जरठत्व *n.* खोंकडपणा *m.*

To **Decry**, *v. a. cry down, clamour against, blame.* हाकाटा *m.*-हाकाटी *f.*-&c. करणें *g. of o.* नांवानें-नांवें बोंब *f.*-हाका *f. pl.*-&c. मारणें-शंख *m.* करणें *g. of o.* नांव *n.*-दोष*m.*-&c. ठेवणें.

Decumbence, &c. See **Recumbence**, &c.

To **Dedicate**, *v. a. devote, consecrate.* वाहणें, अर्पणें, समर्पिणें, नवसणें, प्रतिष्ठणें, प्रतिष्ठा *f.*-उत्सर्ग *m.* करणें *g. of o.* लावणें-देणें *with* कडे *of o.*

2 (one's self). मुंड*n.* मुंडावणें *or* मुंड मुंडावून बसणें-असणें&c.

To d. one's soul, body, and substance. तन मन धन समर्पण*n.* करणें.

3 (a book, &c.). नांवावर-नांवानें नजर करणें-अर्पणें.

Dedication, *n.* v. V. 1.—*act.* वाहणें*n.* समर्पिणें*n.* &c. समर्पण*n.* अर्पण *n.* उत्सर्ग *m.* प्रतिष्ठा *f.*

I. ग्रंथनजर केल्याबद्दल ग्रंथाच्या आरंभीं जो लेख असतो तो.

To **Deduce**, *v. a.* v. To **Infer.** अनुमानानें-तर्कानें-&c. काढणें-घेणें, अनुमान*n.*-तर्क*m.* काढणें-करणें.

Deducible, *a.* v. V. अनुमानानें काढाया जोगा-&c. अनुमेय.

To **Deduct**, *v. a. subtract.* बाद करणें-घालणें, वजा करणें-पाडणें-घालणें, कमी करणें, काटणें, काढणें, घेणें, घालवणें, मिना घालणें.

Deducted, *p.* v. V. बाद केलेला-झालेला-&c. वजा केलेला-झालेला-पडलेला-घातलेला, मिना घातलेला, व्यवकलित.

Deduction, *n.* v. V.—*act.* बाद करणें *n.* वजा करणें *n.* &c. व्यवकलन*n.*

I. *amount deducted.* वजात *f.*

II. See **Conclusion.**

Deductive, *a.* v. To **Deduce.** अनुमानाचा, आनुमानिक, अनुमेय.

Deductively, *adv.* v. A. अनुमानानें, अनुमान करून.

Deed, *n. act,* v. **Action.** काम*n.* कर्म*n.* कार्य*n.* कृत्य*n.* क्रिया *f.*

A virtuous or good d. सुकर्म*n.* सुकृत*n.*

2 *exploit, achievement, feat.* मात *f.* महत्कृत्य *n.* महत्कार्य*n.* अद्भुतक्रिया *f.* शर्तीचें-बशर्तीचें काम *n.* कृतकृत्य *n.* कौतुक *n.* शतक्रतु *m.* पुरुषार्थ *m.* कृतार्थ*m.* दिग्विजय*m.*

Deeds, *feats, exploits.* चरित्र *n.* चरित *n.*

To perform a mighty d. शिखरीं काठी*f.* चढवणें, अटकेस झेंडे *m. pl.* लावणें, गंगेस घोडे*m. pl.* न्हावबवणें, दिग्विजय*m.* करणें.

—in a bad sense. उदव *m.* करणें, उदवणें.

To perform deeds of valor. धार *f.* करणें.

3—in law, v. **Bond.** खत *n.* पत्र *n.* लेख *m.* दस्तऐवज*m.*

D. of acquittance. फारीखत *f.* राजीनामा*m.*

D. of agreement. करारनामा*m.* सम्मतिपत्र*n.*

D. of gift or conveyance. दानपत्र*n.*

D. of lease or tenure. पट्टा *m.*

D. of purchase. खरीदखत*n.* खरीदपत्र *n.* कबाला *m.*

D. of relinquishment, (of divorce, manumission,&c.). सोडखत*n.* सोडचिठ्ठी *f.*

D. of sale. फरोकखत *n.* क्रयलेख्य *n.*

In deed, in very d. v. **Truly.** खराच, खरोखर, वास्तविक.

To **Deem**, *v. a. think, esteem.* मानणें, जाणणें, समजणें, गणणें, लेखणें, धरणें.

Deep, *a.* खोल (*remiss.* खोलट, खोलवट, खोलकट, खोलगट, *deepish*), ओंड *or* ओंढ, सखल (*remiss* सखलवट), कोंडवरा, गैहरा, गंभीर, निम्न.

Very d. अगाध.

2 *occult, &c.* v. **Abstruse.** खोल, सखोल, गूढ, निगूढ.

3 *artful, &c.* v. **Cunning, Insidious.** ओंतल्या गांठीचा, कारस्थानी, कावेदार, कावेबाज, नाटकी, धूर्त, पाताळयंत्री.

4 *grave, solemn.* सखोल, गंभीर.

5—of sound. घन, गंभीर, घोस, उद्दाम, डोर.

6—of color. गैहरा *or* गहिरा.

7 *deep-sunken,*—the eye. कोंझा *or* कोंजा *remiss.* कोंझट *or* [कोंजट.

8—of sleep. घोर, गडद, गाढ, निबिड.

9 *that is in or to a high degree.* फारच, अत्यंत, पराकाष्ठेचा, अतिशयित.

D. silence. सामसूम *n.f.*

Deep, *n. sea.* समुद्र*m.* सागर*m.* दर्या*m.*

2 *dead, &c.* v. **Height.** ऐन (in comp. as a prefix, as ऐनरात्रीं in the d. of night. ऐन हिंवाळ्यांत in the d. of winter, &c.).

To **Deepen**, *v. a. make deeper.* खोलगें, अधिक खोल-ओंड-&c. [करणें.

2 *make brighter, clearer, fuller, &c.* उजरणें, स्पष्ट-व्यक्त-टवटवीत-गैहरा-&c. करणें.

To **Deepen**, *v. n. grow deeper.* अधिक खोल-&c. होणें.

2 *grow brighter, clearer, fuller.* उजरणें, खुलणें, चढणें, स्पष्ट-व्यक्त-टवटवीत-गैहरा-&c. होणें.

Deeply, *adv.* v. A. 1. खोल, ओंड.

I. *profoundly, thoroughly.* खोलगडून, अभिनिवेशपूर्वक, अभिज्ञानपूर्वक.

D. versed, &c. पारंगत.

II. *to or in a high degree.* फारच, अत्यंत, अतिशय, मनापासून, बेंबीच्या देंठापासून.

Deepness, Depth, v. A. 1. खोली *f.* खोलावा*m.* खोलपणा*m.* ओंडपणा*m.* सखलपणा*m.* गांभीर्य*n.*

To get out of one's d. *lit. fig.* खोल पाण्यांत शिरणें.

2 खोलपणा*m.* गूढता *f.* गूढभाव*m.*

Deer, *n.* हरिण*m. pop.* हरण*m.n.* मृग*m.* कुरंग*m.* Some species are चितळ, डांगळ, भेंकर *or* रें, माळशिकारी हरण, रोही, सूकर, ताम्रमृग, कृष्णमृग *or* कृष्णसार, सांबर.

Bounding of a d. चौकडी *f.*

Deer-catcher, *n.* पाशी.

Deer-eyed, *a.* मृगनयन (*f.* ना), मृगलोचन (*f.* ना), मृगनेत्री.

Deer-skin, *n.* हरणाचीकातडी *f.* मृगाजिन *n.*

To **Deface**, *v. a. disfigure, deform.* विरूप-व्यंग-खराब-&c. करणें, बिघडवणें, रूप*n.*-&c. मोडणें *g. of o.* स्वरूपाचा-रूपाचा-&c. नाश*m.* करणें *g. of o.* आकारभंग*m.*-स्वरूपभंग*m.*-&c. करणें *g. of o.*

2 See To **Efface.**

Defalcation, *n. diminution.* तोटा*m.* कमताई *f.* कोताई *f.*

Defamation, *n.* v. V.—*act.* आब्रूघेणें*n.* &c. चहाडी *f.* तुफान*n.* अपवाद*m.* अभिशंसन*n.* विकत्थन*n.*

Defamatory. See **Slanderous.**

To **Defame**, *v. a.* v. To **Asperse.** बदनामी *f.* करणें *g. of o.* आब्रू *f.*-हुरमत *f.*-&c. घेणें *g. of o.* अभिशंसन*n.*-अभिशाप*m.*-विकत्थन*n.*-&c. करणें *g. of o.*

Defamer, *n.* **Defaming**, *p. a.* v. V. *and* **Asperser.** बदनामी करणारा, &c. चहाड, तुफानखोर, चहाडखोर, अपवादक, अभिशंसन-&c. कर्त्ता.

DEFAULT, *n. omission, failure, fault.* अंतर*n.* तफावत *f.* चूक *f.* कसर *f.* गुंजावीस *f.* ढळ*m.* टळ*m.* नास्तिपक्ष*m.*
2 *defect, want.* अभाव*m.*

DEFAULTER, *n.* कामांत-चाकरींत-बोलींत-&c. कसर करणारा-तफावत करणारा, चाकरीचा तफावत्या *or* तफावती, लाजीमदार.
D. in accounts. हिशोबचोर, तजकऱ्या.
2 *one who fails to appear when called in court.* हुकुमाप्रमाणें हाजीर न झालेला मनुष्य.

To DEFEAT, *v. a. beat, overthrow, discomfit.* जिंकणें, मारणें, मोडणें, हर *f.*-पाडाव*m.*-हार *f.*-जय*m.*-पराजय*m.*-पराभव*m.*-अपजय*m.*-अजय*m.*-अपयश*n.*-भंग*m.*-भंजन*n.* करणें *g. of o.* पराभवणें, हरवणें *or* हारवणें, पासला पाडणें, पट्टाधूळ *f.* करणें *g. of o.*
2 *baffle, foil, frustrate, disconcert, &c.* नासणें, मोडणें, भंग *m.*-भंजन *n.*-विघात *m.*- घात *m.*-मनोभंग *m.*-उत्साहभंग *m.*-&c. करणें *g. of o.*—utterly, thoroughly, irrecoverably, &c. Corresponding with *To Defeat*, as bearing this implicaion of *utterness* or *completeness*, there are in English numerous verbs and formations, strong, and striking, and abundantly current; yet, of rather low estimation as vulgar or free. Equally numerous, equally significant, and of equivalent estimation, there are verbs and formations in *Maráthi*. The words therefore corresponding with *To smash, squash, dish, mar, blast, confound, knock on the head, &c. &c.*—as applied to persons, affairs, schemes, measures, &c. we have collected here. The whole answer to the whole in the general import, whilst particular ones agree with particular ones in particular aspect. नासणें, धासळणें, घालवणें, नाश *m.*-सत्यानास *m.*-बिघाड *m.*-विघात *m.* करणें, तजावजा *adv.* करणें, तोंडावर मारणें, कांठावर मारणें, लधडणें *or* लधाडणें, धोबाडणें, डोई *f.* मारणें *g. of o.* हेलपटणें, हुसकटणें, हुसकणें, लटपटवणें, धूळ *f.*-धूळधाणी *f.*-धूळपट *f.*-धूळदशा *f.*-धूळधमासा*m.*-पट्टाधूळ *f.*-विस्थापाक *m.*-मुसभंजन *n.*-तिन्हड *f.*-बचमंगळ *n.*-बदरंग *m.*-बेरंग*m.*-बदशान *or* बच्छान *f.*-वीट *or* विट्ट *m.*-चिवडा *m.*-विचका *m.*-नासाडा *or* नासडा*m.*-नासधूस *f.*-अपयश *n.*-मातेरा *m.*-चंदन *or* गोपचंदन *n.*-माती *f.*-पीठ *n.*-पिठाड *or* पिठडा *m.*-चुना *m.*-&c. करणें, रसातळास नेणें. And corresponding with *To be defeated*, as involving the sense more strikingly expressed by *To be smashed, squashed, dished, &c., To be done for, To go to pot, To end in smoke, &c. &c.* the following are some of the words and phrases. खचणें, खचळणें, गंढारणें, गंढाळणें, जाजावणें, वाहवणें, फसणें, घडघडणें (*intens.* घडाडणें), कोसळणें, धासळणें *or* ढासळणें, बितुळणें, फिसकणें, फिसकटणें, *or* फसकणें, &c. ढवढवणें, धुळींत जाणें, भंगास जाणें, बोंबलणें, रडणें, चसणें, रांडावणें, कांठावरबसणें *imp.* लटपटणें, धकावणें, दगावणें, चबढब *f.*-ढवळा *m.*-ढवळाढवळ *f.*-बचमंगळ *n.*-&c. होणें *g. of s.*

DEFEAT, DEFEATING, *n.* v. V. 1.—*act.* जिंकणें *n.* &c. मोडणी *f.* जिंकणूक *f.* भंजन *n.*—*state.* हर *or* हार *f.* पाडाव *m.* जय *m.* पराजय *m.* पराभव *m.* भंग *m.* अपजय *m.* अजय *m.* अपयश *n.* शिकस्त *f.*
To acknowledge d. by (or inferiority to). अजित जाणें *or* विजित जाणें, हार जाणें-येणें (both phrases with neg. con. and with ला *or* स *of o.*), चीं म्हणणें.
2—*act.* मोडणें *n.* &c. मोडणी *f.* भंजन *n.*—*state.* भंग *m.* नाश *m.* घात *m.* विघात *m.* *See also the numerous nouns given under the Verb.*

DEFEATED, *p.* v. V. 1. जिंकलेला, &c. पाडाव, शिकस्त, पराजित, पराभूत, जित, भग्न.
To be d. हार जाणें, तोंडांत खाणें.
2 नासलेला, मोडलेला, &c.

To DEFECATE, *v. a.* v. TO CLARIFY. शोधणें, मळ *m.* काढणें-छाटणें *g. of o.*

DEFECATION, *n.* v. V.—*act.* शोधणें *n.* शोधन *n.*

DEFECT, *n. imperfection, incompleteness, want of something requisite.* उणेपणा *m.* कमीपणा *m.* उणवाई *f.* कमती *f.* कमताई *f.* कमतर *f.* कमतणूक *f.* कोताई *f.* व्यंग *n.* गुंजावीस *f.* तफावत *f.* तजावुज *n.* तजाबुजू *n.* कसर *f.* अपूर्णता *f.* हीनता *f.* वैकल्य *n.*
Slight d. or excess. कमज्यास्त *n.* कमज्यास्ती *f.* कंपेश *m.*
2 *moral imperfection, failing,* v. FAULT. दोष *m* चूक *f.* अंतर *n.* तफावत *f.* गुंजावीस *f.*
3 *natural imperfection.* दोष *m.* ऐब *m.* खोड *f.*
4 *a d. thing or point wanting.* बिंग *or* बिंगें *n.* छिद्र *n.* व्यंग *n.* उणें *n.* हीण *n.* [णें *n.*

DEFECTION, *n. revolt, &c.* फितूर *m.* फितवा *m.* फितावा *m.* फिट-

DEFECTIVE, *a.* v. N. 1. *imperfect, incomplete, faulty.* उणा, अपुरा, अपुरता, अपूर्ण, अधुरा, अधू, कोता, उणवाईचा, कसरीचा, गुंजाविसीचा, तफावतीचा, &c. हीन, विकल, विकलांग, न्यूनांग, अंगहीन, विधुर, नकटा.
D. verb. गौणक्रियापद *n.* [बदार.
2 v. FAULTY. दोषी, सदोष, दोषयुक्त, कसरीचा, तफावतीचा, ऐ-

DEFECTIVELY, *adv.* v. A. अपुरतेपणीं, कसरीनें, कसरराखून, अपुरा-&c. *decl.*

DEFECTIVENESS. See DEFECT.

DEFENCE, DEFENDING, *n.* v.V. 1.-*act.* राखणें *n.* रक्षणें *n.* &c. रक्षण *n.* राखण *f.*
I. *guard, fence, &c.* आवरण *n.* आवार *m.* निवारक *n.* निवारणसाधन *n.* निवारणोपाय *m.*
II. *shelter, &c. afforded,* v. PROTECTION. आश्रय *pop.* आसरा *m.* शरण *n.* पांघरूण *n.* छाया *f.* छत्र *n.*
III.—in law : *defendant's reply.* उत्तर *n.* जबाब *m.* प्रतिवाद *m.* आंगसुटका *f.*
IV. *defendant's cause or side.* उत्तर पक्ष *m.*
An evidence on the d. उत्तरसाक्षी.

DEFENCELESS, *a. unarmed, exposed, &c.* उघडा, अशस्त्र, शस्त्रहीन-रहित-&c. निरायुध, त्राणसाधनरहित, निराश्रय, रक्षाहीन.

To DEFEND, *v. a. guard,* v. TO PROTECT. राखणें, रक्षणें, रक्षण *n.*-राखण *f.*-त्राण *n.*-बचाव *m.*-&c. करणें *g. of o.*
2 *assert, uphold, vindicate,* v. TO MAINTAIN. संभाळणें, राखणें, प्रतिपादणें.

DEFENDANT, DEFENDER, *n.* v. V. 1. राखणारा, &c. रक्षक, रक्षणकर्त्ता, संरक्षक, त्राता.
I.—in law. प्रतिवादी, उत्तरवादी, प्रतिपक्षी, उत्तरपक्ष, असामी.

DEFENSATIVE. See DEFENCE.

DEFENSIBLE, *a.* v.V.1. राखाया-चा-जोगा-&c. रक्षणीय, रक्ष्य, गो-

पनीय, गोप्य.

DEFENSIVE, *a. serving to defend.* बचावाचेकामाचा, रक्षणाचा, रक्षणोपयोगी. [क.

2 *carried on in defence.* बचावाचा, आत्मरक्षणाचा, आत्मरक्ष-

To DEFER, *v. a. delay, post-pone, put off.* उशीर *m.*-विलंब *m.*-दिरिंग *m.*-दिवसगत *f.*-&c. करणें-लावणें, टाळा *m.* देणें, ढकलणें, लोटणें, टाळणें, घालवणें, मुद्दतीवर-कालांतरावर-दिवसगतीवर-&c. लोटणें-टाळणें-टाकणें, ढकल *f.*-ढकलपट्टी *f.*-ढकलाढकल *f.*-ढकलाढकली *f.*-&c. करणें *g. of o.* उपेक्षणें.

2 See To REFER.

To DEFER, *v. n. yield to another's opinion.* भिडेनें हो म्हणणें-अनुमोदन *n.* करणें-&c. तोंडराखी *f.*- भीडराखी *f.* मुरवतराखी *f.* -&c. करणें.

DEFERENCE, *n. regard, &c.* v. RESPECT. भीड *f.* भीडभाड *f.* भीडराखी *f.* तोंडराखी *f.* मुरवतराखी *f.* मुरवत *f. v.* बाळग, राख, धर, मुलाजा *m.* चाड *f.*

To be restrained or affected by d. भिडावणें.

To pay servile d. unto. नमोनमो *adv.* करणें.

DEFERENTIAL, *a.* v. N.—person. भिडस्त, भिडसारू *or* ळू, मर्यादशीर, मर्यादशील.

2—speech, action, &c. भिडेचा, मुरवतीचा, भिडस्तपणाचा.

DEFERENTIALLY, *adv.* v. A. भिडेनें, भिडस्तपणानें, भीडराखून, मुरवतराखून.

DEFERRED, *p.* v. V. कालांतरावर घातलेला, मुद्दतीवर लोटलेला, दिवसगतीवर लोटलेला, &c. विलंबित.

DEFIANCE, DEFYING, *n.* v. V. 1. युद्धाह्वान *n.* अहंतापूर्वकाह्वान *n.* अहोपुरुषिका *f.*

In d. of. हटकून, हटेंच.

To bid d. See To DEFY.

DEFICIENCY, *n. want.* उणवाई *f.* उणावळ *f.* उणीव *f.* उणावा *m.* बाण *f.* कमती *f.* कमीपणा *m.* कमताई *f.* कमतर *f.* कमतणूक *f.* निवंना *f.* कोताई *f.* नपूर *or* निपूर *f.* अपूर *f.* अपूरनपूर *f.* तूट *f.* तोटा *m.* न्यूनता *f.* खूट *f.*

Slight d. or excess. कमज्यास्त *n.* कमज्यास्ती *f.* फंपेश *m.*

DEFICIENT, *a.* v. WANTING. उणा, कमी, कमती, कमता, अपुरा, अपुरता, अपूर्ण, कोता, न्यून, ऊन, हीन.

DEFICIT. See DEFICIENCY.

DEFILE, *n. long narrow passage or way.* पन्हळ *or* पन्हाळ *m.f. dim.* पन्हळी *or* पन्हाळी *f.* खिंडवाट *f.* एकपावलीवाट *f.* गोंड *f. n.* बारी *f.*

To DEFILE, *v. a. make foul or unclean,* v. To DIRTY. मळवणें, मळकट-मळीण-&c. करणें.

2—*corrupt, vitiate, contaminate, taint.* अपवित्र-मळीण-खराब-लिप्त-लिप्साळा-भ्रष्ट-&c. करणें, बिघडवणें.

3—ceremonially; *pollute, make impure.* विटाळणें, बाटवणें, ओंवळा करणें. [चालणें-जाणें.

To DEFILE, *v. n. go file by file.* एकामागूनएक अशा ओळीनें

DEFILED, *p.* v. V. A.1. *and* DIRTY. मळवलेला, मलकटलेला, मळीण, प्राप्तमल, जातमल.

2 अपवित्र-&c. केलेला, बिघडवलेला,-&c. लिप्त, लिप्साळा, भ्रष्ट.

3 विटाळलेला, बाटवलेला, बाटगा, बाट्या.

To be d. बाटणें, विटाळणें.

DEFILEMENT, *n.* v. V. A 1.—*act.* मळवणें *n.* मळकट करणें *n.* &c.—*state.* मळवलेलेपणा *m.* मळीणपणा *m.* प्राप्तमलता *f.* [भ्रष्टता *f.*

2—*act.* अपवित्र करणें *n.* बिघडवणें *n.* &c.-*state.* अपवित्रता *f.*

3—*act.* विटाळणें *n.* बाटवणें *n.* &c.—*state.* विटाळ *m.* बाट *m.* बाटगेपणा *m.* बाटवडा *m.*

D.-gener. विटाळचंडाळ *m.*

General d. बाटाबाट *f.* भ्रष्टाकार *m.* [मलप्रद.

DEFILER, *n.* DEFILING, *p. a.* v. V.A.1. मळवणारा, &c. मलावह,

2 बिघडविणारा, अपवित्र-भ्रष्ट-&c. कर्त्ता-कारी-कारक.

3 विटाळणारा, बाटवणारा, &c. [लक्षणीय.

DEFINABLE, *a.* v. V. 2. लक्षण करायाजोगा-&c. निर्वचनीय, लक्ष्य,

To DEFINE, *v. a.* See To CIRCUMSCRIBE. 2—in logic. लक्षण *n.* करणें-सांगणें-बांधणें, निर्वचणें, अनुगम *m.*-निर्वचन *n.*-निरुक्ति *f.* करणें *g. of o.*

DEFINED, *p.* v. V. 2. लक्षण बांधलेला, &c. निरुक्त, कृतनिर्वचन, कृतलक्षण, अनुगत.

DEFINITE. See DETERMINATE.

DEFINITION, *n.* v. V. 2. लक्षण *n.* निरुक्ति *f.* निर्वचन *n.*

Justness of d. लक्षणसमन्वय.

DEFINITIVE. See DETERMINATE.

To DEFLECT, DEFLECTION, DEFLEXURE. See To DEVIATE, DEVIATION.

DEFLORATION, DEFLOURING, *n.* v. V.—*act.* चिरा उतरणें *n.* हातलावणी *f.* कौमार्यभंग *m.* कौमार्यनाश *m.* सक्षतीकरण *n.* कन्याधर्षण *n.*

2 उत्तमांशहरण *n.*

To DEFLOUR, *v. a. deprive of virginity.* चिरा *m.* उतरणें-फोडणें *g. of o.* हातलावणी *f.* करणें *g. of o.* असविणें, कौमार्यभंग *m.*-कौमार्यनाश *m.* करणें *g. of o.* क्षत-सक्षत करणें.

2 *take away the prime.* उत्तम अंश *m.*-तत्तामाल *m.*-&c.नेणें.

DEFLUXION, *n.* खालीं वाहणें *n.* अधःप्रवाह *m.*

To DEFORM, *v.a. mar the form, render ugly,* v. To DISFIGURE. विरूप-कुरूप-&c. करणें, रूप *n.* मोडणें *g. of o.* आकारभंग *m.*-रूपभंग *m.*-&c. करणें *g. of o.*

DEFORMED, *a. distorted, &c.* v. UGLY. खुळा *remiss.* खुळपट, व्यंग, विकल, विकलांग, विकृतांग, खेंबडा, अपरूप, विरूप, हीनरूप, अपांग.

D. in all his limbs. अष्टवक्र *pop.* अष्टावक्र.

DEFORMITY, DEFORMEDNESS, *n.* v. A. व्यंग *n.* व्यंगता *f.* वैकल्य *n.* अंगवैकल्य *n.* वैरूप्य *n.* विरूपता *f.* विकलांगत्व *n.*

I. a deformity. व्यंग *n.* ऐब *m.*

To DEFRAUD. See To CHEAT, To DECEIVE.

To DEFRAY, *v. a. bear the expense of.* निस्तारणें, वारणें, फेडणें, करणें, देणें, माथींघेणें, अदा करणें, निर्वाह *m.* करणें *g. of o.*

DEFT, *a. dexterous,* v. EXPERT. दक्ष. [प्राप्त.

DEFUNCT, *a.* v. DEAD. मेलेला, मृत, मयत, लोकांतरगत, लोकांतर

To DEFY, *v. a. call to combat,* v. To CHALLENGE. अहंतापूर्वकाह्वान *n.* करणें, युद्धाह्वान *m.* करणें, अहोपुरुषिका *f.* दाखवणें-करणें.

2 *brave,* v. To DARE. तुच्छ मानणें-करणें, तृणवत् मोजणें, नजुमानणें, कःपदार्थ *m.* समजणें.

DEGENERACY, *n.* v. A. मूलगुणांचा-ऱ्हास *m.* मूलगुणक्षीणता *f.* मूलगुण-ऱ्हास *m.* मूलसत्व-ऱ्हास *m.* मूलगुणापकर्ष *m.* मूलगुणापकृष्टता *f.* मूलगुणभ्रष्टता *f.* मूलधर्मभ्रष्टता *f.* वैगुण्य *n.*

To DEGENERATE, *v. n. decline in goodness.* मूलगुण *m.*-मूलस-

त्व *n.*-&c. सोडणें, गुण-ह्रास *m.*-सत्व-ह्रास *m.*-सत्वक्षीणता *f.*-&c. होणें *g. of s.* उतरणें, बिघडणें, बिचलणें.

DEGENERATE, *a.* DEGENERATED, *p.* DEGENEROUS, *a.* v.V. गुणक्षीण, मूलगुणभ्रष्ट, गुणापकृष्ट, अपकृष्टगुण, कमजात, बिगुण, भ्रष्ट, पतित, अधम.

DEGLUTITION, *n. swallowing.* गिळणें *n.* गिलन *n.* निगरण *n.*

DEGRADATION, *n.* v. V.—*act.* पदवी हलकी करणें *n.* &c.—*state.* मानभंग *m.* माननाश *m.* मान-ह्रास *m.* भ्रंश *m.* च्युति *f.* पदच्युति *f.* स्थानच्युति *f.* &c. अपकर्ष *m.* पातित्य *n.*

To DEGRADE, *v. a. lower in rank, dignity, &c.* पदवी *f.*-योग्यता *f.*-किमत *f.*-मान *m.*-&c. हलका करणें *g. of o.* हलका-&c. करणें, हलके पदवीस-हलके पायरीस-&c. आणणें, मानभंग *m.*-मान-ह्रास *m.*-भ्रंश *m.*-अपकर्ष *m.*-&c. करणें *g. of o.* पदच्युत-पदभ्रष्ट-&c. करणें.

DEGRADED, *p.* v. V. हलके पदवीस आणलेला, &c. पदच्युत, पदभ्रष्ट, स्थानच्युत, स्थानभ्रष्ट, पतित, मानभ्रष्ट, मानच्युत, गतमान, नष्टमान, भ्रष्टमान, गलितमान.

DEGRADING, *a. lowering, disreputable,* v. DISHONORABLE. आब्रूघेणा, इज्जतघेणा, इज्जतखाऊ, अपयशाचा, बेआब्रूचा.

DEGREE, *n. rank, station.* पदवी *f.* पायरी *f.* मरातब *m.f.* पद *n.* दर्जा *m.*

2 *grade, step, stage.* पर्याय *m.* पायरी *f.*

By degrees. पर्यायपर्यायानें, क्रमशः, क्रमतः, अंशतः.

3 See EXTENT, MEASURE.

In the smallest d. जरा बाजरा, अणुमात्र, काडीमात्र, अणुरेणु, किमपि *with neg. con.*

Lowest d. कनिष्ठपक्ष *m.* निरुष्टपक्ष *m.* करंटपक्ष *m.*

To this d. इतपत, इथवर.

4—in geometry. अंश *m.* भाग *m.*

Equation of a d. आप्त *n.*

5 (of latitude). अक्षांश *m.*

6 (of longitude). रेखांश *m.*

7 (at a university). विद्यालयांतली पदवी *f.*

To DEHORT, *v. a. exhort against.* v. To DISSUADE. निवारणार्थ-निवृत्त्यर्थ-&c. बुद्धिवाद *m.* सांगणें-उपदेश *m.* करणें, परावर्त्तन बुद्धि *f.* सांगणें, निवारणोपदेश *m.* करणें.

DEHORTATION, *n.* v. V. निवारणार्थ बुद्धिवाद *m.* निवारणोपदेश *m.*

DEHORTATORY, *a.* निवारणोपदेशाचा, निवारणोपदेशात्मक.

To DEIFY, *v. a.* देव *m.* करणें, देवपद *n.* देणें, देवांत गणणें.

2 See To IDOLIZE.

To DEIGN, *v. n. condescend.* मेहरबानी *f.*-कृपा *f.*-अनुग्रह *m.*-प्रसाद *m.*-&c. करणें, मेहरबान-प्रसन्न-&c. होणें.

DEISM, *n.* केवलेश्वरमत *n.* शास्त्रनिराकृतिकेश्वरवाद *m.*-मत *n.*

DEIST, *n.* केवलेश्वरवादी, केवलेश्वरमतानुसारी, शास्त्रनिराकृतिकेश्वर मतवादी.

DEISTIC, DEISTICAL, *a.* केवलेश्वरमतसंबंधी-विषयक, शास्त्रनिराकृतिकेश्वरमतानुसारी.

DEITY, *n. divinity,* v. GODHEAD. देवपणा *m.* देवत्व *n.* देवता *f.*

2 *the* D. v. GOD. देव *m.* भगवान् *pop.* भगवंत *m.* परमेश्वर *m.* ईश्वर *m.*

3 *a* d. v. GOD. देव *m.* देवता *f.* दैवत *n.*

To DEJECT, *v. a.* v. To DISPIRIT. उत्साहभंग *m.*- मनोभंग *m.*-&c. करणें *g. of o.* खिन्न-उदास-उदासी-&c. करणें.

DEJECTED, *p.* v. V. खिन्न-&c. केलेला-झालेला, खिन्न, उदास, अवसन्न, मलूल.

DEJECTEDLY, *adv.* उदासपणानें, औदासीन्यपूर्वक, विषादपूर्वक.

DEJECTION, DEJECTEDNESS, *n.* v. V.—*state.* उदासपणा *m.* औदासीन्य *n.* खिन्नता *f.* अवसाद *m.* विषाद *m.* विषण्णता *f.*

I. a d. v. STOOL. झाडा *m.* जुलाब *m.*

To DELAY, *v. a. put off,* v. To DEFER. बिलंब*m.*-दिरिंग*m.*-उशीर*m.* करणें-लावणें, वेळ*m.* लावणें, उपेक्षणें, टाळा*m.* देणें, दिवसगतीवर-&c. टाळणें-ढकलणें-घालणें-लोटणें-&c.

2 *stop, detain.* खोळंबवणें, थांबवणें, खोळंबा*m.*-खोटी*f.*-&c. करणें *g. of o.* गतिभंग*m.*-गतिरोध*m.*-&c. करणें *g. of o.*

To DELAY, *v. n.* See To DAWDLE.

DELAY, DELAYING, *n.* v.V.A. 1.—*act.* उशीर लावणें*n.* बिलंब करणें*n.* &c. बिलंब*m.* बिलंबन*n.* घालघसर *f.* ढकल *f.* ढकलपट्टी *f.* टाळा*m.* उपेक्षा *f.* [गतिरोध *m.*

2—*act.* खोळंबवणें *n.* &c.—*state.* खोटी *f.* खोळंबा*m.* गतिभंग*m.*

I. *lateness, &c.* उशीर*m.* वेळ*m.* दिरिंग *or* दिरंग*m.* बिलंब*m.* कालबिलंब*m.* काळगत. *f.* वार*m.f.* देर *f.* विमर्द *m.*

DELAYED, *p.* v. V. A. 1. दिवसगतीवर घातलेला &c. बिलंबित, प्राप्तबिलंब, उपेक्षित.

2 खोळंबवलेला, खोळंबलेला, &c. खोटी, गतिरुद्ध.

To be d. खोळंबणें, खोटी *f.*-खोळंबा*m.* होणें *g. of s.*

DELAYER, *n.* v.V.A.1. बिलंब लावणारा, &c. घालघसऱ्या, उपेक्षक.

DELEBLE, *a. that can be blotted out.* पुसून टाकायाजोगा-&c.

DELECTABLE, DELECTATION. See DELIGHTFUL, DELIGHT.

To DELEGATE, *v. a. intrust,* See To COMMIT. 2 *commission and send.* वकील-&c. करून पाठवणें.

DELEGATE, *n. deputy, agent,* वकील, अखत्यारी, मुनीम, प्रतिनिधि.

DELETERIOUS, *a.* v. DEADLY. घातक, प्राणांतक, प्राणनाशक, निधनकारी.

2 *injurious,* v. HURTFUL. अपकारक, अपकारी.

To DELIBERATE, *v. n. pause and consider, weigh reasons for and against a measure.* विचार*m.* करणें-पाहणें, मसलत *f.*-मनसुबा *m.*-विचारण *n.*-मनन *n.*-&c. करणें, विचारांत असणें, करूं नकरूं पाहणें-करणें.

DELIBERATE, *a. circumspect, thoughtful.* विचारी, विचारशील, विचारवान् *pop.* विचारवंत, विचारानुयायी, सविचार, समीक्ष्यकारी, विमृश्यकारी, संप्रेक्ष्यकारी.

2 *formed or done with deliberation.* विचाराचा, विचारानें केलेला, विचारपूर्वक, विचारसिद्ध, सविचार, सावधगिरीचा.

DELIBERATELY, *adv.* v. A. *and* DESIGNEDLY. विचारानें, विचारकरून, विचारपूर्वक, विचारपुरस्सर, अक्कल हुशारीनें, जाणून, जाणूनबुजून, समजूनउमजून, बुद्ध्या.

DELIBERATENESS, *n.* v. A. विचारशीलता *f.* विचारिता *f.* विचारानुयायित्व *n.* विमृश्यकारिता *f.* समीक्ष्यकारित्व*n.* संप्रेक्ष्यकारिता *f.*

2 विचारपूर्वकता *f.* विचारसिद्धता *f.* सविचारता *f.*

I. See DELIBERATION.

DELIBERATION, *n.* v. V. विचार करणें *n.* विचार पाहणें *n.* विचार *m.* मसलत *f.* मनसुबा*m.* विचारण *n.* विचारणा *f.* मनन*n.* पूर्वापरविचार *m.* मागलापुढला बिचार *m.* आगचामागचा विचार *m.* कर्त्तव्याकर्त्तव्यविचार *m.* कार्याकार्यविचार*m.* आदिपश्चात्विचार*m.*

DELIBERATIVE, *a. having a right, &c. to deliberate.* विचार करण्याचे कामाचा, विचार करण्याचे अधिकाराचा.

DELICACY, DELICATENESS, *n.* v. A. 1. मिजाज *f.* खंत *f.* खोड *f.* चखनटपणा *m.* &c.
2 नाजकाई *f.* नाजूकपणा *m.* सोंगळपणा *m.* हल्वटपणा *m.* &c. सौकुमार्य *n.* सुकुमारत्व *n.* कोमलता *f.*
3 नाजकाई *f.* बारकाई *f.* नाजूकपणा *m.* बारिकपणा *m.* लाघव *n.*
4 मऊपणा *m.* मृदुपणा *m.* मृदुत्व *n.* &c. लाघव *n.*
5 भीड *f.* मुरवत *f.* मर्यादा *f.* मर्यादशीलता *f.* मुखदाक्षिण्य *n.* मुखसंकोच *m.*
I. See DAINTY.

DELICATE, *a. nice in eating,* v. DAINTY. मिजाजखोर, खंतखोर, चखनट, चोखनळ, चोखारी.
2 *tender, soft, not hardy.* नाजूक, कोमल, सुकुमार *or* सकुमार, प्रकृतीचा हल्वट, सोंगळ, सोमल *or* सोंवळ, सूक्ष्म, हल्वट, मुलाईम, तलम, अलकृत, हलुमाळ *or* हलुमळ.
3 *slender, thin, slight, feeble, &c.* v. WEAK. नाजूक, बारीक, हलका, लघु.
4 *soft, fine, &c.* मऊ, मृदु, सूक्ष्म, कोमल, मुलाईम.
5 *paying minute regard to feeling.* भिडेचा, भिडेभाडेचा, मुरवतीचा, भीडमुरवतीचा, भिडस्त, मर्यादेचा, मर्यादशील, मुखसंकोचाचा, मुखदाक्षिण्याचा.
6 *pleasing to the taste, nice.* गोड, रुचिकर, मजेदार.
7 *that requires careful treatment,*—a point, &c. नाजूक, नाजकाईचा, बारीक.
8 *of fine texture.* तलम, तलमसुती.

DELICATELY, *adv.* v. A. 5. भिडेनें, भिडस्तपणानें, भीड-मुरवत राखून.
To live d. *fare daintily.* मिष्टान्न *n.*-पक्वान्नें *n. pl.*-&c. रोजखायालामिळणें *in.con.*

DELICIOUS, *a. luscious.* गोड, रुचिर, रुच्य, रुचिकर, रुचीक, मजेदार, रसभरित, मिष्ट, स्वादु, स्वादिष्ट.

DELICIOUSNESS, *n.* v. A. गोडी *f.* चव *f.* रुच्यता *f.* रुचि *f.* खुमारी *f.* मजेदारी *f.* परितोष *m.*

DELIGHT, *n.* v. PLEASURE. हर्ष *m.* आनंद *m.* उल्लास *m.* संतोष *m.*

To **DELIGHT,** *v. a.* v. To PLEASE. आनंदविणें, हर्षविणें, संतोषविणें, रिझवणें, आनंद *m.*-हर्ष *m.*-&c. देणें, खुश-संतुष्ट-आनंदित-परितुष्ट-&c. करणें.

To **DELIGHT IN,** *v. n.* रमणें, रतणें, रिझणें, रीज *or* रीझ *f.*-शौक *m.*-आवड *f.* असणें *g. of o.* सुख *n.*-आनंद *m.*-हर्ष *m.* पावणें.

DELIGHTED, *p.* v.V.A. हर्षविलेला, &c. हर्षित, आनंदित, उत्साहित, उल्लसित, परितुष्ट.
To be d. *feel glad.* आनंद *m.*-हर्ष *m.*-&c. वाटणें *in. con.*
To be highly d. बाल दाल खुश होणें.

DELIGHTFUL, DELIGHTSOME, *a.* v. V. A. *and* AGREEABLE. आनंदविणारा, &c. हर्षक, सुख-आनंद-हर्ष-&c. दायक-कर-कारक-कारी-&c. रंजक, अनुरंजक, रमणीय, रम्य, रमणीक.

DELIGHTFULLY, DELIGHTSOMELY, *adv. in a manner to receive pleasure.* सुखानें, सुख वाटे असें.
2 *in a manner to give pleasure.* आनंद देण्याजोग्या रीतीनें.

DELIGHTFULNESS, DELIGHTSOMENESS, *n.* v. A. रंजकत्व *n.* हर्षकत्व *n.* आनंददायकत्व *n.* &c.
2 See PLEASURE.

To **DELINEATE,** *v. a. trace the lineaments, sketch, &c.* अंकणें, रेखटणें *or* रेखाटणें, रेखणें, काढणें, अंकन *n.*-अंकणी *f.* नकशा *m.*-आलेख्य *n.*-&c. करणें *g. of o.*
2 v. To DESCRIBE. निरूपिणें, निरूपण *n.* करणें *g. of o.*

DELINEATED, *p.* v. V. 1. अंकलेला, रेखटलेला, &c. लिखित, चित्रगत.
2 निरूपिलेला, &c. निरूपित, वर्णित.

DELINEATER, *n.* **DELINEATING,** *p. a.* v. V. 1. अंकणारा, रेखटणारा, &c.
2 निरूपिणारा, निरूपक, निरूपणकर्त्ता-कारक.

DELINEATION, *n.* v. V. 1.—*act.* अंकणें *n.* रेखणें *n.* &c. अंकणी *f.* अंकन *n.* आलेख्य *n.*
2 निरूपिणें *n.* निरूपण *n.* वर्णन *n.*
I. *draught, sketch, &c.* नकाशा *m.* नकशा *m.* रेखटलेला आकार *m.*

DELINQUENCY, *n. failure in duty, &c.* v. FAULT. अपराध *m.* गुन्हा *m.* तकूशीर *f.* तफावत *f.* कसर *f.*

DELINQUENT, *n. offender.* अपराधी, गुन्हेगार, अपराधकर्त्ता, दोषी, चाकरीचा-&c. तफावती.

To **DELIQUATE.** See To MELT.

To **DELIQUESCE,** To **DELIQUIATE,** *v. n.* हवेंतला ओलावा शोषून विरघळणें-रस *m.* होणें.

DELIQUESCENCE, *n.* हवेंतल्या ओलाव्यानें विरघळणें *n.*-रस *m.* होणें *n.*

DELIQUESCENT, *a.* हवेंतल्या ओलाव्यानें विरघळणारा- रसहोणारा.

DELIRIOUS, *a. raving.* बरळणारा, बरळत-चावळत-&c. पडलेला, प्रलापी, बेशुद्ध, बेसावध, बेहोश.

DELIRIUM, *n.* सर *m. f.* चित्ताचाभ्रम *m.* चित्तविभ्रम *m.* बुद्धिविभ्रम *m.* ज्वरमोह *m.* प्रजल्पावस्था *f.* उन्मत्तवायु *m.*
D. tremens. सतत व पुष्कळ दारू पिऊन जें वेड लागतें तें.

To **DELIVER,** *v. a. liberate, release, set free,* v. To FREE. सोडवणें, सोडणें, बंदखलास-मोकळा-मुक्त-&c. करणें.
2 *rescue, save.* तारणें, उद्धरणें, काढणें, बचावणें, बचाव *m.*-उद्धार *m.*-उद्धरण *n.*-उद्धारगत *f.*-तारण *n.*-&c. करणें *g. of o.*
3 *present, offer,* v. To GIVE. देणें, हातीं देणें, अर्पणें, समर्पणें, निवेदणें, ओपणें, स्वाधीन करणें, पदरीं घालणें.
4 (a woman in child birth). कोन *m.*-प्रसव *m.* करणें *g. of o.* प्रसवविणें, प्रसूत-बाळंत-&c. करणें, सुटका *f.* करणें *g. of o.* सोडवणें, गर्भमोचन *n.* करणें.
5 (address, lecture, &c.) देणें, करणें.
6 up; *give up.* देणें, सोडणें, स्वाधीन करणें, हातीं देणें, पदरीं घालणें.

DELIVERANCE, DELIVERY, *n.* v. V. 1.—*act.* सोडवणें *n.* सोडणें *n.* &c.—*a. or s.* सोडवण *f.* सोडवणूक *f.* बंदखलास *m.* सुटका *f.* मोकळीक *f.*
2—*act.* तारणें *n.* उद्धरणें *n.* &c. तारण *n.* उद्धरण *n.* त्राण *n.* —*state.* उद्धार *m.* उद्धारगत *f.*
3—*act.* देणें *n.* अर्पणें *n.* &c. अर्पण *n.* समर्पण *n.* निवेदन *n.* विधान *n.*
4—*act.* बाळंत करणें *n.* प्रसूत करणें *n.* प्रसवविणें *n.* &c. प्रसवक्रिया *f.* गर्भमोचन *n.*—*state.* v. CHILD-BIRTH. प्रसव *m.* सूति *f.* प्रसूति *f.*
Easy d. सुखप्रसव *m.*
Month of d. सूतिमास *m.*
To be on the point of d. बाळंत व्हायास टेकणें-टेकावणें.
I. See PRONUNCIATION, UTTERANCE.

DELIVERED, *p.* v. V.1. सोडवलेला, सोडलेला, &c. बंदखलास, बंधनमुक्त, मुक्त.
2 तारलेला, उद्धरलेला, &c. तारित, उद्धृत.
3 दिल्हेला, &c. अर्पित, समर्पित, निवेदित, विहित, निहित, न्यस्त.
4 बाळंत केलेला-झालेला, &c. प्रसूत.

A woman d. बाळंतीण *f.* बाळंत *f.* कोन निघालेली *f.* प्रसूतिका *f.* सूतिका *f.*

To be d. बाळंत होणें, कोन *m.* निघणें *g. of s.* प्रसब *m.*-&c. होणे *g. of s.* हातीं पायीं उतरणें-सुटणें, दोन जिवांचा निवाडा *m.* होणें.

DELIVERER, *n.* v. V. 1. सोडवणारा &c. मोचक, मुक्तिकर्त्ता-कारक-&c.

2 तारणारा, उद्धरणारा, &c. तारक, उद्धारक, उद्धर्त्ता, उद्धार-तारण-&c. कर्त्ता.

3 देणारा &c. अर्पक, समर्पक, निवेदक.

DELL, *n. hollow among hills, &c.* खोंडा *m.* कोंडकें *n.* दरा*m dim.* दरी *f.* भुयार *n.*

DELTA, *n.* चिमट्याचा-चिमट्यांतला प्रदेश *m.*

To DELUDE, *v. a.* v. To DECEIVE. फसवणें, वंचणें, झकवणें, छकावणें, दगा *m.*-झोला *m.*- ढोला *m.* देणें.

DELUDED, *p.* v. V. फसवलेला, &c. वंचित.

DELUGE, *n. inundation.* पाणजंजाळ *n.* जगबूड *f.* जगबुडती *f.* जलप्रलय *m.* जलप्लव *m.* संप्लव *m.* एकार्णव *m.*

To DELUGE, *v. a. inundate, flood.* बुडविणें, गर्क करणें, जलमय-जलप्लावित-&c. करणें. [करणारा, &c.

DELUGER, *n.* DELUGING, *p. a.* v. V. बुडविणारा, &c. पाण जंजाळ

DELUSION, *n.* v. V.—*act.* फसवणें *n.* ठकवणें *n.* &c. फसवणूक *f.* वंचन *n.*—*state.* फसगत *f.* फसगपत *f.* फटवण *f.* मोह *m.* भ्रम *m.* भ्रांति *f.*

I. *illusion.* माया *f.* मोह *m.*

DELUSIVE, DELUSORY, *a.* v. V. फसवणारा, &c. ठकाऊ, ठकारू, ठकडा, कपटी, सकपट, फसवणुकीचा, मोहाचा, मायेचा, मोहक, मोहकर्त्ता-कारक-&c. भ्रम-भ्रांति-&c. कर-कारक-&c.

To DELVE See To DIG. [*m.* प्रजानायक.

DEMAGOGUE, *n. leader of the mob.* ग्राम *m.* ग्रामणी *m.* गांवगुंड

DEMAIN, DEMESNE, *n.* स्वाधीनभूमि *f.* स्वसत्ताक्रांत देश *m.*

To DEMAND, *v. a. require of right,* v. To CLAIM. सत्तेचा-सत्तेनें-हक्काचा-&c. मागणें, सत्ता *f.* करणें *with* ला *or* स *of o.* अधिकारपूर्वक मागणें, दावा *m.* करणें *with* वर *of o.*

2 See To ASK.

DEMAND, DEMANDING, *n.* v. V. 1.—*act.* सत्तेचें मागणें *n.* हक्काचें मागणें *n.* दावा *m.* [*f.* अपेक्षा *f.*

I. *call for, requisition.* मागणें *n.* मागणी *f* तलब *f.* आकांक्षा

General or great d. for. हकारा *m.* हकारा *m.* मार *m.* सपाटा *m.* झोड *f.*

II. *price asked.* सांगितलेलें-मागितलेलें मोल *n.*

Exorbitant d. *high terms.* हाक *f.*

DEMANDANT. See PLAINTIFF.

DEMARCATION, *n. marking off.* परिछेद *m.*

2 *limit,* v. BOUND. सीमा *pop.* शींव *or* शींव *f.* हद्द *f.*

To DEMEAN, (one's self). *v. a.* v. To BEHAVE. आचरणें, वागणें, वागणूक *f.*-&c. करणें.

2 (one's self) v. To ABASE. कमीपणा *m.*-हलकेपणा *m.* घेणें.

DEMEANOUR, *n.* v. CONDUCT. आचरण *n.* वर्त्तणूक *f.* चाल *f.*

To DEMENTATE, &c. See To MADDEN, &c.

DEMERIT, *n. ill deserving, &c.* दोष *m.* पाप *n.* नालायकी *f.* असौष्ठव *n.* दंडार्हता *f.* दूष्यता *f.* दौर्गुण्य *n.*

DEMI, *prefix.* अर्ध.

DEMI-GOD, *n.* v. GOD. उपदेव *m.* उपदेवता *f.* देवयोनि *f.*

DEMISE, *n.* v. DEATH. मरण *n.* निवृत्ति *f.* लोकांतरगमन *n.*

To DEMISE. See To BEQUEATH.

DEMOCRACY, *n. government by the people.* लोकांचें राज्य *n.* लोकप्रभुत्व *n.* लोककर्तृकराज्य *n.* बहुनायकी *f.* लोकसाधारणाधिपत्य *n.*

DEMOCRAT, *n.* लोककर्तृकराज्यप्रवर्त्तक-पक्षपाती-&c.

DEMOCRATIC, DEMOCRATICAL, *a.* v. N. लोककर्तृकराज्य संबंधी-विषयक, लोकप्रभुत्वसंबंधी, लोकसाधारणाधिपत्यसंबंधी-विषयक.

To DEMOLISH, *v. a. raze, dismantle,* v. To DESTROY. मोडणें, मोडून टाकणें, पाडणें, पाडून-भंगून टाकणें, मोडून तोडून टाकणें, चपाट *or* सपाट-जमीनदोस्त करणें, निर्दळण *n.*-&c. करणें *g. of o.* निर्दाळणें.

DEMOLISHED, *p.* v. V. मोडलेला, मोडून तोडून टाकलेला, &c. चपाट, चपेट, जमीनदोस्त, निर्दलित.

DEMOLITION, *n.* v. V.—*act.* मोडून टाकणें *n.* मोडून तोडून टाकणें *n.* &c. निर्दळणी *or* निर्दाळणी *f.* निर्दळण *or* निर्दाळण *n.* निर्दलन *n.* निर्दलना *f.* उपहंती *f.* [देवता *f.*

DEMON, *n.* v. DEVIL. देव *m.* भूत *n.* पिशाच *m.* देवयोनि *f.* अप-

2—in mythology, *Titan.* दैत्य *m.* दानव *m.* असुर *m.*

Water d. गिन्हा *m.* आखा *f.*

DEMONIAC, DEMONIACAL, *a.* v. N. 1. *and* DEVILISH. भूताचा, पिशाचाचा, पैशाच, पैशाचिक.

2 असुरी, असुराचा, असुरकृत, असुरसंबंधी, &c. आसुर.

D. possession, influence, &c. भूतबाधा *f.* पिशाचबाधा *f.* &c. See under DEVIL. [नुष्य *n.*

DEMONIAC, *n. possessed person.* भूतग्रस्त मनुष्य *n.* पिशाचग्रस्तम-

DEMONOLATRY, *n.* भूतार्चन *n.* भूतभक्ति *f.* पिशाचभक्ति *f.*

DEMONOLOGY, *n.* भूतपिशाचादिविषयकनिबंध *m.*

DEMONSTRABLE, *a.* v. V. प्रमाणदेऊनसिद्धकरायाजोगा-सारखा-&c. प्रतिपादनीय, प्रतिपाद्य, उपपादनीय.

DEMONSTRANDUM, *n.*—in logic. साध्य *n.*

To DEMONSTRATE, *v. a. prove to be certain.* प्रमाणें देऊन सिद्ध करणें, सिद्धांत *m.* करणें *g. of o.* साधणें, प्रतिपादणें, प्रतिपादन *n.*-उपपादन *n.*-&c. करणें *g. of o.* सिद्धांतित-प्रमाणसिद्ध-सप्रमाण-शाबूत-प्रतिपादित-&c. करणें, खचीत करून दाखवणें.

DEMONSTRATED, *p.* v. V. सिद्ध केलेला, &c. सिद्ध, सिद्धांतित, प्रतिपादित.

DEMONSTRATION, *n.* v. V.—*act.* साधणें *n.* सिद्ध करणें *n.* &c. साधन *n.* प्रतिपादन *n.* उपपादन *n.* सिद्धि *f.* उपपत्ति *f.* प्रतिपत्ति *f.*

I. *matter demonstrated,* v. CONCLUSION. सिद्धांत *m.* खचितार्थ *m.*

II. demonstrations; *imposing indications, preparations, &c.* आव *m.* आवारा *m.* खटाटोप *m.* आडंबर *m.* डौल *m.* मांडणूक *f.* मांडणी *f.* घटाव *m.*

Empty d. मेघाडंबर *m.* *n.* अजायुद्ध *n.*

DEMONSTRATOR, *n.* DEMONSTRATIVE, *a.* v. V. सिद्ध करणारा, सिद्धांत करणारा, सैद्धांतिक, प्रतिपादक, प्रमाता, उद्बोधक.

I. See CONCLUSIVE.

DEMONSTRATIVELY, *adv.* सबलप्रमाणें-प्रमाणें देऊन-दाखवून, उपपत्तिपूर्वक, खातरीहोण्याजोगा-&c. *decl.*

To DEMORALIZE, &c. See To CORRUPT, &c.

DEMULCENT, *a. softening.* मऊ करणारा, मऊ करणाऱ्या गुणाचा, मृदु-&c. कारी.

To DEMUR, *v. n.* v. To HESITATE कांकरणें, कांकूं *f.*-कानकून *f.*-

नानू *f.*-&c. करणें, बुचकळणें or बुचकुळणें, मागें पुढें करणें-घेणें, कुरू नकरू करणें, आक्षेप *m.* धरणें.

2 (in law) नकरार *f.* सांगून थांबणें.

DEMUR, DEMURRING, *n.* v. V. कांकरणें*n.* &c. कांकूं *f.* कानकून *f.* नानू *f.* नचनन्*n.* आक्षेप*m.*

DEMURE, *a. affectedly modest*, v. HYPOCRITICAL. गोमुख्या, भगळी, भगल्या, भगलभावार्थी, बोकेसन्यासी, बकध्यानी.

A d. villain. मिस्कीन मारवाडी, मिस्कीन मात्रागमनी.

2 SEE GRAVE. [स्कीनपणानें.

DEMURELY, *adv.* v. A. 1. बोकेसन्यास घेऊन, बकध्यान धरून, मि-

DEMURENESS, *n.* v. A. 1. *and* HYPOCRISY. भगल *f.n.* बोकेसन्यास *m.* बकध्यान *n.* मिस्कीनपणा *m.*

DEMURRAGE, *n.* गलबत खोळंबविल्या बदलचें देणें *n.*-खुटवा *m.*

DEMY, *n.* कागदाचा एक प्रकार आहे. [ढोल *f.*

DEN, *n.* (of a wild beast). बिल *pop.* बीळ *n.* गुहा *f.* दरी *f.*

Tiger's d. वाघबीळ*n.* [निषेधनीय.

DENIABLE, *a.* v. V. 1. नाकारायाजोगा-सारखा.-&c. निषेध्य,

2 नाकाराया जोगा-&c.

DENIAL, DENYING, *n.* v. V. 1.—*act.* नकारणें *n.* निषेधणें *n.* &c. नकार or नाकार *m.* निषेध *m.* प्रतिषेध *m* अस्वीकार *m.* अनंगीकार *m.* प्रत्याख्यान *n.* निरसन *n.* निरासन *n.* निराकरण *n.* निराकृति *f.* आक्षेप *m.*

2—*act.* नकारणें *n.* निषेधणें *n.* &c. नकार or नाकार *m.* निषेध *m.* निराकरण *n.* निराकृति *f.*

3—*act.* नकारणें *n* &c. नकार or नाकार *m.* अस्वीकार *m.* अनंगीकार *m.* अपह्नुति *f.* अपह्नव *m.*

DENIED, *p.* v. V. 1. नकारलेला, निषेधलेला, &c. निषेधित, निषिद्ध, प्रतिषिध, प्रत्याख्यात, निरस्त, रद्द, आक्षिप्त, अस्वीकृत, अनंगीकृत.

To DENIGRATE. See To BLACKEN

DENIZEN, *n. alien admitted to citizenship.* पौरीकृतजन *m.*

2 *dweller.* राहणारा, वासी *in comp.* स्थ *in comp.*

To DENOMINATE, *v. a. name.* संज्ञा *f.*-नाम *n.*-नांव *n.*-अभिधान *n.* देणें-ठेवणें.

DENOMINATION, *n.* v. NAME. नांव*n.* संज्ञा *f.*

2 v. SECT. पंथ *m.* मार्ग *m.* शाखा *f* गण *m.*

DENOMINATIONAL, *a.* v. N. 2. शाखासंबंधी-विषयक

DENOMINATOR, *n.* (of a fraction). छेद *m.* छेदक *m.*

Common d. समच्छेद*m.* [ज्ञापन *n.*

DENOTATION, *n.* v. V.—*act.* दाखवणें *n.* &c. प्रदर्शन *n.* सूचन *n.*

To DENOTE, *v. a. betoken.* दाखवणें, दर्शवणें, जाणवणें, प्रदर्शन *n.*-उद्बोध *m.*-सूचन *n.*-ज्ञापन *n.*-&c. करणें *g.of o.* चिन्ह *n.*-लक्षण*n.* असणें *in. con. and g.of o.*

DE NOUEMENT, *n.* उलगडा *m.* उकल *m.*

To DENOUNCE, *To* DENUNCIATE, *v. a. declare in a threatening way.* धमकी देऊन-दारूवून सांगणें, धमकीचे बाटेनें सांगणें, हाक *f.*- हाकाटी *f.*मारून ठेवणें *g. of o.* धमकी *f.*-&c. देणें *g.of o.*

2 See To ACCUSE.

DENOVO, See ANEW.

DENSE, *a.*—of liquids, v. THICK. घट्ट, दाट, जाडा, घन.

2—of solids, v. COMPACT. घट्ट, घटमूट, दृढ.

3—of a forest, &c. v. THICK. निबिड, गर्दबाज, सांद्र.

DENSITY, DENSENESS, *n.* v. A. 1. घट्टपणा*m.* दाटपणा*m,* घट्टाई *f.* घनत्व*n.*

2 घट्टपणा*m.* दृढपणा*m.* दृढता *f.*

3 निबिडपणा *m.* गर्दबाजी *f.*

DENT. See DINT. [दांत.

DENTAL, *a. belonging &c. to the teeth.* दांताचा, दंत्य, दंतसंबंधी,

DENTICULATED, *a. set with teeth.* दंती,दात्यांचा, दंतेरा, दंतविशिष्ट.

DENTIFRICE, *n.* दांतवण *n.* दांतण *n.* दारशिणा or दांतचिना *m.* दंतचूर्ण*n.* दंतपवन*n.*

DENTIST, *n.* दंतवैद्य.

DENTITION, *n. teething.* दांत फुटणें *n.* दंतोद्भेद*m.* दंतोद्भव*m.*

To DENUDE. See To STRIP. [निश्चघोषण *n.*

DENUNCIATION *n.* v. V. धमकीदेऊन सांगणें *n.* &c. धमकी *f.* अ-

To DENY, *v. a. disallow, contradict,*—opposed to *admit.* नकारणें or नाकारणें, अमान्य करणें, निषेधणें, प्रतिषेधणें,नाकबूल करणें, नकार or नाकार*m.* करणें *g. of o.* अनंगीकार*m.*-अस्वीकार *m.*-निरसन*n.*- निराकरण*n.*- निराकृति *f.* करणें *g. of o.* कान*m. pl.* झाकणें, कानावर हात*m.* ठेवणें, आक्षेप *m.* करणें-घेणें, कानांत बोट*n.* घालणें, आंगाबाहेर-आंगा निराळा *decl.* करणें.

To d. one's word or engagement. बदलामीवरयेणें.

2 *refuse;*—opposed to *grant.* नकारणें or नाकारणें, निषेधणें, नकार or नाकार *m.* करणें, *g. of o.* ना म्हणणें-सांगणें, नचा फाडा*m.* वाचणें, निराकरण*n.*- निराकृति *f.*-&c. करणें *g. of o.*

To d. flatly. निक्षाडा *m.* देणें, बाटाण्याची अक्षत *f.* लावणें.

To d. one's self. जीव *m.* जाळणें-मारणें.

3 *disown, conceal,*—opposed to *confess.* नकारणें or नाकारणें, नकार or नाकार *m.* करणें *g. of o.* नाकबूल करणें, नाकबूल होणें-जाणें.

DEODAND, *n.* देवासदिल्हेला दंड *m.*

To DEPART, *v. n.* v. To GO. जाणें, निघून जाणें, रवाना-चालता-चालू-मार्गस्थ-&c. होणें, मार्ग *m.*-वाट *f.*-&c. धरणें, वाटेस-&c. लागणें, प्रयाण *n.*-प्रस्थान *n.* करणें.

2 v. To DIE.जाणें, गतणें, गुजरणें.

To d. this life, v. To DIE. जाणें, गतणें.

DEPARTMENT, *n.* खातें *n.* विल्हे *f.* विल्हा *m.* प्रकरण *n.* खिसा *m.*

DEPARTMENTAL, *a.* v. N. प्रकरणाचा, प्रकरणसंबंधी, प्राकरणिक, खात्याचा.

DEPARTURE, *n.* v. V. 1.—*act.* निघून जाणें *n.* &c. चलन *n.* प्रस्थान *n.* प्रयाण *n.* गमन *n.* विगम *m.* अपगम *m.* व्यपगम *m.* अवगति *f.* अपसरण *n.* निस्सरण *n.* निष्क्रमण *n.* निर्याण *n.*

2 See DEATH.

To DEPASTURE, *v. n. graze.* चरणें.

To DEPEND, *v. n. hang from.* v. To HANG. लोंबणें, अवलंबणें*pop.* ओळंबणें, ओंळकंबणें, लटकणें.

2 *be subject to, influenced by, &c. connected with as a cause.* टेंकणें-असणें *with* वर *of o.* लागीं-हातीं-स्वाधीन-&c. असणें*g.of o.*

3 *trust to,rely on,* v. To CONFIDE. अवलंबणें, ओठंगणें, टेंकणें -वसणें-राहणें-जाणें *with* वर *of o.* भरवश्यावर असणें *with g. of o.* अवलंब *m.*-अवलंबन *n.* करणें.

4 *be yet undetermined.* लोंबणें, हिलगणें, भिजत पडणें, अनिर्णीत-&c. असणें.

DEPENDENCE, DEPENDENCY, DEPENDING, *n.* v. V.—*state.* लोंबणें *n.* &c. अवलंब *m.* अवलंबन *n.* आलंब *m.* आलंबन *n.*

2 *and* CONNECTION. संबंध *m.* अधीनता *f.* [ळ टेंकणी *f.*

3 *and* CONFIDENCE. अवलंब *m.* अवलंबन *n.* कपाळटेंक *f.* कपा-

I. *state of being at the disposal of another.* ताबेदारी *f.* परतंत्रपणा *m.* पराश्रय *m.* पराधीनता *f.* परतंत्रता *f.* पारतंत्र्य *n.* अस्वातंत्र्य *n.*

II. dependency. ताब्यांतील प्रांत *m.*-देश *m.*-बेट *n.*-&c.

DEPENDENT, *n. retainer*, v. FOLLOWER. आश्रयी, आश्रित, आश्रयांतला माणूस, पोष्य, अनुगामी, अनुचर, अनुजीवी.

DEPENDER, *n.* DEPENDENT, *a.* DEPENDING, *p. a.* v. V. 1. अवलंबित, लंबित, लंबमान.

2 अधीन, संबंधी.

3 ओठंगणारा, टेकणारा, &c. अवलंबित, अवलंबी.

4 अनिर्णीत, संजाइती *or* संजाईत, उभा, भिजत पडलेला.

I. *at the disposal of another.* ताबेदार, परांकित, अधीन, पराधीन, अन्याधीन, पराश्रय, पराश्रित, नाथवान्.

To DEPICT. See To PAINT, To DESCRIBE.

DEPILOUS, *a. without hair.* केशहीन, विकेश, निर्लोम.

DEPLETION, *n. act of emptying.* रिता करणें *n.* रिक्तकरण *n.* शून्य करण *n.*

DEPLORABLE, *a.* v. LAMENTABLE, WRETCHED. रडूं याया जोगा-जोगता-&c. शोच्य, शोचनीय, रोदनीय, शोकार्ह, शोकोचित.

DEPLORABLY, *adv.* रडूं यायाजोगा-&c. *decl.* खेदवाटाया जोगा *decl.*

To DEPLORE, *v. a.* v. To LAMENT. रडणें, खेद-विपळाप *m.*-शोक *m.*-विलाप *m.*-&c. करणें *g. of o.*

To DEPLOY, *v. n.* See To EXTEND.

To DEPLUME, *v. a.* v. To PLUCK. पिसें *n. pl.* उपटणें *g. of o.*

To DEPONE. See To DEPOSE.

DEPONENT, *n.* v. EVIDENCE. शपथेवर साक्षी, साक्षदेणारा, साक्षीदार.

To DEPOPULATE, *v. a.* v. To DESOLATE. उजाड-ओस-ओसाड-उद्ध्वस्त-निर्जन-निर्मनुष्य-&c. करणें.

DEPOPULATED, *p.* v. V. उजाड-&c. केलेला, निर्जन-&c. केलेला.

DEPOPULATION, *n.—act.* उजाड करणें *n.* &c.*—state* उजाडी *f.* ओसाडी *f.* उद्ध्वस्तपणा *m.*

To DEPORT, *v. a.* (one's self) v. To BEHAVE. वागणें, वर्तणें.

2 See To TRANSPORT.

DEPORT, DEPORTMENT, *n.* v. V. 1. *and* CONDUCT. आचरण *n.* चाल *f.* चर्या *f.* चालचर्या *f.* चालचलणूक *f.*

To DEPOSE, *v. a.* (from the throne). गादीवरून काढणें, राजपदच्युत-राजपदभ्रष्ट-सिंहासनभ्रष्ट-राज्यभ्रष्ट-&c. करणें.

2 (from an office). काढणें, काढून देणें- घेणें, स्थानभ्रष्ट-स्थानच्युत-पदभ्रष्ट-अधिकारभ्रष्ट-&c. करणें.

3 See To DEPOSIT.

To DEPOSE, *v. n. give testimony.* साक्ष *f.*-साक्ष्य *n.*-साक्षी *f.* देणें.—in writing. जबानी *f.* लिहून देणें.

DEPOSED, *p.* v. V. A.1. गादीवरून काढलेला, &c. राज्यभ्रष्ट, भ्रष्टराज्य, सिंहासनभ्रष्ट, राजपदभ्रष्ट.

2 स्थानभ्रष्ट, पदभ्रष्ट, अधिकारभ्रष्ट, भ्रष्टाधिकार.

To DEPOSIT, *v. a. lay down, lodge*, v. To PLACE. ठेवणें, न्यास *m.* करणें *g. of o.* न्यस्त करणें.

2 *place in the keeping of.* ठेवणें, जिम्मेस-दिमतीस-ताब्यांत-&c. ठेवणें-देणें, हवालीं करणें.

3 *lay as a pledge.* गहाण ठेवणें.

DEPOSIT, *n. pledge, pawn.* गहाण *n.* निक्षेप *m.* उपनिधि *m.* आधि *m.* आधान *n.*

Profit from (through the use of) a d. भोगलाभ *m.*

Use of a d. गहाणाचा भोगवटा *m.* आधिभोग *m.*

To relinquish part of a d. in payment of a loan. गहाण *n.* लहान करणें.

2 *thing committed unto.* ठेव *f.* ठेवी *f.* ठेवणूक *f.* ठेवणें *n.* अमानत *or* अनामत *f.* निक्षेप *m.*—compreh. indef. &c. ठेवारेवा *m.* ठेवरेव *f.*

D.-money, *charge for keeping a d.* ठेवगावट *f.*

3 *pledged, &c.—state.* अमानत *f.*

In d. अमानत *or* अनामत, गहाणवट.

4 *matter lodged.* ठेव *f.*

D. of mud, as from a river. साई *f.* पोयटा *m.* गाळा *m.*

DEPOSITARY, *n. person with whom a deposit is placed.* अनामत दार, दिम्मतदार, जिम्मेदार.

DEPOSITED, *p.* v. V. 1. ठेवलेला, न्यस्त, आहित.

2 ठेवलेला, ठेवणाऊ, ठेवणुकी *or* ठेवणुकीचा, ठेवणू, अमानत, अनामत, निक्षिप्त, निहित.

3 गहाण ठेवलेला.

DEPOSITION, *n.* v. V. (To DEPOSE) 1.—*act.* गादीवरून काढणें *n.* &c. राजपदभंग *m.* छत्रभंग *m.*

2—*act.* काढणें *n.* &c. स्थानभंग *m.* अधिकारभंग *m.*

v. V. N. साक्ष *f.* साक्षी *f.* साक्ष्य *n.*

Written d. जबानी *f.*

v. V. (To DEPOSIT.)—*act.* ठेवणें *n.* न्यास *m.* निक्षेप *m.*

DEPOSITORY, DEPOT, *n. place where things are deposited.* निधान *n.* कोठार *n.* कोठा *m.* कोठी *f.* भांडागार *n.* संचयस्थान *n.* संग्रहालय *m.* [विधान *n.*

DEPRAVATION, *n.* v. V.—*act.* वाईटकरणें *n.* &c.—*state.* भ्रष्टता *f.* [दुष्टता *f.*

To DEPRAVE, *v. a. vitiate*, v. To CORRUPT. वाईट-खराब-&c. करणें, बिघडणें, भ्रष्ट-आचारभ्रष्ट-&c. करणें.

DEPRAVED, DEPRAVITY, See WICKED, WICKEDNESS.

To DEPRECATE, *v. a. pray against.* माफी *f.*-क्षमा *f.*-सोडवण *f.*-&c. मागणें *g. of o.* माफ मागणें, निवारणप्रार्थना *f.*- प्रतीकारप्रार्थना *f.*-परिहारप्रार्थना *f.* करणें *g. of o.*

To DEPRECIATE, *v. a. lower the value of.* किमत *f.*-मोल *n.*-दर *m.*- भाव-&c. उतरणें-पाडणें-हलका करणें-&c. *g. of o.*

2 fig. *underrate, undervalue, represent as of little worth.* हलका करणें-दाखवणें, हिणवणें *or* हिणावणें, हलकेपणा *m.* आणणें, उणेपणा *m.*-लहानवी *f.*- अप्रतिष्ठा *f.*-&c. करणें-सांगणें, योग्यता *f.*-किमत *f.*-&c. हलकी करणें-करून दाखवणें *g. of o.* अपकर्ष *m.* करणें *g. of o.*

To DEPRECIATE, *v. n. fall in value.* किमत *f.*-मोल *n.*-दर *m.*-भाव *m.*-&c. उतरणें-पडणें-कमीहोणें-&c. *g. of s.* अपकर्ष *m.* होणें *g. of s.*

DEPRECIATED, *p.* v. V. A. 1. किमत उतरलेला, दर हलका केलेला, &c.

2 हलका करून दाखवलेला, हिणवलेला, &c. अपकृष्ट.

DEPRECIATION, *n.* v. V. A. 1.—*act.* किमत उतरणें *n.* &c.

2 हिणवणें *n.* &c. अपकर्ष *m.* गुणापकर्ष *m.*

To DEPREDATE, DEPREDATOR, &c. See To PLUNDER, &c.

To DEPRESS, *v. a. press down.* दाबणें, दडपणें.

2 *deject, sadden*, v. To DISPIRIT. खिन्न-उदास-उदासी-विषण्ण-&c. करणें, उत्साहभंग *m.*-हर्षभंग *m.*-मनोभंग *m.*-&c. करणें *g. of o.*

3 *make dull or languid*,—trade, &c. मंद-&c. करणें, मंदी *f.*

आणणें, तेजी *f.* कमी करणें *g. of o.*

DEPRESSION, *n.* v. V. 1.—*act.* दाबणें *n.* दडपणें *n.*

2—*state.* उदासपणा *m.* औदासीन्य *n.* उत्साहभंग *m.* हर्षभंग*m.* ग्लानि *f.* अवसाद *m.* विषाद *m.*

3—*act.* मंद करणें *n.* &c.—*state.* मंदी *f.*

I. *a. d. a hollow, a sinking,* v. HOLE. खळगा*m. dim.* खळगी *f.* खोलगा *m.* खोलबा *m.* बस्खळ *f.* दबका *m.*

DEPRIVATION, *n.* v. V. 1.—*act.* नागवणें*n.* &c. नागवणूक *f.* नागवण *f.* नाडणूक *f.*—*state.* नागवण *f.* नागवणूक *f.* नाडणूक *f.* नागवलेलेपणा *m.* नाश*m.* तोटा*m.* हानि *f.* हीनता *f.* नष्टता *f.*

To DEPRIVE, *v. a. bereave.* नागवणें, नाडणें, वेगळा-निराळा-रहित-वांचून-विना-शिवाय-&c. करणें, (as त्या चोरानें मला पागोट्या निराळें केलें that thief deprived me of my turban), नागवा-उघडा-रांडका-बोडका-&c. करणें *with* अंशीं-विषयीं-अर्थी *of o.* (as त्यानें मला पुत्राविषयीं नागवें केलें), मुकविणें, आंचवविणें, नष्ट-भ्रष्ट करणें(in comp. as नष्टबुद्धि करणें to deprive of reason, &c.).

2 (of office or preferment.) अधिकार भ्रष्ट—पदभ्रष्ट-स्थानभ्रष्ट-&c. करणें.

DEPRIVED, *p.* v. V. नागवलेला, नाडलेला, रहित केलेला, &c. नष्ट (in comp. as नष्टबुद्धि, नष्टधैर्य, &c.)

DEPTH, *n.* v. DEEPNESS. खोली *f.* &c.

D. up to the breast. छातीठाव *m.*

D. up to the waist. कमरठाव *m.*

D. above the neck. बुडत ठाव *m.* [er, &c.).

I. v. HEIGHT. ऐन (in comp. as ऐनहिंवाळा the d. of wint-

DEPUTATION, *n.* v. V. —*act.* नेमून पाठवणें *n.* नियुक्त करून पाठवणें *n.* &c. नियुक्तप्रेषण *n.*

I. *body deputed.* नेमून पाठविलेलें मनुष्य *n.* नियुक्तप्रेषित.

To DEPUTE, *v. a. appoint or send as a substitute.* नेमून-नियुक्त करून-वकील करून-अखत्यारी करून पाठवणें, वारचा-वांटचा पाठवणें.

DEPUTY, *n. lieutenant, vicegerent.* वकील, मुनीम, मुतालीक, अखत्यारी, नायब, प्रतिनिधि, प्रतिपुरुष, दुयम.

2 *factor,* v. AGENT. गुमास्ता, कारभारी.

DEPUTYSHIP, *n.* v. N. 1. वकिली *f.* वकालत *f.* मुनिमी *f.*

To DERANGE, *v. a. disarrange, disorder,* v. To CONFUSE. गोंधळणें, गळहाटणें, गफलतणें, उलकटणें, उसकटणें, घालमेल *f.*-धांदल *f.*-गळहाटा *m.*-गोंधळ *m.*-&c. करणें *g.of o.*

2 *disorder in mind.* बुद्धिभ्रंश *m.*-बुद्धिविक्षेप *m.*-चित्तविक्षेप *m.*-चित्तविभ्रम*m.*-चित्तविभ्रंश-&c. करणें *g.of o.* विक्षिप्त करणें.

DERANGED, *p.* v. V. 1. गोंधळलेला, &c. अव्यवस्थित.

2 *and* MAD. बुद्धिभ्रष्ट, विक्षिप्त, विक्षिप्त बुद्धि.

DERANGEMENT, *n.* v. V. 1.—*act.* गोंधळणें*n.* गफलतणें*n.* &c.—*state.* घालमेल *f.* अव्यवस्था *f.* गळहाटा *or* ठा *m.* विसकळ *f.* गोंधळ *m.* घोळ *m.* घोंटाळा *m.* गदळ *m.* गफलत *f.* भानगड *f.* गडबड *f.* उलटापालट *f.* [चित्तविक्षेप *m.*.

2 *and,* MADNESS. बुद्धिभ्रंश *m.* चित्तविभ्रम *m.* चित्तविभ्रंश *m.*

DERBYSHIRE-NECK, *n.* मन्यास्तंभ *m.*

DERELICTION, &c. See ABANDONMENT, &c.

To DERIDE, *v. a. mock, jeer,* v. To RIDICULE. विटंबणें, विटंबना *f.*-उपहास*m.*-थट्टा *f.*-मस्करी *f.*-टर *or* टेर *f.*-&c. करणें*g.ofo.*

DERISION, *n.* v. V.—*act.* उपहास*m.* विटंबना *f.* टर *or* टेर *f.* थट्टा*f.*

I. *laughing stock.* उपहासपात्र *n.* उपहासास्पद *n.* विनोदास्पद *n.* खेळवणा *m.*

DERISIVE, DERISORY, *a.* v. V. विटंबनेचा, उपहासाचा, उपहाससूचक, उपहासात्मक.

DERIVATION, *n.*—in grammar. व्युत्पत्ति *f.* व्युत्पादन *n.*

DERIVATIVE, *a. received from another.* दुसऱ्यापासून पावलेला, अन्यप्राप्त, अन्यलब्ध. [द्धित *m. n.*

DERIVATIVE, *n. word, &c. derived.* कृदंत *n.* साधितशब्द *m.* त-

To DERIVE, *v. a. draw or receive as from a source.* काढणें, धरणें, घेणें, पावणें, येणें *with in con.*

2—in grammar, *trace.* काढणें, व्युत्पत्ति *f.* करणें *g. of o.*

DERIVED, *a.*—in grammar. व्युत्पन्न.

To be d. निघणें.

DERMAL, *a. belonging to the skin.* त्वचेचा, त्वक्संबंधी, त्वाच.

DERNIER, *a. final, ultimate.* v. LAST. शेवटचा, शेवटला, निदानचा, अंतीचा.

To DEROGATE, *v. n. detract from.* हलकेपणा *m.* आणणें, मानऱ्हास *m.*-मानहानि *f.*-तेजोऱ्हास *m.*-तेजोहानि *f.*-&c. करणें *g. of o.* अपकर्ष *m.* करणें.

DEROGATIVE, DEROGATORY, *a.* v. V. आब्रूघेण्या, इज्जतखाऊ, मानऱ्हासक, महत्वऱ्हासक, तेजोहारक, लघुत्वजनक.

DERVISE, *n.* दरवेशी.

To DESCANT, *v. n. discourse, expatiate.* वक्तृत्व *n.*-वाक्पांडित्य *n.*-वाग्जल्प *m.*-वाक्पाटव *n.*-वाक्प्रसर *m.*-&c करणें, गाणें *n.*-पोवाडा *m.*-&c.करणें- गाणें-लावणें.

DESCANT, *n. singing with modulations.* खांचखोंचीचें गाणें *n.*

To DESCEND, *v. n. move, come or go down.* उतरणें, खालीं जाणें-येणें, अवतरणें, डेबणें, डेबरणें, अवरोहण *n.*-अधोगमन *n.*-अवतरण *n.* करणें. [येणें *n.*

2 *proceed from as a source &c.* चालणें, येणें, पावणें, चालून

3 *proceed from an ancestor.* वंशाचा-वंशी-वंशज- &c. होणें, वंशांत उत्पन्न होणें. [येणें.

4 (from generals to particulars) सामान्यावरून विशेषांवर

DESCENDANT, *n.* वंशाचा, वंशी, वंश्य, वंशज, गोत्रापत्य *n.*

DESCENDANTS, v. OFFSPRING. संतति *f.* संतान *n.*—esp. male. अवलाद *f.*

D. of the female branch. अफलाद *f.*

DESCENDED, *p.* v. V. 1. उतरलेला, अधोगत, अवतारित, अवतीर्ण उत्तीर्ण, अवरूढ, अवपन्न.

2 वंशांत उत्पन्न झालेला, &c. परंपरोत्पन्न, वंशोत्पन्न.

DESCENDING, *a. declivous.* उतरता *remiss.* उतरवट.

DESCENT, *n.* v. V. 1.—*act.* उतरणें *n.* उतार *m.* अवरोह *m.* अवरोहण *n.* अधोगति *f.* अवगति *f.* अवतरण *n.* अवतार *m.* अवपतन *n.* अवपात *m.* अधःपात *m.*

2 चालणें *n.* येणें *n.* &c.

D. from time immemorial. अनादिपरंपरा *f.*

D. of a fashion, practice, &c. ओढण *n. f.* धोरण *n.*

3 v. FAMILY. परंपरोत्पत्ति *f.* क्रमोत्पत्ति *f.* गोत्रोत्पत्ति *f.* उत्पत्ति *f.* कुळी *f.*

Of pure d. v. FAMILY. बियांचा, कुलीन, वंशविशुद्ध, सद्वंश.

I. a d. *a declivity.* उतरण *f.* उतरड *f.* उतरडी *f.* उतार *m.* उतरवण *f.* वरंगळ *f.* डेबण *f.* डेबणें *n.* [गा, &c.

DESCRIBABLE, *a.* v. V. अंकाया-चा जोगा-&c. रेखाटाया-चा-जो-

2 वर्णन कराया-जोगता-सारखा-&c. निरूपणीय, निरूप्य, निर्वचनीय, निरूपणयोग्य, निरूपणशक्य, लक्ष्य.

To DESCRIBE, *v. a. mark out, sketch out.* काढणें, रेखटणें *or* रेखाटणें, अंकणें, नकशा *m.* काढणें *g. of o.*

2 *represent, depict, portray.* वर्णणें, निर्देशणें, निरूपिणें, निर्वचणें, वर्णन *n.*-निरूपण *n.*-&c.करणें *g. of o.*

DESCRIBED, *p.* v. V. 1. काढलेला, रेखटलेला, &c. [वर्णन.

2 वर्णन केलेला-झालेला, वर्णित, वर्णगत, निरूपित, निर्दिष्ट, जात-

DESCRIPTION, *n.* v. V. 1.—*act.* काढणें *n.* रेखटणें *n.* &c.

2—*act.* वर्णणें *n.* निरूपिणें *n.* &c. वर्णन *n.* निरूपण*n.* निर्देश*m.* निर्वचन *n.* लक्षण *n.* व्याख्या *f.* गुणन *n.*

I. *sketch, plan, &c.* नकशा *m.* नकाशा *m.*

II. *sort.* v. KIND. जाति *f.* जात *f.* प्रकार *m.* तऱ्हा *f.*

Of what d. कसा.

DESCRIPTIVE, *a.* v. V. 2. वर्णनात्मक, वर्णनरूप, वर्णनाचा, वर्णनकारक, वर्णनपर.

To DESCRY, *v.a. spy out, see from a distance.* दुरून-लांबून-&c. पाहणें-लक्षिणें, दूर-लांब पाहणें.

2 *detect,* v. To DISCOVER. शोध *m.* काढणें-लावणें *g.of o.* शोध *m.* लागणें *in. con.*

To DESECRATE, *v. a. defile.* विटाळणें, बाटवणें, भ्रष्ट करणें, प्रतिष्ठाभंग*m.*- प्रतिष्ठाध्वंस *m.* करणें *g. of o.*

DESECRATION, *n.* v. V. विटाळणें*n.* &c. प्रतिष्ठाभंग *m.* प्रतिष्ठाध्वंस *m.* अपवित्री करण*n.*

DESERT, *n. wilderness, waste, wild.* रान*n.* अरण्य*n.* जंगल*n.* मरुस्थल*n.* मरु *m.* मरुदेश*m.*

DESERT, *a. wild, waste, unpeopled.* जंगली, बेराण *or* न, रखरखीत, रुखा, रुक्ष, ओस, सुना, सुनका, निर्जन, शून्य, शून्याकार.

2 *of or belonjing to a d.* जंगली, जंगलाचा, अरण्याचा, आरण्य, आरण्यक.

To DESERT, *v. a. forsake, leave,* v. To ABANDON. सोडणें, टाकणें, त्यागणें, टाकून-&c. जाणें.

To DESERT, *v. n. run away form one's regiment, &c.* चाकरी *f.* टाकून-सोडून-&c. जाणें, पळून जाणें, निरोप घेतल्यावांचून चाकरी *f.* सोडणें.

DESERT, DESERVING. See MERIT.

DESERTER, *n.* v. V. N. पळून जाणारा, पळया, पळून गेलेला, निरोपावांचून चाकरी सोडलेला.

DESERTION, *n.* v. V. A.—*act.* सोडणें*n.* टाकणें*n.* &c. त्याग*m.* परित्याग*m.*—*state.* सांड *f.* त्यक्तावस्था *f.* त्यक्तदशा *f.* त्यक्तता *f.*

Spiritual d. भगवत्कृपेची निराशा *f.*

v. V. N.—*act.* पळून जाणें*n.* चाकरी टाकून जाणें*n.*

To DESERVE, *v. c. merit, be worthy of.* योग्य-लायक-अर्ह-पात्र-&c. होणें-असणें, *in. con.*

DESERVEDLY, *adv.* यथायोग्य, यथायुक्त, यथान्याय, यथार्ह.

DESERVER, *n.* DESERVING, *p. a. worthy, meritorious.* लायक, चांगला, भला, योग्य, योग्यतेचा, अर्ह (in comp.), पात्र (in comp.).

DESHABILLE. See DISHABILLE.

To DESICCATE, &c. See To DRY, &c.

To DESIDERATE. See To DESIRE, To WANT.

DESIDERATUM, *n. something desired.* इष्ट*n.* अभीष्ट*n.* ईप्सित *n.*

To DESIGN, *v. a. purpose, intend, mean.* उद्देशणें, संकल्पणें, कल्पिणें, अवांकणें, उद्देश*m.*-मनोद्देश *m.*-बेत*m.*-इरादा*m.*- मनोदय*m.* -&c. करणें, मनांत धरणें, मनांत असणें *in. con.* लक्ष*n.*-लक्ष्य*n.*-अभिप्राय*m.* असणें *g. of o.*

2 *plan, scheme, project.* रचणें, योजणें, कल्पिणें, बेत*m.*-योजना *f.*-कल्पना *f.*-रचना *f.*-तजवीज *f.*-&c. करणें.

DESIGN, *n. purpose, intention, mind.* बेत*m.* मन*n.* बुद्धि *f.* मनसुबा *m.* उद्देश*m.* मनोद्देश *m.* मनोरथ *m.* मनोगत *n.* मनोदय *m.* अर्थ *m.* हेतु*m.* उद्देश्य *n.* मतलब*m.* इंगित *n.* मानस *n.* आशय *m.* निमित्त *n.* अभिप्राय *m.* अभिप्रेत *n.* हृदय *n.* हार्द (*pop.* हरद्द *or* हरिद्द *or* हार्द्द) *n.* संकल्प *m.* कल्पना *f.* विवक्षा *f.* चिकीर्षा *f.* विषय *m.*

2 *scheme, plan, project.* कल्पना *f.* अनुसंधान *n.* मसलत *f.* तजवीज *f.* बेत *m.* योजना *f.* युक्ति *f.* ग्रंथ *m.* मूस *f.* (ex. कामाची मूस).

I. *model, plan, sketch.* नमुना *m.* नकशा*m.* नकाशा*m.*

DESIGNATE, *a.* DESIGNATED, *p.* v. V.1. निर्देशलेला, &c. निर्दिष्ट, उपलक्षित, विशेषित, व्यपदिष्ट.

D. by name. नामजात *or* द.

To DESIGNATE, *v. a. point out, distinguish.* निर्देशणें, निर्देश *m.*-व्यपदेश करणें *g. of o.* निर्दिष्ट-व्यपदिष्ट-&c. करणें.

To d. by name. नामनिर्देश *m.* करणें,

2 v. To APPOINT. नेमणें, योजणें, नेमणूक *f.*-योजना *f.*-&c. करणें *g. of o.* नियुक्त करणें.

3 v. To MARK out. अंकून देणें, बेतून देणें, रेखटणें.

DESIGNATION, *n.* v. V. 1.—*act.* निर्देशणें*n.* निर्देश*m.* व्यपदेश*m.*

2—*act.* नेमणें*n.* &c. नेमणूक *f.* योजना *f.*

3—*act.* अंकून देणें*n.* &c. अंकन *n.*

I. *mark, indication.* लक्षण *n.* उपलक्षण *n.*

II. *import,* v. MEANING. अर्थ *m.* भावार्थ *m.*

DESIGNED, *p. & a.* v. V. 1. संकल्पलेला, &c. उद्दिष्ट, मनसोद्दिष्ट, सांकल्पित, अभिप्रेत, चिकीर्षित.

2 योजलेला, रचलेला, &c. योजित, नियोजित.

I. v. INTENTIONAL. ऐच्छिक, सांकल्पिक, संकल्पकृत, बुद्धिकृत.

DESIGNEDLY, *adv.* v. P. 1. जाणून, जाणूनपुसून, जाणूनबुजून, समजून उमजून, बुद्ध्या, बुद्धिपूर्वक, बुद्धिपुरस्सर, मनःपूर्वक, अक्कलहुशारीनें, आदरून, आवर्जून, तात्पुरचा, उदमेखून.

DESIGNER, *n.* DESIGNING, *p. a.* v. V. 1. संकल्पणारा, उद्देश करणारा, &c.

2 योजणारा, रचणारा, &c. योजन-&c. कर्त्ता.

I. *artful, crafty,* v. CUNNING. मतलबी, मतलबदार, कावेदार, कावेबाज, कवाइती *or* दी, कवाईतदार, धूर्त.

DESIGNMENT. See DESIGN.

DESIRABLE, *a.* v. V. 1. इच्छिण्याजोगा-सारखा-&c. काम्य, कमनीय, स्पृहणीय, स्पृह्य, अपेक्षणीय, अपेक्ष्य, अपेक्षितव्य, आकांक्षनीय, आकांक्ष्य, आकांक्षितव्य, वांछनीय, इच्छार्ह, कामार्ह, लोभ्य, लोभनीय, इच्छाविषय, लोभविषय, इच्छास्पद. [इंता *f.*

DESIRABLENESS, *n.* v. A. काम्यता *f.* स्पृहणीयता *f.* &c. इच्छा-

DESIRE, *n. eagerness after.* आशा *f.* आस्था *f.* चहा *f.* हवस *f.* अपेक्षा *f.* चाड *f.* हव्यास *m.* तलब *f.* काम *m.* कामना *f.* स्पृहा *f.* ईषणा *f.* भोगेच्छा *f.*—in high degree; *thirst after, panting or hankering after, longing for, &c.* हांव *f.* भूक *f.* वेड *n.* वळवळ *f.* वळका *m.* धण *f.* नितांत *m.* खुडसणी *f.* कोड *n.* आळ *m.* *f.* चुटपूट *f.* उत्कंठा *f.* उत्कटेच्छा *f.* तृष्णा *f.* तृषा *f.* अभिलाष *m.*

मास m. दुराशा f. उत्सुकता f. औत्सुक्य n. लालसा f. लिप्सा f. आर्त्त f. See also ITCH.

Carnal d. काम m.

Object of d. इष्ट n. इष्टवस्तु n.

Snare, fetters, &c. of d. आशापाश m. आशाजाल n. आशाबंधन n.—Entangled in it. आशाबद्ध.

Void of d. Exempt or free from d. अनिच्छ, निरिच्छ, अनपेक्ष, निरपेक्ष, निराकांक्ष, निःस्पृह, निराश, निर्वासन, निष्काम.

To gratify (intense) d. पारणें n. फेडणें (neut. फिटणें).

To mock or balk d. वासना f. फजीत करणें.

To mortify d. वासना f. मोडणें-फोडणें-मारणें (ex. वासना फोडुनियां चूर्ण केली सुपारी), जीव m. जाळणें-मारणें, इच्छाविनाश m.-इच्छाक्षय m.-इच्छानिवृत्ति f. करणें.

To repress or restrain d. जिभेला चिमटा m. घेणें, इंद्रियनिग्रह m.-इंद्रियसंयमन n. करणें.

2 a d. a wish. इच्छा f. वांच्छा f. वासना f. आकांक्षा f. कांक्षा f. कामना f. मनःकामना f. स्पृहा f. हेतु pop. हेत m. संकल्प m. मानस m. n. मनीषा pop. मनशा or मनसा f. मनेच्छा f. मनेप्सित n. मनोरथ m. ईहा f. मनोदय m. चिंतन n.

According to one's d. (or purpose). इच्छेजोगता, यथाकाम, यथाभिमत.

Evil d. दुर्वासना f. कुवासना f. पापवासना f.

Virtuous or good d. पुण्यवासना f. धर्मवासना f. सद्वासना f.

To grant or fulfil a d. इच्छादान n.-आकांक्षापूरण n.- इष्टवस्तुप्रापण n. करणें.

To obtain a d. इच्छालाभ m.-इष्टवस्तुलाभ m.-इष्टवस्तूपलब्धि f.-इष्टापत्ति f. होणें in. con.

To DESIRE, v. a. wish for. इच्छिणें, वांच्छिणें, आशावणें, चिंतणें, चिंतन n. करणें g. of o. इच्छा f.-आशा f.-आस f.-उमेद f.-वांच्छा f.-&c. धरणें-करणें—in high degree; to crave, to thirst, pant, hanker after, to long for, to be dying for, &c. खवखवणें, धोपणें, नितांनणें or नितांदणें, मरणें, अभिलाषणें, लुलुपणें, लुसुलुसु adv. करणें, जीव m. टांगला असणें g. of s. कंकांतणें, जीव m. वर धरणें. or वरता जीव धरणें, छंद m. धरणें-घेणें, उपीत पिणें-घेणें, झुटझुटणें, तरतरणें or तरारणें, तरवणें, झुटाटणें, खुरखुरणें, धादावणें, भुकेणें, तान्हेणें, लुब्धणें, लोभणें, कंठी प्राण m. धरणें, प्राण m. ओकणें.

2 request, entreat, v. To BEG. प्रार्थणें, विनवणें.

3 bid, v To COMMAND. सांगणें, आज्ञा f. करणें.

DESIRED, p. v. V. 1. इच्छलेला, &c. इच्छित, अपेक्षीत, आकांक्षित, कांक्षित, वांच्छित, इष्ट, अभीष्ट, अभीप्सित, ईप्सित, अभिलाषित, ऐच्छिक, ईहित, मनईप्सित (vulg. मनेप्सित).

DESIRER, n. DESIRING, p. a. DESIROUS, a. v. V. 1. इच्छिणारा, &c. इच्छावान्, साकांक्ष, इच्छु (esp. in comp. as धनेच्छु, विद्येच्छु, मोक्षेच्छु &c.), आकांक्षी (in comp.), हव्यासी, इच्छान्वित, जातस्पृह, लुब्ध,—in high degree; craving, &c. हवळा, मुजरा or मुजीर, उत्कंठित, सोत्कंठ, अभिलाषी, भुकेला, लोभग्रस्त, लोभाविष्ट, लोभान्वित, लोभारूढ, लोलुप, लोभाक्रांत, लोभातुर, लोभाकुल, लोभांध, अतीच्छ, आशाभूत, आशाळभूत.

To DESIST, v. n. stop, leave off, v. To CEASE. राहणें, थांबणें, मोडती f. घेणें, हात m. अटोपणें-काढणें, निवर्त्तणें.

DESISTANCE, DESISTING, n. v. V. राहणें n. हात अटोपणें n. &c. निवर्त्तन n.

DESK, n. लिहिण्याचें सोईचें मेज n.

DESOLATE, a. DESOLATED, p. v. V. उजाड केलेला-झालेला, उजाड, ओस, ओसाड, वैराण or न, पडसर, पडकर, बेचिराग or ख, भगास, सुना, सुनका, उद्वस्त, उद्वस, निर्जन, शून्य, शून्याकार.

I. SEE SOLITARY and DISTRESSED.

To DESOLATE, v. a. depopulate. उजाड-ओसाड-ओस-बेचिराग-निर्जन-&c. करणें, उजाडी f.-ओसाडी f.-&c. करणें g. of o. उठवणें, खरांटा m. फिरवणें with वर of o.

DESOLATION, n. v. V.—state. उजाडी f. ओसाडी f. उद्वस्तता f. वैराणी or नी f. बेचिरागी f. Some strongly significant words and striking phrases and figures expressing this sense are राखरांगोळी f. गोपचंदन n. भणभणाट or भणाण m. राक्षसी पीठ कांडितात, तेथें खरांटा फिरला आहे, त्या देशावर &c. गवत रुजलें आहे (घरावर &c.), घरास कांट्या लागल्या आहेत, तेथें चिट पांखरूं देखील भेटत नाही, दिवा लागत नाहीं (त्या देशांत-गांवांत-&c.), पाटा वरवंटा झाला (देशाचा-गांवाचा), तेथें शुक्क आहे.

DESPAIR, DESPERATION, n. hopelessness. v. DESPONDENCY. निराशा f. नैराश्य n. आशाभंग m. आशाविच्छेद m. आसमोड f. आशानष्टता f.

To DESPAIR, v. n. v. To DESPOND. आशा f. सोडणें-टाकणें-घालवणें, जीव m. टाकणें, प्राण m. सोडणें, आशात्याग m.-आशामोचन n-&c. करणें, निराश-&c. होणें.

DESPAIRER, n. DESPAIRING, p. a. v. V. and DESPONDENT. आशा सोडलेला, आशा सोडणारा, &c. निराश, नष्टाश, गताश, भग्नाश, हताश, आशाहीन.

To DESPATCH, v. a. send off smartly. धाडणें, दवडणें, घालवणें, दामटणें, दपटणें, पिटणें, पिटाळणें, लावणें, पळत लावणें, हकारणें, क्षेपणें, रवानगी f. करणें, क्षेप m.-क्षेपण n. करणें g. of o.

2 perform or execute promptly, dispose of, knock off, rattle off. अटपणें, उरकणें, उरका m. उरकणें g. of o. उलगडणें, झपाटणें, चपाटणें, रपाटणें, रगडणें, फटकारणें, भरकटणें or भरकडणें, भरकांडणें, चरकटणें, फरकटणें, फडफडवणें, उडवणें, बार m. उडवणें with कामाचा &c. चराचर-भराभर adv. करणें i.e. लिहणें-वाचणें-जेवणें-शिवणें-&c. तासणें, उलटणें, उलथणें, सारणें, चुकवणें, त्वरेबर घेणें.

3 put to death, v. To KILL. गत f.-गति f. देणें, गतीस लावणें-मिळवणें, लोकांतरास-ऊर्ध्व पंथास-पितृलोकास-&c. लावणें-पाठवणें, लोकांतरगत करणें.

DESPATCH, n. smartness, expedition. झपाटा m. चपाटा m. झटपट f. शिताबी f. जलदी f.

2 letter sent with expedition, &c. मुजरत-मुद्दाम पाठवलेला कागद m.-खलिता m-&c.

DESPATCHED, p. v. V. 1. धाडलेला, &c.

2 अटपलेला, उरकलेला, &c.

To be d. अटपणें, उरकणें, उलटणें, उलथणें, चराचर adv. होणें.

DESPERADO, n. desperate, furious fellow. अततायी or अतत्यायी, साहसी, साहसिक, कपाळफोड्या, आवसावरचा वाघ m.

DESPERATE, a. despairing, v. DESPONDENT. निराश, आशाहीन, हताश, नष्टाश, नष्टधैर्य, त्यक्ताश.

2 rash, reckless, hot brained, v. MADCAP. जिवावर उदार, साहसी, साहसिक, कपाळफोड्या, साहसकर्मकर्त्ता, राक्षसी, तामस.

3 hopeless, remediless. निरुपाय, उपायातीत, उपायहीन-शून्य-&c. निराशेचा, बेइलाज, उपायाशक्य, लाचार, असाध्य, कठीण.

4 See EXCESSIVE.

DESPERATELY, *adv.* v. A. 2. साहसानें, साहसपूर्वक, जिवावर उदार होऊन, जिवाची आशा न बाळगतां.

4 See EXCESSIVELY.

DESPERATENESS, *n.* v. A. 1. निराशा *f.* नैराश्य *n.* आशाराहित्य *n.* आशाहीनता *f.*

2 साहस *n.* साहसपणा *m.*

3 निरुपायता *f.* उपायहीनता *f.* उपायराहित्य *n.*

DESPERATION, See DESPAIR.

DESPICABLE, *a.* v. V. *and* CONTEMPTIBLE. धिक्कार कराया-जोगा-जोगता-&c. तिरस्कार्य, अवमाननीय, हलका, तुच्छ, कवडीचा, दमडीचा, निकृष्ट, अधम, पाजी.

DESPICABLENESS, *n.* v. A. हलकेपणा *m.* तिरस्कार्यता *f.* अवमाननीयता *f.* अवमानार्हता *f.*

To DESPISE, *v. a.* v. To CONTEMN. तिरस्कारणें, अवगणणें, अवमानणें, अनमानणें, अनादरणें, हलका-तुच्छ-&c. मानणें, कःपदार्थ करणें-मानणें, धिक्कार *m.*-हेळा *f.*-हेळणा *f.*-अवमान *m.*-&c. करणें *g. of o.*

DESPISING, *n.* v. V.—*act.* तिरस्कारणें *n.* &c. तिरस्कार *m.* धिक्कार *m.* अवमान *m.* अनादर *m.* अवगणन *n.* अवगणना *f.*-हेळणा *f.* हेळा *f.* अवहेलन *n.* अवहेलना *f.*

DESPITE, &c. See SPITE, &c.

To DESPOIL, *v. a. rob of,* v. To DEPRIVE, To PLUNDER. नागवा-&c. करणें *with* विषयीं *of o.* वेगळा-वांचून-&c. करणें, लुटणें, नाडणें.

To DESPOND, *v. n. lose hope, despair.* आशा *f.* सोडणें-टाकणें-घालवणें, आशा *f.*-धीर *m.*-धैर्य *n.*-&c. सुटणें *g. of s.* निराशा *f.* होणें *g. of s.* हात पाय *m. pl.* गळणें *g. of s.* पाय *m. pl.* मोडणें *g. of s.* हात *m. pl.* टेकणें, जीव *m.* टाकणें, प्राण *m.* सोडणें, आशात्याग *m.*-आशामोचन *n.*-&c. करणें, निराश-नष्टाश-नष्टधैर्य-&c. होणें.

DESPONDENCY, *n. hopelessness, despair.* निराशा *f.* नैराश्य *n.* गताशा *f.* आशाभंग *m.* आशानष्टता *f.* दौर्मनस्य *n.* विषाद *m.*

DESPONDENT, *a.* DESPONDING, *p. a. hopeless, despairing.* निराश, नष्टाश, हताश, गताश, त्यक्ताश, मुक्ताश, भग्नाश, गतोत्साह, विगतोत्साह, निरुत्साह, हतोत्साह, भग्नोत्साह, विषण्ण, अवसन्न, मनोहत, नष्टधैर्य, दीनचेतन, अवाङ्मुख.

DESPONDINGLY, *adv.* v. A. आशा सोडून, निराश होऊन.

DESPOT, *n. absolute sovereign.* स्वतंत्रराजा, स्वायत्तराजा, स्वाधीन *pop.* स्वस्वाधीन राजा, मुखत्यार राजा.

2 See TYRANT.

DESPOTIC, DESPOTICAL. See ABSOLUTE.

DESPOTISM, *n. absolute power.* स्वतंत्रता *f.* स्वातंत्र्य *n.* अनिर्बंधशासन *n.* अनिर्बंधसत्ता *f.*

2 *an arbitrary government.* स्वतंत्रराजकराज्य *n.* अनिर्बंधकराज्य *n.*

DESSERT, *n. course of fruit after dinner.* जेवल्यानंतरचा फराळ *m.* भोजनोत्तर फलाहार *m.* मुखशुद्धि *f. vulgo* मुखशूद *f.* मुखवास *m.*

To DESTINATE, DESTINE, *v. a. appoint by previous determination.* v. To APPOINT. पूर्वी-पहिल्यानें-&c. योजून ठेवणें, पूर्वयोजना *f.*-पूर्वनियोग *m.*-पूर्वनियोजन *n.* करणें *g. of o.* पूर्वनियोजित करणें.

2 *allot to the future portion of.* दैवीं-दैवांत-प्रारब्धांत-&c. लिहिणें, नशिबानें नेमणें.

DESTINATION, *n.* v. V. 1.—*act.* पूर्वीची योजना *f.* पूर्वयोजना *f.* पूर्वनियोग *m.* पूर्वनियोजन *n.*

I. *purpose for which a thing is destined,* v. END. नियोजित कर्म *n.* नियोजित विषय *m.*

II. *place to which a thing is appointed.* नेमलेलें स्थान *n.* जागा *f.* नियुक्तस्थान *n.*

DESTINED, *p.* v. V. 1. पूर्वी योजून ठेवलेला, &c. पूर्वनियोजित, पूर्वनियुक्त, दैवकृत, दैवपर.

2 दैवीं लिहिलेला, &c.

DESTINY, *n.*—as the power destining, *Fate, Necessity.* दैव *n.* दैविक *n.* अदृष्ट *n.* कृतांत *m.* काळ *m.* कर्म *n.* पूर्वकर्म *n.* कर्मगति *f.* गति *f.* दैवगति *f.* प्रारब्ध *n.* प्राक्तन *n.* प्राक्तनकर्म *n.* नसीब *n.* लक्ष्मी *f.* दैवाचे *or* प्रारब्धाचे *or* नसिबाचे ताळे *m. pl.* पायांचा प्रताप *m.* पायगुण *m.*—considered as absolutely *irresistible, inavertible, &c.* कर्मबलिवंत, कर्मबलोत्तर, कर्मोत्तर, बलवत्तरकर्म, कठिनकर्म, बलियाप्राक्तन, बलवत्तर दैव काळ-&c.

Appointed by D. दैवकृत.

Persecutions of D. Trouble or evil appointed by D. ब्रह्मकपाट *n.* कर्मकचाट *n.* कर्मकपाट *n.* कर्मकटकट *f.*

Subject to D. दैववश, दैवाधीन.

2—as the state &c. destined; *doom, lot, allotment, fortune.* दैवरेषा *or* दैवरेखा *f.* ब्रह्मरेषा *or* ब्रह्मरेखा *f.* ब्रह्मलेख *m.* ब्रह्मलिखित *n.* कपाळरेषा *f.* कपाळपट्टी *f.* कपाळरेखा *f.* कपाळलेख *m.* दैवयोग *m.* दैवदशा *f.* प्रारब्धयोग *m.* ललाटरेषा *or* रेखा *f.* कपाळ *n.* घटित *n.* कर्मफल *n.* कर्मयोग *m.* कालनियोग *m.* विधि *m.* जन्मांतर *n.* पूर्वरेषा *f.* भवितव्य *n.* होतव्य *n.* होयीक *n.*

Fulfilment of d. कर्मभोग *m.*

It was in my d. माझ्यादैवींहोतें *or* लिहिलेंहोतें.

Of high d. v. FORTUNATE. उंचकपाळ्या.

Man must fulfil his d. सटवीनें लिहिलें तें टळणार नाहीं.

Man must labor and fulfil his d. काळा कष्टाचा हक्कमात्र कधीं जात नाहीं.

DESTITUTE, *a. forlorn,* v. FRIENDLESS, POOR. निराश्रय, निराश्रित, अनाश्रय, अनाश्रित, अनाथ, निराधार, निरालंब, अनुत्पन्न, अनुपपन्न, उघडाबोडका, उघडा.

2 *wanting, in want of,* v. WANTING. निराळा-वेगळा-शून्य-हीन रहित-&c. all in comp.

DESTITUTION, *n.* v. A. 1. निराश्रितपणा *m.* उघडेपणा *m.* निराश्रयता *f.* अनाश्रय *m.* निराधारता *f.* आश्रयराहित्य *n.* अनाथावस्था *f.* अनुपपत्ति *f.* अन्नानगत *f.*

2 हीनता *f.* राहित्य *n.* अभाव *m.*

To DESTROY, *v. a. raze, demolish, &c.* मोडणें, मोडून तोडून टाकणें, मोडून-पाडून-भंगून-&c. टाकणें, पाडणें, धुळीस मिळवणें, जमीनदोस्त करणें, चपाट *or* सपाट करणें, विधुळणीस मिळवणें-पाडणें, पाटा वरवंटा *m.* करणें-फिरवणें, ध्वंस *m.*-ध्वंसन *n.*-विध्वंस *m.*-विध्वंसन *n.*-प्रध्वंस *m.*-संहार *m.*-विघात *m.*-विघाटन *n.*-उच्छेद *m.*-&c. करणें *g. of o.* ध्वंसणें, विध्वंसणें, नाहींसा करणें, नष्ट करणें, संहारणें, उच्छेदणें, निर्दाळणें, उपहंती *f.*-संहृति *f.* करणें, गाढवाचा नांगर *m.* फिरवणें.

2—freely; *ruin, spoil, devastate, lay waste, excessively injure, &c.* नासणें, नासून टाकणें, नाश *m.*-विनाश *m.*-सत्यनाश *pop.* सत्यानाश *m.*-नासाड *f.*-नासाडा *m.*- नासाडी *f.*-चंदन *n.*-गोपचंदन *n.*-नासधोस *m.*-नासधूळ *f.*-धूळ *f.*-धूळधाणी *f.*-धूळदशा *f.*-धूळधमासा *m.*-धूळपट *f.*-पट्टाधूळ *f.*-तसनस *or* तसनास *m. f.*-वर्तुळाकार *m.*-माती *f.*-चुना *m.*-पीठ *n.*-पिठाड *m. n.*-पिटडा

m.-राळ *f.*-पटाडा *m.*-रासरांगोळी *f.*-निर्दलन *n.*-निर्दलना *f.*-फन्ना *m.*-&c. करणें, कात्यायन *n.* करणें-काढणें *g. of o.* सप्पा *m.* बळब-णें-उडवणें-करणें, धुमा *or* धुवा *m.* उडवणें-करणें, पस्त *adv.*-नाचूद *adv.* करून टाकणें, रसातळास नेणें (neut. जाणें), भंग *m.*-भंजन *n.*-हानि *f.* करणें *g. of o.*

3 *kill, extirpate, annihilate, &c.* नाहींसा करणें, निपातणें, उ-च्छेदणें, घात *m.*-उच्छेद *m.*-निपात *pop.* निःपात *m.*-निर्मूलन *n.*-निर्दलन *n.*-संहार *m.*-अत्यय *m.*-क्षय *m.*-लय *m.*- नशन *n.*-फन्ना *m.*-तळपट *n.*-लोप *m.* (esp. in comp.)—&c. करणें *g. of. o.* नाचूद *adv.*-पस्त *adv.* करणें, नाचूद *adv.* बुडवणें.

DESTROYED, *p.* v. V. 1. मोडलेला, मोडून तोडून टाकलेला, &c. ध्वंसित, ध्वस्त, विध्वंसित, उच्छिन्न, निर्दलित, संहृत.

2 नासलेला, नासून टाकलेला, &c. जायां, नाशित, विनाशित, खाक झालेला, नष्ट (also, in comp. and with much elegance and expressiveness, as नष्टवीर्य, नष्टधन, नष्टप्रभाव, नष्टबुद्धि, नष्टपराक्रम, नष्टोपाय, &c.), विनष्ट, निर्दलित, भग्न, क्षीण.

3 नाहींसा केलेला, उच्छेदलेला, &c. उच्छिन्न, निर्दलित, संहृत.

DESTROYER, *n.* DESTRUCTIVE, *a.* v. V. 1. मोडणारा, &c. वि-ध्वंसक, विध्वंसा, विघातक, विघाती, संहारक, संहारकर्त्ता-कारक-कारी-&c. भंजक, उच्छेदक.

2 नासून टाकणारा, &c. नाशक, नाशी, नासरा, विनाशक, वि-नाशी, भंजक, घातक, घातकी, क्षयकर, नाशावह, काळ.

3 नाहींसा करणारा, घातक, घातकी, नाश-उच्छेद-&c. कर्त्ता-का-री-&c. निधनकारी, घ्न (in comp. as रोगघ्न, ज्वरघ्न, पितघ्न).

DESTRUCTIBLE, *a.* v. V. 1.—मोडाया-चा-जोगा-जोगता-&c ध्वंस-नीय, विध्वंसनीय, निर्दलनीय, उच्छेदनीय.

2 नासाया-चा-जोगा-जोगता-&c. नाशवंत, क्षयिष्णु, अंतवंत.

DESTRUCTION, *n.* v. V. 1.-*act.* मोडणें *n.* मोडून टाकणें *n.*-&c.ध्वं-सन *n.* विध्वंसन *n.* उच्छेदन *n.* भंजन *n.*—*state.* ध्वंस *m.* वि-ध्वंस *m.* विघात *m.* उच्छेद *m.* संहार *m.* प्रलय *m.*

To sweep with the besom of d. खरांटा *m.* फिरवणें.

2—*act.* नासणें *n.* नासून टाकणें*n.*—*state.* नाश *m.* विनाश *m.* हानि *f.*

3 लय *m.* विलय *m.* अत्यय *m.*

N. B. For more nouns refer to those given under the meanings of the Verb.

Hour of d. विनाशकाल *m.*

The universal d. महाप्रलय *m.* आत्यंतिकप्रलय *m.* प्रकृतिप्रलय *or* प्राकृतिकप्रलय *m.* कल्पांत *m. or* कल्पांतप्रलय *m.*ब्रह्मप्रलय *m.* दैनंदिनप्रलय *m.* प्रलय *m.*

DESUETUDE, *n.* v. DISUSE. गैरबळण *n.* अनभ्यास*m.* अनुपलब्धि*f.*

DESULTORINESS, *n.* v.A. बेतालपणा *m.* क्रमराहित्य*n.* अव्यवस्था*f.*

DESULTORY, *a. passing from one subject to another without order.* उडाणटप्पूचा, मंडूकप्लुतीचा, मंडूकानुवृत्तीचा, अव्यवस्थेचा, बेताल, डावखुरा, अक्रमिक, उच्छृंखल.

To DETACH, *v. a. disunite, disengage,* v. To SEPARATE. सो-डवणें, वेगळा-भिन्न-वियुक्त करणें, उकलणें.

2 (troops, &c.). टोळी *f.*-तुकडी *f.* करून पाठवणें *g. of o.*

To DETACH, *v. n. come off, cease to adhere.* निघणें, सुटणें, उ-करणें. [वियुक्त.

DETACHED, *a. not connected,* v. SEPARATE. अलग, तुटक, स्फुट,

DETACHMENT, *n. body (of troops, &c) detached.* तुकडी *f.* टोळी *f.* सेनाखंड *n.*

To DETAIL, *v. a. relate, &c. in particulars.* तपसील *m.*-बयाद *m.f.*-बयाणा *m.*-&c. सांगणें-लावणें-लिहणें-&c. तपसीलवार-बया-दवार-&c.सांगणें-लिहणें-&c. फाडा *m.* वाचणें *g. of o.* बासलात *f.* लावणें *with* स *or* ला, परिवेदन *n.* करणें.

DETAIL, *n. detailed statement.* तपसील *m.* बयाज *or* द *m f.* ब-यावल *n.* बयाणा *or* ना *m.* बाबत *f.* पान्हेरा *m. v.* दे, उपपत्ति *f.*

In d. तपसीलवार, चितपसील, बयादवार *or* बयाजवार, सविस्तर, जिन्नसवार, रकमवार.

Wearisome d. परवड *f.*

To DETAIN, *v. a. keep back,* v. To RETAIN. ठेवणें, राखणें.

2 *restrain from, hold back,* v. To STOP. रोकणें, अडवणें, खोळंबवणें, गळचिपी *f.* धरणें-आवळणें, खोटी *f.*-खोळंबा *m.*-&c. करणें *g. of o.*

3 *hold in custody.* कैदेंत-बंदींत-अटकेंत-&c. ठेवणें.

To DETECT, DETECTION, &c. See To DISCOVER, DISCOVERY, &c.

DETENTION, DETAINING, *n.* v. V. 1.—*act.* ठेवणें *n.* राखणें *n.*

2—*act.* रोकणें *n.* अडवणें *n.* &c. अडवणूक *f.*—*state.* गुंता*m.* गुता *m.* खोटी *f.* खोळंबा *m.* अटकाव *m.* अटकावा *m.*

3 अटकेंत ठेवणें *n.* &c.

To DETER, *v. a. stop by fear.* भय घालून-भय दाखवून-भिवबून-भयप्रदर्शन करून-&c. अडवणें-अटकावणें-विमुख करणें-पराङ्मुख करणें-&c. [ING, &c.

To DETERGE, DETERGENT, &c. See To CLEANSE, CLEANS-

To DETERIORATE, *v. n. grow worse,* v. To DEGENERATE. उत-रणें, बिघडणें, बिघडतजाणें, गुणग्रास उणावणें-खालावणें, वाईट होणें, गुणऱ्हास *m.*-गुणापचय *m.*-&c. होणें *g. of s.*

To DETERIORATE, *v. a.* खराब-वाईट-&c. करणें, बिघडवणें, गुणऱ्हा-स *m.*-&c. करणें *g. of o.*

DETERIORATION, *n.* v. V. N.—*state.* उतरता पाया *m.* उतरतीक-माण *f.* खचतापाया *m.* अपकर्ष *m.* अपचय *m.* विपर्यास *m.* अधो-गति *f.* अन्यथाभाव *m.* गुणऱ्हास *m.* गुणापचय *m.* ऱ्हास *m.* तेजो-ह्रास *m.*

DETERMINABLE, *a.* v. V. 1· ठरावया-चा-जोगता-&c. निधारणीय, निर्धार्य, अवधारणीय, अवधार्य, निर्णेय.

DETERMINATE, *a. ascertained, settled to be,* v. CERTAIN. नि-खालस, तहकीक, सचीत, निर्धारित, निर्णीत, वास्तविक.

2 *settled, definite, limited, fixed;*—esp. of time. बांधा, बं-दा, सावधि, सावधिक, कृतावधि, इयत्तेचा, नेमाचा, नियमाचा, ठरावाचा, मुद्दतीचा, समर्याद, कृतकाल, परिछिन्न.

3 *conclusive,* v. DECISIVE. निर्णय करणारा, निर्णायक.

DETERMINATELY. See CERTAINLY.

DETERMINATENSS, *n.* v. A. 1. निखालसपणा *m.* निखालसता *f.* सचितपणा *m.* निर्धारितत्व *n.* &c.

2 मान *n.* मिती *f.* परिमिति *f.* प्रमाण *n.* मर्यादा *f.* मोईन *f.* इय-त्ता *f.* सावधिकत्व *n.* &c.

DETERMINATION, *n.* v. V. A. 1.—*act.* ठरावणें *n.* निर्णय *m.* नि-श्चय *m.* ठराव *m.* निर्धारण *n.* अवधारण *n.* निश्चयीकरण *n.* सिद्धि *f.*

2—*act.* ठरावणें *n.* नेमणें *n.* &c. ठराव *m.* निश्चय *m.* नियम *m.*

3—*act.* परिछिन्न करणें *n.* परिछेद *m.*

v. V. N.—*act.* संकल्प करणें *n.* निश्चय करणें *n.* संकल्पिणें *n.*

I. *decision, decidedness, resolution,* v. FIRMNESS. अट *f.* आग्रह *m.* निग्रह *m.* हुकूम *f.* धीर *m.* धैर्य *n.* निकर *m.* प्रागल्भ्य *n.*

II. *a d. a resolve.* निश्चय *m.* निर्धार *m.* संकल्प *m.* करार *m.*

Fixed d. वज्रसंकल्प *m.*

III. *matter determined,* (settled, fixed, &c.). घटित *n.* घटितार्थ *m.* वास्तव *n.*

To DETERMINE, *v. a. ascertain, settle.* ठरावणें, अवधारणें, निर्णय *m.*-निर्धार *m.*-निर्धारण *n.* करणें *g. of o.* निर्णीत-निर्धारित-&c. करणें.

2 *settle, appoint,* v. To FIX. ठरावणें, नेमणें, ठराव *m.*-निश्चय *m*-नियम *pop.* नेम *m.*-&c. करणें *g. of o.* खचीत-निश्चित-निखालस-&c. करणें.

3 *settle judicially,* v. To DECIDE. फैसला *m.*-निवाडा *m.*-&c. करणें *g. of o.*

4 *define, confine, limit.* v. To BOUND. परिच्छेद *m.* करणें *g. of o.* परिच्छिन्न करणें.

5 *resolve.* संकल्प *m.*-निश्चय *m.*-मनांत ठराव *m.*-नेम *m.*-&c. करणें *g. of o.*

6 *give a direction or impulse to.* कल *m.* देणें, रोंख *m.* लावणें.

To DETERMINE, *v. n. resolve.* संकल्पिणें, संकल्प *m.*-निश्चय *m.*-&c. करणें, हाल *f.* बांधणें.

DETERMINED, *p. & a.* v. V. A. 1. ठरावलेला, अवधारलेला, &c. निर्णीत, निश्चित, निर्धारित, अवधारित, सिद्ध.

2 ठरावलेला &c. खचीत केलेला-झालेला, &c.

3 फैसला केलेला, &c.

4 परिच्छेद केलेला, परिच्छिन्न. [लिपक.

5—agent. कृतनिश्चय, कृतसंकल्प.—object. संकल्पित, सांक-

I. *decided, resolute,* v. FIRM. निश्चयाचा, कराराचा, करारी, निर्धारी, निर्धाराचा, अटीचा, धीर, धिराचा, निश्शंक, वज्रसंकल्पी.

DETERMINEDLY, *adv.* दाटून, दाटचळें.

DETERMINER, *n.* DETERMINATIVE, *a.* v.V.A.1. ठरावणारा, &c. निर्णायक, निश्चायक, निर्धारक, निर्णय-&c. कर्त्ता-कारक-कारी.

2 ठरावणारा, &c. खचीत-&c. करणारा.

3 फैसला करणारा, निवाडा करणारा.

4 परिच्छेद करणारा-कर्त्ता, परिच्छेदक.

DETERSION, *n. cleansing* (*a sore*). क्षतशोधन *n.* क्षतविशोधन *n.* क्षतशुद्धि *f.*

DETERSIVE, *a.* v. N. क्षतशोधक, क्षतविशोधक, क्षतशुद्धिकारक.

To DETEST, *v. a.* v. To ABHOR. ओंगळ-&c. मानणें. अतिद्वेष *m.* करणें *g. of o.*

DETESTABLE, *a.* v. HATEFUL. अतिद्वेष्य, अत्यप्रिय.

DETESTATION, *n.* v. ABHORRENCE. अतिद्वेष *m.*

To DETHRONE, *v. a.* गादीवरून काढणें-खालीं करणें, सिंहासनच्युत-सिंहासनभ्रष्ट-राजपदच्युत-राजपदभ्रष्ट-&c. करणें.

To DETONATE, *v. n. explode, burn with a sudden report.* धडकणें, भडकणें, भुरकन-भुसकन-सुरकन-फटफट-&c. उडणें-जाळणें-&c.

To DETORT, &c. See To TWIST, &c.

To DETRACT, *v. a. take away from the reputation or merit of.* हलकेपणा *m.* आणणें, अपकर्ष *m.*-मानऱ्हास *m.*-मानक्षय *m.*-मानहानि *f.*-गुणापवाद *m.*-पाणउतारा *m.*-&c. करणें *g. of o.*

2 *take away from.* घेणें, घेऊनघेणें, हरण *n.*-अपहार *m.* करणें *g. of o.*

DETRACTION, *n.* v. V. 1. *and* ASPERSION. अपकर्ष *m.* गुणापकर्ष *m.* गुणापवाद *m.* गुणदूषण *n.* असूया *f.*

DETRACTOR, *n.* DETRACTORY, *a.* v.V. 1. *and* ASPERSER. अपकर्ष करणारा, अपकर्षकर्त्ता, गुणापकर्षकर्त्ता, गुणापवादक, गुणापवादकर्त्ता, गुणघाती, गुणदूषक, असूयाकारक.

DETRIMENT, *n.* v. LOSS. नुकसान *n. f.* नुकसानी *f.* तोटा *m.* हानि *f.*

2 *damage, injury,* v. HURT. खराबी *f.* नुकसान *n. f.* धक्का *m.* हानि *f.* क्षति *f.* अपकार *m.*

DETRIMENTAL, *a.* v. N. 2 *and* HURTFUL. अपकाराचा, अवगुणकारी, अपकार-&c. करणारा, अपकारक, अपकारी, क्षतिकारक, हानिकारक.

To DETRUDE, *v. a. thrust down.* खालीं ढकलणें-रेटणें-लोटणें-&c. अधःक्षेप *m.* करणें.

DETRUSION, *n.* v. V. खालीं ढकलणें *n.* &c. अधःक्षेप *m.*

DEUCE. See DIE.

DEUTEROGAMIST, *n. one who marries the second time.* बिजवर.

DEUTROGAMY, *n.* दुसरें लग्न *n.* द्वितीयसंबंध *m.* द्वितीयविवाह *m.*

To DEVASTATE, *v. a. waste, ravage, &c.* नासधूस *f.*-नासधूळ *f.*-धूळदशा *f.*-धूळधाणी *f.*-पायमल्ली *f.*-&c. करणें *g. of o.* धुवा *m.*-चंदन *n.*-गोपचंदन *n.* उडवणें-करणें *g. of o.* खटारणें, बैराण-&c. करणें.

DEVASTATED, *p.* v. V. बैराण केलेला, &c. बैराण, उजाड.

DEVASTATION, *n.* v. V.—*act.* नासधूस करणें *n.* &c. खटारणें *n.* अवमर्द *m.* अवमर्दन *n.* उपमर्द *m.*—*state.* पायमल्ली *or* पायमाली *f.* नासधूस *f.* नासधूळ *f.* उपप्लव *m.* बैराणी *f.* उत्पात *m.* अवांडाव *f.* गोपचंदन *n.* चंदन *n.* चुना *m.*

To DEVELOPE, *v. a. unfold, make known, &c.* स्पष्ट-प्रगट-उघड-&c. करणें, उघडीक *f.*-प्रसिद्धि- &c. करणें *g. of o.* उघडदशेस-प्रसिद्धीस-&c. आणणें, उकलणें, उलगडणें. [उलगडणें.

To be developed. बाहेर पडणें, उघडदशेस-प्रसिद्धीस-&c. येणें,

DEVELOPMENT, *n.* v.V.—*act* उघड करणें *n.* &c.—*state.* उलगडा *m.* उकल *m.* उघाडी *f.*

To DEVIATE, *v. n.* lit. fig. *swerve, stray, wander.* चहकणें *or* भकणें, बिचलणें, बिचल *f. m.* खाणें, बिथरणें, आडवाटेंत-आडमार्गांत-आडरानांत जाणें-शिरणें, पाऊल *n. or* पावटा *m.* वांकडा टाकणें *or with g. of s.* पडणें, चळणें, च्यवणें.

DEVIATION, *n.* v. V.—*act.* भकणें *n.* बिचलणें *n.* &c. चळ *m.* च्यवन *n.* व्यभिचार *m.* उत्क्रम *m.* उत्क्रमण *n.* अपथगमन *n.* विपथगमन *n.* विचलन *n.* विगति *f.*

DEVICE, *n. scheme, plan,* v. CONTRIVANCE. युक्ति *f.* कल्पना *f.* बुद्धि *f.* उपाय *m.* जुगूत *f.* शकल *f.* डाव *m.* तोड *f.*

Devices. तोडजोड *f.*

Crooked d. आडवें उभें *n.*

2 *ingenious machine, &c.* करामत *f.* कुलंगडें *n.*

3 See EMBLEM.

DEVIL, *n. fiend, demon, &c.* (For *the Devil—in theology,* the term, though it is much misunderstood, is, of course, शैतान *or* सैतान *m.* from the Arabic). The *Devils* of the Hindus are numerous, and are distinguished into orders and classes. Pretending not to any accurate classification of these beings, we have collected below some names and titles answering generally to *devil, demon, fiend, sprite, goblin.* For the particulars of their natures, offices, haunts, practices, &c., consult the M. & E. Dict. असुर, भूत, पिशाच, प्रेत, राक्षस, वेताळ, आग्यावे-

नाद, चेडा, मोहनभूत, रूद्रपिशाच, कर्णपिशाच, मारका, समा, स-दीत, जिद, चाळा, पुरूस, योगिनी, सोभणी, लांब or लांबसट, टास, विवशी, जर्माण, डाकिनी *pop.* डंखीण, हडळ or ळी, हेडली, असाळी, अवबंन. *See further under* GHOST.

Devils and demons, fiends and goblins,—compreh. भूतप्रेत n. भूतकेत or खेत n.

A very d. *a malignant person.* जिवंतपिशाच, जिनासमंध, जिनी अवदसा, काळाचाकाळ, खवीस, जिद.

Art or business of raising, injecting, or exorcising devils. भुताटकी *f.*—The practiser of it. भुताटक्या.

Ceremony of summoning a d. to occupy and actuate. गऱ्हाण n. v. घाल, माजव.

Ceremonies, gener. to lay a d. शांति *f.* शांतिक *n.*

D.-dealer. देवभक्त्या, देवरुषी, देवलशी, भक्त्या, भगत, भुताळा or ळ्या, भूतवैद्य, भुतारा, पंचाक्षरीकर्म करणारा, पंचाक्षरी, गऱ्हाणेकरी.

D.-dealing, *raising, exorcising, &c. of devils.* देवभक्ति *f.* देवक्की *f.* भगतकी *f.* पिशाचविद्या *f.* भुताटकी *f.* देवरसपण *n.*

D.-incited (to assail). चेष्टावणीचें भूत.

D.-world. D.-creation. *illusions of devils.* भूतसृष्टि *f.* आसुरीमाया *f.*

Disease, affliction, or mischief, gener. ascribed to a d. बाहेरचाधा or बाहेरचीबाधा *f.* पिशाचबाधा *f.* भूतबाधा *f.* बाहेर-लीपीडा *f.* बाहेरवसा *m.* लागीर or लागोर *f.* आडगुण *m.* आड-फांटा *m.* आडवर्ण *m.* उपद्रव *m.* ग्रहपीडा *f.* ग्रहबाधा *f.* देवाधर्मीचा (रोग-बाधा-पीडा-उपद्रव &c.), झपाट्याची (बाधा *f.*-दुखणें&c.).

Haunt or lurking hole of devils. भूतखाना *m.* भूतखाई *f.* थळ *n.*

Influence or working of devils as producing disease or mischief. आडगुण *m.* आडफांटा *m.* आडवर्ण *m.*

Offerings (of food) to some d. (in appeasement,&c.). भक्र *m.* वाडी *f.* सांडणें *n.*

Of or belonging to devils. Produced by devils—esp. of maladies or troubles. पैशाच, पैशाचिक, उपद्रवीक, उपद्रवी, आडगुणाचा, आडफांट्याचा, झपाट्याचा.

Pranks and tricks of devils. भूतचेष्टा *f.*

Stated or established offering to a d. नीम *m.v.*दे, सांड.

String or company of devils. भुतावळ *f.*

Subject of possession (man, &c.) by a d. देवझाड *n.* झाड *n.* झाड्या.—to quit it. भाव *m.* सोडणें, गति *f.* घेणें.

To be d.-blasted, or d.-affected. लागोरणें or लागीरणें.

To bind a d. under engagement (not to molest, &c.). धरबंधावर or धरबंदावर आणणें-बसवणें-&c. कुरीवर बसवणें.

To cast out a d. भूत *n.*-&c. घालवणें-सोडवणें, प्रसारण *n.* करणें. [करणें.

To inject a d. भूत *n.* घालणें-पेसणें, चेष्टावणी *f.*-पेषणूक *f.*

To set up d.-dealing. देव्हारा *m.* or रें *n.* माजवणें-मांडणें-बाडवणें.

DEVILISH, *a. of or belonging to the d.* सैतानाचा, सैतानाच्या संबंधाचा, सैतानानें केलला, &c. The following words, being derivatives respectively of the terms denoting particular orders or classes of Devils (See DEVIL), express of course corresponding shades of the general sense of *devilish.* पैशाच or पैशाचिक (from पिशाच), भौतिक (from भूत), आसुर & असुरी (from असुर), राक्षसी (from राक्षस), पिसाटीक, संबंधीक, पिशाचाचा, भूताचा, असुराचा, &c. पिशाच -&c. संबंधी.

2 See WICKED.

DEVIOUS, *a.* v. V. *and* ERRING. वाटसोडून जाणारा, अपथगामी, अपथवर्त्ती, विपथगामी, अमार्गी.

I. v. IRREGULAR. गैरशिस्त, बेशिस्त, गैरमार्गाचा, बांकड्या मार्गाचा, बांकड्या पावलाचा, गैरराहाचा, आडमार्गाचा, अनृजु.

DEVIOUSNESS, *n.* v. A. I. अमार्ग *m.* अपथ *m.* व्यभिचार*m.* व्यतिक्रम *m.* [कल्प्य.

DEVISABLE, *a.* v. V. 1. योजाया-चा-जोगा-सारखा-&c. कल्पनीय,

To DEVISE, *v. a. excogitate, invent, plan,* v. To CONTRIVE. योजणें, काढणें, कल्पिणें, चिंतणें, कूप्ति *f.*-तजवीज *f.*-&c. काढणें-करणें *g. of o.*

2 See To BEQUEATH.

DEVISING, *n.* v. V. 1.—*act.* योजणें *n.* काढणें *n.* &c. योजना *f.* योजणूक *f.* चिंतन *n.*

DEVOID, *a. not possessing,* v. WANTING. रहित, शून्य, हीन, निराळा, वेगळा, all in comp. रिता, रिक्त.

DEVOIR, *n. act of respect.* सलाम *m.* मुजरा *m.*

To DEVOLVE, *v. a. deliver over.* कोलणें, टाकणें, लोटणें, ढकलणें, टाळणें, सोंपणें, गळ्यांत घालणें (माळखंड-माळ-&c.), गुजरणें.

To DEVOLVE, *v. n. come to, fall on by succession.* आंगावर-माथ्यावर-वर-&c. पडणें-येणें *g. of s.* गळ्यांत येणें (माळखंड *n.* माळ *f.* गोणी *f.*-&c.) गळीं पडणें, आंगावर टेंकणें.

To DEVOTE, *v. a. give by vow,* v. To DEDICATE. नवसणें, वाहणें, अर्पणें, समर्पणें, अर्पण *n.*-समर्पण *n.*-&c. करणें *g. of o.*

DEVOTED, *p. and a.* v. V. नवसलेला, वाहिलेला, अर्पित, समर्पित.

I. *given up to, addicted, intent upon,* v. INTENT. आसक्त, आसक्तचित्त, दृढभक्ति, एकतान, निरत, तत्पर, तल्लीन, परायण & पर (in comp. and forming valuable compounds endlessly, as ईश्वरपरायण, भक्तिपरायण, पुण्यपरायण, धर्मपरायण, पापपरायण, स्त्रीपरायण, विषयपरायण, निंदापरायण, स्तुतिपरायण, &c. or भक्तिपर, पुण्यपर &c.), फिदा, साक्षेपी, संसक्त.

DEVOTEDNESS, *n.* v. P. वाहिलेलेपणा*m.* &c.अर्पितत्व*n.*समार्पितत्व*n.*

I. आसक्ति *f.* भक्ति *f.* दृढभक्ति *f.* निष्ठा *f.* तत्परता *f.* तल्लीनता *f.* &c. साक्षेप *m.* संसक्ति *f.*

DEVOTEE, *n.* v. ASCETIC. योगी *pop.* जोगी, बैरागी, भक्त *pop.* भगत, संत.

Female a. योगिनी *pop.* जोगीण, &c.

DEVOTION, *n.* v. V.—*act.* नवसणें *n.* वाहणें *n.* &c. अर्पण *n.* समर्पण *n.*—*state.* वाहिलेलेपणा *m.* अर्पितत्व*n.* समार्पितत्व *n.*

I. See DEVOTEDNESS I. II. v. DEVOUTNESS. भक्तिभाव *m.* भक्ति *f.* ईश्वरनिष्ठा *f.*

Hollow and interested d. पिलभक्ति *f.*

Spiritual and abstract d. योग *m.*—the practice of it. योगाभ्यास *m.*

III. *or* devotions, *worship.* भजन *n.* पूजा *f.* अर्चा *f.* देवार्चन *n.* देवपूजा *f.* जपजाप्य *n.*

Morning devotions. प्रातःस्मरण *n.*

DEVOTIONAL, *a. relating &c. to worship.* भजनाविषयींचा, भजनाकडचा, भजनसंबंधी-विषयक, देवपूजेचा, भजनाचे उपयोगाचा.

DEVOTIONALIST, DEVOTIONIST, *n. person superstitiously given to d.* देवपिसामाणूस *m.* देवनादी, भजन्या, टाळकुट्या, बोडकीचें सोंवळें करणारा, दिवसभर नाक धरून बसणारा, देवाचें डोकें धरून बसणारा.

To DEVOUR, *v. a.* v. TO EAT. खाऊन टाकणें, खाऊन चट करणें, खाऊन पीठ *n.* करणें *g. of o.* खाऊन कडाचूर *m.* करणें *g. of o.*

To be ready to d. आ वासून असणें.

2 fig. *swallow up*, v. TO CONSUME. खाणें, गिळणें, फस्त *adv.* खाणें-करणें.

DEVOUT, *a. devoted to religious exercises, &c.* भजनी, भजनशील, भक्तिमान् *pop.* भक्तिमंत, भक्तिपरायण, भक्तिपर, भक्तिप्रवण, भक्तिनिष्ठ, भक्तिवेल्हाळ, पारमार्थिक, देवपरायण, देवभक्त, भजनशाली, जपी, जपपरायण, जपपर, भक्तीचाभुकेला, तपोवृद्ध, तपःशाली.

DEVOUTLY, *adv.* v. A. भक्तिभावानें, भक्तीनें, भक्तिपूर्वक, &c.

DEVOUTNESS, *n.* v. V. भक्तिभाव*m.* भक्ति*f.* देवनिष्ठा*f.* भक्तिनिष्ठा*f* ईश्वरनिष्ठा*f.* भजनशीलता*f.* परमार्थबुद्धि*f.*

DEW, *n.* दहिंवर *or* दंवर*n.* दंव*m.* तुषार*m.n.*

To be bedewed दंवारणें.

DEW-DROP, *n.* दंवाचा थेंब*m.* तुषारबिंदु*m.* तुषारकण*m.* हिमकण*m.*

DEW-LAP, *n. the pendant flesh from the throat of an ox.* कांबळी*f.* पोळी*f.* गलकंबल*m.* सास्ना*f.*

DEWY, *a. relating, &c. to dew.* दंवाचा, दहिंवराचा, तुषारमय, तुषारवान्, दंवानें ओला, तुषारसदृश, तुषाराक्त.

DEXTERITY, *n.* v. A. हातोटी *or* हातवटी *f.* हातोळा *or* हातवळा*m.* हाताची सुगराई*f.* हस्तकौशल्य*n.* हस्तलाघव*n.* कौशल्य*n.* कौशल *n.* दाक्षिण्य*n.* दाक्ष्य*n.* दक्षता*f.*

DEXTEROUS, *a. adroit*, v. EXPERT. हाताचा कुशळ, हातवळलेला, हातचानीट, करदक्ष, दक्ष, कुशल. [पूर्वक.

DEXTEROUSLY, *adv.* v. A. हातवटीनें, कौशल्यानें, दक्षतेनें, दक्षता-

DEXTRAL, *a. not left*, v. RIGHT. दक्षिण, अपसव्य.

DIABETES, *n.* बहुमूत्रमेह*m.* बहुमूत्र*n.* उदकमेह *m.* मूत्रातिसार*m.*

D. mellitus. इक्षुमेह*m.* मधुप्रमेह*m.*

DIABOLICAL. See DEVILISH.

DIADEM, *n.* v. CROWN. मुकुट *pop.* मुगूट*m.*

Gem or jewel of a d. मुकुटमणि*m.*

DIAGNOSIS, *n.* रोगभावना*f.* भावना*f.* [चिन्ह*n.*

DIAGNOSTIC, *n. sign or symptom of disease.* रोगलक्षण*n.* रोग-

DIAGONAL, *a.* कर्णाकृति, कर्णरेषाकृति, कोणस्थ, कोणगामी.

DIAGONAL, *n.* कर्ण*m.* कर्णरेषा*f.*

DIAGONALLY, *adv.* कर्णरेषेनें.

DIAGRAM, *n. geometrical, &c. figure.* क्षेत्र*n.* चक्र*n.* भंगी*f.* आकृति*f.* नकशा*m.*

DIAL, *n.* शंकुयंत्र*n.*

Style of a d. शंकु*m.*

DIAL-PLATE, *n.* शंकुवृत्त*n.*

2 घड्याळाची-&c. तबकडी*f.*

DIALECT, *n.* भाषाभेद*m.* देशभाषा*f.* भाषेचा प्रकार*m.*

DIALECTICS, *n.* v. LOGIC. न्यायशास्त्र*n.* तर्कविद्या*f.*

DIALOGISTIC, DIALOGISTICAL, *a. having the form of a dialogue.* संवादरूप, संवादात्मक, प्रश्नोत्तररूप.

DIALOGUE, *n.* संभाषण*n.* संवाद*m.* प्रश्नोत्तर*n.* *or* प्रश्नोत्तरें*n. pl.* जाबसाल*m.* [*f.*वृत्तार्धरेषा*f.*

DIAMETER, *n.* मध्यरेषा*f.* मध्यसूत्र*n.* गर्भसूत्र *n.* व्यास*m.* व्यासरेषा

DIAMETRICAL, *a. describing a diameter.* व्यासरूपी.

2 *direct, downright, outright, flat, &c.* धडक, सडक, धडधडीत, धडाका, निखालस, नीट, थेट, सरळ, खास. Some phrases and sayings expressive of *diametrical opposition* are त्याची पूर्व तर आमची पश्चिम, त्याची उत्तर तर आमची दक्षिण, त्याचा हां तर आमचा नां, त्याचें पांढरें तर आमचें काळें, त्याचें आडवें तर आमचें उभें.

DIAMETRICALLY, *adv.* v. A. 2. धडधडीत, निखालस.

DIAMOND, *n.* हिरा*m.* हीरक*m.* हीर*m.* वज्र*m.* *n.*—in contempt. हिरकूट*n.* The following terms express sorts or varieties. तोरमल्ली, राजावर्त्त, बिल्याण, नथुशाईहिरा.

D. cut with facets. तरतरा*m.* बिल्याण*m.*

D.-bit. हिरकणी*f.*

D.-mine. हिरेखाण*f.* वैरागर*m.* वज्राकर *m.*

D. cut d. यमकाला यमक, प्रासाला प्रास, शेरास सवाशेर.

DIAMOND, *a.* हिऱ्यांचा.

DIAPER, *n.* कापडाचा प्रकार आहे.

DIAPHANOUS. See TRANSPARENT.

DIAPHORETIC, *a. causing perspiration.* स्वेदोत्पादक, घर्मोत्पादक, स्वेदजनक-कारक-&c.

DIAPHORETIC, *n.* घाम उत्पन्न करणारें औषध *n.* स्वेदन *n.* स्वेदोत्पादक औषध *n.*

DIAPHRAGM, *n. midriff.* मधला पडदा *m.*

DIARRHŒA, *n.* हगवण *f.* हगरड*f.* धंडाळी *or* धांडाळी-धेंडाळी-धेंडोळी-ढेंढळ-ढेंढाळी*f.* फोकांडी*f.* हगक *f.* डरंगळ *f.* भसरें *n.* अतिसार*m.* संग्रहणी*f.* ग्रहणी*f.*बहिर्भूमीची व्यथा*f.*परसाकडेचा उपद्रव *m.*

Affected with d. हगवणकर *or* करी *m.*

Violent or general d. ढगळपट्टी*f.* ढेंढळपट्टी*f.* मुसलवादा*m.*

To have a d. पोट *n.* जाणें-सुटणें *g. of s.* धेंडळणें *or* धेंडाळणें *or* ढेंढळणें, डरंगळणें, ढगळणें, ढाळणें, फोकलणें, पोटाचें पाणी *n.* होणें, ढाळ *m. pl.* होणें.

DIARTHROSIS, *n.* चलसंधि *m.*

DIARY, *n. journal* दिनवृत्तपत्र *n.* दिनवृत्तलेख *m.* दिनचर्यालेख *m.* आह्निकपत्रक *n.* रोजच्या वर्तमानाची वही*f.*

DIASTOLE, *n.* (रक्ताशय-धमनी-इत्यादिकांचें) प्रसरण *n.*

DIBBLE, *n.* खणतें *n.* खणतोड*f.* *n.*

To DIBBLE, *v. a.* खुंटळणें, टोंबिणें.

DICE. See DIE.

DICER, DICE-PLAYER, *n.* जुगारी, जुगाऱ्या, जुवेबाज, द्यूतकार.

DICING, DICE-PLAYING, *n.* जुवा *m.* जुवेबाजी*f.* जुगार *m. n.* द्यूत *n.*

To DICTATE, *v. a. tell to be written.* लिह्याचा सांगणें, लिह्ण्याकरितां सांगणें, मजकूर सांगून लिह्वणें.

2 v. TO DIRECT. हुकूम *m.*-आज्ञा*f.*-&c. करणें-देणें.

DICTATE, *n. order, precept, &c.* हुकूम *m.* आज्ञा*f.* विधि *m.* वाक्य *n.* वक्तव्य *n.*

DICTATION, *n.* v. V. 1—*act.* सांगून लिह्वणें *n.* &c.

2 v. ORDER. हुकूम *m.* आज्ञा*f.*

DICTATOR, *n. one invested with absolute authority.* मुखत्यार-अधिकारी, अप्रतिबंधाधिकारी, बंधनाधीनशास्ता.

DICTATORIAL, *a.* See ABSOLUTE.

2 *dogmatical, imperious.* सत्ता चालविणारा, सत्ताधिशी चा-

लविणारा, आपला चक बसवणारा, सत्ताधिशीचा,कदरेचा, जरबेचा, आढ्यतेचा, मुसल्यारासारखा.

DICTATORIALLY, *adv.* v. A कदरेनें, जरबेनें, मुसल्यारासारखा *decl.*

DICTION, *n. phraseology,* v. STYLE. भाषणाची शैली *f.*-सरणी*f.*-चाल *f.*-रीति *f.*-&c. वाक्यरचना *f.*

Good d. सुभाषित *n.* शब्दशुद्धि *f.*

DICTIONARY, *n.* कोश *or* कोष *m.* शब्दकोश *m.* शब्दसंग्रह *m.*

DICTUM, *n.* वचन *n.* वाक्य *n.* उक्तवाक्य *n.* वक्तव्य *n.*

DIDACTIC, DIDACTICAL, *a. preceptive.* उपदेशाचा, उपदेशात्मक, उपदेशरूप.

DIE, *n. gaming cube.* फासा *m.* पाश *m.* अक्ष *m.*

False d. कपटफासा *m.* दुरक्ष *m.* कूटाक्ष *m.*

Mark or dot on a d. पगडा *m.* रेजा *m.*

Of or belonging to dice. अक्षाचा, आक्षिक. A few of the numerous terms used by *dice players* are thrown together here. पव, दुव्वा, दुरूक, चौक, उपरपगडा, उपरपंजा, उपरछक्का, दुड्डी, एकरंगी, कजेल, कजेली, कदली, कदलणें, चव्वा, चारकाने, चारदाणे, तिरपगडा, तिरूक *or* तिरी, तीनकाने, तीनदाणे &c.

2 *coining d.* शिक्का *m.*

3 (of a goldsmith) रवाळ *f.* रवाळणें *n.*

To DIE, *v. n. expire.* मरणें, देवाज्ञा *f.* होणें *in. con.* जाणें, निवर्त्तणें, बारणें, गमावणें, गतणें, गतावणें, निजणें, निमणें, गुजरणें, गनहोणें, देह*m* पडणें-जाणें-&c. *g.of s.* प्राण *m.*-देह *m.* टाकणें-सोडणें-ठेवणें-त्यागणें-&c. The following words and phrases are cant,covert, allusive, &c. but they are too common to be omitted. गुंडाळणें, अटपणें,उरकणें, खपणें, संपणें, उलथणें, खटारणें, खटावणें, घडघडणें,चचणें, चंचरणें, चसणें, जाजावणें, टोळपणें, करोट *m.* होणें *g. of s.* गवाळें *n.* अटपणें, गाशा *m.* गुंडाळणें, डोळे *m. pl.* झांकणें, बिऱ्हाड *n.* अटोपणें, भाव *m.*सोडणें, गठडी *f.* होणें *g. of s.* पंथास पोंहचणें, चसनापुरास जाणें, घोड्याखालीं येणें-राव, रुष्णवर्ण होणें *g. of s.* राम *interj.* म्हणणें, राम *m.* होणें *in. con.* रुप्याचे डोळे *m. pl.* करणें, प्रस्थान *n.* गुंडाळणें-अटपणें-बांधणें, प्रस्थान *n.* चालणें *g. of s.* न येण्याचे वाटेनें जाणें, निजधामास जाणें, वर जाणें, स्वर्गवासी-कैलासवासी-वैकुंठवासी होणें, परलोकगत-लोकांतरगत-दिवंगत-&c. होणें.

To be about to d. मरतडणें.

To d. by inches. तीळतीळ प्राण सोडणें.

To d. suddenly. तडकातडकी *or* तडकाफडकी *adv.* मरणें, ताडातुडी *adv.*-बोलतां बोलतां मरणें, उलथणें.

To d. suddenly (in the height of vigour, plenitude of enjoyment, &c.). खातांजिवतां *or* खातांपितां-चालतां बोलतां मरणें, भरल्या घोसानें मरणें, पुढें वाढलेल्या पानास लात *f.* मारणें. [*g. of s.*

To d. in great numbers. मरामर *f.* चालणें-लागणें-होणें

Dying or extremely sick state (of men, animals, &c.) मरवड *f.* मरतवड *f.* मरतवडा *m.* मरी *f.*

2 away; *fail, cease, &c.* गळणें, निमणें, खचणें, निरसणें.

To DIE, *v. a.* See To DYE.

DIET, *n.* v. FOOD. खाणें *n.* आहार*m.* भक्ष्य *n.*

2—in medicine. पथ्य *n.* युक्ताहार *m.*

Bad d. or regimen. कुपथ्य *n.* अपथ्य *n.*

Change of d. तोंडाचा पालट*m.* जिभेचा पालट*m.* अन्नपरिवर्त्त*m.*

D. and regimen पथ्यपाणी *n.*

Hard and rigid d. or regimen. खडतरपथ्य *n.* वज्रपथ्य*n.*

Milk d. दुग्धाहार *m.* [फसल *f.*

Nutritive and fattening d. रतीब *or* रातीब *m.* खुराक *m.*

Person under d. पथ्यकरी, युक्ताहारी.

Vegetable d. शाकाहार *m.*

3 See ASSEMBLY.

To DIET, *v. a. put on a diet.* पथ्यावर ठेवणें-घालणें, पथ्य*n.*सांगणें.

2 v. To FEED. खायाला घालणें, जेवूं घालणें, पोसणें.

DIET-DRINK, *n.* पथ्याचें पाणी *n.* पथ्योदक *n.* Some of the common *diet-drinks*, answering to *gruel, caudle, posset, sherbet, &c.* are गरगट *m. n.* कांजी *n.* राब *f.* पिटी *f.* सुंठवडा *m.* शिरें *n.* गुळवणी *n.* चिंचवणी *n.* अंबटवणी *n.* सोनवणी *n.* शिकंजी *f.* कणेरी *f.* सांजा *m.*

DIETARY, *n. allowance of food,* v. ALLOWANCE. मोताद *f.* रतीब *m.* चंदी *f.*

DIETARY, DIETETIC, *a. pertaining to diet.* पथ्याचा, पथ्यकर, पथ्यसंबंधी, पथ्यविषयक, पथ्य, पथ्याविषयींचा.

DIFFARREATION, *n.* The ceremony answering to this is काडी मोडून देणें *or* काडी मोडणें (the breaking and mutual giving of a *stick* or *straw*).

To DIFFER, *v. n. be distinct, dissimilar or other; vary, disagree.* भेद *m.*-फारफेर *m.*-फेर *m.*-तफावत *f.*-अंतर*n.*-तारतम्य*n.*-तरतमभाव *m.*-&c. असणें *g. of s. recip.* भिन्न-निराळा-वेगळा-&c. असणें.

2 *be at variance,* v. To DISAGREE. वांकडें *n.*-वैमनस्य *n.*-बिघाड *m.*-&c. असणें-पडणें *g. of s.*

3 (in opinion, &c.) v. To DISAGREE. मतभेद *m.*-द्वैत *n.*-&c. असणें *g. of s.* असम्मत-विसम्मत-विमत-&c. असणें.

DIFFERENCE, DIFFERING, *n.* v. V. 1. फेर *m.* फारफेर *or* फेरफार *m.* फरक *m.*तफावत *f.* अंतर *n.* (also in comp. and much and elegantly, as अर्थांतर, वाक्यांतर &c.), भेद *m.* (also in comp. and much and elegantly, as अर्थभेद, वाक्यभेद, स्थलभेद, गृहभेद, वृक्षभेद), अधिकउणें *n.* निराळेपणा *m.* वेगळेपणा *m.* &c. भिन्नभाव *m.* भिन्नता *f.* न्यूनाधिकभाव *m.* न्यूनाधिक्य *n.* न्यूनाधिक *n.* न्यूनातिरेक *m.* भेदाभेद *m.* तजावूज *or* तजावुजू *n.* तरतम *n.* तारतम्य *n.* वैलक्षण्य *n.* वैगुण्य *n.* वैधर्म्य *n.* वैजात्य *n.* परत्व *n.* द्वैविध्य *n.* असाम्य *n.* असमत्व*n.* पार्थक्य *n.* अनैक्य *n.*

D. great as between black and white. आकाश पाताळाचा भेद, जमीन असमानाची तफावत.

Slight d. (of one thing with another). हेर फेर *m.*

Splitting the d. (in bargains, &c.) खांजणी भांजणी *f.* कवडतावड *f.*

2 *variance, contention,* v. DISAGREEMENT. वांकडें *n.* दुई *f.* द्वैत *n.* द्वैतभाव *m.* द्वैध *n.* [द्वैविध्य *n.*

3 मतभेद *m.* मतांतर *n.* विप्रतिपत्ति *f.* वैमत्य *n.* द्वैत *n.* द्वैध *n.*

I.—in arithmetic. अंतर *n.* उत्तर *n.*

II.—in astronomy; ascensional d. चारकांड *n.*

Sine of ascensional d. चारज्या *f.*

DIFFERENT, *a. other, distinct.* वेगळा, निराळा, न्यारा, दुसरा, इतर, अन्य, भिन्न, अपर, पर, वायला, निखालस, दुजा, एर, परका *or* खा, पारखा, सवता.

2 *dissimilar* v. UNLIKE. असदृश, विसदृश, अतुल्य, बिजातीय, बिगुण, बिलक्षण.

DIFFERENTIAL CALCULUS, *n.* शून्यलब्धि *f.*

DIFFERENTLY, *adv.* v. A. *in a different manner.* निराळें, वेगळें, अन्य-भिन्न-&c. रीतीनें-प्रकारानें, अन्यथा.

DIFFICULT, *a. hard, not easy.* कठिन *pop.* कठीण, अवघड, जड, भारी, बिकट, मुशकील, क्लिष्ट, विषम, जबर, जरब, गडखळ, श्रमसाध्य, कष्टसाध्य, आयाससाध्य, प्रयत्नसाध्य, दुर्घट, दुःसाध्य, दुष्कर, दुर्निर्वह, दुःशक, दौःशक्य, दुर (in comp. as दुर्लभ, दुर्लंघ्य, &c.) —in high degree. दगडफोड, फत्तरफोड, डोईजड, धोंडेफोड, खडेफोड, कडाचूर, सुदुश्चर.

2 (of understanding) v. ABSTRUSE. कठीण, अवघड, गुरु, गुरुगम्य, दुर्गम्य, अगम्य, दुर्ज्ञेय, दुर्बोध.

3 *hard to please or win,* v. CROSS. कठीणमर्जीचा, करडेमर्जीचा, दिकती, दुराराध्य, दुस्सेव्य.

DIFFICULTLY, *adv. with difficulty,* See under DIFFICULTY.

DIFFICULTY, *n.* v. A. 1. कठीणपणा *m.* अवघडपणा *m.* बिकटपणा *m.* &c. काठिन्य *n.* कठिनता *f.* श्रमसाध्यता *f.* &c. दौष्कर्य *n.* दुष्करता *f.* &c.

With d. जुलमानें, जुलमावर, जुलमाजुलमीं, जुलमाजुलमानें, कुच्छ्रेंकरून, संकटानें, श्रमानें, अलेंबलें, जरूर.

2 कठीणपणा *m.* अवघडपणा *m.* गूढता *f.* दुर्ज्ञेयता *f.*

I. a d. *a knotty or hard matter, point, &c.* कूट *n.* गूढ *n.* गूढार्थ *m.* कोडें *n.* मुशकील *f.* डोंगर *m.* गड *f.* [*in. con.*

To feel in a d. पंचाईत *f.*- विचार *m.*-मसलत *f.*-&c. पडणें

II. a d. *scrape, hobble, &c.* v. TROUBLE. संकट *n.* दुःख *n.* कचाट *n.* अडचण *f.* संकष्ट *n.* कोडें *n.* कातर *f.* कुलंगडें *n.* सँकटें *n.* ओकटें *n.* अलगड *f.*

To get into a d. अडकित्यांत सांपडणें. [ढून घेणें.

To draw off from or out of a d. दगडाखालून हात *m.* का-

III.—as made, started, &c. v. OBJECTION. शंका *f.* दिक्कत *f.* आक्षेप *m.* किंतु *m.* फणगडा *m.* फंगरूड *n.* फगाड *m.* आड *f. v.* धर.

Without d. बिनदिक्कत *or* बेदिक्कत.

DIFFIDENCE, *n. want of confidence, distrust,* v. DOUBT. अविश्वास *m.* शंका *f.* आशंका *f.*

2 *distrust of self, want of confidence in one's own ability, &c.* आपणाविषयींचा अविश्वास *m.*-अभरवसा *m.*-संशय *m.*-&c. अधैर्य *n.* स्वगुणशंका *f.* स्वक्षमताशंका *f.* असाहस *n.* साहसाभाव *m.* संशय *m.* शंका *f.* [अधृष्टता *f.*

3 *bashfulness, &c.* v. MODESTY. भीड *f.* लज्जा *f.* संकोच *m.*

DIFFIDENT, *a.* v. N. 1. *and* DISTRUSTFUL. सशंक, साशंक, शंकाशील, अप्रत्ययी.

2 अधीर, आपणाविषयीं सशंक, स्वशंक, आत्मशंकी.

3 v. MODEST. लज्जाशील, संकोची, संकोचशील, भेजूड, भिडस्त, भिडस्तरू *or* सारू, अधृष्ट.

DIFFIDENTLY, *adv.* v. A. 2. आपणाविषयींसशंक होऊन, शंकापूर्वक.

3 भिडेनें, भिडस्तपणानें, &c. लज्जापूर्वक.

To DIFFUSE, *v. a. spread abroad,* v. TO SPREAD. फैलावणें, पसरणें, विस्तारणें, विस्तार *m.*-फैलाव *m.*-प्रसर *or* प्रसार *m.*-प्रसरण *or* प्रसारण *n.*-&c. करणें *g. of o.*

To be diffused around—an odour. दमदमणें.

DIFFUSE, *a.* DIFFUSED, *p.* v. V. विस्तारलेला, फैलावलेला, पसरलेला, विस्तार केलेला, &c. विस्तारित, विस्तीर्ण, प्रसृत, प्रवृद्ध, प्रकीर्ण.

I.—in style, &c. पघळ, विस्ताराचा, विस्तृत, विस्तारयुक्त, पाल्हाळाचा, पाल्हाळीक.

DIFFUSELY, v. A. I. विस्तारानें, ग्रंथविस्तारानें.

DIFFUSION, *n.* v. V.—*act.* विस्तारणें *n.* फैलावणें *n.* &c. प्रसारण *n.* —*state.* विस्तार *m.* पसारा *m.* फैलावा *m.* फैलाव *m.* प्रसार *m.*

I. Diffuseness (of style, &c.). ग्रंथविस्तार *m.* अर्थवाद *m.* प्रपंच *m.*

DIFFUSIVE, *a. having the quality of spreading.* प्रसरणशील, प्रसरणधर्मक, व्यापक.

2 See DIFFUSE.

DIFFUSIVENESS, *n.* v. A. 1. प्रसरणशीलता *f.* व्यापकता *f.*

2 See DIFFUSION.

To DIG, *v. a.* खणणें, खोदणें, खांडणें.

2 up; *break up.* उखणणें.

To DIG, *v. n.* खणण्याचें काम *n.* करणें.

DIGEST, *n. compendium, summary, &c.* v. ABRIDGEMENT. कलमबंदी *f.* सारग्रंथ *m.* समाहार *m.* संहिता *f.*

To DIGEST, *v. n. be digested.* पचणें, जिरणें, पचन *n.* होणें *g. of s.* पचणीं-जिरणीं पडणें.

2—a wound, &c. पिकणें, पक्क होणें.

To DIGEST, *v. a.* (food). पचवणें, जिरवणें, पाचन *n.*-पाक *m.* करणें *g. of o.* पचणीं-जिरणीं पाडणें-घालणें, जीर्ण-पक्क करणें.

2—in chemistry, &c. शिजवणें, क्कथन *n.* करणें, शृत करणें.

3 See TO ARRANGE.

DIGESTED, *p.* v. V. N. पचलेला, &c. जिरणीं-पचणीं-आहारीं पडलेला, पचन झालेला, जीर्ण, पक्क.

v. V. A. 1. पचवलेला, &c. पाचन-&c. केलेला, पचणीं-&c. घातलेला-पाडलेला.

2 क्कथित, शृत.

DIGESTER, *n.* DIGESTIVE, *a.* v. V. A. 1. पचवणारा, &c. जिरणीं-पचणीं पाडणारा-घालणारा, पाचक, पाचन, अग्निवर्द्धक, अग्निप्रद, अग्निद, दीपक, जारण.

Any thing to promote d. जिरवण *n.* [*pl.*

D.—powers. जठराग्नि *m.* जठरानल *m.* कोष्ठाग्नि *m.* पंचोष्मे *m.*

Languor of d. powers. अग्निमांद्य *n.* मंदाग्नि *m.*

DIGESTIBLE, *a.* v. V. N. पचाया-जोगा-जोगता-&c. पचनीय, पच्य, शीघ्रपाक.

DIGESTION, *n.* v. V. A. 1.—*act.* पचवणें *n.* &c. पाचन *n.*—*state.* पाक *m.* परिपाक *m.* पुटपाक *m.*

v. V. N. पचणें *n.* &c. पचन *n.*

Of bad or weak d. मंदाग्नि.

Of good d. दीप्ताग्नि. [करणारा.

DIGGER, *n.* DIGGING, *p. a.* v. V. A. 1. खणणारा, &c. खनन-

Stone d. बेलदार.

DIGGING, *n.* v. V.—*act.* खणणें *n.* &c. खनन *n.* खोदणी *f.* खणती *f. v.* लाव.

DIGIT, *n.* (of the moon's diameter) कला *f.* चंद्रकला *f.* इंदुकला *f.* इंदुरेखा *f.* इंदुदल *n.* चंद्रांश *m.*

2 (of the sun's diameter). अर्कांश *m.*

Decrease of digits (of sun or moon). क्षय *m.*

Increase of digits. वृद्धि *f.*

DIGNIFIED, *a. marked with dignity, noble.* मोठेपणाचा, मोठेप-

णाचें डौलाचा, प्रौढ, प्रौढीचा, थोर, मान्यतेचा, श्रीमंती, श्रीमंती डौलाचा, गौरवाचा.

To DIGNIFY, *v. a. make honorable, illustrious, &c.* मोठेपणा *m.*-थोरपणा *m.*-महत्व *n.*-शोभा *f.*-&c. आणणें-देणें, प्रौढ-थोर-&c. करणें.

DIGNITARY, *n.* मोठ्या पदवीचा-श्रेष्ठपदवीचा मनुष्य *m.*

DIGNITY, *n. honor, greatness, &c.* मोठेपणा *m.* थोरपणा *m.* प्रौढी *f.* मान्यता *f.* गौरव *n.* माहात्म्य *n.* अनुभाव *m.*

2 *high situation, &c.* उंचपदवी *f.* मोठीपदवी *f.* मोठी असामी *f.* मरतबा *m.* दर्जा *m.*

3 *quality of inspiring with awe, commandingness, imperativeness, majesty, &c.* दबदबा *m.* दबाव *m.* दाब *m.* सलाबत *f.* सलाबतपणा *m.*

To DIGRESS, *v. n. depart from one's subject.* फाकणें, रान *n.* घेणें, रानांत शिरणें, रान *n.* सोडणें-बदलणें-पारखें करणें, भटकणें, भडकणें, पाय *m. pl.* फोडणें, फांदडा *m.* फोडणें-घेणें, उडणें, वाहवणें, चाचरणें.

DIGRESSION, v. V.—*act.* फाकणें *n.* रान घेणें *n.* &c.

I. a d. *passage deviating.* फांटा *m.* फांदडा *m.* पागोरा *m.* फांद *f.* पद्दर *m.* शाखा *f.* आडकथा *f.* अवांतरकथा *f.*

DIGRESSIVE, *a.* फाकणारा, रानांत शिरणारा.

DIKE, *n.* v. DITCH. खंदक *m.*

2 *mound*, v. BANK. बांध *m.* धरण *n.*

To DIKE, *v. a.* बांध *m.*-धरण *n.* बांधणें.

To DILAPIDATE, *v. n. go to ruin.* मोडकळीस-मोडीस-पडीस येणें, मोडणें, मोडकळणें.

To DILAPIDATE, *v. a.* मोडकळीस-मोडीस पडीस आणणें.

DILAPIDATED, *p.* v. V. N. मोडकळीस आलेला, &c. मोडावलेला, पडका, पडीत.

DILAPIDATION, *n.* v. V.—*state.* मोडकळीस आलेलेपणा *m.* मोडावलेपणा *m.* मोडतीदशा *f.* पडतीदशा *f.* पडझड *f.*

DILATATION, *n.* v. V. A. 1. पसरणें *n.* &c. प्रसारण *n.*—*state.* प्रसार *m.* फैलावणी *f.*

v. V. N. 1. खुलणें *n.* &c. फुलणी *f.*

To DILATE, *v. a. spread out, expand.* पसरणें, विस्तारणें, फैलावणें, प्रसारण *n.*-प्रसार *m.* करणें, खुलविणें, फुलविणें.

2 *tell or say diffusely.* विस्तारानें-विस्तार करून-विस्तार पूर्वक-&c. सांगणें-कथन *n.* करणें.

To DILATE, *v. n. open, expand, widen.* खुलणें, फुलणें, फुलफुलणें, उमलणें, पसरणें.

2 *speak copiously on.* विस्तार *m.*-ग्रंथविस्तार *m.*-वाक्य विस्तार *m.*-पाल्हाळ *m.*-&c. करणें.

DILATORILY, *adv.* v. A. उशिरानें, उशिरां, उसरीं, उशीर करून-लावून, वेळकरून-लावून, चेंगटाईनें, &c.

DILATORINESS, *n.* v. A. चेंगटाई *f.* चेंगटपणा *m.* दिरिंगेपणा *m.* सावकाशेपणा *m.* &c. दिरंगाई *f.* ढिली *f.* सावकाशी *f.* हयगई *or* हैगई *f.* लिंगस्ताई *f.* सुस्ती *f.* सुस्ताई *f.* चिरकारिता *f.*

DILATORY, *slow, slack, procrastinating,*—of persons. वेळलाव्या, उशिऱ्या, दिरिंग्या, ढिला, ढिल्या, ढील, थिल्लट, सावकाश्या, चेंगट, चेंगटी, चेंगट्या, विलंबी, दीर्घसूत्री, दीर्घसूत्र, मंद, जड, चिरकारी, चिरक्रिय, जडक्रिय, सुस्त, सुस्ता, लिंगशा.

2—of things. ढिला, ढील, चेंगट, चेंगटाईचा, दिरंगाईचा, सावकाशीचा, दीर्घसूत्री, मंद, सुस्ताईचा, &c. थिल्लट.

DILEMMA, *n. vexatious alternative, strait, difficulty, &c.* कातर *f.* चिमटा *m.* विडती *f.* पेच *m.* पेचाटी *f.* दुमारा *m.* दुमारें *n.* कचाट *m.* कचाटी *f.* कच *f.* उभयतः पाशरज्जू *f.* उभयसंभव *m.*

To be in a d. कातरींत-अडकित्यांत-&c. सांपडणें.

To reduce to a d. फांद्यांत घालणें-पाडणें.

DILIGENCE, *n.* v. A. कामसूपणा *m.* कष्टाळूपणा *m.* उद्योगीपणा *m.* &c. उद्योग *m.* परिश्रम *m.* मेहनत *f.* व्यासंग *m.* व्यवसाय *m.* अध्यवसाय *m.* उद्यम *m.* आसक्ति *f.* संसक्ति *f.* सक्ति *f.* साक्षेप *m.* अभ्यास *m.* अनालस्य *n.* निरालस्य *n.* उद्योगिता *f.* उद्योगशीलता *f.* &c.

To give d. use d. &c. उद्योग *m.*-परिश्रम *m.*-&c. करणें, झटणें, लगट *m. f.* करणें.

DILIGENT, *a. assiduous, sedulous, industrious,*—of persons. कामाळू, कष्टाळू, कष्टी, श्रमी, कामीक, कामी, खप्या, खपी, कामसू, उद्योगी, मेहनती, मेहनत्या, कसालती, कामठ, कर्मशील, कर्मशूर, उद्यमी, उद्योगशील, अनलस, निरलस, सोद्योग, यत्नवान्, यत्नी, प्रयत्नवान्, प्रयत्नी, यत्नशील, उपद्व्यापी, व्यासंगी, परिश्रमी, व्यवसायी, श्रामक, अध्यवसायी, आसक्त, संसक्त, साक्षेपी, सक्त.

2—of things, मेहनतीचा, श्रमाचा, परिश्रमाचा, &c. व्यासंगपूर्वक, &c.

DILIGENTLY, *adv.* मेहनतीनें, &c. व्यासंगपूर्वक, &c.

DILL-SEED, *n.* बाळंतशेप *or* शोप *f.* मिश्रेया *f.* शालेय *m.* शीतशिव *m.*

To DILLY-DALLY. See To DALLY.

To DILUTE, *v. a. make thin, weak, &c.* पातळ-सरसरीत-सरबरीत-बरबरीत-&c. करणें.

DILUTE, *a.* पातळ, सरसरीत, सरबरीत, बरबरीत, न्यूनतेजस्क.

DILUVIAN, *a.* जलप्रलयाचा, जलप्रलयसंबंधी-विषयक.

DIM, *a. dim-sighted.* मंददृष्टि, ठोसरदृष्टीचा, दृष्टीचा मंद-जड, फुटक्या डोळ्याचा, मंद.

2 *of dull vision,*—the eye. मंददृष्टि, मंद, फुटका, ठोसर, अधू.

3 *of dull appearance, obscure, indistinct, dull.* पुसका, पुसट, पुसकट, मळकट, ओंधट, अंधक, दुर्दर्श.

4 *not bright or lustrous.* अंधक, मंदज्योति, मंदकांत, मंदतेजस्क, मंदतेजा, न्यूनतेजस्क, अल्पतेजस्क, निस्तेज, अतेज, मिणमिणा *or* ण्या, मलिनप्रभ, न्यूनप्रभ, न्यूनज्योति, न्यूनकांति.

5 *darkish;*—weather, &c. v. DUSKY. ओंधट, धुंद, अंधक.

6 *dull of apprehension*—the understanding, मंद, जड.

To DIM, *v. a.*—the vision. मंद-जड-&c. करणें, मंदत्व *n.* आणणें.

Of dimmed or dullened vision. धुंद.

2 See To OBSCURE. [घनांग *n.*

DIMENSION, *n.* मेज *n.* मोज *n.* पोटमेज *n.* क्षेत्रफल *n.* लांबीरुंदी *f.*

To DIMINISH. See To LESSEN.

DIMINUTION, *n. the act of lessening.* लहान-न्यून-&c. करणें *n.* क्षय-अपचय-&c. करणें *n.*

2 *the state of becoming less.* उतार *m.* क्षय *m.* ऱ्हास *m.* अपचय *m.* अपक्षय *m.* उतरती *f.*

DIMINUTIVE, *a.* v. LITTLE. लहान, लाहनाळा, ऱ्हस्व, लघु, क्षुद्र.

DIMINUTIVENESS, *n.* v. A. लहानपणा *m.* लहानकी *f.*

DIMITY, *n.* दुमेटी *f.* दुमेटीचें कापड *n.*

DIMLY, *adv.* v. A. 3. अंधक, धुंदक, धुरकट, धुरट, धुकट, भुरकट, धुंदुकधुंदुक, धुंदुकमुंदुक, धुंदुसमुंदुस, झुरळूकझुरळूक, तुरळकतुरळक, चांचपड चांचपड.

4 अंधक, मिणमीण.

D. burning-lamp or light. मिणमिणीत.

To burn d. मिणमिणणें. [धुंदी f.

DIMNESS, n. v. A. 1. अंधारी f. दृष्टिमांद्य n. दृष्टिमंदत्व n. मांद्यn.

2 फुटकेपणा m. मंददृष्टित्व n. मांद्य n. मंदत्व n. तिरीम n.

3 पुसकेपणा m. पुसटपणा m. &c. ओंध f.

4 अंधकपणा m. तेजोन्यूनता f. तेजोमांद्य n. कांतिन्यूनता f.

5 ओंधटपणा m. &c. काळोखी f. ओंध f. अंधारी f. काळंबण n. काहूर n. v. ये, उठ.

6 मंदपणा m. जडपणा m. मंदत्व n. तिरीम n.

DIMPLE, n. हनुवटीची खळी f. हनुकूपिका f.

2 (on the cheek) गालाची खळी f. गालकुच्चा m.

DIN, n. *clang, &c.* खणका m. दणका m. ठोका m. ठांठू n. f. टकटक or ठकठक f. घुमटा m. धूम f. धूमधडाका m. धडाका m. तडाका or खा m.—intens. दणदणाट m. दणाण m.

To DIN, *v. a. stun with noise.* कानठळीं or ळें n. pl.-कानठळया f. pl. बसविणें, कान m. pl. फोडणें-बहिरे करणें.

To DINE, *v. n.* v. MEAL. जेवणें, भोजन n. करणें, दिवसाचें मुख्य-भोजन n. करणें.

To d. on or off. जेवणें (as मी भात जेवलों).

To DINE, *v. a.* भोजन n. घालणें, जेवण n. घालणें.

DINED, *p.* v. V. N. जेवलेला, &c. कृतभोजन.

DINGLE, n. *hollow among hills.* खोरा m. or रें n. खोंडा m. आड f. दरा m. *dim.* दरी f.

DINGY, *a. dirty looking.* मळकट, मळमळीत, मजीत.

DINING, DINNER, n. v. MEAL. जेवण n. जेवा m. भोजन n. दिवसाचें मुख्य भोजन n.

Bad (poor, &c.) d. कुभोजन n.

D. of friends. इष्टभोजन n.

D. to Bráhmans. ब्राह्मणभोजन n. ब्राह्मणसंतर्पण n.

Good d. *a blow out, &c.* इच्छाभोजन n. छटाकी f. चक्का m. भरगच्चीचें जेवण n.

Hard pressed for a d. मध्याह्न काळाचें कठीण *g. of s.*

To lay for d. पंगत f. मांडणें.

To make one's d. of a glass of water. थंडा फराळ करणें.

Dinner is waiting. भाकरीला भूक लागली.

2 *entertainment.* जेवणावळ f. भोजनसमारंभ m.

DINING-ROOM, n. जेवणाची खोली f. जेवणघर n.

DINNER-TIME, n. जेवणवेळ f. भोजनवेळ f. भोजनसमय m.

DINT, n. (of the forming hammer). ठोका m. ठसा m. घाव m. घावटा m.

2 *mark of a blow,*—gener. पोचा m. खोंच f. खोंचा m. *dim.* खोंची f. खोंप f. खोंक f. खोमा m. घावटा m. [मठारणें.

To hammer down the dints (of a new metal vessel).

The hammer for doing so. मठारणें n.

3 *power,* v. FORCE. जोर m. बळ n.

To DINT, *v. a. indent.* खोमलणें, ठोका m. or ठोके m. pl.-खोंचा m. or खोंचे m. pl.-&c. पाडणें-मारणें.

DINTED, *p.* v. V. खोमललेला, खोंचे पाडलेला, &c. पोचट, पोचारा, पोचेरा, चेचका.

To be or become d. पोचलणें, खोमलणें.

DIOPTRIC, DIOPTRICAL, *a.* v. N. किरण वक्रीभवनानुशासन शास्त्रसंबंधी-विषयक.

DIOPTRICS, n. किरण वक्रीभवनानुशासन शास्त्र n.

DIOCESE, n. बिशप जो पाद्री त्याच्या अधिकाराखालचा प्रदेश m.

To DIP, *v. n. immerge.* बुचकळणें or बुचकुळणें, डुबकळणें, बुचकळी or बुचकुळी f. -बुटकुळी f. -बुडी f. -बुडकी f. -डुबी f. -डुबकी f.-&c. मारणें-घेणें-खाणें.

2 fig. (into a science or subject). बुचकुळणें or बुचकळणें, डुबणें, ओरखडणें.

3 *incline.* झुकणें, कलणें.

To DIP, *v. a. immerge.* बुचकळणें or बुचकुळणें, बुडवणें, डुबकळणें, बुचकळी or बुचकुळी f.-बुटकुळी f.-&c. देणें, बुडी f.-बुडकी f.-&c. खावविणें.

2 out; *take out by a ladle, &c.* पळीनें-&c काढणें-काढून घेणें.

DIP, DIPPING, n. v. V. N. 1. बुडी f. बुडकी f. बुचकळी or बुचकुळी f. बुटकुळी f. डुबकी f. डुबी f. डूब m. डुबकळी f. पाणबुडी f. मज्जन n. अवगाहन n.

D. or plunge as of a paper kite. गोता m. गोत f.

v. V. A.—*act.* बुचकळणें n. &c. बुचकळी देणें n. &c.

I. *declivity,* v. DESCENT. उतरड f. डेवण n.

DIPHTHONG, n. संधिस्वर m. द्विस्वर m.

DIPLOMA, n. *writing conferring power, privilege, &c.* सनद f. पत्र n. पत्रक n.

DIPLOMACY, n. राजमंत्रीचें कर्तृत्व n. राजदूताचें कर्त्तत्व n. राजदूतकर्म n. राजदौत्य n. [विषयक.

DIPLOMATIC, *a.* राजमंत्रीच्या कर्तृत्वाचा, राजदूतकर्तृत्व संबंधी-

D. body. राजदूतांची मंडळी f. राजदूतसमूह m.

DIPLOMATIST, n. राजदूताचे कामांत कुशल, राजदूतकर्मनिपुण.

DIPPED, *p.* v. V. N. 1. बुचकळलेला, बुचकळी मारलेला, &c. अवगाढ, अवगाहीत, मज्जित.

v. V. A. बुचकळलेला, बुचकळी दिल्हेला, &c.

DIRE, DIREFUL, *a.* v. DREADFUL. भयानक, घोर, भयंकर, उग्र.

DIRECT, *a.* v. STRAIGHT. उजू, नीट, सरल, अवक्र.

2—*as opposed to* reverse. सुलटा, सुफराटा, सुपरीत, अपसव्य, अनुलोम, सलोम.

D. and reverse. सुफराटाउफराटा, सव्यापसव्य, सुपरीतविपरीत, अनुलोमविलोम.

To make d. सुफराटणें.

3 *not circuitous.* नीट, समोरचा, सडक, दोरी धरलेला, दोरी सूत.

4 *not collateral.* एकमाळकेचा, अस्यूतपरंपरेचा, अखंडपरंपरेचा.

5 *not mediate,* v. IMMEDIATE. साक्षात् संबंधाचा, जातीनिशींचा.

6 *express, explicit, not ambiguous,* v. PLAIN. साफ, स्पष्ट, उघडा, धडधडीत.

To DIRECT, *v. a. point against, aim.* रोंखणें, नेमणें, योजणें, लक्षणें, शिस्त f.-निशाण n.-रोंख m.-&c. धरणें *g. of o.* [णें.

2 *prescribe, order.* हुकूम m.-आज्ञा f.-ताकीद f. करणें-देणें, सांग-

3 *point out the way, show the course, &c.* रस्ता m.-वाट f.-मार्ग m.-परिपाटी f.-परिनालिका f.-रीति f.-&c. दाखवणें-सांगणें-लावून देणें, मार्गप्रदर्शन n.-&c. करणें.

4 See To REGULATE, To GOVERN.

DIRECTED, *p.* v. V. 1. रोंखलेला, योजलेला, &c.

2 सांगितलेला, आज्ञप्त, निर्दिष्ट, विध्युक्त, शासित, आदिष्ट, निदिष्ट.

3 निर्दिष्टपद्धति, निर्दिष्टमार्ग.

DIRECTER, n. DIRECTIVE, *a.* DIRECTORY, *a.* v. V. 1. रोंखणारा, योजणारा, &c. प्रयोगी, प्रयोक्ता.

2 *and* DIRECTOR. हुकूम करणारा, निदेष्टा, निदेशी, आदेशी,

शास्ता, अनुशास्ता, शासक, विनेता.

3 रस्ता दाखवणारा, परिणायिका दाखवणारा, &c.

DIRECTION, *n.* v. V. 1.—*act.* रोंखणेंn. नेमणेंn. &c. योजनn. प्रयोगm.

2 *command*, v. ORDER. सांगणी *f.* सांगी *f.* निर्देशm. निदेशm. आदेशm. शासनn. विधि *m.*

Directions, *rules laid down.* धडाm.

3 रस्तादाखवणेंn. &c. मार्गप्रदर्शनn. मार्गदर्शनn.

I. *clew to find.* पत्ताm.

II. *address, superscription.* नांवाचापत्ताm. नांवागांवाचा पत्ताm.

III. *bearing, bent*, v. TENDENCY. रोंखm. झोकm. मोड *f.* मांडणी *f.* संधानn. कल *m.*

IV. *point of the compass.* दिशा *f.*

In every d.—fleeing, &c. दिशांदिशां, दाहीदिशां, दशदिशां, प्रतिदिश, बारावाटां.

DIRECTLY, *adv.* v. A. 1. नीट, उजू, सरळ, &c.

3 नीट, थेट, समोर, सडक, धडक, खास.

5 *and* IMMEDIATELY. जातीनिशीं, साक्षात्.

6 *and* PLAINLY. धड, साफ, स्पष्ट.

I. *instantly*, v. IMMEDIATELY. लागलाच, आतांच, अविलंबें.

DIRECTNESS, *n.* v. A. 1. उजूपणा *m.* निटाई *f.* सरळपणा *m.* सरलता *f.* सारल्य *n.* आर्जव *n.* ऋजुत्व *n.*

2 सुलटेपणा *m.* सुकराटेपणा *m.* अपसव्यता *f.* आनुलोम्य *n.*

3 निटाई *f.* सडकपणा *m.*

DIRECTOR, *n. superintendent, manager*, v. CONDUCTOR. अधिकारी, अध्यक्ष, वहिवाटदार, सुकाण्या, सुकाणदार, नायक, दिम्मतदार, प्रवर्त्तकाचार्य. [comp.

DIRECTORY, *n. book of directions.* पद्धतिग्रंथ *m.* पद्धति *f.* in

DIRECTRESS, DIRECTRIX, *n.* v. DIRECTOR. अधिकारिणी *pop.* अधिकारीण *f.* &c.

DIREFULNESS, DIRENESS, *n.* v. A. घोरपणा *n.* भयानकत्व *n.* भयंकरत्व *n.* उग्रता *f.*

DIRGE, *n. funeral song.* शोकाचें गाणें *n.* मरशा *m.* शोकगीत *n.*

DIRK, *n.* v. DAGGER. खंजीर *m.* सुरा *m.* पालकोयती *f.*

DIRT, *n.* मल *m. n. pop.* मळ *m.* मैल *m.* किट्ट *n.*

Caked or thick d. कट *m.* खट *f.* काट *m.* किटण *n.* किट्ट *pop.* कीट *n.*

That hides d. मळघाऊ *or* ब, मैलखोर.

2 *rubbish, &c.* केर *m.* कचरा *m.* माती *f.* खळमळ *m.* घाण *f.* हेंदर *f.* हेंदरेंदर *f.*

D. and rubbish—compreh. केरकचरा *m.* केरकस्तान *n.*

3 (as amongst grain, sugar, &c.). मातेरा *m. or* रें *n.* मातड *n.* गदळ *m.*

DIRTINESS, *n.* v. A. मळकेपणा *m.* मळीणपणा *m.* &c. मालिन्य *n.*

DIRTY, *a. filthy, foul.* मळका *remiss.* मळकट, मलिन *pop.* मळीण, मळसर, मळखर, हिडीस, हिडशा, घाणेरडा, गदळ, समल, मलयुक्त, मलदूषित, कळकट *or* कळकूट, मिचकूट, मसकट.

Very d.—*black with d.* काळामस.

To become d. मळणें, मळकटणें, कळकटणें, कटणें, काटणें, किटणें, मसकटणें, मिचकटणें *or* मिचकुटणें.

To DIRTY, *v. a.* मळविणें, मळीण-मळका-&c. करणें, मळगावणें *or* मळघावणें, गादवणें *or* गादावणें.

2 *cover with filth, befoul.* हिडसावणें, हिडीस-हिडशा-&c. करणें, भरिवणें, भरणें, घाण *f.* करणें *g. of o.*

DIRTY-LOOKING, *a.* मजीत, मळमळीत.

DIS. This inseparable particle is expressed by दुर्, अ, निर्, ना, विन, गैर, बे, बद, कु, वि, उ, as, दुराग्रह, अकीर्त्ति, अनादर, निरपेक्ष, नापसंद &c., in its senses of *negation, deterioration*, or *depreciation*; and by वि, उ, in its sense of *undoing, nullifying*, or *depriving.* Note. Some words may be sought for in vain under DIS which will be found under IN.

DISABILITY, *n.* See WEAKNESS.

2 *want of qualification.* कार्याक्षमता *f.* अक्षमता *f.* अयोग्यता *f.* नालायकी *f.*

To DISABLE, *v. a.* शक्ति *f.*-बळ *n.*-&c. मोडणें *g. of o.* शक्तिनाशm. -शक्तिभंग *m.*-&c. करणें *g. of o.* निश्शक्त-अशक्त-शक्तिहीन-क्षीणशक्ति-निर्बल-&c. करणें, असमर्थ-अक्षम-&c. करणें.

DISABLED, *p.* v. V. अशक्तकेलेला, &c. नष्टशक्ति, नष्टबल, हतशक्ति, हतबल, क्षीणशक्ति, गतशक्ति, &c.

To DISABUSE, *v. a. undeceive.* भ्रांति *f.*-भ्रम *m.*-&c. काढणें-उडवणें-घालवणें-मोडणें *g. of o.* कान *m. pl.*-डोळे *m. pl.*-कानाचे दट्टे *m. pl.* उघडणें *g. of o.* डोळ्यावरचा धूर *m.* उडवणें *g. of o.* कान *m. pl.* झाडणें *g. of o.*

DISADVANTAGE, *n.* v. LOSS. अहित *n.* अनहित *n.* हानि *f.* खामी *f.* अनिष्ट *n.* नुकसान *n. f.* नुकसानी *f.* [नें विकणें.

To sell to a d. तोटा करून-खाऊन-&c. विकणें, भीतर सवाई-

DISADVANTAGEOUS, *a.* तोटा होण्याचा, नुकसान होण्याचा, गैरनफ्याचा, अहित, अहितावह, अहितकारक-कारी, अहितप्रद, हानिकारक, अनिष्टकारक, कार्यइष्ट-&c. भंजक-नाशक-&c. प्रतिकूल.

DISADVANTAGEOUSLY, *adv.* v. A. तोटा करून, तोटा खाऊन, तोटा सोसून, भीतर सवाईनें, गैरसोईनें, प्रातिकूल्यपूर्वक.

DISADVANTAGEOUSNESS, *n.* v. A. प्रतिकूलता *f.* प्रातिकूल्य *n.*

DISAFFECTED, *a. ill-inclined to.* मन फिरलेला, मन उडालेला, विमनस्क, विमना, विमत, दुर्मनस्क, असंतुष्ट, उडाळ, विरक्त, वीतराग, वांकडा.

DISAFFECTION, *a.* नावड *f.* अनावड *f.* अप्रीति *f.* अभक्ति *f.* असंतोष *m.* विरक्ति *f.* वैराग्य *n.* दौर्मनस्य *n.* वैमनस्य *n.* वैमत्य *n.*

D. to the king. राजद्रोह *m.*

To DISAGREE, *v. n. be diverse, dissimilar, or distinct*, v. To DIFFER. अंतर *n.*-भेद *m.*-फेर *m.*-तफावत *f.*-&c. असणें *g. of s. recip.* भिन्न-निराळा-&c. असणें.

2 *be at variance, differ.* वांकडें *n.*-बेबनाव *m.*-बिघड *m.*-वैमनस्य *n.*-द्वैत *n.*-द्वैतभाव *m.*-&c. असणें *g. of s. recip.* मिळणींत नसणें.

3 (in opinion, &c.). नाकबूल होणें-जाणें, विप्रतिपत्ति *f.*-भिन्नभाव *m.*-मतभेद *m.*-द्वैत *n.*-बिसम्मत *n.*- असम्मत *n.*-&c. असणें *g. of s. recip.* विसम्मत-असम्मत-&c. असणें.

4 *be unwholesome, &c. to.* बाधणें, नावडणें, नडणें, डिवणें, बावडा-बाधक-प्रतिबद्धक-अपथ्य-&c. असणें.

DISAGREEABLE, *a. unpleasant.* नावडता, नावडा, नापसंत, अपसंत, अनिष्ट, नावडीचा, अप्रीतीचा, नापसंतीचा, अप्रिय, अरुचि, अरुच्य, अरुचिर, विप्रिय, अरम्य, असौम्य, अग्राह्य, द्वेष्य, कडू.

DISAGREEABLENESS, *n.* v. A. नावडतेपणा *m.* नावडेपणा *m.* &c. अप्रियत्व *n.* अरुच्यता *f.* &c.

DISAGREEABLY, *adv.* v. A. नआवडेसा *decl.* कंटाळायेण्याजोगा *decl.* त्रासहोण्याजोगा *decl.*

DISAGREEMENT, *n. diversity, dissimilitude,* v. DIFFERENCE. अंतर *n.* फेर *m.* भेद *m.* भिन्नता *f.* भिन्नभाव *m.* बिलग *n.* असाम्य *n.* असमता *f.*

2 *variance, misunderstanding, difference, dissension, discord.* अंतर *n.* वांकडें *n. v.* पड, नपड *f.* बेबनाव*m.* बिघड *or* विघाड *m.* दुई *f.* बांक *m.* नाचक्की *f.* दुसग *f.* दुसगाई *f.* फूट *f.* वैमनस्य *n.* विपट *n.* वितुष्ट *n.* विप्रयोग *m.* खडबड *f.* द्विधा *f.* द्वैत*n.* द्वैतभाव *m.* द्वैध *n.* वैमत्य *n.* भेद *m.* भिन्नभाव *m.* अनैक्य *n.*

3 (of opinion). मतभेद *m.* भिन्नभाव *m.* विप्रतिपत्ति *f.* विसम्मत *n.* विसम्मति *f.* असम्मत *n.* असम्मति *f.* द्वैत *n.* द्वैध *n.* द्वैविध्य *n.* वैमत्य *n.*

4 (in a statement, &c.). v. DISCREPANCY. तफावत *f.* तफावत *f.* तकराळ *f.* फेर *m.* अंतर *n.* वैपरीत्य *n.*

To DISALLOW, DISALLOWANCE, &c. See To DISAPPROVE, To REJECT, &c.

To DISANNUL, &c. See To ANNUL, &c.

To DISAPPEAR, *v. n.* नाहींसा-अदृश्य-दिसेनासा-&c. होणें, जाणें, राहणें, उडणें, अंतर्धान *n.* पावणें, अंतर्धान *n.*-तिरोधान *n.*-&c. होणें *g. of s.* काळें होणें *g. of s.* काळें *n.* करणें.

DISAPPEARANCE, *n.* v. V. नाहींसा होणें *n.* &c. अदर्शन *n.* अलोकन *n.* लोप *m.* अंतर्धान *n.* तिरोधान *n.*

DISAPPEARED, *p.* v. V. नाहींसा झालेला, दिसेनासा झालेला, &c. दृश्यातीत, दर्शनातीत, अंतर्हित, तिरोहित.

To DISAPPOINT, *v. a.* निराशा *f.*-आशाभंग *m.*-आशाखंडन *n.*-&c. करणें *g. of o.* आशा *f.* मोडणें-घालवणें *g. of o.* अंबट करणें, हताश-नष्टाश-भग्नाश-&c. करणें.

DISAPPOINTED, *p.* v. V. आशा मोडलेला, &c. हताश, भग्नाश, नष्टाश, निराश, मनोहत, प्रतिहत, भ्रष्टसंकल्प, खंडिताशंस.

DISAPPOINTMENT, *n.* v. V.—*act.* आशा मोडणें*n.* आशाखंडन *n.* फलखंडन *n.*—*a. or s.* हिरमोड *m. f.* आशाभंग *m.* उत्साहभंग *m.* मनोभंग *m.*—*state.* आशेची निराशा *f.* निराशा *f.* आशानष्टता *f.* नैराश्य *n.*

DISAPPROBATION, DISAPPROVAL, *n.* v. V. नापसंती *f.* अपसंती *f.* अमान्यता *f.* अनंगीकार*m.* अस्वीकार*m.* असम्मति *f.* विसम्मति *f.* विमति *f.* वैमत्य *n.*

To DISAPPROVE, *v. a.* नापसंत-अपसंत-नामंजूर-अमान्य-नाकबूल -&c. करणें, नाकारणें, अनंगीकार*m.*-अस्वीकार*m.*-&c.करणें*g. of o.*

DISAPPROVED, *p.* v. V. नापसंत केलेला, &c. नापसंत *or* द, अपसंत, गैरमान्य, अमान्य, नामंजूर, नाकबूल.

DISAPPROVER, *n.* DISAPPROVING, *p. a.* v. V. नापसंत करणारा, &c. गैरमान्य, नाकबूल, नापसंत, अमान्य, विसम्मत, असम्मत, विमत.

DISAPPROVINGLY, *adv.* दोषदृष्ट्या, दोषबुद्ध्या, असम्मतिपूर्वक, &c.

To DISARM, *v. a.* हत्यारें*n. pl.*-शस्त्रें*n. pl.*-&c. घेणें-काढूनघेणें *g. of o.* अशस्त्र-शस्त्रहीन-निरायुध-&c. करणें, शस्त्रहरण*n.* करणें.

To DISARRANGE, &c. See To DERANGE, &c.

DISARRAY. See DISORDER.

DISASTER, *n. blast of a planet.* संक्रांतीचें बसणें*n.*

2 *mishap,* v. CALAMITY. अनर्थ*m.* अवचट *n.* अनिष्ट *n.* अनिष्टापात*m.* अनर्थापात *m.*

DISASTROUS, *a.* v. CALAMITOUS, UNLUCKY. अनर्थाचा, अभद्र, अरिष्ट, अनिष्टात्मक, अनिष्टरूप.

DISASTROUSLY, *adv.* v. A. अनर्थ होऊन, दुरंतहोऊन.

DISASTROUSNESS, *n.* v.A. अरिष्ट*n.* अभद्र*n.* अभद्रता *f.* अरिष्टता *f.*

To DISAVOW, DISAVOWAL. See To DENY, DENIAL.

To DISBAND, *v. a. dismiss from military service.* मोडणें, तोडणें, बाटेस लावणें, फांटा *m.* देणें.

DISBANDED, *p.* v. V. मोडलेला, तोडलेला, &c. तुटक.

DISBELIEF, *n.* अप्रत्यय *m.* अविश्वास *m.* अमान्यता *f.* नमानणें *n.* अप्रामाण्यग्रह*m.* असत्यग्रह*m.*

To DISBELIEVE, *v. a.* खोटा-असत्य-अप्रमाण-&c. मानणें, अप्रामाण्यग्रह*m.*-असत्यग्रह *m.* होणें-असणें *with* विषयीं *of o. and inv. con.* खोटा-असत्य-&c. वाटणें *inv. con.* अविश्वास*m.*-&c. ठेवणें.

DISBELIEVER, *n.* DISBELIEVING, *p. a.* v.V. खोटा मानणारा, &c. अप्रत्ययी, अविश्वासी, अप्रामाण्यग्राही.

To DISBURDEN, *v. a.* ओझें*n.*-&c. उतरणें-काढणें, ओझ्यापासून-&c. सोडवणें, भारमुक्त करणें, भारमोचन*n.* करणें *g. of o.*

To DISBURSE, &c. See To EXPEND, &c.

To DISCARD, *v. a. turn off, cast away,* v. To DISMISS. गाळणें, घालवणें, काढून देणें, दूर करणें, बाटेस लावणें.

DISCARDED, *p.* v. V. दूरकेलेला, काढून दिलेला.

To DISCERN. See To DISTINGUISH, To DISCOVER.

DISCERNMENT. See DISCRIMINATION, JUDGMENT.

To DISCHARGE, *v. a. disburden, unload.* ओझें *n.*-&c. उतरणें-काढणें *g. of o.* रिकामा-रिता-मोकळा-खाली-&c. करणें, लोटणें, भारमोचन *n.* करणें.

2 *let fly, give vent or issue.* सोडणें, काढणें, विसर्जन*n.* करणें (esp. in comp. as बाणविसर्जन-शस्त्रविसर्जन-मलविसर्जन-मूत्रविसर्जन-&c. करणें).

3 (a gun). सोडणें, डागणें, मारणें, झाडणें, बार *m.* सोडणें-उडवणें-झाडणें.

4 (a debt), *liquidate,* v. To CLEAR. फेडणें, झाडणें, अदा करणें, वारणें, फेड *f.*-बेबारा*m.* करणें *g. of o.* बेबाक करणें.

To d. in part. उरता करणें.

5 v. To DISMISS. निरोप *m.*-&c. देणें, दूर करणें, बरतरफ करणें.

6 *let go,* v. To RELEASE. सोडणें, सोडून देणें, सोडवणें, मोकळा-&c. करणें.

7 *perform, execute.* करणें, बजावणें.

DISCHARGE, DISCHARGING, *n.* v. V.—*act.* ओझें उतरणें *n.* रिकामा करणें*n.* लोटणें*n.* &c. भारमोचन*n.*

D. of the bowels. झाडा *m.*

2—*act.* सोडणें *n.* काढणें *n.* विसर्जन *n.* विसर्ग *m.*

3—*act.* सोडणें *n.* झाडणें *n.* &c. बार *m.*

4—*act.* फेडणें *n.* &c. फेड *f.* फेडणूक *f.* दफेरफे *f.*

5—*act.* निरोप &c. देणें *n.* निरोप *m.* बरतरफी *f*

6—*act.* सोडणें *n.* &c. मुक्त करणें *n.* सोडवण *f.* सोडवणूक *f.* मोचन *n.*—*state.* सूट *f.* सुटका *f.* सोडवण *f.* मुक्ति *f.*

7—*act.* करणें *n.* बजावणें *n.*

I. *flowing or issuing out.* निचरा *m.* स्राव *m.*

II. *matter emitted.* निचरा *m.* स्राव *m.* स्रावितवस्तु *n.*

D. of pus. पू *m.* पूय *m.*

D. of thick and bloody pus. रेंदा *m.*

III. v. ACQUITTANCE. फारखत *n. f.* बेदावा *m.* बेदावापत्र*n.*

DISCHARGED, *p.* v. V. 1. ओझें उतरलेला, &c. लोटलेला, भारमुक्त.

2 सोडलेला, &c. मुक्त.

3 सोडलेला, डागलेला, &c. बार झालेला.

4 केहलेला, &c. बेघाक.

5 निगेप दिल्हेला-घेतलेला, बरतरफ केलेला-झालेला, &c. बरतरफ.

DISCIPLE, *n.* शिष्य, चेला, विद्यार्थी, शागिर्द, छात्र, अनुयायी, अनुगामी.

Female d. चेली *f.*

Head d. पट्टशिष्य.

DISCIPLESHIP, *n.* शिष्यपणा *m.* चेलेपणा *m.* शागिर्दी *f.* शागिर्दपणा *m.* शिष्यत्व *n.* शिष्यदशा *f.*

DISCIPLINARIAN, *n. one strict, or severe in discipline.* कदरखोर, कदरेचा, कदरवाला, धारेवर बागवणारा, जंत्रीं धरणारा.

DISCIPLINE, *n. culture, tuition, &c.* v. EDUCATION. शिकवण *f.* विनय *m.* शिक्षा *f.* शिक्षण *n.* सुशिक्षा *f.* सुशिक्षण *n.*

2 *training, regulating, taming, &c.* बळण *n.* शासन *n.* अनुशासन *n.* शास्तृत्व *n.* नियंतृत्व *n.* नियमन *n.* नियंत्रण *n.* अनुनय *m.* कैद *f.* सुधारणा *f.* सुधारणी *f.* सुधारणूक *f.*

To keep under tight d. धारकसीं धरणें, तरवारेचे धारेवर बागवणें-चालवणें-धरणें (or धारेवर बागवणें-&c.), जंत्रीं धरणें, जत्रांतून ओढणें, जात्याखालीं धरणें, करवतावर धरणें, अटणें.

3 *good order, regularity, subjection to rules, &c.* बंदोबस्त *m.* बंदोबस्ती *f.* व्यवस्था *f.*

4 *chastisement,* v. PUNISHMENT. शिक्षा *f.* शासन *n.*

To DISCIPLINE, *v. a.* See To EDUCATE. To INSTRUCT.

2 *train, regulate, break in, bring into order.* पेटवणें, काढणें, कमावणें, सुधारणें, बंदोबस्त *m.*-सुधारणी *f.*-&c. करणें *g. of o.* बळणांत ठेवणें, बठणीस-बळणीस-&c. आणणें, उगळणें or उगाळणें, बळण *n.* लावणें, पाडगा करणें, शासन *n.*-अनुशासन *n*--नियमन *n.*-&c. करणें *g. of o.*

3 See To PUNISH.

To DISCLAIM, *v. a. disown, disavow,* v. To DENY. आंगावाहेर-आंगा पलीकडे-आंगा निराळा-आंगा बेगळा-&c. टाकणें-करणें, अनंगीकार *m.*-अस्वीकार *m.*-&c. करणें *g.of o.* नाकारणें, निरसन *n.*-निराकरण *n.*-&c. करणें *g. of o.*

To DISCLOSE, *v. a. uncover, lay open to the view.* झांकण *n.*-&c. काढणें *with* पासून *of o.* उघड-उघडा-प्रगट &c. करणें, उजाडीम-उघडदशेस-&c. आणणें.

2 *reveal,* v. To TELL. फोडणें, उघडणें, उहू *m.* करणें, बदणें, काढणें, उघड *f*-उघडीक *f.*- प्रकाश *m.*-&c. करणें *g. of o.*

DISCLOSURE, *n.* v. V. 1.—*act.* उघड करणें *n.* प्रकटीकरण *n.*—*state.* उघड *f.* उघडदशा *f.*

2—*act.* फोडणें *n.* उघडणें *n.* &c. स्फोटन *n.* विख्यापन *n.*—*state.* उजागरी *f.* फोड *f.* उघडीक *f.* उघड *f.*

To DISCOLOR, *v. a.* v. To STAIN. रंग *m.* खराब करणें-फिरवणें *g. of o.* विवर्ण करणें, वैवर्ण्य *n.*-वर्णविकार *m.*-&c. करणें.

DISCOLORATION, *n.* v. STAIN. वैवर्ण्य *n.* वर्णविकार *m.* वर्णविकृति *f.* ठिकें *n.* ठीक *n.* खबला *m.*

Circular d. भोवरी *f.* चकंदळ *n.*

Red d. in the skin. लासें *n.*

DISCOLORED, *p.* v. V. विवर्ण केलेला, विवर्ण, प्राप्तवैवर्ण्य, वर्णविकृत. [&c.

DISCOMFIT, To DISCOMFIT, &c. See DEFEAT, To DEFEAT.

DISCOMFORT, *n.* असुख *n.* असमाधान *n.* अस्वास्थ्य *n.* सुखाभाव *m.* गैरसोई *f.*

To DISCOMMEND. See To BLAME.

To DISCOMMODE. See To INCOMMODE.

To DISCOMPOSE, *v. a. derange, disarrange,* v. To CONFOUND. विसकटणें, विसकळणें, ढबळणें, विसकळ *f.*-घालमेल *f.*-गोंधळ *m.*-अव्यवस्था *f.*-&c. करणें *g. of o.*

2 *disturb, perturb, disquiet, ruffle.* असुख *n.*-असमाधान *n.*-अस्वास्थ्य *n.*-उद्वेग *m.*-हैराणी *f.*-क्षोभ *m.*-व्याक्षोभ *m.*-मनोभंग *m.*-शांतिभंग *m.*-&c. करणें *g. of o.* गढूळ-व्यग्र-व्याकुल-अस्वस्थ-उद्विग्न-संतप्त-क्षुब्ध-&c. करणें, गढुळणें, ढवळणें or डहुळणें, क्षोभवणें, खवळवणें, खळबळवणें, गद्‌ळणें, घडी *f.* बिघडणें-विघडवणें.

DISCOMPOSED, *p.* v. V. 1. विसकटलेला, विसकळलेला, &c.

2 व्यग्र-&c. केलेला, हैराण, व्यग्र, संतप्त, संतापित, तापित, विमना, विमनस्क, दुर्मना, दुर्मनस्क, उद्विग्न, गतधृति, गतगांभीर्य, गतधैर्य.

To be or become d. संतापणें, क्षोभणें, खवळणें, खळबळणें, तळतळणें.

DISCOMPOSURE, DISCOMPOSING, *n.* v. V. 1.—*act.* विसकटणें *n.* विसकळणें *n.* &c.—*state.* विसकळ *f.* घालमेल *f.* गोंधळ *m.* अव्यवस्था *f.* धांदल *f.*

2—*act.* व्यग्र करणें *n.* &c.—*state.* अस्वास्थ्य *n.* असमाधान *n.* असुख *n.* ताप *m.* संताप *m.* उद्वेग *m.* हैराणी *f.* हैराणगत *f.* वैमनस्य *n* क्षोभ *m.* व्याक्षोभ *m.* क्षुब्धता *f.* मनस्ताप *m.* मनोभंग *m.* शांतिभंग *m.* तलखली *f.* तळतळ *f.* तळमळ *f.* डामाडूळ *f.*

To DISCONCERT. See To DEFEAT, To CONFUSE, To DISCOMPOSE.

To DISCONNECT, *v. a.* v. To SEPARATE. वेगळा-पृथक्-भिन्न-&c. करणें, संबंध *m.* तोडणें *g. of o.*

DISCONSOLATE, *a. sad, sorrowful.* दुःखी, दुःखित, खिन्न, उदास, उदासी, असमाधानी, अस्वस्थ, बेदिल, दिलगीर, विमनस्क, विमना.

DISCONSOLATELY, *adv.* v. A. दुःखानें, दिलगिरीनें, उदासपणानें, &c. असमाधानपूर्वक.

DISCONSOLATENESS, *n.* v. A. उदासपणा *m.* उदासी *f.* असमाधान *n.* दिलगिरी *f.* अस्वस्थता *f.*

DISCONTENT, DISCONTENTEDNESS, DISCONTENTMENT, *n.* असमाधान *n.* असंतोष *m.* अतृप्ति *f.* अतुष्टि *f.* असंतुष्टता *f.* अरति *f.*

DISCONTENTED *a.* असमाधानी, असंतोषी, असंतुष्ट, अतुष्ट, अतृप्त, अतृप्तमनस्क, अतृप्तमना.

DISCONTENTEDLY, *adv.* v. A. असंतोषानें, असंतोषवृत्तीनें, असंतोषपूर्वक.

DISCONTINUANCE, To DISCONTINUE, *v. n.* &c. See CESSATION, To CEASE, &c.

To DISCONTINUE, *v. a. leave off.* सोडणें, टाकणें.

2 *stop.* बंदकरणें, मह्कूब करणें.

DISCONTINUITY, *n.* अनैरंतर्य *n.* खंडितत्व *n.* विच्छेद *m.* सव्यवधानता *f.*

DISCONTINUOUS, *a.* अनिरंतर, खंडित, विच्छिन्न, सव्यवधान.

DISCORD, *n.*—in music. स्वरांचा अमेळ *m.* स्वरमेलनाभाव *m.* वैस्वर्य *n.*

2 *a* d. *discordant note.* अपस्वर *m.*

3 *dissension,* v. DISAGREEMENT. बेबनाव *m.* बांकडें *n.* वैमनस्य *n.* भिन्नभाव *m.* द्वैत *n.* द्वैतभाव *m.*

DISCORDANCE, DISCORDANCY, See DISAGREEMENT, INCONSISTENCY.

DISCORDANT, *a. not harmonious.* बेसूर, बदसूर, अपसुऱ्या, विस्वर, अपस्वर, कर्णकटु, कर्णकठोर, कर्कश.

I. See INCONSISTENT.

DISCOUNT, *n. allowance for prompt payment.* सूट *f.* सोड *f.*—among bankers. कटमुदतीचा पैसा*m.*

To DISCOUNT, *v. a.* कटमुदतीनें-कटमितीनें देणें, सूट *f.*-सोड *f.* देणें.

To DISCOUNTENANCE, *v. a. discourage by cold treatment.* पायमोड *f.*-हिरमोड*m.f.* करणें *g.of o.* विमुख-पराङ्मुख-पाठमोरा-&c. होणें *in. con.* पाणी*n.*-विरजण*n.*-पायमोडें*n.* घालणें,पाय*m.* मोडणें.

To DISCOURAGE, *v. a.* v. To DISPIRIT. हिरमोड*m.*-पायमोड *f.*-मनोभंग*m.*-उत्साहभंग*m.*-&c. करणें *g. of o.* हिम्मत *f.* मोडणें*g. of o.* भंगणें.

2 *attempt to repress or prevent.* मोडा*m.*-मोडें*n.*-मोडती *f.*-पाणी*n.*-विरजण*n.*-&c. घालणें, पाय*m.* मोडणें.

DISCOURAGED, *p.* v. V. 1. नष्टोत्साह, हतोत्साह, नष्टधैर्य, हतधैर्य, बेदिल.

DISCOURAGER, *n.* DISCOURAGING, *p. a.* v. V. 1. हिरमोड करणारा, &c. मोड्या, पाय मोडणारा, मनोभंजक, उत्साहभंजक, उत्साहघातक-नाशक-&c. धैर्यभंजक-&c.

DISCOURAGEMENT, *n.* v. V.—*act.* हिरमोड करणें*n.* &c.—*state.* हिरमोड*m.f.* पायमोड *f.* उत्साहभंग*m.* मनोभंग*m.* धैर्यभंग*m.*

I. *discouraging thing or circumstance.* पायमोडें*n.* मोडतें*n.* मोडें*n.* मोडती *f.* [करणें.

To DISCOURSE, *v. n.* v. TO CONVERSE. संभाषण*n.*-संवाद*m.*-&c.

2 *speak, lecture, hold forth.* भाषण*n.* करणें.

DISCOURSE, *n.* v. CONVERSATION. संभाषण*n.* संवाद*m.*

2 *treatise.* ग्रंथ*m.* कवन*n.* निबंध*m.* प्रबंध*m.*

DISCOURTEOUS, &c. See RUDE, UNCIVIL, &c.

To DISCOVER, *v. a. uncover, lay open to view.* झाकण*n.*-पडदा*m.*-&c. काढणें *with* पासून *of o.* उघडा-दिसता-&c. करणें, उघडदेशास-&c. आणणें.

2 *spy, descry, ken,* v. To SEE. लक्षिणें, पाहणें, डोळे*m. pl.* होणें *in. con.*

3 *find out, detect.* उमगणें *or* उमंगणें, काढणें, ताडणें, शोध*m.*-ठिकाण*n.*-ठिकाणा*m.*-टाव*m.*-&c. लावणें-काढणें *g. of o.* शोध*m.*-ठिकाण*n.*- थांग*m.*-&c. लागणें *in. con.* सांपडणें *in. con.*

4 (new things or places). अढळणें-सांपडणें-मिळणें *in. con.* पहिल्यानें पाहणें, दृष्टीस पहिल्यानें पडणें *in. con.*

DISCOVERY, DISCOVERING, *n.* v. V. 1.—*act.* उघड करणें*n.* &c. प्रकटीकरण*n.*

2—*act.* लक्षिणें*n.* पाहणें*n.*

3—*act.* उमगणें*n.* काढणें*n.* &c.

4 अढळणें*n.* &c. अढळ*m.*

DISCREDIT, *n.* v. DISGRACE. अप्रतिष्ठा *f.* अपयश*n.*

2 *want of belief.* अमान्यता *f* अविश्वास*m.* अश्रद्धा *f.*

To DISCREDIT. See TO DISBELIEVE.

DISCREDITABLE, *a.* v. DISGRACEFUL. इजतखाऊ, इजतघेणा, अपयशस्कारक, यशोघ्न.

DISCREET, *a. prudent,* v. WISE. समजदार, समजूतदार, समंजस, समजीक, उचितज्ञ, विवेकी, विवेकाढ्य, सविवेक, सुज्ञ, सदसद्दर्शी.

DISCREETLY, *adv.* v. A. समजीकपणानें, विवेकानें, &c. विवेक पूर्वक, सदसद्विचार पूर्वक.

DISCREPANCE, DISCREPANCY, *n. difference, disagreement.* फेर*m.* तफावत *f.* तजावत *f.* तकराळ *f.* अंतर*n.* फांट*m.* विप्रतिपत्ति*f.* द्वैध*n.* द्वैविध्य*n.* अनैक्य*n.* वैपरीत्य*n.* अर्थविरोध*m.* संदर्भविरोध*m.* वचनविरोध*m.* भावांतर*n.* [विरुद्ध.

DISCREPANT, *a.* v. INCONSISTENT. फारफेराचा, विप्रतिपन्न, संदर्भ-

DISCRETION, DISCREETNESS, *n. prudence, judiciousness.* समजदारी *f.* समजीकपणा*m.* समंजसपणा*m.* विवेक *m.* विचार *m.* तजवीज *f.* सदसद्विचार *m.*सदसद्दर्शन*n.* बुद्धि *f.* उचितज्ञता *f.*

2 *liberty of acting according to one's own judgment.* मुखत्यारी *f.* स्वतंत्रता *f.* यथाप्रसंगवर्त्तनाधिकार*m.* प्रसंगानुसारवर्त्तनाधिकार *m.*

That is arrived at years of d. जाणता, प्रबुद्ध.

DISCRETIONAL, DISCRETIONARY, *a. left to discretion.*विचाराधीन, विवेकाधीन, विचारनिर्णेय, मुखत्यार, मुखत्यारीचा.

To DISCRIMINATE. See To DISTINGUISH.

DISCRIMINATION, *n. discernment,* v. JUDGMENT. विवेक*m.* विचार *m.* तारतम्य*n.* तरतम*n.* तरतमभाव*m.*

2 *mark of distinction.* लक्षण *n.* चिन्ह*n.*

DISCRIMINATIVE, *a. that observes distinction.* विवेकदर्शी, विचारदर्शी, सदसद्दर्शी, तारतम्यविलोकी.

To DISCUMBER. See To DISENCUMBER.

To DISCROWN, *v. a.* मुगुट*m*-&c. काढणें-काढून घेणें.

DISCURSIVE, *a.* See ROVING. 2 See ARGUMENTATIVE.

DISCUS, *n.* चक्र *n.*

To DISCUSS, *v. a.* v. To ARGUE. घाटणें, घोळणें, कुटणें, मंथणें *or* मथणें, वाटाघाट *f.*-घाटाघाट *f.*-खल *m.*-&c. करणें *g. of o.*

2 *resolve*—humors. उतरणें, बसवणें, फांकवणें, वितळवणें.

To be discussed. उतरणें, बसणें, फांकणें, वितुळणें, फाटणें.

DISCUSSION, *n.* v. V. A. 1.—*act.* घोळणें*n.* &c. घाटाघाट *f.* वाटघाट *f.* आलोडन*n.* घर्षण*n.* मंथन*or* मथन*n.* खल*m.*

DISDAIN, *n.* v. CONTEMPT. तिरस्कार *m.* तिटकारा *m.* अनादर *m.* अवज्ञा *f.* अवगणन *n.*

To DISDAIN, *v. a.* v. To CONTEMN. धिक्कारणें,धिक्कार*m.*-तिरस्कार*m.*-&c. करणें *g. of o.* तुच्छ-हलका-&c. मानणें.

DISDAINFUL, *a. scornful,* v. CONTEMPTUOUS. मगरूर, मगरुरीचा, दिमाखाचा, दिमाखदार, ताठल्या डोळ्यांचा, ताठ्याचा.

DISDAINFULLY, *adv.* v. A. तिरस्कारानें, अनादरानें, &c. अवज्ञापूर्वक.

DISDAINFULNESS, *n.* v. A. मगरुरी *f.* दिमाख*m.* ताठा*m.*

DISEASE, *n. morbid state.* रोग*m.* विकार*m.*विकृति *f.* रुग्णावस्था *f.*

Cure or alleviation of d. रोगशांति *f.* रोगोपशम *m.*

2 *a* d.*a malady,* v.DISORDER. रोग*m.*दुखणें*n.*दुःख*n.* आजार*m.*

An inherited or a connate d. जन्माचा रोग*m.*

D. incidental to children. बालरोग*m.*

D. incidental to women. स्त्रीरोग*m.*

The seventy two orders or classes of d. बाहत्तर *or* बहात्तर रोग*m. pl.*

DISEASED, *a.* v. N. *and* DISORDERED. रोगी *remiss.* रोगट, रोगग्रस्त, दुखणेकरी, आजारी, रोगान्वित, व्याधित, रुग्ण.

To DISEMBARK, *v. c.* उतरणें.

DISEMBODIED, *a. divested of the body.* विदेह, विदेही, देहातीत, त्यक्तदेह, मुक्तदेह, त्यक्तकाय-शरीर-&c.

To DISEMBODY, *v. a.* देहानिराळा-विदेह-&c. करणें.

To DISEMBOGUE, *v. n.* (समुद्रांत) मुखद्वारा मिळणें-प्रवेश*m.* होणें.

To DISENABLE. See To DISABLE.

To DISENCHANT, *v. a. free from the force of a charm.* मंत्रमु-

क करणें, मंत्रापासून सोडवणें, मंत्राची उलट *f.*-&c. करणें.

To **Disencumber**, *v. a.* ओझें *n.*-भार *m.*-&c. काढणें-काढून हलका करणें, मोकळा करणें, गुंता *m.*-&c. तोडणें, भारमुक्त करणें.

To **Disengage**, *v. a. disentangle, detach, extricate, withdraw,* v. To Separate. उकलणें, उगवणें, सोडणें, सोडवणें, काढणें, गुंता *m.*-गुताबळ *f.* तोडणें-काढणें-सोडवणें, गुंतागुंत *f.*-गुंताडा *m.* काढणें, वेगळा-निराळा-&c. करणें, सुटका *f.* करणें *g. of o.*

Disengaged, *p.* v. V. उकललेला, सोडलेला, &c. सुटा, उकलींव.

I. *unoccupied, unemployed.* रिकामा, खाली, मोकळा, निरुद्योगी.

Disengagement, *n.* v. V.—*act.* उकलणें *n.* सोडवणें *n.* &c. सोडवण *f.* सोडवणूक *f.* उगवण *f.* उगवणी *f.* उगवणूक *f.* उकलणूक *f.* उकलणी *f.*—*state.* उकल *m.* उकाल *m.* सुटका *f.*

I. *vacancy, leisure.* रिकामपण *n.* रिकामेपणा *m.* मोकळेपणा *m.* निरुद्योग *m.*

To **Disentangle**, *v. a. disengage, extricate.* उकलणें, उगवणें, उलगडणें, सोडवणें, गुंता *m.*-गोवा *m.*-गुंताडा *m.*-गुंतागुंत *f.*-&c. काढणें-सोडवणें.

Disentangled, *p.* v. V. उकललेला, सोडवलेला, &c. उकलींव.

Disentanglement, *n.* v. V.—*act.* उकलणें *n.* उलगडणें *n.* &c. सोडवणूक *f.* उगवण *f.* उगवणी *f.*—*state.* उलगडा *n.* उकल *or* उकाल *m.* निकाल *m.*

To **Disenthral**. See To Free.

Disesteem, *n.* v. Contempt. अपमान *m.* अनमान *m.* हलकाभार *m.* अव्हेर *m.* नाचक्की *f.* बदबोई *f.*

To **Disesteem**, *v. a.* v. To Contemn. अपमानणें, अनमानणें, अनादरणें, अपमान *m.*-&c. करणें *g. of o.*

Disfavor, *n. discountenance.* अवकृपा *f.* करडीमर्जी *f.* करडीकमान *f.* गैरमर्जी *f.* इतराजी *f.* अप्रसन्नता *f.* अप्रसाद *m.* वक्रदृष्टि *f.* कुदृष्टि *f.*

2 *state of unacceptableness.* नापसंती *f.* नावड *f.* नावडतेपणा *m.* अरुचि *f.*

To **Disfigure**, *v. a. deform, &c.* विरूप-कुरूप-व्यंग-बदसुरत-बेडौल-खराब-&c. करणें, रूपनाश *m.*-रूपभंग *m.*-&c. करणें *g. of o.* विरूपकरण *n.* करणें *g. of o.*

Disfigurement, *n.* v. V.—*state.* रूपनाश *m.* रूपभंग *m.* विरूपता *f.* वैरूप्य *n.* नष्टरूपता *f.*

To **Disfranchise**, *v. a.* हक्क *m.*-सनद *f.* काढणें-काढून घेणें *g. of o.*

To **Disgorge**, *v. a. vomit out.* ओकणें, उगळणें, ओकून-उगळून-&c. टाकणें, उद्गीर्ण करणें.

2 *give back.* परत-माघारा-&c. देणें.

Disgrace, *n. disfavored state.* बदरंग *m.* बेरंग *m.* बदबोई *f.* अप्रतिष्ठा *f.* अपयश *n.* अयश *n.* पाणउतारा *m.* बदलौकिक *m.* बदनाम *n.* बदनामी *f.* तेजोभंग, *m.* तेजोहानि *f.* तेजोऱ्हास *m.* मानभंग *m.* मानहानि *f.* च्युति *f.* परिभव *m.*—as involving the sense of *ridiculousness and of ridiculous or pitiable state through ridicule.* Words and phrases conveying this import abound in *Maráthí.* They are mostly of lax or free formation; but they have extensive currency, are in constant use, and bear strong, and vivid, and impressive significance. They would thus but ill render such sober English words as *disfavor, dishonor, derision, ignominy, exposure, shame, scorn, opprobrium, &c.*: yet, than these we are aware of no English words more closely correspondent. They might indeed well represent certain *other* formations; but these being necessarily excluded from the Dictionary, they will be admitted, we apprehend, to have been rightly collected and inserted here. फजिती *f.* फटफजिती *f.* हसें *n.* थुथू *f.* छिथू *f.* धूळ *f.* धूळदशा *f.* धूळधमासा *m.* धूळधाणी *f.* धूळधाण *f.* धूळधूळ *f.* धूळपट *f.* पट्टाधूळ *f.* धूळपट्टी, अब्बस *f.* झील *f.* बचेरी *f.* भंबेरी *f.* रेवडी *f.* भंडवा *or* भंडमा *f.* भुरली *f.* राळ *f.* बिट्ट *or* बीट *m.* उलटी पूजा *f.* बदनकशा *m.* बदरंग *m.* बदशान *or* बच्छान *f.* बदबोई *f.* भगल *f.* टपली *f.* भंड *n.* शेणमार *m.* फत्तरपूजा *f.* फेरघोंगडें *n.* हुरेवडी *f.* हुर्रेवावडी *f.* हुरली *f.* वखवख *f.* भवाडा *m.* विटंबना *f.* शोभा *f.* नाकाटी *f.* नाचक्की *f.*

2 *cause of shame.* अयशाची-अपकीर्त्तीची-&c. गोष्ट *f.*-विषय *m.* अपयशाचें-&c. स्थान *n.*-घर *n.*-कारण *n.* कलंक *m.*

To **Disgrace**, *v. a. put out of favor.* कृपेंतून-मर्जीतून-&c. काढणें-घालवणें, गाळणें, च्युति *f.* करणें *g. of o.*

2 *put to dishonor or shame.* v. To Humble. लाजवणें, लाज *f.*-&c. आणणें, अब्रू *f.*-इजत *f.*-&c. घेणें-घालवणें *g. of o.* मानभंग *m.*-तेजोभंग *m.*-मानहानि *f.*-अपमान *m.*-अप्रतिष्ठा *f.*-पाणउतारा *m.*-&c. करणें *g. of o.* तोंडास काळिमा *m.* लावणें, तोंडावर काळोखी *f.*-&c. आणणें, पागोटें *n.*-नाक *n.* खालीं करणें *g. of o.* खाली पहायास लावणें, शोभा *f.* करणें *g. of o.* शिकुल *f.* उतरणें *g. of o.* निर्माल्यसें करून टाकणें, मेखाट्या *f. pl.* घेणें, शेंदूर *m.* उतरणें *g. of o.* बावडी *f.* करणें *g. of o.* मंजा *m.* उतरणें, साडे *m. pl.* करणें *g. of o.* गुबावरून ओढणें, पोतेरें *n.* करून टाकणें, भुरली *f.*- टपली *f.*-&c. उडवणें *g. of o.*

Disgraced, *p.* v. V.1. मर्जीतून गाळलेला-गळालेला-&c. गाळलेला, गलित, च्युत, पदच्युत, पदभ्रष्ट.

2 अपमान केलेला, लाजवलेला, खालीं पहायास लावलेला, &c. अपमानित, अनादृत, विमानित.

Disgraceful, *a. shameful, dishonorable.* लाजिरवाणा, अपयशस्कर, अपयशस्कर्त्ता, अपयशस्कारी, अपयशोजनक, यशोघ्न, यशोहर, यशोनाशक, &c. कीर्त्तिहर-हारक-हारी-&c. अपमानकारक, अपयशाचा, अपमानाचा, दुष्कीर्त्तीचा, &c. इजतखाऊ, इजतघेणा, इजतघेऊ, अब्रूघेणा, अब्रूगमाबू.

Disgracefully, *adv.* v. A. अपमानानें &c. अपयशपूर्वक.

To **Disguise**, *v. a. conceal by a strange dress, &c.* वेष *pop.* भेस *m.*-सोंग *n.*-कपटवेष *m.*-कपटरूप *n.*-&c. देणें-घेणें, वेष *pop.* भेस *m.* बदलणें-पालटणें, आकारगोपन *n.*-आकारगुप्ति *f.* करणें *g. of o.* लपवणें, पांघरूण *n.* घालणें.

Disguise, Disguisement, Disguising. *n.* v. V.—*act.* सोंग देणें *n.* भेस बदलणें *n.* &c. आकारगोपन *n.* आकारगुप्ति *f.*

I. a d. *a dress, form, &c. covering reality.* सोंग *n.* वेष *m.* कपटवेष *m.* छद्मवेष *m.* कपटरूप *n.* छद्म *n.* छल *m. n.* भेश *or* भेष *or* भेस *m.* व्याज *m. n.* अपदेश *m.*

In d. वेषपालटून-बदलून.

Disguised, *p.* v. V सोंग-वेष दिल्हेला-घेतलेला, कपटवेष, कपटवेषी, छद्मवेषी, कपटरूपी, छद्मवेषधारी, आकारगोपित.

Disgust, *n. loathing, nausea.* वीट *m.* कंटाळा *m.* किळस *f. m.* चिळस *f.* तिरस्कार *m.* त्रास *m.* खंत *f.* खंती *f.* रीस *f.* तिटकारा *m.* विकळी *f.* विकळत *f.* शिसकारी *f.* शिसारी *or* शिसारी *f.* चिकारा *m.* चिणका *m.* चिणकारा *m.* उच्छाद *m.* उचाट *m.* विकृत *f.* विकृति *f.* निर्वेद *m.* बीभत्स *m.* उपरति *f.* विरक्ति *f.* बैताग *m.*

2 See Distaste.

To DISGUST, *v. a.* कंटाळवणें, विटवणें, वीट *m.*-कंटाळा *m.*-किळस *f. m.*-चिळस *f.*-&c. आणणें, दिक्क-जिक्क-विरक्त-&c. करणें.

DISGUSTED, *p.* v. V. कंटाळवलेला, विटवलेला, &c. दिक्क-&c. केलेला. विटका, दिक्क, जिक्क, जिगजीग *or* जिकजीक, सपा, निर्विण्ण, विरक्त.

To be d. with, v. To LOATHE. कंटाळणें, विटणें, *also* विटणें *g. of o.* & सीं *of s.* उचाटणें, बेतागणें, कंटाळा *m.* येणें *g. of o. with in. con.*

DISGUSTFUL, *a.* DISGUSTING, *p. a.* v. V. *and* N. कंटाळवाणा *or* वाणी, किळसवाणा *or* वाणी, चिळसवाणा *or* वाणी, घाणेरा, घाणेला, घाणेरडा, हिडशा, हिडीस, हेंद्रा, कुत्सित, ओसटा, ओसटवाणा, अचकट, अघोरी, ओंगळ, ओंगळवाणा, बीभत्स, अमंगल.

DISH, *n.*—for holding food, &c. ताट *n.* तबक *n.* परात *f.* पात्र *n.* बासन *n.* थाळा *m. dim.* थाळी *f.* भाजन *n.* भांड *n.* सानक *f.*

Dishes and platters—compreh. थाळीठावकें *n.*

Earthen d. मृन्मयपात्र *n.*

Flat, earthen d. सापर *n.*

Wooden d. with a handle. दांडेपाळ *f.* दांडेपाळें *n.* दांडपाळें *n.*

To lick the dishes clean. चाटून पुसून खाणें.

2 *prepartion of food.* प्रकार *or* अन्नाचा प्रकार *m.* अन्न *n.* परी *f.* पर *f.* पक्वान्न *n.* पदार्थ *m.* Some of the common *dishes* are आडवत, आपा, उकडहंडी, उंडा, उंबर, उसळ, ओतींबथालीपीठ, कचोरी, कटकढी, कढी, कण्या, काला, कुटा, केशरीभात, कोडबुळें *or* बोळें, खवणकांकडी, खांडवी *or* वें, खिची, खीर, खुतखुताभात, गांठोडें, घाट, घाटलें, घारकूट, घारगा, घारवीट, घारी, घुटें, चुरमा, चोढ्याचुरमा, डांगर, डाळवांगें, तंपीठ, तवसें *or* तवसोळी, ताकतई, तारफेणी, तिक्रय *or* व, तोंडलीभात, धोंडवाण *or* वायण.

DISH-CLOUT, *n.* शोधणें *or* सोधणें *n.* पुसणें *n.*

DISH-WATER, *n.* रांधवणी *n.* विसळवणी *n. or* विसुळवणी *n.* फळकवणी *n.* लेपवणी *n.*

DISHABILLE, To dress or be in d.—of men. पंचा-आडपंचा-गजा नेसणें *or* नेसून असणें, लहान नेसणें-नेसून असणें.—of women. आडवें-उभें नेसणें-नेसून असणें, वेढून घेणें, लहान नेसणें.

To DISHEARTEN, &c. See To DISPIRIT, &c.

To DISHERIT. See To DISINHERIT.

To DISHEVEL, *v. a. spread loosely, &c.*—the hair. विखरणें, पिंजारणें, फिंदारणें, फिस्करणें *or* पिखुरणें, उभवणें, पिंजारणी *f.* करणें *g. of o.*

DISHEVELLED, *p.* v. V. विखरलेला, पिंजारलेला, &c.

D. tresses or hair. झिंग्या *f. pl.* झिंज्या *f. pl.*

Having d. tresses. झिंपऱ्या.

Long and d. tress. झिंपरी *f.* झोंटी *f.* झिंझोटी *f.*

Of d. hair. विगलितकेश.

To be d. पिंजरणें.

DISHONEST, *a.* v. KNAVISH. लबाड, छट, ठकवरा, लटकुरा, लटका, बेइमानी, हराम, खोटसाळ, अप्रामाणिक *pop.* अप्रमाणिक, असाधु.

2—an employment, profits, &c. हराम, हरामाचा, हरामखोरीचा, लबाडीचा, अप्रमाणिकपणाचा, चोरीचा, अधर्माचा, अमार्गाचा.

DISHONESTY, *n.* v. A. 1. लबाडी *f.* छटपणा *m.* अप्रमाणिकपणा *m.* बेइमान *n.* अप्रामाणिकत्व *n.* असाधुत्व *n.* अधर्म *m.*

DISHONOR, *n.* v. DISGRACE. अप्रतिष्ठा *f.* मानभंग *m.* मानहानि *f.* तेजोभंग *m.* तेजोहानि *f.* तेजोन्हास *m.* अपयश *n.* अयश *n.* अपकीर्त्ति *f.*

To DISHONOR, *v. a.* v. To DISGRACE. अपमान *m.*-अप्रतिष्ठा *f.*-मानभंग *m.*-तेजोभंग *m.*-पाणउतारा *m.*-&c. करणें *g. of o.* अब्रू *f.*-इजत *f.*-हुरमत *f.*-&c. घेणें-घालवणें *g. of o.* हलका भार *m.* करणें. हलका करणें.

2 (a bill of exchange, &c.) नकारणें.

3 *debauch.* भ्रष्ट-दूषित-&c. करणें, दूषण *n.* करणें *g of o.*

DISHONORABLE, *a. disreputable*, v. DISGRACEFUL. अयशस्कर, यशोघ्न, कीर्त्ति हर-हर्त्ता-हारक-हारी, यशो हर-हर्त्ता-&c. अपमानकारक-कारी-&c. इजतखाऊ, इजतघेऊ, इजतघेणा.

2 *destitute of honor.* हलकेवर्त्तणुकीचा, अधम वृत्तीचा, पामरवृत्तीचा, अधमवृत्ति, क्षुद्रवृत्ति, क्षुल्लक वृत्ति, पामरवृत्ति, पाजी.

DISHONORED, *p.* v. V. 1. अपमान केलेला, &c. अपमानित, अनादृत, विमानित.

2 नकारलेला.

3 दूषित.

DISHONORING, *n.* v. V. 1.—*act.* अपमान करणें *n.* मानखंडना *f.* मानभंग *m.* तेजोभंग *m.* पाणउतारा *m.*

2 नकारणें *n.* नकार *m.* नकारणी *f.* नकाराई *f.*

3 दूषण *n.*

DISINCLINATION, *n. want of desire.* अनावड *f.* नावड *f.* अनुत्कंठा *f.* अनुत्साह *m.* निरुत्साह *m.* अनुत्सुकता *f.*

DISINCLINED, *a.* v. N. अनुत्सुक, अनुत्कंठित, विमत.

To be d. to. मन घेत नाहीं-होत नाहीं-धजत नाहीं, मनदेवता-मनपिंगळी लवत नाहीं, नको नको होणें *in. con.*

DISINFECTANT, *a.* साक्रामिकरोगबीजनाशक, दुर्गंधनाशक.

DISINGENUOUS, *a. not open & frank*,—of persons. कुडा, कपटी, मनाचा कुडा-कपटी-कुजका-वांकडा-खोटा, वक्रबुद्धि.

2—of conduct, &c. कपट्याचा, कपटी, कुडेपणाचा, कुडेभावाचा, वक्रबुद्धीचा.

DISINGENUOUSLY, *adv.* v. A. कुडेभावानें, कापट्यानें, वक्रभावानें.

DISINGENUOUSNESS, *n.* v. A. 1. कुडेपणा *m.* कुडाभाव *m.* मनाचा कुजकेपणा *m.* &c. कापट्य *n.* वक्रभाव *m.*

To DISINHERIT, *v. a. cut off from an hereditary right.* बेवारसा *m.*- वृत्तिछेद *m.*-वृत्तिछेदन *n.* करणें *g. of o.* वारसा *m.*-काढणें *g. of o.* बेवारसी-बेवारीस-पितृधनाविभागी-&c. करणें,

DISINHERITING, DISINHERISION, *n.* v. V.—*act.* बेवारसा करणें *n.* बेवारीस करणें *n.* &c. वृत्तिछेद *m.* वृत्तिछेदन *n.* पितृधनाविभागिकरण *n.*—*state.* वृत्तिछेद *m.* बेवारीस केलेपणा *m.* छेदित वृत्तित्व *n.* वृत्तिछेदितत्व *n.*

To DISINTER, *v. a.* थडग्यांतून-कबरेंतून-&c. काढणें, खणून काढणें, खनितोद्धार *m.* करणें.

DISINTERESTED, *a. not selfish*—of persons. निष्काम, निर्लोभ, निर्मम, अस्वार्थिक, अस्वार्थक, मुक्तसंग, अफलाकांक्षी.

2—of acts, &c. निष्काम बुद्धीचा, अस्वार्थबुद्धीचा, &c. निष्काम, निर्लोभ.

DISINTERESTEDLY, *adv.* v. A. निष्कामबुद्धीनें, निष्कामबुद्ध्या, &c.

DISINTERESTEDNESS, *n.* v. A. निष्कामबुद्धि *f.* अस्वार्थबुद्धि *f.* निर्लोभबुद्धि *f.* निष्कामता *f.* निर्ममत्व *n.* निस्पृहता *f.* निरिच्छता *f.* अस्वार्थ *m.* स्वार्थाभाव *m.*

DISINTERMENT, *n.* थडग्यांतून काढणें *n.* &c खनितोद्धार *m.*

To DISJOIN, *v. a.* v. To SEPARATE. वियोग *m.*-भेद *m.*-विश्लेष *m.*

करणें *g. of o.* संबंध *m.* तोडणें *g. of o.* वेगळा-वियुक्त-&c. करणें.

Disjoined, Disjunct, *p.* v. V. *and* Separated. वेगळा केलेला, &c वियुक्त, विश्लिष्ट.

Disjoiner, *n.* **Disjoining,** *p. a.* v. V. वियोग करणारा, &c. वियोगकारी, विश्लेषकारी.

Disjoining, Disjunction, *n.* v.V.—*act.* भेद करणें *n.* &c. वियोजन *n.* विभेदन *n.* भेदन *n.* —*state.* वियोग *m.* विश्लेष *m.*

To **Disjoint,** *v. a. put out of joint, &c.* सांधा *m.*-संधि *m.*-सांध *f.*-&c. उसळणें-उसकटणें-उपटणें-उपडणें-सोडवणें, संधिभंग *m.*-संधिभेद *m.*-संधिविश्लेष *m.*-&c. करणें *g. of o.*

Disjointed, *p.* v. V. सांधा उसळलेला, &c. विसंधित, संधिविश्लिष्ट, संधिच्युत, च्युतसंधि, स्थानच्युत, स्थानभ्रष्ट.

I. See Incoherent.

Disjunctive, *a.*—in grammar. पक्षांतर बोधक.

Disk, *n.* of the sun &c. बिंब *n.* मंडल *n.*

2 See Quoit.

Dislike, *n. aversion, distaste, disrelish, dissatisfaction.* नावड *f.* अनावड *f.* अवडणें *n. v.* ये, पड, अप्रीति *f.* अभक्ति *f.* अरुचि *f.* नाखुशी *f.* निरशी *f.* अरति *f.* अवमति *f.* विमति *f.* अश्रद्धा *f.*

To **Dislike,** *v. a.* नावडता-नापसंत-अप्रिय-&c. असणें-वाटणें *in. con.* नावड *f.*- अनावड *f.*-अप्रीति *f.*-&c. असणें *g. of o. in. con.* नावडणें *in. con.*

Disliked, *p.* v. V. नावडता, नावडीचा, अनावडीचा, अप्रिय, विप्रिय, नापसंत *or* द, अपसंत.

To **Dislocate,** *v. a.* v. To Disjoint. सांधा *m.*-&c. उसळणें.

Dislocation, *n.* v. V.—*act.* सांधा उसळणें *n.* सांध्याची उसळणी *f.*-उसकटणी *f.*-&c.—*state.* संधिभंग *m.* संधिभेद *m.* संधिविश्लेष *m.* संधिच्युति *f.*

To **Dislodge,** *v. a. remove from a place.* स्थळापासून-स्थानापासून-&c. काढणें-उठवून लावणें, स्थानांतर *n.*-स्थानभ्रंश-स्थानच्युति *f.*-&c. करणें *g. of o.* स्थानभ्रष्ट-स्थानच्युत-&c. करणें.

Disloyal, *a.*—of persons. राजद्रोही, राजविद्वेषी, राजशासनाबमानी, राजाभक्त, राजाचा निमकहराम.

2—of acts, &c. राजद्रोहाचा, राजद्वेषाचा.

3 *treacherous.* See False.

Disloyalty, *n.* v. A. 1. राजद्रोह *m.* राजद्वेष *m.* राजाभक्ति *f.*

Dismal, *a. gloomy, dull,*—weather, &c. ओंधट, मळीण, अंधक.

A d. day. दुर्दिन *m. n.*

2 See Dreary. 3 See Sad.

To **Dismantle,** *v. a. deprive of dress* v. To Strip. वस्त्रें *n. pl.* काढणें. [रणें.

2 *deprive of apparatus, &c.* सामान *n.*-&c. काढून घेणें, उस्त-

3 (a town, &c.). शहरपन्हा *m.*-गांवकुसूं *n.*-&c. मोडणें.

To **Dismay,** *v. a. daunt, dishearten,* v. To Dispirit. धैर्यभंग *m.*-धैर्यनाश *m.* करणें *g. of o.* धैर्य *n.*-हिम्मत *f.*-&c. खचविणें *g. of o.* दहशत *f.* देणें-घालणें, भय *n.* घालणें, हवालदिल-नष्टधैर्य-&c. करणें.

Dismay, *n.* v. Fright. दहशत *f.* भय *n.* धाक *m.* जेधा *f.* तिरपीठ *f.* पांचाबर धारण *f. v.* बस.

To **Dismember,** *v.a.* अवयव *m. pl.* सोडणें-छेदणें-संडणें-तोडणें-वेगळे करणें-&c.अवयवछेद *m.*-अंगछेद *m.*-गात्रछेद*m.*-&c. करणें *g.of o.*

To **Dismiss,** *v.a. send away, give leave of departure.* आज्ञा *f.*-हुकुम *m.*-रजा *f.*-निरोप *m.*-रुखसत *f.* देणें, बिदाई *f.*-रवानगी *f.*-विसर्जन *n.*-&c. करणें *g. of o.* बिदा करणें.

To d. an assembly. बरखास करणें.

2 *divest of office or employment, discharge, discard, turn off.* कामावरून-&c. काढणें, काढणें, घालवणें, काढून देणें-टाकणें, दूर-बरतरफ-तगीर-&c. करणें, वाटेस *or* वाटे लावणें, बरतरफी *f.*-तगिरी *f.*-फांटा *m.*-विडा *m.*-तगिरीचें वस्त्र *n.*-पट्टचा *or* ट्टया *f. pl.*-ढाळ *m.* देणें, साडे *m. pl.* करणें *g. of o.* हातीं नारळ *m. or* श्रीफळ *n.* देणें, दुसऱ्याचें घर *n.* दाखवणें, पदच्युत-पदभ्रष्ट-&c. करणें. —promptly or summarily. मेखा *f. pl.*-मेखाट्या *f. pl.* उचलणें-उपटणें- खांद्यावर देणें.

Dismissal, Dismission, *n.* v.V.1.—*act.* आज्ञा देणें *n.*&c. आज्ञा *f.* हुकूम *m.* रजा *f.* निरोप *m.* रुखसत *f.* बिदाई *f.* बिदागी *f.* बिदाइकी *f.* रवानगी *f.* विसर्जन *n.*

D. with sweetmeats, &c. of a company. खिरापत *f.*

Presents on d. बिदाई *f.* बिदागी *f.* बिदाइकी *f.* रवानगी *f.* पाठवणी *f.* पावणूक *f.*

2—*act.* काढणें*n.* वाटेस लावणें*n.* काढून देणें*n.* दूर करणें*n.* &c. बरतरफी *f.* रजा *f.* रुखसत *f.* तगिरी *or* तहगिरी *f.* उठकळ *f.* उठकट *f.*

Dismissed, *p.* v.V. 1. निरोप दिल्हेला, &c. बिदा, विसर्जित, बरखास.

2 वाटेस लावलेला, काढून दिल्हेला, &c. बरतरफ, तगीर *or* तहगीर, जिम्मा पारक, रुखसत, अधिकारच्युत, च्युताधिकार, पदच्युत, पदभ्रष्ट, अधिकारभ्रष्ट.

To be d. वस्त्रें*n. pl.* होणें *in. con.*

To **Dismount,** *v. a.* उतरणें, काढणें, पाडणें, खालीं आणणें-करणें.

To **Dismount,** *v. n. alight.* उतरणें, खालीं येणें, डेबरणें, अबरोह *m.*-अवरोहण*n.* करणें.

Disobedience, *n.* आज्ञाभंग*m.* आज्ञोल्लंघ*m.* आज्ञोल्लंघन *n.* अमान्यता *f.* असेवा *f.*

Disobedient, *a.* हुकूम मोडणारा, हुकूममोड्या, हुकूम तोड्या, बेहुकमी, गैरमान्य, आज्ञाभंजक, आज्ञोल्लंघक, आज्ञात्यागी, आज्ञातिक्रमी.

To **Disobey,** *v. a.* आज्ञा *f.*-हुकूम*m.*-&c. मोडणें-तोडणें, आज्ञाभंग *m.*-आज्ञोल्लंघ*m.*-आज्ञोल्लंघन*n.*-&c. करणें.

To **Disoblige,** *v. a. offend by unkindness.* अनुपकारानें-अकृपेनें -अनुपकारद्वारा-&c. असंतुष्ट-नाखुश-&c. करणें, मरजी *f.* मोडणें--खट्टी करणें *g. of o.*

Disobliging, *p. a.* v. V. अनुपकारी, निरुपकारी, अननुरोधी, अनुपकारशील, उपकारशत्रु, उपकारशठ, उपकारविमुख.

Disorder, *n.* (of things, affairs, &c.). v. Confusion. अव्यवस्था *f.* घालमेल *f.* उलटापालट *or* उलथापालथ *f.* गाबाळ*n.* विसकळ *f.* अफरातफर *f.* गफलत *f.* गडबड *f.* व्युत्क्रम*m.* व्यतिक्रम*m.* भग्नप्रक्रम*m.* धांदल *f.* धांदलपट्टी *f.* धांदलाधांदल *f.* चवचव *f.* चवढव *f.* बचबच *f.* घाण *f.* गुघाण *f.* रळफळ *f.* गदळ*m.*

2 *disturbance, commotion,* v. Tumult. गडबड *f.* बंड़ाळ *or* ळी *f.* गलबल *f.*

3 *derangement of health,* v. Sickness. विकार*m.* विकृति *f.* रोग*m.* असमाधान*n.* अस्वास्थ्य*n.*

D. of the stomach or bowels from indigestion. अन्नविकार*m.* अन्नविकृति *f.*

4 *a* d., *a disease, malady, ailment.* रोग*m.* विकार*m.* दुखणें*n.* दुःख*n.* आजार*m.* व्याधि*m.* बाधा *f.* दरद *f. m.* विकृति *f.* आमय*m.*

Dangerous d. जिवासांड रोग*m.*-दुखणें*n.*-विकार*m.*-&c.

Disorders and diseases,—compreh. रोगराई *f.*

Exacerbated or supervenient d. (through error of regimen). बाचोटn. To be exacerbated, &c.—a d. बाचकुटणें.
Natural d.-*distinguished from* preternatural d.अंगरोगm.
5 (of mind). See DISCOMPOSURE.

To DISORDER, *v. a. disarrange, derange, discompose*, v. To CONFOUND. विसकळणें, ढवळणें, गफलतणें, उलकटणें, उसकटणें, अव्यवस्था *f.*-उलटापालट *or* उलथापालथ *f.*-घालमेल *f.*-धांदल *f.*-&c. करणें *g. of o.*
2 *derange the health.* विकारm.-विकृति *f.*-उपद्रवm.-व्यथा *f.* करणें, बाधणें, रोगm. उत्पन्न करणें.
3 *ruffle, disturb.* See To DISCOMPOSE.

DISORDERED, *p.* v. V. 1. विसकळलेला, &c. विसकळीत, अव्यवस्थित, अस्ताव्यस्त, व्यस्ताव्यस्त, व्यस्त.
2 *ill, ailing*, v. SICK. दुखणाईत, दुखणेकरी, आजारी, विकारी, अस्वस्थ, असमाधानी, आतुर *or* रोगातुर, रुग्ण.

DISORDERLINESS, *n.* v. A. 1. *and* DISORDER. अव्यवस्थितपणा *m.* डावखुरेपणाm. &c. अव्यवस्था *f.* क्रमराहित्यn. क्रमशून्यता *f.*

DISORDERLY, *a. disordered, confused, immethodical, &c.* अव्यवस्थित, अस्ताव्यस्त, व्यस्ताव्यस्त, व्यस्त, डावखुरा, अक्रमिक, क्रमशून्य-रहित, क्रमबाह्य, निरन्वय, बेबंद, बचबचीचा, धांदलाधांदलीचा, चवढवीचा, &c.
2—of persons, &c. बेबंद, गबाळी *or* गबाळया, भांभळ *or* भांबळ्या, भांड्या, भोंगळ, भसभोंगळ, गहाळ.
D. family or circle. टमटमराज्य *n.*
3 *lawless, &c.* v. LICENTIOUS. अशिष्ट, बेशिष्ट, गैरशिष्ट, बेढंगी, ढंगी, ढंग्या, वावगा.

DISORDERLY, *adv.* v. A. 1. *immethodically.* अव्यवस्थेनें, अव्यवस्थितपणानें, &c.
2 *contrarily to good order.* गैरशिष्ट, गैररीतीनें, गैरमार्गानें.

To DISORGANIZE, *v. a.* v. To DISORDER. अव्यवस्था *f.*-&c. करणें *g. of o.* अव्यवस्थित-&c. करणें, रचना *f.* मोडणें, *g. of o.*

To DISOWN, *v. a* v. To DENY. नाकबूल जाणें-होणें, नाकारणें, ना म्हणणें, अस्वीकार *m.*-अनंगीकार *m.*-&c. करणें *g. of o.*

DISOWNED, *p.* v. V. नाकारलेला, &c. अस्वीकृत, अनंगीकृत.

DISOWNING, *n.* v. V.—*act.* नाकारणें *n.* अस्वीकारm.अनंगीकारm.

To DISPARAGE, *v. a. depreciate, undervalue, &c.* हलका-अपकृष्ट-&c. करणें, गुणापकर्ष *m.*-गुणऱ्हास *m.*-अपकर्ष *m.*-&c. करणें *g. of o.* हलकेपणा *m.*-उणेपणा *m.* आणणें, निरस्कारणें, हिणवणें *or* हिणावणें, योग्यता *f.*-&c. हलकी करून दाखवणें *g. of o.*

DISPARAGEMENT. See DISGRACE.

DISPARITY, *n.* v. DIFFERENCE. तफावत *f.* फेर *m.* न्यूनाधिक्य *n.* न्यूनाधिकभाव *m.* असमानता *f.*

To DISPART. See To SEPARATE.

DISPASSION, *n.* v. QUIETISM. शम *m.* शांति *f.*

DISPASSIONATE, *a. calm, impartial,*—of persons. शांत, थंड, निर्मम, निस्पृह, उदासीन, निष्पक्षपात.
2—of proceedings, &c. शमाचा, शमतेचा, निष्पक्षपाताचा.

DISPASSIONATELY, *adv.* v. A. शांतपणानें, थंडपणानें, निष्पक्षपातानें.

DISPATCH. See. DESPATCH.

To DISPEL, *v. a. disperse, &c.* उडवणें, घालवणें, दवडणें, पळवणें, फांकविणें, दूरकरणें, विल्हेवाट *f.* करणें *g. of o.* बाराबाटांस लावणें.

DISPELLED, *p.* v. V. उडवलेला, दवडलेला, &c.

DISPENSARY, *n.* धर्माचादवाखानाm. औषधशाला *f.*

DISPENSATION, *n.* v. V. 1.—*act.* वांटणें*n.* वांटणी *f.* वांटप*n.*
I. *dealing of God with his creatures.* मनुष्यास ईश्वरानें केलेली सुखदुःखाची वांटणी *f.* ईश्वरकर्तृकसुखदुःखनियोग *m.* ईश्वरीव्यवस्था *f.*
II. *license to do what is forbidden or to omit what is commanded.* विधिमोचन*n.* विधिमुक्ति*f.* माफी *f.* प्रतिप्रसव *m.*

To DISPENSE, *v. a. deal out, distribute.* v. To DIVIDE. वांटणें, वांटणी *f.*-वांटप*n.*-&c करणें *g. of o.* [णें, करणें.
2 (laws, justice, &c.) *administer, apply.* वहिवाटणें, चालव-
3 with; *waive, give up, &c.* सोडणें, टाकणें, माफ करणें, माफी *f.*-क्षमा *f.*-सुटका *f.*-&c. करणें-देणें, नको म्हणणें.
I can dispense with it *(can do without it.)* त्यावांचून खोळंबानाहीं. तें नसलें तरी चालेल.

To DISPEOPLE. See To DEPOPULATE.

DISPEPSY. See INDIGESTION.

To DISPERSE, *v. a. dissipate*, v. To SCATTER. उडवणें, उधळणें, फांकवणें, गादवणें *or* गादावणें, मोडणें, घालवणें, दवडणें, पळवणें, जिकडे तिकडे करणें, परागंदा करणें, रानोमाळकरणें, फांकाफांक *f.*-उडवाउडव *f.*-&c. करणें *g. of o.* वाट *f.* लावणें *g. of o.*
2 *diffuse.* See To SPREAD.

To DISPERSE, *v. n. be scattered.* फांकणें, पांगणें, वितुळणें, जिकडे तिकडे जाणें-होणें, बारावाटा *f. pl.* होणें *g. of s.* रानोमाळ होणें, परागंदा होणें.

DISPERSED, *p.* v.V.A.1.उडवलेला, फांकवलेला, &c.परागंदा, विभिन्न.

DISPERSEDLY, *adv.* इतस्ततः, तजावजा, तीनतेरा.

DISPERSION, *n.* v.V. A.1.—*act.* उडवणें*n.* फांकवणें*n.* &c.—*state.* उडवाउडव *f.* फांकाफांक *f.* बाताहत *f.* विल्हेवाट *f.* विधवाट *f.* द्राणादाण *f.*
v. V. N. फांकणें *n.* पांगणें *n.* &c. पांगणी *f.*
General d. पांगापांग *or* गी *f.*

To DISPIRIT, *n. a. dishearten, depress, deject.* मन*n.*-हिम्मत*f*-पाय*m. pl.* मोडणें *g. of o.* उत्साहभंग*m.*-धैर्यभंग*m.*-मनोभंग*m.*-हर्षभंग*m.*-उत्साहनाश *m.*-&c. करणें *g. of o.* हिरमोड *f. m.*-पायमोड *m. f.* करणें *g. of o.* टांके *m. pl.* ढील करणें *g. of o.* उदासखिन्न-बेदिल-मलूल-&c. करणें, भंगणें, मोडणें.

DISPIRITED, *p.* v. V. मन मोडलेला, &c. उदास, उदासी, ग्लान, गतोत्साह, विगतोत्साह, भग्नोत्साह, निरुत्साह, नष्टोत्साह, मलूल, बेदिल, मनोहत, विषण्ण, अवसन्न, दीनचेतन, अवाङ्मुख.

DISPIRITER, *n.* DISPIRITING, *p. a.* v. V. मन मोडणारा, &c. मनमोड्या, हिरमोड्या, पायमोड्या, मनोभंजक, उत्साहभंजक, धैर्यभंजक, उत्साहनाशक-घातक-&c.

DISPIRITING, *n.* v.V.—*act.* उदास करणें *n.* मन मोडणें*n.*&c. हिरमोड *m. f.* पायमोड *m. f.* मनमोड*m. f.* मनोभंग *m.* उत्साहभंग *m.* धैर्यभंग*m.*

To DISPLACE, *v. a. remove from its place.* स्थळ *n.* पालटणें *g. of o.* स्थानांतर*n.*-स्थलांतर *n.* करणें *g. of o.* स्थानभ्रष्ट-स्थानच्युत-स्थलभ्रष्ट-&c. करणें.
2 *derange, &c.* See To CONFUSE. 3 See To DISMISS.

To DISPLAY, *v. a. exhibit, set forth*, v. To MANIFEST. To SHOW. दाखवणें, प्रकाश*m.*-प्रसिद्धि *f.*-&c. करणें *g. of o.* उघडप्रगट-प्रसिद्ध-&c. करणें, बाहेर काढणें.
2 *unfold, expand.* See To SPREAD.

DISPLAY, DISPLAYING, *n.* v.V. 1.—*act.* दाखवणें*n.* प्रगट करणें*n.*

&c. प्रकाशन *n.* आविष्करण *n.* आविष्कार*m.*

I. *imposing array,* v. SHOW. आब *m.* आबारा *m.* थाट *m.* थाटमाट *m.* कटाव *m.* घटाव*m.* टामदूम *or* दुमदाम *f.* जगडंबर *n.*

To make an imposing d. प्रस्थ *n.* माजविणें-वाढविणें.

DISPLEASANT. See DISAGREEABLE.

To DISPLEASE, *v. a.* v. To OFFEND. नाखुश-खपा-असंतुष्ट-रुष्ट-&c. करणें, रुसवणें, मरजी *f.* मोडणें *g. of o.*

DISPLEASED, *p.* v. V. नाखुश केलेला, &c. नाखुश, खपा, खट्टा, खट्टू, खट्टी, रंजीस, इतराज, अप्रसन्न, असंतुष्ट, गैरखुश, गैरखुशी, गैरराजी, खिशाणा.

DISPLEASER, *n.* DISPLEASING, *p. a.* v.V. *and* DISAGREEABLE. नाखुश करणारा, &c. असंतोषक, असंतोषकारक, नावडता, नावडा, अनावड, नापसंत, अनिष्ट.

DISPLEASURE, *n. displeasedness,* v. OFFENCE. गैरमरजी *f.* करडी मरजी *f.* करडीकमान *f.* नाखुशी *f.* इतराजी *f.* असंतोष *m.* अवरुपा *f.* अप्रसन्नता *f.*

To DISPLODE, &c. See To EXPLODE, &c.

To DISPLUME. See To PLUCK.

DISPORT. To DISPORT, See PLAY. To PLAY.

To DISPORT, *v. a.* See To AMUSE.

DISPOSABLE, *a.* v. V. 1. मांडायाचा-जोगा-&c. उपन्यसनीय.

DISPOSAL, *n. act of disposing.* See DISPOSITION. 2 *power or right of disposing, arranging, &c.* हात*m.* सत्ता *f.* आज्ञा *f.* हुकूम *m.* सूत्र*n.* अधिकार *m.* नियंत्रणा *f.* नियंतृत्व *n.* योजनाधिकार *m.* योजनसत्ता *f.*

To DISPOSE, *v. a. arrange, set, lay orderly.* मांडणें, थांगारणें, रचणें, योजणें, लावणें, जुळणें, थाटणें, अडगविणें, जुडणें, व्यवस्था *f.*-रचना *f.*-रचाई *f.*-योजना *f.*-बंदोबस्त*m.*-विन्यास*m.*-उपन्यास*m.*-&c. करणें *g. of o.*

2 *frame the mind or will, incline.* मन वळविणें-लवविणें-तोलविणें-कलविणें-&c. *g. of o.* मनाला झोक*m.*-कल*m.*-ओढ *f.*-&c. देणें *g. of o.* अनुसरवणें, चित्त*n.* लावणें *g. of o.* प्रवर्त्तविणें, प्रवण-उन्मुख-&c. करणें.

3 of; *apply to a particular purpose.* v. To APPLY, To USE. योजणें, कामास-बाटेस-&c. लावणें, व्यवस्था *f.*-वहिवाट *f.*-विनियोग*m.*-&c. करणें *g. of o.* वाट *f.* करणें-लावणें *g. of o.*

4 of; *part with, &c.* v. To SELL. टाळून टाकणें *or* टाळणें, देऊन टाकणें *or* देणें, बाहेर करणें, पिशवींत उतरणें-घालणें-टाकणें.

5 of; *settle, finish, clear off.* निकाल*m.* करणें *g. of o.* उरकणें, उरका *m.* उरकणें, वाट *f.*-व्यवस्था *f.* करणें-लावणें *g. of o.*

DISPOSED, *p.* v.V. 1. मांडलेला, रचलेला, &c. रचित, विरचित, योजित, व्यवस्थापित, व्यवस्थित, उपन्यस्त, विन्यस्त, अनुक्रांत, प्रनिविहित.

2 वळवलेला, &c. प्रवण, प्रवृत्त.

To feel d. मनदेवता *f.*-मनपिंगळा*m.* लवणें-धांवणें-उठणें.

3 योजलेला, &c.

To be d. of. वहिवाटणें, वाट *f.* लागणें *g. of s.*

4 टाळून टाकलेला, देऊन टाकलेला, &c.

5 निकाल केलेला.

To be d. निकाल *m.*-परिणाम*m.*-शेवट *m.*-&c. होणें *g. of s.*

DISPOSER, *n.* v. V. 1. मांडणारा, रचणारा, &c. योजक, व्यवस्थापक, योजना-रचना-&c. कर्त्ता, व्यवस्थाता, व्यवस्था कर्त्ता.

DISPOSING, DISPOSITION, DISPOSAL, *n.* v. V. 1.—*act.* मांडणें*n.* रचणें *n.* योजणें*n.* &c. मांडणी *f.* मांडणूक *f.* मांडावळ *f.* मांडणावळ *f.* मांड*m.* रचना *f.* रचणी *f.* रचणूक *f.* अडगव *f.* अडगवणी *f.* थांगारणी *f.* थांगारणूक *f.* व्यवस्थापन *n.* विनियोग*m.* उपन्यास*m.* विन्यास*m.* प्रतिविधान *n.* अनुसंधान*n.*—*state.* व्यवस्था *f.* बंदोबस्त*m.* बंदोबस्ती *f.* घटाव *m.* कटाव *m.*

Price or cost of d. रचणावळ *f.* रचाई *f.* [*n.*

2—*act.* मन वळविणें*n.* झोक देणें*n.* &c.—*state.* वासना *f.* प्रावण्य

3—*act.* वहिवाट करणें *n.* वाट करणें *n.* वाटलावणें *n.* विनियोग *m.*

4—*act.* देणें *n.* टाळणें *n.* &c.

I. *disposedness of nature,* v. NATURE, TENDENCY. स्वभाव *m.* जन्मस्वभाव *m.* मूलस्वभाव *m.* भाव *m.* शील *n.* ओढ *f.* (स्वभावाची &c.).

II. (of mind or will) *temper, &c.* स्वभाव *m.* प्रकृति *f.* शील *n.* शिलाणें *n.* प्रकृतिभाव *m.* तबियत *f.* मरजी *f.* कदर *f.* खोय *f.* खोयबोय *f.*

D. and temper. शीलशिलाणें *n.*

Evil d. असद्भाव *m.*

Good d. सद्भाव *m.* शील *n.*

Happy d. सुखिस्वभाव *m.* संतोषवृत्ति *f.*

Of an evil d. दुःशील, दुःस्वभाव.

Of a good d. सुशील, शीलवान् *pop.* शीलवंत, शीलाचा.

III. *method,* v. ORDER. क्रम *m.* अनुक्रम *m.* पर्याय *m.*

To DISPOSSESS. See To DEPRIVE.

DISPRAISE, *To* DISPRAISE. See BLAME, To BLAME.

DISPROOF, *n. confutation.* खंडन *n.* असत्त्वस्थापन *n.* अप्रामाण्यस्थापन*n.*

DISPROPORTION, *n. want of proportion, disparity.* तफावत *f.* विजोडपणा *m.* न्यूनाधिकभाव *m.* असाम्य *n.* साम्याभाव *m.* प्रमाणवैकल्य *n.* प्रमाणवैषम्य *n.* विषमभाव *m.*

DISPROPORTIONAL, DISPROPORTIONATE, *a.* v. N. विजोड, विषमपरिणामक, विषमभावाचा, न्यूनाधिकपरिमाणक, असम, असमान.

To DISPROVE, *v. a. confute, &c.* खोटा-लटका-&c. करणें-करून-दाखवणें, खोटेपणा *m.*-खोटाई *f.*-&c. आणणें, खंडन *n.*-असत्त्वस्थापन*n.* करणें *g. of o.*

DISPUTABLE, *a.* v. V. A. वाद करायाजोगा, तकरारी, तकरारीचा, &c. विप्रतिपद्य, प्रत्याख्येय, आलोड्य, विवादार्ह, वादयोग्य, विवादास्पद, विवादस्थान, क्षोदार्ह, क्षोदक्षम.

DISPUTATION, *n.* v. V. N. 1.—*act.* वाद *m.* विवाद *m.* वादप्रतिवाद *m.* वाग्युद्ध *n.* हेतुवाद *m.* खंडनमंडन *n.*

D.-club. वादाचा अड्डा *m.*

D.-rooms. वादाचा अड्डा *m.*

Testimonial awarded at disputations of pre-eminence. अजितपत्र *n.*

DISPUTATIOUS, DISPUTATIVE, *a.* v. V. N. 1. वादकरण्याच्यास्वभावाचा, अतिवादी, विवादी, वादी, वादरत, विवादार्थी, वादप्रिय, वादशील, वादप्रवण, वादासक्त, बोलभांड, पाणी पिंपिऊन वाद करणारा-घालणारा, तकरारी.

Perversely d. खळवादी.

DISPUTATIOUSNESS, *n.* v. A. वादकरण्याचास्वभाव *m.* वादप्रीति *f.* वादासक्ति *f.* वादप्रावण्य *n.*

To DISPUTE, *v. n. contend in argument,* v. To ARGUE. वाद *m.*-विवाद *m.*-वादविवाद *m.*-विप्रतिपत्ति *f.*-&c. करणें-सांगणें-&c.

To d. vehemently. पायावर पाय देऊन वाद *m.* सांगणें.

2 *strive, contend,* v. To FIGHT, To QUARREL. भांडणें, कज्जा *m.*-भांडण *n.*-&c. करणें.

To DISPUTE, *v. a. controvert, contest, call in question.* वाद*m.* -तकरार *f.* घेणें-सांगणें *g. of o.* पंचाईत *f.* सांगणें, आक्षेप *m.*-शंका *f.*-आकांक्षा *f.*-कक्षा *f.*-&c. घेणें *with* वर *of o.* प्रतिपक्ष *m.*-विरुद्धपक्ष *m.*-&c. घेणें-करणें, वाद *m.*-विवाद *m.*-विप्रतिपत्ति *f.*-विप्रतिपादन *n.*-प्रत्याख्यान *n.*-निरसन *n.*-निराकरण *n.*-अस्वीकार *m.*-&c. करणें *g. of o.*

DISPUTE, DISPUTING, *n.* v. V. N. 1. *and* DISPUTATION. वाद *m.* विवाद *m.*

Obstinate & perverse d. खळवाद *m.*

To be under d. वाद *m.* चालणें *g. of s.*

That is beyond d. निर्विवाद.

2 भांडण *n.* कज्जा *m.* झगडा *m.* झोंबट *n.* तकरार *f.*

Take a loss but settle the d. हर मान झगडा तोड.

I. *disputed matter.* खटला *m.* खटलें *n.*

Confused d. भानगड *f.* हिलगड *f.*

DISPUTED, *p.* v. V. A. वादाचा, तकरारीचा, वादग्रस्त, वादास्पद, वादस्थान, विप्रतिपन्न, प्रत्याख्यात, वैकल्पिक, निराकृत, निरस्त, अस्वीकृत.

DISPUTER, DISPUTANT, *n.* v. V. N. 1. वाद करणारा, वादकर्त्ता, वादी, वाद्या, विवदमान.

DISQUALIFICATION, *n.* v.V.—*act.* अयोग्य करणें *n.* &c.—*state.* नालायकी *f.* अयोग्यता *f.* अक्षमता *f.*

I. *that which disqualifies.* नालायकी आणणारी गोष्ट *f.* अयोग्यता प्रापक-&c. विषय *m.*

DISQUALIFIED, *p.* v.V. अयोग्यकेलेला, &c. नालायक, अयोग्य, अक्षम.

To DISQUALIFY, *v. a. make unfit.* अयोग्य-अक्षम-नालायक-&c. करणें, अयोग्यता *f.*-&c. आणणें.

DISQUIET, DISQUIETUDE. See DISCOMPOSURE.

To DISQUIET. See To DISCOMPOSE.

DISQUISITION. See DISCOURSE, TREATISE.

DISREGARD, DISREGARDING, *n.* v. CONTEMPT. अवमान *m.* अनमान *m.* अपमान *m.* अनादर *m.* अव्हेर *m.* उपेक्षा *f.* अनपेक्षा *f.* अवज्ञा *f.* अवज्ञान *n.* अवगणन *n.* अवगणना *f.* अवमति *f.*

To DISREGARD, *v. a. slight, neglect,* v. To CONTEMN. अवमानणें, अनमानणें, अपमानणें, अनादरणें, अव्हेरणें, अवगणणें, उपेक्षणें, उबगणें, उपेक्षा *f.*-अव्हेर *m.*-अवमान *m.*-&c. करणें *g. of o.*

DISREGARDED, *p.* v.V. अवमानलेला, &c. अवमानित, अपमानित, अवगणित, उपेक्षित, अनपेक्षित, अवज्ञात, अनादृत, अवमत.

DISREGARDER, *n.* DISREGARDFUL, *a.* v. V. अवमानणारा, &c. अवमान-&c. कर्त्ता-कारी, उपेक्षक, अनपेक्ष.

DISRELISH, *n.* v. DISLIKE. अनावड *f.* अरुचि *f.* निरशी *f.*

To DISRELISH, *v. a.* v. To DISLIKE. नावडता-&c. असणें-वाटणें *in. con.* नावड *f.*-अप्रीति *f.*-&c. असणें *g. of o. & in. con.*

DISREPUTABLE, *a. mean, dirty, &c.* v. LOW, BLACKGUARDLY. हलका, हुच्चा, अप्रतिष्ठित, अप्रतिष्ठेचा, असंभावित, असभ्य, नापत, गैरअब्रूचा, बेअब्रूचा, जघन्यवृत्तीचा, अनार्य.

2 *causing disrepute,* v. DISGRACEFUL. इजतखाऊ, इजतघेऊ, इजतघेणा, अब्रूघेणा.

DISREPUTE, *n. loss or want of reputation, disesteem, discredit.* अपकीर्त्ति *f.* अकीर्त्ति *f.* दुर्लौकिक *m.* अलौकिक *m.* बदलौकिक *m.* नामोश *f. m.* नामोशी *f.* बदनाम *n.* बदनामी *f.* अपमान *m.* अख्याति *f.* अपयश *n.* अप्रतिष्ठा *f.* हलका भार *m.* बदचोई *f.* नापूस *f.*

DISRESPECT, *n. disesteem,* v. CONTEMPT. अपमान *m.* अनादर *m.* अमर्यादा *f.* असत्कार *m.* असन्मान *m.* अवमान *m.* अवमानना *f.* अवज्ञा *f.* बेअदबी *f.*

DISRESPECTFUL, *a.* v. N. अपमानाचा, अनादराचा, अमर्यादेचा, &c. अवमानी, अपमान-अनादर-&c. कारक-कारी.

DISRESPECTFULLY, *adv.* v.N. अमर्यादा करून, अमर्यादेनें, अनादर-&c. करून, अनादर-&c. पूर्वक.

To DISROBE. See To STRIP.

DISRUPTION. See BREAKING, BREACH.

DISSATISFACTION, *n. discontent.* अतृप्ति *f.* असमाधान *n.* अप्रसन्नता *f.* असंतोष *m.*

DISSATISFACTORY, See UNSATISFACTORY.

DISSATISFIED, *a.* v. DISCONTENTED. असंतुष्ट, असंतोषी, अतृप्त, अप्रसन्न, नाखुश, अपरितुष्ट.

To DISSECT, *v. a. anatomize.* (प्रेत *n.*) फाडणें-कापणें, शवव्यवच्छेद *m.*-&c. करणें.

2 See To ANALIZE.

DISSECTION, *n.* v. V. 1.—*act.* फाडणें *n.* कापणें *n.* शवव्यवछेद *m.*

2 See ANALYSIS.

DISSECTOR, *n.* v. V. 1. प्रेतफाडणारा-कापणारा, शवव्यवछेदक.

To DISSEIZE, *v. a. dispossess wrongfully.* अन्यायानें वेगळा-रहित-&c. करणें, अन्यायानें वहिवाट *f.* काढून घेणें-नाहींशी करणें *g. of o.*

To DISSEMBLE, *v. a. hide under false appearance.* v. To CONCEAL. लपवणें, छपावणें, चोरणें, पांघरूण *n.* घालणें.

To DISSEMBLE, *v. n. act hypocritically.* बहाणा *m.*-मिष *pop.* मीस *n.*-निमित्त *n.*-कपट *n.*-मकर *n.*-&c. करणें, सोंग *n.* दाखवणें.

DISSEMBLER, *n.* v. HYPOCRITE. मिसखोर, वेषधारी, छद्मवेषी, छद्मी, मनांत एक जनांत एक.

DISSEMBLINGLY, *adv.* बहाणाकरून, मिष *pop.* मीसकरून, &c. कपटानें.

To DISSEMINATE, *v. a.* v. To SPREAD. पसरणें, प्रसर *m.*-प्रसार *m.* -प्रचार *m.*-प्रवृत्ति *f.* करणें *g. of o.* पेरणें, प्रसृत-प्रचारित-&c. करणें.

DISSEMINATED, *p.* v. V. पसरलेला, &c. प्रसृत, प्रचारित.

DISSEMINATION, *n.* v. V.—*act.* पसरणें *n.* &c. प्रसार *m.* प्रसारण *n.*

DISSENSION, *n. contention, discord,* v. DISAGREEMENT. कलह *m.* बखेडा *m.* कळ *f.* भेद *m.* खडबड *f.*

Domestic or intestine d. कुटुंबकलह *m.* घरफूट *f.* गृहभेद *m.* घरभेद *m.*

To foment or feed d. आगींत तेल *n.* ओतणें.

To sow d. आग *f.* पाखडणें, फुणगी *f.* टाकणें *or* लावणें, भेद *m.*-भेदन *n.* करणें.

To DISSENT, *v. n. disagree in opinion,* गैरमान्य-अमान्य-असम्मत-विसम्मत-&c. असणें, असम्मति *f.*-अस्वीकार *m.*-&c. करणें *and* असणें *with g. of s.* मतांतर *n.*-मतभेद *m.* असणें *g. of s.*

2 *differ from an established church.* सरकारानें स्थापलेल्या धर्मास अमान्य असणें.

DISSENT, *n.* v. V. 1. अस्वीकार *m.* अनंगीकार *m.* असम्मत *n.* असम्मति *f.* विसम्मत *n.* मतभेद *m.* मतांतर *n.*

2 सरकारानें स्थापलेल्या धर्मास अमान्य असणें *n.*

DISSENTER, *n.* DISSENTIENT, *a.* v. V. 1. नाकबूल, गैरमान्य, गैरराजी, असम्मत, विसम्मत, मतांतरग्राहक-ग्राही, मतांतरावलंबी,

मतांतरधारी.

2 सरकारानें स्थापलेल्या धर्मास अमान्य असणारा.

DISSERTATION, *n. discourse.* ग्रंथ *m.* कवन *n.* निबंध *m.* प्रबंध*m.* बापचना *f.*

To DISSERVE. See To HURT.

DISSERVICE, *n. ill turn, injury.* अपकार *m.* अपकृति *f.* अहित *n.* हानि *f.*

To DISSEVER. See To SEVER.

DISSIDENT. See DISSENTIENT. [भिन्न.

DISSIMILAR, *a.* v. UNLIKE. असदृश, अतुल्य, असमान, असम,

DISSIMILARITY, *n.* v. A. असादृश्य *n.* असदृशता *f.* असाम्य *n.* तफावत *f.* अंतर *n.* भेद *m.*

DISSIMULATION, DISSEMBLING, *n.* v. V. *and* HYPOCRISY. ढोंगाचा-कपटाचा व्यवहार *m.* छद्मव्यवहार *m.* आकारगोपन *n.* होटांत एक पोटांत एक, मनांत एक जनांत एक, अवहित्था *f.* अपलाप *m.* वचस्येकं मनस्येकं *n.*

To DISSIPATE, *v. a. disperse,* v. To SCATTER. उडवणें, उधळणें, फांकविणें, मोडणें, घालवणें, वितुळविणें.

2 See To SQUANDER.

To DISSIPATE, *v. n.* उडणें, फांकणें, वितुळणें *or* वितुळून जाणें.

DISSIPATED, *a.* v. LOOSE.—of persons. व्यसनी, बदफैल, दुर्व्यसनी, विषयलंपट.

2—of life, conduct, &c. बदफैलीचा, दुराचरणाचा, भांगभुरक्याचा, &c.

DISSIPATION, *n. dissolute, irregular course of life.* बदफैली*f.* बेढंग *m.* दुराचरण *n.* भ्रष्टाचार *m.* दुर्वृत्ति *f.* भांगभुरका *m.*

DISSOCIABILITY, *n.* v. A. एकलकोंडेपणा *m.* &c. माणसाची घाण *f.* माणसाचा कंटाळा *m.*

DISSOCIABLE, DISSOCIAL, *a.* v. MISANTHROPIC. एकलकोट, एकलकोंडा, एकाड, माणूस घाण्या, नसनसखवडा.

To DISSOCIATE. See To SEPARATE.

DISSOLUBLE, *a. that may be melted.* वितुळवाया-चा-जोगा-&c. द्रव कराया जोगा-&c. द्राव्य, द्रावणीय, द्रवीकरणयोग्य, द्रावणार्ह.

DISSOLUBILITY, *n.* v. A. द्राव्यत्व *n.* द्रावणार्हता *f.* द्रवीकरणयोग्यता *f.*

DISSOLUTE, *a. licentious,* v. LOOSE.—of persons. बदफैल, ढंगी, ढंग्या, बेढंगी, चौढाळ, व्यसनी, दुर्व्यसनी, भ्रष्टाचारी, दुराचारी, दुर्वृत्त.

A d. or dissipated fellow. चंगी *m.* चंगी मंगी *m.*

2—conduct, &c. बदफैलीचा, दुर्व्यसनाचा, दुराचाराचा, &c. सोदेशाई.

DISSOLUTENESS, *n.* v. A. बदफैली *f.* दुर्व्यसन *n.* बेढंग *m.* भ्रष्टाचार *m.* दुराचार *m.* दुर्वृत्ति *f.* सोदेशाई *f.* सोदेगिरी *f.*

DISSOLUTION, *n.* v. V. A. 1.—*act.* वितुळविणें *n.* विघरवणें *n.* द्रावण *n.* द्रवीकरण *n.*

2—*act.* मोडणें *n.* तोडणें *n.* &c. भंग *m.* भंजन *n.*—*state.* बिघड *m.* भंग *m.* संडलेंतुटलें *n.*

3—*act.* मोडणें *n.* विसर्जन *n.*

v. V. N. 1. वितुळणें *n.* विघरणें *n.* रसहोणें *n.*

2 तुटातुटी *f.* तुटातूट *f.* फूट *f.* फाट *m.* फाटफूट *f.* भंग *m.*बिघड*m.*

I. See DEATH.

DISSOLVABLE. See DISSOLUBLE.

To DISSOLVE, *v. a. liquefy,* v. To MELT. वितुळविणें, विघरवणें, द्रव *m.*-रस *m.* करणें *g. of o.*

2 *disunite, separate, take to pieces, &c.* v. To BREAK. मोडणें, तोडणें, भंजन *n.*-भंग *m.*-&c करणें *g. of o.* विघड *m.* पाडणें-करणें *g. of o.* अवयव *m. pl.* निराळे करणें *g. of o.*

3 (an assembly, &c.) v. To DISMISS. मोडणें, बरखास करणें, विसर्जन *n.* करणें *g. of o.*

4 See To SOLVE.

To DISSOLVE, *v. n.* v. To MELT.वितुळणें, विघरणें, द्रव *m.*-रस *m.* होणें *g. of o.*

2 *break up, be disbanded,* v. To BREAK. तुटणें, फुटणें, फाटणें, फांकणें, सुटणें, भंग*m.*-विघड*m.*-&c. होणें *g. of s.*

DISSOLVENT, *a. that has power to melt.* द्रावक, द्रवकारक-कारी, स्रावक.

DISSONANCE, DISSONANT. See DISCORD, DISCORDANT.

To DISSUADE, *v. a. divert by argument, exhortation, &c.* दोन गोष्टी सांगून-बुद्धिवाद सांगून-उपदेश करून-&c. फिरवणें *or* मन*n.*-बुद्धि *f.*-चित्त*n.*-अंतःकरण*n.*-&c. फिरवणें *g. of o.* बोधपूर्वक परावर्त्तन*n.*-निवृत्ति *f.*-निवारण*n.*-&c. करणें *g. of o.* निवारण्यासाठीं बुद्धिवाद*m.* सांगणें, निवारणोपदेश*m.* करणें.

DISSUASION, *n.* v. V. निवारणोपदेश*m.* निवारणबुद्धिवाद*m.* परावर्त्तनोपदेश*m.* [निषेधार्थक.

DISSUASIVE, *a.* v. V. निवारक, निवारणधर्मक, निवारणोपदेशात्मक,

DISSYLLABIC, *a.* द्व्यच्क.

DISSYLLABLE, *n.* द्व्यच्कशब्द*m.* द्विस्वरशब्द*m.*

DISTAFF, *n.* चरखी *or* की *f.* तर्कुटी *f.*

To DISTAIN, See To STAIN.

DISTANCE, *n. space between.* पल्ला*m.* टप्पा*m.* छट्टा*m.* लांबण *f.* अवधि*m.* अंतर*n.* तफावत *f.* अंतरा*m.* अंतराल*n.*

2 *remoteness, farness.* लांबी*f.* दूरता *f.* दूरत्व*n.* विप्रकर्ष*m.*

At a great d. लांबच लांब, लांबचे लांब, दुरचे दूर.

At or to a great d. लांब, दूर. [पाहणें.

To keep at a d. *be or become cold towards.* दूर धरणें *or*

3 See INTERVAL. 4 See RESPECT. 5 See RESERVE.

To DISTANCE, *v. a. outstrip, leave behind.* मागें-पाठीमागें टाकणें -घालणें-करणें, अंतरणें.

DISTANCED, *p.* v. V. मागें टाकलेला, अंतरलेला, &c.

DISTANT, *a. remote, far;*—of time or space. दूर, दूरचा, दुरील, दुरला, दुरवरचा, लांब, लांबचा, लांबणीचा, मोठ्या अंतराचा, मोठे अवधीचा, दूरस्थित, दूरस्थ.—in high degree. लांबचलांब, लांबचे लांब, सुदूर, विप्रकृष्ट. [पडणें.

To be put off to a d. time. लांबणें, लांबणीवर-लांबणीखालीं

2 v. RESERVED. अनोळख्यासारखा, तिऱ्हाइतासारखा, अनोळखीच्या डौलाचा. [इशत.

3 *remote in view, slight, faint.* लांबचा, अल्प, स्वल्प, किंचित,

DISTASTE, *n. disrelish,* v. DISLIKE. अनावड*f.* निरशी *f.* अवडणें *or* अवढणें*n. v.* पड, ये, अरुचि *f.* अभक्ति *f.* अश्रद्धा *f.* अरति *f.*

DISTASTEFUL, *a. nauseous to the palate.* अरुचिर, अरुच्य, अरुचिकर, अरुचिक, अस्वादिष्ट, कुस्वाद, दुःस्वाद.

2 See UNPLEASANT.

DISTASTEFULNESS, *n.* v. A. 1. अरुच्यता *f.* अस्वादिष्टता *f.* &c.

DISTEMPER, *n. disease, malady,* v. DISORDER. विकार*m.* विकृति *f.* आजार*m.* रोग*m.*

2 (of cattle) लाळ *f. v.* ये, तोंड *n. v.* ये, तोंडलाग*m.*

DISTEMPERED, *a.* v. DISEASED, DISORDERED. व्याधित, रोगान्वित.

To DISTEND, *v. a. stretch out, extend, swell,* v. To STRETCH. फुगवणें, फुलवणें, वासणें, विस्तीर्ण करणें, ताणणें, तणतणीत-तटतटीत करणें. [तणवरणें.

To be distended. तटतटणें *intens.* तटाटणें, तणणें, तणतणणें,

To DISTEND, *v. n.* फुगणें, फुलणें, वासणें, विस्तीर्ण होणें.

DISTENSION, *n.* v. V. A.—*act.* ताणणें*n.*—*state.* तटाटा*m.* ताठा*m.* *v.* ये. ताण*m. v.* ये. तटाटलेपणा*m.* तटतटीतपणा*m.* &c.

D. of belly from flatus. गुबारा *or* गुभारा *m. v.* धर *with* पोटामध्यें, डांभारा*m. v.* धर.

DISTICH, *n. couplet.* दोहरा*m.* बैत *f.*

To DISTIL, *v.a.* (spirits, &c.). भबक्यानें काढणें, संधान*n.*-निस्सारण*n.*-निष्कासन*n.*-&c. करणें *g.of o.* अर्क*m.* काढणें.

2 See To DROP.

To DISTIL, *v. n. fall in drops,* v. To DROP. टपकणें, टिबकणें.

DISTILLATION, DISTILLING, *n.* v. V. A. 1. भबक्यानेंकाढणें*n.* मद्यसंधान *n.* संधान *n.* संधानी *f.* संधिका *f.* मद्यनिस्सारण *n.* आस्रुति *f.* स्रुति *f.*

DISTILLER, *n.* v. V. A. 1. मद्य काढणारा, कलाल, काळण, संधानकर्त्ता, अर्ककार, मद्यकार, शौंडिक. [र *n.*

DISTILLERY, *n.* कलालाची भट्टी *f.* रेंद *m.* रेंदसरा*m.* मद्यसंधानागा-

DISTINCT, *a. other,* v. DIFFERENT. निराळा, वेगळा, जुदा, भिन्न, विलक्षण.

2 *disjunct, not conjunct,* v. SEPARATE. निराळा, वेगळा, जुदा, मोकळा, अलग, पृथक्, निरवालस, भिन्न, असंबद्ध, असंसृष्ट, असलग्न.

3 *plain, conspicuous,* v. CLEAR. साफ, स्पष्ट, व्यक्त, सुव्यक्त.

DISTINCTION, DISTINGUISHING, *n.* v. V. 1.—*act.* भेद पाहणें *n.* &c. विवेचन *n.* विवेचना *f.* विभावन *n.* विभावना *f.* तारतम्यदर्शन*n.* भेददर्शन *n.*

2—*act.* भेदणें *n.* &c. भेद *m.* भेदन *n.* अवच्छेद *m.* परिच्छेद *m.* व्यवच्छेद *m.* पृथक्करण *n.*—*state.* व्यावृत्ति *f.*

D. of own and other, (relations, things, &c.) *regard to meum et tuum.* आपपर *or* स्वपर भाव *m.* आपपर *or* स्वपर बुद्धि *f.*-लक्ष्य *n.*-दृष्टि *f.*-मत *n.*-&c.

D. of persons. उंचनीच-सामान्यविशेष-उच्चावच-&c. दृष्टि *f.* -बुद्धि *f.*-मत *n.*-&c.

Non-d. of persons. सर्वसाधारण-आपामरसाधारण-&c. वृत्ति *f.*-वर्त्तन *n.*-मन *n.*-लक्ष्य *n.*-भाव *m.*-बुद्धि *f.*-दृष्टि *f.*-&c.

I. *diversity,* v. DIFFERENCE. भेद *m.* फेर *m.* फरक *m.* तारतम्य *n.* न्यूनाधिक्य *n.*

II. *holding to be different.* विषमभाव *m.* द्वैतभाव *m.* भेददृष्टि *f.* भेदभाव *m.* तारतम्यभाव *m.* तरतमभाव *m.* विषमदृष्टि *f.*

To treat without d. एका काठीनें हांकणें, एका माळेंत ओवणें, सब घोडे बारा टक्के करणें-मानणें.

III. *note or mark distinguishing.* विशेष *m.*

IV. *eminence, superiority.* मोठेपणा *m.* श्रेष्ठत्व *n.* विशेषता *f.* लौकिक *m.* नांव *n.* प्रतिष्ठा *f.*

DISTINCTIVE, *a. that marks difference.* भेदसूचक-दर्शक-&c.

D. mark. विशेषलक्षण *n.*

DISTINCTLY, *adv.* v. A. 3. साफ, स्पष्ट, सव्यगत, व्यक्त.

DISTINCTNESS, *n.* v. A. 1. निराळेपणा *m.* वेगळेपणा *m.* भिन्नत्व *n.* वैलक्षण्य *n.* [संसृष्टत्व *n.*

2 निराळेपणा *m.* मोकळेपणा *m.* निरवालसपणा *m.* पार्थक्य *n.* अ-

3 स्पष्टता *f.* व्यक्तता *f.*

To DISTINGUISH, *v.a. note the difference of, discern, discriminate.* तारतम्य *n.* पाहणें-ठेवणें-राखणें, भेद *m.*-विशेष *m.*-फेर *m.* -न्यूनाधिक्य *n.*-&c. पाहणें-जाणणें-मनांत आणणें, विवेचन *n.*-विवेचना *f.*-विभावन *n.*-विभावना *f.* करणें *g. of o.*

2 *separate from, make distinct or particular.* भेदणें, भेद *m.*-भेदन *n.*-अवच्छेद *m.*-परिच्छेद *m.*-व्यवच्छेद करणें *g. of o.*

3 (one's self). श्रेष्ठत्व *n.*-वरिष्ठत्व *n.*-यश *n.*-नांव *n.*-प्रतिष्ठा *f.*-&c. मिळवणें-संपादणें.

DISTINGUISHABLE, *a.* v. V. 1. विवेचनीय, विभावनीय, विभाव्य.

2 भेद्य, भेदनीय, विशेषणीय, विशेष्य.

DISTINGUISHED, *p.* v. V. 1. कृतलक्षण, आहृतलक्षण, विवेचित, विविक्त, विभावित.

2 अवच्छिन्न, परिच्छिन्न, व्यवच्छिन्न, पृथक्कृत, विशिष्ट, विशेषित.

3 *eminent, &c.* नांवाचा, नामजात, प्रतिष्ठित, नामांकित, लब्धकीर्त्ति, लब्धयश, लब्धप्रतिष्ठ, असाधारण.

DISTINGUISHER, *n.* DISTINGUISHING, *p. a.* v. V. 1. तारतम्य पाहणारा-ठेवणारा, &c. विवेचक, विवेकी, विवेकाढ्य, भेददर्शक, तारतम्यदर्शक.

2 भेद करणारा, &c. भेदक, अवच्छेदक, परिच्छेदक, व्यवच्छेदक, विशेषक, विशेषण.

To DISTORT, *v. a.* v. To TWIST. मुरडणें, वांकडा-वक्र-विकृत-&c. करणें, पिळे *m. pl.* देणें. [घणें.

2 (a passage, meaning.) v. To WREST. वळवणें, ओढून

DISTORTED, *p.* v.V.1. मुरडलेला &c. खुळा *remiss.* खुळपट, विकृत, विकल, साचीकृत.

To be or become d. तिरपणें *or* तिरपावणें.

2 वळवलेला, ओढून घेतलेला.

DISTORTION, *n.* v. V. 1. —*act.* मुरडणें *n.* वांकडा करणें *n.* &c. —*state.* v. CONTORTIONS. वैकल्य *n.* मुरगाळा *m.* पिळा *m.*

To DISTRACT, *v. a. perplex, bewilder,* v. To CONFOUND. घाबरविणें, बहकावणें, गडबडवणें, ओढाताण *f.*-त्रेधा *f.*-तारांबळ *f.*-धांदल *f.*-ताणाताण *f.*-&c. करणें *g. of. o.*

2 *greatly disturb, or discompose,* v. To MADDEN. वेडा-विक्षिप्त-&c. करणें, चित्तविभ्रम *m.*-चित्तविभ्रंश *m.*-चित्तविक्षेप *m.*-बुद्धिभ्रंश *m.*-&c. करणें *g. of o.*

3 *divert from a point, draw from an object.* फिरवणें, फांकवणें, बहकावणें, काढणें, भ्रष्टवणें.

DISTRACTED, *p.* v. V. 1. घाबरवलेला, घाबरा, विमना, विमनस्क.

2 वेडा केलेला-झालेला, चित्तविक्षिप्त, बुद्धिभ्रष्ट, चित्तविभ्रमी.

3 फिरवलेला, &c.

To be d. दिल *m. n.* फांकणें-फांकटणें *g. of s.*

DISTRACTER, *n.* DISTRACTING, *p. a.* v. V. 1. घाबरविणारा, गडबडविणारा, &c. धांदलीचा, ओढाताणीचा.

DISTRACTION, v. V. 1.—*act.* घाबरवणें *n.* &c. ताणाताण *f.* ओढाताण *f.* कुतरओढ *f.* कुतरतोड *f.*—*state.* तिरपीट *f.* तारांबळ *f.* धांदल *f.* तारातीर *f.* डामाडूळ *f. n.* त्रेधा *f.* तिरडाफांक *f.* वैमनस्य *n.* चित्तवैकल्य *n.* वैचित्य *n.*

2 *and* MADNESS. चित्तविभ्रम *m.* चित्तविभ्रंश *m.* चित्तविक्षेप*m.* बुद्धिभ्रंश *m.*

To DISTRAIN, *v. a. seize for debt.* कर्जाबदल धरणें-घेणें, कोल *m.*

n.-कबज *n.* धरणें.

DISTRESS, *n. affliction*, v. TROUBLE दुःख *n.* क्लेश *m. pl.* कष्ट *m. pl.* श्रम *m. pl.* हैराणी *f.* हैराणगत *f.* ताप *m.* संताप *m.* कासाविसी *f.* कष्टावस्था *f.* कष्टदशा *f.* हैराणदशा *f.* &c.

To be in great d. अर्धाजीव *m.* होणें, कंठीं प्राण *m.* येणें.

2 *miserable state*, v. WRETCHEDNESS. हाल *m. pl.* हालहवाल *m. pl.* हालअपेष्टा *f.* दुर्दशा *f.* हलवंड्या *f. pl.* हवेलंडी *f.* गाळण *f.* हलाकी *f.*

3 *straitness of circumstances*, v. POVERTY. अडचण *f.* चडचड *f.* चणचण *f.* तारंबळ *f.* विपत्ति *f.* अडचणूक *f.* ओढ *f.* ओढगस्ती *f.* गिरिबदारी *f.* हलाकी *f.* वखवख *f.*

To relieve one's d. अडचणूक *f.* मोडणें *g. of o.*

4 *act of distraining.* कबज *n.*

5 *property seized.* कबज *n.*

To DISTRESS, *v. a.* v. To AFFLICT. To TROUBLE. पिडणें, पिडवणें, दुःख *n.*-क्लेश *m. pl.*-कष्ट *m. pl.* देणें, क्लेशणें, हैराणी *f.*-हैराणगत *f.*- &c. करणें *g. of o.* हैराण-&c. करणें.

2 *reduce to want or wretchedness.* हाल *m. pl.*-हालहवाल *m. pl.*-दशा *f.*-हलाकी *f.*-तारंबळ *f.*-अडचण *f.*-&c. करणें *g. of o.* अडचणींत-विपत्तींत-संकटांत-&c. पाडणें-घालणें-आणणें, अडचणवणें.

DISTRESSED, *p.* v. V. 1. दुःखी, दुःखित, श्रमी, कष्टी, क्लेशी, क्लिष्ट, पीडित, कासावीस, व्यग्र, संतप्त, संतापित, प्राप्तदुःख, प्राप्तक्लेश, &c.

2 ओढगस्त, ओढिस्तु, गिरिबदार, दुर्गत, कृच्छ्रगत, आपन्न, विपत्तिग्रस्त, आपत्प्राप्त, आपद्ग्रस्त.

To be d. अडचणणें.

DISTRESSING, *p. a.* DISTRESSFUL, *a.* v. V. 1. पिडणारा, &c. दुःखाचा, कष्टाचा, क्लेशाचा, कष्टदशेचा, हैराणगतीचा, दुःखद, दुःखप्रद, क्लेशद, क्लेशप्रद, क्लेशावह, &c. कष्टकारक-कारी.

2 तारंबळीचा, अडचणीचा, ओढगस्तीचा, विपत्तीचा, हालांचा, हाल अपेष्टेचा.

DISTRESSING, *n.* v. V. 1.—*act.* पिडणें *n.* पिडवणें *n.* क्लेशणें *n.* &c. संतापन *n.* कष्टीकरण *n.*

3 अडचणवणें *n.* अडचण करणें *n.* &c.

To DISTRIBUTE, *v. a. deal out, dispense*, v. To DIVIDE. वांटणें, वांटून देणें, वाढणें, विभागणें, विभागून देणें, वांटणी *f.*-वांटप *n.*-वांटावांट *f.* करणें *g. of o.* [धणें.

To d. into classes, orders, &c. वर्गोपवर्ग *m. pl.* करणें-बांधणें.

DISTRIBUTION, *n.* v. V.—*act.* वांटणें *n.* वांटून देणें *n.* &c. वांटणी *f.* वांटप *n.* वांटावांट *f.*

D. into classes, orders, &c. वर्गोपवर्गीकरण *n.*

I.—in logic. शृंगग्राहिका *f.*

DISTRIBUTIVE, *a.* वांटून देणारा, वांटणी करणारा.

DISTRICT, *n. circuit of authority.* चकला *m.* महला *m.*

2 *division of country*, v. COUNTY. प्रांत *m.* महाल *m.* तालुका *m.* जिल्हा *m.*

Throughout the districts. महालानिहाय.

To DISTRUST, *v. a. be diffident of*, v. To DOUBT. अविश्वास *m.*-अप्रत्यय *m.* करणें-ठेवणें, शंका *f.*-आशंका *f.*-संशय *m.*-&c. धरणें *and with in. con.* असणें *g. of o.*

DISTRUST, *n. diffidence, non-reliance*, v. DOUBT. अविश्वास *m.* शंका *f.* आशंका *f.* अप्रत्यय *m.* कल्प *m.*

DISTRUSTED, *p.* v. V. शंकित, आशंकित, अविश्वसित.

DISTRUSTFUL, *a.* v. SUSPICIOUS. अविश्वासी *or* सू *or* सूक, सशंक, साशंक, शंकाशील, अप्रत्ययी.

2 (of self) See DIFFIDENT.

To DISTURB, *v. a. stir, move, displace.* हालवणें, चाळवणें, ढवळणें, स्थानभ्रंश *m.*-स्थलभ्रंश *m.*-स्थलांतर *n.* करणें *g. of o.*

2 *disquiet, &c.* v. To AGITATE, To DISCOMPOSE. गढुळणें, गदळणें, खंदळणें, गळ्हाटणें, अस्वस्थ-क्षुब्ध-व्यग्र-&c. करणें.

3 *impede*, v. To HINDER. To INTERRUPT. हरकत *f.*-विघ्न *n. m.* करणें, व्याक्षेप *m.* घालणें-आणणें-करणें.

DISTURBANCE, DISTURBING, *n.* v. V. 1.—*act.* हालवणें *n.* ढवळणें *n.* &c. स्थानभ्रंश *m.* स्थलभ्रंश *m.*

2 *and* DISCOMPOSURE.—*act* गढुळणें *n.* गदळणें *n.* &c.—*state.* क्षोभ *m.* व्याक्षोभ *m.* क्षुब्धता *f.* उद्वेग *m.*

3 See HINDERANCE, INTERRUPTION.

I. *commotion, combustion*, v. TUMULT. धांदल *f.* धांदलपट्टी *f.* खूळ *n.* दंगा *m.*

DISUNION, DISUNITING, *n.* v. V. A.—*act.* वेगळा करणें *n.* भेदणें *n.* भेद *m.* भेदन *n.* द्वैधीकरण *n.*—*state.* वियोग *m.* भेद *m.* विश्लेष *m.* वियुक्तता *f.* विश्लिष्टता *f.* विभक्तता *f.*

I. fig. of families, &c. बिघड *m.* तूट *f.* फूट *f.* भेद *m.* वेगळेचार *m. pl.* वेगळीक *f.* वियोग *m.* अनैक्य *n.* भिन्नभाव *m.* विभक्तभाव *m.* द्वैतभाव *m.*

To DISUNITE, *v. a.* v. To SEPARATE. वेगळा-भिन्न-निराळा-&c. करणें, भेदणें, संबंध *m.* तोडणें-मोडणें *g. of o.* भेद *m.*-वियोग *m.*-बिघड *m.*-&c. करणें *g. of o.*

To DISUNITE, *v. n.* वेगळा-&c. होणें, वियोग *m.*-&c. होणें *g. of s.*

DISUSAGE, DISUSE, *n. neglect of use.* गैरवळण *n.* गैरराबता *m.* गैरवहिवाट *f.* अनभ्यास *m.* अनुपस्थिति *f.* अनुपलब्धि *f.* अव्यवहार *m.* लोप (esp. in comp. as आचारलोप, संप्रदायलोप, रीतिलोप, धर्मलोप, &c.), अनाचरण *n.*

That has not fallen into d. उपस्थित.

To fall into d. पडीं पडणें, मागें पडणें, ढळणें.

To DISUSE, *v. a.* वहिवाट *f.*-राबता *m.*-वळण *n.*-अभ्यास *m.*-&c. सोडणें-मोडणें *g. of o.* अनभ्यास *m.*-अव्यवहार *m.*-&c. करणें *g. of o.*

DISUSED, *p.* v. V. *and* OBSOLETE. राबता सोडलेला, &c. अव्यवहारित, अनुपस्थित, लुप्त.

DITCH, *n. trench, &c.* चर *m.* खंदक *m.* खान *n.*

2 *moat.* खंदक *m.* खाई *f.* चर *m. dim.* चरी *f.* परिखा *f.*

DITTO. सदरहू, तथा.

DITTY. See SONG.

DIURETIC, *n.a. medicine to provoke urine.* मूत्रढाळ *m.* बस्तिशोधन *n.* लघ्वीजुलाब *m.* इंद्रियजुलाब *m.* इंद्रियरेचन *n.* इंद्रियशोधन *n.*

DIURETIC, *a.* v. N. मूत्रढाळाचा, मूत्रल, मूत्रक, मूत्रोत्पादक, मूत्ररेचक.

DIURNAL, *a. quotidian*, v. DAILY. दिवसाचा, रोजचा.

2 *belonging to the day.* दिवसाचा, दैनिक, दैन, दिवातन.

D. motion (of the earth) दैनंदिनगति *f.*

DIVAN, *n. council-chamber.* दिवाण *m.* दिवाणखाना *m.*

To DIVARICATE, *v. n. fork, part into two.* फुटणें, दुफांटा *m.*-दुभाग *m.*-&c. होणें *g. of s.*

To DIVARICATE, *v. a. divide into two.* दुभागणें, दुभाग *m.*-दुफोड *f.*-दुफाड *f.*-&c. करणें *g. of o.*

DIVARICATION, *n.* v.V.N. फुटणें *n.* दुफांटा *m.* दुबाळकें *or* दुबेळकें *n.*

To DIVE, *v. n.* बुडी *f.*-डुबकी *f.*-खोलबुडी *f.*-सुरकांडी *f.* मारणें.

2 *go deep into a subject.* पारंगत-प्रवीण-&c. होणें.

Dive, Diving, *n.* v. V. बुडी *f.* डुबकी *f.* पाणबुडी *f.* सुरकांडी *f.* सुरकुंडी *f.*

Diver, *n.* v. V. 1. पाणबुड्या, बुडी-&c. मारणारा.
I.—the bird. पाणबुड्या *m.*

To **Diverge**, *v. n. extend or spread in different directions from the same point.* फुटणें, पसरणें, फांकणें, फांकटणें.

Divergence, *n.* v. V. फांकणें *n.* फांकटी *f.*

Divergent, *a.* v. V. फांकणारा, फुटणारा, फांकट, केंद्रपराङ्मुख.

Divers, *a.* v. Various. नाना, विविध, अनेक, अनेकप्रकारचा.

Divers, Diverse. See Different.

Diversely, *adv. in various ways*, v. Variously. नानापरी, परोपरी, भिन्नप्रकारांनीं, अनेक प्रकारांनीं.

To **Diversify**, *v. a.*v. To Vary. पालटणें, पालट *m.*-फेर *m.*-फेरफार *m.*-भेद *m.*-प्रकारांतर *n.*-पर्यायांतर *n.*-रूपभेद*m.*-रूपांतर*n.*-&c. करणें *g. of o.*

Diversion, Diverting, *n.* v. V. 1.—*act.* फिरवणें *n.* वळवणें*n.* परिवर्त्तन *n.*
2—*act.* रमवणें *n.* रंजविणें *n.* रंजन *n.*
I. *object or cause of d.*v. Play. गमत *f.* करमणूक *f.* विरंगुळा *m.* कौतुक *n.*
II. (in war) हूलदासवून-भूलथाप देऊन-&c. शत्रूचें लक्ष्य दुसरेकडे लागे असें करणें.

Diversity, *n. dissimilitude*,v. Difference. निराळेपणा *m.*&c. भिन्नता *f.* असमता *f.* असाम्य *n.* वैजात्य *n.*
2 See Variety.

To **Divert**, *v.a. turn off.* फिरवणें, वळवणें, मोहरा *m.*-तोंड *n.*-रोंख *m.* फिरवणें-वळवणें *g. of o.* मोड *f.*-वळण *n.* देणें, परिवर्त्तन *n.* करणें *g. of o.* मार्गत्याग *m.* करविणें.
2 *entertain*, v. To Amuse. रमविणें, रंजविणें, विरंगुळा *m.*-करमणूक *f.*-&c. करणें *g. of o.* [मनोरंजक.

Diverting, *a. entertaining*, v. Amusing. गमती, गमतीचा,

To **Divest**, *v. a. denude*, v. To Strip. वस्त्रें *n. pl.* काढणें, नागवणें, उघडा-नागवा-सुना-&c. करणें.
2 v. To Deprive. बेमळा-निराळा-हीन-रहित-&c. करणें.

To **Divide**, *v.a. part, cut.* भेदणें, छेदणें, कापणें, दुभागणें, दुभांगणें, भांगणें, विभागणें, विछेद *m.*-परिछेद *m.*-&c. करणें *g. of o.*
2 *sever, sunder*, v. To Separate. भेद *m.*-भेदन *n.* करणें *g. of o.* वेगळा-निराळा-भिन्न-अलग-&c. करणें-ठेवणें.
3 *deal out, dole, partition, distribute, dispense, share.* वांटणें, वांटून देणें-घेणें, विभागणें, विभागून देणें-घेणें, वाढणें,भांजणें, वांटणी *f.*-वांटप *n.*-&c. करणें *g. of o.* वांटे *m. pl.*-अंश*m. pl.*-&c. करणें *g. of o.* [रणें *g.of o.*
4—in arithmetic. भागणें, भाग *m.* देणें, भांजणें, भाजन *n.* क-

To **Divide**, *v. n.* See To Part.

Divided, *p.* v. V. A. 1. भेदलेला, छेदलेला-&c. छेदित, छिन्न, विछिन्न, परिछिन्न, भिन्न.
2 वेगळा-&c. केलेला, विभक्त.
3 वांटून दिल्हेला-घेतलेला, विभागलेला, &c. विभागित, विभक्त, भाजित, अंशित.
4 भागलेला, भांजलेला, भाजित.

Dividend, *n. share of a divided thing*, v. Share. वांटा *m.*भाग *m.* तकूशीम *f.* हिस्सा *m.*
2—in arithmetic. भाज्य *n.* भाज्यांक *m.*

Divider, *n.* v. V. A. 1. भेदणारा, छेदणारा &c. भेदक, छेदक, विच्छेदक, परिछेदक, छेद-विच्छेद-&c. कर्त्ता-कारक-&c.
2 भेद करणारा, वेगळा-&c. करणारा, &c.
3 वांटणारा, वांटून देणारा-घेणारा, &c. अंशमान.
4 भागणारा, भाजक. [ची विद्या *f.*

Divination, *n.* v. V. प्रश्न-शकुन-ठोका-&c. पाहणें *n. or* पाहण्या-
D. by figures, &c. रमल *n.*

Divine, *a. pertaining &c. to God.* ईश्वरी, ईश्वरीय, ईश्वराचा, देवाचा, ईश्वरसंबंधी, देवसंबंधी, देवकीय, दैव, दैविक, ऐश, ऐशिक, दिव्य, गीर्वाण, गीर्वाणी, ईश्वर (in comp.)
D. favor. भगवत्कृपा *f.* ईश्वरकृपा *f.*
D. power. भगवत्सत्ता *f.* ईश्वरसत्ता *f.*
D. will. भगवदिच्छा *f.* ईश्वरेच्छा *f.*

Divine, *n.*—Christian. ख्रिस्ती धर्मोपदेशक, पाद्री.
—Hindu. उपाध्या, आचार्य, भट.
2 *theologian.* देवज्ञानांत-परमार्थ ज्ञानांत-&c. प्रवीण.
—Hindu. वैदिक, ब्रह्मज्ञानी, वेदशास्त्रसंपन्न.

To **Divine**, *v. a. predict, prognosticate.* प्रश्न*m.*-शकुन*m.*-ठोका *m.*-भाकित *n.* पाहणें-पाहून सांगणें, दैवप्रश्न *m.* पाहणें-सांगणें.
2 See To Guess.

Divinely, *adv. by the agency, &c. of God.* ईश्वराकडून, देवाकडून, ईश्वर in comp. as ईश्वरोपदिष्ट d. instructed. ईश्वरप्रेरित d. prompted, &c.
2 See Excellently.

Diviner, *n.* v. V. 1. शकुन पाहणारा-पाहून सांगणारा, दैवज्ञ, पाहण्या, ठोकजोशी, मेढेजोशी, पिंगळाजोशी, भाकड जोशी, भाडल्याजोशी.

Divinity, *n. deity, godhead.* देवपणा*m.* देवता *f.* देवत्व *n.* ईश्वरत्व *n.* ईशता *f.* ईशत्व *n.*
2 *theology.* देवज्ञान*n.* परमार्थज्ञान *n.* ब्रह्मज्ञान *n.* वेदांत *m.* तत्वज्ञान *n.* अध्यात्मज्ञान *n.* अध्यात्मशास्त्र *n.*
3 *a* d. v. God. देव *m.* देवता *f.* [छेदनीय.

Divisible, *a.* v. V. A. 1. भेदाया जोगा-&c. भेद्य, भेदनीय, छेद्य,
2 भेद कराया जोगा-&c. खंडनीय.
3 वांटाया जोगा-&c. भाज्य, भाग्य, अंश्य, अंशनीय.

Division, Dividing, *n.* v.V.A. 1.—*act.* भेदणें *n.* छेदणें *n.* &c. भेद*m.* भेदन*n.* छेद *m.* छेदन *n.* विभेद *m.* विच्छेद *m.* परिच्छेद *m.* अवच्छेद *m.*
2 भेद करणें *n.* भेद *m.* भेदन *n.* पृथक्करण *n.*
3 वांटणें *n.* वांटून देणें *n.*-घेणें*n.* विभागणें *n.* &c. वांटणी *f.* वांटप *n.* अंशन *n.*
4 भागणें *n.* भाजन *n.* भजन *n.* हरण *n.*
I. See Disagreement, Disunion.
II.—in arithmetic;—the rule. भागाकार *m.* Some of the modes are धावरा भागाकार, बैठा भागाकार.
III. *a* d. *place divided off, a partition.* खण *m.* खाना *m.* खिसा *m.* घर *n.* पड *m. n.* पूड *m. n.* कपा *or* कप्पा *m.* अंखणी *or* अंकणी *f.*
IV. *dividing body*, v. Partition. पडदा *m.* पडदी *f.* भेदसाधन *n.* [शीम *f.*
V. *portion, part*, v. Share. विभाग *m.* भाग *m.* अंश *m.* तकू-
VI. *order, class.* वर्ग *m.* कोटि *f.* भेद *m.*
VII. (as in a bag, &c.) पूड *n.* कप्पा *m.* खिसा *m.*

VIII. (of a book) *section, book, chapter.* अंग *n.* शाखा *f.* खंड *n.* प्रकरण*n.* ग्रंथ *m.* कथाभाग *m.* प्रसंग *m.*

IX. (of an army) सेनाभाग *m.* सेनाशाखा *f.*

DIVISOR, *n.*—in arithmetic. भाजक, हर, हार, हारक, छेदक.

DIVORCE, DIVORCEMENT, *n.* दादल्याबायकोची सुटासूट *f.* विवाहसंबंध मोचन *n.* विवाहसंबंधमुक्ति *f.* दांपत्य मोचन*n.* दांपत्यमुक्ति*f.*

Writing, bill, &c. of d. सोडचिठ्ठी *f.* सांडखत *n.* सूटपत्र *n.*

To DIVORCE, *v. a.* विवाहसंबंध *m.*-दंपतिसंबंध *m.*-&c. तोडणें, काडी *f.* मोडून देणें, विवाहसंबंधमोचन*n.*-&c. करणें.

2 See To SEPARATE.

To DIVULGE, &c. See To PUBLISH, To BLAB, &c.

To DIZEN. See To DECK.

To DIZZEN, *To* DIZZY, *v. a. make giddy.* घेरी *f.*-भोवंड *f.*-भोवळ *f.*-&c. आणणें.

DIZZINESS, *n.* v. A.1. घेरी *f.* भोवंड *f.* भोंड *f.* भोवळ *f.* घायतळ *f.* गिरकी *f.* काजळी *f.* झांज *f.*

DIZZY, *a. giddy.* घेरी-&c. आलेला.

To be or get d. भोवणें *in. con.*डोळे *m.pl.*-कपाळ *n.*फिरणें.

2 *causing giddiness.* घेरी आणणारा, भोवंड आणणारा, &c.

3 *giddy.* See THOUGHTLESS.

To DO, *v. a. perform, act.* करणें.

To be done, *fit, &c. to be done.* करणीय, कर्तव्य, कार्य.

To do carefully, cautiously, mindfully. जपून-संभाळून-&c. करणें.

To do carelessly, indifferently, &c. केलें केलें न केलें न-[केलेंसें करणें.

To do dashingly, grandly, gloriously. गाजवणें, फटकारणें.

To do easily, readily, simply. अनायासें-सहज-चालतां चालतां-जातां जातां-बोलतां बोलतां-&c. करणें.

To do over again. उलटणें, आवृत्ति *f.* करणें *g. of o.*

To do roughly, rudely, coarsely. झोडणें, झोडपणें, भरडणें.

To do smartly, energetically, overpoweringly. फटकारणें, दपटणें, रपाटणें, झपाटणें, रगडणें, सपाटणें, दामटणें.

To do with effort or toil. उरापोटावर उचलणें, उरीं पोटीं करणें, जिवावर करणें, संकटानें-जुलुमानें,-&c. करणें.

2 *transact, execute,* v. To MANAGE. करणें, चालवणें, आचरणें, निर्वाह *m.* करणें *g. of o.*

To have to do with. गांठ *f.*-प्रसंग *m.* असणें *in. con.*

3 *achieve, &c.* v. To ACCOMPLISH. साधणें, संपादणें, घडवणें, उरकणें.

4 *execute & bring to a conclusion,* v. To ACCOMPLISH. करणें, उरकणें, उरक *or* उरका *m.* उरकणें *g. of o.* शेवटास-&c. नेणें.

5 away ; v. To REMOVE. निष्कृति *f.* करणें *g. of o.*

6 with ; *use,* v. To EMPLOY. कामास-उपयोगास लावणें.

Do in the imperative as an emphatic word is represented by च, as घाई करच *do make haste.*

To DO, *v. n. act commonly,* v. To BEHAVE. आचरणें, चालणें, वागणें, वर्त्तणें.

2 *be with respect to health, &c. fare.* असणें (as तुम्ही कसे आहां How do you do?). वर्त्तमान *n.*-प्रकृति *f.*-&c. असणें (as तुमचें वर्त्तमान कसें काय आहे ? &c.).

3 *succeed, serve,* v. To ANSWER. चालणें, उपयोगीं पडणें, कामास येणें-पडणें.

We-&c. can do without it-&c. त्यावांचून खोळंबा नाहीं, तें नसलेंतरी चालेल.

We-&c. cant do without it-&c. त्यावांचून गतिनाहीं-चालायाचें नाहीं-अडेल- खोळंबा होईल.

DOCIBLE, DOCILE, *a. teachable, tractable, ductile,* v. OBEDIENT. सुशिक्ष्य, सुशिक्षणीय, सुशास्य, सुशासनीय, सुखशिक्ष्य-शिक्षणीय-शास्य-&c. शिक्षानुवर्त्ती, सुखनियम्य, प्रणेय, सुशिष्य, शिष्ट, सुबोध, गरीब, सालस, कह्यांत राहणारा-राहायाजोगा.

DOCILITY, *n.* v. A. सुशिक्ष्यता *f.* सुशास्यता *f.* प्रणेयत्व *n.*&c. शिष्टता *f.* गरिबी *f.* सालसपणा *m.*

DOCK, *n.* (for ships). गोद *f.* गोदी *f.*

2 *tail-stump.* लांडेशेंपूट *n.* लंडपुच्छ *n.* लंडपुच्छमूल *n.*

3 *place where a criminal stands in court.* कोर्तांत कैदी उभा राहण्याची जागा *f.* पिंजरा *m.*

DOCK, *n. rumex vesicarius.* लोलिका *f.*

To DOCK, *v. a. cut off the tail.* लांडा-लंड-&c. करणें, कापणें, छेदणें, लंडपुच्छ-&c. करणें.

2 (an account) कापणें, कमीकरणें.

DOCKED, *p.* v. V. 1.—tail, &c. लांडा केलेला, लंड *pop.* लांडा, मुंढा.—the animal. लंडपुच्छ, छिन्नपुच्छ.

DOCKET, *n. bill tied to goods.* अंकपट्टी *f.* बीजक *n.*

2 *abstract statement.* गोष्वारा *or* गोश्वारा*m.*

DOCK-YARD, *n.*गोद *f.* गोदी *f.*

DOCTOR, *n. learned man.* शास्त्री*m.* आचार्य*m.* पंडित *m.* To this word, as prefixed to the names of learned men, agree, आचार्य, शास्त्री, as *affixed* ; as राघवाचार्य, गंगाधरशास्त्री.

2 v. PHYSICIAN. वैद्य *m.* चिकित्सक*m.*

A fig for the d. when cured. गरज सरो वैद्य मरो.

To DOCTOR, *v. a.* v. To PHYSIC. औषध *n.* देणें, औषधोपचार*m.* करणें.

DOCTRINAL, *a. containing or relating to doctrine.* शिक्षेचा, शिक्षासंबंधी, शिक्षाविषयक, मततत्वविषयक, मततत्वसंबंधी, मततत्वप्रतिपादक.

DOCTRINE, *n.* शिक्षा *f.* मत *n.* मततत्व *n.* उपदेश *m.*

Traditional d. संप्रदाय*m.*

2 See KNOWLEDGE.

DOCUMENT, *n.*—in law; *a written evidence.* सड *or* सडी *f.* दाखला *m.* साधनपत्र*n.*—compreh. or gener. दस्तऐवज*m.* लेख*m.* लिखापढा*m.* लेखपढा*m.* लेखपत्र*n.* लेखप्रमाण*n.* लेखपूस *f. or* लिखापुसा*m.*

D. of doubtful meaning or authority. संदिग्धलेख्य*n.*

Forged d. कपटलेख्य*n.* कूटलेख्य*n.*

DOCUMENTAL, DOCUMENTARY, *a.* v. N. लेखप्रमाणाचा, लेखाचा, लेख्यप्रमाणसंबंधी-विषयक-&c.

DODDER, *n.* आकाशवल्ली *f. pop.* आकाशवेल *f.*

DODECAGON, *n.* द्वादशास्त्र*n.*

To DODGE, *v. n. shift place by a sudden start.* दचकूनसरणें, [दचकणें.

2 *play fast & loose.* धरसोड *f.* करणें.

To DODGE, *v. a. evade by a sudden shift of place.* एकेकडे सरून-आंग चोरून-&c. चुकावणें.

DODGE, *n.* v. TRICK, फट *f.* फटवण *f.*

DOE, *n.* हरिणी *pop.* हरणी *or* हरण *f.* मृगी *f.*

DOER, *n.* DOING, *p. a.* v. V. A. 1. करणारा, कर्त्ता, करी (in comp. and in the wide sense of *worker, laborer, dealer* or *occupant in*, as यात्रेकरी,मारेकरी,शेतकरी, भाडेकरी, कापडकरी, भिक्षेकरी, इटेकरी, पट्टेकरी), कर, कारी, कारक, (these three in comp. as *doing good, &c.* हितकर, गुणकारी,*doing or making light, ease, &c.* प्रकाशकर, सुखकर, and आनंदकर, कल्याणकर, कफकारी, पित्तकारी, वातकारी, क्षयकारी, वृद्धिकारी, शांतिकारक, पुष्टिकारक, रोगकारक, शोककारक, तृषाकारक),वाला(in comp. as बोलणेवाला, देणेवाला), वाईक(in comp. as आस्थेवाईक &c.).

To DOFF, *v. a. put off.* काढणें, उतरणें.

DOG, *n.* कुतराm. (राm. रीf. रेंn.)श्वानm.n(शुनीf.)कुक्कुरm. (कुक्कुरी *f. and pop.* कुकरm. n.)श्वाm. ग्रामसिंहm. Some sounds uttered in calling a d. are कुलुलु, यू.

Every d. has his day. चार दिवस सासूचे चार दिवस सुनेचे.

Give a d. a bad name and hang it. एकदां कानफाटी नाम (or बदू नाम *or* बदनाम) पडलें, म्हणजे बाईटच.

Like d. and cat,—agreeing, &c. इळा आणि भोंपळा.

To go to the dogs. चुलींत जाणें, मसनांत जाणें.

To DOG, *v. a. follow closely, indefatigably, &c.* पाठ *f.* घेणें-पुरवणें *g. of o.* पाठलागm. करणें, दुमाल्यावर असणें, पाठीस लागणें, हुंगून पाठीस लागणें *g. of o.*

DOG-CHEAP, *a.* मातीच्या मोलाचा, कवडीच्या मोलाचा.

DOG-DAY, *n.* ज्यादिवसांत लुब्धक ताऱ्याचा उदयास्त सूर्या बरोबर होतो त्यांतला एक दिवस.

DOG-LATIN, *n. gibberish.* पिशाचभाषा *f.* राक्षसीभाषा *f.*

DOG-LOUSE, *n.* गोचीडm. *f. dim.* गोचडी *or* गोचिडी *f.*

DOG-ROSE, *n.* रानगुलाबm.

DOG-SLEEP, *n. wakeful sleep.* कुतऱ्याची झोंप *f.* जागृतनिद्रा *f.* श्वाननिद्रा *f.* सावधझोंप *f.*

DOG-STAR, *n.* लुब्धकm. लुब्धकताराm.

DOG-TOOTH, *n.* सुळाm. सुळादांतm.

DOG-TROT, *n.* कुतरचाल *f.*

DOGGED, *a.* v. SULLEN. कुरठा, कुचर, कुचरस्वभावाचा, घुणा.

DOGGEDLY, *adv. with obstinate resolution.* हटकून, हटूनतटून, हट्ट धरून, दुराग्रहपूर्वक. [दांडकमनn.

DOGGEDNESS, *n.* v. A. कुरठेपणाm. कुचरपणाm. कुचरस्वभावm.

DOGGEREL, *n.* हलकीकविता *f.* अधमकाव्यn.

DOGGISH, *a. snappish,churlish,* v. CROSS. तुसडा, तिडका,खेंकडा.

DOGGISHNESS, *n.* v. A. तुसडेपणा *m.* तिडकेपणा *m.* &c.

DOGMA, *n. principle, tenet.* मतबीजn. मततत्वn. मूलवाक्यn.

DOGMATIC, DOGMATICAL, *a. positive and overbearing in opinion.* मताभिमानी, मतवादी, हठवादी, मताग्रही.

DOGMATISM, *n.* मताभिमान *m.* मतवादm. मताग्रहm. हटवादm.

DOGMATIST, *n.* See DOGMATIC.

To DOGMATIZE, *v. n.* अभिमानानें-&c. मत *n.* सांगणें-देणें.

DOING, *n.* v. V.A. 1.—*act.* करणें *n.* करणी *f.* कृति *f.* करण *n.*(in comp. as *making separate*, पृथक्करण, and निर्मलीकरण, पवित्रीकरण, शुद्धीकरण, व्यक्तीकरण, स्पष्टीकरण), कर्तृत्वn. कर्तव्यn.

At one d. *at one handling, in one act.* एकामी *or* में, एका दमानें, एका अवसानानें, एका हातासरसा. [चेष्टितn.

Doings; *acts, transactions,* v. DEEDS. कृत्यें *n.pl.* चरित्रn.

The doings of the LORD. ईश्वरी करणी *f.* केशव करणी *f.*

DOLE, TO DOLE. See SHARE, TO DISTRIBUTE.

DOLEFUL, DOLESOME, *a. sorrowful,* v. SAD.—persons. रडका, रडकुंडा, रडवा, उतरल्या तोंडाचा,काळ्या तोंडाचा, म्लान, विषण्ण,

D. countenance. रोतीसुरत *f.* रडकें तोंड *n.* रडकी मुद्रा *f.*

2—tidings, &c. v. DOLORIFIC. शोकाचा, शोकावह, शोकप्रद.

3 *dismal.* See DREARY.

DOLEFULNESS, DOLESOMENESS, *n.* v. A. 1. रडकेपणा *m.* रडवेपणा *m.* &c. उतरलेलें तोंड *n.* रडवेंतोंड *n.* रडकेंतोंड *n.*

DOLL, *n. puppet.* पुतळी *f.* खुंटबावली *f.* बाहुली *f.* पुत्रिका *f.*

DOLLAR, *n.* स्पेनदेशांतील व अमेरिकाखंडांतील एक नाणें आहे त्याची किंमत सुमारें सवा दोन रुपयांची आहे.

DOLOR. See GRIEF, PAIN.

DOLORIFIC, *a.* v. AFFLICTIVE. दुःखाचा, शोकावह, शोकप्रद, शोकद, दुःखद, दुःखप्रद, दुःखदायक, शोककारक-जनक-हेतुक, खेदकारक-जनक &c.

DOLOROUS. See DOLEFUL.

DOLPHIN, *n.* शिशुमार *m.*

DOLT, *n. blockhead, &c.* v. FOOL. मूर्ख *c.* दगड *c.* धोंडा *c.* टोणपा *m.* (टोणपी *f.*) ढुम्या *m.* (ढुमी *f.*). नंदी *m.* नंदीपुत्र *m.* शहाण्याची खरबड *f.*

DOLTISH. See STUPID.

DOMAIN, *n. dominion, possession, estate.* राज्य *n.* अधिकाराखालचा देश *m.* वतनीजमीन *f.* स्वसत्ताक्रांत देश *m.* [स *m.*

DOME, *n. cupola.* घुमट *m. dim.* घुमटी *f.* घटाटोप *m.* डेरा *m.* कळ-

DOMESTIC, *n.* v. SERVANT. घरांतला-घरचा-&c. चाकर *m.*-चाकरीण *f.*-कामकरीm.-कामकरीण *f.* घरकाम्या *or* घरकाम्या चाकर *m.* गृहभृत्य *m.* गृहकिंकर *m.*

DOMESTIC, *a. belonging to the house.* घरचा, घरांतला, गृह्य, गृहसंबंधी, गृह in comp.

D. duties. गृहकर्म *n.* गृहकृत्य *n.* गृहकार्य *n.*

D. squabbling. गृहकलह *m.* गृहभेद *m.* यादवी *f.*

2 *not wild.* घरपोशा, ग्राम्य, घर in comp. ग्राम in comp. घरसंबईचा, पाळलेला, पाळींव.

3 *produced or made at home.* घरचा, घरांतला, घरगुती, घराऊ.

4 *belonging to one's own country, not foreign.* मुलकी *or* स्वी, देशी, देशीय, अविदेशीय, अविदेशज.

5 *fond of home.* गृहप्रिय, घर सोडून बाहेर न जाणारा, घरीं बसण्यास सुख मानणारा, गृहासक्त, गृहलंपट, गृहनिमग्न.

To DOMESTICATE, *v. a. tame, accustom to the house.* घर संवईचा-घरसोंकील-घरसंवक्या-माणसळा-&c. करणें, माणसळवणें, घरची सवई लावणें.

DOMESTICATED, *p.* v. V. माणसळवलेला, &c. पाळींव, घर सोंकील, घर संवक्या, घर संबईचा, माणसळा.

DOMICILE. See RESIDENCE.

DOMINANT. See PREDOMINANT.

To DOMINATE. See To RULE.

DOMINATION. See DOMINION.

To DOMINEER, *v. n. lord it haughtily.* कडक अमल *m.*-जलाल अमल *m.*-करडा अमल *m.* करणें-चालवणें, करडी कमाण *f.* चालवणें, जलाली *f.* करणें, पाणी *n.* जाळण, चामचे दाम *m. pl.* चालवणें, सत्ता *f.* करणें, गर्वानें सत्ता *f.* करणें.

DOMINEERING, *a. disposed to bully, &c.* v. OVERBEARING. उद्धत *pop.* उद्धट, शेखीमिरवणारा, आपला झेंडा मिरवणारा, प्रभुसम्मित.

DOMINICAL, *a.* प्रभूचा दिवस-म्हणजे आदितवार-दाखविणारा.

DOMINION, *n.* v. RULE. राज्य *n.* आधिपत्य *n.* ऐश्वर्य *n.* अमल *m.*

2 v. KINGDOM, COUNTRY. राज्य *n.* राष्ट्र *n.* देश *m.* अधिकारासालचा देश *m.* स्वसत्ताक्रांतदेश *m.*

To DON, *v. a. put on.* घालणें, आंगावर घेणें.

DONATION, *n. act of giving.* देणें *n.* दान *n.* [स्वीस *n.*

2 *thing given, grant,* v. GIFT. दान *n.* दाय *m.* देणगी *f.* बक्षीस *n.*

DONATIVE, See GIFT.

DONE, *p.* v. V. 1. केलेला, कृत.

To have done with. *cease to have concern with, withdraw from.* नांव *n.* सोडणें, नांव न घेणें, नांवानें पाणी *n.* सोडणें *g. of o. with all.*

DONKEY. See ASS.

DONOR, *n.* v. GIVER. देणारा, दाता, दानकर्त्ता.

DON'T. नको (नका *pl.*) उंहुं.

DOODLE, *n. simpleton.* भोळानाथ *m.*

DOOLY, *n. litter for sick persons.* डोली *f.* दोला *m. dim.* दोली *f.*

DOOLY-BEARER, *n.* डोलीवाला, डोलकर, भोई.

To DOOM, *v. a.* v. TO CONDEMN, TO SENTENCE. शिक्षा *f.*-शासन *n.*-&c. सांगणें, शिक्षेचा-&c. हुकूम *m.*-आज्ञा *f.*-&c. सांगणें-देणें, शिक्षेस सांगणें, दंडनास नेमणें-देणें.

2 See TO DESTINE.

DOOM, DOOMING, *n.* v. V. 1.—*act.* शिक्षा सांगणें *n.* शिक्षेस सांगणें *n.* दंडनास नेमणें *n.* &c.

1. *sentence.* शिक्षेचा-&c. हुकूम *m.*-आज्ञा *f.*

DOOMSDAY, *n.* जगाच्या न्यायाचा दिवस *m.*

DOOR, *n.* दार *n.* दरवाजा *m.* द्वार *n.* कवाड *n.* कपाट *n.* प्रतीहार *m.*

At, in, to, &c. every d. दारोदार, घरोघर. [दारें *n.*

Back d. परसदार *or* परूसदार *n.* मागीलदार*n.*—of a jakes.

From d. to d. दारोदार, घरोघर. [दार *n.*

Front d. पुढला दरवाजा *m.*उजदार *n.*दर्शनी दरवाजा*m.*पुढील-

In doors. घरीं, आंत.

Leaf or fold of a d. झडप *f.* तलफ *f.n.*द्वारशाखा *f.* कपाट*n.*

Open d. *freeness of access, &c.* मुक्तद्वार *n.*

Out of doors. घराबाहेर, दाराबाहेर, बाहेर.

Secret or private d. चोरदार *n.* चोरदरवाजा *m.*

Shelf or plank over a d. दारशीक *n.*

Shutting up of doors. दारफळण्या *f. pl. or* दारफळणी *f.*

Tenon-slip across a d. नागोस *or* सा *m.* बाटेरपट्टी *f.*

To dance attendance from d. to d. लोकांचीं घरें *or* दारें *n. pl.* पुजणें, द्वारपूजा *f.* करणें.

To lay at the d. of. गळीं *or* गळां बांधणें *g. of o.* माथां *or* माथीं मारणें *g. of o.*

To shew the d. (दुसऱ्याचें) घर *n.* दाखवणें.

DOOR-CASE, DOOR-FRAME, *n.* चौकट *f.*

Cross-piece of a d.—under or upper. उंबरा *m.* उंबऱ्या *m.* उंबरठा *m.* दारबठा *m.*—under. खालचा उंबरा *m.*—upper. वरचा उंबरा *m.* कपाळपट्टी *f.* मस्तकपट्टी *f.*

Jamb of a d. दारकस *f.*

Ornamental slip of wood over a door or window frame. दर्शनपट्टी *f.* दर्शनी पट्टी*f.* [देवडीवाला.

DOOR-KEEPER, *n.* दरवाजकरी, द्वारपाल, दरबान, द्वारी, द्वारस्थ,

DOOR-POST, *n.* बाही *f.* दारकस *f.* सुलका *m.* द्वारस्तंभ *m.*

Tenon of a d. दारकुसूं *n.* कुसूं *n.* [द्वार *n.*

DOOR-WAY, *n.* दार *n.* दरवाजा *m.* दारठण *n. f.* दारबठा *or* बटा *m.*

DORMANT, *a. not in action.* निजलेला, झोंपीं गेलेला, निद्रित, अनुद्भूत, गुप्त, अप्रकट. [गार*n.*

DORMITORY, *n. sleeping room.* शेजघर *n.* शयनालय *n.* शयनागार *n.*

DORSAL, *a. pertaining to the back.* पाठीचा, पाठचा, पृष्ठ्य, पृष्ठसंबंधी.

DOSE, *n.* मोताद *f.* रकम *f.* मात्रा *f.* औषधपरिमाण *n.*

To DOSE. See TO PHYSIC. [*n.* शून्य *n.*

DOT, *n.* पूज *n.* बिंदु *m. dim.* बिंदुकली *f.* बिंदुकलें *n.* बिंदलें *n.* टिंब

To DOT, *v. a.* पूज *n.*-शून्य *n.*-&c. देणें-मांडणें-&c.

DOTAGE, *n. imbecility of mind from old age.* म्हातारचळ *m.*चळ *m.* साठी *f.* साठीबुद्धि *f.* पिसें *n.* बाळें *n.* तारें *n.*

To be getting into one's d. साठळणें.

DOTAL, *a. of or belonging to a dower.* स्त्रीधनसंबंधी-विषयक, यौतकसंबंधी-विषयक.

DOTARD, *n. person in dotage.* म्हातारचळ्या, साठ्या, साठ्याबुद्धीचा, म्हातारबुद्धीचा, पाऊण म्हातारी *f.* भळू *m.* नष्टबुद्धि, नष्टेंद्रिय.

To DOTE, *v. n.* (through age, &c.). बाळेणें, खुळावणें, विकळणें, म्हातारचाळे *m. pl.*-म्हातारचेष्टा *f.* करणें, म्हातारचळ *m.* लागणें *in. con.*

2 *be in love to extremity.* भुलणें, भुलून जाणें, वेडा होणें, तन्मय-तल्लीन-मोहित-अत्यासक्त-&c. होणें.

DOTER, *n.* DOTING, *p. a.* v. V. 1. *and* DOTARD. खुळावलेला, &c. नष्टबुद्धि, नष्टेंद्रिय.

2 भुलून गेलेला, निरत, अन्यासक्त, तन्मय झालेला, &c.

DOTINGLY, *adv. by excessive fondness.* भुलून, वेडा होऊन,अत्यासक्तीनें, &c.

DOTTED, *a. diversified with small detached objects.* मध्येंमध्यें बिंदू प्रमाणें पदार्थ मांडलेला. [*pl.*

DOUBGRASS, *n.* bent grass; *cynodon dactylon.* हरळी *f.* दूर्वा *f.*

DOUBLE, *a. composed of two.* जोडगिरी, जोडगीर, जुळा, जोड (in comp. as जोडनळी a double barrel.)

D.-fruit. जोडफळ *n.* फळाचें जुळें *n. or* जूळ *n.*

D. thing-gener. जूळ *n.* जुळें *n.*

2 *twice as much.* दुपट *or* दुप्पट, दुणा, दुरा, द्विगुण.

D. work or trouble. दुणेंकाम *n.* दुहेरें काम.

3 *two in number, two fold, &c.* दुहेरा, दुहेरी, द्विरूप, द्व्यात्मक, द्विप्रकारक, द्विविध, दु in comp.

4—a letter. (ex. क्क, ग्ग, च्च) द्वित्त.

5 *folded,* v. DOUBLED. दुहेरी, दुहेरा, दुहिरी, दुडना, दुडती.

6 See DECEITFUL.

DOUBLE, *n.* दुपट *or* दुप्पट *f.* दुपटी *f.* दुणी *f.*

2 v. FOLD. घडी *f.* पदर *m.*

3 *thing doubled over.* दुंडा *m.* दुटें *n.* दुट्टा *m.*

4 *artful turn,* v. ARTIFICE. पेंच *m.* डाव *m.*

5 *a turn in running.* बांकण *n.* बळण *n.*

To DOUBLE, *v. a. make twice as much.* दुणणें, दुपट-&c. करणें.

2 *fold over,* v. TO FOLD. दुणणें, दुमटणें *or* दुमडणें, दुंतणें, दुणाविणें, मोडणें.

3 (a cape, a point) बळसा *m.* घालणें, बळसाघेऊन जाणें.

To DOUBLE, *v. n.* दुपट-द्विगुणित-&c. होणें, दुणावणें, दुणारणें.

2 *turn back or wind.* बांकण *n.* घेणें, बांकणानें जाणें.

3 over, under, back, &c. मुरडणें *or* मुरुडणें.

4 up;— as through age. गठडी *f.* खुरमुंडी *f.* होणें *g. of s.*

Double-barrelled, *a.* दुनळी, दुबारी, जोडनळीचा.

Double-dealer, *n.* **Double-dealing**, *a.* v. **Deceitful.** दुधड, द्विजिह्व, दुतोंड्या, दुबोल्या, दुरंगी, दुटप्पी, मनांत एक जनांत एक. [णूक *f.*-&c.

Double-dealing, *n.* दुटप्पी व्यवहार *m.*-व्यापार *m.*-चाल *f.*-वर्त्त-

Double-entendre, *n. a word or expression with a double meaning.* दुरोखी *or* दुटप्पी बोलणें *n.*-भाषण *n.*-वाक्य *n.*-&c. वक्रोक्ति *f.* श्लेष *m.* द्व्यर्थ *m.*

Double-entry, *n.* दुहिरी वहिवाट *f.*

D. book. दुहिरी वहिवाट वही *f.*

Double-faced, *a.* v. **Deceitful.** दुरोखी, दुतोंड्या, दुधड, उभयतोमुख, उभयपक्षीं समान, उभयसाधारण, उभयसामान्य, उभयविध.

Double-minded, *a. unsettled, wavering.* दोन मनांचा, फुटक्या मनाचा, द्विमनस्क, द्विमना.

Double-natured, *a.* द्विस्वभाव, द्विधातुक, उभयविध.

Double-tongued, *a.* द्विजिह्व, अनेकजिह्व.

2—a padlock. दुकांटी.

3 See **Deceitful.**

Doubled, *p.* v.V. A. 1. दुप्पट केलेला, &c. द्विगुणित, द्विगुणीकृत. 2 दुघडी, दुणता, दुमता, दुडता *or* ती, दुहेरा *or* री, दुहिरी, दुरा, मुरडींव.

Doublet, *n. inner garment of a man.* बंडी *or* आंतली बंडी *f.*

Doubleness. See **Duplicity.**

Doubling, *n. duplicature,* v. **Fold.** दुमड *f.* दूण *f.* मोड *f.*

2 (in a rope or string) *curl, loop.* तिढा *m.* तिडा *m.* तीड *f.* मेढा *m.*

3 *edge doubled over.* मुरूड *or* मुरड *f.*

4 *artful turn.* पेच *m.* डाव *m.*

Doubloon, *n.* स्पेन आणि पोर्तुगाल ह्या देशांतील एक नाणें आहे.

Doubly, *adv.* v. A. दुप्पट, द्विगुण, द्विगुणित, दुपटीनें.

Doubt, *n. uncertainty of mind.* संशय *m.* संदेह *m.* शंका *f.* आशंका *f.* किंतू *m.* दुग्धा *f.* भ्रम *pop.* भरम *m.* भ्रांति *f.* वचमा *m.* कल्पना *f.* बानवा *f. m.* कांक्षा *f.* कल्प *pop.* कलप *m.* कलाफ *m.* विकल्प *m.* अंदेशा *m.* अविश्वास *m.* अप्रत्यय *m.*

Of solved or removed d. छिन्नसंशय.

Solution of d. संशयनिवृत्ति *f.*

2 *a* d. *a questioned point.* संशय *m.* किंतू *m.* आकांक्षा *f.* कांक्षा *f.* शंकास्पद *n.* कलाफ *m.*बुचकळा *or* बुचकुळा *m.*

To **Doubt**, *v. a. withhold assent or confidence from; to question, distrust, &c.* संशय *m.*-संदेह *m.*-शंका *f.*-अंदेशा *m.*-&c. धरणें-बाळगणें-घेणें-मानणें *g. of o.* संशय *m.*-शंका *f.*-भ्रांति *f.*-&c. असणें-येणें *g.of o. in. con.* अविश्वास*m.*-अप्रत्यय*m.*करणें-ठेवणें.

To **Doubt**, *v. n. be in suspense, &c.* शंकणें, आशंकणें, भ्रांति *f.*-संदेह *m.*-संशय *m.*-बानवा *m. f.*-&c. असणें-वाटणें *in. con.* साशंक-सशंक-शंकित-&c. असणें.

Doubted, *p.* v. V. A. शंकित, आशंकित, संदिग्ध.

Doubtful, *a. that doubts.* साशंक, सशंक, शंकित, आशंकित, संशययुक्त, संशयापन्न, संशयग्रस्त, शंकाग्रस्त, सांशयिक, भ्रांत, शंकी, संकुचित, संकोचित, जातसंशय, जातशंक, प्राप्तसंशय.

2 *disposed to doubt, ever doubting.* संशयी, संदेही, संशयालु, संशयापन्नमानस, शंकाशील, भ्रांत्या, भ्रांतिष्ट, भ्रांतिखोर, संशयखोर, भ्रांतहृदय, भ्रमिष्ट, भ्रमी, संदिग्धमति, कांक्षी, शंकी, दिक्कती, दिक्कतखोर.

3 *questionable, uncertain, ambiguous, &c.* संशयाचा, संदेहाचा, भ्रांतीचा, &c. संदिग्ध, संशययुक्त, संशयात्मक, सांशयिक, संशयित, संशयस्थ, संशयापन्न, विकल्पात्मक, शंकनीय, भ्रांतिकर, भ्रांतिकट, भ्रांतिवट, भ्रांतवट, मुग्ध, मुग्धा *a. ind.* वैकल्पिक.

To leave d. संशय *m.* ठेवणें *g. of o.*

Doubtfully, **Doubtingly**, *adv.* v. A. 1. संशयानें, दुग्धा, संधेवीं, सशंक, संशय-&c. पूर्वक, शंकेनें, दुग्धेनें.

3 अत्रप *or* ब, अळमटळम, मुग्ध, मुग्धा, अभोगत, अरळ, उभारत.

Doubtfulness, *n.* v. A. 1. *and* **Doubt.** संशय *m.* संदेह *m.* शंका *f.* भ्रांति *f.* दुग्धा *f.* संशययुक्तता *f.* &c.

3 भ्रांतिवटपणा *m.* &c. संदिग्धता *f.* विकल्प *m.* अत्र *n.* अत्रप *n.* अळमटळम *n. f.* अळमटाळ *or* ळी *f.* संशयितपणा *m.*

Doubtless, *adv.* v. **Certainly.** निस्संशय, निस्संदिग्ध, निस्संदेह, निश्चयपूर्वक.

Douceur, *n.* v. **Gift.** बक्षीस *n.* पारितोषिक *n.*

Dough, *n.* मळलेलें पीठ *n.* तिंबलेली कणीक *f.*

Ball of d. thrown into the fire to be baked. संकर *m.*

D. rolled in a leaf and baked. पानगा *m. dim.* पानगी *f.*

Lump of kneaded d. उंडा *m. dim.* उंडी *f.* बोटी *f.*

Puffed mass of d. baked on embers. रोट *m.* रोटगा *m.*

Doughtily, *adv.* v. A. मर्दीनें, शौर्यपूर्वक.

Doughtiness, *n.* v. A. मर्दी *f.* शहामत *f.* प्रतापशालिता *f.*

Doughty, *a. brave, illustrious, &c.* v. **Bold.** गाढा, मर्दा, बहादर, प्रतापशाली. [न.

Doughy, *a.* पिठाळ, पिठूळ, पिठा, पिठ्या, गिचगिचीत *or* गिजगिजी-

To be d.—bread. पिठाळणें *or* पिठुळणें.

To **Douse**, *v. a. plunge into.* डुबकन-कर-दिशी-&c. बुडविणें-घालणें.

Dove, *n.* खबुतर *or* कबुतर *n.* कपोत *m.*

Dove-colored, *a.* खबुतराच्या रंगाचा.

Dove-cot, **Dove-house.** *n.* खबुतरखाना *m.* खुबडी *f.* खुराडें *n.* खुडी *f.* खुडें *n.* धाबळ *f.* कपोतपालिका *f.*

Dove-tail, *n.*—in carpentry, &c. चाळा *m.* कळासी *f.*

To **Dove-tail**, *v. a.* कळासी *f.* जोडणें.

Dow, *n. a particular kind of boat.* डाव *m.* [आहे.

Dowager, *n.* मरण पावलेल्या मोठ्या मनुष्याचे विधवेचा किताब

Dowdy, *n.* नेभळीस्त्री *f.* मुग्धम्मा *f.* जोगम्मा *f.*

Dower, **Dowry**, *n. a woman's wedding portion or jointure.* स्त्रीधन *n.* अंदण *n.* यौतक *n.* स्त्रीभरणधन *n.* स्त्रीदाय *n.*

2 See **Jointure.** 3 *price paid for a bride.* देज *n.* मुलीचा-पैसा *m.* कन्याशुल्क *n.*

Dowlas, *n.* जाड कापडाचा एक भेद आहे.

Down, *n. soft feathers.* लव *or* लंव *f.* मृदुलोम *n.*

Bed of d. *fig.* सुखशेज *f.* सुखशय्या *f.* सुखासन *n.*

2 (of plants). कापूस *m.*

3 *soft wool, hair, &c.* लोंहकर *or* लोंकर *f.* लव *or* लंव *f.* कापूस *m.* फूल *n.*

4 *open plain.* माळ *m.* माळजमीन *f.* माळरान *n.* मैदान *n.*

Down, **Downwards**, *adv. & prep.* खालीं, खालतां *or* तीं *or* तें, अधः (esp. in comp, as अधःपतन, अधःपात, &c.), हेट, अवाक्.

2 *on its mouth, belly, &c.* उपडा, पालथा, थपी.

Downcast, *a. dejected,* v. **Dispirited.** अधोमुख, अधोवदन, अधोदृष्टि, अवाङ्मुख, अवाग्वदन, नम्रमुख, दीनमुख, दीनवदन,

म्लानवदन.

Downfal, *n.* v. **Disgrace**. स्थानभ्रंश *m.* स्थानच्युति *f.* पदच्युति *f.* अधिकारच्युति *f.* अधःपात *m.*

Down-hearted, *a.* v. **Dispirited**. उदास, बेदिल, गतोत्साह.

Down hill, *a.* v. **Declivous**. उतरता, उतरवट.

Down hill, *n.* v. **Declivity**. उतरण *f.* उतरड *f.*

Downright, *a. direct, tending straight.* नीट, धोपट, धोपटमार्गाचा, सरल *or* ळ, वक्रभावरहित-शून्य.

2 *unceremonious, &c.* v. **Blunt**. धोपटमार्ग्या, धोपटमार्गाचा, सरपूस, ससलसीत.

3 See **Arrant**.

Downright, *adv. outright, plump,* v. **Bluntly**. धडधडीत, स्पष्ट, साफ, धादांत, धड.

2 *completely.* निस्तूक, धडधडीत, धड.

Down-ward, *a. tending downwards.* खालचा, खालीं जाण्याचा, अधोगामी, अधःप्रवण.

Downy, *a.* लवेचा, लोंहकरीचा, लोंहकर भरलेला.

2 See **Soft**.

Dowry. See **Dower**.

Dowse. See **Slap**.

Doxology, *n.* v. **Praise**. स्तुतिवाद *m.* स्तुतिपाठ *m.*

To **Doze**, *v. n. sleep lightly.* डुकली *or* डुलकी *f.* घेणें, डुकल्या *f. pl.* घेणें-देणें, डुकली *f.*-गुंगी *f.* येणें *in. con.* डोळ्यांचें कडू *n.* मोडणें, डोळा *m.* लागणें *with g. of s.* डोळे *m. pl.* करंजावणें.

Doze, *n. light sleep.* डुकली *or* डुलकी *f.* हलकी झोंप *f.* अल्पनिद्रा *f.*

Dozen, *n.* बारा, द्वादशक *n.* दोन छकड्या *f. pl.*

D. of years. तप *n.*

Dozen. *a.* बारा, द्वादश.

Dozing, *a.* v. **Sleepy**. डुलकीखोर, झोप्या.

Dozy, &c. See **Sleepy**, &c.

Drab, See **Harlot**. 2 See **Jade**.

Drab, *n.* मळ्या रंगाचें कापड आहे.

Dracunculus, *n guinea-worm.* नारू *m.* दोरा *m.*

Draff, *n.* v. **Refuse**. गबाळ *m. n.* गाळ *m.* गाळा *m.* गदळ *m.n.*

Draffish, **Draffy**. See **Worthless**.

Draft, *n. bill of exchange,* v. **Bill**. हुंडी *f.* हुंडीचिट्ठी *f.*

D. on Aldgate Pump. झोकचिट्ठी *f.* वाऱ्यावर चिट्ठी *f.*

2 See **Draught**.

To **Drag**, *v. a.* v. To **Draw**. ओढणें, फरपट *f.* काढणें, खेंचून ओढणें, अवकर्षण *n.* करणें.

2 (*along, through, over, roughly, &c.*). घसकावणें, फरफरावणें, फरफरिवणें, खरखरावणें, खरडीतओढणें, घसटून-रगडून-खसकावून-&c. ओढणें.

To **Drag**, *v. n. move along on the ground.* फरपटणें, फरपटत-फरपट्यां *adv.* जाणें-चालणें, रखडणें. [रखडणें.

2 *proceed heavily.* रडतरडत *or* रडतखडत *adv.* जाणें-चालणें,

Drag, *n. matter to be dragged.* ओढ *f.*

Track of a d. ओढ *f.* फरपटा *m.* फरपट *f.*

2 v. **Harrow**. कुळव *n.*

3 (of a cart, &c.) *thing to retard progress.* ढकली *f.*

4 गाडीचा एक प्रकार आहे.

Drag-cart. ओढावण *or* णें *n.*

Drag-hook, *n.* गळ *m.*

Drag-net, *n.* महाजाळें *n.* नीर *m.* पाग *m.*

Drag-rope, *n.* ओढ *f.* ओढण *f.* नाडा *m.*

To **Draggle**, *v. a. dirty by drawing on the ground, &c.* लोळवणें, लोंघळावणें, लोळसावणें, लोळवून-&c. मळविणें.

To **Draggle**, *v. n. trail on the ground, in the mud, &c.* लोळणें, लोंघळणें, लोळून-&c. मळणें.

Draggle-tail. v. **Slattern**, **Slut**. लगताळा *or* ळ्या.

Dragoman, *n.* v. **Interpreter**. तरजुमान *m.*

Dragon, *n.* एक कल्पित सपक्ष सर्प आहे.

Dragons blood, *n.* धातुकमृगरक्त *n.*

Dragoon, *n. horse-musketeer.* करोल *m.*

To **Drain**, *v. a. draw off gradually.* निथळणें, निथळून काढणें, निचरून काढणें, काढतां काढतां काढणें.

2 *empty by gradually drawing off the contents.* निथळून कोरडा-&c. करणें.

3 (grouud,). पाट *m*-पळ *f.*-पळवा *m.*-&c. काढणें *or* काढून कोरडा करणें.

4 See To **Filter**.

5 *empty,* v. To **Exhaust**. रिकामा-रिता-कोरडा-&c करणें.

To **Drain**, *v. n. flow off gradually.* निथळणें, निचरणें.

Drain, *n. water course, channel, &c.* नाला *m.* मोरी *f.* पाट *m.* पळ *f.* पळवा *m.* सारणी *f.* प्रणाली *f.* प्राणालिका *f.* नरांडी *f.* जलमार्ग *m.* जलनिर्गम *m.*

Drainer, *n.* (for boiled rice, vegetables, &c.). वेळणी *f.* शिबें *n.*

Drake, *n.* बदकाचा नर *m.* बदक *m.* हंस *m.* कलहंस *m.*

Dram, *n. draught of spirituous liquor.* दारूचा घोंट *m.*-घुटका *m.*

Dram-drinker, *n.* v. **Sot**. दारूबाज *c.* [जिका *f.*

Dram-shop, *n.* दारूचें दुकान *n.* पिठा *m.* पानगोष्ठिका *f.* गंजा *f.* गं-

Drama, *n.* नाटक *n.* रूपक *n.* Style of dramatic representation or composition. वृत्ति *f.* There are four, viz. कौशिकी, भारती, सात्वती, आरभटी. Certain species or varieties of the *drama* are ळीत, भाण, संगीत, समवकार, प्रहसन, डिम, व्यायोग, &c.

Course or arrangement of a d. नाटकप्रपंच *m.*

Denouement of a d. कार्य *n.*

Dramatic recitation. भारती *f.*

Dramatis personæ पात्रें *n. pl.*

Phraseology of the d. नाट्योक्ति *f.*

Religious d. ळीत *n.*

Science (rules and laws) of the d. नाट्य *n.* नाट्यधार्मिक *n.* भरतशास्त्र *n.*

Dramatic, *a.* v. N. नाटकाचा, नाटकी, नाटकीय, नाटकसंबंधी, नाटकविषयक, अभिनयविषयक, अभिनेय.

Dramatist, *n.* नाटककवि, नाटकग्रंथकार. [क्या.

Draper, *n. seller of cloth.* कापडकरी, चाटी *or* चाट्या, कापडवि-

Drapery, *n. cloth-work.* कापड काम *n.*

2 *cloth, &c.* कापडीमाल *m.* कापडी जिन्नस *m.*

3 *dress of a picture.* पैहराव *or* वा *m.* (चित्राचा)

Drastic, *a. powerful, violent,*—a medicine. जलाल, कडक, जबर.

Draught, *n.* See **Drinking**.

2 *quantity drunk at once.* घोट *m.* घुटका *m.*

3 v. **Drawing**. ओढणें *n.*

Beast of d. वाहीम खांद्याचा (बैल &c.)

4 *sketch*, v. DELINEATION. बेत *m.* नकशा *m.*

Rough d. अराखडा *m.* बेनबात *m.* मसुदा *m.*

5 (of a ship). बूड *f.* ओंड *f.*

6 *bill of exchange*, v. BILL. हुंडी *f.* हुंडीचिट्ठी *f.*

7 *drawing force or power*. ओढ *f.* ओढण *f.*

8 *current of air*. वाऱ्याची धार *f.* वाऱ्याचा नेट *m.* वाऱ्याची धांव *f.*

In a d. बारेघशीं, वाऱ्याचे धारेवर-नेटावर, &c. वाऱ्यावर.

9 draughts. सोंकट्या *f. pl.* चौपट *f.* चौसार *m.* चौसारखेळ *m.*

Materials at d. (pieces, board, dice, &c.). सारंगपाट *m.* सारीपाट *m.*

Player at d. सोंकटीबाज.

Piece or man at d. सोंकटी *f.* सोंकटें *n.* सार *f.* सारी *f.*

10 (of fishes.) एका खेपेस जाळ्यांत धरलेले मासे *m. pl.*

DRAUGHT-ANIMAL, *n.* खांद्याचा बैल *m.*-घोडा *m*-&c. वाहीम *n.*

DRAUGHT-BOARD, *n.* पट *m. f.* चौपट *f.*

DRAUGHTSMAN, *n.* नकाशा काढणारा *m.*

DRAUGHTY, *a.* वाऱ्याच्या धारेचा.

To DRAW, *v. a. drag, pull along.* ओढणें, ओढून-खेंचून-&c. नेणें-घेणें, आकर्षणें, कर्षणें, आकर्षण *n.*-कर्षण *n.* करणें *g. of o.*

That draws well—a bullock, &c. ओढीक.

2 *cause to flow from.* काढणें, सोडणें, बाहविणें, स्राव *m.* करणें *g. of o.* धार *f.* पाडणें-काढणें *g. of o.* [निपसणें.

3 (from a scabbard or sheath). काढणें, उपसणें *or* उसपणें,

4 (as with a rope from a well). शेंदणें, शेनणें, काढणें.

Bucket or pail for drawing. शेंदणें *n.*—the rope of it. शेंदवणी *f.*

5 (lines, figures, pictures). अंकणें, काढणें, ओढणें, लिहणें.

6—as a blister, &c. ओढणें. [लाव, घाल.

Application (of leaves or drugs) to d. ओढा *m. v.*

7 out, off, from, &c.—freely. v. To EXTRACT, To EXTRICATE, &c. काढणें, काढून घेणें, निपसणें, उद्धरण *n.*-उद्धार *m.*-&c. करणें *g. of o.*

8 out, up, (a statement, bill, &c.). आकारणें, लिहणें, करणें, घडणें, सजविणें.

9 up, in, together, &c. v. To CONTRACT. अखुडणें *or* अखडणें, आकर्षणें, आवरणें, अटपणें, अटपता घेणें-धरणें, अवटरणें, आवर *m.*-आवरण *n.*-&c. करणें *g. of o.*

10 See To ATTRACT.

To DRAW, *v. n. shrink, &c.* v. To. CONTRACT. अखुडणें *or* अखडणें, ओढणें, अवळणें.

2 *be strained and stiffened,*—the eyes. ताटकळणें, ताठुरणें, ताठणें, टांकळणें *or* टांकुळणें.

3 back; off; out of. पाठीमागें *or* मागें सरणें-फिरणें-घेणें-हटणें, माघार *m f.*-काढ *f.*-काढावा *m.*-माघलट *f.*-मोडती *f.* घेणें, परतणें, काढतें *n.*-निघतें *n.*-मोडतें *n.*-कांकरतें *n.*-&c. घेणें, आंग *n.* काढणें *or* काढून घेणें, बिचल *m. f.* खाणें *or* बिचलणें, कच *f.* खाणें.

That draws back or off. आंग काढ्या, आंग काढू.

4 in; *feel abashed or repressed.* चपापणें, वचकणें, दबणें, कान *m.pl.*-मिशा *f pl.* पाडणें-खाली करणें.

5 off; *go down, subside.* काढणें, उतरणें.

6 on; near, *approach, be close at hand.* जवळ-&c. येणें, भिडणें, नेटणें, लगटणें.

7 up;—the skin, &c. v. To TIGHTEN. अटरणें, अटुरणें *or* अटारणें, अवटरणें, अवटणें, आकसणें.

8 up or in; *contract one's self.* आंग *n.* मारणें *or* चोरणें.

DRAW-BACK, *n. allowance.* सूट *f.* सोडलेला पैका *m.*

2—fig. *deduction from benefit.* बाण *f.* उणीव *f.* व्यंग *n.*

DRAW-BRIDGE, *n.* काढायाचा घालायाचा पूल *m.*

DRAW-WELL, *n.* मोटेचीविहीर *f.*

Apparatus,—collect. over a d. बडव *f.* बडवण *f.*

Basin or receiver of a d. थारोळें *or* थारळें *n.* उरोटा *m.* वाफा *m.*

Bucket of a d. मोट *f.*

Cistern of a d. थारोळें *n.*

Ground watered from a d. मोटस्थळ *n.* मोटस्थळजमीन *f.*

Inclined plane of a d. धांव *f.* ओढव *f.* सारणी *f.* चारी *f.*

Inclined posts of a d. सुळके *m. pl.*—Cross-piece connecting them. कपाळपट्टी *f.*

Rings of a bucket of a d. लाकणें *n. pl.*

Rope of a d. नाडा *m.*

Rope attached to the nose of a bucket of a d. सोंडदोर *or* रा *m.* सोंडसोल *m.*

Side-pieces upon which rests and revolves the कणा or pin. कणेच्या बाहुल्या *f.pl. or* बाहुलीं *n.pl.* बुटल्या *f. pl.*

Wheel of a d. चाक *n.* गाडी *f.*—Axle or pin of the wheel. चाकदांडा *m.* कणा *m.*

DRAWER, *n.* v. V.A. 1. ओढणारा, &c. आकर्षक, कर्षक, आकर्षण कर्ता-कारक, &c.

2 काढणारा, सोडणारा, &c.

3 अंकणारा, &c. चितारी, चित्रकार.

I. (as of a purse, &c.) *draw-string.* ओढदोरा *m.* मंदोरा *m.*

II. *box in a case.* खण *m.* खाना *m.* घर *n.* पड *m.* पूड *n.* ओढखण *m.*

Secret d. चोरखण *m.* चोरघर *n.*

III. drawers.—long. इजार *f.* पायजामा *m.*—short. चोळणा *m.*

DRAWING, *n.* v. V. A. 1.—*act.* ओढणें *n.* &c. आकर्षण *n.* कर्षण *n.*

3—*act.* काढणें *n.* &c. उपसणी *f.* उसपणी *f.*

5—*act.* अंकणें *n.* काढणें *n.* अंकणी *f.*

6—*act.* ओढणें *n.* ओढा *m.* [अवकर्षण *n.*

7—*act.* काढणें *n.* &c. उद्धरण *n.* उद्धार *m.* समुद्धरण *n.* समुद्धार *m.*

9—*act.* आकर्षणें *n.* आवरणें *n.* &c. आवर *m.* आवरण *n.* अटाप *m.* आकर्षण *n.* आकुंचन *n.* उपसंहार *m.*

I. *a* d. *a draught, picture, &c.* नकशा *m.* नकाशा *m.* लिपी *f.* चित्र *n.* आलेख्य *n.*

DRAWINGROOM, *n. room for company.* बैटकीची जागा *f.* रंगमहाल *m.* आरसमहाल *m.* सभामंदिर *n.* दिवाणखाना *m.* सदर *f.*

To DRAWL, *v. n. utter in a slow way.* रेंगत-लांबत-ओढत-&c. बोलणें, ओढूनबोलणें, विल्हळणें, हेल काढून वाचणें-बोलणें-&c.

DRAWL, DRAWLING, *n.* v. V.—*act.* रेंगत बोलणें *n.* विल्हळ *or* विल्हाळ *m.* दीर्घोच्चारण *n.* द्राविडप्राणायाम *m.*

DRAWLER, *n.* DRAWLING, *p. a.* v. V. रेंगत-&c. बोलणारा-वाचणारा, ओढूनबोलणारा, विल्हळ्या, तोंडचाजड.

DRAWN, *p.* v.V.1. ओढलेला, &c. आकर्षित, कर्षित, आकृष्ट, अवकृष्ट.

DRAY, *n.* सामानाची गाडी *f.* छकडा *m.*

DREAD, *n.* v. FEAR. धास्त *f.* धास्ती *f.* हैबत *f.* दहशत *f.* खता *or* खंता *f.* जरब *f.*

DREAD, *a.* See FRIGHTFUL, AWFUL.

To DREAD, *v. a.* v. To FEAR. भिणें, धास्त *f.*-धास्ती *f.*-दहशत *f.*-धाक *m.*-&c. बाळगणें-खाणें-धरणें-घेणें *g. of o.* धास्त *f.*-धाक *m.*-&c. बसणें *g. of o. with in. con.*

DREAD-NOUGHT, *n. a desperado, &c.* v. MADCAP. निर्धास्त, अकुतोभय, संदातटू *m.* उफराट्या काळजाचा, उलट्या काळजाचा, साहसकर्मा.

DREADFUL, *a. terrible,* v. FEARFUL. अकटोविकट, अकराळविकराळ, भेंसूर, भयानक, भयंकर, भैरव, घोर, दारुण, भैम.
2 See SINFUL.

DREADFULLY. See FEARFULLY.

DREADFULNESS, *n.* v. A. 1. भेंसूरपणा*m.* भयानकत्व *n.* दारुणत्व*n.*

DREADLESS, *a. intrepid,* v. FEARLESS. निर्भय, भयरहित-हीन, निर्धास्त. [भयानुभव*m.*

DREAM, DREAMING, *n.* स्वप्न*m. n.* स्वप्नावस्था *f.* दर्शन *n.* निद्रावि-
Bad (inauspicious, &c.) d. दुःस्वप्न *m. n.* दुष्टस्वप्न *m. n.*
Creation of dreams, *the illusory world of Morpheus.* स्वप्नसृष्टि *f.* स्वप्नप्रपंच *m.*
Interpretation of dreams. स्वप्नविचार *m.*
Interpreter of dreams. स्वप्नविचारी.
Like a d. स्वप्नवत्.
State of dreaming. स्वप्नावस्था *f.*

To DREAM, *v. n.* स्वप्न *m. n.* पाहणें, स्वप्न *n. m.* पडणें-होणें *in. con.*
2 *think, imagine.* ध्यानीं मनीं-मनीं मानसीं-स्वप्नीं विचारीं-स्वप्नांत-&c. असणें *in. con.*

To DREAM, *v. a.* स्वप्नांत पाहणें, स्वप्न *n. m.* पाहणें *g. of o.* [*con.*
To d. a dream. स्वप्न *n. m.* पाहणें, स्वप्न *n. m.* पडणें-होणें *in.*
2 away; *waste in idle thoughts.* रिकाम्याविचरांत-मनोरथ करून-&c. घालविणें.

DREAMER, DREAMY. See VISIONARY.

DREAR, DREARY, *a. gloomy, dismal,*—of places. उदास, उदासवाणा *or* णी, भयाण *or* न, भणभणीत, रुखा, रुक्ष, रखरखीत, भडंगळ, शून्याकार, शून्य *pop.* सुना.

DREARINESS, *n.* v.A. उदासपणा*m.* भणभणीतपणा *m.* &c. भयाण *or* न *n.* रखरखाट *m.* रौक्ष्य *n.*

DREDGE, *n.* See DRAG-NET. 2 नदींतला गाळ काढण्याकरितां केलेलें आकर्षण यंत्र *n.* [करणें.

To DREDGE, *v. a.* आकर्षण यंत्रानें गाळ *m.* काढणें *or* काढून खोल

DREGGISH, DREGGY, *a.* v. N. रेंद्याचा, गाद्याचा, &c. रेंदाड, गढूळ, गदळ.

DREGS, *n. lees, grounds, sediment.* गाळ*m.* गाळसाळ *m.* गदळ *n.* रेंदा*m.* रेंदगड *n.* रेंदड *or* रेंदाड *n.* मल *m.n.* मळ *m.* सांका *m.*सांसा*m.* सांसारा *m.* किट्ट*n.* [निपटारा*m.*
D. of society, v. PEOPLE. लोकांचा गाळ, लोकांचें गदळ,

To DRENCH, *v. a. soak, wet thoroughly.* चिंब *or* चिम्म-चिबचिबीत *or* चुबचुबीत *or* चपचपीत-थबथबीत-चीप *or* चींब ओलाचिंब-समीज *adv.* भिजवणें-करणें, उपळवणें.
2 (cattle, &c.). पाजणें, घोट्यानें पाजणें.

DRENCH, *n. physic for a brute.* घोट्यानें-घोट्यानें पाजायाचें औषध*n.*- जुलाब *m.*

DRENCH-HORN, *n.* घोटें *n.* घोटें *n.* नाड*n.* नाडा *m.*

DRENCHED, *p.* v. V. 1. चिंब-चिबचिबीत-थबथबीत-&c. भिजवलेला-भिजलेला केलेला, ओलाचिंब.

To DRESS, *v. a. clothe, attire.* वस्त्र*n.*-वस्त्रें*n.pl.* नेसवणें-पांघरविणें-लेवविणें, पांघरूण*n.* घालणें, परिधान*n.* करविणें, सवस्त्र-वस्त्रविशिष्ट-सचेल-वेषान्वित-&c. करणें.—finely पोशाक *m.* करणें.
2 *set to rights, trim.* ओजवणें, सुधारणें, निटावणें, नीट करणें, उस्तवारी *f.* करणें *g. of o.*
3 *prepare by labor.* कमावणें, मशागत *f.*-मरामत *f.*-कमाई *f.*-कमाविशी *f.*-कमावीस *f.*-संस्कार*m.*-परिष्कार *m.*-&c. करणें *g. of o.* तयारकरणें.
4 (a wound, limb, &c.) धुऊन साफ करून मलमपट्टी *f.*करणें.
5 *prepare victuals,* v. To COOK. स्वयंपाक *pop.* सैंपाक *m.* करणें *g. of o.* सिद्ध करणें.
6 (ground) *manure, &c.* कारवणें, कमावणें, तयार करणें.
7—in the military art. सारखावणें, सारखा-&c. करणें,सुधारणें.
8 up, out. v. To ADORN. सजवणें, सज्जित-सज्ज-&c. करणें.

To DRESS, *v. n. put on one's clothes,* v. To PUT ON. वस्त्र *n.* नेसणें-लेणें, पांघरूण *n.* घेणें-लेणें, वस्त्रपरिधान *n.* करणें, कपडे *m. pl.* करणें.
To d. finely. नटणें.
To be dressed out. बनींबनणें.
To d. sluttishly. आडवें नेसणें *or* लावून घेणें.
2—soldiers. सारखा-नीट-&c. होणें.

DRESS, *n. apparel, garments, &c.* v. CLOTHES. वस्त्र *n. or* वस्त्रें *n. pl.* पांघरुणें *n. pl.*
D. of honor presented. खिलात *f.*
Full-d. दरबारी पोशाक *m.*
2 *habit, garb, costume.* वेष *m.* भेश *or* भेष *or* भेस *m.* पेहराव *m.* पेहरावा *m.* लिभास *m.*
3 See GOWN.

DRESSED, *p.* v. V. N. वस्त्र-&c. नेसलेला, ल्यालेला, पांघुरलेला, सवस्त्र, वस्त्रयुक्त, सचैल.

DRESSER, *n.* v. V. A. 1. वस्त्र नेसवणारा, पांघरूण घालणारा, &c.
2 सुधारणारा, &c.
3 कमावणारा, &c. मशागत-कमाई-&c. करणारा.
I. See TABLE.

DRESSING, *n.* v. V. A. 1.—*act.* वस्त्र-&c. नेसवणें *n.* &c.
2—*act.* ओजवणें *n.* सुधारणें *n.* &c. ओज *f.* [गत *f.*
3—*act.* कमावणें *n.* &c. कमाई *f.* कमाविशी *f.* कमावीस *f.* मशा-
5—*act.* स्वयंपाक *pop.* सैंपाक *m.* पाक *m.* पाकक्रिया *f.*
6—*act.* कारवणें *n.* कमावणें *n.* &c. मरामत *f.* [रण *n.*
v. V. N. 1.—*act.* नेसणें *n.* वस्त्रपरिधान *n.* परिधान *n.* वस्त्रधा-
I. *manure spread.* पसरलेलें खत *n.*

DRESSING-ROOM, *n.* पांघरूण घेण्याची खोली *f.*वस्त्र नेसण्याची खोली *f.* वस्त्रपरिधानालय *n.*

DRESSY, *a. fond of dress.* पोशाकाचा हौशा-आवडता-&c. लिभासी.

To DRIBBLE, *v. n. fall in drops.* ठिपकणें *or* ठिबकणें, टबकणें, टपटप-थेंबथेंब-&c. पडणें-गळणें.
2 See To DRIVEL. [ळणें.

To DRIBBLE, *v. a. throw down in drops.* थेंबथेंब-&c. पाडणें-गा-

DRIBLET, *n.* लहानरकम *f.*
To pay in driblets. अधेल्या दमडीनें-दमडी अधेल्यानें-अधेल्यापैशानें-पैशाटक्क्यानें-&c. फेडणें-देणें-&c.

DRIED, *p.* v. V. A. 1. वाळवलेला, सुखवलेला, &c. शुष्क-&c. केलेला
2 शोषलेला, शोखलेला, शोषित.
v. V. N. वाळलेला, सुखलेला, &c.

Utterly d. up—tank, well, river, &c. कोरडाटांक, कोरडाठणक, कोरडाठणठणीत.
4 वाळका, वाळकुंजा, वाळकुडा.
D. up, parched, &c.—country, soil. रखरखीत.
DRIFT, *n. thing driven along.* लोंढा *m.* लोट *m.*
D. of dust. वावधूळ *f.*
D. of rain or spray. वावझड *f.*
2 *forceful current.* ओढ *f.* ओढा *m.* वाहवटळ *f.*
3 *tendency of action, speech, &c.* v. MEANING. ओढ *f.* ओढा *m.* प्रवाह *m.* ओघ *m.* रोख *m.* झोंक *m.* गम *m.* कटाक्ष *m.* धोरण *n.*
To DRIFT, *v. n. float along.* वाहवणें, ओघाबरोबर वाहून जाणें, लोंढ्यासरसा वाहून जाणें, प्रवाहपतित होणें.
2 *be driven into heaps.* वाऱ्याच्या जोरानें वाहून जाऊन ढीग *n.*-रास *f.*-&c. होणें.
To DRIFT, *v. a.* वाहून नेऊन ढीग *m.*-रास *f.*-&c. करणें *g. of o.*
To DRILL, *v. a. perforate, bore,* v. To PIERCE. भोंक *n.* पाडणें, विंधणें, वेधणें.
2—in the military art. कवाईत *or* कवाईद *f.* शिकवणें, व्यूहशिक्षा *f.* करणें, सैन्यविन्यास *m.* शिकवणें.
DRILL, *n.* v. AUGER. सामता *m.* वेधन *n.* बरमा *m.*
2 *military exercise.* कवाईत *or* कवाईद *f.*
DRILL-PLOUGH, *n.* v. PLOUGH. पाभर *f.*
D. of two tubes. मोघड *m. f. n.* मोघण *n. f.*
D. of three tubes. तिफण *f. or* तिफणी *f. or* तिफणें *n.*
Tube or channel of a d. फण *m.*
Seed-box of a d. चाडें *or* चाढें *n.*
To DRINK, *v. a.* पिणें, पिऊन घेणें, प्राशन *n.*-पान *n.* करणें, प्राशणें.
To d. eagerly and largely. घोटणें, घोटा *m.* लावणें, ढसासणें, ढसासून पिणें.
To give to d. पाजणें.
To d. off. एका खेपेनें पिणें, पिऊन टाकणें.
To d. up. निःशेष पिणें.
To DRINK, *v. n.* पिणें.
2 *be a drunkard.* दारू पिण्याची सवई *f.* असणें *in. con.* दारूबाज-निशाबाज-&c. असणें.
DRINK, *n.* प्यायाचें *n.* पिण्याचापदार्थ *m.* पेय *n.* पानीय *n.*
Acidulated or cooling d. पन्हें *n.* शर्बत *n.* पानक *n.* Some are शिकंजी *f.* चिंचवणी *n.* &c.
DRINK-MONEY, *n.* पोस्त *n.*
DRINKABLE, *a.* v. V. A. प्याया-चा-जोगता-&c. पेय, पानीय, प्राशनीय, प्राशनार्ह, पानयोग्य.
DRINKABLE, *n.* v. DRINK. पिण्याचा पदार्थ *m.*
DRINKER, *n.* v. V. A. पिणारा, प्राशनकर्त्ता, प्राशक, पानी (in comp. as मद्यपानी, मधुपानी, क्षीरपानी), पी (in comp. as मद्यपी), प (in comp. as मधुप, रक्तप, द्विप).
DRINKING, *n.* v. V. A. पिणें *n.* प्राशन *n.* पान *n.* (esp. in comp. as अमृतपान, मधुपान, रसपान, सुरापान, क्षीरपान, मद्यपान).
I. *practice of drinking to excess.* दारू पिण्याची सवई *f.*
To DRIP, *v. n. fall in drops.* टपकणें, ठिपकणें, ठिबकणें, थबथबणें, गळणें, पाघळणें, स्रवणें.
2 *have a liquid falling from it in drops.* टपकणें, ठिपकणें, ठिबकणें, थबथबणें.
DRIP, DRIPPING, *n.* v. V. 1.—*act.* टपकणें *n.* &c. ठिबकणी *f.* टपकणी *f.* ठिपकणी *f.* गळ *f.* गळती *f.* टपका *m.* स्राव *m.* स्रव *m.* स्रवण *n.* श्राव *m.*
I. *matter dripping.* गळ *f.* गळती *f.*
Drippings (from a tree, &c.) after a shower. उधळे *or* ओथळे *m. pl.*
DRIP-STONE, *n. filter.* गळती *f.* जलशोधक यंत्र *n.*
DRIPPING, *p. a.* v. V. टपकणारा, &c. स्रावी & स्रावक (in comp. as जलस्रावी, रक्तस्रावी, दुग्धस्रावी, मधुस्रावी).
D.-wet. ओलाचिंब, थबथबीत, चपचपीत *or* चबचबीत *or* चिबचिबीत, चीप *or* चीब. [णें-होणें.
To be d. चपचपणें, चबचबणें, चिबचिबणें, सभीज *adv.* भिज-
DRIPPINGLY, *adv.* थबथब *intens.* थबाथब *or* बां, टपटप *or* पां *intens.* टपाटप *or* पां, ठिपठिप *or* ठपठप *or* पां, चिबचिब *or* बां.
To DRIVE, *v. a. force along.* दवडणें, दपटणें, दामटणें, लाटणें, लोटणें, रगडणें, रपाटणें, ढकलणें, लाटालाटीनें दपटणें.
2 *force in,* v. To STUFF. खोवणें, खोसणें, ठासणें, खोंचणें, खोंचरणें, भोकसणें *or* भोसकणें, शिरकवणें *or* शिरकावणें, दपटणें *or* दपटून शिरवणें-भरणें-&c. संचारणें.
3 *force in by hammering or beating.* मारणें, ठापरणें, दपटणें, ठोकून रोवणें.
4 *force away, from, off, &c.* हाकणें *or* हांकणें, हाकलणें, हाकून-हाकलून देणें, दवडणें, पिटून लावणें, धुडावणें, दुदावणें, छुकू *or* शुक्रू *interj.* करणें *or* म्हणणें, हुंडारणें, घालवणें, घालवून देणें, सारणें, पिटाळणें, पिटाळणी *f.* करणें *g. of o.*
Particular words or interjections are used in *driving away or off.* Those used—to a beast, gener. हत्त, हुडुत्त.—to a cat. छुकू, छुतू *or* शुकू & शुतू, शिरू.—to birds, हुश्श *or* हुस्स.—to crows, &c. हड्या.—to a dog, हड, हडहड, हडि.
5 (a flock, a beast, &c.). हाकणें *or* हांकणें, हाकून नेणें, हाकवणें, पेलणें.
Particular words or interjections are used in *driving on.* Those used—to a horse or bullock are, इयां, इयांइयां.—to an elephant, धकधक, धगधग, धगेधगे *or* दगेदगे, धा.—to cattle, थेक, हैक, हड.—to fowls, खुड.—to sheep or goats, तिरू *or* थिरू.—pigs, डू.
6 (a vehicle). हाकणें *or* हांकणें, चालवणें.
7 (a trade, a bargain, &c.). हाकणें *or* हांकणें, वाहणें.
8 *urge or impel vehemently.* दवडणें, दपटणें, दामटणें, ढकलणें, पिटाळणें, पिटणें, हकालणें, पिटाळणी *f.* करणें, पेलणें.
9 *take in a carriage.* गाडींत-&c. घेऊन नेणें.
To DRIVE, *v. n. be impelled along.* ओढवणें. [*g. of s.*
2 *aim at or tend to.* ओढ *f.*-ओढा *m.*-धोरण *n.*-&c. असणें *with*
3 *go in a carriage.* गाडींत-&c. बसून जाणें. [जाणें *n.*
DRIVE, *n. an excursion in a carriage.* गाडींत बसून फिरणें *n.*-
2 गाडींत बसून जाण्याचा रस्ता *m.*
DRIVEL, *n.* v. SLAVER. लाळ *f.*
To DRIVEL, *v. n. slaver.* लाळणें, बरबरणें, लाळ *f.* गळणें *g. of s.* लाळ *f.* गाळणें-टाकणें.
2 See To DOTE.
DRIVELLER, *n.* DRIVELLING, *p. a.* v. V. 1. लाळ गाळणारा, &c. लाळ्या, लाळगाळ्या.
2 See DOTARD.
DRIVELLING, *n.* साठी *f.* म्हातारचाळे *m. pl.* म्हातारचळ *m.*

Driven, *p.* v. V. A. 1. दवडलेला, दपटलेला, &c.
2 सोसलेला, ठासलेला, &c.
3 मारलेला, ठोकून रोवलेला, &c.
4 हाकललेला, हाकून दिल्हेला, सारित, निस्सारित.

Driver, *n.* v. V. A. 1. दवडणारा, दपटणारा, लाटणारा, &c.
2 सोबणारा, ठासणारा, &c.
3 हाकणारा, गुरेंहाक्या.
4 *and* Coachman. हांकणारा, गाडीवान, धुरकरी *or* धुरेकरी.

To **Drizzle**, *v. n. rain in small drops.* शितोडणें *or* सितोडणें, पुसारणें, पाऊस *m.*-धुईधुई *f.* येणें, कोंडा पाऊस *m.* पडणें, रिपरीप *f.*-&c. लावणें-लागणें.

Drizzle, *n. small rain.* बुरबूर *f.* बुरंगट *n.* बुरंगें *n.* तुसार *or* तुसारा *m.* तुषार *m.* पावसाचा कोंडा *m.* कोंडा *m.* कोंडा पाऊस *m.*

Drizzling, *n.* v. V.—*act.* मुळमूळ *f.* मिरमीर *f.* रिपरीष *f.* तुषारपात *m.*

Drizzlingly, *adv.* शिरिशिरि, झिरिमिरि, थुईथुई, थिवथिव.

Drizzly, *a.* v. N. बुरबुरीचा, तुसाऱ्याचा.

Droll, *a. odd, comical, facetious,*—of persons. मस्कऱ्या, विनोदी, कौतुक्या, मौज्या, मौजाळा.
2—of things, &c. मौजेचा, कौतुकाचा, तमाशाचा, चमत्काराचा, हसव्या, हास्यजनक.

Droll, *n.* See Buffoon.

Drollery, *n. buffoonery.* मस्करी *f.* थट्टामस्करी *f.*

Dromedary, *n.* v. Camel. एकमदारी उंट *m.* उंट *m.*

Drone, *n.* मधमाशीचानर *m.* मधुमक्षिकानर *m.*
2 For this word in the sense of *an unproductive and burdensome consumer* there are numerous words and phrases. These differ from one another in aspect and reference and exact implication; but they sufficiently convey the general sense just given. घांसखाऊ, तुकडमोड्या, भाकरमोड्या, जेवतागण, ऋणाईत, ऋणकरी, ऋणदार, ऋणाईतरूपी, फुकटखाऊ, फुकट्या, पोटपोशा, आइतोजी, आइतोबा, आयतगब्बू, भोजनभाऊ, भोजन्या, मेजबान, अजगर *or* अजगरवृत्तीचा, आयत्या पिठावर रेघ ओढणारा. There are also some smart proverbs or sayings descriptive of and reprehensive of this character. कन्हतो कुंथतो मलिद्याला उठतो, धणगायाला पाहिजे चांगले दोन शेराचें आणि काम नको करायाला काडीचें, जेवायाला आधीं निजायाला मध्यें कामाला कधीं मधीं, तोबऱ्याला पुढें लगामाला पाठीमागें, खायास काळ घरणीस भार.
3 *hum.* गुणगुण *f.* घुमटा *m.* नाद *m.* नकी *f.*

Dronish. See Lazy.

To **Droop**, *v. n. languish, faint.* गळणें, खचणें, बातडणें, उफटणें, करपणें, मोडणें, बसणें, बळमोड *f. m.* होणें *g. of s.* ग्लान-म्लान--गलित-&c. होणें, ग्लानि *f.*-म्लानि *f.*-&c. येणें *in. con.*
2 *hang the head.* मान *f.* टाकणें, मान *f.* मोडणें-पडणें *g. of s.*

Drop, *n.* थेंब *m.* बिंदु *m.* बुंद *m.* थेंबका *m.* थेंबटा *m.* थेंबडा *m.* टपका *or* ठपका *m.* ठिपका *m.* [थब *or* थां.
By drops; *drop! drop!* ठपटप *or* पां *or* ठपठप *or* पां, थब-
2 (of a sprinkling, spurtling, splashing, of spray, &c.). शिंट *f.* शिटा *m.* शितोडा *m.* छाटा *m.*
3 (of an ornament) *pendant.* चमकी *f.* चमक *f.* लोलक *m.*
4 (of a gallows, &c.) पडतीफळी *f.* पाडलायेईल अशी केलेली फळी *f.*

To **Drop**, *v. a. pour in drops.* थेंब *m.*-बुंद *m.*-ठिपके *m. pl.*-&c. पाडणें-टाकणें-गाळणें, टपटप-थबथब-थेंबथेंब—&c. पाडणें-टाकणें, गाळणें.
2 *let fall.* सांडणें, पाडणें, पाडवणें, सोडणें, टाकणें, पडूंदेणें.
A thing dropped and lost. सांड *n.*
3 v. To Lose. गमावणें, गफलतणें, गलफटणें, सांडणें.
4 *let go, give up, lose regard or care for.* सांडणें, सोडणें, सोडून देणें, गाळणें, टाकणें, नांव*n.*-वार्त्ता *f.*-बाजपूस *f.*-&c. सोडणें *g. of o.* सांड *f.* करणें.
To d. out of mind or memory. सांडणीस टाकणें-घालणें.
5 *omit, leave out.* सोडणें *n.* गाळणें, खाणें.

To **Drop**, *v. n. fall in drops.* टपकणें, ठिपकणें, टिबकणें, गळणें, टपटप-थबथब-थेंबथेंब-&c. पडणें.
2 *fall.* पडणें, गळणें, गलन *n.*-स्खलन*n.*-विस्रंसन*n.* होणें *g. of s.*
To be ready to d. (from fatigue or faintness).पडोपडो साह्णें. [&c. होणें.
3 *cease, come to nothing.* राहणें, पडणें, विरणें, बितुळणें, तकूब-
4 in; *come unexpectedly.* अवचित-अकस्मात्-&c. येणें.
To d. in regularly and constantly. ठेवला-नेमका-टाकला येणें, दत्त म्हणून येणें.

Dropped, *p.* v. V. N. 2. पडलेला, गळालेला, गळींब, गलित विगलित, च्युत, स्रस्त, स्खलित.

Dropping, *n.* v. V. A. 1.—*act.* गाळणें *n.* टपटप पाडणें*n.*
2—*act.* सांडणें*n.* &c. सांड *f.* सांडणूक *f.* सांडणी *f.* गालन *n.*
3—*act.* सांडणें *n.* गमावणें*n.* &c. सांड *f.* सांडणूक *f.* सांडणी *f.*
4—*act.* सांडणें *n.* गाळणें *n.* &c. सांड *f.* सांडणी *f.* सांडणूक *f.* गाळण *f.*
5—*act.* गाळणें *n.* &c. गाळण *f.* [टिबकणी *f.*
v. V. N. 1. टपकणें *n.* गळणें *n.* &c. टपकणी *f.* ठिपकणी *f.*
2 पडणें *n.* गलन *n.* पतन*n.* स्खलन *n.* विस्रंसन *n.*
I. *matter falling in drops.* गळ *f.* गळती *f.*

Dropsical, *a.* v. N. उदरी, उदररोगी, उदररोगाचा, उदररोगसंबंधी.

Dropsy, *n.* उदररोग*m.* उदर *n.* उदरी *f.* Some of the distinctions or varieties are उदकोदर *or* जलोदर, वातोदर, मत्स्योदर, प्लीहोदर, सर्पोदर, रक्तोदर, बद्धगुदोदर, पित्तोदर, कफोदर, त्रिदोषोदर, क्षतोदर.

Dross, *n. recrement of metals.* मल *m. n. pop.* मळ*m.* किट्ट *pop.* कीट *n.* किटण *n.* कलंक *m.* जळ*m. f.*
2 See Rust.
3 v. Dregs. Refuse. गाळ *m.* रेंदाड *n.* किट्ट *n.*

Drossy, *a.* v. N. 1. मलयुक्त, मलविशिष्ट, किट्टयुक्त.
3 See Dreggy.

Drought, *n. want of rain.* सुकवें*n.* सुकवा*m.* अनावृष्टि *f.* अवृष्टि *f.* अवर्षण *n.* जलशोष *m.* अवग्रह*m.*
Crop destroyed by d. सुकवें*n.*
Time of scarcity from d. खरपड *n. f.* सुका दुकळ*m.*
2 *dryness of throat,* v. Fauces. कोरड *f.* शोष *m.*

Droughty, *a. wanting rain.* निपावशा, सुकव्याचा, अनावृष्टीचा, अवर्षणाचा.

Drove, *n. body of cattle driven.* हेड *f.* तांडा *m.* काफला*m.*

Drover, *n. one who drives cattle to market.* हेड्या.

To **Drown**, *v. a.* बुडविणें, बुडवून मारणें-प्राण*m.* घेणें.

To d. one's self. पाण्यांत घालून घेणें.

2 (one's self)—as an act of religion. जलसमाधि *m.f.* घेणें. [असें करणें.

3 (the voice, &c.) बुडविणें, दबविणें, लोपविणें, ऐकूं न जाई

4 See To DELUGE.

To DROWN, *v. n.* बुडणें, बुडून मरणें, जलमरण*n.*-जलमृत्यु *m.* पावणें.

To struggle (sink and rise, &c.) in drowning. गचकळणें, गचकळ्या *f. pl.* खाणें, गचावणें.

To DROWSE, *v. n. be heavy with sleepiness.* झोपेनें गुंगणें, झोपेनें गुंग-जड-&c. होणें-असणें, गुंगी *f.* येणें.

DROWSILY, *adv.* v. A. गुंगत, सुस्तीनें.

DROWSINESS, *n.* v. A. 1. झोपेची गुंगी *f.*-तार *f.*-खरबी *f.* सुरसुरी *f.* सुस्ती *f.* सुमि *f.* तंद्रा *f.*

DROWSY, *a. heavy with sleepiness*, v. SLEEPY. झोपेची गुंगी आलेला, गुंगलेला, गुंग, निद्राग्रस्त. [ग्या.

2 *habitually inclined to sleep*, v. SLEEPY. झोपाळू, झोप्या, गुं-

3 See STUPID.

DROWSY-HEADED. See HEAVY.

To DRUB, *v. a.* v. To BEAT. कुचलणें, कुटणें, कुदवणें, खुबलणें, कुमलणें, कुमकणें, ठोकणें, कुटण *n.*-&c. काढणें.

DRUBBING, *n.* v. V.—*act.* कुचलणें *n.* &c. कुट्टा *m.* कुटण *n.* कुट्टण *n.* कुटघेल *n.* कुंदी *f.* मारकूट *f.*

To DRUDGE, *v. n.* v. To TOIL. हाडें *n. pl.* झिजवणें, हाडांचीं काडें *n. pl.* करणें, हाडांचे मणी *m. pl.* करणें, महारकष्ट *m. pl.*-कबाडकष्ट *m. pl.*-कुत्तेघशी *f.*-&c.करणें, रक्ताचें पाणी *n.* करणें.

DRUDGE, DRUDGER, *n.* v. V. कष्टाळू, कष्टी, कसालती, खप्या, कबाडी *or* ड्या, कबाडकाम्या.

DRUDGERY, *n. hard labor.* कसाला *m.* कसालत *f.* महारकष्ट *m.pl.* कबाडकष्ट *m. pl.* कबाडकाम *n.* कुत्तेघशी *f.* खप *m.*

DRUG, *n. substance used in medicine.* औषधीद्रव्य *n.* औषध *n.* द्रव्य *n.* भेषज *n.*

Drugs. मसाला *m.*

Heating, &c. drugs. गरममसाला *m.*

2 fig. *a commodity of no demand in the market.* सांदोरीस पडलेला माल *m.* पडीतमाल *m.*

To DRUG, *v. a. physic.* औषध *n.* देणें.

2 *tincture with something injurious.* बाधक-अपकारक-विकारकारक-&c.पदार्थ *m.*-द्रव्य *n.* घालणें-मिसळणें.

DRUGGET, *n.* नमदा *m.*

DRUGGIST, *n. seller of drugs.* गांधी, औषधविक्या, पसारी *or* पसाऱ्या, भेषजी.

DRUM, *n.* पडघम *n.* तंबूर *m.* आनक *m.* These three words, though they, in common with the words following, express *kinds* or *sorts*, yet are, preferably to those, to be used in the general sense of *drum.* काळू *m.* खरडी *f.* टिमकी *f.* डंका *m.* डमरु *or* डहूर *or* डौर *m.* ढोल *m. dim.* ढोलक *or* ढोलकी *f.* तबल *m. dim.* तबलक *f.* तबला *m.* ताशा *m.* दमदमा *m.* दमामा *m.* दायरा *m.* पखवाज *m.* मरफा *m.* मांदळा *m.* मृदंग *m.* संबळ *m.*

Brace of a d. माळू *or* माहळू *m.* ओढण *f.* कांकर *m.*

Child's d.—gener. ढमढमें *n.* ढमकें *n. or* ढुमढुमें *n.* ढुमकें*n.*

End or head of a d. पुडा *m.* पूड *n.* तोंडी *f.* नडघें *n.* फेडा *m.*-End which is beaten, वाजता पुडा,-Bass-end, धुमाचापुडा,

Frame of a d. टोपण *n.*

Hour-glass d. डमरु (डहूर *or* डौर) *m.* हुडुक्क *pop.* हुडूक*m.*

Paste applied to the end of a d. शाई *f.*चोहण *or* बोवण*n.*

Roll upon a d. ताशेरा *or* तासेरा *m.*

Swollen as tight as a d.—the belly, v. BELLY. दब्बदबदबीत-दुमदुमीत-टमटमीत-&c. भरलें-झालें.

With drums beating and colors flying, *fig.* धैांशा लावून.

2 (of the ear). कानाचा पडदा *m.*

To DRUM, *v. n.* v. N. 1. पडघम *n.*- तंबूर *m.*-&c. वाजवणें-पिटणें. Numerous formations are in use imitatively expressive of the *sounding* of a Drum. Some of these are दमदम *or* दुमदुम *or* धमधम (dom! dom!); and the verb, दमदमणें *or* दुमदुमणें, and, *intensely*, ढमढम *or* मां, ढमाढम, ढमामा; and the verb, ढमढमणें, ढबढब *or* बां (rub a dub!); and the verb, ढबढबणें *or* ढबढब वाजणें, डिमडिम *or* टिमटिम (tim! tim!—the sound of the *tomtom*), दबदब *or* बदबद (expressive of the flat, dead sound of unbracedness, &c.) and the verbs, दबदबणें, बदबदणें, भदभदणें.

DRUM-STICK, *n.* टिपरूं *or* रें *n.* टिपरी *f.* चोप *f.*

To DRUMBLE, *v. n.* v. To MUDDLE. खंदळणें *or* खंदाळणें.

DRUMMER, *n.* v. V. पडघम-&c. वाजवणारा. The following terms are *particular*, and signify the performers respectively upon the *sorts* of drum, from the names of which they are formed ढोलजी (beater of ढोल), ढोलक्या (beater of ढोलक), तबलजी (beater of तबला), and तंबूरची *or* जी, ताशेकरी *or* तासजी, मरफेकरी, मृदंगी *or* ग्या, पखवाजची *or* जी, संबळ्या, &c.

DRUNK, DRUNKEN, *a. inebriated.* झिंगलेला, मस्त, प्यालेला, दारूचा-&c. कैफ चढलेला, तंबर, छटेला, छाकटा, मत्त, प्रमत्त, पीत, मद्यविव्हल, मद्यग्रस्त, मद्याक्रांत, मद्यवश, तुंद, क्षीब.

Dead d. गुल्ल, लुल्ल, गुंग.

D. pranks. मस्ती *f.*

To be d. झिंगणें, घोड्यावर बसणें, हत्तीवर बसणें, कैफ *m.*-अमल *m.* चढणें-येणें *in. con.* छाकणें. [फी-अमली.

2 *given to liquor.* झिंगा, झिंग्या, मस्ता, मस्त्या, दारूचा-&c. कै-

3—quarrel, acts, &c. कैफांतला, अमलांतला, मदमूलक.

DRUNKARD, *n.* दारूबाज, दारू पिणारा-खाणारा, झिंग्या, झिंगीखोर, मस्ता, मस्त्या, मद्यपी, निशाबाज, अमली.

DRUNKENNESS, *n.* v. A. 1. दारूची नशा *or* निशा *f.* झिंगी *f.* दारूचा-&c. कैफ *m.*-अमल *m.*-तार *f.* मद *m.* [निर्द्रव.

DRY, *a. not moist.* कोरडा, सुका *or* सुका, शुष्क, अनार्द्र, अक्लिन्न,

Stifly d.—a washed cloth. खडक, खडखडीत, चुरचुरीत, सणसणीत, खडंग.

To be or become crisply or stifly d.—cloth, paper, crops, grass, &c. कडकणें, खडंग वाळणें.

2 *not juicy.* सुका *or* सुका *remiss.* सुसट *or* सुकट, शुष्क, नीरस, रसहीन-शून्य-&c, रसातीत, गतरस.

Old & dry—a vegetable. तरडा intens. जूनजून तरडा.

3 *jejune, barren, without pathos, &c.* v. SPIRITLESS. कोरडा, अळणी, रुखा, रूक्ष, बेकस, वाकस, विरस, नीरस.

4—as the hair, *course and stiff.* करडा, रांठ, भरभरीत, निवर.

5—as bread, &c. by itself. कोरडा, सुका *or* सुका, निकळा, नुस्ता *or* निरसा.

6 *unctuous and crumbly.* फुसफुसीत *or* फसफसीत, भसभसीत *or* भुसभुसीन, फळफळीत, भरभरीत.
7—a milch animal. भाकड, अटलेला, उडालेला, बिसका.
To become d. उडणें, अटणें, बिसकणें.
8 *hard, poor, not bland or savory.* रसरसीत, रुखा, रुक्ष.
9 See THIRSTY. 10 *free from rain,&c.* कोरडा, बिनपावसाचा, पर्जन्याभावाचा.
11 See SARCASTIC. [करणें.
To DRY, *v. a.* वाळवणें, सुखवणें *or* सुकवणें, कोरडा-सुखा-शुष्क-&c.
2 up. शोषणें, शोखणें *or* सोखणें, अटवणें.
To DRY, *v. n.* वाळणें, कोरडणें, सुखणें *or* सुकणें, कोरडा-&c. होणें.
Matter (grain, &c.) spread out to d. वाळवण *n.* सुकवण *n.*
2 up. सुखणें, सुखटणें *or* सुकटणें, शोषणें, शोखणें *or* सोखणें, अटणें, कोरडा पडणें, अटणी *f.*-अटणूक *f.* होणें *g. of s.*
3 up; *become meagre,* v. To WASTE. अळणें, अटणें, सुखणें.
4 up; *lose succulence.* सुखटणें *or* सुकटणें, सुखा-&c. होणें, रस *m.* जाणें *g. of s.*
DRY-EYED, *a.* कोरड्या डोळ्यांचा, निरश्रुलोचन.
DRY-LAND, *n.* खुशकी *f.* स्थल *n.*
DRY-NURSE, *n.* आपलें स्तन पाजीत नाहीं अशी जी दाई ती *f.*
DRYAD, *n.* वनदेवी *f.*
DRYAGE, *n.* (of grain, spirits, &c.). वाळवण *n. v.* जा, सुखणावळ *or* सुकणावळ *f.* सुकवण *n.* घट *f.*
DRYING, *n.* v. V. A. 1.—*act.* वाळवणें *n.* सुखा करणें *n.* &c. शुष्की करण *n.*
2—*act.* शोषणें *n.* &c. शोषण *n.* शोष *m.*
DRYNESS, *n.* v. A. 1. कोरडेपणा *m.* सुखेपणा *m.* शुष्कत्व *n.* अनार्द्रता *f.* सुखाडी *f.*
2 सुखेपणा *m.* शुष्कता *f.* रसराहित्य *n.* रसाभाव *m.*
3 कोरडेपणा *m.* रुखेपणा *m.* रुक्षता *f.* रौक्ष्य *n.* नीरसता *f.*
DRYSHOD, *adv. without wetting the feet.* कोरड्या पायांनीं, सुख्या पायांनीं, पाय भिजल्याशिवाय.
DUAL, *a. expressing the number two.* द्विसंख्य, द्विसंख्याक.
DUAL, *n.*—in grammar. द्विवचन *n.*
DUALISM, *n.*—as opposed to Pantheism. भेदवाद *m.* भेदप्रत्यय *m.* भेदबुद्धि *f.* भेददृष्टि *f.* द्वैत *n.* द्वैतवाद *m.* द्वैतमत *n.*
DUALIST, *n.*—as opposed to Pantheist. भेदवादी, द्वैतवादी.
DUALITY, *n. two-ness.* द्वित्व *n.* द्वैगुण्य *n.*
To DUB, *v. a. confer a dignity, &c.* मरातब *f.m.*-किताबत *f.*-पदवी *f.*-&c. देणें, म्हणविणें, करणें.
DUBBER, *n. skin-vessel for oil, ghee, &c.* बुधला *m. or* बुधलें *n. dim.* बुधली *f.* दबडा *or* डबडा *or* डबरा *m. dim.* दबडें *or* डबडें *or* डबरें *n.* डबकें *or* डपकें *n. dim.* डबकी *f.*
DUBIOUS, &c. See DOUBTFUL, &c.
DUCAL, *a.* ड्यूक ह्या पदवीच्या संबंधाचा.
DUCAT, *n.* कितीएक देशांतील एक नाणें आहे.
DUCK, *n.*—tame. बदक *n.*
2—wild. हंस *m.*
3—Muscovy or the Brahmany. चक्रवाक *pop* चकवा *m.*
Ducks and drakes—the play. भाकरीचा खेळ *m.* भाकऱ्या *f. pl.* काकरी *f. pl.*
To make ducks and drakes of money. द्रव्याचे धुडके *m. pl.* उडवणें, चणेफुटाणे *m. pl.* करणें *g. of o.*

4 v. DIP. बुडी *f.* बुडकी *f.*
To DUCK. See To DIP.
DUCK-LEGGED, *a.* आखुड पायांचा, ऱ्हस्वपाद.
DUCKLING, *n.* बदकाचें पिलूं *n.*
DUCT, *n. tube, &c.* नळ *m.* नलिका *f.* वाहिनी *f.*
DUCTILE, *a. capable of expansion.* प्रसारणीय, प्रसारणयोग्य, प्रसरक्षम.
2 *capable of being drawn out.* तारकाढतांयेण्याजोगा, उद्वर्त्तनीय, उद्वर्त्तनयोग्य.
3 See PLIANT.
DUCTILITY, *n.* v. A. 1. प्रसारणयोग्यता *f.* प्रसरक्षमता *f.*
2 उद्वर्त्तनीयता *f.* उद्वर्त्तनक्षमता *f.*
DUDGEON, *n. ill-will, displeasure.* खपीमर्जी *f.* रुसवा *m.* बितुष्ट *n.*
To be in high d. फूं होणें, हटास पेटणें.
DUE, *a. owed.* यायाचा, द्यायाचा, पावायाचा, देय, हक्कहलाल, हक्कहलालाचा.
2 *appropriate, fit,* v. RIGHT. योग्य, यथायोग्य, यथायुक्त, यथान्याय, लायक, बाजवी.
3 (mail, &c.). येण्याचा,यावयाचा, याव्याच्या हक्काचा.
DUE, *n. thing due.* घेणें *n.* घेव *m.* देणें *n.* येणें *n.* पावणें *n.*
2 *legal perquisite, custom, &c.* हक्क *m. n.* हक्कमाल *m.* कानू *f.*
Dues (annually made to idols, beggars, &c.) दायतें *n.*
Dues paid in cash. हक्कटक *m.*
DUE, *adv.* v. EXACTLY. थेट, बरोबर.
DUEL, *n. combat between two.* दोघांचेंयुद्ध *n.* द्वंद्वयुद्ध *n.*
DUELLIST, *n.* द्वंद्वयोद्धा.
DUENESS, *n.* v. A. 2. योग्यता *f.* यथायोग्यता *f.* लायकी *f.*
DUET, *n. song or air for two performers.* जोडीचें गाणें *n.* जोडीचें वाजविणें *n.* द्वंद्वगान *n.*
DUG, *n. teat.* सड *m.* आंचूळ *or* आंचळ *m.* आंसड *m.* दोभ *m.*
DUG, *p.* v. V. खोदलेला, &c. खोदींव, खनित.
DUKE, *n.* बडेलोकांची एक पदवी आहे.
2 v. PRINCE, KING. देशपाल *m.* देशपति *m.*
DUKEDOM, *n.* ड्यूक ह्याचा किताब *m.*
2 ड्यूक ह्याचें राज्य *n.*
DULCET. See SWEET.
To DULCIFY, TO DULCORATE, &c. See To SWEETEN, &c.
DULCIMER, *n.* प्राचीन काळचें एक वाद्य आहे.
DULL, *a.* v. STUPID. जड, मंद, बुद्धीचा जड, मंदमति *or* मतिमंद, मंदबुद्धि, अल्पबुद्धि, अल्पमति, जडबुद्धि, गाफल *or* गाफली.
2 *unready, backward,* v. SLOW, SLUGGISH. सुस्त *or* सुस्ता, मंद *remiss.* मंदट *or* मंदड, जड, मट्ठ *or* मठ्ठा, पड्या, स्तिमित.
D. of hearing. कानाचा जड.
D. of seeing. दृष्टीचा-डोळ्यांचा मंद.
3 *gloomy, dismal, &c.*—of places, v. DREARY. उदास, उदासवाणा *or* णी.
4 *not bright.* मजीत, मळमळीत, अंधक, निस्तेज, कयाहीन.
5 *dim, dusky, gloomy;*—of weather, &c. औंधट, धुंद, अंधक *or* अंधूक, मळीण, अंधारीचा, अंधाऱ्या, ओंधीचा.
6 *not merry, lively, &c.*—meetings, &c. v. SPIRITLESS. मुका, सामसुमीचा, मळमळीत, पळपळीत, उदासीचा, बेरंग, बिरस.
7—trade, business, &c. मंद, थंड, थंडा, हलका, निस्तेज, मंदीचा.
To become d. मंदी *f.* पडणें *g. of s.*

8 *melancholy*, v. SAD. उदास.

9 See BLUNT.

To DULL, *To* DULLEN, *v. a. make dull*, v. To STUPIFY, To DIM, To BLUNT. जड-मंद-निस्तेज-उदास-&c. करणें.

To DULL, *To* DULLEN, *v. n. lose brightness, clearness, freshness.* विटणें, मळणें, झडणें, मळीण होणें, उतरणें.

2 *lose sharpness, smartness, briskness.* बहिरावणें, मेहरणें.

DULLARD. See FOOL. [विटका.

DULLED, DULLENED, *p.* v. V. N. 1. विटलेला, मळलेला, &c.

DULNESS, *n.* v. A. 1. जडपणा *m.* मंदपणा *m.* &c. जडत्व *n.* जाड्य *n.* बुद्धिमांद्य *n.* मतिमांद्य *n.* मंदबुद्धि *f.* मंदमति *f.*

2 सुस्तपणा *m.* जडपणा *m.* मदपणा *m.* जाड्य *n.* स्तिमिताई *f.* अस्फूर्ति *f.*

3 उदासपणा *m.* उदासी *f.* औदास्य *n.*

4 मजितपणा *m.* मळमळितपणा *m.* &c.

5 ओंधटपणा *m.* मळिणपणा *m.* अंधुकपणा *m.* ओंध *f.* अंधारी *f.* आभाळांची झांप *f.*

6 उदासी *f.* मळमळितपणा *m.*

7 मंदी *f.* मंदपणा *m.* थंडाई *f.* थंडी *f.*

8 उदासी *f.* उदासपणा *m.* दौर्मनस्य *n.* दौश्चित्त्य *n.*

DULY, *adv.*v. RIGHTLY. यथोचित, यथायोग्य, यथायुक्त, यथास्थित, यथामार्ग, यथान्याय, यथाविधि. [कु,बाग्रहित.

DUMB, *a. incapable, &c. of speech.* मुका, मोना, मूक, अमू, अवा-

2 *mute.* See SILENT.

DUMB-BELL, *n.—in gymnastics.* मुदगल *m.*

DUMBNESS, *n.* v. A. 1. मुकेपणा *m.* मूकत्व *n.* वाकूशक्तिराहित्य *n.*

DUMBSHOW, *n.*v. PANTOMINE. भाषणरहित हावभाव *m.* मुकाट्यानें केलेली बतावणी *f.*

To DUMFOUND, *v. a. confuse, strike dumb.* बोबडी *f.*-फेपरी *f.* वळवणें *g. of o.* निरुत्तर-अनुत्तर-बीतोत्तर-कुंठित-वाग्रुद्ध-वाकूस्तब्ध-स्तब्धवाक्-&c. करणें, वाग्रोध *m.*-वाकूस्तंभ *m.*-&c. करणें *g. of o.*

DUMMY, *n. dumb partner.* अंगगडी, अंडगडी, पोटगडी, दगड्या, अंधळा तिरळा, पित्या.

Playing at a game with d. अंधळा तिरळा *m.* अंधळें तिरळें *n.*

DUMPINESS, *n.* v. A. चेपटपणा *m.* &c.

DUMPS, *n. gloomy state of mind.* उदासपणा *m.* उदासी *f.* उदासवृत्ति *f.* दौर्मनस्य *n.* दौश्चित्त्य *n.*

DUMPY, *a. squat, low, flattish, &c.* चेपट, चपटा, चपडा, चापट, चपताड *or* डा, चपतळ *or* ळा *or* चपताळा, चिपतळ *or* ळा *or* चिपताळा, बसकीचा, बसकट, बसका, टिल्लू, टिल्लू *or* ल्या, टुल्लू, थपकट *or* टा, थबकड *or* डा, बतखल *or* बदखल, ठेंगू, घुंट, बुटकणा.

DUN, *a.*—the color. जरदा, मळया, कोशा.

DUN, DUNNER, *n.*v.V. तगादा करणारा-लावणारा, तगाददार, तगादगीर, करजकरी.—in allusive, covert, cant, &c. phraseology. धरणकरी *or* धरणेकरी, खपाट्या, गळग्रह, गळेपडू, शनि, बरातदार.

To DUN, *v. a. press to pay a debt.* तगादा *m.* करणें-लावणें-बसवणें, निकड *f.*-तड *f.*-&c. लावणें, तड *f.* ओढणें, तोडणें, बाटाघाट *f.* करणें *g. of o.* In the shade of the sense of this word as appearing under *To sit or fix one's self determinedly and doggedly at a person's door, whether in exaction of payment, or in enforcement of compliance with a demand generally*, there are numerous terms and phrases extensively current and strikingly characteristic; as धरणें *n.* करणें, धरणें बसणें, तगादा *m.* बसणें, तगाद्यास बसणें, खणपट *f.* घेणें *or* खणपटीस बसणें-लागणें-येणें, धुणी *f.* घालून बसणें, गोण *f.* घालून बसणें, खिळण *f.* घेणें-धरणें, ताण *m. n.* देणें, पायासीं पाय बांधून बसणें, खपाटीस बसणें-लागणें, अधिवासन *n.*-अधिष्ठान *n.* करणें, मेखाटणीस-मानगोटीस-गरगोटीस-गळचिपीस-चोकांडीस-&c.-बसणें, गळीं पडणें.

DUNCE, *n. dullard, dolt, thickskull*, v. FOOL. दुधड ओनाम्या, अक्षरशत्रु *m.* दगड *m.* धोंडा *m.* शनि *m.* विकटशास्त्री *m.*

DUNG, *n.*—gener. हग *mf.* गू *m.* विष्ठा *f.* पुरीष *m. n.* मल *m. n.* शकृत् *n.* अमेध्य *n.* मय *m. n.* in comp.

Cloth, &c. befouled with d. हगेरें *n.* भरावलेलें फडकें *n.*-चिरगूट *n.*-&c.

Lump or nodule of d. लेंड *n.* लेंडूक *n. dim.* लेंडी *f.*

2 (of birds). शीट *or* छीट *f.* शेर *f.*

3 (of elephants, horses, asses, mules). लीद *f.*

4 (of the cow, bull, or buffalo) v. COWDUNG. शेण *n.* गोमय *m.n.*

Mass of d. as voided. पोहो *m. dim.* पोहटी *f.* पोंव *m.* पोंथा *m.*

Pit receiving the daily d. of cattle. शेणकई *or* शेणकाई *f.* शेणकी *f.* शेणाडी *f.*

5 (of man). गू *m.*

To DUNG, *v. a. manure.* खत *n.*-&c. घालणें, खतावणें.

To DUNG, *v. n.* हगणें, मलोत्सर्ग *m.*-मलविसर्जन *n.*-मलत्याग *m.*-&c. करणें.

2—birds. शिटणें, शेरणें.

3—the cow, bull, or buffalo. शेणणें.

DUNG-HILL, *a.* See BASE, MEAN.

DUNG-HILL, DUNG-HEAP, *n.* उकरडा *or* उकिरडा *m.* उकरीड *m.* खातेरें *n.* हगरड *f.* नरक *m.*

DUNG-YARD, *n.* नरकाड *f.* नरकाडी *f.* नरकड *f.* नरकांड *f.*

DUNGEON, *n. dark close prison.* अंधार कोठडी *f.* अंधारकोंडी *f.* अंधार खण *m. f.* अंधारखाणी *f.* अंधारी *f.*

DUNNING, *n.* v. V. तगादा *m.* निकड *f.* तड *f.* धरणें *n.*

Order or token (from the creditor, &c.) to stop a d. मनाई *f.* मनाचिठ्ठी *f.* तकूबचिठ्ठी *f.*

Vehement or general d. ओढाओढो *f.* हबक *f.*

DUODECIMALS, *n.* द्वादशांश *m. pl.*

Multiplication of d. द्वादशांश गुणाकार *m.*

DUODECIMO, *a.* द्वादश पत्री सांच्याचा, द्वादश पत्री.

DUODECIMO, *n.* द्वादशपत्री सांच्याचें पुस्तक *n.*-ग्रंथ *m.*-&c.

DUPE, *n. person easily deceived.* फशा, भोळा, भळू.

To DUPE, *v. a.* v. To CHEAT. फसवणें, ठकवणें.

DUPLICATE, *n. copy.* दुसरी प्रत *f.* प्रत्यंतर *n.* नकल *f.* उतारा *m.*

To DUPLICATE, DUPLICATE, See To DOUBLE, DOUBLE.

DUPLICATURE, *n. a doubling*, v. FOLD. दुमड *f.* दूण *f.* मोड *f.*

DUPLICITY, *n. double mindedness*, v. DECEIT. दुजाभाव *m.* दुटप्पीपणा *m.* दुतोंडीपणा *m.* दुरंगीपणा *m.* द्विनिष्ठता *f.*

DURABILITY, DURABLENESS, *n.* v. A. टिकाऊपणा *m.* टिकणेपणा *m.* स्थायित्व *n.* चिरस्थायित्व *n.* स्थिरता *f.*

DURABLE, *a.* v. ENDURING. टिकाऊ, टिकाया-तगाया-चा-जोगता-जोगा-&c. स्थायी, चिरस्थायी, स्थिर, चिरकालिक.

DURABLY, *adv.* v. A. टिकायाजोगा-तगायाजोगा *a. decl.*

DURANCE. See CONFINEMENT.

DURATION, *n.* v. TIME. काल *pop.* काळ *m.* लांबी *f.* स्थितिकाल *m.* कालमान *n.* कालदैर्घ्य *n.* कालमर्यादा *f.*

2 *lasting, continuance*, v. ENDURANCE. टिकाव *m.* टिकावा *m.* स्थिति *f.*

DURBAR, *n.* दरबार *m. n.*

DURESS. See IMPRISONMENT.

DURING, *prep.* जों, जंव, यावत्, पर्यंत, आंत, मध्यें, भर (in comp. as दिवसभर, वर्षभर, आयुष्यभर). It is often expressed by असतां (as ज्वर असतां जवूं नये dont eat during fever).

DUSK, DUSKY, *a. tending to darkness.* ओंधट, धुंद, अंधक *or* अधूक, अंधारीचा, ओंधीचा. [धूसर.

2 *tending to blackness.* काळसर, काळवट, काळानिळा, निस्तेज,

DUSK, *n.* काळोखी *f.* काळवें *n.* अंधारी *f.* ओंध *f.* काळंबण *n.*

D. of evening. राक्षसवेळ *or* राक्षसीवेळ *f.* आसुरी वेला *f.* कानरवेळ *f.* गोधूल *n.*

DUST, *n.* धूळ *f.* धूलि *f.* रेणु *m.* रज *n.* रजी *f.*

Particle of d. रजःकण *m.*

To throw d. उद्धूलन *n.* करणें.

2—as flying in clouds, or as lying in quantity, धुरळा *or* ळा *or* धुराळा *or* धुळोरा *or* धुळारा *or* धुळोरा *m.* धुळवट *f.* धुळवाड *f.* खकाणा *m.* खकाण *f.* [मरणें).

To lay the d. धुरळा *m.* मारणें (and to be laid, धुरळा *m.*

To lay one's mouth in the d. नाकदुराई *f.* काढणें.

To level with the d. धुळीस मिळवणें, विधुळणीस पाडणें-मिळवणें, जमिनीस मिळवणें.

To be mingled with the d. धुळीस मिळणें.

3 v. POWDER. चूर्ण *n.*

4 fig. *row, kick up*, v. TUMULT. गर्दी *f.* धांदल *f.*

To kick up a d. दणका *m.* माजणें.

To DUST, *v. a. free from dust.* धूळ *f.* काढणें-झाडणें-झटकणें-झटकारणें, झाडणें, धूलिशोधन *n.* करणें.

2 *cover or sprinkle with dust.* धूळ *f.* टाकणें.

DUST-BOARD, *n.* धूळपाटी *f.*

DUST-CART, *n.* केराचीगाडी *f.*

DUSTER, *n.* धूळझाडण्याचा रुमाल *m.*-फडकें *n.*

DUSTINESS, *n.* v. A. धुळकटपणा *m.* धुळवटपणा *m.* धूलियुक्तता *f.* धूलिप्राचुर्य *n.*

DUSTY, *a. covered, &c. with dust.* धुळकट, धुळवट, धुळकटलेला, धुळीनें भरलेला, धूळबसलेला, धुळीचा, धूलिमय, धूलियुक्त, धूलिप्रचुर.

DUTEOUS, DUTIFUL, *a.* v. OBEDIENT. हुकमी, हुकुमझल्या, हुकुमचंदा, आज्ञाधारक, आज्ञाधारी, सेवाधर्मपरायण, सेवातत्पर, सेवापर, शुश्रूषातत्पर, स्वधर्मासक्त, स्वधर्मतत्पर.

2 *enjoined or required by duty.* धर्माचा, सेवाधर्माचा, स्वधर्माचा, स्वकर्माचा.

DUTEOUSNESS, DUTIFULNESS, *n.* v. A. हुकमीपणा *m.* सेवाधर्म *m.* आज्ञाधारकत्व *n.* सेवातत्परता *f.* स्वधर्मासक्ति *f.* स्वधर्मतत्परता *f.*

DUTIFULLY, *adv.* v. A. सेवाधर्मपूर्वक, सेवाधर्मपुरस्सर, सेवाधर्मानें.

DUTY, *n.* धर्म *m.* कर्म *n.* काम *n.* आवश्यक कार्य *n.* कार्य *n.*

Daily or regular d. नित्यकर्म *n.* नित्यकृत्य *n.*

Discharge or fulfilment of d. धर्मनिष्पत्ति *f.*

General or common d. साधारण धर्म *m.*

Neglect of one's d. स्वधर्मत्याग *m.*

Proper or peculiar d. स्वधर्म *m.* विशेषधर्म *m.* स्वकर्म *n.*

To become the d. of. भाग *m.* होणें *or* भागास येणें *with* ला *or* स *of s.*

2 *a* d. धर्म *m.*

Minor or inferior d. उपधर्म *m.* गौणधर्म *m.*

3 *toll, tax*, v. CUSTOM. जकात *f.* सायर *n.*

4 (military) पहाऱ्याचें काम *n.* कामगिरी *f.* नोकरी *f.*

DWARF, *n.* वामन *m.* वामनमूर्त्ति *f.* अल्पमूर्त्ति *f.* ऱ्हस्वमूर्त्ति *f.* ऱ्हस्व, भुईचा लहान.—in contempt. भुईठाकूर *m.* ठेंगोजी *m.*—jocosely. वामनावतार *m.* [खुरटवणें.

To DWARF, *v. a. stunt.* वाढ *f.* खुंटविणें *g. of o.* खुजट-&c. करणें,

DWARFISH, *a.* ठेंगणा, ठेंग्या, ठेंगू, खुजा, खुजट, खुरट, टारगा, बुटारणा, बुटुकणा, वामन, वामनमूर्त्ति, ठिलू *or* ठिल्या, टिल्लू, टुल्लू, ठुला, टुरमा, अल्पतनु, खर्व, जामूण.

DWARFISHNESS, *n.* v. A. ठेंगणेपणा *m.* ठेंगूपणा *m.* &c.

To DWELL, *v. n.* v. To RESIDE. राहणें, नांदणें, घर *n.*-वस्ती *f.*-वास *m.* असणें *g. of s.*

2 upon; *make unceasing mention of.* घोकणें, घोकणी *f.* घेणें-मांडणें-लावणें, घोर *m.* घेणें, गावा *m.* गाणें, गीत *n.* गाणें, जप *m.* धरणें-घेणें, जपमाळ *f.* घेणें, गाणें, जपणें, घोष *or* उद्घोष *m.* करणें-लावणें-मांडणें, तांडव *n.* करणें, आंकणकडवें *n.* करणें.

To d. upon, peevishly, &c. बाधंग *m. n.* लावणें-मांडणें-सांगणें-घेणें, गाणें *n.*-टकटक *f.*-किरकीर *f.*-पिरपीर *f.*-रिपरीप *f.*-&c. लावणें-मांडणें. [com.

DWELLER, *n.* v. V. राहणारा, नांदणारा, वस्ती करणारा, वासी in.

DWELLING, *n.* v. V. 1. राहणें *n.* नांदणें *n.* नांदणूक *f.* नांदवट *f.*

2 घोकणें *n.* घोकणी *f.* घोर *m.* घोष *m.* उद्घोष *m.* गावा *m.* चावटाई *f.* [मकाण *or* न *n.*

I. *place of d.* v. RESIDENCE. घर *n.* ठिकाण *n.* ठिकाणा *m.*

DWELLING-HOUSE, DWELLING-PLACE, *n.* v. RESIDENCE. घर *n.* ठिकाण *n.* मकाण *or* न *n.*

To DWINDLE, *v. n. become less.* लहानावणें, लहनाळणें, उणावणें, क्षिणणें, उतरणें, घटणें, ऱ्हास *m.*-क्षय *m.*-&c. होणें *g. of s.* कमी-न्यून-&c. होणें.

DWINDLED, *p.* v. V. लहानावलेला, &c. कमीझालेला, &c. क्षीण.

DYE, *n.* रंग *m.* रंगवणी *n.*

To DYE, *v. a.* रंगणें, रंगवणें, रंग *m.* देणें.

To d. over again, *to give a dip.* डूब *m.* देणें.

2 (by sprinkling). छिडकणें.

DYED, *p.* v. V. 1. रंगवलेला, &c. रंगी, रंगीत.

DYER, *n.* v. V. 1. रंगवणारा, रंग देणारा, रंगारी, रंगरेज, रागी.

DYING, *n.* v. V. To DYE.—*act.* रंगवणें *n.* रंग देणें *n.* &c. रंगरेजी *f.*

Cost or price of d. रंगणावळ *f.* रंगाई *f.*

v. V. To DIE, *and* DEATH. प्राणत्याग *m.* प्राणोत्सर्ग *m.*

DYING, *a. pertaining to death, given, uttered, &c. just before death.* अंतकालचा, मरणकालाचा, मरतेवेळचा.

DYKE. See DIKE.

DYNAMICS, *n.* चलतपदार्थ शास्त्र *n.*

DYNASTIC, *a.* v. N. राजवंशावलि विषयक-संबंधी.

DYNASTY, *n. race or succession of kings.* राजवंशावलि *f.* राजवंशपंक्ति *f.* राजावलि *pop.* राजावळी *f.*

DYSENTERIC, *a.* v. N. अतिसाराचा, आंवरक्ताचा, &c. आमरक्तसंबंधी-विषयक, अतिसारी.

DYSENTERY, *n.* आमरक्त *pop.* आंवरक्त *n.* आमातिसार *m.* अतिसार *m.* संग्रहणी *f.* ग्रहणि *or* ग्रहणी *f.* [कम.

DYSPEPSY, *n.* v. INDIGESTION. अग्निमांद्य *n.* पाककृच्छ्र *n.* मंदपा-

DYSPEPTIC, *a.* अजीर्णविकारी, अजीर्णरोगी.

DYSPNŒA, *n.* v. ASTHMA. धाप *f.* ऊर्ध्ववायु *m.* श्वासावरोध *m.* श्वास *m.*

DYSURY, *n.* मूत्रकृच्छ्र *n.* अश्मरी *f.*

Hot d. उन्हाळें *m. pl.* उन्हाळी *f.* मूत्रदाह *m.*

To be affected with hot d. उन्हाळणें.

E.

E. Of the three sounds of this letter, viz. that in *scene*, that in *men*, and that in *prey, vein*, the first is represented by ई, the second exists not in *Maráthí*, and the third is represented by ए.

EACH, *a. every one,*—singly or distributively. एकएक, एकक, एकएकटा, एकएकला, हरएक, प्रत्येक, प्रति (in comp. as प्रतिदिवस, प्रतिदिन, प्रतिक्षण, प्रतिपद, प्रतिजन,) न (as in घरानघर, झाडानझाड, दिवसानदिवस).

E. other, E. the other. एकमेक.

E. (his, her, its) own. आपआपला. ex. They came *each* bringing *his own* books. ते आपआपलीं पुस्तकें घेऊन आले. *Every one* approves of *his own* disposition. सर्वांस आपआपला स्वभाव चांगला वाटतो, &c.

EAGER, *a. keenly desirous,* v. DESIROUS, EARNEST. उत्सुक, उत्कंठित, हवसदार, सोत्कंठ, अतीच्छ.

2 *impatiently desirous,* v. IMPATIENT. उतावळा, हूड, हवळा, हवळ्या, हुटहुट्या, हुडहुड्या, हुटहुटलेला, हुडहुडलेला.

To be e. हुटहुटणें *intens.* हुटाटणें, हुडहुडणें, उतुतणें, उताटणें, फुरणें, फुरफुरणें, हुडहुडी *f.* भरणें *in. con.* अत्तणें, भुऱ्यावणें, भुऱ्योभुऱ्यो करणें.

EAGERLY, *adv.* v. A. 1. उत्सुकतेनें, उत्कंठेनें, उत्कंठापूर्वक, सोसासोसानें, सोसें.

2 उतावळीनें.

EAGERNESS, *n.* v. A. 1. हांव *f.* हवस *or* हौस *f.* उत्कंठा *f.* उत्साह *m.* औत्सुक्य *n.* उत्सुकता *f.* प्रोत्साह *m.*

2 उतावळी *f.* हुडहुडी *f.* हुटहुटी *f.* हुटहूट *f.* चुळचूळ *f.* चुळचुळमुंगळा *m.* घायकूत *f. n.* उताट *f.* उत्कळ *f.* उभळ *f.* उत्कलिका *f.* संभ्रम *m.*

A flush of e. फुरशी *f.*

To cool, &c. one's e. हुडहुडी *f.*-&c. मोडणें-जिरवणें *g. of o.*

EAGLE, *n.* गरुड *m.*

2 (lesser Indian e.) *aquila fulvescens.* मोरघार *f.*

3 (Sea-eagle) See OSPRAY.

EAGLE-EYED, *a.* v. SHARP-SIGHTED. तिखट डोळ्यांचा, तिखट डोळ्या, सूक्ष्मदर्शी, सूक्ष्मदृष्टि, तीक्ष्णदृष्टि.

EAR, *n.* कान *m.* कर्ण *m.* श्रवण *m. n.* श्रुति *f.* श्रोत्र *n.*

Curved edge of the e. पाळ *f.* कर्णपालि *f.* कर्णपालिका *f.*

Discharge from the e. कर्णस्राव *m.*

Drum of the e. कानाचापडदा *m.*

Dull of hearing—an e. फुटका.

Hollow of the e. श्रवणोदर *n.* कर्णछिद्र *n.*

Hollow or line along the e. कानफट *or* ड *n.* कानशील *n.* कानसल *or* सूल *n.* कानाड *n.*

Inflammation of the e. कर्णपाक *m.*

Lobe of the e. चांपा *m.* चाप *m.* कर्णलतिका *f.*

Matter whispered in the e. कानगोष्ट *f.* कानमंत्र *m.* कानमंत्री *f.* छूमंतर *m.*

Outer e. वेष्टन *n.*

Ringing in the e. Noise in the e. कर्णनाद *m.* कर्णक्ष्वेड *m.*

Root of the e. कर्णमूल *n.* कर्णजाह *n.*

Scabbiness of the ears. कानकिरळी *f.* कानकीड *f.* कानकुरकुटी *f.*

Stoppage of the e. (from cold, &c.). कानांस दट्टा *m. v.* बस, कानांस दादरा *m. v.* बस.

That has passed the e.—a matter. कानावरून गेलेला, कर्णपृष्ट, कर्णारूढ.

That has learned by the e. कान भट्टीचा, ऐक भट्टीचा.

That has been learned by the e. कान भट्टीचा, ऐक भट्टीचा.

To the e.;—drawing a bow. कानाडी, आकर्ण.

To abuse, poison, &c. the e. of. कान *m.* फुंकणें-भरणें-भारणें-भारवणें, कानगच्ची *f.* करणें.

To bore the e. कान *m.* टोचणें, कर्णवेध *m.* करणें.

To give or lend an e. कान *m.*-चित्त *n.*-लक्ष्य *n.*-&c. देणें.

To let in at one e. and out at the other. ह्याकानानें ऐकणें ह्या कानानें सोडणें.

To prick up one's ears. कान *m. pl.* टवकारून पाहणें, कान *m. pl.* उभारणें.

To pull the ears of. कान *m.* उपटणें-धरणें-पिळवटणें, कानचिमळी *f.* घेणें. [करणें.

To set by the ears. लावालाव *or* वी *f.*-शिकवाशिकव *f.*

To stop one's ears against. To turn a deaf e. to. कान *m. pl.* झाडणें-झांकणें, कानझांक *f.*-कानगच्ची *f.* करणें, पाठ *f.* देणें, काना गाडा *m.* करणें.

To whisper in the e. of. कानफुसी *or* कानाफुसी *f.*-कर्णजप *m.*-कर्णमैथुन *n.*-&c. करणें, कानाशीं *or* कानीं लागणें, कानगी *f.* करणें-देणें.

The ears sicken, tire, &c. कान *m. pl.* किटतात.

2 (of a vessel or article) v. HANDLE. कान *m.* कानपा *m.*

3 *spike of corn,*—gener. कणीस *n.* कणिश *n.* सस्यमंजरी *f.* धान्यशीर्षक *n.*

4 (of wheat). ओंबी *f.*

5 (of rice). कणशी *f.*

Full state of the e. तोठरा *m.*

6 (of rice, wheat, &c.) *pendulous ear.* लोंबी *f.* लोंब *f.* लोंग *f.* लोंबट *or* त *n.* (enhanc. लोंबर *n.* लोंगर *n.*), तुरंबी *f.*

7 (of राळा, बरी, सावा, &c.) ओंबट *n.*

To EAR, *v. n. shoot into ears.* निसवणें, पसवणें, कणसें *n. pl* येणें, निसव *f.*-निसवणी *f.*-निसवील *or* निसवेल *f.* होणें, तुरंबणें.

EAR-ACHE, *n.* कानदुखी *f.* कर्णशूल *pop.* कानसूळ *m.*

EAR-LOCK, *n.* झुलूप *n.* काकपक्ष *m.*

EAR-PICK, *n.* कानकोरणें *n.* कानकोरणी *f.*

EAR-RING, *n.* कुंडल *n.* कर्णभूषण *n.* कर्णालंकार *m.* अवतंस *m.* Some of the common ear-rings or ear-ornaments are, कर्णफूल *n.* कवळी *f.* काप *m.* कुडा *m. or* कुडें *n.* कुडूक *m. n.* कुडकी *f.* खिडकबाळी *f.* खुंटबाळी *f.* खुरडू *m.* घोसबाळी *f.* चंद्रबाळी *f.* झुबकेबाळी *or* झुबेबाळी *f.* झुबा *m.* टोपणबाळी *f.* डूल *m.* तळप *m.* ताटंक *n.* तानवड *n.* तोंगलबाळी *f.* दूल *m.* पत्रबाळी *f. or* पत्ता *m.*

पानबाळी *f.* बाळी *f.* बुगडी *or* मुगडी *f.* मासबाळी *f.*

E. made with gold begged. भिकबाळी *f.*

EAR-SHOT, *n.* हाकेचा टप्पा *m.* कर्णपथ *m.*

EAR-WAX, *n.* कानबा *m.* कानमळ *m.* मेंकण *n.* कर्णमल *m.* कर्णगूथ*m.*

EAR-WIG, *n.* कानघोण *f.* कर्णकीटी *f.* कर्णजलूका *f.*

EAR-WITNESS, *n.* कानाचासाक्षी, ऐकींवसाक्षी, श्रवणसाक्षी.

EARED, *a. having ears.* कानाचा, कर्णवान्, सकर्ण, कर्णी.

2—of corn. सकण.

EARING, *n.* v. V. निसवणी *f.* निसव *f.* निसवील *or* निसवेल *f.*

EARL, *n.* इंग्लंदांतील बडेलोकांची एक पदवी आहे.

EARLY, *a. of good or right time.* सकळवाणीचा, सकळवेळींचा, वेळेवारींचा, लवकर झालेला-आलेला-येणारा-&c.

2 *of ancient time.* पूर्वीचा, पूर्वकालचा, पूर्वकालिक, प्राचीन, प्राक्तन.

Earlier. पलीकडचा *or* ला, पलीकडील (or पैलिकडचा &c.).

3 *that ripens sooner.* आगप, आगस, अगांत (disting. from मागप, मागस, मागांत), हळवा *or* हळा (*remiss.* हळवट *earlyish*).

To be early ripe. आगसणें.

EARLY, *adv. soon, betimes.* सकळ, सकाळवणीं *or* वाणीं, सकाळ *or* सकळवेळीं, वेळेवारीं, आदींबिदीं, लवकर, अगांत.

It is still e. अजून लवकर आहे.

To EARN, *v. a.* v. To GET. मिळवणें, कमावणें, संपादणें, उपार्जन *n.*-उपार्जना *f.*-&c. करणें *g. of o.*

EARNER, *n.* EARNING, *p. a.* v.V. मिळवणारा, &c. जोडका, जोडता, कमावता, कमावू.

The earning member of a family. जोडकापूत *m.* जोडकाराम *m.* जोडतापूत *m.* जोडताराम *m.* जोडताराबजी *m.*

EARNEST, *a. ardent, warm, zealous, solicitous.* आस्थेवाईक, आस्थेकरी, आस्थिक, आस्थावान्, दरदी, उदमेखी, मनापासूनचा, पोटागीचा, तिडकीचा, कळकळीचा, उत्सुक, उत्कंठित, उत्साह, उत्साही, उत्साहवान्, सोत्साह, अनुरक्त, अनुरत, आसक्त, तत्पर, तल्लीन.

EARNEST, *n. seriousness.* खरेपणा *m.* सत्यभाव *m.*

In e. सत्यानें.

To take up in e. मनावर घेणें-धरणें.

2 *money, &c. given in token.* इसार *m.* इसारा *m.* सच *m.* सचकार *m.* बयाणा *or* ना *m.*

To pay down in e. तोंडीं लावणें.

3—as in plays; *not fun or sport.* जिंकणा मानी *f.* जिंतणा मानी *f.* जिंकणूक *f.* जीत *f.* जिंतणूक *f.* व्यवहार *m.*

In e. सत्यानें.

EARNESTLY, *adv.* v. A. आस्थेनें, उत्कंठेनें, आस्थापूर्वक, औत्सुक्यपूर्वक, &c. पोटागीनें, &c. साक्षेपें, मनापासून, उदमेखून.

EARNESTNESS, *n.* v. A. आस्था *f.* उत्कंठा *f.* उत्सुकता *f.* उत्साह *m.* उदमेख *m.* पोटाग *f.* कळकळ *f.* तिडीक *f.* आसक्ति *f.* अनुराग *m.* अनुरक्ति *f.* अनुरति *f.*

EARNING, *n.* v. V.—*act.* मिळवणें *n.* संपादणें *n.* &c. संपादन *n.* उपार्जन *n.* उपार्जना *f.*

I. earnings, v. GETTINGS. मिळकत *f.* कमाई *f.* पैदास्त *f.*

EARTH, *n. the terraqueous globe.* पृथ्वी *or* पृथिवी *f.* भूमि *pop.* भुई *f.* भूगोल *n.* भू *f.* भूमंडल *n.* धरित्री *pop.* धरती *and* धरणी*f.* अचला *f.* मही *f.* मेदिनी *f.* वसुंधरा *f.* वसुधा *f.* वसुमती *f.* उर्वी *f.* कुंभिनी *f.* ज्या *f.* धरा *f.* क्षमा *f.* क्षिति *f.* क्ष्मा *f.* क्षोणी *f.* अवनि *or* अवनी *f.* Some descriptive or allusive terms for the *earth,* corresponding with *the habitation of mortals, the theatre of action, the field of labor, the nurse of beings, &c. &c.* are, मृत्युलोक *m.* नरकलोक *m.* मर्त्यलोक *m.* कर्मभूमि *or* कर्मभूमिका *f.* भूतधात्री *f.* भूतग्राम *m.* भूतसंसार *m.* मध्यलोक *m.* जीवाजीवाधार *m.* दिग्चक्र *n.* समुद्रमेखला *f.* सर्वसहा *f.* वसुंधरा *or* नानारत्नवसुंधरा *f.* उदधिमेखला *f.* चतुस्समुद्रवलयांकितपृथ्वी *f.* दुःखसागर *m.* Nine divisions (खंड *m.* वर्ष *m.*) are made of the *earth.* These are इलावृत, भद्राश्व, हरिवर्ष, किंपुरुष, केतुमाल, रम्यक, भरतखंड, हिरण्मय, उत्तरकुरु. [लोक *m.*

Belt of mountains encircling the e. चक्रवाल *m.* लोका-

Burden or load upon the e. भूभार *m.*

Conquering the e. दिग्विजय *m.*

Conqueror of the e. दिग्विजयी.

Corners of the e. चौखुंट *m. pl.*

Face of the e. भूतल *pop* भूतळ *n.* जगतीतल *n.* भूपृष्ठ *n.*

Regions below the e. अधोलोक *m.* अधोभुवन *n.* पाताल *n.* नागलोक *m.*

Serpent upholding the e. शेष *m.*

Shade cast by the e. भूभा *f.*

The umbra of the earth's shadow. भूभाबिंब *n.*

To the uttermost borders of the e. दिगंतीं, दिगंतरीं.

To wander over the e. दिग्भ्रम *m.*-दिग्भ्रमण *n.*-&c. करणें.

To commit to the e. (treasure, &c.). भूमिग्रस्त करणें, माती आड करणें.

2—the element. माती *f.* मृत्तिका *f.* पृथ्वी *f.* Some of the common *earths* are केवटा, खळगा, गंगामृत्तिका, घशा, गोपचंदन, चिकणखडू, तांबडमाती, पांढरमाती, द्वारावती, लांबी, माल्‌, शाडू *or* शेडू, कुरमूज.

Lump of e. मोदळा *or* मोधळा *m.*

3—the present world. जग *n.* जगती *f.* भूलोक *m.* इहलोक*m.*

4 *the ground.* जमीन *f.* धरणी *f.* धरती *f.* भूमि *f.* भुई *f.*

5 *arable land,* v. SOIL. जमीन *f.* भूमि *f.*

To EARTH. See To BURROW.

EARTH-OIL, *n.* मातीचें तेल *n.* भूमितैल *n.*

EARTH-NUT, *n. ground nut.* भुईमूग *m.*

EARTH-PIT, *n.* मातखण *or* खाण *f.*

EARTH-QUAKE, *n.* धरतीकांप *m.* भूमिकंप *m.* भूकंप *m.* धरणीकंप*m.*

EARTH-WORK, *n.* मातकाम *n.*

EARTH-WORM, *n.* गांडूळ *or* गांडोळ *or* गांडवळ *m.n.* दवणा *m.* दवणें *n.* दानवा *m.* दानवें *n.* काडू *m.*

EARTHEN, *a.* मातीचा, मृत्तिकामय, मृन्मय, मृत्तिकारूप, मार्त्तिक, मृदात्मक, पार्थिव.

E. ware. मातीचीं भांडीं *n. pl.*

EARTHLINESS, *n.* v. A. 1. इहलोकसंबंध *m.* भूलोकसंबंध *m.* &c. भौमिकत्व *n.* &c. ऐहलौकिकत्व *n.*

2 ऐहिकदृष्टि *f.* ऐहिकबुद्धि *f.* ऐहिकविषयासक्ति *f.* &c.

EARTHLY, *a. belonging to this earth; mundane, not heavenly.* भूलोकाचा, भूलोकचा, भूलोकींचा, इहलोकचा, &c. भूलोकसंबंधी, भूलोकविषयक, मृत्युलोकचा, &c. ऐहलौकिक, ऐहिक, भौम, भौमिक.

2 *or* EARTHLY-MINDED, v. SENSUAL. ऐहिकदृष्टि, ऐहिकपरा-

यण, ऐहिकलंपट, ऐहिकविषयतल्लीन, &c. प्रपंचनिमग्न. [न्मय.
EARTHY, *a. consisting of e.*v. EARTHEN.मातीचा, मृत्तिकामय,मृ-
2 *belonging to e.* मातीचा, मृत्तिकासंबंधी, मृत्तिकाविषयक.
3 *having e. mingled*—sugar, grain, &c. मातड, मातट, मातेरा, मातमळ.
EASE, *n. quiet, rest, tranquillity.* चैन *n.* समाधान *n.* सुख *n.* खुशाली *f.* कुशल *n.* सुखोपा *m.* सुखापा *m.* सुखावा *m.* सुखबा *m.* स्वस्थता *f.* स्वास्थ्य *n.* सौख्य *n.* संस्था *f.*
At e. In e. सुखानें, सुखाचा *decl.* कुशल, स्वस्थ *com.* स्वस्त, सुस्त *v.* बस, निज, अस, सुचित्त, आराम. [आरामी *f.*
2 *rest from pain.* चैन *n.* सुख *n.* समाधान *n.* आराम *m.*
3 *rest after labor.* विसांवा *m.* विश्राम *m.* विश्रांति *f.*
4 *freedom from difficulty or great labor.* सहजपणा *m.* अनायास *m.* सुख *n.* क्लेशाभाव *m.* आयासाभाव *m.* अक्लिष्टपणा *m.* श्रमराहित्य *n.*
With e. See EASILY.
To EASE, *v. a. alleviate, assuage, mitigate, mollify, allay.* आराम *m.*-सुख *n.*-चैन *n.*-स्वस्थता *f.*-&c. देणें-करणें, आराम *m.*-चैन *n.* पाडणें *or* पडणें *with in. con.* हलका कमी-&c. करणें, शमवणें, शांतवणें, सांत्वन *n. pop.* शांत्वन *n.*-समाधान *n.*-उपशम *m.*-प्रशम *m.*-उपशमन *n.*-&c. करणें *g. of o.*
To e. nature. See under NATURE.
EASEL, *n.*—of a painter. चित्राचीफळी *f.* चित्र फलक *n.*
EASILY, *adv.* v. A. *readily, &c.* सहज, सहजांत, सहजपणानें, सहजपणें, सहजगतीनें, सहजगत्या, सहजरीतीनें, सहजरीत्या, सहजाखालीं, सहजानसार, सहजाबारीं, सहजावृत्या, सहजावृत्तीनें, सहजासहजीं, अनायासानें, अनायासें, आइता *or* ऐता, अक्लिष्टपणें, अक्लेश, अयत्नानें, अयत्नतः, अचानक, सहल, अवलिळा, बिनदिक्कत, चालतां चालतां, जातां जातां, बोलतां बोलतां.
I. *gently, softly, without shaking, &c.* हलक्यानें, हळू, अचळ, अचानक.
II. *leisurely, composedly, not hurriedly, &c.* सावकाश, सावकाशीनें, सावकाशीवर, सावकाशीखालीं.
EASINESS, *n.* v. A. 1. 2. *and* EASE. सुख *n.* सुखीपणा *m.* स्वस्थता *f.* स्वास्थ्य *n.* सौख्य *n.* कुशल *n.* खुशाली *f.* कुशलता *f.* सुखावस्था *f.* कुशलावस्था *f.*
3 (of performance or attainment). सोपेपणा *m.* सौकर्य *n.* सुसाध्यता *f.* सुखसाध्यता *f.* अल्पसाध्यता *f.* &c. सौलभ्य *n.*
4 सोपेपणा *m.* सौगम्य *n.* सुबोधता *f.* बालबोधता *f.* &c.
5 सुरळीतपणा *m.* सरळपणा *m.* सरलत्व *n.*
6 हलकेपणा *m.* मऊपणा *m.* &c.
8 मनाची नरमाई *f.* &c. नरमपणा *m.*भोळेपणा *m.*
EAST, *n.* पूर्वदिशा *f.* पूर्व *f.* उगवत *f.* प्राची *f.*
Lying e. and west,—a building, a field. पूर्वपश्चिम, प्राक्पश्चिम.
Towards the e. सूर्याखालीं, खालीं.
2 *eastern regions.* पूर्वेकडीलदेश *m.* पूर्वदेश *m.* उगवतेकडचादेश.
EASTERLY, EASTERN, *a. of or belonging to the east.* पूर्व, पूर्वेचा, पूर्वदिशेचा, पूर्वेकडचा, पूर्वेकडील, प्राचीन, प्राच्य, पौर्व.
2 *born in the e.* पूर्वज.
3 *facing the e.* पूर्वेचा, पूर्वेकडील, पूर्वाभिमुख, सूर्याभिमुख.
EASTWARD, *adv.* पूर्वेकडे, पूर्वदिशेकडे, उगवत, प्राक्.
EASY, *a. enjoying quiet, rest, tranquillity, &c.* सुखी, सुखरूप, खुशाल, सुचित्त, स्वस्थ, सुस्थ.
To feel e. सुखास पडणें-येणें-वाटणें *v. impers.*
That is in easy circumstances, *that has a comfortable maintenance.* घरचा सुखी, खाताजेवता, खातापिता, निर्द्धात *or* निर्धात.
2 *free from pain.* सुखरूप, आरामी, सुखी.
3 *not difficult.* सोपा, सोपारा, सहज, साहजिक, सुलभ, सवघड, हलका, सुकर, सुशक, सुघटित, हातचा, सहजसिद्ध, असान, सलील, सलीस, अल्पसाध्य, सुसाध्य, अनायाससाध्य, सुखसाध्य, हळूफूल, हलका फूल, फूलासारखा, सु (in comp. forming valuable words endlessly; as *e. of access or passage* सुगम; *e. of apprehension* सुबोध; *e. of cure* सुसाध्य; &c. &c.).
To become e. to from practice. ढाळाखालीं-वळणाखालीं-परिपाटीखालीं-&c. पडणें.
4 (of apprehension) *not abstruse.* सोपा, सुबोध, सुगम, सुगम्य, बालबोध, सुज्ञेय, सुसज्ञेय, लघुगम्य.
5 *unconstrained, unlabored, &c.* सरल *pop.* सरळ, ऋजु *pop.* उजू, सुरळीत, अक्लिष्ट.
6 *gentle, moderate, mild, &c.* in numerous shades. हलका, नरम, मृदु, मऊ, सौम्य, सुमाराचा, सोईचा, सुखाचा. [वह.
7 *that affords ease.* सुखाचा, सुखकर, सुखदायक, सुखप्रद, सुखा-
8 *complying, &c.*, v. SOFT. मनाचा नरम, मनाचा कोंवळा, मनाचा भिडस्त, नरम, भोळा.
To EAT, *v. a.* खाणें, भक्षणें, भक्षण *n.*-अशन *n.*-&c. करणें,—in significant, jocose, or free phraseol. भक्ष्यस्थानीं घालणें, धडांत टाकणें-घालणें-उतरणें, प्राणपूजा *f.*-पोटपूजा *f.*-&c.करणें,—with the power of such phraseologies as *to eat up,to clear the decks, to lick clean the platters, to make clear work, to dispose of, &c.* खाऊन टाकणें, खाऊन लकलकीत *or* लक्क करणें, खाऊन ठार करणें, मटगोळा *m.* करून टाकणें, चाटून पुसून खाणें, निपटून शिपटून खाणें, झडती *f.* लावणें-देणें, चट्टामट्टा *m.*-तळझाडा *m.*-तळपट *n.*-निःपात *m.*-निसंतान *n.*-सफेजंगी *f.*-सप्पा *m.*-निरानिपटा *m.* करणें, चाटून पुसून नाहींसा करणें, कडाचूर *m.* करणें-करून टाकणें, चपेट *or* चपाट *adv.* करणें, फस्त *adv.* खाणें, रपाटणें, झपाटणें, चपाटणें, ताव *m.* देणें *with* वर *of o.* पूज करणें, उपटून खाणें, सप्पा *m.* उडवणें-चळवणें *g. of o.* रगडणें, रपाटणें.
To eat one's words, v. To RETRACT. बोलणें *n.*-बोल *m.*-&c. परत-माघारा घेणें.
He that would eat, must work. खटपट करी तोच पोटभरी, दळील तोच भरील.
2 *corrode.* खाणें, खणणें. [करणें.
To EAT, *v. n. take a meal,* v. MEAL. जेवणें, भोजन *n.*-जेवण *n.*
2 into;—an ulcer, &c. चरणें.
EATABLE, *a.* v. V. A. 1. खाया-भक्षाया-चा-जोगा-जोगता-&c. भक्ष्य, भक्षणीय, भक्षितव्य, भोज्य, भक्षणार्ह, खाद्य, खादनीय, अदनीय.
EATABLE, *n.* खाणें *n.* भक्ष्य *n.* खाद्य *n.* भोज्य *n.* भक्ष *m.*
Eatables—compreh. *or* freely. खाणें जेवणें *n.* भक्ष्यें भोज्यें *n. pl.*-amongst children. खाऊ *m.* खाई *f.*
Light e. (as a fruit, a sweetmeat, &c.) भातुकें *n.* भातकूल *n.* तानलाडू *m.* भूकलाडू *m.*
EATEN, *p.* v. V. A. 1. खाल्लेला, &c. भक्षित, भुक्त, खादित, अशित, गिलित, ग्रस्त, ग्रसित.

Eater, *n.* v. V. A. 1. खाणारा, &c. भक्षण-&c. कर्त्ता, भक्षक *and* भक्षी (in comp. as अन्नभक्षक, मांसभक्षी, &c.), भोजी (in comp. as अन्नभोजी, मांसभोजी, &c.), आशी (in comp. as अन्नाशी, अमृताशी, विषाशी, पथ्याशी, अल्पाशी, मिताशी), भुक् (in comp. as वायुभुक्सर्प, आखुभुक्, अन्नभुक्), खादरा (in comp. and with contemptuous implication,as. अफीम खादरा, भांग खादरा, &c.).

Eating, *n.* v. V. A. 1.—*act.* खाणें *n.* &c. भक्षण *n.* अशन *n.* अदन *n.* खादन *n.*

2 खाणें *n.* खणणें *n.* खणती *f.*

v. V. N. 1. जेवणें *n.* जेवण *n.* भोजन *n.*

To be heavy & listless from over-eating. डेबणें.

Eating-house, *n.* अन्नाचें दुकान *n.* भटारखाना *m.* जेवणावळ *f.*

Keeper of a e. भटचारी *or* भटारी.

Eaves, *n.* वळचणी *f. pl.* पागोळ्या *f. pl.* पावळ्या *f.pl.* हीड *f.*गई *f.*

Eaves-drip, *n.* वळचणीची धार *f.* पागोळी *f.* पावळी *f.*

To **Eaves-drop**, *v. n.* आडून-वळचणींतून-&c. कानवसा *m.*-कानवा *m.*-कानव्हळा *m.* घेणें.

Eaves-dropper, *n.* v. V. आडून-&c. कानवसा-&c. घेणारा.

Ebb, Ebbing, *n. reflux of the tide.* ओहट *m.* ओहटी *f.* ओहटें *n.* सुकती *f.* [*m.*

Extreme e. ebb at the springs. निखार *or* निंखार ओहट

The e. and flow. सुकती भरती *f.*

2 *wane, &c.* v. **Decline**. उतार *m.* उतरती *f.* उतरतापाया *m.*

To **Ebb**, *v. n.* v. N. 1. ओहटणें, ओहट *m.*-ओहटी *f.* चालणें-लागणें.

To e. dry. सुखणें.

Ebb-tide. See **Ebb**.

Ebony, *n. diospyros glutinosa.* टेंभुरणी *f.* आबनूस *m.* तेंदू *or* तेंटू *m.* तिंदुक *m. f.*

Ebriety. See **Drunkenness**.

Ebriosity, *n.*v.A. दारूबाजी *f.* निशाखोरी *f.* झिंगीखोरी *f.* निशाबाजी *f.*

Ebrious, *a. given to drinking.* दारूबाज, मस्ता *or* मस्त्या, अमली, निशाखोर, निशाबाज, झिंगा *or* झिंग्या *remiss.* झिंगट *rather e.* झिंगीखोर.

Ebullition, *n.* v. **Boiling**. कढ *m.* अधण *n.*

Sound *or* noise of brisk e. सळसळ *f.*-intens. सळाळ *m.*

2 (as of tenderness, grief, &c.) *sudden swelling and bursting forth.* उबाळा *m.* उभड *f.* उभडा *m.* उमाडा *m.* उमास *m.* उमासा *m.* उमाळा *m.* उमाळी *f.* उत *m.*

Eccentric, *a. divergent.* केंद्रपराङ्मुख, मध्यत्यागी,

2—in geometry. असमकेंद्र, विषमकेंद्र.

3 fig. *anomalous, devious,* v. **Irregular**. गैरमार्गाचा, गैरचालीचा, एकप्रकार, एकप्रकारचा, एकतऱ्हेचा, गैरशिस्त, बेशिस्त, लोकबाह्य, लोकोत्तर, अन्यथाचारी, अन्यथावर्त्ती.

Eccentricity, *n.* v. A. 1. केंद्रपराङ्मुखता *f.* मध्यत्यागिता *f.*

2 असमकेंद्रता *f.* असमकेंद्रभाव *m.* केंद्रवैषम्य *n.*

3 गैरशिस्तपणा *m.* बेशिस्तपणा *m.* विलक्षणपणा *m.* अन्यथाचार *m.* अन्यथावर्त्तन *n.* वैलक्षण्य *n.* लोकबाह्यता *f.* लोकमर्यादोल्लंघन *n.* लोकमर्यादातिक्रम *m.*

Ecclesiastic, *n. person holding an appointment in the church.* धर्मकर्मनियुक्त मनुष्य *m.* धर्मपदनियुक्त मनुष्य *m.* धर्मोपदेशक *m.*

Ecclesiastical, *a. belonging, &c. to the church or religion.* धर्माविषयींचा,धर्मप्रकरणाचा,धर्मप्रकरणविषयक,धर्मप्रकरणसंबंधी.

Echo, *n.* प्रतिध्वनि *m.* प्रतिनाद *m.* प्रतिशब्द *m.* पडशब्द *m.* पडसाद *m. f.* अनुध्वनि *m.* अनुरणन *n.*

2 fig; *mere repeater of the opinions of another.* तुणतुण्या, बोललेलें बोलणारा.

To **Echo**, *v.n.* प्रतिध्वनि *m.*-प्रतिनाद *m.*-प्रतिशब्द *m.*-&c.होणें, घुमणें, दणदणणें, दणाणणें.

To **Echo**, *v. a.* प्रतिध्वनि *m.*-प्रतिनाद *m.*-प्रतिशब्द *m.*-&c. करणें.

Echoed, *p.* v. V. A. प्रतिध्वनित, प्रतिनादित.

Eclaircissement. See **Explanation**.

Eclat, *n. applause, honor, &c.* v. **Glory**. रंग *m.* नकशा *m.* शोभा *f.* प्रतिष्ठा *f.* गाजावाजा *m.*

Eclectic, *a. selecting, choosing.* निवडून-वेचून-&c. काढणारा.

Eclipse, *n.* ग्रहण *n.* ग्रह *m.* ग्रास *m.* उपराग *m.*—of the sun. सूर्यग्रहण *n.*—of the moon. चंद्रग्रहण *n.*

Day of an e. ग्रहपर्व *n.* राहुपर्व *n.*

Duration of an e. स्थिति *f.*

Immersion or ingress at an e. स्पर्श *m.* वेध *m.*—Ablution at it. स्पर्शस्नान *n.*

Obscuration of an e. खग्रास *m.* राहुग्रास *m.*

Period of a lunar e. चंद्रपर्व *n.*

Rising during e. ग्रस्तोदय *m.*

Setting during e. ग्रस्तास्त *m.*

Total e. मीलन *n.*

Uncovering of an e. उन्मीलन *n.*

To **Eclipse**, *v. a.* ग्रासणें, ग्रास *m.* करणें *g. of o.* ग्रस्त करणें.

2 fig; *darken, obscure, &c.* v. To **Excel**. फिका-माजी-&c. पाडणें, मागें पाडणें, निस्तेज-मजीत-&c. करणें, उणें *n.* आणणें *with* ला *or* स, पाणी *n.* कमी करणें *g. of o.*

Eclipsed, *p.* v. V. 1. ग्रासलेला, राहुग्रस्त.

To be e. ग्रहण *n.* लागणें *in. con.*

2 फिका-&c. पाडलेला, मागें पाडलेला, &c.

To be e. दिपणें, दिपावणें, फिका पडणें, मजीत होणें.

Ecliptic, *n. great circle of the sphere.* क्रांतिवृत्त *n.* क्रांतिमंडल *n.* क्रांतिकक्ष *n.* क्रांतिकक्षा *f.* अयनवृत्त *n.* भवलय *n.* भवृत्त *n.*

Declination of a point of the e. क्रांति भाग *m.*

Inclination (of a planet's orbit) to the e. परमापम *m.*

Motion of the nodes of the e. क्रांतिपातगति *f.*

Nodes of the e. क्रांतिपात *m.*

Obliquity of the e.परमक्रांति *f.*परक्रांति *f.*परमापम *m.*परापम *m.*

Eclogue, *n. pastoral.* मेषपालन विषयक काव्य *n.*

Economical, *a.* v. N. 2. *frugal,*—of persons. काटकसऱ्या, कतरबेती, कतरबेत्या, कारस्थानी, अल्पव्ययी, परिमितव्ययी, विचारव्ययी, व्यवस्थितव्ययी, आडगिराइकीघेणारा, नफेबार-&c. घेणारा.

2—of expenses, &c. काटकसरीचा, कतरबेती, कतरबेताचा, घरजोगाबणीचा, घरजुगुतीचा, अल्पव्ययाचा, मितव्ययाचा.

Economist, *n.* See the **Adjective**.

To **Economize**, *v. n.* बेताबातानें-टापटिपीनें-काटकसरीनें-&c. खर्च *m.* करणें, जितक्यास तितका-टापासटीप गरज *f.* करणें, काटकसर *f.* काढणें, खर्च *m.* करणें-पाहणें, कारकुनी *f.* करणें.

Economy, *n. management, disposition, arrangement, &c.* व्यवस्था *f.* बेत *m.* बेतबात *m.* बंदोबस्त *m.* संजोग *m.* कारस्थान *n.*

Political e. अर्थशास्त्र n. .

2 *discretion of expense, frugality.* काटकसर f. कतरबेत m. काटकसरीचा-&c. खर्च m. घरजुगूत f. घरजोगावणी f. तडजोड f. खर्चाचाबेतबात m.-टापटीप f. कारस्थान n. अल्पव्यय m. परिमितव्यय m. गृहस्थीकावा m.

ECSTACY, *n. absorbed state*;—gener. समाधि m. f. तन्मयावस्था f. मोहावस्था f. आवेश m.

2 *rapture, transport,* v. JOY. परमानंद m. हर्षावेश m. हर्षनिमग्नता f. हर्षसंभ्रम m.

ECSTATIC, *a. rapturous.* हर्षावेशाचा, परमानंदाचा, मोहक.

ECUMENICAL. See UNIVERSAL.

EDACIOUS, EDACITY. See GLUTTONOUS, GLUTTONY.

EDDY, *n. contrary current.* घोटाळा m. फुगें n.

2 *whirlpool.* भोवरा m. आवर्त्त m. चक्र n.

To EDDY, *v. n.* घोटाळणें, कोंडाळणें, गोंधळणें.

EDGE, *n.* (of weapons, &c.). धार f. धारा f. बाड f.

A dull e. पडती धार, बसकी धार.

A sharp e. वाहती धार.

2 *brink, verge, margin.* कड f. कांठ m.किनारा m. कोर f. धार f. बाणी f. दर f. बाजू f. प्रांत m. प्रांतभाग m. कडण f.

Of broken e.—pitcher. &c. कांठफुटका. [पाळ f.

Raised e. (as around wells, mouth of handmill &c.)

To be set on e.—the teeth. अंबणें.

3 (esp. of fields, &c.) *border, margin, &c.* मेर f. मेंड m. दर f. बाजू f. किनारा m. कुपट f.

4 fig. *sharpness of weapons.* पाणी n. तेज n.

To EDGE, *v. a.* (weapons, tools, &c.). धार f. काढणें-करणें, शेवटणें, बाड f. देणें.

2 *sharpen, whet.* धार f. करणें-लावणें-देणें, पाजवणें, पाणी n. देणें, बाड f. लावणें, शेवटणें.

3 on; v. To INCITE. उठाळणी f. देणें-करणें, टोंचणी f. देणें-लावणें, धिग्या f. pl. लावणें.

Person edged on. खंडेराव m. हुणगोबा m.

4 See To BORDER. To FRINGE.

5 *move sideways.* बाजूकडे सरकवणें.

To EDGE, *v. n. move edgewise.* खिसणें, बाजूवर-कडेवर-&c. जाणें-होणें-सरणें- सरकणें.

EDGE-LESS, *a.* v. BLUNT. भिधारी, निधार.

EDGE-TOOL, *n.* धारेचें हत्यार n.-अऊत n.-&c.

EDGE-WISE, *adv.* धारेकडून, कडेकडून, कुडती v. लाव, बसव, ठेव.

EDGED, *a.*—of weapons, tools, &c. धारेचा, धारायुक्त, धाराविशिष्ट, सधार.

2 *having an edge (or border).* धार *or* धारी (in comp. as दुधार *or* दुधारी, तिधारी, चौधारी).

EDGING, *n. lace, fringe, &c. at the edge.* धडी f. किनारी f. कोर f. लकेरी f. मगजी f. गोट m. गोटा m.

That has e. मगजीदार.

EDIBLE, *a.* v. EATABLE. खायाचा, खाद्य, भक्ष्य, भक्षणीय.

EDICT, *n. decree, &c.* v. LAW. राजाज्ञा f. राजशासन n. शासन n. आज्ञापत्र n. निबंध m.

General e. or enactment. सामान्यशासन.

EDIFICATION, *n.* v. V. परमार्थ बुद्धीची वृद्धि f. सन्मार्ग निष्ठेची वृद्धि f. सन्मार्गस्थैर्य n. ज्ञानवृद्धि f.

EDIFICATORY. See EDIFYING.

EDIFICE, *n.* v. BUILDING. इमारत f. इमला m.

To EDIFY, *v. a. instruct, improve.* परमार्थबुद्धि f. देणें-वाढवणें, सन्मार्गनिष्ठा f. स्थापणें-वाढवणें, सन्मार्गस्थैर्यप्रापण n. करणें, उपदेश m. करणें.

EDIFYING, *p. a.* v. V. परमार्थबुद्धि वाढवणारा, सन्मार्गनिष्ठा वाढवणारा, ज्ञानवर्द्धक, उपदेशपर.

To EDIT, *v. a. prepare for publication.* शोधकरून छापण्यास तयार करणें, शोधपूर्वक ग्रंथ प्रकाश m. करणें.

EDITION, *n.*—of a book. आवृत्ति f. छाप m. छापणी f.

EDITOR, *n.* v. V. शोध करून छापण्यास तयार करणारा, शोधपूर्वक ग्रंथ प्रकाशक, ग्रंथप्रकाशक.

2 *conductor of a newspaper.* कर्त्ता.

EDITORIAL, *a.* v. N. 2. कर्त्याचा, कर्त्यानें केलेला-लिहिलेला.

EDITORIAL, *n.* कर्त्यानें केलेला लेख m.कर्त्यानें लिहिलेला मजकूर m.

To EDUCATE, *v. a. instruct, &c.* शिक्षा f. करणें, शिकवणें, लिहिणें पुसणें n. सांगणें, शिक्षित-विद्याकलादिशिक्षित करणें.

2 *bring up, rear.* पाळणें, पोसणें,पाळणूक f.-पालनपोषण n.-&c. करणें, लहानाचा मोठा करणें.

EDUCATED, *p. & a.* v. V. 1. शिकवलेला, &c. शिक्षित.

2 पाळलेला, &c. पोषित.

I. *furnished with knowledge.* पढीक, पढलेला, व्युत्पन्न,अध्ययनसंपन्न, विद्यासंपन्न.

EDUCATION, *n.* v. V. 1.—*act.* शिकवणें n. शिकवण f. शिक्षा f.

I. *state of being furnished with knowledge,* v. LEARNING. विद्या f. व्युत्पत्ति f. अध्ययनसंपन्नता f. अध्ययनसंपत्ति f. अक्षरसंपत्ति f. साक्षरता f.

That has finished his e. कृताध्ययन, अधीत, अभ्यासप्रवीण.

EDUCATIONAL, *a.* शिक्षेचा, शिक्षासंबंधी, शिक्षाविषयक.

E. department. विद्याखातें n. शाळाखातेंn.

To EDUCE, *v. a. bring or draw forth.* काढणें, काढून घेणें-आणणें, निष्कासनn. करणें.

EEL, *n.* वाम f. वांव f.

To EFFACE, *v. a. expunge, obliterate, blot out, erase, cancel.* पुसणें, पुसून टाकणें, पुसकटणें, खोडणें, खोडून टाकणें, बोळा m. फिरवणें, छकणें, छेकाm. मारणें, फांटाm. देणें-मारणें-घालणें, पूजn. घालणें-देणें, काढणें, काढून टाकणें, खरडून-छिलून-&c. काढणें, दिसेनासा करणें. [केलेला, &c.

EFFACED, *p.* v. V. पुसून टाकलेला, खोडून टाकलेला, दिसेनासा

EFFACEMENT, EFFACING, *n.* v. V.—*act.* पुसून टाकणें n. &c.

EFFECT, *n.* v. CONSEQUENCE. कार्यn. गुण m. फल *pop.* फळ n. अर्थ m. जन्य n.

Cause and e. कार्य कारणn.

Evil e. अवगुणm.

In e. *really.* वस्तुतः, वस्तुगत्या.

Relation of cause and e. कार्यकारण भाव m.

Without e. Of no e. निष्फळ, व्यर्थ.

To take e. *succeed.* गुणास येणें, बीं रुजणें, फळणें

To take e. upon. लागणें, लागू होणें.

To take evil e. बाधणें, वठणें.

2 effects; *goods,* v. CHATTELS. मालमत्ता f.

To EFFECT, *v. a. perform, produce, do, make,* v. To ACCOMPLISH. साधणें, संपादणें, सर करणें.

2 *bring about, bring to pass.* घडवून-बनवून-&c. आणणें, घडवणें, करवणें, साधणें, जोडणें, घटवटणा *f*.-&c. करणें.

Effected, *p*. v. V. 1. साधलेला, &c. साधित, सिद्ध, निष्पादित, चरितार्थ.

2 घडवून आणलेला, घडवलेला, साधलेला, &c.

Effecting, *n*. v. V. 1.—*act*. साधणें *n*. संपादणें*n*. &c. साधणूक *f*. साधन*n*. संपादन *n*. निष्पादन *n*. घटना *f*.

2—*act*. घडवून आणणें*n*. घडवणें*n*. &c. घटवटणा *f*. उपस्थापन*n*.

Effective, *a*. *that produces effect*, v. **Efficacious**. गुण कारक-कारी-कर्त्ता, गुणावह, गुणाधायक, गुणोपधायक, कार्यसाधक, कार्यसंपादक, साधनी.

2 *fit for service or use.* उपयोगी, उपयोगाचा, कामाचा, कार्योपयोगी, कार्यक्षम, कार्यसमर्थ, कार्यशक्त.

Effectiveness, *n*. v. A. 1. गुण*m*. गुणकारकत्व*n*. कार्यसाधकत्व*n*. गुणकारिता *f*. &c. कर्मगुण*m*.

2 उपयोगीपणा *m*. उपयोगिता *f*. कार्यक्षमता *f*. कार्यशक्ति *f*.

Effectual, *a*. *that has produced effect.* सफल, अमोघ, सार्थक, सार्थ, कृतार्थ, कृतकृत्य, कृतगुण, प्राप्तफल, फलित.

2 *that produces effect.* See **Efficacious**.

Effectually, *adv*. v. A. फळ*n*.-गुण*m*.-&c. येईल असें.

2 *thoroughly*, v. **Wholly**. पुरतेपणें, अगदीं.

Effectualness, *n*. v.A.1. सफलत्व *n*. साफल्य*n*. अमोघत्व*n*. &c.

To **Effectuate**. See To **Effect**.

Effeminacy, *n*. v. A. रांडेपणा*m*. बाइक्येपणा*m*. बाइलेपणा*m*. नामर्दी *f*. नामर्दपणा *m*. रांडमाणुसकी *f*. स्त्रीबुद्धि *f*. स्त्रीस्वभाव*m*.

Effeminate, *a*. *womanish*. बाइक्या, बाइल्या, नामर्द, रांड्या, स्त्रीबुद्धि, कन्यारास, जनानी, चुलभानवशा, बाईलकाम्या.

An e. person. रांडमाणूस*m*. बाईलमाणूस*m*. रांड्यापुरुष *m*. लंडी *f*. दक्या *m*. रंडापति*m*.

That has an e. voice—a man. बाईलबोल्या.

To **Effervesce**, *v. n. work, bubble and hiss*, v. To **Ferment**. उतणें, ऊत*m*. येणें *in. con.* चिवचिवणें, खतखतणें.

Effervescence, *n*. v. V. उतणें*n*. ऊत*m*. खतखत *f*.

Effervescent, *a*. v. V. खतखतणारा, फणफणणारा, फणफणीत.

Effete. See **Barren**, **Worn out**.

Efficacious, *a*. *productive of effect, powerful of effect.* गुणी, गुणाचा, गुणकारक- कारी-&c. गुणावह, गुणाधायक, गुणदायक, गुणप्रद, गुणोपधायक, गुणोत्पादक, अमोघ, साधनी, कारिगर *or* गार, कार्यसाधक, कार्यसंपादक, जयावह.

Efficaciousness, **Efficacy**, *n*. v. A. सत्व *n*. तेज *n*. गुण *m*. गुणांश *m*. कर्मगुण *m*. गुणकारिता *f*. गुणावहता *f*. बळाबळ *f*. जीव *m*. कार्यकारिता *f*. गुणशक्ति *f*. कार्यसाधकता *f*.

Efficiency. *n*. v. A. कर्त्तृत्व *n*. कर्त्तेपणा *m*. कार्यसाधकत्व *n*.

Efficient, *a*. *that effects or causes*, v. **Causative**. कारक, कार्यसाधक, साधक.

Effigy, *n*. *image, representation.* बाहुला *m*. *or* ली *f*. *or* लें *n*. पुतळा *m*. प्रतिनिधि *m*. प्रतिमा *f*. प्रतिरूप *n*. प्रतिमूर्ति *f*. प्रतिकाय *m*. प्रतिकृति *f*.

Funeral rites performed on an e. (of leaves of Butea frondosa) when the corpse is missing. पालाशविधि *m*.

Efflorescence, *n*.—in medicine; *eruption of humours.* पुरळ *or* पुळूळ *m*. उतणें *n*. उफणणें *n*. उगवण *f*.

2—in chemistry. केनसी *f*. चिती *f*.

Effluvium, *n*. गंधपरमाणु *m*.

Strong, stimulating e. ओरट *or* ओरड *m*. [स्राव *m*.

Efflux, **Effluence**, *n*. *flowing out.* बाहेर येणें *n*. बाहेर निघणें*n*.

To **Efforce**. See To **Force**.

Effort, *n*. *strenuous exertion.* प्रयत्न *m*. आयास *m*. सायास *m*. प्रयास *m*. जुलूम *m*. जबरदस्ती *f*. देवड *f*. बशर्त *f*. भगीरथप्रयत्न *m*. दीर्घप्रयत्न *m*. आटाघाट *m*. *f*. वाटाघाट *m*. *f*. आटाआट *f*. उद्यम *m*. महोद्यम *m*. महोत्साह *m*. अट्टाहास *m*. घोरंकार *m*. *pl*.

With e. यत्नतः, प्रयत्नतः, अटें बळें.

Without e. अयत्नतः *pop.* अयत्नानें *or* अयत्नें.

With many efforts. सातासायासांनीं.

Of this word the sense is further distinguishable into two shades; and there are in *Maráthi* very many and very lively formations involving the sense yet respecting, some, the one shade, and some, the other. Here accordingly, we have collected the formations; and we have distinguished the sense that they might be duly allotted. In the shade of *a vehement and concentrated exertion of strength*—as expressed by such words as *a strain, a heave, a pull*, are यत्न *m*. प्रयत्न *m*. महाप्रयत्न *m*. ताण *m*. *n*. उरस्फोड *f*. नेट *m*. तडक *f*. अवसान*n*. एकगजब *m*. ढई *f*. वेग *m*. पेलाव *m*. धोंशा *m*. अनर्थ *m*. त्राण *n*. लगट *m*. *f*.

With one vehement e. *with all vigor concentrated, with might and main.* भरघोसानें *or* भरल्याघोसानें, मोठ्याजोरानें, मोठ्यापिळानें, बशर्तीनें, सत्राण *or* णें, जीवटाकून-तोडून-देऊन, तिडीक देऊन *or* एके तिडकेनें, आंतडीं कवळून.

To make a last and desperate e. मरतां मरतां हातपाय *m*. *pl*. झाडणें.

In the shade of *a brisk, smart, and short exertion of strength*,—as expressed by such words as *a run, a spurt, a go, a stretch, a rush, a dash, a start, a heat, a snatch, a fit, a brunt*, are झपाटा *m*. तडाका *m*. धडाका *m*. तडक *f*. भलेरी *v*. लाव, घाल, हिरिरी *f*. भराका *m*. भरारा *m*. कढ *m*. *v*. काढ, सूड *m*.

With one brisk e. *upon a stretch, at a run, at one dash, rush, spurt, go, &c. in a breath.* एका झपाट्यानें, एका सपाट्यानें, एका तडाक्यानें, &c. एक ओढ *or* एका ओढीनें, एका दमानें, एका आवेशानें, झपाट्यासरसां, तडाक्यासरसां, भिराक्यासरसां, एक कढ काढून.

To make great e. or exertion. जंजाळ *m*. *n*. तोडणें, जंजीर *f*. तोडणें. [द्वृत्य *n*.

Effrontery, *n*. v. **Impudence**. धिटाई *f*. तिखें *n*. तोंड *n*. औ-

Effulgence, **Effulgent**. See **Brightness**, **Bright**.

To **Effuse**, *v. a. pour out.* ओतणें.

Effusion, *n*. v. V.—*act*. ओतणें *n*. ओतणी *f*.

E. of blood. रक्तपात *m*.

Eger, *n*. *impetuous flood.* घोडा *m*. बाण *m*.

Egg, *n*. अंड *pop.* अंडें *n*. कवट *or* ठ *n*.

Contents of an e. बील *m*. बलक *m*.

Golden e. हत्तीचा पाय *m*.

Produced from e. अंडज.

To drop her eggs—a bird. अंडीं *n*. *pl*. गाळणें.

To EGG. See To INCITE.

EGG-PLANT, *n.* वांगी *f.* वृंताक *m.*

The fruit of the e. वांगें *n.* वृंताक *n.*

EGG-SHELL, *n.* कवंची *f.* कवंठी *f.* कवंटें *n.* अंड्याचें टरफल *n.*

EGOISM, *n. assertion of personality, sense of self.* अहंपणा *m.* मीपणा *m.* मीपण *n.* अहंकार *m.* अहंभाव *m.* अहंमति *f.* अहंमान *m.* अहंममता *f.* अहंपदार्थ *m.*

EGOIST, *n.* अहंमानी, अहंवादी.

EGOTISM, *n. self-conceit, self-praise, &c.* मीपणा *m.* मीपण *n.* आपलीक *f.* आत्मस्तुति *f.* आत्मश्लाघा *f.*

EGOTIST, *n.* EGOTISTICAL, *a.* मीपणा भोगणारा-मिरवणारा-करणारा, बढाईखोर, आपली बढाई सांगणारा, आत्मश्लाघी, आत्मस्तावक.

To EGOTIZE, *v. n.* आपला बडिवार *m.*-आपली बढाई *f.*-आपली बढाइकी *f.*-&c. सांगणें-मिरवणें, आत्मश्लाघा *f.*-आत्मस्तुति *f.*करणें.

EGREGIOUS, *a. eminent, distinguished.* विलक्षण, लोकोत्तर, अलौकिक.

2 v. ARRANT. बिलंद, बिलंदी.

EGREGIOUSLY, *adv. greatly, enormously, &c.* v. EXCESSIVELY. पराकाष्ठेचा, अत्यंत, फारच.

EGRESS, EGRESSION, *n. going or issuing out.* बाहेर जाणें *n.* निघणें *n.* बहिर्गमन *n.* बहिर्गम *m.* निर्गमन *n.* निस्सरण *n.* निष्क्रमण *n.*

EH, *interj.* ए, ये, ओं, उः, अरे, रे.

EIGH, *interj.* हाय, अहा.

EIGHT, *a.* आठ, अष्ट.

Aggregate of e. आठकी *f.* अष्टक *n.*

Consisting of, belonging to, &c. e. आठका.

EIGHTEEN, *a.* अठरा.

EIGHTH, *a.* आठवा.

EIGHTIETH, *a.* ऐशावा.

EIGHTY, *a.* ऐशीं,-one.एक्याऐशीं,एकांयूशीं,-two.ब्याऐशीं,ब्यांयूशीं,-three. त्र्याऐशीं, त्र्यांयूशीं,four.चौऱ्याऐशीं *or* चौऱ्यांयूशीं,five. पंचायूशीं,-six.शांयूशीं,-seven.सत्यांयूशीं,-eight,अठ्यांयशीं,-nine एकुणनव्वद, नव्यांयूशीं.

EITHER, *pron. which soever of two.* अन्यतर, एकतर, हाकींतो.

2 *any one.* कोणी *or* कोण्ही, कोणीही.

EITHER, *adv.* v. OR. कीं. [*m.* करणें.

To EJACULATE, *v. a. dart,* v. To THROW. फेंकणें, टाकणें, निक्षेप

EJACULATION, *n.* v. V.—*act.* टाकणें *n.* &c. निक्षेप *m.*

I. *short prayer, &c.* प्रार्थनेचा उद्गार *m.* उद्गारित प्रार्थना *f.* आकस्मिकालप्रार्थना *f.*

To EJECT, *v. a. cast out,* v. To EXPEL. घालवणें, घालणें, काढणें, काढून देणें-टाकणें, निस्सारण *n.*-निरसन *n.*-&c. करणें *g. of o.*

2 (a demon). काढणें, घालवणें, सोडवणें, प्रसारण *n.* करणें *g. of o.* प्रसारित करणें.

EJECTION, *n.* v. V.—*act.* घालवणें *n.* &c.. बहिष्कार *m.* बहिष्करण *n.* निस्सारण *n.* निरसन *n.* निरासन *n.* निरास *m.*

To EKE OUT, *v. a. make to serve, last, &c.* पुरवणें, पुरवून पुरवून करणें, लांबवणें.

To ELABORATE, *v. a. prepare, work up, &c. with care and diligence.* मोठ्याश्रमानें तयारकरणें, कमावणें, कमावणी *f.*-कमाई *f.*-मशागत *f.*-मरामत *f.*-संस्कार *m.*-परिष्कार *m.*-&c. करणें, परिष्कृत-संस्कृत करणें.

ELABORATE, *a.* ELABORATED, *p.* v. V. मोठ्याश्रमानें केलेला, संस्कृत, संस्कारित, परिष्कृत, मेहनतीचा, मशागतीचा, &c. श्रमसाधित.

ELABORATELY, *adv.* v. V. मोठ्याश्रमानें, मोठ्यामेहनतीनें, संस्कारपूर्वक.

To ELAPSE, *v. n. pass.* जाणें, होऊन जाणें, लोटणें, उडणें, गुजरणें *or* गुदरणें, गत होणें, गतणें.

ELAPSED, *p.* v. V. गेलेला *or* गेला, &c. गत, भूत, गुदस्त *or* गुदस्ता.

ELASTIC, *a. that has the property of returning to the form from which it is bent, &c.* स्थितिस्थापक, पूर्वस्थितिप्रापी, पूर्वस्थितिगामी, वेतसवृत्ति, लवचीक.

ELASTICITY, *n.* v. A. स्थितिस्थापकता *f.* &c. स्थितिस्थापकगुण *m.* लवचीकपणा *m.* वेतसवृत्ति *f.*

To ELATE, *v. a. elevate with success,* v. To PUFF UP. हर्षानें चढवणें-फुगवणें, हर्षपुष्ट-हर्षप्रफुल्लित-&c. करणें.

ELATE, *a.* ELATED, *p.* v. V. हर्षानें चढलेला-फुगवलेला, हर्षपुष्ट, हर्षप्रफुल्लित, हर्षोन्नत.

ELATION, *n.* v. V.—*state.* हर्षविकास *m.* हर्षपुष्टि *f.* हर्षोन्नति *f.*

ELBOW, *n.* कोंपर *m. n.* कूर्पर *m.*

E.-joint. कोपराची खीळ *f.*

2 *flexure or angle.*—gener. कोपरा *m.* वांकण *n.*

Elbows and ears,—compreh. *corners and projections.* कानकोपरे *m. pl.* [रणें-ढोसणें.

To ELBOW, *v. a.* कोंपरखळी *f.*-कोंपरढोसणी *f.* मारणें, कोपरानें मा-

ELBOW-ROOM, *n.* कोंपरपसरण्याला जागा *f.* अवकाश *m.*

ELDER, *a.* वडील, थोरला, ज्येष्ठ, पूर्वज, अग्रिम.

ELDER, *n.* पुरखा, गुरुजन.

Elders, v. ANCESTOR. वडील *or* वाडवडील *m. pl.* मागले *m. pl.* मागील पुरुष *m. pl.*

Elders, *elderly people.* वृद्ध *m. pl.* वृद्धलोक *m. pl.*

Council or meeting of elders. वृद्धसभा *f.* वृद्धसंघ *m.* वृद्धसमुदाय *m.* वृद्धमंडल *n.*

Teach not your elders! मुला तुझ्या सटीच्या न्यां घुगऱ्या खाल्ल्या आहेत.

ELDERLY, *a.* v. OLD. आडम्हातारा, उतारवयाचा, उत्तरवयस्क, वयःस्थ *or* वयस्थ, वयोगत, वयस्क.

ELDERSHIP, *n.* v. A. वडलाई *f.* अग्रजत्व *n.* ज्येष्ठत्व *n.*

ELDEST, *n.* सर्वांहून वडील-ज्येष्ठ-&c. पहिला, वडील.

ELECT, *a.* ELECTED, *p.* v. V. निवडलेला, वरलेला, निवडून नेमलेला, &c. वृत्त, वृत.

To ELECT, *v. a. select, choose.* निवडणें, वरणें, निवडून-वेचून घेणें-काढणें-नेमणें-योजणें-कूम करणें. [वड *f.*

ELECTION, *n.* v. V.—*act.* निवडणें *n.* वेचणें *n.* &c. वरण *n.* नि-

I. *power of choice,* v. CHOICE. निवडण्याची सत्ता *f.*-अधिकार *m.*

ELECTOR, *n.* v. V. निवडूननेमणारा, निवडूनयोजणारा, &c.

ELECTRIC, ELECTRICAL, *a. pertaining, &c. to electricity,* विजेचा, विद्युतेचा, विद्युत्संबंधी, विद्युत्विषयक, वैद्युत.

2 *containing electricity.* विद्युत्वान्, तडित्वान्, विद्युद्गर्भित, तडिद्गर्भित.

ELECTRICITY, *n. electric fluid.* वीज *f.* विद्युत् *f.* विद्युत्तन्मात्र *n.* इरम्मद *m.*

To ELECTRIFY, *v. a. give an e. shock to.* विजेचा धक्का *n.* देणें.

2 *charge with electricity.* वीज *f.* भरणें-घालणें.

3 fig. *shock.* See To SHOCK.

ELECTRIFYING-MACHINE, *n.* धका *or* क्का *m.*

ELECTUARY, *n.*—in medicine. लेह *m.* अवलेह *m.*

ELEEMOSYNARY, *a. living on alms.* भिकेवर पोट भरणारा, भिक्षा-जीवी, भिक्षोपजीवी, भिक्षाशी, घातलेल्या अन्नाचा.

2 *given in alms.* भिकेचा, भिक्षेचा, खैरातेचा, धर्माचा, भैक्ष्य, भिक्षाप्राप्त, भिक्षालब्ध. [च्याप्रकरणाचा.

3 *relating to charitable donations.* धर्मादायाचा, धर्मादाया-

ELEGANCE, *n.* v. A. 1. सुशोभितपणा *m.* सुरेखपणा *m.* शोभा *f.* कांति *f.* श्री *f.* चारुता *f.* लावण्य *n.*

2 प्रौढी *f.* सफाई *f.* लालित्य *n.* पदलालित्य *n.*

ELEGANT, *a.* v. BEAUTIFUL, FINE. शोभिवंत, सुशोभित, शोभेचा, सुरेख, भव्य, दिव्य, चारु, राजस, राजसबाणा.

2—of style; *flowery, figured.* अलंकारी, आलंकारिक, सालं-कार, प्रौढ, प्रशस्त, गद्यपद्यात्मक, सु in comp.

ELEGANTLY, *adv.* v. A. 1. शोभेलसें, शोभेनें, शोभापूर्वक.

2 प्रशस्तपणानें, प्रौढीनें, सफाईनें.

ELEGIAC, *a.* v. N. शोकगीताचा, शोकगानाचा.

ELEGY, *n. mournful song.* शोकगीत *n.* शोकगान *n.* विलापगीत*n.* शोककवन *n.* [मरशा *m.*

E. sung by Muhammadans during their Muharram.

ELEMENT, *n. constituent principle.* धातु *m.* तत्व *n.* मूलतत्व *n.* द्रव्य *n.* कारण *n.*

The seven elements of the body. सप्तधातु *m. pl.* (These are chyle, blood, flesh, fat, marrow, bone, semen; or रस, रक्त, मांस, मेद, मज्जा, अस्थि, शुक्र).

2—as earth, air, &c. भूत*n.* महाभूत*n.*

The five elements (*viz.* earth, water, fire, air, ákásha). पंचभूतें*n.pl.* पंच महाभूतें *n.pl.* पंचतत्वें*n.pl.* पंचता *f.* धातुजात*n.* प्रकृति *f.*

An archetype or subtile rudiment of any of the five elements. तन्मात्र*n.* [पंचीकरण*n.*

Reduction into union and order of the five elements.

Relation of an e. (or the elements) with its (or their) combinations and modifications. प्रकृतिविकृतिभाव*m.*

That lives in (any) two of the elements, *amphibious.* उभयचर, द्विधागति.

The five subtile rudiments of the five elements. पंच-तन्मात्रें*n.pl.* [त्र*n.*

3 *province, sphere, &c.* v. BUSINESS. प्रकरण*n.* विषय*m.* क्षे-

4 elements; v. RUDIMENTS. मूलपीठिका *f.* मूलतत्वें*n.pl.*

5 See INGREDIENT.

ELEMENTAL, ELEMENTARY, *a. belonging, &c. to the elements.* भूतविषयक, भूतसंबंधी, भौतिक, भौत, भूतभाव, भूतस्थ.

2 *produced by, consisting of, &c. the elements or an e.* पंच-भूतांचा, पंचतत्वांचा, पंचभूतात्मक, &c.पांचभौतिक, आधिभौतिक.

3 *initial,* v. RUDIMENTAL. मूलतत्वविषयक, मूलतत्वप्रतिपादक.

ELEPHANT. हत्ती*m.* हस्ती*m.* गज*m.* कुंजर*m.* मातंग*m.* वारण*m.* करी *m.* लंबकर्ण*m.*—in contempt, &c. हतरूड*n.*

Bell of an e. गजघंटा *f.* गजघाट *f.*

Body-cloth of an e. झूल *f.* बुरका *or* खाम.

Carrier of spear before an e. गडेकरी*m.*

Chain or rope of foot of an e. अंदू*m.* [गाडूरा*m.*

Driver or keeper of an e. पीलवान*m.* महात *or* महावत*or*

E. in rut. मदोत्कट (कुंजर, गज, &c.).

E. without tusks. बुकणाहत्ती *or* मुकणाहत्ती*m.*

Elephants—considered as an arm of an army. गजभार *m.* कुंजरभार*m.*

Exudation from the temples of an e. हस्तिमद*m.* मद *m* सिंधु*m.*

Female e. हत्तीण *f.* हस्तिनी *f.* कुंजरी *f.* करेणु *f.*

Foothold for the rider of an e. कलावा *or* किलावा*m.*

Frontal globe on forehead of an e. कुंभ*m.*

Goad of an e. अंकुश*m.*

Head-cloth of an e. श्री *f.*

Large or fine e. गजराज*m.* गजेंद्र*m.* गजपति*m.* गजपुंगव*m.*

Nail of the foot of an e. *It is used medicinally.* गज-नख*m.n.* [महाल*m.*

Place where elephants are tied up. पीलखाना*m.* हत्ती-

Scream or cry of the e. किंकळी *f.* किराळी *f.*

Seat behind the tower of an e. for the page. खवासखाना*m.* खवासा*m.*

Temple of the e. गंड*m.* गंडस्थल*n.* कट*m.*

Tip of the trunk of an e. पुष्कर*n.*

Tower of an e. (canopied). अंबारी *f.* चंवरडोल*m.*

Tower of an e. (without canopy). हौदा*m.*

Troop or body of elephants. गजभार*m.* कुंजरभार*m.* गज-व्रज*m.* गजयूथ*n.*

Young male e. छावा*m.*

ELEPHANT-EARED, *a.* गजकर्णी.

ELEPHANTIASIS, *n.* वारूळ*n.* चाळपुळी *f.* वल्मीक*n.* [न.

ELEPHANTINE, *a.* हत्तीचा, गजाचा, हस्तिसंबंधी, हस्तिविषयक, हास्ति-

To ELEVATE, *v. a.* v. To RAISE. उंच करणें, उंचावणें, चढवणें.

2 *raise to a higher station,* v. To EXALT. मोठा-&c. करणें, वाढवणें, पदवी *f.* वाढवणें *g. of o.*

ELEVATE, *a.* ELEVATED, *p.* v. V. 1. उंच केलेला, उंचावलेला, &c.

2 मोठा केलेला, मोठ्या पदवीस चढवलेला.

ELEVATION. *n.* v. V.—*act.* उंच करणें *n.* &c. चढवणी *f.*

2 मोठा करणें *n.* वाढवणें *n.*

I. See HEIGHT. DIGNITY.

ELÈVE, *n. one brought up by another.* पोष्य, आश्रित.

ELEVEN, *a.* अकरा, एकादश.

ELEVENTH, *a.* अकरावा.

ELF. See DEMON, DEVIL.

To ELICIT, *v. a. draw or strike out, &c.* काढणें, निष्पन्न करणें.

ELIGIBILITY, ELIGIBLENESS, *n.* v. A. ग्राह्यता *f.* ग्रहणीयता *f.* वरणीयता *f.* &c. योग्यता *f.* लायकी *f.*

ELIGIBLE, *a. fit, &c. to be chosen.* घ्यायाचा-चा-जोगता-&c. ग्राह्य, ग्रहणीय, उपादेय, वरणीय, वर्य, परिगणनीय, नियोजनीय, स्वीक-रणीय, अंगीकार्य, योग्य, लायक.

To ELIMINATE, *v. a. expel, thrust out.* काढणें,काढून टाकणें-देणें.

2 (in Algebra) छेकणें, काढून टाकणें.

ELIMINATION, *n.* v.V.1. *act.*-काढणें *n.*—काढून टाकणें *n.* &c.

2 (in Algebra) छेकणें *n.* &c.

ELISION, *n.*—in grammar. लोप *m.* अदर्शन *n.*

Lost by e. गळत.

ELITE, *n. flower, choice portion.* निवड *f.*

ELIXIR VITÆ, *n.* रसायन *n.*
ELK *n.* सांबर *m. n.*
ELL, *n.* कापड मोजण्याचें एक इंग्रेजी मेज आहे.
ELLIPSE. See ELLIPSIS, 2.
ELLIPSIS, *n.*—in rhetoric. पदन्यूनता *f.* पदापेक्षा *f.* पदाकांक्षा *f.*
Supplying of an e. अध्याहार *m.* आकांक्षापूरण *n.*
(Word, clause, &c.) required to supply an e. (पद, वाक्य-&c.) अध्याहार्य.
(Word, clause, &c.) brought to supply an e. (पद, वाक्य-&c.) अध्याहृत.
2—in geometry. अंडाकार *m.* अंडाकृति *f.* दीर्घवर्तुल *n.*
ELLIPTICAL, *a.* v. N. 1. पदन्यूनतेचा, पदापेक्षेचा, पदाकांक्षेचा. 2. अंडाकार, अंडाकृति.
ELLIPTICALLY, *adv.* v. A. 1. कांहीं शब्द सोडून, पदन्यूनतापूर्वक. 2 अंडाकृतीनें.
ELM, *n.* एक झाड आहे.
ELOCUTION, *n. fluent, &c. speech,* v. ELOQUENCE. वक्तृत्व *n.* जबेफराशी *f.* वाक्चातुर्य *n.* शब्दचातुर्य *n.* वाक्पाटव *n.*
ELOGY. See PANEGYRIC, PRAISE.
To ELONGATE, &c. See To LENGTHEN, &c.
To ELOPE, *v. n.* v. To RUN AWAY. पळून जाणें, पळ *f.* काढणें-नेणें.
2—of a female. हात *m.* धरून जाणें, घर *n.* रिघणें-निघणें, लागून जाणें *with* शीं *of o.* बाहेर निघणें.
ELOPEMENT, *n.* v. V. 1. पळणें *n.* पळून जाणें *n.* पलायन *n.* 2 घररिघणी *f.* घरनिघणी *f.* घररिघाव *m.*
ELOQUENCE, *n.* वक्तृत्व *n.* वक्तृत्वशक्ति *f.* जबेफराशी *f.* जिभेची हातोटी *f.* वाचाशक्ति *f.* वाचोयुक्ति *f.* वाक्चातुर्य *n.* शब्दचातुर्य *n.* शब्दपांडित्य *n.* वाक्पाटव *n.* वाक्पटुता *f.* रसवंती *f.* सुप्रलाप *m.*
Goddess of e. (or speech). सरस्वती *f.* वाग्देवी *f.* वाग्देवता *f.* वाग्वल्ली *f.* वाग्विलासिनी *f.* वाग्वल्लरी *f.*
ELOQUENT, *a.* बोलून चांगला, बोलका, वक्ता, तोंडचा चतुर, तोंडचा नीट, सांगसुगरण, जबेफरास, वाग्मी, वाक्पटु, वाक्यविशारद, वाचोयुक्तिपटु, वागीश, वाक्पति, सुभाषित, मधुरभाषी, मंजुलभाषी, सुंदरभाषी, वदान्य.
Some terms for *an e. person (male)* are, बोलून बृहस्पति *or* बृहस्पति *m.* वाग्देवता *f.* वाचस्पति *m.* वक्ता *m.* महारथ *or* महारथी *m.* भाषणाचे छडे उडवणारा *m.*—for *an e. female.* सरस्वती, &c. *See the terms above for* goddess of eloquence. —for *an e. oration or composition.* पुष्पवृष्टि *f.* द्राक्षापाक *m.*
To speak with animated and overpowering e. छर्रे *m. pl.* उडविणें.
ELSE, *pron. one besides,* v. OTHER. दुजा, दुसरा, अन्य.
ELSE, *adv. otherwise.* नाहींतर, अन्यथा, इतरथा, एरवीं, नाहींपेक्षां, नाहींपक्षीं.
2 *beside, except that.* शिवाय, खेरीज, अणखी.
ELSEWHERE, *adv.* इतर ठिकाणीं, दुसऱ्या ठिकाणीं, अन्यठिकाणीं, अन्यस्थलीं, अन्यत्र, इतरत्र.
To ELUCIDATE, *v. a.* v. To EXPLAIN. उघडा- प्रत्यक्ष-स्पष्ट-व्यक्त -प्रकाशित-&c. करणें.
ELUCIDATION. See EXPLANATION.
To ELUDE, *v. a. evade, escape from artfully.* चुकवणें, टाळणें, टाळाटाळ *f.*-चुकवाचुकव *f.* करणें *g. of o.* झोका *m.*-ढोला*m.*-झुगारा*m.*-चुकांडी *f.*-&c. देणें, डोळा*m.* चुकवणें-मारणें, दृष्टि *f.* चोरणें-चुकवणें *g. of o.*
ELUDER, *n.* v. V. चुकवणारा, &c. चुकाऊ *or* चुकावू, दृष्टिचोर, दृष्टिचुकावू, नजरचोर, नजरचुकावू, तोंडचुकावू.
ELUSIVE, ELUSORY, *a.* v. V. *tending to elude.* चुकवणुकीचा, चुकांडीचा, डोळाचुकवण्याचा, झोका देण्याचा, &c.
ELYSIAN, *a.* v. N. स्वर्गाचा, स्वर्गीय, इंद्रभुवनाचा.
ELYSIUM, *n. Indra's pleasure-ground.* इंद्रभुवन*n.* स्वर्ग*m.* नंदन*n.*
To EMACIATE, *v. n. become thin or lean,* v. To WASTE. रोडणें, रोडावणें, झुकणें, झुरणें, आंग*n.* टाकणें-सोडणें, रोड-कृश-&c. होणें-होत जाणें-चालणें, आंगाचा-शरीराचा-पोटाचा चिपोटा*m.* होणें.
EMACIATE, *a.* EMACIATED, *p.* v. V. *and* LEAN. रोड झालेला, झुकलेला, रोड, रोडका, कृश, सुकट्या, सुरवट, लंग, खंगार, क्षीण, झुरतुडला, हडहडीत. [रोडकेपणा *m.*
EMACIATION, *n.* v. V.—*state.* सुखवशी *or* सुकवशी *f.* रोडपणा*m.*
To fall in, or become flat from e. चोपटणें, चोपणें.
EMANANT, EMANATIVE, *a.* v. V. निघणारा, वाहणारा.
To EMANATE. *v. n. issue, flow, proceed from.* निघणें, वाहणें, सुटणें, निस्सरण *n.*-&c. होणें *g. of. s.* निस्सृत-&c. होणें.
EMANATION, *n.* v. V.—*act.* निघणें &c. निस्सरण *n.* निर्याण *n.* निर्गमन *n.*
I. *that which issues.* निस्सृतद्रव्य *n.*-पदार्थ*m.*
To EMANCIPATE, *v. a.* v. To FREE. बंदखुलास *or* खलास*m.*-बंदसुटका *f.*-बंदसूट *f.*-मोकळीक *f.*-सुटका *f.*-बंधमोचन*n.*-&c. करणें, सूट *f.*-सोड *f.* देणें.
2—in theology, *deliver from migratory existence.* मोक्ष *m.*-मुक्ति *f.*- अढळपद*n.*-अक्षयपद*n.* देणें, मुक्त करणें, अढळपदावर बसविणें.
EMANCIPATED, *p.* v. V. 1. बंदखलास, बंधनमुक्त, मुक्त. 2 मुक्त, नित्यमुक्त, लब्धमुक्ति, प्राप्तमुक्ति.
EMANCIPATION, *n.* v.V. 1.—*act.* सोडणें*n.* सोडवण *f.* सोडवणूक *f.* सोड *f.* बंदखलास *m.* बंधमोचन *n.* मोचन *n.*—*state.* सोडवण *f.* सूट *f.* सुटका *f.* मोकळीक *f.* मुक्ति *f.* मुक्तता *f.*
2—*act.* मुक्त करणें *n.* &c.—*state.* v. BEATITUDE, HEAVEN. मुक्ति *f.* मोक्ष *m.* उद्धारगत *f.* उद्धार *m.* अपवर्ग *m.* अपुनरावृत्ति *f.* अपुनर्भव *m.*
Desirous of e. मोक्षार्थी, मुमुक्षु.
Way or course to e. मुक्तिमार्ग*m.*
Working out of e. मुक्तिसाधन *n.*
To EMASCULATE, *v. a. deprive of virility.* खसी करणें, पुरुषत्वभंग*m.*-पुरुषत्वनाश *m.*-पुंस्त्वभंग *m.*-पुंस्त्वनाश*m.*-प्रजननशक्तिभंग *m.*-&c. करणें *g. of o.* नपुंसक-नष्टवीर्य-गतवीर्य-&c. करणें.
EMASCULATE, *a.* EMASCULATED, *p.* v. V. खसी केलेला, &c. नष्टवीर्य, गतवीर्य, नष्टपौरुष. [घालणें-भरणें.
To EMBALM, *v. a.* (a corpse). चिरकाल राहण्यासाठीं मसाला*m.*
To EMBANK, *v. a.* बांधारा *m.*-बांध*m.*-&c. करणें-घालणें.
EMBANKMENT, *n.* v. MOUND. बंधारा*m.* बांध*m.*
EMBARGO, *n. restraint on ships.* गलबताची मनाई *f.*-बंदी *f.*-&c. बंदराची बंदी *f.* गलबतास जाण्यायेण्याचा अटकाव *m.*
To EMBARK, *v. a. put on ship board.* गलबतावर-&c. चढवणें.
2 *engage in an affair.* प्रवृत्त-उद्युक्त करणें. [जाणें.
To EMBARK, *v. n. go on ship board.* गलबतावर-&c. चढणें-चसणें-
2 fig. *engage in a business.* प्रवर्त्तणें, प्रवृत्त होणें, हात*m.* घालणें.
EMBARKATION, *n.* v. V. A.1. गलबतावरचढवणें *n.*

2 v. V. N. 1. गळबनावरचढणें.

To EMBARRASS, *v. a. perplex, bewilder, &c.* v. To ENTANGLE, To CONFOUND. गळफटणें *or* फाटणें, गोफाटणें, गुरपटणें *or* फटणें *or* फाटणें, गुंनवणें, गुंतागुंत *f.*-&c. करणें *g. of o.* पेंचणें, पेंचांत-पेंचाटींत-घोळांत-फेऱ्यांत-&c. पाडणें-घालणें-आणणें-सांपडवणें.

EMBARRASSMENT, *n.* v. V.—*act.* गळफटणें*n.* गुरपटणें*n.* &c.—*state.* गळफटा *or* फाटा*m.* गुरपटा *or* फटा *or* फाटा*m.* पेंच*m.* पेंचाटी*f.* अडचण *f.* अडचणूक *f.* गिरकांडा*m.* पायगोवा*m.* पायखुंटी *f.* पायगुंता*m.*

I. v. TROUBLE, DIFFICULTY. लचांड*n.* झटन*.* लिगाड*n.* कुलंगडें*n.*

II. *encumbrance,* v. CLOG. फास*m.* खोडा*m.* पायखोडा*m.* गळग्रह*m.*

EMBASSADOR. See AMBASSADOR.

EMBASSADORIAL, *a.* वकिलाचा, वकिलाविषयींचा.

EMBASSY, *n. functions, &c. of an ambassador.* वकिली *f.* वकिलात *f.* दूत्य*n.* दौत्य*n.* दूतकर्म*n.* दूतक्रिया *f.*

2 See ERRAND, MESSAGE. [बकीलमंडळी *f.*

3 *an ambassador or body of ambassadors.* बकील*m. or*

4 *dwelling or office of an a.* वकिलाचावाडा*m.* वकिलांचीकचेरी*f.*

To EMBATTLE, *v. a. arrange in order of battle.* फौज*f.* रांगेनें-उभीकरणें, सेनायोजना*f.*-रणयोजना*f.*-रणरचना*f.*-&c. करणें *g. of o.*

To EMBELLISH, *v. a.* v. To ADORN. शोभा *f.* देणें-करणें, सुशोभित-मंडित-&c. करणें, मंडन*n.* करणें *g. of o.*

2 fig. (a story or matter) *dress up, trick out, color, varnish, &c.* बनावणें, बतावून सांगणें, तिखट मीठ*n.* लावून सांगणें, हातपाय *m. pl.* लावणें-फोडणें (and *neut.* लागणें-फुटणें-पसरणें), फुगवणें.

EMBELLISHMENT, *n.* v. V. 1. सुशोभित करणें *n.* मंडन*n.* भूषण*n.*

2 बनावून सांगणें*n.* पल्लव *pop.* पालव & पाल्हाळ*m.* लावा*m.* अर्थवाद*m.* तांडव*n.* टीका *f.* संस्कार*m.*

I. v. ORNAMENT. अलंकार*m.* भूषण*n.*

EMBERS, *n. hot ashes.* फुपाटा *or* फोपेटा*m.* मुंबर *or* मुमर*m.n.* मुमीर *or* मुमूर*m.n.* रसाणें*n.* आहार*m.*

Cake baked on e. आहारोळी *f.* खांकर *or* खाकरा*m.*

Mass of e. फुलझगरें*n.*

To EMBEZZLE, *v. a. fraudulently appropriate.* खाणें, गिळणें, ग्रासणें, चावणें, हरामखोरी *f.*-तनाखोरी *f.*-खग्रास*m.*-चापसाचापसी *f.*-खाद *f.* -अभिलाष*m.* करणें, खादगी *f.* खाणें. गिळंकृतकरणें. Formations and phrases involving the sense of this verb are numerous and exceedingly expressive. दपटणें, जिरवणें, मुरवणें, गटकावणें, पचवणें, चापसणें, हबकणें, गळंत-गप-गडगप-गडलगप-गट-गरक-नाट-उरोमुरो-*adv.* करणें, दम*m.* देणें-मारणें, भक्ष्यस्थानीं घालणें-टाकणें-उतरणें, गळ्याखालीं उतरून देणें, गोळाबेरीज *f.*-काळापात*m.* करणें *g. of o.* खाऊन चकंदळ*n.* करणें *g. of o.* खाऊन पीठ*n.* करणें *g. of o.* अवदान*n.*-डल्ला*m.* मारणें *g. of o.* गिळंकृत *or* सगळंकृत करणें, खाड्यांत उतरणें *or* उतरून देणें, ताव*m.* देणें *with* वर *of o.* (द्रव्यावर-रुपयावर-पैक्यावर-&c.). डल्ला*m.* देणें *g. of o.* धडांत टाकणें-घालणें-उतरणें, बाट *f.* लावणें *g. of o.* आप्यायन*n.*-भानगड *f.* करणें *g. of o.*

To e. daringly, bravingly, &c. गिळून ढेंकर*m.* देणें, तळ*m.* घालून बसणें, तळ मारणें, जिरावणी न मागतां खाणें.

EMBEZZLED, *p.* v. V. खाललेला, ग्रासलेला, &c. ग्रस्त, ग्रसित.

EMBEZZLEMENT, *n. thing embezzled.* खाद *f.* खादगी *f.* हरामखोरी *f.* तनाखोरी *f.*

EMBEZZLER, *n.* v. V. खाणारा, गिळणारा, &c. खादू, गटगील, गटगिळया.

To EMBITTER, *v. a. make bitter or grievous.* दुःखाचा-क्लेशाचा-कठीण-&c. करणें, दुःख*n.*-क्लेश*m.*-&c. देणें, दुःसह-दुःसह्य करणें.

To EMBLAZON, *v. a. adorn with armorial ensigns.* कुलीन चिन्हांनीं सुशोभित करणें.

2 *publish pompously,* v. To BLAZON. धंवश्यानें वर्णन*n.* करणें, धंवशा*m.*-गाजावाजा*m.*-&c. करणें *g. of o.*

EMBLEM, *n. sign, symbol, &c.* चिन्ह *n.* निशाणी *or* नी *f.* खूण *f.* सूचकचित्र *n.*-चिन्ह *n.* ससंकेतचित्र *n.*-चिन्ह *n.*

EMBLEMATIC, EMBLEMATICAL, *a.* v. N. संकेताचा, संज्ञीक, संकेतगर्भित, सांकेतिक, लाक्षणिक, व्यंजक, उद्बोधक, ज्ञापक, सूचक.

EMBODIED, *p.* v. V. 1. देही, देहधारी, देहवान्, शरीरी, शारीरिक, तनुमान्, वपुष्मान्, जातरूप.

2 संग्रह केलेला, &c. संग्रहीत.

To EMBODY, *v. a. invest with a body.* देही-शरीरी-सदेह-&c. करणें, देह *m.*-शरीर *m.*-&c. देणें.

2 *form into a body or system.* संग्रह *m.*-संग्रहण *n.*-संग्रहीकरण *n.*-संहिता *f.* करणें *g. of o.* एकेठिकाणीं आणणें.

3 *form into a military body.* फौजबंदी *f.* करणें *g. of o.* रणरचना *f.* करणें *g. of o.*

To EMBOLDEN, *v. a.* v. To ENCOURAGE. धीर *m.*-दिलासा *m.*-हिम्मत *f.*-&c. देणें.

EMBOLISM, EMBOLISMAL. See INTERCALARY.

To EMBOSS, *v. a.* गेंद *m. pl.*-गोंडे *m. pl.*-&c. लावणें, गेंददार-गोंडेदार करणें.

EMBOSSED, *p.* v. V. गोंडेदार, गेंददार.

To EMBOWEL, *v. a. deprive of entrails.* आंतडीं *n. pl.* निपसणें-काढणें *g. of o.*

To EMBRACE, *v. a. clasp in the arms.* आलिंगणें, कवळणें, कंवटाळणें, वेंगणें, वेंगटणें *or* वेंगाटणें, वेंटाळणें, वेंगाळणें, अवटाळणें, आलिंगून-कवळून-वेंगाडून-&c. धरणें, वेंगेंत-कवेंत-गवेंत-&c. धरणें, उरासीं-पोटासीं धरणें, उरीं पोटीं धरणें, कव *f.*-गव *f.*-मिठी *f.*-अठी *f.*-विळखा *m.*-&c. घालणें, वेंग *f.*-मिठी *f.* मारणें, खेम *f.* देणें, आलिंगन *n.* करणें-घेणें-देणें, कवळणी *f.*-कंवटाळणी *f.*-&c. करणें *g. of o.*

To join in e. भेटणें, भेटाभेट *f.* होणें *g. of s.*—eagerly, &c. कडकडां भेटणें, अवळणें, अंवटाळून-कंवटाळून धरणें.

2 *comprise,* v. To COMPREHEND. कवळणें, कंवटाळणें, आकळणें.

3 *admit, accept, take, &c.* घेणें, पतकरणें, अंगीकारणें, स्वीकारणें, अवलंबणें, आश्रयणें, ग्रहण *n.*-अंगीकार *m.*- स्वीकार *m.* करणें *g. of o.*

EMBRACE, EMBRACING, *n.* v. V. 1.—*act.* आलिंगणें *n.* &c. कवळणी *f.* कंवटाळणी *f.* वेंगाटणी *f.* अंगकवळी *f.* आलिंगन *n.* आश्लेष *m.* श्लेष *m.* कोडीकरण *n.*—*state.* मिठी *f.* खेम *f.* खेव *f.* विळखा *m.*

Close and fast e. *Cornish hug.* माकडमिठी *f.* मगरमिठी *f.*

Friendly e. क्षेमालिंगन *n.* क्षेम *n.*

Mutual e. (on meeting). भेटाभेट *f.* भेट *f.*

2—*act.* कवळणें *n.* आकळणें *n.* &c. आकलन *n.*

3—*act.* घेणें *n.* पतकरणें *n.* पतकर *or* पतकार *m.* अंगीकरण *n.* अंगीकार *m.* स्वीकरण *n.* स्वीकार *m.* ग्रहण *n.* आश्रयण *n.*

I. *comprehension of the arms.* गव *f.* कव *f.* कवळ *n.* कवळा *m.* कवळी *f.* वेंग *f.*

EMBRACED, *p.* v. V. 1. आलिंगलेला, कवळलेला, &c. वेंगेत-&c. धरलेला, आलिंगित, पोटासीं धरलेला, आश्लिष्ट.
2 कवळलेला, आकळलेला, &c. आकलित, व्यापित, व्याप्त.
3 घेतलेला, पतकरलेला, &c. आश्रित, अवलंबित, अंगीकृत, स्वीकृत.

EMBRASURE, *n. opening in a wall for cannon, &c.* जंगी *f.* जंजिरी *f.* तोफेची खिडकी *f.*

To EMBROCATE, *v. a. rub with a lotion.* औषधानें चोळणें, औषध *n.* चोळणें.

EMBROCATION, *n. lotion for rubbing a diseased part.* चोळण्याचें औषध *n.*-पाणी *n.*-&c. मर्दनौषध *n.*

To EMBROIDER, *v. a. ornament with figured work, &c.* कशीदा *m.* काढणें, बुटी *f.*-वेल *f.*-वेलबुटी *f.* करणें-काढणें.

EMBROIDERED, *p.* v. V. बुटीदार, बुटेदार, वेलबुटीचा, कशीद्याचा, बुट्यांचा.
E. with gold. भरमी.
Full-e. भरनकशी.

EMBROIDERY, *n. flowered work.* कशीदा *m.* बुटी *f.* नकशा *m.* नकशी *f.* नकासकाम *n.*

To EMBROIL, *v. a. set a quarrelling,* v. QUARREL. फूट *f.*-तूट *f.*-विघड *m.*-&c. पाडणें, कळ *f.*-आग *f.* लावणें, खजाळी *f.* करणें.

EMBROILER, *n.* v. V. *and* INCENDIARY. कज्जेदलाल, कळलाव्या, कळचेट्या *or* कळचेटव्या, आगलाव्या, दुलाव्या.

EMBRYO, EMBRYON, *n. first rudiments of an animal in the womb.* नुक्ताधरलेला गर्भ *m.*-गाभ *m.* भ्रूण *m.* पिंड *m.* जरायुस्थ गर्भ *m.*
Murder of e. (or fœtus). भ्रूणहत्या *f.*
2 (of a plant.) मूलांकुर *m.* अंकुरबीज *n.* मोग *m.*

EMENDATION, *n. act of correcting*—a writing, &c. चुकाकाढणें *n.* शोभ *m.* शोधन *n.*
2 *an alteration for the better.* शोध *m.*

EMERALD, *n.* पाच *f.* गरुडपाच *f.* मरकत *m.* राजनील *m.* पन्नग *pop.* पन्ना *m.* हरिन्मणि *m.*

EMERALD, *a. of an e. color.* मारकत, जंबुर्दी.

To EMERGE, *v. n. rise out of.* वर येणें, उदय *m.* पावणें, उदय *m.*-उन्मजन *n.*-उद्गमन *n.* होणें *g. of s.* उन्मजन *n.*-उद्गमन *n.* करणें.
2 (from poverty, obscurity, &c.). उदय *m.* होणें *g. of s.* उदयास येणें, जमीन *f.* सोडणें, पाठ *f.* उचलणें, डोकें *n.* काढणें-वर करणें, उसळ *n.* पांढरें होणें *g. of s.*

EMERGENCE, EMERSION, *n.* v. V. 1.—*act.* वर येणें *n.* उदय *m.* उन्मज्जन *n.* उद्गमन *n.*
2 उदय *m.* अभ्युदय *m.*
I. (of a planet). उदय *m.*
Eastern e. पूर्वोदय *m.* Western e. पश्चिमोदय *m.*
II. *occasion, call arisen: exigence, urgency.* उदितकार्य *n.* नैमित्तिक प्रयोजन *n.*-कार्य *n.*-&c. अवसान *n.* आकस्मिक प्रसंग *m.* आकस्मिकोपस्थित प्रयोजन *n.* गरज *f.* निकड *f.* जरूरी *f.* अवचित आलेलें काम *n.* यायी *m.*

EMERGENCY, See EMERGENCE, II.

EMERGENT, *a. suddenly arising, urgent.* निकडेचा, जरुरीचा, आकस्मिक प्रसंगाचा, उदित कार्याचा, आकस्मिकोपस्थित, अकल्पितोपस्थित.

EMERODS. See HEMORRHOIDS.

EMERY, *n.* कुरुंदाचा चूर *m.*

EMETIC, *n.* उलटी *f.* वमन *n.* उलटीचें-वांतीचें औषध *n.*

EMETIC, EMETICAL, *a.* उलटीचा, वांतीचा, वामक, वांतिकारक.

EMIGRANT, EMIGRATE, *a.* v. V. आपला देश सोडून गेलेला, स्वदेशत्यागी, स्वदेशत्यागपूर्वकपरदेशवासी, गयाळ, उठून गेलेला.

To EMIGRATE, *v. n. leave one's country to reside in another.* आपला देश *m.* सोडणें-सोडून जाणें, देशत्याग *m.* करणें, देशांतर *n.* करणें, उठून जाणें.

EMIGRATION, *n.* v. V.—*act.* आपला देश सोडून जाणें *n.* देशत्याग *m.* स्वदेशत्यागपूर्वक परदेशवास *m.*

EMINENCE, *n. rising ground,* v. HILL. उंचवटा *m.* उंचवळा *m.* उमाठा *m.* उंचाड *n.*
2 *exaltedness, celebrity, &c.* v. FAME, GREATNESS. मोठेपणा *m.* मातबरी *f.* प्रतिष्ठा *f.* प्रसिद्धि *f.* श्रेष्ठता *f.* श्रैष्ठ्य *n.* लौकिक *m.* नांवलौकिक *m.* [श्रेष्ठ्य *n.*
3 *excellence.* v. SUPERIORITY. प्रकर्ष *m.* उत्कृष्टता *f.* श्रेष्ठता *f.*
By e. विशेषें करून.

EMINENT, *a. dignified, elevated, exalted,* v. FAMOUS, GREAT. थोर, उंच, मातबर, प्रसिद्ध, श्रेष्ठ, टळक, शिष्ट, वरिष्ठ, प्रतिष्ठेचा, प्रसिद्धीचा, नांवालौकिकाचा.

EMINENTLY, *adv. in a high degree.* विशेषेंकरून, प्रकर्षेंकरून, अतिशय, अतिशयेंकरून.

EMIR, *n.* अमीर *m.* [गुप्तदूत.

EMISSARY, *n.* v. MESSENGER, SPY. दूत, हेर, चार, गूढचार,

EMISSION, *n.* v. V. *act.* सोडणें *n.* पाडणें *n.* टाकणें *n.*

To EMIT, *v. a. send forth, give vent to.* सोडणें, पाडणें, टाकणें, देणें.

EMMENAGOGUE, *n.* ऋतुजनक-प्रवाहक-&c. औषध *n.* ऋतूद्भव *or* ऋतूद्भावक औषध *n.*

EMMET. See ANT.

EMOLLIENT, *a. softening, suppling.* मवाळ करणारा, मवागीचा, मवारीचा, मवाळीचा, मृदुकारी, स्निग्ध.

EMOLLIENT, *n.* मवाळीचें मवारीचें-मवागीचें-&c. औषध *n.* प्रशमन *n.* उपशमन *n.* स्नेहन *n.*

EMOLUMENT, *n.* v. ADVANTAGE, GAIN. फळ *n.* फलश्रुती *f.* मिळकत *f.* लाभ *m.* प्राप्ति *f.*

EMOTION, *n. agitation of mind,* v. DISCOMPOSURE. क्षोभ *m.* व्याक्षोभ *m.* उद्वेग *m.* व्यग्रता *f.* मनस्ताप *m.*
2 *motion or working of the mind.* मनोवृत्ति *f.* चित्तवृत्ति *f.* मनोविकार *m.* मनोविकृति *f.* रस *m.* राग *m.* विकार *m.* विकृति *f.* भाव *m.* हुंडूक *m.*
To be choking under some great e. कंठ *m.* दाटणें-सद्गदित होणें *g. of s.* गदगदून येणें, गहिंवरणें.

EMOTIONAL, *a.* v. N. 2. मनोवृत्तीचा, चित्तवृत्तीचा, &c. मनोविकार विषयक, मनोविकार संबंधी.

To EMPALE, *v. a. spit upon a stake.* सुळावर-सुळीं देणें-चढवणें-घालणें, शूलारोप *m.* करणें.

EMPEROR, *n. supreme monarch.* सम्राट्, सार्वभौमराजा, चक्रवर्ती, चक्रवान्राजा, मंडलेश, मंडलेश्वर, मंडलाधीश, राजेंद्र, राजाधिराज, महाराज.

EMPHASIS, *n. stress of voice in pronunciation.* शब्दावर-&c. नेट *m.*-जोर *m.*-&c. अवधारण *n.* दीर्घोच्चारण *n.* स्वरस *m.* काकु *f.* जिव्हाघात *m.* स्वराघात *m.*

To EMPHASIZE, *v. a.* उच्चारतांना नेटm.-जोरm.-&c. देणें.

EMPHATIC, EMPHATICAL, *a.* v. N. नेटाचा, जोराचा, सावधारण, अवधारणोच्चारित.

EMPHATICALLY, *adv.* v. N. नेटm.-जोरm. देऊन, स्वराघातानें.

EMPIRE, *n. imperial power.* अधिराज्यn. आधिराज्यn. साम्राज्य n. चक्रवर्त्तित्व n. सार्वभौमराज्य n.

2 *region of an emperor.* सार्व भौमाचें राज्यn.- राष्ट्र n. चक्र n. चक्रवर्त्तिराष्ट्रn.

EMPIRIC, *n.* v. QUACK. बाडीवैद्य, नाकाडोळ्याचा वैद्य, अशास्त्रवैद्य.

EMPIRIC, EMPIRICAL, *a.* v. EXPERIMENTAL. अनुभवाचा, आनुभविक *pop.* अनुभवीक, अनुभवसिद्ध, प्रयोगसिद्ध.

To EMPLOY, *v. a. busy, exercise, keep at work.* खपवणें, राबवणें, कामावणें, वापरणें, कामn. करून घेणें.

To e. one's self (in, at, with, amidst). वावरणें.

2 *entertain for service, engage.* ठेवणें, चाकरीस ठेवणें, काम n.-धंदाm.-चाकरी f.-रोजगारm.-&c. सांगणें-देणें.

3 *apply, use.* वापरणें, व्यापारणें, व्यवहारणें, वहिवाटणें, लावणें, कामीं-उपयोगांत-&c. लावणें, संभोगm.-विनियोगm.-योजना f.-&c. करणें, सेवणें, सेवनn.-सेवा f. करणें *g. of o.*

EMPLOYABLE, *a.* v. V. 1. खपवाया-चा-जोगता-&c.

2 ठेवाया-चा-जोगा-&c.

3 वापराया-चा-जोगा-&c. व्यवहार्य, वर्त्तनीय, सेवनीय.

EMPLOYED, *p.* v. V. 1. खपवलेला, राबवलेला, &c.

2 ठेवलेला, चाकरीस ठेवलेला, &c. [सेवित.

3 वापरलेला, लावलेला, &c. व्यवहृत, व्यापृत, युक्त, प्रयुक्त, प्रसक्त,

EMPLOYER, *n.* v. V. 1. खपवणारा, राबवणारा, &c.

2 *and* MASTER. काम सांगणारा, चाकरीस ठेवणारा, &c.

3 वापरणारा, लावणारा, &c. योजक, प्रयोजक. [&c.

EMPLOYMENT, EMPLOY, *n.* v. V. 1.—*act.* खपवणेंn. वापरणेंn.

2 ठेवणेंn. काम सांगणें n. &c.

3 वापरणेंn. &c. विनियोग m. योजना f. सेवन n. सेवा f.

I. *occupation, business, work to do.* काम n. उद्योग m. व्यापार m. धंदाm.

II. *service, trade, &c. means of living,* v. BUSINESS. रोजगार m. चाकरी f. धंदा m. खटला m.

E.—compreh. धंदा रोजगारm.

Fat, rich, lucrative, &c. e. ताजारोजगारm. ताजीरोटी f.

Home or stationary e. बैठारोजगारm.

Public e. (or post). मामलत f. मामला m. हुद्दा m. दिवाण आसामी f. आसामी f.

That has e. or service. रोजगारी, रोजगारशीर, धंदेवाईक.

That is out of e. बेरोजगार, बेरोजगारी, बेकार, रिकामा, रिकामका.

To be out of e. घरीं बसणें, तपीं बसणें, बसणें, मांडीवर मांडी टाकून बसणें, लोळणें, माशा f. pl. मारीत बसणें.

To EMPOISON, EMPOISONED. See To POISON, POISONED.

EMPORIUM, *n. commercial city.* पेंठ f. उतारपेंठ f. पेंठेचा गांव m.

To EMPOVERISH, *v. a. make poor,* v. To BEGGAR. भिकेस आणणें, दरिद्री-कंगाल-निर्धन-निर्द्रव्य-निःकांचन-&c. करणें.

2 (land) *destroy fertility of.* नापीक-मजीत-&c. करणें, नापिकी f.-उर्वरात्वभंग m. करणें.

To EMPOWER, *v. a.* See To ENABLE.

2 v. To AUTHORIZE. मुखत्यारी f.-&c. देणें, मुखत्यार करणें.

EMPRESS, *n.* महाराणी f. सम्राज्ञी f. चक्रवर्त्तिनी f. सार्वभौमी f.

2 *consort of an emperor.* सार्वभौमराजाची पट्टराणी f.

EMPTIED, *p.* v. V. 1. रिकामा-रिता-&c. केलेला, रिकीकृत, रेचित.

EMPTINESS, *n.* v. A. 1. रितेपणा m. रिकामेपणा m. &c. शून्य n. शून्यता f. रिक्तता f. रिक्तभाव m. शून्यभाव m.

2 पोकळपणा m. वायकळपणा m. &c. पोकळी f. पोकळीक f. भोक n. निरर्थकत्व n.

3 रिकामेपणा m. सुनेपणा m. &c. शून्यता f.

4 फांकेपणा m. भाकडपणा m.

EMPTY, *a. containing nothing.* रिकामा, रिकामका, रिता, रिक्त, खाली, शून्य, खुला.

2 *unsubstantial, hollow, &c.* पोकळ, रिकामा, रिकामका, रिता, बावकळ *or* वायकळ, वायकरणी *or* वायकरणीचा, वायफट, वांज *or* वांजा, निरर्थक, वातल *or* वातील, उपरटप्पी, उपरटप्याचा, स्वप्नवत्. [निसोरडा.

3 *unfurnished, unprovided, &c.* रिकामा, सुना, सुनका, शून्य,

4 *blank, barren, void, wanting.* फांका *or* फाका, बावंडा, वांझा *remiss.* वांझट, भाकड, भुकिस्त, भुकड.

To EMPTY, *v. a. make e. or void, evacuate, exhaust, &c.* रिकवणें, रिचवणें, रिकामा-रिता-खाली-&c. करणें.

2 out; (as by baling, ladling, &c.). उसपणें *or* उपसणें, उभरणें, उसपा *or* उपसाm.-उसपण *or* उपसण f.-उसपणी *or* उपसणी f. करणें.

EMPTY-HANDED, *adv.* रिकाम्या हातानें *or* रिकाम्या हातीं.

EMPTY-HANDED, *a.* रिकाम्या हाताचा, रिक्तहस्त, रिक्तपाणि, शून्यहस्त.

EMPTY-HEADED, *a.* v. STUPID. निर्बुद्धि *pop.* निर्बुद्ध, अल्पबुद्धि, अल्पमति.

EMPTYING, *n.* v. V. 1.—*act.* रिकवणें n. रिचवणें n. &c. रिचवण f. रिचवणी f. रिचवणूक f. रिक्तीकरण n. [उपसणी f.

2 उसपणें n. उसपा *or* उपसा m. उसपण *or* उपसण f. उसपणी *or*

EMPURPLED, *a.* जांभळ्यारंगाचा केलेला.

EMPYREAL, EMPYREAN, *a.* v. N. सत्यलोकसंबंधी-विषयक.

EMPYREAN, *n. highest heaven.* सत्यलोक m. सत्यभुवन n.

To EMULATE, *v. a. cope or vie with,* v. To RIVAL. बरोबरी f. -सरोबरी f. करणें, तोलास तोल m. घेणें-देणें, सर f.-सरी f. करणें -लावणें, डाली f. बांधणें *with* सीं *of o.* टक्कर f. मारणें-खाणें *with* ला *or* स *of o.* टाक f. टाकणें, पोटरीस पोटरी f. घासणें, तोलास तोल m. घेणें, सर f.-सरी f. येणें *g. of s.* ला *of o.* स्पर्धणें, तुळणें.

EMULATION, *n.* v. V. देखोदेखी f. चढोवढी f. सरोबरी f. मित्रस्पर्द्धा f. स्पर्धा f. प्रतिस्पर्धा f. *v.* लाव, धर, कर, मांड, हेवादेवा m. तोलदारी f.

I. *desire of equalling.* ईर्ष्या *or* ईर्षा *pop.* ईर f. हेवा m. इसाळ m. इसाळा m. जिगीषा f.

EMULATIVE, EMULOUS, *a.* v. V. ईर्षी, ईर्षेचा, इरेचा, चढोवढीचा, इसाळू *or* ळ्या *or* ळा, प्रतिस्पर्धी, स्पर्धी, स्पर्धालु, हरश्रीचा, जिगीषु, ईर्ष्यालु, ईर्ष्याविष्ट, ईर्ष्यायुक्त.

EMULATIVELY, EMULOUSLY, *adv.* v. A. देखीदेख *or* खी, ईर्षेनें, चढोवढीनें, हेव्यानें, तोलदारीनें, इसाळा इसाळीं.

To ENABLE, *v. a.* शक्ति f.-सामर्थ्य n.-ताकत f.-&c. देणें-आणणें, शक्त-सशक्त-समर्थ-कार्यक्षम -कार्यसमर्थ-शक्तिविशिष्ट -बलसंपन्न -शक्तिसंपन्न-&c. करणें.

To ENACT, *v. a. decree, establish by law.* स्थापन n.-स्थापना f. -व्यवस्थापन n. करणें *g. of o.* स्थापणें, ठराव m.-नियम m.-नि-

बंध m.-कायदा m. करणें, सिद्ध करणें.

ENACTED, p. v. V. स्थापलेला, &c. व्यवस्थापित.

ENACTMENT, n. v. V.—act. स्थापणें n. स्थापन n. स्थापना f. व्यवस्थापन n.—state. सिद्धि f.

I. matter enacted, v. LAW. कायदा m. शासन n.

ENAMEL, n. मिना m.

Bit of e. डाक or डांक m.

2 (of the teeth) दांतांचें लुकण n.

To ENAMEL, v. a. मिना m. चोळणें-लावणें-चढवणें.

ENAMELLED, p. v. V. मिना लावलेला, मिन्याचा, मिनेदार.

ENAMELLER, n. v. V. मिना लावणारा, &c. मिनागार or मिनेगार, मिनेवाला.

ENAMELLING, n. मिनाकारी or मिनेकारी f. मिन्याचें काम n.

ENAMOURED, a. charmed, captivated with. भुललेला, &c. गुणबेल्हाळ, फिदा, वेडा, मोहित, आसक्त, रत (in comp. as स्त्रीरत, विषयरत, कर्मरत, अध्ययनरत), लुब्ध, निरत, अनुरक्त, रागी, अनुरागी, सानुराग. [होणें.

To be e. भुलणें, रंजणें, रंगणें, रिझणें, भाळणें, वेडा-लुब्ध-&c.

To ENCAMP, v. n. pitch tents. डेरे m. pl.-डेरादांडी f.-तळ m. देणें and in. con. पडणें.

ENCAMPMENT, n. v. CAMP. गोट m. [पडण n.

2 place or ground of encamping. तळ m. मुकाम m. पडाव m.

Searching of an e. upon leaving it. तळझाडा m. तळशुद्धि f. तळशोधणी f.

ENCEINTE, a.v. PREGNANT. गरोदर.

To ENCHAIN, v. a. सांखळीनें बांधणें, शृंखलाबद्ध करणें. [विणें.

2 (the attention, &c.) गोवणें, गुंतविणें, गुंतवून घेणें, अडक-

To ENCHANT, v. a. lit. fig. v. To CHARM. भारणें, मंत्रणें or मंतरणें, भारणी f. करणें g. of o. भारणी f. घालणें-टाकणें.

ENCHANTER. See MAGICIAN, SORCERER.

ENCHANTING, a. See CHARMING. [माया f.

ENCHANTMENT, n. v. CHARM. मोहनी f. भाव f. चेटक n. आसुरी-

ENCHANTRESS. See SORCERESS. [णें g. of o.

To ENCHASE, v. a. v. To INLAY. जडणें, जडणी f.-जडाव m. कर-

To ENCIRCLE, v. a. v. To SURROUND. घेरणें, घेरा m.-गरका m.-&c. घालणें-मारणें, आवरणें, वेष्टणें, वलयांकित-आवृत्त-प्रावृत्त करणें.

2 (in the arms) v. To EMBRACE. कंवटाळणें, कवळणें, कवळून धरणें. [यांकित.

ENCIRCLED, p. v. V.1. घेरलेला, वेष्टलेला, &c. आवृत्त, प्रावृत्त, वल-

To ENCLOSE, v. a. shut up by a fence, &c. कुडणें, कुंपण n.-कुडण n.-आवार m. n.-आवरण n. घालणें-करणें.

2 shut in. See To SURROUND.

3 (a letter in a letter or envelope). भिडणें, घालणें, मलफूप करणें, लपेटणें.

ENCLOSURE, n. enclosed place, v. YARD, COURT. अवाड n. आवार m. वाडगें n. वाडकुलें n. वयवाडा m. आवृतस्थल n.

2 (esp. of arable or meadow ground). वाडी f. dim. वाडगें n. वाडकुलें n. कुडलेला कास m. कुडलेलें कुरण n. [रवाडी f.

E. round a house, sown or planted. आगर m. n. आग-

Proprietor of an e. वाडकर.

3 enclosing wall, hedge, &c. v. FENCE. आवार m. n. परिघ m. वेष्टन n. प्राकार m. कुड्य n. [&c.

I. letter, &c. enclosed. लाखोट्यांत घातलेला कागद m.-हुंडी f.-

ENCOMIAST, n. panegyrist. स्तुतिकर्त्ता, स्तावक, स्तवकर्त्ता.

ENCOMIASTIC, a. laudatory. स्तुतीचा, स्तवाचा, स्तुतिविषयक, स्तुत्यात्मक.

ENCOMIUM, n. v. PRAISE. स्तुति f. प्रशंसा f. स्तुतिवाद m.

To ENCOMPASS, v. a. v. To SURROUND. वेरणें, वेढणें, वेष्टणें, घेरा m.-गराडा m.-&c. घालणें.

ENCORE, adv. again. फिरून, मातुक्यान, अणखी.

To ENCOUNTER, v. a. v. To MEET. गांठणें, गांठ f. पडणें in. con. with g. of o. मिळणें in. con. भेटणें in. con. आडवायेणें in. con. चारडोळे m. pl. होणें in. con. संघट्टणें. [ट्टन n.

ENCOUNTER, n. meeting. गांठ f. भेट f. दृष्टादृष्ट f. भेटाभेट f. संघ-

2 See COMBAT, BATTLE.

To ENCOURAGE, v.a. embolden. धीर m.-दम m.-धैर्य n.-अवसान n.-हिम्मत f.-दिलासा m.-दिलभरवसा m.-धिरा m.-&c. देणें, आश्वासणें, आशावणें, अनुमोदणें, अभिनंदणें, उठावणी f.-आश्वासन n.-प्रोत्साहन n.-&c. करणें g. of o.

ENCOURAGED, p. v. V. धीर दिल्हेला, &c. आश्वासित, प्रोत्साहित, अनुमोदित, अभिनंदित, प्राप्तधीर, प्राप्तधैर्य, लब्धधैर्य.

ENCOURAGEMENT, n. v. V.—act. धीर देणें n. &c. उठावणी f. आश्वासन n. अनुमोदन n. अभिनंदन n. प्रोत्साहन n. नाभिकाकार m.—state. encouragedness, assuredness. दिलासा m. दिलदिलासा m. दिलभरवसा m.

ENCOURAGER, n. ENCOURAGING, p. a. v. V. धीर देणारा, धैर्य देणारा, धीर देण्या, दम देण्या, &c. उठावणी करणारा, प्रोत्साहक, आश्वासनप्रद-दायक-कारक-&c. अनुमोदक, अभिनंदक.

ENCREASE, &c. See INCREASE, &c.

To ENCROACH, v. n. intrude on another's rights or possessions. दुसऱ्याच्या कामांत-अधिकारांत-&c. घुसणें-शिरणें, शीम f. दाबणें, मर्यादा सोडून जाणें, सीमोल्लंघन n. करणें, क्रांति f.-आक्रमण n.-&c. करणें.

ENCROACHER, n. ENCROACHING, p. a. v.V. दुसऱ्याच्या कामांत-&c. शिरणारा-&c. शीम दाबणारा.

ENCROACHMENT, n. v. V. दुसऱ्याच्या कामांत शिरणें n. &c. आक्रमण n. क्रांति f.

To ENCUMBER, v. a. v. To CLOG. ओझें-&c. देऊन अवघडवेंण-अडवविणें, पायमोडा m.-पायमोडें n.-खोडा m.- लोढणें n.-&c. घालणें or घालून खोळंबवणें, पायगुंता m.-&c. करणें g. of o.

ENCUMBERANCE, n. v. CLOG. पायखोडा m. मानखोडा m. पायखुंटी f. मानखुंटी f. झट n. गुंता m.

ENCYCLICAL. See CIRCULAR.

ENCYCLOPEDIA, n. circle of sciences. विद्यासंग्रह m.

END, n. extreme part, extremity. शेवट m. अंत m. शेरा m. टोंक n. अग्र n. शेवटचा भाग m. अग्रभाग m. अंत्यभाग m. चरमभाग m. चरमावयव m. प्रांत m. परममर्यादा f. परमावधि m. पर्यंत m. पार m. अंतपार m. उत्तरावधि m. मर्यादा f. शिखर m. n. पोंस n. पोंसट n. पेत m. अघरडा m.

Extreme or very e. सरशेवट m. सरताशेवट m.

At the extreme e. सरत्याशेवटीं, सरशेवटीं, सरतेशेवट.

At the e. of. अंतीं.

From e. to e. आरपार, अहदतहद.

Standing on e. उत्तंभित.

To the e. कडवर.

2 cessation, &c. v. CONCLUSION. शेवट m. अंत m. आखेरी f.

समाप्ति *f.* अवसान *n.* अवसाय *m.* अवधि *m.*

To come to some e. (settlement, stop, &c.). थारास जाणें *or* येणें.

3 *ultimate state.* परिणाम *m.* निर्गम *m.* गति *pop.* गत *f.* तड *or* थड *f.* पर्यवसान *n.* व्यवस्था *f.* प्रांत *m.*

4 *issue, remote consequence.* परिणाम *m.* निर्गम *m.* निगम *m.* पर्यवसान *n.* उदर्कफल *n.* उदर्ककार्य *n.* उदर्क *m.* क्षेत्रफल *n.*

Until the e. आसमाप्ति.

5 *object, aim.* अभिप्राय *m.* आशय *m.* अभिप्रेत *n.* सार्थक *n.* उद्देश *m.* उद्देश्य *n.* लक्ष्य *n.*

To answer its e. सार्थकी लागणें.

Suit your e. to your means. अंथरूण पाहून पाय पसरावे.

END, *a. of or belonging to the end.* शेवटचा, शेवटील, शेवटला.

To END, *v. a. conclude, close, finish, terminate.* समाप्त-तमाम-बंद-&c. करणें, समाप्ति*f.*-अखेर*f.*-अंत*m.*-&c. करणें *g. of o.* संपवणें, उरकणें, अटोपणें, सारणें, शेवट*m.*-तड *f.* घेणें-करणें, शेवटास-समाप्तीस-&c. नेणें-लावणें-आणणें, समापन*n.*-समारोप*m.*-समारोपन*n.*-&c. करणें *g. of o.*—with an implication of completeness, *finish and clear off.* निरानिपटा*m.*-निरानिपटारा*m.* करणें—any religious ceremony. उजविणें.

To END, *v. n. conclude, close, finish, terminate.* संपणें, अटोपणें, उलगणें, उलगडणें, उरकणें, अंत*m.*-शेवट*m.*-अखेरी *f.*-परिणाम*m.*-&c. होणें, समाप्त-अखेर-तमाम-&c. होणें, सूप*n.* फडफडणें *or* वाजणें.

To ENDAMAGE. See To HURT.

To ENDANGER, *v. a. hazard.* भयांत-संकटांत-धोक्यांत-&c. घालणें-पाडणें, काळाचे तोंडींदेणें *or* घालणें, मरणाच्या पारीं बसवणें, मृत्युसदनीं धाडणें, (*and* To be endangered, काळाचेतोंडीं पडणें-जाणें-सांपडणें, मरणाच्या पारीं बसणें, मृत्युसदनीं शिरणें).

To ENDEAR, *v.a.* प्रिय-आवडता-गोड-&c. करणें.

ENDEARMENT, *n. tender affection, lovingness.* प्यार *f.* लाड*m.* लाडीगोडी *f.* लाडुकपणा*m.* लळा*m.* Some of the terms of endearment in use are here collected. For a husband or lover, प्रिय, प्राणनाथ, प्राणवल्लभ, प्राणप्रिय, प्राणेश्वर, प्राणविसावा, प्राणसखा, जिवलग, जीवितेश, जीवितनाथ, जीवितवल्लभ, जीवितोधीश. For a wife or lover, प्रिया, प्राणप्रिया, प्राणवल्लभा, प्राणसखी, प्राणेश्वरी, हृदयंगमा, हृदयविश्रामा, जीवितस्वामिणी, जीवितवल्लभा, &c.

ENDEAVOR, *n.* v. EFFORT. यत्न*m.* प्रयत्न*m.* लाग*m.* उपचार*m.*

To ENDEAVOR, *v.n. make effort or essay*, v. To TRY, To STRIVE. यत्न*m.*-प्रयत्न*m.*-उद्योग*m.*-&c. करणें, झटणें, अजमावणें.

ENDED, *p.* v. V. A. संपवलेला, &c. समापित.

v. V. N. संपलेला, &c. समाप्त, तमाम, खलास, आखेर.

ENDING, *n.* v.V.A.—*act.* संपवणें*n.* शेवट करणें*n.* &c. समापन*n.*—*state.* See END, CONCLUSION.

ENDEMIAL, ENDEMIC, *a. peculiar to a country.* देशीय, तद्देशीय, [तद्देशोत्पन्न.

ENDIVE, *n.* कासनी *f.*

ENDLESS, *a.* v. INFINITE. अनंत, अपार, निरवधि, दुरंत, निस्सीम, [अशेष, निश्शेष.

ENDLESSNESS, *n.* v. A. निस्सीमता *f.* अशेषता *f.* आनंत्य*n.* अनंतत्व*n.* अपारत्व*n.*

ENDOGENOUS, *a. growing from within.* आंतूनवाढणारा, अंतर्व- [र्धिष्णु.

To ENDORSE. See To INDORSE.

To ENDOW, *v. a. furnish with dowry.* यौतक*n.*-अंदण*n.*-&c. देणें, यौतकसंपन्न-यौतकयुक्त-&c. करणें.

2 (with some fund or provision). नेमणूक *f.*-वर्षाशन*n.*-स्वास्थ्य*n.*-वृत्ति *f.*-अग्रहार*m.*-&c. देणें-करून देणें, वृत्तियुक्त-वृत्तिसंपन्न-वृत्तिविशिष्ट-&c. करणें.

3 (with some excellence). गुण*m.* देणें, गुणी-गुणवान्-गुणयुक्त-गुणसंपन्न-सुलक्षण-सुलक्षणिक-&c. करणें.

ENDOWED, (with) *a.* संपन्न, युक्त, संयुक्त, all in comp.

ENDOWMENT, *n. property assigned.* नेमणूक *f.* वृत्ति *f.* स्वास्थ्य*n.* सरंजाम*m.*

Religious e. धर्मादाय*m.* धर्मादाव*m.* अग्रहार*m.*

2 *gift of nature.* गुण*m.* सुलक्षण*n.* ईश्वरीदेणें *n.*

That has good endowment. गुणी, गुणिजन, गुणवान्, सुलक्षणिक, सुलक्षणी, सुलक्षण.

To ENDUE. See To INDUE.

ENDURABLE, *a.* v. V. A. सोसाया-चा-जोगा-सारखा-&c. सह्य, सहनाई, सहनयोग्य, सहनशक्य. [सहन*n.*

ENDURANCE, *n.* v.V. A.1.—*act.* कंठणें*n.* भोगणें*n.* &c. सोसणूक*f.*

2 सोसणें*n.* सोसून घेणें*n.* &c. सहन*n.* क्षमा *f.* क्षांति *f.* तितिक्षा*f.*

v. V. N. टिकणें*n.* ठरणें*n.* निभणें*n.* &c. टिकाव*m.* टिकावा*m.* निभाव*m.* निभावणी *f.* निभावणूक *f.* तगाव *m.* टिकावणूक *f.* नांदणूक *f.* स्थैर्य*n.* स्थिति *f.*

I. *fortitude, patience.* सहनशक्ति *f.* धरम. धीर*m.*

To ENDURE, *v. a.* (pain) *undergo*, v. To SUFFER. सोसणें, कंठणें, भोगणें, काढणें, अनुभवणें, सहन*n.*-&c. करणें *g. of o.*

2 *bear with fortitude or patience*, v. To BEAR. सोसणें *in. con.* सोसून घेणें, साहणें, सोस *m.* धरणें.

To ENDURE, *v. n. last through or out, abide, stand, remain.* टिकणें, ठरणें, राहणें, निभणें, निभावणें, धारणें, धारावणें, स्थिरावणें, तगणें, बहिवाटणें, नांदणें, पार पडणें, टिकणें *n.*-ठरणें*n.*-निभणें *n.*-निभाव *m.*-&c. असणें-होणें, जंग *m.* देणें, धर *m.*-दम *m.* धरणें, धर धरावणें.

As long as sun and moon e. आचंद्रार्क. [&c.

ENDURER, *n.* ENDURING, *p. a.* v. V. A. 1. सोसणारा, भोगणारा,

2 सोसून घेणारा, साहणारा, सहनकर्त्ता, सोसक, कंठक, सोसाळू, सोशीक, धीर, क्षमी, क्षम, क्षांत, तितिक्षु, चिकण.

v. V. N. *lasting, durable, permanent, abiding.* टिकणारा&c. टिकाऊ, स्थायी, स्थायिक (in comp.) चिरस्थायी, चिरकालिक, स्थिर, करारी, अढळ, ध्रुव, स्थाणु, चिक्कण, चिकट, चिवट, सत्वधीर, अक्षय, अविनाशी, अनश्वर.

ENDWISE, *adv. erectly.* उभ्यानें, उभा *decl.*

2 टोंक समोर करून.

ENEMA, *n. an injection.* पिचकारीचें औषध*n.* बस्ति *f. m.*

ENEMY, *n. public foe.* गनीम, शत्रु.

Irruption or the depredations of the e. गनिमाई *f.*

2 *foe, adversary, antagonist, opponent.* शत्रु, वैरी, दुशमन, रिपु, अरि, हरीप *or* फ, दायीज, दावेदार, दावेकरी, दावेदुशमन, विपक्ष, प्रतियोगी, सपत्न.

Captured or overcome by one's e. शत्रुग्रस्त.

Concealed and deadly e. अस्तनींतली आग *f.*

The six enemies of the soul, *viz.* lust, anger, desire, affection, pride, envy. षड्रिपु.

An e. I must expect, but let him be a wise one. दुशमन असावा पण दाणा असावा.

ENERGETIC, ENERGETICAL, *a. spirited, powerful, vigorous.*

उत्साहाचा, तेजाचा, हिंमतीचा, उत्साही, उत्साहवान्, उत्साहसंपन्न, सोत्साह, सतेज, तेजवान्, तेजश्शाली, ऊर्जस्वी, जिवट, जिवदार, रगदार, रग्या, रगेल, खमक्या, खमशा, खरमरीत, ससखसीत, संदा, प्रगल्भ.

ENERGETICALLY, *adv.* v. A. उत्साहानें, उत्साहपूर्वक.

ENERGY, *n. vigor, force, &c.* v. SPIRIT, POWER. धमक *f.* धमकी *f.* हिंमत *f.* जीव *m.* दम *m.* उत्साह *m.* जोत *f.* वेग *m.* तेज *n.* जोम*m.* औत्सुक्य*n.*

2 (of a deity) *active power personified as his wife.* शक्ति *f.* प्रकृति *f.* मातृ *or* मातृका *f.*

To ENERVATE, *v. a.* v. To WEAKEN. निर्बल-दुर्बल-निश्शक्त-शक्तिहीन-शक्तिक्षीण-कमजोर-&c. करणें, वीर्य*n.*-शक्ति *f.*-&c. कमी-करणें *g. of o.*

2 (a horse) घोड्याचीशीर *f.*-शिरा *f. pl.* तोडणें.

ENERVATION, *n.* v. V. 1. बलहानि *f.* शक्तिक्षय *m.*

To ENFEEBLE. See To WEAKEN.

To ENFORCE. See To COMPEL, To FORCE.

2 *put into execution by force.* बळानें-बळ करून-&c. चालवणें-चालू करणें-प्रवृत्तकरणें.

ENFORCED, *p.* v. V. 2. बळानें चालवलेला-&c.

ENFORCEMENT, *n.* v. V. 2. बळानें चालवणें *n.* &c.

To ENFRANCHISE, *v. a.* See To FREE. 2 (a town, &c.) सनद *f.* देणें.

To ENGAGE, *v. a. enlist, bring into a party or affair.* ठेवणें, शिरवणें, प्रवृत्त-उद्युक्त-&c. करणें.

2 *win and attach, gain.* मनावणें, वळवणें, आपलासा-वश-आसक्त-&c. करणें, मोहणें.

3 *bind by agreement.* वचनांत-वचनानें-वचनीं-&c. गोवणें-गुंतवणें-बांधणें-गोवून घेणें-बांधून घेणें-&c. प्रतिज्ञाबद्ध-प्रतिज्ञाधीन-&c. करणें.

4 *hold under occupation, use, &c., employ.* गोवणें, गुंतवणें, कामांत-&c. गोवणें, गोवून- &c. घेणें.

5 See To PLEDGE. 6 *enter into battle with.* लढाई *f.* देणें, लढाई *f.*-युद्ध *n.*-&c. सुरू करणें *with* शीं *of o.* [द्ध *n.* करणें.

To ENGAGE, *v. n. conflict with,* v. To FIGHT, लढाई *f.* देणें, यु-

2 *embark in any business.* पडणें, शिरणें, प्रवर्त्तणें, प्रवृत्त-उद्युक्त होणें, हात*m.* घालणें, डोई *f.* देणें, डोकें*n.* घालणें.

3 *promise, agree, pledge one's self.* वचन*n.*-भाक *f.*-शब्द*m.*-&c. देणें, प्रतिज्ञा *f.*-बोली *f.*-करार*m.* करणें, हाल *f.* बांधणें.

ENGAGED, *p.* v. V. A. 1. ठेवलेला, प्रवृत्त, उद्युक्त.

2 मनावलेला, वळवलेला, वश केलेला, &c.

3 वचनानें गुंतवलेला-गुंतलेला, &c. वचनबद्ध, प्रतिज्ञाबद्ध, &c.

4 *and* BUSY. कामांत गुंतवलेला-गुंतलेला-&c.रुद्ध.

To be e. गुंतणें, रुधणें.

v. V. N. 2. प्रवर्तमान, प्रवृत्त, सन्निविष्ट, उद्युक्त, युक्त.

ENGAGEMENT, *n. promise, &c. made,* v. AGREEMENT. पण *m.* बोली *f.* करार *m.* वायदा *m.* प्रतिज्ञा *f.* संकेत *m.* नियम *m.* ठेप *f.*

E. upon oath. आण भाक *or* प *f.* शपथपूर्वकवचन *n.*

Faithful to e. सत्यप्रतिज्ञ, सत्यसंध.

Written e. कबुलात *f.* कबुलायत *f.* मुचलका *m.* कौलनामा *m.* करारनामा *m.* इकरारनामा *m.* प्रतिज्ञापत्र *or* पत्रक *n.*

Written e. with fixedness of time. वायदेरोखा *m.* वायदेचिट्ठी *f.*

2 *occupation,* v. BUSINESS. काम *n.* उद्योग *m.*

3 v. FIGHT. लढाई *f.* संग्राम *m.*

ENGAGING. See CHARMING, PLEASING. [उत्पन्न करणें.

To ENGENDER, *v. a.* v. To BEGET. जनन *n.*-प्रजनन *n.* करणें,

2 *produce, occasion,* v. To CAUSE. उत्पन्न करणें, कारणभूत-होणें-असणें *in. con.*

ENGINE, *n. machine, &c.* यंत्र *n.*

2 See INSTRUMENT. [णणारा.

ENGINEER, *n.* यंत्रफिरवणारा-चालवणारा-&c. यंत्रांचें काम जा-

2 See CIVIL-ENGINEER.

ENGINEERING, *n.* यंत्रांचें काम *n.* यंत्रें चालविण्याचें काम *n.*

ENGLISH, *a.* इंग्रेजी, इंग्लिश, इंग्लंददेशाचा, बिलायती, बिलायतसंबंधी, बिलायतचा.

ENGLISH, *n.*—the people. इंग्रेजलोक *m. pl.* इंग्रेजीलोक *m. pl.* इंग्लिश लोक *m. pl.*

Rule or sway of the E. इंग्रेजी *f.*

2—the language. इंग्रेजी *f.*

To ENGRAVE, *v. a. carve, &c.* कोरणें, खोदणें, किरवणें, नकासणें.

2 *imprint,* v. To IMPRESS. ठसवणें, बिंबविणें.

ENGRAVED, *p.* v. V. 1. कोरलेला, &c. कोरींव, खोदींव, नकसींव.

ENGRAVER, *n.* v. V. 1. खोदणारा, &c. खोदकाम्या, खोदींव काम करणारा. [रणी *f.*

ENGRAVING, *n.* v. V. 1.—*act.* कोरणें *n.* खोदणें *n.* खोदणी *f.* को-

I. *thing engraved.* नकशा*m.*नकशी*f.*नकास काम*n.*खोद काम *n.*

To ENGROSS, *v. a. take the whole of.* सगळ्याचा सगळा-साऱ्याचा सारा-साऱ्याचें सारें *n.*-&c. घेणें.

2 *engage wholly,* v. To ABSORB. ग्रासणें, वेढणें, वेष्टणें, गरक-तल्लीन-&c. करणें.

3 *write in large letters.* मोठ्या अक्षरांनीं लिहिणें-प्रत *f.*करणें.

ENGROSSED, *p.* v. V. 2. ग्रासलेला, &c. गरक, निमग्न, तत्पर, तल्लीन, तन्मय, नादाळ, नादिष्ट, नादी, कडाचूर, आविष्ट (in comp. as कामाविष्ट, लोभाविष्ट, विषयाविष्ट).

To be e. निमग्णें, गडणें, गडून जाणें, नादावणें.

To ENGULF, &c. See To INGULF.

To ENHANCE, *v. a. advance, raise, &c.* v. To INCREASE. वाढवणें, अधिक करणें, किम्मत *f.*-मोल *n.*-&c. वाढवणें-चढवणें*g.of o.*

To ENHANCE, *v.n. rise,advance,* v. To INCREASE. वाढणें,चढणें.

ENHANCEMENT, *n.* v. INCREASE. वाढ *f.* चढ *m.* वृद्धि *f.*

ENIGMA, *n. riddle, &c.* उखाणा *m.* गूढ *n.* कोडें *n.* दृष्टकूट *n.* कूट*n.* डुमाणें *n.* अंतर्लापिका *f.* प्रहेलिका *f.* प्रवल्हिका.

ENIGMATICAL, *a.* v. N. कूटाचा, कोड्याचा, कूटार्थक, गूढार्थक, भावगर्भ, व्यंग्योक्तीचा, व्याजोक्तीचा.

E. speech. अप्रशिखा *f.* व्यंग्योक्ति *f.* व्याजोक्ति *f.*

To ENJOIN, *v. a. charge, &c.* v. To COMMAND. खरावणें, बजावणें, खरावून-बजावून-हटकून-हुडसून-खडसून-&c.सांगणें-हुकूम*m.* करणें-आज्ञा *f.* देणें, तटकारणें, जतावणें, ताकीद *f.* करणें-देणें, आज्ञापणें.

ENJOINED, *p.* v. V. खरावलेला, खरावून सांगितलेला, &c. विहित, आज्ञापित, आदिष्ट, चोदित.

ENJOINING, *n.* v. V. *and* INJUNCTION. बजावणें *n.* &c. ताकीद *f.* सांगी *f.* आज्ञापन *n.* विधान *n.*

To ENJOY, *v. a. feel with pleasure.* भोगणें, भोग *m.* घेणें-करणें *g. of o.* सुख *n.* घेणें-पाहणें-अनुभवणें *g. of o.* सुख *n.*-संतोष *m.*-

हर्ष *m.*-&c. पावणें *with* पासून *of o.* सुख *n.*-&c. वाटणें *g. of o. with in. con.*

2 *hold fruition of.* भोगणें *both direct and in. con.* उपभोगणें, बहिवाटणें, अनुभवणें, भोग *m.*-उपभोग *m.* घेणें-करणें, अनुभव *m.* घेणें-करणें, भोगवटा *m.*-बहिवाट *f.* करणें, भोग भोगवटा *m.* करणें.

To e. and communicate. त्याग भोग *m.* करणें.

3 (one's self). रमणें, सुखांगणें, सुख *n.*-आनंद *m.*-&c. पावणें, सुख *n.*-&c. वाटणें *in. con.* सुखी-&c. असणें, सुखास वाटणें-येणें-पडणें *imper.*

Enjoyable, *a.* v. V. 2. भोगाया-चा-जोगा-&c. भोग घ्याया-चा-जोगा-&c. भोग्य, उपभोग्य, भोक्तव्य.

Enjoyed, *p.* v. V. 1. भोगलेला, &c.

2 भोगलेला, &c. उपभुक्त, भुक्त, अनुभूत, अनुभविक, अनुभवी.

Enjoyer, *n.* v. V. 1. भोगणारा, भोगी, संभोगी, भोक्ता.

2 भोग घेणारा-करणारा, &c. उपभोगी, भोगी, भोक्ता, उपभोक्ता, भुक् (in comp. as ऐश्वर्यभुक्, सुखभुक्, वृत्तिभुक्, श्रीभुक्).

Enjoyment, *n.* v. V. 1.—*act.* भोगणें *n.* भोग *m.* संभोग *m.*

2—*act.* भोगणें *n.* उपभोग *m.* भोगवटा *m.* भोग्य *n.* भुक्ति *f.* अनुभव *m.* बहिवाट *f.*

I. *agreeable feeling,* v. Pleasure, Happiness. सुख *n.* आनंद *m.* हर्ष *m.*

II. *sexual e.* संभोग *m.* अंगसुख *n.* उपभोग *m.*

III. *sensual e.* विषयभोग *m.* विषयसुख *n.* भोगविलास *m.*

To Enkindle, See To Kindle.

To Enlarge, *v. a.* v. To Increase. वाढवणें, मोठा-प्रशस्त-&c. करणें, वृद्धि *f.*-विस्तार *m.* करणें *g. of o.* विस्तारणें.

2 See To Release.

3 *dilate, expand*—as with joy, &c. खुलवणें, फुलवणें.

To be enlarged, फुलणें, खुलणें.

To Enlarge, *v. n.* v. To Increase. वाढणें, अधिक होणें, वृद्धि *f.*-विस्तार *m.* होणें *g. of s.*

2 *expatiate.* विस्तार *m.*-वाक्यविस्तार *m.*-ग्रंथविस्तार *m.*-फैलाव *m.* करणें-करून सांगणें-लिहणें, पाल्हाळ *m.* लावणें-करणें.

Enlarged, *p.* v. V. A. 1. वाढवलेला, &c. विस्तारित, प्रवृद्ध.

Enlargement. See Increase.

To Enlighten, *v. a.* lit. उजेड *m.*-प्रकाश *m.* करणें-पाडणें, प्रकाशणें, प्रकाशित करणें, प्रकाशन *n.*-द्योतन *n.*-&c. करणें.

2 fig. *instruct.* प्रकाश *m.* करणें, तमोहरण *n.*-तमोभंग *m.*-तमोनाश *m.*-आंध्यभंग *m.*-आंध्यदूरीकरण *n.*-ज्ञानदान *n.*-&c. करणें.

Enlightened, *p.* v. V. 1. प्रकाशलेला, प्रकाशित, प्रकाशयुक्त, द्योतित.

2 सुज्ञ, ज्ञानी, जातज्ञान, प्राप्तज्ञान, हततिमिर, हृतांध्य, हतांधकार.

Enlightener, *n.* Enlightening, *p. a.* v. V. 1. प्रकाश करणारा-पाडणारा, प्रकाशक, द्योतक.

2 तमोहर-हर्त्ता-हारक-हारी, अंधकारघ्न, ज्ञानदाता.

Enlightening, Enlightenment, *n.* v. V. 1.—*act.* प्रकाशणें *n.* प्रकाशन *n.* प्रकाश *m.* द्योतन *n.*

2—*act.* प्रकाश *m.* प्रकाशन *n.* तमोहरण *n.* तमोभंग *m.* तमोनाश *m.* तिमिरभंग *m.* अंध्यभंग *m.* अंधकारभंग *m.* ज्ञानदान *n.* ज्ञानसंपत्ति *f.*

To Enlist, *v. a. engage in public service by entering the name in a register.* नांवनिशी *f.* मांडणें *g. of o.* नांवनिशींत घेणें, पट्टांत-पट्टावर-पट्टास मांडणें-घालणें-दाखल करणें-&c. *or* मांडून-घालून-&c. चाकरीस ठेवणें, कलमजारी *f.*-कलमबंदी *f.*-&c. करणें *g. of o.*

2 fig. *engage in a cause.* प्रवर्त्तविणें, प्रवृत्त-उद्युक्त-&c. करणें.

To Enlist, *v. n.* पट्टावर-&c. आपलें नांव लिहून-लिहवून-चढवून-&c. चाकरीस राहणें.

2 *engage in a cause.* प्रवर्त्तणें, प्रवृत्त-उद्युक्त-&c. होणें.

Enlisting, *n.* v. V. A. 1.—*act.* पट्टावर मांडणें *n.* &c. जमाबंदी *f.* कलमजारी *f.* कलमबंदी *f.*

To Enliven, *v. a. make alive.* सजीव-जिवंत-जिता-&c. करणें, जीवदान *n.*-प्राणदान *n.* करणें.

2 *make vigorous, vivacious, lively, &c.* v. To Animate. जीव *m.*-दम *m.*-उत्साह *m.*-तेज *n.*-तेजगी *f.*-रंग *m.*-&c. आणणें-देणें, जिवट-जीवदार-&c. करणें.

En-masse, *adv. in a body.* संघशः

To tumble e. कोसळणें, धासळणें.

Enmity, *n. ill will, &c.* द्वेष *m.* शत्रुपणा *m.* वैर *n.* दुशमनी *f.* दुशमनगिरी *f.* दावा *m.* शत्रुत्व *n.* शत्रुभाव *m.* द्वेषभाव *m.* सापत्न्य *n.* विरोध *m.*

Deep and deadly e. हाडवैर *n.* खडाष्टक *n.* बारावा बृहस्पति *m. g. of s. recip.*

Secret e. अंतर्वैर *n.*

Enneagon, *n. figure with nine angles.* नवास्र आकृति *f.* नवकोणाकृति *f.*

To Ennoble, *v. a.* अमीर करणें, अमिरी *f.*-अमिराची पदवी *f.* देणें, मरातबेस चढवणें, बडे लोकांचे पट्टावर नांव *n.* घालणें *g. of o.*

2 See To Exalt.

Ennui, *n. lassitude, weariness.* उचाट *m.* उच्छाद *m.* विषाद *m.* ग्लानि *f.* त्रास *m.*

Enormity, *n. wrongness,* v. Wickedness. अतिदुष्टता *f.* अतिदुष्टत्व *n.*

2 *an* e. *an atrocity.* मोठें पाप *n.* महापातक *n.* अघोर पातक *n.*

Enormous, *a. atrocious,* v. Wicked. अतिदुष्ट, महापातकाचा.

2 *immense, monstrous,* v. Large. जरब, जबर, अवाढव्य.

Enormously, *adv.* v. Excessively. अतिशय, अमर्याद.

Enough, *a.* v. Sufficient. पुरता, पुरा, पुराया जोगा.

Enough, *n.* पुरवटा *or* टा *m.* पर्याप्ति *f.* पुरव *f.*

E. and plenty. पुरेपुरे.

E. and to spare. ऊरपूर *f.* त्यागाभोगापुरता (पैका-संपत्ति-द्रव्य-&c.). पुरपुराट *m.*

To give e. of it. पुरपुरे होई असें (मारणें-ठोकणें-घोळणें-&c.).

Enough, *adv.* पुरे, बस, मक्का.

To be e. and over. पुरून उरणें.

Enough ! पुरपुरे, पुरेपुरे, बहुत, बसभाई.

To Enquire. See To Inquire.

To Enrage, *v. a.* v. To Anger. रागास आणणें, तापवणें, कोपविणें, संतप्त करणें, खिजवणें *or* खिजावणें.

Enraged, *p.* v. V. *and* Angry. रागावलेला, संतप्त, संतापित, कोपित, कोपाकुल, जातामर्ष.

To Enrapture, *To* Enravish, *v. a.* v. To Rejoice. आनंद माईनासा (*or* मावेनासा) करणें, फारच संतोषविणें, आनंदोत्कर्ष *m.* करणें, आल्हादणें, प्राल्हादणें, परितोषण *n.*-संतोषण *n.*-परमानंदन *n.* करणें *g. of o.* आल्हादित-परितुष्ट-परमानंदित-&c. करणें.

Enraptured, Enravished, *p.* v. V. फारच संतोषवलेला, &c. परमानंदित, परितुष्ट, आनंदभरित, आनंदमग्न, आनंदमय, हर्षाविष्ट.

To Enrich, *v. a.* सधन-धनिक-धनवान्-धनसंपन्न-&c. करणें, आढ्यंकरण *n.* करणें.

2 v. To FERTILIZE. सुपीक-पिकाऊ-&c. करणें, पिकाऊपणा *m.* आणणें.

ENRICHED, *p.* v. V. 1. सधनकेलेला, &c.

ENRICHER, *n.* ENRICHING, *p. a.* v. V. 1. सधन करणारा, &c. धनद, धनप्रद, धनावह, धनदायक, संपत्तिदायक.

To ENROL, *v. a. enter on a roll, register.* नांवनिशी *f.* करणें-मांडणें, घालणें, नांवनिशींत घेणें-आणणें, नांव *n.* लिहणें, पट्टांत-पट्टावर-&c. मांडणें-घालणें-दाखल करणें.

ENROLMENT, *n.* v. V. नांवनिशी *f.* कलमबंदी *f.* कलमजारी *f.*
I. See REGISTER.

ENS, *n.* v. ENTITY. वस्तु *n.*

ENSAMPLE. See EXAMPLE.

ENSANGUINED, *a. stained with blood.* रक्तानें भरलेला, रक्तबंबाळ.

To ENSCONCE, *v. a. shelter, cover, secure.* लपवणें-लपवून घेणें *with* आड *of the object.*

To ENSHRINE, *v. a. enclose in a chest, &c.* सुरक्षित राहण्यासाठीं पेटींत-&c. बसविणें.
To e. in ones affections. देव्हा यांत बसविणें-मांडणें.

ENSIGN, *n.* v. FLAG. बावटा *m.* निशाण *or* न *n.* ढाल *f.* ध्वज *m.*
2 *badge, sign,* v. MARK. चिन्ह *n.* लक्षण *n.*
3 फौजेंतील एक हुद्देदार आहे.

ENSIGN-BEARER, *n.* निशाणदार, निशाणबर्दार, पताक्या, ध्वजधारी.

To ENSLAVE, *v. a.* दास-गुलाम-&c. करणें, गुलामकींत-दासदशेंत-दास्यांत-दास्यावस्थेंत-दासकोटींत आणणें, दासत्वापन्न-दास्यापन्न-&c. करणें, दासीकरण *n.* करणें *g. of o.*

ENSLAVED, *p.* v. V. दासकेलेला, &c. दासत्वापन्न, दास्यापन्न.
E. by his passions. इंद्रियदास, इंद्रियवश, इंद्रियजित.

To ENSNARE, &c. See To INSNARE, &c.

To ENSUE, *v. a.* v. To FOLLOW. पाठीस लागणें *g. of o.* पाठलाग *m.* करणें *g. of o.*

To ENSUE, *v. n. succeed in a train of events or course of time.* मागून-नंतर-&c. होणें, मागचा-पाठीमागचा येणें.
2 *follow as a consequence.* होणें, उद्भवणें, घडणें, फळ *n.*-परिणाम *m.*-&c. होणें.

ENSUING, *a. next following.* येणारा, येता, पुढला.

To ENSURE. See To INSURE.

To ENTAIL, *v. a.* (an estate, &c.). वंशपरंपरा भोग्य देणें, वंशपरंपरागत करणें, दानविक्रयातीत करून देणें.
2 *fix unalienably.* न निघेसा जडवणें-ठेवणें.

To ENTANGLE, *v. a. twist, interweave.* गोवणें, गुंतवणें, गळफटणें *or* गळफाटणें, गुरपटणें, गोंधरणें *or* गोंधविणें, गुतागूत *f.*-गुंतागुंत *f.*-गळफटा *m.*-गुरपटा *m.*-गुताडा *m.*-&c. करणें *g. of o.*
2 *involve in difficulties.* गोवणें, गुंतवणें, गोवून-&c. घेणें, फांसीं देणें, फासणें, पेंचणें, गोफाटणें, गळफटणें, गोफाट्यांत-पेंचांत-&c. घालणें-सांपडवणें-पाडणें-धरणें.

ENTANGLED, *p.* v. V. 1. गोवलेला, &c.
To be e. गुतणें, गोंधळणें, गोंधवणें, गोंधरणें.
2 गोवलेला, गोफाट्यांत घातलेला, &c.
To be e. फसणें, गोफाट्यांत सांपडणें-पडणें, पेंचाटींत सांपडणें.

ENTANGLEMENT, *n.* v. V. 1.—*state.* गूत *f.* गुतागूत *f.* गुंतागुंत *f.* गुंताडा *m.* गुथडा *m.* गुथडागुथड *f.* गळफटा *or* गळफाटा *m.* गुरपटा *m.* गुंडाळा *m.*
2—*state.* गोवा *m.* पायगोवा *m.* पायगुंता *m.* पायगुंत *f.* पायखुंटी *f.* पायखोडा *m.* गळफटा *or* गळफाटा *m.* गुतागूत *f.* गुरपटा *or* फटा *or* फाटा *m.*

To ENTER, *v. a.* (upon a roll, list, bill, &c.). बार करणें, लिहणें, रुजू करणें, मांडणें, घालणें, दाखल करणें, चढवणें, धरणें, नेसवणें.

To ENTER, *v. a. come or go in.* आंत जाणें-येणें, शिरणें, शिरकणें, रिघणें, प्रवेशणें, प्रवेश *m.* करणें, दाखल-प्रविष्ट होणें.
2 *engage in, embark upon.* प्रवर्त्तणें, हात *m.*-पाय *m.* घालणें-शिरवणें-ठेवणें, पाऊल *n.* ठेवणें, प्रवृत्त होणें.
3 *take possession of,*—a devil. शिरणें, वतरणें *or* वतारणें, संचरणें, संचारणें, रेवणें.
4 (into the system). संचरणें, संचारणें, भिनणें, भिनरणें *or* भिनारणें, भेदणें *or* भेदून जाणें, रेवणें.

To ENTER INTO, *v. n. See the verb active.*

ENTERED, *p.* v. V. A. बार केलेला, &c. रुजू, बार, समाविष्ट.
v. V. N. 1. आंतगेलेला, दाखलझालेला, प्रविष्ट, निविष्ट.

ENTERPRISE, *n. bold or hazardous undertaking.* अचाटकाम *n.* जोखीम *n.* जोखमाचें काम *n.* जिवावरचें काम *n.* कचाट *n.* साहसकर्म *n.* दुर्गकर्म *n.*

ENTERPRISING, *a.* v. ADVENTUROUS. कचाटी *or* ट्या, उलेढाल्या, अचाट करणारा, अचाट बुद्धि खेळवणारा, अचाट उद्योगी, साहसी, खटपट्या, उत्पाती.

To ENTERTAIN, *v. a. engage, hire.* ठेवणें, चाकरीस-चाकरीवर-&c. ठेवणें, चाकर-&c. ठेवणें.
2 *receive hospitably, treat, feed.* पाहुणचार *m.*-पाहुणेर *m.*-आतिथ्य *n.*-मेजवानी *f.*-मेजवानकी *f.*-आगतस्वागत *n.*-आदर आतिथ्य *n.*-आतिथेय *n.* करणें, परामर्श *m.* घेणें-करणें, जेवूं घालणें, जेवण *n.* देणें.
3 *please, divert,* v. To AMUSE. रमविणें, रंजविणें, रमणूक *f.*-करमणूक *f.*-&c. करणें *g. of o.*
4 (in the mind). बाळगणें, धरणें, ठेवणें.

ENTERTAINING, *a.* v. AMUSING. गमती *or* गमत्या, करमणुकीचा, करमणुक्या. [&c.

ENTERTAINMENT, *n.* v. V. 1.—*act.* ठेवणें *n.* चाकरीस ठेवणें *n.*
2 पाहुणचार *m.* पाहुणेर *m.* आतिथ्य *n.* आतिथेय *n.* मेजवानी *f.* मेजवानकी *f.*
E. daily upon a general invitation. नित्यावळ *f.*
3 रमवणें *n.* रंजवणें *n.* रंजन *n.* अनुरंजन *n.*
4 बाळगणें *n.* धरणें *n.*
I. v. FEAST. जेवणावळ *f.* मेजवानी *f.* मेजवानीचें जेवण *n.*

To ENTHRAL. See To ENSLAVE.

To ENTHRONE, *v. a.* गादीवर-सिंहासनावर-&c. बसवणें, सिंहासनारूढ-नृपासनारूढ-राजपदस्थित-&c. करणें.

ENTHRONED, *p.* v. V. गादीवर बसवलेला, &c. सिंहासनारूढ, राजपदारूढ, राजपदस्थित, राजासनारूढ.

ENTHUSIASM, *n. fervor or excitement of mind in pursuit of an object.* आवेश *m.* अत्युत्साह *m.* परमोत्साह *m.* महोत्साह *m.* अत्यासक्ति *f.* अनुराग *m.* अभिनिवेश *m.* शौक *m.*
2 (religious). देवपिसें *n.* देववेड *n.* देववारें *n.* साक्षात्काराभास *m.* देवसंचारभान *n.*

ENTHUSIAST, *n.* See the Adjective.

ENTHUSIASTIC, ENTHUSIASTICAL, *a.* v. N. 1. आवेशी, आवेशाचा, अनुरागी, अनुरागाचा, सानुराग, अळका, अळकुवा (as गाण्याचा अळकुवा, &c.), वेडा, तीक्ष्ण, शौकी, आवेशपूर्वक, आ-

बेशपुरस्सर. [चारभानी.

2 देवपिसा, देवबेडा, साक्षात्काराभासी, साक्षात्कारभानी, देवसं-

ENTHUSIASTICALLY, *adv.* v. N. 1. आवेशानें, अनुरागानें, शौकानें, &c. आवेशपूर्वक, अनुरागपूर्वक.

ENTHYMEME, *n.* लुप्तैकावयव न्याय *m.*

To ENTICE, *v. a.* v. To ALLURE. लोभ *m.* दाखवणें, प्रलोभन *n.* करणें *g. of o.* मोह *m.* घालणें, अंबोण *n.* देणें.

ENTICEMENT. See ALLUREMENT.

ENTIRE, *a. unbroken, undivided, &c.* v. WHOLE. पुरा, पूर्ण, सबंध, संपूर्ण, अव्यंग, अखंड, साद्यंत, समस्त.

2 *full, complete*, पुरा, पुरता, पूर्ण, संपूर्ण, साद्यंत, सकल, समस्त, समग्र, अशेष, कृत्स्न, सांग, यथासांग.

ENTIRELY, *adv. completely*, v. WHOLLY. अशेषतः, निश्शेष, तमाम, झाडून, बिलकूल, यच्चयावत्, सर्वभावें, अवच्छेदकावच्छेदें करून.

ENTIRENESS, ENTIRETY, *n.* v. A. 1. पुरेपणा *m.* पूर्णता *f.* संपूर्णता *f.* साकल्य *n.* सामग्र्य *n.*

2 पुरेपणा *m.* पूर्णता *f.* संपूर्णत्व *n.* पूर्त्ति *f.* &c. साकल्य *n.* सामग्र्य *n.* अशेषता *f.*

To ENTITLE, *v. a. give title or right to.* अधिकार *m.*-सत्ता *f.*-हक्क *m.*-दावा *m.*-योग्यता *f.*-&c देणें, अधिकारी-साधिकार-अधिकारसंपन्न-&c. करणें.

2 See To NAME.

ENTITLED, *p.* v. V. 1. अधिकार दिल्हेला, अधिकारी केलेला, &c. अधिकारी, साधिकार, अधिकारसंपन्न.

ENTITY, *n.* v. BEING. अस्तित्व *n.* सत्व *n.* वस्तुता *f.*

2 *an* e. *a being.* वस्तु *n.* सत्व *m. n.* अर्थ *m.* अधिभूत *n.*

To ENTOMB, *v. a.* v. To BURY. थडग्यांत-&c. घालणें, गाडणें.

To e. alive. चिणणें, चिणून टाकणें.

ENTOMOLOGY, *n.* विभक्तांगकीटकविद्या *f.* विभक्तांगकीटकवर्णन *n.*

ENTRAIL, *n. an intestine.* अंतडी *f.* अंतडें *n.* आंत *n.* अंत्र *n.*

ENTRANCE, ENTERING, *n.* v. V.A.—*act.* बार करणें*n.* बारनिशी*f.*

Double e. or entry. दुबेरजी हिशेब *m.*

v. V. A. 1. आंत येणें *n.*-&c. प्रवेश *m.* प्रवेशन *n.* निवेश *m.* समावेश *m.* रीघ *f. m.* रिघाव *or* रिघावा *m.* शिरकाव *m.*

J. *avenue, passage*, v. DOOR. द्वार *pop.* दार *n.* वाट *f.* मार्ग *m.* तोंड *n.* प्रवेशसाधन *n.*

Front or main e. सिंहद्वार *n.*

ENTRANCED. *a. put into a trance or ecstacy.* तन्मय केलेला-झालेला, तन्मयावस्थापन्न, तन्मयावस्थ, समाधिस्थ.

To ENTRAP, *v. a.* v. To DECEIVE. फाशांत धरणें-आणणें-पाडणें-सांपडवणें, फशीं देणें-पाडणें, फसगत*f.*-फसगपत*f.*-&c. करणें *g. of o.*

To be entrapped. फशीं पडणें, फसणें.

To ENTREAT, *v. a. solicit*, v. To BEG. विनवणें, काकळूत*f.*-मिनत *f.*-मिनती *f.*-मिनतवारी *f.*-विनंती *f.*-&c. करणें *g. of o.* खिनतबार-&c. अर्ज*m.* करणें, मागणें.

2 See To TREAT. 3 *bring over, &c.* v. To PERSUADE. समजावणें, मनावणें.

ENTREATY, *n.* v. V. 1. विनवणी *f.* विनंती *f.* मिनत *f.* मिनती *f.* मिनतवारी *f.* मिनतमाना*m.* काकळूत *f.*

ENTRY. See ENTRANCE.

To ENUMERATE, *v. a.* v. To COUNT. गणणें, गणना *f.*-गणती *f.*-&c. करणें-सांगणें *g. of o.*

ENUMERATION, *n.* v. V. गणना *f.* गणती *f.* गणन*n.* मोजणी *f.*

To ENUNCIATE. See To UTTER.

To ENVELOP, *v. a. wrap.* आवरणें, लपेटणें, वेष्टणें, आवरण*n.*-वेष्टन *n.*-&c. करणें, वेष्टित-&c. करणें.

ENVELOPE, *n. wrapper.* आवरण*n.* वेष्टन*n.* वासन*n.*

E. to a letter. लाखोटा*m.* लिफाप*m.* पोलक *m.* गलिचा*m.*

ENVELOPED, *p.* v. V. लपेटलेला, &c. वेष्टित, परिवेष्टित.

To ENVENOM, *v. a. poison.* विषयुक्त-विषाक्त-विषान्वित-लिप्त-&c. करणें, विष*n.* घालणें-लावणें.

ENVIABLE, *a.* v. V. स्पृहणीय, स्पृह्य, ईर्ष्याविषय, ईर्ष्यापात्र, ईर्ष्याजननशक्तिक.

ENVIER, *n.* ENVIOUS, *a.* v. V. इरेचा, हेव्याचा, मत्सराचा, देखदुखी *or* ख्या, मत्सरी, समत्सर, मात्सर, अन्यशुभद्वेषी, असोशा *or* असोशी, असोशीक, अदेख, हेवेखोर, दृष्टीचा पापी *or* खोटा, वक्रदृष्टि, ईर्ष्यायुक्त, ईर्ष्यालु, ईर्ष्यमाण, ईर्ष्याधीन, ईर्ष्यावान्, ईर्ष्यामय, अक्षम, अक्षांत.—in high degree. ईर्ष्यावश, ईर्ष्यान्वित, मत्सराविष्ट.

ENVIOUSLY, *adv.* v.A. हेव्यानें, मत्सरानें, &c. ईर्ष्यापूर्वक *or* पुरस्सर.

To ENVIRON, *v. a.* v. To SURROUND. घेरणें, वेढणें, वेष्टणें, वेढा*m.*-घेरा*m.* घालणें, गरका*m.* मारणें.

ENVIRONS, *n. neighbouring places.* आसपासचादेश*m.* आसमंतात्देश*m.* भोंवरगांव*m. pl.* भोंवरदेश*m.* सामंतदेश*m.* घेरा*m.*

ENVOY, *n. ambassador.* वकील, दूत.

ENVOYSHIP, *n.* वकिली *f.* दौत्य*n.*

ENVY, *n.* ईर्ष्या *or* ईर्षा *pop.* ईर *f.* हेवा*m.* इसाळ*m.* मत्सर*m.* मात्सर्य*n.* अदेखाई *f.* पोटदुखी *f.* वक्रदृष्टि *f.* अक्षमा *f.* अक्षांति *f.* असहन*n.* असूया *f.* अन्यगुणद्वेष*m.* अन्यशुभद्वेष*m.* परोत्कर्षासहन*n.*

To ENVY, *v. a.* ईर्ष्या *or* ईर्षा *pop.* ईर *f.*-हेवा*m.*-मत्सर*m.*-&c. करणें, पोट*n.* दुखणें *g. of s.* डोळे*m. pl.* जळणें *g. of s.* पोटांत सलणें, पोटांतशूळ*m.* उठणें, पोटदुखी *f.* होणें *g. of s.* [ब्दांतर*n.*

EPACT, *n. excess of the solar year above the lunar.* सौरचांद्रा-

EPHEMERAL, *a. lasting one day.* एकदिवसाचा, ऐकाहिक, दिनायु, एकाहजीवी. [शी.

2 *short lived.* दोनदिवसांचा, अठवडेपाईक *or* वाईक, उत्पन्नविना-

EPIC-POEM, *n.* पंवाडा *or* पोंवाडा*m.* माहात्म्य*n.* वीरोपाख्यान*n.*वीरचरित्र*n.*

EPICEDIUM, *n.* v. ELEGY. शोकगीत*n.* विलापकवन*n.*

EPICENE, *a. common to both genders.* उभयलिंगक, उभयलिंग, उभयविध.

EPICURE, *n. one given to luxuries of the table.* पोटबाबू, पुखानंद, स्वादूनंदन, गोडघाशा, जीभशिंदळ, भोजनसुखतत्पर-आसक्त-&c. पोटार्थी.

2 v. SENSUALIST. भोगी, विलासी, विहारी.

EPICYCLE, *n.* प्राकूचक्र*n.* परिधि*m.* नीचोच्चवृत्त*n.*

EPIDEMIC, *n. disease which seizes many people.* मरी *f.* जरीमरी *f.* मरगी *f.* महामारी *f.* धाम *f.* पटकी *f.* लपेट *f.* सांत *or* ती *f.* वारें *n.* मारक*m.*

EPIDEMIC, EPIDEMICAL, *a.* v. N. सांतीचा, पटकीचा, धामीचा, वाऱ्याचा, &c. बहुमारक, बहुग्राहक, बहुव्यापक, धाडीचा.

E. fever. जरलपेट *f.* जरी *f.*

EPIDERMIC, *a.* बाहेरील त्वचेचा. [कू *f.*

EPIDERMIS, *n. outer skin.* बाहेरलीत्वचा *f.* बहिस्त्वक् *f.* बाह्यत्व-

EPIGASTRIC, *a.* v. N. वरलेपोटाचा, मणिपूरसंबंधी.

EPIGASTRIUM, *n. upper part of the abdomen.* वरलेंपोट *n.* मणि-

पूर *n.* पूर्वबस्ति *f.*

EPIGEUM. See PERIGEE.

EPIGLOTTIS, *n.* श्वासमार्गाचा पडदा *m.* कंठद्वारपाल *m.*

EPIGRAM, *n. pointed, lively piece of poetry.* नोक झोकीची कविता *f.* नोकीची कविता *f.* चुटका *m.* साकूत कविता *f.*

EPILEPSY, *n.* अपस्मार *m.* फेपरें *n.* फुरें *n.* मरगी *f.* मिरगी *f.* घुरें *n.* मरक *m.* ग्रहामय *m.* भूतविक्रिया *f.*

Fit of e. गिरकें *n.* फेपरें *n.*

EPILEPTIC, *a. affected with epilepsy.* फेपरेकरी, फेपऱ्या, अपस्मारी, अपस्मार रोगी, मिरग्या.

2 *belonging to e.* अपस्माराचा, फेपऱ्याचा, अपस्मारसंबंधी, अपस्मारविषयक.

EPILOGUE, *n. poem, &c. at the end of a play.* अंत्यमंगल *n.* नाटकांत शेवटले मंगलश्लोक *m.*

2 *recapitulation.* उपसंहार *m.*

EPINICION, *n. song of triumph.* जयगान *n.* जयगीत*n.*जयघोष*m.*

EPISCOPACY, *n.* बिशपांची सत्ता *f.* बिशपांचा अधिकार *m.*

EPISCOPATE, *n.* बिशपांचावर्ग *m.*

EPISODE, *n. separate incident in a poem or story.* उपकथा *f.* अवांतरकथा *f.* आडकथा *f.* पताका *f.* फरडूक *n.* फरडुकें *n.*

EPISODIACAL, *a.* v. N. उपकथेचा, &c. प्रासंगिक, प्रसंगोपात्त, उपकथेसंबंधी. [मलबद्धरोग *m.*

EPISTASIS, *n. suppression of urine &c.* मूत्रावरोध *m.* आनाह *m.*

EPISTLE, *n.* v. LETTER. पत्र *n.*

EPISTOLARY, *a.* v. N. पत्रोपत्रींचा, कागदोपत्रींचा, पत्रसंबंधी, पत्रविषयक, पत्रद्वारक.

EPITAPH, *n. inscription on a tomb stone.* थडग्यावरचा लेख *m.*

EPITHALAMIUM, *n. nuptial song.* लग्नगीत *n.* विवाहगीत *n.* वैवाहिकमंगलगीत *n.* लग्नाचा पोंवाडा *m.*

EPITHET, *n. adjective.* विशेषण *n.* गुणवाचकशब्द *m.* गुणनाम *n.*

2 *title,* v. NAME. उपाधि *m.* संबोधन *n.* [द्वार *m.*

EPITOME, *n.* v. ABRIDGMENT. सारांशग्रंथ *m.* सारसंग्रह *m.* सारो-

To EPITOMIZE, &c. See To ABRIDGE, &c.

EPOCH, *n. fixed point from which time is computed.* शकादि*m.* शकमूल *n.* शकारंभ *m.* ध्रुव *m.*

EQUABILITY, *n.* v. A. 1. सारखेपणा *m.* एकसारखेपणा *m.* समभाव *m.* समानभाव *m.* समानता *f.* साम्य *n.*

2 समानवृत्ति *f.* समवृत्ति *f.* समवृत्तित्व *n.* समचित्तता *f.*

EQUABLE, *a. of uniform tenor, equal, even.* सारखा, एकसारखा, समान, सम, अन्यूनाधिक, अन्यूनानतिरिक्त, समस्थ.

2 *equanimous.* समचित्त, समवृत्ति, समानवृत्ति, समतोल.

3—temperament, &c. समधात, समरस, सात्म्याचा.

EQUABLY, *adv.* v. A. 1. एकसारखा, सारखा, सारखेपणानें, &c.

EQUAL, *a.* सारखा, समान, सम, तुल्य, बराबर, बराबरचा, बराबरीचा, सममात्र.

2 *uniform.* See EQUABLE.

3 *matching, par.* बराबरीचा, जोडीचा, तोलाचा, एकतोलाचा, समतोल, समकक्ष, समानकक्ष. [समसमान.

4 *exactly correspondent, answering colsely.* तंत, तंतोतंत,

5 *adequate to,* See COMPETENT.

EQUAL, *n. match, fellow.* बराबरचा, बरोबरीचा, जोडीचा, तोलाचा, समतोल, समकक्ष, तोड *f.* तुलना *f.*

To EQUAL, *v. a. be equal to.* सारखा-बराबर-सम-तुल्य-&c. असणें -होणें, तुळणें, बरोबरी *f.*-सरोबरी *f.*-सर *f.*-&c. येणें *g. of s.* ला *or* स *of o.* [&c. करणें.

2 *make equal to.* सारखावणें, सारखा-बरोबर-बरोबरीचा-सम-

EQUALITY, *n.* v. A. 1. सारखेपणा *m.* बरोबरी *f.* तुलना *f.* तुळा *f.* सरोबरी *f.* तौल्य *n.* साम्य *n.* समता *f.* समभाव *m.*

To claim e. with. मांडीसमांडी *f.* टेकून बसणें, टाक *f.* टाकणें, बराबरी *f.* आणणें.

To EQUALIZE, *v. a. make equal.* बराबर-सारखा-सम-समान-समतोल-&c. करणें, सारखावणें, समीकरण *n.* करणें *g. of o.*

EQUALIZED, EQUALLED, *p.* v. V. सारखा-&c. केलेला, समीकृत, तुलीत.

EQUALLY, *adv.* v. A. सारखा, एकसारखा, बरोबर, बरोबरीनें.

EQUANIMITY, *n. evenness of mind.* समानवृत्ति *f.* समवृत्ति *f.* समभाव *m.* समानभाव *m.* समानप्रकृति *f.*

EQUANIMOUS, *a.* v. N. समानवृत्ति, समवृत्ति, समचित्त, समरस, समानप्रकृतिक.

EQUATION, *n. making equal.* समीकरण *n.*

2—in algebra. समीकरण *n.*समीक्रिया *f.*

Reduced to an e. समीकृत.

The side of an e. पेटा *m.*

To put a problem in equations. समीकरण *n.* घालणें—To solve it. समीकरण सोडणें.

EQUATOR, *n.*—terrestrial. विषुववृत्त *n.* विषुवचक्र *n.* विषुवरेखा *f.* विषुवमंडल *n.* भूमध्यरेषा *f.* भूचक्र *n.* विषुवद्वृत्त *n.* भूपरिधि *m.* निरक्ष *m.*

Country along the e. निरक्षदेश *m.*

Radius of e. भूकरण *m.*

2—celestial. नाडीमंडल *n.* नाडीवलय *n.* नाडीवृत्त *n.*

EQUATORIAL, *a.* v. N. 1. विषुववृत्ताचा, विषुवचक्राचा, &c. विषुववृत्तसंबंधी, भूमध्यरेषासंबंधी.

EQUERRY, *n.* राजाच्या घोडशाळेचा अधिकारी, पाग्या, खासदार.

EQUESTRIAN, *a. pertaining to horses.* घोड्यांचा, घोड्याविषयींचा, अश्वसंबंधी, अश्वविषयक, आश्विक.

2 *mounted.* अश्वारूढ, अश्वारोही, अश्वारोह, तुरंगी. [तुरंगी.

EQUESTRIAN, *n.* v. HORSEMAN. घोडेस्वार, अश्वसादी, अश्वचारी,

EQUIANGULAR, *a.* समकोण, समकोणक.

EQUIDISTANT, *a.* सारख्या अंतराचा, समांतर.

EQUILATERAL, *a.* सारख्या बाजूंचा, समभुज.

An e. triangle. समत्रिभुज *m.*

EQUILIBRATION. See EQUIPOISE.

EQUILIBRIUM, *n.* v. EQUIPOISE. समतोल *m.* समतुलना *f.* समता *f.* तुलासाम्य *n.* तुलासमता *f.*

In e. with. भारोभार, भारंभार, समतोल, तोलोतोल.

EQUINE, *a. relating, &c. to a horse.* घोड्याविषयींचा, अश्वसंबंधी, अश्वविषयक, आश्विक, आश्व.

EQUINOCTIAL, *a.* v. N. विषुवसंबंधी, विषुवरेखासंबंधी.

E. circle or line, v. EQUATOR. विषुवरेखा *f.* विषुवद्वृत्त *n.* विषुवचक्र *n.*

E. point. विषुव *n.*

E. points. क्रांतिपात *m.*

Entrance of the sun into an e. point. संपात *m.*

EQUINOX, *n.* विषुव *n.* विषुप *n.* विषुवत् *n.*

Autumnal E. विषुवपद *n.* जलविषुव *n.* सषड्भक्रांतिपात *m.*

Day of the e. विषुवदिन *n.*
Interval between the equinoxes. अयनकाल *m.*
Precession of the equinoxes. अयनचलन*n.* क्रांतिपातगति *f.* अयनांश*m.*
Shade cast at noon by a gnomon at the e. पलभा *f.* विषुवच्छाया *f.*
Vernal E. महाविषुव*n.* हरिपद*n.*
Festival held about the vernal e. होळी *f.* शिमगा*m.*—Dust-day after the burning of *Holi.* धुळवड *f.* रंगपंचमी *f.* —Holy-day after the day of burning. शितळ शिमगा*m.*—Light rain which falls about this time. होळीचें शिंपणें*n.* —Mud-pit for sporters to kick and dance in. राड *f.*—Obscene verses sung at the festival. सख्या *f. pl.*—Pile arranged to be kindled.होळी, हुताशनी *f.*—Powder thrown about. गुलाल*m.*— Glass-ball filled with it. गुलालगोटा*m.* कुमकुमा*m.*—Right of placing the cake upon the pile. होळीची पोळी *f*—Scattering of colored powders. रंगशिंपणें *n.*शिंपणें*n.*—Song in eulogy of the festival.होरी *f.*—Sport of dust-throwing. धूलिवंदन*n.*—Sport and fun on the last day. कोकट होळी,—Sporter or fun-maker during the festival. होळकर *or* होळीचा होळकर.—To burn the *holi.* होळी *f.* करणें.

To Equip, *v. a. accoutre.* सजवणें, सज्जणें *or* सजणें, संजोगणें, सज्ज-सिद्ध-&c. करणें, सजणी *f.*-&c. करणें *g. of o.*

Equipage, *n. attendants, train,* v. Retinue. सवारी *or* स्वारी *f.* इतमाम *m.* लवाजिमा *m.* आराबा *m.*
E. of a chieftain. खाससवारी *f.*
2 See Carriage.
3 *furniture, &c. of an army.* फौजेचें-&c. साहित्य *n.*- सामान *n.*-&c. युद्धोपकरणें *n. pl.* युद्धोपसाहित्यें *n. pl.* युद्ध सामग्री *f.*

Equipment, *n.* v. V.—*act.* सजवणें *n.* सजणी *f.* सजवणी *f.* सजवणूक *f.* सज्जन *n.* सज्जना *f.* सज्जीकरण *n.* [म*m.*
I. *necessaries,* v. Apparatus. साज*m.* सरंजाम*m.* साजसरंजा-

Equipoise, *n. equality of weight, equilibrium.* समतोल *m.* समतुलना *f.* भारसमता *f.* भारसाम्य *n.* तुलासाम्य *n.* तुलासमता *f.* समतौल्य *n.*
In e. with. भारोभार, भारंभार, समतोल, तोलातोल.
To hold in e. पासंगावर-काट्यावर-धड्यावर-&c. धरणें-राखणें -ठेवणें.

Equipollence, Equipollent. See Equivalence.

Equiponderance, *n.* v. Equipoise. वजनाची बरोबरी*f.* समतोल *m.* भारसाम्य *n.* समतौल्य *n.* समतुकभाव *m.*

Equiponderant, *a. of the same weight.* समतोलाचा, एकतोलाचा, एकवजनी, समतोल, समभार, तोलाचा.

To Equiponderate, *v. n. be equal in weight.* समतोलाचा-समतोल-समभार-&c. असणें-होणें.

Equipped, *p.* v.V. सजलेला, सजवलेला, &c. सज्ज, सज्जित, सज्जीकृत, सज्य, शिलेपोस, कडीकोट, जैयत.

Equitable, *a. due, right,* v. Just. नीतीचा, न्यायाचा, यथान्याय, न्याय्य, यथार्ह, यथायोग्य, उजू, मार्गाचा, रास्त.
2—of persons, v. Just. इनसाफी, न्यायी, न्यायाचा, नीतीचा, न्यायनिष्ठ, नीतिमान् *pop.* नीतिवान, नीतिवंत, &c. प्रामाणिक.

Equitableness, *n.* v. A. 1. प्रमाणिकपणा *m.* न्याय *m.* यथान्यायता *f.* न्यायानुगुण्य *n.* न्यायानुकूल्य *n.* उजूपणा*m.*
2 प्रमाणिकपणा*m.*न्यायिता*f.*न्यायनिष्ठा*f.*प्रामाण्य*n.*प्रामाणिकत्व*n.*

Equitably, *adv.* v. A. न्यायेंकरून, यथान्याय, न्यायपूर्वक, न्यायानुसार, न्यायतः.

Equitation. See Riding.

Equity, *n.* v. Justice. न्याय *m.* इनसाफ *m.* नीति *f.*
Court of e. युक्तायुक्तविचार-सदसद्विचार-&c. करून न्याय करण्याची सभा *f.*

Equivalence, *n.* v. A. 1. मोलाची-किमतीची बरोबरी *f.* समतोल *m.* बरोबरी *f.*

Equivalent, *a. equal in value or worth,* lit. fig. एका मोलाचा, एकेकिमतीचा, तोलाचा, एका तोलाचा, समतोलाचा, समतोल, एका वजनाचा, बरोबरचा, बरोबरीचा, सममूल्य, एकमूल्य.
2 *of the same import.* एकार्थाचा, एकार्थक, समानार्थक.

Equivalent, *n. that which is equal in value, &c.* बरोबरीचा-तोलाचा-एकतोलाचा-&c. पदार्थ*m.*-विषय*m.*-&c. समानमूल्यद्रव्यांतर *n.*

Equivocal, *a. ambiguous.* दोन अर्थांचा, द्व्यर्थ, द्व्यर्थक, उभयार्थक, दुटप्पी, दुभावाचा, उभयपक्षींसमान, उभयसाधारण, उभयसामान्य, द्व्यामुष्यायण, दोहोंडगरींवरचा, अळमटळम, श्लिष्ट, व्यधिकरण.
E. generation. अयोनिसंभव, अयोनिज, स्वेदज.

Equivocality, Equivocalness, *n.* v. A. द्व्यर्थता *f.* द्व्यर्थकत्व *n.* दुटप्पीपणा *m.* द्व्यर्थभाव *m.*

Equivocally. See Ambiguously.

To Equivocate, *v. n. speak ambiguously, use terms which admit of different senses.* दुटप्पी बोलणें-दुभावाचें बोलणें *n.*-दोहोंडगरींवरचें बोलणें *n.*-&c. बोलणें, अकडंतिकडं *n.*-इधरतिधर*n.*-अळमटळम *f.*-कंगुमंगु *or* कंगमंग *f.*-&c. करणें, बावंद्या *f. pl.*-भावांस्त्र *m. pl.* लावणें-घेणें-फोडणें, पर्याय *m.* सांगणें-फोडणें.

Equivocation, *n.* v. V. दुटप्पी बोलणें *n.* द्व्यर्थक भाषण *n.* अकडंतिकडं *n.* वाक्छल *m.* इदरतिधर *n.*

Equivoque, *n. ambiguous speech.* वक्रोक्ति *f.* श्लेष *m.*

Era, *n.* See Epoch.
2 *succession of years proceeding from a fixed point.* शक *m.* शाक *m.*
Founder of an e. शककर्त्ता, शाकेश्वर.
In, from, &c. the e. शके (as शकेसतराशें बावन), सन (as सन १८४७)

To Eradicate, *v. a.* v. To Root out. मुळासुद्धां उपटून-उपडून काढणें-टाकणें, निर्मूळ करणें, उत्पाटणें, समूलोत्पाटन *n.*-समूलोत्पाट *m.*-निर्मूलन *n.*-निर्मूल *n.* करणें.

Eradication, *n.* v. V.—*act.* मुळासुद्धां उपटणें *n.* &c.समूलोत्पाटन *n.* समूलोत्पाट *m.* निर्मूलन *n.* निर्मूल *n.* उत्पाटन *n.* उन्मूलन*n.*

To Erase, *v. a.* v. To Efface. खोडणें, खोडून-छिणून-छिलून-खरडून-&c. काढणें, पुसून टाकणें.
To e. much, confusedly, &c. खोडाखोड *f.* करणें.
To e. completely. तळसून काढणें.

Erasing, Erasure, *n.* v. V.—*act.* खोडणें *n.* &c. लोप *m.*
I. *place where a word has been erased.* खोडलेलें स्थळ *n.*

Ere. See Before.

Ere long. See Soon.

To Erect, *v. a. raise upright.* उभा करणें, उभारणें, उंचावणें.

2 v. To BUILD. बांधणें, रचणें.
3 *institute*, v. To ESTABLISH. उभारणें, स्थापणें.
ERECT, *a. upright, not leaning.* उभा, नीटउभा, सरळउभा, नीट, सरळ, सताड.
Rigidly e. तरतरीत उभा. [उत्थापन *n.*
ERECTION, *n.* v. V. 1.—*act.* उभा करणें *n.* उभारणें *n.* उभारणी *f.*
E. of the hairs of the body. रोमांच *m.* लोमांच *m.*
2—*act.* बांधणें *n.* रचना *f.* रचणूक *f.*
3—*act.* उभारणें *n.* &c. स्थापना *f.*
I. an e. v. BUILDING. इमारत *f.* इमला *m.*
ERECTNESS, *n.* v. A. उभेपणा *m.* सरळउभेपणा *m.* सरळपणा *m.*&c.
EREMITE. See HERMIT.
ERGO, *adv.* म्हणून, तस्मात्, अतएव, अतः.
ERMINE, *n.* एक लहान जनावर आहे, व त्याची कातडी.
EROTIC, *a.* v. AMATORY. शृंगारी, शृंगारिक *pop.* शृंगारीक, शृंगाररससंबंधी.
To ERR, *v. n. deviate, stray,* v. To WANDER. चुकणें, बहकणें *or* भकणें, चुकून जाणें.
2 *mistake, blunder.* चुकणें, बहकणें *or* भकणें, घसरणें, चळणें, वाहवणें, भ्रमणें, भुलणें, चकणें, चकरणें, चूक *f.* करणें, झक *f.* मारणें.
ERRAND, *n. message, something to be told or done by a messenger.* निरोप *m.* संदेश *pop.* संदेसा *m.* प्रेष *m.* दौत्य *n.* दूतकर्म *n.* संदिष्टकर्म *n.*
Empty e. or trip. हेलपटा *or* हेलपाटा *m.* झोका *m.* झोकचिट्ठी *f.* गोता *m.* खेटे *m. pl.*
Running on an empty e. येरजार *or* झार *f.* येरधार *f.*
Running about on empty errands. तिरस्थळी *f.* हेलपटनिशी *f.* हेलपायकी *f.*
To send upon an empty e. हेलपटणें, भडकावणें.
ERRAND-BOY, *n.* निरोप्या *m.*
ERRANT, ERRATIC, ERRING, *a,* v. WANDERING. भ्रमी, भ्रमणकर्त्ता, भ्रमणकारी, &c. ओढाळ, परागंदा, स्खलित.
2 *deviating, straying.* चुकर, चुकार, चुकूर, भ्रमी, भ्रमिष्ट, भ्रांत, विभ्रांत.
ERRANTRY, *n.* v. A. 1. फिरणें *n.* भ्रमण *n.* पर्यटन *n.*
ERRATUM, *n.* अशुद्ध *n.* चूक *f.*
Correction of errata. शोध *m.*
Sheet of errata. शोधपत्र *n.* शुद्धिपत्र *n.* [नस्य *n.*
ERRHINE, *n. medicine administered through the nose.* नथ *f.*
ERRONEOUS, *a. erring, mistaking.* चुकणारा, चुकलेला, भ्रांत, भ्रमी, भ्रमिष्ट. [भ्रमाचा, अशुद्ध.
2 *false, mistaken,* v. WRONG. चुकलेला, चुकीचा, भ्रांतीचा,
ERRONEOUSLY, *adv.* चुकून, भ्रांतीनें, भ्रांति-भ्रम-मतिभ्रमपूर्वक, चुकतचुकत, चुकतमाकत *or* वाकत, चुकूनमाकून *or* वाकून.
ERRONEOUSNESS, *n.* v. A. 2. खोटेपणा *m.* खोटाई *f.*
ERROR, *n. wandering from truth.* भ्रम *m.* भ्रांति *f.* मतिभ्रम *m.* मतिभ्रांति *f.* भ्रमज्ञान *n.* संभ्रम *m.* विभ्रम *m.* मिथ्यामति *f.* अविद्या *f.*
The two grand sources of *error* are आवरण and विक्षेप or *the covering or concealing* (*by the object contemplated*) *of its real nature or quality*; and *the casting forth of an appearance or seeming different from reality.*
2 *mistake, blunder, inaccuracy.* चूक *f.* चुकी *f.* अशुद्ध *n.* अबद्ध *n.* दोष *m.* तफावत *f.* गुंजाबीस *f.* भोळें *n.* भोळाभासा *m.*
Errors and omissions,—compreh. चूकभूल *f.* चळचूक *f.*
"Errors excepted." चूकभूल द्यावी घ्यावी, भोळा भासा द्यावा घ्यावा.
ERST. See BEFORE. FORMERLY.
ERUCTATION, *n.* v. BELCH. ढेकर *or* ढेकूर *m.*
A low or soft e. दचकळी *f.*
ERUDITE, *a.* v. LEARNED. विद्वान्, पढीक, पढलेला, व्युत्पन्न, अध्ययन संपन्न, अधीत.
ERUDITION, *n.* v. LEARNING. विद्या *f.* विद्वत्ता *f.* पांडित्य *n.* ज्ञातृत्व *n.* व्युत्पत्ति *f.* अध्ययनसंपत्ति *f.* अक्षरसंपत्ति *f.*
ERUPTION, *n. breaking forth.* फुटणें *n.* स्फोट *m.* जोरानें बाहेर-निघणें *n.* सवेगनिस्सरण *n.*
2—in medicine. उतणें *n.* उफणणें *n.* उगवण *or* उगण *f.* पुरळ *or* पुरूळ *m.* फुटकळ्याचा *or* फुटकुळ्याचा दाथर *m.*
E. after fever. काटे *m. pl.*
Fulness, copiousness of an e. लाहडा *m.* (as देवीचा-गोंवराचा-खरजेचा-&c. लाहडा).
3 (as of ants, gnats &c.) *sudden swarming.* ऊत *m.* उद्धीज *n.* झुंडार *n.* पेंव *n.* v. फुटणें.
ERYSIPELAS, *n.* धावरें *n.*
ERYTHEMA, *n.* इसप *or* व *m.* विसर्प *m.* विसर्पिका *f.*
ESCALADE, ESCALADING, *n.* v. V. शिड्या लावून चढणें *n.*
To ESCALADE, *v. a. scale.* शिड्या लावून चढणें.
To ESCAPE, *v. a. avoid, obtain security or exemption from.* चुकवणें, टाळणें, टळविणें, झुकविणें, हुकविणें.
To be avoided. चुकणें (as हें तुम्ही केलें असतें तर माझें किती दुःख चुकलें असतें).
2 *pass unobserved.* चुकवणें, दृष्टि *f.*-नजर *f.*-&c. चुकवणें, चुकूनराहणें, नजरेंतून-दृष्टींतून जाणें.
To ESCAPE, *v. n. flee and be secure.* सुटणें, सुटून जाणें, निघून जाणें, अंतरणें, पळून-&c. निभावणें-वहिवाटणें.
2 *pass unharmed.* तरणें, पारपडणें, निभावणें, वहिवाटणें, जगणें, वांचणें, धड-सुधा-अपूट-कोरा-&c. राहणें.
To find a way to escape. तरल्या पंथास लागणें.
To set on a way to escape. तरल्या पंथास लावणें.
ESCAPE, ESCAPING, *n.* v. V. A. 1.—*act.* चुकवणें *n.* टाळणें *n.*&c. टाळणी *f.* टाळणूक *f.* निस्तरण *n.* निस्तार *m.*—*state.* आंगसुटका *f.* बचाव *m.* उद्धार *m* उद्धारगत *f.* तरणूक *f.* सुटका *f.*
Means of e. तरणोपाय *m.*
v. V. N. 1. पळून जाणें *n.* सुटून जाणें *n.* &c.
2 निभाव *m.* निभावणी *f.* निभावणूक *f.*
ESCHAROTIC, *a. caustic.* मांसदाहक, दाहकारी.
ESCHAROTIC, *n.* अवसादन *n.*
ESCHEAT, *n. land, &c. which reverts to the state through failure of heirs.* बेहतनमाल *or* बेतनमाल *m.* बेवारीसमाल *m.* बेवारीस जिंदगी *f.* मयतमाल *m.* अदायादरिक्त *n.*
To ESCHEW. See To AVOID.
ESCORT, ESCORTING, *n.* v. V.—*act.* बोळवणें *n.* बोळवण *f.* बोळवणी *f.* बोळवणूक *f.*
I. *attendant protecting body.* बलावा *or* बल्हावा *m.* बोळावा *m.* पावणी *f.*
A light e. सडीसवारी *f.*
Cost or hire of an e. बलावा *or* बल्हावा *m.*

To ESCORT, *v. a. attend and guard by land.* बरोबर-संगें- &c. जाऊन पावणें-पोहोंचविणें-पावणें *n.* करणें, &c. बोळवणें, बोळवण *f.*-बोळवणी *f.*-बोळवणूक *f.* करणें *g. of o.* [य, भोज्य.

ESCULENT, *a.* v. EATABLE. खाया-चा-जोगता-&c. भक्ष्य, भक्षणी-

ESCUTCHEON, *n.* कुलमानद्योतकध्वजादि चिन्हांचें चित्र *n.*

ESOPHAGUS, *n. gullet.* अन्नाची नळी *f.* अन्नमार्ग *m.*

ESOTERIC, *a. private.* गुप्त, गुप्तोक्त, एकांतोपदिष्ट, रहःकथित.

E. doctrine. चोरविद्या *f.*

ESPECIAL. See SPECIAL.

ESPECIALLY, *adv.* विशेषें करून, विशेषतः, विशेषात्कारें, मुख्यत्वें करून, प्राधान्यें करून.

ESPIONAGE, *n. employment of spies.* चारद्वारकावलोकन *n.* चारद्वारकदर्शन *n.* चारचक्षु *n.* पैशुन्य *n.*

ESPLANADE, *n.* किल्ल्याचें पुढचें मैदान *n.*

ESPOUSAL, ESPOUSING, *n.* v. V. I.—*act.* वाग्दान *n.* वाचादान*n.* मागणी *f.*

2 वरणें *n.* वरण *n.* परिणय *m.* परिणयन *n.* पाणिग्रहण *n.*

3 स्वीकारणें *n.* &c. स्वीकार *m.* अंगीकार *m.* कैवार *m.*

4 कैवार *m.* कासेस मारणें *n.* &c.

To ESPOUSE, *v. a.* v. To BETROTH. वाग्दान *n.*-वाग्निश्चय *m.*-&c. करणें *g. of o.*

2 *wed*, v. To MARRY. उद्वाहणें, परणणें *or* प्रणणें, वरणें, परिणय *m.*-परिणयन*n.*-पाणिग्रहण *n.* करणें *g. of o.*

3 *adopt, take up* (*to maintain, &c.*). आदरणें, अंगीकारणें, स्वीकारणें, धरणें, घेणें, अभिमानणें *or* अभिमान *m.* धरणें *g. of o.* कैवार *m.* घेणें-करणें, पक्ष *m.* धरणें, मनावर घेणें *or* धरणें, डोईवर घेणें.

4 *take under protection.* कासेस-काखाटीस-बगलेस मारणें-घेणें, कासेंत-बगलेंत घेणें, कैवार *m.* घेणें-करणें, पक्ष *m.* धरणें.

ESPRIT, *n.* अभिमान *m.*

E. de corps. स्वगणाभिमान *m.*

E. de parti. स्वपक्षाभिमान *m.* स्वमताभिमान *m.*

E. de pays. देशाभिमान *m.*

To ESPY. See To SPY.

ESQUIRE, *n.* एक किताब आहे. [जाणें.

To ESQUIRE, *v. a. attend, chaperon.* संभाळण्याकरितां बरोबर

ESSAY, *n. attempt*, v. TRIAL. यत्न *m.* प्रयत्न *m.* उद्योग *m.*

I. *tract.* निबंध *m.* स्वल्पप्रबंध *m.*

To ESSAY, *v. n. attempt*, v. To TRY. यत्न *m.*-प्रयत्न*m.*-उद्योग *m.* &c. करणें, करून पाहणें-बघणें.

2 See To ASSAY.

ESSAYIST, *n. writer of essays.* निबंध रचणारा.

ESSENCE, *n. constituent substance*, v. NATURE. तत्व *n.* सत्व *n.* आत्मा *m.* प्रकृति *f.* प्रकृतिस्वभाव *m.* तन्मात्र *n.*

Oneness or identity of e. तादात्म्य *n.* तदात्मकता *f.*

2 *main substance or virtue of.* कस *m.* सार *m. n.* सारांश *m.* तत्व *n.* तत्वांश *m.* [त्कर्ष*m.*

3—in medicine, v. EXTRACT. काढा*m.* कषाय*m.* अर्क*m.* नि-

Fragrant e.—gener. अत्तर*n.*

4 *substance, virtue, pith, marrow, cream, flower.* सार*m.n.* सारांश*m.* गर्भ*m.* तात्पर्य *n.* तात्पर्यार्थ*m.* तत्व*n.* तत्वार्थ*m.* तात्विक*n.* तत्तामाल*m.* सत्व*n.* निर्गलितार्थ*m.* गोळाबेरीज *or* गोळीबेरीज *f.* गोशेरा*m.* गोष्वारा*m.* गोष्वारा*m.* नीस*m.* *v.* काढ, इत्यर्थ*m.* इदमित्थ*n.*

5 See BEING.

ESSENTIAL, *a.* v. N. 1. *pertaining naturally.* स्वभावसिद्ध, स्वाभाविक, प्रकृतिसिद्ध, निसर्गसिद्ध.

2 *necessary to the existence of.* स्वभावसिद्धिसाधक, स्वभावसिद्धीचा, अविनाभावाचा, अविनाभूत, प्रवृत्तिनिमित्तभूत, नांतरीयक, अव्यभिचारी, अस्तित्वैकहेतुक, सत्तैकहेतुक, सत्तोपादान.

Essential and inherent character. अविनाभाव*m.*

3 *highly necessary, and important.* जरूरीचा, फार जरूरीचा, आवश्यक, नियतावश्यक, अवश्योपयोगी.

ESSENTIAL, *n. constituent principles.* See NATURE.

2 *chief point, point of great importance.* जरूरीची गोष्ट *f.*आवश्यकविषय*m.*-&c. [निसर्गतः.

ESSENTIALLY, *adv.* v. A. 1. स्वभावेंकरून, स्वभावानें, स्वभावतः,

To ESTABLISH, *v. a. settle, fix, set, place.* स्थापणें, थावरणें, थारावणें, थिरावणें, घालणें, स्थापन*n.*-स्थापना *f.*-आधान *n.*-अधिष्ठान *n.*विधान*n.* करणें *g. of o.* स्थापित-स्थिर-&c. करणें.

2 *set up, institute.* स्थापणें, संस्थापणें, मांडणें, उभारणें, स्थापन *n.*-स्थापना *f.* करणें *g. of o.*

3 *substantiate, evince, evidence*, v. To PROVE. स्थापणें, सिद्धकरणें, खरा करून देणें-दाखवणें, स्थापन*n.*-स्थापना *f.*-&c. करणें *g. of o.*

4 See To CONFIRM, To RATIFY.

5 (as a rule or law) v. To APPOINT. नेमणें, नेमूनदेणें.

ESTABLISHED, *p.* v. V. 1. स्थापलेला, थावरलेला, &c. स्थापित, अधिष्ठित, आहित, काईम, मुस्तकीम, नियत.

2 स्थापलेला, &c. स्थापित, संस्थापित, उत्थापित.

3 स्थापलेला, सिद्ध केलेला, &c. स्थापित, सिद्ध, साबूत *or* साबीत, उपपन्न.

ESTABLISHER, *n.* v. V. 1. स्थापणारा, &c. आधायक, विधायक, विधाता, विधानकर्त्ता.

2 स्थापणारा, &c. स्थापक, संस्थापक, उत्थापक.

3 स्थापणारा, &c. स्थापक, स्थापनकर्त्ता, &c. निर्वाहक.

ESTABLISHMENT, *n.* v. V. 1.—*act.* स्थापणें*n.* स्थापन*n.* स्थापना*f.* जडाव*m.* आधान*n.* विधान*n.* निवेशन *n.*—*state.* जडाव*m.* निवेश*m.* अधिष्ठान*n.*

2 स्थापणें*n.* &c. स्थापन*n.* स्थापना *f.* संस्थापन*n.* संस्थापना *f.* उत्थापन*n.*—*state.* प्रतिष्ठा *f.*

3—*act.* स्थापणें*n.* साधन*n.* स्थापन*n.* स्थापना *f.* मंडन*n.* निर्वाह *m.*—*state.* उपपत्ति *f.* सिद्धि *f.*

Document or writing in e. साधनपत्र*n.*

E. of a position. साध्यसिद्धि *f.*

Means of establishing (a charge, claim, suit, &c.). साधनसूत्र*n.*

I. *appointed allowance.* नेमणूक *f.*

II. *body* (*as of officers, servants, &c.*) *established.* नेमणूक *f.* नेमणुकीची मंडळी *f.* कारखाना*m.*

State or domestic e. इतमाम*m.* लबाजमा*m.* खटला*m.* खटलें*n.*

III. Worldly e. *one's fortune, business, retinue, train, &c.* संसार*m.* खटला*m.* खटलें*n.* आराबा*m.* अरस्तूल*m.* संसाराचा गाडा *m.* गाडानाडा*m.* जोजार*m.* तेगार*m.* फडफडागत *f.* फडफडाव*m.*

Large e. लंगरखाना *m.* फाकडपसारा *m.* ब्रह्मांडकारखाना *m.* ब्रह्मांडसंसार *m.* गंजीकोटकारखाना *m.*

Encumbered with a large e. जोजारी.

To have a large e. or family. जोजारणें *or* जोजावणें.

ESTATE, *n. land, possessions, &c.* वतन *n.* वतनदारी *f.* वृत्ति *f.*

E. in land. जमीन *f.* मिरास *f.*

E. and establishment,—compreh. *lands and cattle, family and followers.* फडफडागत *f.* फडफडाव *m.* खटला *m.* खटलें *n.*

Extensive or great e. हत्तीसारखें वतन *n.*

Rise or falling to of an e. आगम *m.*

2 See EFFECTS. 3 See STATE.

To ESTEEM, *v. a.* v. To VALUE. गणणें, मोजणें, मेजणें, लेखणें.

2 *value highly, prize.* चांगला-&c. समजणें-मोजणें-गणणें-मानणें, फार मानणें-मोजणें-&c.

ESTEEM, *n. high regard or value for.* योग्यताबुद्धि *f.* मान्यताबुद्धि *f.* योग्यताग्रह *m.* मान्यताग्रह *m.* योग्यतादृष्टि *f.* मान्यतादृष्टि *f.* मान्यता *f.* गणती *f.*

2 *judgment.* See ESTIMATION.

ESTEEMED, *a.* v. ESTIMABLE. मान्य, योग्य.

ESTIMABLE, *a. worthy of regard or good opinion.* मान्य, माननीय, आदरणीय, मानार्ह, मानपात्र, भला, चांगला, योग्य.

ESTIMABLENESS, *n.* v. A. मान्यता *f.* योग्यता *f.* मानार्हता *f.*

To ESTIMATE, *v. a. adjust the worth of, rate.* जोखणें, तोलणें, मोजणें, गणणें, जोखून-तोलून-&c. ठेवणें.

2 (expenses, amount, &c.) *compute, rate.* अजमासणें, अजमावणें, अटकळणें *in. con.* अटकळून सांगणें-बोलणें-पाहणें-&c. आकारणें, अडसट्टा *m.* पाहणें, अटकळ *f.* करणें, शुमार *m.* पाहणें-काढणें-बांधणें-करणें.

ESTIMATE, ESTIMATION, *n.* v. V. 1—*act.* जोखणें *n.* तोलणें *n.* &c. तुलना *f.* गणती *f.* मोजणी *f.* हिशेब *m.*

2 अजमासणें *n.* अजमावणें &c. आकारणी *f.*

I. *computation made.* अजमास *m.* अजमाव *m.* अडसट्टा *m.* आकार *m.* अटकळ *f.* ठोकताळा *or* थोकताळा *m.*

Precise and exact e. सूक्ष्ममान *n.*

Random e. बारेमाप *n.* अटकळ पंचविशी *f.*

Rough e. कच्चा आकार *m.* स्थूलमान *n.* अटोंका *or* अटंका *m.* ठोकताळा *m.* अनुमानधपका *m.* अनुमानोक्ति *f.* शुमार *m.* तगदमपट्टी *f.* तगदमा *m.* अटकळपंचविशी *f.*

Upon a rough, &c. e. सरासरी.

II. *weight, regard.* मान *n.* पाड *m.* लेखा *m.* हिशेब *or* हिशोब *m.* गणती *f.* गणना *f.* केवा *m.*

Light e. हलकाभार *m.*

Of little e. हलका, अवगणित, अगणित.

Of the lowest e. कडेलोट, कडेशेवटचा.

III. *judgment,* v. OPINION. मत *n.* बुद्धि *f.* हिशेब *m.* गणती *f.*

ESTIVAL, *a. relating, &c. to summer.* ग्रीष्मकालाचा, ग्रीष्मर्तुसंबंधी, ग्रैष्मिक, ग्रीष्मकालिक.

To ESTRANGE, &c. See To ALIENATE, &c.

ESTUARY, *n. frith.* खाडी *f.*

ET CÆTERA. This phrase is well rendered by आदि & इत्यादि. आदि means *first,* इति means *thus.* आदि is used in comp. and, at the end; as आम्रादि mangoes, *et cætera;* फलादि, पुष्पादि, वृक्षादि, मनुष्यादि, सुवर्ण रौप्यताम्रादि, काम क्रोध लोभादि, i. e. Fruit *being first,* flowers *being first.* इत्यादि stands alone, closing the sentence; as आकाश अग्नि वायु जल इत्यादि *A'kásha,* fire, air, water, *thus first, these being principal or precedent.* To इत्यादि the letter क is often added. *See* आदि, इत्यादि, *and* आदिकरून in M. & E. Dict. Frequently the Persian वगैरे (وغيره *and the others*) is used.

The et cæteras. इतरविशेष.

To ETCH, *v. a.* तांब्यावर खुणा करून खोदून काढणें.

ETERNAL, *a. without beginning or end.* अनाद्यंत, अनाद्यनंत, अनादिनिधन, आद्यंतरहित-शून्य, आदिमध्यांतरहित, नित्यसिद्ध, सदातन, सनातन.

2 *without beginning.* अनादि, अनादिसिद्ध, विभु.

3 *without end, everlasting, endless.* सर्वकाळ राहणारा, अनंत, शाश्वत, शाश्वतिक, सतत, संतत, अशेष, नित्य, अनश्वर, अविनाशी, अनिधन, अमर, नित्यस्थायी, निरंतर, सर्वकालस्थायी, अनंतकालस्थायी.

ETERNAL, *n.* See GOD.

ETERNALLY, *adv. without end, constantly,* v. EVER. सतत, निरंतर.

ETERNITY, *n. duration without beginning or end.* अनाद्यंतत्व *n.* अनाद्यंतता *f.* अनाद्यनंतत्व *n.* आद्यंतशून्यता *f.*

2 *exemption from commencement.* अनादित्व *n.* अनादिता *f.* अनादिसिद्धि *f.*

Succession or series from e. अनादिपरंपरा *f.*

2 *duration without end.* अनंतत्व *n.* आनंत्य *n.* शाश्वती *f.* शाश्वत *f. n.* सातत्य *n.* सांतत्य *n.* शाश्वतता *f.* नैरंतर्य *n.* अनंतकालस्थायित्व *n.*

To ETERNIZE. See To PERPETUATE. To IMMORTALIZE.

ETHER, *n.*—the element. आकाश *n.*

2—in chemistry. एक अर्क आहे.

ETHEREAL, *a.* v. N. 1. आकाशाचा, आकाशीय, आकाशी, आकाशज, आकाशमय, आकाशस्वरूप.

2 v. HEAVENLY. दिव्य.

ETHIC, ETHICAL, *a.* v. N. नीतीचा, नीतिशास्त्राचा, नीतिसंबंधी-विषयक, नीतिशास्त्र-&c. संबंधी-विषयक.

ETHICS, *n. science of morals.* नीति *f.* नीतिशास्त्र *n.* नीतिविद्या *f.* दंडनीति *f.* नय *m.* नयशास्त्र *n.* नयविद्या *f.* अर्थशास्त्र *n.* बार्हस्पत्य *n.*

ETHNOLOGY, *n.* नृजातिविद्या *f.*

ETIQUETTE, *n. forms of ceremony.* सभ्याचारपद्धति *f.* शिष्टाचारपद्धति *f.* शिष्टाचाररीति *f.* आदरोपचाररीति *f.*

Royal e. राजोपचार *m.*

ETUI, *n. case of instruments.* नाचकंड *or* कण *n.*

ETYMOLOGICAL, *a.* v. N. व्युत्पत्तीचा, शब्दसाधनविद्यासंबंधी-विषयक, व्युत्पत्तिसंबंधी-विषयक, &c.

ETYMOLOGY, *n. derivation, analysis, &c. of words.* शब्दसाधनविद्या *f.* व्युत्पत्ति *f.* प्रक्रिया *f.* शब्दसाधनिका *f.* पदभंजन *n.* शब्दनिरुक्ति *f.*

ETYMON, *n. primitive word.* मूलशब्द *m.* शब्दयोनि *f.* शब्दबीज *n.*

EUCHARIST, *n.* प्रभुभोजन *n.*

2 स्तुतिवाद *m.* स्तुतिपाठ *m.*

EUCHARISTIC, EUCHARISTICAL, *a.* v. N. 1. प्रभुभोजनाचा, प्रभुभोजनविषयक-संबंधी.

EUCRACY, *n.*—in medicine. समधातुक प्रकृति *f.* धातुसाम्य *n.*

EULOGIST, *n.* स्तुतिकरणारा, प्रशंसक, स्तुतिपाठक.

EULOGISTIC, *a.* स्तुतीचा, स्तुतिमय.

To EULOGIZE. See To PRAISE.

EULOGY, *n. writing of praise*, v. PANEGYRIC. स्तोत्र *n.* स्तुतिपाठ *m.* स्तुतिवाद *m.*

2 See PRAISE.

EUNUCH, *n.* षंड *or* शंड *m.* खोजा *m.* नपुंसक *m.* राशी *m.* क्लीब *m.* छिन्नमुष्क *m.* छिन्नांड *m.* तृतीयप्रकृति *f.*

EUPHONIC, EUPHONOUS, *a. agreeable in sound.* कानासगोड, सुस्वर, कर्णमधुर, सुश्राव्य, श्रवणमंगल.

EUPHONY, *n. smooth enunciation of sound.* कर्णमाधुर्य *n.* सुस्वरोच्चार *m.* मधुरोच्चार *m.*

EUPHORBIA,—antiquorum or tirucalli. शेर *m.* चिकाडा *m.* निवळ *f.* निवळी *f.* काडेहुरा *or* काड्याहुरा *m.*—tortilis. निवडुंग *or* निवडंग *m. n.* निवडगुंगट *m. n.* निवलकांडें *n.*

EUROPEAN, *a.* युरोपखंडाचा, युरोपखंडांतला, युरोपखंडसंबंधी, विलायती, विलायतचा.

EUROPEAN, *n.* फिरंगी, टोपीवाला, टोपीकर, टोपकर.

EUTHANASIA, *n. easy death.* सुखाचें मरण *n.* सुखमरण *n.* सुमरण *n.*

To EVACUATE, *v. a. eject, void, discharge.* टाकणें, सोडणें, उत्सर्ग *m.*-उत्सर्जन *n.*-विसर्ग *m.*- विसर्जन *n.*-त्याग *m.*- निस्सारण *n.*-&c. करणें *g. of o.*

2 *void by stool.* गुदद्वारा उत्सर्ग *m.*-&c. करणें *g. of o.* हगणें.

To be evacuated. पडणें.

3 See To EMPTY, To PURGE.

EVACUATION, *n.* v. V.—*act.* टाकणें *n.* &c. उत्सर्ग *m.* उत्सर्जन *n.* विसर्ग *m.* विसर्जन *n.* त्याग *m.* त्यजन *n.*

2—*act.* मलविसर्ग *m.* मलविसर्जन *n.* मलोत्सर्ग *m.* मलोत्सर्जन *n.* मलशुद्धि *f.* शौच *n.* झाडाझडका *m.*

The evacuations. मलमूत्रोत्सर्ग *m.*

I. *an* e. v. PURGE. झाडा *m.* ढाळ *m.*

To EVADE, *v. a. escape, avoid, elude.* चुकवणें, टाळणें, झुकविणें, झुकाटी *f.*-झुकांडी *f.*-झुकापुरी *f.*-झुगारा *m.*-झोका *m.*-धोका *m.*-&c. देणें.

2 *elude, divert, turn off.* चुकवणें, टाळणें, उडवणें, झुलवणें, झुकविणें, झुकविणें, ढाळ *m.* देणे, टाळाटाळ *f.*-चुकवाचुकव *f.*-उडवाउडव *f.* करणें *g. of o.* चुकांडी *f.*-झोंकपट्टी *f.*-झुगारपट्टी *f.* देणें.

EVADER, *n.* EVASIVE, *a.* v. V. 1. चुकवणारा, टाळणारा, झोका देणारा &c. झोक्याचा, झुकापुरीचा, झुगाऱ्याचा, &c.

2 चुकवणारा, टाळणारा, उडवणारा, &c. उडाऊ, छप्पू, उडाऊछप्पी, उडवाउडवीचा, चुकवाचुकवीचा, झुगारपट्टीचा.

EVANESCENT, *a.* v. TEMPORARY. लवकर नाहींसा होणारा, अचिर, अचिरस्थायी, क्षणस्थायी.

2—of colors. कच्चा, उडाऊ.

EVANGELICAL, *a. according to the gospel.* सुवार्त्तानुयायी, सुवार्त्तानुसंधानी, शुभवर्त्तमानानुसारी.

EVANGELIST, *n. writer of the gospel.* सुवार्त्तालेखक-रचक, शुभवर्त्तमानलेखक-रचक.

2 *preacher of the gospel.* सुवार्त्ताघोषक.

To EVAPORATE, *v. a. convert into vapour.* वाफ *f.* करणें *g. of o.* वाफ करून-वाफेनें उडवणें-नेणें-आकर्षणें-सुखवणें, बाष्पभूत-बाष्प परिणामक-&c. करणें.

To EVAPORATE, *v. n.* वाफ *f.* होणें, वाफेनें-वाफ होऊन उडणें-अटणें-सुखणें, उडणें, उडून जाणें.

EVAPORATION, *n.* v. V. A.—*act.* वाफ करणें *n.* &c. बाष्पीकरण *n.* v. V. N. वाफ होऊन उडणें *n.* बाष्पभवन *n.*

EVASION, *n.* v. V. 1.—*act.* चुकवणें *n.* टाळणें *n.* &c.

2 चुकवणें *n.* उडवणें *n.* &c. उडवणी *f.* उडवणूक *f.*

I. *means of evading, shift, subterfuge.* सोडवण *f.* सबड *f.* सिडकी *f.* दार *n.*

II. *evasive speech or arts.* अळमटळम *n. f.* अकडंतिकडं *n.* इधर तिधर *n.* गड्डेपड्डे *m. pl.* घटपट *n.* हिला *m.* हिलाहरकत *f.* पेंचपाच *m.* हुज्जत *f.*

EVASIVE. See EVADER.

EVE, EVEN, *n.* See EVENING.

2 *evening before a holiday.* पूर्वसंध्या *f.*

3 *period just preceding.* अदलादिवस *m.*

EVEN, *a. level, equal, plain.* सपाट, सारखा, एकसारखा, बराबर, साफ, निढाळ, तळवट, समान, सम, समस्थ, समसमान, न्यहार.

2 *level with, parallel to.* बराबर, सारखा, सम *all with* शीं *of o.* समसमान.

3 *not odd.*—of number. सम, युग्म.

An e. number. बेकी *f.*

EVEN, *adv. notwithstanding.* जरी.

2 *so much as.* देखील, देखीत, सुद्धां.

3 *also, likewise.* ही, देखील, देखीत, सुद्धां, बलक, बलकी.

4—as a word of exaggeration or emphasis. ही, देखील, देखीत.

To EVEN. See To LEVEL.

EVEN-HANDED. See IMPARTIAL.

EVEN-TEMPERED, *a.* समचित्त, समवृत्ति, समानवृत्ति.

EVENING, *n.* सांज *or* झ *f.* सायंकाल *m.* संध्याकाल *m. pop.* संध्याकाळ *f.* सांजवेळ *f.* संध्या *f.* तिनसांजा *f. pl.* तिनीसांजा *f. pl.* सवसांज *f.* सायाह्न *m.* साय *m.* दिनावसान *n.* दिनांत *m.* दिनमर्यादा *f.* प्रदोष *m.* प्रदोषकाल *m.* नक्षत्रदर्शन *n.* गोधूल मुहूर्त्त *m.* गोरजमुहूर्त्त *m.* कातरवेळ *f.* राक्षसवेळ *or* ळा *f.*

About the time of e. twilight. सवेसांजचा *ad. decl.*

In the e. सांजे, सांजवेळीं, संध्याकाळीं, साये.

In the dusk of e. डोळे उजेडीं.

To become or to draw towards e. सांजवणें *or* सांजळणें *or* सांझळणें.

EVENING, *a.* सांजचा, संध्याकाळचा, सांध्य, प्रादोष.

EVENING-SONG, EVENSONG, *n.* संध्याकाळचें स्तोत्र *n.*

EVENING-STAR, *n.* शुक्र *m.*

EVENLY, *adv.* v. A. 1. सारखा *decl.* बराबर.

EVENNESS, *n.* v. A. 1. सारखेपणा *m.* सपाटी *f.* साफी *f.* समता *f.* साम्य *n.* समानता *f.*

2 बराबरी *f.* सारखेपणा *m.* साम्य *n.* समता *f.*

3 साम्य *n.* समता *f.*

EVENT, *n. incident*, v. OCCURRENCE. घडूनआलेली गोष्ट *f.* गोष्ट *f.* वृत्त *n.*

Novel or strange e. अघटितघटना *f.* अपूर्वगोष्ट *f.* अद्भुतगोष्ट *f.*

2 *result, issue, upshot*, v. CONSEQUENCE. फल *pop.* फळ *n.* परिणाम *m.* परिपाक *m.*

EVENTFUL, *a. full of incidents.* उलटापालटीचा, घडामोडीचा, अद्भुतवृत्त-विशेषवृत्त-वर्णनीयवृत्त-&c. विशिष्ट-युक्त, विशेषवृत्तात्मक &c. विशेषवृत्तपरिपूर्ण, विशेषवृत्तांतप्रचुर.

EVENTIDE. See EVENING.

EVENTUAL, *a. happening as a consequence.* अन्यकार्यानुयायी, अन्यकार्याधीन, अन्यकार्य परिणामभूत, कार्यरूपफलीभूत, आनुषंगिक.

2 See FINAL.

EVENTUALLY, *adv.* शेवटीं, परिणामीं.

EVER, *adv. at any time.* कधीं, कद्दीं, कोणत्यातरी काळीं, कोणत्यातरी वेळीं, केव्हांतरी, कदापि (*with neg. con.*).

2 *at all times, constantly, continually.* सर्वकाल,सदा, सदासर्वदा, नित्य, निरंतर, नेहमी, हमेश, हमेशा, नित्यानें, नित्यनित्यश:,सदैव, सदोदित, सतत, संतत,अक्षयीं, अजस्त्र,—emphatically; corresponding with *morning, noon, and night, night or day, summer or winter, early or late, &c.* सदासर्वकाळ, सदासर्वदा, बारामहिने तेराकाळ, येतां जातां, येऊन जाऊन, उठतांबसतां, उठल्याबसल्या, ऊठपाय *or* उठापायीं, जेव्हां तेव्हां, नित्यानित्य, नित्यनियमानें, नित्यांत, नित्यदा, नित्यउठून, रोजउठून, हरहमेश, हरहमेशा, हरघडी, हरवखत, घडीघडी, घडोघडी,अष्टाप्रहर, रात्रंदिवस, वेळ अवेळ, उत्तरामात्रां *or* त्रीं, अहोरात्र, निशिदिनि, अहर्निश, प्रतिपद, पदोपदीं, पदेपदे, आंगोघडी *or* ड्या, सपसप *or* सबसब.

E. and anon. जेव्हांतेव्हां, हरघडी, वारंवार, येरयेरां.

For e. सर्वकाल, अनंतकाल, शेवटवर,शेवटपर्यंत, आकाल मर्याद.

EVERGREEN, *a.* सदाहिरवा, सदाहरितपर्ण, सदार्द्रपर्णक.

EVERLASTING, *a. ever during,* v. ETERNAL, PERPETUAL. सर्वकाळ राहणारा, नित्य, नित्यस्थायी, सर्वकालस्थायी, शाश्वत, शाश्वतिक, अनंत, अविनाशी.

2—the deity, *existing from e. to e.* v. ETERNAL. नित्यसिद्ध, अनादिनिधन, अनाद्यनंत.

3—time or duration, *ever and continuously flowing.* अखंड दंडायमान.

EVERLIVING, *a.* v. ETERNAL, IMMORTAL. नित्यजीवी, अमर.

EVERMORE. See EVER.

EVERY, *a.* हरएक, हर, प्रत्येक. [एकएकला.

2—singly or distributively, v. EACH. एकएक, एकएकटा,

E. body. E. one. हरकोण्ही, एकूनएक, एकानएक. In enhancement of this sense there are in English the expressions, *all without exception, the whole world, tout le monde, high and low, rich and poor, great and small, old and young, &c. &c.* The correspondent expressions in *Maráthí* are collected here. आबालवृद्ध, बाळगोपाळ, लहानमोठे, लहानथोर, महारपोर *m. pl.* आपामरसाधारण, चांडालांत, समाकुळ पांढर *f.* रावरंक, मनुष्यमात्र, यावन्मनुष्य, यच्चयावत्.

E. one for himself(on his own bottom, &c.). आंगोपती.

To, by, per, &c. e. one,—singly. असामीवार, आंगोगडी *or* आंगागवडी.

EVERY-DAY, *adv.* v. DAILY. रोज रोज, प्रति दिवशीं, रोजउठून.

EVERY-DAY, *a.* v. DAILY. प्रतिदिवसाचा, नित्याचा.

EVERYWHERE, *adv.* जिकडेतिकडे, जिथेंतिथें, सर्वत्र, सरीसर्वत्र, सर्वत:, सर्वठिकाणीं, हर एकठिकाणीं, विश्वत:, विष्वक्.

EVIDENCE, *n. manifestness,* v. CLEARNESS. व्यक्ति *f.*

2 *proof.* प्रमाण *n.* गमक *n.* मुद्दा *m.* The e. of *sense* (perception) is प्रत्यक्षप्रमाण *n. or* प्रत्यक्ष *n.*—of *reasoning* (inference) अनुमान *n.*—of *comparison* or *analogy* उपमान *n.* —*testimony* शब्द *m.* And, (as in cases of disputed property), the e. of *possession or fruition* is भोगप्रमाण *n. or* भोग *m.*—of a *grant* or other *document* (documentary) लेखप्रमाण *n. or* लेख *m.* सड *or* सडी *f.*—of *witnesses to the right* (testificatory) साक्ष्यप्रमाण *n. or* साक्ष्य *n.*—of an *appeal by ordeal,* दिव्यप्रमाण *n. or* दिव्य *n.* And,e.—compreh. (documentary, oral, circumstantial, &c.),दाखला मुकाबला *m.* साधनसूत्र *n.* or—compreh. and freely (proof, presumption,argument,ground,&c.),मुद्दापत्ता *or* पत्तामुद्दा *m.*

Ocular e. प्रत्यक्ष *n.* चाक्षुष *n.* चाक्षुषज्ञान *n.* दृक्प्रत्यय *m.*

Oral e. जबानी *f.*

With due e. and proof. पत्त्यामुद्यानिशीं *or* मुद्यापत्त्यानिशीं.

To have ocular e. of. दृष्टोत्पत्तीस येणें *g. of s.*

3 *witness, testimony.* साक्ष *f.* साक्षी *f.* शाहिदी *f.* ग्वाही *f.* जबानी *f.* साक्ष्य *n.*

Corroborative e. पडसाक्ष *f.* प्रतिसाक्ष्य *n.* प्रत्यंतर *n.*

False e. कूटसाक्ष्य *n.*

With or upon e. साक्षमोज्यानें, साक्षीनिशीं.

4 *witness,*—of persons. साक्षी, साक्षीदार, साक्ष, ग्वाही, ग्वाहीदार, शाहिदी, शाहिदीदार, शाहीद, साक्षीमोज्या.

Corroborative e. पडसाक्षी, पडसाक्ष, प्रतिसाक्षी.

False e. कूटसाक्षी.

5 *sign, indication, thing evidencing.* लक्षण *n.* निशाणी *or* नी *f.* दाखला *m.* पत्तामुद्दा *m.* मुद्दा पत्ता *m.*

To EVIDENCE. See TO MANIFEST, TO PROVE.

EVIDENT, *a.*v. PLAIN. उघड, उघडा, स्पष्ट, साफ, प्रत्यक्ष, प्रकट *pop.* प्रगट, प्रसिद्ध.

EVIDENTLY, *adv.* v. PLAINLY. उघड, साफ, प्रत्यक्ष, प्रत्यक्षत:, साक्षात्, निवळ, धडधडीत, धादांत.

EVIL, *a. ill,*—gener. v. BAD. वाईट, दुष्ट, खराब, कुत्सित.

2 v. WICKED, SINFUL. पापी, पापिष्ट, पापाचा, कु (in comp. as कुकर्म, &c.), असत् (in comp. as असत्कर्म, असज्जन, असत्संग, &c.), दुर (in comp. as दुर्जन, दुर्गुण, &c.).

3 *distressful, afflictive, &c.* v. CALAMITOUS. दु:खाचा, अरिष्टाचा, दुष्ट, अभद्र, दु:खदायक, दु:खप्रद, दु:खावह.

EVIL, *n. ill,*—gener. v. BADNESS. वाइटपणा *m.* दुष्टपणा *m.* दुष्टाई *f.* दुष्टता *f.*

2 v. WICKDNESS, SINFULNESS. पाप *n.* कुकर्म *n.* दुष्टाई *f.* दुर्मति *f.* दुर्बुद्धि *f.* कुडें *n.* कुडाभाय *m.* मल *m. n.*

To stir up the e. in. खोड *f.* काढणें *g. of o.*

3 *adversity, &c.* v. CALAMITY. अनिष्ट *n.* अरिष्ट *n.* अभद्र *n.* अपाय *m.*

E. to him who e. thinks. *Honi soit qui mal y pense.* ज्याचें कुडें त्याचें पुढें.

To anticipate an e. उद्याचें मरण आज आणणें.

To be waiting to do e. unto. दर्भ घेऊन उभा असणें.

To put off an e. आजचें मरण उद्यांवर लोटणें.

Provide your remedy before the e. आसवला आधीं किंक फोडावी, पाण्या आधीं बळण बांधावें.

4 *mischief,* v. INJURY. अपाय *m.* अपकार *m.*

EVIL, *adv.* For this adverb and some of its compounds, EVIL-AFFECTED, EVIL-FAVORED, &c. See ILL.

EVIL-DISPOSED, *a.* मनाचा वांकडा-खोटा-कुडा-कुटिल-वक्र-&c. दु:शील, वक्रदृष्टि, कुड्यापाबड्याचा.

EVILDOER, *n.* कुकर्मी, अकर्मी, अकर्मा, दुष्कर्मी, दुष्कर, कुजन.

EVIL-DOING, *n.* अपकृति *f.* दुष्कृत *n.* दुष्कृति *f.*

2 *an e. a sin.* कुकर्म*n.* अकर्म*n.* अकार्य*n.* दुष्कर्म*n.* दुष्कृत*n.* अपकर्म*n.*

EVIL-EYE, *n.* blast or stroke from. दृष्टि *f.* [र्णे, दृष्टावणें.
To suffer the blast of an e. दृष्टि *f.* पडणें-लागणें-होणें,दृष्टाळ-
To remove (by charms &c.) the blast of an e. दृष्टि *f.* काढणें-उतरणें-ओवाळूनटाकणें.
A mark made with soot or lamp-black to avert the influence of an e. तीट *f. m.*

EVIL-EYED, *a.* दृष्टीचा पापी *or* खोटा, पापदृष्टि, नजरपापी.

EVIL-GENIUS, *n.*—considered as pursuing, &c. मैंदगिऱ्हा*m.* ब्रह्मकपाट*n.*

EVIL-MINDED, *a.* v. WICKED. बुद्धीचा खोटा, मनाचा कपटी, कुड्याभावाचा, कुडया पावड्याचा, दुर्बुद्धि, दुर्बुद्ध, दुष्टबुद्धि, दुष्टात्मा, दुरात्मा, दुष्टमानस, दुष्टचेता, दुष्टमति, कपटमति, दुर्मति, कुमति, पापमति, कुबुद्धि, पापबुद्धि, दुर्हृदय, दुर्हृद.

EVIL-MINDEDNESS, *n.* v. A. कुबुद्धि *f.* कुमति *f.* कुभाव*m.* दुष्टभाव *m.* दुष्टबुद्धि *f.* दुर्बुद्धि *f.* दुर्मति *f.* द्वेषभाव*m.* काळें*n.* काळेंबेरें*n.* काळेंमेलें*n.* कुडें*n.* कुडाभाव*m.* कुडेंपावडें*n.* दौरात्म्य*n.* दौर्मनस्य*n.*

EVIL-SPEAKING, *n.* v. SLANDER. उणें काढण्याचें बोलणें*n.* चाहडी *f.* अपवाद*m.*

EVIL-SPIRIT, *n.* v. DEVIL. अपदेवता *f.*

To EVINCE. See To MANIFEST, To PROVE.

To EVISCERATE, *v. a. take out the entrails.* अंतडीं*n. pl.* काढणें *g. of o.*

To EVOKE, *v. a. call forth,* v. To CALL. बोलावणें, आव्हानणें, आव्हान*n.* करणें *g. of o.*

EVOLUTION, *n.*—in arithmetic. मूळकर्म*n.*

To EVOLVE, &c. See To DISENTANGLE, To OPEN, &c.

EWE, *n.* मेंढी *f.* मेषी *f.*

EWER, *n.* तस्त*n.* ताम्हण *or* न*n. dim.* ताम्हणी *f.*

EXACERBATION, *n. paroxysm.* भरतें*n.* चढ*m.* प्रवृत्ति *f.* लाहडा*m.* प्रकोप*m.*
E. and remission. चढउतार*m.*

EXACT, *a. nice, correct;*—of matters done, v. ACCURATE. बरोबर, तवताक, रेखला, बेताबाताचा, टापटिपेचा, बंदिस्त, बंदिस्तीचा, स्पष्ट.
2 *closely careful, strictly observant;*—of persons, v. ACCURATE. बेतबात्या, सूत्रक, सूत्रा, सूत्री, सुती.

To EXACT, *v. a. extort.* जुलमानें घेणें-काढणें, बळकावणें, पिळणें, पिळून-खणून-&c. काढणें.
2 *demand of right, & by authority.* सत्तेनें-हक्कानें-सत्तापूर्वक-अधिकार पूर्वक-&c. मागणें-घेणें.

EXACTION, *n. unjust requisition, extortion.* जोरलब *f.* खंड*m.* खंडणी *f.* धोंड *f.* Certain common *exactions* of official personages are, कमरखुलाई *f.* खुराकी *f.* घासदाणा*m.* मसाला*m.*

EXACTLY, *adv.* v. A. 1. बराबर, नेमका, तुळाधार, तारंतार, खास, यथावत्, यथासूत्र.
I. *precisely, strictly, closely.* बरोबर, थेट, तसाच, तंत, तंतोतंत, केवळ, हुबहू, अविच्छिन्न, चरब.

EXACTNESS, *n.* v. A. 1. तवताकपणा*m.* रेखलेपणा*m.* टापटीप*f.* खराई *f.*
2 सुत्रेपणा*m.* सुतीपणा*m.* सुयंत्रता *f.*

To EXAGGERATE, *v. a. heighten in representation.* फुगवणें, फुगवून-वाढवून-&c. सांगणें, तिखटमीठ*n.*-मीठमिरची *f.* लावणें-लावून सांगणें, हातपाय*m. pl.* लावणें-फोडणें *or* लावून-फोडून सांगणें, कांट्याचा नायटा*m.*-मोहरीचा मेरु*m.*-राईचा पर्वत*m.*-पराचा पारवा *m.*- पराचाकावळा*m.*-रजाचा गज*m.*-एकाचीं दोन*n. pl.*-अंगुष्ठावरून दशशीर *m.*-&c. करणें-करून सांगणें.

EXAGGERATION, *n.* v. V.—*act.* फुगवणें *n.* फुगवून सांगणें*n.* अत्युक्ति *f.* अतिशयोक्ति *f.* तांडव*n.* अतिरिक्तकथन*n.* अर्थवाद*m.*

To EXALT, *v. a.*v. To RAISE. उभारणें, उंचकरणें.
2 *elevate, dignify, ennoble, &c.* मोठा-उंच करणें, चढवणें, वाढवणें, मोठेपणा*m.*-थोरपणा*m.*-&c. देणें, मोठेपणास आणणें, पदवी *f.* वाढवणें *g. of o.* मोठी पदवी *f.* सांगणें-देणें, मोठे पदवीस चढवणें, प्रतिष्ठा *f.* देणें, शील *f.*-शिक्कल *f.*-&c. चढवणें *g. of o.* शीड*n.* चढवणें-उभारणें *g. of o.* न्यहाल करणें.
3 See To PRAISE. 4 See To ELATE.

EXALTAION, *n.* v. V. 2.—*act.* चढवणें *n.* वाढवणें *n.*&c. सरफराजी *f.* तेजोवृद्धि *f.*मानवृद्धि *f.*प्रतिष्ठावृद्धि *f.*—*state.* See GREATNESS.

EXALTED, *p.* v. V. 2. चढवलेला, मोठेपणास आणलेला, &c.
I. See LOFTY, SUBLIME. [च्छा *f.*

EXAMINATION, *n.* v. V. 1.—*act.* पुरशीस *or* पुरसीस *f.* पूस *f.* पृ-
2—*act.* शोधणें *n.* तपासणें *n.* &c. तपासणी *f.* तपास *m.* शोध*m.* शोधणूक *f.* चौकसी *f.* छडा *m.* छडाछड *f.* छडणूक *f.* वास्तपुस्त *f.* बाजपुशी *or* बाजपूस *f.* सूड *m.* तलाश *m.* तिसड *f.* विचार *m.*विचारपूस *f.* विचारणा *f.* विचारण *n.* परीक्षण *n.* परीक्षा *f.* विचक्षणा *f.* समीक्षण *n.* संवीक्षण *n.* गवेषण *n.* अन्वेषण *n.* विमर्श *m.* विभावन *n.* विभावना *f.* परीष्टि *f.*
Public and open e. फडपूस *f.*
3—*act.* पारखणें *n.* &c. पारख *f.* परीक्षा *f.* कसोटी *f.*
4—*act.* निहाळणें *n.* &c. निहाळणी *f.* हेर *f.* हेरणी *f.* टेहळणी *f.* कसोशी *f.* निरीक्षण *n.* निरीक्षा *f.*

To EXAMINE, *v. a. interrogate, question.* पुरशीस *or* पुरसीस *f.*-प्रश्न *m. pl.*-सवाल *m. pl.* घालणें-करणें, पुस्तापास्त *f.*-पृच्छा *f.*-&c. करणें *g. of o.*—closely, strictly, &c. छडा *m. or* छडाछड *f.* काढणें-लावणें, छडणें, घोळणें *or* घोळ घोळून घेणें, खोदून-खोदखोदून-खोलून-&c. विचारणें-पुसणें-&c. खोरसणी *f.* घेणें, कसणें.
2 *investigate, scrutinize, explore, inquire into.* शोधणें, चौकसणें, तपासणें, पाहणें, परीक्षणें, शोध *m.*-सूड *m.* घेणें-काढणें-करणें *g. of o.* छडा *m.*-छडणूक *f.*-छडाछड *f.* काढणें-पाहणें-लावणें *g. of o.* अन्वेषणें, चौकसी *f.*-तपास *m.*-तपासणी *f.*-विचारपूस *f.*-&c. करणें *g. of o.*
3 *try by experiment.* पारखणें, पाहणें, कसणें, पारख *f.*-परीक्षा *f.*-करणें-पाहणें घेणें *g. of o.* कसोटी *f.* पाहणें *g. of o.* चौकसणें.
4—closely, narrowly, &c. *inspect, survey, explore.* निहाळणें, निरेखणें, हेरणें, टेहळणें, हेरणी *f.*-टेहळणी *f.*-&c. करणें, निरीक्षणें, डोळेभर *or* दृष्टिभर पाहणें, डोळ्यांत तेल घालून पाहणें, दिव्या वातीनें शोधणें, कांठ कोणा *m.* मोजणें.
5 (schools, scholars, &c.) परीक्षा *f.* घेणें *g. of o.*

EXAMINED, *p.* v. V. 1. पुरशीस घातलेला, पुस्तपास्त केलेला-झालेला, &c. जातपृच्छ.
2 शोधलेला, तपाससेला, &c. विचारित, परीक्षित, अन्वेषित, अन्विष्ट, निरीक्षित, विभावित.
3 पारखलेला, कसलेला, &c. परीक्षित, जातपरीक्ष.
4 निहाळलेला, निरेखलेला, &c. निरीक्षित.

EXAMINER, *n.* v. V. 1. पुरशीस घालणारा, &c. पृच्छक.
2 शोधणारा, चौकसणारा, &c. शोधक, परीक्षक, अन्वेषी.

3 पारखणारा, &c. परीक्षा करणारा, परीक्षा कर्त्ता, परीक्षक.
4 निहाळणारा, निरेखणारा, &c. हेऱ्या, टेहळया.
5 परीक्षा घेणारा. [मोना m.

EXAMPLE, n. *pattern, ensample, model.* कित्ता m. नमुना or न-
Following an e. अनुकरण n. अनुकार m. अनुक्रिया f.
To follow the e. of. वळणावर-कित्त्यावर जाणें.
To set an e. कित्ता m. घालून देणें.
2 *instance, precedent.* प्रतीक n. अढळ m. दाखला m. उदाहरण n. दृष्टांत m. निदर्शन n.
3—in grammar. उदाहरण n. निदर्शन n.
4 See SAMPLE.

EXANIMATE, a. v. DEAD, LIFELESS. निर्जीव, प्राणरहित, निःप्राण.

EXANIMO, v. HEARTILY. मनापासून.

To EXASPERATE, &c. See To EXCITE, To ANGER, &c.

To EXCAVATE, v. a. *make hollow, scoop out.* पोखरणें, कोरणें, पोकळ-&c. करणें, उकरणें.

EXCAVATION, n. v. V.—*act.* पोखरणें n. कोरणें n. उकरणें n.
Price or cost of an e. उकराई f.
I.—the cavity formed. पोखर f. n. पोखारा m.

To EXCEED, v. a. *go beyond, be greater or more than.* पलिकडे -वर-&c. होणें-असणें-जाणें-&c. अगळा-अधिक-वरचा-अतिरिक्त-&c. असणें, अतिक्रम m.-अतिक्रमण n.-&c. करणें.
2 *surpass.* See To EXCEL.

To EXCEED, v. n. *go too far, pass the bounds of propriety.* मर्यादा f. सोडणें-सोडून जाणें, अगळी f.-अगळीक f. करणें, मर्यादातिक्रम m.-मर्यादातिक्रमण n.-मर्यादोल्लंघन n.-&c. करणें.

EXCEEDER, n. EXCEEDING, p. a. v. V. A. 1. पलिकडे जाणारा-&c. अधिक, (and, in comp. as एकाधिकशत, एकाधिकसहस्र, त्र्यधिकलक्ष, पंचाधिककोटि, एकाधिक विंशति, &c.), उत्तर (in comp. as पंचोत्तरशत, क्रोशोत्तर योजन, अंगुलोत्तरहस्त), अधिक आगळा, अगळा (ex. शेर अगळा मण, मण अगळी खंडी), अतिरिक्त (esp. in comp. as एतदतिरिक्त, तदतिरिक्त), पर (in comp. as परःशत, परःसहस्र, परोलक्ष, &c.).

EXCEEDING, EXCEEDINGLY, *adv. to a great degree.* अतिशय, अतिशयित, अत्यंत, फारच, पराकाष्ठा, पराकाष्ठेचा a. decl. अति- (in comp. as अतिसुंदर, &c.).

To EXCEL, v. a. *outgo, outdo, exceed, surpass, transcend.* मागें टाकणें-पाडणें-सांडणें, जिंकणें, अंतरणें, माजी पाडणें, मागसांडणें, पगडी f.-पागोटें n. घेणें g. of o. कान m. pl. कापणें g. of o. अवली f. साधणें, उणें n. आणणें *with* ला or स, अगळा-अधिक-श्रेष्ठ-&c. होणें, चढ m.-अतिक्रम m.-अतिक्रमण n.-&c. करणें.

To EXCEL, v. n. *be preëminent.* वरचढ-वर्चस्वी-उत्कृष्ट-श्रेष्ठ-&c. असणें, चढ m.-वर्चस n.-वर्चस्व n.-वर्चस्वता f. असणें g. of s.

EXCELLED, p. v. V. A. मागें टाकलेला, &c. जित.

EXCELLENCE, EXCELLENCY, n. v. A. उत्कृष्टपणा m. उत्तमपणा m. उत्कृष्टता f. श्रेष्ठता f. गुण m. सत्व n. सौष्ठव n. उत्कर्ष m. प्रकर्ष m. गुणोत्कर्ष m. गुणाधिक्य n. गुणातिरेक m. [n. भूषण n.
2 *an* e. *a virtue, good quality, &c.* गुण m. सद्गुण m. सुलक्षण
3 एक किताब आहे.

EXCELLENT, a. v. GOOD. फार चांगला, उत्तम, वरिष्ठ, श्रेष्ठ, उत्कृष्ट, प्रकृष्ट, प्रकांड, खासा, लोकोत्तर, शिलका.
Most e. सर्वोत्तम, अत्युत्तम, परमवरिष्ठ, परात्पर, परमोत्कृष्ट, सर्वोत्कृष्ट, बरीयान्.

EXCELLENTLY, *adv.* v.A. फार चांगला a. decl. उत्तम, उत्तमरीतीनें.

EXCEPT, p. *exclusively of.* शिवाइ, वांचून, विना, वेगळ or ळा, खेरीज, खेरीज करून, सोडून, वेगळा करून, वघळून.

To EXCEPT, v. a. *leave out.* खेरीज-वेगळा-निराळा-वर्ज-वर्जित-&c. करणें, वर्जणें, वघळणें, सोडणें, गाळणें. [रणें.
2—in grammar. व्यावृत्ति f.-अवच्छेद m.-व्यवच्छेद m.-&c. क-

To EXCEPT, v. n. See To OBJECT.

EXCEPTED, p. v. V. A. 1. खेरीज केलेला, वर्जलेला, वघळलेला, &c. वर्ज, वर्जित, व्यतिरिक्त, अपवादित, खेरीज.
2 अवच्छिन्न, व्यवच्छिन्न, व्यावृत्त, विधिसंकुचित, विधिसंकोचित.

EXCEPTER, n. v. V. A. 1. खेरीज करणारा, वर्जणारा, वर्जक, वर्जन कर्त्ता-कारी.
2 व्यावृत्ति करणारा, अवच्छेदक, व्यवच्छेदक, व्यावर्त्तक.

EXCEPTING. See EXCEPT.

EXCEPTION, n. v. V. A. 1.—*act.* वर्जणें n. वघळणें n. &c. व्यतिरेक m. वर्जन n. बहिष्कार m. बहिष्करण n. अपवाद m.
2 अवच्छेद m. व्यवच्छेद m. व्यावृत्ति f. विधिसंकोच m. ग्रहण n.
I. *matter or point excepted.* विधिभंजक n. विधिसंकोच m. विपक्ष c. अपवाद m.
II. See OBJECTION. [य, दूष्य.

EXCEPTIONABLE, a. v. OBJECTIONABLE. रुबाध, बाध्य, दूषणी-

EXCEPTIONAL, a. *constituting an exception.* अपवादाचा, अपवादरूप, अपवादभूत.

EXCEPTIOUS. See CAPTIOUS.

EXCESS, n. *greaterness or moreness,* gener. विशेष m. वरताळा m. आधिक्य n. प्राधान्य n. सौष्ठव n. [तसवाई.
By great e. *to a degree much beyond.* सातसवाईनें or सा-
E. and deficiency. कमज्यास्त n. कमज्यास्ती f. कमपेश m. न्यूनाधिक्य n. न्यूनाधिकभाव m.
A slight e. is expressed by. कांकण भर or दोन कांकणें.
2 *superabundance, superfluity.* पराकाष्ठा f. अधिकाई f. अतिरेक m. अतिशय m. अतिरिक्तता f. आतिरेक्य n. आतिशय्य n.
3 (of action). In this sense there are numerous and forcible words of combinations. Corresponding with these, there are in English but few single words, and the combinations, to which the English idiom inclines, though abundantly strong and striking, have of course no place in a Dictionary. Ideas, however, and judgments, and thoughts, and feelings, are, when expressed in English, expressible in *Maráṭhí:* and the exhibition of the mode of expressing them, howsoever it may violate the forms and rules of Lexicography, cannot but be acceptable to the scholar who is in earnest. For this sense then, or, as more comprehensively and more strikingly expressed under *vehemence and ardency,* or *violence and intenseness of action,* and, as conveyed by such words and combinations as *extravagance, exorbitance, outrageousness, wild intemperance, furious vehemence, &c. &c.* are, पराकाष्ठा f. अतिरेक m. हद्द f. बेहद्द f. शर्त्त f. कहर m. गजब or एकगजब m. अनर्थ m. दंगा m. सीमा *pop.* शिमा f. जुलूम m. आकांत m. धूम f. धुमाळी f. धुमड f. प्रलय m. शेवट m. तुफान n. अवधंडा m. सतम f. n. घमशान n. शिंबड or डी f. झोड f. वेडाचा पाऊस m. ढकलपंच्यासी f. मार m. मारामार

f. गर्दी f. अत्याचार m. अतिशय m. अतिप्रसंग m.

To carry to e. बाकी f. न ठेवणें g. of o.

Excessive, a. v. N. 1. *exceeding.* अतिमर्याद, अमर्याद, निर्मर्याद, मर्यादातीत, उन्मर्याद, लंघितमर्याद, अतिक्रांतमर्याद, बेहद्द, अतिशय, अतिशयित, आत्यंतिक, लंघितनियम, अतिक्रांतनियम, निस्सीम, अतिमान, अति (in comp. as अतिक्रम, &c.)

2 *superabundant, &c.* बेसुमार, अति (in comp. as अतिवाद, अतिरेक, &c.), अत्यंत, अतिशय, अतिरिक्त, अतिशयित, अनिवार, दुरंत, बेमार.

3—of actions or agents. As this is the general sense borne by the following and many other extensively and emphatically used words, *extravagant, exorbitant, outrageous, intemperate, wild, mad, &c.* here are collected the *Maràthi* words which the most closely render them. पाराकाष्टेचा, शर्त्तीचा, जरब, भारी, कहरी, मनस्वी, अत्यंत, अनर्थाचा, आकांताचा, अपरिमित, अमित, अनिवार, नितांत, अतोनात or स्त, अमर्याद, अतिमर्याद, निर्मर्याद, अतिशय, प्रचंड, प्रकांड, अतिशयित, बेहद्द, बेसुमार, बेताल, अबीट, बळकट, अचाट, अतिमान, आत्यंतिक.

Excessively, *adv.* v. A. 1. अतिशय, अमर्याद, अति, अत्यंत, पराकाष्टेचा (*a. decl.*) पराकाष्टा, फारच, भारी, बेसुमार, बेताल, &c. अवासवा, अवाचेसवा, अतोनात, अतीव.

To **Exchange**, *v. a. give for, barter, truck.* बदल-बदला-&c. देणें, प्रतिदान n.-परिदान n.-विनिमय m.-निमय m.-&c. करणें.

2 *interchange.* बदलाबदल f.-अदलाबदल f.-सदलाबदल f.-फेरमोबदला m.-फेरबदली f.-&c. करणें g. of o. ऐवज मोबदला करणें.

3 (monies or currencies). बटवणें or बटावणें or बटावणें.

Exchange, Exchanging, *n.* v. V. 1. बदला देणें n. &c. परिदान n. प्रतिदान n. विनिमय m. निमय m. व्यतिहार m.

2 बदलाबदल f. अदलाबदल f. मुबदला or मुबादला m. फेरमोबदला m. or मोबादला m. फेरबदली f. हेबडदेवड f.

I. *traffic with monies.* सट्टा m. सट्टाबट्टा or बट्टासट्टा m.

II. *balance of currencies.* बटाव or बटाव m. बट्टा m. बटाई f. बटणावळ f.

Surplusage or gain on e. बरबट्टा m. वर्त्ताळा m.

III. *person changing with.* इसममुबादला m.

IV. (as of a watch, a body of troops, &c.). बदली f.

V. *place where merchants, &c. transact business.* उदमीलोकांचा फड m.-अड्डा m. चौक m.

Exchequer, *n.* जमाबंदीची कचेरी f. राजकोष m.

Excisable, *a.* जकातीचा, जकाती.

Excise, *n.* v. Custom. जकात f. सायर n. शुल्क n.

E. booth, box, stand. सायर n.

Exciseman, *n.* जकात्या, जकातदार, [च्छेदन n.

Excision, *n. cutting off.* अवच्छेद m. अवकर्त्तन n. उच्छेद m. उ-

Excitable, *a.* v. V. 1. चेतवायाजोगा-&c. उद्दीपनीय, उद्दीप्य, उत्तेजनीय, उद्बोधनीय.

2 चेतवाया-चा-जोगा-&c. &c. संतापनीय, संताप्य,

I. *soon excited.* शीघ्रोत्सुक, शीघ्रोत्कंठी.

Excitation, Excitement, *n.* v. V. 1.—*act.* उचलणें n. उठवणें n. चेष्टवणें n. &c. उचल f. उठावणी f. उद्दीपन n. उत्तेजन n. उत्थापन n. उद्बोधन n. प्रबोधन n. बोधन n. उद्बोध m. प्रबोध m. क्षोध m. इंद्रियबोधन n.—*state.* चेतव m. उत्तेजितत्व n. उद्बोधितत्व n. उद्बुद्धता f. प्रबुद्धावस्था f. &c. आवेश m. आविष्टता f.

2—*act.* खिजवणें n. चेतवणें n. &c. खिजवणी f. चेष्टावणी f. चिडवणी f. खवंडाळी f. संतापन n. क्षोभण n.—*state.* खाजवाखाजव f. खवळाखवळ f. संताप m. क्षोभ m. आवेश m. व्याक्षोभ m. क्षुब्धता f.

3—*act.* गडबडवणें n. तळमळवणें n. &c.—*state.* तळतळ f. *intens.* तळतळाट m. तळमळ f. तलखली f. आवेश m. संभ्रम m. आवेग m. संवेग m. See also Impatience.

To **Excite**, *v. a. arouse, stir up.* चेतवणें, चेष्टवणें, उठवणें, उचलणें, ठोठावणें, चेतव m. आणणें, चेताळणें, उचल f.-उठावणी f.-उत्तेजन n.-उद्दीपन n.-उद्बोधन n.-प्रबोधन n.-उद्बोध m.-प्रबोध m. -&c. करणें g. of o. जागा-जागता-जागृत-&c. करणें.

2 *provoke, enrage, exasperate,* v. To Anger. खिजवणें or खिजावणें, खाजवणें, चेतवणें, चितावणें, चेष्टवणें, चेतळवणें, खलसलावणें, फुंकणें or फुंकून देणें, संतापवणें, क्षोभवणें, खवंदळणें, खोड f. काढणें g. of o. खवंडाळी f. करणें g. of o.

3 *disorder, flurry,* v. To Agitate. गडबडवणें, तळमळवणें, गडबड f.-तळमळ f.-तळतळ f.-संभ्रम m.-&c. करणें g. of o.

Excited, *p.* v. V. 1. उचललेला, उठवलेला, चेष्टवलेला, &c. उत्तेजित, तेजित, उत्थापित, प्रबोधित, प्रबुद्ध, उद्बुद्ध, समुत्सुक, उदित.

2 चेतवलेला, खिजवलेला, &c. तप्त, संतप्त, संतापित, क्षुब्ध, क्षोभित.

To be or become e. चेतळणें or चेताळणें, आवेशणें, क्षोभणें, खवंदळणें, खवळणें, झांज जाणें, अणीबाणीवर येणें.

3 गडबडवलेला, &c. डामाडूल, संभ्रांत.

Exciter, *n.* **Exciting**, *p. a.* v. V. 1. उठवणारा, चेष्टवणारा, &c. उचल-&c. करणारा, उत्थापक, उत्तेजक, उद्दीपक, दीपक, उद्बोधक, प्रबोधक, उत्तेजन-उद्दीपन-&c. कर्त्ता-कारी.

2 चेतवणारा, खिजवणारा, संतापवणारा, &c. संतापक, संतापनकारी-&c.

3 गडबडवणारा, &c. संभ्रमकारक, आवेगकारक, &c.

To **Exclaim**, *v. n. call out, vociferate,* v. To Bawl. मोठ्यानें बोलणें, ओरडून-कडकून-&c. बोलणें-&c.

2 (against). हाकाटा m.-हाकाटी f. करणें, नांवानेंबोंब f. मारणें g. of o. गिल्ले m. pl. सांगणें g. of o.

Exclamation. See Outcry, Interjection.

To **Exclude**, *v. a. shut out, &c.* lit. fig. आंत येऊं न देणें, आंत येण्याची बंदी f. करणें g. of o. प्रवेशावरोध m.-प्रवेशप्रतिबंध m. -प्रवेशवर्जन n.-&c. करणें g. of o. वर्जणें, वर्ज-वार्जित-खेरीज-&c. करणें, वर्जन n.-बहिष्कार m.-बहिष्करण n.-&c. करणें g. of o.

Excluded, *p.* v. V. वर्ज केलेला, &c. वर्ज, वर्जित, खेरीज, बहिष्कृत, व्यावृत, अवरुद्धप्रवेश, रुद्धप्रवेश, प्रतिबद्धप्रवेश.

Excluder, *n.* **Exclusive**, *a.* v. V. वर्जकरणारा, &c. वर्जक, वर्जन-&c. कर्त्ता-कारी-&c. व्यावर्त्तक, प्रवेशावरोधक, प्रवेशनिरोधक, प्रतिबंधक-&c.

Excludible, *a.* v. V. वर्ज करायाजोगा-&c. वर्जनीय, वर्ज्य, व्यावर्त्य.

Exclusion, *n.* v. V.—*act.* आंत येऊं न देणें n. &c. प्रवेशावरोध m. प्रवेशनिरोध m. प्रवेशप्रतिबंध m. वर्जन n. बहिष्कार m. बहिष्करण n. व्यावृत्ति f.

Exclusive, *a. possessed to the exclusion of others.* अन्याग्राह्य, इतराग्राह्य, अन्यव्यावृत्त, इतरव्यावृत्त, अनन्यग्राह्य.

Exclusively, *adv.* v. A. दुसऱ्यांस-इतरांस-अवांतरांस-&c. वर्जून, खेरीज करून.

To **Excogitate**, *v. a. strike out by thinking.* मनन करून यो-

जणें-रचणें-काढणें, कल्पिणें, चिंतणें.

EXCOGITATION, *n.* v. V.—*act.* कल्पना *f.* मननपूर्वक योजना *f.*

To EXCOMMUNICATE, *v. a. expel from communion.* धर्मातून काढणें-घालवणें, धर्मबहिष्करण*n.*-धर्मबहिष्कार*m.*-धर्मबहिष्कृति *f.*-&c. करणें *g. of o.* वाळ *f.*-वाळीत*n.* घालणें-पाडणें, धर्मबहिष्कृत-धर्मबाह्य-अपांक्त-बहिष्कृत-&c. करणें.

EXCOMMUNICATED, *p.* v. V. धर्मातून काढलेला, &c. धर्मबहिष्कृत, वाळीत, बहिष्कृत, अपांक्त.

EXCOMMUNICATION, *n.* v. V.—*act.* धर्मातून काढणें*n.* &c. धर्मबहिष्कार *m.* धर्मबहिष्करण. धर्मबहिष्कृति *f.* वाळ *f.* वाळीत*n.*

EXCORIATION, *n. abraded skin.* सालडें *n.* सालपट *n.* साल *f. n.* सातारडें*n.* चट्टा *m.* पोपेटा*m. v.* जा.

EXCREMENT, *n.* v. DUNG. विष्ठा *f.* किट्ट*n.* मल*m. n. pop.* मळ *m.* अन्नमल*m. n.* आहारमल *m. n.* पुरीष*n.*

E. of birds. शीट *f.*

Human e. गू *m.*

Smell of e. खचरटाण *f.*

EXCREMENTAL, *a. belonging, &c. to e.* अन्नमलाचा, किट्टाचा, अन्नमलसंबंधी, किट्टसंबंधी, उत्सर्जितमलसंबंधी-विषयक.

EXCREMENTITIOUS, *a. containing e. &c.* किट्टरूप, किट्टात्मक, त्यक्तमलात्मक, उत्सर्जितमलरूप, देहोत्सृष्ट, देहत्यक्त.

EXCRESCENCE, *n.* (upon the body) v. WEN. वृद्धि *f.* मांसवृद्धि *f.* अवाळू *n.* गुल्म*m.*

2 (upon a tree,&c.). गुळुंब *or* भ *or* गुळूम *n.* टुंग *n.* टुंगर *n.* टुंगळ*n.* टुंगूळ *n.* टेंगूळ*n.* टुंबर *n.* गुंज *f. n.*

EXCRETION, *n. evacuation.* त्याग*m.* उत्सर्ग*m.* विसर्ग *m.*

2 See EXCREMENT.

EXCRETIVE, EXCRETORY, *a.* मलोत्सर्जक, मलत्याजक, किट्टोत्सर्जक, किट्टत्याजक.

To EXCRUCIATE, See To TORMENT.

EXCRUCIATING, *a. extremely painful or distressing.* अतिवेदनेचा, अतिवेदना कारक, जिवावरचा, जिवापरता, जीवघेण्या, प्राणहर, जिवापाडीचा.

To EXCULPATE, *v. a.* v. To ABSOLVE. निरपराध-निर्दोष ठरविणें-करणें, दोष*m.*-&c. उडवणें, दोषमोचन*n.*-दोषमुक्ति *f.*-दोषनिरसन*n.*-&c. करणें.

EXCULPATED, *p.* v. V. निरपराध ठरवलेला, &c. दोषमुक्त.

EXCULPATION, *n.* v. V.—*act.* दोषमोचन *n.* दोषनिरसन *n.* दोषमुक्ति *f.*

EXCULPATORY, *a.* v.V. दोषउडवणारा, &c. दोषमोचक, निर्दोषकारी.

EXCURSION, *n. ramble, jaunt, trip, tour.* सहल *f.* सफर *f.* फेरफटका *m.* फेरा*m.* पर्यटन*n.*

2 See DIGRESSION.

EXCURSIVE. See RAMBLING.

EXCUSABLE, *a.* v. V. 3. माफ करायाजोगा, सोडायाजोगा, क्षमा करायाजोगा, क्षमापात्र.

To EXCUSE, *v.a. extenuate, palliate.* निमित्त*n.*-सबब *f.*-&c. सांगून उडवणें-घालवणें-कमी करणें, हुज्जत *f.*-निमित्त*n.*-बहाणा *m.*-&c. सांगणें.

2 *disengage from obligation.* सोडणें, सुटका *f.*-मोकळीक *f.*-सोडवण *f.*-सोडवणूक *f.*-सोड *f.*-क्षमा *f.*-&c. करणें-देणें, माफ करणें, माफी *f.* देणें. [मा *f.* करणें.

3 *pardon,* v. To FORGIVE, To PASS OVER. माफ करणें, क्ष-

EXCUSE, *n. apology, plea.* सोडवण *f.* सोडवणूक *f.* निमित्त *n.* दोषपरिहारक भाषण *n.* परिहारक *n.*

False e. मीस *n.* मिष *n.* निमित्त *n.* हुजत *f.* बहाणा *m.* खिडकी *f.* तपसील *m.*

Framer of excuses. निमित्तखोर, हुजतखोर, हुजनी.

String of excuses. बाबत *f. v.* सांग, लाव, बयाणा *m.* बयाद *m. f. v.* सांग, वाच.

EXECRABLE, *a. very bad, vile,* v. HATEFUL. अतिदुष्ट, कुत्सित, अतिनिंद्य, घाणेरडा.

To EXECRATE, &c. See To CURSE, &c.

To EXECUTE, *v. a. perform, do,* v. To ACCOMPLISH. करणें, करून टाकणें, साधणें, संपादणें, सिद्ध करणें, सर करणें, बजावणें, अनुष्ठणें.

2 *punish capitally.* जीव *m.*-प्राण *m.* घेणें *g. of o.* वधशिक्षा*f.*-मरणदंड *m.*-देहांतदंड *m.*-देहांतदंडन *n.*-वधदंड *m.*-वधदंडन *n.*-करणें, देहांत करणें. [जावणें.

3 (a decree or process of a court) अमलांत आणणें, ब-

4 (a law paper) *sign & seal.* सहीशिक्का *m.*-सईनशिक्का *m.* घालणें-देणें. [ष्ठित.

EXECUTED, *p.* v. V. 1. साधलेला, संपादलेला, &c. साधित, अनु-

2 देहांतदंडित, प्राणांतदंडित, वधदंडित, जातवधदंड.

3 अमलांत आणलेला, &c.

4 सईन शिक्का घातलेला, &c.

EXECUTION, *n.* v.V.1.—*act.* साधणें *n.* संपादणें *n.* &c. साधन *n.* साधणूक *f.* अनुष्ठान *n.*

2—*act.* देहांतदंडन *n.* प्राणांतदंडन *n.* वधदंडन *n.* वध *m.*

Place of e. वधभूमि *f.* वधस्थान *n.*

3 अमलांत आणणें *n.* &c.

4 सईनशिक्का घालणें *n.* &c.

EXECUTIONER, *n.* v. V. 1. *and* AGENT, PERFORMER. 2 मांग*m.* अंतक *m.* प्राणांतक *m.* वधपाशी *m.*

EXECUTIVE, *a. that administer the laws.* राज्यविधि-राज्यनियम-&c. प्रवर्त्तक-प्रवर्त्तनाधिकारी.

EXECUTOR, *n.* (to a will). मृत्युपत्र-मृत्युलेख-मृतलेख-&c.चालवणारा-बजावणारा, मृत्युलेख प्रवर्त्तक. [णारी स्त्री*f.*

EXECUTRESS, EXECUTRIX, *n.* मृत्युलेख-&c. चालविणारी-बजावि-

EXEGESIS, EXEGETICAL. See EXPLANATION. EXPLANTORY.

EXEMPLAR. See EXAMPLE.

EXEMPLARY, *a. worthy of imitation* . कित्त्याचा, कित्ता घ्यायाजोगता-&c. दाखला घ्यायाजोगता, दृष्टांतास योग्य, अनुकरणीय, अनुकार्य, अनुसार्य, अनुकरणार्ह, अनुसरणार्ह, अनुगम्य, उत्तम, भला.

2 *such as may give warning to others.* दहशत-धाक-जरब-&c.बसवायाचा-बसायाचा-बसवायाजोगा-&c. जरबेचा.

EXEMPLIFICATION, *n.* v. V.—*act.* दाखला देणें*n.* दृष्टांतसमर्थन*n.*

I. See COPY.

EXEMPLIFIED, *p.* v. V. दाखल्यानें स्पष्ट केलेला, &c. दाखलेवाईक, दृष्टांत समर्थित, उदाहृत.

To EXEMPLIFY, *v. a. illustrate, example.* उदाहरण*n.*-दाखला*m.*-दृष्टांत *m.*-&c. देणें *or* देऊन सिद्ध-स्पष्ट-&c. करणें, द्योतवणें.

To EXEMPT, *v. a. give immunity to.* सोडणें, सुटका *f.*- मोकळीक *f.*-माफी *f.*-&c. देणें, माफ करणें.

EXEMPT, *a.* EXEMPTED, *p.* v. V. सुटा, सोडलेला, माफ, माफीचा,

पाळणुकीचा. [पाळणुकीचा.

E. from tax or duty. गैरदस्त, गैरदस्ती, दस्तीबाद, पाळ,

EXEMPTION, *n. immunity.* माफी *f.* मोकळीक *f.* सुटका *f.* मुक्ति *f.*

To EXENTERATE, *v. a. take out the bowels of.* अंतडीं *n. pl.*-*&c.* बाहेर काढणें. [बंधी.

EXEQUIAL, *a.* v. N. उत्तरकार्याचा, &c. और्ध्वदेहिक, उत्तरक्रियासं-

EXEQUIES, *n. funeral rites*, v. OBSEQUIES. क्रिया *f.* कर्मांतर *n.* क्रियाकर्मांतर *n.* उत्तरकार्य *n.* उत्तरक्रिया *f.* अंत्येष्टि *f.* और्ध्वदेहिक *n.*

EXERCISE, *n. practising*, v. PRACTICE. अभ्यास *m.* कसरत *f.* फेरफटका *m.* अभ्यसन *n.* सराव *m.*

Military e. कवाईत *or* द *f.*

2 *employing, working, &c.* वापरणें *n.* व्यापार *m.* व्यवहार *m.*

3 *labour for health, &c.* सहल *f.* व्यायाम *m.*

4 See LESSON, TASK.

To EXERCISE, *v. a. exert, use, put in use.* कामीं-उद्योगास-&c. लावणें, व्यापार *m.*-व्यवहार *m.*-खर्च *m.*-&c. करणें *g. of o.* खेळवणें, चालवणें.

2 *employ, engage, work at, in, &c.* वापरणें, व्यापारणें, व्यवहारणें, वहिवाटणें, घोळणें.

To e. one's self at, in, &c. वापरणें, वहिवाटणें.

3 (authority, power, &c.) करणें, चालवणें.

4 *practice habitually*, v. To PRACTICE. अभ्यासणें, अभ्यास *m.*-&c. करणें.

EXERCITAION. See EXERCISE.

To EXERT, *v. a. put forth, use.* कामीं लावणें, खर्चणें, करणें, प्रयोग *m.* करणें *g. of o.* लावणें, खर्च *m.*-व्यय *m.*-&c. करणें *g. of o.*

To e. one's self, v. To STRIVE. श्रम *m.*-मेहनत *f.* घेणें, नेटणें, झटणें, बळ *n.* करणें, दांतीं बळ *n.* धरणें, दंड *m. pl.* पेलणें.

EXERTION, *n.* v. V.—*act.* कामीं लावणें *n.* &c. प्रयोग *m.*

I. *strenuous effort*, v. EFFORT. प्रयत्न *m.* आयास *m.* प्रयास *m.* सायास *m.* कष्ट *m.* नेट *m. n.* नेटपाट *m.*

EXHALATION, *n.* v. V. 1.—*act.* बाष्परूप त्याग *m.* बाष्परूपोत्सर्ग*m.*

I. *that which is exhaled*, v. VAPOUR. बाफ *f.* बाष्प *n.*

To EXHALE, *v. a. emit, send out—as vapour.* बाफेच्या रूपानें सोडणें-टाकणें, बाफ करून सोडणें, बाष्परूप त्याग *m.*-बाष्परूपोत्सर्ग *m.*-&c. करणें, सोडणें.

2 *draw out*—as vapour. See To EVAPORATE.

To EXHAUST, *v.a. drain, consume, use wholly.* खर्चणें *or* निश्शेष खर्चणें, शोषणें *or* शोखणें, उडवणें, अटवणें, फडशा *m.*-फन्ना *m.*-सप्पा *m.*-&c. करणें-उडवणें *g. of o.* फडशाफारीक *f.*-निझाडा*m.*-निःपात *m.*-झाडा *m.*-निसांठा *m.*-&c. करणें *g. of o.* सारणें, कोरडाखलास-फारीक-&c. करणें.

2 *tire out, consume the strength of*, v. To TIRE. भागवणें, शिणवणें, श्रमवणें, हायास-जिकिरीस-जेरीस-चिरकीस-&c. आणणें, शीण *m.*-भागवटा *m.*-&c. आणणें, चुरा*m.*-चुराडा *m.*-&c. करणें *g. of o.* भूस *n.*-भूर *m.* काढणें-पाडणें *g. of o.* बेजार-बेदम-जेर-&c. करणें.

EXHAUSTED, *p.* v.V.1. निश्शेष खर्चलेला, उडवलेला, खलास, समाप्त, फारक *or* फारीक *or* ख.

To be e. संपणें, सरणें, होणें, खपणें, अटपणें, उरकणें, उडणें, अटणें, रुमाप्ति *f.* होणें *g. of s.* टाळ *m.* बाजणें *g. of s.*

Certain phrases and free formations in this sense, and answering to *To be out, done, up, clean gone, &c.* are धाव्वा *m.*-घंटा *f.*-शंख *m.* बाजणें *g. of s.* नांवानें पूज *n.* पडणें *g. of s.* तळ *m.* लागणें-पडणें *g. of s.* बराबर होणें, बियाण्यास नसणें, बाट *f.* लागणें*g. of s.* निरानिपटा *m.*-धुबाधार *f.*-निझाडा *m.*-निसांठा *m.*-निःपात *m.*-फन्ना *m.*-आखरी *f.* होणें *g. of s.* बाढणें.

2 भागवलेला, &c. बेजार, बेदम, हलाक *or* ख, चकनाचूर *or* चकाचूर, तुटार, दिक्क, निशाण, लचलालवंगला, परिश्रांत,क्लांत,सुश्रांत.

To be e. दमणें, शिणणें, भागणें, बेंघणें *or* बेंगणें, अटणें *or* जीव *m.* अटणें, टणकारणें, टणकणें, चिरकीस येणें, जेरीस येणें, जिकिरीस येणें, कडोसरीस येणें, उरीं फुटणें, नाडी *f.* अटपणें *g. of s.* हायास येणें, किर्र *adv.* होणें, जीव *m.* तुटणें *g. of s.* उताणा पडणें, नाकीं नऊ येणें, मट्यास येणें, भूस *n.*-मुसकट *n.*-भूर *m.*निघणें-पडणें *g. of s.* घोडें *n.* थकणें *g. of s.* रेंगळणें, हेंगणें, तरसणें, कलमलणें *impers. or with* जीव, डोकें, *&c. as s.* डोई *f.* टेंकणें, मरोपुरेसा होणें, सुश्रांतणें.

EXHAUSTER, *n.* EXHAUSTING, *p. a.* v. V. 1. निश्शेष खर्चणारा, फडशा करणारा-उडवणारा, निसांठा करणारा, &c.

2 भागवणारा, शिणवणारा, &c. भागवट्याचा, शिणाचा, &c. परिश्रांतिकारक.

EXHAUSTION, *n.* v. V. 1.—*state.* समाप्ति *f.* निसांठा *m.* निझाडा *m.* आखरी *f.* निःपात *m.* लय *m.* For the expression of this sense, and with particular implications and significancies well worthy of observation, there are some lively and striking formations. ठणठणाट *m.* ठणठणपाळ *m.* खडखडाट *m.* खडबडखुंटा *m.* घणघण घंटा *f.* बालोबाल निसंतान*n.* खसखसाट *m.* नकार घंटा *f.* अस्त *n.* फना *or* न्ना *m.* घळघळघंटा *f.* थाळा वाटी *f.* चणचण *f.*

2 भागवटा *m.* भागलीक *f.* शीण *m.* शिणोटा *m.* ताण *m.n.* मोडकळा *m.* तुटारी *f.* आट *f.* आटाआट *f.* आटाघाट *f.* आटापीट *f.* हलाकी *or* खी *f.* पिठाड *m. n.* पिठडा *m.* पीठ *n.*आटापिटा *m. or* टी *f.* वाटाघाट *m. f.* बूर *m. v.* काढ, निघ, पड, तिरपीट *f.* टेंक *f.* बेजारी *f.* खुरदमा *m.* चकनाचूर *or* चकाचूर *m.* टणक *or* ठणक*m.* टणकारा *m.* घुमा *m.* भुसडा *or* भुसाडा *m.* भूस *n.* भुसा *m.* कलमल *f.* आयास *m. pl. v.* हो, क्लांति *f.* परिश्रांति *f.* त्रेधा *f.*

EXHAUSTLESS. See INEXHAUSTIBLE.

To EXHIBIT, *v. a.* v. To SHEW, To MANIFEST. दाखवणें, दर्शविणें, प्रदर्शविणें, प्रदर्शन *n.*-&c. करणें *g. of o.*

2 (medicine) *administer.* देणें, चारणें, प्रयोग *m.* करणें *g. of o.*

EXHIBIT, *n.* v. VOUCHER. दाखला *m.* लेख *m.*

EXHIBITION, *n.* v. V. 1.—*act.* दाखवणें *n.* &c. प्रदर्शन *n.* आविष्करण *n.* आविष्कार *m.*

2 देणें *n.* &c. प्रयोग *m.*

I. *allowance to a student.* विद्यार्थ्याची नेमणूक *f.*

EXHIBITIONER, *n.* नेमणुकीचा विद्यार्थी *m.*

To EXHILARATE, *v. a.* v. To ANIMATE, To CHEER. खुश-आनंदित-हृष्टचित-आल्हादित-&c.करणें, उल्हास*m.*-उत्साह*m.*-&c.आणणें.

EXHILARATION, *n.* v. V. *and* JOY. उल्हास *m.*उल्हासवृत्ति *f.* खुशी *f.* आनंद *m.*

To EXHORT, *v. a.* v. To CHARGE, To ADVISE. बजावणें, सांगणें, सांगी *f.* करणें, बुद्धि *f.*-बुद्धिवाद *m.* सांगणें, उपदेश *m.*-बोध *m.*-&c. करणें.

EXHORTATION, *n.* v.V.—*act.* सांगी *f.* सांगणी *f.* उपदेश *m.* बुद्धिवाद *m.* उद्बोध *m.* बोध *m.* बोधन *n.*

EXHORTATIVE, EXHORTATORY, *a. containing exhortation.* उपदेशाचा, उपदेशात्मक, उपदेशरूप, उपदेशपर, उद्बोधक, प्रबोधक.

EXHUME. See To DISINTER.

EXIGENCE, EXIGENCY, *n. want, need, distress.* गरज *f.* ओढ *f.* ओढगस्ती *f.* अडचण *f.* तारंबळ *f.* तान *m.* गिरिबदारी *f.* अबाळ *f.*

EXILE, *n.* See BANISHMENT. 2 *banished person.* देशनिकाल्या, देशपार केलेला, देशबहिष्कृत.

To EXILE. See To BANISH.

To EXIST, *v. n. to be.* असणें, जिणें.

2 See To LIVE.

EXISTENCE, *n.*v. V. आहेपणा *m.* असतेपणा *m.* अस्तित्व *n.* सत्व *n.* सत्ता *f.* भाव *m.* स्थिति *f.* विद्यमानता *f.*

Attainment of the end of e. जन्मसार्थक *n.* जन्मसाफल्य *n.* जीवसाफल्य *n.*

Prior e. प्राग्भाव *m.*

EXISTENT, *a.* EXISTING, *p. a.* v. V. असणारा, अस्तित्वविशिष्ट, विद्यमान, भौतिक, सात्विक, सत्ववान्, सत्तावान्.

E. and non-existent. सदसत्, भावाभावविशिष्ट.

I. *extant.* प्रसिद्ध, उपलभ्यमान, उपलभ्य.

EXIT, EXODUS. See DEPARTURE.

EX OFFICIO. अधिकारपरत्वें *or* परत्वेंकरून. [धिष्णु.

EXOGENOUS, *a. growing from without.* बाहेरून वाढणारा, बहिर्व-

To EXONERATE, *v. a. free from a charge or blame.* मोकळा-मुक्त-निर्मुक्त-&c. करणें, दोषानिराळा-बेठपका-&c. करणें, दोष *m.* -ठपका *m.* उडवणें.

2 See To DISBURDEN.

EXONERATED, *p.* v. V. 1. मोकळा केलेला, &c. दोषमुक्त.

EXONERATION, *n.* v. A. 1. मोकळा करणें *n.* &c. दोष मोचन *n.* दोषमुक्ति *f.* [*n.* अमर्यादता *f.*

EXORBITANCE, EXORBITANCY, *n.* v. A. अतिशयता *f.* आतिशय्य

EXORBITANT, *a.* lit. fig. v. EXCESSIVE. अतिशयित, अमर्याद, निर्मर्याद, निस्सीम, अतिमान, बेठिकाणा, बेसुमार.

2—of price. जबर, जरब, भारी, अक्रीत.

To EXORCISE, *v. a.* v. DEVIL. झाडणें, घालवणें, काढणें, प्रसारण *n.*-भूतनिस्सारण *n.* करणें.

EXORCISER, EXORCIST, *n.* v. V. भूतकाढ्या, पंचाक्षरी, देवरुषी *or* शी, देवलशी, मांत्रिक, जाणता.

EXORCISM, *n.* v. V. भूतकाढणें *n.* भूतप्रसारण *n.*

EXORDIUM, *n.* v. PREFACE. उपोद्घात *m.* उपन्यास *m.* वाङ्मुख *n.*

EXOSSEOUS, *a. boneless.* हाडांनिराळा, अस्थिरहित.

EXOTERIC, *a.* v. PUBLIC. प्रसिद्ध, लोक प्रसिद्ध, बाह्यात्काराचा.

EXOTIC, *a.* v. FOREIGN. बिदेशीय, विदेशी, विदेशज, अन्यदेशज, देशांतरज.

EXOTIC, *n.* विदेशीय-&c. वृक्ष *m.*-वनस्पति *m. f.*-औषधी *f.*-&c.

To EXPAND, *v. a. spread out,* v. To SPREAD. पसरणें, विस्तारणें, फैलावणें, फैलावणी *f.*-फैलाव *m.*-&c. करणें *g. of o.*

2 *open out, dilate.* खुलवणें, फुलवणें, उमलवणें.

To EXPAND, *v. n. spread out.* पसरणें, प्रसरणें, रुंदावणें, फैलावणें.

2 *dilate, open out.* खुलणें, फुलणें, उमलणें, विकसणें, उकलणें.

3 fig.—with delight, &c. फुलणें, फुलफुलणें, खुलणें, खुलावणें, कळी *f.* उमलणें *g. of s.*

EXPANDED, *p.* v. V. A. & V. N. 1. पसरलेला, विस्तारलेला, &c. पसरट, विस्तारित, विस्तीर्ण, विस्तृत, विसृत, प्रवृद्ध, प्रकीर्ण.

2 खुललेला, उकललेला, &c. सविकाश, प्रफुल्ल, प्रफुल्लित, उन्मीलित, विकसित.

3 फुलफुललेला, खुलावलेला, &c. प्रफुल्ल, प्रफुल्लित. [वट *n.*

EXPANSE, *n. wide extent.* मोठाविस्तार *m.* सपाटी *f.* तळ *m.* तळ-

EXPANSION, *n.* v.V. A.—*act.* पसरणें *n.* विस्तारणें *n.* &c. फैलावणी *f.* प्रसार *m.* प्रसारण *n.*

2 खुलवणें *n.* &c.

v. V. N. 1.—*state.* विस्तार *m.* फैलाव *m.* पसारा *m.* प्रसार *m.* प्रसरण *n.* प्रसर *m.* विस्तृति *f.* प्रपंच *m.* वृद्धि *f.* [न *n.*

2—*act.* खुलणें *n.* फुलणें *n.* &c. विकास *m.* उन्मीलन *n.* विकस-

EXPANSIVE, *a.* पसरावयाजोगा-जोगता-&c. पसारा व्हावयाजोगा-&c. प्रसरणीय.

EX PARTE. एकतर्फी, एकतर्फा, एकपक्षी.

E. statement. एकतर्फामजकूर *m.*

E. view-opinion-statement. एकदेशी मत *n.*-कल्पना *f.*-लक्ष्य *n.*-तर्क *m.*-वाद *m.*-मजकूर *m.*-&c.

To EXPATIATE, *v. n. range at large.* मोकळ-मोकार-मोकाट-मोकळेपणीं-&c. फिरणें, स्वैरगमन *n.* करणें.

2 *enlarge in discourse,* v. To ENLARGE. विस्तार *m.*-फैलाव *m.* -तांडव *n.*-&c. करणें *or* करून बोलणें-लिहणें.

To EXPATRIATE, *v. a.* See To BANISH. 2 (one's self). स्वदेशत्याग *m.*-देशत्याग *m.*-स्वदेशविसर्जन *n.* करणें.

To EXPECT, *v. a. wait or look for.* वाट *f.* पाहणें *g. of o.* वाट *f.*-मार्ग *m.* लक्षिणें *g. of o.* प्रतीक्षा *f.*-प्रतीक्षण *n.*-मार्गप्रतीक्षा *f.*-&c. करणें *g. of o.* प्रतीक्षणें.—intently, anxiously, &c. टाटकळया *f. pl.* देत बसणें, टाटकळणें, वाटेस डोळे *m. pl.* लावणें.

2 *have a previous apprehension of.* अगा *f.*-घांग *f.*-संभव *m.*-संभूति *f.*-सुमार *m.*-&c. असणें *g. of o. with in. con.*

EXPECTABLE, *a.* v. V. प्रतीक्ष्य, प्रतीक्षणीय, अपेक्षणीय, अपेक्ष्य.

EXPECTANCY, EXPECTATION, *n.* v. V. 1.—*act.* वाट पाहणें *n.* मार्गप्रतीक्षा *f.* प्रतीक्षा *f.* प्रतीक्षण *n.* निरीक्षण *n.* निरीक्षा *f.* अपेक्षा *f.* आशा *f.* टाटस्थ्य *n.*

2 अगा *f.* घांग *f.* भास *m.* संभव *m.* संभूति *f.*

To hold in anxious e. ताणणें.

To wait or stop in e. टटणें, तिष्ठणें.

EXPECTANT, *a.* EXPECTER, *n.* v. V. 1. वाट पाहणारा, मार्गप्रतीक्षा-&c. कर्त्ता-कारी-&c. टटस्थ, प्रतीक्षक, प्रतीक्षी, अपेक्षी, अपेक्षक, निरीक्षमाण, प्रतीक्षमाण.

EXPECTED, *p.* v. V. 1. अपेक्षित, प्रतीक्षित, निरीक्षित.

2 चित्तकलित.

To EXPECTORATE, *v. n. discharge phlegm by coughing.* खाकरणें, कफोद्गिरण *n.* करणें, कफ *m.* पडणें *in. con.* कफ *m.* पाडणें.

EXPECTORATION, *n. discharge of phlegm by coughing.* कफनिष्कासन *n.* कफनिःसारण *n.* कफहरण *n.*

EXPECTORATIVE, EXPECTORANT, *a.* कफघ्न, कफनाशक, कफसारक, कफनिःसारक, कफहारक, कफनिष्कासक, कफोद्गिरणप्रवर्त्तक.

EXPEDIENCE, *n.* v. A. उपयोग *m.* कार्योपयुक्तता *f.* योग्यता *f.* औचित्य *n.* लायकी *f.*

EXPEDIENT, *a. proper for the purpose or object.* कार्योपयोगी, कार्योपयुक्त, योग्य, उपयोगी, उचित, लाजीम, लायक.

EXPEDIENT, *n.* v. REMEDY. उपाय *m.* तोड *f.* युक्ति *f.* गति *f.* गत *f.* सद्गत *f.* शकल *f.* सेंकटें *n.* कृमि *f.* [युक्तिमान्.

Fertile in expedients. उपायज्ञ, साधनी, युक्त्या, उपायकुशल,

To Expedite, *v. a. hasten.* त्वरेबर-जलदीवर-शीघ्रगतीवर-&c. घेणें-आणणें, शीघ्रगति *f.*-त्वरितगति *f.* करणें *g. of o.*

Expedition, *n. despatch, haste.* जलदी *f.* त्वरा *f.* झटपट *f.*

2 *light, &c. armament.* सडी फौज *f.*

3 *military enterprise.* मोहीम *f.* दौड *f.*

Expeditious, *a. quick, smart, speedy;*—of persons. जलद, तासहा or ताकडा, झटपट्या, शिताब, शीघ्रकारी, आशुकारी.

2 *quickly executed or done*—of matters. ताबडतोबीचा, झटपटीचा, जलदीचा, त्वरेचा, शिताबीचा.

Expeditiously, *adv.* जलदीनें, त्वरेनें, झटकन-कर-&c. झटपट, चटपट.

To Expel, *v. a. drive out, eject.* काढणें, काढून देणें-टाकणें, घालवणें, घालणें, दवडणें, दूर करणें, वाटेस लावणें, निष्कासन*n.*-निस्सारण*n.*-बहिष्करण*n.*-बहिष्कार*m.*-&c. करणें *g. of o.*

Expelled, *p.* v. V. काढलेला, काढून दिल्हेला, बहिष्कृत, निस्सारित, निःकासित or निष्कासित, निराकृत, निर्वासित.

To Expend, *v. a. lay out, disburse,* v. To Spend. खर्चणें, वेचणें, खर्च*m.*-व्यय*m.* करणें *g. of o.*

2 *use, consume, employ upon.* खर्चणें, लावणें, खलास करणें, सारणें, खपवणें, संपवणें.

Expended, *p.* v. V. 1. खर्चलेला, &c.

To be e. खर्ची पडणें. [ख.

2 *and* Exhausted. खर्चलेला, &c. खलास, फारक or फारीक or

To be e. संपणें, खपणें.

Expenditure, Expending, Expense, *n.* v. V. 1—*act.* खर्चणें*n.* खर्च*m.* वेच*m.* (esp. in comp. with the word खर्च, as खर्चवेच), व्यय*m.* (also, in comp. as धनव्यय, आयुष्यव्यय, बलव्यय).

Right e. सद्व्यय*m.*

Uncalled for e. नस्ता खर्च*m.*

Unproductive e. बुडीतखर्च*m.*

Wrong e. असद्व्यय*m.*

I. *money expended.* खर्च*m.*

Contingent e. सादिलवार खर्च.

Extra or odd e. शिवायखर्च, खेरीजखर्च.

Minor or miscellaneous e. आडखर्च, वरखर्च, बाजेखर्च, किरकोळखर्च, गैरखर्च, उपखर्च.

Original or main e. ऐनखर्च.

Expensive, *a. given to expense,* v. Extravagant. खर्चीक, धोताल, धोताल्या, अतिव्ययी, बहुव्ययी, व्ययशील.

2 *costly.* मोठ्या मोलाचा, बहुमोलाचा, किम्मतीचा, किमतदार, पैसेसाऊ, बहुमोली, बहुमूल्य, जरब, जरबकिमतीचा, मातबर, बहुव्ययसाध्य, धनहर-हारक-हर्त्ता.

Expensively, *adv. at great cost.* बहुतखर्च करून, अतिव्ययपूर्वक.

Expensiveness, *n.* v. A. 1. खर्चीकपणा*m.* धोतालपणा*m.* &c. धोताली *f.* व्ययशीलता *f.*

2 उंची *f.* मोठें मोल*n.* &c. बहुमूल्यता *f.* &c.

To Experience, *v. a. know experimentally; suffer, feel, enjoy.* अनुभवणें, भोगणें, उपभोगणें, अनुभव*m.*-भोग*m.*-परीक्षा *f.*-प्रचीत *f.*-&c. घेणें-करणें-पाहणें *g. of o.* पाहणें, परीक्षणें, दृष्टांतास-दाखल्यास-अनुभवास-निदर्शनास-दृष्टोत्पत्तीस येणें *in. con.* साक्षात्कार *m.* करणें-करून पाहणें-घेणें, दृष्टांत*m.*-दाखला*m.*-&c. होणें *g. of o. with in. con.* अढळांत असणें *g. of s.* विज्ञान*n.* असणें-घडणें *g. of o. with in. con.*

Experience, Experiencing, *n.* v. V.—*act.* अनुभवणें *n.* भोगणें *n.* &c अनुभव *m.* भोग *m.* उपभोग *m.* परीक्षा *f.*

I. *experimental knowledge.* प्रतीति *pop.* प्रतीत or प्रचीति or प्रचीत*f.* प्रत्यय *m.* अनुभव *m.* परीक्षा *f.* साक्षात्कार *m.* दृष्टांत *m.* दृष्टावा*m.* दाखला *m.* अनुभूति *f.*

By or through e. निदर्शनीं.

Personal e. स्वानुभव *m.* स्वानुभूति *f.*

That is under e. अनुभूयमान.

Universal or general e. सर्वानुभूति *f.*

Within one's personal e. डोळ्या देखत or तां, जाणोपरी, स्वदृष्टीच्या अमलांत.

To agree with the e. of. दाखल्यास उतरणें.

To bring under e. निदर्शनास आणणें.

To come under e. दृष्टोत्पत्तीस-निदर्शनास-प्रतीतीस-&c. येणें, निदर्शनीं कळणें-समजणें.

Experienced, *p.* v. V.—agent. अनुभव घेतलेला, अनुभवलेला, &c. अनुभवी, अनुभूत, उपभुक्त, अनुभवरसिक, साक्षात्कृत.—object. अनुभवलेला, &c. अनुभवाचा, प्रतीतीचा, &c. अनुभूत, आनुभविक *pop.* अनुभवीक, उपभुक्त, अनुभवारूढ, इंद्रियारूढ, परीक्षित, प्रतीत.

I. *exercised, practised, knowing, &c.* बहिवाटलेला, वापरलेला, घसवटलेला, जाणसळलेला, जाणता, केलेला, केलाभोगलेला, केलाधरलेला, केलासवरलेला, वाकबदार, वाकबगार, घटींव, पक्क *pop.* पक्का, शेकलेला, बहुदृष्ट, व्यवहारज्ञ, ज्ञानवृद्ध, व्यवहारवृद्ध, कृतकर्मा, परिज्ञाता, गरमनरम पाहिलेला, सोळा संस्कार झालेला.

Experiencer, *n.* Experiencing, *p. a.* v. V. अनुभवणारा, &c. अनुभव घेणारा, &c. भोगी, उपभोक्ता, भोक्ता.

Experiment, *n. trial.* पारख *f.* परीक्षा *f.* अजमाव *m.* प्रयोग *m.* क्रिया *f.* कृति *f.* [हणें.

To Experiment, *v. n.* परीक्षा *f.*-प्रयोग *m.*-&c. करणें-करून पा-

Experimental, *a. pertaining to e.* परीक्षेचा, परीक्षासंबंधी, परीक्षा विषयक.

2 *knowable by or on e.* अनुभवाचा, परीक्षेचा, अनुभवानें-&c. कळायाचा, अनुभवगम्य, अनुभववेद्य, अनुभवज्ञेय.

3 *known by or on e.* अनुभवाचा, परीक्षेचा, आनुभविक *pop.* अनुभवीक, अनुभवसिद्ध-स्थापित-निश्चित, अनुभवशीर, परीक्षासिद्ध-स्थापित-&c. अनुभवपूर्वक, अनुभवपुरस्सर.

Experimentalist, Experimenter, *n.* परीक्षा करणारा, परीक्षा करून पाहणारा, परीक्षक, परीक्षा कर्त्ता.

Experimentally, *adv.* v. A. परीक्षेनें, अनुभवानें, अनुभवेंकरून, परीक्षापूर्वक, अनुभवपूर्वक, &c.

Expert, *a. dexterous, adroit, skilful.* कुशल, हाताचा कुशळ, हातवळलेला, हातचा नीट, ताखडा, सुघड, कसरतीचा, सराईत, कसबी, खबरदार, दक्ष, करदक्ष, पटु, कृती, कृतकर्मा.

Expertly, *adv.* कुशलतेनें, कौशलानें, कौशल्यपूर्वक, कसरतीनें, &c.

Expertness, *n.* v. A. हातवळा or हातोळा *m.* हातवटी or हातोटी *f.* सुगराई *f.* सुगरावा *m.* ओज *f.* कसरत *f.* कसब *n.* कुशलता *f.* कौशल *n.* कौशल्य *n.* हस्तकौशल्य *n.* हस्तलाघव *n.* हस्तचापल्य *n.* दाक्ष्य *n.* शिक्षाशक्ति *f.*

To Expiate, *v.a. atone for.* प्रायश्चित्त*n.*करणें *g. of o.* प्रायश्चित्त घेऊन-करून घालवणें, निरपणें, निपटणें, निस्तरणें or निस्तारणें, धुवून टाकणें, परिमार्जन*n.*-प्रक्षालन*n.*-निरसन *n.*-&c.करणें*g.of o.*

Expiation, *n.*—*act.* प्रायश्चित्तानें घालवणें *n.* निरपणें *n.* &c. प्रायश्चित्त *n.* परिमार्जन *n.* प्रक्षालन *n.* निष्कृति *f.* निरसन *n.* पा-

पापनुति *f.*

General e. *expiation at once of all.* सर्वप्रायश्चित्त.

I. *means of expiation.* प्रायश्चित्त *n.*

EXPIATORY, *a.* प्रायश्चित्तरूप, प्रायश्चित्तात्मक, प्रायश्चित्तार्थक, पापनिष्कृतिकर-कारक.

EXPIRATION, *n.* v. V. A. 1. निश्वास *pop.* निसास *m.* प्रश्वास *m.*

I. See END.

To EXPIRE, *v. a. breathe out.* श्वास *m.*-निश्वास *pop.* निसास *m.* देणें-टाकणें-सोडणें.

2 See To EXHALE.

To EXPIRE, *v. n.* v. To DIE. मरणें, प्राण *m.* सोडणें-टाकणें, प्राणत्याग *m.*-प्राणोत्सर्ग *m.*-&c. करणें.

2 *end, terminate.* मुद्दत *f.*-अवधि *m. f.* भरणें-संपणें-&c. *g. of s.* भरणें, पुरणें, संपणें, पुरा-पूर्ण-&c. होणें.

3 *fail, come to nothing,* v. To PERISH. नष्ट होणें, बुडणें.

To EXPLAIN, *v. a. expound, interpret, clear by note or comment.* विवरणें, अर्थ *m.* करणें-सांगणें *g. of o.* विवृति *f.*-विवरण *n.*-व्याख्या *f.*-व्याख्यान *n.*-टीका *f.*-&c. करणें *g. of o.*

2 *elucidate, illustrate, make plain or clear.* उकलणें, उलगडणें, उगवणें, उकलून-&c. देणें, समजावणें, बोधवणें, समजावून-समजून देणें, उघडा-स्पष्ट-व्यक्त-प्रत्यक्ष-प्रकाशित-&c. करणें, उकाल *or* उकल *m.*-उलगडा *m.*-फाड *m.*-प्रकाश *m.*-&c. करणें *g. of o.* प्रकाशणें, द्योतवणें, उद्घाटन *n.*-प्रकाशन *n.*-द्योतन *n.*-&c. करणें *g. of o.*

EXPLAINABLE, *a.* v. V. 1. विवरणाया जोगा-सारखा-&c. विवरणयोग्य, विवरणशक्य, व्याख्येय.

2 उलगडायाजोगा-सारखा-&c. प्रकाश्य.

EXPLAINED, *p.* v.V. 1. विवरलेला,&c. विवृत, व्याख्यात, उपन्यस्त.

2 उकललेला, स्पष्ट केलेला, &c. स्फुट, स्फुटित, प्रकाशित, उद्घाटित, स्पष्टीकृत, द्योतित.

EXPLAINER, *n.* v. V. 1. विवरणकरणारा, व्याख्याकरणारा, विवरणकार, व्याख्याता, व्याख्याकार.

2 उकलून देणारा, समजावून देणारा, &c. प्रकाशक, द्योतक.

EXPLANATION, *n.* v. V. 1.—*act.* उकलणें *n.* &c. विवरण *n.* विवृति *f.* विख्यापन *n.* व्याख्यान *n.* व्याख्या *f.* उपन्यास *n.*

2—*act.* उकलणें *n.* समजावणें *n.* स्पष्ट करणें *n.* &c. स्पष्टीकरण *n.* व्यक्तीकरण *n.* उद्घाटन *n.* परिस्फोट *m.* फाड *m.* प्रकाशन *n.* प्रकाश *m.* द्योतन *n.*—*state.* उलगडा *m.* उकल *or* उकाल *m.* प्रपंच *m.* प्रकाश *m.*

Minute and tiresome e. *a long and dull story in e.* भारूड *n.v.* लाब, लापण्णिका *f.* [मजूत *f.*

Popular or familiar e. कुलवाड समजाविशी *f.* कुलवाड स-

I. *explanation given.* व्याख्या *f.* टीका *f.* अर्थ *m.*

II. *removal of differences: good understanding effected.* समजूत *f.* समजी *f.* समजाविशी *f.* समजावीस *f.*

EXPLANATORY, *a.* v. V. 1. टीकेचा, टीकारूप, विवरणरूप, विवरणात्मक, व्याख्यारूप, व्याख्यात्मक, अर्थसूचक-&c.

2 समजावण्याचा, उलगडा करणारा, उलगड्याचा, परिस्फोटकारक, प्रकाशकारक.

EXPLETIVE, *n. word used to fill a vacancy, or for ornament.* वाक्यालंकार *m.* पादपूरण *n.* वाक्यपूरक-पादपूरक शब्द *m.* पालवपद *or* पालुपद *n.* The expletives in general use are परता, आपला, मग, बेटा *or* बेटी *or* बेट्याचा, रांडेचा, शिनळीचा.

EXPLICABLE. See EXPLAINABLE.

To EXPLICATE, *v. a. unfold,* lit. fig. v. To OPEN, To EXPLAIN. उलगडणें, उकलणें, उगवणें, उलगडा *m.*-फाड *m.*-परिस्फोट *m.*-&c. करणें *g. of o.*

EXPLICATION. See EXPLANATION.

EXPLICIT, *a. express, plain.* साफ, स्पष्ट, उघड, चरचरीत, सरपूस, खसखसीत, अगूढ, अगर्भित.

EXPLICITLY, *adv. expressly, plainly,* v. BLUNTLY. उघड,निवळ, निक्षूण, परिछिन्न, स्पष्ट, साफ, धडधडीत, बोलून चालून, त्रिवार.

EXPLICITNESS, *n.* v. A. उघडपणा *m.* &c. स्पष्टता *f.*

To EXPLODE, *v. a. reject with noise or contempt.* उडवणें, धुत्कारणें, हिडसावणें *or* हेडसावणें, झिडकारणें, झिडकावणें, हुर्योहुर्यो करणें.

2 उडवणें, बार *m.* उडवणें *g. of o* [*g. of s.*

To EXPLODE, *v. n. burst with a sudden report.* बार *m.* उडणें, सुटणें, उडणें, आवाजा बरोबर फुटणें-उडणें, धडकणें, भडकणें, भुरकन-सुरकन-&c. उडणें. [महत्कार्य *n.*

EXPLOIT, *n. feat, &c.* v. DEED. मात *f.* कौतुक *n.* कृतकृत्य *n.*

To perform great exploits. पराक्रम *m.* करणें-दाखविणें, झेंडा *m.* लावणें.

To EXPLORE, See To EXAMINE, To SEARCH.

EXPLOSION, *n.* v.V.N. उडणें *n.* आवाजाबरोबर फुटणें *n.* बार *m.*

Of one e.—squib, cracker, &c. एकबारी,—of two दुबारी, &c. [*m.*

I. *loud sound of e., report.* बार *m.* धडाका *m.* भडाड *m.* धडाड

EXPLOSIVE, *a. causing explosion.* बाराचा, बार करणारा-उडवणारा, बार करण्याचा, बार होण्याचा.

EXPONENT, *n.*—in algebra. घातप्रकाशक *m.*

To EXPORT, *v. a. carry out of a country in traffic.* भरून नेणें, विकायासाठीं देशांतरास नेणें- पाठवणें-&c. वणंजेस नेणें.

EXPORT, *n. commodity sent to a foreign market.* वणंजेस न्यायाचा-नेलेला माल *m.* देशांतरास नेण्याची वणंज *f.* रवानगी *f.*

A pass for exports. रवानगी चिट्ठी *f.* [चा.

EXPORTABLE, *a.* v. V. विकायासाठीं देशांतरास न्यायाचा-पाठवाया-

To EXPOSE, *v. a. lay open or out.* उघडा टाकणें-पाडणें-सोडणें-मांडणें-ठेवणें-करणें, बाहेर टाकणें, मांडणें, दिसता ठेवणें.

2 (to ridicule, &c.). v. To DISGRACE. उघडा पाडणें, बावडी *f.*-रेवडी *f.*-फजिती *f.*-&c. करणें *g. of o.* धिड *f.*-धिंडवडा *m.*-&c. काढणें-भोवडणें *g. of o.* उखळ बेरीज *f.* काढणें *g. of o.*

3 (follies, foibles, faults,) v. FAULT. उघडा पाडणें-करणें, उघडिकेस-उघाडीस-&c. आणणें, उचकटणें, विचकणें, विचका *m.*-विदारणी *f.*-विदारण *n.*-विदारणा *f.*-उद्घाटन *n.*-&c. करणें *g. of o.*

4 *put in an exposed place or state.* उघड्यावर-उघडवासन्यांत-&c. ठेवणें-टाकणें. [ति *f.*

EXPOSITION, *n.* v. EXPLANATION, 1. व्याख्या *f.* विवरण *n.* विवृ-

I. *book containing expositions &c.* व्याख्यारूप ग्रंथ *m.* टीका *f.*

EXPOSITOR, *n.* v. EXPLAINER. व्याख्याकार, विवरणकार, व्याख्याता. [टीका *f.*

I. *book containing expositions &c.* व्याख्यारूप ग्रंथ *m.*

EXPOSITORY. See EXPLANATORY.

To EXPOSTULATE, *v. n. remonstrate.* कान उघडण्यासाठीं बोलणें-भांडणें, भांडून कान *m.pl.* उघडणें, भांडणें, भांडण *n.*-वाद *m.* करणें, भांडून पुसणें, कान *m. pl.* झाडणें, कानाचे किडे *m. pl.* झाडणें,

चारगोष्टी *f. pl.* सांगणें.

EXPOSTULATION, *n.* v. V. कानझाडणी *f.* कानउघडणी *f.* औपदेशिक वाद*m* सोपदेश मित्रकलह*m.*

EXPOSURE, EXPOSING, *n.* v. V. 1.—*act.* उघडा टाकणें *n.* बाहेरटाकणें *n.* &c.—*state.* उघडपसारा *m.* उघडीक *f.* उघडदशा *f.*

2 *and* DISGRACE. धिंड *f.* धिंडवडा*m.* रेवडी *f.* टेर *f.* भंड*n.* भंडमा *f.* भंडावा*m.* भंडाळी *f.* भुरली *f.* ढवढव*f.* धांगोडा *m.* विटंबना *f.* उभस्वना *f.*

3—*act.* विचकणें*n.* &c. विचकणी *f.* उसळबेरीज *f.* टमटमनगरी *f.* उद्घाटन*n.* दोषोद्घाटन*n.* दोषोद्घोष *m.* दोषोद्भावन *n.* विदारण *n.* विदारणा *f.* विदारणी *f.* व्याख्या *f.*—*state.* विचका *m.*

To EXPOUND, *v.a.*v. To EXPLAIN. विवरण*n.*-विवृति *f.*-व्याख्या *f.* -&c. करणें *g. of o.*

To EXPRESS, *v. a. utter, declare,* v. To TELL. उच्चारणें, सांगणें, तोंडावाटे काढणें, मुखद्वारा-शब्दद्वारा प्रगटकरणें, बोलून दाखवणें, उल्लेख*m.*-उल्लेखन*n.*-&c. करणें. [नाहीं.

"I can not express." सांगतां पुरवत नाहीं, पुसतां गरज

2 *indicate,* v. To SHOW. दाखवणें, दर्शवणें, सुचवणें.

3 *represent in painting, &c.* काढणें, हुबहू काढणें-उतरणें.

4 *squeeze out.* काढणें, पिळणें *or* पिळून-&c. काढणें.

EXPRESS, *a.* v. EXPLICIT. साफ, स्पष्ट, चरचरीत.

EXPRESS, *n. messenger sent on purpose.* मुजरद पाठवलेला-मुद्दाम -पाठवलेला-ताबडतोबीचा-&c.जासूद*m.*-निरोप्या*m.*-गाडी *f.*-&c.

EXPRESSED, *a.*—in grammar, &c. *opposed to* understood. वाचनिक.

EXPRESSION, *n.* v. V. 1.—*act.* उच्चारणें*n.* &c. उच्चार*m.* उच्चारण*n.* उल्लेख*m.* उल्लेखन*n.*

4—*act.* काढणें*n.* पिळणी *f.* पिळण *f.* निष्कासन*n.* निस्सारण*n.*

1. (of features.). पाणी*n.* ठेवण *f.* ठेव *f.* मजादारी *f.* विभंग*m.* मुद्रा *f.*

An angry e. क्रोधमुद्रा *f.* A placid e. शांतमुद्रा. A happy e. हर्षमुद्रा *f.* &c. [प्रयोग *m.*

II. *phrase, term,* v. WORD. शब्द *m.* वाक्य *n.* प्रयोग *m.*शब्द-

Authorized e. अभियुक्त प्रयोग *m.*

Figurative e. व्यंजना *f.*

EXPRESSIVE, *a. significant of.* वाची, वाचक *or* वाचिक (in comp. as गुणवाची, कालवाची, देशवाचक, धर्मवाचक), बोधक, उद्बोधक (in comp.), अर्थक (in comp. निंदार्थक), अभिधायक, शक्त.

2 *full of meaning,* v. SIGNIFICANT. अर्थवान्, अर्थान्वित.

EXPRESSLY, *adv. plainly, explicitly.* उघड, स्पष्ट, साफ, परिछिन्न.

2 *with special design.* तात्पुरचा, मुद्दाम, मुजरत *or* द, आवर्जून, आक्षेपून, उदमेखून, हटकून, हुकमें, उद्देशकरून, उद्देशून, उद्देशतः, आदरून, अवग्रून.

EXPULSION, *n.* v. V. To EXPEL.—*act.* काढणें *n.* &c. बहिष्कार *m.* बहिष्करण *n.* निःकासन *or* निष्कासन *n.* निःकाशन*n.*निस्सारण *n.* निराकरण *n.* निर्वासन *n.* उच्चाटन *n.*

EXPULSIVE, *a. having the power of expulsion.* निष्कासक, निस्सारक, निष्कासनशक्तिविशिष्ट, निष्कासनसमर्थ, &c.

To EXPUNGE, *v. a.* v. To EFFACE. पुसून टाकणें-काढणें, बोळा *m.* फिरवणें-घालणें, शाई *f.* घालणें, भांजून टाकणें.

To EXPURGATE, &c. See To PURGE, &c.

EXQUISITE, *a. consummate, being in the highest degree.* पराकाष्टेचा, परमावधीचा, परममर्यादेचा.

2 *very excellent.* फार चांगला, उत्कृष्ट, अत्युत्तम.

EXQUISITE, *n.* See FOP.

EXQUISITELY, *adv.* v. A. पराकाष्टेचा, &c.

2 फारचांगल्या रीतीनें.

EXTANT, *a. not extinct, forgotten, &c.* चालता, जिता, जागता, जिवंत, प्रसिद्ध, उपस्थित, जागृत, उभा, वर्त्तमान, विद्यामान, उपलभ्य, उपलभ्यमान. [*f.* उपलब्धि *f.*

EXTANTNESS, *n.* v. A. चालतेपणा *m.* जागतेपणा *m.* &c. उपस्थिति

EXTEMPORANEOUS, EXTEMPORARY, *a. made, &c. at the time, unpremeditated.* प्रसंगीं सुचलेला, समयोपस्थित, समयकल्पित, समयस्फूर्त्त पूर्वविचाररहित-शून्य.

EXTEMPORANEOUSLY, EXTEMPORARILY, EXTEMPORE, *adv.* v. A. पूर्वविचाररहित, समयोपस्थितीनें, समयस्फूर्त्तीनें.

To EXTEMPORIZE, *v. n.* पूर्वीच्या विचाराबांचून-समयस्फूर्त्तीनें-&c. बोलणें-भाषण *n.* करणें-व्याख्यान *n.* करणें-&c.

To EXTEND, *v. a. stretch out.* लांब करणें, लांबविणें, पुढें करणें.

2 *spread abroad.* पसरणें, विस्तारणें, फैलावणें, फैलावणी *f.*-फैलाव *m.*-&c. करणें *g. of o.*

3 *continue, carry on.* लांबविणें, वाढवणें.

4 *confer, impart, &c.* v. To GIVE. देणें, प्रापण *n.* करणें, उपधान *n.* करणें.

To EXTEND, *v. n. stretch out.* लांबणें.

2 *spread abroad.* पसरणें, पसारा *m.*-विस्तार *m.*-&c. होणें *g.of s.*

3 *reach.* पोहोंचणें, जाणें, येणें.

EXTENDED, *p.* v. V. A. 1. लांब केलेला, लांबवलेला, पुढें केलेला.

2 पसरलेला, &c. पसरट, विस्तारित, विस्तृत, विसृत.

3 लांबवलेला, वाढवलेला.

EXTENSION, *n.* v. V.A.1.—*act.* लांबविणें *n.* लांब करणें *n.*—*state.* लांबवलेलेपणा *m.*

2—*act.* पसरणें *n.* &c. फैलावणी *f.* प्रसारण *n.* प्रसरण *n.*—*state.* फैलाव *m.* प्रसार *m.*

v. V. N. 1.—*state.* लांबी *f.*

2—*state.* पसरलेपणा *m.* &c. पसारा *m.* विस्तार *m.* विस्तृति *f.* विस्तर *m.* प्रसर *m.*

EXTENSIVE, *a. wide, large.* लांब, लांबरुंद, लांबीरुंदीचा, प्रशस्त, विशाल *or* ळ, विस्ताराचा, मोठ्या विस्ताराचा, विस्तीर्ण.

2—as used of business, establishments, &c. पसरट, पसाऱ्याचा, फैलावाचा, अलाई, आलिज्याहा.

An e. business or concern. फाकडपसारा *m.* फापटपसारा*m.*

EXTENSIVENESS, *n.* v. A. 1. मोठा विस्तार *m.* प्रशस्तपणा *m.* प्रशस्तता *f.* प्राशस्त्य *n.* विशाळपणा *m.* विस्तीर्णता *f.*

EXTENT, *n. degree to which a thing is extended.* सीमा *f.* मर्यादा *f.* अवधि *m. f.* व्याप्ति *f.* पहोंच *m. f.*

To such an e. एथपर्यंत, एथवर.

To what e. कोठपर्यंत, कोठवर.

2 v. LENGTH. लांबी *f.*

To EXTENUATE, *v. a. palliate.* कमी-कम-हलका-न्यून-&c. करणें-करून दाखवणें-&c. हलकेपणा *m.*-न्यूनता *f.*-&c. आणणें.

2 *make thin, rare, &c.* पातळ-सूक्ष्म-क्षीण-&c. करणें.

EXTENUATION, *n.* v. V. 1.—*act.* हलका करणें *n.* हलकेपणा आणणें *n.* &c. न्यूनीकरण *n.*

EXTERIOR, EXTERNAL, *a.* v. OUTER. बाहेरचा *or* ला, बाहेरील, बाहेरल्या आंगाचा, बाह्य, बहिर्भागाचा.

2. *relating to foreign countries.* बाहेरील देशांच्या संबंधाचा, परदेशचे संबंधाचा.

EXTERIOR, *n.* v. OUTSIDE. बाहेरलें आंग *n.* बरघाट *m.* बहिर्भाग*m.*
2 *outward deportment.* बाहेरील चाल *f.* बाह्यवर्त्तन *n.*

To EXTERMINATE, *v. a. extirpate, destroy utterly.* उपटून टाकणें-काढणें, नाहींसा करणें, निपातणें, निसंतान *n.* करणें-उडवणें, बी *f.* मोडणें-नाहींसा करणें *g. of o.* तळपट *n.*-ताळावाट *f.*-उन्मूलन *n.*-उत्पाटन *n.*-निःपात *m.*-&c.करणें *g. of o.* समूलनाश *m.* करणें *g. of o.*

EXTERMINATION, *n.* v. V.—*act.* उपटून टाकणें *n.* &c. उन्मूलन *n.* उत्पाटन *n.* उच्छेदन *n.* संहार *m.* ध्वंसन *n.*—*state.* समूलनाश*m.* ध्वंस *m.* निःपात *m.* तळपट *n.* ताळावाट *f.*

EXTERNALLY. See OUTWARDLY.

EXTERNALS, EXTERIORS, *n. outward parts.* बाहेरील-बाहेरचे भाग *m. pl.* बाहेरचें आंग *n.*

EXTINCT, *a.*—a family, &c. मालवलेला, नाहींसा झालेला, मयत *or* मैयत, निर्बीज, बियाण्यास नाहीं असा, विनाशित, विनष्ट, निर्गत. [हींसा होणें.
To be e. नकल *f.* होणें *g. of s.* नावनट *adv.* होणें-बुडणें, ना-
2 *ceased, passed away, &c.* नाहींसा झालेला, मालवलेला, गतझालेला, नाबूद झालेला.

EXTINCTION, *n.* (of a family, &c.). निर्बीज *n.* निर्बी *f.* निर्बीं*n.* बींबूड *f.* निपात *pop.* निःपात *m.* निपोताशांति *or* निपुताशांति *f.* तळपट *n.* समुच्छेद *m.* क्षय *m.* लय *m.* बिलय *m.* लोप *m.* विनाश *m.* समूलनाश *m.*

To EXTINGUISH, *v. a.* v. To QUENCH. विझवणें, विझण*n.* घालणें, शांतवणें, मालवणें.
2 *put an end to, make to pass away,&c.*नाहींसा करणें,मोडणें.

EXTINGUISHER, *n.* दिवा-बत्ती विझविण्याचें साधन आहे.

To EXTIRPATE, &c. See To ROOT OUT, &c.

To EXTOL, *v. a.* v. To PRAISE. वाखाणणें, गुणवर्णन *n.*-कीर्त्तन *n.* करणें *g. of o.* कीर्त्तणें.

To EXTORT, *v. a. draw from by force or injustice.* बळजोरीनें-जुलमानें-जबरीनें-बलात्कारानें-अन्यायानें-&c.घेणें-काढणें-हरण करणें-&c. अक्रीत घेणें, बळकावणें, पिळणें, पिळून-मुरदाडून-मुरगाळून-खणून-&c. घेणें-काढणें.

EXTORTION, *n.* v. V.—*act.* बळजोरीनें-&c. घेणें *n.* जुलूमजास्तीचें घेणें *n.* बलात्कारपूर्वकहरण *n.* अन्यायपूर्वकहरण*n.*
Open e. दिवसा दरवडा *m.*
Wealth acquired by e. हपापाचा माल *m.*
I. *unjust compulsion,* v. FORCE. जुलूम *m.* जुलूमदस्ती *f.*

EXTORTIONER, *n.* v. V. जुलमानें-&c. घेणारा-पिळणारा-&c.अक्रीत घेणारा, हपापानें दौलत मिळवणारा.

EXTRA. This prefix, in its sense of "*over and above*" is rendered by शिवाई (as शिवाई जमा, शिवाई खर्च) खेरीज (as खेरीज-जमा, खेरीज खर्च), अभिजित् &c. and in its sense of "*beyond, by, miscellaneous, non-descript, &c.*" by आड (as आडखर्च, आडकाम, आडसांठा), गैर, फुटका.

To EXTRACT, *v.a. draw from or out,*—gener. काढणें, काढून घेणें, निपसणें, निष्कासन *n.*-अवकर्षण *n.*-निर्हार *m.*-&c. करणें *g. of o.*
2—in chemistry. निष्कर्ष *m.*-निष्कासन *n.*-&c. करणें *g. of o.*
3 a root—in arithm. or algebra. मूळ *n.* काढणें.
4 (from a book, &c). वेंचा *m.*-उतारा *m.* घेणें.

EXTRACT, *n. subtance extracted, essence.* काढा *m.*कषाय *m.* अर्क *m.* निष्कर्ष *m.* निर्यास *m.* द्रव्य *n.*
Vegetable e. शिरा *m.* [उतारा*m.*
2 *passage extracted.* वेंचा *m.* टाणेटोणे *m. pl.* ग्रंथोद्धृतांश *m.*-
Book of extracts. वेंचा *m.* बहाड *or* बाड *n.* गबाळग्रंथ *m.*

EXTRACTION, *n.* v. V. 1.—*act.* काढणें *n.* &c. निष्कासन *n.* निर्हार *m.* निर्हरण *n.* अवकर्षण *n.* अभ्यवकर्षण *n.*
2 निष्कर्ष *m.* निष्कासन *n.*
I. *descent, birth,* v. FAMILY. कुळी *f.* उपज *m.* वंश *m.*

EXTRA-HUMAN, *a.* अमानुष, अपौरुष.

EXTRANEOUS, *a.* See FOREIGN.
2 v. IRRELEVANT. बाहेरचा *or* ला, अप्रस्तुत, अप्रकृत, अप्रासंगिक, अप्राकरणिक.
E. discourse or matter. आडकथा *f.* इकडच्या तिकडच्या गोष्टी *f. pl.* इकडंतिकडं *n.* इधरतिधर *n.*

EXTRAORDINARINESS, *n.* v. A. 1. अलौकिकपणा *m.* &c. अपूर्वाई *f.* अपरूपपणा *m.* वैलक्षण्य *n.* वैजात्य *n.*

EXTRAORDINARY, *a.* v. STRANGE. अधिकोत्तर, विलक्षण, विलक्षणीक, विशेष, नवलविशेष, लोकोत्तर, लोकाधिक, अलौकिक.
2 See SPECIAL.

EXTRA-PROVISION, EXTRA-STOCK, *n. reserve, &c.* उपराळा *m.*

EXTRAVAGANCE, *n.* v. A. 1. *and* EXCESS. पराकाष्ठा *f.* अमर्यादा *f.* अनर्थ *m.* ढकलपंच्यासी *f.* नियमातिक्रम *m.*
2 *and* SQUANDERING. उधळपट्टी *f.* उधळमाधळ *f.* अतिव्यय*m.* अपव्यय *m.* बहुव्यय *m.* उफानगिरी *f.*

EXTRAVAGANT, *a. outrageous, &c.* v. WILD, EXCESSIVE. अमर्याद, निर्मर्याद *m.* गैरशिस्त, बेताल, अन्योविन्य, अद्वातद्वा, बाष्कळ.
2 *prodigal, profuse, lavish.* उधळा, उधळ्या, उडव्या, उडाऊ, खर्चीक, अतिव्ययी, व्ययशील, अपव्ययी, अपरिमितव्ययी. Some terms for a prodigal and wasteful person—*a spend thrift, squanderer, scatterling, &c.*—are उधळखोर, उधळपट्या, उधळमाणक्या, उधळमाधळ्या, उधळवाढ्या.
3 *copious, profuse,* v. EXUBERANT. उधळपट्टीचा, घळघळीत, चळचळीत, चंगळपट्टीचा, रगडीचा, अतिव्ययाचा.

EXTRAVAGANTLY, *adv.* v. A. 1. मर्यादासोडून, अमर्याद, बेताल, अत्यंत, अतिशय.
2 उधळपट्टीनें, खर्चीकपणानें, अतिव्ययपूर्वक.

EXTRAVASATED, *a.* नाडिबहिर्भूत, नाडिबहिष्कृत.

EXTRAVASATION, *n.* नाडिबहिष्करण *n.*

EXTREME, *a. outermost, last.* शेवटचा *or* ला, शेवटील, कडेशेवटचा, सरतेशेवटचा, सरशेवटचा, अग्रवर्त्ती, सरता, चरम.
2 *utmost, of the highest degree.* पराकाष्ठेचा, परममर्यादेचा, परमावधीचा, आत्यंतिक, अतिशयित, अतिमात्र, प्रचंड.
3 *belonging to extremity.* शेवटचा, निर्याण, निर्वाणींचा, अंतींचा, निदानचा, निदानींचा, परिणामींचा, परमावधिक.

EXTREME, *n. extremity,* v. END. शेवट *n.* अंत *m.* अग्र *n.* शेवटचा भाग *m.* टोक *n.*
2 (of an arithm. or geom. progression)—the first. आदिधन *n.* आदिपद *n.* आदिवदन *n.*—the last. अंत्यधन *n.* अंतपद *n.*
3 *utmost point, highest degree.* पराकाष्ठा *f.* बेहद्द *f.* हद्द *f.* सीमा *f.* परममर्यादा *f.* परमावधि *m. f.* कळस *m.*

Avoid extremes. अतिसर्वत्रवर्जयेत्.

To reach its e. सीमा f.-मर्यादा f.-शेवट m.-&c. होणें g. of s.

EXTREMELY, adv. in the utmost degree, v. EXCESSIVELY. पराकाष्ठेचा, अत्यंत, अति, फारच, परम (in comp. as परमकठिन, परमकठोर, परमनिर्दय, परमचतुर).

EXTREMITY, n. utmost part, end. टोंक n. शेवट n. अग्र n. सरशेवट m. अग्रभाग m. परममर्यादा f. परमावधि m. f. पर्यंत m. शेंडा m. शिखर n. शेरा m. पोंख n. पोंखट n. पोन m. अघरडा m. अंत m. प्रांत m. चरमावयव m. उत्तरावधि m. चरमभाग m.

2 utmost point, highest degree, v. EXTREME. पराकाष्ठा f. परममर्यादा f.

3 extreme distress or necessity. निदान n. निदान बाजू or निदानचीबाजू f. कडेशेवटचीबाजू f. निर्वाण n. चरमावस्था f. चरमदशा f.

At the last e. निदान.

Reserved for (or useful for) one's e. निर्वाणींचा, निदानींचा, निदानचा.

Saviour, friend, helper, &c. in e. निर्वाणींचा or निदानींचा त्राता तारणारा-पाठराख्या-&c.

The last e. articulum mortis. प्राणांतीकn.

To be in e. डचघाईस or डफघाईस येणें, नाकीं सूतn. धरणें.

To be reduced to e. रक्तरक्त होणें, त्राहित्राहि होणें.

To EXTRICATE, v. a. v. To FREE. सोडवणें, तारणें, उद्धरणें, मोकळा करणें, सोडवणूक f.-उद्धारm.-समुद्धारm.-&c. करणें g. of o.

EXTRICATED, p. v.V. सोडवलेला, तारलेला, &c. तारित, समुद्धृत.

EXTRICATION, n. v.V.—act. सोडवणेंn. &c. सोडवणूक f. तारणn. उद्धारm. उद्धरणn. समुद्धारm. समुद्धरणn.

EXTRINSIC, EXTRINSICAL, a. v. OUTER. बाहेरचा, बाहेरला, बाहेरील, बाह्य.

EXTRINSICALLY, adv. from without. बाहेरून.

To EXTRUDE, &c. See To EXPEL, &c.

EXUBERANCE, n. v. A. 1. माजm. मातm. वाढीचा भरm. उफाड्याची वाढ f. अतिवृद्धि f. वृद्धिबाहुल्यn.

2 पुष्कळपणाm. पूरm. क्रूरपूर f. पुरपुराटm. चळचळाटm. अतिरेकm. बहुत्वn.बाहुल्यn. विपुलता f. वैपुल्यn. प्रचुरता f. प्राचुर्यn. उद्रेक m. समृद्धि f. उत्कर्षm. प्रकर्षm. Conveying this sense there are words and phrases absolutely endless. They are lax and licentious through all the gradations, and they may, by some, be termed low, gross, vulgar, &c., but they are in the general, strongly and strikingly expressive, and they are strictly constituents of a popular tongue. They are to be held as rendering the English words lots, piles, heaps, bushels, oceans, power, &c. महामूर or महामुरी f. उपट f. घमंड or डी f. चंगळ or ळी f. चंगळपट्टी f. चंगाल f. मात f. रगडपट्टी f. रगड f. रगाडी f. घबूक f. चंगळवटी f. रेंगळ f. रेड f. गजक f. गचक f. रेल or ळ f. रेलचेल f. लयलूट f. मार m. लूट f. शरत f. आबादानी f. अमनचैन f. जईन चईन f. गरदी f. धिंवडी f. ठेल f.बहार f. बस f. पराकाष्ठा f. सीमा f. चमचमाटm. चळचळाटm. चेल or चेळ or चेहल f. चेकळ f. गडगंज f. घमशानn. झिंवड or डी f. ठेल f. झोड f. दिवाळी f. डू m. v. गाज, धुमड f. धूम m. धुमशान n. धुमश्चक्री f. भडिमार m. मारामार f. ढसर or ढस्सर f. लखलूट f. लखलोटm. f. शीगलोट f. झुंबड f. देवड or देव्हड f.चौकळ f. चेकळ f. झगड f. लोटm.

EXUBERANT, a. of rich growth, v. LUXURIANT. उफाड्याचा, उफाट्याचा, उफाड्याच्या वाढीचा, वाढीच्या भराचा.

2 over-abounding, copious, profuse पुष्कळ, बहुत, प्रचुर, बहुल, बहळ, मुबलक or ख, उदंड, अतिशय, अतिशयित, अतिरिक्त, समतिरिक्त, यथेच्छ, यथेष्ट, उद्रिक्त, समृद्ध, अतिमान. There are numerous vulgar words expressing this sense; and these as vulgar, should, ordinarily be omitted. The omission however of vulgar words from a Dictionary of the language of a people of which the higher classes stand but obscurely distinguished from the lower, and which indulge themselves, not infrequently, in the use of them, is a measure of somewhat questionable propriety. We insert them then with this introduction. लय or लै, मस्त, मोप, अमुप or अमोप, उमाप or उमोप, ढीग, चौकळ, मुराद, मनमुराद, मनस्वी, मनस्वार, अमोज, चमचमीत, चळचळीत, महामूर, भरपूर, गडगंज, मांयदळ or ळा, अमनचैन or अमीनचमीन, पोक, or पोका, भक्रम , घळघळीत, घवघव, अघळपघळ, चंगळपट्टीचा, रेलचेलीचा, राट, रगडपट्टीचा, &c.

EXUDATION, n. v. V.—state. पाझरm. ओहळm. गळ f. निचराm. स्रावm. स्रवm.

I. matter exuding, v. OOZE, SWEAT. चिहाळ m. चेहळm. चिल्हाट m. निचराm. निर्यासm.

To EXUDE, v. n. ooze from or out. ओहळणें, ओघळणें, पाझरणें, स्रवणें, गळणें, निचरणें, वाहणें.

To EXULT, v. n. v. To TRIUMPH. अत्यानंद m. पावणें, कास्रा f. pl. वाजवणें, टिरी f. pl. पिटणें-बडविणें-थोपटणें, टाळ्या f. pl. पिटणें, नागवा नाचणें, उल्लासणें.

EXULTATION. See TRIUMPH.

EXUVIÆ, n. प्राण्यांनीं टाकलेलें कातडें n.-कवच n. m.-&c.

EYE, n. डोळा m. नेत्र n. चक्षु n. नयन n.लोचन. n. अक्षि n. दृष्टि f. वीक्षण n. दृक् f. (in comp. as दृक्कर्म, दृग्गोचर, दृग्विषय, कमलदृक्, दोषदृक्).

Apple of one's e. जिबाचा ताईत m. गळ्याचा ताईत m.

To keep like the apple of one's e. तळहाताचे फोडासारखें वागवावें or वाळगावें.

Before one's. eyes. डोळ्यादेखत or तां.

Black of the e. pupil and iris. बुबूळ or काळें बुबूळ n.

Coat or humor of the e. डोळ्याचा पडदा m. अक्षिपटल n.

Cooling application to inflamed eyes.निवणn. निवळणn.

Darkness coming over the e. अंधारी f.

Drawnness, strainedness or stiffness of the e. ताटकळी f. ताठा m.

Dull of vision—an eye. फुटका.

Dusky suffusion over the e. भूर f. भुरी f.

Evil e. पापदृष्टि f. विषदृष्टि f. Blast from an evil e. दृष्टिपात m. दृष्टिविकार m. Having an evil e. दृष्टीचा पापी, पापदृष्टीचा, दृष्टाळा, पापदृष्टि, विषदृष्टि. To remove the blast of an evil e. दृष्टि f. काढणें-उतरणें-ओवाळून टाकणें. To suffer the blast of an evil e. दृष्टावणें, दृष्टळणें or दृष्टाळणें, दृष्टि f. पडणें-लागणें-होणें-&c. in. con.

E. of favor. कृपादृष्टि f. कृपावलोकन n. कृपाकटाक्ष m.

E. of the mind. Intellectual e. ज्ञानचक्षु n. ज्ञानदृष्टि f. दिव्यचक्षु n.

E. of sense. Material e. चर्मचक्षु n. चर्मदृष्टि f.

Film over the eyes. पडदा *m.* पटल *pop.* पडळ *n.*
Flushedness of the eyes. नेत्रराग *m.*
Glaze of the eyes (as in death). चंद्री *f. v.* लाग.
Gum or mucus of the e. डोळ्याचा गू *m.* चिपड *n.* चिपडा *m.* चिपडी *f.* चिपडें *n.* ढेर *f.* भेंड *n.* भेरड *n.* चिपाट *or* ड *n.* उकीर *m.* कांबरें *n.* Covered or foul with it. चिपटा, शेफ्या.
Homunculus of the. e. बाहुली *f.*
Judgment of the e. नजर पारख *f.*
Language of the eyes. नेत्रपल्लवी *f.*
Magical application to the e. अंजन *n.*
Of upturned eyes. वरडोळ्या.
Of large, round, &c. full eyes. गटगटीत डोळ्या.
Outer corner of the e. नेत्रपर्यंत *m.* नेत्रप्रांत *m.* अपांग*m.*
Red spot on the white of the e. कुरुंद *m.*
Sealedness of the eyes under stupor. झांप *f.* झांपड *f.* झांपण *f.* झांक *f.* झांज *f. v.* पड, घाल. [रखरा *m.*
Shooting or painful throbbing of the e, खरखर *f.* ख-
Skill to judge by the e. नजरपारख *f.*
Speck on the e. कोकी *f.*
That draws or strains the e. डोळेफोड, दृष्टिफोड.
That has come under one's own e. दृष्टीच्या अमलांतला.
That offends or pains the e. डोळेफोड, दृष्टिफोड.
White of the e. पांढरें बुबूळ *n.*
With one's own eyes. दृष्ट्या.
Work to catch the e. दर्शनी काम.
To be in one's e. लक्षांत-नजरेंत-&c.असणें.
To be inflamed, look fiery, &c.—the eyes. डोळे *m. pl.* चढणें-साराबणें.
To be gummy,—the eyes. चिपडणें, ढेरणें. [जळणें.
To be pained at the sight of,—the eyes. डोळे *m.pl.*
To close in sleep,—the eyes. डोळ्यासीं डोळा *m.* लागणें, डोळे *m. pl.*-मिटणें*n.*
To fear to meet the e. of. दोहों डोळ्यांची मुरवत *f.*राखणें.
To feast the eyes upon. डोळ्यांचें पारणें *n.*फेडणें, डोळे*m. pl.* भरून पाहणें, दृष्टिभर पाहणें.
To get heavy (from want of sleep, &c.)—the eyes. तारवटणें, तारकटणें. [च्छा पाहणें.
To have one's eyes about one. मागें पुढें पाहणें, आगा पि-
To have a twitching in the eyes. डोळे *m. pl.* लवणें.
To have atoms (*or muscæ volitantes*) float before the eyes. डोळ्यापुढें लकलक करणें *v. imp.* डोळ्यांपुढें काजवे *m. pl.* येणें.
To keep an e. upon. शोध *m.* ठेवणें *g. of o.*
To obtain the desire of one's eyes. डोळे *m. pl.* निवणें*or* थंड होणें. [*pl.* उघडणें.
To open the eyes (to one's folly). डोळे *m. pl.*-कान *m.*
To see with the corner of the e. आडव्यादृष्टीनें पाहणें.
To set the eyes and glare,—a dying person. डोळे *m. pl.* फाडणें.
To shut one's eyes (to, against). डोळे *m. pl.* झांकणें, डोळ्यांवर कातडें *n.* ओढणें.
To sink into their sockets,—the eyes. डोळे *m. pl.* पाताळांत जाणें, डोळे *m. pl.* पोंढळणें.
To strain one's eyes. डोळ्यांची वात *f.* करणें, डोळेफोड *f.* करणें. [णी *n.* ढाळणें.
To stream,—the eyes. डोळे *m. pl.* ढाळणें, डोळ्यांतून पा-
To throb—the eyes. खरखरणें.
To turn up the white of the eyes. डोळे *m. pl.* ग्र्याचे करणें, डोळे *m. pl.* मोडणें-उफराटणें-उफरांडणें.
To wander idly—the eyes. फांकणें, तरळणें.
To wipe or dry the eyes of. डोळे *m. pl.* पुसणें *g. of o.*
We can see the mote in our brother's e. but cannot see the beam in our own. दुसऱ्याचे डोळ्यांतलें कुसळ (दिसतें) आपल्या डोळ्यांतलें मुसळ (दिसत नाहीं).
2 (as of a peacock's tail, of a potatoe, a cocoa-nut, a grain of corn, &c.). डोळा *m.* नाक *n.*
3 (of a needle, &c.). नेडें *or* नेढें *n.* बेज *n.* नाक *n.*
4 *catch for a hook.* डोळा *m.* फासा *m.* तुकमा *m.*
5 *small hole through.* डोळा *m.* डोळू *m.* डोळूक *m.* पात *m.*
To Eye, *v. a.*—wistfully or wishfully. टुकटुकणें, टुकणें, टोकणें, टक-टकटक-टकमक-टकाकां *adv.* पाहणें, तलपणें.
2—intently and pointedly. रोखून पाहणें.
3—fiercely, &c. v. To Glare. डोळे *m. pl.* गुरकावणें-पिंजारणें-फाडणें *or* गुरकावून-&c. पाहणें. [नेत्रपिंड *m.*
Eye-ball, *n.* बुबूळ *n.* अक्षिगोल *m.* अक्षिगोलक *m.* अक्षिकूटक *n.*
Eye-brow, *n.* भ्रू *f. pop.* भंवई *or* भुंवई *f.* भ्रुकुटी *f.* कोदंड *n.*
Intimation by twitch of the e. भ्रूसंकेत *m.*
To knit the e. भंवयांस गांठी *f. pl.*-अढी *f.* घालणें, भंवया *f. pl.* चढविणें.
Eye-drop, *n.* v. Tear. असूं *n.* अश्रु *m. n.*
Eye-lash, *n.* पापणीचे केश *m. pl.* पक्ष्म *n.*
Eye-lid, *n.* पापणी *f.* पात *f. n.* पातें *n.* पुट *m. n.*
Eruption on the inside of the upper e. घुमड *m.* खुपरी *f.*
Hair shooting from the e. internally—a disease.पडपापण्या *f. pl.* पडकेश *m.pl.* [चा चाकर.
Eye-servant, *n.* डोळ्यापुढचा-दृष्टीपुढचा-दृष्टीपुढला चाकर, दृष्टी-
Eye-service, *n.* डोळ्यापुढची-दृष्टीपुढची चाकरी *f.*
Eye-sight, *n.* v. Sight. दृष्टि *f.*
Eye-sore, डोळ्याचा कांटा *m.* नेत्रशल्य *n.* नेत्रकंटक *m.*
To be an e. unto. डोळ्यांत खुपणें *or* सलणें, खुपणें, सलणें.
Eye-tooth, *n. dens caninus.* सुळा *m.* सुळका *m.*
Eye-wink, *n.* नेत्रसंकेत *m.*
Eye-witness, *n.* साक्षी, प्रत्यक्षदर्शी, साक्षाद्द्रष्टा, साक्ष *m.*
Eyed, *a. having eyes.* डोळस, डोळ्यांचा, चक्षुष्मान्.
Fine e. सुलोचन, चकोरदृक्.
Large e. गटगटीत डोळ्या, वटवटीत डोळ्या, वटवट्या.
Little e. चिमण डोळ्या, लिरव्या डोळ्यांचा.
Eyelet, *n.* डोळा *m.* नेडें *or* नेढें *n.* बेज *n.* नाक *n.* डोळू *m.* डोळूक*m.*
Eyrie, Eyry, *n.* हिंस्र पक्ष्यांची घरटें बांधण्याची जागा *f.*

F.

F. This letter has no corresponding symbol in Marāthī. The sound of फ approximates the nearest to its sound.
Fable, *tale*, &c. v. Story. कल्पित कथा *f.* कथानक *n.*

2 *idle story*. जनकथा *f.* दंतकथा *f.* लोककथा *f.*

3 *an untruth*, v. FALSEHOOD. खोटीगोष्ट *f.* अनृत *n.*

FABRIC, *n.* See BUILD, BUILDING. 2 v. TEXTURE. वीण *f.* विणकर *f.*

3 v. CLOTH. कापड *n.*

To FABRICATE, *v. a.* See To BUILD, To FORM.

2 *forge, devise falsely*. रचणें, करणें, बनावणें, खोटा-&c. रचणें.

FABRICATED, *p.* v. V. 2. बनावलेला, खोटा रचलेला, &c. बनावट, बनाऊ.

FABRICATION, *n. forged story, false device*, v. MACHINATION. कुभांड *n.* कुफरांड *or* कुफराण *n.* कुष्मांड *n.* कुदांड *n.* कवंटाल *or* ळ *n.* कंडी *f.* थोतांड *or* थोथांड *n.* तोतया *m.* तकराळ *f.* तरकट *n.* *v.* घे, सांग, बगल्यांड *or* ठ *n.* कचाट *n.* खेंकटें *n.* पाखंड *n.*

2 *false report*. कंडी *f.* कंडाळी *f.v.* उठ, उड, पिक, नीळ रांप *m.f.*

FABRICATOR, *n.* v. V. 2 (of lies, &c. to injury). कुभांडी *or* ड्या, कुभांडखोर, कुफरांडी *or* ड्या, कुफराणी, कुदांडी *or* ड्या, कुदांडखोर, कवंटाल्या *or* ळ्या, थोतांडी, पाखंडी.

FABULIST, *n.* कथारचक, कादंबऱ्या.

FABULOUS, *a. fictitious, founded on fable*. पंचोपाख्यानी, कल्पित, कल्पिनकादंबरींतला, दंतकथासिद्ध.

FACE, *n. surface of the fore part of the head*. तोंड *n.* मुख *n.* आनन *n.* वदन *n.* वक्त्र *n.* तुंड *n.*—in contempt. मुसकट *or* ड *n.* मुसकूट *n.* मुसकाड *n.* मुसकं *n.* मुसकुरी *f.* मुसकाडी *f.* श्रीमुख *n.* —in poetry, &c. मुखकमल *n.* मुखचंद्र *m.* मुखडा *m.*

Before one's f. तोंडापुढें, तोंडासमोर, समक्ष.

F. to f. तोंडातोंडीं, तोंडचेतोंडीं, रूबरू *or* रूबुरू, समक्ष, समोरासमोर, सवडे, सवड्या.

Fair and soft to one's f. तोंडावर गोड, तोंडापुरता गोड.

Hairs along each side of f. काजण्या *f. pl.*

Of averted f. पराङ्मुख, विमुख.

Pouting or puffed out f. तोंबरा *m.*

Rigidity of the muscles of the f. and neck. अनंतवात *m.*

Side of the f.—specially with reference to slapping it, or with some reproach. कानफट *or* ड *n.* कानशील *or* कानसल *or* सूल *n.* खोकाड *n.* खोकडी *f.* थोबाडी *f.* थोबाड *n.* थोतरी *f.*

Side of the f. including the temple. गंड *m.*

Stripe along the f. (esp. of the horse). मुखपट्टा *m.*

That is in one's f.—wind, sun, tide, &c. तोंडाचा.

To one's f. In the f. of. तोंडावर, डोळेउजेडीं.

To be afraid to look in the f. दोहों डोळ्यांची मुरवत *f.* राखणें.

To fall upon one's f. तोंडघशीं पडणें.

To give a smack in the f. तोंडांत-तोंडावर-कानफडांत-&c. मारणें, तोंड *n.*-कानफड *or* ट *n.*-कानशील *n.*-कानसल *or* सूल *n.*-कानाड *n.*-&c. मारणें-फोडणें-सुजवणें, मुसकटणें, तोंड *n.* रंगवणें, श्रीमुखांत देणें, श्रीमुखावर चाखवणें-चळवणें, थोबाडींत मारणें, तोंडावर लगावणें. [*g. of o.*

To smack the f. of loudly & forcibly. खोकडी *f.* गुंगविणें

To hide the f. in a cloak. मुसकटणें, मुसकणें.

To meet f. to f. तोंडावर तोंड *n.* पडणें-दणें.

To set one's f. against. तोंड *n.* देणें.

To shew the f. *appear publicly*. तोंड *n.* बाहेर काढणें.

To throw in one's f. (favors, obligations). तोंडीं काढणें.

To throw upon one's f. तोंडघशीं देणें-पाडणें.

2 *cast of features, countenance, look*. तोंड *n.* मुख *n.* चेहरा *m.* चेहरामोरा *m.* मोहरा *m.* सुरत *f.* तोंडवळण *n.* तोंडवळा *m.* रूप *n.* वदन *n.* आनन *n.*

Bold f. उघडा माथा *m.*

Confusion of f. तोंडास काळोखी *f.*

Long (whining, rueful, &c.) *f.* रडत तोंड *n.* रोतीसुरत *f.*

To get confusion of f. नाकावर पदर *m.* येणें *g. of s.*

To make a long f. तोंड पसरणें-वासणें-वेंगडणें-वाईट करणें, रडकुंडीस येणें *or* परतणें.

To make wry faces. दांत *m. pl.*-तोंड *n.* विचकणें, तोंड *n.* वांकडें करणें.

To make faces at. टिवल्याबाव्हल्या *f. pl.* करणें, वेंकावल्या *f. pl.*-वांकुल्या *f. pl.*-वेटावण्या *f. pl.* दाखवणें.

3 v. SURFACE. तल *m.* पाठ *f.* आंग *n.* [ग *m.*

4 *fore part*, v. FRONT. तोंड *n.* मुख *n.* अग्र *n.* मुखभाग *m.* अग्रभा-

On its f. थपी *v.* लाव, बसव.

That lies with its f. upwards. उताणा, उलथा.

To fall upon its f. चित *or* चीत *adv.* पडणें—as *opposed to* To fall with its f. upwards. पट *adv.* पडणें.

5 *confidence, assurance, effrontery*. नाक *n.* तोंड *n.* धिटाई *f.* तिखें *n.*

6 (as of a cut, gem or other polygon). पयलू *or* पैलू *m.*

To FACE, *v. a. meet in front*. तोंडास तोंड *n.*-तोंडावर तोंड *n.* देणें.

2 *stand opposite to*. समोर-सन्मुख-सम्मुख-सम्मुखीन-&c. असणें-राहणें.

To FACE, *v. n. turn the f.* तोंड *n.* फिरवणें, तोंड *n.* फिरवून असणें.

FACE-CLOTH, *n.* मुखवस्त्र *n.*

FACE-WIPER, *n.* तोंडपुसणें *n.* मुखवस्त्र *n.*

FACED, *a.* तोंडाचा, मुखाचा, तोंडी.

FACET, *n.* पयलू *or* पैलू *m.* कण *m.*

Having facets—gem, &c. पैलूदार.

FACETIOUS, *a. jocular, witty*—of persons. गतक्या, गमती, ख्याली, ठट्ठेखोर, ठट्ठेबाज, ठट्ठेबाईक, विनोदी, रसिक.

2—of sentiments. विनोदाचा, ठट्ठेचा, रसिक, विनोदरूप, विनोदात्मक.

FACETIOUSLY, *adv.* v. A. विनोदानें, ठट्ठेनें, विनोदपूर्वक.

FACETIOUSNESS, *n.* A. 1. विनोद *m.* ठट्ठेबाजी *f.* रहस्य *n.* रसिकता *f.*

FACIAL, *a. pertaining, &c. to the face*. तोंडाचा, मुखाचा, मुखाच्या संबंधाचा.

FACILE. See EASY.

To FACILITATE, *v. a. make easy*. सोपा-सोपारा-सुसाध्य-सुलभ-सुगम-सुप्राप्य-&c. करणें, सौकर्य *n.* करणें *g. of o.*

FACILITY, *n. freedom from difficulty*, v. EASINESS. सोपेपणा *m.* सुसाध्यता *f.* सौकर्य *n.*

2 *ease in performing*, v. EXPERTNESS. हातवटी *f.* हातवळा *m.* हात *m.* कसरत *f.* टूक *f.*

3 *means by which performance is rendered easy*. सोई *f.* साधन *n.* सुसाध्यसाधन *n.*

4 v. SOFTNESS. मनाचा कोवळेपणा *m.*-नरमपणा *m.*

FACING, *a. having the face towards*. समोर, अभिमुख.

FAC SIMILE, *n. an exact copy*. हुबहू काढलेली प्रत *f.*

FACT, *n. thing done or occurred*. घडलेली *or* घडून आलेली गो-

ए *f.* झालेलें कार्य*n.*
Founded on f. ठिकाणबद्ध.
2— in law, *the matter of f.* भूत *n.*
Facts of a case. हकीकत *f.* कैफियत *f.*
Recital of facts. बयाणा *or* नाम*m.* मजकूर*m.*
3 *actuality, reality.* तथ्यता *f.* सत्यता *f.* वास्तविकपणा *m.*
In f. वस्तुतः, वस्तुगत्या, तथ्य, तत्वतः.

FACTION, *n. party.* तट*m.* तड*m.* फळी *f.* पक्ष*m.* [दंगा*m.*
2 *dissension, public discord.* तट*m.* द्वैत *n.* बंडाळी *f.* बलवा*m.*

FACTIOUS, *a. given to faction.* दंगेखोर, बंडखोर, फिसादखोर, फिसादी, बंडी, बंड्या, फंदी, वितंडवादी.
2 *proceeding, &c. from faction.* फंदफितुराचा, बंडाळीचा, फळी बांधण्याचा.

FACTIOUSLY, *adv.* v. A. बंडाळी फंदफितूर*m.*-&c. करण्याचे बुद्धीनें.

FACTIOUSNESS, *n.* v. A. दंगेखोरी *f.*-बंडखोरी *f.*-बंडाळी *f.*-&c. करण्याची बुद्धि *f.*

FACTITIOUS, *a.* v. ARTIFICIAL. केलेला, कृतीचा, कृत्रिम, यौगिक.

FACTOR, *n.* v. AGENT. अडत्या, गुमास्ता, कारभारी.
2—in arith. or algebra. गुण्यपद *or* गुणकपद*n.* पद*n.*

FACTORAGE, *n.* v. N. अडत *f.*

FACTORSHIP, *n.* v. N. गुमास्तेपणा *m.* गुमास्तेगिरी *f.*

FACTORY, *n.* अडत्यांचा अड्डा *m.* कोठी *f.* मांडवी *f.*
2 v. MANUFACTORY. कारखाना *m.*

FACTOTUM, *n.* हरकामी *or* म्या, कामाचा गाडा *m.*

FACULTY. See ABILITY, POWER.

FACUND, FACUNDITY. See ELOQUENT, ELOQUENCE.

To FADDLE. See To FIDDLEFADDLE.

To FADE, *v. n. wither.* कोमणें, कोमजणें, कोमेजणें, कोमावणें, कोमाइणें, झेंबणें *or* झेमणें, बाकुटणें, बावणें, रंग *m.* जाणें *g. of s.* उतरणें.
2—of colors, &c. विटणें, उडणें, उतरणें, रंग *m.* उडणें-उतरणें *g. of s.* झडणें, विटकर-फिका-मजीत-&c. होणें. [होणें.
3 *faint, disappear,* v. To VANISH. दिसेनासा होणें, नाहींसा-

FADED, *p.* v. V. 1. कोमलेला, रंग गेलेला, &c. म्लान, बावका.
2 विटलेला, फिका झालेला, रंग उतरलेला, &c. विटका, उभरंग, उभरा, बाणढाळ, मजीत, उतरल्या रंगाचा, नीरक्त.

FADING, *a. that quickly fades.* विटकर, विटका. [थ *m.n.*

FÆCES, *n. excrement.* मल *m. n. pop.* मळ *m.* गू *m.* पुरीष *n.* गू-
Colorless or white f. अरक्तमल *n.*
Frothy and mucous f. फेनिल आंव *f.*
Thin and watery f. ढगळ *f.* फोक *m.* फोकलण *f.*
2 See DREGS, DIRT.

To FAG, *v. n.* v. To TOIL. खपणें, कटणें, कष्ट *m. pl.*-श्रम *m. pl.* -&c.करणें, अटाआट *m.*-अटाघाट *m. f.*-&c. करणें.
2 *grow wearied,* v. To TIRE. दमणें, श्रमणें, थकणें.

To FAG, *v. a.* See To TIRE.

FAG, *n.* See DRUDGE.

FAG-END, *n.*—of cloth, &c. दशा *f. pl.* चाल *m. f.*
To twist or secure the f. रेवड *f.* घालणें, वरवड *f.* घालणें.
2 See REFUSE.

FAGGING, *n.* v. V. N. 1.—*act.* खपणें *n.* अटाआट *m. f.* अटाघाट *m. f.* अटापिटा *m.* अटापिटी *f.* अटापीट *f.* आंगमोड *f.* कबाडकष्ट *m. pl.* कुत्तेघशी *f.* अट्टाहास *m.*

FAGOT, *n.* मोळी *f.* लांकूड भारा *m.* भारी *f.* गोयला *m.*

FAGOT-SELLER, *n.* मोळविक्या, मोळक्या, मोळीवाला.

To FAIL, *v. n. fall short, become deficient.* खुटणें, तुटणें, कमी -उणा-न्यून-&c. पडणें, तूट *f.*-खूट *f.*-तोटा *m.*-कमती *f.*-&c. पडणें *g. of s.*
2 *become extinct.* राहणें, उडणें, सरणें, मरणें, बुडणें, जाणें, गळणें, नाहींसा होणें.
3 *sink, decline, decay, &c.*—hopes, spirits, strength, &c. मोडावणें, मोडकळणें, *or* मोडकळीस येणें, खचणें, खचळणें, तुटणें, मोडणें, भागणें, गळणें, जाणें, बसणें, उतरणें, राहणें, झरणें, थकणें, गंढारणें, मेटें *n. pl.* बसणें *g. of s.* लेंड्या *f. pl.* गाळणें.
4—eyes, ears, &c. *become impaired.* फुटणें, क्षय *m.*-ऱ्हास*m.* -&c. पावणें.
5 *yield, give way,* v. To GIVE. भागणें, फचकणें, कचणें, बसणें, घसरणें, डगागणें.
6 *miss, miscarry,* v. To DEFEAT. चुकणें, खचणें, खचळणें, हरणें, फसणें, बिथरणें, फिसकणें, फिसकटणें, लटपटणें, थकणें, बिनसणें, अनुपपत्ति *f.*-कार्यविपत्ति *f.* होणें *g. of s.*
7 *be deficient in duty.* चुकणें, टळणें, ढळणें, खिचणें, नाट *adv.* जाणें *or* येणें, अंतर *n.*-तफावत *f.*-गुंजावीस *f.*-कसर *f.*-&c. करणें, and with *g. of s.* होणें-पडणें.
8 *become bankrupt.* थकणें, तुटणें, मोडणें, बसणें, डगागणें.

To FAIL, *v. a. forsake, leave in the lurch.* अंतर *n.* देणें, फशीं देणें-पाडणें, तोंडघशीं देणें.

FAIL, FAILING, FAILURE, *n.* v. V. N. 1. *and* DEFICIENCY. तुटणें *n.* तूट *f.* खूट *f.* तोटा *m.* नपूर *f.* अपूर *f.*
2 बूड *f.* बिबूड *f. n.* फन्ना *m.*
3 *and* DECLINE. मोडणें *n.* &c. मोड *m.* मोडकळ *f.*
6 बिचका *m.* फसाव *m.* फसणूक *f.* भंग *m.* लटपट *f.* धूट *f.* धूळमाती *f.* बिथरणी *f.*
7 चूक *f.* ढळ *m.* कमतर *f.* कसर *f.* गुंजावीस *f.* अंतर *n.* तफावत *f.* तजावूज *or* तजावुजू *n.*
8 थकणें *n.* बुडणें *n.* फसणूक *f.*
I. *a. f. a weakness, &c.* v. FAULT. उणें *n.* हीण *n.*
Without fail, v. CERTAINLY. खचीत, अवश्य.

FAIN. See GLAD, GLADLY.

To FAINT, *v. n. swoon.* मूर्च्छना *f.*-मूर्च्छा *f.*-कलम *m. f.* येणें *in. con.* मूर्च्छागत-मूर्च्छित होणें, अंधेरी *or* अंधारी *f.* येणें.
2 *lose courage, ardor, &c.* v. COURAGE. धीर *m.*-अवसान*n.* -&c. सोडणें, गळणें, खचणें, कमर *f.* खचणें मोडणें-बसणें *g. of s.* मेटें *n. pl.* बसणें *g. of s.* टिरी *or* टिऱ्या *f. pl.* कांपणें *g. of s.*
3 See To VANISH.

FAINT, *a. of sinking spirits; inclined to swoon.* कलमललेला, कलमल आलेला, मूर्च्छावान्, मूर्च्छोन्मुख, मूर्च्छनोन्मुख, ग्लान, म्लान, अवसन्न.
To be f. कलमलणें. [उभरा.
2—of colors. फिका *remiss.* फिकट, अंधक, पुसका, उभरंग,
3—of sounds. मंद, हलका, बारीक, दुःश्राव्य.
4 *slack, sluggish, unanimated, languid.* मंद, ढिला, ढील, मळमळीत, मिणमिणा, निर्जीव, शिथिल, सुस्त, थंड, थंडा, थंडाईचा, ढिलीचा.
5 *weak, slight, little in degree.* पातळ, हलका, लघु, अल्प, स्वल्प, न कळत *or* कळत न कळत *or* कळे नकळे इतका, कळे न

कळेसा.

FAINT-HEARTED, *a.* v. COWARDLY. निर्वीर्य, न्यूनधैर्य, अल्पधीर, विषादी, मनमरू.

FAINTED, *p.* v. V. 1. मूर्च्छा आलेला, &c. मूर्च्छित, मूर्च्छागत, मूर्च्छापन्न, प्राप्तमूर्च्छ.

FAINTING, *n.* v. V. 1. मूर्च्छा *f.* मूर्च्छना *f.* कलम *m.* झीट *f.*

FAINTLY, *adv.* v. A. 3. मंद, मंदमंद.

4 मंद, सुस्ताईवर, ढिलाईवर, थंडपणानें, मिणमीण.

5 हलका, कळे न कळेसा *a. decl.* कळत न कळत.

FAINTNESS, *n.* v. A. 1. फलमल *f.* ग्लानि *f.* म्लानि *f.*

4 मंदपणा *m.* ढिलेपणा *m.* मळमळीतपणा *m.* थंडाई *f.* सुस्ताई *f.* ढिलाई *f.*

FAIR, *a.* (of complexion) *or*—the complexion. गोरा *remiss.* गोरटा and गोरटेला and गोरेला *fairish,* सावळा *or* सांवळा, गोमटा, गोरा गोमटा, उजळ, गौर, उजवट, ताम्र *or* ताम्रवर्ण (and *atributively* ताम्रमुख).—intens. *fair as the lily, the snowdrop, &c.* गोराधमक, धमधमीत *or* धवधवीत गोरा, गोरा गोरापीठ, गोरा गोरा पान, पांढरा धोप, हळदीचा गाभाच.

Fairish, *v. supra.* निमगोरा, गोरासा.

2—of weather. उघडा, सुकेडीचा, सुसाडीचा, उघाडीचा, उजाडीचा, निरभ्र.

Interval of f. weather. उघाड *f.* उघाडी *f.*

3—of wind. पाठीमागचा, मागचा, पाठचा, अनुकूल *pop.* सानकूल, सोईचा, चांगला.

4 *equal, equitable, reasonable,* v. JUST. बरोबर, वाजवी, नीट, रास्त, प्रामाणिक *pop.* प्रमाणिक, उजू, मार्गाचा, सोईचा, योग्य, यथार्थ, बाळबोध, बाळबद.

By f. means. गुणेगोविंदें *or* गुणेगोविंदानें.

F. and foul. सव्यापसव्य.

F. but false. लटका पण नेटका.

F. words. गोडगोड बोलणें *n.* गुळपापडी *f.*

5 *upright, honorable,*—of persons. प्रामाणिक *pop.* प्रमाणिक, इमानी, इमानदार, खऱ्याव्यवहाराचा, खऱ्याचालीचा, सुरळीत, साळढाळ, सरल *pop.* सरळ, साधा, नेकीचा, नेतीचा.

6 *moderately, good.* बरा, बरासा, नेमस्त, बराबाईट.

7 *handsome,* v. BEAUTIFUL. सुंदर, रूपवंत, खुबसुरत.

Fair one, v. BEAUTY. सुंदरी *f.* रूपवती *f.*

The fair, the fair sex, *women.* बायका *f. pl.* स्त्रिया *f. pl.* स्त्रीजाति *f.*

8 See LEGIBLE.

FAIR, *n. great market.* मेला *or* मेळा *m.* हट्ट *pop.* हाट *or* हट *m.* जत्रेचा बाजार *m.* उरुसाचा बाजार *m.*

FAIR, FAIRLY, *adv.* v. A. 4. न्यायानें, नीतीनें, उजूपणानें, सरलपणानें, नेकीनें, लवाडीवांचून, वाजवी, बरोबर, मार्गानें, रीतीनें, &c. प्रमाणिकपणानें.

1. *completely,* v. WHOLLY. साफ, निस्तूक.

FAIRING, *n.* मेळ्यांतून विकत आणलेली देणगी *f.*

FAIRNESS, *n.* v. A. 1. गोरटाई *f.* गोरेपणा*m.* &c. गौरत्व*n.*

2 उघडेपणा*m.* निरभ्रता *f.* अभ्रवातराहित्य*n.*

3 सानकूलपणा*m.* अनुकूलता *f. corr.* अनकुलता *f.* आनुकूल्य*n.*

4 प्रमाणिकपणा*m.* उजूपणा*m.* न्याय्यत्व*n.* [चकपणा*m.*

5 प्रमाणिकपणा*m.* नेक *f.* नेत *f.* सुरळीतपणा*m.* साधेपणा*m.* अवं-

FAIR-SPOKEN, *a.* गोडबोल्या, मिष्टभाषणी, तोंडचा गोड, बोलून सुघड -भला-चांगला-गोड-मिठा.

FAIRY, *n.* परी *f.* कल्पितदेवता *f.*

FAIRY, *a.* परींचा, परीच्या संबंधाचा.

FAITH, *n. belief of revealed religion.* शास्त्रश्रद्धा *f.* शास्त्रभक्ति *f.*

2 *trust in God.* भाव*m.* देवश्रद्धा *f.* देवनिष्ठा *f.* परमेश्वरश्रद्धा *f.* परमेश्वरनिष्ठा *f.*

3 *trust,*—gener. v. BELIEF. विश्वास*m.* श्रद्धा *f.* इतबार*m.* निश्चय*m.* भरवसा*m.*

Done with f. श्रद्धाकृत.

Strong f. *steady belief.* एकनिश्चय*m.*

To break *f.* विश्वासघात*m.* करणें.

4 *a f. religious system.* धर्म*m.* मत*n.* मार्ग*m.* पंथ*m.* संप्रदाय*m.*

5 See FAITHFULNESS.

FAITH-BREACH, *n.* विश्वासघात*m.*

FAITH-BREAKER, *n.* विश्वासघातकी, विश्वासघातक.

FAITHFUL, *a. firm in belief of religion.* शास्त्रमानी, शास्त्रपरायण, शास्त्रनिष्ठ, धर्मपरायण, श्रद्धावान्, श्रद्धान्वित.

2 *trusting in God.* परमेश्वरावर-देवावर-&c. विश्वासठेवणारा-विश्वासी, ईश्वरविश्वस्त.

3 *stanchly adherent, &c.* इमानी, इमानदार, इमानाचा, निमकहलाल, दृढभक्ति, प्रभुभक्त, स्वामिभक्त, खरा.

4 *keeping faith, observant of promise, &c.* कराराचा, करारी, सत्यवचनी, सत्यप्रतिज्ञ, सत्यव्रत, प्रामाणिक *pop.* प्रमाणिक, खरा, सत्य. [इत्थंभूत.

5 *conformable to truth,* v. TRUE. खरा, सत्य, यथातथ, यथार्थ

FAITHFULLY, *adv.* v. A. 3 इमानानें, इमानें इतबारें, दृढभक्तिपूर्वक.

4 सत्य राखुन, खरेपणा राखुन, खरेपणानें, &c.

5 इत्थंभूत, यथावृत्त, यथावत्.

FAITHFULNESS, *n.* v. A. 3. इमान*n.* खरेपणा*m.* इमानीपणा*m.* इमानदारी *f.* निमकहलाली *f.* दृढभक्ति *f.* प्रभुनिष्ठा *f.* प्रभुभक्ति *f.*

4 खरेपणा*m.* खराई *f.* प्रमाणिकपणा*m.* &c. सत्य*n.* सत्यता *f.* सत्यप्रतिज्ञता *f.* सत्यवचनता *f.*

5 खरेपणा*m.* सत्यता *f.* याथातथ्य*n.* यथार्थता *f.* याथार्थ्य*n.*

FAITHLESS, *a. unbelieving.* अविश्वासी, श्रद्धाहीन-शून्य-&c. भावशून्य-&c. [निमकहराम.

2 *perfidious,* v. FALSE. खोटा, बेइमान, हाडाचा खोटा-वाईट,

FAITHLESSNESS, *n.* v. A. 1. अविश्वास*m.* अविश्वासिता *f.* विश्वासाभाव*m.* श्रद्धाशून्यता *f.* भावशून्यता *f.* &c.

2 खोटाई *f.* खोटेपणा*m.* बेइमानी *f.* निमकहरामी *f.*

FALCHION, *n.* v. SWORD. तेगा*m.*

FALCON, *n.* बहिरीससाणा*m.* ससाणा *or* ना*m.* बहिरी*m.* श्येन*m.*

FALCONER, *n.* बहिरीससाणेवाला, बहिरीससाणा घेऊन शिकार करणारा.

FALCONRY, *n.* बहिरीससाणा घेऊन शिकार करणें *n.*

To FALL, *v. n.* पडणें, गळणें, पतन*n.*-&c. होणें *g. of s.* च्यवणें.

To f. asleep. झोंप *f.* लागणें *in. con.*

To f. along senseless. फलें*n.* पडणें *g. of s.*

To f. suddenly or with agitation. दुबकणें, सोबकणें.

2 *subside, decline from intenseness,* v. To ABATE. पडणें, उतरणें, उणावणें, हलकावणें, बसणें.

3 *be degraded, ruined, &c.* खचणें, खचळणें, बसणें, बुडणें, भ्रंश *m.*-च्युति *f.*-&c. होणें *g. of s.* पतित-भ्रष्ट-च्युत-गलित-&c. होणें.

4—leaves, blossoms, fruits, hair, &c. झडणें, गळणें, फटाफ-

ट *adv.* पडणें, गळ *f.*-गळती *f.*-झड *f.*-फटाबळ *f.*-पाभळ *f.* लागणें *g. of. s.* [गतणें.
5 (in battle) *be killed.* पडणें, कटणें, कामास येणें, गमावणें,
6 away; *grow lean*, v. To WASTE. चोपणें, चोपटणें, ढकलणें, आंग *n.* टाकणें-सोडणें-सांडणें, अचांगणें, अचांगी *f.* भरणें-होणें, लंगणें *or* लंघणें, रंगळणें, झडणें, चुंबणें, घसरणें, सांडवणें.
7 in; *sink in, be depressed.* खोलगटणें, खोलटणें, बसणें, पोंढळणें, आंत जाणें.
8 off; *become worse or less.* तुटणें, घसरणें, बिचलणें, बिघडणें.
9 on; to; *set to eagerly.* पडणें, लागणें, जुडणें, उठावणें, घसरणें, झडझडणें, मार *f.* पडणें.
10 on; upon; v. To ATTACK. तुटून पडणें *with* वर, आंगावर तुटून पडणें, आंगावर येणें, गळीं पडणें, चालून जाणें, उडणें *with* वर, उपटणें, घसरणें, तोंडीं *or* तोंडास लागणें.
11 out; v. To QUARREL, तुटणें, बिघड *m.*-विघड*m.* पडणें *g. of s.* घडी *f.* विघडणें.
12 short of. अंतरणें, कमी पडणें, तुटणें, अपूर *f.*-नपूर *f.*-तोटा *m.*-कसर *f.*-&c. असणें.
13 to; *apply one's self to.* झटणें, जुडणें, पडणें, लागणें, उठावणें, सुटणें. [डणें *g. of o.*
14 under; *be ranged or reckoned with.* खालीं ओढणें-मो-
15 in with; v. To MEET. गांठ *f.* पडणें.
16 See also To APOSTATIZE, To REVOLT, &c.

FALL, FALLING, *n.* v. V.1.—*act.* पडणें *n.* &c. पतन *n.* पात *m.* गलन *n.* च्यवन *n.* च्युति *f.* भ्रंश *m.* स्रंसन *n.*विस्रंसन *n.* अधःपात *m.* विनिपात *m.* विगलन *m.* स्खलन *n.*
F. of rain. वर्षाव *m.* पावसाचा वर्षाव *m.* वृष्टि *f.*
2 उतार *m* ओसार *m.* ओसारा *m.*
F. and rise. उतारचढ *m.*
3—*act.* खचणें *n.* &c.—*state.* v. DEGRADATION. च्युति *f.*भ्रंश *m.* पदच्युति *f.* पदभ्रंश *m.* स्थानभ्रंश *m.* माननाश *m.* मानभंग *m.*
4 झडणें *n.* &c. झडणी *f.* झडणूक *f.*
Great & rapid f. पटका *m.* पटाडा *m.* फटाबळ *f.*
I. See WATERFALL.

FALLACIOUS, *a. sophistical, deceptive.* आभासाचा,आभासात्मक, भ्रामक, भ्रमजनक, भ्रांतिजनक, सिद्धांताभासक, सिद्धांतप्रतिभासक, खोटसाळ.
2 *not well founded, mocking expectation.* भ्रांतीचा, नादाचा, फसविण्याचा, भ्रांतिमूलक.

FALLACY, *n. sophism, &c.* आभास *m.* सिद्धांताभास *m.*

FALLEN, *p.* v. V. 1. पडलेला, &c. पतित, च्युत (esp. in comp. as स्थानच्युत, पदच्युत, अधिकारच्युत,) गलित *or* विगलित (esp. in comp.as tooth-fallen विगलितदंत, hair-fallen विगलितकेश, and विगलितनख, विगलितेंद्रिय, विगलितवीर्य, &c.), भ्रष्ट, भ्रंशित, स्रस्त, स्खलित.

FALLIBILITY, *n.* v. A. चुकायाजोगेपणा *m.* &c. भ्रमयोग्यता *f.* &c. भ्राम्यता *f.* भ्रांतिधर्म*m.*

FALLIBLE, *a. liable to err.* चुकाया जोगता-जोगा-&c. घसराया जोगता-जोगा-&c. भ्राम्य, भ्रमयोग्य, भ्रमाई, भ्रमपात्र, भ्रांतिधर्मा, संभावित-भ्रमक.
Man is f. भ्रांतेःपुरुषधर्मत्वं.

FALLING SICKNESS, *n.* v. EPILEPSY. मरगी *or* मिरगी *f.*

FALLOW, *a.*—ground. पडीत,पडीक, नाकीर्द,बिनलागवडीचा,पडकर.
F. for years. सनवात पडीत. [चून ठेवलेला.
2 *left unsowed after ploughing.* नांगरल्यावर बीं पेरल्यावां-

FALLOW, *n. ground at rest.* पड *f.* पडीत जमीन *f.*

To FALLOW, *v. a.* नांगरल्यावर बीं पेरल्यावांचून ठेवणें.

FALLOWDEER, *n.* एक जातीचा हरिण *m.* आहू.

FALSE, *a. not true,*—morally. खोटा, असत्य, लटका, लटीक, लबाड, खोटसाळ, खोटारा, लबाडीचा, &c. मिथ्या, सकपट, कपटसंध, गैररास्त, वितथ, मृषा, अलीक,—freely, indef. &c. लटका लांडा, लटका फटका, लबाडलचाड, लबाडलाताड, लबाडलाताळ.
2 *not true,*—physically. खोटा, लटका, लटीक, मिथ्या, असत्य, गैरवास्तवीक, अवास्तविक, अवास्तव.
3 *treacherous, perfidious, faithless.* खोटा, खोटसाळ, खोटारा, लटका, लटकुरा *or* कोरा, कपटी, मनाचा कपटी, मनाचा कुजका, मनाचा खोटा, &c. निमकहराम, बेइमान, अप्रामाणिक *pop.* अप्रमाणिक, सकपट, कपटमति, कृत्रिमी, असत्यप्रतिज्ञ, कुडा, कूड, हाडाचा खोटा-वाईट-&c.—freely, indef. &c. लटका लांडा, लटकाफटका, लबाडलाताड.
F. but fair looking. लटका पर नेटका.
4 *counterfeit, not real.* खोटा, खोटसाळ, मिथ्या, केलेला, नकली, कृतीचा, कृत्रिम, कपटी, कपटाचा, सोंगाचा, तकलुबी, बनाऊ, बनावलेला, आरोपित.
The f. and debased (rupees, money, &c.). खोटानाटा (पैसा, रुपया &c.).

FALSE-HEARTED, *a.* v.FALSE. मनाचा कपटी, मनाचा खोटा, मनाचा कुजका, कपटमति.

FALSEHOOD, FALSENESS, FALSITY, *n.* v. A. 1. लबाडकी *f.* लबाडी *f.* खोटाई *f.* खोट *f.* खोटेपणा *m.* &c. असत्यता *f.* कपट *n.* कापट्य *n.* कृत्रिम *n.* अलीक *n.* मृषावाद *m.*—freely, indef. &c. लबाडीलचाडी *f.* लबाडीलताडी *f.* लबाडीलकारी *f.* लांडीलबाडी *f.* लांडेंलटकें *n.*
2 खोटेपणा *m.* &c. खोटाई *f.* खोट *f.* असत्यता *f.*
3 खोटाई *f.* खोट *f.* खोटेपणा *m.* &c. कपट *n.* कापट्य *n.* बेइमानी *f.*बेइमानकी *f.*मनाचा कुजकेपणा*m.*&c. निमकहरामी *f.*—freely, indef. &c. लबाडीलचाडी *f.* लबाडीलाताडी *f.* लबाडीलकारी *f.* लांडीलबाडी *f.* लांडेंलटकें *n.*
4 खोटेपणा *m.* &c. खोटाई *f.* खोट *f.*
I. a f. *an untruth.* लबाडी *f.* अनृत *n.* मिथ्याभाषण *n.*मिथ्यावचन *n.* मिथ्योक्ति *f.*

FALSELY, *adv.* v. A. 1. खोटा, *a. decl.* लबाडीनें, खोटेपणानें, &c. असत्य, मिथ्या, गैररास्त, मृषा.
2 मिथ्या.
3 लबाडीकरून, लबाडीनें, बेइमानीनें, कपटानें.

To FALSIFY, *v. a. render false by interpolation, &c.* खोटा करणें, नवा-बाहेरचा-&c. शिरवून खोटा करणें, कूटक्षेपविपर्यस्त करणें.
2 *prove false.* खोटा-असत्य-&c. करणें-पाडणें-करून दाखवणें, खोटेपणा *m.*-वैपरीत्य *n.*-&c. आणणें.
2 *violate, break by falsehood.* खोटा करणें-पाडणें, खोट *f.*-&c. आणणें, मोडणें. [गणपति *m.*

FALSTAFF, *n. fat and happy fellow,* v. FAT. गुळाचा गणेश *or*

To FALTER, *v. n. hesitate in utterance,* v. To HESITATE. अडखळणें *or* अडखुळणें *or* अडकळणें, कांचकळणें, गुटमळणें, गुपटणें, लागणें, गचकळया *f. pl.* खाणें, बोबडी *f.*-फेंपरी *f.* वळणें *g. of s.*
2 *fail, yield, sink under.* कचणें, कचकणें, कचकरणें, कचरणें,

काचावणें, गचावणें, खचणें, घसरणें, गळणें, गंढारणें, कच *f.* खाणें.

Fame, *n. reputation, renown, celebrity.* कीर्त्ति *f.* लौकिक *m.* नाम *pop.* नांव *n.* नांवलौकिक *m.* आख्या *f.* ख्याति *f.* प्रख्या *f.* प्रख्याति *f.* प्रसिद्धि *f.* नांवरूप *n.* नावसकी *f.* नामना *f.* नामोश *m.* प्रतिष्ठा *f.* यश *n.* प्रथा *f.* प्रथिति *f.* विश्रुति *f.* रूढि *f.* अस्करा *m.* गाजावाजा *m.* अगाजा *m.* डंका *m.* भुमका *m.v.* उड, उठ, अवाबा *m.*

To acquire f. नांवास चढणें, नांव *n.*-यश *n.*-&c. मिळवणें, यशाची गुढी *f.* उभारणें, कीर्त्ति *f.*-नांव*n.*-धौंसा *m.*-&c. गाजवणें, शक *m.* गाजवणें, झेंडा *m.*-तुरा *m.*-ध्वज *m.*-&c. लावणें, अस्करणें *or* अस्कारणें.

To lose one's f. शिक्कल *f.* गमावणें.

2 *rumour, talk, bruit,* v. Report. अवई *or* अवाई *f.* अफवा *f.* बोलवा *f. m.* आख्या *f.* वदंता *f.* वार्त्ता *f.*

Famed, *a.* v. Famous. प्रख्यात, प्रसिद्ध, कीर्तिमान्.

Familiar, *a. of or belonging to a family.* घरचा, गृहसंबंधी, गृहविषयक.

2 *unceremonious, free, easy.* खळबळीत, घळघळीत, घळबळीत, घळमळीत, अळबळीत *or* हळबळीन, हळबळा, अळबळीत गळबळीत.

To become f. भीड *f.* चेपणें *g. of s.*

3 *well versed in, accustomed to, &c.* v. Conversant. वहिवाटलेला, वागलेला, राबलेला, वापरलेला, &c. भेदी, भेया, भुम्या, माहितगार, वाकबगार, वाकचदार.

4 *well known.* घसवटीचा, घसवटींतला, परिपाठांतला, माहितीचा, माहितगारीचा, परिचयाचा, परिचयांतला, परिचित, दखल.

5 *intimate.* सलगीचा, सलगी, घसणीचा, गट्टीचा, गटपटीचा, घळीमेळीचा *or* घळामेलीचा, खेळीमेळीचा, संसर्गी, संसक्त.

Familiar, *n. intimate.* सखा, खेळीमेळीचा मित्र.

Familiarity, *n.* v. A. 2. खळबळीतपणा *m.* घळघळीतपणा *m.* &c.

3. 4 खांद *m.* खांदा *m.* दखलगिरी *f.* माहितगारी *f.* माहीत *f.* जाणसाळ *f.* वाकबदारी *f.* अभ्यास *m.* सवई *f.* राबता *m.* घसवट *or* घसट *f.* जाणीव *f.*

5 जवळीक *f.* घसण *f.* घसणी *f.* खेळीमेळी *f.* गोडी गुलाबी *f.* रहासाळी *f.* गट्टी *f.* गटपट *f.* संसक्ति *f.*

F. breeds contempt. नात्याची जसी जवळीक तसी आदराची कोवळीक.

To **Familiarize**, *v. a. habituate,* v. To Accustom. घसणीखालीं-वहिवाटीखालीं-वहिवाटींत-राबत्यांत-&c. आणणें-पाडणें, राबता *m.*-सराव *m.*-&c. पाडणें, रांबवणें.

To become familiarized. रांबणें, जाणसळणें, सवई *f.* लागणें *in. con. with g. of o.*

Familiarly, *adv.* v. A. 2. खळबळीतपणानें, &c. खळबळीत, घळघळीत, &c. मुखसंकोचावांचून, मुखदाक्षिण्यावांचून.

5 खेळीमेळीनें, स्नेहभावानें, सख्यभावानें.

Family, *n. household, &c.* कुटुंब *n.* घरदार *n.* घर *n.* घरचे लोक *m. pl.* घरचींमाणसें *n. pl.* परिग्रह *m.* परिवार *m.* रांडपोर *n.* खटला *m.* खटलें *n.* कबिला *m.* मुलेंमाणसें *n. pl.* बाईलभिडंग *n.* बाइलबडगा *m.* जोजार *m.* [चार*m.*

Custom or course of procedure of a f. घरचार *m.* गृहा-

F.-quarrel. गृहकलह *pop.* घरकलह *m.* घरतंटा *m.* घरखटला *m.* गृहभेद *m.* गृहछिद्र *n.* घरफूट *f.* कुटुंबकलह *m.*

F.-cares and anxieties. बाळंदा *or* बाळंधा *m.*

F. of little ones. बाळंदा *or* बाळंधा *m.*

F.-circle. घरमंडळी *f.* घरगुतीमंडळी *f.* घरमेळ *m.*

F.-stock or store. घरबेगमी *f.* घरोटी *f.*

Of the f. घरचा, अंतरंग, अंतरंगींचा, अंतरींचा, स्वकीय.

Pension or provision granted by Government to a family. बाळपरवेशी *f.* बाळपरवरशी *f.*

That has a family; *a family man.* कुटुंबी, कुटुंबाळा, कुटुंबवत्सल, सकुटुंब, घरबारी, खटलेकरी, खटलेवाईक, जोजारी, कबीलदार.

That is the earning (or sustaining) member of a family. जोडता, जोडका, कुटुंबकबाडी, जोडतापूत, कमावता, कमावतापूत.

2 v. Offspring, Children. मुलेंबाळें *n. pl.* मुलेंलेंकरें *n. pl.* पोरेंबाळें *n. pl.* [ळा.

That has a family. लेंकुरवाला *or* ळा, पोरवाला, कच्चेबच्चेवा-

3 *house, lineage, race, tribe.* कुल *pop.* कूळ *n.* वंश *m.* गोत्र *n.* घर *n.* घराणा *m.* घराणें *n.* जाति *pop.* जात *f.* बिल्हय *f.* खूम *n.* खांदान *f.* खानवटा *m.* अवलाद *f.* अन्वय *m.*

An emigrated or extinct f. गतकूळ *n.*

Extinction or ruin of a f. कुललोप *m.* वंशलोप *m.* कुलक्षय *m.* कुलनाश *m.* घरबूड *f.* गृहभंग *m.* कुलोच्छेद *m.* वंशोच्छेद *m.* गृहोच्छेद *m.* बींबूड *f. n.* तळपट *n.* थाळावाटी *f.* दारफळणी *f.*

F.-practice or rite. कुलाचार *m.* कुलधर्म *m.* वंशसमाचार*m.* वंशानुचरित *n.* वंशीकसंप्रदाय *m.* वंशीकरीति *f.* &c.

F.-honour or respectability. कुलमर्यादा *f.* कुलोत्कर्ष *m.*

F.-quality, trait, &c. बसलात *f.*

F.-pride. कुलाभिमान *m.*

F.-ties and connections. अनुबंध *m.*

F.-priest or spiritual director. कुलगुरु *m.* कुलोपाध्याय *m.* कुलाचार्य *m.*

F.-tale. कुळकट *f.* खणकत *f.*

Head or chief of a f. कुलपति *m.* कुलनाथ *m.*

History of a f. वंशचरित्र *n.*

Line, order or succession of a f. कुलपरंपरा *f.*वंशपरंपरा*f.*

That is of a good or ancient f. v. Gentle. कुलीन, जातीचा, जातिवंत, पिढीजाद *or* जादा, असल, असील, घरंदाज, सुवर्ण, खांदानीचा, खाणीचा, आर्य.

That is of a low f. v. Base. हीनकुल.

Of the f. of. वंशी, वंशीय, वंश्य.

Religion or a religious observance of a f. कुलधर्म *m.*

Tutelar divinity of a f. कुलदेवता *f.*कुलदैवत*n.*कुलस्वामी*m.*

To be reduced—a f. घर *n.* बसणें.

Such designations as *ornament of the family, glory of the house, lustre of the tribe, light, honor, grace, &c. of the race or line,* are answered by कुलदीपक, कुलभूषण, कुळाचा टिकला *or* टिळा, कुलतिलक, कुलरत्न, कुलावतंस. And as applied to females by कुलांगना, कुलवधू, कुलस्त्री. Such designations as *prop, pillar, stay, defence, &c. of the family, house, race, &c.* are answered by घराचाखांब, घराचाधारण, धरणखांब, दौलतीचा खांब, घराचें पांघरूण, मेढ्या, and espec. with ironical implication जोडकापूत *m.* जोडताराम *m.* Such designations as *ruin, bane, pest, evil genius, &c.* of the *family or race,* are rendered by कुलनाश, कुलांगार, मुळावर येणारा *or* बसणारा, दिवटा, पांढऱ्या पायाचें संतान.

Terms answering to *brand, blot, scandal, reproach, disgrace, &c.* of the family are, दिवटा, पागोटें खालीं करणारा, कुपुत्र, कुसंतान, दक्षिणेचादिवा, नांवावर पाणी घालणारा; and as restricted to females, कुलटा.

4 *birth, extraction, descent.* कुळी *f.* खाण *f.* उपज *m.* उत्पत्ति *f.* विल्हय *f.* विल्हा *m.*

5 (of animals, plants, &c.) जाति *pop.* जात *f.* वर्ग*m.*

Famine, *n.* v. Scarcity. दुष्काल *pop.* दुकळ *or* दुकाळ *m.*काळ *m.* दुर्भिक्ष *n.* महागाई *f.*

F. occasioned by excessive rain. ओला दुकळ *or*दुकाळ*m.*

F. occasioned by drought. सुका दुकाळ *m.*कोरडा दुकाळ*m.*

To **Famish**, *v. a.* v. To Starve. उपासी मारणें.

To **Famish**, *v. n.* v. To Starve. उपासी मरणें, दुकळणें, अन्नावांचून मरणें.

Famous, *a. celebrated, renowned.* नांवकरी, नामधारी, नामदार, नामांकित, नामजात *or* द, नांवाचा, नामी, कीर्त्तीचा, प्रतिष्ठेचा, &c. कीर्त्तीमान्, ख्यात, आख्यात, प्रख्यात, विख्यात, प्रतिष्ठित, प्रसिद्ध, सुप्रसिद्ध, यशवंत, यशस्वी, प्राप्तयश, यशोवृद्ध, यशस्वान्, नावसता, हकाट्याचा, असकऱ्याचा, रूढ, विश्रुत, प्रथित, आख्यासंपन्न, दिग्विभावित.

Famously, *adv. finely, &c.* उत्तमप्रकारें, नामी, उत्कृष्ट.

Famousness. See Fame.

Fan, *n.* पंखा *m.* विंझुणा *or* विझुणा *m.* व्यजन *n.* फटकणें *n.* झडपण *n.* धवित्र *n.* [फटफटें *n.*

F. of bamboo matting for fanning a fire. फटफटणें*n.*

2 *winnowing basket.* सूप *n. dim.* सुपली *f.* शूर्प *n.*—deprecative or diminutive. सुपडें *n.*

To **Fan**, *v. a.* पंखा *m.* वारणें, पंख्यानें वारा *m.* घालणें, विंझुणवारा *m.* घालणें, फटकणें, झडपणें, झटकणें, झटकावणें, हडपणें, झाडणें.

2 See To Winnow.

Fanatic, Fanatical, *a.* v. N. of persons. धर्मपिसा, धर्मवेडा, धर्मखुळा, देवताळा, देवपिसा.

2—of opinions, &c. धर्मवेडाचा, &c.

Fanaticalness, Fanaticism, *n. religious phrenzy.* धर्मपिसें *n.* धर्मवेड *n.* धर्मखुळ *n.* देवताळें *n.* देवपिसें *n.*

Fancied, *p.* v. V. कल्पित, मनःकल्पित, भावित.

Fanciful, *a. whimsical, humoursome,*—of persons. मनमौज्या, छंदखोर, छंदी, छंदिष्ट, छांदिष्ट, तऱ्हेबाज, लहरी, लहरीदार, तबियती, ख्याली, उचल चावडा, मिजाजखोर, चिकित्सखोर, आडकांट्या, मनस्वी.

2—of matters. स्वछंदाचा, मनस्वी, मानसिक, मनःकल्पित, ऐच्छिक, स्वछंदःकल्पित, तऱ्हेचा, तऱ्हेदार, तऱ्हेवाईक, लाडका.

Fancifulness, *n.* v. A. 1. छंदीपणा *m.* छंदिष्टपणा *m.* &c. मिजाजखोरी *f.* खोड *f.* मनोलौल्य *n.*

Fancy, *n. imagination.* कल्पनाशक्ति *f.* कल्पनासामर्थ्य *n.* कल्पकत्व *n.* तर्कशक्ति *f.*

Creation of the f. मानससृष्टि *f.* मनोरथसृष्टि *f.*

Play of f. बुद्धिविलास *m.*

2 *a f. notion, a thought.* कल्पना *f.* आभास *m.* भास *m.* तर्क *m.* वितर्क *m.* तरंग *m.* कांक्षा *f.* चिकित्सा *f. v.* ये.

Fancies, *fantasies, phantoms.* कल्पनासृष्टि *f.*

Pretty f. बूट *m.* चुटका *m.* नुकता *m.*

Wild f. Crude f. क्लिष्टकल्पना *f.* कुतर्क *m.* वितर्क *m.* वेड *n.*

3 *taste, conception.* मन *n.* मर्जी *f.* स्वाद *m.* कल्पना *f.*

4 *a whim, a humour.* लहर *f.* तरंग *m.* खोड *f.* छंद *m.* मौज *f.* मनमौज *f.* मुंगा *m.* तबियत *f.* उत्कलिका *f.* असद्ग्रह *m.* [खाणें.

To indulge fancies. छंदछंद *m. pl.* करणें, मनीं मांडे *m. pl.*

To indulge the fancies of. लळा *m.*-छंद *m. pl.*-लाड *m.*-&c. पुरवणें-चालवणें *g. of o.*

To **Fancy**, *v. n.* कल्पना *f.* करणें, कल्पना *f.* मनांत येणें *in. con.* वाटणें *in. con.* मनदेवता *f.*-मनपिंगळी *f.* धांवणें. [*g. of o.*

To **Fancy**, *v. a. imagine.* कल्पिणें, कल्पना *f.*-भावना *f.*-&c. करणें

2 *like, approve.* मर्जीस-पसंतीस-उचितास-मनास-&c. येणें-पडणें *in. con.* आवडणें *in. con.*

Fane, *n.* v. Temple. देवालय *n.*

Fanfaron. See Hector.

Fang, *n. pointed tooth, &c.* सुळा *m.* सुळका *m.* सुळादांत *m.* शूलदंत *m.* विषाण *m. n.*

Fanged, *a.* v. N. सुळ्यांचा, सुळ्यादांतांचा, शूलदंती.

Fangled. See Gawdy, Showy.

Fantastic, Fantastical, *a.* See Fanciful, Imaginary.

Fantasy. See Fancy.

Far, *adv.* दूर, लांब, दूरवर, लांबवर.

As f. as. जिथपर्यंत, जिथपावेतों, जिथवर, *or* जेथपर्यंत &c.

As f. as this. एथपर्यंत, एथपावेतों, एथवर, एतावत.

By f. v. Much. बहुत, फार.

From f. दुरून, लांबून. [दूर.

How f. कोठपर्यंत, कोठपावेतों, कोठवर, कितपत, केथूवर, किंवे-

Of f. and near. इकडचा तिकडचा.

So f. तेथपर्यंत, तेथपावेतों, तेथवर.

Far, *a. remote, distant.* दूरचा, लांबचा, दुरांदूरचा, दुरील, दूरस्थ.

Far-aimer, *n.* दीर्घसंधानी.

Far-aiming, *n.* दीर्घसंधान *n.*

Far-fetched, *a.* v. Forced. क्लिष्ट, अवघड, बळेंचा, ओढून ताणून आणलेला.

Far-piercing, *a.* दूरवेधी.

Farsighted, Far-seeing, *a.* दीर्घदृष्टि, दीर्घदर्शी, दूरदृष्टि, दूरदर्शी, पोहचेला.

Farce, *n.*—in the Drama. प्रहसन*n.*

Farcial, *a.* v. N. प्रहासी, प्रहसनसंबंधी, प्रहसनविषयक.

Farcy, *n.* गर *f.* लूत *f.* अश्वकुष्ठ *n.*

Fardel. See Bundle. [जन*n.*

Fare, Faring, *n. feeding, living.* खाणें*n.* अन्न*n.* जेवण*n.* भो-

Coarse or hard f. आलापाला*m.* कोंडा भोंडा*m.* अरबचरब*n.* अरबट चरबट *n.* अचरपचर*n.* अचरटपचरट*n.* अबरचबर*n.* अरकसबरकस*n.* रबर*n.* चणवणी मिठवणी *n.* कुभोजन *n.* कदन्न*n.*

Dainty f. *good pudding, &c.* गोडजेवण*n.* गोडघास *m.* मिष्टान्न*n.* आप्यायन *n.*

Poor f. ताककण्या *f. pl.* ताकपाणी *n.*

Rich f. *nutritious diet.* खुराक*m.* स्वाद *f.*

Sumptuous f. भरगच्ची जेवण*n.*

Good fare's a good Doctor. स्वाद हरी व्याध.

2 *passage-money.* भाडें*n.* मोल *n.* हेलम*n.*

3— by ship or boat. नोर*m.*

To **Fare.** See To Go, To Be, To Feed.

Farewell, *adv.* v. Adieu. स्वस्ति, कल्याण असो, क्षेम असो.

FAREWELL, *n.* v. LEAVE. निरोप*m.* आज्ञा *f.*

FARINA, *n.*—in botany. पुष्परेणु*m.* पराग*m.*

2 *flour.* पीठ *n.* पिष्ट *n.*

FARINACEOUS, *a. mealy.* पिठाचा, पिष्टमय, पिष्टात्मक, पिष्टगुणक.

FARM, *n. land leased on rent.* धान्यानें घेतलेली जमीन *f.* धान्याचीं शेतें *n pl.* शेतगणा*m.* कुणबावा*m.* कुणबीक *f.* शेतीक*n.* थळ *n.*

Out f. *f. out of the parish.* ओवंडा*m.*

Out f. holder. ओवंडेकरी.

2 (of the revenue, customs, &c.). इजारा *m.* गुत्ता *m.* गुतका*m.* हुंडबा *or* हुंडा*m.* खंडणूक *f.*

Roll or schedule of farms. इजारपट*m.*

To FARM, *v. a.* (the revenues, customs, &c.). *lease out.* खंडणें, खंडून देणें, तोडूनदेणें, मक्ता*m.*-इजारा*m.*-&c. करून देणें, मक्त्यानें-&c. देणें.

2 *take on lease.* खंडून घेणें, तोडून घेणें, मक्ता *m.*-इजारा *m.*-हुंडा*m.*-&c. करणें-करून घेणें, मक्त्यानें-इजाऱ्यानें-&c. घेणें.

3 *till*, v. To CULTIVATE. नांगरणें ढुणणें.

FARM-HOUSE, *n.* शेतकऱ्याचें रहायाचें घर*n.*

FARM-YARD, *n.* शेतकऱ्याच्या घराचे सभोंवतालचें वाडगें *n.*

FARMER, *n.*—(of fields). धारेकरी, उपरी (esp. as opp. to थलकरी *or* थलवाईक landed proprietor), शेतकरी, कुणबी, क्षेत्रजीवी. See also AGRICULTURIST.

2 (of the revenues, customs, &c.), v. CONTRACTOR. इजारदार, खोत.

FARMING. See AGRICULTURE.

2 (of the revenues, &c.). खोती *f.* खोतकी *f.*

FARNESS. See DISTANCE.

FARRAGINOUS, *a.* v. MEDLEY. पंचभेळीचा, पंचमेळीचा, घेडगुजरीचा, मिश्र.

FARRAGO. See MEDLEY.

FARRIER, *n. horse-shoer.* नालबंद.

2 *horse-doctor.* घोड्याचावैद्य*m.* साळोत्तरी, अश्ववैद्य, अश्वचिकित्सक, शालिहोत्री.

FARRIERY, *n.* v. N. 1. नालबंदी *f.*

2 घोड्याची वैद्यकी *f.* अश्वचिकित्सा *f.* अश्ववैद्यक *n.* साळोत्तर *or* साळोत्र*n.* शालिहोत्र*n.*

FARROW, *n. litter of pigs.* डुकराचें वेत*n.*

FART, *n.* पाद*m.* अपानवायु*m.* अधोवायु *m.* पश्चिमवायु *m.* श्रद्धा *f.* टरका*m.* टारादुरी *f.* फुसकुली *f.*

Fetor of a f. पादघ्राण *f.*

To FART, *v. n.* पादणें, पर्दन*n.* करणें, पाद*m.*सोडणें, टरका*m.* मारणें.

FARTHER, *a. more remote.* अधिकदूर, दूरतर, उत्तर (in comp. as, F. half. उत्तरार्ध. F. or concluding part of the night उत्तररात्र. F. or ulterior division, side, country, &c. उत्तरभाग, उत्तरखंड, उत्तरपक्ष, उत्तरांग, उत्तरदेश, उत्तरवय, &c.) अपर (in comp. as अपरार्ध, अपररात्र).

FARTHERMOST, FARTHEST, *a.* सर्वांहून-सर्वांपेक्षां दूर, दूरतम, कडेशेवटचा, अतिदूरचा. See FURTHER, &c.

FARTHING, *n.* इंग्लंदांत हलक्या किमतीचें एक तांब्याचें नाणें आहे.

To FASCINATE, *v. a.* v. To CHARM, lit. fig. भारणें, मोह *m.* घालणें, मोहणें, दृष्टि *f.* बंद करणें *g. of o.* नजरबंदी *f.* करणें *g. of o.* मोहित- &c. करणें.

FASCINATED, *p.* v. V. भारलेला, &c. मोहित, चकित, चक, चकमूल, वश, वशीकृत.

To be f. चकणें, चौकडी *f.* भुलणें *or* गुंग होणें *g. of s.*

FASCINATION, *n.* v. V.—*act.* भारणें *n.* &c. भारणी *f.* मोहन *n.* वशीकरण *n.* वशक्रिया *f.*—*state.* मोह *m.* नजरबंदी *f.* चित्तभ्रम *m.* भुरळ *f.* भुरळें *n.* भुलवण *f.* भूल *f.*

FASHION, *n. make, cast,* &c. v. FORM. आकार *m.* डौल *m.* घडण *f.* घडणी *f.* घडवण *f.* घाट *m.* भंगी *f.*

2 *cut of clothes, &c.* बेत *m.* बेतणी *f.* कातरणी *f.*

3 *general practice,* v. CUSTOM. चाल *f.* रीति *pop.* रीत *f.* ओळ *f.* ओळा *m.* वळण *n.* परिपाठ *m.* पाठ *m.* प्रघात *m.* लोकप्रचार *m.* लोकप्रघात *m.* प्रथा *f.*

To go out of f. ढळणें, पडीं पडणें.

4 See MANNER.

To FASHION. See To FORM.

FASHIONABLE, *a. popular, current, established by custom,* v. CUSTOMARY. लोकचालीचा, जनरूढीचा, लोकसिद्ध, लौकिक, जनाचारसिद्ध, व्यवहारसिद्ध, बहुमत.

2 *observant, &c. of the mode.* सभ्यसंप्रदायाचा, सभ्यरीतीचा, शिष्टसंप्रदायाचा, &c. सभ्यसांप्रदायिक, सभ्यसंप्रदायानुयायी, सभ्यरीत्यनुसारी, सभ्यसंप्रदायावलंबी.

To FAST, *v. n. go without food.* अन्नावांचून-अन्नावेगळा-अन्नानिराळा-&c. असणें-राहणें, उपास*m.*-अनशन*n.*-अनाहार*m.*- &c. करणें *and* असणें-घडणें *in. con.* अन्नवर्जन*n.* करणें.

To sink and form hollows—the flanks and belly from fasting. खपाटें *n. pl.*-खपाट्या *f. pl.*-भकाटें*n. pl*-&c. बसणें, पोट*n.* भकाटीस *or* भकाळीस जाणें, पोटाला भकाळी*f.*पडणें, पोटाची भकाळी *f.* होणें.

2—religiously. उपास*m.*-उपवास*m.*-उपोषण*n.*-&c.करणें.

3—dietetically. लंघन*n.* करणें.

FAST, FASTING, *n.* v. V. 1.—*act.* अन्नावांचून राहणें*n.* अनशन*n.* अनाहार*m.* निरशन*n.* अन्नवर्जन *n.*

2 उपास*m.* उपवास*m.* उपोषण*n.* निराहार*m.* निराहारव्रत*n.*अनशनव्रत*n.* निरशनव्रत *n.* रोजा *m.* (among Muhammadans).

3 लंघन*n.*

Breaking of a f. पारणें*n.* पारणा *f.* पारण*n. v.* फेड, कर.

Fastings and austerities, compreh. उपास आनास *m.* उपासतापास *m.*

F. and eating on alternate days. धारण पारण *or* धारणें पारणें *n.*

F.-day. *a Banyan or hungry day.* फांका *or* फाका*m.*

F. to death. प्रायोपवेशन*n.*—That is fasting to death. प्रायोपविष्ट.

Rigid or utter f. निश्चक्र उपोषण*n.* निरशन*n.* निराहार उपास*m.*

FAST, *a. fixed, firm, tight.* घट्ट, ठाम, ठास, अंवळ, अढळ, अचल, काईम, स्थिर.

To play fast and loose. धरसोड *f.* करणें.

2 (a color) पक्का, करारी.

3 (of sleep) v. SOUND. गाढ, निबिड.

4 v. SWIFT. जलद, जलदीचा.

FAST, *adv. fixedly, firmly.* घट्ट, गच्च, गळपट, दाट, पच्ची, बळकट, बळकटून, मजबूत *or* द, खच्च, दृढ.

F. asleep. गाढ-घुरघूस-&c. निजलेला.

To sit f. *press together.* सेटणें.

2 *swiftly,* v. QUICKLY. लौकर, जलद, वेगी.

F. by. See NEAR.

FAST-DAY, *n.* उपवासाचा-उपोषणाचा-&c. दिवस *m.*उपोषणदिन*m.n.*

FAST-HANDED, *a.* v. MISERLY. हाताचा जड, बद्धमुष्टि.

To FASTEN, *v. a. make fast,*—gener. बांधणें, बळकट-घट्ट-दृढ-मजबूत-&c. करणें, नहालेसा-ननिवेसा-नउघडेसा-&c. करणें, खिळणें, गांठणें.

2 *make fast to, tie up, &c.* v. To TIE. बांधून टाकणें, गोवणें, जखडणें *or* जखडून बांधणें, जवकणें *or* जवकून बांधणें, तांगडणें, गबसून टाकणें.

3 up; *secure by closing, locking, bolting, &c.* लावणें, लावून गच्च करणें, लावून बंदोबस्त करणें.

4 together; v. To LINK. सांगडणें, गांठणें, बांधणें.

To FASTEN, *v. n. fix one's self.* चिकटून-बिलगून-झोंबून-&c. धरणें-राहणें.

FASTENED, *p.* v. V. A. 1. बांधलेला, घट्ट केलेला, &c. खिळींव.

2 जखडलेला, जखडून बांधलेला, &c.

FASTENING, *n.* v. V. 1.—*act.* बांधणें *n.* &c. खिळण *f.* बंधन *n.*

I. *that binds or fastens.* बंधन *n.*

FASTER, *n.* FASTING, *p.a.*v.V.1. अन्नावांचून राहणारा, &c. उपासी, उपवासी, उपोषित, अनाहारी, अभुक्त.

2 उपासकर *or* करी, उपोषित, उपोषण-&c. कर्त्ता, निराहारी, अनशनी, अनशनव्रती.

FASTIDIOUS, *a. squeamish, nice,* v. DAINTY. कंटाळखोर, खंतखोर, खोडकर, मिजाजखोर, मिजाजी, चोखनळ, चोखारी, चोखांदळा, सोंगळ, सोड्याळ, तिटकारी, तिरस्कारी, चिळसखोर, चिळसी.

FASTIDIOUSNESS, *n.* v. A. मिजाज *f.* मिजाजखोरी *f.* नाजकाई *f.* सोंगळपणा *m.* &c. [बुदी *f.*

FASTNESS, *n.* v.A. 1. गच्चपणा *m.* घट्टपणा *m.* &c. बळकटी *f.* मज-

2 पक्केपणा *m.* &c.

3 गाढपणा *m.* &c.

4 जलदी *f.*

FASTNESS. See FORT, CASTLE.

FAT, *a. having fat, plump, fleshy.* पुष्ट, परिपुष्ट, मेदस्वी, पीन, पीवा, पीवर, मांसभरू, मांसल *pop.* मासाळ, मांसपुष्ट, मांसशील, मांसभरित, मेदोवृद्ध, दुलदुलीत, गबगबीत *or* गुबगुबीत, दुमदुमीत, तुंद, ताजालठ, खुराकाचा, दुहेरी पासोळीचा, दुहेरीहाडाचा, —reproachfully, with the power of *gross, bloated, corpulent, bulky and flabby, full-fed and sluggish.* कापशा, धोनशा, पोंधा, फोपशा, पोशा, पोस्ती *or* पोस्त्या, फेंदू, भस भोंगळ, ढमाल *or* ढमाल्या, ढोण्या, गदेल्या, मस्त, झोजा, नेभळा, वृथापुष्ट. Appellatives or designations involving this sense and implication, and thus answering to *fatty, porpoise, pig, stalled-ox, barrel-belly, tun, butt, &c.* are धूड *n.* ढोणसकड *n.* ढोण *n.* ढेर *f.* अगडबंब, अगडधू, बोका, बोंगा, मोधळा, दुड्या, भोपळ्यारोगी, पेजपात्र, पोंथा, लोथ, लोधा, लोधडा, आधोड, शेणपा, ढब्बू, तोलंबा, अचळोजी, अचळोचा.

F. and happy. साळाधाला, तुष्टपुष्ट, हृष्टपुष्ट, तुंद.

To become f. and flabby. कापूस *m.* सवंगकरणें, कापूस *m.* सस्ताहोणें *g. of s.* कापुसणें, बेंबीचें उखळ *n.* होणें *g. of s.* मेण*n.* चढणें *g. of s.*

To get f. पोसणें.

To get f. and saucy. माजणें, मातणें.

2 *oily, unctuous, rich, &c.* चिकण, स्निग्ध, स्नेही, स्नेहाळ.

3—of soil. चिकण, चिकणवट.

FAT, *n.* चरबी *f.* मांदें *n.* मेद *m.* वसा *f.* मांससार *m.* मांसतेज *n.* मांसस्नेह *m.* स्नेह *m.*

To FAT. See To FATTEN.

FAT-WITTED, *a.* v. STUPID. घृतबुद्धि, मंदबुद्धि, जेनबुद्धि.

FATA MORGANA, *n.* गंधर्वनगर *n.* गंधर्वसृष्टि *f.*

FATAL, *a. of or belonging to fate.* दैवाचा, दैविक, दैवसंबंधी, अदृष्टाचा, अदृष्टसंबंधी, दैवाधीन, अदृष्टाधीन, दैववश, दैवकृत, दैवहेतुक.

2 *mortal, killing,* v. DEADLY. जीवघेणा, प्राणघेणा, घातक, घातकी, प्राणघातक, प्राणघातकी, घातपरिणामक, नाशपरिणामक.

FATALISM, *n. the doctrine of inevitable necessity.* दैववाद *m.* प्रारब्धवाद *m.* दैवचिंता *f.* दैवकर्तृमत *n.* दैवचालकमत *n.* दैवकर्तृवाद *m.* दैवैकवाद *m.*

FATALIST, *n.* दैववादी, प्रारब्धवादी, अदृष्टवादी, दैष्टिक, दैवचिंतक, दैवपर, दैवकर्तृवादी, दैवैकवादी.

FATALITY, *n. invincible necessity.* दैवाधीनता *f.* दैवपरत्व*n.* दैवायत्तता *f.* दैववशता *f.*

2 See FATE.

FATALLY, *adv.* v. A. 1. दैवानें, दैवयोगानें.

2 नाश घडेसा, नाशहोईसा, नाशपर्यंत, नाशपरिणामक.

FATE, *n.* v. DESTINY. दैव*n.* दैवगति *f.* कर्म*n.* कर्मगति *f.* प्रारब्ध*n.* प्राक्तन*n.* प्राक्तनकर्म*n.* कृतांत*m.* काल*m.*

Drawn by one's f. दैवानें ओढवलेला, कालाकृष्ट.

Stroke of f. अपघात*m.*

Speech, promise, &c. as sure as f. ब्रह्मलेख*m.* ब्रह्मलिखित *n.* ब्रह्मरेखा *f.*

2 *appointment of destiny,* v. DESTINY. कपाळ*n.* कपाळरेषा *f.* दैवरेषा *or* रेखा *f.* दैवयोग*m.* घटित*n.*

FATE-CONTROLLED, *a.* दैववश, दैवाधीन, दैवायत्त.

FATED. See DESTINED.

FATHER, *n.* बाप*m.* पिता*m.* जनक*m.* जनिता*m.* ज्ञाति*m.* तात*m.*—as a compellation of respect. बाबा*m.* तीर्थरूप*m.* तीर्थ*n.* तीर्थपाद*m.* गुरु*m.* गुरुजन*m.*—familiarly, as PAPA, PA. बा.

House of one's f. पितृगृह*n.*

Like f. like son. यथापिता तथापुत्रः, यथाबीजं तथा अंकुरः, जसीखाण तसीमाती. [शिकवतो

The children are wiser than their fathers. आज्यास नातू

To FATHER, *v. a.* See To ADOPT.

2 *ascribe to one as his offspring.* बापपणा*m.* स्थापणें-दाखवणें, पितृत्वस्थापन*n.*-पितृत्वारोप*m.*-&c. करणें.

FATHER-IN-LAW, *n.* सासरा*m.* श्वशुर*m.*

Father of one's f. आजेसासरा*m.*

F. of one's son or daughter. विवाही *pop.* व्याही*m.*

Mother of one's f. आजेसासू *f.*

Sister of one's f. आतेसासू *f.*

The respectful compellation for f. (wife's father) is मामा; and (husband's father) मामाजी *or* मामंजी *used plurally.*

FATHER-HOOD, *n.* बापपणा*m.* पितृत्व*n.* जनकत्व*n.*

FATHER-LESS, *a. whose f. is dead.* बापपोरका, पितृहीन, मृतपितृक, गतपितृक.

2 *whose f. is not known.* निबाप्या, अपितृक.

Fatherly, *a.* बापासारखा, पितृवत्, पितृसदृश, पितृसमान.

Fathom, *n.*—the measure. व्यामm. *pop.* वांव *f. or* वोवाm.

To **Fathom**, *v. a. encompass with the arms.* कवळणें, कवटाळणें, वेंगणें.

2 *sound, try the depth.* ठावm.-तळm. पाहणें-मोजणें-लावणें-घेणें.

3 fig. *find the bottom of.* थांगm.-ठिकाणn.-ठिकाणाm.-शोधm. -&c. लावणें and *in. con.* लागणें. [लस्पर्श.

Fathomless, *a. bottomless.* अथाक, अथांग, बेठाव, अगाध, अत-

Fatigue, *n. weariness.* श्रमm. कष्टm. टणकm. भागवटाm. भागलीकf. शीणm. मांदगीf. श्रांतिf. परिश्रम m. ग्लानिf. क्लांतिf.आयासm.—generally or freely. शीणभागm.

2 *toil*, v. Labor. श्रमm. कष्टm.

To **Fatigue**, *v. a. weary*, v. To Tire. श्रमवणें, शिणवणें, थकवणें, दमवणें, भागवणें, टणकm.-शीणm.-भागवटाm.-&c. आणणें-देणें, श्रमी-कष्टी-&c. करणें, कंकातणें.

Fatigued, *p.* v. V. श्रमवलेला, &c. *or* श्रमलेला-शिणलेला-दमलेला -&c. श्रमी, कष्टी, मांदा, श्रांत, परिश्रांत, ग्लान, क्लांत.

To be f. v. To Tire. श्रमणें, कष्टणें, टणकणें, शिणणें, भागणें, हायास-मट्टयास येणें.

Fatness, *n.* v. A. 1. पुष्टि *f.* परिपुष्टि *f.* पुष्टता *f.* मेदोवृद्धि *f.* दुलदुलीतपणा *m.* गबगबीतपणा *m.* &c. मांसलत्व *n.*

2 चिकणाई *f.* चिकणपणा *m.* स्निग्धता *f.* स्नेह *m.* स्नेहाळपणा *m.*

To **Fatten**, *v. a.*v. A. 1. पोसवणें, पुष्ट-ताजा-दुलदुलीत-&c.करणें, भरवणें *or* आंगानें भरवणें.

To **Fatten**, *v. n.* पोसणें, आंगानें भरणें, आंगn.धरणें-घेणें, तरतरणें, तणसरणें, माजणें.

Fattener, *n.* **Fattening**, *p. a.* v. V. A. पुष्ट करणारा, पोसवणारा, &c. पौष्टिक, पुष्टिकारक-जनक-&c. बृंहण, मेदोवर्धक.

Fatuity, **Fatuousness**, *n.* v. A. चळ *m.* खूळ *n.* पिसें *n.* चित्तभ्रंश *m.* दुष्टबुद्धि *f.* दुर्बुद्धि *f.* दुर्मति *f.*

Fatuous, *a.* v. Foolish. खुळा, चळेल, नष्टबुद्धि.

Fauces, *n.* v. Throat. गळा *m.* कंठ *m.*

Dryness of f. कोरड *f.* कंठशोष *m.*

Fault, *n. defect, absence, default.*v. Want. अभावm. हीनताf.

2 *defect, imperfection, flaw.* दोष *m.* ऐब *m.* बिंग *or* बिंगें *n.* खोड *f.* कसर *f.* गुंजावीस *f.* व्यंग *n.* छिद्र *n.* गोम *f.* फांट *f. v.* घे, रध्र *n.*

To find f. v. To Blame. दोष *m.* देणें-काढणें-लावणें-ठेवणें-आणणें, खोडणें, खोड *f.* ठेवणें, दूषणें, बिंग *or* गें *n.* पाडणें-करणें, टूं *n.* ठेवणें.

3 *omission of duty, failure, neglect, &c.* अपराध *m.* अन्याय *m.* अन्याव *m.* दोष *m.* चूक *f.* चुकी *f.* तकसीर *f.* गुन्हा *m.* ढळ *m.* टळ *m.* खता *f.* गुंजावीस *f.* कसर *f.* कमतर *f.*अंतर *n.* तफावत *f.* क्षुद्रक *n.* क्षुल्लक *n.*

4 *ill quality, evil, vice.* दुर्गुणm.दुर्लक्षणn.ऐब *m.* खोड *f.*दोषm.

5 *mistake, blunder*, v. Error. चूक *dim.* चुकी *f.* अशुद्ध *n.*

6 *failing, foible, weakness.* उणें *n.* हीण *n.* छिद्र *n.* रंध *n.* वर्म *n.* मर्म *n.* छद्म *n.*

Fault, foibles, &c.—as ripped up or dragged to light. उखाळ्या पाखाळ्या *f. pl.* उखाळ्या *f. pl.v.* काढ, वर्मेंकर्में *or* कर्मेंवर्में *n. pl. v.* काढ, उच्चार, बोल, खुसपटें *n. pl. v.* काढ, कुरापती *f. pl. v.* काढ, कुरेंपिष्टें *n. pl. v.* काढ, सांग, कुरपृष्टें *n. pl.* कुळपटें *n. pl.* नालिस्ती *f. pl. v.* सांग, धुसकींफुसकीं *n. pl.* खोऱ्याळ *or* ळी *f. v.* काढ, कफावती *f. pl. v.* काढ, घे.

That is fond of spying out faults, v. Censorious. दोषदृष्टि, दोषदर्शी, छिद्रदर्शी, छिद्रान्वेषी, छिद्रानुसारी, रंधान्वेषी.

To bring up (against) one's faults, foibles, &c. खुसपटें *n. pl.* रचणें-मांडणें, नालिस्ती *f. pl.* सांगणें, कुचानिंदा *f.*-कुचानिंदी *f.*-कुचबिंध्या *f. pl.*-कुचाळकी *f.*-&c. करणें *g. of o.*

To expose or disclose one's secret faults. मर्मछेद *m.*-वर्मभेद *m.*-मर्मोद्घाटन *n.*-दोषोद्घाटन *n.*-दोषोद्घोष *m.*-दोषोद्भावन *n.*-&c. करणें, विदारण *n.*-विदारणी *f.*-बिचका *m.*-उखळबेरीज *f.*-टमटम नगरी *f.* करणें, पैशून्य *n.* काढणें, कुरापती *f. pl.*-खुसपटें*n. pl.*-छिद्रें *n. pl.*-मर्में *n. pl.*-छद्में *n. pl.* काढणें.

To watch for or spy out one's faults. पैशून्य *n.* पाहणें, रंधान्वेषण *n.*-छिद्रान्वेषण *n.* करणें, छिद्रें *n. pl.*-मर्में *n. pl.*-छद्में *n. pl.* पाहणें.

7 *puzzle.* See Perplexity. To be at f. थकणें, तरंगणें, कुंठित असणें, चक्री *f.* गुंग होणें-भुलणें.

Faultily, *adv.blunderingly.* चुकतचुकत, चुकतमाकत *or* वाकत.

Faultiness, *n.* v. A. 1. उणेपणा *m.* अपुरतेपणा *m.* &c. हीनता *f.* विकलता *f.* वैकल्य *n.* अंगवैकल्य *n.*

2 खोडकरपणा *m.* &c. दोष *m.* ऐब *m.* सदोषता *f.* सबाधता *f.*

3 अपराधीपणा *m.* &c. सदोषता *f.* सापराधता *f.* &c. दोष *m.* अपराध *m.*

4 कसर *f.* तफावत *f.*

Faultless, *a.* v. N. 1. *and* Complete. पुरता, पूर्ण, बिनकसर, निर्दोष, सांग, अन्यूनातिरिक्त.

2 *and* Perfect, Sound. बिनखोड, अखोड, निखोड, अव्यंग, निर्दोष, बिनऐब, निर्बाध, चोखाळ, नितोड, निकोप *or* पी, निर्दुष्ट, नखीं दोष नाहीं (purus, castus, &c. *ad unguem*).

3 *and* Innocent. निरपराध, अनपराध, अनपराधी, बिनअपराध, निर्दोष, निरत्यय.

Faultlessness, *n.* v. A. 1. पुरतेपणा *m.* पूर्णता *f.* निर्दोषता *f.*

2 बिनखोडपणा *m.* &c. बिनखोडी *f.* निर्दोषता *f.* दोषराहित्य *n.*

3 निरपराधपणा *m.* &c. निरपराधता *f.* &c. अपराधराहित्य *n.* दोषराहित्य *n.*

Faulty, *a.* v.N.1. *imperfect, incomplete, wanting*, v. Defective. उणा, कोता, अपुरता, अपूर्ण, हीन, बिकल, विकलांग, न्यूनांग, अंगहीन.

2 *having defects, imperfections, blemishes, flaws.* खोडकर, दोषवान्, सदोष, दोषी, दोषिक, दोषयुक्त, कसरीचा, तफावतीचा, सबाध, ऐबदार.

3 *guilty of faults*, v. Criminal. अपराधी, अन्यायी, सदोष, दोषी, सापराध.

4 *having ill qualities.* दुर्गुणी,-दुर्लक्षणी, अवगुणी, खोडील, खोडकर, खोडाळ, खोड्या, खोड्यारा, खोड्याळ, ऐबदार.

5 *having errors*, v. Erroneous. अशुद्ध, सदोष, अबद्ध.

Faun, *n.* कल्पित बनदेवतेची एक जात.

Favor, *n. kind regard, &c.* लोभ *m.* मेहरबानी *or* बानगी *f.* मेहर *f.* कृपा *f.* कृपादृष्टि *f.* कृपावलोकन *n.* अनुग्रह *m.* दृष्टि *f.* नजर *f.* मर्जी *f.* खुशमर्जी *f.* प्रसाद *m.* शिफारस *f.* हिमाईत *f.* कूर्मदृष्टी *f.*

F. and affection. दयामाया *f.*

Given as a token of f. प्रसादी, प्रासादिक *pop.* प्रसादिक,

In f. of—legal decision, &c. तरफेनें, बतीं *or* बतीनें,

Object of f. कृपापात्र *n.* कृपाभाजन *n.*
To creep into f. with. पोटांत शिरणें.
2 *a* f. *an act of kindness.* उपकार *m.* आभार *m.* असान *or* एहसान *n.* कृतोपकार *m.*
Return-f. प्रत्युपकार *m.*
To upbraid or taunt with favors. नेरेभार *m.* लावणें, तोंडीं काढणें, टेपर *m. n.*-टेपरण *n.* ठेवणें, अस्मारा *m.* टाकणें, उस्मा *or* उश्रामा *m.* करणें.
3 *token of f.* प्रसाद *m.* प्रीतिदान *n.*
4 v. PARTIALITY. तरफदारी *f.*

To FAVOR, *v. a. befriend, &c.* कृपा *f.*-मेहरबानी *f.*-&c. करणें, कृपादृष्टि *f.*-नजर *f.*-डोळा *m.*-&c. ठेवणें-करणें-देणें, हिमाईत *f.*-मदद *f.*-&c. देणें-करणें, पाठ *f.* राखणें *g. of o.* हात *m.* देणें, बाहिदारी *f.* करणें, अनुकूल-&c. होणें. [असणें.
2 *afford advantage.* सोई *f.* करणें-देणें, उपयोगी-उपकारी-&c.

FAVORABLE, *a. propitious, kind.* मेहरबान, अनुकूल, धारजणा- *or* जिणा, बहाल, प्रसन्न, सुप्रसन्न, उपकारी, अनुग्राही, सुमना *or* सुमनस्क, अभिमुख.
To become f.—fortune, &c. उघडणें, भरभरणें, मळमळणें, धारजण्यास येणें.
2 *promotive, helpful, &c.* v. CONDUCIVE. उपयोगी, उपकारक, उपकारी, उपयुक्त.
3—of planets, aspects, &c. v. AUSPICIOUS. इष्ट, अभीष्ट, अनुकूल, भद्रकारक, भद्रकारी, शुभ, शुभकर, सु in comp.

FAVORABLENESS, *n.* v. A. 1. प्रसन्नता *f.* सुप्रसन्नता *f.* आनुकूल्य*n.* अनुकूलता *f.* कृपा *f.* बहाली *f.* सौमनस्य*n.* आभिमुख्य *n.*
2 उपयोगीपणा*m.* उपकारिता *f.* उपयुक्तता *f.*
3 इष्टत्व*n.* आनुकूल्य*n.* बल *n.* (esp. in comp. as चंद्रबल, ताराबल, ग्रहबल, &c.) शुभ*n.* [&c. होऊन.

FAVORABLY, *adv.* v. A. 1.कृपेनें, मेहरबानीनें, &c. अनुकूल-प्रसन्न-

FAVORED, *p.* v.V.1. अनुगृहीत, आभारी, उपकृत, कृपापात्र, कृपाभाजन, प्राप्तानुग्रह, जातानुग्रह.
Ill-favored, v. UGLY. कुरूप, कुलक्षण.
Well-favored, v. HANDSOME. सुरूप, सुलक्षण.

FAVORER, *n.* v. V. 1. कृपा करणारा, कृपादृष्टि ठेवणारा, हिमाईत देणारा, &c. अनुग्रह-&c. कर्त्ता, अनुग्राहक, सुहृत् *or* द्.

FAVORITE, *a.* v. DARLING. आवडता, आवडीचा, लाडका, प्रिय,प्रीतीचा, प्रीतींतला.

FAVORITE, *n.*v. DARLING. कृपापात्र*n.* प्रीतिपात्र*n.* नाकाचाबाल *m.*
Discarded f. निर्माल्य*m. n.*

FAVORITSIM, *n. partiality.* तरफदारी *f.* पक्षपात*m.* प्रपंच*m.* न्यूनाधिकबुद्धि *f.*

FAWN, *n.*हरणाचेंपोर *n.* पाडस *n.*

FAWN-EYED, *a.* हरणडोळ्या, मृगनयन, कुरंगनयन, मृगनेत्र, मृगलोचन.

To FAWN, *v. n. cringe, make servile court, bow and scrape,* v. To FLATTER. जी *or* जीजी *interj.*-हांजी *interj.* करणें-म्हणणें, नाक*n.* घासणें, पुढच्यापुढें नाचणें, भजनीं *or* भजनास लागणें, आर्जवणें, थुंका*m. or* थुंकी *f.* झेलणें, तोंड*n.* चाटणें, आर्जव*n.*-लवण भंजन*n.*-नमोनमो *adv.* करणें.

FAWNER, *n.* FAWNING, *p. a.* v. V. जीजी करणारा-म्हणणारा-&c. आर्जवी, आर्जवू, आर्जवाचा, तोंडचाट्या, तोंडपुज्या.

FAWNING, *n.* v. V.—*act.* जीजी म्हणणें*n.* &c. जीजीपणा*m.* आर्जव *n.* थुंकी झेलणी *f.* तोंडपूजा *f.* तोंडपुजेपणा*m.* लवणभंजन*n.* नमोनमो करणें*n.* [&c.

FAWNINGLY, *adv.* v.V. आर्जवानें, आर्जवकरून, लवण भंजनकरून,

FEALTY, *n.* v. LOYALTY. प्रजाधर्म*m.* निमक हलाली *f.* स्वराजनिष्ठा *f.*

FEAR, *n. emotion excited by the apprehension of evil.* भय*n.* भीति *f.* त्रास*m.* दर*m.* वित्रास*m.* भी *f.*
Sudden f. See FRIGHT.
Through f. भेणें.
2 *dread, awe, reverence.* दबदबा*m.* दाब*m.* दबाव*m.* दरदरी*m.* दरारा*m.* दगदगा*m.* धास्त *or* धास्ती *f.* धडकी *f.* धाक*m.* धडकण *f.* हैबत *f.* दहशत *f.* जरब *f.* बचक*m.* बचका*m.* बाज*m.* चक*m.* दर्प*m.* जुमान*m.* जुमास*m.* जूम*m. v.* खा.
F. of man. लोकभय*n.* लोकभीति *f.* लोकलज्जा *f.* लोकलाज *f.* जनभीति *f.* जनलज्जा *f.*
3 *apprehension, misgiving, anxious anticipation.* शंका *f.* आशंका *f.* अंदेशा*m.* संशय*m.* वसवसा*m.* घोर*m.* धोका*m.* धासरा *or* धोसरा*m.* दहशत *f.* भेदरा*m.* हैबत *f.* बचक*m.* खत्ता *or* खतरा*m.*
To apply to the fears of. भय*n.* दाखवणें, भयप्रदर्शन*n.* करणें.

To FEAR, *v.a. apprehend, dread.* भिणें, भय*n.*-शंका *f.*-&c. असणें *g. of o. with in.con.* शंकणें, आशंकणें, वसवसा *m.* जाणें *in. con.* बचक *or* बचका*m.* खाणें-बाळगणें—and, *with in. con.* जाणें.
2 *stand in awe or dread of, care for, regard as reverend, formidable, &c.* भिणें, भय*n.*-धाक*m.*-धास्त *f.*-&c. धरणें-बाळगणें -खाणें, धास्त *f.*-धाक*m.*-&c. बसणें *g. of o. with in. con.* जुमानणें, -जुमानून असणें *neg. con.* जुमान*m.*-जुमास*m.*-जूम*m.* खाणें-पावणें, *with g. of o. and neg. con.* भिडावणें, बचकणें, बचकून असणें, बचक *or* बचका*m.* बाळगणें *with g. of o.* थरत *or* थरथरांभिणें.

To FEAR, *v. n. be afraid.* भिणें, भय*n.*-&c. असणें-वाटणें *in. con.* बचकणें, भिडावणें.

FEAR-STRICKEN, *a.* v. FRIGHTENED. भयचकित.

FEARED, *p.* v. V. A. 1. शंकित, आशंकित.

FEARFUL, *a. timorous, timid, apprehensive.* भितरा, भिकट, भिकूट, भेंकड *or* भेंकूड, भयाळू, भेजूड, भीरु, भिभिस्त, भिड्डड, भ्याट *or* भ्याड, भेड, भेदड, भेसूड, भयशील, भयस्वभाव, कातर.
2 *afraid,* v. FRIGHTENED. भयभीत, भययुक्त, सभय, जातभय, प्राप्तभय, शंकित, आशंकित, सशंक, साशंक, शंकामय.
3 *dreadful, frightful, formidable, tremendous, terrible, terrific, horrible, horrid.* अकटोविकट, अकराळ, विकराळ, अघोर, भयंकर, भयानक, विकट, विकराल, कराल, भैरव, दारुण, उग्र, रौद्र, भयावह, भयकारक, भयजनक, भेंसूर, भ्यासूर, त्रासकर-कारककारी, त्रासदायी, भीषण, भीम. [होऊन.

FEARFULLY, *adv.* v. A. 2. भिऊन, भयधरून, भयानें, भयभीत-&c.
3 धाक-भय &c. बसवायाजोगा *decl.*
I. See EXCESSIVELY.

FEARFULNESS, *n.* v. A. 1. भितरेपणा *m.* भ्याडपणा *m.* &c. भीरुता *f.* भयशीलता *f.* भयस्वभाव *m.* [भ्यालेपणा *m.*
2 *and* FEAR. भय *n.* भीति *f.* भयभीनपणा *m.* भयावस्था *f.*
3 अकराळपणा*m.* विकराळपणा*m.* भयानकत्व*n.* भयजनकत्व*n.*&c

FEARLESS, *a. intrepid,* v. BOLD. निर्भय, अभय, अभीरु, अशंक, बेपरवा. [अप्राप्तभय.
2 *not afraid.* बिनघोर, बिनधोक, विशंक, अशंक, अजातभय,

FEARLESSLY, *adv.* v. A.1. निर्भय, बेधडक, बेजरब, बेलाशक, बेबसवसा, बेचरक, निधड.
2 निर्भय, निश्शंक, बिनघोर, बिनधोक, निघोर *or* निर्घोर.

Fearlessness, *n.* v.1. निर्भयता *f.* अभीति *f.* अभीरुता *f.* भयराहित्य *n.* भयशून्यता *f.*

Feasibility, Feasibleness, *n.* v. A. घडायाजोगेपणा *m.* &c. करणीयता *f.* साध्यता *f.* &c. संभावना *f.* संभाव्यता *f.* घटनीयता *f.* ओल *f. n.* ओलावा *m.* ओलास्रा *m.* सौकर्य *n.* सौगम्य *n.*

Feasible, *a. practicable, &c.* घडाया-व्हाया-&c. जोगा-सारखा-&c. करायाजोगता-जोगा-&c. करणीय, घटनीय, साध्य, सवघड, सुकर, सुगम, गमनीय, संभावनीय, संभाव्य, सुलभ.

Feast, *n. treat, entertainment.* जेवणावळ *f.* मेजमानी *or* मेजवानी *f.* भोजनसमारंभ *m.* भोजनोत्सव *m.*

2 *day of rejoicing,* v. Festival. सण *m.* सणवार *m.* सणाचा दिवस *m.* पर्व *n.* [रणें-देणें.

To **Feast**, *v. a. entertain, treat.* मेजमानी *or* मेजवानी *f.* क-

2 *delight, gratify.* पारणें*n.* फेडणें, धणी *f.*-हौस *f.* पुरवणें*g.ofo.*

To **Feast**, *v. n. eat sumptuously.* गोडजेवण *n.*-उत्तम भोजन *n.* करणें, सण *m.*-दिवाळी *f.*-घमंडी *f.*-घमशान *n.*-चमचमाद *m.*-&c. करणें, धणंगणें, पात्र *n.* नाचवणें.

Feastful. See Festive. [*m.*

Feat, *n. exploit,* v. Deed. मात *f.* महत्‌कृत्य*n.* कृतकृत्य *n.*पराक्रम

Feather, *n.* पीस *m. n.* पिसारा *m.* पर *m.* पंख *m.* पिच्छ *n.*

Feathers. पिसारा *m.*

" Birds of a feather " एका माळेचेमणी *m. pl.*

F. of an arrow. पक्ष*m.* पिसारा*m.*

Stuff manufactured from feathers. पंखी *f.*

To get a f. in one's cap. तुरा *m.* लावणें.

Feathered, *a.* पिसाऱ्याचा, पिसांचा, सपक्ष, सपिच्छ, पिच्छिल.

Featherless, *a.* निपिसा, अपिच्छ, अपक्ष, अजातपक्ष.

Feathery, *a. like, &c. feathers.* पिसाऱ्या सारखा.

Feature, *n. lineament of the face.* रूपलक्षण *n.* रूपचिन्ह *n.* मुखलक्षण *n.* मुखचिन्ह *n.*

Features. तोंडवळण *n.* तोंडवळा *m.* तोंड घडण *f.* तोंड बाग *f.* मुखवटा *m.* चेहरा *m.* रूपरेषा *f.* रूपरेखा *f.* रूप *n.*

Featured, *a.* सुलक्षण, लक्षणयुक्त-विशिष्ट.

Bold-f. उदारलक्षण.

Ill-f. कुरूप, कुलक्षण.

Well-f. सुरूप, रूपवान्, सुलक्षण, चेहरेदार, चेहरेबाज.

Febrific, *a. causing fever.* ज्वरप्रद-दायक-जनक-कारक-&c.

Febrifuge, *a. subduing fever.* ज्वरनाशक, ज्वरघ्न, ज्वरांतक,ज्वरहंता, ज्वरापह, ज्वरहर-हर्त्ता-हारक-हारी.

Febrifuge, *n.* तापाचें-ज्वराचें औषध *n.* ज्वरनाशक-&c. औषध*n.*

Febrile, *a. of or belonging to fever.* तापाचा, ज्वराचा, ज्वरसंबंधी.

2 *indicating fever.* ज्वरसूचक, ज्वरदर्शक.

F. symptoms, v. Feverishness. कणकणी *f.*

February, *n.* इंग्रेजीवर्षाचा दुसरा महिना *m.*

Fecal, *a.* मळाचा, मलमय, पुरीषमय.

Feculence, *n. foulness, muddiness.* गढूळपणा *m.* रेंदाळपणा *m.* मलिनता *f.* कलुषता *f.* कालुष्य *n.*

2 *lees, dross, recrement,* v. Dregs, Dirt. मल *m. n. pop.* मळ *m.* गदळ *n.* गाळ *m.* रेंदा *m.* किट्ट *n.* रेंदगड *m.*

Feculent, *a.* v. N. गदळ, गढूळ, रेंदाड, रेंदाळ, गाळाचा, रेंद्याचा, &c. मलिन, समल, कलुषित, किट्टमय.

Fecund, &c. See Fruitful, &c.

Fed, *p.* v. V. 1. पोसलेला, पाळलेला, &c. पोषित, पुष्ट.

Federal, *a. pertaining, &c. to a league or compact.* कराराचा, संकेताचा, नियमाचा, समयसंबंधी, समयविषयक, सामयिक, सांकेतिक, सांविद.

Federary. Federate. See Confederate.

Fee, *n. fief, feud.* कुणबावा*m.* ?

2 (as of office) *perquisite.* दस्तुरी *f.* हक्क*m.* For legal fees the word फी *f.* from the English is commonly used.

F. of a visiting physician. पायफोडणी *f.*

Retaining f.—of a wakil. सचकार*m.*

Fees. बालाई याफ्त *f.*

Fee-farm, *n.* मोकासा*m.* कुणबावा*m.*

To **Fee**, *v. a.* फी *f.*-&c. देणें.

Feeble, *a.* v. Weak. अशक्त, निर्बल, दुर्बल, कमजोर, कमकुवत, शक्तिक्षीण, हलका.

Feeble-minded, *a.* हलकेबुद्धीचा, उणेबुद्धीचा, कोवळयाबुद्धीचा, बुद्धीचा हलका-दुर्बल-जड-&c.

Feeble-tongued, *a.* जिव्हेचा जड, अडव्याजिभेचा, मुखदुर्बल*or*ळ.

Feebleness, *n.* v. A. कमजोरी *f.* अशक्तता *f.* दुर्बलता *f.* निर्बलता *f.* शक्तिक्षीणता *f.*

Feebly, *adv.* दुर्बलतेनें, दौर्बल्यानें, कमजोरीनें, &c. हलका *a. decl.*

To **Feed**, *v.a.* खायाला घालणें-देणें, पोसणें, पाळणें, पोषणें,अन्न*n.* देणें, खाऊं-जेवूं घालणें, पालनपोषण*n.*-&c. करणें *g. of o.*

To f. (child, &c.) by the hand or with a spoon. भरविणें.

2 (cattle, &c.) *administer food.* चारणें, चारा*m.* घालणें-देणें.

3 v.To Supply. पुरवणें, पुरवणूक *f.*-&c. करणें *g. of o.*

To **Feed**, *v. n. subsist by eating.* खाणें, चरणें, जीवन*n.* करणें-पावणें, पोट*n.* भरणें, आहार *m.* करणें *with g. of o.* (also in comp. as दुग्धाहार-फलाहार-&c. करणें), उपजीवन*n.*-उपजीविका *f.*-&c. करणें *with* वर *or* नें *of o.*

Feed, Feeding, *n.* v. V. A. 1.—*act.* पोसणें*n.* &c. पोषण*n.* पाळणूक *f.* पालन *pop.* पाळण*n.*

v. V. N. 1. खाणें *n.* आहार*n.* (in comp. as अन्नाहार, फलाहार, धान्याहार, दुग्धाहार, मत्स्याहार, मांसाहार, तृणाहार, अल्पाहार, मिताहार).

I. See Food.

II. (of horses, camels, &c.) *regular allowance.* चंदी *f.* रतीब *or* रातीब *m.*

Feeder, *n.* v. A. V. 1. पोसणारा, खायाला घालणारा, &c. पालणवाला, पोषक, अन्नदाता.

v. V. N. खाणारा, आहारी (in comp. as अन्नाहारी, फलाहारी, धान्याहारी, दुग्धाहारी, मत्स्याहारी, मांसाहारी, तृणाहारी, अल्पाहारी, मिताहारी-&c.), जीवी (in comp. as अन्नजीवी, मांसजीवी, &c.), उपजीवी (in comp. as अन्नोपजीवी, &c.).

To **Feel**, *v. a. perceive by the touch.* स्पर्शणें, स्पर्श*m.* करणें,स्पर्शज्ञान*n.*-&c. होणें *in.con. with g. of o.* स्पर्शेंद्रियानें-स्पर्शेंद्रियद्वारा-&c. समजणें.

To f. the pulse. नाडी *f.* पाहणें.

3 *try by the touch, press and squeeze, &c.* चापणें, चाचपणें, चापसणें, चापसून-चाचपून-&c. पाहणें, रांपणें.

To be feeling one's way; *to beat about the bush.* चांचपडणें, चांचपणें, चापणें, चांचपडत जाणें-बोलणें.

3 *have perception or sensation of.* वाटणें *in. con.* समजणें *in. con.* सोसणें, भोगणें, अनुभव*m.*-&c.होणें *g. of o. with in. con.*

4 (mentally) *be affected by.* घेणें, मानणें, जुमानणें, लागू पडणें *in. con.* भिनणें *in. con.* ठसणें.

To FEEL, *v. n. have perception by the touch.* स्पर्श *m.* कळणें-समजणें-&c. *in. con.* स्पर्शज्ञान *n.*-&c. होणें *in. con.*

2 *appear to the touch.* स्पर्शास वाटणें-लागणें *in. con.* वाटणें, लागणें.

3 *have perception mentally.* वाटणें, लागणें, भासणें, समजणें *all with in. con.*

To f. well. जिवास बरें वाटणें *in. con. with g. of s.* समाधान *n.*- &c. वाटणें.

To f. pleasant or agreeable to. भावणें *in. con.*

To f. sore. बरमणें.

4 *have sensibility excited.* द्रवणें, पाझरणें, कळवळणें, द्रव *m.*-पान्हा *m.*-कळकळ *f.*-कळवळ *f.*-कळकळा *m.*-&c. येणें.

FEEL, FEELING, *n. sense of feeling,* v. TOUCH. स्पर्श *m.* स्पर्शेंद्रिय *n.* त्वगिंद्रिय *n.*

2 *sensation, effect of perception.* ज्ञान *n.* समज *m.* बोध *m.* वेदना *f.* कलना *f.* स्पर्शज्ञान *n.* स्पर्शबोध *m.*

3 *sensibility, susceptibility.* कन्हवाळूपणा *m.* करुणा *f.* दया *f.* करुणार्द्रता *f.* द्रव *m.* पाझर *m.* कळवळा *m.*

To force f. खाजवून पान्हा *m.* आणणें.

4 *emotion, passion,* v. SENTIMENT. भाव *m.* रस *m.* मनोधर्म *m.* मनोवृत्ति *f.*

FEELERS, *n.*—tentacula of animals. मिशी *f.*

FEELING, *a. sensible, susceptible.* हृदयवान्, हृदयालु, सहृदय, करुणामय, करुणार्द्र, कन्हवाळू, कोंवळ्या मनाचा, मनाचा कोंवळा, कोमलमनस्क, नवनीतमनस्क, कोमलांतःकरण.

2 *expressive of feeling.* कळकळ आणायाजोगा, कळवळयाचा, करुण, कारुणिक, कारुण्याचा, करुणात्मक, करुणापर, करुणारसप्रधान.

FEELINGLY, *adv.* v. N. 3. करुणापूर्वक, दयापूर्वक.

To FEIGN, *v. a.* v. To INVENT. कल्पिणें, रचणें, योजणें.

2 *make show of, pretend, sham.* गतक *n.*-सोंग *n.*-ढोंग *n.*-मीस *n.*-कोंग *n.*-बहाणा *m.*-&c. करणें-घेणें *g. of o.* हूल *f.*-धोप *f.*-डौल *m.*-&c. दाखवणें.

FEIGNED, *p.* v. V. 1. रचलेला, &c. कल्पित, मनःकल्पित, आहार्य.

2 गतक केलेला, &c. गतकाचा, सोंगाचा, मिसाचा, हुलीचा, हुलकावणीचा, &c.

FEIGNEDLY, *adv.* v.A. 2. सोंगानें, मिसानें, &c. सोंगाचा *decl.* &c.

FEIGNER, *n.* v. V. 1. कल्पिणारा, रचणारा, &c. कल्पक, रचक, योजक. [गतक्या, गतकाळ्या.

2 गतक घेणारा, &c. ढोंगी, मिसखोर, मिसकरा, कोंगी, कोंग्या,

FEIGNING, *n.* v.V. 1.—*act.* कल्पिणें *n.* रचणें *n.*&c. आहार्यारोप *m.*

2 *and* FEINT. गतक घेणें *n.* सोंग घेणें *n.* &c.

FEINT, *n. pretence, sham.* ढोंग *n.* मिष *pop.* मीस *n.* कोंग *or* कोंघ *n.* हिल्ला *m.* गतक *n.* हूल *f.* हुलकावणी *f. v.* दाखव, छल *m.* अपदेश *m.*

2 *mock stroke, &c.* चमक *f.* पेच *m.* हूल *f.* हुलकावणी *f. v.* दाखव, हुणूक *f. v.* दाखव, दावल *f. v.* दाखव, धोप *f.*

Feints. डावपेंच *m. pl.*

To FELICITATE, *v. a. make happy.* सुखी-&c. करणें.

2 See To CONGRATULATE.

FELICITOUS, FELICITY. See HAPPY, HAPPINESS.

FELINE, *a. belonging, &c. to cats.* मांजराचा, वैडालिक, विडालजातीय. [दय.

FELL, *a. savage, &c.* v. CRUEL. क्रूर, निर्दय, उग्र, दारुण, मांगहृ-

FELL, *n.* See HIDE.

To FELL, *v. a. cause to fall.* पाडणें, पाडून टाकणें, तोडणें, तोडून टाकणें, निजवणें, जमीनदोस्त करणें.

FELLNESS, *n.* v. A. क्रूरता *f.* क्रौर्य *n.* उग्रता *f.* &c.

FELLOE, See FELLY.

FELLOW, *n. associate, companion, consort, comrade, partner, &c.* सोबती, संगति *pop.* संगती *or* संगाती, साथी, भाऊ *m.* बंधु *m.* गडी, सलगी, संगवयी, सवंगडा, सवंगडी, सहाय, सचिव, भिडतू *m.* पंक्तीचा.

2 *equal, peer,* v. MATCH. बराबरचा, तोड *f.* जोडा *m.* भाऊ *m.* & बहीण *f.* are constantly used in the sense.

3 *one of a pair.* जोडा *m.* यमल, यम.

This is (his, her, its) f. (in lying, folly, villany). हा त्याचा भाऊ (*or* ही त्याची बहीण), त्याच्या पायासीं हा बांधावा.

4 *person, body, hand, one*;—familiarly. गडी *m.* माणूस *m.* *n.* भाई *m.*

Bold and heroic f. मर्दगाजी *m.* मर्द *m.* मर्दमाणूस *m.*

Fellows—compreh. *chaps, hands.* गडीमाणूस *m. pl.*

Fine (splendid, dashing, &c.) f.—ironic. उजेडाचा माणूस *m.*

Some f. or other. गवत्या गोमाजी.

Some fellows, some half dozen fellows or other. अलबते गलबते *m. pl.* गवते गोमाजी *m. pl.* गोमाजी सोमाजी *m. pl.* साळकोजी माळकोजी *m. pl.* साळके गोळके *m. pl.* ऐगू बैगू *m. pl.* अलते भलते *m. pl.*

You f. अरे.

5 *rascal, vagabond, dog*;—revilingly. सुडका *m.* सुडकें *n.*

6 *wight, wretch, &c.*—compassionately. बापडा, बिचारा.

7 (of a college, &c.) फेलो from the English. सभासद. [&c.

Fellow is expressed in composition by स, सह, सम, एक,

FELLOW-STUDENT, FELLOW-SCHOLAR, *n.* गुरुबंधु *m.* गुरुभाऊ *m.* सहाध्यायी, सतीर्थ्य, सतीर्थ.

FELLOW-SUFFERER, *n.* एकदुःखी, समदुःखी.

FELLOWSHIP, *n. companionship, &c.* सोबत *f.* संगत *f.* साथ *f.* संग *m.* सहवास *m.* साहाय्य *n.* साचिव्य *n.* अनुषंग *m.* साहचर्य *n.* साहित्य *n.*

2 (of table). पंक्ति *pop.* पंगत *f.* एकपंक्ति *or* एकपंगत *f.* पंक्तिव्यवहार *m.* भोजनव्यवहार *m.* अन्नव्यवहार *m.*

Fit for f. पंक्तीचा.

To admit into f. पंक्तीस घेणें.

To hold f. with. पंक्तीस बसणें *g. of o.*

3—in arithm. सर्कत *f.* सर्कतवांटणी *f.*—Single f. एकेरीसर्कत *f.* Double f. दुहेरीसर्कत *f.*

4 (in a college, &c.) फेलोची जागा *f.*-पदवी *f.*-नेमणूक *f.*

FELLY, *n.*—of a wheel. अढकड *n.* वांक *or* वाक *n.* पाटा *m.* Cord connecting over a gap two fellies. वांकाळा *m.*

FELON, *n. one guilty of felony.* अततायी, उत्तमसाहसापराधी, उत्तमसाहसी, महापराधी, वधोद्यत, साहसिकापराधी.

2 See WHITLOW. [चा.

FELONIOUS, *a.* v. WICKED. पापबुद्धीचा, पापवासनेचा, पापसंकल्पा-

FELONY, *n. capital or heavy crime.* आततायीपणा *m.* साहस *n.*

साहसिकापराध *m.* उत्तमसाहसापराध *m.* घोरसाहस *n.*

Felt, *n.* जेन *or* जीन *n.* बुरणस *or* बुरणूस *m.* नमदा *m.*

A piece of f. छाप *f.*

Made of, belonging to, &c. f. बुरणुसी.

To form (roll out) f. जेन *n.*-बुरणूस *m.* लाटणें.

Female, *n.* v. Woman. स्त्री *f.* बायकोमाणूस *f.* बाईलमाणूस *f.* रांडमाणूस *f.* स्त्रीजन *m.* अंगना *f.* अंगनाजन *m.*

2 (of animals or plants). मादी *f.* बायको *f.* स्त्री *f.* महिला *f.*

Female, *a. not male*,—noting sex. स्त्रीजातीचा, स्त्रीजातीय, स्त्रीव्यक्तिक, स्त्रैण.

2 *belonging to woman*, v. Feminine. स्त्रीचा, बायकोचा, स्त्रीजातीचा, स्त्रीजातिसंबंधी, स्त्रीजातिविषक.

F. code. बायकांचें शास्त्र *n.*

The F. sex. स्त्रीजात *f.* बायकांची जात *f.*

Feminality, *n. female nature.* बायकोपणा *m.* स्त्रीत्व *n.* स्त्रीधर्म *m.* स्त्रीभाव *m.* [जनानी, स्त्रैण.

Feminine, *a.*—noting sex. स्त्रीजातीचा, स्त्रीजातीय, स्त्रीव्यक्तिक, 2 *belonging, &c. to woman.* स्त्रीचा, स्त्रीजातीचा, स्त्रीसंबंधी, स्त्रीजातिसंबंधी, स्त्रैण, जनानी, स्त्रीवत्.

3—in grammar. स्त्रीलिंग, स्त्रीलिंगक. [ऊरुगत.

Femoral, *a. belonging to the thigh.* मांडीचा, ऊरुसंबंधी, ऊरुस्थ,

Fen, *n. marsh, &c.* पाणथळ *n.* पाणदळ *n.* पाणथर *n.* झिलाण *n.* दलदल *f.* अनूपभूमि *f.*

Fence, *n. guard against*,—gener. आवरण *n.* आवार *m.* निवारक *n.* निवारणोपाय *m.* निवारणसाधन *n.*

2 *hedge, paling, &c.* कुपण *n.* वई *or* वही *or* वै *f.* कुडण *n.* कुंप *m.* आडा *m.* आवरण *n.* आवार *m.* आडकूट *or* आडकूड *n.* वेष्टन *n.* परिघ *m.*

Dividing f. अंतर वही *f.*

Gap in a f. बोळक *m.*

To **Fence**, *v. a. secure by a fence.* कुपण *n.*-कुडण *n.*-वही *f.*-&c. घालणें-घालून राखणें, कुडणें.

2 See To Guard.

To **Fence**, *v. n. play with foils, &c. at attack and defence.* दांडपट्टा *m.* खेळणें, शस्त्राभ्यास *m.*- शस्त्रक्रीडा *f.*-&c. करणें.

Fencer, *n.* v. V. N. दांडपट्टा खेळणारा, दांडपट्टेवाला, पट्टाईत.

Practising stick of a f. दांड *m.* गदगी *f.* [&c.

Fencing, *n.* v. V. A.—*act.* कुडणें *n.* कुडण *n.* कुपण घालणें *n.*

Price or cost of f. कुडणावळ *f.*

v. V. N.—*act.* दांडपट्ट्याचाखेळ *m.* शस्त्रक्रीडा *f.*

To **Fend**, *v. a. keep off*, v. To Ward. वारणें, निवारणें.

Fender, *n.*—of a fire place. चुलीची पाळ *f.*

Fennel, *n.*—sweet. बडीशोप *f.*

F.—seed. कृष्णजीरक *m.*

Having the smell of f.—mangoes, &c. मिरमिरा.

Fenny, *a. marshy, &c.* पाणथळाचा, पाणवळाचा, अनूप.

Fenugreek, *n.* मेथी *f.*

F.-water. मेथवणी *n.*

Sweet-meat of seed of f. मेथोडा *m.*

Ferine. See Savage, Wild.

To **Ferment**, *v. n. work, effervesce.* घुमणें, चिबचिबणें, उमळणें, *impers.* उनणें, खतखतणें, करणें, फणफणणें, फिणफिणणें, फिदफिदणें, फदफदणें, उफणणें.

Ferment. See Heat, Agitation.

Fermentation, *n.* v. V. घुमणें *n.* &c. उमाळा *m.* पाक *m.*

F. of dough, &c. खमीर *m.*

Fern, *n.* नेचा *m.* नेचरी *f.*

Ferocious, *a.* v. Fierce, Cruel. क्रूर, उग्र, उग्रबागरा, दारुण, कजाख, हिंसालु, हिंसक, हिंस्र, व्याघ्रमुख, आसुर.

Ferociousness, **Ferocity**, *n.* v. A. क्रूरपणा *m.* उग्रपणा *m.* उग्रता *f.* क्रूरता *f.* क्रौर्य *n.* दारुणता *f.* [लोह.

Ferreous, *a. made, &c. of iron.* लोखंडाचा, लोखंडी, लोहमय,

Ferret, *n.* एक लहान जनावर आहे.

To **Ferret out**, *v. a. hunt and search for.* हुडकून-शोधून-उकरून-खणून-&c. काढणें.

Ferriage, *n. fare at a ferry.* उतार *m.* उतारा *m.* उतरणावळ *f.*

Ferruginous, *a. partaking, &c. of iron.* लोखंडाचा, लोखंडी, लोहविशिष्ट, लोहधर्मक.

Ferrule, *n. ring round a stick, &c.* वसू *dim.* वसवी *f.* मांडळ *f.* विडी *f.* मायणी *f.*

To **Ferry**, *v. n.* पार करणें *or* तरी पार करणें-नेणें, उतरणें.

Ferry, *n. passage to be crossed.* तर *f.*

2 *ferry-boat.* तर *f.*

Ferry-boat, *n.* तर *f.*

F. ferrying gratuitously. धर्मनाव *f.* धर्मनौका *f.*

Ferry-man, *n.* उतारी *m.* उताऱ्या *m.* ताऱ्या *m.* तऱ्या *m.*

Fertile, *a. producing abundantly.* पिकाऊ *or* व, पिकाचा *or* फारपिकाचा, उत्पन्नाचा, बहुपिकी, सुपीक, सुपिकी, हरपिकी, बहुसस्य, बहुसस्योत्पादक, बहुफलदायक, बहुप्रसव.

F. soil. उर्वरा *f.*

2 See Inventive, Ingenious.

Fertileness, **Fertility**, *n.* v. A. 1. पिकाऊपणा *m.* सुपीकपणा *m.* &c. बहुसस्यत्व *n.* उर्वरात्व *n.* बहुसस्योत्पादकत्व *n.* बहुप्रसवत्व *n.* [*m.*-&c. आणणें.

To **Fertilize**, *v. a.* पिकाचा-सुपीक-बहुसस्य-&c. करणें, पिकाऊपणा

Ferule, *n.*—of schoolmasters. थापटी *f.*

Fervency, **Fervor**, **Fervidness**, *n.* v. A. 1. उष्णता *f.* तलखाई *f.* तिखटाई *f.* तलखली *f.* तीव्रता *f.* तीक्ष्णता *f.*

2 उदमेख *m.* तलखली *f.* हौस *f.* उत्साह *m.* उत्कंठा *f.* औत्सुक्य *n.*

Fervent, **Fervid**, *a. hot, vehement*, v. Ardent. उष्ण, तलख, तलखल्या, तिखट, तीव्र, तीक्ष्ण, चंड, प्रचंड.

2 *eager, warm, impassionate*, v. Earnest. उदमेखी, उत्सुक, उत्साही, हौसदार, पोटागीचा, तिडकीचा, कळकळीचा, सोत्साह.

Fervently, *adv.* v. A. 2. उत्कंठेनें, उत्सुकतेनें, औत्सुक्यपूर्वक, हौशीनें, मनापासून, तलखलीनें.

Festal, **Festival**, **Festive**, *a.* सणाचा, सणसुदीचा, सोहळ्याचा, उत्सवाचा, उत्सवाविषयींचा, सणाविषयींचा, &c. उत्सवसंबंधी, शुभ, मांगलिक.

F. occasion.—as a marriage, &c. कारण *n.* कार्य *n.* प्रयोजन *n.* निमित्त *n.* शुभकर्म *n.* शुभकार्य *n.* मंगलकार्य *n.* मंगल *n.* मांगल्य *n.* मांगलिक *n.* सोहळा *m.* सोहाळा *m.* मंडन *n.* शोभन *n.* लग्नकार्य *n.* लग्नमुहूर्त *m.* वीध *f.*

F. rite or act,—gener. सोहळा *m.* सुखसोहळा *m.*

Presents (articles of apparel) upon f. occasions. आहेर *m.* Suitable to be given as such. आहेराऊ, आहेरी.

To **Fester**, *v. n. rankle, grow virulent*,—a scratch, &c. चिडणें,

चरणें.

2 fig.—mentally. सलणें, खुपणें.

FESTIVAL, n. *feast, festive occasion*, v. HOLYDAY. सणm. सणवारm. सणाचा दिवसm. निमित्तn. प्रयोजन n. कारण n. सोहळा *or* सोहाळाm. पर्वn. पर्वणी *f.* पर्वदिवसm. उत्साहm. उत्साव *or* उत्सव m. उत्साहाचा दिवसm.—of Muhammadans, ईद *f.*

F. with illuminations. दीपोत्सवm.

Flowers, sweetmeats, &c. distributed at the close of a religious f. महाप्रसादm.

Great f. *or* great rejoicings. महोत्सवm. महोत्साहm.

Money, &c. given to dependents at a f. पोस्तm.n.

Presents (to Bráhmans) at a f. देकारm.

Solar f. सूर्यपर्वn.

FESTIVITY, n. See FESTIVAL.

2 *social rejoicing*. उत्साहm. उत्सवm. आनंदउत्साहm.

FESTOON, n.—in architecture. वेलबुटी *f.* वेलबूट *or* बुट्टाm.

To FETCH, v. a. v. To BRING. जाऊन आणणें, आणणें.

2 *bring as its price*. किंमत *f.* येणें *in. con.*

3 See To REACH.

FETCH, n. *trick*, v. ARTIFICE. डावपेचm.

FETE CHAMPETRE, n. रानजेवणn. वनभोजनn.

FETID, a. v. STINKING. वासट, वाशेळा, घुरट, दुर्गंधी.

FETIDNESS, FETOR, n. v. STINK. घाण *f.* घुरटाण *f.* घुरष्टाण *f.* ओरढाण *f.* दौर्गंध्यn. दुर्गंधm. पूतिगंधm.

FETLOCK, n. नेवराचे केशm. *pl.* किंवा ते असतात तीजागा *f.*

FETTER, n. *chain for the feet*. बिडी *f.* अर्गला *or* ळाm. निगडm.n. पादबंधनn.

To FETTER, v. a. v. N. बिडी *f.*-&c. घालणें.

2 See To CLOG.

FETUS, FETAL. See FŒTUS, FŒTAL.

FEUD, n. *contention, &c.* तडm. तटm. कलहm. भांडणn.

To be the occasion of a f.—a matter. तडास-तटास लागणें.

Family f. कुटुंबकलहm. गृहकलहm.

2 *fief, fee*. मोकासाm. कुणबावाm.

FEUDAL, a. *held, &c. in fee*. मोकाशाचा, जाहगिरीचा.

FEUDARY, FEUDATORY, n. मोकासी, मोकासदार, जाहागीरदार.

A feudatory prince or chieftain. सामंतm.

FEVER, n. तापm. ज्वर *vulg.* जरm. जाळm.

Ardor of f. तापाचा लाहडाm.

Bilious f. पित्तज्वरm.

Cold fit of a f. हिंव *or* हींव n.

Common f. प्राकृत ज्वर m.

Eruptions after f. तापउतणें n. जर उतणें n.

F. ascribed to vitiation of the *bile*. पित्तज्वर ;—of the humour *phlegm*, कफज्वर ;—of the humour *wind*, वातज्वर; —of the three humours, त्रिदोषात्मक ज्वर, सन्निपातज्वर—of the bile and air, पित्तवात ज्वर; —of the bile and phlegm, पित्त कफ ज्वर.

F.—petechial or putrid. वेडामधुरा m.

F.—quartan. त्र्याहिकज्वर, तिजारें n.

F.—quintan. चातुर्थिक ज्वर.

F.—quotidian. ऐकाहिकज्वर.

F.—tertian. द्वयाहिकज्वर, दुजारें n.

F. seated in the bones. हाडजर m. हाडकुरकुटी *f.*

F. with ague. हिंवज्वर m. हिंवताप m. हुडहुडाजर m. हुडहुडाताप m. हिमज्वर m. शीतज्वर m. [जातज्वर.

F.—patient. F.—subject. तापकरी, जरकरी, ज्वरी, ज्वरित,

Hot paroxysm of f. तापाचा लाहडा m. ज्वराग्नि m.

Illusions of f. ज्वरसृष्टि *f.*

Inflammatory f. दाहज्वर m.

Intermittent f. अंतऱ्या ताप m. [*v.* ये.

Prostration of strength in f. मुरमुशी *f. v.* ये, कडमोड m.

Recovered from f. गतज्वर.

Remittent or irregular f. विषम ज्वर, ऐकाहिक ज्वर.

Rigor of f. कडमडी *f.*

Scarlet f. उदर्द m. n.

Slow creeping f. चोरताप m.

Slow or lingering f. जीर्णज्वर m.

Sprinkling of holy water over f.-patient. उदकशांति *f.*

Typhus f. काळज्वर m.

Violent f. with delirium & syncope. सन्निपात m.

To stop a f. by incantations. ज्वर *or* जर m. बांधणें.

FEVERISH, a. *having a slight fever*. कणकणी आलेला, आंग मोडून आलेला, कसर आलेला, &c. मंदज्वरार्त्त, ज्वरोन्मुख.

F. excitement. संताप ज्वर m.

To feel f. कणकणणें, कडमडणें, (हिंवानें, तापानें, &c.) कडमडीत असणें-पडणें-निजणें-&c. कडांगी *f.*-कडमोड m. येणें-भरणें-लागणें *in. con.* आंग n. मोडून येणें, आंग n. खरवणें.

2 *disposed to fever*. ज्वराचे प्रकृतीचा, ज्वरस्वभाव, ज्वरशील.

FEVERISHNESS, n. v. A. 1. कणकणी *f.* कणकण *f.* कुरकुटी *f.* कडकडी *f.* खरब *f.* खरबी *f.* कडंग *f.* कडांगी *f.* कसर *f.* काहिली *f.* ज्वरांश m. ज्वराग्नि m. धमका m. धमकी *f.* तलखली *f.* तलखी *f.*

FEVEROUS, a. *having fever*. ज्वरकरी, तापकरी, ज्वरित, ज्वरी, जातज्वर, सज्वर, प्राप्तज्वर, ज्वरयुक्त-विशिष्ट, ज्वरार्त्त.

FEW, a. कितीएक *or* कित्येक, कांहीं, थोडाबहुत, थोडा, थोडका, दोनचार, चार, पांच, चारपांच, अल्प, स्वल्प.

FEWNESS, n. v.A. थोडकेपणा m. थोडेपणा m. अल्पता *f.* स्वल्पता *f.* क्काचित्कत्व n.

FIAT, n. *decree*. आज्ञा *f.* हुकूम m. उक्तवाक्य n.

FIB, *To* FIB. See LIE, To LIE.

FIBRE, n. *small thread or filament*. तंतु m. *pop.* तांत *or* तांथ *f.* तांतू m. सूत्र *pop.* सूत n.

2 (of a leaf, of wood, &c.). शिरा m. शीर *f.* हिरका m. हीर m. रेषा *f.* शंकु m.

Of soft f.—wood, ढिसळ, ढिसाळ, ढिसूर, ढिसूळ.

Fibres (as of mangoes, &c.). चुचर n. चुचरट n. (*or* चोंचर &. चोंचरट) लोंकर *f.* जरगुड n.

Fibres (of hemp, *ambádi, &c.*) clotted. बट *f.*

3 (of a root). पाळ n. पागोरा m. कुडी *f.* कुडें n.

FIBROUS, a. *consiting, &c. of fibres*. तांतूचा, तंतुमय, सूत्रमय, जरगुडी.

FIBULA, n. *outer bone of the leg*. बहिर्जंघास्थि n.

FICKLE, a. v. CHANGEABLE. चंचल *pop.* चंचळ, चपल, उडलटप्पू, उडाणटप्पू, उचलचावडा, चंचलवृत्ति, चंचलचित्त, क्षणिकचित्त, क्षणिकबुद्धि.

FICKLENESS, n. v. A. चंचळपणा m. चांचल्य n. चापल्य n. चपल-

ता *f.* चंचल-&c. बुद्धि *f.*

Fiction, *n. false report, &c.* v. **Fabrication**. थोतांड *n.* तरकट *n.* कंडी *f.* कंडाळी *f. v.* उड, उठ, पिक.
2 *romance, novel, fable, &c.* v. **Story**. कल्पितकथा *f.* कल्पितगोष्ट *f.* कल्पितकादंबरी *f.* कादंबरी *f.*
3 *thing feigned*,—gener. कल्पना *f.* रचना *f.* बनावलेली-रचलेली &c. गोष्ट *f.*

Fictitious, *a. feigned, imaginary.* कल्पित, कल्पिलेला, रचलेला, कल्पनेचा, काल्पनिक, मनःकल्पित, बौद्ध, अवास्तविक.
2 *counterfeit, not real*, v. **False**. खोटा केलेला, कृत्रिम, मिथ्या, बनाऊ, कपटाचा.

Fictitiously, *adv.* v. A. कल्पून, रचून, &c. सकृत्रिम, सकपट, कापट्यपूर्वक. [अवास्तविकत्व *n.*

Fictitiousness, *n.* v. A. 1. काल्पनिकत्व *n.* कल्पितत्व *n.* &c.
2 खोटेपणा *m.* खोटाई *f.*

Fiddle, *n.* सारंगी *f.* रबक *n.* रबाब *n.*
F. of one string. किनरी *f.*—player on it, किनऱ्या *m.*

To **Fiddle**, *v. n. play upon a fiddle.* सारंगी *f.*-&c. वाजवणें.
2 See To **Fiddle-faddle**.

Fiddle-stick, *n.* गज *m.* कमान *f.*

Fiddle-string, *n.* सारंगीची तार *f.*

Fiddle-faddle, *n.* Of this word the sense or acceptation seems, notwithstanding the Dictionaries, to be *light and reiterate and unmeaning action*; and to be sufficiently expressed by the words *trifling, idling, playing, fiddling, piddling, &c.* Under this view of it the corresponding words in *Maráthí* are numerous and expressive. They have of course differing particular aspects and bearings. उकलाउकल *f.* उलगा घाल *f.* काढ घाल *or* घालकाढ *f.* उठाठेव *f.* सोडबांध *f.* फिरवाफिरव *f.* उसपाभर *f.* उघड झांक *f.* झांकउघड *f.* उचला उचल *f.* उचलासांचल *f.* उचला डेबर *f.* उटारेंटा *m.* उटारेंटी *f.* खुटुबुटू *f.* चांचपाचांचप *f.* चापीचोपी *f.* नस्ताकारभार *m.* रिकामा कारभार *m.* रिकामचेष्टा *f.* हातचाळा *m.*

To **Fiddle-faddle**, *v. n.* v. N. उकलाउकल *f.*-उचलाउचल *f.*-उठाठेव *f.*-चापीचोपी *f.*-&c. मांडणें-करणें, नस्ताकारभार *m.*-रिकामाकारभार *m.*-रिकामचेष्टा *f.*-&c. करणें, शेण *n.* खाणें, माशा *f. pl.* मारणें-गिळणें.

Fiddler, *n.* v. V. 1. सारंगी वाजवणारा, सारंग्या, सारंगी वाला.

Fidelity, *n.* v. **Faithfulness**. इमान *n.* इमानीपणा *m.* खरेपणा *m.* प्रमाणिकपणा *m.* प्रामाणिकत्व *n.* [निष्ठा *f.*
F. to a master or lord. स्वामिभक्ति *f.* प्रभुभक्ति *f.* स्वामि-
F. to a husband. पातिव्रत्य *n.*

To **Fidget**, *v.n. be restless, move about irregularly.* चळवळणें, चुळबुळणें, चुळमुळणें, वळवळणें, सुळसुळणें, चुळबूळ *adv.* मुंगळा *m.* लागणें *in. con.* वळवळ *f.*-चळचळ *f.*-चुळबूळ *f.*-&c. लागणें-सुटणें *in. con.* उठबैस *f.* करणें.

Fidget, Fidgeting, *n.* v. V. *and* **Fidgetiness**. चळवळणें *n.* &c. उठाबशी *f. pl.* उठबैस *f.* उटेरेंटे *m. pl. v.* लाग.

Fidgetiness, *n.* v. A. चुळबूळ *f.* चळवळ *f.* वळवळ *f.* सुळसुळ *f.* चुळचूळ *f.* चुळमूळ *f.* नाचरी *f. v.* लाग, उठपळ *f.* उठबैस *f.* लटपूट *f.* चांचल्य *n.*—intens. चुळबुळाट *m.* चळवळाट *m.* सुळसुळाट *m.* वळावळ *f.*

Fidgety, *a. restless, &c.* चुळबुळा *or* चुळबुळ्या, चुळचुळा *or* ळ्या, चळवळ्या, वळवळ्या, चंचल, चपल, तिरतिरा *or* ऱ्या.

Fie, *interj.* छ, छत्, छा, छिः, छिछी, छुः, धिक्.
Fie! Fie! शिवशिव.
To cry f. फट म्हणणें, थु-थुथु-छिथु-&c. करणें.

Fief. See **Feud**.

Field, *n. enclosure for tillage or pasture.* वावर *n.* वाडी *f. dim.* वाडगें *n.* वाडकुलें *n.* आवार *m.* ठिकें *n.*
2 *cultivated tract.* शेत *n.* वावर *n.* क्षेत्र *n.*
Blank spot in a f. of corn. ओसा *m.*
Boundaries of a f. क्षेत्रसीमा *f.*
Continuous course or range of fields. सजा *or* सज्जा *m.*
Division of or in a f. मळी *f.* भांगा *m.* कुणगा *m.*
F.-business; *agricultural operations.* शेतकी *f.* शेती *f.* शेतभात *n.*
Fields—collect. शेतगणा *m.*
Fields, enclosures, &c.—compreh. *or* gener. शेतवाडी *f.*
Fields, plantations, arable grounds—compreh. *or* gener. शेतमळा *m.* शेतपोत *n.* शेतभात *n.* शेतसरी *f.*
Living in the fields (as during harvest). शेतवस्ती *f.*
Owner of a f. शेतकरी, शेती.
Person employed to work in the fields. शेतकरी, शेतखप्या, शेतकाम्या.
Setting of a f. or plantation. लावणी *f.*
Small f. कडतरी *f.*
Stand in a f. for the watcher. माळा *m.* माळोंचा *m.*
To carry a f. *carry or haul.* खळवटणें.
Unsown f. नापेर *n. f.*
Victuals taken by laborers in the f. शिदोरी *f.* दिवातें *n.* वाढणें *n.* वाळण *n.* वाढलें *n.*
Water-pipe fixed in the bank of a f. भोंगळी *f.*
3 *wide expanse, open tract.* मैदान *n.* पटांगण *n.* भूमि *f.*
F. of battle. रणांगण *n.* रणभूमि *f.*
Taking the f. मुलुकगिरी *f.*
4 *space for action or operation.* जागा *f.* स्थल *n.*
F. of vision. पाहण्याचा आटोका *m.*-टप्पा *m.*

Field, *a. raised in fields.* शेताचा, जिराइती, क्षेत्रज.

Field-book *n.* जंगल खरडा *m.*

Field-day, *n.* कवाईत करण्याचा दिवस *m.*

Field-house, *n.* शेतघर *n.*

Field-marshal, *n.* लशकरांत एक पदवी आहे.

Field-officer, *n.* जो लशकरी सरदार कपतानाच्या वर असून जनरलाच्या खालीं आहे त्यास संज्ञा आहे.

Field-piece, *n.* स्वारीची तोफ *f.* चालती तोफ *f.*

Field-produce, *n.* जिराईत *n.* शेतपीक *n.*

Field-sports, *n.* शिकार *f.* मृगया *f.*

Fiend, *n.* v. **Devil**. पिशाच *m. n.* भूत *n.* राक्षस *m.*

Fiend-like, Fiendish, *a.* v. **Fierce**. राक्षसी, आसुर, संबंधीक.

Fierce, *a. savage, violent, furious, outrageous.* उग्र, उग्रबागरा, खपती, जहाल *or* झाल, जालीम, जलाल, आग्या, कजाख, कट्टा, कडक, खंदा, दारुण, उग्रकर्मा, जाज्वल्य, प्रखर, चंड, प्रचंड, राक्षसी, आसुर, व्याघ्रमुख. Some terms and phrases for *a fierce, furious, ferocious, formidable fellow*, and corresponding with *ogre, devil, fiend, blue-beard, giant maul,*

&c. are यम, यमरूप, यमरूपी, यमस्वरूप, यमदूत, कालमूर्त्ति, कालपुरुष, कालस्वरूप, कालरूप, कालरूपी, कल्पांतकाल or कर्जेतकाळ, कृतांत काल *pop.* करदन काळ, कृतांत, प्रलयकाल, राक्षस, भडे राक्षस, आग्यावेताळ, रुद्रावतार, आकरावारुद्र, जहरी मोहरा, आबसावरचा वाघ, तुफान, पंचानन, कजाख, जितासमंध, दैत्यांशी.
2—as flame, &c. तिखट, तिखट डोंब, कणखर, जलाल, चणचणीत, कडक, खरमरीत, तीक्ष्ण, तीव्र, प्रचंड.

FIERCELY, *adv.* v. A. 1. उग्रपणानें, कडकपणानें, &c. उग्रतापूर्वक, उग्रस्वभावानें, &c.
2 कडकपणानें, &c. तीक्ष्णतापूर्वक, &c.

FIERCENESS, *n.* v. A. 1. उग्रपणा *m.* उग्रता *f.* उग्रस्वभाव *m.* रुद्रस्वभाव *m.* राक्षसस्वभाव *m.* &c. कडकपणा *m.* जहाली *f.* जलाली *f.* कजाखी *f.* नाकावरराग *m.*
2 तिखटाई *f.* जलाली *f.* तलखाई *f.* चणचणीतपणा *m.* कडकपणा *m.* &c. तीक्ष्णता *f.* तैक्ष्ण्य *n.* तीव्रता *f.*

FIERINESS, *n.* v. A. 1. अग्निता *f.* अग्निस्वभाव *m.* अग्निधर्म *m.*
2 उष्णता *f.* जहाली *f.* जलाली *f.* तलखी *f.* तलखली *f.* कजाखी *f.* तापडाई *f.* तापटप्रकृति *f.* &c. नाकावर राग *m.*
3 उष्णता *f.* जळजळीतपणा *m.*

FIERY, *a.* *belonging to fire.* आगीचा, अग्नीचा, अग्निमय, आग्नेय, अग्निवत्.
2 *irascible,* v. HOT, PASSIONATE. आग्या, उष्ण, खपती, तापट or तापड, जहाल or झाल, जलाल, तलख, तलखल्या, चंड, खंक, खंदा, आसुर, जाज्वल्य. [त, तलख.
3 *biting, stinging, &c.* v. PUNGENT. आग्या, उष्ण, जळजळी-

FIERY-EYED, *a.* ज्वलितनयन.

FIFE, *n.* पोंवा or पांवा*m.* बांसरी *f.* मुरली *f.* वेणु*m.*

To FIFE, *v. n.* पोंवा-&c. वाजवणें.

FIFER, *n.* पोंवा-&c. वाजवणारा, वेणुवादक.

FIFTEEN, *a.* पंधरा, पंचदश.
An aggregate of f. पंधरकी *f.*

FIFTEENTH, *a.* पंधरावा.

FIFTH, *a.* पांचवा.

FIFTH, *n.* पांचवा हिस्सा*m.* पंचमांश*m.*

FIFTIETH, *a.* पन्नासावा.

FIFTY, *a.* पन्नास.—one, एकावन or न्न.—two, बावन्न.—three, तिरपन्न or त्रेपन्न.—four, चौपन्न.—five, पंचावन.—six, छप्पन्न.—seven, सत्तावन्न.—eight, अठ्ठावन्न.—nine, एकुणसाठ.
Aggregate of f. पन्नासी *f.*
Age of f. पन्नासी *f.*

FIG, *n.*—garden, *ficus carica.* अंजीर*m.* —Indian f. *ficus Indica.* वड*m.* वट*m.*—*f. glomerata.* उंबर *m.* उदुंबर *m.*—(the fruit उंबर)—holy f. *f. religiosa.* पिंपळ *m.* अश्वत्थ *m.*—*ficus scabriuscula.* बोखाडा *m.* काळाउंबर *m.*—*ficus benjamina.* नांदरूख *f.* [पार *m.*
Mass raised around the f. religiosa and f. Indica, &c.
Ceremony of raising this mass. अश्वत्थोद्यापन*n.*
Descending shoot of f. Indica. पारंबी *f.* [फें.
A f. for you and your father too. तुला फें तुझ्या बापाला

FIG-COLORED, *a.* अंजिरी, अंजिराच्या रंगाचा. [करणें.

To FIGHT, *v. n.* *contend in battle.* लढणें, लढाई *f.*-युद्ध*n.*-&c.
2 v. To CONTEND, To QUARREL. झुंजणें or जुजणें or झुंजणें.

FIGHT, FIGHTING. *n.* v. V. 1. लढणें *n.* लढाई *f.* युद्ध *n.* रण *m.* *n.* संग्राम*m.* संगर*m.* समर*m.* विग्रह*m.* विदारणा *f.* संप्रहार *m.* शस्त्रव्यवहार*m.*
Ardor for the f. युद्धकंडू *f.*
Close f. बाहुयुद्ध*n.* घनचक्र*n.*
Fair f. धर्मयुद्ध *n.*
Tumultuous and furious f. तुमुल *pop.* तुंबळ*n.*
2 झुंजणें or झुंजणें*n.* मारामार or मारामारी *f.* हणमार *m.* हणामारी *f.* जुंज or झुंज *n.* कुटाकुटी *f.* द्वंद्वयुद्ध*n.*
F. for sport. क्रीडाकलह *m.*
F. (setting to fight) of animals for a wager. प्राणिद्यूत*n.*
Height or heat of the f. ऐनलढाई *f.* ऐनमारामारी *f.*
Sharp or brisk f. कट्टीलढाई-मारामारी-&c. लटपट *f.* कचाकची *f.*
To itch to f. बाह्या *f. pl.* फुरारणें *g. of s.*

FIGHTER, *n.* FIGHTING, *p. a.* v. V. लढाई-युद्ध-&c. करणारा.
I. *fit for war.* लढाऊ, लढाईच्या कामाचा, लढवई or वाई, युद्धोपयोगी. [रचलेली गोष्ट *f.*

FIGMENT, *n.* *invention, fiction.* कल्पना *f.* रचना *f.* कल्पिलेली-

FIGURABLE, *a.* *that may be brought into a shape.* आकार करायासयोग्य-&c. आकार करणशक्य, आकारयोग्य.

FIGURATE, *a.* *having shape or form.* आकाराचा, आकारी, आकारवान्, आकारविशिष्ट, साकार, मूर्त्तिमान्, मूर्त्तिमंत, मूर्त्त.

FIGURATIVE, *a.* *typical.* लाक्षणिक, अन्यप्रतिरूपक, अन्यप्रतिबिंबक, अन्यदर्शक, उद्बोधक, संज्ञीक.
2 *not literal.* लाक्षणिक, औपचारिक, उपचारसिद्ध.
3—of style; *full of figures.* अलंकारी, आलंकारिक, सालंकार, अलंकारयुक्त.
F. language or speech. उपचार*m.*
F. style. व्यंजना *f.* व्यंजनावृत्ति *f.*

FIGURATIVELY, *adv.* v. A. 2. लक्षणेंकरून. [*m.* रूप*n.*

FIGURE, *n.* *shape,* v. FORM. आकार *m.* आकृति *f.* बळण *n.* बेत
2 *a f.* *a form, a definite thing.* मूर्त्ति *f.* रूप *n.* आकृति *f.* आकार *m.* बिंब *n.*
Composition (of talc, gum, &c.) for raising figures on cloth. खडी *f.* काट *m.*
Figures, figured work (of vines, flowers, &c.) drawn, embossed, &c. बुटी or बुट्टी *f.* वेलबुटी or ट्टी *f.* वेलबूट or वेलबुट्टा *m.* बुटे or बूट *m. pl.* फुल्या *f. pl.* नकशी *f.* नकशा *m.* नकासकाम *n.* बिरवण *f.*
Figures drawn (upon occasions) over the floor and walls. रांगोळया *f. pl.* भोंडला *m.*
Ornamented with figured work. नकशीदार.
To make figured work. नकसणें.
To adorn with figured work. बिरविणें. [चितरणें.
To cover with figures & images (a wall, floor, &c.)
3 *person, exterior,* v. FORM. रूप *n.* मुद्रा *f.* रूपरेषा *f.* रूपरेखा *f.* शरीराचीमूस *f.*
Fine, elegant, &c. f. रूपडें *n.*
Of fine f. छबदार.
4 *statue, image.* पुतळा *m.* *dim.* or *of a female.* पुतळी *f.* बाहुला *m.* or लें *n.* *dim.* or *of a female.* बाहुली *f.* चित्र *n.* प्रतिमा *f.* [यंत्र *n.* चित्र*n.*
5 (as of a heavenly body, &c. in explaining it). भंगि*f.*

6—in geometry. क्षेत्र *n.* आकृति *f.*

7 *character in arithmetic.* अंकडा *m.* अंक *pop.* अंस *or* आंसम.

Figures. *cyphering.* हिशेब *or* हिशोब *m.*—Place of figures. अंकस्थल *n.* [दर्शकचिन्ह *n.*

8 *emblem, symbol, type.* प्रतिरूप *n.* प्रतिरूपक *n.* प्रतिबिंब *n.*

9—in rhetoric. अलंकार *m.* उपचार *m.* रूपक *n.* Some of the common *figures* in rhetoric are. उपमा, अनन्वय, रूपक, परिणाम, आक्षेप, उल्लेख, अनुप्रास, प्रास, स्मृति, भ्रांति, संदेह, अपन्हुति, उत्प्रेक्षा, अतिशयोक्ति, विशेषोक्ति, विनोक्ति, सहोक्ति, तुल्ययोगिता, दीपक, व्यतिरेक, भाविक, सार, श्लेष, सामान्य, सम, प्रतीप, चर्वणा.

Figures & tropes generally—as distinguished from शब्दालंकार Verbal ornaments, अर्थालंकार *m.*

10 *distinguished appearance, &c.* रंग *m.* शोभा *f.* नकशा *m.*

To cut a f. *cut a dash.* छान *f.* मारणें, फड *m.* मारणें-संपादणें, चमचमाट *m.* करणें, चमकावणें, आंग *n.* दाखवणें, राजणें, विराजणें, विलसणें, भलें सोंग *n.* आणणें.

To FIGURE, *v. a.* आकार *m.*-&c. करणें.

2 *work figures &c.* वेलबुट्टी *f.*-&c. काढणें, बुटीदार-&c. करणें, नकासकाम *n.*-&c. करणें.

3 See To IMAGINE.

To FIGURE, *v. n. make a figure, be distinguished.* नकशा *m.* करणें, राजणें, विराजणें. See also under FIGURE.

FIGURED, *a. figurate.* साकार, रूपवान्, मूर्त्तिमान्, मूर्त्तिमंत, मूर्त्त.

2 *having figures (carved, drawn, &c.).* बुटीदार, नकशी, नकशीदार, फुलकारी, चित्रित.

3 *numbered by figures.* अंकी, अंसी.

FILACEOUS, *a. consisting of threads.* तंतुमय, सूत्रमय.

FILAMENT, *n.* सूत्र *n.* तार *f.* केसर *m.* तंतु *vulg.* तांतु *m.* किंजल्क *m.*

Pendulous filaments from a dirty roof, &c. जळमटें *n.pl.*

FILAMENTOUS, *a. like a filament.* सूत्रसदृश, तंतुवत्, तंतुतुल्य.

2 *consisting of filaments.* तंतुमय, सूत्रमय.

FILBERT, *n.* कंवटीचें एक फल आहे.

To FILCH, &c. See To STEAL, &c.

FILE, *n.* (as of soldiers). माळका *f.* रांग *f.* कतार *f.*

2—the instrument. कानस *f.* [use. तबलक *f.*

3 (of papers, documents, &c.) फेल *n. f.* is in common

4 See LIST.

To FILE, *v. a. rub with a f.* कानसणें, कानसीनें घासणें.

2 (papers, &c.) फेलावर *or* फेलीवर घालणें-लावणें-ठेवणें, फेरिस्ताला-&c. लावणें.

To FILE, *v. n.* एका मागून एक अशारीतीनें चालणें.

FILIAL, *a.*—as used of a son. पुत्राचा, पुत्रसंबंधी-विषयक, पुत्रीय, पुत्रधर्माचा, पुत्रधर्मक.—as used of a daughter. कन्येचा, लेकींचा, पुत्रीचा, पुत्रिकाधर्माचा, पुत्रिकाधर्मक.—as used of a child, without reference to sex. अपत्याचा, अपत्यधर्माचा.

F. affection. पितृस्नेह *m.* पितृभक्ति *f.* with reference to one's father. मातृस्नेह *m.* मातृभक्ति *f.* with reference to one's mother.

F. duty. पुत्रधर्म *m.* पुत्रिकाधर्म *m.* अपत्यधर्म *m.*

FILIATION, *n.* पुत्रत्व *n.* सुनत्व *n.*

2 See ADOPTION.

FILINGS, *n.* कीस *m.* चूर्ण *n.* (esp. in comp. as लोहचूर्ण *n.*&c.).

To FILL, *v. a.* भरणें, भरून देणें, भरणी *f.*-भरण *n.*-&c. करणें *g. of o.* भरित-&c. करणें.

To f. full. डब्ब-तुंद-भरपूर-&c. भरणें.

2 See To SATISFY, To GLUT. [*in. con.*

3 (an office, &c.) करणें, असणें *with* चा *or* कडे *of s.* and

4 up; *occupy.* अटवणें, रोधवणें, गुंतवणें.

To be filled by. भरणें, अटणें, गुंतणें, अटोपणें.

5 up; *supply cavities, &c.* भरणें, बुझणें, ओहरणें, माचणें.

6 up or in;—tables, columns, &c. भरणें.

To FILL, *v. n. grow full.* भरणें, भरून जाणें.

2 out; *become fleshy or pulpous.* आंगीं फुटणें-भरणें, आंग *n.* धरणें, भरणें, फुगणें, पुष्टहोणें,

FILL, *n. fullness, satisfaction.* भरती *f.* भरित *n.* भरण *n.* धालेपणा *m.* तृप्ति *f.* पर्याप्ति *f.*

To the f. आतृप्ति.

To eat one's f. पोटभर-पोटभरून जेवणें.

To get one's f. of. तुंबडी *f.* भरणें *g. of s.*

To take one's f. of. भर *m.* घेणें *g. of o.* धण *f.* घेणें.

FILLED, *p.* v. V. 1. भरलेला, भरित, पूरित, पूर्ण, परिपूर्ण, पूर्त्त, पूरकृत, पर्याप्त.

F. full. भरपूर.

F. with (thoroughly occupied and overborne by). आकुल (in comp. as हर्षाकुल, शोकाकुल, भयाकुल, क्रोधाकुल, लोभाकुल).

F. state. भरती *f.* भरगत *f. n.* भरताड *f.*

FILLET, *n. band.* पट्टी *f.* रकटा *m.*

Front f. कपाळपट्टी *f.*

To FILLET, *v. a.* पट्टी *f.* बांधणें.

FILLING, *a.*—as an article of food. पुरवटेसार, पुरवट्याचा.

2 *becoming pulpous, ripening,*—fruit. गारशेल, गदरेल.

FILLING, *n.* v. V. A. 1.—*act.* भरणें *n.* भरणी *f.* भरण *n.* भरती *f.* पूरण *n.* परिपूर्ण *n.*

F. and emptying. भरउभर *f.*

To FILLIP, *v. a.*—with the finger. टिचकणें, टिचणें, टिच *f.*-&c. मारणें, तटकारणें.

FILLIP, FILLIPPING, *n.* v. V. टिंच *or* टीच *f.* टिचकी *f.* टचका *m.*

With a f. टिच-कन-कर-&c.

FILLY, *n.* शिंगी *f.* बछेरी *f.*

2 *boisterous girl,* v. ROMP. घोडी *f.* धिंगड *n.* तट्टाणी *f.*

FILM, *n. pellicle.* तवंग *m.* सारा *m.* सायरा *m.* कोशेटा *m. dim.* कोशेटी *f.* कोशेरा *m.* तव *n.* तरंग *m.* तरंज *f.*

2 (over the eye). कवडा *m.* पटल *pop.* पडळ *n.* तवंग *m.* तरंग *m.* सायरा *m.* सारा *m.* पदर *m.*

3 fig. *blind, covering, &c.* अंतर्धान *n.*

To FILTER, *v. a. purify by a filter.* गळतीनें गाळणें-छाटणें-&c.

To FILTER, *v. n. percolate.* पाझरणें, गळणें, क्षरणें.

FILTER, *n. strainer for water.* गळती *f.* गलंतिका *f.*

To FILTRATE. See To FILTER.

FILTH, *n. foul matter, nastiness.* घाण *f.* मल *pop.* मळ *m.* खस्त *n.* खळमळ *m.* तन्हाण *n.* हेंदर *f. n.* चिखल *m.* कल्मष *n.* किल्बिष *n.* [आशौच *n.*

FILTHINESS, *n.* v. A. 1. मळकेपणा *m.* मळीणपणा *m.* मालिन्य *n.*

2 ओंगळपणा *m.* ओंगळपणा *m.* &c.

FILTHY, *a. foul, &c.* v. DIRTY. मळका *remiss.* मळकट, मलिन *pop.* मळीण, हेंदरा, समळ.

2 *nauseating, loathsome, &c.* v. DISGUSTING. ओखटा, ओंगळ, हिडशा *or* हिडसा, हिडीस, हेंदरा, ओंगळवाणा.

FILTRATION, *n.* गळतीनें गाळणें *n.* गाळणी *f.*

FIN, *n.* माशाचा पर *m.* मत्स्यपक्ष *m.*

FINABLE, *a.* v. V. धनदंडार्ह, धनदंड्य.

FINAL, *a. ultimate,* v. LAST. शेवटचा *or* ला, शेवटील, अंत्य, आंत, अंतिम, चरम.

FINALÉ, *n. end, closing scene, &c.* उद्यापन *n.* निष्ठा *f.* अंत *m.*

FINALITY, *n. final state.* शेवटली अवस्था *f.* चरमत्व *n.*

FINALLY, *adv.* v. A. शेवटीं, अंतीं, अवसानीं, अखेर.

I. *utterly,* v. WHOLLY. अगदीं, निस्तूक.

FINANCE, FINANCES, *n.* v. REVENUE. वसूल *m.* हाशील *m.* जमा *f.* जमा वसूल *m.*

FINANCIAL, *a.* v. N. वसुलाचा, हाशिलाचा, वसुलाविषयींचा, वसूल [प्रकरणाचा.

FINANCIER, *n.* जमा वसुलाचे कामांत कुशल-दक्ष.

To FIND, *v. a. obtain, attain.* पावणें, मिळणें, लागणें, लब्ध होणें, प्राप्त होणें, पडणें *all with in. con.*

2 (something lost). सांपडणें, मिळणें, गवसणें, गावणें, *all with in. con.*

3 *meet with, fall upon.* मिळणें, सांपडणें, भेटणें, अढळणें *all* [*with in. con.*

4 *know by experience.* दाखला *m.*-अनुभव *m.*-प्रत्यय *m.*-&c. येणें-होणें *g. of o. with in. con.* अनुभवानें-&c. समजणें-जाणणें -&c. अनुभवानें-&c. मालूम पडणें-ठाऊक होणें-समजणें *in. con.*

5 *detect, discover, apprehend* (faults, excellencies).काढणें.

6 *discover by study, &c.* काढणें. [उलगडणें.

7 See To SUPPLY, 8 out; *unriddle, solve.* ताडणें, जिंकणें,

9 out; v. To INVENT. काढणें.

10 out; *detect, discover, trace, bring to light.* उमगणें *or* उमंगणें, काढणें, शोध *m.* काढणें-लावणें *g. of o.* ठायीं-&c. पाडणें, ठिकाणा *m.*-ठिकाण *n.*-थांग *m.*-&c. लावणें-पाडणें *g. of o.* हुंगणें.

To be found out, *be brought to light.* उमगणें, उमटणें *or* उमठणें, उमग *m.*-उमट *m.* पडणें *g. of s.* शोध *m.*-ठिकाणा*m.*-&c. लागणें *g. of s.*

11—as a jury. ठराव *m.*-निर्णय *m.*-निवाडा *m.*-&c. करणें.

12 fault with; v. To BLAME. ठपका *m.* ठेवणें, बोल *m.* लावणें-ठेवणें.

How do you find yourself? कसेआहां ? कायवर्तमान आहे?

FINDING, *n. verdict.* ठराव *m.* निर्णय *m.* निवाडा *m.*

A revised f. or decision. परत फैसला *m.*

FINE, *a. not coarse.* बारीक, बारकस, तलम,—compreh. *or* indef.

F. and small, &c. बारीकसारीक.

2 *of fine texture.* बारीक, तलम, बारीकसुती, तलमसुती, बारीकसुताचा, तलमसुताचा.

3 *subtil, rare, tenuous.* बारीक, नाजूक, सूक्ष्म, तनु.

4 *large and splendid, substantial and showy.* छानीचा, छानदार, शानदार, ढबदार, ठळक, ठोकळ, घवघवीत, घसघशीत, घोंस, घोस, उद्दाम, भव्य, शोभिवंत, सश्रम.

5 *splendid, dashing, gorgeous, garish, gaudy, flash.* छानीचा, छानदार, शानदार, पोशाकी *or* खी, देखणाऊ, देखाऊ, घवघवीत, भळभळीत, झळक, टूमदार, टुमीचा, अयटबाज, छालछबीला, सुभावणा, शोभवणा, शोभान्वित, जरकबरक, भडक, भबूक, भडकीचा, थाटाचा, थाटमाटाचा, मिरवणुकीचा, विराजमान, विराजित, विलसित.

F. and showy but worthless. पोशाकी *or* खी *or* गी.

6 *good, excellent, capital, grand, splendid, superb, noble, &c.*—freely. चांगला, उत्तम, सुंदर, बेश, खासा, बेशखासा, भला *or* ला, खुबीदार, मजेदार, नगीना, नामी, फर्माशी *or* सी, सरस, नादर, उमदा, उदार, चोख, चोखट, चोखा, चखोट, शेलका, तोफा, शिरां, उत्कृष्ट, बुंद, बुंदडा, गुलजार, नमूद *or* नमोदा, चांग, अनवा, दाणा, घवघवीत, घोंस, दिव्य, दीप्त.

7—a reasoning, &c. *subtil.* बारीक, सूक्ष्म, लघु.

8 See PURE, REFINED.

FINE, *n. mulct.* खंड *m.* खंडणी *f.* दंड *m.* गुन्हेगारी *f.* तावण *f.* धनदंड *m.* फुरई *f.* दंडफुरई *f.* नागवण *f.* जुलमाना *m.*

Fines and forfeits,—compreh. खंडदंड *m.* खंडगुन्हेगारी *f.*

F. to be paid to the king. राजदंड *m.*

F. to be paid to a bráhman. ब्रह्मदंड *m.*

Vexatious or unjust f. भुरदंड *m.*

To FINE, *v. a. mulct.* दंड *m.*-धनदंड *m.* करणें, दंड *m.*-धनदंड *m.*-&c. घेणें, दंडणें.

2 See To PURIFY, To REFINE.

To FINE-DRAW, *v. a.* बेमालूम रफू करणें.

FINE-EYED, *a.* दिव्यचक्षु, दिव्यदृष्टि.

FINE-LOOKING, *a.* v. HANDSOME. देखणा, दर्शनीय, उदारलक्षण.

FINELY, *adv.* v.A. 5. *splendidly, showily, gorgeously,&c.* नटून-थटून, खूब, छानीनें, डौलानें, टुमीनें.

FINENESS, *n.* v.A. 1. 2. बारकाई *f.* बारिकपणा*m.* तलमाई *f.*

3 बारकाई *f.* बारिकपणा*m.* बारकावा*m.* नाजकाई *f.* नाजुकपणा*m.* सौक्ष्म्य*n.* सूक्ष्मता *f.* [&c.

4 छान *f.* शान *f.* छानदारी *f.* ढब *f.* ढबदारी *f.* घवघवितपणा*m.*

5 छान *f.* शान *f.* छानदारी *f.* टूम *f.* टुमदारी *f.* भळभळाट*m.* भडक*f.* झळक *f.* v. मार, भळभळितपणा *m.*

6 सुंदरपणा*m.* सौंदर्य*n.* सरसपणा*m.* उमदेपणा*m.* चोखपणा*m.* &c.

7 बारिकपणा*m.* बारकाई *f.* सूक्ष्मता *f.* सौक्ष्म्य*n.* [दारी *f.*

FINERY, *n. show, splendor.* छान *f.* शान *f.* छानदारी *f.* टूम *f.* टूम-

2 *fine clothes.* दरबारीपोशाक*m.* लग्नाचा-वरातीचा-शिलंगणाचा-नवऱ्याचा-&c. पोशाक*m.* छानछुकीचें वस्त्र*n.*

FINESSE, *n.*v. ARTIFICES. पेचपाच *or* पाचपेच *m pl.* डावपेच *m.pl.* हिलाहरकत*f.*

FINGER, *n.* बोट*n.* अंगुलि *pop.* अंगुळी *or* अंगाळी *f.* करशाखा *f.*

F. in, *part or concern in,* आंग*n.*

Five fingers.—collect. अंगुलिपंचक*n.*

Fore f. तर्जनी *f.* प्रदेशिनी *f.*—little f. अंगठी *f.* करंगळी *or* करंगुळी *f.* कनिष्ठिका*f.*—middle f.मधलेंबोट*n.* मध्यमा*f.*कर्णिका*f.* —ring-f. third-f. अनामिका *f.*

Space between the fingers. गेचक*n.* गेचकळ*n.*

Talking with the fingers. करपल्लवीभाषा *f.* करपल्लवी *f.* अंगुलिसंदेश*m.*

That is at one's fingers ends. तोंडपाठ, मुखपाठ, हातखडा.

To burn one's fingers, fig. आंच *f.*बसणें *in. con.*

To crack the f.-joints. बोटें*n. pl.* मोडणें, अंगुलि भंग*m.*-अंगुलिमोटन*n.*-अंगुलिस्फोटन*n.* करणें.

To get a f. in. बोट*n.* शिरकणें, चंचुप्रवेश*m.* करणें.

To point out with the f. बोट*n.* करणें-दाखविणें, अंगुलि नि-

देंश *m.* करणें.

To twist round one's f. बोटावर नाचवणें.

2 *finger's breadth.* बोटn. अंगुल *pop.* अंगूळ*n.*

To the extent of a f. बोटभर.

To FINGER, *v. a. get into one's hand or possession.* दस्तावणें, दस्त*m. n.*करणें, हस्तगत करणें, हातांखालीं घालणें.

2 *mess by fingering and pressing.* बोटळणें *or* बोटाळणें.

3—furtively or peculatingly, v. To EMBEZZLE. चापसणें, दपटणें.

FINGER-RING, *n.* अंगूळवेंढें*n.* अंगुलीयक*n.*

FINGERED, *a. having fingers.* बोटाचा, सांगुलिक, बोट्या (in comp. as एकबोट्या, दुबोट्या, &c.).

Six f. सांगळ्या, अधिकांगुल.

FINGERLESS, *a.* निबोट्या, अंगुलिहीन.

FINICAL, *a. fastidiously or affectedly nice.* ठाकठिक्या, टापटिप्या, चापचोप्या, चाकचोप्या, बेतचाल्या, चोखनळ, टापटीप-&c. करणारा.

FINICALNESS, *n.* v. A. ठाकठिकेपणा*m.* टापटिपेपणा*m.* &c. टापटीप *f.* चाकचोप *f.* चाकचोपी *f.*

FINIS, *n.* v. END. इतिश्री *f.* समाप्ति *f.*

To FINISH, *v. a. complete.* v. To ACCOMPLISH. पुरता-पूर्ण-तमाम -&c. करणें, आखेरी *f.* मारणें, शेवटास-सिद्धीस-&c. नेणें.

2 *conclude.* v. To END. संपवणें, उलगडणें, आटोपणें.

3 *give the last touch, polish, perfect.* ओजवणें, सुधारणें, आखेरी *f.* संभाळणें-साधणें, ओज *f.* करणें *g. of o.* सफाई *f.*-झिलाई *f.*-ओप *f.*-&c. आणणें, परिष्कार *m.*-संस्कार *m.*-&c. करणें *g. of o.* घासणें, घासपूस *f.* करणें, नेपाळणें.

4 *consume, expend, come to the end of*, v. To EXHAUST. संपविणें, सारणें, फडशा*m.*-&c. करणें *g. of o.*

To be finished. सरणें, संपणें, फडशा*m.*-&c. होणें *g. of s.*

FINISH, FINISHING, *n. last touch (polish, &c.) given.* ओज *f.* सफाई *f.* ओप *f.* झिलाई *f.* लाघव*n.*

FINISHED, *p.* v.V. 1. पुरता-&c. केलेला, शेवटास-&c. नेलेला, सिद्ध,

2 संपवलेला, समाप्त.

3 ओजवलेला, &c. परिष्कृत, संस्कारित, संस्कृत.

4 संपवलेला *or* संपलेला, &c.

FINITE, *a. limited, bounded.* सावधि, सावधिक, समर्याद, ससीम, अंतवान् *pop.* अंतवंत, सांत, आद्यंतवान्, संपन्न (in comp. as कालसंपन्न, देशसंपन्न).

FINITENESS, *n.* v. A. सावधित्व *n.* सावधिकत्व *n.* समर्यादत्व *n.* ससीमता *f.* सांतता *f.*

FINLESS, *a.* पक्षहीन.

FINNY, *a.* सपक्ष.

FIR, *n.* देवदारु *m. n. pop.* देवदार *m.*

FIRE, *n.* आग *f.* अग्नि *m.* विस्तव *or* विस्तू *m.* अनल *m.* (also in comp. as f. of lust कामानल, f. of hunger क्षुधानलand क्रोधानल, लोभानल, मदानल &c.).

By a slow f.—cooking, &c. मंदाग्नीं.

Fall of meteorous f. अग्न्युत्पात *m.* दिव्यउत्पात *m.*

F. fabled to be in the ocean. वडवाग्नि *m.* वडवानल *m.*

Flint, steel, &c. for striking f. चकमक *f.*

Roaring f. Blazing f. कल्लोळ *or* ळ *m.* भडका *or* भडाका*m.* लोळ *m.* धोकाळ *m.* धोदराट *m.* धगाटा *m.*

Sacred or sacrifical f. इन *n.* होमाग्नि *m.* गुप्ताग्नि *m.*—hole, enclosed space, or vessel for preserving it. अग्निकुंड *n.* कुंड *n.* होमशाला *f.* होमकुंड *n.*—maintainer of it. अग्निहोत्री.—maintenance.अग्निहोत्र*n.*—particular wood used for kindling it. अरणि *or* गणिकारिका *f.* (Premna spinosa). पलाश *m.* (Butea frondosa). खदिर *m.* (Mimosa catechu). —stick used in kindling it. समिध् *pop.* समीध *f.*

Sheet of f. धोत *m.* लोळ *m.* गलूल *m.*

Widower's sacred f. विधुराग्नि *m.*

To be on f. आग *f.* लागणें, जळणें, लागणें.

To expose to the action of f. (medical compounds, &c.). अग्निपुट *n.*-आंच *f.* देणें.

To place over a slow f. मवाग्नीं टाकणें.

To set on f. आग *f.* लावणें, पेटवणें, शिलकावणें *or* शिलगावणें.

To take f. To catch f. पेट *m.* घेणें, चेत *f.* घेणें, शिलकणें *or* शिलगणें.

2 *a f. a kindled heap of sticks, logs, coals, &c.* आगटी *or* आकटी*f.* आगटें *or* आकटें *n.* शेकोटी *or* शेकाटी *f.* धकटी *or* धगटी *f.* धकटें *or* धगटें *n.* धगें *n.* परसा *m.*

3 *burning of a house, &c.* v. CONFLAGRATION. आग *f.* v. लाग.

4 (from guns, &c.) v. FIRING. गोळीमार *m.*मारा *m.* मार*m.*

Range or reach of f. मारा *m.*

To come within reach of f. माऱ्याचे आंत येणें.

5 See ARDOR, PASSION. चुडी *f.* लावणें.

To FIRE, *v. a.* v. To KINDLE. पेटवणें, आग *f.* लावणें, चूड *f.*-[चुडी *f.* लावणें.]

2 v. To CAUTERIZE. डागणें *or* दागणें, लासणें, दाहन *n.* करणें.

3 *discharge a gun or firepiece.* मारणें, सोडणें, डागणें *or* दागणें, उडवणें, झाडणें, बार *m.* सोडणें-उडवणें-झाडणें *g. of o.*

To FIRE, *v. n. take f.* v. To KINDLE. पेट *m.* घेणें, पेटणें, चेतणें.

2 fig. *get angry*, v. ANGRY. पेटणें, चेतणें, तापणें, संतापणें, कोपणें, रागास चढणें.

3 *discharge guns.* बार *m.* सोडणें.

To f. away animatedly and continuously. झडणें.

FIRE-ARMS, *n.* v. MUSKET, GUN, &c. अग्न्यस्त्रें *n. pl.*

FIRE-BALL, *n.* अग्निगोलक *m.* उल्का *f.* [*f.* उल्मुक *n.*]

FIRE-BRAND, *n.* कोलती *f.* कोलीत *n.* अंगार *m.* अग्निकाष्ठ *n.* उल्का *f.* उल्मुक *n.*

F. in the hand of a madman. पिशाच्या हातीं कोलीत.

2 fig. v. INCENDIARY. आगलाव्या, आगघाल्या, चूडलाव्या.

FIRE-ENGINE, *n.* आगविझविण्याचें यंत्र *n.* बंब *m.*

FIRE-FLY, *n.* काजवा *m.* खद्योत *m.* प्रभाकीट *m.* तमोमणि *m.*

FIRE-LOCK, *n.* चापीबंदूक *f.* चापाची बंदूक *f.*

F. with a flint, as disting. from match lock. गार भांड *or* डें *n.*

FIRE-NEW, *a.* v. NEW. घणकोरा, घणाखालचा, नवघड.

FIRE-PAN, *n.* शेगडी *f.* आगटी *f.* आगटें *n.*

FIRE-PLACE, *n.* चूल *f. dim.* चुलाणें *n. and intens.* चुला *m.* चुलवान *or* ण *n.* चुलाण *n.*

F. of a ship or boat. चुलदान *n.*

Hob of a f. अवेल *n.* वाईल *or* बैल *m. n.*

Large & rude f. चुलवा *m.*

Raised back of a f. भाणोसा *or* भानोसा *m.*

Range of fire-places. चुलवान *or* ण *n.* चुलांगण *n.*

FIRE-PROOF, *a.* v. INCOMBUSTIBLE. पेटघ्यायाचा नाहीं असा, अदाह्य.

FIRE-STONE, *n.* अग्निप्रस्तर *m.*

Fire-wood, *n.* v. Fuel. जळण *n.* जळवण *n.*
F. merchant. लकडवाला. [रू *f.*
Fire-work, *n. composition of gunpowder, &c.* दारूकाम *n.* दा-
Certain *fire-works* are घडेबाजी, भुइनळा, नळा, चंद्रजोत, तारा, चापा, चिचुंदरी, जांतीण, पेटी, फुलझडी, फुलझाड, फुलबाजी, महताब, शिंगट, सुरसुरी, हातनळा, लंका, दारूचा डल्ला.
Various fireworks put together and fired. भुताळें *n.* भुइनळा *m.*
2 *diversion with fireworks.* आतसबाजी *f.* अग्निक्रीडा *f.* लंका *f.*
Fire-worship, *n.* अग्नीचीउपासना *f.*-भक्ति *f.*-&c.
Firing, *n.* v. V. A. 2. See Cautery.
3 गोळीमार *m.* मारा *m.* मार *m.* मारगिरी *f.*
Brisk or furiuos f. (of ordnance, musketry, stones, and, *fig.* of abuse, &c.). देवडमार *m.* भडमार *or* भडिमार *or* भडेमार *m.* धडाधडी *f.*
Double f. दुमारा *m.* दुमारें *n.*
Line of f. मारा *m.*
Mutual f. गोळागोळी *f.*
I. v. Fuel. जळण *n.* जळवण *n.* सर्पण *n.*
Firkin, *n.* एककैली माप आहे.
Firm, *a. closely compressed, hard, compact.* घन *pop.* घण, घट्ट, घटमूट, दाट, दृढ, कणखर, टणक, कठिन *pop.* कठीण, निबर, सक्कस, खंबीर, खम्माल, कुब्बल, सदृढ, सुदृढ, घनीकृत, जंजीरबंद.
F. (from ramming or beating) *hard.* ठास, ठाम.
To grow f. and compact. घटणें.
2 *steady, determined, decided, resolute.* धिराचा, कराराचा, करारी, निश्चयाचा, नेटाचा, नेटक, निर्धाराचा, निर्धारी, धीर, स्थिर, अटीचा, टेकीचा, चिकट, चिकट्या, खमशा, दमदार, निश्शंक, निग्रही, धक्क, सुधीर, सत्वधीर, स्थिरबुद्धीचा, स्थिरमनस्क, दृढसंकल्प, वज्रसंकल्पी, दृढनिश्चय, स्थिरनिश्चय, धैर्यवान्, धारिष्टवान्, धैर्यशाली, स्तब्ध, मजबूत. [वळ.
3 *tight, close, fast.* घट्ट, ताठ, ठाम, गाढ, साबीत *or* साबूत, अ-
4 *fixed, stable,* v. Enduring. अढळ, स्थिर, अचल, ध्रुव, स्थाणु.
5 *substantial and strong,*—esp. of edifices. बळकट, जोराचा, खंबीर, खम्माल, धक्क, खबरदार, अकुतोभय, भक्खम, भक्कम, बंदिस्त, कुब्बल, संगीन, साबूत, जंजीरबंद, मजबूत.
Firm, *n. partnership or house.* घर *n.* अड्डा *m.* मंडळी *f.*
Firmament, *n. region of the air,* v. Heaven. आकाशमंडल *n.* नक्षत्रमंडल *n.* मेघमंडल *n.* घनाश्रय *m.* [तरीक्ष.
Firmamental, *a.* v. N. आकाशमंडलाचा, आकाशमंडलसंबंधी, आं-
Firman, *n. royal mandate, &c.* फर्मान *or* फरमाना *m.*
Firmly, *adv.* v. A. 2. धैर्यानें, चिकटपणानें, धैर्यपूर्वक, दृढनिश्चयपूर्वक, निग्रहपूर्वक, &c.
4 घट्ट, गच्च, खच, बळकट, दृढ, पची, कडकडून, कडकावून.
Firmness, *n.* v. A. 1. घट्टाई *f.* घट्टपणा *m.* कठीणपणा *m.* &c. टणकाई *f.* खंबिरी *f.* काठिन्य *n.* दृढता *f.* दृढिमा *m.* दाढ्यं *n.*
2 धैर्य *n.* धीरता *f.* अट *f.* नेट *m.* निग्रह *m.* चिकटपणा *m.* चिकटाई *f.* धारणा *f.* धारिष्ट *n.* धृति *f.* हिय्या *m.* निर्बंध *m.* स्थैर्य *n.* हुरूम *f.* दम *m.*
5 जोर *m.* खंबिरी *f.* खबरदारी *f.* बळकटी *f.* मजबुती *f.*
First, *a.* पहिला, पहिलील, प्रथम, आद्य, आदि, आदिम, पूर्व, अवल, मुख्य, प्राथमिक, अपूर्व.
At or for the f. time. पहिल्यानें *or* पहिल्यान्.
From the f. (part, &c.) to the last. आद्यंत.
I am the F. and the Last. अहं आद्यंतः.
2 See Chief.
First, *adv.* पहिल्यानें, पहिलें, अगोदर *or* अगोधर, आदीं, आदौ, प्रथम, प्रथमतः, पुरः (in comp. as पुरस्सर, पुरोगामी).
At f. पहिला, पहिल्यान्, पूर्वीं, अवल.
As at f. पूर्ववत्.
F. and foremost. पुढच्या पुढें. [विधीं.
F. of all. पुढच्या पुढें, आदींचेविदीं *or* आदींविदीं *or* आधीं-
From f. to last. अवलआखर, आद्यंत.
From the f. पहिल्यापासून, पूर्वीपासून, अवलपासून.
First-born, *a.* प्रथमजात, अग्रजात, प्रथमोत्पन्न, ज्येष्ठ.
First-fruit, *n. annats.* नवाळी *f.* नवीनवाळ *or* नवीनव्हाळ *f.* नवान्न *n.* नवधान्य *n.*
Feast of the f. नवें *n.* नवान्न *n.* Day of it. नवान्नपुनव *f.* नवान्नपूर्णिमा *f.* नव्याची पुनव *f.*
Firstling, *a.* पहिलेविणीचा, पहिलेवेताचा.
First-rate, **First-sort**, *a.* अवल, अवलराशीचा, उत्तमप्रतीचा.
Firth. See Frith.
Fiscal, *n.* See Revenue.
Fiscal, *a.* v. N. वसुलाचा, वसुलाविषयींचा.
Fish, *n.* मासा *m.* *dim.* मासळी *or* मासोळी *f.* मच्छ *m.* मत्स्य *m.* मीन *m.* जलचर *m.*—in cant or free phraseol. पाणशेंग *f.* बंदरीजिन्नस *m.*—as exposed for sale or lying in quantities. मासळी *f.* माहुरें *n. pl.* Some kinds of *fish* are बोंबील, हलवा, शिंगाडा, केंड, खिरड, गादा, घोगरा, चिंबणें, डांकू, निवटा, बोटी, सुकट, मरल.
Basket-work let down to catch f. बोकशी *f.*
Odd f. *a queer fellow.* जलचर, तमाशाचा माणूस.
Shoal of f. मत्स्यसंघात *m.*
To **Fish**, *v. n.* मासे *m. pl.* मारणें-धरणें, माशांची शिकार *f.* करणें, मत्स्यधारण *n.*-मत्स्यघात *m.* करणें.
2 fig. युक्तीनें मिळविण्याचा यत्न करणें.
To **Fish**, *v. a.* up. ओढून काढणें.
Fish-bone, *n.* कांटा *m.* कंटक *m.* मत्स्यकंटक *m.*
Fish-hook, *n.* गळ *m.* बडिश *n.* गरी *f.* मत्स्यवेधन *n.*
Fish-monger, *n.* मासेविक्या, मत्स्यविक्रयी.
Fish-net, *n.* माशांचें जाळें *n.* मत्स्यजाल *n.*
Fish-pond, *n.* माशांचा हौद *m.* मत्स्यकुंड *n.*
Fish-wife, **Fish-woman**, *n. woman who sells fish.* मासेविकणारी *f.* मासेविकी *f.*
Fisher, **Fisherman**, *n.* मासा धरणारा-मारणारा, मत्स्यधारक, मत्स्यग्राहक. The words following denote *castes* of fishermen. धीवर *pop.* ढिवर, कोळी, गाबती *or* दी *or* गाबीद, दालदी, भोई, कैवर्त्त *or* कैवर्त्तक *m.* [-&c. दालद *n.*
Fishery, **Fishing**, *n.* मासे धरण्याचा धंदा *m.*-काम *n.*-कारखाना *m.*
Fishing, *a.* मासे धरण्याचे कामाचा, दालदी.
Fishy, *a.* माशाचा, माशासारखा, मत्स्यवत्.
Fissure, *n.* v. Crack. भेग *f.* भेर *f.* रेभ *f.* भळ *f.* सांड *f.* तडा *m.* तीर *m.*
Fist, *n.* मूठ *f.* मुष्टि *f.* मुष्टिका *f.*—jocosely. मुष्टिमोदक *m.*
Blow with the f. मुटका *m.* *v.* मार, दे, ढुसा *m.* बकांदी *f.* गुद्दा *m.* मुष्टिप्रहार *m.*

Blow with the side of the f. बुकी *f.* बुकांदा *or* बकांदा*m.* बुकांदी *or* बकांदी *f.* बुकाडा *m.* बुतका *or* बुदका*m.*

Clenching the f. मुष्टिबंध*m.*

F. as raised to strike. मुटका *m. v.* उगार.

F. to f. मुष्टीमुष्टि.

Free of the f. *given to striking.* हाताचा फटकळ.

Huge f. Mutton f. बुकाडा *m.*

Iron (or hard) f. वज्रमुष्टि*m. f. pop.* वज्रमूठ *f.*

Of an iron f. वज्रमुष्टि.

Striking with the f. मुष्टिप्रयोग*m.*

To beat with the side of the f. बुदकणें.

Fistful, *n.* मूठभर (used with a noun). मुष्टि *f.*

Fisticuffs, *n.* मुष्टामुष्टी *f.* हातपिटी *f.* धप्पाधप्पी *or* धब्बाधब्बी *f.* कुटाकुटी *f.* कुटाकूट *f.* मुष्टीमुष्टि *f.*

To come to f. हातपिटीवर-हातघाईवर-&c. येणें.

Fistula, *n.*—in ano. भगंदर*m. pop.* भगेंद्र*n.* नाडीव्रण*m.* नाडी *f.*

2—lachrymalis. नासूर*m.* अश्रुनाली *f.*

Fistulous, *a.* नाडिरूप, नाड्याकार.

F. sore. नाडिव्रण*m.* [हर *f.* वेग *m.*

Fit, *n. sudden affection or attack.* झटका*m.* झपाटा *m.* सर *f.* ल-

F. of anger. भिरड *f.* भिरडी *f.* भिरकंडा *m.* भिरकांडें *n.* झणका *m.* झणकारा*m.* रागाचीसर *f.* तैष*m.* तेख*m.*

F. of sullenness, doggedness, &c. खळ *f. v.* घे, हट *m.v.*घे.

When the fit's over the doctor comes. भोग फिटे आणि वैद्य भेटे.

2 *return after intermission.* फेरा *m.* पाळी *f.* पालट *m.*

By fits and remissions. असून असून, राहून राहून, खळून-खळून, विसवून विसवून.

By fits and starts. सोडून सोडून, धरून सोडून, टंगळमंगळ, खंडळमंडळ, तालताल.

3 (of epilepsy, &c.). फेपरें *n.* भिरकें *n.* गिरकें *n.*

Fit, *a. qualified,*—of persons. योग्य, उपयोगी, लायक, क्षम, उपयुक्त, लाजीम, अर्ह.

2 *decent, becoming, suitable.* योग्य, जोगता *or* जोगा (in comp. as राजाजोगता, भिक्षुकाजोगता, पहायाजोगता, करायाजोगता, &c.), उचित, शिस्त, शिस्तवार, लायक, लाजीम, युक्तिसार, युक्त, उपयुक्त, समर्पक. [कार्याकार्य.

F. and unfit, *proper and improper.* युक्तायुक्त, सदसत्,

3 *adapted, serviceable or suitable for.* जोगता *or* जोगा (in comp. as पायांजोगता जोडा, आंगाजोगा आंगरखा), बरोबर, लायक, अर्ह (in comp. as पूजनार्ह, भक्षणार्ह, दानार्ह, ग्रहणार्ह &c.), अनुरूप.

To **Fit**, *v. a. make qualified.* योग्य-उपयुक्त-लायक-&c. करणें, योग्यता *f.*-&c. आणणें-देणें.

2 *accommodate to, suit with, adapt.* मिळवणें, लावणें, मेळ*m.*-जवा *m.*-जम *m.*-&c. बसवणें-पाडणें, जुळणी *f.*-&c. करणें.

3 *suit, become.* शोभणें, घटणें, सजणें, साजणें.

4 out; up; *furnish, &c.* संजोगणें, सज्जणें *or* सजणें, सजवणें, सज्जना *f.*-&c. करणें *g. of o.* सज्ज-सज्जित-&c. करणें.

To **Fit**, *v. n. be fitting or proper.* शोभणें, साजणें, योग्य-ठीक-&c. होणें-दिसणें.

2—*a garment.* आंगाबरोबर होणें, आंगांत बसणें.

3 with; *suit, sit with.* मिळणें, जुळणें, लागणें, बसणें.

Fitly, *adv.* v. A. 2. योग्य, यथायोग्य, ठीक, दुरूस्त.

Fitness, *n.* v. A. 1. योग्यता *f.* लायकी *f.* अर्हता *f.* क्षमता *f.*

2 योग्यता *f.* लायकी *f.* शिस्तपणा *m.* शिस्तवारी *f.* औचित्य *n.* योग *m.* युक्ति *f.*

F. of things. नीति *f.*

3 काम *n.* उपयोग *m.* लायकी *f.*

Fitting, *a.* See **Fit.**

Five, *a.* पांच, पंच.

Aggregate of f. पंचकडी *f.* पंचक *n.* फाड *n.* पांडव *m.* (as there were five *Pándawas*).

F.-armed,—warrior, &c. *also,*—of wild beasts. पंचहत्यारी.

F.-faced. F.-sided. पंचानन, पंचमुखी.

F. fold. पांचपट.

Surplusage of f. (per cent, in buying *karbá*, mangoes, &c.). पंचोतरी *f.* पंचोतरा *m.*

Fives, *n.* एक खेळ आहे.

To **Fix**, *v. a. make fast or firm.* ठाम-गच्च-गट्ट-बळकट-&c. बसवणें-लावणें-&c. खिळणें, न हालेसा-न ढळेसा-न निघेसा-&c. करणें, स्थिर-अढळ-अचल-&c. करणें, पच्ची करणें, खिळण *f.* करणें *g.ofo.*

2 *plant, place, set.* लावणें, घालणें, नेमणें, नेमवणें, स्थापणें, स्थापना *f.*-आधान *n.*-विधान *n.*-अवस्थापन *n.*-प्रस्थापन *n.*-&c. करणें *g. of o.*

To f. one's self at. तळ *m.* घालून बसणें.

3 *settle, appoint, determine, establish.* ठरावणें, स्थापणें, नेमणें, बांधणें, नियम *or* नेम *m.*-ठराव *m.*-निश्चय *m.*-&c. करणें *g. of o.* स्थापन *n.*-&c. करणें *g. of o.* इयत्ता *f.* करणें *g. of o.* ठाम-मुकरर-नियमित *or* नेमित-निश्चित-सचीत-मोयीन-&c. करणें.

4 *confine, restrain, stay.* स्थिरावणें, थांबवणें, राहवणें, बसवणें, स्तंभन *n.*-स्तंभ *m.* करणें *g. of o.* स्थिर-&c. करणें.

To **Fix**, *v. n. rest, stay, stop,* v. To **Settle.** बसणें, स्थाकरणें, स्थिरावणें, थावरणें.

2 (as in death)—the eye. थिजणें.

3 on; *determine on.* नेम *m.*-ठराव *m.*-निश्चय *m.*-&c. करणें.

Fixed, *p. & a.* v. V. A.1. खिळलेला, न हालेसा केलेला, &c. खिळींव, ठाम, ठास, धीर थावर, काईम, अढळ, अचल, मसमू, मुसूम, मुस्तकीम. [पित, प्रस्थापित.

2 लावलेला, नेमलेला, स्थापलेला, &c. स्थापित, आहित, अवस्था-

3 ठरावलेला, नेमलेला, &c. निश्चित, नियमित, बांधा, बंदा, मोयीन, मसमू, मुसूम, मुस्तकीम, ठाम, ठास, नियत.

To be f. ठरणें.

4 स्थिरावलेला, &c. स्थिर, स्तंभित, स्तब्ध. [स्थाणु.

I. *stationary.* अढळ, स्थावर, अचर, अचल, निश्चंचल, ध्रुव,

II.—in law. *as opposed to* moveable. स्थावर.

Fixedness, *n.* v. P. 1. ठामपणा *m.* ठासपणा *m.* खिळलेपणा *m.* गच्चपणा *m.* &c. अढळपणा *m.* स्थैर्य *n.* स्थिरता *f.* काइमी *f.*

3 ठामपणा *m.* ठासपणा *m.* सचितपणा *m.* &c. निसालसता *f.* नियमितत्व *n.* निश्चितत्व *n.* &c.

4 स्थिरावलेलेपणा *m.* &c. स्तंभितत्व *n.* स्तब्धता *f.*

Fixer, *n.* v.V.A. 1. गच्च-&c. बसवणारा, खिळणारा, &c. लावणारा, &c. स्थापक, अवस्थापक, प्रस्थापक, आधान-विधान-अवस्थापन-&c. कर्त्ता, आधायक.

3 नेमणारा, ठरावणारा, &c. मुकरर करणारा, &c.

4 स्थिरावणारा, &c. स्तंभनकर्त्ता.

FIXTURE, *n. fixed furniture.* स्थावर माल *m.* स्थावरद्रव्य *n.*

To FIZZ, *To* FIZZLE, *v. n. make a hissing noise.* फदफदणें *or* फिदफिदणें, फसफसणें, फणफणणें, फिणफिणणें.

FIZZING, *n.* v. V. फदफदणें *n.* &c. फिणफिण *f.* फणफणणी *f.* —intens. फणफणाट *m.*

FLABBINESS, *n.* v. A. फोपशेपणा *m.* &c. थोंतली *or* थोंथली *f.* धोनशी *f.* धोदसी *f.* शोफ *m.* शोफा *f.* थलथल *f.*

FLABBY, *a. soft, loose, &c. not firm.* फोपशा *or* सा, थलथलीत *or* थिलथिलीत, लफलफीत, दलदलीत, थोंतील *or* थोंथील, सुटलेला, कापशा, धोनशा, भेंगळ, भसभेंगळ, शिथिल, वाहवरा, फदूल, फपोला, ढिसळ *or* ढिसूळ *or* ढिसाळ.

That is f. सुटल्या आंगाचा, फोपशा आंगाचा.

To grow f. कापुसणें.

FLACCID, *a. not stiff, not tense, &c.* बिलबिला, बिलबिलीत, लिबलिबीत, बिळबिळीत, मिसमिसीत, गिलगिलीत, ढिला, ढोल, शिथिल, सैल.

FLACCIDITY, FLACCIDNESS, *n.* v. A. बिलबिलेपणा *m.* लिबलिबीतपणा *m.* शिथिलपणा *m.* &c. शैथिल्य *n.* शिथिलता *f.*

To FLAG, *v. n. hang loose, &c.* ढिला-ढोल-सैल-&c. होणें-होऊन पडणें, पडणें, लेंबकळणें, झोळंबणें, झोल *m.* येणें *in. con.*

2 fig. *languish, &c.* v. To DROOP. थंडावणें, मंदावणें, हलकावणें, सुस्तावणें, गळणें, उतरणें.

FLAG, *n. colors, ensign.* निशाण *or* न *n.* बावटा *or* बाहुटा *m.* झेंडा *m.* पताक *f.* पताका *f.* ध्वज *m.* ध्वजा *f.* केतु *m.* बैरक *f.*

Grand f. of an army (directing its march and encampments). ढाल *f.* Bearer of it. ढालाईत, ढाल्या, ढालकरी.

The streamer or pennon of the grand flag of the Peshwà. जरीपटका *m.*

2 *flat stone for pavements.* फरशी *f.* फरशा दगड *m.*-धोंडा *m.*

3 पाण्यांतील एक वनस्पति आहे.

To FLAG, *v. a.* फरसबंदी *f.* करणें.

FLAG-STAFF, *n.* ढालकाठी *f.* काठी *f.* ध्वजस्तंभ *m.*

Tuft or bunch at the end of f. हरडा *or* हिरडा *m.*

To FLAGELLATE, FLAGELLATION. See To WHIP, WHIPPING.

FLAGEOLET, *n. pipe.* अलगुजें *n.* [शैथिल्य *n.*

FLAGGINESS, *n.* v. A. ढिलेपणा *m.* सैलपणा *m.* &c. शिथिलाई *f.*

FLAGGY, *a. lax, limber.* ढिला, ढील, सैल, शिथिल, झोलआलेला.

FLAGITIOUS, &c. See WICKED, &c.

FLAGON, *n.* v. VESSEL. जांब *or* जाम *m.* सुरा *f.* सुरई *f.* चंबू *m.*

FLAGRANCE, FLAGRANCY, *n.* v. A. उघडपणा *m.* धडधडीतपणा *m.*

FLAGRANT, *a. glaring, notorious.* ठळक, उघड, धडधडीत, टळटळीत, ढळढळीत.

FLAIL, *n.* झोडण्याची काठी *f.* [ल *m. f.*

FLAKE, *n.* (of fire). किटाळ *n.* कोजळी *f.* पोळा *m.* फुणगी *f.* गू-

FLAM, *n. trick, lie.* फटवण *f.* फसवण *f.* ठकवण *f.*

FLAMBEAU, *n.* v. TORCH. टेंभा *m.* दिवटी *f.* कांकडा *m.*

FLAME, *n.* ज्वाला *f. pop.* जाळ *m.* ज्वाळ *f.* ज्वाळा *f.* अग्निशिखा *f.* अग्निज्वाला *f.* कील *f.*

Fierce, glowing f. भडका *m.* भडाका *m.*

Spire or tongue of f. आगीची जीभ *f.* आगिबळा *m.* आगिबळी *f.* अग्निशिखा *f.*

To set in a f. (a town, country, &c.). fig. फुंकणें *or* फुंकून देणें (गांव, देश &c.).

2 See ARDOR, PASSION.

To FLAME, *v. n.* ज्वाला *f. pop.* जाळ *m.*-ज्वाळ *f.*-ज्वाळा *f.* होणें-येणें- उठणें *g. of s.* भबकणें.

FLAME-COLORED, *a.* निखाररंगी, अग्निवर्ण.

FLAMING, *p. a.* v. V. ज्वाली, ज्वलित, जाज्वल्यमान, जाज्वल्य, दीप्तिमान्, देदीप्यमान.

I. *fervent, vehement,* v. ARDENT. आवेशाचा, तलख.

FLAMINGO, *n.* हंसक *m.* [अंक *m.*

FLANK, *n. side, near the thigh.* कड *f.* कट *m.* कडसणी *f.* कटि *f*

Sunkenness or hollowness of the f. (from fasting, &c.) v. BELLY. भकाटी *f.* भकाळी *f.* पाखल *f.* बाखल *f.*

2 (as of an army). बाजू *f.* पार्श्वभाग *m.* पार्श्वांग *n.*

To FLANK, *v. a. attack the flank.* बाजूवर हल्ला *m.* करणें.

2 *turn the flank.* बाजूला फेरा घालून जाणें.

3 दुतर्फा उभे करणें, बाजूवर उभे करणें.

FLANNEL, *n.* धुशा *or* सा *or* धोसा *m.* but the word commonly used is फलानेल *f.* from the English.

FLAP, *n. thing to flap with ; fan, &c.* झडपण *n.* झडपणें *n.* झडपणी *f.* फटकणें *n.* हडपणें *n.* बिंझुणा *m.*

2 (of trowsers, &c.). खिस्तक *n. f.*

3 v. FLAPPING. झटका *m.* झटकारा *m.* झणकार *or* रा *m.*

4 (of a coat, &c.). *skirt.* झोल *m.* घेर *m.*

To FLAP, *v. a. beat with a flap.* झडपणें, फटकणें, हडपणें, झटकणें, झटकावणें, झटका *or* झटकारा *m.* देणें.

To f. out, (a light). पालवणें, पालव *m.* करणें-टाकणें, झणकाऱ्यानें विझवणें-मालवणें-&c.

2 *move with a flapping noise.* फडफडवणें *or* फडफडाविणें.

To FLAP, *v. n. ply the wings noisily.* फडफडणें, झडफडणें, फडत्कार *m.* करणें. [*adv.* वाजणें.

2 *make a flapping noise.* फडफडणें, फडकणें, फडफड-झडफड

FLAP-EARED, *a.* गजकर्ण.

FLAPPER, *n. fan, &c.* v. FLAP. झडपण *n.* फटकणें *n.*

FLAPPING, *n.* v. V. A. 1. झडपणें *n.* &c. झडपणी *f.* झटका *m.* झटकारा *m.* झणकार *or* रा *m.*

A general f. झडपाझडपी *f.*

2 फडफडवणें *n.* फडफडवणी *f.* फडफडावणी *f.*

v. V. N. 1. फडफडणें *n.* &c. फडफड *f.* फडफडणी *f.*

2 फडफडणें *n.* &c.

I. *noise of f.* फडत्कार *m. intens.* फडफडाट *m.* फडाड *m.*

FLAPPINGLY, *adv.* फटफट *or* टां, फडफड *or* डां, चरचर *or* रां-*intens.* फटाफट, फटाटां, फडाफड, फडाडां, चराचर, चरारां.

To FLARE, *v. n. burn fiercely or blazingly,*—a light, &c. ढणढणणें, ढळढळणें, ढणढण-ढळढळ-&c. जळणें.

2 *glitter with painful splendor,* v. To GLARE. रसरसणें, रणरणणें, झळकणें, भडक *f.* मारणें.

FLARING, *p. a.* v. V. ढणढणीत, ढळढळीत.

2 रसरसीत, रणरणीत.

I. *flashy, showy, &c.* भडक, भबूक, झळक, भळभळीत.

FLARINGLY, *adv.* v. A. ढणढण, ढळढळ *or* ळां *intens.* ढळाढळ *and* ढळाळां, ढणाढण *or* णां.

FLASH, FLASHING, *n.* v. V. चक्क *n.* लक्क *n.* झग *n.* चमक *f.* झगमग *f.* झळझळ *f.*—*intens.* vivid f. dazzling f. &c. चमच-

माट *m.* झकझकाट *m.* झलाल *m.* झकाकी *or* झगागी *f.* चकाकी *f.* चकाचकी *f.*

F. and no fight. अजायुद्ध *n.* दंपतिकलह *m.* मेघाडंबर *n.*

With a f. चक्-कन-कर-&c. झक-कण-कर&c.लक्कण,लक्कर,&c.

2 *glaring and transient display.* टिमटीम *f.* टिरटीर *f.* टुरटूर *or* टुरटुरू *f.*

A brilliant f. and then a prison,—the Prodigal's course. तुरतुरं फुरफुरं तीनमासं चंदनंबंदनं तीन मासं लपनं छपन तीन मास शृंखला बंधनं तीन मासं.

To FLASH, *v. n. glitter with a transient flame.* चकमकणें, चमकणें, चकचकणें *intens.* चकाकणें, लकलक *adv.* करणें, लकलकणें *intens.* लकाकणें, तळपणें, झगमगणें,झकझकणें *intens.* झकाकणें, लवणें.

To f. in the pan. रंजक *f.* पिणें-उडणें.

FLASHINESS, *n.* v. A. 1. बाहेरची ढब *f.* बाहेरून गोजरेपणा *m.*

2 लकलकीतपणा *m.* भळभळीतपणा *m.* भडक *f. v.* मार, झळक *f. v.* मार, भळभळाट *m.*

FLASHY, *a. showy but empty.* देखणाऊ, देखाऊ, टिकमिरवणा, अहेराऊ, अहेरी, ढबदार, फूलझधारा, डौल्या, बाहेरच्याडौलाचा, बाहेरचेढबेचा, बाहेरून गोजरा-भव्य, इंजाई.

2 *showy, gaudy,* v. FINE. लकलकीत, लक्क, लकीलक्क, झळक, भडक, भडकीचा, ढबदार, भळभळीत, उद्दाम, दर्शनी.

FLASK. See BOTTLE, VESSEL. 2 See POWDER-FLASK.

FLAT, *a. level, even.* सपाट, समान, सारखा, सम, पाणसाळ.

2 *not rising high, extended.* चपटा, चापट, बसका, बसकट, चपताड, चपताडा, चपतळ, चपतळा.

3 *level with the ground, lying, fallen.* चपाट, चपेट, सपाट, जमीनदोस्त, भुईबरोबर.

To lay f. पाडून टाकणें, बिछावणें, चीत *adv.*-जमीनदोस्त *adv.* करणें, लंबा *adv. decl. or* लंबे *adv.* करणें.

4 *dead, vapid, spiritless.* फिका *or* फिक्का *remiss.* फिकट, पाणचट, पचपचीत, पचकळ, पचरट,मळमळीत, मिटमिटीत, बाकस *or* बाकूस, हिमळ, बेकस, अळणी, निस्सत्व, निस्सार, मुळमुळीत *or* मिळमिळीत, असार, अरसिक, गतरस, गतस्वाद, गतसार, गतसत्व, निर्जीव, निर्वीर्य, नीरस, रुक्ष, उमळा *or* उंबळा, पचाल *or* ळ.

5—of sounds. तरळ, बोद, बदबदीत, ढबढबीत.

To sound f.—relaxed drum, &c. डबडबणें *intens.* डबाबणें.

6 *downright, outright,* v. POSITIVE. साफ, उघड, निखालस.

F. refusal. निझाडा *m. v.* दे.

FLAT, *n. level tract.* v. PLAIN. पटंगण *or* पटांगण *or* पाटंगण *n.* पाटा *m.* माळ *m.*

2 (on hilly ground). भाटलें *n.* माळी *f.*

3 *shallow.* भाट *f. n. dim.* भाटी *f.*

FLAT-NOSED, *a.* चपणी, नतनासिक.

FLAT-ROOFED, *a.* धाब्याचा.

FLAT-WISE, *adv.* थपी.

FLATLY, *adv. downright, peremptorily,* v. A. 6. निक्षूण, साफ, परिछिन्न, निझाडून.

To reply or state f. तटका *m.* तोडणें-तोडून टाकणें.

FLATNESS, *n.* v.A. 1. सपाटी *f.*सपाटपणा*m.*सारखेपणा*m.*समानता*f.*

2 चपटेपणा *m.* बसकेपणा *m.* &c. [*f.* गतसारता *f.*

4 फिकेपणा *m.* पाणचटपणा *m.* मळमळितपणा *m.* &c. गतरसता

To FLATTEN, *v. a.* चापटणें, चेपणें, चेगठणें, चपटा-&c. करणें.

FLATTENED, *p.* v. V. चापटलेला, &c. चापट, चपटा, चपडा, चेपट.

To FLATTER, *v.a. court by praise, blandishments, obsequiousness, &c.* मुखस्तुति *f.*-आर्जव *n.*-खुशामद *or* खुशामत *f.* करणें, तोंड पाहून-तोंडासारखें-तोंडापुरतें-तोंडदेखलें-तोंडदेखणें-तोंडदेखें-&c. बोलणें, जी-जीजी-हांजी *adv.* करणें-म्हणणें.

To f. one's self, pride one's self on. अकड *f.*-अभिमान *m.* बाळगणें-भोगणें-धरणें *g. of o.*

2 *gratify, &c.* v. To PLEASE. संतोषविणें, संतुष्ट-&c. करणें.

FLATTERER, *n.* FLATTERING, *p.a.* v. V. 1. खुशामद-&c. करणारा, खुशामती *or* खुशामदी, खुशामत्या, खुशामदखोर, तोंड पाहून बोलणारा, तोंडासारखें-&c. बोलणारा, आर्जवी, आर्जवू, जीजी-&c. करणारा-म्हणणारा, मिथ्याप्रशंसक.

2 संतोषविणारा, संतोषकारक.

FLATTERY, *n.* मुखस्तुति *f.* खुशामद *or* खुशामत *f.* आर्जव *n.* स्तुतिवाद *m.* लाडीगोडी *f.* मिथ्या प्रशंसा *f.* तोंडासारखें बोलणें *n.* तोंडदेखलें बोलणें *n.* तोंडापुरतें बोलणें*n.*—With the power of such words as, *butter, soap, palaver, blarney, flummery.* गूळखोबरें *n.* गूळपापडी *f.* गूळगूळधापडी *f.* घमटगुळवणी *n.* लभगोष्टी *f. pl.* व-हाडगोष्टी *f. pl.* धातुपोषणाचें बोलणें *n.*-गोष्टी *f. pl.*

FLATULENCE, FLATULENCY, *n. windiness in the stomach.* वायु *m.* वातरोग *m.* वायुरोग *m.* आमवात *m.* आमवायु *m.* कुपितवायु *m.* कोष्ठवायु *m.* आध्मात *m.* आध्मान *n.*

Bilious f. पित्तवायु *m.* [जंतबातालें *n.*

F. occasioned by worms. कृमिबातालें *or* किरीमबातालें *n.*

F. with heat. उष्णवायु *m.*

FLATULENT, *a. producing wind, windy.* बावडा, वातूल *or* ळ, वायुबद्धक, वातिक, वातकर-कारक.

2—of the state or habit of body. वातप्रकृतीचा, वातूल *or* ळ, वातबद्ध, वायुबद्ध, वायुग्रस्त, वातप्रधान, वातप्रकृतिक.

FLATUS, See FLATULENCE.

To FLAUNT, *v. n. make a display of finery, &c.* छानछुकी *f.* मिरवणें, छानछुकीची मिरवण *f.*-मिरवणूक *f.* करणें, भडक *f.*-&c. मारणें.

FLAUNTING, *p. a.* v. V. *and* FINE. भडक मारणारा, भडक, भडकीचा, भळभळीत.

FLAVOR, *n.* v. TASTE. चव *f.* मजा *f.* स्वाद *m.* रुचि *f.* रूच *f.* आस्वाद *m.* बोई *f.* रस *m.*

To FLAVOR, *v. a.* चव *f.*-स्वाद *m.*-&c. देणें.

FLAVORLESS, *a.* v. TASTELESS. निचव, बेचव, अरुचिकर.

FLAVORED, FLAVOROUS, *a.* v. TASTEFUL. चवदार, मजेदार, स्वादिष्ट, रुचिकर, रसिक.

Exquisitely f. षड्रस.

FLAW, *n. crack.* दोरा *m.* दोरबा *m.* चीर *f.* तडा *m.* बाल *m.* फूट *f.*

Having a f. फुटक, फुटकर, पिचका, फाटफूट.

2 *blemish, imperfection, defect,* v. FAULT. बिंग *or* बिंगें *n.* गोम *f.* व्यंग *n.* फांट *m.* छिद्र *n.* दोष *m.* खोड *f.* ऐब *m.*

3 (in a rupee, &c.). फाटफूट *f.* खोड *f.*

Having a f. फुटक, फुटकर, पिचका, फाटफूट, कच्ची.

FLAWLESS, *a.* निखोड, अखोड, निकोप, निकोपी, निर्दोष, साफ, अछिद्र, अव्रण.

FLAWY, *a.* v. N. 1. फुटक, फुटकर, पिचका, फाटफूट.

2 खोडकर, खोडीचा, ऐबदार, बिंगी, गोमीचा.

Flax, *n.* *linum usitalissimun.* जवस *m. n.* जवशी *f.* अळशी *or* सी *f.* अतसी *f.*
 2–the fibre. जवसाचे दोर *m pl.*
Flaxen, *a.* जवसाचा.
To **Flay**, *v. a. skin.* सोलणें, कातडी *f.*-चामडी *f.* लोंबवणें-काढणें, टोपसाल *n.* काढणें-उडवणें *g. of o.* उधडणें. [स्वच.
Flayed, *p.* v. V. सोललेला, टोपसाल काढलेला, &c. सोलींव, नि-
Flea, *n.* पिसू *f.* पीस *f.* पुशी *f.*
Fleabane, *n.*—purple. काळीजिरी *f.* कडूकारळी *f.*—seed. कालेंजिरें *n.* कडूकारळें *n.* काळेंरें *n.*
Flea-bite, *n.* पिसूचा दंश *m.*
Fleam, *n.* घोड्याचें रक्त काढण्याचें नख्तर *n.*
Fleawort, *n.*—plant or seed. इसपगोल *m.*
Flecked. See **Speckled.** [जातपक्ष, ग्रामपक्ष.
Fledge, Fledged, *a. furnished with feathers.* पंख फुटलेला,
 To be or become f. पंख *m. pl.* फुटणें.
To **Flee**, *v. n.* पळणें, पळून जाणें, पळ *m. f.* काढणें, पाठ *f.* दाखवणें-देणें, यः पलायाचें *n.* करणें, पोबारा *m.* करणें-म्हणणें.
 To f. wildly, as in rout, fright, &c. उधळणें, पळ *m. f.* काढणें, भणभणणें, दिशांदिशां *adv.* पळणें.
Fleece, *n.* एके मेंढीची एके खेपेस कातरलेली लोंकर *f.*
To **Fleece**, *v. a. shear off wool.* लोंकर *f.* कातरणें-कातरून काढणें.
 2 *pill, pluck,* v. To **Plunder.** बोडणें, टोपसाल *n.* काढणें, बोडकावणें, घासणें, घासटणें, मुंडणें, घर *n.* घेणें, घर *n.* धुणें.
Fleecy. See **Woolly.**
To **Fleer**, &c. See To **Mock**, &c.
Fleet, *a. swift-going,* v. **Swift.** धावरा, पळका, चालक, चालूक, जलद, जंघाल *pop.* जंघाळ, पायसूट, अतिवेगी, जवी, वेगवान्.
Fleet, *n.* (of ships of war). अरमर *or* अरमार *n.* लढाऊ गलबतांचा समुदाय *m.*
Fleeting, *a. transient,* v. **Temporary.** अस्थायी, क्षणिक, चल, उत्पन्नविनाशी. [रून.
Fleetly, *adv.* v. A. *and* **Swiftly.** जलद, जलदीनें, अतिवेगेंक-
Fleetness, *n.* v. A. धावरेपणा *m.* जलदी *f.* जंघाळपणा *m.* वेग *m.* त्वरा *f.* अतिवेग *m.*
Flesh, *n.* मांस *pop.* मास *n.* आमिष *n.* क्रव्य *n.*—contemptuously. मासकंड *n.* मासकण *n.* मासगंड *n.* मासुरडा *m.* मासुरडें *n.*
 Dead or proud f. मुडदारमास *n.* पूतिमांस *n.*
 Marks burned into the f. तप्तमुद्रा *f.*
 Way of all f. महापथ *m.*
 To lose f. आंग *n.* टाकणें-सांडवणें-सोडणें.
 To turn into f.—food. आंगीं *or* आंगास लागणें.
 2 *flesh meat, animal food.* मांस *pop.* मास *n.* सागुती *or* सागोती *f.* आमिष *n.*
 3 *carnal appetites.* विषयबुद्धि *f.* विषयासक्ति *f.* विषयवासना *f.* विषयतल्लीनता *f.* विषयसेवा *f.* विषयव्यासंग *m.*
 4 *carnal state.* इंद्रियाधीनता *f.* इंद्रियवशता *f.*
 5 v. **Body.** शरीर *n.* देह *m.*
 6 *mankind.* मनुष्यजाति *f.* मनुष्यमात्र *n.*
Flesh-diet, *n.* मांसाहार *m.*
Flesh-meat. See **Flesh.**
Fleshiness, *n.* v.A.1. मासाळपणा *m.* गबगबीतपणा *m.* &c. मांसपुष्टि *f.* मांसशीलता *f.*
Fleshliness, *n.* v. A. 1. विषयबुद्धि *f.* विषयासक्ति *f.* विषयपरता *f.*
Fleshly, *a. carnal,* v. **Sensual.** विषयाचा, विषयी, विषयासक्त, इंद्रियवश, रजोगुणी.
 2 *human, not divine.* मनुष्याचा, मानवी, मनुष्यजातीचा.
Fleshy, *a.* v. **Plump, Fat.** मांसल *pop.* मासाळ, मासभरू, मांसशील, मांसपुष्ट, गबगबीत *or* गुबगुबीत, टमटमीत *or* टुमटुमीत, खुराकाचा.
 2 *pulpous.* गरभरू, गाभडा, भरदार.
 3 *belonging to flesh.* मासाचा, मांससंबंधी. [पणा *m.*
Flexibility, Flexibleness, *n.* v. A. 1. लवचीकपणा *m.* लवके-
 2 मऊपणा *m.* मृदुता *f.* नमनशीलत्व *n.*
Flexible, Flexile, *a. pliable, pliant, supple, limber, lithe.* लवचीक, लवका, नमनशील.
 2 *soft, easy, &c.* मऊ, मृदु, नमनशील, सुनम्य.
Flexous. See **Winding.**
Flexure. See **Bend, Bent.**
Flicker, Flickering, *n.* v.V.1.—*act.* टिकटीक *n.* टिकटिकी *f.* लुकलुकी *f.* धुगधुगी *f.* धुगधूग *f.*
To **Flicker**, *v. n. quiver,*—as a light, life, &c. टिकटिकणें, लुकलुकणें, लिकलिकणें, लकलकणें, लिकलीक *adv.*-लुकलूक *adv.*-टिकटिक *adv.*-मरूंमरूं *adv.*-झिरूमिरू *adv.* करणें, जायास करणें, घुटमळणें *or* मुळणें.
 2 See To **Flutter.**
Flickerer, *n.* **Flickering**, *p. a.* v. V. 1. टिकटिकणारा, टिकटीक करणारा, &c. लिकलिकीत, लुकलुकीत, झिरूमिरू.
Flickeringly, *adv.* टिकटिकी, टिकटीक, झिरूमिरू.
Flight, *n.* v.V.—*volation.* उडणें *n.* उड्डाण *n.* [पलायन *n.*
 I. *or* **Fleeing.** पळणें *n.* पळून जाणें *n.* पळण *or* पळणी *f.*
 General f. पळ *m. f.* पळण *n.* पळणी *f.* पळपट *f.* पळापळ *f.* धांवाधांव *f.* भणाण *m.*
 To put to f. पळविणें, पळायास लावणें.
 To take to f. पळ *m. f.* काढणें.
 II. (of birds) v. **Flock.** झुंड *f.* साईर *f.*
 III. (of arrows, &c.) See **Volley.**
 IV. (of stairs or steps) जिना *m.* सोपान *n.* सिडी *or* शिडी *f.* सिढी *or* शिढी *f.*
Flightiness, *n.* v. A. वायचळ *m.* चंचळपणा *m.* चंचलता *f.*
Flighty, *a. wild, fanciful, disordered in mind.* वायचळ्या, चंचल *pop.* चंचळ, अचपळ, उडलटप्पू, उडाणटप्पू, लहरी, लहरीदार, अव्यवस्थितबुद्धि.
Flimsiness, *n.* v. A. नादानी *f.* नादानकी *f.* लुकसानी *or* लुसकानी *f.* फुसकेपणा *m.* &c.
Flimsy, *a. weak, of slight texture, worthless, &c.* फुसका, फुसकुला, गलतान, पादरफुसका, धुसका फुसका, नादान, नुकसान *or* नी *or* लुकसान *or* लुसकान, कमतणूक, कमजोर, निर्जीव, कागदी, जुजबी, लेंचीपेची, लेंचापेंचा, अचकूल, बाजेगिरी, अलबेला, इंजाईत, वालथर, लुंगा, थिसूळ, शेणामेणाचा, झाबू *or* झाबू, हाडाचा खोटा वाईट-&c.
 A f. thing. आयाबाया *f.*
To **Flinch**, *v. n. draw back, shrink,* v. To **Draw-back.** कचणें, कचकणें, कचकरणें, कच *f.* खाणें, घसरणें, हटणें, मागें पाहणें-होणें, माघार *f.*-&c. घेणें, मोडतें *n.*-काढतें *n.*-&c. घेणें, पाऊल *n.* मागें काढणें.

FLINCHER, *n.* v. V. कचखाणारा, घसरणारा, हटणारा, &c. आंगकाढ्या, आंगकाढू, माघार-&c. घेण्या.

FLINCHING, *n.* v.V.—*act.* कचणें*n.* घसरणें*n.* &c. कच *f.* माघार *f.*

To FLING, *v. a.* v. To CAST. झोकणें, फेंकणें, घालणें, टाकणें, फिगारणें.

2 (in wrestling) v. To THROW. पाडणें, चीत करणें.

3 out; (a limb, &c.). असडणें, झटकावणें, असडा*m.*-हिसडा*m.*-झटका*m.*-झटकारा*m.* देणें.

4 open. झपाट्यासरसा-झोकासरसा-झोक्यानें-झपाट्यानें-&c. उघडणें.

To FLING, *v. n. kick, &c.* v. To FLOUNCE. आदळ आपट *f.* करणें, हातपाय*m. pl.* पासडणें-आपटणें-आदळणें-झाडणें.

2 out; *lash out.* दुगाण्या *f. pl.*-दुलाच्या *f. pl.*-दुमच्या *f. pl.*-लात्या *f. pl.*- पिछाड्या *f. pl.* झाडणें.

FLING, FLINGING, *n.* v. V.A. 1.—*act* .झोकणें*n.* फेंकणें*n.*&c.क्षेप *m.* प्रक्षेप *m.* [टेपरण *n.*

I. v. SARCASM. टोला*m.* तुक्का*m.* आक्षेप*m.* अवक्षेप *m.* टेपरा *m.*

FLINT, *n.* गार *f.* गारगोटा *m. dim.* गारगोटी *f.* चकमकीचा धोंडा *m.* फतरी *f.* अग्निप्रस्तर *m.*

A f. and steel for striking fire. चकमक *f.*

To get milk from a f. दगडास पान्हा*m. or* पाझर*m.* आणणें, स्वांबाला डीक*m.* पाहणें, दगडाचा दोर *m.* काढणें.

FLINT-HEARTED, *a.* v. PITILESS. पाषाणहृदय, कठिनहृदय.

FLINTY, *a.* गारगोटी, गारगोट्यांचा.

FLIPPANCY, FLIPPANTNESS, *n.* v. A. 1. पातळजीभ *f.* तोंडचा चपळपणा *m.* वाक्चापल्य *n.*

FLIPPANT, *a. voluble,* v. GLIB. तोंडचा चपळ, पातळजिभेचा, पातळजिभ्या, लुबलुब बोलणारा, वाकूचपल, चपलवाकू, चपलजिह्व.

2—of speeches, &c. तोंडचे चपळपणाचा, पातळजिभेचा, वाकूचापल्याचा.

FLIPPANTLY, *adv.* v. A. पातळजिभेनें, वाकूचापल्यपूर्वक.

FLIRT, *n. giddy, &c. girl.* नाचणघुगरी *f.* नाचरी *f.* टेवखोर *f.* नखरेबाज *f.*

To FLIRT, *v. a.* See To JERK.

To FLIRT, *v. n. act with coquetry.* नखरा*m.*-अदा *m.*-हाव*m.pl.* करणें-दाखवणें.

2 See To SNEER.

FLIRTATION, *n.*v.V. N.1.—*act.* नखरेबाजी *f.* नखरा*m.* हाव*m.pl.*

To FLIT, *v. n. fly away.* उडून जाणें, उड्डाण*n.*-प्रडीन*n.* करणें.

2 *migrate.* घर*n.*—जागा *f.*-&c. पालटणें, थारेपालट *m.*-थळपालट*m.*-स्थानांतर*n.*-&c. करणें.

3 See To FLUTTER.

FLITCH, *n.* डुकराचा वाळवलेला पार्श्वभाग*m.*

To FLOAT, *v. n. swim or be borne on the surface.* तरणें, पोवणें, तरंगणें, तिरणें, तरावणें *or* तऱ्हावणें, तरण*n.*-प्लवन*n.* होणें *g. of s.*

2 along, down, &c. वाहवणें, वाहणें, वाहून जाणें.

To FLOAT, *v. a.* वाहवून नेणें.

2 See To INUNDATE.

FLOAT, *n. raft.* ताफा*m.* तर *f.* तरण*n.*

F. composed of gourds. पेटें*n.* पेटा*m.*

F. composed of two canoes or boats. सांगड *m.f.*—that works it. सांगड्या.

2 *timbers, &c. set to float down.* ताफा *m.*

FLOATING, *p. a.* v. V. N. 1. तरता.

FLOCK, *n.* (of sheep or goats). कळप *m.* खिल्लार *n.* झुंड *f.* कुळ *n.* यूथ *n.* सागा *m.* खांड *n.* थवा *m.*

2 (of birds). पल्ला *m.* साईर *f.* झुंड *f.* झांक *f.*

3 *body or crowd of people.* थोट *m.* गट्टा *m.* घोळका *m.* घोळ *m.* गोल *m.*

4 *lock of wool.* लोंकरीचा बुचका *m.*-पुंजका *m.*

To FLOCK, *v. n. gather in a company or crowd.* जमणें, एकवटणें, गोळा-जमा होणें, मेळा *m.* जमणें *g. of. s.*

To FLOG, *v. a. beat with a whip, &c.* छडी *f.*-चाबूक *m.*-कोरडा *m.*-कमची *f.*-चमकी *f.*-&c. मारणें-चमकावणें, फटके *m.pl.*-फटकारे *m. pl.* मारणें, चमकावणें.

FLOOD, *n. body of water.* लोंढा *m.* लोट *m.* लाट *f.*

A f. of tears. अश्रुधारा *f.*

2 *inundation,* v. DELUGE. पाणजंजाळ *n.* जलप्रलय *m.*

3 (of the tide) *flow, flux.* भरती *f.* जोर *m.*

To FLOOD, *v. a.* v. To DELUGE. जलमय-&c. करणें.

FLOOD-GATE, *n.* उघडी *f.* सांडवा *m.* सांड *f.*

FLOODED, *p.* v. V. *deluged, inundated.* जलमय केलेला, &c. जलाकीर्ण, जलाक्रांत, जलमय, जलाप्लुत.

FLOODING, *n. excessive discharge from the uterus.* विटाळाचा लोंढा *m.*-लोट *m.* लोंढ्यासारखा विटाळ *m.*

FLOOK, *n.* (of an anchor). पावडा*m.* फाळ*m.* कांटा*m.* आंकडा*m.*

FLOOR, *n.*—of planks. कडिपाट *m.* पाटणी *f.* पटाई *f.* तक्तपोशी *f.*—of earth. जमीन *f.*भुई *f.*भूमि *f.*कृत्रिमभूमि *f.*—of chunam. गच्ची *or* चुनेगच्ची *f.*—of paved stone. फरस*m.*फरसबंदी *f.*

A well beaten terrace or f. चीण *f.*

Earthen f. of an upper story, loft, &c. पेंड *m.*

F.-patter or beater. चोपण *or* णी *f. or* णें *n.* भुरवणें *n.*

Laying a f. of planks. पटाई *f.*

To flatten (by beating) a f. चोपणें, चोपटणें.

To smooth a f. नेपाळणें.

2 See STORY.

To FLOOR, *v. a. cover with a floor,*—of planks. पाटणें, कडेपाट *m.*-तक्तपोशी *f.*-तक्तबंदी *f.* करणें,—of earth. जमीन *f.*-भुई *f.* करणें.

2 *knock down.* पाडून टाकणें, बिछावणें, लोळवणें, पछाडणें, चीत *adv.*-जमीनदोस्त *adv.*-लंबा *or* लंबे *adv.* करणें.

3 *silence, pose, &c.* कुंठित-निरुत्तर- &c. करणें, तोंड *n.* बंद करणें *g. of o.*

FLOOR-CLOTH, *n.* जाजम *n.*

FLOORED, *p.* v. V. 1. पाटलेला, कडेपाट केलेला, &c.

2 पाडून टाकलेला, लोळवलेला, &c. चीत, जमीनदोस्त, लंबा *adv. decl.* लंबे *adv.*

3 कुंठित केलेला, &c. कुंठित, निरुत्तर.

FLOORING. See FLOOR.

FLOP, *interj.* डुब-कन-कर-&c.चुट-कन-कर-&c. घसंवकर.

Flop! Flop! *floppingly.* डकडक *or* कां, डचडच *or* चां, थलथल *or* लां.

To FLOP, *v. n. shake about with a noise.* लफलफणें, सळबळणें, डचमळणें, डचडचणें, थलथलणें, डुचमळणें.

2 over. हिसळणें.

FLOPPER, *n.* FLOPPING, *p. a.* v. V. 1. डचमळणारा, &c. डळडळीत, डचडचीत, थलथलीत.

FLORAL, *a. pertaining to flowers.* फुलांचा, पुष्पांचा, पौष्प, पुष्पसंबंधी, सौमनस.

FLORID, *a. brightly red.* लालचुंद, लालभडक, भडक, लाल.
2—of style, &c. *brilliant.* अलंकारी, अलंकारिक, अलंकारयुक्त, अलंकारप्रचुर, अलंकारप्रधान.

FLORIDITY, FLORIDNESS, *n.* v. A. 1. लालभडकपणा *m.* &c. लाली *f.* रक्तिमा *m.* [रप्राधान्य *n.*
2 आलंकारिकत्व *n.* अलंकारप्राचुर्य *n.* अलंकारबाहुल्य *n.* अलंका-

FLORIFEROUS, *a. producing flowers.* पुष्पावह, पुष्पप्रद.

FLORIN, *n.* एक नाणें आहे.

FLORIKIN, *n. otis aurita.* मोठा तनमोर *m.*

FLORIST, *n. cultivator of flowers.* फूलमाळी *m.* फुलारी*m.* माळी*m.*

FLOSS, *n. downy substance.* कापूस *m.*

FLOSS-SILK, *n.* कच्चें रेशीम *n.*

FLOTAGE, FLOTSON, FLOTSAM, *n.* फुटल्या तरांड्याचा माल *m.* सारीमाती *f.* अस्वामिक तरितद्रव्य *n.*

FLOUNCE, *n.* झालरीसारखा झग्याचा झोल *m.*

To FLOUNCE, *To* FLOUNDER, *v. n. struggle, fling about with violence.* धडपडणें *or* फडणें *or* बडणें, चडफडणें, तडफडणें, हातपाय *m. pl.* पासडणें-आदळणें-आपटणें-झाडणें-नाचवणें, नाचणें, आदळआपट *f.* करणें.

FLOUNCING, FLOUNDERING, *n.* v. V.—*act.* धडफडणें *n.* &c. तडफड *f. intens.* तडफडाट *m.* धडपड *or* फड *or* बड *f. intens.* धडफडाट *m.* चडफड *f. intens.* चडफडाट *m.*

FLOUR, *n.* पीठ *n.* पिष्ट *n.* धान्यचूर्ण *n.*
Balls of f. fried. बुंद्या *f. pl.*
Bread, &c. made of coarsely ground f. जाडीभरडी भाकर *f.*-पोळी *f.*-&c.
F. and water sugared. पीठपाणी *n.*
F. of pulse and rice coarsely ground together. भरडा*m.*
F. boiled (for various purposes). उकड *f.* धुली *f.* पिठी *f.* खळ *f.*
F. cast over cakes in rolling out. लाटण *n.*
F. of various grains parched and ground together. भाजणी *f.* [टवा *m.*
F. rolled up by the finger. गव्हुला *m.* बोटवा *m.* घोळबो-
F. sprinkled (to be soured). आंबतें *n.*
F. used to thicken. कणी *f.*
Fine rice f. पिठी *f.*
Gram f. बेसन *m. n.*
Rolls of pulse f. fried. शेव *f.*
Wheaten f. कणीक *f.*
Coarse wheaten f. सांजा *m.*
Fine wheaten f. मैदा *m.* कणकीचा गरा *m.* सोजी *f.* सपिठी *f.* सपीठ *n.* रवा *m.*

To FLOURISH, *v. n.*—of plants, &c. पोसणें, तरतरणें, टवटवणें, जिवट-जीवदार-&c. होणें, जिवटणें, जीव *m.* धरणें.
2 of persons, affairs, &c. *thrive,* v. To PROSPER. वर्धणें, तरतरणें, तरारणें, रंगास चढणें, जमणें, सतेज असणें, भरभर *f. intens.* भरभराट *m.*-चलती *f.*-चालताकाळ *m.*-&c. असणें *g. of s.*
3—as a town, country, &c. आबाद *or* आबादान होणें, आबादानी *f.*-आबादी *f.* असणें *g. of s.*
4 (with a pen, &c.). बिरखडणें *or* बिरखुडणें, भरकंडणें, भरकांडे *m. pl.* मारणें, बिरखड्या *f. pl.*-खिरबिट्या *f. pl.*-काढणें-मारणें, फरगडे *m. pl.* फोडणें.

To FLOURISH, *v. a. wave,* v. To BRANDISH. परजणें, चमकावणें.
2 (the arms—in oratory). पट्टा *m.* परजणें, हातवारे *m. pl.* करणें.
3—in rhetoric, v. To EMBELLISH. बनावून सांगणें, बतावणी *f.* करणें *g. of o.* पाल्हाळ *m.*-अर्थवाद *m.*-&c. करणें *g. of o.*

FLOURISH, *n. figure scribbled with a pen.* भरकडा *or* भरकंडा*m.* भरकांडा *m.* फरकटा *or* डा *or* फरगडा *m.* बिरखड्या *or* बिरखुड्या *f. pl.* खिरबिट्या *f. pl.*
2—in rhetoric, *bold figure, &c.* बोलण्याचा भरकांडा *m.* अर्थवाद *m.* [रीत.

FLOURISHING, *p. a.* v. V. N. 1. टवटवीत, जिवट, जीवदार, तरत-
2 *and* PROSPEROUS. खातापिता, गबरू, श्रीमंत, श्रीकार, श्रीमान्, श्रेयस्वान्, भरभरीचा, &c. समृद्ध, संपन्न, वर्धित, वर्धमान.
F. or happy state. बेहबुदी *f.*
Prosperous or f. state. भरभर *f.*—*intens.* भरभराट *m.*
F. or failing, *thriving or sinking,*—of trades, affairs, &c. तरता बुडता.
F. or ascendant period. अमदानी *f.*
3 आबाद, आबादान, आबादानीचा, आबादीचा.

FLOUT. See SARCASM.

To FLOUT, *v. a.* v. To CONTEMN. झिडकावणें, झिडकारणें, झिटकारणें, तिटकारणें, तिरस्कारणें, हिडसणें *or* हिडसावणें *or* हेडसावणें, तिटकारा *m.*-छिथु *f.*-थुथु *f.* करणें, खुडकाविणें, खुडका *m.* देणें, निरस्कारणें, जोपारणें, ढांगळणें.

FLOUTING, *n.* v. V. झिडकावणें *n.* &c. झिडकार *m.* झिडकारणी *f.*

To FLOW, *v. n.* वाहणें, प्रवाहणें, चालणें, ओघळ *m.*-प्रवाह *m.*-&c. होणें-चालणें *g. of s.*
To f. gushingly & noisily. भळभळणें, भळभळ-&c. वाहणें, *intens.* मळाळणें. [णें-होणें.
2—*opposed to* ebb. भरणें, भरती *f.*-जोर *m.*-वीळ *f.* लागणें-ये-
3 *pass smoothly, swimmingly, &c.* सरळ-सुरळीत-अस्खलित-प्रवाहरूप-धारारूप-&c. चालणें, सरणें, प्रवाह *m.* चालणें *g. of o.*
4 *abound.* वाहणें, धार *f.* पडणें *g. of s.* लोटणें, भरून चालणें, फुलून निघणें, फुलणें, प्रचुर होणें. [निघणें.
5 from; *proceed, issue, run.* वाहणें, गळणें, पाझरणें, स्रावणें.
6 off; *run down,*—a river, &c. ओसरणें, उतरणें, ओसारा *m.* होणें *g. of s.* [होणें *g. of s.*
7 over. उचंबळणें, उपरांडणें, वरसांडणें, बरसांड होणें, उत्सेक *m.*.
To f. over from boiling. उतणें, ऊत *m.* होणें.

FLOW, FLOWING, *n.* v. V. 1.—*act.* वाहणें *n.* &c. ओघ *m.* प्रवाह *m.*
F. of speech. वाक्सरणि *f.* वाग्धारा *f.*
2 भरती *f.* भरतें *n.* वीळ *f.* जोर *m.*
3 प्रवाह *m.* संसर्प *m.*
4 भरती *f.* भरतें *n.* बहर *m.* भर *m.* पूर *m.*

FLOWER, *n.* फूल *n.* पुष्प *n.* कुसुम *n.* माल्य *n.* सुमन *n.* प्रसून *n.*
Chaplet or garland of flowers. फुलोरा *or* फुलवरा *m.*
Compound or flosculous f. केंसर *n.*
Cultivator and seller of flowers. फूलमाळी, फुलारी, माळी.
Exudation of a f. पुष्पद्रव *m.*
Farina of a f. पुष्परेणु *m.* पराग *m.*

Nectar or honey of flowers. मधु *n. pop.* मध *m.* मद *m.* पुष्परस *m.* मकरंद *m.* सुधा *f.* पुष्पनिर्यास *m.* पुष्पसार *m.* पुष्पस्वेद *m.*

Presenting of flowers in the hands. पुष्पांजलि *m. f.*

2—as carved, painted, worked, &c. फुली *f.* बुटा *m.* बूट *m.*

3 (as of grain) *blossom.* फुलोरा *or* फुलवरा *m.*

4 v. PRIME. बहर *m. f.* बहार *m. f.* ऐनभर *f.*

The f. of youth. भरजवानी *f.*

5 *best part, choice.* निवड *f.* उत्तमांश *m.*

6 flowers. See MENSES. 7 (of speech) See FIGURE.

To FLOWER, *v. n. blossom, bloom,* v. To BLOW. फुलणें, फुलें *n. pl.* येणें, विकसणें, मोहरणें (used esp. of the mango).

To FLOWER, *v. a. adorn with figures of flowers.* बूट *m.*-&c. काढणें, बुटीदार-&c. करणें.

FLOWER-GARDEN, *n.* फूलबाग *m. f.* पुष्पवाटिका *f.* पुष्पवाटी *f.*

FLOWER-POT, *n.* कुंडी *f.*—large कुंडा *m.*

FLOWER-TREE, *n.* फूलझाड *n.* पुष्पवृक्ष *m.*

FLOWERED, *p.* v. V. फुललेला, &c. पुष्पी, पुष्पित, कुसुमित.

I.—a cloth, &c. v. FIGURED. फुलकारी, बुटीदार, वेलबुटीचा.

F. work. बुटी *f.* वेलबुटी *f.* वेलबूट *m. n.* वेलबुट्टा *m.*

FLOWERINESS, *n.* v. A. 1. पुष्पमयता *f.* पुष्पाकीर्णता *f.* पुष्पप्रचुरता *f.* पुष्पबाहुल्य *n.*

2 अलंकारिता *f.* अलंकारप्राचुर्य *n.* अलंकारबाहुल्य *n.*

FLOWERY, *a. full, &c. of flowers.* फुलांचा, पुष्कळफुलांचा, पुष्पमय, पुष्पाकीर्ण, पुष्पसंकुल, पुष्पप्रचुर, पुष्पविशिष्ट, सौमनस.

2—of style, &c. अलंकारी, आलंकारिक, अलंकृत, अलंकारविपुल, अलंकारप्रचुर.

FLOWING, *p. a.* v. V. 3. *smooth, fluent,*—speech. धारावाही, धारावाहिक, सरळ, सुरळीत.

I.—a garment, &c. घोळदार, घेरदार.

FLOWINGLY, *adv. smoothly, swimmingly, &c.* तडक *or* का, कडक *or* का, सुरळीत, सरळ, घमघम *or* मां *intens.* घमाघम, घवघव, अनुधार, सुदामत, अलग, अलगत, अचानक, अलिप्तपणें, सरिरास.

To FLUCTUATE, *v. n.*—water, &c. हेलकावणें, हेलकावा *m.* खाणें -देणें.

2 *be irresolute,* v. To HESITATE. गुटमळणें, गुपटणें, धरसोड *f.* करणें, लटपटीत असणें.

3 *rise and fall, be unsettled.* चढउतार *m.* असणें *g. of s.* एका रंगावर-एके स्थितीवर-&c. नसणें, अस्थिर असणें, फिरणें.

FLUCTUATION, *n.* v. V. 1. हेलकावा *m.*

2 गुटमळणें *n.* &c. धरसोड *f.*

3 चढउतार *m.* अस्थिरता *f.* चंचलता *f.*

FLUE, *n.* v. CHIMNEY. धुराडें *n.*

2 *soft down.* लव *f.* मृदुलोम *n.*

FLUENCY, *n.* v. A. 1. बोलकेपणा *m.* जिभेचा चपळपणा *m.* वाकूचापल्य *n.* वाक्सरणि *f.* वाग्धारा *f.*

2 सरळपणा *m.* सुरळितपणा *m.*

FLUENT, *a. free, voluble*—speaker. बोलका, जिभेचा चपळ, चपलजिह्व, चपलवाक्, वाक्चपल.

2—speech. धारावाही, धारावाहिक, सरळ, सुरळीत, रथासारखा.

FLUENTLY, *adv. volubly, glibly.* चुरचूर, चुणचूण, चुरचुरां, चरचर *intens.* चराचर.

FLUID, *n.* द्रवद्रव्य *n.* द्रवपदार्थ *m.* प्रवाहीपदार्थ *m.*

FLUID, *a.* सद्रव, द्रव, द्रवरूप, प्रवाही, वहनशील.

FLUIDITY, *n.* v. A. द्रवता *f.* द्रवत्व *n.* द्रवभाव *m.* प्रवाहित्व *n.* वहनशीलता *f.*

FLUMMERY, *n.* अंबील *f.* आंबवें *n.* कांजी *n.* लापशी *f.*

F. parched and caked. अंबोळी *f.*

FLUOR ALBUS, *n.* पांढरवणी *n.* धुपणी *f.* पांढरी धुपणी *f.* होळणी *f.* प्रदर *pop.* पदर *m.*

FLURRIED, FLUSTERED, FLUTTERED, *p.* v. V. गडबडवलेला, डामाडूळ, संभ्रांत, व्याकुल, व्याकुलमना, व्यग्र, व्यग्रमनस्क, संविग्न, संविग्नमानस.

To FLURRUP, *v. a. sup up noisily.* ओरपणें, भुरकणें, फुरकणें, भुरका *m.*-फुरका *m.* मारणें.

FLURRUPING, *n.* v. V.—*act.* ओरपणें *n.* &c. भुरका *m.* फुरका *m.*

FLURRY, *n.* v. V.—*state.* गडबड *f.* लगबग *f.* धांदल *f.* डामाडूळ *f.* संभ्रम *m.* संवेग *m.* ओढाताण *f.* आवेग *m.* व्याकुलता *f.*

I. *sudden gust of wind.* वाऱ्याचा झटकारा *m.*-झटका *m.*

To FLURRY, *v. a. agitate, commove.* गडबडवणें, घाबरवणें, गडबड *f.*-धांदल *f.*-डामाडूळ *f.*-संभ्रम *m.*-&c. करणें *g. of o.* संभ्रांत-व्याकुल-व्यग्र-&c. करणें.

To FLUSH, *v. n. flow copiously.* भळभळ-भळभळां-भडभड-भडभडां वाहणें-निघणें-&c.

2—the face, &c. लाली *f.* येणें, तांबडालाल होणें, तांबरणें.

To FLUSH, *v. a. redden, &c.* लाली *f.* आणणें, तांबडालाल करणें.

To be flushed. तांबरणें, तांबुसणें.

FLUSH, *n. sudden and copious afflux.* लोट *m.* लोंढा *m.* उधान *n.* ऊत *m.* बहर *m.* लहर *f.*

2 (of eagerness, desire, &c.) *ardor, glow.* हुरशी *f.* v. धर, सुट, ये, चढ, हुरूप *m. f.* गुरमी *f.* गुरमाई *f.* गुरमा *m.* फणका *m.* कढ *m.* उकळी *f.* वेग *m.*

3 तोंडावर-&c. अकस्मात आलेली लाली *f.*

FLUSH, *a. fresh looking,* v. FRESH. टवटवीत, तुकतुकीत.

2 (in cash) भरपूर, संपन्न, तळींरामगार.

FLUSTER, To FLUSTER. See FLURRY, To FLURRY.

FLUTE, *n.* बांसरी *f.* मुरली *f.* मोहरी *f.* पोंवा *or* पांवा *m.*

2 (of a pillar, &c.). खांचणी *f.* बलकी *f.*

FLUTING, *n.* (of a pillar, &c.). खांचणी *f.* बलकी *f.*

To FLUTTER, *v. n.*—as a bird, a flag, &c. फडफडणें, फडकणें, चरचरणें *intens.* चराडणें, झडफडणें, पंख *m. pl.* झाडणें.

2—the heart, v. To PALPITATE. धुगधुगणें, धडकणें, धडधडणें.

To FLUTTER, *v. a.* See To FLURRY.

FLUTTER, FLUTTERING, *n.* v. V. N. 1. फडफडणें *n.* &c. फडकणी *f.* खुडखुड *f.* फडत्कार *m.*

2 धडकी *f.* धडधडी *f.* धडधड *n.* धुगधुगी *f.* धुगधुग *f.* डुगडुगी *f.* डुगडुग *f.* डागडूग *f.* धाकधूक *n.*

v. V. A. See FLURRY.

FLUTTERINGLY, *adv.* फडफड *or* डां, फरफर *or* रां, चरचर *or* रां, —*intens.* फडाफड, फडाडां, फराफर, फरारां, चराचर, चरारां.

FLUVIAL, *a. belonging, &c. to rivers.* नदीसंबंधी.

FLUX, *n.* See FLOW. 2 v. DIARRHŒA. ढेंढळ *f.* ढेंढाळी *f.* (or घेंडाळी *f.* &c.) ढगळ *f.* ढंगळ *f.*

Bloody f. रक्तओढ *f.* रक्तस्राव *m.*

To have a f. पोट *n.* जाणें-सुटणें *g. of s.* ढाळ *m. pl.* होणें *g. of s.* ढाळणें, ढगळणें.

To FLUX. See To MELT.

To FLY, *v. n. move through the air.* उडणें, उड्डाण *n.*-उड्डीन *n.*-प्रडीन *n.*-डीन *n.* करणें, पक्षिगतीनें-आकाशगतीनें जाणें.
2 *rise in air.* उडणें.
3 *pass rapidly.* लवकर जाणें-निघून जाणें-गुजरणें-&c.
4 at;*fall upon.* v. To ATTACK. उडणें *with* वर, तुटून पडणें *with* वर, आंगावर तुटून पडणें, आंगावर येणें, घसरणें.
5 out; *break out into passion,* v. To RAGE. उधळणें, उसळणें, उसळी *f.* खाणें, कातावणें, ढेंकणें, दांतीं येणें, उपायीं येणें.
6 up;—powders by a blast, &c. भबकणें.
7 See To FLEE.
With flying colors. धोशालावून.
To let fly. v. To DISCHARGE. सोडणें.

To FLY, *v. a. shun,* v. To AVOID. चुकवणें, टाळणें, दूर टाकणें.
2 *quit by flight.* पळून जाऊन सोडणें, पळून जाणें *with* पासून, &c. *of o.*

FLY, *n.* माशी *f.* मासूक *n.* मक्षिका *f.*
Stinging f. गांध *f.* गांधीण *f.* गांधील *m. n.* गांधीलमाशी *f.* डांस *m.* आघीमाशी *or* आघी *f.*
Swarm of flies. मास *f.*
Wild f. रानमाशी *f.* वनमक्षिका *f.*

FLY-BLOW, *n.* सडी *f.* असडी *f.*

FLYCATCHER, *n.*—the bird. शिपाई *m.*

FLY-LEAF, *n.* मलपृष्ठ *n.* [*n.* डीन *n.*

FLYING, *n.* v. V. N. 1.—*act.* उडणें *n.* उड्डाण *n.* उड्डीन *n.* प्रडीन

FOAL, *n.* शिंगरूं *n.* बछेरा *m.* अश्वशाव *m.*
That is with f.—mare or she ass. सबर *or* सभर.

To FOAL, *v. c.* पसवणें.

FOAM, *n.* फेन *pop.* फेण *m.* फेंस *m.* कफ *m.*—in cant phraseol. मुखरस *m.* [*con.*

To FOAM, *v. n.* फेणणें, फेंसणें, फेंसळणें, फेण *m.*-फेंस *m.* येणें *in.*

FOAMER, *n.* FOAMING, *p. a.* FOAMY, *a.* v. V. फेंसळलेला, &c. फेंसाळ, फेंसट, फेनयुक्त, फेनल, फेनिल.

FOB, *n. pocket, &c.* घड्याळ ठेवण्याचा खिसा *m.*-कपा *or* कप्पा *m.*

To FOB. See To CHEAT.

FOCAL, *a.* केंद्राचा, केंद्रसंबंधी.

FOCUS, *n.*—in geometry. केंद्र *n.* नाभि *m.*
2—in optics. किरण एकत्र जमण्याचें स्थान *n.* तेजस्संकर्षदेश *m.*
3 (of a ray of light) *focal point.* अग्रकर *m.* अग्रांशु *m.*

FODDER, *n.* वैरण *f.* चारा *m.* गवतकाडी *f.* घासपात *m.*
Litter of f. चघळ *m. n.* चघळबघळ *m. n.* गोखरें *n.*

To FODDER, *v. a.* वैरण *f.*-चारा *m.*-&c. घालणें.

FOE. See ENEMY. [it. मेथी *f.*

FŒNUGREEK, *n.*—the grass. मेथी *f.*—the grain or seed of

FŒTAL, *a.* v, N. गर्भाचा, गर्भसंबंधी, गार्भ.

FŒTUS, *n.* गर्भ *pop.* गाभ *m.* भ्रूण *m.*
Dead f. मूढगर्भ *m.* नष्टगर्भ *m.*
Dead f. remaining in the womb. शल्य *pop.* सल *n.*
Instrument for extracting a dead f. गर्भशंकु *m.*
Motion of f. in utero. गर्भचलन *n.*
Murder of a f. भ्रूणहत्या *f.*
Murderer of a f. भ्रूणहत्यारा.
Pain suffered by a f. whilst in the womb. गर्भयातना *f.*

FOG, *n.* मुऱ्हें *n.* धुई *f.* धुकें *n.* धुमें *n.* धुकट *n.*

FOGGINESS, *n.* v. A. धुरकट *n.* धुरट *n.*

FOGGY, *a.* धुक्याचा, धुरकटाचा, धुरटाचा.

FOH, *interj.* इश्यो, इश्शो, इश्श.

FOIBLE, *n.* v. FAULT. उणें *n.* हीण *n.* छिद्र *n.* क्षुलक *n.* क्षुद्र *n.* क्षुद्रक *n.*

To FOIL, *v. a. frustrate, &c.* v. To DEFEAT. मोडणें, हारवणें, हेलपटणें, थकवणें, वाहवणें, लटपटवणें, चालेनासा करणें.

FOIL, *n. leaf for gilding, &c.* बरख *m.* पत्र *n.* (सुवर्णपत्र, रौप्यपत्र &c.), पत्रा *m.* (सोन्याचा-रुप्याचा पत्रा), पान *n.* (सोनेरीपान &c.).
2—among jewellers. डांक *m.* तवा *m.* पूट *or* पूठ *n.*
3 *blunt fencing sword.* निधारी-बुळा-बोथी-&c. तरवार *f.*-पट्टा *m.* दांड *m.*
4 See DEFEAT. 5 आरशाचे पाठीवरची कल्हई *f.*

FOILED, *p.* v. V. मोडलेला, &c. नष्टोपाय, हतोपाय, प्रतिहत, भग्नसंकल्प, खंडिताशंस.

FOIN. &c. See THRUST, &c.

To FOIST, *n. a. insert surreptitiously.* खुपसणें, घुसडणें, खुपसून-&c. घालणें, घालघुसड *f.* करणें.

FOISTER, *n.* v.V. खुपसणारा, &c. खुपशा, घुसड्या.

FOISTING, *n.* v.V. खुपसणें *n.* &c.खुपसणी *f.*घुसडणी *f.*घालघुसड *f.*

FOISTY. See FUSTY.

FOLD, *n. enclosure for sheep, &c.* कोंडवाड *f.* कोंडवाडा *m.*कोंडी *f.* कोंडण *f.* मेंढवाडा *m.* वाडा *m.*
2 (for calves, kids, &c.). गोठी *f.* माची *f.*
3 *double, complication, ply.* घडी *f.* पदर *m.* चुणी *f.* निरी *f.* पट्टी *f.* पडदा *m.*
Bagging or bellying f. ओंचा *m.*
Flowing or undulating f. (in draperies, &c.). लहर *f.*
Of one and a half f. दिडका.
Upper or outer f. घडीपदर *m.*
4 (in comp. as, two fold, seven fold, &c.). गुण, पट, (in comp. as द्विगुण, सप्तगुण, दुपट, सातपट).
5 *folded cloth, paper, &c.* घडी *f.* (as दुघडी, तिघडी, चौघडी).
Three cornered f. रुमालीघडी.
6 (as of cakes, crusts, onions, &c.) *layer, coat.* पदर *m.* पडदा *m.* पापुद्रा *m.* पातोडा *m.*
7—of a rope, &c. v. TURN. विळखा *m.*

To FOLD, *v. a. shut up in a fold.* कोंडवाडींत-वाड्यांत-&c. कोंडणें-घालणें, बंद करणें. [ळणें.
2 *lay up in folds.* घडी *f.* घालणें *n. or* घालून ठेवणें, मुरडणें, जु-
3 *double.* दुमडणें *or* दुमटणें, दुणणें, दुंतणें, घडी *f.* करणें.
4 (the arms) एकावरएकठेवणें, विळखा *m.* घालणें.
5 (in the arms) v. To EMBRACE. वेंगटणें, वेंगाळणें, कंवटाळणें.

FOLDED, *p.* v.V. 2. मुरडलेला, &c.
3 दुडता *or* दुडती घडीव, घडी (in comp. as दुघडी, तिघडी, चौघडी), पदरी (in comp. as एकपदरी, दुपदरी, तिपदरी, चौपदरी).
F. state, *foldedness.* घडी *f.* (esp. in comp. as, once foldedness एकघडी *f.* and दुघडी, तिघडी, चौघडी, &c.) पट *f.*

FOLDING, *a.*—of doors, &c. दुतलफी, दुझडपी, दुफळी.

FOLIAGE, *n. leaves.* पानें *n. pl.* पाला *m.* पल्लव *m.* विस्तार *m.*
Tuft of f. पालव *m.*
New f. पालवी *f.*
Of rich and luxuriant f. सातारा *or* सातेरा. [डबरणें.
To be covered with f.—tree or plant. सातरणें, डवडवणें,

To **Foliate**, *v. a.* (a looking glass) पान्याची कल्हई *f.* करणें, पारा *m.* चढवणें.

Folio, *n. folio-sheet.* दुबंदीपान*n.* दुबंदी कागद*m.*

2 *folio-book.* दुंड्यांचें पुस्तक*n.* &c.

Folk, *n.* v. People. लोक*m. pl.* आलम*n.* आलमदुनया *f.* गोमाजी सोमाजी *m. pl.*

To **Follow**, *v. a. go after, pursue, &c.* मागें-पाठीमागें-मागून-पाठीमागून-&c. जाणें-येणें-चालणें-&c. पाठीस लागणें *g. of o* पाठ *f.* घेणें *g. of o.* अनुगमन*n.*-अनुयान*n.*-पश्चाद्गमन*n.*-&c. करणें.

2 *attend as a dependant.* मागें चालणें *g. of o.* अनुगमन*n.*-अनुवर्त्तन*n.*-अनुवृत्ति *f.*-अनुचरण*n.*-&c. करणें.

3 *observe, copy.* v. To Imitate. वळणावर जाणें *g.of o.* वळण*n.*-मोड *f.* धरणें-घेणें *g.of o.* अनुसरणें, अनुवर्त्तणें, अनुवर्त्तन*n.*-अनुसरण*n.*-&c. करणें *g. of o.*

4 (a course, &c.) *observe, practise.* आचरणें, पाळणें, सेवणें, वाहणें, अनुसरणें, अनुवर्त्तणें, आश्रयणें, आचरण*n.*-सेवन *n.*-सेवा *f.*-&c. करणें *g. of o.*

5 *be consequential.* अनुगत-&c. होणें, फलरूप होणें, सिद्ध होणें, घडणें, होणें, फळ *n.*-परिणाम *m.*-&c. होणें. [घडणें-असणें.

6 *come after, succeed in order of time.* मागून-&c. होणें-

Followed, *p.* v. V. 1. पाठलाग केलेला, &c.अनुयात, अनुगत.

3 अनुसरलेला, &c.अनुसृत.

4 आचरलेला, &c.आचारित, सेवित.

Follower, *n.* **Following**, *p. a.* V. 1. मागें-&c. येणारा-जाणारा-&c. अनुगामी, अनुयायी, अनुचर, अनुग, अनुगत, पश्चाद्वर्त्ती.

2 पाठीमागें-मागें चालणारा, जिलीबदार, अनुगामी, अनुयायी, अनुचर, अनुचारी, पार्श्वक, आश्रित, अनुजीवी, अनुग.

Followers, *retainers, domestics.* चाकरनफर *m.pl.* चाकरपेशा *m.* आराबा *m.* लवाजिमा *m.* सेवकवर्ग *m.* अनुयायिवर्ग *m.* लोक *m. pl.* परिवार *m. pl.* हशम *n.* परिग्रह *m.*

3 अनुसरणारा, &c. अनुसारी, अनुयायी, अनुगामी, अनुवर्त्ती.

4 आचरणारा, &c. सेवक, सेवी, सेवमान. [पुढील.

I. *that comes after, that is next,* v. Next. पुढचा, पुढला,

Following, *n.* v. V. 1.—*act.* मागें-&c. जाणें-येणें *n.* अनुगमन*n.* अनुगम *m.* अनुयान *n.* अनुचरण *n.* अनुचार *m.* अनुसरण *n.*

2 अनुगमन *n.* अनुचरण *n.* अनुचर्या *f.* अनुवर्त्तन *n.*

3 अनुसरणें *n.* &c. अनुसरण *n.* अनुवर्त्तन, *n.* अनुवृत्ति *f.*

4 आचरणें *n.* &c. आचरण *n.* सेवन *n.* सेवा *f.* अनुसरण *n.*आश्रय *m.* आश्रयण *n.* पालन *n.* अनुवृत्ति *f.*

Folly, *n. foolishness, &c.* वेड *n.* वेडेपण *n.* मूर्खपणा *n.* बेकुबी *f.* अज्ञान *n.* मूर्खता *f.* मूढता *f.* मौर्ख्य *n.* मौढ्य *n.* मोह *m.*

2 *a* f. *a wild scheme, &c.* वेडेंकाम *n.* वेड *n.* कुतर्क *m.* वितर्क *m.* कुकल्पना *f.*

Follies. वेडेचार *or* वेडेवेडेचार *m. pl.*

To **Foment**, *v. a. embrocate, &c.* शेकणें, शेक *m.* देणें-घेणें, शेकणी *f.* करणें, शेकशेगडी *f.* करणें, ऊब *f.* देणें,

2 (dissension). फुंकणें *or* फुंकून देणें, चेतवणें, पेटवणें, तेल *n.* घालणें-ओतणें, गोंवरी *f.*-पेंढी *f.* घालणें-लावणें-टाकणें, फुंकर *m.* घालणें, चेतवाचेतव *f.*-&c. करणें.

Fomentation, *n.* v. V. 1.—*act.* शेकणें *n.* &c. शेकणी *f.* शेक*m.*

2 फुंकणें *n.* चेतवणें *n.* &c. चेतवाचेतव *f.* [*m.*

I. *heated leaves, &c. applied to foment.* उपणा*m.*पेंड *m.*कवल

Fond, *a. affectionate, tenderly kind, &c.* v. Loving. ममताळु *or* ळू, ममतेचा, स्नेहाळ, स्नेहाळू, प्रीतिमान्, वत्सल, प्रेमल *or* ळ. —as the language of a child. लाडका.

2 *loving, liking, delighting in.* लाहडी, आवडता (*as* ताकाचा-गाण्याचा-&c. आवडता), शोखी *or* शौकी, तलबी *or* तलफी, आसक्त, लंपट, आशीक, इष्की.

To be f. of. चाहणें.

3 See Foolish.

To **Fondle**, *v. a. caress, smooth, stroke, &c.* लाडकणें, पोटाळणें, जोंबाळणें, चोंबाळणें, गोंजारणें, अंजारणें, कुरवाळणें, लाड *m.*-लडिवाळ *m.*-लाडीग *m.*-प्यार *m. f.*-कोडकौतुक *m.*-लालन *n.*-वात्सल्य *n.*-&c. करणें *g. of o.* जयजयकार *m. pl.* करणें *g. of o.* लालित करणें.

Fondler, *n.* **Fondling**, *p. a.* v. V. लाड-&c. करणारा, लडिवाळ, लाडका, लाडाचा.

Fondling, *n.* v. V. लाडकणें *n.* &c. लाड *m.* लडिवाळ *m.* लाडूकपणा *m.* लाडीगोडी *f.* लाडकी *f.* लाडीग *m.* लालन *n.*कोडकौतुक *n.* कोड *n.* अलोलकी *f.* अलोलीक *n.*

I. *person fondled.* लाडका, प्यारा, क्रीडामृग, प्रीतिपात्र.

Fondly, *adv.* v. A. 1. लाडानें, लाडुकपणानें, लाडें कोडें, लाड-&c. करून, मोहबुद्ध्या, मोहदृष्ट्या.

3 See Foolishly.

Fondness, *n.* v. A. 1. प्रीति *f.* ममता *f.* ममताळूपणा *m.* लळा *m.* *v.* लाव, वाळग, कर, प्यार *f.*

2 आवड *f.* चाड *f.* भक्ति *f.* प्रीति *f.* रति *f.* आसक्ति *f.* छंद *m.* चाळा *m.* उल्लास *m.*

Acquired liking or f. चट *f.* चटक *f.*

Font, *n.* बाप्तिस्म्याचें पाणी ठेवण्याचें पात्र*n.*

Fontanel, *n. issue.* पोत *m. n.* [अशन*n.*

Food, *n.* अन्न*n.* खाणें*n.* भक्ष्य*n.* आहार*m.* भोजन*n.* खाद्य *f.* खाण*n.*

Article of f. भक्ष्य *n.* भोज्य*n.* खाद्य *n.*

Coarse, unsavory f. v. Fare. अरबटचरबट*n.* अरकसबरकस*n.* कदन्न *n.*

Consisting or composed of f. अन्नमय.

Daily f. शेर*m.*

Distribution of f. अन्नशांति *f.* अन्नसंतर्पण*n.*

Dressed f. स्वयंपाक*m.* सिद्धान्न*n.* पक्वान्न*n.* शिदोरी *f.* बोनें*n*,

Dressed f. given in alms to Bráhmans. माधुकरी *f.*

Dressing of f. स्वयंपाक *pop.* सैंपाक*m.*

Extra or odd articles of f. आडखाणें*n.* आडखाद्य *f.*

F. and clothing. अन्नवस्त्र*n.* अन्नाच्छादन*n.* ग्रासाच्छादन*n.*

F. burned in the cooking. करप *f.* राखुंडी *f.*

F.—compreh. or indef. भाकर तुकडा*m.* अन्नपाणी*n.* अन्नोदक*n.* खाणेंपिणें*n.*

Form or modification of f. अन्नविकार *m.* अन्नविकृति *f.* अन्नप्रकार*m.* अन्नपरिणाम*m.*

Heavy f. जडान्न*n.*

Incompatible f. विरुद्धभोजन*n.* विरुद्धान्न*n.*

Leavings of f. अन्नशेष*m.*

Loathing of f. अन्नद्वेष*m.* अन्नविकार*m.* अन्नविरुति *f.*

Non-observant of the distinction of f. सर्वभक्ष, सर्वभक्षक, सर्वान्नभक्षक, सर्वान्नभोजी.

Nutritious f. खाद्य *f.*

Rich and savory f. मिष्टान्न*n.* खुराक*m.*

Undressed f. शिधा *m.*

Wholesome f. सत्वान्न *n.*

Wonted quantity of f. आहार *m.* जेवण *n.* खाणें *n.* खादगी *f.*

FOOL, *n.* मूर्ख *c.* बेडामाणूस *m.* (बेडी बायको *f.* &c.), यथाजात मनुष्य *n.* See under FOOLISH.—freely, for *calf, dolt, blockhead, jackass, numskull, &c. &c.* बैल, गाढव, अक्कलेचा गधडा, धोंडा, नंद, नंदी, नंद्या, नांद्या, नरपशु, घोरड, दगड, खुळेश्वर, टोणपा, टोणपनाथ, टोणपशुद्ध, टोणपेश्वर, ठोंबा *or* ठोंब्या, उल्लू, पथर, बांठीचापिता, नरपशु, देवापुढें देव *or* देवापुढचा देव, ढुम्या, देवानांप्रिय, शंख, शुंट *or* शुंठ, माठ्या, शामाठ्या, शतमूर्ख, शुद्धस्फटिक, शुद्धबुद्ध, राजा, ढ, शाहाण्याची खरवड, गाढवाचा खरारा, बुद्धीचा नवसागर, बुद्धीचा खंदक, माणसाचा कांदा, माणसाचा अवतार, माणसाचा लेंक, घोड्याचा पूत *or* लेंक, झळझळीत मूर्ख, निपटमूर्ख, ठणठणपाळ, गाढवीचा, मूर्खशिरोमणि, गाबदी, बेडीहळद, शेंड्यावर बसून झाड तोडणारा, महादेवाचें वाहन, आरुश.

A learned f. पढतमूर्ख.

An arrant f. शतमूर्ख.

F.'s phiz. बावळीमुद्रा *f.* गाबाळमुद्रा *f.*

F.'s errand. हिसका *m.*

To make a f. of. v. To DECEIVE. झकवणें, भोंदणें, धाब्यावर बसवणें. [मारणें.

To make a f. of one's self. नकशा *m.* गमावणें, झक *f.*

Better be a wise man's servant than a fool's master. शाहण्याचा व्हावें चाकर पण वेड्याचा होऊंनये धनी.

2 See BUFFOON. [*f. pl.* मारणें.

To FOOL, *v. n. trifle, toy, idle.* गमणें, खेळणें, शेण *n.* खाणें, माशा

To FOOL, *v. a.* v. To DECEIVE. छकवणें, झकवणें, भोंदणें, धाब्यावर बसवणें, तोंडींपानें *n. pl.* पुसणें.

To f. away one's money. पैक्याचा-&c. भांगभुरका *m.* करणें, पैका *m.*-&c. भांग भुरक्या खालीं उडवणें.

FOOL-HARDINESS, *n.* v. A. विषमसाहस *n.* दुःसाहस *n.* कुसाहस *n.*

FOOL-HARDY, *a.* v. MADCAP. दुःसाहसिक, उरफाट्या काळजाचा, उलट्या काळजाचा.

FOOLERY, *n.* वेडेपण *n.* वेड *n.* वेडेचार *or* वेडेवेडेचार *m. pl.*

FOOLISH, *a.*—of persons. खुळा (*remiss.* खुळसर, खुळसट खुळकट), वेडा (*remiss.* वेडसर, वेडगळ, वेडका,) पिसा, चळेल, बेकूब *or* बेवकूब, भळू, बावळा, माठ्या, मूढ, मूर्ख, निर्बुद्ध, अचरट, हीनबुद्धि, नष्टबुद्धि, बुद्धिहीन-रहित-शून्य–&c. ज्ञानरहित-हीन–शून्य-&c. अल्पबुद्धि, अल्पमेधा, अल्पधी, अल्पमति, मंदमति, मुग्ध, यथाजात, मूढात्मा.

To make to look f. फजीत करणें-पाडणें.

To turn f. चवणें, चळणें.

2—of actions. मूर्खपणाचा, वेडेपणाचा, बेकुबीचा, अज्ञानाचा, अविचाराचा, बावटळ *or* बावटूळ, बावकळ.

FOOLISHLY, *adv.* मूर्खपणानें, वेडेपणानें &c. मूर्खावाणी, मूर्खापरी, वेड्यावाणी, &c.

FOOLISHNESS, *n.* v. A. 1. वेड *n.* वेडेपणा *m.* वेडेपण *n.* &c. बेकुबी *f.* अज्ञान *n.* मूर्खपणा *m.* मूर्खता *f.* मूढता *f.* मौर्ख्य *n.* मौढ्य *n.* ज्ञानराहित्य *n.* बुद्धिहीनता *f.* &c. ज्ञानाभाव *m.*

FOOLSCAP, *n.* एक प्रकारचा कागद आहे.

FOOT, *n.* पाय *m.* पाऊल *n.* चरण *m. n.* पद *n.* पाद *m.* पग *n.*

An evil f. पायचळ *m. f.* पायचाळा *m.* पायरवा *m.*

Artistic position or cast of the foot in fencing, dancing, &c. पावटा *m.*

Covering for the feet. पादत्राण *n.* पादरक्षा *f.*

Fallen at the feet of. चरणगत, चरणपतित, पादलग्न.

Fidgeting with the feet. पायचाळा *m.* [पायांचा.

Having foul (mud-clogged, dusty, &c.) feet. भरल्या

Heavy of f. पायाचा जड.

Hollow of the f. तलहृदय *n.*

Light of f. पायसूट.

On f. v. AFOOT. पायीं, पायउतारां, पादचालीनें, पादचालीं.

Going on f. पादचाल *f.* चरणचाल *f.*

On the f of पायीं *g. of. s.*

Touching the f. or feet (in reverence). पादग्रहण *n.*

Treading under f. पायमळी *or* पायमाली *f.* पादाक्रमण *n.*

Trodden under f. पादाक्रांत. [र्घ्य *n.*

Water presented to wash the hands and feet. पाद्या-

With feet yet foul from the road. भरल्या पायांनीं.

To burn the feet (by walking on hot ground, &c.). पायांच्या पोळ्या *f. pl.* करणें.

To get on one's feet (after sickness, &c.). जमिनीस पाय *m. pl.* लागणें *g. of s.* जमीन *f.* सोडणें.

To get on f. (into vogue). लागणें, पडणें.

To set on f. मांडणें, उठवणें, लावणें, उभा करणें, चालू-प्रवृत्त-&c. करणें.

To strike the f. (against a stone, &c.). ठेंस *f.*-ठोकर *f.* खाणें- (*in. con.*) लागणें.

To wash the feet. पादप्रक्षालन *n.*-पाद्य *n.* करणें.

2—the measure. बाराइंचांचें माप *n.* फूट *m. f.*

3 *lower part,* v. BOTTOM. पाय *m.* बुडखा *m.* बुडूख *n.* तळ *n.* *pop.* तळ *m.* बुंध *n.*

4 (of a table, &c.). पाय *m.* खूर *m.*

5 (of a bed, field, hill, &c.). पायतें *n.* पायगत *n.* पाय *m.* पायांस *n.* पायींत *n.*

6 *infantry.* पायदळ *n.*

7 (of a verse). पाद *m.* चरण *m.* गण *m.* N. B. Maráthí prosody requires three syllables to make a गण.

8 See FOOTING.

To FOOT. See To DANCE, To WALK.

FOOT-BALL, *n.* लातचेंडू *m.*

FOOT-BOY, *n.* पोऱ्या *m.* नफर *m.* खिदमतगार *or* खिदमतदार *m.*

FOOT-FALL, *n. sound of a foot-step.* पायरव *m.* सांचल *or* सांचोल *f. m.* सांचोळा *m.* चाहूल *f.* खडका *m.*—as considered the cause of evil. पायचळ *m. f.* [काढणें.

To listen for a f. खडका *m.*-सांचल *f. m.*-&c. घेणें *or*

FOOT-HOLD, *n.* v. FOOTING. पाय ठेवायाला आधार *m.* पाय टेंकणें *n.* आश्रय *pop.* आस्रा *m.* धार *or* धारा *m.*

FOOT-HOT, *adv. immediately.* पायांच्या धुळीसुद्धां, पायांची धूळ असतां-न झाडतां-न पुसतां.

FOOT-MAN, *n.* प्यादा *m.* पदाति *m.*

2 *attendant on foot, messenger, &c.* पाईक *or* पायक *m.* पट्टेकरी *m.* पट्टेवाला *m.* पदाति *m.*

FOOT-MARK, FOOT-PRINT, *n.* पाऊल *n.* पावटी *f.* पदचिन्ह *n.* पदांक *m.* पद *n.*

FOOT-MAT, *n.* पायपुसणें *n.* पायपुसें *n.* पायद्दाज *n.*

Foot-note, *n.* पृष्ठाचे खालीं लिहिलेली टीप *f.*

Foot-pace, *n.* पाय चाल *f.* पाऊल चाल *f.* पावंडचाल *f.*

Foot-pad, *n.* वाटमाऱ्या.

Foot-path, *n.* पायवाट *f.* पाऊलवाट *f.* पायरस्ता *m.* पायमार्ग *m.*

Foot-soldier, *n.* प्यादा *m.* पदाति *m.*—loosely, lightly, freely, &c. प्यादा जवादा *m.*

Foot-stalk, *n.* देंठ *m.* वृंत *n.*

Foot-step, *n.* पाऊल *n.* पावला *m.* पावंडा *m.* पद *n.*

2 *sound of a foot.* पायरव *m.* सांचल *or* सांचोल *f. m.* सांचोला *m.* खडका *m.*

3 *vestige.* See Trace.

Foot-stool, *n.* पीठ *n.* पादपीठ *n.* पदासन *n.*

Footed, *a. having feet.* पायांचा, सपाद, पादविशिष्ट, पादयुक्, पाद (in comp. as अश्वपाद, &c.), पद (in comp. as द्विपद, चतुष्पद, &c.).

Large-f. बृहत्पाद.

Swift-f. पायांचा पारवा.

Footing, *n. ground for the foot, place to tread on.* पाय ठेवायाला आधार *m.*-आस्रा *m.*-&c. पाय टेंकणें *n.* पाबटा *m.* पांवडा *m.* पायवटणी *f.* पायठेवण *f.* थार *or* थारा *m.*

2 *foundation, warrant,* v. Ground. जागा *f.* थार *or* थारा *m.* आधार *m.* आश्रय *pop.* आस्रा *m.*

3 *entrance, establishment.* पाया *m.* पायंडा *m.* पांवडा *m.* पगडा *m. all with v.* पड, प्रवेश *m.* पैवस्ती *f.* पायशिरकाव *m.*

Firm f. अढळपद *n.*

To get f. (in an office, &c.). जडणें, नांगी *f.* लागणें *g. of s.* भुईसीं पाय *m.* लागणें *g. of s.* पगडा *m.* पडणें *g. of s.* पगडा *m.* घालणें, नखी *f.* रुतणें *g. of s.* पाळें *n.* घेणें, टांकी *f.* लागणें *g. of s.* [नेमणूक *f.*

4 *state, condition, settlement.* व्यवस्था *f.* स्थिति *f.* बंदोबस्त *m.*

Friendly f. रहसाळी *f.* रहस्य *n.* सुलूक *or* ख *m.* सलोगा *m.* संवित्ति *f.* सोहलत *f.* सौरस्य *n.*

Fop, *n. coxcomb.* अकडबाज, नखरेदार, नखरेबाज, कुर्रेदार, कुर्रेबाज, अलबेला, छैलछबेला, छेला.

Foppery, Foppishness, *n.* v. N. अकडबाजी *f.* नखरेदारी *f.* नखरेबाजी *f.* छानछुकी *or* छोकी *f.* शानशुकी *or* शोकी *f.* अलबेलीछान *f.* कुर्रा *m.*

Foppish, *a.* v. Fop. अलबेला, अकडबाजीचा, नखरेदारीचा.

For, *prep. because of, on account of.* मुळें, साठीं, करितां, खब, बाबत, बाबें.

2 *in the place of.* जागीं, जाग्यावर, स्थानीं, स्थानावर, बदल *or* ला, बारीं, बारचा *decl.* बांटचा *decl.*

3 *for the sake of.* खातर, साठीं, करितां, खब, बदलखातर, अर्थ (in comp. as स्नानार्थ, भोजनार्थ, प्रीत्यर्थ).

For, *conj.* कांतर, कांकीं.

For as much. ज्यापक्षीं, ज्यापेक्षां, अर्थात्.

Forage, *n.* कहीचीलूट *f.* लुटून आणलेलें तृणकाष्ठ *n.*

To **Forage**, *v. n.* कही *f.* करणें, तृणकाष्ठ *n.* लुटून आणणें-नेणें.

Forage-party, *n.* कही *f.*

To **Forbear**, *v. n. refrain, &c.* v. To Abstain. धिरणें, खळणें, दम *m.*-धीर *m.* धरणें, राहणें, थांबणें.

Forbear ! नको.

To **Forbear**, *v. a. spare, &c.* v. To Forgive. गम *m. f.* खाणें, गई *f.* करणें, सोडणें, तोल *m.* देणें.

Forbearance, Forbearing, *n.* v. V. N. थांबणें *n.* राहणें *n.* धीरधरणें *n.* &c. व्यापारवर्जन *n.* भोगवर्जन *n.* याम *m.* संयम *m.* संयाम *m.* संयमन *n.* यम *m.*

v. V. A. गम *m. f.* गई *f.* क्षमा *f.* क्षांति *f.* मुलाजा *m.*

Forbearer, *n.* **Forbearing**, *p. a.* v. V. N. धिरणारा, धीरधरणारा, दमधरणारा, थांबणारा, धिमा *or* म्मा. [क्षंता, क्षम.

v. V. A. गम खाणारा, गई करणारा, &c. गहीन, क्षमी, क्षमावान्,

To **Forbid**, *v. a. prohibit, interdict.* मना करणें, नको म्हणणें, वारणें, निवारणें, निषेधणें, प्रतिषेधणें, वर्जकरणें, बंदी *f.*-मनाई *f.*-निषेध *m.*-प्रतिषेध *m.*-&c. करणें *g. of o.*

God forbid देवकरो (as, God forbid that I should see him. देवकरो आणि त्याचें दर्शन न होवो).

2 See To Hinder.

Forbidden, *p.* v.V.1. निवारलेला, वर्जकेलेला, &c. मना, वारित, निवारित, निषेधित, निषिद्ध, प्रतिषिद्ध, वर्जित, परिवर्जित, प्रत्याख्यात.

I.—as used of food, &c. हराम.

Forbidder, *n.* **Forbidding**, *p.a.* v.V.1. मना करणारा, निषेध करणारा, &c. निवारक, निवारण-&c. कर्त्ता-कारक-&c. वर्जक, परिवर्जक.

I. *repulsive.* अप्रीतिजनक, अभक्तिजनक, त्रासजनक, अमंगल, अप्रसन्न.

Forbidding, v.V.1.—*act.* निवारणें *n.* &c. मनाई *f.* वारण *n.* निवारण *n.* निषेध *m.* प्रतिषेध *m.* परिवर्जन *n.* प्रत्याख्यान *n.*

By way of f. निषेधमुळें.

Force, *n.* v. Strength, Power. बल *pop.* बळ *n.* जोर *m.* जोम *m.* बळाबळ *f.* आंगवण *f.*

Brute f. *as opposed to* art *or* skill. आंगबळ *n.* आंगजोर *m.* आंगधटाई *f.* आंगधिटाई *f.* आंगमरदाई *or* आंगमरदी *f.* बाहुबल *n.* भुजबल *n.* [ळकटी *f.* तेज *n.*

2 *virtue, validity, &c.* जीव *m.* शक्ति *f.* बल *n.* बळाबळ *f.* ब-

That is in f. चालता, चालू, जिता, जागता, जिवंत, उपस्थित, अमलांत आलेला, प्रवर्त्तमान, वर्त्तमान.

Through the f. of. परत्वें *or* परत्वेंकरून (in comp. as जातिपरत्वें, संप्रदायपरत्वें, लोकाचारपरत्वें, कालपरत्वें, देशपरत्वें, दैवपरत्वें).

To be in f. चालणें, बागणें, वर्त्तणें, चलती *f.*-चाल *f.*-&c. असणें *g. of s.* चालू-&c. असणें.

3 *compulsion, violence.* जोर *m.* जोराबा *m.* जोरावरी *f.* जोरा *m.* जोरजबरी *f.* बळजोरी *f.* बळात्कार *m.* जुलूम *m.* जुलूमज्यास्ती *f.* जबरदस्ती *f.*

By f. v. Compulsively. बळें, जुलमानें *or* जुलमावर.

To come to f. बळास येणें.

To use f. बळ *n.* करणें.

4 (as of a disease, of winds, heat, &c.). *violence, vehemence.* जोर *m.* बल *pop.* बळ *n.* उग्रम *m.* जोम *m.* गंड *m.* v. मोड, जिरव, रग *f.* झपाटा *m.* वेग *m.* [दलभार *m.*

5 *a f. an armament.* सैन्य *n.* बळ *n.* सैन्यभार *m.* सेनाभार *m.*

Light armed f. खडीफौज *f.*

6 See Momentum.

To **Force**, *v. a. constrain,* v. To Compel. बळ *n.*-बळजोरी *f.*-जोर *m.*-जबरी *f.*-&c. करणें *with* वर *of o.* गळ *m.* घालणें.

2 *drive by force.* दामटणें, ढकलणें, दपटणें.

3 v. To Ravish. दपटणें, जुलूम *m.*-बळजोरी *f.*-बळात्कार *m.*-&c. करणें *with* वर *of o.*

4 *wrest, strain, distort*. ओढणें, ओढून ताणून आणणें, ओढून काढणें-आणणें.

5 (a business, &c. upon). पाठीवर गोणी *f.* घालणें, डोकीवर धोंड *f.* देणें-चढवणें-बळवणें, गळां *adv.* बांधणें.

6 (a passage). दपटून-जबरीनें-&c. शिरणें, रिघणें, घसणें, धसकणें, घुसडणें, घुसणें, शिरकणें, रिघाव *or* वा *m.*-रीघ *m.f.*करणें.

7 (fruit, &c.) *cause to ripen soon*. बळें-मारून मुटकून पिकविणें.

FORCED, *p.* v.V. 4. ओढून ताणून आणलेला, &c. बळेंचा, बळें बळेंचा *or* बळयां बळयांचा, क्लिष्ट, अवघड.

FORCEPS, *n.* वैद्याचा चिमटा *m.*

FORCEFUL, FORCIBLE, *a.* v. STRONG, POWERFUL. बळकट, बळाचा, जोराचा, जोरदार, सबल, प्रबल.

FORCIBLENESS, *n.* v. A. बल *pop.* बळ *n.* बळकटी *f.* जोरदारी *f.* सबलता *f.* प्रबलता *f.*

FORCIBLY, *adv. by force.* बळें *or* बळानें, बळेंकरून, बळकरून, जोरानें.

2 *powerfully.* बळकटीनें.

FORD, *n.* उतार *m.* पायउतार *m.* उतरण *f.* पार *m.*

Deep or difficult f. दांडगा उतार *m.*

F. for carriages. गाडेउतार *m.*

To FORD, *v. a. cross by wading.* पाय उतारानें उतरणें, पायानें-पायीं उतरणें.

Too deep to be forded—water. पोहणी, पोहनाव.

FORDABLE, *n.* v. V. पायानें-पायीं उतराया-चा-जोगा-&c. पायउतार.

FORDABLENESS, *n.* v. A. उतार *m.* तारा *m.*

FORE, *a. anterior.* पुढचा *or* ला, पुढील, मोहरचा *or* ला, मोहरील, समोरचा *or* ला, समोरील, अगला, अग्रिम, अग्रवर्त्ती, पुरोवर्त्ती, अग्र (in comp. as, forepart अग्रभाग, foreteller अग्रसूचक, and अग्रवर्त्ती, अग्रगामी, &c.), पूर्व (in comp. as पूर्वसूचक, पूर्वज्ञापक, &c.). Numerous compounds with *fore* are not so current as the equivalent compounds with *pre*. Most of such are omitted.

The f. and the hinder. आगलामागला.

FORE-ARM, *n.* कोपर आणि मणगट ह्यांच्या मधला हात *m.*

To FORE-BODE. See To BODE.

FORE-CAST, *n. previous contrivance.* आगोदरची तजवीज *f.* पूर्वयोजना *f.* पूर्वसंधान *n.*

To FORE-CAST, *v. n. contrive beforehand.* अगोदर तजवीज *f.*-&c. करणें-करून ठेवणें, पूर्वी बेतबात *m.*-योजना *f.*-बंदोबस्त *m.*-&c. करणें-करून ठेवणें, पूर्वयोजना *f.*-पूर्वसंधान *n.*-&c. करणें.

FORE-CASTLE, *n. forward part of a ship.* गलबताचा-&c. पुढलाभाग *m.*

FORE-CHOSEN, *a.* अगोदर निवडलेला.

FORE-CITED, *a. before mentioned.* मशारनिल्हे, मजकूर.

FORE-END, *n. fore-part.* पूर्वभाग *m.*

FORE-FATHER, *n.* v. ANCESTOR. वडील, पूर्वज.

Forefathers. बाडवडील *m. pl.* बापदादे *m. pl.* आजेपणजे *m. pl.* पितर *m. pl.*

To FORE-FEND. See To AVERT.

FORE-FINGER, *n.* पुढलें बोट *n.* तर्जनी *f.* प्रदेशिनी *f.*

FORE-FOOT, *n.* पुढला पाय *m.*

FOREFRONT, *n.* v. FRONT. पुढचाभाग *m.*

To FORE-GO, *v. a.* v. To GIVE UP. सोडणें, त्यागणें, निवृत्ति *f.* करणें *g. of o.*

FORE-GOING. See ANTECEDENT.

FORE-GONE, *a.* पूर्वीठरवलेला, पूर्वसंकल्पित.

FORE-GROUND, *n.* पूर्वभाग *m.* अग्रभाग *m.*

FORE-HEAD, *n.* कपाल *pop.* कपाळ *n.* माथा *m.* भाल *n.m.* निढळ *or* निढाळ *n.* ललाट *n.* अदृष्ट *n.*

Sectarial mark on the f. टिकला *m. dim.* टिकली *f.* टिका *m.* टिळा *m.* टिळक *m.* तिलक *m.* अक्षत *f.* छप्पा *m.* पुंड्र *m.*

Vertical mark on the f. नाम *n.*

To FORE-KNOW, *v. a.* अगोधर-पहिलेंच-पूर्वी-&c. जाणणें-समजणें-जाणून ठेवणें, भविष्यज्ञान *n.*-&c. असणें *in. con. g. of o.* पूर्वज्ञात-&c. असणें with विषयीं *of o.*

FORE-KNOWER, *n.* v. V. अगोधर जाणणारा-जाणून ठेवणारा, &c. भविष्यज्ञ, भविष्यदर्शी, दैवज्ञ.

FORE-KNOWING, FORE-KNOWLEDGE, *n.* भविष्यज्ञान *n.* भविष्यद्दर्शन *n.* भाविज्ञान *n.*

FORE-LAND. See CAPE.

FORE-LOCK, *n.* कपाळावरचे-टाळूवरचे केश *m. pl.* टाळूवरची बट *f.* भ्रमरक *m.* भ्रमरालक *m.*—of a horse शेंडी *f.*

To take time by the f. वेळ *f.*-सवड *f.*-&c. साधणें-साधून घेणें.

FORE-MAN, *n.* v. CONDUCTOR, LEADER. कारभारी, कारखानदार, मोहरा, मोहरक्या, दिवाणजी, मुनीम.

FORE-MAST, *n.* पुढची डोलकाठी *f.*

FORE-MENTIONED, *a.* वर म्हटलेला, मशारनिल्हे *or* निल्हे, मजकूर, पूर्वोक्त, पूर्वोदित, पूर्वचोदित.

FORE-MOST, *a.* सर्वांपुढचा-पुढला-पुढील, मोहरचा, मोहरला, अग्रिम, अग्रस्थित, अग्रवर्त्ती, अग्रेसर.

FORE-NAMED, *a.* वर म्हटलेला, मजकूर, पूर्वोक्त, पूर्वोदित.

FORE-NOON, *n.* दुपारचे पूर्वीचीवेळ *f.* पूर्वाह्ण *m.* चढतीवेळ *f.* प्राह्ण *m.*

FORE-PART, *n.* पुढलाभाग *m.* अग्र *n.* अग्रभाग *m.* मुख *n.* तोंड *n.* मोहर *f.*

F. and back part. आगापिछा *m.*

FORE-RUNNER, *n.* lit. पुढें धावणारा, अग्रगामी, प्राग्गामी.

2 fig. अग्रसूचक, लक्षण *n.*

To FORESEE, *v. a.* भविष्य *n.*-भविष्यार्थ *m.* पाहणें-पाहून ठेवणें-करणें-करून ठेवणें-समजणें, अगोधर-पहिलेंच-पूर्वी-&c. पाहणें-पाहून ठेवणें, भविष्य दर्शन *n.*-&c. असणें *in. con. and g. of o.* प्रबेक्षण *n.* करणें.

To FORE-SHOW, *v. a.* अगोधर- पूर्वी-&c. दाखवणें-दाखवून देणें, भविष्यसूचन *n.*-अग्रसूचन *n.*-पूर्वसूचन *n.*-&c. करणें *g. of o.*

2 See To FORETELL.

FORE-SHOWER, *n.* v. V. 1. पूर्वी दाखवणारा-दाखवून देणारा, &c. भविष्यसूचक, भविष्यसूची.

FORE-SIGHT, *n,* दूरदर्शन *n.* दूरदृष्टि *f.* भविष्यदर्शन *n.* भविष्यदृष्टि *f.* दीर्घदर्शन *n.* दीर्घदृष्टि *f.*

FORE-SKIN, *n.* पुढली चामडी *f.* टोपी *f.* शफाग्रचर्म *n.*

To FORE-STALL, *v. a. anticipate.* अवली *f.*-आघाडी *f.* साधणें-मारणें *g. of o.* आगपाई *f.* साधणें-करणें *g. of o.*

FORE-TASTE, *n.* पूर्वभोग *m.* आदिभोग *m.* पूर्वानुभव *m.* कालापकर्षभोग *m.* बानगी *f.*

To FORE-TELL, *v. a. predict, prophesy.* भाकीत *n.*-भविष्य *n.*-भविष्यार्थ *m.*-भवितव्य *n.* करणें-करून ठेवणें-सांगणें-&c. भाकणें, कथून ठेवणें, अगोधरच-&c. कथून ठेवणें, भविष्यकथन *n.*-भाविकथन *n.*-&c. करणें.

Foreteller, *n.* v. V. भविष्य सांगणारा, भाकणारा, &c. भविष्य-कथक, भविष्यद्वक्ता, दैवज्ञ.

Fore-telling, *n.* v. V. भाकणें *n.* भाकणूक *f.* भविष्यकथन *n.* भाविकथन *n.* अग्रनिरूपण *n.*

Fore-thought, *n.* पूर्वविचार *m.* दूरदर्शन *n.* दूरदृष्टि *f.* दीर्घदर्शन*n.* दीर्घदृष्टि *f.* अगा *m. f.*

Fore-tooth, *n.* चौकटीचा दांत *m.* राजदंत *m.*

To **Fore-warn**, *v. a.* अगोदर-पहिल्यानें-पूर्वी-&c. जतावणें-सुच-विणें-&c. ताकीद *f.* करणें-देणें, तटकारणें.

Foreign, *a. of a foreign country.* बाहेरच्या देशचा, बाहेरचा, परदेशाचा, परदेशी, परमुलुखचा, परमुलखी, परदेशीय, विदेशी, वि-देशीय, वैदेशिक, अन्यदेशीय, भिन्नदेशीय, पर, दुरांदूरचा, दूरस्थ, बिराणा, वहिश्चर.

2 *extraneous, remote, unconnected, &c.* बाहेरचा *or* ला, अ-प्रकृत,अप्रस्तुत, अप्रासंगिक, अप्राकरणिक, भिन्न, असंबद्ध, असंदर्भ.

Foreigner, *n.* v. **Foreign**. परदेशी, विदेशी, परमुलखी माणूस, परदेशचें माणूस.

Foreignness, *n.* v. A. 2. अप्रासंगिकत्व *n.* अप्राकरणिकता *f.* &c. भिन्नभाव *m.* असंबद्धभाव *m.*

Forensic, *a. belonging to a court of judicature.* न्यायसभेचा, न्यायसभासंबंधी-विषयक.

Forest, *n.* अरण्य *n.* वन *n.* रान *n.* जंगल *n.* कांतार *m. n.* कानन *n.* दाव *m.* अटवी *f.* वृक्षजाल *n.*

Conflagration of a f. वणवा *m.* दावानल *m.* दावाग्नि*m.* दाव*m.*

Dweller in a f. वनवासी, वनस्थ, वनाश्रय.

Forest, *a. of or belonging to a forest.* अरण्याचा, वनाचा, रा-नाचा, आरण्य, आरण्यक, वान.

Forest-roving, *a.* वनचर, वनेचर.

Forester, *n.* वनवासी, रान्या, रानकरी.

Forfeit, *n. that which is lost by a fault, &c.* दंड *m.* गुन्हेगा-री *f.* तावण *f.* [*f.* अड *f.*

2—as attached to engagements or bonds. अट *f.* अटक

To **Forfeit**, *v. a. lose by a fault, &c.* दंडास देणें, दंड *m.* देणें.

To be forfeited. दंडास जाणें.

Forfeitable, *a.* दंडास जाण्याजोगा.

Forfeiture, *n.* v. V. दंडास देणें*n.* दंडास जाणें.

2 See **Forfeit**.

Forge, *n.* लोहाराची साळ *f.*-भट्टी *f.* लोहाराचा कारखाना*m.*

To **Forge**, *v. a. work, form by the hammer, &c.* घडणें, घडणी *f.*-घडणूक *f.*-घटन*n.*-घटना *f.*-&c. करणें *g. of o.*

Metal to be forged. घडीत*n.*

2 *make falsely, counterfeit.* बनाऊ-बनावटीचा-खोटा-खोटसाळ-कृत्रिम-&c. करणें, बनावणें.

Forged, *p.* v. V. 1. घडलेला, घडींव.

2 बनाऊ केलेला, बनावलेला,बनाऊ, बनावटीचा, बनावणीचा, खो-टा, खोटसाळ, काल्पनिक, कूट in comp. as कूटशासन.

Forger, *n.* v. V. 1. घडणारा, घडकामी *or* म्या.

2 बनावणारा, बनाऊ-&c.करणारा.

Forgery, Forging, *n.* v. V. 1.—*act.* घडणें*n.* घडणी *f.* घडणू-क *f.* घडण *f.* घटना *f.* घटन*n.*

2 बनाऊ करणें*n.* &c.

I. *art or business of f.* घडकाम *n.*

II. *forged writing.* बनावलेला-बनाऊ-&c. कागद *m.*लेख*m.*-&c. कपटलेख*m.*कपटलेख्य*n.* कूटलेख्य*n.*

To **Forget**, *v. a.* विसरणें, विसर*m.*-विस्मृति *f.*-विस्मरण*n.* होणें-पडणें *in. con. g. of o.* आठवण *f.* न राहणें, भुलणें, भोळा भासा जाणें, भूल *f.*-मोह*m.* पडणें *in. con.*

To f. one's self. भुलणें, भांबवणें *or* भांचावणें.

Forgetful, *a.* विसराळू,विसऱ्या, स्मरणाचा-आठवणीचा-&c.फुटका.

2 *negligent, neglectful, heedless, &c.* विसराळू, घळया, ग-हाळ, भांब्या, भांबळ *or* ळया, गफलती,गफलत्या, झांबऱ्या, झावळ.

Forgetfulness, *n.* v. A. 1. विसराळूपणा*m.* विसर*m.* विस्मरण*n.* विस्मृति *f.* मोह*m.* भूल *f.* अस्मरण*n.* अस्मृति *f.*

Through f. and ignorance. विसरभोळ्या खालीं.

2 गहाळपणा*m.* भांबळपणा*m.* &c. गफलत *f.* अन्हेर *m.*

To **Forgive**, *v. a. pardon.* माफ करणें, सोडणें, बक्षीस*n.* करणें, माफी *f.*-क्षमा *f.*-क्षांति *f.*-&c. करणें *g. of o.* दंड*m.*-अपराध*m.*-अन्याय*m.*-&c. सोडणें *g. of o.*

Forgiven, *p.* v. V. सोडलेला, माफ केलेला, माफ, क्षांत.

Forgiveness. See **Forgivingness, Pardon.**

Forgiving, *a. ready to forgive.* क्षमी, क्षमावान्, दयालु *pop.* ळू, दयाशील, क्षमाशील, क्षमापर, क्षमिना, क्षम, क्षंता, क्षांत.

Forgivingness, *n.* v. A. क्षमा *f.* दया *f.* क्षांति *f.* दयाशीलता *f.* क्षमाशीलता *f.*

Forgotten, *p.* v. V. विसरलेला, विस्मृत, अस्मृत.

Fork, *n. furcation.* दुखांदा *m.* नांगें*n.* दुबेळकें*n.* गेचक *n.* गेचकळ*n.* बेळकें*n.* बेचक*n.* बेचकूल*n.* बेचकें*n.* बेचांगळें*n.* दुफांटा*m.* फांदा*m.*

2 *forked thing.* डेळकें *or* ढेळकें*n.* डेळकी *f.* डेळी *f.* केल*n.*

3—table f. कांटा*m.* [येणें.

To **Fork**, *v. n.*—as corn, a tree, &c. फांकणें, फांदीस-पातीस

2—a road, &c. दोन फांटे *m. pl.* फुटणें *g. of s.*

Forked, Forky, *a.* डेळक्याचा, दुबेळक्याचा, दुफांट्याचा, द्विशाख, द्विकंटक.

Forlorn, *a.* v. **Friendless.** निराधार, निराश्रय, अनाश्रय, अ-नाथ, अगतिक, गतिहीन. [अनाश्रय *m.*

Forlornness, *n.* v. A. आश्रयहीनता *f.* आश्रयराहित्य *n.* &c.

Form, *n. fashion, figure, shape.* आकार *m.* आकृति *f.* घडण *f.* घडणी *f.* घडवण *f.* बांधा *m.* घाट *m.* घडीत *n.* डौल *m.* उभारणी *f.* रूप *n.* छब *f.* बेत *m.* बळण *n.* विध *m.* (in comp. as द्विवि-ध),—as involving the power of the freely used words *cut, make, mould, stamp, cast, build, bent, turn.* बेत *m.* तोड *f.* मोड *f.* ठेव *f.* ठेवण *f.* घटाव *m.* घाटी *f.* घाटणी *f.* घाट *m.* डौल*m.* बांधा *m.* बांधणी *f.* बांधाबळ *f.* भट्टी *f.*मासला *m.* रूप *n.* बळण*n.* *Form*, in comp. is neatly rendered by आकार, as *moon-form* चंद्राकार, *egg-form, oval* अंडाकार,*circle-form, circular* चक्राकार, मंडलाकार, वृत्ताकार, बलयाकार, *sphere-form* गोला-कार,*leaf-from, pitcher-form, &c.* ad libitum. पर्णाकार, कल-शाकार, गृहाकार, वृक्षाकार, पुस्तकाकार, करंडाकार, पीठाकार, &c.

Human f. नररूप.

Of one f. एके प्रतिमेचा. [बिंब *n.* मूर्त्ति *f.*

2 *a* f. *a shape, definite thing.* आकार *m.* आकृति *f.* रूप *n.*

3 *particular modification.* विकार*m.* विकृति*f.* परिणाम*m.* रूपांतर*n.*

4 *prescribed method.* पद्धति *pop.* पद्धत *f.* बेत *m.* क्रम *m.* परिपाटी *f.* विधि *m.*

In due f. यथा विधि, पद्धतवार. [उपचार *m.*

5 *ceremony, ceremonial,* v. **Rite.** रीति *pop* रीत *f.* संस्कार*m.*

To go through the f. of. वरवर *adv.* करणें, शास्त्रार्थ *m.* करणें, शिष्टाचार *m.* करणें, गरजेचें *n.* करणें, टाकणें *n.* टाकणें.
6 *external appearance*, v. APPEARANCE, SHOW. रूप *n.* आकार *m.* डौल *m.*
7 (as for an official paper). दस्तूर *n.*
A f. lying ready to be filled as wanted. डौळ *m.*
A form-sheet. डौळपत्रक *or* डौळापत्रक *n.*
8 (of students, &c.,) *class.* वर्ग *m.*
9 *make, cast, or air of the body.* आंगबळण *n.*आंगलट *f.* आंगलोट *m.* आंगवटा *or* ठा *or* आंगोठा *m.* आंगलवण *f.* आंगबांधा *m.* ठाणमाण *n.* रूपरेषा *f.* रूपरेखा *f.* शरीराची मूस *f.* शरीराची काठी *f.* आंगकाठी *f.* अंगयष्टि *f.* हाडगात *n.* धज *f.*
10 (as of a verb or noun). रूप *n.*
11 *bench.* बांक *m.*
12 *sort, kind,* v. MANNER. प्रकार *m.*
13 (of a hare) ससा बसायाची निजायाची जागा *f.*

To FORM, *v. a. make, model, shape, fashion.* घडणें, वळवणें, उतरणें, काढणें, करणें.
2 *combine and dispose*, v. To ARRANGE. रचणें, बांधणें, रचना *f.*-रचणूक *f.*-बंदोबस्त *m.*-&c. करणें *g. of o.*
3—mentally, v. To CONCEIVE. धरणें, बांधणें.
4 *constitute, make,* v. To COMPOSE. अंगभूत-अवयवभूत-&c. असणें *in. con.* बनावणें.

To FORM, *v. n. assume the due form.* वळणें.
2 *rise, appear, take being, come up, out, &c.* धरणें, बनणें, उठणें, येणें, निघणें, पडणें, चढणें, उचलणें.
3—the hand, in writing, drawing, &c. वळणें.

FORMAL, *a.* v. CEREMONIOUS. आदरोपचारी, आदरोपचाराचा, आदरोपचारनिष्ठ, आदरसत्कारी.
2 *done according to form.* बेताचा, बेतींव, कायदेशीर, यथापद्धति, यथामार्ग, यथाविधि, आचारशुद्ध, संप्रदायशुद्ध, सौत्र.
3 *having the form but not the essence,* v. EXTERNAL. बाहेरचा, बाहेरच्या डौलाचा, वरवरचा, बाह्याकाराचा. [क्रियानिष्ठ.

FORMALIST, *n. observer of forms,* v. CEREMONIOUS. कर्मनिष्ठ,
2 *mere observer of form and outward appearance.* बाह्योपचारी, बाह्यधर्मनिष्ठ, बाह्यधर्मवृत्ति.

FORMALITY, *n.* v. A. 1. आदरोपचारनिष्ठा *f.* आदरोपचारभक्ति *f.* आदरोपचारसेवा *f.*
2 कायदेशीरपणा *m.* यथामार्गता *f.* विध्यनुयायिता *f.* विध्यानुकूल्य *n.*
I. *a* f. v. FORM, RITE. उपचार *m.* रीति *f.* संस्कार *m.*

FORMALLY, *adv.* v.A. 1. आदरोपचारानें, आदरानें, आदरपूर्वक, &c.
2 पद्धतवार, यथापद्धति, यथाविधि, विधिवत्.

FORMATION, FORMING, *n.* v.V.A. 1.—*act.* घडणें *n.* काढणें *n.*&c. घडणी *f.* घडणूक *f.* घटना *f.* घटन *n.*
2—*act.* रचणें *n.* &c. रचणूक *f.* रचना *f.*
v. V. N. 2. *and* PRODUCTION. उत्पत्ति *f.* उद्भव *m.*
I.—in grammar (of words, &c.). व्युत्पत्ति *f.*
II. *make, structure,* v. FORM. बनावट *f.* घडण *f.* घडवण *f.*

FORMED, *p.* v. V. A. 1. घडलेला, &c. घडींव, घटित in comp.
To be f. upon. वळणावर जाणें *g. of o.*
2 रचलेला, रचित.
I.—in grammar,—a word, &c. व्युत्पन्न, यौगिक.

FORMER, *n.* FORMING, *p. a.* v. V. A. 1. घडणारा, काढणारा, करणारा, &c. कर्त्ता, जनक.

FORMER, *a. foregoing, prior, previous, preceding, anterior, antecedent.* मागचा *or* ला, मागील, अधींचा, अधील, पेशजींचा, माजी, पूर्व, पूर्वीचा, अगोदरचा, अगोदरील, प्राचीन, पूर्वकालीन, प्राक्तन, पूर्वतन, पौर्व. [भूतपूर्व.
2 *that was before, that has been.* पेशजींचा, गत, गतकालचा,
3 *immediately preceding.* अदला, आगला, गेला, पहिला.

FORMERLY, *adv.* v. A. *anciently, in time past.* मागें, पूर्वी, मागल्या काळीं, गेल्या काळीं, जुन्या काळीं, पहिल्या काळीं, पूर्वकालीं, गतकालीं, पेशजीं, पहिल्यान्, पहिला *adv. decl.* पुरः, पुरा.
As f. यथापूर्व, पूर्ववत्.

FORMICATION, *n.*—the tingling or sensation. मुंग्या *f. pl. v.* ये, चढ, झुळझूळ *f. intens.* झुळझुळाट *m.* विरविरी *or* विरवीर *f.* रवरवी *or* रिंवरीव *f.* [राल, घोर.

FORMIDABLE, *a.* v. FEARFUL. भयंकर, भयजनक, भयोत्पादक, क-

FORMIDABLENESS, *n.*v.A. भयंकरत्व *n.*भयजनकता *f.* [बेडौल.

FORMLESS, *a.* निराकार, निराकृति, आकारहीन-शून्य-रहित, अमूर्त्त,

FORMLESSNESS, *n.* v. A. अमूर्त्ति *f.* निराकारता *f.* आकारशून्यता *f.*

FORMULA, *n. prescribed form or method.* पद्धति *pop.* पद्धत *f.* विधि *m.* विधान *n.* रीति *pop.* रीत *f.* [संग्रह *m.*

FORMULARY, *n. book of forms.* पद्धति *f.* विधानमाला *f.* विधान-

To FORNICATE, *v. n.* v. N. 1. अविवाहितस्त्रीशींगमन-अनूढागमन *n.*-कन्यागमन *n.*-वेश्यागमन *n.*-&c. करणें.
3 शिंदळकी *f.*-छिनाली *f.*-रांडबाजी *f.*-&c. करणें.

FORNICATION, *n. commerce of a man with an unmarried woman.* अविवाहितस्त्रीशींगमन *n.* अनूढागमन *n.* कन्यागमन *n.* वेश्यागमन *n.* अविवाहितागमन *n.*
2 *incontinence of an unmarried woman.* अनूढाव्यभिचार *m.*
3 *unlawful intercourse of the sexes*—gener. शिंदळकी *f.* छिनाली *f.* छिनाला *m.* रांडबाजी *f.* जारकर्म *n.* व्यभिचार *m.* बदअमल *m.* बदकर्म *n.*—in cant or covert phraseology. बाहेरख्याल *m.* बहिर्द्वार *n.* बहिर्व्यसन *n.* Note. As Hindus all marry, fornication as distinguished from adultery is rare.

FORNICATOR, *n.* v. N. 1. अविवाहितस्त्रीशींगमन करणारा, अनूढागामी, कन्यागामी, वेश्यागामी, &c.
3 शिंदळ-छिनाल-रांडबाज-&c. पुरुष-मनुष्य-&c. शिंदळकी-&c. करणारा, बाहेरख्याली, बहिर्व्यसनी. [णी *f.*

FORNICATRESS, *n.* v. N. 2. अनूढव्यभिचारिणी *f.* अनूढकामचारि-
3 शिंदळ-छिनाल-&c. बायको *f.*-स्त्री *f.* शिंदळकी-&c. करणारी.

To FORSAKE, *v. a.* v. To ABANDON. सोडणें, सोडून जाणें, टाकणें, टाकून जाणें, त्याग *m.*-परित्याग *m.*-&c. करणें *g. of o.*

FORSOOTH, *adv. in truth.* तर खरा *a. decl.* तर सई, तर होय.

To FORSWEAR, *v. a. renounce on oath.* शपथ *f.* वाहणें-खाणें-करणें *with g. of o. or* विषयीं. आण *f.* वाहणें *with g. of o.* शपथ-आण वाहून सोडणें, शपथपूर्वक सोडणें, सशपथत्याग *m.* करणें *g. of o.*
2 *deny on oath.* शपथ करून-शपथपूर्वक-सशपथ-&c. नाकारणें, अपन्हव *m.* करणें, अपलाप *m.* करणें.
3 (one's self) *commit perjury.* खोटी शपथ *f.* करणें-वाहणें, क्रिया भ्रष्ट करणें.

FORT, *n.* कोट *or* कोठ *m.* क़िल्ला *m.* दुर्ग *m.*
Country on outside of a f. बाहेरकोट *m.*
Crest or highest works of a f. बालेकिल्ला *m.* [णी *f.*
Earth heaped up against the wall of a f. रेवण *f.* रेव-

F. on the plain.—as disting. from a hill-f. भुईकोट *m.*
F. surrounded by the sea. जंजीरा *m.*
Governor or keeper of a f. किल्लेदार *m.* दुर्गाधिकारी *m.* दुर्गाध्यक्ष *m.*
Hill-f. गड *m.* Accountant of a hill-f. गडनीस *m.* (his office or business. गडनिविसी *or* निसी *f.*). Soldier or Peon serving in a hill-f. गडकरी *m.*
Impregnable or strong f. बांका किल्ला *m.*
Investing or besieging a f. दुर्गावरोध *m.*
Outer-f. बाहेर कोट *m.*
Small f. गढी *f.* चौबुरजी *f.*
The upper f. बालेकिल्ला *m.*
To kindle the jungle round a f. किल्ला *m.* नेसवणें.
Town belonging to a f. पेठ *f.*
Wall of a f. कोट *m.* कोठ *m.* तड *m.* फांद *m.* प्राकार *m.*—
Second or outer wall of a f. पडकोट *or* परकोट *m.*
2 *or* forte: *that in which one excels.* बिरीद *n.* बिरुद *n.* बाणा *m.* बाण्याची वस्त *f.* कुलदैवत *n.*

Forth, *adv. onward, forward.* पुढें.
And so forth. इत्यादि, वगैरे.
2 *abroad.* बाहेर.

Forth, *prep. out of.* आंतून. [जिता, जागता.

Forth-coming, *a. ready to appear.* हाजीर, तयार, सिद्ध, जिवंत,

Forthwith, *adv. immediately.* लागलाच, तेव्हांच, तत्क्षणीं, तसाच, आतांच, असाच, एव्हांच, ताबडतोब.

Fortieth, *a.* चाळिसावा.

Fortification, *n.* v. V.—*act.* तटबंदी *f.* कोटबंदी *f.*
I. *place fortified*, v. Fort. कोट *m.* किल्ला *m.* [या *f.*
II. *science of military architecture.* दुर्गप्राकारादिरचनवि-
Fortifications, *works of a fort.* तटबंदी *f.*

To **Fortify**, *v. a.* तटबंदी *f.*-कोटबंदी *f.*-&c. करणें, तटबंदीनें मजबूत करणें, दुर्गप्राकारादिदृढ करणें.
2 See To Confirm, To Strengthen.

Fortitude, *n. strength or firmness of mind.* धीर *m.* धैर्य *n.* छाती *f.* धारिष्ट *n.* हिय्या *m.* वीर्य *n.* धारणा *f.* धर *m.* धृति *f.* सहनशक्ति *f.*

Fortnight, *n.* पंधरवडा *m.* द्विसप्ताह *n.* अर्धमास *m.* मासार्ध *n.*
Lunar f. पक्ष *m.*

Fortress, *n.* v. Fort. कोट *m.* गढी *f.* चौबुरजी *f.*

Fortuitous, *a.* v. Accidental. आगंतुक, दैवघटित, दैवजात, दैवोपस्थित, यदृच्छाजात.

Fortuitousness, **Fortuity**, *n.* v. A. दैवयोग *m.* यदृच्छा *f.* दैवघटितत्व *n.* आगंतुकत्व *n.* &c.

Fortuitously, *adv.* v. A. *and* Accidentally. दैवयोगें करून, दैवयोगानें, दैववशात्.

Fortunate, *a. lucky, happy, successful,*—of persons. भाग्याचा, दैवाचा, मोठ्या दैवाचा, सुदैवाचा, &c. सदैव, भाग्यवान् *pop.* भाग्यवंत, दैववान् *pop.* दैववंत, नसीबवंत *or* नसीबवान, सभाग्य, बहुभाग्य, धन्य, पद्महस्ती, वरदहस्ती, भाग्यशाली, दैवशाली, यशस्वी, यशवंत, अदृष्टवान् *pop.* अदृष्टवंत, श्रीमान्, बखतवार, तालेवार, तालेवंत, सुभग, उंचकपाळ्या, होंड्या कपाळाचा.
2 *coming by good luck, bringing some unexpected good.* सुभाग्याचा, सुदैवाचा, मंगल , शुभकर, श्रेयस्कर, शुभावह.
3 See Auspicious. [दैवयोगानें.

Fortunately, *adv.* सुभाग्यानें, सुदैवानें, भाग्यबलानें, भाग्योदयानें,

Fortunateness, *n.* v. A. 1. सौभाग्य *n.* यश *n.* बखतवारी *f.* तालेवारी *f.* सद्दी *f.* सलाबतपणा *m.* सभाग्यता *f.* भाग्यशालित्व *n.* दैवशालिता *f.*

Fortune, *n.*—as the power allotting, v. Destiny. दैव *n.* प्रारब्ध *n.* नसीब *n.* कर्म *n.* कपाळ *n.* दैविक *n.* दैवाचे-प्रारब्धाचे-नसिबाचे-&c. ताले *m.pl.* साधलाध *or* द *f.*—as the Genius of prosperity or success, रंगदेवता *f.* लक्ष्मी *f.* श्री *f.* Of *Fortune* as a divinity or power as much notice is taken by the Maráthá's as by other people. The opening, smiling, or becoming propitious of F. is expressed by दैव *n.*—भाग्य *n.*-नसीब *n.*-&c. उघडणें-खुलणें-उपटणें-उभें राहणें-उदित होणें-उजेडणें-&c. कपाळाची रेघ *f.*-रेषा *f.* उघडणें-उपटणें, दैव *n.*-भाग्य *n.*-&c. उदय *m.* पावणें-उदयास येणें, भाग्याचा-दैवाचा-&c. उदय *m.* होणें *g. of. s.* लक्ष्मी *f.* अवतरणें *with* वर *of o.*
The turning, frowning, or becoming adverse of F. is expressed by. दैव *n.*-भाग्य *n.*-नसीब *n.*-&c. फुटणें-माघारणें-अस्त होणें.
The increasing propitiousness of F. is rendered by दैवानें- &c. उपट *f.* खाणें.
The taking of a run by F. (of good or evil) is दैवानें-&c. धांव *f.* घेणें.
The constraining by F. (to some evil) is दैवानें-&c. ओढ *f.* घेणें *or* दैव *n.*-&c. ओढवणें. [ळफळणें.
The showering down of favors by F. is दैव *n.*-&c. फ-
Dawn of good f. भाग्योदय *m.*
Favorite of F. भाग्यपुरुष *m.* ऐश्वर्याचा प्राणी *m.* दैवाचा-प्राणी, दैवाचा पुतळा *m.*
F.'s favors. रंगदेवतेचा प्रसाद *m.*
Gusts of F's favors. घोवें *n.* गोवें *n.* घबाड *n.*
Offerings to F. from a meal to preserve her favors. लक्ष्मी रावण *f.*
Sport of F. *poor wight.* भाग्याचा भोपळा *m.* दैवाचा भोपळा, अकाबाईचें बाळ *n.* [डगें *n.*
Wheel of F. दैवचक्र *n.* कालचक्र *n.* संसारचक्र *n.* रहाटगा-
Worship of F. लक्ष्मी पूजन *n.*
Through labor and the aid of F. काळा कष्टानें.
F. favors the bold. धारिष्टास दैव धाजणें.
You may outrun all, but F. will outrun you. सर्वांपुढें धाववेल पण दैवापुढें धाववत नाहीं.
2 *allotment, lot,* v. Destiny. दैवरेषा *f.* दैवदशा *f.* दैवाचे ताले *m. pl.* दैव *n.* कपाळ *n.* भाग्य *n.* प्रारब्ध *n.* भोग *m.* भोक्तृत्व *n* भवितव्य *n.* होतव्य *n.* होयीक *n.* होष्य *n.* होष्यमाण *n.*
3 *luck, success,* (good or bad). लाभालाभ *m.* यश अपयश *n.* सुख दुःख *n.* बरें वाईट *n.*
Good f. सुदैव *n.*
Ill f. दुर्दैव *n.* नाट *n.*
4 *property, possessions, wealth.* धन *n.* संपत्ति *f.* दौलत *f.* लक्ष्मी *f.* मत्ता *f.* वित्त *n.* वित्तविषय *m.*
Of blasted fortunes. हतश्री, हतैश्वर्य.
That has made his f. प्राप्तश्री.

To make or be making one's f. दैव*n.* काढणें, दैवास चढणें-येणें, तरतरणें, पिकणें *g. of s.* भरभरणें *g.of s.* भळभळणें *g. of s.* डोई *f.* हालिवणें, टेंभा *m.* पाजळणें.

To FORTUNE, *v. n.* v. To HAPPEN. घडणें, दैवानें घडणें-घडून येणें.

FORTUNE-BOOK, *n.* शकुनवंती *f.*

To FORTUNE-TELL, *v. a.* दैव *n.*-दैवरेषा *f.*-भवितव्य *n.*-होतव्य *n.*-&c. सांगणें-भाकणें *g. of o.*

FORTUNE-TELLER, *n.* v. V. दैव सांगणारा, होतव्य सांगणारा, &c. जोशी *or* ठोकजोशी, मेढेजोशी, डाकोचा *or* डाकोताजोशी, कुडबुडा *or* कुडमुडाजोशी, सर्वदा *or* सरोदा जोशी, पिंगळा जोशी, डौऱ्या जोशी, कालबेला *or* ल्या, नक्षत्रसूची, दैवज्ञ, दैवलेखक.

FORTUNE-TELLING, *n.* v. V. दैव सांगणें *n.* दैव भाकणें *n.* &c. कालबेल *f.* उपश्रुति *f.* There are various systems of *fortune-telling, interpreting omens, &c.* of which some are मेढेमत *or* मेढगमत *n.* भाडळीमत *n.* सहदेवमत *n.* गोरखमत *n.*

FORTY, *a.* चाळीस.—one, एकताळीस, एकेचाळ, एकचाळीस, एकेताळ, एकताळीस.—two, बेताळीस, बेचाळीस, बेचाळ.—three, त्रेताळीस, त्रेचाळीस.—four, चव्वेचाळ, चव्वेचाळीस, चव्वेताळ, चव्वेताळीस.—five, पंचेताळ, पंचेताळीस, पंचेचाळ, पंचेचाळीस, पस्ताळ.—six, शेताळ, शेताळीस, शेचाळ, शेचाळीस.—seven, सत्तेताळ, सत्तेताळीस, सत्तेचाळ, सत्तेचाळीस.—eight, अठ्ठेताळ, अठ्ठेताळीस, अठ्ठेचाळ, अठ्ठेचाळीस.—nine, एकुणपन्नास.

Aggregate of f. चाळसी *f.* चाळिसा *m.*

Age of f. चाळसी *f.*

Dimness of vision about the age of f. चाळसी *f.*

FORWARD, FORWARDS, *adv.* पुढें, मोहरें.

Right f. सरधोपट.

To come f. *advance.* पुढावणें, पुढारणें, सरसावणें, सरळणें, सरकणें, सरकावणें. 2 *offer one's self, volunteer.* धजणें *or* धजावणें, धज *f.* देणें.

To put one's self f. *be obtrusive.* आपलें घोडें *n.* ढकलणें, पुढेंपुढें करणें.

2 *towards the fore part.* पुढल्याभागाकडे.

FORWARD, *a. eager, ardent, zealous,* v. EARNEST. उत्सुक, उत्कंठित, उत्साहवान्, उत्साही, सोत्साह, धजदार.

2 *pert, impudent, wanting in modesty, &c.* धीट, निर्भीड, धृष्ट, असंकोच, संकोचहीन-रहित-&c. मुखसंकोचहीन-रहित-&c. अगळिकीचा, उद्दाम, अविनय, लुबरा, लुडबुड्या, लघाळ, लचाळ, लचाड.

To be officiously f. पुढच्या पुढें करणें-नाचणें.

3 *advanced beyond the usual degree.* आगसलेला, पुढारलेला, पुढें गेलेला.

4 *advanced towards completion.* समाप्ती जवळ आलेला, आसन्नसमाप्तिक, उपसमाप्तिक. [पोंचविणें.

To FORWARD, *v. a. send forward, transmit.* पुढें पाठवणें, पेंड *m.*

2 See To PROMOTE. [उत्कंठा *f.*

FORWARDNESS, *n.* v. A. 1. उत्सुकता *f.* उत्साह *m.* औत्सुक्य *n.*

2 धिटाई *f.* धीटपणा *m.* निर्भीडपणा *m.* अमर्यादा *f.* लचाळकी *f.* लचाडकी *f.* मुखसंकोचाभाव *m.* मुखसंकोचराहित्य *n.* अगळीक *f.* अगळी *f.* अगळीत *f.*

FOSSE. See DITCH.

FOSSIL, *n. substance dug from the earth.* खणतीचें द्रव्य *n.* धातु *m.* उपधातु *m.*

FOSSIL, *a. that is dug from the earth.* पृथ्वींतून खणून काढलेला, खननोद्भूत, आकरोद्भूत.

FOSSILIST, *n.* धातुवादी, धातुवेत्ता. [आपंगणें.

To FOSTER, *v. a. nurse, feed,* v. To NOURISH. पोसणें, पाळणें,

2 *cherish, harbor, indulge.* वाहणें, बागवणें, बाळगणें, राखणें.

FOSTER-BROTHER, *n.* दूधभाऊ *m.* दाईभाऊ *m.*

FOSTER-CHILD, *n.* पाळक-पोसका *or* गा-पोसणा *or* पोष्णा मुलगा*m.*-मुलगी *f.*-लेंक *m. f.*-&c.

FOSTER-DAUGHTER, *n.* पाळकलेंक *f.* पाळकबेटी *f.* पालककन्या *f.*

FOSTER-FATHER, *n.* पाळकबाप *m.*

FOSTER-MOTHER, FOSTER-DAM, *n.* v. NURSE. पाळक आई *f.* पालकमाता *f.* धात्री *f.*

FOSTER-SISTER, *n.* दूधबहीण *f.* दाई बहीण *f.*

FOSTER-SON, *n.* पाळकलेंक *m.* पाळकबेटा *m.* पालकपुत्र *n.*

FOSTERED, *p.* v. V. 1. पोसलेला, &c. पोसका *or* गा, पोसणा *or* पोष्णा, परिपालित.

FOSTERER, *n.* v. V. 1. पोसणारा, &c. पोसिंदा *or* पोशिंदा.

FOUL, *n. disease of the clefts of the hoofs of cattle.* खुरखूत *or* खुरकूत *n.* खुरगुटी *f.*

To be affected with it. खुरखुतणें *or* खुरकुतणें.

FOUL, *a. filthy,* v. DIRTY. मळका *remiss.* मळकट, मलिन *pop.* मळीण, मळसर, मलदूषित, कलुष.

2 *loathsome,* v. DISGUSTING. घाणेरा, घाणेरडा, ओंगळ, ओखटा, मुरदाड *or* मुडदार, अमंगल. [चकट.

3—hands, &c. after eating, culinary vessel, &c. उष्टा, मि-

To be f.;—hands, &c. करबडणें, करकटणें, मिचकटणें.

4 *unfavorable,*—of wind. उलटा, तोंडचा, समोरचा, प्रतिकूल.

5 *unfair, inequitable.* अप्रामाणिक, असरल, अनृजु, कुटिल.

6 See IMPURE. 7—weather, v. STORMY. जोळी, वारेवादळाचा.

8—a rope, &c. hindered from motion. अडकलेला, अडलेला.

To fall f. of. आंगावर येणें.

FOUL-MOUTHED, FOUL-SPOKEN, FOUL-TONGUED, *a.* v. ABUSIVE. तोंडाळ, तोंडाचा फटकळ, तोंडाचा वाईट, काळदांत्या, काळजिभ्या, अडबे जिभेचा, दुर्मुख, वाग्दुष्ट, कुबट.

2 *given to obscene language.* तोंडशिंदळ, जीभशिंदळ *or* तोंडाचा-&c. शिंदळ.

To FOUL, *v. a.* v. To DIRTY. मळवणें, मळका-मळीण-&c.करणें.

FOUL-PLAY, *n.* दगा*m.*

Suspicion of f. दगा*m.*

FOULED, *p.* v. V. मळलेला, भरलेला, &c. मजीत.

FOULNESS, *n.* v. A. 1. मळकेपणा*m.* मळीणपणा*m.* &c. मल *pop.* मळ*m.* मळकटी *f.* मालिन्य*n.* कल्मष*n.* कलुषता *f.*

To FOUND, *v. a. lay the basis of; establish, set up, build.* पाया*m.* घालणें, स्थापणें, संस्थापणें, स्थापना *f.*-स्थापन*n.*-&c. करणें *g. of o.* स्थापित-&c. करणें.

2 *form by melting, &c.* ओतणें.

FOUNDATION, *n.* v. V. 1.—*act.* स्थापणें*n.* &c. स्थापन*n.* स्थापना *f.* संस्थापन*n.* संस्थापना *f.*

I. *basis or lower parts.* पाया*m.* बुडखा*m.* बुडूख *n.*

To lay a firm f. चिरेबंदी पाया*m.* घालणें.

II. *footing, warrant, &c.* v. GROUND. धार*m.* धारा*m.* आधार*m.* आश्रय *pop.* आस्रा*m.*

III. v. ENDOWMENT. धर्मादाय *m.* धर्मादाव *m.*

FOUNDED, *p.* v. V. 1. स्थापलेला, &c. स्थापित, संस्थापित.
2 ओतलेला, ओतींव.

FOUNDER, *n.* v. V. 1. स्थापणारा, &c. स्थापक, संस्थापक, स्थापन- &c. कर्त्ता, प्रयोजक.
2 ओतणारा, ओतारी.
I. (of a religious order or sect). आचार्य *m.* प्रवर्त्तकाचार्य*m.* संस्थापक, धर्मस्थापक.
II. (of a race). मूलपुरुष*m.* मूल*n.* गोत्र*m.*

To FOUNDER, *v. a.*—a horse, &c. पायांनीं-पायांचा अधू-&c. करणें, लंगडा करणें.

To FOUNDER, *v. n. sink*—ship, &c. बुडणें, बसणें, फसणें, गर्क [होणें.

FOUNDERY, *n. place, &c. for melting metal.* धातू ओतण्याचा कारखाना*m.* भटारखाना*m.* कुप्यशाला *f.*

FOUNDLING, *n. deserted child found.* गवर्शेमूल*n.* निवाप्या, अज्ञातपितृक, अपविद्ध.

FOUNT, FOUNTAIN, *n.* (of water) v. SPRING. झरा *or* झिरा*m.* झरी *f.* जलाकर*m.*
A corrupt f. cannot send forth fresh streams. आडांत पाणी खारट तर पोहऱ्यांत कोठून गोड येईल ! कोळ्याचा कोळी होईल न होईल तरी पांच डाग घेऊन उठेल.
2 playing f. कारंजें*n.* फवारा*m.*
3 v. SOURCE. मूल*n.* आदि*m.* [स्थान*n.*

FOUNTAIN-HEAD, *n.* v. SOURCE. जिव्हाळा*m.* सरचश्मा*m.* मुख्य-

FOUR, *a.* चार, चौ (in comp. as चौकट, चौकडा, चौकोनी), चतुर, चहुं (in comp. as चहुंकडे, चहुत्रा), चौघे*m.pl.* (चौघी *or* घ्या *f. pl.* चौघें *or* घीं *n. pl.* This word is used only of human beings).
Aggregate of f. चौकडी *f.* चतुष्क*n.* चतुष्टय*n.*
Aggregate of f. (cowries or pice). गंडा*m.*
Of f. kinds, sorts, ways. चतुर्विध.

FOUR-FOLD, *a.* चौपट, चतुर्गुण.

FOUR-FOOTED, *a.* चौपायी, चार पायांचा, चतुष्पद.

FOUR-SCORE, *a.* चार विसा.

FOUR-SQUARE, *a.* v. QUADRANGULAR. चतुरस्र.

FOUR-TWISTED, *a.* चौपदरी.

FOUR-WHEELED, *a.* चार चाकांचा, चौचाकी, चार चाकी.

FOURTEEN, *a.* चौदा, चतुर्दश.

FOURTEENTH, *a.* चौदावा.

FOURTH, *a.* चौथा, चतुर्थ, तुरीय.
To make the subject of a f. operation (to plough, read, &c. the fourth time.) चौसारणें *or* चौसरणें, चौसारणी करणें.

FOURTH, *n.* चौथाई *f.* पावकें *n.* चौथा वांटा *m.* चतुर्थांश *m.* चोतकर *or* चौतकर *m.*—of a cake, jack fruit, &c. चतकोर *m. f.* चतकर *m. f.*
Excess by a f. सवाई *f.*
That exceeds by a f. सवा, सवाई.

FOWL. *n.* See BIRD.
2—gallinaceous. कोंबडा (डा *m.* डी *f.* डें *n.*) कुक्कुट *n.*
F.—house. खुडी *f.* खुडें *n.* खुराडें *n.* [*f.* करणें.

To FOWL, *v. a. catch fowls for game.* पाखरांची-पक्ष्यांची पारध

FOWLER, *n.* v. V. पाखर पारधी, फांसेपारधी, बाघरी, पाशी.

FOWLING-PIECE, *n.* शिकारीची-पारधीची बंदूक *f.*

FOX, *n.* खोंकड *or* कोंकड *f. n.*
Flying f. वडवाघूळ *n.*

FOX-GLOVE, *n.* एकवनस्पति आहे.

FRACTION, *n.* (of an integral). अपूर्णांक *m.* अपूर्ण *m.* अंश *m.* भाग *m.* भिन्न *n.* राशिभाग *m.*
Vulgar fractions. व्यवहारी अपूर्णांक *m.pl.* शुद्ध अपूर्णांक*m.pl.*
Addition of fractions. भिन्न संकलन *n.*
Common measure of a f. अपवर्त्तक *m.* अपवर्त्त *m.*
Compound fractions. प्रभाग जाति *f. pl.* प्रभाग जाति अपूर्णांक *m. pl.*
Cube of a f. भिन्नघन *n.*
Decimal f. दशांश अपूर्णांक *m.*
Denominator of a f. छेदक *m.* छेद *m.*
Division of fractions. भिन्नभाजन *n.* भिन्नभागहर *m.*
Improper f. विषम अपूर्णांक *m.*
Multiplication of fractions. भिन्नगुणन *n.*
Numerator of a f. अंश *m.*
Proper f. सम अपूर्णांक *m.* [अंशसवर्णन*n.*
Reduction of f. to a common denominator. सवर्णन *n.*
Reduction of f. to a lower denomination. अपवर्त्तन *n.*
Simple fractions. भागजाति *f. pl.* भागजाति अपूर्णांक*m.pl.*
Square of a f. भिन्नवर्ग *m.*
Subtraction of fractions. भिन्नव्यवकलन *n.*

FRACTIONAL, *a.* अपूर्णांकाचा, अपूर्णांकसंबंधी, भागिक.

FRACTIOUS, *a. apt to quarrel*, v. CROSS. तुटक, तुटसाळ, तुडस, तुसडा.

FRACTURE, *n.* फूट *f.* भंग *m.* भंजन *n.*

To FRACTURE, See To BREAK.

FRAGILE, *a. brittle, weak*, v. FRAIL. फुटरा, फुटीर, नाजूक, भंगुर, भंगशील, भंजनशील, अशक्त, कांचेच्या भांड्यासारखा.

FRAGILITY, *n.* v. A. भंगुरता *f.* भंगशीलता *f.* नाजुकपणा *m.*

FRAGMENT, *n. piece broken*, v. BIT. तुकडा *m. dim.* तुकडी *f.* खंड *m.* कुटका *m.*
Fragments, *bits, pieces, shivers, fritters.* चाराचुरा *m.* चकनाचूर *or* चकाचूर *m.* चुरा *m.* चूर *m.* चूरचार *m. pl.* चुराडा *m.* कुटा *m.* खुर्दा *m.*
Fragments (of rice, pulse, &c.), *broken grains.* आडकणी *f.* कणोर *or* कणबर *m.*
In fragments. खंडशः.

FRAGMENTARY, *a.* तुकड्यांचा, खंडमय.

FRAGRANCE, *n.* v. A. सुवास*m.* सुगंध*m.* सुगंधि*m.* गोडी *f.* खुशबोई *f.* सौरभ्य *n.* सुरभि *m.* परिमल *pop.* परिमळ *m.* माधुर्य *n.* स्वाद*m.*
I. a f. *fragrant substance.* गंध*m.* सुरभि*m.* सुगंधिद्रव्य*n.* परिमलद्रव्य*n.*
A widely diffused f. दमदमाट*m.* घमघमाट*m.*
To have a diffusive f. दमदमणें, घमघमणें, घवघवणें.
Strong, sweet, &c. diffusive,—a f. घमघमीत, घवघवीत.

FRAGRANT, *a. sweet of smell.* सुवासाचा, सुगंधाचा, सुवासिक, सुगंधिक, सुगंधि, गोड, खुशबोईचा, सुरभि, इष्टगंध, परिमलयुक्त-विशिष्ट.

FRAIL, *a. fragile, weak.* भंगुर, क्षणभंगुर, भंजनशील, भंगशील, क्षणविध्वंसी, नश्वर, नाजूक, अशक्त, दुर्बल, निर्बल, फुटरा, फुटीर, निर्जीव.

2 *weak in resolution, liable to err.* अधीर, अस्थिर, अस्थिरबुद्धि, चलबुद्धि, स्खलनशील, भ्रमशील.

Frail, *n. basket of rush.* ल्व्हाळयाची टोपली *f.*

Frailness, Frailty, *n.* v.A. 1. भंगुरता *f.* भंगशीलता *f.* नश्वरता *f.* नैश्वर्य *n.* अशक्ति *f.* अशकता *f.* दुर्बलता *f.* दौर्बल्य *n.*

2 अस्थिरबुद्धि *f.* चलबुद्धि *f.* अस्थिरता *f.* स्खलनशीलता *f.* भ्रमशीलता *f.*

I. *a* f. *a foible.* v. **Fault.** चूक *f.* चुकून घडलेली गोष्ट *f.*

To **Frame**, *v. a.* (an account, &c.) आकारणें, करणें, घडणें.

2 See To **Form.** 3 *adjust, adopt, &c.* जम *m.*-जवा *m.*-&c. बसवणें, जुळूनदेणें.

Frame, *n.* (as of a picture, &c.). चौकट *f.* घर *n.* सांचा *m.*

2 (as of a drum, tabor, saddle, &c.). खोड *n.* गाडा *m.* पूड *n.*

3 (of the mind). चित्तवृत्ति *f.* वृत्ति *f.* मनोविकार *m.* मनोवृत्ति *f.* प्रकृति *f.* भाव *m.*

4 (of the body). v. **Form.** शरीराची काठी *f.* आंग काठी *f.* आंगबांधा *m.* अंगरचना *f.* अंगयष्टि *f.* हाडगात *n.*

Of high f.—used of beasts. उभ्याकुडीचा.

5 *empty frame, skeleton.* सांगाडा *or* सांकाटा *m.* सटारा *m.* आंगकाठी *f.* मांडणी *f.* मांडणूक *f.* मांडणावळ *f.* मांडावळ *f.*

6—to support boxes, casks, &c. घोडा *m. dim.* घोडी *f.* घडवंची *f.* माचोळी *f.*

A f. (of wood or iron) in which pitchers are carried on beasts. लगड *f.*

7 cradle, bed, &c.—gener. घोडी *f.*

8—as matted or wattled, and as for a window-shutter, gate of an enclosure, &c. ताटी *f.* तकेंट *or* तटकें *n.* तटकी *f.* झापा *m.* झडपा *m.*

F. or erection in a field, or on a tree, &c. for watching the crops. माच *m.* माचाळ *n.*

F. work of bamboos, sticks, &c. for roofs, decks, &c. साट *m.* साटी *f.*

F. for stacks of hay. माच *m. dim.* माचोळी *f.* माची *f.*

Frame-work, *n.* See **Frame**, 1. 5.

Franchise, *n.* सरकारानें दिलेला अधिकार *m.*

2 *exemption.* सूट *f.* माफी *f.* मोकळीक *f.*

3 *asylum*, v. **Sanctuary.** आश्रयस्थान *n.*

Frangible, &c. See **Fragile**, &c.

Frank, *a. open, ingenuous, candid,*-of persons. मनाचा मोकळा, मनाचा साफ, निष्कपट, अकपट, अकृत्रिम, मनाचा निर्मळ, निर्मळ मनाचा, निवळ मनाचा, साळढाळ, निष्प्रांजल, प्रांजल, मनाचा पाक, दिलपाक, हळवळा, हळवळीत, प्रशस्त, सालस, सरल, सरलबुद्धि, खडखडीत, खणखणीत, घळघळीत, घळवळीत, घळमळीत, शुद्धमति.

2—of speech, &c. प्रशस्तपणाचा, सरळभावाचा, सालसपणाचा, निष्कापट्याचा, &c. [पडूं न देणें.

To **Frank**, *v. a.* (a letter) पत्रावर सही करून डाकेचें हांसील

Frankincense, *n.* ऊद *m.* लोभानीऊद *m.* चंद्रसेनीऊद *m.* धूप *m.*

Ashes of f. उदी *f.*

Coal to kindle f. धुपांगरा *m.*

Oil of f. उदेल *n.*

Perfumed with the smoke of f. उदेला.

Soot or condensed smoke of f. फूल *n.*

Stick, &c. set with lights of f. झाड *n.*

Wick or stick covered with f. ऊदकाडी *f.* ऊदबत्ती *f.* धूपकाडी *f.* अगरबत्ती *f.*

To fumigate with f. उदवणें, धुपवणें.

Frankly, *adv.* v.A. निष्कपट, कपट सोडून, निष्कपटानें, मोकळया मनानें, मन मोकळें करून, प्रांजळ, निवळ, सालसपणानें, सरलभावानें, प्रशस्तमनानें, निष्प्रांजळपणानें. [*n.*

Frankness, *n.* v.A. मनाचा मोकळेपणा *m.* दिलपाकी *f.* निष्कापट्य अकापट्य *n.* प्राशस्त्य *n.* सालसपणा *m.* सरलभाव *m.* अकृत्रिम *n.*

Frantic, *a. raving, furious, &c.* v. **Mad.** तग्रवग्र, कावराबावरा, तारकाबारका, वेडापिसा, मारकावेडा.

Franticly, Frantically, *adv.* v. A. कावराबावरा-&c. होऊन, वेड्यासारखा *decl.*

Franticness, *n.* v. A. कावरे बावरेपणा *m.* &c.

Fraternal, Fraternity. See **Brotherly, Brotherhood.**

To **Fraternize**, *v. n.* भाऊपणानें-भाऊबंदीनें-&c. जमणें-मिळणें-असणें.

Fratricidal, *a.* v. N. भ्रातृहत्यासंबंधी, भ्रातृहत्याविषयक.

Fratricide, *n.*—the act. भ्रातृहत्या *f.* भ्रातृवध *m.* भ्रातृघात *m.*

2—the agent. भ्रातृहत्यारा, भ्रातृघाती, भ्रातृहंता.

Fraud, *n.* v. **Deceit.** ठकबाजी *f.* लबाडी *f.* कपट *n.* कापट्य *n.* छल *m.* छद्म *n.* मकर *n.* धौर्त्तिका *f.* धौर्त्य *n.* कैतव *n.* व्याज *m.*

Fraudful, Fraudulent, *a.* v. N. *and* **Deceitful.** कपटी, मकरी, सकपट, धूर्त्त, छट, शठ, कपटवृत्ति.

2—of things, &c. कपटाचा, ठकबाजीचा, मकराचा, &c.

F. dealing or doing. ठकधंदा *m.* ठकव्यापार *m.* ठकसौदा *m.* लगतग *f.*

F. arts. ठकविद्या *f.*

Fraudfulness, Fraudulence, *n.* v. A. ठकबाजी *f.* खोटेपणा *m.* कापट्य *n.* धूर्त्तता *f.* शठत्व *n.* शाठ्य *n.*

Fraudfully, Fraudulently, *adv.* v. A. कपटानें, कपटपूर्वक, कपट करून, ठकबाजीनें, &c.

That trades or deals f. घालू *or* घाल्या, घालपाडू.

Fraught. See **Freight.**

Fraught, *a.* v. **Filled.** भरलेला, पूर्ण, परिपूर्ण.

Fray. See **Fight, Brawl.**

To **Fray.** See To **Frighten.** 2 See To **Rub.** [वेड *n.*

Freak, *n. whim, fancy.* लहर *f.* तरंग *m.* मौज *f.* छंद *m.* डुक्की *f.*

2 *frolic, trick*, v. **Prank.** चाळा *m.*

Freaks, *frolics, pranks.* ख्याल *m. pl.* चार *m.pl.* चोज *m. pl.* चाळा *m.* [*f.* करणें.

To indulge or play freaks. लहरा *f.pl.* मारणें, तऱ्हातऱ्हा

Freakish, Freakful, *a. fanciful, &c.* लहरी, लहरीदार, तबियती, छंदखोर, छंदी, छंदिष्ट, छांदिष्ट, मनमौज्या, छांदसवृत्ति, ख्याली, मनस्वी.

Freakishness, Freakfulness, *n.* v. A. छंदखोरी *f.* छंदिष्टपणा *m.* मनोलौल्य *n.*

Freckle, *n. spot on the skin.* ठिकें *n.* ठीक *n.* चिथडा *m. dim.* चिथडी *f.* तिल *pop.* तीळ *m.* मस *f.* तिलक *m.*

Freckled, Freckly, *a.* v.N. ठिक्याचा, गव्हळा, तिलकी, ठिकें-&c. आलेला, सतिल, तिलयुक्त.

Free, *a. enjoying liberty.* मोकळा, स्वतंत्र, स्वतंत्रेच्छ, स्वेच्छ, स्वेच्छाचारी, स्वाधीन, स्ववश, अनन्याधीन, अन्यानधीन, स्वायत्त, आत्माश्रय, आत्माश्रयाचा, स्वैर, स्वैरवृत्त, कामचार.

To set f. v. To FREE. मोकळा-बंदखलास-&c. करणें.

2 *unrestrained, unconstrained.* मोकळा, सुटा, मुखत्यार, निर्विघ्न, निर्बंध, अबंध, ऐच्छिक, स्वसंतोषाचा, आपखुशीचा, खुलाशाचा, फकड.

3 *open, not forbidden, &c.* मोकळा, उघडा, निर्बंध, अप्रतिबंध, प्रतिबंधरहित-शून्य, मुक्तद्वार.

F. and open. *exposed freely to the public.* मोकळा ढोंकळा, मोकळा चाळका.

4 *ingenuous, candid,* v. FRANK. मनाचा मोकळा, मोकळ्यामनाचा, निष्कपट. [घळमळीत.

5 *intimate,* v. FAMILIAR. सळबळीत, घळघळीत, घळबळीत,

6 *clear from, exempt.* मोकळा, मुक्त, सुटा, वेगळा *or* निराळा (as दोषानिराळा, &c.), रहित-हीन-&c. in comp. [शाचा.

7 *costing nothing,* v. GRATUITOUS. फुकटा, फुकटशाई, बिनपै-

8—of style, *not cramped or stiff.* मोकळा, विसकळ, साफ, प्रशस्त, सरल, सुरळीत, ऋजु.

9 *unengaged, unemployed, &c.* सुटा, रिकामा, मोकळा.

10 *liberal.* See GENEROUS.

To FREE, *v. a. set free, liberate.* मोकळणें *or* मोकलणें, सोडणें, सोडून देणें, मोचणें, मोकळा-मुक्त-बंधमुक्त-बंदखलास-&c. करणें, मोकळीक *f.*-सुटका *f.*-सोडवणूक *f.*-&c. करणें *g. of o.* बंधन *n.* तोडणें *g. of o.* मोचन *n.*-&c. करणें *g. of o.*

FREE-AGENCY, *n.* स्वतंत्रता *f.* स्वातंत्र्य *n.* स्वेच्छा *f.*

FREE-BOOTER, *n.* लुटारू, लुटारी, पुंड, पुंडपाळ.

FREE-SPOKEN, FREE-TONGUED, *a.* v. BLUNT. तोंडाचा पट्टा सुटलेला, निर्भीड बोलणारा, खणखणीत, अबद्धमुख, कामबाद, स्पष्टवक्ता, स्पष्टवादी, जिभेस हाड नाहीं असा.

FREED, *p.* v. V. सोडलेला, मोकळा केलेला, &c. मुक्त, मोचित, बंदखलास, बंधमुक्त, निर्मुक्त.

FREED-MAN, *n.* गुलामगिरींतून-दास्यांतून-&c. सुटलेला मनुष्य *m.*

FREEDNESS, *n.* v. P. मुक्ति *f.* मुक्तता *f.* विमुक्ति *f.* मोक्ष *m.*

FREEDOM, FREENESS, *n.* v. A. 1. मोकळेपणा *m.* स्वातंत्र्य *n.* स्वतंत्रता *f.* स्वाधीनता *f.* स्वेच्छाचार *m.* स्वेच्छाचारिता *f.*

2 मोकळेपणा *m.* मुखत्यारी *f.* मुक्ति *f.* बंधनाभाव *m.* बंधनराहित्य *n.*

FREEHOLD, *n.* वतन *n.* जमीनदारी *f.* स्वसत्तेचा-&c. क्षेत्र *n.*-वतन *n.* -&c. मिरास *f.*

FREEHOLDER, *n.* थळकरी, जमीनदार, मिरासदार.

FREEING, *n.* v. V.—*act.* सोडणें *n.* मोकळणें *n.* &c. सोडवण *f.* सोडवणूक *f.* मोचन *n.* मोक्षण *n.* मुक्ति *f.* विमोचन *n.*

FREELY, *adv. unobstructedly, &c.* v. FLOWINGLY. अलग, अलगन, सुरळीत, सरळ. [पखुशीनें.

2 *without constraint,* v. SPONTANEOUSLY. स्वसंतोषानें, आ-

3 *readily, securely, &c.* खुशाल, सुखरूप, सुखेनैव, सुदामत.

4 v. GRATUITOUSLY. फुकट, फुकटवारी.

5 *frankly.* मन मोकळें करून, मोकळ्या मनानें.

6 *copiously.* See ABUNDANTLY.

FREEMAN, *n.* स्वतंत्र-स्ववश-&c. मनुष्य *m.*

FREER, *n.* v.V. सोडणारा, मोकळा-&c. करणारा, &c. मोचक (esp. in. comp. as भवमोचक, ऋणमोचक, पापमोचक, &c.), मोचन-&c. कर्ता.

FREE-SCHOOL, *n.* धर्मार्थ घातलेली साळ *f.*

FREETHINKER, *n.* v. INFIDEL. चार्वाक, शास्त्रद्वेषी.

FREEWILL, *n. power of directing one's own actions.* मुखत्यारी *f.* अखत्यारी *f.* स्वेच्छाकर्तृत्व *n.*

Doctrine of f. पौरुषवाद *m.* प्रयत्नवाद *m.*—Maintainer of it. पौरुषवादी, प्रयत्नवादी.

2 *spontaneity.* स्वसंतोष *m.* आपखुशी *f.*

To FREEZE, *v. n. be congealed with cold.* थंडीनें गोठणें-जमणें-थिजणें, गारटणें *or* गारठणें.

To FREEZE, *v. a. congeal with cold.* गारटवणें *or* गारठवणें, थिजवणें, गोठवणें.

To FREIGHT, *v. a. load, lade.* लादणें, भरती *f.*-भरताड *f.*-भरगत *f.*-&c. करणें *g. of o.*

FREIGHT, *n. cargo, lading.* भरगत *f.* भरीत *n.* भरत *f.* भरताड *f.* भरवण *n. f.* भरतक *n.* बारदान *n.*

2 *cost of freight.* नोर *m.* भाडें *n.*

FREIGHTED, *p.* v. V. लादलेला.

FRENCH, *a.* फ्रांस देशचा किंवा त्यांतील लोकांचा.

FRENCH, *n.* फ्रांस देशची भाषा *f.*

FRENCHMAN, *n.* फ्रांस देशचा मनुष्य *m.* फरासीस *m.*

FRENZY, *n.* v. MADNESS. उन्माद *m.* उन्मादवायु *m.* कावरेबावरेपणा *m.*

FREQUENCY, *n.* v. A. वारंवार झालेलेपणा *m.* पौनःपुन्य *n.* आभीक्ष्ण्य *n.* असकृत्त्व *n.* पुनःपुनर्जातत्व *n.*

F. of coming and going. राब *m.* राबता *m.*

FREQUENT, *a. often done, &c.* वारंवार घडणार-होणार-&c. *or* घडलेला-झालेला, वारंवारचा, पौनःपुनिक, अभीक्ष्ण.

To FREQUENT, *v. a. resort to.* वारंवार-&c. जाणें-येणें, खेटे *m. pl.*-खेपा *f. pl.*-पैरव *m.*-पैरवी *f.* घालणें, येवाजावा *m.*-जावायेवा *m.*-&c. करणें, जाण्याचा-येण्याचा-&c. राबता *m.*-राब *m.*-रफ्त *m.* असणें *g. of s. with in. con.* व्याप *m.* असणें *in. con.*

FREQUENTED, *p.* v. V. राबलेला, रांबलेला, बहिवाटीचा, राबत्याचा, राबाचा.

FREQUENTER, *n.* v. V. वारंवार जाणारा-येणारा, खेपा-&c. घालणारा, &c. खेप्या, खेपा *or* खेटे घाल्या, खेट्या, येरजाऱ्या.

FREQUENTING, *n.* v. V. जावायेवा *m.* येवाजावा *m.* येणें जाणें *n.* पैरव *m. or* पैरवी *f.* गमनागमन *n.* व्याप *m.* संगति *f.*

FREQUENTLY, *adv.* v. OFTEN. वारंवार, अनेकवार, फारवेळ, फारदां, प्रायः, प्रायशः, इजाबिजातिजा, असकृत्.

FRESCO, *n.* भिंतीवरचीं चित्रें *n. pl.*

FRESH, *a. not stale.* गोड, ताजा, ताथा, तत्ता, ताथोट, साजूक, अनसूट, लोणकडा *or* कढा, अनुच्छिष्ट. [क्षार.

2 *not salt.* गोड, गोडा, अलवण, अलवणी, अळणी, निखार, अ-

3 *clear, lively, healthy-looking;*—of countenance, plants, &c. टवटवीत, टकटकीत, टुकटुकीत, टकमकीत, तुकतुकीत, लुसलुसीत, रसरसीत, तजेलदार.

To look f. टवटवणें.

4 *brisk, not tired, &c.* ताजा, हुशार, जिबट, असुदा.

F. and brisk. ताजातवाना, ताजातवान.

5 *new, unpractised.* नवा, नवखा, नवशिका, असुदा, कोरा, बिनवहिवाटीचा, रांपलेला नाहीं, घसवटलेला नाहीं.

6 *recent.* See NEW, LATE.

7 of wind. जोराचा, वेगाचा.

FRESH, *n.* (to a river). पूर *m.* रेल *f.* पुरवणी *f.* हौर *m.*

Sticks and rubbish brought down by a f. पुराड *or* पुराट *n.* गजरी *f.* बसण *n.*

To FRESHEN, *v. a. make fresh.* गोडावणें, गोडा-&c. करणें, सारटपणा *m.* काढणें. [चढणें.

To FRESHEN, *v. n. grow fresh or vigorous.* बळावणें, जोरावणें,

FRESHMAN, *n.* विद्यालयांत नवाआलेला विद्यार्थी *m.*

FRESHNESS, *n.* v. A. 1. गोडी *f.* ताजगी *f.* ताजेपणा *m.* साजूकपणा *m.* ताथेपणा *m.* &c.

2 गोडी *f.* गोडेपणा *m.*

3 टवटवी *f.* टकटकी *f.* टुकटुकी *f.* तुकतुकी *f.* लुसलुसी *f.* कला *f.* नवली *f.* नूर *m.* कांत *f.* तेजगी *f.* तजला *or* तजेला *m.* तजेली *f.* पाणी *n.* तरतरी *f.*

4 ताजेपणा *m.* हुशारी *f.* तेजगी *f.* अश्रम *m.*

5 नवेपणा *m.* असुंदपणा *m.* कोरेपणा *m.* [थंडी *f.*

I. *pleasing coolness,*—of the air. गुलाबी थंडी *f.* कोवळी

To FRET, *v. a. rub away,* v. To ABRADE, To RUB. चोळवटणें, चोळटणें, चोळणें.

2 *irritate, vex,* v. To ANGER. खाजवणें, खिजवणें *or* खिजावणें, चिथावणें, चिडवणें.

3 *agitate, make to ripple.* क्षोभविणें, क्षुब्ध-&c. करणें.

To FRET, *v.n. rub away,* v. To RUB. घाराबटणें, घासटणें, घासणें.

2 *be in vexation, chafe, boil,* v. To FUME. चोळणें, चिवचिवणें, तळतळणें, कुढणें *or* मनांत कुढणें, धुसधुसणें, धुसमुसणें, चुरमुरणें, चुळमुळणें, उबगणें.

3 after; *grieve after.* चटपटणें, हुरहुरणें, खंत *f.* घेणें *g. of. o.* टोकळा *or* टुकळा *m.* धरणें-करणें *g. of o.* ढासरा *or* ढोसरा *m.* धरणें *g. of o.* चुरमुरणें, रुणा *m.* घेणें *g. of o.* or *inversely* लागणें *g. of s.* आपल्या जिवाला खाणें, खुरखुर *f.*-हुरहूर *f.*-&c. करणें *g. of o.* or *inversely* लागणें, मंगळ *n.* गातबसणें, चुरमुरे-*m. pl.* खाणें-खात बसणें-देत बसणें.

4—the skin, through a blister. तडतडणें.

FRETFUL, *a.* v. PEEVISH. चिरखोड, चिडचिड्या, पिरपिरा, पिरपिऱ्या, किरकिरा, चटपटी *or* ट्या, खंती. [पणा *m.*

FRETFULNESS, *n.* v. A. चिरखोडी *f.* किरकिरेपणा *m.* &c. चिडणे-

FRETTING, *n.* See FRICTION. v. V. N. 2. तळतळ *f.* तळमळ *f.* तडफड *f.* चिवचीव *f.* धुसधूस *f.* धुसमूस *f.* चुरमूर *f.*

3 चटपट *or* चुटपूट *f.* खुरखूर *f.* रुखरूख *f.* खुतखुत *f.* खुतपूत *f.* खुदखुद *f.* खुणखुण *f.* हुरहूर *f.* चुरमूर *f.* बळबळ *f.*—intens. खुरखुराट *m.* चुरमुराट *m.* रुखरुखाट *m.* [चूर्णयोग्यता *f.*

FRIABILITY, *n.* v. A. पिठेपणा *m.* पिठुळपणा *m.* &c. चूर्णधर्म *m.*

FRIABLE, *a. soft, crumbling.* पिठा *or* पिठ्या, पिठूळ, खुसखुसीत, खुटखुटीत, फुसका, फुसकुला, फुसफुशीत, भुसभुशीत, विरणा, विरका, आशुचूर्णनीय, चूर्णधर्मी, चूर्णधर्मक.

FRICTION, *n. rubbing.* चोळणें *n.* चोळणी *f.* घासणें *n.* घासणी *f.* चाळे *f.* संघर्षण *n.* संघर्ष *m.* संघट्टन *n.* संहर्ष *m.*

FRIDAY, *n.* शुक्रवार *m.* भृगुवार *m.*

FRIED, *p.* v. V. तळलेला, तळींव, तळका, तळकट.

FRIEND, *n.* मित्र, स्नेही, इष्ट, सखा, दोस्त, दोस्तदार, निसखा, यार, सुहृत् *or* सुहृद्, अर्धांग, सुखादुःखाचा सोबती, एकदुःखसुखी *or* एकदुःखसुख, सख in comp.

Acquired f. कृत्रिममित्र.

Contest of friends. मित्रयुद्ध *n.* मित्रकलह *m.*

False f. दुर्मित्र, कपटमित्र, असन्मित्र, किंसखा.

Female f. सखी *f.* मैत्रीण *or* मित्रीण *f.* सजणी *f.* सहेली *f.* दोस्तदारीण *f.* आली *f.*

F. in need. वेळाईत.

Friends, relatives, and connexions—compreh. or gener. सखे सोयरे *or* सगे सोयरे *m. pl.* सुहृत्संबंधी *m. pl.* इष्ट आप्त *m. pl.*

Friends and acquaintances. इष्टमित्र *m. pl.*

Interested f. मतलबीयार, साकांक्षित स्नेही.

Of one's friends and acquaintances. ओळखी पाळखीचा, ओळखी पाळखी, ओळखी देखीचा, ओळखी देखी.

A f. in need is a f. indeed. निर्वाणींचा दाता तोच दाता.

Real friends are not easily set by the ears. काठीनें पाणी हाटलें तर दोन ठिकाणीं होत नाहीं (or पाण्यांत काठी मारली तर का पाणी दोन जागां होईल ?).

With provisions in store we've friends by the score. जों जवळ आयरा तों जग सोयरा, असतील शितें तर मिळतील भुतें.

2—the compellation. गडी, मित्र.

3 See PATRON.

FRIENDLESS, *a. destitute, forlorn.* उघडा, उघडाबोडका, अनाश्रय, अनाश्रित, निराश्रय, निराश्रित, अनाथ, बिचारा, पंगु *pop.* पंगू, नागवा, नंगा, निजोर, निराधार, निरवलंब, निरालंब, अगतिक, गतिहीन, असहाय, अनावृत, निखोरडा, निधूत.

Friend of the f. अनाथनाथ, अगतिकगति.

FRIENDLINESS, *n.* v. A. दोस्तदारी *f.* दोस्ताई *f.* गोडी गुलाबी *f.* मित्रत्व *n.* मित्रता *f.* सोलत *or* सोहलत *f.* रहस्य *n.* रहश्श *n.* स्नेह *m.* स्नेहभाव *m.*

F. of terms or footing. गोडी गुलाबी *f.* रहसाळी *f.*

FRIENDLY, *a.* स्नेहाचा, स्नेहभावाचा, स्नेही, मैत्रीचा, मैत्र, मैत्रेय, मित्र, स्नेहाळू, सख (in comp. as एतत्सख, तत्सख, इंद्रसख), इखलासी, अनुकूल.

FRIENDLY, *adv.* मित्रबुद्ध्या, मित्रदृष्ट्या, मित्रभावानें.

FRIENDSHIP, *n.* मैत्रकी *or* मैत्रिका *f.* मैत्री *f.* मित्रभाव *m.* स्नेह *m.* स्नेहभाव *m.* दोस्ती *f.* दोस्तदारी *f.* दोस्ताई *f.* इखलास *f.* इष्टत्व *n.* सख्य *n.* सखित्व *n.* साख्य *n.* साचिव्य *n.* सौहार्द *n.* सौहृद *n.* घटित *n.*

Breach of f. मित्रभेद *m.*

Close f. जाळी *f.* जंगडी *f.* सांगड *f.* गट्टी *f.* यारी *f.* अद्वैत *n.* अद्वैतभाव *m.* दाटी *f.* घणदाटी *f.* जीवश्चकंटश्च *n.* गळश्चकंठश्च *n.* स्नेहबाद *m.*

Formation of f. मित्रलाभ *m.* मित्रलब्धि *f.*

Interested f. साकांक्षित स्नेह *m.*

To form a close f. मतकूट *n.* मिळणें *g. of s.*

FRIER, *n.* v. V. तळणारा, तळपी.

FRIEZE, *n.* लोंकरी कापडाची एक जात आहे.

FRIGATE, *n.* लढाऊ गलबताचा एक प्रकार आहे.

FRIGHT, *n. sudden fear, terror.* वचक *or* वचका *m.* बाज *or* बाच *m.* धास्त *or* धास्ती *f.* अपधाक *m.* ढासरा *m.* हैबत *f.* भेदरा *m.* आंच *f.* धडकी *f.* धबका *m.* दचका *m.* दचक *f.* त्रास *m.* वित्रास *m.*—in high degree; as expressed by *alarm, amazement, horror, consternation, dismay, &c.* गात्रभंग *m.* अंडत्रास *m.* त्रेधा *f.* तिरपीट *f.* तिऱ्हड *f.* भयभर *m.* घोरभय *n.* धैर्यभंग *m.* विक्षेप *m.* वैचित्य *n.*

To take or conceive f. वचक *or* वचका *m.*-बाच *or* बाज *m.* खाणें and *in. con.* जाणें-बसणें, धास्त *or* धास्ती *f.*-हैबत *f.* घेणें,

खाणें, डासरा *m.* धरणें, त्रास *m.* पावणें, आंच *f.* बसणें *in. con.* दचक *f.*-दचका *m.*-धडकी *f.*- धबका *m.* बसणें-भरणें *in. con.* इचकणें *or* दचकणें, बचकणें, बाचटणें, बाचकणें, अपधाकणें, धास्तावणें, भेदरणें, भिणें, गोळा *m.* येणें *in. con.* घाबरणें, गांगरणें *or* (गेंगारणें, गेंगरणें, गोंगरणें,), गांगावणें, छळणें.—in high degree; as expressed by such phrases as *to be frightened out of one's wits—out of one's seven senses, to be terror-struck, to be struck aghast, &c.* आंड *m.* ब्रह्मांडास *or* कपाळीं जाणें *g. of s.* भुलीचें झाड *n.* भेटणें *in. con.* देव्हाऱ्यांत देव नाहींसा होणें, गर्भगळीत होणें, धाबें *n.* दणाणणें *g. of s.* गांड *f.* फाटणें *g. of s.* मलमूत्र *n.* होणें *in. con.* मृतप्राय होणें, गतप्राण होणें, लेंडी *f.* गाळणें, हगूट *m.* लागणें *in. con.* त्यागणें, हांवभरी होणें, पांचावरधारण *f.* बसणें *g. of s.* हगमूत *f.* लागणें-सुटणें *in. con.* तजावजा *adv.* होणें, छाती *f.*-ऊर *m.* फाटणें *g. of s.* जीव *or* प्राण *m.* कालवणें *g. of s.* चकरी *f.* गुंग होणें *g. of s.* चकरी *f.* भुलणें, चकरमकर *f.* भुलणें *g. of s.* हातापायाचे ढीग *m. pl.* होणें *g. of s.* बावरणें, धादरणें, हगुटणें, काव्हणें *or* कहावणें.

2 *a f. a frightful woman, &c.* भूतखान *n.* जखीण *f.*

To FRIGHT, *To* FRIGHTEN, *v. a.* v. N. भिवविणें, भिवणें, भेडावणें, भेडसावणें, भेदरावणें, दचकवणें, वचकवणें, &c. भय *n.*-भेदरा *m.*-&c. घालणें, धडकी *f.*-&c. भरविणें-बसवणें, भयप्रदर्शन *n.* करणें, भयभीत-भयान्वित-&c. करणें, बुजविणें *or* बुजाविणें,—in high degree, *terrify, frighten out of one's wits, &c.* पांचावर धारण *f.* बसवणें *g. of o.* त्रेधा *f.*-तिरपीट *f.* करणें *g. of o.* देव्हाऱ्यांत देव नाहींतसे करणें *g. of o.* धाबें *n.* दणाणविणें, घराचीं कौलें *n. pl.* हालविणें-पळविणें *g. of o.* खालचें पाणी *n.* वर करणें *g. of o.* माटमूट करायास लावणें, मृतप्राय-भयाकुल-भयाक्रांत-&c. करणें.

To f. into. मानेवर सुरी ठेवून करविणें.

FRIGHTENED, *p.v.* V. भेडावलेला, &c. भ्याला, घावरा, भयभीत, भययुक्त, भयान्वित, सभय, जातभय, प्राप्तभय, भीत, त्रासित, वित्रासित, त्रस्त, वित्रस्त, त्रासयुक्त-&c. शंकित, आशंकित, शंकान्वित, सशंक, साशंक.—in high degree; *filled with—swallowed up by—overcome by—&c. fear.* भयाक्रांत, भयग्रस्त, भयातुर, भयाकुल, भयार्त्त, भयपीडित, भयविह्वल, भयविप्लुत, भचचकित, भयाविष्ट, भयाधीन, शंकामय, हौलदिल, हगीरमुतीर, बावरा, कावराबावरा, नष्टेंद्रिय.

FRIGHTFUL, *a.* v. FEARFUL. भयंकर, भयानक, भयजनक, अकटोविकट, अकराळ, अकराळ विकराळ, घोर, दारुण, कराल *pop.* कराळ.

FRIGHTFULNESS, *n.* v. A. भयंकरपणा *m.* अकराळ विकराळपणा *m.* भयजनकत्व *n.* घोरता *f.* भीष्मता *f.* रौद्रता *f.*

FRIGID, FRIGIDITY. See COLD, &c.

FRIGORIFIC, *a. causing cold.* हिमकर, हिमजनक, हिमोत्पादक, शीतजनक, शीतोत्पादक, शीतावह.

FRINGE, *n.* झालर *f.* लकेरी *f.* झल्लर *f.*

To FRINGE, *v. a.* झालर *f.*-&c. लावणें.

FRINGED, *p. and a.* v. V. झालरदार, झालर लावलेला.

FRIPPERY, *n. old clothes, &c.* जुनेरीं *n. pl.* जुनींपानीं *n. pl.* जुनींपुराणीं पांघरुणें *n. pl.* जुनवन *f.* [र *m.*

2 जुनीं पांघुरणें *n. pl.*-&c. विकण्याची जागा *f.* जुनेऱ्यांचा बाजा-

To FRISK, *v. n.*—a deer, horse, &c. ठिकणें, नाचणें.

2—dogs, kittens, kids, &c. बागडणें, नाचणें.

3—gener. *dance about, jump and leap, skip and caper.* खिदडणें *or* खिदाडणें, खिदळणें *or* खिदाळणें, घुरदळणें, घुरदळा *m.*-खिदडा *m.* घालणें, टिणटिण *adv.* उड्या *f. pl.* मारणें, नाच *m.* मांडणें, नाचणें, डुंदडणें, बाकुदणें, बोकलणें, बागडणें, उल्हाळणें *or* उल्हाळणें.

To f. wildly, boisterously, &c. धिंगडणें, धिंगाणा *m.*-धिबडी *f.*-तातकथय्या *m.*-ताथय्या *m.*-&c. मांडणें-घालणें-करणें.

FRISK, FRISKING, *n.* v. V. 1. ठिकणें *n.* नाचणें *n.*

2 बागडणें *n.* नाचणें *n.*

3 खिदडणें *n.* &c. उड्या मारणें *n.* खिदडा *m.* घुरदळा *m.* घुरदळें *n.* घुरदळी *f.* घुरदळ *f.* भोरीप *n.*

Wild, boisterous, &c. f. धिंगाणा *m.* धिबडी *f.* तातकथय्या *m.* ताथय्या *m.* थैथय्या *m.*

FRISKER, *n.* FRISKING, *p. a.* FRISKY, *a.* v. V. 1. नाचणारा, ठिकणारा, नाचरा, ठिकरा.

2 बागडणारा, नाचणारा.

3 *and* FROLICSOME. खिदळणारा, नाचणारा, उड्या मारणारा, उड्या, नाचरा, मौजा मारणारा, रग्या, रगदार, रगेल, खिलाडी *or* डू, खुशमौजा, मोज्या, मौजाळा.

FRISKINESS, *n.* v. A. 3. नाचरेपणा *m.* उडेपणा *m.* मस्ती *f.* खिलाडीपणा *m.* मोज्येपणा *m.*

FRITH, *n. strait of the sea.* खाडी *f.*

FRITTER, *n.* मासाचा तळलेला तुकडा *m.*

2 *fragment, &c.* v. BIT. तुकडा *m.* कुटका *m.*

To FRITTER, *v. a.* तुकडे *m. pl.* करणें.

FRIVOLITY, FRIVOLOUSNESS, *n.* v. A. 1. हलकेपणा *m.* छिछोरी *or* चिचोरी *f.* छिछोरबुद्धि *f.*

2 हलकेपणा *m.* पोकळपणा *m.*

FRIVOLOUS, *a.*—of persons, v. LIGHT. हलका, छिछोर *or* चिचोर, छिछोरबुद्धीचा. [क्षुल्लक, क्षुद्र.

2—of subjects, v. LIGHT. हलका, हलकट, फुसका, पोकळ,

FRIZZLE, &c. See CURL, &c.

FRO, *adv. to and fro.* इकडे तिकडे, एथून तेथवर तेथून एथवर.

To walk to and fro. पांजण्या *f. pl.* घालणें.

FROCK, *n.* (of children) आंगडी *f. or* डें *n.* आंगी *f.* झगलें *n.* झबलें *n.*

2 (of men) आंगरखा *m.*

3 See GOWN.

FROCK-COAT. See COAT.

FROG, *n.* बेडूक *m. dim.* बेडकी *f.* बेडकुळी *or* बेटकुळी *f.* भेंक *m.* मंडूक *n.* दर्दुर *m.*

Female f. बेडकी *f.*

F. in a well. आडांतला बेडूक *m.* कूपांतला मंडूक *m.*

2 (of a horse's hoof). बेडकी *f.* पुतळी *f.*

FROLIC, *n. sport, &c.* v. FUN. खेळ *m.* खुशाली *f.* ख्यालीखुशाली *f.* मौज *f.* कौतुक *n.*

Frolics, v. PRANKS. ख्याल *m. pl.* चार *m. pl.* चोज *m. pl.*

To FROLIC, *v. n. sport, gambol, play pranks.* उड्या *f. pl.*-लहरा *f. pl.*-मौजा *f. pl.* मारणें, कौतुक *n.* करणें.

FROLICSOME, *a.* v. N. मौजाळा, मौज्या, खुशमौज्या, कौतुकी, कौतुक्या, ख्यालीखुशालीचा, ख्याली, खिलाडी *or* डू, रग्या, रगेल, रगदार, उड्या, उडीमाऱ्या, लहरी, रंगेल, रंगेला, रंगेली, चाळक.

FROLICSOMENESS, *n.* v. A. खिलाडीपणा *m.* खेळकरपणा *m.* ख्यालीखुशाली *f.*

FROM, *prep.* पासून, जवळून, कडून, हून in comp. ऊन in comp.

F. and unto. अहदतहद.

Front, *n. face, fore part.* तोंडn. मुखn. मोहराm. मोहर *f.* पुढाm. पुढोसा *or* पुढवसाm. अघाडी *f.* समोरचा-पुढचा भागm.-आंगn. दिसतें आंगn. अग्रn. अग्रभागn. पुरोभागm.

Brazen f. तिखैंn.

Exactly in f. of. पुढच्यापुढें.

F. and rear. आगापिछाm. अघाडीपिछाडी *f.*

F. to f. समोरासमोर.

From in f. of. मोहरून, समोरून.

From the f. पुढून.

In f. पुढें, समोर.

In f. of. समोर, मोहरें.

In f. and in rear. अघाडी पिछाडी.

To set out in f. मोहर *f.* धरणें.

Unblushing f. उघडा माथाm.

To **Front**, *v. a. be opposite to.* समोर-सम्मुख-&c. असणें-उभा-राहणें *g. of o.* समक्षता *f.* करणें *g. of o.*

Frontal, *a. belonging to the forehead.* कपाळाचा, ललाटसंबंधी.

Frontier, *n. confines.* पालवm. लत्ताm. लगताm. सारद *or* सरहद्द *f.* प्रांतभागm.

F. district. कड *or* कडेमहालm. कडप्रांतm.

Frontier, *a.* लत्यावरचा, लत्याचा, लगत्याचा, &c.

Fronting, *p. a.* v. V. समोरचा *or* ला, मोहरचा *or* ला, मोहरील, समोरील, सन्मुख *or* सम्मुख, अभिमुख, पुरोवर्त्ती.

Frontispiece, *n.* पुस्तकाच्या प्रारंभींचें चित्रn. ग्रंथाग्रवर्तिचित्र n. 2 See **Front**.

Frontlet, *n.* कपाळपट्टी *f.*

Frost, *n.* पाणी थिजविणारी थंडी *f.* हिमn. नीहारm. इंद्राग्निधूमm. 2 See **Hoar-frost**.

Frost-bitten, *a.* हिंवानें करपलेला-जाळलेला, हिमग्रस्त, हिमदग्ध.

Frosty, *a.* हिमाचा, हिमवान् *pop.* हिमवंत, हिम्य, हैम, हैमन, तुषार.

Froth, *n.* फेसm. फेन *pop.* फेणm. कफm.

2 *vain or empty display.* बुटटकी *f.* फुशारकी *f.* फुशारी *f.*

To **Froth**, *v. n.* फेणणें, फेसणें, फेसळणें, फेसटणें, फेस *m.*-फेण *m.* येणें *in. con.*

To **Froth**, *v. a.* फेसणें, फेणवणें, फेसवणें, फेसm.-&c. आणणें.

Frothiness, *n.* v. A. 1. फेंसटपणा *m.* फेंसाळपणाm. &c.

Frothy, *a full of froth, made of froth, &c.* फेंसट, फेंसाळ, फेसाचा, फेनल *or* फेनिल, सफेन, फेनयुक्त-विशिष्ट.

2 *empty, trifling,* v. **Light**. पोकळ, फोल, फुसकुला, छिछोर *or* चिचोर.

3 *consisting of empty display.* फुशारकीचा, फुशारीचा, बुटटकीचा.

Frouziness, *n.* v. A. उबटपणा *m.* उबटाण *f.* उभसाण *f.*

Frouzy, *a. musty, &c.* उबट, कुबट, सापट, उबटलेला, सांपलेला.

To get f. उबटणें, कुबटणें.

Froward, *a.* v. **Perverse**. अडफांट्या, अकरनकर, करनकर, करनकऱ्या, जिद्दखोर.

Frowardness, *n.* v. A. अकरनकर *f.* जिद्द *f.* जिद्दखोरी *f.*

To **Frown**, *v. n.* भवया *f. pl.* चढवणें-वर नेणें, भवयांस-कपाळास गांठी *f. pl.*-अठी *f.*-अठ्या *f. pl.* घालणें-आणणें, झिमोटा *m.* मारणें-घालणें, कपाळास तिडीक *f.* येणें-उठणें *in. con.*

Frown, Frowning, *n.* v. V. अठी *f.* भ्रुकुटीभंग *m.* भ्रूभंग *m.* भ्रुकुटी *f.* झिमोटा *m.* भ्रूक्षेप *m.* भ्रूविक्षेप *m.*

I. *look of displeasure.* कटाक्ष *m.* क्रोधमुद्रा *f.*

Frozen, *p.* v. V. थंडीनें थिजलेला-गोठलेला-&c. गारठलेला, हिमस्तब्ध, हिमस्तंभित, हिमग्रस्त.

Fruable, *a. to be enjoyed.* भोग्य, उपभोग्य, भोक्तव्य.

Fructiferous, *a. that bears fruit.* फळाचा, फलवान्, फली, फलद.

Fructification, *n.* v. V. A. सफल करणें *n.* सफली करण *n.*

I. वनस्पतीचे फलोत्पादक भाग *m. pl.*

To **Fructify**, *v. a. make fruitful, or productive.* फलवान्-सफल-सुपीक-सुपिकी-&c. करणें, सफलत्व *n.*-उर्वरात्व *n.*-&c. आणणें, उर्वरात्वप्रापण *n.*-साफल्यप्रापण *n.*-&c. करणें. [&c. होणें.

To **Fructify**, *v. n. become fruitful.* सुपीक-सफल-फलवान्-फली-

Fructivorous, *a.* फळभक्षी, फलभोजी, फलाशी.

Fructuous, &c. See **Fruitful**, &c.

Frugal, *a.* v. **Economical**. काटकसऱ्या, कतरबेती, अल्पव्ययी, परिमितव्ययी, कतरबेताचा, काटकसरीचा.

Frugality, *n.* v. A. घरजोगावणी *f.* घरजुगूत *f.* काटकसर *f.* कतरबेत *m.* कारस्थान *n.* अल्पव्यय *m.* परिमितव्यय *m.*

Frugally, *adv.* v. A. काटकसरीनें, कतरबेतानें.

Fruit, *n.* फल *pop.* फळ *n.* मेवा *m.*

Crop of f. coming in the season. मिठाबार *m.*

Crop of f. coming after the season. सट्टाबार *m.*

Fallen f. पाड *m.*

Falling of f. (from ripeness, in a storm, &c.). गळती *f.* पाड *m. v.* लाग.

Hook with netting to gather f. आंसी *f.* झेला *m.* घळ *m.*

Knocking down or gathering of f. पाडा *m.* फलपातन *n.*

Layers of straw, &c. for ripening f. अढी *f.* भट्टी *f.* To ripen in such layers,—f. उतरणें *or* अढींत उतरणें.

Straw, &c. used to ripen f. पिकवण *n.*

That bears good f. सुफल.

Topmost f. शेंडफळ *n.*

Unripe (hard, green, &c.) f. दोडा *m.* काकडा *m.* बोरा *m.*

To be plump and blooming,—f. उतळणें.

To yield f. lit. fig. फळणें.

2 fig. v. **Consequence**. फल *or* फळ *n.* फळश्रुति *f.* अर्थm. परिपाकm.

Fruit-tree, *n.* फळझाड *n.*

Fruitage, *n. fruit collectively.* फळफळावळ *or* फळावळ *f.* फळें *n. pl.*

Fruiterer, *n.* फळविक्या, फलविक्रयी.

Fruitery, *n.* See **Fruitage**. 2 *repository for fruit.* फळाची कोठी *f.* फलालय *n.* फलागार *n.*

Fruitful, *a. that bears fruit, productive.* फलवान्, सफल, सुफल, फलित, फलद, फलप्रद, बहुफल, अमोघ, फलद्रूप.

2 *prolific, not barren.* प्रसवशील, बहुप्रसव, गर्भधारणशील, अवंध्य. [द्रवn. &c.

Fruitfulness, *n.* v. A. 1. साफल्यn. सफलता *f.* बहुफलता *f.* फल-

2 प्रसवशीलता *f.* बहुप्रसवत्वn. बहुप्रजत्वn. अवंध्यत्वn.

Fruition, *n.* v. **Enjoyment**. उपभोगm. भोगm. भोगवटाm.

Fruitless, *a. vain, unproductive.* निष्फल, फलहीन-रहित-शून्य -&c. रिकामा, रिकामका, रिता, व्यर्थ, निरर्थक, पोकळ, कोरडा, निष्कारण, अफल, विफल.

Fruitlessly, *adv.* v. A. व्यर्थ, वृथा, फुकट, निरर्थक, शुष्काशुष्क, शुष्काशुष्की, उगा.

FRUITLESSNESS, *n.* v. A. पोकळपणा*m.* &c. निष्फलता *f.* नैष्फल्य*n.* फलराहित्य*n.* &c वैफल्य*n.* विफलता *f.*

FRUMENTY, *n.* गव्हांची खीर *f.* क्षिप्रा *f.*

FRUSH, *n.*—in a horse's foot. बेडकी *f.* पुतळी *f.*

FRUSTRATE. See VAIN, USELESS.

To FRUSTRATE, *v. a.* v. To DEFEAT. निष्फल-व्यर्थ-निरर्थक-&c. करणें, मोडणें, भंग*m.* करणें *g. of o.* हेलपटणें, लटपटवणें, विफलीकरण*n.* करणें *g. of o.*

2 (a deed, &c.) *annul.* रद्दकरणें, निरर्थक-&c. करणें.

FRUSTRATED, *p.* v.V. 1. निष्फळ केलेला, मोडलेला, हेलपटलेला, &c. विफलीकृत.

FRUSTRATION, *n.* v. V. 1.—*act.* मोडणें*n.* &c. भंग*m.* विघात*m.* विफली करण*n.*

FRY, *n. matter frying or fried.* तळण*n.* तळप*n.*

2 *crowd of small fish.* चिंगळ्यांचा थवा*m.*-जमाव*m.*-&c.

To FRY, *v. a. cook in a frying pan.* तळणें, तळण*n.*-तळप*n.* करणें *g. of o.*

To f. (corn, pulse, chillies, &c.) with oil, &c. सातळणें, सातळणी *f.* करणें.

The smell of an article frying. तळसाण *f.*

To FRY, *v. n. be cooked in a frying pan.* तळणें. [तळपणें.

2 *suffer under the action of heat.* तळणें, तळतळणें, पोळणें,

FRYING, *n.* v. V. A.—*act.* तळणें*n.* तळण*n.* तळप*n.*

FRYING-PAN, *n.* तळणी *f.* कढई *f.* तळण *f.* तळणाटोप*m.* तेलवा*m.*

To fall out of the f. into the fire. फुपाट्यांतून निघून आगींत पडणें, गळ्यांत गोणी *f.* येणें.

To FUDDLE, *v. a. make drunk.* झिंगवणें, उलू-मस्त-&c. करणें.

To FUDDLE, *v. n. drink to excess.* झिंगणें, उलू-&c. होणें.

FUDGE, See STUFF, NONSENSE. [फांटीं*n. pl.*

FUEL, *n.* सरपण*n.* जळण*n.* जळवण*n.* इंधन*n.* समिध *f.* लाकूडफाटें*n.*

Dry crackling f. भडस *f.* भुरकाड्या *f. pl.* भुरकाड*n.* भड *f.* भरकाड *or* भरकांड*n.*

Fit for f. जळाऊ, जाळाऊ, जाळींव.

Wood split into logs for f. फिटा*m.*

To add f. to the flame. आगींत*n.*-जळत्यांत पेंढी *f.* टाकणें.

FUGACIOUS, &c. See FUGITIVE, &c.

FUGH, *interj.* इश्यो, इश्श, इशो. [पळता.

FUGITIVE, *a. flying, running away.* पळणारा, पळपटा, पळका,

2 *wandering, vagrant.* हिंडफिऱ्या, परागंदा.

3 *not durable, not stationary.* अस्थायी, अचिर, चर, क्षणिक, भंगुर. [पळया.

FUGITIVE, *n. person who runs from his station, &c.* पळपट्या,

Fugitives. पळ*m.* पळपटे*m. pl.*

FULCRUM, *n.*—of a lever. तरफेची अट *f.* टेंकू *m.*

To FULFIL, *v. a.* (a wish, promise, intention, declaration, &c.). v. To ACCOMPLISH, पुरवणें, पुरा-पूर्ण-पार-खरा-सत्य-सिद्ध-&c. करणें, शेवटास-सिद्धीस नेणें.

2 (a prophecy, &c.). पुरा-पूर्ण-खरा-सत्य-&c. करणें-करून देणें, अनुभवास-निदर्शनास-&c. आणणें.

3 (a term, period, &c.) भरणें, पुरा-पुरता-पूर्ण-&c. करणें.

FULFILLED, *p.* v. V. 1. 2. पुरा केलेला-झालेला, पूर्ण, पुरता, परिपूर्ण, पूर्त, चरितार्थ, कृतार्थ, कृतकृतार्थ.

To be f. पुरणें.

3 पुरा केलेला-झालेला, भरलेला, पुरा, पूर्ण, परिपूर्ण.

To be f. भरणें.

FULFILLER, *n.* v. V. 1. पुरा-&c. करणारा, पूर्णकर्त्ता.

FULFILLING, FULFILMENT, *n.* v. V. 1.—*act.* पार करणें *n.* &c. परिपूरण *n.* उक्तनिर्वाह *m.*—*state.* सिद्धि *f.* सार्थक*n.* सार्थक्य *n.* चरितार्थ *m.* पूर्त्ति *f.* परिपूर्त्ति *f.*

FULGENT. See SHINING, BRIGHT.

FULL, *a. having no space void.* भरला, भरलेला, भरपूर, पूर्ण, पूर्त्त, भर (in comp. as भरपेला), अनवकाश, पूरित, भरित (in comp.).

2 *abounding in.* मय (in comp. as धान्यमय, जलमय, तेजोमय, अग्निमय, पर्वतमय,), प्रचुर (in comp. as पुष्पप्रचुर, वृक्षप्रचुर, &c.), गडगंज, घवघवीत, उदार.

3 *sated, satisfied.* अभर झालेला, धालेला, तृप्त, परितृप्त.

4—of relations; *not half, step, in law, &c.* सखा, सगा.

5—a color. गहिरा *or* गैहरा, पक्का.

6—a voice. भरपूर, भरदार, उद्दाम.

7 *well filled, plump, pulpous, swelling.* भरदार, गबगबीत *or* गुबगुबीत, ठसठसीत *or* ठुसठुसीत, घवघवीत, घसघसीत.

8 *not defective or partial,* v. COMPLETE. पुरा, पुरता, पूर्ण, परिपूर्ण, संपूर्ण, सांग, सांगसंपूर्ण, पक्का, भर in comp.

9 *not profile*—a picture. दुचष्मी, दुहसबी.

FULL, *n. highest state or degree,* v. HEIGHT. भर *f.* भरती *f.* भरतें *n.* पराकाष्ठा *f.* सीमा *f.* मर्यादा *f.* भर (in comp. as a prefix, as भर हिंवाळा, भरउन्हाळा, भरदौलत, भरजवानी).

To reach its f. पराकाष्ठा *f.*-सीमा *f.*-&c. होणें *g. of s.*

2 *complete measure.* पुरतेपणा *m.* पूर्णता *f.* पूर्त्ति *f.*

FULL, *adv. quite, to the same degree, without diminution.* तंत, तंतोतंत, बरोबरीचा, तसाच, टांकोटांक, समसमान.

2 *exactly,* बरोबर, तंत, थेट.

3 *to equality with, to the quantity or amount of.* भर (as गाडीभर a cart full, मूठभर a hand full, शेरभर a ser-full, &c.).

4 *completely.* पुरतेपणीं, पुरेपणीं, पुरता, पुरा, पूर्ण,—with the power of good, quite, regular, tight, bouncing, &c. implying *completeness, ampleness, liberal, flowing* measure, भर (in comp.) तब्बल, ताठ, ताठर, घळघळीत, घसघशीत, चरचरीत, चरब.

To FULL, *v. a.* (clothes) यंत्रानें घट करून स्वच्छ करणें.

FULL-BLOWN, *a.* पुरा फुललेला, पूर्णविकसित.

FULL-DRESS, *n.* भरपोषाक *m.*

In f. भरपोषाकानें, भरपोषाकानिशीं.

FULL-EYED, *a.* भोंकरडोळ्या, प्रफुल्लनयन, मृगनयन. [तोंडाचा.

FULL-FACED, *a.*—*opp. to* profile. दुहसबी, दुचष्मी, समोरच्या

FULL-GROWN, *a.* पुरेवाढीचा.

FULL-TONED, *a.* घोंस, डोर, झार.

FULLER, *n.* v. WASHERMAN. रजक, वस्त्रधावक.

FULLER'S EARTH, *n.* खारी माती *f.*

FULLY, *adv.* See FULL.

To FULMINATE. See To THUNDER, To DETONATE.

FULNESS, *n.* v. A. 1. भरलेपणा *m.* पुरतेपणा *m.* &c. पूर्णता, पूर्त्ति *f.* पूर्त्तता *f.* परिपूर्त्ति *f.*

2 *and* ABUNDANCE. भर*m.* प्राचुर्य*n.* प्रचुरता *f.*

3 भर*m.* धालेपणा*m.* ढेर *f.* तृप्ति *f.* पर्याप्ति *f.* पूर्त्ति *f.*

8 पुरेपणाm. &c. पूर्णताf. &c. भरतेंn. भरm. भरणn.

FULSOME, *a. nauseous, offensive*, v. DISGUSTING. ओखटा, ओंगळ, अमंगल, चिळसवाणा, कंटाळवाणा, बीभत्स.

FULSOMENESS, *n.* v. A. ओखटेपणाm. ओंगळपणाm. &c.

To FUMBLE, *v. n. do awkwardly.* अडाण्यावाणी-अनाड्यावाणी-हेंगाड्यावाणी-&c. करणें, कांचकळणें, चांचपडणें, चांचपणें, लडबडणें.

FUMBLER. See BUNGLER.

FUME. See SMOKE, STEAM.

To FUME, *v. n. smoke, steam.* धुमणें, धुमसणें, धुपणें.

2 *chafe, fret, boil, &c.* v. To RAGE. कडकडणें, जळफळणें, फुणफुणणें, खुणखुणणें, धुगसणें, धुसमुसणें, धुसधुसणें, मुसमुसणें, कुरबुरणें, कुरमुरणें, चुरमुरणें, कुरमणें, काव्हणें, जळणें, जळपणें, चवतळणें *or* ताळणें, चाचावणें, चिवचिवणें, तवतवणें, तातवणें, तळतळणें, चडफडणें, नाकफुड्या *f. pl.* पिंजारणें-फुगवणें- फुरफुरवणें, फूं *adv.* होणें, चुरमुरे *or* कुरमुरे*m. pl.* खाणें-खात बसणें-दांत बसणें, जळफळ*f.*-चडफड*f.*-&c. करणें.

To FUMIGATE, *v. a.* धूर*m.*-धुरी*f.*-धुकटी*f.*-बाफारा*m.*-&c. देणें.

FUMIGATION, *n.* v. V.—*act.* धूर देणें *n.* &c. बाफारा*m.* धूर *m.* धुरी *f.* धुकटी *f.*

FUMING, *n.* v. V. 1. धुमसणें*n.* &c.

2 जळफळणें*n.*&c. जळफळ *f.* धुसमूस *f.* धुसधूस *f.* चडफड *f.*तडफड *f.* जळफळ *f.* कुरबूर *f.* कुरमूर *f.* खुणखुण*f.* अंतर्दाह *m.*

FUN, *n. sport, frolic, &c.* खुशाली *f.* ख्याली खुशाली *f.* खेळीमेळी *f.* खेळी *f.* मौज *f.* खेळ *m.* तमाशा *m.* रंग *m.* मजा *f.* कौतुक*n.* क्रीडा *f.* लीला *f.* कुतूहल *n.* विनोद *m.* रमूज *f.*

2—*as opposed to* earnest; *joke, sport.* मस्करी *f.* खेळ *m.* ठट्टा *f.* विनोद *m.* खेळ कुडी *f.*

FUNCTION, *n. employment*, v. OFFICE, BUSINESS. काम *n.* कर्म *n.* कार्य *n.* अधिकार *m.* व्यापार *m.*

Proper or peculiar f. स्वकर्म *n.* स्वधर्म *m.*

2 *faculty, power.* शक्ति *f.* गुण *m.* [बंधी.

FUNCTIONAL, *a.* v. N. कामाविषयींचा, कार्याविषयींचा, व्यापारसं-

FUNCTIONARY, *n.* v. OFFICER. कामगार, कामदार, अमलदार, अधिकारी.

FUND, *n. capital*, v. STOCK. पुंजी *f.* भांडवल *or* भांडोल *n.* गांठोडें *n.* गठडें *n.* केवा *m.* गठ्ठा *m.* ऐपत *f.* फंड *n.* (*from the English*).

2 funds. *money lent to government.* सरकारास कर्जी दिलेला पैका *m.*-धन *n.*-&c.

To FUND, *v. a.* फंडांत भरणें.

2 फंड *n.* जमविणें.

FUNDAMENT, *n. bum, breech.* गांड *f.* गुदप्रदेश *m.* अधोदेश *m.* अधःप्रदेश *m.* अधोभाग *m.*

FUNDAMENTAL, *a. pertaining to the foundation, essential, not accidental.* मूलभूत, मूलरूपी, मूलविषयक-संबंधी,आधारभूत, प्रवृत्तिनिमित्तभूत, सत्तैकहेतुक, आवश्यक. [&c.

FUNDAMENTAL, *n. primary principle.* मूलभूतविषय *m.*-गोष्ट *f.*-

FUNEBRIAL, FUNERAL, FUNEREAL, *a. belonging, &c. to a funeral.* उत्तरकर्माचा, प्रेतकर्माचा, &c. प्रेतकर्मसंबंधी, क्रियासंबंधी, क्रियाविषयक, और्ध्वदेहिक.

A f. pile. चिता *f.*

Ascending the f. pile. चितारोहण *n.*

Bursting of the skull of the corpse on the f. pile. कपालमोक्ष *m.*

F. ashes. चिताभस्म *n.*

F. fire. चिताग्नि *m.*

F. fire accompanied by the proper rites. मंत्राग्नि *m.*

F. rites and ceremonies, v. OBSEQUIES. क्रिया *f.* क्रियाकर्मांतर *n.* प्रेतकर्म *n.* प्रेतकार्य *n.* उत्तरक्रिया *f.*

The officiating Bràhman at f. rites. दर्म्या *m.*

Unhallowed f. fire. भडाग *f.* भडाग्न *f.* भडाग्नि *m.*

FUNERAL, *n.* v. OBSEQUIES. शवसंस्कार *m.* प्रेतसंस्कार *m.*

2—*the procession.* प्रेतयात्रा *f.* शवयात्रा *f.* स्मशानयात्रा *f.* मसणबोळावा *m.* [सारखा.

FUNGOUS, *a. like a fungus.* अळंब्यासारखा, वाढलेल्या मासा-

FUNGUS, *n.* v. MUSHROOM. अळंबें *n.*

2—in surgery. वाढलेलें मास *n.* मुरदाड मास *n.*

To FUNK, *v. n.*—from fear. हगुटणें, लेंड्या *f. pl.* गाळणें, गांड *f.* फाटणें *g. of s.* गंढारणें, कंबटें *n.* घालणें.

FUNKER, *n.* v. V. हगरा.

FUNNEL, *n. inverted hollow cone with a pipe.* गळणी *f.* नरसाळें *n.* नाळचें *n.* चिमणी *f.* [तायन *n.*

2 *vent for smoke, air, &c.* धुराडें *n.* धारें *n.* गवाक्ष *m. n.* वा-

FUNNY, *a. droll, comical.* मौजेचा, कौतुकाचा, तमाशाचा, चमत्काराचा, चमत्कारिक. [केश *m.*

FUR, *n. skin with hair.* लोंकरीची कातडी *f.* सलोमचर्म *n.* दाना-

2 *soft hair.* लोंकर *f.* लंव *f.* लोम *n.* [खरस*f.*शेवाळ*f.n.*

3 (as upon the tongue, &c.). बुरसी *f.* बुरसा *m.* बुरा *m.*

To be covered with f.—teeth, tongue, &c. बुरशेणें, बुरसणें, बुरसावणें, बुरबुरणें, शेवाळणें.

To FURBISH, *v. a.* v. To POLISH. उजळणें, निसळणें, सिकल *f.* करणें, उजळा *m.*-ओप *f.*-ओपसरा *m.*-झील *f.*-झिलाई *f.* देणें, ओपवणी *f.* करणें *g. of o.*

FURBISHER, *n.* v. V. उजळणारा, &c. सिकलगर *or* गार *or* शिकलगर &c. शस्त्रमार्ज, असिधावक, असिधाव.

FURCATION, *n.* v. FORK. डेळी *f.* डेळकी *f.* डेळकें *or* ढेळकें *n.* फेल *n.*

FURIOUS, *a. wildly raging, outrageous*, v. RAGING. तग्रबग्र, कावरा बावरा, तारका बारका, उगरा बागरा, आततायी, काहिरी, साहसी, साहसिक.

2 *violent, vehement*, v. EXCESSIVE, IMPETUOUS. चंड, प्रचंड, जबर, जबरा, अनर्थाचा, अवधंड्याचा, जोराचा, झपाट्याचा, तडाख्याचा, विकोपास गेलेला. [घोर.

3—of battle or fighting, v. HOT. दारुण, तुमुल *pop.* तुंबळ,

FURIOUSLY, *adv.* v. A. 1. कावरेबावरे पणानें, &c.

2 जोरानें, तडाख्यानें, चंड, आवेशानें, अनर्थानें, अवधंड्यानें.

FURIOUSNESS, *n.* v. A. 1. तग्रबग्रपणा *m.* &c. सतम *f. n.* साहस*n.* साहस बुद्धि *f.*

2 सुसाटेपणा *m.* तडाखा *m.* धडाका *m.* चंडत्व *n.* प्रचंडत्व *n.* सतम *f. n.* अनर्थ *m.* अवधंडा *m.* कहर *m.*

To FURL, *v. a. roll up* (*a sail*). बात *f.* बळणें *g. of o.* गुंडाळून बांधणें, सुरळी *f.* करणें *g. of o.*

FURLONG, *n.* मैलाचा आठवा हिस्सा *m.*

FURLOUGH, *n.* v. LEAVE. रजा *f.*

FURNACE, *n.* भट्टी *f.* चुला *m.* चुलवाण *n.* चुलाण *n.*

To come up out of the f. (of affliction, &c.). दिव्यां-

तून *or* दिव्यास उतरणें.

2 (of goldsmiths). आगटी *f. or* टें *n.* बागेसरी *f.*

To FURNISH, *v. a. supply with.* पुरवणें, संजोगणें, सजवणें, सजन *n.*-&c. करणें *g. of o.* सज्ज-सज्जित-संपन्न-विशिष्ट-&c.करणें.

To f. a house. घर *n.* मांडणें.

2 *supply, give.* देणें, पुरवणें, पुरावा *m.*-पुरवणी *f.*-भरणा*m.*-भरती *f.*-साहित्य *n.* करणें *g. of o.*

FURNISHED, *p.* v. V. 1. सजवलेला, &c. सज्ज, सज्जित, सज्जीकृत, कडीकोट.

2 दिल्हेला, पुरवलेला.

FURNISHING, *n.* v. V. 1.—*act.* पुरवणें *n.*&c. पुरावा *m.* सज्जन *n.* सज्जना *f.* सज्जीकरण *n.*

2 देणें *n.* पुरवणें *n.* पुरावा *m.* पुरवणी *f.*

FURNITURE, *n.* सामान *n.* साहित्य *n.* सरंजाम *m.* सामग्री *f.*

FURRED, *a. covered with fur.* बुरसावलेला, बुरशेला, &c. बुरा चढलेला, बुरा वाढलेला.

FURRIER, *n. dresser of leather.* ढोर *m.* चाम्हार *m.*

FURROW, *n.* (for seed). तास *n.* हरळ *m.*

2 *trench, channel, groove, &c.* खांचणी *f.* कोरणी *f.* खोबण *or* खोबणी *f.* [नरांडी *f.*

3—as torn up by water, v. GULLY. घळ *f.* घळण *f.* घळय *f.*

To be torn or worn into furrows. घळणें.

4 See WRINKLE.

To FURROW, *v. a.* तास *n.*-&c. पाडणें.

2 खांचणी *f.*-&c. पाडणें.

3 See To WRINKLE.

FURTHER, *a. beyond this.* परता, पलीकडचा *or* ला, पलीकडील(*or* पैलीकडचा &c.), उत्तर (in comp.).

2 See ADDITIONAL.

FURTHER, *adv.* एथून-तेथून पुढें, पुढें, उत्तरत्र.

F. and f. उत्तरोत्तर.

2—as used in discourses, &c. दिगर, दिगर मजमून.

To FURTHER, &c. See To PROMOTE, To HELP, &c.

FURTHERMORE, *adv. moreover.* अणखी.

FURTHERMOST, FURTHEST, *a.* सर्वांच्या पलीकडचा, सर्वांच्या बाहेरचा, कडेशेवटचा.

At the f. असें करतां, यथाकथंचित्.

FURTIVE, *a. stolen.* चोरीचा, चोरींब.

FURTIVELY, *adv.* चोरीनें, चोरून, अंधारीकुंधारी.

FURY, *n.* v. RAGE, ANGER. जळप*m.*प्रकोप *m.*वणवा *m.*तैष*m.*तेख*m.*

2 *vehemence, violence, &c.*—of a storm, &c. तडाका *or* खा*m.*

3 *a* f. *a furious woman.* चंडिका *or* चंडी *f.* हडळ *or* ळी *f.* बजास *or* ग *f.* घोडसठवी लागलेली, आगजाळी *f.* शूर्पनखा *f.* तुफान *n.* जिवंत पिशाच *n.*

FURZE, *n.* एक झाड आहे.

To FUSE, *v. a.* v. To MELT. वितुळविणें, रस *m.* करणें *g. of o.* गालन *n.*-&c. करणें *g. of o.*

To FUSE, *v. n.* v. To MELT. वितुळणें, रस *m.* होणें *g. of s.*

FUSEE, FUSIL, *n.* लहान बंदूक *f.*

FUSIBILITY, *n.* v. A. द्राव्यता *f.* गालनीयता *f.* द्रवीकरणीयता *f.* द्रवीकरणयोग्यता *f.*

FUSIBLE, *a.* वितळायाजोगा, द्राव्य, गालनीय, द्रवीकरणयोग्य, द्रवीकरणशक्य, सद्रव, द्रवीकरणीय.

FUSILEER, *n.* लहानबंदूक धरणारा शिपाई.

FUSION, *n.* v. V.—*act.* अटणें *n.* गाळणें &c. गालन *n.* द्रावण *n.* द्रवीकरण *n.*—*state.* द्रव *m.* द्रवत्व *n.* द्राव *m.*

FUSS, *n. ado, pother, &c.* v. BUSTLE. खटपट *f.* खटखट *f.* खवट्व *f.* खस्ता *f. pl.* v. काढ, गडबड *f.* उपद्व्याप *m.*

F. and row about. अवांव *n.* तांडव *n.*

FUSSY, *a.* v. N. खटपट्या, गडबड्या.

FUST, *n. musty smell.* उबटाण *f.* उबसाण *f.*

To FUST, *v. n.* उबटणें, उबट-&c. होणें.

FUSTIAN, *n.* सुती कापडाचा प्रकार आहे.

2 See BOMBAST.

FUSTIAN, *a.* See BOMBASTIC. [उबसाण *f.*

FUSTINESS, *n.* v. A. उबटपणा *m.* केनसटपणा *m.* &c. उबटाण *f.*

FUSTY, *a. mouldy, &c.* उबट, केनसट, सापट, बाशेळा, वासकट, वासका.

To get f. उबटणें.

FUTILE, *a. trifling, worthless.* हलका, बावगा, बावकळ, पोकळ.

2 v. INEFFECTUAL. निष्फल, निरर्थक.

FUTILITY, *n.* v. A. 1. हलकेपणा *m.* पोकळपणा *m.* पोकळी *f.*

FUTURE, *a.* पुढचा *or* ला, पुढील, मोहरचा *or* ला, पुढें व्हावयाचा, &c. भविष्य, भावी, भाविक, आगामी, आगंतव्य, आगमिष्यमाण, भव्य, भाव्य, भवनीय, भविता, अनागत, एष्य, जन्य, जनिष्यमाण.

F. and fixed, *certain to come.* अवश्यंभावी.

F. state. उदर्कावस्था *f.*

2 *that has time intervening.* सावधि, सावधिक.

FUTURE, FUTURITY, *n. time future.* पुढला काल *m.* भविष्य काल *m.* भाविकाल *m.* उत्तर काल *m.* उदर्क काल *m.* उदर्क *m.* भवितृत्व *n.* आयति *f.*

In f. पुढें.

2 *a. future event.* होईक *n.* होतव्य *n.* भवितव्य *n.* भविष्य *n.* होष्य *n.* होष्यमाण *n.*

FY, *interj.* छी, धिक्, छिः.

G.

G. This letter is represented as to its hard sound by ग, and as to its soft sound by ज.

GAB, GABBLE, *n.* v. PRATE. बरळ *f.* गलगल *f.* गबगब *f.* गबगबा *m.* बडबड *f.* बडबडाध्याय *m. f.* जल्प *m.* जल्पना *f.* वाग्जल्प *m.* वाग्जल्पना *f.*

Gift of the g. जिभेची हातोटी *f.*

To GABBLE, *v. n.* v. To PRATE. बडबडणें, बकबकणें, फात्या *f. pl.* करणें-मारणें-फाडणें.

GABION, *n.* बिनबुडाची टोपली *f.*

GABLE, *n.*—of a house. चांदई *or* चांधई *f.*

GABY, *n. silly, weak person,* v. WEAK. रेमेडोक्या*m.* मेषपात्र *n.*

GAD. See GOAD, POINT.

To GAD, *v. n. idly rove.* हिंडणें, भटकणें, उनाडणें, हिंडणवारे*m. pl.*-हिंडफेरा*m.*-उनाडकी *f.* करणें, भटकया *f. pl.* मारणें-मारीत फिरणें.

GAD ABOUT, GADDER, *n.* These words, as restricted to *females,* are rendered by नगरभवानी, भटक भवानी, गांवभवानी, हिंडफिरी, गांव गाई, पायांवर नक्षत्र पडलें असी, बारावरची बिल्ली,

जिच्या पायास भिंगरी असती *or* भोवरा पडलेला आहे.—and as used of *males*. हिंडफिऱ्या, भटक भैरव *or* भैरोबा, पायांवर *or* पायीं भोवरा पडलेला, ज्याचा तळ थांबत नाहीं, यथेष्टचारी.

GADFLY, *n.* गोमाशी *f.* घंघाळी *f.* डांस*m.* दंश*m.*

GAFFER, *n.*—the compellation. बावा*m.* बा*m.*

A little g. बडलोबा*m.*

To GAG, *v. a. stop the mouth.* तोंडांत बोळा*m.*-चोंबा*m.* घालणें -कोमणें, तोंड*n.* कोंडणें-बांधणें-बंद करणें.

To g. with a clout. चोंदी *f.* देणें.

GAG, *n. something put into the mouth to hinder speech.* तोंड कोंडण्याचा बोळा*m.*

GAGE, *n. pledge.* पैजेची खूण *f.* पैजेचा विडा*m.* प्रतिज्ञाचिह्न*n.*

To GAGE. See To PLEDGE.

GAGGLE, &c. See CACKLE, &c.

GAIN, *n. profit, emolument, gettings, earnings.* मिळकत *f.* प्राप्ति *f.* कमाई *f.* पैदास्त *f.* किफायत *f.* सरफा *or* सरिफा*m.* नफा*m.* लाभ *m.* मिळताव*m.* उत्पन्न*n.* आय*m.* आदाय*m.* अदा*m.* जोड *f.* मीळ *f.* उपज*m.* निपज*m.* कमाविसी *f.* गाऊल*n.* गबान*n.* गबानी *f.* आमदानी *f.* प्राप्त्यंश*m.* प्राप्तव्यांश*m.* लभ्यांश *m.* लभ्य*n.*—gener. *or* loosely. लाभागोभा*m.*

By way of g. नफेवारीं, सरिफेवारीं.

Dishonest g. लुचपत *f. v.* खा.

G. and loss. लाभालाभ*m.*

Prospect of g. लाभदृष्टि *f.*

Unexpected or rare g. अलभ्यलाभ*m.* घोबें*n.* घबूक*n.*

2 *advantage, benefit*, v. ADVANTAGE. हित*n.* फायदा*m.* नफा*m.* सरफा *or* सरिफा*m.* फळ*n.* फळश्रुति *or* फळ श्रूत *f.* लाभ*m.* स्वार्थ*m.*

To GAIN, *v. a. obtain, procure,* v. To GET. मिळवणें *or* मेळवणें, पैदा करणें, संपादणें, मिळणें *in. con.* प्राप्त होणें *in. con.*

2 *obtain as profit or advantage.* कमावणें, मिळवणें *or* मेळवणें, संपादणें, अर्जणें, मिळकत *f.*-किफायत *f.*-कमाई *f.* करणें *g. of o.* उपार्जना *f.*-उपार्जन*n.*-&c. करणें *g. of o.* राशी पुंजीस येणें *in.con.*

3 *attain, make,* v. To REACH. पावणें, अटपणें, सई करणें.

To g. ground. See To ADVANCE.

To GAIN, *v. n. have advantage or profit.* लाभ *m.* होणें *in. con.* लाभणें, लाधणें.

2 on; *encroach.* पुढेंयेणें-जाणें-सरणें.

3 on. आटोपत-गांठीत-&c. जाणें-चालणें.

GAINED, *p.* v. V. A. 1.मिळवलेला, &c. प्राप्त, पैदा, उपलब्ध, लब्ध, आपन्न (in conp.), आप्त (in comp.), अवाप्त (in comp.).

2 मिळवलेला, कमावलेला, &c. संपादित, उपार्जित, अर्जित.

GAINER, *n.* v. V. A. 1. मिळवणारा, संपादणारा, &c.

2 मिळवणारा, कमावणार, &c. नफेकरी, कमाऊ.

GAINFUL, *a.* v. N. 2. *lucrative.* मिळकतीचा, नफ्याचा, किफायतीचा, &c. किफायतवार, किफायती, नफेवार, सरफेवार, सरफेवाईक, लाभदायक, सफल, फलद्रूप. [णी *f.*

GAINING, *n.* v. V. A. 1.—*act.* मिळवणें*n.* &c. मिळवणूक *f.* मिळव- 2—*act.* कमावणें *n.* &c. उपार्जन *n.* उपार्जना *f.* अर्जन *n.* अर्जना *f.* संपादणूक *f.* संपादन *n.*

To GAINSAY, *v. a. contradict, controvert.* खंडणें, वाद *m.* घेणें *g. of o.* उलट *adv.* बोलणें-सांगणें, उलट *m. f.*-उलटा *m.* घेणें *with* वर *of o.* प्रत्याख्यान *n.*-विपरीत कथन *n.*-विरुद्ध कथन *n.* करणें.

GAIRISH, *a. gaudy*, v. FINE. भडक, झळक, भडकीचा.

GAIRISHNESS, *n.* भडकपणा *m.* &c. भडक *f. v.* मार.

GAIT, *n. air or manner of walking.* गति *f.* चाल *f.* चालण्याची नोक *f.*-ढब *f.*

Solemn or stately g. गजगति *f.*

GALA-DAY, *n.* छानछोकीचा दिवस *m.*

GALANGAL, *n. alpinia g.* कोळंजन *or* कोळिंजन *n.* [दी *f.*

GALAXY, *n.* v. MILKY WAY. आकाशगंगा *f.* आकाशनदी *f.* सुरन-

GALBANUM, *n.*—the gum-resin. गंधाबिरुजा *or* गंधाबेरोजा *m.*

GALE, *n. vehement wind.* वावटळ *or* वावटूळ *f.* ढोसण *f.* जवळ *or* जौळ *n.* महावात *m.* वातूल *m.* वात्या *f.*

2 See PASSION.

GALL, *n. bile.* पित्त *n.*

2 *galled place*, v. EXCORIATION. नाळ *f.*

GALL-BLADDER, *n.* पित्ताची कुपी *f.*-पिशवी *f.*

GALL *or* GALL-NUT, *n.* मायफळ *n.* माजूफळ *n.* माजा *m.*

Black g. काळामाजा *m.*

White g. गोरामाजा *m.*

GALL-STONE, *n.* पित्ताच्या पिशवींतला खडा *m.*

To GALL, *v. a. fret the skin.* चोळटणें, चोळवटणें, घासणें, घासटणें, सोलणें, लागणें.

2 *annoy, vex,* v. To TEASE. जाचणें, छडणें, छळणें, जाचणी *f.* -जाचणूक *f.* करणें, इजा *f.*-दुःख *n.*-उपद्रव *m.* देणें.

GALLANT, *a. gay,* v. FINE. भडक, भडकीचा, छानदार, छानीचा.

2 *spirited*, v. BRAVE. रगदार, रगेल, रग्या, दिलदार, शौर्यशाली, प्रतापशाली.

3 *courtly to ladies.* स्त्रीसन्मानी, स्त्रीजनतोषी, स्त्रीजनानुवर्ती, स्त्र्यादरी, स्त्रीसत्कारी, स्त्रीप्रेमी, स्त्रीसन्मानपर.

GALLANT, *n. paramour, &c.* v. LOVER. धगड, जार, उपपति, इश्कबाज, इश्की, दोस्त.

Rival g. सवतळा *or* सवताळा.

GALLANTLY, *adv.* v. A. 2. दिलदारीनें, मोठे छातीनें, शौर्यपूर्वक.

3 स्त्रीजनानुवृत्तीनें, स्त्रीसन्मानपूर्वक, स्त्रीसत्कारबुद्धीनें.

GALLANTRY, *n.* v. A. 1. See FINERY.

2 दिलदारी *f.* जवानमर्दी *f.* मर्दाई *f.*

3 स्त्रीजनानुवृत्ति *f.* स्त्रीसत्कार *m.* स्त्रीसन्मान *m.*

I. *vicious* g. इष्कबाजी *f.*

GALLED, *p.* v. V. 1. चोळवटलेला, लागलेला, &c.

Having a g. or sore back. नाळी, नाळ्या, नाळपड्या.

2 जाचलेला, &c.

GALLERY, *n. covered terrace outside of a house.* सज्जा *m.*

2 (in a church, theatre, &c.) पायऱ्याप्रमाणें खांबांवर केलेली चढत्या बैठकांची जागा *f.*

GALLEY, *n.* गलबताचा एक प्रकार आहे.

2 *cook room of a ship of war.* लढाऊ गलबतावरचा ओवरा *m.*

GALLEY-SLAVE, *n.* गलबतावर वल्हें मारणारा गुलाम.

GALLIMATIA, *n.* v. NONSENSE. अगडतगड *n.* अगडबगड *n.* अकडंतिकडं *n.* इधरतिधर *n.* [बील *f.*

GALLIMAUFRY, *n.* v. MEDLEY. खिचडी *f.* खिचडमिचड *n.* गोतां-

GALLING, *p. a.* v. V. 2. जाचणारा, &c. जाचक, छळक.

GALLI POT, *n.* औषध ठेवायाचें एका प्रकारचें भांडें आहे.

GALLON, *n.* एक कैली माप आहे.

To GALLOP, *v. n.* चौकणें, चौखूर *adv.* उडणें-धावणें-उडत चालणें-

जाणें, चौकाबर जाणें-येणें, भरधांव चालणें-पळणें.

To GALLOP, *v. a.* दबडणें, दामटणें, पिटणें, दपटणें, पिटाळणें, हकारणें, फेकणें, दौड *m.* काढणें *g. of o.*

To g. up and down. फेरणें, फेर *m.*-फेरफटका *m.* देणें.

To g. violently. ताण *m.* देणें.

GALLOP, GALLOPING, *n.* v. V. A. दबडणें *n.* पिटणें *n.* &c.

To put out into a g. चौखूर-भरधांव-चौपायीं-चौफेर-&c.काढणें, घोडा *m.* फेकणें-हकारणें-चौकावर आणणें. [सुटणें-&c.

To set off at a g.—a horse. चौपायीं-चौफेर-&c. निघणें-

I.—the pace. चौक *m.* चौकचाल *f.* दबडचाल *f.* भरदपट *f.* भरधांव *f.* भरझ्याल *f.* दुडाण *n.* दुडाणचाल *f.*

In a g. भरदपट, भरधांव, भरझ्याल, चौखूर.

GALLOPIN, *n. servant for the kitchen.* खटपट्या.

To GALLOW. See To FRIGHTEN.

GALLOWAY, *n. small sized horse.* आडघोडा *m.*

GALLOWS, *n.* फांशी देण्याचा खांब *m.* गळाचीं लांकडें *n. pl.*

To GAMBLE, *To* GAME, *v. n. play at dice, cards, &c. for a stake.* पणाचा खेळ *m.*-पैजेचा खेळ *m.*-हारजितीचा खेळ *m.*-&c. करणें, फांसे *m. pl.*-जुवा*m.*-जुगार *m. n.*-द्यूत *n.*-&c. खेळणें, जुवेबाजी *f.* करणें.

GAMBLER, GAMESTER, *n.* v. V. पणाचा खेळणारा, पैजेचा खेळणारा, &c. जुवाखेळणारा, फांसेखेळणारा, &c. जुगारी *or* ऱ्या, जुवेबाज, द्यूतकार, अक्षद्यू, अक्षद्यूत, अक्षधूर्त्त, कितव.

GAMBLING, GAMING, *n.* v. V.—*act.* जुवा खेळणें *n.* फांसे खेळणें *n.* &c. जुगार *m. n.* जुवा *m.* जुवेबाजी *f.* द्यूत *n.* पणाचा-पैजेचा-हारजितीचा-मांडणीचा-&c. खेळ *m.*

GAMBLING-HOUSE, *n.* जुवाखेळण्याचा अड्डा *m.*.फड *m.* जुव्याचा-जुगाराचा- जुगाऱ्याचा-&c. अड्डा *m.* द्यूतशाला *f.*

GAMBOGE, *n.* रेवाचिनीचा शिरा *m.* रेवंदसार *m.*

To GAMBOL, *v. n.* v. To FRISK, To PLAY. खिदडणें, खिदळणें *or* खिदाळणें, बोकलणें, उड्या *f. pl.* मारणें, नाचणें, बागडणें, हुंदडणें.

2—in the water. डुंबणें *or* डुंमणें, डुबकणें, बुडकणें.

GAMBOL, GAMBOLING, *n.* v. V. 1. खिदडणें*n.* &c. खिदडा *m.* उड्या *f. pl.* नाच *m.*

Wild g. बोकंदळ *n.*

GAMBRELS, *n. hind legs of a horse.* पिन्छाडी *f.*

GAME, *n. sport,* v. PLAY. खेळ *m.* क्रीडा *f.* कौतुक *n.*

To make game of. See To MOCK.

2 *jest, not earnest.* मस्करी *f.* खेळ *m.*

3 *match at play.* डाव *m. v.* खेळ, बाजी *f. v.* खेळ.

Full g. lit. fig. भरडाव *m.*

Losing g. उतार बाजी *f.*

4 *animals of game.* पारध *f.* शिकार *f.* मृगया *f.*

To GAME. See To GAMBLE.

GAME-COCK, *n.* लढाऊ कोंबडा *m.* पैजेचा कोंबडा *m.*

GAMESOME, *a.* See PLAYFUL.

GAMESTER. See GAMBLER.

GAMMER, *n.*—the compellation. बया *f.*

GAMMON, *n. hoax.* झोका *m.* झोला *m.* झोल। *m.*

To GAMMON, *v. a. to hoax.* झोका *m.*-झोला *m.*-&c. देणें.

GAMUT, *n. musical scale.* ग्राम *m.* स्वरग्राम *m.* सरिगमपधनी *f.*

The notes of the *gamut* are:—षड्ज, ऋषभ, गांधार, मध्यम, पंचम, धैवत, निषाद *pop.* निखाद.

Chanting the notes of the g. सरिगम *f.*

Running down the notes of the g. अवरोह *m.*

Running up the notes of the g. डगर *f. v.* घे.

GANDER, *n.* हंस *m.* कलहंस *m.* वरट *m.*

GANG, *n.* v. BAND. टोळी *f.* थवा *m.* चुंग *f.* झुंड *f.* गट *or* गट्ट *m.* गठ्ठा *m.* मुठाण *n.*

GANG-WAY, *n.* जहाजावर जाण्याचें दार *n.*

GANGES, *n.* गंगा *f.* भागीरथी *f.* देवनदी *f.* त्रिवेणी *f.*

G. of heaven. v. MILKYWAY. आकाश गंगा *f.*

G. of the infernal regions. भोगवती *f.*

Spot on which the g. descends. गंगोत्री *f.* [TIFY.

GANGRENE, *To* GANGRENE. See MORTIFICATION, To MOR-

GAOL, *n. prison.* बंदिखाना*m.* कैदखाना *m.* बंदखाना*m.* तुरुंग*m.* बंदिशाल*f.* कारागार*n.* कारागृह*n.*—in covert phrase. ज्ञानमठ*m.*

To GAOL. See To IMPRISON.

GAOL-DELIVERY, *n.* बंदखलास *m.*

GAOLER, *n.* बंदिखान्यांचा-तुरुंगाचा-&c. अधिकारी, बंदिशालाध्यक्ष, कारागृहाधिकारी, कारापति.

GAP, *n.* खिंड *f. dim.* खिंडकुली *f. or* लें *n. or* खिंडुकली *f. or* लें *n. and enhanc.* खिंडार *or* रें *n.* खांड *f. enhanc.* खांडार *n.* भोकू *m.* संधि *m. f.*

Large g. भगदड *or* ळ *or* भगदाड *n.* भगाड *n.* भगास *n.* भोंकसा *or* भोसका *m.* भोसकट *or* टें *n.* खांडार *n.* खिंडार *or* रें *n.*

G. in the teeth. खांड *f.* बोंथरखिंड *f.* बोंथरखेंडें *n.*

2 fig. *intermitted day or time,* v. BREAK. खाडा *m.* नागा *m.* खंड *m.*

3 *flaw, defect.* छिद्र *n.*

GAP-TOOTHED, *a.* दांत पडका *or* गा, बोंथरा, बोंचरडा, बोथरखंड *or* डा, बोथरखिंड्या, बोंथरा.

To GAPE, *v. n. yawn.* जांभई *f.*-जांभळी *f.* घेणें-देणें, *or with in. con.* येणें, जृंभणें.

2 *open widely,*—a plank, a fruit, the ground, &c. उकलणें, वासणें, विचकणें, भेगलणें, भेतलणें, तडणें, तडकणें, भळ *f.*-भेग *f.* पडणें *in. con.*

3 *open the mouth from wonder, &c.* आ *m.* पसरणें-वासणें, तोंड *n.* वासणें-विचकणें.

GAPE, GAPING, *n.* v. V. 1. जांभई *f.* जांभळी*f.* जृंभा *f.* जृंभण*n.*

GAPER, *n.* GAPING, *p. a.* v. V. 3. आपसऱ्या, तोंडवास्या, आ पसरलेला, तोंडवासलेला.

GARB, *n.* v. CLOTHES, DRESS. वेष *m.* पेहराव *m.* लिभास *m.*

GARBAGE. See REFUSE.

To GARBLE, *v. a. sift, separate, pick, &c.* गाळणें, गाळागाळ *f.* करणें-करून सांगणें *g. of o.* गाळून गाळून सांगणें-लिहणें.

GARBLED, *p.* v. V. गाळलेला, &c. गाळागाळीचा.

GARDEN, *n.* बाग *m. f. dim.* बगीचा *m.* वाटी*f.* वाटिका *f.* उपवन *n.* कृत्रिमवन *n.* आराम *m.* उद्यान *n.*

Flower g. फुलबाग *m. f.* पुष्पवाटिका *f.* [चे *m. pl.*

Gardens—compreh. *gardens, plantations, &c.* बागबगी-

G.—fruits. बागाईती फळें *n. pl.*

Kitchen g. मळा *m.* बागाईत *n.*

Of or belonging to a g. बागाइती. [मीन *f.*

GARDEN-GROUNDS, GARDEN-LAND, *n.* बागाईत *n.* बागाइती ज-

GARDEN-PLOT, *n.* तक्ता *m.* क्यारी *f.* ताटवा *m.* वाफा *m.*

GARDEN-STUFF, *n.* बागाईत *n.* बागाईती *f.* माळवें *n.*

Portion of g. exacted as market-toll. शेव *f.*

GARDENER, *n.* माळी, बागवान, काछी, कुंजरा *or* कुंजडा *m.*

Flower-g. फुलमाळी.

Gardeners ward, quarter, &c. माळवाडा *m.* माळी आळी *f.*

Kitchen-g. मळेकरी. [नी *f.*

GARDENING, *n.* बागकाम *n.* माळीपणा *m.* बागवानपणा *m.* बागवा-

GARGARISM, GARGLE, *n.* *wash for the throat.* गुळणा *m.* गुळणी *f.* गुरळा *m.* कुळी *f.* गुळण्याचें-&c. औषध *n.* गंडूष *m.* आचमनीय *n.*

To GARGARIZE, *To* GARGLE, *v. a.* गुळणे *m. pl.*-गुळण्या *f. pl.*-&c. करणें, खुळखुळावणें, खुळबुळावणें, खुळबूळ *f.* करणें, गंडूष *m.* करणें.

GARLAND, *n.* हार *m.* माला *pop.* माळ *f.* माला *f.* (in comp. as पुष्पमाला, पर्णमाळा, शाखामाला), गजरा *m.* घोंसा *m.* चीप *f.* माल्य *n.* स्रक् *or* स्रग् *f.*

G. of wild flowers. वनमाला *f.*

2 *collection of printed pieces.* ग्रंथमाला *f.*

GARLIC, *n.* लसूण *m. f.* लशुन *n.*

Clove of g. लसूणबी *f.* पांकळी *f.* बोंवा *m.* लसूण *n.* बोय *f.*

GARMENT, *n.* v. CLOTHING, CLOTHES. पांघरूण *n.* वस्त्र *n.* प्रावरण *n.* [टकुरें *n.*

A tattered mantle or g. फटकर *or* फटकूर *n.* फटकुरी *f.* फ-

G. of patches. कंथा *f.* वाकळ *f.* गोदडी *f.*

GARNER, *n.* v. GRANARY. कोठी *f.* कोठार *n.* धान्यागार *n.*

To GARNER, *v. a.* कोठींत-कोठारांत-&c. ठेवणें.

GARNET, *n.* याकूत *m.*

To GARNISH, *v. a. decorate.* सजणें, सजवणें, साजरा-सुशोभित-&c. करणें.

GARNISHMENT, GARNITURE. See ORNAMENT.

GARRET, *n. room at the top of a house.* शेवटचे माडीवरची-मजल्यावरची खोली *f.* माळ्यावरची खोली *f.*

GARRISON, *n.*—the place. तटबंदीचा गांव *m.*-किल्ला *m.*-&c. ठाणें *n.*

2—the troops. ठाण्यांतील-तटबंदीच्या गांवांतील-&c. शिपाई *m. pl.* किल्ल्याचे रखवालीस ठेवलेलीं माणसें *n. pl.* किल्लेराखण *f.*

To GARRISON, *v. a. furnish with soldiers for defence.* रखवालीस शिपाई *m. pl.*-&c. ठेवणें.

GARRULITY, *n.* v. A. वाचाळपणा *m.* बटबटेपणा *m.* &c.

GARRULOUS, *a.* v. TALKATIVE. बोलगाडा, वाचाळ, बटबट्या, बहुभाष.

GARRULOUSLY, *adv.* v. A. वाचाळपणानें, वाचाळहोऊन.

GARTER, *n.* पायमोजा बांधावयाची पट्टी *f.* मोजेबंद *m.*

GAS, *n.* वायुरूप एक प्रवाही पदार्थ आहे, ग्यास *m.*

GASCONADE, *n.* v. V. BOAST. शेखी *f.* शेखीचें बोलणें *n.*

To GASCONADE, *v. n.* To BOAST. शेखी *f.* मिरवणें, बल्गना *f.* करणें, दंदेदरफडे *m. pl.* गाणें.

GASEOUS, *a.* v. N. वायुरूप, वातरूप.

GASH, *n. deep and wide cut.* भोकसा *or* भोसका *m.* भगदड *n.* मोठी जखम *f.* वार *m.* घाव *m.*

To GASH, *v. a.* घाव *m.*-वार *m.*-&c. करणें.

To GASP, *v. n.* v. To PANT. धापा *f. pl.* देणें-दाटणें, धापलणें, धापणें, लाहक्या *f. pl.*-अहाळण्या *f. pl.* देणें, कांसळणें.

GASP, GASPING, *n.* v. V. धाप *f.* लाहकी *f.* आहळणी *f.* दम *m.* कासश्वास *m.* ऊर्ध्व *m.* उदान *n.*

The last g. घुट्ट *n.* [*g. of s.*

To be at the last g. तंतीं-कंठीं-दंतीं प्राण *m.* उरणें-लागणें-

GASTRIC, *a. belonging to the belly or stomach.* जठराचा, जाठर, जठरसंबंधी.

G. juice. जठराग्नि *m.* जठरानल *m.* कोष्ठाग्नि *m.* (These words mean literally *fire of the belly*). [गोपुर *n.*

GATE, *n.* (of a city, palace, &c.). द्वार *pop.* दार *n.* दरवाजा *m.*

Building over the g. गोपुर *m. n.*

Front or grand g. सिंहद्वार *n.* महाद्वार *n.* [दरवाजा *m.*

2 (of a village or ward, &c.). वेस *f.* फटका *m.* फाटक *n.*

3 (of an enclosure, in a fence, &c.). झडपा *m.* झांपा *m.* तकटें *or* तटकें *n. dim.* तटकी *f.* कवाडी *f.* ताटी *f.* वेस *f.* फाटक *n.* फांकट *n.*

GATE-KEEPER, *n.* (of a village). वेसकर, द्वारपाल.

GATE-WAY, *n.* दरवाजा *m.* देवडी *or* देवढी *f.* गोपुर *n.*

To GATHER, *v. a. collect.* गोळा करणें, एकवटणें, मिळवणें, गोळावणें, साचडणें, जमा करणें, जमविणें, एकवट-एकत्र करणें, कवळणें, जमावणें, गुंडाळणें, गवसणें, संग्रह *m.*-संचय *m.*-&c. करणें *g. of o.*

2 *crop, pluck.* तोडणें, काढणें, तोडून घेणें, उतरणें, तोडणी *f.*-तोडा *m.*-&c. करणें *g. of o.*

3 *draw together, into narrow compass, &c.* सावरणें, अटपणें, आवरणें, अखुडणें, सापसारणें, अटोप *m.*-अटप *m.*-आवर *m.*-आवरण *n.*-&c. करणें.

4 v. To PUCKER. मुरुडणें *or* मुरडणें, सुरकुतविणें.

5 (sums due, &c.). उगवणें, उकळणें, वसूल करणें, उगारणें, उगावा *m.*-उगावागा *m.*-&c. करणें *g. of o.*

Monies gathered in. उगवण *f.* उगवणी *f.* उगवा *m.* उगावा *m.* उगवील *f.* उगारणी *f.*

6 *collect logically.* अनुमान *n.*-तर्क *m.* करणें, हाशील *n.* घेणें, तर्कानें-तर्क करून-अनुमान करून-&c. काढणें, सिद्ध करणें, सिद्धांत *m.*-&c. काढणें.

To GATHER, *v. n. come together, collect, assemble.* एकवटणें, मिळणें, गोळा होणें, जमणें, एकवट-एकत्र होणें, जुटणें, जुडणें.

2 v. To PUCKER. सुरकुतणें, मुरुडणें *or* मुरडणें, अखुडणें.

3 *generate pus.* पुवळणें, पुलेणें, पुलेजणें, पुवारणें, पुळणास येणें, ओढून येणें.

GATHER, *n.* v. PUCKER. सुरकुती *f.* चिरमी *f.* झुरळी *f.*

GATHERED, *p.* v. V. A. 1. गोळा केलेला, एकवटलेला, &c. जमा, सांचीव, संगृहीत, संचित, समवेत, समाहित, संहित, मिलित, एकस्थ.

2 तोडलेला, &c. उतरींव.

3 सावरलेला, अटपलेला, &c.

4 मुरडलेला, &c. मुरडींव. [कर्त्ता.

GATHERER, *n.* v. V. A. 1. गोळा करणारा, &c. संचय-संग्रह-&c.

GATHERING, *n.* v. V. A. 1.—*act.* गोळा करणें *n.* &c. जमाव *m.* संग्रहण *n.* संग्रह *m.* एकीकरण *n.* चयन *n.* चय *m.* समाहरण *n.* समाहार *m.* संहार *m.*

G. from all quarters. जमवाजमव *f.*

2 तोडणें *n.* &c. तोडणी *f.* तोडा *m.* ओढा *m.*

3 सांवरणें *n.* &c. सावरणी *f.* अटोपणी *f.* अटोप *m.* अटप *m.* आवरण *n.* आवर *m.*

4 मुरडणें *n.*
5 उगवणें *n.* उगवण *f.* उगवणी *f.* उकळीत *f. n.* उकळा *m.*उगावा *m.* उगवील *f.* उगावागा *m.* उग्राणी *f.*
I. *a* g. *a puckering.* चिरमी *f.* सुरकुती *f.*
II. *a tumor, &c.* टुसरूं *n.*
GAUD. See ORNAMENT, TRINKET.
GAUDERY. See FINERY.
GAUDILY, *adv.* v. A. छानीनें, टुमीनें, भडकमारून.
GAUDINESS,*n.*v. A. छान*f.* शान*f.*भडक *f. v.* मार, भळभळाट*m.*टूम*f.*
GAUDY, *n.* v. FINE. देखणाऊ, देखाऊ, टुमदार,भडक, भबूक, भडकीचा, टिकमिरवणा, शानदार, छानीचा.
To GAUGE, &c. See To MEASURE, &c.
GAUNT, *n.* v. LEAN. रोड, रोडका, सडकपातळ, काठंग्या, रोडांग्या, पातळांग्या, हाडगळ, हाडळ,-एकपासोळीचा.
Tall and g. धांडळ *or* ढांडळ.
GAUNTLET, *n.* दस्ताना*m.* वज्रमुष्टि *pop.* वज्रमूठ *f.*
To take up the g. पण*m.* उचलणें, विडा*m.* उचलणें.
To throw the g. पण*m.* मांडणें-स्थापणें-रोवणें.
GAUZE, *n.* कपरधूल *or* धूरकपूर*m.*
GAWK. See FOOL.
GAWKY, *a.* v. AUKWARD. अनाडी, आडाणी.
GAY, *a. airy, blithe, lively,* v. MERRY. आनंदी, आनंदवृत्ति, उल्हासी, उल्हासवृत्ति, खुशदिल,खुशमौजा, खुशमौजी.
2 *fond of amusements and sports.* रंगेल, रंगेला, रंगेली, रंगी, रंगिला, ख्याली, चयनी, कौतुकी, गुलहौशी *or* हौशा, खुशालचंद, बिलासी.
3 v. INE. छानीचा, छानदार.
GAYETY, GAYNESS, *n.* v. A. 1. आनंदवृत्ति *f.* आनंदस्वभाव*m.* उल्हासवृत्ति *f.*
I. See MERRIMENT, MIRTH. II See PLEASURE.
GAYLY, *adv.* v. A. 1. आनंदानें, उल्हासानें, उल्हासवृत्तीनें.
3 v. FINELY. छानीनें, छानदारीनें.
To GAZE, *v. n. look intently.* टक-टकटक-टकमक-टकाकां-मुटमुट *adv.* पाहणें, टक *f.*-टकळी *f.* लावणें-लावून पाहणें, टुकटुकणें, टुकणें, टोकणें.
GAZE, GAZING, *n.* v. V. टकमक पाहणें*n.* &c. टक *f.* टकळी *f.* एकाग्र दृष्टिपात*m.*
GAZELLE, *n.* v. DEER. मृग*m.*
GAZETTE, *n. newspaper.* अखबार *f.* वर्त्तमानपत्र*n.*
To GAZETTE, *v. a.* वर्त्तमान पत्रांत छापणें-प्रसिद्ध करणें.
GAZETTEER, *n.* See. GAZETTE.
2 देश नगर नदी इत्यादिकाच्या वर्णनाचा ग्रंथ*m.* [*or* कां.
GAZINGLY, *adv.* v. V. टक, टकटक *or* कां *intens.* टकाकां, टकमक
GAZING-STOCK, *n.* दृष्टिपात्र*n.* उपहासदर्शनास्पद*n.*
GEAR, *n.* (of a cart, plough, &c.) *harness, tackle.* ब्रेठण*n.* तेगार*m.* सरंजाम*m.* सामान*n.*
2 See DRESS.
GELATINE, GELATINOUS, *a. resembling gelly, viscous.* चिकीचा, चिकीसारखा, चिकचिकीत. [करणें *g. of o.*
To GELD, *v. a. castrate.* खसी करणें, अंड*m.* कापणें, मुष्कछेदन*n.*
2 (by pounding the testicle) बडविणें, चेचणें.
GELLY. See JELLY.
GELT, GELDING, *n. animal gelt.* खसी केलेला-खसी-भादा *or* भाद्या घोडा-&c.
GEM, *n. precious stone.* रत्न*n.* मणि *or* मणी*m.* जवाहीर*n.* मणका*m.*
G.-mine. रत्नाकर*m.*
Hidden g. *fig.* झाकलें माणीक*n.*
Jewels or gems-compreh. खडेकंकर*m. pl.*
Judge or connoisseur of gems. रत्नपारखी.
Middle g. of a string. मध्यनायक *pop.* मदनायक*m.*
Small ruby, diamond, or other g. चूण *f.* चुणी *f.*
The nine gems. नवरत्नें*n. pl.*
Of or belonging to a g. जवाहिरी.
Set or studded with gems. रत्नजडीत, रत्नखचित.
Socket of a g. कोंदण *n.*
String of gems. मणिमाला *f.* मणिसर*m.* [ठिकडें*n.*
The g. or boss as the middle of a finger ring. ठीक*n.*
To mount gems. कोंदण*n.* करणें.
2 See BUD.
To GEM, *v. a.* रत्नखचित-रत्नजडीत-&c. करणें.
GEMINI, *n.*—the zodiacal sign. मिथुन*n.* युग्म*n.* द्वंद्व*n.*
GEMMARY, GEMMEOUS, *a. pertaining, &c. to gems.* रत्नाचा, जवाहिरी, रत्नसंबंधी, रत्नविषयक, मणिसंबंधी.
GENDER, *n.*—in gram. लिंग *n.*
Feminine. g. स्त्रीलिंग *n.*
Masculine g. पुल्लिंग *n.*
Variation (of words) through g. लिंगकार्य *n.*
To GENDER. See To BEGET. To COPULATE.
GENEALOGICAL, *a.* v. N. वंशचरित्राचा, वंशानुक्रमविषयक, वंशानुक्रमसंबंधी, वंशावळीचा, &c.
GENEALOGIST, *n.* कुलाचार्य्य, कुलक्रम-वंशक्रम-&c. दर्शक, कुलक्रमज्ञ.
GENEALOGY, *n. history of a pedigree.* वंशचरित्र*n.* वंशानुचरित*n.* वंशावलिवर्णन *n.* कुलक्रमचरित्र *n.* [कुलपरंपरा *f.*
2 *pedigree.* वंशावळ *f.* वंशानुक्रम *m.* कुलक्रम *m.* वंशपरंपरा *f.*
GENERAL, *a. belonging to the genus, generic.* जातीचा, जातिमात्राचा, साधारण, सामान्य, जातिमात्रविषयक, जातिमात्रसंबंधी.
2 *not particular, not specified.* साधारण, सामान्य, औत्सर्गिक, मोघम *or* मोहगम, अवछिन्न, अपरिछिन्न, अविशेष, अप्रतिपदोक्त.
3 *usual, customary,* v. COMMON. रूढीचा, रूढींतला, व्यावहारिक *pop.* व्यवहारिक, प्रायिक. [बेसाधारण.
4 *public, relating to all* v. COMMON. सर्वांचा, सर्वसंबंधी, स-
GENERAL, *n. commander of an army.* सेनापति, सैन्याध्यक्ष, सैन्याधिपति, सेनाकर्त्ता, बखशी *or* षी *or* बक्षी.
2 See WHOLE.
In general. See GENERALLY.
GENERALISSIMO, *n.* मुख्यसेनापति *m.*
GENERALITY, GENERALNESS, *n.* v. A. 1. साधारण्य *n.* सामान्य*n.* साधारणत्व *n.* सामान्यता *f.* जातित्व *n.* जातिस्वभाव *m.*
2 साधारण्य *n.* साधारणत्व *n.* सामान्य *n.* साधारणभाव *m.* सामान्यभाव *m.* अविशेषत्व *n.*
3 रूढि *f.* प्रचार *m.* प्रायिकत्व *n.*
I. See MAIN, MAJORITY.
To GENERALIZE, *v. a.* साधारण्य *n.* आणणें, साधारण्य आणून करणें-वहिवाटणें, साधारण्यांत आणणें.
GENERALLY, *adv.* v. A. 2. साधारणरूपानें, सामान्यरूपानें, साधारणरीतीनें, सामान्येंकरून, सामान्यानः, उत्सर्गात, उत्सर्गतः, ण.

विशेषतः, सदर.

3 बहुतकरून, प्रायः, प्रायशः, सामान्यतः, बहुधा, बहुशः.

GENERALSHIP, *n. office of a general.* सेनापतित्व *n.* बख्शीगिरी *f.*

2 *military skill.* युद्धकौशल्य *n.* युद्धदाक्षिण्य *n.* रणपटुत्व *n.*

To GENERATE, *v. a.* v. To BEGET. उत्पन्न करणें, उत्पादणें, जनन *n.* -प्रजनन *n.* करणें.

GENERATION, *n.* v. V.—*act.* उत्पादणें *n.* जनन *n.* प्रजनन *n.*

Male or female organs of g. उपस्थ *m. n.* गुह्य *n.*

Male organ of g. शफ *n.* शिश्न *n. m.*

I. *a* g. *single succession.* पिढी *f.* पुस्त *m.* पुरुष *m.* डोई *f.*

From g. to g. पिढीदरपिढी, पुस्तदरपुस्त, पिढीपेस्तर.

GENERATIVE, *a. that has the power of propagation.* जननशक्तियुक्त, जननशक्तिविशिष्ट, जननशक्तिक.

GENERIC, GENERICAL, *a.* v. GENERAL. जातीचा, जातिसंबंधी, साधारण, सामान्य.

GENERICALLY, *adv.* v. A. सामान्यतः, जातीसंबंधीं, जातीविषयीं.

GENERICALNESS, *n.* v. A. जातित्व *n.* जातिस्वभाव *m.* साधारण *n.* साधारण्य *n.* सामान्य *n.*

GENEROSITY, GENEROUSNESS, *n.* v. A. 1. दातेपणा *m.* उदारपणा *m.* सढळपणा *m.* धौताली *f.* औदार्य *n.* उदारत्व *n.* दातृत्व *n.* दानशौर्य *n.* दानशूरता *f.* दानशीलता *f.* दानोत्साह *m.*

2 मनाचीथोरवी *f.*

GENEROUS, *a. liberal, bountiful.* उदार, दाता, धौताल, प्रदाता (esp. in comp. as धनप्रदाता, अन्नप्रदाता, विद्याप्रदाता), दानशूर, दानशील, त्यागशील, हातचा सुटा, हाताचा मोकळा, सढळ, उदारवृत्ति, उदारस्वभावाचा, औदार्यशाली, दातार, दायी, दानी (esp. in comp.), दातृत्वशाली, वदान्य, बहुप्रद.

Some terms for *a generous person*, are कर्ण *or* कर्णाचा अवतार, देवबा, दुपती धेनु, दानशूर, दानवीर, वीर, दानशौंड.

Person generous with the property of another. आईजीच्या दोंदावर बाईजी उदार असा.

2 v. MAGNANIMOUS. मनाचा थोर, महात्मा.

GENEROUSLY, *adv.* v. A. 1. सढळपणानें, औदार्यानें, औदार्यपूर्वक, मोकळ्या हातानें, &c.

2 उदारमनानें, मोठ्यामनानें.

GENIAL, *a. that agrees with one's constitution.* मानणारा, प्रकृतीस मानणारा, अनुकूल, अनुगुण, सात्म्याचा, प्रकृत्यनुगुण.

2 See MERRY.

GENITAL, *a. pertaining to generation.* जननविषयक, जननसंबंधी, प्रजननसंबंधी, प्रजोत्पादनसंबंधी.

GENITALS, *n. parts belonging to generation.* उपस्थ *m. n.* जननांग *n.* जननाव्यव *m.* घड *m.*

GENITIVE, *n.*—the case. संबंध कारक *n.* षष्ठी कारक *n.* षष्ठी *f.*

GENITURE, *n.* v. BIRTH. जन्म *m. n.*

Lord of the g.—in astrology. जन्मनक्षत्र *n.*

GENIUS, *n. protecting power, &c.* देवता *f.* (as ग्रामदेवता, स्थलदेवता, वनदेवता, &c.) दैवत *n.* माहात्म्य *n.* (as स्थानमाहात्म्य, ग्राममाहात्म्य, देशमाहात्म्य).

G. of a place. स्थलदेवता *f.* क्षेत्रपाल *m.*

G. of dwelling places. वास्तुदेवता *f.* वास्तुपुरुष *m.*

2 *mental power.* बुद्धिवैभव *n.* बुद्धिपाटव *n.* प्रज्ञा *f.* सुधी *f.* कल्पनाशक्ति *f.*

3 *disposition of mind.* बुद्धि *f.* बुद्धीची धांव *f.* मनाची ओढ *f.*

4 *a* genius. See CLEVER.

GENTEEL, *a. polite, of good manners, &c.*—persons. शिष्ट, सभ्य, चालीचा, शिष्टसंप्रदायी, सभ्यसंप्रदायी, शिष्टाचार, सभ्याचार, शिष्टाचारसंपन्न, सभ्याचारसंपन्न.

2—of manners, customs, &c. v. GENTLEMANLY. गृहस्थी, शिष्ट, सभ्य, शिष्टाचाराचा.

GENTEELNESS, *n.* v. A. 1. मनुष्यपणा *m.* माणुसकी *f.* गृहस्थपणा *m.* गृहस्थगिरी *f.* शिष्टाई *f.* शिष्टाइकी *f.* सभ्यता *f.* शिष्टता *f.*

GENTIAN, *n. g. cherayta.* किरात *pop.* किराईत *n.* किराईत कोडकी *f.* किराईत फुलकी *f.* चिराईत *n.*

Stick or dried g. काडेचिराईत *n.*

GENTILE, *a.* यहूदी नाहीं असा.

2—in grammar. जातिवाचक.

GENTILITY, *n. good extraction.* कुलीनता *f.* आभिजात्य *n.* वर्णश्रेष्ठता *f.* वर्णश्रैष्ठ्य *n.* कुलश्रैष्ठ्य *n.* सद्वंशता *f.* वंशविशुद्धि *f.*

2 See GENTEELNESS.

GENTLE, *a. well-born, of good birth.* पिढीजाद *or* जादा, कुलवंत, जातिवंत, असल, असील, जातीचा, कुलीन, कुलज, घरंदाज, वंशज, वंश्य, वंशविशुद्ध, सद्वंश, अभिजात, खांदानीचा, खाणीचा, वर्णश्रेष्ठ, सुवर्ण, सुजात, आर्य.

2 *meek, peaceable,* v. MILD. गरीब, धिमा *or* धिम्मा, संत *or* संथ, स्वभावाचा सौम्य-शांत-&c. सौम्य, सौम्यवृत्ति, शांत, नरम, मिसकीन, अक्रूर, बापडा, बापुडवाणा *or* णी.

3 *moderate, mild.* नरम, सौम्य, मृदु, कोमल.

G. measure. सामोपचार *m.*

4—a breeze, &c. हलका, मंद, संत *or* संथ.

GENTLE-FOLK, *n.* पांढरपेशा *m.* पांढरपेशाचे लोक *m. pl.* पांढरपेशेलोक *m. pl.* गृहस्थलोक *m. pl.* सभ्यलोक *m. pl.* कुलीनलोक *m. pl.*

GENTLE-MAN, *n.* गृहस्थ *m.* साहेब *m.* सज्जन *m.* सुजन *m.* सुमनुष्य *m.* सभ्यजन *m.* सभ्यपुरुष *m.*

GENTLE-MANLIKE. See GENTLEMANLY.

GENTLE-MANLINESS, *n.* v. A. 1. माणुसकी *f.* मनुष्यपणा *m.* गृहस्थगिरी *f.* गृहस्थपणा *m.* सुजनता *f.* सुजनत्व *n.* सौजन्य *n.* सभ्यवृत्ति *f.* सौजन्यवृत्ति *f.*

GENTLE-MANLY, *a. polite, courteous, &c.*—person. सभ्य, शिष्ट, चालीचा, सभ्यवृत्ति, शिष्टवृत्ति, सुजनवृत्ति, सौजन्यवृत्तीचा, सभ्याचार, सभ्याचारसंपन्न, शिष्टाचार, शिष्टाचारसंपन्न.

2 *becoming a gentleman; polite, &c.*—acts, customs, &c. गृहस्थी, गृहस्थगिरीचा, शिष्ट, सभ्य, सौजन्याचा, सभ्याचाराचा, शिष्टाचाराचा, गृहस्थास योग्य, गृहस्थोचित, गृहस्थाई, सभोचित.

GENTLE-WOMAN, *n. lady.* कुलीनस्त्री *f.* कुलस्त्री *f.* कुलवधू *f.* कुलांगना *f.*

GENTLENESS, *n.* v. A. 1. *and* GENTILITY. कुलीनता *f.* आभिजात्य *n.* वर्णश्रेष्ठता *f.*

2 गरीबी *f.* धिमाई *or* धिम्माई *f.* नरमाई *f* भलाइकी *f.* भलाई *f.* माधुर्य *n.* संथपणा *m.* शांति *f.* शांतस्वभाव *m.* शांतवृत्ति *f.* सौम्यवृत्ति *f.* सौम्यप्रकृति *f.* स्वभावमार्दव *n.*

3 नरमाई *f.* मंदी *f.* मृदुता *f.* कोमलता *f.* सौम्यता *f.* मांद्य *n.*

4 हलकेपणा *m.* मंदी *f.* मांद्य *n.* मंदता *f.*

GENTLY, *adv.* v. A. 2. धिमेपणानें, संतपणानें, नरमाईनें, &c. सौम्यरीतीनें, सौम्यवृत्तीनें, शांतवृत्तीनें.

I. *softly, without force or violence.* हलक्यानें, हळू, धिरे, धिरेधिरे, धिराधिरे, हळूच, हळूकण, हळूकर, हळूदिशी, थंडेंथंडें.

GENTRY. See GENTLE-FOLK.

GENTU, See HINDU.

GENUFLECTION. See KNEELING.

GENUINE, *a. not counterfeit, not spurious, real.* खरा, असल, असील, थेट, सत्य, अकपट, अकृत्रिम, चोख, बियांचा, खाणीचा, हाडखरा. हाडाचा खरा *or* चांगला, खऱ्या हाडाचा, खरारोकडा.

GENUINENESS, *n.* v. A. खराइ *f.* खरेपणा *m.* असलपणा *m.* असलाइ *f.* चोखपणा *m.* थेटपणा *m.*

GENUS, *n. class.* जाति *f.* जात *f.* जातिपक्ष *m.* गण *m.* वर्ग *m.*

GEOGRAPHER, *n.* v. N. भूगोलविद्यावेत्ता, भूगोलविद्याकवि.

GEOGRAPHICAL, *a.* v. N. भूगोलविद्येचा, भूगोलविद्यासंबंधी, भूगोलविद्याविषयक.

GEOGRAPHY, *n.* भूगोलविद्या *f.* भूगोलवर्णन *n.*

GEOLOGICAL, *a.* v. N. भूरचनाशास्त्र संबंधी-विषयक, &c.

GEOLOGIST, *n.* भूरचनाशास्त्रवेत्ता, क्षितिरचनावेत्ता.

GEOLOGY, *n. science of the structure of the earth.* भूरचनाशास्त्र *n.* क्षितिरचनाशास्त्र *n.* भूफवचशास्त्र *n.* भूगर्भशास्त्र *n.*

GEOMANCER, *n.* v. N. रमलपाहणारा, रमली.

GEOMANCY, *n. divination by figures, &c.* रमल *m.*

GEOMETER, GEOMETRICIAN, *n.* v. N. रेखागणिती, रेखागणित्या, रेखागणक.

GEOMETRICAL, *a.* v. N. रेखागणिताचा, क्षेत्रतत्वविद्येचा, क्षेत्रतत्वविद्यासंबंधी.

GEOMETRY, *n. science of the mensuration of lines, surfaces, &c.* रेखागणित *n.* रेखाकोणगोलादिविद्या *f.* क्षेत्रतत्वविद्या *f.*

2 *mensuration of the earth.* ज्यामिति *f.* भूमिति *f.* भूमापन *n.* क्षेत्रमापन *n.*

GERANIUM, *n.* एक फूल झाड आहे.

GERM, *n. sprout.* अंकुर *m.* कोम*m.* मोड *m.* कोरक *m.*

2 fig. बीज *n.* मूळ *n.*

GERMAN, *n. first cousin.* भाऊ *m.* (बहीण *f.*) बंधु *m.* बंधुजन *m.* बांधव *m.*

To GERMINATE, *v. n.* v. To SPROUT. अंकुरणें, फुटणें, मोड *m.*-&c. येणें, मोडावणें. [उद्भिज्ज.

GERMINATED, *p.* v. V. अंकुरलेला, &c. मोड आलेला, अंकुरित,

GERMINATION, *n.* v. V.—*act.* अंकुरणें *n.* फुटणें *n.* &c. मोड *m.* अंकुर *m.*

GESTATION, *n. pregnancy.* गर्भाचें वाहणें *n.* गर्भधारण *n.* गर्भवहन *n.* गर्भारपणा *m.* गाभणपणा *m.* (of beasts).

To GESTICULATE, *v. n. make gestures.* हावभाव *m. pl.*- अंगविक्षेप *m.*-अभिनय *m.*-&c. करणें, भाव *m.pl.* दाखवणें.

GESTICULATION, *n.* v. V.—*act.* हावभाव करणें *n.* &c. अंगविक्षेप *m.* अंगहार *m.* आंगिकचेष्टा *f.* अभिनय *m.* अभिनीति *f.*

GESTICULATORY, *a. representing in gestures.* अंगविक्षेपाचा, आंगिक.

GESTURE, *n. movement of the body or limbs.* हावभाव *m. pl.* इंगित *n.* अंगविक्षेप *m.* अंगभंग *m.* अदा *or* आदा *m.* सूची *f.*

Manual gestures. हातवारे *m.pl.*

To GET, *v. a. procure, obtain, gain.* मिळवणें *or* मेळवणें, संपादणें, जोडणें, घेणें, पावणें, मिळणें, लाभणें, लाधणें, लाहणें, गावणें (*these five with in. con.*), हस्तगत-प्राप्त करणें *or* होणें *in. con.* संपादणी *f.*-संपादणूक *f.*-&c. करणें *g. of o.*

To get a beating. मार *m.*-&c. खाणें, तोंडांत खाणें.

2 *gain as profit, earn, acquire,* v. To GAIN. मिळवणें, कमावणें, अर्जणें, अर्जन *n.*-उपार्जन *n.*-&c. करणें *g. of o.*

3 *prevail on,* v. To INDUCE. वळवणें, मन *n.* मनावणें.

4 See To BEGET. 5 See To HAVE.

To GET, *v. n. arrive at,* v. To REACH. पावणें, पोहोंचणें.

2 v. To BECOME. होणें.

3 off, v. To ESCAPE. सुटणें, निस्तरण *n.* *or* निस्तार *m.* होणें *g. of s.*

4 on; *proceed smoothly.* चालणें, सरणें.

5 out; v. To GO, To SET OUT. निघणें, चालणें.

Get out with thee! जाय गड्या, हत्त्.

6 over, through; *pass through well.* निभणें, निभावणें, उतरणें, तरणें, पार पडणें, बहिवाटणें, तरणूक *f.*-निभाव *m.*-&c.-होणें *g. of s.*

7 up, from bed; v. To RISE. निजून उठणें, उठणें.

GETTER, *n.* v. V. A. 1. मिळवणारा, संपादणारा, &c. संपादक, संपादन कर्त्ता.

2 मिळवणारा, कमावणारा,&c. अर्जक, अर्जनकर्त्ता, &c.

GETTING, *n.* v. V. A. 1.—*act.* मिळवणें *n.*&c. संपादणी *f.* संपादणूक *f.* संपादन *n.* लाहो *m.* आसादन *n.*

2 मिळवणें *n.* उपार्जन *n.* उपार्जना *f.* अर्जन *n.* अर्जना *f.*

I. See GAINS.

GEWGAW. See TOY, BAWBLE.

GHASTLINESS, *n.* v. A. मडेकळा *f.* प्रेतकळा *f.* प्रेतछाया *f.*

GHASTLY, *a. death-like.* मुरद्या सारखा, प्रेतकळेचा, मडेकळेचा, प्रेतछायेचा, मुतासारखा, प्रेतवत्, मृतवत्.

GHOST, *n.* See SPIRIT. 2 *disembodied spirit,* v. DEVIL. भूत*n.* पिशाच *m.n.* पिसाट *n.*—of a *Bráhman.* ब्रह्मराक्षस *m.* ब्रह्मपिशाच*m.n.* ब्रह्मग्रह *m.* ब्रह्मपुरुष*m.* ब्रह्मसंबंध*m.* महापुरुष *m.* संबंध*or*समंध*m.* मुंज्या*m.*—of a *Muhamadan.* खवीस*m.* झोटिंग*m.* जिंद *m.*—of a *Shudra.* डांब *f.* तळखांबा*m.*—of a widow. हेडली *f.* लांव *f.* लांवसट *f.*—one of an extinct family. निर्वंशीकलम *n.*—of a female dying violently. जखीण *f.* हडळ *or* हडळी *f.*

To give up the g. v. To DIE. प्राणत्याग *m.*-प्राणोत्सर्ग*m.*-प्राणविसर्जन *n.*-&c. करणें, प्राण *m.*-भाव *m.* सोडणें.

To see or fall in with a g. भुलीचें झाड*n.* भेटणें *in. con.*

GHOSTLY, *a. spiritual.* परमार्थाचा, पारमार्थिक, परमार्थसंबंधी, परमार्थविषयक.

2 *relating to ghosts.* भूतसंबंधी-विषयक, पिशाचसंबंधी-विषयक.

GIANT, *n.*—in mythology. दैत्य *m.* दानव *m.* असुर *m.*

2 *man of great stature,* v. HULK. दिग्गज पुरुष *m.* धिप्पाड माणूस *m.* बृहत्काय-बृहच्छरीर-&c. मनुष्य *m.* महाकाय.

GIANTESS, *n.* धिप्पाड बायको *f.*

GIANT-LIKE. See GIGANTIC.

GIBBERISH, *n. unintelligible language.* पिशाच भाषा *f.* रांगडी-हेंगाडी-कोंगाडी-कानडी-&c. बोली *f.*-भाषा *f.* रांगडी घिसघीस *f.* गुडुबुडू *n.* कुडबूड *n.*

GIBBERISH, *a.* रांगडा, हेंगाडा.

GIBBET. See GALLOWS.

To GIBBET, See To HANG.

GIBBOSITY, GIBBOUSNESS, *n.* v. A. उंचवटेपणा*m.* फुगोटेपणा*m.*

2 पोंगेपणा*m.* पोंकेपणा*m.* कुबडेपणा*m.*

I *a* g. पोंग*n*.

GIBBOUS, *a. protuberant, swelling*. उंचवट्याचा, फुगीर, फुगींव, फुगाऱ्याचा, फुगोट्याचा, खंडमंडल.

2 *hump-backed*. पोंग्या *or* पोंगा, पोंक्या *or* पोंका, कुबडा.

GIBE, &c. See SNEER, &c.

GIDDINESS, *n.* v. A. 1. घेरी *f.* गिरकी *f.* भोवंड *f.* भोवळ *f.* झीट *f.* तिरमी *f.* तिरमिरी *f.* तव *f.* तवर *f.* घायतळ *f.* घायकूतन. चक्कर *n.* आंधेरी *f.*

Fit of g. भिरकंडा *or* भिरकांडा *m.* भिरकंडी *or* कांडी *f.* भिरकांडें *n.* भिरकें *n.* भिरभिरी *f.* भिररी *f.*

3 छिछोरी *or* चिचोरी *f.* अविचारीपणा *m.* चांचल्य *n.* चंचलता *f.* चापल्य *n.* चपलता *f.* अविचारिता *f.*

GIDDY, *a. vertiginous*. घेरी-भोंवळ-&c. आलेला.

To be or become g. कपाळ *n.*-डोसकें *n.*-&c. फिरणें-भोवणें *g. of s.* तिरमिरणें, मिरणें.

2 *causing giddiness*,—a height, &c. भोवंड.-&c. येण्याजोगा, भोवंड-&c. आणण्याजोगा.

3 *volatile, airy*, v. THOUGHTLESS, LIGHT. अविचारी, अविवेकी, हीनविचार, विचारमूढ, न्यूनविचार, छिछोर *or* चिचोर, चंचल, चपल, बुद्धीचा चंचळ, बावगा, अविमृश्यकारी, अविचार्यकारी, सहसाकारी.

GIDDY-BRAINED, GIDDY-HEADED. See GIDDY 3.

GIFT, *n.* v. GIVING. देणें *n.* दान *n.*

2 *thing given*. दान *n.* देणगी *f.* देणें *n.* दत्त *n.* बक्षीस *or* बक्षीस *n.* इनाम *n.* दत्ति *f.*

Bad (unlawful to receive) g. कुदान *n.*

G. from a saint, idol, &c. प्रसाद *m.* वर *m.*

G. in return for a g. प्रतिदान *n.*

Humble g. तुलसीपत्र *n.*

Resumer of a g. दत्तापहारक, दत्तापहारी.

Resumption of a g. दत्तापहार *m.* दत्ताप्रदान *n.* [क्षता *f.*

3 *right of giving*. देण्याचा अधिकार *m.* दानाधिकार *m.* दानाध्य-

4 *faculty, talent, endowment*. गुण *m.* कला *f.* करामत *f.*

GIFTED, *a. talented, endowed, of parts and attainments*, v. CLEVER. गुणवान्, गुणवंत, गुणी, गुणकर, गुणाढ्य, बहुगुणी, गुणिजन, सुलक्षणी, सुलक्षणिक, सुलक्षण, प्रयुक्त (in comp.). Some terms for a person full of gifts and graces are गुणग्राम, गुणनिधि, गुणपात्र, गुणनिधान, गुणराशि, गुणाकर, गुणसागर, गुणाचीरास, गुणाचीखाण.

GIG, *n. buggy*. बगी *f.* is commonly used.

2 See WHIRLIGIG. 3 *small swift boat of a ship*. जहाजाची जलद चालणारी होडी *f.*

GIGANTEAN, GIGANTIC, *a. very large*,—of persons, v. LARGE. बृहत्काय, बृहच्छरीर, बृहदंग, स्थूलांग, स्थूलकाय, स्थूलशरीर, महाकाय.

2—of things. अवाढव्य, अफाट, पर्वतवत्, भीमविग्रह.

To GIGGLE, *v. n. laugh idly, titter*. खिदखिदणें, हिहिहि *adv.*-हिहि-खिदखिद *or* दां-&c. हांसणें, हिहि *adv.*-&c. करणें, खसखस *f.* पिकणें *g. of s.*

GIGGLER, *n.* GIGGLING, *p. a.* v. V. खिदखिद्या, खिदखिदहस्या, खिदखिद हांसणारा, &c.

GIGGLINGLY, *adv.* v. V. हिहिहि, हिहि, फदफद *or* दां *or* फिदफिद *or* दां, खिदखिद, खिखि, खिसखिस, खोखो.

GIGLOT, *n.* v. WANTON. नाचणघुगरी *f.* नाचरी *f.*

To GILD, *v. a. overlay with gold*. मुलामा *m.* करणें-चढवणें-देणें, सोनें *n.* चढवणें-ढाळणें, सोन्याचें पाणी *n.*-सोन्याचा ढाळ *m.*-सोन्याचा लेप *m.*-सोन्याचा धूर *m.*-सोन्याची ओप *f.* देणें.

2 *make bright, illumine*. तेजस्वी-प्रकाशित-&c. करणें, द्योतन *n.* करणें *g. of s.*

GILDED, GILT, *p.* v.V. 1. मुलामा केलेला, &c. मुलामी, मुलाम्याचा, मुलामा दिल्हेला, सोन्याचा ढाळ दिल्हेला, &c.

GILDER, *n.* v.V. 1. मुलामा चढवणारा-देणारा-&c.

GILDING, *n.* v. V. 1.—*act*. मुलामा देणें *n.* &c.

I *a g. gold laid on*. सोनेरीलेप *m.* सोन्याचाधूर *m.* सोन्याचें पाणी *n.* सोन्याची ओप *f.* मुलामा *m.* पाणी *n.*

GILL, *n.*—of a fish. कल्ला *m.* मत्स्याचें श्वासेंद्रिय *n.*

2—of a fowl. गळचुंडी *f.*

3—the measure. एक लहान केली माप आहे.

GIM, GIMMY. See SPRUCE, SMART.

GIMCRACK, *n. toy, pretty piece of mechanism*. जुगूत *f.* टूम *f.* बूट *m.* कुलंगडें *n.* कळ *f.*

GIMLET, *n.* सामता *m.* बरमा *m.* टोपण *n.* चौरशी *f.* वेधन *n.*

GIN, *n. trap*. सांपळा *m.* पाश *pop.* फास *m.*

2 *engine*. यंत्र *n.* ओझीं उचलण्याचें यंत्र *n.*

3 cotton gin. कापसाच्या सरक्या काढण्याचें यंत्र *n.*

4 एके प्रकारचें मद्य आहे.

To GIN, *v. a.* यंत्रानें सरक्या *f. pl.* काढणें.

GINGER, *n.*—the plant or green root. सुंठ *f.* शुंठी *f.* अलें *n.* आर्द्रक *n.* सर्वशाक *f.*—the dry root. सुंठ *f.* शुंठी *f.*

Decoction of g. G.-water. सुंठवणी *n.*

Mango-smelling g. आंबेहळद *f.*

Preserved g. अलेपाक *m.*

GINGER-BREAD, *n.* सुंठवड्याची वडी *f.*

GINGERLY, *adv. cautiously*. जपून, संभाळून, युक्तीनें.

GINGLE, &c. See JINGLE, &c.

GINJALL, *n. a kind of gun*. जेजाल *f.*

GIRAFFE, *n.* एक जनावर आहे.

To GIRD, *v. a. bind round*. वेटाळणें, गुंडाळणें, वेष्टणें, लपेटणें, बांधणें, *or* गुंडाळून-वेष्टून-&c. बांधणें, भिडणें, भिडविणें.

2 (a cart, plough, &c.). वेठणें, वेठण *n.* गुंडाळणें.

3 See To SURROUND.

GIRDER, *n.*—in architecture. तुळई *f.*

GIRDLE, *n. band for the waist*. कमरबंद *m.* कमरपट्टा *m.* पट्टा *m.* पटका *m.* माजपट्टा *m.* कांची *f.* मेखला *pop.* मेखळा *f.* कटिबंध *pop.* कटिबंद *m.* कटिबंधन *n.* कटिसूत्र *n.* कटिवेष्टन *n.* करगोटा *m.* करदोरा *or* करधोटा *m.* दाब *m. f.* दाभ *f.* [girdles.

N. B. Some of these words express different kinds of

2 See ENCLOSURE. 3 See ZODIAC.

4 *plate for baking*. तवा *m.*—for *polis*. पोळतवा *m.*

Earthen g. drilled. रान्हें *n.*

To GIRDLE, *v. a.* कमरपट्टा *m.*-&c. बांधणें.

2 See To SURROUND.

GIRDLE-STEAD, *n.* कडोसरी *or* कडोसो *f.* कणबट *f.*

GIRL, *n.* मूल *dim.* मुलगी *f.* पोर *dim.* पोरगी *f.* पोंगडी *f.* कन्या *f.* कन्यका *f.* कुमारी *f.* कुंवार *f.* चेड *n.* चेडू *n.* बरदा *f.* धीदा *f.*

GIRLHOOD, *n.* मुलीची-&c. अवस्था *f.* कुंवारपण *n.* कौमार्य *n.*

GIRLISH, *a.* पोरीचा, मुलीचा, मुलीसारखा, कन्यावत्.

GIRTH, *n. compass*, v. CIRCUMFERENCE. घेरा *m.* घेर *m.* फेरा *m.* फेर *m.* वेढ *m.*

G. of the body. आडगात *n.*

2 (of a saddle). तंग *m.*

That has his girths tightened (ready to be mounted)—a horse. तंगबार.

Narrow g. तंगी *f.*

GIST, *n. main point.* मुख्यगोष्ट *f.* मुख्यविषय *m.*

To GIVE, *v. a. bestow, confer.* देणें, दान *n.*-&c. करणें *g. of o.* निवेदणें, अर्पणें, समर्पणें, बहाल करणें, प्रतिपादणें, अर्पण *n.*-समर्पण*n.*-&c. करणें *g. of o.* अर्पित-&c. करणें, प्रापण *n.*-उपधान*n.*-&c. करणें, पदरीं घालणें.

2 away. देणें, देऊन टाकणें-सोडणें, स्वत्वनिवृत्ति *f.* करणें *g. of o.* सत्तेबाहेर-हाताबाहेर-&c. करणें-घालवणें.

3 back; v. To RETURN. परत देणें-करणें, वळता देणें, पाठीमागें देणें, परतणें.

4 (it to soundly); v. To SCOLD. भला घेणें, कचकावणें.

5 (one's self out for). म्हणविणें.

6 (one's self up to); v. To ADDICT. छंदास लागणें, भरणें, नादीं भरणें-लागणें, भरीं भरणें.

7 up; *resign, renounce.* सोडणें, सोडून देणें, वर्जणें, विसर्जणें, टाकणें, टाकून देणें, वाहणें, नांव *n.* सोडणें *g. of o.* पाणी *n.*-उदक *n.* सोडणें-देणें *with* ला *or* स *of o.* सांडणें, तिलांजलि *m. f.* देणें, हात *m. pl.* झाडणें *with* विषयीं-&c. *of o.* शपथ *f.* वाहणें *g. of o.* त्याग *m.*-वर्जन *n.*-विसर्जन*n.*-विसर्ग *m.*-उत्सर्ग *m.*-उत्सर्जन*n.*-&c. करणें *g. of o.*

8 ear to; v. To ATTEND. ऐकणें, कान *m.*-लक्ष्य *n.*-&c. देणें.

9 forth; out, v. To PUBLISH. जाहीर-प्रसिद्ध-&c. करणें.

To g. place to; *make room for.* जागा *f.* घेणें, ओसर *m.* घेणें-देणें.

To g. chase to, v. To PURSUE. पाठीस लागणें.

To give over to. सोंपणें, हवालीं करणें.

To GIVE, *v. n. yield, give way.* कचणें, कचकणें, कचकरणें, कचरणें, दबणें, दबकणें, डगणें, डगागणें, घसरणें, सरकणें, सरणें, सरसावणें, बसणें, नमणें, लपणें, लब खाणें, भागणें, सचणें, सचळणें, मोडावणें, जाणें, दणावणें, चेपणें.

2—a wall, &c. *yield and incline.* रेलणें.

3 in; See To SUBMIT.

4 over; See To CEASE, To STOP.

GIVEN, *p.* v. V. A. 1. दिल्हेला, &c. दत्त, निवेदित, प्रतिपादित, अर्पित, समर्पित.

G. and resumed. दत्तापहृत.

G. and taken. दत्तादत्त.

6 लंपट, लागट, लाहडी, लबूद.

7 वर्जित, विसर्जित, उत्सर्जित, उत्सृष्ट, विसृष्ट.

GIVER, *n.v.* V. A. 1. देणारा, दान कर्त्ता, दाता, प्रदाता.

To express the sense of *giver* in some of its numerous shades (*conferer, bestower, imparter, afforder, presenter, &c.*), compounds may be freely formed with द, प्रद, दाता, प्रदाता, दानी, दायक & दायी, उपधायक, प्रापक, आवह, (as सुखद, दुःखद, फलद, [illegible], अन्नदाता, विद्यादाता, द्रव्यप्रदाता, वस्त्रप्रदाता, मोक्षदानी, कैवल्यदानी, [illegible], सौख्यदायी, शत्रुपधायक, हर्षोपधायक, हितप्रापक, अहितप्रापक, सुखावह, दुःखावह, &c. &c.).

GIVING, *n.* v. V. A. 1.—*act.* देणें *n.* &c. दान *n.* प्रदान *n.* उपधान *n.* निवेदन *n.* प्रतिपादन *n.* विसर्ग *m.* वितरण *n.*

To express the sense of this word in some of its numerous shades (*conferring, bestowing, imparting, communicating, affording, presenting, &c.*), compound formations may be made *ad libitum* with दान *n.* प्रदान *n.* उपधान *n.* प्रापण*n.* अर्पण *n.* समर्पण*n.*(as सुखदान, दुःखदान, अन्नप्रदान, वस्त्रप्रदान, फलोपधान, गुणोपधान, हितोपधान, कल्याणोपधान, धनोपधान, लाभोपधान, ज्ञानोपधान, विनयोपधान, इष्टप्रापण, अनिष्टप्रापण), &c. &c.

7 सोडणें *n.* वर्जणें *n.* &c. वर्जन *n.* विसर्जन *n.* उत्सर्जन *n.* उत्सर्ग *m.* (esp. in comp. as वृक्षोत्सर्ग, कूपोत्सर्ग, गृहोत्सर्ग, मूलोत्सर्ग, लोभोत्सर्ग, अभिमानोत्सर्ग, अधिकारोत्सर्ग), त्याग *m.* (esp. in comp.).

GIZZARD, *n.* पाखराचा कोठा *m.*

GLACIAL, *a. icy.* बर्फाचा, हिम्य, हैम.

GLACIER, *n.* बर्फाचें माळरान *n.*

GLACIS, *n.* किल्ल्याबाहेरची उतरती जमीन *f.* रेवण *f.* रेवणी *f.*

GLAD, *a. expressing or giving joy*, v. JOYFUL. आनंदाचा, हर्षाचा, आनंदप्रद, आनंदकारक-&c. सानंद, आनंदयुक्त, हर्षयुक्त.

2 *rejoiced*, v. PLEASED, JOYFUL. खुश, आनंदित, हर्षित, सानंद.

To be or feel g. आनंद *m.*-हर्ष *m.* वाटणें *in. con.* आनंदणें.

To GLAD, *To* GLADDEN, *v. a.* v. To REJOICE. आनंद *m.*-संतोष *m.*-&c. देणें-करणें, संतुष्ट-हर्षयुक्त-खुश-&c. करणें, हर्षविणें, संतोषविणें, आनंदविणें, आल्हादणें, हर्षण *n.*-&c. करणें *g. of o.*

GLADE, *n. opening in a wood.* अरण्यांतली-राईंतली-झाडींतली-&c. बखळ *f.*

GLADIATOR, *n.* तरवारीनें खेळ करणारा *m.*

GLADLY, *adv.* v. A. आनंदानें, संतोषानें, संतोषेंकरून, आनंदेंकरून, आनंदेशीं, आनंदाशीं, प्रसन्न अंतःकरणेंकरून.

GLADNESS, *n.* v. A. *and* JOY. आनंद *m.* हर्ष *m.* संतोष *m.* खुशी *f.* सानंदता *f.*

GLADSOME. See JOYFUL.

GLAIR, *n. white of an egg.* पांढरा बील *m.* अंड्यांतली सफेदी *f.*

To GLANCE, *v. n. shoot or dart a ray.* चमकणें, चमक *f.* मारणें.

2 *fly off obliquely.* ओझरता *adv.*-झांजरता *adv.*-कातरता-*adv.*-कसरता *adv.* जाणें-पडणें-&c.

3 *play the eye.* कान्या डोळ्यानें पाहणें, दृष्टिविक्षेप *m.*-नेत्रविक्षेप *m.*-&c. करणें, कटाक्षावेक्षण *n.* करणें.

4 at; *take a transient view of.* डोळा *m.* घालणें, डोळ्याखालीं-घालणें, ओझरता पाहणें.

GLANCE, *n.* (of light) चमक *f.* v. मार.

2 (of the eye). दृष्टिविक्षेप *m.* नेत्रविक्षेप *m.* नेत्रकटाक्ष *m.* कटाक्ष *m.*

Amorous glances. गमजे *m. pl.*

3 *glimpse, transient view.* देखवा *m.* ईषद्दर्शन *n.* झुळूक *f.* धोप *f.* ओशेटा *m.*

GLANCINGLY, *adv.* v. V. 1. ओझरता, झांजरता, कातरता, कसरता.

GLAND, *n.*—in anatomy. मांसपिंड *m.* पिंड *m.* मांसग्रंथि *m.*

GLANDERS, *n.*—the disease. शेंब *or* शेम *f.* शेंबा *m.*

GLANDULAR, GLANDULOUS, *a.* v. N. मांसग्रंथिविशिष्ट, मांसग्रंथिमय.

To GLARE, *v. n. shine dazzlingly or oppressively.* चकाकणें, झकाकणें *or* झगागणें, झळकणें, झळझळणें, झळाळणें, लकाकणें, तकाकणें.

2 *look fiercely, &c.* टौंकारणें *or* टौंकारून पाहणें, गुरकावून पाहणें, डोळे *m. pl.* फाडणें-गुरकावणें-पिंजारणें-बटारणें-फिदारणें-वढवणें-तरारणें-वासणें-टौंकारणें, चांदण्या *f. pl.* तरारणें, फडी *f.* फिंदारणें.

GLARE, GLARING, *n.* v. V. 1. *and* BRIGHTNESS, BRILLIANCY. चकाकी *f.* झकझकाट *m.* झकाकी *f.* झगागी *f.* झळाळ *m.* झळाळी *f.* झळझळाट *m.* अही *f.* अहळी *f.* अतितेज *n.* अतिप्रकाश *m.*

2 गुरकी *or* गुरकाई *f.* गुरगुरीत दृष्टि *f.* क्रोधदृष्टि *f.*

GLARER, *n.* GLARING, *p. a.* v. V. 1. झळक फळक, झडकफडक, झळझळीत, जरकबरक, जाज्वल्यमान, जाज्वल्य, देदीप्यमान, अतिदीप्त, अतिदीप्यमान.

2 टौंकारणारा, गुरकावणारा, &c. गुरगुरीत.

I. *notorious, strikingly evident,* v. CLEAR. धडधडीत, उघड, जागरूक, उद्दाम, ढळढळीत, टळटळीत, झळझळीत.

GLARINGLY, *adv.* v. A. 1. धडधडीत, उघड, ढळढळीत.

GLASS, *n.* काच *m. pop.* कांच *f.*

Pane, sheet, or piece of g. भिंग *n.* ताव *m.* तावदान *n.*

2 *a g. a g.-vessel.* कांचेचा पेला *m.* काचपात्र *n.* काचकुपी *f.* काचघटी *f.* गलास *n.* from the English is now common.

Musical g. जलतरंग *m.*

3 *looking glass.* आरसा *m. dim.* आरसी *f.* दर्पण *n.* आदर्श *m.*

GLASS, GLASSY, *a. made of g., like g.* कांचेचा, काचमय, काचरूप, काचनिर्मित, काचवत्, काचसदृश.

G. door or window. तावदान *n.*

GLAUCOMA, *n.* टीक *f.* ? कांचबिंदु *m.* ?.

To GLAZE, *v. a. furnish with glass.* कांच *f.* जडवणें-बसवणें-लावणें, तावदानें *n. pl.* बसवणें-&c.

2 (pots, &c.). लाखटणें, लाखलोटा करणें, लाख *f.*-रोगण *n.* देणें-लावणें.

Material for glazing. लाखवण *n.*

3 *give a smooth surface to.* झिलई *f.*-सफई *f.*-&c. देणें.

GLAZIER, *n.* v. V. 1. कांच बसवणारा, तावदानवाला, कांचवाला.

G's putty. चिकी *f.*

To GLEAM, *v. n.* v. To SHINE. चकचकणें, चकमकणें, चमकणें, झकझकणें, झगमगणें, लकलकणें, चकचक *adv.*-लकलक *adv.* करणें, —intens. चकाकणें, झकाकणें *or* झगागणें लकाकणें.

GLEAM, GLEAMING, *n.* v. V. चमक *f.* लक्क *n.* चक्क *n.* झगमग *f.* झगमगी *f.* झळझळ *f.*—intens. चकाकी *f.* झकाकी *or* झगागी *f.* झकझकाट *m.* झळाळ *m.* झळझळाट *m.*

With a sudden g. चक्क-कन-कर-&c. झक-कर-कन-&c.

GLEAMINGLY, *adv.* v. V. चकचक, लकलक, झक-कन-कर-&c.

To GLEAN, *v. a.* (stalks and ears of corn). सरवा *m.* वेंचणें, दाणे *m. pl.* टिपणें-वेंचणें, उंछ *n.*-उंछन *n.* करणें.

2 fig. *gather by little here and there.* वेंचून वेंचून घेणें, टिपून टिपून घेणें-काढणें-जमविणें.

GLEANER. *n.* v. V. 1. सरवा वेंचणारा, दाणे टिपून घेणारा, &c. उंछवृत्ति, उंछशील.

GLEANING, *n.* v. V. 1. वेंचणें *n.* टिपणें *n.* टिपून घेणें *n.* &c. उंछन. उंछन *n.* शिलोंच्छवृत्ति *f.*

I. *matter gleaned.* सरवा *m.* निसरवा *m.*

Subsistence upon g. उंच्छवृत्ति *f.*

GLEBE, *n.* v. SOIL. काळी *f.* जमीन *f.*

2 *land belonging to a living.* उपाध्यायाच्या वृत्तीची जमीन *f.*

GLEE, *n.* v. JOY. आनंद *m.* हर्ष *m.* उल्हास *m.* खुशी *f.*

GLEEFUL, GLEESOME, *a.* v. JOYFUL. हर्षित, हर्षयुक्त.

GLEET, *n.* परमा *m.* परमें *n.* गळ *f.* होळणी *f.* स्रवण *n.* स्रव *m.* स्राव *m.*

G. in the form of threads. सूतपरमें *n.*

GLEN, *n. hollow between hills.* खोरा *m.* खोरें *n.* आड *f.* दरा *m.*

GLIB, *a. smooth, flowing.* गुळगुळीत, सुळसुळीत, निसरडा.

2 *flippant, voluble.* तोंडाचा-जिभेचा चपळ, पातळजिभेचा, पातळजिभ्या, लुबलूब-चुरचूर--&c. बोलणारा, चपल, वाक्चपल, चपलवाक्, चपलजिह्व.

To GLIB, *v. a.* See To CASTRATE.

2 *make smooth.* गुळगुळीत-सुळसुळीत-&c. करणें.

GLIBLY, *adv.* v. A. 1. सुळ-कन-कर-&c. सुळसूळ.

2 चुरचूर, चुणचूण, तुरतूर, सुळसूळ, सुरळीत.

GLIBNESS, *n.* v. A. 1. गुळगुळीतपणा *m.* सुळसुळीतपणा *m.* निसरडेपणा *m.*

2 जिभेचाचपळपणा *m.* सुरळीतपणा *m.* गौल्यता *f.* वाक्चापल्य *n.*

To GLIDE, *v. n. flow gently.* वाहणें, सरणें, संथ *or* संत वाहणें-चालणें, संसर्प *m.* करणें.

2 *move smoothly along.* सुळकणें, सरपटणें, सरकटणें, सरणें, सरपट्या-सरपटत-सरकत-सुळकण-&c. जाणें-चालणें.

GLIM. See LIGHT.

To GLIMMER, *v. n. give a faint, &c. light.* मिणमिणणें, झुगझुगणें, टिकटिकणें, टुकटुकणें, टिकटीक-मिणमीण-&c. जळणें-करणें-तेवणें.

GLIMMER, GLIMMERING, *n.* v. V. टिकटीक उजेड *m.* मिणमिणीत उजेड *m.* अंधकप्रकाश *m.* मंदप्रकाश *m.* ईषत्प्रकाश *m.*

I. *indistinct view.* झुळूक *f.* छाया *f.* ईषद्दर्शन *n.*

GLIMMERING, *p. a.* v. V. टिकटीक जळणारा-करणारा, &c. मिणमिणा *or* ण्या, मिणमिणीत.

GLIMMERINGLY, *adv.* मिणमीण, चांचपड चांचपड, अंधक, टिकटीक.

GLIMPSE, *n. faint light.* टिकटीक उजेड *m.* मिणमिणीत उजेड *m.* अंधकप्रकाश *m.*

2 *transitory view.* झुळूक *f.* ईषद्दर्शन *n.* दृष्टिभेट *f.* डोळेभेट *f.*

To afford a g. of. देखवा *m.* दाखवणें, निसुरता दाखविणें.

To catch a g. of. ओझरता *adv.* पाहणें, निसुरता पाहणें-देखणें and with *in. con.* दिसणें.

To GLISTEN, *To* GLISTER, *v. n.* v. To GLITTER. लुसलुसणें, टवटवणें, तकतकणें, चकचकणें, चकमकणें.

GLISTENING, GLISTERING, *p. a.* v. V. लुसलुसणारा, चकचकणारा, &c. लुसलुसीत, चकचकीत, तकतकीत, पांढुरका.

To GLITTER, *v. n. sparkle with light.* चकचकणें, लकलकणें, लुकलुकणें *or* लिकलिकणें, लखलखणें, चकमकणें, चमकणें, तकतकणें, झकझकणें, झगमगणें, झळकणें, झळझळणें, झळक *f.*-भडक *f.* मारणें, तकतक *adv.*-लकलक *adv.* करणें *or* होणें, स्फुरणें.—intens. *to glare.* चकाकणें, लकाकणें, तकाकणें, झकाकणें *or* झगागणें.

GLITTER, GLITTERING, *n.* v. V. *and* BRILLIANCY, BRIGHTNESS. लकलकी *f.* लुकलुकी *f.* लखलख *f.* झगझगी *f.* झगमगी *f.* तकतकी *f.* चमक *f.* झळक *f.* झळझळ *f.* स्फुरण *n.* जिलहई *f.* कांत *f.* चाकचक्य *n.* औज्ज्वल्य *n.*—intens. *glare.* झकाकी *f.* झगागी *f.* तकाकी *f.* लकाकी *f.* झकझकाट *m.* लकलकाट *m.* झगझगाट *m.* चकचकाट *m.* झळझळाट *m.*

GLITTERER, *n.* GLITTERING, *p. a.* v. V. *and* BRILLIANT. ल-

कलकीत, लिकलिकीत, लक, झकझकीत, तकतकीत, झळझळीत, झळकफळक, उजळ, उजळपाजळ, जरकबरक.

GLITTERINGLY, *adv.* चकचक, झकझक, झगझग, लकलक.

To GLOAT. See To GAZE.

GLOBATE, GLOBATED. See GLOBULAR. [तुंल *n.*

GLOBE, *n. round body, ball, &c.* गोळा *m.* गोल *m.* गोलक*m.* ब-

Celestial g. खगोल *m.* आकाशमंडल *n.*

Terrestrial g. भूगोल *m.*

2 *the earth.* भूगोल *m.* भूमंडल *n.* [मल *or* माल *n.*

GLOBE-AMARANTH, *n.* मखमल *or* मखमाल *f.*—the flower. मख-

GLOBE-THISTLE,*n. echinops echinatus.* कांटेचुबक*m.n.*ऊंटकटार*m.* ऊंटकटारी *f.* ब्रह्मदंड *m.* ब्रह्मदंडी *f.*

GLOBOSE, GLOBULAR, GLOBULOUS, *a. spherical, round.* वाटोळा, गोलाकार, गोटोळा,गोल, वर्त्तुल, वर्त्तुलाकार.

GLOBOSITY, *n.* v. A. गोल *m.* गोलपणा *m.* गोलत्व *n.* गोलभाव *m.*

GLOBULE, *n. small round body.* गोळी *f.* रवा *m.*

To GLOMERATE, *v. a. gather into a ball.* गोळा *m.*-गुंडा *m.*-&c. करणें *g. of o.* गुंड्याच्या आकाराचा करणें.

GLOOM, *n.* (*of weather*). अंधारी *f.* ओंध *f.* धुंदाई *f.* काहूर *n.* v. ये, उठ, काळोखी *f.* धुंदी *f.* काळंबण *n.* [रानंद*m.*

2 *heaviness of mind.* उदासपणा *m.* उदासी *f.* औदासीन्य*n.*नि-

GLOOMINESS, *n.* v. A. 1. *and* GLOOM, 1. ओंध *f.* काळोखी *f.*झांपड *f.* झांक *f.* झांप *f.* झांकाळ *f.* v. घाल.

2 घुमेपणा *m.* उदासी *f.* उदासपणा *m.* औदासीन्य *n.* उदासवृत्ति *f.* औदासीन्यवृत्ति *f.* विषाद *m.*

3 कुडुकपणा *m.* मुखमालिन्य *n.* मुखमलिनता *f.*

GLOOMY, *a.*—weather, the heavens, &c. ओंधट, अंधक *or* अंधुक, धुंद, अंधारीचा, काळोखीचा, झांकाळीचा, काळोखमय, मळीण, उदास, न्यूनप्रभ, न्यूनतेज, न्यूनज्योति.

2 *sullen, melancholy,* v. LOW-SPIRITED. घुणा *or* घुण्या, घुम्या, उदास, उदासीन.

2 *cloudy of look,* v. GLUM. कुडूक, कुडूकवाणी, काळतोंड्या, रडतोंड्या, रडवा, मुखरोगी, मलिनमुख, खिन्नवदन.

GLORIFICATION, *n.* v. V. 1. मोठेपणा देणें *n.* &c.

2 परम्पद देणें *n.* &c. परम्पदप्राप्ति *f.*

GLORIFIED, *p.* v. V. 1. मोठेपणा दिल्हेला, &c.

2 परम्पद दिल्हेला, &c. परम्पद प्राप्त.

To GLORIFY, *v. a. render glory to,* v. To HONOR, To PRAISE. मोठेपणा *m.*-&c. देणें, गौरव *n.* करणें *g. of o.* स्तुति *f.*-स्तवन *n.*-स्तव *m.*-&c. करणें *g. of o.*

2 *exalt to glory, or heavenly bliss.* दिव्यपदवी *f.*-परम्पद *n.*-&c. देणें, दिव्यभोग *m.* देणें, परम्पदास नेणें, दिव्यशोभान्वित करणें.

GLORIOUS, *a. illustrious, resplendent, &c.* तेजवान्, तेजवंत, तेजस्वी, तेजोमय, तेजाळ, तेजशाली, प्रतापी, प्रतापवान्, प्रतापशाली, प्रतापान्वित, विभवशाली.

GLORIOUSNESS, *n.* v. A. तेज *n.* प्रताप *m.* प्रभाव*m.* विभव *m. pop.* वैभव *n.* श्री *f.* मोटेपणा *m.* महिमा *m. f.* माहात्म्य *n.*

GLORY, *n. renown, credit,* v. HONOR. जयश्री *f.* वीरश्री *f.* श्री *f.* प्रताप *m.* तेज *n.* प्रतिष्ठा *f.* यश *n.* Corresponding to this word in the free applications made of it involving with varying aspect and intensity the general sense of such words as *honor, credit, splendor, lustre, brilliance, show, figure, dash, flash, glare, glitter, eclat,* are रूप *n.* रंग *m.*नकशा *m.* मात *f.* यश *n.* गाजावाजा *m.* शोभा *f.* रोशनाई *f.* कांत *f.* वीरश्री *f.* झळक *f.* भडक *f.* छान *f.* शान *f.* थाट *m.* थाटमाट *m.*

Glory ! (to thee, &c.). जय, जयजय, जयजया.

2 *illustriousness, &c.* v. GLORIOUSNESS. तेज *n.* प्रभाव *m.* प्रताप *m.* मोठेपणा *m.*

3 *rays around a head.* अंशुमाला *f.*

4 See PRAISE.

5 *heavenly felicity,* v. BEATITUDE, HEAVEN. मोक्ष *m.* निर्वाण *n.* अपवर्ग *m.* परमपद *n.*

To GLORY. See To BOAST.

GLOSS, *n. comment.* टीका *f.* टिप्पणी *f. pop.* टिप्पण *n.* भाष्य *n.* विवरण *n.* विवृति *f.* व्याख्या *f.*

2 *polish, lustre.* झिलाई *f.* जिल्हई *f.* झील *f.* सफाई *f.* सफाईदारी *f.* तजला *or* तजेला *m.* तजेली *f.* ओप *f.* लकेरी *f.* कांत *f.* औज्वल्य *n.*

3 (upon paper, cloth, &c. through rubbing). मोहरा *m.*

To GLOSS, *v. a. explain by comment.* विवरणें, विवरण *n.*-व्याख्या *f.*-व्याख्यान *n.* करणें *g. of o.*

2 *give a polish to.* जिल्हई *f.*-झिलाई *f.*-&c. देणें, सफाई *f.*करणें.

GLOSSARIST, *n.* टीका करणारा, &c. टीकाकार, भाष्यकार.

GLOSSARY, *n. dictionary of difficult terms.* अप्रसिद्धशब्दांचा कोश *m.* कूटार्थशब्दकोश *m.* गूढशब्दार्थबोधिनी *f.*

GLOSSINESS, *n.* v. A. 1. लुसलुशी *f.* तिळतिळी *f.* नितळाई *f.* तकतकी *f.* चकचकी *f.* चाकचक्य*n.*

GLOSSY, *n. smooth and shining.* तिळतिळीत *or* तुळतुळीत, नितळ, नळनळीत, लुसलुशीत, उजळ, उजळपाजळ, सोज्वल, तकतकीत, गुळगुळीत, चकचकीत, जिल्हईदार, सफाईदार, तजलेदार *or* तजेलदार, मोहरेदार.

2—of colors. तेल्या.

3—of boils, grapes, &c. *full and glowing, tense and glistening.* टळटळीत *or* टिळटिळीत *or* ठळठळीत, डळडळीत *or* ढळढळीत, नळनळीत.

GLOTTIS, *n.* श्वासमार्ग*m.* श्वासमार्गद्वार*n.*

GLOVE, *n.* हाताचा मोजा*m.* हातमोजा*m.* पंजा*m.*

Leathern g. or shackle. चामोटा*m. dim.* चामोटी *f.* v. खिळ.

To GLOW, *v. n. burn fiercely or vehemently, blaze.* धगधगणें, धडकणें, धडधडणें, भडभडणें, भडाडणें, खबखबणें, रसरसणें, तापणें, तपणें, संतापणें, जळफळणें, फणफणणें, रणरणणें, रणरण *adv.* करणें, रसरस *adv.* करणें, भभकणें *or* भबकणें, भडकणें, भणाणणें.

2 *be bright, shining, &c.* झळकणें, झळझळणें, झळाळणें, झकाकणें, चकाकणें. [कणें.

3—the countenance, plants, &c. लुसलुसणें, टवटवणें, टकट-

4—the mouth, &c. from hot substances. तिखटावणें, तिखावणें, धगधगणें, भगभगणें, फणफणणें, झणझणणें, झणक्या *f. pl.* मारणें—intens. फणाणणें, झणाणणें.

5—the heavens at dawn. भणभणणें, भडकणें, फुलणें.

6—a live coal. निखारणें.

GLOW, GLOWING, *n.* v. V. 1. धक *or* धग *f.* धगधग *f.* रणरण *f.* डोंब *or* आगीचा डोंब*m.* भडका *or* भडाका*m.* जळफळ *f.* फणका*m.* फणकारा*m.* अहळी *f.* अही *f.* निघा*m.* आंच *f.* आग*f.* ताप*m.* संताप *m.*—intens. धोदाट *or* धोधाट *or* टा*m.* धोदराट*m.* धगाटा*m.* भडभडाट*m.* भडाड*m.* फणफणाट*m.* फणाण*m.*

2 झळाळ*m.* झळझळाट*m.* झळाळी *f.* झकाकी *f.* चकाकी *f.*

3 लुसलुशी *f.* टवटवी *f.* टकटकी *f.* टुकटुकी *f.* तुकतुकी *f.*
4 तोंडचा डोंब*m.* धगधग *f.* भडका*m.* भकभक*or*भगभग *f.* फणफणणी *f.* फणका*m.* फणकारा*m.* झणी *f.* झणझणी *or* झणझण *f.* झणकी *f.or* झणक्त्या *f.pl.—intens.* भगभगाट *m.* फणाण*m.*फणफणाट *m.* झणझणाट*m.*

I. (after a meal, of passion, &c.). गुरमी *f.*

GLOWING, *p. a.* v.V. 1. धगधगीत, ढणढणीत, रणरणीत, फणफणीत, रसरसीत, कडकडीत, कडक, खरमरीत, चणचणीत.
2 जाज्वल्य, जाज्वल्यमान, दीप्तिमान, देदीप्यमान, अग्निदीप्त, अग्निमय, दीप्त, ज्वाली, ज्वलित.
3 लुसलुसीत, टवटवीत, टकटकीत, टुकटुकीत, तुकतुकीत.
4 भळभळीत, भणभणीत, फणफणीत.

GLOW-WORM, *n.* सोनकिडा*m.*

To GLOZE. See To FAWN.

GLUE, *n.* सरस *m.* चिकटवण*n.* डकवण*n.*

To GLUE, *v. a. join with glue.* सरस*m.* लावणें, सरसानें जोडणें.

GLUM, *a. sullen, sour of look.* हिंपुटी *or* हिंपूट *or* हिमट, हिमटतोंड्या, काळतोंड्या, कुडूक, कुडूकवाणी, उतरल्या तोंडाचा, मुखरोगी, मलूल, मलिनमुख, दुर्मुख, खिन्नवदन.
To look g. तोंड*n.* उतरणें, तोंड*n.* बाईट करणें *or, g. of s.* तोंड *n.* बाईट होणें, पायपोसासारखें तोंड*n.* करणें.

GLUME, *n.*—of grain, &c. खपला*m.*

To GLUT, *v. a. cloy, sate.* उपट *f.*-टेर *f.*-टेक *f.*-निशा *f.*-&c. करणें -पाडणें *g. of o.* अमर *f.*-मर *f.* करणें, ओकारी *f.* आणणें, कंठापर्यंत घालणें-आणणें-वाढणें.
To g. one's self with. अभरवण *f. n.*-उपट *f.* घेणें.

GLUT, *n. superabundance.* रेड *f.* ठेल *f.* रेळ *f.* रेळचेळ *f.* उपट *f.*
2 *glutted state, gluttedness.* अभर *f.* टेर *f.* टेक *f.* धालेपणा*m.* उपट *f.* मनशामोड *f.* निशा *f.*

GLUTEN, *n.*—of vegetables, &c. चीक*m.* बलक*m.*

GLUTINOUS, *a. viscous.* चिकाचा, चिकट, चिकण.

GLUTINOUSNESS, GLUTINOSITY, *n.* v. A. चिकटपणा *m.*चिकचीक *f.* चिकटण *f.*

GLUTTON, *n.*—*See the adjective.* Here are collected the terms and phrases correspondent with *gorger, gormandizer, greedy gut, belly god, heliogabalus, cormorant, gully gut, gobble gut, &c. &c.* अगस्ति, उदरपिशाच, कुक्षिंभरि, खाण्याला काळ, खादाडमाबसा, खादाडकुरकुला, पोटबाबू, पोट्या, पोटार्थी, पोटभरू, पोटभऱ्या, खादू, खादूनंदन, खाबू, पुखानंद, रावणाची खाई, राक्षस, लाहंचर, पोटांतब्रह्मराक्षस बाळगणारा, भीम, बकासुर, उदरंभरि *pop.* उदरंभर.

To GLUTTONIZE, *v. n.* v. To STUFF. ओ येईतों खाणें-जेवणें, दपटून जेवणें, नळीचें बऱ्हाड *n.* करणें, तोंड *n.* हातीं धरणें, आकंठ भोजन *n.* करणें.
To feel heavy and listless from gluttonizing. जेवण*n.*-अन्न *n.*-&c. हातीं पायीं येणें-डेवणें-रेवणें *g. of s.*

GLUTTONOUS, *a. given to excess in eating.* खादाड, खाऊखादाड, अधासी, अधोडी, अघोरी, दपटून-रपाटून-&c. जेवणारा, बळकट जेवणारा, खाणोरा *or* री, दपट्या, खाऊपासरी, बहुभक्ष, बहुभक्षी, बहुभोजी, बहुभुक्, बह्वाशी, अत्याशी, अत्याहारी, अमितभक्षी, अमितभोजी, अतिभोजी, वृकोदर, उदरप्रधान, उदरपरायण, घासानें आगळा, खयाशा, घस्मर, औदरिक. *See also the noun.*
A g. or greedy woman. खाऊधेवडी *f.* खादाडमाबशी *f.*

GLUTTONOUSNESS, GLUTTONY, *n.* v. A. खादाडपणा *m.*आधासीपणा *m.* &c. पोटपूजा *f.* उदरसेवा *f.* अतिभोजन *n.* बहुभक्षण *n.* अतिभक्षण *n.* अत्याशन *n.* अत्याहार *m.*

To GNARL. See To GROWL.

GNARLED, GNARLY, *a. knotty.* गांठींचा, गांठळ *or* गांठाळ, ग्रंथिल.

To GNASH, *v. n.* v. To FUME, To RAGE. दांत *m.pl.* खाणें, दांत ओंठ *m.* खाणें, दांतावणें, दांतीं येणें, कचकचणें, खिसणें, खेसणें, खेकणें, कडकडणें, निथणणें, चबताळणें.
To g. and spit at—a monkey. खेंकणें, खेंकाटणें, खेंसणें.

To GNASH, *v. a.* (the teeth). दांत *m. pl.* खाणें-कडकडा *adv.* खाणें-करकरावणें-चावणें-रगडणें, दांत ओंठ *m.pl.* खाणें *or* चावणें, किरकीट *or* दांतकिरकीट *f.* करणें, दांतकिरकिटी *f. pl.* देणें.

GNASHING, *n.* v. V. A. दांतखाणें *n.* कचकच *f.* कडकड *f.* दांतकिरकीट *f.*—intens. कचाच *m.* कचकचाट *m.*

GNASHINGLY, *adv.* कडकडां *or* करकरां, कचकचां.

GNAT, *n.* चिलट *n.* केंबरें *n.* मुरकूट *or* मुरकट *n.f.* मत्सर *m.* मशक*m.*

To GNAW, *v. a. eat away, corrode.* खाणें, खणणें, खांडणें.
2 *eat or tear with the teeth.* करांडणें *or* करंडणें, कंडारणें, कुरकुटणें, कुरकुडणें, तोडणें, कातरणें, डासळणें.
3—as remorse, &c. खाणें, खोचणें, खुपणें, टोचणें, डोचणें, सलणें, डाचणें *or* डांसणें.
4 *or* be a gnawing (in the belly). पोटांत चावणें-डाचणें-किंबचणें-खांडणें *v. impers.*

GNAWING, *n.* v. V. 1. खाणें *n.* खणणें *n.* &c. खणती *f.*
2 करांडणें *n.* तोडणें *n.* &c. करांडणूक *f.*
3 डाचणें *n.* &c. चुरचूर *f.* (*intens.* चुरचुराट *m.*) खवखव*f.*

GNOMON, *n. style of a dial.* शंकु *m.* कील *m.*
The shadow cast by the g. शंकुछाया *f.* प्रभा *f.*

To GO, *v. n.* जाणें, चालणें, चालता-चालू होणें-असणें, गमन *n.*-यात्रा *f.* करणें.—with the power and implication of such words and phrases as, *to be off, to make off, to make one's self scarce, to take one's self off.* तोंड *n.* काळें करणें, काळापात *m.* करणें, आसन *n.* गुंडाळणें.
About to go. गंतुकाम, गमनोन्मुख.
To feel an impulse to go. पाय *m.* घेणें-वाहणें.
To go and come. To go to and fro. जाणें येणें *n.*-जावायेवा *m.*-गमनागमन *n.*-गतागत *n.*-यातायात *n.* करणें, गिरट्या *f. pl.* घालणें.
2 by; *pass away, cease, become no more, &c.* जाणें, मागें पडणें, गुजरणें *or* गुदरणें, गत होणें, गतणें, निरसणें, नाहींसा होणें, निघणें, गेला मेला गतलासा होणें. [ळणें, चालणें.
3 down with; *pass with.* पुरवणें, साहणें, सोसणें, पचणें, गि-
4 in;—an eruption. पोटीं उतरणें.
5 off;—a gun, &c. उडणें, सुटणें, बार *m.* होणें *g. of s.*
6 off well; *be done or pass with eclat.* रंग *m.*-छान *f.* उतरणें-उडणें *g. of s.* बहर *or* बहार *f.* उडणें *g. of s.*
7 off; *obtain sale.* खपणें, विकणें, खप *m.*-&c. होणें *g. of s.*
8 on;—clothes on the body, &c. चढणें.
9 out, from, forth. निघणें, निर्गम *m.*-निर्याण *n.*-निस्तरण *n.*-उत्क्रमण *n.*-&c. होणें *g. of s.* निर्गत-निर्यात-उत्क्रांत-&c. होणें.
10 out; *be extinguished.* जाणें, मालवणें, विझणें, विझून जाणें.
11 over again. दुसारणें *or* दुसरणें, दुहारणें, आवृत्ति *f.* करणें *g. of o.*—a third time. तिसारणें *or* तिसरणें,—a fourth time.

चौसारणें *or* चौसरणें.

12 through (a study, &c.). निभणें, पारायण *n.*-&c. करणें.

13 with,—carnally. संगतीं जाणें, संग *m.* करणें.

GO-BETWEEN, *n.* दरम्यान *c.*

2—female. दूती *or* दूतिका *f.* कुट्टनी *pop.* कुंटण *or* कुंटीण *f.* संचारिका *f.*

GO-CART, *n.* पांगूळगाडा *m. dim.* पांगूळगाडी *f.*

GOAD, *n. prick.* आर *f.* अरी *f.* पराणी *f.*

An elephant g. अंकुश *m.*

To GOAD, *v. a.* v. N. आर *f.* लावणें-टोंचणें, टोंचणें, डोंचणें.

2 fig. See To URGE.

GOAL, *n. mark or bound of a race.* दवडीची हद्द *f.*-मर्यादा *f.* अवधि *m. f.* धावनमर्यादाचिह्न *n.* धावनसीमास्तंभ *m.* टिपण *n.* निशाण *n.*

To reach the g. बेडा *m.* पार जाणें-असणें-होणें-करणें,&c.

2 *starting post.* धावनारंभस्तंभ *m.* धावनारंभस्थान *n.* अवधि *m.f.*

3 See END.

GOAT, *n.* बकरा *m.* (रा *m.* री *f.* रें *or* रूं *n.*) बोकड *m.* बस्त *m.* शेरडूं *or* शेळडूं *n.* (शेरडी *or* शेळी *f.*)अज *m.* (अजा *f.*) छाग *m.* (छागी *f.*)

GOAT-HERD, *n.* शेळक्या, शेरडुक्या, अजापाल, अजापालक, अजाजीव, अजाजीवी.

GOAT-SKIN, *n.* सागळ *f.*

G.—dressed (for shoes, &c.). नरी *f.*

GOATISH, *n.* बोकडा सारखा ज्याचा वास आहे तो.

2 See LUSTFUL.

GOB, *n.* (of phlegm.). खाकरा *or* खाकेरा *m.* बडका *or* बेडका *m.* बडस *m.* डेलकर *n.* डरकल *n.*

To GOBBET, *To* GOBBLE, *v. a. eat noisily, hastily, and in large pieces.* मटकावणें, मटमटावणें, बकबक *or* बकाबक-चराचरगपागप-मटमट-&c. *adv.* खाणें, मटगोळा *m.*-गटगोळा *m.*-गटाणा *m.* करून टाकणें, बकाणा *or* बोकाणा *m.*-गोळा *m.* मारणें, बोकांदणें.

2 up ; *devour greedily, &c.* v. To EAT. बोकांदणें, चपाटणें, रपाटणें, रगडणें.

GOBBET, *n. large mouthful.* बकाणा *or* बोकाणा *m.* बोकणा *m.* बोकणी *f.* बोबका *m.*

GOBBLINGLY, *adv.* v. V. 1. गप-कन-कर-&c. गपगप *or* पां,—intens. गपागप, गपापां.

GOBLET, *n.* v. VESSEL. जांब *or* जाम *m.* पंचपात्र *n.*

GOBLIN, *n.* v. GHOST. भूत *m. n.* पिशाच *n.* प्रेत *n.* भोंदगिन्हा *m.*

G.-HALL. भूतखाना *m.*

GOD, *n.*—the Supreme Being. देव, भगवान् *pop.* भगवंत *m.* परमेश्वर, ईश्वर, प्रभु, आदिपुरुष, ठाकूर *or* ठाकूरजी. There are numerous *descriptive names* or *epithets* of God. Some are अखंडदंडायमान, अकळ, अगाध, अगोचर, अंतर्यामी, अनागत विधाता, अनादि *or* अनादिसिद्ध, अनाद्यंत, अनाद्यनंत, अपरंपार, अलक्ष्य, अविनाशी, अव्यक्त, अस्वप्न, आदिकर्त्ता, आदिकारण, आदिपुरुप, ऋणहर्त्ता, कर्ममोचन, कर्मसाक्षी, कर्माध्यक्ष, गतिदाता, चित्, चित्साक्षी, चित्तचालक, चित्स्वरूप, चिद्घन, चिन्मय, चिन्मात्र, चिद्रत्न, चिदानंद, चिद्विलास, चिद्रूप, चैतन्य, चिदाकार, जगज्जीवन, जगत्कारण, जगदात्मा, जगदीश, जगदीश्वर, जगदुद्धार, जगद्गुरु, जगद्वंद्य, जनार्दन, जीवितेश, तेजोरूप, त्रिकालदर्शी, त्रिकालज्ञ, त्रैलोक्य विस्तार, दीनवत्सल, देवाधिदेव, नर, निग्रहानुग्रहसमर्थ, निजरूप, निजमूर्त्ति, नित्यमुक्त, नित्यसिद्ध, निजानंद, निमित्तकारण, निरंजन, निराकार, निरालंब, निराधार, निरामय, निर्गुण, निर्विकार, निर्विकल्प, निर्वाणींचा तारू *or* त्राता, निस्संग, पतितपावन, परमतत्व; परमात्मा, परमपुरुष, परपुरुष, परवस्तु, परमवरिष्ठ, परमहंस, परमेश्वर, पुराणपुरुष, पुरातनपुरुष, पूर्णघन, भक्तकाजकैवारी, भक्तवत्सल, भक्तकाजकल्पद्रुम, भक्तजनाभिमानी, भवभंजन, भवांतक, भवनिवारण, भवदायक, महापुरुष, महालय, मायावी, विराट्देही, विराट्स्वरूप, विश्वनेत्र, विश्वेश्वर, विश्वाधार, विश्वव्यापक, विश्वकुटुंबी, विश्वंभर, विश्वरूप, विश्वात्मा, सगुण, साकार, सर्वसाक्षी, सर्वसुख, स्वानंद, सच्चिदानंद, सकलगुणकंद, सत्य, सन्, सत्यसंकल्प, सर्वतोमुख, सर्वभूतभूतांतर, सर्वेश्वर, सर्वोत्तम, सर्वोत्कृष्ट, सोहम्मूर्त्ति, स्थूलसूक्ष्म, स्वयंभू, हंस.

G. of gods. देवाधिदेव.

God as possessing attributes. सगुण, साकार.—Worship of God as such. सगुणोपासना *f.* God as destitute of attributes. निर्गुण, निराकार.—The worship of God as such. निर्गुणोपासना *f.*

Chain or course of God's government. ईश्वरसूत्र *n.* ईश्वरतंत्र *n.* ब्रह्मसूत्र *n.*

For the love of g. ईश्वरप्रीत्यर्थ.

Power—as upholding and ruling, of God. ईश्वरसत्ता *f.*

Recitation of the names of God. नामोच्चारण *n.* कीर्त्तन*n.*

Will of God. ईश्वरेच्छा *f.* ईश्वरी इच्छा *f.*

Wrath of God. ईश्वरीक्षोभ *m.*

God's path is through the deep waters. ईश्वरी कर्त्तृत्व [गहनगति आहे.

Keep God in your thoughts whilst engaged in your work. कामामध्यें काम भजभज मना राम.

2 *a. g. a deity, an idol.* देव *m.* देवता *f.* दैवत *n,* आदित्य *m.* गीर्वाण *m.* सुर *m.* विबुध *m.* सुमन *m.* Some of the classes or orders of *gods, demigods, devils. &c.* (See DEVIL) are अध्वर,अनिल, आदित्य, कामरूपी, किन्नर, कूष्मांड, खेचर, गंधर्व, ग्रह, चाळा, देवचार, नाग, भूत, मारुत, यक्ष (यक्षिणी *f.*), रुद्र, वसु, वालखिल्य, विद्याधर, विश्व, साध्य, सिद्ध.

Some of the common names of *Brahmá* are ब्रह्मा, ब्रह्मदेव, धाताविधाता, प्रजापति, प्रजोत्पादक, आदिकर, आदिकर्त्ता, आदिकवि.

—of *Wis'hnu.* विष्णु, नारायण, आदिनारायण, जगन्नाथ, जनार्दन, अनंत, वसंतमाधव, हरि, कल्की.

Black stone sacred to *Wis'hnu.* शालिग्राम *m.*

—of *Shiwa.* शिव, महादेव, ईश्वर, जटिल, जटाधारी, नीलकंठ, पंचानन, पशुपति, भैरव, भोळानाथ, भोळाशंकर, शंकर, शंभु, महेश्वर; रुद्र, सदाशिव, सोम, अर्धनारीनटेश्वर, हर, शूळी.

Bull of S. नंदी *m.* बसवा *or* बसवण्णा *m.*

Lingam of S. लिंग *n.* बाण *m.*—Worshipper of it. लिंगाईत.—Stone bearing it in the centre,(of the shape of the योनि,) शाळुंका *or* खा *m.*—Female energy counter-part of phallus of S. शक्ति *f.*—Worship of it. शाक्तभक्ति *f.* शाक्तपूजा *f.* शाक्तधर्म *m.* &c.—Worshipper of it. शाक्त.

Worshipper. of S. शैव.

—of *Dewi.* देवी, पार्वती, गौरी, चंडी *or* चंडिका, अंबा, उमा, काली *or* कालिका, दुर्गा, भगवती, काळकाई, जगदंबा, भद्रकाली,

भवानी, भैरवी, मंगलागौरी, ज्येष्ठागौरी, महादेवी, महामाया, शाकरी, शाकंभरी, शांभवी, षष्ठी (*pop.* सठी, सठवी, &c.)

—of *Saraswati.* सरस्वती, शारदा, वाणी, वाग्वल्ली, वाग्विलासिनी, वाग्लहरी.

—of *Ganesha.* गणेश, गणपति, गजानन, चिंतामणी, मंगळमूर्ति, विनायक, लंबोदर, विघ्नहर, विघ्ननाशक, विघ्नराज, रंगदेवता, शूर्पकर्ण.

Certain other divinities male and female, are व्यंकटेश (*pop.* व्यंकोबा), उपांगललिता, काळभैरव *or* भैरव, रुत्या, जीवंतिका (*pop.* जीवती), वज्रेश्वरी (*pop.* वज्रा, वज्रयोगिनी), मोहिनी. And others, viewed of the wretched idolaters themselves as *two penny gods and goddesses*, are, म्हैसासुर *or* म्हसोबा, खळनाथ, बापदेव *or* बापा, मेसादेवी, मायराणी, निगळ, पुरूस, आजादेवी, चिंध्यादेवी—and the whole bundle comprehensively, भूताबळी *f.* जाखाई जुखाई *f.*

Attendant g. अंगदेवता *f.*

Artist or architect of the gods. विश्वकर्मा, सुकर्मा.

Court or assembly of the gods. देवसभा *f.*

Gods set up to preside (upon festival, &c. occasions). देवक *or* देवदेवक*n.*—Setting up of them. देवकप्रतिष्ठा *f.* देवकस्थापन*n.*—Dismissal of them. देवकोत्थापन*n.* देवतोत्थापन*n.* उद्वासन*n.* देवताविसर्जन*n.*

Inferior g. उपदेव*m.* उपदेवता *f.*

Local g. स्थलदेवता *f.* क्षेत्रपाल*m.* अधिदेव*m.* भूदेवी *f.* भुमका *f.*

Mother of the gods. अदिति *f.*—of the Titans or devils. दिति *f.*

Physician of the gods. धन्वंतरि*m.*

Preceptor of the gods. सुरगुरु*m.* सुराचार्य*m.*

Presiding g. अधिदेव*m.* अधिदेवता *f.* अधिदैवत*n.*

Tutelar g. of. इष्टदेव*m.* इष्टदेवता *f.*—Present to it. राखण*f.*

To set up rites in propitiation of the gods. देवपण *n.* करणें, देवधर्म*m.* उठवणें-मांडणें-आरंभणें.

To seek direction from the gods. देवीं धर्मीं विचारणें.

3 *thing idolized, an idol.* देव्हारें*n.* दैवत*n.*

GODDESS, *n.* देवी *f.* भगवती *f.*

GOD-FATHER, *n.* धर्म पिता*m.*

GODHEAD, *n.* v. DIVINITY. देवपणा*m.* देवपण *n.* देवता *f.* देवत्व *n.*

GODLESS, *a.* v. WICKED. देवलंड, देवभक्तिविमुख, अधर्मी, देवघाण्या, धर्मविमुख.

GODLIKE, *a.* See DIVINE.

2 *of divine form.* देवरूपी, देवस्वरूपी.

GODLINESS, *n.* v. A. ईश्वरभक्ति *f.* ईश्वरनिष्ठा *f.* ईश्वरपरायणत्व*n.* परमार्थबुद्धि *f.*

Path of g. भक्तिमार्ग*m.*

GODLY, *a. pious, religious,*—of persons. ईश्वरभक्त, ईश्वरमनस्क, ईश्वरनिष्ठ, ईश्वरपरायण, धर्मनिष्ठ, धर्मपरायण, धार्मिक, पारमार्थिक.

2—of things. ईश्वरभक्तीचा, ईश्वरनिष्ठेचा.

GOD-MOTHER, *n.* धर्ममाता *f.*

GODOWN, *n. store-room.* जिन्नसखाना*m.* गुदांव*n.*

GOER, *n.* GOING, *p. a.* v. V. 1. जाणारा, &c. चालता, चालू, चारी (in comp. as वनचारी, ग्रामचारी, जलचारी), ग & गामी (in comp. as खग, जलग, भूमिग, आकाशगामी, पातालगामी), सरक.

GOGGLE, *a.*—the eye. बटबटीत, बटबट्या, गटगटीत.

To GOGGLE, *v. a. strain the eyes.* डोळे*m. pl.* बटारणें.

GOGGLE-EYED, *a.* बटबट्या, बटबटीत डोळ्या, भोकरडोळ्या.

GOGLET, *n.* v. VESSEL. चंबू*m.* गिंडी *f.* अपकरा*m.*

GOING, *n.* v. V. 1.—*act.* जाणें*n.* चालणें*n.* चाल *f.* गमन*n.* गति *f.* विगम*m.* प्रस्थान*n.* प्रयाण*n.* यात्रा *f.* यान*n.* सरण*n.* अपसरण*n.*

G. & coming. जावा येवा*m.* जायें *f.* जाणें येणें*n.* गमनागमन*n.* गतागत*n.* यातायात *f.*

To set a g. चालीस लावणें, चालता-चालू करणें.

GOITRE, *n. tumor on the throat.* गलगंड*m.* गडु*m.* मन्यास्तंभ*m.*

GOITROUS, *a.* गडुकंठ.

GOLD, *n.* सोनें*n.* सुवर्ण*n.* कनक*n.* कांचन*n.* हिरण्य*n.* हेम *n.* स्वर्ण*n.* जांबूनद*n.*

Alloyed g. कूटस्वर्ण*n.*

Better even than g. सोन्याहून पिवळा.

Color of g. (as appearing upon heating it). ताव*m.*

G. and such like valuables,—compreh. *or* carelessly. सोनेंवानें *n.*

Pure (very pure) g. बावनकसी सोनें*n.*

GOLD, *a.* See GOLDEN.

GOLD-DUST, *n.* सोन्याचीमाती *f.* कनकपराग*m.*

GOLD-FINCH, *n.* पिवळ्यारंगाचा एक पक्षी आहे.

GOLD-FINDER, *n.* झारेकरी, झाऱ्या.

GOLD-FISH, *n.* पिवळ्यारंगाचा एक मासा आहे.

GOLD-MOHUR, *n.*—the flower tree. गुलतुरा *m.* सोनतरवड*m.*

GOLD-LEAF, *n.* सोनेरी पत्र *n.* सोनेरी बरख *m.*

GOLD-SMITH, *n.* सोनार, सुवर्णकार.—in contempt. सोनारडा, कथीलकुट्या, ठोकडा *m.* ठोक्या*m.*—in allusive and reproachful phraseology. देखतचोर, सुवर्णस्तेयी, पश्यतोहर.

Anvil of a g. for forming beads &c. मणखुरा*m.*

Burnisher of a g. नितळणा *m.*

Business or art of a g. सोनारकी *f.* सोनारकाम *n.*

Furnace or chafing dish of a g. आगटी *f. or* टें*n.* बागेसरी *f.*

Hammer of a g. घांट्या*m.*

Nippers or tongs of a g. सवाणा *or* ना *m.* सांडस *m. dim.* सांडसी *f.* सांडणी *f.* Some other implements of *goldsmiths* are करडा, कंडारणें, कांकणा, तुत्या, दबकें, पानसळई.

GOLD-THREAD, *n.* जरतार *f. n.* जर *f. m.*

GOLDEN, *a. of or belonging to gold.* सोन्याचा, सोनेरी, सुवर्णाचा, सुवर्णसंबंधी, सुवर्णमय, सुवर्णात्मक, सौवर्ण, कनकमय, हैम.

2 *of the color of gold.* सोन्याचे रंगाचा, सुवर्णरंगी, सोन्याचा.

3 *excellent, valuable.* सोन्याचा, लाखा रुपयांचा, लाख्या.

GOLF, *n.* एका खेळाचें नांव आहे.

GONE, *p.* v. V. 1. गेला, रवाना, गत, निर्गत, अवगत, अपगत, उत्क्रांत, निर्वाण, प्रस्थित, यात, अपसृत, अंतरित, वीत, अतीत, गत & विगत (useful in comp. as विगतैश्वर्य, &c.).

GONG, *n. plate of iron struck as a bell.* घड्याळ *n.* तास *m.* घंटा *f.* घडी *f.* झेंगट *n.*

Person appointed to strike a g. घड्याळची *or* जी, तासजी.

Stick, &c. to strike a g. टिपरूं *n.*

GONORRHŒA, *n.* परमा *m.* परमें *n.*

GOOD, *a.* चांगला, बरा, उत्तम, चोख, चोखट *or* चखोट, चोखटा, चोखावेश, खासा, बरवंटा, बरवा, चंगा, चांग, चांगट, चिलखी, हित.—intens. *extremely g., excellent, superexcellent, precious,* भला, लाखा

रुपयांचा, लाल्या, बावनकसी, सर्वोत्तम, सर्वोत्कृष्ट, राजपसंद, उत्तमोत्तम, बेशखासा, सुष्ट, ऊरुसत्व, विनीचा.

The g. and the bad. बराबाईट, सारासार, सदसत्.—Consideration of the g. and the bad. सारासार विचार *m.* सदसद्विचार *m.*—Discrimination between the g. and the bad. सदसद्विवेक *m.*—Separating the g. from the bad. क्षीरनीरविभाग *m.*

G. for nothing person. अजागलस्तन *pop.* अजागल *or* ळ, हरळी प्रसाद *m.* झुरडफुंक्या.

Pretty g. बरा, बरासा.

Very g. बेशखासा.

To give one as g. as he brings. तोलास तोल *m.* देणें.

To seem g. unto. धर्मास-उचितास-विचारास येणें *g. of s.*

2 *sound, strong, firm, substantial; having strength, pith, spirit, virtue.* कसदार, जीवदार, दळदार, खबरदार, सकस, ससार, सतेज, सात्विक, जिवट, ऐवजदार, सक्ष्म *or* शक्ष्म, धड, धडका.

3—of signs, aspects, seasons, &c. *not inauspicious.* शुभ, शुद्ध, इष्ट, मंगल, सु (in comp. as सुकाल, सुमुहूर्त्त-&c.).

G. and bad. शुभाशुभ, सुष्टासुष्ट, स्वाडद्वाड.

4—morally, v. VIRTUOUS, &c. चांगला, भला, नेकीचा, नेक, साधु, सत्वशील, सत्वसंपन्न, सात्विक, सत्वस्थ, सत्ववृत्ति, सद्वृत्ति, धार्मिक, धर्मी, धर्मिष्ट, साधुवृत्ति, सत्(in comp. and abundantly, as सत्कर्म, सत्संग, सद्गुण, सद्धर्म सन्मार्ग, सज्जन).

G. (godly, virtuous, &c.) man. सत्पुरुष, सुजन, सुमनुष्य, सद्गृहस्थ, पुण्यपुरुष, पुण्यप्राणी, पुण्यात्मा.

G. (simple, mild, &c.) man. देवभोळा, देवमाणूस, ईश्वरीपुरुष, भजनी.

5 *benevolent,* v. KIND. परोपकारी, उपकारी. [निर्मळ.

6—pieces of money. सणसणीत कोरा, सणसणीत, खणखणीत,

To make good, *supply a loss.* भरून देणें.

GOOD, *n. a good thing.* श्रेय *n.* श्रेयाची-कल्याणाची-&c. गोष्ट *f.*

Fugitive g. पळतें पीक *n.*

The supreme g. *summum bonum.* परमार्थ *m.*

2 *benefit, profit,* v. ADVANTAGE. फायदा *m.* फल *n.* हित *n.* बरें *n.* उपकार *m.* गुण *m.*

3 *weal, well being.* कल्याण *n.* श्रेय *n.* बरें *n.* हित *n.* अभीष्ट *n.*

To wish or seek the g. of. कल्याणचिंतन *n.*-अभीष्टचिंतन *n.*-&c. करणें. *g. of o.* बरें मागणें *with* ला *or* चा *of o.* बऱ्याबर असणें *g. of o.*

4 *moral qualities,* v. VIRTUE. नेकी *f.* श्रेय *n.*

5 goods; *wares,* v. COMMODITIES. माल *m.* जिन्नस *m. pl.* जिन्नसपानस *m. pl.*

Goods taken from a shop to be retained or returned as may suit. जांगड *f.*

Perishable goods. नासकें केणें *n.*

6 goods; *goods and chattels.* माल *m.* मालमत्ता *f.* इस्ताद *f.* सामान *n.* चीजबस्त *f.* जिंदगी *f.* इलाखिला *m.* चरद्रव्य *n.*

GOOD, *adv.* बरें, बेश.

GOOD-BREEDING, *n. politeness.* सुजनत्व *n.* सौजन्य *n.* सभ्यता *f.* विनय *m.* सुविनय *m.*

GOOD BY! v. ADIEU. सुखी ऐस, स्वस्ति.

GOOD HUMOUR, *n.* खुशमर्जी *f.*

GOOD HUMOURED, *a.* खुशमर्जी.

GOOD MAN, *n. master of a household.* घरकरी, घरधनी, घरचा.

GOOD-LOOKING, *a.* v. HANDSOME. सुरतपाक, सुरूप.

GOOD NATURE, GOOD TEMPER, *n.* सुशील *n.* सुस्वभाव *m.* सालसाई *f.* सद्वृत्ति *f.* सुवृत्ति *f.* संतोषवृत्ति *f.* आनंदवृत्ति *f.* सौशील्य *n.*

GOOD NATURED, GOOD TEMPERED, *a.* शीलाचा, सुशील, सत्वशील, शीलवान् *pop.* शीलवंत, सालस, संतोषवृत्ति, सद्वृत्ति, सुवृत्ति.

G. fellow. गुळाचा गणेश *or* गणपति.

GOODWILL, *n.* मर्जी *f.* खुशमर्जी *f.* रुपा *f.* सौमनस्य *n.*

To acquire the g. of. मर्जी *f.* संपादणें, पोटांत शिरणें.

To lose the g. of. मर्जीतून उतरणें, मनांतून उतरणें.

To preserve the g. of. मर्जी *f.* राखणें.

GOOD WIFE, GOOD WOMAN, *n.* घरकरीण *f.* घरधनीण *f* घरचारिणी *f.* सवाशीण *f.* घरची *f.* अयो *f.*

GOODLINESS, *n.* v. A. साजरेपणा *m.* &c. सौंदर्य *n.* लावण्य *n.* सुरूपता *f.* खुमास *m.*

GOODLY, *a. comely, graceful, handsome, &c.* सुरूप, सुंदर, गोरागोमटा, साजरा, गोजरा, गोजिरवाणा, देखणा, सुदर्शन, सुभावणा.

GOODNESS, *n.* v. A. 1. चांगुलपणा *or* चांगलेपणा *m.* चोखटपणा *m.* गुण *m.* तेज *n.* सत्व *n.* सत्ता *f.* सौष्टव *or* सौष्ठव *n.*

2 *soundness, firmness, vigour, heartiness, pluck, &c.—as opposed to* rottenness, decrepitude, debility, &c. and as remaining in articles or animals. कस *m.* सत्व *n.* जीव *m.* ऐवज *m.* वीर्य *n. pop.* वीर *and* विरी *f.* तेज *n.* स्वारस्य *n.* जीवनपाणी *n.*

3 शुद्धि *f.* शुभ *n.* शुभता *f.* &c.

4 चांगुलपणा *m.* नेकी *f.* भलाई *f.* भलाइकी *f.* भलेपणा *m.* साधुपणा *m.* साधुत्व *n.* साधुवृत्ति *f.* सत्व *n.*

5 रुपा *f.* उपकार *m.*

GOODY, *n.*—the compellation. अबा *or* अबाजी *f.* आऊ *f.* बाई *f.*

Little g. बडलाई *f.* बडलाबाई *f.*

GOOSE, *n.* हंसी *f.* बरटी *f.*

Cry of the g. *cackle.* हंसनाद *m.*

Flight or flock of geese. हंसमाला *f.*

2 See FOOL.

GOOSEBERRY, *n.* एक फळ आहे.

GORBELLIED, *a.* v. POTBELLIED. दोंदाळ, दोंदी, ढेऱ्या, तुंदिल.

GORBELLY, *n.* v. POTBELLY. ढेर *f.* दोंद *n.*

GORE, *n.* v. BLOOD. रक्त *n.* गोठलेलें रक्त *n.* रक्ताचीं चकलें *n. pl.*

2 (of a garment). कळी *f.* बचा *m.*

To GORE, *v. a. pierce with a horn.* शिंगटणें *or* शिंगाटणें, शिंग *n.* मारणें, भोकसणें *or* भोसकणें, भसकावणें.

Scratch or mark of a goring. कांखर *m.*

GORGE, *n.* v. THROAT. गळा *m.* कंठ *m.*

2 *narrow pass between hills.* खिंड *f.* खिंडकुली *f. or* लेंन. घोल *m.*

3 *full meal, glut.* अभरवण *f. n.* पुखा *m.*

To GORGE, *v. n.* v. To STUFF. दपटून जेवणें, उपट जेवणें, अभरवण *f.* घेणें, नळीचें वऱ्हाड *n.* करणें, पुखा *m.* पाडणें-उरकणें, आकंठ जेवणें-भोजन *n.* करणें, मळभ भर खाणें, धणंगणें.

To GORGE, *v. a.* See To GOBBLE. 2 See To GLUT.

GORGEOUS, *a.* v. FINE. भडक, जरक बरक, भळभळीत, घवघवीत, झळक फळक, झळझळीत, विलसित, बिराजमान, विराजित.

GORGEOUSNESS, *n.* v. A. भडक *f.* v. मार *f.* शान *f.* झळझळ *f.* झळझळाट *m.* भळभळाट *m.*

GORGER, *n.* v. V. N. *and* GLUTTON. रपाटून-दपटून-&c. जेवणारा, बळकट जेवणारा, दपट्या.

GORGET, *n. armor for the throat.* पदक *n.* जुगणी *f.* कंठत्राण *n.*

To GORMANDIZE, *v. n.* v. To STUFF. दपटून-रपाटून-रगडून-&c. जेवणें, उपट जेवणें, मळभ भर खाणें, अभरवण *f. n.* घेणें, धणंगणें.

GORMANDIZER, &c. See GLUTTON, &c.

GORY, *a.* v. BLOODY. रक्तबंबाळ, रक्तानें भरलेला, रक्ताक्त.

GOSLING, *n.* हंसाचा बच्चा *m.*

GOSPEL, *n.* सुवार्त्ता *f.* शुभवार्त्ता *f.* शुभवर्त्तमान *n.*

GOSSAMER, *n.* म्हातारी *f.* वानतूल *n.*

GOSSIP, *n. tattling person,* v. PRATER. खबऱ्या, गपांछाट्या, बात्या, बातखबात्या, बात्यारा, खबात्या, गप्पीनाथ, गप्पीदास, गप्पी, गप्प्या, गोष्टीलंपट, गोष्टिप्रिय.

2 *gadding and tattling female.* नगरभवानी *f.* भटकभवानी *f.* गांवगाई *f.* गांवघांट *f.* हिंडफिरी चावट बायको *f.* लघाळमावशी *f.* लघाळभवानी *f.* [लघाळकी *f.*

3 *mere tattle.* गप *f.* गपसप *f.* खबर बखर *f.* खबर बाता *f. pl.*

GOSSIP-STAND, *n.* For this term as signifying *spot of meeting of gossips, news-mongers, loungers, and of idlers and scamps generally,* and as generic of *reading-room, club, lounge, barber's shop, alehouse, village tree, scandal point,* and similar designations, are, अखाडा *m.* अड्डा *m.* फड *m.* चवाठा *m.* चावडी *f.* रिकामचावडी *f.* रिकाम्यांचा फड *m.*

To GOSSIP, *v. n. tattle,* v. To PRATE. गपा *f. pl.* छाटणें, बाता *f. pl.* कुटणें-खबालणें-छाटणें-मारणें, फात्या *f. pl.* मारणें.

GOT, GOTTEN, *p.* v. V. A. 1. मिळवलेला, संपादलेला, &c. संपादित, संपन्न, प्राप्त, संप्राप्त, लब्ध, उपलब्ध, हस्तगत, आपन्न, व्याप्त, अवाप्त, करप्राप्त, यात, अधिगत, आसादित.

2 मिळवलेला, &c. उपार्जित, अर्जित.

Ill-g. Dishonestly g. हराम, हरामाचा, अन्यायोपार्जित.

Well-g. Honestly g. हलाल, हलालाचा, न्यायोपार्जित.

GOTHAMIST, *n.* v. WISEACRE. चतुरसाबाजी, दीडशाहणा.

GOUGE, *n.* v. CHISEL. विंधण्याचें अऊत आहे.

To GOUGE, *v. a.* (डोळा) बोटानें उपटून काढणें.

GOURD, *n.* भोंपळा *m.*

Bitter g. कडूभोपळा *m.* कटुतुंबी *f.* कटुकालाबु *m.*

Bottle shaped g. तुंबा *m.* तुंबी *f.* अलाबु *m.*

Young g. घटा *m.* Some other kinds are घणसा, डांगर, तवशी, नारिंगी तवशी, धेंडशी, परवर, पेटा *or* पेठा.

GOURMAND, *n.* v. GLUTTON. पोटबाबू, खादूनंदन, कुक्षिंभरि.

GOUT, *n.* v. RHEUMATISM. वातरोग *m.* वायु *m.* संधिवायु *m.* शूल *m.*

GOUTY, *a. diseased with the gout.* वातरोगी, संधिवायुग्रस्त, संधिवायुरोगी. [वायुसंबंधी.

2 *of or belonging to gout.* वातरोगाचा, संधिवायुरोगाचा, संधि-

To GOVERN, *v. a.* (a people, &c.). राज्य *n.*-अमल *m.*-अधिकार *m.*-हुकमत *f.*-हुकूम *m.*-&c. करणें-चालवणें.

2 *rule, regulate, control.* हुकमांत ठेवणें-चालवणें, आवरणें, अटपणें *or* अटोपणें, बंदोबस्त *m.*-बंदोबस्ती *f.* राखणें-ठेवणें *g. of o.* आवरण *n.*-आवर *m.*-अटोप *m.*-शासन *n.*-नियमन *n.*-&c. करणें *g. of o.*

GOVERNABLE, *a.* v. V. 2. आवराया-चा-जोगता-जोगा-&c. अटोपायाजोगा-&c. नियम्य, नियमनीय, शास्य, शासनीय, वश्य.

GOVERNED, *p.* v. V. 2. आवरलेला, &c. शासित, नियमित, नियत, नियंत्रित.

GOVERNESS, *n. female ruler.* नायकीण *f.* स्वामिनी *pop.* स्वामीण *f.* अधिकारिणी *pop.* अधिकारीण *f.* शासनकारिणी *f.*

2 *female teacher.* शिकवणारीण *f.* उपदेशिका *f.* उपदेष्ट्री *f.*

GOVERNMENT, *n.* v. V. 1.—*act.* राज्य *n.* अमल *m.* हुकमत *f.*

2—*act.* नियमन *n.* नियम *m.* नियंत्रण *n.* नियंत्रणा *f.* शासन *n.* अनुशासन *n.* अटोप *m.* आवरण *n.* आवर *m.* नियंतृत्व *n.* शास्तृत्व *n.* —*state.* बंदोबस्त *m.* बंदोबस्ती *f.* आळा *m.* आळाबांधा *m.* आळेबंद *m.*

I. *governing body.* सरकार *n.* [धिकार *m.*

II. (as of a district, colony, &c.). मामलत *f.* मामला *m.* अ-

III.—in grammar. अधिकार *m.* कारक *n.* [लेला.

GOVERNMENTAL, *a.* सरकारचा, सरकारच्या संबंधाचा, सरकारानें के-

GOVERNOR, *n.* (of a district, of a town, &c.). हाकीम, मामलतदार, मामलेदार, सुभेदार, अधिकारी.

The g. बडेसाहेब *m. pl.* गवर्नर साहेब *m.*

2 *ruler, regulator, &c.* नियंता, नियामक, शासक, शास्ता, शासन-नियमन-&c. कर्त्ता, अनुशास्ता.

GOVERNORSHIP, *n.* v. N. 1. हाकिमी *f.* हाकिमाई *f.* मामलतदारी *f.* मामलेदारी *f.*

GOWK. See FOOL.

GOWN, *n. woman's upper garment.* पेशवाज *m.*

2 *long robe*—gener. झगा *m.* जामा *m.* [लिपुट *m. n.*

GOWPEN, *n.* अंजलि *m. pop.* अंजळी *f.* ओंझळ *or* ओंजळ *f.* अंज-

GRAB. (This is corrupted from غراب *Arabic*). गुराब *f.*

To GRAB, *v. a.* v. To SEIZE. झोंबाडणें, झोंबाडा *m.* घालणें.

To GRABBLE. See To GROPE. 2 See To GROVEL.

GRACE, *n.* v. FAVOR. कृपा *f.* अनुग्रह *m.*

Object of g. कृपापात्र *n.* आनुग्राह्य.

To get into one's good graces. पोटांत शिरणें.

To get out of one's good graces कृपेंतून-मर्जींतून-मनांतून उतरणें.

2 *divine favor.* ईश्वरी कृपा *f.* ईश्वरी अनुग्रह *m.*

3 *divine influence.* ईश्वरी प्रेरणा *f.* ईश्वर प्रेरित बुद्धि *f.*

4 v. BEAUTY. शोभा *f.* कला *f.* छब *f.* लावण्य *n.* रूप *n.*

5 v. GRACEFULNESS. छब *f.* छबदारी *f.* धज *f.*

6 a g. *a virtue, an excellence.* सुलक्षण *n.* भूषण *n.* अलंकार *m.* रत्न *n.* गुण *m.*

7 *a short prayer or praise before or after meal.* भोजनापूर्वी किंवा भोजनानंतर करायाची ईश्वराची प्रार्थना *f.*-स्तुति *f.*

A "grace before meal" used by Hindus. त्रिसुपर्ण.

To GRACE, *v. a.* v. To ADORN. सुशोभित करणें, शोभा *f.* देणें-आणणें, शोभन *n.*-मंडन *n.* करणें *g. of o.*

2 *dignify, honor, &c.* मोठेपणा *m.*-&c. देणें, मोठा-&c. करणें.

GRACEFUL, *a.* v. BEAUTIFUL, HANDSOME. छबदार, छबडा, साजरा, गोजरा, गोजिरवाणा, छबीला *or* छबेला, कांतीव, कांतींबकोरींव, ललित. [खुबीनें.

GRACEFULLY, *adv.* v. A. छबीनें, डौलानें, डौलदारीनें, छानीनें,

GRACEFULNESS, *n.* v. A. छब *f.* छबी *f.* छबदारी *f.* छान *f.* खुबी *f.* साजरेपणा *m.* गोजरेपणा *m.* &c. कांति *f.* लालित्य *n.* लावण्य *n.*

GRACELESS, *a. reprobate, abandoned.* देवाधर्मानें टाकलेला, त्यक्तधर्म, धर्मत्यक्त, कोडगा, देवाधर्मानें ओवाळलेला.

GRACIOUS, *a. favorable, condescending,* v. KIND. कृपाळ *or* ळू, कृपेचा, कृपायुक्त, कृपादृष्टीचा, अनुग्रहाचा, अनुग्राही, अनुग्राहक, बहाल, उपकारी.

2 v. Merciful. दयालु *or* ळू, दयावंत, सकरुण.

Graciously, *adv.* v. A. 1. कृपेनें, कृपापूर्वक, कृपापुरस्सर, कृपादृष्टीनें, &c.

2 दयेनें, दयापूर्वक, &c.

Graciousness, *n.* v. A. 1. कृपाळूपणा *m.* कृपा *f.* कृपादृष्टि *f.* कृपाकटाक्ष *m.* बहाली *f.* अनुग्रह *m.* प्रसाद *m.* कृपालुता *f.*

Gradation, *n. order, regular process by degrees.* अनुक्रम *m.* क्रम *m.* क्रमिकगति *f.* आनुपूर्व्य *m.*

In regular g. क्रमक्रमानें, यथाक्रम, क्रमशः.

2 *step of a series.* पर्याय *m.* पायरी *f.*

Grade, *n. step, degree.* पायरी *f.* पर्याय *m.* रुतबा *m.*

Gradient, *a.* साररुया प्रमाणानें चढणारा किंवा उतरणारा.

Gradient, *n.* चढाचें किंवा उताराचें प्रमाण *n.*

Gradual, *a. proceeding by dejrees.* क्रमानुक्रमाचा, क्रमक्रमाचा, क्रमिक, अल्पाल्प.

Gradually, *adv.* v. A. क्रमक्रमानें, क्रमानुक्रमानें *or* क्रमानुक्रमें, क्रमेंकरून, क्रमशः, तीळतीळ. The sense of this word is very idiomatically supplied by the repetition of the present participle as करतां करतां केलें. He did it gradually. होतहोत होईल, जातां जातां जाईल, &c. &c.

G. and gently, as one is able. सोईसोईनें.

To Graduate, *v. a.* अंश *m. pl.*-भाग *m.pl.* मांडणें-पाडणें.

2 *confer a degree on.* विद्यालयांतली पदवी *f.* देणें.

To Graduate, *v. n.* विद्यालयांतली पदवी *f.* मिळविणें.

Graduate, *n.* विद्यालयांतली पदवी ज्यासमिळालीआहे तो.

Graduated, *p.* v. V. A. 1. अंश पाडलेला &c. [शिडाइत *n.*

Graff, Graft, *n. shoot, &c. inserted in a tree.* कलम *n.*

To Graff, *To* Graft, *v. a. insert a shoot.* क़लम *n.* लावणें-करणें, पैवंद *n.* करणें. [शिडाइती.

Graffed, Grafted, *a. bearing grafts.* कलमी, पैवंदी *or* धी,

G. tree or stock. इसाड *n.* ईस *n.*

2 *produced by a grafted tree.* कलमी, कलमाचा, पैवंदी *or* धी.

Grain, *n. corn.* धान्य *pop.* धान *n.* दाणा *m.* गल्ला *m.* अन्न *n.* कण *m.* दाणागोटा *m.* सस्य *or* शस्य *n.* The *Hindus* divide their grains into two classes.—1st. The *Grains* अठरा धान्यें. (These are, गहूं, तूर, जव, जोंधळा, वाटाणा, लांक, साळ, हरभरा, मसूर, जवस, मूग, राळा, तीळ, हरीक, कुळीत *or* थ, सांवा, उडीद, चवळी). And 2d. the *Inferior grains,* उपधान्यें *or* कुधान्यें *or* कदन्न *n.* (These are, सजगुरा, भादली, वरी, नाचणी, वरग, कांग, खपले गहूं, मका, कर्डी, राजगिरा, मटकी, पावटा, मुगी, वाल, कारळें, देवभात, सातू, अंबाडी). Note. Some *Pandits* give lists which differ from the above in a few grains.

A husked g. बेटका *m.* [कोरान्नकरी.

Alms of undressed g. कोरान्न *n.*—Person that begs it.

Awned or bearded g. शूकधान्य *n.*

Broken g. आडकणी *f.* आडदाळ *f.* कणव्रर *or* कणोर *m.* फूट *f.* फुटळ *f. n.* [ससकर *m.*

Dirty (earth-mingled) g. मातकण *n.* मातेरा *m.* मातेरें *n.*

Early grains—collect. अग्रधान्य *n.* अगात *n.*

Full and good g. or ears of corn. कणदार.

G. as just trodden out. मदन *m. pl.*

G. as a premium upon money lent. काढा *m.*

G. for consumption of an army. रसद *f.*

G. (pulse or corn) coarsely ground. भरडा *m.*

G. taken to be coarsely ground. भरडण *n.*

G. (or corn) which bursts or breaks readily. फुटाळू दाणा *m.* फुटीर *or* फुटरा दाणा *m.*

Late grains—collect. पश्चिमधान्य *n.*

Lending g. at interest. धान्यबर्द्धन *n.*

Mixed g. ससकर *m.*

Parched g. चबिना *m.* लाह्या *f. pl.*

Receptacle for g.—general. कोथळा *m. dim.* कोथळी *f.*

Receptacle for g. in a wall. अंबार *n.* बळद *n.*

Sack or case for g. भोत *m.* [उमलें *n.*

Soaked or steeped g. भिजाणे *m. pl.* भिजण *f.* उंबलें *or*

Store of g. धान्यसंग्रह *m.*

Undressed g. (esp. as given to Bráhmans, &c.). आमान्न *n.* उलफा *m.* शिधा *m.*

Unhusked g. boiled. घुगऱ्या *f. pl.*

To be g.—surfeited,—horse, &c. दाणावणें.

2 *single corn.* दाणा *m.* कण *m.*

Empty through excessive rain— ears of corn, or a grain. पाणपिसा.

Hollow or light g. फोल *n.* फोलकट *n.* फुंकणी *f. or* ण *n. or* णूं *n.* चिंबचळें *n.* चिंबफोल *n.* कुणी *f.* पोंकण *n.* फुलकें *n.*—through much rain. पाणफोल *n.* पाणपिशी *f.*

Hollow or light grains. मुकण *n.* फोल *n.* खोकस *n.* पुंजट *n.* पुंजरट *n.* [मुकाणा, मुका.

That remains hard after soaking or steeping—grain.

3 (of gunpowder, sugar, sand, &c.). रवा *m.* कण *m.* बिराणा *m.* [णी *f.*

4 (of wood, &c.). हिरका *m.* हीर *m.* and *fig.* मोड *n.* मोड-

Against the g. बिलोम, प्रतिलोम.

Agreement with the g. आनुलोम्य *n.*

Contrariety to the g. वैलोम्य *n.* प्रातिलोम्य *n.*

That is with, and against the g. अनुलोम बिलोम.

With the g. अनुलोम.

5 एक लहान वजन आहे.

6 *atom, jot, iota, &c.* v. Bit. कण *m. dim.* कणी *f.* कला *f.*

7 grains. अर्क काढलेल्या धान्याचा चोथा *m.*

Grain-cellar, *n.* पेव्र *or* पेंव *n.*

Grain-dealer, *n.* भुसारी, मोदी.

Grain-parcher, *n.* भडभुंज्या, भुजारी, भुजारा, भाजपी.

Gram, *n. Cicer arietinum.* चणा *m.* हरभरा *m.*

Acid obtained from g.-plants. आंब *f.*

Flour of g. बेसन *n.*

Flour of g. boiled and spiced. अळण *n.*

Flour of g. spiced and fried. फुरफुरी *f. or* रें *n.*

G. soaked and parched. फुटाणा *m.* चणे फुटाणे *m. pl.*

Green pods of g. parched. हवळा *or* हुळा *or* उळा *m.*

Green gram plants given to fatten horses. फसल *f.*

Pod of g. घाटा *m.* [तृणसदृश.

Gramineal, Gramineous, *a.* गवताच्याजातीचा, तृणजातीय,

Graminivorous, *a. feeding on grass.* तृणभक्षी, तृणाहारी, तृणाद, तृणजीवी.

GRAMMAR, *n.*—the science. व्याकरण *n.* शब्दशास्त्र *n.*
Rules of g. शब्दशासन *n.*
2—a book on it. व्याकरण *n.* व्याकरणाचें पुस्तक *n.*

GRAMMARIAN, *n.* व्याकरणी, वैयाकरणी, वैयाकरण, व्याकरणकार, शाब्दिक.
Mere g. केवल वैयाकरण, शुद्धवैयाकरण.

GRAMMATICAL, *a. relating to grammar.* व्याकरणाचा, व्याकरणसंबंधी, व्याकरणविषयक, वैयाकरण.
2 *according to grammar.* व्याकरणशुद्ध, व्याकरणसिद्ध, व्याकरणानुसारी, शब्दशास्त्रसिद्ध, शब्दशास्त्रानुसारी.
G. accuracy. शब्दशुद्धि *f.*
G. error. अपशब्द *m.*

GRAMMATICALLY, *adv.* v. A. व्याकरणानुसार, व्याकरणानुरूप, व्याकरण संभाळून, लिंगविभक्ति संभाळून.
If looked at g. व्याकरणदृष्टीनें पाहिलें असतां.

GRANARY, *n. store-house for grain.* कोठा *m.* कोठार *n. dim.* कोठी *f.* कोष्ठ *m.* कोष्ठक *m. n.* दास्तान *n.* धान्यशाला *f.* धान्यागार *n.* धान्यकोष्ठक *m. n.* अन्नकोष्ठ *m.* अन्नकोष्ठक *m. n.*
Subterraneous g. पेंव *n.*—lining of it (composed of bundles of holcus). भेळा *m.*

GRAND, *a. illustrious, &c.* v. GREAT. मोठा, थोर, महान्, वैभवाचा, वैभववान्, वैभवशाली.
2 *splendid, magnificent, &c.* v. FINE. भव्य, थाटाचा, थाटमाटाचा, ढबदार, टूमदार, धजदार, विराजमान, विराजित, देदीप्यमान *pop.* दैदीप्यमान, नामी, खासा, उमदा, आलिजाह्मं, धनत्तर, उदार.
3 *principal,* v. CHIEF. मुख्य, श्रेष्ठ, अग्रगण्य.

GRANDCHILD, *n.*—in male or female line. नातरूं *n.* नातवंड *or* नातुंड *or* नातोंड *n.*
G. of g. निपणत्वंड *n.*
Great g. पणतुंड *or* पणतोंड *or* पणत्वंड *n.*

GRANDDAUGHTER, *n.*—in male or female line. नात *f.* नातीण *f.*—*son's daughter.* पौत्री *f.*—*daughter's daughter.* दौहित्री *f.*
Great g. पणत *or* ती *or* थी *f.* पणतोली *f.* प्रपौत्री *f.*
Husband of g. नातजावाई *m.*

GRANDFATHER, *n.*—paternal. बाप आजा *m.* प्रपिता *m.* पितामह *m.* पितृपिता *m.*—paternal *or* maternal. आजा *m.*—maternal. माय आजा *m.* मातामह *m.* मातृपिता *m.*
Brother of g. चुलत आजा *m.*—his wife. चुलत आजी *f.*
Compellation for g. अजोबा.
G. of g. निपणजा *m.* वृद्ध प्रपितामह *m.*
G. of great g. खापर पणजा *m.*
Grandmother of g. निपणजी *f.* [प्रमातामह *m.*
Great g.—pat. पणजा *m.* प्रपितामह *m.*—mat. पणजा *m.*
House of mat. g. आजूळ *or* आजोळ *n.*
House of g. of g. निपणजूळ *or* निपणजोळ *n.*

GRANDMOTHER, *n.*—pat. बापआजी *f.* पितामही *f.*—pat. *or* mat. आजी *f.*—mat. माय आजी *f.* मातामही *f.*
Great g.—pat. पणजी *f.* प्रपितामही *f.*
G. of g. निपणजी *f.*

GRANDSIRE. See GRANDFATHER.

GRANDSON, *n.*—in male or female line. नातू *m.* नत्ता *m.*—*son's son.* पौत्र *m.*—*daughter's son.* दौहित्र *m.*
G. of great g. खापरपणतू *m.*
Grandchild of great g. खापरपणतोंड *or* त्वंड *n.*
Wife of g. नातसून *f.*
G. of g. निपणतू *m.*
Great g. पणतू *m.* प्रपौत्र *m.*
Wife of great g. पणतसून *f.*

GRANDEE, *n. nobleman.* सरदार *m.* अमीर *m.* मोठा मनुष्य *m.* बडालोक *m.* उमराव *m.* उंचपदवीचा मनुष्य *m.*

GRANDEUR, GRANDNESS, *n.* v. A. 1. मोठेपणा *m.* थोरी *f.* थोरवी *f.* बडेजाव *f.* ऐश्वर्य *n.* वैभव *n.* विभव *m.* भूति *f.* विभूति *f.*
2 भव्यपणा *m.* ढब *f.* ढबदारी *f.* छान *f.* थाट *m.* थाटमाट *m.* शानदारी *f.* डौल *m.* डौलदारी *f.* भव्यता *f.*

GRANGE, *n. a farm with buildings, &c.* शेतकीच्या घरांसुद्धां जमीन जुमला *m.*

GRANITE, *n.* एक जातीचा दगड आहे.

GRANIVOROUS, *a. subsisting on grain.* अन्नभक्षी, अन्नभोजी, अन्नाशी, अन्नजीवी, अन्नाहारी, धान्यभक्षक, शस्यभक्षक.

GRANNY, *n.* v. GRANDMOTHER. आजीबाई.

To GRANT, *v. a. concede, allow,* v. To ADMIT. कबूल-मान्य करणें, कबूल-मान्य-&c. असणें *with* स *or* ला *of o.* स्वीकार *m.*-रुकार *m.*-&c. करणें *g. of o.*
2 v. To GIVE. देणें, दान *n.* करणें, बक्षीस *n.* करणें.

GRANT, *n. gift by deed, &c.* इनाम *m. n.* इनामत *f.* शासन *n.*
Deed of g. v. DEED. इनामपत्र *n.* सनद *f.* शासनपत्र *n.*
Forged g. कूटशासन *n.*
Grants—compreh. इनाम इक्राम *n.*
G. of land. जाहगीर *f.* इनामत *f.*
G. of lands or tenements viewed as a means of subsistence. सानक *f.*
Holder of a g. इनामदार, जाहगीरदार.
Resumption of a g. दत्तापहार *m.*
Tax upon a g. इनामपट्टी *f.*
Voucher of a g. इनामपत्र *n.*

GRANTEE, *n. person to whom a grant is made.* इनाम घेणारा-पावणारा, प्रतिगृहीता.

GRANTOR, *n. person who grants.* इनाम देणारा, दाता.

GRANULAR, GRANULARY, *a.* दाण्याचा.

To GRANULATE, *v. n.*—as a healing sore. माठळणें, माठणें, मठारणें, शेजेस येणें, किरळ *m.* फुटणें.

GRANULATION, *n.* (of a sore). अंगूर *m.* किरळ *m.*
Medicaments to effect g. माठवण *n.*

GRANULE, *n. little grain or particle.* दाणा *m.* कंकर *m.* कण *m.* कणी *f.* कणिका *f.*
2 (of congealed honey, oil, &c.). रवा *m.* रवका *m.* कण्या *f. pl.*

GRANULOUS, *n.* v. N. 1. दाणेदार, कणीदार.
2 रवाळ, रवेदार, कणदार.

GRAPE, *n.*—the vine. द्राक्षा *pop.* द्राक्ष *f.* द्राक्षी *f.*—the fruit. द्राक्ष *n.* अंगूर *n.*
Some kinds are, फकिरी द्राक्ष, बेदाणा, साहेबी, सुलतानी.
Black g. काळें द्राक्ष *n.*
Juice of the g. द्राक्षारस *m.*

GRAPE-SHOT, *n.* कुलपीगोला *m.*

Graphic, Graphical, *a. well described.* उत्तम वर्णनाचा, सुवर्णनात्मक, सुवर्णित, सुनिरूपित, प्रत्यक्षसदृशबोधक, स्वरूपदर्शक, स्वरूपबोधक.

Graphically, *adv.* v. A. उत्तमवर्णनानें, मनांत भरेसा-ठसेसा *decl.*

Grapnel, *n. small anchor.* लोली *or* लोयली *f.* रोयली *f.*

To **Grapple**, *v. a.* v. To Seize. झोंबणें, झोंबाडणें, पकडणें.

To **Grapple**, *v. n. contend in close fight.* झोंबणें, झोंबी *f.*-पकड *f.* घेणें.

To **Grasp**, *v. a.* v. To Seize. मुठींत-पंज्यांत-कवज्यांत-हातांत-हातानें-&c. धरणें, धरणें, पकडणें, झोंबणें, झोंबाडणें, झोंबाडा *m.* घालणें-मारणें.

To g. at. धरूं-पकडूं-&c. पाहणें. [डाम.

Grasp, Grasping, *n.* v. V.—*act.* धरणें *n.* पकडणें *n.* &c. झोंबा-

I. *reach, power of mind,* v. Capacity. अवांका *m.* अटोंका*m.* आटंका *m.* आक्रमशक्ति *f.* आकलनशक्ति *f.* आव *m.* कव *f.*

II. *gripe, power,* v. Clutches. डाव *m.* आवडाव *m.* घावडाव *m.* अवांका *m.*

Grasping, *a.* v. Greedy. अधाशी, आशाळभूत.

Grass, *n.* गवत *n.* घास *m.* तृण *n.* तण *or* तन *n.* The common *grasses* are, करड, कशेट*or* कसई, काश, कुंजरा, कुत्रें, कुंदा, कुंभा, केणा, कोथेर *or* रें, गोंडाळ, गोप, गोपुर, चिकटा, चिमचारा *or* चिमणचारा, डांग, तांबेट, धापा, धुपा, निरा, पाटिंग, पंदें *or* धें, पयोधर, पुत्येण, बेर, बेरकी, बोबडा, बोर, भद्रमोथा, माकडशेंडा, माचळ, मारवेल, मुंज, मेथी, मोथ *or* मोथा, लव्हा *or* लव्हाळा, लोसंडीचार, लोहाळा, शिंपी, शेडें, साज, हड.

Bent g. *Agrostis linearis.* दुर्वा *f. pop.* दुरवा *f.* हरळी *f.*

Bits and ends of g. तणस *f.*

Blades of young g. चारकूट *n.*

The good grasses.—compreh. शाळूगवत *n.*

G. fit to be cut. कापींव गवत *n.* कापींव घास *m.*

G. sickle. खराळी *f.*

Green g. as growing on moist patches. जिताडा *or*रा*m.*

Implement for grubbing up g. खुरपें *n.* हातखुरपें*n.*रंभा*m.*

Sacrificial g. *Poa cynosuroides.* कुश *m. n.* दर्भ *pop.* दाभ*m.*

Stalk of g. तणसडी *or* खुडी *or* तणसरी *f.*

Young and green g. हिरवळ *f.* हिरवें *n.* चार *f.* शष्प *n.*

To become covered with g.—a field, &c. गवताळणें.

Grass-cloth, *n.* गवतीकापड *n.*

Grass-cutter, *n.* गवतकाप्या, गवत्या, घासकाप्या, घासवाला.

Grass-hopper, *n.* गवत्याटोळ *m.* टोळ *m.* नाकतोडा *or* ड्या *m.*ऊंट*m.*

Grass-plot, *n.* गवताची-चारीची-&c. सपाट जागा *f.*

Grassiness, *n.* v. A. गवताळपणा *m.* तृणाछादितत्व *n.* &c. तृणविपुलता *f.*

Grassy, *a. covered with grass.* गवताचा, गवताळ, गवताळा, तृणमय, तृणाकीर्ण, तृणाक्रांत, तृणाछादित, तृणव्याप्त.

Grate, *n. frame of bars.* गजांची जाळी *f.*

2 (of a fire place). गजांची शेगडी *f.* बसविलेली आगटी *f.*

To **Grate**, *v. a. wear by rubbing,* v. To Scrape. किसणें, घासून कीस *m.* काढणें. [डणें, खरारणें.

To **Grate**, *v. n. make a harsh noise.* करकरणें, खडखडणें, खडा-

2 fig. *be irritating.* बाईट-कर्कश-&c. लागणें.

Grated, *a. furnished with a grate.* गजांचे जाळीचा.

Grateful, *a. thankful.* उपकारी, आभारी, निमकहलाल, कृतज्ञ, उपकारज्ञ, उपकारस्मर्त्ता.

2 v. Agreeable. गोड, सुखप्रद, सुखद, सुखावह, हृदयंगम.

Gratefully, *adv.* v. A. 1. उपकार मानून-जाणून-आठवून-स्मरून, कृतज्ञतापूर्वक.

Gratefulness, *n.* v. A. 1. *and* Gratitude. निमकहलाली *f.* कृतज्ञता *f.* उपकारज्ञता *f.*

2 गोडी *f.* रंजकत्व *n.* सुखदायकत्व *n.*

Grater, *n. coarse scraper.* किसणी *f.*

Gratification, *n.* v. V. 1.—*act.* संतोषवणें *n.* &c. संतोषण *n.* संतोषीकरण *n.*—*state.* संतोष *m.* संतुष्टाई *f.*

2—*act.* पुरवणें *n.* संतर्पणें *n.* संतर्पण *n.*

I. *a g. a recompense,* v. Reward. हरकी *f.* पारितोषिक*n.*

II. See Pleasure.

Gratified, *p.* v. V. 1. संतोषवलेला, &c. संतोषित, संतुष्ट.

To be g. संतोषणें.

2 पुरवलेला, फेडलेला, &c. संतर्पित.

Gratifier, *n.* **Gratifying**, *p. a.* v. V. 1. संतोषवणारा, संतोष करणारा-देणारा, &c. संतोषकारक, सुखप्रद.

To **Gratify**, *v. a. delight,* v. To Please. संतोषवणें, संतोष*m.* करणें *g. of o.* संतोष*m.* देणें, खुश-संतुष्ट-संतोषित-&c. करणें.

2 *indulge,* v. To Satisfy. पुरवणें, पूर्ण-तृप्त-&c. करणें, फेडणें, संतर्पणें, संतर्पण*n.*-&c. करणें *g. of o.*

Grating, *n. harsh sound.* करकर *f.*—*intens.* करकराट*m.* खडखडाट*m.* खडाड*m.* खराड*m.* खरखराट*m.*

2 *or* **Gratings**; *matter grated.* कीस*m.*

Grating, *a. harsh sounding.* कर्कश, कर्णकटु, कर्णकठोर.

Gratingly, *adv. with a grating noise.* खडखड *or* डां *intens.* खडाखड, खरारां.

Gratis, *adv. for nothing.* फुकट, फुकटवारी, मुफत, फुकटाफुकट *or* टी, फुकटफाकट, फुका, फुकटफुका, एरवी.

Gratitude, *n. thankfulness, &c.* उपकारस्मरण*n.* उपकारस्मृति*f.* उपकारज्ञान*n.* कृतज्ञता *f.* उपकारज्ञता *f.* निमकहलाली *f.*

Gratuitous, *a. costing nothing.* फुकटचा, मुफतचा, फुकटा *or* ट्या, फुकटशाई, मुफती, बिनपैशाचा, एरवींचा.

Gratuitously. *adv.* v. Gratis. फुकट, फुकटवारी.

Gratuity, *n. present.* बक्षीस*n.* पारितोषिक*n.* संतोषदान*n.* इनाम*n.*

To **Gratulate**, &c. See To Congratulate, &c.

Grave, *a. solemn, serious, sober.* गंभीर, गंभीरमनाचा, सखोल, भरकुंब *or* भरकूम *or* खूम, गंभीरमनस्क, दीर्घ, धीर, प्रगल्भ.

2 See Weighty.

3—of sounds. *not acute.* प्लुत.

Grave, *n.* प्रेताची गार *f.* प्रेताचा खाडा*m.* प्रेतकुंड*n.* शवगर्त्ता *f.*

To be brought to the brink of the g. खाड्याच्या कडेसहोंड्याच्या डेंगेस येणें.

To **Grave**, *v. a. carve.* खोदणें, कोरणें.

Grave-clothes, *n.* प्रेतवस्त्र*n.* शववस्त्र*n.*

Gravel, *n.* कंकर*m.* रेंव *f.* रेंवा*m.* रेंवडा*m.* वाळू *f.* वालुका *f.* शर्करा *f.*

Heap of g. रेंवठा*m.*

2—the disease. मूतखडा*m.* शर्करा *f.* अश्मरी *f.* सिकता *f.*

Gravelly, *a.* v. N. रेंवट, रेंवसाळ, शर्करावान्, शार्कर, शार्करीय.

Gravely, *adv.* v. A. 1. गंभीरपणानें, भरकूमपणानें, गांभीर्यपूर्वक, गंभीरतेनें, हसल्यावाचून, नहसतां.

Graven, *p.* v. V. कोरलेला, &c. कोरींव.

GRAVENESS, GRAVITY, *n.* v. A. गंभीरपणा*m.* गांभीर्य*n.* गंभीरता *f.* भरकुमी *f.* भरकूमपणा*m.* धीरता *f.*

I. *heaviness*, v. WEIGHT. भार*m.* गौरव*n.* गरिमा*m.* गुरुत्व*n.* जाड्य*n.* भारमान*m.*

II. See GRAVITATION.

GRAVID. See PREGNANT.

To GRAVITATE, *v. n. tend to the centre.* गुरुत्वाकर्षण*n.* पावणें, गुरुत्वाकृष्ट होणें, मध्याभिसरण *n.*-मध्याभिगमन*n.*-केंद्राभिसरण*n.*-केंद्राभिगमन*n.* करणें. [&c.

GRAVITATION, *n.* v. V. गुरुत्वाकर्षण*n.* गुरुत्वहेतुकमध्याभिसरण*n.*

GRAVY, *a. juice of dressed meat.* भिजवण*n.* पक्वमांसरस*m.*

GRAY, *a. dirty white.* कबरा, कर्बुर, कसरा, धूसर.

Iron-g. करडा.

2—the eye. कैरा *or* खैरा.

3—hair. करडा, करड, पिकलेला.

To get g. फुलणें.

GRAY-EYED, *a.* कैरा.

GRAY-HEADED, पांढऱ्या केशांचा, पिकलेल्या केशांचा, रुपेरी केशांचा.

GRAY-HAIRED, *a.* पक्वकेश, पलित.

GRAYNESS, *n.* v. A. 1. कबरेपणा *m.* कसरेपणा *m.* &c. [णें.

To GRAZE, *v. a.* (cattle). चारणें, चारणीवर-चारणीस घालणें-ठेव-

2 *rase.* घसटणें, घसवटणें, घासटणें, चाटणें, चरवटणें, झाजरणें, चाटून-घासटून-घसवटून-&c. जाणें.

To GRAZE, *v. n.*—cattle. चरणें.

GRAZED, *p.* v. V. A. 2. घसटलेला, &c.

To be g. खरचटणें, घासटणें.

GRAZIER, *n. feeder, &c. of cattle.* गुरेंचारणारा, गुराखी, गुराख्या, गोवारी, राखणा, पशुपालक, पशुपाल, चारक.

GRAZIERY, GRAZING, *n.* राखणावळ *f.* पाशुपाल्य *n.*

G. of cattle at night. पसरा *m.*

GREASE, *n.* चरबी *f.* माखण *n.* ओशट *n.* स्नेह *m.* [टा *m.*

2—as adhering to lamps, oil vessels, &c. मेणकट *n.* चिक-

To be smeared with this g. मेणकटणें.

3 (for axles). ओंगण *n.*

4—disease in the horse. मेंडी *f.*

To GREASE, *v. a.* चरबी *f.*-&c. लावणें, माखणें, बुळबुळावणें, चुळबुळावणें, चुळबुळीत-मिळमिळीत-&c. करणें.

2 (axles, &c.). ओंगणें, ओंगण *n.* लावणें-घालणें.

GREASINESS, *n.* v. A. 1. ओशट *n.* बुळबूळ *f. intens.* बुळबुळाट*m.* चिकणाई *f.* तेलटपणा *m.* स्निग्धता *f.* बुळबुळीत*n.*

2 चुळबुळीतपणा *n.* मेणकटपणा *m.* &c. मिळमीळ *f. intens.* मिळमिळाट *m.* [स्निग्ध.

GREASY, *a. oily, fat.* चिकण, चिकणवट, बुळबुळीत, तेलट, तेलकट,

G. or unctuous article of food. ओशट *n.* [तेलकट.

2 *smeared with g.* चुळबुळीत, मिळमिळीत, ओशट, मेणकट,

To be or become g. चुळबुळणें.

GREAT, *a.* v. LARGE. मोठा, थोर, थोरला, महान् (महती *f.* महत् *n.*), महा (in comp.), स्थूल *or* ळ, गुरु, बृहत्.

As g. जेवढा, जितका.

How g. केवढा.

So g. तेवढा, तितका.

So g. एवढा, इतका.

2 *of a high degree; high, much, intense, &c.* मोठा, भारी, महा (in comp.), परम (in comp.), फार, अतिशय.

A g. deal. See MUCH.

3 *important, weighty.* मोठा, भारी, महा (in comp.), वजनदार, वजनाचा.

4 *of high rank, noble, illustrious, exalted, grand, mighty, &c.* मोठा, थोर, थोरवट, थोरवीचा, बडा, श्रीमान्, श्रीमंत, बुद्रुख, प्रौढ, तेजस्वी, तेजवंत, तेजोमय, प्रतापी, प्रतापवान्, प्रतापशाली, उमदा, ठळक, असाधारण, नरवर, मानवृद्ध, राजमान्य (in notes and writings).

A g. man. मानभाजन *n.* महाजन *m.* बडालोक *m.* वृंद *n.* बीर *m.* व्यक्ति *f.*

Contest with the g. समर्थस्पर्धा *f.* [ला *m.*

Connection (interest) with the g. वशिला *m.* वगवशि-

Dependent on the g. महदाश्रय.

The g. बडेलोक *m. pl.* थोरलोक *m. pl.*

The g. and small, rich and poor, high and low. हालीमवाली *m. pl.* लहानथोर, लहानमोठे *m. pl.* छोटा मोटा.

To become a g. man. शिष्टावणें.

To play the g. man. बडाई *f.*-बडिवार *m.* हाकणें, फुशारकी *f.* मिरवणें-मांडणें-करणें. [नीचा.

5 *splendid, magnificent, grand.* मोठा, उमदा, शानदार, छा-

6 *familiar, thick*, v. INTIMATE. सलगीचा, खेळीमेळीचा.

7 *hard, grievous.* जड, कठीण, मुशकील.

8 See PREGNANT.

GREAT, *n.* SEE GROSS, LUMP.

By the g. उक्ता *decl.*

GREATER, *a.* अधिक मोठा-थोर-&c. थोरला, सरस, अधिक, विशेष.

GREATEST, *a.* सर्वांहून *or* सर्वांपेक्षां मोठा-थोर-&c. अवल.

GREATLY, *adv. in a great degree*, v. VERY. फार, बहुत, अति, अतिशय, पराकाष्ठेचा.

2 SEE NOBLY.

GREATNESS, *n.* v. A. मोठेपणा *m.* महत्व *n.* महिमा *m.* महिमान *n.* स्थूलता *f.* स्थौल्य *n.* बृहत्व *n.*

2 मोठेपणा *m.* भारीपणा *m.*

3 मोठेपणा *m.* भारीपणा *m.*

4 मोठेपणा *m.* थोरपणा *m.* थोरवी *f.* थोरी *f.* थोराई *f.* थोरवकी *f.* ऐश्वर्य *m.* माहात्म्य *n.* श्रीमंती *f.* मातबरी *f.* बडेजाव *f.* विभव *m.pop.* वैभव *n.* महिमा *m.f.* महंता *f.* महती *f.* प्रभव *m.* भभाव *m.* भूति *f.* विभूति *f.*

GREAVES, *n. armour for the legs.* जंघात्राण *n.*

GREED, GREEDINESS, *n.* v. A. 1. खादाडपणा *m.* अधासीपणा *m.* &c. खाखा *f.* खाखाई *f.* बखबख *f.* खवखव *f.*

2 लोभ *m.* सोस *m.* हिरस *or* हिरीस *f.* बखबख *f.* खवखव *f.* हावरेपणा *m.* हिरसीपणा *m.* अहोपीपणा *m.* &c.

GREEDILY, *adv.* v. A. 1. खाखाईनें, घाईघाईनें, हावरेहावरे.

2 लोभानें, लोभबुद्ध्या, लोभदृष्ट्या, लोभभावानें.

GREEDY, *a. ravenous, voracious*, v. GLUTTONOUS. खादाड, अधासी, अधोडी, अधोरी, बखबख्या.

2 *vehemently desirous*, v. COVETOUS. लोभी, लोभिष्ट, हावरा, हिरसी, बखबख्या, अहोपी, सोशी *or* सोसी, आशाळभूत, लोभान्वित, लोभाविष्ट.

GREEDY-EYE, *a.* v. COVETOUS. आशाभूत, आशाळभूत.

GREEN, *a.* हिरवा, *remiss.* हिरवट *greenish*, हरित.

Dark g. हिरवागार, हिरवाचार.

Of a pea-green, or darkish g. निबुरडा. [निळा.

2—of plants; *succulent, sappy.* ओला, कोवळा, सरस, रसाळ,

G. food (grass, leaves, &c.) for cattle. आलें n. ओलें पालें n. झाडपाला m. नीळवट f. हिरवें n. हिरवळ f. चार f. भुइंचार f. हिरवीचार f.

G. grass, g. corn, g. crops. निळें n. नीळवट f.

3—of wood, *not dry.* हिरवा, ओला, आंग ओला, दमट, दमसार, चिंबट, आर्द्र.

G. sticks, logs, or billets. ओलट or ओलवट f.

4 *raw, unripe, unprepared,* lit. fig. हिरवा, हिरवंडा, हिरवस, कच्चा, अपक्क, अपरिपक्क.

GREEN, n.—the color. हिरवा रंग m. हरितवर्ण m.

2 *grassy plain.* ओलवण f. गवताड n. f. नीळवट f. हिरवें n.

3 greens. भाजी f. भाजी पाला m.

Greens and roots, *rude fare.* आला पाला m. आलें पालें n. झाड पाला m.

G. kept cropped. खुंटभाजी f.

4 *verdure.* हिरवळ f. हिरवट f. नीळवट f. सबजी f.

GREEN GROCER, n. माळवेविक्या, काछी, कुंजरा.

GREEN-HORN, n. *raw, inexperienced person.* कच्चा, अजाण, अल्लड, अपेट, नवा, अव्यवहार.

GREEN HOUSE, n. कोवळीं झाडें राखण्याकरितां केलेलें घर n.

GREEN MARKET, n. माळसात f. माल्हट m. मंडई f.

GREENNESS, n. v. A. 1. हिरवेपणा m. सबजी f.

2 कोवळेपणा m. ओलेपणा m.-&c. कोवळीक f. ओलावा m.

3 हिरवेपणा m. ओलेपणा m. दमसरपणा m. ओलावा m.

4 हिरवेपणा m. कच्चेपणा m. अपक्कता f. अपक्कदशा f.

GREEN ROOM, n. नेपथ्य n. नेपथ्यशाळा f.

To GREET, v. a. v. To SALUTE. नमस्कार m.-रामराम m.-सलाम m.करणें-सांगणें, कुशलप्रश्न m.-क्षेमप्रश्नm.-अभिवादनn.-&c. करणें.

To GREET. v. n. See To WEEP.

GREETING. See SALUTATION. [कलापस्थ.

GREGARIOUS, a. *going in flocks.* अनेकचर, संगचर, समूहचर,

GRENADE, n.—the missile. अनार m. n. नळा m. हिंगणबेट n.

GREY. See GRAY.

GREY-HOUND, n. शिकारी कुत्र्यांची एक जात आहे.

GRIDDLE, n. *girdle or plate for baking.* तवा m.

GRIDIRON, n. मास भाजण्याचें एक साधन आहे.

GRIEF, n. *sorrow,* v. AFFLICTION. दुःखn. खेदm. शोकm. झुरहूर f. मनस्ताप m.

2 *cause of sorrow.* दुःख n. दुखास कारण n.

GRIEVANCE, n. *cause of grief.* दुःख n. दुखाची गोष्ट f. दुःख देणारी गोष्ट f. संकट n. अनिष्ट n. दुःखास्पद n. गौरव n.

To GRIEVE, v. a. *distress, pain,* v. To AFFLICT. दुःख n.-क्लेश m.-&c. देणें, दुःखी-खिन्न-श्रमी-&c. करणें, दुखवणें or दुखावणें, रडवणें, श्रमवणें.

To be grieved. दुखारणें, दुःखी-खिन्न-&c. होणें.

To GRIEVE, v. n. *sorrow.* रडणें, दुःख n.-खेद m.-शोक m.-&c. करणें, चिंतावणें, दुखारणें, दुःखी-श्रमी-कष्टी-&c. होणें.

To g. excessively. प्राण m. ओकणें.

To g. over. खेद m. मानणें g. of o.

2 (for a person or thing lost or gone), v. To FRET. चुरमुरणें, मंगळ m. गातवसणें, ढासरा or ढोसरा m. धरणें g. of o. टोकळा or टुकळा m. धरणें-करणें g. of o. झुरझुरणें, रुणा m. घेणें g. of o. or, *inversely,* लागणें g. of o.

GRIEVED, a. v. SORROWFUL. दुःखी, खिन्न, दिलगीर, खेदयुक्त.

GRIEVER, n. GRIEVING, p. a. v. V. A. दुःख देणारा, दुःखद, दुःखप्रद, दुःखदायक.

v. V. N. रडणारा, &c. दुःखी, दुःखित, खिन्न, खेदित, दिलगीर, रंजीस, खेदयुक्त, समुत्सुक.

GRIEVING, n. v. V. A.—*act.* दुःख देणें n. &c. दुःखप्रापण n.

v. V. N. रडणें n. रड f. v. घे, खेद m. शोक m.

2 खुरखुर f. चुरमूर f. झुरहूर f. चुटपूट f. रुखरूख f. अपसोस m.

GRIEVOUS, a. *painful, burdensome,* v. AFFLICTIVE. जड, कठीण, अवघड, भारी, जबर, जरब, दुःखकारक, दुःखद, दुःखप्रद, &c. सखत, दुःसह, क्लेशकारक, क्लेशद, &c.

To feel g. अवघड-जड-&c. वाटणें *in. con.*

2—of faults, &c. भारी, मोठा, गुरु, महा (in comp.).

3—of complaints. अतिदुखाचा, परमसंकटाचा.

GRIEVOUSNESS, n. v. A. 1. कठीणपणा m. अवघडपणा m. भारीपणा m. &c. दुःसहता f. गौरव n.

GRIFFIN, n. v. GREEN-HORN. नवा, नवा आलेला.

To GRILL, v.a. *broil.* भाजणें, भाजण n.-भर्जन n.-भाजप n. करणें g. of o.

GRILL, n. a. *grilled article or dish.* भाजण n. भाजणें n. भाजप n. भाजलेला पदार्थ m.

GRILLED, p. v. V. भाजलेला, भाजका, भाजींव, भर्जित, भृष्ट.

GRILLING, n. v. V.—*act.* भाजणें n. भर्जन *pop.* भाजण n.भाजप n. भाजणूक f.

GRIM, GRIM-FACED, a. *fierce looking, ill-looking.* भयंकरतोंडाचा, तोंडाचा भयंकर, उग्र, उग्रमुद्रेचा, उग्रमुख, उग्रवदन, कालस्वरूप, क्रूरमुख, व्याघ्रमुख, विकटमूर्त्ति.

GRIMACE, n. *wry face.* माकडचेष्टा f. वांकुली f. विचकुली f.

To make grimaces. वांकुल्या f.pl.-वेंटावण्या f.pl.-वेडावणें n.-विचकुल्या or वेचकुल्या f. pl.-वानरविचकुल्या f.pl.-&c. दाखवणें.

GRIME, n. *deeply insinuated dirt.* कीट n. खट f. कट m. काटm. किटण n. कलच m.

To GRIME, v. a. v. N. किटवणें, काटवणें, कटवणें.

To be grimed. किटणें, काटणें, कटणें.

GRIMLY, *adv.* v. A. उग्रतोंडानें, उग्रमुद्रेनें, &c. उग्रमुख करून, &c.

GRIMNESS, n. v. A. तोंडाचा उग्रपणाm.-&c.उग्रमुखता f.मुखक्रौर्यn.

GRIMY, a. v. N. किटलेला, कटलेला.

To GRIN, v. n. दांत m.pl. विचकणें-काढणें-दाखवणें or विचकून-काढून-दाखवून हासणें, बत्तिसी f. दाखवणें, कवळ्या f.pl.-कवड्या f. pl. बाहेर काढणें-दाखवणें, खिसखीस हासणें.

GRIN, GRINNING, n. v. V.—*act.* दांत विचकणें n. &c. दांत विचकणी f. खिसाणा m. v. मांड, दंतप्रदर्शन n.

To GRIND, v. a. दळणें, पिसणें, पेसणें or पेषणें, दळण n.-दळप n.-दलन n.-पेषण n. करणें g. of o.

2—coarsely. भरडणें, घरटणें or घरडणें, चरडणें, घसाडणें.

Grain, &c. taken to be coarsely ground. भरडण n.

3 *rub upon a stone.* वाटणें.

4 *sharpen upon a stone.* सहाणेवर घासणें-लावणें-पाजणें.

Grinding wheel (for knives, scissors, &c.) चरकी or सीf.

5 *chew.* चावणें, चर्वणें, चर्वण n. करणें g. of o.

6. v. To OPPRESS. घाण्यांत-चरकांत-&c. घालणें.

7 (the teeth) करकराविणें.

GRINDSTONE, *n.* सहाण *f.* शाण *m.*

GRINDER, *n.* v. V. 1. दळणारा, &c. दळणकरी, दळपी, दळ्या, दलनकर्त्ता, पेषणकर्त्ता.

I. *back-tooth.* दाढ *f.* [पेषण *n.*

GRINDING, *n.* v. V. 1. दळणें *n.* &c. दळण *n.* दळप *n.* दलन *n.*

G. and pounding, — compreh. दळाकांडा *or* कांडादळा *n.* दळण कांडण *n.* कांडाभरडा *m.*

Mill for g. जातें *n.*

Price or cost of g. दळणावळ *f.* दळाई *f.* दळप *n.* पिसणावळ *f.* पिसाई *f.*

2 भरडणें *n.* &c. भरडण *n.* चरडभरड *f.*

Noise of rough g. घरडा *m.* घराडा *m.*

3 वाटणें *n.* वाटण *n.* मलन *n.* विमर्दन *n.*

GRINNER, *n.* GRINNING, *p. a.* v. V. दांत दासवून हांसणारा, दांत विचकणारा, &c. दांतविचक्या, दांतकाढ्या.

GRINNINGLY, *adv.* दांत विचकून, दांत दासवून, खिसखीस.

To GRIPE, *v. a. grasp, &c.* v. To SEIZE. मुठींत- कवज्यांत-चिकाटींत-&c. धरणें, धरणें, पकडणें, झोंबणें, झोंबाडणें.

2 *hold fast.* गच्च-बळकट-&c. धरणें.

3 (the bowels). पोटांत मुरडा *m.*-तिडीक *f.*-शूळ *m.*-&c.करणें.

GRIPE, GRIPING, v. V. 1.—*act.* धरणें *n.* &c. झोंबाडा *m.* v.घाल, मार, कबज *n.* पकड *f.* मिठी *or* हाताची मिठी *f.* चिकाटी *f.*

I. (of an opponent in argument). चिकाटी *or* चिकोटी *f.*

II. *grasp, power,* v. CLUTCHES. डाव *m.* आवडाव *m.* अवांका *m.* [परिणामशूल *m.*

III. gripes; *colic.* मुरडा *m.*मरोडा *m.* पोट दुखणें *n.* पोटदुखी *f.*

To have the gripes. पोटांत मुरडणें-मुरडून येणें *v. imper.* वेंट *m. pl.* फिरणें *in. con.* [मुखक्रौर्य *n.*

GRISLINESS, *n.* v. A. अकराळपणा *m.* विकराळपणा *m.* उग्रता *f.*

GRISLY, *a. hideous, frightful,* v. FEARFUL. अकराळ, विकराळ, भयंकर, भयानक, भीमदर्शन, उग्रदर्शन.

GRIST, *n. corn to be ground.* दळण *n.* दळप *n.* भरडण *n.* घाणा *m.* घाणी *f.* वैरण *n.* घास *m.*

To pour in g. वैरणें. [*n.* नलक *n.*

GRISTLE, *n. cartilage.* कूर्चा *f.* तरुणास्थि *n.* मृद्वस्थि *n.*कोमलास्थि

GRISTLY, *a.* v. N. तरुणास्थिमय, तरुणास्थिरूप.

GRIT, *n.* (of meal). भरड *m.* भरडा *m.* सांजा *m.* कण्या *f. pl.*

A g. रवा *m.* तरीं *n.*

Husks and grits in meal. चरड *n.* चरंडा *m.*

2 *sand, rough particles.* रेंव *f.* रेंवाळें *n.* रेंवा *m.*

A g. सकेरा *or* सकिरा *m.*

GRITTINESS, *n.* v. A. रेंवटपणा *m.* रेंवाळ *m.* &c. किचकिचीतपणा *m.* &c. कच *f.*

GRITTY, *a. having grit.* रेंवट, रेंवाळ, रेंवड, कचकचीत, किचकिचीत, शर्करावान्.

GRIZZLE, *n. mixture of white and black.* करडारंग*m.* कबरारंग*m.*

GRIZZLED, GRIZZLY, *a. turning grey.* करडा, काळापांढरा, कबरा, धूसर, मोरा. [रवणें.

To GROAN, *v. n.* कन्हणें, कुंथणें, विळवणें *or* विल्हाळणें, हुंबणें, प-

GROAN, GROANING, *n.* v. V. कन्हणें *n.* कुंथणें *n.* विळवणें *n.* &c. कन्हें *n.* कुन्हती *f.* विळवणी *f.* विल्हाळ *m.* हायहूय *f.* हायाहूया *m.*

GROANER, *n.* GROANING, *p. a.* v. V. कन्हणारा, &c. विळव्या, विल्हाळ्या.

GROAT, *n. four pence.* गंडा *m.*

GROCER, *n. seller of grocery.* पसारी, किराण्या, वाणी.

Green g. माळवें विक्या, बागवान, कुंजडा *or* कुंजरा.

GROCERY, GROCER'S WARE, *n. sugars, spices, &c.* किराणा *m.* खाजें *n.* वाणजिन्नस *m.* वाणसौदा *m.*

GROIN, *n.* मांडीचा सांधा *m.* ऊरूसंधि *m.* ऊरूमूल *n.* गोडें आंग *n.* आडसंधि *m. f.* आडसांधा *m.* वंक्षण *m.* कटिसंधि *m.* ढेसण *n.* ढेंसें *n.* जांघ *f.*

GROOM, *m. attendant on a horse.* घोडक्या, मोतद्दार *or* मोतादार, नफर *m.* खासदार, घोडेवाला *esp. of Europeans.*

Business of a g. घोडकी *f.* मोतद्दारी *f.* खासदारी *f.*

2 See SERVANT. 3 See BRIDEGROOM.

To GROOM, *v. a.* v. N. 1. चाकरी *f.*-मालीश *f.*-खरारा *m.* करणें *g. of o.* पाठ *f.* पुसणें-चोळणें *g. of o.* [माल *m.*

Lip-rope used in grooming. होटाळी *or* ओटाळी *f.* पुज-

GROOVE, *n. channel or hollow cut by a tool.* खाजणी *f.* खंचणी *f.* कोरणी *f.* खोवण *or* णी *f.* खचरा *m.*

A sliding or running g. अखोटा *n.* थिरणी *f.*

To GROOVE, *v. a.* v. N. खांचणी *f.*-&c. करणें-पाडणें-खोदणें.

A grooving plane. खचरा *m.* पिलपील *f.* चिरणी *f.*

GROOVE-SLIP, *n.* ओंदण *n.*

To GROPE, *v. n. feel along, feel about.* चांचपडणें, चांचपणें *or* चांपचणें, चांपणें, चांपत -चांचपडत -चांचपत-&c. जाणें-पाहणें-&c. रांपणें.

GROPINGLY, *adv.* चांपत, चांचपडत, चांचपत.

GROSS, *n. the bulk, the mass, the lump.* भररास *f.* ठोकरास *f.* ठोकमाल *m.* ठोकजमा *f.*

In the g. By the g. v. LUMP. ठोक *or* एकठोक, सकट *or* सगट, सकटासाली, एकरकम, उक्ता *decl.* उक्तें.

2 *number of twelve dozen.* चोवीस छकड्या *f. pl.*

GROSS, *a. coarse, rough, thick, &c.* v. COARSE. मोटा, मोटाधाटा, स्थूल, भसाडा, रटाला, रटेल, ऐवट, जाडा.

2 *dense, not refined, &c.* स्थूल, जड.

3 *enormous, great, &c.*—of faults, &c. भारी, मोठा, गुरु, महा (in comp.), भोपळा एवढा.

4 *dull.* स्थूल, स्थूलबुद्धि, स्थूलमति.

5 *indelicate, obscene, vulgar, &c.* अचकट विचकट, विचकट, बाष्कळ, बीभत्स, कुत्सित, अवाच्य. [र, बळकट.

6 *palpable, great,*—ignorance, &c. गाढ, निबिड, दाट, घो-

7 *whole.* कच्चा, ठोक.

GROSSNESS, *n.* v. A. 1. मोठेपणा *m.* भसाडेपणा *m.* रटालेपणा *m.* स्थूलत्व *n.* स्थौल्य *n.*

2 स्थूलत्व *n.* स्थौल्य *n.*

3 भारीपणा *m.* मोठेपणा *m.* &c.

4 स्थूलता *f.* स्थूलबुद्धि *f.* स्थूलमति *f.*

5 विचकटपणा *m.* बाष्कळपणा *m.*

GROTESQUE, *a. of wild or whimsical figure.* वेडाविद्रा, वेडाविपारा, वेधूड, अपरूप, विलक्षण, वक्राकृति.

GROTESQUENESS, v. A. वेडेविद्रेपणा *m.* &c. अपरूपता *f.*

GROTTO, GROT, *n.* v. CAVE. गुहा *f.* गव्हर *n.*

GROUND, *p.* v. V. 1. दळलेला, &c. दलित, चूर्णीत, चूर्णकृत.

2 भरडलेला, &c. भरडींव, भरडी, भरड.

3 बाटलेला, बाटींव.

GROUND, *n.* भुई *f.* भूमि *f.* जमीन *f.* धरणी *f.* धरती *f.*

Along the g. भुईसरपट.

An abandoned or waste piece of g. सराबा *m.*

G. obtained from the sea. खार *f.* खारट *n. f.*

G. saturated with moisture. उपळवट *f.* उपळवटा *m.*

Holy g. देवभूमि *f.* पुण्यभूमि *f.* पुण्यक्षेत्र *n.*

Level g. सपाटी *f.* समथळ*n.* तवा*m.* समभूमि *f.*

Low g. दचका*m.*

Rising g. उंचवटा*m.* उंचवळा*m.* उंचाड*n.*

Off or free from the g.—a weight under raising. भुइसांड. जमीनसांड, तळसांड.

To gain g. v. To ADVANCE. सरशी *f.*-सरशीबाजू *f.*-सरसाई *f.*-&c. होणें *g. of s.*

To run aground. तळास-भुईस-&c. लागणें.

To lose g. See To DECLINE.

To shift or leave one's g. *fig.* रान*n.* बदलणें-सोडणें, पारखें *n.* होणें *g. of s.*

2—esp. with reference to agriculture, v. LAND. काळी *f.*

Black g. काळीजमीन *f.* काळवट जमीन *f.*

Dry. g. g. without moisture. निपळ *f.* [पाण्याचा.

Raised by the moisture of the g. ओलाचा, निपाणी, नि-

3 *land occupied*, v. FIELD, ENCLOSURE. शेत*n.*

Grounds—compreh. *all fields and enclosures, &c.* जमीनजुमला*m.* शेतवाडी *f.* शेतपोत*n.* शेतभात*n.* [वर*m.*

4 *floor.* जमीन *f.* भूमि *f.* भुई *f.* तल*n.* *pop.*तळ*m.* भुईसर*n.* पर-

On the g. भुईसर.

5 (of an encampment, &c.). तळ*m.*

To break g. प्रस्थान *or* अंगप्रस्थान*n.* करणें. [तवा*m.*

6 (of a picture, a garment, &c.). जमीन *f.* भूमि *f.* भुई *f.*

7 *foundation, footing, warrant, authority, &c.* जागा *f.* पाया *m.* ठिकाण*n.* ठिकाणा*m.* थार *or* थारा*m.* बीज*n.* हेतु*m.* लाग*m.* प्रमाण*n.* गमक*n.* मुद्दा*m.* आधार*m.* आश्रय*m.* मूळ*n.* उपष्टंभ*m.*

Having g.—a story, &c. ठिकाणबद्ध.

8 *place of action.* See FIELD.

9 grounds; v. DREGS. गाळ*m.*गाळसाळ*m.* सांका*m.* रेंदा*m.*

To GROUND, *v. a. lay or set on the ground.* भुईवर-&c. ठेवणें-टेंकणें.

2 *found.* आधार*m.*-आश्रय*m.*-&c. धरणें-घेणें-सांगणें-&c. आधारानें-आश्रयानें-आधारावरून-&c. करणें-सांगणें-&c.

3 *settle in first principles.* मूलग्रंथांत पक्का करणें, मूलतत्वप्रवीण-मूलतत्वपारंगत-परिभाषाभिज्ञ-&c. करणें.

To GROUND, *v. n. run aground.* तळास-भुईस-तळावर-कोरड्यावर-&c. लागणें-लागून असणें.

GROUND FLOOR, *n.* तळ*m.* तळचा मजला *m.*खालचा मजला*m.*

GROUND-NUT *n.* भुईमूग*m.*

GROUND-PLAN, *n.* दुर्ते*n.*

GROUND-RENT, *n.* भुईभाडें*n.* भुईदेणें*n.*

GROUND-WORK. *n. base-part*, v. FOUNDATION. पाया*m.* बुडखा*m.*

2 *initial steps or stages.* मूल *or* ळ*n.* मूळपीठिका *f.* पठार*m.* *v.* घाल, पावटा*m.* पायंडा*m.*

GROUNDLESS, *a. unreasonable, &c.* v. CAUSELESS. अकारण, निःकारण, निर्निमित्त, नाधाणी *or* नी. [निराश्रय.

2—a report, &c. ठिकाणावांचूनचा, निर्मूल, निर्बीज, निराधार,

GROUNDLESSLY, *adv.* v. A. 1. कारणावांचून, &c. निःकारण, निर्निमित्त, नाधाणी *or* नी, उगा *decl.*

GROUNDLESSNESS, *n.* v. A. 1. अकारणत्व*n.* निःकारणत्व*n.*

2 निर्मूलता *f.* निराधारता *f.* &c. प्रमाणाभाव*m.* आधाराभाव*m.* आधारराहित्य*n.* &c.

GROUP, *n. cluster, assemblage.* गट्ट*m.*गट्टा*m.*जमाव*m.*टोळी *f.*

To GROUP, *v. a.* एकेठिकाणीं जमविणें, जमाव*m.*-&c. करणें *g. of o.*

GROUSE, *n.* पक्ष्यांची एक जात आहे.

Rock g. पकोरडी *f.*

GROUT, *n. coarse meal.* सांजा*m.*

2 grouts. See LEES.

GROVE, *n. wood.* राई *f.* वन*n.* बन *n.* उपवन *n.* वृक्षवाटिका *f.* कानन*n.* उद्यान*n.* वृक्षजाल*n.*

To GROVEL, *v. n.* भुई *f.*-जमीन *f.*-&c. धरणें-धरून असणें-धरून चालणें, रांगणें.

GROVELLING, *a. mean, undignified,* v. Low. हलका, नीच, अधम, निकृष्ट, पाजी, जघन्य.

To GROW, *v. n. be produced by vegetation.* रुजणें *or* रुझणें, उपजणें, निपजणें, उत्पन्न होणें.

2 *advance to maturity.* वाढणें, वाढणीस-वाढीस लागणें, चढणें, मोठा होत जाणें, थोरावणें, उचलणें.

3—rapidly, vigorously; *shoot up.* उफाटणें, उफाट्यानें-धुमाऱ्यानें वाढणें, गरगरां *adv.* वाढणें, गरगरणें, उफणणें *or* उफाणणें, बोकडणें, सरसावणें, सरळणें, उचलणें, उसळणें.

That grows or has grown rapidly—animal or plant. वाढाळ, वाढाळू, उसुलवार, उद्दाम.

4 *increase, enlarge,* v. To INCREASE. वाढणें, वाढत जाणें-चालणें, वर्धणें, लांबणें, पुच्छ *n.* फुटणें-वाढणें-लांबणें *in. con.*

5 v. To BECOME. होणें, होतजाणें.

6 together. मिळून-लागून जाणें.

7 up; *arrive at manhood.* वयांत येणें, लहानाचा मोठा होणें.

To GROW, *v. a. raise by cultivation.* पिकवणें, निपजविणें, उत्पन्न करणें.

GROWER, *n.* GROWING, *p. a.* v. V. N. 2. वाढणारा, वाढता, वाढीस लागणारा, वाढीस लागलेला, &c.

4 वाढणारा, वाढत चालला, &c. वाढता, वर्धमान, वृद्धिंगत, वर्धिष्णु.

GROWING, GROWTH, *n.* v. V. N. 1. रुजणें *n.* &c.

2 वाढणें *n.* &c. वाढ *f.* वाढणी *f.* वृद्धि *f.* अभिवृद्धि *f.*

Made to allow for g.—a garment. वाढत्या आंगाचा.

4 वाढणें *n.* &c. वाढ *f.* वाढणी *f.* वर्धन *n.* वृद्धि *f.*

I. v. PRODUCE. उपज *m.* निपज *m.*

To GROWL, *v. n.*—as a dog, &c. गुरकणें, गुरकावणें, गुरगुरणें, गुरगुरावणें (*or* घुरघुरणें, घुरघुरावणें), गुरगूर *f.*-&c. करणें.

2 *murmur*, v. To GRUMBLE. कुरकुरणें, बुरबुरणें, कुरमुरणें, कुरकूर *f.*-पुटपूट *f.*-&c. करणें-लावणें.

GROWL, GROWLING, *n.* v. V. 1.—*act.* गुरकणें *n.* &c. गुरकणी *f.* गुरकावणी *f.* गुरगुरावणी *f.* गुरगूर *f.* *or* घुरघूर *f.* *intens.* गुरगुराट *or* घुरघुराट *m.*

2 कुरकुरणें *n.* &c. कुरकूर *f.* कुरमूर *f.* पुटपूट *f.*

GROWLER, *n.* GROWLING, *p. a.* v. V. 1. गुरकणारा, &c. गुरक्या.

2 कुरकुरणारा, कुरकूर करणारा, &c. कुरकुऱ्या, कुरमुऱ्या.

GROWN, *p.* v. V. N. 1. रुजलेला, उपजलेला, &c.
2 वाढलेला, मोठा झालेला, &c. वृद्ध.
4 वाढलेला, &c. वृद्ध, वर्धित, समृद्ध.
7 वयांत आलेला, पूर्ण वाढलेला, भरवाढीचा, प्रौढ, प्रवृद्ध.

GROWTH. See GROWING.

GRUB. See WORM.

To GRUB, *v.a. root out by digging.* खुरपणें, खुरपून टाकणें-काढणें, खुरप्यानें काढणें, चोखळून काढणें, तळसून काढणें.

GRUB-AXE, GRUB-HOE, *n.* खुरपें *dim.* हातखुरपें *n.* रंभा *m.* रंभापुतळी *f.* दावली *f.*

GRUB-GRASS, *n. short grass.* खरडा *m.*

To GRUDGE, *v. a.* See To ENVY. 2 *give unwillingly.* मोठ्या संकटानें-दुःखानें-कष्टानें-जुलमानें-&c. देणें.

GRUDGE, *n. sullen malice,* v. MALICE. अकस *m. f.* खुनस *m.* अदावत *f.* चुरस *f.* कुन्हा *m. v.* धर, दावा *m.* आड दावा *m.* डाव *m.* हट *m.* मुकादावा *m.* कोर *f.* कोरबंदी *f.* पीळ *m.* डौंक *m. v.* राख, धर, शल्य *pop.* सल *n.* गुबारा *or* गुभारा *m.* गांठ *f.* गोवरीची आग *f.* कुपित्थ *n.* मानसहिंसा *f.* अंतर्दाह *m.*
To gratify a g. दावा *m.* उगवणें, वैरोद्धार *m.*करणें.
To maintain a g. मनांत गांठ *f.* ठेवणें.

GRUDGE-BEARING, *a. spiteful.* अकसखोर, अकसी, कुन्हेवाईक, दावेदार, दावेकरी, दीर्घद्वेषी, मेण्यासाप, आडगांठ्या, कुधण.

GRUDGINGLY, *adv.* v. V. असंतोषानें, मोठ्या संकटानें, दुःखानें, कष्टानें, जुलमानें, &c.

GRUEL, *n.* (esp. of rice). पेज *f.*—(of parched rice). मंड *m.* —(of bits of rice). कणेरी *f.*
Sour g. कांजी *f.* This word is improperly used by Ladies and Ayas for gruel.

GRUFF, *a. rough, surly.* तुटक, तुटक बोलणारा, खट्याळ, खट्या, दाष्ट, दाष्टीक, रुक्षवदन, कठोरवाक्, रुक्षवाक्, रुक्षवाणि, परुषवाक्.

GRUFFLY, *adv.* v. A. रुक्षवाणीनें, कठोरपणानें, परुषवाणीनें, &c.

GRUFFNESS, *n.* v. A. दाष्टपणा *m.* वाक्कठोरता *f.* वाक्रौक्ष्य *n.* वचनपारुष्य *n.*

To GRUMBLE, *v. n. murmur.* कुरकुरणें, कुडकुडणें, कुरबुरणें, कुरमुरणें, कुणकुणणें, धुसमुसणें, बुरबुरणें, मुरमुरणें, कुरकूर *f.*-कुरबूर *f.*-&c. करणें-लावणें.
2—as the bowels. कुरकुरणें, कुरमुरणें, कुरमणें, गरबरणें, गुरगुरणें, गुडगुडणें, घुरघुरणें, घुळघुळणें, कुटकुटणें, खळखळणें. (Most of these verbs are also *impersonal*).

GRUMBLER, *n.* GRUMBLING, *p. a.* v. V. 1. कुरकुरणारा, &c. कुरकुऱ्या, कुरबुऱ्या, कुणकुण्या, &c. घसघशा, कुडकुडा,कुडकुड्या, कुडकुडवाणा.

GRUMBLING, *n.* v. V. 1.—*act.* कुरकुरणें *n.* &c. कुरकूर *f.* कुडकूड *f.* कुरबूर *f.* कुरमूर *f.* कुणकूण *f.* बुडबूड *f.* बुरबूर *f.* मुरमूर *f.* घसघस *f.* पुटपूट *f.* धुसमूस *f.*
2 गुरगुरणें *n.* गरबरणें *n.* &c. गुरगूर *f.* कुटकूट *f.*

GRUME, *n. thick consistence, clot, &c.* गुठळी *or* गोळुली *f.*

GRUMOUS, *a.* v. N. गुठळ्यांचा, चाकळांचा.

To GRUNT, *v. a.*—the pig. डुरडुरणें, डुरडूर *f.* करणें, बुरकणें.
2—the buffaloe. रेंकणें, बुरकणें, बुरंगळणें *or* बुरंगाळणें.

GRUNT, GRUNTING, *n.* v. V. 1. डुरडुरणें *n.* डुरडुरणी *f.* डुरडूर *f.* सूकरशब्द *m.* [जिम्मेदार.

GUARANTEE, GUARANTY, *n.*—the person. हामीदार, जामीन,
2—the warranty. हामी *f.* जामिनी *f.* जिम्मा *f. m.*

To GUARANTEE, *To* GUARANTY, *v. a. warrant, be security for.* जिम्मा *f. m.*-हामी *f.*-&c. घेणें, जिम्मेदार-हामीदार-&c. होणें.

To GUARD, *v.a. defend, keep.* राखणें, रक्षणें, राखण *f.*-रखवाली *f.* -रक्षण *n.*-संरक्षण *n.*-&c. करणें *g. of o.* [वध राहणें.

To GUARD, *v. n. be in a state of caution.* जपणें, संभाळणें, सा-

GUARD, GUARDING, *n.* v. V. A. राखणें *n.* &c. राखण *f.* रक्षण *n.* संरक्षण *n.* चौकी *f.* चौकीदारी *f.* पाहरा *m.* रखवाली *f.* खबरदारी *f.*
To keep g. चौकी *f.*-चौकीदारी *f.*-पाहरा *m.* करणें.
I. *body guarding.* चौकी *f.* पाहरा *m.*
Hire of a g. चौकीदारी *f.*
II. *person guarding, watchman, &c.* चौकीदार, पाहरेकरी, रखवालदार, राखणदार, राखणाईत, राखणा, राखण.
Hire of a g. राखण *f.* राखणावळ *f.*
III. *thing guarding, fending, &c.* वारण *n.* निवारण *n.* निवारक *n.* त्राण *n.* (in comp. as जंघात्राण).
IV. *state of caution and vigilance.* हुशारी *f.* सावधगिरी *f.*
To be on one's g. जपणें, संभाळणें.
V. (of a sword hilt). खोबळा *m.*

GUARDED, *p.* v. V. A. राखलेला, रक्षलेला, रक्षित, संरक्षित.
I. *a. circumspect,* v. CAUTIOUS. सावध, सावधगिरीचा.

GUARDEDNESS, *n.* v. A. सावधगिरी *f.*

GUARDER, *n.* v. V. A. राखणारा, रक्षक, रक्षण-&c. कर्त्ता.

GUARDIAN, *n. warden, one that has the care of.* दिम्मतदार, रखवालदार, राखणदार, राखण.

GUARDSMAN, *n.* गाडदी. [*m.* जमरूद *m.*

GUAVA, *n.*—the tree. पेरू *m.* जांब *m.*—the fruit. पेरू *m.* जांब

GUDGEON, *n.* एक मासा आहे.
2 See GULL.

GUERDON. See REWARD.

To GUESS, *v. a. conjecture.* तरकणें, अटकळणें, तर्क *m.*-अटकळ *f.*-अनुमान *n.* करणें, कल्पना *f.* बांधणें-करणें.
2 out, *hit upon, discover.* जिंकणें, जितणें, ताडणें, ओळखणें.
3 *form an estimate or judgment of,* v. To ESTIMATE. अटकळणें, अजमासणें, अजमावणें, अडसट्टा *m.* पाहणें, अजमास *m.* बांधणें, अटकळ *f.* करणें *g. of o.*

GUESS, GUESSING, *n.* v. V. 1. अटकळणें *n.* &c. अटकळ *f.* तर्क *m.* कल्पना *f.* अनुमान *n.*
2 जिंकणें *n.* &c. ताडबाजी *f.*
3 अटकळणें *n.* &c. अटकळ *f.* अजमास *m.* अडसट्टा *m.*
Rough g. अटकळ पंचविसी *f.* अनुमानधपका *m.* अटोंका *or* अटंका *m.*

GUESSER, *n.* v. V. 1. अटकळणारा, अटकळ-तर्क-&c. करणारा.
That is a good guesser, *shrewd at guessing.* ताडबाज, तर्कबाज, तर्की, तार्किक, अटकळबाज, अनुमानी, अजमासी.

GUEST, *n. a person dropping in for hospitality.* पाहुणा (णा *m.* णी *f.* णें *n.*), अतिथि, अभ्यागत, आला गेला *m. or* आलें गेलें *n.* मेहमान *m.* प्राघुणिक.
Attention to a g. (as at a feast). परामर्श *m. v.* घे, कर.
G.—compreh. *or* loosely. पहीपाहुणा.
Honors, &c. paid to a g. आदरउपचार *m. pl.* संभावना *f.* संभ्रम *m.* मधुपर्क *m.*
Proper for a g. आतिथ्य, आतिथेय.

2 *a person invited to an entertainment.* बोलाविलेलें मनुष्य *n.* मेजवान, मेहमान. [मंत्रण्या.

G.-summoner or caller. बोलावणेकरी, बोलावण्या, आ-

GUEST-RITES, *n.*v. HOSPITALITY. पाहुणचार *m.* अतिथिपूजन *n.* आतिथ्य *n.* मेजवानकी *f.* मेजवानी *f.*

To GUGGLE. See To GURGLE.

GUIDAGE, *n. reward given to a guide.* वाटदाखवणावळ *f.*

GUIDANCE, GUIDING, *n.* v. V. 1.—*act.* वाट दाखवणें *n.* &c. मार्गप्रदर्शन *n.* नयन *n.* नय *m.* नीति *f.*

2 वळवणें *n.* &c. ओढा *m.* ओढ *f.* प्रेरणा *f.*

3 चालवणें *n.* &c. चालवणी *f.* वहिवाट *f.* निर्वाह *m.*

To GUIDE, *v. a. direct in one's way.* वाटेनें-&c. नेणें, वाट *f.*-रस्ता *m.*-मार्ग *m.*-&c. दाखवणें, वाट *f.*-रस्ता *m.*-&c. दाखवून नेणें, पावणें, पाववणें, नय *m.*-नयन *n.*-मार्गप्रदर्शन *n.*-&c. करणें.

2 *influence, give direction to.* वळवणें, ओढणें, प्रेरणें.

3 *direct, manage*; v. To CONDUCT. चालवणें, वहिवाटणें, बलवणें.

GUIDE, GUIDER, *n.* v. V. 1. वाटेनें नेणारा, वाट दाखवून नेणारा, &c. वाटाडी *or* ड्या, वाटकाढू *or* काढ्या, मार्गप्रदर्शक, नेता, विनेता, नयनकर्त्ता.

Spiritual g. गुरु *m.*

GUIDE-POST, *n.* वाट-रस्ता-मार्ग-&c. दाखविणारा खांब.

GUILD, *n.* सनदी मंडळी *f.*

GUILE, *n.* v. CUNNING, DECEIT. कपट *n.* दगा *m.* कावा *m.* काबादावा *m.* माव *f.* कृत्रिम *n.* चेटक *n.* कपटविद्या *f.*

GUILEFUL, *a.* v. CUNNING. कपटी, दगेखोर, सकपट, छद्मी, कावेदार, कृत्रिमी, मायावी, कपटाचा, दग्याचा.

GUILELESS, *a.* v. HONEST, SIMPLE. निष्कपट, निष्कृत्रिम, अकृत्रिम, निष्प्रपंच, अकपट, अमायी, अमायिक, अमाय, अवक्र.

GUILELESSNESS, *n.* v.A. निष्कपटपणा *m.* भोळेपणा *m.* अकृत्रिम*n.* अमाया *f.* निष्कापट्य *n.*अकापट्य *n.*कपटाभाव*m.* कपटराहित्य *n.*

GUILLOTINE, *n.* शिर छेदण्याचें साधन आहे.

GUILT, *n. criminality.* दोष *m.* पाप *n.* पापीपणा *m.* दोषीपणा *m.* सापराधता *f.* सदोषता *f.* दुष्टाईना *f.* [पराधिता *f.*

GUILTINESS, *n.* v. A. दोषीपणा *m.* सदोषता *f.* सापराधता *f.* अ-

GUILTLESS, *a. innocent.* निर्दोष, निरपराध, दोषरहित-शून्य-&c. अपाप, निर्मल, निष्कलंक, धुतल्या मोत्यासारखा.

GUILTLESSNESS, *n.* v. A. निर्दोषता *f.* निरपराधता *f.* दोषराहित्य*n.*

GUILTY, *a.* v. CRIMINAL. दोषी, सदोष, पापी, सपाप, कृतपाप, कृतापराध.

GUINEA, *n.* सोन्याचें एक नाणें आहे.

GUINEA-WORM, *n.* नारू *m.*—in covert or cant phraseol. नारायण *m.* नारोपंत *m.*

GUISE. See MANNER, DRESS. [सोटा *m.*

GUITAR, *n. lute.* वीणा *pop.* विणा *m.* रुद्रविणा *m.* सरोदा *m.* सुर-

Bowl of a g. भोपळा *m.*

G. with three strings. सतार *f. n.*

G. with six strings. छतार *m.*

Turkish g. with four strings तंबुरा *m. dim.* तंबुरी *f.*

GULF, *n. bay.* आखात *n.* मोठी खाडी *f.*

2 *deep place in the earth, abyss.* अगाध दरा *m f.* मोठाचर*m.*

To GULL, *v. a.* v. To DECEIVE. भोळावणें, भोळसावणें, छकवणें, मुंडवण *f.* घालणें *g. of o.* तोंडावरून हात *m.* फिरवणें *g. of o.* गळा *m.* कापणें *g. of o.* धुरी *f.* देणें.

To be gulled. छकणें, मुंडवण *f.* पडणें *g. of s.*

GULL, *n. simple fellow, gudgeon, cully, coney, bubble.* भजनी, भळू, भोळा, फशा, थापडबाईक.

GULL-CATCHER, GULLER, *n.* v. V. *and* DECEIVER. छकवणारा, फसवणारा, &c.

GULLET, *n.* v. THROAT. गळा *m.* गळघांटी *f.* घसा *m.* अन्नाची नळी *f.* अन्नमार्ग *m.*

GULLY, *n. rugged chasm or furrow.* घळ *f.* घळय *f.* घळण *f.* खांचर *n.* ओघळ *f.* ओघळी *f.* ओहळ *f.* नरांडी *f.* खांडा *m.* बेहेड *n.*

To GULP, *v. a.* (liquids). घोटणें, गटगट-घोटघोट-घुटघुट *adv.*-*&c.* पिणें, ढोसणें.

2 (solid substances) v. To BOLT. गोळा *m.* मारणें.

GULP, GULPING, *n.* v.V.1. घोटणें *n.* घोट *m.* गुटका *or* घुटका *m.*

By gulps, *gulpingly.* घटघट *or* टां, घटाघट *or* टां, घटाटां (*or* गटगट, गटागट, &c.), घुटघुट, ढसढस *or* सां.

Expiring g. Last g. घुट्ट *n.*

With a g. गट-कन-कर-&c. घुट-कन-कर-&c. घुट्ट.

GUM, *n.* डिंक *or* डीक *m.* चीक *m.* गोंद *m.*

G. Arabic. बाभळीचा डीक *or* गोंद *m.*

G. water. डिकवणी *n.*

2 (of the teeth). हिरडी *f.* दंतमांस *n.*

Rubber for the g. (of a child). चोपण *or* णी *f. or* णें*n.* चुंफणी *f.* [उकीर *m.*

3 (of the eyes) v. EYE. डोळ्याचा गू *m.* चिपडा *m.* चिपडें*n.*

To be covered with g.—the eyes. चिपडणें.

To GUM, *v.a. smear with gum.* डिकवणें, डीक *m.*-गोंद *m.* लावणें.

GUMBOIL, *n.* हिरडीचा फोड *m.* द्विजव्रण *m.*

GUM-STAND, GUM-BOTTLE, *n.* गोंददाणी *f.* डिंकदाणी *f.*

GUMMY, *a. consisting of gum.* डिकाचा, गोंदाचा, चिकाचा.

2 *producing gum.* डिकाचा, डिका, डिकेरा, चिकाळ *or* चिकाळा *or* चिकाळ्या.

3 *sticky, &c. with gum.* चिकट *or* चिकण, चिकचिकीत.

4—the eyes. चिपडा, शेण्या.

GUN, *n.* v. CANNON. तोफ *f.* उल्हाटयंत्र *n.*

G. carried on a camel. सुतरनाल *f.*

2 v. MUSKET. बंदूक *f.*

Sight of a g. मखी *f.* माशी *f.* मासकी *f.*

Report of a g. पेट *m.* बार *m.*

That has a long reach or range—a g. पल्लेदार.

GUN-BOAT, *n.* एकतोफी नाव *f.*

GUN-CARRIAGE, *n.* तोफेचा गाडा *m.* रणगाडा *m.*

GUNFIRE, *n.* सकाळची किंवा संध्याकाळची तोफ सुटण्याची वेळ *f.*

GUN-POWDER, *n.* दारू *f.*

Ball of g. (to be kindled and thrown). दारूचा डल्ला*m.*

G. granulated. बिराण्याची दारू *f.*

GUN-SHOT, *n. reach or range of a gun.* गोळीचा टप्पा *m.* गोळीची मारणी *f.* (*or* गोळयाचा टप्पा *&c.*).

GUN-SHOT, *a.* गोळीलागून झालेला.

GUN-SMITH, *n.* बंदुका करणारा लोहार.

GUN-WALE, GUNNEL, *n.*—of a ship or boat. बहाण *or* बहाणी*f.* बाण *f.* बाणी *f.*

GUNNER, *n. cannonier.* गोलंदाज, खलासी.

GUNNERY, *n.* गोलंदाजी *f.* उल्हाटयंत्रविद्या *f.*

To GURGLE, *v. n. run or flow with a purling noise.* घुळघुळणें, खळखळणें, बुडबुडणें, घुळघूळ-भुळभूळ-बुडघूड-*adv.* निघणें-वाहणें.

GURGLER, *n.* GURGLING, *p. a.* v. V. घुळघूळ वाजणारा, खळखळीत.

GURGLING, *n.* v. V.—*act.* घुळघुळणें*n.* &c. खळखळ*f. intens.* खळखळाट*m.*

GURGLINGLY, *adv.* खळ-कन-कर-&c. खळखळ *or* ळां, खुळखूळ *or* ळां, घुळघूळ *or* ळां, भुळभूळ *or* ळां, झुरुझुरु, झुरझुर *or* रां, दुरुदुरु, बुडबूड *or* डां, भुडभूड *or* डां,—*intens.* खळाखळ *or* ळां, खुळाखूळ *or* ळां.

To GUSH, *v. n. flow or rush out with violence.* भडभडणें, फळफळणें, भडभड-भळभळ-फळफळ-घळघळ-&c. *adv.* निघणें-सुटणें-वाहणें-बाहेर पडणें, उभडा*m.*-&c. सुटणें-निघणें-होणें *g. of s.* उफाळणें, उफाळा*m.* निघणें-येणें *g. of s.*—*intens.* भडाडणें.

GUSH, GUSHING, *n.* v. V. भडभडणें*n.* &c. उभड*m.* उभडा*m.* उमाडा*m.* भडका*m.* भडाका*m.* उबाळा*m.*

GUSHER, *n.* GUSHING, *p. a.* v. V. भडभडणारा, फळफळणारा, भडभड-&c. वाहणारा-&c.

GUSHINGLY, *adv.* भडभड *or* डां, फळफळ *or* ळां, भळभळ *or* ळां, भुळभूळ *or* ळां, घळघळ *or* ळां.—*intens.* फळाफळ, फळाळां.

GUSSET, *n.* चिडी *f.* बगल *f.* [सोंसाटा*m.*

GUST, *n. blast, puff.* झटका*m.* झटकारा*m.* घुगी *f.* झुक्की *f.* सोंसा*m.*

In gusts. सोंसों.

That comes in sudden gusts—wind. सोशा.

2 (of flame, hot wind, &c). भयका *or* भयकारा*m. dim.* भयकी*f.*

3 v. TASTE. स्वाद*m.* रुचि *f.*

GUSTY, *a. blowing in gusts.* सोशा, सुसाट्याचा *or* सोसाट्याचा.

GUT, *n.* v. BOWELS. आंतडें*n.*

To GUT, *v. a. take out the entrails of.* आंतडीं*n. pl.* निपसणें-काढणें *g. of o.*

2 (a house, &c.) v. To PLUNDER. लुटणें, धुणें, धुऊननेणें.

GUTTA SERENA, *n.* कांचबिंदु*m.* कांचबिंब*m.n.* काच*m.* तिमर*n.*

GUTTER, *n. channel for water.* पन्हळ*m. dim.* पन्हळी *f.* सारणी *f.* नरांडी *f.* नाला*m.* प्रणालिका *f.* प्रणाली *f.* गटर*n.* from the English word is becoming common.

2—esp. as through a wall. मोहरी *or* मोरी *f.* नाहणी *f.*

To GUTTLE, *v. n. eat greedily,* v. To STUFF. मटमटावणें, मटकावणें, मटमट-मटकमटक-गळगळ *or* ळां-गटगट *adv.* खाणें, गटाणा *m.* करून टाकणें *g. of o.* [मूलीय.

GUTTURAL, *a. pronounced in the throat.* कंठ्य, कंठस्थ, जिव्हा-

G. or deep sound. कंठ*m.*

To GUZZLE, *v. n. drink largely and greedily.* धोटणें, ढोसणें, झोकणें, गटगटणें, गळगळ-ढसढस-गटगट-&c. *adv.* पिणें, धोटा*m.* लावणें.

GYMNASIUM, *n. place of exercise.* तालीमखाना *m.* असाडा*m.* मल्लभूमि *f.* मल्लांगण*n.* मल्लयुद्धशाला *f.* रंगभूमि *f.* रंगांगण*n.* रंग*m.*

Some of the exercises of the *Gymnasium* are उठबैस, एकलंगीपेंच, कंबरफोडापेंच, कसोटापेंच, घिस्सापेंच, चक्रदंड, चकरदंड, जोरकशी *or* जोर, तबकफाडपेंच, दंड, दस्ती पेंच, दांडपटा, दुलंगीपेंच, मल्लखांब, लंगोटपेंच, लुक्कणपेंच, स्वारीपेंच.

Certain articles of the apparatus or furniture of the *Gymnasium*, and certain of the weapons or implements used by the Athletæ are अंतरपगडी, कारलें, गदगा, जोडनाल, फावडी *or* पावडी, फरी, बाळगुंडा, मल्लखांब, मल्लतूर्य, मुद्गर *pop.* मुदगल, लेजीम, वज्र, मुष्टि, हत्ता.

Lessons in the exercises of the g. तालीम *f.*

Testimonial of pre-eminence (in the feats of the g.). अजितपत्र*n.*

Wrestling pit in a g. हवदा *or* हौदा*m.*

GYMNASTIC, *a. pertaining to athletic exercises.* तालीमबाजीचा, मल्लयुद्धाचा, &c. मल्लयुद्धसंबंधी-विषयक, मल्लक्रीडासंबंधी-विषयक, व्यायामसंबंधी-विषयक.

GYMNASTICS, *n.* तालीमबाजी *f.* मल्लयुद्ध *n.* मल्लक्रीडा *f.* व्यायाम *m.*

GYNARCHY, GYNŒOCRASY, *n. female government.* स्त्रीराज्य *n.* स्त्रीप्राधान्य *n.*

GYNECEUM, *n. female apartments.* जनानखाना *m.* अंतःपुर *n.* अंतर्गृह *n.* महाल *m.* स्त्र्यगार *m.*

GYRATION, GYRE, *n. circle.* गिरकांडा *m.* गिरकी *f.v.* मार-दे-खाघे, फेरा *m.* फेरी *f.* वेढा *m.* आवर्त्त *m.* भ्रम *m.*

GYVES. See FETTER.

H.

H. This letter is represented by ह्.

HA, *interj.* हा, हाहा.

Ha, ha, ha. हहह *or* हाहाहा.

HABERDASHER, *n.* फीत, सुया, सुताच्या गुंड्या वगैरे जिन्नस विकणारा.

HABERGEON, *n.* v. ARMOUR. बख्तर *or* बक्तर *n.*

HABILIMENT. See DRESS.

HABIT, *n.* (of body). भावना *f.* प्रकृति *f.* तबियत *f.* देहस्थिति *f.*

2 *disposition, &c. from practice.* सवई *or* सवय *f.v.* पड, लाग, सराव *m. v.* पड, अभ्यास *m.* परिपाठ *m.v.* पड, रीति *pop.* रीत *f.* ढाळ *m. f.* चांप *m. f.* आदत *f.*

Habits—gener. *or* compreh. स्थिति रीति *f.* स्थीत रीत *f.*

To get into a h. of. सवई *f.*-&c. लागणें, पाठ*m.* पडणें *in.con.*

3—in an ill sense; *trick, way.* खोड *f.* चटक *f.* चवणा *or* चौणा *m.* लकब *f.* तलब *f.* व्यसन *n.* दुर्व्यसन *n.* छंद *m.*

Light habits or ways. चार*m.pl.* चारचार*m. pl.*—addicted to such. चारकट *or* चारगट.

Low disreputable h. भिकारखोड *f.* भिकारचाळा *m.*

Of ill habits. खोडकर, छंदी, दुर्व्यसनी, व्यसनी, व्यसनीक.

To break an ill h. खोड *f.* मोडणें.

To contract an ill h. खोडणें, चटावणें.

4 *constant practice.* राबता *m.* राब *m.* रफ्त *m.* वहिवाट *f.*

Skill or familiarity acquired by h. कसरत *f.* सांद*m.* सवई *f.*

5 v. DRESS. वेष *m.* भेष *m.* पेहराव *m.*

To HABIT, &c. See To DRESS, &c.

HABITABLE, *a. fit for residence.* राहाया-जोगा-जोगता-&c. वास्तव्य, वास्तेय, वासयोग्य, वासार्ह, आजीव्य. [सार्हता *f.*

HABITABLENESS, HABITABILITY, *n.* v. A. वासयोग्यता *f.* वा-

HABITANT. See INHABITANT.

HABITATION, *n. act of residing,* v. RESIDENCE. राहणें*n.* वस्ती*f.*

2 *place of abode,* v. RESIDENCE. वस्ती *f.* वास्तु *n. f.* वसति *f.* वसन *n.* निवासस्थान *n.*

HABITUAL, *a.* v. CUSTOMARY. सवईंतला, अभ्यासांतला, पाठांतला,

नित्यपाठांतला, राबत्यांनला, संवईचा, &c.

To become h. to. ढाळासाली-अभ्यासाखाली-सराबाखाली-&c. पडणें, सवई f.-&c. लागणें g. of o. पाठ m. पडणें g. of o.

HABITUALLY, *adv.*v.A.नेमी *or* नेहमीं, नेमानें, नित्य,नित्य नेमानें.

To HABITUATE, *v. a.*v. To ACCUSTOM. सवंई *or* सवय *f.*-अभ्यास *m.*-&c. लावणें-पाडणें, सवईंत-राबत्यांत-&c. आणणें.

To be habituated. सवई *f.*-&c. लागणें *g. of o.* खांद *m.*-खांदा *m.* पडणें.

HABITUATED, *p.* v. V. सवईचा, अभ्यासाचा, अभ्यासी, सबई लागलेला, &c. अभ्यस्त, कृताभ्यास.

HABITUDE. See HABIT.

To HACK, *v. a. cut irregularly and badly, notch*, v. To MANGLE. अचकट विचकट तोडणें, चोचाबून-झाझावून-&c. तोडणें, खांडणें, खापलणें, सडकणें, तोडणें, छिंदणें.

To h. and hew. धसकावणें, धसधस *adv.* तोडणें, झाजाविणें, सपासपी *f.* करणें.

To h. to pieces. कुचा *or* खुरचा *f. pl.* पाडणें, खांडोळी *f.*-खांडोळीं *n. pl.* करणें *g. of o.*

2 See To HESITATE.

HACK, HACKNEY, *n. hired horse.* भाड्याचा घोडा *m.*

2 *horse*—in contempt. घोडकट *n.* घोडकें *n.* भट्टाचा तट्टू *m.* हरदासीघोडा *m.*

HACKING, *a.*—cough. दबत दबत येणारा.

To HACKLE, *v. a. dress* (flax, &c.) पिंजणें, पिंजारणें, उगविणें.

HACKLE, *n. instrument for dressing flax, &c.* पिंजणी *f.*फणी*f.*

To HACKNEY, *v. a. practice, accustom, harden.* राबवणें, रांपवणें, निरडणें *or* निरढणें, पुरढणें.

To be hackneyed. रांपणें, राबणें, निरडणें. [करणें.

2 *make trite or common.* सर्वांतोंडीं करणें, उष्टा-जनोच्छिष्ट-&c.

HACKNEY-COACH, *n.* भाड्याची गाडी *f.*

HACKNEYED, *p.* v. V. 1. राबवलेला *or* राबलेला, रांपविलेला *or* रांपलेला, निरडलेला, &c.

2 सर्वांतोंडीं केलेला-झालेला, उष्टा, प्राकृत, जनोच्छिष्ट, लोकोच्छिष्ट.

HADDOCK, *n.* समुद्रांतला एक मासा आहे.

HADES, *n* v. HELL. अधोभुवन *n.* अधोलोक*m.*

HAFT, *n. handle.* दांडा *m.* मुठ्या *m.* मूठ *f.* थरू *n.* कबजा *m.* परज *m.* सरू *m.*

To HAFT, *v. a.* मूठ *f.*-&c. बसविणें, मुठींत-&c. बसविणें.

HAG, *n. witch, beldam, fright.* जखीण *f.* डंखीण *f.* हडळ *or* हडळी *f.* भूतखान *n.* भूतखाना *m.* हेडंबा *f.* लांव *f.* लांबसट *f.*

HAGGARD, *a.* v. LEAN. खप्पड, खल्लड, थेरडा, मलूल, मन्या.

2 See INTRACTABLE.

To HAGGLE, *v. n. dispute in bargaining.* ओढणें, ओढून धरणें, घासणें, घासाघास *or* घासाघीस, *f.*-घसघस *or* घिसघीस *f.*-&c. करणें, अबणापाबणा *decl.* करणें-करून घेणें *or* देणें-विकणें.

To HAGGLE, *v. a.* See To HACK.

HAGGLER, *n.* v. V. N. ओढून घेणारा, घासणारा, ओढक, घसघशा, घासाघिशा, घासघीस-&c. करणारा, खाराखिऱ्या, ओढताण्या.

HAGGLING, *n.* v. V. N. ओढून घेणें *n.* घासणें *n.* &c. घासाघास *or* घासाघीस *f.* घसघस *or* घिसघीस *f.* खाराखार *or* खाराखिरी *f.* ओढ *f.* ओढाताण *f.*

HAIL, *interj.* v. SALUTATION. जयजय, जयजया, नमस्कार, नमो, नमोनमः, स्वस्ति.

HAIL, *n.* गारा *f. pl* करका *f.* मेघगर्भ *m.*

To HAIL, *v. a. call to*, v. To CALL. हटकणें, हाक *f.* मारणें.

To HAIL, *v. n.* गारा *f. pl.*-&c. पडणें.

HAIL-STONE, *n.* गार *f.* करका *f.*

HAIL-STORM, *n.* गारांचा पाऊस *m.*

HAILY, *a.* गारांचा.

HAIR, *n.*—a hair. केश *pop.* केस *m.* बाल *m.*—the hair केश *pop.* केस *m. pl.* बाल *m. pl.*

Against the h. (or grain). बिलोम, प्रतिलोम.

Circlet of h. preserved around the *shendi.* भोवरा *m.* संजाप *or* व *m.*

Clotted h. बट *m.*

Combings of h. गुथ *f.*

Composition to blacken the h. कलप *or* फ *m.*

Dishevelled and dirty lock of h. केसुरडी *f.* केसटी *f.*

Dressed or tufted h. बुचडा *m.* केशपाश *m.*

Falling off of the h. इंद्रलुप्त *m. n.* चाई *f.* उंदरी *f.*

First crop of h. of a child. जावळ *n.* नरककेस*m.*

H. loosely bundled up and tied. जोंबडा *m.*

Having the h. (hairy side) inwards. अंतर्लोम.

Line made along the head by parting the h. भांग *m.* शिंता *m.* शिंतें *n.* सीमंत *m.*—Ceremony of adjusting it (during gestation, &c.) सीमंतोन्नयन*n.*—Pin or wire used in making it. भांग सळयी *or* भांगसळ *f.*

Lock of h. left on the crown at tonsure. शेंडी *f.* चूडा *f.* शिखा *f.* शिखंड *m.* टाळू *f.*

Loose tress of h. झिटी *f.* झिंजी *f.* झिपटी *f.* झिंपरी *f.* झिंपोरडी *f.* बाबरी *f.* बाबर झोंटी *f.* झोंट *f.* झोंटी *f.* भिंसटी *f.*

Matted or clotted tress of h. पेलू *f.*

Pulling the h. (in squabbling). झोंट धरणी *f.*

Rope of h. केसारी *f.* वाळ्याची दोरी *f.*

The hair knot (of women). गोफा *m.*

Topknot of matted h. जटाजूट *m.* जटाभार *m.*

Tress of matted h. जटा *f.* जट *f.*—Person wearing matted tresses. जटाधारी, जटिल, जटिली, जटाळ्या.

White hairs, *old age.* पांढरे केस*m. pl.*

With the h. (or grain). अनुलोम, सलोम.

2 (of the body or limbs). रोम*m. n.*लोम *n. m.* लव *or*लंव*f.*

Line of h. along the belly. रोमावलि *f.*

Ring of h. भोवरा *m.*

3 *filament* (of a plant) केसर *pop.* केंसर *n.* [a noun.

HAIR-BREADTH, *n.* केसाचें अंतर*n.* केसाएवढें अंतर*n.* केसभर with

HAIR-BRUSH, *n.* केशमार्जनी *f.*

HAIR-LACE, HAIR-TIE, *n.* अगवळ *or* आगवळ *m. n.*

HAIRINESS, *n.* v. A. 1. केसाळपणा*m.* केशबाहुल्य *n.* बहुकेशता *f.*

HAIRLESS, *a.* केशहीन, अकेश.

HAIRY, *n. abounding with hair.* केसाळ *or* ळू, बहुकेश, केशबहुल, केशमय, रोमश, रोमवान्, लोममय, लोमश.

2 *made of hair.* केसाचा, केसाचा केलेला, केशमय, केशनिर्मित.

HALBERD, *n.* v. SPEAR. भाला *m.*

HALBERDIER, *n.* भालेवाईक, भालेकरी, भालेवाला.

HALCYON, *n. king fisher.* डिचा *m.*

HALCYON, *a. still, quiet, &c.* v. CALM. शांत.

H. days. fig. सुवत्ताकाळ *m.* सुबत्ता *f.* अमृतवेळ *or* ळा *f.* अमृताची घटका *f.*-घडी *f.*

To HALE. See To DRAG.

HALE, *a. stout and healthy.* धडाखडा, धडसा, धडका, धडस, धडसाखडसा, खडखडीत, खुडखुडीत, खडस, खडसा, खणखणीत, धट्टाकट्टा *or* खट्टा, धडधाकट *or* ड, धडधोप, धडधोपट, तवाना, धड, कडक, दोनटक्यांनीं धड, टणकटणका, पाडकुला, कटाक्ष, अरोग.

HALENESS, *n.* v. A. धडेखडेपणा *m.* धडसपणा *m.* &c. आरोग्य *n.* टणकाई *f.*

HALF, *n.* अर्ध *n.* निमा *m.* निमे *f.* अर्धूक *n.* अर्धल *or* अर्धेल *f.* अर्धभाग *m.* निमाई *f.* निमखाई *f.* निमशाई *f.* ढवक *n.* अर्धांश *m.* दल *or* ळ *n.*

About h. निमेसिमे, अर्धामर्धा *or* मुर्धा, अर्धासा.

By halves, in halves. निमेनिम *or* निमोनिम, अर्धोअर्ध, अर्धोर्ध.

Better h. (wife). अर्धांग *n.*

Composed of one and a h. दिडका *or* दिडता.

Exceeding by one and a h. दिडका *or* दिडता.

H. of a load. निमकें *n.*

H. of a rupee. अधेली *f.*

H. of a pice. अधेला *m.*

Half in conjunction with numerals is as follows:— One and a h. दीड. Two and a h. अडीच ; and for Three and upwards, साडे as Three and a h. साडेतीन ; Four and a h. साडेचार, &c. &c.

HALF, *adv.* अर्ध *pop.* अर्धा *or* आधा, निमे, अर्धवट, अर्ध (in comp. as h.–assent, अर्धांगीकार *m.* h.-boiled, अर्धशिजा. h.-bruised, अर्धबोवडा. h.-dead, अर्धमेला. h.-dined, अर्धजेवा. h.-learned, अर्धबाट. h.–mad, अर्धवेडा. h.–ripe, अर्धकच्चा, &c. &c.) निम (in comp. as निमशिजा, निमकच्चा, &c.)

H. brother or sister (by the father's side). भिन्नोदरभाऊ *m.*-बहीण *f.* सावत्र-सापत्न भाऊ *m.*-बहीण *f.* (by the mother's side). भिन्नपितृकबंधु *m.*-बहीण *f.* अधला भाऊ *m.* अधलीबहीण *f.*

HALL, *n. a room at the entrance of a house.* हवेलींत-वाड्यांत जातांना पहिल्यानें जी खोली लागते ती *f.* दाराजवळची खोली *f.* गृहमुखशाला *f.*

2 (of justice) दिवाणखाना *m.* धर्मसभा *f.* न्यायसभा *f.*

3 (for public business). कचेरी *f.* सदर *f.* सरकारवाडा *m.*

4 (of audience). दिवाणखाना *m.* दरबार *n.m.* सदर *f.* सभा *f.* भद्र *n.*

5 *public or large room.* दिवाणखाना *m.* दलान *or* दालन *n.* माजघर *n.* मध्यगृह *n.* अड्डा *m.* अखाडा *m.*

HALLIARD, *n. rope for hoisting, &c. a sail.* कांड *n.* यारी *f.*

To HALLOO, *v. n.* v.To CALL. ललकारणें, कुकारणें, सादवणें *or* सादावणें, कुकारा *m.*-आरोळी *f.*-हाक *f.*-&c. मारणें, साद *m.* घालणें-देणें-हाकणें, बोंभाणें, बोंभावणें.

HALLOO,—exclamation calling attention. अरे, अहो, हें वहा, &c.

HALLOO-BELLOW, *n. general shouting.* हाकाटा *m.* हाकारा *m.*. हाकारी *f.* हाकाहाक *f.* रोराण *n.*

HALLOOING, *n.*v.V.—*act.* ललकारणें *n.* &c. ललकारी *f.* ललकारणी *f.* साद *m.* कुकारा *m.* पुकारा *m.*

To HALLOW, *v. a. make holy, reverence as holy.* पवित्र करणें-मानणें, पवित्रीकरण *n.* करणें *g. of o.*

2 See To CONSECRATE.

HALLUCINATION, *n. error, mistake.* चूक *f.* भूल *f.* भ्रम *m.*

HALO, *n. circle round the sun or moon.* खळें *n.* परिवेष *m.* परिधि *m.* अंशुमाला *f.*—large h. तळें *n.*

Lunar h. पाणकोंबडा *m.* पाणकोंबडें *n.*

To HALT, *v. n.* v. To LIMP. लंगडणें, लंगणें, टिंगणें, पाय *m.* काढणें.

2 *stop.* उभा राहणें, ठेपणें, थोपणें, थांबणें.

3—in a march; *encamp.* मुकाम *m.* करणें, तळ *m.* देणें.

4 See To HESITATE.

To HALT, *v. a.* उभा करणें, थोपविणें.

HALT, *a.* v. LAME. लंगडा.

HALT, HALTING PLACE, *n.* मुकाम *m.* पडाव *m.* पडण *n.* तळ *m.*

HALTER, *n. rope, or cord, for a horse, &c.* काढणी *f.* वागदोर *m.*

2 *hanging rope.* फासींदेण्याची दोरी *f.*-तांत *f.*

To twist a h. for one's own neck. उपटून सूळ *m.* खांद्यावर घेणें.

To HALTER, *v. a.* काढणी गळ्यांत घालणें.

To HALVE, *v. a. divide into two equal parts.* अर्धार्ध-निमेनिम *or* निमोनिम करणें, दुधड-दुखंड-द्विभाग-&c. करणें, दोन तुकडे *m. pl.* करणें.

2 *share equally.* समान-समसमान-&c. वांटून घेणें, निमशाई *f.* करणें.

HALVED, *p.* v. V. 1. अर्धार्ध केलेला, &c. अर्धकृत, सामीकृत.

HAM, *n. inner or hind part of the knee.* ढोपराचा-&c. आंतला भाग *m.* पायाची लवण *f.*

2 खारावलेली व वाळवलेली डुकराची मांडी *f.*

HAME, *n. collar.* शिवळ *f.*

HAMLET, *n.* वाडी *f.* खेडें *n.* पाडा *m.* पाडें *n.* गांवढें *or* धें *n.* गांवढेगांव *m.* आडगांव *m. n.* कोंड *m.* मजरा *m.* ग्राम *m.*

HAMMER, *n.* हतोडा *m. dim.* हतोडी *f.*

Sledge-h. घण *or* घन *m.*—wielder of it. घणकरी *m.*

2 (of goldsmiths, braziers, &c.). घाटचा *m.*

To HAMMER, *v. a.* हतोड्यानें ठोकणें-मारणें-घडणें-&c.

To smooth-h. मटारणें.

2 out; v. To EXCOGITATE. मनन करून योजणें-&c.

HAMMOCK, *n. swinging bed.* चोपाळा *m.* झोंपाळा *m.* झुला *m.* झुलावा *m.*

HAMPER, *n.* v. BASKET. पेटारा *m. dim.* पेटारी *f.*

To HAMPER, *v. a. shackle, embarrass, hinder.* गळफट्यांत-घोळांत-अडचणींत-फेऱ्यांत-&c. घालणें-पाडणें, गोवणें, गोवून घेणें, अटकावणें.

To be hampered. अवघडणें, अडचणणें.

To HAMSTRING, *v. a. hough.* कुच्या *f. pl.*-मांडीच्याशिरा *f. pl.* तोडणें *g. of o.*

HAND, *n.* हात *m.* हस्त *m.* कर *m.* पाणि *m.* पंचा *m.*—poetic. करपल्लव *m.* हस्तकमल *n.*

Action with the h. *manual gesticulations.* हातवारे *m.pl.*

Back of the h. पालथा हात *m.* करपृष्ठ *n.*

Free of the h. हातचा सुटा, हातचा सढळ, हातचा मोकळा.

Gone into the hands of. हस्तगत, करप्राप्त.

Hands, the hands. करद्वय *n.*

H. as spread abroad or opened out. पंजा *m.*

H. contracted and hollowed. पसा *m.* कुडचा *or* ता *m.* चुळका *m.* चूळ *m.f.* खोंगा *m.* प्रसृति *m.*

H. curved as to clutch. अर्धचंद्र m.

Hands hollowed and joined. अंजलि m. pop. ओंजळm. f. अंजलिपुट n. संपुट m. सिंहतल n. करपुट n.

H. in, part in. आंग n. कर m.

H. inverted and fingers pointing down. बचक f. बुचकुली f. डवक or डोंक f. —Quantity brought up by the h. so held. बुचकुली f. डवक or डोंक f.

H. over h. हातोहात, हातोहातीं.

Of whom the hands reach to the knees; *longimanus.* आजानुबाहु.

On one h. *in one view, &c.* एकपक्षीं.

Ready to h. *ready-made, &c.* आयता.

Slip of the h. हस्तदोष m.

Taking the h.—in marriage. पाणिग्रह m. पाणिग्रहण n.

That has a h. in (some evil work, &c.). लिप्त, लिप्ताळा.

That holds or bears in the h. पाणि (in comp. as दंडपाणि, वेत्रपाणि, वज्रपाणि).

That is in h.—a work, &c. हाताखालीं or हातीं असणारा, हाताखालचा, घटमान, प्रवर्त्तमान, प्रकृत, प्रस्तुत.

That is off one's hands, *finished, done.* हातानिराळा, हातावेगळा, उलथलेला, उलटलेला.

That lives from h. to mouth. उत्पन्नभक्षी.

Under the h. of. *in subjection unto.* हाताखालीं.

Whether with one's own h. or through the h. of another.—giving, doing, &c. हस्तें परहस्तें.

Whilst the h. is in. हातासरसा, लगेहात, खेपेसरसा or खेपेनें, तापल्या पाठीनें.

With a. high h. with a strong h. &c. पराक्रमानें. [णि.

With empty h. रिकाम्या हातानें or हातीं, रिक्तहस्त, रिक्तपा-

With one's own h. आपहस्तें, आपहस्तकीं.

To be at h. v. To Come. हातावर or हाताबोटावर येणें, आंगावर येणें, भिडणें, बितणें, नेटणें, नेहटणें, टेकणें, टेकावणें.

To be h. and glove. To be h. in h. गळश्च कंठश्च होणें, संगें मगें adv. असणें.

To clap the hands together. टाळी f. मारणें-पिटणें-वाजवणें, ताल m. मारणें.

To come to h.—monies, &c. पावणें, पोंहचणें, पावती f.-पोंहच f. होणें g. of s. पावता-पोंहचता होणें.

To draw in one's h. *cease, &c.* हात m. अटोपणें-आवरणें.

To drop the hands. हातपाय m. pl. गाळणें.

To fall or come to h. हातीं चढणें.

To fold the hands together—in respectful attention. हात m. pl. जोडणें, अंजलिपुट n. जोडणें.

To have the upper h. मात्रा f. वर असणें in. con. [होणें.

To have one's hands full. अवघडणें, गाड्याला जुंपलेलासा

To lay hands upon (as to seize, &c.). हात m. pl. घालणें-टाकणें-करणें, दस्त m. करणें.

To lay (rapacious or furtive) hands upon. हात m. मारणें-देणें, दस्तावणें, दस्तकरणें. [णें-मारणें.

To lend a helping h. हात m. देणें, आंग n. देणें, डोई f. दे-

To lie upon one's hands. गळीं पडणें, आंगावर पडणें.

To live by the labor of one's hands. हातावर संसार m. करणें or पोट n. भरणें, हातावर मिळवणें.

To put one's h. to. हात m. घालणें.

To restrain one's h. हात m. राखणें.

To shake one's hands of, *give up.* हात m. pl. झाडणें *with* विषयीं-&c. *of o.* [चेपणें.

To squeeze one's hands, *to bribe.* हात m.-मूठ f. दाबणें-

To strike hands, *make a bargain.* हातावर हात m. मारणें, टाळी-पटकी f. करणें, टाळी f. मारणें.

To strike with the back of the h. अडव्या हातानें मारणें.

To take in h. हाताखालीं घालणें.

To tie the hands behind. मुसक्या f. pl. बांधणें, जेल m. pl. बांधणें, चतुर्भुज करणें.

To tie one's hands up. हातपाय m. pl. गुंडाळणें, बोकांडी f. धरणें, गळा m. बांधणें, गळा m. गोवणें, गोकटी f. धरणें.

To toss or deliver from h. to h. हातोपात or हातोहात *adv.* टाकणें-देणें.

To walk upon one's hands with one's feet in the air. गलदूम f. टाकणें-चालणें-करणें. [देणें.

To wash one's hands of. हात m. pl. धुणें, तिलांजलि m. f.

To withdraw one's h. (or self) from. हात उगावा m.करणें.

A flowing h. keeps friends friendly. हात ओला तर मैत्र भला नाहींतर पडला अबोला.

2 *hand breadth.* चौंगा m. पांच अंगुळें n. pl. पांच बोटें n. pl.

3—at cards. हात m. दस्त m. दस्ता m. डाव m. बाजी or बाजू f.

4 *character of writing.* हातवळा m. वळण n. अक्षर n. लिपि f. अक्षरांची मोड f.

5 *person, workman, &c.* गडी m. माणूस n. कामकरी.

At h. See Near.

To Hand, *v. a. give, &c. with the hand.* हातानें देणें, हातीं घेऊन-उचलून-&c. देणें, देणें, हातावर देणें, हस्तार्पण n. करणें.

2 *lead or guide by the hand.* हात देऊन नेणें, हात धरून नेणें.

3 down; *transmit in succession.* परंपरेनें-परंपरा-&c. चालवणें.

4 on ; *pass from one to another.* हातोहात-हातोपात-&c. नेणें-पोंचविणें-&c.

Hand-bell, *n.* हातघांटी f. घांटी f.

Hand-bellows, *n.* हातभाता m.

Hand-bill, *n.* जाहिरात f.

Hand-breadth, *n.* चौंगा m. पांच अंगुळें n. pl.

Hand-cuff, *n.* हातबेडी or बिडी f.

To Hand-cuff, *v. a.* हातबेडी f. खिळणें-ठोकणें- घालणें.

Hand-full, *n.* पसा m. खोंगा m. मूठ f. मुष्टिमात्र n. भर used with a noun.

Double h. ओंझळ f. m. धोत f.

(In, at, with) one h. एकमुठीं.

Mere h. *a few.* ईनमीन सवातीन, ईनमीन साडेतीन.

To the extent of a h. मूठभर, पसाभर, &c.

Hand-gallop, *n.* साधीचौक चाल f.

Hand-high, *a. reachable by the hand.* हातपावा.

Hand-kerchief, *n.* रुमाल m. दस्तरुमाल m. छाटी f. अचला m.

Hand-language, *n.* करपल्लवी भाषा f. करपल्लवी f.

Hand-maid, *n.* दासी f. परिचारिका f.

Hand-mill, *n.* जातें n. जातीण or जातण f. *dim.* जातली or जातुली f. घरट m. *dim.* घरटी f. चक्की f.

Bushel (iron lining of the mouth) of a h. मानी f.

Chiseller or re-chiseller of a h. जातें उकट्या, टंकारी, टांकेकरी.

Edge around the mouth of a h. पाळ *f.* पाळें *n.*

First grindings upon a h. उकटी *f.*

Flour adhering to the h. चिकटा *or* चिकोटा *m.*

Incision made upon a h. with a chisel. टांकी *f.*

Leaf or slab of a. h. तळी *f.*

Pin of a h. कील *m.* खुंटा *m.*

Slip of iron on the upper leaf of a h. पाटी *f.*

To chisel or re-chisel a h. उकटणें, टांकणें.

To turn or ply a h. जातें ओढणें. [णें, घरडणें.

To husk, or grind coarsely in the h. (*gharat*). घरट-

HAND-OAR, *n.* हातवल्हें *n.*

HAND-SAW, *n.* हातकरवत *m. dim.* हातकरवती *f.*

HAND-WRITING, *n. signature.* हस्ताक्षर *n.* दस्तखत *n.* दस्तूर *n.*

One's own h. स्वदस्तूर *n.* स्वाक्षर *n.*

2 *manner of writing.* हातवळा *m.* वळण *n.* अक्षर *n.* लिपि *pop.* लीप *f.* अक्षरांची मोड *f.*

Good h. खुशखत *n.* मुक्ताफल *n.*

HANDICRAFT, *n. manual occupation.* कला *pop.* कळा *f.* घडकाम *n.* हातकाम *n.* हुनर *m.* शिल्प *n.* शिल्पकर्म *n.* शिल्पविद्या *f.*

HANDICRAFTSMAN, *n. mechanic, &c.* घडकामी *or* म्या, शिल्पी, शिल्पकार, शिल्पकर्मी.

HANDINESS, *n.* v. A. 1. हाताची सुगराई *f.* हातोटी *f.* हातवळा *m.* हस्तचापल्य *n.* हस्तलाघव *n.* हस्तचातुर्य *n.* हस्तकौशल्य *n.*

HANDIWORK, *n.* हातकाम *n.* कारिगरी *f.* करणी *f.* हस्तकर्तृत्व *n.* घटना *f.* हस्तक्रिया *f.* हस्तकृति *f.* हस्तकर्म *n.*

HANDLE, *n.* दांडा *m.* दांडी *f.* मूठ *f.* मुठ्या *m.* मुष्टि *f.* कान *m.* थरू *or* थेरू *n.* परज *m.* कबजा *m.* आंकडा *m.*

2 (of a plough, harrow, &c.) रुमणी *or* रुम्हणी *f.* रुमणें *or* रुम्हणें *n.*

To HANDLE, *v. a. take into the hand.* हातांत घेणें-धरणें, हात *m.*-बोट *n.* लावणें.

2 *manage with the hand, wield.* वापरणें, वहिवाटणें, धरणें.

3 *discuss, consider.* घोळणें, घाटणें, घाटाघाट *f.*-घाटाघाट *f.*-घोळ *m.* करणें *g. of o.*

4 See To TREAT.

To h. roughly. घोळमाडणें, घोळसावणें, घोळणें.

HANDSEL, *n. first sale of.* बोहणी *f.* प्रथमविक्रय *m.*

HANDSOME, *a. beautiful, elegant.* सुंदर, रूपवान्, स्वरूपवान्, रूपस, छबदार, छबडा, छबिला *or* छबेला, गोजरा, गोजिरवाणा, गोरा गोमटा, राजस, राजसवाणा, देखणा, दर्शनी, दर्शनीय, आकारशुद्ध, आवशुद्ध, कातींव, कातींवकोरींव, भव्य, उदारांग, उदारलक्षण, सुरेख, सुशोभित, सुभावणा, शोभनांग.

A h. person. राजमोहरा *m.* राजपिंड *m.* राजपिंडा *m.* राजबिंडा *m.*

2 See LIBERAL, NOBLE.

HANDSOMENESS, *n.* v. A. 1. सुरेखाई *f.* सुरेखी *f.* छब *f.* छबी *f.* छबदारी *f.* आकारशुद्धि *f.* गोजरेपणा *m.* &c. सौंदर्य *n.* अंगसौष्ठव *n.* लवलक्षण *n.* खुमास *f. n.* खुमाशी *f.*

HANDY, *a. ready, dexterous,* v. EXPERT. हाताचा कुशळ, दक्ष, सुघड, हरकामी *or* म्या, हस्तपटु, करदक्ष.

2 *convenient, &c.* v. USEFUL. उपयोगी, उपयोगाचा, सोईचा, कारणी, कारणीक.

To HANG, *v. a. suspend, &c.* लोंबवणें, लटकावणें, टांगणें, हिलगणें, हिलगावणें, लोंबत बांधणें-ठेवणें.

2 on; up. अडकवणें, ठेवणें.

3 *execute by hanging.* फांशीं देणें, गळीं देणें, गळीं अडकवणें, फांशीं-गळीं चढवणें, गळफांस *m.* देणें.

To h. one's self. फांसघालून जीव *m.* देणें, फास *m.* घालून घेणें, गळफांस *m.* घेणें.

To h. fire (a gun) बंदुकेंतली दारू लवकरपेट *f.* नघेणें.

4 down; *let fall, &c.* खालीं घालणें.

To HANG, *v. n. be suspended.* लोंबणें, लटकणें.

2 *depend loosely,* v. To DANGLE. हिलगणें, अलगणें, ओळकंबणें, झोळकंबणें, ओथंबणें, लोंबकळणें.

3—a person; *be dependent on.* कच्छपीं *or* कासेस लागणें *g. of o.* आश्रयास-आश्रयीं लागणें *g. of o.* दुमाला *m.* धरून असणें *g. of o.* लोंबणें, अवलंबणें, ओथंबणें.

4—a matter; *be dependent on, rest upon.* गुंतणें, अडकणें, बांधलेला असणें, राहणें-असणें *with* वर *of o.*

5—a business or work; *linger, remain unsettled, &c.* लोंबणें, हिलगणें, हिलगडणें, अंबर पडणें *or* असणें, भिजत पडणें, भिजत कांबळें *or* घोंगडें *n.* पडणें *g. of s.* तरंगणें, अर्धोदयीं पडणें, तगीं लागणें.

6 back; *hold back, stickle, be reluctant, &c.* ओढणें *or* ओढून धरणें, ओढ *f.*-ओढण *f. n.* घेणें, ओढतें घेणें, खेंचून धरणें, खिळण *f.* घेणें-धरणें, खिळणीसयेणें, खुटणें *or* खुटून बसणें, पड *f.* घेणें-पत्करणें, आक्षेप *m.* धरणें.

7 down;—a loaded branch, &c. ओथंबणें.

8 upon; in enforcement, supplication, &c. पाठ *f.*-पिच्छा *m.* -&c. घेणें-पुरवणें, पाठीस लागणें, खणीखापटीस *or* खणपटीस बसणें-येणें-लागणें, गळचिपी *f.* अवळणें-धरणें, गळचिपीस-बगोटीस-बोकांडीस-गरगोटीस-गोकटीस-मानेस-मेखाटणीस *or* मेखाटीस-नरडीस-&c. बसणें, दुमाल्यावर-पल्ल्यावर-पिच्छयावर-&c. असणें, गळग्रह *m.* घालणें, गळीं पडणें-लागणें, खपाटीस बसणें-लागणें, खणती *f.* घेणें, खणपट *f.* घेणें *or* घेऊन बसणें, लणकुदळ *f.* घेणें, राशीस लागणें-बसणें, बगोटी धरणें, दुमची पुरवणें, टाचळणें, धोंडावणें, डोंचणें, खटाळणें, त्वष्ट *m. n.* करणें.

HANGMAN, *n.* फांशीं देणारा मनुष्य *m.*-मांग *m.*-डोंब *m.* दंडपाशिक.

HANG-NAIL, *n.* नर *m.*

HANGED, *p.* v. V. A. 1. लोंबवलेला, टांगलेला, &c.

2 अडकवलेला, &c.

3 फांशीं दिल्हेला, &c.

To be h. फांशीं जाणें-पडणें, &c.

HANGER, *n.* HANGING, *p. a.* v. V.N. 1. लोंबणारा, &c. अवलंबित, आलंबित, आलंबी, लंबित, लंबमान.

3 hanger on. v. FOLLOWER. आश्रयाचा, आश्रित, पोष्य.

Idle h. पंक्तिबारगीर, पंक्तिपठाण, भोजनभाऊ, जेवनागण, पात्रेसंमित.

6 ओढक.

I. *that merits the punishment of hanging*—a crime. फांशीं जाण्याचा, गळीं जाण्याचा.

II. *that by which a thing hangs.* अंकडा *m.*

HANGER, *n.* v. SWORD. निमचा *m.*

HANGING, *n.*—against a wall, &c. झालर *f.*

HANK, *n.* v. SKAIN. कुकडें *n.* पाष्ट *n.*

To HANKER, *v. n.* v. To DESIRE. छंद *m.* घेणें-धरणें, सोस *m.* घेणें, सवसवणें, कंकातणें, नितांतणें *or* नितांदणें, लुलुपणें, जीव*m.* टांगला असणें.

HANKERING, *n.* v. V. *and* DESIRE. छंद *m.* सोस *m.* सवलव *f.*

HAP, HAP-HAZARD. See FORTUNE, CHANCE.

HAPLESS, *a.* v. WRETCHED. दुर्भाग्य, दुर्दैव, भाग्यहीन.

HAPLY. See PERHAPS.

To HAP, *To* HAPPEN, *v. n. come to pass.* घडून-होऊन-बनून-&c. येणें-जाणें-घडणें, होणें, पडणें, निघणें, उपस्थित होणें, वर्त्तणें.

To h. occasionally.अवसे पुनवेस-सठीसामाशीं-सणावाराला-तिथिपर्वणीला-&c. येणें-घडणें. [होणें.

2 unto; *betide*, v. To BEFALL. भिडणें, भोवणें, लगटणें, प्राप्त

HAPPENING, *n.* v. V. 1. घडणें *n.* घडून येणें *n.* घटना *f.* घटन *n.* उपस्थान*n.* भवन *n.*

HAPPILY, *adv.*v.A.1. सुखानें, सुखेंकरून, सुखरूप, सुखेनैव, यथासुख. I. *fortunately.* सुभाग्यानें, सुदैवानें, दैवबलानें, भाग्योदयानें.

HAPPINESS, *n.* v. A. 1. सुख *n.* खुशाली *f.* कुशल *n.* कौशल *or* कौशल्य *n.* आनंद *m.* सौख्य *n.* सुखिता *f.* सुखावस्था *f.* क्षेम *m.* कल्याण *n.* श्रेय *n.* भद्र *n.* शर्म *n.*

True h. सदानंद *m.*

H. is found only in the path of holiness. जें सदाचरणास वांकडें तें समाधानास वांकडें.

HAPPY, *a. in a state of felicity*, v. BLESSED. सुखी, सुखरूप, कुशल, सुखसंपन्न, खुशाल, प्राप्तसुख, प्राप्तकल्याण, प्राप्तार्थ, प्राप्तेष्ट, खुशवखत, स्वस्थ, सानंद, क्षेमवान्, क्षेम, कुशली, क्षेमसंपन्न.

H. fellow. सुखापुरी.

2 *of a happy disposition.* आनंदी, उल्हासी, संतोषी, आनंदवृत्ति, संतोषवृत्ति, सदानंद *or* सदानंदी, नित्यानंद. [शस्वी.

3 *lucky, successful*, v. FORTUNATE. पद्महस्ती, वरदहस्ती, य-

4—of rites, observances, &c. *good, joyous, festal.* शुभ, मंगल, भद्र, सु (in comp.).

5 *that supplies pleasure*,—condition, &c. सुखाचा, सुखद, सुखावह, &c.

HARANGUE, *n. oration, set speech.* भाषण *n.* वाकूप्रबंध *m.*प्रवचन *n.* उपन्यास *m.* सोपपत्तिकसालंकारभाषण *n.* सालंकारभाषण *n.* सुवचनात्मकभाषण *n.*

To HARANGUE, *v. n.* v. N. भाषण *n.*-सालंकारभाषण *n.*-&c.करणें.

To HARASS, *v. a.* v. To TIRE. भागवणें, कष्टी-श्रमी-&c. करणें, श्रमवणें, दमवणें, कष्ट *m.*-श्रम *m.*-&c. देणें.

2 *worry, distress, torment, &c.* v. To TEASE. गांजणें, जाचणें, घोळणें, सतावणें, बेजार करणें, कांतावणें, दुःख *n.*-क्लेश *m. pl.*-श्रम *m. pl.*-&c.देणें, श्रमी-कष्टी-बेजार-&c. करणें.

HARASSED, *p.* v. V. 1. श्रमवलेला, &c. श्रमी, कष्टी, बेजार, बेदम.

2 गांजलेला, जाचलेला, &c. श्रमी, कष्टी, बेजार, उपद्रुत.

HARASSER, *n.* HARASSING, *p. a.* v. V. 1. श्रमवणारा, &c. कष्टदायक, कष्टप्रद.

2 जाचणारा, गांजणारा, उपद्रवकारक-दायक-&c. उपद्रवी, क्लेशद.

HARASSING, HARASSMENT, *n.* v. V. 1. —*act.* श्रमवणें *n.* &c. भागवणूक *f.*

2 गांजणें *n.* &c. गांजणूक *f.* जाचणी *f.* जाचणूक *f.* गाळण *f.* बाटाघाट *m. f.* इजा *f.* उपद्रव *m.* उपसर्ग *m.* उपद्व्य *m.* उच्छाद*m.*

HARBINGER, *n. forerunner, &c.* पुढले तयारीचा खटपट्या, अग्रदूत, अग्रगंता, आगमसूचक.

HARBOUR, *n.*—for ships. नांगरवाडा *m.* बंदर *n.*

Floating (deep-water) h. तरतें बंदर *n.*

Open h. वाहतें बंदर *n.*

The space opposite to the mouth of a h.बारा*m.*

2 *shelter*, v. ASYLUM. आश्रय *pop.* आस्रा *m.* थारा *m.* आश्रयस्थान *n.*

To HARBOUR, *v. n. go into harbour.* बंदर *n.* करणें.

To HARBOUR, *v. a. shelter, give asylum or protection to.* आश्रय *m.*-आस्रा *m.*-थारा *m.*-ठाव *m.*-स्थान *n.*- &c. देणें.

2 (in the mind) *entertain.* बाळगणें, धरणें, ठेवणें, मनांत राहूं देणें.

HARD, *a. firm, &c.*कठिन *pop.*कठीण, निबर, सक्कस, टणक, दृढ, सखत, कठिनस्पर्श, कठोर, संगीन, वज्र, वज्रप्राय.—intensely h. सुदृढ, अतिकठिन, अतिकठोर. [त, ताठर.

2 (through dryness) *stiff, rigid.* कडक *or* खडक, खडखडी

3—wood, stone, &c. चिकण, चिंबट *or* चेंबट, कणखर, निबर, कडक, रठ *or* रंठ, दृढ, वज्र, वज्रप्राय.

4 *not solved in boiling* ;—rice. चटचटीत *or* चडचडीत, सटसटीत *or* सडसडीत, धडधडीत, फडफडीत, बुटबुटीत, फळफळीत, कांकड.

5 *not bland or unctuous.* भरभरीत, रसरसीत, रुखा, रुक्ष, अस्नेह, अस्निग्ध, स्नेहांशरहित.

Hard fare. See FARE.

6—a regimen or diet. निकंठ, कडक, कडकडीत, वज्रपथ्य.

7—a business or work, v. DIFFICULT. कठीण, अवघड, बिकट, भारी, मुसकील, दगड फोड, दुष्कर, दुःसाध्य, गडसळ.

H. work, v. TOIL. दगदग *f.* कष्ट *m.* कसाला *m.*

8 *grievous, rigorous, &c.* v. SEVERE. कठीण, अवघड, सखत, जड, जबर, जबरा, जालीम, जुलमाचा.

9 *unreasonable, unjust.* अन्यायाचा, अन्याय्य, गैरवाजबी, जुलमाचा.

10 *difficult to the mind*, v. OBSTRUSE. कठीण, अवघड, दुर्ज्ञेय, दुर्बोध. [ठीण.

11 (winter, &c.), *intense*, v. SEVERE. कडक, कडकडीत, क-

12 *unfeeling, pitiless*, v. CRUEL. निर्दय, दयाहीन.

13—as water. जड.

HARD, *adv. violently, forcibly, vehemently. &c.* बळफट, रगडून, रपाटून, झपाटून, कचकावून, जोरानें.

2 *with close application, laboriously.* श्रमानें, सखतमेहनतीनें, श्रम करून, मेहनत करून, &c. आयासपूर्वक, जीव *m.* लावून-तोडून-देऊन.

To keep h. at. ताणणें, अंबवणें, आंबडणें, चरकीं धरणें.

3 See NEAR.

HARD-CASH, HARD-COIN, *n.* रोकड *f.* सोनें नाणें*n.* रोख पैसा *m.*

HARD-EARNED, *a.* कष्टाचा, श्रमाचा, निढळच्या घामाचा, श्रमसाधित, श्रमोपार्जित, कष्टोपार्जित, नबानबसाचा, लोंबी झोंबीचा.

HARD-FEATURED, *a.* रांठ, रांठ तोंडवळयाचा.

HARD-HEARTED, *a.* v. CRUEL. कठिनहृदय, कठिनांतःकरण, पाषाण हृदय, दगडाच्या हृदयाचा, कठोर, निष्ठुर.

HARD-HEARTEDNESS, *n.* v. A. कठोरपणा *m.* नैष्ठुर्य*n.* दयाहीनता *f.* दयाराहित्य *n.*

HARD-WARE, *n.wares made of iron, &c.* लोखंडीमाल *m.*-डागिने *m. pl.*-जिन्नस *m.*- सामान *n.*

Old and broken h. मोडे *f.* मोडतोड *f.*

Hard-working, *a.* v. **Laborious.** कष्टाळू, कष्टी, कसालती, मशागती, काटक.

To **Harden**, *v. n. become hard.* कठीण-घट्ट-दृढ-&c. होणें, दृढावणें, घटावणें, गोठणें.

2 (in wickedness). निरडणें *or* निरढणें, पुरढणें.

3 *grow hardy*;—the body, &c. घटणें, अटणें, जमणें, कसणें.

4—a fruit, a boil, &c. *grow dry, tough, shrivelled.* दाठरणें, दाढरणें, जारटणें. [ठवणें.

To **Harden**, *v. a. make hard.* कठीण-घट-दृढ-&c. करणें, गो-

2 (in wickedness). निरडणें *or* निरढवणें, पुरढवणें.

3 *make firm, hardy, &c.* घट्ट-सुदृढ-बळकट-&c. करणें, घटवणें.

Hardened, *p.* v. V. N. 1. कठीण-&c. झालेला.

2 निरडलेला, पुरढलेला, निचाडा.

3 घटलेला, &c. घटींव, कडवा.

4 जारटलेला, &c. जारट.

Hardihood, Hardiness, *n.* v. A. 1. बळकटपणा *m.* टणकपणा *m.* कणखरपणा*m.* &c. टणकाई *f.* रांकटाई *f.* बळकटी *f.* सहनशक्ति *f.* सहिष्णुता *f.* कटाक्ष *m.*

2 धिटाई *f.* धीटपणा *m.* दुःसाहस *n.* साहस *n.* धारिष्ट *n.* धाष्टर्य *n.*

Hardly, *adv. not easily, with difficulty, scarcely.* कष्टें-दुःखें-आयासें-कृच्छ्रें-&c. करून, सायासें, जुलमानें *or* जुलमावर, जरूर, जसातसा *or* जसेंतसें करून. [नाहीं.

2 *scarcely, almost not.* जरूर, क्वचित्, विरळा, बहुतकरून

The sense is often idiomatically expressed by the reduplication of a verb; as, मी घरास पोंहचलों न पोंहचलों इतक्यांत पाऊस आला, I had hardly got home when the rain came.

Hardness, *n.* v. A. 1. कठीणपणा *m.* निबरपणा *m.* &c. टणकाई *f.* काठिन्य *n.* दृढता *f.* दाढर्य *n.* द्रढिमा *m.*

I. (of the times) v. **Dearth.** चडचड *or* चणचण *f.* (*or* अन्नाची-खाया प्यायाची-&c. चडचड *f.*).

Hardship, *n. injustice, hard case.* कठीण-अवघड-जड-&c. गोष्ट *f.* ओझें *n.* गौरव *n.*

2 *suffering, trials.* दुःख *n.* कष्ट *m. pl.* श्रम *m. pl.* हाल *m. pl.* वनवास *m.* कटास *m.*

To suffer hardships. श्रम *m. pl.*-हाल *m. pl.*-&c. काढणें-भोगणें, कटासणें.

Hardy, *a. strong, not delicate, not sickly, &c.* कणखर, टणक, बळकट, टणका, रांकट, रांठ, चिकट, चिकण, कडवा, काटक, खडसा, धडसा, घणसर, घणघाव, कटाक्ष, नेटदार, लोखंडी, सहिष्णु, वज्रदेही, वज्रशरीरी, आयासक्षम, अवीट.

H. and iron frame. वज्रदेह *m.* वज्रशरीर *n.*

2 *daring, bold, impudent.* धीट, साहसी, साहसिक, धारिष्टवान्, अवीट.

Hare, *n.* ससा *m.* खरगोस *m.* शश *or* शशक *m.* लंबकर्ण *m.*

Hare-brained. See **Madcap.**

Hare-lip, *n.* रावखंडें *n.* रावखंडा होंट *m.*

Hare-lipped, *a.* रावखंडा, रांवा, ओंठतुट्या.

Harem. See **Seraglio.**

Hark, *interj.* ऐक, ऐका.

To **Hark.** See **To Listen.**

Harlequin. See **Buffoon.**

Harlot, *n. woman who prostitutes her body for hire, courtezan, &c.* रंडी *f.* कसबीण *f.* कलवंतीण *f.* कंचनी *f.* वेश्या *f.* रांड *f.* बाजारीण *f.* बाजारबसवी *f* बसवी *f.* बाजारची खाट *f.* साधारणस्त्री *f.* सामान्या *f.* सामान्यस्त्री *f.* बेसवा *f.* गणिका *f.* वारांगना *f.* वारस्त्री *f.* वारवधू *f.* रूपाजीवा *f.* सर्ववल्लभा *f.* मालजादी *f.* उष्टीपत्रावळ *f.*

2 *woman guilty of lewdness, whore, strumpet, &c.* छिनाल *f.* शिनळबायको *f.* शिंदळबायको *f.* व्यभिचारिणी *f.* पुंश्चली *f.* कुलटा *f.* असती *f.* असाध्वी *f.*

Harlotry, *n. trade, &c. of a harlot.* कसब *n.* वेश्यावृत्ति *f.* भगवृत्ति *f.* वेश्याजीविका *f.* भगजीविका *f.*

2 *lewdness; whoredom, &c.* छिनाली *f.* शिनळकी *f.* शिंदळकी *f.* छिनाला *m.* शिंदळचार *m. pl.* शिंदळचाळे *m. pl.*

Harm, *n. crime, wickedness, wrong.* बाईट *n.* अन्याय *m.* अनीति *f.* प्रत्यवाय *m.* अपराध *m.* पाप *n.* बाध *m.* दोष *m.*

2 *detriment, mischief,* v. **Hurt.** खराबी *f.* नुकसानी *f.* हानि *f.* अपकार *m.* क्षति *f.*

What harm does it do to you? त्यांत तुझें काय जातें?

To **Harm**, *v. a.* v. To **Hurt.** खराबी *f.*-नुकसानी *f.*-बाईट *n.*-अपकार *m.*-&c. करणें *g. of o.* उपद्रव *m.* करणें, दुखापत *f.* देणें-करणें.

Harmful. See **Hurtful.**

Harmless, *a.*—of persons; *unprovoking,* v. **Inoffensive.** बापडा, बापुडवाणा *or* णी, मिसकीन, गरीब, गरंगील, अद्वेष, अद्वेषी, अद्वेषबुद्धि.

2 *not detrimental, not injurious.* अविकारी, अबाधक, निर्बाधक, निरुपद्रवीक, अनपकारी.

3 *unharmed.* अपूट, कोरा, अभंग, अक्षत, अप्राप्तापकार, अप्रहत.

Harmlessness, *n.* v. A. 1. बापडेपणा *m.* मिसकीनपणा *m.* गरीबी *f.* अद्वेषिता *f.* अद्वेषबुद्धि *f.*

2 अविकारीपणा *m.* अविकारिता *f.* अनपकारिता *f.*

Harmonic, Harmonical, *a. relating, &c. to harmony.* स्वरमेळाचा, स्वरमिळणीचा, स्वरैक्याचा, स्वरैक्यसंबंधी.

Harmonica, *n.* जलतरंग *m.*

Harmonious, *a. concordant, musical, symphonious.* स्वरमेळाचा, स्वरमिळणीचा, स्वरैक्याचा, स्वरैक्यविशिष्ट, तालशुद्ध, समताल, समस्वर, समानस्वर.

2 *concordant,* v. **Consistent.** संगतवार, सुसंगत, संदर्भाचा, मिलाफाचा, जव्याचा, जमाचा, सुयुक्त, सुरळीत.

Harmoniousness, *n.* v. A. 1. *and* **Harmony.** स्वरमेळ *m.* स्वरैक्य *n.* तालसमता *f.* [संदर्भशुद्धि *f.*

2 तालामाला *m.* ताळा *m.* ताळमेळ *m.* जम *m.* जवा *m.* जुगल *f.*

Harmonium, *n.* एक वाद्य विशेष आहे.

To **Harmonize**, *v. n. agree in sounds.* स्वरांचा मेळ *m.*-स्वरांची मिळणी *f.*-स्वरमेळ *m.*-&c. असणें-होणें *g. of s. recip.*

2 v. To **Agree.** जमणें, जुळणें, बनणें, मिळणींत असणें, संभवणें, तालामाला *m.*-जवा *m.*-जम *m.*-जुगल *f.*-&c. असणें *g. of s.*

To **Harmonize**, *v. a. cause to agree.* जमविणें, जम *m.*-जवा *m.*-जुळणी *f.*-&c. बसवणें *g. of o. recip.*

Harmony, *n. musical concord.* स्वरमेळ *m.* स्वरमिळणी *f.* स्वरांची मिळणी *f.*-स्वरांचा बनाव *m.*-जमाव *m.*-&c. तानमान *n.* सुरभरणा *m.* स्वरमेलन *n.* स्वरैक्य *n.* स्वरसमता *f.* तालसमता *f.*

2 *concord,*—gener. v. **Agreement.** मेळ *m.* मिलाफ *m.* तिळागुणी *n.* बनाव *m.* घटाव *m.* ऐक्य *n.* एकोपा *m.* सौरस्य *n.*

3 (as of books, statements, &c.). एक वाक्यता *f.* ताळा *m.* जडप *n.* v. वस.

Harness, *n. traces, &c. of a horse.* गाडीच्या घोड्याचा सरंजाम *m.* ओढ *f.* ओढण *f.* गळसूत्रें *n. pl.* अश्वसामग्री *f.*

To **Harness**, *v. a. get ready for draught.* सरंजाम *m.* घालणें, जुंकायास तयार करणें.

2 See To Equip. [Lute.

Harp, *n.* The Maráthás have not the harp. See Lyre, Jew's h. मोरचंग *m.* चंग *m.*

To **Harp**, *v. n.* upon, fig. v. To Dwell. घोकणें, गाणें *or* गावा *m.* गाणें, जपमाळ *f.* घेणें, जपणें, आंकण कडवें *n.* करणें *g. of o.* चाबटाई *f.* करणें *g. of o.* घोकणी *f.* करणें-घेणें-&c. *g. of o.* घोप *m.* घेणें-लावणें *g. of o.*

Harpoon, *n.* मासा मारण्याची बरची *f.*

To **Harpoon**, *v. a.* बरचीनें मारणें.

Harpsichord, *n.* एक तंतुवाद्य आहे.

Harpy, *n. rapacious person.* गिधडा *m.* गिधाड *n.*

Harridan, *n.* उद्दीपत्रावळ *f.* वृद्धवेश्या *f.*

Harrier, *n.* सशाचे शिकारीचा कुतरा *m.*

Harrow, *n.* The following words express *kinds.* दंताळें *or* दांताळें *or* दांताळ *n.* कुळव *m.* गुठा *m.* गुठें *n.* दांता *m.* फांसाटी *or* फेंसाटी *f.* मैंद *m.* फण *m.* अळें *n.* इंगा *m.* झोंपा *m.* बखरा *m.* बखर *m. n.*

To **Harrow**, *v. a.* v. N. पाळी *f. or* कुळवाची पाळी *f.* घालणें *or* कुळवणें (draw over the कुळव), गुठावणें (draw over the गुठा), फेंसाटणें (to use the फेंसाटी), इंगा *m.* फिरवणें, बखरणें *or* बखारणें (to use the बखर.)

2 fig. (the soul, &c.). कांट्यावर ओढणें-घालणें, फांसाटीवर घालणें, काळिजाला घरे *m. pl.*-छिद्रें *n. pl.* पाडणें, काळीज *n.* फाडणें-फोडणें.

To **Harry**. See To Tease.

Harsh, *a.* (to the taste) *austere, acerb,* v. Sour, Rough. अंबटा *or* ट्या, अंबट ढाण, खट्टा *or* ट्या, रुक्ष *pop.* रुखा, अस्नेह, अस्निग्ध.

2 (to the ear). कर्णकठोर, कर्णकटु, कर्कश, कठोर, रांठ, कर्णफोड, कानफोड, दुःश्राव्य.

3 (to the feelings). अणखर, सखत, निष्ठुर, कठोर, कठीण, परुष, अस्निग्ध, अस्नेह, स्नेहभावरहित. [दाष्टीक, करडा.

4—of persons, v. Rude, Cross. उग्र, खाष्टी, कडवा, दाष्ट,

Harshness, *n.* v. A. 1. अंबटाई *f.* अंबटेपणा *m.* &c. रौक्ष्य *n.* रुक्षता *f.*

2 रांठपणा *m.* कर्णकटुता *f.* कार्कश्य *n.* दुःश्राव्यता *f.*

3 सखती *f.* सखतपणा *m.* कठीणपणा *m.* कठोरपणा *m.* &c. पारुष्य *n.*

4 खाष्टीपणा *m.* कडवेपणा *m.* &c. करडीमर्जी *f.* दुःस्वभाव *m.* दुःशीलता *f*

Hart, *n. male deer.* हरिण *pop.* हरण *m.*

Hartshorn, *n.* हरणाचें शिंग *n.*

Harumscarum, *a. wild, wanton, flighty, &c.* धांदली *or* ल्या, धांदला, धांधलीचा, घोंटाळ्या, हूड, धडबड्या, उत्पाती.

A h. fellow, v. Madcap. शेलचिल्ली.

Harvest, *n. season of gathering the crops.* फसलहंगाम *m.* पिकदाब *m.* कापणीची वेळ *f.* कापणीचे दिवस *m. pl* पिकलें *n.* पिकाराड *or* पिकाळाड *f.* कापण्याची घात *f.* घात *f.* हंगाम *m.* फसल *f.* सुगी *f.*

Corn given to mendicants at h. धान्यभिक्षा *f.*

2 *ripe crops.* पीक *n.* फसल *f.*

Abundant h. सुपीक *n.*

Autumnal h. खरीफ *or* प *n.*—Relating to it. खरिफी *or* पी.

Vernal h. रब्बी *or* रबी *f.* रबीधान्य *n.*

Harvest-home, *n. feast at harvest.* फसल हंगामाचें जेवण *n.* नवें *n.* नवीनवाळ *f.* खलयज्ञ *n.*

To **Hash**, *v. a. chop into small pieces.* फोडी *f. pl.*-खुरचा *f. pl.* पाडणें *g. of o.* चोचावून तुकडे *m. pl.* करणें *g. of o.*

Hash, *n.*—of meat. खिमा *m.*

Hasp, *n.* कडी *f.*

Haste, *n.* v. Hurry. घाई *f.* जलदी *f.* उतावळ *or* ळी *f.* त्वरा *f.* झटपट *f.* आवेग *m.* [सो गंभीर.

The more h. the less speed. उतावळा सो बावळा धीर

To **Haste**, *To* **Hasten**, *v n.* जलदी *f.*-त्वरा *f.*-&c करणें.

2 *move with hurry.* लगबग-लगेलगे-लगबगीनें-&c. जाणें-चालणें-येणें.

To **Haste**, *To* **Hasten**, *v. a.* जलदीवर-त्वरेवर-&c. घेणें-आणणें, जलदी *f.*-त्वरा *f.*-&c. करणें *g. of o.* शीघ्रगति *f.*-त्वरितगति *f.* करणें *g. of o.* [*or* गां, लगेलगे.

Hastily, *adv.* v. A. 1. जलदीनें, त्वरेनें, घाईनें, लगलग, लगबग

2 उतावळीनें, उतावळेपणानें, मागेंपुढें पाहिल्यावांचून, विचार केल्यावांचून, हूडपणानें.

3 तापटपणानें, रागांत, राग येऊन, संतापानें.

Hastiness, *n.* v. A. 1. आगपाई *f.*

2 उतावळी *f.* उतावळेपणा *m.* हूडपणा *m.* अविमृश्यकारिता *f.*

3 तापटपणा *m.* तापडपणा *m.* नाकावर राग *m.* गरमप्रकृति *f.* जलद्प्रकृति *f.*

Hasty, *a. quick, not dilatory.* जलद, जलदीचा, त्वरेचा, सत्वर, शीघ्र, शीघ्रगामी.

2 *precipitate, rashly prompt.* उतावळा, उतावळीचा, उतावळेपणाचा, हूड, अविमृश्यकारी, जाल्म.

3 *quick of temper, passionate.* जलद, तापड, तापट, शीघ्रकोपी, पित्तवेगी, नाकावर रागाचा.

4 See Early.

Hasty-pudding, *n.* आयता *m.*

Hat, *n.* टोपी *f.*

The eighteen hats. The European or h.-wearing nations. अठराटोपी, अठराटोपकर. See Turban.

To **Hatch**, *v. a.* (eggs). फोडणें, अंडें *n.* फोडून काढणें.

2 See To Contrive.

Hatch, *n. brood.* कोंबडीचे पिलांची वीण *f.*-वेत *n.*

Hatch, **Hatchway**. *n.* गलबता वरील मजल्याचें दार *n.* गलबताच्या एका मजल्यावरून दुसऱ्या मजल्यास जाण्याचा रस्ता *m.*-मार्ग *m.*-&c. [*m. pl.*

2 hatches. गलबता वरील मजल्याच्या दारांबर ठेवायाचे दादर

To **Hatchel**, **Hatchel**. See To Hackle. Hackle.

Hatchet, *n.* कुऱ्हाड *f.* कुऱ्हाडी *f.* कुऱ्हाडें *n.* परशु *pop.* परश *m.* तबल *m.*

To **Hate**, *v. a.* द्वेष *m.*-दुशमनी *f.*-वैर *n.*-&c. करणें-राखणें-ठेवणें, द्वेषणें—intensely; *detest, &c.* v. To Abhor. ओंगळ-ओखटा-&c. मानणें, अत्यंतद्वेष *m.* करणें *g. of o.* डोळ्यांत सलणें *in, con.*

Hate, **Hatred**, *n.* दावा *m.* अदावत *f.* वैर *n.* द्वेष *m.* द्वेषभाव *m.*

विद्वेषm.
Concealed h. गोवरीची आग f.
Dire and deadly h. (between two parties). बिजें बारें g. of s. recipr. बाराबा बृहस्पति g. of s. recipr.
Fixed and deadly h. उभादावाm. उभेंवैरn. उभाद्वेषm. हाडवैरn. बद्धवैरn. खडाष्टकn. बद्धकटाक्षm. अर्कद्वेषm.
Innate or instinctive h. जातिवैरn.

HATED, p. v. V. द्वेषलेला, द्विष्ट, विद्विष्ट.

HATEFUL, a. detestable, odious. खंबचट, द्वेष्य, द्वेषणीय, द्वेषार्ह, द्वेषयोग्य, द्वेषपात्र, द्वेषभाजन, द्वेषविषय, द्वेषास्पद, द्वेषायतन, द्वेषक्षेत्र, द्वेषलक्ष्य, विद्वेष्य, विद्वेषणीय, अक्षिगत, खल, शठ, दुर्जन, कुटिल, कुटाळ, कुचाळ, कुचर, दुईद्.—in high degree; abominable, detestable, loathsome, &c. अतिद्वेष्य, अत्यप्रिय, अतिद्वेषास्पद, अतिद्वेषविषय, अतिद्वेषार्ह, अतिद्वेषयोग्य, अतिद्वेषपात्र, &c. अमंगल, ओंगळ, ओखटा, केवलविष, विषतुल्य, विषप्राय, कुत्सित, कुत्सनीय.

HATEFULNESS, n. v. A. खंबचटपणाm. &c. द्वेषार्हताf. द्वेषयोग्यता f. कौटिल्यn.—in high degree. अमंगळपणाm. ओंगळपणाm. &c. अतिद्वेषार्हताf. अतिद्वेषयोग्यताf. अतिद्वेष्यताf. अत्यप्रियता f. विषतुल्यता f. कुत्सनीयता f. कौत्सित्यn.

HATER, n. v. V. द्वेष करणारा, &c. द्वेषक, द्वेषी, विद्वेषी, विद्वेष्टा, द्रोही (in comp. as पितृद्रोही, मातृ-गुरु-मित्र-स्वामि-&c. द्रोही).

HAUGHTILY, a. v. A. गर्वानें, दिमाखानें, मगरुरीनें, &c.

HAUGHTINESS, n. v. A. and PRIDE. गर्वm. अभिमानm. ताठाm. मगरुरी f. दिमाखm. दमm. आढ्यता f. v. बाळग, मिरव, ओढ, इशीम f. v. बाळग, भोग, तोराm. रग f. स्तोमm. n. खट्टाm. बदमस्ती f. प्रतिष्ठा f. v. बाळग, मिरव.

HAUGHTY, a. v. PROUD.—of persons. गर्वी, गर्विष्ट, गर्वित, अभिमानी, मगरूर, पिळदार, रगदार, ऊर्ध्वदृष्टि, चढेल, दिमाखी, दिमाखदार, तोरेदार, दिमाखाचा, मानी, बदमस्त, उदगा, उदगामादगा, उन्नतशिरा, अविनय.
2—of things. गर्वाचा, दिमाखाचा, मगरुरीचा, &c.

To HAUL, v. a. v. To DRAW. ओढणें, खेंचणें, ओढून-खेंचून नेणें.

HAUM. See STRAW.

HAUNCH, n. thigh. मांडी f. मांड f.

To HAUNT, v. a. frequent. येणें जाणेंn. करणें, जाण्या येण्याची रहाळ f. असणें in. con. उठपायीं-उतरा मातरा-&c. जाणें, फेरी f. टाकणें-घालणें, बैठक f. करणें.
2—ghosts, goblins, &c. भूतn. लागणें, भूत संचारm.-पिशाच संचारm. असणें in. con.
To be haunted. पिसाटणें.
Haunted house or place. भुतवाडाm. भुतखानाm. भुतखेळेंघरn. उपद्रवीक घरn.-जागा f.-&c.

HAUNT, n. place of resort. बैठक f. बसण्याचा अड्डाm. रहाळीची जागा f. फेरीटाकण्याची-घालण्याची जागा f.

HAUTBOY, n.—the instrument. सनयी or य f.

HAUTEUR, n. v. PRIDE. गर्वm. ताठाm. दर्पm. मगरुरी f.

To HAVE, v. a. possess, hold, &c. धरणें, राखणें, बाळगणें, असणें in. con. जवळ असणें in. con. and g. of s. हातीं असणें g. of s. गांठीस असणें g. of s.
Not to h. in one. अष्टांगीं नसणें-गांवीं नसणें with g. of s. and in. con.
2 be under a necessity or obligation. असणें, लागणें, भाग असणें, पाहिजे all with in. con. (as मला तिकडे जायाचें आहे, मला तिकडे जाणें भाग आहे, &c.).
3 take, accept, receive, &c. घेणें, पतकरणें, स्वीकारणें.
4 at; assail. See To ATTACK.
5 on; wear. आंगावर असणें in. con. धारण n. करणें.

HAVEN, n. v. HARBOUR. बंदर n. नांगरवाडा m.

HAVER, n. HAVING, p. a. v. V. 1. धाता.
Having, holding, bearing, &c. are incessantly used in English to form Attributives or Predicates. In this use they are neatly and expressively represented by words (single or compound) having क affixed. Ex. Having the title of Pandit, पंडितोपनामक. Bearing the surname of Jagannàth, जगन्नाथोपनामक. Having joy for its subject (speech,) आनंदविषयक (वाक्य). Having the five elements as its consistence or essence (the earth). पंचभूतात्मक (पृथ्वी, जग, &c.). Having gold as its base or subject (a trinket), सुवर्णात्मक (अलंकार). Having sin as its root or spring (pain) पापमूलक(दुःख). Having a father alive (a man), जीवत्पितृक (पुरुष). Having a river for its mother, nurse, fosterer, &c. (a country), जलमातृक or नदीमातृक (देश). Bearing design, or intention, (an act, a speech), बुद्धिपूर्वक (कृत्य, भाषण). Bearing concern, hope, &c. आस्थापूर्वक, आशापूर्वक, &c. and स्तुत्यात्मक, निंदात्मक, गद्यपद्यात्मक, त्रिदोषात्मक, त्रिगुणात्मक, पुण्यात्मक, पापात्मक, पुण्यमूलक, (सुख, &c.), स्त्रीमूलक (कलह, &c.), आकाशमूलक (वायु), आदरपूर्वक (भाषण, वर्त्तन, &c.), शपथपूर्वक (साक्षी, &c.), इच्छापूर्वक (यत्न, प्रार्थना, &c.), अंतःकरणपूर्वक (भक्ति, &c.), लोभविषयक, कामविषयक, न्यायविषयक, व्याकरणविषयक, &c. &c. And, in comp. esp. with Persian and Hindoostanee words, by दार & बरदार (ex. pointed, अणीदार; having strength, जोरदार; bearing a mace चोबदार, and भालदार, चौकीदार, रंगदार, गोलदार, बेलेबरदार, शिकेबरदार, निशाणबरदार, &c. &c.)
Having, in the sense possessing, is, through various shades, rendered by युक्त in comp. (as having anxiety, चिंतायुक्त, क्रोधयुक्त, &c.); by वाला (as पैकेवाला, आम्बूवाला, &c.); by मान् or मंत and by वान् or वंत (as बुद्धिमान्, शक्तिमान्, द्रव्यवान्, भाग्यवान्, &c.); by संपन्न (as विद्यासंपन्न, धन-ज्ञान-पुण्य-&c. संपन्न); by करी, (as पैकेकरी, &c.).

HAVING, n. v. V. 1.—act. धारण n. धरण n.

HAVOCK, n. slaughter, devastation, &c. v. DESTRUCTION. कत्तल f. पटाडा m. अनर्थ m. सप्पा m. तुफान n. कंदाळी f. नासधूस f. नासधूळ f. प्रलय m. उत्पात m. उपप्लव m.

To HAVOCK. See To DESTROY.

To HAW, v. n. hem and haw. v. To HESITATE. हांहूं n.f.-कांकूं n.f.-नांनूं n.f.-&c. करणें.

HAWK, n. ससाणा m. बहिरी ससाणा m. शिकरा m. श्येन pop. शेन m.
Female h. श्येनी pop. शेनी f.

HAWK-EYED, a. of acute sight. काकदृष्टि, दीर्घदृष्टि, दूरदृष्टि.

HAWK-NOSED, a. गरुडनाक्या, गरुडनासिक, शुकनासिक.

To HAWK, v. n. make an effort to bring up phlegm. खाकारणें or खाकेरणें.
2 practice falconry. बहिरी ससाणा घेऊन शिकार f. करणें.

To HAWK, *v. a.* up (phlegm). खाकरणें *or* खाकेरणें, खंकारणें, खाकरून-&c. काढणें, खाकरी *or* खाकारी *f.* काढणें.
2 *sell by proclaiming in the streets.* फेरीनें विकणें, घरोघर-दारोदार-&c. विकणें.

HAWKER, *n.* v. V. A. 2 *and* PEDLER. फेरीवाला.

HAWSER, *n.* v. ROPE, CABLE. दोर *m.*

HAY, *n.* वाळलेलें गवत *n.* सुखा घास *m.* घास *m.* पह्याण *n.* पेण *n.*
To make h. while the sun shines. वाहत्या गंगेंत हात धुणें, कल्पवृक्षासालीं बसून झोळीला गांठी कां द्याव्या ?

HAY-RICK, HAY-STACK. *n.* तणारा *m.* वाळलेल्या गवताचा गंज*m.* गवताचें उडवें *n.*

HAZARD, *n. chance of harm.* v. DANGER. भय *n.* धोका *m.* जोखीम *n.* खत्रा *m.*
To run the h. तवकल *f.* करणें.

To HAZARD, *v. a. expose to danger.* जोखमांत-भयांत-धोक्यांत-संकटांत-&c. घालणें-पाडणें.

HAZARDOUS, *a.* v. DANGEROUS. जोखमी, जोखमाचा, तवकलीचा, भयाचा, धोक्याचा, सभय.

HAZE, *n.* धुकें *n.* धुमें *n.*

HAZEL, *n.* एक झाड आहे.

HAZEL, *a.*—the eye. भोरा.

HAZILY, *adv.* धुरकट, धुरट, अंधक. [री *f.*

HAZINESS, *n.* v. A. धुई *f.* धुकें *n.* धुमें *n.* धुरकट *n.* धुरट *n.* अंधा-

HAZY, *a.* धुक्याचा, धुम्याचा, &c. धुंद.

HE, *pro.* तो (*that* male). हा (*this* male).
2 *any man,* he who. जोकोणी, जोमनुष्य.

HEAD, *n.* डोई *f.* डोकी *f.* डोकें *n.* मस्तक *m. n.* शिर *n.* डोकसी *f.* डोसकी *f.* डोकसें *n.* डोसकें *n.* डोकूल *n.* डोचकी *f.* डोचकें *n.* मुंड *n.* मुंडी *f.* मुंढी *f.* मुंडकी *f.* मुंडकें *n.* मूर्धा *m.* शीर्ष *n.* मौलि *or* मौली *m.* उत्तमांग *n.*—as separated from the body, रुंड *pop.* रुंढ *n.*—in contemptuous, cant, or light phraseol. as *sconce, noddle, pate, poll, crop, pow, cranium, costard,* टांगें *n.* टकली *f.* टकलें *n.* टाळकें *n.* टाकुलें *n.* डोंबल *n.* बोढ *n.* बोडकूल *n.* बोडकें *n.* बोडसें *n.* बगोटें *n.* तरटें *n.* बेलटी *f.* बेलटें*n.* खोपरी *f.* नारळ *m.*
Blow or bump with the h. ढुंडका *m.* ढुंदडा *m.*
From h. to foot. आपादमस्तक, आपादतलमस्तक, नखशिखपर्यंत, आनखशिख, नखशिखांत.
H. and tail, fig. *beginning & end.* शेंडा बुडखा*m.*शेंडाबुंधा*m.*
Made out of one's own h. बगलेंतून काढलेला, स्वकपोलकल्पित.
Shaking of the h. (as in palsy, &c.). शिरःकंप *m.*
That is at the h. of, *that is first or chief.* पहिला, मुख्य, अग्रगण्य. [&c.) शिरी *f.*
The ornamental cloth on the h. (of elephants, horses,
Upper half of the h. ब्रह्मांड *n.*
Wind in the h. ज्ञानवायु *m.*
With the head poked or thrust forward,—looking. ढुंकून, डोकावून. [रोवेष्टन *n.*
Wrapper or girding for the h. टापशी *f.* कानपट्टी *f.* शि-
To be knocked on the h. v. To FAIL. घडघडणें,घडाडणें, वाहवणें, कोसळणें, लटपटणें.
To be wrong in the h. मस्तक *m. n.*-&c. फिरणें *g. of s.*
To begin to hold up the h. मान *f.* वर करणें, डोकें *n.*-डोई *f.*-&c. काढणें.
To bind h. and foot. सुरमुंडी *f.* करणें *g. of o.*
To bow down one's h. मस्तक *n. m.* ठेंगणें करणें.
To get above or over one's h. डोक्यावर बसणें.
To get heaviness in the h. डोक्यास *or* मस्तकास भारें *m.* चढणें *g. of s.*
To hang the h. मान *f.* खालीं घालणें, अवाङ्मुख-नतमुख-नतमूर्द्धा-&c. होणें, विरवणें. [नतशिरा होणें.
To hold a high h. आढ्यता *f.* मिरवणें-ओढणें-बाळगणें, उ-
To hold up the h. again. पाठ *f.* उचलणें.
To lose one's h. *become bewildered.* बाचलणें.
To rise into the h. चढणें.
To shave the h. डोई *f.* करणें.
To turn round the. h. मुरडणें, डोसकें *n.*-&c. मुरडणें.
2 (as of fish, snakes, lizards, certain birds, &c.). डोळूक *m.* टोंकरी *f.*
3 *chief leader,* v. CONDUCTOR. नायक, नांगन्या, नाक *n.* सरदार *f.* शिरोभाग *m.* मुरब्बी *m.*
4 (as of a body of guides, dooley-bearers, &c.) v. CAPTAIN. मुकद्दम, नायक, हवालदार, जमादार, मिरधा.
5 *most eminent person of.* शिखामणि *m.* शिरोमणि *m.* चूडामणि *m.* मुकुटमणि *m.* शिरताज *m.*
6—in comp. with such words as head-constable, head-master, &c. सर (ex. सरनायक, सर देशमुख, सर कमाविसदार), ऐन (ex. ऐनकारभारी, &c.).
7 *highest member or part,* v. TOP. माथा *or* माथ्या*m.* शेंडा *m.* मस्तक *m. n.*
8 *froth, &c. on top.* शीग *f.*
9 (of a bed). उशागत *n.* उशेगत *n.* उसें *n.*
10 *topic, department, &c.* प्रकरण *n.* विल्हय *or* विल्हे *f.* कलम *n.* खातें *n.* आसन *n.*
11. (as of cattle) *single one.* सर*m.* शेपटी*f.* शेपडी *f.*ढाय *m.* खुंट *m.*—of camels, नफर.—of elephants, नग.—of horses, पुठा *or* पुट्ठा *m.* रास *m.*—of goats & sheep माच (above 20), बुद्द (below 20.)
12 *an individual.* डोई *f.*
13 (of a boil, pustule, &c.). तोंड *n.* मुख *n.* [पोत *m.*
14 (of a spear, lance, dart, arrow). भाल *or* भलn. फल*n.*
15 See UNDERSTANDING. 16 (of corn, &c.) v. EAR. लोंग *f.* लोंबी *f.* लोंब *f.* लोंबट *n.*
A stunted or diminutive h. लुंगस *n.* लुंगू *n.*

To HEAD, *v. a. take the lead, conduct. &c.* पुढाकार *m.*-पुढार*m.*-पुरस्कार *m.*-&c. करणें, पुढारी-पुढाईत-अधिपति-&c. असणें *in. con.* पुढाईत-&c. होऊन चालवणें-नेणें.

HEAD-ACHE, *n.* कपाळशूळ *m.* माथाशूळ *or* माथेसूळ *m.* कपाळदुखी *f.* मस्तकशूल *m.* शिरःपीडा *f.* [*of s.*
To have a h. मस्तक *n.*-डोकें *n.*-डोई *f.*-&c.-उठणें-चढणें *g.*
To give a h. मस्तक *n.*-डोकें *n.*-डोई *f.*-&c. उठविणें.

HEAD-BAND, *n.* कानपट्टी *f.* शिरोवेष्टन *n.*
2 (of a horse). पुंजी *f.*

HEAD-DRESS, *n.* टोपी *f.* शिरोवेष्टन *n.*

HEAD-LAND, *n.* टोंक *n.* भूशलाका *f.*

2—of a field. कडपट्टी *f.*

HEAD-LESS, *a.* मस्तकहीन, अशिरस्क.

HEAD-LOAD, *n.* डोई ओझें *n.* शिरभारा *m.* शिरभारी *f.*

HEAD-LONG, *a. heady, precipitate,* v. RASH, IMPETUOUS. गळदट, शिरजोर, धडफडीचा, धडबडीचा, हाडकपाळी *or* ळ्या, हुरमट, हूड.

2 See STEEP.

HEAD-LONG, *adv.* v. A. 1. उतावळीनें, उतावळेपणानें, हुर्योंहुर्यों करून, हुरळून, दाटबळें, हूडपणानें, विचारकेल्यावांचून, मागेंपुढें पाहिल्यावांचून, धसकावून.

I. *with the head foremost.* डोईकडून, अधोमुख.

HEAD-MAN, *n.* v. CHIEF, CONDUCTOR, &c. मुकद्दम, हाकीम, अधिकारी, मुखरण, अध्यक्ष (in comp. as ग्रामाध्यक्ष, स्थानाध्यक्ष).

HEAD-MONEY, *n.* मनुष्यपट्टी *f.* डोईपट्टी *f.*

HEAD-MOST, *a. foremost.* सगळयां पुढचा, सर्वाग्रगामी.

HEAD-ORNAMENT, *n.* शिरोभूषण *n.*

HEAD-PIECE, *n. armor, &c. for the head.* शिरस्त्राण *n.* शिरस्क *n.*

2 See UNDERSTANDING.

HEAD-QUARTERS, *n.* सेनापति-मुख्य अधिकारी-&c. राहण्याची जागा *f.*

HEAD-ROPE, *n.* (of a horse). आघाडी *f.* दावासन *n.*

HEADSHIP, *n.* मुख्यता *f.* प्रधानता *f.* श्रेष्ठत्व *n.*

HEAD-STALL, *n.* सरदारी *f.* मोहरकी *f.* शिरदाली *f.*

HEAD-STRONG, *a. heady, precipitate, &c.* v. IMPETUOUS, SELFWILLED. शिरजोर, हाडकपाळी *or* ळ्या, गळदट, दांडगा, अडेल, आपढंगी, आपगंड, हेंकट, हेंकड, हेंकेखोर, दंड, सैरट.

HEAD-WORK, *n. intellectual labor.* बुद्धीचें काम *n.* मानसिक श्रम *m.*

HEADINESS, *n.* v. A. शिरजोरी *f.* शिरजोरपणा *m.* दांडगाई *f.* दांडगावें *n.* दांडगाबा *m.* हूडपणा *m.* आपढंग *m.*

HEADING, *n.* सदर *n.*

Marginal epitomizing h. बिना *m.* बिनी *f.*

HEADY, *a. headstrong, headlong, hasty, &c.* v. RASH, IMPETUOUS. हाडकपाळी *or* ळ्या, कपाळफोडया, शिरजोर, गळदट, हुरमट, हूड, उनाड, दांडगा, धसक्या, मुसांड्या, दंड, हेंकट, अविमृश्यकारी, सैरट.

2 See INTOXICATING. [देहें-करणें.

To HEAL, *v. a.* v. To CURE. निरोगी-बरा-&c. करणें, आरोग्य *n.* देणें-करणें.

2 (disputes, variance, &c.) v. To RECONCILE. मिलाफ *m.*-समेट *m.*-&c. करणें.

To HEAL, *v. n.* भरणें, माठळणें, माठणें, बरा-&c. होणें.

HEAL-ALL, *n. fig.* त्रैलोक्यचिंतामणि *m.*

HEALING, *a. of healing virtue.* रोगघ्न, औषधी, ओखदी, रोगशांतिकारक.

HEALTH, *n.* (of body). शरीरसंपत्ति *f.* शरीरस्वास्थ्य *n.* आरोग्य *n.* अरोग *m.* शरीरसमाधान *n.* अनामय *n.*

2 *feeling of body as respects health.* तबियत *f.* प्रकृति *f.* शरीरप्रकृति *f.* भावना *f.*

Accounts of h. (and doings)—as communicated. कुशलार्थ *m.* भलीभलाई *f.*

Enquiries after h. and welfare. कुशलप्रश्न *m.* परामर्श *m.* *v.* घे-कर, (esp. among females), पुसणें *n.*

3 (of mind, spirit, &c.). चित्तसमाधान *n.* स्वास्थ्य *n.* स्वस्थता *f.* खुशाली *f.*

4 *wish of health & happiness.* आरोग्याची-कल्याणाची-खुशालीची इच्छा *f.*

To drink a h. अमक्याचें नांव घेऊन त्याचें आरोग्य असो असें म्हणून कांहीं पिणें.

HEALTHFUL, HEALTHY, *a.* (of a body). अरोगी, अरोग, नीरोग *pop.* निरोग *or* निरोगी, निरामय, तवाना, स्वस्थ, सुस्थ, शरीरसंपन्न, धडधाकट *or* ड, दोन टक्यांनीं धड, टणक, टणका, अव्रण.

2 (of look) *fresh, clear, glowing, lively, &c.* टवटवीत, तुकतुकीत, टवटवीत-&c. तोंडाचा, मुखश्रीसंपन्न, मुखरागसंपन्न.

3 (of mind, spirit, &c.) चित्तसमाधानी, स्वस्थ, सुस्थ, खुशाल.

4 *salubrious, salutary.* शरीरास चांगला, आरोग्यप्रद, आरोग्यदायक, आरोग्यवर्द्धक, निरामय, हितकर.

HEALTHFULNESS, HEALTHINESS, *n.* v. A. 1. निरोगीपणा *m.* आरोग्य *n.* अरोगिता *f.* स्वस्थता *f.* स्वास्थ्य *n.* विकाराभाव *m.* विरुत्यभाव *m.* विकारराहित्य *f.* अरोग *m.* अनामय *n.*

2 काया *or* कया *f.* नूर *m.* कांत *f.* मुखश्री *f.* मुखराग *m.* कला *f.* तुकतुकी *f.* तजला *or* तजेला *m.* तजली *or* तजेली *f.*

HEAP, *n. pile, &c.* ढीग *m.* ढिगर *m.* ढिगार *or* ढिगारा *m.* राशि *m.* *pop.* रास *f.* एकराशि *m.* गोळा *m.* जमाव *m.* पुंज *m.* पुंजा *m.* गंज *m.f.* पिंड *m.* सांठ *m.* सांठा *m.* मेळावा *m.* संग्रह *m.* संचय *m.* चय *m.* संघात *m.* संचित *n.* संभार *m.* संघ *m.* समूह *m.* समुच्चय *m.* संदोह *m.* समवाय *m.* स्तोम *m.* वार *m.* वृंद *n.* एकपुटा *m.*

H. as scratched up (by ants, rats, &c.). उकर *or* उकीर *m. dim.* उकरी *f.*

Heaps, *lots, &c.* v. EXUBERANCE. ढीग, मोप, मस्त.

The h. *the gross collection.* भररास *f.*

To fall in heaps, *drop and die, or be sick, suddenly and by multitudes.* चेंदा *m.*-धापा *m.* वळणें *g. of s.*

2 (esp. of grain). पुंज *m. dim.* पुंजी *f.* डुंग *m. dim.* डुंगी *f.* डुंगा *m.* डिंग *m. dim.* डिंगोरा *m.* & डिंगोळी *f.*

3 (of things loosely heaped). दुडपा *m.* मोकळ *f.*

To HEAP, *v. a. pile up.* सांचवणें, सांठवणें, गोळा करणें, पुंजी करणें, ढीग *m.*-ढिगारा *m.*-रास *f.*-&c. करणें *g. of o.* एकपुठा *m.* जमवणें *g. of o.* संचय *m.*-संग्रह *m.*-&c. करणें *g. of o.*

To h. up above the measure. शीग *f.* भरणें.

HEAPED, *p.* v. V. सांचवलेला, &c. संगृहीत, संचित, उपचित, चित, संकलित, समुदित, पिंडित, राशीकृत, एकराशीभूत, राशिगत.

HEAPER, *n.* v. V. सांचवणारा, &c. संग्रही, संग्राहक, संग्रह-संचय-&c. कर्त्ता.

HEAPING, *n.* v. V.—*act.* सांचवणें *n.* &c. संचयन *n.* चयन *n.* चय *m.* संकलन *n.* राशीकरण *n.* पिंडीकरण *n.*

To HEAR, *v. a.* ऐकणें, आकर्णणें, श्रवण *n.*-&c. करणें, कानीं-कानावर पडणें-येणें *in. con.* परियेसणें *or* परिसणें.

To be able to h. ऐकूं येणें *in. con.*

To refuse to h. कान *m. pl.* झाडणें.

2 *hearken, obey.* ऐकणें, मानणें, मनावर घेणें, परियेसणें *or* परिसणें.

HEARD, *p.* v. V. 1, ऐकलेला, ऐकींव, आकर्णित, श्रुत, कर्णारूढ, कर्णधृष्ट, कानावरून गेलेला.

To be able to be h. ऐकूंजाणें, ऐकूंयेणें.

HEARER, *n.* v. V. 1. ऐकणारा, &c. श्रवणकर्त्ता, श्रोता.

HEARING, *n.* v. V. 1.—*act.* ऐकणें *n.* आकर्णन *n.* श्रवण *n.* श्रुति *f.*

I.—the sense. श्रवणेंद्रिय *n.* श्रवण *n.* श्रुति *f.* कर्ण *m.* श्रवणशक्ति *f.*

Hard of h. कानाचा जड, फुटक्या कानाचा.

Loss of h. अश्रवण *n.*

Sharp, quick, &c. of h. कानाचा तिखट, श्रवणपटु.

II. *apprehension or note by the ear.* ऐकीव n. ऐकणें n.

III. *reach of the ear.* कानाचा टप्पा m. ऐकण्याचा टप्पा m.

To HEARKEN. See To LISTEN.

HEARSAY, n. v. REPORT. सांगासांगी f. तोंडातोंडीची गोष्ट f. कर्णोपकर्णीं आलेली गोष्ट f. श्रुति f.

Known through h. ऐकून ठाऊक.

HEARSE, n. मुड्याची or मुरद्याची गाडी f. प्रेतरथ m. शवयान n.

HEART, n. काळजाचा बोका m. (or *pop.* काळीज n. which *properly* means the Liver), हृदयकमल n. रक्ताशय m. हृत् or हृद् (in comp. as हृद्रोग, हृत्कमल).

To have the h. at the lips. घुटवळणें.

2—as the seat of the affections. चित्त n. मन n. हृदय n. दिल m. n. अंतःकरण n. बुद्धि f. पोट n. मानस n. अंतर n. अंतर्याम n. अभ्यंतर n. हृदयमंदिर n. चिच्छक्ति f.

Ability of learning by h. पाठशक्ति f.

From the bottom of the h. बेंबीच्या देंठापासून.

The h. and the life. अंतर्बाह्य n.

In the recesses of the h. मनच्या मनीं.

Known by h. तोंडपाठ, मुखपाठ, मुखीं बसलेला, पाठ, मुखोद्गत.

Knower of the secrets of the h. अंतर्ज्ञानी, अंतरसाक्ष, अंतरसाक्षी.

Knowledge of the secrets of the h. अंतर्ज्ञान n.

A property or attribute of the h. मनोधर्म m.

Purification or purity of h. अंतःशौच n.

Quick at learning by h. पाठी.

Singleness of h. अनन्यभाव m.

State or affection of the h. मनोविकार m. मनोविकृति f.

That has by h. पाठी.

To one's heart's content. पोटभर, धनवर, मनमुराद, धणपुरेस्तूर, इच्छातृप्त, आतृप्ति, आतृप्त, यथातृप्ति, यथातृप्त, यथेच्छ, यथेष्ट, मनेच्छ, मनेच्छा.

With all one's h. and soul and strength. काया वाचा मनेंकरून, सबाह्याभ्यंतर, पंचप्राणानें, जीवादारभ्य, सर्वात्मना, जिवाभ्यास or जिवाभ्यासानें. [भावेंकडून.

With full purpose of h. मनोभावें or मनोभावानें or मनो-

With h. and hand. In h. and deed. सबाह्याभ्यंतर.

To follow the desires of one's h. मन मानतें तेंच करणें.

To give one one's h. काळीज n. काढून देणें, मन n. अर्पणें.

To have it in one's h. मनांत असणें. [m. सोडणें.

To have one's h. sink. काळजानें ठाव m. सोडणें or धीर-

To have one's h. in one's mouth (to be alarmed and distressed) कंठीं प्राण m. येणें.

To have or get a heavy h. ऊर m. दडपणें *g. of s.*

To learn by h. पाठ-मुखपाठ-&c. करणें.

To press to one's h. जिवासीं-उरासीं-पोटासीं धरणें.

To set one's h. upon. प्राण m. ठेवणें, जीव m. टांगणें.

To take to h. काळजीं लागणें *in. con.* काळजी f.-तिडीक f. -&c. लागणें *in. con. g. of o.* [ठाऊक.

The h. knows its own plague. अळवाची खाज अळवास

3 *core, inner part.* गर्भ *pop.* गाभा m. मोख m.

At h. *at the core or bottom.* हाडीं (ex. हाडीं शुद्ध-खरा-खोटा-चांगला-वाईट-&c.).

4 (of timber). केत m. साड m. नार m.

5 (of a boil, &c.). बीं n. गाईर f. मोख m.

6 *spirit,* v. COURAGE. धैर्य n. अवसान n.

To lose h. धैर्य n.-अवसान n.-&c. सोडणें-टाकणें.

To take h. धैर्य n.-अवसान n.-दम m.-&c. धरणें.

HEART-ACHE, n. हृद्रोग m. मनोदुःख n. मनोव्यथा f. चिंताज्वर m.

HEART-BREAKING. See HEART-RENDING.

HEART-BURN, n. अम्लपित्त n. तीक्ष्णाग्नि m. हृद्रोग m.

HEART-BURNING, n. *secret enmity.* आंतूनवैर n. मुकादावा m. अंतर्दाह m. अंतर्वैर n.

HEART-FELT, a. *cordial.* पोटांतला, आंतड्याच्या पिळाचा, बेंबीच्या देंठाचा, अंतर्यामीचा, अंतर्यामी, हृद्य.

HEART-PEA, HEART-SEED, n. पिंगवी f.—its seed पिंगवें n.

Oil of h. पिंगवेल n.

HEART-PIERCING, a. हृदयवेधक, हृदयाविंधु.

HEART-RENDING, a. *deeply afflictive.* फारच दुःख देणारा, परमशोकप्रद, अतिशोकप्रद.

HEART-SEARCHING, a. मनकवडा, अंतर्यामी, अंतरसाक्ष, अंतरसाक्षी, चित्तसंव्य.

HEART-STEALING, HEART-ALLURING, &c. a. चित्तचोर, चित्तचोरटा, चित्तभ्रमी, मारू.

HEARTH, n. *place for fire on a floor.* शेकाटीची-परशाची-आगटीची-&c. जागा f.

HEARTILY, *adv.* v. A. 1. मनोभावें or मनोभावेंकरून, जिवाभावानें, मनापासून, बेंबीच्या देंठापासून, मनःपूर्वक, जीवादारभ्य, पंचप्राणानें, नेट देऊन, साक्षेपें. [मारून.

I. *to one's heart's content,* v. HEART. पोटभर, कचकावून,

HEARTINESS, n. v. A. 1. उद्मेख m. पोटाग f. आस्था f. उत्सुकता f. औत्सुक्य n. साक्षेप m. अनुरक्ति f. अनुराग m.

2 ऐवज m. टणकाई f. खणखणितपणा m. खडखडितपणा m.

HEARTLESS, a. *spiritless.* निरुत्साह, निरुत्साही, अनुत्साही, निर्जीव, निर्वीर्य, धैर्यहीन, उत्साहहीन, अनास्थ.

2 *insincere.* वरकरणी, वरकर्मी, वरवंचाईचा.

HEARTLESSNESS, n. v. A. 1. अनुत्साह m. अनास्था f. अनुत्साहता f. निरुत्साहता f. &c. उत्साहाभाव m.

2 वरवरपणा m. वरकरणीपणा m.

HEARTY, a. *warm, cordial, zealous, earnest,* v. SINCERE. उद्मेखी, उत्सुक, साक्षेपी, अंतःकरणापासूनचा, आस्थेचा, जिवाभावाचा, मनापासूनचा, जिव्हाळ्याचा, अंतर्यामीचा, पोटागीचा, नाभिकमळापासूनचा, हृद्य, अनुरक्त, अनुरत.

H. in offices of hospitality. टेंकदार, टेंकीचा.

2 *in full health,* v. HALE. टणक, टणका, खणखणीत, खडखडीत, खडस, खडसा, पाडकुला.

To make a h. meal. दपटून-पोट भरून-&c. जेवणें, चांगला-पुष्कळ जेवणें.

HEAT, n.—the sensation. गरमी f. दाह m. डाह m.

2—as in objects. उष्णता f. उष्ण n. उष्मा m. ऊब f. गरमी f. ताप m. तेज n.

Red h. अग्निवर्ण m.

Heating to a red h. ताव m. To heat to a red h. तावणें.

3 (of weather). ऊन n. ऊन्ह n. उष्ण n. उष्णता f. ऊब f. उष्मा m. उबाळा m. उन्हाळा m. उन्हाळी f. उकाडा m. गरमा m. ताप m.

Eruption or pimple from h. घामोळी f. घामोळें n.

In the h. (of the day). उन्हातान्हाचा *decl.* दुपारतिपारचा *decl.* दुपारींतिपारीं.

Temperate h. सरदगरमी *f.*

To be affected by h. उन्हाळणें.

4 (in the system). उष्ण *n.* उष्णता *f.* गरमी *f.* जळजळ *f.* डाह *m.* काहिली *f.* डोंब *or* आंगाचाडोंब *m.* थाळ *f.* थळण *f.* अंतर्दाह *m.* अंतर्ज्वलन *n.*

Prickly h. घामोळें *n.*

5 *flush, excitement, agitation, passion.* गुरमी *f.* तापm. संताप *m.* जळजळ *f.* तळतळ *f. intens.* तळतळाट *m.* जहाली *or* ज्याली *f.* आवेश *m.* घाई *f.* गडबड *f.*

6 (as in animals) *desire of the other sex.* माजm. मस्ती *f.* उधानn. भरm.—of mares, she asses, &c. हत्याणn.

To be in h. माजm. करणें, उधानणें.

7 *effort, stretch, bout.* दमm. हिररी *f.* एलगारm.

In one h. एकेझपाट्यानें, एकदम, एकातडाक्यानें. [पणाm.

8 (of temperament). गरमी *f.* रागिटपणाm. तापटपणाm. कडक-

9 (as of drugs, art. of food), *heating quality.* उष्णता *f.*

10 *vehemence, violence, &c.* झपाटाm. तडाका *or* खाm. कडाखाm. आवेशm. [णें, कढवणें.

To Heat, *v. a. make hot.* तावणें, तापवणें, ऊन-उष्ण-तप्त-&c. कर-

2 *set to heat.* उन्हत ठेवणें.

To Heat, *v. n. become hot.* तापणें, ऊन-&c. होणें.

To h. and spoil. उबणें. [पित, संतप्त.

Heated, *p.* v. V. A. 1. तावलेला, तापवलेला, तापित, तप्त, संता-

Heath, *n.* एकझाडआहे.

2 *place overgrown with bushes.* रानn.

Heathen, *n. pagan, idolater, &c.* मूर्तिपूजक, असद्धर्मी, असत्यधर्मी.

Heathenism, *n.* मूर्तिपूजा *f.* मूर्तिपूजनn. असद्धर्मm.

Heather. See Heath, 1.

Heating, *a. of heating quality,*—medicines, &c. उष्ण, उष्णवीर्य, उष्णशक्तिक. [तावm.

Heating, *n.* v. V. A. 1.—*act.* तावणेंn. &c. तापनn. संतापनn.

A h. (as of a pot to purify it). आगिवळाm. आंच *f.*

H. of gold and plunging of it into water. पाणतावm.

To Heave, *v. a. lift,* v. To Raise. उचलणें, उठवणें.

To h. a sigh. उमासाm.-उसासाm.-&c. टाकणें.

2 *throw,* v. To Cast. झोकणें, फेंकणें.

To Heave, *v. n.* v. To Pant. धापा *f. pl.* देणें-दाटणें, धापलणें, धापणें, लाहक्या *f. pl.* देणें. [सणें.

2 *swell and rise.* उमासm.-उमासाm.-उसासाm.-&c. येणें, उसा-

To h. and sob. उसंबणें.

3 *keck.* उमळणें, कळमळणें, कळकळणें, उमदळणें, उचलणें, पोटांत कालवणें, खंबदळणें, ढवळणें, मळमळणें, उन्मळणें, मळमळ *f.* करणें. (All these verbs are *impersonal* and *with* as well as *without* the word पोटांत).

4 in sight; *appear.* दृष्टीस पडणें, डोळ्या पुढें येणें.

Heave, Heaving, *n.* v. V. N. 1. धापलणेंn. उराचें उडणेंn. ऊर उडणेंn. लाहकी *f.* ऊर्ध्वm. ऊर्ध्ववायुm.

2 उमासm. उमासाm. उमाडाm.

3 कळमळ *f.* उमासm. उमासाm. उमाडाm. उमळ *f.*

Heaven, *n. the regions above, sky.* आकाशm. *n.* आस्मानn. गगनn. अंतरिक्षn. अभाळn. अंतराळn.—the Heavens, generally. आकाशमंडलn. नभोमंडलn. गगनमंडलn. नक्षत्रमंडलn. खगोलm. तारामंडलn. तारांगणn. ऊर्ध्वलोकm. ज्योतिश्चक्रn. घनाश्रयm.

Calamitous visitation from h. अस्मानचपेटाm. अस्मानी *f*

Flush or glow of the heavens. दिग्दाहm.

Heavenly car. आकाशयानn. आकाशवहनn.

H. of heavens. ध्रुवलोकm.

In the midst of h. अंतरिक्ष, अंतराळ, अधांतरीं *or* त्रीं.

Sphere of the h. खगोलm.

Voice from h. आकाशवाणी *f.* देववाणी *f.* अशरीरिणी *f.*

To be flushed with the coming day,—the heavens. दिशा *f. pl.* फांकणें-फुलणें.

2 *seat of the blessed.* उत्तमलोकm. दिव्यलोक, देवलोक, परलोक, पुण्यलोक, उर्ध्वलोक.

There are, according to the Hindus, different *Heavens,* the seats respectively of different deities with their beatified worshippers. The *Heaven of Brahmá is,* ब्रह्मलोक, सत्यलोक, देवलोक.—of *Vishnu.* वैकुंठn. विष्णुलोक.—of *Shiva.* कैलासm. शिवलोक.—of *Indra.* स्वर्गm. स्वर्गलोक, स्वर्लोक, इंद्रलोक, देवलोक, सुरलोक, सुरालय *n.*

A courtezan of the h. of Indra. अप्सरा *f.*

A female or nymph of the h. of Indra. सुरांगना *f.*

For *Heaven* as a *state,*—as the final beatitude of mortals, and as held to consist in *Emancipation from migratory being and absorption into the Divine Essence,* some terms are, मुक्ति *f.* मोक्षm. अपवर्गm. कैवल्यn. उद्धारm. उद्धारगत *f.* उद्धरण *n.* सिद्धि *f.* विमुक्ति *f.* निर्याण *n.* ब्रह्मसुख *n.* ब्रह्मसायुज्य *n.* ब्रह्मनिर्वाण *n.* निर्वाण *n.* ब्रह्मप्राप्ति *f.* निःश्रेय *n.* श्रेय *n.* निःश्रेयस *n.* महोदय *m.* कैवल्य *n.* निर्वृति *f.* निवृत्ति *f.* अपुनरावृत्ति *f.* अपुनर्भव *m.* शम *m.* शिव *n.* For *Heaven* simply as *the final beatitude,* some terms are, परमगति *or* परमागति *f.* उत्तमगति *f.* परमपद *n.* सर्वदुःखक्षय *m.* परमपदस्थिति *f.* The four *graduated states of heavenly bliss* (चतुर्विधामुक्ति), are, सलोकता *f. or* सालोक्य *n.* (Residence in heaven with the Deity). सरूपता *f. or* सारूप्य *n.* (Bearing of the likeness of the Deity in heaven). समीपता *f. or* सामीप्य *n.* (Being ever near or in the presence of the Deity). सायुज्य *n.* (Absorption into the esssence of the Deity).

That has attained any of these states. मुक्त, सिद्ध, सिद्धपुरुष, प्राप्तमोक्ष.

3 See God.

Heaven-kissing, *a.* गगनचुंबित, नभोलिह. [दैविक.

Heaven-sent, *a.*—of calamitous visitations. आस्मानी, दैवकी,

Heavenly, *a. belonging to the heavens or sky.* आकाशाचा, आस्मानाचा, गगनस्थ, अंतरिक्षस्थ, आकाशमंडलसंबंधी, गगनमंडल-नभोमंडल-&c. संबंधी.

2 *inhabiting or belonging to Heaven.* देवलोकाचा, परमलोकाचा, उत्तमलोकाचा, &c. देवलोकवासी, उत्तमलोकवासी, &c. स्वर्ग-&c. संबंधी, स्वर्गीय, आमुष्मिक, दिव्य, दिविष्ठ, दिविज, दिवोद्भव.

3 *divine, super-excellent.* दिव्य, अत्युत्तम, सर्वोत्तम.

Heavenly-minded, *a.* v. Spiritually-minded. परमार्थबुद्धि, परमार्थदृष्टि, परमार्थी, पारमार्थिक, परमार्थासक्त, परमार्थनिष्ट, परनिष्ठ.

Heavenly-mindedness, *n.* v. A. परमार्थबुद्धि *f.* परमार्थदृष्टि *f.*

परमार्थीपणा *m.* परमार्थासक्ति *f.* परमार्थनिष्ठा *f.* परलोकनिष्ठा *f.* परनिष्ठा *f.*

HEAVILY, *adv.* v. A. 2. भारी, फारच, फार दुःख होईसा *decl.* फार श्रम होईसा *decl.* &c.
3 सुस्त, जड, जडप्राय, &c.
7 The words expressing this sense differ of course in their particular implications, and thus they correspond with, *in torrents, peltingly, dashingly, scouringly, sweepingly.* झिम, धुमाधार, धुवाधार, झमझम *or* मां, झमाझम, धोधोधो, सटसट *or* टां, सटासट, सटाटां, बळकट.

HEAVINESS, *n.* v. A. 1. भारीपणा *m.* जडपणा *m.* जडता *f.* जाड्य *n.* गुरुत्व *n.*
2 भारीपणा *m.* जडपणा *m.* दुःसहता *f.*
3 सुस्ती *f.* सुस्तपणा *m.* &c. आंगसुस्ती *f.* जडता *f.* जाड्य *n.*
4 उदासपणा *m.* उदासी *f.* अनुत्साह *m.* उत्साहाभाव *m.*
6 जडपणा *m.* जडता *f.* जाड्य *n.* गुरुत्व *n.*
10 गुंगी *f.*

HEAVY, *a. ponderous,* v. WEIGHTY. भारी, जड, गुरु, जडशील, जडधोंडा, जडशिळा, जडगोळा, the three last indeclinable, गरिष्ठ.
To be h.—the limbs, head, &c. भारावणें, भार *m.* उतरणें -वाटणें-&c. (पायांस, हातांस), भार*m.* चढणें (डोक्यास, मस्तकास).
To be h. and dull—eyes from want of sleep. तारवटणें.
2 *grievous, afflictive.* जड, भारी, सख्त, दुःसह, दुःखद, दुःखप्रद, &c.
3 *dull, sluggish, torpid, &c.* सुस्त, जड, अंगजड, जडप्राय, मंद, मद्द, मठ्या, जडधोंडा *ind.* निस्तेज, मलूल, स्तिमित.
To be h. from eating. सुरसुरी *f.* येणें, सुरसुरणें.
4 *dejected, dull,* v. DISPIRITED. उदास, उदासवाणी, निरुत्साह, भग्नोत्साह, मलूल, बेदिल, दुर्मना, दुर्मनस्क.
5 *not merry, not lively, wanting spirit, &c.*—meetings, &c. उदासीचा, बेरंगी, विरस, पळपळीत, मळमळीत, निस्तेज.
6 *of difficult digestion.* जड, गुरु, गरिष्ठ, दुःपच्य.
7—as rain. मुसळधार, शिळाधार, दगडफोड, बळकट, जबर, निबिड, गडद, घन *or* घण.
8—as sleep. गाढ, गाढमूढ, गरक, गडद, घोर, घनघोर, घोरांदर, निबिड. [ठीण.
9—road, land, &c. चिकटपणामुळें गाडी वगैरे चालण्यास क-
10 (as under intoxication, sleep, grief, &c.) गुंग.
To be h. गुंगणें, गुंगारणें,—To render h. गुंगविणें.
That is h. गुंगी *or* गुंग्या.

HEAVY-HEARTED, *a.* v. DISPIRITED. दुर्मना *or* दुर्मनस्क.

HEAVY-LADEN, *a.* भाराक्रांत, भारव्याकुल.

HEAVY-LIMBED, *a.* आंगजड.

HEAVY-WITTED, *a.* v. DULL. स्थूलबुद्धि.

HEBDOMAD, HEBDOMADAL. See WEEK, WEEKLY.

HEBREW, *a.* इब्री.

HEBREW, *n.* इब्रीभाषा *f.*

HECATE, *n.* v. FURY. चंडिका *or* चंडी *f.*

HECATOMB, *n.* शंभर बैलांचा यज्ञ*m.* शतक्रतु *m.* (of horses).
Hecatombs of slain. पूर्णाहुति *f.*

HECTIC, *n.* क्षयज्वर *m.* जीर्णज्वर *m.*

HECTIC, *a.* क्षयज्वराचा, क्षयज्वरसंबंधी.

HECTOR, *n.* Under this word in the sense of *blustering pretender to valour,* and as synonymous with *bully, swingebuckler, swashbuckler; swasher, swaggerer, gascon, thraso, fanfaron, &c.* are collected the words and phrases corresponding in *Maráthí.* तिसमारखान, धारराव, अरेराव, शेंदाडशिपाई, इमामदांडगा, वीरपीर, शमशेरबहादूर, तरवारबहादूर, अडूमाडू, पंचहत्यारी, खणक्या, शतंभीष्म, शूरमानी, शूरम्मन्य, ढेंगोजी, टेंकोजी, धोट *or* धोठ, रगडमल्ल, लंड, लहूनिरंजन, लठ्ठभारती.

To HECTOR, *v. n.* v. TO BLUSTER, TO BOAST. घटंपटं *n.*-अरेरावकी *f.*-रगडमली *f.*-चढाईच्या गोष्टी *f. pl.*-&c. करणें-सांगणें.

HEDDLE-BAR, *n.*—of a loom. पावठणी *f.*

HEDGE, *n.* वई *f.* कुंपण*n.* कुडण*n.* कुंप*n.* आडा*m.*आवरण*n.*आवार*m.*
Thorn-h. कांटेवई *f.*

To HEDGE, *v. a. enclose with a hedge.* कुडणें,कुडण *n.* करणें, कुडण *n.*-कुंपण *n.*- &c. घालणें.
2 up. See To OBSTRUCT.
3 in. See To SURROUND.

HEDGEHOG, *n.* एक जनावर आहे.

HEDGE-ROW, *n.* ताटी *f.* in comp. ताट *f.* in comp.

To HEED, *v. a. mind, regard.* ऐकणें, मानणें, पुसणें, जपणें, मनावर घेणें, ध्यानांत आणणें-धरणें-ठेवणें, लक्ष्य *n.* देणें.

HEED, *n. attention, regard, advertence.* ध्यान *n.* अवधान *n.* भान *n.* लक्ष *n.* लक्ष्य *n.* मनोयोग *m.*
To take h. जपणें, संभाळणें.

HEEDFUL, *a. attentive.* सावध, सावधान, सावचित, सुचित्त.

HEEDLESS, *a.* v. CARELESS. गाफल, गाफली, गफलती *or* त्या, गाफली, बेफाम, झांवळ, झांबऱ्या, असावध,असावधान,अनवधान, प्रमादी. [नानें, प्रमादतः.

HEEDLESSLY, *adv.* v. A. गाफलपणानें, &c. गफलतीनें, अनवधा-

HEEDLESSNESS, *n.* v. A. गफलत *f.* गाफलपणा *m.* &c. अनवधान *n.* अनवधानता *f.* प्रमाद *m.*

HEEL, *n.* टांच *f.* खोंट *f.* पादमूल *n.* पार्ष्णि *m.*
A tumor on the h. टांचरूं *n.*
The great tendon above the h. *tendo achillis.* धोंडशीर *f.* दवणशीर *f.* घोडशीर *f.*
To be close at the heels of. नेटणें *or* नेहटणें, लगोलग *adv.* असणें, दुमाल्यावर असणें.
To cool one's heels (as in waiting). अंबणें (and *causally* अंबवणें), अंबत बसणें, कुजत-बाळत-सुकत बसणें.
To show the heels, To take to one's heels, v. To FLEE. पाठ *f.* दाखवणें, पळ *m.*काढणें, इस्या*f.* करणें, झुरकणें.
To urge or strike with the h. टांचळणें *or* टांचाळणें, दुमणी *f.* देणें-करणें, एड *f.* देणें.
2 (of a shoe or sandal). खुरा *m.* खुरें *n.*

To HEEL, *v. a. lay on one side.* कलावर ठेवणें, कलंडत ठेवणें.

To HEEL, *v. n. lie over on a side.* कलंडणें, कलणें, टळणें, कल *m.* जाणें *g. of s.* एकारणें, करोटणें.
That has heeled over. कलंडेा, कलता *or* कलथा.

HEEL-ROPE, *n.* पायबंद *m.* पिच्छाडी *f.*

HEGIRA, *n.*—the epoch. हिजरी *f.* हिजरा *m.*

HEIFER, *n. young cow.* गुजी *or* गोजी *f.* कालवड *f.*

HEIGH HO, v. INTERJECTION. अहा.

HEIGHT, *n.* उंचीf. उंचपणा m. उन्नता f. उन्नति f.

2 *highest or greatest degree.* भर m. भरतें n. For this sense, as expressed by such words as *meridian, zenith, heyday, acme, summit, pinnacle, tiptop, plenitude, fulness, full tide, &c.* the corresponding words are, बहर or बहार m. ऐन (in comp. as a prefix, as ऐन उन्हाळा, ऐन हिंवाळा, ऐन पावसाळा, ऐन दोनप्रहर, ऐन भर, ऐन जवानी, ऐन दौलत, ऐन ऐश्वर्य, ऐन हंगाम, ऐन आमदानी, ऐन मारामारी&c.), भर (in comp. as a prefix, as भरहिंवाळा, भरउन्हाळा, &c.), कळस m. पराकाष्ठा f. सीमा f. मर्यादा f. लहरबहर f. भरडाव m. समा m. जोर m. जोरगत f. उधान n. पर्व n. पर्वकाळ m. पर्वणीf.

In the h. (the meridian or plenitude of). ऐन (in comp.), भरघोसानें or भरल्या घोसानें. [साधणें.

To reach the h. (acme, pinnacle, &c.).सीमा f. संपादणें-

3 *eminence,* v. HILL. उंचवटा m. उंचाड n.

4 *elevation of rank, greatness.* थोरवी f. थोरी f. थोरपणा m. उंच पदवी f. श्रेष्ठत्व n.

To HEIGHTEN, *v. a. raise high,* v. To RAISE. उंच करणें, उंचावणें, चढवणें, वाढवणें.

2 *enhance, augment, &c.* v. To INCREASE.To AGGRAVATE. वाढवणें, उत्कर्ष m.-आधिक्य n.-&c. करणें g. of o. उत्कृष्ट करणें.

HEINOUS, *a. atrocious, &c.* v. WICKED. अघोर, घोर, उग्र, अतिदुष्ट. [ष्टत्व m.

HEINOUSNESS, *n.* v. A. घोरपणा m. &c. अतिदुष्टता f. अतिदु-

HEIR, *n.* दाईज or दायजी, दायाद, वारिसदार or वारसेदार, वारीस, धनाधिकारी, उत्तराधिकारी.

Co-resident h. after partition. संसृष्टि.

Co-residence of heirs after partition. संसृष्टत्व n.

H.-apparent, to a throne. युवराज or युवराजा—His office, &c. यौवराज्य n. [निवारशीक.

That is without h. or rightful claimant. निवारशी or

HEIRESS, *n.* v. HEIR. दायजीण f. वारसीण f. वारिसदारीण f. धनाधिकारिणी f. उत्तराधिकारिणी f.

HEIRLESS, *a.* दायादहीन, अदायिक. [घरबुड़f.

HEIRLOOM, *n.* वंशपरंपरेनें मिळणारा पदार्थ m.-वस्तु n.-चीजf.-&c.

HEIRSHIP, *n.* वारसा m. वारीस m. n. धनाधिकार m. उत्तराधिकार m.

HELD, *p.* v. V. A. 1. धरलेला, &c. धृत.

HELIACAL, *a. solar.* सूर्याचा, सौर्य, सौर, सूर्यसंबंधी.

HELIOSCOPE, *n.* सूर्य पाहण्याची दुर्बीण f.

HELIOTROPE, *n.* एक फूल आहे.

HELIX, *n. a circumvolution.* पेच m. [लोक m.

HELL, *n. region under the earth.* पाताल n. अधोभुवन n. नाग-

There are seven *Pàtàlas* (सप्तपाताल) enumerated, viz. अतल, वितल, सुतल, तलातल, रसातल, महातल, पाताल.

2 *place of punishment after death.* नरक m. निरय m. नारक m.

The Hindus suppose *Narak* or Tartarus to contain many divisions or different places of torture. Some are, अंधतामिस्र, अवीची, असिपत्रवन, कुंभीपाक, तपन, तप्तवालुका, तामिस्र, महारौरव, रौरव, लोहसूर्मि, संघात.

Abiding in H. नरकवास m.

Going to H. अधोगति f. अधःपात m. अधःपतन n.

Judge of H.—यम;—familiarly, यमाजी भास्कर, यमाजीपंत, यमाजी बाबाजी.—His Messenger. यमदूत.

Pains of H. यमदंड m. यमयातना f. यमजाचणी f. यमशिक्षा f. कालदंड m. यातना f. नरकयातना f.

Pit of H. नरककुंड n.

River of H.— वैतरणी f.

Road to H. नरकमार्गm. अधःपथm. धूम्रमार्गm.(i. e. smoky and dark through sin or ignorance).

Watch dogs of H. श्याम and शबल.

3 See GAMBLING HOUSE.

HELLEBORE, *n.*—black. कुटकी or काळीकुटकी f. कटुरोहिणी f.

HELLISH, *a.* v. HELL 2. नरकाचा, नरकसंबंधी, नारक, नारकी, नारकीय, नरकाई.

HELM, *n.* (of a ship). सुकाण or नn. सुकाणूn. कर्णm.

HELMS-MAN, *n.* सुकाण्या or न्या, सुकाणदार, बाबेकरी, नावाडी or ड्या, कर्णधार, नाविक, कर्णग्राह. [म n. f.

HELMET, *n.* लढाऊ टोपी f. टोपी f. शिरस्त्राणn. जंजीरटोपm. झिल्ली-

To HELP, *v. a. aid, assist, succour.* कुमक f.-साह्यn.-साहाय्यn.-मदद f.-मददगारी f.-बाहीदारी f.-पुस्तपन्हाm.-&c. करणें, आंगn.-डोई f.-बाही f.-खांदm.-हातm.-पाठ f.-&c. देणें, पाठीशीं घेणें-घालणें.

2 *better, alleviate, &c.* v. To REMEDY. उपायm.-इलाजm.-&c. करणें.

3 to ;—at table. घालणें, वाढणें.

4 *forbear, refrain.* See To ABSTAIN. [असणें.

To HELP, *v. n.* v. To CONDUCE. सहाय-सहकारी-&c. होणें-

HELP, HELPING, *n.* v. V. A. 1.—*act.* कुमक करणें n. हात देणें n. &c. मददगारी f. सहकार m. उपकार m.

To come to the h. of. उभा राहणें *with* ला or स *of o.*

To cry out Help ! Help ! धांवा m. करणें-मारणें, त्राहित्राहि *interj.* करणें, रक्षरक्ष *interj.* करणें.

3 वाढणें n. वाढणी f.

I. *helping cause,* v. HELPER. सहकारी, सहाय, मददगार.

Present h. in trouble (or need). वेळाईत.

II. *aid afforded.* कुमक f. मदद f. साह्य n. साहित्य n. साहाय्य n. दुमाला m. गुडघा m. पुस्तपन्हा m.

System of rendering mutual help, esp. in agricultural operations. सांवड f. देवड f. विरजीक f.

III. *remedy, &c. presented.* उपाय m. इलाज m. गति f. गत्यंतर n. तरणोपाय m.

HELP-MATE, *n.* v. MATE. हस्तक्या, हातसंड, हात खुरपणें n.

HELPER, *n.* HELPING, *p. a.* HELPFUL, *a.* v. V. A. 1.मदद-&c. करणारा, मददगार, सहकारी, सहाय, साहाय्यकर्त्ता-कारी-&c. पठंगा or पठिंगा or पठिंबा, बाहीदार, उपकारी, उपकर्त्ता, उपकारक.

3 वाढणारा, वाढपी or वाढप्या.

HELPLESS, *a. wanting power to succour one's self.* नाबर, नबळा, अबळा, दुर्बल, दुबळा, बिचारा, लाचार, गोळेकारी, मोघागोळा, अगतिक, हातपाय स्वाधीन नाहींत असा, पराधीन, परवश, पराधीनशरीर, देहधर्माक्षम, देहवृत्यक्षम.

To be or become h. उताणा पडणें, तळावर बसणें-राहणें, रक्षरक्ष *interj.* होणें, उठवणीस येणें or उठवण f. घेणें, गठडी or हातापायांची गठडी f. होणें, हातापायांचे ढीग m. pl. पडणें, and, *causally,* to make h. पाडणें-बसवणें-खिळणें or खिळून टाकणें-करवणें-आणणें-करणें-पाडणें.

2 *remediless.* निरुपायाचा, नाइलाजाचा, अनुपायाचा, निरुपाय, अनुपाय, गतिहीन, बेइलाजाचा, बेईलाज, नाइलाज.

HELPLESSNESS, *n.* v. A. 1. नबळेपणा *m.* अबळेपणा *m.* &c. उठवण *f.* लाचारी *f.* बिचारेपणा *m.* लाचारपणा *m.* पराधीनता *f.* परवशता *f.* हातापायांची गठडी *f.* हातापायांचें ढीग *m. pl.*

2 निरुपाय *m.* नाइलाज *m.* निरुपायता *f.* गतिहीनता *f.*

HELTER-SKELTER, *adv. confusedly and tumultuously.* तजावजा, अफरातफरीनें, तीनतेरा, सैरा वैरा, इतस्ततः.

HELVE, *n.* v. HANDLE. दांडा *m.* [बन *f.*

HEM, *n.* (of a garment). गोट *m.* लेड *or* लेढ *f.* मुरड *f.* दा-

2 *noise uttered in clearing the throat.* खांकरणें *n.* खांकरा *m.* खांकारा *m.* खांकरण्याचा शब्द *m.*

To HEM, *v. a.* (a garment or cloth). तुरपणें, तुरपगिरी *f.*-तुरपणी *f.*-&c. करणें.

2 *environ,* v. To SURROUND, घेरणें, वेढणें.

To HEM, *v. n. make a noise by violent expulsion of the breath.* खांकरणें *or* खाकिरणें, खंकारणें, खांकरा *m.*-खांकारा*m.* देणें.

To clear the throat by hemming. गळा *m.* खांकरणें.

2 fig. *hem and haw,* v. To HESITATE. हांहूं *n.f.*-कांकूं *n.f.*-नांनूं *n.f.*-नचननु *n.*-&c. करणें. [करणें.

3—as to arouse, to give notice of presence, &c. चांचूं *n.*

HEMICRANY, *n. pain affecting half the head.* अर्धशिशी *f.* अर्धशीर्ष *m.*

HEMIPLEGY, *n. palsy affecting one side.* अर्धांग *n.* अर्धांगवायु *m.* पक्षाघात *or* पक्षघात *m.* पक्षवात *m.* पक्षवायु *m.*

2 (of the face and neck). अर्दित*or* अर्दितवात*m.*अर्दितवायु*m.*

HEMISPHERE, *n. half the globe.* निमगोल *m.* अर्धगोल *m.*

The Eastern h. पूर्वकपाल *n.* प्राक्कपाल *n.* पूर्वगोलार्ध *n.*

The Western h. पश्चिमकपाल *n.* पश्चिमगोलार्ध *n.*

HEMISPHERICAL, *a.* v. N. निमगोल, अर्धगोल, अर्धगोलाकृति.

HEMISTICH, *n.* अर्धा केलेला श्लोक *m.* श्लोकार्ध *n.*

HEMLOCK, *n.* एक वनस्पति आहे.

HEMOPTYSIS, *n.*—plethorica. रक्तपित्त *n.*

HEMORRHAGE, *a. flux of blood.* रक्तप्रवाह *m.* रक्तस्राव *m.* रक्तपित्त *m. n.* अस्रपित्त *m. n.*

HEMORRHOIDS, *n. piles.* मूळव्याध *or* मूळव्याधि *f.* गुदरोग *m.* अर्शोरोग *pop.* अर्शरोग *m.*

Figs or excrescences in the h. मोड *m.pl.* गुदांकुर *m.pl.*

HEMP, *n. Cannabis sativa, or Crotolaria juncea.* ताग *m.* शण *pop.* सण *m.* भंगा *pop.* भांग *f. or* भंग *f.* भृंगा *f.* भृंगी *f.*—in cant phraseology. हिरवी तमाखू *f.* भकारी *f.* गुरुप्रसाद *m.* ज्ञानवल्ली *f.* शांभवी *f.* विजया *f.*

Addicted to the use of the intoxicating potion prepared from h. भांग्या, भंग्या, भंगी, भांगखाऊ, भंगट *or* भंगड.

Dry leaves of h. ground in water with spices. घोटा*m.*

Exudation of the flowers of h. prepared as a drug. चरस *m.*

H. tops, *fructification of h.* गांजा *m.* हिरवा *m.* बूट *m.* —dry and crumbled do. गरदा *m.*

H.-leaves. पत्ती *f.* [*of h.* माजुमी.

H.-eater, *eater of some or other of the preparations*

Intoxicating potion prepared from h. भांग *f.*

Leaves of h. ground in milk with sugar and spices. दुधिया *or* दुध्या *m.* [&c. तळी *f.*

Powder of h. prepared by roasting, washing, sugaring,

Preparation of h. with sugar, spices, &c. माजूम *f.* याकुती *f.* सबजी *f.*

Preparer and vender of *bháng.* भंगेरा, भंगेरी.

Smoker of h. tops. गांजेकस, हिरवा, हिरवट.

Stalk of h. जोसी *f.*

Stripped stem of the h. plant. सणकाडी *f.*

Thread or string of h. शणसूत्र *n.*

2 *Hibiscus cannabinus.* अंबाडी *f.* अंबाडा *m.*—the seed of it. अंबाडी *f.*—the fibrous integuments of it. अंबाडी *f.* अंबाडा *m.*—the leaves of it. अंबाडी *f.*

HEMPEN, *a.* v. N. 1. तागाचा, सणाचा, शाण.

2 अंबाडीचा.

HEN, *n.*—domestic. कोंबडी *f.* कुकुटी *f.*

2 *female of fowls*—gener. मादी *f.*

HEN-BANE, *n.*—black. खुरासनी *or* खुरासानी ओंव्याचें झाड *n.*—the seed. खुरासानी *or* खुरासनी ओंवा *m.*

HEN-COOP, HEN-HOUSE, *n.* खुराडें *or* खोराडें *n.* खुडी *f.*

HEN-PECKED, *a. that is governed or led by his wife.* बाइलबंदा, बाइलबुद्ध्या, बाइल्या, बाइलबांध्या, स्त्रीजित, स्त्रीबुद्धि, स्त्रीवश, स्त्र्यंकित, स्त्र्यधीन, दयिताधीन.

HENCE, *adv. from this place.* इकडून, इकडणें, एथून. [थून.

2 *from this time.* आतांपासून, ह्याकाळापासून, एव्हांपासून, ए-

3 *for this reason.* म्हणून, ह्यामुळें-साठीं-&c. ह्यावरून.

HENCE-FORTH, HENCE-FORWARD, *adv.* एथूनपुढें, एथून, एथपासून, ह्याउपर, इतउपर, इतउत्तर, अतःपर, इतःपर.

HEPATIC, HEPATICAL, *a. belonging to the liver.* काळजाचा, यकृत्संबंधी.

HEPATITIS, *n. inflammation of the liver.* यकृत् *m. n.*

HEPTAGON, *n. figure of seven sides or angles.* सप्तकोन *n.* सप्तास्र *n.* सप्तकोणाकृति *f.*

HEPTAGONAL, *a.* v. N. सप्तकोन, सप्तास्र.

HER, *poss. pro.* हिचा *or* इचा, तिचा.

HERALD, *n. proclaimer, &c.* नकीब, शिंगाड्या, बंदिजन, बंदी, स्तुतिपाठक, चारण, चार.

HERB, *n.* ओषधि *f.* औषधि *f.* वनस्पति *f.* बुटी *f.*

Herbs and simples. जडीबुटी *f.* झाडपाला *m.*

Pot-h. शाक *f.* भाजी *f.*

Pot-herbs and vegetables. शाकभाजी *f.* [धिविषयक.

HERBACEOUS, *a. belonging, &c. to herbs.* ओषधिसंबंधी, ओष-

HERBAGE, *n.* v. PASTURE. झाडपाला *m.* हिरवळ *f.* हिरवें *n.*

HERBAL, *n. book on plants.* ओषधिकल्प *m.*

HERBALIST, *n. one skilled in plants.* ओषधिवेत्ता, वनस्पतिवेत्ता.

HERBARIUM, *n.* शुष्कोषधिसंग्रह *m.* [जीवी.

HERBIVOROUS, *a.* वनस्पतीवर उपजीविका करणारा, शाक तृणादि-

HERCULEAN, *a. very difficult, requiring great effort.* महत्प्रयासाचा, भगीरथप्रयत्नाचा, महत्प्रयत्नसाध्य.

2 *great.* See LARGE.

HERD, *n.* v. FLOCK. कळप *m.* झुंड *f.* खिल्लार *n.* कुल *n.* यूथ *m. n.*

Noon-resting spot of pasturing herds. गोठण *f.* आखर *m.*—To collect the herds at it गोठाविणें

That keeps with the h. कळपगुद्द.

2 (esp. of wild animals). साईर *f.*

3 (of people) *rabble*, v. PEOPLE. जंगमढवळें *n.*

To HERD, *v. n. keep or move in companies.* कळपानें-कळपाचा कळप-&c. फिरणें-राहणें.

2 See To ASSOCIATE. [पशुरक्षी.

HERDS-MAN, *n.* खिल्लारी, राखणा, धनगर, गोप, जांगळी, पशुपाल,

Hire or wages of a h. राखणावळ *f.*

HERE, *adv.* एथें, इकडे, अत्र.

H. and beyond. अईलपईल *or* ऐलपैल.

H. and there,—round about. आजूबाजू *or* आजूबाजूस, अरतापरता, आरापारा, इकडेतिकडे, जिकडेतिकडे, जेथें तेथें, ठायीं ठायीं.—with intermissions or intervals. मध्यें मध्यें, जागोजाग, ठायीं ठायीं, खंडळ मंडळ, टंगळमंगळ,तुरळक.—dispersedly. इतस्ततः, जागोजाग.

Of h. there and every where; *of near and far, &c.* इकडचा तिकडचा.

Nor h. nor there. अरत्र ना परत्र, इह ना पर.

2 *in this life.* इहजन्मीं, इहजन्मांत, इहलोकीं.

HEREABOUTS, *adv.* सुमारें ह्याठिकाणीं, ह्याठिकाणच्या जवळपास-आसपास. [लीं.

HEREAFTER, *adv. in time to come.* पुढें, पुढल्या काळांत, उत्तरका-

2 *in the next world.* परलोकीं.

HEREAFTER, *n. future state.* परलोक *m.*

HEREDITARY, *a. that has descended from an ancestor.* वंशपरंपरागत, वंशपरंपरायात, वडीलपरंपरागत, पिढीचा, पिढीजाद, पितृक्रमायात, पैतृक, पितृप्राप्त, वडिलोपार्जित, वतनाचा, परंपरीण, वंशीक, दायोपागत, दायलब्ध, दायप्राप्त.

H. disposition, quality, &c. वसलात *or* द *f.*

H.-estate, office, profession, &c. वतन *n.* मिरास *f.*

H. officer. वतनदार.

Fellow h.-officer. वतन बंधु, वतनभाऊ.

2 *descendible to one's heirs.* पिढीजाद चालायाचा, पिढीदरपिढी-वंशपरंपरेनें-&c. चालायाचा, वंशपरंपरोपभोग्य, वंश्योपभोग्य.

3 *transmitted from a parent to a child,* disease, &c. आईबापापासून-वडिलापासून-&c. आलेला-जडलेला.

HEREOF, *a.* एथचा *or* ला, एथील, अत्रत्य, एतत्स्थानिक, एतत्स्थानीय.

HERESY, *n. heterodox doctrine.* पाखंड *n.* पाखंडमत *n.* ठोंगमत *or* ठेंगमत *n.* धोतांडमत *n.* ठेंगा *m.* अपथ *m.* कुपथ *m.* कुमार्ग *m.*

HERETIC, *n.* v. HETERODOX. पाखंडी, कुमार्गी, कुमार्गगामी, धोतांडमती, ठोंगमती, ठेंग्या. [मताचा.

HERETICAL, *a.* v. N. पाखंडी, पाखंडमताचा, धोतांडमताचा, ठोंग-

HERETOFORE, *adv.* v. FORMERLY. मागें, पूर्वी.

HEREUPON, *adv.* ह्याजवर.

HEREWITH, *adv.* ह्या बरोबर-सहित-&c.

HERITABLE, *a. capable of inheriting.* रिक्थहारी.

2 *that may be inherited.* वारिसपणानें भोगायाचा-भोगायाजोगा, उत्तराधिकारोपभोग्य.

HERITAGE, *n.* v. INHERITANCE. वतन *n.* वारसा *m.* वारीस *m. n.*

HERMAPHRODITE, *n.*—male. हिजडा *m.* ढवा *m.*—female. हिजडी *f.* अर्धनार *f.* जनानी *f.*—gener. नपुंसक *n.* हिजडें *n.*

HERMAPHRODITIC, *a. partaking of both sexes.* उभयलिंगक.

HERMETIC, HERMETICAL. See CHEMICAL.

HERMIT, *n. anchoret, recluse.* वनवासी, अरण्यवासी, वानप्रस्थ.

HERMITAGE, *n. habitation of a hermit.* गुंफा *f.* पर्णकुटी *f.* पर्णशाला *f.* आश्रम *m.* मठ *m. dim.* मठी & मढी *f.* अरण्यवास *m.*

HERMITESS, *n.* वनवासी बायको *f.* वनवासिनी *pop.* वनवासीण *f.* अरण्यवासिनी *f.* वानप्रस्था *f.*

HERNIA, *n. rupture.* अंतर्गळ *m.* अंत्रवृद्धि *f.*

Umbilical h. बेंड *n.* बेंबट *n.* नाभिवर्द्धन *n.*

That has umbilical h. बेंडा, बेंड्या.

HERO, *n. man of distinguished valor.* वीर, शूर, मर्द, मर्दमाणूस, गाजीमर्द, मर्दगाजी, गाजी, जवानमर्द, धारराव, धारकरी, युद्धवीर, योद्धा, रणशूर, रणधीट, रणधीर, रणसिंह, अतिरथ *or* रथी, महारथ, तरवारबाहादूर, शमशेरबहादूर, दिग्विजयी, बावनबीर, अप्रतिभट, धेंड *n.* भारतीबीर, बाघमान्या, परशुराम, युद्धिष्ठिर, भीष्म, वज्र, तोंडीं लागणारा, शूरशिरोमणि.

Drinking of heroes in battle. वीरपान *n.*

Heroes—compreh. अतिरथी महारथी *m. pl.*

Hero's badge (bracelet). वीरकंकण *n.*

Post in battle wished for by heroes. वीराशंसन *n.*

2 (of a drama or poem). नायक *m.*

HEROIC, HEROICAL, *a. belonging, &c. to a hero; brave, daring, &c.* शूर, शूराचा, वीराचा, दिलदाराचा, बहादराचा, मर्दाईचा, वीर्यवान्, वीर्यशाली, रणधीट, शौर्यशाली, शौर्याविष्ट, प्रौढप्रताप, निर्वाणी.

HEROICALLY, *adv.* v. A. मर्दाईनें, मर्दुमकीनें, &c. शौर्यपूर्वक.

HEROINE, *n. female h.* बहादरस्त्री *f.* बहादरीण *f.* वीरा *f.*

2 (of a drama or poem). नायका *f.*

HEROISM, *n.* v. N. वीर्य *n.* जवान मर्दी *f.* मर्दी *f.* मर्दुमकी *f.* मर्दुमी *f.* मर्दाई *f.* बहादरी *f.* शौर्य *n.* वीरत्व *n.* वीरश्री *f.* वैर *n.* विक्रम *m.*

HERON, *n.* बगळा *m.* बगळी *f.*

HERPES, *n.*—farinosus. दादर *m.* दाथर *m.* दाथरा *m.* इसप *or* विसप *m.* विसर्पिका *f.* विसर्प *m.* दद्रु *or* दर्द्रु *m.* पामा *f.*

2—exedens. ओला नायटा *m.* ओला इसप *m.* लूत *f.*

HERPETIC, *a.* v. N. दादराचा, &c. दर्द्रुरोगी.

HERRING, *n.* समुद्रांतला एक मासा आहे.

HESITANCY, See HESITATION, 1.

To HESITATE, *v. n. demur, waver, be in doubt or suspense.* कांकरणें, गुळमुळणें, गुरमळणें, घुरमुळणें, गुटमळणें, आशंकणें, अवांकणें, गणबणणें, गणमणणें, कुडकुडणें, गुपटणें, तरंगणें, घोटाळणें, डगणें, डळमळणें, अडखळणें *or* अडखुळणें, बुचकळणें *or* बुचकुळणें, मागें पुढें पाहणें-करणें, कांकू *f.*-कासकूस *f.*-नानू *f.*-कंगुमंगु *or* कंगमंग *f.*-कानकून *f.*-कुडकूड *f.*-धरसोड *f.*-&c. करणें, करूंनकरूं करणें, दहीं खाऊं मही खाऊं करणें, आंत बाहेर होणें, मन *n.* खाल वर होणें *g. of s.*

2 (in speech). गुटमळणें *or* घुटमळणें, गुरमळणें, अटकळणें, अडकळणें, अडखळणें *or* अडखुळणें, गुपटणें, कांचकळणें, चांचपडत बोलणें, लागणें, गचके *m. pl.*-गचक्या *f. pl.*-गचकळ्या *f. pl.* खाणें, बोलतां बोलतां चाचरी *f.* खाणें, गच्चाबुच्चाबोलणें.

To h. and stammer. बोबडी *f.* वळणें *g. of s.*

HESITATER, *n.* HESITATING, *p. a.* v. V. 1. कांकरणारा, &c. गुळमुळणारा, कांकूं-&c. करणारा, ओढक, कांक्षी, कांक्षाखोर, आशंकित, गुरमळ्या, घोंटाळ्या, दोलायमान, फुटक्यामनाचा.

2 अडखळणारा, अडखळून बोलणारा, चांचपडत बोलणारा, &c.

HESITATINGLY, *adv.* v.V. 1. धरून सोडून, संधेवीं, मागेंपुढें, कांकू, मन खालवर होऊन, कासकूस-&c. करून, टंगळमंगळ.

HESITATION, *n.* v. V. 1. काकूं *or* काकूं *f.* कासकूस *f.* कसाकुशा *f.* धरसोड *f.* आशंका *f.* नांनू *f.* नचननु *f.* टंगळमंगळ *f.* भावसंधि*m.* दुग्धा *f.* आक्षेप*m.* दिक्कत *f.*

Without h. or scruple. बेवसवसा, बेधडक, बिनदिक्कत.

2 गुटमळणें*n.* अटकळणें*n.* अडकळणें *n.* &c. गचका*m.*गचागुचा*m.*

HESPERIAN, *a.* पश्चिमेकडील, पश्चिम. [ह्यस्त्य.

HESTERNAL, *a. belonging &c. to yesterday.* कालचा, ह्यस्तन,

HETEROCLITE, HETEROCLITICAL, *a.*—in grammar. विधिभंजक.

HETERODOX, *a. heretical, holding untrue doctrine.* पाखंडी, कुमार्गी, कुमार्गानुयायी, कुमार्गगामी, अपथगामी, अपथवर्ती, वाममार्गी, वाममार्गानुयायी, विधर्मी.

2 *contrary to the true doctrine.* पाखंडाचा, पाखंडमताचा, कुमार्गाचा, वाममार्गाचा, &c. अशास्त्र, अशास्त्रीय, अवैध.

HETERODOXY, *n. untrue doctrine, heresy.* पाखंड*n.* पाखंडमत*n.* कुपथ*m.* अपथ*m.* कुमार्ग*m.* वाममार्ग*m.* विधर्म*m.*

HETEROGENEITY, *n.* v. A. वैगुण्य*n.* वैजात्य*n.* वैधर्म्य*n.* वैवर्ण्य*n.* विजातीयता *f.*

HETEROGENEOUS, *a. opposite in nature, &c.* विजातीय, विगुण, विधर्म, विधर्मक, विवर्ण.

To HEW, *v. a.* (trees, &c.). तोडणें.

Price of hewing. तोडणावळ *f.*

To h. roughly (stones). डगळणें *or* डघळणें.

2—gener. *chop, hack, &c. violently.* खांडणें, खापलणें, छिंदणें, धसकावणें, खुरचा *f. pl.* पाडणें *g. of o.* चटणी *f.*-छिंद *f.* करून टाकणें *g. of o.*

HEWER, *n.* v. V. 1. तोडणारा, तोड्या, तबलदार.

HEWN, *p.* v. V. 1. तोडलेला, तोडींव.

Roughly h. (or chiselled)—a stone. मेटींव, डगळींव,

HEXAGON, *n. figure of six angles.* षट्कोणाकृति *f.*

HEXAGONAL, *a.* षट्कोण, षडस्त्र.

HEY, *interj.* ये, ए.

HEY, hey there! हां.

HEYDAY, *n.* v. HEIGHT. भर*m.* ऐनभर*m.* बहर *or* बहार*m. f.* लहरबहर *f.* उधान*n.* पर्व*n.* पर्वणी *f.*

HIATUS. See GAP.

HIBERNAL, *a. of or belonging to winter.* हिंवाळ्याचा, शैशिर, शिशिरऋतुसंबंधी. [विणें.

To HIBERNATE, *v. n.* एकांतस्थळीं जाऊन राहून हिंवाळा*m.* घाल-

To HICCOUGH, *v. n.* v. N. उचकी *f.*-गुचकी *f.*-उडकी *f.*-हिक्का *or* हेक्का *f.* येणें-लागणें *in. con.*

HICCOUGH, HICKUP. *n. convulsion of the stomach.* उचकी *f.* गुचकी *f.* उडकी *f.* हिक्का *or* हेक्का *f.* गंभीरा *f.*

HID, HIDDEN, *p.* v. V. 1. लपवलेला, &c. गुप्त, गोपित, आच्छादित, आच्छन्न, प्रच्छादित, प्रच्छन्न, छन्न, संगुप्त, तिरोहित.

To lie h. v. To HIDE. दडणें.

To HIDE, *v. a. conceal, &c.* लपवणें, छपवणें, झांकणें, ढापणें, ढाकणे, दाबणें, झांकळणें *or* झांकाळणें, दाबा*m.* धरणें-देणें, चोरणें, आच्छादणें, प्रच्छादणें, गुप्त-&c. करणें-ठेवणें, दाबादाबी *f.* करणें, आच्छादन *n.*-प्रच्छादन*n.*-गोपन*n*-संगोपन *n.*-तिरोधान*n.*-&c. करणें *g. of o.*

To HIDE, *v. n. lie hid.* लपणें, छपणें, लिकणें, दडणें, दडून-लपून-&c. बसणें, दडा*m.* *or* दडी *f.* मारणें, लपण *f.* धरणें-घेणें.

HIDE, *n. skin,*—of an animal. चामडें*n.* कातडी *f.* चरसा*m.* सालटी *f.* सालटें*n.* साल *f. n.* चर्म*n.* आधोड *or* आधवड *f.*

Cow's h. गोचर्म *n.*

HIDE AND SEEK, *n.* लपंडाव *m.* लिकंडाव *m.* लपंडाई *f.* दडकुली *f.* डोळे झांकणी *f.*

HIDEOUS, *a.* v. FEARFUL. अकटोविकट, अकराळ विकराळ, विकट विकराळ, कौ न बौ, कांहीं न बाहींच, आसुर, भीमदर्शन, करालवदन.

A h. person. काळरूप *or* पी, काळस्वरूप, यमरूप *or* पी, यमस्वरूप, असुर. [&c.

HIDEOUSNESS, *n.* v. A. अकटोविकटपणा*m.* अकराळ विकराळपणा*m.*

HIDER, *n.* HIDING, *p. a.* v. V. A. लपवणारा, झांकणारा, &c. आच्छादक, प्रच्छादक, आच्छादन *n.*-गोपन-&c. कर्त्ता.

v. V. N. दडणारा, दडून बसणारा, &c.

HIDING, *n.* v. V.A.—*act.* लपवणें *n.* &c. लपवणी *f.* लपवणूक *f.* छपवणी *f.* आच्छादन *n.* गोपन*n.* संगोपन *n.* प्रच्छादन *n.* तिरोधान *n.* [दडी *f.*

v. V. N.—*act.* दडणें *n.* दडण *f.* लपण *f.* लिकण *f.* दडा *m.*

HIDING-PLACE, *n.* लपण *f.* लिकण *f.* दडण *f. n.*

HIE, *interj.* लगे.

To HIE, *v. n.* v. To HASTE. लगेलगे जाणें.

HIERARCH, *n.* धर्मसंबंधी मुख्य अधिकारी *m.* मुख्य आचार्य *m.*

HIERARCHAL, *a.* धर्मसंबंधी मुख्य अधिकाऱ्याचा.

HIERARCHY. *n.* धर्मसंबंधी मुख्य अधिकार *m.*

2 धर्मसंबंधी अधिका यांची मंडळी *f.* आचार्यसमूह *n.*

HIEROGLYPHIC, *n. emblematic figure, &c.* सांकेतिक चित्र *n.* सांकेतिकाक्षर *n.*

HIEROGLYPHIC, HIEROGLYPHICAL, *a.* v. N. संज्ञीक, सांकेतिक, संकेतात्मक.

To HIGGLE, *v. n.* v. To HAGGLE. ओढाताण *f.*-घासाघास *f.*-खाराखीर *or* खाराखिरी *f.* करणें.

2 See To HUCKSTER.

HIGGLEDY-PIGGLEDY, *adv. confusedly, &c.* उलटापालट, एकबाट, अस्तव्यस्त, व्यस्ताव्यस्त, मागेंपुढें, इकडचा तिकडे, तिकडचा इकडे, आदिपश्चात्, आदिम्रग.

HIGGLER, *n.* v. V. 1. घसाघशा, घासघिशा, खाराखिऱ्या.

HIGH, *a. lofty, tall.* उंच *remiss.* उंचवट *or* उंचट *highish,* उंचाड, उच्च, उन्नत, धिपाड *or* धिप्पाड, तुंग.

2—a vessel, a turban, &c. *not low, flat, or spreading.* उभार, उभांग, उभट, उभेंटा. [पहाड.

3—a note or tone. उंच, चढा, किनरा *or* किन्हरा, उदात्त,

4 *of great altitude.* ऊर्ध्वस्थ, ऊर्ध्वस्थित.

5—of wind. जोराचा, जोमाचा, बळकट, सुसाट्याचा.

6 *of a high degree.* बळकट, भराचा, भरजोराचा, पराकाष्ठेचा.

7 See GREAT. 8 See DEAR. 9 See CHIEF.

10 *elevated, sublime, &c.* v. LOFTY. उंच, प्रौढ, प्रगल्भ, प्रशस्त.

11— as meat v. TAINTED. लागरा, लागलेला, वासट.

H. day. H. noon. ऐनदोन प्रहर *or* पहार, भरदोन प्रहर, खडी दुपार.

The most h., The Supreme. परात्पर, परमवरिष्ठ.

HIGH-BIRTH, *n.* कुलीनता *f.* आभिजात्य *n.* [अभिजात.

HIGHBORN, *a.* v. WELL-BORN. कुलीन, कुलज, वंशज, जातिवंत,

HIGH-MINDED, HIGH-SPIRITED, *a.* मानी, महामति, महामना,

महामनस्क, उदारचेता, उद्धतमनस्क *or* उद्धतमना, दर्पी, तवरी.

High-seasoned, *a.* v. Pungent. तिखटडोंब, भगभगीत, झणझणीत, सणसणीत, जळजळीत.

2 v. Piquant. खमखमीत, खमंग, चमचमीत.

High-tide, High-water, *n.* समा *m.* भरतीची सीमा *f.* सवारी *or* सवारी *f.*

High-way, *n.* राजमार्ग *m.* घंटापथ *m.* हमरस्ता *m.* हमरहा *m.* सडक *f.* महापथ *m.* राजपथ *m.*

High-way-man, *n.* वाटमाऱ्या, वाटपाडू *or* ड्या.

High-words. See Altercation.

Highland, *n.* पहाडी देश *m.* डोंगरी देश *m.*

Highlander, *n.* पहाडी, पहाड्या, डोंगरकरी.

Highly, *adv. in a great degree,* v. Very. फार, बहुत, अति.

Highness, *n.* v. A. 1. उंचपणा *m.* उंची *f.* उच्चता *f.*

I. कांहीं राजे रजवाडे व बडेलोक ह्यांचा किताब आहे.

Hilarity. See Mirth.

Hill, *n.* डोंगर *m. dim.* डोंगरी *f.* पर्वत *m.* पहाड *m.* गिरि *m.* अग *m.* अचल *m.* नग *m.* भूधर *m.* अद्रि *m.*—As understood in such words as *height, rising ground, rising, mount, eminence , hillock, ascent, knoll, knap, &c.* डोंगरी *f.* टेकड *or* डें *n.* टेकडी *f.* टेकाड *n.* उंचवटा *m.* उंचवळा *m.* उमाठा *m.* उंचाड *n.* उटिंबरा *m.* डुंग *m.n.* डुंगा*m.* डुंगी *f.* बिंडा *m.* ढिमा *m.* खडपा *m.*

Cleared patch on the side of a h. (for corn, &c.). डोंगरदळें *n.* दळा *m. or* दळें *n.* तुरवठें *n.*

Foot of a h. पायतें *n.* पायतर *or* रा *m.* पायधर *or* रा *m.* पायथा *m. or* थें *n.* पायगत *n.* पायबंस *n.* पायीत *n.*

Hills and mountains—compreh. डोंगर कंगर *m.* डोंगर गिंगर *m.* डोंगर बिंगर *m.*

Hilly country, hilly tracts. डोंगर रान *n.*

Level plat upon the slope of a h. माजवी *f.* माची *f.* माळी *f.* पेढ *or* पेढ *n.*

Level ground on the summit of a h. पठार *n.*

Precipitating one's self from the summit of a h. भृगुपात *m.* कडेलोट *m.*

Recess or deep hollow between hills, v. Cavern. खीरें *n.* खोंडा *m.* घोल *or* घोळ *m. n.* खोचार *or* ड *n.*

Side of a h. तट *m.* कडसर *f.*

Skirts of a h. डोंगरकांठ *m.* डोंगरकिनारा *m.* डोंगरकठडा *m.*

Summit of a h. डोंगराचा माथा *m.*

Waist of a h. आडवण *n.*

Hillock, *n. gentle protuberance on the ground, mound, bump, &c.* उटंगळ *n.* उटंबरा *or* उटिंबरा *m.* उटंगर *m.n.* टेंक *n.* टेप *n.* टेपरा *m.* टेपर *n* ढुंग *n.* टुंगर *n.* टुंगूळ *or* टेंगूळ *n.* टुंबर *n.* टेंब *m.* टेंभा *m.* ढेमूस *n.* डुंगा *m.* बिंडा *m.* [टेपटाप *m. pl.*

Hillocks—compreh. *ant-hills, mounds, &c.* टापटेप *or*

2 *small hill, mount, &c.* See Hill, [वंतमय.

Hilly, *a.* डोंगरी, डोंगरवट, डोंगराचा, डोंगराळ, पहाडी, पर्वतीय, प-

Hilt, *n.* v. Handle. कबजा *m.* परज *m.* मूठ *f.*

Himself, *pron.* आपण, खुद.

By h. v. Alone. एकटा.

Hind, *n. female deer.* हरिणी *f.* मृगी *f.* एणी *f.*

Hind, *n. swain,* v. Countryman. शेतखण्या.

Hind, Hinder, *a.* मागचा *or* ला, मागील, पाठीमागचा *or* ला.

The h. parts. पिच्छा *m.* पिच्छाडा *m.* पिच्छाडी *f.*

To Hinder, *v. a. obstruct, impede, stop.* अडवणें, अटकवणें, अटकावणें, अडथळणें, अडकवणें, नडणें, अवरोधणें, रोधणें, कुंठविणें, अडवा करवत *m.* घालणें, मोडा *m.*-मोडती*f.*-अडती *f.*-&c. घालणें, अटकेंत घालणें, अडवा येणें, बाधणें, अटकाव *m.*-अडथळा *m.*-हरकत *f.*-विघ्न *m. n.*-अवरोध *m.*-&c. करणें *g. of o.*

Hinderance, Hindering, *n.* v. V.—*act.* अडवणें *n.* अटकवणें *n.* &c. अडवण *f.* अडवणूक *f.* अवरोधन *n.* संरोध *m.*—*state.* अटकाव *m.* अटकावा *m.* अडथळा *m.* हरकत *f.* अवरोध *m.* व्याघात *m.* व्याक्षेप *m.*

I. *impediment, obstacle, that which hinders.* अडती *f.* अडथळा *m.* अटकाव *m.* नड *f.* नडाव *m.* अड *m.* अडवण *f. n.* अडवणूक *f.* अडकें *n.* अडकाठी *f.* विघ्न *m. n.* हरकत *f.* बाध *m.* वेध *m.* वारण *n.* अडखूळ *n.* खेंव *m.* अंतराय *m.* गुंता *or* गुता *m.* गुतारुता *m.* व्यवधान *n.* व्याघात *m.* व्याक्षेप *m.*

Hindered, *p.* v. V. अडवलेला, अटकावलेला, &c. अवरुद्ध, रुद्ध, अपरोधित, विघ्नित, व्याहत, स्तंभित, स्तब्ध.

To be h. अडणें, अपरोधणें.

Hinderer, *n.* v. V. अडवणारा, अटकावणारा, &c. अडती-&c. घालणारा, अडवण्या, अडव्या, मोडया, अवरोधक, अवरोधी, व्यवधायक, हरकती, हरकतखोर, विघ्नकर्त्ता-कारी, मुजाहीम (only in letters, passports, &c.).

Hindermost, Hindmost, *a.* सर्वांमागचा *or* ला, सर्वांच्या पाठीमागचा *or* ला.

Hindu', *n.* हिंदू *m.*

Of or belonging to a h. हिंदवानी, हिंदवी.

Hinge, *n.*—jointed ; *jimmers.* बिजागरें *n.*—consisting of a spike and ring. नरमादी (the male member is नर, the female मादी).

To Hinge, *v. a.* बिजागरीं *n. pl.* बसविणें-लावणें.

To Hinge, *v. n.* v. To Depend. टेंकणें-असणें *with* वर *of o.*

To Hint, *v. a. bring to mind by a slight mention, allude to.* सुचवणें, खुणावणें, दर्शवणें, नोक *f.*-चुणूक *f.* दाखवणें-मारणें *g. of o.* इशारा *m.*-इशारत *f.*-सूचना *f.*-सूचन *n.*-दिक्प्रदर्शन *n.*-&c. करणें-देणें *g. of o.* दिशा *f.* दाखवणें, आडपडद्यानें बोलणें, ध्वनित-&c. करणें.

Hint, *n.* सूचना *f.* इशारत *f.* इशारा *m.* इंगित *n.* खूण *f.* नोक *f.*

Hinter, *n.* v. V. सुचवणारा, &c. इशारा-&c. देणारा, सूचक, सूचना-सूचन-&c. कर्त्ता.

Hip, *n.* पायाची खीळ *f.* कमरेचा खबाटा *m.* पायाचा-मांडीचा खुबा *m.* कटि *f.* कट *m. n.*

H. and loins. जघन *n.* कटितट *n.* कटस्थल *n.* कटिदेश *or* कटिप्रदेश *m.* श्रोणि *f.* [रेवर घेणें.

To carry on the h. (a child, &c.). कडेवर-बेंगेवर-कम-

Hip-bone, *n.* कमरेची फळी *f.* श्रोणिफलक *n.*

Hippopotamus, *n.* जलघोटक *m.* विदु *m.*

Hircarrah, *n. messenger.* हरकारा *m.*

To Hire, *v. a. procure or engage for hire.* भाड्यानें घेणें-ठेवणें, भाड्याचा *a. decl.* घेणें, भाडें *n.* देऊन घेणें.

2 *entertain in service for hire.* वेतनानें ठेवणें.

2 See To Let.

One who hires out (cattle, vehicles, &c.) भाडेकरी.

HIRE, *n.* भाडें *n.* किराया *m.* मोल *n.* भाटक *n.*—loosely or indefinitely. भाडेंतोडें *n.*

H. merely to convey and deposit. टाकभाडें *n.*

Return-h. परतभाडें *n.*

2 v. WAGES. अजुरा *m.* मजूरी *f.* मुशारा *m.* वेतन *n.*

HIRED, *p.* v. V. 1. भाड्यानें घेतलेला, भाड्याचा.

2 वेतनानें ठेवलेला, वेतनाचा.

HIRELING, *n.* lit. fig. मोलकरी, मुशारखोर, मजुरदार, भाडेकरी, वेतनी, वेतन्या, अजुरदार, मजूर.

Business, wages, &c. of a h. अजुरदारी *f.*

The h. fleeth, but will the shepherd (owner) flee? गुराख्यानें गुरें टाकलीं पण धनी टाकील काय ?

HIRSUTE, *a.* v. HAIRY, SHAGGY. केसाळ, बहुकेश, लोमश.

HIS, *poss. pro.* त्याचा, ह्याचा, आपला.

HISS, *interj.* घिस.

To HISS, *v. n.*—snakes, &c. फुसकारणें, फुसफुसणें, फुंपणें, फूत्कारणें, फोंफावणें, फुंकारा *m.*-&c. टाकणें-मारणें, शेळ *f.* घालणें, शेसाळणें.

2 —a substance under fermentation or effervescence. फसफसणें, चरचरणें *intens.* चराडणें.

3—rockets, &c. v. To WHIZZ. झुरझुरणें, सणसणणें.

4—a cat, &c. फिसकारणें.

To HISS, *v. a. hoot off or out.* हिश्श or हुश्श *adv.* करणें, हिसफिस-धिसफिस *adv.* करणें, हुसकटणें, हुसकणें, धिसपिटावणें, छिथू *n.* करणें, हुयोंहुयों करणें.

HISS, HISSING, *n.* v. V. N. 1. फुस्स *n.* फुसफूस *f.* धुसधुस *f.* धुधुकार *m.* फुसकारा *m.* फूं *n.* फुंकार *m.* फुंकारा *m.* फूत्कार *m.* धूत्कार *m.* शेळ *f.*

HISSINGLY, *adv.* फिस्स, फसफस or सां, चरचर or रां,—*intens.* फसाफस, फसासां, चराचर, चरारां.

HIST, *interj.* चुप or चिप or चप.

HISTORIAN, *n.* बखर करणारा-&c. वृत्तांत कर्त्ता, इतिहास कर्त्ताकार-रचक-ग्रथक-&c.

HISTORICAL, *a.* v. N. 1. बखरीचा, वृत्तांताचा, इतिहासाचा, इतिहासविषयक, इतिहाससंबंधी, ऐतिहासिक.

HISTORIOGRAPHER. See HISTORIAN.

HISTORY, *n. narration of past events,* v. ACCOUNT. बखर *f.* इतिहास *m.* किताबत *f.* वृत्तांत *m.* आख्यायिका *f.* पुरावृत्त *n.*

2 (esp. of kings and great men). पुरवणा *m.* पोंवाडा *m.* चरित्र *n.*

3 *knowledge of history.* इतिहासज्ञान *n.* पुरावृत्तज्ञान *n.*

4 See DESCRIPTION.

HISTRIONIC, HISTRIONICAL, *a.* नाटकाचा, नाटकीय, नाट्यसंबंधी, नाट्यविषयक.

To HIT, *v. a.* v. To STRIKE. मारणें, हनन *n.* करणें, हाणणें, आघात *m.*-&c. करणें.

2 *strike the mark.* मारणें, टिचणें, टिपणें, वेधणें.

To HIT, *v. n. strike against.* लागणें, थडक *f.*-धडक *f.* लागणें-बसणें *g. of s.* [धणें.

2 *hit the mark, succeed.* लागणें, उतरणें, चोट *f.*-लाग *m.* साधणें.

HIT, *n.* v. STROKE. आघात *m.* टचका *m.*

2 *lucky chance.* लाग *m.* चोट *f.* *v.* साध.

3 *stroke of satire.* ठोसरा *m.* ठोंबरा *m.* ठोमणा *m.* टोमणा *m.* or णें *n.* टोला *m.* तुक्का *m.* टेपरा *m.* टेपरण *n.* टेपण *n.* टेपरें *n.*

HIT, *p.* v. V. A. 1. मारलेला, &c. हत, आहत, उपहत, अभिहत.

To HITCH, *v. a. hook or complicate in.* गुतवणें, गोवणें, हिलगणें, हिलगडणें, अडकविणें.

To HITCH, *v. n. become hooked in; become entangled.* गुंतणें, हिलगणें, हिलगडणें, अडकणें, लागणें.

HITCH, *n. impeded or interrupted state.* हिसका *m.* तिढा *m.* तिढी *f.* तीड *f.*

HITHER, HITHERWARD, *adv.* इकडे, ऐलीकडे or स, अलाड, अरता.

H. and thither. इकडेतिकडे, ततस्ततः, इतस्ततः.

HITHER, *a. that is towards this part.* इकडचा or ला, इकडील, ऐलीकडचा or ला, एथचा or ला, एथील.

HITHERMOST, सर्वांच्याऐलीकडचा, सर्वांच्याइकडचा.

HITHERTO, *adv.* एथपर्यंत, एथपावेतों, एथवर, अजून or ण, अद्यापि *pop.* अद्याप, हाकाळ, हाकाळपर्यंत or पावेतों, हाकाळ मर्यादा, आजपर्यंत-पावेतों-वर-तंव, अद्ययावत्, अद्यावधि.

HIVE, *n. artificial habitation of bees.* मधमाशांसाठीं केलेलें घर *n.* कृत्रिम मधुमक्षिकालय *n.*

To HIVE, *v. a.* केलेल्या घरांत राहविणें-राहतसेंकरणें.

HO, *interj.* हो, अहो, अरे, रे.

Ho you ! अरे, ए.

HOA, *interj.* हो.

HOAR, HOAR-FROST, *n. congelation of dew.* दंवाचे थिजलेले बिंदु *m. pl.* बर्फ *n.* नीहार *m.* हिम *n.* तुषार *m.* तुषारकण *m. pl.*

HOAR, *a.* See WHITE, GRAY.

HOARD, *n.* v. STORE. सांठा *m.* ठेव *f.* ठेवी *f.* ठेवा *m.* ठेवणें *n.* जोड *f.* डबुलकें or गें *n.* डबुलें or डबोलें *n.* निधान *n.* निधि *m.* डला *m.* बांधलीगांठ *f.* संचय *m.* (as द्रव्यसंचय, धनसंचय, धान्यसंचय, अन्नसंचय, &c.).

To HOARD, *v. a. lay up, store.* सांचवणें, सांठवणें, सांठवण *n.*-संचय *m.*-&c. करणें, जोडणें, जोड *f.* मिळवणें-संपादणें-जोडणें.

HOARDING, *n.* v. V.—*act.* सांचवणें *n.* &c. सांठवण *n.* संचयन *n.*

A general h. सांठवासांठव *f.*

HOARSE, *a. having the voice rough from a cold.* घोगरा, घोगऱ्यागळ्याचा, बसलेल्या गळ्याचा, स्वरभग्न, भग्नस्वर, भिन्नस्वर.

To become h. गळा *m.*-&c. फुटणें-बसणें *g. of s.* घसा *m.* बसणें *g. of s.* [करणें.

To make one's self h. *lit. fig.* गळा *m.* फोडणें, गळेफोड *f.*

HOARSENESS, *n.* v. A. घोगरेपणा *m.* स्वरभंग *m.* स्वरभग्नता *f.*

HOARY, *a. gray with age,* v. GRAY-HAIRED. पिकल्या केशांचा, पलित.

HOAX, *n. trick, deception.* फटवण *f.* झोका *m.* झोला *m.* ढोला *m.*

To HOAX, *v. a. trick,* v. To DECEIVE. झोका *m.*-झोला *m.*-&c.देणें.

HOB, *n. side of a cooking stove.* अवेल or अवील *m. n.* वाईल or वैल *m. n.* निवणें *n.*

Cooking stove having a h. अवेलचूल *f.* वाईलचूल or वैलचूल *f.*

HOBBARD DE HOY, *n.* v. STRIPLING. आडवाप्या, आडगोसमा, आडमानई.

To HOBBLE, *v. n.* v. To LIMP. लंगडणें, कुलपणें or गुलफणें, कुलपत-लंगडत चालणें.

2 fig.—a work, &c. रखडणें, रेंगतचालणें.

HOBBLE, *n. limping gait.* लंगडशाई *f.* लंगडशादी *f.*

2 *scrape, difficulty,* v. TROUBLE. लचांड *n.* कचाट *n.* कचा-

टी *f.* खेंकटें *n.* झेंगट *n.* पेंच *m.* चक्र *n.* कच *f.* ओकटें *n.* अलगड *f.* भारूड *n.*

HOBBLINGLY, *adv. with stops and pauses.* रडतरडत *or* रडतखडत, रुटुखुटू *or* खुटुरुटू, तुनुमुनुकरून *or* तुनुमुनू, झरतमरत.

HOBBY, HOBBY-HORSE, *n. stick of children.* घोडा *m.* काठीचा घोडा *m.* काठघोडा *m.*

2 *favorite pursuit, &c.* दैवत *n.* कुलदैवत *n.* हौशीचा विषय*m.* खेळ *m.* खेळणा *m.* क्रीडामृग *m.* [बौ *m.*

HOBGOBLIN, *n. goblin, &c.* चेडा *m.* पिशाच *n.* प्रेत *n.* बाऊ *or*

HOBNAIL, *n.* मोठ्यागुलाचा खिळा *m.*

HOCK, *n.* गुडघा व नेबर ह्यांच्या मधला पाय *m.*

To HOCK. See To HAMSTRING.

HOCUS-POCUS, *n. jugglery.* फांफू *n.* छांछू *n.* तंत्रमंत्र *or* थंतरमंतर *n.* जंतरमंतर *n.* धंतरमंतर *n.* थातुमातुं *n.* थातुरमातूर *n.* ताडातोडा *m.* टाणाटोणा *or* टोणाटाणा *m.* धंदराधंदरं (प्रवर्त्तते).

HOD, *n. mason's tray,* कोळंबे *n.* गबेलें *n.* गमेल *n.*

HODGE-PODGE, HOTCH-POTCH, *n.* v. MEDLEY. पंचभेळ *f.* खिचडी *f.* खिचडमिचड *f.*

HODIERNAL, *a. of this day.* आजचा *or* ला, अद्यतन.

HOE, *n.* कुदळ *f.* कुदळें *n.* कुदळी *f. enhanced.* कुदळा *m.* पावडें *or* फावडें *n. dim.* फावडी *f.* केगरें *n.* कुद्दाल *m.* खनित्र *n.*

A dung and rubbish h. खोरें *n.* खोरण*n.* खोरणी *f.* खोरणें*n.*

Raised by the h.—grain, &c. कुदळयाचा.

To HOE, *v. a.* v. N. कुदळणें, कुदळीनें-&c. खणणें.

HOG, *n.* डुकर *m. f. n.* शूकर *m.* सूकर *m.*

Domestic or tame h. घरडुकर *n.*

To HOG, *v. a. cut the hair short.* केस *m. pl.*-अयाल *f.* कातरणें.

HOG-PLUM, *n. spondias mangifera.* अंबाडा *or* अमडा *m.* रानआंबा *m.*

HOG-STYE, *n.* डुकराचेंघर *n.* डुकरवाडा *m.*

HOGGISH, *a.* डुकरासारखा, शूकरवत्, शूकरसदृश, सौकर.

HOGGISHNESS, *a.* v. A. डुकरपणा *m.* सौकर्य *n.* शूकरत्व *n.* शूकरसादृश्य *n.*

HOGSHEAD, *n. barrel.* एक कैलीमाप आहे, पीप *n.*

HOIDEN, *n.* v. ROMP. धांगड *n.* घोडी *f.* घोडसी *f.* जानी *f.* भोपळदेवता *f.*

To HOIDEN. See To ROMP. [करणें.

To HOIST, *v. a.* v. To RAISE. उचलणें, उंचावणें, उभारणें, उंच

To h. sail. शीड *n.* हकारणें.

To HOLD, *v. a. grasp, clutch, &c.* धरणें, अवलंबणें.

To h. or grasp firmly. कचकावून-करकचून *adv.* धरणें.

2 *keep, retain.* धरणें, राखणें, ठेवणें.

3 *maintain as an opinion.* धरणें, आश्रयणें, बाळगणें, अवलंबणें, आश्रय *m.*-आश्रयण *n.* करणें *g. of o.*

To h. pertinaciously. धरून बसणें. [भावणें.

4 *regard, view,* v. To CONSIDER. धरणें, मानणें, मोजणें,

5 v. To CONTAIN. मावून-सांठवून घेणें, समावेश *m.* होणें *g. of o. and in. con.*

6 (office, place, &c.) असणें.

7 (court, council, meeting, &c.) करणें, भरणें, जमविणें.

8 *refrain, withhold,* v. To RESTRAIN. आटपणें, आवरणें.

9 in; v. To RESTRAIN. आवरणें, अटोपणें, रोखणें, रोखून धरणें.

10 on; v. To CONTINUE. चालवणें, चालूठेवणें.

11 out; *extend, stretch forth.* लांब करणें, पुढें करणें.

12 up;—the head. ताठून धरणें, ताठ-ताठला धरणें, उंच करणें. उंचावणें.

To hold one's tongue or peace. मौन्य *n.* धरणें, उगाचचुप-&c. राहणें, जीभ *f.* आटपणें-आवरणें.

To HOLD, *v. n. be true, apply.* लागूपडणें-होणें, लागणें.

2 *continue unimpaired,* v. To ENDURE. ठरणें, टिकणें.

3 *refrain.* थांबणें.

Hold! hold! हां! हाहां! थांबा. [*n.* घेणें.

4 back; v. To HANGBACK. ओढून धरणें, ओढ *f.*-ओढण *f.*

5 on; v. To DEPEND. अवलंबणें, अवलंब *m.*-अवलंबन *n.* करणें,

6 together, v. To CONSIST. संभवणें, जुळणें, जमणें, मिळणें.

7 up;—rain. उघडणें, अखुडणें *or* अखडणें, उभणें, राहणें, खुलणें, काढणें, झडपणें, हडकणें, निखारणें, ताण *m.* देणें. [हांटला.

The rain has held up. पावसानें झाडलें, पावसानें निखारा

To h. good, To h. true. लागूपडणें.

HOLD, *n. grasp, clutch.* धर *m.* कबज *m.*

To lay h. To take h. v. To SEIZE. धरणें, हातांत धरणें.

To obtain firm h.—a disease, &c. धर *m.* धरणें.

2 *holding power,* v. CAPACITY. धर *m.*

3 *something to hold by.* आस्त्रा *m.* आश्रय *m.* आधार *m.*

4 *custody.* कैद *f.* बंदी *f.*

5 (of a ship). कोठी *f.* दास्तान *n.*

6 *stop, clasp, &c.* v. CATCH. अडकण *n.* अडकवण *n.*

7 See FORTRESS. CASTLE.

HOLDER, *n.* v. V. A. 1. धरणारा, धारी & धारक & धर & धर्त्ता (in comp.).

HOLDING, *n.* v. V. A. 1.—*act.* धरणें *n.* &c. धारण *n.* धरण *n.* v. V. N. 7. उघड *f.* उघाड *f.* उघाडी *f.* ताण *m.*

HOLE, *n. pit, cavity, depression.* खळगा *m. dim.* खळगी *f.* खळी *f.* खांच *f.* खांचर *n.* खाडा *m.* खोलगा *m.* खोलवा *m.* खंदक *m.* होंडा *m.* खाड्टें *n.* गार *f.* गर्त्ता *f.*

Holes and hollows,—compreh. खांचखळगे *m. pl.* खांचखोबळे *m. pl.* खांचर खळगे *m. pl.*

H. to creep out at, *fig.* सवड *or* संवड *f.* खिडकी *f.* फट *f.*

Large irregular h. भोकसा*m.* भोसका*m.* भोसकू*m.* खांचाड*n.* भगळ *f.* भगदड *or* भगदाड*n.* भगाडन. भगदळ*n.* भगास*n.* भदाड*n.*

2 (in cloth, &c.) *perforation, bore.* भोंक *n.* छिद्र *n.* छेद *m.* डोळू *n.* डोळूक *n.* डोळा *m.* मुखी *f.* मुखरी *f.* भोंसकट *or* टें *n.* भोकसा *m.* भोसका *m.* वेध *m.* विध *n.* रंध्र *n.* भोंकू *m.* घरका *m.* घरा *m.* तितूर *m.* ढोबळा *m.* बुराख *m.*

A h. bored in coins or ornaments to ascertain the purity of the metal. सुलाख *m.*—To test in this way. सुलाखणें.

Full of holes. शतच्छिद्र.

That is fond of picking holes, v. CENSORIOUS. छिद्रान्वेषी, रंध्रान्वेषी.

That has a h. in his coat. आंगीं उणा.

To enlarge a bore or h. by working something about in it. भुरळणें, भुरळणी *f.* करणें.

To pick a h. in (one's coat, &c.) v. FAULT. छिद्र *n.* पाहणें, छिद्रान्वेषण *n.*-रंध्रान्वेषण*n.* करणें.

3 *hollowed or hollow place,* v. HOLLOW. पोखर *n.* पोखारा*m.*

सांचर *n.* साडा *m.* विवर *n.*

4 *cell of an animal.* घर *n.* बिल *pop.* बीळ *n.* विवर *n.*

5 (through a wall, &c. as an outlet for water). मोंकू *m. n.* काना *m.* मोहरी *or* मोरी *f.*

6—as made in a smooth surface. खोंच *f. dim.* खोंची *f.* खोबळा *m. dim.* खोबळी *f.* छेद *m.* खोवी *f.* खांच *f.* टोंचा *m.* टोंची *f.*

7—as made in the flesh (by a boil, &c.). घरका *m.* घरडा *m.* घरा *m.* घरटा *m.*

8 (in the ground,—as for a post, &c.). दर *m.* टोब *m.* नेम *n. m.*

To fix in a h. (a post, &c.) नेमविणें.

HOLIDAY. See HOLY-DAY.

HOLINESS, *n.* v. A. 1. पवित्रपणा *m.* पवित्रता *f.* शुद्धि *or* मनःशुद्धि *f.* विशुद्धि *f.* परिशुद्धि *f.* अंतःशौच *n.* अंतःशुद्धि *f.* अंतःपावित्र्य *n.* अंतःशुचिता *f.* साधुता *f.* निष्पापता *f.* पापराहित्य *n.*

2 सोवळेपणा *m.* पवित्रपणा *m.* पवित्रता *f.*

To HOLLA, &c. See To HALLOO, &c.

HOLLOW, *a. not solid.* पोकळ.

2fig. *unsound, unreal, unsubstantial, &c.* v. EMPTY. पोकळ, रिकामा, रिकामका, रिता, बायकरणी *or* बायकरणीचा, मावेचा, वरवंचाईचा, रिक्त, फुसका, फुसकुला.

3 *insincere, perfidious,* v. FALSE. कुजका, मनाचा कुजका, हाडाचा खोटा-बाईट-&c.

4—ground; *sunken, depressed,* v. Low. खसल, बदखल, खोलगट *or* खोलकट, खसलबट.

5—as the eye. कोंजा *or* कोंझा.

6—grains, &c. पोलकट, पोलट, बांझा *dim.* बांझट.

7—as the voice. खोल गेलेला, ओढलेला, अंतर्गल.

HOLLOW, *n. cavity, concavity.* खळगा *m. dim.* खळगी *f.* &खळी *f.* खोबळा *m. dim.* खोबळी *f.* खोलगा *m.* खोलबा *m.* पुट *n.* खांच *f.*

2 *sinking ground; a bottom, a low place.* लवण *n.* बतखल *or* बदखल *n. f.* दबका *m.* खसल *n.* खसलबट *n.* ओंडण *n.* बसक *f.*

3 (in a hill, rock,&c.) ढोल *m. dim.* ढोली *f.* खबदड *n.f.* खबदडी *f.* कपार *n. f.* दरा *m.* घाव *f.* घोबर *n.* पोखर *n.* पोखारा *m.* पोखार *m.* विवर *n.* खोपड *f.* खोपाड *n.* कंदर *m.n.* [पोकळ करणें.

To HOLLOW, *v. a. scoop out, &c. excavate.* पोखरणें, टोंकरणें,

2 *make concave or deep.* खोलवणें.

To HOLLOW, *v. n. sink, fall in.* खोलटणें, खोलगटणें.

HOLLOW-EYED, *a.* कोंझा, कोंझट.

HOLLOW-HEARTED, *a.* v. FALSE. मनाचा कुजका.

HOLLOW-SOUNDING, *a.* खबखबीत. [लाघा *m.*

HOLLOWNESS, *n.* v. A. 1. पोकळी *f.* पोकळीक *f.* पोकळपणा *m.* खो-

2 पोकळी *f.* पोकळीक *f.* पोकळपणा *m.* रिकामेपणा *m.* &c. भोक *n.*

3 कुजकेपणा *m.* &c.

HOLLY, *n.* एक झाड आहे.

HOLLY-HOCK, *n.*—the Chinese & Persian h. गुलखैरा *or* रूम.

HOLME, *n. island in a river.* जूं *n.* जुंबा *m.*

HOLOCAUST, *n. burnt offering.* होम *m.*

Of or belonging to a h. होम्य. [पिशवी *f.*

HOLSTER, *n.* पिस्तूल ठेवण्या करितां खोगरा पुढें लावलेली कातड्याची

HOLY, *a. pure, immaculate, &c.* मनाचा पवित्र-शुद्ध-निर्मल-&c. पवित्र, शुद्ध, विशुद्ध, परिशुद्ध, मनःशुद्ध, अंतःशुद्ध, अंतःशुचि, निर्मल, पापरहित-शून्य-हीन, निष्पाप, साधु.

2 *hallowed.* पवित्र, सोवळा, पवित्रीकृत.

A h. spot or place. पुण्यक्षेत्र *n.* पुण्यतीर्थ *n.* पुण्यभूमि *f.* पुण्यस्थान *n.* देवस्थल *n.* देवस्थान *n.* देवद्वार *n.* क्षेत्र *n.*

H. time or season. पुण्यकाल *m.* पुण्यावसर *m.*

HOLY-DAY, *n. religious festival.* सण *m.* सणवार *m.* सणाचा दिवस *m.* पर्व *n.* पर्वणी *f.* पर्वदिवस *m.* पर्वदिन *m. n.* सणसुदी *f.* सणसुदीस *m.* सणसूद *f.* मोठादिवस *m.* देवतवार *or* देउतवार *m.* उत्साह *m.* उत्सव *m.* उत्साव *m.* सोहळा *m.* पुण्यदिन *m.n.* उत्साहदिवस *m.* उत्साहदिन *m.n.* पुण्याह *m.n.*

Present made on a h. सण *m.*

Victuals given (to retainers, &c.) on a h. सण *m.*

To keep h. सण *m.* करणें.

Certain of the *Holydays, Saints' days, Festivals, &c.* are अदुःखनवमी *or* अयोनवमी, अविधवानवमी, अहेवनवमी, अक्षयतृतीया, ऋषिपंचमी, कपिलाषष्ठी, कराष्टमी, कालाष्टक, कालाष्टमी, कोजागर *or* कोजागरीपूर्णिमा, गजछाया, गुढीपाडवा, गोकुलाष्टमी, गौरीतृतीया, घातचतुर्दशी, घायाळचतुर्दशी, चंपाषष्ठी, चंपाष्टमी, चुडीपुनव, चौथभरणी, जन्माष्टमी, टवळी अमावास्या *or* अंवस, तुलसीविवाह, त्रिपुरीपुनव *or* पौर्णिमा, त्रिपुरोत्सव, दत्तात्रेयजयंती, दवणीपुनव *or* पौर्णिमा, दशरथललिता, दशाहरा, दसरा, दंडिपौर्णिमा, दिवई, दिवाळी, दिव्याची अमावास्या, धनतेरस, धर्मराजाची बीज, नरसिंहजयंती, नवरात्र, नवान्नपूर्णिमा *or* नव्याचीपुनव, नरकचतुर्दशी, नागदिवाळी, नागपंचमी, नारळीपौर्णिमा *or* पुनव, परिवर्तनी, पवित्रीपुर्णिमा, पिठोरी, पोवतीपुर्णिमा, पोळा, प्रबोधिनी, प्रबोधोत्सव, बहीणबीज *or* बहीणतीज, बेंदुर, भरणीचौथ (*or* चौथभरणी) भाऊबीज, भानुसप्तमी, मकरसंक्रमण *or* संक्रांति, मत्स्यजयंती, महानवमी, महाष्टमी, महाशिवरात्र *or* रात्रि, रथोत्सव, रंगपंचमी, रामजयंती, रामनवमी, ललितापंचमी, वत्सद्वादशी *or* वागबारस *or* वसुबारस, वडपुनव *or* वटपूर्णिमा, वसंतपंचमी, वांझीपुर्णिमा *or* पुनव, विजयादशमी, बेळअंवस, वैकुंठचतुर्दशी, शयनी, शारदीयनवरात्र, शिमगा, शिवरात्रि *or* रात्र, शिळासप्तमी, शीतळ शिमगा, सोमवती, हरितालिका, होळीपुनव. [दिवस *m.*

2 *day of liberty.* सुटी *f.* सुटीचा दिवस *m.* खेळणी *f.* खेळणीचा

HOLY-WATER, *n.* गंगा *f.* गंगोदक *n.* तीर्थ *n.*

Vessel for h. गंगाजळी *f.* तीर्थगंडी *or* गिंडी *f.* तीर्थकुंडी *f.* तीर्थपात्री *f.* तीर्थोटी *or* तीर्थवटी *f.*

To make oath upon h. गंगाजळी *f.* घेणें-उचलणें.

HOMAGE, *n. obeisance, reverence, respect paid to one's lord.* उपासना *f.* सेवा *f.* मुजरा *m.* राजवंदन *n.* राजाभिवंदन *n.* प्रभुवंदन *n.* बादशाही मुजरे *m. pl.*

H. of the heart and affections. भावभक्ति *f.*

HOME, *n. own house.* आपलें घर *n.* निजगृह *n.* निजधाम *n.* निजालय *n.* स्वगृह *n.*

At h. and abroad. घरींरानीं, घरींदारीं, जनींवनीं.

Service or employment at h. बैठा रोजगार *m.* बैठी चाकरी *f*

To drive (by incantations) from house and h. उच्चाटन *n.* करणें *g. of o.* [*or* लोक *of o.*

To drive from house and h. वनवास *m.* आणणें *with* स-

To keep at h. घर *n.* धरणें.

2 *own country.* आपला देश *m.* स्वदेश *m.*

Absent from h. प्रवासी, प्रोषित.

HOME, *a. domestic, not foreign.* घरचा, घरगुती, गृह्य, मुलकी *or* खी, देशी, देशीय.

Home, Homewards, *adv. to own house, country, &c.* घरीं, घरास, घराकडे, आपल्या घरीं, &c. स्वगृहीं, गांवीं, गांवास, &c. स्वदेशास, स्वग्रामास.

2 *close to one's own feelings, concerns, &c.* जिव्हारीं, जिव्हाळीं, आंगीं, हाडीं.

To bring h. unto. आंगीं *or* आंगास लावणें, पदरीं घालणें *or* पदरीं माप *n.* घालणें, लागू करणें, (*and,* To come or be brought h. to लागणें-पडणें-येणें-होणें.).

To come h. to.—a trouble or evil. आंगीं *or* आंगास येणें, जिव्हारीं लागणें, हाडीं घाव *m.* होणें-येणें-लागणें.

To be at h. in,—*to be conversant with.* परसांतील भाजी असणें *in. con.*

To feel at h. (in an office, &c.) बस *m.* बसणें *g. of s.*

Home-bird, *n. one fond of staying at home.* घरकोंबडा *m.* कूपमंडूक *m.*

Home-bred, Home-raised, Home-made, &c. *a.* घरगुती, घराऊ, घरघराऊ, घरचा, पाळींव, घरपोसा, गांवठी, मुलकी *or* खी.

Homeliness, *n.* v. A. 1. गांवरानीपणा *m.* &c. साधपणा *m.* असभ्यता *f.*

Homely, *a. not fine or elegant.* गांवरानी, गांवठी, कुणबाऊ, कुणबीवजा, साधा, असभ्य, धडवती, धडवतीचा, ग्राम्य, निर्वाहाचा.

2 (of features), v. Plain. साधारणरूपाचा, साध्यारूपाचा, दहाजणांसारखा.

Homeopathy, *n.* रोग विरुती प्रमाणें विरुति उत्पन्न करून रोग दूर करण्याचा मार्ग *m.*-विद्या *f.*

Homicide, *n.*—the act. खून *m.* नरहिंसा *f.* नरवध *m.*

2—the agent. नरहिंसक *c.* नरघ्न *c.* नरहंता *m.*

Homily, *n.* श्रोत्यांनीं ऐकावें म्हणून धर्मसंबंधी केलेलें भाषण *n.*

Homogeneity, Homogeneousness, *n.* v. A. साजात्य *n.* साधर्म्य *n.* सावर्ण्य *n.* आनुगुण्य *n.* एकजातीयता *f.* सजातीयता *f.*&c.

Homogeneous, *a. of the same kind or nature.* एकजातीय, सजातीय, स्वजातीय, समजातीय, सधर्म, समधर्मक, एकधर्मक, सवर्ण, सविध, अनुगुण, निर्भेल.

Homologous, *a.* समपरिमाण, तुल्यपरिमाण.

Hone, *n.* शीळ *f.*

To **Hone,** *v. a.* शिळेवर लावणें-पाजवणें.

Honest, *a. true, sincere, honorable, guileless, &c.* खरा, सत्य, इमानी, इमानदार, इमानाचा, सात्विक, सत्वशील, सत्ववृत्ति, सत्यव्रत, सरल *pop.* सरळ, ऋजु *pop.* उजू, प्रामाणिक *pop.* प्रमाणिक, निष्कपट, निष्कृत्रिम, अकृत्रिम, प्रांजल *or* निष्प्रांजल, अकपट, भावार्थी, निष्प्रपंच, रहारास्त, साळढाळ, साळसूद *or* ध, साळा भोळा.

2 *fair, just, equitable.* नेकीचा, सचोटीचा, साखीचा, प्रामाणिक *pop.* प्रमाणिक, प्रमाणिकपणाचा, सरलभावाचा, भला, खरेव्यवहाराचा, अकूटव्यवहार.

3—an employment, profits, &c. हलाल, हलालाचा, सत्य, साधु, सत् in comp.

4 See Chaste.

Honestly, *adv.* v. A. 1. खराईनें, खरेपणानें, इमानानें, &c.

2 प्रमाणिकपणानें, सचोटीनें, नेकीनें, &c.

Honesty, *n.* v. A. 1. खराई *f.* खरेपणा *m.* सत्य *n.* इमान *n.* इमानदारी *f.* प्रमाणिकपणा *m.* सारल्य *n.* सत्ववृत्ति *f.* सालसाई *f.* साळशी *f.* भावार्थ *m.* निष्कापट्य *n.* परमार्थबुद्धि *f.* सावपणा *m.*

2 सचोटी *or* सचवटी *f.* नेक *f.* नेत *f.* साख *f.* प्रमाणिकपणा *m.* प्रामाणिकत्व *n.*

H. is the best policy. अति शाहणा त्याचा बैल रिकामा, भोळा भाव सिद्धीस जाव.

Honey, *n.* मधु *n. pop.* मध *m. f.* माक्षिक *n.* क्षौद्र *n.*

H. water. मधवणी *n.*

Rivers of h. मधुकुल्या *f. pl.*

Honied words and killing deeds. हातावर साखर आणि मानेवर कातर, गोड बोलणें आणि साल सोलणें.

Honey-comb, *n.* मधपोळें *n.* पोळा *m.* पोळें *n.* पोळ *n. dim.* पोळी *f.* मधशिसा *m.* चरवी *f.* मधुकोश *m.* Some kinds or forms of h. are काट्याळें *n.* (the cells environing a stick), काळवें *n.* (a rich kind), फोंगें *n.* (long kind), सातेरूं *n.* (it has seven cells), मुरकुट्यें *n.* (made by the मुरकुटी माशी), पोयें *or* पोवें *n.* (formed in the hollow of a stone, tree, &c.).

Division of the h. which contains the honey. कांदा *m.*

Division of the h. containing the bees or their young. पाकडी *or* पेंकडी *f.* [ना *m.*

Honey-moon, Honey-month, *n.* लग्न झाल्यावरचा पहिला महि-

Honey-mouthed, Honey-tongued, *a.* गोडबोल्या, मधुरभाषी, प्रियवादी, प्रियंवद.

Honeyed, *a.* मधाचा, मधुमय.

Honor, *n. dignity, greatness, rank, &c.* थोरपणा *m.* मोठेपणा *m.* थोरवी *f.* थोरी *f.* मातबरी *f.* प्रतिष्ठा *f.* गौरव *n.*

2 *credit, character, name,* v. Reputation. आबरू *f.* इज्जत *f.* नांव *n.* नामोश *m.* हुरमत *f.* पाणी *n.*

To become bound in h. इरेस पडणें. [ऊणें.

To keep one's h. पागोटें *n. or* पागोट्याचे पेंच *m. pl.* संभा-

To lose one's h. नाक *n.* गमावणें, पाणी *n.* जाणें *g. of s.*

To stain the h. of. पागोटें *n.* खालीं करणें.

To take concern for the h. of. अभिमान *m.* धरणें *g. of o.*

3 *nobleness or grandeur of mind; sense of h. &c.* मनाचा थोरपणा *m.* प्रशस्तपणा *m.* सत्ववृत्ति *f.* सत्वासक्ति *f.* सत्वशीलता *f.* अभिमान *m. v.* बाळग-भोग-धर-मान, लाज *f. v.* राख, खंत *f.*

To be jealous or watchful of one's h. सत्वास जागणें.

4—as rendered or paid; *reverence,* v. Respect. मान *m.* सन्मान *m.* सत्कार *m.* मान्यता *f.* आदर *m.* गौरव *n.* संभ्रम *m.* स्फीति *f.*

Honors, v. Civilities. आदर उपचार *m. pl.* आदरमान *m.* आदरसत्कार *m.* मानसन्मान *m.*

Chief honors (as paid at assemblies). अग्रपूजा *f.*

5 *credit, eclat, lustre,* v. Glory. बोज *m.* यश *n.* नावरूप *n.* झील *f.* शिकल *f.* रया *f.*

To **Honor,** *v. a. reverence, glorify, magnify, &c.* थोर जाणणें-समजणें, गौरवणें, भजणें, उपासणें, मान *m.*-मर्यादा *f.* राखणें-ठेवणें. [मोठा-&c. करणें.

2 *dignify, ennoble, &c.* v. To Exalt. मोठेपणा *m.*-&c. देणें,

3 (a bill, &c.). सकारणें, आदर *m.* करणें *g. of o.* पटविणें *or* पटाविणें

4 *receive or treat with honor.* सत्कारणें, सन्मानणें, आदरणें, गौरवणें, मान *m.*-सन्मान *m.*-आदर *m.*-सत्कार *m.*-गौरव *m. n.*-&c. करणें *g. of o.* ताजीम *f.* देणें.

To h. by investing with robes, &c. तसरीफ *f.* करणें *g. of o.* तसरीफ *f.* देणें.

HONORABLE, *a. worthy of honor, illustrious, noble, &c.* आबरूचा, इजतीचा, प्रतिष्ठेचा, मान्य, हुरमतीचा, हुरमती, हुरमतदार, नामदार, नेकनामदार, माननीय, आदरणीय, उपास्य, संभावनीय, संभाविन, मातबर, प्रतिष्ठित, शिष्ट, गुरु, गरिष्ठ, यशस्वी.

2 *noble of mind, actuated by principles of honor, &c.* मनाचा थोर-प्रशस्त-उदार-&c. थोरमनाचा, सत्ववृत्तीचा, सत्ववृत्ति, सत्वशील, सत्वसंपन्न, सात्विक, सत्वस्थ, उदारचेता, उदारमनस्क, महामना, महामनस्क.

3 *bearing or bringing honor, creditable.* आब्रूचा, प्रतिष्ठेचा, इजतीचा, यशस्कर, इजती, प्रतिष्ठित, कीर्तिप्रद-दायक, मानप्रद, मानद, हलाल.

4 *proper, right, honest,* v. JUST, FAIR.प्रामाणिक *pop.* प्रमाणिक, यथायोग्य, यथान्याय, नेकीचा, नेतीचा.

HONORABLENESS, *n.* v. A. 1. मानमान्यता *f.* मान्यता *f.* इजत *f.* हुरमत *f.* गौरव *n.* मातबरी *f.* शिष्टाइकी *f.* शिष्टाई *f.* वकर *m.*

2 मनाचा थोरपणा *m.*-प्रशस्तपणा *m.*- &c. सत्व *n.* सत्य *n.* सत्वशीलता *f.* सत्ववृत्ति *f.* सत्वासक्ति *f.* लाज *f. v.* राख.

4 प्रमाणिकपणा *m.* नेक *f.* नेत *f.* प्रामाणिकत्व *n.*

HONORABLY, *adv.* v. A. 2. थोरमनानें, मनाच्या थोरपणानें, सत्वासक्तिपूर्वक.

I. *with tokens of honor.* आदरानें, सन्मानानें, सन्मान करून, सन्मानपूर्वक, आदरपूर्वक.

II. *reputably.* आब्रूनें, आब्रू राखून.

HONORARY, *a. conferring, &c. honor.* आब्रूचा,प्रतिष्ठेचा, प्रतिष्ठासूचक, यशस्कर. [रितां नेमलेला.

2 *performing duty without pay.* पगाराशिवाय केवळ प्रतिष्ठेक-

3 *having a place without pay or duty.* पगाराशिवाय व कामाशिवाय प्रतिष्ठेकरितां नेमलेला.

HONORED, *p.* v. V. 1. भजलेला, उपासलेला, &c. उपासित,

3 सकारलेला, &c. आदृत.

To be h. पटणें.

4 आदरलेला, &c. सत्कारित, सम्मानित, सन्मानित, सन्मानी, मानित, सत्कृत, आदृत, प्रतिष्ठित, संभ्रमी.

HONORER, *n.* HONORING, *p. a.* v. V. 1. भजणारा, &c. उपासक, उपासनाकर्त्ता-&c.

2 मोठेपणा देणारा, &c. मानद, मानप्रद.

4 सत्कारणारा, &c. सत्कार-सन्मान-&c. करणारा-कर्त्ता.

HONORING, *n.* v. V. 1.—*act.* उपासणें *n.* &c. भक्ति *f.* उपासना *f.*

3 सकारणें *n.* सकार *m.* आदरण *n.* [सत्क्रिया *f.*

4 सत्कारणें *n.* आदरणें *n.* &c. आदरण *n.* सम्मानन *n.* संभ्रम *m.*

HOOD, *n. covering of the head.* टोपी *f.* घुंगट *n.*

Cloak or mantle with a h. घुगी *f.*

2 (of a snake). फडा *f.* फडी *f.* फण *m. f. n.* फणा *f.*

3 (of a carriage.) दमन *n.*

4—as used in comp. denoting state, quality, &c. पणा *m.* पण *n.* ता *f.* त्व *n.* &c.

HOODED, *a. of a hooded or curved head,*—nails, ladles, &c. नागफणी, अंकडेदार.

To HOODWINK, *v. a. blind by covering the eyes.* डोळ्यांला पाटा *m.*-पडदा *m.* बांधणें, डोळे *m. pl.* बांधणें, अंधारी *f.*-पटल *n.* घालणें.

2 fig. See To BLIND. [शफ *m. n.*

HOOF, *n. horny cover of a beast's foot.* खुर *pop.* खर *m.* क्षुर *m.*

A division of a cloven h. गेळ *n.* गेळी *f.*

To be born with two hoofs (or legs) white—a calf or colt. दोहोखुरीं (*or* दोहो पायांनीं) उतरणें.

To be born with the four hoofs (or legs) white—a calf or colt. चौखुरीं (*or* चहूं पायांनीं) उतरणें, चौखुरणें.

To shew the cloven h. गुण *m.* दाखवणें *or* गुणावर येणें, गुण *m.pl.* उधळणें *g. of s.* आपल्या ढंगावर येणें, वायद्यावर येणें *or* सरणें.

2 (esp. of a horse or ass). सुंब *m.*

Bumps on the side of a h. रसुली *f.*

Paring of the h. सुंबतराशी *f.*

Thin and delicate h. गाजर सुंब *m.*—Delicate-hoofed. गाजरसुंब्या.

HOOK, *n. curved end.* अंकडा *m.* अंकडी *f.* केल *n.*

By h. or by crook; *by some means or other.* अलेंबलें, कसेंतरी, कसेंहीकरून, जसातसा, जसेंतसें करून, जेमतेम, अडपझडप, युक्ती प्रयुक्तीनें.

2 (of a staple). कडी *f.*

H. and staple. कडी कोयंडा *m.*

H. and eye. फासा *m.*

That has a h. and eye. फासेदार, सफाशी.

3—for fish. गळ *m.* गरी *f.*

4 (of devotees). *swinging hook.* गळ *m.* [बगाड *n.*

The act of swinging by a h. बगाड *n.*—the apparatus.

5 *bill-hook,* v. BILL. कोयता *m. dim.* कोयती *f.* बोडसा *m.* बोडसें *n.*

To HOOK, *v. a. fasten with or to a h.* अंकड्यांत अडकवणें, अकड्यास अडकवणें.

2 *catch with a h.* गळानें धरणें.

3 See To INSNARE.

HOOK-NOSED, *a.* गरुडनाकया, गरुडनासिक, शुकनासिक.

HOOKED. See CROOKED.

HOOP, *n. band of wood or metal.* आटा *m.* विडी *f.* कडें *n.*

2 (as of a sieve, tambourine, &c.). कडें *n.*

To HOOP, *v. a.* कडें *n. or* कडीं *n. pl.* घालणें.

To HOOP, *v. n.* See To SHOUT.

HOOPING-COUGH, *n.* डांग्या खोकला *m.* सुसी *f.*

HOOPOE, *n. upupa minor.* सुतार *m.* [भावणें.

To HOOT, *v. n.*—the owl. घुंघु *f.* करणें, घुमणें, बोभाणें *or* बों-

2 *halloo at or after.* हुर्यो हुर्यो *adv.*-हेडसफेडस *adv.* करणें.

To HOOT, *v. a. drive with shouts of contempt.* हुडकावणें, धुडकणें *or* धुडकावणें, धुडावणें, धुतकारणें, हडवडावणें, हडहडावणें, हिडसावणें *or* हेडसावणें, धुवकाविणें, धिसपिटावणें, हुर्र *f.*-हुररेबडी *f.*-हुरली *f.*-&c. करणें *g. of o.*

HOOT, HOOTING, *n.* (of the owl). घुघु *f.*

2 *hallooing at or after.* हुर्र *f.* हुररेबडी *f.* हुरबाबडी *f.* हुरली *f.* हडहड *f.* धिस *f.*

HOOT, *interj.* हत्त, हुडुत्त, हुर्र, थू.

To HOP, *v. n. leap on one leg.* एकापायानें-एकापायावर चालणें-जाणें-उडणें, लंगडी *f.* घालणें. [चालणें.

2 *skip lightly, bound, &c.* उडणें, उडत *or* उडतउडत जाणें-

3 See To DANCE. [प्लुति *f.*

HOP, HOPPING, *n.* v. V. 1.—*act.* एकापायाची उडी *f.* लंगडी *f.*

HOP, *n.* एक लता आहे.

HOPABED, *n.*—the play. अकुटें दुकुटें *n.*

HOPE, *n.* आशा *f.* आस *f.* आस्था *f.* उमेद *f.*

Frustration of h. आशाभंग *n.* नैराश्य *n.*

Renewal or revival of h. पुनराशा *f.*

Unreasonable h. दुराशा *f.* अत्याशा *f.*

To throw up h. v. COURAGE. आशा *f.*-दम *m.* टाकणें-सोडणें.

Whilst there's life there's h. (*or* Dum spiro spero). श्वास तों आस.

2 *object of h.* आशा *f.* आशाविषय *m.*

To HOPE, *v. n.* आशा *f.*-आस्था *f.*-आस *f.* ठेवणें-धरणें-बाळगणें-राखणें, अपेक्षा *f.* करणें, आशावणें, आसावणें.

HOPEFUL, *a. full of hope.* आशावान्, आशान्वित, आशाविष्ट, आशाबद्ध, आशायुक्त, आस्थेकरी, आस्थापूर्वक, आस्थापुरस्सर, साश, उमेदवार.

2 *giving h. promising.* व्हायासारखा, सफल व्हायासारखा, सिद्धीसजायासारखा, होतकर, होतकरू, फलोदर्क.

HOPEFULLY, *adv.* v. A. आस्थेनें, &c. आस्थापूर्वक, आस्थापुरस्सर.

HOPEFULNESS, *n.* v. A. 1. आस्था *f.* उमेदवारी *f.* उमेद *f.* आशाविष्टता *f.*

2 व्हायासारखेपणा *m.* होतकरपणा *m.*

HOPELESS, *a. wanting hope,* v. DESPONDENT. निराश, आशाहीन-रहित-&c. आसतुटा, हताश, भग्नाश, नष्टाश.

2 *giving no hope,* v. DESPERATE. निरुपाय, उपायहीन, निराशेचा.

HOPELESSNESS, *a.* v. A. 1. निराशा *f.* नैराश्य *n.* आशाराहित्य *n.*

2 निरुपायता *f.* उपायराहित्य *n.*

HOPPER, *n.* (of a mill). घैरणें *n.*

HOPPERS, HOPSCOTCH, *n.*—the play. लंगडशाई *or* लंगडशादी *f.* [लंगडी *f.*

HORAL, HORARY, *a. relating to an hour or the hours.* होरासंबंधी, होराविषयक, होरेय.

HORDE, *n.* फिरता थवा *m.* फिरती झुंड *f.*

HORIZON, *n.*—rational or real. क्षितिज *n.* अंबरांत *m.* दिगंत *m.* आकाशकक्षा *f.* भूगर्भक्षितिज *n.*

2—sensible or visible. काळी धार *f.* धार *f.* बांदरी *f.* दृष्टिमर्यादा *f.* चक्रवाल *n.* मंडल *n.* उदयाचल *m.* अस्ताचल *m.* भूपृष्ठ क्षितिज *n.*

Glow of the h. दिग्दाह *m.*

HORIZONTAL, *a. parallel to the h.* काळे धारेबरोबर, क्षितिजैकसूत्र, क्षितिजसमसूत्र.

H. angle. समपृष्ठकोन *m.*

HORN, *n.* शिंग *n.* शृंग *n.* विषाण *n.*—in contempt. शिंगट *n.*

Bow of h. शार्ङ्ग *n.*

Cord attached to a h. शिंगोटी *f.*

Flattish h. पताडें *n.* [*or* म्या.

Of back turned horns. हुंडा *or* होंडा, पाठशिंगी *or* गाम्या.

Horn for holding powder. शिंगडा *m.* [*or* ड्या.

Of long or large horns. शिंगाळ *or* ळ्या *or* ळू, शिंगाडा *or* ड्या.

The horns—collectively. शिंगाडा *m.*

To draw in one's horns. कान *m. pl.* पाडणें, नाक *n.* गुंडाळणें.

To strike with the horns. शिंगटणें *or* शिंगाटणें.

2 (of the moon). शृंग *n.* कोराचें अग्र *n.*

3—instr. of music. शिंग *n.* शृंग *n.* The most common are करणा *m.* (Blower of it करणेकरी), तुतारी *f.* (Blower of it तुतारजी, तुताऱ्या), बांका *m. dim.* बांकी *f.* (Blower of it बांकेकरी), शिंग *n.* (*dim.* शिंगी *f.*) (Blower of it शिंगाड्या, शिंगकरी), मोरशिंग, रणशिंग.

HORN-BOOK, *n. primer.* मुलांची पहिली पोथी *f.*

HORNED, *a. having horns.* शिंगाचा, शृंगी, शृंगयुक्त, शृंगविशिष्ट.

H. beast,—compreh. शिंग शिंगोटी *f.* शिंगोटी *f.*

Fee on the purchase of a h. beast. शिंगोटी *f.*

Short h. अखुडशृंगी *or* शिंगी.

2 *of sprouted or shotten horns.* शिंगाळू.

HORNET, *n.* मोठ्या जातीची गांधील *f.* गांधील माशी *f.* साळखादें *n.* तुंबसर *or* तुंबसळ *m.*

HORNLESS, *a.* अशृंग, शृंगहीन,

HORNY, *a. made of horn.* शिंगाचा, शृंगमय, शृंगनिर्मित, शार्ङ्ग.

2 *hard,* v. CALLOUS. कठीण.

HOROLOGE, *n. chronometer.* कालमानयंत्र *n.*

HOROMETRY, *n. art of measuring time.* कालमिति *f.* कालमान *n.*

HOROSCOPE, *n. scheme of the signs of the zodiac at a birth.* जन्मकुंडली *f.* जन्मलग्नकुंडली *f.* ग्रहकुंडली *f.*

Appeasement of a boding h. जननशांति *f.*

Determination from the h. of the fortunes of a person. जातक *n.*

Disagreement or enmity of the h. (of two parties). गणवैर *n.*

Diversity of h. गणमध्य *n.*

Identity or amity of h. (of two parties). गणमैत्री *f.* गणैक्य *n.* ग्रहमैत्री *f.* वश्य *n.* राशिघटित *n.* घटित *n.*

The paper on which are recorded the particulars of a h. जन्मपत्र *n.* जन्मपत्री *f.* जन्मपत्रिका *f.*

HORRIBLE, HORRID, *a.* v. FEARFUL. घोर, अघोर, अकटोविकट, अकराळ विकराळ, भयंकर, भयानक, भयजनक.

HORRIBLENESS, HORRIDNESS, *n.* v. A. घोरपणा *m.* &c. भयानकत्व *n.*

HORRIFIC. See HORRIBLE.

To HORRIFY, *v. a. strike with horror,* v. To SHOCK. धस *m. n.*-धसका *m.*-धडकी *f.*-&c. बसवणें, रोमांच *m. pl* उभे करणें, कांटा *m.*-कांटे *m. pl.* आणणें.

To be horrified. रोमांच *m. pl.* उभे राहणें, कांटा *m.* येणें.

HORRIPILATION, *n. erection of the hairs of the body.* कांटे *m. pl.* रोमांच *m.* लोमांच *m.* थरकांटा *m.* पुलक *m.*

From joy. रोमहर्ष *m.* लोमहर्ष *m.* पुलक *m.*

From fear. थरकांटा *m. v.* उठ.

That is under h. रोमांचित, पुलकित.

HORROR, *n.* v. FRIGHT. महाभय *n.* अतिभय *n.*

To be struck with h. उरांत धस *m. n.* होणें.

2 (preceding fever). शिसारी *f.* कांटे *m. pl.*

3 horrors. *distressing scenes.* भयंकरप्रसंग *m. pl.*

4 horrors. *delirium tremens.* सतत व पुष्कळ दारू पिऊन जें वेड लागतें तें.

HORROR-STRICKEN, *a.* उरांत धसझालेला, भयचकित, त्रस्त.

HORSE, *n.* घोडा *m.* (डा *m.* डी *f.* डें *n.*) वारू *m.* अश्व *m.* वाजी *m.* तुरंग *m.* तुरंगम *m.* घोटक *m.* नर *m.* सैंधव *m.* हय *m.*—in contempt, &c. and answering to *rip, jade, hack, &c.* घोडकट *n.* घोडकें *n.* पंचकल्याण *or* णी घोडें *n.* हरळीप्रसाद *m.*—in endearment or admiration. गाजीमर्द *m.* घोडपुत्र *m.*

The colors of the *Horse* are, करडा iron grey. गंगा white with reddish patches. चितोडा roan. तांबडा बोर chesnut. तेल्याबोर bay. निळा white. सारंगा dark bay.

The paces are, साधीचाल *f.* चवडचाल *f.* चौकचाल, टांकणचाल, तुरकीचाल, दबडचाल, दुडकीचाल, धावरीचाल, भरधांवचाल, सात्रकचाल, रहिवालचाल, कोकरचाल, बाजीचाल, हदडूकचाल.

Some of the faults or blemishes are, असनकुहा, उतरंड, खुंटउपट *or* उपाड, गोम, दलभंजन, बाशिंग, सर्पीण, हरदावळ.

Some of the auspicious marks are. खुंटेगाड, गंगापाट, देवमणि (*pop.* देवमण) पंचकल्याण, पद्म, रणशूर, शामकर्ण.

Some of the diseases are, बरसात *or* बरसाती, भेंडी, मुंगा, असुढाळ.

Arab h. ताजी *or* तेजी *m.*

Bedding of a h. शेज *f.*—To lie down on it. शेजेस येणें.

Body-cloth of a h. झूल *f.* भुरका *m.* भुरकी *f.*

Connoisseur or knowing one in horses. अश्वपरीक्षक.

Defluxion or catarrh of the h. शेंबा *m.*

Fore ropes of a h. दवासन *n.*

Furniture of a h. तंगतोबरा *m.*

Grazing of horses. घोडेखाद *f.*

Head-bands of a h. (of tape or cotton rope). पुंजी *f.*

Head-ropes of a h. आघाडी *f.* दवासन *n.*

Head-and heel-ropes of a h. आघाडी पिछाडी *f.*

Heel-ropes of a h. पिछाडी *f.*

Heel-leather of h. मुज़ामा *m.*

Hirer out of horses. घोडेखोत.

H. having the five auspicious marks. पंचकल्याणी घोडा *m.*

Kick or stroke with the foot of a h. टापर *or* टाफर *f.*

Leading rope of a h. बागदोर *m.* बाग *f.*

Leavings in the nose bag of h. उरदाणा *m.*

Line or row of horses picketed. घोडवळ *f.* तबेला *or* तवेला *m.*

Lip-rope of a h.—(used in grooming &c.). होंटाळी *or* ओंठाळी *f.* पुजमाल *m.*

Necessaries of a h.—compreh. तंगतोबरा *m*

Nose-bag of a h. तोबरा *m.*

Of puny & sorry breed—a h. यारदा *or* यारदी.

Ornaments for the head of a h. कंडा पट्टा *m.*

Pace of a h. चाल *f.* गति *f.* धारा *f.*

Plume for the head of a h. झुम्मा *m.*

Riding h. बसता घोडा *m.* पाठाळ *n.* पाठवळ *m.*

Sacrifice of a h. अश्वमेध *m.*

Small or under sized h. आडघोडा *m.*

Stroke from the fore foot of h. टाप *f.* टाफ *f.*

Tail of a h. दांडी *f.*

Tying the fore legs of a h. इचकला *m.* कळवा *m.*

To become mature (i. e. of five year's age).—a h. पंचारणें *or* पंजारणें.

To be cat-hammed—a h. टाळ *m. pl* वाजणें *g. of. o.* टाळकुट्या-टाळघाशा असणें.

To get gourdiness in the extremities,—a h. रसींउतरणें.

To seize and twist round the upper lip of a h, मुंगा *m.* धरणें.

Look not a gift-h. in the mouth. धर्माची गाई दांत कांगी नाहीं.

When the h. is stolen shut the stable-door. बैल गेला (धंडीनें मेला) आणि झोंपा केला.

2 *stand, frame, &c.* घोडा *m.* घडोंची *or* घडवंची *f.*

3 *cavalry.* तुरूकस्वार *m. pl.* घोडदळ *n.* अश्वभार *m.* तुरंगभार *m.*

Body of h. under one commander. पनक *n.* पागा *f.*—Commander of it. पनक्या, पाग्या.—Writer attached. पागनीस *m.*

H. of the king or state. हुजूरपागा *f.* खासपागा *f.*

Horse-back, *n.* on horse-b. घोड्यावर.

Seat on h. मांडी *f. or* मांड *f. v.* साध, आसन *n.*

That is mounted on h. सवार *or* स्वार, अश्वारूढ, अश्वारोह.

Horse-boy, *n.* घोडक्या *or* घोडका, महार पोरगा.

Horse-breaker, *n.* चाबुकस्वार, अश्वशिक्षक.

Horse-breaking, *n.* चाबुकस्वारी *f.* अश्वशिक्षा *f.*

Horse-cloth, *n.* झूल *f.*

Horse-dealer, *n.* घोड्यांचा व्यापारी *m.*

Horse-doctor, *n.* साळोत्तरी *or* शाळोत्री, जाणता, अश्ववैद्य, अश्वचिकित्सक, अश्वपरीक्षक.

Horse-dung, *n.* लीद *f.*

Heap or hill of h. लिदाड *n.*

Horse-emmet, *n.* घोडमुंगी *f.* घोडमुंगळा *m.*

Horse-faced, *a.* v. Ugly. घोडतोंड्या.

Horse-fly, *n.* घोडमाशी *f.*

Horse-glove, Horse-rubber, *n.* हातालें *n.* हातणी *f.* हात्या *m.*

Horse-hair, *n.* घोड्याचेकेस *m. pl.* अश्वलोमा *m.*

Horse-keeper, *n.* v. Groom. घोडक्या *or* घोडका *m.* मोतद्दार *m.*

Horse-laugh, *n.* *loud boisterous laugh.* मोठें हासणें *n.* महाहास *m.* अतिहास *m.* अट्टहास *m.*

Horse-man, *n.* *rider.* सवार *or* स्वार, स्वारी, घोडेस्वार, घोड्याचा, सादी, अश्वसादी, तुरंगसादी, तुरंगी, अश्वबार.

2 *one skilled in riding.* मांडसाधलेला, मांडजमलेला, चढाईत, अश्वारोहकुशल.

3 *horse-soldier.* सवार *m.* तुरुक (*or* तुर्क) सवार *m.* राऊत *m.*

Horse-manship, *n.* सवारकी *f.* सवारी *f.* अश्वारोहविद्या *f.*

Horse-musketeer, *n.* करोल *or* करवल *m.*

Horse-musketeering, *n.* करोली *or* करवली *f.*

Horse-play, *n.* v. Romps. धांगडधिंगा *m.* धाबडधिंगा *m.* धिंगामस्ती *f.* खरमस्ती *f.* धुमड *f.* धुमाळी *f.* धुरळ्या *f. pl. v.* घाल, खिदडा *or* खिदाडा *m.*

Horse-race, *n.* घोड्याची दौड *f.*-शर्यत *f.*

Horse-radish tree, *n.* *hyperanthera morunga.* शेगवा *m.* शेगट *m.* शोभांजन *m.*

Decoction of the pods or leaves of h. शेगटवणी *n.* शेकटवणी *n.*

Horse-shoe, *n.* नाल *m.*

Nail of h. नालमेख *f.* मेख *f.*

Set of horse shoes. नालडबा *m.*

Horse-shoer, *n.* नालबंद.

Horse-shoeing, *n.* नालबंदी *f.*

H. on the four feet. चौबंदी *f.*

H. on two feet. दुबंदी *f.*

Price of h. नालबंदी *f.*

To perform h. नाल *m. pl.* बांधणें (घोड्याला).

To perform half h. *open shoes.* खोलबंदी *f.* करणें.

HORSE-SOLDIER, *n.* सवार, तुर्कसवार, राऊत.

H. who provides his own horse. शिलेदार.

H. equipped by his employer. बारगीर.

HORSE-STALL, *n.* ठाण *or* ठाणें *n.*

HORSE-WAY, *n.* घोडेवाट *f.*

HORSE-WHIP, *n.* चाबूक *m.*

To HORSE-WHIP, *v. a.* चाबूक *m. pl.* लगावणें-मारणें-हाणणें, चाबुकाचा मार *m.* देणें, चाबुकणें *or* चाबकणें.

HORTATIVE, HORTATORY, *a. giving advice.* उपदेशाचा, बुद्धिवादाचा, उपदेशक, बुद्धिवादक, बुद्धिप्रद, प्रबोधक.

HORTICULTURAL, *a.* v. N. बागकामाचा, बागकामाविषयींचा, बागाइताचा.

HORTICULTURE, *n. cultivation of a garden.* बागकाम *n.* बागाईतकाम *n.* बागाईत *n.* उद्यानकर्म *n.* उद्यानविद्या *f.*

HORTICULTURIST, *n.* बागकाम करणारा-जाणणारा, बागाइत्या, उद्यान कर्मवेत्ता.

HOSE, HOSIERY. See STOCKINGS.

HOSPITABLE, *a. given to hospitality.* अतिथिपूजक, अतिथिसत्कारी, अतिथिप्रिय, अतिथिवत्सल, आतिथेय, आतिथ्युत्सुक, आतिथ्यतत्पर, आतिथ्यासक्त.

2 *relating to hospitality.* पाहुणचाराचा, अतिथिपूजनाचा, आतिथ्याचा, &c. अतिथिपूजनविषयक-संबंधी.

HOSPITABLENESS, *n.* v. A. 1. अतिथिप्रीति *f.* अतिथिवात्सल्य *n.* आतिथ्यासक्ति *f.*

HOSPITABLY, *adv.* v. A. 1. पाहुणचार करून, आगतस्वागत करून, आतिथ्यपूर्वक.

HOSPITAL, *n. building for the sick.* रोगिशाला *f.* रोग्याश्रय *m.* रोग्यालय *n.* बिमारखाना *m.* इस्पिताळ *f. n.* corrupted from the English is common.

2 *place of refreshment for paupers or wayfarers.* धर्मपोई *f.* [पोई *f.*

3 *alms house.* धर्मशाला *pop.* धर्मसाळ *f.*

HOSPITALITY, *n. entertainment of strangers.* पाहुणचार *m.* आगतस्वागत *n.* अतिथिपूजन *n.* आतिथ्य *n.* आतिथेय *n.* आदर आतिथ्य *n.* आतिथ्यादर *m.* अतिथिसेवा *f.* अतिथिसत्कार *m.* मेजबानकी *f.* मेजबानी *f.* बरदास्त *f. v.* कर, राख, मनुष्ययज्ञ *m.*

HOST, *n. entertainer.* यजमान, मेजबान, आतिथ्यकारी-कर्त्ता, आतिथ्यस्वामी, आतिथेय, परधनी *m.*

2 *forces,* v. ARMY. सैन्यदल *n.* चक्र *n.* सेनाभार *m.* दलभार *m.*

3 *great number,* v. MULTITUDE. झुंड *f.* चुबका *m.* चुंग *f.* चुंब *f.* राष्ट्र *n.* वृंद *n.* चक्र *n.*

4—as a term of praise for an eminent person. कोटि *f.* प्रकरण *n.* वृंद *n.* एकांगवीर *m.* एकांड्या *m.* प्रस्थ *n.* प्रस्थान *n.*

HOSTAGE, *n. person delivered as a pledge.* ओल *f.* शरीरबंधक *m.*

To give as a h. ओलीस ठेवणें.

HOSTESS, *n.* यजमानीण *f.* आतिथ्यकारिणी *f.* घरधनीण *f.*

HOSTILE, *a.* v. ADVERSE. वैरी, द्वेषी, शत्रुभावाचा, शत्रुपणाचा, दुशमनगिरीचा, वांकडा, प्रतिकूल, विपक्षी, प्रतिपक्षी, शात्रवीय.

HOSTILELY, *adv.* v. A. शत्रुपणानें, शत्रुभावानें, वैरभावानें, शत्रुत्वपूर्वक.

HOSTILITY, *n.* v. A. *and* ENMITY. शत्रुभाव *m.* वैर *n.* दुशमनगिरी *f.* दुशमनी *f.* प्रातिकूल्य *n.*

Hostilities. See WAR.

HOSTLER. See GROOM.

HOT, *a.*—objects, gener. ऊन, ऊन्ह, उष्ण, गरम.

Boiling h. Burning h. Scalding h. &c. उनून *or* उन्हून, कढत, जळत, जळजळीत, कडकडीत, धगधगीत, सणसणीत, जळफळीत, रसरसीत, लसलसीत, गरमागरम, अत्युष्ण, सद्यस्तप्त.

Red h. अग्निवर्ण.

To be h. and sweltering. उकडणें, उबाबणें, उमगणें, उचलें, डगडगणें (All *impersonal*).

It is glowing h. ऊन लाही करतें, रणरणतें, सणसणतें, रणरण-सणसण *adv.* करतें.

2—weather. रणरणीत, सणसणीत.

3 v. PASSIONATE. खपती, उष्ण, आग्या, तापट *or* ड, तपीळ, गरम, तलक, जहाल, *or* झाल.

4 *ardent, vehement.* तलखल्या, तलख, तिखट, तीक्ष्ण, तीव्र, प्रखर, जहाल *or* झाल, आवेशी.

5 *piquant, biting, &c.* v. ACRID, PUNGENT. तिखट, तलख, खवरा, खंबिरडा, खरमरीत, जळजळीत, झणझणीत, सणसणीत, भगभगीत, कडक, तीक्ष्ण, तीव्र, तिक्त, उष्णवीर्य, प्रखर.

6—battle, fighting; *furious, vehement.* तुंबळ, दारुण, घोरांदर, निर्वाण, घनघोर *or* घनाघोर, कट्टा.

HOT-BED, *n. bed for ripening fruits, &c.* भट्टी *f.* अढी *f.*

HOT-BRAINED, HOT-HEADED, *a.* v. MADCAP. साहसी, साहसिक, दुःसाहसिक, दुःसाहसी.

HOT-HOUSE, *n.* उष्ण हवेंतील झाडें ठेवण्यासाठीं केलेलें घर *n.*

HOTCH-POTCH, *n.* v. MEDLEY. खिचडी *f.* धेडगुजरी *f.* गोतांबील *f.*

H. of many kinds of grain boiled. चित्रान्न *n.*

HOTEL, *n.* पोस्तखाना *m.* होटेल *n.* is getting common.

HOTLY. See VEHEMENTLY.

HOTNESS. See HEAT.

HOUGH, *To* HOUGH. See HAM, TO HAMSTRING.

HOUND, *n.* शिकारी कुत्रें *n.*

HOUR, *n.* (of 60 minutes). तास *m.* होरा *f. m.* अवर *m.* (the English word).

2 (of 24 minutes). घटका *f.* घडी *f.* घटिका *f.* घटी *f.* नाडी *f.*

An h. or so. घडीएक.

At all hours. वेळ अवेळ.

Auspicious, &c. h. सुमुहूर्त्त *m.*

Every h. (or moment). घडीघडी, घडोघडी, हरघडी, हरवख्त.

The golden h. सोन्याची घटका *f.* अमृतवेळ *f.* सोनवेळ *f.*

H.-cup. घटका *f.*

H.-plate, v. GONG. घंटा *f.* घटी *f.* घड्याळ *n.* तास *m.*

Whose h. is come. प्राप्त काल.

The h. is full; *the time is up, out, &c.* घटका भरली.

HOUR-GLASS, *n.* डमरु यंत्र *n.* वाळूचें घड्याळ *n.*

HOUR-HAND, *n.* अवरकांटा *m.*

HOURLY, *a.* हरघडीचा, घडीघडीचा, घडोघडीचा.

HOURLY, *adv.* हरघडी, घडीघडी.

HOUSE, *n.* घर *n.* गृह *n.* मकाण *or* न *m. n.* महाल *m.* मंदिर *n.* भवन *n.* आलय *n.* गेह *n.* शाला *pop.* शाळ *f.* धाम *n.* सदन *n.* सद्म *n.* अगार *n.* in comp.—in contempt or disparagement, answering to *hovel, hut, anchoret's cell, shed, cell, hole, &c.* तिवांशी घर *n.* तिवांशी खोपट *n.* मठी *f.* पर्णकुटी *f.* पर्णशाला *f.* उन्हाळ सावली *f.*

N. B. For the houses of Europeans बंगला is commonly

used, but among themselves the Marâṭhâs apply this word to a summer or pleasure house.

A deserted or desolate h. पडघर *n.*

At, in, to, &c. every h. घरोघर.

Born in one's h.—a slave. खानाजाद.

Central portion of a h. माजघर *m.n.* मधलेंघर *n.* मधघर *n.* मध्यगृह *n.*

Ceremony of occupying a new h. घरभरणी *f.* घररिघणी *or* घररिघवणी *f.* गृहप्रवेश *m.* वास्तुप्रवेश *m.*

Ceremonies in purification of a h. गृहशुद्धि *f.* वास्तुशांति *f.*

First entrance, by a wife, of the h. of her husband. घरभरणी *f.* घररिघणी *or* घररिघवणी *f.* गृहप्रवेश *m.*

H. having flat roof of earth. धाबें *n.*

Inner apartments of a h. अंतःपुर *n.* अंतर्गृह *n.* गृहांतर *n.* गृहाभ्यंतर *n.*

Large and stately h. *mansion.* वाडा *m.* हवेली *f.*

Master of the h. घरकरी *m.* घरधनी *m.*

Mistress of the h. घरकरीण *f.* घरधनीण *f.* घरचारिणी *f.* घरण *f.* गृहांगना *f.*

Open h. *hospitable mansion.* धर्मपुरी *f.* देवपुरी *f.*

Person taking care of a h. घरराख्या, घरासराखण.

Pleasure h. Summer h. बंगला *m.*

Rain water from the roof of a h. घरवणी *n.*

Register of the houses (of a town or village). घरटीप *f.* घरगणती *f.* खाने सुमारी *f.*

Shutting up of a h. or houses. दारकळणी *f.*

Site of a h. गृहभूमि *f.*

Site of a h. (esp. of a ruined h.) घरठण *or* घरठाण *n.* घरठा *m.* घरबंद *m.*

Thatching a h. घरशाकारणी *f.* घरशिवणी *f.*

To ransack the houses. घरडोळ *f.* घेणें.

To roof in a h. घर *n.* नेसवणें.

To set out or to furnish a h. घर *n.* मांडणें.

To set up or keep h. घर *n.* करणें, संसार *m.*-प्रपंच *m.*-&c. करणें-पाहणें. [घेणें-काढणें.

To take the run of (go over all) the houses. घरटीप *f.*

To turn the h. out of window. घर *n.* डोईवर घेणें.

You may judge of the h. from the yard. घराची ओज आंगण सांगतें.

2 *firm, &c.* v. COMPANY. घर *n.* पेढी *f.*

3 *race, lineage,* v. FAMILY. घर *n.* घराणा *m.* घराणें *n.*

4 *household,* v. FAMILY. घर *n.* कुटुंब *n.*

5 *station of a planet.* घर *n.*

6 *square of a chess-board, &c.* घर *n.*

To HOUSE, *v. a. shelter.* रहायास जागा *f.*-घर *n.*-ठिकाण *n.*-&c. देणें, आस्रा *m.*-आश्रय *m.* देणें. [स्थित करणें.

2 *put under cover.* घरांत ठेवणें-राखणें, निगळल्यास ठेवणें, गृह-

To HOUSE, *v. n. take shelter.* आस्रा *m.*-आश्रय *m.* करणें, राहणें.

HOUSE-BIRD, *n. person who stops always in the house.* घरकोंबडा, घरकुबडा, घरकुचा, घरकुंडा, घरबशा, गेहेमेही.

HOUSE-BREAKER, *n.* घरफोड्या, भिंतफोड्या, गृहभेदक, संधिभेत्ता, संधिचोर.

HOUSE-BREAKING, *n.* घरफोडणें *n.* भिंत फोडणें *n.* संधिचौर्य *n.*

HOUSE-HERO, HOUSE-HECTOR, *n. person valiant among the women and children at home.* गोहेशूर, घरगोहो, गेहेशूर, गेहेनर्द्दी.

HOUSE-HOLD, *n.* v. FAMILY. घरदार *n.* घर *n.* कुटुंब *n.*

H.-expenses or consumption. घरखर्च *m.*

H. deity. घरचा देव *m.* कुलस्वामी *m.* कुलदेवता *f.* आराध्यदेवता *f.* आराध्यदैवत *n.* Room appropriated for it. देवखोली *f.* देवघर *n.* देव्हार घर *n.*

Of or beloging to h. घरचा, घराऊ *or* घरघराऊ, घरगुती, अंतरींचा, अंतरंग, अंतरंगींचा.

Quota (of a collection, &c.) due from each h. घरटी *f.*

To invite (to entertainment) a whole h. चुलीस अक्षत *f.* लावणें.

2 *domestic management or economy.* घरसंजोग *m.* घरसंजोगणी *f.* घरजोगावणी *f.* घरजुगूत *f.* घरदार *n.* घरसवर *f.*

H.- affairs. गृहकार्य *n.* गृहव्यापार *m.*

H.-jobs or work (viz. sweeping, cow-smearing, scouring, bringing water, cooking, &c.). घरखटला *m. or* लें *n.* घरकाम *n.* गृहकर्म *n.* गृहकृत्य *n.* घरधंदा *m.* केरपाणी *n.* केरपोतेरें *n.* शेणपोतेरें *n.* शेणकुंडा *m.* ओढा *m. v.* ओढ, वावर *m.* सम्मार्जन *n.* सडासंमार्जन *n.*

To do the h. jobs. केरवार *m.* करणें.

HOUSE-HOLD, *a.* घरचा, घरगुती, घराऊ, घर in comp. गृह in comp.

HOUSE-HOLDER, HOUSE-KEEPER, *n.* घरबारी, कुटुंबी, खटलेवाईक, खटलेकरी, घरंदाज, गृहस्थ, घरवासी, घरवाला, गृहस्थाश्रमी, गार्हस्थ्याश्रमी.

HOUSE-KEEPER, *n.* घरांतली कारभारीण *f.*

HOUSE-KEEPING, *n.* घर करणें *n.* घरचार *m.* घरदार *n.* घरसंसार *m.* संसार *m.* गृहस्थ धर्म *m.*

HOUSELESS, *a.* गृहशून्य, गृहहीन, निराश्रय.

HOUSE-MAID, *n.* घरकामी *f.* घरांतील कामकरीण *f.* घरखपी *f.*

HOUSE-RENT, *n.* घरभाडें *n.*

HOUSE-ROOM, *n.* घरांत राहायाला जागा *f.*

HOUSE-SERVANT, HOUSEBOY, *n.* घरकाम्या, घरखप्या.

HOUSE-STOCK, HOUSE-STORE, *n.* घरबेगमी *f.* घरबेजमी *f.*

HOUSE-TAX, *n.* घरदेणें *n.* घरपट्टी *f.* घरटका *or* घरटक्का *m.* घरसारा *m.* घरवण *f.* उंबरसारा *m.*

HOUSE-TOP, *n.* माळवद *n.* धाबें *n.*

Chunamed terrace on a h. गच्ची *f.* अटाली *f.*

HOUSE-TRESPASSING, *n.* अंदरघुशी *f.*

HOUSE-WARMING, *n. feast on entering a new house.* घरभरणी *f.* घररिघणी *or* घररिघवणी *f.* गृहप्रवेश *m.*

HOUSE-WIFE, *n. mistress of a house.* घरकरीण *f.* घरधनीण *f.* घरचारिणी *f.*

Notable, thrifty, &c. h. सुगरीण *or* सुगरण *f.* अन्नपूर्णा *f.*

2—the case or bag. चंची *f.*

HOUSE-WIFERY, *n.* घरकाम *n.* घरधंदा *m.* घरखटला *m. or* लें *n.* गृहकर्म *n.* गृहकृत्य *n.*

HOUSE-YARD, *n.* आंगण *n.* [टा *m.*

HOUSING, *n. quantity of houses.* घरबंद *m.* घर *n.* उंबरा *m.* घर-

2 (of a saddle). गाशा *m.* पाखर *f.*

HOVEL, *n.* v. HUT. खोपट *n. dim.* खोपटी *or* डी *f.* कुटीर *n.*

To HOVER, *v. n. hang over or around, move backwards and forwards.* घिरट्या *f. pl.*-भोवंडया *f. pl.*-गिरट्या *f. pl.*-&c.

घालणें-मारणें *with* वर *or* भोवतालाा *of o.* भोवंडणें, भोवणें, तरंगणें, तरंगत राहणें, घोटाळणें, गुटमुळणें *or* घुटमळणें, घरमळणें *or* घुरमळणें.

How, *adv. in what manner?* कसा, कसकसा, केवीं.
 2 *by what means?* कसा.
 H. great? H. large? केवढा.
 H. many? H. much? किती, केवढा.

Howbeit, However, Howsoever, *adv. in whatsoever manner or degree.* कसाही, कितीही.
 2 *nevertheless, yet, still.* परंतु, तरीं, तत्रापि, तथापि, अथापि.

Howda, *n.* हौदा *m.*

Howitzer, *n.* गरनाळी सारखी एक प्रकारची तोफ आहे.

To Howl, *v. n.*—as a dog, &c. केंकणें, केंकटणें, केंकावणें, कोंकणें, कोकलणें, रडणें, बोभाणें *or* बोंभावणें.
 2 *cry in distress, wail.* v. To Cry. हेल काढून-गळा काढून-&c. रडणें, आकांत *m.* करणें, आक्रंदणें, आकांतणें, धायमाय *f.* मोकलणें-फोडणें. [वणी *f.* &c.

Howl, Howling, *n.* v. V. 1. केंकणें *n.* &c. केकणी *f.* केंकाव-
 2 गळा काढून रडणें *n.* &c. आकांत *m.* आक्रंदन *n.* आक्रोश *m.* घोर *or* एकच घोर *m.*

Howling, *a.*—wilderness. भणभणीत, घोर.

Hoy, *n.* एक प्रकारची नाव आहे.

Hubble-bubble, *n. particular smoking apparatus.* गुडगुडी *or* गुरगुडी *f.*
 Bubbling sound of a h. गुडगूड *f.* झुरुझुरू *n.*
 Standing tube of a h. मेरु *m.*

Hubbub, *n.* v. Uproar. गलका *m.* गलबा *m.* गलबल *f.* गलबला *m.* गवगव *f.* गवगवा *m.* गूल *f.* कोलाहल *m.* घोर *m.* कल्ला *m.* बलवा *m.*

Huckster, Hucksterer, *n. retailer of small articles.* मोडकावाणी, तुटपुंज्यावाणी, घेवारी, पसारी, डाळपिठ्या-हिंगमिऱ्या वाणी.

To Huckster, *v. n.* लहानसहान जिन्नसांचा व्यापार *m.*-तुटपुंज्या-व्यापार-हलकाव्यापार *m.* करणें, डाळपीठ *n.*-हिंगमिरें *n. pl.*-&c. विकणें.

To Huddle, *v. a. throw together confusedly,* v. To Confound. गोबडणें, गोंधळणें, गोंधळून टाकणें, भानगडणें, गफलतणें, गलफटणें, गडबड *f.*-घोंटाळा *m.*-घालमेल *f.*-&c. करणें *g. of o.*
 2 *perform in a hurry,* v. To Slubber over. गडबडवणें, गडबडगुंडा *m.* करणें *g.of o.* गडबडघोंटाळ्याचा करणें, गुंफाटणें, चरकटणें.

To Huddle, *v. n. crowd together,* v. To Crowd. खेटणें, खेटाखेट *f.*-&c करणें-असणें.

Huddle, *n.* v. Confusion. घालमेल *f.* घपाघोळ *or* घप्पाघोळ *m.* घोंटाळा *m.* गोंधळ *m.* गदळ *m.* गलत *f.* गफलत *f.* शबल *m. f.* गचपण *n.*

Hue, *n. color.* रंग *m.* वर्ण *m.* वाण *m.*
 2 *hue and cry.* पुकारा *m.* हाकाटा *m.* हाकाटी *f.* हाकाहाक *f.* ओरडा ओरड *f.*

Huff, *n. offence, &c.* खीज *f.* चीढ *f.* चिरड *f.* रीस *f.* रुसवा *m.* खपीमर्जी *f.* इतराजी *f.*

To Huff, *v. n. take huff.* खिजणें, चिडणें, रुसणें, खंतणें, चिथणें, अबटा *m.* धरणें.
 2 See To Bluster.

Huffer, *n.* Huffish, *a.* Huffy, *a.* v. V. *that soon takes offence.* चिडखोर, चिरडखोर *or* चिरडीखोर, रुसका, चिडचिड्या, चिडरा, कोरबंद.

Huffiness, *n.* v. A. चिरड *f.* चीढ *f.*

To Hug, *v. a.* v. To Embrace. उरासीं-पोटासीं धरणें, आलिंगणें, उरीं पोटीं धरणें, गळ्यास मिठी घालणें, मिटका *m.* मारणें.

Hug, Hugging, *n.* v. V. आलिंगणें *n.* &c. आलिंगन *n.* मिठी *f.* खेम *f.* खेव *f.* आंगकवळी *f.* बळप *f.*
 Cornish h. मगरमिठी *f.* माकडमिठी *f.*
 Friendly h. क्षेमालिंगन *pop.* खेमालिंगन *n.* प्रेमालिंगन *n.*
 To give a cornish h. कडकडां भेटणें.

Huge, *a immense, vast, monstrous,* v. Large. फारमोठा, बृहत्, कुब्बल, जबर, ऐवट, औजड *or* औजाड, अवाढव्य, डाचाळ, दूघाड, जगड्वाळ, बताणा, बताडा, धनत्तर, कचक, बंबाळ, दांडगा.

Hugeness, *n.* v. A. ऐवटपणा *m.* औजडपणा *m.* &c. बंबाळी *f.*

Hugger mugger, *n. clandestine secrecy, concealment.* लिकाचोरी *f.* गुपचुपी *f.* अडआड *f.*
 In h. लपूनछपून, लिकूनचोरून, लिकाचोरीनें, अडपझडप.

Hulk, *n. body of an old ship.* जुन्यागलबताचा सांगाडा *m.* काठारा *m.*
 2 *bulky, burly, strapping fellow.* The terms bearing this general sense are numerous. They have of course particular implications, and unequal intensity; but, in thus varying, they agree closely with *giant, monster, colossus, goliath, &c.* here therefore they are collected. लठ्ठ्या, लठ्ठभारती, लठ्ठामिश्र, लठ्ठाश्रम, लठ्ठेश्वर, ढील *or* ढेल *n.* धूड *n.* जुंगाड *n.* ढोण *n.* धिप्पाड माणूस, सांगाडा *m.* लोळ *m.* माणसाचा खटारा *m.* दिग्गजपुरुष, दिग्गज, बोका, रावण, धसमुसळा *or* ळ्या, धोंकडा, अजस्र *or* अजस्त्र *n.*

Hull, *n.* v. Husk. टरफल *n.* सालपट *n.* फोल *n.*
 2 *body of a ship.* सांगाडा *m.* पोट *n.* काठारा *m.*
 3 *mere frame.* खटारा *m.* सांगाडा *m.*

To Hull, *v. a.* v. To Husk. सोलणें, सालपट *n.* काढणें *g. of o.*

Hum, *interj.* हां, हूं.

To Hum, *v. n.* v. To Buzz. गुंगणें, भणभणणें *intens.* भणाणणें, कोकावणें, रुणरुणणें.
 2 (in speaking). गुंगत बोलणें, गुंगणें.

To Hum, *v. a. sing in a low voice.* गळ्यांत-गळ्यांतल्यागळ्यांत गाणें.
 To h. a tune. अलापणें, अलाप *m.*-अलापचारी *f.*-तानबाजी *f.*-तानकर्म *n.*करणें, तननं *or* तनाना *adv.*करणें, गुणगुणणें, गुंगणें.

Hum, Humming, *n.* v. V. N. 1. गुंगणें *n.* &c. गुंगणी *f.* भणभण *or* भिणभीण *f.* गुणगूण *or* गिणगीण *f.* गुंजारव *m.* भणका *m.*
 H. or buzz of people speaking. गजबज *f.* कुणकूण *f.* गुणगूण *f.* नाद *m.*

Human, *a. belonging, &c. to mankind.* मनुष्याचा, मनुष्यजातीचा, मानुष, मानुषी, मानवी, मानव, पौरुष, पौरुषेय, नार, नररूप, मनुष्यधर्मी, मनुष्यधर्मक.
 H. art. मनुष्यकला *f.*
 H. being. मनुष्य *pop.* माणूस *n.*

Human-kind, *n.* v. Mankind. मनुष्यजाति *f.*

Humane, *a.* v. Pitiful, Benevolent. दयाळू, दयावान्, सकरुण, करुणावान्, करुणात्मक, हृदयवान्, हृदयालु.

Humanely, *adv.* v. A. दयेनें, दयाळूपणानें, दयापूर्वक, कारुण्यपूर्वक.

Humaneness, Humanity, *n.* v. A. दया *f.* करुणा *f.* कारुण्य *n.*

दयाळूपणा *m.* मनुष्यपणा *or* माणुसपणा *m.* जनदया*f.* लोकदया *f.* भूतदया *f.*

I. *human nature.* मनुष्यत्व *n.* मनुष्यधर्म *m.* मानुष्य *n.*

To HUMANIZE, *v. a. soften, make gentle, &c.* नरम-लीन-नम्र-सदय-&c. करणें.

HUMANLY, *adv.* (speaking) मनुष्यज्ञानाप्रमाणें, मनुष्यबुद्धीप्रमाणें.

HUMBLE, *a. not proud.* नम्र, गरीब, निगर्व *or* निगर्वी, गर्वहीन-रहित-विरहित-विहीन-शून्य, अहंकारा वेगळा-निराळा, निरभिमान, अनभिमानी, निरहंकार, अनहंकार, अनहंकारी, नम्रबुद्धि, नम्रमनस्क, नम्रवृत्ति, लीन, लीनवृत्ति, नम्रतेचा, दीनतेचा, लीनतेचा, &c. दीन, दीनवदन, दैनवाणा, दीनवाणी, अगर्व, अमानी, निरहंमान, मान-&c. वर्जित, प्रणत, लहीन, सविनय, विनयी, विनत, विनयस्थ, विनीत, सानुनय.

2 *not lofty or grand; mean, suited to the poor.* गरीबीचा, गरीबाचे योग्यतेचा, गरीबीलायक, हलके पदवीचा, हलकेयोग्यतेचा, अप्रभ, न्यूनप्रभ.

To HUMBLE, *To* HUMILIATE, *v. a. abase, bring low.* नमवणें, खालावणें, हलकावणें, नम्र-&c. करणें, उतरणें, मोडणें, अभिमान *m.*-&c. मोडणें *g. of o.* पाणउतारा *m.*-रगमोड *f.*-मानखंडन *n.*-अभिमानखंडन *n.*-मानभंग *m.*-तेजोभंग *m.*-मानविध्वंस *m.*-&c. करणें *g. of o.*—With the power or general sense of such words and phrases as, *To mortify, to bring down the pride of, to take the conceit out of, to take the shine out of, to take down a notch, to take down a peg, to bring to his bearings, to make to look sheepish, &c. &c.* लाजावणें, लाज *f.*-&c. आणणें, रग *f.*-रेंच *m.*-खोड *f.*-माज *m.* मोडणें-उतरणें *g. of o.* खई *f.*-खुमखुम *f.*-मोडशी *f.*-ऊब *f.*-भोवळ *f.*-खट्टा*m.*-&c. जिरवणें *g. of o.* मस्तक *n.* टेंगणें करणें *g. of o.* मान *f.*-नाक *n.*-नागोटें *n.* खालीं करणें *g. of o.* खालीं पहायास लावणें, खट्टा *m.*-वरगडा *m.* मोडणें *g. of o.* ऊट *f.*-शिक्कल *f.*-शोभा *f.*-मोठेपणा *m.*-महत्व *n.*-मंजा *m.*-शेंदूर *m.*-शीड *n.* उतरणें *g. of o.* कान *m. pl.* पाडणें, बोड *n.* करणें, बोडणें, बोडंती *f.*-फजिती *f.*-मुखभंजन *n.*-मुखमार्जन *n.*-दर्पोपशांति *f.*-&c. करणें *g. of o.* पट्टी *f.* काढणें *g. of o.* पाण्यापेक्षां पातळ करणें, नाककाटणी *f.* करणें *g. of o.*

To be humbled, *brought down, &c.* पारडें*n.* उतरणें-बसणें *g. of s.* भोवळ*f.*-&c. जिरणें *g. of s.* शीड*n.*-&c. उतरणें *g. of s.* नाक *n.* खालीं पडणें-गुंडाळणें *g. of s.*

2 (one's self) v. To ABASE. कमीपणा *m.* घेणें, नमणें, नीचपणा *m.*-&c. अंगीकारणें, नम्र-&c. होणें.

HUMBLE-BEE, *n.* भुंगा *m.* भ्रमर *m.* भृंग *m.*

HUMBLED, HUMILIATED, *p.* v. V. 1. नमवलेला, नम्र केलेला, उतरलेला, मोडलेला, रग मोडलेला,&c. नष्टाभिमान, खंडिताभिमान.

2 See ABASED.

HUMBLER, *n.* HUMBLING, HUMILIATING, *p. a.* v. V. 1. नमवणारा, खालावणारा, मोडणारा, नम्र करणारा, &c. रगमोड्या, रेंचमोड्या, खोडमोड्या, खईजिरव्या, ऊबजिरव्या.

HUMBLING, HUMILIATION, *n.* v. V. 1.—*act.* नमवणें *n.* खालावणें *n.* &c. बोडणी *f.* बोडंती *f.* अभिमानखंडन *n.* मानखंडन *n.* मानखंडना *f.* मुखभंजन *n.* मुखमार्जन *n.*—*a. or s.* रगमोड *f.* खईमोड *f.* छानमोड *f.* मानभंग*m.*तेजोभंग *m.* मानविध्वंस*m.*—*state.* See DISGRACE.

2 v. ABASEMENT. नमलेपणा *m.* नम्रता *f.* लघुत्वस्वीकार *m.*

H. one's self in the dust. नाकदुराही *f.*

HUMBLY, *adv.* v. A. 1. नम्रपणानें, नम्रतेनें, नम्रबुद्धीनें, गर्वावाचून, अहंकार सोडून, लीनतापूर्वक, विनयपूर्वक, &c.

2 गरीबीच्या रीतीनें, गरीबीच्या चालीनें, गरीबीलायक.

HUMBUG, *n.* v. DECEIT. गुळ खोबरें *n.* पैठणी आदर *m.* वरकमी आदर *m.* गड्डे पद्दे *m. pl.* झोकपट्टी *f.* झुगारपट्टी *f.* लम्पगोष्टी *f. pl.* फोल *n.* भुलताप *or* थाप *f.* बाड *f.* मावेचें मंथन *n.* इधरतिधर *n.* चाम्हारफट *f.*

2 *humbugging person.* गोडबोल्या, लपोडशंख, भुलथापी *or* भुलथाप्या, बाड्या, भोंदू *or* भोंद्या.

To HUMBUG, *v. a.* v. TO DECEIVE. धंदरणें, भुलताप *or* थाप *f.* करणें-देणें, बाड *f.* करणें-मारणें, झुगारपट्टी *f.*-&c. देणें.

HUMDRUM, *a.* v. STUPID. माठ्या, मठ्ठ्या, मळमळीत.

HUMERAL, *a. belonging to the shoulder.* खांद्याचा, स्कंधाचा, स्कंधसंबंधी.

HUMID, *a.* v. MOIST. ओलसर, ओलट.

2—a soil. दमदार, दमाचा.

HUMIDITY, *n.* v. A. 1. ओल *f. n.* ओलावा*m.* ओलासरा*m.* ओलेपणा*m.*

2 दम*m.*

HUMILITY, HUMBLENESS, *n.* v. A. नम्रता *f.* लीनता *f.* गर्वराहित्य*n.* निरभिमानता *f.* निरहंकारता *f.* निरहंमानिता *f.* अमानित्व*n.* दैन्य*n.* दीनता *f.* निर्वेद*m.* नम्रवृत्ति *f.* लीनवृत्ति *f.* विनय*m. f.* विनति *f.*

HUMOR, *n.* (of the body). दोष*m.* धातु*m.* रस*m.*

The three *humors* are. कफ*m.* पित्त*n.* वात*m.* (phlegm, bile or choler, wind).

Disorder or vitiation of any of them. दोष*m.* धातुनाश*m.*

Disorder or vitiation of them all. त्रिदोष*m.* दोषत्रय*n.* त्रिदोष वायु*m.* सन्निपात*m.*

Disorder ascribed to the vitiation of the h. *phlegm.* is, कफविकार*m.* कफरोग*m.*—of the h. *bile,* पित्तविकार*m.*पित्तरोग*m.*—of the h. *wind,* वातविकार*m.* वातरोग*m.* वायुविकार*m.* वायु*m.*

Discharge of humors. रोगवणी*n.*

Excess of any of the three humors. प्रकोप*m.* उल्बण*n.*

2 *present temper, mood.* वृत्ति *f.* भाव*m.* तबियत *f.*

To be in the h. for. स्वर*m.pl.* भजणें-वाहणें *g. of s.*

3 *jocularity, pleasantry, wit.* रहस्य*n.* ठट्ठेबाजी *f.*

4 v. WHIM, FANCY. छंद*m.* तरंग*m.* लहर *f.*

To HUMOR, *v. a.* v. TO INDULGE. लळा*m.*-लाड*m.*-&c. चालवणें *g. of o.* छंदोनुवर्त्तन*n.*-छंदोनुवृत्ति *f.*-छंदोनुरोध*m.* करणें *g. of o.*

HUMORAL, *n. pertaining, &c. to the humors.* कफपित्तवातात्मक, कफपित्तादिजन्य.

HUMORIST, *n.* See HUMOROUS.

HUMOROUS, *a. facetious, waggish, jocular.* ख्याली, विनोदी, विनोदवृत्ति, रसाळ, रसिक, खारटतुरट, ठट्ठेखोर, ठट्ठेबाज, रमुजी *or* रमोजी.

2 *humorsome,* v. FANCIFUL, WHIMSICAL. छंदी, छांदिष्ट, छंदिष्ट, छांदसवृत्ति, तऱ्हेबाज, तबियती.

HUMOROUSNESS, *n.* v. A. 1. विनोदवृत्ति *f.* ठट्ठेखोरी *f.* ठट्ठेबाजी *f.*

2 छांदिष्टपणा*m.* &c. छांदसवृत्ति *f.*

HUMORSOME, See FANCIFUL, WHIMSICAL.

HUMP, *n.* (on the back). कुबड*n.* कोंक*n.* कोंग*n.* खोंद*n.* पोंक *or* गन.

2 (on a bullock's back). कोळ*n.* कोहळें *or* काहाळें *or* कोळें*n.*

कोळखंड *n.* कोळखांदा *m.* वशिंड *or* वशेंड *or* बसंड*n. f.* वृषांस *m.* ककुद*m. n.*

3 (on a camel's back). मदार *f.*

Hump-back, *n.* कुबड*n.* पोंक *or* पोंग*n.* कोंग*m.* कोंक*n.* पेंक*n.*

To have or get a h. पोंकणें, पोंगणें.

Hump-backed, *a.* कुबडा *or* कुबड्या, खोंया, पोंक्या *or* पोंग्या, पेंका *or* क्या, कुब्ज.

Hunch, *n.* See Hump.

2 *thick piece.* ठोकळा*m.* कोंडका*m.* कोंडकें*n.*

Hunch-backed. See Hump-backed.

Hundred, *a.* शंभर (confined to express *one* h. To express plurality शें is used with a numeral prefix as, एकशें, दोनशें, तीनशें), शत.

Aggregate of a h. शेंकडा*m.* शतक*n.*

By hundreds. शेंकडों, शेंकडोशः *or* शेंकडोशा, शतशः, दरसद्दे.

In or by the h. शेंकडा *or* डां, दरसद्दे.

Hundred, *n. division of a country,* v. County. महाल *m.*

Hundredth, *a.* शंभरावा.

Hunger, *n.* भूक *f.* क्षुधा *f.* बुभुक्षा *f.* अन्नेच्छा *f.*—in high degree, agreeing with *craving, ravening, &c.* वखवख *f.* रखरख *f.* रखरखाट*m.* खासा *or* खायखाय *f.* खवखव *f.* लखलख *f.* बाळभूक *f.* क्षुद्बोध*m.*

To allay h. भूक *f.* मारणें, भूकमोड*m. f.*-क्षुधाशांति *f.*-क्षुधाध्वंस*m.*-&c. करणें. [कठीण आहे.

H. is harder than death. अंतकालापेक्षां माध्याह्न काल

H. needs no sauce, sleepiness no pillow. भुकेला कोंडा झोंपेला धोंडा.

To die of h. भुकें मरणें.

To have one's h. appeased or satisfied. भूक *f.* धरणें.

Terms for a person wild with h. are बरगळ भूत *n.* बरगळेल भूत *n.*

2 See Desire.

To Hunger, *v. n.* भूक *f.*-क्षुधा *f.*-&c. लागणें *in. con.* उपासीं *or* उपासीं पोटीं *or* उपवासीं असणें, भुकेणें, भुकेजणें, भुकावणें—in high degree, *to crave, raven, &c.* वखवखणें, खासा *f.* सुटणें, रखरखणें, रखाकणें, लखलखणें, चणचणणें, चणाणणें, खासावणें, धादावणें, कंकातणें *or* कंक्रांतणें, कळकळणें, पोटांत ब्रह्मराक्षस*m.* असणें-उठणें *g. of s.* ठिकरी *f.* तापणें *g. of s.* लाहो*m.* घेणें, पोटांत कावळे*m. pl.* ओरडणें, पोटांत वणवा *m.* पेटणें, खाईनखाईन करणें, पोटांत कल्पांत*m.* होणें. [*f.* काढणें.

To h. and thirst. *bear want and privations.* उपास तान

To sit hungering. दांतास दांत लावून बसणें, चुरमुऱ्यांचे लाडू*m. pl.* खाणें-खातबसणें.

Hungry, *a.* भुका, भुकेला, उपासी, क्षुधित, बुभुक्षित, क्षुधान्वित—in high degree; as expressed by *keen-set, sharp-set, craving, ravenous, famishing, half-starved, hunger-bitten,* क्षुधाकुल, क्षुधातुर, क्षुधाविष्ट, क्षुधाग्रस्त, क्षुधाक्रांत, क्षुधार्त्त, क्षुधांध, क्षुधाविव्हल, क्षुधाधीन, क्षुधापीडित, क्षुधानलविदग्ध, दग्धोदर, हवळा.

H. and needy, भुकेकंगाल.

That is ever h. भुकाळू, घोडभुक्या, भुकेचीखाण *f.* भुकेचेंघर *n.* भुकेचागड्डा*m.*

2 *wanting, barren, meagre, &c.* भुकिस्त, भुकड.

Hunks. See Miser. [करणें *g. of o.*

To Hunt, *v. a.*—in the chase. पारध *f.*-शिकार *f.*-मृगया *f.*-&c.

2 *follow close,* v. To Pursue. पाठीस लागणें *g. of o.*

3 out; v. To Search. हुडकणें, हुडकून काढणें, धुंडाळणें, धुंडाळून काढणें. [&c. जाणें.

To Hunt, *v. n.* पारध *f.*-शिकार *f.*-&c. करणें, पारधीस-शिकारीस-

2 *look for,* v. To Search. शोध*m.* करणें.

To h. every where. घरघर-देशदेश-गांवगांव-&c चाळणें.

Hunt, Hunting, *n.* v. V. N. 1. पारध*f.* शिकार *f.* आखेट*m.* मृगया *f.*

2 See Search.

I. *game, &c. hunted.* शिकार *f.*

Hunter, Huntsman, *n.* v. V. शिकाऱ्या, शिकारबाज, पारधी, मृगयाकार, मृगयु, व्याध, लुब्धक.

Hunter, *n. horse used in the chase.* शिकारीचा घोडा*m.*

Huntress, *n.* शिकारकरणारीस्त्री *f.* मृगयाकारिणी *f.*

Hurdle, *n. crate.* ताटी *f.* सांकाटा*m.* सांपडा*m.*

Hurdy-gurdy, *n.* एक तंतुवाद्यआहे.

To Hurl, *v. a.* v. To Cast. जोरानें फेंकणें-झुगारणें-झोकणें-&c. हौलगडण*n.* हौलपटणें, होडगणें.

Hurl, Hurling, *n.* v. V. जोरानें फेंकणें*n.* हौलगडणें*n.* &c.

I. See Tumult.

Hurly-burly, *n.* v. Tumult. घोळ*m.* घोळंकार*m.* घप्पाघोळ*m.* गोंधळ*m.* धामधूम *or* धुमधाम *f.* धडाका*m.*

Hurra. See Huzza. [प्रचंडवात *m.*

Hurricane, *n. storm of wind.* वादळ *n.* तुफान *n.* चंडवात *m.*

Hurriedly, *adv.* तांतडीं, लगेलगे, लगेतगे करून.

Hurriedness, *n.* v. Hurry. घाई *f.* तांतड *or* डी *f.* लावतोड *f.*

Hurrier, *n.* v. V. A. 1. घायतावणारा, &c. हुलहुल्या, घायकुत्या.

2 गडबडवणारा.

To Hurry, *v. a. urge, hasten.* घायतावणें, गडबडवणें, ताधरानणें, तांतडवणें, नाचवणें, घायकूत *f.*-घाई *f.*-उतावळी *f.*-त्वरा *f.*-हुळहूळ *f.*-हुटहूट *f.*-चुळचूळ *f.* करणें, मुळका *m.* लावणें.

2 over *or* through, v. To Slubber over. गडबडवणें, गडबडगुंडा *m.* करणें *g. of o.* लगेतगे करून *adv.* करणें, गडबड घोंटाळ्याचा करणें.

To Hurry, *v. n. or To be* Hurried. तांतडणें, गडबडणें, हडबडणें, उतावळ *f.*-घाई *f.*-&c. करणें, तांतडी-लगेलगे-लगेतगे करून *adv.* होणें-असणें, उतावळीनें चालणें-जाणें-&c. त्वरणें.

Hurry, *n. violent commotion, &c.* v. Tumult. गडबड *f.* गडबडी *f.* हडबड *f.* घोळ *m.* घोळंकार *m.* झटापटी *f.*

2 *confused eagerness.* घाई *f.* उतावळी *f.* उतावळ *f.* लगबग *f.* लगलग *f.* लगेलगे *f.* तांतड *f.* तांतडी *f.* आगघाई *f.* घालमेल *f.* लावतोड *f.* जलदी *f.* घायकूत *f. n.* संभ्रम *m.* आवेग *m.* संवेग *m.*

To be in a violent h. घाई *f.*-&c. असणें, मुंगळा *m.* लागणें *in. con.* उपीत *n.* पिणें *or* घेणें.

Hurrying, *n.* v. V. A. 1. घायतावणें *n.* &c. घायकूत *f.* चालढकल *f.* हुळहूळ *f.* हुटहूट *f.* चुळचूळ *f.* अफरातफर *f.* मुळका *m.*

Hurry-skurry, *n. bustle, confusion.* दौडादौडी *f.* धांवाधांव *f.* घाई *f.* धामधूम *or* धुमधाम *f.* लावतोड *f.* झटापट *or* टी *f.*

To Hurt, *v. a. harm, injure, impair, damage.* नासणें, बिघडणें, नडणें, खराव करणें, विनासणें *or* बिनसणें, खराबी *f.*-नुकसानी *f.*-&c.-करणें *g. of o.* उपद्रव *m.* करणें.

2 v. To WOUND. दुखापत *f.* करणें-देणें, दुखावणें, घातपात *m.* करणें *g. of o.*

HURT, *n. harm, mischief, damage, detriment, injury.* नुकसान *f. n.* नुकसानी *f.* खराबी *f.* खराबा *m.* नाश *m.* उपद्रव *m.* ढक्का *or* धक्का *m.* अपकार *m.* अपाय *m.* अरिष्ट *n.* अनिष्ट *n.* बाईट *n.* क्षति *f.* हानि *f.*

2 *bruise, &c.* v. WOUND. दुखापत *f.*

To receive h.—a limb, &c. दुखवणें *or* दुखावणें.

HURT, *p.* v. V. 1. नासलेला, &c. अपकृत, प्राप्तापकार, जातापकार, उपहत, विगलित, जायबंदा *or* जायबंदी, लंगडा.

2 दुखावलेला, दुखवलेला, घायाळ, क्षत.

HURTER, *n.* HURTFUL, *a.* v. V. 1. नासणारा, खराबकरणारा, &c. अपकारक, अपकारी, अपकर्त्ता, अपकारकारक-कर्त्ता-&c. अहितकारक-कारी-&c. बाधक, दुष्ट, बाईट, बावडा, उपद्रवकारक-कर्त्ता-&c.अनिष्टकारक-कारी-&c. अपायकारक-जनक-&c.घातक, घातकी.

I.—article of food, v. UNWHOLESOME. अपथ्य, बावडा, बाधक, उपद्रवी, उपद्रवीक, अवगुणी.

HURTFULNESS, *n.* v. A. प्रत्यवाय *m.* अपकारकत्व *n.* अपकारिता *f.* अपकारकभाव *m.*

I. अवगुण *m.* बाधकपणा *m.* बाधकत्व *n.*

HUSBAND, *n.* दादला *m.* दादव्या *m.* नवरा *m.* भर्त्ता *pop.* भ्रतार *or* भर्त्तार *m.* पति *m.* वर *m.* धव *m.* कांत *pop.* कंथ *m.*—in familiar phraseology. गोहो *m.* धगड *m.*—in amatory or poetic phraseology, v. LOVER. प्राणाधिनाथ *m.* रमण *m.* वल्लभ *m.*

Chooser of her h. स्वयंवरा *f.*

Choosing of one's h. स्वयंवर *m. n.*

Duty of h. and wife. स्त्रीपुंधर्म *m.* दंपतीधर्म*m.* दांपत्यधर्म*m.*

Fixing upon a person to be the h. of. वरनिश्चय *m.* वरयोजना *f.*

H. and wife, *married pair.* दादलाबायकें *or* लें *n.* दादला बायको *f.* स्त्रीपुरुषें *n. pl.* स्त्रीपुरुष *m.* दंपती *m. n.* दंपत्य *n.*

H.'s brother. भावा *m.* दीर *m.* देर *m.* देवर *m.* भावो *or* भावोजी *m.*

H.'s brother's wife. जाऊ *or* जावू *f.*

H.'s father. सासरा *m.* श्वशुर *m.*

H.'s father's house. सासरें *n.* सासरघर *n.* सासुरवाड *f.*—Girl resident in it. सासुरवासीण *f.*—Residence in it. सासुरवास *m.*

H's mother. फुइजी *or* फुई *f.* सासू *f.*

H.'s paternal aunt. आतेसासू *f.*

H.'s sister. नणंद *f.* नंदा *f.* वनसें *n. & f. pl.*

Woman whose h. is alive. सुवासिनी *pop.* सुवाशीण *f.*सभर्तृका *f.* सनाथा *f.*

Taking a second h. पाट *m.* न्हावेर *m.*

To run from one's h. and dwell with another man. घर *n.* निघणें, घर *n.* रिघणें.

While the h. struts abroad the wife starves at home, टिळे पट्टे नायकांचे, घरांत हाल बायकांचे.

To HUSBAND, *v. a. manage with frugality.* कतरबेतानें-तडजोडीनें-संजोगानें-&c. खर्च *m.* करणें, संजोग *m.* करणें-ठेवणें.

HUSBAND-HOOD, *n.* दादलेपणा *m.* भर्तृत्व *n.*

HUSBAND-MAN, *n.* v. AGRICULTURIST. शेतकरी, शेतीमाती, शेती, कृषिक, कृषीवल.

HUSBANDRY, *n.* v. AGRICULTURE. शेतकाम *n.* कृषि *f.* कृषिकर्म*n.*

Instruments of h.—gener. or collect. अऊत भरणा *m.*

2 *domestic economy,*v. FRUGALITY. घरजोगावणी *f.*घरजुगूत*f.*

HUSH, *interj.* चुप, उगाच, बोलूंनको.

To HUSH, *v. a. quiet, still.* शांत-थंड-चुप-&c. करणें, शांति *f.*-शम *m.* करणें *g. of o.*

2 hush up; *suppress.* दाबणें, दाबादाब *f.*-चेपाचेप *f.* करणें *g. of o.* दपटणें, छपवणें.

HUSH-MONEY, *n.* v. BRIBE. तोंडदाबणें *n.* मुखपिंड *m.* मुखलेप *m.*

HUSK, *n. external cover, rind, skin, hull.* टरफल *n.* फोल *n.* साल *n.* सालपट *n.*

Husks;—*chaff.* भुसा*m.*भूस*n.* भुसकट*n.* भुसकटा*m.*भुसकूट*n.* भुंशी*f.* भुसी *f.*फोल *n.* खोकस *n.*भोंडें *n.pl.* तुष *m.pop.* तूस *m. n.*

2 (of नाचणी, हरीक, &c.) फरळ *n.*

3 (of legumes). कठाण *or* काठण *n.* गुळीं *n.* गुळें *n.* काड *n.*

To HUSK, *v. a.* v. N. सोलणें, साल *n.*-सालपट *n.*-&c. काढणें *g. of o.* [त्वच.

HUSKED, *p.* v. V. सोललेला, &c. सोलींव, निस्तुष, निस्तुषित, नि-

HUSKY. See HOARSE.

HUSSAR. See TROOPER.

To HUSTLE. See To JUMBLE.

HUSWIFE, HUSSY, *n. term of contempt for a woman.*घरडुकर*n.* रांड *f.* रांडरू *n.*

HUT, *n. cot, crib, cabin, hovel.* खोपट *n. dim.* खोपटी *f.* खोप *or* खोंप *f.* कोपट *n.* खोपड *n. dim.* खोपडी *f.* झोंपडी *f.* झोंपा *m.* झोंपडें *n.* छप्पर *n. dim.* छप्परी *f.* अडघर *n.* कुटीर *n.* पर्णशाला *f.* पर्णकुटी *f.*

HUTCH. See BIN.

HUZZA, *interj.* जयजय, जयजया, जयजयकार, वाहवा.

HUZZA, *n. shout of joy.* गजर *m.* जयजय *m.* जयशब्द *m.* जयघोष *m.* जयजयकार *m.* जयजयशब्द *m.* भलेरी *f.*

To HUZZA, *v. n.* जयशब्द *n.*-&c. करणें.

HYACINTH, *n.* एक वनस्पति आहे.

HYBRID, *a.* v. MONGREL. दोगला, मिश्रजातीय, संकरजातीय.

HYDATIDES, *n. watery vesicles.* काचफोड *m. pl.*

HYDRAULIC, *a.* जंगमजलविद्यासंबंधी-विषयक.

HYDRAULICS, *n. science of fluids in motion.* जंगमजलविद्या *f.* चलज्जलविद्या *f.*

HYDROCEPHALUS. *n.* जलमस्तक.

HYDROCELE, *n. dropsy of the testicles.* कोषवृद्धि *f.* अंतर्गळ *m.*

HYDRODYNAMICS, *n.* उदकगतिस्थितिशास्त्र *n.*

HYDROGEN, *n.*उदकजनकवायु *m.*हैड्रोजिन *n.*(from the English).

HYDROGRAPHER, *n.* समुद्रसरोवर वगैरेचे नकाशे काढणारा.

HYDROGRAPHY, *n.* समुद्रसरोवर वगैरेचे नकाशे काढण्याची विद्या *f.*

HYDROMEL, *n. honey-water.* मधपाणी *n.* मधवणी *n.*

HYDROMETER, *n.* द्रव द्रव्यांचें विशेष गुरुत्व जाणण्याचें साधन *n.*

HYDROPATHY, *n. water treatment.* जलोपचार *m.*

HYDROPHOBIA, *n.* पिसाळलेल्या कुत्र्याचा विखार *m.* विक्षिप्तश्वदंशरोग *m.* अलर्क *m.*

HYDROPICAL. See DROPSICAL.

HYDROSTATICS, *n. science of the weight, &c. of fluids.* उदकस्थितिनिबंध *m.* उदकस्थितिशास्त्र *n.*

HYEMAL, *a. relating to winter.* हिंवाळ्याचा, हिम्य, हैम, हैमन.

Hyena, *n.* तरस *m.* तरक्षु *m.*

Hygrometer, *n.* हवेंतील ओलावा मोजण्याचें साधन *n.*

Hymeneal, Hymenean, *n. marriage song.* विवाहगान *n.* मंगलगीत *n.* [विवाहविषयक.

Hymeneal, Hymenean, *a. nuptial.* विवाहाचा, विवाहसंबंधी,

Hymn, *n. religious song.* सद्गीत *n.* स्तोत्र *n.* अभंग *m.* भजन *n.*

To **Hyp**, *v. a. make low spirited.* उदास-उदासी-विमनस्क-&c. करणें, उदासपणा *m.*-औदासीन्य *n.*-&c. आणणें.

Hyperbole, *n.*—in rhetoric. अतिशयोक्ति *f.* अत्युक्ति *f.* अधिक *n.*

Hyperbolic, Hyperbolical, *a.* v. N. अतिशयोक्तीचा, अत्युक्तीचा, अतिशयोक्तिविशिष्ट, अतिशयोक्तिरूप, अतिशयोक्तिपूर्वक.

Hyperbolist, *n.* अतिशयोक्ति वक्ता-वादी-कर्त्ता, अतिवादक, पिसाचा कावळा करणारा.

Hyperborean, See **Northern**.

Hypercritic, Hypercritical, *a. over critical*, v. **Captious**. चिकित्सखोर, दिक्कतखोर, दिक्कती.

Hypercriticism, *n. excess of criticism*, v. **Captiousness**. चिकित्सा *f.* अतिचिकित्सा *f.*

Hypnotic, *a. soporific.* झोंप आणणारा, निद्राकारक, निद्राजनक.

Hypochondre, *n.* v. **Side**. बख *m. f.* बखाडी *f.*

Hypochondria, Hypochondriasis, *n.* v. **Melancholy**. कुपितवायु *m.* विषाद *m.*

Hypochondriac, Hypochondriacal, *a.* v. **Melancholy**. सदाविषादी, नित्यविषादी, विषादवृत्ति.

Hypocrisy, *n.*—gener. ढोंग *n.* दंभ *m.* डंभ *m.* भगल *f. n.* दांभिक *n.* होटांत एक पोटांतएक *n.* कुहना *f.* आकारगोपन *n.* आकारगुप्ति *f.* वचस्येकंमनस्येकं *n.*

2—religious. बकध्यान *n.* बकव्रत *n.* बोकेसन्यास *m.* बंड *n.* घणघणघंटा *m. f.* धर्मध्वज *m.*

Hypocrite, *n.*—gener. v. N. ढोंगी *or* ग्या, दंभी, दांभिक, डंभी, भगली *or* ल्या, मकरी, वेषधारी, जनांत एक मनांत एक, मिसा, मिसखोर, मिषकर्त्ता. In that shade of the sense of this word denoted by the current terms and phrases *cat, wolf in sheep's clothing, saint-looking ruffian, demure blood-hound, butter-faced cut throat, meekeyed villain, honey-tongued scoundrel, (one looking) as if butter would not melt in his mouth, sanctimonious fellow, lamb-like wolf*,—i. e. *one of soft and mild aspect, but of dark and fell purpose*, there are in *Marāṭhi* numerous terms and phrases equally current and equally significant. गायतोंड्या, गोमुख्या, साडे भावार्थी, भगलभावार्थी बकध्यानी, बकव्रती, बोकेसन्यासी, बैडालव्रतिक, शांतिब्रह्म, गोमुखव्याघ्र, मेंग्या मारवाडी *or* मेण्यामारवाडी, हासतां हासतां दांत पाडणारा, साखरेची सुरी, हातावर साखर आणि मानेवर कातर देणारा, मानभाव, गोडबोल्या आणि सालसोल्या, तोंडावर गोड *or* तोंडापुरता गोड, इंद्रावण *or* इंद्रावणीचें फळ, गुळदगड *or* गुळधोंडा, मिसकीन मारवाडी, मिसकीन मात्रागमनी, सात्विकचांडाल. [णारा.

2—religious. धर्मध्वजी, सर्वलिंगी, मिल्हा, सदानाक धरून बस-

To play the h. कानांत तुळसी *f.* घालणें, प्रस्थ *n.* माजवणें *or* वाढवणें, देव्हारा *m. or* रें *n.* माजवणें *or* वाढवणें.

Hypocritical, *a.* v. **Hypocrite**. ढोंगी, &c. ढोंगाचा, दंभाचा, दांभिकवृत्ति, सदंभ.

H. tricks. ढोंग धत्तुरा *m.*

Hypogastric, *a.* v. N. खालच्या पोटाचा, बास्तेय, बस्तिसंबंधी.

Hypogastrium, *n. lower region of the belly.* खालचें पोट *n.* ओंटी *f.* निरण *n.* बस्ति *or* बस्ति *m. f.* उत्तरबस्ति *f.* बांदन *n.* नाभ्यधोभाग *m.* उपस्थोर्ध्वभाग *m.*

Hypostasis, *n. subsistence, substance.* सत्त्व *n.* अस्तित्व *n.*

Hypotenuse, *n.*—in geometry. कर्ण *m.* श्रवण *n.*

Hypothesis, *n. supposition, principle, &c. assumed.* कल्पना *f.* इष्टकल्पना *f.* अनुभव *m.* अटकळ *f.* अनुमान *n.* अनुमितिकरण *n.* अनुमितिहेतु *m.* संभावना *f.*

Hypothetical, *a.* v. N. कल्पनेचा, अटकळीचा, अनुमानाचा, काल्पनिक, आनुमानिक.

Hypt. See **Hypochondriac**.

Hysterics, *n.* वायुगोळा *m.*

Hysteron-proteron, *adv. reversely.* मागेंपुढें, पुढचामागें, आदिपश्चात्, आदिमग.

I.

I. This vowel is represented in its short sound by इ, in its long sound by ई, and in its diphthongal sound by ऐ.

I, *pron.* मी.

Ice, *n. congealed fluid.* बर्फ *n.* थंडीनें थिजलेलें-गोठलेलें पाणी *n.*-&c.

2 *concreted sugar.* घट्टझालेलीसाखर *f.* साखरेचापाक *m.*

To break the i. *fig.* उपक्रम *m.*-आरंभ *m.*-&c. करणें-काढणें, उट्ट *m.* काढणें.

To **Ice**, *v. a.* बर्फलावून-घालून-&c. थंड करणें.

2 साखरेचापाक *m.* घालणें-चरलावणें.

Ice-berg, *n.* बर्फाचाडोंगर *m.*

Ichneumon, *n.*—vivena. मुंगूस *m. n.* नकुल *m.* बभ्रु *m.* सर्पारि *m.*

Ichor, *n. sanious flux.* रगतपू *m.* लस *f.* पूयरक्त *n.* पूयशोणित *n.*

Ichorous, *a. serous, watery.* रगतपूचा, लसेचा, लसेसारखा, पूयरक्तवत्.

Ichthyology, *n. description, &c. of fishes.* मत्स्यवर्णन *n.*

Ichthyophagous, *a. feeding on fish.* मत्स्यभक्षक, मत्स्याहारी, मत्स्यभोजी.

Ichthyophagy, *n. living on fish.* मत्स्याहार *m.* मत्स्यभोजन *n.*

Icicle, *n. ice-pendent.* हिमकण *m.* तुषारकण *m.*

Iconoclasm, *n. image breaking.* मूर्तिभंग *m.*

Iconoclast, *n.* मूर्तिफोडणारा, मूर्तिभंजक.

Icy, *a. made, &c. of ice.* बर्फाचा, हिमवान्, हिम्य, हिमशीतल, हिममय, हिमप्रचुर.

2 *cold like ice.* बर्फासारखाथंड.

Idea, *n. mental image.* कल्पना *f.* भान *n.* प्रतिभास *m.* आकार *m.*

Distinct i. स्पष्ट प्रतिपत्ति *f.* [ग्रह *m.*

2 *conception, thought*, v. **Notion**. तर्क *m.* भान *n.* भास *m.*

Abstract i. भाव *m.*

Under the i. of. बुद्धीनें.

Ideal, *a. existing in idea*, v. **Intellectual, Mental**. मनींचा, मनोगत, चिद्गत, मानसिक, मनोमय.

2 *visionary*, v. **Imaginary**. मानसिक, काल्पनिक, मनःकल्पित, कल्पित, बौद्ध.

I. world. मानससृष्टि *f.*

IDEALISM, *n. doctrine of the unreality of matter.* माया *f.* योगमाया *f.* अविद्या *f.* अविद्यावाद *m.* अविद्यामत *n.* अजा *f.*

IDEALIST, *n.* v. N. मायावादी, अविद्यावादी.

IDEALLY, *adv.* v. A. 1. and MENTALLY. मनांत.

IDENTIC, IDENTICAL, *a. the same.* तोच, एकही, तन्मय, अभिन्न, अनन्य, अभेद, एकरूप, तद्रूप, केवल.

IDENTICALNESS, IDENTITY, *n.* v. A. ऐक्य *n.* ऐक्यभाव *m.* तादात्म्य *n.* अभिन्नता *f.* अभिन्न भाव *m.* अभेद *m.* अनन्यता *f.* अनन्यभाव *m.* तद्रूपता *f.* ताद्रूप्य *n.* एकरूपता *f.*

Personal i. आत्मौपम्य *n.*

To IDENTIFY, *v. a. prove to be the same.* तोचतो-ह्याचतो-&c. करून दाखवणें, अनन्यनिदर्शन *n.*-तादात्म्य प्रदर्शन *n.* करणें.

2 *treat as the same, make to be the same.* एककरून दाखवणें, एक करून मानणें.

IDIOCRACY, *n. peculiarity of constitution.* आत्मभाव *m.* प्रकृतिस्वभाव *m.* प्रकृतिविशेष *m.* विशेषप्रकृति *f.*

IDIOCY, *n. natural defect of understanding.* जन्माचा वेडेपणा *m.* जन्माचें वेड *n.*-खूळ *n.* उपजतवेडेपणा *m.* &c.

2 *imbecility of mind*—gener. चळ *m.* खूळ *n.* वेड *n.* पिसें *n.* खुळेपणा *m.* बावळेपणा *m.* &c. भोळसर बुद्धि *f.* बुद्ध्यभाव *m.*

Causing i. by magic. उच्चाटन *n.*

Feigned i. घालवेड *n.*

IDIOM, *n. peculiarity of phraseology.* बोलण्याचा प्रकार *m.*-रीति *f.*-चाल *f.*-&c.- भाषणसंप्रदाय *m.* संप्रदाय *m.* भाषणाचा पर्याय *m.*

2 *the genius or cast of a language.* भाषेची-&c. शैली *f.*-रहाटी *f.*- मोडणी *f.*

IDIOMATICAL, *a. relating to idiom.* भाषणसंप्रदायाचा, भाषणसंप्रदाय संबंधी-विषयक, सांप्रदायिक.

2 *according to idiom.* संप्रदायशुद्ध, भाषणसंप्रदायानुसार.

IDIOMATICALLY, *adv.* v. A. भाषणसंप्रदायानें, यथासंप्रदाय, बोलण्याचा संप्रदाय-&c. संभाळून.

IDIOSYNCRACY, *n. peculiarity of constitution.* आत्मभाव *m.* विशेष प्रकृति *f.* प्रकृतिविशेष *m.* प्रकृतिविशिष्टता *f.*

IDIOT, *n.* v. IDIOTIC. खुळा-&c. माणूस, जन्माचा मूर्ख, उपजत मूर्ख, गावदी, अर्भक *m.n.* नंद *m.* वेडीहळद *f.* See also FOOL.

Sham-i. घालवेडा.

IDIOTIC, IDIOTICAL, IDIOTISH, *a.* v. FOOLISH. खुळा, खुळकट, खुळसट, खुळसर, बावळा, वेडाचा, चळाचा, &c. भोळा, भोळवट, भोळसर, भळू, गयाळ, गयाळी, यथाजात.

I. look. बावळी मुद्रा *f.* गाबाळाची मुद्रा *f.*

IDIOTISM, IDIOTCY, *n.* v. IDIOCY. चळ *m.* खुळ *n.*

IDLE, *a. averse from labor,* v. LAZY. आळशी, सुस्त, निरुद्योग, उद्योगशत्रु, उद्योगविमुख.

2 *not engaged,*—person, &c. रिकामा, निकामी, बेकार, खाली, निरुद्योग, निरुद्योगी, सुटा, मोकळा, घरीं बसलेला.

3 *not occupied*-time, &c. v. VACANT. रिकामा, रिकामपणाचा.

4 *trifling, light, silly, &c.* पोकळ, रिकामा, रिकामका, रिता, हलका, वायकरणी, वायकरणीचा, निरर्थक, अनर्थक, वायफट.

To IDLE, *v. n.* v. To DAWDLE. गमणें, जोगवणें, माशा *f.pl.* मारणें *or* मारीत बसणें, हातपाय पांघरून बसणें *or* पोटाळून बसणें, रमणें, रेंगणें, रेंगळणें.

To IDLE-AWAY, *v. a. spend in idleness.* रिकामपणाखालीं-रिकामपणांत-&c. घालवणें, गमावणें.

IDLENESS, *n.* v. A. 1. आळस *m.* सुस्ती *f.* आलस्य *n.* उद्योगद्वेष *m.*

2 रिकामेपणा *m.* बेकारपणा *m.*&c. बेकारी *f.* अनुद्योग *m.* निरुद्योगिता *f.* उद्योगाभाव *m.* उद्योगराहित्य *n.*

4 पोकळपणा *m.* रिकामेपणा *m.* &c. निरर्थकता *f.*

IDLER, *n.* v. V. N. गमणारा, &c. गमदसडा *or* दासडा *or* दासरा, गम्या, रिकामटवळा, खेळगड्या.

Meeting place of idlers. रिकामचावडी *f.*

Troop or band of idlers. कतवार *n.*

IDLING, *n.* v. V. N.—*act.* गमणें *n.* जोगवणें *n.* &c. जोगवण *f.* जोगवणी *f.* जोगवणूक *f.* गमणूक *f.* गमटम *f.* रिकामचेष्टा *f.*

IDLY, *adv.* v. A. 1. आळसानें, आळसीपणानें, &c.

2 रिकामेपणानें &c. उद्योगावांचून, कामावांचून, रिकामा बसून.

4 *without a purpose or an object, merely, lightly.* उगा, उगीच, उगीचचे उगीच, एरवीं, सहज, सहजगतीनें, सहजगत्या, सहजरीतीनें, सहजरीत्या, साहजिक, स्वभावीक, तूष्णीम्.

IDOL, *n. image to be worshipped.* मूर्ति *f.* देव *m.* कृत्रिमदेव *m.* अर्चा *f.* तांदळा *m.*

Ablution (by distillation or streaming) of an i. अभिषेक *m.*—Vessel for effecting it. अभिषेकपात्र *n.* पंचधारें *n.*

Ablution-water of an i. नाह्वणी *n.* नाह्वण *n.*

Apartment (in a temple) of an i. देवखुली *f.* गाभारा *m.*

Articles for the *pújá* of an i. पूजा *pop.* पुजा *f.* बलि *m.*

Ashes of a substance burned before an i. अंगारा *m.*

Blessing or token of favor granted by an i. प्रसाद *m.*

Canopy over an i. मंडपी *or* मांडवी *f.* माळी *f.* छत्र *n.*

Cloth spread over an i. after worship. मुखवस्त्र *n.*

Cloth thrown over an i. मलवस्त्र *n.*

Constitution of an i. देवस्थापन *n.* देवस्थापना *f.* देवतावाहन *or* आवाहन *n.* देवप्रतिष्ठा *f.* चरप्रतिष्ठा *f.* प्रतिष्ठापन *n.* प्रतिष्ठा *f.* अधिवासन *n.*

Drip-pitcher over an i. गळती *f.*

Face (of silver, brass, &c.) for an i. मुखवटा *or* मुखोटा *m.*

Favorable response from an i. उजवी *f.*

Great and extraordinary worship of an i. महापूजा *f.*

Hymn, &c. sung by devotees before an i. पंचपदी *f.*

I. for processions. उत्साहमूर्त्ति *f.* भोगमूर्त्ति *f.* चरमूर्त्ति *f.*

Image of an i. impressed upon a plate. टांक *m.*

Lamp before an i. नंदादीप *m.*—For this there are numerous names, as there are numerous diversities in the composition of the wick. अकरें *n. or* रुद्रवात *f.* अनंतवात *or* विष्णुवात *f.* बेलवात *f.* बोटवात *f.* फुलवात *f.* माणिकवात *f.* काडवात *f.* शिवरात्रवात *f.*

Lamp-dish before an i. निरंजन *n.*

Litter for an i. (when carried in procession, &c.). डोल्हारा *m.* डोला *m.*

Metal cups arranged before an i. नक्षत्रमाला *f.*

Offerings to an i. नैवेद्य *n.* प्रसाद *m.* बोनें *n.*

Offerings of food to an i. after morning-worship. बाळभोग *m.*

Offerings to an i. and priests on or after pilgrimages, &c. देवब्राह्मण *m.*

Particulars and points of i.-worship. पूजोपचार *m.pl.*

There are sixteen (षोडशोपचार).

Periodical festival in honor of an i. जत्रा *f.* यात्रा *f.* झुडा *m.*—Pilgrims or multitude attending it. जत्रा *f.*

Petition or prayer to an i. गऱ्हाणें *n. v.* घाल, कर.

Plate at the back of an i. प्रभावळ *f.*

Procession of an i. देवयात्रा *f.*—around the town. नगरप्रदक्षिणा *f.* छबिना *or* शबिना *m.*

Purification of an i. अर्चाशुद्धि *f.* अर्चा *f.*

Purification of an image in order to constitute it an i. अर्चाशुद्धि *f.* अर्चा *f.*

Railing before an i. गातडी *f.*

Remains of an offering to an i. निर्माल्य *m. n.*

Rice, areca-nut, &c. stuck upon an i. when it is consulted. विणती *f.* कौल *m.* गुढ्या *f. pl.* प्रसाद *m.*

Smearing of an i. (with oil, red lead, &c.). माजण *n.* माखण *n.*

Stand for an i. देवपाट *m.*

String of cocoanuts, &c. around an i. तोरण *n.*

String of flowers, &c. around an i. फुलवरा *or* फुलोरा *m.*

Submersion of an i. जलाधिवासन *n.*

Thread thrown around an i. and thence taken and worn. पवित्र *n.* पोंवतें *n.*—Ceremony of throwing it &c. पवित्रारोपण *m.*

Tumultuous drumming before an i. देवघाई *f.*

Unfavorable response from an i. डावी *f.*

Vessel (of flowers &c.) presented in begging for an i. तळी *f.*

Vessels and articles used in i.-worship. उपकरणीं *n.pl.*

Visit to an i. देवदर्शन *n.* श्रीदर्शन *n.*

Vow to an i. मानणूक *f.* मानत *f.* मानता *f.* माननूक *f.* मानसिक *n.* जाप *m.*

Waving of incense (with lamps) around i. धुपारती *f.*

Woman prostituted to the service of an i. भावीण *f.* भक्तीण *f.* मुरळी *f.*

Worship of an i. देवपूजा *f.* पुजा *f.*

Worship of an i. by offering 100,000 (fruits, flowers, grains, &c.) लाखोली *f.* लक्षपूजा *f.*

To circumambulate an i. on one's right hand. उजवी *f.*-प्रदक्षिणा *f.* घालणें (देवास &c.),—on one's left hand. डावी *f.* घालणें (देवास &c.).

To decorate an i. with flowers. पुजा *f.* बांधणें.

To offer to an i. 1000 (leaves, &c.). सहस्र नाम *n.* वाहणें.

To prostitute herself to an i.—a woman. तेल *n.* घेणें.

To wave around an i. (a fan, brush, &c.). ढाळणें.

2 fig. v. DARLING. देव्हारें *n.* दैवत *n.* पुतळा *m.* कंठमणि *m.*

IDOLATER, *n.* मूर्त्तीची पूजा करणारा, मूर्त्तिपूजक, प्रतिमापूजक.

IDOLATRESS, *n.* मूर्त्तीचीपूजा करणारी *f.*

IDOLATROUS, *a pertaining, &c. to idolatry.* मूर्त्तिपूजेचा, मूर्त्तिपूजासंबंधी, मूर्त्तिसेवेचा, मूर्त्तिभक्तीचा.

2 *addicted to idolatry.* मूर्त्तिपूजा करणारा, मूर्त्तिपूजारत, मूर्त्तिपूजातत्पर, मूर्त्तिपूजापरायण.

3 *partaking of excessive attachment or reverence.* अतिभक्तीचा, अतिमानाचा, अतिप्रीतीचा.

IDOLATRY, *n. worship of idols.* मूर्त्तिपूजा *f.* मूर्त्तिपूजन *n.* मूर्त्तिसेवा *f.* मूर्त्तिभक्ति *f.* प्रतिमासेवा *f.* कृत्रिमदेवसेवा *f.* भक्ति *f.*

2 *excessive attachment or reverence.* अतिभक्ति *f.* अतिप्रीति *f.* अतिमान *m.*

To IDOLIZE, *v. a. love, &c. to excess.* देव्हारें *n.* करणें *g. of o.* अतिप्रीति *f.*-- अतिभक्ति *f.* करणें-ठेवणें, देव्हाऱ्यांतमांडणें-बसवणें.

IDONEOUS, *a.* v. FIT. योग्य, युक्त.

IDYL, *n.* पशुपालनादिविषयक क्षुद्रकाव्य *n.*

I. E. (id est) म्हणजे.

IF, *conj.* जर, जरका, जरकां, जरकरितां, जरकाय, जरीं, यदि.

Even if. जरीं, यद्यपि, यद्यपिचेत्.

If perhaps. कदाचित्, यदाकदाचित्.

IGNEOUS, *a. consisting, &c. of fire.* अग्नीचा, आग्नेय, अग्निमय, अग्निरूप, अग्निसदृश, अग्नितुल्य.

IGNIS FATUUS, *n.*—the meteor. भुतकोलीत *n.* पिशाचदीपिका *f.*

To IGNITE, IGNITION, &c. See To KINDLE, &c.

IGNOBLE, *a. of low birth.* हीनकुळीचा, गल्लीकुचीचा, कमअस्सल, कमजात, अकुलीन, हीनकुल, दौष्कुलेय, हीनजात, दुष्कुलीन, दुर्योनि, प्राकृत.

2 *not honorable, not worthy,* v. MEAN. नीच, हलका, पाजी, अधम, पामर.

IGNOBLENESS, *n.* v. A. 1. कमजातपणा *m.* &c. अकुलीनता *f.* हीनकुळी *f.* कमजात *f.* हीनजातिता *f.*

2 पाजीपणा *m.* &c. पामरता *f.*

IGNOBLY, *adv.* v. A. 2. पाजीपणानें, दौर्जन्यानें, पामरवृत्तीनें.

IGNOMINIOUS, *a. shameful, disreputable, &c.* v. DISGRACEFUL. लाजिरवाणा, अपयशस्कर, यशोहर-&c. अपयशाचा.

IGNOMINY, *n.* v. DISGRACE. अपयश *n.* अपमान *m.* अप्रतिष्ठा *f.* अपकीर्त्ति *f.*

IGNORAMUS, *n. an ignorant person.* निरक्षर, अनक्षर, अक्षरशत्रु, शंख, शंख्या, शंखोबा, शंखध्मा, नरपशु, शेतखप्या, पंडितंमन्य, पंडितमानी, शुद्धस्फटिक, शुद्धबुद्ध.

Sturdy or rude i. टोणपा, टोणा, ठोंब *or* ठोंबा, गलेलठ्ठ, लठ्ठनिरंजन, लठ्ठभारती, लठ्ठमिश्र, लठ्ठेश्वर, लठ्ठाश्रम *or* लोठाश्रम.

IGNORANCE, *n. want of knowledge.* अज्ञान *n.* नादानी *f.* नादानकी *f.* नेणतेपणा *m.* नेणतपण *n.* गैरमाहिती *f.* अविद्या *f.* अज्ञानिता *f.* अज्ञानता *f.* मौढ्य *n.* मौर्ख्य *n.* ज्ञानाभाव *m.* ज्ञानराहित्य *n.* ज्ञानशून्यता *f.*

Gross i. गाढ अज्ञान *n.* घनाज्ञान *n.*

Spiritual i. अज्ञान *n.* अविद्या *f.* मोह *n.* अहम्मति *f.*

IGNORANT, *a. destitute of knowledge, uninstructed, illiterate, &c.* अज्ञान, मूढ, अज्ञानी, अज्ञानात्मक, नेणता, अकळता, अजाण, अजाणता, अनक्षर, अक्षरशून्य, अविद्वान, अविद्य, हीनज्ञान, ज्ञानहीन-शून्य-&c. विद्याहीन-शून्य-&c. मूर्ख, अज्ञ, अविज्ञ, तामस, तमस्वी. [ज्ञ.

2 *unacquainted with.* गैरमाहीत, गैरमाहितगार, अजाण, अनभि-

IGNORANTLY, *adv.* v. A. अज्ञानानें, नादानीनें, गैरमाहितीनें, &c. अज्ञानपूर्वक.

To IGNORE, *v. a. be ignorant of.* नेणणें.

2 *pretend not to know or see.* ठाऊक नाहीं असें दाखवणें.

3 (a bill of indictment) साक्षीपुरावा पुरा नसल्यामुळें रद्द करणें.

IGUANA, *n.* घोरपड *f.* नक्र *m.* गोधा *f.*

ILIAC, *a. pertaining to the lower bowels.* खालच्या आंतडीचा.
I. passion. उदावर्त्त *m.*
That has the i.passion. उफराट्या आंतडीचा, उदावर्त्तरोगी.

ILL, *a.* See EVIL. 2 *sick, unwell.* दुखणेकरी, दुखणाईत, दुखणारू, आजारी, बीमार, काहिला, अस्वस्थ, असमाधानी.
To be i. निजणें, पडणें, निजून असणें, पडून असणें, अंथरूण *n.* धरणें.

ILL, *n.* See EVIL.

ILL, *adv. not well, not rightly,*—gener. वाईट, खराब.
2 *not easily, with pain, &c.* रुछेंकरून, जुलमानें, जुलमावर.

ILL-ACCORDING, ILL-AGREEING, *a.* विलग, विजोड.

ILL-ADVISED, *a.* कुमंत्रित, कूपदिष्ट.

ILL-ARRANGED, *a.* दुष्क्रम, दुष्क्रमाचा, अव्यवस्थित, अव्यवस्थेचा.

ILL-BEHAVED, *a.* v. MISBEHAVED. बेचालीचा, बदचालीचा, &c. अशिष्ट, गैरशिस्त, अशील, दुःशील, दुर्वृत्त, दुर्णीत, दुर्विनीत.

ILL-BEHAVIOR, *n.* v. MISCONDUCT. बेचाल *f.* बदचाल *f.* गैरवर्त्तणूक *f.* दुराचरण *n.* दुराचार *m.*

ILL-BEING, *n.* अकल्याण *n.* अश्रेय *n.* अहित *n.* अकुशल *n.*

ILL-BETOKENING, ILL-BODING, ILL-OMENED, &c. *a.* कुलक्षणी, कुलक्षण, दुर्लक्षणी, अभद्र, अमंगल.

ILL-BLOOD, *n.* v. ENMITY. द्वेष *m.* द्वेषभाव *m.*

ILL-BRED, *a.* अशिष्ट, असभ्य, दुर्वृत्त, अविनय.

ILL-BREEDING, *n.* अशिष्टता *f.* असभ्यता *f.*

ILL-DISPOSED, *a.* v. ADVERSE. वांकडा, वांकड्या मनाचा, विमना, विमनस्क, विमत.

ILL-FAVORED, ILL-FEATURED, *a. ugly, &c.*अवलक्षणी, दुलक्षणी, कुलक्षण, कुलक्षणी, मुद्राहीन, खुरट्या तोंडाचा, विरूप, विद्रूप.

ILL-FLAVORED, *a.* विस्वाद, कुस्वाद.

ILL-FORMED, *a.* बेडौल, कदाकार, विरुताकार, विरुताकृति.

ILL-FORTUNE, ILL-LUCK, *n.* दुर्दैव *n.* दुर्भाग्य *n.* निर्दैव *n.*अरिष्ट *n.* अवदसा *f.* ब्रह्मकपाट *n.*

ILL-LOOKING, *a.* v. UGLY. कुरूप, विरूप.

ILL-MATCHED, ILL-PAIRED, &c. *a.* विजोड, विलग.

ILL-NATURE, *n.* दुष्प्रवृत्ति *f.* असद्वृत्ति *f.* दुःस्वभाव *m.*

ILL-NATURED, *a.* दुःशील, दुःस्वभाव, कर्कश.

ILL-REGULATED, *a.* अव्यवस्थित, अशिष्ट.

ILL-SMELLING, *a.* दुर्गंध, दुर्गंधी.

ILL-SPOKEN, *a.* वाग्दुष्ट, दुर्भाषी, तोंडाचा फटकळ.

ILL-STARRED, *a.* v. WRETCH. भद्र्या *or* ज्याच्या कपाळीं भद्रा *m.* *or* भद्र्या कपाळाचा.

ILL-TEMPER, *n.* दुष्टस्वभाव *m.* दुष्प्रवृत्ति *f.* असद्वृत्ति *f.*

ILL-TEMPERED, *a.* दुष्टस्वभावाचा, कुशील, दुष्प्रवृत्ति, असद्वृत्ति.

ILL-TONED, *a.* बदस्वराचा, बदसुऱ्या, अपसुऱ्या, अपस्वर, बदसूर.

ILL-TRAINED, ILL-TAUGHT, &c. *a.* दुर्विनीत, दुर्णीत, अशिष्ट.

ILL-WILL, *n.* v. ENMITY, MALICE. दुष्टावा *m.* दुष्टाई *f.* दुष्टाइकी *f.* दुष्टभाव *m.*

ILL-WISHER, *n.* अनिष्टचिंतक, अकल्याणचिंतक, हितशत्रु.

ILLAUDABLE, *a. not worthy of praise.* अश्लाघ्य, अश्लाघनीय, अप्रशंसनीय, अप्रशंस्य, अस्तुत्य.

ILLEGAL, *a. contrary to law.* कायद्याबाहेरचा, गैरकायद्याचा, राजनियमविरुद्ध, विधिविरुद्ध, स्मृतिविरुद्ध, अस्मार्त्त, अशास्त्र, राजनिषिद्ध.

ILLEGALITY, *n.* v. A. राजनियमविरोध *m.* विधिविरोध *m.* स्मृतिविरोध *m.* अशास्त्रता *f.*

ILLEGALLY, *adv.* v. A. गैरकायद्यानें, कायदा मोडून-सोडून, विधिविरोधपूर्वक.

ILLEGIBLE, *a. that cannot be read.* वाचायास अवघड-कठीण-&c. गिचमीड, अपठनीय, दुष्पठनीय, पठनाशक्य.

ILLEGIBILITY, *n.* v. A. अपठनीयता *f.* दुष्पठनीयता *f.*

ILLEGITIMACY, *n.* v. A. *and* BASTARD. अनौरसता *f.* जारजता *f.* जारजावस्था *f.* अविधिजन्म *n.* विजन्म *n.* विजन्मता *f.*

ILLEGITIMATE, *a.* v. BASTARD. अनौरस, जारज, व्यभिचारज, अधर्मजात, अपत्नी जात-भव-&c. अदंपत्युत्पन्न, अदंपतीजात, अदंपत्युद्भव, अविधिजात, अशास्त्रजात, अन्योत्पन्न.—in cant phraseol. अकरमाशा.
2 See UNLAWFUL. 3 See ILLOGICAL.

ILLIBERAL, *a. not munificent, &c.* v. MISERLY. अदाता, अनुदार, अवदान्य, अदानशील, अदत्त. [क्षुद्रमनस्क.
2 *not generous, noble, &c.* अप्रशस्त, अप्रशस्तमनाचा, अनुदार,

ILLIBERALITY, *n.* v. A. 1. अदातृत्व *n.* अवदान्यता *f.* अनुदारता *f.*
2 अप्राशस्त्य *n.* अनुदारता *f.* औदार्याभाव *m.*

ILLICIT. See UNLAWFUL. [अप्रमेय.

ILLIMITABLE, *a. boundless,* v. INFINITE. अपरंपार, निस्सीम,

ILLITERACY, ILLITERATENESS, *n.* v. A. अविद्या *f.* अविद्वत्ता *f.* अविद्यता *f.* अनधीतत्व *n.*

ILLITERATE, *a. unlettered, unlearned.* निरक्षर, अनक्षर, अक्षरशून्य, अनधीत, अविद्य, अविद्वान्, अपंडित, विद्याहीन, विद्याशून्य, ढ.
An i. person, v. IGNORAMUS. अक्षरशत्रु, नरपशु.

ILLNESS, *n.* v. DISORDER. दुखणें *n.* रोग *m.* आजार *m.*

ILLOGICAL, *a. contrary to the rules of reasoning.* प्रमाणासिद्ध, अन्यायी, अयुक्तिक, युक्त्यसिद्ध, युक्तिविरुद्ध. [कैकत्व *n.*

ILLOGICALNESS, *n.* v. A. युक्तिविरुद्धता *f.* युक्तिविरोध *m.* अयु-

To ILLUDE, *v. a.* v. To DECEIVE, फसवणें.

To ILLUMINATE, *To* ILLUMINE, *v. a.* v. To ENLIGHTEN. प्रकाशणें, प्रकाश *m.* पाडणें-करणें, प्रकाशन *n.* द्योतन *n.* करणें *g. of o.* उजळणें, प्रकाशित करणें.
2 (with festal lamps, &c.). रोशनाई *f.* करणें, चिरागदान *n.* लावणें-करणें.
3 (paper, &c.). पत्ररंजन *n.* करणें.

ILLUMINATION, *n.* v. V. 1. प्रकाशणें *n.* प्रकाशन *n.* द्योतन *n.*
I. *an* i. *a display of festal lights.* रोशनाई *f.* लक्षदीप *m.* *pl.* चमचमाट *m.* दीपावलि *f.* दीपोत्सव *m.*

ILLUMINATOR, *n.* v. V. 1. प्रकाशणारा, प्रकाशनकारी-कर्त्ता-&c. कांतिकर, तेजस्कर.

ILLUSION, *n.* v. DECEIT. प्रपंच *m.* मोह *m.* [अविद्या *f.*
2—philosophical, *idealism.* माया *f.* योगमाया *f.* अज्ञा *f.*

ILLUSIVE, ILLUSORY, *a.* v. DECEITFUL. मावेचा, मायेचा, मोहाचा, मावीक, मायावी, मायावान् *or* मायावंत, मायिक, मायारूप, मायामय, मोही, अतात्त्विक, ऐंद्रजालिक *pop.* इंद्रजालिक, स्वप्नवत्.
The material world considered as i. मायाचक्र *n.*

ILLUSTRABLE, *a.* v. V. 1. प्रकाश करायाजोगा-&c. प्रकाश्य, प्रकाशनीय, प्रकाशितव्य, द्योत्य. [त्सायोग्य.
2 दाखला द्याया जोगा-&c. उपमेय, उत्प्रेक्षणीय, उत्प्रेक्ष्य, उत्प्रे-

To ILLUSTRATE, *v. a. elucidate,* v. To EXPLAIN. प्रकाश *m.*-

&c. करणें *g. of o.* प्रकाशणें, द्योतवणें.

2 (by a simile). दाखला *m.*-दृष्टांत *m.*-उदाहरण *n.*-&c. देणें-देऊन स्पष्ट करणें, उत्प्रेक्षणें, उत्प्रेक्षा *f.* घेणें.

3 चित्रें *n. pl.*-&c.देणें-देऊन स्पष्ट करणें.

ILLUSTRATED, *p.* v. V. 1. प्रकाशलेला, प्रकाशित, द्योतित.

2 दाखला दिल्हेला, &c. उपमित, उत्प्रेक्षित, उदाहृत, दार्ष्टांतिक.

3 चित्रें दिल्हेला, &c.

ILLUSTRATER, *n.*ILLUSTRATING, *p.a.* ILLUSTRATIVE, *a.*v.V.1. प्रकाशणारा, प्रकाशक, प्रकाशनकर्त्ता-कारक, द्योतक, स्पष्टीकरणोपयुक्त.

ILLUSTRATION, *n.* v. V. 1.—*act.* प्रकाशणें*n.* प्रकाशन*n.* प्रकाश*m.* द्योतन *n.* स्पष्टीकरण *n.*

2 दाखला देणें *n.* उत्प्रेक्षण *n.*

3 चित्रें देणें *n.*

I. *simile, &c.* दाखला *m.* दृष्टांत *m.* उपमा *f.* उत्प्रेक्षा *f.* उदाहरण *n.* उपमान *n.*

Subject of an i. उपमेय *n.* उपमेयभूत अर्थ *m.* बिंब *n.*

II. *picture,* चित्र *n.*

ILLUSTRIOUS, *a. conspicuous. eminent, &c.* v. GREAT. तेजवान्, तेजवंत, तेजस्वी, तेजाळ, उमदा, यशस्वी, तेजोमय, तेजश्शाली, नामदार, नामजाद, श्रीमान्, श्रीमंत, प्रतिष्ठित, प्रसिद्ध, प्रसिद्धीचा, नांव लौकिकाचा.

IMAGE, *n.*v. STATUE, PICTURE, FIGURE. पुतळा *m. dim.* पुतळी*f.* बाहुला *m. or* ली *f. or* लें *n.* मूर्त्ति *f.* बिंब *n.*

2 v. IDOL. मूर्त्ति *f.*

3 *likeness.* बिंब *n.* प्रतिमा *f.* प्रतिरूप *n.* प्रतिकाय*m.* प्रतिकृति*f.*

Reflected i. प्रतिबिंब *n.*

IMAGERY, *n. forms of fancy.* मानससृष्टि *f.* कल्पनासृष्टि *f.*

2 *lively description.* मूर्त्ति पुढें उभी राहण्याजोगें वर्णन *n.*

IMAGEWORSHIP. See IDOLATRY.

IMAGINABLE, *a.*v. V. कल्पना करायास योग्य-&c. कल्पनीय, कल्प्य, कल्पितव्य, भावनीय, विभावनीय.

IMAGINARY, *a. ideal, fancied, visionary, not real.* मनःकल्पित, मानसिक, कल्पनेचा, कल्पित, काल्पनिक, कल्पनासिद्ध, कल्पनारूप, कल्पनाकृत, बौद्ध, अतात्त्विक,अवास्तविक.

IMAGINATION, *n.*—the faculty, v. FANCY. कल्पनाशक्ति *f.* कल्पना *f.*

2 *mental image, idea.* कल्पना *f.* भावना *f.* आकार *m.*

Evil i. *wicked thought.* कुकल्पना *f.* कुतर्क *m.* कुसृष्टि *f.*

3 *device,* v. CONTRIVANCE. कल्पना *f.* युक्ति *pop.* जुगूत *f.*

IMAGINATIVE, *a.* v. V. कल्पक, कल्पनाबाज, कल्पनाचतुर, कल्पनाकुशल, कल्पनापटु, भावनापर.

To IMAGINE, *v. a. form mentally, fancy.* कल्पिणें, कल्पना *f.*-भावना *f.* करणें *g. of o.* मनांत आणणें-धरणें.

2 See To CONTRIVE.

To IMAGINE *v. n.* See To THINK.

IMBECILE, *a. impotent, weak, &c.* v. WEAK. नाकर्त्ता, अकर्त्ता, नबळा, बावर, दुर्बल *or* ळ, अक्षम, हीनशक्तिक.

IMBECILITY, *n.*v.A. नबळेपणा*m.* दुर्बळपणा *m.*&c. अतेज*n.* तारें*n.* दौर्बल्य*n.* अक्षमता *f.*

To IMBIBE, *v. a. drink in.* पिणें, शोषणें, पिऊन-शोषून घेणें, शोषण*n.* करणें *g. of o.*

2 (into the mind). जडणें *in. con.* घेणें, स्वीकारणें, स्वीकारून घेणें, ग्रहण*n.* करणें.

To IMBITTER, IMBOLDEN, &c. See To EMBITTER, &c.

To IMBRUE, *v. a. steep.* भिजवणें, भरवणें, लिप्तकरणें.

To IMBUE, *v. a. tincture,* fig. व्याप्त-युक्त-विशिष्ट-गुणमय-&c.करणें.

IMITABILITY, *n.* v. A. अनुकरणीयता *f.* अनुसरणीयता *f.*

IMITABLE, *a.* v. V. 1. उतराया-चा-जोगा-सारखा-&c. अनुसरणीय, अनुकरणीय, अनुकार्य, अनुगम्य, अनुगमनीय.

To IMITATE, *v. a. copy, &c.* उतरणें, नकल *f.*-उतारा *m.* करणें *g. of o.* मखी *f.* उतरणें *g. of o.* ठाकी *or* थाकी *f.*-टाप *f.*-&c. उतरणें-साधणें-आणणें *g. of o.* कित्ता *m.*-वळण *n.* घेणें *g. of o.* वळणावर जाणें *g. of o.* चाल *f.* धरणें *g. of o.* अनुसरणें, धरणें, घेणें, अनुसरण *n.*-अनुकरण *n.*-&c. करणें *g. of o.*

To i. servilely. कपाळासीकपाळ *n.* घासणें.

2 See To COUNTERFEIT. 3 *mimic, ape, take off, &c.* नकल *f.* करणें-उतरणें *g. of o.* ठेव *f.*-ठेवण *f.*- धाटी *f.*-धाटणी *f.*-टीप *f.*-टाकी *f.*-थाकी *f.*-&c. उतरणें-साधणें-आणणें *g. of o.* विडंबन *n.* करणें *g. of o.*

IMITATED, *p.* v. V. 1. उतरलेला, &c. अनुकृत, अनुसृत.

IMITATION, *n.* v. V. 1.—*act.* उतरणें *n.* &c. अनुसरण *n.* अनुगम *m.* अनुगमन *n.* अनुलक्ष्य *n.* अनुकरण *n.* अनुकार *m.* अनुवृत्ति *f.* अनुवर्त्तन *n.* अनुकृति *f.* देखोदेखी *f.* देखोवेखी *f.*

Made in i. of. नकली.

I. *imitating thing, copy.* नकल *f.* उतारा *m.* अनुसृष्टि *f.*

II. *loose translation, &c.* छायानुहरण.

IMITATIVE, *a.* v. V. 1. *disposed to copy.* उतरणारा, नकल करणारा, नकल्या, अनुकारी, अनुसारी, अनुगामी, अनुवर्त्ती, अनुकरण-&c. कर्त्ता-कारी, अनुकरणशील, अनुकरणस्वभाव, गतानुगतिक, संप्रेक्ष्यकारी.

Men are i. गतानुगतिकोलोकः.

I.—in gram. I. sound or word. अनुकरण *n.*अनुकरणशब्द *m.*

I. verb. अनुकरण धातु *m.*

IMITATOR, *n.* v. V. 1. उतरणारा, नकल करणारा, &c. अनुकारी, अनुसारी, अनुवर्त्ती, अनुकरणकारी, अनुकरणकर्त्ता, &c.

IMMACULATE, *a.*v. PURE.पवित्र, निष्कलंक,निर्दोष, निर्मळ,परिशुद्ध.

IMMACULATENESS, *n.* v. A. पवित्रता *f.* निर्दोषता *f.* &c.

IMMANENT. See INHERENT.

IMMATERIAL, *a. distinct from matter.* अमूर्त्त, अमूर्त्तिमान्, अशरीरी, अदेही, अपांचभौतिक, अप्राकृत, अप्रकृतिविकार, निराकार, अमात्रवत्.

An i. entity. अजडांश *m.*

2 v.UNIMPORTANT. हलका, अनाग्रहाचा, अनिर्भराचा, औदासीन्याचा, लघु, अमुख्य, अप्रधान, साधारण.

IMMATERIALISM, *n. doctrine of the existence of immaterial substances.* देहभिन्नात्मवाद *m.* देहभिन्नात्ममत *n.* आत्मास्तित्ववाद *m.* आत्मास्तित्वमत *n.*

IMMATERIALIST, *n. professor of immaterialism.* आत्मास्तित्ववादी, आत्मास्तिक, देहभिन्नात्मवादी.

IMMATERIALITY, *n.* v. A. 1. अपांचभौतिकता *f.* अमूर्त्ति *f.* अप्राकृतत्व *n.* निराकारता *f.* अमात्रवत्त्व *n.*

IMMATURE, *a.* v. RAW. कचा, कोवळा, अपक्व.

2 (of understanding, &c.). अप्रौढ, अप्रबुद्ध, अप्रगल्भ, अधुरा, बालिश.

3 See PREMATURE.

IMMATURELY. See PREMATURELY.

IMMATURITY, *n.* v. A. 1. कच्चेपणा *m.* कोवळेपणा *m.*&c. कोवळीक *f.* अपक्वता *f.* अपक्वदशा *f.*

2 अप्रौढी *f.* अप्रौढता *f.*

IMMEASURABLE, *a. immense,* v. INFINITE. अमोज, अप्रमेय, अपरिमेय, अमेय, दुष्प्रमेय.

IMMEASURABLENESS, *n.* v. A. अप्रमेयता *f.* &c.

IMMEDIATE, *a. not mediate; proximate, &c.* प्रत्यक्षकारी, साक्षात्कारी, जातीनिशींचा, साक्षात्संबंधाचा, साक्षात्संबंधी, परंपरासंबंधरहित-शून्य-&c.

2 *instant, present.* तेव्हांचा, एव्हांचा, तत्कालचा, अव्यवहितकालिक, तत्क्षणिक, तात्कालिक.

IMMEDIATELY, *adv.* v. A. 1. प्रत्यक्ष, साक्षात्, परंपरासंबंधावांचून, जातिनिशीं, खासगत.

2 लागलाच, तेव्हांच, एव्हांच, तत्क्षणीं, तत्काल, असाच, तसाच, अविलंब, उशीर नलावितां, हातच्या हातीं, अविलंबतः.

IMMEDIATENESS, *n.* v. A. 1. साक्षात्संबंधिता *f.* परंपरासंबंधाभाव *m.* परंपरासंबंधराहित्य *n.* सांतरसंबंधाभाव *m.*

2 तात्कालिकता *f.* तत्क्षणिकत्व *n.* व्यवहितकालाभाव *m.*

IMMEMORIAL, *a. beyond memory.* स्मार्त्तकालातीत, स्मृतिकालातीत, अस्मार्त्तकालिक, अस्मार्त्तकालीन, अस्मार्त्त, अतिप्राचीन.

IMMENSE, *a. unlimited,* v. INFINITE. निस्सीम, अमर्याद, अपरिमेय, अपरिमित, अवारपार. [अवजड.

2 *vast, huge,* v. GREAT. ऐवट, अवाढव्य, अफाट, गरिष्ठ, उद्भट,

IMMENSELY, *adv. vastly, &c.* v. VERY. फारच, अतिशय, अत्यंत.

IMMENSENESS, IMMENSITY, *n.* v. A. 1. निस्सीमता *f.* अपरिमेयत्व *n.*

2 ऐवटपणा *m.* अवाढव्यपणा *m.*

I. *infinite space.* महाकाश *m.*

Filling of i. त्रैलोक्यविस्तार *m.*

That filleth i. त्रैलोक्यव्यापक-व्यापी.

IMMENSURABLE. See IMMEASUREABLE.

To IMMERGE, *To* IMMERSE, *v. a. plunge.* बुडवणें, मज्जन *n.* निमज्जन *n.* करणें *g. of o.* मग्न-निमग्न-मज्जित करणें.

2 *engage deeply,* v. To ABSORB. गुंग-गरक-निमग्न-&c. करणें.

IMMERGED, IMMERSED, *p.* v. V. 1. बुडवलेला, मग्न, निमग्न, मज्जित, अवगाढ, अवगाहित.

2 गुंग, गरक, निमग्न, मग्न, तल्लीन, आप्लुत (esp. in comp. and in figur. uses; as I. in grief. शोकाप्लुत *and* आनंदाप्लुत, स्नेहाप्लुत, ममताप्लुत, खेदाप्लुत, &c.).

I.—a heavenly body. मूढ. [मज्जन *n.*

IMMERSION, *n.* v. V. 1.—*act.* बुडवणें *n.* अवगाहन *n.* निमज्जन *n.*

2—*state.* गुंगपणा *m.* &c. गुंगी *f.* निमग्नता *f.* तल्लीनता *f.* लय *m.n.*

I. (of a planet). अस्त *m. n.* मौढ्य *n.*

Eastern i. पूर्वास्त *m. n.*

Western i. पश्चिमास्त *m.n.*

IMMETHODICAL, *a. that is without method,* v. DISORDERLY. अव्यवस्थित, दुष्क्रम, अक्रमिक, निरन्वय, ढावखुरा.

IMMETHODICALLY, *adv.* v. A. क्रमावांचून, क्रम सोडून, &c. अव्यवस्थेनें.

IMMETHODICALNESS, *n.* v. A. अव्यवस्था *f.* गोंधळ *m.* उत्क्रम *m.* क्रमाभाव *m.* दुष्क्रमता *f.*

IMMINENT, *a. impending, threatening.* खेटलेला, नेटलेला, नेटून आलेला, नेट बाजीचा, आसन्नोपस्थित.

IMMISCIBILITY, *n.* v. A. अमिश्रणीयता *f.* &c. मिश्रणाक्षमता *f.*

IMMISCIBLE, IMMIXABLE, *a. not capable of being mixed.* अमिश्रणीय, अमेलनीय, अमेल.

IMMITIGABLE, *a.* अप्रशमनीय, अप्रशाम्य.

IMMOBILITY, *n. unmovableness, fixedness.* अचालनीयत्व *n.* स्थावरत्व *n.* अचलता *f.* स्थावरभाव *m.* अचलभाव *m.* स्थावरधर्म *m.*

IMMODERATE, *a.* v. EXCESSIVE. अतिमर्याद, अमर्याद, उन्मर्याद, मर्यादातीत, अपरिमित, अमित, अतिशयित.

IMMODERATELY, *adv.* v. A. अमर्याद, अति, अतिशय, पराकाष्ठेचा, बेसुमार.

IMMODERATENESS, IMMODERATION, *n.* v. A. *and* EXCESS. अतिशय *m.* पराकाष्ठा *f.* अपरिमितत्व *n.*

IMMODEST, *a. wanting in decency, delicacy, &c.* निलाजरा, निर्लज्ज, बेशरम, बेहया, लज्जाहीन-शून्य-&c. त्रपाहीन, विलज्ज, अत्रप, अपत्रप, त्यक्तलज्ज, त्यक्तत्रप, लज्जातीत.

2 *exorbitant,* v. IMMODERATE. अमर्याद, अतिमर्याद.

IMMODESTLY, *adv.* v. A. 1. लाज टाकून-सोडून-&c. निलाजरेपणानें, लज्जेवांचून, &c.

IMMODESTY, *n.* v. A. 1. निलाजरेपणा *m.* निर्लज्जता *f.* अपलज्जा *f.* लज्जाभाव *m.* लज्जाराहित्य *n.* लज्जाहीनता *f.* अत्रपत्व *n.*

To IMMOLATE, *v. a.* v. To SACRIFICE. बलि *m.* करणें *g. of o.* बलिदान *n.* करणें *g. of o.*

IMMOLATION, *n.* v. V. बलि करणें *n.* बलिदान *n.*

IMMORAL, *a.*—of persons, v. WICKED. अनीतीचा, दुराचारी, असदाचारी, अनाचारी, दुर्वृत्त, दुष्कर्मी, अन्यायवर्त्ती, अधर्मचारी, अनय, असाधु, धर्मघ्न, कर्मदुष्ट, दुश्चरित्र.

2—of acts. अनीतीचा, अन्यायाचा, दुराचाराचा, अनाचाराचा, &c. धर्मविरुद्ध, नयातीत, असत्, असाधु.

IMMORALITY, v. A. 1. दुष्कर्मीपणा *m.* दुराचारिता *f.* अनाचारिता *f.* &c. असाधुता *f.*

2 अन्यायपणा *m.* असाधुता *f.* अनीतिता *f.* अन्यायता *f.*

I. *immoral act or practice.* अधर्म *m.* अनीति *f.* अनाचार *m.* असदाचार *m.* अन्यायवर्त्तन *n.* अन्यायवृत्ति *f.* अनय *m.* दुर्वृत्ति *f.*

IMMORTAL, *a. exempt from death.* अमर, अमृत, अमरणीय, अमर्त्य, अजरामर, निर्जर, जरातीत, मरणातीत.

2 See IMPERISHABLE.

IMMORTALITY, *n.* v. A. अमृत *n.* अमरता *f.* अमरत्व *n.* अमृतता *f.* अमरणीयत्व *n.* अमृत्यु *m.* मरणाभाव *m.*

Writ of i. *grant of exemption from death.* अमरपटा *or* पट्टा *m.* अमरपत्र *n.*

To IMMORTALIZE, *v. a. make immortal.* अमर-मरणातीत-जरातीत-&c. करणें. [*g. of o.*

2 *exempt from oblivion.* नाम *n.*-कीर्ति *f.*-&c. शाश्वत करणें

IMMOVABILITY, IMMOVABLENESS, *n.* v. A. अढळपणा *m.* अचलता *f.* निश्चलता *f.* &c.

IMMOVABLE, *a.* अढळ, अचर, अचल, निश्चल, स्थावर.

IMMOVABLE, *n.* स्थावर *n.* स्थावरमाल *m.* [माफी *f.*

IMMUNITY, *n. exemption.* सोड *f.* सोडवणूक *f.* सूट *f.* मोकळीक *f.*

To IMMURE, *v. a.* v. To IMPRISON. कोंडून घालणें-ठेवणें, कोंडीत-&c. घालणें.

2 *enclose alive and build in.* चिणणें, चिणून टाकणें.

IMMUTABILITY, *n.* v. A. निर्विकारता *f.* अविकारता *f.* अविकार्यता *f.* विकाराक्षमता *f.* अविकार *m.*

IMMUTABLE, *a. invariable, unchangeable.* निर्विकार, फेरफाराबेगळा, फेरफारानिराळा, निर्विकल्प, अविकार, अविकार्य, विकारातीत, अविक्रिय, कूटस्थ, नित्यसम.

IMMUTABLY, *adv.* v. A. न ढळेसा *decl.* न फिरेसा *decl.* फेरफार न होईसा *decl.*

IMP. See DEVIL, BRAT.

IMPACABLE, &c. See IMPLACABLE, &c.

IMPACT. See TOUCH.

To IMPAIR, *v. a.* v. To HURT, To LESSEN. हानि *f.*-खराबी *f.*-नुकसानी *f.*-&c. करणें *g. of o.* खराब करणें.

IMPAIRED, *p.* v. V. उपहत, विगलित, विकल, शिथिलीकृत, जायबंदा *or* जायबंदी, लंगडा.

To IMPALE, *v. a. fix on a stake.* सुळीं देणें, सुळावर देणें-चढवणें-घालणें, शूलारोपण *n.* करणें *g. of o.*

Impaling stake. शूल *pop.* सूळ *m.*

Worthy to be impaled. शूल्य.

IMPALEMENT, IMPALING, *n.* v. V. सुळींदेणें *n.* &c. शूलारोपण*n.*

IMPALPABILITY, *n.* v. A. अस्पृश्यता *f.* दुःस्पर्शता *f.*

IMPALPABLE, *a. not perceptible to the touch.* अस्पृश्य, अस्पर्शनीय, दुःस्पर्श, स्पर्शाशक्य, त्वगिंद्रियातीत, त्वगिंद्रियागोचर, स्पर्शाज्ञेय, अतिसूक्ष्म.

To IMPANNEL, *v. a.* (a jury) जुरीच्या असाम्यांचीं नांवें *n. pl.* पटावर मांडणें-लिहणें.

IMPARITY. See INEQUALITY.

To IMPART, *v. a. communicate, &c.* देणें, दान *n.*-प्रदान *n.*-उपधान *n.*- &c. करणें *g. of o.*

2 *tell, make known.* कळवणें, जाणवणें, विदित करणें.

IMPARTIAL, *a. not partial, not biassed.* निष्पक्षपात, निष्पक्षपाती, निष्पक्षपाताचा, उभयपक्षीं समान, उभयसाधारण, उभयसामान्य, उदासीन, पक्षपातरहित-शून्य, समदृष्टि, समदर्शी, सुमानवृत्ति, निस्पृह *pop.* निस्पृही.

IMPARTIALITY, *n.* v. A. निष्पक्षपात *m.* समान-सम-अपामरसाधारण-&c. वृत्ति *f.*-वर्त्तन *n.*-लक्ष्य *n.*-दृष्टि *f.*-बुद्धि *f.*-मन *n.*-भाव *m.*-&c. अपक्षपात *m.* पक्षपातराहित्य *n.* &c. उभारतपणा *m.* औदासीन्य *n.* [दृष्टीनें, &c.

IMPARTIALLY, *adv.* v. A. पक्षपात सोडून, पक्षपातावांचून, समान-

IMPASSABLE, *a. not admitting passage.* जाण्यास फार कठीण-अवघड-&c. दुर्लंघ्य, अलंघनीय, अलंघ्य, अगम्य, दुर्गम, दुस्तर, सुदुस्तर, दुरुत्तर. [र्य *n.*

IMPASSABLENESS, *n.* v. A. दुर्लंघ्यता *f.* अगम्यता *f.* &c. दौस्त-

IMPASSIBILITY, IMPASSIVENESS, *n.* v. A. दुःखायोग्यता *f.* दुःखासंग *m.* दुःखासंगिता *f.*

IMPASSIBLE, IMPASSIVE, *a. not susceptible of pain or suffering.* दुःखाबेगळा-निराळा, दुःखातीत, वेदनातीत, अदुःखज्ञ, दुःखासंगी, दुःखास्पृश्य, दुःखास्पृष्ट, नित्यमुक्त, दुःखायोग्य.

IMPASSIONATE, IMPASSIONED, *a. strongly affected, excited, &c.* रागी, रागवान्, रागान्वित, अनुरागी, सानुराग.

IMPATIENCE, *n.* v. A. 1. असोशिकपणा *m.* अधैर्य *n.* असहन *n.* असहनता *f.* असहिष्णुता *f.* धैर्यहीनता *f.* अक्षमा *f.* अक्षांति *f.*

2 उतावळी *f.* खुरखुर *f.* हुटहूट *or* हुटहुटी *f.* उत्कळ *f.* उताट *f.* खवखव *f.* वळका *n.* उत्कंठा *f.* औत्सुक्य *n.* अमर्ष *m.* विलंबासहन *n.*

IMPATIENT, *a. not enduring.* असोशीक, अधीर, अधर, अधिऱ्या, हीनधैर्य, धैर्यहीन, असहिष्णु, असहन, असह, असहनशील, असहमान, अक्षम.

2 *hasty, eager, not enduring delay.* उतावळा, हवळा, हवळ्या, हुटहुट्या, हुडहुड्या, अधिऱ्या, उत्कंठित, हुटहुटलेला, उत्सुक, सोत्कंठ, अमर्षी, अकालसह, विलंबासह.

To be i. after. नितांतणें *or* नितांदणें.

IMPATIENTLY, *adv.* v. A. 1. असोशिकपणानें, &c. अधैर्यपूर्वक, अक्षांतिपूर्वक. [हनपूर्वक.

2 उतावळीनें, उत्कंठेनें, हुटहुटीनें, &c. औत्सुक्यपूर्वक, विलंबास-

To IMPAWN. See To PLEDGE.

To IMPEACH, *v. a.* v. To ACCUSE. दोषारोप*m.*-दोषारोपण*n.* करणें.

2 v. To BLAME. वाईट म्हणणें, दोष *m.* देणें.

IMPECCABILITY, *n.* v. A. पापासंभव *m.* पापासंभावना *f.*

IMPECCABLE, *a. not liable to sin.* पापसंभावनातीत, पापसंभवशून्य-रहित-&c. असंभाव्यपाप, पापसंभवाभावी, पापातीत, पापावश, पापासंगी.

To IMPEDE, *v. a.* v. To HINDER. अटकावणें, अटकाव *m.*-अडथळा *m.*-विघ्न *m. n.*-&c. करणें, मोडा *m.*-अडती *f.*-&c. घालणें.

IMPEDIMENT, *n.* v. HINDERANCE. अटकाव *m.* अड *f.* नड *f.* विघ्न *m. n.* अडथळा *m.* अडखूळ *n.* अंतराय *m.*

I. in speech. वाक्स्खलन *n.*

To have an i. in speech, v. To HESITATE. अडखळणें.

To IMPEL, *v. a.* v. To DRIVE, To PUSH. पुढें लोटणें, चालवणें, दपटणें, दामटणें, सारणें.

To IMPEN, *v. a.* कोंडींत- कोंडवाडींत- &c. कोंडणें-कोंडूनठेवणें.

To IMPEND, *v. n. hang over.* डोईवर टेंकणें, पडायाच्या लागास-संधानास असणें, पतनोन्मुख होणें. [वणें.

2 *be near at hand.* येऊन खेटणें-टेकणें-नेटणें-बितणें-ठेपणें, टेका-

IMPENDENT, *a.* IMPENDING, *p. a.* v. V. 1. डोईवर टेंकलेला, &c. पतनोन्मुख.

2 See IMMINENT.

IMPENETRABILITY, IMPENETRABLENESS, *n.* v. A. अभेद्यता *f.* अभेदनीयता *f.* निर्भेद्यता *f.* &c.

IMPENETRABLE, *a. that connot be pierced.* अभेद्य, अभेदनीय, अवेधनीय, निर्भेद्य, भेदनाशक्य, वेधनाशक्य, अप्रवेश्य.

IMPENITENCE, *n. absence of repentance.* अननुताप*m.* अपश्चात्ताप *m.* अनुतापाभाव *m.* पश्चात्तापाभाव *m.* अनुतापराहित्य *n.* &c.

IMPENITENT, *a.* v. N. अननुतापी, अपश्चात्तापी, अनुतापशून्य-&c. पश्चात्तापशून्य-&c.

IMPERATIVE, *a. expressive of command.* दृढाज्ञासूचक-बोधक-ज्ञापक, अवश्य कर्त्तव्य, अवश्यमाननीय.

2—in grammar. आज्ञावाचक.

IMPERATIVELY, *adv.* v. A. 1. दृढाज्ञा करून.

IMPERCEIVABLE, IMPERCEPTIBLE, *a. that cannot be perceived.* समजण्यांत न येण्याजोगा, बेमालूम, अगोचर, इंद्रियागोचर, इंद्रियायाह्य, इंद्रियाज्ञेय, अतींद्रिय, इंद्रियातीत, इंद्रियाविषय, दुर्लक्ष, दुर्लक्ष्य, दुर्दर्श, अविभावनीय, अव्यक्त.

IMPERCEPTIBLENESS, IMPERCEPTIBILITY, *n.* v. A. बेमालूमपणा *m.* बेमालुमी *f.* अगोचरता *f.* इंद्रियागोचरता *f.* &c. अविभावना *f.* [नकळत.

IMPERCEPTIBLY, *adv.* v. A. कळेनकळेसा *decl.* नकळत, कळत

IMPERFECT, *a. unfinished.* अधुरा, अपुरा, अपुरता, अपूर्ण, असमाप्त, असिद्ध, अनिष्पन्न, कच्चा.

2 *wanting a part*, v. DEFECTIVE. उणा, न्यून, हीन, विकल, विकलांग, न्यूनांग, अंगहीन, कसरीचा, विधुर.

IMPERFECTION, IMPERFECTNESS, *n.* v. A. *and* DEFECT. कच्चेपणा *m.* अधुरेपणा *m.* &c. कसर *f.* वैकल्य *n.* व्यंग *n.* गौण *n.* गुंजावीस *f.*

I. *an* i. v. FAULT. उणें *n.* विंग *or* विंगें *n.* हीण *n.* खोड *f.* ऐब *m.* दोष *m.* गोम *f.*

IMPERFECTLY, *adv.* v A. अपुरतेपणें, अपुरा-अपुरता-&c. *decl.* कच्चा, कसरीनें, कसर राखून.

IMPERFORATE, *a. not pierced.* अवेधित, अभेदित, अविद्ध, अभिन्न, नीरंध्र.

IMPERIAL, *a. belonging to an emperor, or to an empire.* आधिराजिक, सार्वभौमिक, सार्वभौमराज्यसंबंधी, साम्राजिक.

2 v. KINGLY. बादशाही *or* पादशाही.

To IMPERIL. See To ENDANGER.

IMPERIOUS, *a. domineering, haughty, commanding.* कदरखोर, कदरेचा, कदरवाला, कठोणकैदेचा, जालीम, कडक, करडा, करडे अमलाचा, सत्ता चालवणारा, चक्र बसवणारा, उद्धत.

IMPERIOUSLY, *adv.* v. A. कदरेनें, करडे अमलानें, कडकपणानें.

IMPERIOUSNESS, *n.* v. A. कदर *f.* कदरखोरी *f.* जालीमपणा *m.*

IMPERISHABLE, *a. not liable to perish.* अविनाशी, अनश्वर, अक्षय, अनाश्य, अजर, निर्जर, अजर्य्य, अक्षर, अव्ययात्मा, अजरामर.

IMPERISHABLENESS, *n.* v. A. अविनाशिता *f.* अक्षय *m.* अजर्य्य *n.* अव्ययीभाव *m.* अजरभाव *m.* अक्षयभाव *m.*

IMPERMANENCE, *n.* v. A. अस्थिति *f.* अस्थायिता *f.* अनित्यता *f.*

IMPERMANENT, *a. not enduring.* अनित्य, अशाश्वत, अस्थायी, अध्रुव.

IMPERMEABILITY, IMPERMEABLENESS, *n.* v. A. द्रवागम्यता *f.* द्रवाभेद्यता *f.*

IMPERMEABLE, *a. not to be passed through by a fluid.* द्रवागम्य, द्रवरोधक, द्रवाभेद्य, जलाभेद्य.

IMPERSONAL, *a.*—verb. अकर्तृक.

IMPERSONALITY, *n. indistinction of personality.* अव्यक्ति *f.* अव्यक्तिता *f.*

IMPERSUASIBLE, *a. not to be moved by argument.* असमजुती *or* त्या, दुराराध्य, दुराकलनीय.

IMPERTINENCE, IMPERTINENCY, *n.* v. A. 1. अप्रासंगिकत्व *n.* अप्रस्तुतता *f.* अनन्वय *m.*

2 धीटपणा *m.* धिटाई *f.* उद्धटपणा *m.*

IMPERTINENT, *a. not pertinent or relating*, v. IRRELEVANT. अन्वया बाहेरचा, अप्रासंगिक, अप्रस्तुत, अप्राकरणिक, अप्रसक्त.

2 *pert, saucy, &c.* v. IMPUDENT, DISRESPECTFUL. धीट, दांड, धट, उद्धत *pop.* उद्धट.

3 See OBTRUSIVE. 4. See TRIFLING.

IMPERTINENTLY, *adv.* v. A. 1. अप्रसंगवशात्, अप्रसंगोपात्त, अन्वयसोडून, अन्वयाबाहेरचा *decl.*

2 धिटाईनें, धीटपणानें, अमर्यादेनें.

IMPERTURBABLE, *a. that cannot be agitated.* अक्षोभ्य, अक्षोभणीय, नित्यशांत.

IMPERTURBATION, *n.* v. A. अक्षोभ्यता *f.* नित्यशांति *f.*

IMPERTURBED, *a. undisturbed.* अक्षुब्ध.

IMPERVIABLE, IMPERVIOUS, *a. impenetrable.* अभेद्य, अभेदनीय, निर्भेद्य, भेदनायोग्य, भेदनाशक्य, अगम्य, अप्रवेश्य, अप्रवेशनीय, निबिड, गहन.

IMPERVIOUSNESS, *n.* v. A. अभेद्यत्व *n.* अगम्यता *f.* &c. अभेद्यभाव *m.* निबिडपणा *m.* झुडपी *f.* जुंगाड *n.*

IMPETUOSITY, IMPETUOUSNESS, *n.* v. A. 1. झपाटा *m.* तडाका *or* ख्या *m.* कडाका *or* ख्या *m.* सवेगगति *f.* सवेगगमन *n.* सवेगता *f.*

2 तलखली *f.* तलखी *f.* जहाली *or* ज्याली *f.* कडकपणा *m.* कडकी *f.* रगडपट्टी *f.* रगडमल्ली *f.* लांठाई *f.* धडफड *f.* धडबड *f.* धूमधडाका *m.* सतम *f. n.* अमर्ष *m.*

IMPETUOUS, *a. moving with force.* झपाट्याचा, तडाक्याचा, &c. वेगवान्, सवेग, सवेगगामी.

2—of persons; *vehement, furious, &c.* कडक, तलख, तलखल्या, जहाल *or* ज्याल, जलाल, उष्ण, जाज्वल्य, तीव्र, वज्रप्राय, अमर्षवान्, अमर्षी, कटु, उदीर्णवेग.

An i. person. For this sense as amplified or enhanced under such terms, combinations, and epithets as, *A violent and headlong fellow, a rapid and vehement, a rude, heedless, reckless, precipitate, tearing, rattle-through, push-along, drive-apace, dash-away fellow,* there are numerous formations equally significant. रगड्या, रपाट्या, रगडमल्ल, दपट्या, दपटनंदन, धसकट्या, धसक्या, धसकधप्या, धसकनंदन, धसमुसळा *or* ळ्या, धसमसूळ, धडबड्या, धडफड्या, धशा *or* धश्शा, लाट्या, लाटण्या, लाट्यागंगाजी, ढुरमट, हूड, हुंदडा, कपाळफोड्या, ढुर्योंढुर्यो करणारा, उड्या, खमक्या, खणक्या, खमशा, संदा, संदातट्टू, फट्या, फट्याबावरा, भसकचाटू, भसक्या, सडाधस.

IMPETUOUSLY, *adv.* v. A. 1. भरभरां, भरारां, झपाट्यानें, तडाख्यानें.

2 तलखलीनें, जहालीनें, कडकपणानें, &c.

This sense viewed as intended or as emphatic, and as conveyed under such words as *violently, headlong, heedlessly, recklessly, tearingly, slapdash,* is expressed by numerous and striking formations. रगडून, रपाटून, खसाटून, दपटून, तडकावून, तडकून, कडकावून, कडकडून, धशाफशा, धडकून, सडकून, घसरून, भरारून, धडक, धूमधडक, धडकां, तडकां, चराबर, फटकर, बेधडक, बेलाशक, बेनिसबत, दाटबळें, भरार *or* रां, धशाफशा, धसकफसक.

And the *verbs* of this sense and power, agreeing with *to dash on, tear along, drive away, rattle through, &c.* are रगडणें, रपाटणें, धडकावणें, धसकावणें, तडकावणें, सडकावणें, झडकावणें, कडकावणें.

IMPETUS, *n. force of motion.* गतीचा वेग *m.* जोर *m.* झपाटा *m.* तडाका *m.*

To IMPINGE, *v. n.* v. To STRIKE. लागणें.

IMPIETY, IMPIOUSNESS, *n.* v. A. अधर्म *m.* देवनिंदा *f.* धर्मनिंदा *f.* अभक्ति *f.* अनुपासना *f.* ईश्वरानिष्ठा *f.*

2 *act of wickedness.* अधर्म *m.* अधर्मकार्य *n.* अधर्मकृत्य *n.*

IMPIOUS, *a. irreligious.* अधर्मी, अधार्मिक, अधर्माचा, अधर्मनिष्ठ, देवलंड, देवनिंदक, धर्मनिंदक, देवनिंदात्मक.

IMPIOUSLY, *adv.* v. A. देवनिंदाबुद्धीनें, देवनिंदापूर्वक, &c.

IMPLACABILITY, IMPLACABLENESS, *n.* v. A. अप्रसाद्यता *f.* अशाम्यता *f.* &c. दीर्घद्वेषिता *f.*

IMPLACABLE, *a. not to be appeased.* अप्रसाद्य, अशाम्य, असमाधेय, दुःप्रसाद्य, दुःशाम्य, दुराराध्य, दुःसमाधेय, दीर्घद्वेषी, असम.

To IMPLANT, *v. a. plant, infix*, fig. लावणें, लावून ठेवणें, स्थापणें, आधान *n.*-उपधान *n.* करणें.

IMPLANTATION, *n.* v. V.—*act.* लावणें *n.* &c. स्थापना *f.* आधान *n.* उपधान *n.*

To IMPLEAD. See To PROSECUTE.

IMPLEMENT, *n.* v. TOOL. अऊत *n.* बिस्तंड *n.* उपकरण *n.* यंत्र *n.*

To IMPLICATE, *v. a.* v. To INVOLVE. गोवणें, गुंतवणें, गोवून-गुंतवून घेणें.

IMPLICATED, *p.* v. V. गोवलेला, गुंतवलेला.
Criminally i. लिप्त, लिप्ताळा.—To be c. i. लिप्ताळणें.

IMPLICATION, *n.* v. V. To IMPLY. फलितार्थानें दाखवणें *n.* &c. ध्वनन *n.* फलितदर्शन *n.* ध्वनितदर्शन *n.* आक्षेप *m.*
I. *matter implied.* भाव *m.* फलित *n.* फलितार्थ *m.* ध्वनि *m.* ध्वन्यर्थ *m.* ध्वनितार्थ *m.* लक्ष्यार्थ *m.*
II. v. ENTANGLEMENT. गुतागूत *f.* गुताडा *m.*

IMPLICATIVE, *a.* IMPLYING, *p. a.* v. V. फलितार्थाचा, ध्वनितार्थाचा, हेतुगर्भ, संकेतगर्भित.

IMPLICIT, *a. unreservedly confiding, full, &c.*—faith, obedience, &c. पुरा, पूर्ण, निर्विकल्प, अनन्यभावाचा, निस्तोष, बिनदिक्कतीचा, साफ, निखालस.
2 See IMPLIED. [बिनदिक्कत.

IMPLICITLY, *adv.* v. A. 1. अनन्यभावानें, सर्वात्मना, सर्वभावानें,

IMPLIED, *p.* v. V. फलितार्थानें दाखवलेला, &c. अर्थसिद्ध, फलित, ध्वनित, गर्भित, उपलक्षित, आर्थिकार्थसिद्ध, गतार्थ.

To IMPLORE, *v. a. beseech, entreat*, v. To BEG. पायां पडून-हातीं पायीं पडून-दाढीस हात लावून-पदर पसरून-&c. मागणें-&c. काकळूत *f.* करणें *g. of o.* मिनत *f.*-मिनतवारी *f.*-&c. करणें *with* शीं *of o.* [कळूत करून.

IMPLORINGLY, *adv.* मिनतवार, मिनतीवार, मिनत-&c. करून, का-

To IMPLY, *v. a. involve by inference.* फलितार्थानें-फलितार्थेंकरून-&c. दाखवणें-दर्शवणें-सुचवणें-सिद्ध करणें, फलित-गार्भित-&c. करणें, ध्वनन *n.*-आक्षेप *m.* करणें *g. of o.*
To be implied. फलित-गार्भित-&c. असणें.

IMPOLICY, *n. bad policy, &c.* अयुक्ति *f.* बाधकत्व *n.* असमंजसपणा *m.* दुर्नीति *f.* दुर्नय *m.*

IMPOLITE, *a.* v. RUDE. अशिष्ट, असभ्य. [वांचून.

IMPOLITELY, *adv.* v. A. अमर्यादेनें, धट्टाईनें, मर्यादेवांचून, मुरवती-

IMPOLITENESS, *n.* v. A. असभ्यता *f.* अशिष्टता *f.* अनीति *f.*

IMPOLITIC, *a. unwise*—of persons. अविवेकी, अदूरदर्शी, अदीर्घदर्शी, अपरिणामदर्शी, दुर्नीत. [दुर्नीतीचा.
2—of measures. कार्यबाधक, बाधक, अयुक्तिक, अविवेकाचा,

IMPONDERABILITY, IMPONDEROUSNESS, *n.* v. A. तोलनाशक्यता *f.* अतोलनीयता *f.* अतिलघुता *f.*

IMPONDERABLE, IMPONDEROUS, *a. not having sensible weight.* v. LIGHT. वजन करितां येत नाहीं इतका हलका, अतिलघु, तोलनाशक्य.

IMPOROSITY, *n.* v. A. घनता *f.* अतिघनता *f.*

IMPOROUS, *a. quite close of texture.* नीरंध्र, निरंतरावयव, घन, अतिघन, घनावयवक.

IMPORT, *n.* (into a country, &c.). बंदरी जिन्नस *m.* तारवटी जिन्नस *m.* देशांतराहून आणलेली वणंज *f.* आवरदा *m.* or आवरदे *m. pl.*
Revenue from imports. आवरदाजमा *f.*
2 v. MEANING. अर्थ *m.* अभिप्राय *m.* भाव *m.* भावार्थ *m.*
3 See IMPORTANCE.

To IMPORT, *v. a.* देशांतराहून आणणें.
2 *bear as meaning*, v. To MEAN. अर्थ *m.*-&c. असणें.
3 *be of moment*, v. To SIGNIFY. भार *m.*-भारदस्ती *f.*-&c. असणें *g. of o. with in. con.*

IMPORTANCE, *n. consequence, moment*, v. WEIGHT. भार *m.* वजन *n.* भारदस्ती *f.* भारदारी *f.* प्रत्यवाय *m.* केबा *m.* गौरव *n.* कथा *f.* मामलत *f.*

IMPORTANT, *a.* v. WEIGHTY. भारी, मोठा, वजनदार, भारदस्त, भारदार, भारदस्तीचा, प्रधान.

IMPORTATION, *n. act of importing.* देशांतराहून आणणें *n.*
I. importations; *wares imported*, v. IMPORT. देशांतराहून आणलेला माल *m.*

IMPORTED, *p.* v. V. देशांतराहून-&c. आणलेला, तारवटी, तारवट.

IMPORTUNATE, *a. urgent, pertinacious.* लोंचट or ड, चिकट, चिकट्या, चिवट, चेंगट, चामट, वातट or ड, आग्रही, अत्याग्रही, मिन्नतीचा, मिन्नतवारीचा, आग्रहाचा, &c. लांबोरा, खपाट्या, घायकुत्या.
The words following are applied particularly to children or to the common beggar, and they bear an implication either of wearisome persistency or of abject or piteous whining. गळेपडू, गळचिप्या, गळग्रह, हातींपायीं पडणारा or लागणारा, खणपटीस बसणारा, गळचिपी *f.* &c. धरणारा, जीवघेणा or घेण्या, किरकिन्या, पिरपिन्या, रिपरिप्या, जिगजिग्या or जिकजिक्या, जिकिरी, दांत विचक्या, रडूंरडूं करून मागणारा.

IMPORTUNATELY, *adv.* v. A. आग्रहानें, आग्रह धरून, मिन्नतवार, मिन्नतीनें, &c. गळांपडून, खणपटीस बसून, गळचिपी-&c. धरून. *See the Verb.*

IMPORTUNATENESS, IMPORTUNITY, *n.* v. A. लोंचटपणा *m.* चेंगटपणा *m.* &c. आग्रह *m.* अत्याग्रह *m.* मिन्नत *f.* मिन्नतमाना *m.* नेट *m.* मिन्नतवारी *f.* चिकटपणा *m.* &c. चेंगटाई *f.*—esp. of children and beggars. आळ *f.* अळी *f.* जिगजीग or जिकजीक *f.* रिपरीप *f.* जिकीर *f.* चेंगटाई *f.* गळचिपी *f.* गळग्रह *m.* माथाकूट *f.* माथेफोड *f.*

To IMPORTUNE, *v. a.* or *To be* IMPORTUNATE, v. To HANG UPON. मिन्नत *f.*- मिन्नतमाना *m.*-मिन्नतवारी *f.* करणें or करून मागणें, आग्रह *m.* धरणें-धरून मागणें, खणकुदळ *f.* घेणें, धरणें *n.* घेणें, गळ *m.* घालणें.—esp. of children and beggars. गळीं पडणें or लागणें, गळचिपीं बसणें, गळचिपी *f.* आवळणें-धरणें, गळग्रह *m.* घालणें, आळ *f.* घेणें, दांत *m.* विचकणें, खणपट *f.* घेणें, भिरगोरें *n.* लावणें-देणें-मांडणें, दुमची *f.* पुरवणें, पायांवर कुतरीं मांजरें *n. pl.* घालणें.

To IMPOSE, *v. a. lay upon.* घालणें, ठेवणें, स्थापणें, आरोपणें.
2 *lay on as a burden or duty.* बसवणें, घालणें, स्थापणें, टाकणें, सोंपणें, माथां मारणें *g. of o.*
3 on; *cheat*, v. To DECEIVE. फसवणें, ठकवणें, वंचणें.
To be imposed on. फसणें.

IMPOSING, *a. calculated to impress*, v. FINE, GRAND. डौलाचा, ढबदार, ठळक.

IMPOSITION, *n.* v. V. 1.—*act.* घालणें *n.* ठेवणें *n.* &c. स्थापन *n.* स्थापना *f.* आरोप *m.* आरोपणें *n.*
2—*act.* बसवणें *n.* सोंपणें *n.* &c. स्थापन *n.* स्थापना *f.*
I. *imposture*, v. DECEIT, TRICK. फटकण *f.* कूट *m. n.*
II. *tax, &c. imposed.* बसवलेला कर *m.*-दस्त *m.*-&c.

III. *supernumerary task as a punishment.* शिक्षा म्हणून ज्यास्त घातलेला धडा m.-शिकणें n.-&c.

IMPOSSIBILITY, *n.* v. A. असंभवm. असंभावना f. असंभाव्यताf. अशक्यता f. असाध्यता f.

I. *an i. that which cannot be*, v. CHIMERA. असंभावित गोष्ट f. अशक्यविषय m.

To assert impossibilities or absurdities. नाहीं तेंच बोलणें-सांगणें-&c.

To attempt impossibilities. नाहींतेंच करणें, बचकेंत पाणी n. धरणें, मृगजलस्नान n. करणें, धोंड्याचा दोर m. काढणें, जेनाच्या पदरीं गांठ f. देणें-मारणें.

IMPOSSIBLE, *that cannot be, &c.* घडायाचा नाहीं, व्हायाचा-जोगा-&c. नाहीं, अशक्य, असाध्य, असंभवित,असंभावित,असंभावनीय, असंभाव्य, असंभवीक, असंभवी, अघटमान, खपुष्पायमाण, मृगजलवत्, शशशृंगायमाण.

IMPOST, *n.* v. TAX. दस्त m. सरकार देणें n.

IMPOSTHUME. See ABSCESS. [षधांरी.

IMPOSTOR, *n.* v. DECEIVER, ठक, फसव्या, भोंदू, पाखंडी, कूटवे-

General i. or cheat. घरभोंदू, देशठक, धुतारा.

IMPOSTURE, *n.* v. TRICK. भगल f. n. फटवण f. कूट m. n. छल m. n. पाखंड n.

IMPOTENCE, *n.* v. A. 1. कमजोरी f. कमजोरपणा m. नाकर्तेपणा m. &c. बलराहित्य n. &c. निर्बलता f. दुर्बलता f. दौर्बल्य n.

2 बुळेपणा m. नामर्दी f. फतुलाई f. प्रजननाशक्ति f. ध्वजपात m. ध्वजभंग m. पौरुषराहित्य n. भग्नध्वजत्व n. पौरुषाभाव m. क्लैब्यn.

IMPOTENT, *a.* v. WEAK. निर्बल, दुर्बल, हीनबल, हीनसामर्थ्य, हीनशक्तिक, नाकर्त्ता, अकर्त्ता, नबळा, शिळपट.

2 *incapable of propagation.* बुळा, निर्धात, नामर्द, निर्वीर्य, अवीर्य, कमरेचा ढिला, मेंगा *or* मेंग्या, प्रजननाशक, प्रजननाक्षम, फतुला, भागूबाई, निरिंद्रिय, नपुंसक, खाडू, क्लीब, शंड, भग्नध्वज, गतवीर्य, विगतवीर्य, हतवीर्य, पुरुषत्वहीन, अपौरुष, पाउणे आठ, राशा.

To IMPOUND, *v. a. confine in a pen, &c.* कोंडणें, कोंडून ठेवणें, कोंडवाडींत-&c. घालणें, कोंडी f.-कोंडणी f. करणें *g. of o.*

To IMPOVERISH, *v. a. reduce to poverty.* दरिद्र-भिकारी-निर्धन-&c. करणें, भिकेस लावणें-आणणें.

2 *exhaust the strength of.* बळमोड m. f.-बलऱ्हास m.-बलहानि f.-सत्वनाश m.-सत्वहानि f.-&c. करणें *g. of o.* दुबळा-दुर्बळ-निःसत्व-&c. करणें.

IMPOVERISHED, *p.* v. V. 1. दरिद्री-&c. केलेला.

2 नष्टार्थ, नष्टधन, नष्टद्रव्य, नष्टबल, नष्टवीर्य, नष्टसत्व, गतवीर्य.

IMPOVERISHING, IMPOVERISHMENT, *n.* v. V. 1. दरिद्रकरणें n. दरिद्री करण n. धन हरण n.

2 सत्वनाश n. सत्वहानि f. [दौष्कर्य n.

IMPRACTICABILITY, *n.* v. A. 1. असाध्यता f. अशक्यता f. &c.

IMPRACTICABLE, *a.* v. IMPOSSIBLE. असाध्य, असाधनीय, दुःसाध्य, दुरतिक्रम, अशक्य, अघटनीय, बेलाग.

2 *untractable*, v. PERVERSE. अकरनकर, शिरजोर.

3 (road, &c.) See IMPASSABLE.

IMPRANSUS, *a. that has not had his meal.* अभुक्त, अकृतभोजन, नजेवलेला.

To IMPRECATE, IMPRECATION. See To CURSE, CURSE.

IMPREGNABLE, *n. not to be taken,*—fort, &c. दुर्धर, दुर्जेय, अजेय, अजिंक, दुःसाध्य, बिकट, बेलाग, गडसल.

To IMPREGNATE, *v. a. make pregnant.* गर्भार-सगर्भ m.-&c. करणें, गर्भस्थापन n.-गर्भस्थापना f.-गर्भाधान n.-&c. करणें.

2—as used of female animals. गाभण करणें, फळवणें.

3 (flowers) रज n.-पराग m. ठेवणें.

4 *communicate the virtues of one thing to another.* गुण m.-धर्म m.-&c. देणें, in comp. गुणयुक्त-गुणान्वित-&c. करणें.

IMPREGNATE, *a.* IMPREGNATED, *p.* v. V. *and* PREGNANT. गर्भार, सगर्भ.

I. *having received a communication of the virtue of.* गुणयुक्त, गुणमिश्रित.

IMPREGNATER, *n.* IMPREGNATING, *p. a.* v. V. 1. गर्भार करणारा, &c. गर्भकर, गर्भद, गर्भस्थापक, गर्भोत्पादक.

IMPREGNATION, *n.* v. V. 1.—*act.* गर्भस्थापन n. गर्भस्थापना f. गर्भाधान n. गर्भोत्पादन n.

To IMPRESS, *v. a. print, stamp.* ठसवणें, छापणें, उमटवणें, ठसाm.-&c. मारणें, मुद्रित करणें, बेटणें. [उपतिष्ठवणें.

2 *fix deeply,* fig. ठसवणें, बिंबवणें, भिनवणें, भरवणें, बाणणें,

To be impressed. ठसणें, बिंबणें, भिनणें, भरणें, उपतिष्ठणें; also, inversely, *to be impressed by,* as; त्याची गोष्ट माझ्या मनांत ठसली.

3 *force into service.* See To PRESS.

IMPRESSED, *p.* v. V. 1. ठसवलेला, &c. बेटींव, मुद्रित.

2 ठसवलेला, बिंबवलेला, &c. उपतिष्ठित.

IMPRESSION, IMPRESS, IMPRESSURE, *n. mark made, stamp.* ठसा m. छाप m. छापा m. मुद्रा f. मुद्रिका f. आकार m.

Indelible i. चिऱ्यावरची *or* दगडावरची रेघ f.

Transient i. पाण्यावरची-वाळवेबरची रेघ f.

To take off an i. बेटणें.

To come off well—an i. बठणें, बेटणें.

2 (upon a coin). मोहर f.

3 mental i; *idea, &c.* भास m. आभास m. भान n. वचक m. v. जा, उमज m.

4 *sense impressed, awe, &c.* छाप f. धाग f. ठसका m. उसाm.

To make an i. ठसणें, भिनणें.

5 See EDITION.

IMPRESSIVE, *a. that makes a deep impression on the mind.* मनांत ठसण्या जोगा, मनांत भरण्याजोगा, चित्तभेदक, हृद्भेदक, हृद्गामी, हृदयंगम, भावोत्पादक.

IMPRESSIVELY, *adv.* v. A. मनांत ठसण्याजोगा *decl.* &c.

IMPRIMIS, *adv. in the first place.* पहिल्यानें, आदि, आदौ, प्रथमतः.

To IMPRINT. See To IMPRESS. 2 See To PRINT.

To IMPRISON, *v. a. confine in a prison, &c.* तुरुंगांत- बंदीखान्यांत-&c. घालणें-टाकणें, कोंडणें, कोंडून ठेवणें, कैद-बंद-कारागारबद्ध-&c.-करणें, बंदांत-बंदींत-कैदेंत-अटकेंत-&c. घालणें, कोंडणीf.-कोंडी f.-&c. करणें *g. of o.*

IMPRISONED, *p.* v. V. बंदांत घातलेला, &c. कैद, कारागारबद्ध, कारागुप्त. [कोंडी f.

IMPRISONMENT, *n.* v. V.—*state.* कैद f. बंदी f. बंद m. अटक f.

IMPROBABILITY, *n.* v. A. असंगति f. असंगतत्व n. असंभव m. असंभावना f.

IMPROBABLE, *a. not likely to be, &c.* व्हायाजोगा-सारखा-&c. नाहीं, असंभव, असंभवी *pop.* असंभवित, असंभवीक, असंभव-

नीय, असंभाव्य, असंगत, अवघड, दुर्घट, अघटित, दुःसंभाव्य, अघटनीय, कठीण, बिकट, दूर, दूरापास्त *pop.* दुरापस्त, असत्यसन्निभ.

IMPROBITY, *n.* v. DISHONESTY. लबाडी *f.* अप्रमाणिकपणा *m.* अप्रामाण्य *n.* अप्रामाणिकत्व *n.* प्रामाण्यभाव *m.* असाधुता *f.*

IMPROMPTU, *adv. off hand.* विचारकेल्यावांचून, पूर्वविचाररहित, समयोपस्थितीनें.

IMPROMPTU, *n. extemporaneous composition.* शीघ्रकविता *f.* शीघ्रकवन *n.* प्रासादिककविता *f.*

IMPROPER, *a. unfit, unsuitable, unadapted, unqualified.* अयोग्य, अनुपयोगी, निरुपयोगी, अयुक्त, अनुपयुक्त, निरुपयुक्त, निर्युक्तिक, अयथातथ, कार्याक्षम, नालायक.

2 (to be done) v. UNJUST, WRONG. करायाजोगा-&c. नाहीं, अकार्य, अयोग्य, अनुचित, गैरवाजबी, गैरशिस्त, अन्याय्य, अयुक्त, अकर्त्तव्य.

IMPROPRIETY, *n.* v. A. 1. अयोग्यता *f.* अनुपयोगिता *f.* अयुक्तता *f.* अनुपयुक्तता *f.* अयुक्ति *f.* निर्युक्ति *f.* नालायकी *f.*

2 अकार्यता *f.* अयोग्यता *f.* गैरशिस्त *f.* अनीति *f.* अनौचित्य *n.* आनुचित्य*n.* अयुक्ति *f.* अन्याय*m.* अन्यायत्व*n.*

IMPROVABLE, *a.* v. V. A. 1. चांगला कराया-व्हाया-&c. जोगा-जोगता- सारखा, सुधारायाजोगा-&c.

To IMPROVE, *v. a. make better, advance in good qualities.* अधिक चांगला-&c. करणें, गुण*m.*-&c. वाढवणें *g. of o.* गुणवृद्धि *f.*- गुणवर्द्धन*n.*-सत्ववर्द्धन*n.*-गुणोत्कर्ष*m.*-गुणाभिवृद्धि *f.*-गुणसंवर्द्धन-&c. करणें.

2 *employ to good purpose, use to advantage, turn to account, &c.* फळ येईसा *decl.* करणें, सार्थक-सफळ होईसा *decl.* करणें-वापरणें, चांगला *decl.*-चांगल्या रीतीनें-&c. वहिवाटणें, चांगल्या गोष्टीस लावणें, सद्व्यापार*m.* करणें *g. of o.*

To IMPROVE, *v. n. better, &c.* चांगला होत जाणें, चढणें, रंगास-रूपास चढणें-चढत चालणें, वाढणें, गुण*m.*-&c. वाढणें *g. of s.* उत्तरोत्तर चांगला होणें.

IMPROVEMENT, *n.* v. V. A. 1.—*act.* गुण वाढवणें*n.* &c. संवर्द्धन*n.* गुणवर्द्धन*n.* गुणसंवर्द्धन*n.* सत्ववर्द्धन*n.*

v. V. N.—*state.* चढती कळा *f.* गुणवृद्धि *f.* सत्ववृद्धि *f.* गुणसंवृद्धि *f.* गुणाभिवृद्धि *f.* शुभाभिवृद्धि *f.* संवृद्धि *f.*

IMPROVIDENCE, *n.* v. A. अदूरदृष्टि *f.* अदूरविचार*m.* अदीर्घदृष्टि *f.*

IMPROVIDENT, *a. wanting forecast.* अदूरदर्शी, अदूरदृष्टि, अदीर्घदर्शी, अदीर्घदृष्टि, अपरिणामदर्शी, भाव्यविचारी. [चा.

IMPROVING, *p.a.* v. V. N. चांगला होणारा, चढता, वाढता, चढते कळे-

IMPRUDENCE, *n.* v. A. अविवेक*m.* अविचार*m.* अदूरदृष्टि *f.* अविचारिता *f.* अविमृश्यकारिता *f.* अनालोचना *f.*

IMPRUDENT, *a. indiscreet, &c.*—of persons. अविचारी, अविवेकी, अविचारशील, विचारमूढ, विचारहीन-शून्य-&c. हीनविचार, अदूरदर्शी, अदूरदृष्टि, पूर्वापरादर्शी, असमंजस, अविमृश्यकारी, अपर्यवसानदर्शी. [पुरस्सर.

2—of acts. अविचाराचा, अविवेकाचा, अविचारपूर्वक, अविचार-

IMPRUDENTLY, *adv.* v. A. 1. अविवेकानें, &c.

IMPUDENCE, *n.* v. A. धिटाई *f.* धठाई *f.* औद्धत्य*n.* तिसें *n.* तोंड *n.* नाक *n.* अभयमुद्रा *f.* वैयात्य*n.* धार्ष्ट्य*n.*

IMPUDENT, *a. shameless, saucy, &c.* धीट, धट्ट, निर्भीड, निर्लज्ज, निलाजरा, दांडगा, उद्धत, बेचाड, समुद्धत, धृष्ट, वियात.

IMPUDENTLY, *adv.* v. A. धिटाईनें, नाक लावून *or* उंचे नाकानें, तुरा लावून.

To IMPUGN, *v. a. oppose.* विरुद्ध बोलणें, दूषण*n.* देणें, दूषित करणें, विप्रतिपत्ति *f.*-विप्रतिपादन*n.*-विरुद्धकथन *n.* करणें.

IMPULSE, *n.* v. BLOW, FORCE. आघात*m.* धक्का*m.*

2 *emotion towards.* उकळी *f.* कढ*m.* चव *f.* चेव*m.* कंडू *f.* कंडी *f.* उत्कलिका *f.* वेग*m.* स्फुरशी *f.* स्फुरूप*m. f.*

A sudden i. सतसत*m.*

Acting upon i. लाडकाव्यवहार*m.*

That follows his impulses. मनस्वी *or* मनसोक्त वर्त्तणारा-वागणारा-चालणारा-&c. यथाकामी, कामकामी, कामचार, यथेच्छ.

Upon, according to, &c. i. मनसोक्त.

IMPULSIVE, *a. moving, impellent.* चालवणारा, सारणारा, चालक, सारक.

IMPUNITY, *n. exemption from punishment.* अदंड *m.* अदंडन *n.* दंडाभाव*m.* दंडनाभाव*m.* दंडविरहितत्व*n.* अताडन*n.*

2 *exemption from injury.* अनपकार*m.* अपकाराभाव *m.*

Assurance of i. अभय*n.* अभयवचन*n.*

Bond of i. अभयपत्र *n.*

IMPURE, *a. foul, feculent, &c.* v. DIRTY. मळका *remiss.* मळकट, मलिन *pop.* मळीण, समल.

2 *unholy, unclean, unchaste, sinful.* मलिन *pop.* मळीण, अपवित्र, अशुद्ध, अपूत, नापाक, अमंगल, पापाचा, पापी, पापबुद्धीचा, अचकटविचकट.

3 *unclean, defiled,*—ceremonially. अपवित्र, विटाळलेला, विटाळाचा, अशुद्ध, अशुचि, आशौची (*See under* IMPURITY). अमेध्य, अपूत, अमंगल, नापाक.

I. from a birth. सुवेरतुला, सूतकी *pop.* सुतकी, सुवेरकरी.

I. through a death. सुतकतुला, सुतकाळा *or* ळ्या, सुतकी, सुतकील.

4—language, style. अशुद्ध, अप्रशस्त.

IMPURENESS, IMPURITY, *n.* v. A. 1. मळकेपणा*m.* मळिणपणा*m.* मालिन्य*n.* समलता *f.*

2 अपवित्रता *f.* मळिणपणा*m.* मालिन्य*n.* अशुद्धि *f.*

3 अपवित्रपणा*m.* अपवित्रता *f.* विटाळ*m.* अशुद्धि *f.* अशुचि *f.* अशुचिता *f.* आशौच*n.* This word, though it signifies impurity *generally*, is, when uncompounded, understood *especially* of that impurity which arises in consequence of a *death.* When in composition its sense is determined by the power of the component word prefixed; as, जननाशौच, मृताशौच, ग्रहणाशौच, अतिक्रांताशौच, &c.

I. during an eclipse. ग्रहणाशौच*n.*

I. from childbirth or miscarriage. सुवेर*m.* सूतक*n.* सूत्याशौच*n.* जननाशौच*n.* विरधाळें*n.* वृद्धि *f.* जाताशौच*n.*

I. from a death or a miscarriage in the family. कडूविटाळ*m.*

I. from the touch of stale things. उष्टाविटाळ*m.*

I. through a death. मृताशौच*n.* शावाशौच*n.* मृतक*n.* अवरोध*m.* सूतक*n.*

To spread one's i. विटाळ*m.* कालवणें.

4 अप्रशस्तता *f.* अशुद्धि *f.* [रोप्य.

IMPUTABLE, *a.* v. V. 1. आरोप करायास योग्य, आरोपणीय, आ-

IMPUTATION, *n.* v. V. 1.—*act.* आरोपणें*n.* आरोपण*n.* आरोप*m.* अभियोग *m.*

2 v. BLAME. ठपकाm. शब्दm. अपवादm.

To IMPUTE, *v. a. attribute, assign,* v. To ASCRIBE. आरोपणें, अभियोगm.-आरोपणn.-आरोपm. करणें *g. of o.*

2—in an ill sense.आंगावर घालणें, माथां *adv.* मारणें, ठपका *m.* ठेवणें-आणणें.

IN, *prep.* or *adv.* आंत, मध्यें, मधीं, भितर, माजीं, माझारीं, आंतउतां *or* तीं.

In, as a privative or negative is rendered by अ, निर, दुर, as अशुद्ध, निर्दोष, दुरंत, &c. Of those English words to which sometimes *In* is prefixed and sometimes *Un*, such as are not found here should be looked for under *Un*.

INABILITY, *n. want of power.* अशक्ति *f.* असामर्थ्य*n.* अक्षमता *f.* अपराक्रम*m.* कार्याक्षमता *f.* अनिर्वाहकत्व*n.*

INACCESSIBILITY, INACCESSIBLENESS, *n.* v. A. अगम्यता *f.* दुर्गमता *f.* दौर्गम्य *n.* दुष्प्राप्यता *f.*

INACCESSIBLE, *a. not to be reached, &c.*पावाया जोगा-&c. नाहीं, अगम्य, दुर्गम, बेलाग, दुष्क्रम, दुष्प्राप्य, गहन.

INACCURACY, *n.* v. A. अशुद्धता *f.* चूक *f.* चुकी *f.* अंतर*n.* तफावत *f.* गुंजावीस *f.*

INACCURATE, *a. erroneous, not correct.* अशुद्ध, चुकीचा, तफावतीचा, नादुरुस्त, गैरराास्त, सदोष, अयथार्थ.

INACTION, *n. want of action.*अव्यापार*m.* अनुद्योग*m.* व्यापाराभाव *m.* उद्योगाभाव*m.* अचेष्टा *f.*

INACTIVE, *a. not acting or busy.* निर्व्यापार, रिकामा, पडलेला, व्यापारहीन-विहीन-रहित-विरहित.

2 *not active,* v. INDOLENT. अनुद्योगी, निरुद्योगी, सुस्त, ढिला, अव्यवसायी, अव्यवसायवान्. [हित्य*n.*

INACTIVITY, *n.* v. A. 1. रिकामपणा*m.* निर्व्यापारता *f.* व्यापाररा-

2 सुस्ती *f.* ढिलेपणा*m.* अनुद्योगिता *f.* निरुद्योगिता *f.* अव्यवसाय*m.*

INADEQUACY, INADEQUATENESS, *n.* v. A. नपूर *or* निपूर *f.* निपुरेतपणा *m.* निपुरेपणा *m.* अपुरतेपणा *m.* &c. अयोग्यता *f.* अनुपयुक्तता *f.* असामर्थ्य *n.* अपर्याप्ति *f.* अक्षमता *f.*

INADEQUATE, *a. not sufficient.* निपुरता, निपुरा, अपुरता, अपुरा, अपूर्ण, अपर्याप्त,अयोग्य,अनुपयुक्त,असमर्थ, अक्षम, कार्याक्षम, अपूरक.

INADEQUATELY, *adv.* v. A. न पुरेसा, तोटा येईसा, अपुरता, अपुरा, *all declinable.*

INADMISSIBILITY, *n.* v. A. अग्राह्यता *f.* अनादेयता *f.* &c.

INADMISSIBLE, *a. not proper to be allowed or received.* मानायाजोगा-सारखा-&c. नाहीं, अग्राह्य, अस्वीकार्य, अनंगीकार्य, अनादेय, स्वीकारानर्ह.

INADULT, *a. not grown up.* अप्राप्तयौवन, अज्ञातयौवन.

INADVERTENCE, *n.* v. A. गफलत *f.* अनवधान *n.* अनवधानता *f.* असावधानता *f.* दुर्लक्ष्य *n.* अलक्ष्य *n.* अलक्ष *n.* प्रमाद *m.*

INADVERTENT, *a. inattentive.* असावधान, गैरसावध, अनवधान, गाफल *or* गाफील *or* गाफली, प्रमादी, दुर्लक्ष, बेफाम.

INADVERTENTLY, *adv.* v. A. गफलतीनें, गैरसावधपणानें, प्रमादानें, &c. चुकून माकून *or* वाकून, अवचुकून, कळत न कळत, न कळून, अनवधानपूर्वक, प्रमादतः, प्रमादातः.

INALIENABLE, *a. that cannot be transferred, &c. to another.* परादेय, अन्यादेय, अदेय, वंशमात्रोपभोग्य, वतनी.

INALIENABLENESS, *n.* v. A. परादेयता *f.* अन्यादेयता *f.* &c.

INALIMENTAL, *a. affording no nourishment.* अपुष्टिकर, अपौष्टिक.

INAMORATA, *n.* रागिणी *f.* प्रिया *f.*

INAMORATO, *n.* रागी *m.* प्रिय *m.*

INANE. See EMPTY.

INANIMATE, INANIMATED, *a.* v. LIFELESS. निर्जीव, निचेष्ट, निश्चेष्ट, अचेतन, निष्प्राण, जड.

Animate and i. चेतनाचेतन. [रिक्तता *f.*

INANITION, *n.*—in medicine. अनाहार *m.* आहाराभाव *m.* उदर-

INANITY. See EMPTINESS. [मान्द्य *m.*

INAPPETENCE, *n. want of appetite.* अरुचि *f.* अक्षुधा *f.* क्षुद-

2 *want of desire.* अनिच्छा *f.* अलोभ *m.* अनभिलाष *m.*

INAPPLICABILITY, *n.* v. A. अयोग्यता *f.* अनुपयुक्तता *f.* अप्रयोज्यता *f.*

INAPPLICABLE, *a. not proper to be applied.* लावायास अयोग्य, लावायाजोगा नाहीं, अयोग्य, अप्रयोज्य, अनुपयुक्त.

INAPPLICATION, *n.* v. INDOLENCE. अनुद्योग *m.*

INAPPOSITE, *a. not pertinent.* अप्रासंगिक, प्रसंगानुचित, अयोग्य, असमर्पक. [गा.

INAPPRECIABLE, *a.* किंमत *f.*-मोल *n.*-योग्यता *f.*-&c. नसमजायाजो-

INAPPREHENSIBLE, *a. not to be apprehended.* अग्राह्य, अग्रहणीय.

INAPPREHENSIVE, *a.* अशंकान्वित.

INAPPROPRIATE, *a.* v. IMPROPER. अयोग्य, अनुपयुक्त, अनुपयोगी, अयुक्त, निर्युक्तिक.

INAPPROPRIATENESS, *n.* v. A. अयोग्यता *f.* अनुपयुक्तता *f.* अनुपयोगिता *f.* [पयुक्तता *f.*

INAPTITUDE, INAPTNESS, *n. want of fitness.* अयोग्यता *f.* अनु-

INARABLE, *a. not fit to be plowed.* लागवडीचा नाहीं, नांगरायास अयोग्य, अकर्षणी.

INARTICULATE, *a. not distinct.* अव्यक्त, अस्पष्ट, गुळमुळीत, किडमिडा, अस्पष्टोच्चारित, अस्पष्टोच्चाराचा, क्लिष्ट, अविस्पष्ट.

INARTICULATELY, *adv.* v. A. अस्पष्टोच्चारानें, &c. अस्पष्ट, अव्यक्त, गुळमुळीत.

That speaks i. बोबडा. [च्चार *m.*

INARTICULATENESS, *n.* v. A. अस्पष्टता *f.* अव्यक्तता *f.* अस्पष्टो-

INARTIFICIAL, *a. not done by art; natural.* अकृत्रिम, अकल्पित, स्वयंकृत, स्वयंभू, स्वयंजात, स्वतःसिद्ध. [भाबडा.

2 *framed without art.* साधा, साधारण, भोळा, साळाभोळा,

INATTENTION, *n. want of attention.* अनवधान *n.* अनवधानता *f.* असावधानता *f.* गैरसावधपणा *m.* दुर्लक्ष *n.* अलक्ष्य *n.* अलक्ष *n.* आनाकानी *f.* [प्रमाद *m.*

2 *neglect.* अबाळ *f.* अबजतन *n.* अवनिगा *or* घा *f.* हयगयी *f.*

INATTENTIVE, *a. not attending, not heeding.* अनवधान, असावध, बेसावध, गैरसावध, बेफाम, गाफल *or* गाफील, गाफली, दुर्लक्ष, अनवहित, अदत्तांतःकरण, अतन्मनस्क, अप्रस्तुतलक्ष.

2 *not attentive,heedless, neglectful,* v. CARELESS. गफलती, गफलत्या, गाफली, प्रमादी.

INATTENTIVELY, *adv.* v. A. 1. दुर्लक्षानें, अनवधानपूर्वक.

INAUDIBLE, *a. that cannot be heard.* दुःश्राव्य, कष्टश्राव्य, दुःस्वश्राव्य, अश्राव्य, श्रवणाशक्य.

INAUDIBLY, *adv.* v. A. ऐकूं येईनासा, ऐकूं न येईसा, ऐकूं जाईनासा, कानीं पडेनासा, *all decl.*

INAUGURAL, *a. pertaining, &c. to inauguration.* प्रतिष्ठेचा, प्रति-

ष्ठासंबंधी, प्रतिष्ठाविषयक.

INAUGURATION, *n.* v. V. प्रतिष्ठा *f.* प्रतिष्ठापन *n.*

To INAUGURATE, *v. a. induct into an office with ceremonies,* v. To INSTALL. प्रतिष्ठा *f.*-प्रतिष्ठापन *n.* करणें *g. of o.*

INAUSPICIOUS, *a. ill omened, &c.*अमंगल, अशुभ, अनिष्ट, अभद्र, दग्ध, दग्धहस्त, दुर्लक्षणी, नेष्ट, नाट, नाटाळ *or* नाठाळ *or* नाठ्याळ, खष्ट, खडतर, खट्याळ.

To be i. वक्रीं असणें.

INAUSPICIOUSNESS, *n.* v. A. अमंगळपणा *m.* अमंगलता *f.*अशुभ*n.*

INAUTHENTICITY, *n. want of authenticity.* खोटेपणा *m.* अप्रामाण्य *n.* प्रमाणाभाव *m.* [दुरत्यय.

INAVERTIBLE, *a.* अनिवार, अनिवार्य, दुर्निवार, दुर्वार, अपरिहार्य,

INBEING, *n. inherence.* अंतःस्थिति *f.* अंतस्सत्ता *f.* अंतर्भाव *m.*

INBORN, INBRED, *a.* v.INHERENT, NATURAL. अंतर्जात, अंतर्भव.

INCALCULABLE, *a. that cannot be computed.*अगणनीय, अगणेय, अगण्य, अगणित, असंख्यात, बेसुमार.

INCANDESCENCE, *n.* अत्युष्णता *f.*

INCANTATION, *n. enchantment,* v. CHARM. मंत्र *m.*

I. to kill. मारण *n.*

I. to kill or injure,—gener. जारणमारण *n.*

I. to produce impotency or disease. जारण *n.*

Rites in acquiring an i. पुरश्चरण *n.*

INCANTATORY, *a.* v. N. मंत्राचा, मांत्रिक, मंत्रसंबंधी, मंत्रपाठक, मंत्रपाठी.

INCAPABILITY, INCAPABLENESS, *n.* v. A. नाकर्तेपणा *m.* &c. अशक्ति *f.* असामर्थ्य *n.* अशकता *f.* अक्षमता *f.* नालायकी *f.*

INCAPABLE, *a. incompetent.* नाकर्त्ता, अकर्त्ता, अशक्त, असमर्थ, अयोग्य, अक्षम, कार्याक्षम, नाकूस, नालायक, निर्गुणाचा.

INCAPACIOUS *a.* v. NARROW. अप्रशस्त, अल्पावकाश, अडचणीचा.

To INCAPACITATE, *v. a. disable, disqualify.* असमर्थ-अक्षम-अशक्त-&c. करणें, योग्यताहीन-क्षमताहीन-&c.करणें, सामर्थ्यहरण*n.*-क्षमताहरण *n.*-योग्यताहरण *n.*-&c. करणें.

INCAPACITY, *n. want of power.* See INABILITY. 2 *stupidity.* बुद्धिमांद्य *n.* बुद्धिजाड्य *n.* बुद्ध्यभाव *m.*

To INCARCERATE, &c. See To IMPRISON, &c.

INCARNATE, *a. invested with a body.* देहधारी, देही, शरीरी, देहधृत, अवतारी, अवतीर्ण, मूर्त्तिमान्.

To become i. अवतरणें.

INCARNATION, *n. act of taking a human body.* अवतार *m.*देहधारण *n.* There are particularly ten *Incarnations* of Vishnu (दशावतार) viz. मत्स्य, कूर्म, वराह, नृसिंह, वामन, परशुराम, राम, कृष्ण, बुद्ध, कल्की. Of these nine are considered to be past.

Anniversary of an i. जयंती *f.*

I. of an emanation. अंशावतार *m.*—as distinguished from an i. of the deity in full. पूर्णावतार *m.*

Marvels or tales of the incarnations. अवतारचरित *n.* अवतारकथा *f.*

Player representing the incarnations. दशावतारी.

Recounting the exploits of the incarnations. चर्चा *f.*

To INCASE. See To ENCLOSE. [मादी, गाफल.

INCAUTIOUS, *a.* v. CARELESS. असावध, गैरसावध, असावधान, प्र-

INCAUTIOUSLY, *adv.* v. A. असावधपणानें, &c. प्रमादपूर्वक, असावधानपूर्वक, प्रमादतः. [माद *m.*

INCAUTIOUSNESS, *n.* v. A. असावधपणा *m.* गैरसावधपणा *m.* प्र-

INCENDIARISM, *n.* घरजाळणें *n.* आगारदाह *m.*

INCENDIARY, *n.* lit. घरजाळणारा, आगलाव्या, आगलावणारा, आगारदाही, जळत्या, अग्निद.

2 *fomenter of dissension.* Appellatives, allusive terms, expressise phrases, &c. bearing this sense, and answering to *make bate, breed bate, embroiler, inflamer, firebrand, boute feu, broil-breeder, quarrel-kindler, setter by the ears, &c.* are numerous and extensively current. Some are here collected. आगलाव्या, जळत्या, नारद *or* कळीचा नारद, नारदमुनि, कज्जेदलाल, कळलाव्या, कळचेट्या, कळचेटव्या, फुणगीलावणारा *or* टाकणारा, फुंकणारा, कैपती, बीर भरणारा *or* देणारा, दुलावा *or* व्या, लावालावी करणारा, गृहभेदी, घरभेदी *or* द्या, घरघालू *or* ल्या, घरनाशी *or* शा, घरफोड्या, घरमारू *or* ऱ्या, खाजाळ *or* ळा *or* खजाळ, खेळ्या, चेरगडी, (लोकांच्या) घरांवर कुतरें चढवणारा, दाणे टाकून कोंबडे झुंझवणारा.

INCENSE, *n. perfume exhaled by fire.* धूप *m.*

To INCENSE, *v. a. perfume with incense.* धूप *m.* दाखवणें-देणें, उदवणें, धूपवासित-धूपित-&c. करणें, वासन *n.* करणें.

2 *enrage, provoke,* v. To ANGER, To EXCITE. कोपविणें, संतापवणें, संतप्त-&c. करणें, संतापन *n.* करणें *g. of o.* पित्त *n.* तापविणें *g. of o.*

INCENSED, *p.* v.V. 1. धूपदिल्हेला, &c. धूपित, धूपवासित, धूपायित. 2 संतापवलेला, &c. तप्त, तापित, संतप्त, संतापित, कोपज्वलित, कोपदीप्त.

INCENTIVE, *n. inciting cause,* v. INCITEMENT. उत्तेजन *n.* उत्तेजक *n.* उद्बोधक *n.*

INCENTIVE, *a.* v. INCITING. उत्तेजक, प्रवर्तक, प्रयोजक, प्रवृत्तिकारक, प्रोत्साहक.

INCEPTION. See BEGINNING. [विषयक.

INCEPTIVE, *a. beginning.* उपक्रमाचा, औपक्रमिक, उपक्रमसंबंधी-

INCESSANT, *a.* v. CONTINUAL. निरंतर, एकसारखा, संतत.

INCESSANTLY, *adv.* v. CONTINUALLY. निरंतर, एकटक, एकसारखा.

INCEST, *n. prohibited cohabitation.* अगम्यागमन *n.*(as committed by a male). अगम्यगमन *n.* (as committed by a female). गोत्रगमन *n.*

Female, connection with whom is i. अगम्या *f.*

I. with one's father's or guru's wife. गुरुतल्पगमन *n.* गुरुतल्प *n.*

I. with one's mother. मातृगमन *vulg.* मात्रागमन *n.*

INCESTUOUS, *a.* v. N. गोत्रगमनी, गोत्रगामी, अगम्यागामी, अगम्यागमनाचा, अगम्यागमनसंबंधी.

I. with father's wife. गुरुतल्पग, गुरुतल्पी.

I. with mother. मातृगामी *vulg.* मात्रागमनी.

Some terms for an incestuous person are. गोत घोडा*m.* गोत्र कुठार *m.* गोत्रकुदळ *m.*

INCH, *n.*—the measure. अंगुल *pop.* अंगूळ *n.* (8 barley corns put side by side). तसू *n.* इंच *m.* from the English is common.

A quarter of an i. पाइड *or* पाइड *f.* पाईण *f.*

By inches, by inchmeal. थोडाथोडा *decl.* जातांजातां, होतांहोतां, थोटथोट.

To INCHOATE, INCHOATE, &c. See To BEGIN, BEGUN, &c.

INCIDENCE, *n. falling.* पडणें *n.* पतन *n.* 2 See INCIDENT.

INCIDENT, INCIDENTAL, *a. casual, fortuitous, &c.* v. OCCASIONAL. प्रासंगिक, नैमित्तिक, कादाचित्क, अनित्य.

To be in. to. पाठीमागें असणें.

2 *happening by accident,* v. ACCIDENTAL. आगंतुक, दैवघटित, दैवजात, असमवायी.

3 *apt to happen.* घडून येण्याजोगा-सारखा-&c. पाठीमागें असणारा, प्रसंगानें व्हावयाचा.

INCIDENT, *n.* v. AFFAIR. घडून आलेली गोष्ट *f.* गोष्ट *f.* वृत्त *n.* उदितकार्य *n.*

INCIDENTALLY, *adv.* v. A. 1. प्रसंगानें, प्रसंगानुसार, प्रसंगवशात्, प्रसंगवशें, प्रसंगतः.

INCIPIENT, *a. commencing.* उपक्रमाचा, प्रारंभींचा, आदींचा, पहिला, आरंभक, औपक्रमिक, पूर्वावस्थक.

INCIRCUMSPECTION, *n. want of caution.* गैरसावधपणा *m.* असावधपणा *m.* असावधान *n.* असावधानता *f.*

INCISION, INCISURE, *n. cut, gash, &c.* घाव *m.* घाय *m.* फाड *m.* फासणी *f.* चीर *f.* छेद *m.*

INCISOR, *n. foretooth.* चौकीचादांत *m.* चौकडीचा दांत *m.*

INCISORY, *a.* कापणारा, छेदक.

INCITATION, INCITEMENT, *n.* v. V.—*act.* उचलणें *n.* प्रेरणें*n.*&c. उठावणी *f.* उठावणूक *f.* उभारणी *f.* उचल *f.* उटाळणी *f.* उत्तेजन *n.* प्रवर्त्तन *n.* प्रोत्साहन *n.* उट्टंकण *n.* प्रेरणा *f.* प्रेरण *n.* उद्दीपन *n.* टोंचणी *f.*

2 *inciting cause, incentive.* उत्तेजन *n.* प्रेरक *n.* उत्तेजक *n.* उत्तेजनहेतु *m.* उत्तेजनकारण *n.* प्रयोजन *n.*

To INCITE, *v. a. instigate, stimulate, stir up, prompt, &c.* उचलणें, चढवणें, चढास *or* चढींदेणें, चढ *m.* देणें, भरवणें, उभारणें, शिकवणें, चेहरावणें, प्रेरणें, भर *f.* देणें-घालणें, फूस *f.* देणें, ईर्षा *f.* देणें, धिग्या *f. pl.* लावणें, टोंचणी *f.* देणें-लावणें, बीर *m.* भरणें-देणें, उटाळणी *f.*-उठावणी *f.*-उचल *f.*-उत्तेजन*n.*-&c.करणें *g.of o.*

INCITED, *p.* v. V. उचललेला, प्रेरलेला, &c. प्रवर्त्तित, प्रोत्साहित, प्रेरित.

INCITER, *n.* INCITING, *p. a.* v. V. उचलणारा, उठावणी करणारा, &c. उत्तेजक, प्रवर्त्तक, प्रयोजक, प्रोत्साहक, प्रेरक, प्रेरिता, प्रेरयिता, प्रेरण-उत्तेजन-&c. कर्त्ता-कारी.

INCIVILITY, *n.* v. RUDENESS. अविनय *m.* अननुनय *m.* अशिष्टता *f.* असभ्यता *f.* दौर्जन्य *n.* दुर्जनता *f.* अशिष्टाचार *m.*

INCLEMENCY, *n.* v. A. कठिणपणा*m.* कठोरपणा*m.* निर्दयपणा*m.*&c.

INCLEMENT, *a. pitiless, harsh, severe.* निर्दय, कठीण, कठोर, रुक्ष, कडकडीत, करडा.

INCLINABLE, *a. leaning, tending,* lit. fig. कलाचा, झोकाचा, कलण्याजोगा, प्रवण.

INCLINABLENESS, *n.* v. A. कल *m.* झोक *m.* प्रावण्य *n.*

INCLINATION, *n.* v. V. N. 1. कल *m.* झोक *m.* तोल *m.* रोंख *m.*

I. (of a planet's orbit) to the ecliptic. परमापम *m.*

2 मनाची ओढ *f.* मनाचा तोल *m.* मनाचा कल *m.* &c. मन *n.* आकांक्षा *f.* वासना *f.* कांक्षा *f.* प्रावण्य *n.* मति *f.* मनधावणी *f.* भर *m.*

To follow one's own i. मनमानतें तेंच करणें, आपल्या भ-[रानें चालणें.

To INCLINE, *v. n. lean, tend, bend.* कलणें, झुकणें, झोकणें, तोलणें, वळणें, ओणवणें, वांकणें, कलता-झुकता-&c. होणें, तोल*m.*-झोक *m.*-कल*m.*-रोंख*m.* जाणें *g. of s.*

2 *be desirous or disposed.* कलणें, झुकणें, तोलणें, वळणें, ओढणें, भावणें *impers.* तोल*m.*-झोक*m.*-&c. जाणें-असणें *g. of s.* मन*n.*-&c. घेणें-लवणें *g. of s.* ओढ *f.*-&c. येणें, स्वर*m. pl.* वाहणें-भजणें *g. of s.* मन *n.* असणें-बसणें-लागणें *g. of s.* ओढवणें.

To INCLINE, *v. a. give a leaning to.* झुकवणें, कलवणें, तोलवणें, लववणें, वांकविणें, कलावर-तोलावर-&c. धरणें, कल*m.*-तोल*m.*-&c. देणें.

2 *turn the will,* v. To DISPOSE. वळवणें, मन*n.* वळवणें-लववणें-&c. अनुसरवणें, प्रवण-&c. करणें.

INCLINED, *p.* v.V. N. 1. कललेला, झुकलेला, &c. तोल-&c. गेलेला.

An i. plane. उतरण *f. n.*

2 वळलेला, &c. प्रवण, शील in comp.

To be or feel i. मन*n.*-मनदेवता *f.*-मनपिंगळा*m.* लवणें-धावणें [*g. of s.*

To INCLOSE, INCLOSURE. See To ENCLOSE, &c.

To INCLUDE, *v. a.* See To ENCLOSE. 2 *comprise,* v. To COMPREHEND. आकळणें, धरणें, आकलन*n.*-समावेश*m.* करणें *g. of o.* अंतर्गत-अंतर्भूत-&c. करणें.

INCLUDED, *p.* v.V. 2. आकळलेला, धरलेला, पोटचा, अंतर्गत, अंतर्वर्त्ती, अंतर्भूत, अंतःपाती (in comp.).

To be i. under. मोडणें, ओढणें.

INCLUSION, *n.* v. V. 2—*act.* आकळणें*n.* धरणें*n.* &c. आकलन*n.* —*state.* समावेश*m.* अंतर्भाव*m.*

I. of both (dates and places). अभिविधि*m.*

INCLUSIVE, *a. that is comprehended,* v. INCLUDED. धरलेला.

INCLUSIVELY, *adv.* v. A. धरून (as सोमवार धरून Monday inclusively), सुद्धां, सकट.

INCOG, INCOGNITO, *adv. in a disguise of the real person.* गुप्तरूपानें, गुप्तवेषानें, अज्ञातरूपानें, अज्ञातवेषानें.

Living i. अज्ञातवास *m.*

INCOGITABLE, *a. inconceivable.* अचिंत्य, अचिंतनीय, अकल्प्य, अकल्पनीय.

INCOGITANCY, *n. want of thought.* अचिंतन *n.* अचिंता *f.* चिंतनाभाव *m.*

INCOGITANT, INCOGITATIVE, *a. wanting the power of thought.* अमनस्क, अचिंत, चिंतनरहित. [नाहीं.

INCOGNIZABLE, *a. that cannot be recognised.* ओळखतां यावयाचा

INCOHERENCE, INCOHERENCY, *n.* v. A. 1. असलग्नता *f.* असंयोग *m.* असंसक्ति *f.*

2 अनन्वय *m.* असंगति *f.* असंदर्भ *m.* संदर्भाशुद्धि *f.*

INCOHERENT, *a.*—lit. *wanting cohesion, not joined to each other.* असलग्न, असंयुक्त, तुटका, तुटक.

2—fig. v. INCONSISTENT. तुटक, तुटका, बिचूक, असंगत, असंबद्ध, अनन्वित, संदर्भविरुद्ध, संदर्भाशुद्ध, अन्योविन्य, असंभूत.

I. talk. अकडंतिकडं *n.* ढांचेंढूंचें *n.*

INCOHERENTLY, *adv.* v. A. 2. कांहींचें बांहीं, यद्वातद्वा *pop.* अद्वातद्वा, वांकडेंतिकडें, रिकाम्या रानीं, बिचूक, अकडंतिकडं, ढांचेंढू *or* ढांचेंढूंचें.

To talk i. वडाची साल पिंपळास लावणें.

INCOMBUSTIBILITY, INCOMBUSTIBLENESS, *n.* v. A. अदहनीयता *f.* अदाह्यता *f.*

INCOMBUSTIBLE, *a. that will not burn.* पेट घ्यायाचा नाहीं, अदहनीय, अदाह्य, दहनाशक्य, दहनानर्ह, ज्वलनानर्ह.

INCOME, *n. revenue.* जमा *f.* उत्पन्न *n.* प्राप्ति *f.* आय *m.* अदाई *f.*

आदाय *m.* अदा *m.* उदय *m.* अमदानी *f.* मिळकत *f.*
I. and expenditure. आयव्यय *m.*
That is without i. अनुत्पन्न, अनुपपन्न.

INCOMMENSURABILITY, INCOMMENSURABLENESS, *n.* v. A. असमपरिमाणत्व *n.* असमानत्व *n.*

INCOMMENSURABLE, *a. having no common measure.* असमपरिमाण, असमान, भिन्नपरिमाणक, असमपरिमेय.

INCOMMENSURATE, *a. not of equal extent.* न्यूनपरिमाण.

To INCOMMODE, *a. give inconvenience to.* अडचण *f.*-अडचणूक *f.*-&c. करणें, अडचणींत घालणें-पाडणें, उपद्रव *m.*-इजा *f.* करणें-देणें.
To be incommoded. अवघडणें, अडचणणें.

INCOMMODIOUS, *a. inconvenient.* गैरसोईचा, अडचणीचा, अप्रशस्त, अनुपयुक्त, अननुकूल.

INCOMMODIOUSNESS, *n.* v. A. गैरसोई *f.* अडचण *f.* अप्रशस्तता *f.* &c.

INCOMMUNICABILITY, INCOMMUNICABLENESS, *n.* v. A. 1. अनिवेद्यता *f.* अनिवेदनीयता *f.*
2 अन्यादेयता *f.* अनन्यदेयता *f.*

INCOMMUNICABLE, *a. that cannot be told, &c.* सांगायास योग्य-शक्य-&c. नाहीं, अनिवेद्य, अनिवेदनीय, अज्ञापनीय, अप्रकाश्य, अनन्यवेद्य.
2 *that cannot be imparted or given.* अन्यादेय, अनन्यदेय.

INCOMMUNICATIVE, *a. reserved, taciturn.* तोंडाचा जड, आंतल्या गांठीचा, खोल, मख्ख, अबोलका, अबोल्या, गहन, कथाविरक्त, भाषणविरक्त.

INCOMPACT, *a. not close, solid, &c.* अघन, अदृढ.

INCOMPARABLE, *a. that admits not of comparison.* अनुपम, निरुपम, अनुपमेय, अतुलनीय, अप्रतिम, सर्वोत्तम, सर्वोत्कृष्ट.

INCOMPARABLENESS, *n.* v. A. अनुपमता *f.* निरुपमता *f.* अनौपम्य *n.* सर्वोत्कृष्टता *f.*

INCOMPARABLY, *adv. beyond comparison.* अनुपम, निरुपम, सर्वोत्कृष्ट, अनौपम्यानें, अनौपम्यपूर्वक.

INCOMPASSIONATE, *a. pitiless,* v. CRUEL. निर्दय, दयाहीन.

INCOMPATIBILITY, *n.* v. A. विजोडपणा *m.* वैरुद्ध्य *n.* वैपरीत्य *n.* असंभव *m.* असंभावना *f.*

INCOMPATIBLE, *a. inconsistent.* विजोड, विलग, विरुद्ध, विपरीत, व्यधिकरण, असमानाधिकरण, असंभावनीय, असंभाव्य, असंभावित, अयथातथ. [*f.* असामर्थ्य *n.*

INCOMPETENCY, *n.* v. A. 1. अयोग्यता *f.* नालायकी *f.* अक्षमता
2 अपुरतेपणा *m.* &c. नपूर *f.* निपूर *f.* अपूर्ति *f.*

INCOMPETENT, *a. wanting faculties or qualifications,* v. UNABLE, UNFIT. अयोग्य, अक्षम, कार्याक्षम, नालायक, नाकर्त्ता, नाकूस, गलतान, असमर्थ. [नपुरा, अपूर्ण.
2 *inadequate,* v. INSUFFICIENT. अपुरता, अपुरा, निपुरा *or*

INCOMPLETE, *a. unfinished.* अपुरता, अपुरा, अधुरा, असंपूर्ण, असमाप्त, अनिष्पन्न, अकृत.
2 *imperfect, defective.* अपुरता, अपुरा, अपूर्ण, तुटक, कसरीचा, विकल, विकलांग, अंगविकल, अंगहीन, न्यूनांग, हीनांग.

INCOMPLETENESS, *n.* v. A. 1. अपुरतेपणा *m.* अपुरेपणा *m.* अधुरेपणा *m.* असमाप्ति *f.* असिद्धि *f.* अनिष्पत्ति *f.*
2 अपुरतेपणा *m.* &c. अपूर्णता *f.* वैकल्य *n.* कसर *f.* गुंजाबीस *f.*

INCOMPLIANCE, *n. non-compliance.* अस्वीकार *m.* असम्मति *f.* अननुवर्त्तन *n.* अननुरोध *m.*

INCOMPREHENSIBILITY, INCOMPREHENSIBLENESS, *n.* v. A. अज्ञेयत्व *n.* दुर्ज्ञेयता *f.* दुर्बोधता *f.* &c.

INCOMPREHENSIBLE, *a. inapprehensible by the understanding.* अज्ञेय, अविज्ञेय, दुर्ज्ञेय, दुर्बोध, दुरवबोध, अलक्ष्य, दुर्लक्ष, दुर्लक्ष्य, बोधातीत, बोधागम्य, बोधागोचर, बोधाविषय, बुद्ध्यतीत, ज्ञानातीत, अनधिगम्य, अकल, निगूढ, गहन, दुरूह. [*f.* &c.

INCOMPRESSIBILITY, *n.* v. A. असंकोचनीयता *f.* असंक्षेपणीयता

INCOMPRESSIBLE, *a. not to be compressed.* असंकोचनीय, अनाकुंचनीय, आकुंचनाशक्य, असंक्षेपणीय.

INCOMPUTABLE, &c. See INCALCULABLE, &c.

INCONCEALABLE, *a. not to be hid.* अगोपनीय, गोपनाशक्य, गोपनाक्षम.

INCONCEIVABLE, *a. that cannot be conceived by the mind.* अचिंत्य, अचिंतनीय, अतर्क्य, अवितर्क्य, अकल्पनीय, अभावनीय, निराभास, दुरूह, असंभावनीय, असंभाव्य. [संभावना *f.*

INCONCEIVABLENESS, *n.* v. A. अचिंत्यता *f.* अतर्क्यता *f.* &c. अ-

INCONCLUSIVE, *a. not settling a question.* अनिश्चयकारी, असिद्धांतकारी, अनिर्णयकारी, अनिश्चायक, अनिर्णायक, अनियामक, अप्रमापक, अपसिद्धांतकारी.

INCONCLUSIVENESS, *n.* v. A. अनिश्चयकारिता *f.* अनिश्चायकत्व *n.* अप्रमापकत्व *n.* &c. अयुक्ति *f.*

INCONGRUITY, *n.* v. A. विजोडपणा *m.* विलग *n.* असंबद्धता *f.* असंबंध *m.* अनन्वय *m.* असंभव *m.* असंभावना *f.*

INCONGRUOUS, *a.* v. INCONSISTENT. विजोड, विलग, असंबद्ध, असंगत, असंभाव्य, असंभावित, असंभावनीय.

INCONSEQUENCE, *n.*—in logic. अनन्वय *m.* असमन्वय *m.* असिद्धांत *m.* सिद्धांताभाव *m.*

INCONSEQUENT, INCONSEQUENTIAL, *a. not following from the premises.* अनन्वित, असमन्वित, सिद्धांतरहित, असंबद्ध.

INCONSIDERABLE, *a. little, trifling,* v. LIGHT. अगण्य, उपेक्षणीय, हलका, थोडा, लहान, अल्प, जमेस धराया जोगा-&c. नाहीं.

INCONSIDERABLENESS, *n.* v. A. हलकेपणा *m.* थोडकेपणा *m.* &c. लहानवी *f.*

INCONSIDERATE, *a. thoughtless, imprudent.* अविचारी, अविचारशील, अविवेकी, हीनविचार, हीनविवेक, विचारहीन-रहित-शून्य-&c. हूड, परिणामादर्शी, अविमृश्यकारी.
2 *proceeding from thoughtlessness.* अविचाराचा, अविवेकाचा, विचाराभावाचा, &c. अविचारमूलक.

INCONSIDERATELY, *adv.* v. A. अविचारानें, अविचारपूर्वक &c. विचारकेल्यावांचून, मागेंपुढें पाहिल्यावांचून, भुलून, सहसा.

INCONSIDERATENESS, INCONSIDERATION, *n.* v. A. अविचार *m.* अविवेक *m.* विचाराभाव *m.* विवेकाभाव *m.* अचिंता *f.* अतर्क *m.* विचारराहित्य *n.* अविचारिता *f.*

INCONSISTENCE, INCONSISTENCY, *n.* v. A. 1. विजोडपणा *m.* विरोध *m.* वैपरीत्य *n.* बेबनाव *m.* विसंगति *f.* असंगति *f.* असंगतता *f.* असंभावना *f.* असंभव *m.* अयुक्ति *f.* वैजात्य *n.* वैलक्षण्य *n.* वैधर्म्य *n.* वैगुण्य *n.*
2 अनन्वय *m.* असमन्वय *m.* असंदर्भ *m.* संदर्भविरोध *m.* असंगति *f.* पूर्वापरविरोध *m.* संदर्भाशुद्धि *f.*

INCONSISTENT, *a. incompatible, incongruous, not agreeing with.* विजोड, विलग, विरुद्ध, विरोधी, विपरीतधर्मक, विगुणक, विसंगत, असंगत, असंभावनीय, असंभाव्य, असंभवित *or* असंभावित, असंभवी, असंभूत, अनुपयोगी, अनुपयुक्त, विजातीय, विलक्षण.

2 *incoherent, not agreeing with itself.* असंगत, विसंगत, असंबद्ध, अनन्वित, असमन्वित, संदर्भाशुद्ध, संदर्भविरुद्ध, असंदर्भ, संदर्भ विरहित, पूर्वापरविरुद्ध, विचूक.

INCONSISTENTLY, *adv.* v. A. 2. ताळ-धरबंध-धारबोल-&c. सोडून, अकडंतिकडं,विचूक.

INCONSOLABLE, *a. not to be consoled.* असांत्वनीय, सांत्वनाशक्य, दुःसांत्वनीय, शोकान्वित.

INCONSONANT. See INCONSISTENT, DISCORDANT.

INCONSPICUOUS, *a.* दुर्दर्श, अव्यक्त, असहज दृश्य.

INCONSTANCY, *n.* v. A. चंचलपणा*m.* चंचलता *f.* चांचल्य*n.* अस्थिरता *f.* अस्थैर्य*n.*

INCONSTANT, *a. unstable, fickle*, v. CHANGEABLE. चंचल, अस्थिर, अधीर, अस्थायी, क्षणिकचित्त, क्षणिकबुद्धि, चंचलवृत्ति, हरिद्राराग.

INCONTESTABLE, *a.* v. INDISPUTABLE. अविवाद्य, अविवदनीय, विवादाशक्य, निर्विवाद, अखंडनीय, अबाध्य, निराबाध्य.

INCONTESTABLY, *adv.* v. A. निर्विवाद, बेतकरार.

INCONTINENCE, INCONTINENCY, *n.* v. A. इंद्रियानिग्रह*m.* इंद्रियासंयम*m.* इंद्रियासंयमन*n.* इंद्रियानियमन *n.* इंद्रियानिग्रहिता *f.* इंद्रियासंयमिता *f.* &c.

INCONTINENT, *a. not restraining the passions.* इंद्रियानिग्रही, इंद्रियासंयमी, इंद्रियादमी, अनधीनेंद्रिय, अजितेंद्रिय, कासोट्याचाढिला-हलका-&c. व्यभिचारी, जारकर्मी.

INCONTROVERTIBLE, *a.* v. INDISPUTABLE. अविवदनीय, अखंडनीय, विवादाशक्य, अबाध्य, निर्विवाद, प्रमाणानपेक्ष.

INCONVENIENCE, INCONVENIENCY, *n.* v. A. गैरसोई *f.* अडचण*f.* अयुक्तता *f.* अयुक्ति *f.* अनुपयुक्तता *f.*

I. *an* i. अडचण *f.* अडणूक *f.* गैरसोई *f.* गौरव *n.*

To INCONVENIENCE, *v. a.* v. To INCOMMODE. गैरसोई *f.*-&c. करणें *g. of o.* अडचणींत घालणें.

INCONVENIENT, *a. incommodious, unsuitable.* गैरसोईचा, अडचणीचा, अनुपयोगी, अनुपयुक्त, अयुक्त, अयुक्तिक, दुःखद, दुःखप्रद-जनक-&c. क्लेशद, क्लेशप्रद-&c.

INCONVENIENTLY, *adv.* v. A. गैरसोईचा *decl.* गैरसोईनें, गैरसोई होईसा *decl.*

INCONVERSANCY, *n.* v. A. अनभ्यास *m.* गैरराबता *m.* गैरमाहिती *f.* अपरिज्ञान *n.* अनैपुण्य *n.* अप्रावीण्य *n.* अनालोड्य *n.*

INCONVERSANT, *a. not versed, not familiar.* गैरमाहीत, गैरमाहित्या, गैरमाहितगार, अनभ्यासी, अनभ्यस्त, अनिपुण, अप्रवीण, अनिष्णात.

INCONVERTIBLE, *a. that cannot be changed into some thing else.* द्रव्यांतर करणाशक्य,रूपांतरकरणाशक्य,पदार्थांतरकरणाशक्य.

INCORPORAL. See INCORPOREAL.

To INCORPORATE, *v. a.* See To EMBODY. 2 *mix and make into one body.* मिसळणें, मिळवणें, मिसळून-&c. एककरणें, एकाकार *m.*-संपर्क *m.*-&c. करणें *g. of o.*

3 *form into a legal body.* सनदीमंडळी *f.* करणें.

To INCORPORATE, *v. n.* मिळणें, मिळून-&c. एकहोणें.

INCORPOREAL, *a. that has not a material body.* विदेही, अदेह, अशरीर, अशरीरी, अशारीरक, अनंग, अविग्रह, निराकार.

INCORPOREALNESS, INCORPOREITY, *n.* v. A. विदेहत्व *n.* अशरीरत्व *n.* &c. देहाभाव *m.* शरीराभाव *m.* वैदेह्य *n.* अशरीरभाव *m.*

INCORRECT, *a. inaccurate*, v. WRONG. अशुद्ध, चुकीचा, सदोष, दोषी, गैरवास्तवीक, गैरास्त, नादुरुस्त.

Altogether i. सर्वाशुद्ध.

INCORRECTLY, *adv.* v. A. अशुद्ध, चूक करून, अन्यथा.

INCORRECTNESS, *n.* v. A. अशुद्धता *f.* अशुद्धि *f.* गैरवास्तविकपणा *m.* सदोषता *f.* नादुरुस्ती *f.*

INCORRIGIBLE, *a. depraved beyond correction*, v. SHAMELESS, WICKED. कोडगा, घाय कटार, निगरगटा, शिक्षातीत, अशिक्षणीय, अगदी कामांतून गेलेला, माणसांतून उठलेला, अतिदुष्ट.

INCORRIGIBLENESS, *n.* v. A. कोडगेपणा *m.* &c. [वित्र.

INCORRUPT, *a.* v. PURE. अदुष्ट, अदूषित, अभ्रष्ट, शुद्ध, स्वच्छ, प-

INCORRUPTIBILITY, *n.* v. A. अनाश्यता *f.* अविनाशिता *f.* अविकारिता *f.* विकाराक्षमता *f.*

INCORRUPTIBLE, *a. not susceptible of corruption or decay.* अनाश्य, अविनाश्य, अविनाशी, अविकार, अविकार्य, अविकारी, अनश्वर, विकाराक्षम, विकाराशक्य, अजरामर, अपकर्षाक्षम.

INCORRUPTION, INCORRUPTNESS, *n.* v. A. अविकार *m.* अविकृति *f.* विकाराभाव *m.* अदुष्टता *f.* अभ्रष्टता *f.* स्वच्छता *f.*

To INCRASSATE, &c. See To THICKEN, &c.

To INCREASE, *v. n. grow greater or more.* वाढणें, चढणें, वर्धणें, ज्यास्त-अधिक-&c. होणें, वाढ *f.*-वृद्धि *f.*-&c. होणें *g. of s.* वृद्धि *f.* पावणें, थोरावणें, अधिकावणें.

2 (in force or intenseness). जोरावणें, जडावणें, जडकावणें, बळावणें.

To INCREASE, *v. a. make greater or more.* वाढवणें, चढवणें, अधिक-ज्यास्त-&c. करणें, वाढ *f.*-वृद्धि *f.*-&c. करणें *g. of o.*

INCREASE, INCREASING, *n.* v. V. N. वाढणें *n.* वाढ *f.* वाढवा *or* वाढावा *m.* वाढणूक *f.* चढ *m.* चढती *f.* बढती *f.* वृद्धि *f.* अभिवृद्धि *f.* वर्धन *n.* संवर्धन *n.* उपचय *m.*

v. V. A. वाढवणें *n.* वाढवणूक *f.* वर्धन *n.* संवर्धन*n.*

I. *increment.* वाढवा*or* वाढावा*m.*वाढ *f.* वाढा*m.* वृद्धि *f.* संवृद्धि*f.*

INCREASED, *p.* v. V. N. वाढलेला, &c. वर्द्धित, संवर्द्धित, वृद्ध, प्रवृद्ध.

v. V. A. वाढवलेला, &c. वर्द्धित, संवर्द्धित.

INCREASER, *n.* INCREASING, *p. a.* v.V. N. 1. वाढणारा, &c. वाढता, चढता, चढाचा, वर्द्धमान, वृद्धिंगत.

v. V. A. वाढवणारा, वर्द्धक, वृद्धिकर-कर्त्ता-कारक-&c. संवर्द्धक.

INCREDIBILITY, *n.* v. A. अश्रद्धेयता *f.* विश्वासानर्हता *f.* विश्वासायोग्यता *f.*

INCREDIBLE, *a. that cannot be believed.* खरामानायाजोगा-&c. नाहीं, अश्रद्धेय, अविश्वसनीय, अविश्वास्य, विश्वासानर्ह, विश्वासायोग्य.

INCREDULITY, *n.* v. A. अश्रद्धा *f.* अभक्ति *f.* अविश्वास*m.* अश्रद्धालुता *f.*

INCREDULOUS, *a. indisposed to believe.* अश्रद्धावान्, अश्रद्धालु, अभक्ति, मंदश्रद्ध, मंदप्रत्यय.

INCREMENT, *n. increase, addition.* वाढ *f.* वाढा *m.* वाढवा *or* वाढावा*m.* वृद्धि *f.*

To INCRIMINATE. See To CRIMINATE.

To INCRUST, *To* INCRUSTATE, *v. a. cover with a crust or hard coat.* पूट *or* पुट*n.*-कवच*n.*-&c. चढवणें-देणें, किटवणें, सपुट-सकवच-पुटयुक्त-&c. करणें.

INCRUSTATION. See CRUST.

To INCUBATE, *v. n. sit on eggs, to hatch.* अंडीं *n. pl.* उबवणें, अंड उबारा*m.* करणें.

INCUBATION, *n.* v. V. अंडीं उबवणें*n.*

INCUBUS, *n. night mare.* कुस्वप्न*m. n.* अजीर्णप्रयुक्तस्वप्न*m. n.*

To INCULCATE, *v. a. teach by frequent repetitions.* वारंवार सांगून शिकवणें-बिंबवणें-भरवणें-उपतिष्ठवणें, पौनःपुन्योपदेश *m.* करणें *g. of o.* उगाळणें, वाटाघाट *f.*-वाटावाटी *f.*-घासाघास *f.*-त्रिवारबोध*m.*-&c. करणें *g. of o.*

INCULCATED, *p.* v. V. वारंवार सांगितलेला, &c.

INCULCATION, *n.* v. V.—*act.* वारंवार सांगणें*n.* &c. पौनःपुन्योपदेश*m.* वाटावाट *f.* वाटावाटी *f.* घासाघास *f.* त्रिवारबोध*m.*

INCULPABLE. See UNBLAMABLE.

To INCULPATE, &c. See To CRIMINATE, To BLAME, &c.

INCUMBENCY, *n.* v. A. 2. आवश्यकता *f.* कर्त्तव्यता *f.* आवश्यक*n.* ओझें*n.* भार*m.*

INCUMBENT, *a. lying or resting on.* वरराहणारा-असणारा, उपरिस्थित, आधेय.

2 *lying on as a duty.* आवश्यक, अवश्यकर्त्तव्य, कर्त्तव्य, लाजीम, जरूर, अकरणेप्रत्यवाय.

To be i. on. भाग असणें-येणें-पडणें (ex. मला बोलणें भाग आहे), प्राप्त असणें.

INCUMBENT, *n. holder of a benefice or office.* धर्मवृत्तिभोगी, धर्मवृत्तिधारी, वृत्तिभोगी.

To INCUR, *v. a. bring on one's self, make one's self liable to.* पदरीं घेणें-बांधणें-बांधून घेणें, आपणावर आणणें-ओढणें-ओढून घेणें, पात्र *n.* होणें *g. of o.* घेणें, योग्य-अर्ह-&c. होणें *in. con.* (in comp.).

INCURABLE, *a. that cannot be cured, &c.* असाध्य, असाधनीय, दुस्तर, अचिकित्स्य, चिकित्सातीत, चिकित्साबाह्य, अपरिहार्य, अप्रतीकार्य, निरुपाय, उपायातीत, बेलाग.

INCURABLENESS, INCURABILITY. *n.* v. A. असाध्यता *f.* असाधनीयता *f.* अचिकित्स्यता *f.* &c. निरुपायता *f.*

INCURABLY, *adv.* v. A. बरा न होईसा *decl.*

INCURIOSITY, INCURIOUSNESS, *n.* v. A. अजिज्ञासा *f.* अबुभुत्सा *f.* बोधेच्छाभाव *m.*

INCURIOUS, *a. not curious.* अबुभुत्सु, अजिज्ञासु, श्रवणदर्शनानुत्सुक, अल्पशोधी, विकौतुक. [आक्रमण *n.*

INCURSION, *n. inroad, invasion.* स्वारी *f.* दौड *f.* क्रांति *f.* आक्रम*m.*

INCURSIVE, *a.* स्वारी-&c. करणारा, आक्रमण-&c. कारी.

To INCURVATE, &c. See To BEND, &c. [ऋणबद्ध.

INDEBTED, *a. being in debt.* ऋणी, देणेदार, देणेकरी, ऋणकरी,

2 *laid under obligation.* बांधलेला, बांधीव, बांदा, विकलेला, उपकारी, उपकारबद्ध. [लज्जाभाव*m.*

INDECENCY, *n.* v. A. निलाजरेपणा *m.* निर्लज्जता *f.* लज्जाराहित्य*n.*

I. *indecent behaviour.* गैरशिष्टचाल *f.* अशिष्टाचार *m.*

INDECENT, *a. offensive to modesty, delicacy, &c.* निलाजरा, निर्लज्ज, लाजिरवाणा, लाजलावणा, लाजलाव्या, निलाजरेपणाचा, निर्लज्जतेचा, हीनलज्ज, लज्जाकारक, लज्जाप्रद, लज्जावह, बेशरमेचा, लज्जाहीन, लज्जारहित, अशिष्ट, अचकट विचकट, बीभत्स, कुत्सित.

INDECENTLY, *adv.* v. A. निलाजरेपणानें, निर्लज्जतापूर्वक, लाज टाकून.

INDECISION, *n. want of firmness.* अधीर *m.* अधैर्य *n.* धरसोडपणा *m.* धरसोड *f.* मनश्चांचल्य *n.* मनस्तारल्य *n.*

INDECISIVE, *a. not decisive.* अनिश्चयात्मक, अनिर्णयात्मक, अनिश्चायक, अनिर्णायक, पळपळीत, अळमळीत, गुळमुळीत,

2 *undecided, wavering.* अधीर, धरसोड्या, अस्थिर.

INDECLINABLE, *a.*—in grammar. अव्यय, अविकारी, अविभक्तिक, अव्ययात्मक, अव्ययरूप.

I. compound. अव्ययी भाव *m.*

I. word. अव्यय *n.*

INDECOROUS, *a. unbecoming.* अशिष्ट, अशिष्टाईचा, अशिष्टाचाराचा, अमर्यादेचा, &c. अयोग्य, अनुचित, अन्यायी, अन्याय्य, अविनय.

INDECOROUSLY, *adv.* v. A. अशिष्टाईनें, अमर्यादेनें, अमर्यादापूर्वक, अशिष्टाचारपूर्वक, शिष्टाचार सोडून.

INDECOROUSNESS, INDECORUM, *n.* v. A. अशिष्टाई *f.* अमर्यादा *f.* अन्याय *m.* अनौचित्य *n.* अविनय *m.* असभ्यता *f.* अशिष्टाचार *m.* असभ्याचार *m.* शिष्टाचारातिक्रम *m.*

INDEED, *adv. verily, really, actually,* v. TRULY. सत्य, वास्तवीक, खराच, खरोखर, खचीत, अवश्य, भावार्थ, सई *or* सही, बरीक.

INDEFATIGABLE, *a. unwearied, not yielding to fatigue.* धकायाजोगा-&c. नाहीं, अश्रमणीय, अश्रांत, अक्लांत, परिश्रमी, मेहनती, अश्रमी, कसालती, खप्या, परिश्रमाचा.

INDEFATIGABLY, *adv.* v. A. परिश्रमानें, परिश्रमपूर्वक.

INDEFEASIBILITY, *n.* v.A. अनिवार्यता *f.* अपरिहार्यता *f.* &c.

INDEFEASIBLE, *a. that cannot be set aside.* अनिवार्य, अपरिहार्य, अखंडनीय, अच्छेद्य, अच्छेदनीय, खंडनाशक्य, छेदनाशक्य.

INDEFECTIBILITY, *n.* v. A. अविकारता *f.* अक्षयता *f.* &c.

INDEFECTIBLE, *a. not liable to decay.* अविकार, अविकार्य, अक्षय *pop.* अक्षयी, अक्षय्य, क्षयानर्ह, क्षयायोग्य, अनाश्य, अविनाश्य.

INDEFENSIBILITY, *n.* v. A. अरक्ष्यता *f.* अरक्षणीयता *f.* &c.

INDEFENSIBLE, *a. that cannot be maintained.* राखायास-संभाळायास अयोग्य- अशक्य-&c. अरक्ष्य, अरक्षणीय, रक्षणायोग्य, रक्षणाशक्य, अशक्यरक्ष.

2 *that cannot be supported or vindicated.* अप्रतिपाद्य, अप्रतिपादनीय, प्रतिपादनाशक्य, अशक्यप्रतिपादन, अव्यवस्थापनीय, व्यवस्थापनाशक्य, अव्यवस्थाप्य, अनुत्तर, अदेयोत्तर.

INDEFINABLE, *a. not to be defined.* अनिर्वचनीय, अनिर्वाच्य, निर्वचनाशक्य, अलक्षणीय.

INDEFINITE, *a.* v. INDETERMINATE. अनिश्चित, अनिर्धारित, अनियमित, अनवधारित, अनियत, मोघम *or* मोहगम, संजाइती, संजाईत, अभोगत, मुग्ध, मुग्धा.

2 *exceedingly great, &c.* v. INFINITE. अमर्याद, बेहद्द, बेसुमार, बेठिकाण, बेथांग, अप्रमेय.

INDEFINITELY, *adv.* v. A. 1. मोघम *or* मोहगम, अभोगत, नपुत्रोनपुत्री, अनियमपूर्वक.

2 अमर्याद, बेसुमार, &c.

INDEFINITENESS, *n.* v. A. 1. मोघमपणा *m.* अभोगतपणा *m.* &c. अनिश्चितत्व *n.* &c. अनियम *m.* अळमटळम *n. f.*

INDELIBILITY, INDELIBLENESS, *n.* v.A. अमार्जनीयता *f.* अमार्ज्यत्व *n.* &c.

INDELIBLE, *a. not to be effaced, &c.* पुसून जायाचा नाहीं, जायाचा नाहीं, अमार्ज्य, अप्रमार्ज्य, अमार्जनीय, पक्का बसलेला, वज्रलेपायित, वज्रप्राय.

INDELICACY, *n.* v. A. 1. बेमुरवत *f.* बेमुलाजा *m.* निर्भीड *f.* निर्भिडपणा *m.* असंकोच *m.* संकोचराहित्य *n.*

2 v. INDECENCY. अशिष्टाई *f.* अशिष्टता *f.* अशिष्टाचार*m.* मर्यादातिक्रम *m.*

INDELICATE, *a. void of fine feeling or delicacy.* बेमुरवतीचा,

बेमुलाज्याचा, निर्भीड, निर्भिडेचा, असंकोच, असंकोचाचा, संकोचहीन-रहित-&c. अमर्यादशील.

2 v. INDECENT. लज्जाकारक, लज्जाप्रद, लज्जावह, लाजलावणा.

INDELICATELY, *adv.* v. A. 1. बेमुरवत, बेमुलाजा.

INDEMNIFICATION, *n.* v. V. 1. तोट्यावांचून राखणें *n.* &c.

2 भरून देणें *n.* &c. नुकसान भरणी *f.* हानिपूरण *n.* क्षतिपूरण*n.*

To INDEMNIFY, *v. a. secure against loss.* तोट्यावांचून राखणें, तोटा न येण्याची हामी *f.* देणें.

2 *re-imburse.* भरून देणें, नुकसान*n.*-&c. भरून देणें, हानिपूरण*n.*-क्षतिपूरण*n.*-&c. करणें.

INDEMNITY, *n. security against loss.* तोटा न येण्याची हामी *f.* तोटा न होऊं देण्याची हामी *f.*

Paper, &c. of i. नुकसानचिट्ठी *f.* हानिपूरणपत्र*n.*

2 *security against punishment.* शिक्षा न होण्याची हामी *f.*

Paper, &c. of i. दंडाभयपत्र*n.* अदंडपत्र*n.* अभयपत्र*n.*

INDEMONSTRABLE, *a.* असाध्य.

To INDENT, *v. a. notch, scollop.* खांडे *m. pl.*-खांडी *f. pl.*-&c. पाडणें, करवती कांठी-क्रकचाकार-&c. करणें.

2 *bind out by contract.* करारानें-&c. ठेवणें-&c.

To INDENT, *v. n. bargain.* See To CONTRACT.

2 *make a requisition for supplies.* मागणी *f.* करणें.

INDENT, *n.* See INDENTATION.

2 *official requisition for supplies.* मागणी *f.*

INDENTATION, *n. notch, &c.* खांडा*m.* खांड *f.* खांडोरें*n.* खाप *f.n.*

I. as of the edge of an unfinished wall, thatch, &c. चाल *f.*

INDENTED, *p.* v.V. खांडे पाडलेला, करवती कांठी, कातरकुतर, अनुक्रकच, क्रकचाकार.

2 करारानें ठेवलेला.

INDENTURE, *n. covenant, writing of contract.* करारनामा*m.* नियमपत्रक*n.*

To INDENTURE, &c. See To INDENT, &c.

INDEPENDENCE, INDEPENDENCY, *n.* v.A. 1. स्वातंत्र्य*n.* स्वतंत्रता *f.* स्वाधीनता*f.* अपराधीनता*f.* अवशता*f.* अपारतंत्र्य*n.* मुखत्यारी*f.*

2 असंबंध*m.* संबंधाभाव*m.* संबंधराहित्य*n.* अनन्यसंबंध*m.* अन्यसंबंधाभाव*m.*

3 अनन्यानुवर्त्तन*n.* स्वमतानुगमन*n.* स्वमतानुयायिता *f.* स्वमतानुसारिता *f.* स्वमतानुसरण *n.*

4 घरचा सुखीपणा*m.* घरची संपत्ति *f.* घरची संपन्नता *f.* अनन्योपजीविका*f.*

INDEPENDENT, *a. not under the control of others.* स्वतंत्र, स्वाधीन *pop.* स्वस्वाधीन, स्ववश, अपराधीन, अपरतंत्र, अनन्याधीन, अवश, स्वायत्त, अनायत्त, मुखत्यार, स्वैर, स्वैरी, स्वैरगामी.

2 *not connected with, or dependent on others.* अनन्यसंबंधी, अनन्यसंबंधाचा, अन्यसंबंधरहित- शून्य-&c. निरवलंब, निरालंब.

3 *not obsequious.* अनन्यानुवर्त्ती, अन्याननुवर्त्ती, स्वतांचा, स्वबुद्ध्यनुसारी, स्वमतानुगामी, स्वमतानुयायी, स्वायत्त.

4 *possessing a competence.* घरचा सुखी-स्वस्थ-संपन्न-खातापिता-&c. खाऊन जेवून खुशाल, अनन्योपजीवी.

INDEPENDENTLY, *adv.* v. A. 1. स्वतंत्रपणानें, &c. स्वातंत्र्यपूर्वक, &c. मुखत्यारीनें.

2 अनन्यसंबंधानें,अन्यसंबंधावांचून, अन्यसंबंधाभावपूर्वक, शिवाई.

3 आपल्या बुद्धीनें, स्वमतानुसरणपूर्वक, &c.

INDESCRIBABLE, *a.* अवाच्य, अनिर्वाच्य, अनिर्वचनीय, अनिरूपणीय, अकथनीय, अवर्णनीय, शब्दातीत.

INDESERT, *n. want of merit.* गुणाभाव*m.* योग्यताभाव*m.* असौष्ठव *n.* योग्यताराहित्य*n.* [याभाव*m.*

INDESTRUCTIBILITY, *n.* v. A. अविनाश्यता *f.* &c. अक्षय*m.* क्षयाभाव*m.*

INDESTRUCTIBLE, *a.* अविनाश्य, अनाश्य, अविनाशी, नाशाशक्य, अक्षय, अक्षय्य, अक्षर, अव्यय, अनश्वर, अविनश्वर.

INDETERMINABLE, *a.* अनिश्चेय, अनिर्धार्य्य, अनिर्धारणीय, अनवधार्य्य, अनिर्णेय, अप्रमेय.

INDETERMINATE, *a. not definite; vague, lax, loose.* अनिश्चित, अनिर्धारित, अनवधारित, अनियमित, मोघम *or* मोहगम, संजाइती, संजाईत, अभोगत, धरसोडीचा, डळमळीत, पळपळीत, पुळपुळीत, पुळपुळा, गुळमुळीत, बुळबुळीत, अळमळीत, अळमळीत गुळमळीत, अलबेला, भोंगळ, भसभोंगळ, बुळका, मुध, मुग्धा.

INDETERMINATELY, *adv.* v. A. मोघम *or* मोहगम, अभोगत, अळमळीत, अळमटळम, दुग्धा, धरून सोडून, अत्रप *or* ब, उभारत.

INDETERMINATENESS, *n.* v. A. मोघमपणा *m.* &c. अनिश्चितत्व*n.* &c. अनियम *m.* अत्र *n.* अत्रप *or* ब *n.* तथा *f. neg. con.* दुग्धा *f.*

INDETERMINATION, *n. unsettled state of mind.* अनिश्चय *m.* अनिर्धार *m.* निश्चयाभाव *m.* धरसोडपणा *m.*

INDEVOTION, *n. want of devotion to.* अभक्ति *f.* अनासक्ति *f.* अनिष्ठा *f.*

2 v. IRRELIGION. अभक्ति *f.* ईश्वराभक्ति *f.* भक्त्यभाव *m.* ईश्वरानिष्ठा *f.* अश्रद्धा *f.*

INDEVOUT, *a. not having devout affections.* भक्तिहीन-शून्य-&c. भक्तिभावहीन-&c. अभक्त, अभक्तिमान्, ईश्वरानिष्ठ, अनीश्वरपरायण.

INDEX, *n. pointer out.* प्रदर्शक *n.* दर्शक *n.* सूचक *n.* ज्ञापक *n.*

2 *table of contents.* अनुक्रमणिका *f.* सूचीपत्र *n.* सूची *f.* सूचिका *f.* जंत्री *f.*

3 *fore finger.* तर्जनी *f.*

4 (in algebra, &c.) घातप्रकाशक.

INDEXTERITY, *n. want of skill.* अदक्षता *f.* अदाक्ष्य *n.* अदाक्षिण्य *n.* अनैपुण्य *n.*

INDIA, *n.* हिंदुस्थान *n.* भरतखंड *n.* भारत *n.* भरतवर्ष *n.* जंबुद्वीप *n.*

INDIAN, *a.* हिंदुस्थानचा, भरतखंडचा, हिंदुस्थानांतला, &c.

INDIAN CORN, *n.* मका *m.*

Grain of i. मकाणा *m.*

Straw of i. मकाण *n.*

I. parched. मकाणे *m. pl.*

INDICANT, INDICATORY. See INDICATIVE.

To INDICATE, *v. a. point out,* v. To SHEW. दाखवणें, दर्शवणें, प्रदर्शवणें, सुचवणें, बोधवणें, प्रदर्शन *n.*-बोधन *n.*-&c. करणें *g. of o.*

INDICATED, *p.* v. V. दाखवलेला, &c. प्रदर्शित, दार्शित, बोधित, निर्दिष्ट, उद्दिष्ट, आविर्भूत.

INDICATION, *n.* v. V.—*act.* दाखवणें *n.* &c. प्रदर्शन *n.* बोधन *n.* बोध *m.* निर्देश *m.* उद्देश *m.* सूचन *n.* सूची *f.*

I. of a passion, &c. by gesture or action. आविर्भाव *m.* अभिनय *m.* आकार *m.* सूची *f.*

II. *sign, symptom, token.* लक्षण *n.* खूण *f.* चिन्ह *n.* निशाणी *or* नी *f.* छाया *f.* सूचक *n.* व्यंजन *n.* पूर्वरूप *n.*

INDICATIVE, *a.* v. V. दाखवणारा, प्रदर्शक, दर्शक, सूचक, बोधक,

उद्बोधक (all used esp. in comp.), सूची (in comp.), दर्शी (in comp.).
I.—in grammar. स्वार्थ.

To INDICT, *v. a. charge in a writing.* लेखनाभियोग *m.*-लेखाभियोग *m.* करणें, दोषारोप *m.* करणें.

INDICTED, *p.* v. V. लेखनाभियुक्त, लेखाभियुक्त.

INDICTMENT, *n.* v. V. अभियोगलेख *m.* अभियोगपत्र *n.* दोषारोपपत्र *n.* भाषालेख *m.*

INDIFFERENCE, *n.* v. A. 1. *equipoise of mind.* उदासीनपणा *m.* समभाव *m.* समदृष्टि *f.* समानदृष्टि *f.* औदासीन्य *n.* उदासीनभाव *m.* समपक्षता *f.* ताटस्थ्य *n.*
2 *unconcern.* अनास्था *f.* अनुत्साह *m.* अनुत्कंठा *f.* औदासीन्य *n.* उदासीनवृत्ति *f.* अनपेक्षा *f.* निरपेक्षा *f.* अनिच्छा *f.* हैगई *f.* बेपरवाई *f.* अनमान *m.* आळस *m.* अनादरबुद्धि *f.* कानाडोळा *m.* आनाकानी *f.*
3 सारखेपणा *m.* बराबरी *f.* समता *f.* समतोलता *f.* आग्रहाविषयता *f.* रुतारुतत्व *n.*

INDIFFERENT, *a. neutral, not inclining.* उदासीन, समदृष्टि, समचित्त, समपक्ष, निःस्पृह, तटस्थ.
2 *unconcerned.* उदास, उदासीन, उदासीनवृत्ति, अनास्थ, निरुत्साह, निःस्पृह, अनिच्छ, निराश, निरीह, निचाड, अजुर्दा, बेपरवा, बेदर्दी, बेफिकीर, निःकाळजी *or* निकाळजी, अनपेक्ष, उपेक्षाबुद्धि, नीरत, सोपेक्ष.
3 *without preponderance or preferableness.* सारखा, बराबर, सम, समतोल, उदासीनपणाचा, अनाग्रहाचा, आग्रहाविषय, रुतारुत.
4 *common, badish.* सामान्य, मध्यमप्रतीचा, अधलंड मधलंड, खैराती, खैरीशैरी, तसाच, तशासारखा, तादृश *neg. con.*

INDIFFERENTLY, *adv.* v. A. 1. उदासीनपणानें, औदासीन्यानें, समदृष्टीनें, समभावानें, समपक्षतेनें.
2 अनास्था-अनुत्साह-&c. पूर्वक, टंगळमंगळ.
3 सुमाराचा *decl.* कसातरी, जेमतेम, जसातसा *decl.* सरासरी.

INDIGENCE, INDIGENCY, *n.* v. POVERTY. अनुपपत्ति *pop.* अनुपत *f.* गरीबी *f.* कंगाली *f.* दारिद्र्य *n.* नातवानी *f.* ददात *f.*

INDIGENOUS, *a. native, not exotic.* मुलकी *or* खी, देशचा, देशांतला, देशी (in comp.), देशीय & देश्य (in comp.), देशज, दैशिक. [नातवान, बुभुक्षित.

INDIGENT, *a.* v. POOR. अनुत्पन्न, अनुपपन्न, गरीब, दरिद्र, कंगाल,

INDIGESTED, *a. not concocted in the stomach.* नपचलेला, अपक्व, अजातपाक, अपाक, अपचन.
2 *not regularly arranged, &c.* अजातव्यवस्थ, अभूतव्यवस्थ, अव्यवस्थित.

INDIGESTIBLE, *a. not easily converted into chyme.* दुष्पच, दुष्पच्य, दुष्पचनीय, कष्टपच्य, दुर्जर, जड, अजीर्णकारक.

INDIGESTION, *n. dyspepsy.* अजीर्ण *n.* अजीर्णता *f.* अजीर्णविकार *m.* अन्नविकार *m.* अन्नविकृति *f.* अपाक *m.* अपचन *n.*
Flatulent i. विदग्धाजीर्ण *n.*
Slight i. अजीर्णांश *m.*
Weight on the stomach from i. जाड्य *n.*

To INDIGITATE, *v. a. point out with the finger.* बोट *n.* करणें-करून दाखवणें, बोट *n.* दाखवणें. [मानकुद्ध.

INDIGNANT, *a.* v. ANGRY. तप्त, संतप्त, कोपज्वलित, क्रुद्ध, अभिमानक्रोध*m.*

INDIGNATION, *n.*v. ANGER. कोप*m.* रोष*m.* तेष*m.* संताप*m.* जळ*m.*

INDIGNITY, *n. contumely, &c.* v. CONTEMPT. अपमान*m.* अनादर*m.* अव्हेर*m.* हेलना *f.* हेला *f.* अवज्ञा *f.*

INDIGO, *n.*—the plant. नीळ *f.* नीली *f.* गुळी *f.* नीलिनी *f.* नीलिका *f.* निळंबी *f.*
2—the colour obtained. नीळ*f.* गुळी *f.* काळीगुळी *f.* नीली*f.*

INDIRECT, *a. not direct or straight,* lit. असरल, अनृजु, बांकडा, फेऱ्याचा, वळणाचा.
2 fig. *oblique, not express, &c.* आडमार्गाचा, आडवाटेचा, आडरस्त्याचा, वांकडे वाटेचा, द्वारांतराचा, आडपडद्याचा,पडद्याचा, पर्यायाचा.
3 *devious, dishonest.* वांकडा, वक्र, गैरमार्गाचा, गैररितीचा, अमार्गाचा, कुटिल, अनृजु.

INDIRECTLY, *adv.* v. A. 1. *and* OBLIQUELY. ओझरता.
2 आडमार्गानें, आडवाटेनें, आडरस्त्यानें, पर्यायानें, पर्यायेंकरून, द्वारानें, द्वारांतरानें, आडपडद्यानें, परभारां, परभारें.
3 गैरमार्गानें, गैररितीनें, अमार्गानें.

INDIRECTNESS, *n.* v. A. 1. असरलता *f.* वांकडेपणा *m.* अनृजुता*f.*
3 वांकडेपणा *m.* वक्रता *f.*

INDISCERNIBLE, *a. not perceptible.* अलक्ष्य, दुर्लक्ष्य, इंद्रियातीत, इंद्रियागोचर, अतिसूक्ष्म.

INDISCERNIBLENESS, *n.* v. A. अलक्ष्यता *f.* इंद्रियागोचरता *f.*

INDISCERPTIBILITY, *n.* v. A. अभेद्यता *f.* अच्छेद्यता *f.* &c.

INDISCERPTIBLE, *a. incapable of separation.* अभेद्य, अभेदनीय, अच्छेद्य, अच्छेदनीय.

INDISCIPLINABLE, *a.* अशिक्ष्य, अशिक्षणीय, शिक्षणाशक्य, अशक्यशिक्ष, अशक्यशासन.

INDISCIPLINE, *n.* अशिक्षा *f.* अशासन *n.* अशिक्षण *n.*

INDISCOVERABLE, *a.* शोधून काढायास अशक्य, अलक्ष्य, दुर्लक्ष्य.

INDISCREET, *a.* v. IMPRUDENT. अविचारी, अविचारशील, अविवेकी, विचारशून्य-रहित-&c. अविचाराचा,अविवेकाचा, असमंजस.

INDISCRETION, *n.* अविचार *m.* अविवेक *m.* विचाराभाव *m.* विवेकाभाव *m.*

INDISCRIMINATE, *a. made or done without discrimination, confused, general.* अविचाराचा, अविवेकाचा, योग्यायोग्यविचार-तारतम्यविचार-पात्रापात्रविचार-&c. रहित-हीन-शून्य, अविविक्त, निर्विशेष.
2 See INDISCRIMINATING.

INDISCRIMINATELY, *adv.* v. A.1. अविवेकानें, अभेदानें,योग्यायोग्यविचार-तारतम्यविचार-&c. न करून-केल्यावांचून, अविशेषतः, निर्विशेषतः.

INDISCRIMINATING, *a. that does not distinguish.* अविवेकी, हीनविवेक, हीनविचार, विवेकशून्य, अविशेषज्ञ, तारतम्यादर्शी, भेदादर्शी, स्थूलदर्शी, स्थूललक्ष्य.

INDISCRIMINATION, *n.* अविवेक *m.* अविचार *m.* अविवेचना *f.* विवेकाभाव *m.* विवेचनाभाव *m.* विशेषाविचार *m.* तारतम्याविचार *m.* अनालोचना *f.*

INDISPENSABLE, *a. that cannot be spared or omitted.* अगत्याचा, आवश्यक, जरूर, जरूरीचा, अत्याज्य, अमोक्तव्य, नांतरीयक, अनन्यथासिद्ध, नाप्राप्त.
It is not i. त्यावांचून खोळंबा नाहीं. [अत्याज्यता *f.*

INDISPENSABLENESS, *n.* v. A. अगत्य *n.* जरूरी *f.* आवश्यकता *f.*
Asserting or holding the i. of. अगत्य *n.* अगत्यवाद *m.*

Assertor or holder of the i. of. अगत्यवादी.

INDISPENSABLY, *adv.* v. A. अवश्य, अगत्य, अगत्यरूप, अगत्यपूर्वक, जरूर.

To INDISPOSE, *v. a. disincline.* फिरवणें, मन *n.* फिरवणें *g. of o.* परतिवणें, पराङ्मुख-विमुख-पाठमोरा-अनुत्साही-&c. करणें, उलटवणें, पालटवणें, अनुत्साह *m.* करणें *g. of o.* निरशी *f.* आणणें.

2 *disorder slightly.* विकृति *f.*-विकार *m.*-असमाधान *n.*- अस्वास्थ्य *n.* करणें, अस्वस्थ करणें.

INDISPOSED, *p.* v. V. 1. पराङ्मुख, विमुख, पाठमोरा, अनुत्साही, गैरराजी, गैरखुशी, नाकबूल, अमान्य, विमत, विरुत, विरक्त, प्रतिकूल.

2 v. SICK. अस्वस्थ, असमाधानी, विकारी, मांदा, असुस्थ.

INDISPOSITION, *n.* v. V. 1.—*state.* अनावड *f.* नावड *f.* निरशी *f.* विरुत *n.* विरुती *f.* अनुत्साह *m.* निरुत्साह *m.* गैरखुशी *f.* अनुत्कंठा *f.* अनुत्सुकता *f.* विरक्ति *f.*

2 *slight disorder.* विकार *m.* असमाधान *n.* अस्वास्थ्य *n.* अस्वस्थता *f.* मांदगी *f.* मांद्य *n.* समाधानाभाव *m.*

INDISPUTABLE, *a.* अविवाद्य, अविवदनीय, निर्विवाद, विवादाशक्य, अखंडनीय, खंडनाशक्य, अबाधित, अबाध्य, निराबाध्य, निराबाध, बे तकरार, साधनानपेक्ष, प्रमाणानपेक्ष.

INDISPUTABLY, *adv.* v. A. *and* CERTAINLY. निर्विवाद, बेतकरार.

INDISSOLUBILITY, INDISSOLVABLENESS, *n.* v. A. 1. अद्रावणीयत्व *n.* अद्राव्यत्व *n.* द्रावणाशक्यता *f.*

2 अखंडनीयत्व *n.* अभेद्यता *f.* दृढता *f.* सुदृढता *f.*

INDISSOLUBLE, INDISSOLVABLE, *a. not capable of being melted, &c.* अद्रव, अद्रावणीय, अद्राव्य, द्रावणाशक्य, द्रावणानर्ह, अगलनीय.

2 *that cannot be broken; firm, lasting.* अखंडनीय, अखंड्य, अभेद्य, भेदनाशक्य, अभेदनीय, दृढ, सुदृढ, भंजनाशक्य, अशक्यभंजन, वज्र, वज्रप्राय. [स्फुट, क्लिष्ट.

INDISTINCT, *a. not clear, &c.* v. OBSCURE, अस्पष्ट, अव्यक्त, अ-

INDISTINCTLY, *adv.* v. A. अंधक, अस्पष्ट.

INDISTINCTNESS, *n.* v. A. अस्पष्टता *f.* अव्यक्तता *f.*

INDISTINGUISHABLE, *a.* अपरिच्छेद्य, अपरिच्छेदनीय, अव्यवच्छेद्य, अविशेषज्ञेय, अपृथक्ज्ञेय, अपृथक्क्रिय.

INDISTURBANCE, *n.* v. CALMNESS. अक्षोभ *m.* क्षोभाभाव *m.*

To INDITE, *v. a. compose.* करणें, रचणें, बांधणें, कवणें, रचना *f.* करणें *g. of o.*

2 See To DICTATE.

INDIVIDUAL, *a. single, one.* एकटा, एकट्याचा, व्यक्तीचा, पृथगात्मक, पृथग्व्यक्तिक, भिन्नव्यक्तिक.

INDIVIDUAL, *n. single person.* जण *m. f. n.* (The plural is जण *m.* जणी *f.* जणें *n.*) असामी *f. m.* व्यक्ति *f.* एकमनुष्य *n.* नफर *m.* विशेष *m.*

The individuals (of a species)—collect. व्यक्तिपक्ष *m.*

INDIVIDUALITY, *n.* पृथक्त्व *n.* पार्थक्य *n.* व्यक्तिता *f.* पृथगात्मकता *f.* पृथगात्मिका *f.* कैवल्य *n.*

I. *essential and constituting quality.* स्वत्व *n.* विशेष *m.*

INDIVIDUALLY, *adv. separately.* असामीवार, एकएक, व्यक्तितः, व्यक्तिशः.

INDIVISIBILITY, INDIVISIBLENESS, *n.* v. A. अविभाज्यता *f.* अविभजनीयता *f.*

INDIVISIBLE. *a.* अविभाज्य, अविभजनीय, विभजनाशक्य, अवि-

भक्तव्य, अपृथक्करणीय, अभेद्य.

INDOCILE, *a. unteachable.* अशिक्षणीय, अशिक्ष्य, अनुपदेश्य, दुःशिक्ष्य, दुःशिक्षणीय, अशक्यशिक्ष, कुशास्य, दुःशास्य.

2 *untractable.* See OBSTINATE.

INDOCILITY, *n.* v. A.1. अशिक्ष्यत्व *n.* दुःशिक्ष्यता *f.* अनुपदेश्यत्व *n.* कुशास्यता *f.* &c.

To INDOCTRINATE, &c. See To TEACH, &c.

INDOLENCE, *n.* v. A. आळस *m.* आळसीपणा *m.* सुस्ती *f.* सुस्तपणा *m.* आलस्य *n.* उद्योगद्वेष *m.* उद्योगशत्रुता *f.* निरुद्योगिता *f.* अनुद्योगिता *f.* अव्यवसाय *m.*

INDOLENT, *a. idle, indisposed to labor,* v. LAZY. आळसी, आळसट, सुस्त, अनुद्योगी, निरुद्योगी, निरुद्योग, निरुत्साह, ढिला, ढील, आंगजड, जड, शिथिल, अलस, उद्योगशत्रु, उद्योगविमुख, अव्यवसायी, अव्यवसायवान्.

To grow i. आळसणें, आळसावणें.

INDOLENTLY, *adv.* v. A. आळसानें, आळस करून, सुस्तीनें, आळसट, आलस्य-&c. पूर्वक.

INDOMABLE, INDOMITABLE, *a. that cannot be tamed.* अदम्य, अदमनीय, दुर्दम्य, अजिंक, दुर्ज्ञेय, दुर्धर, अनाधृष्य, दुराधर्ष.

To INDORSE, *v. a. write on the back of* (a bill, order, &c.). पाठीवर नांव *n.* लिहणें, पाठीवर सही *f.* करणें, नांव लिहून सकारणें, सही *f.* करून सकारणें.

INDORSEMENT, *n.* v. V. पाठीवरची सही *f.*

INDRAUGHT, *n. inlet.* खाडी *f.*

INDUBITABLE, *a.* v. CERTAIN. निस्संशय, निस्संशयाचा, निस्संदिग्ध, असंदिग्ध, निश्चयात्मक, खचीत. [निश्चयात्मक.

INDUBITABLY, *adv.* v. CERTAINLY. खचीत, निभ्रांत *or* निर्भ्रांत,

To INDUCE, *v. a. influence, persuade.* मनावणें, वळवणें, मन *n.* मानवणें-वळवणें-ओढणें-&c. *g. of o.* प्रवृत्त करणें, उत्तेजन *n.* करणें-देणें.

2 *cause, produce, occasion.* आणणें, ओढून आणणें, उद्भावणें, उठवणें, आवंतणें.

INDUCED, *p.* v. V. 1. मानवलेला, वळवलेला, &c. प्रवृत्त, उत्तेजित.

2 आणलेला, ओढून आणलेला, &c.

INDUCEMENT, *n. inducing cause; motive, &c.* उत्तेजन *n.* उत्तेजक *n.* प्रयोजन *n.* प्रयोजक *n.* प्रवर्त्तक *n.* प्रलोभन *n.* सबब *f.*

To INDUCT, *v. a. introduce into an office.* पदावर-&c. बसवणें, यथाविधिस्थापना *f.* करणें, संस्कारपूर्वक अधिकृत करणें.

INDUCTION, *n.* v. V.—*act.* पदावर बसवणें *n.* &c. यथाविधिस्थापना *f.* संस्कारपूर्वकस्थापना *f.*

I. *inference,* v. CONCLUSION. अनुमान *n.* सिद्धांत *m.*

II. *reasoning from particulars to generals.* विशेषपरीक्षापूर्वकसर्वसाधारणनिश्चय *m.* विशेषपरीक्षापूर्वकसाधारणानुमान *m.* विशेषपरीक्षापूर्वकसाधारणकल्पना *f.*

INDUCTIVE, *a. leading to.* प्रवर्त्तक, प्रवृत्तिकारक.

2 *proceeding by induction.* विशेषपरीक्षापूर्वकसाधारणानुमानाचा, विशेषपरीक्षापूर्वकसाधारणकल्पनेचा.

To INDUE, *v. a. clothe.* See To INVEST, 2 *endow.* देणें, प्रदान *n.* करणें, युक्त-विशिष्ट-संपन्न-अन्वित-समन्वित-&c. (all in comp.) करणें.

INDUED, *p.* v. V. 2. विशिष्ट केलेला, &c. संपन्न, युक्त, विशिष्ट, अन्वित, समन्वित, प्रयुक्त.

To INDULGE, *v. a. permit to be or continue; not to check or restrain.* बाळगणें, ठेवणें, राखणें, अनावरण *n.*-अनावर *m.*-अनाकलन *n.*-&c. करणें *g. of o.* मोकळा सोडणें.

2 *gratify, grant, comply with.* पुरा-पूर्ण-परिपूर्ण-तृप्त-संतृप्त-&c. करणें, पुरवणें, चालवणें, फेडणें.

3 *humor, cocker, pamper, &c.* लाडकणें, लाडकावणें, लाडावणें, लाड *m.*-लडिवाळ *m.*-लळा *m.*-लाडकी *f.*-लाडीग *f.*-कोडकौतुक *n.* पुरवणें-चालवणें-पाळणें *g. of o.* लालन *n.* करणें *g. of o.* छंदोनुवर्त्तन *n.*-छंदोनुवृत्ति *f.*-छंदोनुरोध *m.*-&c. करणें *g. of o.*

4 *favor.* कृपा *f.* करणें, कृपा करून देणें.

To INDULGE, *v. n. yield to the enjoyment or practice of without restraint.* असंयतभोग *m.*-अनियतभोग *m.*-यथेच्छभोग *m.*-&c. करणें, यथेच्छप्रवृत्ति *f.* करणें.

INDULGED, *p.* v. V. A. 1. बाळगलेला, &c. मोकळा सोडलेला, अनावृत, अनाकलित, अनियमित.

2 पुरा केलेला, पुरवलेला, &c.

3 लाडकावलेला, लाडावलेला, &c. लालित.

INDULGENCE, *n.* v.V. 1.—*act.* बाळगणें*n.* अनावरण*n.* अनावर *m.* अनाकलन*n.* अनियमन*n.* असंयम*m.*

3 लाडकावणें*n.* लाडावणें *n.* &c. लाडनणूक *f.* लाड*m.* लाडकी *f.* कोड*n.* कोडकौतुक*n.* लालन*n.* छंदोनुवर्त्तन*n.* छंदोनुवृत्ति *f.* छंदोनुरोध*m.*

I. *favor granted.* प्रसाद*m.* प्रीतिदान*n.* मेहरबानगीची देणगी *f.*

INDULGENT, *a. yielding to wishes, ready to gratify,* v. FOND, KIND. लाडपुरव्या, लाडचालव्या, लडिवाळ पुरवणारा, छंदोनुवर्त्ती *pop.* छंदानुवर्त्ती, छंदोनुसारी *pop.* छंदानुसारी, छंदोनुयायी *pop.* छंदानुयायी.

2 *lenient, not severe,* v. MILD. सौम्य, कोमल, नरम, क्षमापूर्वक, क्षमापुरस्सर, क्षमावान्, सौम्यदृष्टि, दयादृष्टि, सदय, दयार्द्र.

INDULGENTLY, *adv.* v. A. 2. कृपादृष्टीनें, दयार्द्रदृष्टीनें, क्षमापूर्वक, क्षमापुरस्सर.

To INDURATE, INDURATION. See To HARDEN, &c.

INDUS, *n.*—the river. सिंधुनद*m.* सिंधु*m.*

INDUSTRIAL, *a. consisting in industry, &c.* परिश्रमाचा, उद्योगाचा, मेहनतीचा, उद्योगमय.

INDUSTRIOUS, *a.* v. DILIGENT. कामसू, कामट, सप्या, कष्टाळू, कष्टी, मेहनती, उद्योगी, उद्योगशील, अनलस.

INDUSTRIOUSLY, *adv.* v. A. मेहनतीनें, मेहनतकरून, उद्योगपूर्वक, परिश्रमपूर्वक.

INDUSTRIOUSNESS, INDUSTRY, *n.* v. A. *and* DILIGENCE. मेहनत *f.* परिश्रम*m.* अनालस्य*n.* निरालस्य*n.* अनलसता *f.* उद्योगशीलता *f.* [स्थिति *f.*

INDWELLING, *n.* v. RESIDENCE. अधिष्ठान*n.* अधिष्ठिति *f.* अंतः

INDWELLING, *a. inherent.* अंतस्थ, अंतःस्थित, अधिष्ठित.

To INEBRIATE, &c. See To INTOXICATE, &c.

INEDIBLE, *a.* v. UNEATABLE. अखाद्य, अभक्ष्य.

INEFFABLE, *a.* v. UNSPEAKABLE. अनिर्वाच्य, अनिर्वचनीय, अवाच्य, वचनागोचर, अकथनीय, अकथ्य, शब्दातीत.

INEFFABLENESS, *n.* v. A. अकथनीयता *f.* अकथ्यता *f.* &c.

INEFFECTIVE, INEFFECTUAL, INEFFICACIOUS, INEFFICIENT, *a. not producing effect, &c.* कार्यासाधक, कार्याकारी, कार्यासमर्थ, कार्याक्षम, कार्यासंपादक, अगुणकारी, अगुणक, फलाजनक, व्यर्थ, निरर्थक, निष्फल, विफल.

INEFFECTIVELY, INEFFECTUALLY, *adv.* v. A. व्यर्थ, निरर्थक, वांयां, वृथा, बेलाग.

INEFFECTIVENESS, INEFFICACY, INEFFICIENCY, *n.* v. A. कार्यासाधकत्व*n.* कार्याकारिता *f.* कार्याक्षमता *f.* कार्यासामर्थ्य*n.*&c. गुणराहित्य*n.* गुणाभाव*m.*

INELASTIC, *a.* अस्थितिस्थापक.

INELEGANCE, *n.* v. A. अशोभा *f.* असौंदर्य*n.* शोभाभाव*m.* सौंदर्याभाव*m.* विशोभा *f.* शोभाराहित्य*n.*

INELEGANT, *a. wanting beauty, polish, &c.* बेडौल, बेढब, शोभारहित, विशोभित, सौंदर्यरहित, अप्रशस्त.

INELIGIBILITY, *n.* v.A. अग्राह्यता *f.* ग्रहणानर्हता *f.* अवरणीयता *f.* अयोग्यता *f.* नालायकी *f.*

INELEGIBLE, *a. not capable of being chosen, not suitable.* अग्राह्य, ग्रहणानर्ह, ग्रहणायोग्य, अवरणीय, अनुपादेय.

INELOQUENCE, *n.* v. A. 1. जिभेचा जडपणा*m.* मुखदौर्बल्य*n.* जिव्हाजाड्य*n.* हीनवक्तृत्व*n.* अवक्तृत्व*n.*

INELOQUENT, *a.*—a speaker. जिभेचा जड, आडव्याजिभेचा, मुखदुर्बल, हीनवक्ता, हीनवाक्, अवक्ता, वागपटु, वागजड, जडजिह्व.

2—speech, &c.वक्तृत्वहीन-शून्य-&c. वक्तृत्वपाटवरहित-शून्य-&c. वाक्पटुतारहित-&c.

INENARRABLE, *a. that cannot be told.* अनिवेद्य, अनिवेदनीय, अनिर्वचनीय, अनिर्वाच्य, अकथनीय, अवर्णनीय.

INEPT, &c. See UNFIT, &c.

INEQUALITY, *n.* v. A. UNEQUAL, 1. उंचसखलपणा *m.* उंचनीचपणा *m.* उखरवाखरपणा *m.* &c. वैषम्य *n.*

2 *and* DIFFERENCE. असमता *f.* असादृश्य *n.* असमानता *f.* वैषम्य *n.* विषमभाव *m.* असमंजस *m.*

INEQUITABLE, *a. unjust.* अन्याय्य, अप्रामाणिक, अयथार्थ, अयथान्याय, असमंजस.

INERRABLE, &c. See INFALLIBLE, &c.

INERT, *a. destitute of the power of motion.* जड, अचेष्ट, अचेतन, चेष्टाहीन.

2 *dull, &c.* v. SLUGGISH. सुस्त, आंगजड, जड, ढिला, अनुष्ण, शिथिल, अनुद्योगी.

INERTIA, *n.* जडता *f.* जाड्य *n.*

INERTION, *n. want of action, &c.* अनुद्योग *m.* अव्यापार *m.* अचेष्टा *f.* अप्रवृत्ति *f.* उद्योगाभाव *m.* व्यापाराभाव *m.*

INERTNESS, *n.* v. A. 1. जडता *f.* जाड्य *n.* अचेष्टा *f.* चेष्टाराहित्य*n.*

2 सुस्ती *f.* सुस्तपणा *m.* ढिलेपणा *m.* शैथिल्य *n.* अनुद्योगिता *f.*

INESCULENT, *a.not eatable.* अखाद्य, अभक्षणीय,अभक्ष्य, अभोज्य

INESTIMABLE, *a.* v. INVALUABLE. अमूल्य, अमोलिक, अमोल, अनर्घ, मूल्यातीत.

INEVITABILITY, *n.* v. A. अनिवार्यता *f.* अपरिहार्यता *f.* निवारणाशक्यता *f.*

INEVITABLE, *a. that cannot be avoided.* अनिवार्य, अनिवार, अपरिहार्य, अवारणीय, निवारणाशक्य, बिनतोड.

INEXCITABLE, *a.* अक्षोभ्य, अक्षोभणीय, क्षोभणाशक्य.

INEXCUSABLE, *a. not to be palliated.* अनिवार्यदोष, अपरिमार्जनीयदोष, अपरिमार्जनीय, अकारणोत्तर, निमित्तानिस्तार्य, निमित्तापरिहार्य.

2 *not to be borne or passed over.* माफ करायास अयोग्य, अक्षम्य, अक्षमणीय, क्षमाकरणायोग्य, अक्षंतव्य.

INEXHAUSTIBLE, *a.* अक्षय, व्ययक्षयशून्य, अशक्यव्यय, अपार, अनंत.

INEXHAUSTIBLENESS, *n.* v. A. अक्षयता *f.* अनंतता *f.*

INEXISTENCE, *n. want of being.* असत्व *n.* असत्ता *f.* अभाव *m.*

INEXISTENT, *a. that is not in being.* असत्, अविद्यमान, अवर्त्तमान, अप्रसिद्ध.

INEXORABILITY, INEXORABLENESS, *n.* v. A. दुराराध्यता *f.* दुराराधनीयता *f.* &c. कठोरपणा *m.* कठिणपणा *m.*

INEXORABLE, *a. not to be moved by intreaty.* दुराराध्य, दुराराधनीय, आराधनाशक्य, असमजुती *or* त्या, कठोर, कठोरचित्त, कठीण, पाषाणहृदय, कणक्या, खपाट्या.

INEXPECTANT, *a. not looking for.* अप्रतीक्षक, अप्रतीक्षमाण, अनपेक्षक, अनपेक्षी.

INEXPECTATION, *n.* अप्रतीक्षा *f.* अनिरीक्षा *f.* अनपेक्षा *f.* निरपेक्षा *f.*

INEXPEDIENCE, INEXPEDIENCY, *n.* v. A. अयोग्यता *f.* अनौचित्य *n.* अनुपयुक्तता *f.* अकार्यता *f.* अकर्त्तव्यता *f.* नालायकी *f.*

INEXPEDIENT, *a. not expedient, not fit.* अयोग्य, अनुचित, अनुपयुक्त, अकर्त्तव्य, अकार्य्य, नालायक.

INEXPERIENCE, *n. want of experience or experimental knowledge.* अननुभव *m.* निरनुभव *m.* अप्रत्यय *m.* अननुभूति *f.* कच्चेपणा *m.* गैरमाहिती *f.* अजाणपणा *m.* कोवळेपणा *m.* अल्लडपणा *m.* &c. व्यवहाराज्ञान *n.* व्यवहाराज्ञता *f.*

INEXPERIENCED, *a. not having experience.* अजाण, अजाणता, गैरमाहीत, गैरमाहितगार, अपेट, असडा, अल्लड, कच्चा, कोवळा, नवेउमेदीचा, अप्रबुद्ध, अव्यापार, बालिश, व्यवहाराज्ञ.

INEXPERT, *a. unskilful,* v. AWKWARD. नाकसबी, अनाडी, अकुशल, अदक्ष, अपटु, हीनकौशल्य, घसक्या, घसट्या.

INEXPERTNESS, *n.* v. A. अनाडीपणा *m.* अकौशल *n.* अदक्षता *f.*

INEXPIABLE, *a. that admits not of atonement.* प्रायश्चित्तानर्ह, प्रायश्चित्तायोग्य, प्रायश्चित्तातीत, निष्कृत्यशक्य, निष्कृत्ययोग्य, अनिष्कृतिक, दुस्त्यज, दुस्त्याज्य, अमोचनीय, अपरिमार्जनीय, अविशोधनीय, अप्रतिसमाधेय.

INEXPLAINABLE, INEXPLICABLE, *a.* ज्याचा उलगडा व्हायाचा नाहीं, अव्याख्येय, अविवरणीय, अस्फोटनीय, अनुद्घाटनीय, विवरणाशक्य.

INEXPLICABILITY, *n.* v. A. अविवरणीयता *f.* &c.

INEXPRESSIBLE, *a. unutterable.* अनिर्वेद्य, अनिर्वेदनीय, अनिर्वचनीय, अनिर्वाच्य, अकथनीय, अनुच्चार्य, अनुच्चारणीय.

INEXPRESSIVE, *a. unanimated, dull.* अळणी, फिक्का, मळमळीत, अलवण.

INEXTANT, *a.* अनुपस्थित, अविद्यमान, अनुपलभ्यमान, अनुपलभ्य.

INEXTINGUISHABLE, *a. that cannot be quenched.* अशमनीय, अप्रशमनीय, प्रशमनाशक्य, अविझा, न विझता.

INEXTIRPABLE, *a. that cannot be rooted out.* अनुत्पाटनीय, अनुत्खातनीय, उत्पाटनाशक्य.

INEXTRICABLE, *a. not to be disentangled.* गुंता काढायास अशक्य, अमोचनीय, मोचनाशक्य.

To INEYE, *v. a. inoculate,*—a bud. पैवंद करणें, पिवंदी *f.* करणें.

INFACUNDITY, *n.* v. INELOQUENCE. मुखदौर्बल्य *n.* अवक्तृत्व *n.*

INFALLIBILITY, *n.* v. A. 1. अभ्रांतिधर्म *m.* भ्रमायोग्यता *f.* अस्खलितबुद्धि *f.* अस्खलितमति *f.* स्खलनासंभव *m.*

2 अमोघता *f.*

INFALLIBLE, *a. not capable of erring.* अचूक, भ्रमातीत, स्खलनातीत, भ्रमायोग्य, अभ्रांतिधर्मा, अस्खलितमति, अस्खलितबुद्धि, असंभाव्यभ्रम, प्रमादातीत.

2 *not liable to fail,* v. SURE. अचूक, अचूकसंधानी, अमोघ.

INFALLIBLY. See CERTAINLY, SURELY.

INFAMOUS, *a. notoriously vile,*—of persons. बदलौकिकाचा, दुर्लौकिकाचा, दुष्कीर्तीचा; अपकीर्तीचा, बदनामीचा, बदनाम, बट्ट्याचा, बट्टेखोर, कुख्यात, अयशा.

To become i. दिवा *m* लावणें, धुळीचे दिवे *m. pl.* लावणें.

2 *that renders infamous,* v. DISGRACEFUL. अपयशस्कर, अपयशाचा, इजतखाऊ, इजतघेणा, अपकीर्त्तिकारक.

INFAMOUSNESS, INFAMY, *n.* v. A. 1. अप्रतिष्ठा *f.* अपकीर्त्ति *f.* अकीर्त्ति *f.* दुर्लौकिक *m.* बदलौकिक *m.* दुष्कीर्त्ति *f.* बदनामी *f.* बदनाम *n.* अपयश *n.* अयश *n.* कुख्याति *f.* नाम *pop.* नांव *n.* v. ठेव.

INFANCY, *n. childhood.* तान्हेपणा *m.* बाळपण *n. and* पणा *m.* लहानपण *n. and* पणा *m.* बालत्व *n.* बाल्य *n.* बालावस्था *f.* शैशव *n.* बालदशा *f.*

2—in law. See MINORITY.

INFANT, *n. babe.* तान्हेंमूल *n.* आंगाबरचें-कडेवरचें मूल *n.* लहानमूल *n.* लहानबाळ *n.* बाल *or* बाळ *n.* बालक *or* बाळक *n.* उत्तानशय, डिंभ.

Chubbiness or plumpness of an i. बाळसें *n.* v. घे-ये.—To get it. बाळसावणें.

2—in law. v. MINOR. अप्राप्तव्यवहार, अज्ञातव्यवहार.

INFANT, *a.* बाल (in comp.) बालदशेचा, बालदशेंतला.

INFANTICIDE, *n.*—the act. बालहत्या *f.* बालहिंसा *f.* बालवध *m.* बालघात *m.*

2—the agent. बालहत्यारा, बालहंता, बालहिंसक.

INFANTILE, INFANTINE, *a. belonging, &c. to infancy or an infant.* बाळपणाचा, बाल्यदशेचा, बालकीय, बालावस्थेचा, बाल्यसंबंधी, बालकसंबंधी.

INFANTRY, *n. foot soldiers.* पायदळ *n.* पायभार *m.* पदातिभार *m.*

To INFATUATE, *v. a. make foolish, deprive of judgment.* बेडाबेडगळ-खुळा-नष्टबुद्धि-नष्टविवेक-हतज्ञान-&c. करणें, खूळ *n.*-बेड *n.* &c. लावणें, वेडावणें, खुळवणें, भुलविणें, बुद्धिभ्रंश *m.*-ज्ञानभ्रंश *m.*-&c. करणें *g. of o.* मोहांत घालणें-पाडणें.

To become or get infatuate. बेडगळणें, गुंगणें, भुलणें, बुद्धिभ्रंश *m.*-&c. होणें *g. of s.*

INFATUATED, *p.* v. V. *and* MAD. बेडावलेला, बेडगळ केलेला-झालेला, &c. नष्टबुद्धि, नष्टविवेक, नष्टज्ञान, हतज्ञान, भ्रष्टबुद्धि, बुद्धिभ्रष्ट, गुंग, धुंद, मूढचेता.

INFATUATION, *n.* v. V.—*state.* बेडावलेलेपणा *m.* &c. खूळ *n.* बेड *n.* धुंदी *f.* गुंगी *f.* भूल *f.* भुलवण *f.* भुरळें *n.* भुरळ *f.* मोह *m.* बुद्धिभ्रंश *m.* ज्ञानभ्रंश *m.* नष्टविवेकता *f.* &c. मूढग्राह *m.*

I. as betokening misfortune. अकाबाईचा पाया *m.*

INFEASIBILITY, INFEASIBLENESS, *n.* v. A. असाध्यता *f.* दुःसाध्यता *f* दौष्कर्य *n.* अशक्यता *f.*

INFEASIBLE, *a. impracticable,* v. IMPOSSIBLE. असाध्य, दुष्कर, दुःसाध्य, अशक्य.

To INFECT, *v. a. taint, affect with communicated qualities.* आपले गुण देऊन रोगी-दुष्ट-&c. करणें, आपला रोग *m.*-आपलें दुःख *n.*-&c. देणें, स्वरोगाक्रांत-स्वरोगसंसृष्ट-रोगसंक्रमित-संसर्गदूषित-&c. करणें.

INFECTED, *p.* v. V. रोग दिल्हेला-घेतलेला, &c. रोगाक्रांत, रोगसंक्रमित, रोगसंसृष्ट, संसर्गदूषित, संसर्गदुष्ट, सांसर्गिकरोगी, रोगसंसर्गी.

INFECTION, *n. infectious matter, infecting cause.* रोगाची बाफ *f.*

रोगाचा गंध *m.* लस *f.* रंध *f.*

2 *infected state.* संसर्गदोष *m.* स्पर्शदोष *m.*

INFECTIOUS, *a.* v. CONTAGIOUS. स्पर्शानें-वाफेनें-गंधानें-&c. लागणारा, स्पर्शसंचारी, सांसर्गिक, सांक्रामिक.

INFECTIOUSNESS, *n.* v. A. स्पर्शसंचारिता *f.* सांसर्गिकत्व*n.* सांक्रामिकत्व*n.* [अफल.

INFECUND, *a.* *barren*, v. UNFRUITFUL. वांझ, वांझा, अफलवान्,

INFECUNDITY, *n.* v. A. *and* UNFRUITFULNESS. वांझपणा*m.* वंध्यत्व *n.* अफलता *f.* अफलत्व.

INFELICITY, *n.* v. UNHAPPINESS. दुःख*n.* अकल्याण*n.* कल्याणाभाव *m.*

To INFER, *v. a.* *deduce from premises.* अनुमान*n.*-तर्क*m.*-तार्किक*n.*-ऊह*m.*-उन्नयन*n.*-&c. करणें *g. of. o.* अनुमानणें, ताडणें, तर्कानें-अनुमानानें-&c. काढणें-घेणें-सिद्ध करणें.

INFERABLE, *a.* v. V. अनुमेय, तर्कवेद्य, तर्कसाध्य, तर्कगम्य, अनुमानसाध्य, साध्य, अनुमानगम्य, अनुमानवेद्य.

INFERENCE, *n.* *a truth drawn from another*, v. CONCLUSION. तर्क*m.* अनुमान*n.* अनुमिति *f.* तर्कनिश्चय*m.* तर्कसिद्धांत*m.* अनुमानसिद्धांत *m.*

I. from circumstances. अर्थापत्ति *f.*

Subject of an i. व्याप्य.

That leads to an i. अनुमापक, उन्नायक.

INFERENTIAL, *a.* *gathered by inference.* आनुमानिक, अनुमानसिद्ध, तर्कसिद्ध.

INFERIOR, *a.* *lower in place.* खालचा, खाला, खालील, अधर, अधम, अधःस्थ.

2 *lower in station, rank, &c.* खालचा, खाल्या *or* खालच्या पायरीचा-पदवीचा-योग्यतेचा-ओळीचा-प्रतीचा-&c. कनिष्ठप्रतीचा-पदवीचा-&c. जेर, जेरदस्त.

3 *of little excellence or value.* हलका, नीचा, निंचा, निरस, हलक्या किमतीचा, उणा, उणास, उणेकिमतीचा, कनिष्ठप्रतीचा, निकृष्ट, अपकृष्ट.

4 *of less importance*, v. SECONDARY. गौण, अप्रधान, अमुख्य, अन्यथासिद्ध.

INFERIOR, *n.* *a person in a lower station, &c.* खालच्या पायरीचें-पदवीचें-&c. मनुष्य *n.*

INFERIORITY, *n.* v. A. 2. खालची योग्यता *f.* खालची पदवी *f.* कनिष्ठता *f.* कनिष्ठभाव *m.*

To allow one's i. कमीपणा*m.* घेणें, हार जाणें-विजितजाणें *with* स *or* ला.

3 उणेपणा *m.* कमीपणा *m.* हलकेपणा *m.* निरसपणा *m.* उणासपणा *m.* &c. निरसाई *f.* निरसी *f.* अपकृष्टता *f.*

I. in stature, size, age, &c. धाकुटपण *n.* धाकुटपणा *m.*

4 गौणता *f.* गौणभाव *m.* अप्रधानता *f.*

INFERNAL, *a.* *belonging to the lower regions.* पाताळचा, पातालसंबंधी, अधोभुवनसंबंधी.

I. regions, v. HELL. पाताल *n.* अधोभुवन *n.*

2 See HELLISH.

INFERNAL, *n.* *inhabitant of the lower regions.* पातालवासी, नरकवासी, पातालसंस्थ, नरकसंस्थ, नरकस्थ.

INFERRED, *p.* v. V. ताडलेला, &c. आनुमानिक, अनुमानसिद्ध.

INFERRIBLE. See INFERABLE.

INFERTILE, *a.* v. BARREN. नापीक, अफल, अफलवान्, वंध्य.

INFERTILITY, *n.* v. A. नापीकपणा *m.* अफलता *f.* वंध्यता *f.*

To INFEST, *v. a.* *annoy, harass*, v. To TROUBLE. उपद्रव *m.*-इजा *f.*-तस्दी *f.*-पीडा *f.*-उपसर्ग*m.*-उपप्लव*m.*-&c.करणें-देणें-लावणें.

INFESTATION, *n.* v. V. *and* MOLESTATION. उपद्रव *m.* नड *f.* नडाव *m.*

INFIDEL, *n.* *disbeliever in the christian scriptures.* ख्रिस्तीशास्त्राविश्वासी, ख्रिस्तीशास्त्राश्रद्ध.

2 *rejecter of revealed religion*,—gener. शास्त्राविश्वासी, शास्त्राश्रद्ध, शास्त्रनिंदक, शास्त्रद्वेषी, नास्तिक, धर्मनिंदक.

INFIDEL, *a.* v. N. 2. शास्त्रनिंदेचा, शास्त्राश्रद्धेचा, शास्त्रनिंदात्मक.

INFIDELITY, *n.* *disbelief of religion.* शास्त्राविश्वास *m.* शास्त्राश्रद्धा *f.* शास्त्रनिंदा *f.* धर्मनिंदा *f.*

2 *unfaithfulness to the marriage bond.* व्यभिचार *m.* जारकर्म *n.* विवाहसम्बिद्व्यतिक्रम *m.* विवाहसमयभंग *m.* विवाहप्रतिज्ञोल्लंघन *n.*

I. on the part of a husband. असाधुता *f.*

I. on the part of a wife. अपातिव्रत्य *n.* पातिव्रत्यभंग *m.*

INFINITE, *a.* *unbounded, unlimited.* अपार, अनंत, अनंतपार, अपरंपार, निरवधि, निरवधिक, असीम, निस्सीम, अमर्याद, अनियत्ताक. For this word as made, in the rather free phraseology of multitudes, to convey the general sense of *Immense, immeasurable, illimitable, incalculable, unfathomable, bottomless, boundless, endless, numberless, &c. &c.* i. e. *exceeding all bounds and all computation, conception, and thought*, there are numerous words and phrases. These though well agreeing with *Infinite*, both in the sense just exhibited and in extensiveness of currency and use, have, as their English representatives above, differing *particular* implications and aspects. Some are here collected. अगाध, अनिवार, अमर्याद, निर्मर्याद, अवारपार, दुरंत, अतिशय, अतिशयित, पराकाष्ठेचा, अपरिमित, अमित, अपरिमेय, अप्रमेय, असंख्य, अगणनीय, अगण्य, अगणित, बेसुमार, बेसुमाराचा, बेहद्द, अशेष, निश्शेष.

INFINITELY, *adv.* v. A. अपार, अमर्याद, &c. फारच, अतिशय.

INFINITENESS. See INFINITUDE. [सूक्ष्म.

INFINITESIMAL, *a.* *indefinitely small.* अत्यल्प, अलिपष्ठ, अति-

INFINITIVE, *n.*—in grammar. साधारणरूप *n.* सामान्यरूप *n.* तुमुन्नतपद *n.* भाववचन *n.*

INFINITUDE, INFINITY, *n.* v.A. अपरंपारपणा *m.* आनंत्य *n.* अनंतता *f.* अपारता *f.* सीमाभाव *m.* असीमत्व *n.* सीमाराहित्य *n.* निरवधिभाव *m.* अवध्यभाव *m.*—in free phraseology, &c. पराकाष्ठा *f.* बेहद्दपणा *m.* बेसुमारपणा *m.* &c.

INFIRM, *n.* *not firm, stable, &c.* अस्थिर, लटपटीत, डळमळीत, डगमगीत, खिळखिळा, लुसकान *or* लुकसान, नादान, अध्रुव, अदृढ.

2 *feeble, &c.* v. WEAK. निर्बळ, दुर्बळ, नबळा, अशक्त, कमजोर, कमकुवत, लुसकान *or* लुकसान, अक्षम *pop.* अखम.

I. from age,—an animal. जखूख, जखूखल, जखूखड म्हातारा, लुळाखुडा *or* लुडाखुडा.

I. of purpose, v. IRRESOLUTE. धरसोडीचा, चंचळमनाचा.

INFIRMARY, *n.* v. HOSPITAL. बीमारखाना *m.* रोगिशाला *f.*

INFIRMITY, INFIRMNESS, *n.* v. A. 1. डळमळितपणा *m.* &c. अस्थिरता *f.* अध्रुवत्व *n.* अदृढता *f.* लुसकानी *or* लुकसानी *f.* नादानी *f.*

2 निर्बळपणा *m.* नबळेपणा *m.* कमजोरपणा *m.* &c. अशक्ति *f.* अशक्तता *f.* शक्तिन्यूनता *f.* बलन्यूनता *f.* दौर्बल्य *n.* बलहीनता *f.*

I. *weakness, failing, foible.* उणें *n.* व्यंग *n.* लंगडें *n.* गोम *f.*

II. *malady*, v. DISORDER. दुखणें *n.* रोग *m.* व्याधि *pop.* व्याध *f.*

To INFIX, *v. a. fix by thrusting in, &c.* खुपसणें, खोवणें, खोंसणें, रोवणें, खुपसून-खोसून-&c. बसवणें.

2 See To INLAY. 3. See To IMPLANT.

To INFLAME, *v. a. set on fire*, lit. fig. v. To KINDLE. चेतवणें, पेटवणें, संतापवणें, तापवणें, उद्दीपन *n.*-प्रदीपन *n.*-&c. करणें *g. of o.* संतापन *n.*-&c. करणें *g. of o.* उद्दीप्त-प्रदीप्त-संतप्त-संतापित-&c. करणें.

2 *make hot, angry, and painful.* संतप्त-कुपित-क्रुद्ध-दाहयुक्त-&c. करणें, संतापन *n.*-&c. करणें *g. of o.* बिकोपास नेणें.

INFLAMED, *p.* v. V. 1. चेतवलेला, &c. उद्दीप्त, प्रदीप्त, दीपित, संतप्त, संतापित, तापित.

To be or become i. चेतणें, पेटणें, तापणें, संतप्त-&c. होणें.

To be i. with anger or lust. जळफळणें.

2 संतप्त-&c. केलेला-झालेला, संतप्त, कुपित, क्रुद्ध, दाहयुक्त.

That is i.—an eye. खुपरा.

INFLAMER, *n.* INFLAMING, *p. a.* v. V. 1. चेतवणारा, संतापवणारा, &c. उद्दीपनकर्त्ता-कारी-&c. प्रदीपनकर्त्ता-कारी-&c. संतापनकर्त्ता-कारी-&c.

INFLAMMABILITY, INFLAMMABLENESS, *n.* v. A. ज्वलनशीलता *f.* दहनशीलता *f.* ज्वालाग्राहिता *f.*

INFLAMMABLE, *a. that may be set on fire.* पेट घेणारा, पेट घेण्या, ज्वलनशील, दहनशील, ज्वालाग्राही, ज्वलनधर्मक, दाह्य.

INFLAMMATION, *n.* v. V. 1.—*act.* चेतवणें *n.* &c. उद्दीपन *n.* प्रदीपन *n.* दीपन *n.* तापन *n.* संतापन *n.*—*state.* ताप *m.* संताप *m.* प्रदीप्तता *f.* उद्दीप्तता *f.* संतप्तता *f.* [संतप्तता *f.*

2—*state.* आग *f.* दाह *m.* बिदाह *m.* अंतर्दाह *m.* अंतर्ज्वलन *n.*

INFALMMATORINESS, *n.* v. A. 1. दाहजनकत्व *n.* दाहोत्पादकत्व *n.* विदाहित्व *n.* &c.

INFLAMMATORY, *a. tending to excite inflammation.* दाह करणारा, दाहजनक, दाहोत्पादक, दाहकारक, दाहक, बिदाही, तापजनक-कारक-&c.

2 *accompanied with morbid heat.* सदाह, दाहयुक्त, दाहविशिष्ट, दाहिक, दाह in comp. (as दाहज्वर i. fever).

3 *tending to incense.* संताप करणारा, संतापक, संतापकारक-जनक-&c.

To INFLATE, *v. a. swell with wind.* फुगवणें, फुगीर-वातफुल्ल-आध्मात &c. करणें.

2 fig. *puff up.* फुगवणें, फुलवणें, माजवणें, मातवणें, फुगेसा-माजेसा-&c. करणें, उन्मत्त-&c. करणें.

INFLATED, *p.* v. V. 1. फुगवलेला, फुगीर, फुगरा *remiss.* फुगट, वातफुल्ल, ध्मात, आध्मात. [विदग्ध.

2 फुगवलेला, &c. फुगरा, पत्रासी *or* जी, उन्मत्त, मदान्वित, दु-

INFLATION, *n.* v. V. 1.—*act.* फुगवणें *n.* फुगवणी *f.* फुगवणूक *f.* फुगवण *f.* आध्मान *n.* ध्मान *n.*—*state.* फुगवशी *f.* फुगोशी *f.* फुगारा *m.* फुगोटा *m.* फुगोटी *f.*

2—*state*, v. CONCEIT. माज *m.* पत्रास *or* पत्राज *f.* दिमाख *m.* आढ्यता *f.* ऊत *m.*

To INFLECT, *v. a.* v. To BEND. बांकवणें, लवणें, झोकवणें, कलवणें, झोक *m.*-&c. देणें.

2—in grammar. विभक्ति *f.*-शब्द *m.*-रूप *n.*-&c. चालवणें, विभक्ति *f.* करणें-जोडणें, रूपांतर *n.* करणें.

INFLECTED, *p.* v. V. 1. बांकवलेला, झोकवलेला, &c.

2 विभक्त्यंत, सविभक्तिक, जातरूपांतर, प्राप्तरूपांतर.

INFLECTION, *n.* v. V. 1.—*act.* बांकवणें *n.* &c. बांकवणी *f.*

2 विभक्ति *f.* विभक्तिकार्य *n.* कार्य *n.* लिंग कार्य *n.* रूपांतर *n.*

A plural i. (of a noun, verb, &c.). अनेक वचन *n.*

String or series of the inflections (of a noun or verb). रूपावलि *pop.* रूपावळी *f.*

INFLECTIVE, *a. having the power of bending.* बांकवणारा, लववणारा, वक्रीकरणक्षम.

INFLEXIBILITY, INFLEXIBLENESS, *n.* v. A. ताठा *m.* ताठ *m.* ताठरपणा *m.* अनमनीयता *f.*

2 चिकटपणा *m.* चिवटपणा *m.* आग्रहीपणा *m.* आग्रह *m.* निग्रह *m.* नेट *m.* दृढसंकल्पता *f.* निर्विकल्पता *f.* &c.

3 हेंका *m.* हेंकडपणा *m.* दुराग्रह *m.* दुराग्रहीपणा *m.*

INFLEXIBLE, *a. that cannot be bent.* ताठ, ताठर, अनमनीय, अनाम्य, नमनाशक्य.

2 *not to be swerved in mind*, v. FIRM, RESOLUTE. चिकट, चिवट, आग्रही, निग्रही, दृढसंकल्प, निर्विकल्प, अविकल्प.

3—in an ill sense. v. OBSTINATE. हेंकट *or* हेंकड, दुराग्रही, हट्टखोर, हट्टी.

INFLEXIBLY, *adv.* v. A. 2. चिकटपणानें, &c. आग्रहपूर्वक, निग्रहपूर्वक, दृढसंकल्पपूर्वक, दृढनिश्चयपूर्वक.

To INFLICT, *v. a. lay on, impose*, (pain, evil, &c.). लावणें, घालणें, देणें, करणें, भोगवणें, भोगायास लावणें.

INFLICTION, *n.* v. V.—*act.* लावणें *n.* देणें *n.* &c. उपधान *n.* (in comp. as दंडोपधान, &c.), आधान *n.* (in comp. as दंडाधान, &c.).

I. See PUNISHMENT.

INFLUENCE, *n. physical power.* शक्ति *f.* बल *pop.* बळ *n.* कर्तृत्वशक्ति *f.* करणशक्ति *f.* गुणकारिता *f.*

2 *moral power, weight, authority, prevalence, &c.* वजन *n.* वजनदारी *f.* भार *m.* भारदस्ती *f.* चलती *f.* चाल *f.* चलवल *f.* चालचलाव *m.* बोज *m.* तोल *m.* जड *f.* बग *f.* मान्यता *f.* गौरव *m. n.* आबदाब *m.* ओढ *f.* ओढा *m.*

To exert one's i. with. भिडेस घालणें, भीड *f.* घालणें *with* स *or* ला *of o.*

To have i. on. भार *m.*-&c. पडणें.

To INFLUENCE, *v. a. act on, affect physically.* कार्य *n.*-कर्तृत्व *n.*-&c. करणें, गुण *m.* करणें-देणें, चालणें, लागणें, चालू होणें *with* वर *of o.*

2 *induce, lead, &c.* v. To MOVE. वळवणें, मनावणें, ओढणें, वळवून-&c. घेणें, ओढ *f.*- ओढा *m.* लागणें *in. con.*

INFLUENTIAL, *a. that has power to influence*, v. N. 2. *and* WEIGHTY. वजनदार, वजनशीर, भारदस्त, भारदस्तीचा, बगीदार, तोलदार, डोईजड, भिडेचा, बगीचा, चलतीचा, &c.

INFLUENZA, *n. epidemic catarrh.* धामीचें-सांतीचें पडसें *n.*-&c.

INFLUX, *n. act of flowing in.* आंत वाहणें *n.* अंतर्वहन *n.* अंतःप्रवहण *n.* अंतःप्रवाह *m.* [येणें *n.*

2 fig. *coming or importation in abundance.* धव्याचा धवा

To be a great i. (of men, animals, &c.). पेंव *n.*-भोम *n.*

&c. फुटणें.

To INFOLD, *v. a. involve, inwrap,* v. To WRAP. वेष्टणें, गुंडाळणें, वेटाळणें, लपेटणें.

2 See To EMBRACE.

To INFOLIATE, *v. a. cover with leaves.* पालवी *f.*-पल्लव *m.*-&c. आणणें-देणें, सपर्ण-सपल्लव-सपत्र-&c.करणें.

To INFORM, *v. a. give life to,* v. To ANIMATE. सजीव-सचेतन-&c. करणें.

2 *acquaint, apprise, advise, advertize.* कळवणें, जाणवणें, सांगणें, सुचवणें, समजावणें, बोधवणें, बुझवणें *or* बुझावणें, ज्ञापवणें, विज्ञापणें, उपदेशणें, खबर *f.*-बातमी *f.*-वर्त्तमान *n.*-वार्त्ता *f.*-&c. देणें, जाण *f.*-सूचना *f.* करणें-देणें, बोध *m.*-प्रबोध *m.*-ज्ञापन *n.*-विज्ञापन *n.*-&c. करणें, माहितगार-माहीत-जाणता-बोधित-ज्ञात-सूचित -&c. करणें, माहीत -श्रुत-&c. करणें. Note. The student will observe that of many of the above verbs the *matter to be told* is the object.

To INFORM, *v. n. give intelligence of crime.* अपराधाची-&c. खबर *f.*-बातमी *f.*-&c. देणें.

INFORMAL, *a. not according to form,* v. IRREGULAR. बेकायद्याचा, गैरकायद्याचा, अविधि, अशास्त्र, अयथाविधि, विधिविरुद्ध.

INFORMALITY, *n.* v. A. अविधिता *f.* अशास्त्रता *f.* विधिविरोध *m.* विधिविपर्यास *m.* अपरीति *f.* अविधि *m.*

INFORMALLY, *adv.* v. A. विधि सोडून-मोडून-वर्जून-&c. अयथाविधि, विधिविपर्यासपूर्वक.

INFORMANT, *n.* v. V. A. 2. कळवणारा, जाणवणारा, सुचवणारा, खबर देणारा, &c. खबऱ्या, बातमीदार, सूचनकर्त्ता, &c. बोधक, प्रबोधक, सूचक, ज्ञापक, विज्ञापक.

v. V. N. अपराधाची खबर देणारा, अपराधाचा खबऱ्या-बातमीदार-&c. मुद्दई, मुदाईम, अन्यायसूचक.—reproachfully or allusively, जोडका पूत, जोडतापूत, जोडताराम, कानलाग्या, द्विजिह्व.

INFORMATION, INFORMING, *n.* v. V. A. 2.—*act.* कळवणें *n.* जाणवणें*n.* बोधवणें *n.* &c. बोध *m.* प्रबोध *m.* बोधन*n.* प्रबोधन*n.* सूचन *n.* सूचना *f.* ज्ञापन *n.* विज्ञापन *n.* विज्ञप्ति *pop.* विज्ञाप्ति *f.* v. V. N.—*act.* अपराधसूचन *n.* अपराधसूचना *f.* अन्यायसूचन *n.* अन्यायसूचना *f.*

I. *notice, news, advice, &c. communicated,* v. INTELLIGENCE. खबर *f.* बातमी *f.* सूचना *f.*

II. *knowledge.* बोध *m.* प्रबोध *m.* ज्ञान *n.* विज्ञान *n.*

INFORMED, *p.* v. V. A. 2. जाणवलेला, माहितगार केलेला, &c. सूचित, बोधित, प्रबोधित, ज्ञापित, विज्ञापित, विज्ञप्त, उपदिष्ट, उपदेशी.

INFORMER. See INFORMANT.

INFORMIDABLE, *a. not fearful.* अभयानक, अभयंकर, अभयावह.

INFRACTION, *n. infringement.* मोड *m.* भंग *m.* उल्लंघ *m.* उल्लंघन *n.* खंडन *n.*

INFRANGIBLE, *a. not to be broken, &c.* अभंग, अभेद्य, अभेदनीय, असंड्य, असंडनीय.

INFREQUENCE, INFREQUENCY, *n.* v. A. विरळपणा *m.* विरळेपणा *m.* विरलता *f.* क्काचित्कत्व *n.* अनाभीक्ष्ण्य *n.* अपौनःपुन्य *n.*

INFREQUENT, *a. rare, uncommon.* विरल *pop.* विरळ, विरळा, विरलागत, क्काचित्क, अपौनःपुनिक, अनाभीक्ष्ण.

INFREQUENTLY, *adv.* v. A. क्कचित्, विरळ.

To INFRINGE, *v. a. break, violate.* मोडणें, तोडणें, उल्लंघणें, भंग *m*-उल्लंघ *m.*-उल्लंघन *n.*-&c. करणें. [लंघित.

INFRINGED, *p.* v. V. मोडलेला, तोडलेला, &c. भग्न, विच्छिन्न, उ-

INFRINGER, *n.* INFRINGING, *p. a.* v. V. मोडणारा, तोडणारा, &c. भंगकर्त्ता-कारी, भंजक, विच्छेदक.

INFRINGEMENT, *n.* v. V.—*act.* मोडणें *n.* &c. मोड *m.* भंग *m.* भंजन *n.* उल्लंघ *m.* उल्लंघन *n.* विच्छेद *m.* अतिक्रम *m.* अतिक्रमण *n.*

INFRUABLE, *a. not to be used or enjoyed.* अभोग्य, भोगानर्ह.

To INFURIATE, *v. a. render furious, enrage.* तापवणें, संतापवणें, कोपविणें, संतप्त-संतापित-कोपान्वित-तप्तबप्त-&c. करणें, वेड *n.* भरवणें.

INFURIATE, *a. mad with rage, furious,* v. RAGING. रागानें वेडा झालेला, तप्तबप्त, संतप्त, संतापित, कोपान्वित, कोपज्वलित, क्रोधांध, क्रोधविक्षिप्त.

To INFUSCATE, INFUSCATION. See To BLACKEN, To DARKEN.

To INFUSE, *v. a. pour in, instil.* ओतणें, घालणें.

2 fig. *pour into the mind.* घालणें, भरविणें, ठेवणें, आधान*n.*-स्थापन *n.*-निक्षेप *m.*-न्यास *m.*-&c. करणें *g. of o.*

3 *steep.* भिजवणें, भिजत-भिजूं घालणें-ठेवणें, भावना *f.*-रसपुट *n.*-&c. देणें.

INFUSIBLE, *a. not fusible.* अद्राव्य, अद्रावणीय, द्रावणाशक्य.

INFUSION, *n.* v. V. 1.—*act.* ओतणें *n.* घालणें *n.*

2—*act.* घालणें *n.* भरवणें*n.* &c. उपधान *n.* आधान*n.* न्यास *m.* निक्षेप *m.*

3 भिजवणें *n.* &c. भावना *f.*

I. *liquor made by infusing.* काढा *m.* कषाय *m.* रस*m.* फांट *n.* पाणी *n.* काढ *m.*

Cold i. हिम *m.* शीत *m.* शेळ *n.*

INGATHERING. See HARVEST.

INGELABLE, *a. that cannot be congealed.* थिजवायास-&c. अयोग्य-अशक्य, घनीकरणाशक्य, घनीकरणानर्ह.

To INGENDER. See To ENGENDER.

INGENIOUS, *a. possessing the faculty of invention, inventive.* कल्पक, योजक, कल्पनाबाज, कल्पनेचा, उपायी, चतुर, युक्त्या, युक्तिमान्, युक्तिवान्, साधनी, लागलाव्या, लाग्या, अनुसंधानी, संधानी, करामती, हिकमती *or* त्या, हुनरी, हरहुनरी, इलमी, इलमबाज, उपायज्ञ, मार्मिक.

2 *of curious design, &c.* करामतीचा, युक्तीचा, कळाकुसरीचा, कलाकुशलतेचा, कलाचातुर्याचा, हुनरबाजीचा, चातुर्याचा, युक्तिनिष्पन्न. [चातुर्यानें.

INGENIOUSLY, *adv.* v.A. 1. युक्तीनें, युक्तीकरून, युक्तिवता, युक्त्या,

INGENIOUSNESS, INGENUITY, *n.* v. A. 1. कल्पनाशक्ति *f.* कल्पना *f.* युक्ति *pop.* युगत *f.* चतुराई *f.* चातुर्य *n.* कला *f.* हिकमत *f.* हुनर *m.f.* इलम *m.* कडासणी *f.* [कुलंगडें *n.*

2—as in works, acts, &c. करामत *f.* युक्ति *f.* कारागिरी *f.*

INGENUOUS, *a. open, candid, fair,* v. FRANK. मनाचा मोकळा-साफ-&c. निष्कपट, अकपट, निष्पांजल, दिलपाक, प्रशस्त, सरळ, साळढाळ, घळघळीत, घळवळीत, घळमळीत.

2 See MAGNANIMOUS, NOBLE.

INGENUOUSLY, *adv.* v. A. 1. निष्कपटपणानें, कपट सोडून, &c. प्रशस्त मनानें, दिलपाकीनें, सरलभावानें, &c.

INGENUOUSNESS, *n.* v.A. 1. मनाचा मोकळेपणा *m.* निष्कापट्य *n.*

प्राशस्त्य *n.* दिलपाकी *f.* सरलभाव *m.* सरलता *f.* सारल्य *n.*

INGLORIOUS, *a. that brings no glory or fame.* अकीर्त्तीचा, अयशाचा, अलौकिकाचा, अकीर्त्तिकर, अकीर्त्तिद, अयशस्कर, अयशःप्रद, अश्रीमान्.

2 See DISGRACEFUL. [अप्रसिद्धि *f.*

INGLORIOUSNESS, *n.* v. A. अकीर्ति *f.* अयश *n.* कीर्त्तिराहित्य *n.*

INGOT, *n.*—of gold or silver. लोट *f.* इंट *f.* गट *m.* राळ *f.*

INGOT-MOULD, *n.* ईषीका *f.* तूलिका *f.*

To INGRAFT, &c. See To GRAFT, &c.

To INGRAIN, *v. a. dye before manufacture.* विणण्यापूर्वी रंगविणें. 2 *work into the natural texture.* भिनवणें, भिद्वणें, हाडींखिळवणें.

INGRATE, INGRATEFUL. *a.* See UNGRATEFUL.

INGRATE, *n. an ungrateful person.* Ordinarily, one language is rendered into another by word being placed with word; but where in the one language *words* are used to convey sentiments and thoughts and truths and in the other *phrases*—where, of the one the genius leans to plain and simple and direct speech, and of the other, to figured and flowery and emblematic expression, there it seems clearly to be demanded that figures and phrases and proverbs and idioms, if they justly and vividly represent the word which stands to be represented, be viewed as equivalent with single words, and be used as copiously and freely. Accordingly, designative or allusive of, or involving the idea of, *Ingrate* or *Ingratitude*, some phrases or sayings are. खाऊनिंदक, खादनिंदक, गाईचागोहोरा, अस्तनींतला साप, खाल्ल्या घरचे वांसे मोजणारा, खाल्ल्या अन्नावर उठणारा, खाल्ल्या अन्नावर माती घालणारा, बारावर्षें खांद्यावर वागविलें तरीं आस्ते उतार, दूधपिऊन विष ओकणारा, पोसल्या पोरा काय करशी तर म्हातारीचे डोळे काढशी, ज्याचा मंत्र त्याच्या मस्तकावर हात ठेवणारा, जेथें खाल तेथें हगाल, वाळूवर मुतल्यानें फेस ना पाणी ओली ना खोली, आइच्या खाटेवर चढणारा.

To lavish favors on an i. अळवावर आंचवणें.

To INGRATIATE, *v. a. get into favor.* रुपा *f.*-मर्जी *f.*-आर्जव *n.*-&c. संपादणें, मर्जी *f.* संपादन करणें, रुपासंपादन *n.* करणें, पोटांत शिरणें.

INGRATITUDE, *n. unthankfulness.* निरुपकारीपणा *m.* अनुपकारीपणा *m.* अकृतज्ञता *f.* कृतघ्नता *f.* निमकहरामी *f.* अनुपकारिता *f.* निरुपकारिता *f.* प्रत्युपकाराभाव *m.*

INGREDIENT, *n. component part of a mixture.* वाना *m.* वान *n.* द्रव्य *n.* उपचार *m.* जिन्नस *m.* प्रकार *m.* साधन *n.* उपकरण *n.* घटकावयव *m.*

Ingredients—of compositions in general. मसाला *m.*

Compound of 32 ingredients. बत्तिशी *f.*—of 36 do छत्तिशी *f.*

INGRESS, *n. entrance,* lit. fig. प्रवेश *m.* निवेश *m.* समावेश *m.* सन्निवेश *m.* संचार *m.*

I. of a luminary at an eclipse. वेध *m.*

INGUINAL, *a. belonging to the groin.* मांडीच्या सांध्याचा, ऊरुसंधीचा, वंक्षणसंबंधी.

To INGULF, *v. a. swallow up.* गर्क-गडप-गहद-&c. करणें,

To be ingulfed. गर्क-&c. होणें.

INGUSTABLE, *a. not perceptible to the taste.* रसनेंद्रियातीत, रसनेंद्रियागोचर, रसनेंद्रियाविषय.

To INHABIT, *v. n.* v. To RESIDE. राहणें, बसणें, नांदणें, वास *m.*-वसति *pop.* वस्ती *f.*-निवास *m.*-&c. करणें, घर *n.*-&c. असणें, अधिष्ठणें.

To INHABIT, *v. a. dwell in.* राहणें, &c. (See the V. N.) with the object in the locative case.

INHABITABLE, *a.* v. V. *fit for residence.* राहयाजोगता-सारखा-&c. राहण्या लायक, वास्य, वसितव्य, वसनीय, वासार्ह, वासयोग्य.

INHABITANT, INHABITER, *n.* v. V. राहणारा, राहणार, वस्तीकरणारा, वासकरणारा, नांदणारा, बसणारा, रहिवासी, वस्तीकर, कर *or* करी (as attached to the name of a town or place, as पुणेकर an i. of Poona, काशीकर an i. of *Kàshi,* गांवकरी an i. of the village, &c.), वासी (in comp. as वनवासी, नगरवासी, गृहवासी, &c.), निवासी (in comp. as द्वारकानिवासी, &c.), स्थ (in comp. as ग्रामस्थ, क्षेत्रस्थ, &c.), संस्थ (in comp. as जलसंस्थ, स्वर्गसंस्थ, &c.), अंतस्थ, अंतस्थित, अधिष्ठित.

INHABITATION, *n.* v. RESIDENCE. राहणें *n.* वास *m.* वसति *pop.* वस्ती *f.* अधिष्ठान *n.* अधिष्ठिति *f.*

INHABITED, *a. that has inhabitants, not empty or desolate.* नांदता, वसता, रावता, वसातीचा.

INHALABLE, *a.* v. V. श्वासाबरोबर घ्यायाचा-प्यायाचा-खायाचा-&c. प्राशनीय, पानीय.

INHALATION, *n.* v. V. श्वासाबरोबरघेणें *n.* &c. प्राशन *n.*

To INHALE, *v. a. draw into the lungs.* श्वासाबरोबर घेणें-खाणें-पिणें, पिणें, खाणें, घेणें, ओढणें.

INHALED, *p.* v. V. श्वासाबरोबर घेतलेला, &c. प्राशित.

INHARMONIOUS, *a.* v. UNMELODIOUS. बेसूर, बदसूर, अपस्वर.

2 v. INCONSISTENT. बिसंगत, असंगत, संदर्भविरुद्ध, असंदर्भ.

To INHERE, *v. n. exist, or be fixed in.* राहणें, बसणें, अधिष्ठणें, धरून-अधिष्ठून असणें, स्थिति *f.*-&c. करणें, स्थिति *pop.* स्थीत *f.*-अधिष्ठान *n.*-अधिष्ठिति *f.*-&c. असणें *g. of s.*

INHERENCE, *n.* v. V. स्थिति *pop.* स्थीत *f.* अधिष्ठान *n.* अधिष्ठिति *f.* अंतःस्थिति *f.* संस्था *f.* संस्थिति *f.* निष्ठा *f.* समवाय *m.* समवायसंबंध *m.* अंतर्वर्त्तन *n.* अंतर्वृत्ति *f.*

INHERENT, *a.* v. V. स्थित, अधिष्ठित, अंतस्थित, अंतस्थ, अंतरस्थ, अंतर्वर्त्ती, निष्ठ (in comp. as घटनिष्ठ, देहनिष्ठ, &c.), संस्थ, समवेत, समवायसंबंधी.

I. *naturally pertaining to,* v. NATURAL. स्वाभाविक *pop.* स्वभाविक, औत्सर्गिक, नैसर्गिक, सांसिद्धिक, सहज.

An i. quality or attribute. अनुगत धर्म *m.*

To INHERIT, *v. a. receive by inheritance.* वारीस-वारिसदार-&c. होऊन पावणें-भोगणें-घेणें-&c. वारिसपणानें-वारशानें-वारिसदारीनें-&c. पावणें-भोगणें-घेणें-&c. वारीस-वारिसदार-&c. होणें *g. of o.* वारसा *m.*-&c. येणें *g. of o. with* कडे *of s.*

2 *receive by nature from a progenitor.* बापापासून-वडिलापासून-&c. येणें-जडणें *in. con.* पिढीचा-पिढीजाद-वसलातीचा-पित्रागत-&c. असणें *in. con.*

INHERITABLE, *a.* v. V. 1. वारिसपणानें-&c. भोगायाचा-भोगायाजोगा-&c. पितृपुत्र परंपरा भोग्य, उत्तराधिकारोपभोग्य,

INHERITANCE, INHERITING, *n.* v. V. 1.—*act.* वारिसपणानें पावणें *n.* &c. वारिसपणाचा-&c. भोग *m.* रिक्थग्रहण *n.* रिक्थग्रह *m.* रिक्थप्राप्ति *f.* रिक्थदान *n.*
Obtained by i. वतनी.
Right of i. उत्तराधिकार *m.*
I. *heritage, patrimony.* वारसा *m.* वारीस *m. n.* वतन *n.* वतनवाडी *f.* दाय *m.* बापरोटी *f.*
One entitled to share in an i. दायजी *c.*
Portioning or portion of i. दायभाग *or* दायविभाग *m.* रिक्थविभाग *m.*
Share of an i. v. SHARE. वंत *m.* अंश *m.*

INHERITOR, *n.* v. V. 1. *and* HEIR. वारिसपणानें भोगणारा, &c. वारीस, वारिसदार *or* वारसेदार, उत्तराधिकारी.
Joint i. वतनबंधु *m.* वतनभाऊ *m.*

INHERITRESS, INHERITRIX. See HEIRESS.

INHESION, *n.* v. INHERENCE. अंतःस्थिति *f.* अधिष्ठान *n.* अधिष्ठिति *f.* [&c.

To INHIBIT, INHIBITION, &c. See To RESTRAIN, To FORBID,

INHOSPITABLE, *a. not disposed to entertain guests.* अतिथिद्वेषी, अतिथिशत्रु, अभ्यागतद्वेषी, अभ्यागतशत्रु, अतिथिविमुख, अतिथिपराङ्मुख, अनातिथेय.
2—a country, &c. परक्यास गैरसोईचा, अभ्यागताशरण, अभ्यागतानुपकारी, अभ्यागताहित, परानिर्वाहक.

INHOSPITABLENESS, INHOSPITALITY, *n.* v. A. 1. अतिथिद्वेष *m.* अभ्यागतद्वेष *m.* अभ्यागतद्रोह *m.* अनातिथ्य *n.* आतिथ्यनादर *m.* अतिथ्यसत्कार *m.* [थिद्वेषपूर्वक.

INHOSPITABLY, *adv.* v. A. अतिथिद्वेषानें, अनातिथ्यपूर्वक, अति-

INHUMAN, *a.* v. CRUEL.—of persons. निर्दय, दयाहीन, दयाशून्य, निर्घृण, क्रूर, राक्षसी, राक्षसधर्मा, मनुष्यविधर्मा.
2—of acts. क्रूरपणाचा, निर्दयपणाचा, क्रूर.

INHUMANITY, *n.* v. A. निर्दयपणा *m.* निर्दयपण *n.* निर्दयता *f.* क्रूरता *f.* क्रौर्य *n.* मनुष्यवैधर्म्य *n.*

To INHUMATE, *To* INHUME. See To BURY.

INHUMATION, *n.* v. BURIAL. भूमिनिक्षेप *m.* भूमिनिवेशन *n.* क्षितिन्यास *m.*
Self i. जिवंत समाध *f.*

INIMICAL, *a. unfriendly,* v. ADVERSE. द्वेषी, वैरी, अमित्र, असख, असुहृद्, अस्निग्ध, विमना, अहितमना, हितशत्रु.

INIMICALLY, *adv.* v. A. शत्रुबुद्ध्या, शत्रुदृष्ट्या, शत्रुभावानें.

INIMITABILITY, *n.* v. A. अनुपमेयता *f.* अप्रतिमता *f.* अद्वितीयता *f.* अनन्यसाध्यता *f.*

INIMITABLE, *a. surpassing imitation.* अनुपमेय, अद्वितीय, अप्रतिम, उपमातीत, अनन्यसाध्य, अनन्यशक्य, अन्यासाध्य, अन्याशक्य, अननुकार्य, अनुकरणाशक्य, अभविष्यदुपम.

INIQUITOUS, *a.* v. UNJUST. WICKED. अन्यायाचा, अनीतीचा, अधर्माचा, अन्यायी, अधर्मी, अधार्मिक, अधर्मचारी, अयथान्याय, अनय, हराम.

INIQUITOUSNESS, *n.* v. A. अन्याय *m.* अनीति *f.* अधर्म *m.* दुर्नीति *f.* अनय *m.* पाप *n.* अन्यायिता *f.* अधार्मिता *f.* अयथान्यायता *f.* नीतिविरोध *m.* नीतिविरुद्धता *f.* नीतिविपर्यास *m.*

INIQUITY, *n. injustice.* See INIQUITOUSNESS.
2 *act of injustice,* v. SIN. पाप *n.* अन्याय *m.* अधर्म *m.* अनीति *f.*
The cup or measure of i. is full. पापाचा घडा भरला, पापाची पायली भरली.

INITIAL, *a. placed at the beginning.* पहिला, प्रथम, आद्य, पूर्व, आदिम, प्राथमिक.
2 See INCIPIENT. [द्याक्षर *n.*

INITIAL, *n. first letter of a name.* नांवाचा पहिला वर्ण *m.* नामा-

To INITIATE, *v. a. introduce into a sect or society, &c. by ceremonies.* दीक्षा *f.*-अनुग्रह *m.* देणें, संस्कार *m.*-मंत्रोपदेश *m.*-उपदेश *m.* करणें, दीक्षा देऊन-संस्कार करून-&c. घेणें, दीक्षित-संस्कृत-&c. करणें, मुंडणें.
2 *instruct in rudiments or principles; make acquainted with.* पहिलीशिक्षा *f.*-प्रथमशिक्षा *f.* देणें, उपदेश *m.*-प्रथमोपदेश *m.* करणें, विद्यारंभ *m.*-विद्योपक्रम *m.*-&c. करविणें, मूलपीठिका *f.* सांगणें-लावणें-लावून देणें, विद्याप्रविष्ट-विद्याभिनिविष्ट-&c. करणें.
3 *begin upon.* उपक्रम *m.*-प्रारंभ *m.*-&c. करणें.

INITIATED, *p.* v. V. 1. दीक्षा दिल्हेला, &c. दीक्षित, संस्कारित, संस्कृत, जातसंस्कार, जातदीक्ष, कृतसंस्कार, कृतदीक्ष, उपदिष्ट, मंत्रवान्.
2 पहिली शिक्षा दिल्हेला, &c. कृतविद्योपक्रम, जातविद्योपक्रम, विद्याप्रविष्ट, विद्याभिनिविष्ट.

INITIATION, *n.* v. V. 1. दीक्षा देणें *n.* &c. दीक्षा *f.* संस्कार *m.* उपदेश *m.* मंत्रोपदेश *m.*
2 पहिलीशिक्षा *f.* प्रथमशिक्षा *f.* विद्याप्रवेश *m.* अभिनिवेश *m.*

INITIATIVE, INITIATORY, *a. tending to initiate.* दीक्षाकरणसंबंधी, दीक्षाकरणविषयक, दीक्षाकरणोपयोगी.

INITIATIVE, *n. introductory step or measure.* उपक्रम *m.*
To take the i. पेरणें.

To INJECT, *v. a. throw or dart in.* आंत टाकणें-घालणें-&c. अंतःक्षेप *m.*-अंतःप्रक्षेप *m.*-अंतःक्षेपण *n.*-&c. करणें *g. of o.* अंतःक्षिप्त-&c. करणें.
2 (with a syringe). पिचकारी *f.* मारणें, बस्ति *m. f.* देणें.

INJECTION, *n.* v. V. 1.—*act.* आंत टाकणें *n.* &c. अंतःक्षेप *m.* अंतःप्रक्षेप *m.* अंतःक्षेपण *n.* अंतःप्रक्षेपण *n.* [औषध *n.*
I. *medicine to be injected.* बस्ति *m. f.* पिचकारीनें घालायाचें

INJUDICIOUS, *a.* v. UNWISE.—of persons. असमजीक, असमजदार, असमंजस, अविवेकी, असूज्ञ, उचितानभिज्ञ.
2—of acts. अविवेकाचा, असमंजसपणाचा, असमजिकपणाचा.

INJUDICIOUSLY, *adv.* v. A. अविवेकानें, असमजिकपणानें, अविवेकपूर्वक. [अविवेक *m.*

INJUDICIOUSNESS, *n.* v. A. असमजिकपणा *m.* असमंजसपणा *m.*

INJUNCTION, *n. order, precept,* v. COMMAND. हुकूम *m.* आज्ञा *f.* ताकीद *f.* आदेश *m.* विधान *n.*
Writ or letter of i. ताकीदचिठ्ठी *f.* ताकीदपत्र *n.*

To INJURE, *v. a. hurt unjustly, wrong.* अपकार *m.*-अन्याय *m.*-अपराध *m.*-बाईट *n.*-नुकसान *n.*-द्रोह *m.*-&c. करणें *g. of o.* नाहक दुःख *n.* देणें, जुलूम *m.* करणें.
2 *harm, damage, &c.* v. To HURT. खराब-जायां-जायबंदी-&c. करणें, खराबी *f.*-नुकसानी *f.*-नुकसान *n.*-अहित *n.*-&c. करणें *g. of o.*

INJURED, *p.* v. V. 1. अपकार केलेला, &c. जातापकार, प्राप्तापकार, अपकृत, कृतापकार, दत्तापकार. [कार.
2 खराब केलेला- झालेला, &c. जायां, जायबंदी, जायबंदा, प्राप्ताप-

INJURER, *n.* INJURING, *p. a.* INJURIOUS, *a.* v. V. 1. अपकार करणारा, अन्याय करणारा, जुलूम करणारा, &c. अन्यायकारी, परापकारी, परापकारक, परानिष्टकारी, द्रोही, द्रोहकारी, द्वेषी.

2 *and* Hurtful. खराब करणारा, नुकसान करणारा, &c. अपकारक, अपकारी, अहितकारक, अहितकारी, घातक, घातकी, क्षतिकर-कारक-प्रद-&c. हानिकर-कारक-प्रद-&c. द्वेषी.

To be injurious. बाधणें, बाधक असणें.

Injuriously, *adv.* v. A. 1. अन्यायानें, अन्यायेंकरून, विनापराध, निरपराध, नाहक, द्रोहपूर्वक.

Injury, *n. hurt without justice.* अन्याय*m.* बाईट*n.* अपराध*m.* जुलूम*m.* अपकार*m.* अपकृति *f.* द्रोह*m.*

To be seeking the i. of. बाइटावर असणें *g. of o.*

2 *hurt, harm, detriment.* अपकार*m.* नुकसान*n.* नुकसानी *f.* खराबी *f.* नाश*m.* हानि *f.* क्षति *f.* अपाय*m.* धका *or* धक्का *m.* तकस *m.*

3 (to a limb, member, &c.). दुखापत *f.* दुःख*n.* अपकार*m.*

To receive i. दुखवणें *or* दुखावणें.

Injustice, *n. iniquity, wrong,* v. Iniquitousness. अन्याय*m.* अनीति *f.* दुर्नीति *f.* अनय *m.* अधर्म *m.* बेइनसाफ *m.* नीतिविपर्यास*m.*

2 an *i. a wrong.* अन्याय*m.* अपराध*m.* बेदाद *f.* जुलूम*m.*

Ink, *n.* शाई *f.* मषी *f.*—made of lamp-black, lac, &c. लाखीशाई *f.*

Red i. (i. e. the dye of *lac, lodhra, &c.* so used). अलित !*m.* अळता*m.* अलक्तरस*m.* अलक्त*m.*

Cake of red i. (i. e. cotton steeped in the dye of *lac, lodhra, &c.*), पोळी*f.* अळता *m.*

Piece of rag put into i. सोपा*m.* सोपें*n.*

Seller, &c. of i. शाईवाला, शाईविक्या, रकवानू.

To Ink, *v. a.* शाईनें भरणें-भरवणें-माखणें-&c.

Ink-horn, Ink-stand, *n.* दऊत *or* दौत *f.* मसिकूपी *f.* मसिधानी *f.* मसिपात्र*n.*

Piece of rag usually kept in the i. पोस्त*n.*

Inkle, *n. tape.* नवार *f.*

Inkling, *n. slight knowledge of.* चुणूक *f.* झुणूक *f.* आभास*m.* भास*m.* झुळूक *f.* वास*m.* गंध*m.* गंधवास*m.*

To divine the whole from an i. सुतानें स्वर्गास जाणें.

To give an i. दिशा *f.* दाखवणें, दिक्प्रदर्शन*n.* करणें.

To have an i. चुणूक *f.*-वास*m.*-&c. समजणें, वास*m.*-गंध*m.* -&c. येणें.

2 See Inclination, Desire.

Inky, *a.* शाईचा, शाईसा, शाईसारखा.

Inlaid, *p.* v. V. जडावकेलेला, &c. खचित.

Inland, *a. interior, remote from the sea.* समुद्राहून दूरचा, मध्यदेशचा, मध्यदेशस्थ, देशमध्यस्थ, देशमध्यवर्त्ती, असमुद्रतीरस्थ, समुद्रदूरस्थ. [अविदेशज.

2 *not foreign; domestic.* देशी, मुलकी, देशीय, अविदेशीय,

To Inlay, *v. a. infix.* जडणें, खचणें, जडणी *f.*-जडण *f.*- जडाव*m.* करणें *g. of o.* खचित-&c. करणें.

Inlay, *n. inlaid or set state.* जडाव*m.* [म्या.

Inlayer, *n.* v. V. जडणारा, &c. जड्या, जडावकाम्या, कोंदणका-

Inlaying, *n.* v. V.—*act.* जडणें, &c. जडण *f.* जडणी *f.* जडणकाम*n.*

Inlet, *n. place of ingress, entrance.* वाट *f.* द्वार *pop.* दार*n.* प्रवेशमार्ग*m.*

2 *creek, &c.* खाडी *f.* वांकण*n.* ओहर*m.*

To Inlist. See To Enlist.

Inly. See Inward.

Inmate, *n. one who lives in the same house.* सहवासी, सहस्थायी, एकस्थलस्थ, एकनिवासी.

Inmost, *a. farthest in.* सर्वांहून आंतला *or* चा, अत्यभ्यंतरस्थ, अत्यभ्यंतरवर्त्ती, अत्यंतस्थित.

Inn, *n. house for the reception of travellers.* भटारखाना *m.* सराई *f.* उतारवाडा *m.* जेवणावळीचें घर *n.*

Inn-keeper, *n.* भटाऱ्या, भटारी.

Innate, *a. inborn,* v. Natural. जातीचा, जन्माचा, स्वाभाविक *pop.* स्वभाविक, स्वभावसिद्ध, स्वभावज, सहज, नैसर्गिक, निसर्गज, प्रकृतिस्थ, अंतर्जात, अंतर्भव.

An i. vice or evil propensity. जन्मखोड *f.*

Innateness, *n.* v. A. स्वाभाविकत्व *n.* नैसर्गिकत्व *n.* &c. अंतर्भाव*m.*

Innavigable, *a. impassable by ships, &c.* अनाव्य, अनौतार्य, नौगमनानर्ह, नौगमनाशक्य.

Inner, *a. interior, not outward.* आंतला, आंनचा, आंतील, आंतल्याबाजूचा, आंतल्या आंगचा, आंतल्या कडचा *or* ला, आंतल्या घडचा *or* ला, आंतल्याकडील, आंतल्याधडील, आभ्यंतर, अंतरंग, अंतस्थित, अंतर्वर्त्ती, आंतर, गर्भस्थ.

I. part. अभ्यंतर *n.*

Innermost. See Inmost. [खाजण*n.*

Innings, *n. lands recovered from the sea.* खार *f.* खारट *n.*

Innocence, Innocency, *n.* v. A. 1. निरपराधिपणा *m.* निरपराधता *f.* अनपराधता *f.* निर्दोषता *f.* &c. अपराधराहित्य *n.* दोषराहित्य *n.* दोषशून्यता *f.* निष्कलंकता *f.* पाकी *f.* दिलपाकी *f.* पापाज्ञान*n.* अज्ञातपापावस्था *f.*

2 अविकारिपणा *m.* निरुपद्रविकपणा *m.* सात्विकपणा *m.* &c. अविकारिता *f.* निर्विकारता *f.* अनपकारिता *f.* &c. अनपकार *m.* सात्विकता *f.* सत्वगुण *m.*

3 बापुडेपणा *m.* गरीबी *f.* निष्कपटपणा *m.* दिलपाकी *f.* सालसाई *f.* निष्कापट्य *n.* अकापट्य *n.*

Innocent, *a. free from guilt.* निरपराध *pop.* निरपराधी, अनपराध *pop.* अनपराधी, निर्दोष, दोषरहित-शून्य-&c. अपराधरहित-शून्य-&c. अदोष, अपाप, अज्ञातापराध, अज्ञातपाप, अज्ञातपाप, निष्कलंक, अलिप्त, निर्मल, पाक.

2 *not hurtful; innocuous.* अविकारी, निर्विकारी, निरुपद्रवीक, अबाधक, निर्बाधक, अनपकारी, अनपकारक, निरपकारी, अविकारकारी, अनुपद्रवकारी, अनहितकारी, अन्यथाकारी, अदुष्ट, सात्विक, कोमल.

3 *guileless, &c.* v. Simple. गरीब, बापुडा, निष्कपट, निष्कृत्रिम, दिलपाक, सालस.

Innocently, *adv.* v. A. 1. दोषावांचून, अपराधावांचून, दोषघडल्यावांचून, अदोषानें, निर्दोषतः.

3 निष्कपटपणानें, निष्कापट्यानें, दिलपाकीनें, अदोषबुद्धीनें, &c.

Innocuous, *a. not hurtful,* v. Innocent. अविकारी, निर्विकारी, अनपकारी.

Innocuousness, *n.* v. A. अविकारिपणा *m.* अविकारिता *f.* निर्विकारिता *f.* अनपकार *m.*

To Innovate, *v. a. change by introducing novelties.* नवीरीत *f.*-नवीचाल *f.*-नवामार्ग *m.*-&c. करणें-पाडणें-&c. *or* करून-पाडून-&c. फिरवणें-पालटणें, नवेंजुनें *n.* करणें-करून फिरवणें, फेरफार *m.*-फिरवाफिरव *f.*-परिपाठ्यंतर *n.*-रीत्यंतर *n.*-&c. करणें.

Innovation, *n.* v. V.—*act.* फिरवणें *n.* पालटणें *n.* &c. फिरवाफिरव *f.* रीत्यंतरस्थापन *n.* पाठांतरस्थापन *n.*

I. *change made.* नवीरीत *f.* नवीचाल *f.* नवामार्ग *m.* नवापरिपाठ *m.* &c.

INNOVATOR, *n.* v. V. नवेंजुनें करणारा, नवीरीति करणारा, &c. नवसंप्रदाय प्रवर्त्तक, नवसंप्रदायाचार्य, मतांतर स्थापक.

INNOXIOUS, INNOXIOUSNESS. See INNOCUOUS, &c.

INNUENDO, *n. oblique hint.* नोक *f. v.* मार-दासब, रळी *f.* व्यंग्योक्ति *f.* व्यंग *n.* पर्यायोक्ति *f.* भंग्युक्ति *f.* वक्रोक्ति *f.* अन्योक्ति *f.*

INNUMERABILITY, INNUMERABLENESS, *n.* v. A. अगणनीयता *f.* अगण्यता *f.* &c.

INNUMERABLE, *a. that cannot be counted.* अगणनीय, अगण्य, अगणितव्य, अगणेय, असंख्येय, असंख्य, अगणित, बेसुमार, कोट्यवधि, गणनाशक्य, गणनातीत, संख्यातीत.

INNUTRITION, *n. want of nutrition.* अपुष्टि *f.*

INNUTRITIOUS, *a. not nourishing.* अपुष्टिकर, अपुष्टिद, अपोषक, अपौष्टिक.

INOBSERVABLE, *a. that cannot be observed or seen.* अलक्ष्य, दुर्लक्ष, दुर्लक्ष्य, लक्ष्यागोचर, सूक्ष्मतर.

INOBSERVANT, *a.* असावधानदृष्टि.

INOBSERVATION, *n.* दुर्लक्ष *n.* अलक्ष *n.* अलक्ष्य *n.*

To INOCULATE, *v. a.* (a tree &c.). पिवंदी करणें.

2 (for the small pox). देवी *f.* काढणें-देणें, फोडया *f. pl.* काढणें, तोडगा *m.* करणें, शिक्का *m.* देणें, छापणें.

INOCULATED, *p.* v. V. 1. पिवंदी केलेला, पिवंदीचा.

2 देवी काढलेला, तोडगा केलेला-&c. तोडग्याचा.

I. small pox. कुंभाराच्यादेवी *f. pl.*-माता *f. pl.*

INOCULATION, *n.* v. V. पिवंदी *f.*

2 देवी काढणें *n.* &c. तोडगा *m.* तोटगा *m.* शिक्का *m.*

INOCULATOR, *n.* v. V. 2. देवी काढणारा, शिक्का देणारा, &c. तोडगेकरी, तोटगेकरी.

INODOROUS, *a. that has no smell.* निर्गंध, अगंध, गंधरहित-शून्य-हीन-&c.

INOFFENSIVE, *a. unprovoking, harmless.* गरीब, बापडा, बापुडबाणा *or* णी, मिस्कीन, अद्रोह, निद्रोह, अद्रोही, निर्द्रोही, अपरद्रोही, अद्वेष, अद्वेषी, अद्वेषबुद्धि, अद्वेष्टा, अनुपद्रवकारी, अपरदुःखद, अहिंस्र, अहिंसक, अघातुक, सात्विक, सत्ववृत्ति, सत्वशील, सत्वस्थ, सालस, साळसूद *or* ध, गरंगील. Some significant terms and appellatives for *an inoffensive person* are अजातशत्रु, भोळानाथ, भोळाशंकर, भोळासांब, धर्मराज, गोब्राह्मण, गोगलगाय, रामाय स्वस्ति रावणायस्वस्ति म्हणणारा, गंगा गये गंगादास मथुरा गये मथुरादास असा.

2 *not injurious or hurtful*, v. INNOCENT. अविकारी, अनपकारी, निरुपद्रवीक, अबाधक.

INOFFENSIVENESS, *n.* v. A. 1. गरीबी *f.* बापडेपणा *m.* साळसुदी *f.* सात्विकपणा *m.* अद्रोह *m.* अद्वेष *m.* अहिंसा *f.* अद्वेषिता *f.* अद्वेषबुद्धि *f.* सत्ववृत्ति *f.* सत्वशीलता *f.* &c.

2 अविकारिपणा *m.* अविकारिता *f.* अनपकारिता *f.* अबाधकता *f.* अनपकार *m.*

INOFFICIAL, *a.* सरकारी नात्याचा नाहीं, अनाधिकारिक, अनधिकार प्रयुक्त.

INOPERATIVE, *a producing no effect.* अकार्यकारी, अकार्यकारक, अगुणकारी, अकार्यसाधक, अकिंचित्कर.

INOPPORTUNE, *a.* v. UNSEASONABLE. अवकाळा *or* ळ्या, अकाळ्या, अवेळेचा, अवेळींचा, अनवसर, अप्राप्तकाल, असामयिक, अकालीन, अप्रसंगोपात्त.

INOPPORTUNELY, *n.* v. A अवकाळीं, अकाळीं, अवेळीं, असमयीं,

INOPPORTUNENESS, *adv.* v.A. अवेळेपणा *m.* अकालीनता *f.* असामयिकत्व *n.* अवेळ *f.* अनवसर *m.*

INORDINACY, INORDINATENESS, *n.* v. A. *and* EXCESS. अमर्यादपणा *m.* बेसुमारपणा *m.* बेहद्द *f.* मर्यादाराहित्य *n.* अमर्यादा *f.* मर्यादातिक्रम *m.*

INORDINATE, *a. not limited to rules or bounds prescribed*, v. EXCESSIVE. अमर्याद, अतिमर्याद, उन्मर्याद, मर्यादातीत, लंघितमर्याद, अतिक्रांतमर्याद, लंघितनियम, बेसुमार, अनिवार.

INORDINATELY, *adv.* v. A. अमर्याद, अतिमर्याद, बेसुमार, बेहद्द.

INORDINATION, *n. deviation from rule*, v. IRREGULARITY. व्यभिचार *m.* नियमातिक्रम *m.* अविधि *m.*

INORGANIC, INORGANICAL, *a. devoid of the organs of life.* जीवितसाधनरहित-शून्य-&c. जड, निर्जीव, अप्राणी, प्राणवायुसंचाररहित, निरवयव, जीव्यंगरहित.

INOSCULATION, *n. union of two bodies at their extremities.* अग्रद्वयसंधि *m.* अग्रसंयोगसंधान *n.*

INQUEST, *n. enquiry, investigation*, v. EXAMINATION. चौकशी *f.* शोध *m.* सूड *m.* तपास *m.* तलाश *or* स *m.* सुगावा *m.*

INQUIETUDE, *n. uneasiness, &c.* असमाधान *n.* अशांति *f.* अस्वास्थ्य *n.* अस्वस्थता *f.* बेआरामी *f.* खुणखुण *f.* खुतखुत *f.*

To INQUIRE, *v. a.* v. To ASK. पुसणें, प्रश्न *m.*-&c. करणें-घालणें, विचारणें.

2 about; after; for, (one's health, &c.). पुसणें, विचारणें, पाचारणें, वर्त्तमान *n.*-खबर *f.*-समाचार *m.*-&c.पुसणें-विचारणें-घेणें.

3 into; *investigate*, v. To EXAMINE. तपासणें, शोधणें, चौकसणें, चौकशी *f.*-तपास *m.*-शोध *m.*-&c. करणें-लावणें-घेणें, छडा *m.*-छडाछड *f.*-&c. काढणें-लावणें-&c.

INQUIRER, *n.* INQUIRING, *p. a.* v. V. 1. पुसणारा, विचारणारा, &c. पुस्ता, पृच्छक, प्रष्टा.

2 पुसणारा, खबरघेणारा, वर्त्तमानविचारणारा, &c.

3 तपासणारा, शोधणारा, &c. शोधक, शोधकर्त्ता.

INQUIRY, *n.* v. V. 1.—*act.* पुसणें *n.* &c. पुस्तपास्त *f.* पुरशीस *f.* विचारपूस *f.* पृच्छा *f.*

2 पुसणें *n.* पाचारणें *n.* &c. विचारपूस *f.*

3 तपासणें *n.* &c. चौकशी *or* सी *f.* तपास *m.* तलाश *or* स *m.* तजवीज *f.* शोध *m.* बाजपुशी *f.* बाजपूस *f.* बास्तपुस्त *f.* छडा *m.* छडाछड *f.* अन्वेषण *n.* विचक्षणा *f.*

Public and open i. फहपूस *f.*

INQUISITION, *n. inquest, inquiry, &c.* चौकशी *or* सी *f.* तपास *m.* सूड *m.* तलाश *or* स *m.* समीक्षण *n.* संवीक्षण *n.* विचक्षणा *f.*

2 *court for inquiring into religion.* धर्मसमीक्षणसभा *f.*

INQUISITIVE, *a. given to inquiry*, v. CURIOUS. चौकसदार, चौकस, तलाशी, शोधक, बहुशोधी, जिज्ञासु, विचक्षण, गवेषणासक्त.

INQUISITIVENESS, *n.* v. A. शोधकबुद्धि *f.* शोधकत्व *n.* जिज्ञासा *f.* गवेषणासक्ति *f.*

INQUISITORIAL, *a. pertaining to inquisition.* चौकशीचा, तपासकरण्याचा, शोधकरण्याचा, शोधलावण्याचा, समीक्षणसंबंधी.

INROAD, *n. incursion.* दौड *f.* स्वारी *f.* धाड *f.* आक्रमण *n.*

INSALUBRIOUS, *a. unfavorable to health*, v. UNHEALTHY. रोगी, रोगाचा, रोग आणणारा, रोगकारक-जनक-प्रद-&c. बाधक, असात्म्य-अस्वास्थ्य कारक-जनक-&c. असमाधान कारक-जनक-&c.

INSALUBRIOUSNESS, INSALUBRITY, *n.* v. A. रोगीपणा *m.* रोगजनकत्व *n.* असात्म्य *n.* असात्म्यता *f.*

INSANABLE. See INCURABLE.

INSANE, *a. unsound in mind*, v. MAD. पिसा, वेडा झालेला, विक्षिप्त, विक्षिप्तमनस्क, बुद्धिभ्रष्ट, उन्मत्त, उन्मादी.

INSANENESS, INSANITY, *n.* v.A. बुद्धिभ्रंश *m.* बुद्धिभ्रष्टता *f.* विक्षिप्तता *f.* उन्माद *m.* उन्मत्तता *f.* उन्मत्तवायु *m.*

INSATIABLE, INSATIATE, *a. that cannot be satisfied.* असोशी *or* सी, हावरा, वखवरूया, अधासा *or* सी, अतर्पणीय, अतर्प्य, तर्पणाशक्य, अशमनीय, दुर्भर.

INSATIABLENESS, INSATIABILITY, INSATIETY, *n.* v.A. असोशी *or* सी *f.* हावरेपणा *m.* लाहो *m.* वखवख *f.* अतर्पनीयता *f.* तर्पणाशक्यता *f.* &c.

INSATISFACTION, *n.* असमाधान *n.* असंतोष *m.* अतृप्ति *f.*

INSATURABLE, *a. that cannot be saturated or filled.* अपूरणीय, पूरणाशक्य.

To INSCRIBE, *v. a. write on, engrave.* लिहणें, कोरणें, खोदणें, 2 *dedicate.* नांवानें-नांवावर-&c. नजर करणें-अर्पणें, नामांकनपूर्वक अर्पण *n.* करणें.

INSCRIPTION, *n. a. writing on a stone, &c.* लेख *m.* लिपि *f.* पाषाण लेख *m.* शिलालेख *m.* अंकितलेख *m.* मुद्रितलेख *m.*

2 See TITLE.

INSCRUTABLENESS, INCRUTABILITY, *n.* v. A. अतर्क्यता *f.* दुर्ज्ञेयता *f.* दुर्लक्षता *f.* &c.

INSCRUTABLE, *a. unsearchable, &c.* v. INCOMPREHENSIBLE. अकळ, अतर्क्य, दुर्ज्ञेय, दुर्लक्ष, दुर्लक्ष्य, अलक्ष्य, बुद्ध्यतीत, बोधागम्य, अनधिगम्य, गहन, अगाध, खोल.

INSECABLE, *a. that cannot be divided.* अच्छेद्य, अच्छेदनीय, छेदनाशक्य.

INSECT, *n.*—in zoology. किडा *m.* किडूक *n.* कीड *f.* कीट *m.* कीटक *m.* कृमि *m.* विभक्तांगकीटक *m.*

INSECTILE, *a. having the nature of insects.* किड्याचे जातीचा, किडीचे जातीचा, कीटजातीय, कीट धर्मक.

INSECTIVOROUS, *a. feeding on insects.* कीटभक्षक, कीटजीवी, कीटाशी.

INSECURE, *a. not confident of safety.* भयसंशयी, भयसंशयात्मा, भयशंकापन्न, सभय, सशंक, भयशंकान्वित, संकटशंकी, भयसंभव. 2 *not safe.* भयाचा, धोक्याचा, जोखमाचा, संशयाचा, खऱ्याचा, &c. जोखमी, संशयात्मक, शंक्य, भयशंक्य, भयशंकनीय, शंकास्पद, अभरवशाचा.

INSECURITY, *n.* v. A. 1. भयशंका *f.* भयसंशय *m.* भयसंशयिता *f.* भयसंभव *m.* सभयता *f.* सशंकता *f.* भयसंशयापन्नता *f.*

2 *and* DANGER. भय *n.* धोका *m.* खत्रा *m.* जोखीम *f. n.*

INSENSATE, *a. stupid*, v. SENSELESS. बुद्धिवेगळा *or* निराळा, निर्बुद्धि, बुद्धिहीन-शून्य-&c.

INSENSIBILITY, INSENSIBLENESS, *n.* v. A. 1. अगोचरता *f.* इंद्रियागोचरता *f.* इंद्रियाग्राह्यता *f.* बेमालुमपणा *m.*

2 सुनेपणा *m.* &c. बधिरत्व *n.* सुप्ति *f.* स्पर्शाज्ञान *n.* स्पर्शानभिज्ञता *f.* नष्टेंद्रियता *f.*

3 अजाणपणा *m.* अग्राहकत्व *n.* गुणाग्राहकत्व *n.* गुणानभिज्ञता *f.* गुणाज्ञान *n.* गुणज्ञानमूढता *f.* अदृक्चित्त *n.*

4 बेसावधपणा *m.* बेहोषपणा *m.* निचेतनपणा *m.* निचेष्टितपणा *m.* &c. धुंदी *f.* अचेतनता *f.* निश्चेष्टता *f.* असंज्ञा *f.* गतसंज्ञता *f.*

INSENSIBLE, *a. not discoverable by the senses*, v. IMPERCEPTIBLE. अगोचर, इंद्रियागोचर, इंद्रियाग्राह्य, इंद्रियाविषय, इंद्रियातीत, अतींद्रिय, अलक्ष्य.

2 *wanting corporeal sensibility.* बहिरा, सुना, बधिर, सुप्त, नष्टेंद्रिय, स्पर्शानभिज्ञ.

3 *void of feeling, insusceptible of emotion.* अजाण, अग्राहक, अगुणग्राहक, गुणाग्राहक, गुणानभिज्ञ, गुणाज्ञ, गुणज्ञानमूढ, अदृक्चित्त.

4 *inconscious.* निचेतन, निश्चेतन, निचेष्टित, अचेतन, धुंद, बेसावध, बेहोष, बेशुद्ध, शुद्धिबुद्धिहीन, देहभानरहित, असंज्ञ, गतसंज्ञ, मृतकल्प.

INSENSIBLY. See IMPERCEPTIBLY.

INSENTIENT. See INSENSIBLE.

INSEPARABLE, *a. that cannot be disjoined or parted.* अभेद्य, अभेदनीय, भेदनाशक्य, अवियोज्य, वियोजनाशक्य, वियोजनानर्ह, अपृथक्करणीय, नित्यसहवर्त्ती, नित्यसंबंधी, समवायसंबंधी.

INSEPARABLENESS, INSEPARABILITY, *n.* v. A. अभेद्यता *f.* अभेदनीयता *f.* भेदनाशक्यता *f.* भेदनानर्हता *f.* &c. नित्यसंबंध *m.* समवायसंबंध *m.*

To INSERT, *v. a. enter among others, set in or among.* घालणें, भिडवणें, शिरवणें, शिरकावणें, संचारणें, समावेश *m.*-प्रवेश *m.*-&c. करणें *g. of o.* अंतर्गत-दाखल-प्रविष्ट-&c. करणें, अन्यांतर प्रविष्ट-अन्यांतरस्थित-&c. करणें.

INSERTED, *p.* v. V. भिडवलेला, शिरकावलेला, प्रविष्ट केलेला, &c. अन्यांतर प्रविष्ट, अन्यांतरस्थित.

INSERTION, *n.* v. V.—*act.* घालणें *n.* भिडवणें *n.* संचारणें *n.* &c. शिरकावणी *f.* शिरवणूक *f.* शिरकाव *m.* निवेश *m.*

INSIDE, *n. interior part.* आंतली बाजू *f.* आंतला भाग *m.* आंतलें आंग *n.* अंतरंग *n.* अभ्यंतर *n.* गर्भ *m.*

In the i. and on the outside. अंतर्बाह्य.

INSIDE, *adv.* आंत, आंतल्या बाजूस, आंतल्या आंगीं, आंतल्याकडेस *or* धडेस, आंतल्या आंत, अंतरीं, अंतरंगीं.

INSIDE, *a.* आंतले बाजूचा, आंतला.

INSIDE-OUT, *a.* उफराटासुफराटा, उफराटसुफराट, उलटासुलटा, [उलटा.

INSIDIOUS, *a. deceitful, sly, treacherous.* कपटाचा, काव्याचा, दग्याचा, पकडीचा, धडपकडीचा, पेचपांचाचा, &c. कपटी, छद्मी, लाघवी, दगेखोर, कावेखोर, कुडा.

INSIDIOUSLY, *adv.* v A. कपटानें, काव्यानें, दग्यानें, &c. कावा करून, कपट करून, पेचपांच करून, &c. पकडधरून, कपटपूर्वक, छद्मपूर्वक, &c.

INSIDIOUSNESS, *n.* v. A. कपट *n.* कापट्य *n.* कावा *m.* कावादावा *m.* कावित्र *n.* लाघव *n.*

INSIGHT, *n. thorough knowledge.* प्रवेश *m.* निवेश *m.* परिचय *m.* गम्य *n.* परिज्ञान *n.* अभिज्ञान *n.* आलोचना *f.*

INSIGNIA, *n. marks, badges.* v. SIGN. चिह्नें *n. pl.* लक्षणें *n. pl.*

I. of royalty. राजचिन्हें *n. pl.*

INSIGNIFICANCE, INSIGNIFICANCY, *n.* v. A. 1. अनर्थकत्व *n.* निरर्थकत्व *n.* अर्थशून्यता *f.* अर्थहीनता *f.* अर्थाभाव *m.*

2 हलकेपणा *m.* एरशेरपणा *m.* &c. लघुत्व *n.* क्षुल्लकत्व *n.* अगण्यता *f.*

3 हलकेपणा *m.* लहानवी *f.* एरशेरपणा *m.* &c. लघुत्व *n.* लाघव *n.* क्षुल्लकत्व *n.* अगण्यता *f.*

INSIGNIFICANT, *a. void of meaning.* अनर्थक, निरर्थक, निरर्थ, अर्थशून्य-हीन-रहित-&c. अर्थावाचक.

2 *unimportant, having no weight or effect.* हलका, लहान,

एर, एरशेर, एरळ, अगण्य, लघु, क्षुल्लक, अल्पप्रभाव.

3 *without weight of character*, v. MEAN. हलका, लहान, किसान, एर, एरशेर, एरळ, अगण्य, क्षुल्लक, आकिंचित्कर.

INSINCERE, *a. dissembling, hypocritical, false.* कपटी, कृत्रिमी, छद्मी, मकरी, दुभावाचा, दुरंगी, दुतोंड्या, खोटा, मनाचा खोटा, सकपट, अनृजु, असरल, अप्रांजल.

2 *hollow*, v. EMPTY. वायकरणी, बायकरणीचा, बायकळ, बावकळ, वरकरणी, वरबंचाईचा, कपटाचा.

INSINCERELY, *adv.* v. A. 1. कपटानें, कपट करून, कपट भावानें &c.

INSINCERITY, *n.* v. A. 1. खोटेपणा *m.* लबाडी *f.* दुरंगीपणा *m.* &c. कापट्य *n.* कपटभाव *m.* दुजाभाव *m.* दुभाव *m.* असारल्य *n.*

2 वायकरणीपणा *m.* वरकरणीपणा *m.* वावकळपणा *m.* &c.

To INSINUATE, *v. a. introduce gently.* खोवणें, खोसणें, खुपसणें, युक्तीनें शिरवणें-शिरकावणें-प्रविष्ट करणें-&c.

2 *push or work into favor*, (with recip. pro.). पोटांत शिरणें, कृपा *f.*-मर्जी *f.*-आर्जव *n.*-&c. संपादणें, मर्जी *f.* संपादन करणें.

3 *hint ; suggest by remote allusion.* दर्शिवणें, सुचविणें, नोक *f.* दाखवणें *g. of o.* नोकीखालीं दाखवणें, व्यंग्योक्तीनें-पर्यायोक्तीनें-छेकोक्तीनें-अन्योक्तीनें-&c. सांगणें-दर्शिवणें-दाखवणें-कळवणें-&c. सूचना *f.* करणें *g. of o.* अवक्षेप *m.* करणें *g. of o.* खुणावणें.

To INSINUATE, *v. n. steal into, enter gently, &c.* युक्तीनें शिरणें-शिरकणें-प्रवेश *m.* होणें, शिरत शिरत शिरणें, जात जात जाणें, घुसणें.

INSINUATED, *p.* v. V. A. 1. खोवलेला, युक्तीनें शिरवलेला, &c.

3 नोकीखालीं दाखवलेला, दर्शिवलेला, पर्यायोक्तीनें सांगितलेला, &c. अवक्षिप्त.

INSINUATER, *n.* INSINUATING, *p. a.* INSINUATIVE, *a.* v. V.A. 2. मर्जी संपादणारा, आर्जवी, लाघवी, लाघवणा, मनधरणीचा, मनमिळाऊ, मनोहारी, फुसलाव्या.

v. V. N. शिरत शिरत शिरणारा, &c. सूक्ष्म, सूक्ष्मगामी.

INSINUATION, *n. power of pleasing.* लाघवीपणा *m.* लाघव *n.* वशीकरण गुण *m.*

2 *sly suggestion, distant allusion.* नोक *f.* खाेी *f.* व्यंग्य *n.* व्यंग्योक्ति *f.* व्यंग्यार्थ *m.* पर्यायोक्ति *f.* छेकोक्ति *f.* उपरोध *m.* खोंच *f.*

INSIPID, *a. tasteless, flat, vapid,* lit. fig. निचव, बेचव, विरस, पाणचट, कवकवीत, कचकचीत, पचपचीत, मळमळीत, गळगळीत *or* गिळगिळीत, सपक, पचकळ, फिक्का, अळणी, अरस, नीरस.

INSIPIDITY, INSIPIDNESS, *n.* v. A. निचवपणा *m.* पाणचटपणा *m.* कवकवितपणा *m.* विरसपणा *m.* पचपचितपणा *m.* &c. विरसता *f.* वैरस्य *n.* अरसता *f.* आरस्य *n.* नीरसता *f.* आलवण्य *n.*

To INSIST, *v. n. press for, persist, &c.* आग्रह *m.*-अट *f.*-आड *f.* -अडती *f.*-हट *m.*-&c. करणें-धरणें-धरून बसणें, अडून बसणें, धाया *m.* घेणें-घेऊन बसणें, आटछाट *f.* करणें-धरणें-लावणें, खपाटीस-खणपटीस-&c. बसणें-लागणें, खणपट *f.* घेणें.

2 (in discourse, &c.), v. To DWELL. घोर *m.* घेणें, घोकणी *f.* घेणें-मांडणें-लावणें, घोष *m.*-उद्घोष *m.*-&c. करणें-लावणें- मांडणें.

INSITIENCY, *n. freedom from thirst.* अतृषा *f.* तृषाभाव *m.* पिपासाराहित्य *n.*

To INSNARE, *v. a. entrap,* lit. fig. फांसानें-फांशानें धरणें, फासणें, फांसटणें, फांशांत धरणें, फशीं देणें-पाडणें, फसवणें, फसगत *f.*-फसगपत *f.*-फसगयवत *f.* करणें *g. of o.* जालबद्ध-पाशबद्ध-&c. करणें.

To be insnared. फसणें, फशीं पडणें, फसगत *f.*-&c. होणें *g. of s.*

INSNARED, *p.* v. V. फांसलेला, फांसटलेला, फशीं दिल्हेला-पडलेला, &c. जालबद्ध, पाशबद्ध.

INSOBRIETY, *n. intemperance.* अतिपान *n.* अतिप्राशन *n.*

INSOCIABLE, *a. averse to conversation,* v. UNSOCIAL. माणुसघाण्या, घुम्या, अनालापी, असंलापी, संभाषणशत्रु, संभाषणविमुख-पराङ्मुख.

To INSOLATE, *v. a. expose to the sun, &c.* उन्हत ठेवणें, उन्हांत ठेवणें-घालणें, उन्ह *n.* देणें-दाखवणें, सूर्यपुट *or* पुठ *n.*-सूर्यकिरणपुट *n.* देणें.

INSOLATION, *n.* v. V. सूर्यपुट *or* पुठ *n.* सूर्यकिरणपुट *n.*

Heated, &c. by i. सूर्यपुटी *or* पुठी.

INSOLENCE, *n.* v. A. 1. उद्धटपणा *m.* दांडगेपणा *m.* उरमटपणा *m.* &c. दांडगाई *f.* मगरूरी *f.* आढ्यता *f.* धट्टाई *f.* उन्माद *m.* बदमस्ती *f.* वैयात्य *n.* औद्धत्य *n.*

INSOLENT, *a. haughtily contemptuous and disdainful.* मगरूर, उद्धत *pop.* उद्धट, दांड, दांडगा, उरमट, बदमस्त, मस्त, मस्तवाल, शिरजोर, उन्मत्त, चढेल, पिळदार, माजोरी, शेफारलेला, माजलेला, मानी, अविनय. [णाचा, &c.

2 *proceeding from insolence.* मगरुरीचा, दांडगाईचा, दांडगेप-

INSOLENTLY, *adv.* v. A. 1. मगरुरीनें, दांडगाईनें, दांडगेपणानें, उद्धटपणानें, &c. नाकलावून, उंचानाकानें, तुरालावून.

INSOLIDITY, *n.* अघनता *f.* अघनत्व *n.*

INSOLUBLE, INSOLVABLE, *a. not to be resolved or cleared.* उलगडायास अशक्य-&c. उलगडायाचा नाहीं असा, अनुद्घाटनीय, अनुद्घाट्य, उद्घाटनाशक्य, अस्फोटनीय, अव्याख्येय, अनिर्वाह्य, कठिन *pop.* कठीण, अवघड, बिकट, गूढ.

2 *indissolvable.* द्रवायाचा नाहीं असा, अद्राव्य, अद्रावणीय, अगालनीय, द्रावणाशक्य.

3 *heavy, hard, that will not become soft,*—grains, pulse, &c. चहाट, कुचर, जड.

INSOLUBILITY, INSOLVABLENESS, *n.* v. A. 1. उलगडायास अशक्यपणा *m.* &c. अनुद्घाटनीयता *f.* अनुद्घाट्यता *f.* उद्घाटनाशक्यता *f.* कठिणपणा *m.*

2 अद्राव्यता *f.* द्रावणाशक्यता *f.* &c.

3 चहाडपणा *m.* कुचरपणा *m.* जाड्य *n.*

INSOLVENCY, *n.* v. A. नादारी *f.* नादारपणा *m.* नातवानी *f.* ऋणमोचनाशक्ति *f.* ऋणमोचनासामर्थ्य *n.*

INSOLVENT, *a. unable to pay debts.* नादार, बसलेला, थकलेला, मोडकळीस आलेला, उठवणीस आलेला, ऋणमोचनाशक्त, ऋणमोचनासमर्थ, ऋणापकरणासमर्थ, परिक्षीण.

To become i. थकणें.

INSOLVENT, *n.* See BANKRUPT.

INSOMUCH, *adv. to that degree.* एथपर्यंत, एथपावेतों.

To INSPECT, *v. a. look into, &c.* v. To EXAMINE. पाहणें, बघणें, निरखणें, टेहळणें, निहाळणें, पाहणी *f.* करणें, शोधणें, निरीक्षणें, हेरणें, शोध *m.*-समीक्षण *n.*-&c. करणें *g. of o.*

2 See To SUPERINTEND.

INSPECTED, *p.* v. V. 1. पाहिलेला, निरखलेला, &c. निरीक्षित, समीक्षित, अवेक्षित.

INSPECTION, *n.* v. V.—*act.* पाहणें *n.* &c. पाहणी *f.* शोध *m.* हेर *m.* निरीक्षण *n.* निरीक्षा *f.* समीक्षण *n.* समीक्षा *f.* अवेक्षण *n.* अवेक्षा *f.*

INSPECTOR, *n.* INSPECTING, *p. a.* v. V. 1. पाहणारा, निरेखणारा, पाहणीकरणारा, &c. निरेख्या, टेहळ्या, हेऱ्या, निरीक्षक, समीक्षक, अवेक्षक, समीक्षण-&c. कर्त्ता, अवेक्षमाण, निरीक्षमाण, समीक्षमाण.

2 *and* SUPERINTENDENT. चौकसनीस (his office चौकसनिशी *f.*), अमीन (his office अमिनी *f.*), पुसणारा, पुस्ता. the English word is also used.

INSPERSION, *n. sprinkling on.* छिडकाव *or* छिटकाव*m.*शिडकाव*or* बा*m.* अभिषिंचन *n.* प्रोक्षण*n.* [श्वास *m.*

INSPIRATION, *n.* v.V.N. श्वास घेणें *n.* श्वासग्रहण *n.* श्वासादान *n.* v. V. A. 1.—*act.* फुंकणें *n.*

2 श्वासाबरोबर घेणें *n.* &c.

4 भरिवणें *n.* बुद्धिदेणें *n.* &c. आधान *n.* स्थापन *n.* निक्षेप *m.*

5 ईश्वरसूचना *f.* ईश्वरप्रेरणा *f.* ईश्वरसंचार *m.* अवसर *m.* वारें *n.*

Note. The two last words are commonly used of the afflatus of an inferior god or of a devil.

By i. वारें येऊन.

To INSPIRE, *v. n. draw in breath.* श्वास *m.* घेणें.

To INSPIRE, *v. a. breathe into.* फुंकणें. श्वासभरित-श्वासपूरित-&c. करणें.

2 *draw into the lungs.* श्वासाबरोबर घेणें-खाणें-पिणें-&c. श्वासमार्गानें आकर्षण करणें.

3 *infuse by breathing.* फुंकून-फुंकरानें-फुंकेसरसा-फुंकाऱ्याबरोबर-&c. घालणें-स्थापणें.

4 *infuse into the mind.* भरिवणें, बुद्धि *f.*-वासना *f.*-कल्पना *f.* -&c. देणें, प्रेरणा *f.* करणें, आधान *n.*-स्थापन *n.*-निक्षेप *m.*-&c. करणें.

5 (supernaturally). भरिवणें, सुचविणें, मनांत प्रेरणा *f.* करणें, अवसर *m.*-वारें*n.* येणें-शिरणें-भरणें-संचारणें *in. con.* वारें *n.* -&c. शिरवणें-भरिवणें-घालणें.

INSPIRED, *p.* v. V. A. 5. ईश्वरप्रेरित, ईश्वरसूचित, देवसंचाराचा, अवसर आलेला.

To be i. वारें *n.*-अवसर *m.* येणें.

To INSPIRIT, *v. a. enliven, cheer, encourage, &c.* v. To ANIMATE. जीव *m.*-दम *m.*-धैर्य *n.*-उत्साह *m.*-&c. आणणें-देणें, प्रोत्सहन *n.*-प्रोत्साहन *n.*-&c. करणें *g. of o.* उत्सुक-&c. करणें.

INSPIRITED, *p.* v. V. दमआणलेला, &c. प्रोत्साहित, उत्साहित, प्राप्तोत्साह, जातोत्साह.

INSPIRITER, *n.* INSPIRITING, *p. a.* v. V. दम आणणारा-देणारा-&c. प्रोत्साहक, प्रोत्सहनकर्त्ता-कारी-&c. उत्साहजनक-कारक-&c. उत्साहप्रद.

INSPIRITING, *n.* v. V.—*act.* दम देणें *n.* जीव आणणें *n.* &c. प्रोत्सहन *or* प्रोत्साहन *n.* उत्साहप्रापण *n.* उत्साहजनन *n.*

To INSPISSATE, INSPISSATION. See To THICKEN, &c.

INSTABILITY, *n.* v. A. अस्थिरता *f.* अस्थैर्य *n.* अस्थायित्व *n.* अधैर्य *n.* चंचलता *f.* चांचल्य *n.* अनवस्था *f.* अनवस्थिति *f.* अनवस्थान *n.*

INSTABLE. See UNSTABLE.

To INSTALL, *v. a. instate in an office, &c. with the customary ceremonies.* संस्कार करून-संस्कारानें-संस्कारपूर्वक-&c. स्थापणें-बसवणें-&c. टिका*m.* लावणें, वस्त्रें *n. pl.* देणें, प्रतिष्ठणें, प्रतिष्ठापन *n.*-प्रतिष्ठा *f.* करणें *g. of o.* अधिकारारूढ-पदारूढ-अधिकृत-&c. करणें.

2 (a king, &c.). अभिषेकणें, अभिषेक *m.*-मूर्धाभिषेक *m.*-पट्टाभिषेक *m.* करणें *g. of o.*

INSTALLATION, *n.* v. V. 1.—*act.* टिका लावणें *n.* वस्त्रें देणें *n.* प्रतिष्ठणें *n.* संस्कारपूर्वकस्थापन *n.* प्रतिष्ठापन *n.* प्रतिष्ठा *f.* पदस्थापना *f.* पदस्थापन *n.*

2 अभिषेक *m.* मूर्धाभिषेक *m.* पट्टाभिषेक *m.*

INSTALLED, *p.* v. V. 1. संस्कारानें स्थापलेला, वस्त्रें दिल्हेला, &c. संस्कारपूर्वकस्थापित, प्रतिष्ठित, प्रतिष्ठापित, अधिकारस्थ, पदारूढ, जातप्रतिष्ठ, कृतप्रतिष्ठ, लब्धप्रतिष्ठ.

2 अभिषिक्त, मूर्धाभिषिक्त, पट्टाभिषिक्त, जाताभिषेक, प्राप्ताभिषेक, कृताभिषेक, लब्धाभिषेक.

INSTALMENT, *n. part of a sum paid at one time.* खिस्त *f.*हप्ता*m.*

Payment by instalments. खिस्त *f.*

Settlement for the payment of a sum by instalments. हप्तेबंदी *f.* खिस्तबंदी *f.*

2 See INSTALLATION.

INSTANCE, *n. urgency, insisting, &c.* v. IMPORTUNITY. आग्रह *m.* अत्याग्रह *m.* मिन्नती *f.* मिन्नतवारी *f.*

2 *example, precedent, case.* उदाहरण *n.* दाखला *m.* दृष्टांत *m.* अढळ *m.* प्रतीक *n.* स्थल *n.* लक्ष्य *n.*

In the first instance, *at first.* पहिल्यानें, प्रथम.

To INSTANCE, *v. a.* उदाहरण *n.*-दाखला *m.*-&c. देणें-सांगणें-म्हणून देणें.

INSTANT, *a. urgent, insisting,* v. IMPORTUNATE. आग्रह धरलेला, आग्रही, निग्रही, अत्याग्रही, मिन्नत्या.

2 *immediate, without intervening time.* एव्हांचा, तेव्हांचा, तत्कालिक, अव्यवहितकालिक, अनंतरकालिक, अनंतरकालीन, तत्क्षणिक.

3 See QUICK. 4 *current,*—of months. चालता, वर्त्तमान.

INSTANT, *n. moment, twinkling.* क्षण *m.*पल *pop.* पळ *n.* चिपडी *f.* लहम *n.* मात्रा *f.* निमिष *or* निमेष *m.* त्रुटि *f.* पलस *n.* विपल*n.*

Every i. क्षणोक्षणीं, अनुक्षणीं.

At that i. तत्क्षणीं, तत्काल *pop.* तात्काल, तसाच, तेव्हांच.

This i. लागलाच, एव्हांच, आतांच.

INSTANTANEOUS, *a. occurring without apparent succession.* तात्कालचा, तत्कालिक, तत्क्षणिक, अव्यवहितकालिक, अव्यवहितकालीन, आकालिक.

INSTANTANEOUSLY, *adv. in an instant.* एकाक्षणांत, एकापळांत, एकापळामध्यें, पळमारतांच, &c.

INSTANTER, *adv.* See INSTANTLY, 2.

INSTANTLY, *adv.* v. A. 1. आग्रह करून-धरून, मिन्नतीनें, &c. आग्रहपूर्वक, &c.

2 आतांच, आतांचेआतांच, एव्हांच, अशाचेअसाच, सद्यः, उशीर न लागतां *or* न लावितां, अव्यवहितकालीं,—with reference to returning. उभ्यापायानें, आल्यापायानें, मागल्यापायीं, ह्यापाउलीं, उभ्यांउभ्यां, उभाउभी.

I. after, I. upon. लागलाच, तसाच, तशाचेतसाच, हालोहाल, हातच्याहातीं.

To INSTATE, *v. a. set or place in a rank or condition.* कामावर-अधिकारावर-&c. बसवणें-स्थापणें-स्थापना *f.* करणें *g. of o.* पदस्थ-पदारूढ-&c. करणें.

INSTATED, *p.* v. V. अधिकारावर बसवलेला, &c. पदस्थ, पदारूढ.

INSTEAD, *adv.* or *prep. in the place of.* जागीं, जागां, जागें, ठि-

काणीं, ऐवजीं, बदल *or* बदला, मुबदला *or* मुबादला, वारचा *decl.* वारीं.

INSTEP, *n.*—of the foot. धूर *or* पायाची धूर *f.* धुरी *f.* पायाचा-शिरदळ *m.* पदोपरिभाग *m.*

To INSTIGATE, *v. a. set on, prompt, &c.* v. To INCITE. उचलणें, चढवणें, शिकवणें, चढीं देणें, भरिवणें, बीर*m.* भरणें-देणें, भर*f.*-फूस *f.* देणें, उचल *f.*-उठावणी *f.*-उत्तेजन *n.*-&c. करणें.

INSTIGATED, *p.* v. V. उचललेला, चढवलेला, &c. उत्तेजित, प्रवर्तित, प्रोत्साहित, प्रेरित.

INSTIGATION, *n.* v. V.—*act.* उचलणें *n.* &c. शिकवणी *f.* शिकवण *f.* उठावणी *f.* उटाळणी *f.* उटाळा *m.* उचल *f.* उठावा*m.* प्रेरणा *f.* प्रेरण*n.* उत्तेजन*n.* प्रवर्तन*n.* प्रोत्साहन*n.*

INSTIGATOR, *n.* INSTIGATING, *p. a.* INSTIGATORY, *a.* v. V. उचलणारा, बीर भरणारा, उठावणी करणारा, &c. उत्तेजक, प्रवर्तक, प्रेरक, प्रोत्साहक, प्रयोजक, उद्बोधक, प्रवर्तन-उत्तेजन-&c. कर्त्ता-कारक-कारी.

I. to an evil act. कुप्रवर्तक, कौंशा.

To INSTIL, *v. a. infuse by drops.* थेंब थेंब घालणें-ओतणें.

2 *infuse gradually into the mind.* थोडथोडा-अल्पअल्प-अल्पशः- &c. भरवणें-ठसवणें-घालणें-&c.

INSTILLATION, INSTILLMENT, *n.* v. V. 1. थेंब थेंब घालणें*n.*&c.

2 थोडथोडा भरवणें *n.* &c.

INSTINCT, *n. natural knowledge or directing power.* आंगचें ज्ञान *n.* आंगची बुद्धि *f.* आंगचें शहाणपण *n.* &c. अंगस्वभाव*m.* औत्पत्तिक-स्वाभाविक-साहजिक-&c. ज्ञान*n.*-बुद्धि *f.*-गुण*m.*-&c. उपज्ञा *f.* पशुबुद्धि *f.*

INSTINCT, *a. moved, animated, &c.* उत्तेजित, प्रेरित.

INSTINCTIVE, *a. prompted by instinct.* आंगचे बुद्धीचा, आंगच्या शहाणपणाचा, साहजिकधर्माचा, &c. स्वाभाविक, प्रकृतिसिद्ध, स्वाभाविकज्ञानसिद्ध, &c.

INSTINCTIVELY, *adv.* v. A. आंगचे बुद्धीनें, आंगच्या ज्ञानानें, &c. स्वभावतः, निसर्गतः.

To INSTITUTE, *v. a. establish, set up, appoint.* स्थापणें, संस्थापणें, नेमणें, नेमून देणें, घालणें, लावणें, लावून देणें, पाडणें, चालू-प्रवृत्त-&c. करणें, स्थापन*n.*-संस्थापन*n.*-&c. करणें *g. of o.*

2 *commence, set on foot, &c.* चालवणें, आरंभणें, मांडणें, प्रवर्तणें, चालू-सुरू-प्रवृत्त-&c. करणें.

3 See To INSTRUCT.

INSTITUTE, *n. established law or order.* नियम *pop.* नेम*m.* विधि*m.* विधान *n.*

Institutes of religion, law, or letters,—esp. as considered of divine origin. शास्त्र *n.* [हिता *f.*

Compendium or collection of laws and institutes. सं-

INSTITUTED, *p.* v. V. 1. स्थापलेला, संस्थापलेला, नेमलेला, &c. स्थापित, संस्थापित, विहित, वैध, प्रवर्तित.

2 चालवलेला, आरंभलेला, चालू केलेला, &c. प्रवर्तित.

INSTITUTION, *n.* v. V. 1.—*act.* स्थापणें*n.* &c. स्थापन*n.* स्थापना *f.*संस्थापन*n.* संस्थापना *f.* प्रवर्तन *n.*

I. *established law,* v. INSTITUTE. विधि*m.* नियम*m.*

II. *system, plan, society, &c. established.* स्थापित-संस्थापित-&c. मंडळी *f.*-सभा *f.*-मार्ग*m.*-&c. कारखाना *m.*

INSTITUTIONAL, *a.* वैधिक, नैयमिक.

INSTITUTOR, *n.* v. V. 1. स्थापणारा, संस्थापणारा, &c. स्थापक, संस्थापक, स्थापन-संस्थापन-&c. कर्त्ता-कारी, विधाता, विधायक, प्रवर्तक, प्रयोजक.

To INSTRUCT, *v. a. educate, inform,* v. To TEACH. शिकवणें, सांगणें, पढवणें, उपदेश *m.*-शिक्षा *f.*-अध्यापन *n.*-&c. करणें, उपदेशणें, शिक्षणें, बोधवणें, बोध *m.*-बोधन *n.*-&c. करणें.

2 *enjoin, direct,* v. To ORDER. सांगणें, आज्ञा *f.*-हुकूम *m.* करणें देणें, आज्ञापणें.

INSTRUCTED, *p.* v. V. 1. शिकवलेला, पढवलेला, &c. अध्यापित, शिक्षित, बोधित, उपदिष्ट, उद्बुद्ध.

2 आज्ञापलेला, आज्ञापित, आज्ञात, आज्ञप्त.

INSTRUCTION, *n.* v. V. 1.—*act.* शिकवणें *n.* पढवणें *n.* &c. अध्यापन *n.* शिक्षण *n.* शिक्षा *f.* उपदेश *m.* बोधन *n.* उद्बोध *m.* उद्बोधन *n.*

2 आज्ञापणें *n.* आज्ञापन *n.* [बोध *m.*

I. *precepts conveying knowledge.* उपदेश *m.* हितवाद *m.* हित-

II. *direction, order,* v. COMMAND. हुकूम *m.* आज्ञा *f.*

Instructions. धडा *m.* पाठ *m.*

Code of instructions. सूत्र *n.*

INSTRUCTIVE, *a. conveying instruction.* उपदेशाचा, बोधाचा, उपदेशावह, उपदेशप्रद, बोधावह, उपदेशपर, बोधकारी, बोधपर, ज्ञानोत्पादक, ज्ञानप्रवर्त्तक, उपदेश (in comp.), बोध (in comp.).

INSTRUCTOR, *n.* INSTRUCTING, *p. a.* v. V. 1. शिकवणारा, पढवणारा, सांगणारा, &c. शिक्षक, उपदेशक, उपदेष्टा, उपदेशकर्त्ता-कारी, अध्यापक.

INSTRUMENT, *n. tool, implement.* अऊत *n.* हतेर *or* हत्यार *n.* शस्त्र *n.* किरंड *n.* साधन *n.* कर्मसाधन *n.* करण *n.* उपकरण*n.* यंत्र*n.*

A case of instruments. गंज *m.*

2 *doer, agent, means.* कार्यकर्त्ता, कार्यकारक, कार्यसाधक, प्रयोज्यकर्त्ता, प्रयोज्य, निमित्त *n.* निमित्तकारण *n.* साधन *n.* कारण*n.*

3 *deed, writing, &c.* v. BOND. लेख *m.* खत *n.* पत्र *n.* पत्रक *n.* पट्टा *m.* [*n.* तूर्य *n.*

4—of music, v. MUSIC. वाद्य *n.* वाजंत्र *n.* वाजंत्रें *n.* वादित्र

Animated sound of musical instruments. धूम *f.* ठांदू *n.* ठांका *m.* टाळघोळ *m.* वाद्यघाई *f.*

Beating of musical instruments. बाजा *m.*

I. of martial music. रणवाद्य *n.*

I. sounded by the mouth. मुखवाद्य *n.*

I. stringed. तंतुवाद्य *n.* तंत्रीवाद्य *n.* [चर्मवाद्य *n.*

I. covered with skin, (drum, tabor, tambourine, &c.).

I. suitable to festive occasions. मंगलवाद्य *n.*

Wind of a musical i. दम *m.*

INSTRUMENTAL, *a. conducive as an instrument or means.* साधनी, साधक, कार्यसाधक, साधनीभूत, साधनभूत, कारणभूत, निमित्तकारणभूत, प्रयोजक, उपकारी, सहकारी, कारणी.

2 *effected by instruments.* शस्त्रांचा, शस्त्रसाधित, शस्त्रसिद्ध, शस्त्रकृत, शस्त्रसंपादित.

3 *made by instruments; not vocal.* वाद्यांचा, वाद्यसंबंधी, वाद्योत्पन्न, वाद्यसिद्ध, वाद्यजनित.

INSTRUMENTALITY, INSTRUMENTALNESS, *n.* v. A. 1. साधकत्व *n.* कार्यसाधकत्व *n.* कारकत्व *n.* करणत्व *n.* साधनत्व*n.* निमित्तत्व*n.*

I. (of persons) *medium.* गुजारत *f.* मारफत *f.*

INSUAVITY, *n. want of pleasantness of manner.* तुसडेपणा *m.* कुरठेपणा *m.* द्रुष्पणा *m.* कठोरपणा *m.* पारुष्य *n.*

INSUBJECTION. See INSUBORDINATION.

INSUBORDINATE, *a. not submissive to authority, unruly.* शिरजोर, बेहुकमी, अनावर, अनिवार, अवश, आज्ञानधीन, अनाज्ञावश, अविनीत, अविधेय, स्वाम्यनधीन, अवशवर्त्ती, शासनविमुख, शिक्षाविमुख.

INSUBORDINATION, *n.* v. A. बेहुकमीपणा *m.* &c. अवशता *f.* आज्ञानधीनता *f.* स्वाम्यनधीनता *f* अविनय *m.* अविधेयता *f.* अविनीतता *f.* शासनविमुखता *f.* &c.

I. *insubordinate conduct.* आज्ञाभंग *m.* आज्ञातिक्रम *m.* आज्ञातिरस्कार *m.* आज्ञावगणन *n.*

INSUBSTANTIAL, *a. not real,* v. UNREAL. अवास्तविक, अवास्तव.

INSUBSTANTIALITY, *n.* v. A. अवस्तुता *f.* अवस्तु *n.* असत्यता *f.*

INSUFFERABLE, *a intolerable,* v. INSUPPORTABLE. सहायास अशक्य-अयोग्य-&c. असह्य, असहनीय, दुःसह, सहनाशक्य.

INSUFFERABLENESS, *n.* v. A. असह्यता *f.* असहनीयता *f.* सहनाशक्यता *f.* दौःसह्य *n.*

INSUFFICIENCE, INSUFFICIENCY, *n.* v. A. अपुरतेपणा *m.* निपुरतेपणा *m.* &c. अपूर *f.* नपूर *f.* निपूर *f.* वाण *f.* अपर्याप्ति *f.*

2 अपुरतेपणा *m.* &c. नालायकी *f.* अक्षमता *f.* कार्याक्षमता *f.* कार्यासामर्थ्य *n.*

INSUFFICIENT, *a. not enough.* अपुरता, अपुरा, अपूर्ण, निपुरा, निपुरता, अपर्याप्त, निर्वाहाक्षम.

2 *wanting in ability, &c. incapable, incompetent.* अपुरता, अपुरा, नालायक, अयोग्य, अक्षम, कार्याक्षम, कर्माक्षम, कार्यासमर्थ, अनुपयुक्त.

INSUFFICIENTLY, *adv.* v. A. 1. अपुरतेपणीं, अपुरता *decl.* निपुरा *decl.* &c. कमी, अपूर्ण.

INSUFFLATION, *n. breathing upon.* फुंकर घालणें *n.* फुंकरणें *n.* श्वासप्रक्षेप *m.* श्वासन्यास *m.* [द्वीपविषयक.

INSULAR, *a. belonging to an isle.* बेटाचा, द्वीपाचा, द्वीपसंबंधी,

2 *surrounded by water.* पाण्यानें वेढलेला, जलवेष्टित, द्वीपाकार, द्वीपरूप.

INSULARITY, *n.* v. A. 2. द्वीपता *f.* द्वीपाकार *m.* द्वीपाकृति *f.* जलवेष्टितत्व *n.* द्वीपरूप *n.*

INSULATED, *a. standing by itself.* तुटक, अलग, फटकून राहिलेला, असंलग्न, अनन्यसंयुक्त, अनन्यलग्न, पृथक्स्थित.

INSULT, *n. act or speech of insolence or contempt,* v. ABUSE. हेटाळणी *f.* निंदा *f.* अपमानाची करणी *f.* बेअदबी *f.* अपमान *m.* अनादर *m.* अपमानभाषण *n.* अपमानक्रिया *f.* भर्त्सना *f.* निर्भर्त्सना *f.* अवज्ञा *f.*

To INSULT, *v. a. treat with abuse, insolence, contempt, &c.* हेटाळणें, हेळणें, निर्भर्त्सणें, भर्त्सणें, आबू *f.* जाईसें बोलणें-करणें, *g. of o.* अपमान *m.*-अनादर *m.*-निर्भर्त्सना *f.*-&c. करणें *g. of o.*

INSULTER, *n.* INSULTING, *p. a.* v. V. अपमानकरणारा, हेटाळणारा, अपमानाचा, अनादराचा, &c. निर्भर्त्सक, भर्त्सक, निंदक.

INSULTINGLY, *adv.* v.A. हेटाळणीकरून, &c. अपमानपूर्वक, अवज्ञापूर्वक.

INSUPERABILITY, *n.* v. A. दुर्लंघ्यता *f.* अलंघ्यता *f.* अजेयता *f.* लंघनाशक्यता *f.* &c. दुस्तरता *f.* दौस्तर्य *n.*

INSUPERABLE, *a. insurmountable, not to be overcome.* दुर्लंघ्य, अलंघ्य, अलंघनीय, लंघनाशक्य, दुस्तर, दुरतिक्रम, अजेय, दुर्निवार्य, अनिवार्य, दुरधिगम.

INSUPPORTABLE, *a. that cannot be borne, endured, &c.* सोसायास अशक्य-अयोग्य-&c. असह्य, असहनीय, दुःसह, दुःसहनीय, सहनाशक्य, सहनानर्ह, निःसह, दुर्निर्वह, अतिकठिन.

INSUPPORTABLENESS, *n.* v. A. असह्यता *f.* असहनीयता *f.* सहनाशक्यता *f.* &c.

INSUPPRESSIBLE, *a. not to be suppressed, &c.* आवरायास-दाबायास-&c. अशक्य-अयोग्य-&c. अनिवार, दुर्निग्रह, निग्रहणाशक्य, शमनाशक्य. [मा *m.*

INSURANCE, *n. assurance against loss or damage.* विमा *or* वि-

2 *cost or charge of insuring.* विमा *m.*

To INSURE, *v. a. contract for a consideration to secure from loss.* विमा *m.* करणें.

2 *purchase security for from loss.* विम्यांत ठेवणें, विम्यानें देणें, विमा *m.* उतरणें. [विमेकरी.

INSURER, *n.* INSURING, *p. a.* v. V. 1. विमा करणारा, विमेदार,

INSURGENT, *n. one who has risen against authority.* सरकारावर उठलेला, बंडवाला, बंड्या.

Band of insurgents. बंड *n.* खूळ *n.* मवास *m.*

INSURMOUNTABLE, *a.* v. INSUPERABLE. दुर्लंघ्य, दुस्तर *intens.* सुदुस्तर, अनिवार्य, दुर्निवार्य.

INSURMOUNTABLENESS, *n.*v.A.दुर्लंघ्यता *f.* दुस्तरता *f.*&c. दौस्तर्य *n.*

INSURRECTION, *n. a. seditious rising.* सरकारावर उठणें *n.* उठावणी *f.* बंड *n.* दंगा *m.* खूळ *n.* बेदा *m.* ठेंगा *m.* गेर *f. m.* मवासी *or* शी *f.* राजविरुद्ध संभूयसमुत्थान *n.*

INSURRECTIONARY, *a* v. N. बंडाचा, बंडी, बंड्या, दंग्याचा, ठेंग्या.

INSUSCEPTIBILITY, *n.* v. A. अजाणपणा *m.* अग्राहकत्व *n.* ग्रहणाक्षमता *f.* वेदनाशक्ति *f.*

INSUSCEPTIBLE, *a. not capable of receiving impression, &c.* अजाण, अग्राही, अग्राहक, ग्रहणाक्षम, ग्रहणशक्तिरहित, वेदनाशक्त, वेदनशक्तिरहित.

INTACT. See UNTOUCHED.

INTACTABLE, *a. not perceptible to the touch.* अस्पृश्य, अस्पर्शनीय, स्पर्शागम्य, स्पर्शाज्ञेय, स्पर्शागोचर, स्पर्शाविषय.

INTANGIBILITY, INTANGIBLENESS, *n.* v. A. अस्पृश्यता *f.* दुःस्पृश्यता *f.* स्पर्शाविषयता *f.* स्पर्शानर्हता *f.* &c.

INTANGIBLE, *a. that cannot or may not be touched.* स्पर्श करायास अशक्य-अयोग्य-&c. अस्पृश्य, अस्पर्शनीय, दुःस्पर्श, दुःस्पृश्य, स्पर्शाविषय, स्पर्शागोचर, स्पर्शायोग्य, स्पर्शानर्ह.

INTEGER, *n.a whole number.* पूर्णांक*m.*अभिन्नांक*m.*रूप*n.*अभिन्न*m.*

INTEGRAL, *a. entire,* v. WHOLE. संपूर्ण, अखंड, अभिन्न, अविकल, अत्रुटित, अन्यून, सांग.

2 *not fractional.* बंदा, बांधा, सबंध, पूर्ण, अभिन्न.

INTEGRITY, *n. entireness.* संपूर्णता *f.* पूर्णता *f.* अखंडत्व *n.* अभिन्नत्व *n.* अभिन्नभाव *m.* साकल्य *n.* सांगता *f.*

2 *honesty, probity, uprightness, &c.* प्रमाणिकपणा *m.* खरेपणा *m.* खराई *f.* नेकी *f.* नेक *f.* नेत *f.* सचोटी *f.* प्रामाणिकत्व *n.* प्रामाण्य *n.* सत्य *n.* सत्व *n.*

INTEGUMENT, *n. natural covering or coating.* आवरण *n.* वेष्टन *n.* पदर *m.*पडदा *m.*पापुद्रा *or* पापोद्रा *m.*पापोडा *m.*शरीरावरण *n.*

INTELLECT, *n.*v. UNDERSTANDING. बुद्धि *f.*धी *f.*चित् *f.*चिच्छक्ति *f.*

INTELLECTION, *n. act of understanding.* ज्ञान *n.* बोध *m.* बुद्धिग्रह *m.* ज्ञप्ति *f.*

INTELLECTIVE. See INTELLECTUAL.

INTELLECTUAL, *a. relating to the understanding.* बुद्धीचा, बुद्धी-

विषयींचा, ज्ञानाचा, ज्ञानशक्तीचा, चित्ताचा, मनाचा, &c. ज्ञानसंबंधी-विषयक, बुद्धिसंबंधी-विषयक, चित्तसंबंधी-विषयक, मानस, मानसिक.

2 *perceived by the intellect; existing in the understanding.* मानसिक, बुद्धिगम्य, मनोगम्य, चिद्गत, मनोगत.

3 *endowed with understanding.* चिच्छक्तिक, ज्ञानशक्तिक, ज्ञानशक्तिसंपन्न, ज्ञानशक्तिविशिष्ट, चिच्छक्तिविशिष्ट, बुद्धिविशिष्ट, ज्ञानपात्र, बुद्धिपात्र, बुद्ध्यधिकरण, सज्ञान.

INTELLIGENCE, *n. notion, information, tidings.* बातमी *f.* खबर *f.* वर्त्तमान *n.* वार्त्ता *f.* सूचना *f.* समाचार *m.*

Authentic or official i. खासबातमी *f.* खित्तीम बातमी *f.* खासखबर *f.*

I. received from an emissary at a foreign court. अकबर or अखबर or अखबार *f.*

Secret i. चोरबातमी *f.* गूढभाषित *n.*

2 *understanding, sense, sharpness.* बुद्धि *f.* ज्ञान *n.* जाणीव *f.* चतुराई *f.* चातुर्य *n.* हुशारी *f.* वकूब *m.* चेतना *f.* चैतन्य *n.*

Glow or lustre of i. जाणतीकळा *f.*

3 an *intelligence, a spirit.* चिद्व्यक्ति *f.* ज्ञानव्यक्ति *f.* बुद्धि-[रूपव्यक्ति *f.*

INTELLIGENCER, *n. one who sends intelligence.* बातमीदार, खबऱ्या, वार्त्ताहर, वार्त्तिक, वार्त्तावह.

2 (at Courts). अकबर or अखबर or अखबारनवीस or नीस.

INTELLIGENT, *a. endowed with understanding.* v. INTELLECTUAL. ज्ञानशक्तिक, बुद्धिविशिष्ट.

2 *knowing, understanding, clever, &c.* v. WISE. जाणता, सुजाण, शाहणा, समजदार, समंजस, ज्ञानी, बुद्धिमान्, मतिमान्, खबरदार, सुबुद्ध or सुबुद्धि, चतुर, हुशार, चौरस, चप्पू, सुज्ञ, प्राज्ञ, मेधावी, सुमेधा, विज्ञ, विदुर.

INTELLIGENTIAL, *a. consisting of unbodied mind.* चिदात्मक, चिद्रूप, चिन्मय, चिद्घन.

2 See INTELLECTUAL.

INTELLIGIBILITY, INTELLIGIBLENESS, *n.* v. A. बुद्धिगम्यता *f.* बुद्धिग्राह्यता *f.* ज्ञेयता *f.* &c.

INTLLIGIBLE, *a. possible to be understood.* समजायाजोगा-सारखा-&c. मनांत-ध्यानांत-&c. यायाजोगा-सारखा-&c. बुद्धिगम्य, ज्ञानगम्य, बोधशक्य, ज्ञेय, बुद्धिग्राह्य, शक्यबोध, यथाबोध.

Easily i. Very i. v. PLAIN. बाळबोध, सुबोध, स्पष्ट, सुस्पष्ट.

INTELLIGIBLY, *n.* v. A. समजायाजोगा-&c. *decl.* ध्यानांत यायाजोगा-&c. *decl.* साफ, स्पष्ट, यथाबोध.

INTEMPERANCE, INTEMPERATENESS, *n.* v. A. 1. बेसुमारपणा *m.* अमर्यादा *f.* अतिशय *m.* पराकाष्ठा *f.* मर्यादाराहित्य *n.*

2 अमितभोग *m.* अनियतभोग *m.* विहारानियम *m.* आहारविहारानियम *m.* असंयम *m.* असंयमन *n.* अनियतवर्त्तन *n.* असंयतवर्त्तन *n.* अनियतवृत्ति *f.* असंयतवृत्ति *f.* असंयताचार *m.* अनियताचार *m.*

3 अत्याहार *m.* अतिभक्षण *n.* अतिभोजन *n.* अत्यशन *n.*

4 अतिपान *n.* अनिप्राशन *n.*

INTEMPERATE, *a. exceeding the due degree,* v. EXCESSIVE. बेसुमार, बेहद्द, अतिमर्याद, अमर्याद, अतिशयित, अमित, अपरिमित, अतिमान.

2 *immoderate in enjoyment,*—gener. अमितभोगी, अमितविहारी, अनियतभोक्ता, अपरिमित भोगी-विहारी-&c. अनियतेंद्रिय, असंयमी, अनियतवर्त्ती, अनियतवृत्ति, अनियताचारी, असंयताचारी, अत्याचारी, अनियमवान्, अनियमी.

3 (in eating), v. GLUTTONOUS. अतिभोजी, अमितभोजी, अमितभक्षी, अत्याहारी, अत्याशी.

4 (in drinking), v. DRUNKARD. अतिपानी, अतिप्राशक.

5 See PASSIONATE.

INTEMPERATURE, *n. excess of some quality.* वैषम्य *n.* गुणवैषम्य *n.* धातुवैषम्य *n.* असमधातुता *f.*

INTENABLE. See UNTENABLE, INDEFENSIBLE.

To INTEND, *v. a.* lit. *stretch, strain, distend.* ताणणें, तणावा *m.* -ताण *m.* देणें-बसवणें, तणतणीत- तटतटीत-&c. करणें.

To be intended. तटतटणें, तणणें, तणतणणें, तणबरणें,—*intens.* तटाटणें.

2 fig. *make intense, increase.* वाढवणें, चढवणें, प्रकर्ष *m.*-उत्कर्ष *m.*-&c. करणें *g. of o.* अधिक-भारी-जबर-जोराचा-&c. करणें.

3 *mean, design.* मनांत योजणें-धरणें-लक्षिणें-नेमणें-&c. मनांत असणें *in. con.* इरादा *m.*-बेत *m.*-मनोरथ *m.*-&c. करणें-धरणें *g. of o.* अभिप्राय *m.*-&c. असणें *g. of o. and in. con.* अवांकणें.

5 See To SUPERINTEND.

To INTEND, *v. n. grow intense.* जोरावणें, जडावणें, जडकावणें, बळावणें, अधिक-भारी-जोराचा-&c. होणें.

INTENDANT, *n. supervisor, director, &c.* v. SUPERINTENDENT. अध्यक्ष, उपद्रष्टा, अमीन.

INTENDED, *p.* v. V. A. 1. ताणलेला, तणावा दिल्हेला, &c.

2 *and* INTENSE. वाढवलेला, चढवलेला, भारी केलेला, &c.

3 मनांत योजलेला, &c. उद्दिष्ट, मनसोद्दिष्ट, मानसोद्दिष्ट, अभिप्रेत, चिकीर्षित, संकल्पित, विवक्षित.

INTENSE, *a.* lit. *strained, stretched.* ताणलेला, तटतटलेला, तणतणलेला, &c. तटतटीत, तणतणीत, ताठ.

2 fig. *close, strict, severe, of assiduous application.* ताणाचा, लगटाचा or लगटीचा, व्यासंगाचा, अभिनिवेशपूर्वक, व्यासंगपूर्वक.

3 fig. *raised to a high degree; vehement, excessive, severe, &c.* भारी, जबर, अतिशयित, पराकाष्ठेचा, कडक, कडकडीत, चणचणीत, तिखट, तीव्र, तीक्ष्ण, तलख, जलाल, जालीम, प्रचंड, प्रकृष्ट.

4 *anxiously attentive.* See INTENT.

INTENSELY, *adv.* v. A. 2. लगट करून, नेटानें, चित्त एकतानकरून, अभिनिवेशपूर्वक, व्यासंगपूर्वक.

3 भारी, फारच, पराकाष्ठेचा *decl.* अति, अतिशय, अतिशयेंकरून.

INTENSENESS, INTENSITY, *n.* v. A. 1. ताण *m.* ताठर *m.* तणावा *m.* ताणलेपणा *m.* तणतणितपणा *m.* &c.

2 ताण *m.* लगट *m. f.* नेट *m.* अभिनिवेश *m.* व्यासंग *m.*

3 भारीपणा *m.* कडकपणा *m.* तिखटपणा *m.* &c. पराकाष्ठा *f.* अतिशय *m.* कडका *m.* जलाली *f.* तीव्रता *f.* तीक्ष्णता *f.* &c. प्रकर्ष *m.* आतिशय्य *n.*

To INTENSIFY, *v. a. raise to a higher degree, make intense.* वाढवणें, चढवणें, प्रकर्ष *m.*- उत्कर्ष *m.*- &c. करणें *g. of o.* अधिक-भारी-&c. करणें.

INTENSION, *n.* v. V. A. 1.—*act.* ताणणें *n.* ताण देणें *n.* ताणणी *f.* —*state.* ताण *m.* ताठर *m.* तणावा *m.* ताणलेपणा *m.*

2—*act.* वाढवणें *n.* चढवणें *n.* वाढवणी *f.* वाढवणूक *f.* वर्द्धन *n.* —*state.* वृद्धि *f.* प्रकर्ष *m.* उत्कर्ष *m.* प्रकृष्टता *f.*

INTENSITIVE, INTENSIVE, *a. serving to give force or emphasis to a word.* प्रकर्ष-उत्कर्षकरणारा, प्रकर्षकारक-ज्ञापक-द्योतक, उत्कर्षकारक-ज्ञापक-द्योतक, अर्थविशेषकारक-ज्ञापक-&c. Certain words and particles are employed to intend the sense of other words. They are, some prefixed, some affixed, some significant, some non-significant. As many of them as could be inserted under sufficiently corresponding words in English, have been inserted accordingly : but both those and the others remaining are collected here.

आग, affixed to तिखट hot, pungent, &c. (Hot as fire).

कढत, aff. or pre. to ऊन. (Boiling hot).

करकरीत, aff. to कोरा, नवा, ताजा and other words signifying "new." (Bran new).

काजरा, aff. to कडू. (Bitter as the काजरा nux vomica).

कुळकुळीत, कूट, किट्ट *or* कीट, कोळसा, aff. to काळा black. (Black as coal, black as soot, &c.).

खडखडीत, aff. to कोरडा dry. (Stiff dry).

खारट, pref. to मीठ salt. (Very salt).

गार, aff. to हिरवा green, to ओला wet, and to थंड cold.

गुंज, aff. to लाल red.

गोड, pre. or aff. to मिठा sweet. (Sweet as sugar).

घूस, aff. to काळा black.

घोट, aff. to खारट salt.

चटक, aff. to पिवळा yellow.

चार, aff. to हिरवा green. (Green as grass).

चिंच, aff. to आंबट sour. (Sour as tamarinds).

जर्द, aff. to पिवळा yellow, to तांबडा red.

जहर, aff. to कडू bitter.

जळजळीत pre. to ऊन hot.

जाळ, aff. to तिखट hot, pungent. (Hot as fire).

जोत, aff. to लाल red.

झणझणीत, pre. to तिखट hot, acrid, &c. [&c.).

झळझळीत, aff. or pre. to पांढरा white.(Glittering white,

टांक, ठणठणीत, aff. to कोरडा dry, empty.

ठिक्कर, aff. to काळा black.

डसाण, डहाण, डाण, ठाण्या, aff. to आंबट sour.

डोंब, aff. to तिखट, &c. acrid, pungent.

डोह, aff. to काळा black (applied to the water of rivers, &c.)

ढुस्स, *or* धुश्श *or* धुस्स, aff. to काळा black.

ढाण, aff. to काळा black, and to निबर tough, stiff.

तरडा, aff. to जून old, dry, &c.

ततरीत, aff. and pre. to उभा upright. (Bolt upright, straight as an arrow, &c.).

धमक, aff. धमधमीत, aff. or pre. धवधवीत, aff. or pre. धोप aff. to पिवळा yellow, गोरा fair, पांढरा white.

पान, पीठ, aff. to गोरा fair. (Fair as a lily, white as flour).

फटक *or* फटीक, फटफटीत, फेक, aff. to पांढरा white. (White as chrystal).

फूल, aff. to पांढरा and भना white.

बिबवा, aff. to काळा black.

बुंद, aff. to लाल, and तांबडा red.

बेरड, भिल्ल, मांग, हबशी, aff. to काळा black. (Black as a negro, moorman, &c.).

भडक, भबूक, aff. to लाल, and तांबडा red.

भोर, aff. to काळा black.

मस, मोदळा, aff. to काळा black. (Black as soot).

रसरसीत, aff. and pre. to ऊन Hot; aff. to पिवळा yellow.

लाल, aff. to तांबडा.

लुसलुसीत, pre. and aff. to कोंवळा tender.

विखल, aff. to कडू bitter (esp. as reduplicated कडूकडू विखल).

शंख, aff. to निवळ and other epithets of pellucidness.

सफेत *or* द, aff. to पांढरा white.

Intent, *a. having the mind fixed or bent on.* एकचित्त, एकतान, एकनिष्ठ, एकरोंखी, एकाग्र, एकाकार, एकाग्रचित्त, सापेक्षी, अभिनिवेशी, अभिनिविष्ट, तत्पर, तल्लीन, तन्मनस्क, आसक्त, संसक्त, अनन्यवृत्ति, अनन्यमना, अनन्यमनस्क, अभिमुख, नियत, युक्त, आसक्तचित्त, आसक्तचेता, आसक्तमना, लुब्ध, आविष्टचित्त, आविष्टचेता, आविष्टमना.

To be i. upon. लुबकणें.

Intent, *n. intention, purpose,* v. **Design.** आशय *m.* अभिप्राय *m.* मतलब *m.*

To all intents. सर्वस्वीं, सर्वस्वें, सर्वथैव, सर्वार्थी, सर्वार्थतः.

Intention, *n. purpose, &c.* v. **Design.** आशय *m.* अभिप्राय *m.* मतलब *m.* बेत *m.* इरादा *m.* इंगित *n.* खुलासा *m.* तात्पर्य *n.* कल्पना *f.* आकांक्षा *f.* चिकीर्षा *f.* विवक्षा *f.*

Purity of i. चित्तशुद्धि *f.* अंतःकरण शुद्धि *f.*

2 *intentness, fixedness of mind.* एकाग्रता *f.* एकचित्तता *f.* एकतानता *f.* &c. एकनिष्ठा *f.* आसक्ति *f.* संसक्ति *f.* तत्परता *f.* अनन्यवृत्ति *f.* अभिनिवेश *m.*

Intentional, *a. done with design.* संकल्पाचा, इराद्याचा, &c. संकल्पानें-मतलबानें-&c. केलेला, बुद्धिकृत, संकल्पकृत, ज्ञानकृत, कामकृत, ऐच्छिक, बुद्धिपुरस्सर, अभिप्रायपुरस्सर, &c. बुद्धिपूर्वक, &c. साभिप्राय, सांकल्पिक, अर्थवान्.

Intentionally, *adv.* v. A. *and* **Designedly.** बुद्ध्या, जाणून, जाणून बुजून, बुद्धिपूर्वक, बुद्धिपुरस्सर.

Intentive. See **Intent.**

Intently, *adv.* v. A. *with close attention or application.* निष्ठेनें, एकनिष्ठेनें, एकाग्रतेनें, सापेक्षपानें, एक लक्ष्यानें, मन एकाग्रकरून, सापेक्षें करून, सापेक्ष धरून, लयलावून, लक्षलावून, &c. निष्ठापूर्वक, &c.

Intentness, *n.* v. A. एकाग्रता *f.* निष्ठा *f.* एकनिष्ठा *f.* एकनिष्ठता-*f.* एकचित्तता *f.* आसक्ति *f.* संसक्ति *f.* अभिनिवेश *m.* अनन्यवृत्ति *f.*

To **Inter**, *v. a.* v. To **Bury.** पुरणें, गाडणें, माती आड करणें, भूमिगत-&c. करणें.

Intercalar, Intercalary, *a. inserted, added,*—day or month. अधिक, धोंड in comp. सौराब्दपूरक.

The i. month. धोंडा *m.* धोंडमास *m.* धोंडमहिना *m.* पुरुषोत्तममास *m.* मलमास *m.* अधिकमहिना *m.* अधिकमास *m.* अधिमास *m.* अधिमासशेष *m.* असंक्रांतिकमास *m.*

To **Intercalate**, *v. a.* (a month). अधिकमास *m.*-मलमास *m.* -&c. घेणें-घालणें-धरणें.

2 (a day). अधिकदिवस *m.*-&c. घेणें-&c.

To **Intercede**, *v. n. pass between.* See To **Intervene.**

2 *act between two parties*, v. To MEDIATE. मध्यस्थपणा *m.*-मध्यस्थी *f.*-&c. करणें.

3 for ; *plead in favor of.* मध्यें पडून *or* येऊन रदबदली *f.*-विनंती *f.*-प्रार्थना *f.*-&c. करणें, मध्यस्थ होऊन-मध्यस्थीनें-&c. विनंती *f.*-रदबदली *f.*-&c. करणें, भीड *f.* घालणें, परार्थप्रार्थना *f.*-परार्थविनति *f.*-&c. करणें.

INTERCEDENT, *a.* INTERCEDER, *n.* v. V. 2. *and* MEDIATOR. मध्यस्थ, मध्यवर्ती. [प्रार्थक.

3 मध्यस्थपणानें-मध्यस्थ होऊन-&c. रदबदली करणारा, परार्थ

To INTERCEPT, *v. a. stop on its passage, obstruct in progress.* वाटेंत-रस्त्यांत-&c. धरणें, वाट *f.* मारणें-अडवणें, गतिभंग *m.*-गतिरोध *m.*-रोध *m.*-अवरोध *m.*-&c. करणें *g. of o.*

INTERCEPTED, *p.* v. V. वाटेंत धरलेला, &c. रुद्ध, अवरुद्ध.

INTERCEPTION, *n.* v. V.—*act.* वाटेंत धरणें *n.* &c. वाटमारणी *f.* वाटमारा *m.* वाटअडवणी *f.* गतिभंग *m.* गतिरोध *m.* रोध *m.* अवरोध *m.* प्रतिबंध *m.* [स्थी *f.*

INTERCESSION, *n.* v. V. 2. मध्यें येणें *n.* मध्यस्थपणा *m.* मध्य-

3 मध्यस्थपणानें रदबदली *f.* मध्यस्थीनें विनंती *f.* परार्थप्रार्थना *f.* परार्थविनति *f.*

INTERCESSOR, *n.* v. V. 2. *and* MEDIATOR. मध्यस्थ, मध्यवर्ती.

2 मध्यस्थपणानें रदबदली करणारा-विनंती करणारा-भीडघालणारा, परार्थ प्रार्थक.

INTERCESSORY, *a. containing or relating to intercession.* मध्यस्थीचे रदबदलीचा, मध्यस्थपणाचे विनंतीचा, परार्थ प्रार्थना संबंधी, परार्थ प्रार्थना विषयक.

To INTERCHANGE, *v. n. succeed alternately*, v. To ALTERNATE. एक आड एक येणें-&c. परस्परानुगमन *n.*-&c. होणें *g. of s.*

To INTERCHANGE, *v. a. give and take mutually, change*, v. To EXCHANGE. बदलाबदल *f.*- अदलाबदल *f.* -सदलाबदल *f.* -&c. करणें *g. of o.*

2 *reciprocate.* परस्पर देणेंघेणें *n.*-परस्पर देवाणघेवाण *n.*-घेवदेव *m. f.*-दानप्रतिदान *n.*-&c. करणें, परस्पर घेणें-देणें-करणें. &c.

INTERCHANGE, *n.* v. V. N. *and* ALTERNATION. पालट *m. f.* परस्परानुगमन *n.*

v. V. A. 1. बदलाबदल *f.* अदलाबदल *f.* सदलाबदल *f.*

2 देणेंघेणें *n.* देवघेव *f.* देवाणघेवाण *n.* विनिमय *m.* आदानप्रदान *n.* दानप्रतिदान *n.* [रामी *f.*

I. of compliments or salutations. सलामासलामी *f.* राम-

INTERCHANGEABLE, *a.* v.V. N. *and* ALTERNATE. परस्परानुगामी, अन्योन्यपृष्ठानुगामी.

v. V. A. 1. अदलाबदल करायाजोगा, बदलाबदलीजोगा, सदलाबदलव्हावयाजोगा, &c.

2 परस्पर द्यायाघ्यायाजोगा-सारखा-&c. देवघेव करायाजोगा, परस्पर कराया-द्याया-&c. जोगा-&c. विनिमयार्ह.

INTERCHANGEABLY. See ALTERNATELY. [मध्यस्थ.

INTERCOSTAL, *a. placed between the ribs.* बरगड्यांमधला, बंकि-

INTERCOURSE, *n. connection by mutual communications or dealings.* जाणेंयेणें *n.* येणेंजाणें *n.* जावायेवा *m.* येवाजावा *m.* पायरव *m.* बोलणेंचालणें *n.* सहवास *m.* रहवास *m.* वळघटा *m.* वळण *n.* वळवट *f.* ढळण *or* दळण *n.* दळणवळण *n.* दळवट *f.* दळवटा *m.* दंडक *m.* घसरट *f.* वहिवाट *f.* वाग *f.* वागणूक *f.* रुळणी *f.* रकूत *m.* परिचय *m.* संघट्टन *n.* संसर्ग *m.*

Close or familiar i. रहाळ *f.* रहाळी *f.* घसण *f.* घसणी *f.* घसटणी *f.*

Sweetness of i. रहसाळी *f.*

To establish i. or a footing with. पायंडा *m.* पाडणें-घालणें-करणें. and, To be established. पायंडा *m.* पडणें-होणें.

To refuse all i. with. वारा *m.* न घेणें-न पडूं देणें *g. of o.* वाऱ्यास न उभा राहणें *g. of o.* सावली *f.* न पडूं देणें.

INTERCUTANEOUS, *a. being within or under the skin.* कातडीच्याआंतचा *or* आंतला, त्वगंतर्भूत, त्वगंतर्गत, त्वगंतःस्थित, त्वगंतर्वर्ती.

To INTERDICT, *v. a. prohibit*, v. To FORBID. मना करणें, निषेधणें, मनाई *f.*-निषेध *m.*-आसेध *m.* करणें *g. of o.*

INTERDICT, INTERDICTION, *n.* v. V. मनाकरणें *n.* निषेधणें *n.*&c. मनाई *f.* निषेध *m.* प्रतिषेध *m.* आसेध *m.*

I. (of use, or sale, &c.) in the name of the king or state. द्वाही *or* दुराही *f.* [*m.* थापटी *f.*

Mark or sign of an i. द्वाही *f.* जोंबडा *m.* द्वाहीचा जोंचडा

Written i. मनाचिठ्ठी *f.*

To disregard an i. दुराही *f.*-&c. मोडणें.

To lay an i. द्वाही *f.*-दुराही *f.* घालणें-देणें-बांधणें-बांधून टाकणें.

INTERDICTORY, *a. serving to prohibit.* निषेधाचा, मनाईचा, निषेधक, निषेधकारक, निषेधरूप, निषेधबोधक-ज्ञापक-&c. निषेधार्थक.

INTEREST, *n. good, advantage.* बरें *n.* हित *n.* कल्याण *n.* लाभ *m.* फायदा *m.*

2 *influence over, prevalence with*, v. INFLUENCE. चलती *f.* भार *m.* वजन *n.* गौरव *n.*

3 *regard to private profit.* स्वार्थ *m.* लाभलोभ *m.* लाभालोभा *m.* स्वार्थदृष्टि *f.* स्वहितावलोकन *n.*

4 *lively feeling about*, v. CONCERN. आस्था *f.* कळकळ *f.* काळजी *f.* जिव्हाळा *m.* दरद *m. f.* होष *m.* परवा *f.*

5 *share, part or connection in with reference to loss or gain.* भागी *f.* पाती *f.* लाभालाभाविषयीं अंश *m.*-संबंध *m.*-सामलात *f.*

6 *premium on the use of money, usury.* व्याज *n.* वृद्धि *f.* मिती *f.* वार्धुष्य *n.* कलांतर *n.*

At i. कर्जी.

Calculating and drawing out the i. accruing upon sums at broken periods. व्याजकटावणी *f.*

Casting up an i.-account (of Dr. and Cr.) and drawing out the balance. व्याजफैलावण *or* णी *f.*

Compound i. चढतें व्याज *n.* चक्रवाढ *f.* चक्रावळ *f.* चक्रवृद्धि *f.*

I. at the rate of half per cent per mensem. अर्धोत्रा *m.* —at one per cent. एकोत्रा *m.*—at one and a half. दिढोतरा *or* दिढोत्रा *m.*—at two. दुहोतरा *or* दुहोत्रा *m.*—at three. तिहोतरा *or* तिहोत्रा *m.*—at four. चहुत्रा *or* चहोत्रा *m.*—at five. पंचोतरा *or* पंचोत्रा *m.*—at six. साहोतरा *or* साहोत्रा *m.*—at seven. सातोतरा *or* सातोत्रा *m.*—at eight. आठोतरा *or* आठोत्रा *m.*—at nine. नवोतरा *or* नवोत्रा *m. or* नहोत्रा *m.*—at ten. दाहोतरा *or* दाहोत्रा *m.*—at eleven. अकरोतरा *or* अकरोत्रा *m.*—at twelve. बारोतरा *or* बारोत्रा *m.*—at twenty. विसोतरा *or* विसोत्रा *m.*

Exorbitant i. ठकव्याज *n.*

Inclusively of i. सव्याज, व्याजासुद्धां.

I. on broken periods. कटतें व्याज *n.*

Simple i. सरळव्याज *n.*

That bears i.—money. व्याजाऊ *or* व्याजाव, व्याजी *or* व्याजू, व्याजाचा.

That does not bear i. बिनव्याजी, बिनव्याजाचा, अवृद्धिक.

The 12th part of the amount of i. due. बारोत्राm.

To regulate the i. of a debt according to the broken periods, (periods of part liquidation). तुटमितीनें *or* तुटमुद्दतीनें व्याज *n.* करणें, कटमितीनें *or* कटमुद्दतीनें व्याज *n.* करणें.

7 *connection with great persons.* वशिलाm. वगf.वगवशिलाm.

8 *interestingness; power to interest or please.* रस *m.* मनोरंजकता *f.* मनोरंजनशक्ति *f.* चित्तवेधकता *f.*

To INTEREST, *v. a. excite emotions in, move or affect towards.* कळकळ *f.*-आस्था *f.*-पोटाग *f.*-ओढ *f.*-&c. लावणें-आणणें-जडिवणें-उत्पन्न करणें, आस्थायुक्त-&c. करणें.

2 *engage the attention or curiosity of.* मनn.-चित्तn.-लक्ष्यn.-&c. वेधणें, मनास ओढ *f.*-ओढाm. लावणें, कौतुकn. वाटणें *in. con.*

3 *give an interest or share in.* भागी *f.*-पाती *f.*-भागm.-अंशm.-&c. देणें, भागीदार-अंशी-&c. करणें.

4 (one's self). अगत्यn.-आस्था *f.*-पोटाग *f.*-&c. धरणें *and with in. con.* असणें, मनावर घेणें.

INTERESTED, *p. and a.* v. V. 1. कळकळ आणलेला, &c. आस्थेकरी, आस्थिक, आस्थेवाईक, आस्थावान्, आस्थापूर्वक, आस्थापुरस्सर, दरदी, पोटागीचा, कळकळीचा, आस्थेचा, &c.

3 भागीदार, पातीदार, अंशी, संबंधी.

I. *desirous of advantage or gain*, v. SELFISH. लाभलोभी, लाभदृष्टि, अलगरजी, मतलबी, सकाम.

INTERESTEDNESS, *n.* v. A. 1. लाभलोभ *m.* लाभलोभा *m.* लाभदृष्टि *f.* फलाशा *f.* सकामता *f.* अपेक्षा बुद्धि *f.*

INTERESTING, *p. a.* v.V. 1. कळकळ आणणारा, आस्थालावणारा, ओढलावणारा, &c. [रंजक.

2 मनवेधणारा, &c. चित्तवेधक, लक्ष्यवेधक, &c. हृदयंगम, मनो-

To INTERFERE, *v. n. interpose, intermeddle.* मध्यें पडणें-येणें-शिरणें, हातm.-तोंडn. घालणें, तिसरा-तृतीय होणें.

2—idly, officiously, &c. v. To MEDDLE. लुडबुडणें, लांडाकारभारm.-बुचाकारभारm.-&c. करणें, लटलटणें.

3 *come in collision*, v. To CLASH. आडवा येणें, नडणें, घासाघास *f.*-&c. होणें.

4—a horse. नेवर *n. m.* लागणें.

INTERFERENCE, *n.* v. V. 1.—*act.* मध्येंपडणेंn. &c. मध्यस्थी *f.* मध्यस्थपणा *m.* अंतरागमन *n.*

2 लुडबुडणेंn. लुडबूड *f.* लांडाकारभार *m.* बुचाकारभारm. नस्ताकारभार *m.* [कमकf.

3 आडवायेणें *n.* &c. घासाघास *f.* घासाघीस *f.* कचाकची *f.* च-

4 नेवर लागणें *n.*

INTERFERER. See MEDDLER.

INTERFLUENT, INTERFLUOUS, *a. flowing between.* मध्यें वाहणारा, मध्यप्रवाही.

To INTERFUSE, *v. a. form or spread between.* मध्येंमध्यें घालणें-ओतणें-टाकणें.

INTERIM, *n. intervening time.* मधलाकाळ *m.* आंतलाकाळ *m.* मध्यकाल *m.* अंतर्गतकाल *pop.* अतरितकाळ *m.*

In the i. इतक्यांत, इतक्यामध्यें. [आंतर.

INTERIOR, *a.*v. INNER. आंतचा, आंतील, आंतला, आंतल्याकडचा,

2 See INLAND.

INTERIOR, *n. internal part, inside.* आंतला भाग *m.* आंतली बाजू *f.* आंतलेंआंग *n.* अंतरंग *n.* अभ्यंतर *n.* गर्भ *m.* अंतःप्रदेशm.

2 (of a house). माजघर *m. n.* आंतवार *n.* अभ्यंतर *n.* अंतर्गृह *n.* मध्यगृह *n.*

3 (of a country). देशाचा मध्यभाग *m.* देशमध्य*n.* मध्यदेशm.

INTERJACENCY, *n.* v. A. मध्यस्थिति *f.* मध्यवर्त्तित्व *n.*

INTERJACENT, *a. lying between.* मध्यें पडलेला, मध्यस्थित, मध्यवर्त्ती, अंतर्वर्त्ती.

To INTERJECT, *v. a. cast between or in.* मध्यें टाकणें-घालणें-&c. मध्यप्रक्षेपण *n.*-मध्यप्रक्षेप *m.*-मध्यक्षेपण *n.*-&c. करणें.

INTERJECTED, *p.* v. V. मध्यें टाकलेला-घातलेला-&c. मध्यप्रक्षिप्त, मध्यक्षिप्त.

INTERJECTION, *n.* v. V.—*act.* मध्यें टाकणें *n.* &c. मध्यप्रक्षेपण *n.* मध्यप्रक्षेप *m.* मध्यक्षेपण *n.* मध्यक्षेप *m.*

I. *exclamation, ejaculation.* उद्गार *m.*

The interjections of admiration, astonishment, or surprise are, आहा, आहाहा, अहा, अहो, अहाहा, अबब, बबब, आबाबय, अबाबा, अब्ब *or* अब्बा, अतत;—of sudden admiration, sudden reminiscence, &c. ओहो;—of amazement or dismay, ललल, अलल, अलाला;—of contempt, &c. छ, छत्, छिः, छिछी, छी, धिक्, फें, कःपदार्थ;—of disgust, &c. इश्श, इश्यो, इश्शो, फिश्श, फिश्शो, फिस, फूं, थत्तु, शिव;—of displeasure, reproach, &c. हून्, उदव, हा, हांहां, अहा, छी;—of grief or sorrow, अरेरे, रेरेरेरे, अललल, अहा, अहाहा, हाय हाय, अहाय अहाय, अहह, कटा, कटकटा, कपाळमाळा;—of joy, exultation, &c. डियो, हां, अहाहा,—of negation, prohibition, &c. उंहुं, ऊंहुं;—of pain, उस, हुंहुं, आये, ओय;—of unconcern, &c. अंः. Some interjections peculiar to females, are अगई, अगगई, अईअई.

To INTERLACE, *v. a. insert one thing with another*, v. To INTERMIX. मध्येंमध्यें घालणें-गांठवणें-मिळवणें, मिसळणें, जडणें, मिश्रित-&c. करणें.

To INTERLARD, *v. a. insert between*, v. To INTERMIX. मध्यें-मध्यें घालणें-&c. मिसळणें.

2 *diversify by mixture.* भेळ *f.*-मिसळ *f.*-&c. घालणें-घालून विचित्र करणें.

To INTERLEAVE, *v. a. insert blank leaves in.* मध्येंमध्यें कोरीं पानें *n. pl.* घालणें-घालून बांधणें.

To INTERLINE, *write in alternate lines.* एक आड ओळ करून-एकआड ओळीनें-एकांतऱ्या ओळीनें-&c. लिहणें, एकांतर पंक्तीनें लिहणें, ओळीस ओळ लिहणें.

2 *write between the lines.* ओळींच्या मध्यें लिहणें-घालणें, पंक्तिद्वयमध्यलेखन *n.* करणें.

INTERLINEAR, INTERLINEARY, *a.* v. V. 1. *written in alternate lines.* एकआड ओळ करून लिहिलेला, एकांतऱ्या ओळीनें लिहिलेला, &c. [लिहिलेला.

2 *written between lines before written.* ओळींच्या मध्यें

INTERLINEATION, *n. writing inserted between written lines.* ओळींच्या मध्यें घातलेला-लिहिलेला-&c. शब्द *m.*-वाक्यn.-लिहिणेंn.-शोध *m.*-&c.

To INTERLINK, *v. a. connect by uniting links.* कडीस कडी *f.* अडकवणें, परस्पर गांठवणें, परस्परग्रंथित करणें.

INTERLOCUTION. See DIALOGUE. [संवादी.

INTERLOCUTOR, *n. one who speaks in dialogue.* संवादकर्त्ता,

INTERLOCUTORY, *a. consisting of dialogue.* संवादाचा, संवादरूप, संवादात्मक.

To INTERLOPE, *v. n. intrude into the trade or privileges of another.* नाहक्क मध्यें पडणें-शिरणें, सत्ता नसतां दुसऱ्याच्या व्यापारांत-कामांत-&c. शिरणें-घुसणें-&c. सत्तेवांचून-&c.अधिकार *m.*-व्यापार *m.*-धंदा *m.*-&c. करणें.

INTERLOPER, *n.* INTERLOPING, *p. a.* v. V. नाहक्क मध्यें पडणारा, &c. खुपशा, घुशा, जड्या, उपरी, अनधिकारी, असत्ताकव्यापारी, आयत्या बिळांत नागोबा.

INTERLUDE, *n. diversion between acts of a play.* नाटकाचे अंकांच्या मधला तमाशा *m.* उभय प्रवेशांतर्गत कौतुक *n.*

INTERLUNAR, INTERLUNARY, *a. belonging to the time when the moon is invisible.* अमावास्येचा, अमासंबंधी, अमावास्याकालिक.

INTERMARRIAGE, *n. marriage between two families, when each takes one and gives another.* बदलाचें लग्न *n.* सार्टेलोटेंन. प्रत्युद्वाह *m.*

Confused connection through i. गोरख सांखळी *f.*

I. of three families. तिरकूट *n.* तिसुती *f.*

To INTERMARRY, *v. n.* v. N. बदलाचें लग्न *n.*-&c. करणें.

2 *make marriages with one another.* परस्पर कन्याव्यवहार *m.*-विवाहव्यवहार *m.*-&c. करणें, कन्याव्यवहार *m.*-विवाहव्यवहार-&c. असणें *g. of s. recip.*

To INTERMEDDLE, INTERMEDDLER, &c. See To MEDDLE, &c.

INTERMEDIAL, INTERMEDIARY, INTERMEDIATE, *a. situate between, lying between.* मधचा, मधला, मध्य, मध्यम, मध्यस्थित, मध्यवर्त्ती, अंतरालस्थित, उभयमध्यस्थित.

INTERMEDIATELY, *adv.* v. A. मधच्या मध्यें, दर्म्यान.

INTERMENT. See BURIAL.

INTERMINABLE, INTERMINATE, *a. boundless, endless,* v. INFINITE. निरवधि, अनंत, निस्सीम, निश्शेष, असमापनीय, असमाप्य.

INTERMINABLENESS, INTERMINATENESS, *n.* v. A. निरवधिता *f.* आनंत्य *n.* &c. सीमाराहित्य *n.* मर्यादाराहित्य *n.*

To INTERMINGLE, &c. See To MIX, &c.

INTERMISSION, *n.* v. V. A.—*act.* ठेवणें *n.* राहवणें *n.* तकूब करणें *n.* &c. मंडूकानुवृत्ति *f.*

v. V. N.—*state.* खोळंबा *m.* नागा *m.* खाडा *m.* तकूब *n.* तकुबी *f.* विराम *m.* व्यवधान *n.*

I. *break, pause.* खंड *m.* खाडा *m.* नागा *m.* खळ *m.* मोडा *m.* व्यवधान *n.* अंतर *n.*

INTERMISSIVE. See INTERMITTENT.

To INTERMIT, *v. a. cause to cease for a time, suspend.* कांहीं काळपर्यंत ठेवणें-राहवणें, मध्यें ठेवणें-राहवणें, खळवणें, थांबवणें, तकूब करणें-ठेवणें, खाडा*m.*-खळ *m.*-खंड*m.*-&c. पाडणें, विराम*m.*-&c. करणें.

To INTERMIT, *v. n. cease for a time.* कांहीं काळपर्यंत राहणें, मध्यें राहणें, खळणें, थांबणें, थोपणें, खाडा *m.*-खळ *m.*-नागा *m.*-&c. पडणें-होणें *g. of s.*

2—a fever. मध्यें मध्यें जाणें-राहणें-&c. असून असून-राहून राहून-टाळून टाळून-&c. येणें.

INTERMITTED, *p.* v. V. A. कांहीं काळपर्यंत राहवलेला, राहवलेला, तकूब ठेवलेला, &c. स्खलित *or corr.* खलीन.

INTERMITTENT. See INTERMITTING.

INTERMITTER, *n.* INTERMITTING, *p. a.* v. V. A. कांहीं काळपर्यंत राहवणारा, खळवणारा, थांबवणारा, &c. विराम करणारा.

v. V. N. 1. कांहीं काळपर्यंत राहणारा, मध्यें राहणारा, खळणारा, &c. येताजाता, काढता लागता, तुटक, फुटकर, फुटक, सविच्छेद. 2 येता जाता, येता निघता, अंतरित.

INTERMITTINGLY, *adv. with intermissions.* राहून राहून, असून असून, विसवा विसवीनें, खंडळ मंडळ, अडातुडी.

To INTERMIX, *v. a. mix together,* v. To MIX. मिळवणें, मिसळणें, भिसळणें, मिळवामिळव *f.*-भिसळाभिसळ *f.*-मिसळामिसळ *f.*-&c. करणें, मिश्रित-&c. करणें.

To INTERMINGLE, *v. n. be mixed together.* v. To MIX. मिसळणें, मिळणें, मिळून जाणें, मिसळाभिसळ *f.*-&c. होणें *g. of s.*

INTERMIXING, INTERMIXTURE, *n.* v. V. A.—*act.* मिळवणें *n.* मिसळणें *n.* &c. मिळवामिळव *f.* कालवाकालव *f.* मिश्रण *n.* मिश्रीकरण *n.*—*state.* भिसळाभिसळ *f.* मिसळामिसळ *f.* मिसळ *f.* मिसळा *m.* भिसळ *f.* भेळ *f.*

I. *mass formed by mixing.* मिसळ *f.* मिसळा *m.* भिसळ *f.*

II. *additament mixed.* भेळ *f.* मिसळ *f.*

INTERMONTANE, *a. being between mountains.* पर्वतांमधला, पर्वतमध्यस्थित, गिरिमध्यस्थ.

INTERMUNDANE, *a. being between worlds.* भुवनांमधला, भुवनमध्यस्थित.

INTERMURAL, *a. lying between walls.* भिंतींच्या मधला, प्राकारांतर्वर्त्ती, प्राचीरांतर्वर्त्ती. [भ्यंतर.

INTERNAL, *a.* v. INWARD. आंतचा, आंतला, आंतील, आंतर, आ-

2 See INTRINSIC. 3 See DOMESTIC.

INTERNALLY, *adv.* v. A.1. आंत, आंतल्याकडेस, आंतल्या बाजूस.

I. *mentally, &c.* आंत, मनांत, अंतःकरणांत, पोटांत.

INTERNATIONAL, *a.* देशादेशाचे परस्परव्यवहाराचा, परस्परदेशांचा, देशपरस्पर.

INTERNODATION, INTERNODE, *n.*—in botany; *portion between two knots.* कांडें*n.* पेर *n.* पेरें*n.* ग्रंथिद्वयमध्य *m.* पर्वद्वयमध्य *m.*

INTERNUNCIO, *n.* v. MESSENGER. उभयपक्षदूत, उभयवार्त्ताहर.

To INTERPOLATE, *v. a. add or insert spuriously, foist in.* खुपसणें, घुसडणें, दपटणें, क्षेपक घालणें, क्षेप *m.*-क्षेपण *n.* करणें *g. of o.*

INTERPOLATED, *p.* v. V. खुपसलेला, घुसडलेला, क्षेपकेलेला, क्षिप्त.

INTERPOLATION, *n.* v. V.—*act.* खुपसणें *n.* &c. खुपसणी *f.* घुसडणी *f.* घालघुसड *f.* क्षेप *m.* क्षेपण *n.* [&c.

I. *matter interpolated.* क्षेपक *m.* खुपसलेला ग्रंथ *m.*-वाक्य*n.*-

INTERPOLATOR, *n.* v. V. खुपसणारा, घुसडणारा, &c. खुपशा, घुशा, क्षेपणकर्त्ता.

INTERPOSAL. See INTERPOSITION.

To INTERPOSE, *v.a.place between.* मध्यें-आड ठेवणें-करणें- घालणें. 2 See To INTRUDE.

To INTERPOSE, *v. n. step in between parties, mediate.* मध्यें पडणें-होणें-येणें, आड होणें-येणें, मध्यस्थी *f.*- &c. करणें.

INTERPOSED, *p.* v. V. A. 1. मध्यें ठेवलेला, आडकेलेला.

INTERPOSER, *n.* INTERPOSING, *p. a.* v. A. 1. मध्यें ठेवणारा, आड करणारा, &c.

v. V. N. *and* MEDIATOR. मध्यें येणारा-पडणारा-&c.

INTERPOSITION, *n.* v. V. A. 1.—*act.* मध्यें ठेवणें *n.* मध्यें घालणें *n.* &c.

v. V. N. मध्यें येणें *n.* मध्येंपडणें *n.* मध्यस्थी *f.* मध्यस्थगिरी*f.* अंतरागमन *n.* अंतरागतकृत्य *n.* अंतरागतयत्न *m.*

To INTERPRET, *v. a. explain, unfold, make clear.* अर्थ *m.* करणें-सांगणें *g. of o.* उलगडा *m.*-परिस्फोट*m.*-विवरण *n.*-व्याख्या *f.*-&c. करणें *g. of o.* उघडा-स्पष्ट-&c. करणें, विवरणें.

2 *translate.* भाषांतर *n.*-तर्जुमा *m.* करणें *g. of o.*

INTERPRETATION, *n.* v. V. 1.—*act.* अर्थसांगणें *n.* विवरणें*n.* &c. व्याख्या *f.* व्याख्यान *n.* विवरण *n.* विवृति *n.* अर्थकरण *n.* स्पष्टीकरण *n.* विख्यापन *n.*

I. *meaning given.* अर्थ *m.* टीका *f.* व्याख्या *f.*

Doubtful i. संदिग्धार्थ *m.* [चिंध्या.

Far fetched, &c. i. क्लिष्टार्थ *m.* अर्थाचे तुकडे भागवताच्या

II. *translation.* भाषांतर *n.* तर्जुमा *m.*

INTERPRETED, *p.* v. V. 1. अर्थ केलेला, विवरलेला, &c. विवृत, जातविवरण, कृतविवरण.

INTERPRETER, *n.* INTERPRETING, *p. a.* v. V. 1. अर्थ करणारा-सांगणारा, &c. विवरण-&c. कर्त्ता-कारी.

2 भाषांतर करणारा, &c. दुभाषी *or* दुभाष्या, तर्जुमान.

INTERRED, *p.* v. V. पुरलेला, गाडलेला, &c.

INTERREGNUM, *n. time of a throne being vacant.* अनायक *n.* निर्नायकी *f.*अराजक*n.*अराज्य*n.*राजद्वय मध्यगत अराजककाल*m.*

To INTERROGATE, *v. a. question, ask,* v. To EXAMINE. पुसणें, सवाल *m.*-प्रश्न *m.* करणें-घालणें, पुस्तापास्त *f.*-पुरशीस *f.*-&c. करणें -घालणें-पाडणें.

INTERROGATION, *n.* v. V.—*act.* पुसणें *n.* &c. पुसणी *f.* पुसापुसी *f.* पुसापूस *f.* पुस्तापास्त *f.* पुरशीस *f.* पृच्छा *f.*

I. *a question.* प्रश्न *m.* सवाल *m.* पृच्छा *f.*

Mark or note of i. प्रश्नचिन्ह *n.*

INTERROGATIVE, *a. denoting a question, &c.* प्रश्न करण्याचा, प्रश्नाचा, प्रश्नरूप, प्रश्नार्थक, प्रश्नात्मक, प्रश्नसूचक. [सर्वनाम*n.*

INTERROGATIVE, *n. word used in asking a question.* प्रश्नार्थक-

INTERROGATOR, *n.* v. V. पुसणारा, प्रश्न करणारा, &c. पुसता, प्रश्नकर्त्ता, पृच्छक, प्रष्टा.

INTERROGATORY, *a.* v. INTERROGATIVE. प्रश्नरूप, प्रश्नार्थक.

INTERROGATORY, *n.* v. QUESTION. प्रश्न *m.* सवाल *m.*

To INTERRUPT, *v. a. break and hinder.* मोडणें, मोडा *m.*-मोडती *f.*-अडथळा *m.*-अटकाव *m.*-हरकत *f.*-&c. मध्यें घालणें-मध्यें करणें-&c. मोड *m.*-भंग *m.*-गतिभंग *m.*-खंडन *n.*-विच्छेद *m.*-&c. करणें *g. of o.* खंडित-विच्छिन्न-&c. करणें.

INTERRUPTED, *p.* v. V. मोडलेला, मोडा घातलेला, &c. खंडित, विच्छिन्न, तुटक, तुटका, स्खलित *or corr.* खलीत.

INTERRUPTER, *n.* v. V. मोडणारा, मोडा घालणारा, &c. मोड्या, खंडनकर्त्ता, विघ्नकर्त्ता-कारी, &c.

INTERRUPTION, *n.* v. V.—*act.* मोडणें *n.* भंग *m.* खंडन *n.* विच्छेद *m.*—*state.* मोड *m.* मोडा *m.* मोडती *f.* अडथळा*m.* अटकाव*m.* हरकत *f.* खळव *m.* गतिभंग *m.* गतिरोध *m.*

I. See INTERMISSION.

To INTERSECT, *v. a. cut or cross so as to divide.* फोडून जाणें, दुभागणें, छेदणें, भेदणें, *or* दुभागून-छेदून-भेदून जाणें.

To INTERSECT, *v. n. cut and cross mutually.* परस्पर छेदून जाणें-भेदून जाणें-&c. परस्पर छेदन *n.* करणें.

INTERSECTED, *p.* v. V. A. दुभागलेला, छेदूनगेलेला, &c.

INTERSECTION, *n.* v. V. A.—*act.* फोडून जाणें*n.* भेदणें*n.* छेदणें*n.* &c. भेदन *n.*

Point of i. छेदनबिंदु *m.*

v. V. N. परस्परछेदन *n.*

To INTERSERT, *v. a.* v. To INSERT. मध्यें घालणें-ठेवणें.

To INTERSPERSE, *v. a. scatter or set among other things.* मध्येंमध्यें फोकणें-फेंकणें-टाकणें-विकिरणें-लावणें-घालणें, प्रतिमध्यावकिरण *n.*-&c. करणें.

INTERSPERSED, *p.* v. V. मध्येंमध्यें फोकलेला, &c.

INTERSPERSION, *n.* v. V.—*act.* मध्येंमध्यें टाकणें *n.* &c. प्रतिमध्यावकिरण *n.* अंतरांतरावकिरण *n.*

INTERSTELLAR, INTERSTELLARY, *a. situate among the stars.* तारामंडलांतःस्थित, तारागणांतर्गत, तारामंडलमध्यवर्त्ती.

INTERSTICE, *n. narrow space between.* फट *f.* सांध *f.* चिरण *f.* संधि *m. f.* अंतर *n.*—as between layers of stones &c. दर्ज*f.*

Any dark i. अंधारी *f.* [सुटा.

INTERSTITIAL, *a. containing interstices.* फटींचा, सांधींचा, सांतर,

To INTERTANGLE. See To ENTANGLE.

INTERTEXTURE, See INTERWEAVING.

To INTERTWINE, *To* INTERTWIST, *v. a. twine or twist one with another.* एकमेकांत-एकांतएक-&c. गुंफणें-गुंतवणें-गांठवणें-ग्रथित करणें.

INTERVAL, *n. time or space between.* अंतर *n.* अंतरा *m.* अंतराल *or* ळ *n.* संधि *m. f.* तफावत *f.* मध्यांतर *pop.* मध्यंतर *n.*

At intervals. मध्येंमध्यें.

2 *time between.* मधला काळ *m.* मधलीवेळ *f.* वेळ *f.* अवकाश *m.* अंतरावसर *m.* मध्यावसर *m.* अभ्यंतर काल *m.* विमर्द *m.*

3 *time yet to pass between.* अवधि *m. f.* अवध *f.* अवकाश *m.* उशीर *m.* वेळ *m.* फुरसत *f.* विलंब *m.* दिरिंग *m.*

4 *space between,* v. SPACE. अवकाश *m.* तफावत *f.* फरक *m.*

5 *space yet to be crossed,* v. DISTANCE. अवधि *m. f.* अवध *f.* अवकाश *m.*

6 (of ease, &c. between paroxysms). संधि *m.* मधला मधला काळ *m.*

To INTERVENE, *v. n. come, be, or happen between.* मध्यें येणें-पडणें-घडणें-असणें-उपस्थित होणें-&c. आड येणें-&c. मध्यस्थित-मध्यवर्त्ती-&c. असणें.

INTERVENIENT, *a.* INTERVENING, *p. a.* v. V. मध्यें येणारा-पडणारा-घडणारा *or* मध्यें आलेला-पडलेला-&c. आड येणारा-असणारा-आलेला-&c. व्यवधायक, अंतर्धायक, अंतर्गत, व्यवहित.

INTERVENTION, *n.* v. V. मध्यें येणें *n.* मध्यें पडणें *n.* मध्यें असणें *n.* आड येणें *n.* &c. व्यवधान *n.* मध्यवर्तित्व *n.* मध्यस्थिति *f.*

I. *interposition,* v. MEDIATION. मध्यस्थी *f.* अंतरागमन *n.*

INTERVIEW, *n. mutual view or sight, meeting.* भेट *f.* मुलाखत *f.* दृष्टादृष्ट *f.* नजर *f.* नजर गुजारत *f.* नजरगुजारा *m.* नजरानजर *f.* अन्योन्यदर्शन *n.*

Dying i. जिवंत भेट *f.* डोळे भेट *f.*

Hurried, brief, &c. i. डोळे भेट *f.* दृष्टिभेट *f.*

To INTERVOLVE, *v. a. involve one with another.* एकामेकांत-

एकांतएक-परस्पर-&c. गुंतवणें-गांठवणें-गांथणें, गुतागुत *f.*-परस्परग्रथन *n.*-&c. करणें *g. of o.* [गांथणें.

To INTERWEAVE, *v. a.* v. To PLAT. विणणें, गांथणें, एकांत एक

INTERWEAVING, *n.* v. V. विणणें *n.* गांथणें *n.*

INTESTABLE, *a. not qualified to make a will.* मृत्युपत्रकरण्यास अयोग्य-&c. मृत्युपत्रानधिकारी, मृतलेखकरणाक्षम.

INTESTACY, *n. state of dying without making a will.* अकृतमृतपत्रता *f.* स्वानिर्बंधमरण *n.*

INTESTATE, *a. that has died without a will.* मृत्युलेख केल्यावांचून मेलेला, मृत्युपत्र न केलेला, अकृतमृत्युपत्र, अकृतमृतलेख, स्वानिर्बंधमृत, अकृतव्यवस्थमृत.

I. property. निवारस माल *m.*

INTESTINAL, *a. belonging to the intestines.* अंतड्यांचा, अंत्रसंबंधी, आंत्रिक.

INTESTINE, *n. bowel.* अंतडें *n.* अंतडी *f.* अंत्र *n.*

INTESTINE, *a.* v. INWARD. आंतचा, आंतला, आंतील.

2 *not foreign,* v. DOMESTIC. देशी, देशीय, अविदेशज, स्वदेशांतर्गत.

I. war. आपसांतली लढाई *f.* यादवी *f.*

To INTHRAL. See To ENSLAVE.

To INTHRONE. See To ENTHRONE.

INTIMACY, v. A. 2. सलग *f.* सलगी *f.* लगत *f.* जवळीक *f.* घसण *f.* घसणी *f.* घसट *f.* घसटणी *f.* दाटी *f.* घणदाटी *f.* घणदाट *n.* दाटमैत्री *f.* गटपट *f.* गट्टी *f.* घरोबा *m.* दोस्ती *f.* खेळीमेळी *f.* बापभावकी *f.* सख्यभाव *m.* दांडापेंडा *m.* दांडापेंढोळा *m.* संघट्टन *n.* परिचय *m.* प्रत्यासत्ति *f.* संसक्ति *f.*

INTIMATE, *a. near, close.* जवळचा, अंतरंग, अंतरंगींचा, अंतरींचा, जिवींचा.

2 *close in friendship,* v. FAMILIAR. खेळीमेळीचा, सलगीचा, गट्टीचा, घसणीचा, घळामेळीचा, अंतर्यामी, दाट, संसक्त, संसर्गी.

To be i. लाळ *f.* गळणें *g. of s. recip.* रस *m.* पाघळणें-गळणें *g. of s. recip.*

3 See INWARD.

INTIMATE, *n. crony.* सलगी, सलगीचा, खेळमेळ्या, सखा, जिवींचा जिव्हाळा *m.* जिवींचा मित्र.

To INTIMATE, *v. a. make known indirectly or slightly.* सुचवणें, दर्शिवणें, जाणवणें, सूचना *f.*-&c. करणें *g. of o.* खबर *f.*-&c. देणें *g. of o.*

INTIMATED, *p.* v. V. सुचवलेला, दर्शिवलेला, &c. सूचित.

INTIMATER, *n.* INTIMATING, *p. a.* v. V. सुचवणारा, दर्शिवणारा, &c. सूचक, दर्शक, सूचन-&c. कर्ता.

INTIMATION, INTIMATING, *n.* v. V.—*act.* सुचवणें *n.* &c. सूचना *f.* सूचन *n.* सूची *f.*

I. *intimation given.* सूचना *f.* सुचें *n.* खबर *f.* बातमी *f.*

To INTIMIDATE, *v.a. make fearful, dishearten, daunt.* भिववणें, भेडसावणें, भेडावणें, भय *n.*-दहशत *f.*-&c. घालणें-बसवणें, हिम्मत *f.*—&c. मोडणें *g. of o.* धैर्यभंग *m.*-धैर्यनाश *m.*-उत्साहभंग*m.*-&c. करणें *g. of o.* भयभीत-सभय-भययुक्त-&c. करणें.

2 *threaten, scold, snub, &c. in order to frighten.* दटावणें, दबावणें, दाबणें, धमकावणें, भय *n.*-धाक *m.*-&c. दाखवणें-घालणें, भयप्रदर्शन *n.* करणें, डरावणें, डरकावणें, दरडावणें, गुरकावणें, दडवडावणें, खमकावणें, खरकावणें, दवकावणें, दामटणें, धडकावणें, खडसणें, खडसावणें, ललकारणें, दबावणी *f.*-धमकावणी *f.*-&c. करणें *g. of o.*

INTIMIDATED. *p.* v. V. 1. भेडसावलेला, भेडावलेला, &c. दबेल, नष्टधैर्य, नष्टोत्साह, गतधैर्य, गतोत्साह, जातभय, प्राप्तभय, जातशंक, प्राप्तशंक.

INTIMIDATION, *n.* v. V. 1.—*act.* भिववणें *n.* भेडसावणें *n.*&c. भेडावणी *f.* भयप्रदर्शन *n.*—*state.* भेडावलेलेपणा *m.* धैर्यनाश *m.* धैर्यभंग *m.* उत्साहभंग*m.* जातभयता *f.*

2—*act.* दटावणें *n.* दबावणें *n.* &c. दबावणी *f.* दटावणी *f.* धमकावणी *f.* &c. धमकी *f.*दाब*m.* दबाव*m.* दाबदुबी *f.* दाबीदुबी *f.* दाबदूब *f.* दाबदडप *f.* दाडदपट *f.* दरडाई *f.*

Empty intimidations. मेघाडंबर *or* मेघडंबर *n.*

INTIRE, INTIRENESS. See ENTIRE, &c.

INTO, *prep.* मध्यें, आंत.

INTOLERABLE, *a. unbearable.* सोसवेनासा, नसोसवेसा, असह्य, असहनीय, सहनाशक्य, निःसह, दुःसह, दुर्निर्वह, दुर्विषह.

INTOLERABLENESS, *n.* v. A. असह्यता *f.* असहनीयता *f.* सहनाशक्यता *f.* दुःसहता *f.* दौःसह्य *n.*

INTOLERABLY, *adv.* सोसवेनासा *decl.* नसोसवेसा *decl.*

INTOLERANCE, *n.* v. A. 1. असोशिकपणा *m.* असहनशीलता *f.* असहिष्णुता *f.* असहन *n.* अक्षमा *f.* अतितिक्षा *f.* क्षमाभाव *m.*

2 परमतासहन *n.* अन्यमतासहन *n.* परमतासहिष्णुता *f.* परमतातितिक्षा *f.*

INTOLERANT, *a. unable to bear.* असोशीक, असहनशील, असहिष्णु, असह, असहन, अक्षम.

2 *not enduring difference of opinion.* परमतासह, अन्यमतासह, परमतासहिष्णु, अन्यमतातितिक्षु, परमतासूयक.

To INTOMB, *v. a. deposit in a tomb.* समाधींत ठेवणें, समाधिस्थ-समाधिनिक्षिप्त-&c. करणें.

INTONATION, *n. modulation of the voice.* स्वरभेद *m.*

To INTONE, *v.a.* स्वरावर-चालीवर-धाटणीवर-&c.म्हणणें-वाचणें-&c.

To INTORT. See To TWIST.

To INTOXICATE, *v. a. inebriate.* कैफ *m.*-माद *m.*-तार *f.*-गुंगी *f.*-मस्ती *f.*-&c. आणणें, माजवणें, गुंगवणें, मस्त-मत्त-&c. करणें.

2 fig. मस्ती *f.*-माज *m.*-माद *m.*-उन्माद *m.*-&c. आणणें, मस्त-उन्मत्त-प्रमत्त-&c. करणें.

INTOXICATE, *a.* INTOXICATED, *p.* v. V. 1.कैफ आलेला, &c.मस्त.

Stupidly i. निशाधुंद.

To be i. कैफ *m.*-अमल *m.*-तार *f.*-&c. चढणें *in. con.* तारवटणें, तारकटणें, झिंगणें. [मगनमस्त.

2 माज आलेला, &c. मत्त, उन्मत्त, बदमस्त, मदान्वित, मदोन्मत्त,

To be i. माजणें, उतणें.

INTOXICATER, *n.* INTOXICATING, *p. a.* v. V. माजवणारा, कैफ आणणारा, &c. अमलाचा, कैफाचा, &c. कैफी, अमली, मादक, उन्मादक, घुमरा.

Addicted to the use of i. articles. अमली.

I. drug or substance. कैफ *m.* निशा *f.* अमलीपदार्थ *m.*

I. substances,—compreh. or gener. निशापाणी*n.* Some *intoxicating potions or preparations* are कुसुंबा, घोटा, चरस, तल्ली, मदंती, माजूम, याकुती, सबजी.

2 उन्मत्त करणारा, &c. उन्मादक, &c.

INTOXICATION, *n.* v.V.1.—*act.* माजवणें *n.*गुंगवणें*n.*&c.—*state.* निशा *f.* झिंगी *f.* मस्ती *f.* कैफ *m.* अमल *m.* तार *f.* गुंगी *f.* माजणें *n.* माद *m.*

2—*state.* दौलतीची-द्रव्याची-&c. मस्ती *f.*-गुंगी *f.*-धुंदी *f.*-&c.

The i. (of drugs, riches, honors, &c.) *intoxicating influence.* अमल *m.* कैफ *m.* निशा *f.* मस्ती *f.* ऊब *f.* मद *m.* माद *m.* उन्माद *m.*

INTRACTABILITY, INTRACTABLENESS, *n.* v. A. निक्षीपणा *m.*अडेलपणा *m.* &c. अनिवार्यता *f.* दुःसाध्यता *f.* दुर्धर्षता *f.* &c.

INTRACTABLE, *a. unmanageable, refractory,* v. OBSTINATE, PERVERSE. निकशी *or* निक्षी, करनकर, अडेल, अनिवार, अनिवार्य, अवश्य, दुःसाध्य, दुराधर्ष, दुर्धर्ष, दुःशासन, दुःशास्य.

INTRANSIENT, *a.* v. PERMANENT. अक्षणिक, चिरस्थायी, सुस्थिर.

INTRANSITIVE, *a.*—in grammar. अकर्मक.

INTRANSMUTABILITY, *n.* v. A. अविकार्यता *f.*

INTRANSMUTABLE, *a. incapable of change into another substance.* अविकार्य, विकाराशक्य, अपरिणामी, परिणामांतराक्षम, अवस्थांतराक्षम.

To INTRENCH, *v. a. break with hollows.* खळगे *m. pl.*-खांची *f. pl.*-&c. पाडणें, परिखाविशिष्ट-&c. करणें.

2 *fortify with a trench.* खंदक *m.*-&c. खाणणें *or* खणून मोरचा *m.* बांधणें-घालणें, परिखाश्रित करणें.

To INTRENCH, *v. n.* v. To ENCROACH. शीम *f.*-शीव *f.*-&c. दाबणें *or* दाबून येणें-जाणें, क्रांति *f.*-आक्रमण *n.* करणें.

INTRENCHMENT, *n. ditch and parapet.* खंदक मोरचा *m.*

Intrenchments. मोरचा *m.*

INTREPID, *a. fearless,* v. BOLD. छातीचा, छातीदार, दिलदार, धाडसी, निर्भय, अभीत, अज्ञातभय, धारिष्टवान्.

INTREPIDITY, *n.* v. A. छाती *f.* धाडस *n.* दिलदारी *f.* काळीज *n.* हिय्या *m.* धारिष्ट *n.* [धैर्यपूर्वक.

INTREPIDLY, *adv.* v. A. छातीकरून, हिय्या करून, छातीनें, &c.

INTRICACY, INTRICATENESS, *n.*v. A. गुंतागुंत *f.* गुंतागूत *f.* गुंताडा *m.* गुंतावळ *f.* सुताड गुताड *n.* गोंधवागोंधव *f.* गांदागोंद *f.* भानगड *f.* लपेट *f.* लपेटी *f.*

Intricacies and involution of a plot, poetical piece, &c. घडमोड *f.* घडामोड *f.* छक्के पंजे *m. pl.*

INTRICATE, *a. complicated, perplexed, involved.* गुंताड्याचा, गुंतागुंतीचा, गांठागांठीचा, अढ्यांचा, सुताडगुताडाचा, घोटाळ्याचा, भानगडीचा, लपेटी, लपेटीचा.

An i. case or affair. गोंध *f.* गुतवळ *f. n.* सुताडें *n.*

INTRIGUE, *n. complicated plot or scheme.* फंद *m.* कुलंगडें *n.* कारस्थान *n.* कंत्राण *n.* कंत्राट *n.* कंत्राड *n.* कचाट *n.* चक्रव्यूह *m.*

2 *complication or involution of a plot, &c.* घडमोड *f.* घडामोड *f.*

3 See AMOUR. [रचणें-करणें.

To INTRIGUE, *v. n. plot, &c.* कंत्राण *n.*-कारस्थान *m.*-फंद *m.*-&c.

INTRIGUER, *n.* INTRIGUING, *p. a.* v. V. कंत्राण-&c. रचणारा-करणारा, कंत्राणी, फंदी, कारस्थानी, कचाट्या.

INTRINSIC, INTRINSICAL, *a. inward, essential, not accidental,* v. NATURAL. जातीचा, आंगचा, मुळचा, स्वाभाविक *pop.* स्वभाविक *or* बीक, स्वभावसिद्ध, प्राकृतिक, सांसिद्धिक.

INTRINSICALLY, *adv.* v. V. *and* NATURALLY. जातीचा *decl.* जातीनें, स्वभावाचा *decl.* स्वभावेंकरून, जातितः, प्रकृतितः.

To INTRODUCE, *v. a. bring into use, notice, &c.* रुढींत-वहिवाटींत-लौकिकांत-प्रवृत्तींत-&c. आणणें, रूढि *f.*-प्रवृत्ति *f.*-प्रचार *m.*-&c. पाडणें-करणें *g. of o.* काढणें, स्थापणें, चालू-प्रवृत्त-&c. करणें.

2 (to the presence or acquaintance of). भेट *f.*-मुलाखत *f.*-ओळख *f.*-&c. करवणें-करून देणें, भेटवणें, रुजू करणें.

3 *cause to enter.* शिरवणें, शिरकवणें, घालणें, प्रवेश *m.*-&c. करवणें *g. of o.* प्रविष्ट-&c. करणें.

4 *make first mention of.* उद्दू *m.* काढणें *g. of o.*

INTRODUCED, *p.* v. V. 1. चालू केलेला, प्रवृत्त केलेला, स्थापलेला, काढलेला, &c. प्रवृत्त, प्रवर्त्तित.

3 शिरवलेला, शिरकवलेला, &c. निविष्ट, प्रविष्ट.

INTRODUCTION, *n.* v. V. 1.—*act.* वहिवाटींत आणणें *n.* काढणें *n.* स्थापणें *n.* &c. स्थापन *n.* स्थापना *f.* प्रवर्त्तन *n.*—*state.* प्रवृत्ति *f.* प्रसिद्धि *f.* प्रचार *m.*

2—*act.* भेटवणें *n.* भेट करून देणें *n.* &c.

Letter of i. भेटीची चिठ्ठी *f.* ओळखीची चिठ्ठी *f.* भलावण *f.*

3—*act.* शिरवणें *n.* शिरकवणें *n.* &c.

I. *preface, &c.* प्रस्तावना *f.* प्रस्तावन *n.* उपोद्घात *m.* उपन्यास *m.* पूर्वांग *n.* परिभाषा *f.*

INTRODUCTIVE, *a. serving to introduce, being preparatory to.* प्रवेश-निवेश-प्रवृत्ति-&c. साधक, प्रवेशमार्गसाधक.

INTRODUCTORY, *a. preliminary, prefatory.* प्रस्तावनेचा, उपोद्घाताचा, &c. प्रस्तावनारूप, उपोद्घातरूप.

INTROGRESSION, *n. entrance.* प्रवेश *m.* निवेश *m.*

INTROMISSION, *n.* v. V. आंतसोडणें *n.* &c. निवेशकरण *n.*

To INTROMIT, *v. a. let in, admit, be the medium of entrance.* आंतसोडणें, येऊं देणें, निवेशन *n.*-प्रवेशन *n.*-&c. करणें *g. of o.* प्रवेशद्वार *n.*-प्रवेशसाधन *n.* असणें.

To INTROMIT, *v. a.* See To MEDDLE.

INTROSPECTION, *n. looking within.* अंतरवलोकन *n.* अंतर्दर्शन *n.* अंतर्दृष्टि *f.* [अंतर्निष्ठ.

INTROSPECTIVE, *a.* v. N. अंतर्दृष्टीचा, अंतर्मुख, अंतर्दृष्टि, अंतर्दर्शी,

To INTROVERT, *v. a. turn inwards.* आंत-आंतल्याकडे-&c. फिरवणें-करणें, अंतर्मुख करणें.

To INTRUDE, *v. n. enter without invitation, permission, or right.* न बोलावतां येणें-जाणें-शिरणें-&c. कामावांचून-सत्तेवांचून-&c. येणें जाणें-शिरणें-&c. घुसणें, घुसडणें, अनधिकार पूर्वक प्रवेश *m.*-असत्ताकागमन *n.*-&c. करणें.

To INTRUDE, *v. a. force in without invitation or right.* कामावांचून-सत्तेवांचून-बळेंच-&c. शिरवणें-शिरकवणें-पदरीं घालणें-प्रविष्ट करणें, खुपसणें. [लेला.

INTRUDED, *p.* v. V. A. बळेंच-&c. घातलेला-शिरवलेला-&c. खुपस-

INTRUDER, *n.* INTRUSIVE, *a.* v. V. N. न बोलावतां येणारा-आलेला-&c. घुसणारा, घुशा, अनधिकारी, आगंतुक, अनाहूतागंता.

v. V. A. बळेंच घालणारा-शिरवणारा.

INTRUSION, *n.*v.V.N.—*act.* बोलावल्यावांचून येणें*n.*-जाणें*n.*-शिरणें*n.*-&c. घुसणें*n.* घुसडणें*n.* अनधिकारपूर्वक प्रवेश*m.* असत्ताकागमन*n.* अनाहूतागमन*n.*

v. V. A.—*act.* बळेंच घालणें*n.* सत्तेवांचून शिरवणें*n.* &c.

To INTRUST, *v. a. deliver in trust,* v. To COMMIT. सोपणें, ओपणें, हवालणें, विश्वासणें, पात्यवणें.

2 See To TRUST.

INTUITION, *n. instantaneous knowledge or perception.* साहजिकज्ञान*n.* सहजोपलब्धज्ञान*n.* प्रमाणनिरपेक्षज्ञान*n.* तात्कालिकज्ञान*n.* अंतर्ज्ञान*n.*

INTUITIVE, *a. received or seen without arguments.* पाहतांच

कळायाजोगा-कळून यायाजोगा, तेव्हांच कळायाजोगा-&c. प्रमाणनिरपेक्षज्ञेय, सहजज्ञेय, अंतर्ज्ञानाचा.

2 *seeing clearly, seeing without arguments.* पाहतांच जाणणारा, सहजज्ञ, अयत्नज्ञ, प्रमाणनिरपेक्षज्ञ, अंतर्ज्ञानी, अंतर्ज्ञानाचा.

INTUITIVELY, *adv.* v. A. अंतर्ज्ञानानें, तेव्हांच, सहजच.

INTUMESCENCE, INTUMESCENCY, INTURGESCENCE, *n.* v. SWELLING. सूज *f.* शोथ*m.* शोफ*m.* सुमार*m.* आध्मान*n.*

To INTWINE, *v.a. twine or twist together.* गुंफणें, विणणें, गांथणें.

INUENDO. See INNUENDO.

INUNCTION, *n.—act.* v. ANOINTING. माखणें*n.* उटणें*n.* अभ्यंग*m.* अभ्यंजन*n.—state.* अभ्यंग*m.* माखलेलेपणा*m.*

Ablution after i. अभ्यंगस्नान*n.* [हूं घालणें.

To wash (children, &c.). after i. न्हाण*n.* घालणें, ना-

To INUNDATE, *v. a. overflow, deluge.* बुडवणें, जलमय-जलप्लुत-जलप्लावित-जलव्याप्त-&c. करणें, जलप्रलय*m.*-जलप्लावन*n.*-&c. करणें *g. of o.*

2 fig. *fill with an overflowing abundance.* बुडवणें, रेलचेल *f.* -समृद्धि *f.*-&c. करणें *with the locative of o. and g. of s.*

INUNDATED, *p.* v. V. बुडवलेला, जलमय केलेला, &c. जलमय, जलप्लुत, जलप्लावित.

INUNDATION, *n. overflow of water.* जलप्रलय*m.* जलप्लाव *m.* जलप्लावन*n.* प्रलय*m.*

Partial or transitory i. खंडप्रलय*m.*

INURBANITY. See RUDENESS.

To INURE, *v. a. habituate, accustom, harden by use.* सवईंत-घसवटींत-&c. आणणें, घसवटीखालीं-सवईखालीं-&c. पाडणें, सवईचा-घसवटीचा-&c. करणें, घटवणें, वळसावणें, रव्हाटवणें, रांववणें, वहिवाटणें, वहिवाटवणें, निरडणें *or* निरढणें, दळवटणें, अभ्यस्त करणें.

To be or get inured. घटणें, घसवटणें, मुरणें, निरडणें *or* निरढणें, राबणें, दळवटणें.

INURED, *p.* v. V. घसवटींत आणलेला- आलेला, सवईखालीं पाडलेला-पडलेला, राबलेला, घटलेला, घसवटलेला, वळसावलेला, &c. कडवा, अभ्यस्त.

INUTILITY, *n. uselessness.* अनुपयोग*m.* निरुपयोग*m.* अनुपयोगिता *f.* निरुपयोगिता *f.* निरर्थकत्व*n.* वैयर्थ्य*n.*

INUTTERABLE, *a. inexpressible.* अवाच्य, अवचनीय, अनिर्वचनीय, अनुच्चारणीय, अनुच्चार्य.

To INVADE, *v. a. assail, assault,* v. To ATTACK. चालून-चढूनजाणें-येणें *with* वर *of o.* चढ*m.*-चढाई*f.*-चढाव*m.*-चाल *f.* करणें *with* वर *of o.*

2 (a country). धाड *f.* घालणें-मारणें *with* वर *of o.* दौड *f.* -स्वारी *f.*-चाल*f.*-चढाई *f.*-&c. करणें *with* वर *of o.* चढून-चालून येणें-जाणें *with* वर *of o.* आक्रमणें, आक्रमण*n.* करणें, आक्रांत करणें.

INVADER, *n.* INVADING, *p. a.* v. V. 1. चालून येणारा-जाणारा, चढून येणारा-जाणारा, &c.

2 धाड घालणारा, दौड करणारा, स्वारी करणारा, &c.आक्रमण कर्त्ता.

INVALID, *a. of no force or cogency,* v. WEAK. निर्जीव, निर्बल, निस्तेज, अप्रमाण.

2 *void, null.* अनुपयोगी, निरुपयोगी, पोकळ, व्यर्थ.

INVALID, *n. sickly person.* रोगाळा, रोगेला, रोग्या, रोगाड्या, कुरणेकरी, कुरण्या.

2 *worn out soldier, &c.* जायां झालेला शिपाई *m.*-खलाशी *m.*

To INVALIDATE, *v. a. render of no force or effect,* v. To ANNUL, To WEAKEN. निर्बल- निर्जीव-पोकळ -व्यर्थ-रद्द-&c. करणें, माजी पाडणें, अप्रामाण्य *n.* आणणें.

INVALIDITY, *n.* v. A. 1. निर्बलता *f.* दुर्बलता *f.* &c. अप्रामाण्य*n.*

2 पोकळपणा *m.* पोकळी *f.* अप्रामाण्य *n.*

INVALUABLE, *a. inestimable.* बेकिम्मत, अमोलिक, अमोल, मोलाआगळा, किम्मती आगळा, अमूल्य, मूल्यातीत, अनर्घ.

INVARIABLE, *a. that does not vary or change.* स्थिर, सुस्थिर, नियत, फेरफारा निराळा, फेरफारा वेगळा, अचल, अचंचल, एकचंदाचा, एकसारखा, निर्विकार, निर्विकल्प.

INVARIABLENESS, *n.* v. A. स्थिरता *f.* सुस्थिरता *f.* सुस्थैर्य *n.* फेरफारा निराळेपणा *m.* &c.

INVARIABLY, *adv.* v. A. नित्यनियमानें *or* नेमानें, नियतनियमानें, एकसारखा *decl.*

INVASION, *n.* v. V. 1.—*act.* चालून येणें *n.* &c. चाल *f.* चढाई *f.* चढाव *m.* चढ *m.*

2—*act.* धाड घालणें *n.* दौड करणें *n.* &c. स्वारी *f.* चाल *f.* धाड *f.* चढाई *f.* चढाव *m.* चढ *m.* आक्रमण *n.* अधिक्रम *m.* अधिक्रमण *n.* क्रांति *f.* परचक्र *n.*

Ravages, &c. of an i. राजक्रांति *f.* राजक्रांत *n.* राजीक *n.* गनिमाई *f.* गल्मिाई *f.*

INVECTIVE, *n. railing speech or expression,* v. ABUSE. निंदा *f.* निंदोक्ति *f.* निर्भर्त्सन *n.* निर्भर्त्सना *f.* कुत्सा *f.* गर्हा *f.* परिभाषण *n.*

INVECTIVE, *a. abusive, railing,* v. N. निंदेचा, निंदात्मक, कुत्सात्मक, गर्हात्मक, निंदारूप.

To INVEIGH, *v. n. exclaim or rail against.* निंदा *f.*-निर्भर्त्सना *f.*-कुत्सा *f.*-गर्हा *f.*-&c. करणें *g. of o.* तोंड *n.* सोडणें-टाकणें *with* वर *of o.* नांवें बोंब *f.* मारणें, शंख *m.* करणें-रडणें *g. of o.*

To INVEIGLE, *v. a. entice, wheedle.* फुसलावणें, भुलताप *or* थाप *f.* देणें-घालणें *or* देऊन-&c. नेणें, मोह *m.*-भूल *f.*-भुरळ *f.*- भुरळें *n.*-भुलवण *f.*-&c. घालणें *or* घालून नेणें, तंतरणें.

INVEIGLER, *n.* INVEIGLING, *p. a.* v. V. फुसलावणारा, &c. फुसलाव्या, भुलथाप्या, भुलथापेचा.

INVEIGLEMENT, INVEIGLING, *n.* v. V. फुसलावणें *n.* &c. फुसलावणी *f.* मोह *m.* प्रलोभन *n.*

To INVENT, *v. a. find out, contrive, devise.* काढणें, योजणें, कल्पिणें, नवा रचणें, योजणूक *f.*-योजना *f.* करणें *g. of o.* युक्ति *f.*-कल्पना *f.* काढणें *g. of o.*

2 *forge, fabricate, contrive falsely.* रचणें, पदरचा रचणें, कल्पिणें, बनावणें, खोटा करणें-रचणें, बगलेंतून-खाकेंतून-खिशांतून-&c. काढणें. [बोद्ध.

INVENTED, *p.* v. V. 1. काढलेला, योजलेला, &c. कल्पित, क्लृप्त,

2 रचलेला, बनावलेला, बगलेंतून काढलेला, &c.

INVENTING, *p. a.* INVENTOR, *n.* v. V. 1. काढणारा, योजणारा, &c. योजक, कल्पक, योजन-&c. कर्त्ता-कारी.

2 रचणारा, पदरचा रचणारा, बगलेंतून काढणारा, &c.

INVENTION, *n.* v. V. 1.—*act.* काढणें *n.* योजणें *n.* &c. योजणूक *f.* योजना *f.* योजन *n.* कल्पना *f.*

2—*act.* रचणें *n.* &c. रचणूक *f.*

Of one's own i. स्वकपोलकल्पित.

I. *inventive genius,* v. INGENUITY. कल्पना *f.* कल्पनाशक्ति *f.*

उपाय *m.* युक्ति *f.*

II. *matter invented.* नवी कल्पना *f.* नवी युक्ति *f.* कृति *f.*

Inventions and devices,—compreh. कळाकुसरी *f.pl.*

III. *matter forged or feigned.* कल्पना *f.* रचलेली गोष्ट *f.*

I. to deceive, injure, &c. v. FABRICATION. थोतांड*n.* बलांट *n.*

INVENTIVE, *a.* v. V. 1. *and* INGENIOUS. कल्पक, कल्पनाबाज, उपायी, युक्त्या, युक्तिमान्, युक्तिवान्, करामती.

INVENTOR, *n.* v. V. 1. काढणारा, योजणारा, युक्ति-&c. काढणारा.

INVENTORY, *n. list of articles or goods.* याद *f.* यादी *f.* झडती *f.* फेरिस्त*n.* टीप *f.*

INVERSE, *a. inverted, contrary.* उलटा, उफराटा, उलटा पुलटा, उलटा सुलटा, व्युत्क्रमाचा, व्यत्ययाचा, विपर्यस्त, व्यत्यस्त, व्यस्त.

INVERSELY, *adv.* v. A. उफराट्यानें, उफराट्या क्रमानें, व्युत्क्रमानें, विपर्यस्त क्रमानें, &c. मागेंपुढें.

INVERSION, *n.* v.V.—*act.* उलटणें*n.* उफराटणें*n.* उलटा करणें*n.* व्यस्तीकरण*n.*—*state.* उलटलेलेपणा*m.* उलटलेपणा*m.* व्यतिक्रम *m.* व्युत्क्रम*m.* व्यत्यय*m.* विपर्यय*m.* विपर्यास*m.*

To INVERT, *v. a. change the order or place of.* उलटणें, उफराटणें, उफराटा-उलटा-&c. करणें, मागेंपुढें करणें, क्रम*m.*-अनुक्रम*m.*-&c. फिरवणें *g. of o.* व्युत्क्रम *m.*-व्यतिक्रम*m.*-व्यत्यय*m.*-&c. करणें *g. of o.* [क्रांत.

INVERTED, *p.* v. V. उलटलेला, उलटा केलेला, &c. व्यतिक्रांत, व्यु-

INVERTEDLY, *adv. in a contrary order.* मागेंपुढें, व्युत्क्रमानें, व्यतिक्रमपूर्वक.

To INVEST, *v. a. dress, clothe.* नेसवणें, पांघरवणें, परिहित-परिवृत-प्रावृत-&c. करणें. [ल करणें.

2 (with an office, &c.) v. To INSTAL. वस्त्रें*n. pl.* देणें, बहा-

3 *clothe figuratively, indue, &c.* युक्त-विशिष्ट-संपन्न-&c. करणें.

4 (a fort, &c.) *enclose.* गराडा*m.*-घेरा *m.*-वेढा *m.*-&c. घालणें, वेष्टणें, गोट*m.* घालणें-देणें, परिवेष्टन*n.*-परिवेषण*n.* करणें *g. of o.* परिवेष्टित करणें.

5 (money) घालणें, घालून-गुंतवून-&c. ठेवणें.

INVESTIGABLE, *a.* v. V. शोधायाजोगा-जोगता-&c. विचारणीय, विचार्य, विचारयोग्य, विचारार्ह.

To INVESTIGATE, *v. a. search into, enquire into,* v. To EXAMINE. शोधणें, तपासणें, चौकसणें, चौकशी *f.*-तपास *m.*-&c. करणें *g. of o.* शोध*m.* घेणें-करणें-काढणें *g. of o.* सूड*m.*-सुदावा*m.*-सुगावा *m.*-छडा*m.*-छडणूक *f.* लावणें-काढणें *g. of o.* विचारण*n.*-विचारणा *f.* करणें *g. of o.*

INVESTIGATED, *p.* v. V. शोधलेला, तपासलेला, &c. विचारित, अन्वेषित, अन्विष्ट, परीक्षित.

INVESTIGATER, *n.* INVESTIGATING, *p. a.* v. V. शोधणारा, तपासणारा, &c. शोधक, विचारक, परीक्षक, अन्वेषक, अन्वेषी.

INVESTIGATION, *n.* v. V.—*act.* शोधणें, तपासणें *n.* &c. शोध*m.* चौकशी *or* सी *f.* तपास*m.* तपासणी *f.* तलाश*m.* सूड*m.* सुगावा*m.* सुदावा *m.* वाजपुशी *f.* वाजपूस *f.* तजवीज *f.* दर्याफ्त *f.* परीक्षा*f.* परीक्षण *n.* गवेषण*n.* अन्वेषण *n.* विचार*m.* विचारण*n.* विचारणा *f.* विचक्षणा *f.* खाराखिरी *or* खारासीर *f.*

INVESTIGATIVE, *a. curious in researches.* शोधक, परीक्षक, चौकस, चौकसदार.

INVESTING, INVESTITURE, *n.* v. V. 1.—*act.* नेसवणें *n.* &c.

2 वस्त्रें देणें *n.* पदस्थापन *n.* पदस्थापना *f.* प्रतिष्ठापन*n.* प्रतिष्ठा *f.*

4 गराडा घालणें *n.* वेष्टणें*n.* &c. परिवेष्टन *n.* परिवेषण *n.*

INVESTMENT, *n.* See INVESTING. 2.—of goods. साटें*n.* खेप*f.* खरीदी *f.* वांडें *n.*

A whole i. वांड्याचें वांडें *n.*

Deed of the purchase of an i. साटेखत *n.* साटेपत्र *n.*

To buy up the whole of an i. साटें *n.* मारणें-घेणें.

INVETERACY, INVETERATENESS, *n.* v. A. 1. जडलेलेपणा *m.* रेबलेलेपणा *m.* जुनाटपणा *m.* &c. बहुकालिकत्व *n.* बद्धमूलता *f.*

INVETERATE, *a. deep rooted, of long standing.* जडलेला, रेबलेला, जुनाट, जून, बहुतदिवसांचा, बहुतदिवसी, बहुकालिक, बद्धमूल, दृढमूल.

To become i. जडणें, जुनावणें, हाडीं खिळणें, जखडणें, रेबणें.

2 *having fixed habits.* सवईलागलेला.

INVIDIOUS, *a.* v. ENVIOUS. देखदुखी, मत्सरी, समत्सर.

2 *likely to cause envy or hatred.* मत्सर व्हायाजोगा, ईर्ष्याकर-जनक, ईर्ष्योत्पादक, मत्सरावह, द्वेषप्रद-जनक-&c.असूयाजनक, असूयोत्पादक. [समत्सर.

INVIDIOUSLY, *adv.* v. A. 1. मत्सरानें, हेव्यानें, &c. मत्सरपूर्वक,

2 मत्सर व्हायाजोगा *decl.* असूयाजनक बुद्धीनें, द्वेषजनक बुद्धीनें.

INVIDIOUSNESS, *n.* v. A. 1. मत्सर *m.* हेवा *m.* मात्सर्य *n.*

2 ईर्ष्याजनकत्व *n.* द्वेषजनकत्व *n.* असूयाजनकत्व *n.*

INVIGILANCE, *n. want of watchfulness.* गैरसावधपणा *m.* गैरहुशारी *f.* अनवधान *n.*

To INVIGORATE, *v. a. give vigor to,* v. To STRENGTHEN. पुष्टकरणें, पुष्टि *f.*-तेजोवृद्धि *f.*-बलवर्धन *n.*-पुष्टीकरण *n.*-&c. करणें *g. of o.* बळकटी *f.*-&c. आणणें.

INVIGORATED, *p.* v. V. पुष्टकेलेला, &c. वार्धितबल.

INVIGORATER, *n.* INVIGORATING, *p. a.* INVIGORANT, *a.* v. V. पुष्ट करणारा, पौष्टिक, पुष्टिकारक, धातुपुष्ट, बलवर्धक, तेजस्कर.

INVIGORATION, *n.* v. V.—*act.* पुष्ट करणें *n.* बलवर्द्धन *n.* तेजोवर्द्धन *n.* पुष्टीकरण *n.*—*state.* बलवृद्धि *f.* तेजोवृद्धि *f.*

INVINCIBILITY, INVINCIBLENESS, *n.* v. A. अजिंकपणा *m.* अजेयता *f.* अदम्यता *f.* अपराभाव्यता *f.* &c.

INVINCIBLE, *a. not to be conquered or overcome.* अजिंक, अजेय, दुर्जय, दुर्जेय, अजय्य, अदम्य, अपराभाव्य, दुर्निवार.

INVIOLABILITY, INVIOLABLENESS, *n.* v. V. 1. अबाध्यता *f.* अबाधनीयता *f.* अनपकार्यता *f.* &c.

2 अनुलंघ्यता *f.* अलंघनीयता *f.* अलंघ्यता *f.* अनतिक्रमणीयता*f.* अतिक्रमणानर्हता *f.*

3 अलंघनीयता *f.* अलंघ्यता *f.* भंगानर्हता *f.*

INVIOLABLE, *a. not to be injured or hurt.* अबाध्य, अबाधनीय, अनपकार्य, अपकारायोग्य, अपकारानर्ह, विकारायोग्य, विकारानर्ह.

2 *not to be profaned, or treated irreverently.* अनुल्लंघनीय, अनुल्लंघ्य, अलंघनीय, अलंघ्य, उल्लंघनायोग्य, अनुल्लंघ्यमर्याद, अनतिक्रमणीय, अतिक्रमणायोग्य, अतिक्रमणानर्ह.

3 *not to be broken.* मोडायास अयोग्य, भंगायोग्य, भंगानर्ह, अलंघनीय, अलंघ्य, अभेद्य, अभंग.

INVIOLATE, *a. unbroken, uninjured.* अभंग, अबाध, अबाधित, अभेदित, अलंघित, अभग्न.

INVIOUS, *a. impassable.* अगम्य, गमनाशक्य, गमनायोग्य, दुर्गम.

To INVISCATE, *v. a. daub with glue, &c.* चीक *m.*-&c. लावणें, चिकटावणें.

INVISIBILITY, INVISIBLENESS, *n.* v. A. अदृश्यता *f.* दृष्ट्यगोच-

रता *f.* परोक्षता *f.* अलोकनीयता *f.* अलक्ष्यता *f.* &c. अलोकन *a.* अदर्शन *n.*

INVISIBLE, *a. that cannot be seen.* अदृश्य, अनवलोकनीय, अवलोकनीय, अलक्ष्य, दुर्लक्ष्य, दुर्लक्ष, दुर्दर्श, दृष्ट्यगोचर, दृष्ट्यविषय, दर्शनातीत, परोक्ष, असाक्षात्, अचाक्षुष.

INVITATION, *a.* v. V. 1.—*act.* बोलावणें *n.* अवंतणें *n.* पाचारणें *n.* &c. आमंत्रण *n.* निमंत्रण *n.* पाचारण *n.* आकारण *n.* आह्वान *n.*

Countermand of an i. निमंत्रण *n.*

To INVITE, *v. a. bid, call, ask to come.* बोलावणें *or* बलावणें, सांगणें, आमंत्रणें, आकारणें, पाचारणें, अवंतणें, आवाहणें, बाहणें, निमंत्रणें, आमंत्रण *n.*-&c. करणें *g. of o.*

2 *draw to, tempt to come, allure.* मन *n.*-चित्त *n.*.&c.ओढणें-ओढून घेणें *g. of o.* ओढणें, ओढून घेणें, चित्ताकर्षण *n.*-प्रलोभन *n.*-&c. करणें *g. of o.*

INVITED, *p.* v. V. 1. बोलावलेला, पाचारलेला, &c. आमंत्रित, निमंत्रित, आकारित, आहूत.

The servant who summons to a feast the invited guests. बोलावणेकरी, आमंत्रण्या. [भित.

2 ओढलेला, ओढून घेतलेला, आकृष्टमनस्क, आकृष्टचित्त, प्रलो-

INVITER, *n.* INVITING, *p. a.* v. V. 1. बोलावणारा, पाचारणारा, &c. आमंत्रक, निमंत्रक, आमंत्रण-&c. कर्त्ता. [र्त्ता.

2 चित्त ओढणारा, मन ओढून घेणारा, चित्ताकर्षक, प्रलोभन क-

To INVOCATE. See To INVOKE.

INVOCATION, *n.* v. V. 1.—*act.* धांवा करणें *n.* धांवणें करणें *n.* नांव घेणें *n.* धांवा *m.* नामोच्चारण *n.* नामस्मरण *n.* आह्वान *n.* आवाहन *n.*

INVOICE, *n. list of merchandise consigned.* पाठविलेल्या मालाची याद *f.* बीजक *n.* थेटपट्टी *f.*

To INVOKE, *v. a. call on in prayer.* नांव *n.* घेणें *g. of o.* धांवा *m.*-धांवणें *n.* करणें-मारणें *g. of o.* स्मरणें, आवाहणें, नामस्मरण *n.*-नामोच्चारण *n.*-स्मरण *n.*-आवाहन *n.* करणें *g. of o.*

2 (blessings on) . v. To BLESS. दुवा *m.*-बरें *n.* मागणें.

INVOKED, *p.* v. V. 1. धांवा केलेला, &c. आवाहित, आहूत.

INVOKER, *n.* INVOKING, *p. a.* v. V. 1. नांव घेणारा, धांवा करणारा, &c. आवाहन-&c. कर्त्ता-कारी.

INVOLUNTARILY, *adv.* v. A. 2. स्वसंतोषावांचून, सुखसंतोषावांचून.

3 अनिच्छापूर्वक, इच्छानधीनतापूर्वक. [स्वैरगामिता *f.*

INVOLUNTARINESS, *n.* v. A. 1. अस्वाधीनता *f.* अस्वैरिता *f.* अ-

2 स्वसंतोषाभाव *m.* असंतोष *m.* संतोषाभाव *m.*

3 इच्छानधीनता *f.* इच्छाबाह्यता *f.* अनैच्छिकता *f.*

INVOLUNTARY, *a. not having will or choice.* अस्वाधीन, अस्वैरगामी, अस्वैरी, अस्वेच्छ, अनिच्छ, गैरमुखत्यार.

2 *not proceeding from choice ; unwilling.* स्वसंतोषावांचूनचा, सुखसंतोषावांचूनचा, गैरखुशीचा.

3 *independent of will or choice.* इच्छेबाहेरचा, इच्छानधीन, इच्छाबाह्य, अनैच्छिक, अस्वेच्छाजात. [&c. वेष्टन *n.*

INVOLUTION, *n.* v. V. 1.—*act.* गुंडाळणें *n.* वेष्टणें *n.* लपेटणें *n.*

2—*act.* ध्वनन *n.*

3—*act.* जोडणें *n.* मिळवणें *n.* &c.

4—*act.* घेणें *n.* ओढून घेणें *n.* आकलन *n.* [वागोंधव *f.*

6—*state,* v. INTRICACY. गुंता *m.* गुतागूत *f.* गुताडा *m.* गोंध-

I. of speech, &c. कडोविकडी *f. pl.* लपेट *f.* लपेटी *f.*

7 (in arithm. or algebra) घात *m.* घातकर्म *n.*

To INVOLVE, *v. a. inwrap, &c.* गुंडाळणें, वेष्टणें, लपेटणें, वेढणें, वेष्टन *n.* करणें *g. of o.*

2 v. To IMPLY. ध्वनन *n.*करणें *g.of o.*ध्वनित-गर्भित-&c.करणें.

3 *entwine, unite.* जोडणें, मिळवणें, गुंतवणें, बांधणें.

4 *take in, draw in, catch, conjoin.* घेणें, ओढून घेणें, बरोबर ओढून घेणें, माळेस-माळेंत धरणें-घेणें-मिळवणें-गुंतवणें-सांपडवणें, आकलन *n.* करणें *g. of o.* आकलित-&c. करणें.

5—in difficulties, &c. v. To ENTANGLE. गुंतवणें, गोवणें, गुंतागुंत *f.*-&c. करणें *g. of o.* गळा *m.* गोवणें *g. of o.*

6 *complicate, make intricate.* गुंतवणें, गुरपटणें *or* गुरफटणें, गळफटणें, गुंताडा *m.*-गुतागूत *f.*-गोंदागोंद *f.*-सुताडें *n.*-गुनबळ *f.*-&c. करणें-करून टाकणें *g. of o.*

7 (in arithmetic or algebra). घात *m.* देणें.

INVOLVED, *p.* v. V. 1. गुंडाळलेला, लपेटलेला, &c. वेष्टित.

2 ध्वनित, गर्भित, अर्थसिद्ध, आर्थिकार्थसिद्ध.

4 ओढून घेतलेला, सांपडवलेला, माळेंत मिळलेला, &c. आकलित

To be i. सांपडणें, गुंतणें.

5 गुंतवलेला, गोवलेला, &c.

To be i. सांपडणें.

6 *and* INTRICATE. गुरपटलेला, &c. गुंताड्याचा, गुंतागुंतीचा, लपेटी, लपेटीचा. [चा, अनासत्तिक.

—as a sentence or style. दूरान्वयाचा, दूरान्वयी, अनासत्ती-

Artfully involved & ambiguous. लपेटीचा.

INVULNERABILITY, INVULNERABLENESS, *n.* v. A. अभेद्यता *f.* अछेद्यता *f.* क्षतानर्हता *f.*

INVULNERABLE, *a. that cannot be wounded.* अभेद्यदेह, अछेद्यदेह, अभंगदेह, क्षतानर्ह, असंभाव्यक्षत, वज्रदेह, वज्रशरीर, वज्रांगी.

INWARD, *a. internal, interior, &c.* आंतल्याकडचा *or* ला, आंतल्याकडील, आंतला,आंतचा, आंतील,आंतल्या बाजूचा, आंतल्या धडचा, आंतर, आंतरिक, अंतरस्थ, अंतर्वर्त्ती.

Truth or purity in the inward parts. अंतःशौच *n.*

2—letters, papers, &c. आवक.

INWARD, INWARDS, *adv.* v. A. आंतल्याकडे, आंतल्याबाजूस, आंतल्याधडेस, आंत.

INWARDLY, *adv.* See INWARD. 2 *in the heart or mind.* आंत, मनांत, पोटांत, मनच्यामनीं, आंतून, अंतरंगीं.

INWARDS, *n. pl. viscera.* पोटांतले अवयव *m. pl.* पोटांतली अंगें *n. pl.* अंतडीं *n. pl.*

To INWEAVE, *v. a. intermix by weaving.* विणून मिळवणें-भरवणें-मिश्रित करणें, एकत्र विणणें.

To INWRAP, INWRAPPING. See To WRAP, &c.

To INWREATH, *v. a. surround as with a wreath.* माळ *f.* घालणें- बांधणें, मालावेष्टित-मालाविशिष्ट-&c. करणें.

INWROUGHT, *a. set with.* जडीत,खचित,भरित all used in comp.

IOTA. See JOT.

IRASCIBILITY, IRASCIBLENESS, *n.* v. A. रागिटपणा *m.* &c. तापडाई *f.* शीघ्रकोप *m.* शीघ्रकोपिता *f.* क्रोधशीलता *f.* पित्तप्रकृति *f.* पित्तस्वभाव *m.* क्रोधस्वभाव *m.* राग *m.* चिरड *f.* चीड *f.*

IRASCIBLE, *a. fiery, easily angered,* v. PASSIONATE. रागीट, तापट *or* ड, जलद, क्रोधशील, क्रोधी, क्रोधिष्ट, कोपिष्ट, कोपी, कोपट, संतापी, शीघ्रकोपी, तामस *pop.* तामसी, तामसगुणी, पित्तस्वभावाचा.

IRE, *n.* v. ANGER. क्रोधm. कोपm. संताप *m.*

IREFUL, *a.* v. ANGRY. क्रोधिष्ट, क्रोधी, क्रोधान्वित, संतप्त.

IRIS, *n.* v. RAINBOW. इंद्रधनुष्य *n.*

2—of the eye. बुबूळn. नेत्रतारकामंडलn. कनीनिकामंडल *n.* कनीनिकापरिधि *m.*

To IRK, *v. a. weary, give pain to.* दुःख *n.* वाटणें *g. of s. with in. con.* कंटाळा *m.* येणें *g. of s. with in. con.* अवघड-कठीण-&c. वाटणें *in. con.*

IRKSOME, *a. wearisome, tedious.* कंटाळा यायाजोगा, कंटाळवाणा, कंटाळ्याचा, त्रासावह, त्रासद, त्रासकारी-कारक-जनक-दायक-&c. दुःखद, क्लेशद.

IRKSOMENESS, *n.* v. A. कंटाळा *m.* त्रास *m.* उबग *m.*

IRON, *n.* लोखंड *n.* लोह *n.* आयस *n.*

Green sulphate of i. हिराकस *m.* धातुशेखर *m.* पुष्पकासीशm. नयनौषध *n.*

I. filings. लोखंडाचा कीसm. लोहचूर्ण *n.*

I. ore. बीडn. लोखंडाचा दगडm. लोखंडाचीमाती *f.*—the common pyritic i-ore. सुवर्णमुखी *f.* सुवर्णमाक्षिक *n.* विटमाक्षिक *n.*

Medicinal preparation from the rust of i. मंडूर *m.n.*

Mounted with i. (rings, tags, &c.) लोहांगी.

Red sulphate of i. धातुकासीस *n.*

Rust of i. किटणn. लोहकिट्टn. अयोमलn. लोहभस्म *n.*

Rust-eaten i. कीटn. किटणn.

Smelter of i. धवड *or* धावड, लोहकार.

Sulphate of i. हिराकसm.

Sulphuret of i. ताप्यn. पांशुकाशीसn.

Tipped or pointed with i. अयोमुख.

2 *instrument or utensil made of i.* लोखंडी डागिना *m.* लोखंडीसामान *n.*

Smoothing i. इस्त्री *f.*

3 irons; See CHAIN, FETTER.

IRON, *a.* लोखंडाचा, लोखंडी, धावडी, लोहमय, अयोमय, लौह, लोहात्मक, आयस.

I. boiler or vessel. लोखंडी *f.*

I. balance. लोहतुला *or* तुळा *f.*

I. work, *portion (of a building, machine, &c.) which consists of iron.* लोखंड काम *n.*

To IRON, *v. a. smooth with an i.* इस्त्री *f.* करणें.

2 *shackle.* बेडी *f.*-बेड्या *f. pl.*-शृंखला *f.*- सांखळदंड *m.*-&c. घालणें, शृंखलाबंधन *n.* करणें *g. of o.*

IRON-FISTED, *a.* वज्रमुष्टि.

IRON-FRAMED, *a.* वज्रदेह, वज्रशरीर.

IRON-HEARTED, *a.* वज्रहृदय, अयोहृदय.

IRON-MONGER, *n.* लोखंडी सामान विकणारा, लोखंडाचा बेपारी.

IRON-MOULD, *n.* लोखंडाचा डाग *m.* लोहचिन्हn.

IRON-WOOD, *n.* अंजनी *f.*

IRONIC, IRONICAL, *a. expressing irony.* विपरीत लक्षणेचा, उपरोधाचा, उपरोधी, उपरोधीक, औपरोधिक, उपरोधात्मक, साक्षेप.

IRONING, *n.* v. V. 1. इस्त्री *f.*

IRONY, *n. speech of which the meaning intended is contrary to the words.* उपरोध *m.* व्याजोक्ति *f.* आक्षेप *m.* विपरीतलक्षणा *f.*

2 *blame under the guise of praise.* निंदास्तुति *f.* निंदापरस्तुति *f.* व्याजस्तुति *f.* निंदाफलकस्तुतिवाक्य *n.* मृषावाद *m.* सोल्लुंठन *n.* *v.* बोल.

IRRADIANCE, IRRADIANCY, *n.* v. BRILLIANCE. दीप्ति *f.* कांति *f.* प्रभा *f.* द्युति *f.*

To IRRADIATE, *v. a.* v. To ENLIGHTEN. प्रकाश *m.*-प्रकाशन *n.*-द्योतन *n.*-&c. करणें *g. of o.* प्रकाशित-दीप्त-&c. करणें.

IRRADIATION, *n.* v. V.—*act.* प्रकाशन *n.* द्योतन *n.*

I. See SHINING.

IRRATIONAL, *a. void of reason.* अजाण, अज्ञान, ज्ञानावेगळा-निराळा, बुद्धीवेगळा-निराळा, बुद्धिहीन-शून्य-रहित-&c. ज्ञानशक्ति रहित-शून्य-&c. ज्ञानसाधनरहित-&c. अज्ञानपात्र, पशुवत्.

2 *contrary to reason, absurd, foolish.* मूर्खपणाचा, वेडेपणाचा, मूर्खत्वाचा, अज्ञानाचा, &c. असमंजस, असमर्पक, असंबद्ध, अयुक्तिक, युक्त्यसिद्ध, युक्तिविरुद्ध, अयुक्त, बुद्धिविपर्यासाचा.

An. i. quantity, *a surd.* करणी *f.* करणीपद *n.*

IRRATIONALLY, *adv.* v. A. 2. मूर्खपणानें, वेडेपणानें, असमंजसपणानें, &c. युक्तिविरुद्ध, पशुवत्.

IRRATIONALITY, *n.* v. A. 1. अज्ञान *n.* ज्ञानराहित्य *n.* बुद्ध्यभाव *m.* ज्ञानशक्तिराहित्य *n.*

IRRECLAIMABLE, *a. not to be recovered from vice.* मार्गावर आणायास अशक्य, हातांतून गेलेला-सुटलेला, माणसांतून उठलेला, उपदेशबाह्य, दुष्कर्मापरावर्त्तनीय.

IRRECONCILABLE, *a. not to be brought back to amity,* v. IMPLACABLE. असमजुती *or* त्या, असमजुतीचा, अशमनीय, अशाम्य, शमनाशक्य, अशक्यशम.

2 *that cannot be made to agree,* v. INCONSISTENT. मिलाफ करण्यास अशक्य, बेबनावाचा, असंगत, परस्परविरुद्ध, असंभावनीय, असंभाव्य.

IRRECONCILABLENESS, *n.* v. A. 2. *and* INCONSISTENCY. परस्परविरोध *m.*

IRRECOVERABLE, *a. not to be regained.* फिरून हातास लागायाजोगा नाहीं, हातांतून पारगेलेला, नमिळायाचे वाटेनें गेलेला, गेलागतलेला, पुनरप्राप्य, अपुनःप्राप्य, पुनरलभ्य, अपुनर्लभ्य, असमाहार्य.

2 *not to be remedied,* v. IRREMEDIABLE. उपाया बाहेरचा, निरुपाय.

IRRECOVERABLENSS, *n.* v. A. 1. पुनरप्राप्यता *f.* पुनरलभ्यता *f.* असमाहार्यता *f.*

IRREFRAGABLE, IRREFUTABLE, *a. that cannot be refuted or disproved.* खंडन करायास अशक्य, अखंडनीय, खंडनाशक्य, खंडनायोग्य, समाधानाशक्य, अप्रतिसमाधेय, असमाधेय, अपरिहार्य, अनिवार्य, दुरुद्धर, वज्रप्रमाण.

IRREFRAGABLENESS, IRREFUTABLENESS, *n.* v. A. अखंडनीयता *f.* खंडनाशक्यता *f.* &c.

IRREGULAR, *a. not according to rule, &c.* बेकायद्याचा, कायद्याबाहेरचा, बेशिस्त, गैरशिस्त, गैररितीचा, गैरचालीचा, गैरमार्गाचा, अशास्त्र, अविधि, अवैध, विधिभंजक, विधिहीन, विधिविरुद्ध, अयथाशास्त्र, अयथाविधि, अयथामार्ग, उत्सूत्र, अनृजु, अनाचारिक.

2 *immethodical.* डावखुरा, अक्रमिक, क्रमशून्य-रहित-&c. क्रमबाह्य, उच्छृंखल.

3 *deviating from the rules of moral rectitude.* अनाचारी, अमार्गी, असन्मार्गी, आडमार्गी, आडवाट्या, अशिस्त, गैरचालीचा, गैरमार्गाचा, &c. विपथगामी, अपथगामी, अपथवर्त्ती, अन्यथाचारी, अन्यथाकारी, आचारवर्जित.

4 *uneven,unequal.* उंचनीच, उंचसखल, असम, विषम.
5 (troops)निराळ्या कायद्याचा.
6—in grammar. व्यभिचारी.

IRREGULARITY, *n.* v. A. 1. बेशिस्तपणा *m.* गैरशिस्तपणा *m.* गैरशिस्त *f.* बेकैद *f.* अशास्त्रता *f.* अविधिता *f.* अवैधत्व *n.* &c. अविधान *n.* अविधि *m.* व्यभिचार *m.* अपथ *m.* अमार्ग *m.* व्यतिक्रम *m.* उत्क्रम *m.* नियमातिक्रम *m.* नियमोल्लंघन *n.*
An i. in diet or regimen. कुपथ्य *n.* अपथ्य *n.*
2 अक्रम *m.* उत्क्रम *m.* व्यतिक्रम *m.* क्रमाभाव *m.* व्यत्यास *m.* अव्यवस्था *f.* अन्याय *m.*
3 अनाचार *m.* अनाचरण *n.* गैरचाल *f.* गैरवर्त्तणूक *f.* कुपथ *m.* अपथ *m.* कुपथगमन *n.* विपथगमन *n.* [षम्य *n.*
4 उंचनीचपणा *m.* उंचसखलपणा *m.* असमता *f.* विषमता *f.* बे-

IRREGULARLY, *adv.* v. A. 1. बेकायदा, कायदासोडून, गैररितीनें, गैरमार्गानें, &c. विधिभंगकरून, अयथाशास्त्र, अयथाविधि, &c. अविधानतः.
2 क्रमसोडून, क्रमावांचून, &c.

IRRELATIVE, *a. without relation or connection.* असंबंधी, निःसंबंध, असंग, निस्संग, संबंधरहित, सुटा.

IRRELEVANCY, *n.* v. A. अप्रासंगिकत्व *n.* प्रसंगबाह्यता *f.* अप्रस्तुतता *f.* &c. अप्रसंग *m.* अनन्वय *m.* अन्वयाभाव *m.* संबंधाभाव *m.*

IRRELEVANT, *a. not applicable or pertinent.* प्रसंगाबाहेरचा or ला, अप्रस्तुत, अप्रकृत, अप्रासंगिक, अप्रसक्त, अप्राकरणिक, प्रसंगबाह्य, अनन्वित, असंगत, अन्योविन्य, इकडचातिकडचा.
I. discourse or matter. अकडंतिकडं *n.* इधरतिधर *n.* आडकथा *f.* आडरान *n.* फगरूड *n.* फगाड *m.* ढांचेंढूं or ढांचेंढूंचें *n.*

IRRELEVANTLY, *adv.* v. A. संबंध-अन्वय-&c. सुटून-सोडून, संबंधावांचून, &c. अकडंतिकडं, इधरतिधर, ढांचेंढूं or ढांचेंढूंचें, अन्योविन्य. [पायहीन.

IRRELIEVABLE, *a.* v. IRREMEDIABLE. निरुपाय, निरुपायाचा, उ-

IRRELIGION, *n. impiety.* अधर्म *m.* धर्मलंडाई *f.* देवलंडाई *f.* कर्मलंडाई *f.* भ्रष्टपणा *m.* अनाचार *m.* भ्रष्टाचार*m.* दुराचार *m.* कर्मभ्रष्टता *f.* धर्मलोप *m.*

IRRELIGIOUS, *a. impious.* अधर्मी, अधार्मिक, धर्मलंड, देवलंड, कर्मलंड, धर्मलंडाईचा, देवलंडाईचा, &c. अनाचारी, भ्रष्टाचारी, दुराचारी, भ्रष्टाचाराचा, &c. कर्मभ्रष्ट, आचारभ्रष्ट, देवाधर्मावेगळा-निराळा, त्यक्तधर्म.

IRREMEABLE, *a. not admitting return.* अपुनरागम्य, परावृत्त्यशक्य, अपरावृत्तीचा, अपुनरावृत्तीचा.

IRREMEDIABLE, *a. admitting of no remedy.* निरुपाय, निरुपायाचा, अनुपाय, उपायहीन-शून्य-&c. उपायातीत, उपायाबाहेरचा, बेइलाज, बेइलाजाचा, बिनतोड, अपरिहार्य, परिहाराशक्य, उपायाशक्य, प्रतीकाराशक्य, अप्रतीकार्य, अशक्यप्रतीकार, दुरत्यय.

IRREMEDIABLENESS, *n.* v. A. निरुपाय *m.* नाइलाज *m.* बेइलाज *m.* निरुपायता *f.* उपायराहित्य *n.*

IRREMISSIBLE. See UNPARDONABLE.

IRREMOVABLE, *a. that cannot be removed.* अपरिहार्य, परिहाराशक्य, निस्सारणाशक्य, दुरुद्धर, अचल, स्थिर, स्थायी.

IRREPARABLE, *a. that cannot be repaired or mended,* v. IRREMEDIABLE. सुधारायास अशक्य, सुधारायाजोगा-जोगता-&c. नाहीं, बेइलाजाचा.
2 See IRRECOVERABLE.

IRREPREHENSIBLE, *a.* v. BLAMELESS. निर्दोष, अदूष्य, अदूषणीय, अनिंद्य, दोषशून्य, निर्बाध, अदोषपात्र.

IRREPRESSIBLE, *a.* v. IRRESTRAINABLE. आवरतांयेईनासा, अटोपतांयेईनासा, अनावर, अपरिहार्य.

IRREPROACHABLE, *a.* v. BLAMELESS. अनिंद्य, अनिंदनीय, अदूष्य, निर्दोष, निर्बाध, निष्कलंक, अवाच्य, अपरिवाद्य, परिवादानर्ह, अनपवाद्य.

IRREPROVABLE, *a.* v. BLAMELESS. अनिंद्य, अदूष्य, अदूषणीय, दूषणायोग्य, दूषणानर्ह, निर्दोष, बिनठपक्याचा.

IRRESISTANCE, *n. non-resistance.* अनिवारण *n.* अवारण *n.* निवारणाभाव *m.* अप्रतीकार *m.*

IRRESISTIBILITY, IRRESISTIBLENESS, *n.* v. A. अप्रतीकार्यता *f.* प्रतीकाराशक्यता *f.* अनिवार्यता *f.* &c.

IRRESISTIBLE, *a. resistless.* अप्रतीकार्य, प्रतीकाराशक्य, अनिवार्य, अनिवार, निवारणाशक्य, वारणाशक्य, दुर्वार, असंहार्य, अबाधित.

IRRESOLUBLE, See INDISSOLUBLE.

IRRESOLUTE, *a. not firm or resolute, wavering.* मनाचा चंचल, चंचल मनाचा, धरसोड्या, धरसोडीचा, अधीर, अदृढबुद्धि, अस्थिरबुद्धि, अस्थिर मनस्क, अस्थिरचित्त, चंचलवृत्ति, अधैर्य, फुटकेमनाचा.

IRRESOLUTELY, *adv.* v. A. धरूनसोडून, धरसोडकरून, धरसोडीनें, अधैर्यपूर्वक, अस्थैर्यपूर्वक, &c.

IRRESOLUTION, *n. want of firmness of mind.* धरसोड *f.* अधैर्य*n.* अधीरता *f.* चंचलबुद्धि *f.* चित्तचांचल्य*n.*अस्थैर्य *n.* अस्थिरबुद्धि *f.*

IRRESPECTIVE, *a. not regarding circumstances.* अनपेक्ष, निरपेक्ष, अन्यानपेक्ष, अपेक्षाहीन.

IRRESPECTIVELY, *adv.* v. A. अपेक्षेवांचून, निरपेक्ष, अनपेक्ष.

IRRESPONSIBILITY, *n.* v. A. पृच्छानर्हता *f.* प्रश्नायोग्यता *f.* पृच्छानधीनता *f.*

IRRESPONSIBLE, *a. not answerable for consequence.* बिनमोसब्याचा, बिनमोसबी, पृच्छानर्ह, प्रश्नायोग्य, पृच्छानधीन.

IRRESTRAINABLE, *a. not to be kept back.* आवरतांयेईनासा, अटोपतां येईनासा, अनावर, अनिवार्य, निवारणाशक्य,अनिवार, अनियम्य, अवकळ,अपरिहार्य,दुर्निवार, दुर्वार, दुर्निग्रह, दुराकलनीय.

IRRETENTIVE, *a. not apt to retain.* धारणाशक्तिहीन-रहित-&c. धारणाहीन-रहित-&c. अधारक, अधारणापटु. [अनुपाय.

IRRETRIEVABLE, *a.* v. IRREMEDIABLE. निरुपाय, निरुपायाचा,
2 v. IRRECOVERABLE. अपुनःप्राप्य, पुनराप्राप्य.

IRREVERENCE, *n. want of respect or veneration,* v. DISRESPECT. अनादर *m.* अपमान *m.* अवज्ञा *f.* अनादरबुद्धि *f.* अपमानबुद्धि *f.*

IRREVERENT, *a. wanting in reverence,* v. DISRESPECTFUL. अनादराचा, अनादरबुद्धीचा, अनादरी, अनादरकर्त्ता-कारी, अनादरबुद्धि, अपमानकर्त्ता-कारी-&c. अवज्ञाकारी. [दरबुद्धीनें.

IRREVERENTLY, *adv.* v. A. अपमानानें, &c. अनादरपूर्वक, &c. अना-

IRREVERSIBLE, *a. that cannot be altered or repealed.* फिरवायास अशक्य-&c. रद्दकरायाजोगानाहीं, अपरावर्त्तनीय, अपरावर्त्त्य, अनिवर्त्तनीय, अनिवर्त्त्य, परावर्त्तनाशक्य, परावृत्त्यनर्ह, लोपाशक्य, अलोप्य, अखंड्य, अटळ.

IRREVERSIBLENESS, *n.* v. A. अपरावर्त्तनीयता *f.* परावर्त्तनाशक्यता *f.*

IRREVERSIBLY, *adv.* v. A. फिरवतांयेईनासा*decl.* उलटतांयेईनासा*decl.*

IRREVOCABLE, *a. not to be revoked or repealed,* v. IRREVERSI-

BLE. अपरावर्त्तनीय, अपरावर्त्य, अलोप्य.

To IRRIGATE, *v. a. water by causing a stream to flow over.* पाटानें पाणी *n.* देणें, पाटाचें पाणी *n.*-दंडाचें पाणी *n.* देणें, पाट*m.*-दंड *m.*-&c. सोडणें, पन्हळीचें शिंपणें *n.*-प्रणालिकासिंचन *n.* करणें.
2 See To WATER, To WET.

IRRIGATION, *n.* v. V. 1.—*act.* पाट सोडणें *n.* पाटाचें पाणी देणें*n.* पन्हळीचें शिंपणें *n.* प्रणालिकासिंचन *n.*
By i. (raised, &c.). आडव्यापाण्यानें.
Grain raised by i. in the hot weather. गिमवस*f.* गिमवा*m.*
Raised by i. आडव्यापाण्याचा, पाणभरणीचा, पाणभरीत, पाणभरिताचा.
Requiring i.—grain. पाणभरा *or* पाणीभरा.
Scuttle used in i. झेला *m.*
Water (of rivers, tanks or wells) employed in i. आडवें पाणी *n.*

IRRISION, *n.* v. RIDICULE. उपहास *m.*

IRRITABILITY, *n.* v. A. 1. रागिटपणा *m.* &c. क्रोधशीलता *f.* पित्तप्रकृति *f.* क्रोधस्वभाव *m.* शीघ्रकोपित्व *n.* चिरड *f.* चीढ *f.*

IRRITABLE, *a. easily angered,* v. PASSIONATE. कोपी, कोपिष्ट, शीघ्रकोपी, चिरडखोर, चिरडीखोर, चिडखोर, चिडचिड्या, चिडरा, कोरचंद, काविरडा.
2—a wounded limb, &c. झुळझुळा.

IRRITANT. See IRRITATING.

To IRRITATE, *v. a. provoke, &c.* v. To ANGER. खिजवणें *or* खिजावणें, चितावणें, चिडवणें, कातावणें, चिढीस आणणें-देणें-नेणें, खवंडाळी *f.* करणें *g. of o.*
2 (a sore, &c.). चिडवणें, आग *f.* करणें *g. of o.* झुळझुळवणें, संतापवणें, संतप्त-&c. करणें.

IRRITATED, *p.* v. V. 1. खिजवलेला, चिडवलेला, चिढीस आणलेला-आलेला, &c.

IRRITATER, *n.* IRRITATING, *p. a.* v. V. 1. खिजवणारा, चिडवणारा, &c. खिजवणीचा, चिडवणुकीचा, चिडवणीचा, खवंडाळीचा.
2 चिडवणारा, संतापवणारा, &c. संतापक, दाहकारक.

IRRITATION, *n.* v. V. 1.—*act.* खिजवणें *n.* चिडवणें *n.* &c. खिजवणी *f.* चिडवणी *f.* चिडवणूक *f.* खवंडाळी *f.*—*state.* चिरड *f.* चीढ *f.* चिणकारा *m.* संताप *m.* संतप्तता *f.* रागाचा आवेश *m.* क्रोधावेश *m.*
2 चिडवणें *n.* &c.—*state.* आग *f.* संताप *m.* दाह *m.*

IRRITATIVE. See INFLAMMATORY.

IRRUPTION, *n. a bursting in.* आंत पडणें *n.* आंत येणें *n.*
2—*hostile incursion.* दौड *f.* धाड *f.* कहात *f.*

ISCHURETIC, *n. that relieves ischury.* मूत्रावरोधनाशक-हारक.

ISCHURY, *n. stoppage of urine.* मूत्रावरोध *m.* मूत्रावष्टंभ *m.* विष्टंभ *m.* विबंध *m.* आनाह *m.*

ISH. With this particle as added to adjectives and as conveying the sense of *diminution,* correspond the affixes सर, सा, कट *or* गट, ट, स, (as कडसर bitter*ish*, मोठासा larg*ish* काळवट black*ish*, हिरवट green*ish*, खोलगट deep*ish*, पिवळट yellow*ish*, हिरवस raw*ish*,) and the prefixes (though these to *Sanscrit* words only) आ, ईषत् (as ओष्णम् warm*ish*, ईषदुष्ण warm*ish*, &c.). With *ish* as added to nouns, and as conveying the sense of *participation in* any quality or character, correspond the affixes टा, आ, का, गळ, (as चोरटा thiev*ish*, वेडा fool*ish*, बेडका fool*ish*, &c.).

ISLAND, ISLE. *n.* टापू *m.* बेट *n.* द्वीप *m. n.*—contemptuously. बेटाड *n.*
2 (in a river or inlet). जूं *n.* जुयटें *n.* जुवें *n.* ढेला *m.* [गड्डा *m.*

ISLAND, *a. belonging, &c. to an island.* बेटाचा, &c. द्वीप्य, द्वैप्य, द्वीपस्थ, द्वीपसंबंधी.

ISLANDER, *n.* बेटांतला राहणारा, बेटकरी, द्वीपवासी, द्वीपनिवासी, द्वीपी, द्वीप्य, द्वैप्य, द्वीपस्थ.

ISLET, *n. litle isle.* लहान बेट *n.* उपद्वीप *m. n.*

ISOCHRONAL, ISOCHRONOUS, *a. of equal duration.* समसंख्यकालिक, समसंख्यकाल, समकालिक, समानकालिक.

To ISOLATE *v. a. place by itself.* सुटा-बेगळा-&c. ठेवणें-करून ठेवणें.

ISOLATED, *p.* v. V. सुटा ठेवलेला, &c. सुटा, अलग, तुटक, बेगळा, निराळा, असंग, निस्संग, अनन्यलग्न, अनन्यसंयुक्त.

ISOLATION, *n.* v. V.—*state.* निराळेपणा*m.* बेगळेपणा*m.*

ISOSCELES, *a. having two equal legs.* समद्विपार्श्व.
An i. triangle. द्विसमत्रिभुज*m.*

ISRAELITE, *n.* इस्राएलाच्या वंशांतला मनुष्य*m.*

ISRAELITISH, *a.* इस्राएलाचा, इस्राएली.

ISSUE, *n. egress, passing out.* निकाल*m.* निस्सरण*n.* निर्याण*n.* बहिस्सरण*n.*
I. of blood. रक्तस्राव*m.*
2 *event, result, termination.* परिणाम*m.* निगम*m.* निर्गम*m.* गति *pop.* गत *f.* उतारा*m.* वासलात *or* द *f.*
Happy i. निर्गम*m.* सद्गति *pop.* सद्गत *f.* निर्गति *pop.* निर्गत *f.* परिणाम*m.* v. लाग *esp. with neg. con.*
3 *fontanel.* पोत *or* पोंत *or* पोंथ*m. f. n.*
4 *progeny.* संतान*n.* संतति *f.* बीज*n.* प्रजा *f.* अपत्य*n.*
5 (in a case at law) मुद्दा*m.*

To ISSUE, *v. n. pass or flow out.* निघणें, सुटणें, वाहणें, फुटणें, निर्गम*m.*-&c. होणें *g. of s.* निर्गत-&c. होणें.
2 *come out.* निघणें, बाहेर येणें-जाणें-पडणें.
3 *proceed from, be produced.* निघणें, उत्पन्न होणें, उपजणें, निपजणें, उगवणें, उद्भवणें.
4 *close, end, result in.* परिणाम*m.*-शेवट*m.*-अंत*m.*-पर्यवसान*n.*-&c. होणें *g. of s.*

To ISSUE, *v. a. send out, put into circulation.* चालू-&c. करणें, चलणीस काढणें, व्यवहारांत-देवघेवांत-देण्याघेण्यांत- &c. घालणें- आणणें.
2 *send out, deliver from authority.* करणें, देणें, फरमावणें, सादर करणें, प्रसिद्ध करणें.
3 *deliver for use, give out from store.* देणें, वांटणें.

ISSUELESS, *a.* v. CHILDLESS. असंतान, अप्रज, अनपत्य.

ISTHMUS, *n.* संयोगीभूमि *f.* लग*m. f.*

IT, *pro.* तें, हें.

ITS. त्याचा, ह्याचा.

ITCH, *n.*—the disease. खरूज *f.* खाज *f.* कंडू *f.* कंड *f.* पामा *f.* खर्जू *f.*
Dry i. सुकी खरूज *f.*
I. or scab of cattle. कथला*m.* कथली *f.* [जाई *f.*
Goddess worshipped by persons who have the i. खर-
Purulent or running i. ओली खरूज *f.* बेलखरूज *f.* लसीखरूज *f.* [होणें.
To have the hand stiff with the i. हाताचे लाडू*m. pl.*

2 *an itching.* खाजf. खाजव f. कंडू pop. कंड f. गुदगुदी f. झुळझूळ f. चिणचीण f.

Sudden and violent itching. खरजेचा खरकाm.-बळका m. खरखर f. खरखराm.

Violent & hot itching. घायकूत f. n. v. ये.

3 *eager desire, panting, thirsting after, impulse for, &c.* खाज f. कंडू f. कंडाm. सबसब f. खुरखुर f. intens. खुरखुराटm. खुदखुद f. खुटखुटी f. वळवळ f. झुळझूळ f.मुंगाm. सळकाm.चवm. चेवm. कढm. उकळी f. धाम f. धामाm. खुमखुम f.इष्कm. फुरणn.

To ITCH, *v. n.*v.N. 2. खाजणें, झुळझुळणें, गुदगुदणें, कंड f. खाणें, खाज f.-कंड f.-&c. सुटणें, खाज f. पडणें, खाज f. करणें imp. खरखर f. लागणें-येणें. [खाजरा.

That affects the throat with an itching sensation. 3 खवखवणें, खुरखुरणें, झुळझुळणें, वळवळणें, सळसळणें, खाज f.-&c. सुटणें in. con. नक्षत्रn. पडणें.

To i. to speak,—the tongue. लुवलुवणें or लवलवणें.

ITCHY, *a. affected with the itch.* खरजुडा, खरजुला, खरज्या, कंडू रोगी, पामी.

2 *prone to contract the i.* खरजुडा, खरजुला.

ITEM, *n. article, separate particular.* कलमn. रकम f. बाब f. बाबत f. प्रकरणn.

An extra i. खेरीजकलमn.

I. by item. रकमवार, रकमबंद.

2 *piece, article.* डागm. डागिणा or नाm.

Items. इलाखिलाm.

ITEM, *adv. also.* अथच, अपरं.

To ITERATE, *v.a. utter again,* v. To REPEAT. दुसऱ्यानें-फिरून -&c. बोलणें- सांगणें, पुनरुक्ति f. करणें g. of o.

2 *do again,* v. To REPEAT. दुसऱ्यानें-फिरून-&c. करणें, दुसारणें, दुणावणें, पुनःपुनः करणें. [पुनर्वचन n.

ITERATION, *n.* v. V. 1.—*act.* दुसऱ्यानें बोलणें n. &c. पुनरुक्ति f. 2—*act.* दुसारणें n. &c. दुसारणी f. पुनःकरण n. पुनरावृत्ति.

ITINERANT, *a. wandering, not settled.* फिरस्ता, फेरेकरी, फेरीदार, फेरीचा, फिरता.

ITINERANT, *n.* See the Adjective.

ITINERARY, *n. book of travels.* मार्गक्रमणलेख m. प्रवासवृत्तलेखm.

To ITINERATE, *v.n. travel from place to place.* गांवगांव m.-देश m.फिरणें, फिरणें, फेरी f. करणें, देशपर्यटन n.-देशभ्रमण n. करणें.

IVORY, *n.* हस्तिदंत m. गजदंत m.

IVORY, *a.* हस्तिदंताचा, हस्तिदंती.

IVY, *n.* एक लता विशेष आहे.

J.

J. This letter is represented by ज.

To JABBER, *v. n.* v. To PRATE. बचबच or बचाक्चां adv. बोलणें-करणें, बटबटणें, बकणें, जाबडणें, बडबडणें, अगडतगड n.-अगडबगड n. बोलणें.

JABBER, JABBERING, *n.* v. V.—*act.* बडबडणें n. &c. बडबड f. बटबट f. बकबक f. लवलव f.

JABBERER, *n.* JABBERING, *p. a.* v. V. बडबडणारा, &c. बडबड्या, बटबट्या, बकबक्या.

JACENT, *a. lying at length.* पडलेला, निजलेला.

JACK, *n.*—the tree. फणसm.निचूळ m. डगूळ m.—the fruit.फणसm. निचूळ m. महाफल n.—the seed. आंठल f.आंठीळ f. आंठोळी f.

End -piece of the fruit of the j. टेबळी f.

Fungus on the j.-tree. फणसचें or फणसांबें n. फणसांबा m.

Juice of the j.-fruit. मध m. f.

Lump of pulp of the j. गरा m.

Pulp of the fruit mashed and rolled out into a cake. फणसपोळी f. फणसाचा साठा m. फणसाचें साट n.

Seedless lump of the pulp of the j. fruit. चांपें n.

Shreds or filamentous portion around the pulp of the j. fruit. चार m. f. चिवर n. सांगूळ f.

Young unripe j. कुइरी or कुंवरी f. पारा m.

Two grand distinctions are made of this fruit, *viz.* कापा फणस (hard or firm jack), and बरका or रसाळ फणस (soft, flaccid, oozy, &c. jack): and to these is added a third, *viz.*सकल्या फणसexpressive of the middle quality.

JACKANAPES. See MONKEY, COXCOMB.

JACK-ASS, *n.* v. ASS. गाढव.

JACK OF THE WHEEL, *n.* जांतीण f.

JACK-PUDDING, *n.* v. BUFFOON. हंडीबाग, भांड.

JACKAL, *n.* कोल्हा m. (कोल्ही f. and without ref. to sex कोल्हें n.) जंबूक m. सृगाल or शृगाल m. n. (शृगाली f.) शिवा f.

Cry. of the j. कुई f. कुकी f. हूकf. कोल्हेहूक f. कोल्हेभूक f.

Old j. purveyor (as believed) to the tiger. भालू f. भलूकm.

JACKET, *n.* बंडी f. कुडती f. कुडतें n. डगलें n. चोळा m. कंचुक m.

JACONET, *n.* मलमलीचा प्रकार आहे.

JADE, *n. sorry horse, rip, &c.* घोडकें n. घोडकट n.

2 *sorry woman.* बायरूं n. रांडरूं n. सांडरूं n.

To JADE, *v. a.* v. To FATIGUE. श्रमवणें, शिणवणें, भागवणें, श्रमी-कष्टी-&c. करणें.

To JADE, *v.n.become wearied,* v.To TIRE. वेंगणें, काचावणें, काचणें, लंघणें, श्रमणें, रेंगळणें, गांड f. फुटणें g. of s.

JADED, *p.* v. V. A. श्रमवलेला, भागवलेला, &c. v. V. N. वेंगलेला, श्रमलेला, &c. लचलालबंगला, ग्लान.

JADEDNESS, *n.* v. P. खुरदमा m. खुरदा m. खुंदला m. आट m.आटा आट f. आटाघाट f. आटापिटा m. आटापटी f.आटापीट f.

To JAG, *v. a. notch, &c.* खाडी f. pl.-खांडे m. pl.-सड m. pl.-&c. पाडणें.

JAG, *n. notch, indentation.* खांड f. खांडा m. dim. खांडोरेंn. सड m. कातरा m. हीर m. [खरे m. pl.

Jags or indentations (as of a roughened sickle).

JAGGED, *p.* v. V. खांडे पाडलेला-पडलेला, &c. खांडींचा.

JAGHIRE, *n. grant of land from Government.* जाहगीर f.

Holder of a j. जाहगीरदार.

JAIL, *n. prison.* तुरुंग m. (from the Portug.) बंदिखाना m. कैदखाना m. बंदिशाळा f. बंधनागार n. कारागार n. कारागृह n.—in allusive, covert, or cant phraseol. बिन भाड्याचें घर n. ज्ञानमठ m. पंडितखाना m.

JAILER, *n.* तुरुंगावरचा अधिकारी m. बंदिखान्याचा-&c. नायक-हवालदार-कामगार-&c. कारागृहाधिपति, कारागृहाध्यक्ष.

JAKES, *n.* v. PRIVY. शेतखाना m. पायखाना m. शौचकूप m.

Cleaner of j. हलालखोर.

JALAP, *n.* एका प्रकारचा जुलाब आहे.

JAM, *n. conserve of fruits.* मुरंबा *or* मुरब्बा *m.*

To JAM, *v. a. squeeze, press.* चिरंगटणें, चेंगरणें, चिरडणें, बेचकुळींत धरणें-सांपडवणें, &c.

JAMB, *n.*—of a door. दारकस *f.* बाही *f.* सुळका *m.*

JAMMED, *p.* v. V. चिरंगटलेला, चेंगरलेला, बेचकुळींत धरलेला, &c.

To be j. दाटणें, बेचकुळींत सांपडणें.

To JANGLE, *v. n.* v. To WRANGLE. किलकिलणें, किलबिलणें, खटपटणें, कटकट *f.*-खटपट *f.*-कचकच *f.*-&c. करणें, *and, with in. con.* चालणें *g. of s.*

JANGLE, JANGLING, *n.* v. V.—*act.* किलकिलणें *n.* &c. कटकट *f.* खटपट *f.* कचकच *f.* कलकल *m. f.* (*intens.* कलकलाट *m.*) किलकील *f.* किलबील *f.* रसकस *f.*

JANITOR, *n.* v. DOOR-KEEPER. देवडीवाला, द्वारपाल, द्वाररक्षक.

JANTILY, *adv. gaily.* नटूनथटून, छानीनें, छानछुकीनें, गमज्यानें, कटावानें.

JANTINESS, *n.* v. A. छान *f.* छानछुकी *f.* कटाव *m.* [बाचा.

JANTY, *a. airy, showy, fine.* छानदार, छानीचा, छानछुकीचा, कटा-

JANUARY, *n.* इंग्रेजी सनाचा पहिला महिना *m.* पौषमाघ *m.*

To JAPAN, *v. a.* जपानच्या रीतीनें रोगण *n.* लावणें.

To JAR, *v. n. grate, &c.* करकरणें, करकर-कर्कश-&c. बाजणें, कर्कशशब्द *m.*-&c. करणें, नादावणें.

2 fig. *clash, interfere, be inconsistent.* विजोड-विलग-विसंगत-&c. असणें-पडणें, बेबनाव *m.*-&c. असणें *g. of s.* जम *m.*-जवा *m.*-जुगल *f.*-&c. न बसणें *g. of s.*

3 See To SQUABBLE, To QUARREL.

JAR, *n. jarring sound.* करकर *f.* कर्कशशब्द *m.*-नाद *m.*-&c.

2 *earthen vessel.* घडा *m.* मडकें *n. dim.* मडकूल *n.* कुंडी *f.* घागर *f.* घट *m.* कुंभ *m.* The common *jars* are बरणी *f.* माठ *m.* माथण *f.* मांद *f.* मांदण *f. n.* नांद *f.* कलसा *m.* कळसुली *f.* रांजण *n. dim.* रांजणी *f.*

JARGON, *n.* v. GIBBERISH. कानडें *n.* हेंगाडी-कोंगाडी-रांगडी-&c. बोली *f.* राक्षसी भाषा *f.* पिशाच भाषा *f.*

2 *barbarous mixture of languages.* खिचडी *f.* धेडगुजरी *f.*

JARGONIST, *n.* v. N. 2. धेडगुजऱ्या, मिश्रभाषी.

JASMINE, *n.* जाई *f.* जाती *f.*

Arabian j. मोगरी *f.*

American j. इष्कपेंच *m.*

Eared j. जुई *f.*

Yellow j. सोन जुई *f.* Some other kinds are कुंद *m.* j. multiflorum or pubescens. चमेली j. grandiflorum. मोगरा *m.*-बट मोगरा *m.*-मोगरी *f.*-मोगर *f.* j. zambac. मोतिया *or* मोतिया मोगरा *m.* कटिमोगरी *f.*

JASPER, *n.* एकमणी आहे.

Porphyritic j. किरमिजी *f.*

JAUNDICE, *n.* पांडु *pop.* पंडु *m.* पांडुरोग *m.* कामीण *f.* कामला *pop.* कामळ *f.* कावीण *f.* काबीळ *f.* कवळ *f. n.* हळद्या *m.*

Incipient j. पंडुछाया *f.*

JAUNDICED, *a. that has j.* पंडुरोगी, पांडुरोगग्रस्त-विशिष्ट-युक्त-&c.

JAUNT, *n. ramble,* v. EXCURSION. सहल *f.* सफर *f.* सैर *f.*

JAVELIN, *n. spear.* सैती *f.* बरची *f.* सांग *f.* भल्ली *f.* शक्ति *f.* शलाका *f.*

JAW, *n.* जबडा *or* जावडा *or* चावडा *m.* जांभाड *n.* जांभाडें *n.* दाभाड *n.* चाभाड *n.* दाढ *f.* हनु *f.* बचेळी *or* बच्याळी *or* बेचाळी *f. or* ळें *n.*—in cant or covert phraseol. दांताळपुरी *f.*

Articulation of the j. दांताची खीळ *f.*

The jaws. चव्हाळें *n.* टाळी *n.pl.* [भ *m.*

Locked j. दांतखिळी *or* खीळ *f.* v. बस, हनुग्रह *m.* हनुस्तं-

To lock one's j. (as by a charm). दाढ *f.* बांधणें.

2 *clatter, rattle, jabber,* v. PRATE. बडबड *f.* बकबक *f.* बकवा *m.* बटवट *f.* अगडतगड *n.* अगडबगड *n.*

To put in one's j. तोंड *n.* घालणें, मध्येंलबलब *or* लुबलब *adv.* बोलणें, आपलें घोडें *n.* ढकलणें.

To stop one's j. दाढ *f.* बांधणें.

To JAW, *v. n.* v. To PRATE. जाबडणें, बडबडणें, बटवटणें, तोंड *n. n.* करणें-वाजवणें.

JAW-TOOTH, *n.* दाढ *f.* दंष्ट्रा *f.*

JAY, *n.*—the blue j. *Coracias indica.* चाष *pop.* चास *m.* मणिकंठ *m.* नीलकंठ *m.*

2—*Gracula religiosa.* मयना *or* मैना *m.*

JEALOUS, *a. apprehensive of rivalship, impatient of another's success.* मत्सरी, समत्सर, मत्सराचा, सवतमत्सराचा, सापत्नभावाचा, &c. अन्यशुभद्वेषी, परोत्कर्षद्वेषी, परोत्कर्षासह, परोत्कर्षासूयक, परयशोसह, परोत्कर्षाशंकी, अन्यशुभाशंकी, वक्रदृष्टि.

2 *suspicious in love.* प्रीतीचा संशय आलेला, प्रेमविपर्यासशंकी, प्रीतिव्यत्ययाशंकी, प्रीतिव्यभिचाराशंकी, प्रेमसंशयी.—a husband of a wife, परपुरुषाशंकी, परपुरुषशंकित, जारशंकित.—a wife of a husband, परस्त्रीशंकित.

3 *careful or concerned for the honor of.* अभिमानी.

JEALOUSY, *n.* v. A. 1. मत्सर *m.* सवतमत्सर *m.* सापत्नभाव *m.* सापत्न्य *n.* अन्यशुभद्वेष *m.* परोत्कर्षद्वेष *m.* परोत्कर्षासहन *n.* परोत्कर्षासूया *f.* अन्यशुभाशंका *f.* परोत्कर्षाशंका *f.* वक्रदृष्टि *f.*

2 प्रीतीचा संशय *m.* प्रेमसंशय *m.* &c. प्रेमविपर्यासाशंका *f.* प्रीतिव्यत्ययाशंका *f.* प्रीतिव्यभिचाराशंका *f.*—of a husband respecting a wife, परपुरुषाशंका *f.* जारशंका *f.*— of a wife respecting a husband, परस्त्रीशंका *f.*

3 अभिमान *m.*

To JEER, *v. a. mock, deride,* v. To RIDICULE, To CONTEMN. उपहास *m.*-ठट्टा *f.*-खिक्या *or* खिख्या *f. pl.*-कुचविंध्या *f. pl.*-कुचाळी *f.*- उपाळी *f.*-ढवाळी *f.*-ढवाळकी *f.*-टवाळी *f.*-&c. करणें *g. of o.* उपहासणें.

JEER, JEERING, *n.* v. V.—*act.* उपहास *m.* ढवाळी *f.* ढवाळकी *f.* कुचविंध्या *f. pl.* कुचाळी *f.* टर *or* टेर *f.*

JEERER, *n.* JEERING, *p. a.* v. V. उपहास करणारा, &c. उपहासक, टवाळ, ढवाळ, ढवाळखोर. [पूर्वक, &c.

JEERINGLY, *adv.* उपहासानें, उपहास करून, टवाळीनें, &c. उपहास-

JEJUNE, *a. barren, dry, &c.* रुखा, रुक्ष, बेकस, भुकिस्त, भुकड, निर्जीव, नीरस, रसहीन-शून्य, हीनरस.

JEJUNENESS, *n.* v. A. रुखेपणा *m.* रुक्षता *f.* रौक्ष्य *n.* रसराहित्य *n.* रसाभाव *m.* नीरसता *f.*

JELLY, *n.*—of fruit. मुरब्बा *m.* फलपाक *m.*

2—of flesh. मांसघननिष्काथ *m.*

3 *viscous substance.* चिकी *f.*

To JEOPARD, *To* JEOPARDIZE, *v. a. hazard, expose to danger.* जोखमांत-भयांत-संकटांत-&c. घालणें-पाडणें.

To j. one's life. काळाच्या तोंडीं *or* दाढेंत जाणें *or* पडणें.

To j. another's life. काळाच्या तोंडीं *or* दाढेंत घालणें *or* देणें.

JEOPARDOUS, *a. hazardous,* v. DANGEROUS. जोखमी, जोखमाचा.

JEOPARDY, *n. hazard,* v. DANGER, RISK. जोखीम *n.* भय *n.* धोका *m.* खत्रा *m.*

2 (of life). प्राणसंकट *n.* प्राणसंदेह *m.* प्राणांत *m.* प्राणावरचा लाग *m.* जिवावरचा लाग *m.* अपमृत्यु *m.* जिवावरची पाळी *f.* सुळावरची पोळी *f.* जिवावरची गोष्ट *f.* प्राणासींगांठ *f.* जिवासीं *or* प्राणासीं सापका *m.*

To be in j. प्राणावर *or* जिवावर बितणें-येणें *impers. con.* प्राणासीं *or* जिवासीं गांठ *f.* पडणें *or* सापका *m.* पडणें *g. of s.* अडकित्यांत सांपडणें, उखळांत डोसकें *n.* असणें *g. of s.*

To JERK, *v. a. twitch, &c.* असडणें *or* हसडणें *or* हिसडणें, आंचकणें, कचकणें, हिसका *m.*-हिसडा *m.*-असडा *m.*-आंचका *m.*-झटका *m.*-झटकारा *m.*-&c. देणें.

To be jerked, *sustain a jerk or shock.* गचकणें, कचकणें, हिसका *m.*-&c. बसणें.

2 *fling with a quick smart motion.* झटकारणें, झटकारून-झटकून-&c. फेंकणें-टाकणें, आडहातानें फेंकणें-मारणें-&c.

JERK, *n. sudden pull, push, &c.* हिसका *m.* हिसडा *m.* असडा *m.* आंचका *m.* झटका *m.* झटकारा *m.*

JESSAMINE. See JASMINE.

To JEST, *v. n. joke, &c.* ठट्टा *or* थट्टा *f.*-ठट्टेबाजी *f.*-ठट्टामसकरी *f.*-मस्करी *f.*-मजाख *f.*-विनोद *m.*-&c. करणें.

JEST, *n. joke,* ठट्टा *or* थट्टा *f.* ठट्टेचें भाषण *n.* मस्करीचें भाषण *n.* परिहासोक्ति *f.* विनोदोक्ति *f.* विनोदभाषण *n.*

Jests and jokes. ठट्टेबाजी *or* थट्टेबाजी *f.* ठट्टामस्करी *f.* मस्करी *f.* मजाख *f.*

To turn into j. ठट्टा *f.* करून टाकणें *g. of o.*

2 *object of laughter or sport.* विनोदास्पद *n.* विनोदपात्र *n.* उपहासपात्र *n.* उपहासास्पद *n.*

3 opposed to *earnest*; *game, sport, fun.* खेळ *m.* मस्करी *f.* ठट्टा *f.* खेळकुडी *f.*

JESTER, *n.* JESTING, *p. a.* v. V. ठट्टा-&c. करणारा, ठट्टेबाज, ठट्टेखोर, मस्कऱ्या, विनोदी, विनोदकारी, विनोदभाषी, विदूषक.

I. *zany, merry andrew,* v. BUFFOON. खुशमस्कऱ्या, भांड, क्रीडामृग *m.*

King's j. रायविनोदी.

JESTINGLY, *adv.* ठट्टेनें, ठट्टेवारी, विनोदानें, &c.

JESUIT, JESUITICAL, JESUITISM, *fig.* See CUNNING, &c.

JET, *n. jet-d'eau.* कारंजें *n.* फवारा *m.*

Basin made for the water of a j. हौद *m.*

Elevated cistern for a j. धमधमा *m.*

Thousand streamed j. हजारी कारंजें *n.*

2 *black stone.* कार *m.*

To JET. See To JUT.

JET-BLACK, JETTY, *a.* See BLACK.

JETTY, *n. pier, mole.* धका *or* धक्का *m.*

JEU D'ESPRIT, *n. witticism.* चुटका *m.*

JEW, *n.* यहूदी, इस्राएल, शनवाऱ्या तेली.

J.'s harp. चंग *or* मोरचंग *m.* मुखवाद्य *n.*

JEWEL, *n. precious stone, &c.* रत्न *n.* मणि *or* मणी *m.* जवाहीर *n.*

Jewels, v. JEWELRY. जडीत *n.* जडिताचे *or* जडावाचे दागिने *or* डागिने *m. pl.* जवाहीर *n.*

Relating to gems or jewels. जवाहिरी.

J. worn in a crest. चूडामणी *m.*

2—as a term of endearment. रत्न *n.* परीस *m.* जिवडा *m.*

JEWEL-HOUSE, JEWEL-OFFICE, JEWELRY, *n.* जवाहीरखाना *m.* रत्नशाला *f.*

JEWEL-MINE, *n.* रत्नाची खाण *f.* रत्नखनि *f.* मणिभूमि *f.* रत्नभूमि *f.*

JEWELLER, *n.* जवाहिरी *vulg.* जोहरी, मणिकार *pop.* मणेर *or* मणेरी *or* मण्यार, जड्या.

JEWELRY, *n. jewels.* जडीत *n.* जडिनाचे *or* जडावाचे डागिने *m.pl.* गहना *or* गहिना *m.* वस्तवानी *f.* डागिने *or* दागिने *m.pl.* जवाहीर *n.*

2 v. JEWEL-HOUSE. रत्नशाला *f.*

JEWESS, *n.* यहूदीण *f.*

JEWISH, *a.* यहूदी *or* यहूद्यांचा, यहूदीचा, यहूदी संबंधी.

JEWRY, *n. Jews' quarter.* यहूद्यांचा महल्ला *m.*

JIB, *n.*—the sail. जीभ *f.* फांगी *f.*

The-jib-sheet. जिभांगें *n.*

JIFFY. See TRICE.

JIG. See DANCE.

JILT, *n. woman who trifles with her lover.* ठकडी बायको *f.* प्रतारिका *f.* संकेतितान्यगामिनी *f.*

To JILT, *v. a. trick in love,*—a woman. ठकवून टाकणें-सोडणें, झोका *m.* देणें.

JIMMERS, *n. jointed hinges.* बिजागरें *n. pl.* बिजागरीं *n. pl.*

To JINGLE, *v. n. clink, sound with a rattle.* खळखळणें, घणघणणें, छणछणणें, छमकणें, झणझणणें, झणत्कारणें.—*intens.* घणाणणें, छणाणणें.

2—toe-ornaments, &c. रुणझुणणें.

JINGLE, *n. clinking sound.* खळखळ *f.* झणकार *m.* झणकारा *m.* झणत्कार *m.* झंकार *m.* छणछण *f.*—*intens.* घणघणाट *m.* छणछणाट *m.* छमछमाट *m.* खळखळाट *m.*

2 (of toe-ornaments, &c.). रुणझुण *f.* झमझम *f.* छमाछमी *f.*—*intens.* झमझमाट *m.* छणछणाट *m.*

JINGLING, *p. a.* v. V. खळखळणारा, छणछणणारा, &c. खळखळीत.

JINGLINGLY, *adv.* छणण, खळ-कन-कर-&c. खळखळ, घणघण *or* णां, छणछण, झमझम *or* मां, चमचम.—*intens.* छणाणां, घणाणां, छणाछण, घणाघण, चमाचम, झमाझम, खळाखळ.

2—bells, &c. on the toes. छमकन-कर-&c. छमछम, झमझम *or* मां, झुणझुण, रुणझुण *or* रुमझुम.

JINJALL, *n.* जेजाल *or* जंज्याळ *f.*

JOB, *n. piece of chance work.* आडकाम *n.* अडपझडपकाम *n.* किरकोळ काम *n.*

By the j. उक्ता.

Errand jobs. लव *f.* लवै *f.* लवेचें काम *n.*

J.-boy. आडखप्या.

2 *work set on foot for private profit or ends.* स्वार्थाचें काम *n.*-कार्य *n.* स्वार्थमात्रोद्देश्य कार्य *n.*

To JOB, *v. n. do jobs.* आडकाम *n.*-अडपझडपकाम *n.* करणें.

JOBBER, *n.* v. V. आडकाम करणारा, &c. आडकामी, आडकाम्या, कामकरी.

JOBBERNOWL, *n.* v. FOOL. गाढवाचा खरारा *m.* माठ्या.

JOCKEY, *n. rider, breaker in, &c. of horses.* चाबुकस्वार, अश्वशिक्षक, अश्वोपजीवी.

2 See ROGUE.

To JOCKEY, *v. a. cheat, trick*, v. To DECEIVE. फसवणें, छकवणें, धूर *m.* देणें, डोईवर हात *m.* फिरवणें.

JOCOSE, *a.* v. JOCULAR. ठट्ठेखोर, ठट्ठेबाज, गतक्या.

JOCOSELY, *adv.* v. A. ठट्ठेनें, विनोदानें, ठट्ठेवारी, हसतहसत, ठट्ठेचे रितीनें, &c.

JOCOSENESS, *n.* v. A. ठट्ठेबाजी *f.* ठट्ठेखोरी *f.*

JOCOSERIOUS, *a. partaking of mirth and seriousness.* विनोदमिश्रित.

JOCULAR, *a. facetious, jocose*,—of persons. ठट्ठेखोर, ठट्ठेबाज, ठट्ठेवाईक, मस्कऱ्या, गतक्या, विनोदी, विनोदकारी, ख्याली, रसिक, गोष्टीविल्हाळ, विदूषक.

2—of sentiments, &c. विनोदाचा, मस्करीचा, ठट्ठेचा, विनोदी, रसिक, विनोदात्मक, विनोदावह, विनोदास्पद.

JOCULARITY, *n.* v. A. 1. ठट्ठेबाजी *f.* ठट्ठेखोरी *f.* विनोद *m.* रसिकता *f.* रहस्य *n.*

JOCUND, *a. gay, lively, gladsome*, v. MERRY. आनंदी, उल्लासी, आनंदाचा, उल्लासाचा, आनंदवृत्ति, उल्लासवृत्ति, खुशदिल, खुशमोजा. [आनंदीपणा *m.*

JOCUNDITY, JOCUNDNESS, *n.* v. A. आनंदवृत्ति *f.* उल्लासवृत्ति *f.*

To JOG, *v. a. push or shake slightly.* आंचकणें, हबकणें, धक्का *m.*-हिसका *m.*-आंचका *m.*-&c. देणें-मारणें.

2 *prick or touch hintingly.* टोचणें, डवचलणें, डोंचणें, खटाळणें, *or* खट्याळणें, ठोठाविणें, टुमणी *f.* लावणें.

To JOG, *v. n. move heavily, slowly, &c.* खुटुरुटु-रुटुखुटु-रुटुघुटु-जुगजुग-रडतखडत-&c. जाणें-चालणें.

To j. on with, *shift, manage, &c. with.* जोगवणें, जोगवण *f.*-जोगवणी *f.* करणें, गरज *f.* करणें.

JOG, JOGGING, *n.* v. V. A. 1.—*act.* आंचकणें *n.* &c. धका *or* धक्का *m.* ढका *m.* आंचका *m.* हबका *m.* हिसका *m.*

2—*act.* टोचणें *n.* &c. टुमणी *f.* ढुसणी *f.* उटाळा *m.*

JOGGINGLY, *adv. heavily, slowly, &c.* खुटुरुटू, रुटुखुटू, रुटुघुटू, रडतखडत, रडतरडत, जुगजूग, तुनुमुनू, तुनुमुनुकरून.

To JOGGLE, *v. a.* See To JOG, *v. n.* See To SHAKE.

JOGTROT, *n.* खुद्दक खुद्दक चाल.

JOHN A NOKES and TOM A STILES. देवदत्त.

To JOIN, *v. a. unite, combine, put together.* जोडणें, जडणें, मिळवणें, सांधणें, सांधपणें, एक करणें, सांधप *n.*-जडप *n.*-संयोग *m.*-संयोजन *n.*-&c. करणें *g. of o.* संयुक्त-संयोजित-&c. करणें.

2 to; *add unto.* जोडणें, जडणें, जुळणें, लावणें.

A piece joined on. सांधा *m.* जोड *m. f.*

To JOIN, *v. n. unite, become one with.* मिळणें, एकहोणें, संयोग *m.*-&c. असणें *g. of s.* सांधणें.

2 *be contiguous.* लगता *m.*-लगत *f.* असणें *g. of s. recip.* लगत-असणें, लगटून-लागून-चिकटून-भिडून-&c. असणें.

3 *confederate*, v. To COMBINE. मिळणें, जुडणें, जुटणें, जुगणें.

To j. in with in singing, *second.* सूर *m.* धरणें, झेलणें, जोडगिरी *f.* करणें.

To j. *be begun*—battle. जुंपणें, बितणें.

JOINED, *p.* v. V. A. 1. जोडलेला, मिळवलेला, सांधलेला, &c. सांधींव, योजित, संयोजित.

2 जोडलेला, &c. जडींव.

v. V. N. 1. मिळालेला, &c. युक्त, संयुक्त, लग्न, विलग्न, संलग्न, युत.

JOINER, *n.* JOINING, *p. a.* v. V. A. 1. जोडणारा, मिळवणारा, सांधणारा, &c. सांधकाम्या, जोडकाम्या, जडकाम्या, सांधपी, सांधप्या, योजक, संयोजक, योजन-संयोजन-संयोग-&c. कर्त्ता-कारी.

2 जोडणारा, जडणारा, &c.

v. V. N. 2. लगत्याचा, लगतचा, लगतीचा, संसर्गी, संसक्त, उपश्लिष्ट, अनुयोगी.

I. v. CARPENTER. सुतार, सूत्रधार.

JOINERY, *n. art and business of joining.* जोडकाम *n.* जडकाम *n.* सांधकाम *n.*

Price or cost of j. जडणावळ *f.* जडण *f.* जोडाई *f.*

JOINING, *n.* v. V. A. 1.—*act.* जोडणें *n.* मिळवणें *n.* सांधणें *n.* &c. जोडणी *f.* जोडणूक *f.* जडण *f.* जडणी *f.* जोडप *n.* जडप *n.* सांधप *n.* सांधणी *f.* योजणूक *f.* योजन *n.* योजना *f.* संयोजन *n.* संयोजना *f.* समाहरण *n.* समाहार *m.*

2—*act.* जोडणें *n.* &c. जोडणी *f.* जोडणूक *f.* जडणी *f.* जडण *f.*

I. See JOINT.

JOINT, *n. articulation, knuckle, knot, &c.* सांध *f.* सांधा *m.* संधि *m. f.* संध *f.* पेर *n.* पेरें *n.* पर्व *n.* कांडें *n.* गांठ *f.* सील *f.* बंद *m.* ग्रंथि *m.* चाळा *m.* अस्थिसंधि *m.*

Knob or prominence of a j. खुबा *m.*

To be out of j. सांधा *m.* उखळणें.

2 *line or point of junction.* सांध *f.* सांधा *m.* जोड *m.* संधि *m. f.*

3 *portion included between two articulations*, v. INTERNODATION. कांडें *n.* पेर *n.* पेरें *n.*

4 *limb of an animal cut up by the butcher.* खाटिकानें निराळा केलेला जनावराचा अवयव *m.*

JOINT, *a. shared by two or more.* समईक *or* समाईक, सामाजिक *pop.* समाजीक, साधारण, अनेकस्वामिक, अनेकसत्ताक, बिरजुमाली.

2 *united in the same office, duty, possession, &c.* संगतीचा, सोबतीचा, एककार्यकारी, एकाधिकारी, सह (in comp. as सहभोगी j. possessor. सहस्वामी j. proprietor. सहाधिकारी j. official, &c. &c.), सद्वितीय, भाज and बंधु (in com. as वारिसभाज j. heir).

3 *united, combined.* जुटीचा, जमातीचा, जुळणीचा, मिलाफाचा, &c. चौघांचा, संभूयसमुत्थानाचा, संभूयसमुत्थानक.

To JOINT, *v. a. form with articulation.* सांध्यांचा करणें, सांध्यांनीं जोडणें, संधिविशिष्ट करणें.

2 *divide in the joints.* सांधा *m. or* सांधे *m. pl.* तोडणें-सोडवणें, संधिभंग *m.*-संधिभेद *m.* करणें.

JOINTED, *p.* v. V. 1. सांध्यांचा केलेला, सांध्यांचा, सांधींव, संधित, संधियुक्त, संधिविशिष्ट.

2 सांधेसोडवलेला, &c. संधिभेदित.

JOINTER, *n.*—*large plane.* दर्ज *m.*

JOINTLY, *adv. together, in concert*, v. CONJOINTLY. मिळून, जुटीनें, मिळणीनें, युगपत्, योगतः, बिरजुमाल.

JOINTRESS, *n.* रांडरोटा-&c. जिलाआहे ती.

JOINTURE, *n. woman's settlement.* बाईलबांटा *m.* रांडरोटा *m.* रांडरोटी *f.* भर्तृदत्तविधवावेतन *n.*

JOIST, *n.*—of a building. कडी *f.* बरगा *m.* दांडा *m.*

Consisting of joists. कडीबंद.

To JOIST, *v. a.* कडीपाट *m.* करणें.

JOKE, *n.* v. JEST. ठट्ठा *f. or* थट्टा *f.* ठट्ठेचें भाषण *n.* विनोदोक्ति *f.* विनोदभाषण *n.* गतक *n.*

Practical j. हाताचीथट्टा *f.*

2—opposed to *earnest.* खेळ *m.* मस्करी *f.* खेळकुडी *f.*

To JOKE, *v. n.* v. To JEST. ठट्टा *f.*-मस्करी *f.*-&c. करणें.

JOKER, *n.* v. V. *and.* JESTER. ठट्ठा-&c. करणारा, मस्कऱ्या, विनोदी.

JOLE. See CHEEK.

JOLLINESS, JOLLITY, *n.* v. A. 1. उल्हासीपणा *m.* आनंदीपणा *m.* उल्लासिता *f.* उल्लासवृत्ति *f.*

I. See MERRIMENT.

JOLLY, *a. jovial, gay, lively, &c.* v. MERRY. उल्लासी, आनंदी, घमंड्या, गमत्या, चयनी, मौज्या, हौशा, रंगेला.

2 *plump, sleek.* टमटमीत *or* टुमटुमीत, गुबगुबीत, गुमगुमीत, ताजा, ताज्या आंगाचा.

To JOLT, *v. a. shake with sudden jerks.* आंचकणें, हबकणें, हादरणें, हिसडणें, हिसकणें, हांदुळणें *or* हावदुळणें, धक्के *m. pl.*-हिसके *m. pl.*-गचके *m. pl.*-&c. बसवणें.

To be jolted. गचकणें, हादरणें, गचका *m.*-धक्का *m.*-हिसका *m.*-&c. बसणें *in. con.*

To JOLT, *v. n. shake with a short motion.* हिसकणें, हिसकावणें, हांदुळणें, हिंदळणें, हिंदकळणें, हिसका *m.*-&c. खाणें.

JOLT, *n. shock or shake from a jerk.* धक्का *or* धका *m.* ढका *m.* हिसका *m.* आंचका *m.* हबका *m.* गचका *m.* गचकी *f.*

JOLTHEAD, *n.* v. FOOL. ढुम्या, टोणपा.

To JOSTLE, *v. a. shake by running against.* रेंटणें, रेंटून जाणें, धक्का *m.*-हिसका *m.*-&c. देणें-लावणें-मारणें *or* देऊन-&c. जाणें.

JOSTLING, *n.* v. V.—*act.* रेंटणें *n.* &c. रेंटाई *f.*

J. and shouldering (in a crowd). मुंडपघुसणी *f.*

JOT, *n.* v. BIT. लेश *m.* लवलेश *m.* बिंदु *m.* अणु *m.* रजःकण *m.* तिलमात्र *n.*

To JOT, *v. a. note down.* टाचणें, टिपणें, टाचून-टिपून ठेवणें.

JOTTING, *n.* टाचण *n.* टिपण *n.* टिपणी *f.*

JOURNAL, *n. diary.* रोजच्या वर्तमानाची वही *f.* रोजनामा *m.* दिनचर्यालेख *m.* दिनवृत्तपत्र *n.*

2 (of a merchant) *book framed from the* WASTE-BOOK *and introductory to the* LEDGER. पक्का खरडा *m.* पक्कीवही *f.* खनावणी *f.* बतावणी *f.*

Note. Where, as in single entry, only two books are used, viz. Journal or Day-book, and Ledger or Post-book, there the terms wanted to express this word must be sought under *Day-book* or *Waste-book* and the terms given here must be added to those under *Ledger.*

A particular account in the j. खातें *n.*

3 See NEWSPAPER.

JOURNEY, *n. travel by land.* सफर *f.* वाट *f.* मार्ग *m.* रस्ता *m.* (as तीन दिवसांची वाट, चार दिवसांचा रस्ता &c.) यात्रा *f.* मार्गक्रमण *n.* देशभ्रमण *n.* पर्यटन *n.*

Halting or alighting on a j. पेणें *n.*

J. to and from, *trip.* खेप *f.*

Money taken to defray the expenses of a j. वाटखर्च *m.* वाटखर्ची *f.*

To accomplish the object of one's j. सफर *f.* साधणें.

To JOURNEY, *v. n.* v. N. चालणें, वाट *f.*-मार्ग *m.*-रस्ता *m.* चालणें-क्रमणें, मुसाफरी *or* मुशाफरी *f.*-मार्गक्रमण *n.*-यात्रा *f.*-&c. करणें.

JOURNEYER, *n.* JOURNEYING, *p. a.* v. V. *and* TRAVELLER. वाट चालणारा, वाटसरू, वाटमार्गी, मार्गस्थ.

JOURNEYING, *n.* v. V.—*act.* वाट चालणें *n.* रस्ता चालणें *n.* &c. चाल *f.* मार्गक्रमण *n.* यात्रा *f.* यान *n.*

JOURNEYMAN, *n. hired workman.* दुसऱ्याच्या हाताखालचा कामकरी, हस्तक्या, कामकरी, वेतनी कामकरी, वेतनी कामदार, हातकाम्या.

JOURNEYWORK, *n.* हातकाम *n.*

JOUST. See JUST.

JOVIAL, *a. jolly, &c.* v. MERRY. घमंड्या, चयनी, उल्लासी, सदानंदी, नित्योत्सवी, मौज्या.

JOVIALITY. See MERRIMENT.

JOWL. See CHEEK.

JOY, *n. gladness, delight, exultation, &c.* आनंद *m.* हर्ष *m.* हर्ख *m.* संतोष *m.* उल्लास *m.* खुशी *f.* उत्साह *m.* आल्हाद *m.* प्राल्हाद *m.* प्रमोद *m.* परितोष *m.* आनंदवृत्ति *f.* हर्षवृत्ति *f.*—as intensed, and expressed by *rapture, transport, ecstacy, &c.* अत्यानंद *m.* परमानंद *m.* महानंद *m.* अतिहर्ष *m.* अतिसंतोष *m.* महाहर्ष *m.* ब्रह्मानंद *m.* ब्रह्मसुख *n.* महाल्हाद *m.* हर्षसंरंभ *m.* रोमहर्ष *m.* रोमांच *n.* बालोबालखुशी *f.* बालोबालसुख *n.* रोमरोमहर्ष *m.* हर्षावेश *m.*

To give one j. See To CONGRATULATE.

To JOY, *v.n. be glad,* v. To REJOICE. आनंद *m.*-&c. पावणें, आनंदित-&c. होणें, आनंद *m.*-&c. वाटणें *in. con.* हर्षणें, आनंदणें.

To JOY, *v. a. make glad,* v. To REJOICE. आनंदविणें, हर्षविणें, आनंदित- &c. करणें.

2 See To CONGRATULATE.

JOYFUL, *a. glad, exulting.* खुश, आनंदयुक्त, हर्षयुक्त, हर्षान्वित, सानंद, आनंदमय, हर्षात्मक, हर्षमाण.—in high degree, as expressed by *enraptured, enravished, overjoyed, transported, in ecstacy, &c.* आनंदमय, आनंदाप्लुत, हर्षाक्रांत, हर्षाकुल, हर्षाविष्ट, हर्षग्रस्त, बालोबालसुखी, रोमरोमसुखी, बालोबालखुश, रोमांचित.

Ever j. नित्यानंद *pop.* नित्यानंदी, सदानंदी.

2 *causing joy.* आनंदाचा, हर्षाचा, आनंदप्रद-कारक-दायक, हर्षावह, हर्षद, हर्षप्रद-कारक-&c. उत्साहकर-कारक-&c.

JOYFULLY, *adv.* v. A. 1. आनंदानें, हर्षानें, आनंदेंकरून, आनंदेंशीं, आनंदपूर्वक, &c.

JOYFULNESS, *n.* v. A. *and* JOY. आनंदवृत्ति *f.* सानंदत्व *n.*

JOYLESS, *n. void of joy.* निरानंद, आनंदहीन-शून्य-रहित-&c. हर्षहीन- शून्य-रहित-&c. उदास, निरुत्साह.

2 *yielding no joy.* असुखप्रद, असुखद, अहर्षद, अनुत्साहकर, निरुत्साहाचा.

JOYLESSLY, *adv.* v. A. 1. आनंदावांचून, हर्षावांचून, हर्षहीन-&c.

JOYOUS, *a. glad, joyful,* v. MERRY. आनंदी, उल्लासी, आनंदवृत्ति.

2 *giving joy,* v. JOYFUL. आनंदाचा, हर्षाचा, हर्षप्रद.

JOYOUSLY. See JOYFULLY.

JOYOUSNESS. See JOY.

JUBILANT, *a. shouting with joy.* जयशब्दोच्चारी, जयशब्दकारी-वादी-घोषी.

JUBILEE, *n. season of great festivity.* सण *m.* महोत्साह *m.* महोत्सव *m.*

JUDGE, *n. officer who hears and determines causes.* न्यायाधीश, न्याय पाहणारा-करणारा-तोडणारा, इनसाफ-न्यायाधिशी-&c. करणारा, मनसुबदार, खटला पाहणारा, मुनसफ, धर्माधिकारी, धर्माध्यक्ष, प्राड्विवाक, अक्षदर्शक, जज्ज from the English is used for a European judge.—among Muhammadans. काजी.

Criminal j. फौजदार.

2 *connoisseur, &c.* पारखी, परीक्षक, जाणता, जाण, ग्राहक, ग्राही, गुणग्राहक, चिकित्सक, परीक्षावंत, रसज्ञ.

To JUDGE, *v. n. form an opinion or judgment.* निर्धार *m.*-निश्चय *m.*-तजवीज *f.*-&c. करणें, अनुमान *n.*-तर्क *m.*-&c. करणें, मत *n.*-समजूत *f.*-&c. असणें *g. of s.*

2 *consider accurately, discern, distinguish.* विचार *m.*-विचारण *n.*-दर्याफ़्त *f.*-दर्याफ़्ती *f.*-तजवीज *f.*-&c. करणें, पाहणें, ताडणें.

3 *hear and determine causes.* खटला *m.*-न्याय *m.*-इनसाफ*m.* -&c. पाहणें-तोडणें-निवडणें, न्यायाधिशी *f.* करणें, वाद *m.*-तंटा*m.*-खटला *m.*-&c. तोडणें.

To JUDGE, *v. a. try, examine and decide on.* न्याय *m.* पाहणें-करणें-तोडणें-निवडणें-मनास आणणें *g. of o.* न्यायाधिशी *f.*-इनसाफ *m.*-मनसुबी *f.*-निर्णय *m.*-निवाडा *m.*-&c. करणें *g. of o.* —Expressing the sense of this word as appearing under the phrases *to call to account, to take to task, to reckon with, to haul over the coals,* are the following पुसणें, पुसून घेणें, विचारणें, हिशोब *m.*-झाडा *m.*-झडती *f.*-झाडाझडती *f.* घेणें, पाहून घेणें, बाटाबाट *f.*-बाटाबाटी *f.*-&c. करणें, घोळणें, घोळून घेणें, छडा *m.*-छडाछड *f.* काढणें-लावणें.

2 *reckon, think, consider.* मोजणें, गणणें, लेखणें.

3 v. To RULE. अनुशासणें, शासन *n.*-अनुशासन *n.* करणें *g. of o.*

JUDGESHIP, *n.* न्यायाधिशी *f.* मुनसफी *f.* धर्माधिकार *m.*

JUDGMENT, *n. faculty of judging, discrimination.* बुद्धि *f.* समज *m. f.* तर्क *m.* ज्ञान *n.* विचार *m.* विवेक *m.* विवेकता *f.* तजवीज *f.* तारतम्य *n.*

According to one's j. यथाबुद्धि, यथामति.

2 *thought, notion,* v. OPINION. मत *n.* बुद्धि *f.* विचार *m.* तजवीज *f.*

3 *determination of the mind, decision.* निर्धार *m.* निश्चय*m.* धडा *m.* अवधारण *n.*

To strive against one's better j. बुद्धीसीं वैर *n.* करणें.

4 *sentence, award.* निवाडा *m.* निर्णय *m.* फैसला *m.* हुकूम *m.*

5 *right of sentencing.* न्याय करण्याचा अधिकार *m.*-सत्ता *f.*-योग्यता *f.*

6 *divine infliction.* ईश्वराचा गजब *m.* ईश्वराचा कहर *m.*

JUDGMENT-DAY, *n.* जगाचा न्याय करण्याचा दिवस *m.*

JUDGMENT-HALL, *n.* न्यायसभा *f.* धर्मसभा *f.*

JUDGMENT-SEAT, *n.* न्यायाधिशाची गादी *f.* न्यायासन*n.* धर्मासन*n.*

JUDICATORY, *n. court of justice.* अदालत *f.* न्यायसभा *f.* धर्मसभा *f.* नीतिसभा *f* धर्मशाला *f.* धर्माधिकरण *n.* न्यायागार *n.*

JUDICATORY, *a. dispensing justice.* न्यायकरण्याचा, न्यायपाहण्याचा.

JUDICATURE, *n. power of distributing justice.* न्याय पाहण्याचा-करण्याचा अधिकार *m.* न्यायदर्शनाधिकार *m.* न्यायाधिकार*m.* धर्माधिकरण *n.* न्यायाधिशी *f.*

2 See JUDICATORY.

JUDICIAL, *a. pertaining, &c. to the administration of justice.* न्यायाधिशीचा, न्याय करण्याचा-पाहण्याचा, न्यायप्रकरणाचा, न्यायदर्शन संबंधी.

2 *relating, &c. to the practice of courts of justice.* व्यवहाराचा, व्यवहारिक *or* व्यावहारिक, व्यवहारी, व्यवहारसंबंधी-विषयक.

J. procedure. व्यवहार *m.* क्रिया *f.*

3 *inflicted as a penalty or in judgment.* शिक्षाहेतुक, दंडरूप, न्यायदर्शनकृत, न्यायदर्शन प्रयुक्त.

JUDICIOUS, *a. possessing sound judgment, acting according to sound judgment,* v. WISE. विवेकी, समजदार, समजीक, समंजस, समजूतदार, सुजाण, सविवेक, विवेकाढ्य, सुज्ञ, प्राज्ञ, ज्ञानचक्षु, ज्ञानदृष्टि, सदसद्दर्शी, उचितज्ञ.

2 *accordant with sound judgment,* v. WISE. विवेकाचा, शाहणपणाचा, समजुतीचा, समंजसपणाचा, समंजस, सुयुक्त, सुयुक्तीचा, समर्पक, सविवेक, विवेकयुक्त, विवेकानुसार.

JUDICIOUSLY, *adv.* v. A. समंजसपणानें, शाहणपणानें, समजुतीनें, सविवेक, विवेकानुसार.

JUDICIOUSNESS, *n.* v. A. 1. समजदारी *f.* समजूतदारी *f.* समंजसपणा *m.* &c. विवेक *m.* सुज्ञता *f.* प्राज्ञता *f.* &c.

2 समंजसपणा *m.* समर्पकपणा *m.* सुयुक्तता *f.* सुयुक्ति *f.*

JUG, *n.* v. VESSEL. चंबू *m.* सुरई *f.* कुजा *m.*

A glass j. शिसा *m.*

To JUGGLE, *v. n. play tricks by sleight of hand.* गौडबंगाल *n.*-गारूड *n.*-बाजेगरी *f.*-नजरबंदी *f.*-दृष्टिबंधन *n.*-दृष्टिबंध *m.*-हातचलाकी *f.*-&c.करणें.

2 *practise artifices.* गारूड *n.*-भानामती *f.*-लपंडाव *m.*-लपंडाई *f.*- लप्पंछप्पं *n.*-&c. करणें-खेळणें. [झोका *m.*

JUGGLE, *n. trick, deception.* फट *f.* फटवण *f.* ठकवण *f.* ढोला *m.*

JUGGLER, *n.* JUGGLING, *p. a.* v. V. 1. *and* CONJURER. गौडबंगाल करणारा, &c. गारुडी *or* गारोडी, गौडबंगाली, भानामत्या, नजरबंद, बाजेगर, ढंगधोत्रेकरी, ऐंद्रजालिक, मायाजीवी.

The gibberish, mummery, &c. of a j. ढंगधोत्र *n.*

2 लपंडाव करणारा-खेळणारा,&c. भानामत्या, लपंडाव्या.

JUGGLERY, JUGGLING, *n. act or practice of legerdemain.* गारूड *n.* गौडबंगाल *n.* भानामती *f.* भानामतीचा खेळ *m.* बाजेगरी*f.* नजरबंदी *f.* दृष्टिबंधन *n.* दृष्टिबंध *m.* इंद्रजाल *n.* छांछू *f.* जंतर मंतर *m.* हातचलाकीचा खेळ *m.* हस्तलाघव *n.* माया *f.* भूतसृष्टि *f.*

2 *underhand work, artifices, tricks.* गारूड *n.* भानामती *f.* लपंडाव *m.* लपंडाई *f.* लप्पंछप्पं *n.* काळेमेळें *n.*

JUGULAR, *a. belonging to the neck.* गळ्याचा,कंठसंबंधी,कंठस्थ.

JUICE, *n. sap of plants and fruits.* रस *m.* पाणी *n.* द्रव *m.* निर्यास *m.* सुधा *f.*

Neat or pure j. अंगरस *m.* आपरस *m.* स्वरस *m.*

JUICELESS, *a.* नीरस *pop.* निरस, विरस, रसहीन-रहित-शून्य, शुष्क.

JUICINESS, *n.* v. A. रसाळपणा *m.* सरसता *f.* रसबाहुल्य *n.*

JUICY, *a. succulent.* रसाळ, रसभरू, रसभरित, सरस, रसबानू.

JUJUB, JUJUBE, *n.*—the tree. बोर *f.* बोरी *f.* बदरी *f.* सौबरी *f.* —the fruit. बोर *n.* बदर *n.*

Branch of the j. tree broken off. बोरकांटी *f.* बोराटी *f.*

Fruit of the j. dried and pounded. बोरकूट *n.*

Stone or seed of the j. आंटीळ *f.* आंठोळी *f.*

JULY, *n.* इंग्रेजी सालाचा सातवा महिना *m.* आषाढ श्रावण *m.*

To JUMBLE, *v. a. mingle confusedly,* v. To CONFOUND. ढवळणें, गोंधळणें, भानगडणें, गोबडणें, गोंधळ *m.*-गोंधळागोंधळ *f.*-घालमेल *f.*-ढवळाढवळ *f.*-&c. करणें *g. of o.*

JUMBLE, *n. state of confused mixture,* v. CONFUSION. गोंधळ *m.* घोळ *m.* घालमेल *f.* घप्पाघोळ *m.* गदळ *m.* एकवाट *m. f.* गफलत *f.* गलत *f.* शबल *n.* संकर *m.* गडबडगुंडा *m.*

2 *confused mass*, v. MIXTURE. सटरफटर *n.* लटरफटर *n.* गोतांबील *f.* गोह्योत *n.*

JUMBLED, *p.* v. V. ढवळलेला, गोंधळलेला, &c. गदळ, शबल, संकीर्ण.

JUMBLER, *n.* JUMBLING, *p. a.* v. V. गोंधळणारा, &c. घालमेल्या, गोंधळ्या, भानगड्या.

To JUMP, *v. n. leap.* कुदणें, उडणें, उडी *f.* मारणें.

To j. about, v. To FRISK. टिणटिण *adv.* उड्या *f. pl.* मारणें, खिदडणें, खिदाळणें.

2 See To AGREE.

JUMP, JUMPING, *n.* v. V. 1.—*act.* कुदणें *n.* उडी *f.* उड्डान *n.*

A j. or leap with the legs closed. चिपी उडी *f.*

JUNCTION, *n. act of joining*, See JOINING. 2 *joinedness, union, combination, connection.* जोड *m.* जडण *f.* मिलाफ *m.* योग *m.* संयोग *m.* समायोग *m.* जूट *m.f.* जवा *m.* मिळण *f.* लगत *f.* लगता *m.* संगत *f.* संगति *f.* संगम *m.* संग *m.* संधि *m.* समागम*m.* संधान *n.* संपर्क *m.* संसर्ग *m.* संसक्ति *f.* सक्ति *f.* संश्लेष *m.* युक्तता *f.* संयुक्तता *f.* युक्ति *f.* युति *f.* [संधिस्थान *n.*

3 *point of union.* सांधा *m.* सांध *f.* जोड*m.* संधि *m. f.* संध *f.*-

JUNCTURE, *n. line of junction.* सांधा *m.* सांध *f.* जोड *m.f.* संधि *m.f.* संध *f.*

2 *articulation*, See JOINT. 3 *point of time, crisis.* संधि *m. pop.* संध *f.* टिपण *n.* ढासण *n.* गव *f.* आणी *f.* बाणी *f.* अवसान *n.* अवसर *m.* गडसंद् *or* ध *f.* प्रसंग *m.*

Perilous j. सापका *m. v.* पड, कच *f.*

Unseasonable j. आडसंधि *f.*

JUNE, *n.* इंग्रेजी सालाचा साहवा महिना *m.* ज्येष्ट-आषाढ *m.*

JUNGLE, *n. forest, wild place, &c.* जंगल *n.* रान *n.*

JUNGLE, *a. inferior, common,*—of trees. रायवळ, जंगली.

JUNGLY, *a.* जंगली, जंगलाचा.

JUNIOR, *a. younger.* धाकटा, बयानें लहान, कनिष्ठ.—as distinguished from *senior* (बुद्रुक), खुर्द.—as used of member of a family—धाकटा, पाठचा, पाठीचा, मागचा, खालचा, अनुज, अवरज.

2 *inferior in rank.* खालचा, खालचे पायरीचा, लहान.

JUNIPER, *n.* एक झाड आहे.

JUNKET, *To* JUNKET. See FEAST, To FEAST.

JUNTA, JUNTO, *n. cabal.* v. BAND. कट *m.* गट *or* गट्ट *m.* जूट *m.*

JUPITER, *n.*—the planet. बृहस्पति *m.* गुरु *m.*

JURIDICAL, *a. used in courts of justice.* अदालतीचा, अदालती, न्यायसभेचा, न्यायसभासंबंधी, व्यवहाराचा, व्यवहारिक, व्यावहारिक.

JURIDICALLY, *adv. according to forms of law.* न्याय पाहण्याच्या कायद्याप्रमाणें, न्यायदर्शनसंप्रदायानुसार.

JURISCONSULT, *n. one who gives opinion on points of law.* धर्मशास्त्रसांगणारा, धर्मशास्त्री, धर्मशास्त्रज्ञ, धर्मप्रवक्ता.

JURISDICTION, *n. power or right of exercising authority, &c.* अधिकार *m.* हुकूम *m.* अमल *m.* अमलदारी *f.*

That belongs to the j. of. अमलांतला, इलाख्यांतला.

JURISPRUDENCE, *n. science of law.* व्यवहारशास्त्र*n.* व्यवहारज्ञान*n.* धर्मशास्त्र *n.* स्मृतिशास्त्र *n.* [धर्मशास्त्रज्ञ.

JURISPRUDENT, *a. understanding law.* व्यवहारज्ञ, व्यवहारवेत्ता,

JURIST, *n. one learned in the law.* धर्मशास्त्री, व्यवहारज्ञ,व्यवहारवेत्ता, धर्मज्ञ.—among Muhammadans. मुल्ला *or* मुलना *or* मुलाणा.

JUROR. See JURYMAN.

JURY, *n.* पंच *m.pl.* ज्युरी *f.* (from the English).

JURYMAN, *n.* पंच, पंचाईतदार, पंचाईत, ज्युरीची असामी *f.* ज्युरीवाला, ज्युरींतलें मनुष्य.

JUST, *a. upright, equitable, honest, fair*—of persons. न्यायी, इनसाफी, न्यायाचा, नीतीचा, नेकीचा, नेतीचा, सचोटीचा, खऱ्या व्यवहाराचा, न्यायनिष्ठ, न्यायनिष्ठुर, न्यायशील, न्यायपर, न्यायाचारी, न्यायपरायण, न्यायानुसारी, न्यायानुवर्त्ती, न्यायानुयायी, प्रामाणिक *pop.* प्रमाणिक, धर्मी, रास्त, खरा, रहारास्त, नीतिमान् *pop.* नीतिवान, नीतिवंत, नीत, परनिष्ठ, याथार्थिक, अकूट व्यवहार. Some terms employed to express directly,allusively, appellativelly, &c. *An eminently just person*, and thus answering to *Aristides, Nuoshirwan, &c.* are, धर्मराज, धर्मावतार, धर्ममूर्त्ति, धर्मात्मा, धर्मरूपी, न्यायमूर्त्ति, न्यायरूपी, न्यायपुरुष.

2 *according to equity, right, proper, good*—of acts, &c. न्यायाचा, नीतीचा, इनसाफाचा, हिशेबाचा, नीट, ठीक, वास्तविक, न्याय्य, यथान्याय, यथानीति, न्यायसिद्ध, रास्त, उजू, वाजबी, हिशेबी *or* हिशोबी, तात्विक, याथार्थिक, प्रमाण, प्रमाणभूत.

3 *correct, suitable, appropriate.* बराबर *or* बरोबर, ठीक, लायक, वाजवी, रुईचा, रीतीचा, हिशोबाचा,योग्य, यथायोग्य, समर्पक, युक्तिसार, युक्त, सुयुक्त.

4 *exact, fair, full*—of measures, weights, &c. नक्की *or* निकी *or* निका, खरा, रास्त, बराबर.

JUST, *adv. exactly, nicely.* बराबर, थेट, खास, केवल *or* ळ, च.

Just as it was, *wholly unaltered*, जशाचा तसा, जसेचा तसा. [ल्लीं,नुक्ता *decl.*

2 *near or nearly*, —in time. आतां, आतांशी, इतक्यांत, हा-

J. as, *in the instant that.* तसाच.

3 *merely, barely.* नुस्ता *decl.* फक्त, केवल *or* ळ, मात्र.

4 *narrowly, barely*, this sense is best rendered by adopting another construction, as I just escaped drowning. मी बुडतां बुडतां वांचलों, *or* मी बुडायाचा वांचलों.

JUST, *n. tilt.* करवली *f.* सादीक्रीडायुद्ध *n.*

JUSTICE, *n.*—the virtue. न्याय *m.* नीति *f.* धर्मन्याय *m.* धर्म *m.* न्यायशीलता *f.* न्यायनिष्ठा *f.* परनिष्टता *f.* न्यायासक्ति *f.*

2 *right, redress of wrong.* न्याय *m.*इनसाफ *m.*दाद *f.* न्याव*m.*

3—as opposed to mercy; *merited punishment.* योग्यशिक्षा *f.* युक्तदंड *m.* न्यायदंडन *n.* यथापराधदंड*m.*यथापराधशासन*n.*

4 *equity, justness, agreeableness to right.* उजूपणा *m.* खरेपणा *m.* रास्तपणा *m.* योग्यता *f.* यथायोग्यता *f.* न्याय्यता *f.* यथार्थता *f.* याथार्थ्य *n.*

5 *administrator of justice.* न्यायाधीश, न्यायपाहणारा, धर्माध्यक्ष, धर्माधिकारी.

JUSTICIARY, *n. administrator of justice*, v. JUDGE. न्याय पाहणारा, न्यायाधीश, न्यायाध्यक्ष, धर्माध्यक्ष, न्यायदर्शी, धर्माधिकारी.

JUSTIFIABLE, *a. that may be proved to be right; allowable, proper.* निर्दोष दाखवायाजोगा, दोषनिराकरणार्ह, दोषनिराकरणशक्य, निराकरणीयदोष, योग्य, वाजबी, न्याय्य, न्यायानुसार, न्यायाधार, सन्याय.

JUSTIFICATION, *n.* v. V. 1.—*act.* निर्दोष करणें *n.* &c. निर्दोषीकरण *n.* न्यायीकरण *n.* दोषमोचन *n.* दोषमार्जन *n.*—*state.* उ-

जवता माथा *m.* उजळमाथा *m.* उजळतोंड *n.* उघडामाथा *m.* मार्जितापराधता *f.* दोषमुक्तता *f.* आरोपितदोषमुक्ति *f.*

2—*act.* प्रपादणें *n.* &c. संपादणी *f.* संपादणूक *f.* दूषणप्रतिहार *m.* दोषप्रतीकार *m.* दोषनिराकरण *n.* दोषनिवारण *n.*

JUSTIFIED, *p.* v. V. 1. निर्दोष केलेला-ठरवलेला-&c. निर्दोषीकृत, मुक्तदोष, दोषमुक्त, निवृत्तदोष.

JUSTIFIER, *n.* JUSTIFYING, *p. a.* v. V. निर्दोष करणारा-ठरवणारा-&c. निर्दोषीकरणकर्त्ता-कारी-&c.दोषमोचन-&c.कर्त्ता-कारी-&c.

To JUSTIFY, *v. a. clear from guilt.* निर्दोष-निर्बाध-निष्कलंक-निरपराध-दोषमुक्त-&c. करणें-ठरवणें-करून दाखवणें, उजळता माथा *m.*-उजळमाथा *m.*-उजळतोंड *n.*-&c. करणें *g. of o.* निर्दोषीकरण *n.*-&c. करणें *g. of o.*

2 *show to be right or proper, maintain, vindicate.* दोष*m.*-&c. उडवणें *g. of o.* चांगला-योग्य-निर्दोष-&c. करून दाखवणें, प्रपादणें, संपादणी *f.*-संपादणूक *f.*-सफेती *f.*-&c. करणें *g. of o.* दूषण प्रतिहार*m.*-दोष प्रतीकार*m.*-दोषनिराकरण*n.*-&c.करणें *g.of o.*

To JUSTLE. See To JOSTLE.

JUSTLY, *adv.* v. A. 1. 2. न्यायानें, न्यायेंकरून, इनसाफानें, नीतीनें, रास्तीनें, &c. यथान्याय, यथानीति, न्यायतः, धर्मतः, न्यायपरायण, धर्मपरायण.

J. or unjustly. हक्कनाहक्क, हक्कनाक.

3 बराबर, योग्य, यथायोग्य, ठीक, लायक, वाजवी, समर्पक, यथास्थित, तुळांधार, तारंतार.

I. See JUST.

JUSTNESS, *n.* v. A. 2. खरेपणा *m.* रास्तपणा *m.* खराई *f.* न्याय्यता *f.* यथार्थता *f.* याथार्थ्य *n.*

3 योग्यता *f.* यथायोग्यता *f.* लायकी *f.* युक्तता *f.* सुयुक्तता *f.* समर्पकता *f.* युक्ति *f.*

To JUT, *v. n. shoot forward, project.* बाहेर *adv.* येणें-जाणें-पडणें-वाढणें. [तारुण्यकालीन.

JUVENILE, *a.* v. YOUTHFUL. तरुण, तारुण्याचा, तारुण्यकालिक,

J. pastime or sport. बालक्रीडा *f.* बालचरित्र *pop.* बालचरित *n.* बाललीला *f.* [नावस्था *f.*

JUVENILITY, *n.* v. A. तारुण्य *n.* तारुण्यावस्था *f.* यौवन *n.* यौव-

JUXTAPOSITION, *n. state of being placed by each other.* लगत *f.* लगता *m.* निकटानिकटी *f.* नैकट्य*n.* उपन्यास*m.* उपश्लेष*m.*

K.

K. This letter is represented by क.

KALE, *n.* कोबीचा एक भेद आहे.

KALENDAR. See CALENDAR.

To KAW, *v. n. cry as a crow, &c.* करकरणें, कावकावणें, कोकावणें, करकर *f.*-कावकाव *f.* करणें. [काकरव *m.*

KAW, *n. cry of the crow, &c.* करकर *f.* कावकाव *f.* काकशब्द*m.*

To KECK, *v. n. heave.* उमळणें, उमदळणें, उचलणें *all three impersonal.* उमट *m.* *n.*-उमास *m.*-उमासा *m.*-उमाळा *m.* येणें *in. con.*

KEDGER, *n.* v. ANCHOR. लोली *f.* लंगर *m.*

KEEL, *n.* (of a boat, &c.). कणा *m.* अडें *or* आडें *n.* कचोरा *m.* गाड्या *m.*

KEEN, *a. sharp, well edged.* पाणीदार, तिखट, तीक्ष्ण, तीव्र,कडक, जलद, धांवता, पातळ, पातळधारेचा, चरचर, चरचरीत.

2—as cold. कडक, कडक्याचा, कडाक्याचा, तिखट, तीव्र, हाडफोडा.

3—as hunger, desire, &c. कडक, कडकडीत, चणचणीत, तिखट, प्रखर, तीक्ष्ण, तीव्र. [खी, हौसदार.

4 *eager, warm, &c.* v. EARNEST. उत्साही, प्रोत्साही, उदमे-

5 *acute of mind,* v. SHARP. चणचणीत, तीक्ष्ण, तीक्ष्णबुद्धि, तीव्रबुद्धि, जलद, कुशाग्रमति. [दंशी.

6 *bitter,* v. ACRIMONIOUS. तीक्ष्ण, तीव्र, कटु, झोंबायाचा,

KEENNESS, *n.* v. A. 1. पाणी *n.* तेज *n.* तेजगी *f.* तिखटाई *f.* तीक्ष्णता *f.* तीव्रता *f.* पातळ धार *f.*

2 कडकपणा *m.* कडका *m.* तिखटपणा *m.* तीव्रता *f.*

3 कडकपणा *m.* कडकडीतपणा *m.* &c. तीक्ष्णता *f.* तीव्रता *f.* &c.

4 उत्साह *m.* उदमेख *m.* आसक्ति *f.* अनुराग *m.*

5 चणचणीतपणा *m.* बुद्धितीक्ष्णता *f.* बुद्धितैक्ष्ण्य *n.* कुशाग्रमति *f.*

6 खंवटपणा *m.* तीक्ष्णता *f.* कटुता *f.* &c. [उरवणें.

To KEEP, *v. a. retain, preserve.* राखणें, ठेवणें, धरणें,धरून असणें,

2 *hold in custody or charge.* राखणें, ठेवणें, दिम्मतीस ठेवणें, दिम्मतीस असणें *in. con.*

3 *take care of, preserve in security,* (things). राखणें, राखून ठेवणें, जतनावणें, जतन ठेवणें, जोपासणें, जोपासून ठेवणें, जोपावणें, संभाळणें, संभाळून ठेवणें, जतन *n.*-संगोपन *n.*-जोपासना *f.*-&c. करणें *g. of o.* मावजत *f.* ठेवणें *g. of o.*

4 *protect, guard.* राखणें, रक्षणें, संरक्षिणें, राखण *f.*-रखवाली *f.*-रक्षण *n.*-संरक्षण *n.*-खबरदारी *f.*-&c. करणें *g. of o.*

5 *detain, restrain, hinder.* थांबवणें, खोळंबवणें, राहवणें, ठेवून घेणें, राहून घेणें, अटकावणें, खोटी *f.*-खोळंबा *m.*-&c. करणें *g.of o.*

To k. till late. उशिरावर धरणें.

6 *tend, look after, &c.* (animals). राखणें, जोपासणें, जोपावणें, जोंबाळणें, जतनावणें, पाळणें, राखण *f.*-रखवाली *f.*-बरदास्त *f.*-&c. करणें *g. of o.*

7 *retain in any state or place.* राखणें, ठेवणें, धरणें, पाळणें.

8 *continue a state or tenor.* राखणें, ठेवणें, धरणें, पाळणें.

9 *observe* (season, festival, &c.). पाळणें, करणें, आचरणें, साधणें. [करणें *g. of o.*

10 *observe, regard, obey.* पाळणें, राखणें, मानणें, उपासना *f.*

11 *entertain, retain.* राखणें, ठेवणें, बाळगणें, पाळणें.

12 (promise,word, &c.) *fulfill.* राखणें, पाळणें, संभाळणें, खरा-सत्य-पूर्ण-&c. करणें.

14 *support, maintain, feed.* पाळणें, पोसणें, संभाळणें, पालन *n.*-पोषण *n.*-पालनपोषण *n.*-&c. करणें *g. of o.*

15 *hold as one's concubine or paramour.* राखणें. [ठेवणें.

16 back; *reserve, withhold.* राखणें, ठेवणें, चोरणें, चोरून-

17 back ; v. To RESTRAIN. आवरणें, आकळणें, अटोपणें.

18 under ; *hold in subjection.* वश-स्वाधीन-हुकमांत-&c. ठेवणें, दाबणें.

To k. house. घरदार *n.* करणें.

To k. hard at. जंत्रीं धरणें.

To k. one's bed, v. BED. खाट *f.*-अंथरूण *n.*-&c. धरणें.

To k. a school. शाळ *f.* घालणें, शाळ *f.*-&c. असणें *g. of s.*

To KEEP, *v. n. continue, remain, stay.* राहणें.

2 *last, remain without injury.* राहणें, चांगला-&c.राहणें, नासल्यावांचून राहणें, टिकणें, तगणें, दम *m.* धरणें.

3 to; *adhere to, &c.* fig. चिकटणें, चिलगणें, चिकटून-चिलगून-धरून-पकडून-&c. असणें.

4 on; *persevere, continue.* राहणें-जाणें-चालणें used with the present participle of another verb, as तो गात राहिला He kept on singing. [रण *n.*

KEEP, KEEPING, *n.* v. V. A. 1.—*act.* राखणें*n.* ठेवणें*n.* &c. धा-

2 v. CHARGE. दिम्मत *f.* रखवाली *f.*

3 राखणें*n.* &c. जतन*n.* संगोपन*n.* जोपासना *f.* जोपाशीर *f.* जोपासणी *f.* जोपाशील *f.* निगा *f.*

4 राखण *f.* रक्षण*n.* संरक्षण*n.* रखवाली *f.* राखणावळ *f.* खबरदारी *f.* रक्षा *f.*

6 राखणें*n.* &c. राखण *f.* रखवाली *f.* राखूळ *or* राखोळ *f.* राखीळ *f.* राखणावळ *f.* पालन *pop.* पाळण *n.* जोपासणी *f.* जोपासना *f.* जोपाशीर *f.* जोपाशील *f.* बरदास्त *f.*

9 पाळणें*n.* पालन *pop.* पाळण*n.* &c.

10 पाळणें*n.* पालन *pop.* पाळण*n.* उपासना *f.*

14 पाळणें*n.* पोसणें*n.* पालन *pop.* पाळण*n.* पोषण*n.* पाळणपोषण.

I. *price of keeping or feeding.* पाळणावळ *f.* पोसणावळ *f.* राखणावळ *f.*

II. v. DUNGEON. अंधारकोंडी *f.* अंधारी *f.*

III. *consistency,* v. AGREEMENT. घटाव*m.* बनाव*m.* जम*m.* जुळणी *f.*

KEEPER, *n.* v. V. A. 1. राखणारा, ठेवणारा, &c. धारणकर्त्ता.

2 राखणारा, &c. दिम्मतदार, दिम्मतवाला, जिम्मेदार.

4 राखणारा, &c. रखवालदार, राख्या, राखणदार, राखणा, राखण, राखणाईत, रक्षक, संरक्षक, रक्षण-&c. कर्त्ता, रक्षण.

Hire or wages of a k. राखणावळ *f.* राखण *f.*

6 राखणारा, राख्या, पाळणारा, पालक, पालनकर्त्ता, पाल (in comp. as पशुपाल, &c.).

Hire or wages of a k. राखणावळ *f.* राखण *f.* राखूळ *or* राखोळ *f.* राखील *f.*

10 पाळणारा, मानणारा, &c. पालक-धारक-धारी (in comp. as आज्ञापालक, आज्ञाधारक &c.).

KEEP-SAKE, *n. thing to be kept in remembrance of the giver.* आठवणीसाठीं दिलेली वस्त *f.* यादगारी *f.* यादगिरी *f.* आठवणूक *f.*

KEG, *n. small barrel.* लहान पीपन*n.*

To KEN, *v. a. descry.* लांब-दूर-&c. पाहणें, लांबून-दुरून-&c.पाहणें.

2 v. TO KNOW. जाणणें.

KEN, *n. reach of sight.* दृष्टीचा-नजरेचा-&c. आटोका*m.*-अमल*m.*-अडसट्टा*m.*-टप्पा*m.*

2 *reach of knowledge.* बुद्धीचा आटोका*m.*-अडसट्टा*m.*-अमल*m.*-अवांका*m.* बुद्धीची धांव *f.* बुद्धि *f.*

KENNEL, *n. dog-house.* कुत्र्याचें घर*n.*-खोपट*n.* कुत्तेखाना*m.* श्वशाला *pop.* श्वानशाला *f.*

2 *pack of hounds.* शिकारी कुत्र्यांचा कळप*m.*

3 *burrow* (of a fox, &c.) बीळ*n.*

4 v. GUTTER. नाला*m.*

KERCHIEF, *n.* रुमाल*m.*

KERMES, *n.*—the insect. कृमि*m.*

KERN, *n. hand mill.* जांतें*n.* जांतीण *f.* घरट*m.*

KERNEL, *n.*—of a nut, &c. गर्भ*m.* गर*m.* गीर*m.* मगज*m.* मोख*m.*

2 *seed of pulpy fruit.* बी *f.* बीज*n.* अठी *f.* अठळी *f.* आंठीळ *f.* आंठोळी *f.* अष्टि *f.*

KESTREL. See HAWK.

KETCH, *n. two masted vessel.* दुकाठीमहागिरी *f.* दुकाठीगलबत*n.*

KETTLE, *n. pot, boiler, &c.* देग *or* डेग *f.* हंडा *or* हांडा*m.* *dim.*हंडी *or* हांडी *f.* काईल *or* कावील *f.* कढई *f.* कटाह*m.* उदस्थाली *f.* हौद*m.* सतेल*n.* The English word *kettle* is nearly naturalized as केतली *f.*

KETTLE-DRUM, *n.* नगारा*m.* धोंशा *or* धौंसा *m.* डंका *m.* दमदमा *m.* दमामा *m.* नौबत *f.* भेर *f.* भेरी *f.* तुडुंब *or* तुडूम*n.* दुंदुभि *m.*

Frame of a k. पडगें *or* पडघें*n.*

Grand k. (of processions, &c.). साहेब नौबत *f.*

K.–band. चौघडा*m.*

Closing peal on the k.–band. उतारबाजी *f.* उतारबाजा*m.*

KETTLE-DRUMMER, *n.* नगारची *or* नगारजी.

KEY, *n.* किल्ली *f.* चावी *f.* कुंजी *f.*

False k. चोरकिल्ली *f.* चोरचावी *f.* चोरकुंजी *f.*

Master k. गुरुकिल्ली *f.*

2—in music. घर*n.*

3 *explanation, secret, trick of,* v. ART. किल्ली *f.* कला *pop.* कळ *f.* उतारा*m.*

4 keys, (of a musical instrument). घर*n.*

5 See QUAY.

KEY-HOLE, *n.* किल्लीचें घर*n.* कुलपाचें तोंड*n.* भोंक*n.*

KEY-STONE, *n.* कमाणीचा दट्टा*m.*-दाटा*m.* कमाणीच्या वरचा मधला दगड*m.* [पादिका *f.*

KIBE, *n. sore, chilblain.* थंडीची भेग *f.* फूट *f.* तडा*m.* कातरा*m.* वि-

KICK, *n.* लात *or* लाथ *f.* लत्ता *f.* लत्ताप्रहार*m.* पादप्रहार*m.*

K. from a beast. लाताड*n.* लाताडी *f.*

K. out, *fling or jerk of the foot.* झटका*m.* झटकारा*m.*

K. up, *row, uproar.* गर्दी *f.* धांदल *f.* धुमाळी *f.*

Kicks and knocks, kicks and thumps. खबेटोणपे*m. pl.* टकेटोणपे*m.pl.* *v.* खा-घे-भोग.

2 *recoil.* झिंजारा *or* झिंजाडा*m.*

To KICK, *v. n. throw out the foot with violence.* पाय*m.* झाडणें-टाकणें-उचलणें.

To k. and flounder. हातपाय*m.pl.* खोडणें.

2 (up or out)—a horse, &c. लात *f.* झाडणें-मारणें, दुलाच्या *f.pl.*-दुमच्या *f.pl.*-दुगाण्या *f.pl.* झाडणें, लातळणें *or* लाताळणें.

3 *lash out,*—cow, &c. आसडी *f.* मारणें.

4—a gun; *recoil.* झाडणें, झिंजारणें *or* झिंजाडणें.

To KICK, *v. a. strike with the foot.* लात *f.* मारणें, पादप्रहार*m.*-पादाघात*m.* करणें.

To k. with the heel. टांच *f.*-खोट *f.* मारणें.

To k. soundly. लथडणें *or* लथाडणें *or* लातडणें, लातळणें *or* लाताळणें, लाता *f.pl.* सडकणें *or* सडकून-कचकून-रगडून-रपाटून-&c. देणें, पाद्याचें*n.* घालणें-करणें, पायपूजा *f.* करणें.

To k. and thumb soundly. लाताबुक्यांनीं तुडवणें.

KICKED, *p.* v. V. A. लातमारलेला, पादाहत, पादताडित, लत्तित.

Well-k. लातडलेला, लथडलेला *or* लथाडलेला.

KICKER, *n.* KICKING, *p. a.* v. V. N. 1. 2. *given to kicking,*—a horse, cow, &c. लातड *or* लाताड, लातडा, लाताळ, लातरा, पायाचा फटकळ, मारका, मारकणा.

KICKING, *n.* v.V. A.—*act.* लातमारणें*n.* पादप्रहार*m.* पादाघात*m.* लत्ताप्रहार*m.*

K. and pommelling. लातबुकी *f.* [लातालेंन.

Vehement and general k. (as of many horses, &c.).

Kickshaw, *n.* चीज *f.*

Kid, *n.* बकऱ्हंn. करडूंn. कराडूंn. करडेंn.

Female k. पाठ *f.*

To **Kid**, *v. n.* विणें.

Kidder, *n. an engrosser of merchandise, one who buys in wholesale.* अडत्या, अडतीचा वाणी-व्यापारी.

Kidling, *n. young kid.* लहान करडूंn.

To **Kidnap**, *v. a. steal* (a human being). उचलून-चोरून-धरून -&c. नेणें, हरणें, हरण करून नेणें, मनुष्यस्तेयn. करणें.

Kidnapper, *n.* v. V. (मुलास-मनुष्यास-&c.). उचलून नेणारा, मनुष्यस्तेयी, नरस्तेयी.

Kidney, *n.* मूत्रपिंडm. गुर्दm.

Kidney-bean, *n. phaseolus radiatus.* उडीदm.

Fields of or for k. उडदावळ *f.*

Kilderkin, *n.* एक लहान पीप आहे.

To **Kill**, *v. a. deprive of life.* मारणें, जिवेंमारणें, जिवानूशी मारणें, मारून टाकणें, जीव *m.*-प्राण *m.* घेणें *g. of o.* बधणें, हिंसणें, हाणणें, वध *m.*-हिंसा *f.*-हत्या *f.*-खून *m.*-&c. करणें *g. of o.* निवटणें, विदारणें, मथणें *or* मंथण, गत *or* गति *f.* देणें, गतीस लावणें-मिळवणें, लोकांतरास-ऊर्ध्वपंथास-पितृलोकास-&c. लावणें-पाठवणें, लोकांतरगत-&c. करणें.—cruelly, ferociously, in numbers, &c. with the power of *to butcher, to massacre, to slaughter, to cut to pieces, &c.* काटणें, कापणें, कापून काढणें, छाटणें, सांकटणें, खापलणें, कत्तल *f.*-कट्टा *m.*-काटाकाटी *f.*-&c. करणें *g. of o.* मारून खस्त-फस्त-पस्त-&c. करणें, सप्फा *or* सप्पा *m.*-सफेजंगी *f.* उडवणें-करणें *g. of o.* पूर्णाहुती *f.* करणें *g. of o.* बळी *m.* देणें, सूदणें, निकृंतणें, निकृंतन *n.*-निकंदन *n.*-सूदन *n.*-कदन *n.*-&c. करणें *g. of o.* खांडोळीं *n. pl.*-लेखण्या *f. pl.* करणें *g. of o.* लोथी *or* लोदी *f. pl.*-कुचे *m. pl.* पाडणें *g. of o.*—esp. for food, or in sacrifice. हलाल करणें, जबेकरणें. [तोडणें.

To k. by inches. तीळ तीळ जीव *m.* घेणें, सांडसानें मास *n.*

To k. outright. ठार *adv.* मारणें, पाणी *n.* मागूं न देणें, एकघाव दोन तुकडे *m. pl.* करणें, चीतकरणें.

2 (time). घालवणें, दवडणें, टाळणें, लोटणें, काढणें.

3 (quicksilver). मारणें.

To be killed—quicksilver. मरणें.

Killed, *p.* v. V. 1. मारलेला, जिवें मारलेला, &c. हतप्राण, हतजीव, हतचैतन्य, नष्टप्राण, नष्टचैतन्य, मारित, घातित, हत.

Killer, *n.* **Killing**, *p. a.* v. V. 1. मारणारा, जिवें मारणारा, &c. मारक, बधक, हिंसक, घातक, हंता, हत्यारा (in comp. as स्त्रीहत्यारा, &c.) बध-&c. कर्त्ता.

I. *life endangering.*—work, &c. जिवासांड, जिवापरता, जीवत्रेणा, प्राणघेणा.

II.—as used of eyes, charms, blandishments, &c. मारू, मारक, अतिमोहक.

Killing, *n.* v. V. 1.—*act.* मारणें *n.* जिवें मारणें *n.* &c. वध *m.* घात *m.* हत्या *f.* हिंसा *f.* प्राणघात *m.* हनन *n.* क्षणन *n.* मारणn. विदारण *n.* विदारणा *f.* कदन *n.* सूदन *n.* सूना *f.* मथन *or* मंथन *n.* मर्दन *n.* विमर्दन *n.* निकृंतन *pop.* निकंदन *n.*

Kiln, *n.*—for bricks, lime, &c. भट्टी *f.*

2—of a potter. अवा *m.*

3—for parching corn, &c. भट्टी *f.* भाड *n.*

Kilt, *n.* घागऱ्यासारखें पुरुषाचें नेसण आहे.

Kin, *n.*v. **Relationship.** गोत्र *n.* गोत्रसंबंध *m.* एकगोत्रसंबंध *m.* नातें *n.* सापिंड्य *n.*

Of k. गोत्री, गोत्रज, गोत्रसंबंधी, गोती, सजातीय.

2 *kindred*, v. **Relations.** भाऊबंद *m. pl.* गोत *n.* गोतपत *or* गोतपात *n.* गोतवळा *m.*

Kin, *a.* v. **Kindred.** सजातीय, सवर्ण.

Kind, *a. disposed to do good to others, benevolent, benign.* कृपालु *pop.* कृपाळ *or* कृपाळू, कृपावान् *pop.* कृपावंत, कृपाशील, कृपायुक्त, कृपाविशिष्ट, कृपान्वित, उपकारक, उपकारी, उपकारशील, उपकारपर, परोपकारी, परोपकारक, परोपकारशील, लोकोपकारी, लोकोपकारशील, &c. उपकारबुद्धि, परोपकारबुद्धि, मेहरबान, अनुग्राहक, हृदयी, हृदयालु, सुहृदय, लोकहितेच्छु, लोककल्याणेच्छु. —*intens.* कृपाभरित, कृपापूर्ण, कृपासंपन्न, कृपाढ्य, कृपापूरित, कृपाविष्ट, कृपाप्रचुर, कृपामय. Some appellatives or designations for *a kind (gracious, favoring) person*, are कृपानिधि, कृपासागर, कृपासमुद्र, कृपासिंधु, कृपाब्धि, कृपार्णव, कृपाकर, कृपानिधान, कृपाराशि, कृपामूर्त्ति, कृपापुरुष, कृपाघन, कृपारूप, कृपाभूत.

2 *proceeding from kindness.* कृपेचा, उपकाराचा, परोपकराचा, मेहरबानीचा, कृपाळू, उपकारबुद्धीचा, परोपकारबुद्धीचा.

Kind, *n. genus, race.* जाति *pop.* जात *f.* ज्ञात *f.*

Man-k. मनुष्य जाति *f.*

Nature or constitution of the k. जातिस्वभाव *m.*

Woman-k. स्त्रीजाति *f.*

2 *sort.*—in a sense more loose than genus. जात *f.* प्रकार *m.* विधि *m.* तऱ्हा *f.* पर *f.* भात *f.* विध in comp. तोड *f.* प्रत *f.*

A different k. विजात *f.*

Difference of k. वैजात्य *m.*

Of a different k. विजातीय.

Of different kinds. तऱ्हेतऱ्हेचा, परीपरीचा, परोपरीचा, जातीजातीचा, भांतोभांतीचा.

Of every k. हरजिनशी *or* सी, हरभांत.

Of a particular k. (ज्या *or* त्या) प्रतीचा, जातीचा, पडोशाचा, ताड्याचा.

Of two kinds. उभयविध.

3 *manner, way*, v. **Manner.** पर *f.* प्रकार *m.* डौल *m.* चाल *f.* रीति *pop.* रीत *f.*

4—in revenue; *products of the soil.* ऐनजिन्नस *m.*

Kind-hearted, *a.* v. **Kind.** हृदयी, हृदयालु, हृदयवान्, चित्तवान्, सुहृदय.

To **Kindle**, *v. a. fire, set on fire, light*, lit. fig. चेतवणें, पेटवणें, पेटेसाकरणें, पेटता करणें, शिलकावणें *or* शिलगावणें, उजळणें, पाजळणें, लावणें, आग *f.* लावणें, चूड *f.*-चुडी *f.* लावणें, प्रदीपन *n.*-उद्दीपन *n.*-&c. करणें *g. of o.* प्रदीप्त-&c. करणें.

To be kindled—lights, fire, &c. लागणें.

Straws, sticks, &c. used for kindling. पेटवणn.चेतवणn.

To **Kindle**, *v. n. catch fire.* पेटणें, चेतणें, चेतवणें, चेतावणें, शिलकणें *or* शिलगणें, पेट *m.*-चेत *m.* घेणें, तेवणें.

Kindled, *p.* v. V. A. पेटवलेला, चेतवलेला, &c. दीपित, प्रदीपित, उद्दीपित, दीप्त, प्रदीप्त, उद्दीप्त, प्रज्वलित, उज्ज्वलित.

KINDLER, *n.* KINDLING, *p. a.* v. V A. पेटवणारा, चेतवणारा, &c. दीपक, प्रदीपक, उद्दीपक, दीपन-&c. कर्त्ता.

KINDLING, *n.* v. V. A.—*act.* पेटवणें *n.* चेतवणें *n.* &c. शिलकावण *or* शिलगावण *f.* शिलकावणी *or* शिलगावणी *f.* दीपन *n.* प्रदीपन *n.* उद्दीपन *n.* प्रज्वलन *n.* उज्ज्वलन *n.* These are chiefly in comp.

v. V. N. पेटणें *n.* चेतणें *n.* &c. पेट *m.* घेणें *n.* चेत *m.*

KINDLINESS, *n.* See KINDNESS.

2 *friendliness and pleasantness of intercourse.* रहसाळी *f.* रहस्य *n.* रहश्श *n.* स्नेहभाव *m.* प्रीतिभाव *m.* गोडीगुलाबी *f.*

KINDLY, *a. congenial, genial, &c.* समशील, समानशील, समधर्मक, समभाव, समानभाव, सात्म्याचा, अनुगुण, अनुकूल.

2 *bland, mild, gentle.* कोमल *or* ळ, सौम्य, सात्विक, सात्म्याचा.

KINDLY, *adv.* v. A. KIND. कृपाकरून, मेहरबानी करून, मेहर करून, मेहरबानीनें, स्नेहभावानें, कृपाबुद्ध्या, कृपादृष्ट्या, अनुकूल होऊन, &c.

2 v. A. KINDLY. सुदामत, सुरळीतपणें, सुरळीतपणानें, सरलभावानें, ऋजुभावानें, बऱ्याबोलानें.

KINDNESS, *n.* v. A. कृपा *f.* अनुग्रह *m.* कृपाळूपणा *m.* मेहरबानी *f.* मेहरबानगी *f.* मेहर *f.* मोहबत *f.* इनायत *f.* कृपाशीलता *f.* कृपालुता *f.* परोपकारिता *f.* लोकोपकारिता *f.* &c. उपकारशीलता *f.* उपकारबुद्धि *f.* परोपकारबुद्धि *f.* लोकोपकारबुद्धि *f.* परहितबुद्धि *f.* जनकृपा *f.* लोककृपा *f.* लोकहितेच्छा *f.* जनसौहृद *n.* भलाई *f.* भलाइकी *f.* भलीभलाई *f.* भलमाणसाई *f.* माणूसपणा *m.* सौजन्य *n.* रायत *or* रायात *f.*

I. *an act of k. a favor, &c.* उपकार *m.* परोपकार *m.* कृतोपकार *m.* उपकृति *f.* एहसान *n.* इनायत *f.* [संबंध *m.*

KINDRED, *n.* v. RELATIONSHIP. नातें *n.* संबंध *m.* गोत्र *n.* गोत्र-

2 v. RELATIONS. भाऊबंद *m. pl.* गोत *n.* गणगोत *n.* गोतवळा *or* गोतोळा *m.* गोतपत *or* पात *n.* गोत्रसमुदाय *m.* बंधुवर्ग *m.* बंधुजन *n.* [नातलग.

KINDRED, *a. related.* गोत्री, गोत्रज, एक गोत्रज, सगोत्र, सवर्ण,

2 *of the like nature or properties.* सवर्ण, सजातीय, समानशील, समभाव, सधर्मक, समधर्मक, सात्म्याचा, साधर्म्याचा.

KINE, *n. cows.* गायी *f. pl.* गाया *f. pl.* गायगुरें *n. pl.* पाडुकें *n. pl.*

KING, *n.* राजा, राव, राय, राणा, छत्रपति, नरेंद्र, नरेश्वर, नरदेव, नरपति, नराधिप, नृप, नृपति, भूपाल *or* ळ, महीपाल, भूप, भूपति, लोकपाल *or* ळ, पार्थिव, प्रजापति, इंद्र (in comp. as नरेंद्र, भूतेंद्र, मृगेंद्र, खगेंद्र, &c.).

Some terms of honor or panegyric for *kings* are, राजतिलक, राजमुकुट, राजमुकुटमणि, राजदीपक, राजरत्न, राजचूडामणि, राजसूर्य.

Daughter of a k. राजकुमारी *f.* राजकुंवरी *f.* राजकन्या *f.*

King of kings. राजाधिराज, राजराज, राजाधिप, राजेंद्र.

K. and beggar. रावनीरंक.

Like k. like people. यथाराजा तथा प्रजा.

Line of kings. राजावलि *f.*

Son of a k. राजकुमार, राजकुंवर, राजपुत्र.

That is without a k. or head. अराजक, अनायक.

KING-CRAFT, *n. art of governing, skill in governing.* राज्यनयन विद्या *f.* राज्यकर्तृत्व *n.* राज्यचातुर्य *n.*

KINGS-EVIL, *n.* गंडमाळा *f. pl.* [बळा *m.*

KING-FISHER, *n.* डिचा *m.* ढिसा *m.* गण्या *m.* खंज्या *m.* पाणका-

KINGDOM, *n.*—country. राज्य *n.* राष्ट्र *m. n.*

2 *government.* राज्य *n.* राज्याधिकार *m.*

The animal k. जीवजाति *f.* जीवगण *m.* जीवकोटि *f.*

The mineral k. धातुजाति *f.*-गण *m.*-कोटि *f.*

The vegetable k. वनस्पति जाति *f.*-गण *m.*-कोटि *f.* तृणजाति *f.* उद्भिज्ज कोटि *f.*

KING-HOOD, KINGSHIP, *n.* राजत्व *n.* नृपत्व *n.* राज्य *n.* राजाधिकार *m.* राजपद *n.*

KING-LIKE, KINGLY, *a. belonging to a k. suitable, &c. to a k.* राजाचा, राजकीय, राजसंबंधी, राजयोग्य, राजोचित, राजार्ह, राजपदवीयोग्य, पादशाही, बादशाही.

2 v. MONARCHIAL. एकराजसत्ताक, एकाधिपत्याचा.

KINS-FOLK, *n. kindred,* v. RELATIONS. भाऊबंद *m. pl.* गोत *n.* बंधुजन *n.* बंधुवर्ग *m.* दाईजगोत्रज *m. pl.*

KINSMAN, *n. man of the same race or family.* भाऊबंद, गोतभाऊ, गोती, कुलपुरुष, गोत्रबंधु, गोत्रपुरुष, ज्ञाती, दायाद, दाईज, दायजी, स्व. बंधु, बंधुजन, स्वजन, कुटुंबी, सपिंड, सगोत्र, सनाभि, समानोदक, सकुल्य.

KINSWOMAN, *n.* गोतबहीण *f.* गोत्रबहीण *f.*

KIRK. See CHURCH.

To KISS, *v. a.*—actively, *take a kiss.* चुंबणें, मुका *m.*-चुंबन *n.* घेणें *g. of o.* चुंबन *n.* करणें.—To suffer one's self to be kissed, let one have a kiss is मुका *m.*-चुंबन *n.* देणें.

KISS, *n.* मुका *m.* चुंबन *n.*

KISSED, *p.* v. V. मुका घेतलेला, चुंबित.

KISSER, *n.* KISSING, *p. a.* v. V. मुका घेणारा, चुंबणारा, चुंबन कर्त्ता, चुंबक & चुंबी (in comp. as मुखचुंबी, गगनचुंबक).

KISSING-CRUST, *n.* चिकटलेल्या पोळ्यांचा वण *m.*

KIT, *n.* v. BAGGAGE, TRAPS. खटलें *n.* बाडबिशात *f.* इत्रा खित्रा *m.* गबाळें चबाळें *n.*

KITCHEN, *n. cooking room.* स्वैपाकघर *n.* ओबरा *or* ओयरा *m.* ओंनारा *m.* मुतबखm. मुतबखखानाm. बावरचीखानाm. पाकशाला *f.* पाकगृह *n.* रंधनागार *n.*

Clerk of the k. बाकनीस, मुतपाकाचा कारभारी, पाकगृहाधिकारी.

KITCHEN-GARDEN, *n.* मळा *m.* भाजीमळा *m.* परसू *n.* शाकवाटिका *f.*

KITCHEN-MAID, KITCHEN-WENCH, *n.* खटपटी *or* खटपटीण *f.* आइतें करणारी-करूनदेणारी.

KITCHEN-WORK, *n.* स्वैपाक घरांतलेंकाम *n.*

KITE, *n.* घार *f.* घारूड *or* घारवड *n.* चिल्ह *m.*

Flock of kites. घारूड *or* घारवड *n.*

2 *paper-kite.* वावडी *f.* पतंग *m.* कनकावळाm. तुकूल *f.* दुकूल *f.* घार *f.* N. B. These words express different sorts of paper kites.

Dip of a k. गोता *m.*

Streamer (of paper) tied to a k. चंग *m.*

KITTEN, *n.* मांजराचें पिलूं *n.*

To KITTEN, *v. n.* विणें.

To KLICK. See To CLICK.

To KNAB, *v. a. bite, gnaw.* चावणें, कडकड-खुटखुट-&c. खाणें.

KNACK, *n. knickknack, toy.* खेळ *m.* खेळणा *m.* जुगूत *f.*

2 *readiness, dexterity.* हातोटी *f.* युक्ति *f. pop.* जुगूत *or* युगूत *f.* टूक *f.* कडासणी *f.* ओज *f.*

3 *art, trick, secret.* हिकमत *f.* कळ *f.* टूक *f.* युक्ति *f. pop.* युगूत *or* जुगूत *f.* किल्ली *f.* कल्पना *f.* घडमोड *or* घडामोड *f.*

KNAG, *n. knot in wood.* गांठ *f.* ग्रंथि *m.* गुळुंब *or* गुळुंभ *n.* गुळूम *n.*

KNAGGY, *a.* v. N. गांठळ *or* गांठाळ, ग्रंथिल.

2 *fig. crabbed.* खट्याळ, द्वाड, खडतर. [टेंगूळ *m.*

KNAP, *n. eminence, protuberance.* टेंकड *or* टेंकाड *n.* टेंकडी *f.*

To KNAP, *v. a. break short*, v. To SNAP. मोडणें, कटकन-कटकर-पटकन-नटकन-&c. मोडणें.

KNAPPY, *a. full of knaps.* टेकाळ, टेंगळांचा.

KNAPSACK, *n. soldier's bag.* थैली *f.* भाता *m.*

KNAR, *n. knot in wood.* See KNOT.

KNAVE, *n. dishonest person, cheat*, v. ROGUE. ठक, ठग, ठकबाज, दगाबाज, दगेखोर, सोदा, काशीकर, काबूयार, हिल्लेबाज, वंचक, गुंडा.

An arch k. A slippery k. बाटोळागोळा *m.* बाटोळागोटा *m.* बाटोळाधोंडा *m.* पांढरापरीस *m.*

A pack or crew of knaves. चांडाळ चौकडी *f.* धूर्त्तमंडल *n.* शकुनिचतुष्टय *n.*

2—at cards. गुलाम *m.*

KNAVERY, KNAVISHNESS, *n. dishonesty, &c.* ठकपणा *m.* ठकडेपणा *m.* छटपणा *m.* लटकेपणा *m.* लबाडी *f.* काबूयारी *f.* धूर्त्तता *f* धूर्त्ताई *f.* शाठ्य *n.* धौर्त्य *n.* धौर्त्तिका *f.*

3 *knavish practices*, v. ROGUERY. ठगाई *f.* ठकाई *f.* ठकबाजी *f.* ठकविद्या *f.* ठकूविद्या *f.* दगाबाजी *f.* दगलबाजी *f.* धतुरा *or* धत्तुरा *m. v.* दाखव.

KNAVISH, *a. dishonest, fraudulent.* ठकाऊ, ठकावू, ठकारू, ठकबरा, ठकव्या, ठकू, ठकडा, फसव्या, खटनट, नटखट, दगाबाज, दगलबाज, दगेखोर, लबाड, लटका, लटकुरा, खोटसाळ, छट, धूर्त्त, शठ, वंचक, ठकबाजीचा, दगलबाजीचा, ठकविद्येचा, ठकपणाचा, असाधु, कितव, अप्रामाणिक, धौर्त्तिक, हरामी, हरामजादा, हराम.

2 See MISCHIEVOUS.

To KNEAD, *v. a. work and press with the hands.* मळणें, मर्दणें, कमावणें, चिवळणें, अवळणें, चुरणें, कुसकरणें *or* कुसकुरणें, कामाई *f.*-मळणी *f.*-&c. करणें *g. of o.*—(wheaten dough) तिंबणें.

To k. and squeeze (clothes in washing them). चुबकणें, चुबकणी *f.* करणें. [अवमर्दित.

KNEADED, *p.* v. V. मळलेला, कमावलेला, &c. मार्दित, उपमर्दित,

KNEADING, *n.* v.V.—*act.* मळणें *n.* कमावणें *n.* &c. कमाई *f.* मळणी *f.* मरामत *f.* उपमर्द *m.* उपमर्दन *n.* अवमर्द *m.* अवमर्दन *n.* मर्दन *n.*

K. the limbs. चप्पी *f.* संवाह *m.* संवाहन *n.*

KNEADING-TROUGH, *n.*—of wood. काठवट *f.*—of metal. परात *f.* पितळी *f.*

KNEE, *n.* गुडघा *m.* ढोंपर *n.* ढोपा *m.* डोका *m.* जानु *m.*

A bump with the k. ढोपर खळी *f. v.* मार.

Hollow on either side of the k. डोळा *m.*

Inflammation at the k. गुडघी *f.* ढोपरी *f.*

To bump with the k. गुडघा *m.* मारणें.

To have the knees sink under from age, &c. ढोपरखुटीसयेणें.

KNEED, *a.* गुडघ्याचा, ढोंपराचा.

KNEE-DEEP, *a.* गुडघ्याइतका, ढोपराइतका, गुढघाभर, गुडघ्याबराबर.

KNEE-JOINT, *n.* ढोपराची-&c. खीळ *f.* जानुसंधि *m.*

KNEE-PAN, *n.* गुडघ्याची-ढोपराची-&c. वाटी *f.* वाटी *f.* जानुफलक *n.*

To KNEEL, *v. n.* गुडघे *m. pl.*-&c. टेंकणें, मेटें *n. pl.* टेंकणें, मेटेखुंटीस-ढोपरखुंटी *adv.* बसणें. [ध्वनि *m.*

KNELL, *n. sound of a bell at a funeral.* प्रेतनयनकालिक घंटा-

KNICK KNACK, *n. a trifle or toy.* खेळ *m.* खेळवणा *m.* खेळणें *n.* जुगूत *f.*

KNIFE, *n.* सुरी *f.* छुरिका *f.* Some of the sorts as used for various purposes are बकई *f.* नारकत *n.*

A large k. सुरा *m.*

Clasp k. मोडसुरा *m.*—*dim.* मोडसुरी *f.*

Pen-k. चाकू *m.*

KNIGHT, *n.*—the title. सरदार बहादूर *m.*

2—at chess. घोडा *m.*

Check mate with the k. घोडमात *f.* घोडशह *m.*

KNIGHT-HOOD, *n.* सरदारबहादुरी *f.*

To KNIT, *v. a. weave without a loom.* हातांनीं विणणें.

2 *unite*, v. To JOIN. जोडणें, मिळवणें.

3 (the brows) *contract.* मोडणें, मुरडणें, अढी *f.* घालणें.

4 See To TIE.

KNIT, *n. texture.* विणकर *f.* वीण *f.*

KNIT, *p.* v. V. 1. हातांनीं विणलेला.

2 जोडलेला.

Strong-k. Well-k. v. COMPACT. दृढसंधि, वळींब.

KNITTING-NEEDLE, *n.* सळई *f.* विणण्याची सुई *f.* [कसा *m.*

KNITTLE, *n. draw-string.* ओढदोरा *m.* मणदोरा *m.* उघडदोरा *m.*

KNOB, *n. protuberance, bunch, boss.* बोंड *n.* बोंडी *f. dim.* बोंडूक *n.* बोंडस *n.* गेंद *m.* गोंडा *m.* झुबका *m.* झुमका *m.* माथा *m.* माथ्या *m.*

2 (as in wood) *knot.* गांठ *f.* गुळुंब *or* गुळुंभ *n.* गुळूम *n.* गुंज *f. n.* गुंजट *n.* ग्रंथि *m. f.*

KNOBBY, *a.* v. N. 2. *and* KNOTTY. गांठाळ, गांठळगुंजट, गांठळगुंठळ, ग्रंथिल.

To KNOCK, *v. n. hit, strike against.* लागणें, धडकणें, धडक *f.*-भडक *f.*-धडका *m.*-भडका *m.*-&c. लागणें-बसणें.

2 *knock at.* ठोकणें, ठोठावणें, थाप *f.* मारणें.

3 under; *submit*, v. To YIELD. दबकणें, मेटें *n. pl.* टेंकणें, बें *n.* करणें-म्हणणें, हारींजाणें, अजिंक जाणें.

4 up; *become fatigued*, v. To TIRE. थकणें, वेंगणें, काचावणें, लंघणें, घोडें *n.*-घोडा *m.* थकणें *g. of s.* नाडी *f.* अटपणें *g. of s.* टांके *m. pl.* ढील होणें *g. of s.* उरीं फुटणें, चकनाचूर-चकाचूर होणें.

To KNOCK, *v. a. strike, hit.* मारणें, पिटणें, ठोकणें, ठोठावणें, ठोक *m.*-ठोका *m.*-&c. देणें.

2 down; *fell, prostrate.* पाडणें, जमीनदोस्त करणें, चीत करणें, बिछावणें, निजवणें, लोळवणें.

3 off; *rattle off, do sharply*, v. To DESPATCH. ठोकणें, झपाटणें, फटकारणें, भरकटणें *or* भरकडणें, भरकाडणें, रपाटणें, रगडणें, तासणें, चरकटणें.

4 up; *fatigue*, v. To TIRE. भागवणें, श्रमवणें, हायास आणणें, हाडें *n. pl.* घुसळणें, खोमलणें, घुसळणें, पादवणें, चकाचूर करणें, अटारा *m.* पाडणें *g. of o.*

To be knocked up. टणकणें, भागणें, थकणें, मरगळीस *or* मरळीस येणें, हायास येणें, हदहूवणें, आंगाचा चकनाचूर *m.* होणें *g. of s.* अटारा *m.* पडणें *g of s.*

5 about; *use or treat roughly, violently, heedlessly, &c.* घुसडणें, घुसटणें, पुदडणें, पुदलणें, पुदाळणें.
6 on the head, lit. See To KILL, fig. *frustrate*, v. To DEFEAT. मोडणें, हेलपटणें, व्यर्थ-&c. करणें, पासला-पालथा पाडणें.

KNOCK, KNOCKING, *n.* v. V. N. 1.—*act.* लागणेंn. धडकणेंn. धडक *f.* धडका*m.* धडक *f.* धडका*m.*
v. V. A. 1. ठोकणेंn. &c. ठोका*m.* ठोक *m.* प्रहार *m.* आघात*m.*
3 फटकारणें *n.* &c. फटकारणी *f.*

KNOCK-KNEED, *a. of knees that approach each other.* गुडघेघाशा, संहत जानु, संहत जानुक, संज्ञु.

KNOCKER, *n.*—of a door, &c. ठोकणी *f.* ठोकणें *n.*

To KNOLL, *v. n. sound,*—a bell. वाजणें.

KNOLL, *n. eminence, hillock.* टेंकड *n.* टेंकडें *n.* टेंकडी *f.* टेंकाड*n.* खडपा *m.* उटंगर *m. n.* उटंगळ *n.*

KNOP. See KNOB.

KNOT, *n. complication.* गांठ *f.* गूत *f.* ग्रंथि *m. f.* ग्रंथिका *f.*
Bow-k. आसुडगांठ.
Common single k. निरगांठ.
Common slip k. सुरगांठ, सुटगांठ, आसुडगांठ.
Closing k. formed with the strands. पोकळगांठ.
Grandam's k. अडाणी गांठ, बाईलगांठ.
K. tied to aid remembrance. खूणगांठ.
Reef k. चाडेगांठ. [सरगांठ.
Running k. शेसरगांठ, पाश *m.* सरकफांस *m.* सरक गांठ,
Slip k. निसरगांठ.
The sacred or holy k. ब्रह्मगांठ.
To tie a k. गांठ *f.* देणें-मारणें.
2 *bond of union.* गांठ *f.* ग्रंथि *m. f.*
An indissoluble k. जन्माची गांठ *f.* रेशमाची गांठ *f.*
3 *articulation, knuckle,* v. JOINT. कांडें *n.* गांठ*f.* ग्रंथि *m f.* पर्व *n.*
4 *gang, crew,* v. BAND. गट्ट*m.* गट्टा *m.* चुंग *f.* मुठाण *n.*
5 *tuft, bunch, clump.* चुबका *m.* झुबका *m.* झुमका *m.* बेट *n.* गुच्छ *m.* स्तबक *m.*
6 *ball, gathering, lump.* गांठ *f.* गुठळी or गोठळी *f.*
7 *knotty point, intricacy, difficulty.* अठी *f.* अढी *f.* गांठ *f.* गुढी *f.* कोडें *n.* गूढार्थ*m.* पीळ *m.*
8 (in the mind) *a prejudice.* अट *f.* अढी *f.* अठी*f.* गांठ*f.*

To KNOT, *v.a. complicate or tie in a knot.* गांठणें, बांधणें, गांठ *f.* देणें-मारणें. [बांधणें-धरणें.

To KNOT, *v. n. form knots.* गांठळणें, कांडळणें, पेरें *n.*-कांडें*n.*-&c.

KNOTTINESS, *n.* v. A. 1. गांठळपणा*m.* गांठळगुंठळपणा *m.* &c.

KNOTTED, KNOTTY, *a. full of knots.* गांठळ or गांठाळ, गांठळगुंजट, गांठळगुंठळ, ग्रंथिल, ग्रंथिप्रचुर, ग्रंथिमय, ग्रंथिविशिष्ट.
2 fig. *full of knotty points,* v. INTRICATE. गुंतागुंतीचा, गुंताड्याचा, खचरट, खडतर.
A k. affair. गोंध *f.*
A k. point. कोडें *n.* कूट *n.* खडकळ *n.* गूढार्थ *m.*

To KNOW, *v. a. have knowledge of.* जाणणें, समजणें, कळणें, ठाऊक-माहीत-&c. असणें *in. con.* ज्ञान *n.*-परिज्ञान*n*-&c. असणें *g. of o. & in. con.*
Who knows? कोण जाणे, नजाणे.
To become known. अवगणें, समजणें.
2 *recognize.* ओळखणें, जाणणें, ओळख *f.*-&c. पटणें *g. of o. with in. con.*
3 *be familiar or acquainted with* (persons). जाणणें, ओळखणें, ओळख *f.*-परिचय*m.*-&c. असणें *in. con.*
4 *be acquainted with* (things). जाणणें, समजणें, येणें *in.con.* माहितगारी *f.*-गम्य *n.*-&c. असणें *in. con. g. of o.*
5 (carnally). जाणणें, भोग *m.* घेणें-देणें, जवळ जाणें.

To KNOW, *v. n. have knowledge.* जाणणें, समजणें, ज्ञान *n.*-&c. असणें *in. con.*
Not to know, *nescire.* नेणणें.

KNOWABLE, *a.* v. V. A. 1. जाणायाचा-जोगता-&c. ज्ञेय, विज्ञेय, ज्ञातव्य, वेदनीय, वेद्य, ज्ञानगम्य, बुद्धिगम्य, परिचय गम्य.

KNOWER, *n.* KNOWING, *p. a.* v. V. A. 1. जाणणारा, &c. ज्ञाता, विज्ञाता, वेत्ता.
4 *and* V. N. जाणणारा, &c. जाण, जाणता, माहितगार, माहितदार, माहीत,वाकब, वाकबदार,वाकबगार, जातज्ञान, प्राप्तज्ञान, लब्धज्ञान.
I. *skilful, clever, proficient, &c.* जाण, जाणता, शहाणा, कुशल, ज्ञानी, जाणसळ or जाणसाळ, पक्का, चतुर, विचक्षण, हुशार, खबरदार, समजदार, अभिज्ञ, प्रवीण, विशारद.
II. *shrewd, cunning, sharp, not to be taken in.* पक्का,खबरदार, चत्रा, पोक, पोका, काबू, गुंडा, नागर, बाट, बाटगा, बंदर, पंजाबी, छपन्नी or छपन्न्या, छतिशा, बाराबंदरचें पाणी प्यालेला, छप्पनदेश फिरलेला, बाटोळा धोंडा, बाटोळा गोटा, मारवाडी.

KNOWING, KNOWLEDGE, *n. certain perception.* ज्ञान *n.* परिज्ञान *n.* विज्ञान *n.* बोध *m.* प्रबोध *m.* अवबोध *m.* उद्बोध *m.* अवगम *m.* ज्ञप्ति *f.* वेदन *n.* प्रतीति *f.* प्रमा *f.* प्रमिती *f.*
2 *recognition.* ओळख *f.* प्रत्यभिज्ञान *n.* प्रत्यभिज्ञा *f.*
3 *acquaintance* (with persons). ओळख *f.* जाणपछान *f.* पछान *f.* परिचय *m.* जाणसाळ *f.* दंडक *m.*—indef. loosely, &c. ओळखपाळख *f.* ओळखदेख *f.*
K. by sight. तोंड ओळख *f.*
4 *acquaintance, conversancy, versedness in,* (science, &c.). ज्ञान *n.* परिचय *m.* माहितगारी *f.* माहिती *f.* माहीत *f.* वाकबदारी *f.* वाकबगारी *f.* दसलगिरी *f.* गम्य *n.* गति *f.* वासना *f.* प्रवेश *m.* अभिज्ञान *n.* अभिज्ञता *f.* प्रवीणता*f.* प्रावीण्य *n.* नैपुण्य*n.* आलोड्य *n.*
5—opposed to ignorance; *information respecting.* ज्ञान *n.* खबर *f.* माहिती *f.*माहितगारी *f.*माहीत *f.* वेत्तृत्व*n.*ज्ञातृत्व*n.*
According to one's k. यथाज्ञान, यथाज्ञानें.
Before one's k. or time. जाणोपरीचे अगोधर.
Within one's k. जाणोपरी.
Without the k. of. नकळत *with* स or ला.
6 *learning, science.* ज्ञान *n.* विद्या *f.* विज्ञान *n.*
Divine or spiritual k. ब्रह्मज्ञान *n.* ब्रह्मविद्या *f.* तत्वज्ञान *n.* आत्मज्ञान *n.* आत्मविद्या*f.* अध्यात्मज्ञान*n.* अध्यात्मविद्या *f.* परमार्थज्ञान *n.* परमार्थविद्या *f.* ज्ञानविद्या *f.* अध्यात्म *n.*
Instruction in divine k. ब्रह्मोपदेश *m.* ज्ञानोपदेश *m.* ब्रह्मदान *n.* आत्मबोध *m.*
Sacred and profane k. ज्ञानविज्ञान.
Thirst after k. जिज्ञासा *f.*
Thirsty after k. जिज्ञासु.

KNOWINGLY, *adv. wittingly, &c.* जाणून, समजून, उमजून, जा-

णून बुजून, जाणून पुसून, जाणून सवरून, समजून उमजून, जाणत, or जाणतजाणत, कळत, बुद्धिपूर्वक, बुद्धिपुरस्सर.

KNOWN, *p.* v. V. A. 1. जाणलेला, &c. ठाऊक, माहीत, ठावका, माहूम, विदित, ज्ञात, परिज्ञात, विज्ञात, परिचित, वित्त, अवगत.

Publicly k. v. NOTORIOUS. प्रसिद्ध, जाहीर, महशूर, उघड.

Universally k. जगत्प्रसिद्ध *pop.* जगप्रसिद्ध, जगजाहीर.

To be k. to. कळणें, ठाऊक-माहीत-&c. असणें, समजणें.

KNUCKLE, *n. joint of a finger.* बोटाची सांध *f.*-सांधा *m.*-संधिम. *f.*-पेरें *n.*-पेरकें *n.* पर्व *n.* बंद *m.*

To knock on the head with one's knuckles. टाप *f.*-टापर *f.* मारणें.

To strike with a k. टिंच *f.* मारणें, टिचकणें.

To KNUCKLE, *v. n. submit,* v. To YIELD. मेटें*n. pl.* टेकणें, चीं*f.* म्हणणें, बें*n.* करणें-म्हणणें.

L.

L. This letter is represented by ल.

LA, *interj.* पहा.—as used by a woman. अगई.

LABDANUM, *n. cistus ladaniferus.* लादन*n.*

LABEL, *n. slip of paper, &c. attached to any thing shewing its contents.* चकती *f.* खूणचिट्ठी *f.* चिठ्ठी *f.*

2—as attached to shew the number and price severally. अंकपट्टी *f.* बीजक*n.*

To LABEL, *v. a.* v. N. चकती *f.* &c. लावणें-बांधणें-मारणें.

LABIAL, *a. belonging to the lips.* ओठांचा.

2 *formed by the lips,*—letters. ओष्ठ्य.

LABIODENTAL, *a. formed by the lips and teeth.* दंतोष्ठ्य or दंतौष्ठ्य, दंत्योष्ठ्य.

LABOR, *n. toil, travail, trouble, pains, wearisome exertion.* मेहनत *f.* श्रम*m.* कष्ट*m.* क्लेश*m.* मशागत *f.* उद्योग*m.* उपद्व्याप *m.* आयास*m.* प्रयास*m.* सायास*m.* परिश्रम*m.* अटाआट*m. f.* अटाघाट *m. f.* अटापिटा*m.* अटापिटी *f.* अटापीट *f.*

L.—compreh. labor and pains, toil and trouble. मेहनत मशागत *f.*

Day-l. मजुरी *f.* रोजमजुरी *f.* मजूरकाम*n.* मोलमजुरी *f.* हेलपाटी *f.*

Forced l. बिगार *f.* वेठ *f.*

Fruitless l. गजस्नान*n.* कुंजरशौच*m.* तुषकंडन*n.* जलताडन*n.* बोकेढुंज *f.* बोकेफोड *f.*

Hard l. सखत मेहनत *f.* कसालत *f.* कसाला*m.* कष्टीमेहनत*f.*

Hard and toilsome l. दगडफोड *f.*

Low or servile l. *drudgery.* कबाडकाम*n.* कबाडकष्ट*m.*

Manual or bodily l. आंग मेहनत *f.* व्रात*m.*

Price or wages of l. मशागत *f.* मेहनत *f.* मजुरी *f.* मोल*n.*

Toilsome and vexatious l. दगदग *f.* खस्ता *f. or f. pl.* धकाधक*f.* कडाकूट*f.* कपाळकूट*f.* कपाळफोड*f.* डोईफोड*f.* माथाकूट*f.* माथेफोड *f.* उरस्फोड *f.*

With great l. सातासायासानें, जुलमाजुलमीं or जुलमाजुलमानें, जुलमानें, जुलमावर.

2 *work to be done, or done,* v. WORK. काम *n.* मेहनत घेऊन केलेलें-कराव्याचें काम*n.*

3 *travail,* v. CHILD-BIRTH. प्रसववेदना *f.* प्रसूतिवेदना *f.* गर्भवेदना *f.*

To LABOR, *v. n. toil, work hard.* खपणें, श्रम*m.*-कष्ट*m.*-मेहनत*f.*-&c. घेणें-करणें.—as enhanced. जिवावर-छातीवर-&c.काम*n.* करणें, दंड*m.* काढणें, अटाआट*m.f.*-आटाघाट*f.*-डोईफोड *f.*-कपाळकूट *f.*-उरस्फोड *f.*-&c. करणें, मरून-जीवदेऊन-जीवतोडून-&c. काम*n.* करणें, जीव*m.* अर्धाकरणें, रक्ताचें पाणी*n.* करणें, हाडें*n. pl.* झिजवणें, हाडांचीं काडें*n. pl.* करणें, हाडांचे मणी*m.pl.* करणें.

2 *do work.* खपणें, राबणें, राबडणें, काम*n.* करणें.

3 *be in distress, strife, struggling, &c.* अब्दणें, कुचंबणें, अडचणणें, अवघडणें, कुचंबत जाणें-&c.

4 *be in child-birth.* वेणा*f. pl.*-तिडका *f. pl.* देणें, प्रसवांत-प्रसूतींत-प्रसववेदनेंत-प्रसवावस्थेंत-&c. असणें.

To LABOR, *v. a. form or prosecute with labor; elaborate.* श्रमानें-कष्टानें-श्रम घेऊन-कष्ट घेऊन-&c. करणें, मशागत *f.*-&c. करणें *g. of o.*

LABORATORY, *n. work-room.* कारखाना*m.* उद्योगगृह*n.*

LABORED, *p.* v.V.A. श्रमानें केलेला, कष्टसिद्ध, श्रमसिद्ध, मशागतीचा.

LABORER, *n.* LABORING, *p. a.* v.V. N. 1. खपणारा, श्रम घेणारा-करणारा, मेहनत करणारा, श्रमकर्त्ता, कष्टकारी, &c.

2 खपणारा, खप्या, कामकरणारा, कामकरी, कष्टकरी.

A day-l. मजूर, मजूरकर, मजूरकरी, मजूरदार, मजूरवाला, रोजकरी, रोजकाम्या, रोजदार, बेगारी or बिगारी.

Business of a day-l. मजुरी *f.* रोजमजुरी *f.* मजूरकाम *n.*

Wages of a day-l. मजुरी *f.* रोजमजुरी *f.* रोजी *f.*

A l. man, *one of the laboring class.* मशागती or त्या, आंगमेहनती or त्या, कबाडकष्टी, कबाडकाम्या, मोलकरी, घोंगड्या, कांबळ्या, पायकाळा, लंगोटबंद, काळीप्रजा *f.* व्रातीन.

A l. lad. आडखप्या.

An idle l. दिवसभऱ्या, महिनेभरू.

The l. class,—compreh. कुणबीमाळी *m. pl.*

LABORIOUS, *a. assiduous, industrious,* v. DILIGENT. कामी, कामाळू, कामसू, खप्या, मेहनती or त्या, मशागती, कसालती, कष्टाळू, उद्योगी, आयासी, श्रामिक, उपद्व्यापी.

A l. person. कामाचा गाडा *m.*

2 *requiring labor, toilsome.* मेहनतीचा, मशागतीचा, कसालतीचा, कष्टाचा, श्रमाचा, दगडफोड, दगडफोडीचा, उरस्फोडीचा, कठीण, सखत, कष्टसाध्य, श्रमसाध्य, आयाससाध्य, सकष्ट.

LABORIOUSLY, *adv.* v. A. श्रम घेऊन, कष्ट घेऊन, मेहनत घेऊन, श्रम-कष्ट-&c. करून, यत्नतः, प्रयत्नतः, आयासपूर्वक.—as enhanced. जीव तोडून, जीव देऊन, सातासायासांनीं, मरून, रक्ताचें पाणी करून, आटाआट-आटाघाट-&c. करून.

LABORIOUSNESS, *n.* v. A. 1. *and.* DILIGENCE. कामाळूपणा *m.* कामसूपणा*m.* कष्टाळूपणा *m* उद्योग *m.* उद्यम *m.* उद्योगशीलता *f.*

2 कठीणपणा *m.* सखतपणा *m.* कष्टसाध्यता *f.* श्रमसाध्यता *f.*

LABYRINTH, *n. place or road full of windings.* नागमोडीची जागा *f.*-वाट *f.* गोल्यांची-लपंडावाची-गिरकांड्याची-गुंतागुंतीची-&c. जागा *f.* घोंटाळा*m.* घोटाळ्याची जागा *f.* सातबांकी जागा*f.*-वाट *f.* चक्रव्यूहाचा वाडा *m.*

2 fig. *an intricate case or matter.* चौऱ्याशीचा फेरा *m.*

LAC, *n.*—the dye, or insect (coccus lacca) which forms it. लाख *f.* राक्षा *f.* लाक्षा *f.* अलिता or अळता *m.* अलक्त *m.* अलक्तक *m.*

A stick of l. लाखाचीकारी *f.* लाखाडी *f.*

Cake l. चपड़ा or चोपडा or चोपडी लाख *f.*

Earthen pot smeared with l. लाखलोटें *n.* लाखाळें *n.*
Liquified l. dye. अलक्तरस *m.*
Of the color of l., dyed with l. लाखी.
Pouring l. into a socket (in preparation for the gem.). लाखपाड *m.* [खाळें *n:*
Ring or trinket bearing its gem in l. लाखपाड *m.* ला-
Stuffed or filled with l. लाखी, लाखट. [*f.* करणें.
To besmear with l. लाखटणें, लाखणें, लाखटणी *f.*-लाखण *n.*
2 See LACK.

LACE, *n. texture of interwoven threads.* जाळी *f.* दाल *m.*
2 *gold or silver lace.* कलाबतू *m. f.* तुई *or* तोई *f.*
Gold l. सोनेरी कलाबतू *m. f.*
Silver l. रुपेरी कलाबतू *m. f.*
Gold or silver l. तुई *or* तोई *f.*
3 *string for fastening clothes.* फीत *f.* नाडी *f.*

To LACE, *v. a. fasten or bind with a lace or tape.* विणणें, फितीनें-नाडीनें बांधणें, नाडी *f.* लावणें-घालणें-देणें.
To l. (a bedstead, &c.) with broad tape. नवारणें.—with twists of cocoanut fibres. सुंभणें.
2 *border, &c. with lace.* कलाबतू *m. f.* लावणें, कलाबतूची पट्टी *f.* बांधणें, जरीकांठ *m.* लावणें, किनारी *f.* देणें-लावणें.
3 v. To BEAT. सडकणें, ठोकणें, चोपणें, झोडणें.

LACE-MAN, *n.* जाळीवाला, जाळीविक्या.

LACED, *p.* v. V. 1. विणलेला, &c. विणीव.
2 कलाबतू लावलेला, &c. कलाबतूकांठी, जरीकांठी.

To LACERATE, *v. a. rend,* v. To TEAR. फाडणें, टरकावणें, विदारणें, विदारण *n.*-&c. करणें *g. of o.*
2 v. To SCRATCH. ओरपणें, ओरखडणें, ओरबडणें.

LACERATED, *p.* v. V. 1. फाडलेला, &c. विदारित, विपाटित.
2 ओरपलेला, ओरखडलेला, &c.

LACERATION, *n.* v. V. 1.—*act.* फाडणें *n.* विदारणें *n.* &c. फाडणी *f.* विदारण *n.* विदारणा *f.* विपाटन *n.*
2—*act.* ओरपणें *n.* &c.
I. *the rent made.* फाळा *m.* चीर *f.*
II. See SCRATCH.

LACHRYMAL, *a. pertaining to tears.* आंसवांचा, अश्रुसंबंधी.
2 *secreting, &c. tears.* अश्रूत्पादक, अश्रुजनक, अश्रुवाहक.

LACHRYMOSE, *a.* अश्रुमय.

To LACK, *v. a.* v. To WANT. उणीव *f.*-वाण *f.*-कमती *f.*-न्यूनता *f.*-&c. असणें *in. con. & g. of o.* उणा-&c. असणें *with* नें *of o.* (as तो संतानानें उणा आहे he lacks offspring), हीन-रहित-&c. असणें.

To LACK, *v. n. be in want.* अडचणींत-अडचणुकींत-तंगचाईंत-&c. असणें, अडचण *f.*-अडचणूक *f.*-अबाळ *f.*-तंगचाई *f.*-&c. असणें *in. con.* गरजू-गरजवंत-&c. असणें, अनुत्पन्न असणें.
2 *be wanting.* उणा-कमी-न्यून-&c. असणें, अभाव *m.*-शून्याकार *m.*-वाण *f.*-उणीव *f.*-न्यूनता *f.*-&c. असणें *g. of s.* पूज *n.* असणें *with* वर *of s.*

LACK, *n.* v. WANT. उणीव *f.* वाण *f.* न्यूनता *f.* गरज *f.* अभाव *m.* शून्याकार *m.* ठणठणपाळ *m.* ठणठणाट *m.* ददात *f.*
2 *one hundred thousand.* लाख *m.* लक्ष *m.*
Assemblage of a l. (of flowers, fruits, &c.). लाखोली *f.*
By lacks. लाखों, लाखोंशा, लक्षावधि, लक्षशः.
Lacks upon lacks. लाखोंलाख. [पति *m.*
Possessor of a l. of rupees. लक्षेश्वर, लक्षपति *pop.* लख-
That is worth a l. *superexcellent.* लाख्या, लाखोरुपयांचा.

LACKADAY, *interj.* v. ALAS. हाय हाय, कटकटा.

LACKBRAIN, *n.* v. FOOL. ठणठणपाळ, ढ, ढंढंणा, मठ्या.

LACKER, *n. varnish.* लाख *f.* लाक्षा *f.* रोगण *n.*

To LACKER, *v. a. smear with lacker.* रोगण *n.* देणें-लावणें-करणें, लाखटणें, लाख *f.* लावणें.

LACKERED, *p.* v. V. रोगण लावलेला, लाखटलेला, &c. रोगणी.
A. l. ornament. लाखाळें *n.*

LACKEY, *n. foot boy.* खिदमतगार *or* दार, पोऱ्या, नफर, खवास, पार्श्वानुचर.

LACKLUSTRE, *a.*—the countenance. कायाहीन, कळा (*pop.* कळा) हीन, निस्तेज, तेजोहीन, मंदकांत, उफट *or* आंफट.
2—a pearl. खरडेवजा *a. ind.* वाणढाळ, मजीत, नरम.

LACONIC, LACONICAL, *a. brief, concise,*—speaker. थोडक्यांत-बोलणारा, संक्षिप्तवक्ता, संक्षिप्तभाषी, मितभाषी, परिमितभाषी, अविस्तृतवक्ता.
2 *expressed in few words,*—speech. संक्षिप्तोक्त, संक्षिप्तोक्तीचा, संक्षेपोक्तीचा, अल्पशब्दक, मित. [पोक्ति *f.*

LACONISM, *n. concise speech.* संकलितोक्ति *f.* संक्षिप्तोक्ति *f.* संक्षे-

LACQUER. See LACKER.

LACRYMOSE, *a.* v. WEEPING. रडता.

LACTAGE, *n. produce of milch animals.* दुपतें *or* दुभतें *n.* पेजें *n.* गोरस *m.* गव्य *n.* [रविशिष्ट.

LACTARY, *a. having juice like milk.* दुध्या, दुधाचा, क्षीरी, क्षी-

LACTARY, *n.* v. DAIRY. दुभत्याचें घर *n.* दुभत्याची जागा *f.* गोरसशाला *f.*

LACTATION, *n. act of giving milk.* थान पाजणें *n.* थान देणें *n.*

LACTEAL, *a. milky.* दुधाचा, दुग्धसंबंधी, दुग्धवत्, दुग्धमय.
2 *conveying chyle.* अन्नरसवाहक, अन्नरसचालक.

LACTEAL, *n. vessel of the body that conveys chyle.* अन्नरसवाहिनी *f.* रसायनी *f.*

LACTEOUS, *a. milky.* दुधाचा, दुग्धसंबंधी, दुग्धमय.
2 *conveying chyle.* अन्नरसवाहक, अन्नरसचालक.

LACTESCENT, *a. producing milk, or a milky juice.* दुधाचा, दुध्या, दुग्धोत्पादक, क्षीरी, क्षीरवान.

LACTIFEROUS, *a. that conveys milk.* दुग्धवाहक, दुग्धप्रवाहक.

LAD, *n.* v. STRIPLING. पोरगा, पोऱ्या, बाप्या, बाप्यामाणूस, आडबाप्या, आडगोखमा, आडमानई *or* आडमानाय, मानई, बाल, किशोर.
3 *fellow, chap, boy,*—familiarly. गडी, जवान, गोह्रो.

LADDER, *n.* शिडी *or* शिढी *or* सिडी *or* सिढी *f.* निशीण *f.* निसण *f.* सोपान *n.* [णें.

To LADE, *v. a.* v. To LOAD. लादणें, ओझें *n.* भरणें-घालणें, भर-
2 See To LADLE.

LADEN, *p.* v. V. 1. लादलेला, भरलेला & भारयुक्त, भारवान्.

LADING, *n.* v. V. 1.—*act.* लादणें *n.* &c. लादणी *f.* लदाव *m.*
I. *load, cargo,* v. FREIGHT. भरगत *f.* भरीत *n.* बारदान *n.*

LADLE, *n.* पळा *m. dim.* पळी *f.* चमचा *m.* थावर *m.* कडची *f.* दिवली *f.* दर्वी *f.*
Bowl of a l. बोंड *n.* पळूं *n.* टवळें *n.* माथळा *m.*
L. with perforations. झारा *m.*

L. for ladling out boiled rice. ओगराळें n. मुदाळें n.

L. made of a piece of cocoa-nut, hollowed mango-stone, &c. डब m. डबला or डोला m. dim. डबली or डोली f. डफली f. [or ड्या.

Suitable to be served out with a *pali* or l. पळीबाडा

Wooden l. डाव f. चाटू m.

To LADLE, *v. a. empty out with a ladle, &c.* उसपणें, उसपणी f.-उसपा m.-&c. करणें g. of o. पळ्यानें-&c. काढणें.

To l. out (boiled rice,) *serve it out on the leaf-plates.* ओगरणें.—the mass thus turned out. ओगरm. [ण n.

LADLING, n. v. V.—*act.* उसपणें n. उसपणी f. उसपा m. उसप-

LADY, *n. woman of family or of good breeding.* सभ्यस्त्री f.-बायको f.-&c. शिष्टस्त्री f.-बायको f.-&c. कुलवधू f. कुलस्त्री f. कुलांगना f. कुलजा f. कुलीना f.

2—as a title. बाई f. नायका f.

A Muhammadan l. बीबी f. बुबू f. बेगम f.

LADY-BIRD, LADY-BUG, LADY-COW, LADY-FLY, n. कुंकुवाचा किडा m. सोनकिडा m. इंद्रगोप m. इंद्रकीट m. ताम्रकृमि m.

LADY-LIKE, a. v. GENTEEL. सभ्य, शिष्ट.

2 *becoming a lady.* शिष्टस्त्रीस योग्य, सभ्यस्त्र्युचित.

LAG, *n. lowest class, fag end, &c.* गाळ m. गदळ m. n. केर m. शेंडेफळ n. [वणें.

To LAG, *v. n. hang behind.* मागें पडणें-राहणें, मागसणें, मागसा-

LAGGER, n. LAGGING, *p. a.* v. V. मागें पडणारा, मागसणारा, &c. पायचोर.

LAGOON, LAGUNE, n. खार f.

LAIC, LAICAL, *a. not clerical,* v. LAY. गृहस्थी, गृहस्थ, गृहस्थ कोटींतला, गृहस्थकोटिसंबंधी-विषयक.

LAIC, *n. layman.* गृहस्थ m.

LAIR, *n. bed or resting place* (of a wild beast). पशु-श्वापद बसायाची निजायाची जागा f. कपा or कोपा m. कुपी f. बसक f. आखर m. गोठण f. जाळी f.

LAITY, *n. the body of the people distinguished from the clergy.* गृहस्थवर्ग m. गृहस्थकोटि f.

LAKE, n. सरोवर n. कासार m. ऱ्हद m. जलाशय m. पुष्करिणी *pop.* पुष्करण & पोखरण f.

LAMB, n.—male. कोंकरा m.—female. कोंकरी f.—gener. without reference to sex. कोंकरूं n.

A female l. about a year old. लाव्हर or लाहोर f.

LAMBATIVE, *a. taken by licking.* चाटायाचा, लेह्य, अवलेह्य.

LAMBATIVE, *n. a medicine taken by licking.* चाटण n. लेह m. अवलेह m.

LAMB-KIN, n. कोंकरूं n. लहान कोंकरूं n.

LAMBENT, *a. playing about, &c.* खेळता, चाटता.

LAME, *a. cripple, &c.* लंगडा, पांगळा, पांगा, पांगूळ, पंगु *pop.* पंगू, पायानें अधू, पायाचा अधू, व्यंग, लंगडखुट, विकलांग, खंज.

A l. person. लंगडशाई or लंगडशादी c. लंगडदीन c.

2 fig. *imperfect, not satisfactory.* लंगडा, अधू, व्यंग, विकल, लेचापेचा, लगडीतगडीचा.

To LAME, *v. a. make lame.* पांगळा-लंगडा-&c. करणें.

LAMELLAR, LAMELLATED, *a. covered, &c. with thin plates or scales.* खवल्या, खवलांचा.

LAMELY, *adv.* v. A. 1. लंगडत, लंगडतलंगडत, लुचपत, लुचपत लुचपत, कुलपतकुलपत, लंगड्याचाणी, पांगळ्याचाणी.

To go l. लंगडणें.

2 fig. लगडतगड, तुनुमुनू or तुनुमुनू करून.

LAMENESS, n. v. A. 1. लंगडेपणाm. पांगळेपणाm. अधुपणाm. अंगवैकल्य n. पंगुत्व n. [कसर f.

2 लंगडेपणा m. अधुपणा m. विकलता f. वैकल्य n. विकलभाव m.

To LAMENT, *v. a. bewail, deplore, regret.* रडणें, शोचणें, खेद m.-दुःख n.-शोक m.-&c. करणें-धरणें-मानणें g. of o. हायहाय f. करणें g. of o. विलाप m.-शोचन n.-&c. करणें g. of o.

To LAMENT, *v. n. mourn, wail, &c.* रडणें, र f.-रर f. करणें, विपलापणें, आक्रंदणें, आक्रोशणें, आकांतणें, आक्रंदन n.-आक्रोश m.-विलाप m.-हायहाय f.-रुदन n.-रोदन n.-&c. करणें, रचीबारस्त्रडी f. वाचणें, रचाफाडा m. वाचणें, रुदंती f. करणें.

LAMENTABLE, a. v. V. A. रडाया-चा-जोगा-जोगता-&c. शोच्य, शोचनीय, शोचितव्य, शोकार्ह, शोकयोग्य, शोचनार्ह, शोकविषय, दुःखविषय, खेदास्पद, शोकास्पद.

I. *expressing sorrow, &c.* See MOURNFUL.

LAMENT, LAMENTATION, n. v. V. A.—*act.* रडणें n. शोचणें n. खेद करणें n. &c. शोक m. शोचन n.

v. V.N. रडणेंn. आक्रंदणेंn. &c. र f. आक्रंदनn. आक्रोशm. हायहाय f. धाय f. धायमाय f. विलाप m. विपलापm. रुदनn. रोदनn.

To cry with loud lamentations. धायधाय रडणें-ओरडणें.

LAMENTER, n. LAMENTING, *p. a.* v. V. A. रडणारा, शोचणारा, &c. विलाप-शोक-&c. कर्त्ता.

LAMINA, *n. thin plate or scale.* पत्र n. पत्रा m. पडदा m. चीप f. पदर m. कातळा m. [कातळ्याचा.

LAMINATED, *a. consisting of thin plates, &c.* पडद्याचा, पत्र्याचा,

To LAMM, *v. a. cudgel,* v. To BEAT. टोणपणें, टोणकावणें.

LAMP, n. दिवाm. दीप m. दीपकm. चिरागm.—in covert, &c. phrase. सूर्यपिलूं n. Some kinds of *lamp* are दिवा m. लामण or लाम्हण or लांबणदिवा, रोमण or रोवणदिवा, रोवणदिवी or दिवली f. रोमणी f. दिवटी or दिवली or दिवी f. दीपिका f. कैंपत f. हिलाल m. ठाणवई or ठाणवी f.

Branched or forked l. दुशाख f.

By, in, &c. l.-light. दिव्याउजेडीं.

Cluster of lamps. झुंबर m. झाड n.

Door-l. *lamp in a doorway.* दारचा दिवा m. दारठणचा दिवा m. देहलीदीप m.

Earthen saucer form l. कोंडें n. पणती *dim.* पणतोली f. चिकोरी or शिकोरी f.

Evening l., lamp lighted every evening in a temple. सांजदिवा m. सांजवात f.

Flame of a l. दिव्याची जोत f. दीपशिखा f.

Frame or erection for a row of lamps. चिरागदान n.

Hanging l. हंडी or हांडी f. कंदील m.

L. hung in the air. आकाशदिवा m. आकाशदीप m.

Lighting up of the lamps (in a temple, &c.). दिवेलावणी f. दिवेबात f. दीपबात f.

Metal and upright l. समई or समय f.—the saucer of it for the oil and wicks, or to receive the drippings. चाडें n. ठवळें n. माठलें n.

Obeisances paid to the lamps at lighting. दीपदर्शनn.

Obeisances, salutations, (to Rájás, &c.) paid at l.

lighting. दिवटी जोहार *m.* दिवटी सलाम *m.* दिवटीमुजरा *m.*

Oil of an extinguished l. दिपुष्ट *or* दिपोष्ट *n.*

Operations—compreh. of preparing, and lighting a l. दिवाबात *f.* तेलघात *f.*

Place (in a house) for the suspension of the great l. दिवठण *or* दिवठाण *n.*

Row or range of lamps. दीपावलि *pop.* दिपावळी *f.* दीपमाळ *f.* [लें *n.*

Saucer for the oil and wicks of a l. दिवेलावणें *n.* माठ-

Stand or stem of a l. ठाणवई *or* ठाणवी *f.*

Stink of an extinguished l. दिपुशाण *f.*

String or loop to suspend a hanging l. ओलाणी *f.* ओलाणें *n.* ओलण *f.* [गण *f.*

Time of l. lighting. दिवेलावण *or* दिवेलावणी *f.* दिवेला-

To extinguish a l. दिव्यास निरोप *m.*-पदर *m.*-फूल *n.*-शेव *f.* देणें, दिवा *m.* काढणें-पालवणें.

To freshen or brighten a l. दिवा *m.* सरसा करणें.

LAMP-BLACK, *n.* मस *f.* काजळ *n.* मशेरी *f.* कज्जल *n.* मषी *f.* दीपकिट्ट *n.*

LAMP-LADDER, *n.* घडोंची *f.* घोडा *m.*

LAMP-LIGHT, *n.* दिव्याचा उजेड *m.*-प्रकाश *m.*

By l. दिव्याउजेडीं.

LAMP-STAND, *n.* दिवा *m.* दीप *m.* ठाणवई *or* ठाणवी *f.* दीपवृक्ष *m.* दीपिका *f.* शिखातरु *m.*

LAMPASS, *n.*—the disease. मुंगा *m.* ठाळबेलें *n.*

LAMPOON, *n. satirical piece.* निंदेचा पोवाडा *m.* निंदाख्यापक वाक्य *n.*- लेख *m.*

LANCE, *n.* v. SPEAR. भाला *m.* बरची *f.* नेजा *m.*

To LANCE, *v. a.* भाला *m.*-बरची *f.* मारणें.

2 *cut, &c. with a lancet.* नस्तरानें फाडणें-कापणें-छेदणें, फाडणें, फाड *m.* करणें, फांसणी *f.* घालणें-मारणें-टाकणें.

LANCER, *n.* भालेकरी *m.* बरचीवाला *m.*

LANCET, *n.*—the surgical instrument. नस्तर *n.*

Cut or opening made by a l. फाड *m.* फांसणी *f.*

To LANCH, *v. a. throw, dart.* फेंकणें, टाकणें, मारणें.

To LANCINATE, *v. a. rend,* v. TO TEAR. फाडणें, चिरणें.

LANCINIATED, *a. fringed.* झालरीचा.

LAND, *n. country, region.* देश *m.* मुलूख *m.* प्रांत *m.* राष्ट्र *n.*

2—as opposed to water and air. जमीन *f.* भुई *f.* खुशकी *f.* स्थल *pop.* स्थळ *n.*

L. and water. जलस्थल *n.*

Confusion of l. and water (as through inundation). जलस्थलभ्रम *m.*

L.-carriage, *price paid for transport by l.* खुशकी कडील भाडें *n.* स्थलमार्गाचें-पायरस्त्याचें-&c. भाडें *n.*

Neck of l. दांडा *m.* दांडी *f.*

The main l. खुशकी *f.*

The way by l.—as opposed to *the way by water.* पायमार्ग *m.* पायरस्ता *m.* पायवाट *f.* खुशकी *f.* स्थलमार्ग *m.*

3 *ground, earth, soil,*—with reference to agriculture. जमीन *f.* भुई *f.* भूमि *f.* काळी *f.*

Arable l. शेतजमीन *f.* जिराईत *n.* ढेप *n.* क्षेत्रभूमि *f.*

Arable lands—collect. शेतगणा *m.*

Arid or sterile l. भुकाड *n.* निखरड *n.* बरडजमीन *f.* मानट *n.*

Burning of l. in agriculture. भाजावळ *f.* भाजवट *f.*

Burning of l.—compreh. पोळभाज *or* भाजपोळ *f.* जाळपोळ *f.* जाळभाज *f.* जाळापोळी *f.* [मोड *f.*

Clearing of l. in bringing it under cultivation. तण-

Cultivated l. लागवड *f.* लागवडजमीन *f.* वहीतजमीन *f.* सागली *f.*

Cultivated throughout-land. सबंधवहीत.

Elevated & dry level spot in arable l. भाट *n.* भाटलें *n.* —that abounds in such. भाटवळ.

Hill-l. just cleared and burned (for cultivation). सरवा *m.* सरवट *n.*

Inspector and assessor of l. जमीननीस *m.*

L. inundated by excessive rain. पाणबुडीत *n.*

L. watered by irrigation. पाणथळ *n.*

L. irrigated by water courses. पाटस्थळ *n.* पाडथळ *n.*

L. irrigated from a draw-well. मोटस्थळ *n.*

L. unirrigable. कुडथळ *n.* कोरडवाही *or* वाहू (*or* कोरडवाव) जमीन *f.*-शेत *n.*-&c. निपाणीजमीन *f.*

L. newly brought under irrigation. पाणभरजमीन *f.*

L. just reduced under cultivation. नवरान *n.*

L. burned and prepared for plants. दाढ *f.* भाजावळ *f.* भाजवट *f.* तरवा *m.* राब *m.*

Loppings strewed over l. to be burned. राब *m.* दाढ *f.* कवळ *n.* भइस *f.*—Dry grass, rubbish, &c. strewed over the loppings. बडी *f.* तणवर *m.* लेबट *m.* लेवणें *n.* खर *f.*—Litter remaining of the burned loppings. विरपल *f.*

Moist (as opposed to arid) l. पाणथल *n.* पाणबळ *n.* पाणदव *n.*

Plants growing on burned l. दाढ *f.* राब *m.* तरवा *m.*

Range of cultivated l. सज्जा *m.*

Range of uncultivated and unproductive l. माळजमीन *f.* माळरान *n.* [*f.* कीर्द *f.*

Reducing waste l. under cultivation. लावणी *f.* लागवड

Rising tax upon l. इस्तावा *m.*

Slip or strip of l. पट्टी *f.* फाळी *f.* फाळकी *f.*

Survey of arable l. पैमाशी *f.* ढेपपाहणी *f.*

Waste l. रानवा *m.* रान *n.* आडरान *n.* खराबा *m.*

Waste or fallow l. of the crown. सरकार खराबा *m.*

Waste l. amidst tilled l. पोटखराबा *m.* [आणणें.

To reduce l. under cultivation. लागवडीस आणणें, कीर्दीस

4 *estate, grounds.* जमीन *f.* शेत *n.*

Crown-lands. खालसा *or* खालिसा *m.* शेरी *f.* [णी *f.*

Grain paid by the sublessee to the land holder. खंड

L. lying in another village. ओवंडा *m.*—holder of it. ओवंडे करी *m.* ओवंडकरू *m.*

L. reversionary to the state. शेरी *f.*

Lands tenanted from the state. रकमी जमीन *f.*

Lands and tenements. compreh.—*the whole estate.* जमीन जुमला *m.*

L. held on sublease. खोनसज्जा *m.*

Landed proprietor. मिरासदार, मिरासी.

Land-farmer of the Crown. खोत, शेरीकरी.—balance in kind due from the tenants to him. खोनबाकी *f.*—waste lands made over to him. सोतसराबाm.

Under-tenant or sublessee of l. संडकरीm.

To LAND, *v. a. set on shore.* उतरणें, तरीस-किनाऱ्यास-कांठास-&c. लावणें, कांठीं उतरणें.

To LAND, *v. n. go on shore.* उतरणें, तरीस लागणें-उतरणें.

LAND-ANIMAL, *n.* भूचर, भूमिचर, स्थलचर.

LAND-BREEZE. See LAND-WIND.

LAND-FLOOD. See INUNDATION.

LAND-FORCE. See ARMY.

LAND-HOLDER, *n. proprietor of land.* जमीनदार, मिरासदार, मिरासी, थलकरी, थलवाईक, थलभरी, कुणबावेदार.

LAND-LADY, *n. woman who has tenants.* घराची मालकीण *f.*-धनीण *f.* घरवाली *f.* मालकीण *f.* घरधनीण *f.*

LAND-LOCKED, *a. encompassed by land.* खुशकींत सांपडलेला, भूप्रतिबंधित, भूवेष्टित.

LAND-LORD, *n. owner of land who has tenants under him.* जमिनीचा मालक,जमीनदार,क्षेत्रपति,क्षेत्रधनी,क्षेत्रस्वामी,भूस्वामी.
2 *owner of a house who has tenants.* घराचा मालक, घरधनी, घरवाला.
3 *keeper of an inn.* भटाऱ्या.

LAND-MARK, *n. mark to designate a boundary.* शिंवेचीखूण *f.* मेरेचीखूण *f.* खूण *f.* शींव *f.* हद्द *f.* क्षेत्रसीमाचिन्ह *n.* क्षेत्रमर्यादाचिन्ह *n.*

LAND-MEASURE, *n.* v. MEASURE. जमिनीचेंमान*n.* क्षेत्रपरिमाण*n.*

LAND-MEASUREMENT, *n.* जमीनमोजणी *f.*-मसाद *f.*

Relating to l. मसादी.

LAND-REGISTER, *n.* जमीन झाडा *m.* थलझाडा *m.*

LANDS-MAN, *n.* खुशकींतलामाणूस, खुशकीवाला, नवा सफरी.

LAND-SURVEY, *n.* जमीन मोजणी *f.* जरीब *m. pl.*

LAND-TAX, *n.* शेतसारा *m.* सारा *m.* धारा *m.* भूमिकर *m.*

L.—freely. सारादोरा *m.*

Mitigated l. धारे एहसान *n.* [डेकरी.

LAND-WAITER, *n.*—the officer of the customs. घाटावरचा झा-

LAND-WIND, *n. wind blowing from the land.* तडीचा-किनाऱ्याचा-&c. वारा *m.* मुईवरला वारा *m.* मतलई *f.*

LANDED, *a. having an estate in land.* शेतकरी, शेती, जमीनदार, कुणबावेदार, क्षेत्रधन, क्षेत्रसंपन्न, भूमिधनसंपन्न, स्थावरधनसंपन्न.
2 *consisting in land.* शेताचा, जमिनीचा, कुणबाव्याचा, क्षेत्रधनाचा. [दर *n.*

LANDING, LANDING-PLACE, *n.* घाट *m.* उतरण्याची जागा *f.* बं-
2 (of a stairs or flight of steps). जिन्यावरचीसपाटी *f.* पटांगणाची पायरी *f.* जिन्याची तबकडी *f.*

LANDSCAPE, *n. the land which the eye can comprehend in a single view.* डोळ्याच्या टप्प्यांतला-दृष्टींतला-दृष्टिपातांतला-&c. देश *m.*-प्रदेश *m.* दृष्टिपातांतर्गतदेश *m.*
2 *picture of scenery.* भूप्रदेशाचें चित्र *n.*

LANDSLIP, *n. slip down of land from a mountain.* पर्वताचाभागकोसळूनपडणें *n.*
2 *the land slipped.* कोसळून पडलेला पर्वताचा भाग *m.*

LANE, *n. narrow road between houses or fields.* गल्ली *f.* अळी *f.* बीद *or* बीध *f.* बिदी *or* बिधी *f.*बोळ *m.* शेरी *f.* गोंड *f.* पाणंद *or* पाणंध *f.* पांद *f.* आळ *f.* वाठार *f.*

Lanes, alleys, &c. compreh. गल्लीकुची *f.* सिंडगोंडी *f.*

In every l. and alley. आळो आळीं.

LANGUAGE, *n.* v. SPEECH. वाणी *f.* वाचा *f.* [उक्ति *f.*
2 *speech, thoughts expressed.* बोलणें *n.* भाषण *n.* बोल *m.*
Bad l. दुरुक्ति *f.* दुर्भाषण *n.* दुरुत्तर *n.* दुर्वचन *n.* दुर्वाक्य *n.*
Classical or polished l. संस्कृतोक्ति *f.*
3 *a language.* बोली *f.* भाषा *f.*
A foreign l. भाषांतर *n.*
4 *style, diction.* भाषणाची शैली *f.*-सरणी *f.*-रीति *f.*-&c. वाक्यरचना *f.* वाक्सरणि *f.*

LANGUID, *a. of drooping spirits, indisposed to exertion.* मांदा, मंद, सुस्त, सुस्ता, जड, ग्लान, म्लान, मजीत, अनवसान, क्लांत, क्लांतमनस्क, अवसन्न, अवसादित.
2 *weak, feeble, dull, slack, slow, &c.*—of business, motion, &c. मंद, ढिमा *or* धिमा, ढील, ढिला, सुस्त, सुस्ता, शिथिल, स्तिमित, मेणचट, मेण्या.
3 *indifferent, cold, &c.* थंड, थंडा, उदासीन, उदास, अनास्थ, निरास्थ, आस्थाहीन-रहित-&c. अनुत्सुक, निरुत्सुक, शीत.

LANGUIDLY, *adv.* v. A. 1. 2. 3. मंद, मंदमंद, आळसत आळसत, रेंगत रेंगत, सुस्त, सुस्ताईवर, ढिलाईवर, मिणमीण,थंडपणानें, अळमटळम, अळमळीत.

LANGUIDNESS, *n.* v. A. 1. *and* LANGUOR. मांदेपणा *m.* सुस्तपणा *m.* सुस्ती *f.* मांद्य *n.* ग्लानि *f.* म्लानि *f.*
2 मंदपणा *m.* ढिमेपणा *m.* ढिलेपणा *m.* शिथिलपणा *m.* ढिलाई *f.* ढिल्ली *f.* ढील *f.* स्तिमिताई *f.* मांद्य *n.* शैथिल्य *n.* शिथिलता *f.*
3 थंडपणा *m.* थंडाई *f.* उदासपणा *m.* अनास्था *f.* आस्थाराहित्य *n.* अनुत्सुकता *f.* औदासीन्य *n.* कानाडोळा *m.*

To LANGUISH, *v.n.*v. To PINE, To DROOP. रोगणें, लंघणें *or* लंगणें, ग्लान-&c. होणें, ग्लानि *f.*-&c. येणें *in. con.*
2 *proceed slackly, with diminished vigor.* मंदावणें, मंदपडणें, आळसावणें, सुस्तावणें, रेंगतचालणें, रेंरें चालणें, ढिलाईवर-मंदाईवर-सुस्ताईवर-आळसावर-&c. पडणें-चालणें.
3 *look softly and tenderly.* कामालसदृष्टीनें-कामार्द्रदृष्टीनें-प्रणयमंजुलदृष्टीनें-&c. पाहणें.

LANGUISHER, *n.* LANGUISHING, *p. a.* v. V. 1. लंघणारा, ग्लान झालेला, ग्लानि आलेला, &c. ग्लान, म्लान.
2 मंदावलेला, मंदपडलेला, ढिलाईवर-&c. पडलेला.
3 कामार्द्र दृष्टीनें पाहणारा, &c.कामालस दृष्टीचा, कामार्द्र दृष्टीचा.

LANGUISHMENT, *n. softness of look, &c.* ललित *n.* लालित्य *n.* कोमलावलोकन *n.* ललितावलोकन*n.*काममंददृष्टि *f.* कामार्द्रदृष्टि *f.*

LANGUOR, *n. lassitude, listlessness, heaviness.* मांदगी *f.* मांदेपणा *m.* मांद्य *n.* सुस्ती *f.* सुस्तपणा *m.* ग्लानि *f.* म्लानि *f.* ग्लानता *f.* म्लानता *f.* क्लांति *f.* कलमल *f.* मंदता *f.* शिथिलता *f.* शैथिल्य *n.* जडत्व *n.* जाड्य *n.* स्तैमित्य *n.* क्लम *m.* अवसाद *m.* अवसन्नता *f.* विषाद *m.* तंद्रा *f.* अंगभंग *m.* [त्पादक.

LANIFEROUS, LANIGEROUS,*a.producing wool.* लोमजनक, लोमो-

LANK, LANKY, *a. not plump, thin,* v. LEAN. पातळ, सडपातळ, सडकपातळ, सडसडीत, टुकड, काटचाळा, एकशेवडी, कांकीट, पातळांगी, खपाटें बसलेला.

Tall & lanky. धांडळ *or* ढांडळ,ढांगळ,लंबाड *or* ड्या, लेसाटा.
2 *lax, not distended,* v. LOOSE. ढिला, सैल, शिथिल.

LANKNESS, LANKINESS, *n.* v.A. 1.पातळपणा*m.* पातळाई *f.* सडसडितपणा *m.*
2 ढिलेपणा *m.* सैलपणा *m.* शिथिलपणा *m.*

LANTERN, *n.* फाणस *or* फाणूस *m. n.* कंद्या *m.* कंदील *m.*

LANTERN-JAWED, *a.* v. N. गालचिंबा, चापटतोंड्या, गालबशा, बसक्या गालांचा.

LANTERN-JAWS, *n. thin visage.* चापटतोंड *n.*

LANUGINOUS, *a. covered with down or soft hair.* लोमश, लोममय, सलोम. [घेर *m.* झोल *m.*

LAP, *n.* (of a garment) *loose flowing part.* पदर *m.* घोळ *m.*
2 (of a petticoat, &c.). ओंटा *m.* ओंटी *f.* ओंटला *m.*
3 *part over the thighs; or the thighs in a sitting posture.* ओसंग *m.* ओसंगा *m.* ओसंगळा *m.* मांडी *f.* उत्संग *m.* अंक *m.*

To LAP, *v. a. wrap around,* v. To WRAP. लपेटणें, गुंडाळणें, वेष्टणें.
2 *wrap in,* v. To WRAP. गुंडाळणें, वेष्टणें.
3 *lick up.* चाटूनपिणें, चकचक पिणें-पिऊन टाकणें.

To LAP, *v.n. to be turned over.* चढणें, वाढणें, चढून-वाढून असणें.
2—as the dog, &c. चकचक पिणें.

LAP-DOG, *n.* कुलंगाकुत्रा *m.* (fem. कुलंगी कुत्री *f.*) पशमी कुत्रा *m.* (कुत्री). These words express varieties.

LAP-FUL, *n.* ओंटी *f.*
As much as a l. ओंटी भर.

LAPIDARY, LAPIDIST, *n. a. preparer and seller of precious stones.* मणिकार *pop.* मणेर *or* मणेरी *or* मण्यार, घासारी, जवाहिरी *or* जोहरी, मणिपरिष्कारक, रत्नपरिष्कारक, रत्नोपजीवी, रत्नविक्रयी.

LAPIDEOUS, *a.* v. STONY. दगडाचा, पाषाणमय, पाषाणात्मक.

LAPIDESCENCE, *n. turning into stone.* दगडहोणें *n.* पाषाणभूय *n.*

LAPIS-LAZULI, *n. azure stone.* वैदूर्य *pop.* बैडूर्य *n.* नीलोपल *m.* असिताश्मा *m.* असितोपल *m.*

LAPLING. See SENSUALIST.

LAPPET, *n.* See LAP 1.

LAPSE, LAPSING, *n.* v. V. 1.—*act.* वाहणें *n.* प्रवाह *m.* गति *f.* संतगति *f.* संतप्रवाह *m.*
L. of time. कालगति *f.*
2 घसरणें *n.* चळणें *n.* &c. चळ *m.* ढळ *m.* स्खलन *n.* च्यवन *n.* च्युति *f.* भ्रंश *m.*

To LAPSE, *v. n. glide, flow, pass slowly.* प्रवाह *m.*-गति *f.*-संतगति *f.*-&c. होणें *g. of s.* वाहणें, निसरणें.
2 fig. *slip, fall, err.* घसरणें, ढळणें, चळणें, ढळ *m.*-चळ *m.* होणें *g. of s.* स्खलन *n.*-च्यवन *n.*-&c. होणें *g. of s.* स्खलित-&c. होणें.
3 *fall or pass on from one proprietor to another.* एका मालकाकडून दुसऱ्या मालकाकडे जाणें, मूळच्या मालकाकडे-वरच्या मालकाकडे जाणें.

LAPSED, *p.* v. V. 2. चळलेला, घसरलेला, &c. स्खलित, च्युत.

LAPSUS LINGUÆ, *n. mistake in speaking.* जिव्हादोष *m.* मुखदोष *m.* वाग्दोष *m.*
It was a l. जीभ चळली.

LAPSUS MANUS, *n. mistake in writing.* हस्त दोष *m.*

LAPWING, *n.* टिटवी *f.* टिट्टिभ *m.* कोयष्टि *m.* पंककीर *m.*
Red wattled l. पाणटिटवी *f.*

LARBOARD, *n. left hand side of a vessel.* डावेंचोडद *n.*

LARBOARD, *a.* डावेचोडदाचा, डावेबोडदाकडील.

LARCENY, *n.* v. THEFT. चोरी *f.* स्तेय *n.* चौर्यकर्म *n.*

LARCH, *n.* देवदारूच्या जातीचा एक वृक्ष आहे.

LARD, *n.* डुकराची चरबी *f.*

To LARD, *v. a. baste with lard.* डुकराची चरबी *f.* लावणें-मारवणें.
2 *fatten.* पुष्ट करणें.
3 *interlard,* v. To INTERMIX. भेळ *f.*-भिसळ *f.*-&c. घालणें-घालून विचित्र करणें.

LARDER, *n. room where meat is kept.* सागुती ठेवायाची खोली *f.* मांसखाद्यशाला *f.* भक्ष्यमांसागार *n.* भोज्यशाला *f.*

LARGE, *a. big, great, &c.* मोटा *or* मोठा, थोर, थोरला, मोठाथोरला, टणक, महान् (महती *f.* महत् *n.*), महा (in comp.), स्थूल *or* ळ, गुरु, बृहत् (esp. in comp. as बृहच्छरीर, बृहदुदर), आकारमहत्वाचा,—as enhanced, and as conveying the general sense of *big, bulky, burly, stout, strapping, &c.* as used of men or animals. धडेल, धडल्याव, धडंग *or* धडिंग, धजेल, धडेलमोला, मोटाड, थोराड, गबदूल, गबदुला, मोटाधाटा, मोटाझपाटा, लडदू *or* धू, गडदू, भलेलह, गलेलह, रट, रटेल, रटाला, भक्कम, जबर, जबरा, रचूक, ढमाल *or* धमाल, ढमाल्या, अगडबंब, मस्त, मातबर, बोका, गजेंद्र,—as expressing the idea of disproportionate size, answering to *huge, vast, monstrous, enormous, massy, massive, &c.* बोजड, अवजड *or* अवजाड, झांबड, बंब, अगडबंब, अफाट, अवाढव्य, जगड्वाळ, अढाळ, बंबाळ *or* बोंबाळ, मरखम, भक्कम, रवेद *or* त, रमढोल, ऐवट, कचक, विशाल *or* ळ, दन्ना, धनत्तर, धक्कर, लटारणा, सटारणा, सटारा, बताणा, बताडा, दृघाड.—and, with a shade of difference, to *swinging, bouncing, whacking, banging, strapping, thumping, whapping, &c.* रट, रटाला, रटेल, लह, लट्ठा *or* ट्ठ्या, लठारणा, बताडा, बताणा, कंडारणा, दंडारणा, रपाटा, झपाटा, जरब, जबर, जबरदस्त, जबरा, ठस्स, ठसठशीत, घस्नर, पोक, पोका, गंजीबक्ष, र. Some terms for *a large thing,* agreeing with the free formations *whacker, whapper, thumper, &c.* are रपाटा *m.* झपाटा *m.* धपाटा *m.* रपाटखान *m.* रट्ट *m.* रट्टा *or* रट्या *m.* रगडमल्ल *m.* रामढोल *m.* लोळ *m.* ढेर *f.* अजस्र *n.*
How l. केवढा, कितवा.
L. and fine. कंडारणा, टपकळ, धजदार.
L. and lubberly. पोशा, पोस्ती *or* पोस्त्या, बंद्या, बोकंदळ.
Larger. अधिक.
L. relatively, *large-sized.* टकोर *or* टकोरा, टपोर *or* टपोरा, टबोणा, टिकोर *or* टिकोरा, इगळ *or* इघळ, थोरवट.
So l. एवढा, इतका.
So l. as. तेवढा, तितका.
2 *extensive, wide.* मोठा, लांबरुंद, लांबीरुंदीचा, प्रशस्त, विशाल *or* ळ, पसाऱ्याचा, मोठ्या विस्ताराचा, विस्तीर्ण, ऐसपैस, अघळपघळ, ऐसापैसाचा, पैस.
3 *liberal, munificent,* v. GENEROUS. प्रशस्त, उदार.
4 *copious, plentiful,* v. ABUNDANT. पुष्कळ, प्रशस्त, विपुल, मुबलक *or* ख.
At large, *without restraint.* मोकार, मोकाट, मोकळा *a. decl.* मोकळेपणीं, उनाड. 2 *roomily.* ऐसपैस. 3 *diffusively.* विस्तारानें, विस्तारें करून, सविस्तर. [काच.

LARGE-BODIED, *a.* बृहच्छरीर, बृहदंग, स्थूलशरीर, स्थूलांग, स्थूल-

LARGE-HEADED, *a.* बृहच्छिरा, स्थूलशिरा, बृहच्छीर्ष.

LARGE-LIMBED, *a.* बृहदंग.

LARGELY, *adv.* v. A. 3. प्रशस्तपणीं, उदारपणीं, मोकळ्या हातानें.
4 पुष्कळपणीं, प्रशस्तपणीं.

1. *diffusively.* प्रशस्तपणीं, विस्तारानें, विस्तारेंकरून, विस्तारपूर्वक.

LARGENESS, *n.* v. A. 1. मोठेपणा *m.* &c. महत्व *n.* स्थूलता *f.* स्थौल्य *n.*

2 मोठेपणा *m.* प्रशस्तपणा *m.* विशाळपणा *m.* &c. प्रशस्तता *f.* प्राशस्त्य *n.*

3 प्रशस्तपणा *m.* उदारपणा *m.* प्रशस्तता *f* प्राशस्त्य *n.* औदार्य *n.*

4 पुष्कळपणा *m.* &c. विपुलता *f.* वैपुल्य *n.* बाहुल्य *n.*

LARGESS, *n.* v. GIFT. बक्षीस *n.* बक्षिशी *f.* पारितोषिक *n.* दान *n.*

LARK, *n.* कुक्कुटकुंभा *m.* कुंभारकुकडा *or* कुंभारकुकूड *m.* भारद्वाज *m.*

2 crested l. चेडवळ *m.*

3 See SPORT. [सूचना *f.*

LARUM, *n. alarm given,* v. ALARM. हाक *f.* कुई *f.* आसन्नभय-

2—bell, &c. v. ALARM-BELL. हुलीचें जंगट *n.*

LARYNGOTOMY, *n. cutting the larynx.* कंठनाल छेदन *n.*

LARYNX, *n. upper part of the wind pipe.* नरडी *f.* नरडें *n.* मणका *m.* कंठनाल *m.* घांट *f.* घांटी *f.*

LASCAR, *n. Indian sailor.* खलाशी.

2 *Indian artillery man.* खलाशी.

LASCIVIOUS, *a. lewd, wanton,* v. LUSTFUL. कामी, कामुक, सकाम, कामातुर, कामासक्त, व्यवायी, स्त्रीव्यसनी, स्त्रीलंपट, कामप्रवण.

2 *proceeding from lust, indicating lust, &c.* कामबुद्धीचा, कामदृष्टीचा, कामभावाचा, सकाम, काममूलक, कामहेतुक, कामसूचक.

LASCIVIOUSLY, *adv.* v. A. कामुकपणानें, कामभावानें, कामपूर्वक, कामभावपूर्वक, कामबुद्ध्या, कामदृष्ट्या.

LASCIVIOUSNESS, *n.* v. A. 1. कामीपणा *m.* &c. कामुकता *f.* सकामता *f.* कामासक्ति *f.* कामबुद्धि *f.* कामदृष्टि *f.* कामभाव *m.*

LASH, *n. thong of a whip.* काकडा *m.* पागोरा *m.* फुसडी *f.* वादा *m.*

2 *stroke or stripe with a whip, &c.* फटका *m.* फटकारा *m.* चटकणी *f.* Note. The name of the instrument with which a stripe is given is commonly used to express a lash with it, as पांच कोरडे मार, पांच छड्या लावल्या, &c.

3 *a stroke of satire.* ठोमणा *m.* ठोसरा *m.* ठोसा *m.*

To LASH, *v. a. scourge,* v. To WHIP. फटके *m. pl.* मारणें, सडकणें, सडकावणें, फटकावणें, फडफडवणें. [करणें.

2 *satirize.* ठोमणे *m. pl.*-&c. देणें, बोडणें, बोडणी *f.*-बोडंती *f.*

3 *tie up to.* जखडणें, तांगडणें, हिलगावणें.

To LASH, *v. n. ply the whip.* चाबूक *m.*-&c. फडफडवणें.

2 out,—a horse, &c. मागलेपाय *m. pl.*-पिछाडी *f.*-दुलाच्या *f. pl.*-दुमच्या *f. pl.*-दुगाण्या *f. pl.* झाडणें.

3 out;—fig. *become extravagant, run into excess.* मर्यादा *f.*-सीमा *f.*-अवधि *m.*-बाकी *f.*-&c. सोडणें-न ठेवणें, बंधारण *n.* सोडणें, उधळणें, भडकणें.

LASS, *n. girl, young woman.* पोर *f.* पोरगी *f.* पद्रकरीण *f.* आडबायको *f.*

LASSITUDE, *n.* v. LANGUOR. मांदगी *f.* सुस्ती *f.* ग्लानि *f.* मांद्य *n.* कलमल *f.* विषाद *m.* अवसाद *m.* सैथिल्य *n.* तंद्रा *f.*

Subject to l. तंद्रालु.

To have the l. which precedes fever. आंग *n.* कसकसणें-कसणें-मोडून येणें, आंगमोडे *m. pl.* येणें, कसकस *f.*-कडमड *f.*-कडमोड *f.* येणें-भरणें.

LASSO, *n.* रानघोडे धरण्यासाठीं फांसाची दोरी *f.*

LAST, *a. latest, that comes after all the others.* सगळ्यांच्या-&c.मागचा-पाठीमागचा, शेवटचा, कडेशेवटचा, चरमागत, आगतांत्य.

2 *hindmost.* सर्वांच्या-&c. शेवटचा, शेवटील.

3 *concluding, final, beyond which there is no more.* शेवटचा, शेवटला, शेवटील, शेवटींचा, सरतेशेवटचा, अंतचा, अंतींचा, अखेरीचा, समाप्तीचा, सरता, अंतिम, अंत्य, चरम.

L. (dying) request. निर्वाणींची प्रार्थना *f.*

L. (dying) instruction, injunction, &c. निर्वाणींचा बोध *m.*-उपदेश *m.*-भाषण *n.*-&c.

L. but one. उपांत्य.

4 *next before the present.* गेला, मागला, मागचा, गुदस्त.

L. night. कालरात्रीं, कालचे रात्रीस.

L. year. सालगुदस्तां.

5 *utmost, extreme.* निर्वाणचा, निर्वाणींचा, निदानचा निदानींचा, कडेशेवटचा.

At l. शेवटीं, शेवटाखालीं, आखर *or* आखेर, शेलीं, सरतेशेवट, सरतेशेवटीं, निदान, निदानीं, निदानचा *decl.* एकदांचा *decl.*

LAST, *adv. the last time.* मागले *or* गेले खेपेस-वेळेस-प्रसंगास. The meaning of this adverb is best expressed by adopting another construction, as, when I last saw my mother आईचे मागले भेटीस *at my last interview with my mother, &c.*

2 *in conclusion.* शेवटीं, आखर *or* आखेर.

LAST, *n.* (of a shoe). जोड्याचा सांचा *m.* कलबूत *m. n.* शिंगोटी *f.*

To LAST, *v. n. remain, continue, hold out.* राहणें, टिकणें, ठरणें, तगणें, चालणें, पुरणें, टिकाव *m.*-टिकावा *m.*-तगाव *m.*-तगावा *m.*-तगवणी *f.*-तगवणूक *f.* होणें *g. of s.* टिकाव *m.*-&c. धरणें.

To make to l. तगविणें.

2 (through or out) *endure, come well out of.* निभणें, निभावणें, बहिवाटणें, पार पडणें, निभाव *m.*-निभावणी *f.*-निभावणूक *f.* होणें *g. of s.*

LASTING, *p. a.* v. V. 1. *durable.* टिकणारा, &c. टिकाऊ, तगाऊ, तगवणा, टिकाव्याचा, तगाव्याचा, तगवणीचा, अवीट, पुरवटेसार, चिरस्थायी, कल्पांतस्थायी, ध्रुव.

LASTINGNESS, *n.* v. A. टिकाऊपणा *m.* तगाऊपणा *m.* &c. चिरस्थायिता *f.*

LASTLY, *adv. finally, in conclusion.* शेवटीं, अंतीं, अवसानीं, सरतेशेवट, सरतेशेवटीं.

LATCH, *n.*—of a door. खिटीची कडी *f.* फिरकी *f.*

To LATCH, *v. a.* (a door). खिटी *f.* घालणें, फिरकी *f.* फिरवणें.

LATCHET, *n. tie.* बंद *m.* बंध *m.* बंधन *n.* बाद *m.* बादी *f.*

LATE, *a. not soon or early, long delayed.* उशिरां-उशिरानें-&c. आलेला, मागसून आलेला, उशिराचा, कालातिक्रमाचा, अतिकालाचा, अतिकालींचा, अतिवेळाचा *or* अतिवेळेचा, विलंबागल, समयातीत.

That is usually l. अतिकाळ्या.

To be l. *be long delayed.* मागसणें.

2 *late ripening, late sown, &c.*—a product of the season. मागस, मागप, मागांत, (distinguished from आगस, आगप, आगांत).

3 *that ripens late.* गरवस, गरवा, गरा, महान्.

4 *last or recently in any place, office, &c.* मागला, मागचा, माजी, गेला.

5 *recent, modern.* नवा, नूतन, नवसर, नवथर, ऐलीकडचा *or* ला, ऐलीकडील, थोडे दिवसांचा, आधुनिक, अर्वाचीन, सद्यस्क, सद्यस्कालीन.

Of l. times, *of modern date.* ऐलीकडचा *or* ला.

Of l. *in time not long past.* ऐलीकडे *or* अलीकडे, थोडके दिवसांचे आंत, महिना पंधरा दिवसांचे आंत, दोचों महिन्यांत, अर्वाचीन काळीं.

6 *deceased,* v. DEAD. लोकांतरगत, परलोकगत, मयत.

LATE, *adv. after delay, after the proper time.* उशिरानें, वाटकोळानें, उशिरां, उसरी, उस्रां, वाटकोळां, वाडवेळां, वाढोळां, उशीर-वेळ-बिलंब-देर-&c. करून, अतिकालानें, अतिवेळेनें, अतिकाल-&c. करून. [गेला, &c.

It is too l. अतिकाल झाला, अतिवेळ झाली, वेळ गेली, समय

To keep l. *to detain long.* उशिरावर धरणें.

2 *at a later period, after the proper season.* मागून, मागाहून, मागसून, मागस, वेळ-घात-&c. टाळून.

3 See LATELY. 4 *far in the day.* दिवस फार चढल्यावर, दिवस फार आल्यावर,—in the night रात्र फार गेल्यावर, रात्र फार झाल्यावर.

It is l. (in the day). दिवस फार चढला-गेला, दिवस थोडा राहिला. [थोडी राहिली.

It is l. (in the night). रात्र फार गेली-झाली, रात्र

LATELY, *adv. recently, only a little while ago.* नुक्ता *decl.* निकता *or* निका *decl.* नवसर, नवथर, नूतन, नेटका *decl.* थोडक्या दिवसांमागें, थोडे दिवस झाले.

LATENCY, *n.* v. A. गुप्तता *f.* गूढता *f.* गुप्तभाव *m.* अप्राकट्य *n.*

LATENESS, *n.* v. A. 1. अतिकालता *f.* अवेळपणा *m.* कालातिक्रमता *f.*

I. *time far advanced.* उशीर *m.* अतिकाल *m.* अतिवेळ *m. f.* अवेळ *f.* कालातिक्रम *m.* [अप्रकट.

LATENT, *a. secret, not seen,* v. HID. गुप्त, गूढ, अदृश्य, अदृष्ट,

LATER, *a. more recent, &c.* ऐलीकडचा-ऐलीकडला *with* पेक्षांहून-&c. थोड्या दिवसांचा.

LATERAL, *a. belonging, &c. to the side.* बाजूचा, पार्श्वाचा, पार्श्वसंबंधी, पार्श्विक, पार्श्व, अनुपार्श्व, पार्श्वस्थ.

LATERALLY, *adv. by the side.* बाजूस, बाजूला, अनुपार्श्वें.

LATH, *n. narrow slip of wood, bamboo, &c. for plastering, &c.* कांबट *or* कांबीट *f. n.* कारव *f.*-कारवी *f.* (made of the tree of this name).

Wall made of l. and plaster. कूड *m.*

2 (for roof). रीप *f.* ओंबणाची काठी *f.*

3 fig. *thin person.* काठांग्या, काठ्याळा, लकड्या, कागदी ज्वान.

To LATH, *v. a. cover with laths.* ओंवणें, ओंबण *n.*-रिपार *m. n.* -रीप *f.* घालणें-करणें. [प *f.*

LATH-WORK, LATHING, *n.* ओंबण *or* ओमण *n.* रिपार *m. n.* री-

LATHE, *n.*—turner's instrument. चरक *or* चरख *m.* नारंद *m.*

Shavings from the l. कांत *m.*

To form on the l. कांतणें.

To turn in the l. चरखीं धरणें.

LATHER, *n. foam of soap.* साबुणाचा फेंस *or* फेण *m.*

To LATHER, *v. a.* v. N. साबुणाचा फेंस *m.* लावणें.

LATHY, *a. lanky,* v. LEAN. काठांग्या, काठ्याळा, लकड्या.

LATIN, *n.* लातिनभाषा *f.*

LATITANCY, *n.* v. A. गुप्तता *f.* गुप्तभाव *m.* दडी *f.* दडा *m. v.* मार.

LATITANT, *a. concealed, lying hid,* v. HID. गुप्त, दडलेला, दडीमारलेला.

LATITUDE, *n. breadth.* रुंदी *f.* रुंदावा *m.*

2—celestial. विक्षेप *m.* शर *m.*

3—terrestrial. विषुववृत्तापासून अंतर *n.* अक्ष *m.*

A degree of l. अक्षांश *m.* अक्षभाग *m.*

Argument of the l. अक्षकर्ण *m.* पतनकेंद्र *n.*

Circle or parallel of l. अक्षवृत्त *n.* अक्षांशवृत्त *n.* स्वदेशमध्यपरिधि *m.*

The complement of the l. of. लंब *m.* लंबक *m.*

Sine of the l. अक्षज्या *f.* पलज्या *f.*

The cosine of the l. of a place. लंबज्या *f.*

4 *freedom from rules, laxity.* मोकळेपणा *m.* मोकळीक *f.* खुलेपणा *m.* शिथिलपणा *m.* शैथिल्य *n.* अनिर्बंध *m.* निर्बंधराहित्य *n.* निर्बंधापेक्षा *f.* नियमापेक्षा *f.*

LATITUDINAL, *a. pertaining to the breadth.* रुंदीचा, रुंदाव्याचा.

LATITUDINARIAN, *a. not confined by precise limits.* मोकळिकेचा, मोकळे पायांचा, मोकळे चरणांचा, मोकळचरणी, निर्बंधापेक्षक, शास्त्रशैथिल्यानुयायी, शास्त्रशैथिल्यानुवर्ती, नियमापेक्षक.

LATITUDINARIANISM, *n. laxity of opinion, &c.* निर्बंधापेक्षा *f.* निर्बंधापेक्षाबुद्धि *f.* मतशैथिल्य *n.*

LATTER, *n. later,*—opposed to former. पाठीमागचा *or* ला, मागचा *or* ला, दुसरा, उत्तर (in comp. as उत्तरार्ध, उत्तरभाग, उत्तरराग, उत्तरपूजा, the l. half, the l. part, &c.), अपर (in comp. as अपररात्र *pop.* अपरात्र, अपराह्ण, &c.), अंत्य, अंतिम.

2 *modern, belonging to recent time.* ऐलीकडचा *or* ला, ऐलीकडील, अर्वाचीन, अर्वाचीन कालचा. [क.

3 *second mentioned.* दुसरा, मागला, मागून उच्चारलेला, उत्तरो-

LATTERLY, *adv. of late, in recent time.* ऐलीकडे *or* अलीकडे, ऐलीकडच्या दिवसांत, थोडक्या दिवसांचे आंत, अर्वाचीन कालीं, अर्वाक्.

LATTER-MATH. See AFTER MATH. [गवाक्षजाल *n.*

LATTICE, *n. net work, &c.* जाळीदार काम *n.* जाल *n.* कटंजन *n.*

LAUD. See PRAISE.

To LAUD, *v. a.* v. To PRAISE. स्तवणें, वाखाणणें, कीर्त्तणें, वंदणें, वाणणें, वर्णणें.

LAUDABILITY, LAUDABLENESS. *n.* v. A. स्तवनीयता *f.* वंदनीयता *f.* वंद्यता *f.* &c. स्तवनार्हता *f.* स्तवनयोग्यता *f.*

LAUDABLE, *a.* v. V. स्तवाया-चा-जोगता-&c. स्तुत्य, स्तवनीय, कीर्त्तनीय, वंदनीय, वंद्य, वर्णनीय, गेय, श्लाघनीय, श्लाघ्य, स्तवार्ह.

I. See HEALTHY.

LAUDABLY, *adv.* v.A. स्तवायाजोगा *decl.* स्तुति करायाजोगा *decl.*

LAUDANUM, *n.* अफूचा अर्क *m.*

LAUDATORY, *a. containing praise.* स्तुतीचा, स्तुतिपाठक, स्तावक, स्तुत्यात्मक, स्तवनात्मक, स्तुतिप्रद, स्तुतिरूप, स्तुतिपरायण.

LAUDED, *p.* v. V. स्तवलेला,&c. स्तुत, प्रशंसित, वंदित, वर्णित, कीर्तित, संकीर्तित.

LAUDER, *n.* LAUDING, *p. a.* v. V. स्तवणारा, &c. स्तावक, वंदक, स्तुति-स्तवन-वंदन-&c. कर्त्ता-कारक-&c.

LAUDING, *n.* v. V.—*act.* स्तवणें *n.* &c. वाखाणणी *f.* वाखाणणूक *f.* वर्णणूक *f.* स्तवन *n.* वंदन *n.* वर्णन *n.* वर्णना *f.* कीर्त्तन *n.* संकीर्त्तन *n.*

2 निर्बाध, निर्दोष, ठपक्यावांचून, प्रत्यवायावांचून, योग्य, यथायोग्य. [हित्य *n.*

Lawfulness, *n.* v. A. 2. निर्बाधपणा *m.* निर्दोषता *f.* प्रत्यवायरा-

Lawgiver, Lawmaker, *n.* कायदेकरणारा, विधिस्थापक, विधिप्रवर्त्तक, विधिकर्त्ता, स्मृतिकार, बिधायक, बिधायी.

Lawless, *a. unrestrained by law*,—of persons, v. **Licentious**. बेकैद, बेकैदी, बेकायद्याचा, अनर्गल *or* ळ, बेशिस्त, गैरशिस्त, मनस्वी, पुंड, टोंग, मवास, मवासी, आचारभ्रष्ट, आचारहीन, विधिनिषेधातीत, विध्यतिवर्त्ती, शास्त्रातिवर्त्ती.

2 *contrary to law*,—of acts. बेकैदी, बेकायद्याचा, टोंगाईचा, पुंडाईचा, मनस्वी, विध्यतिवर्त्तनाचा, शास्त्रातिवर्त्तनाचा.

Lawlessness, *n.* v. A. 1. बेकैदीपणा *m.* अनर्गळपणा *m.* बेशिस्तपणा *m.* &c. बेकैद *f.*

I. *licentious, law-braving conduct.* पुंडाई *f.* टोंगाई *f.* दांडगाई *f.* मवासी *f.* विध्यतिवर्त्तन *n.* शास्त्रातिवर्त्तन *n.*

Lawn, *n. open space in a wood.* रानांतली-झाडींतली-&c. बखळ *f.* -सपाटी *f.* रानांतलें मैदान *n.*-पटांगण *n.*

2 एक जातीचें बारीक कापड आहे.

Law-suit, *n.* खटलें *n.* खटला *m.* मुकदमा *m.* व्यवहार *m.* विवाद *m.* वाद *m.* कार्य *n.* अक्ष *m.* [वेत्ता.

Lawyer, *n. one versed in the laws.* धर्मशास्त्री, धर्मज्ञ, धर्मशास्त्र-

2 *pleader in a court of justice.* अदालतीचा-अदालतींतिला-अदालती-&c. वकील *m.* व्यवहारानुवादी.

Lax. See **Loose.**

Laxative, *a. mildly purgative.* पोट *or* कोठा मोकळा करणारा, मलावष्टंभघ्न, मलावरोधनाशक, मलावष्टंभभंजक, सारक.

Laxative, *n.* पोट मोकळें करणारें औषध *n.* सुखढाळ *m.* मलावष्टंभघ्न-सारक-&c. पदार्थ *m.*-औषध *n.*

Laxity, Laxly. See **Looseness, Loosely.**

To **Lay**, *v. a. place, put, reposit, dispose, &c.* ठेवणें, घालणें, स्थापणें, टेकणें, रचणें, मांडणें, योजणें, स्थापन *n.*-स्थापना *f.*-न्यास *m.*-निक्षेप *m.* करणें *g. of o.*

2 *beat down.* पाडणें, निजवणें, बसवणें, पासला पाडणें.

3 *spread on a surface.* लावणें, चढवणें, देणें, माखणें.

4 *settle, still, compose,* lit. fig. शांत-थंड-&c. करणें, शमवणें, बसवणें, शमन *n.*-सांत्वन *n.*-शांति *f.*-&c. करणें *g. of o.*

5 (a ghost, &c.). खिळवणें, गाडणें, गाडून टाकणें, बसवणें.

6 *stake, wager.* पण *m.* करणें-घालणें *g. of o.* होड *f.*-पैज *f.* करणें-घालणें-मारणें *g. of o.* टाकणें, लावणें, मांडणें, पणाला-&c. घालणें-ठेवणें-&c.

7 (eggs). घालणें, गाळणें, टाकणें.

8 *apply.* घालणें, चढवणें, लावणें, योजणें.

9 *impose* (a tax, duty, charge, &c.). बसवणें, स्थापणें, घालणें, ठेवणें, टाकणें, आरोपणें.

10 *impute, charge* (a crime, &c.). टाकणें, घालणें, आरोपणें.

11 aside; *put off or away.* ठेवणें, टाकणें, काढून-&c. ठेवणें.

12 by; *put aside, put up.* ठेवणें, एकीकडे ठेवणें, लावून ठेवणें, हातानिराळा-वागीनिराळा-वहिवाटीनिराळा *decl.*-बाहेर-&c. ठेवणें.

To l. by carefully, to preserve. जतन ठेवणें-करणें, जतनेस ठेवणें-घालणें, पुजून ठेवणें. [डून ठेवणें.

13 by; *reserve for a future time.* ठेवणें, राखणें, निराळा का-

14 down; *state,* v. To **Propose.** उपपादणें, उपपादन *n.* करणें *g. of o.*

15 down (a load) ठेवणें, डेवरणें.

16 hold; v. To **Catch.** धरणें.

17 in; *store.* घेऊन ठेवणें, सांठवणें, सांचवणें, संग्रह *m.*-&c. करणें *g. of o.* सांठ्यास-सांटप्यास-संग्रहास-&c. ठेवणें, बेगमी *f.*-बेजमी *f.*-बरव *or* बरू *f.* करणें-करून ठेवणें *g. of o.*

18 out; *set forth, spread, dispose.* मांडणें, ठेवणें, रचणें, टाकणें.

19 out ; *expend.* खर्चणें, वेचणें, लावणें, खर्च *m.*-&c. करणें *g. of o.*

20 on; (blows, a whip, &c.). चढवणें, लगावणें, लावणें, तडकाविणें, तडतडविणें.

21 to heart. मनावर घेणें-धरणें-आणणें.

22 up; *confine to bed, &c.* निजवणें, पाडणें, बसवणें, खाटेस-अंथरुणास-&c. खिळवणें.

To be laid up. पाठ *f.* भुईसलागणें *g. of s.* निजणें, पडणें, अंथरूण *n.* धरणें-धरून असणें, खाटेस खिळणें.

23 up; *hoard, store.* सांठवणें, सांचवणें, संग्रह *m.*-&c. करणें *g. of o.*

To **Lay**, *v. n. produce eggs.* अंडीं *n. pl.* घालणें.

Lay, *n. stratum.* See **Layer.** 2 *meadow,* See **Lea.** 3 *song, poem.* गीत *n.* कविता *f.*

Lay, *a. not clerical.* गृहस्थी, गृहस्थाचा, गृहस्थकोटिसंबंधी, गृहस्थकोटिविषयक, धर्मपदस्थातिरिक्त, धर्मपदारूढातिरिक्त, भिक्षुकातिरिक्त, धर्माधिकारदीक्षाहीन, अजातधर्माधिकारदीक्ष.

Lay-land, *n. fallow ground.* पड *f.* पडित जमीन *f.*

Lay-man, *n.* गृहस्थ *m.* गृहस्थ कोटींतला मनुष्य *m.*

Lay-stall, *n. dung-heap.* खातेरें *n.* उकिरडा *m.*

Layer, *n. stratum.* थर *m.* पडदा *m.* परवड *f.* तह *m.*

Detached l. (as of onions, &c.). पदर *m.*

L. of earth & stones (as over a dam, &c.) धरणी *f.*

Laying, *n.* v. V. A. 1.—*act.* ठेवणें *n.* स्थापणें *n.* घालणें *n.* &c. रचणूक *f.* रचना *f.* स्थापन *n.* स्थापना *f.* न्यास *m.* आसादन *n.* निक्षेप *m.* योजणूक *f.* योजना *f.*

10 आरोपणें *n.* आरोपण *n.* आरोप *m.* (esp. in comp.as दोषारोप &c.). [णावळ *f.*

18 मांडणें *n.* &c. मांडणी *f.* मांडणूक *f.* मांड *m.* मांडावळ *f.* मांड-

Lazar, *n. leper, &c.* कोड्या, रक्तपित्या, गलत्कुष्टी, गलत्कुष्ठ्या, महाव्याधिग्रस्त.

Lazar-house, Lazaretto, *n.* कोडवाडा *m.* कोड्यांचें इस्पिताल *n.* कुष्टीशाला *f.* महाव्याधिस्थशाला *f.*

Lazarly. See **Leprous.**

Lazily, *adv.* v. A. आळसानें, आळस करून, आळसत आळसत, गमत गमत, टंगळमंगळ, अळमटळम, अळमळीत, आलस्यपूर्वक.

Laziness, *n.* v. A. आळस *m.* आळशीपणा *m.* सुस्ती *f.* सुस्तपणा *m.* ढिलेपणा *m.* आलस्य *n.* अलसता *f.* निरुद्योगिता *f.* अनुद्योगिता *f.* अव्यवसाय *m.* उद्योगद्वेष *m.* कार्यप्रद्वेष *m.* उद्योगशत्रुत्व *n.* कार्यानुत्साह *m.* उद्योगविमुखता *f.*

Lazy, *a. idle, indolent, slothful, sluggish.* आळसी *or* शी, आळसट, आळसडा, सुस्त, ढिला, ढील, पड्या, कामचुकाऊ, उठबळ, आंगजड, जड, शिथिल, अलस, निरुद्योग, निरुद्योगी, अनुद्योगी, निरुत्साह, उद्योगविमुख, उद्योगपराङ्मुख, उद्योगद्वेष्टा, कार्यानुत्साही, उद्योगशत्रु. Some terms and phrases for a *very lazy person* are सातांळशी, शताळशी *or* सी, आळशांचा राजा, आळशांचा मायबाप, उटावरून शेळ्या वळणारा, काठीनें पाणी शिवणारा, काठीनें संध्या करणारा, पिकल्या झाडाखालीं उपाशी मरणारा.

Superlatively l. शताळशी.

To become l. आळसणें, आळसटणें, आळसावणें, सुस्तावणें.

Lea, *n. meadow land.* कुरण *n.* कास *m.*

A salt marsh or l. बहाड *n.*

Lead, *n.* शिसें *n.* सीस *or* सीसक *n.* वंग *n.*

Red l. शेंदूर *m.* सिंदूर *n.* शोण *n.* सौभाग्य *n.*

Of the color of red l. शेंदरा, शेंदरी, शेंदऱ्या.

White l. सफेता *or* सफेदा *m.*

2 (for sounding water). बुडीद *m.* गळ *m.*

3 leads. *flat roof covered with lead.* शिशाचें धाबें *n.*

To **Lead**, *v. a. guide by the hand.* हात *m.* धरून नेणें *g. of o.* हातीं धरून नेणें-फिरवणें-घेऊन जाणें.

2 *conduct, guide to.* नेणें, घेऊन जाणें, वाटदाखवून-&c. नेणें, वाटेनें नेणें, पावणें, पाववणें, नय *m.*-नयन *n.*-प्रापण *n.*-&c. करणें *g. of o.*

3 *conduct, head.* पुढें जाऊन-पुढाईत-&c. होऊन नेणें-चालवणें, पुढाकार *m.*-&c. करणें *g. of. o.* पुढार *m. f.* काढणें-घेणें *g. of. o.* पुढारी-पुढाईत-&c. असणें *in. con.* पुरोनयन *n.* करणें.

4 *draw, entice, allure.* फुसलावून नेणें, मोह घालून नेणें, प्रलोभन *n.* करणें, तंतरणें.

5 *influence, induce,* v. To Move. मनावणें, ओढणें, ओढून घेणें, वळवणें, प्रवर्त्तवणें, ओढ *f.*-ओढा *m.* लागणें *in. con.*

6 (time, life, &c.) *spend, pass.* काढणें, घालवणें, लोटणें, गुजराण *f.*-गुजारा *m.* करणें *g. of o.*

To **Lead**, *v. n. go first, &c. shew the way.* पुढें जाणें-होणें, पुढें जाऊन वाट *f.* दाखवणें, पुढाइती *f.*-पुढाइतपणा *m.*-मोहरपी *f.*-पुरस्कार *m.*-&c. करणें, आगा *m.*-आघाडी *f.*-पुढार *m. f.* घेणें.

2 to; *bring about, bring on.* ओढीस आणणें, ओढीस येणें *in. con.*

Lead, Leading, *n.* v. V. N. पुढाइतपणा*m.* पुढाइती *f.* पुढाकार*m.* पुढारकी *f.* मोहरपी *f.* पुरस्कार *m.* पुढार *m. f.*

To take the l. See To Lead.

Leaden, *a. made, &c. of lead.* शिशाचा, सीसमय.

Leader, *n.* **Leading**, *p. a.* v. V. A. 1. हात धरून नेणारा, हातीं धरून नेणारा.

2 नेणारा, वाटेनें-वाट दाखवून-&c. नेणारा, नयन-&c. कर्त्ता, नेता.

3 & V. N. *head, chief,* v. Conductor. नायक, पुढाईत, पुढाकारी, पुढारी, मोहरपी, मोहर काढ्या, पुरस्कर्त्ता, अग्रगामी, अग्रेसर, मुखरण, मुखरीण, बिनीचा, प्रमुख, (in. comp.) पुरस्सर (in. comp.).

L. of a religious order or sect. आचार्य.

L. of a team or train. मोहर काढ्या, मोहरवड्या, मोहरपी, मोहरचा, मोहरला, मोहरा, चाव्ह्ऱ्या, सरजा, अगली *or* ल्या. (bullock) नायका बैल.

Lead-pencil, *n.* शिशाची-चें पेन्सिल.

Leadership, *n.* See Lead.

Leadwort, *n.* Ceylon l. चित्रक *m.* चित्रमूळ *f.*

Leaf, *n.* (of a plant). पान *n.* पर्ण *n.* पत्र *n.* दल *or* दळ *n.*

Dry and littered leaves. पातेरा *m.* पाचोळा *m.*

L. used as a dish or plate. जेवणवत *n.*

Load of leaves (esp. of those used as dishes). पानभारा *m.* पानपेंडा *m.*

Pinnate or long-shaped l. पात *n. f m.* पाती *f.* पातें *n.*

Tripartite l. निकटें *n.* तिवण *f.*

Vender or bringer of leaves for dishes. पानारी.

Plate or dish made of leaves. पत्रावळ *f.* पुट *n.*—a small one. ठिकोळें *or* ठिगोळें *n.*

Unblown spike of leaves. शिगरी *f.*

To be shed or cast—leaves of a tree. खडणें.

2 (of a book). पान *n.* पत्र *n.* पत्रक *n.* वरख *m.*

3 (of a folding door, &c.). फळी *f.* कवाड *n.* कपाट *n.* तलफ *n.* फरदा *m.* झडप *n.*

L. of a table. खालवर करण्याची फळी *f.*

4 (of a hand mill). पेड *or* पेढ *n. f.* तळी *f.*

5 *thing foliated.* वरख *m.* पत्रा *m.* पत्र *n.*

To **Leaf**, *v. n. shoot out leaves.* पानें *n. pl.*-पालवी *f.* फुटणें-येणें *in. con.* पालेणें, पालेजणें, पालवणें.

Leafage, *n.* पानें *n. pl.* पाला *m.* पालवी *f.* पल्लव *m. pl.*

Leaf-metal, *n.* तकट *or* तकटें *n.*

Leafiness, *n.* v. A. पर्णबाहुल्य *n.* पर्णप्राचुर्य *n.*

Leafless, *a bare.* निपाणी, सडसडीत, निष्पर्ण, निष्पत्र, अपत्र, पर्णशून्य.

A l. tree. खराटा *m.*

Leaflessness, *n.* v. A. निष्पर्णता *f.* निष्पत्रता *f.* पर्णशून्यता *f.*

Leaflet, *n.* लहान पान *n.*

Leafy, *a. having many leaves.* दाटपानाचा, बहुपानी, बहुपर्ण, पर्णबहुल, पर्णप्रचुर, पर्णवान्, पर्णमय.

League, *n. alliance, confederacy, &c.* v. Combination. संधि *m.* एकोपा *m.* ऐक्य *n.* एकवळा *m.* जूट *m.* जट *m.* कट *m.* कटाव *m.* कूट *n.*

2 *measure of three miles.* दीड कोस *m.*

To **League**, *v. n. confederate,* v. To Combine. जुटणें, जटणें, जुडणें, जूट *m.*-&c. करणें, मिळून असणें.

Leagued, *p.* v. V. जुडलेला, जुटलेला, &c. [बुळकी *f.*

Leak, *n. hole or crevice that admits water.* गळतें *n.* गळती *f.*

To stop a l. गळतें *n.* काढणें.

To spring a l. फूट *f.* घेणें, झरा *m.* लागणें *in. con.*

2 v. Ooze. पाझर *m.* [वाहणें.

To **Leak**, *v. n. let water in.* गळणें, झरणें, पाझरणें, ठिपकणें,

2 (a boat, &c.). पाणी *n.* घेणें.

Leakage, *n. fluid that enters by leaking.* पाझर *m.* गळतें *n.* गळीत *n.* गळण *f.*

2 *loss by leakage.* घट *f.* घस *f.*

Leakiness, *n.* v. A. गळकेपणा *m.*

Leaking, *p. a.* **Leaky**, *a.* v. V. गळणारा, गळका, गळता, पाझरता, पाणी घेणारा, मुतरा.

To **Lean**, *v. n. leave the perpendicular,* v. To Incline. कलणें, झुकणें, तोलणें, कलता-झुकता-&c. होणें, रेळणें, एकारणें.

2 fig. *tend, propend,* v. To Incline. कलणें, लवणें, झुकणें, वळणें, मोडणें, कल *m.*-झोक *m.*-&c. असणें. [णें.

3 *bend, be in a bending posture.* लवणें, ओणवणें, ओणवा हो-

4 *incline against, rest on, recline.* टेंकणें, ओठंगणें, ठेपणें.

To **Lean**, *v. a. incline, cause to lean.* टेंकणें.

Lean, *n.*—of flesh. तांबडें मास *n.*

Lean, *a. wanting flesh, thin, meagre, lank, gaunt.* रोड, रोडका, रोडंग, रोडंगा, पातळ, सडकपातळ, सडपातळ, काटकुळा *or* कोळा, पातळांगी, पातळांग्या, लुकड, लुकडा *or* ड्या, लुक्कड, तंतारा, तंता-

रीक, कांकीट, किडकिडीत, किरकाडा, किचकाड, किचकाडा, किचकाडी, किचकाट, कमतनूक, सुकट्या, सुखट, हडहडीत, सडसडीत, हाडळ, हाडगळ, वाळका, वाळकुंजा, वाळकुंडा, रंगाळा, कृश, कृशांग, क्षीण, शुष्क, शुष्कांग. Some terms and epithets for a *very lean person*, agreeing wtih *starveling, skeleton, bare-bones, a lath, bag of bones, &c.* are रोडांग्या, रोड्या, लकड्या, काठंग्या, काठ्याळा, फाटक्या आंगाचा, एकेरी आंगाचा, एकशेवडी, पातकिरला, अर्ध्याजिवाचा, एकफांसोळीचा, झुरझुरपंजर, मरकाड्या, मरतुकडा, मरणा, मरतमडें *n.* बांगडीसारखा, खपाटें बसलेला, पाठीस पोट लागलेला, झुडतर, जरत्कारू, कांबा *m.* दिपाचा कवडा *m.* हाडांचा पिंजरा *m.* पाप्याचा पितर *m.*

To become l. *waste away, fall away, become emaciate, gaunt, meagre, &c.* रोडणें, रोडावणें, रोडंगणें, रोडेणें, क्षिणणें, गळणें, आंग *n.* टाकणें, सुखणें, वाळणें, अटणें, अळणें, झडणें, सांडवणें, मरीस जाणें, खंगणें, काचणें, काचावणें, डगागणें, हडवंगणें *or* हडवांगणें, हडहडणें, ढकलणें, आंग *n.*-शरीर *n.*-&c. जाणें *g. of s.* कापूस *m.* महाग करणें.

In the rather varied sense *to be emaciated, to be (having become)lean and meagre*, and as expressed by various phrases; such as, *to be reduced to a skeleton, to be mere skin and bone, to be a mere bag of bones, to be as thin as a lath, to be as thin as a whipping post, to be as lean as death, &c. &c.* there are numerous phraseologies in Maráthì ; as चुंबणें, चोपटणें, चोपणें, झुकणें, तंगणें, लंगणें *or* लंघणें, बठणें, हातापायांचें पडवळ *n.* होणें, हातापायांच्या-हाडांच्या फुंकण्या होणें, आंगाचें पाणी होणें, हाडांचे मणी होणें, भालूसारखा असणें, पाठीस पोट *n.* लागणें, पोटाची पन्नावळ आणि हाता पायांचें पडवळ होणें, पाठ आणि पोट एक होणें, खपाटें *n. pl.* बसणें, कडप *n.* बळणें *g. of s.* हातापायांचा ढीग होणें, संक्रांत *f.* बसणें *in. con.* पोट वाढणें आणि हातापायांच्या काड्या होणें.

2 *barren, spiritless,* v. Jejune. भुकिस्त, रुखा, रुक्ष.

Leaning, See Inclination.

Leanness, *n.* v. A. 1. रोडपणा *m.* रोडकेपणा *m.* &c. पातळाई *f.* लुकडाई *f.* कृशत्व *n.* कार्श्य *n.* क्षीणता *f.* कृशांगता *f.*

2 भुकिस्तपणा *m.* &c.

To Leap, *v. n. spring, jump, &c.* उडणें, कुदणें, उडी *f.* मारणें-घालणें, फांदणें, ठिकणें, क्षेप *f.*-झाप *f.* मारणें-घालणें-टाकणें, लाग *f.* मारणें. [न जाणें.

To Leap, *v. a. pass over by leaping.* उडून जाणें, उडी *f.* मारू-

Leap, Leaping, *n.* v. V. N.—*act.* उडणें *n.* उडी *f.* लंघन *n.* उड्डाण *n.*

L. with the legs closed. चिपी उडी, चुबकती उडी.

L. heels over head. गोल्हांट *f. n.*

L. with the legs caught up. मोटकुळी उडी.

L. with the four legs. चौखुरी उडी.

Look before you leap. पाऊल जपून टाकावें-ठेवावें, फुंकून पाय टाकावा, पाय धुऊन टाकावा.

Leaper, *n.* Leaping, *p. a.* v. V. N. उडणारा, &c. उड्या, उड्डाण करणारा.

Leap-frog, *n.*—the play. कुदाकुदी *f.* बेडूककुदी *f.*

Leap-year, *n.* अधिकदिवसाचें वर्ष *n.*-साल *n.* अधिक दिनवत्सर *n.*

To Learn, *v. a. acquire by study.* शिकणें, शिकून घेणें, अभ्यास *m.* करणें *g. of o.* येणें *in. con.*

To l. by heart. पाठ करणें.

2 *gain the knowledge of, become informed of.* माहिती *f.*-माहितगारी *f.*-&c. करून घेणें *g. of o.* समजणें, ऐकणें, श्रुत-अवगत-&c. करणें, कळणें-समजणें *in. con.* बातमी *f.*-&c. लागणें *g. of o. with in. con.* ऐकण्यांत येणें *in. con.*

3 See To Teach.

To Learn, *v. n. acquire knowledge, study.* शिकणें, पढणें, म्हणणें, अभ्यास *m.*-विद्याभ्यास *m.* करणें.

To l. to read and write. पढणें *n.*-म्हणणें *n.*-लिहणें पुसणें *n.*-लिहणें पढणें *n.*-लिहणें म्हणणें *n.*-&c. शिकणें.

2 of ; *take pattern.* पाहून करणें, कित्ता *m.*-वळण *n.* घेणें *g. of o.*

Learned, *p. & a.* v. V. A. 1. शिकलेला, शिकून घेतलेला, &c. शिकणाऊ, शिकाऊ, शिक्षित, ऐकलेला, समजलेला, ऐकण्यांत आलेला.

I. *read, versed in science, &c.* पढलेला, पढीक, शिकलेला, विद्वान्, विद्याविशिष्ट, साक्षर, अक्षरस्थ, शिक्षित, व्युत्पन्न, विद्यासंपन्न, अध्ययनसंपन्न, अक्षरसंपन्न, विद्यावान्, लब्धविद्य, अभ्यस्तविद्य, कृतविद्य, विद्यावृद्ध, विद्याशाली, अधीत, बहुज्ञ, बहुविद्य.

A l. man. पंडित, पंडितजन, विद्वज्जन.

A l. fool. पढत मूर्ख.

II. *skilled in, versed in,* v. Conversant. जाण, जाणता, माहितदार, माहितगार, वाकबदार, अभ्यस्त, वहिवाटलेला, निपुण, प्रवीण, विशारद.

III. *containing learning.* पांडित्याचा, खोलबुद्धीचा, खोल, गहन, गूढ, शास्त्रीय, व्युत्पादक.

Learnedly, *adv. with erudition.* पांडित्यानें, पांडित्य करून, पांडित्य दाखवून, विद्वत्तेनें.

Learner, *n.* v. V. A. 1. शिकणारा, शिकून घेणारा, &c.

v. V. N.1. *and* Scholar. शिकणारा, पढणारा, अभ्यास करणारा, विद्यार्थी, शिकणाऊ, शिकाऊ. [त्यनवा.

One ever learning without coming to knowledge. नि

Learning, *n.* v. V. A. 1.—*act.* शिकणें *n.* शिकून घेणें *n.*

v. V. N. शिकणें *n.* पढणें *n.* म्हणणें *n.* अध्ययन *n.* अभ्यास *m.* विद्याभ्यास *m.* शिक्षा *f.*

I. *knowledge of literature, &c.* विद्या *f.* व्युत्पत्ति *f.* पांडित्य *n.* ज्ञातृत्व *n.* विद्वत्ता *f.* वेत्तृत्व *n.* विद्यासंपत्ति *f.* अध्ययनसंपत्ति *f.* अक्षरसंपत्ति *f.* साक्षरता *f.* शिकणें *n.* पढणें *n.* म्हणणें *n.* अध्ययन *n.*

An ignorant and obtrusive pretender to l. लुडबुडापंडित.

Obtrusive and empty pretence to l. पांडित्य *n.v.* मिरव.

Piece-l. टाणेटोणे *m. pl.*

II. *literature.* विद्या *f.* अक्षर *n.* [वन *n.*

Cultivation of l., pursuit of l. विद्याभ्यास *m.* विद्यानुसे-

Patronising l. विद्यानुपालन *n.*

That cultivates l. विद्यानुसेवी.

Leasable, *n.* v. V. कौलानें द्यावा-चा-जोगा-जोगता-सारखा-&c.

Lease, *n. contract for a number of years.* कौल *m.* कौलनामा *m.* पत्ता *m.*

Cost of procuring a l. कौलावण *f.*

To Lease, *v. a. let by lease.* कौलानें देणें.

To Lease, *v. n.* See To Glean.

Lease-hold, *a. held by lease.* कौली, कौलाचा, कौलानें घेतलेला.

Lease-holder, *n.* कौली मक्तेदार, कौलदार, कौल्या. [फ *f.*

Leash, *n. cord or thong for a dog, &c.* काढणी *f.* सडा *m.* सड-

2 *tierce.* तिकडी *f.* त्रिक *n.*

To LEASH, *v. a.* v. N. 1. काढणीनें-&c. बांधणें.

LEASING. See FALSEHOOD.

LEAST, *a. smallest, &c.* सर्वांपेक्षां-सगळ्यांपेक्षां-&c. लहान-धाकटा-&c. सर्वांहून-सगळ्यांहून-&c. लहान-धाकटा-&c. कनिष्ठ, अल्पिष्ठ, लघिष्ठ. [थोडा *decl.*

LEAST, *adv. in the smallest degree.* सर्वांहून-सर्वांपेक्षां-&c. कमी-

At l. *not to say more.* तरीं, तर, तरस्तरा *a. decl.* तरसई, तरहोय, Ex. त्याला वक्तृत्व जरी नाहीं बोलतां येतें तर खरें. Though he be not eloquent he is at least able to speak.

At the l. किमानपक्ष, कनिष्ठपक्ष, निरुष्टपक्ष, निदान, निदानपक्ष, करंटपक्ष, कडेशेवट, गेलामेला (*a. decl.*) तरीं, गेलागनला (*a. decl.*) तरीं, काहीं नाहींतरीं, अगदीं नाहींतरीं, थोडातरीं, गेला बाजार तरीं.

Not in the l. कांहींच नाहीं, किमपि नाहीं, बालाग्र नाहीं.

LEATHER, *n.* कमावलेलें कातडें *n.* कातडें *n.* चामडें *n.* चाम *n.* चर्म *n.*

Strap or tie of l. वादी *f.* चामोटा *m.* बरत्रा *f.* तस्मा *m.*

Worker in l. (comprehending currier, tanner, &c.). चाम्हार, ढोर, चर्मकार, चर्मक.

2 *skin as pulled off.* साल *f. n.* सालडें *n.* सालपट *n.* कातडी *f.*

To lose l. साल *f. n.*-सालडें *n.*-&c. जाणें *g. of s.*

To LEATHER. See To BEAT.

LEATHER-DRESSER, *n.* चाम्हार, ढोर, चर्मकार.

LEATHER, LEATHERN, *a. made, &c. of leather.* कातडयाचा, चामड्याचा, चर्माचा, चर्मी, चार्म, चर्ममय, चर्मनिर्मित.

LEAVE, *n. permission, assent.* परवानगी *f.* आज्ञा *f.* हुकूम *m.* मोकळीक *f.* सुटी *f.* अनुज्ञा *f.* अभ्यनुज्ञा *f.*

2 *permission to depart.* निरोप *m.* आज्ञा *f.* हुकूम *m.* रजा *f.*

To take l. घेणें, निरोप *m.*-आज्ञा *f.*-&c. घेणें.

3 (of absence). रजा *f.* निरोप *m.* रुखसत *f.* सुटी *f.*

To LEAVE, *v. a. quit, depart from.* सोडणें, सोडून जाणें, सोडून देणें, वर्जणें, विसर्जणें, विसर्जन *n.*-&c. करणें *g. of o.*

2 *forsake,* v. To ABANDON. टाकणें, सोडणें, सांडणें, त्याग *m.*-&c. करणें *g. of o.*

3 *suffer to remain.* सोडणें, ठेवणें, राखणें, राहूं देणें, शेषठेवणें, न घेणें, न नेणें. [रणें.

4 *bequeath.* मृतपत्रांत-मृतलेखांत-&c. देणें, मृत्युलेखदत्त-&c. क-

5 alone; *cease from, &c.* सोडणें, सोडून जाणें, सोडून देणें, पाठ *f.* सोडणें, सोड *f.* देणें, सांड *f.* करणें.

6 alone ; *not to touch.* हात *m.* न ठेवणें, हात *m.* न लावणें, हात *m.* काढणें.

7 off ; *cast aside or away.* टाकणें, सोडणें, घालायाचा *a. decl.* सोडणें, वर्जणें.

8 off ; *desist from.* सोडणें, टाकणें, वर्जणें. [वर्जणें.

9 out ; *omit.* सोडणें, गाळणें, टाकणें, वगळणें, सांडणें, अंतरणें,

To LEAVE, *To* LEAVE off, *v. n.* See To CEASE, To STOP.

LEAVED, *a. having leaves.* पानांचा, पर्णाचा, सपर्ण, पर्णी, पानी in. comp.

Two-leaved, opposite leaved. द्विपर्ण.

2 *having leaves or folds.* फळ्यांचा.

Two-leaved. दुफळी.

LEAVEN, *n. fermenting matter to raise dough.* आंबवण *n.* फुगवण *n.* समीर *n.*

To LEAVEN, *v. a. affect by leaven.* फुगवण *n.*-आंबवण *n.*-समीर *n.*-&c. घालणें-घालून फुगवणें, आंबवणें, आंबवून फुगवणें.

LEAVENED, *p.* v. V. फुगवण घातलेला, फुगवलेला, &c. फुगवणाचा.

LEAVER, *n.* LEAVING, *p. a.* v. V.1 सोडणारा, टाकणारा, &c. विसर्जन-वर्जन &c. कर्त्ता. [न *n.*

LEAVING, *n.* v. V. 1. 2. सोडणें *n.* &c. त्याग *m.* वर्जन *n.* विसर्ज-

LEAVINGS, *n. things left ; remnants, refuse,*—gener. उरलीं-सुरलीं *n. pl.* उरवण *f.* उरवा *m.* गदळ *n.* शेष *m.* अवशेष *m.*

2—of food. उष्टें *n.* अन्नशेष *m.* भुक्तशेष *m.* उच्छिष्ट *n.* उच्छिष्टान्न *n.* भुक्तसमुच्छिन्न *n.*

L.—compreh. *scraps, crumbs, dirty dishes, &c.* उष्टवळ *f.* उष्टवड *f.* उष्टावळ *f.* खरकटवळ or खरकटावळ *f.* खरकटवड *f.* खरकटवाडा or वडा *m.* उष्टींपाष्टीं *n. pl.* उष्टींमाष्टीं *n. pl.*

LECHER, *n. man given to lewdness,* v. WENCHER. रांडबाज, रांडछंदी, रांडव्यसनी, लंपट, इष्कबाज, बिसनी. Some phrases used of an inveterate l. are. ह्यास माय मावशी नाहीं, तो माय मावशी पाहत नाहीं, तो आई बहीण पाहत नाहीं, तो लेक सून पाहत नाहीं.

To LECHER, *v. n.* रांडबाजी *f.*-इष्कबाजी *f.*-&c. करणें.

LECHEROUS, *a. addicted to lewdness,* v. LUSTFUL. कामी, संभोगी, स्त्रीव्यसनी, रांडव्यसनी, रांडछंदी, स्त्रीलंपट, स्त्रीपर, स्त्रीरत, स्त्रीव्यासंगी, स्त्रैण, बहिर्व्यसनी, व्यवायी, व्यवायपरायण.

LECHEROUSNESS, *n.* v. A. *and* LUST. कामीपणा *m.* रांडव्यसन *n.* रांडछंद *m.* स्त्रीव्यसन *n.* स्त्रीव्यासंग *m.* कामासक्ति *f.*

LECHERY, *n. practice of lewdness.* रांडबाजी *f.* इष्कबाजी *f.* कटिशूलाचें *n.* बदफैली *f.* बाहेरख्याल *m.* बहिर्व्यसन *n.*

LECTION, *n. a reading, variation of copies.* पाठ *m.* पाठांतर *n.* पाठभेद *m.*

LECTURE, LECTURING, *n.* v. V. A. 1.—*act.* पाठसांगणें *n.* पाठन *n.* अध्यापन *n.* व्याख्यान *n.*

2 तोंडचीशिक्षा *f.* शब्दाचामार *m.* वाग्दंड *m.* वाग्शासन *n.*

v. V. N. पाठसांगणें *n.* पाठ *m.*

To LECTURE, *v. a. instruct formally.* पाठ *m.* सांगणें *with* स *or* ला *of o.* पाठन *n.*-अध्यापन *n.*-&c. करणें.

2 *reprimand.* तोंडची शिक्षा *f.*-शब्दाचा मार *m.*-&c. करणें-देणें, वाग्दंड *m.*-वाग्शासन *n.* करणें, कानास खडा *m.* लावणें, कान *m. pl.* उघडणें-उपटणें.

To be constantly lecturing. कानीं कपाळीं रडणें-ओरडणें.

To LECTURE, *v. n. read a lecture.* पाठ *m.* सांगणें.

LECTURER, *n.* v. V. A. 1. पाठसांगणारा, अध्यापक, पाठक, पाठन-अध्यापन करणारा. [कर्त्ता.

2 कानास खडालावणारा, &c. शब्दाचा मार करणारा, वाग्दंड-&c.

v. V. N. पाठ सांगणारा, पाठक.

LED, *p.* v. V. A. 1. हातीं धरून नेलेला, &c.

2 नेलेला, वाटेनें नेलेला, &c. नीत, प्रापित.

3 पूर्वक *and* पुरस्सर (in comp. as अकारपूर्वक वर्ण, मनुष्यपूर्वक प्राणी, सिंहपूर्वक श्वापद, गरुड पुरस्सर पक्षी, &c.).

LED-HORSE, *n. horse led for show.* कोतवालघोडा *m.* कोतवाल *m.* कोतल *m.*

LEDGE, *n. layer, stratum.* थर *m.* परवड *f.*

2 *ridge, projecting part.* जई *or* जै *f.* चिरणी *f.* छपेली *or* सपेली *f.* कंगोरा *m.* कड *f.*

LEDGER, *n. book framed from the journal,*—of a merchant. पक्कीखतावणी *f.* खातेवही *f.* See Note under JOURNAL.

Account abstracted from the l. तालेबंद *m.*

Entering into the l. बार करणें*n.* सतावणी *f.*

Lee, *n. sediment*, See **Lees**. 2 *side toward which the wind blows.* वाऱ्याचे समोरची दिशा *f.*-जागा *f.*-बाजू *f.* वाताभिमुख-दिशा *f.*

L.-side of a ship. दमान *n.*

Under the l. of. निवाऱ्यांत, अडोशांत.

Lee-ward, *adv.* वाऱ्यासमोरचे दिशेकडे, वाऱ्यासमोर.

Lee-ward, *a.* वाऱ्यासमोरचे दिशेकडचा, वाऱ्यासमोरचा,वायुसन्मुख.

Leech, *n. blood-sucker.* जळू *f.* जोख *f.* जलौका *f.* जलूका *f.*

A female that applies leeches. जोखीण *f.*

2 See **Physician**.

Leek, *n.* कांदा *m.*

Leer, *n. oblique or arch look.* बांकडा-आडवा डोळा*m.* आडवीदृष्टि *f.* कटाक्ष *m.* नेत्रकटाक्ष *m.* अपांगदर्शन *n.*

Leers. गमजे *m. pl.*

To **Leer**, *v. n.* v. N. आडवे दृष्टीनें-अर्धे दृष्टीनें-बांकड्या डोळयानें-काण्या डोळयानें-&c. पाहणें, डोळे *m. pl.* मोडणें, अपांगदर्शन *n.*-कटाक्षावेक्षण *n.*-कटाक्षवीक्षण *n.*-कटाक्षावलोकन *n.*-&c. करणें.

Leerer, *n.* **Leering**, *p. a.* v. V. आडवेदृष्टीनें पाहणारा, डोळे मोडणारा,&c. नजरबाज, अपांगदर्शी, कटाक्षवीक्षी, कटाक्षावलोकी.

Leering, *n.* V.—*act.* आडवे दृष्टीनें पाहणें *n.* &c. अपांगदर्शन *n.* कटाक्षावेक्षण *n.* कटाक्षवीक्षण *n.* कटाक्षावलोकन *n.* नेत्रपल्लवी *f.*

Leeringly, *adv.* डोळे मोडून, बांकड्या डोळयानें, आडवेदृष्टीनें, &c.

Lees, *n. dregs, sediment.* गाळ *m.* गाळा *m.* रेंदा *m.*

Left, *p.* v. V. 1. सोडलेला, सोडून दिल्हेला, &c. वर्जित, विसर्जित, रहित, विरहित.

2 सोडलेला, टाकलेला, &c. त्यक्त, परित्यक्त, उज्झित.

3 सोडलेला, ठेवलेला, शेषठेवलेला, &c. उरता, बाकी, अवशिष्ट, उर्वरित.—orts, &c. उरला सुरला, उरला पुरला, उरसूर.

L. of a meal. उष्टा, उच्छिष्ट.

To be l. v. To **Remain**. उरणें, वांचणें.

4 मृतपत्रांत दिल्हेला, मृत्युलेख दत्त.

9 सोडलेला, गाळलेला, &c. अंतरित, अंतरीक, वर्ज, वार्जित.

Left, *a.*—not the right. डावा, डावका, वाम, सव्य, चपना.

L. arm. वामबाहु *m.*

L. hand. वामहस्त *m.* सव्य *n.*

L. side. वामांग *n.* वामकुक्षि *m.*

To cast or leave on the l. hand (an object in passing it). डावलणें, डावी *f.*-डावा *m.* घालणें. [डावा.

2 *that is on the left hand.* डाव्याहातचा, डाव्याहाताकडचा,

Left-handed, *a.* डावखुरा *or* खोरा, डावरा, डावका, चपना.

Left-handedness, *n.* v. A. डावखुरेपणा *m.* डावरेपणा *m.*

Leg, *n.* पाय *m.* टांग *f.* टांगडी *f.* तांगडी *f.* तंगडी *f.* तंगड*n.* डोंका *or* डोका*m.*

Born with the legs foremost. पायाळ *or* ळू.

Swelling of the legs. श्लीपद *n.*

That has one l. shorter than the other. दीड पायाचा.

That is upon his last legs. उठवणकर.

Worked off one's legs. लचला लवंगला. [घेणें.

To be upon one's last legs. उठवणीस येणें, उठवण *f.*

To give leg-bail, *run off.* पोबारा *m.* करणें-म्हणणें, झ्या *f.* करणें-म्हणणें.

To set firm upon one's legs. उठवण *f.* मोडणें.

To stand upon one's legs again. पाठ *f.* उचलणें, भुईसीं पाय *m.* लागणें.

To stand upon one's own legs. स्वबलावर-आपल्या जोरावर-आपल्या आधारानें-&c. उभा राहणें.

To stretch one's legs. पाय *m.* मोकळा करणें.

2 (of a table, chair, &c.). पाय *m.* खुर *m.*

Legacy, *n. bequest.* मृत्युलेखार्पितदान *n.* मृत्युपत्रस्थदान *n.* मृत्युलेखदान *n.*

Legal, *a. that is conformable to law.* कायदेशीर, कायद्याचा, कायद्यास बरोबर-रुजू-लायक-&c. स्मृतिशास्त्रसम्मत, धर्मशास्त्रसम्मत, धर्मशास्त्रानुमत, धर्मशास्त्रानुयायी, धर्मशास्त्रानुसारी, धर्मशास्त्रानुरूप, धर्मशास्त्रप्रोक्त, व्यवहारविधिसम्मत, व्यवहारविधिप्रोक्त, &c. राज्यनियमानुमत, राज्यनियमसम्मत, &c. राज्यव्यवस्थासम्मत, राज्यव्यवस्थानुयायी, &c. स्मार्त्त, सौत्र.

2 *of or belonging to law.* व्यवहाराचा, व्यवहार संबंधी-विषयक, व्यवहार मार्गाचा, व्यवहार विधीचा, व्यावहारिक, स्मार्त्त.

3 *enjoined, prescribed, constituted, &c. by law.* कायद्यानें-शास्त्रानें-कायद्यांत-शास्त्रांत-&c. सांगितलेला, शास्त्रोक्त, स्मृतिशास्त्रविहित, स्मृतिशास्त्रप्रोक्त, राज्यनियमविहित, राज्यनियमानुसार, व्यवहारविधिप्रोक्त, व्यवहारविधिविहित.

4 *that looks to works for salvation.* कर्ममार्गी, कर्ममार्गाचा, कर्ममार्गाश्रयी, कर्ममार्गावलंबी, कर्ममार्गसेवी-धारक-&c. कर्मशील, कर्मठ.

Legalist, *n. one who rests on works.* कर्ममार्गी, &c. See A. 4.

Legality, **Legalness**, *n.* v. A. 1, स्मृतिशास्त्रानुयायिता *f.* धर्मशास्त्रानुयायिता *f.* व्ययहारविध्यनुयायिता *f.* राज्यनियमानुयायिता *f.* धर्मशास्त्रानुकूल्य*n.* धर्मशास्त्रनुसारिता *f.* स्मृतिशास्त्रानुकूल्य*n.* &c.

4 *reliance, &c. on works.* कर्ममार्गनिष्ठा *f.* कर्ममार्गसेवा *f.* कर्ममार्गाश्रयण *n.*

To **Legalize**, *v. a. make lawful, authorize.* कायद्यांत-विधींत-&c. घेणें-आणणें, कायद्यानें स्थापणें, हुकूम *m.*-आज्ञा *f.*-मोकळीक *f.*-मुबा *f.*-&c. करणें-देणें *g. of o.* आचारिक-विहित-विधेय-अनिषिद्ध-विधिगत-विधिप्रविष्ट-अप्रत्यवाय-निर्दोष-&c. करणें.

Legally, *adv.* v. A. 1. कायद्याप्रमाणें, कायद्यावरहुकूम, कायदेशीर, स्मृतिशास्त्रानुसार, धर्मशास्त्रानुसार, व्यवहारविध्यनुसार, राज्यनियमानुरूप-&c.

4 कर्ममार्ग आश्रयून, कर्ममार्गसेवन पूर्वक, कर्ममार्गनिष्ठेनें.

Legate, *n. ambassador.* वकील, दूत.

Legatee, *n. one who has a legacy left to him.* मृत्युलेखदानाधिकारी, मृत्युलेखदानग्राही.

Legation. See **Embassy**.

Legator, *n. one who leaves a legacy.* मृत्युलेखदानकारी.

Legend, *n. narrative of a saint, holy place, &c.* माहात्म्य *n.* चरित्र *n.* कथा *f.* अनुसंधान *n.* आख्यायिका *f.*

Reciter of legends. कथेकरी, हरिदास *pop.* हरदास, अनुसंधानी, कथिक, गोसावी.

Sweetmeats distributed at the close of a recitation of a l. प्रसाद *m.* खिरापत *f.*

2 *incredible, unauthentic tale, &c.* दंतकथा *f.* जनकथा *f.* लोककथा *f.*

Legendary, *a. existing in legend, fabulous.* हरदासी, जुनेक-

धेनन्धा, कथीक, कथाशेप, पुराणकथित, पुराणोक, पुराणांतरचा, कथोपलब्ध, पंचोपाख्यानी.

LEGENDARY, *n. reciter of legends.* कथेकरी, हरिदास *pop.* हरदास, कथड्या *or* कथाड्या, अनुसंधानी, कथिक, गोसावी.

LEGERDEMAIN, *n.* v. JUGGLERY. हातचलाकीचा खेळ *m.* हस्तलाघव *n.* गारूड *n.* गोडबंगाल *n.* इंद्रजाल *n.*

LEGGED, *a. having legs.* पायांचा, पायी (in comp. as दुपायी), पद (in comp. as द्विपद).

LEGGING, *n.* पायावर बांधायाचें कातडें *n.*

LEGIBILITY, *n.* v. A. 1. बाचायाजोगेपणा *m.* &c. पठनीयता *f.* पठनशक्यता *f.* पठनयोग्यता *f.*

2 बाचायास सोपेपणा *m.* सुवाच्यता *f.*

LEGIBLE, *a. possible to be read.* बाचायाजोगा-जोगता-सारखा-&c. पठनीय, पाठ्य, पठनयोग्य, पठनशक्य. [सुपाठ्य.

2 *easy to be read.* बाचायास सोपा, साफलिहलेला, सुवाच्य,

LEGIBLY, *adv.* v. A. 2. साफ अक्षरांनीं, साफ, स्पष्ट, सुवाच्य.

LEGION, *n.*—military body. सेनादल *n.* सैन्यदल *n.* सेनाभार *m.* सेनाभाग *m.* [चक्र *n.*

2 *great number*, v. MULTITUDE. झुंड *f.* झुबका *m.* वृंद *n.*

To LEGISLATE, *v. n. enact laws.* कायदे *m. pl.*-कानू *f. pl.*-नियम *m. pl.*-&c. करणें-स्थापणें-बांधणें-रचणें, कायदेबंदी *f.*-कानूबंदी *f.*-&c. करणें, कैदकानू *f.*-कानूजाबता *m.* करणें.

LEGISLATION, *n.* v. V.—*act.* कायद्यांची रचणूक *f.* &c. कायदेबंदी *f.* कानूबंदी *f.* जाबतेबंदी *f.* नियमस्थापना *f.* विधिस्थापना *f.*

LEGISLATIVE, *a. law-making.* कायदे रचण्याचा, कायदे करण्याचा, कायदे करणारा, जाबतेबंदीचा, &c. नियमस्थापक, विधिस्थापक-रचक-&c.

LEGISLATOR, *n.* v. A. कायदे-कानू-कानूजाबता-&c. करणारा-रचणारा-&c. नियम स्थापक, विधिस्थापक,-&c.

LEGISLATURE, *n. the power or body which makes laws.* कैदकानू-कायदे-&c. करण्याच्या अधिकाराची सभा *f.*-मंडळी *f.*-&c. विधिस्थापनाधिकारी सभा *f.* राज्यव्यवस्थानियमकारी *m. pl.* सरकार *n.*

LEGIST. See LAWYER.

LEGITIMACY, *n.* v. A. 1. औरसता *f.* औरसत्व *n.* उरस्यता *f.* धर्मपत्नीजत्व *n.* सुजन्म *n.* धर्मपत्नीजन्म *n.* दंपतिजन्म *n.* दंपत्युद्भव *m.*

2 असलपणा *m.* खरेपणा *m.* खराई *f.*

LEGITIMATE, *a. born in wedlock.* औरस, धर्मपत्नीज, दंपतिजात, दंपत्युत्पन्न, दंपत्युद्भव, सुजन्मा, असल, असील, विधिजात.

2 *not false ; just, proper*, v. RIGHT. खरा, असल, असील, बाजवी, वास्तविक, यथान्याय.

To LEGITIMATE, *v. a. invest with legitimacy.* औरसपणा *m.*-औरसत्व *n.*-&c. देणें-प्रापण करणें, औरसांत-औरसवर्गांत घेणें-आणणें, असलसा करणें, औरससम-औरसायित-&c. करणें.

LEGITIMATELY. See LAWFULLY, RIGHTLY.

LEGUME, *n.* See POD. 2 *pl.* LEGUMES, v. PULSE. काठण *n.* काड *n.* कडदण *n.* द्विदल *pop.* द्विदळ *n.* द्विदल धान्य *n.*

LEGUMINOUS, *a. pertaining, &c. to pulse.* कडदणाचा, द्विदलजातीचा, द्विदल जातीय, द्विदलांतर्गत.

LEISURABLE, *a. vacant, not occupied,*—time, &c. अवकाशाचा, फुरसतीचा, फावतीचा, रिकामा, रिकामपणाचा, रिकामवेळेचा.

LEISURE, *n. freedom from business.* अवकाश *m.* वेळ *f.* फुरसत *f.* रिकामपणा *m.* रिकामकी *f.* फावती *f.* अवसर *m.* वाव *m. f.*

At l. फावेल तेव्हां, फावेल तसा, फावल्या वेळेस, फावतीनें, यथावकाशें, अवकाशानुरूप.

Interval of l. सवड *f.* संधि *m. f.* फट *f.* उसंत *or* उसंथ *f.* उसरत *f.* उसरव्त *f.* उसंधि *f.*

Period of l. रिकामवेळ *f.*

That is without l. अनवकाश, निरवकाश.

Want of l. अनवकाश *m.* अनवसर *m.*

To find l. फावणें *in. con.*

LEISURELINESS, v. A. सावकाशी *f.* थंडाई *f.*

LEISURELY, *a. done without hurry.* सावकाशीचा, सावकाशीनें-&c. केलेला, फुरसतीचा, थंडाईचा, धिमाईचा.

2 *slow, not hasty*, v. DILATORY, DAWDLER. सावकाशी, सावकाशीनें करणारा, चेंगट, वेळलाव्या, दिरिंग्या, धिमी.

LEISURELY, *adv.* v. A. 1. सावकाशीनें, धिमाईनें, धिमेपणानें, थंडाईनें, &c. सावकाश, रमत रमत, रमतेरमते. [घेणें.

To take (a work, &c.) l. सावकाशीवर घेणें, थंडाईवर

LEMAN. See GALLANT.

LEMMA, *n. a previous proposition proved.* पूर्वसिद्धांतित गोष्ट *f.* पूर्वगृहीत सिद्धांत *m.*

LEMON, *n. citrus acida,*—the tree. निंबूण *or* लिंबूण *f.* निंबुणी *or* लिंबुणी *f.* निंबोणी *or* लिंबोणी *f.*—the fruit, निंबू *or* लिंबू *n.*

LEMON-GRASS, *n.* गवती चहा *m.* पातीचा चहा *m.* कढी गवत *n.* कढी पात *f.* रोहिष *n.*

LEMONADE, *n.* निंबाचें-लिंबाचें सरबत *n.*-पन्हें *n.*

To LEND, *v. a. give to be returned in kind.* उसना-उसनवट-उसनवार देणें, उसणवारी देणें.

To l. just for a moment. हात उसना देणें.

2 *afford the temporary use of.* जायजणा-जायांचा-मागणीचा-याचितक देणें, जायां *adv.*-जायांस देणें, दोनदिवस-चार दिवस -&c. देणें.

3 (money, at interest). कर्जी-कर्जास-व्याजास-&c. देणें, कर्ज *n.*-ऋण *n.* देणें, कर्जाऊ-व्याजू-&c. देणें, व्याजानें-काळांतरानें-सावकारीनें देणें.

4 See To AFFORD, GIVE.

LENDER, *n.* v. V. 3. *and* CREDITOR. धनको, धनकोनाम.

LENDING, *n.* v. V. 1.—*act.* उसनवारी देणें *n.* &c.

2 जायांस देणें *n.* &c.

3 कर्जदेणें *n.* व्याजानें देणें *n.*

L. and borrowing. देघे *f.* देणेंघेणें *n.* देवघेव *f.* देवाघेवा *m.* देवाण घेवाण *n.* देवालेवा *m.*

LENGTH, *n.* लांबी *f.* दैर्घ्य *n.* आयाम *m.*

At full l. (lying, &c.). लंबा *adv. decl.* लंबे.

L.—in land measurement. तूळ *m. n.*

2 *extent of space.* लांबी *f.* लांबण *f.* दूरता *f.*

3 *extent of duration, space*, v. DURATION, TIME. वेळ *m.* काल *or* ळ *m.*

3 *great duration or space.* लांबण *f.* दैर्घ्य *n.*

At l. *at its full extent.* संक्षेप केल्यावांचून, सविस्तर, सुविस्तर, असंक्षेपतः.

At l. *after long delay*, v. AT LAST. शेवटीं, निदानीं,

To such l. एथवर, एथपर्यंत-पावेतों.

To LENGTHEN, *v. a. make longer, elongate.* लांबवणें, लांब-अधिकलांब करणें, लांबीकडे-लांबीवर वाढवणें.

2 *prolong, protract, continue.* लांबवणें, वाढवणें, दीर्घ करणें.

3 out; लांबता धरणें, लांबीवर धरणें, लांबण *f.* लावणें.

To be lengthened out. लांबीवर-लांबणीवर पडणें.

To LENGTHEN, *v.n.grow longer.* लांबणें, लांबावणें, वाढणें,लांब होणें.

LENGTHENED, *p.* v. V. A. 1. लांबवलेला, अधिक लांबकेलेला &c.

LENGTHWISE, *adv. in the direction of the length.* लांबीनें, लांबीकडून, दीर्घतेनें, लंबा *decl.*

L. and breadthwise. औरसचौरस.

LENGTHY, *a.* v. LONG. लांबचलांब, बराचलांब.

LENIENT, LENITIVE, *a. assuasive, emollient.* नरम-मऊ-&c. करणारा, शमक, उपशमक.

2 *mild, clement,* v. MILD. कोमल *or* ळ, सौम्य, मृदु, सौम्यपणाचा, दयेचा, नरम, सामाचा, सामोपचाराचा, सामोपायाचा, सामोपचारी, सामोपायी, सामोपायक,सदय,दयाळू, अपरुष, अनुग्र.

L. measure. सामोपचार*m.* सामोपाय *m.*

LENIENT, LENITIVE, *n. a medicine or application that eases.* उपशमक पदार्थ *m.*-औषध *n.*-&c. सामोपचार *m.* उपशमन *n.* प्रशमन *n.* [पूर्वक.

LENIENTLY, *adv.* v. A. 2. सामानें, सामोपचारानें, सौम्यतेनें, क्षमा-

LENITY, LENIENCY, *n.* v.A. 2. कोमळपणा*m.*सौम्यता *f.* नरमाई *f.* सामबुद्धि *f.* सामोपचारबुद्धि *f.* अपरुषत्व *n.*

L.—opposed to severity. अल्पदंड *m.*अल्पदंडन*n.*अल्पशिक्षा *f.*

LENS, *n.* दुर्बीन वगैरे यंत्रांतील कांच *f.*

LENT, *p.* v.V. 2. उसना दिल्हेला, उसनावारी दिल्हेला, &c. उसना.

2 जायजणा दिल्हेला.

3 कर्जीदिल्हेला, &c. कर्जाऊ, कर्जाचा, ऋणाचा.

LENTIGO, *n. scurfy eruptions.* सुरमा *m.* ? शिबें *n.* ?

LENTIL, *n.*—the plant. मसूर *f.*

LEO, *n.*—the zodiacal sign. सिंह *m.*

LEONINE, *a. belonging, &c. to a lion.* सिंहाचा, सिंहसंबंधी, सैंह, सैंहिक, सिंहधर्मक, सिंहसदृश.

LEOPARD, *n.* चिता *or* चित्ता *m.* चित्रक *m.* खड्याबाघ *or* खड्या *or* खरडा *m.* डाहण्याबाघ *m.* दिवट्या बाघ *m.*

LEPER, *n.* v. A. कोढी, कोढ्या, कुष्ठ्या.

LEPORINE, *a. belonging, &c. to a hare.* ससाचा, शशसंबंधी.

LEPROSY, *n.* कोढ *or* कोड *n.* कुष्ठ *n.* कुष्ठरोग *m.* The Medical Shástras enumerate 18 kinds,viz.7 severe and 11 milder.

Black l. रक्तपिती *f.* रक्तकुष्ठ *n.* व्याधि *m.* महाव्याधि *m.* महारोग *m.*—Person afflicted with it. रक्तपित्या, रक्तकुष्ठी, व्याधिष्ठ, महारोगी.

L. with circular spots. मंडल *n.*

Purulent or running l. ओलें कुष्ठ.

Wasting l. गलत्कुष्ठ *n.*

White l. पांढरें कोड *n.* श्वेतकुष्ठ *n.*

LEPROUS, *a.*कोढ्या, कोढी *or* कोडी, कुष्ठी, कुष्ठ्या, कोढेला, कुष्ठरोगी.

L. with serous runnings. लशाकोढ्या.

LESS, *a.—comparative of little.* लहान, कमी, कम, कमती, थोडा, न्यून, अल्प, all used with हून-पेक्षां-&c.

To grow or become l. लहानावणें, लहानाळणें.

2—in height, length, age, &c. *lower, shorter, smaller, younger.* धाकटा, लहानगा;—as distinguished from वुड्ढा *or* क (the greater) खुर्द.

3 *short of.* उणा, कम.

The privative termination *less* is rendered by हीन, शून्य, रहित, विरहित, विहीन, व्यतिरिक्त affixed (all used in comp. as मतिहीन witless, द्रव्यशून्य pennyless, &c. &c.); by बे and बिन prefixed to words of Persian or Hindustani origin (as बेइमान faithless, बेकस sapless, बिनतोड faultless); and by the particles अ and निर्, नि, &c. prefixed (as अबाध, निर्दोष, निरपराध-&c. &c.).

L. or more. उणापुरा, न्यूनाधिक, न्यूनातिरेक.

LESS, *adv.* v. A. कमी, थोडा, &c.

LESSEE, *n. one who takes on lease.*कौलीमक्तेदार, कौल्या, कौलदार.

To LESSEN, *v. a. make less, diminish in bulk, quantity, &c.* लहान-कमी-थोडा-थोडका-उणा-न्यून-&c. करणें, ऱ्हास *m.*-मानऱ्हास *m.*-मानक्षति *f.*-महत्वऱ्हास *m.*-स्थौल्यऱ्हास *m.*-&c. करणें *g. of o.* लघुकरण *n.*-न्यूनीकरण *n.* करणें *g. of o.*

2 *diminish in degree, &c. abate.* उतरणें, उतरवणें, कमी-हलका-उणा-न्यून-मंद-&c. करणें, उतार *m.*- उपशम *m.*-&c. करणें *g. of o.* निववणें, ऱ्हास *m.*-क्षय *m.*-क्षति *f.*-&c. करणें *g. of o.*

To LESSEN, *v. n. become less in bulk, quantity, &c.* लहान-कमी-थोडा-&c. होणें, थोडकावणें,लहानावणें,लहानाळणें, तुटणें, घटणें, ऱ्हास *m.*-क्षति *f.*-मानऱ्हास*m.*-महत्वऱ्हास*m.*-&c. होणें*g.of s.*

2 *become less in degree; abate,* v. To DECREASE. उणावणें, हलकावणें, थोडकावणें, उतरणें, मंदावणें, खालावणें, बसणें, निवणें, हलका-मंद-&c. पडणें-होणें, उतार *m.*-उपशम *m.*-ऱ्हास*m.*-क्षय *m.*-&c. होणें *g. of s.* [घुरुत, क्षीण.

LESSENED, *p.* v. V. A. 1. लहान केलेला, थोडका केलेला, &c. ल-

2 उतरलेला, हलका केलेला, &c.

v. V. N. 1. लहान झालेला, थोडकावलेला, लहानावलेला, &c.

2 उणावलेला, हलकावलेला, &c.

LESSENER, *n.* LESSENING, *p. a.* v. V. A. 1. लहान करणारा, &c. लघुकारक, न्यूनकारक, ऱ्हासकारक, &c.

2 उतरणारा, हलका करणारा, &c. उपशम-&c. कर्त्ता.

LESSENING, *n.* v. V. A. 1.—*act.* लहान करणें *n.* &c. लघुकरण*n.* न्यूनीकरण *n.*—*state.* ऱ्हास *m.* क्षय *m.* क्षति *f.* मानऱ्हास *m.* मानक्षति *f.* महत्वऱ्हास *m.* महत्वक्षति *f.* स्थौल्यऱ्हास *m.*

2 *and* V. N. 2. See ABATEMENT, DECREASE.

LESSER, See LESS.

LESSON, *n. thing read, &c.* धडा *m.* पाठ *m.* व्याख्यान *n.*

L. to be read. वाचणी *f. v.* सांग, शिक.

L. to be conned. संथा *f.* घोकणी *f.*

2 *matter inculcated.* उपदेश *m.* शिक्षा *f.*

Lessons (as in gymnastics, accomplishments, &c.). तालीम *f. v.* दे, घे.

To learn a l. *get instruction from experience.* अक्कल*f.*-अद्दल *f.* घडणें *in. con.*

To get a severe l. पटकी *f.* खाणें, टेंच *f.* खाणें *or in. con.* लागणें, पटकी *f.* बसणें *in. con.* [*g. of o.*

To take a l. from, *copy, &c.* दाखला *m.*-धडा *m.* घेणें

To LESSON, *v, a. tutor, prompt, put up to,* v. To TEACH. शिकवणें, शिकवण *f.*-शिकवणी *f.* करणें, बार *m.* भरणें-देणें, कान *m.* फुंकणें-भरणें-भारणें *g. of o.*

LESSONED, *p.* v. V. शिकवलेला, &c. घोकीव, घोक्या.

Lessor, *n. one who lets on lease.* कौलानें देणारा, कौल देणारा, सडानें देणारा.

Lest, *conj.* कदाचित्, यदाकदाचित्, म्हणी, नजाणो.

To **Let**, *v. a. suffer, allow*, v. To Permit. देणें, परवानगी *f.*-मोकळीक *f.*-हुकूम *m.*-&c. देणें.

2 *put to hire.* भाड्यानें-भाड्यास देणें-लावणें, भाडें*n.*घेऊन देणें.

3 *obstruct*, v. To Hinder. अडथळा *m.*-अटकाव *m.*-प्रतिबंध *m.*-&c. करणें.

4 alone; See To Leave alone. 5 in; See To Admit.

6 loose. सोडणें, मोकळा-&c.सोडणें.

7 off; *discharge, fire.* सोडणें, उडवणें, मारणें, बार *m.*सोडणें, झाडणें, डागणें.

8 off, v. To Pardon. सोडणें, माफ करणें.

9 out; *suffer to escape.* सोडणें, सुटूं-जाऊं-&c. देणें.

10 out; v. To Farm. खडून देणें, मक्त्यानें-&c. देणें.

To let blood, v. To Bleed. रक्त *n.*-शीर *f.* काढणें.

To let fly, v.To Discharge. सोडणें, विसर्जन*n.*करणें*g.of o.*

Let there be! व्हावा.

Let, *n. obstacle*, v. Hinderance. अड *f.* अट *f.* अटकाव*m.* आडकाठी *f.* नड *f.* प्रतिबंध *m.* वेध *m.*

Let, *p.* v. V. 2. भाड्यानें दिल्हेला.

Lethal, *a. mortal*, v. Deadly. प्राणनाशक-हारक.

Lethargic, Lethargical, *a. morbidly drowsy and heavy* —persons. मोठा झोपाळू-झोप्या, झापड पडलेला, &c. अतिनिद्रालु, जड, उठवळ.

2 *heavy, &c.*—sleep. गाढ, गाढमूढ, घोर, कुंभकर्णी.

Lethargy, *n. morbid drowsiness.* झांक *f.* झांप *f.*झांपण *f.* झांपड *f.* अतिनिद्रा *f.* कुंभकर्णी झोप *f.*

Lethe, *n. oblivion.* विस्मृति *f.*

Lethean, *a.causing oblivion.* विसर पाड्या, विस्मृतिजनक-कारक.

Lethiferous, *a.* v. Deadly. मृत्युजनक, प्राणनाशक-हारक.

Letter, *n.* (of the alphabet). अक्षर *n.*वर्ण *m.*हरफ *m.*मातृका*f.*

Compound l. जोड अक्षर *n.* संयुक्ताक्षर *n.* संध्यक्षर *n.*

Euphonous union or coalition of letters. वर्णसंधि *m.* संधि *m.*

Fully sounded or aspirated l. महाप्राण *m.*

Knowledge of the letters. अक्षर ओळख *f.*

L. by letter. अक्षरशः.

Letters drawn upon the sand board in learning to write. धुळाक्षर *n.*

Simply sounded or unaspirated l. अल्पप्राण *m.*—aspirated l. महाप्राण *m.*

The setting (of a child) to his letters. अक्षरारंभ *m.*

To form letters (in learning to write) by drawing a dry pen through the letters of the copy. घोंटविणें, घेरविणें, घोंटाळणें.

2 *epistle.* पत्र *n.* कागद *m.* लिखित*n.* लेख *m.* पत्रिका *f.* पत्रक*n.*

Letters and notes—compreh. कागदपत्र*m.n.*चिठ्ठीचपाटी *f.*

By l. *through epistolary communication.* कागदोपत्रीं, पत्रद्वारा.

Envelope of a l. लाखोटा *m.* लिफाप *m.*

L. sealed or closed with gum, a wafer, &c. लाखोटा *m.*

L. without a separate envelope. लगत लाखोटा *m.*

Letters patent. सनद *f.*—That is held, &c. by letters patent. सनदी.

The address or complimentary commencement of a l. v. Address. मयना *or* माना *m.* अलकाब *f.*

Upon sight of the l. पत्रदर्शनीं, पत्र पाहतांच, पत्र पाहतांक्षणीं.

To become a dead l. ढळणें, टळणें, माजी पडणें.

Letters to and from certain of the offices and relations of life bear significant names. A letter to a father, mother, elderly relation, superior, &c. is विज्ञापनापत्र, विज्ञप्तिपत्र, विनंतीपत्र.—to a son or daughter, younger brother, &c. आशीर्वादपत्र.—from a superior officer. आज्ञापत्र.

Some of the lowly designations assumed by the writer in letters are पोष्य, पोष्यांतर्गत, आश्रित, आश्रितांतर्गत, चरणरज, चरणधूलि *or* चरणधूळ, दासानुदास, आज्ञाधारक, आज्ञांकित.

3 *literal meaning.* वाच्यार्थ *m.* पदार्थ *m.* शब्दार्थ *m.* प्राथमिकार्थ *m.* अक्षरार्थ *m.*

4 letters; *literature.* अक्षर *n.* चार अक्षरें *n. pl.* विद्या *f.*

5 *type.* अक्षर *n.* अक्षराचा ठसा *m.* अक्षरमुद्रा *f.*

To **Letter**, *v.a. mark with letters.*अक्षरें *n.pl.* लिहणें *with*वर *of o.* अक्षरांकित-अक्षरचिह्नित-अक्षरमुद्रित-अक्षरयुक्त-अक्षरविशिष्ट-&c. करणें.

Letter-carrier, *n.* कागदी, कागद्या.

Lettered, *p. and a.* v. V. अक्षरांकित-युक्त-मुद्रित-विशिष्ट.

I. *literate*, v. Learned. साक्षर, अक्षरस्थ, विद्वान्.

II. *belonging to learning.* विद्येचा, विद्येंतला, विद्यासंबंधी-विषयक.

Leucophlegmacy, *n. dropsical habit.* कफोदर *n.* कफशोथ*m.*

Leucorrhea, *n. fluor albus*,v. Whites. पांढरवणी*n.* श्वेतप्रदर*m.*

Levee, *n.*—of a great man. दरबार *m. n.* सभा *f.*

Level, *a. equal, plain*, v. Even. सारखा, बरोबर, सपाट, निढाळ, सम, समान, सुती.

Very l., uniformly l. सरसपाट.

2 *equal with, on the same plane with.* सारखा, बरोबर, समदेशस्थ, समभूमिस्थ.

Level, *n. even or plain surface.* सपाटी *f.* सारखीजमीन *f.* समस्थल *pop.* समथळ *n.* समभूमि *f.* समदेश *m.*

2 *rate, standard.* दर *m.* धडा *m.* भाव *m.*

3 *state of equality.* बरोबरी *f.* सारखेपणा *m.* समता *f.* समानता *f.* साम्य *n.* समसमानता *f.* तुलना *pop.* तुळणा *f.*

4 (of masons). पाणसळ *or* साळ *f.* साधन *f.* साधनी *f.*

5 *line of aim, vision, &c.* शिस्त *f.* लक्ष्य *n.* धोरण *n.* संधान*n.* लक्ष्यदेश *m.* लक्ष्यसूत्र *n.*

6 *rule, plan.* बेत *m.* नियम *pop.* नेम *m.*

To **Level**, *v. a. make even, &c.* सारखा-बरोबर-साफ-सपाट-समान-&c. करणें, सारखावणें.

2 *make equal with.* बरोबर-सारखा-&c. करणें *with* सीं.

3 *lay flat.* जमिनीस मिळवणें,जमिनीबरोबर-भुईबरोबर-भुईसपाट-&c. करणें, जमीनदोस्त करणें, पाडणें.

4 *aim.* लावणें, नेमणें, रोंखणें, योजणें, शिस्त *f.*-&c.धरणें-करणें-बांधणें *g. of o.*

Levelled, *p.* v. V. 1. 2. सारखा केलेला, सपाट केलेला, &c. सारखावलेला, समीकृत.

3 जमिनीस मिळवलेला, &c. जमीनदोस्त, चपाट *or* चपेट.

Leveller, *n.* **Levelling**, *p. a.* v. V. 1. 2. बरोबर-सारखा-सपाट-सम-&c. करणारा.

I. *one who destroys distinctions in society.* लहान मोठे सारखे करणारा, उच्चनीचभावविघातक, एकाकाठीनें हाकणारा एका माळेंत ओवणारा.

Levelling, *n.* v. V. 1. 2.—*act.* सारखावणें *n.* बरोबर करणें *n.* &c. समीकरण *n.*

Levelness, *n.* v. A. 1. सारखेपणा *m.* बरोबरी *f.* सपाटी *f.* साम्य *n.* समता *f.* समानता *f.*

Uniform l. सरसपाटी *f.*

2 सारखेपणा *m.* बरोबरी *f.* समभूमिस्थभाव *m.*

Lever, *n.*—in mechanics. तीर *m.* तरफ *f.* उटाळी *f.* उटाळा *m.* उटाळणी *f.* टेका *m.* टेकावा *m.* लबाडी *f.*

To raise with a l. उटाळणें.

Leveret, *n. young hare.* सशाचें पिलूं *n.* शशवत्स *m. n.*

Leviathan, *n.*—the fish. देवमासा *m.*

To **Levigate**, *v. a. grind or rub to a powder.* वाटणें, घोंटणें, उगाळणें, गरगटणें, पिसणें.

Levigated mass or matter. उगाळा *m.* कल्क *m.*

Levigating stone. घाटवाईन *n.*

Matter to be levigated. वाटण *n.*

Levigated, *p.* v. V. वाटलेला, उगाळलेला, &c. वाटींव, घोंटींव.

Levigation, *n.* v.V.—*act.* वाटणें *n.* &c. उगाळणी *f.* वाटण *n.* घोंटणी *f.*

Levity. See **Lightness.**

To **Levy**, *v. a. raise, collect,*—troops. जमवणें, मिळवणें, जमाबंदी *f.* करणें. [करणें.

2 *raise by assessment.* पट्टी करून वसूल करणें-मिळवणें-जमा

Levy, Levying, *n.* v. V. 1.—*act.* जमवणें *n.* &c. जमाबंदी *f.*

2 पट्टीनें जमवणें *n.*

I. *troops raised.* जमाबंदी *f.*

II. *money raised.* पट्टी *f.*

Lewd, *a. libidinous,* v. **Lustful.** कामी, कामुक, सकाम, कामभावाचा, बदफैल, बदख्याल, व्यवायी, कामासक्त, स्त्रीलंपट, स्त्रीव्यसनी, स्त्रीव्यासंगी.

Lewdly, *adv.* v. A. कामीपणानें, कामुकपणानें, कामभावानें, कामबुद्ध्या, कामदृष्टीनें, &c.

Lewdness, *n.* v. A. कामीपणा *m.* कामुकपणा *m.* कामुकता *f.* सकामता *f.* कामासक्ति *f.* कामभाव *m.* कामबुद्धि *f.* कामदृष्टि *f.*

I. *lewd practice.* इष्कबाजी *f.* बदकर्म *n.* बदफैली *f.* बदख्याली *f.* बाहेरख्याल *m.* कटिशूलाचें *n.*

Lexicographer, *n. maker of a lexicon.* कोशकर्त्ता, कोशकार, अभिधानकर्त्ता. [कोशकरण *n.*

Lexicography, *n. dictionary making.* शब्दकोशरचना *f.* शब्द-

Lexicon, *n. dictionary.* शब्दकोश *m.* कोश *m.* अभिधान *n.*

Liable, *a. subject to, exposed to, having a tendency to.* जोगा, योग्य, वश, स्वाधीन, अधीन (in comp. as रोगाधीन, मरणाधीन, &c.), शील (in comp. as भंगशील).

2 *answerable,* v. **Responsible.** मोसबेदार, जिम्मेदार, जाब-उत्तर-मोसबा-&c. देणारा.

Liableness, Liability, *n.* v. A. 1. जोगेपणा *m.* योग्यता *f.*

2 मोसबेदारी *f.* जिम्मेदारी *f.*

Liar, *n. wilful utterer of falsehood.* लबाड, खोटें बोलणारा, असत्यवादी, असत्यवक्ता, मिथ्याभाषी, मिथ्यावादी, मृषावादी, अनृतवादी, अनृतभाषी.

A great l. सातलबाड, लबाडांचा राजा, द्विजिह्व, अनेकजिह्व, लबाडांचा बाप, लबाडशिरोमणि, असत्यचूडामणि.

Some strong lively terms or combinations for *a liar* are, खऱ्याचें खांड, ज्याचे जिभेस हाड नाहीं,हा लबाडवांचून नव्हे, वडाची साल पिंपळाला पिंपळाची साल वडाला लावणारा, कुत्र्याचा पाय मांजरावर मांजराचा पाय कुत्र्यावर घालणारा.

Libation, *n.*—the act. तर्पण *n.* देवतोद्देशें पेयनिषेक *m.*-पेयत्याग *m.*-रसनिषेक *m.*

2—wine, &c. poured. तर्पणद्रव्य *n.* तर्पणोदक *n.* निषेच्यरस *m.*

Libel, *n. defamatory writing.* अपवादकलेख *m.*-पत्र *n.* अपवादलेख *m.* अपवादपत्र *n.* निंदालेख *m.* निंदापत्र *n.*

To **Libel**, *v. a. defame in writing.* लेखानें-कागदोपत्रीं निंदणें-निंदा *f.* करणें *g. of o.* निंदा *f.* लिहणें *g. of o.* निंदापत्र *n.*-निंदालेख *m.*-&c. लिहणें. [निंदित.

Libelled, *p.* v. V. कागदोपत्रीं निंदलेला, &c. पत्रनिंदित, लेखन-

Libeller, *n.* **Libelling**, *p. a.* v. V. कागदोपत्रीं निंदणारा,&c. निंदापत्र-निंदालेख-&c. लिहणारा.

Libellous, *a.* निंदेचा, &c. अपवादक, निंदक, अभिशंसक.

Liberal, *a. of good birth,* v. **Gentle.** कुलीन, कुलज, वंशज, सद्वंश, अभिजात, सुजात.

2 *munificent, generous, lavish.* उदार, धोताल, सढळ, हाताचा सढळ, हाताचा सुटा, हाताचा मोकळा, मोकळ्या हाताचा, उदारमनाचा, मोठ्यामनाचा, दाता, वदान्य, दानशील, दानबुद्धि, दानशूर, ढसळ *or* ढसाळ, ढिसळ *or* ढिसाळ, ढस्सर, धिंग, खर्चक, खर्चिक, व्ययी, बेचक, व्ययशील, व्ययबुद्धि, त्यागशील, प्रशस्त, मुक्तहस्त, उदारहस्त, उदारधी, दानशौंड, दातृत्वशाली, औदार्यशाली, स्थूललक्ष.

3 *copious, abundant, profuse,* v. **Exuberant.** प्रशस्त, सढळ, घळघळीत, चळचळीत, गडगंज, मुबलक *or* स.

4 *not selfish, not contracted,* v. **Candid.** प्रशस्त, उदार, उदारमनाचा, प्रशस्तपणाचा, प्रशस्तमनाचा, मोकळ्या मनाचा, मनाचा मोकळा, उदारधी.

5 *free to excess,* v. **Licentious.** बेकैद, बेताल *or* ळ, मर्यादातीत, मर्यादातिवर्त्ती, मर्यादातिक्रमी, विध्यतिवर्त्ती, विध्यतिक्रमी.

Liberality, *n.* v. A. 2. उदारपणा *m.* सढळपणा *m.* हाताचा मोकळेपणा *m.* खर्चिकपणा *m.* &c. औदार्य *n.* दानशीलता *f.* दानबुद्धि *f.* व्ययबुद्धि *f.*

3 प्रशस्तपणा *m.* घळघळितपणा *m.* सढळपणा *m.* &c. प्राशस्त्य *n.*

4 प्रशस्तपणा *m.* उदारपणा *m.* प्राशस्त्य *n.* औदार्य *n.*

To **Liberalize**, *v. a. free from narrow views, &c.* प्रशस्त-प्रौढपोक्त-&c. करणें, प्रशस्तपणा *m.*-प्राशस्त्य *n.*-प्रौढता *f.*-&c. देणें-आणणें. [पणानें, &c.

Liberally, *adv.* v. A. 2. उदारपणानें, मोकळ्या हातानें, सढळ-

3 घळघळीत, चळचळीत, छणछण, प्रशस्तपणानें, सढळपणानें.

4 उदारमनानें, प्रशस्तमनानें, प्रशस्तपणानें, &c.

To **Liberate**, &c. See **To Free, To Deliver**, &c.

Libertine, *n. dissolute, licentious person, rake, &c.* सोदा,

लुच्चा, फंदी, चंगी, चंगीभंगी, इष्कबाज, इष्की, रांडबाज, व्यसनी, विसनी, स्त्रीव्यसनी, शृंगारी, वल्ली.

LIBERTINE, *a. licentious, dissolute*, v. LOOSE. सोदा, लुच्चा, लुफ्फा, कुश्चळ, खोटचाल, बदफैल, बदनेत, सोदेशाई, सोदेगिरीचा, लुच्चेगिरीचा, सोदेशाईचा, दुर्व्यसनी, स्त्रीव्यसनी, रांडव्यसनी, स्त्रीव्यसनाचा.

LIBERTINISM, *n.* v. A. सोदेगिरी *f.* लुच्चेगिरी *f.* सोदेशाई *f.* सोदाई *f.* सोदावें *n.* लुच्चाई *f.* लुच्चेशाई *f.* बदफैली *f.* बदकर्म *n.* स्त्रीव्यसन *n.* रांडव्यसन *n.* रांडबाजी *f.* इष्कबाजी *f.*

LIBERTY, *n.*—as *opposed to* slavery. स्वतंत्रपणा *m.* स्वतंत्रता *f.* स्वातंत्र्य *n.* स्ववशता *f.* स्वाधीनता *f.* स्वायत्तता *f.* स्वेच्छाचारिता *f.* अदास्य *n.* अदासत्व *n.*

2—as *opposed to* necessity. मुखत्यारी *f.* अखत्यारी *f.* अदृष्टानधीनता *f.* अदैवाधीनता *f.*

To be at l. (to act, speak, &c.). मोकळीक *f.*-मुखत्यारी *f.* असणें *in. con.*

With free will & full l. रजावंतीनें *or* रजावंदीनें.

3 *freedom*—gener. मोकळेपणा *m.* सुटेपणा *m.* मोकळीक *f.* मुक्ति *f.* बंधनाभाव *m.* बंधनराहित्य *n.*

At l. मोकाट, मोकार.

That is at l. v. FREE. मोकळा, सुटा.

To set at l. v. To FREE. मोकलणें, मोकळा-&c. करणें, मोकळीक *f.* देणें.

4 *privilege, immunity.* सोडवणूक *f.* सूट *f.* माफी *f.* माफीची-&c. गोष्ट *f.* माफीचा-&c. विषय *m.*

5 *leave*, v. PERMISSION. परवानगी *f.* मोकळीक *f.* सुटी *f.* मुवा *or* मुभा *f.*

Open & full l. राजरुशी *or* राजरोशी *f.*

With perfect l. or permission. सुखेनैव.

6 *transgression of decorum.* अगळीक *f.* अमर्यादा *f.* मर्यादोल्लंघन *n.* मर्यादातिक्रमण *n.* मर्यादातिवर्त्तन *n.* मर्यादातिचार *m.*

To take the l. of doing, *do without special license.* पुसल्यावांचून-आज्ञाघेतल्यावांचून-&c. करणें.

LIBIDINOUS, &c. See LUSTFUL, &c.

LIBRA, *n.*—the zodiacal sign. तुला *pop.* तूळ *f.*

LIBRARIAN, *n.* किताबखान्यावरचा अधिकारी, पुस्तकशालाधिकारी, पुस्तकशालाध्यक्ष, पुस्तकशालाधिपति.

LIBRARY, *n. collection of books.* पुस्तकांचा भरणा *m.* ग्रंथांचा भरणा *m.* पुस्तकसंग्रह *m.*

2—the building. किताबखाना *m.* पुस्तकशाला *f.* पुस्तकालय *n.* पुस्तकसंग्रहागार *n.*

To LIBRATE, *v. a. hold in equipoise*, v. To BALANCE. समतोल-&c. धरणें, पासंगावर-कांट्यावर-&c. धरणें-राखणें.

LICENSE, *exorbitant liberty.* अनर्गळपणा *m.* बेकैदपणा *m.* अनर्गलता *f.* निरंकुशता *f.* अनर्गलावस्था *f.* विधिनिषेधातीतता *f.* विधिनिषेधातीतभाव *m.*

2 *leave*, v. PERMISSION. परवानगी *f.* हुकूम *m.* आज्ञा *f.*

Full and perfect l. राजरोशी *f.* मुवा *f.*

To allow great l. to. सैलदोरी *f.* देणें.

3 *warrant of permission.* सनद *f.* परवाना *m.* परवानगीची चिट्ठी *f.* हुकूमनामा *m.*

To LICENSE, *v. a. permit by a license*, v. To PERMIT. सनद *f.*-परवाना *m.*-परवानगीची चिट्ठी *f.*-&c. देणें, परवानगी *f.*-हुकूम *m.*-आज्ञा *f.*-&c. देणें.

LICENSED, *p.* v. V.—person. सनद दिल्हेला-मिळालेला, सनदी, सनदेचा—article. परवानगीचा, अभ्यनुज्ञात.

LICENTIATE, *n. one who has a license.* सनदी, सनदवाला.

LICENTIOUS, *a. using license, disorderly, unruly, unrestrained, lawless, &c.*—of persons. बेकैद, बेकैदी, बेबंद, अनर्गल *or* ळ, व्यभिचारी, अमर्याद, निर्मर्याद, बारगळ, बारगा, बारबंडा, बाष्कळ, दांडगा, उद्धत, बावगा, निरंकुश, बेशिस्त, गैरशिस्त, अशिष्ट, मनस्वी, मवास, मवाशी, स्वच्छंदी, स्वेच्छाचारी, स्वैरी, स्वैरगति, कामाचारी, यथेष्टाचारी, कामवृत्त, दुराचारी, अनाचारी, भ्रष्टाचारी, अत्याचारी, आचारहीन, आचारभ्रष्ट, आचारवर्जित, कर्मभ्रष्ट, वल्ली, विधिनिषेधातीत, विध्यतिवर्त्ती, शास्त्रातिवर्त्ती, विधि निषेधातिवर्त्ती, मर्यादातिचारी, मर्यादातिवर्त्ती, मर्यादातिक्रमी, त्यक्तबंधन, त्यक्तनिर्बंध.

2 *profligate, libertine, dissolute, rakish, &c.* सोदा, लुच्चा, ढंगी, ढंग्या, बेढंग, बेढंगी, व्यसनी, दुर्व्यसनी, बाजिंदा, बटाऊ, बदनेत, बदफैल, बदख्याल, दुर्वृत्त, स्त्रीव्यसनी, दुराचारी, अनाचारी, चौढाळ, खोटचाल, कुश्चळ, टवाळ, टवाळखोर, अकर्मान्वित, सर्वाबद्ध.

3 *exceeding the limits of propriety, law, &c.*—acts. &c. बेकैद, बेबंद, बेकैदी, अनर्गल *or* ळ, बेताल *or* ळ, अमर्याद, मर्यादातीत, मनस्वी, ऐच्छिक, स्वेच्छाचाराचा, स्वैरगतीचा, मर्यादातिचाराचा, मर्यादातिक्रमाचा, व्यभिचाराचा, विध्यतिवर्त्तनाचा, शास्त्रातिवर्त्तनाचा, शास्त्रातिक्रमाचा.

LICENTIOUSLY, *adv.* v. A. 1. 3. बेकैदपणानें, बेबंदपणानें, अनर्गळपणानें, &c. बेकैद, बेताल, बेबंद, मनस्वी, विध्यतिवर्त्तन-शास्त्रातिवर्त्तन-शास्त्रातिक्रमण-&c. करून.

2 बेढंगीपणानें, बाजिंदेपणानें, &c.

LICENTIOUSNESS, *n.* v. A. 1. बेकैदपणा *m.* बेबंदपणा *m.* अनर्गळपणा *m.* बेशिस्तपणा *m.* &c. बेकैद *f.* बेकैदी *f.* निरंकुशता *f.* अनर्गलता *f.* मवासी *f.* अनाचार *m.* व्यभिचार *m.* कामाचार *m.* अत्याचार *m.* विधिनिषेधातीतता *f.* मर्यादातिक्रम *m.* मर्यादातिवर्त्तन *n.* विध्यतिवर्त्तन *n.* शास्त्रातिवर्त्तन *n.* शास्त्रातिक्रम *m.* नियमातिवर्त्तन *n.* निमातिक्रम *m.*

2 लुच्चेशाई *f.* लुच्चेगिरी *f.* टवाळकी *f.* टवाळी *f.* बदफैली *f.* बदख्याली *f.* ढंग *m.* बेढंग *m.* थेर *m. n.* अजागळी *f.* भ्रष्टाचार *m.* अनाचार *m.* दुराचार *m.* दुर्वृत्ति *f.*

LICHEN, *n.* दगडावरची शेवाळ *f.*

To LICK, *v. a.*—with the tongue. चाटणें, लेहन *n.*-अवलेहन *n.*-&c. करणें *g. of o.*

2 See To LAP. 3 v. To BEAT. टोला *m.* देणें-मारणें.

LICK, *n.* v. BLOW. टोला *m.* चपाटा *m.* रट्टा *m.*

LICKERISH, *a.* v. DAINTY. खोराकी, खोराक्या, चोखांदळा, चोखाळा, चोखारी.

2 *eager to taste or enjoy.* लाळघोट्या, जिभळ्या *or* जिभाळ्या, चाट्या *or* चाटणारा, मिटक्या मारणारा, भोगोत्सुक.

LICKERISHNESS, *n.* v. V. 1.—*act.* चोखांदळेपणा *m.* चोखाळेपणा *m.*

LICKING, *n.* v. V. 1.—*act.* चाटणें *n.* लेह *m.* अवलेह *m.* लेहन *n.* अवलेहन *n.*

LICK-SPITTLE, *n. a meanly obsequious person*, v. OBSEQUIOUS. थुकीझेलणारा, थुकीझेल्या.

LICORICE, *n.*—the plant. ज्येष्ठमध *or* ज्येष्ठीमध *f.* ढोरगुंज *f.* रतनगुंज *f.* मधुयष्टिका *f.* यष्टिमधु *n.* मधुक *n.*

LID, *n.* v. COVER. ढांकण *n.* झांकण *n.* झांपण *n.* टोपण *n.* सरपोस *m.* पिधान *n.*

That has a l.—a pot &c. झांकींव.

2 (of the eye). पापणी *f.* नेत्रकपाट *n.*

LIDLESS, *a.* बिन झांकणाचा, उघड्यातोंडाचा.

LIE, *n. falsehood.* लबाडी *f.* खोटीगोष्ट *f.* खोटेंबोलणें *n.* अनृत *n.* लटीक वाद *m.* मिथ्योक्ति *f.* मिथ्यावाद *m.* मिथ्यावचन *n.* मिथ्याभाषण *n.*

To LIE, *v. n. rest horizontally, &c.* पडणें, निजणें.

2 *press upon.* पडणें, बसणें, दडपण होऊन राहणें, दडपणें, दडकण पडणें, दडकणें.

3 *be reposited or laid up.* पडणें, असणें, संग्रहीं असणें.

4 *remain fixed or still, be placed, situated, &c.* पडणें, बसणें, राहणें, असणें.

5 *remain unfinished or unexecuted.* पडणें, राहणें.

6 *sit or stay lazily, inactively, helplessly, &c.* पडणें, बसणें, पायावर पाय घालून-डाळून-चढवून-&c. बसणें, अढ्याला पाय घालून-लावून बसणें, आसनमांडी घालून बसणें, चोहोंचा आंस घालून बसणें, दंडासन *n.* घालणें. [वा *m.* घेणें.

7 by; *intermit labor,* v. To REST. बिसावणें, विसवणें, विसा-

8 down; *recline for rest.* निजणें, लवंडणें, आडई *or* आडव *f.* घेणें, आडवरणें *or* आडवारणें, आडवा होणें, आंग *n.*-पाठ *f.* टाकणें-लावणें, पासल *f.* घेणें, पासलपट्टी *f.* करणें, पासलणें, पहुडणें.

10 in; *be in child bed.* कोनीं निघणें, कोन *m.* निघणें-होणें *g. of s.* बाळंत होणें.

Lying-in chamber. बाळंतखोली *f.* सूतिकागृह*n.* सूतिगृह*n.*

11 over; *heel, incline on one side.* कलंडणें, कलणें, कलथणें, लवंडणें, करोटणें, एकारणें, कलंडा-&c. होणें.

12 over; *stand over, be suspended.* राहणें, खुंटीस-धसास-&c. अडकणें-लागणें, तकूब-महकूब पडणें, भिजत पडणें.

13 to;—a ship, &c. बाकसी *f.* घेणें.

14 up; *keep in doors, keep in a recumbent position, &c.* निजून-पडून-बसून-&c. राहणें, अंथरूण-&c. धरून राहणें, घर धरून राहणें, आडई घेऊन राहणें.

To be laid up, *keep one's bed from sickness,* v. BED. जमीन धरून असणें, जमिनीस पाठ *f.* लागणें *g. of s.*

15 upon; *be incumbent on,*—a duty. पडणें, बसणें, टेकणें, उराबर-गळ्यांस-मानेस-माथां-माथीं-शिरीं -शिरावर-डोईवर-आंगावर-&c. बसणें-पडणें-असणें *g. of s.*

16 with; *have carnal knowledge of.* निजणें *with* शीं-जवळ-पाशीं *of o.* एकशयन *n.*-एकशय्या *f.*-सहशय्या *f.* करणें.

To l. about; *be lying about unused,*—articles, &c. लोळणें, लुडबुडत पडणें.

To l. littering about. पडला झडला असणें.

To l. in wait, v. To LURK. दडणें, लिकणें, टपणें, दबा *m.* धरणें-मारणें.

To l. in wait for a pretext. निमित्तास टेंकणें.

To l. on one side. कानोडणें *or* कानवडणें, कानवडा *or* कानोडा होणें.

To LIE, *v. n. utter falsehood.* लबाडी *f.* बोलणें-सांगणें, खोटें-लबाड-लटकें-&c. बोलणें, मिथ्योक्ति *f.*-&c. करणें-बोलणें.

LIEF, *adv.* See WILLINGLY.

LIEGE, *a. bound to be faithful, loyal, &c.* हुकमी, हुकमती, हुकुमबंदा, ताबेदार, सेवाधर्मी, प्रजाधर्मी.

3 *sovereign.* सत्तेचा, सत्तेवाईक, सत्ताधारी, सत्ताधीश, सत्तावान्.

LIEGE, *n.* See LORD, SOVEREIGN.

LIEGE-MAN, *n.* v. A. हुकुमबंदा, ताबेदार.

LIEN, *n. legal claim.* कायदेशीर हक्क *m.* कायदेशीर दावा *m.* [राचा.

LIENTERIC, *a. pertaining to a lientery.* भसऱ्याचा, आमातिसा-

LIENTERY, *n. diarrhœa in which food is passed undigested.* भसरा *m.* भसरें *n.* आमातिसार *m.*

LIEU, *n.* v. STEAD. जागा *f.*

In l. of. मोबदला, बदला, ऐवजीं.

LIEUTENANCY, *n. office, &c. of a lieutenant.* मुतालकी *f.* मुतालका *m.* नायबी *f.* प्रतिनिधित्व *n.*

2 फौजेंतला अगरअरमारांतला एक अमलदार आहे. [नायब.

LIEUTENANT, *n. deputy, locum tenens.* प्रतिनिधि, मुतालीक,

L. of a king, *Lord-l.* राजप्रतिनिधि.

LIFE, *n. vitality, vital faculty or principle.* जीव *m.* प्राण *m.* जीवित *n.* जीवित्व *n.* चेतना *f.* चैतन्य *n.* दम *m.* जीवकला *or* कळा *f.* जीवन कला *or* कळा *f.* प्राणवायु *m.* पंचप्राण *m. pl.* जीवात्मा *m.* भूतात्मा *m.* प्राणात्मा *m.* ओज *n.*—emphatically, *life and soul.* जीव प्राण *m.* पंचप्राण *m. pl.*

Breath of l. प्राणवायु *m.*

2 *existence, living.* जीव *m.* प्राण *m.* जिणें *n.* जीवित *n.* जीवन *n.* प्राणन *n.* जीवदशा *f.* वांचतीदशा *f.* जीवद्दशा *f.*

Abandonment, resigning, &c. of l. प्राणोत्सर्ग *m.* प्राणत्याग *m.* जीवोत्सर्ग *m.*

Danger of one's l. जिवावरचा लाग *m.* जिवावरची पाळी *f.* जिवावरचें संकट *n.* प्राणसंकट *n.* प्राणाशीं गांठ *f.* प्राणांतीक अवस्था *f.*

Deprived of l. हतप्राण, हतजीवित, नष्टजीवित.

Dearer than l. जिवापरता, प्राणापरता.

Granting of l. जीवदान *n.* प्राणदान *n.*

Impatience of l. जिवाचा-प्राणाचा-देहाचा-&c. कंटाळा *m.* जीवनत्रास *m.* जीवनद्वेष *m.* मुमूर्षा *f.*

Love of l. जीविताशा *f.* जिजीविषा *f.*

Maintaining or keeping of l. प्राणधारण *n.* प्राणरक्षण*n.* प्राणजीवन *n.* [शिरावर उदार.

Reckless of l. जिवावर उदार, प्राणावर उदार, देहावर उदार,

Saving of one's l. जीवदान *n.* प्राणदान *n.*

The first half of human l. पूर्ववय *n.*—That is in the first half of l. पूर्ववयस्क.

The latter or declining half of l. उत्तरपराई *or* पऱ्हाई *f.* उत्तरवय *n.*—That is in the decline of l. उत्तरवयस्क.

The thread of l. आयुष्याची दोरी *f.* [जीवनहेतु*m.*

The end, purpose, object, &c. of l. जन्माचें सार्थक*n.*

To be tired of l. मरो पुरेसा होणें.

To bring into l. जन्मास घालणें, जन्म *m. n.* देणें.

To enter into public l. लौकिकांत येणें, चौघांत येणें, लोकव्यवहारांत येणें.

To lose one's l. प्राणानूशी-जिवानूशी-जिवें जाणें, प्राणास-जिवास मुकणें, प्राणास आंचवणें.

To rise against one's l. जिवावर उठणें.

To take one's l. in one's hand. शिर *n.* हातावर घेणें, जीव *m.* मुठींत धरणें. [पडणें.

To threaten one's l. जिवावर येणें-बितणें, जिवाशीं गांठ

To trust one's l. to the honor of. मांडीवर मान *f.* ठेव-

णं, मांडीचें उसें *n.* करणे.

3 *mundane existence, present being.* जन्म *m. n.* मृत्युलोकची-भूलोकची-इहलोकची-&c. वस्ती *f.* इहलोकवास *m.* भूलोकवास *m.* संसार *m.* संसरण *n.* संसृति *f.* भव *m.*

Active or secular l. प्रवृत्ति *f.* प्रवृत्तिमार्ग *m.* प्रवर्त्तन *n.* संसारमार्ग *m.* (as opposed to retired and contemplative l. निवृत्ति *f.* निवृत्तिमार्ग *m.* परमार्थ मार्ग *m.*).

The present l. इहकाल *m.* इहजन्म *m. n.*—In the present l. इहजन्मीं,इहजन्मांत.

The sea of l. भवसमुद्र *m.* भवसागर *m.* भवार्णव *m.*

The cares and troubles, toil and turmoil of l. संसाराची सटपट *f.*-खवदव *f.*-उलेंढाळें *n.*-दगदग *f.*-ढवेंढाळ *n.*-&c.

The vicissitudes or wheel of l. संसारचक्र *n.* भवचक्र *n.* काळचक्र *n.*

The transiency and uncertainty of l. There are some lively figures involving this sense as, घटकेचें घड्याळ, कमळणीवरचा बिंदु, अळवावरचें पाणी, पाण्यावरची रेघ*or*रेषा, दुपारची सावली, खुंट्यावरला कावळा.

The two states or conditions of l. अवस्थाद्वय*n.*—They are, *happiness*, सुखावस्था *f.* सुखदशा *f.* and *misery.* दुःखावस्था *f.* दुःखदशा *f.*

The three states or modes of l. अवस्थात्रय *n.* They are, *waking state,* जाग्रदवस्था; *dreaming state,* स्वप्नावस्था; and *state of sound sleep,* सुषुप्त्यवस्था. Another account makes five, viz. जागृति, स्वप्न, सुषुप्ति, तुरीया, उन्मनी.

4 *conduct, living and acting.* चाल *f.* चालचर्या *f.* चालचलणूक *f.* वर्त्तणूक *f.* आचरण *n.* रहणी *f.* स्थितिरीति *f.* स्थीत *f.*

Holy living or l. धर्माचरण *n.* धर्मचर्या *f.* धर्मानुष्ठान *n.*

5 *condition, life with respect to happiness or misery.* जिणें *n.* नांदणूक *f.* वागणूक *f.* वर्त्तणूक *f.* स्थिति *pop.* स्थीत *f.*

High l. श्रीमंती *f.*

Low l. गरीबी *f.*

6 *age, term of living.* आयुष्य *n.* आयु *n.* आयुष्यमर्यादा *f.* जन्म *m. n.* हयात *f.* जीवितकाल *m.* आयुर्दाय *m.* आयुर्मान *n.* जीवमान *n.* जन्मकाल *m.* परमायु *n.* उमर *f.*

Companion for l. (husband, wife, &c.). जन्माचा सोबती, जिवाचा सोबती, जन्माचा जोडा *m.*

Connection or tie for l. जन्माची गांठ *f.* जन्मगांठ *f.*

During l., all one's l., for l., while l. lasts. जन्मभर, जन्मपर्यंत, तहांहयात, यावज्जीव, यावजन्म, यावद्देह, आमरण, आमरणांत, आजन्मांत.

For once in one's l. जन्माचे कर्मी.

In all one's l. *since one was born.* आल्या जन्मांत, जन्मापासून, बापजन्मांत, बापजन्मीं *neg. con.* जन्मतः, जन्मादारभ्य. [शिदोरी सरली.

L. is ended. आयुष्याची दोरी तुटली-सरली, आयुष्याची

Provision or maintenance for l. जन्माची भाकर *f.*-बेगमी *f.*-शिदोरी *f.*

7 *human affairs, common course of things.* प्रपंच *m.* संसार *m.* लौकिक*m.*संसरण*n.*संसृति *f.* संसारयात्रा *f.* लोकयात्रा*f.*भव*m.*

8 *briskness, vivacity, &c.* v. SPIRIT. जीव *m.* तेज *n.* तेजगी *f.* पाणी *n.* जीवनपाणी *n.* रंग *m.* रोशनाई *f.*

To get fresh l. जीव *m.* धरणें.

9 *narrative of the life of, memoir.* चरित्र*n.*चरित*n.*आख्यान*n.*

10—as a term of endearment. जिवडा, जिवलग, प्राण *m.* जीव *m.* प्राणविसांवा *m.*

From the l. यथाप्रति *pop.* यथाप्रत.

To the l. *with exact resemblance.* हुबहू *or* हुबेहू.

LIFE-BOAT, *n.* फुटलेल्या गलबतावरील माणसें वांचविण्या करितां केलेली नाव *f.*

LIFE-GIVING, *a.* जीवन दायक-प्रद-प्रदाता-&c. जीवदाता.

LIFE-GUARDS, *n. troops about the royal person.* हुजरात *f.*

LIFE-LESS, *a. deprived of life,* v. DEAD. गतप्राण, गतासु, गतचेष्ट, निःप्राण, प्राणविरहित.

2 *inanimate.* निर्जीव, अप्राण, निष्प्राण, अजीव, अचेतन, अचेष्ट, निचेष्ट, जड.

3 *without fire, energy, salt, &c.* v. SPIRITLESS. निर्जीव, निस्तेज, विरस, निस्सार, निस्सत्व, मळमळीत, पळपळीत, फुसका, फुसकुला.

LIFELESSLY, *adv.* v. A. 3. अळमळीत, मळमळीत, पळपळीत.

LIFE-TIME, *n. term of living,* v. LIFE, 6. आयुष्य *n.* जन्म*m.n.* जीवितकाल *m.*

All one's l. *during life,* v. LIFE. जन्मभर, जन्मपर्यंत.

LIFE-WEARY, *a.* जिवास त्रासलेला-कंटाळलेला, मरोमरोसा झालेला, जीवनत्रस्त.

To LIFT, *v. a.* v. To RAISE. उचलणें, उचलून घेणें, उठवणें, उंचकरणें-घेणें, वर करणें.

To l. from the ground. भुईसांड-जमीनसांड करणें.

2 *snap up and pocket,* v. To STEAL. उचलणें, उपटणें.

3 up; *swell with pride,* v. To PUFF UP. चढवणें, शेपारवणें, माजवणें, फुगवणें, शीड *n.* चढवणें *g. of o.* गजस्कंधीं-गंडस्थळीं-घोड्यावर-हत्तीवर-&c. बसवणें.

To be lifted up. चढणें, माजणें, उतणें, फुगणें, शेरडावणें, शीड *n.* चढणें *g. of s.* गजस्कंधीं-गंडस्थळीं-घोड्यावर-हत्ती वर-&c. बसणें, आसन *n.*-ढोंगण *n.*-&c. जड होणें *g. of s.*

To l. up the voice. See To CRY.

LIFT, LIFTING, v.V.A.1.—*act.* उचलणें *n.* उठवणें *n.* उत्थापन *n.*

To give a l. See To HELP.

LIFTER, *n.* LIFTING, *p. a.* v. V. 1. उचलणारा, &c.

2 उचलणारा, उचल्या.

LIGAMENT, *n.* v. TIE. बंधन *n.*

2—in anatomy. संधिबंधन *n.* संधिबंध *m.*अस्थिबंधन *n.*

LIGATURE, *n. band, bandage.* बंद *m.* बंधन *n.* पट्टी *f.* कसणी *f.* आळा *m.*

LIGHT, *n.* उजेड*m.* प्रकाश*m.* तेज*n.* ज्योति *f. pop.* ज्योत *f.* जोत *f.* कांति*f.* दीप्ति*f.* प्रभा *f.* आभा*f.* भा *f.* शोभा *f.* छवि *f.* आलोक*m.*

2 See DAY LIGHT, DAWN. 3 *knowledge.* ज्ञान *n.* प्रकाश *m.* बोध *m.* अवगम *m.*

4 *public notice, open view, state of being known.* उजेडी *f.* उघडीक *f.* प्रसिद्धि *f.* उजागरी *or* उजागिरी *f.* लौकिक *m.*

To come to l. *become known, be found out, &c.* उमटणें, उमगणें *or* उभगणें, उमट *m.*-उमग *m.* पडणें *g. of s.* उजेडास-उजाडीस-उजेडीस-प्रसिद्धीस-उदयास-उमाळ्यास-उमाळीस -उमाळयास-&c. येणें, ठायीं पडणें, बाहेर पडणें.

To bring to l. उजेडास-उजाडीस-प्रसिद्धीस-&c. आणणें, ठायीं-ठिकाणीं-&c. पाडणें, बाहेर आणणें, उमग *m.* पाडणें *g. of o.*

5 (of a picture). चित्रावर उजेडाची जागा *f.* प्रकाशितचित्रांश *m.* चित्रस्थ प्रकाशितस्थल *n.*

6 *point of view.* दृष्टि *f.* लक्ष्य *n.* दृष्टिसूत्र *n.* दृष्टिपातसूत्र *n.* लक्ष्यसूत्र *n.* दृष्टिपातमार्ग *m.*

If you look at it in this light. असें पाहिलें असतां.

7 *any thing that gives light, a lamp, candle, &c.* उजेड *m.* दिवा *m.* दीप *m.* दीपक *m.* चिराग *m.*

A huge, flaring, swaling l. अंबा बाईचा पेात *m.*

LIGHT, *a. not heavy.* हलका, थोड्यावजनाचा, हलू, लघु, अल्पप्रमाण, सुवाह्य, कमतोल.

Lightest. लघिष्ठ.

2 *not afflictive.* हलका, हलुवट *or* हलवट, लहान, थोडा, लघु, सुसह्य, सुवाह्य, सुवह.

3 *not difficult,* v. EASY. हलका, सोपा, सुसाध्य, सुशक, सुवाह्य, सुघटित, हलू फूल, फुलासारखा.

4 *easy of digestion.* हलका, लघु, सुपच, सुखपच्य.

5 *not encumbered, not heavily armed, &c.*—a force. सडा, सडासांटा, सडासांठ.

6 *nimble, agile, &c.* v. ACTIVE. चपल *or* ळ, आंगाचा हलका, आंगाचा चपळ, चपळा, आंगसूट, चलाक *or* ख.

L. and tight, *compact and dapper.* सुटसुटीत, लुटलुटीत, अटपता, अटस, अटोपशुद्ध, अटकर, सुबक.

7 *slight, small, trivial, inconsiderable.* हलका, लहान, थोडा, लघु, अल्प, क्षुल्लक, क्षुद्र, हलुवट *or* हलवट, उपेक्षणीय, अगण्य, तुच्छ, जमेस धराया जोगा नाहीं, पोकळ, फुसका, फुसकुला.

To make l. of, To set l. by, v. To CONTEMN. हलका-तुच्छ-&c. करणें-मानणें, थेर *n.* करणें *g. of o.* अमान्य करणें.

8 *not dense, not gross, &c.* पातळ, बारीक, विरलावयव, शिथिलावयव, अस्थूल, अघन.

9 *airy, trifling, wanting dignity, sobriety, steadiness, &c.* हलका, मनाचा हलका, हलक्या मनाचा, पचकळ, पचरट, पचाल *or* ळ, छिछोर *or* चिचोर *or* छचोर, एर, एरशेर, बावकळ *or* बायकळ, बावगा, बायघळ, गैरी, किसान, ओल्सा, चटोर, टौर, टारगा, चाट, हुचा, कमतोल, तुच्छ, गांभीर्यरहित-शून्य-&c. अप्रगल्भ, लघुचित्त, लघुचेता.

10 *wanting reason ; silly, inconsiderate.* गयाळ, गलतान, खैरी शैरी, गैरी, गैदी.

11 *lightsome, not dark.* उजेडाचा, उजेडीचा, सप्रकाश, प्रकाशयुक्त, प्रकाशबहुल, प्रकाशमय, सोज्वल.

12 *pale, whitish, fair, &c.* उजळ, पांढरा, सांवळा, निमगोरा.

13 *not intense, not deep,*—of colors. हलका, फिका, उभरंग.

14 *cheerful, not oppressed, &c.,* v. MERRY. आनंदाचा, उल्लासाचा, आनंदवृत्तीचा, सानंद. [शुद्ध.

15—used of the fortnight of the waxing moon. शुक्ल,

To LIGHT, *v. a. give light to.* उजेड *m.*-प्रकाश *m.* देणें-करणें-दाखवणें.

2 *illuminate,* v. To ENLIGHTEN. प्रकाशणें, उज्वलन *n.*-प्रकाशन *n.*-द्योतन *n.*-&c. करणें *g. of o.* प्रकाशित-द्योतित-उज्वलित-&c. करणें.

3 *set on fire,* v. To KINDLE. पेटवणें, चेतवणें, शिलगावणें, उजळणें, उज्वलन *n.*-प्रज्वलन *n.*-&c. करणें *g. of o.* उज्वलित-&c. करणें.

4 See To LIGHTEN.

To LIGHT, *v. n. fall on, happen to find.* मिळणें-गांठणें-सांपडणें-भेटणें *in. con.* ठेपणें, लागणें, पडणें, बसणें. [भिडणें.

2 *fall, alight, strike on.* पडणें, बसणें, लागणें, उतरणें, ठेपणें,

3 *stoop from flight.* उतरणें, अवतरणें, खालीं येणें.

4 *descend,* v. To DISMOUNT. उतरणें, अवरोह *m.* करणें.

5 v. To KINDLE. पेटणें, चेतणें, लागणें.

LIGHT-ARMED, *a.* हलक्या हत्यारांचा, आडहत्यारी, आडहत्यारबंद.

LIGHT-FINGERED, *a. addicted to petty thefts.* हाताळ, हाताळू, हातलाव्या, दपट्या, रपाट्या.

LIGHT-FOOTED, *a.* पायसूट, पायाचा चपळ-जलद, पायस्वार.

LIGHT-HANDED, *a. that has a quick, &c. hand.* हलक्या हाताचा, हाताचा चपळ, चपळ हाताचा, लघुहस्त.

LIGHT-HEADED, *a. delirious.* बायचळलेला, बावचळलेला, बायचळ्या, विक्षिप्त, बेशुद्ध, बेसावध, बेहोष.

To get l. बायचळणें, बावचळणें *or* बावचळणें.

2 See THOUGHTLESS.

LIGHT-HEADEDNESS, *n.* v. A. 1. बायचळ *m.*

LIGHT-HEARTED, *a.* v. MERRY. आनंदी, उल्लासी, आनंदवृत्ति, सुमनस्क.

LIGHT-HOUSE, *n. building with a light to guide seamen.* मनोरा *m.* दीपस्तंभ *m.* दीपगृह *n.* [चा, लघु.

LIGHT-MINDED, *a.* v. LIGHT, 9. मनाचा हलका, हलक्या मना-

To LIGHTEN, *v. n. flash, &c.* चमकणें, चकाकणें, लकाकणें, चकमकणें, जोवणें, स्फुरणें.

To LIGHTEN, *v. a.* See To ENLIGHTEN. 2 *lessen the burden of.* हलका करणें, हलकावणें, कांहीं ओझें *n.* काढणें, कांहीं रिता-&c. करणें, न्यूनभार-अल्पभार-&c.करणें.

3 *make less heavy.* हलका-कमी-&c. करणें, हलकावणें.

LIGHTER, *n.*—the boat. पडाव *m.*

LIGHTLY, *adv.* v. A. 1. हलका *decl.* हलू, हलक्यानें.

2 हलका *decl.* हलू, थोडा, सोसेसा *decl.* सोसतसोसत, साहतसाहत.

3 *without difficulty, of course,* v. EASILY. सहज, सहजगतीनें, सहजगत्या.

5 सड्यानें, सड्यानूशीं, सड्यानिशीं, सडेसामानानिशीं, सडेस्वारीनिशीं, पायगुंत्यावांचून.

6 See NIMBLY. 9 हलकेपणानें, हलकेचालीनें, हलकेरितीनें, छिछोरीनें, चटोरपणानें, चटोरीनें, अशिष्टाईनें, &c.

13 आनंदवृत्तीनें, आनंदेंकरून.

I. *without proper grounds.* उगाच, एरवी, विनाकारण, निःकारण *or* निष्कारण, निष्प्रयोजन.

LIGHTNESS, *n.* v. V. 1. हलकेपणा *m.* लघुत्व *n.* लघिमा *m.* लाघव *n.* भाराभाव *m.* भारहीनता *f.*-राहित्य *n.*-&c.

2 हलकेपणा *m.* &c. सुसह्यता *f.* सुवहता *f.*

3 हलकेपणा *m.* सोपेपणा *m.* सुसाध्यता *f.* सुशकता *f.*

6 आंगचा चपळपणा *m.* &c. अंगचापल्य *n.* [पणा *m.*

7 हलकेपणा *m.* हलकाभार *m.* लघुता *f.* लघुत्व *n.* लाघव *n.* पोकळ-

9 हलकेपणा *m.* मनाचा हलकेपणा *m.* छिछोरी *or* चिचोरी *f.* चिचोरपणा *m.* (*or* छचोरी *f.* &c.) पचकळपणा *m.* चटोरपणा *m.* &c. चटोरी *f.* अशिष्टाई *f.* अशिष्टाइकी *f.* लाघव *n.* लघुत्व *n.* अप्रगल्भता *f.* गांभीर्यराहित्य *n.*-हीनता *f.*-&c.

LIGHTNING, *n.* वीज *f.* बिजली *f.* विद्युल्लता *f.* विद्युत् *f.* चपळा *f.* सौदामिनी *f.* रोहिणी *f.* तडित् *f.* वज्र *m.n.* जोव *f.*

Forked or zigzag l. विद्युल्लता *f.* असिलता *f.*

The falling or darting of l. विद्युत्पात *m.*

LIGHTS, *n. lungs of brute animals.* जनावराचा फुप्फुस *pop.* फुपूसm. फोपसm.

LIGHTSOME, *a. not dark, luminous.* उजेडाचा, सप्रकाश, प्रकाशयुक्त, प्रकाशमय, सुप्रकाश, तेजस्वी, सोज्वल, दीप्तिमान्.

2 *cheerful, exhilarating.* हर्षप्रद-दायक-&c. आनंदकारक-प्रद-&c. सुखावह, खेदहंता.

3 *gay, light,* v. MERRY. आनंदी, उल्लासी, आनंदवृत्तीचा.

LIGHTSOMENESS, *n.* v. A. 1. उजेडी *f.* रोशनाई *f.* सप्रकाशता *f.* प्राकाश्य*n.* सोज्वलता *f.* औज्ज्वल्य *n.*

2 रोशनाई *f.*

3 आनंदवृत्ति *f.* हर्षवृत्ति *f.*

LIGNEOUS, *a.* v. WOODEN. लाकडाचा, काष्ठमय, काष्ठरूप.

LIKE, *a. of the same quantity, quality, &c.* v. EQUAL. बरोबर, बरोबरचा, सारखा, समान, सम, तुल्य, तसा and तसला (correl. of जसा and जसला).

2 *resembling, similar.* सारखा, बरोबर, तुल्य, सम, समान, सारसा, सदृश, तुल्यरूप, अनुरूप, सवर्ण, सरूप, सन्निभ, सदृश, प्रातिभासिक, रूप and रूपी (in comp. as पितृरूप,देवरूपी, &c.), वत् (in comp. as सुवर्णवत्, देववत्, &c.), वजा (in comp. as ब्राह्मणवजा, कुणबीवजा, &c.), उपम (in comp. as सुर्योपम), प्रतिम (in comp. as सूर्यप्रतिम, सिंहप्रतिम);—as adjunct to nouns converting them into adjectives the word is rendered by सा,as देवसा god-like, वीरसा warriorlike, &c. दाखल (as पुत्रादाखल like a son).

3 *probable,* See LIKELY.

LIKE, *n. match, fellow,* v. EQUAL. तोड *f.* जोडीचा, बरोबरीचा.

2 See LIKING.

L. and dislike. आवड नावड *f.*

LIKE, *adv. in the same manner.* सारखा *decl.* प्रमाणें, बरोबर, वाणी (as वेड्यावाणी, थोरावाणी, &c.), परी (as बापापरी, लेंकरापरी, &c.), गत (as वेड्याचे गत), वजा (as ब्राह्मणवजा, कुणबीवजा &c.), वारीं (as तृणावारीं,&c.), वार (in comp.with Hindustani words as, तपसीलवार, बयादवार,&c.), बरहुकूम.

L. as. जसा (antecedent of तसा), ज्याप्रमाणें, &c.

See LIKELY.

To LIKE, *v. a. have a liking for.* चाहणें, इच्छिणें, चांगला-बरा-गोड-प्रिय-&c. वाटणें *in. con.* आवडणें *in. con.* भावणें *in. con.* आवड *f.*-गोडी *f.*-&c. असणें *g. of o. & in. con.* आवड *f.*-&c. करणें *g. of o.*

2 *be pleased with.* v. To APPROVE. पसंत-मान्य-कबूल-&c. करणें, पसंत-&c. होणें *in. con.* मानवणें *in. con.*

To be liked. पटणें, पसंत होणें, मर्जीस उतरणें-पटणें.

To LIKE, *v. n. list, choose, please.* आवडणें-चाहणें-गमणें-रुचणें-भावणें-बरें वाटणें-मर्जीस येणें-पडणें-&c. *all with in. con.* खुशी *f.*-मर्जी *f.*-&c. असणें *g. of s.* मन *n.* मानवणें *g. of s.* कल *m.*-मनदेवता *f.*-मनपिंगळा *m.*-मनपिंगळी *f.* वाहणें-लवणें.

LIKE-MINDED, *a.* समानशील, समस्वभाव.

LIKELIHOOD, LIKELINESS, *n.* v. A. लाग *m.* रंग *m.* धोरण *n.* आकार *m.* डौल *m.* घाट *m.* सुमार *m.* मांड *m.* संभावना *f.* संभव *m.*

LIKELY, *a. probable.* जोगा-जोगता-सारखा-सा-&c. (used with the verb indicated as, घडाया जोगा. L. to happen. पडायासारखा. L. to fall, तो यावा सा आहे. He is l. to come.) संभावनीय, संभाव्य, संभावनात्मक. The sense is also expressed by the use of the past participle with असावा *or* असेल ; as तो काल आला असावा *or* तो काल आलाअसेल.

LIKELY, *adv. probably.* अधिक करून, अधिक बांट्यांनीं, तीन बांट्यांनीं *or* बांटे, नऊ बांट्यांनीं *or* बांटे.

Most l. बहुतकरून, नव्याण्णव बांट्यांनीं *or* बांटे, हजार बांट्यांनीं *or* बांटे, प्रायः, प्रायशः.

To LIKEN, *v.a. compare.* उपमा *f.*-तुलना *f.*-बरोबरी *f.*-&c. करणें-देणें, उपमणें, तुळणें *or* तोलणें.

LIKENED, *p.* v. V. उपमित, तुलित.

LIKENER, *n.* v. V. उपमा देणारा-करणारा.

LIKENESS, *n.* v. A. 2. सारखेपणा *m.* सारखवट *f. n.* सारखवटा *m.* सादृश्य *n.* सदृशता *f.* सारूप्य *n.* समरूपता *f.* साम्य *n.* आनुगुण्य *n.* आनुधर्म्य *n.* तुलना *f.* तुला *f.* तौल्य *n.* औपम्य *n.* आभास *m.* अनुकार *m.* आनुरूप्य *n.* अभ्युपगम *m.*

I. *form, semblance, appearance.* रूप *n.* स्वरूप *n.* आकार *m.* आकृति *f.* डौल *m.*

II. *picture, image, &c. resembling a person or thing.* प्रतिमा *f.* प्रतिरूप *n.* प्रतिरूपक *n.* प्रतिकृति *f.* प्रतिबिंब*n.* चित्र *n.* तस्वीर *f.*

LIKEWISE, *adv. in like manner.* तसाच, तथा, तद्वत्.

2 *also, too.* ही, देखील *or* देखीद, पण, अणखी.

LIKING, *n. fondness for, pleasure in.* चहा *m. f.* चाड *f.* आवड *f.* गोडी *f.* प्रीति *f.* गोडवी *f.* अभिरुचि *f.* इष्क *m.* शोख *or* शोक *m.*—esp. as contracted, चट *f.* चटक *f.* चवणा*m.* छंद*m.* चाळा *m.* सवई *f.* लचक *f.* लचका *m.*

L. and disliking. आवडनावड *f.* प्रियाप्रिय *n.*

To contract a l. for. चटावणें, चकसणें, चट *f.*-&c. लागणें *in. con.* मन *n.* बसणें-लागणें *g. of s.* संवकणें *or* सोंकणें, सोंकावणें.

To lose one's l. for मन *n.* उठणें-तुटणें *g. of s.* चट *f.*-&c. जाणें.

2 *mind, choice, wish respecting.* मन *n.* चित्त *n.* खातर *f.* ध्यान *n.*

To (according to) the l. of. इच्छेसारखा-जोगा-&c. मनासारिखा-जोगा, आवडीसारखा-&c.

3 *state of body, case, condition.* देहभावना *f.* देहस्थिति *f.*

That is in good l. दुलदुलीत, ताजा, पुष्ट, टमटमीत.

LILIPUTIAN, *n.* v. DWARF. वामनमूर्ति *f.*

LILY, *n.* कणेल *n.* ? भुईकमळ *n.*

Water l. See LOTUS.

LIMATURE, *n. filings.* कीस *m.*

LIMB, *n. member.* अंग *pop.* आंग *n.* अवयव *m.* गात्र *n.*

To have an aching of the limbs. आंग *n.* मोडून येणें.

Trembling of the limbs. गात्रभंग *m.*

2 *border,* v. EDGE. कड *f.* किनारा *m.*

3 See BRANCH.

LIMBED, *n.* आंगाचा, अंगी, अवयवी, सावयव, सांग.

Large l. Ample l. उदारांग, बृहदंग, बृहदवयव.

Light l. सुटसुटीत *or* सुडसुडीत आंगाचा, आंगाचा सुटसुटीत, आंगसूट.

LIMBER, *a. pliant.* लवचीक, लवका, लवसर, लवकिरा.

LIMBERNESS, *n.* v. A. लवचिकपणा *m.* लवकेपणा *m.* &c.

Limbless, *a.* निरवयव, निरंग, अंगहीन-शून्य-&c. अवयवहीन-&c.
Limbo, See **Hell**, **Prison**.
Lime, *n.* चुना *m.* चूर्ण *n.* सुधा *f.*
Fine l. well levigated to lay over and finish a chunam work. संदला *or* संधला *m.* निरू *m.* [पट्टी *f.*
Leaf which holds the l. eaten with betel leaves. चुन-
L. made from shells. शिंपीचा चुना *m.*
Nodule of l. खडा *m.* चुनखडा *m.* [टिपगारी *f.*
Pointing with l.—a wall, &c. दर्जंगिरी *f.* टिपगिरी *or*
Pot for holding the l. eaten with betel leaves. चुनाळ *m.* चुनोटा *m.* चुनोटी *f.*
Pure fine l. कळीचा चुना *m.*
Well ground l. संधला *m.*
2 *bird-lime.* चिकोटा *m.* चिकटा *m.* चिकोटी *f.*
Stick covered with l. चिकाटी *f.*
Lime, *n. citrus limonum*,—the tree. निंबुणी *f.* निंबूण *f.* निंबोणी *f.* निंबी *f.* Note; all these words are popularly spelt with लि instead of नि. ईड्*f.* जाभीर*f.*—the fruit. निंबू*n.* अंबटनिंबू *n.* ईडलिंबू *n.* जाभीर *n.* [बोटी *f.*
Half of a l. (esp. as roasted, sugared, and spiced) निं-
The sweet l.—the tree. साखरनिंबी *f.*—the fruit, साखरनिंबू *n.*
The small thin skinned l. कागदीनिंबू *n.*
To **Lime**, *v. a. smear with bird lime.* चिकटा*m.*-&c. लावणें-लेपणें, चिकट करणें. [लणें.
2 See To **Insnare**. 3 *manure with lime.* चुन्याचें खत घा-
Lime-burner, *n.* लोणारी, चुनाभाजणारा, चूर्णकार.
Lime-kiln, *n.* चुन्याची भट्टी *f.* चुनभट्टी *f.*
Lime-mill, *n.* घाणी *f.* चुन्याचा घाणा *m.*
Wheel rut of a l. घाणा *m.* घाणी *f.* घाण *f.*
Lime-quarry, *n.* चुनेखाण *or* चुनखाण *f.*
Lime-stone, *n.*—a nodule of. चुनखडा *m. dim.* चुनखडी *f.* चूर्णखंड *n.* चूर्णोपल *m.*
A burnt l. चुनकळी *f.* कळी *f.*
Abounding in l.—ground. चुनखडी.
Lime-water, चुनवणी *n.*
Limit, *n. boundary, border*, v. **Bound**. सीमा *f. pop.* शींव *f.* शीम *f.* शिमा *f.* हद्द *f.* अवधि *m.* अवसान *n.* वेला *f.*
That forms the l. of. अवधिभूत.
2 limits (of a prison). मोकळिकीची हद्द *f.*
To **Limit**, *v. a. set bounds to*, v. To **Bound**. सीमा *f.*-शींव *f.*-अवधि *m.*-हद्द *f.*-&c. बांधणें-करणें-देणें-घालणें, ससीम-सावधिक-&c. करणें.
2 *confine within certain bounds; restrict.* मर्यादा *f.*-हद्द *f.*-इयत्ता *f.*-परिमिति *f.*-&c. करणें-ठेवणें, आळा *m.*-आळाबांधा *m.*-धरबंद *or* बंध *m.*-बंधारण *n.*-बंद *m.*-बंध*m.*-&c. करणें-करून देणें-घालणें-&c.
Limitation, *n.* v. V. 2.—*act.* मर्यादा करणें *n.* &c.—*state.* आळा *m.* आळाबांधा*m.* बंधारण *n.* बंद *m.* बंध *m.* बंधन *n.* धरबंद *m.* इयत्ता *f.* परिमितता *f.*
Limitative. See **Limiter**. [सावधिक.
Limited, *p. and a.* v. V. 1. शींव घातलेला, &c. समर्याद, ससीम,
2 आळा घातलेला,&c. समर्याद, ससीम, सावधिक.
I. *confined*, v. **Narrow**. सांकड, संकोचाचा, अडचणीचा, अप्रशस्त. [णारा, &c. सामंत.
Limiter, *n.* **Limiting**, *p. a.* v. V. 1. सीमा करणारा, हद्द बांध-
2 मर्यादा करणारा, इयत्ता ठेवणारा, आळा बांधणारा, &c.
Limitless, *a.* v. **Infinite**. बेहद्द, निरवधि, निस्सीम.
To **Limn**, *v. a. paint, draw.* चित्र *n.*-नकशा*m.*-तस्बीर *f.*-&c. काढणें *g. of o.* काढणें.
Limner, *n.* v. V. चित्र काढणारा, &c. चितारी, चित्रकार.
Limous. See **Muddy**.
To **Limp**, *v. n. walk lamely.* लंगडणें, कुलपणें, गुलफणें, लचकणें, लचंगणें, लुचपणें, टिंगणें, पेंगणें, लंगणें, पाय *m.* काढणें, लंगडत-कुलपत-लुचपत-लचकत-&c. चालणें-जाणें, लंगडशाई *f.*-लंगडशादी *f.*-लंगडी *f.* घालणें.
Limp, **Limping**, *n.* v. V.—*act.* लंगडणें *n.* कुलपणें *n.* &c. लंगडशाई *f.* लंगडशादी *f.* लंगडी *f.* पेंगणी *f.* लंगडणी *f.*
Limper, *n.* **Limping**, *p. a.* v. V. लंगडणारा, लंगडत चालणारा, &c. लंगडा, लंगडखूट, खंज.
Limpid, *a.* v. **Clear**. निवळ, नितळ, स्वच्छ, काचेसारखा.
Limpidity, **Limpidness**, *n.* v. A. निवळपणा *m.* नितळपणा*m.* नितळाई *f.* स्वच्छता *f.*
Limpingly, *adv.* v. A. लंगडत लंगडत, कुलपत, लुचपत, &c.
Limsy, **Limpsy**. See **Flaccid**. [प्रचुर.
Limy, *a. containing lime.* चुनखडी, चुनखडीचा, चुन्याचा, चूर्ण-
2 *relating, &c. to lime.* चुन्याचा.
3 *viscous.* चिकोट्याचा, चिकट्याचा.
Linch-pin, *n. pin to confine a wheel on the axletree.* चाकाचीखीळ *f.* आंसाची खीळ *f.* अक्षाग्रकीलक *m.*
Lincture, **Linctus**, *n. medicine taken by licking.* चाटण *n.* अवलेह *m.* लेह्य *n.* [*or* णी *f.*
Line, *n. longitudinal extension.* रेसा *f.* रेषा *f.* धारणी *f.* सरणि
Right l. सरल रेषा *f.*
2 *string, cord.* दोरी *f.* सडक *f.* चऱ्हाट *n.* रस्सी *f.*
L. stretched for hanging clothes. ओलाणी *f.*
3 *thread, &c. extended to direct operation.* सूत *n.* सूत्र *n.*
By l. and rule. यथासूत्र.
4 (in the face, hands, &c.) *lineament.* रेखा *f.* रेषा *f.* रेष *f.* खत *n.* There are certain *lines* supposed to be auspicious or otherwise designative. Some are, आयुष्यरेषा, ऊर्ध्वरेषा, कातर, गोत्ररेषा, चक्र, यव *pop.* जब, जवमाळा, धनरेषा *or* धनरेघ, पद्म, पुत्ररेषा, भांडार, शंख, सर्पिणी, खीरेषा, स्वस्तिक.
5 (of writing or print). ओळ *f.* *or* वळ *f.* वळी *f.* पंक्ति *pop.* पंगत *f.*
6—as drawn with a pen, &c. रेघ *f.* ओळ *or* वळ *f.* वळी*f.* रेसा *f.* रेषा *f.* खत *n.* लेखा *f.*
A waving l. लहर *f.*
L. as drawn through a word, letter, &c. फांटा *m.*
Lines and figures drawn (along a wall, &c.). खतकशी*f.*
To draw a l. or stroke. ओळ *f.* फोडणें.
There are certain *lines* drawn in accounts and letters which have particular significances and particular names. Some of the second kind are, दुरकानी रेघ *or* ओळ, तिरकानी रेघ *or* ओळ, चौरकानी रेघ *or* ओळ. For those of the first kind See **Account**.

7 *rank, row.* ओळ or बळ *f.* बळी *f.* पंक्ति *pop.* पंगत *f.* सर *f.* सरद *f.* फरा *m.* रांग *f.* माला *pop.* माळ *f.* हार *f.* आवलि *f.* श्रेणी *f.* दंड *m.* पात *f.*

A l. (of men or animals) in procession. रव *f.* रवण *f. n.* भरड *f.* तांडा *m.* लाघाबळ *f.*

A close l. फळी *f.*

To break through a close l. फळी *f.* फोडणें- फोडून जाणें.

In one l. or row. एकसरीं or एकसरें, एकसर, एकशेज.

8 *disposition, method.* क्रम *m.* अनुक्रम *m.* शेज *n. f.* पर्याय *m.* परिपाटी *f.*

9 v. EQUATOR. विषुववृत्त *n.* भूमध्यरेषा *f.*

10 *ascending or descending series of a family.* वंश *m.* वंशावलि *pop.* वंशावळ *f.* वंशपरंपरा *f.* कुलपरंपरा *f.* परंपरा *f.* रव *f.* आवलि *f.*

L. of ancestors. वडीलपरंपरा *f.*

11 (of soldiers, &c.) रांग *f.* फरा *m.*

To form in l. फरा *m.* धरणें-धरून उभे राहणें.

12 lines; *trenches.* खंदकमोरचा *m.*

13 lines; *rows of military huts.* छावणी *f.*

14 (of conduct or procedure) *course.* तंत्र *n.* ओळ *f.* ओळा *m.* मोड *f.* मोडणी *f.*

Straight-forward l. of conduct. उभादांडा *m.*

15 *department or course of business.* पेशा *m.* धंदा *m.*

To LINE, *v. a. cover on the inside.* मढणें, मढवणें.

To l. with cloth. कापडणें.

2 *put lining to* (a garment). अस्तर *n.* लावणें-देणें.

3 *impregnate* (used of irrational animals) गाभण करणें.

4 (with soldiers.) शिपाई *m. pl.* रांगेनें उभे करणें.

LINEAGE, *n. house, race, &c.* v. FAMILY. वंश *m.* घर *n.* घराणा *m.* गोत्र *n.*

2 See OFFSPRING, 3 See LINE 10.

LINEAL, *a. composed of or relating to lines.* रेघांचा, रेखांचा, &c. रेखामय, रेषामय, रेषारूप.

2 *descending, &c. directly.* परंपरेचा, परंपरेनें आलेला, परंपरागत, परंपरायात, क्रमागत, क्रमायात, क्रमप्राप्त, पारंपरिक.

LINEALLY, *adv.* v. A. 2. परंपरेनें, परंपरापूर्वक, वंशानुक्रमानें, कुलानुक्रमानें, गोत्रक्रमानें.

LINEAMENT, *n. feature.* रूपचिह्न *n.* रूपलक्षण *n.* अंगलक्षण *n.*

Lineaments, *outlines, figure, &c.* वळण *n.* रूपरेषा *f. pl.* आंगलट *f.* आंगलोट *m.* [रूप, पांक.

LINEAR, *a. consisting of lines.* ओळींचा, पंक्तींचा, पंक्तिमय, पंक्ति-

LINED, *p.* v. V. 1. मढवलेला, &c. मढींव.

LINEN, *a. made, &c. of flax.* तागाचा, सणाचा, तागाचे सुताचा, सणाचे सुताचा, शाण.

LINEN, *n.* तागाचें-सणाचें कापड *n.* शाणवस्त्र *n.*

2 See CLOTHES.

LINEN-DRAPER, *n.* v. CLOTH-MERCHANT. कापडकरी, चाटी or चाट्या, बजाज.

LINGAM, *n.* v. PHALLUS. लिंग *n.*

Worshipper of the l. लिंगाईत, लिंगवंत—in contempt. लिंगडा, लिंग्या.

To LINGER, *v. n. remain about, stay long, loiter,* v. To DAWDLE. गमणें, रेंगणें, रेंगळणें, वेळ *m. f.* -देर *f.*- उशीर *m.*-&c. लावणें.

2 *proceed sluggishly, heavily, &c.*—a work, &c. रखडणें, रेंगणें, रखडत-रेंगत-झरतमरत-&c.चालणें, लांबणीवर पडणें, भिजत पडणें.

3 (in sickness). रेंगणें, रखडणें, खितपणें or खिरपणें, खितपणीस पडणें-लागणें, रेंगत-मरत-&c. पडणें, खिबदणें, पचणें, पचणीस पडणें, खाटेस खिळणें, अंथरूण *n.* धरणें.

4—a sickness. रेंगणें, खितपणीस पडणें-लागणें, धुपणें, घुमणें, खिळणें, हाडीं खिळणें, चेंगटाईखालीं पडणें, लांबणीवर-लांबणीखालीं पडणें, खिपरी बसणें.

5 *hang in doubt,* v. To HESITATE. गुटमुळणें, गुळमुळणें, गुटमळणें, घुरमुळणें.

6—a sound, &c. *last long, hang on.* घुमणें.

LINGERER, *n.* LINGERING, *p. a.* v. V. 1. गमणारा, &c. गमदसडा or दासडा, चेंगट.

2 रखडत चाललेला, &c. चेंगट, चेंगटाईचा.

4 खितपणीचा, चेंगट, चेंगटाईचा, झिरणीचा.

LINGERINGLY, *adv.* v. A. 2. रेंगतरेंगत, रखडतरखडत.

3 खिरपत, खितपत.

LINGET, *n. small mass of metal.* धातूचीकांडी *f.* लगड *f.*

LINGLE, *n. shoemaker's thread.* चाम्हाराचा धागा *m.*

LINGO, *n.* v. LANGUAGE. बोली *f.* भाषा *f.* [दंत्य.

LINGUA-DENTAL, *a. formed by the tongue and teeth.* जिव्हा-

LINGUA FRANCA, *n. mixed language.* खिचडी *f.* घेडगुजरी *f.*

LINGUAL, *a. relating, &c. to the tongue.* जिभेचा, जिव्हेचा, जिव्हासंबंधी.

LINGUIST, *n. person skilled in languages.* अनेकभाषा जाणणारा, बहुभाष्या, बहुभाषावेत्ता, अनेकभाषाज्ञ.

2 See INTERPRETER.

LINIMENT, *n. soft or liquid ointment.* चोळण्याचें औषध *n.*-पाणी *n.* लेप *m.* स्नेहन *n.* द्रवमर्दनौषध *n.*

LINING, *n.* v. V. 2—*act.* मढणें *n.* मढवणें *n.* मढणी *f.* मढवणी *f.* मढवणूक *f.* मढण *n.*

Price or cost l. मढणावळ *f.* मढवाई *f.*

I. *covering that lines.* मढ *f.* मढण *n.* मढणी *f.*

II. (of a garment) अस्तर *n.*

LINK, *n.* (of a chain). कडी *f.* दुवा *m.* घुणा *m.* [ग्रंथि *m.*

2 *tie, bond,* v. CONNECTION. लग *f.* लगा *m.* लगाबांधा *m.*

3 v. TORCH. मशाल *f.* दिवटा *m.* दिवटी *f.*

L. of rolls of coarse cloth. पोत *m.*

To LINK, *v. a. join, connect, concatenate.* सांगडणें, जोडणें, लांकणें, जोड *f. m.*-सांगड *f.*-लांख *f.*-जूळ *f.*-जुगल *f.*-&c. घालणें-लावणें *g. of o. recip.* जांगड *f.* घालणें-करणें, संबंध *m.*-संबंधन *n.*-&c. करणें, शृंखलाबद्ध करणें.

LINK-BOY, *n.* मशालची or जी, दिवट्या. [अतसीबीज *n.*

LINSEED, *n. seed of flax.* अळशी *f.* जवस *m. n.* उमाबीज *n.*

LINSEED OIL, *n.* जवसाचें तेल *n.*

LINSEY-WOOLSEY, *a. made of linen and wool mixed.* कांहीं तागाचा कांहींलोंकरीचा, शाणोर्ण, क्षौमोर्ण.

LINSTOCK, *n.*—of gunners. तोडा *m.* बत्ती *f.* [कीस *m.*

LINT, *n.* See FLAX. 2 *linen scraped.* सण कापडाचा-तागाचा.

LINTEL, *n.* (of a door frame &c.). वरचा उंबरा *m.* उंबरठा *m.* उंबत्रा *m.* दारवंठा *m.* कपालपट्टी *f.* गणेशपट्टी *f.* तोरण *n.*

LION, *n.* सिंह *m.* केसरी *m.* मृगराज *m.* मृगेंद्र *m.*
 Roar of the l. सिंहनाद *m.*
 2 *object of interest or curiosity.* कौतुक *n.* पाहण्याजोगा चमत्कारिक पदार्थ *m.*
LIONESS, *n.* सिंहीण *f.* सिंही *f.*
LION-HEARTED, LIONLIKE, *a.* सिंहस्वभाव, सिंहहृदय, सैंहिक.
LIP, *n.* ओठ *m.* होट *or* होंट *m.* ओष्ठ *m.*
 The lips. अधर *m.* अधरपुट *n.*
 The lower l. अधर *m.* अधरोष्ठ *m.*
 Drinking the nectar of the lips. अधरपान *n.*
 Nectar of the lips. अधरामृत *n.* ओष्ठामृत *n.*
 Of blobber or large lips. ओठाळ.
 Red lips. बिंबाधर *m.*
 Smacking of the lips. मिटकी *f.* मिटका *m. v.* मार.
 Sticking together of the lips. मिटकी *f.* मिटका*m. v.* बस.
 To bite the lips at. दांतओठ*m.* खाणें-चावणें, दांताेंवणें, अधर *m.* चावणें-चावूनखाणें.
 To open one's lips. जीभ *f.*-ओठ *m.* हालवणें, जिव्हा *f.* [विटाळणें.
 To pass one's lips. तोंडावाटे-वाणीवाटे-ओठाबाहेर-&c. निघणें.
 To pollute one's lips. जिव्हा *f.* विटाळणें.
 2 (of a cup, &c.) v. EDGE. कांठ*m.* कड *f.*
To LIP. See To KISS.
LIP-DEVOTION, *n.* तोंडची भक्ति *f.* बरबर भक्ति *f.* बरची-बरपंगी-[&c. भक्ति *f.*
LIP-LABOUR, *n.* ओठापासूनचें बोलणें *n.* गळ्यावरचें बोलणें *n.* वरपंगी बोलणें *n.* वरकरणी बोलणें *n.*
LIP-WISDOM, *n.* तोंडचें ज्ञान *n.* हरदासी ज्ञान *n.*
LIPOTHYMY, *n.* v. FAINTING. मूर्च्छा *f.* मूर्च्छना *f.* ग्लीट *f.*
LIPPED, *a. having lips,* v. N. 1. ओठाचा, ओष्ठवान्, ओष्ठी, ओष्ठ (in comp. as भग्नोष्ठ, &c.).
 2—a vessel. वळलेले कांठाचा, वळींव कांठी, गलथेदार.
LIPPITUDE, *n. blearedness.* चिपडेपणा *m.*
LIQUABLE, LIQUEFIABLE, *a.* v. V. A. द्रव करायाजोगा-जोगता-&c. द्राव्य, द्रावणीय, द्रावणार्ह.
 v. V. N. द्रव व्हायाजोगा, &c. द्रवार्ह, गलनीय, सद्रव.
LIQUEFACTION, *n.* v. V. A.—*act.* द्रवविणें *n.* पाघळविणें *n.* &c. द्राव *m.* द्रावण *n.* द्रवीकरण *n.*—*state.* द्रवत्व *n.* द्रावितत्व *n.* द्रावितावस्था *f.*
LIQUEFIED, *p.* v. V. A. द्रववलेला, &c. द्रावित, द्रवीकृत.
 v. V. N. द्रवलेला, पाघळलेला &c. द्रुत.
To LIQUEFY, *v. a.* v. To MELT. द्रवविणें, पाघळविणें, रस *m.*-द्रव *m.*-&c. करणें *g. of o.* द्रावण *n.*-द्रवीकरण *n.* करणें *g. of o.*
To LIQUEFY, *v. n.* v. To MELT. द्रवणें, पाघळणें, पघळणें, सद्रव होणें, द्रव *m.* होणें *g. of s.*
LIQUESCENCY, *n. aptness to melt.* गलनशीलता *f.* गलनस्वभाव*m.*
LIQUESCENT, *a. melting.* द्रवणारा, सद्रव, द्रवमाण.
LIQUID, *n. liquor.* रस *m.* द्रवद्रव्य *n.* सद्रव पदार्थ *m.*
LIQUID, *a.* v. FLUID. सद्रव, द्रव, द्रवरूप, प्रवाही, प्रवाहधर्मक.
To LIQUIDATE, *v. a. pay off, discharge,* v. To CLEAR. फेडणें, झाडणें, वारणें, फडशा *m.*-&c. करणें *g. of. o.* अदा-फारीक-&c. करणें, फैसल करणें, ऋणशोधन *n.* करणें *g. of o.*
 To be liquidated. फिटणें.
LIQUIDATED, *p.* v. V. फेडलेला, &c. फारक, फारीक *or* फारीस, फिटंफाट, रफेदफे, अदाई, वारीद *or* वारीत.
LIQUIDATION, *n.* v. V.—*act.* फेडणें *n.* झाडणें *n.* &c. फेड *f.* फेडणी *f.* फेडणूक *f.* शोधन *n.*—*state.* फडशा *m.* बेबारा *m.* फैसल *m. f.* फैसला *m.* फीट *f.* फिटाफीट *f.* बेबाक *f.* झाडबाकी *f.* रफेदफे *f.* वारापाणी *n. f.*
 L. of debts, रदकर्ज *n.*
LIQUIDITY, LIQUIDNESS, *n.* v. A. सद्रवपणा *m.* द्रवत्व *n.* द्रवभाव *m.* रसता *f.* प्रवाहधर्म *m.*
LIQUOR, *n. fluid.* द्रवद्रव्य *n.* सद्रव पदार्थ *m.* रस *m.*
 2 v. DRINK. पेय *n.* पेयद्रव्य *n.*
 Drinker of spirituous, &c. l. मद्यपी, मद्यप.
 Spirituous or vinous l. दारू *f.* शराब *m.* मद *m.* मद्य *n.* मदिरा *f.* सुरा *f.* सीधु *f.*
LIQUOR-AMNII, *n. the waters.* पाणमोट *f.* पाणमोटली *f.* मोट *f.*
LIQUOR-SHOP, *n.* दारूचें दुकान *n.* दारूखाना *m.* मदिरागृह *n.*
To LISP, *v. a. speak with a whistling sound.* शीळ *or* शिवळ घालून बोलणें, भग्नदंतोच्चारण *n.* करणें.
LISP, LISPING, *n.* v. V. शिळीचें बोलणें *n.* भग्नदंतोच्चारण *n.*
LISPER, *n.* LISPING, *p. a.* v. V. शीळ घालून बोलणारा, भग्नदंतोच्चारण कर्त्ता, जडजिव्हेचा, जिव्हेचा जड, अस्फुटवाक्, लोहल.
LIST, *n. catalogue, roll.* फेरिस्त *n.* अनुक्रमानें याद *f.* नांवनिशीवार याद *or* यादी *f.* फर्द *m.* पट *m.* नांवनिशी *f.* टीप *f.*
 To run over a l. (of grievances). फाडा *m.* वाचणें.
 2 lists: *ground enclosed for combats, tilts, &c.* रंगांगण *n.* रंगण *n.* रंगभूमि *f.* मल्लभू *f.* अखाडा *m.*
 To enter the l. against. रंगणांत येणें.
 3 *strip of cloth.* धांद *f.* धांदोटी *f.* चिंधी *f.* चिंधोटी *f.* पट्टी *f.*
 4 *border of cloth.* बनातीचा कांठ *m.*
 5 *desire, liking.* इच्छा *f.* स्पृहा *f.* मन *n.*
To LIST, *v. n. desire, choose,* v. To LIKE. चाहणें *in. con.* आवडणें *in. con.* इच्छेस-मनास-मर्जीस-&c. येणें *in. con.*
 2 See To ENLIST.
To LIST, *v. a.* See To ENLIST. 2 See To LISTEN.
To LISTEN, *v. n. lend the ear.* ऐकणें, कान *m.* देणें-लावणें, लक्ष्य *n.* देणें-लावणें.
 2 (surreptitiously, privily, &c.). कानोसा *m.*-कानवा*m.*-कानव्हळा *m.*-सांचोल *m.*-सांचोला *m.*-&c. घेणें.
 3 *lend the mind ; heed, obey.* ऐकणें *g. of o.* मानणें, मन *n.* देणें-लावणें, मनावर घेणें.
LISTENER, *n.* LISTENING, *p. a.* v. V. 1. ऐकणारा, कान देणारा, &c. श्रवणकर्त्ता, श्रोता.
 2 कानोसा घेणारा, &c. कानोश्या, कानलाव्या, सांचोल्या.
LISTENING, *n.* v. V. 1.—*act.* ऐकणें *n.* &c. श्रवण *n.*
 2 कानोसा *m.* कानवा *m.* कानव्हळा *m.* सांचोल *m.* सांचोला *m.*
LISTLESS, *a. apathetic, indifferent, &c.* v. CARELESS. अनास्थ, अनुत्सुक, आस्थाहीन, उदास, उदासीन, निस्पृह, निरिच्छ.
 2 *indisposed to exertion,* v. LANGUID. मांदा, सुस्त, जड, अनवसान.
LISTLESSLY. See LANGUIDLY.
LISTLESSNESS, *n.* v. A. 1. अनास्था *f.* अनुत्साह *m.* अनुत्सुकता *f.* उदासपणा *m.* अनीहा *f.* अनिच्छा *f.* अननुराग *m.*
 2 *and* LANGUOR. मांदेपणा *m.* सुस्तपणा *m.* मांद्य *n.*
LITANY, *n.* प्रार्थनेची पद्धति आहे.
LITERAL, *a. following the letter.* मूलशब्दानुसारी, मूलशब्दानुया-

र्था, यथाशब्द, मूलपदानुसारी, अवयवार्थानुसारी.
2 *consisting of letters.* अक्षरी, अक्षरांचा.
3 *not figurative, &c.* मूलार्थक, मुख्यार्थक, शक्य.

LITERALLY, *adv.* v. A. 1. मूलशब्दाप्रमाणें, मूलशब्दानुसार, मूलशब्दानुरूप, यथामूलशब्द.
2 अक्षरांनीं, अक्षरशः.
3 मूलार्थाप्रमाणें, मूलार्थानुसार, मुख्यार्थानुसार.
L. and liberally. शब्दतः अर्थतः.

LITERARY, *a. pertaining to literature.* विद्येचा, विद्याविषयक, विद्यासंबंधी, विद्याप्रकरणाचा, विद्याप्रकरणसंबंधी.
2 *fond of literature, &c.* विद्याप्रिय, विद्यानुरागी, विद्याव्यसनी, विद्यालंपट, विद्याव्यवसायी.

LITERATE, *a. versed in sciences,* v. LEARNED. विद्वान्, विद्यासंपन्न, व्युत्पन्न, साक्षर, अक्षरस्थ.

LITERATI, *n. pl.* पंडितमंडळी *f.* विद्वत्समाज *m.* विद्वद्वृंद *n.*

LITERATURE, *n.* v. LEARNING. विद्या *f.* अक्षर *n.* पढणें *n.*
Branch of l. उपशास्त्र *n.*

LITHARGE, *n. semivitreous oxyd of lead.* मुडदारशिंग *or* शेंग *n.*

LITHE, LITHESOME, *a. limber,* v. PLIANT. लवचीक, लवका.

LITHENESS, *n.* v. A. लवचिकपणा *m.* लवकेपणा *m.*

To LITHOGRAPH, *v. a.* दगडी छापावर-शिळाछापावर छापणें.

LITHOGRAPH, *n.* शिळाछापावर-&c. छापलेलें चित्र *n.*-&c.

LITHOGRAPHY, *n.* शिळाछापाची विद्या *f.* दगडी छापाची विद्या *f.*

LITHOMARGE, *n.* सुफेद जहर मोहरा *m.*

LITHONTRIPTIC, *a. that dissolves the stone in the bladder.* मुतखडा दूरकरणारा, अश्मरीघ्न, अश्मरीहर, मूत्राश्मनाशक.

LITHOTOMY, *n.* मुतखडा काढणें *n.* मूत्राश्मोच्छेद *m.*

LITIGANT, *n. person engaged in a lawsuit.* खटलेकरी, वादी, वाद्या, वादकरणारा, विवादार्थी.

LITIGANT, *a. contending at law.* वादकरणारा, चाललेल्या वादाचा-खटल्याचा-&c. विवदमान, व्यवहारिक, व्यवहारी.

To LITIGATE, *v. a. contest at law.* खटलें *n.*-खटला *m.*-वाद *m.*-&c. करणें-उभाकरणें-सांगणें-घालणें-उपस्थित करणें.

LITIGATED, *p.* v. V. वादाचा, विवादाचा, &c. वादग्रस्त, वादानुगत, विवादानुगत. [वहार *m.*

LITIGATION, *n.* v. V.—*and* LAWSUIT. वाद *m.* विवाद *m* व्य-
That is under l. वादग्रस्त.

LITIGIOUS, *a. inclined to go to law.* खटलेखोर, विवादी, विवादशील, वादरत, विवादप्रिय, विवादप्रवण, विवादबुद्धि, लडथड्या.
2 *disputable.* वादाचा, विवादाचा.

LITIGIOUSNESS, *n.* v. A. 1. विवादासक्ति *f.* विवादप्रीति *f.* विवादबुद्धि *f.* वादबुद्धि *f.* [चंवरडोली *f.*

LITTER, *n. vehiculary bed.* डोली *f.* पाळणा *m.* महापा *or* माफा *m.*
2 *brood of young.* वीण *f.* वेत *n.* वीत *n.* खोप *f.*
3 *a birth of animals.* वेत *n.* वीण *f.* वीत *n.*
4 *bed of animals.* गवताची शेज *f.* तृणशय्या *f.*
5—*of things lying about.* पडझड *f.* अडगळ *f.* केर *m.* ऐचण *n.* पसारा *m.* विखरा *m.* गल्हाटा *or* ठा *m.* गळंगा *m.* पखरडा *m.* पखेडा *m.* उगाळ *f.* रेंद *f.* रेंदा *m.* राडा *m.* घाण *f.* पसळ *f.* पसळण *f.* गचपण *n.*

To LITTER, *v. a. bring forth.* विणें, प्रसवणें *pop.* पसवणें, वीत *n.*-वेत *n.* होणें *in. con.*
2 *cover with straw, &c.* गवत *n.* टाकणें-पसरणें, तृणास्तृत-आस्तृत तृण-स्तृण-&c. करणें.
3 (*a room, &c. by casting about*). पसारा *m.*-पखरडा *m.*-विखारा *m.*-रामायण *n.*-ऐचण *n.*-&c. करणें-करून टाकणें *g. of o.* विखरणें-पखरणें *or* विखरून-&c. टाकणें, भरून टाकणें.
4 *scatter, strew about disorderly.* विखरणें, पखरणें, पसारा *m.*-विखरा *m.*-पखरडा *m.* करणें-करून टाकणें *g. of o.*

LITTLE, *a. of small extent.* लहान, विस्तारानें लहान, अल्प, अल्पविस्तृत, अल्पविस्तार.
Somewhat l. लहानसर, अल्पस्वल्प.
2 *small, diminutive, short.* लहान, ठेंगा, ठेंगणा, लहानावळ, लहानाळ, आकाराचा-आकारानें लहान, मटगा, सखल, जामूण, गिड्डा, चिक्कर, चिघूर, लघु, तनु, बुटुकणा, किरकोळ, क्षुद्र, क्षुद्रक, क्षुल्लक, ऱ्हस्व, सूक्ष्म. Expressive of *littleness with neatness, little and comely, short and tight, dapper, &c.* some words are ठेंगणा ठुसका, ठेंगणा रेंगणा, चिमणा, चिमका, चिमकुला.
L. and stout. बेंडू.
Somewhat l. लहानसर, सखलवट.
3 *not much, not many.* थोडका, थोडा, कांहीं, अल्प, इवला, इलिसा, इवलासा, इवलिसा.
Very l. स्वल्प, अल्पाल्प, कळे न कळे इतका, कळे न कळेसा.
4 *of small dignity, importance, &c.* हलका, लहान, हलक्या किमतीचा, लहान किमतीचा, हलक्या योग्यतेचा, क्षुल्लक, क्षुद्र, लघु.
6 *some, not none.* कांहीं, कांहींबाहीं.

LITTLE, *adv. in a small quantity or degree.* अमळ, अमळसा *decl.* जरासा *decl.* थोडा *decl.* जरा, जराकसा *decl.* जराक, इवला-इलिसा-विलासा-इवलिसा *all decl.* कांहीं, कांहींसा *decl.* थोडासा *decl.* किंचित्, यत्किंचित्, ईषत् in comp. अल्पशः.

LITTLE, *n. small space.* थोडकी जागा *f.* थोडा-थोडका (used with the noun required).
In a l. *in a short time or space.* थोडक्यांत.
2 *small part, proportion, or quantity.* थोडा अंश *m.* अल्पांश *m.* अल्पमात्र *n.* मात्रा *f.* किंचिदंश *m.*
By l. and l. *in small quantity at a time.* थोडथोडा, थोडथोडका, थोडाथोडा, थोडकाथोडका-&c. *all decl.* तीळतीळ.
3 *slight affair.* थोडीगोष्ट *f.* हलकीगोष्ट *f.* क्षुद्रगोष्ट *f.* &c.

LITTLENESS, *n.* v. A. 1. लहानपणा *m.* लहानवी *f.* अल्पत्व *n.* अल्पविस्तार *m.*
2 लहानवी *f.* लहानपणा *m.* ठेंगणेपणा *m.* &c. लघुता *f.* &c. लाघव *n.* लघिमा *m.* सौक्ष्म्य *n.*
3 थोडकेपणा *m.* थोडेपणा *m.* &c.
4 लहानपणा *m.* हलकेपणा *m.* हलकीकिम्मत *f.* हलकीयोग्यता *f.* लघुत्व *n.* लाघव *n.* [तीरस्थ.

LITTORAL, *a. belonging to the shore.* थडीचा, तडीचा, तटस्थ,

LITURGICAL, *a.* v. N. समाजप्रार्थनापद्धतिसंबंधी-विषयक-रूप-&c.

LITURGY, *n. formulary of public prayers.* समाजप्रार्थनापद्धति *f.* समाजभजनपद्धति *f.* सामाजिकभक्तिपद्धति *f.*

To LIVE, *v. n. be in animation.* जिणें, जिवणें *or* जीवणें, चेतणें, सजीव-जीवंत *or* जिवंत-&c. असणें, जीवनदशेंत-जीवनावस्थेंत-&c. असणें, जीवनदशा *f.*-&c. असणें *g. of s.*
2 *pass life.* वागणें, वापरणें, वावरणें, नांदणें, वर्त्तणें, राबणें, संसरणें, दिवसलोट *m.*-दिवसलोटी *f.* करणें.
To l. in style. शान *f.*-दूम *f.*-चमचमाट *m.* करणें.

To l. securely and happily. रामराज्य *n.* करणें.

3 *continue in life.* वांचणें, जगणें.

I will not live. मी प्राण ठेवणार नाहीं.

If we live and meet again. ह्यात मुलाखत असली तर.

4 *be subsisted or maintained.* उदरनिर्वाह*m.*-निर्वाह*m.*-प्रपंचनिर्वाह*m.*-गुजराण *f.*-गुजारा*m.*-रोजगुजारा*m.*-रोजगुजराण *f.*-&c. करणें, प्रपंच*m.*-संसार*m.*-प्रपंचनिर्वाह*m.*-उपजीविका *f.*-उपजीवन *n.*-दिनचर्या*f.*-रोजी *f.*-पोटाचें *n.*-पोटापाण्याचें *n.*-रोजकीर्द *f.*- &c. चालवणें, *or with g. of s.* चालणें. [करणें.

5 upon; See To Feed. 6. v. To Dwell. राहणें, वस्ती *f.*

7 through or out. वांचणें, जगणें.

Live. See Living.

Livelihood, *n. subsistence, support of life, living.* उपजीविका *f.* उपजीवन*n.* गुजारा*m.* गुजराण *f.* उदरनिर्वाह*m.* प्रपंचनिर्वाह*m.* निर्वाह*m.* चरितार्थ*m.* जिनगी*f.* जिनगाणी *f.* जिंदगी *f.* जगणूक*f.* जीवन*n.* जीविका *f.* प्राणधारण*n.* प्राणजीवन*n.* वर्त्तन*n.*

Bare or mere l. *shifting with a pittance.* गुजारा*m.* गुजराण *f.* गुजर*m.* दिनचर्या *f.* दिननिर्वाह*m.*

To have or get a l. पोट *n.*-पोटाचें *n.*-पोटापाण्याचें-&c. चालणें *g. of s.* भाजी भाकर *f.* मिळणें *in. con.* तोंडीं घास*m.* येणें *g. of s.*

2 *means of subsistence, maintenance, living.* उपजीविका *f.* उपजीव्य*n.* पोटगी *f.* पोटस्त*n.* पोटस्थ*n.* अन्नपाणी*n.* दाणापाणी*n.* आटापाणी*n.* अन्नोदक*n.* शेर*m.* भाकर *f.* पांचशेरी *or* पासेरी *f.* जिंदगी *f.* जिनगी *f.* जिनगाणी *f.* जीवनोपाय*m.* जीवनसाधन*n.* उपजीवनसाधन*n.* जीवनार्थ*m.* वृत्ति *f.* जीवनवृत्ति *f.*

Bare or scanty l. *mere pittance.* अर्धीभाकर *f.* अर्धीकोर *f.* अर्धी नितकोर *f.* अर्धीचतकोर *f.* ग्रासाच्छादन*n.* अन्नाच्छादन*n.*

To take away the l. of. पोटावर पाय*m.* देणें, अन्नांत माती *f.* कालवणें-घालणें, अन्नावर पाणी*n.* घालणें.

Live-coal, *n.* इंगळ *or* इंगोळ*m.* इंगळा*m.* निखारा*m.* जिवंत कोळसा *or* जित कोळसा *or* जिता कोळसा*m.*

Live-stock, *n. cattle, &c.* जीवधन *n.*चर्मधन *n.* [चपळाई *f.*

Liveliness, *n.* v. A. l. जिवटपणा*m.* जिवसपणा*m.* &c. हुशारी*f.*

2 आनंदीपणा*m.* आनंदवृत्ति *f.* उल्लासवृत्ति *f.* आनंदिता *f.*

4 दणदणितपणा*m.* &c. रंग*m.* रोशनाई *f.*

Livelong, *a. long in passing, tedious.* लांबणीचा, चेंगट, बारा प्रहरांचा, दीर्घकालाचा, दीर्घकाल, दीर्घकालिक.

Lively, *a. vivacious, vigorous.* जिवट, जिवस, जीवदार, रगदार, रग्या, रगेल, हुशार, खबरदार, चपळा.

2 *sprightly, gay, blithe, buxom,* v. Merry. आनंदी, उल्लासी, आल्हादी, रंगदार, रंगी, आनंदवृत्ति, उल्लासवृत्ति, हास्यमुख, हास्यवदन, खुशदिल, खुशालीचा.

3 *representing life.* हुबहूचा, खऱ्याखुऱ्यासारखा, जशाचा तसा, सत्याभासी, तत्प्रतिरूपक, प्रत्यक्षसदृश, प्रत्यक्षप्राय.

4 *noisy, animated, &c.*—of entertainments, &c. v. Merry. दणदणीत, दणक्याचा, कडकडीत, रोशनाईचा, रंगाचा.

5 *swarming, full of bustle*—house, town, &c. गजगजीत, गजबजीत.

To be l. गजगजणें, गजबजणें.

Liver, *n.* Living, *p. a.* v. V. l. जिणारा, &c. जिता, जीवंत *or* जिवंत, सजीव, जीवदार, सप्राण, जिवा, जीवित, चेतित, प्राणमय, जीवमय, सचेष्ट, चेतन, जीवभूत, आयुष्मान्, भवी.

2 वर्ती (in comp. as सद्वर्ती virtuous liver, कुवर्ती ill-liver, &c.).

4 उपजीवी, उपजीवक, जीवी, जीव (all in comp. as कृष्युपजीवी that lives by agriculture, विद्योपजीवी that lives by science, शस्त्रोपजीवी & शस्त्राजीव that lives by arms, &c.).

I. *vigorous, strong, &c.* v. Lively. जीवदार, जिवट, बळकट, सुदृढ.

II. *running, not stagnant.* जिता, जिवंत *or* जीवंत, जितासु.

Liver, *n.—the organ.* काळीज*n.* यकृत्*m.n.* पित्ताशय*m.* काळखंड*n.*

Chronic complaint of the l. यकृत्गुल्म *m. n.*

Enlargement of the l.—a disease of children. डबा *m.*

Inflammation of the l. यकृत् *m. n.* जरंडी *f.*

Liver-color, *a.* काळिजाच्या रंगाचा, यकृद्वर्ण.

Liverwort, *n.*—Indian. ऐरण भैरण *f.*

Livery, *n. particular or appropriate dress.* पेहरावा *or* पैरावा *m.* पेहराव *or* पैराव *m.* वेष *m.* लिभास *m.* बाणा *m.* [-&c.

2 *appropriate dress of servants.* चाकरांचा बाणा *m.*-पैराव *m.*

Liverystable, *n. stable in which horses are kept for hire.* घोड्यांचा अड्डा *m.*

2 *stable in wich horses are fed at a certain rate.* ज्यांत घोडे राखणीस असतात असा तबेला *m.*

Livid, *a. black and blue.* हिरवानिळा, हिरवा पिवळा, काळा निळा, काळवटलेला, उफट, ओफट, काळवटीचा, &c.

Lividity, Lividness, *n.* v. A. हिरवे निळेपणा *m.* काळेनिळेपणा *m.* &c. काळवटी *f.* काळवंडी *f.* काळवण *f.* कालिमा *m.* मडेकळा *f.* प्रेतकळा *or* कळा *f.* [चलनवलन *n.* चेष्टा *f.*

Living, *n.* v. V. 1. जिणें *n.* &c. जिणी *f.* प्राणधारण *n.* जीवन *n.*

2 वागणें *n.* &c. वाग *f.* वागणूक *f.* नांदणूक *f.* वर्त्तणूक *f.* वर्त्तन*n.*

3 वांचणें *n.* जगणें *n.* जगणूक *f.* वांचणूक *f.*

4 उदरनिर्वाह *n.* प्रपंचनिर्वाह *m.* गुजारा *m.* गुजराण *f.* जिंदगी *f.* जिनगानी *or* णी *f.* जिनगी *f.* उपजीविका *f.* उपजीवन. (also in comp. as विद्योपजीवन living by learning, कृष्युपजीवन living by husbandry, &c.).

I. *means of living,* v. Livelihood. उपजीविका *f.* उपजीवन*n.* उपजीव्य *n.* जीवन *n.* वृत्ति *f.*

That has a l. वृत्तिवंत, वृत्तिमान्.

To devour or waste the l. of. घर *n.* धुणें.

Good l. *rich fare.* खुराक *m.* रतीब *m.* रातब *m.* खिरीपुरी *f.*

Lixivial, *a.* v. N. खारवण्याचा, क्षारविशिष्ट.

Lixivium, *n. lye.* खारेंपाणी *n.* खारवणी *n.*

Lizard, *n.* Some kinds are, चोपई *f.* धापट *m.* सरड *or* सरडा *m.* सरडी *f.* गणपत *f.* पल्लि *pop.* पाल *f.* (house lizard), घोरपड *f.* (ignuana), सापसुरळी *f.* विसाप *m.*

Cry of the house l. चुकचूक *f.*

To utter its cry—the house l. चुकचुकणें.

Lo, *interj.* पहा, पहा बरें.

Load, *n. burden, freight.* ओझें *n.* भरगत *n.* भरीन *n.* भरताड *f.* *n.* हेल *m. f.* बोजा *or* बोझा *m.* भार *m.* लादणी *f.* [झें *n.*

A tight (i. e. large and heavy) l. ताठ ओझें *n.* ताठर ओ-

Bullock or horse-l. (of fuel, fodder, &c.). कबाड *n.*

Fit for or employed in bringing loads, (of fuel, &c.) —a bullock. कबाडा *or* कबाड्या.

Half (or side) of a bullock or horse l. आखें *n.*

L. to be carried on the head. डोई ओझें *n.*

L. of grass, &c. पेंडका *m.* भारा *m.* बरंड *f.* विरड *f.*

L. carried by men pressed. पेंड *m.*—The carrier of it. पेंडाऱ्या. [कस *m.*

Rope with which to confine a l. on a beast, &c. भार-

2 See BUNDLE. 3 fig. (of cares, &c.). ओझें *n.* भार *m.* गोण *f.* गोणी *f.* धोंड *f.* लकडा *m.*

To relieve one's mind of a l. जिवावरचें अधण *n.* उतरणें.

4—of a gun, &c. *charge.* बार *m.* पेट *m.*

To LOAD, *v. a. lade, freight.* लादणें, ओझें *n.*-भरगत *f.*-भरीत *n.*-&c. भरणें-घालणें-ठेवणें-टाकणें, लादणी *f.* करणें *g. of o.* भरणें, भर *f.*-भरती *f.*-भरताड *f.*-&c. करणें *g. of o.*

2 *encumber, burden.* लादणें, ओझें *n.*-भार *m.*-&c. घालणें-लादणें, भारग्रस्त-भाराक्रांत-&c. करणें.

3 (a gun, &c.). भरणें, बार *m.* भरणें.

LOADED, *p.* v. V. 1. लादलेला, भरलेला, &c. भारवान्.

2 लादलेला, भारग्रस्त, भाराक्रांत, भारपीडित.

3 भरलेला, बारभरलेला.

LOADER, *n.* v. V. 1. लादणारा, भरणारा, &c. लाद्या.

LOADING, *n.* v. V. 1.—*act.* लादणें *n.* भरणें *n.* लादणी *f.* भरती *f.*

I. See FREIGHT, LOAD. [*m.* अयस्कांत *m.*

LOAD-STONE, *n.* लोहचुंबक *m.* चुंबक *m.* चुंबकमणि *m.* लोहकांत

LOAF, *n.* v. BREAD. पांव *m.* रोट *m.* रोटी *f.*

LOAFER, *n. idle vagrant sponger.* तुकड्या, आगंतुक्या, उंडीउकल्या, उंडी बकाल.

LOAM, *n.*—the earth. चिकणमाती *f.* लुकणीमाती *f.*

LOAMY, *a.* v. N. चिकण, चिकणमातीचा.

LOAN, *n. thing lent or borrowed.* उसना-उसनवार दिल्हेला *or* घेतलेला-मागून घेतलेला-&c. डागिना *m.*-पदार्थ *m.*-विषय *m.*-वस्त *f.*-&c. उसनें *n.*

2 *state of being lent.* उसनवारी *f.* उसनवट *f.*

On l. उसनवार, उसनवट, उसनवारी. [पासनें.

By way of loan. जायां, जायांस, उसन्यानें, उसनें, उसनें-

3 (of money on interest), v. DEBT. कर्ज *n.* ऋण *n.* व्याजीं दिल्हेला-घेतलेला-&c. पैका *m.*-&c.

To LOAN. See To LEND.

LOATH, *a. averse, reluctant,* v. UNWILLING. नाराजी, नाखूश, पराङ्मुख, विमत, विमुख, रंजीस.

To LOATHE, *v. a. abominate, detest,* v. To ABHOR. अतिद्वेष *m.*-अतिद्वेषण *n.*-&c. करणें, ओंगळ-ओखटा-&c. मानणें, विष मानणें.

2 *be disgusted with, be tired of.* कंटाळणें, उचाटणें, विटणें, किळसणें, त्रासणें, खंतावणें, ओकणें, बेतागणें, उबगणें, संतापणें, विटणें *with g. of o. and* सीं *of s.* कंटाळा *m.*-किळस *m. f.*-चिळस *f.*-वीट *m.*-ओकारा *m.*-ओकारी *f.*-त्रास *m.*-&c. येणें *in. con. & g. of o.*

LOATHING, *n.* v. V. 1.—*act.* अतिद्वेषण *n.* अतिद्वेष *m.*

2 *and* DISGUST. कंटाळा *m.* वीट *m.* चिळस *f.* किळस *f.* उचाट *m.* ओकारा *m.* उच्छाद *m.* खंत *f.* विषाद *m.*

LOATHENESS, *n.* v. A. नाखुशी *f.* विमति *f.* विमुखता *f.*

LOATHESOME, *a.* v. DISGUSTING, HATEFUL. कंटाळवाणा, चिळसवाणा, किळसवाणा, ओंगळ, ओखटा, घाणेरडा, घाणेरा, घाणेला, कुत्सित.

LOATHSOMENESS, *n.* v. A. ओंगळपणा *m.* ओखटेपणा *m.* घाणेरडेपणा *m.* &c. कौत्सित्य *n.* कुत्सितभाव *m.*

LOBBY, *n. ante-room, passage, &c.* ढेलज *or* ढेलेज *f.* ओटी *f.* देवडी *or* ढी *f.* ओसरी *f.* सदरेची पुढची खोली *f.*

LOBCOCK, LOB, *n. heavy, sluggish person,* v. LUBBER. मठ्या, भैंद, लाधेडा, लाधा.

LOBE, *n. division of the lungs.* फुफुसाचा भाग *m.*

2 (of the ear). कानाचा चापा *m.* कानाचें चापें *n.*

LOBSTER, *n.* समुद्रांतला खेंकडा *m.*

LOCAL, *a. relating, &c. to a place.* स्थानाचा *or* स्थानचा, देशाचा *or* देशचा, स्थानसंबंधीचा, देशसंबंधी, देशसंबंधक, स्थानसंबंधी, स्थानीय, देश्य, स्थानिक, देश *in comp.* स्थान *in comp.*

2 *limited to a particular place, topical.* एकदेशी, एकदेशीय, एकस्थानिक, विशेषस्थानिक, एकस्थानस्थ.

LOCALITY, *n.* v. A. 1. देशसंबंध *m.* स्थानसंबंध *m.* देशता *f.* स्थानता *f.* देशभाव *m.*

I. *position, situation,* v. PLACE. जागा *f.* स्थान *n.*

LOCALLY, *adv.* v. A. 1. देशाविषयीं, स्थानाविषयीं, &c. स्थानसंबंधानें, देशसंबंधानें.

To LOCATE, *v. a.* v. To PLACE. ठेवणें, बसवणें, वसवणें, स्थान *n.*-स्थिति *f.*-अवस्थान *n.*-&c. करणें *g. of o.*

LOCATED, *p.* v. V. ठेवलेला, बसवलेला, वसवलेला, वसलेला, &c. स्थित, स्थानस्थित, अवस्थित.

LOCATION, *n.* v. V.—*act.* ठेवणें *n.* बसवणें *n.* &c.

I. v. SITUATION. जागा *f.* स्थान *n.* अवस्थान *n.* स्थिति *f.*

II.—in grammar. अधिकरण *n.*

LOCH. See LAKE.

LOCK, *n.*—for a door, box, &c. कुलूप *n.* टाळें *n.* ताला *m.* तालक *n.* तालयंत्र *n.* N. B. All these words mean Padlock as well as Lock. When a distinction is wanted, the word आंगचें *or* पेटीचें is prefixed to signify a lock not a padlock.

Handle of a door l. फिरकी *f.*

Tongue or bolt of a l. or padlock. कांटा *m.*

To put by under double l. and key. सात गांठी देऊन ठेवणें, साता गांठी पलीकडे ठेवणें.

2 (as of a joint) *articulation.* खीळ *f.* (as कोपराची-मणगटाची-&c. खीळ), चाळा *m.*

3 (of a gun). चाप *m.*

That has a l.—a gun. चापी.

4 *hug, grapple.* पकड *f.* पेच *m.* डाव *m.*

5 (of hair). केशाचा झुबका *m.*-झुमका *m.*-बुचका *m.*-जुडगा *m.*-&c.

Curly l. झुलूप *n.*

Dishevelled and dirty l. केसटी *f.* केसुरडी *f.*

Matted or clotted l. बट *f.* जट *f.* जटा *f.*

Mass of matted locks tufted on the crown. जटाभार *m.*

Side l. (left when the head is first shaved). काकपक्ष *m.* शिखंड *m.*

Tuft or l. left on the crown at tonsure. शेंडी *f.*

6 (of wool, &c.). लोंकरीचा झुबका *m.*

7 (for a wheel, &c.) उटाळें *n.* उटी *f.* ऊट *f.* अडकण *n.*

To LOCK, *v. a. fasten with a lock.* कुलूप *n.* लावणें-करणें-मारणें, ताला *m.*-टाळें *n.* देणें-मारणें, किली कुलूप *n.* करणें-लावणें, किली *f.* करणें, ताला-&c. फिरवून बंद करणें.

2 *shut up by locking in.* कुलपांत-टाळयांत-किलींत ठेवणें, कुलूप-&c. लावून-देऊन बंद करणें.

3 (in the arms) v. To EMBRACE. अवटाळणें, कंबटाळणें.

To LOCK, *v. n. unite by mutual insertion.* एकमेकांत लागून गुंतणें, एकमेकांत लागून जुडणें.

LOCKED, *p.* v. V. A. 1. कुलूप लावलेला, &c.

2 कुलपांत ठेवलेला, &c.

L. jaw. दांतखीळी *f.* दांत खीळ *f. v.* बस.

LOCKER, *n.* v. DRAWER. खण *m.*

L. of a boat. पयाळ *f.* [लूपबंदी *f.*

LOCKING, *n.* v. V. A. 1. कुलूप लावणें *n.* &c. कुलूपलावणी *f.* कु-

LOCKET, *n.* v. CATCH. फांसा *m.* अडकवण *n.* मुदन *f. n.* मुदनी *f.*

LOCKSMITH, *n.* लोहार, करजकर *or* करचकर.

LOCK UP, *n.* कोंडी *f.*

LOCOMOTION, *n. act of moving from place to place.* एका जागेंतून दुसऱ्या जागेंत जाणें *n.* स्थानांतरगमन *n.* स्थलांतरगमन *n.* स्थानांतरकरण *n.* स्थलांतर करण *n.* स्थानांतर *n.* स्थलांतर *n.*

2 *the power of moving from place to place.* एकेजागेंतून दुसऱ्या जागेंत जाण्याची शक्ति *f.* स्थानांतरगमनशक्ति *f.* स्थलांतर करणशक्ति *f.* &c. चलनशक्ति *f.* गमनशक्ति *f.*

LOCOMOTIVE, *a. having the power of motion.* चलनशक्तिक, चलनधर्मक, चलनशील, चर, चल, चरिष्णु, जंगम.

LOCUM-TENENS, *n. deputy, &c.* प्रतिनिधि, मुतालीक.

LOCUST, *n.* टोळ *m.* शलभ *m.* शरभ *m.* The species denominated gryllus crestatus, gryllus erridissimus, &c. bear the general names नाकतोडा *or* तोडया *m.* गवताचा उंट *m.*

Attack of locusts. टोळधाड *f.* टोळक्रांत *f.* टोळक्रांति *f.*

Depredations of locusts. टोळखाद *f.*

Swarms of locusts. टोळी *f.*

LODE, *n. metallic vein.* धातुरेषा *f.*

To LODGE, *v. a. house temporarily.* बिऱ्हाड *n.* देणें, जागा *m.f.*-ठाव *m.*-स्थान *n.*-&c. देणें.

2 *plant, place, fix, set.* बसवणें, वसवणें, ठेवणें, घालणें, लावणें, स्थापणें, स्थापना *f.*-न्यास *m.*-&c. करणें. *g. of o.* न्यस्त-&c. करणें.

To LODGE, *v. n. reside temporarily.* बिऱ्हाड *n.* करणें-देणें-लावणें, राहणें, जागा *m. f.*-स्थल *pop.* स्थळ *n.*-मुकाम *m.*-&c. करणें.

2 *lie, rest, sit, remain, stay.* बसणें, राहणें, पडणें, धारणें, धारावणें, थिरावणें, स्थिरावणें, स्थावरणें, घर *n.* घेणें-करणें, थारा *m.*-&c. धरणें.

LODGE, *n.* See HOUSE, HUT.

LODGER, *n.* LODGING, *p. a.* v. V. N. 1. बिऱ्हाड करणारा, &c. बिऱ्हाडकरी, बिऱ्हाडकरू, बिऱ्हाडू, वसतकरू, वस्तीकरू.

I. *one who hires a room, &c. in the house of another.* भाडोत्री, भाडेकरी, बिऱ्हाडकरू, बिऱ्हाडू, बिऱ्हाडकरी.

LODGING, *n.* See LODGMENT. 2 *temporary habitation.* बिऱ्हाड *n.* मुकाम *m. n.* उतारघर *n.*

L.-expenses. बिऱ्हाडखर्च *m.*

Residence in a l. बिऱ्हाड *n.* [तळशोधणी *f.*

Search of a l. on leaving it. तळझाडा *m.* स्थलशुद्धि *f.*

To make a l. घर *n.* करणें-घेणें.

LODGMENT, *n.* v. V. A. 2.—*act.* बसवणें *n.* स्थापणें *n.* &c. स्थापन *n.* संस्थापन *n.* संस्थापना *f.*—*state.* संस्थिति *f.* स्थिति *f.*

LOFT, *n. upper room or floor.* माडी *f.* माळा *m.* माळूचें *n.* माळोंचा *m.*

LOFTILY. See PROUDLY.

LOFTINESS, *n.* v. A. 1. उंचपणा *m.* उंची *f.* [गरूरी *f.*

2 *and* PRIDE. गर्व *m.* अभिमान *m.* ताठा *m.* आढ्यता *f.* म-

3 मोठेपणा *m.* प्रौढी *f.* प्राशस्त्य *n.*

LOFTY, *a. high.* उंच.

2 *haughty.* v. PROUD. गर्वी, अभिमानी, मानी, चढेल, वरडोळ्या, ऊर्ध्वदृष्टि, उन्नतशिरा.

3 *elevated, exalted, sublime.* थोरपणाचा, थोरवीचा, मोठेपणाचा, उंच, प्रशस्त, प्रौढ, प्रौढविषयात्मक.

LOG, *n. shapeless piece of wood.* कोंडका *m.* कोंडकें *n.* करंडा *m.* करंडें *n.* ढोण *n.* ढोणकूर *n.* ढोणप *n.* टोणी *f.* टोणकें *n.* टोटकें *n.* ओंडा *m.* ओंडी *f.* भिंतळा *m.* फांटें *n.* फोड *f.* दुकांड *f.* उसळपा *or* सळपा *m.*

Logs cleft for fuel. फिटा *m.*

A pile of fuel logs. औट *m.*

2 (of a ship). गलबताची-&c. गति मापण्याचें यंत्र *n.* नौकागतिमापक यंत्र *n.*

3 logbook. गलबताचा-&c. रोजनामा *m.*

4 *sluggard, &c.* आर, मठ्या, मैंद, ढोण *n.* ढोण्या, ढोणसकड *n.* आळसभोंडारा. Some terms for a man lying senseless or helpless *like a log* are, गठडी *f.* मोट *f.* मोधागोळा *m.* गोळा *m.*

LOGARITHM, *n.* The English word is used as लाग्रतम *n.*

LOGGERHEAD, *n. dolt, blockhead, &c.* v. FOOL. माठ्या, ढोण्या, टोणपा, टोणपशुद्ध, टोणपनाथ *m.* टोणपेश्वर *m.* शाहण्यांची खरवड *f.* गाढवाचाखरारा *m.* अक्कलेचागधडा *m.*

To fall or go to loggerheads. हातघाईवर-लातबुकीवर-झोटधरणीवर-मारकुटीवर-&c. येणें.

LOGGISH, *a. heavy, dull, &c.* v. STUPID. मठ, माठ्या, ढोण्या.

LOGIC, *n. art of reasoning.* तर्क *m.* न्याय *m.* तर्कशास्त्र *n.* तर्कविद्या *f.* न्यायशास्त्र *n.* निरूह *m.* Some of the terms of *Logic* are अतिव्याप्ति *f.* (over extension or comprehension—of a definition), अव्याप्ति *f.* (under extension or comprehension—of a definition), अभिव्याप्ति *f.* (universal extension or comprehension—of a definition), अव्याप्यवृत्ति *f.* (peculiarity—of application or existence), उत्थाप्याकांक्षा, उपलप्रक्षेप, कैमर्थ्य, प्रवृत्तिनिमित्त, प्रसक्ति, व्याप्य, व्याप्यकोटि, व्यासज्यवृत्ति, सिद्धसाधनदोष.

Logical acumen. तार्किक्य *pop.* तार्किक *n.*

LOGICAL, *a. relating, &c. to logic.* तर्कविद्येचा, तर्कशास्त्राचा, तर्कविद्यासंबंधी, तर्कविद्याविषयक, तर्कशास्त्रविषयक, तार्किक.

2 *skilled in logic.* तर्की, तर्कबाज, तार्किक, तर्कविद्यावेत्ता, तर्कविद्याप्रवीण, तर्कशास्त्रज्ञ.

3 *according to the rules of logic.* तर्कशास्त्रशुद्ध, तर्कशास्त्रसिद्ध, न्यायशास्त्रशुद्ध, न्यायशास्त्रसिद्ध, तर्कशास्त्रसम्मत, न्यायशास्त्रसम्मत. [शास्त्राचे बलानें.

LOGICALLY, *adv.* v. A. 1. तर्कशास्त्रानुसार, तर्कशास्त्रानुरूप, तर्क-

LOGICIAN, *n. person skilled in logic.* तर्की, तर्कबाज, तार्किक, तर्कशास्त्री, न्यायशास्त्री, तर्कविद्यावेत्ता, नैयायिक.

A mere l. केवलनैयायिक. [शब्दयुद्ध *n.*

LOGOMACHY, *n. dispute about words.* शब्दवाद *m.* शब्दविवाद *m.*

LOGWOOD, *n.* पतंग *m.* ?

LOIN, LOINS, *n.*—the part of the body. कमर *f.* माजाड *n.*

कास *f.* कटिदेश *m.* कटितट*n.* कटि *f.*—contemptuously. पेकट *or* पेंकट *m.* पेकाड *n.* पेगट *n.*

Cloth worn round the l. covering the privities. लंगोटी *f.*

Cloth-girdle for the l. कांचा *m.* पंचा *m.*—of a short and narrow size. गज्या *or* गज्जा *m.* गजवें *or* गज्जें *n.*

Cord or chain (of silk, silver,&c.) worn round the l. कडदोरा *m.* कटदोरा *m.* करगोटा *m.* करदोडा *or* रा *m.* करधोटा or डा *m.* कटिसूत्र *n.*

Girding up the l. कमरबंदी *f.* कमरबस्ता *m.*

Of girded l. बांधल्या कमरेचा, कमरबंद.

Of the l. of. पोटचा.

Sprung from one's own l. अंगज.

Strained in the l.—horse, camel, &c. कमरी.

To gird up one's l. कमर *f.* बांधणें, कांचा *m.* भिडवणें-पिटणें, कास *f.* घालणें.

To spring from the l. of. पोटीं जन्मणें *g. of s.*

To LOITER, *v. n. linger, be slow in progress,* v. To DAWDLE. चालतांना रेंगणें-रेंगळणें-खेळणें-&c. गमणें, रमणें, रमतरमत-रमतेरमते-&c. चालणें, चेंगटाई *f.*-&c. करणें, गमटम *f.* मांडणें-करणें.

To LOITER, (away), *v. a. waste by loitering.* खेळण्याखालीं-गमण्याखालीं-&c. घालवणें-दवडणें.

LOITERER, *n.* LOITERING, *p. a.* v. V. N. चालतांना रेंगणारा, गमणारा, &c. गमदसडा *or* गमदासडा *or* गमदासरा, गम्या, चेंगट, खेळगड्या. [गटाई *f.* गमटम *f.*

LOITERING, *n.* v. V. N. गमणें *n.* &c. जोगवण *f.* जोगवणी *f.* चें-

LOITERINGLY, *adv.* v. A. रमतरमत, रमतेरमते.

To LOLL, *v. n. lean lazily, &c.* आळसी होऊन-आळसत-आळसानें-&c. पडणें-टेंकणें-आंग *n.* टाकणें.

2—as the tongue, &c. लळलळणें, लवलळ *adv.* करणें.

To LOLL, *v. a. thrust out*—the tongue. काढणें, बाहेर काढणें, लळलळीत करणें.

LOLLING, *n.* v. V. N. 1. आळसानें आंग टाकणें *n.*

L. and languishing—as indicative of the tender passion. ललित *n.* लालित्य *n.*

LONE, LONELY, *a. solitary, unfrequented.* आडवळणी, आडवळणाचा, बिनराबत्याचा, गैरराबत्याचा, बिनवहिवाटीचा, निर्जन, विजन, न्यूनसंचार, हीनसंचार, विविक्त.

2 *single, sole.* एकला, एकटा, एकाकी, असंग, असहाय, सडा.

3 *addicted to solitude.* एकलकोंडा, एकलकोट, एकांतप्रिय, एकांतसेवी, विविक्तसेवी.

4—in feeling. उदास.

To feel l. उदास वाटणें.

LONELINESS, LONENESS, *n.* v. A. 1. आडवळणीपणा *m.* &c. निर्जनता *f.* विजनता *f.* विविक्तता *f.* संचारन्यूनता *f.* संचारहीनता *f.*

2 एकलेपणा *m.* एकटेपणा *m.* सडेपणा *m.* असंगता *f.*

3 एकलकोंडेपणा *m.* एकांतप्रीति *f.* एकांतरुचि *f.* एकांतभक्ति *f.*

LONESOME, *a. dismal from solitariness.* उदास, भणभणीत, भयाण *or* न.

LONESOMENESS, *n.* v. A. उदासपणा *m.* भणभणितपणा *m.* भणभणाट *m.* भणाण *m.* असकड *n.*

LONG, *a.*—of time or space. लांब, लांबणीचा, लांबीचा, दीर्घ, लंब, लंबायमान, आयत.

Longish. लांबट, लांबसर.

Very l. लांबचलांब, लांबचेलांब, लंबचेड, लंबछोड.

In the l. run. परिणामीं, शेवटीं, आखेरीस.

2—of space. लांब, लांबीचा, लांबणीचा. To express the idea of *tediously long, wearily long,* the word म्हसर is used with certain nouns, as, म्हसरमैदान *n.* म्हसररान, म्हसर रस्ता, &c. &c.

Gracefully tall or l. लांबलचक *or* का.

3—of time. लांब, फार, पुष्कळ.

4 *not soon ceasing.* लांब, लांबणीचा, फार वेळचा, बहूत काळचा, दीर्घकालिक, चिरकालिक.

5 v. DILATORY. दिरंग्या, उशिऱ्या, उशीरलाव्या, चेंगट, विलंबकारी, विलंबी, दीर्घसूत्री.

6 v. TEDIOUS. लांबणीचा, लांबलेला, चेंगट, चेंगटाईचा.

7—a vowel, &c. दीर्घ, गुरु.

LONG, *adv. to a great extent in space.* लांब, दूर, दूरवर, लांबवर.

2 *to or from a great extent in time.* बहूत काळ, बहूत काळापासून, बहूत काळपर्यंत, चिरकाल, बहुकाल, फार वेळपर्यंत-पावेतों-वर, फार वेळापासून, फार वेळानें,—as used restrictedly to a time within the passing day. वाटकोळ, वाढोळ, वाढवेळ, वाटकोळचा *decl.* वाढोळचा *decl.* [वर.

3 *throughout, through the duration of.* भर, पर्यंत, पावेतों,

As l. as. जंव *or* जों, जोंपर्यंत, जेथ *or* जिथवर, जेथ *or* जिथपर्यंत, जेथ *or* जिथपावेतों, जेढवळ, जेढोळ, जावत्, जावत्काल. [अचिर, अचिरात्.

Ere l. थोडक्या काळांत, थोडक्या दिवसांत, थोडके वेळेंत,

How l. कोठवर, कोठपर्यंत, कोठपावेतों.

L. ago. बहूत काळ झाला, फार दिवस झाले, बहूत वर्षें झालीं, मागेंच, कधींच.

So l. तेथ *or* तिथवर, तेथ *or* तिथपर्यंत, तेथ *or* तिथपावेतों, तेढवळ *or* तेढोळ.

To LONG, *v. n. desire intently,* v. To DESIRE. लोभणें, लुब्धणें, नितांतणें *or* नितांदणें, धोपणें, धादावणें, आशावणें, भुकेणें, तान्हेणें, कंकांतणें, मरणें, खवखवणें, आरेणें, खुरखुरणें, संतावणें, कंठीं प्राण *m.* धरणें, प्राण *m.* सोखणें *g. of s.* जीव *m.* टाकणें, प्राण *m.* ओकणें, जीव *m.* टांगला असणें *g. of s.*

2—a woman in pregnancy. डोहळे *m. pl.* लागणें-होणें *in. con.*

LONG-ARMED, *a.* लांब हात्या, लंबहस्त, आजानुबाहु.

LONG-BELLIED, *a.* लांब पोट्या, लंबोदर.

LONG-EARED, *a.* लांब कान्या, लंबकर्ण.

LONG-FACED, *a.* लांब तोंड्या, दीर्घमुख, लंबतुंड.

LONG-HEADED, *a.* v. WISE, CLEVER. बुद्धिमान्, अनुसंधानी, दीर्घसंधानी, संधानी, लागलाव्या, लाग्या. [स्थायी.

LONG-LASTING, *a.* बहूत काळाचा, चिरकालिक, दीर्घ कालिक, चिर-

LONG-LEGGED, *a.* लांबटांग्या, ढेंगाळ, ढांगळ, टांगळ.

LONG-LIVED, *a.* चिरंजीवी, दीर्घायु, चिरायु, दीर्घायुष्य, दीर्घजीवी, आयुष्मान्. Some appellatives or allusive attributives for *a long-lived person* are, जांबुवंत, मार्कंडेय, जुना कपि.

LONG-NECKED, *a.* लांबमान्या, उंटमान्या.

LONG-NOSED, *a.* लांबनाक्या.

LONG-SIGHTED, *a.* दीर्घदर्शी, दूरदर्शी, दीर्घदृष्टि.

LONG-SIGHTEDNESS, *n.* v. A. दीर्घदृष्टि *f.* दूरदृष्टि *f.* दूरदर्शन *n.*

LONG-SOME. See TIRESOME.

Long-sufferance, Long-suffering, *n.* v. Patience. सोसिकपणा*m.* सहनशीलता *f.* क्षमा *f.* क्षांति *f.*

Long-suffering, *a.* v. Patient. सोसीक, सहनशील, सहिष्णु, चिरसहिष्णु, क्षमावान्, क्षांत.

Long-winded, *a. tedious in narration,*—person, v. Proser, Prolix. चघळ, चावनट, चावट, बयादी, चेंगट, दीर्घसूत्री.

2—speech, &c. चघळपणाचा, चावटाइचा, चरपटपंजरीचा, चेंगटाइचा.

Long-wise, *adv. in the direction of the length.* लांबीप्रमाणें, लांबीवर, लांब, लंबा *decl.* लांबींत, लांबीनें.

Longer, *n.* **Longing,** *p. a.* v.V. l. *and* Desirous. नितांतलेला, लुब्ध झालेला, &c. सुजरा, आशाभूत.

Longer, *a.* अधिकलांब.

Longest, *a.* सर्वांहून-सर्वांपेक्षां-&c. लांब.

Longeval, Longevous, *a.* v. Long lived. चिरंजीवी, दीर्घायु, चिरायु, आयुष्मान्.

Longevity, *n.* v.A. चिरायु*n.*दीर्घायुष्य*n.* चिरायुष्य*n.* चिरंजीवित्व*n.*

Longimanous, *a. long-handed.* लांबहात्या, लंबहस्त.

Longimetry, *n. measurement of distances.* दूरत्वमिति*f.* दूरत्व मापन*n.* दैर्घ्यमापन*n.* [आळ*m. f.*

Longing, *n.* v. V. l. *and* Desire. नितांत*m.* आशा *f.* भूक *f.*

The anguish of separation and the l. for the return of. चटक *f.* चटका*m. v.* लाग, बस.

2 डोहळे*m. pl.* दोहद*n.* [ळतुली *f.*

A pregnant woman beginning to have longings. डोह-

Feasting and merry making on the appearance of longings. डोहळे जेवण*n.*

Longingly, *adv.* v.A. जीवटांगून, जीव तोडून, लाहोलाहो करून, पंचप्राण *or* प्राण लावून, प्राण ओकून, टक लावून.

Longitude, *n. length.* लांबी *f.* [रिंधि *m.*

2 (of the earth). रेखांश*m.pl.* रेखागण*m.* रेखासमूह *m.* रेखाप-

A degree of l. रेखांश *m.* [रेखावृत्त*n.*

A meridian or circle of l. याम्योत्तरवृत्त*n.* रेखांशवृत्त*n.*

3 *position to east or west.* रेखांश*m.* रेखांतर*n.*

Difference of l. रेखांतर*n.*

4 (celestial.) भोग*m.*

Longitudinal, *a. running lengthwise.* लांबीचा, लांबीवरचा.

Longitudinally. See Long-wise.

Looby. See Clown.

To **Look,** *v. n. direct the sight.* पाहणें, बगणें *or* बघणें, दृष्टि *f.* घालणें-लावणें-देणें-करणें, देखणें, प्रेक्षणें, अवलोकणें, विलोकणें, अवलोकन*n.*-&c. करणें. [करणें, ठेवणें.

To l. about. खालवर पाहणें, खालवर दृष्टि *f.*-नजर *f.*-&c.

To l. closely or intently. टकणें, टक लावून पाहणें, टेहळणें, निहाळणें *or* न्याहाळणें, निरखणें, निहाळून-निरखुन-&c. पाहणें, रोंखणें, रोंखुन पाहणें.

To l. in, *put the head in to look.* डोकावणें, डोकावून पाहणें.

To l. wistfully. टुकणें, टुकटुकणें, टुकटुक-&c. पाहणें.

2 *seem, appear.* दिसणें, दिसून येणें, नजरेस येणें, वाटणें, भासणें, दिसायास-पहायास-दिसण्यांत-पाहण्यांत-&c. असणें, रंग*m.*-डौल *m.*-आकार*m.*-रूप*n.*-&c. असणें, *in. con.*

It looks as if it would rain. पावसाचा रंग-&c. दिसतो, पावसानें मांड घातला.

3 *have a particular air, appearance, &c.* दिसणें, रंग*m.*-रूप*n.* -डौल*m.*-&c. असणें.

To l. well. शोभणें.

4 See To Expect. 5 after; *attend to, take care of.* पाहणें, संभाळणें, जोपासणें, जोंचाळणें, संभाळ *m.*-जोपाशीर *f.*-जोपाशील *f.*-जोपास *f.*-निगा *f.*-निगादास्त *f.*-बरदास्त *f.*-ओज *f.*-खबरदारी *f.*-देखरेख *f.* करणें-ठेवणें, शोध *m.*-चौकशी *f.*-वास्तपुस्त *f.*-वाजपुशी *f.*-&c. ठेवणें-राखणें, खबर *f.*-समाचार *m.*-&c.घेणें.

6 after; See To Search. 7 for; v. To Expect. वाट *f.* पाहणें, मार्ग *m.*-वाट *f.*-&c. लक्षिणें.

8 for; See To Search. 9 into; v. To Examine. पाहणें, चौकशी *f.*-विचार *m.*-&c. करणें.

To l. and wait for as indispensable. आक्षेप *m.* धरणें *g. of o.* उरता *f.* धरणें *g. of o.*

10 on, upon; *consider, esteem, think.* मोजणें, गणणें, मेजणें, मानणें, लेखणें.

11 on; *be a mere spectator.* पाहणें, तमाशा *m.*-&c. पाहणें, तमाशगीर-&c. असणें.

12 over; See To Examine. 13 out; v. To Search. शोध *m.*-तलाश *m.*-&c. करणें-ठेवणें.

14 out; *be on the watch.* जपणें, लक्षिणें, टपणें, जपत-टपत-लक्षीत असणें, टेहळणें.

15 upon; *behold.* पाहणें, लक्षिणें.

To l. down upon. See To Contemn.

To l. up to. See To Regard, To Revere.

Look, *n. air of the face, cast of countenance.* चेहरा *m.* मुद्रा *f.* सुरत *f.* चर्या *f.* रूप *n.* स्वरूप *n.*

A fixed l. टक *f. v.* लाव, लाग.

Angry or hard l. कटाक्ष *m.*

Idiotic & slovenly l. गाबाळमुद्रा *f.*

Casting lewd looks. कटाक्षावेक्षन *n.*

Side l. कटाक्ष *m.* अर्धवीक्षन *n.*

To have one's lofty looks brought down. नाक *n.* खालीं पडणें *g. of s.*

2 *aspect or appearance,*—gener. आकार *m.* रूप *n.* डौल *m.* रंग *m.* घाट *m.* छाया *f.*

3 See Looking.

Look, *interj.* पहा, बघा.

Looker, *n.* **Looking,** *p. a.* v. V. 1. पाहणारा, दृष्टि लावणारा, अवलोकणारा, &c. प्रेक्षक, वीक्षक, आलोचक, द्रष्टा, दर्शी (in comp. as दीर्घदर्शी, &c.), अवलोकन-विलोकन-&c. कर्त्ता.

2 *spectator.* तमाशगीर.

Looking, *n.* v. V. 1. पाहणें *n.* बगणें *n.* &c. दृष्टि *f.* दृष्टिपात *m.* दर्शन *n.* अवलोकन *n.* विलोकन *n.* आलोचन *n.* प्रेक्षण *n.* प्रेक्षा *f.* वीक्षण *n.* संदर्शन *n.*

5 after. संभाळ *m.* जोपासणी *f.* जोपाशीर *f.* जोपाशील *f.* जोपासणूक *f.* जोपावणी *f.* जोपावणूक *f.* जोपा *f.* निगा *f.* निगादास्त *f.* बरदास्त *f.* ओज *f.* संगोपन *n.*

Looking-glass, *n. mirror.* आरसा *m. dim.* आरसी *f.* ऐना *or* अयना *m.* दर्पण *n.* आदर्श *m.*

Look out, *n.* देश पाहण्या करितां घरावर बांधलेला बंगला *m.*

Loom, *n.* (of a weaver). माग *m.*

Cross stick of a l. पालवट *m.*

Fresh from the l.—cloth. नव्या ताण्याचा.

Hole for the descent of the foot at a l. मागम्.

Pin confining the beam of a l. ओढपट्टी *f.*

Step of a l. पाठवणी *f.* Some words for other parts or members of *a loom* are, सुतारा,हातखुंटा, हात्या.

To LOOM, *v. n. appear indistinctly*—as a thing at a distance. दुरून अस्पष्ट दिसणें, दिसणें.

LOON, *n.* v. RASCAL. हरामजादा, हरामी, दुर्जन.

LOOP, *n. noose, &c.* मुदन *f.* फासा *m.* वाळा *m.* तुकमा *m.* कानी *f.*

LOOP-HOLE, *n. aperture in a wall.* जंगी *f.* धारें *n.* गवाक्ष *n.* रंध्र *n.*

2 *shift, salvo, evasion.* खिडकी *f.* सोडवण *f.* सबड *f.*

To leave a l. (for escape). सबड *f.* वाट *f.*-&c. ठेवणें, निसर गाठ *f.* देऊन ठेवणें, सोडवून ठेवणें.

LOORY, *n.*—the bird. नुरी *f.*

To LOOSE, *To* LOOSEN, *v. a. unbind, untie, make loose.* सोडणें, मोकळा-&c. करणें, फेडणें, सोडणूक *f.*-&c. करणें *g. of o.* उकलणें, मोचन *n.*-&c. करणें *g. of o.*

2 *liberate, free.* सोडणें, सोडून देणें, मोकळा-मुक्त-&c. करणें-सोडणें, मोचणें, मोकलणें, सुटका *f.*-सोडणूक *f.*-मोचन *n.*-विमोचन *n.*-&c. करणें *g. of o.* सुटका *f.*-&c. देणें.

3 *relax, slacken, luxate.* ढिलावणें, निसळणें, ढिला-ढील-ढिलता-शिथिल-&c. करणें.

To LOOSE, *To* LOOSEN, *v. n. become slack, relaxed, &c.* ढिलावणें, सैलावणें, सैल-ढील-ढिला-शिथिल-पोकळ-बुळका-&c. होणें, सुटणें, उकलणें.

2 *set sail, leave a port.* हकारणें, बंदर *n.* सोडणें, निघणें.

LOOSE, *a. unbound, untied, unconfined.* मोकळा, सुटा, मोकारा, अबद्ध, अनिगृहीत, बंधनरहित-शून्य-&c.

To become l. सुटणें.

To break l. सुटणें, सुटून जाणें.

To let or set l. सोडणें, सोडून देणें, मोकळा सोडणें.

2 *not fast or fixed, not tight.* ढिला, ढील, ढिलता, खिळखिळा, खिळखिळीत, सैल, लांपट, पोकळ, शिथिल, उसू, गटगटीत, लटपटीत, बुळका, लिबका, अरळ, सलम.

L. or slack through use. चघळ, चाबट.

To get l.—a tie, &c. सुटणें, फिटणें.

3 *not tight*—a garment. ढिला, ढील, ढिलता, सैल, शिथिल, पोकळ, सलम, डगळ *or* डघळ, श्लथ. [भोंगळ.

L. and bagging. लसफशीत *or* सीत, घळघळीत, भसभोंगळ,

To become l. and bagging. घळघळणें.

4 *not crowded or close.* विरल *or* ळ, मोकळा, सुटा, पातळ, विसकळ, विरूळ, बरळ, बरगळ.

Of very l. texture. मासेगाळणा. [टका, स्फुट.

5 *separate, detached, not of.* फुटकळ, मोकळा, सुटा, तुटक, तु-

6 *not concise, close, &c. diffuse.* पघळ, अघळपघळ, विस्ताराचा, विस्तारात्मक, विस्तारयुक्त, पाल्हाळाचा.

7 *not precise; lax, vague, &c.* v. INDETERMINATE. पळपळीत, मळमळीत, डळमळीत, अळमळीत, गुळमुळीत, धरसोडीचा, धरसोड्या, भसभोंगळ, भोंगळ, मुग्ध, मुग्धा.

8 *not costive.* पोटाचा अदळ-ढिला, ढिल्या पोटाचा, कासोट्याचा अदळ, हगरा, हगवणकर *or* करी, मृदुकोष्ठ.

9 *wanton, licentious, dissolute, rakish, libertine, &c.* सोदा, लुचा, लुच्चा, कुश्चळ, खोटचाल, बेढंग, बेढंगी, सोदेशाई, सोदेगिरीचा, लुच्चेगिरीचा, सोदेशाईचा, चौढाळ, स्त्रीव्यसनी, रांडव्यसनी, दुर्व्यसनी, स्त्रीव्यसनाचा, रांडबाजीचा, बटाऊ, व्यभिचारी, व्यभिचाराचा, दुर्वृत्त, बदफैल, बदफैलीचा, बदख्याल, इष्की, इष्कबाजीचा, फकड *or* फक्कड, धिंग, छटेल, छटेला, चटोर, चारगट, चाट, बावगा, खुदरापादरा, शृंगाररसात्मक, शृंगाररसप्रधान. For terms for *a loose, licentious person,* See under LIBERTINE.

To become l. चवणें, वायकळणें.

LOOSE, *n.* See LIBERTY, FREEDOM.

LOOSE-JOINTED, LOOSE-SET, *a.* लुंगा, ढिल्या.

LOOSE-TONGUED, *a.* कानाचा हलका, तोंडाचा हलका, फटकळ.

LOOSED, LOOSENED, *p.* v. V. A. 1. सोडलेला, फेडलेला, मोकळा-केलेला, मुक्त-निर्मुक्त-&c. केलेला, मोचित.

2 सोडलेला, सोडून दिल्हेला, &c. मुक्त-&c. केलेला, मोचित, छिन्नबंधन, बंधमुक्त, मुक्त, विमुक्त, निर्मुक्त, विनिर्मुक्त.

3 ढिलावलेला, ढिलाकेलेला, &c. शिथिलीकृत.

LOOSELY, *adv.* v. A. 1. मोकळा *decl.* सुटा *decl.* मोकळेपणीं, बांधल्यावांचून, मोकळ, मोकार, मोकाट.

2 ढिला, &c. *decl.* ढील, सैल, अरळ, पोकळ, &c.

3 ढिला, &c. *decl.* पोकळ, ढील, &c. घळघळ *or* ळां, घळघळाट.

4 विरळ, पातळ, पैस, ऐसपैस, विसकळ, अंतरानें, तुरळक.

6 पघळ, अघळपघळ.

7 पळपळीत, मळमळीत, &c. मोघम *or* मोहगम, अळमटळम, अळमळीत, धरूनसोडून, अनियमपूर्वक. [पूर्वक.

9 सोदेगिरीनें, &c. खोटचालपणानें, &c. स्त्रीव्यसनपूर्वक, दुर्व्यसन-

LOOSENER, *n.* v.V. A. 1. 2. सोडणारा, मोकळा-&c. करणारा, &c. मोचक, मोचन-&c. कर्त्ता.

LOOSENESS, *n.* v. A. 2. ढिलेपणा *m.* खिळखिळेपणा *m.* उसूपणा *m.* शिथिलपणा *m.* &c. ढिलाई *f.* ढील *f.* खिळखिळी *f.* शैथिल्य *n.*

3 ढिलेपणा *m.* &c. ढिलाई *f.* ढील *f.* शैथिल्य *n.* शिथिलता *f.*

4 विरळपणा *m.* पातळाई *f.* मोकळेपणा *m.* वैरल्य *n.* विरलता *f.* विरलभाव *m.*

6 पघळपणा *m.* अघळपघळपणा *m.*

7 पळपळितपणा *m.* मळमळितपणा *m.* &c. अळमटळम *n. f.*

8 v. DIARRHŒA. पोटाचा अदळपणा *m.*- ढिलेपणा *m.*-&c. हगवण *f.* ढेंढळ *f.* ढेंढाळी *f.* ढगळ *f.* डरंगळ *f.* शौचाचा उपद्रव *m.*-व्यथा *f.*-&c. मृदुकोष्ठ *m.*

To have a l. पोट *n.* चालणें-जाणें.

9 सोदावें *n.* सोदेगिरी *f.* लुच्चेगिरी *f.* लुच्चाई *f.* सोदेशाई *f.* इष्कबाजी *f.* स्त्रीव्यसन *n.* रांडव्यसन *n.* दुर्व्यसन *n.* बदफैली *f.* बदख्याल *m.* बाहेरख्याल *m.* बदकर्म *n.* व्यभिचार *m.*

LOOSENING, LOOSING, *n.*v.V.A. 1. 2.—*act.* सोडणें *n.* फेडणें *n.* सोडणूक *f.* मोचन *n.* विमोचन *n.* & निर्मोचन *n.* विमोक्षण *n.* मोक्षण *n.* मुक्ति *f.* मोक्ष *m.*

3 ढिलावणें *n.* निसळणें *n.* निसळणूक *f.* शिथिलीकरण *n.*

To LOP, *v. a. chop off, cut off.* तोडणें, धसकावणें, धपकावणें, छाटणें.

2 (trees) *cut off the branches.* खडसणें, खचीकरणें, डुसणें, कलम *n.* करणें *g. of o.* खडसणी *f.*-&c. करणें *g. of o.*

To l. off the crop and branches. शेंडाबुडखा *m.* करणें.

LOPPED, *p.* v. V. 1. तोडलेला, छाटलेला, &c.

2 खडसलेला, &c. खची *or* खच्ची.

L. and cropped. लुंडाबुचा.

LOPPING, *n.* v. V. 1.—*act.* तोडणें *n.* &c. तोडणी *f.* छाटणी *f.*

2 खडसणें *n.* &c. खडसणी *f.* कलम *n.*

I. loppings; *matter lopped off.* छाटm. छाटछूटm f. काटकूट f.
II. (of bushes, &c.). काट m. काटकवळn. कवळn. कवळकाटीf.
टहाळ m. n. डहाळ m. n.

A bundle of leaves and loppings. शिरड f.

A single stick of a bundle of loppings. शिरें n. कांट f.

Loquacious, *a.* v. **Talkative**. बोलका, वाचाल *or* ळ, बोलवे-
वडा, बोलगाडा, चावट, बहुभाष, बहुभाषी.

Loquaciousness, Loquacity, *n.* v. A. बोलकेपणा *m.* वाचा-
ळपणा *m.* चावटाई *f.* अतिशयोक्ति *f.* वाचालता *f.*

Lord, *n. ruler, master.* धनी, पति, खावंद, प्रभु, स्वामी, ईश, ईश्वर,
नाथ, अधीश, अधीश्वर, अधिप, अधिपति.

Universal l. सर्वस्वामी.

Who made you l. over us? तूं माझा देव मी तुझा भगत ?

2 *nobleman, grandee.* सरदार, अमीर, उमराव, राव.

My L., your lordship. खावंद, खुदावंत, सरकार, आपण,
साहेब, स्वाम.

3—the **Lord**, v. **God**. भगवान्, परमेश्वर, स्वामी.

4 v. **Husband**. पति.

To **Lord**, *v.n. domineer.* सत्ता *f.*-धनीपणा*m.*-खावंदी *f.*-रावकी *f.*-
साहेबी *f.*-&c. करणें-मिरवणें *with* वर, शक *m.*-मात्रा *f.*-&c. ठे-
वणें-चालवणें, चढ *m.* ठेवणें-करणें, उपर *m.* ठेवणें, शिकारोखा *m.*
करणें-दाखविणें-मिरविणें. [होऊं लागणें.

To begin to l. it (over, with). देव होऊं लागणें, बाप

Lording, Lordling, *n.*—a lord in contempt. राजटलें *n.* रा-
वटलें *n.* राजें *n.*

Lordlike, Lordly, *a. like or becoming a lord.* रावास-सर-
दारास-&c. योग्य, रावास-सरदारास-&c. शोभणारा.

2 *haughty, imperious,* v. **Proud**. गर्वी, अभिमानी, चढेल,
मगरूर, ताठ्याचा, दिमाखाचा.

Lordliness, *n.* v. A. 2. मगरुरी *f.* दिमाख *m.* आढ्यता *f.* ताठा*m.*

Lordship, *n. rulership, mastery.* धनीपणा *m.* स्वामीपणा *m.*
खावंदी *f.* साहेबी *f.* स्वामित्व *n.* स्वाम्य *n.* आधिपत्य *n.* प्रभुत्व*n.*

2 *state &c. of being a lord.* रावकी *f.* रावपणा *m.* खावंदी *f.*
अमिरी *f.* [सत्ताक्रांतदेश *m.*

3 *domain, manor.* जमीनदारी *f.* जाहगिरी *f.* जाहगीर *f.* स्व-

4 Your Lordship ! खावंद, सरकार, स्वाम.

Lore. See **Learning**.

Lorn. See **Forlorn**.

To **Lose**, *v. a.*—as *opposed to* win. हरणें *or* हारणें, हार जाणें,—
in cant phraseology. उदीम करणें, हासील करणें.

To be lost. हारीस जाणें.

2 *let go, drop, miss, mislay, &c.* हारवणें, हरपणें *or* हारपणें,
गमावणें, सांडणें, गहाळणें *or* गाहाळणें, गफलतणें, गळफटणें *or*
गळफाटणें, गळहाटणें.

To be lost. हरपणें *or* हारपणें, गलबलणें, सांडणें, गमावणें,
गलफटणें *or* गलफाटणें, गफलतणें.

To l. one's way. वाट *f.*-&c. चुकणें *g. of s.* गलफटणें *or*
गलफाटणें, गहाळणें.

To l. one's self. दिशाभूल *f.*-दिग्भूल *f.*-दिग्भ्रम *m.*-&c.
होणें *g. of s.*—fig. भुलणें, दृष्टि *f.* चकणें *g. of o.* गलफटणें *or* ग-
लफाटणें.

3 *suffer the cessation, departure, deterioration, &c. of.* मु-
कणें, आंचवणें, अंतरणें, सुटणें, अंतरणें *in. con.* नुकसान *n.*-नुक-
सानी *f.*-तोटा *m.*-&c.होणें-बसणें-पडणें *in. con. with g. of o.*

To be lost. गरक-गडप-गडद *adv.* होणें, नाबूद *adv.* होणें-
जाणें, नाहींसा होणें,—money, as in trade, bad debts, &c.
थकणें, बुडणें, फसणें.

To l. one's life. प्राणास-जिवास मुकणें.

4—as *opposed to* keep. जाणें, गतणें, गुदरणें, सुटणें, बुडणें;
all these mean *to be lost unto.* अंतरणें *in. con.*

5 *squander, throw away.* हरवणें *or* हारवणें, घालवणें, दवडणें,
खोवणें.

To be lost. पोकळीखालीं-पोकळीस-फुकट-पाण्यांत-&c. जाणें.

To **Lose**, *v. n. be out of pocket.* तोटा *m.*-&c. खाणें, तोटा *m.*-
नुकसान *n.*-&c. येणें-होणें-बसणें, पदर *m.* गमावणें-भरणें-घालणें,
पदर *m.* भरीस घालणें, पागोटें *n.* गमावणें, घासटणें, पदरास खार
m. f. लागणें, पाटीचें साल *n.* जाणें.

Loser, *n.* **Losing**, *p. a.* v. V. A. 1. हारणारा, हाऱ्या, हारखाऊ.
2 हारवणारा, &c. सांड्या, गमाव्या, गमाऊ, गहाळ्या.

I. as *opposed to* lucrative. तोट्याचा, तोटा येण्याचा, &c.
आंगावर येण्याचा, पदरभरण्याचा, अहितावह.

A losing concern. बुडस्थळ *n.* तोट्याची बाब *f.*

Losing, *n.* v. V. A. 1. हरणें *n.* हर *f.* हार *f.*

2 गमावणें *n.* हरपणें *n.* सांडणें *n.* सांड *f.* हरवण *f.* हरपण *f.*

5 हरवणें *n.* दवडणें *n.* &c घालवण *f.* हरवण *f.*

Loss, *n.*—as *opposed to* wonness. हार *f.* हर *f.*

2 *detriment, damage,*—as *opposed to* gain. तोटा*m.*नुकसान*n.f.*
नुकसानी *f.* धका *or* धक्का *m.* हिसका *m.* ढोला*m.* गोता*m.* धोका*m.*
झोका*m.* खांच *f.* बुडण *f.* बुडणूक *f.*खोंच *f.* खोट *f.* ठेच *f.* चोट *f.*
नहाघ*m.* नहाची *f.* नाकस्ता *m.* खत्ता *f.* चट्टा *m.* चट्टी *f.* घसण *f.*
घांसण *f.* घस *f.* घसरा *m.* भोकसा *or* भोसका *m.* चपेट *f.* छकड*f.*
तोहमत *f.* मूर *f.* मुरवण *f.* खामी *f.* हानि *f.*-ऱ्हास *pop.* हरास*m.*
अपचय *m.* अपाय *m.* क्षति *f.* Note. The verbs बसणें-येणें-ला-
गणें-खाणें are used with most of the above words.

A dead l. बुडीत *n.* बूड *f.* बुडीत खर्च *m.*

A heavy l. धोंड *f.*

Losses, *monies sunken.* बुडीत *n.* बुडीतखर्च *m.* बूड *f.*

To cause a l. unto. पदरास खार *m. f.* लावणें, टोपी *f.*-पा-
गोटें *n.* घालणें.

To incur or sustain a l. See To **Loose**, *v. n.*

3 *privation, deprivation.* नाश *m.* हानि *f.* क्षति *f.* अंतर *n.*
v. पड, वियोग *m.* गेलेपणा *m.* अभाव *m.* [बूड *f.*

4 *perdition, perishing,* v. **Destruction, Ruin**. नाश *m.*

Utter or great l. नासाड़ा*m.* नासाडी *f.* नासडा *m.* नासाड*f.*

5 *lost or mislaid state.* सांड *f.* हरवण *f.* हरपण *f.* गळहाटा *m.*
देवगत *f.* गफलत *f.* गलफटा *m.* गलबल *f.*

6 *wastage, &c.* v. **Waste**. घस *f.* घट *f.* तूट *f.*

7 *useless application,* v. **Waste**. फुकटखर्च *m.* वृथाव्यय*m.*
असद्व्यय *m.* अपव्यय *m.* नाश *m.*

To be at a l. *be puzzled, &c.* चक्री *f.* गुंग होणें *or* भुलणें
g. of s. तरंगणें, थकणें, गलफटणें, कुंठित असणें.

Lost, *p.* v. V. A. 1. हरलेला, हारीस गेलेला.

2 गमावलेला, हरपलेला, सांडलेला, &c. गहाळ *or* गाहाळ.

3 नष्ट, गरक, गडप झालेला, नाबूद झालेला, नाहींसा झालेला.

4 गेलेला, अंतरलेला, &c. गत, विगत.

5 घालवलेला, दवडलेला, पोकळीस गेलेला, फुकट गेलेला, &c.

I. *stray.* चुकलेला *or* चुकला, भकलेला, चुकार, चुकर, सांड, चुकारीचा, गहाळ *or* गाहाळ झालेला, दिग्भ्रांत.

II.—in astonishment,&c. *bewildered, amazed, confounded.* चक्र, चकभूल, थक्क, थकीत, थक्कित, चुकार, बावरा, भ्रांत, भ्रमयुक्त.

Lost to shame, &c. See SHAMELESS.

LOT, *n. fortune, state assigned,* v. DESTINY. भाग्य *n.* दैवदशा *f.* पाळी *f.* भोग *m.* भोक्तृत्व *n.* भोग्य *n.* भागधेय *n.*

To fall to one's l. कपाळास-दैवास-भागास-विभागास-वांट्यास-&c. येणें *g. of o.* उपतिष्ठणें.

2 *die, or any thing used in determining a fate or portion.* शकुन *m.* फांसा *m.* प्रश्नफांसा *m.* चिठ्ठी *f.*

To cast lots. चिठ्या *f. pl.* टाकणें-काढणें.

3 *portion, parcel.* प्रत *f.* जुळी *f.* गट्टा *m.* पुड्ठा *m.* सांटें *n.* गट्ट *m.* भाग *m.*

4 (of ground) *patch, parcel.* ठिकें *n.*

5 *proportion or share of taxes.* सरकारदेण्याची वांटणी *f.* बर्गत *f.* बर्गणी *f.* सापणी *f.*

6 See MULTITUDE, NUMBER.

Lots, *heaps, piles, &c.* v. EXUBERANCE. उपट *f.* चेल *f.* रेल *or* रेळ *f.* चेकळ *f.* लूट *f.* धमंडी *f.* गजक *f.*

To LOT. See To ALLOT.

LOTH, &c. See LOATH, &c. [पाणी *n.*

LOTION, *n. medicinal wash.* औषधधुवण *n.* धुवणी *n.* औषधी-

LOTOS, LOTUS, *n.*—the plant. कमळीण *f.* कमलिनी *f.* पद्मिनी *f.* —the flower. कमल *or* कमळ *n.* पद्म *n.* पंकज *n.* सारस *n.* सरोज *n.* सरोरुह *n.* Certain species or varieties are काळें कमळ, पांढरें कमळ (*or* पुंडरीक *n.*), तांबडें कमळ (*or* रक्तकमल), सूर्यकमळ, निळेंकमळ (नीलकमल), कुमुद *n.*—the seed. कमलाक्ष *m.*—the seed vessel. कमळगट्ट *m.*—the stalk भिसें *n.* मृणाल *a.*—the pericarp. कर्णिका *f.*

Figure of the leaf of a l. अष्टदल *or* दळ.

L. which grows on the dry ground. स्थलकमल *n.*

LOTTERY, *n.* सोडत *f.*

L.-ticket. सोडतीची चिठ्ठी *f.*

LOUD, *a. high sounding, striking the ear with force.* मोठा, उंच, उंचस्वराचा, भारी, मोठ्या शब्दाचा, मोठ्या नादाचा, बंबाळ, तृतीयस्वनाचा, महास्वरक, महाध्वनिक, महाध्वनिकर, महानादी.

2 v. CLAMOROUS. गलबल्या, गोंगाट्या, ओरड्या.

LOUD, LOUDLY, *adv.* v. A. 1. मोठ्यानें, उंचस्वरानें, उंचशब्दानें, शब्द मोठा करून, आरोळी मारून.

2 गलबलीनें, गलबल करून, &c.

LOUDNESS, *n.* v. A. 1. मोठेपणा *m.* उंचपणा *m.* भारीपणा *m.* &c. मोठाशब्द *m.* मोठाध्वनि *m.* मोठानाद *m.* उच्चस्वर *m.*

2 *clamour,* v. UPROAR. गलबा *m.* गलगल *f.* गलबल *f.*

To LOUNGE, *v. n. spend time idly.* रिकामा-&c. बसणें-फिरणें-पडून राहणें, रिकामचेष्टा *f.*-रिकामटवाळी *f.*-&c. करणें, रिकामचावडीवर-रिकामटेकडीवर-&c. बसणें-फिरणें.

To LOUNGE, *v. a.* (a horse). चक्रावर-मंडलावर धरणें.

LOUNGE, *n. place of lounging.* फड *m.* रिकामचावडी *f.* रिकामटेकडी *f.* चावडी *f.*

2—in the manege. चक्कर *n.*

LOUNGER, *n.* LOUNGING, *p. a.* v. V. N. रिकामा पडून राहणारा, &c. रिकामटवळा, रिकामटेंकडा, रिकामशाई, सदरबारगीर.

LOUSE, *n.* ऊ *or* ऊं *or* उं *f.* यूका *f.*—of cattle, dogs, hogs, &c. कोळ्ळ *f.* गोचडी *f.* गोचिडी *f.* गोचीड *f.* चामीगोचीड *f.* धागऱ्याघोचीड *m.*—do. of a red color. तांब *f.*—l. bred on the body. चामऊ *f.*—found on cloth. चिरू *f.* [ढेण्या *m.*

Large and fat l. टेणा *or* टेण्या *m.* टोणा *or* टोण्या *m.*

Sore on the head breeding lice. टिचर *or* रें *n.* टिचें *n.*

Swarming of lice. बुचबूच *f.*—*intens.* बुचबुचाट *m.* खुतखुत *m. f.* लुवलूव *m. f.*—*intens.* लुवलुवाट *m.*

Young l. or the egg of a l. लीख *f.* लिक्षा *f.*

To swarm with lice. बुचबुचणें, खुतखुतणें.

To LOUSE, *v. a. clean from lice.* उवा *f. pl.* काढणें-मारणें-पाहणें.

LOUSINESS, *n.* v. A. 1. उलेपणा *or* उइलेपणा *m.* उवेरेपणा *m.* उबोडेपणा *m.* बुचबुचलेपणा *m.* खुतखुतलेपणा *m.*

LOUSY, *a. swarming with lice.* उला *or* उइला *or* उवला, उवेरा, बुचबुचलेला, खुतखुतलेला. [अधम, पाजी.

2 *mean, dirty, &c.* v. LOW. शिटाऊ, हटाऊ, लिदबळ, घाणेरडा,

LOUT, *n. sturdy blockhead, dolt,* v. LUBBER. ठोंबा, ठोंब, गोखमा, शुंठ *or* शुंट, धुंभ, म्हैसा, कंठाळ्या माणूस.

LOUTISH, *a.* v. N. ठोंब्या, ढोण्या, धडेल, गलेलठ्ठ, दगडघाशा, अडमुठ्या, कणशा.

LOUTISHNESS, *n.* v. A. ठोंबेपणा *m.* &c.

LOUVER, *n. aperture for smoke.* धारें *n.* धुरांडें *n.* धुराणें *n.* सोनें *n.*

LOVAGE, *n. lingusticum ajwaen.* अजमोदा *m.* अजवान *m.* यवानी *f.*

To LOVE, *v. a. regard with affection.* प्रीति *f.*-प्रीत *f.*-प्रेम *n.*-&c. ठेवणें-करणें-&c. *with* वर *of o.* प्रीति *f.*-प्रीत *f.*-&c. धरणें-बाळगणें-&c. *g. of o.* प्रीति *f.*-प्रेम *n.*-&c. असणें *in. con. with g. of o.* प्रिय-प्यारा-&c. जाणणें-मोजणें-&c.

2 (as the sexes). स्त्रीपुरुषप्रेमभावानें रिझणें-आसक्त होणें.

3 *delight in, like.* चाहणें, आवड *f.*-गोडी *f.*-&c. असणें-वाटणें *in. con. & g. of o.* चांगला-बरा-&c. वाटणें *in. con.*

LOVE, *n. affection, fondness.* प्रीति *pop.* प्रीत *f.* प्रेम *n.* प्यार *m.* आवड *f.* ममता *f.* माया *f.* मोह *m.* चाड *f.* लोभ *m.* प्रेमा *m.* प्रणय *m.* स्नेह *m.* प्रीतिभाव *m.* प्रेमभाव *m.* स्नेहभाव *m.*

L.—gener. *affection, tenderness, &c.* मायाममता *f.*

The overflowing or swelling of l. or tenderness. प्रेम *n.* प्रेमा *m.*

To win the l. of. प्रीति *f.* लावणें-लावून घेणें.

2 (of the sexes). स्त्रीपुरुषप्रेम *n.* स्त्रीपुरुषप्रेमभाव *m.* शृंगार *m.* शृंगाररस *m.* शृंगारभाव *m.* इषक *m.* रति *f.* रतिभाव *m.* मदन *m.*

Illicit l. दोस्ती *f.*

Of or belonging to l. शृंगाराचा, शृंगारी, शृंगारीक,

Subdued by l. मदनवश.

The art of l. कामशास्त्र *n.* कोकशास्त्र *n.*

The airs and arts of l. हाव *m. pl.* हावभाव *m. pl.*

To make l. See To COURT.

3 *delight in, fondness for, attachment to, liking, taking, passion.* प्रीति *pop.* प्रीत *f.* आवड *f.* भक्ति *f.* भक्तिभाव *m.* लजत *f.* हौस *f.* शोख *or* शौक *m.* इषक *m.* स्नेह *m.* रति *f.* रुचि *pop.* रूच *f.* निष्ठा *f.* आसक्ति *f.* संसक्ति *f.* अनुरति *f.* अनुराग *m.* अनुरक्ति *f.* अनुशीलन *n.*

Undivided l. (of the Deity, &c.). अनन्यभक्ति *f.*

To fall in l. with. रिझणें, रंजणें, रंगणें, मोहित-&c. होणें.

To quench or cool l. स्नेहावर-स्नेहांत पाणी *n.* घालणें.

LOVE-APPLE, *n.*—the plant. बेलवांगी *f.* बिलायतीवांगी *f.*—the fruit, बेलवांगें *n.* &c. [मदनलेख *m.*

LOVE-LETTER, *n.* इषकाचें पत्र *n.* शृंगाराचें पत्र *n.* प्रीतिपत्र *n.*

LOVE-MATCH, *n.* प्रीतिविवाह *m.* प्रीतिसोइरीक *f.* प्रीतिसंबंध *m.*

LOVE-QUARREL, *n.* प्रीतिकलह *m.* लाडझगडा *m.* लाडझगडें *n.* प्रणयकोप *m.*

LOVE-SICK, *a.* कामरोगी, मदनरोगी, कामविह्वल-पीडित-&c. मदनविह्वल-पीडित-&c. विरहरोगी.

LOVE-SONG, *n.* शृंगाराचें गाणें *n.* लावणी *f.* (distinguished into कलगी लावणी *and* तुरा *m.*).

A verse of a l. तूक *n.*

LOVE-TALE, *n.* शृंगाराची गोष्ट *f.* शृंगारकथा *f.* शृंगारव्याख्यान *n.*

LOVE-TOKEN, LOVE-TOY, *n.* इष्काची-प्रीतीची-&c. यादगारी *f.*-देणगी *f.*-&c.

LOVE-TRICK, *n.* हाव *m.* हावभाव *m. pl.*

LOVEABLE, *a.* v. V. 1. *and* PLEASING. आवडायाजोगा-सारखा-&c. आवडल्यागुणाचा, प्रीतियोग्य, प्रीत्यर्ह, प्रियगुणक.

LOVELINESS, *n.* v. A. सुंदरपणा *m.* सौंदर्य *n.* लावण्य *n.* रूपलावण्य *n.* लालित्य *n.* कमनीयता *f.* मनोहरता *f.* प्रियंकरत्व *n.* प्रियगुणकत्व *n.*

LOVELY, *a.* v. BEAUTIFUL, CHARMING. सुंदर, अतिसुंदर, कामरूपी, कमनीय, रमणीय, रम्य, मनोहर, मनोज्ञ, मंजु, प्रियंकर, प्रियगुणक, लावण्यवान्, लावण्यशाली, लावणिक, कांत, ललित.

LOVER, *n.* LOVING, *p.a.* v. V.1. प्रीति ठेवणारा-करणारा-&c. प्रेमल *or* ळ, प्रेमाळू, मायाळू, ममताळू, प्रेमवान् *pop.* प्रेमवंत, मायावान्, मायाशील, प्रीतिमान्, ममताशील, वत्सल, स्नेहाळ, स्नेहाळू, प्रणयी, प्रणयवान्, स्नेहाचा, प्रीतीचा, ममतेचा, &c. प्रीतियुक्त, स्नेहयुक्त, स्नेहाप्लुत.

3 भक्तिमान् *pop.* भक्तिमंत, अनुरत, अनुरक्त, अनुरागी, रक्त, रागी, रत,—in high degree, निरत, आसक्त, मोहाक्रांत, मोहाकुल, मोहातुर, मोहार्त्त, मोहाविष्ट, मोहांध.

I. *sweet heart, gallant, &c.*—the man. प्रिय, दोस्त, दोस्तदार, बेल्हाळ, गुणबेल्हाळ, दिलभर, कांत, कंथ, नायक, प्राणजीवन, प्राणाचावाली, प्राणनाथ, प्राणपति, प्राणेश, प्राणप्रिय, प्राणसखा, प्राणविसांवा, जिवाचा वाली-सखा-&c. पिहू, रमण, राघू *or* राघो, राजअंबीर, राजहंस, दयित, बल्लभ, सजण *or* साजण, जीवितेश, प्रीतिपात्र *n.* प्रियतम, यार.—the female. प्रिया, नायका, बल्लभा, प्राणसखी, कांता, &c.

LOVING-KINDNESS, *n.* v. KINDNESS. कृपा *f.* दया *f.* माया *f.* वात्सल्य *n.* अनुग्रह *m.*

LOVINGLY, *adv.* v. A. 1. प्रीतीनें, प्रीतिभावानें, प्रेमभावानें, स्नेहभावानें, &c. आवडीनें, प्रीतिपूर्वक, स्नेहपूर्वक, &c. प्रेमदृष्ट्या, प्रेमबुद्ध्या.

LOVINGNESS, *n.* v. A. 1. *and* LOVE. प्रेमळपणा *m.* मायाळूपणा *m.* &c. वात्सल्य *n.* माया *f.* ममता *f.*

LOW, *a. not high or elevated.* नीच, सखल, खालपट, खालसर, उच्चत्वन्यून, न्यूनोच्चत्व, अधम, अधर.

Very l.—*along the ground.* भुईसरसा, भूसन्निध.

To lay l. लंबा करून देणें.

To be laid l. लंबा होणें.

2 *not rising high, short,* v. LITTLE. ठेंगणा, लहान, सखल (remiss. सखलवट), खालपट, गिड्डा, ऱ्हस्व, अल्प (in comp.).

3 *descending downwards,* v. DEEP. खोल, ओंड, सखल, निम्न.

4—of ground, *sunken, &c.* सखल, सखलवट, खोलकट *or* खोलगट, खोलवट, खोलट, बतखल *or* बदखल, बसकीचा.

5 *squat, flattish,* v. DUMPY. बसकट, बसका, बदखल *or* बतखल.

6—of the water, tide, &c. ओसरलेला, उतरलेला, ओहटलेला, उथळ, निखार.

L. water. सुकती *f.*

L. water and high water. सुकती भरती *f.*

7 *not noisy or loud.* हलका, हळू, मंद, नीचस्वराचा, नम्रस्वराचा, नीच, नम्र.

8—price. हलका, थोडा, मंद, कमी.

9 (of price). v. CHEAP. हलक्या दराचा, उतरल्या दराचा, मंददराचा, नीच, लहान.

10 *dejected, downcast.* उदास, उदासी, उदासीन, खिन्न, दिलगीर, मलूल, विषण्ण, अवसन्न, सविषाद, विमनस्क, विमना.

L. spirits. विषाद *m.*

To become l. विरंबणें.

11 *of mean station, rank, birth, &c.* नीच, हलका, लहान, हलके पदवीचा, पाजी, पामर, अधम, प्राकृत, निकृष्ट, हीन, हीनजातीचा, हीनकुलाचा, क्षुद्र, क्षुल्लक, अकुलीन, अकुलज, हीनकुल, हीनजात, कमजात, नीचकुल, हीनजाति, इतर, सडासारवण्या, झाडलोट्या, पोतेऱ्या, हटाऊ, शिटाऊ, बाजारी.

12 *mean, base, vulgar, disreputable, &c.* हलका, नीच, हलके किमतीचा, हलके योग्यतेचा, हलके भाराचा, उणा, उणादुणा, प्राकृत, ओंत्सा, अर्वाच्य, क्षुद्र, क्षुल्लक, जघन्य, निकृष्ट, अपकृष्ट, अधम, पाजी, जघन्य, जघन्यवृत्तीचा, पामरवृत्तीचा, असंभावित, गैरसाळ, हटाऊ, लिद्वल, झुच्चा, भिकारी, भिकारलक्षणाचा, भिकारचाळ्याचा, बिगीत.

L. life. जघन्यवृत्ति *f.*

13 *not sublime, not exalted.* हलका, हलके योग्यतेचा, पोरका, साबडा, साबळा, अप्रौढ, अप्रगल्भ, अप्रशस्त, चिचोर, एर.

14 *submissive, &c.* v. HUMBLE. नम्र, दीनवाणा *or* वाणी, दीनवदन, नम्रतेचा, सविनय.

15 *not rich, not nourishing,*—diet. हलका, लघु, निरसत्व, कर्शक, कृशकारी. [खालीं, खालें.

LOW, *adv.* v. A. 1. *not on high.* खालता *decl.* खालतीं, खालतें,

2 *at a low price.* हलके किमतीनें. [कुल, &c.).

3 *in a mean condition.* हीन (in comp. as हीन जात, हीन-

4 *near the ground or bottom.* भुईकडे, तळाकडे, बुडाकडे.

5 *not loudly.* हलका *decl.* हलक्यानें, हळू, उपांशु.

6 *in subjection, disgrace, &c.* खालीं, खालें.

To LOW, *v. n.*—a cow. हंबरणें *or* हंबारणें *or* हुंबरणें, हुंबरडा *m.* -&c. फोडणें.

LOW-BORN, *a.* v. LOW. हीनकुल, हीनजात, कमजात, कमअसल.

LOW-PRICED, *a.* हलके किमतीचा, हलका, उणारख, अल्पमोली.

LOW-SPIRITED, *a. not lively or sprightly.* विषादी, सविषाद, बेदिल, मलूल, दुश्चित्त, दुर्मना, दुर्मनस्क, विमना, विमनस्क, उद्विग्नमनस्क, क्लांतमना, उदासवृत्ति, औदासीन्यवृत्ति.

LOWER, *a. of less height, &c.* धाकटा, धाकला, अधिक ठेंगणा.

2 *of or belonging to the lower part.* खालचा, खालला, खालील, अधर, अधस्तन.

To LOWER, *v. a. make lower.* उतरणें, खालीं-खालतें-&c. करणें-आणणें, नीच करणें.

2 *dishonor,* v. TO DISGRACE. मान *m.* कमी करणें *g. of o.*

पाणउतारा *m*.-मानभंग *m*.-मानखंडना *f*.-मानहानि *f*.-&c. करणें *g. of o.*

3 *abate, &c.* v. To LESSEN. उतरवणें, कमी-हलका-&c. करणें, उतार *m*.-&c. करणें *g. of o.*

To LOWER, *v. n. grow less, weaker, milder, &c.* v. To DECREASE. उतरणें, हलकावणें, मंदावणें, हलका-&c. होणें-पडणें, उतार *m*.-&c. होणें *g. of s.*

To LOWER, *v. n. be dark and gloomy, to threaten a storm.* डोरणें *or* डवरणें, डवडवणें, अंधारणें *or* अंधारून येणें, काहूर *n*. येणें-उठणें, अंधारी *f*.-ओंध *f*. होणें, पाऊस *m*. मांडणें, मेघांनीं *or* पावसानें ओंध *f*. घालणें-मांडणें, भरून येणें, झांकळून येणें, मांडून येणें, झांपड *f*. घालणें.

2 *be gloomy, sullen, &c. to pout.* फूं होणें-होऊन बसणें, तोंड *n*. फूं होणें *g. of s.* दुर्मुखणें, काळमुसणें, अंटरणें, फुरकटणें *or* फुरगटणें *or* फुरगुटणें.

LOWER, LOWERING, *n.* v. V. N. 1. डवरणें *n*. भरून येणें *n*.&c. अंधारी *f*. काहूर *n*. ओंध *or* ओंद *f*. काळंबण *n*.

2 फुरकट *or* फुरगूट *n*. दुर्मुखलीचर्या *f*. क्रोधमुद्रा *f*. क्रोधवर्ण *m*. क्रोधछाया *f*.

LOWERED, *p.* v. V. A. 1. उतरलेला, कमी केलेला, &c.

2 मान कमी केलेला, &c. अपकृष्ट.

3 उतरवलेला, कमी केलेला, &c. [आलेला.

LOWERING, *a. gloomy, threatening.* ओंधट, अंधारीचा, भरून

LOWER-MOST, LOWEST, *a.* सर्वांहून खालचा-खालला-&c. सर्वांचे खालचा-&c. अधस्त. [कोटीचा.

2 *inferior to all.* कनिष्ठ, कनिष्ठप्रतीचा, शेवटचेप्रतीचा, चरम-

At the lowest. निदान, निदानपक्ष,कनिष्ठपक्ष, किमानपक्ष,कडे शेवट, गेला बाजारतरी. [डा *m*.

LOWING, *n.* v. V. हुंबरणें *n*. हंबा *m*. हुंबरडा *or* हंबरडा *or* हंबार-

A general or great l. हुंबरड *f*.

LOWLAND, LOWLANDS, *n.* हेटपांत *m*. तळघाट *m*. खालचा देश *m*. तळजमीन *f*.

LOWLANDER, *n.* हेटकरी, तळघाटी.

LOWLILY, *adv.* नम्रतेनें, नम्रबुद्धीनें, नम्रभावानें, दीनतेनें, निरभिमानानें, अभिमानत्यागपूर्वक.

LOWLINESS, *n.* v. A. 1. गरीबी *f*. नम्रता *f*. नम्रबुद्धि *f*. नम्रभाव *m*. निरभिमान *m*. लीनता *f*. दीनता *f*.

2 साधेपणा *m*. साबडेपणा *m*. साळेभोळेपणा *m*.

LOWLY, *a. free from pride,* v. HUMBLE. नम्र, नम्रबुद्धि, गरीब, निरभिमान, निरभिमानाचा, निरहंकार.

2 *not lofty, sublime, &c.* साधा, साबडा *or* साबळा, साधाभोळा, साळाभोळा, अप्रौढ, अप्रगल्भ.

LOWLY, *adv. humbly.* See LOWLILY. 2. See LOW, *adv.*

LOWNESS, *n.* v. A. 1. सखलपणा *m*. नीचपणा *m*. &c. नीचता *f*. उच्चत्वन्यूनता *f*.

3 v. DEPTH. सखलपणा *m*. खोलपणा *m*.

4 सखलपणा *m*. खोलवटपणा *m*.

7 हलकेपणा *m*. &c. मंदत्व *n*.

8 हलकेपणा *m*. &c.

10 उदासपणा *m*. &c. औदासीन्य *n*. विषाद *m*. विषण्णता *f*. अवसन्नता *f*. वैमनस्य *n*. विमनस्कता *f*. दौर्मनस्य *n*.

11 नीचपणा *m*. हलकेपणा *m*. पाजीपणा *m*. &c. हीनकुलता *f*.

12 हलकेपणा *m*. नीचपणा *m*. उणेपणा *m*. हलकी योग्यता *f*. हलकी किम्मत *f*. हलकाभार *m*.

LOW-SPIRITS, *n.* v. LOWNESS, 10. उत्साहाभाव *m*. उदासपणा *m*. विषाद *m*. वैमनस्य *n*. विमनस्कता *f*. दौर्मनस्य *n*.

LOYAL, *a. faithful to one's sovereign.* राजाचा निमकहलाल, स्वराजभक्त-सेवी-निष्ठ-तत्पर-&c. स्वस्वामिभक्त-सेवी-& स्वप्रभुभक्त-सेवी-&c. स्वराजाज्ञावर्त्ती, स्वराजासक्त, प्रजाधर्मपरायण-तत्पर-निष्ठ-&c.

2—as a wife. पतिव्रता, सती, साध्वी.

3—as a husband. स्वदारनिरत, स्वदारैकतान.

LOYALIST, *n.* See LOYAL.

LOYALLY, *adv.* v. A. 1. निमकहलालीनें, राजभक्तिपूर्वक, स्वराजनिष्ठापूर्वक, &c.

LOYALTY, *n.* v. A. 1. राजाची निमकहलाली *f*. स्वराजनिष्ठा *f*. स्वराजभक्ति *f*. स्वराजासक्ति *f*. स्वस्वामिभक्ति *f*. &c. स्वप्रभुभक्ति *f*. &c. प्रजाधर्मनिष्ठा *f*.

2 पातिव्रत्य *n*. सत्त्व *n*. साधुत्व *n*.

3 स्वदारनिरतत्व *n*. स्वदारनिरति *f*. स्वदारनिष्ठा *f*.

LOZENGE, *n.*—the sweet meat. पदक *n*. साखरवगैरेची वडी *f*.

LUBBARD, LUBBER, *n. sturdy, heavy, ignorant, lazy fellow.* लठ्ठेश्वर, लठ्ठाश्रम, लोठाश्रम, लट्ठामिश्र, वृथापुष्ट, ठोंबा, ठोंब्या, ठोंब, अबळ्याबंब, शुंभ, लोधडा, लोधा, सोट, सोटबहिरी, सोटेपीर, सोटेबारगीर, सोटेभैरव, म्हशा *or* म्हैशा, म्हशागुग्गूळ, मठ्या, पोळ, नंदी, रेडा, आर, मैंद, ढब्बू, अचळोजी, अचळोबा, कंठाळ्या माणूस, मसणखुंट.

LUBBERLY, *a. large and lazy.* ठोंब्या, मठ्या, बहुचा, घोणशा, ढोण्या, धडेल, गलेलठ्ठ, धडल्याब, बोजड, धस्समसूळ, धसमुसळा *or* मुसळ्या, मोघळा, रट, रटाळा, रटेल.

LUBBERLY, *adv.* See AWKWARDLY.

LUBRIC, &c. See SLIPPERY, &c.

To LUBRICATE, *v. a. make smooth and slippery.* गुळगुळीत-बुळबुळीत-मऊसूत-&c. करणें, मवागी *f*.-मवाळी *f*.-&c. लावणें *or* लावून मऊ करणें.

LUBRICATED, *p.* v. V. गुळगुळीत केलेला, &c.

LUBRICATION, *n.* v. V. गुळगुळीत करणें *n*. &c.

LUCENT. See SHINING.

LUCERN, *n.*—the plant. विलायती गवत *n*.

LUCID, *a. shining,* v. BRIGHT. लकलकीत, लख्ख, लकीलख्ख.

2 *pellucid,* v. CLEAR. स्वच्छ, निर्मल *or* ळ, सोज्वल.

3 *perspicuous,* v. CLEAR. सुबोध, सुखबोध, अक्लिष्ट.

4 *not darkened by delirium.* शुद्धीचा, सावधपणाचा, हुशारीचा.

LUCIDITY, LUCIDNESS. See BRIGHTNESS, CLEARNESS.

LUCIFER. See VENUS. 2 See SATAN. 3 See MATCH.

LUCIFEROUS, LUCIFIC, *a.* प्रकाशजनक, प्रकाशोत्पादक.

LUCK, *n.* v. FORTUNE, DESTINY. दैव *n*. नसीब *n*. भाग्य *n*. दैवयोग *m*. दैवदशा *f*. दैवगति *pop.* दैवगत *f*. साधलाद *or* साधलाध *f*. लाभालाभ *m*.

By hard labor and with good l. काळाकष्टानें.

Good l. सुभाग्य *n*. सुदैव *n*. भाग्य *n*. यश *n*.

Ill l. q. v. दुर्भाग्य *n*. दुर्दैव *n*.

L. in making money. द्रव्यादृष्ट *n*.

To be in l. दैव *n*.-&c. उघडणें-उदयास येणें *g. of s.* भाग्योदय *m*. होणें *g. of s.* होताकाळ *m*.-होतीवेळ *f*. असणें *g. of s.*

LUCKILY, *adv.* v. A. 1. भाग्यानें, भाग्योदयानें, भाग्यबलानें, भा-

ग्याच्या जोरानें, भाग्योत्कर्षानें.

Luckiness, *n.* v. A. 1. सलाबतपणा *m.* बखतवारी *f.* सलाबत *f.* सद्दी *f.* सभाग्यता *f.* भाग्यशालित्व *n.*

Luckless, *a.* v. Unfortunate. दुर्दैवाचा, अभागी, उणेदैवाचा, अपयशी, भाग्यहीन, हीनभाग्य, अभाग्य, अभाग्यवान्, दग्धहस्ती, कपाळ फुटका, फुटक्या कपाळाचा, दैवफुटका, कपाळकरंटा, करंट्या कपाळाचा, करटा, करंटा, खापरतोंड्या, पांढऱ्या पाचाचा, हाडकपाळी *or* कपाळ्या.

Lucklessness, *n.* v. A. दैवाचा-&c. करंटेपणा *m.* करंटेपणा *m.* &c. दुर्दैव *n.* दुर्भाग्य*n.* कंवखती *f.* दौर्भाग्य*n.* भाग्यहीनता *f.* अपयश*n.*

Sign or mark of l. करंटें लक्षण *n.*

Lucky, *a.* v. Fortunate. दैवाचा, मोठ्या दैवाचा, सुदैवाचा, भाग्याचा, सलाबतीचा, &c. भाग्यवान् *pop.* भाग्यवंत, भाग्यशाली, यशस्वी, बखतवार, सभाग्य, पद्महस्ती, वरदहस्ती, होंड्या कपाळाचा.

L. at making money. द्रव्यादृष्टि.

2 *of favorable influence, auspicious.* शुभ, शुभकर, बरकतीचा, लाभाचा, सु in comp. [र्मसंयोग *m.*

L. conjunction, union of merit and fortune. कर्मध-

Lucrative, *a.* v. Gainful. मिळकतीचा, नफ्याचा, सरफ्याचा, सरफेवार, किफाइती, किफाइतवार, ओला, ओलाव्याचा, आर्द्र, हितावह. [आर्द्रता *f.*

Lucrativeness, *n.* v. A. ओलावा *m.* ओलावा *m.* ओलेपणा *m.*

Lucre, *n.* v. Gain. प्राप्ति *f.* नफा *m.* लाभ *m.*

To **Lucubrate**, *v. n. study by candle light or at night.* दिव्यानें अध्ययन *n.*-अभ्यास *m.*-&c. करणें, निश्यध्ययन *n.*-रात्र्यध्ययन *n.*-&c. करणें.

Lucubration, *n. any thing composed by candle light, &c.* रात्रीस-दिव्यानें-&c. केलेला ग्रंथ-पुस्तक-&c. रात्रीचें कवन *n.*

Ludicrous, *a exciting laughter, laughable.* हसें यायाजोगाजोगता-&c. हसें आणाया जोगा-&c. हास्यजनक, हास्यकर, हास्यकारक, हास्योत्पादक, हास्यप्रद, हास्यरसप्रधान.

Ludicrously, *adv.* v. A. हसें यायाजोगा-&c. *decl.*

Ludicrousness, *n.* v. A. हास्यरस *m.* हास्यजनकता *f.* हास्योत्पादकता *f.* हास्यजननशक्ति *f.*

Lues venerea, *n.* उपदंश *m.* गर्मी *f.*—in cant or covert phraseology. बाहेरची पीडा *f.* बाहेरबाधा *f.* वीसनखीची बाधा *f.* वीसनखीचा उपद्रव *m.* दुःख *n.* ओलांडा *or* ओलंडा *m.* बहिर्विकार *m.*

Afflicted with l. उपदंशी, दुरखेरा, दुरखारा, दुखभऱ्या.

Eruption into purulent sores from l. कथली व्याध *or* व्याधि *f.* कथलें दुःख *n.* कथल्यारोग *m.*

Lug. See Ear.

To **Lug**, *v. a. hale,* v. To Drag. धरून ओढणें, खेचून ओढणें-नेणें, फरफरावणें *or* फरफरिवणें.

To l. by the ears. कान धरून ओढणें-नेणें.

To l. out.—a sword. उपसणें, नागवा करणें.

Lug-sail, *n.* धंडा *m.* ?

Luggage, *n.* v. Baggage. सामान *n.* खाटखडबड *f.* बाडबिशात *f.* पडतल *or* पडदळ *n.*

Lugubrious, *a. mournful,* v. Sorrowful. रडवा, रडका.

Luke-warm, *n. mildly warm.* कोमट *or* कोंबट, ओंबट, सोमट, सोमाळा, शिळवळा, कातामोडलेला, अंगउबारा, मोहजळ *or* मोहचूळ, मंदोष्ण, कोष्ण, ईषदुष्ण, नरम, निमगरम, गरमनरम, सरगरम.

2 *not zealous. ardent, &c.* v. Indifferent. आस्थेचा कमी, कमी आस्थेचा, उद्योगाचा धंडा, उदास, अनास्थ, मंदोत्कंठ, मंदोत्साह.

Luke-warmly, *adv.* v. A. 2. उदासपणानें, कमीआस्थेनें, आळसानें, थंडाईनें, अनास्थापूर्वक, मंदोत्साहानें, उपेक्षाबुद्धीनें.

Luke-warmness, *n.* v. A. 1. कोमटपणा *m.* ओंबटपणा *m.* &c. कोमटाई *f.* निमगरमी *f.*

2 कमीआस्था *f.* अनास्था *f.* उदासपणा *m.* अनुत्कंठा *f.* अनुत्साह *m.* थंडाई *f.* थंडी *f.* आळस *m.* आलस्य *n.* मंदोत्साह *m.*

To **Lull**, *v. a. compose to sleep.* शेजेस आणणें, अंगाई *f.* करणें-करून निजवणें, झोप *f.*-नीज *f.*-नीद *f.*-&c. आणणें.

2 *soothe, appease, quiet, &c.* v. To Compose. शांतवणें *or* सांतवणें, शांतकरणें, आळवणें, आळवून घेणें, सांत्वन *pop.* शांतवन *n.*-&c. करणें *g. of o.*

To **Lull**, *v. n. subside,*—wind. पडणें, बसणें, शांत होणें.

Lull, *n. temporary cessation of wind.* वाऱ्याचीबंदी *f.*- शांति *f.* वायु विराम *m.* वायुस्थैर्य *n.* वायुशांति *f.*

Lullaby, *n. song to put infants to sleep.* पाळणा *m.* हळआई *or* हल्ई *f.*अंगाई*f.*गाई *f.*गाऊ*f.* जोजो *ind.* उरोमुरो *ind.* डिगडिग *ind.*

Lumbago, *n. pain in the loins.* टिचरें *or* टिचें *n.v.* भर, एलकी *f.* उसण *f,* करक *f.* all with *v.* भर, पाठनळ *m. pl. .v.* ताठ, कटिवात *m.*

To get l. कमर *f.* भरणें *or* धरणें *g. of s.*

Lumbal, Lumbar, *a. pertaining to the loins.* कमेरचा,माजाचा, माजाडाचा, कटिदेशाचा, कटिदेशसंबंधी.

L. region. माजाड *n.* चौक *m.*

Lumber, *n. things useless or cumbersome, things heaped together.* खेलखाना *m.* अडगळ *f.* अगडतगड *or* अगडबगड *n.* अटरफटर *n.* सटरफटर *n.* जकिरा *or* जकेरा *m.* रिकामी अडचण *f.* गाबाळ *m. n.* कतवार *n.*ऐचण *f.*गचपण*n.*अनुपयोगी सामान*n.*

L. room. गंजीखाना *m.* जकीरखाना *m.*

To **Lumber**, *v. a. heap together disorderly.* घोळ करून-गळ्हाटा करून-&c. ठेवणें-मांडणें, ढीग-ढिगारा-&c. करून ठेवणें-घालून ठेवणें.

2 *fill with lumber.* अडगळीनें-&c. भरणें, अडगळ *f.*-&c. भरणें *with locative case of o.* अडगळ भरून चेंदणें.

Luminary, *n. body which gives light,* v. Light. दीप *m.* दीपक *m.* प्रकाशक पदार्थ *m.*-वस्तु *n.*-&c.

2 fig. तेजःपुंज *m.* तेजोराशि *m.*

Luminous. See Bright, Shining.

Lump, *n. small mass.* डळा *m.* गरा *m.* गड्डा *m.* भेला *m.* भेली *f.* खडा *m.* रवा *m.* रवका *m.* डिखळ *or* डिखूळ *n.* डिखळी *f.* डिखोळी *f.* डिखुळणी *f.* पिंड *m.*

L. of hardened fæces or scybala. लेंड*n.* लेंडी *f.* गुठळी *or* गुठोळी *f.* पिटकी *f.*

L. or nodule of dung. लेंड *n.* लेंडी *f.* लेंडूक *n.*

2 (esp. of something soft). लबका *or* लपका *m.* लादा *m.* लगदा *m.* लाखोटा *m.* [लंबथा *m.*

L. of flesh, &c. as torn of. लवका *m.* लचका *m.* लोधा *m.*

3 *shapeless mass.* गोळा *m.* गड्डा *m.* गड्डा *m.* डळा *m.* ठेप *f.* भेंडा *m.* पेंड *m.* खाप *f.* पिंड *m.* गोल *m.*

In one l. एकथोक, एकथोप, एकरकम. [बांठा *m.*

4 *collection,* v. Clot. गोठळी *or* गुठळी *or* गुठोळी *f.* डळा *m.*

5 *whole, gross.* भररास *f.* ठोकमाल *m.* ठोकजमा *f.* ठोकबेरीज *f.*

In the l. or gross. एकठोक, एकथोक, ठोक *or* थोक, सकट *or* सगट, सकटनिकट *or* सगटनिगट, सरसकट *or* सरसगट, सकटासाली, सगटाईनें, सकटांत, सकटामध्यें, सरनिसर, उचलक *or* ल, एकंदर, उक्ता *decl.* उक्तें, उधड, उधडा *decl.* एकरकम, घाऊक.

Sale in the gross or l. एकंदर बिकरी *f.*

To pay, lend, give, *or* borrow, receive, &c. in a l. एकमूठ-एकेमुठीनें देणें-घेणें-&c.

To LUMP, *v. a. throw into a mass or body.* एकगोळा *m.*-एकरास *f.*-एकढीग *m.*-&c. करणें *g. of o.* एकंदर करणें, एकठोक-एकथोप-&c. ठेवणें-मांडणें-घालणें, पिंडीकरण *n.* करणें *g. of o.*

2 (sums, items, particulars, &c.) एकरकम *f.*-एककलम *n.*-&c. लिहणें-सांगणें-मांडणें.

LUMPED, *p.v.*V.1. एकगोळा केलेला, एकठोक ठेवलेला, &c. पिंडीकृत.

LUMPING, *a. thumping, whacking, &c.* v. LARGE. रटाला, रटेल, रट्ट, लट्ठ, लठ्ठा, रपाटा, बताडा, कंडारणा. [लबुद्धि.

LUMPISH, *a. dull, heavy, gross.* lit. fig. जड, स्थूल, मठ्ठया, स्थू-

LUMPISHNESS, *n.* v. A. जडपणा *m.* स्थूलपणा *m.* जडता *f.* स्थूलता *f.* स्थौल्य *n.* स्थूलबुद्धि *f.*

LUMPY, *a. having lumps.* गुठळयांचा, डिखळयांचा, गठ्ठ्यांचा, ढेपाळ, डिफळी.

LUNACY, *n.* v. MADNESS. बेडन. उन्मादm. उन्मादवायु *m.*

LUNAR, LUNARY, *a. relating, &c. to the moon.* चंद्राचा, &c. चंद्रसंबंधी, चांद्र, चांद्रिक, सौम्य, सौमिक, ऐंदव.

Lunar day. तिथि *pop.* तीथ *f.* The l. days (whether of the waxing or of the waning moon) are, 1st प्रतिपदा *f.* पाडवा *m.*–2nd. द्वितीया *f.* बीज *f.*–3rd तृतीया *f.* तीज *f.*–4th चतुर्थी *f.* चौथ *f.*–5th पंचमी *f.*–6th षष्ठी *f.* सट *f.*–7th सप्तमी *f.*–8th अष्टमी *f.*–9th नवमी *f.*–10th दशमी *f.*–11th एकादशी *f.* एकादस *f.*–12th द्वादशी *f.* बारस *f.* बारशी *f.*–13th त्रयोदशी *f.* तेरस *f.*–14th चतुर्दशी *f.* चौदस *f.* The day of new moon is, अमावस्या *or* अमावास्या *f.* अवस *f.* अमा *f.* The day of full moon is, पूर्णिमा *or* पौर्णिमा *f.* पुनव *f.* पौर्णमासी *f.* The 11th day of each waxing and waning moon is particularly holy, and has a particular name indicatory of some observance commanded and blessing annexed, or allusive to some recorded event upon it. The following are the names or titles of the two एकादशी of each month:—

चैत्र,	१	कामदा,	२	पापमोचनी,
वैशाख,	१	मोहिनी,	२	वरूथिनी,
ज्येष्ठ,	१	निर्जला,	२	अपरा,
आषाढ,	१	शयनी,	२	योगिनी,
श्रावण,	१	पुत्रदा,	२	कामिका,
भाद्रपद,	१	परिवर्तिनी,	२	अजा,
आश्विन,	१	पाशांकुशा,	२	इंदिरा,
कार्त्तिक,	१	बोधिनी,	२	रमा,
मार्गशीर्ष,	१	मोक्षदा,	२	फलदा,
पौष,	१	प्रजावर्द्धिनी,	२	सफला,
माघ,	१	जयदा,	२	षट्तिला,
फाल्गुन,	१	आमलकी,	२	विजया,

The figure 1 denotes the एकादशी of the शुद्धपक्ष or waxing moon, and the figure 2 that of the वद्यपक्ष or waning moon.

The एकादशी of the शुद्धपक्ष of the months आषाढ and कार्त्तिक are both called महाएकादशी. On the first Vishnu goes to sleep and on the second he awakes.

Difference of solar and l. days. क्षयतिथि *f.*

Inauspicious l. day. घाततिथि *f.* दग्धतिथि *f.*

L. day having no ceremony or rite commanded for it. वांझतिथि or वांझतीथ *f.*

L. eclipse. चंद्रग्रहण *n.*

L. mansion. नक्षत्र *n.*

L. measurement. चांद्रमान *n.*

L. month. चांद्रमास *m.*

L. year. चांद्र वर्ष *n.*

Observance of the fasts and rites of the several l. days. तिथिपालन *n.*

The L. dynasty. चंद्रवंश *m.* सोमवंश *m.*

LUNATED, *a. formed like a half moon.* अर्धचंद्राकार, अर्धचंद्राकृति.

LUNATIC, *a.* v. MAD. वेडा, पिसा, विक्षिप्त, पिसाटलेला, भुताटलेला. —Note; Lunacy is often attributed to demons.

LUNATION, *n. revolution of the moon.* चंद्रभगण *n.* भगणावृत्ति *f.* भगणभोग *m.* चंद्रपरिवर्त्तन *n.*

LUNCH, LUNCHEON, *n. food taken between meals.* चावा *m.* चबिना *m.* फराळ *m.* उपहार *m.*

To LUNCH, *a. n.* फराळ *m.*-उपहार *m.* करणें.

LUNGS, *n.* फुप्फुस *pop.* फुफूस *n.* फोपीस *n.*

To strain one's l. शिरा ताणून बोलणें.

LUNT, *n. match cord to fire a cannon.* जामगी *f.* तोडा *m.*

LURCH, *a. sudden roll of a ship.* गलबताचा-&c. गोता *m.* गलबताची-&c. लवंड *f.*

To fetch a l. गोता *m.*-लवंड *f.* खाणें.

To leave in the l. तोंडघशीं-दांतघशीं-फशीं-होमकुंडीं-&c. देणें-पाडणें, अभरवशीं-अधस्तापीं-अधःपातीं घालणें-पाडणें.

To be left in the l. तोंडघशीं-दांतघशीं-&c. पडणें.

That leaves in the l. अवसानघातकी, आइते वेळेस घात करणारा.

To LURCH, *v. n.*—a ship. लवंड *f.*-गोता *m.* खाणें, लवंडणें.

LURE, *n. bait, allurement, enticement.* आमिषn. खाऊm. पेंडीचा खडाm. लांच *f.* लालूच *f.* प्रलोभनn. लल्लाm.

To hold out a l. सासर *f.* पेरणें-पसरणें, लालूच *f.*-खाऊm.-अंबोण *f.*-&c. दाखवणें-देणें.

To LURE, *v. a. entice,* v. To ALLURE. मोहणें, लालूच *f.*-लोभm.-लाभm.-खाऊm.-&c. दाखवणें, सासर *f.* पसरणें, प्रलोभनn.-&c. करणें *g. of o.*

LURED, *p.* v. V. मोहित, प्रलोभित.

LURID. See DISMAL, GLOOMY.

To LURK, *v. n. lie in wait, lie close.* दडणें, लिकणें, छपणें, लपणें, दडून-लिकून-छपून-&c. बसणें, दडाm.-दडी *f.*-दबा *m.*-&c. मारणें-मारून बसणें.

LURKER, *n.* LURKING, *p. a.* v. V. दडणारा, लिकणारा, दबा मारणारा, &c. दड्या, दडीमाऱ्या.

LURKING, *n.* v. V.—*act.* दडणेंn. &c. दडाm. दडी *f.*

LURKING-PLACE, *n.* दडण *f.* लिकण *f.* लपण *f.*

LURKINGLY, *adv.* v. V. लपूनछपून, लपतछपत, लिकून चोरून.

Luscious, *a. sweet so as to nauseate.* भारी गोड, गोड तोंडफिरवणारा, मिठी बसवणारा, गोड, अतिमिष्ट.

2 *very sweet and rich, delicious.* बहुतगोड, फारगोड, फारमजेदार, फाररुचिर, स्वादिष्ट, अतिमधुर.

Lusciousness, *n.* v. A. 1. भारी गोडपणा*m.* मिठी बसवणारी गोडी *f.* अत्यंतगोडी *f.* अतिमिष्टता *f.*

2 फारगोडी *f.* मोठीगोडी *f.* अत्यंतगोडी *f.* माधुर्य*n.* मधुरता *f.*

Lusory, *a.* v. Playful. खेळाचा.

Lust, *n. longing desire,* v. Desire. सोस*m.* हांव *f.* लाहो*m.* हवस *or* हौस *f.* तृष्णा *f.* लालसा *f.* लिप्सा *f.*

2 *depraved desire.* दुष्टवासना *f.* पापवासना *f.* कुवासना *f.* दुर्वासना *f.* असद्वासना *f.*

3 *carnal desire, appetence.* काम*m.* मदन*m.* मदनेच्छा *f.* विषयसुखाभिलाष*m.* मैथुनेच्छा *f.* रमणेच्छा *f.* विषयवासना *f.* कामाग्नि*m.* कामानल*m.*

Inflamed with, mad with, blind from, &c. l. मदनमस्त, कामातुर, कामांध, कामार्त्त, कामाकुल, कामाक्रांत, कामाविष्ट, कामग्रस्त, कामाधीन, कामान्वित, कामयुक्त, कामजित, मदनविह्वल, &c.

To **Lust**, *v. n. desire vehemently, long,* v. To Desire. लोभणें, लुब्धणें, नितांतणें, धापणें, जीव*m.* टाकणें, प्राण*m.* ओकणें, जीव *m.* टांगला असणें *g. of s.*

2 *have depraved desires.* दुष्टवासना*f.*-पापवासना*f.*-कुवासना *f.* -&c. धरणें-बाळगणें-&c. *and with in. con.* होणें.

3 *desire carnally.* काम*m.*-मदन*m.*-&c. होणें- उत्पन्न होणें *in. con.* सकाम-&c. होणें, कामपूर्वक-मदनपूर्वक इच्छिणें.

Lustful, *a.* v. N. l. *and* Covetous. सोशी *or* सोसी, लोभी, हावरा *or* हवरा, हवसदार *or* हौसदार, कामी.

2 पापवासनेचा, कुवासनेचा, &c.

3 कामी, कामुक, कामबुद्धीचा, कामभावाचा, कामदृष्टीचा, &c. सकाम, संभोगी, कामबुद्धि, कामदृष्टि, काममय, कामात्मा, कामप्रवण, कामवृत्ति, कामासक्त, कामवृत्त, कामारूढ, जातकाम, स्त्रीलंपट, स्त्रीव्यसनी, स्त्रीव्यासंगी, स्त्रीछंदी, रांडछंदी, खजाळ, खाजाळा *or* खाजाळू, फेटाळ, स्त्रीपर, स्त्रीरत, व्यवायी, व्यवायपरायण, व्यवायपर, कामाभिलाषी, कामेच्छु, मदनेच्छु, रजोगुणी, राजस. Some terms for *a lustful person*, answering to *lewdster, lecher, &c. &c.* are व्यसनी, बिसनी, संभोगी, इष्कबाज, कासोट्याचा हलका *or* ढिला, बाहिरख्याली, बाहेरव्यसनी, खाजाळू, खाजाळा, खजाळ. See also Libertine.

Lustfully, *adv.* v. A. 3. कामबुद्धीनें, कामदृष्टीनें, कामभावानें, कामबुद्ध्या, कामदृष्ट्या, कामानें, कामपूर्वक, कामभावपूर्वक.

Lustfulness, *n.* v. A. 3. कामीपणा *m.* &c. कामुकता *f.* कामिता *f.* सकामता *f.* कामासक्ति *f.* कामबुद्धि *f.* कामदृष्टि*f.* कामभाव*m.*

Lustily, *adv.* v. A. जीव तोडून, जीव खर्चून, जीव देऊन, बळकट.

Lustiness, *n.* v. A. जोम *m. n.* जोमदारी *f.* बळकटी *f.* आंगाची बळकटी *f.*-खबरदारी *f.*

Lustral, *a. relating to, or used in purification.* शुद्धीचा, शुद्धीच्या उपयोगाचा, शुद्धिकर, शुद्धिकारक, शुचिकर, शुचिकारक.

To **Lustrate**, *v. a.* v. To Purify. शुद्ध-&c. करणें, शुद्धि *f.*-शुद्धिकरण *n.*-शुचिकरण *n.*-&c. करणें *g. of o.*

Lustration, *n.* v. V.—*act.* शुद्धिकरण *n.* शुचिकरण *n.*—*state.* शुद्धि *f.*

Lustre, *n.* v. Brightness. कांति *f. pop.* कांत *f.* तेज *n.*

2 (of a gem). पाणी*n.* जोत *f.* ढाळ *m.* तेज*n.* तेजगी *f.* कूट *f.* ओज *n. f.*

That has the l. of the planet Venus. शुक्री.

To shed it's l.—a pearl, &c. ढाळणें.

3 *eminence, eclat, renown, &c.* शोभा *f.* प्रतिष्ठा *f.* तेज *n.* रंग *m.* रूप *n.* नांव *n.* नांवरूप *n.* झील *f.* शिक्कल *f.*

Lustrous, *a.* See Bright, Brilliant. 2—a gem, &c. पाण्याचा, ढाळाचा, जोतीचा, &c. पाणीदार, ढाळदार, जोतदार, तेजाळ, तेजवान् *pop.* तेजवंत.

Lustrum, *n. period of five years.* वर्षपंचक *n.* अब्दपंचक *n.* युग *n.*

Lusty, *a. strong, vigorous, able of body, healthy,* v. Stout. धट्टाकट्टा *or* खट्टा, जोधा, जोमदार, घटमूट, जाड, जाडगा, ताजालठ, ताजातवाना, ताजाजवान, कट्टा, जवानकट्टा, जानजवान, धाटामोटा, कुप्पा, जमदाडा *or* ढा, गडदू, दोनटक्यांनीं धड-बळकट-&c.

Lutanist, *n. player on the lute.* विणेकरी, तंबुऱ्या, तंबुरची *or* जी, वीणावादक, वैणिक.

Lutarious, *a. pertaining, &c. to mud.* चिखलाचा, चिखलांतला, पंकस्थ, कर्दमस्थ.

2 *of the color of mud.* चिखलाच्या रंगाचा, पंकवर्ण.

Lute, *n.*—musical instr. वीणा *f. pop.* विणा *m.* तंबुरा *or* तंबोरा *m. dim.* तंबुरी *f.* बीन *m. n.*

Bridge of a l. तारदानी *f.*

L. of one string. तुणतुणें *n.* किन्नरी *f.*

Luter, Lutist. See Lutanist.

Lutulent. See Muddy.

To **Luxate**, *v. a.* v. To Disjoint. जोड *m.*-सांधा *m.*-&c. उखळणें, टांके *m. pl.* ढिले करणें *g. of o.*

Luxation. See Dislocation.

Luxuriance, Luxuriancy, *n. rank or excessive growth.* माज *m.* मात *m.* ऊत *m.* उफाड्याची वाढ *f.* वाढीचा भर *m.* अतिवृद्धि *f.* वृद्धिबाहुल्य *n.* वृद्ध्याधिक्य *n.*

Luxuriant, *a.* v. N. उफाड्याचे वाढीचा, वाढीच्या भराचा, माताचा, वृद्धिबाहुल्याचा, &c. माजलेला, वाढाळू, वाढाळ, उद्दाम.

Luxuriantly, *adv.* v. A. उफाड्यानें.

To **Luxuriate**, *v. n. grow exuberantly.* माजणें, मातणें, ऊत *m.* येणें, उतणें, वठणें, फांपावणें *or* फोपावणें, बांबलणें, डवरणें, डगळणें *or* डघळणें, मसण माजणें.

2 *live luxuriously, revel.* बहर *f.* मारणें-उडवणें, सुखांगणें, सुंखाडणें, धणंगणें.

Luxurious, *a. indulging in gratifications, voluptuous.* भोगी, बिलासी, विहारी, चयनी, सुखवासी, सुखाभिलाषी, विषयभोगाभिलाषी, सुखभोगासक्त, भोगासक्त, सुखभोगपरायण. Some terms for *a voluptuous person* are, सुखानंद, सुखापुरी, सुखबाबु, खुशालचंद.

2 *administering to luxury.* ऐशआरामाचा, सुखाचा, बिलासाचा, सुखोपभोगाचा, सुखकारक, सुखभोगकर, सुखभोगसाधक, सुखभोगावह, विलाससुखप्रद.

Luxuriously, *adv.* v. A. 1. सुखानें, बिलासानें, सुखभोगपूर्वक, विलासभोगपूर्वक, ऐशआरामानें, ऐशआरामींत.

Luxuriousness, *n.* v. A. 1. सुखभोगासक्ति *f.* विषयभोगासक्ति *f.* भोगारासक्ति *f.* भोगलंपटता *f.* सुखभोग *m.* विषयभोग *m.* विषयोपसेवा *f.* विषयसेवा *f.* सुखसेवा *f.*

Luxury, *n.* See Luxuriousness. 2.—a luxury, v. Dainty. मिष्टान्न *n.* स्वाद्वन्न *n.*

3 *any thing gratifying to the senses.* सुखभोगाचा-विलासाचा-ऐशआरामाचा-&c. पदार्थ *m.*-जिन्नस *m.*-&c. विषयसुखसाधन *n.* सुखसाधन *n.* सुखसाहित्य *n.* विषयसुखसाहित्य *n.*

LYE, *n.*—the impregnated water. खारपाणी *n.* खारवणी *n.* क्षारोदक *n.*

LYING, *n. uttering falsehood,* v. LIE. खोटें बोलणें *n.* मिथ्योक्ति *f.*

LYING, *a. mendacious,* v. LIAR. खोटें बोलणारा, असत्यभाषी, असत्यवादी, असत्यवक्ता, मिथ्यावादी, मृषावादी, अनृतभाषी, अनृतवादी, अनृतसंध.

LYING OVER, *a.* कलंडा, कलता, कलथा.

LYMPH *n.*—in anatomy. पाणी *n.* उदकधातु *m.*

LYMPHATIC, *n.*—the vessel. शरीरांतर्गत जलवाहिनी *f.* मेदोवह *n.*

LYNX, *n.* कोळिसरा *or* कोळिस्ता *m.* कोळसुंदा *or* कोळसुना *m.* कोळीस *m.*

LYRE, *n.* v. LUTE. वीणा *f. pop.* विणा *m.*

LYRIC, LYRICAL, *a.* विण्यावर गाण्याचा-जोगा-&c. वैणिक.

LYRIST, *n.* विणावाजविणारा, विणेकरी.

M.

M. is represented by म.

MA. See MOTHER.

MACE, *n. ensign of authority.* छडी *f.* काठी *f.* वेत्र *n.*

2 *club, &c.* v. CUDGEL. सोटा *m.* सोडगा *m.* गदा *f.*

An iron m. लोहदंड *m.*

3—the spice. जायपत्री *f.* पत्री *f.* जातीपत्री *f.* थोरलीपत्री *f.*

Spurious m. कायपत्री *f.* मायपत्री *f.* रामपत्री *f.*

MACE-BEARER, *n.* छडीबरदार, छडीदार, चोबदार, भालदार, सोटेबरदार, ढालाईत, वेत्रधर, वेत्रधारी, वेत्रपाणि, दंडधारी, दंडधर.

The mace-bearers, &c.—the pursuivants generally of a great man. चोबदारभालदार.

To MACERATE, *v. a. make thin, waste.* रोडवणें, खंगवणें, झिजवणें, गळहाटणें, क्षीण-कृश-रोड-&c. करणें, कर्शन *n.*-&c. करणें *g. of o.*

2 *steep.* भिजूं-भिजत घालणें, भिजवणें, भीज *f.* करणें *g. of o.*

MACERATED, *p.* v. V. 1. रोडवलेला, क्षीणकेलेला, &c. क्षीण, कृश.

2 भिजत घातलेला, भिजवलेला.

MACERATION, *n.* v. V. 1.—*act.* रोडवणें *n.* &c. कर्शन *n.* कृशीकरण *n.* क्षीणकरण *n.*

2 भिजवणें *n.* &c. भिजवणी *f.* भीज *f.*

To MACHINATE, *v. a. plan, scheme,* v. To CONTRIVE. योजणें, रचणें, बांधणें, जोडणें, योजना *f.*-&c. करणें *g. of o.*

MACHINATION, *n.* v. V.—*act.* योजणें *n.* रचणें *n.* &c. योजणूक *f.* रचणूक *f.* योजना *f.* रचना *f.*

I. *malicious plot or scheme, device to injure.* कुभांड *n.* कुष्मांड *n.* कुदांड *n.* कुफरांड *n.* कुफराण *n.* कंडाळी *f.* व्यूह *pop.* विभू *or* विहू *m.* कचाट *or* किचाट *n.* लचंड *or* लचांड *n.* सेंकटें *n.* तरकट *n.* बगलाट *n.* कुलंगडें *n.* कुबेडें *n.* थोतांड *n.* कंवटाल *or* ळ *n.* कंवटल *or* ल्य *n.* भारूड *n.* कैपत *f.* कुसृष्टि *f.* कुकल्पना *f.* तकराळ *f.* पाखंड *n.* लिगाड *n.*

MACHINATOR, *n.* v. V. योजणारा, रचणारा, &c. योजक, रचक.

I.—*of malicious devices, &c.* कुभांडी *or* कुभांड्या, कुभांडखोर, कुदांडी *or* कुदांड्या, कुदांडखोर, कुफरांडी *or* कुफरांड्या, कुफराणी, तरकटी, तरकट्या, तरकटबाज, थोतांडी, पाखंडी, लिगाडी, कंवटाल्या *or* ळ्या, कैपती *or* कैपत्या.

MACHINE, *n. engine.* यंत्र *pop.* जंत्र *n.*

MACHINERY, *n. combination of mechanical powers.* कळसूत्र *or* कळासूत्र *n.* कीलकांटा *m.* यंत्रसाहित्य *n.*

2 *machines in general.* यंत्रें *pop.* जंत्रें *n. pl.*

Made or done by m. यंत्री, जंत्री. [यंत्रकार.

MACHINIST, *n. constructor &c. of machines.* यंत्र करणारा,

2 *one versed in machines.* यंत्रांचा माहितगार, यंत्रविद्यानिपुण.

MACKEREL *n.* समुद्रांतला एक मासा आहे.

MACROCOSM, *n. the universe.* विश्व *n.* त्रिभुवन *n.*

MACULA, *n.* v. SPOT, STAIN. डाग *m.* ठिकें *n.* ठिपका *m.* लांच्छन *n.* कलंक *m.*

MAD, *a. disordered in mind, crazed, deranged, insane, lunatic, &c.* वेडा (*remiss.* वेडसर, वेडगळ, वेडपा, वेडका,) पिसा, दिवाना, वेडलागलेला, वायचळलेला, *&c.* खुळा, पिसाटीक, चळेल, नष्टबुद्धि, भ्रष्टबुद्धि, हतबुद्धि, विक्षिप्त, विक्षिप्तमनस्क, विक्षिप्तबुद्धि, विक्षिप्तमति, बुद्धिभ्रष्ट, नष्टेंद्रिय, मत्त, उन्मत्त, उन्मादी, सोन्मद, उन्मादवान्, धंद्र, धंद्रट ;—as intensitive, *frantic, furious, raving, raging, outrageous, &c.* मारकावेडा, धोंडेमारणारा-फोडणारा, दगडमारणारा, पिसळलेला, पिसेंलागलेला, भरतेंआलेला ;—loosely or compreh. *mad, fatuous, foolish, &c.* वेडाखुळा,—freely, *mad, furious, &c.* वेडापिसा.

Stark m. धडधडीत-झळझळीत-&c. वेडा.

To drive m. वेड *n.* भरवणें-भरणें, वेडवणें *or* वेडावणें.

To go m. *become deranged, crazed, &c.* वेड *n.*-चळ *m.n.*-&c. लागणें *in. con.* वेडावणें, वेडाळणें, वेडगळणें, चळावणें, पिसळणें, पिसाटणें, चवणें *or* चेवणें, चळणें, वायचळणें, निकळणें, फांटा *m.* फुटणें-भरणें *in. con.* वांव *f.* चढणें *in. con.* धोंडे-दगड-&c. मारूं लागणें, दगडमारायास सुटणें, धोंडे *m. pl.* फोडूं लागणें.

To run m.—a dog, jackall, &c. पिसळणें.

2 *proceeding from madness, indicating derangement.* वेडा, वेडेपणाचा, वेड्याचा, वेडेचाराचा, बुद्धिभ्रंशसूचक-ज्ञापक-बोधक.

Some phrases expressive of *mad proceedings, wild excesses, &c.* are, वेड पिकणें, वेडाचा पाऊस पडणें.

3 *furious, enraged.* काव्हलेला, खवळलेला, क्षोभलेला, तमवम, खावरा बावरा *or* कावरा बावरा, तारका बारका *or* तारखा बारखा, मदोत्कट.

4 *vehemently desirous, &c.* वेडा, पिसा, (as गाण्याचापिसा, पुराणाचा वेडा), अळका, अळकुवा.

MAD-BRAINED. See MAD.

MADCAP, *n.* Under this word as bearing the general sense of *a wild and recklessly daring person,* and as comprehending the varied import of such terms and designations as *madman, mad fellow, dreadnought, dare devil, wild fire, desperado, a madbrained, crackbrained, harebrained, neck or nought fellow,* we have collected the correspondent *Marathi* terms and phrases. अवतार, अवतारी, अवतार घेतलेला, वेडापीर, कपाळफोड्या, पिसाट, उरफाट्या काळजाचा, उफराटें काळीज, आततायी *or* अतत्यायी, भस्मासुर, उत्पाती, साहृ-

सी, साहसिक, साहसकर्मा, उग्रकर्मा, घोरकर्मा, राक्षस, जिवावर उदार, ज्याचें काळीज पाठीस आहे, पाठीच्या काळजाचा, रगड्या, रपाट्या, खंदातटू, शेखचिल्ली, ओलीभांग, दिग्विजयी, मंत्रचळया, बळी, मारीन कीं मरेन म्हणणारा, नाहीं तेंच करणारा, हातावर शीर घेऊन असणारा, शेंडी तुटो कीं पारंबी तुटो म्हणणारा, देहं वापातयेत् अर्थंवासाधयेतम्हणणारा. [क्षागारn.

MAD-HOUSE, *n.* वेड्यांचा बंदीखाना *m.* विक्षिप्तालय *n.* विक्षि-

MADMAN. See MAD. 1.

MADAM, *n.* v. LADY. बाई *f.* साहेब. The English word under the form of मडम *or* मडमसाहेब is common.

To MADDEN, *v. a. make mad.* वेड *n.* भरवणें-भरणें, वेडवणें *or* वेडावणें, वेडा-&c. करणें, बुद्धिभ्रंश *m.*-&c. करणें *g. of o.*

2 See To EXCITE. To ANGER.

To MADDEN, *v. n. become mad.* वेडा-&c. होणें, वेड *n.*-&c. होणें-लागणें-भरणें *in. con.* बायचळ *n.* होणें, वेडवणें *or* वेडावणें, वेडगळणें, वेडाळणें, बांव *f.* चढणें *in. con.* बुद्धिभ्रंश *m.*-&c. होणें *g. of s.*—esp. from demoniac influence. भुताटणें, पिसावणें, पिसाटणें, पिसळणें.

MADDER, *n.*—the plant. मंजिष्ठ *m. n.* [मित.

MADE, *p.* v. V. 1. उत्पन्न केलेला, केलेला, &c. कृत, उत्पन्न, नि-

2 घडलेला, केलेला, &c.

3 केलेला, बनावलेला, चा (used with the noun, as मातीचा made of earth, सोन्याचा made, of gold, &c.) मय, आत्मक घटित—all in comp.

4 केलेला, कृत्रिम केलेला, &c. कृत्रिम.

M. up. *fabricated.* बनावट, बनींव.

MADLY, *adv.* v. A. 1. वेडानें, वेडेपणानें, वेड्यासारखा, वेड्यावाणी, वेडा होऊन, बुद्धिभ्रंशपूर्वक.

MADNESS, *n.* v. A. 1 वेड *n.* पिसें *n.* खूळ *n.* वेडेपणा *m.* &c. सर *m.* चळ *m.* (as धनचळ, कामचळ, स्त्रीचळ, &c.), बायचळ *m.* बुद्धिभ्रंश *m.* बुद्धिभ्रम *m.* मतिभ्रम *m.* बुद्धिविक्षेप *m.* उन्मत्तवायु *m.* उन्माद *m.* उन्मादवायु *m.* मद *m.*

M. arising from joy. हर्षवायु *m.* आनंदवायु *m.*

Sham m. or idiocy. घालवेड*n.* घालपिसें *n.*

Shammer of m. or idiocy. घालवेडा, कुडावेडा, घालपिसा.

To feign m. वेड घेऊन पेडगावांस जाणें.

To provoke or vex to m. वेड *n.* भरवणें.

3 काव्हलेलेपणा *m.* खवळलेलेपणा *m.* कावरेबावरेपणा *m.* &c.

4 वेड *n.* पिसें *n.* चळ *m. f.* [वेडेपणा*m.*

I. *mad tricks and pranks.* वेडेचार *m. pl.* वेडेवेडेचार *m. pl.*

MÆNORRHAGIA, *n.* धुपणी *f.* प्रदर *pop.* पदर *m.* होळणी *f.* असुक *n.* योन्यर्श *n.* स्त्रीरोग *m.*

MAGAZINE, *n. store house, &c.* कोठा *m.* कोठी *f.* कोठार *n.* कोठारी *f.* भांडागार *n.* भांडारगृह *n.* [*n.* शस्त्रागार *n.*

2 *arsenal, armory.* तोफखाना *m.* शिलेखाना *m.* युद्धद्रव्यागार

3 (of powder). दारूखाना *m.*

4 अनेकविषयांवर केलेलें नियतकाळीं निघणारें पुस्तक *n.*

MAGGOT, *n.* v. WORM. किडा *m.* अळी *f.* अळई *f.* सूत *n.* किर्म *or* किरीम *m.*

A maggoty sore. किवण *n.* किणा *m.*—Bullock, &c. affected with it. किवण्या.—Charm curing it. किवण *n.* उकवण*or*उकवीण *n.*—Swarm of flies producing it. सडी *f.*

To swarm with maggots. बुचबुचणें.

2 See FANCY. [बुचबुचाट*m.*

MAGGOTINESS, *n.* v. A. 1. किडकेपणा *m.* &c. बुचबूच *f. intens.*

MAGGOTY, *a. having maggots.* किडका, किडवळ, किडेला, किडक.

2 See FANCIFUL.

MAGIC, *n. sorcery, enchantment.* जादू *f.* जादूगिरी*f.* चेटक *n.* इलम*m.* बीरविद्या *f.* शाबरीविद्या *f.* पिशाचविद्या *f.* असुरीविद्या *f.* कुविद्या *f.* असद्विद्या *f.* जारण मारणाची विद्या*f.* शाबर*pop.* साबर *n.* अभिचार *m.* अभिचारविद्या *f.*—compreh. जादूटोणा *m.*

Magical formula. See CHARM.

Magical device—gener. (against demoniac influence or disease). तोटगा *or* तोडगा *m.* कुबेडें *n.* कुडें *n.* कुडेंपाबडें *n.* कुडबंडें *n.*

Magical process to injure. कंबटाल *or* ळ *n.* जारण *n.* जारणमारण *n.* अभिचार *m.*

MAGIC, MAGICAL, *a. of or belonging to magic.* जादूचा, जादूगिरीचा, बीरविद्येचा, &c. शाबरी, अभिचारी, अभिचारिक.

2 *done, &c. by magic.* जादूचा, जादूनें केलेला, पिशाचविद्येचा, पिशाचविद्येनें केलेला, शाबरकृत, शाबरी, शाबरीविद्येनें केलेला, अभिचारी.

MAGICALLY, *adv.* v. A. 1. जादूनें, जादूगिरीनें, बीरविद्येनें, &c.

MAGICIAN, *n. one that practises magic; sorcerer, enchanter, wizard, &c.* जादूगीर, जादूखोर, जादूवाला, इलमबाज, इलमी, बीरमंत्री, बावनबिऱ्या, चेटकी, चेटकाळया, कंबटाल्या *or* ळ्या, पिशाचविद्या जाणणारा, कुविद्या जाणणारा, अभिचारी, अभिचारिक, चित्रकर्मा, मूठमाऱ्या (caster of the charmed palmful of grain), गारपगार *or* गारपगारी (hailcausers), जांगुलिक (snake doctors), पाहण्या (finder of lost things).

MAGISTERIAL, *a. of or belonging to a magistrate.* फौजदारीचा, फौजदारीप्रकरणांतला, फौजदाराकडचा, माजिस्त्रेटाकडचा, फौजदारीसंबंधी, धर्माधिकारिसंबंधी, धर्माध्यक्षसंबंधी.

2 *such as suits a master, authoritative.* प्रभुपणाचा, धनीपणाचा, प्रभुत्वाचा, सत्ताविशिष्ट, प्रभुत्वविशिष्ट.

3 *arrogant, hauhty,* v. PROUD. अभिमानी, चढेल, मगरूर, धनीपणाच्या डौलाचा, ताठ्याचा, दिमाखाचा, आढ्यतेचा.

MAGISTERIALLY, *adv.* v. A. 1. फौजदारीच्या नात्यानें, फौजदारीच्या अमलानें, फौजदारीच्या संबंधानें, धर्माधिकारपरत्वेंकरून.

2 प्रभुपणानें, धनीपणानें, &c.

3 अभिमानानें, धनीपणाच्या डौलानें, अहंकारपूर्वक, अभिमानपुरस्सर, दर्पपूर्वक.

MAGISTERIALNESS, *n.* v. A. 2. धनीपणा *m.* प्रभुपणा *m.* प्रभुत्व *n.*

2 धनीपणाचा डौल*m.* आढ्यता *f.* चढेलपणा *m.* ताठा*m.* मगरुरी *f.*

MAGISTRACY, *n. office or dignity of a magistrate.* फौजदारी *f.* फौजदारी पाहण्याचा अमल *m.* माजिस्त्रेटाचाहुद्दा *m.* धर्माधिकार *m.* धर्माधिपत्य *n.*

2 *body of magistrates.* धर्माधिकारी *m. pl.* धर्माधिकारीमंडळी *f.* धर्माध्यक्षसमूह *m.*

MAGISTRAL. See MAGISTERIAL 2.

MAGISTRATE, *n.* फौजदारीपाहणारा, फौजदार, न्यायाधीश, धर्माधिकारी, धर्माध्यक्ष, दंडनायक. The English word, under the form of माजिस्त्रेट, is commonly used.

MAGNANIMITY, *n.* v. A. 1. मनाचा थोरपणा *m*-मोठेपणा *m.*-&c. मनाची थोरवी *f.* माहात्म्य*n.* मनोमहत्व *n.* मनःप्रौढता *f.* मनःप्रागल्भ्य *n.* औदार्य *n.* शौर्य *n.*

MAGNANIMOUS, *a. great of mind.* मनाचा थोर-मोठा-&c. थोरमनाचा, मोठ्यामनाचा, उदारमनाचा, प्रशस्तमनाचा, महामनस्क, महात्मा, महात्मिक, महाशय, उदारचेता, शूर.
2 *dictated, &c. by magnanimity.* थोरमनाचा, उदारमनाचा, &c. मनाच्याथोरवीचा, औदार्याचा, शौर्याचा, औदार्यपुरस्सर.

MAGNANIMOUSLY, *adv.* v. A. मोठ्यामनानें, उदारमनानें, &c. मनाचे थोरवीनें, मोठेंमनकरून, औदार्यपूर्वक.

MAGNATE, *n.* v. GRANDEE. उंचपदवीचामनुष्य *m.*

MAGNET, *n.* v. LOADSTONE. लोहचुंबक *m.*

MAGNETIC, MAGNETICAL, *a. of or belonging to the magnet.* लोहचुंबकाचा, लोहचुंबकसंबंधी, लोहचुंबकविषयक, लोहचुंबनधर्मक.
2 v. ATTRACTIVE. आकर्षक, आकर्षणधर्मक.

MAGNETISM, *n. power of the magnet.* लोहचुंबनधर्म *m.* लोहचुंबनगुण *m.* आकर्षणशक्ति *f.*

To MAGNETISE, *v. a.* लोहचुंबनधर्म *m.*-लोहचुंबनशक्ति *f.* देणें-आणणें, लोहचुंबन धर्म युक्त-&c. करणें.

MAGNIFIC, MAGNIFICAL. See MAGNIFICENT, FINE.

MAGNIFICENCE, *n.* v. A. शोभा *f.* छान *or* शान *f.* शानदारी *f.* उमदेपणा *m.* भव्यपणा *m.* थाट *m.* थाटमाट *or* थाटमांड *m.* अराष *or* अरास *f.* भव्यता *f.*

MAGNIFICENT, *a. grand, splendid,* v. FINE. उमदा, भव्य, छानदार, शानदार, छानीचा, नामी, धनत्तर, शोभिवंत, थाटाचा, सुभावणा, आलिज्याहां.
2 *fond of splendor.* छानीचा-थाटमाटाचा-&c. हौशी-शौकी.

MAGNIFICENTLY, *adv.* v. A. 1. छानीनें, छानदारीनें, मोठेशोभेनें, थाटमाट करून.

MAGNIFIED, *p.* v. V. 1. मोठाकरून दाखवलेला, मोठा दाखवलेला.
2 वाखाणलेला, &c. कीर्तित.

MAGNIFIER, *n.* MAGNIFYING, *p. a.* v. V. 1. मोठा करून दाखवणारा, मोठादाखवणारा, &c.
2 वाखाणणारा, थोरपणादेणारा, &c. कीर्त्तन-वर्णन *n.*-वर्णना *f.*-&c. कर्त्ता-कारी-&c.
I. *magnifying glass.* पदार्थ मोठा करून दाखविणारें भिंग *n.* स्थूल दर्शक भिंग *n.*

To MAGNIFY, *v. a. increase the apparent bulk of.* मोठा करून दाखवणें, मोठा दाखवणें, मोठा भासवणें, मोठा दिसेसा करणें.
2 *extol, laud, glorify,* v. To PRAISE. वाखाणणें, वर्णणें, कीर्त्तणें, थोरपणा *m.*-मोठेपणा *m.*-&c. देणें, वर्णणूक *f.*-&c. करणें *g. of o.*
3 v. To EXAGGERATE, To AMPLIFY. फुगवून-वाढवून-मोठाकरून-&c. सांगणें, अत्युक्ति *f.*-अतिशयोक्ति *f.*-&c. करणें-करून सांगणें, पिसाचा पारवा *m.* करणें.
4 (one's self) *raise in pretension.* मोठेपणा *m.*-वर्चस *n.*-वर्चस्व *n.*-वर्चस्वता *f.*-&c. मिरवणें-दाखवणें.

MAGNIFYING, *n.* v. V. 1.—*act.* मोठा करून दाखवणें *n.* &c.
2—*act.* वर्णणें *n.* &c. वाखाणणी *f.* वाखाणणूक *f.* वर्णणूक *f.* वर्णन *n.* वर्णना *f.*
3 फुगवून सांगणें *n.* अत्युक्ति *f.* अतिशयोक्ति *f.*

MAGNILOQUENCE, *n.* v. BOMBAST. ढबदारीचें बोलणें *n.*-भाषण *n.*

MAGNITUDE, *n.* See GREATNESS. 2 *size, quantity, bulk.* आकारमान *n.* महत्वमान *n.* आकृतिमान *n.* मान *n.* परिमाण *n.* प्रमाण *n.* परिमिति *f. pop.* परिमीत *or* परमीत *f. n.* लांबीरुंदी *f.*

MAGPIE, *n.* एक पक्षी आहे.

MAHOGANY, *n.* एक वृक्ष आहे.

MAID, MAIDEN, *n. young girl, virgin.* कन्या *f.* कुमारी *f.* कन्यका *f.* कुमारिका *f.* बाला *f.* गौरी *f.* अक्षता *f.* रोहिणी. Some words for girls have reference to particular ages. A maid of 5 or 6 years old is, कुमारी *f.* कुमारिका *f.*—from 5 or 6 to 8 or 9, कन्या *f.* कन्यका *f.*—of about 9, रोहिणी *f.*—from 10 to puberty, गौरी *f.* गौरिका *f.* नग्निका *f.* बाला *f.*—of the age of puberty, मध्या *f.* मध्यमा *f.* मुग्धा *f.*
2 *unmarried female,* v. SPINSTRESS. अवरठी *f.* अवरा *f.* निवरा *f.* अविवाहिता *f.* अनूढा *f.*
3 *female attendant.* चाकरीण *f.* सेवकीण *f.* परिचारिका *f.* सहचारिणी *f.* सहचरी *f.*
Hired m. सैरंध्री *f.* मोलकरीण *f.*
The maids and children. रांडापोरें *n. pl.* [कीण *f.*

MAID-SERVANT, *n.* v. MAID, SLAVE-GIRL. चाकरीण *f.* सेव-

MAIDEN, *a. belonging, &c. to a maid.* कुमारीचा, अवरठीचा, &c. कुमारिकासंबंधी, कुमारिकाविषयक, अविवाहितदशेचा, कौमार.
2 *consisting of maidens.* कुमारींचा, कन्यांचा, कन्यामय, कुमारिका गणाचा.
3 *fresh, unused, new.* कोरा, घणकोरा, घणाखालचा, अनुच्छिष्ट *pop.* अनसूट, अपूट, अपूर्व, अजातोपभोग.

MAIDENHEAD, MAIDENHOOD, MAIDHOOD, *n. virginity.* चिरा *m.* कौमार्य *n.* कुमारीदशा *f.* कुमारित्व *n.* कुमारिता *f.* कन्यात्व *n.* कुमारिकाभाव *m.* [नवत्व *n.*
2 *freshness, newness.* कोरेपणा*m.* अनसूटपणा*m.* अपूटपणा*m.*

MAIDENLIKE, MAIDENLY, *a. like a maid, becoming a maid, &c.* कुमारीसारखा, कुमारीसदृश, कुमारीतुल्य, कुमारिकावत्, कुमारिकोचित, कुमारिकानुरूप.

MAIL, *n.* v. ARMOUR. चिलखत *n.* कवच *m. n.* बक्तर *n.*
2 *post.* डांक *f.* टप्पाल *or* टपाल *n.*

To MAIL, *v. a.* चिलखत *n.*-&c. घालणें.

MAIL-COACH, MAIL-CART, *n.* डाकेची-टप्पालाची गाडी *f.*

MAILED, *p.* v. V. चिलखत घातलेला, कवची, सकवच.

MAIM, *n. privation of a limb.* व्यंग *n.* अधूपणा *m.* अंगवैकल्य *n.* वैकल्य *n.* अंगछेद *m.*

To MAIM, *v. a. cripple, disable.* लंगडा-अधू-पंगू-व्यंग-विकलांग-हीनांग-&c.करणें, लंगडेपणा *m.*-वैकल्य *n.*-&c. आणणें.

MAIMED, *p.* v. V. लंगडा-&c. केलेला, पंगु *pop.* पंगू, थोटा, व्यंग, विकलांग, हीनांग, न्यूनांग, छिन्नांग, अंगहीन, अंगविकल.

MAIMEDNESS, *n.* v. P. अधूपणा *m.* &c. व्यंगता *f.* अंगवैकल्य *n.*

MAIMING, *n.* v. V.व्यंगकरणें *n.* &c. व्यंगीकरण *n.* विकलीकरण *n.*

MAIN, *a. principal, &c.* v. CHIEF. मोठा, मुख्य, श्रेष्ठ, प्रधान, प्रमुख, प्रवर.
2 *gross, greatest, containing the chief part.* मोठा, मुख्य, प्रधान, ठोक, ठोकठोक, भरण्याचा.

MAIN, *n. bulk, gross, greater part.* मोठाभाग *m.* मुख्यभाग *m.* प्रधान भाग *m.* मुख्य अंश *m.* भरणा *m.*
For the m. *for the most part.* बहुतकरून, फारकरून, सामान्यतः. [मान्यतः.
In the m. *in the whole taken together.* ठोक, एकंदर, सा-
2 *ocean.* समुद्र *m.* सागर *m.* महासागर *m.*
3 *violence,* v. FORCE. जोर *m.* बल *pop.* बळ *n.* [तोडून.
With might and m. v. EFFORT. मोठ्या जोरानें, जीव

MAIN-LAND, *n. the continent*—as distinguished from an *isle.* मुख्यभूमि *f.* भूखंड *m. n.* पृथ्वीखंड *m. n.*

MAIN-MAST, *n.* मोठा डोल *m.* मधला डोल *m.* मोठी *or* मधली डोल काठी *f.* [मुटा *m.*

MAIN-SAIL, MAIN-SHEET, *n.* शीड *n.* मोठें शीड *n.* अवजार *n.*

MAINLY, *adv.* v. A. बहुत करून, फार करून, प्राधान्यें करून, मुख्यत्वेंकरून, मुख्यशः, प्राधान्यतः, सामान्यतः.

To MAINTAIN, *v. a. preserve or keep in any particular state.* राखणें, ठेवणें, धरणें.

2 *keep up, continue, not suffer to cease.* चालवणें, चालता-चालू-सुरू-उभा-&c. ठेवणें.

3 *defend, hold, not lose or surrender.* राखणें, संभाळणें, रक्षणें, संरक्षणें, संभाळ *m.*-रक्षण *n.*-संरक्षण *n.*-&c. करणें *g. of o.* स्वाधीन-हातीं-&c. ठेवणें.

4 *vindicate, assert, support, make good.* संभाळणें, राखणें, स्थापणें, पुरवणें, पुरवून देणें, प्रपादणें, प्रतिपादणें, पुरवणी *f.*-निर्वाह *m.*-प्रतिपादन *n.*-समर्थन *n.*- स्थापन *n.*-व्यवस्थापन *n.*-&c. करणें *g. of o.*

5 *support the expense of.* खर्च*m.* चालवणें-भागवणें, निर्वाह*m.* *or* खर्चाचा निर्वाह *m.*-निभाव *m.*-&c.करणें *g. of. o.* पारपडणें, तड *f.* घेणें *g. of o.*

6 *support with food, &c.* v. To SUBSIST. पाळणें, पोषणें *or* पोसणें, संभाळणें, बाळगणें, वाहणें, चालवणें *with* चें *of o.* खर्च *m.* चालवणें *g. of o.* अन्नवस्त्र*n.* देणें, योगक्षेम *m.* करणें-चालवणें *g. of o.* पालन पोषण *n.*-&c. करणें *g. of o.*

7 (one's self) v. To LIVE. पोट *n.*-उदरनिर्वाह *m.*-&c. चालवणें.

To MAINTAIN, *v. n.* See To AFFIRM.

MAINTAINABLE, *a.* v. V. A. 3. संभाळायाचा-जोगा-जोगता-सारखा-&c. रक्ष्य, संरक्ष्य, रक्षणीय, रक्षणशक्य, शक्यरक्ष.

4 संभाळायाजोगा-सारखा-&c. स्थापनीय, स्थाप्य, प्रतिपादनीय, प्रतिपाद्य, निर्वाह्य, समर्थनीय, प्रतिपादनशक्य, &c.

6 पाळायाजोगा-सारखा-&c. पालनीय, पोषणीय, पोष्य.

MAINTAINED, *p.* v. V. A. 1. राखलेला, ठेवलेला, &c.

2 चालवलेला, चालता ठेवलेला, &c.

3 राखलेला, &c. रक्षित, संरक्षित.

4 संभाळलेला, प्रपादलेला, प्रतिपादित, स्थापित, समर्थित.

6 पाळलेला, पोसलेला, प्रतिपालित, पालित, पोषित.

MAINTAINING, MAINTENANCE, *n.* v. V. A. 1—*act.* राखणें *n.* ठेवणें *n.* चालवणें *n.* चालता ठेवणें *n.*

3—*act.* राखणें *n.* &c. राखण *f.* संभाळ *m.* रक्षण *n.* संरक्षण *n.*

4—*act.* संभाळणें*n.* &c. पुरवणी *f.* निर्वाह*m.* स्थापन*n.* स्थापना*f.* प्रतिपादन*n.* समर्थन*n.* व्यवस्थापन*n.*

6—*act.* पाळणें*n.* पोसणें*n.* &c. पाळणूक *f.* संभाळ*m.* पाळग्रहण*n.* पालन*n.* पोषण*n.* पालनपोषण*n.* भरण*n.* भरणपोषण*n.* योगक्षेम*m.n*

7—*act.* जिंदगी *f.* जिनगानी *f.*उदरनिर्वाह*m.* निर्वाह*m.* प्राणजीवन*n.* प्राणधारण*n.* उपजीवन*n.* जीवन*n.*

I. *a* m. v. LIVELIHOOD. जिंदगी *f.* जिनगी *f.* उपजीविका *f.* उपजीवन*n.* जीवनोपाय*m.*

MAIZE, *n. Indian corn.* मका *f. m.*

A single grain of m. मकाणा*m.*

A head of m. बोंड*n.* मुटा *or* मुट्टा*m.*

M. parched. मकाणे*m. pl.*

Stalks or straw of m. मकण *or* मकाण *or* मकवण*n.*

MAJESTIC, MAJESTICAL, *a.* v. N. l. राजतेजाचा, राजसत्तेचा, पादशाही, प्रतापाचा, थोरवीचा, &c. थोर, थोरवट, प्रतापवान्, प्रतापशाली, तेजश्शाली, ऐश्वर्यवान्, ऐश्वर्यशाली, प्रभाववान्, प्रभावशाली, भगशाली.

MAJESTICALLY, *adv.*v.A. राजतेजानें, तेजानें,प्रतापानें, वैभवानें,&c.

MAJESTY, *n. dignity, grandeur, greatness.* राजतेज*n.* राजश्री *f.* राजसत्ता *f.* तेज*n.* प्रताप*m.* वैभव*n.* थोरवी *f.* ऐश्वर्य*n.* महिमा*m.* माहात्म्य*n.* भग*n.* इज्जत *or* इभ्रत *f.* सलाबत *f.* सलाबतपणा*m.* भूति *f.* विभूति *f.* विभव*m.* प्रभव*m.* प्रभाव*m.* अनुभाव*m.*

2—the title. राजश्री, महाराज.

His m.,Your m. हुजूर, महाराज.

MAJOR, *a. greater in number, quantity, &c.* मोठा, मुख्य, अधिकसंख्य, अधिकपरिमाणक. [श्रेष्ठ.

2 *greater in dignity, &c.* v. CHIEF. मोठा, मुख्य, प्रधान,

Major and minor (especially as used to distinguish villages bearing the same name) are rendered by बुजूर्ग *or* बुद्रूग and खुर्द.

MAJOR, *n. one of full age*—in law. व्यवहाराधिकारी, जातव्यवहार, प्राप्तव्यवहार, लब्धव्यवहार, व्यवहारयोग्य, व्यवहारार्ह, व्यवहारज्ञ.

2—in logic. प्रतिज्ञा *f.*

3 फौजेंत एक पदवी आहे.

MAJOR DOMO, *n. house steward.* घरकारणी, घरकारभारी.

MAJORITY, *n. moreness.* आधिक्य *n.* अधिकत्व *n.*

2 *the greater number.* मोठी संख्या *f.* अर्धाधिक संख्या *f.* अधिकपक्ष *m.* पाऊण वांटा *m.* पाऊण हिस्सा *m.* तीनवांटे *m. pl.* तीनहिस्से *m.* The sense is often idiomatically rendered by adopting another construction, Ex. बहुतकरून हिंदू होते *or* हिंदूंची संख्या मोठी होती, the majority were Hindus.

3 *full age*—in law. व्यवहार्यवय *n.* व्यवहार्यावस्था *f.* व्यवहारक्षमवय *n.* ज्ञातव्यवहारावस्था *f.*

To MAKE, *v. a. create.* उत्पन्न-पैदा-निर्माण-&c. करणें, करणें, उत्पादणें, निर्मिणें, बनावणें, उत्पादन *n.*-&c. करणें.

2 *form, fashion.* घडणें, करणें, काढणें, उतरणें.

3 *compose, constitute.* असणें-होणें *in. con. with g. of s.* as हें भांडें मातीचें आहे, अंगभूत-अवयवभूत-अंशभूत असणें *in. con.* करणें, बनावणें.

4 *form by art.* करणें, बनावणें, कृत्रिम-&c. करणें.

5 *produce, occasion.* करणें, करविणें.

6 *do, perform, commit.* करणें.

7 *cause to be.* करणें.

8 *constrain, force,* v. To COMPEL. बळ *n.*-बळजोरी *f.*-&c. करणें-चालवणें *with* वर *of o.* This sense is usually expressed by the causal form of the verb, to which बळेंच is frequently added, Ex. बळेंच चालवणें to m. to go. बळेंच बोलवणें to m. to speak.

9 *raise as profit.* मिळवणें, कमावणें, उत्पन्न करणें, पैदा करणें, मागें टाकणें, मारणें, प्राप्ति *f.*-मिळकत *f.*-&c. असणें *g. of o.*

10 *reach, gain, arrive at.* पावणें, पहोंचणें, सई करणें, अटपणें, येणें.

11 *incline to,* v. To DISPOSE. बळवणें.

12 away; v. To KILL. सपवणें, संपवणें, नाहींसा करणें, नाबूद करणें, घात *m.* करणें *g. of o.*
13 away with; v. To EMBEZZLE. लांबविणें, गुंगवणें, लुंघवणें, गरक करणें, पळविणें.
14 good; v. To MAINTAIN. संभाळणें, संभाळ*m.*-&c. करणें *g. of o.*
15 good; v. To FULFIL. खरा-पुरा-&c. करणें-करून देणें, पुरवून देणें, सिद्ध करणें.
16 good; *repay, compensate.* भरणें, भरून देणें.
17 light of; v. To CONTEMN. तुच्छ-हलका-&c. करणें-मानणें.
18 love. See To COURT.
19 merry. ख्यालीखुशाली *f.*-आनंद *m.*-&c. करणें.
20 much of; *treat with fondness.* सोपस्कार *m.* करणें-लावणें *g. of o.* अलोलकी *f.*-अलोलीक*n.*-अलोलीकतालोलीक *n.* करणें *g. of o.*
21 oath; v. To SWEAR. शपथ *f.* वाहणें.
22 of. See To UNDERSTAND. [देऊनटाकणें.
23 over; v. To COMMIT. निरवणें, ओपणें, हवाल्लणें, गुजरणें,
24 out; v. To UNDERSTAND. अर्थ*m.* काढणें-करणें, समजणें.
To be made out. अर्थ*m.* उमगणें-निघणें *g. of s.*
To m. out a person—*discover his disposition and way.* पाऊल *n.* ओळखणें.
25 up; *reconcile.* मिटवणें, सांधणें.
26 up; *get together,* v. To COLLECT. जथणें, जमवणें, जथापत *f.* -जमवाजमव *f.* करणें *g. of o.*
27 up; *repair, put to rights.* सुधारणें, निटावणें, सुधारणी *f.* -सुधारणूक *f.*-निटावणी *f.*-&c. करणें *g. of o.*
28 up; *make good.* भरणें, भरून देणें.
29 water; v. To URINE. मुतणें. 2 v. To LEAK. गळणें.
To m. up one's mind, v. To RESOLVE. निश्चय*m.* करणें.

To MAKE, *v. n. tend, move towards.* जाणें, चालणें.
2 *contribute, conduce.* उपयोगी-कामाचा-&c. होणें, उपयोगीं-कामास-&c. पडणें.
3 as if; *carry appearance.* आकार*m.*-डौल*m.*-धोप *f.*-ढूल*f.*-&c. दाखवणें, वरवर करणें.
4 off; v. To DECAMP. तोंड *n.* काळें करणें, इया *f.* म्हणणें, यःपलाय *n.* करणें. [*m.* पाडणें.
5 up for; *compensate for.* पुरती *f.*-पुरी *f.* करणें-पाडणें, विसर

MAKE, *n. structure, build, &c.* v. FORM. बांधा *m.* बांधावळ *f.* बांधणावळ *f.* घाट *m.* ठेवण *f.* बनावट *f.* घडण *f.* घडणी *f.* घडवण *f.* ठाणमाण *n.* घडमोड *f.* घडामोड *f.*

MAKE-BATE, *n.* v. INCENDIARY. आगलाव्या, कळलाव्या, कज्जेदलाल, कळीचा नारद, चेरगडी.

MAKE-BELIEVE, *n. mere show or pretence.* अनागोंदी कारभार *m.* अनागोंदीजमाखर्च *m.* दसऱ्याचें सोनें *n.*

MAKE-PEACE, *n. peace maker.* कळमोड्या, कळमिटव्या.

MAKE-WEIGHT, *n.* पासंग *m. n.*

MAKER, *n.* v. V. A. 1. करणारा, उत्पन्न करणारा, निर्माण करणारा-&c. उत्पन्न &c. कर्त्ता, कर्त्ता, जनिता, जनक, उत्पादक.
M. of the universe. जगत्कर्त्ता, जगत्स्रष्टा.

MAKING, *n.* v. V. A. 1.—*act.* करणें *n.* उत्पन्न करणें *n.* &c. निर्माण *n.* निर्मिति *f.* उत्पादन *n.*
2 घडणें *n.* &c. घडणी *f.* घडणूक *f.* घटना *f.*
Price of m. घडणावळ *f.* करणावळ *f.*

I. *structure.* See MAKE. [&c.

MAL OR MALE. This prefix is rendered by अ, दुर, बद, गैर,

MAL-ADMINISTRATION, *n.* बदअमल *m.* बदमामली *f.* बदमामला *m.* बदमामलत *f.* दुःशासन *n.*

MAL-APROPOS, *a.* v. UNSEASONABLE. अप्रासंगिक, अप्रस्तुत, अप्रकृत, अप्रसंग, अप्रसंगोपात्त. [म्य *n.*

MAL-CONFORMATION, *n.* विलग *or* विजोड बांधा *m.* अवयववैष-

MAL-CONTENT, *a.*—gener. v. DISCONTENTED. गैरराजी, गैरखुशी.
2 *dissatisfied with the government.* अमलनाखूश, राजमार्गासंतुष्ट, राजमार्गासंतोषी, राजकृतासंतुष्ट.

MAL-FORMATION, *n.* विलग *or* विजोड बांधा *m.*

MAL-PRACTICE, *n. evil practice, practice contrary to rule.* गैरचाल *f.* गैररीत *f.* गैरमार्ग *m.* गैरहा *f.* बदचाल *f.* अकार्य *n.* दुराचार *m.* दुराचरण *n.*

To MAL-TREAT, *v. a. ill use, misuse, treat ill.* गैररीतीनें-गैरचालीनें-गैरमार्गानें-&c. वापरणें-वहिवाटणें-राबविणें, घुसडणें, घुसटणें, खुंदळणें, घुसडा *m.*-भुसडा *m.*-भुसाडा *m.*-भुसा *m.*-घुसडाघुसड *f.*-खुंदळणी *f.*-&c. करणें *g. of o.* असद्व्यापार *m.*-असद्व्यवहार *m.*-&c. करणें *g. of o.*

MAL-TREATMENT, *n.* v. V.—*act.* घुसडणें *n.* &c. घुसडणी *f.* खुंदळणी *f.* घुसडा *m.* घुसडाघुसड *f.* असद्व्यापार *m.* असद्व्यवहार *m.* कुव्यवहार *m.*

MAL-VERSATION, *n. misconduct.* गैरवर्त्तणूक *f.* बदचाल *f.* गैरचाल *f.* खोटसाळ व्यापार *m.* असद्व्यापार *m.* ढंग *m.* बदनेत *f.* असदाचार *m.* असदाचरण *n.*

MALADY, *n. disease,* v. DISORDER. रोग *m.* आजार *m.* विकार *m.* व्याधि *f. m.*

MALAPERT, *a. saucy,* v. IMPUDENT. धीट, धट्ट, चंचीवाग, हुंडीवाग.

MALAPERTNESS, *n.* v. A. धिटाई *f.* धीटपणा *m.*

MALARIA, *n. noxious exhalation.* रोग करणारी वाफ *f.*

MALE, *n.*—of animals. पुरुष *m.* नर *m.* बाप्या माणूस *m.* दादल्या माणूस *m.* पुंव्यक्ति *f.* पुमान् *m.* पुम्प्राणी *m.*
A. m. and female. जोडा *m.* मिथुन *n.* युग्म *n.*
Desire of the m. माज *m.*
2—in botany. पुरुष *m.*
3—a screw. नर *m.*
M. and female. नरमादी.

MALE, *a.*—noting sex. पुरुषजातीचा, पुरुषजातीय, पुंजातीय, पुंव्यक्तिक, पुं (in comp. as पुंसंतान *n.* &c.), पुरुष in comp. नर in comp.
2 *belonging, &c. to males.* पुरुषाचा, पुरुषजातीचा, मर्दानी, पुरुषजातिसंबंधी-विषयक.

MALEDICTION, *n. imprecation, execration, curse.* शाप *m.* अभिशाप *m.* हपाप *m.* दांतांचें विष *n.* बत्तिशी *f.* अमंगलवचन *n.* अकल्याणवचन *n.*

MALEFACTOR, *n.* v. CRIMINAL. अन्यायी, कुकर्मी, दुष्कर्मी, अकर्मी, गुन्हेगार.

MALEVOLENCE, *n. ill-will, disposition to hurt others.* दुष्टभाव *m.* दुष्टबुद्धि *f.* द्वेषभाव *m.* द्वेषबुद्धि *f.* द्वेष *m.* कुडाभाव *m.* कुभाव *m.* कुबुद्धि *f.* कुडें *n.* दौरात्म्य *n.* अपकारेच्छा *f.* अनिष्टेच्छा *f.*

MALEVOLENT, *a. illdisposed to others.* दुष्टभावाचा, द्वेषभावाचा, कुडेभावाचा, &c. दुर्बुद्धि, दुष्टबुद्धि, दुरात्मा, घातपाती, अपकारार्थी, अनिष्टार्थी, दुष्टचेता, अनिष्टचेता, अनिष्टचिंतक.

MALEVOLENTLY, *adv.* v.A. दुष्टभावानें, कुडेभावानें, दुष्टबुद्धीनें, &c. अपकारेच्छापूर्वक, &c.

MALICE, *n. malevolence, spite, malignity, &c.* दुष्टभाव *m.* द्वेषभाव *m.* कुडाभाव *m.* कुडें *n.* कुडेंपावडें *n.* कुडेंकपट *n.* कुढापा *m.* काळें *n.* काळेंबेरें *n.* काळेंढवळें *n.* कालकूट *n.* द्वेष *m.* अकस *m. f.* खुनस *m.* चुरस *f.* अदावत *f.* बरकशी *f.* बरकस *f.* कपट *n.* दौरात्म्य *n.* कोर *f.* कोरबंदी *f.* कुन्हा *m.* दावा *m.* डाव *m.* दांत *m.* दंश *pop.* डंश & डंख & डेाख *m.* द्रोह *m.* कुपित्थ *n.* मानसहिंसा *f.*

M. prepense. द्रोहचिंतन *n.*

Meditating m. द्रोहचिंतन *n.*

Secret m. मुकादावा *m.* मानसहिंसा *f.* अंतर्दाह *m.*

To be inflamed with m. against. डावींपेटणें *with g. of o.*

To conceive m. डाव *m.* धरणें. [करणें.

To gratify one's m. दावा *m.*-&c. उगवणें, वैरोद्धार *m.*-&c.

To meditate m. against. दावे *m. pl.* गाणें-सांगणें *with* वर *of o.* दर्भ घेऊन उभा असणें.

MALICIOUS, MALIGN, MALIGNANT, *a. harbouring malice.* दुष्टभावाचा, द्वेषभावाचा, कुडेभावाचा, &c. मनाचा कुडा *or* कुढा, कुडाकपटी, मनाचा कुजडा, अकसखोर, अकसी, अदावती, अदावत्या, चुरसखोर, चुरसी, दावेदार, दावेदारी, दावेखोर, खुनसी, कपटी, द्रोही, द्वेषी, द्वेष्टा, द्वेषक, दंशी *pop.* डंशी & डंसी, आनखानी, कुटिल *pop.* कुटीळ, दुरात्मा, दुष्टचेता, अनिष्टचेता, अरिष्टसंतोषी, दुष्टबुद्धि, दुर्बुद्ध, दुर्बुद्धि, वैरसंध, तामस, विषहृदय.

2 *proceeding, &c. from malice.* कुडेभावाचा, द्वेषभावाचा, अदावतीचा, चुरसीचा, खुनसाचा, दंशाचा, &c. द्रोहमूलक, द्वेषमूलक, द्रोहहेतुक, द्वेषहेतुक.

3—in astrology, v. INAUSPICIOUS. नाट, नाटाळ *or* नाठाळ, नेष्ट, खष्ट, खडतर.

4—an ulcer, sore, fever, &c. v. VIRULENT. दुश्चिकित्स्य, दुश्चिकित्स, दुर्धर, दुःसाध्य, काल *pop.* काळ (in comp. as कालज्वर *m.* काळफोड *m.* काळपुळी *f.*).

M. fever. सन्निपातज्वर *m.* कालज्वर *m.*

MALICIOUSLY, MALIGNANTLY, *adv.* v. A. 1. कुड्याभावानें, द्वेषभावानें, दुष्टभावानें, कपटभावानें, द्वेषबुद्ध्या, द्वेषदृष्ट्या.

3 वक्री.

MALICIOUSNESS, MALIGNANCY, *n.* V. A. 1. 2. *and* MALICE. कुडाभाव *m.* द्वेषभाव *m.* कुटिलपणा *m.* दौरात्म्य *n.* कौटिल्य *n.* दुर्बुद्धि *pop.* दुर्बुद्ध *f.*

3 नाट *m. n.* नाट बाट *m.* खष्टपणा *m.* खडतरपणा *m.*

To bind, counteract, &c. the m. of. नाट *m.* भाजवणें *g. of o.*

To MALIGN, *v. a. traduce, slander,* v. To ASPERSE. तुफान *n.*-बालंट *n.*-कुफराण *n.*-अदावत *f.*-कुभांड *n.*-&c. घेणें-रचणें *with* वर *of o.* अपवाद *m.*-अभिशंसन *n.*-विकत्थन *n.*-&c. करणें *g. of o.*

MALIGNED, *p.* v. V. तुफान घेतलेला, &c. अपवादित, अभिशप्त, अभिशस्त, विकत्थित.

MALIGNER, *n.* MALIGNING, *p. a.* v. V. तुफान घेणारा, अदावत करणारा, कुभांड रचणारा, &c. अदावती, अदावत्या, तुफानी, कुभांडी, कुभांड्या, कुफराणी, &c. अपवादक, अभिशंसन कर्त्ता.

MALIGNITY. See MALIGNANCY.

To MALINGER, *v.n.* चाकरी चुकविण्या करितां दुखण्याचें मीस करणें.

MALKIN, *n. mop.* बोळा *m.* पोतेरें *n.*

2 *a dirty woman.* पोतेरें *n.* तेलीण *f.* लोणारीण *f.*

MALL, *n. wooden beetle.* मोगरा *m.* मोगर *m.* मुद्गल *m.*

To MALL, *v. a.* v. To BEAT. कुदकणें, कुचलणें, कुमकणें, कुमलणें, कुंदी *f.* काढणें *g. of o.*

MALLARD. See DRAKE.

MALLEABILITY, MALLEABLENESS, *n.* v. A. घनवर्धिष्णुता *f.* घनवर्धनीयत्व *n.* ताडनवर्धनीयत्व *n.*

MALLEABLE, *a. capable of being spread by beating.* घनवर्धिष्णु, घनवर्धनीय, ताडनवर्धनीय. [ताडनवृद्धि *f.*

MALLEATION, *n. extension by beating.* घनवर्धन *n.* घनवृद्धि *f.*

MALLET, *n. wooden hammer.* मेखचू *or* मेखसू *m.* मोगर *m.* मोगरा *m. dim.* मोगरी *f.* ठोकणी *f.* ठोकणें *n.* टापरणें *n.*

Carpenter's m. कुडती *f.*

MALT, *n.* सातूचें वाळवलेलें उंबलें *n.*

MAM, MAMMA, *n.* v. MOTHER. माई *f.* ब *f.* बये *f.*

MAMMALIA, *n. pl.* सस्तन प्राणी *m. pl.* स्तन पाजणारे प्राणी *m. pl.*

MAMMET, *n. dressed figure, puppet.* नेसवलेली पुतळी *f.* बाहुलें *n.*

MAMMIFORM, *a. having the shape of paps.* स्तनाच्या आकाराचा, स्तनाकार, स्तनाकृति, कुचाकार, कुचाकृति.

MAMMILLARY, *a. pertaining to the paps.* स्तनाचा, स्तनसंबंधी, कुचसंबंधी.

MAMMOCK, *n. shapeless piece.* ढोण *n.* ढोणपा *m.* ठोकळा *m.*

MAMMON, *n. wealth, or the deity of wealth,* v. RICHES. लक्ष्मी *f.*

Worship of m. (as by bankers, &c.). लक्ष्मीपूजन *n.*

The world bows to m. द्रव्येण सर्वेवशाः.

Ye cannot serve God and m. द्रव्यसंपादन आणि ईश्वरभजन तंत्रानें होत नाहींत.

MAMMONIST, *n. person devoted to the acquisition of wealth.* धनार्थी, द्रव्यार्थी, धनलोभी.

MAN, *n. mankind.* मनुष्य *n.* माणूस *n.* मनुष्यजाति *f.* लोक *m. pl.* मानव *m.* पुरुष *m.* जन *m.*

The fear of m. जनभीति *f.* लोकेषणा *f.* जनमर्यादा *f.*

To be accustomed to m., be tame and familiar—wild animals. माणसळणें, माणसावणें.

To become ravenous after m.—a tiger, &c. that has tasted human blood. माणसळणें, माणसावणें.

2 *a man, a male.* पुरुष *m.* बाप्या *m.* बाप्यामाणूस *m.* माणूस *m.* मनुष्य *m.* मानई *m.* मानव *m.* मानुष *m.* जन *m.* नर *m.* मनु *m.* मनुज *m.* पुंव्यक्ति *f.* पुमान् *m.* मर्त्य *m.* गडी *m.* (in comp. with a designation, as, ब्राह्मणगडी, भटगडी, सिपाईगडी).

To know m. carnally. पुरुषाला जाणणें-ओळखणें, पुरुषज्ञान *n.*-पुरुषप्राप्ति *f.*-पुरुषदर्शन *n.*-&c. होणें *in.con.* आंगाखालीं जाणें.

3 *adult, not a boy.* पुरुष *m.* बाप्या *m.* गडी *m.* मानई *m.* पणांत-वयांत आलेलामाणूस *m.* गोखमा *m.* गोहो *m.*

A m.'s height or stature. पुरुष *m.* पौरुष *n.*

4 *a human being.* माणूस *n.* मनुष्य *n.* जण *m. f. n. with a numeral prefixed.* असामी *f.* मूर्त्ति *f.*

M. by man. असामीवार.

5 *male servant, attendant, &c.* माणूस *m.* गडी *m.* चाकरमाणूस *m.* गडीमाणूस *m.*

6—familiarly, *person, fellow, chap, &c.* माणूस *n.* गडी *m.* जवान *m.* भाई *m.*

7—eminently. मनुष्य *m.* मर्द *m.* मर्दगाणी *m.*

8—at chess, draughts, &c. नरद *f.* सार *f.* सारिका *f.*

9 *master, possessor, owner, &c.* करी *m.* (in comp. as, गाडेकरी cart man. पेकेकरी a monied man. घरकरी master of the house, &c.),वाला (in comp. as, दूधवाला milk man,&c.).

To MAN, *v. a. furnish with men.* माणसें *n.pl.* ठेवणें-भरणें, माणसांचा भरणा *m.*-माणसांची भरती *f.*-&c. करणें, मनुष्यभरित-&c. करणें. [नरभोजी, &c.

MAN-EATER, *n. cannibal.* मानवाद, मनुष्याद, नराशी, मनुष्यभक्षी,

MAN-EATING, *n. cannibalism.* मनुष्यादन *n.* पुरुषाशन *n.* नरभक्षण *n.* मनुष्य भक्षण *n.* &c.

MAN-HATER, *n.* MAN-HATING, *a.* माणूसगंध्या, माणूसगंधारा, माणूसघाण्या, मनुष्यशत्रु, मनुष्यवैरी, मनुष्यद्वेषी, मनुष्यद्वेष्टा, मनुष्यद्रोही.

MAN-HATING, *n.* मनुष्यद्वेष *m.* मनुष्यत्रास *m.* [हंता,

MAN-KILLER, MAN-SLAYER,*n.* मनुष्यघातक, मनुष्यवधक, मनुष्य-

MAN-KILLING, MAN-SLAUGHTER, MAN-SLAYING, *n.* मनुष्यघात *m.* मनुष्यवध *m.* मनुष्यहत्या *f.*

2—in law. असमीक्ष्यवध *m.* असमीक्ष्यहत्या *f.* अहेतुकृतहत्या *f.*

MAN-STEALER, *n.* मनुष्यचोर, मनुष्यस्तेयी.

MAN-STEALING, *n.* मनुष्यचोरी *f.* मनुष्यचौर्य *n.* मनुष्यस्तेय *n.*

MANACLE, *n. hand-cuff.* हातबेडी *or* विडी *f.* हातकुलूप *n.* हातखोडा *m.*

To MANACLE, *v. a.* v. N. हातबेडी *or* विडी *f.*-हातकुलूप *n.* or *plurally* हातबेड्या-हातकुलपें घालणें.

To MANAGE, *v. a. carry on, direct the concerns of*, v. To CONDUCT. चालवणें, वहिवाटणें,वावरणें, हाकणें,वलावणें,आचरणें.

2 *govern, rule, control, direct.* अटपणें, आवरणें, वागवणें, चालवणें, सुतांत-हातांत-कह्यांत-हुकुमांत-शब्दांत-लगामांत-&c. ठेवणें-धरणें-वागवणें.

3 *wield,use easily, have under command.* वापरणें, वहिवाटणें, चालवणें, वागवणें, झेपणें, झोकणें.

4 *perform, get through with, carry through.* साधणें, निभावणें, निर्वाहणें, अटपणें, तोलणें, पेलणें, झोकणें, झेपणें, रेटणें, चाल करणें.

5 See To TRAIN. 6 *treat with judgment, direct with address.* युक्तीनें वागवणें-वहिवाटणें-चालवणें.

To MANAGE, *v. n. direct affairs, carry on business.* काम *n.*-कारभार *m.*-&c. पाहणें-करणें-चालवणें-संभाळणें.

2 (in domestic affairs). घर *n.* करणें-पाहणें-चालवणें, संसार *m.*-&c. करणें-पाहणें.

3 with; *contrive to get on, shift.* चाल *f.*-चालढकल *f.*-निर्वाह *m.*-&c. करणें, गरज करणें, चाल करणें, जोगवणें, जोगवण *f.*-जोगवणी *f.*-&c. करणें.

MANAGEABLE, *a.* v. V.A. 1. चालवायाजोगा-सारखा-&c. हांकायाजोगता-&c. अटपता, अटपसार, संजुकता *or* संजुगता, खुटखुटीत, सुटसुटीत.

2 वागवायास सोपा, &c. लगामीं धरायाजोगा, &c. वळणीचा, सुतांतला, हातांतला, &c. सुधर्ष.

3 वापरायास सोपा, झेपायास सोपा, &c. झेपायाजोगा, &c.

4 साधायाजोगा-सारखा-&c.झोकायाजोगा-&c. रेंटायाजोगा-&c.

MANAGED, *p.* v. V. A. 3. चालवलेला, वहिवाटलेला,&c. आचरित.

2 आवरलेला, &c. सुतांत ठेवलेला-वागवलेला, &c.

3 वापरलेला, झेपलेला, &c.

To be m. by. ओठंगणें.

4 साधलेला, रेंटलेला, &c. निर्वहित.

MANAGEMENT, MANAGING, *n.* v. V. A. 1.—*act.* चालवणें *n.* &c. वहिवाट *f.* वलावणी *f.* आचरण *n.*

2-*act.* अटपणें *n.* आवरणें *n.* &c. आवरण *n.*—*a. or s.* आवर *m.* अटोप *m.* आळाबांधा *m.* बंदोबस्त *m.*बंदोबस्ती *f.*

3—*act.* वापरणें *n.* झेपणें *n.* &c.

4 साधणें *n.* अटपणें *n.* रेंटणें *n.* &c. निर्वाह *m.*

v. V.N. 3. जोगवणें *n.* &c. जोगवण *f.* जोगवणी *f.* चाल *f.* चालढकल *f.*

I. *skill in managing*, v. ADDRESS. आवर *m.* आवरणशक्ति *f.* आवरआटोप *m.* ओज *f.* युक्ति *pop.* जुगत *f.* वहिवाट *f.*

II. (in domestic matters). *economy.* घरजुगत *f.* घरजोगावणी *f.* [हिम्मत *f.*

III. *authority over, direction of*, v. CONTROL. तैनात *f.*

MANAGER, *n.* MANAGING, *p. a.* v. V. A. 1. *and* CONDUCTOR. चालवणारा, वहिवाटणारा, वलवणारा, &c. वहिवाटदार, कारभारी, दिवाणजी, मुनीम, घटक, कर्त्ता, कारणी.

Head m. ऐनकारभारी.

M. of a festive occasion. संपादक. [वागवणारा-&c.

2 अटपणारा, आवरणारा, आवरण करणारा,आवरक, सुतांत-&c.

v. V. N. 3. जोगवणारा, चाल करणारा, &c. निर्वाहक, निर्वाह-जोगवण-&c. करणारा.

I. *smart in managing, of address and despatch.* अटोपी, अटोपसार, अटोपाचा, आवरशक्तीचा, युक्त्या, साधनी.

II. (in domestic economy) *frugal*, v. ECONOMICAL. काटकसऱ्या, कतरबेती, कतरबेताचा. [आदेश *m.*

MANDATE, *n. order, precept*, v. COMMAND. आज्ञा *f.* हुकूम *m.*

MANDATORY, *a. containing, &c. a command.* आज्ञेचा, आज्ञासूचक, आज्ञाबोधक.

MANDIBLE. See JAW.

MANDRAKE, *n.* लक्ष्मणा *f.* पुत्रदात्री *f.*

To MANDUCATE. See To CHEW.

MANE, *n.*—of a horse. अयाल *or* अयाळ *or* ऐयाल *f.*

2—of a lion. सिंहकेशर *m.* सटा *f.*

MANEGE, *n. school for teaching horsemanship.* घोड्यांचा तालीमखाना *m.* अश्वशिक्षाशाला *f.*

2 *art of training horses.* चाबुकस्वारी *f.*

MANES, *n.* v. GHOST. प्रेत *m. n.*

A deceased person to whom m. one must make an offering. पितर *m.* (when used plurally, *neuter*).

Body of m. (ancestors)—collect. पितृगण *m.*

Business of offering to the m. पितृकर्म *n.* श्राद्धकर्म *n.*

Day sacred to the m. of. पितृतिथि *pop.* पितृतीथ *f.* पितरांचा दिवस *m.*

Giving gifts in honor of the m. पितृतर्पण *n.*

Heaven of the m. पितृलोक *m.*

Oblations to the m. श्राद्ध *n.* पिंड *m.* कव्य *n.*—The oblations are made twice in the year; viz. on the anniversary of the death, and on the same lunar day of the waning half of the month भाद्रपद.

Oblations to the m. of the slain. घायाळ *n.*—The day on which they are made, घायाळतीथ *f.* It is the 14th of भाद्रपदवद्य.

Offering of a ball to the m. of a relative. सपिंडी *f.*

The fortnight of the waning moon of the month भाद्रपद, particularly appointed for the offerings to m. पितृपक्ष *m.* पितरपाट *or* ठ *m.* पितरपाख *m.* The oblations made in this fortnight are called पक्ष *m.* महालय *m.*

Certain *orders* of manes are, अग्निष्वात्त, अर्यमा, कव्यवाहन, पितृमान्, सोम, &c.

Certain oblations to or certain acts or points relating to the *manes* are, एकोद्दिष्टश्राध, उदकुंभश्राद्ध, चौथभरणी, तिलतर्पण, तिलांजलि, दशपिंड, दौहित्र, धर्मपिंड, नांदीमुख, नांदीश्राद्ध, नित्यश्राद्ध, पार्वण, प्रीतिश्राद्ध, हिरण्यश्राद्ध, आमश्राद्ध, पाथेयश्राद्ध.

MANFUL, *a. manly*, v. BOLD. मर्दपणाचा, मर्दुमकीचा, मर्दाना, दिलदार, दिलदारीचा.

MANFULLY, *adv.* v. A. मर्दपणानें, मर्दाईनें, दिलदारीनें, गाजीपणानें, &c. धैर्यपूर्वक, &c. [*m.* दिलदारी *f.*

MANFULNESS, *n.* v. A. मर्दपणा *m.* मर्दी *f.* मर्दुमकी *f.* गाजीपणा

MANGANESE, *n.* एक धातु आहे. [खेडकरधान्य *n.*

MANG-CORN, *n. mixed corn.* बेवड *f.* धान्यांची मिसळ *f.* खेड *f.*

MANGE, *n.*—in horses. गर *f.* खवडे *m. pl.*

2—in cattle. कधला *m.* कधली *f.*

3—in dogs. लूत *f.* खरूज *f.*

MANGELWURZEL, *n.* एक कंद आहे. [कोटंबा *m.*

MANGER, *n. trough for horses' corn.* घोड्यास दाणा चारायाचा

To MANGLE, *v. a. cut in a bungling or tearing manner, hack.* विचकटणें, विचकडणें, झाझाविणें, अचकटविचकट-विचकटविचकट-चोचावून-चाचावून-झाझावून-वेडाबांकडा *decl.*-छिन्नभिन्न-अवासवा-&c. तोडणें-मारणें-खांडणें, विचकण *f.* करणें *g. of o.* छिंदणें.

2 (clothes). कुंदी *f.* करणें, कुंदलणें, घड्या *f. pl.* चोपणें-चेपणें.

MANGLE, *n. instrument for smoothing clothes.* पांघरुणाच्या घड्या चोपण्याचें *or* चेपण्याचें यंत्र *n.*

MANGLED, *p.* v. V. 1. विचकटलेला, चोचावून तोडलेला, &c. छिन्नभिन्न, क्षतविक्षत.

2 कुंदी केलेला, कुंदललेला, &c.

MANGLER, *n.* MANGLING, *p. a.* v. V. विचकटणारा, चोचावून तोडणारा, अचकटविचकट मारणारा, वेडाबांकडा *decl.* तोडणारा, विचकण करणारा.

2 कुंदी करणारा, कुंदलणारा, &c. [&c. विचकण *f.*

MANGLING, *n.* v. V. 1.—*act.* विचकटणें *n.* चोचावून तोडणें *n.*

2 कुंदी *f.*

MANGO, *n.*—the tree. अंबा *or* आंबा *m.* आम्र*m.*—the fruit अंबा *or* आंबा—in contempt. फूट *n.*

Some species or varieties of m. are अफोस (alphonso) आंब, आंबीण, कुरेल अंबा, कुलास, केळ आंबा, गाडगे आंबा, गोटली, गोटीआंबा, गोदडी आंबा, घागऱ्या आंबा, जरंबा, डिखळ्या आंबा, दह्यांबा, बंदछोड, शेंदऱ्या आंबा, शेप्या आंबा, साखरगोटी, सीताफळ्या आंबा.

Blossom of the m. मोहर *m.* (To blossom मोहरणें).

Cake of the mashed pulp of mangoes. साट *n.*

Cluster or tuft of leaves of the m. आम्रपल्लव *m.*

Expressed juice of mangoes. आंबरस *m.*

Fallen m. पडीचा आंबा *m.*

Fallen and burst m. फूट *n.* फुटाळ *n.*

Fine, full, glowing m. रतनकुंड *n.* रतनकूप *m.*

Hook and net with which mangoes are gathered. आंखी *f.* झेलणी *f.* झेला *m.* घळ *m.* झारगें *n.* झेलगें *n.*

Kernel of the m. कोय *f.*

M. that has ripend too quickly. बांबूट *f.* चिभाड *n.*

M. on the tree nearly ripe. शाख *f.*

Mangoes just formed. तोंबर *m.*

Mangoes that have fallen, *as opposed* to mangoes ripened in straw. पड *f.*

M.–stone. कोय *f.* बांठ *dim.* बांठी *f.* बांठा *m.* कोयंडा *m.*

M. stone just formed. कांचोळी *f.*—To have the stone just formed. कांचोळणें, काथवणें.

M. having the stone fully formed. बाठळ *or* बाठाळ आंबा.—To have the stone fully formed. बाठळणें *or* बाठाळणें, बांधटणें.

M. having the kernel just formed. कोयाळ आंबा.—To have the kernel just formed. कोयाळणें.

M.–dinner or meal. रसभोजन *n.*

M. sauce. तक्कु *n.*

M.–water. आंबवणी *n.* [*f.* खटाई *f.*

Mangoes sliced and dried. आंबकटी *or* काठी *f.* अंबोशी

Mangoes sliced & pickled. चिरांबा *m.*

M.–grove. आंबराई *or* आमराई *f.* अंबिवन *n.* [रणी *f.*

Net in which mangoes are kept. गांझ्या *m.* सारण *f.* सा-

Pickled m. उकडअंबा *or* उकडंबा *or* उकडांबा *m.* वेसवाराचें लोणचें *n.*

Preserved m. गुळांब *or* गुळांबा *m.*

Wild m.–tree, *spondias magnifera.* खटांबा *m.*

Young, unripe m. कैरी *f.* बाळअंबा *m.* करंबुटी *f.* कुइरी *f.* कुवली *f.* तोर *n.*

Young m. stoned and preserved. कोयाडें *n.*

Young m. preserved in a salt pickle. लोणांबी *f.* लोणांबा *m.* बिहांबा *m.* बिहांबी *f.* बेहंबी *f.* बियंबी *f.*

MANGO-FISH, *n.* तपस्वी *m.*

MANGOSTEEN, *n. garcinia cambogia*—the plant. कोकंब *f.* कोकंबी *f.* रातंबी *f.* भिरंड *f.*—the fruit. कोकंब *m. n.* रातंबें *n.* रातंबा *m.* भिरंड *n.*

Dried rind of the m. कोकंबसाल *or* सोल*n.* साल*n.* आंबसोल*n.*

Infusion of dried rind of the m. सोलवणी*n.*

Oil extracted from the m. कोकंबेल*n.* रातंबेल*n.* भिरंडेल*n.*

MANGROVE, *n.* तिवर *n.* [खवड्या.

MANGY, *a. afflicted with mange*—a horse. गरीचा, गरभरलेला,

2—cattle. कथला भरलेला, कथल्या, खवड्या.

3—dog. लुतीचा, लूतभरलेला. [*n.* मानुष्य*n.*

MANHOOD, *n. human nature.* माणुसपण*n.* माणुसपणा*m.* मनुष्यत्व

2 *virility, not womanhood.* पुरुषपणा*m.* पुरुषत्व*n.* पौरुष*n.* पुंस्त्व*n.* पुरुषधर्म*m.* पुंभाव*m.* पुरुषभाव*m.* घोवकी *f.* घोवपणा*m.*

3 *not boyhood.* प्रौढपणा*m.* प्रौढदशा *f.* पण*n.* उमर *f.* उमेद *f.* पुरुषदशा *f.* व्यवहारावस्था *f.* दाढीमिशांचें वय*n.*

4 *valor, fortitude, &c.* v. COURAGE. मर्दपणा*m.* मर्दी *f.* मर्दुमी *f.* पुरुषत्व*n.* पौरुष*n.* [वायु*m.* मद*m.*

MANIA, *n.* v. MADNESS. वेड*n.* उन्माद*m.* उन्मादवायु*m.* उन्मत्त-

MANIAC, MANIACAL, *a.* v. MAD. वेडा, वेडापिसा, पिसळलेला. &c. उन्मादवान्.

MANIAC, *n. madman.* See MAD.

MANIFEST, *a. clear, open, apparent,* v. PLAIN. उघड, उघडा, स्पष्ट, प्रकट *pop.* प्रगट, प्रसिद्ध, प्रत्यक्ष, व्यक्त, सुव्यक्त, जाहीर, आविर्भूत, प्रादुर्भूत, उद्भूत, स्फुट, प्रस्फुट.

To become m. प्रकटणें *or* प्रगटणें, आविर्भवणें, उद्भवणें.

MANIFEST, *n. public declaration.* जाहिरात *f.* जाहिरनामा *m.* प्रसिद्धिपत्र *n.*

2 *invoice.* गलबतांत भरलेल्या मालाची याद *f.*

To MANIFEST, *v. a. make apparent, show clearly.* उघड-प्रगट-प्रसिद्ध-स्पष्ट-जाहीर-&c. करणें-करून दाखवणें, दाखवणें, प्रकटणें *or* प्रगटणें, प्रगटवणें, प्रकाश *m.*-प्रसिद्धि *f.*-उघडीक *f.*-&c. करणें *g. of o.* उघडदशेस-उघडिकेस-प्रसिद्धीस-&c. आणणें, प्रकटीकरण *n.* -स्पष्टीकरण *n.*-व्यक्तीकरण *n.*-आविष्करण *n.*-आविर्भवन *n.*-आविर्भाव *m.*-&c. करणें *g. of o.*

MANIFESTATION, *n.* v. V.—*act.* उघड करणें *n.* प्रगटणें *n.* &c. आविष्करण *n.* प्रादुष्करण *n.* आविर्भवन *n.* उद्भावन *n.* स्पष्टीकरण *n.* व्यक्तीकरण *n.* प्रकटीकरण *n.* प्रकाशकरण *n.*—*state.* उघडीक *f.* उघडदशा *f.* प्रकाश *m.* प्रसिद्धि *f.* जाहिरात *f.* व्यक्ति *f.* प्राकट्य *n.* आविर्भाव *m.* उद्भव *m.* प्रादुर्भाव *m.* [*n.* आद्यपीठ *n.*

Seat or place of the first m. of a divinity. आद्यस्थान

MANIFESTED, *p.* v. V. उघड केलेला, प्रसिद्धीस आणलेला, &c. प्रकटित, प्रकटीकृत, स्पष्टीकृत, व्यक्तीकृत, आविष्कृत, प्रादुष्कृत, प्रस्फुटित, स्फुटित.

MANIFESTER, *n.* MANIFESTING, *p. a.* v. V. उघड करणारा, प्रसिद्धीस आणणारा, &c. प्रकाशक, व्यक्तीकरण-प्रकटीकरण-&c. कर्त्ता, अभिव्यंजक.

MANIFESTLY, *adv.* v. A. उघड, प्रसिद्ध, प्रसिद्धपणें, प्रत्यक्ष, साक्षात्, प्रत्यक्षतः, बोलूनचालून, धडधडीत.

MANIFESTNESS, *n.* v. A. उघडपणा *m.* प्रगटपणा *m.* प्रसिद्धपणा *m.* &c. प्रसिद्धि *f.* प्राकट्य *n.* व्यक्ति *f.* सुव्यक्ति *f.*

MANIFESTO. See MANIFEST, 1.

MANIFOLD, *a. of several kinds, many.* बहुत प्रकारचा, बहुत तऱ्हांचा, विविध, बहुविध, नानाविध, बहुप्रकार, बहुगुण.

2 *appearing in various ways.* बहुरूप, अनेकरूप.

MANIKIN, *n. little man.* वामन *m.*-ऱ्हस्वमूर्ति *f.* माणव *m.* माणवक *m.*

2—The anatomical preparation. मनुष्याचे शरीरांतील अवयव दाखविण्या करितां केलेला पुतळा *m.*

To MANIPULATE, *v. a. work with the hands.* हातानें-हस्तव्यापारानें-&c. करणें, हस्तव्यापार *m.* करणें. [व्यापार *m.*

MANIPULATION, *n. work by hand.* हातकाम *n.* हस्तकर्म *n.* हस्त-

MANKIND, *n. the human race,* v. MAN. मनुष्यजाति *f.* मानवजाति *f.* मनुष्यजन *m.* मनुष्यगण *m.* मनुष्यें *n. pl.* माणसें *n. pl.* जग *n.* जगती *f.* जन *m.* जहान *n.*

3 *race of males.* पुरुषजाति *f.* नरजाति *f.* बाप्यांची जात *f.*

MANLIKE. See MANLY.

MANLINESS, *n.* v. A. 1. मर्दपणा *m.* मर्दी *f.* मर्दाई *f.* मर्दुमकी *f.* पुरुषत्व *n.* पौरुष *n.* पुंस्त्व *n.*

MANLY, *a. manlike, firm, brave.* मर्दा, मर्दाना, मर्दाचा, शूर, दिलदार, दिलदारीचा, मर्दाईचा.

2 *of or belonging to a man.* पुरुषजातीचा, पुरुषाचा, मर्दानी, पौरुष, पौरुषेय.

MANNA, *n.*—of the bamboo. तवकीर *or* तवखीर *n.* तवकील *or* तवखील *n.* वंशक्षीर *n.* वंशलोचन *n.*—Persian m. तुरंजबीन *m.*

MANNER, *n. method, mode, way of doing.* रीति *pop.* रीत *f.* चाल *f.* पर्याय *m.* पद्धति *f.* परिपाटी *f.* मार्ग *m.* पंथ *m.* तऱ्हा *f.* रुति *f.* कृप्ति *f.* मांड *f.* मोडणी *f.* क्रिया *f.*

After this m. येणें प्रमाणें.

After the same m. त्या प्रमाणें, तसाच *deel.*

2 *fashion, habit, way,* v. CUSTOM. चाल *f.* रीति *pop.* रीत *f.* परिपाठ *m.* शिरिस्ता *m.*

Manners and customs. रीतभांत *f. or* रितीभांती *f. pl.*

—of a country, देशाचार *m.*

3 *sort, kind.* जात *f.* प्रकार *m.* तऱ्हा *f.* भांत *f.* विधि *m.*

4 *imposingness of action.* ढब *f.* डौल *m.* डौलदारी *f.* आब *m.* घनावट *f.* धजाब *m.*

Pleasing manner or air. छब *f.*

5 *peculiar way, mode, style, fashion, &c.* ढेव *f.* ढेवण *f.* ढब *f.* शैली *f.* पर्याय *m.* बाणी *f.* धरनी *f.* धाटणी *f.* धाटी *f.* धोरण *n.* गति *pop.* गत *f.* तऱ्हा *f.*

Affected m. झोंक *f.*

6 manners; *way of life,* v. CONDUCT. चाल *f.* चालचर्या *f.* वर्त्तणूक *f.* वागवागणूक *f.* स्थितिरीति *pop.* स्थीतरीत *f.* वृत्त *n.*

Good m. सुनीति *f.*

Ill m. अनीति *f.* [रीत *f.*

Manners and morals—compreh. स्थितिरीति *pop.* स्थीत-

7 manners; *ceremonious behaviour,* v. CIVILITY. माणुसपणा *m.* मनुष्यपणा *m.* गृहस्थगिरी *f.* शिष्टाचार *m.* शिष्टाइकी *f.* रीतरवेस *m. f.* अइन *f.*

8 *carriage, deportment, outward behaviour.* वागणूक *f.* वागण्याची पद्धत *f.* रहाणी *f.*

MANNERLINESS, *n.* v. A. शिष्टता *f.* शिष्टाइकी *f.* सभ्यता *f.* गृहस्थगिरी *f.* शिष्टाचारसंपन्नता *f.*

MANNERLY, *a. ceremonious, polite,* v. CIVIL. शिष्ट, सभ्य, शिष्टाचाराचा, शिष्टसंप्रदायी, शिष्टाचारसंपन्न.

MANNISH. See MASCULINE.

MANŒUVRE, *n. skilful move, measure, &c.* युक्ति *f.* युक्तीचा उपाय *m.* हिकमत *f.* डाव *m.* *v.* खेळ, पेच *m.*

Manœuvres. डावपेच *n. pl.* छकडभेद *m. pl.* छक्केपंजे *m. pl.* शकटभेद *m. pl.* युक्तिप्रयुक्ति *f. pl.*

Military manœuvers. कवाईत *or* कवाईद *f.*

To MANŒUVRE, *v. n.*—in mlitary exercise. कवाईत *f.* करणें-खेळणें, व्यूह *m.* करणें-रचणें.

2 *act with art and address.* युक्ति *f.* करणें-चालवणें-खेळणें-लढवणें, कवाईत *f.* चालवणें-करणें-खेळणें-लढवणें.

MAN OF WAR, *n.* सरकारी लढाऊ गलबत *n.* अरमार *n.*

MANOR, *n. land or estate of a lord, &c.* जमीनदारी *f.* जाहगीर *f.* देशमुखीची जमीन *f.*

Lord of the m. जमीनदार, जाहगिरदार, देशमुख, ग्रामणी.

MANORIAL, *a. pertaining, &c. to a manor.* जमीनदारीचा, देशमुखीच्या जमिनीचा, देशमुखीचा, देशमुखी.

MANSION, *n. gentleman's residence,* v. HOUSE. वाडा *m.* हवेली *f.* महाल *m.*

2 (of the moon). नक्षत्र *n.* There are twenty seven, viz. अश्विनी, भरणी, कृत्तिका, रोहिणी, मृग, आर्द्रा, पुनर्वसु,

पुष्य, आश्लेषा, मघा, पूर्वा, उत्तरा, हस्त, चित्रा, स्वाती, विशाखा, अनुराधा, ज्येष्ठा, मूल, पूर्वाषाढा, उत्तराषाढा, श्रवण, धनिष्ठा, शततारका, पूर्वाभाद्रपदा, उत्तराभाद्रपदा, रेवती. A twenty eighth (अभिजित) is added sometimes, which is composed of the last quarter of the 21st and the fifteenth part of the 22nd. Some significant or allusive terms for certain of them (esp. with reference to the rain which falls under them) are, मांजऱ्या (for अनुराधा), चीत and कड्या (for चित्रा), दडप्या (for स्वाती), उंदऱ्या (for विशाखा), तरणा *or* धाकटा कुंवर (for पुष्य), थोरला कुंवर or म्हातारा (for पुनर्वसु), हत्ती (for हस्तनक्षत्र), वळवा (for those *nakshatras* of the rains which follow पूर्वा). Of the asterism or mansion, हस्तनक्षत्र, four feet or divisions (चारचरण) are supposed, and named, from the (as supposed) positively bad and thence improving quality of the rain which falls respectively under them, लोखंडाचा चरण *or* पाय, तांब्याचा पाय, रुप्याचा पाय, सोन्याचापाय. Astrologers make three divisions (गण) of the27 *nakshatras*, consisting of nine each. They are named देवगण, राक्षसगण, मनुष्यगण.

Blind, dark, &c. m. अंधळें नक्षत्र *n.*

Inauspicious m. घातनक्षत्र *n.*

MANSUETE, MANSUETUDE. See TAME, TAMENESS.

MANTEL-PIECE, MANTLE-TREE, *n. projecting ledge, &c.* चिरणी *f.* जई *f.* जै *f.*

MANTLE, *n.* v. CLOKE. घुगी *f.* दुलई *f.* रजई *f.* घुंगरू *m.*

To MANTLE, *v. a. cloke,* v. To HIDE. लपवणें, पांघरूण*n.* घालणें.

To MANTLE, *v. n. joy, revel.* बहर *m.*-मौजा *f. pl.*-&c. मारणें, खुसांगणें.

2 *spread luxuriantly.* डवरणें, वठणें, बाचलणें, फांपावणें, माजणें, फैलावणें.

3 *ferment, work, gather froth.* फेणणें, फेंसळणें, फेनयुक्त होणें, लसलसणें, लसलस *adv.* करणें.

MANTUA, *n. gown.* पेशवाज *m.*

MANTUA-MAKER, *n.* स्त्रीचें पांघरूण शिवून करणारा.

MANUAL, *a. belonging to the hand.* हाताचा, हातचा, हस्तसंबंधी, हस्त्य.

2 *done by the hand.* हाताचा *or* हातचा, हातकामाचा, हस्तव्यापाराचा, &c. हातानें केलेला, हस्तसाध्य.

M. business or work. हातकाम *n.* हस्तक्रिया *f.* हस्तकर्म *n.*

M. skill or ability. हातोटी *f.* हातवळा *m.* हस्तकौशल्य*n.* हस्तकौशल *n.*

M. quickness and smartness. हस्तचापल्य *n.* हस्तलाघव*n.*

Sign m. हस्ताक्षर *n.* हातची सई *f.*

MANUAL, *n. small book or compilation.* पद्धति *f.* सारग्रंथ *m.* सारसंग्रह *m.* संक्षिप्तशास्त्र *n.* [त्रगृह *n.*

MANUFACTORY, *n.*—the place. कारखाना *m* शिल्पशाला *f.* यं-

MANUFACTURE, *n.* v.V. 1.—*act.* शिल्पानें करणें *n.* &c.

I. *thing manufactured.* शिल्पानें-शिल्पक्रियेनें-कसबानें-&c. केलेला पदार्थ *m.*-दागिना *m.*-वस्तु *n.*-वस्त *f.* शिल्प *n.*

—of cloth. सनंग *n.*

To MANUFACTURE, *v. a. form by workmanship.* शिल्पानें-शिल्पक्रियेनें- कारिगिरीनें-&c. करणें-निर्मिणें-निर्माण करणें-सिद्ध करणें-&c.

2 *work up raw materials.* तयार-सिद्ध-&c. करणें, ओजवणें, कमावणें, संस्कार *m.*-कमाई *f.* करणें *g. of. o.*

MANUFACTURED, *p.* v. V.1. शिल्पानें केलेला, &c. शिल्पनिर्मित, शिल्पकृत, कारिगिरीचा.

MANUFACTURER, *n.* MANUFACTURING, *p. a.* v. V. 1. शिल्पानें करणारा, कारिगिरीनें सिद्ध करणारा, &c. कारिगर, शिल्पकार, शिल्पी.

MANUMISSION, *n.* v. V.—*act.* सोडणें *n.* सोडवण *f.* दास्यमोचन *n.*—*a. or s.* सोड *f.* सुटका *f.* सूट *f.* दास्यमुक्ति *f.*

To MANUMIT, *To* MANUMISE, *v. a. release from slavery.* दास्यापासून सोडणें,सूट *f.*-सोड *f.*-&c.देणें, सुटका *f.*-मोकळीक*f.*-दास्यमोचन *n.*-दास्यमुक्ति *f.*-&c. करणें *g. of o.* अदास-दास्यमुक्त-&c.करणें. [मुक्तदास्य.

MANUMITTED, *p.* v. V. दास्यापासून सोडलेला, &c. दास्यमुक्त,

To MANURE, *v. a. dung, apply manure.* कारवणें, खतावणें, खताळणें, खत *n.*-खात *m. n.*-कार*m.*-&c.घालणें-टाकणें.

MANURE, *n. dung or compost to fatten land.* खत *n.* खात *m. n.* खप *m.* खत्रप *n.* कार *m.* खतमूत *n.*

M. of fish. कुटा *m.* कूट *n.*

M. of human ordure. सोनखत *n.*

Rich from m.—a field. खतोड, खतवड, खताड, खातवट.

That smells of the m.—a vegetable. खातूस.

MANURED, *p.* v. V. कारवलेला, खतावलेला, &c. कारीक, खतमुताचा, खतवड.

Raised upon m. lands. खतमुताचा.

MANUSCRIPT, *n. book or paper written with the hand or pen.* हातानें लिहिलेला कागद *m.*-पुस्तक *n.*-&c. हस्तलेख *m.*

Outer sheet or cover of a m. मुखवस्त्र *n.*

MANUSCRIPT, *a.* v. N. हातानें लिहिलेला, हस्तलिखित.

MANY, *a.* फार, बहूत *or* बहुत, पुष्कल *pop.* पुष्कळ, अनेक, बहुतेक, विपुल, बहुल, बहु (in comp. as बहुपाद, बहुभुज, &c.).—*intens.* लक्षानलक्ष, कोट्यवधि, कोट्यानकोटि, समातिरिक्त.

For numerous *vulgar* words See EXUBERANT.

As m. as. जितका, जेवढा, यावत्.

How m. किती, किति, केवढा, कितीक, कितेक, कितका.

In m. places. बहुठिकाणीं, बहुत्र, अनेकत्र.

In m. ways or sorts. बहुप्रकारें, बहुधा.

M. a one. कितीएक *or* कित्येक, कैक.

M. times. बहुदा, बहुवार, बहुवेळ.

So m. as. तितका, तेवढा, तावत्.

MANY, *n. multitude.* समुदाय *m.* समाज *m.* समूह *m.*

MANY-COLORED, *n.* बहुरंगांचा, बहुरंगी, चित्रविचित्र, नानावर्ण, नानाराग.

MANY-CORNERED, *a.* बहुकोण.

MANY-FIBRED, *a.* बहुतंत्री.

MANY-HEADED, *a.* बहुमस्तक, बहुशिरस्क, बहुमूर्द्धा.

MANY-STREAMED, *a.* बहुप्रवाह.

MANY-STRINGED, *a.* बहुत तारांचा, बहुतंत्रिक.

MANY-TIMES. See OFTEN.

MAP, *n.* नकाशा *m.* नकशा *m.* देशालेख्यपत्रक *n.* देशचित्र*n.*

To MAP, *v. a.* नकाशा *m.*-&c. काढणें *g. of o.*

To MAR, *v. a. injure, damage,* v. To SPOIL. बिघडणें, बिघडवणें, बिघाडणें, नासणें, नासवणें, नाश *m.*-बिघड *m.*-बि-

घात *m.*-खिचका *m.*-&c. करणें *g. of o.*

2 *disconcert, &c.* v. To DEFEAT. मोडणें, हुसकटणें, हुसकणें, हिसकणें. [सडी *f.*

MARASMUS, *n. wasting disease*, v. CONSUMPTION. क्षयरोग *m.*

MARAUDER, *n. rover for plunder.* लुटारा, लुटारी, लुटारू, पुंड.

Ravages of marauders. अवाडाव *f.*

MARAUDING, *n. roving for plunder.* लुटीसाठीं फिरणें *n.* लुटीची स्वारी *f.* चिप्याचोळीची स्वारी *f.*

MARBLE, *a. made, &c. of marble.* संगमरवरी, संगमरवराचा.

2 *colored like marble.* संगमरवरी रंगाचा.

MARBLE, *n.* संगमरवर *m.*

2—playing marble. गोटा *m.* गोटी *f.* मंज्या *m.*

Hole or pit at marbles. आगळ *f.* गल *or* गल्ल *f.*

Large m. बट *m.* टप *m.*

M. of lac. गजरा *m.*

The ring at marbles. बद *m.*

The pit-game. आगळडाव *m.* आगळगोटी *f.* गलगोटी *f.*

The ring-game. कोंड डाव *m.* Some of the terms at *marbles* are, एकलकाजा, कानघुशी *or* कानघुसणी, कोंड, कोपरघुसणी, कोंपरी. Some of the plays at *marbles* are, आगळगोट्या, कुरगोट्या, ढोपरगोट्या. [दय.

MARBLE-HEARTED, *a.* v. CRUEL, PITILESS. पाषाणहृदय, वज्रहृ-

MARBLE-PLASTER, *n.* वज्रलेप *m.*

MARCASITE, *n.* सुवर्णमुखी *f.* सुवर्णमाक्षिक *n.* आवर्त्त *m.*

MARCH, *n.*—the month. इंग्रेजी सालाचा तिसरा महिना *m.* फाल्गुनोत्तरार्ध चैत्रपूर्वार्ध *n.* [ची चाल *f.*

2 *military step or movement.* कवाइती चाल *f.* कदमबराबरी-

3 *journey of soldiers.* कूच *n.* सैनिकगमन *n.* सैनिकयात्रा *f.*

4 *grave or stately march.* डौलाची-थाटाची-मिरवण्याची-&c. चाल *f.* गजगति *f.*

To MARCH, *v. n.* as soldiers; *move by steps and in order.* कवाइतीचे चालीनें चालणें, कदम बराबरीनें-कदम बराबरीचे चालीनें चालणें.

2 *journey,*—troops. कूच *n.*-&c. करणें.

3 *march gravely, statelily, &c.* डौलाचे चालीनें-थाटाचे चालीनें-&c. चालणें, मिरवणें, ठमकणें, मिरवत-ठमकत-&c. चालणें, गजगतीनें चालणें.

To MARCH, *v. a.* कवाइतीचे चालीनें-&c. चालवणें.

2 *cause to journey.* कूच *n.* करवणें *g. of o.*

MARCHES, *n. pl. borders*, v. CONFINES. हद्दीचादेश *m.* प्रांतदेश*m.*

MARCHING, *a.* कूच करण्याचा, कुचाचा.

MARE, *n.* घोडी *f.* दुगांडी *f.* अश्विनी *f.* तुरंगिणी *f.* वडवा *f.*

Got out from a m.—offspring. काढाऊ, काढींव.

Large & fine m. मादरवान *f.*

M. kept for breeding. पसू *f.* पसूघोडी *f.*

To bring a m. to the male, or to get offspring from a m. काढवणें.

MARGARITE, *n.* v. PEARL. मोतीं *n.*

MARGIN, *n. brink, border, verge,* v. EDGE. कांठ *m.* किनारा*m.* कड *f.* दर *f.* बाजू *f.* काठार*n.* कांठारा*m.* कुपट *f.* प्रांत*m.* प्रांतभाग*m.*

Along the m. प्रांततः.

2 (of a book or writing). पुस्तकाची-&c. कड *f.* समास *m.*

To leave a margin, *fig.* कूस *f.*-जागा *f.* ठेवणें-राखणें.

MARGINAL, *a. inserted in the margin.* कडचा, समासाचा, समासस्थ, समास्थ, समासलिखित.

M. note. बिना *m.* बिनी *f.*

MARGINALLY, *adv. along the margin.* प्रांताच्या-&c. ठाईं, प्रांततः.

MARIGOLD, *n.*—the flower. झेंडू *m.* झेंडूफूल *n.* मखमल *f. n.*

2 French m. गुलजाफिरी *f.* गुलछडी *f.*

MARINE, *a. relating, &c. to the sea.* समुद्राचा, समुद्रसंबंधी, सागरसंबंधी, समुद्रविषयक, सामुद्र, समुद्रिय, सैंधव, सिंधुक, समुद्रज, समुद्रोद्भव.

2 *relating, &c. to sea affairs.* गलबतांवरच्या कामाविषयींचा, जाहजांचे प्रकरणाचा.

MARINE, *n. sea affairs.* गलबतांकडचें काम *n.* जहाजांचेंकाम *n.*-प्रकरण *n.* अर्मारीकाम *n.* नाविकप्रकरण *n.* जलयानप्रकरण *n.*

2 *soldier employed on board ship.* गलबतावरील शिपाई, अर्मारी शिपाई.

MARINER, *n.*v. SAILOR. गलबती-&c. माणूस *m.* जहाजकरी, जहाजवाला, सफरी, सामुद्र, समुद्रयायी.

MARITAL, *a. belonging to a husband.* भ्रताराचा, भर्त्याचा, &c. भर्तृसंबंधी, भर्तृविषयक, पतिसंबंधी.

MARITIME, *a.* See MARINE. 2. *bordering on the sea, situated on the coast.* समुद्राचे तीरावरचा, तटस्थ, समुद्रतीरस्थ, समुद्रतटस्थ.

MARJORAM, *n. origanum majorana.* मरवा *or* मुरवा *m.*

MARK, *n. token, sign, stamp, &c.* निशाणी *or* नी *f.* खूण *f.* चिन्ह *n.* निशाण *n.* ओळखण *f.* लक्षण*n.* अंक *m.* लिंग *n.* लांच्छन *n.* अभिज्ञान *n.* व्यंजन *n.* व्यंजक *n.*

Marks, stamps, &c.—compreh. खूणमुद्रा *f.* खूणखाण *f.*

Auspicious, &c. m. शुभचिन्ह *n.* शुभलक्षण *n.* सुलक्षण *n.* सुचिन्ह *n.*

An unlucky, inauspicious, &c. m. अशुभचिन्ह*n.* अशुभलक्षण *n.* कुलक्षण*n.* अवलक्षण*n.* अपलक्षण *n.* दुर्लक्षण*n.*दुश्चिन्ह*n.*

A secret or inner m. चोरअंक *m.* अंतरखूण *f.*

A secret or private m. (of traders) आंतील आंख.

M. made by a hot iron. डाग *m.* लास *m.*

That has auspicious, &c. marks. सुलक्षणी, सुलक्षणिक, सुलक्षण. [लक्षण.

That has unlucky, &c. marks. कुलक्षणी, अवलक्षणी, कु-

2 (on the body) *spot, line, &c.* सामुद्रिकलक्षण *n.* सामुद्ररेषा *f.* सामुद्रचिन्ह *n.* सामुद्र*n.*

Belonging or relating to marks. सामुद्रिक.

Divination or interpretation of marks. सामुद्रिक *n.*

Diviner or interpreter of marks. सामुद्रिक.

That has auspicious marks, &c. सुलक्षणी, सुलक्षणिक.

3 *butt, object, aim.* निशाण *n.* टिपण *n.* हिंदुण *or* न *n.* लक्ष्य *n.* वेध्य *n.*

Hitting the m. *lit. fig.* लक्ष्यभेद *m.*

So as just to hit the m. टापासटीप. [णें-देणें.

To strike the m. निशाण *n.* उतरणें, निशाणीं घाव *m.* घाल-

4 (as a substitute for a signature). हातचीखूण *f.*-निशाणी *f.* सहीची निशाणी *f.*

5 एक नाणें आहे.

A man of m. v. EMINENT. प्रसिद्ध, नांवालौकिकाचा.

To MARK, *v. a. put a mark on.* खूण *f.*-निशाणी *f.*-चिन्ह*n.*-&c.

करणें-देणें-लावणें-घालणें-&c. ओळख *f.* ठेवणें-करणें, अंकणें, चिन्हित-अंकित करणें.

2 (cattle, &c. by a cauterizing iron). डागणें, लासणें, डाग *m.*-लास *m.* देणें, लासणी *f.* करणें.

3 *note, take notice of.* पाहणें, लक्षिणें, लक्ष्य *n.*-ध्यान *n.*-चित्त *n.*-&c. देणें-लावणें-ठेवणें, लक्ष्यांत-ध्यानांत-&c. आणणें.

4 off, *define, &c.* v. To BOUND. परिच्छेद *m.* करणें *g. of o.* परिच्छिन्न करणें.

5 out ; *trace the figure, outlines, &c. of.* बेतणें, बेतून देणें, अंकणें, अंकून देणें, रेखटणें *or* रेखाटणें, रेखणें, काढणें, रेखटणी *f.*-अंकन *n.*-&c. करणें *g. of o.*

To MARK, *v. n. note.* लक्ष्यांत-ध्यानांत-&c. आणणें-ठेवणें.

MARKED, *p.* v. V. A. 1. खूण दिल्हेला, &c. अंकलेला, अंकित, चिन्हित, लांछित, कृतलक्षण, लक्षित.

2 डागलेला, लासलेला, डाग दिल्हेला, &c. लाशा.

3 पाहिलेला, लक्षिलेला, &c.

4 परिछेद केलेला, परिछिन्न.

5 बेतलेला, अंकून दिल्हेला, &c.

MARKER, *n.* MARKING, *p. a.* v. V. A. 1. खूण देणारा, निशाणीकरणारा, अंकणारा, &c. अंकन-&c. कर्त्ता-कारक-&c.

2 डागणारा, डाग देणारा, &c. डाग देण्याचा.

3 लक्षिणारा, &c. लक्ष्य देणारा, &c. लक्ष्यांत आणणारा, &c.

4 परिछेद करणारा, परिछेदक.

5 बेतून देणारा, अंकून देणारा, रेखटणारा, &c.

MARKET, *n.* बाजार *m.* हट्ट *m. dim.* हट्टी *f. pop.* हट *or* हाट *m.* गंज *m.*—compreh. & indef. &c. हाटबाजार *m.*

A green m. मंडई *f.* माळहट *m.* माळसात *f.*

A moveable m. हट्ट *pop.* हट *or* हाट *m.*

Afternoon or evening m. गुजरी *f.* गुजरीचा बाजार *m.*

Clerk of the m. निरखी *or* निरख्या, निरख पाडणारा.

Custom or usage of the m. बाजार शिरस्ता *m.*

Current in the m. बाजारचलन *or* चलनी.

M.-court. चावडी *f.*

M.-intelligence. पेंठ *f.*

M.-tattle, report, &c. बाजारअफवा *f.* बाजारबातमी *f.*

Public measurer of a m. मापारी *or* मापाडी.

Stale or after m. शिळाबाजार *m.* अडबाजार *m.*

Stale or refuse m.-commodities. पड केणें *n.*

Tax or duty paid for a booth, stand, &c. in a m. बसकी *f.* बसक *f.* बैठक *f.* बाजार बैठक *f.*

2 *vent, sale.* खप *m.* विकरा *m.* विकरी *f.* विक्रय *m.* ओप *m.*

MARKET, *a.* v. N. बाजारी, बाजारचा.

To MARKET, *v. n.* बाजार *m.*-हाटबाजार *m.*-सौदा *m.*-सौदासूत *n.*-&c. करणें.

MARKET-DAY, *n.* बाजारचा दिवस *m.*-वार *m.* बाजारदिवस *m.* हाटदिवस *m.*

MARKET-FOLK, *n.* बाजारचीं माणसें *n. pl.* बाजारकरी *m. pl.* बाजारकरी लोक *m. pl.*

MARKET-MAN, *n.* बाजारकरी *m.* हाटकरी *m.*

MARKET-PLACE, *n.* बाजारची जागा *f.* बाजारवाडा *m.*

MARKET-PRICE, MARKET-RATE, *n.* बाजारभाव*m.* भाव*m.* पाड*m.* पेंठ *f.*—as fixed by the police. निरख *m.* बाजारनिरख *m.*

Regulator of the m.-rate. निरख्या.

Roll or paper of the m.-rate. निरखबंद *m.*

MARKET-TOWN, *n.* बाजारगांव *m.* पेंठ *f.* पेंठेचा गांव *m.*

MARKET-WOMAN, *n.* बाजारकरीण *f.* हाटकरीण *f.*

MARKETABLE, *a. saleable.* बाजार करायाचा, खपाऊ, विकाऊ, खपायाजोगता-सारखा, क्रेय, विक्रेय.

2 *current, &c. in the market.* बाजारी, बाजारचा.

MARKETING, *n.* बाजार करणें *n.* बाजार *m.* हाटबाजार*m.* सौदा *m.* सौदासूत*n.*

MARKING, *n.* v. V. A. 1.—*act.* खूण करणें *n.* निशाणी देणें *n.* अंकणें *n.* &c. अंकणी *f.* अंकन *n.*

2 डागणें *n.* लासणें *n.* डागणी *f.* लासणी *f.*

3 पाहणें *n.* लक्षिणें *n.* &c.

4 परिच्छेद *m.*

5 बेतणें *n.* अंकणें *n.* &c. बेतणी *f.* अंकणी *f.* रेखटणी *or* रेखाटणी *f.* रेखणी *f.*

MARKING-IRON, *n.* डागणी *f.*

MARKING-NUT, *n.*—the plant. बिबी *or* बिब्बी*or*बिबवी *f.* भल्लातक *m.*कलिद्रुम *m.*—the nut. बिबा *or* बिब्बा *or* बिबवा *m.* भल्लातक*m.*—covertly or cautly. काळा *m.*

Calyx of the m. बिबट *n.* बिबोटी *f.*

Oil obtained from the m. बिबवेल *n.* बिबेल *n.*

Seed of the m. बिबटें *n.*

Spot or dot resembling the m. बिबटें *n.* बिबट *n.*

MARKSMAN, *n. one skilful to hit a mark.* निशाण मारणारा, निशाणमाऱ्या, नेमाड्या, लक्ष्यवेधी, संधानी, अचूकसंधानी.

2 सहीची निशाणी-&c.करणारा.

MARL, *n.*—the earth. चिकणमाती *f.*

MARL-PIT, *n.* चिकणमातीची खाण *f.*

MARMOREAN, *a. made of marble.* संगमरवरी, संगमरवराचा.

MARQUIS, *n.* विलायतेंतील एक पदवी आहे.

MARRED, *p.* v. V. 1. बिघडलेला, नासलेला, &c.

2 मोडलेला, हिसकटलेला, &c.

MARRER, *n.* v.V. 1. बिघडणारा, नासणारा, &c. बिघाड्या, नाशक, विनाशक, विघातक, विघाती. कार्यविनाशक, &c.

2 मोडणारा, हुसकटणारा, &c. मोड्या, विचकट्या, कार्यविघातक,

MARRIAGE, *n. legal union of a man and a woman.* विवाह*m.* लग्न *pop.* लगन*or*लगीन*n.* वऱ्हाड*n.* परिणय*m.* परिणयन *n.* लग्नकार्य*n.* पाणिग्रह*m.* पाणिग्रहण*n.* पाणिपीडन*n.* उद्वाह*m.* उद्वहन*n.* उपयम*m.* उपयाम*m.* हस्तेकरण*n.* There are amongst the Hindus numerous rites and observances relating to *marriage.* The words expressing them, as they can appear under no English words, and, as they will be duly valued by persons studying the language, customs, and fashions of the Hindu body, are inserted here. For explanation of them turn to the M. and E. Dictionary. अरतवण परतवण, अक्षतारोपण, अंबाशिंपणें, आजेचीर *or* आजेवाण, आतेचीर *or* आतेवाण *or* आतेगौरव, आंगठेदाम,उडदामुहूर्त्त, ओहर, करणी, कुरवंडी, गडकनेर *or* केळवण, गांठदाम*or* गांठीचादाम, गांठसोडवण, गिऱ्हे पूजन, गृहप्रवेश, गोडजेवण, घटिकास्थापन, घाणा, दसवंदन, दिवाळसण, देवदर्शन, द्विरागमन,परतवण, पावण, पोटक्षांकणें, फलप्रदान, बोळवण, मांडवपरतणी, मासवंदन, मुहूर्तपूजा, रुखवत, लज्जाहोम, लक्ष्मीपूजन, सप्तपदी *or* सप्तपदीक्रमण, सवेण्या, साडे, साखरपुडा, सुवर्णाभिषेक. Certain *forms* of *marriage* are,—आसुरविवाह, आर्षविवाह, गांधर्वलग्न *or* गांधर्वविवाह, दैविकविवाह, पैशाचविवाह, पाट, प्राजापत्यविवाह, प्रीति-

विवाह, ब्राह्मविवाह, मनमेळलग्न or विवाह, राक्षसविवाह. Some of the terms expressing *things* used at *marriages* are,—अहिरी, उष्टीहळद, ऐरिणी, औक्षवण, कंकण, कऱ्हा, कळसवणी, चौकपासोडा, डाबू or डाऊ, दिवा, नंदाचा पासोडा or नंदाचा शेला, नक्षत्रमाळा or माळ, पाटपासोडा, पालछत्र, पोटक्षाकणें, शेलामुदी, बही. Some of the terms expressing *persons* or *offices* are,—करवला, करवली, कानपिळा or पिळ्या, पावण, पावता, बरधावा. Some of the *ablutions* (of bride, bridegroom, mother of either, &c.) connected with a m. are,—आउन्हाण, दसन्हाण, सोळन्हाण, मासन्हाण, रासन्हाण. Some of the terms expressing *presents*, *courtesies*, *&c.* are, अंगठ्याचा मान, अंबोण, अष्टपुत्री, अष्टायन or अष्टवाणें, आस्वाडपाटी, आंचणी, ज्येष्ठासन, तळी, तिळवण, तेलफळ or तेलसाडी, दंपतिपूजन, दंपतिभोजन, दिंड, बडभोजन, पावण, मधुपर्क, मांडीचेपणें, लगनसाडा, शिष्टाचार, श्रावणपाटी, सीमांतपूजन *pop.* शेवतीपूजन. Other terms expressing various points and particulars are,—जानवसा, जानवसघर, दारढवळणें, दारधरणें, मुहूर्त्तमेढ, सुनमुख. In the solemnization of marriage to say "*I take* (*this woman, this man,*) *to my* (*wife, husband*)" is well rendered by ममम्हणणें.

Ablution at m. मंगलस्नान*n.*

A huddled or hurried m. गडबडगुंडा*m.*

Altar or raised seat at a m. बहुलें or बोहलें*n.*

A shabby m. निर्लेपलग्न*n.*-विवाह*m.* &c.

Asking a girl in m. मागणी *f.* मागी *f.*

Auspicious (season, month, lunar day, *nakshatra,*) for m. लग्नसराई *f.* लग्नमास*m.* लग्नतिथि *f.*

Auspicious juncture (for joining hands, &c.) at a m. लग्नघटिका *f.* लग्नमुहूर्त्त*m.*—The time-cup determining it. लग्नघटिका *f.*—Astrologer's paper stating it. लग्नचिठ्ठी *f.* लग्नपत्रिका *f.*—Roll of such auspicious junctures. लग्नटीप *f.*

Cloth or screen interposed at a m. between the bride and bridegroom. अंतःपट *m.* जमनीक *f.* नंदीचा-नंदाचा-नांदीचा शेला *m.* पासोडा *m.*

Company and attendants at a m. वरात *f.* वऱ्हाड *n.*

Cord with which the height of a proposed bride or bridegroom is ascertained. प्रमाणसूत्र *n.* ब्रह्मसूत्र *n.*

Father of the bridegroom. ओहोबाप—the mother ओहोमाय.

Fee to the priest at a m. मांडवखंडणी *f.*

Interchange between families of daughters in m. बदल *n.* or बदलाचें लग्न *n.* बदलावण *n.*

Joining of the hands at a m. पाणिग्रह *m.* पाणिग्रहण *n.*

Letter of invitation to a m. लग्नचिठ्ठी *f.*

Making up or bringing about a m. घटवटणा *f.*बराबर *f.*

M.-contract. वाग्निश्चय or वाङ्गनिश्चय *m.*

M.-tax. लग्नटका or टक्का *m.*

M.-license. लग्नचिठ्ठी *f.*

M.-feast. लग्नप्रयोजन *n.* प्रस्थ *n.*

M.-festivities. लग्नसोहळा *m.*

M.-offering (to the tutelar deity of a place). तांबूलआवणी *f.* तांबूलशेरणी *f.*

M.-procession. वऱ्हाड *n.* वरात *f.*

M.-service. विवाहोपचार *m.*

M.-string. (It is a string with a bit of gold strung on it; it is put round the neck of the bride, who wears it till she becomes a widow, when it is broken). मंगलसूत्र *n.* सौभाग्यतंतु *m.* मांगल्यतंतु *m.* अहेवतंतू *m.*

Man in or entering into his first m. प्रथमवर (vulg. or pop. पथवर),—his second m. विजवर,—his third m. तिजवर.

Party of the bride at a m. वधूपक्ष *m.* वऱ्हाडणी *f. pl.*

Party of the bride-groom at a m. वरपक्ष*m.*—in a procession. प्रस्थानी वऱ्हाडी. [पारिबर्ह *n.*

Presents made to a bride at her m. अंदण *n.* सुदाय *n.*

Procession of the bride to the m. आगती *f.*

One related by m. सोयरा *m.*

Relation by m. सोयरगत *f.* सोयरीक *f.*

Second m. द्वितीयसंबंध *m.*

Second m. of a *shúdra* woman, or of a *shúdra* man with a *shúdra* widow. पाट *m.* मुहूर्त्त *m.* मोहतूर *m.*

Shed or awning for a m. लग्नमंडप *m.*

Suitable for occasions of m.—cloth &c. लग्नाऊ.

Unduly conducted & therefore invalid m. मंगळ *n.*

To be proposed for m.—a female. सांगून येणें.

To choose in m. वरणें.

To fix on a time for a m. लग्न *n.* काढणें.

To dissolve a m.—a husband and wife. काडी *f.* मोडून देणें, पालव *m.* कापून देणें. [*n.* पाहणें.

To match (child with child) in m. मणगटासारखे मणगट

To be undergoing the ceremony of m. हळद *f.* लागणें *with* स or ला *of s.*

Marriageable, *a. fit for wedlock.* वऱ्हाडायाजोगा, लग्नाजोगा, विवाहाजोगा, &c. विवाह्य, उद्वाह्य, विवाहयोग्य, विवाहोचित, विवाहोपयुक्त, परिणेय, विवाहवयस्क.

A m. boy. नवरा *m.*

A m. girl. नवरी *f.*

M. and yet unmarried. उपवर.

Married, *p.* v.V. N. वऱ्हाडलेला, लग्नझालेला, लग्नाचा, विवाहित, उद्वाहित, ऊढ, कृतविवाह, जातविवाह, परिणीत, जातोपयम, कृतोपयम.

A m. couple, v. Couple. दंपती *n. m.* वहूवर *n.*

A m. man.—*man who has a wife.* सभार्य, सपत्नीक, सकुटुंब, कबीलदार, स्त्रीमान्, सदार, चतुर्भुज.

A m. woman,—*woman who has a husband.* सुवासिनी *pop.* सवाशीण or सवाष्ण or सवाष्ट *f.* अहेव *f.* सभर्तृका, सपत्निका, सधवा, पतिवत्नी.

Marrow, *n.* (of the bones or flesh). मेंदू *m.* मेद *m. n.* मज्जा *f.* वपा *f.* वसा *f.* अस्थिसार *n. m.* देहसार *m. n.*

2 *pith, inner portion.* गर *m.* गीर *m.*मगज*m.*सार*m.*गर्भ*m.*दळ*n.*

Marrow-bone, *n.* मेंदूचें हाड *n.*

2 See Knee.

To **Marry**, *v. a. join in wedlock.* लग्न *n.*-विवाह *m.*-&c. लावणें-चालवणें, विवाहकर्म *n.*-विवाहक्रिया *f.*-विवाहसंस्कार *m.*-लग्नक्रिया *f.*-&c. करणें.

2 *dispose of in marriage.* देणें, लग्नाला देणें, लग्न करून देणें.

3 *take for husband or wife.* विवाहणें, वरणें, उद्वाहणें, परणणें, परिणय *m.*-परिणयन *n.*-पाणिग्रह *m.*-पाणिग्रहण *n.*-&c. करणें.

4 *take to wife.* बायको *f.*-नवरी *f.* करणें-करून घेणें, परिणय *m.*-परिणयन *n.* करणें. [घेणें.

5 *take to husband.* दादला *m.*-नवरा *m.*-पति *m.* करणें-करून

To MARRY, *v. n.* लग्न *n.*-विवाह *m.*-&c. करणें, बऱ्हाडणें, लग्न *n.*-&c. होणें *g. of s.*—with jocose implication. दोहों हातांचे चार हात *m. pl.* करणें, चतुर्भुज होणें, आणा मागें लागणें *g. of s.* चार हात *m. pl.* होणें *g. of s.* पायांत बिडी *f.* पडणें, गळ्यांत माळ *f.* पडणें, नाकांत वेसण *f. n.* पडणें, हाडें *n. pl.* भाजणें *g. of s.*

MARS, *n.*—the planet. मंगल *m.* भौम *m.* अंगारक *m.*

2 The Hindu Mars or God of war is कार्त्तिकेय *or* कार्त्तिक स्वामी.

MARSH, *n. fen, watery tract of land.* दलदल *f.* चिबड *or* चिबीड *f.* झिलाण *n.* पाणथळ *n.* पाणदळ *n.* पाणथळरान *n.* चिबडरान *n.* बेंद *f.*

Salt m. or meadow. खारस्थळ *n.*

To MARSHAL, *v. a. dispose in order,* v. To ARRANGE. रचणें, योजणें, रचना *f.*-योजना *f.*-योजणूक *f.*-व्यवस्थापन *n.*-स्थितिस्थापन *n.*-&c. करणें *g. of o.*

MARSHAL, MARSHALLER, *n.* v. V. रचणारा, &c. योजक, रचक, स्थितिस्थापक, व्यवस्थापक.

I. लशकरांतली एक पदवी आहे.

MARSHY, *a fenny, wet.* दलदलीत, चिबड *or* चिबीड, पाणथळाचा, पाणदळाचा, जलाढ्य, जलमय, जलप्रचुर, जलप्राय.

MART, *n. place of public traffic.* पेंठ *f.* उतारपेंठ *f.* गंज *m.* विक्रयस्थान *n.*

MARTIAL, *a. pertaining, &c. to war.* युद्धाचा, लढाईचा, रणाचा, युद्ध विषयक, युद्धसंबंधी, रणसंबंधी, रणविषयक, युद्धाविषयींचा, &c. युद्धप्रकरणाचा, सांग्रामिक, सामरिक.

2 *suitable for war, useful in war.* युद्धाच्या कामाचा, युद्धाच्या उपयोगाचा, लढाऊ, लढवई *or* बाई, युद्धोपयोगी, रणोपयोगी.

3 *warlike, given to war.* लढाऊ, लढवई *or* बाई, लढता, जुंजार *or* झुंजार, वीरश्रीचा, रणासक्त, रणवीर.

MARTIAL LAW, *n.* लशकरी कायदे *m. pl.*

MARTINET. See DISCIPLINARIAN.

MARTINGAL, *n.* जेरबंद *m.*

MARTYR, *n. one who dies in defence of any cause.* आपल्या मतासाठीं-आपल्या पक्षासाठीं-आपल्या धर्मासाठीं-&c. प्राण देणारा *or* प्राण दिल्हेला-मरण पावलेला, स्वमतार्थ-धर्मार्थत्यक्तप्राण, धर्मार्थार्पितप्राण, स्वधर्मार्थ-स्वमतार्थमृत.

2 *one who suffers much from a disease.* कूळ *n.* गिऱ्हाईक *c.* असामी *f.* पात्र *n.* धारा *m.* घर *n.*

MARTYRDOM, *n.* धर्मासाठीं मरणें *n.* स्वमतासाठीं प्राण देणें *n.* स्वधर्मार्थ प्राणार्पण *n.*

MARTYRED. See MARTYR.

MARVEL, *n.* v. WONDER. नवल *n.* कौतुक *n.* चमत्कार *m.* चोज *n.* नवलाई *f.* नवलपरी *f.* नवलअद्भुत *n.* नवलविशेष *n.*

To MARVEL, *v. n.* v. To WONDER. आश्चर्य *n.*-नवल *n.*-&c. करणें, नवल *n.*-आश्चर्य *n.*-&c. वाटणें *in. con.* चमत्कारणें, साश्चर्य-आश्चर्ययुक्त-&c. होणें.

MARVEL of Peru, *n.* गुलबास *f. m.* सायंकाळी *f.* (the plant) सायंकाळें *n.* (the flower).

MARVELLOUS, *a.* v. WONDERFUL. नवल, नवलाचा, आश्चर्याचा, चमत्काराचा, अद्भुत, आश्चर्यकारक, आश्चर्यकर, चमत्कारिक.

MARVELLOUSLY, *adv.* v. A. नवल वाटायाजोगा *decl.* आश्चर्य वाटायाजोगा *decl.* चमत्कारिकरीतीनें, अद्भुतरूपानें.

MARVELLOUSNESS, *n.* v. A. नवलपणा *m.* नवलाई *f.* अपूर्वाई *f.* अद्भुतता *f.*

MASCULINE, *a. male.* पुरुषजातीचा, पुरुषजातीय, पुंजातीय, पुंव्यक्तिक, पुं *in comp.* पुरुष *in comp.*

2 *belonging to males, fit for males, &c.* पुरुषाचा, पुरुषजातीचा, मर्दानी, पौरुष, पौरुषेय.

3 *resembling a man.* पुरुषधर्मक, पुरुषस्वभावाचा, पुरुषचालीचा, पुरुषवृत्तीचा, नरवत्, पुंवत्, पुरुषवृत्ति, पुंप्रकृति, पुरुषायित, मर्दानी.

4—in grammar. पुल्लिंग.

MASCULINENESS, *n.* v. A. 3. पुरुषस्वभाव *m.* पुरुषवृत्ति *f.* पुंप्रकृति *f.*

MASH, *n. a mixture of things mingled or beaten together.* चेंदा *m.* काला *m.* चिवडा *m.*

M. of ground rice and bran boiled. खिचडा *m.* खिचडें *n.*

M. of tamarinds, mangoes, &c. कोळ *m.* [होत *n.*

2 (for cattle) अंबोण *n.* खिचडा *m.* खिचडें *n.* घाटा *m.* गो-

3 *mashed, crushed, bruised state.* चेंदा *m.* चेंदामेंदा *m.* चेंदूमेंदू *m.* चेंदू *m.*

To MASH, *v. a. bruise, crush, beat into a mess.* कोळणें, चिवडणें, चेंदणें, चेंदरणें, मर्दणें, चेंदामेंदा *m.*-&c. करणें *g. of o.*

2 (as with a ladle or spoon,) अहाटणें, घाटणें.

MASHED, *p.* v. V. 1. चेंदरलेला, &c. चेंदामेंदा केलेला, मर्दित.

2 अहाटलेला, अहाटीव.

MASHINESS, *n.* v. A. गलगलितपणा *m.* &c.

MASHING, *n.* v. V.1.—*act.* कोळणें *n.* चेंदरणें *n.* &c. कोळणी *f.* चेंदणी *f.* मर्दन *n.*

2—*act.* अहाटणें *n.* घाटणें *n.* घाटण *n.*

MASHY, *a. soft, squashy, &c.* गलगलीत *or* गिलगिलीत, बिलबिलीत, बिलबिला, दबदबीत.

MASK, *n. visor.* मुखवटा *m.* रुपडें *n.* कृत्रिममुख *n.* छद्मास्य *n.*

2 *pretence, pretext, cover.* बहाणा *m.* निमित्त *n.* हिला *m.* सोंग *n.* मिष *pop.* मीस *n.* व्याज *m.*

To drop the m. गुण *m. pl.* दाखवणें, गुणावर-गतीवर-गतीसस्वभावावर-रंगावर-ढंगावर-&c. येणें.

To MASK, *v. a. disguise with a mask.* मुखवटा *m.* लावणें-घालणें-घालून लपविणें, मुखवट्यानें लपवणें-झांकणें-&c.

2 *cover, conceal,* v. To HIDE. छपवणें, छपावणें, लपवणें, आच्छादन *n.*-गोपन *n.*-&c. करणें *g. of o.*

MASKED, *p.* v. V. मुखवटा लावलेला, छद्ममुखी, कृत्रिममुखी, कपटमुखी, कपटवेष, छद्मवेषी.

2 छपवलेला, &c. गोपित, आच्छादित.

MASKER, *n.* MASKING, *p.a.* v. V. 1. मुखवटा घालणारा-लावणारा, मुखवट्या, मुखवटाघाल्या.

2 छपवणारा, &c. आच्छादक.

MASLIN. See MESLIN.

MASON, *n.* गवंडी *or* गौंडी, गवंड्या, राज, पिद्रेल (from the Portuguese.)

The instrument of a m. for patting plaster. थापटणें *n.* थापटी *f.*

MASONRY, *n. craft or occupation of a m.* गवंडीपणा *n.*
2 *work done by a mason.* गवंडीकाम *n.* राजकाम *n.*
Solid m. *stone work.* चिरेबंदी *f.*
MASQUERADE, *n.* मुखवट्यांचाखेळ *m.* छद्मवेषसमारंभ *m.*
MASS, *n. lump, body.* गोळा *m.* गड्डा *m.* डळा *m.* गढ्ढा *m.* पेंड *m.* ढबक *n.* ढबका *m.* ढेप *f.* पिंड *m.* गोल *m.* [गदा *m.*
Kneaded and messed or soft m. लादा *m.* लगदा *m.* लु-
M. of wood, stone, &c. धूड *n.* धुडप *n.*
2 *aggregated mass, congeries, assemblage.* जमाव *m.* रट्ट *m.* गट *or* गट्ट *m.* गट्टा *m.* गोल *m.* जुंबाड *n.* झुंड *f.* स्तोम *m.*
A m. falling or fallen from a wall, &c. ढबक *n.* ढक *n.*
Moving m. (of air, water, and *fig.* of men). लोट *m.* लोंढा*m.* मुसंडा *or* मुसांडा *m.*
3 *heap, &c.* ढीग *m.* ढिगार *or* ढिगर *m.* ढिगारा *m.* रास *f.*
4 *gross body, the bulk, the body.* राशि *m. pop.* रास *f.* ढीग *m.* मुख्यभाग *m.* प्रायोभाग *m.* प्रायोराशि *m.*
By the m. In the m. एकथोक, एकठोक, उधड, उक्त.
To MASSACRE, *v. a. butcher,* v. To KILL. कत्तल *f.*-काटाकाटी-*f.*-&c. करणें *g. of o.* सूदन *n.*- सूना *f.*- कदन *n.*-&c. करणें *g. of o.* सप्पा *m.* करणें-उडवणें *g. of o.* सूदणें, निरुंतणें, मारून स्वस्त करणें.
To be massacred. मरून स्वस्त होणें, कटून भरणें.
MASSACRE, MASSACRING, *n.* v. V. कत्तल *f.* काटाकाटी *f.* सप्पा-*m.* कट्टा *m.* सूदन *n.* सूना *f.* निरुंतन *n.* निकंदन *n.*
MASSINESS, MASSIVENESS, *n.* v. A. जडपणा *m.* ऐवटपणा *m.* मोठेपणा *m.* भारीपणा*m.* घणवटपणा *m.* &c. स्थूलत्व *n.* स्थौल्य*n.*
MASSIVE, MASSY, *a. ponderous, thick and heavy.* जड, भारी, जडशील, जडगोळा, जडधोंडा, ऐवट, औजड *or* औजाड *or* अवजड *or* अवजाड, जरब, जबर, मोठा, स्थूल, ठळक, घस्मर, घणवट, घ-णघाव, भक्कम, उद्दाम.
MAST, *n.*—of a ship. डोल *m.* डोलकाठी *f.* डोलखांब *m.* शीडकाठी *f.* काठी *f.* [तिरकती.
That has two masts. दुकाठी.—that has three. तिरकाठी,
MASTER, *n.*—correl. with servant. धनी, खावंद, स्वामी, प्रभु, यजमान, सेव्य, साहेब.—compreh. or loosely. धनीगोसावी.
That serves two masters. उभयस्वामिक, उभयवेतन.
That is his own m. आंगचा धनी, स्वतांचा धनी, स्वतांधनी, आपधनी.
Like m. like man. यथाराजातथाप्रजा.
2 *director, governor, ruler, lord.* अधिकारी, पति, अध्यक्ष, अधिप, अधिपति, वहिवाटदार, नाथ (esp. in comp.), ईश in comp. ईश्वर in comp. नायक, यजमान, अध्वर्यु.
3 *owner, possessor.* धनी, मालक *or* मालीक, स्वामी, खावंद, पति, वाली, करी (in comp. as घरकरी), वाला in comp.
4 *head,* v. CHIEF. नायक, मुख्य.—as used before such words as carpenter, mason, &c. मेस्त्री.
5 (of a ship). नाखवा *or* नाखोदा, मालीम, तांडेल, नौकाधिपति.
6—correl. with scholar or pupil. गुरु, शिक्षक, अध्यापक.
Assistant m. उपगुरु.
M. of a school. पंतोजी.
M. or instructor in science. विद्यागुरु.
7 *teacher of an art or science.* गुरु, वस्ताद (as नृत्याचा वस्ताद, dancing m. गाण्याचा वस्ताद, singing m. &c.).
Business of a m. *or* teacher. वस्तादगिरी *f.*
8 *skilful person.* वस्ताद, जाणता, स्त्रष्टा, पट्टाईत, धुरंधर.
9 *one uncontrolled.* मुखत्यार, स्वतंत्र, धनी, राजा.
Absolute m. कुलमुखत्यार.
To MASTER, *v. a. overcome,* lit. fig. जिंकणें, सर करणें, वश करणें, हस्तगत करणें, स्वाधीन करून घेणें, सत्तेखालीं आणणें, साध्य करणें, अटोपणें, हकाटफांत आणणें.
MASTER-HAND, *n.* वस्तादाचा हात *m.*
MASTER-KEY, *n.* अनेककुलपें उघडणारी किल्ली. This is a m. key. ही किल्ली वस्ताद आहे.
MASTER-PIECE, *n. excellent performance.* मोठ्या कसबाचें-वस्तादीचें-अतिकौशल्याचें-अतिचातुर्याचें-&c. काम *n.* कौशल्याची-चातुर्याची खाण *f.*
This is a m. piece. ह्या कामांत कौशल्याची पराकाष्ठा झाली.
MASTER-STROKE, *n.* वस्तादीचा-वस्तादगिरीचा-मोठ्या कसबाचा-&c. डाव *m.*-खेळ *m.*-उपाय *m.*
MASTERLINESS, *n.* v. A. वस्तादी *f.* वस्तादगिरी *f.* कारिगरी *f* कसबदारी *f.* कसब *n.* छाप *m. f.* छापी *f.* हातोटी *f.* हातवळा *m.* सफाई *f.* कौशल्य *n.* चातुर्य *n.* लाघव *n.*
MASTERLY, *a. formed &c. with skill, clever.* वस्तादीचा, वस्तादगिरीचा, कारिगरीचा, कसबाचा, कसबदारीचा,वस्तादाच्या हातचा, कौशल्याचा, कुशल. [रीचा *decl.*
MASTERLY, *adv.* v. A. वस्तादीनें, &c. वस्तादीचा *decl.* वस्तादगि-
MASTERSHIP, MASTERY, *n. dominion, rule.* धनीपणा *m.* स्वामित्व *n.* आधिपत्य*n.* प्रभुत्व *n.* खावंदी *f.* सत्ता *f.* साहेबसत्ता *f.* साहेबी *f.*
2 *pre-eminence,* v. SUPERIORITY. वरचढपणा *m.* वर्चस्व *n.* चढ *m.* उपर दवडा *m.* उपराळा *m.* शक *m.* श्रैष्ठ्य *n.* प्राधान्य *n.*
3 *ownership.* धनीपणा *m.* मालकी *f.* स्वामित्व *n.* स्वाम्य *n.*
4 See SKILL. [चर्वणाई, चर्वणशक्य.
MASTICABLE, *a.* v. V. चावायाजोगा-जोगता-&c. चर्व्य, चर्वणीय,
To MASTICATE, *v. a. chew.* चावणें, चर्वणें, चर्वण *n.* करणें *g. of o.*
MASTICATED *p.* v. V. चावलेला, चर्वित.
MASTICATION, *n.* v. V.—*act.* चावणें *n.* चर्वण *n.* चर्वणक्रिया *f.* चर्वण व्यापार *m.* [चर्वणौषध *n.*
MASTICATORY, *n. medicine to be chewed.* चावण्याचें औषध *n.*
MASTICATORY, *a. adapted for mastication.* चावण्याच्या कामाचा, चर्वणोपयोगी, चर्वणसाधक.
MASTICH, MASTIC, *n.*—the gum. रुमामस्तकी *f.*
MASTIFF, *n.* एका जातीचा कुत्रा आहे.
MASTLIN, *n.* v. MESLIN. धान्याची बेवड *f.* ससकर *m.*
MAT, *n.* चटई *f.* अंथरी *or* हंतरी *f.*—of date tree spikes. बोऱ्या *m.*—of bamboo. डाली *f.* तट्या *m.* [*f.* तळकर*n.*
An old m. or a piece of one. तळकट *n.* तळका *m.* तळकटी
Sleeping or sitting m. अंथरूण *n.* [अंथरणें.
To MAT, *v. a. cover with matting.* चटई *f.*-&c. टाकणें-घालणें-
2 *twist, plat.* विणणें, वळणें.
MATCH, *n. equal, one able to cope with.* बरोबरीचा, तोलाचा, तोड *f.* तुलना *f.*—in familiar phraseology. *masterer, teacher, man for, lad for, boy for, &c.* गोहो *m.* पीर *m.* धगड *m.* मारतापीर *m.* वस्ताद *m.* शस्त्र *n.*
Of a m. समतोल, समकक्ष, समानकक्ष. [शेरास शेर.
M. with m. यमकाला यमक, प्रासाळा प्रास, जशास तसा,

2 *one that tallies.* बरोबरीचा, बरोबरचा, जोडीचा, तोडीचा, प्रतीचा, जोडा *m.* प्रत *f.*

3 v. MARRIAGE. विवाह *m.* लग्न *n.* विवाह संबंध *m.*

Scheming to effect a m. संदर्भ *m.*

4 *contest, game.* बाजी *f.* डाव *m.*

5 *fire match.* गंधकाडी *f.* सणकाडी *f.* काडी *f.* दिवेसळई *f.* दिव्याचें कांडें *n.* आगीची-दिव्याची काडी *f.* [or दा *m.*

6 (of a gun). तोडा *m.* शेवट *n.* जामगी *f.* बत्ती *f.* पलिता

7 (of a rocket, squib, &c.). रंजक *f.*

To MATCH, *v. n. suit, tally, correspond.* जुळणें, जमणें, मिळणें, जुळणीचा-मिळणीचा-जुटीचा-जोडीचा-&c.असणें, मेळ*m.*-जवा*m.*-जम *m.*-जुगल *f.*-मिलाफ *m.*-&c. बनणें-बसणें-पडणें-जमणें *g. of s. recip.* [बंध *m.* करणें.

2 *unite in marriage.* बऱ्हाडणें, लग्न *n.* लावणें-करणें, विवाहसं-

To MATCH, *v. a. be equal to.* बरोबरी *f.*-तुलना *f.*-समता *f.*-साम्य *n.*-&c. करणें-पावणें *g. of o.* बरोबरी *f.*-सरोबरी *f.*-सर *f.*-&c. येणें *g. of s. with* स *or* ला *of o.* तुळणें, बरोबर-सारखा-&c.असणें.

2 *oppose as equal.* तोड *f.*-मुकाबला *m.*-धगड *m.*-पीर *m.*-&c. उभा करणें *g. of. o.* बरोबरीचा-तुलनेचा-साम्याचा-समतोल-&c. म्हणून आणणें.

3 *suit, adapt, proportion.* जुळणें, जमवणें, मेळ *m.*-जम *m.*-जवा *m.* जुगल *f.*-&c. बसवणें-मिळवणें *g. of o. recip.*

4 *marry, give in marriage.* देणें, लग्न करून देणें, लग्न *n.* लावणें *g. of o.*

MATCHLESS, *a. having no equal.* बिनतोडीचा, अनुपम, अप्रतिम, अद्वितीय, असदृश, निस्तुल—in a bad sense. निर्तुला.

MATCHLESSNESS, *n.* v. A. अनुपमता *f.* अनौपम्य *n.* अप्रतिमता *f.*

MATCH-LOCK, *n.* तोड्याची बंदूक *f.* रंजकेची बंदूक *f.*

Iron of the match of a m. सरजा *m.*

Match-box attached to a m. गुलदान *n.*

MATCH-MAKER, *n. maker of marriages.* घटक, वरेकज्या, वरावरकरणारा, मध्यस्थ.

2 *maker of fire matches.* गंधकाड्या-&c. करणारा.

MATCH-MAKING, *n. making up marriages.* वरावर *f.* वरेकज *f.* घटवटणा *f.* [बती.

MATE, *n. companion, equal,* v. FELLOW. गडी, जोडपी, साथी, सो-

2 *male or female of.* जोडा *m.* जोडपा *m.* जोडपी *m.* जोडपीण *f.*

3 *assistant.* हाताखालचा, गडी, बगल्या, हस्तक्या, हातखुरणें *n.* आडखप्या, पडचाकर, पोटगडी, अंडगडी, भेडतू. [अमलदार.

4 See CHECKMATE. 5 (of a ship). नाखव्याच्या हाताखालचा

To MATE. See To MATCH.

MATER-FAMILIAS, *n. mistress of a family.* घरबासीण *f.* घरकरीण *f.* घरवारीण *f.*

MATERIAL, *a. consisting of matter, not spiritual.* पंचभूतात्मक, पांचभौतिक, आधिभौतिक, पंचभूतकार्य, पंचभूतविकार, पंचतत्वात्मक, भौतिक, भूतकार्य, भूतविकार, प्राकृतिक, प्राकृत, द्रव्यमय, अनात्म, घन.

A m. body. जड *n.* जडांश *m.*

2 *important, momentous.* भारी, मोठा, विशेष, भाराचा, भारदस्तीचा, जरुरीचा, आवश्यक, प्रधान, मुख्य, हाशिलाचा.

3 *not formal; substantial, real, &c.* प्रकृतीचा, प्राकृतिक, वास्तविक, वास्तव.

M. cause. उपादान *n.* उपादान कारण *n.* समवायि कारण *n.*

MATERIAL, *n. ingredient.* बान *n.* बाना *m.* जिन्नस *m.* द्रव्य *n.* पदार्थ *m.* साधन *n.*

Materials. साहित्य *n.* सामान *n.* सामग्री *f.* सरंजाम *m.* संच *m.* उपकरणीं *n. pl.*—compreh. मालमसाला *m.*

Materials and implements (as of worship, sacrifice, &c.)—collectively. संभार *m.*

MATERIALISM, *n. doctrine of the denial of spirit.* देहात्मवाद *m.* अनात्ममत *n.* अनात्मवाद *m.* चार्वाकमत *n.* लोकायत *n.*

MATERIALIST, *n. denier of spirit.* देहात्मवादी, अनात्मवादी, चार्वाकमती, लोकायतिक, विषयी, विषयायी.

MATERIALITY, MATERIALNESS, *n.* v.A. 1. पांचभौतिकत्व *n.* भौतिकत्व *n.* &c. पंचभूतात्मकभाव *m.* पांचभौतिकभाव *m.*

MATERIALLY, *adv.* v. A. 1. प्रकृतितः.

2 फार, विशेष, अतिशयेंकरून, भारी, अवश्य, अगत्येंकरून.

3 वस्तुतः, वस्तुगत्या.

MATERIATE. See MATERIAL.

MATERNAL, *a. of or belonging to a mother.* आईचा, मातेचा, आईकडला, आईकडचा, आईकडील, मातृसंबंधी, मातृक, मातृधर्मक.

M. affection. माउलपण *n.* माउलपणा *m.* अपत्यस्नेह *m.*

M. duty. मातृधर्म *m.* [मातृत्व *n.*

MATERNITY, *n. character or relation of mother.* आईपणा *m.*

MATHEMATIC, MATHEMATICAL, *a. pertaining, &c. to mathematics.* गणिताचा, संख्यापरिमाणविद्येचा, गणितसंबंधी-विषयक, संख्यापरिमाणविद्यासंबंधी-विषयक.

2 *according to the principles of mathematics.* गणितनियमानुसारी, गणितानुरूप, गणितप्राय.

MATHEMATICIAN, *n. one versed in mathematics.* गणिती, संख्यापरिमाणविद्यावेत्ता, गणितशास्त्रज्ञ.

MATHEMATICS, *n. science of magnitude and number.* गणित *n.* गणितशास्त्र *n.* संख्यापरिमाणविद्या *f.* मानविद्या *f.* रेखाबीजादिगणित *n.*

MATIN, *a. pertaining to the morning.* प्रातःकालचा, प्रातःकालिक, प्रातःकालसंबंधी, औषस, औदयिक.

MATINS, *n. morning worship.* प्रातर्भजन *n.* प्रातःस्मरण *n.*

MATRICE, *n.* v. WOMB. गर्भाशय *m.*

2 *mould.* सांचा *m.* मूस *f.*

MATRICIDE, *n.*—the act. मातृवध *m.* मातृहत्या *f.* मातृघात *m.*

2—the agent. मातृहत्यारा, मातृघाती, मातृघ्न, मातृहंता.

To MATRICULATE, *v. a. admit into a college by registering the name.* नांवनिशीमांडून-नांवलिहून-&c. पाठशाळेंत घेणें, संस्कारपूर्वक शाळेंत घेणें, संस्कारपूर्वक विद्यालय प्रविष्ट करणें, मुंडणें.

MATRICULATED, *p.* v. V. संस्कारपूर्वक शाळेंत घेतलेला, संस्कारपूर्वक विद्यालय प्रविष्ट, &c.

MATRICULATION, *n.* v. V. नांव लिहून पाठशाळेंत घेणें *n.* &c. संस्कारपूर्वक विद्यालय प्रवेश *m.*

MATRIMONIAL, *a. of or belonging to marriage.* लग्नाचा, विवाहाचा, &c. लग्नसंबंधींचा, लग्नाविषयींचा, लग्नाकडचा, &c. वैवाहिक, औद्वाहिक, विवाहसंबंधी, लग्नसंबंधी. [स्था *f.*

MATRIMONY, *n.* v. MARRIAGE. विवाह *m.* उद्वाह *m.* विवाहितावस्था *f.*

MATRIX. See MATRICE.

MATRON, *n. a respectable and mature married woman.* घरदाराची बायको *f.* घरवारीण *f.* गरत *f.* प्रौढस्त्री *f.* प्रौढा *f.* प्रगल्भा *f.* मोरीम्हातारी *f.* पतिपुत्रवती *f.*

2 *female superintendent.* कारभारीण *f.* नायकीण *f.* मुकद्दमीण *f.*

MATRONAL, MATRONLY, *a. pertaining, suitable, &c. to a matron.* प्रौढस्त्रीचा, प्रगल्भस्त्रीचा, प्रौढस्त्रीसंबंधी, प्रगल्भस्त्रीसंबंधी, पोक्की लायक, पोक्कीजोगा, प्रगल्भस्त्र्युचित.

2 *elderly.* वयाचा, वयस्क, वयातीत.

MATTED, *p.* v. V. 2. विणलेला, वळलेला, विर्णीव, वळींव.

To be m.—hair. पेंड *m.* वळणें-होणें *g. of s.* चिकटा *m.*-चिकटी *f.* येणें *in. con.*

MATTER, *n.*—not spirit; *body, substance, any thing visible or tangible.* दृश्यस्पृश्यपदार्थ *m.* दृश्यस्पृश्यवस्तु *n.* पंचभूतात्मकवस्तु *n.* द्रव्य *n.* अनात्मा *m.* साकारपदार्थ *m.*-वस्तु *n.*-&c.

Distinguishing between m. and spirit. आत्मानात्मविचार *m.* आत्मानात्मविवेक *m.*

2 *substratum of the universe.* प्रकृति *f.* माया *f.* प्रधान *n.*

3 *that of which any thing is composed.* साधन *n.* साधनभूतवस्तु *n.* द्रव्य *n.* उपादान *n.* प्रकृति *f.*

4 *subject, thing treated.* विषय *m.* प्रकरण *n.* वृत्तांत *m.*

5 *concern, business,* v. AFFAIR. काम *n.* कार्य *n.* गोष्ट *f.* मुकद्दमा *m.* विषय *m.* बाब *f.* प्रकरण *n.*

Matters, *affairs, event.* हकिकत *f.*

By-gone m. गतगोष्ट *f.* गतकथा *f.*

A disputed or unsettled m. *an unclosed business with.* लडथड *f.* लांझा *m.* लफडा *m.* लढा *m.* लाजिमा *m.* खरकटें *n.* लेंभें *n.* लेशपंड *n.* वांझा *m.* वांझें *m.*

Small or light m. हलकी-क्षुद्र-&c. गोष्ट *f.*

Statement or account of matters. वाका *m.* हकिकत *f.*

6 *subject of complaint or suit.* वादाचा-खटल्याचा-&c. विषय *m.* वादविषय *m.*

7 *cause or ground of disturbance, &c.* गडबडीचें-&c.कारण *n.* अस्वास्थ्यकारण *n.* अस्वास्थ्यहेतु *m.*

What's the matter? काय आहे? काय झालें?

8 *import, consequence, moment.* मुजाख *f.* or मुजाखा *m. with neg. con.* प्रत्यवाय *m.* विशात or विशाद *f.* हिशेब *m.*

No m. चिंता नाहीं, परवा नाहीं.

9 *thing, object.* गोष्ट *f.* विषय *m.* अर्थ *m.*

10 *pus.* पू *m.* पूय *m.*

To MATTER, *v. n. be of consequence.* मुजाख *f.*-मुजाखा *m.*-&c. असणें *g. of s.* [णें.

2 *generate pus.* पुवळणें, पुवारणें, पुलेजणें, पुलेणें, पूयगर्भित होणें.

MATTERY, *a. purulent.* पुवाचा, पुवळलेला, &c. बरबरीत, सपूय, पूययुक्त, पूयविशिष्ट, पूयस्रावी.

MATTING, *n.* चटई *f.*—esp. of bamboo. तट्या *m.*

MATTOCK, *n. grubbing instrument.* खुरपें *n.*

2 *hoe.* कुदळ *f.* कुदळा *m. dim.* कुदळी *f.* कुदळें *n.* कुद्दाल *m.*

MATTRESS, *n. bed, bedding.* लेप *m. n.* लेपडी *f.* (contemptuously, लेपडें *n.*) न्याहली or न्याहाली *f.* सुपेती *f.* गदेला *m.* बिछाना *m.*

To MATURATE. See To RIPEN, To SUPPURATE.

MATURATION, *n. ripening, suppuration.* पाक *m.* परिपाक *m.* पचन *n.*

MATURATIVE, *a. conducive to suppuration.* पिकाऊ, पाककारक, पूयकारक. [परिपक्क.

MATURE, *a.* lit. fig. v. RIPE. पक्का, पक्क, प्रौढ, पोक, पोक्का, प्रगल्भ,

To MATURE, *v. a.* See To RIPEN, 2. *bring to perfection.* सिद्ध-ठाम-पक्का-&c. करणें, सिद्धदशेस-पक्कदशेस आणणें. [बर.

MATURELY, *adv. with full deliberation.* पोक्तपणें, पुरतेपणीं, खोलबर.

MATURENESS, MATURITY, *n.* v. A. *and* RIPENESS. पोक्तपणा *m.* पोक्तेपणा *m.* प्रौढी *f.* पक्कता *f.* पक्कदशा *f.* सिद्धदशा *f.* पाक *m.* परिपाक *m.*

MATUTINAL, MATUTINE, *a. belonging to morning.* प्रातःकालचा, प्रातःकालिक, प्रातःकालसंबंधी, औषस, औदयिक.

MAUDLIN, *a. tipsy, fuddled.* झिंगलेला, तारवटलेला, तारचढलेला, मत्तकल्प.

MAUGRE, *adv. in spite of, notwithstanding.* न मानतां, गुंडाळून, गुंडाळून टाकून-ठेवून, झुगारून, धाब्यावर बसवून.

MAUL, *n. mall.* मोगरा *m.* मोगर *m.*

To MAUL, *v. a.* v. To BEAT. चेंचून-ठेंचून-&c. मारणें, कुटणें, घुमा *m.* घालणें, चेंदा *m.*-धिरडें *n.* पाडणें-करणें *g. of o.*

2 *treat roughly.* घुसडणें, चोळवटणें, चुरडणें, घुसडून-&c. टाकणें, हेबाळणें, धुडगूस *m.* घालणें.

MAUND, *n.*—the Indian measure. मण *m.*

About a m. मणखाण, मणखंड.

A m.-measure. मणका *m.*

M. of 12 páylí. बारुलामण *m.*

Quantity equalling a m. मणका *m.*

Weight determining the m. मणका *m.* मणकी *f.*

That is of the weight or capacity of half a m. अदमणका, अदमणा.

To MAUNDER, See To MURMUR, To GRUMBLE. [चा, &c.

MAUSOLEAN, *a. belonging to a mausoleum.* छत्रीचा, मोठे कबरेचा, &c.

MAUSOLEUM, *n. large tomb or monument.* छत्री *f.* मोठी कबर *f.* माठें *n.* रौजा *m.* समाधि *pop.* समाध *f.* चिताचूडक *m.*

MAUVAISE-HONTE, *n. bashfulness.* सभाकंप *m.* जनभीति *f.* जनलज्जा *f.*

MAW, *n. stomach.* कोठा *m.* पोटाची पिशवी *f.*-गाईर *f.*-गार *f.*

2 fig. *vast receptacle, abysm, &c.* उदरदरी *f.* रावणाची खाई *f.* घबाडमाप *n.*

3 *craw of birds.* गचूर *m.* चुनाळ *m.*

MAWKISH, *a. insipid.* पचपचीत, पाणचट, पाणबळ, निचव, बेचव, निरस, मिटमिटीत.

MAWKISHNESS, *n.* v. A. पचपचितपणा *m.* पाणचटपणा *m.* &c.

MAXILLAR, MAXILLARY, *a. belonging to the jaw.* दाभाड्याचा, जांभाड्याचा, हनुसंबंधी.

MAXIM, *n. established principle, axiom.* न्याय *m.* नीति *f.* वचन *n.* वाक्य *n.* सूत्र *n.* There are many *maxims* or *rules of conduct* current among the Maráthás and often quoted. Some of the following are very common, others are used only by the classic scholar. अंधपरंपरान्याय, काकतालीयन्याय, काकाक्षिगोलकन्याय, कैमुतिकन्याय, कपिंजलन्याय, कंटकोद्धारन्याय, दग्धपटन्याय, दग्धाश्वनष्टरथन्याय, देहलीदीपन्याय, घट्टकुटीप्रभात न्याय, तक्रकौडिन्यन्याय, अंधोपरछन्न्याय, गृहकुक्कुटन्याय, मातापुत्रन्याय, पितापुत्रन्याय, स्त्रीभर्तृन्याय, नीरक्षीरन्याय, मत्स्योदकन्याय, वत्सधेनुन्याय, मंडूकप्लुतिन्याय, मध्यमणिन्याय, समसूत्रन्याय, सिंहावलोकनन्याय, जामात्रर्थंश्रपितसूपन्याय, याचितमंडनन्याय, त्यजेदेकंकुलस्यार्थेइत्यादिन्यायः, शतमध्यंधानांकूपंप्रविशतीतिन्यायः, प्रक्षालनाद्धिपंकस्य दूराद-

स्पर्शनंबरं इतिन्यायः, पिशाचभाषयापिशाचो बोधनीय इतिन्यायः.

MAXIMUM, *n. the greatest number or quantity.* परमावधीचें परिमाण *n.* परमावधीची संख्या *f.*

MAY, *n.*—the month. इंग्रेजी सालाचा पांचवा महिना *m.* बैशाखोत्तरार्ध ज्येष्ठपूर्वार्ध *n.* [year's day.

MAY-POLE, *n.* गुढी *f.* is a pole erected on the Hindu new
2 fig. *tall and slender woman.* दिपमाळ *f.* रामकांटी *f.* शेलांटी *f.* गडसा *m.* गडसी *f.*

MAYOR, *n. chief magistrate of a city.* हाकीम, कोतवाल, नगराध्यक्ष, नगराधिकारी. [कोतवाली *f.*

MAYORALTY, *n. office, &c. of a mayor.* हाकिमी *f.* हाकिमाई *f.*

MAYORESS, *n. wife of a mayor.* हाकिमीण *f.* कोतवालीण *f.* नगराधिकारिणी *f.*

MAZARD, *n.* v. FACE. मुसकुरी *f.* मुसकड *n.* मुसकल*n.* मुसकाड*n.*

MAZE, *n. labyrinth.* नागमोडीची जागा *f.*-वाट *f.* घोंटाळा *m.* घोंटाळ्याची जागा *f.*-&c. सातबांकी जागा *f.*-वाट *f.* बेंटाळयांची जागा *f.*-&c.असमानगति *f.*
2 *confused state of things,* v. PERPLEXITY. फिरका *m.* फिरकंडा *m.* फिरकंडी *f.* घोंटाळा *m.* चौऱ्याशीचा फेरा *m.* चौऱ्याशी चागरका *m.*

To MAZE. See To BEWILDER.

MAZY, *a. intricate, perplexed with windings.* घोंटाळ्याचा, नागमोडीचा, सातबांकी, सातबांकांचा, बेंटाळयांचा.

MEACOCK, *n. effeminate man.* रांड्या, रांड्या राघोबा, बाइल्या, बाइक्या.

MEAD, *n. drink of honey and water.* मधवणी *n.* मधुपानक *n.* मधुनीर *n.* [कास *m.*

MEAD, MEADOW, *n. tract of pasture land.* कुरण *n.* वावर *n.*
2 *low land along the banks of rivers, &c.* नहेर *n.* भाटी *f.*
A salt m. or marsh. खाजण *n.* बहाड *n.*

MEADOWY, *a.* कुरणाचा.

MEAGER, MEAGRE, *n. bare of flesh,* v. LEAN. रोडका, किचकाडा, किचकाडी, किडकिडीत, सडसडीत, काठ्याळा, पातळांग्या, कृश, सलफ.
2—of soil, &c. *poor, barren.* भुकिस्त, भुकड, बरड *or* भरड, रुक्ष, निझर. [रडा, शुष्क.
3 *without strength, richness, &c.* बेकस, निकस, निरस, को-

MEAGRENESS, *n.* v.A. 1. किडकिडितपणा *m.* सडसडितपणा *m.*&c. कृशता *f.* कार्श्य *n.*
2 भुकिस्तपणा *m.* बरडपणा *m.* &c.
3 बेकसपणा *m.* निकसपणा *m.* &c. [गडसी *f.*

MEAK, *n. hook with a handle.* अंकडी *f.*अंकुशी *f.* गडसा *m. dim.*

MEAL, *n.* v. FLOUR. पीठ *n.* पिष्ट *n.*
Husks and grits in m. चरड *n.*
The coarse part of m. सांजा *m.*
2 *repast, stated eating.* जेवण *n.* जेवा *m.* भोजन *n.* आहार *m.*—in cant, &c. phraseology, ज *or* जचें *n.* ओदनाचें *n.* भुकीचें *n.* The *meal* or *taking the meal* is with Hindus, and especially with the Bráhman-portion, a matter of religion. Numerous ceremonies and acts preparatory and subsequent pertain to it. Of these the names or terms can scarcely by any classification or introduction be suitably introduced. They may be wanted however by him who would speak or write about their social and religious system,and for him they are here collected. अंचवण, अन्नसमर्पण, अन्नस्तुति, आचमन, आपोशन, आहुति घालणें, उत्तरापोशन, चित्राहुति *pop.* चित्रावती, नेत्रस्पर्शन, नैवेद्य दाखवणें, परिवेषण, परिषिंचन, पात्रप्रक्षालन, पात्रस्थापन, प्राणाहुति *pop.* प्राणावती, मंडल करणें, मौनधारण, शिरामोचन *pop.* शेंडीसोडणें, स्थलशुद्धि *f.* स्थलशोभा *f.* The terms following relate to *fellowship of meal*—to fellowship as permitted or forbidden, and to the particulars and points appendant or emergent. For the signification of any one, consult, of course, the M. and E. Dict. अन्नव्यवहार, पंक्तिदोष, पंक्तिपावन, पंक्तिप्रपंच, पंक्तिभेद, पंक्तिव्यवहार, पंक्त्यंतर, पांक.
At one m. एका भुकेस. [उपास *m.*
Fasting after a m. that has been interrupted. उष्टा-
Good m. *meal to one's heart's content.* इच्छाभोजन *n.*
Light m. फराळ *m.* अल्पाहार *m.* लघ्वाहार *m.* फलाहार *m.*
Line or row at a m. पंक्ति *pop.* पंगत *f.*
Making a m. जेवण *n.* जेवा *m.* भोजन *n.* भुक्ति *f.*—in light phraseology. अन्नसंस्कार *m.* अन्नसंपर्क *m.* प्राणपूजा *f.* —compreh. or careless. जेवणखाण *n.*
M. in the morning. प्रातभोजन *n.* प्रातराशन *n.*—at noon. माध्यान्हिक *n.* माध्यानकाळचें *n.* —at night. रात्रिभोजन *n.* निशिभोजन *n.*
M. taken out (from home.). परान्न *n.*
M. upon parched grain. धान्यफराळ *m.*
M.—time, M.-hour. जेवणवेळ *f.* भोजनवेळ *f.* भोजनसमय *m.* अन्नकाल *m.*
M. of a sanyásí. पुडी *f.*
Nap after one's m. वामकुक्षि *f. v.* कर, हो.
Poor m. *meal on poor fare.* कुभोजन *n.*
Rice, &c. given for a m. जेवा *m.*
Solid and substantial m. चिरेबंदी *f.* [करी.
Summoner of the guests to the ready m. बोलावणे-
Taking one's meals at irregular hours. विषमभोजन*n.*
Taking a meal at night only. नक्तभोजन *n.* नक्त *n.*
The fragments, scraps, dirty dishes, &c. remaining where a m. has been made. खरकट *f.* खरकटवड *or* वाड *f.* खरकटवडा *or* वाडा *m.* खरकटवळ *or* खरखटावळ *f.*
Walk (of a hundred paces) after a m. शतपावली *f.* शतपदी *f.*
Washing the mouth and hands after a m. अंचवण *n.*
That has taken his meal. कृतभोजन.
To take one's m., to make a m. जेवणें—To take a slight m. The sense of this phrase as varied by the particular phrases *To take a snack, to eat a morsel, to take a few mouthfuls, &c.* is expressed by, भूक *f.* मारणें, उष्टा होणें, उष्टावणें, तोंड उष्टें करणें, पाण्यास आस्रा *or* आधार*m.* करणें, चारघास *or* ग्रास*m. pl.* घेणें.—To take a full m. *gorge, cram one's maw, &c.* v. To STUFF. बट्ट्याचें *n.* करणें, कोंदणें, दपटणें (as आज त्यानें खुबकोंदलें *or* दपटलें.), बळकट-कचकावून-रगडून-&c. जेवणें.
To achieve (obtain cleverly) a m. जेवा *m.* पाडणें-उप-

टणें-साधणें.

To hit (be in time for) the m. पंगत *f.* साधणें.

To lay for (lay the leaves, draw the lines, &c.) for the m. पंगत *f.* मांडणें, पात्रें *n. pl.* वाढणें.

To manage to make a m. निपटून शिपटून जेवणें.

To miss (be too late for) the m. पंगत *f.* (*or* पंगतीस) चुकणें. [वाढणें.

To serve the m. (help the company). पंगत *f.* वाढणें,

To sit at m. पात्रीं बसणें.

MEALINESS, *n.* v. A. 1. पिठेपणा *m.* पिठुळपणा *m.* &c. भगरा*m.*

MEALY, *a. soft, dry and crumbling.* पिठा, पिका, पिठूळ, भुगाळ.

2 *overspread with powder like meal.* पिठाळ, कोंडाळ, पिका.

3 *not firm and luscious*—mangoes, melons, &c. पिठूळ.

MEALY-MOUTHED, *a. that is afraid to speak out; that uses softening terms.* मेलतोंड्या, मेमलतोंड्या, दीनवदन,गायतोंड्या, डाळपिठ्या, वचनसंकोची.

MEAN, *a. of low birth, rank, or station,* v. LOW. नीच, हलका, हलके पदवीचा, अकुलीन, कम असल, कमसल, कमजात, हीनकुळ, हीनजात, निकृष्टजातीचा, असंभावित.

2 *low-minded, base, ungenerous.* पाजी, पामर, अधम, हुच्चा, पामरवृत्तीचा, अधमवृत्तीचा, पामरवृत्ति, अधमवृत्ति, जघन्यवृत्ति, पामराचा, कुत्सितमनाचा, हीनआचाराचा, हीन, कृपण.

3 *petty, contemptible, insignificant, worthless.* हलका, हलके किमतीचा, हलके योग्यतेचा, ओत्सा, तुच्छ, यारदा, यारदी, लघु, क्षुल्लक, निकृष्ट, केविलवाणा *or* णी, किलवाणा *or* णी, दरिद्री, भिकारी.

4 *middle, moderate.* मध्यम, मध्य, मधलंड, मध्यमप्रतीचा, मध्यप्रमाणाचा, मध्यपरिमाण. [वर्ती.

5 *intervening, intermediate.* मध्य, मध्यम, मध्यस्थित, मध्य-

Meanwhile; in the mean time. इतक्यांत, इतक्यामध्यें, मध्येंच, मध्यावसरांत.

6 (in mathematics). मध्य, मध्यम.

MEAN, *n. middle rate, mediocrity.* मध्यमपरिमाण *n.* सामान्यपरिमाण *n.* सामान्यपक्ष *m.* साधारणपक्ष *m.* मधलापक्ष *m.*

2 *interval, interim.* मधलीवेळ *f.* मध्यांतर *pop.* मध्यंतर *n.* मध्यावसर *m.* मध्यावधि *m.* अवधि *m.f.* गडसंधि *f.*

3 *instrument, medium.* साधन *n.* उपचार *m.* उपाय*m.* उपकरण *n.* कारण *n.* कर्मसाधन *n.* कार्यसाधन *n.* कार्यसाधक *n.* द्वार*n.* योग *m.* [साधणूक *f.*

Means. सामान *n.* सामग्री *f.* साहित्य *n.* साधनसामग्री *f.*

Minor means. उपसामग्री *f.* [प्रकारें.

By all means, *in all ways.* सर्वथा, सर्वथैव, सर्वोपरी, सर्व

By all means, v. CERTAINLY. अवश्य, निखालस.

By fair means. गुणेगोविंदें, गुणेगोविंदानें.

By no means, *not at all.* सुतराम् नाहीं, नितराम् नाहीं, सर्वात्मना नाहीं, निखालस नाहीं, परिछिन्न नाहीं.

By means of. द्वारा, द्वारें.

By some means or other. कसेंकरून, कसेंहीं,कसेंही करून, जसातसा, कोणेप्रकारें.

By these means. अशानें, असल्यानें, असें करून, येणेंकरून.

By what means. कशानें, कसेंकरून, कसकसा.

The four means of war (means of prevailing in it). उपायचतुष्टय *n.*—these are, साम, दाम, दंड, भेद.

To lay means and measures. लाग *m. pl.* लावणें.

4 means; *fortune, income.* अदा *m.* ऐपत *f.* ऐवज *m.* अवकात *or* द *f.* द्रव्यबल *n.* द्रव्यशक्ति *f.* द्रव्यसामर्थ्य *n.* शक्ति *f.* सामर्थ्य *n.* आय *m.* अदाय *m.* [थाविभव.

Accordingly with one's m. यथाशक्ति, यथासामर्थ्य, य-

To live on one's own m. पदर मोडून खाणें, पदर *m.* खर्चणें-मोडणें.

5 (in geometry). सम *n.*

To MEAN, *v. n. purpose, intend.* मनांत असणें *g. of. s.* अभिप्राय *m.*-उद्देश *m.*-इरादा *m.*-&c. असणें *g. of s.* मनांत धरणें-आणणें, अवांकणें.

To MEAN, *v. a. intend, purpose,* v. To DESIGN. उद्देशणें, संकल्पणें, लक्षिणें, मनांत योजणें-धरणें, चिंतणें, उद्देश *m.*-&c. करणें *g. of o.*

2 *have meaning or signification.* अर्थ *m.* असणें *g. of s.* अर्थ *m.* धरणें-दाखवणें-बोधवणें-सुचवणें.

MEANDER, *n. winding, turn, maze.* फेरा *m.* वांक *m. n.* वळण *n.* वेंटोळें *n.* वेंटाळी *f.* असमानगति *f.*

To MEANDER, *v. n. proceed in a flexuous course.* वळशांनींनागमोडीनें-&c. चालणें, कोंडाळणें, कोंडाळून चालणें, वळसे घेऊनवळसे मारून-&c. चालणें.

MEANDERING, *p. a.* MEANDRIAN, MEANDROUS, *a. winding, flexuous.* वांकांचा, वळशांचा, नागमोडीचा, वळणाचा.

MEANING, *n. purpose, intention.* अभिप्राय *m.* उद्देश *m.* भाव*m.* अर्थ *m.* तात्पर्य *n.* अभिप्रेत *n.* आशय *m.* इंगित *n.* हेतु *m.* खुलासा *m.* मानस *m. n.* हृदय *n.* हार्द *pop.* हरद्र *or* हरिद्र *or* हार्द्र *n.* गण *m.* [तात्पर्यार्थ *m.*

2 (esp. of a speaker or speech). विवक्षा *f.* विवक्षित *n.*

Hidden or secret m. अंतर्गर्भ *m.*

3 *sense, signification.* अर्थ *m.* भाव *m.* भावार्थ *m.* अभिप्राय *m.* खुलासा *m.* मयना *or* माना *m.* गर्भ *m.*

Involved or implied m. गर्भार्थ *m.* गर्भितार्थ *m.*

Latent m. of. मर्म *n.*

Literal m. अवयवार्थ *m.* पदार्थ *m.*

MEANING, *a.* See SIGNIFICANT.

MEANLY, *adv.* v. A. 1. हलक्यावाणी, गरीबावाणी, दरिद्र्यासारखा *decl.* भिकारपणाचा *decl.* भिकाररीतीचा *decl.* &c. [मदृष्ट्या.

2 पाजीपणानें, अधमदृष्टीनें, अधमबुद्धीनें, &c. अधमबुद्ध्या, अध-

4 मध्यमपरिमाणाचा *decl.* मध्यमप्रतीचा *decl.* मध्यमपक्षाचा *decl.* सामान्य पक्षाचा *decl.* &c.

I. *without respect or high estimation of.* हलक्या बुद्धीनें, तुच्छ बुद्धीनें, यःकश्चितूपणानें, यःकश्चित् बुद्धीनें, अनादर बुद्धीनें, लघुत्व बुद्धीनें.

MEANNESS, *n.* v. A. 1. हलकेपणा *m.* नीचपणा *m.* हलकीपदवी *f.* हीनकुलता *f.* निकृष्टजाति *f.* कम असलाई *f.*

2 पाजीपणा *m.* पामरपणा *m.* हुच्चेपणा *m.* मनाचा हलकेपणा *m.* &c. हीण *n.* हीनता *f.* अधमता *f.* पामरता *f.* &c. मनोहीनता *f.* सद्वृत्त्यभाव *m.* [*n.* लाघव *n.* निकृष्टता *f.*

3 हलकेपणा *m.* &c. हलकी किम्मत *f.* हलकी योग्यता *f.* लघुत्व

MEANT, *p.* v. A. 1. उद्दिष्ट, अभिप्रेत, विवक्षित.

MEASLED, *a. infected with the measles.* गोवराचा, गोवर आलेला.

MEASLES, *n.*—the disease. गोवर*m.* गोवरें*n.*—in covert phraseology. शुभा *f.*

M. of which the pustules do not come to a head. मुकागोबर*m.*

MEASURABLE, *a.* v. V. 1. मापायाजोगा-जोगता-&c. मापघ्यायाजोगा-&c. परिमेय, प्रमेय, मेय, मापनीय. [*f.*

MEASURE, *n. extent, dimensions.* माप*n.* मेज *n.*मोज*n.* लांबीरुंदी

To take the m. of. बेतणें, बेतणी *f.* करणें.

2 *thing by which to measure.* माप *n.* मंजन*n.* मोज *n.* मान*n.* परिमाण *n.* प्रमाण *n.*

Fair or just m. नकी *or* निर्कमाप *n.*

Head or peaked rising (of grain, &c.). above the m. शीग *f.*—To reduce it with the strickle. शीग *f.* मोडणें.

M. of capacity. माप *n.* कैलीमाप *n.*

M. of weight. वजनीमाप *n.*

M. good and running over. शीगलीट, ढळता (हात-काटा-तराजू-माप-&c.).

Of short m. अल्पप्रमाणक.

Scanty m. (in selling corn, &c.). भुसार माप *n.*

With over flowing m. शीगवर.

To have one's m. (of desires, &c.). full. टोवणें *n.* भरणें *g. of s.*

To have one's m. (of iniquities, life, &c.) filled. माप *n.*-घडा *m.*-पायली *f.*-&c. भरणें *g. of s.*

The measures of this country differ so widely from those of England that they cannot be put down as corresponding terms to each other. We refer the student who desires full and particular information on the comparison of one with the other to the useful tables of Mr. Prinsep and to the work of Major T. B. Jervis, while for the general student we subjoin the following collection.

Measures of Weight.

तोळा, टंक *or* टांक $\frac{1}{72}$ of a sher.—छटांक, छटांकी, चौवटकें *or* चवाटकें, चवटांक $\frac{1}{16}$ of a sher.—नवटांक, नवटकें *or* नवाटकें, अदपाव $\frac{1}{8}$ of a sher.—पावशेर $\frac{1}{4}$ of a sher.—अछेर *or* अदशेर, रत्तल $\frac{1}{2}$ of a sher.—शेर, This measure greatly varies. The Bombay sher is 11 oz. $3\frac{1}{3}$ dr. avoirdupois. The Poona sher is 1 lb. 15 oz. $8\frac{1}{2}$ dr. The latter is equivalent to 80 Poona rupees.—अडशेरी *or* अडिशेरी $2\frac{1}{2}$ sher.—पांचशेरी *or* पांसरी 5 sher.—धडा 10 sher, 12 sher.—अदमण, अदमणी $\frac{1}{2}$ a *man* or maund.—मण, मणकी. This measure greatly varies. The Bombay maund of 40 seers is 28 lb. avoir. The Poona maund of $12\frac{1}{2}$ sher is 24 lb. 10 oz. $4\frac{1}{2}$ d; the maund of 14 sher is 27 lb. 9 oz. $9\frac{2}{3}$ d; the maund of 40 sher is 78 lb. 13 oz. 4 dr.; the maund of 48 sher is 94 lb. 9 oz, 8 dr.——पल्ला 120 sher, it is 236lb. 9 oz. 2 dr.—खंडी, खारी 20 maunds.

Measures of Capacity.

त्रिळवें $\frac{1}{32}$of a sher.—निळवें, चौटकें *or* चवाटकें, छटांक, छटांकी $\frac{1}{16}$ of a sher.—कोळवें, निपटें, अदपाव, पिटकें $\frac{1}{8}$ of a sher.—चिपटें, पावशेर, शिरीद् $\frac{1}{4}$ of a sher.—मागडें, अठवा, निठवें, अच्छेर, अटकें *or* आठकें *or* आठवें $\frac{1}{2}$ of a sher.—शेर, चोथवा sher. The Bombay sher for liquids, equal to 60 Bombay Rs. is 1 lb. 8 oz. $8\frac{1}{4}$ dr. avoir.—अधोली, अडशेरी, दुशेरी, 2 sher.—पायली, चौशेरी, 4 sher.—अदमण, अदमणी $\frac{1}{2}$ *a man* or maund.—फुडव $\frac{1}{8}$ of a maund.—मण maund.—पल्ला 120 sher.—रोवळा $\frac{1}{6}$ of a candy.—पंचकड 5 maund. —भरा 10 maund.—खंडी (candy), खांडी 20 maund.—The following are also in use in Bombay टिपरी $\frac{1}{4}$ of a sher.—फरा 12 or 16 payli. The following are met with in books. प्रस्थ 48 double handfuls. आढक 4 *prasth* गोष्पद् measure of a cow's foot.

Money Weight.

जव, यव $\frac{1}{16}$ of a *màsá.*—गुंज, रति $\frac{1}{8}$ of a *màsà.*— वाल $\frac{1}{4}$ of a *másá.*—मासा, माष, *másá*; it is of various amount. The common weight is about 17 grains troy.—धरण 3 *màsà.*—तोळा tola; it is of various amount, 180, 184, 187, grains troy.—कर्ष 16 *màsh.*—पल *or* पळ, 4 *karsha.*—तुला 100 *pala.*—भार 20 *tulà.*

Cloth Measure.

जव, यव barley corn.—पैन *or* पाइंन, पाइंड 4 *jaw*; about $\frac{1}{4}$ inch—अंगुल *or* अंगूळ, बोट, 8 *jaw*; finger's breadth.—तसू 2 *angul* or $\frac{1}{24}$ of a *gaj.*—गिरा 3 *angul.*—चवंगा *or* चौंगा hand's breadth—टींच, प्रादेश, 10 *angul*; span measured by the thumb and forefinger.—वीत, वितस्ति 12 *angul*; span measured by the thumb and little finger.—मुंढाहात,रत्नि, 18 *angul*; cubit measured from the elbow to the end of the hand closed.—अरत्नि 21 *angul*; cubit measured from the elbow to the tip of the little finger. हात, हस्त, 24 *angul*; hand or cubit, measured from the elbow to the tip of the midle finger.—गज 24 *tasu*; it is of various amount. It is commonly about 2 feet.—वांव, व्याम$3\frac{1}{2}$ *hát* ; fathom.

Land Measure.

मूठ, मुष्टि, चवंगा *or* चौंगा fist or hand breadth.—हात, हस्त, काकिणी, hand or cubit, 6 *mushti.* It is usually about 18 inches.—दंड, धनुष्य rod of 4 *hát* or cubits.—काठी, pole of 5 *hàt* and 5 *mushti*, or 5 cubits and 5 hand-breadths. —निवर्त्तन 200 square *hát.*—पांड 20 square *kàthis*, $\frac{1}{20}$ of a *bighà.*—बिघा, *bighà.* It is of varying amount. The standard *Bighá* of some parts is 3025 square yards or $\frac{5}{8}$ of an acre ; in other parts the *bighá* is variously estimated at $\frac{7}{10}$ $\frac{3}{4}$ of an acre.—परतन from 4 to 6 *bighás*, *i. e.* as much as is usually ploughed by one going and returning of the plough.—गोचर्म as much as can be comprehended by a cow's hide. मण 6 *bighás.*—रुका 10 *bighas.*—तिरुका, पैसा 3 *rukas* or 30 *bighás.*—सणी, सापिका, सजगणी *or* गाणी, 6 *rukás* or 60 *bighás.*—चवटांक छटांक 60 *bighás.*—पाइंण 30 square *bighás.*—दोरी 20 *partan* or 80-120 *bighás.*—खंडी, चाहूर *or* चाऊर, टका 120 square *bighás*, नवटांक 120 *bighás*, पावशेर 2 *cháurs* or 40 *bighás.*—अछेर 4 *cháurs* or 480 *bighás.* शेर.—Note. The student will observe that some of the above terms used to express land measure are denominations of measures of capacity and weight, and some of monetary subdivisions.

Itinerary Measures.

हात, हस्त, काकिणी hand or cubit.—धनुष्य, दंड rod of 4

hát.—कास. *or* कोश, कोश, according to some 8000, but according to others only 4000 hát or cubits.—गोकोश, गोकोश reach of a cow's lowing.—गव्यूति 2 *kos.*—योजन, गांव, ग्राम 4 *kos.*

3 *rule, standard.* परिमाण *n.* प्रमाण *n.*

4 *proportion, quantity settled.* मेज *n.* मोज *n.* मान *n.* परिमाण *n.* प्रमाण *n.* मिति *f.* परिमिति *pop.* परिमीन *f. or* परमित *f. n.* इयत्ता *f.* मोताद *f.*

Agreeably to m. प्रमाणतः.

In, with, up to, &c. the m. of. प्रमाणें.

5 *allotment.* वांटा *m.* भाग *m.* भोग *m.*

6 *degree, quantity.* मान *n.* प्रमाण *n.* परिमाण *n.*—Note. This sense is usually, and most idiomatically, rendered by the adjectives, *large, much, little, small, &c.* as मोठें शहाणपण a large m. of wisdom. थोडें ज्ञान a small m. of knowledge, &c. &c.

In a great m. फारकरून, बहूतकरून.

In some m. कांहीं, कांहींसा *decl.*

7 *moderation, limit.* मर्यादा *f.* सीमा *f.* सुमार *m.* मिति *f.* परिमिति *f.* प्रमाण *n.* नेमस्तपणा *m.* इयत्ता *f.*

Beyond m. बेसुमार, अमर्याद.

8 *musical time.* ताल *m.* टाळ *m.* मात्रा *f.* Some of the *Times* or *measures* are, दुताल, तिताल, चौताल, ठका, धमार, मोहरा, सवारी. [बद्ध, तालशुद्ध.

Being in musical m. स्वरबद्ध, स्वरशुद्ध, तालबद्ध *pop.* टाळ-

9 *metre.* छंद *n. m.* पद्य *n.* वृत्त *n.* वेद *m.* Certain of the *metres* or *measures* are, अनुष्टुप्, आर्या, ओवी, कटिबंध, कुररी, गीति, ग्रंथ, घनाक्षरी, चर्पटिका, जगती, दंडक *or* दंडी, धुमाळ, नाटक, पंक्ति, पद, प्रकृति, प्रतिष्ठा, प्रबंध, प्रभावती, पृथ्वी, प्रहर्षिणी, मध्यमा, मालिनीवृत्त, शार्दूलविक्रीडित, शिखरणी, सवाई, स्कंध, स्रग्धरा, हरिणी.

False m. छंदोभंग *m.*

10 *means, step.* उपाय *m.* उपचार *m.* साधन *n.* लाग *m.* युक्ति *f.* तजवीज *f.* योग *m.* क्रिया *f.* गत *f.*

A mild or gentle m. सामोपाय *m.* सामोपचार*m.* सौम्योपचार*m.* बालोपचार *m.*

Soothing coaxing, &c. measures. सामदान *n.*

To take mearsures. लाग *m.pl.* लावणें, विहू *m.pl.* रचणें.

To Measure, *v. a. take the measure of.* मापणें, मेजणें, मोजणें, माप *n.*-मेज *n.*-मोज *n.*-&c. घेणें *g. of o.* मापन *n.*-&c. करणें *g. of o.*

To m. or weigh with . उमापणें, उमाणणें.

2 *adjust proportion.* मोजणें-मापणें *with* मापानें-*&c.of recip. noun* (ex. संपत्तीच्या मापानें इच्छा मोजावी, इच्छेच्या मापानें संपत्ति मोजूं नये measure your desire by your fortune, not your fortune by your desire). बरोबरी *f.*-तुलना *f.*-तोल*m.*-&c. करणें *with* बरोबरीनें-तोलानें-&c. *of recip. noun.* मोजणें-धरणें *with* बरोबर *of recip. noun.*

3 *give by measure.* मापून-मेजून-मोजून-&c. देणें.

To Measure, *v. n.be of a certain extent.* भरणें, मेज *n.*-माप *n.*-&c. असणें *g. of s.*

Measured, *p. & a.* v. V. A. 1. मापलेला, मोजलेला, &c. मोजीव, मेजीव, मापी, मापित, मित, परिमित, प्रमित.

2 बरोबर धरलेला, बरोबर मोजलेला, &c.

3 मापून दिल्हेला, &c.

I. *limited, restricted.* मेजला, मोजला, मोजका, परिमित, मित, परिमिताचा, बेताचा, बेताबाताचा, रजपजाचा. [कलेला, सम.

II. *uniform, steady.* नियमाचा, नेमाचा, बांधलेला, रेखलेला, आं-

III. *set in musical time.* तालबद्ध *pop.* टाळबद्ध.

Measureless, *a. immeasurable.* अपरिमेय, अपरिमित, अमोज, अमूप, अमर्याद, निस्सीम.

Measurement, Measuring, *n.* v. V. A. 1.—*act.* मापणें*n.* मोजणें*n.* &c. मोजणी *f.* माप*n.* मेज*n.* मोज*n.* मोजप*n.* मापन*n.* परिमाण*n.* मिति *f.* प्रमिति *f.*

Gross or rough m. स्थूलमान*n.*

Minute and exact m. सूक्ष्ममान*n.*

Random m. वारेमाप*n.*

I. *measure ascertained,* v. Measure. मेज*n.* मोज*n.* माप*n.*

Measurer, *n.* Measuring, *p. a.* v. V. A. 1. मापणारा, मोजणारा, मेज घेणारा, &c. मापक, मापनकर्त्ता.

The m. rod of masons or builders. दुतें *n.*

Meat, *n. flesh meat.* मांस *pop.* मास*n.* सागुती *or* सागोती *f.* आमिष*n.*—jocosely, &c. तांबडी भाजी *f.*

2—gener. v. Food. अन्न*n.*

M. and drink. अन्नोदक*n.* अन्नपाणी*n.* [पाडणें*g. of o.*

To make mince meat of, fig. *cut to pieces.* खुरचा *f.pl.*

To Meaw, To Meawl. See To Squall.

Mechanic, Mechanical, *a. pertaining, &c. to machines, or to work done by them.* यंत्राचा, यंत्री, यंत्राच्या कामाचा, यंत्राविषयींचा, यंत्राच्या प्रकरणाचा, यंत्रविषयक, यंत्रसंबंधी, शिल्पकर्माचा, शिल्पविद्येचा, शिल्पिक, शिल्पी.

2 *constructed, performed, &c. according to the rules of mechanics.* यंत्रशास्त्रानुयायी, यंत्रशास्त्रानुरूप, यंत्रनिर्बंधानुसारी, यंत्रनिर्बंधानुरोधी, यंत्रविद्यानुसारी-&c. यंत्रशास्त्रसिद्ध, शिल्पशास्त्रसिद्ध, शिल्पविद्यासिद्ध, यौक्तिक.

3 *employed in mechanical labor.* शिल्पकर्म करणारा, शिल्पी, शिल्पिक, शिल्पजीवी, शिल्पोपजीवी.

Mechanic, *n. artisan.* शिल्पकर्म करणारा, शिल्पी, कारिगर *or* कारागीर, शिल्पकार, शिल्पोपजीवी, कर्मार.

Mechanically, *adv.* v. A. 2. यंत्रशास्त्रानुरूप, यंत्रशास्त्रानुसार, &c.

I. *by the mere laws of motion, without design, &c.* यंत्राच्यासारखा, सहजामध्यें, सहजाखालीं, विचार न लागतां, लक्ष्य न लागतां, यंत्रप्राय.

Mechanician, *n.* यंत्रशास्त्रवेत्ता, यंत्रविद्यावेत्ता.

Mechanics, *n.*—the science. यंत्रशास्त्र *n.* यंत्रविद्या *f.* यंत्रनिर्बंध *m.* शिल्पशास्त्र *n.* शिल्पविद्या *f.*

Mechanism, *n. construction of a machine.* यंत्राची रचना *f.* कला *pop.* कळ *f.* युक्ति *f.* कुलंगडें *n.*

2 *action of a machine.* यंत्रक्रिया *f.* यंत्रचेष्टा *f.* यंत्रव्यापार *m.*

Mechanist, *n. maker of machines.* यंत्रें करणारा, यंत्रकार.

2 *one skilled in machines.* यंत्रें जाणणारा, यंत्रज्ञ.

Meconium, *n.*—of poppies. खसखसीचा चीक *m.*

2 *first excrement of children.* बाळलेंड *n.*

Medal, *n. stamped piece of metal given in honor of some person or event.* पदक *n.* प्रतिष्ठामुद्रा *f.* कीर्त्तिमुद्रा *f.* बिरदाची मुद्रा *f.* बिरुदमुद्रा *f.*

MEDALLION, *n.* मोठी मुद्रा *f.* [मुद्राविद्.

MEDALLIST, *n.* *one skilled in medals.* मुद्रापारखी, मुद्रापरीक्षक, 2 *one who wears a medal or badge of merit.* बिरदाईत, बिरुदमुद्राधारी, प्रतिष्ठामुद्राधारी, &c.

To MEDDLE, *v. n.* *have to do with.* शिरणें, पडणें, घुसणें, मध्यें पडणें, हात *m.* लावणें-घालणें, हातीं धरणें-घेणें, आंग *n.*-हात *m.*-पाय *m.*-बोट *n.*-&c. असणें *g. of s.* *with locative of o.* अधींमधीं *or* अध्यामध्यांत *or* अधेंमधें-&c. असणें-पडणें.

2 *interpose officiously.* कामावांचून मध्यें पडणें, लडबडणें, लुडबुडणें, सुडबुडणें, लटलटणें, लडबड *f.*-लुडबूड *f.*-दलामालकी *f.*-बुचाकारभार *m.*-&c. करणें-मांडणें, पुढच्यापुढें करणें-नाचणें, उचमपचम *n.* करणें.

MEDDLER, *n.* MEDDLING, *p. a.* v. V. 1. शिरणारा, पडणारा, &c. 2 लडबडणारा, &c. लडबड्या, लुडबुड्या, घालमेल्या, लुबरा, लांबरा, लाभरा, नाचरा, पुढच्यापुढें नाचणारा, बुचाकारभारी, लांडाकारभारी.

MEDDLESOME, *a.* v. MEDDLER, 2. लुबरा, लुडबुड्या.

MEDDLESOMENESS, *n.* v. A. *and* MEDDLING. लुडबुडपणा *m.* लुबरेपणा *m.* नाचरेपणा *m.* &c.

MEDDLING, *n.* v. V.—*act.* शिरणें *n.* &c.

2 मध्यें पडणें *n.* लुडबुडणें *n.* &c. लुडबूड *f.* लडबड *f.* बुचाकारभार *m.* लांडा कारभार *m.* नस्ता कारभार *m.* दलामालकी *f.* अनधिकारचर्चा *f.*

Curious or idle m. उठाठेव *f.* उलगाघाल *f.*

To MEDIATE, *v. n.* *interpose between two parties, intercede, &c.* मध्यें येणें-पडणें, मध्यस्थ होणें, मध्यस्थपणा *m.*-मध्यस्थगिरी *f.*-माध्यस्थी *f.*-मध्यस्थी *f.*-&c. करणें.

2 *be between,* v. To INTERVENE. मध्यें असणें-येणें-पडणें, मध्यस्थित-मध्यवर्त्ती-&c. असणें.

To MEDIATE, *v. a.* *effect by mediation.* मध्यें पडून-मध्यें होऊन-&c. करणें-करविणें, मध्यस्थपणानें-मध्यस्थीनें-मध्यस्थरीतीनें-&c. करणें-करविणें. [मध्यवर्त्ती.

MEDIATE, *a.* *middle, intervenient.* मधचा, मधला, मधील, मध्यस्थ,

MEDIATELY, *adv.* *by means, by a secondary cause, &c.* परंपरेनें, परंपरासंबंधानें, द्वारानें, अन्यद्वारा, अन्याकडून, सांतरसंबंधानें.

MEDIATION, *n.* v. V. N. 1.—*act.* मध्यें असणें *n.* &c. मध्यस्थपणा *m.* मध्यस्थगिरी *f.* मध्यस्थी *f.* माध्यस्थी *f.* माध्यस्थ *n.* मध्यवर्तित्व *n.* अंतरागमन *n.* डाकपट्टी *f.* *v.* घाल.

2 मध्यें असणें *n.* मध्यवर्त्तन *n.* मध्यस्थिति *f.* मध्यवर्तित्व *n.*

MEDIATOR, *n.* v. V. N. 1. मध्यस्थ, मध्यस्थपणा करणारा, &c. मध्यवर्त्ती, माध्यस्थ.

MEDIATORIAL, MEDIATORY, *a.* v. N. मध्यस्थाचा, मध्यस्थीचा, मध्यस्थासंबंधीचा, मध्यस्थसंबंधी, मध्यस्थविषयक.

MEDIATORSHIP, *n.* *office of a m.* मध्यस्थी *f.*

MEDICABLE, *a.* v. CURABLE. उपायसाध्य, चिकित्स्य, वैद्योपचारसाध्य, उपक्रमसाध्य, उपक्रमणीय.

MEDICAL, *a.* *belonging to the art of healing.* वैद्यकीचा, वैद्यकाचा, &c. वैद्याचा, वैद्य, वैद्यकसंबंधी, वैद्यकविषयक, चिकित्सासंबंधी, वैद्यक्रियासंबंधी, आयुर्वेदी.

M. aid or treatment. वैद्योपचार *m.* औषधोपचार *m.*

M. treatment of children. बालोपचार *m.*

MEDICAMENT, *n.* *medicine, drug, &c.* औषधीद्रव्य *n.* औषध *n.* मसाला *m.* द्रव्य *n.* भेषजद्रव्य *n.* भेषज *n.* आयुर्द्रव्य *n.*

Baking of medicaments coated over with cloth and earth. कापडलेप *m.* मातकापड *n.*

Medicaments tied up in a corner of a cloth to be dabbed on the eye or other part. पोतर्डा *f.*

MEDICASTER. See QUACK.

To MEDICATE, *v. a.* *impregnate with something medicinal.* औषधी करणें, औषधगुणक-औषधसंस्कृत-औषधगुणविशिष्ट-&c. करणें.

MEDICATED, *p.* v. V. औषधी केलेला, औषधी, औषधसंस्कृत.

MEDICATION, *n.* v. V.—*act.* औषधी करणें *n.* &c. औषधसंस्करण *n.* औषधसंस्कार *m.* औषधगुणाधान *n.*

MEDICINABLE, MEDICINAL, *a.* *of healing virtue.* औषधी *pop.* आंखदी, औषधाच्या उपयोगाचा, औषधाच्या कामाचा, औषधोपयोगी, औषधीय, रोगहर-हारी-&c. रोगांतक.

2 *belonging to medicine.* औषधाचा, औषधाविषयींचा, औषधसंबंधी, भेषजसंबंधी.

MEDICINE, *n.* *physic.* औषध *pop.* ओखद *n.* दवा *m. f.* भेषज *n.*

Medicines, or medical measures—gener. औषधपाणी *n.* औषधोपाय *m. pl.* औषधोपचार *m. pl.*

To employ medicines. औषध *n. or* औषधें *n. pl.*-औषधोपचार-&c. करणें.

2—the science. वैद्यक *n.* आयुर्वेद *n.*

A *shástra* or treatise on m. वैद्यक *n.*

3—the practice. वैद्यकी *f.* वैद्यक *n.* वैद्यपणा *m.* वैद्यक्रिया *f.* चिकित्सा *f.* उपचार *m.* उपचर्य्या *f.* उपक्रम *m.*

MEDIEVAL, *a.* मध्यकालीन, मध्यकालिक.

MEDIOCRAL, MEDIOCRE, *a.* v. MIDDLING. मध्यम, मध्यममानाचा, मध्यमपक्षाचा, साधारणपक्षाचा.

MEDIOCRITY, *n.* *middle state or degree.* मध्यमपक्ष *m.* साधारणपक्ष *m.* सामान्यपक्ष *m.* मध्यममान *n.* मध्यमप्रत *f.*

2 See MODERATION.

To MEDITATE, *v. a.* *plan, scheme.* कल्पिणें, योजणें, चिंतणें, कल्पना *f.*-योजना *f.*-योजणूक *f.*-&c. करणें *g. of o.* बेत *m.* करणें *g. of. o.*

To MEDITATE, *v. n.* *muse, contemplate.* ध्यान *n.*-चिंतन *n.*-मनन *n.*-&c. करणें, ध्यानांत-&c. असणें.

To m. upon. ध्यानास लागणें *g. of o.*

MEDITATED, *p.* v. V. A. कल्पिलेला, योजलेला, &c. चिंतित, ध्यात.

MEDITATION, *n.* v. V. A.—*act.* योजणें *n.* &c. कल्पना *f.* योजणूक *f.* योजना *f.*

v. V. N. ध्यान *n.* मनन *n.* चिंतन *n.*

Absorbed in m. ध्यानस्थ, समाधिस्थ.

Aspect or air of m. ध्यानमुद्रा *f.*

Posture for m. (on the deity). ब्रह्मासन *n.*

Profound and abstract m. ध्यान *n.* योग *m.* ध्यानयोग *m.* अंतर्ध्यान *n.* अंतर्निष्ठा *f.* अनुध्यास *m.* समाधि *f. m.* *pop.* समाध *f.*—Absorbed in it. समाधिस्थ.

MEDITATIVE, *a.* *addicted to meditation.* ध्यानी, ध्याननिष्ठ, ध्यानशील, ध्यानपर, ध्यानतत्पर, ध्यानपरायण, चिंतनशील.

MEDITERRANEAN, *a.* *encircled by land.* भुईनें घेरलेला-वेढलेला-&c. भूवेष्टित, भूमध्य, भूवलयांकित.

2 *remote from the sea,* v. INLAND. मध्यदेशस्थ, समुद्रासमीप, दूरसमुद्र, असमुद्रतीरस्थ.

Medium, *n. middle place or degree, mean.* मध्यमपरिमाण*n.* मध्यमपक्ष*m.* साधारणपक्ष*m.* सामान्यपक्ष*m.*
2 *means, instrument.* साधन*n.* कर्मसाधन*n.* योग*m.*
3 *channel, way, vehicle.* द्वार *pop.* दार*n.* मार्ग*m.* वाट *f.*योग*m.*
4 (of persons) *instrumentality.* गुजारत *f.* मारफत *f.* विद्यमानता *f.*

Medley, *n. mingled and confused mass.* v. **Mixture.** पंचमेळ *f.* पंचमेळ *f.* पंचमिसळ *f.* बेरड *f.* गोहोत*n.* गोतांबील*n.* घेडगुजरी *f.* खिचडी *f.* खिचडमचड*n.* गिजगिंदा*m.* संकर*m.*

Medley, *a. composed of confusedly mixed things.* पंचमेळीचा, पंचमेळीचा, धेडगुजरीचा, बेरडीचा, काल्व्याचा, मिश्र, नानाजातीय, संकरजातीय, विजोड.

Medullar, Medullary, *a. belonging, &c. to marrow.* मेंदूचा, मेदाचा, मेदसंबंधी, मज्जासंबंधी, अस्थिसारसंबंधी.

Meed, *n.* v. **Reward.** फळ*n.* प्रतिफल*n.*

Meek, *a. gentle, soft, submissive,* v. **Mild.** गरीब, स्वभावानेंगरीब, दीन, सौम्य, सौम्यवृत्ति, मिसकीन, विनयी, विनीत, लीन, गहीन.

Meek-eyed, *a.* मृदुनेत्र, मृदुलोचन.

Meekly, *adv.* v. A. गरीबीनें, लीनतेनें, सौम्यपणानें, &c. विनयपूर्वक, अक्रोधपूर्वक.

Meekness, *n.* v. A. गरीबी *f.* सौम्यपणा*m.* सौम्यता *f.* लीनता *f.* विनय*m.* दीनता *f.* दैन्य*n.* अक्रोध*m.*

Meet, *a. proper, suitable,* v. **Fit.** योग्य, लायक, बरोबर, उचित.

To **Meet**, *v. a. come face to face, confront.* सामोरा-आडवा येणें-जाणें-भेटणें.
2 *come together, encounter.* मिळणें *in. con.* भेटणें, *in. con.* गांठणें, भेट *f.*-चारडोळे*m. pl.*-&c. होणें *in. con. g. of o.* गांठ *f.* पडणें *in. con. g. of o.* नजरानजर *f.*-दृष्टादृष्ट *f.*-&c. करणें *with* सीं *of o.*
3 *find, incur, get.* गावणें, लाधणें.—as used inversely. मिळणें, गावणें, लागणें, प्राप्त होणें.
To m. the wishes of. इच्छेस-मनासयेणें *in. con.*

To **Meet**, *v. n. close face to face.* भेटणें, मिळणें, समोर-समोरा-समोर-सामोरा-&c. भेटणें, आडवा येणें.
2 *come together in a place, encounter.* भेटणें, मिळणें, भेट *f.* -गांठ *f.*-भेटाभेट *f.*-नजरानजर *f.*-चारडोळे*m. pl.*-&c. होणें *g. of s.*
3 *congregate, assemble.* मिळणें, जमणें, एकवटणें, एकटणें, एकारणें, जुडणें, जुटणें, एकत्र होणें. [टणें, भिडणें.
4 *come to and join.* मिळणें, जमणें, जुडणें, जुटणें, जुळणें, मि-
5 with; *light on, find.* मिळणें, सांपडणें, अढळणें, जाणें *all with in. con.* अढळ*m.* होणें *in con. & g. of s.*
6 with; *incur, suffer, receive.* होणें, लागणें, मिळणें, बसणें, येणें, *all with in. con.*
To m. with the approbation of. मनासयेणें-वाटणें *in.con.* मनासारखा असणें.

Meeting, *n.* v. V. N. 2. *and* **Interview.** गांठ *f.*भेट*f.* नजरानजर*f.* दृष्टादृष्ट *f.* भेटाभेट *f.* चारडोळे*m. pl.* मुलाखत *f.*
3 मिळणें*n.* जमणें*n.* बैठक *f.* प्रसंग*m.*
4 मिळणें*n.* जमणें*n.* &c. मिळणी *f.* संगम*m.* संयोग*m.* योग*m.*
5 अढळ*m.*
I. *public concourse,* v. **Assembly.** मंडळी *f.* सभा *f.* बैठक *f.* मेला *f. pop.* मेळा*m.* मजलस *f.* मजालस *f.*
Full m. भर मजलस *f.* भर मजालस *f.*

Meetly, *adv.* v. A. ठीक, योग्य, यथायोग्य, लायक.

Meetness, *n.* v. A. योग्यता *f.* लायकी *f.* औचित्य *n.*

Megrim, *n. hemicrany.* अर्धशिशी *f.*

Meiosis, *n.*—in rhetoric. न्यूनालंकार *m.* [त्तघ्न औषध *n.*

Melanagogue, *n. medicine to carry off black bile.* कृष्णपि-

Melancholic, Melancholy, *a. depressed, dejected,* v. **Dispirited.** उदास, खिन्न, खेदयुक्त, मलूल, दिलगीर, विषण्ण, अवसन्न.
2 *subject to melancholy, hypochondriac.* विषादी, सदाविषादी, सदाखेदी, विषादवृत्ति, नित्यविषण्ण, नित्यविषादी, विषण्णवृत्ति, खेदवृत्ति, नित्यावसन्न.
3 *expressive, &c. of melancholy, mournful.* शोकाचा, खेदाचा, &c. खेदसूचक, विषादप्रधान, विषादप्रचुर, विषादात्मक.
4 *causing sorrow.* खेदकारक, खेदजनक, खेदप्रद, विषादप्रद, विषादजनक, दुःखप्रद.

Melancholic, Melancholist, *n.* v. A. विषादी, सदाविषादी.

Melancholy, *n. low spirits.* उदासपणा *m.* औदासीन्य *n.* खिन्नता *f.* विषाद *m.* अवसाद *m.* अवसन्नता *f.* विषण्णता *f.* विषादभाव *m.* विषादवृत्ति *f.* विषण्णवृत्ति *f.*

Melée, *n. tumultuous assembly.* दंगल *m. f.* एकबाट *m. f.*
M. of a fight. रणसंकुल *n.* तुमुल युद्ध *n.*

To **Meliorate, Melioration.** See To **Improve**, &c.

Melliferous, *a. productive of honey.* मधुप्रद, मधुजनक, मधूत्पादक.

Mellification, *n. production of honey.* मधुकरण *n.* मधुक्रिया *f.*

Mellifluence, *n.* v. A. मधुस्राव *m.* अमृतस्राव *m.* मधुप्रवाह *m.* वाङ्माधुर्य *n.*

Mellifluent, Mellifluous, *a. honied, sweet,*—speech, voice, &c. मधुस्रावी, अमृतस्रावी, द्राक्षापाकाचा, मधुराक्षर, गोड, मधुर, मिष्ट.
M. speech. द्राक्षापाक *m.* साखरेचा रवा *m.*

Mellow, *a. soft with ripeness.* पिकून मऊ झालेला, मुरलेला, मवाळ, परिपक्व, पक्वमृदु.
That is over-m. *soft and flabby.* बिलबिला, बिलबिलीत.
To get m. मुरणें, निवळणें.
To smell m. वासळणें.
2 *soft in sound.* मृदुनादाचा, कोमलध्वनीचा, &c. मृदुनाद, कोमलनाद, मृदुशब्द, मृदु, मंजुल *pop.* मंजूळ.
3 *merry from liquor.* पिऊन आनंदी झालेला.

To **Mellow**, *v. a.* v. To **Ripen.** पिकवणें, मुरवणें, परिपक्वदशेस आणणें, परिपक्व करणें.

To **Mellow**, *v. n.* v. To **Ripen.** मुरणें, निवळणें, उतरणें, गोडावणें, परिपक्वदशेस येणें.

Mellowness, *n.* v. A. 1. मुरलेलेपणा *m.* &c. परिपक्वता *f.* परिपक्वदशा *f.* पक्वमृदुता *f.*
2 नादाचा कोमळपणा *m.* &c. मंजुळपणा *m.* नादमार्दव *n.* मृदुनादता *f.* नादकोमलता *f.* मंजुलत्व *n.*

Melodious, *a. containing melody; sweet, &c.* मंजुल *pop.* मंजूळ, गोड, मधुर, मंजुळवाणा, सुश्राव्य, सुस्वर, श्रोत्रसुख, मधुराक्षर, सुचारुस्वन.

Melodiously, *adv.* v. A. मधुर स्वरांनीं, मंजुलस्वरांनीं.

Melodiousness, *n.* v. A. मंजुळपणा *m.* गोडी *f.* मंजुलता *f.* मधुरता *f.* माधुर्य *n.* सुश्राव्यता *f.*

Melody, *n. agreeable succession of sounds.* स्वरांची गोडी *f.* सुस्वरानुपूर्वी *f.* सुस्वरानुक्रम *m.* स्वरानुक्रममाधुर्य*n.* गोडी*f.* माधुर्य*n.*

Melon, *n.* musk melon,—the plant. खरबूज*f. n.* खरबुजी *f.*—the fruit. खरबूज *n.*

Plantation of musk melons. पालज *f.* Some varieties of *musk melon* are, आकरमाशी, खरडा, खिरणी, टकमकें, नारंगी बारमाशी खरबूज, भोपळीखरबूज.

2 water melon,—the plant. तरबूज *or* टरबूज *f. n.* कलिंगण *f.* कलिंगडी *f.* कलिंगड *f. n.* कालिंगी *f.*—the fruit. तरबूज *or* टरबूज *n.* कलिंगड *n.* कलिंगडें *n.*

A young m. घटा *m.*

Plantation of water melons. काशी *f.*

To **Melt**, *v. a. make liquid ; dissolve, fuse, &c.* अटणें, पाघळविणें, द्रवविणें, वितुळविणें, विघरणें, विरवणें, चेहळविणें, विरघळविणें, कढविणें, कितुळेसा-विरेसा-&c. करणें, द्रव *m.*-रस *m.*-पाणी *n.*-&c. करणें *g. of. o.* द्रावण *n.*-गालन *n.*-द्रवीकरण*n.*-&c.-करणें *g. of o.* सद्रव करणें.

2 *soften. to love, pity, &c.* द्रवविणें, पाघळविणें, पाझरविणें, विरघळविणें, पान्हा *m.*-ओलावा *m.*-घाम *m.*-&c. आणणें, सार्द्रकरणें.

To **Melt**, *v. n. become liquid or fluid.* पघळणें, चिघळणें, चेहळणें *or* चिहळणें, वितुळणें, विघरणें *or* विघुरणें, पाघळणें, द्रवणें, विरणें, विरघळणें, तेवणें, द्रव*m.*-रस *m.*-पाणी *n.*-&c. होणें *g. of s.* गलन *n.*-&c. होणें *g. of s.*

2 *be softened to pity or tenderness.* द्रवणें, पाझरणें, पघळणें, विरघळणें, वितुळणें, पाकुळणें, कन्हवळणें, द्रव*m.*-पान्हा*m.*-घाम*m.*-ओलावा-*m.*-कन्हवळा *m.*-&c. येणें *in. con.*

Melted, *p.* v. V. A. 1. अटलेला, पाघळविलेला, &c. द्रावित, गालित, द्रवीकृत, [जळीत *n.*

Waste (of metals, &c.) on being melted. जळ*f.* जळप*f.*

2 द्रवविलेला, &c. पान्हा आणलेला.

v. V. N. 1. पघळलेला, द्रवलेला, &c. गलित, द्रवीभूत, द्रुत.

Melter, *n.* **Melting**, *p. a.* v. V. A. 1. अटणारा, द्रवविणारा, पघळविणारा, &c. द्रावक, द्रवकर्त्ता.

2 द्रवविणारा &c. द्रव आणणारा, पान्हा आणणारा-फोडणारा, द्रावक, हृदयवेधक, हृदयंगम, करुण, करुणापर.

Melting, *n.* v. V. A. 1.—*act.* अटणें *n.* &c. अटणी *f.* द्रावण *n.* गालन *n.* द्रवीकरण *n.* द्राव *m.*

Price of m. अटणावळ *f.* अटाई *f.*

2 द्रवविणें *n.* द्रव आणणें *n.* &c.

v. V. N. 1. पघळणें *n.* द्रवणें *n.*&c. द्रव *m.*गलन *n.*

2 द्रवणें *n.* &c. द्रव *m.* पान्हा*m.* घाम *m.* पाकुळकी *f.* कन्हवळा*m.* काकळूत *f.*

Member, *n.* (of the body) *limb.* अंग *pop.* आंग *n.* अवयव *m.* गात्र *n.* शरीरांग *n.* प्रत्यंग *n.*

A deficient m. न्यूनांग *n.*—That is deficient in a m. न्यूनांग, हीनांग. [अपांग *n.*

A deficient, imperfect, or distorted m. विकलांग *n.* That is deficient, &c. विकलांग, अपांग.

An excessive or supernumerary m. अधिकांग*n.*—That has one अधिकांग.

A minor m. प्रत्यंग *n.* उपांग *m.*

That has all its members, *entire*, सांग.

That has members or appendages. अंगी, अवयवी.

2 (of a discourse, &c.). अंग *n.* प्रकरण *n.* खंड *m. n.*

3 *part, portion.* अंग *pop.* आंग *n.* अवयव *m.* अंश *m.*

Member by m. अवयवशः.

Forming a m. or part. अंगभूत.

4 (of a community, &c.). v. Individual. असामी *f. m.*व्यक्ति *f.* This sense is often rendered by the use of the adjective एक (as तो पंचांतला एक आहे he is a m. of (or *one of*) the committee). It is rendered also by वाला.

5—esp. of an assembly, council, &c. सभासद,सभ्य, सदस्य, सामवायिक, सामाजिक, सभास्तार, हाजिरमजालस.

Membrane, *n.* आंतली त्वचा *f.* आवरकत्वक् *f.* अंतरत्वक् *f.*

Membraneous, *a.* v. N. आंतले त्वचेचा, आवरक त्वचेचा.

Memento, *n. memorial.* यादगिरी *f.* यादगारी *f.* आठवणूक *f.* स्मरण *n.* ओंळख *f.* ओळखण *f.*

Memoir, *n. history.* चरित्र *n.* बखर *f.*

Memorable, *a. worthy to be remembered.* आठवायाजोगा-सारखा-&c. स्मरायाजोगा-&c. स्मरणीय, स्मरणार्ह, स्मरणयोग्य, स्मर्य.

Memorandum, *n. note to help the memory.* टाचण *n.* टिपण*n.* टाचणी *f.* याद *f.* स्मरण *n.*

To make memoranda. टाचणें, टिपणें.

2 *paper containing memoranda.* याद *f.* यादी *f.* टाचण *n.* टिपण *n.*—compreh. यादबूद *f.*

Memorial, *a. preservative of the memory of.* स्मरणदेणारा, याददेणारा, यादगिरीचा, स्मारक, स्मृतिजनक, स्मरणार्थक.

Memorial, *n. memento, something to preserve memory.* यादगिरी *f.* यादगारी *f.* अठवणूक *f.* स्मरणदेणारी वस्तू *f.* स्मरण *n.* ओळख *f.* ओळखण *f.* स्मारकविषय *m.*

2 *memorandum.* टाचण *n.* टिपण *n.*

3 *petition, address.* अर्जी *f.* अर्जदास्त*f.* याद *f.* यादी *f.*विनंतीपत्र *n.* विज्ञापना पत्र *n.*

Memorialist, *n.* अर्जदार, अर्जी लिहून देणारा.

To **Memorialize**, *v. a.* अर्जी *f.*-&c. देणें.

Memory, *n.*—the faculty. स्मरण *n.* स्मरणशक्ति *f.* स्मृति *f.* धारणाशक्ति *f.* धारणा *f.*

Of a retentive m. आठवणीचा-यादीचा-&c. धड-अटोकाट-बहादूर-खबरदार-&c. पाठी.

Retentiveness of m. धर *m.* धारणा *f.*

The tablets of m. दिलदफ्तर *n.*

2 v. Remembrance. आठवण *f.* आठव *m.* स्मरण *n.* स्मृति *f.* ध्यान *n.*

Readiness of m. समयस्फूर्ति *f.*

Rising to m. स्फूर्ति *f.*

That can recite from m. पाठी That can recite from once hearing एकपाठी;—from twice, दुपाठी; and so onwards, तिपाठी, चौपाठी, &c.

That is committed to m. पाठ.

To arise to m. come into the m. आठवणें, स्मरणें, स्फुरणें.

To commit to m. *learn by heart.* पाठ करणें.

To fix or engrave on one's m. मनांत गांठ *f.* बांधणें, पदरास गांठ *f.* बांधणें-मारणें.

To impress on the m by conning over. पट करणें.

To keep in m. आठवण *f.*-स्मरण *n.*-&c. ठेवणें, ध्यानांत ठेवणें.

To recite from m. पाठ *n.* म्हणणें.

To speak from m. *speak without book.* तोंडानें सांगणें.

MEN-PLEASER, *n.* तोंडदेखा *or* देख्या, जनरंजक, लोकरंजक, जनानुसारी.

To MENACE, *v. a. threaten.* भय *n.*-धाक *m.*-&c. दाखवणें, भय *n.*-दहशत *f.*-दाब *m.*-&c. घालणें, धमकावणें, धमकी *f.* देणें, दटावणें, भेडसावणें, भेडावणें, भिवविणें, दट्टा *m.* देणें, भयप्रदर्शन *n.* करणें.

MENACE, MENACING, *n.* v. V. धमकावणें *n.* &c. धमकावणी *f.* दटावणी *f.* भेडसावणी *f.* धमकी *f.* दट्टा *m.* भयप्रदर्शन *n.*

MENAGE, MENAGERIE, *n. a collection of animals.* पशुपक्ष्यांचा भरणा *m.* पश्वादिसंग्रह *m.* पशुपक्षिसंग्रह *m.* शिकारखाना *m.*

MENAGOGUE, *n.* सुखार्त्तवौषध *n.*

To MEND, *v. a. repair.* नीट-दुरूस्त-&c. करणें, तांगडणें, सुधारणें, डागडुजी *or* डागडोजी *f.*-मरामत *f.*-&c. करणें *g. of o.* जीर्णोद्धार *m.* करणें *g. of o.*

To patch and m. तांगडातांगड *f.*-सांदासांद *f.*-जोडाजोड *f.*-&c. करणें *g. of o.*

2 *correct, set right.* चांगला-नीट-शुद्ध-&c. करणें, सुधारणें, सुधारणें, सावरणें, निटावणें, सुधारणूक *f.*-&c. करणें *g. of o.* स्थितीवर-वाटेवर-&c. आणणें.

3 *make better,* v. To IMPROVE. अधिक चांगला-&c. करणें, गुणवृद्धि *f.*-गुणवर्धन *n.*-&c. करणें *g. of o.*

4 See To HASTEN.

To MEND, *v. n. improve, grow better.* बरा होत जाणें-चालणें, सुधारणें, निटावणें, सावरणें, वाटेवर-&c. येऊं लागणें.

MENDACIOUS, *a. lying,* v. LIAR. खोटा, लबाड, खोटें बोलणारा, असत्यभाषी, अनृत भाषी, असत्यवादी.

MENDACITY, *n.* v. A. *and* FALSEHOOD. लबाडी *f.* लबाडकी *f.* खोटाई *f.* असत्य भाषण *n.*

MENDICANCY, MENDICITY, *n.* v. BEGGARY. भीक मागणें *n.* भिकारीपणा *m.* कंगाली *f.* भिक्षावृत्ति *f.* याचकी *f.* याचकाई *f.* याचनावृत्ति *f.* याचकवृत्ति *f.* भिक्षुकवृत्ति *f.* भिक्षाटन *n.* भैक्षजीविका *f.* भैक्ष *or* भैक्ष्य *n.* भैक्षचर्या *f.*—of a Muhammadan. फकिरी *f.*

To take to m. *turn beggar,* v. BEGGAR. चौपदरी *f.* करणें-घेणें, हातीं भोपळा *m.* घेणें, करोटी *f.*-नरोटी *f.* हातांत घेणें.

MENDICANT, *a. poor to a state of beggary.* भिकारी, भीक मागण्याचा, कंगालीचा, भिक्षोपजीवी, भिक्षाजीवी.

2 *that practises begging,* v. BEGGAR. भीक मागणारा, भीक माग्या, भिक्षेकरी. [भिक्षार्थी.

MENDICANT, *n.* v. BEGGAR. भिकारी, भीकमाग्या, भिक्षेकरी,

Bowl or dish of a m. तुंबडी *f.*

Bell or plate of a m. जंगट *n.*

Undressed corn or pulse given to mendicants. उलफा *m.*

2—religious m. जोगी, गोसावी, अतीत, तडीतापडी, यति *or* यती,—Muhammadan *m.* फकीर. Some of the *orders, sects, or classes* of religious *mendicants* are, अघोरपंथ *or* अघोरमार्ग *m.* अयाचित, अरण्य *n.* अवघडपंथ *m.* अवधूत *or* दत्तात्रेय अवधूत, आश्रम *m.* इंद्र *m.* कालबेला, खरखरमुंडा, खाकी *or* खाक्या, गोसावी, जती, जोगी, डफगाण, डोईफोड्या, त्रिदंडी, दंडी, दंडीगाण *m.* दिंडीगाण *m.* दावलमलीक, दिगंबर, नागडगोसावी, नाथपंथी, पांगूळ, पुरी, बाळसंतोष, बैरागी *or* बेरागी, भुत्या, भैरवजोगी, मेंडजोगी, बन, वासुदेव, शेवडा *m.* संत. See also ASCETIC.

Feasting of a body of religious mendicants. भंडारा *m.*

Religious mendicants compreh. अतीत अभ्यागत, गोसावी बैरागी, फकीर फुकरा. Some of the *invocations* used by them when they beg are, अलख, उदव, एळकोट, जोगबा, दोमदोम, पाऊड, बंमहादेव, बाळसंतोष, वारी. Some of the *weapons* carried about by them are, गुरगूज *or* घुरघूस *m.* घोळ *m.* झेंडा *m.* त्रिशूळ *m.*

MENDING, *n.* v. V. A. 2.—*act.* नीट करणें *n.* तांगडणें *n.* &c. सुधारणी *f.* सुधारणूक *f.* डागडुजी *or* डागडोजी *f.* मरामत *f.* जीर्णोद्धार *m.*

2 सुधारणें *n.* सुधारणी *f.* सुधारणूक *f.* निटावणी *f.*

MENIAL, *n. domestic servant.* घरचाकर, नफर, घरकाम्या, शागिर्दपेशा, झाडसारव्या, झाडलोट्या, भृत्य *pop.* भृत्या, गृहदास.

Menials. चाकरनफर *m. pl.* चाकरचुकर *m. pl.* चाकरपेशा *m.* शागिर्दपेशा *m.*

MENIAL, *a. belonging, &c. to a domestic servant.* घरचाकराचा, घरकामाचा, शागिर्दपेशाचा, चाकरपेशाचा, भृत्याचा, गृहदाससंबंधी, गृहदासविषयक.

M. occupation. चाकरीचा पेशा *m.*

MENISEUS, *n.* अर्धचंद्राकार *m.* अर्धचंद्राकृति *f.*

MENOLOGY, *n. register of months.* मासविवरण *n.*

MENSAL, *a. belonging to, transacted at, meals.* पात्रावरचा, पात्रावरला, जेवणावरचा, भोजनप्रसंगींचा.

MENSES, *n. cattamenia.* विटाळ *m.* पुष्प *n.* रज *n.* ऋतु *m.* स्त्रीधर्म *m.*

First appearance of the m. नहाण *n.* ऋतुदर्शन *n.* रजोदर्शन *n.*

The event is allusively communicated to a husband or father by आपणास पुत्र झाला, वडिलांस नातू झाला, &c.—Ceremonies on the first appearance. ऋतुशांति *f.*—Feast upon the event. नहाणाचा सोहळा *m.* ऋतूत्सव *m.*—Victuals sent to the woman. वाढण *n.* वाढलें *n.* वाढणें *n.*

Immoderate flow of the m. उपळ *m.* धुपणी *f.*

Irregularity of the m. असुख *or* असूख *n.*

Purified from the m. through bathing. ऋतुस्नाता.

Woman having the m. for the first time. नाहणवली *or* नाहणुली.

Woman having the m. regularly. नहातीधुती.

Woman who has ceased to have the m. विरजा, गतरजस्का, गतरजा, गतार्त्तवा, विगतार्त्तवा.

To arrive at the age of menstruation. नहाण पदास येणें.

To have the m. for the first time. नहाण *n.* येणें *in. con.* ऋतु *m.* प्राप्त होणें, जन्म *m.* देखणें-पाहणें, नाहूं लागणें.

To have the m. regularly. नाहणें.

MENSTRUAL. See MONTHLY.

To MENSTRUATE, *v. n. be menstruous,* v. N. विटाळ *m.*-&c. होणें-येणें *in. con.* विटाळशी-&c. होणें;—allusively, तांब्या पालथा पडणें *g. of s.* घटीं बसणें, पाळी *f.* येणें.

MENSTRUOUS, *a. pertaining to the menses.* विटाळाचा, विटाळाविषयींचा, स्त्रीधर्माचा, ऋतुसंबंधी, ऋतुविषयक, रजस्संबंधी, स्त्रीधर्मविषयक, आर्त्तव.

A m. woman. विटाळशी or स्त्री, पुष्पवती, रजस्वला, दुरशी or स्त्री, ऋतुमती, स्त्रीधर्मिणी, सरजा, बाहेरची, बाहेरली, अस्पर्शा, शिवूं नयेशी or स्त्री. The significant terms for a m. woman in the first, second, third, and fourth days respectively of her menstruation are, चांडाली, ब्रह्मघातिणी, रजकी, and शूद्री.

MENSTRUUM, *n. solvent.* द्रावकरस *m.* द्रावण *n.*

MENSURABILITY, *n.* v. A. परिमेयत्व *n.* मापनीयत्व *n.* मेयत्व *n.* मापनक्षमता *f.*

MENSURABLE, *a. measurable.* परिमेय, मापनीय, मेय, मापनशक्य, मापनक्षम. [विषयक.

MENSURAL, *a. relating to measure.* मानाचा, मानसंबंधी, मान-

To MENSURATE. See To MEASURE.

MENSURATION. See MEASUREMENT, MEASURE.

MENTAL, *a. belonging, &c. to the mind.* मनाचा, मनचा, मनींचा, मनांतला, मनःसंबंधी, मनस्थ, मानसिक, मानस, मनोगत, मनोभव, मनोज, मनोमय, मनःकल्पित.

MENTALLY, *adv.* v. A. मनीं, मनांत, मनाचेठाईं, मनच्यामनीं, मनांतल्यामनांत.

To MENTION, *v. a. name, speak of, bring forward orally or in writing.* बोलणें, म्हणणें, सांगणें, काढणें, नांव *n.* घेणें-काढणें *g. of o.* उल्लेख *m.*-उहूम. काढणें-करणें *g. of o.* गोष्ट *f.*-मजकूर *m.*-चर्चा *f.*-प्रसंग *m.*-उकळी *f.*-वार्त्ता *f.*-&c. काढणें *g. of o.* उद्देश *m.*- नामनिर्देश *m.* करणें *g. of o.*

To be mentioned. गोष्ट *f.*-&c. निघणें *g. of s.*

MENTION, MENTIONING, *n.* v. V.—*act.* बोलणें *n.* नांव घेणें *n.* &c. कथन *n.* मजकूर *m.* चर्चा *f.* उल्लेख *m.* नामनिर्देश *m.* उद्देश*m.*

By special m. कंठरवेंकडून.

Delivered by special m. कंठरवोक्त.

No m. whatever. गंधवार्त्ता *f.*-गंधलेश *m.*-&c. *with negative.*

MENTOR, *n. adviser.* उपदेश करणारा, उपदेशक, उपदेष्टा, जांबुवंत*m.*

MENTORIAL, *a.* उपदेशाचा, उपदेशपर.

MEPHITIC, *a. stinking, noxious.* घाणीचा, दूषकगंधी, पूतिगंधी, पूतिगंधात्मक, पूतिविष.

MERCANTILE, *a. relating to trade or traders.* व्यापाराचा, उदिमाचा, व्यापारसंबंधींचा, सावकारी, सौदागरी, सौदागरीचा, वाणिज्यसंबंधी, व्यवहारसंबंधी.

M. travelling. वणज *f.* गस्तंगिरी *f.*

MERCATURE, *n. buying and selling.* क्रयविक्रय *m.*

MERCENARILY, *adv.* v. A. 2. लाभलोभानें, लाभदृष्टीनें, लाभबुद्धीनें, लाभबुद्ध्या, लाभदृष्ट्या.

MERCENARINESS, *n.* v. A. 2. लाभलोभ *m.* लाभलोभा *m.* लाभदृष्टि *f.* लाभबुद्धि *f.* फलाशा *f.* सकामबुद्धि *f.*

MERCENARY, *a. hireling, serving for mere gain.* पैका घेऊन कामकरणारा, मोलकरी, भाडेकरी, मुशारखोर, मजूरदार, भृतक, वैतनिक, वेतनभृत्.

2 *venal, actuated by desire of gain.* लाभलोभी, लाभदृष्टि, लाभबुद्धि, लालचखोर, लांचखोर, सकाम.

MERCENARY, *n.* v. A. 1. मोलकरी, मुशारखोर, मुशारदार.

MERCER, *n. dealer in silks.* रेशमीकापड विकणारा, रेशमीकापडकरी, कौशेयवणिक्.

MERCERY, *n. silk goods.* रेशमी कापड *n.* पट्टवस्त्रें *n. pl.*

MERCHANDISE, MERCHANDRY, *n.* v. TRADE. उदीम *m.* व्यापार *m.* व्यवहार *m.* व्यवसाय *m.* वाणिज्य *n.* सौदागरी *f.* सौदा *m.*

2 *wares, goods.* सौदा *m.* माल *m.* जिन्नस *m.* पण्यद्रव्य *n.*—compreh. or indef. सौदासुत *m. n.* [वानोळा *m.*

An article of m. जिन्नस *m.* केणें *n.* सौदा *m.* वाना *m.*

To MERCHANDISE. See To TRADE.

MERCHANT, *n.* v. TRADER. उदमी, बेपारी, व्यापारी, सौदागर, महाजन, सावकार, वणिक्. Some respectful compellations for a *merchant* are, शेट or शेठ, शेटजी.

MERCHANT-MAN, *n. trading vessel.* जिन्नसी गलबत *n.*-तारूं *n.*-&c. बारकस *n.* महागिरी *f.*

MERCHANTABLE, *a. fit to be bought or sold.* विकाऊ, खपाऊ, खपायाजोगा-&c. विक्रेय, क्रय.

MERCIFUL, *a. compassionate, disposed to forgive.* दयाळ, दयालु *pop.* दयाळू, दयावान् *pop.* दयावंत, दयाशील, दयामय, सदय, दयाबुद्धि, दयादृष्टि, क्षमाशील, क्षमावान् *pop.* क्षमावंत.

2 *not cruel; tender, &c.* v. PITIFUL. कृपाळ, कृपालु *pop.* कृपाळू, कृपाशील, कृपाबुद्धि, कृपावान् *pop.* कृपावंत, करुणाशील, कारुणिक, अनुकंपाशील, अनुकंपावान्.

MERCIFULLY, *adv.* v. A. दयेनें, कृपेनें, &c. दयाबुद्धीनें, दयादृष्टीनें, दयाबुद्ध्या, दयादृष्ट्या, दयापूर्वक, &c.

MERCIFULNESS, *n.* v. A. 1. दया *f.* दयाळूपणा *m.* दयाळपणा *m.* &c. दयाशीलता *f.* दयालुता *f.* दयादृष्टि *f.* दयाबुद्धि *f.* सदयता *f.* क्षमाशीलता *f.* क्षमाबुद्धि *f.*

2 कृपा *f.* दया *f.* कृपाळूपणा *m.* कृपाळपणा *m.* &c. कृपाशीलता*f.* कृपालुता *f.* कृपाबुद्धि *f.* अनुकंपा *f.* घृणा *f.*

MERCILESS, *a. pitiless, cruel.* निर्दय, दयाहीन, दयाशून्य, निर्घृण, कठीण, कठोर, पाषाणहृदय, निष्कृप. [पारदमय.

MERCURIAL, *a. consisting of mercury.* पाऱ्याचा, पारदात्मक,

2 *volatile,* v. CHANGEABLE. चंचल, चपल or ळ, चपळा, क्षणिकबुद्धि, तरलप्रकृतीचा, तरलप्रकृति.

MERCURY, *n.*—the planet. बुध *m.* सौम्य *m.*

2 *quicksilver.* पारा *m.* पारद *m.* रसधातु *m.* रस *m.*

Calx or oxid of m. पारदभस्म *n.* रसभस्म *n.*

Sulphuret of m. कज्जली *pop.* काजळी *f.*

White sublimate or submuriate of m. रसकर्पूर *pop.* रसकापूर *m.*

3 *messenger.* निरोप्या.

A m. *a good hand at walking.* पायांचा पारवा *m.*

MERCY, *n. disposition to forgive offences,* v. MERCIFULNESS. 1. दया *f.* दयाळूपणा *m.* दयाशीलता *f.* दयाबुद्धि *f.* क्षमाबुद्धि *f.*

2 *compassion, tenderness,* v. PITY. दया *f.* कृपा *f.* कृपाळूपणा *m.* करुणा *f.* अनुकंपा *f.* घृणा *f.*

Fountain of m., Ocean of m., &c. दयासागर, दयासमुद्र, दयाब्धि, दयानिधि, करुणासागर, करुणाकर, &c.

Vessel of m. कृपापात्र *n.* दयापात्र *n.* दयाभाजन *n.* कृपाभाजन *n.* अनुग्राह्य.

To be at the m. of, *be in the power of,* v. CLUTCHES. हातांत-कबजांत-&c. सांपडणें, स्वाधीन असणें *g. of o.*

To shew m. दया *f.*-&c. करणें.

3 *pardon, pardoning.* दया *f.* क्षमा *f.* माफी *f.* गई *f.*

Mercy! Mercy! त्राहि त्राहि.

MERCY-SEAT, *n.* दयासन *n.*

MERE, *a. this or that only, pure.* केवळ or ळ, नुस्ता or नुस्था or

निखा, शुद्ध *pop.* सुद्धा.

MERE, *n.* See LAKE.

MERELY, *adv.* v. A. *only, solely, purely, &c.* केवल or ळ, फक्त, मात्र, शुद्ध, एकजात, निखालस, निखळ, निस्तूक, निकूखळ or निखळ, निश्चंक.

M. for nothing. उगा, उगाच, उगीच, उगेच, एरवीं.

MERETRICIOUS, *a. pertaining, &c. to prostitutes.* कसबिणीचा, कंचनीचा, वारांगनीय, वेश्यासंबंधी.

2 *alluring by false show.* कृत्रिम शोभेचा, कसबे शोभेचा, कंचनीच्या सारखा, कसबिणीच्या सारखा, ढबदार, ढबीचा, दिखाऊ, कल्हेगिरीचा.

To MERGE, *v. a.* v. To IMMERSE. बुडविणें, गर्क करणें.

To MERGE, *v. n. be sunk or swallowed up.* गर्क-गडद-&c. होणें, मिळून जाणें. [दुपार *f.*

MERIDIAN, *n. noon.* मध्याह्न *m.* मध्याह्नकाल *m.* दोनप्रहर *m. pl.*

2—in geography and astronomy. मध्याह्नरेषा *f.* याम्योत्तरवृत्त *n.* याम्योत्तररेषा *f.* खमध्य *m.* [तर *n.*

Distance (E. or W.) from the first m. रेखांतर *n.* देशांतर *n.*

Distance between meridians. स्पष्टपरिधि *m.*

3 fig. *highest point or degree.* भर *m.* भरतें *n.* बहर or बहार *m.* कळस *m.* मधभरणी *f.*

MERIDIAN, *a. relating &c. to the meridian line.* मध्याह्नरेषेचा, याम्योत्तररेषेचा, &c. मध्याह्नरेषासंबंधी, याम्योत्तरवृत्तसंबंधी, खमध्यसंबंधी. [कालसंबंधी.

2 *relating, &c. to noon.* मध्याह्नकालाचा, दोनप्रहरचा, मध्याह्नकालसंबंधी.

MERIDIONAL. See MERIDIAN, SOUTHERN.

MERIT, *n. desert, worth.* गुण *m.* योग्यता *f.* लायकी *f.*

Acknowledging or appreciating m. गुणग्रहण *n.*

2 merits; *character with respect to good or ill.* गुणागुण *m. pl.* गुणदोष *m. pl.* मर्मे *n. pl.*

Test or investigation of m. गुणदोषपरीक्षण *n.*

3—in the Hindu religious system; *the desert acquired through works.* पुण्य *n.* पुण्याई *f.* सुकृत *n.* पुण्यसामग्री *f.* श्रेय *n.* तप *n.* धर्म *m.*

Acquisition of m. पुण्यसंपादन *n.* श्रेयस्संपादन *n.*

Acquired by m. पुण्यार्जित, पुण्यविजित.

Fruit or reward of m. पुण्यफल *n.*

M. acquired in some former birth. पूर्वपुण्य *n.*

Mightiness or prevalence of m. पुण्यप्रताप *m.* Some terms, appellatives, &c. for a person of great *merit* are, पुण्यनिधि, पुण्यनिधान, पुण्यसागर, पुण्याब्धि, श्रेयोनिधि, पुण्यपुरुष, पुण्यात्मा, पुण्यराशि, पुण्यमूर्त्ति.

4 *the desert of works whether as good or evil.* संचित *n.* अपूर्व *n.* पूर्वीचा ठेवा *m.*

To MERIT, *v. a. deserve.* योग्य-लायक- पात्र-अर्ह (in comp.) असणें *g. of o.* पुण्यानें-योग्यतेनें-गुणानें-&c. मिळवणें-संपादणें-&c.

MERITORIOUS, *a.* v. N. 1. योग्य, चांगला, लायक, योग्यतेचा, उत्तम, गुणी, गुणवान् *pop.* गुणवंत, गुणसंपन्न, अर्ह (in comp.), पात्र (in comp.).

2 v. N. 3. पुण्यवान् *pop.* पुण्यवंत,पुण्यसंपन्न,पुण्यशाली, पुण्यात्मक, पुण्यरूप, पुण्य (in comp.), तेजःपुंज, सुकृत, सुकृती, कृतपुण्यपुंज. [गुणसंपन्नता *f.*

MERITORIOUSNESS, *n.* v. A. 1. योग्यता *f.* लायकी *f.* गुणिता *f.*

2 and MERIT. पुण्यसंपन्नता *f.* पुण्यसंपत्ति *f.* पुण्यशालिता *f.*

MERMAID, *n.* जळमाणूस *m. n.* मत्स्यकन्या *f.* ?

MERRILY, *adv.* v. A. ख्यालीखुशालीनें, ख्यालीखुशालीखालीं, मौजांखालीं, मौजामारून, खेळीमेळीं or खेळेंमेळें, नाचतमाशानें, हास्यविनोदाखालीं, दणक्यानें, दणक्याखालीं.

MERRIMAKE, *n. meeting for mirth.* ख्यालीखुशालीची-खुशालीची -&c. बैठक *f.*-&c. गोंधळ *m.* उत्सव *m.* उत्साव *m.* उत्साह *m.* दणका *m.*

MERRIMENT, MERRIMAKING, *n. mirth, festivity, merry pranks, frolic, laughing, &c.* ख्यालीखुशाली *f.* खुशाली *f.* ठट्टामस्करी *f.* हास्य *n.* हंसाबाजी *f.* रागरंग *m.* हास्यविनोद *m.* हास्यरंग *m.* खेळीमेळी *f.* रहस्य *n.* मौजा *f. pl.* कौतुक *n.* रंग *m.* तमाशा *m.* नाचतमाशा *m.* उत्सव *m.* उत्साह *m.* उत्साव *m.*

Tumultuous or boisterous m. धिंबडी *f.* झिंबड *f.* झिंबडी *f.* घमशान *n.* धुमाळी *f.* धुमश्चक्री *f.* धुमकूस *m.* धुमाकूळ *m. f.* धुमड *f.* धुमशा *m.* धुमशान *n.* थैथय्या or थैथैया *m.* थैथयाट or थैथैयाट *m.*

MERRINESS, *n.* v. A. 1. हास्यमुखता *f.* हास्यवृत्ति *f.* उल्लासवृत्ति *f.* उल्लासिता *f.* सानंदता *f.* [&c.

2 खुशमौजेपणा *m.* हसरेपणा *m.* रंगेलपणा *m.* &c. सदानंदिता *f.*

MERRY, *a. exhilarated to laughter, gay, happy, joyful.* हास्यमुख, हसतमुखी or मुख्या, हास्यवदन, हास्यविनोदी, हास्यवृत्ति, उल्लासवृत्ति, खुशवखुत, आनंदी, उल्लासी, रंगी, रंगेल, रंगेला, रंगेली, विनोदी, खुशदिल, हृष्टचित्त, सानंद, आनंदयुक्त, आनंदभरित, हास्यभरित.

To get m. रहस्यांत येणें.

To make m. ख्यालीखुशाली *f.*-&c. करणें.

2—of disposition; *fond of fun and frolic, given to laughter and merriment.* खुशमौज्या, मौज्याळा, मौजी or मौज्या, हसरा, हशा, ख्याली, ख्यालखुशाल्या, आनंदी, सदानंदी, आनंदवृत्ति, उल्लासी, उल्लासवृत्ति, रागरंगी, रंगदार, रंगी, रंगेल, रंगेला, रंगेली, कौतुकी, गमत्या, घमंड्या, चयनी, हास्यबुद्धि, विनोदबुद्धि.

3 *causing laughter or mirth.* विनोदी, विनोदाचा, हास्यविनोदाचा, हास्यजनक, हास्योत्पादक, हास्यकारक, विनोदकारक.

M. stories & jests. चटक्या *f. pl.*

4 *lively, animated,*—a festivity, &c. दणक्याचा, दणदणीत, कडाख्याचा, धडाक्याचा, कडकडीत.

MERRY-ANDREW, *n.* v. BUFFOON. हंडीबाग, भांड, कैकाडी, डोंबारी, Note. The two last words signify *castes* who are tumblers and Merry Andrews.

MERRY-MEETING, *n. meeting for mirth.* ख्यालीखुशालीची-खुशालीची-रागरंगाची-&c. बैठक *f.*-&c. उत्सव *m.* उत्साव *m.* उत्साह *m.*

MERSION. See IMMERSION.

MESARAIC. See MESENTERIC.

MESEEMS, *v. imp.* मला वाटतें, मला भासतें.

MESENTERIC, *a.* v. N. आंतड्यांच्या पिशवीचा, अंत्रपेशीसंबंधी, अंत्रपेशी विषयक.

MESENTERY, *n. membrane of the intestines.* आंतड्यांची पिशवी *f.* अंत्रपेशी *f.* अंत्रावरणत्वक् *f.*

Enlargement of the m. प्लीहा *m.*

MESH, *n. interstice of a net.* जाळीचें भोंक *n.* जाळीची खिडकी *f.*-&c. जालांतर *n.* जालरंध्र *n.*

MESHY, *a. reticulated.* जाळीदार, खिडकीदार.

MESLIN, *n. mixed corn or grain.* धान्याची मिसळ *f.* मिसळीचें धान्य *n.* बेवड *f.* बेरड *f.* खेड *f.* खेडकरधान्य *n.* ससकर *m.* मिश्रान्न *n.* भेलधान्य *n.*

MESNE, *a.*—in Law. मध्यवर्त्ति, मध्यस्थित.

MESS, *n. dish of food.* ठाव *m.* ठाय *m.* पात्र *n.* पान*n.* अन्न *n.*

M. prepared for a number of persons in common. गणान्न *n.*

2 *number of persons eating together and sharing the expense.* बिसी *or* भिसी *f.* मलई *f.* सहभोजनपंक्ति *f.* जग्धिपंक्ति *f.* गणान्नपंक्ति *f.*

3 *pickle, plight, trim, &c.*—of persons, affairs, things. दुर्गति *pop.* दुर्गत *f.* दुर्दशा *f.* गति *pop.* गत *f.* फजिती *f.* फटफजिती *f.* हाल *m. pl.* हालहवाल *m. pl.* हालअपेष्टा *f.* बुरेहाल *m. pl.* हल्ल *m. pl.* बदनकशा *or* नक्षा *m.* चवढव *f.* चबढब *f.* चवचव *f.* ढवढव *f.* बचबच *f.* बच्छानू *f.* परवड *f.* भवाडा *m.* बचेरी *f.* घाण *f.* गुघाण *f.* हबेलंडी *f.* हलबेलंडी *f.* फावडी *f.* गुडाकू *or* खु *f.* गळ्हाटा *or* ठा *m.* घप्पाघोळ *m.* चिवडा *m.* बिपत्त्य *m. pl.*

4 *slop, filth, nastiness, &c.*—freely. घाण *f.* ढाण *n.* तऱ्हाण *n.* चेंद *f.* चेंदाड *f.* चेंदा *m.* चेंदरड *f.* हेंदर *f. n.* चिखल *f.* कर्दम *m.*

5 (of things lying about) v. LITTER. रेंद *f.* रेंदा *m.* राडा *m.* पसळ *f.* पसळण *f.*

6 *squeezed, picked, &c. mass.* चिवडा *m.* विचका *m.* चबढब *f.* कचमा *m.* अवडचिवड *f.* अवडा चिवडा *m.*

To MESS, *v. a. mash, squeeze, &c. make into a mess.* कचंबणें *or* कचमणें, कचमळणें, चिंबडणें *or* चिवडणें, किचवटणें, किचबंदणें, किचविंदणें, किवंचणें, मसदणें, मसंदळणें, मुटकळणें, चिवडा *m.*-&c. करणें *g. of o.*

To MESS, *v. n. eat together sharing the expense.* भिसीनें *or* बिसीनें-भिसींत-&c. जेवणें, सहभोजन *n.*-एकपंक्ति भोजन *n.*-&c. करणें, जग्धि *f.* करणें, वर्गणीचें-भिसीचें-&c. जेवण *n.* करणें.

MESS-MATE, *n. one who messes at the same table.* एकताटी, एकाताटांतला सोबती, भिसीचा सोबती, एकपंक्तीचा, समपंक्तीचा, पंक्तिभाऊ, सहभोजी.

MESSAGE, *n. errand, notice sent.* निरोप *m.* संदेश *m.* संदेसा *m.* सांगणें *n.* प्रेष *m.* दूत्य *n.*

M.-bearing, errand business. लब *f. v.* कर, मार, लबेशाई *f.*

To give a m. निरोप *m.* सांगणें.

MESSENGER, *n. person who carries a message.* निरोप्या, जासूद, हरकारा, कासीद, दूत, चार, कागदी, संदेशहर, वार्त्ताहर, वाचिकहर.

Business or office of a m. जासुदी *f.* जासुदगिरी *f.* दौत्य *n.*

Couple or pair of messengers. जासुदजोडी *f.*

Pay or hire of a m. जासुदी *f.* अजूरा *m.*

To dispatch a m. जासूद *m.*-शिपाई *m.*-&c. फेंकणें.

2 (of a paper kite). जासूद *m.*

MESSIAH, *n.* मशीहा, अभिषिक्त.

MESSING, *n.* v. V. A.—*act.* चिवडणें *n.* कचंबणें *n.* किचवटणें *n.* &c. v. V. N. बिसीचें *or* भिसीचें जेवण *n.* एकान्न जेवणें *n.* गणान्नाचें जेवण *n.* एकान्न *n.* सहभोजन *n.* अन्नव्यवहार *m.* पंक्तिव्यवहार *m.*

MESSUAGE, *a. house and adjoining land.* घरवाडी *f.* गृहवाटिका *f.*

METACARPAL, *a.* v. N. हाताच्या चवड्याचा, करभसंबंधी, करभविषयक.

METACARPUS, *n. the hand from the wrist to the fingers.* हाताचा चवडा *or* चौडा *m.* करभ *m.*

Tumour on the m. बाघचौडा *or* बाघचवडा *m.*

METACHRONISM, *n. chronological error of placing an event after its real time.* न्यूनकालनिरूपण *n.* न्यूननिरूपणिक कालव्यत्यय *m.* न्यूननिरूपितकाल *m.*

METAL, *n.* धातु*m. f.*

Chisel to divide ingots or bars of m. रसखुंटणा*m.*

Factitious m. करणीचा (or ची) धातु*m. f.* कृत्रिमधातु*m.*

Fused m. रस*m.*

Fusing of metals together. आवर्त्तन*n.*

Inferior or secondary m. उपधातु*m.*

M. beaten into a plate or leaf. तकट*n.* तकटें *n.* चकली *f.*

Mass of m. *ingot or wedge.* खोट *f.*

Old m. vessels. नाळ *f.* नाळीक*n.*

That is made of a mixture of metals. पंचरसी, भटोर.—A vessel made of mixed metals. भटोरें*n.*

The metals,—collect. धातुजात*n.* Eight are enumerated. (अष्टधातु). They are सुवर्ण, रौप्य, ताम्र, पित्तल, कांस्य, त्रपु, सीसक, लोह; *or, pop.* सोनें, रूपें, तांबें, पितळ, कांसें, कथील, शिसें, लोखंड.

Waste of metals in fusing. जळ *f.*

2 (for a road) रोडी *f.* उगाळी *f.* खडी *f.*

METALLIC, METALLICAL, *a. belonging, &c. to metals.* धातूचा, धातुसंबंधी, धातुरूप.

2 *made of metal.* धातूचा, धातुमय, धातुरूप, धातुनिर्मित.

METALLIFEROUS, *a. producing metals.* धातूत्पादक, धातुजनक.

METALLINE, *a. impregnated with metal.* धातुधर्मक, धातुगुणक.

2 *consisting, &c. of metal.* धातूचा, धातुमय, धातुनिर्मित.

METALLIST, *n. one skilled in metals.* धातुपारखी *or* ख्या, धातुपरीक्षक, धातुज्ञ, धातुवेत्ता.

2 *worker in metals.* धातूचें काम करणारा, धातुकर्मकारी.

METALLOGRAPHY, *n. account of metals.* धातुवर्णन*n.* धातुविचार*m.*

METALLURGIST, *n. worker in metals.* धातूचें काम करणारा, धातुशोधक, धातुशोधन कर्त्ता.

METALLURGY, *n. art of separating and working metals.* धातुशोधनविद्या *f.* धातुशोधन*n.* धातुपृथक्करण*n.*

To METAMORPHOSE, *v. a. change the form, &c. of.* रूपांतर*n.*-देहांतर*n.*-परिणामांतर*n.*-रूपभेद*m.*-&c. करणें, रूप*n.*-स्वरूप*n.*-&c. फिरवणें-पालटणें *g. of o.*

METAMORPHOSED, *p.* v. V. रूपांतर केलेला, &c. रूपविकृत, &c. विकृताकार, विकृताकृति, विकृत, वैकृत, भिन्नरूप.

METAMORPHOSIS, *n.* v. V. रूपांतर*n.* देहांतर*n.* परिणामांतर*n.* स्वरूपांतर*n.* रूपभेद*m.* स्वरूपभेद*n.* आकारविकार*m.* आकारविकृति*f.* परिणाम*m.* विकार*m.* विकृति *f.*

M. of man into a (tiger, wolf, horse, dog, &c.). करणीचा (वाघ-लांडगा-घोडा-कुत्रा-&c.).

METAPHOR, *n. figurative word.* रूपक*n.* रूपकालंकार*m.* आरोप*m.* उपचार*m.* जहल्लक्षणा *f.* जहत्स्वार्था *f.* उपमा *f.*

METAPHORIC, METAPHORICAL, *a.* v.N. लाक्षणिक, औपचारिक, आरोपाचा, आरोपित, सरूपक.

METAPHRASE, *n. mere verbal translation.* शब्दास शब्द भाषांतर *n.* यथाशब्द भाषांतर*n.*

METAPHRAST, *n. literal translator.* शब्दास शब्द उतरून भाषांतर

करणारा, यथाशब्द भाषांतर कर्त्ता.

Metaphysic, Metaphysical, *a. relating, &c. to metaphysics.* आन्वीक्षिकीसंबंधी, आन्वीक्षिकीविषयक, आन्वीक्षिक्यनुयायी, अर्थतत्वशास्त्रसंबंधी, अध्यात्म विद्यासंबंधी.

Metaphysician, *n.* आन्वीक्षिकीवेत्ता, अर्थतत्ववेत्ता.

Metaphysics, *n. science of the principles and causes of things, science of mind.* आन्वीक्षिकी *f.* अमूर्तविषयविज्ञान*n.* अर्थतत्वशास्त्र*n.* अर्थतत्वविद्या *f.* अध्यात्मविद्या *f.* आत्मतत्वशास्त्र *n.* आत्मतत्वविचार*m.* मानसविद्या *f.*

Metastasis, *n. change of place of a disease.* रोगस्थलांतर*n.*

Metatarsal, *a.* v. N. पायाच्या चवड्याचा, प्रपदसंबंधी.

Metatarsus, *n. part of the foot between the ankle and toes.* पायाचा चौडा *or* चवडा*m.* पाऊलाचा मध्यभाग*m.* प्रपद*n.*

Tumour on the m. वाघचवडा *m. or* डें *n.*

Metathesis, *n. transposition of the letters or syllables of a word.* अक्षरांचा फेरफार *m.* वर्णविपर्यय *m.* वर्णव्यत्यय *m.* वर्णव्यत्यास *m.* अक्षर विपर्यय *m.*

To **Mete,** *v. a.* v. To Measure. मेजणें, मोजणें, मापणें.

Mete-wand, Mete-yard, *n.* मेजकाठी *f.* मानदंड *m.*

Metempsychosis, *n. transmigration.* जन्मांतर *n.* जन्मजन्मांतर *n.* अन्यजन्म *n.*

Meteor, *n. luminous body flying or floating in the atmosphere.* उल्का *f.* तारा *m. f.*—considered as a portent. उत्पात *m.* दिव्य उत्पात *m.* [यक.

Meteoric, *a. belonging, &c.to meteors.* उल्कासंबंधी, उल्काविषयक. 2 *proceeding from a meteor.* उल्केचा, उल्कोद्भव, उल्कोत्पन्न, उल्काजात.

Meteorologic, Meteorological, *a.* v. N. विद्युदुल्कादिविद्येचा, दिव्युद्भवविषयसंबंधी, आकाशोद्भववस्तुसंबंधी.

Meteorology, *n. science of the atmosphere and its phenomena.* विद्युदुल्कादिविद्या *f.* आकाशोद्भववस्तुविद्या *f.* अंतरिक्षोद्भवविषयविद्या *f.* वायुचक्रशास्त्र *n.*

Meteorous, *a. of the nature of a meteor.* उल्काधर्मक.

Meter, *n. measurer.* मापणारा, मापक.

Metheglin, *n.* मधाची दारू *f.*

Methinks, *v. imp.* मला वाटतें, मला भासतें, मला सुचतें.

Method, *n. regular disposition or arrangement,* v. Order. क्रम *m.* अनुक्रम *m.* बेत *m.* व्यवस्था *f.* आनुपूर्वी *f.* आनुपूर्व्य *n.* 2 *order of doing, process,* v. Manner. मार्ग *m.* रीति *f.* रीति *pop.* रीत *f.* क्लृप्ति *f.* पद्धति *f.* क्रिया *f.*

Methodical, *a. that acts with method,* v. Orderly. बेताचा, बेतबाती *or* त्या, व्यवस्थित, नियमाचा *or* नेमाचा, नियमी *or* नेमी, नियमशील, क्रमानुकारी.

2 *arranged in method,* v. Orderly. क्रमाचा, बेताचा, बेताबाताचा, बेतीव, व्यवस्थेचा, नियमाचा *or* नेमाचा, व्यवस्थित, सासमुरत, यथानुक्रम, यथाक्रम.

M. procedure or business. परवडीचें काम *n.*

Methodically, *adv.* v. A. 2. क्रमानें, अनुक्रमानें, बेतानें, &c. यथाक्रमानें, यथाक्रमें, यथानुक्रमें, यथाक्रम, क्रमश :.

Methodicalness, *n.* v. A. 1. व्यवस्थितपणा *m.* व्यवस्था *f.* नियमशीलता *f.* क्रमानुकारिता *f.*

2 क्रम *m.* बेतबात *m.* व्यवस्था *f.* व्यवस्थितपणा *m.* ठाकठिकी *f.* यथानुक्रमता *f.*

Methodism, *n. strictness in religious observances.* नियमनिष्ठा *pop.* नेमनिष्ठा *f.* कर्मठपणा *m.* नियमशीलता *f.* नियमासक्ति *f.* कर्मनिष्ठा *f.*

Methodist, *n. one strict in religious observances.* नियमी *or* नेमी, नियमनिष्ठ *or* नेमनिष्ठ, नेमनिष्ठेचा, नियमशील, कर्मठ.

Methodistical, *a. relating to methodism or methodists.* नेमनिष्ठेचा, कर्मनिष्ठेचा, नियमासक्तीचा.

To **Methodize,** *v. a. bring into method or order.* व्यवस्था *f.* -व्यवस्थापन *n.*-&c. करणें *g. of o.* क्रम *m.*-अनुक्रम *m.*-&c.. बांधणें-रचणें-लावणें *g. of o.* व्यवस्थित-&c. करणें, सुधारणें, सापसारणें.

Methought, *v. imp.* मला वाटलें, मला भासलें, मला दिसलें, &c.

Metonymical, *a.* v. N. अजहत्स्वार्थेचा, अजहल्लक्षणेचा, अजहत्स्वार्थलाक्षणिक, अजहल्लक्षण, अजहल्लाक्षणिक. [&c.

Metonymically, *adv.* v. N. अजहत्स्वार्थेनें, अजहत्स्वार्थेकरून,

Metonymy, *n. use of one word for another.*—in rhetoric. अजहत्स्वार्था *f.* अजहल्लक्षणा *f.*

Metre, *n. measure, verse,* v. Measure. छंद *n.* वृत्त *n.* पद्य *n.* वेद *m.* Some varieties of *metrical composition* are, अभंग, आर्या, आरती, ओवी, ग्रंथ, ध्रुपद, प्रबंध, भुपाळी, लावणी, श्लोक.

Harmonic pause in m. यति *f.*

Violation of the laws of m. छंदोभंग *m.*

Metrical, *a.* v. N. छंदोबद्ध, छंदोविशिष्ट, छंदोरूप, पद्यरूप, पद्यात्मक, स्वरबद्ध, तालबद्ध.

Metropolis, *n. capital city.* मुख्यशहर*n.* राजधानी *f.* राजनगरी *f.*

Metropolitan, *a.* v. N. राजधानीचा, राजधानीसंबंधी.

Metropolitan, *n* .विशपांवरचा मुख्य विशप.

Mettle, *n. pluck, &c.* v. Spirit. रग *f.* धमक *f.* पाणी *n.* कंडी *f.* कंडू *m. f.*

To try the m. of. पाणी *n.* जोखणें *g. of o.* दम*m.*-धूम *f.*-&c. पाहणें *g. of o.*

Mettlesome, Mettled, *a.* v. Spirited. रगदार, रगेल, रग्या, रगीचा, पाणीदार, खंदा, खंक, खंकाळ, तापट, तापड, खेंदडा, जलद, तलख, स्वरमस्त.

Mettlesomeness, *n.* v. A. रगेलपणा *m.* खंदेपणा *m.* रग *f.* मस्ती *f.* स्वरमस्ती *f.* तलखी *f.* खुमखुम *f.* सै *f.*

Meum et tuum. This is expressed by आपपर (आप and अपर *own* and *other*). Accordingly " regard to meum et tuum" and similar phrases will be, आपपरबुद्धि *f.* आपपरभाव*m.* आपपरदृष्टि *f.*-भेद *m.*-लक्ष्य *n.*-विचार *m.*-मत *n.*-वृत्ति *f.*-वर्त्तन *n.*-&c. स्वपरभेद *m.* स्वपरभाव *m.* &c. भेददृष्टि *f.* भेदबुद्धि *f.* दुजाभाव *m.* भिन्नभाव *m.*

Mew, *n. place of confinement.* कोंडी *f.* कोंडवाडी *f.*

To **Mew,** *v. a. shut up.* कोंडणें, कोंडून ठेवणें, कोंडींत घालणें.

To **Mew,** *v. n.*—the cat. म्यांव *or* म्यौ *n.* करणें.

Mew, Mewing, *n.* v. V. N. म्यांव *n.* म्यौ *n.*

The purring m. of a cat. घुरम्यांव *n.*

To **Mewl,** *v. n. cry as a little child.* टेंटें *n.*-केंकें *n.*-ट्याहां *adv.* करणें, टेंटावणें.

Miasm, Miasma, *n. noxious effluvia.* कुजटाण *f.* सडवाण *f.* वायुदूषक पूतिगंध *m.* रोगजनक पूतिवात *m.* पूतिवाष्प *m.*

Mica, *n.* अभ्रक *m. n.*

Dark colored m. काळा अभ्रक.

Grey m. पांढरा अभ्रक.

MICROCOSM, *n. little world.* सूक्ष्मजगत् *n.*

Man is a m. पिंडीं तें ब्रह्मांडीं.

MICROMETER, *n. instrument to measure small spaces.* अल्पांतरमापकयंत्र *n.*

MICROSCOPE, *n.* पदार्थास मोठा दिसवणारें भिंग *n.* सूक्ष्मदर्शक यंत्र *n.* जवळच्या पदार्थास मोठा भासविणारें यंत्र *n.*

MICROSCOPIC, MICROSCOPICAL, *a. belonging &c. to a microsscope.* सूक्ष्मदर्शकयंत्राचा, सूक्ष्मदर्शकयंत्रसंबंधी.

2 *that can be seen only by a m.* सूक्ष्मदर्शक यंत्राच्या योगानें मात्र दिसणारा, अतिसूक्ष्म.

MID, *a.* v. MIDDLE. मध्य, मध्यस्थित, मध्यवर्त्ती.

MID-AGE, *n.* मधलें वय*n.* मधली उमर *f.* मध्यवय*n.* आयुर्मध्य*m.n.*

MID-COURSE, *a.* मार्गार्ध *n.* मार्गमध्य *m. n.*

MID-DAY, *n.* v. NOON. दुपार *f.* मध्याह्न *m.* दिनमध्य *m. n.*

The m.-meal. मध्याह्नचें *n.* मध्याह्नकाळाचें *n.*

To become or be m. सावली *f.* पायांखालीं येणें-असणें.

MID-HEAVEN, *n.* खमध्य *m. n.*

MID-LEG, *n.* जंघामध्य *m. n.*

MID-MOST. See MIDDLEMOST.

MID-NIGHT, *n.* मध्यानरात *or* रात्र *f.* दोनप्रहर रात्र *f.* मध्यरात्र *f.* अर्धरात्र *m. f.* निशीथ*m.*

MID-STREAM, *n.* ओघाचा मध्य *m.* प्रवाहमध्य *m. n.*

MID-SUMMER, *n.* उन्हाळ्याचा मध्य *m.* ऐनउन्हाळा *m.* भरउन्हाळा *m.* ग्रीष्मकालमध्य *m. n.*

MID-TWILIGHT, *n.* सांजेचा मध्य *m. n.* कातरवेळ *f.*

MID-WAY, *n.* अर्धी वाट *f.* निमरस्ता *m.* मार्गमध्य *m. n.* मार्गार्ध *n.*

MID-WAY, *adv.* अर्धेवाटेवर, निमरस्त्यावर, मधेंच.

MID-WINTER, *n.* हिंवाळ्याचा मध्य *m.* ऐन हिंवाळा*m.* भरहिंवाळा*m.* शीतकालमध्य *m. n.*

MID-WOOD, *n.* काष्टमध्य *m. n.*

MIDDLE, *n. central part.* मध्य *m. n.* मधला प्रदेश *m.* माज *m.* मध्यदेश *m.* मध्यभाग *m.* गर्भ *m.* गर्भी *f.*

From the m. मधून.

In the m. मध्यें, मधीं, मध्यत:.

In the very m. मधोमध, मधच्या मध्यें. [धचामधचा.

Of the places or parts about the m. अधील मधील, अ-

MIDDLE, *a. of or belonging, &c. to the middle.* मधचा, मधला, मधील, मध्य, मध्यम, मध्यमीय, मध्यवर्त्ती, मध्यस्थ, मध्यस्थित, गर्भस्थ, गर्भस्थित. [मधिबला.

The m. one—used of brothers and sisters. मधवा,

MIDDLE-AGED, *a.* मध्यवयाचा, मध्यमवयाचा, मध्यमवयी, मध्यवयस्क, मध्यमवयस्क.

MIDDLE-EARTH, *n.* v. WORLD. मध्यलोक *m.* मध्यभुवन *n.*

MIDDLE-MAN, *n.* v. MEDIATOR. मध्यस्थ.

MIDDLEMOST, *a. middle.* मधोमधचा, मधला, मधचा, मध्यस्थ.

MIDDLE-SIZED, *a.* मध्यम आकाराचा, मध्यम आकृतीचा, मध्यमाकार, मध्यमाकृति.

MIDDLING, *a. of middle rank, state, or qualities.* मध्यमप्रतीचा, सामान्यप्रतीचा, साधारणप्रतीचा, मधभरणीचा, मध्यपरिमाणाचा, मध्यम, साधारण, सामान्य, नेमस्त, सुमाराचा, सुमारमाफक, रासबट, राशि, मधलंड, अधलंड मधलंड, अधलंड, अर्धलंड-मर्धलंड, माफक, बराबाईट, छोटेखानी, बादशाहीसा.

MIDDLINGLY, *adv.* v. A. साधारण, सामान्य, मध्यमप्रतीचा *decl.* &c. सामान्यत:, साधारणत:.

MIDGE, *n. gnat, eye-fly.* केंबरें *n.* किंबरूं *n.* घुंगुरटें *or* डें *n.* घुंगरूट *or* घुंगरट *n.* चिलट *n.*

MIDLAND, *a.* v. INLAND. मध्यदेशस्थ, मध्यदेशस्थित.

MIDRIFF, *n.* पोटाचा मधला पडदा *m.* पिंजरोदरमध्यत्वक् *f.*

MIDST, *n.* v. MIDDLE. मध्य *m.*

From the m. मधून.

In the m. मध्यें, मधीं.—As involving the sense of surrounded by, overwhelmed by, involved in, in the thickest part, in the depth, &c. गर्क असतां, गढला-बुडालेला-&c. असतां, भर *or* ऐन with the locative case of the noun.

MIDWIFE, *n. woman that assists at parturition.* सुवीण *or* सुईण *f.* दाई *f.* कोनकरणारी *f.* प्रसवकारिणी *f.*

Man-m. v. ACCOUCHEUR. प्रसवकारीवैद्य.

MIDWIFERY, *n.* सुवीणकाम *n.* सुवीणपणा *m.* दाईपणा *m.* प्रसवकरण *n.* सूतिकरण *n.* गर्भमोचन विद्या *f.*

MIEN, *n. air, look, external appearance, &c.* आकार *m.* डौल *m.* चर्या *f.* चेहरा *m.* मुद्रा *f.* रूप *n.* नूर *m.* ध्यान *n.*ढब *f.* छब *f.* चाल *f.*

MIGHT, *n.* v. FORCE, STRENGTH. बल *pop.* बळ *n.* जोर *m.* जोरा *m.* पराक्रम *m.* सामर्थ्य *n.* तकवा *m.* कुवत *f.* मगदूर *m.*

With m. and main, v. EFFORT. जीव लावून-तोडून-टाकून, मोठ्यादमानें, भरघोसानें, भरल्याघोसानें, भर *or* भरल्या घोसानिशीं, अनर्थ करून, सत्राण, साता सायासांनीं.

To work with m. and main. अनर्थ *m.* करणें-मांडणें.

MIGHTILY, *adv.* v. A. 1. बळानें, बळेंकरून, पराक्रमानें, पराक्रमपूर्वक.

3 *greatly, in a great degree.* फारच, अतिशय, पराकाष्ठेचा *decl.* बळकट, अतोनात *or* अतोनास्त, अनर्थ, अनर्थ करून.

MIGHTINESS, *n.*v.A.1. पराक्रम *m.* जोरा *m.* सबलता *f.* प्रबलता *f.*

2 थोरवी *f.* प्रताप *m.* प्रतापशालिता *f.*

MIGHTY, *a. strong,* v. POWERFUL. बलवान् *pop.* बळवान *or* बळवंत, बळकट, जोरदार, बलिष्ठ, बलाढ्य, पराक्रमी.

2 *great, august, &c.* मोठा, थोर, थोरवीचा, प्रतापी, प्रतापवान्, प्रतापशाली, पराक्रमी, प्रभावशाली.

3 *vast, huge, enormous, excessive, prodigious, &c.*—freely. जबर, जबरा, जबरदस्त, बळकट, भारी, अफाट, अनर्थाचा, कहराचा, कुश्चल, संबीर, खम्माल, प्रचंड, चंड, उद्दट.

4 *important, momentous.* मोठा, भारी, वजनदार, भारदस्तीचा.

MIGHTY, *adv. very,* v. EXCESSIVELY. अति, फारच, पराकाष्ठेचा. *decl.*

To MIGRATE, *v. n. remove for residence from one country, &c. to another.* देशांतर*n.*-स्थानांतर *n.*-&c. करणें, देशांतरीं जाणें, देश *m.*-मुलूख *m.*-&c. पालटणें, ठाणपालट *m.*-धारपालट *m.*-&c. करणें.

MIGRATION, *n.* v. V. देशांतर करणें *n.* &c. देशपालट *m.* ठाणपालट *m.* धारेपालट *m.* देशाटन *n.* देशभ्रमण *n.* देशांतर *n.* दिग्भ्रमण *n.* दिग्भ्रम *m.* विदेशगमन *n.*

MIGRATORY, *a.* v. V. देशांतर करणारा, ठाणपालट करणारा.

MILCH, *a. that gives milk.* दुभता *or* दुपता, दुधाचा, दोग्धा.

M. animals—compreh. दूधदुभतें *n.*

A m. animal that yields her milk to the hand. हातकरीण;—that yields it on having her calf presented, वासुरकरीण;—that yields it on the presentation of food. पान्हवणकरीण.

To become m. again,—a female beast. वळणें.

MILD, *a. gentle, tender, soft, not harsh or severe,*—of persons. गरीब, कोमल or ळ, मऊ, सौम्य, सौम्यवृत्ति, सात्विक, सात्विकप्रकृतीचा, कोमळस्वभावाचा, कोमलस्वभाव, कोमलांतःकरण, नरम, गहीन, मृदु, शांत, थंड, शमी, गोडा, अनुग्र, सामोपचारी, सामोपायी, मिस्कीन, सदय, दयार्द्र. Some terms for *a mild person* are, गाय, केवळ गाय, गायरूं, गोगलगाय, पाण्यापेक्षां शितळ.

2 *lenient, gentle, soft, &c.*—of measures, government, &c. मऊ, नरम, मृदु, सौम्य, सौम्यतेचा, सौम्यपणाचा, दयेचा, सामोपचाराचा, सामोपायाचा, अनुग्र.

M. treatment. राजसी उपचार *m.*

3 *gentle, slight, soft, not violent, &c.*—of qualities. कोमल or ळ, कोवळा, मृदु, मवाळ, सौम्य, संत or संथ, सात्विक, मंद, हलका, गोडा, सत्वगुणी, सत्वगुणक, मृदुवीर्य.

M. cold. गुलाबी थंडी *f.*

M. heat. सरदगर्मी *f.*

MILDEW, *n.* v. BLIGHT. मेकाड *n.* मेकाडा *m.* ताका or टाका *m.* भिरड or भेरड *m.*—To be affected by it. भिरडणें or भेरडणें.

2—as on cloth or paper. चिती *f.*

To be mildewed. सरदणें, सरदावणें.

MILDLY, *adv.* v. A. 1. 2. कोमळपणानें, गरीबीनें, सौम्यतेनें, मृदुत्वानें, कोमलभावानें, &c. मवाळीमवाळीनें, गोडीगुलाबीनें.

2 मंद, हलक्यानें, हळू.

MILDNESS, *n.* v. A. 1. कोमळपणा *m.* मऊपणा *m.* &c. गरीबी *f.* नरमाई *f.* कोमलता *f.* मृदुता *f.* सौम्यता *f.* &c. कोमलस्वभाव *m.* मार्दव *n.* माधुर्य *n.* शांति *f.* थंडप्रकृति *f.* भलाई *f.* भलाइकी *f.* सात्विकप्रकृति *f.* सत्व *n.*

2 मऊपणा *m.* नरमपणा *m.* &c. मृदुता *f.* सौम्यता *f.* अनुग्रता *f.* &c.

3 कोमळपणा *m.* संथपणा *m.* कोवळेपणा *m.* सात्विकपणा *m.* &c. कोवळीक *f.* मवाळी *f.* सत्वगुण *m.* सत्वधर्म *m.* सत्व *n.*

MILE, *n.* कोस or कोश *m.* (varying from 1½ to 3 English miles). मैल *m.* from the English is becoming familiar.

A weary long m. घोड्याच्या पाठीवरचा कोश *m.*

MILESTONE, *n.* मैलाचा दगड *m.* देवारणें *n.* कोशमान पाषाण *m.*

MILIARY, *a. accompanied with an eruption like millet seed,*—fever. मसुन्या ? पिटिकायुक्त.

MILITANCY. See WARFARE.

MILITANT, *a. engaged in warfare.* लढता, लढणारा, युद्धप्रवृत्त, संग्रामप्रवृत्त, युद्धोद्युक्त, युद्धोद्यत, संग्रामोद्युक्त, संग्रामारूढ.

MILITARY, *a. belonging to soldiers or to the profession of arms.* शिपायांचा, शिपाईगिरी, शिपाईगिरीचा, शिपाईच्या पेशाचा, शिपाई *in comp.* लश्करी, लढाईच्या कामाचा, युद्धाच्या कामाचा, युद्धाविषयींचा, युद्धप्रकरणाचा, युद्धविषयक-संबंधी, सैनिक, सांग्रामिक, सामरिक.

M. conduct. क्षत्रधर्म *m.* क्षात्रधर्म *m.*

The m. profession. शिपाईगिरीचा पेशा *m.* शिपाईगिरी *f.* शिपाईपेशा *m.* शिपाईबाणा *m.*

2 *following the profession of arms.* शिपाईच्या पेशाचा, शिपाईगिरीच्या धंद्याचा, आयुधजीवी, शस्त्रोपजीवी.

A m. man. शिपाई.

MILITARY, *n. soldiery, the army.* शिपाईलोक *m. pl.* शिपाई *m. pl.* फौज *f.* शिपाईमंडळ *n.*

To MILITATE, *v. n. be opposed to.* वांकडा-आडवा-विरुद्ध-प्रतिकूल-&c. असणें-येणें, वांकडेपणा *m.*-वैर *n.*-विरुद्धभाव *m.*-&c. असणें *g. of s. recip.*

MILITIA, *n.*—as opposed to regular soldiery. शिबंदी *f.*

Landed m. शेतसनदी शिपाई *m. pl.*

MILK, *n.* दूध *n.* दुग्ध *n.* क्षीर *n.* पय *n.* स्तन्य *n.*

Any m. (given to an infant) as distinguished from milk of the breast वरदूध *n.*

Curdled *m.* डिखळ or डिखूळ *n.*

M. and water. दुधवणी *n.*

M.—as watery. खळखळवणी or कळकळवणी *n.*

M. conglobated or inspissated by boiling. खवा *m.* खोवा *m.* मावा *m.*

M. half coagulated. अदमुरें *n.* गोवें *n.*

M. coagulated firmly and uniformly. चक्का *m.*

M. spiced and given to infants. घुटी *f.*

M. warm from the udder. धारोष्ण *n.*

M.-diet. दुग्धाहार *pop.* दुधाहार *m.*—That is on milk diet. दुग्धाहारी *pop.* दुधाहारी, दुधाधारी.

Pure (i. e. unmixed and unheated) m. निरेंदुध *n.* निरशी or निरसें दूध *n.*

Smell of burned m. वाळगष्ठाण *f.*

Sop steeped in m. for an infant. चिरटोळी *f.*

Sudden spurting forth of m. (from the breast or udder) चीळ *f. v.* फुट.

Thickety m. बासुदी *f.*

That yields m. plentifully. दुधाळ, दुधाळू, बहुदुधी.

That yields m. scantily. अल्पदुधी, मिदुधी, पावशेरी (that gives ¼ of a sher), अधशेरी (½ a sher), नैवेद्याची, गोकर्णी, शंखिनी, होमी.

Vessel for heating m. दुधणी or दुधवणी *f.* दुधाणी *f.* दुधाणें *n.*

To be in m. दुभणें.

To cease to be in m. *to dry.* अटणें, उडणें, विसकणें.

To improve in the quantity of m. दुधास फुटणें.

To fall off in the quantity of m. दुधास तुटणें.

2 *milky or white sap.* दूध *n.* दुग्ध *n.* क्षीर *m.* चीक *n.*

To MILK, *v. a.* दूध *n.*-धार *f.* काढणें-पिळणें *g. of o.* पिळणें, दोहणें, दुहणें, दोहन *n.*-&c. करणें.

To m. from the four dugs. चौखूर दूध काढणें.

MILK-BUSH, *m. euphorbia antiquorum or tirucalli.* शेर *m.* चिकाडा *m.* काड्या or काडेहुरा *m.* काड्यानिवडुंग *m.* हुरा *m.* काडा *m.* निबली or नौली *f.*

Hedge or fence of m. शेरताटी *f.*

A spike of the m. नांगी *f.*

MILK-FEVER, *n.* दुधाचा ताप *m.* दुग्धज्वर *m.*

MILK-LIVERED. See COWARD.

MILK-MAID, *n.* धारकरीण *f.* गवळीण *f.*

MILK-MAN, *n. seller, &c. of milk.* दूधवाला, गवळी, गोप.

MILK-PAIL, *n.* चरवी *f.* धारेचें भांडें *n.* दोहनपात्र *n.*

MILK-PAN, *n.* दुधाचें भांडें *n.*

MILK-POTTAGE, *n.* काला *m.* दूधभाकर *f.*

MILK-SOP, *n. feeble minded person,* v. WEAK. लंडी *f.* दुधखुळा *m.* कुकोचा *m.* रांडमाणूस, रांड्या, मेशपात्र *n.* कन्याराशि.

MILK-TOOTH. दुधाचा दांत *m.*

MILK-WHITE, *a.* v. WHITE. पांढरा सफेद, पांढरा फूल, गोरापान, बगळयाच्या पंखासारखा.

MILK-WOMAN, *n.* दूधवाली *f.* गवळीण *f.* [दोह्य.

MILKABLE, *a.* v. V. पिळायाजोगता-सारखा-&c. दुह्य, दोहनीय,

MILKED, *p.* v. V. पिळलेला, &c. दोहित.

MILKER, *n.* v. V. दूध काढणारा, धार काढणारा-पिळणारा, &c. दोहनकर्त्ता, &c. दोग्धा.

MILKINESS, *n.* v. A. 2. दुग्धसादृश्य *n.* दुग्धधर्म *m.*

MILKING, *n.* v. V.—*act.* धारकाढणें *n.* पिळणें *n.* &c. पिळणूक *f.* पिळणी *f.* दोहन *n.* दोह *m.*

Price of m. दुहणावळ *f.* [निर्मित.

MILKY, *a. made of milk.* दुधाचा, दुधाचा केलेला, दुग्धमय, दुग्ध-

2 *resembling milk.* दुधासारखा, दुग्धसदृश, दुग्धवत्, दुग्धधर्मक.

3 *yielding milk.* दुधाचा, दुधाळ, दुग्धप्रद.

MILKY-WAY, *n. galaxy.* आकाशगंगा *f.* आकाशनदी *f.* देवनदी *f.* सुरनदी *f.* स्वर्गंगा *f.* स्वर्नदी *f.* मंदाकिनी *f.* वियद्गंगा *f.* स्वर्धुनी *f.*

MILL, *n. engine for grinding.* दळण्याचें यंत्र *n.* पेषणयंत्र *n.*

2 *hand-mill.* जातें *n. dim.* जांतुली *f.* चक्की *f.*

Large hand m. घरट *m.* घरटी *f.*

Nether stone of a m. तळखंड *m.*

Ring that binds the handle of a hand-m. विडी *f.* माणी *f.*

To reset or rechisel (a mill) टांकणें.

3 (for oil). घाणा *m.*

Beam of m. to which the beast is yoked. अडाणा *m.*

4 (for sugar cane). चरक *m.* रगाडा *m.*

5 See WATERMILL, WINDMILL.

To MILL, *v. a.* v. To GRIND. दळणें, पिसणें.

2 (coins). छापणें, शिक्का *m.*-ठसा *m.*-छापा *m.*-&c. मारणें-बठवणें, बेटणें *or* बेटव्रणें.

MILL-HORSE, *n.* घाण्याचा बैल *m.* (lit. *ox*).

MILL-STONE, *n.* तळी *f.* पेढ *or* पेड *n.* दृळ *n.*

MILL-TOOTH, *n. grinder.* दाढ *f.*

MILLENARIAN, MILLENARY, *a. consisting of a thousand.* सहस्री, साहस्र, हजारी, सहस्रसंख्याक.

MILLER, *n.* v. V. 1. दळणारा, पिसणारा.

MILLESIMAL, *a. thousandth.* सहस्रांशात्मक, सहस्रांशरूप, सहस्रांशसंबंधी, सहस्रतम.

MILLET, *n. panicum miliaceum.* बरग *m.* बरज *m.* सांवा *m.*

A seed of m. बरग *m.*

MILLINER, *n. maker and seller of women's bonnets, &c.* स्त्रियांच्या टोप्या पट्ट्या इत्यादि करणारा-विकणारा, स्त्रीपरिछदोपजीवी.

MILLINERY, *n. articles made or sold by milliners.* स्त्रियांच्या टोप्यापट्ट्या इत्यादिसामान *n.*

MILLION, *n.* दहालाख *m.* दशलक्ष *m.* प्रयुत *n.*—Ten m. कोटि, कोट, क्रोड, नियुत.—Hundred m. अर्बुद.—Thousand m. महा अर्बुद, अब्ज, अर्ब.—Ten thousand m. खर्ब.—Hundred thousand m. निखर्व, महापद्म.—Million of m. महापद्म.—Ten millions of m. महाशंकु.

Millions upon millions. कोट्यानकोटी, कोट्यवधि,

By tens of millions, *by crores.* कोटिशः.

One of a m. *a man superlatively good.* लाखाचा माणस.

MILLIONAIRE, *n. man with a million.* दाहालाख्या, दशलक्षसंपन्न.

MILT, *n. spleen.* पाणथरी *f.* प्लीहा *m.*

2 (of fishes). मत्स्यवीर्य *n.*

MILTER, *n. male fish.* नरमासा *m.* पुरुषजातीचा मासा *m.*

MIME, MIMER. See MIMIC.

MIMELIC, MIMELICAL. See MIMIC.

MIMIC, MIMICAL, *a. imitative, disposed, &c. to copy.* नकल करणारा, नकल्या, अनुकरणकारी, अनुकारी, अनुकरणशील, अनुकरणस्वभाव, विडबनकारी, संप्रेक्ष्यकारी.

2 *consisting of imitation.* नकलेचा, नकल्या, नकली, अनुकरणात्मक, अनुकरणरूप, विडंबनरूप. [विनोदी.

MIMIC, *n. mime, buffoon.* भांड, नकल्या, मस्कऱ्या, हंडीबाग, राय-

2 v. IMITATOR. नकल करणारा-उतरणारा, ठेव-ठाकी-&c. उतरणारा.

To MIMIC, *v.a. imitate for sport,* v. To MOCK. नकल *f.* उतरणें *g. of o.* ठाकी *f.*-ठेव *f.*-थाकी *f.*-धाटी *f.*-धाटणी *f.*-&c. उतरणें-साधणें-आणणें *g. of o.* उतरणें, वेंटावणें, वांकुल्या *f. pl.*-&c. दाखवणें, विडंबन *n.*-&c. करणें *g. of o.*

MIMICRY, *n.* v. V. नकल *f.* ठाकी उतरणें *n.* &c. वांकुल्या *f. pl.* वेंचकुल्या *f.* वेंकावल्या *f. pl.* अनुकार *m.* अनुकरण *n.* अनुकृति *f.* विडंबन *n.*

MINARET, *n.*—in architecture. मनोरा *m.* शिखर *n.*

MINATORY, *a. threatening.* धमकीचा, डराबणीचा, &c. भयप्रदर्शक, भयसूचक, भयप्रेरक.

To MINCE, *v. a. chop into small pieces.* बारीक बारीक तुकडे *m. pl.* करणें *g. of o.* फोडी *f. pl.*-फोडें *n. pl.*-छिंद *f.* करणें *g. of o.* खुर्चा *f. pl.* पाडणें.

2 *diminish in speaking, extenuate in representation.* टेवून सांगणें, गुळणी धरून-धरून सोडून-मुळमुळीत-अळमळीन-अळमटळम-&c. बोलणें-सांगणें, गुळगुळ थापडीचें बोलणें-गुळगुळथापडी *f.* करणें.

3 (words, &c.). *clip.* खाऊन बोलणें, अर्धोच्चार *m.* करणें.

To MINCE, *v. n. walk affectedly or with nicety.* ठमकणें, नटणें, चमकणें, ठमकत-नटत चालणें, मिजाजीनें-ठमक्यानें चालणें.

2 *speak affectedly or with nicety.* चासतमाखत बोलणें, मिंजाजीनें-डौलानें-&c. बोलणें.

MINCE, *n. thing chopped or minced.* छिंद *f.* फोडी *f. pl.*

To make m. meat of. *fig.* चटणी *f.*-छिंद *f.*-कोशिंबीर *f.*-&c. करून टाकणें *g. of o.*

MIND, *n. understanding, the intellectual power.* मन *n.* चित्त *n.* अंतःकरण *n.* मानस *m. n.* जाणीव *f.* चित्तवृत्ति *f.* चित्कला *f.* चिच्छक्ति *f.* मनोवृत्ति *f.* चिदाभास *m.* सच्चिदंश *m.* पोट *n.* अंतर *n.* अभ्यंतर *n.* ध्यान *n.*—viewed as a *divinity, motive principle,* or *personification* generally, मनदेवता *f.* मनपिंगळी *f.* मनपिंगळा *m.* or jocosely मनुबाई *f.* मनाजीपंत *m.* मनसाराम *m.*

Application of the m. मनोयोग *m.*

Arising into the m. उपस्थिति *f.* स्फूर्त्ति *pop.* स्फूर्त *f.*

Come to a right m. शुद्धीवर आलेला, लब्धचेता.

Ease of m. चित्तसमाधान *n.*

Exercise or working of the m. मनोव्यापार *m.*

Faculty or power of the m. मनोधर्म *m.*

In the recesses of the m. मनच्यामनीं.
Of collected and fixed m. एकचित्त, एकश्चित.
Out of one's m. अव्यवस्थितचित्त, अव्यवस्थितबुद्धि.
Reach of m. मनोगति *f.*
To come to a right m. शुद्धीवर येणें.
To come into one's m. सुचणें, स्फुरणें.
It never entered my m. ध्यानीं मनीं नव्हतें.
There is no testimony like that of one's own m. मनाएवढागाही त्रिभुवनांत नाहीं.
2 *seat of the affections*, v. HEART. मन *n.* अंतःकरण *n.* चित्त *n.* पोट *n.* दिल *m. n.* हृदय *n.* अंतर *n.* अंतरंग *n.* अभ्यंतर *n.* हृद् *in comp.*
Composing the (angry, afflicted, &c.) m. मनसमजावणी *f.* मनसमजाविशी *f.*
Conquest of the m. मनोजय *m.* [मनोविकृति *f.*
Frame or working of the m. चित्तवृत्ति *f.* मनोविकार *m.*
Governing and restraining the m. मनोदंड *m.* मनोनिग्रह *m.* [धांव *f.*
Leaning, bearing or bent of m. मनाची ओढ *f.* मनाची-
Peace or quiet of m. मनश्शांति *f.*
To give the m. (the attention or affection) to. मन *n.* घालणें-देणें-लावणें.
To press or lie on one's m. उरावर बसणें.
3 *liking, inclination, will, pleasure.* मन *n.* मर्जी *f.* खुशी *f.* मरजीचा कल *m.* खातर *f.* मानस *m. n.* मनोरथ *m.* मनोदय *m.* मनोत्साह *m.* इच्छा *f.* वासना *f.* आकांक्षा *f.* बुद्धि *f.* मति *f.* ध्यान *n.* जीव *m.* [चा, मनोनुकूल.
According to one's m. मनासारखा, इच्छेजोगता, खातरी-
Change of m. बुद्धिभेद *m.*
As the m. may incline. मनमानेल तसें.
4 *thoughts, sentiments.* मन *n.* मनोगत *n.* मनोदय *m.* मनोभाव *m.* मत *n.* मनसमजूत *f.* हृदय *n.* हार्द *pop.* हार्द्द *or* हरद्द *n.* हृय *n.* हृद्गत *n.*
Of one and the same m. समभाव, एकचित्त.
Opening the m. पोटउकल *f.*
To break, vent, let out one's m. गुळणी *f.* सोडणें.
To know the m. of. डोळा ओळखणें *g. of o.*
To refrain one's m. गुळणी *f.* धरणें.
5 *intention, determination*, v. DESIGN. मन *n.* मनोरथ *m.* मनोदय *m.* मनोद्देश *m.* [मन *n.*
6 *memory*, v. REMEMBRANCE. आठवण *f.* स्मरण *n.* ध्यान *n.*
Flashing across one's m. स्फूर्त्ति *f.* स्फुरण *n.*
To be out of m. मागें पडणें, आठवण न राहणें *g. of. s.*
To call to m. आठवणें, आठवण *f.*-स्मरण *n.*-संस्मरण *n.*-&c. करणें.
To flash across one's m. स्फुरणें.
To put in m. आठवण *f.*-&c. देणें.
To recur to m. सुचणें, आठवणें. [वणें.
To wipe from the m.—knowledge, a friend, &c. बोल-
To MIND, *v. a. fix the thoughts on, attend to.* मन *n.*-लक्ष्य *n.*-चित्त *n.*-ध्यान *n.*-&c. देणें-लावणें, मनांत-ध्यानांत-&c. आणणें-ठेवणें, मनावर-&c. घेणें-धरणें.
2 *regard with submission, heed.* मानणें, ऐकणें, मान्य करणें, गणणें, विचारणें, जमेस धरणें, धरणें, घेणें, मनावर धरणें, चूज *f.* राखणें.
3 *take care of*, v. To LOOK after. पाहणें, संभाळणें, जोपासणें.
4 See To REMIND.
To MIND, *v. n. incline, be disposed.* मन *n.*-मनधावणी *f.*-&c. असणें *g. of s.* मनदेवता *f.*- मनपिंगळा *m.*-&c. लवणें-वळणें-धावणें *g. of s.*
2 *take heed.* संभाळणें, जपणें, सावध असणें.
Mind! खबरदार.
MINDED, *p.* v. V. N. 1. मनाचा, बेताचा, बेतांतला, &c. प्रवृत्त, प्रवण, मनस्क in comp. as गमनमनस्क.
I.—in compos. मनाचा; as *high minded*, मोठ्या मनाचा.
MINDFUL, *a. attentive, heedful, bearing in mind, observant.* मनांत ठेवणारा-धरणारा, ध्यानांत ठेवणारा, ऐकणारा, मानणारा, सावध, सावधान, सावचित्त. [त्तानें.
MINDFULLY, *adv.* v. A. मन देऊन, ध्यान लावून, सावधान चि-
MINDFULNESS, *n.* v. A. ध्यान *n.* अवधान *n.* भान *n.* आठवण *f.* यादगारी *or* यादगिरी *f.*
MINDLESS. See CARELESS, REGARDLESS.
MINE, *a.* माझा (possessive case of मी), मम (poss. case of अस्मद्), मदीय, मत् (in comp. as मत्पुत्र, मद्गृह, &c.).
MINE, *n.* (of ores, fossils, &c.). खाण *f.* खाणी *f.* खनि *f.* आकर *m.*
2 fig. (of virtues, graces, talents, &c.). See above. *also*, आगर *m. n.* घर *n.* निधि *m. pop.* नीध *f.* आस्पद (in comp. as, गुणास्पद, &c.).
3—in the military art. सुरंग *or* सुरुंग *m.* खोबें *n.* संधि *m.*
To MINE, *v. n. dig a mine.* खाण *f.*-&c. खोदणें-खणणें-उकरणें.
2 *form a burrow.* बीळ *n.* करणें-पाडणें-खोदणें-उकरणें, जमीन *f.* &c. पोखरणें. [पाडणें, खणणें.
To MINE, *v. a. undermine.* सुरंग *or* सुरुंग *m.*-बीळ *n.*-विवर *n.*-&c.
MINER, *n.* (for ores, &c.). खाण खणणारा, बेलदार, खनिकर.
2—military. सुरंग्या *or* सुरंग्या, सुरंगपाड्या.
MINERAL, *n. fossil body.* धातु *m.* उपधातु *m.* खनिजवस्तु *n.* आकारजवस्तु *n.* आकरीयद्रव्य *n.*
The m. kingdom. धातुजाति *f.* धातुजात *f.* धातुकोटि *f.*
MINERAL, *a. produced, &c. in a mine.* खाणींतला, आकरीय, आकरी, आकरज, खनिज, आकरोद्भव.
2 *impregnated with minerals.* धातुगुणक, धातुधर्मक, धातुगुणान्वित, धातुसंसर्गी.
MINERALIST, MINERALOGIST, *n. one versed in minerals.* धातुवादी, धातुवेत्ता, आकरीयद्रव्यपरीक्षक, आकरीयवस्तुवेत्ता.
MINERALOGY, *n. science of minerals.* धातुविद्या *f.* धातुपरिज्ञान *n.* धातुवाद *m.* धातुविचार *m.* आकरीयद्रव्यपरिज्ञान *n.*
To MINGLE, MINGLING, &c. See To MIX, MIXTURE.
MINIATURE, *n. portrait on a small scale.* लहान आकाराची तस्वीर *f.* लघ्वाकारचित्र *n.*
MINIKIN, *a.* v. SMALL. लहानखुरा, लहानआकाराचा, लहानआट्याचा-बांध्याचा-&c. बुटका, बुटारणा, बुटुंगा, गिड्डा, चिलवाण *or* णा.
MINIKIN, *n.* See MINION.
MINIM, *n.*—in music. दीर्घस्वर *m.* [ऱ्हस्वव्यक्ति *f.*
2 *small person or thing.* बुटबैंगण *n.* बुटकुला *m.* ऱ्हस्वमूर्त्ति *f.*
3 v. DROP. थेंब *m.* बुंद *m.*
MINIMUM, *n. the smallest number or quantity in a case.*

कनिष्ठपक्षाची संख्या *f.* अवरसंख्या *f.* कनिष्ठमान *n.*

MINIMUS, *n. being of the smallest size.* अत्यल्पपरिमाणकव्यक्ति *f.*-मूर्त्ति *f.* ऱ्हस्वतम मूर्त्ति *f.*

MINION, *n. obsequious favorite.* कृपेंतली असामी *f.* चिरंजीवांतली असामी *f.* नाकचाबाल *m.* लेंकबळा, बगल्या, पोशा, होयबा, क्रीडामृग *m.*

MINISTER, *n.* See SERVANT. 2 *agent, delegate, official, &c.* कामगार, कामदार, कामकरी, चालवणारा, प्रवर्त्तवणारा, वकील, गुमास्ता, कर्मकर, कार्यसाधक, कार्यनिर्वाहक, कर्मसचिव.

3 (of state or government). कारभारी, राजकारभारी, मंत्री, राजमंत्री, प्रधान, सचिव, अमात्य.

Prime m. दिवाण, दिवाणजी, मुख्यप्रधान, प्रधानमंत्री, प्रधानामात्य, महामंत्री, पट्टाधिकारी, वजीर.

Office or business of a prime m. दिवाणगिरी *f.* प्रधानकी *f.* मुख्यप्रधानकी *f.* वजिरी *f.* वजिरात *f.* पट्टाधिकार *m.*

The eight ministers (अष्टप्रधान) are, अमात्य, दबीर, न्यायाधीश, पंडितराव, मंत्री, राजाज्ञा, सचिव, सुमंत. Note. There are other lists which vary slightly from this.

4 *ambassador.* राजाचा वकील, राजदूत.

5 (of religion). उपाध्याय *pop.* उपाध्या *m.* भट *m.* भटपणा करणारा, याज्ञिक *m.* धर्मकृत्य चालविणारा, सेवेकरी *m.* पाद्री is used by all classes for a Christian minister.

To MINISTER, *v. a.* v. To GIVE, To SUPPLY. देणें, पुरवणें, पुरवणूक *f.*-पुरवणी *f.*-&c. करणें *g. of o.* प्रापण *n.* करणें.

To MINISTER, *v. n. attend on, wait on,* v. To SERVE. चाकरी *f.* करणें-काढणें *g. of o.* सेवा *f.*-शुश्रूषा *f.*-&c. करणें *g. of o.*

2 *supply things needful, give relief to, &c.* चालवणें *with g. of o.* पाहिजे तें पुरवणें, खर्च *m.*-निर्वाह *m.*-&c. चालवणें-पुरवणें *g. of o.* समाचार *m.*-खबर *f.*-&c. घेणें *g. of o.*

3 *perform sacerdotal &c. functions.* उपाधीक *n.*-उपाध्यपणा *m.*-भटपणा *m.*-याज्ञीक *n.*-याज्ञिकी *f.*-&c. करणें.

4 See To ADMINISTER. [अनुवर्त्ती.

MINISTERIAL, *a. attendant, subservient.* उपकारक, उपकारी,

2 *pertaining, &c. to an agent, executive.* काम करणाऱ्याचा, कामकरण्याचा, बजावण्याचा, कामदाराचा, &c. कार्यसाधक, कार्यनिर्वाहक, कार्यप्रवर्त्तक, कर्मकरसंबंधी, कार्यसाधकविषयक.

3 *pertaining, &c. to a minister of state.* प्रधानाचा, मंत्र्याचा, कारभाऱ्याचा, &c. मंत्रिसंबंधी.

4 *pertaining, &c. to a minister of religion.* उपाध्याचा, भटाचा, याज्ञिकाचा, पाद्रीचा, &c. उपाध्यपणाचा, &c. याज्ञिकी.

MINISTRANT. See SERVING.

MINISTRATION, MINISTRY, *n.* v. V. A.—*act.* देणें *n.* पुरवणें *n.* पुरवणी *f.* पुरवणूक *f.* प्रापण *n.* [*f.* शुश्रूषा *f.*

v. V. N. 1. *and* SERVICE. चाकरी करणें *n.* &c. चाकरी *f.* सेवा

I. *office or functions of a minister of state.* प्रधानकी *f.* कारभार *m.* कारभारीपणा *m.* अमात्यपणा *m.* मंत्रीपणा *m.* साचिव्य *n.* मंत्रित्व *n.*

Prime m. v. MINISTER. दिवाणगिरी *f.* पट्टाधिकार *m.*

II. *time of ministration, administration.* कारकीर्द *f.* कारभार *m.* अमल *m.* राजवटा *m.* राजवट *f.*

III. *body of ministers of state.* प्रधानमंडळी *f.* अष्टप्रधान *m. pl.* मंत्रिसमाज *m.*

IV. *office, function, &c. of a minister of religion.* उपाधीक *n.* उपाध्यपण *n.* or पणा *m.* भटपणा *m.* याज्ञीक *n.* याज्ञिकी *f.* याजन *n.*

V. v. AGENCY, INSTRUMENTALITY. करणत्व *n.* कारकत्व *n.*

MINIUM, *n. red lead.* शेंदूर *m.* सिंदुर *m.* सौभाग्य *n.*

MINNOW, *n.* नदींतला एक लहान मासाआहे.

MINOR, *a. less, smaller, inferior.* लहान, लघु, कनिष्ठ, गौण.

M. or weaker side. गौणपक्ष *m.*

Minor, as opposed to major (बुजुर्ग or बुद्रूग), in designating a village &c. is rendered by खुर्द.

2 *inconsiderable, small,* v. PETTY. हलका, लघु, किरकोळ or किरकूळ, एर, अडपडप, आड (prefixed to words as, आडखर्च, आडवाणें, &c.). [&c.). कचा.

3—used of measures (of capacity, weight, distance,

MINOR, *n. person under age.* अप्राप्तव्यवहार, अजातव्यवहार, अज्ञातव्यवहार, अप्राप्तकाल, क्रियाबाल, व्यवहारायोग्य, बाल, किशोर.

2 (in logic). उपनय *m.* उत्तरपक्ष *m.*

MINORITY, *n. state of a minor.* बालावस्था *f.* बालदशा *f.* शैशव *n.* अप्राप्तव्यवहारता *f.* अप्राप्तव्यवहारदशा *f.*

2 *lessness.* न्यूनता *f.* न्यूनत्व *n.*

3 *the smaller number.* लहान-&c. संख्या *f.* अर्धोनसंख्या *f.* अल्पपक्षमंडळी *f.* अल्पपक्ष *m.* This sense is often best rendered by varying the construction; as, त्या सभेंत हिंदू थोडे होते or त्या सभेंत हिंदूंचा जमाव थोडा होता. The Hindus were in a minority in that meeting.

The m. must be ruled by the majority. घरासारखा पाहुणा होतो पाहुण्यासारखें घर होत नाहीं.

MINOTAUR, *n. a being half man half bull.* म्हैसासूर *m.* नरसिंह (half man half lion).

MINSTREL, *n. a singer and player.* वैतालिक *m.* वादित्रगायक, वादित्रगायक, मागध.

2 See MUSICIAN.

MINT, *n. mentha sativa.* पुदिना *m.* [टांकसाळ *f.*

2 *place where money is coined.* टंकशाला *pop.* टंकसाल or

Fresh from the m. घणकोरा, घणाखालचा.

To MINT. See To COIN.

MINT-MASTER, *n.* टांकसाळ्या, टंकशालाध्यक्ष, टंकशालाधिकारी.

MINUS, *n.*—in algebra. क्षय *m.* ऋण *n.*

To be m. *come short of, lose.* खालतें or खालीं येणें, हलका होणें. [क्षुद्र, तनु.

MINUTE, *a.* v. LITTLE, SMALL. लहान, अल्प, बारीक, सूक्ष्म,

2 *attending to small things, particular,*—of persons. बारीक पाहणारा, सूक्ष्मदृष्टि, सूक्ष्मदर्शी, अल्पदृष्टि, सूक्ष्मद्रष्टा.

3—of examination, inquiry, &c. बारीक, सूक्ष्म, बारीकमोठ्याचा, लहानमोठ्याचा, बारकाईचा, छडाछडीचा.

MINUTE, *n. sixtieth part of an hour.* पल *pop.* पळ *n.* is the 60 th part of a घटिका or Indian hour, of which 2½ go to an English hour, so that अडीच पळें *n. pl.* or 2½ *pals* are equal to a minute. क्षणपाद *m.* क्षणचतुर्थांश *m.* (क्षण is equal to 30 कला or 4 minutes).

2 *small portion of time*—gener. क्षण *m.* पळ *n.* लहम *f. n.* लहज *m.* निमिष *m.* निमेष *m.*

A m. afterwards. क्षणांतर *n.*

3 (of a degree). कला *f.*

4 *note or memorandum of.* टांचण *n.* टिपण *n.* याद *f.*
5 *written expression of opinion.* शेरा *m.* स्वमतलेख *m.* स्वाभिप्रायलेख *m.*

To MINUTE, *v. a. note, make memorandum of.* टांचणें, टिपणें, टांचून-टिपून ठेवणें-घेणें.

MINUTELY, *adv.* v. A. 2. 3. बारकाईनें, बारीकदृष्टीनें, सूक्ष्मदृष्टीनें, केसानकेस, बालबाल, काडीनकाडी, तिळानतीळ, सड्यानसडा, सडानसडा.
I. v. CIRCUMSTANTIALLY. तपसीलवार.

MINUTELY, *adv.* v. N. *at every minute.* क्षणोक्षण, क्षणोक्षणीं, प्रतिक्षणीं, दरक्षणास.

MINUTENESS, *n.* v. A. 1. बारीकपणा *m.* बारकाई *f.* बारकावा *m.* सूक्ष्मता *f.* सौक्ष्म्य *n.* अल्पता *f.*
2 बारीकपणा *m.* बारकाई *f.* सूक्ष्मता *f.* बारीकदृष्टि *f.* सूक्ष्मदृष्टि *f.*

MINUTIÆ, *n. the smaller particulars.* बारीकगोष्टी *f. pl.* बारीकविचार *m. pl.* सूक्ष्मविचार *m. pl.* अंडींपिलीं *n. pl.* वर्मेंकर्में *n. pl.*

MINX, *n. pert, forward girl.* नाचरी पोर *f.* चंचुबाग मुलगी *f.* बडलाई *f.* बडलाबाई *f.* मानम्हातारी *f.*

MIRACLE, *n. wonder, act or effect beyond human power.* चमत्कार *m.* अद्भुतकर्म *n.* करामत *f.* अमानुषकर्म *n.* देवकृति *f.* देवकृत्य *n.* निसर्गातीतकर्म *n.* प्रकृत्यतीतकर्म *n.*

MIRACULOUS, *a. supernaturally performed.* अद्भुतकर्माचा, करामतीचा, देवकृत्याचा, देवकृतीचा, अद्भुत, अमानुषशक्तिसाधित.
2 *competent to work miracles.* अद्भुतशक्तिक, अमानुषशक्तिक, अद्भुतकारी, अमानुषकर्मकारी.

MIRACULOUSLY, *adv.* v. A. 1. देवकृतीनें, देवकृत्यानें, अमानुषश- [क्तीनें.

MIRAGE, *n.*—the optical illusion. मृगजल *n.* मृगतृष्णा *f.* जलाभास *m.* चित्र *n.*

MIRE, *n.* v. MUD. चिखल *m.* रेंदा *m.* चेंदा *m.* गाळ *m.* रेबड *f.*

MIRINESS, *n.* v. A. चिडचीड *f.* चिबचीब *f.* चिगचीग *f.* चिखल *f.* चेंदाड *f.*

MIRROR, *n. looking glass.* आरसा *m. dim.* आरसी *f.* दर्पण *m. n.* [आदर्श *m.*
2 *pattern, exemplar.* आदर्श *m.* कित्ता *m.* नमुना *or* नमोना *m.* सांचा *m.*

MIRTH, *n.* v. MERRIMENT. हास्य *n.* हसाबाजी *f.* हास्यक्रीडा *f.* हास्यविनोद *m.* ठट्टामस्करी *f.* परिहास *m.*

MIRTHFUL, *a.* v. MERRY. हसतमुखी, हास्यमुख, हशा, खुशमौजा, रंगी, रंगदार, हास्यविनोदाचा.

MIRTHLESS, *a. without mirth, &c.* बेरंगी, बेरंग, उदास.

MIRY, *a.* v. MUDDY. चिडचिडीत, चिडचिडा, चिखलाचा, रेंद्याचा, रेबडीचा, &c. रबरबीत, सकर्दम.
M. and sticky. पेंडबळना, चिगचीग.

MIS. This prefix is rendered by गैर, कु, दुर्, &c. as in the examples that follow.

MIS-ACCEPTATION, *n. understanding wrongly.* गैरसमजूत *f.* असमजूत *f.* विपरीतग्रह *m.* विपरीतग्रहण *n.* अन्यथाग्रह *m.*

MIS-ADVENTURE, *n. mishap,* v. CALAMITY. अवचट *n.* अनिष्टापात *m.* अनर्थापात *m.* आपत्ति *f.*

MIS-ADVISED, *a.* कुमंत्रित, कूपदिष्ट.

MIS-AFFECTED, *a. ill-disposed,* v. ADVERSE. आडवा, विपरीत, विमना, विमनस्क, असख.

To MIS-ALLEDGE, *v. a. state erroneously.* गैरवाका *m.*-गैरहकिकत *f.*-भलतावाका *m.*-&c. सांगणें-समजावणें, अन्यथाकथन *n.*-विपरीतकथन *n.*-&c. करणें. [किकत *f.*

MIS-ALLEGATION, *n. erroneous statement.* गैरवाका *m.* गैरह-

MIS-ALLIANCE, *n. improper association.* दुःसंबंध *m.* कुसंबंध *m.* अयुक्तसंबंध *m.*

MISANTHROPE, MISANTHROPIST, *n. hater of mankind.* जनशत्रु, जगवैरी, जगतूशत्रु *pop.* जगशत्रु, विश्वशत्रु, जनद्वेष्टा, विश्वद्रोही.

MISANTHROPIC, MISANTHROPICAL, *a.* v. N. माणुसगंध्या, माणुसगंधारा, माणुसघाण्या, नसनसखडा, एकलकोंट, एकलकोंडा, पुरुषद्वेषी, जनद्वेषी, विश्वद्वेषी, सर्वद्वेषी, जननिंदक, जनापकारबुद्धि.

MISANTHROPY, *n. hatred to mankind.* माणसाची घाण *f.* माणसाचा कंटाळा *m.* जनद्वेष *m.* विश्वद्वेष *m.* जगत्द्वेष *pop.* जगद्वेष *m.* विश्वद्रोह *m.* मनुष्यत्रास *m.* जनापकारबुद्धि *f.*

MISAPPLICATION, *n.* v. V. असत्प्रयोग *m.* असद्विनियोग *m.* असद्व्यय *m.* अन्यथाव्यय *m.*

To MISAPPLY, *v. a. apply to wrong purposes.* प्रयोग *m.*-खर्च *m.*-&c. अन्यथा करणें *g. of o.* बेजाखर्च *m.* करणें *g. of o.* असत्प्रयोग *m.*-असद्व्यय *m.*-अन्यथाव्यय *m.*-&c. करणें *g. of o.*

To MISAPPREHEND, &c. See To MISUNDERSTAND, &c.

MISAPPROPRIATION, *n.* असद्विनियोग *m.* अन्यथाविनियोग *m.*

To MISBECOME, *v. a. not to become, to suit ill.* न शोभणें, न साजणें, हिणवणें, अयोग्य-नालायक-विशोभित-&c. असणें *in. con.* विशोभा *f.*-&c. आणणें.

MISBECOMING, *a.* अयोग्य, अनुचित.

MISBEGOT, MISBEGOTTEN, *a.* v. BASTARD. शिंदळकीचा, व्यभिचाराचा, जारज, कुजन्मा, कुजात, अशास्त्रजात.

To MISBEHAVE, *v. n.* गैरशिस्त-गैरचाल-गैरचालीनें-&c. चालणें, बदचाल *f.*-दुराचार *m.*-दुराचरण *n.*-&c. करणें.

MISBEHAVED, *a. ill-behaved, rude.* गैरचालीचा, कुचालीचा, बेचालीचा, &c. गैरशिस्त, गैरसाळ, अशिस्त, दुराचरणी, दुराचारी, अनाचारी, दुर्वृत्त, अन्यथाकारी, अन्यथाचारी, दुर्णीत, दुर्विनीत.

MISBEHAVIOR, *n.* v. MISCONDUCT. बेचाल *f.* गैरचाल *f.* बदचाल *f.* कुचाल *f.* गैरचलन *n.* दुराचरण *n.* दुराचार *m.* दुश्चरित *n.*

MISBELIEF, *n. erroneous belief.* असत्श्रद्धा *f.* अन्यथाश्रद्धा *f.* कुश्रद्धा *f.* असद्धर्मश्रद्धा *f.*

MISBELIEVER, *n.* v. N. असत्श्रद्धाकारी, अन्यथाश्रद्धाकारी.

To MISCALCULATE, *v. a.* गणतींत-बेरजेंत-हिशोबांत-आकारांत-&c. चूक *f.* करणें-चुकणें-बहकणें-&c. चुकीचा-गैरबेताचा-&c. गणणें-आकारणें-&c.

To MISCALL, *v. a. name wrongly.* चुकून-चुकीनें-भ्रांतीनें-चुकीचा-&c. म्हणणें, चुकीचें नांव *n.* देणें.

MISCARRIAGE, *n.* v. MISCONDUCT. दुराचरण *n.* दुराचार *m.* असदाचरण *n.* कदाचार *m.*
2 *failure, unfortunate event.* असिद्धि *f.* फसाव *m.* फसगत *f.* विचका *m.* कार्याची अनुपपत्ति *f.* कार्यविपत्ति *f.*
3 v. ABORTION. गर्भपात *m.* दुवेत *n.* गर्भपतन *n.* गर्भस्राव *m.* गर्भस्रव *m.* Note. To the fourth month it is गर्भस्राव *m.* from the fourth month गर्भपात *m.*

To MISCARRY, *v. n. not to succeed,* v. To FAIL. फसणें, लटपटणें, वाहवणें, गळ्हाटणें, फिसकणें, फिसकटणें, हरणें, खचणें, रेवणें, शेवटास-&c. न जाणें, फसगत *f.*-फसाव *m.*-&c. होणें *g. of s.*
2 *have abortion.* दुवेतणें, नासावणें, गर्भस्राव *m.*-गर्भपात *m.*-&c. होणें *g. of s.* उमळणें *or* पोटचें उमळणें *g. of s.* पोटचें पडणें *g. of s.*

3—as used of cattle. गाभाटणें, गाभडणें, गाभसांडणें, गाभ *m.* सांडणें-टाकणें. [करधान्य *f.*

MISCELLANE, *n. mixed grain*, v. MESLIN. बेरड *f.* खेड *f.* खेड-M. of rice and pulse. खिचडा *m.*

MISCELLANEOUS, *a. composed of various kinds.* अनेक प्रकारचा, अनेक जातीचा, जिन्नसवार, नानाविध, अनेकविध, नानाविषयक, अनेकजातीय, विजातीय, संकीर्ण, प्रकीर्ण, सान्निपातिक.—with the implication of pettiness and indeterminateness. किरकोळ, ऐलपैल *or* अईलपईल, अवांतर, किता, अगडबगड, अगडतगड, अडपझडप, चिल्हड *or* चिल्हड.

M. or minor profits. अवांतर प्राप्ति *f.* अवांतर मिळकत *f.*

MISCELLANEOUSNESS, *n.* v. A. संकीर्णता *f.* प्रकीर्णता *f.*

MISCELLANY, *n. miscellaneous collection or mass.* अनेकवस्तूंचा संग्रह *m.* अनेकसंग्रह *m.* नानाविषयकसंग्रह *m.* मिसळा *m.*—with an implication of trumperiness. अगडतगड *n.* अगडबगड *n.* सट्टरफट्टर *n.* खटर पटर *n.*

Miscellanies, *sundries.* ऐलपैलवस्तू *f. pl.*

2—book, &c. अनेकसंग्रहग्रंथ *m.* प्रकीर्णग्रंथ *m.* प्रकीर्णक *n.* प्रकीर्ण *n.*

MISCHANCE. See MISFORTUNE.

MISCHIEF, *n. harm, injury, damage*, v. HURT. नुकसानी *f.* खराबी *f.* वाईट *n.* अपकार *m.* अपाय *m.* हानि *f.* क्षति *f.*

2 *harm, injury*—as designed. घात *m.* घातपात *m.* अरिष्ट *n.* द्रोह *m.*

3 *ill, evil, vexatious affair.* वाईट गोष्ट *f.* वाईट *n.*

MISCHIEF-MAKER, *n.* v. INCENDIARY. आगलाव्या, कळलाव्या, कज्जेदलाल, खेळ्या, खजाल.

MISCHIEF-MAKING, *n. exciting quarrels.* कळलावणी *f.* लावालाव *f.* मित्रभेद *m.* सुहृद्भेद *m.* खजाळी *f.* कुचोद्य *n.*

MISCHIEVOUS, *a. noxious, injurious*, v. HURTFUL. अपकारी, अपकारक, बाधक, अहितकारी, अहितकारक.

2 *injurious, making mischief, inclined to evil.* घातक्या, घातक, घातकी, घातुक, घातपाती, अपकारी, अपकारक, नासरा, नाशा, नासाड्या, उपद्रवी, अवगुणी, खेळ्या, अनिष्टकारी, कुचाळ, कुटाळ, कुटिल, कुटील, खजाळ, नाठाळ *or* नाट्याळ, द्रोही, द्रोहबुद्धि, अपकारबुद्धि, अहितबुद्धि. Some terms and phrases for a *mischievous person* (a malignant mischief maker) are, कंटक, दाहावाग्रह, दशम ग्रह, ग्रह, कुचोद्याचें पांसरूं.

3 This word in the sense of *disordering, injury-doing*, and *trouble giving*, is constantly, and with amplifying mind and angry emphasis, applied to children. Closely corresponding with it in sense, intention, and in application, are the following words in *Maráṭhí*. For words therefore and combinations answering to *prankish, roguish, wild and wanton, set upon tricks and mischief, full of rude freaks and frolics, &c.* the student is to seek here. चेष्टेखोर, चेष्टेबाज, खोडकर, छंदी, छंदिष्ट, छांदिष्ट, छांदस, कुचेष्टखोर, खोटसाळ, टवाळ, टवाळखोर, द्वाड, इब्लत, टारगा, टार, टोर, तंताळ, चारगट, उत्पाती, दुर्गुणी, अचपळ, झटेल, झटेली, चाळक, कारटा, कारटापोरटा, ढंगी, ढंग्या, विजवटा, धांदली, धांदल्या, व्रात्य, स्वतछंदी, अपस्मारी, उपदव्यापी, उपसळा, विपसळा, अवचित्या, अवचिंद, अवचिंद्या. Here also are collected the terms and phrases conveying the sense *A mischievous child*, and agreeing with *plague, pest, imp, urchin, troublesome brat, &c.* अवतार, अवतारी, धाड *f.* अतत्यायी, विजवटा, विजात, आडजात, अपस्मार, पलिस्त, जिवंतपिशाच, खवीस, उपाधव्याधि, अवधात, व्यतीपात, व्यतीपातावर झालेला, कुलनाश, जन्मकुऱ्हाड, जन्मांतरींचा वैरी, चूड, विस्तव, खूळ.

Mischievous tricks or arts. चेष्टा *f.* कुचेष्टा *f.* ढंग *m.* कुढंग *m. pl.* कुचोदी *f.* चाळा *m.* द्वाडचाळा *m.* छंद *m.* छंदफंद *m.* छंदविछंद *m.* मस्ती *f.* उत्पात *m.* थेर *m. n.* अरिष्ट *n.* टवाळी *f.* टवाळकी *f.* अवाडाव *f.*

MISCHIEVOUSNESS, *n.* v. A. 1. अपकारीपणा *m.* बाधकपणा *m.* अपकारिता *f.* बाधकत्व *n.*

2 घातकेपणा *m.* घातकपणा *m.* अपकारीपणा *n.* नासरेपणा *m.* &c. कुचालकी *f.* कुटाळकी *f.* कुटाळी *f.* कुचाली *f.* द्रोहबुद्धि *f.* अपकारबुद्धि *f.*

MISCIBILITY, *n.* v. A. मिसळायाजोगेपणा *m.* &c. मिश्रणीयता *f.* मिश्रणार्हता *f.* मिश्रणयोग्यता *f.*

MISCIBLE, *a. fit, possible, &c. to be mixed.* मिसळायाजोगा-जोगता-&c. मिश्रणीय, मिश्रणार्ह, मिश्रणयोग्य.

MISCOMPUTATION, *n.* चुकीचा-भ्रांतीचा-चुकभुलीचा आकार *m.*-&c.

MISCONCEIT, MISCONCEPTION, *n.* v. V. *and* MISUNDERSTANDING. गैरसमजूत *f.* असमजूत *f.* विपरीतग्रह *m.* विपरीतग्रहण *n.* असद्ग्रह *m.* अयथार्थबोध *m.* अन्यथाबोध *m.* भ्रम *m.* भ्रांति *f.* भ्रमज्ञान *n.* भावाभास *m.*

To MISCONCEIVE, *v. a. have a false notion of*, v. To MISUNDERSTAND. गैरसमजूत *f.*-उलटीसमजूत *f.*-अन्यथाबोध *m.*-&c. असणें *in con. with g. of s. and* विषयीं *or g. of o.* उलटा *de.l.* -विपरीत-&c. समजणें.

To MISCONDUCT, *v. a.* v. To MISMANAGE. वाईट रीतीनें-&c. वहिवाटणें-वापरणें-चालवणें, गैरवहिवाट *f.*-असन्निर्वाह *m.*-&c. करणें *g. of o.*

2 (one's self) *behave ill.* गैरचाल *f.*-कुचाल *f.*-बदचाल *f.*-&c. करणें, गैरचालीनें-गैररीतीनें-कुमार्गानें-&c. चालणें- वागणें, गैरचाल *adv.*-बेचाल *adv.*-&c. चालणें, दुराचरण *n.*-दुराचार *m.*-असदाचार *m.*-&c. करणें.

MISCONDUCT, *n.* v. V. 1. *and* MISMANAGEMENT. गैरवहिवाट *f.* गैरचालवणें *n.* दुर्नयन *n.* असन्निर्वाह *m.* अन्यथाकरण *n.*

2 *ill behaviour.* गैरचाल *f.* बदचाल *f.* कुचाल *f.* गैरचलन *n.* गैरवर्त्तणूक *f.* बदकर्म *n.* बदअमल *m.* दुराचरण *n.* दुराचार *m.* असदाचरण *n.* असदाचार *m.* अनाचार *m.* कदाचार *m.* दुर्वृत्ति *f.* दुर्नय *m.* दुर्नीति *f.* अन्यथाचार *m.* अन्यथाचरण *n.*

MISCONJECTURE, *n.* चुकीची-भ्रांतीची-भुलीची-&c. अटकळ *f.*

MISCONSTRUCTION, *n.* v. V. गैरसमजूत *f.* उलटीसमजूत *f.* विपरीतग्रह *m.* विपरीतग्रहण *n.* अन्यथाग्रह *m.* अन्यथाबोध *m.*

To MISCONSTRUE, *v. a. interpret or understand erroneously.* अर्थ *m.*-भाव *m.*-उलटा समजणें-घेणें, गैरसमजूत *f.* घेणें, विपरीतग्रह *m.*-विपरीतग्रहण *n.* करणें, गैरसमजूत *f.* होणें *g. of o. with in. con.* उलटा-विपरीत-&c. समजणें-जाणणें.

To MISCOUNT, *v. a.* मोजण्यांत-&c. चूक *f.* करणें-चुकणें.

MISCREANCE, *n. misbelief.* असत्श्रद्धा *f.* असद्धर्मश्रद्धा *f.* कुश्रद्धा *f.* अन्यथाश्रद्धा *f.*

MISCREANT, *n.* See INFIDEL, HEATHEN. 2. *vile wretch.* देवलंड, पितृलंड, दुरात्मा, दुर्जन, खल, कुटिल, शठ.

MISDEED, *n.* v. CRIME. कुकर्म *n.* दुष्कर्म *n.* दुष्कृति *f.* बदकर्म *n.*

अकर्म *n.*

To MISDEEM. See To MISJUDGE.

To MISDEMEAN. See To MISCONDUCT, 2.

MISDEMEANOR, *n.* v. MISCONDUCT. दुराचरण *n.* दुराचार *m.* असदाचरण *n.* असदाचार *m.* [तकशीर *f.*

2 *a m. slight offence*, v. FAULT. चूक *f.* चुकी *f.* गुंजावीस *f.*

MISDEVOTION, *n.* असद्भक्ति *f.* अन्यथाभक्ति *f.* भ्रांतीची भक्ति *f.*

To MISDIRECT, *v. a. direct wrongly.* चुकीचा मार्ग *m.* सांगणें, अन्यथामार्गप्रदर्शन *n.*-विपरीतमार्गप्रदर्शन *n.* करणें.

2 (a letter). चुकीचा पत्ता *m.* लिहणें.

MISDOER, *n.* v. CRIMINAL. कुकर्मी, दुष्कर्मी, अन्यायकारी, अन्यथाकारी, अन्यथाचारी.

MISDOING, *n.* v. CRIME. दुष्कर्म *n.* कुकर्म *n.*

To MISEMPLOY, *v. a. employ to no purpose, or to a bad purpose.* घालवणें, व्यर्थ घालवणें, असत्प्रयोग *m.*-असदूव्यापार *m.*-असदूव्यय *m.*-असतूक्षेप *m.*-असदूप्रक्षेप *m.*-&c. करणें.

MISEMPLOYMENT, *n.* v. V. घालवणें *n.* असत्प्रयोग *m.* कुप्रयोग *m.* असदूव्यापार *m.* कुव्यापार *m.* असदूव्यय *m.* असदूविनियोग *m.* असत्क्षेप *m.* असदूप्रक्षेप *m.*

MISER, *n.* v. MISERLY. कृपण, दानशत्रु, अदाता, अदत्त, कदर्य *and* कदर्यु *pop.* कद्रू. In the sense of this word, and with the implication and power of *catch-penny, skin-flint, close-fist, love-gold, scrape-penny, pinch-penny, pinch-fist, hunks, pelter, grip-groat, mammonist, churl, curmudgeon, niggard, snudge*, and numberless similar formations, are numerous and equally expressive formations in *Marâthi.* कौडीटंक, कौडीचुंबक, कौडीपूत, दमडीपूत, दामचुंबक, लोहचुंबक, कंजूस, झारेकरी, सोनार, सराफ, किडेमारी, माशी चोखणारा, कर्णाचा अवतार, उदारकर्ण, कर्ण, वेरूळचा निचाड्या, मड्याचे टाळूचें लोणी खाणारा, गाडगेंधुऊन कढी करणारा, आंगचें पाप न देणारा, आंगचा मळ न देणारा, हा पाप देणार नाहीं पुण्य कोठून देणार, हा चमडी देईल पण दमडी देणार नाहीं.

The prince of misers. अदत्तांचा राजा, अदत्तशिरोमणी, अदत्तशिखामणी.

MISERABLE, *a. unhappy*, v. WRETCHED. दुःखी, दुःखाचा, दुःखांत पडलेला, आपदूग्रस्त, विपदूग्रस्त, विपत्प्राप्त, दुःखापन्न, दुरवस्थ, दुर्दशापन्न, आपन्न, विपन्न.

2 *paltry, trumpery, poor, mean, &c.* v. WORTHLESS. खराब, नाकारा, नादान, फुसका, फुसकुला, फाटका, यारदा, यारदी, एर, एरशेर, मुडदार *or* मुरदाड, कुत्सित, आकिंचित्कर, किलवाणा *or* णी.

3 *despicable, worthless, mean,*—of persons. हलका, पाजी, हलकेयोग्यतेचा, हलकेकिंमतीचा, हुचा, हीन, अधम, कृपण, भिकार, भिकारी, किलवाणा *or* णी.

MISERABLENESS. See MISERY.

MISERABLY, *adv. meanly.* भिकारपणानें, भिकार रीतीनें.

MISERLINESS, *n.* v. A. कृपणपणा *m.* चिकटपणा *m.* चिकटेपणा *m.* किरटेपणा *m.* चप्पूपणा *m.* &c. कृपणत्व *n.* कार्पण्य *n.* कार्पण्यबुद्धि *f.* कृपणबुद्धि *f.* कृपणभाव *m.* अदातृत्व *n.* बारीकदृष्टि *f.* बारीकनजर *f.* व्ययद्वेष *m.* वित्तशाठ्य *n.*

MISERLY, *a. covetous, niggardly, parsimonious.* कृपण, किचटा, लोभी, लोभिष्ट, चिकण, चिकट, चिकटा, चिकू, चप्पू, चक्कू, किरटा, केड, केवटा, केवटी, कद्रू, दरिद्री, हाताचा जड, जड हाताचा, हाताचा चिकट, मिटमिट्या, मिटमिटीत, नजीस, नजूस, फिरमाडी, किडमाकडा, हिमटा *or* ट्या, हिमटी, हिचुटा, ओंढीक, बारीक पाहणारा, बारीकदृष्ट्या, अदाता, अदत्त, अनुदार, छट, शठ, वित्तशठ, दृढमुष्टि, बद्धमुष्टि, अव्यय, अवेच, व्ययशत्रु, व्ययशंकित, अल्पदृष्टि, दातृत्वहीन, हीनदातृत्व, दानभीरु, कदर्य, कीकट, नतद्रूस, किंपच, किंपचान.

MISERY, *n. distress*, v. WRETCHEDNESS, TROUBLE. दुःख *n.* दुखीपणा *m.* कष्ट *m. pl.* हाल *m. pl.* हालहवाल *m. pl.* हालअपेष्ट *f.* अकल्याण *n.* दुःखावस्था *f.* दुर्दशा *f.* आपत्ति *f.* आपदा *f.*

2 *a m. cause of wretchedness*, v. CALAMITY. दुःख *n.* विपत्ति *f.* आपत्ति *f.* आपदा *f.* अनिष्ट *n.* अरिष्ट *n.*

MISFORTUNE, *n. ill fortune.* दुर्दैव *n.* दुर्भाग्य *n.* निर्दैव *n.* कुभाग्य *n.* अरिष्ट *n.* अशुभ *n.* कंबख्ती *f.*—as personified. अलक्ष्मी *f.* अबलक्ष्मी *f.* अवदसा *f.* अकाबाई *f.* महामाया *f.* विंबशी *f.* नरकदेवता *f.*

Sign or token of m. अवदसचिह्न *n.* [*m.*

The rounds or general visitation of m. अकाबाईचा फेरा

2 *a m. a disaster, &c.* v. CALAMITY. विपत्ति *f.* आपत्ति *f.* विपदा *f.* आपदा *f.* आपत् *f.* अनिष्ट *n.* अरिष्ट *n.* बलाय *f.*

That is suffering m. आपदूग्रस्त, आपत्प्राप्त.

To be suffering m. आपदावणें. [वर.

To have a heavy m. befal one. आभाळ *n.* कोसळणें *with*

Misfortunes never come singly. एकादशीचे घरीं शिवरात्र, दुकळांत तेरावा महिना.

To MISGIVE, *v. a. fill with doubt,*—used with the reciprocal pronoun, and with heart or mind as agent. शंका *f.*-आशंका *f.*-संशय *m.*-कल्पना *f.*-विकल्प *m.*-&c. घेणें, दिक्कत *f.* खाणें.

MISGIVING, *n.* v. V. *and* DOUBT. शंका घेणें *n.*&c. शंका *f.* आशंका *f.* संशय *m.* दिक्कत *f.* धोका *m.* कल्पना *f.* विकल्प *m.* आकांक्षा *f.* कुतर्क *m.* कलाफ *m.* किंतु *pop.* किंतू *m.*

MISGOTTEN, *a. unjustly acquired.* अन्यायाचा, हरामाचा, हपापाचा, हरामखोरीचा, लांडीलबाडीचा, अन्यायोपार्जित, अन्यायार्जित, अन्यथासंपादित.

To MISGOVERN, *v. a. rule or administer ill.* वाईट रीतीनें-&c. चालवणें-वहिवाटणें, बदअमल *m.* करणें-चालवणें, गैरवहिवाट *f.*-असन्निर्वाह *m.*-&c. करणें, कुशासन *n.* करणें.

MISGOVERNANCE, MISGOVERNMENT, *n.* v. V. बदअमल *m.* गैरवहिवाट *f.* कुशासन *n.* अन्यथाशासन *n.*

To MISGUIDE. See To MISLEAD.

MISHAP, *n. misfortune*, v. CALAMITY. अनिष्टापात *m.* अरिष्टापात *m.* विपत्ति *f.* लाग *m.* विजोगत *f.*

An unlooked for m. अवचट *n.*

To MISIMPROVE, MISIMPROVEMENT. See MISEMPLOY, &c.

To MISINFER, *v. n. infer wrongly.* चुकीचें-भ्रांतीचें-अयुक्तिक-&c. अनुमान *n.* करणें, मिथ्यानुमान *n.*-अन्यथानुमान *n.* करणें.

To MISINFORM, *v. a. inform wrongly.* चुकीची बातमी *f.*-भ्रांतीची बातमी *f.*-खोटें वर्तमान *n.*-&c. सांगणें-देणें, गैरसमजावणें, गैरवाका *m.*-गैरमजकूर *m.* सांगणें, भ्रम *m.*-भ्रांति *f.* घालणें.

To MISINTERPRET, *v. a. translate erroneously.* खोटा तर्जुमा *m.*-अयथार्थभाषांतर *n.*-&c. करणें.

2 *understand in a wrong sense*, v. To MISCONSTRUE. अर्थ *m.*-भाव *m.*-&c. उलटा समजणें-घेणें *g. of o.*

MISINTERPRETATION, *n.* v. V. 1. खोटा तर्जुमा *m.* अयथार्थभा-

षांतर *n.* अन्यथाभाषांतर *n.*

2 उलटी समजूत *f.* विपरीतग्रह *m.* अन्यथाग्रह *m.*

To MISJUDGE, *v. a. form a false opinion of.* गैरसमजूत *f.*-असत्कल्पना *f.*-असद्भावना *f.*-अन्यथासंभावना *f.*-असत्तर्क *m.*-&c. करणें, विपरीत-&c. समजणें.

MISJUDGMENT, *n.* v. V. गैरसमजूत *f.* असत्कल्पना *f.* असत्तर्क *m.* अन्यथासंभावना *f.* असद्भावना *f.*

MISLAID, *p.*v.V. गमावलेला, सांडलेला, हरपलेला, ठावचूक झालेला, &c. ठावचूक, ठायचूक, गहाळ.

To be m. गैरविल्हेस लागणें-पडणें, गोंधळणें, गडबडणें, गलबलणें, गफलतणें *or* गलफतणें, ठावचूक-&c. होणें, आडवळणीस-आडसांठ्यास पडणें.

To MISLAY, *v. a. lay in a place not recollected, to lose.* गमावणें, गवाळणें *or* गावाळणें, गहाळणें, गफलतणें, हरपणें *or* हारपणें, सांडणें, गळफटणें *or* गळफाटणें, गळहाटणें.

To MISLE, *v. n. rain in fine drops, drizzle.* कोंडेपाऊस*m.* पडणें, बुरंगट*n.*-बुरगें*n.*-बुरबूर *f.*-&c. लागणें.

To MISLEAD, *v. a. lead astray, guide into error, deceive, &c.* lit. fig. गैरमार्गानें-भलत्यामार्गानें-&c. नेणें, गैरमार्गास-भलत्या वाटेस-&c. लावणें, बहकावणें *or* भकावणें, वाट *f.*- रस्ता*m.*-&c. चुकविणें-बहकविणें *g. of o.* कुमार्गप्रवृत्त-विपथगामी-&c. करणें, कुमार्गनयन*n.*-कुशिक्षा *f.*-&c. करणें, फसवणें, भुलविणें, भ्रमांत पाडणें-घालणें.

MISLEADING, *n.* v. V. बहकावणें*n.* भुलवणें*n.*&c. बहकावणी*f.* कुमार्गनयन *n.* कुशिक्षा *f.* असदुपदेश*m.*

MISLED, *p.* v. V. गैरमार्गानें नेलेला, गैरमार्गासलावलेला, &c. कुशिक्षित, कुमार्गप्रवृत्त.

MISLIKE, *To* MISLIKE. See DISLIKE, To DISLIKE.

MISLUCK, *n.* v. MISFORTUNE. दुर्भाग्य*n.* दुर्दैव*n.* अभाग्य*n.*

MISLY, *a. that comes in thin drops,*—rain. कोंड्याचा, बुरंगटाचा, बुरबुरीचा.

To MISMANAGE, *v. a. manage ill.* गैररीतीनें-गैरमार्गानें-&c. बहिवाटणें-चालवणें-वापरणें-आचरणें, गैरवहिवाट *f.*- असन्निर्वाह*m.*-अन्यथाचरण*n.*-&c. करणें *g.of o.* अन्यथा करणें, घाण*f.*-बिघाड *m.*-&c. करणें *g. of o.*

MISMANAGED, *p.* v.V. गैररीतीनें-&c. बहिवाटलेला-चालवलेला-&c.

MISMANAGEMENT, *n.* v. V. गैरवहिवाट *f.* असन्निर्वाह*m.* अन्यथाचरण*n.* दुर्नय*m.* दुर्नयन*n.* असत्कर्तृत्व*n.* असन्नेतृत्व*n.* असत्क्रिया *f.* अव्यवस्था *f.*

To MISMATCH, *v. a.* विजोड जोडणें, असमयोग*m.*-विषमयोग*m.*-&c. करणें, हिणवर*m.* करणें.

To MISNAME, *v. a. miscall.* चुकून-चुकीनें-भ्रांतीनें-चुकीचा-&c. म्हणणें, चुकीचें-भ्रांतीचें नांव*n.* देणें, खोटें नांव*n.*-अन्यथा नाम *n.* -मिथ्यानाम*n.*-&c. ठेवणें-देणें.

MISNOMER, *n. wrong name given.* चुकीचें नांव*n.* भ्रांतीनें दिल्हेलें नांव*n.* अन्यथा नाम*n.*

MISOGAMIST, *n. hater of marriage.* विवाहद्वेषी, उद्वाहद्वेषी, विवाहनिंदक.

MISOGAMY, *n.* विवाहद्वेष*m.* उद्वाहद्वेष*m.* विवाहनिंदा *f.*

MISOGYNIST, *n. hater of women.* स्त्रीद्वेषी, स्त्रीद्वेष्टा, स्त्रीनिंदक, स्त्रीशत्रु.

MISOGYNY, *n. hatred of women.* स्त्रीद्वेष*m.* स्त्रीनिंदा *f.* स्त्रीवैर*n.*

To MISPEL, MISPEND, &c. See To MISSPEL, MISSPEND,&c.

MISPERSUASION, *n. wrong notion or opinion.* गैरसमजूत *f.* उलटीसमजूत *f.* अन्यथासंभावना *f.* विपरीतभावना *f.* भ्रमज्ञान*n.*

To MISPLACE, *v. a. put in a wrong place.* भलत्याठिकाणीं-जागीं-&c. ठेवणें.

2 *place on an improper object.* अनाठायीं-भलत्याठिकाणीं-गैरठिकाणीं-अयोग्यठिकाणीं-भलतठायीं-अपात्रीं-&c.ठेवणें. In this sense are the English phrases *to throw away, to give to the winds, to toss to the dogs, to cast upon the sands, &c.* and corresponding to them in *Maráthí are*, अनाठायीं घालणें, वाऱ्यावर टाकणें, केरबारा*m.*-वारापाणी*n.*-&c. करून टाकणें *g. of o.* केरावाऱ्यांत-केरावाऱ्यानिशीं देणें-टाकणें, विधुळणीस पाडणें-मिळवून टाकणें, चुलींत टाकणें.

To be misplaced. आनाठायीं पडणें-जाणें.

MISPLACED, *p. v.* V. 1. भलत्या ठिकाणीं ठेवलेला, &c.

2 अनाठायींठेवलेला-घातलेला.

MISPRINT, *n. mistake in printing.* छापण्याचा-छापण्यांतला दोष *m.* छापण्यांतली चूक *f.* अशुद्धछाप*m.*

MISPRISON, *n. concealment of a crime.* अपराधाची-&c. छपावणी *f.* कानाडोळा*m.* अपराधगोपन*n.*

To MISPRONOUNCE, *v. a.* अशुद्धउच्चार*m.* करणें *g. of o.* अशुद्धोच्चारण*n.*-असदुच्चारण*n.*-&c. करणें *g. of o.*

MISPRONUNCIATION, *n.* v. V. अशुद्ध उच्चार *m.* अशुद्धोच्चार *m.* अशुद्धोच्चारण*n.* असदुच्चारण*n.* अवाक्षरोच्चारण*n.* अन्यथोच्चारण*n.*

MISPROPORTIONED, *a.* विषमप्रमाणाचा, विषमप्रमाणक, असमप्रमाणक, अन्यथाप्रमाणक.

MISRELATION, MISREPORT, *n. erroneous narration.* अशुद्ध-चुकीचा-&c. मजकूर *m.* असन्निवेदन *n.* असत्कथन *n.* अन्यथाकथन *n.*

To MISREPRESENT, *v. a. give a false representation of.* फेरफार करून-फिरवून-&c. सांगणें, खोटामजकूर *m.*-गैरबाका *m.*-खोटीहकिकत *f.*-&c. सांगणें-समजावणें-लिहिणें-&c. असद्वर्णन *n.*-अन्यथावर्णन *n.*-असत्कथन *n.*-&c. करणें.

MISREPRESENTATION, *n.* v. V.—*act.* फिरवणें *n.* फेरफार *m.* उलटापालट *f.* असन्निवेदन *n.* असत्कथन *n.* अन्यथानिवेदन *n.* असद्वर्णन *n.* अन्यथावर्णन *n.* मिथ्यावर्णन *n.*

I. *a* m. गैरबाका *m.* खोटाबाका *m.* फिरवलेला-फेरफाराचा-&c. बाका *m.* गैरहकिकत *f.* खोटीहकिकत *f.* खोटाकरिणा *m.*

MISRULE, *n. confusion and disorder from insubordination.* अंधाधुंदी *or* धी *f.* बचबच *f.* (राज्यांत, &c.) भालेराई *f.* झोटिंगपादशाही *f.* बेदाद *f.* बंडाळी *f.* बंडाळ *f.*

All is confusion and misrule. उठीतो कुटी, कोणाचा पायपोस कोणाच्या पायांत नाहीं.

2 *unjust rule.* v. TYRANNY. बदअमल *m.* कुशासन *n.*

To MISS, *v. a. not to hit*, lit. fig. निशाण *n.*-संधान *n.*-लक्ष्य*n.*-&c. चुकणें *g. of s.* न लागणें.

To m. one's way, *be astray.* वाट *f.* चुकणें-भुलणें, गलफटणें, गलबलणें.

2 *fail of obtaining.* अंतरणें, मुकणें, न पावणें.

3 *fail to meet.* चुकविणें, चुकणें *in. con.* चुकामूक *f.* होणें-पडणें *g. of s. recip.*

4 *discover to be wanting.* नाहीं असा पाहणें-समजणें, नाहींपणा *m.*-अभाव *m.*-अदर्शन *n.*-&c. समजणें-जाणणें *g. of o.* अभावज्ञान *n.*-&c. होणें *in. con. g. of o.*

5 *perceive the want of.* नाहींसापणा *m.*-उणीव *f.*-उणेपणा*m.*-वाण *f.*-अंतर *n.* वाटणें-समजणें *in. con. with g. of o.*

6 *omit, pass.* बगळणें or वेगळणें, गाळणें, सोडणें, अंतरणें.

To MISS, *v. n. fail to hit.* चुकणें, न लागणें.

2 *not to succeed, to miscarry, to fail,* v. To DEFEAT. चुकणें, हरणें, फसणें, फिसकणें.

3 *fail to obtain, &c.* चुकणें, अंतरणें.

MISS, MISSING, *n.* v. V. A. 1. चूक *f.*

A m. is as good as a mile. अंतरंमहद्दंतरं.

3 चूक *f.*

Mutual m. चुकामुकी *f.* चुकामूक *f.*

5 See WANT.

MISS, *n. young woman.* आडबायको *f.* वधूटी *f.* चिरंटी *f.*

MISSING, *a. lost, stray, not in the place where it should be.* ठावचूक, ठायचूक, गहाल, गफलतलेला, गबाळलेला.

To be m. गफलतणें, गलबलणें, सांडणें, गमावणें, हरपणें or हारपणें, हरवणें or हारवणें, गळफटणें or गळफाटणें, जाणें, गलत *adv.*-गप्प *adv.* होणें, भसकटणें or भांसकटणें, भांसकणें.

MIS-SHAPED, MIS-SHAPEN, *a. ill formed,* v. UGLY. बेढब, बेडौल, ढोबळ, ढोबळा, ओबडधोबड, कुरूप, विरूपक, विरुताकार, विरुताकृति.

MISSILE, *a. that may be thrown.* फेंकायाचा, फेंकून मारायाचा, &c. क्षेपणीय, क्षेप्य.

MISSILE, *n. weapon to be thrown.* फेंकायाचें शस्त्र *n.* सोडायाचें शस्त्र *n.* क्षेप्यायुध *n.*

MISSION, *n. sending.* पाठवणें *n.* धाडणें *n.* पाठवणूक *f.* पाठवणी *f.* प्रेरण *n.* प्रेषण *n.*

2 *state of being sent, commission.* दूतपणा *m.* दूतत्व *n.* दौत्य *n.* प्रैष्य *n.* प्रेरितत्व *n.* प्रेषितत्व *n.* संदेशहरत्व *n.*

3 *body of persons sent.* दूतांची-वकिलांची मंडळी *f.* प्रेरितसमूह *m.* दूतसमूह *m.* दूतमंडळी *f.*

MISSIONARY, *n. one sent to propagate religion.* धर्म शिकविण्यासाठीं पाठवलेला मनुष्य, धर्मसंदेशहर, धर्मकथक दूत, मिशनारी पाद्री is becoming common for a Christian Missionary.

MISSIVE, *a. sent.* पाठवलेला, प्रेरित.

2 See MISSILE.

To MIS-SPEAK, *v. n. err in speaking.* बोलण्यांत घसरणें-चूक *f.* करणें-&c. घसरत-चुकतचुकत-&c. बोलणें.

To MIS-SPEAK, *v. a.* See To MISPRONOUNCE.

To MIS-SPELL, *v. a.* अक्षर फिरवून लिहणें-बोलणें, अशुद्ध लिहणें-बोलणें, अक्षरव्यत्यय *m.*-अक्षरव्यत्यास *m.*-&c. करून लिहणें.

MIS-SPELLING, *n.* अवाक्षर *n.* अक्षरव्यत्यय *m.* अक्षरव्यत्यास *m.* अक्षरविपर्यास *m.*

To MIS-SPEND, *v. a. spend to no purpose or to a bad purpose, waste.* अनाठायीं-अपात्रीं-&c. खर्च *m.* करणें-घालणें-घालवणें-&c. असद्व्यय *m.* -दुर्व्यय *m.* -अपात्रव्यय *m.* -अन्यथाव्यय *m.* -&c. करणें, उडवणें, दवडणें, घालवणें, होगाडणें.

MIS-SPENDING, *n.* v. V.—*act.* अनाठायीं घालणें *n.* उडवणें *n.*&c. उडवणी *f.* असद्व्यय *m.* दुर्व्यय*m.* अपात्रव्यय*m.* अन्यथाव्यय *m.* अपव्यय *m.* अयुक्तव्यय *m.*

MIS-SPENT, *p.* v. V. अनाठायीं घातलेला, उडवलेला, &c. असद्व्ययित, दुर्व्ययित, अन्यथाव्ययित. [&c.

To MIS-STATE, MIS-STATEMENT. See To MIS-REPRESENT,

MIST, *n. haze, fog, &c.* धुई *f.* धुकें *n.* धुमें *n.* धुकट *n.* धुराडी *f.* धुन्हें *n.* धुसें *n.* तुषार *m.* मेघधूम्र *m.* धूमिका *f.*

2 fig. धूर *m.* (गर्वाचा-दौलतीचा-& धूर) धुंदी *f.* अंधारी *f.* मद *m.*

To MISTAKE, *v. a. misapprehend.* See To MISUNDERSTAND.

2 *take one thing or person for another.* चुकून-चुकीनें-भ्रांतीनें-&c. मानणें-घेणें, भ्रम *m.*-भ्रमाभास *m.*-&c. वाटणें *in. con. and g. of o.*

To MISTAKE, *v. n. err, blunder.* चुकणें, भुलणें, घसरणें, बहकणें or भकणें, चूक *f.* करणें.

MISTAKE, *n. misconception,* v. ERROR. चूक *f.* भ्रम *pop.* भरम *m.* गैरसमजूत *f.* भ्रांति *f.* मतिभ्रम *m.* आरोप *m.*

3 *blunder, inaccuracy.* चूक *f.* चुकी *f.* अशुद्ध *n.* कसर *f.* अंतर *n.* तफावत *f.* गुंजावीस *f.*

MISTAKEN, *p.* v. V. N. *that is in error.* भ्रम पडलेला, भ्रांत, भ्रांतियुक्त, जातभ्रम, प्राप्तभ्रम.

To be m. भ्रम *m.* पडणें-होणें *in. con.* भुलणें. [भ्रमपूर्वक.

MISTAKINGLY, *adv. erroneously.* चुकून, भ्रांतीनें, भ्रांतिपूर्वक,

MISTER, *n.* साहेब.

To MISTIME, *v. a. do, &c. at a wrong time.* अकालीं-अवेळीं-&c. करणें-योजणें, अकालयोजना *f.*-&c. करणें.

MISTINESS, *n.* v. A. तुषारयुक्तता *f.* सतुषारता *f.* तुषारभाव *m.* मेघधूम्रव्याप्ति *f.*

MISTION. See MIXTURE.

MISTLETOE, MISLETOE, See PARASITE. [1. &c.

To MISTRANSLATE, MISTRANSLATION. See MISINTERPRET,

MISTRESS, *n.*—correl. with servant. धनीण *f.* स्वामिनी *pop.* स्वामीण *f.* यजमानीण *f.* साहेब or साहेबीण *f.* सेव्या *f.*

2 (of a family or house). घरकरीण *f.* घरधनीण *f.* कुटुंब *n.* कबिला *m.* गृहस्वामिनी *pop.* घरस्वामीण *f.* घरण *f.* गरत or घरत *f.* बाई *f.* गृहिणी *f.*

3 *proprietrix.* धनीण *f.* मालकीण *f.* स्वामिनी *pop.* स्वामीण *f.*

4 *chief, ruler, &c.* स्वामिनी *f.* मुखरण *f.* नायिका *pop.* नायकीण *f.*

5 (of a school). शिकवणारी *f.* शिक्षक *f.* पंतोजीण *f.* अध्यापिका *f.* शालानायिका *f.*

6 *woman skilled in.* सुगरण or सुगरीण *f.* जाणती *f.* बस्ताद *f.*

7 *sweetheart, &c.* v. BELOVED. प्रिया *f.* दयिता *f.* कांता *f.* कामिनी *f.* प्रमदा *f.* अर्धांग *n.*

An offended m. मानिनी *f.* मानवती *f.*

8 *concubine, kept woman.* राख *f.* रक्षा *f.* सोयरी *f.* दासी *f.* भुजिष्या *f.* अवरुद्धा *f.*—in cant phrase. उपवस्त्र *n.* अंगवस्त्र *n.* आंगासालची *f.*

9 *dame, &c.*—the compellation of courtesy to *Shúdra* women. आऊ *f.* अवाजी *f.* अवा *f.*

MISTRUST, *n. want of confidence.* अविश्वास *m.* शंका *f.* आशंका *f.* संशय *m.* कुभाव *m.* कुडाभाव *m.* कुडें *n.* विश्वासाभाव *m.*

To MISTRUST, *v. a. suspect, have doubts of.* शंका *f.*-आशंका *f.* -संशय*m.*-&c. करणें-धरणें *g. of o.* शंकणें, आशंकणें, अविश्वास*m.*-शंका *f.*-&c. असणें *in con. with g. of o.*

MISTRUSTED, *p.* v. V. शंकित, आशंकित, अविश्वस्त.

MISTRUSTFUL, *a.* v. SUSPICIOUS. अविश्वासी, संदेही, संशयी.

MISTRUSTFULLY, *adv.* v. A. अविश्वासानें, &c. संशय धरून, संशयपूर्वक.

MISTRUSTFULNESS, See MISTRUST.

MISTY, *a. overspread, &c. with mist.* धुईचा, धुक्याचा, बांबाळीचा *or* बांबळीचा, बामाळीचा *or* बामळीचा, तुषारयुक्त, सतुषार, तुषारव्याप्त, मेघधूम्रव्याप्त.

M. and raw weather. बांबाळ *or* बांबळ *f.* बामाळ *or* बामळ *f.*

To MISUNDERSTAND, *v. a. take in a wrong sense, misapprehend, misconceive, mistake, &c.* गैरसमजूत *f.*-उलटीसमजूत *f.*-विपरीतग्रह *m.*-अन्यथाग्रह *m.*-&c. होणें *g. of o. with in. con.* अर्थ *m.*-भाव *m.*-&c.उलटा समजणें-घेणें, उलटा *decl.*-विपरीत-&c. समजणें-घेणें, विपरीतग्रह *m.*-अन्यथाग्रह *m.*-विपरीतार्थ *m.*-अर्थविपर्यास *m.*-&c. करणें.

MISUNDERSTANDING, *n.* v. V. गैरसमजूत *f.* उलटीसमजूत *f.* असमजूत *f.* विपरीतबोध *m.* विपरीतग्रह *m.* अन्यथाबोध *m.* विपरीतग्रहण *n.* असद्ग्रह *m.* अन्यथार्थबोध *m.* भ्रम *m.* भ्रांति *f.* भ्रमज्ञान *n.*

I. *ill terms, variance,* v. DISAGREEMENT. वांकडें *n.* वांकडेपणा *m.* बांक *or* वाक *m. n.* बेबनाव *m.* तिडा *m.* तीड *f.* तिसकूट *f.* बिपट *n.* [&c.

MISUNDERSTOOD, *p.* v. V. उलटा समजलेला, विपरीत समजलेला,

MISUSAGE, MISUSE. See MAL-TREATMENT, MISEMPLOYMENT.

To MISUSE. See To MAL-TREAT. To MISEMPLOY.

MITE, *n. small insect.* सूत *n.* किडा *m.*

2 *small quantity,* v. PARTICLE. सुतळीचा तोडा *m.* सुपारीचें खांड *n.* सुईच्या शेंड्यावरची माती *f.*

3 *proverbial expression for a small coin.* कौडी *f.* फुटकीकौडी *f.* नचकल *f.* छदाम *m.* बदाम *m.* कपार्दिका *f.* कपर्दीक *m.*

A widow's m. सुदाम पोहे *m. pl.*

To give one's m. फूल नाहीं फुलाची पाकळी *f.* देणें.

MITHRIDATE, *n. antidote.* विषभंजन *n.* विषापहारक औषध *n.*

MITIGABLE, *a.* v. V. 1. प्रशमन करायाजोगा-सारखा-&c. प्रशमनीय, प्रशाम्य, उपशमनीय, उपशाम्य, प्रशमनयोग्य, &c.

MITIGANT, *n. mitigating thing.* प्रशमन *n.* उपशमन *n.*

To MITIGATE, *v. a. alleviate, assuage, &c.* v. To EASE. हलका-&c. करणें, शमवणें, शांतवणें, प्रशमन *n.*-उपशमन *n.*-उपशांति *f.*-&c. करणें *g. of o.*

2 *make less rigorous or severe,* v. To LIGHTEN. हलका-कमी-सुसह लघु-अल्प-स्वल्प-नरम-मृदु-&c. करणें.

MITIGATED, *p.* v. V. 1. शमवलेला, &c. शमित, प्रशमित, उपशांत.

2 हलका केलेला, &c.

MITIGATER, *n.* MITIGANT, MITIGATIVE, *a.* v. V. 1. शमवणारा, &c. उपशम-शमन-प्रशमन-&c. कर्त्ता-कारी.

MITIGATION, *n.* v. V. 1.—*act.* शमवणें *n.* &c. शमवणूक *f.* सांतवणूक *f.* उपशमन *n.* प्रशमन *n.*—*state.* उतार *m.* उपशांति *f.* उपशम *m.* [पणा *m.* न्यूनता *f.*

2 हलका करणें *n.* &c. लघुकरण *n.* न्यूनीकरण *n.*—*state.* हलके-

MITRE, *n. crown of a bishop, &c.* धर्माध्यक्षाचा-&c. मुकुट *m.*

MITTEN, *n.* बिनबोटांचा हातमोजा *m.*

MITTIMUS, *n. warrant of commitment to prison.* बंदिखान्यांत घालण्याचा हुकूमनामा *m.*

To MIX, *v. a. mingle, blend, unite.* मिळवणें, मिसळणें, भिसळणें, भेलणें *or* भेळणें, एकवटणें, एकवट करणें, भिसळ *f.*-मिसळ *f.*-मिसळा *m.*- भेल *or* भेळ *f.*-&c. करणें *g. of o.* मिसळण *f. n.*-सम्मेलन *n.*-सम्मिश्रण *n.*-&c. करणें *g. of o.* मिश्र-मिश्रित-&c. करणें.

To mix with for the sake of concealment. लगटणें.

2 *jumble, intermingle confusedly,* v. To COMPOUND. गोंधळणें, एकवटणें, एकवट करणें, मिसळामिसळ *f.*-गोंधळ *m.*-घालमेल *f.*-संकर *m.*-&c. करणें *g. of o.*

3 up;—by stirring, &c. कालवणें, ढवळणें, मिळवणें.

To MIX, *v. n. become united or blended.* मिळणें, मिसळणें, भिसळणें, भेलणें, मिळून जाणें, समावणें, रमणें, गोत *n.* मिळणें *g. of s. recip.* भिसळ *f.*-भेल *f.*-&c. होणें *g. of s.*

2 (In company, society, &c.). मिळणें, येणें.

MIXED, *p.* v. V. A. 1. मिळवलेला, मिसळलेला, &c. मिसळ, मिसळीचा, भेळीचा, &c. मिश्र, मिश्रित, सम्मिश्र, संकीर्ण, संयुक्त, संयुत, मिलित, समवेत.

2 गोंधळलेला, &c. संकलित, संकीर्ण.

I.—grain, खेडकर.

MIXER, *n.* MIXING, *p. a.* v. V. A. 1. मिळवणारा, मिसळणारा, मिसळ करणारा, &c. सम्मेलन कर्त्ता-कारी, सम्मिश्रण कर्त्ता-कारी.

2 गोंधळणारा, &c. गोंधळ करणारा, &c. घालमेल्या.

MIXTURE, MIXING, *n.* v. V. A. 1.—*act.* मिळवणें *n.* मिसळणें *n.* &c. मिळवणूक *f.* मिसळणूक *f.* मिळवणी *f.* मिसळणी *f.* मिसळण *f.* सम्मिश्रण *n.* सम्मीलन *n.* सम्मेलन *n.* संयोजन *n.* एकीकरण *n.* मिश्रीकरण *n.*—*state.* मिसळ *f.* मिसळा *m.* भिसळ *f.* भेल *or* भेळ *f.* खेड *f.* भेळाभेळ *f.* आमेज *m.* मिश्रभाव *m.* मिश्रीभाव *m.* संपर्क *m.* संभव *m.* संयोग *m.* अनुषंग *m.*

2—*act.* गोंधळणें *n.* &c. गोंधळणूक *f.* संकलन *n.*—*state.* गोंधळ *m.* गोंधळागोंधळ *m. f.* मिसळामिसळ *f.* कालवाकालव *f.* संकर *m.*

M. of castes. वर्णसंकर *m.* एक मंगळ *n.* एकबाट *m.*

3 कालवणें *n.* कालवणी *f.* कालवणूक *f.*

v. V. N. मिळणें *n.* मिसळ *f.* भिसळ *f.* मिलन *n.*

I. *mixed mass, medley, miscellany.* मिसळ *f.* मिसळा *m.* भिसळ *f.* मिळवण *n.* भेरड *f.* खेड *f.* पंचमिसळ *f.* पंचभेळ *f.* पंचमेळ *f.* गोतांबील *n.* गोहोत *n.* खिचडी *f.* धेडगुजरी *f.* खिचडमिचड *n.* गिजगिंदा *m.* कालवा *m.* संकर *m.*

A m. of rice & split pulse. खिचडी *f.*

A m. of languages. धेडगुजरी *f.* खिचडी *f.* [भेलण *n.*

II. *ingredient added and mixed.* भेल *or* भेळ *f.* मिसळ *f.*

MIZMAZE. See MAZE.

MIZZEN, *n.*—the sail. कळंबी *f.*

2—the mast. मागला डोल *m.* मागली डोलकाठी *f.*

MIZZLE, *n. small rain, drizzle.* कोंडेपाऊस *m.* कोंड्याचापाऊस *m.* बुरंगट *n.* बुरगें *n.* बुरबूर *f.* [लागणें, बुरबुरणें.

To MIZZLE, *v. n. drizzle.* कोंडेपाऊस *m.*-&c. पडणें, बुरंगट *n.*&c.

MNEMONIC, *a. assisting the memory.* स्मृतिसहाय, स्मृतिप्रवर्त्तक.

MNEMONICS, *n. art of memory.* आठवण ठेवण्याची विद्या *f.* स्मरणशास्त्र *n.* स्मरण विद्या *f.*

To MOAN, *v. n. groan.* कन्हणें, विल्हळणें *or* बिल्हाळणें, विवळणें, इवळणें, परवणें, चुळमुळणें, कुंथणें, विणवणें, कन्हेरी *f.*-हायहूय *f.*-&c. करणें-मांडणें.

To m. and whine. पिरंगणें.

To sit moaning and fretting. चुरमुरत बसणें, चुरमुरे *m. pl.* खात बसणें-देत बसणें.

MOAN, MOANING, *n.* v. V. कन्हणें *n.* &c. परवणी *f.* कन्हें *n.* विल्हाळ *or* विल्हळ *m.* किळकिळी *f.* विणवणी *f.* इवळणी *f.* हायहू-

य *f.* आयाओया *f. n.* चुळमूळ *f.*

MOANER, *n.* MOANING, *p. a.* v. V. कन्हणारा, &c. कन्हा, विल्हळ्या *or* विल्हाळ्या, पिरंगा, पिरंग्या.

MOANFULLY, MOANINGLY, *adv.* v. N. कन्हतकन्हत, चुळमूळ.

MOAT, *n. ditch round a fort.* खंदक *m.* चर *m.* खाई *f.* चरिसा *f.* परिसा *f.*

MOB, *n. rabble, tumultuous assemblage,* v. CROWD, PEOPLE. रट्ट *m.* दंगल *m.* लुळें *n.* वंडाळीची मंडळी *f.* अव्यवस्थितसभा *f.*

To MOB, *v. a. harass tumultuously.* गर्दी *f.* करणें *with* वर *of o.*

MOBILE, MOBILITY, *n. canaille, the mob,* v. PEOPLE. महारपोर *m. n.* बाजारबुणगें *n.* लुळें *n.* आडजात *f.* अडाणजात *f.* गबाल्लोक *m. pl.* [ग्यता *f.*

MOBILITY, *n. susceptibility of motion.* गमनयोग्यता *f.* गतियो-

To MOCK, *v. a. imitate in derision, deride by mimicry.* वेंटावणें, वेडावणें, वेंटविणें, वेडावणें *n.*-वेंटावण्या *f. pl.*-वांकुल्या *f. pl.*-विचकुल्या *f. pl.*-वेंचकुल्या *f. pl.*-वेंकावल्या *f. pl.*-&c. दासवणें, ढवाळी *f.*-ढवाळकी *f.*-नकल *f.*-चेष्टा *f.*-कुचेष्टा *f.*-विडंबन *n.*-&c. करणें *g. of o.*

2 *deride, laugh at,* v. To RIDICULE. हासणें, उपहासणें, विडंबणें, उपहास *m.*-थट्टा *or* ठट्ठा *f.*-मस्करी *f.*-टेर *f.*-टर *f.*-बचेरी *f.*-फजिती *f.*-&c. करणें *g. of o.*

3 *tantalize, disappoint, befool,* v. To DECEIVE. चाळवणें, फजीत करणें, चाळवण *f.*-चाळवणूक *f.* करणें *g. of o.* धूर *m.* देणें, तोंडीं पान *n.* पुसणें, धूप *m.* दासवणें,

MOCK, *n.* See MOCKERY, RIDICULE.

MOCK, *a. not real, counterfeit, false.* खोटा, लटका, कपटाचा, कृत्रिम, मिथ्या, नकली, सोंगाचा, मिसाचा, लुटुपुटूचा,

MOCK-FIGHT, *n.* क्रीडायुद्ध *n.* तमाशा *m.*

MOCKED, *p.* v. V. 1. वेंटावलेला, &c. विडंबित.

2 उपहासलेला, उपहसित, जातोपहास.

3 चाळवलेला, फजीतकेलेला, धूरदिल्हेला, &c. फजीत,

MOCKER, *n.* MOCKING, *p. a.* v. V. 1. वेंटावणारा, वेंटावण्या दासवणारा, कुचेष्टा करणारा, &c. टवाळ, टवाळखोर, ढवाळ, ढवाळखोर, विडंबनकर्त्ता-कारी, विडंबक.

2 उपहासणारा, विटंबणारा, &c. उपहासक, उपहासकर्त्ता.

MOCKERY, MOCKING, *n.* v. V. 1.—*act.* वेंटावणें *n.* वेंटावणी *f.* वेडावणें *n.* कुचाळी *f.* ढवाळी *f.* ढवाळकी *f.* टवाळी *f.* टवाळकी *f.* कुचविंध्या *f. pl.* वांकुल्या *f. pl.* विचकुल्या *or* वानरविचकुल्या *f. pl.* वेंचकुल्या *f. pl.* वेंटावण्या *f. pl.* वेंकावल्या *f. pl.* विडंबन *n.*

2—*act.* उपहासणें *n.* हासणें *n.* &c. उपहास *m.* थट्टा *or* ठट्ठा *f.* मस्करी *f.* टेर *f.* टर *f.* बचेरी *f.*

3—*act.* चाळवणें *n.* चाळवण *f.* चाळवणूक *f.* &c.

I. *butt or subject of mockery.* उपहासास्पद *n.* हास्यस्थान *n.* उपहासविषय *m.*

II. *counterfeit appearance, false show.* सोंग *n.* मिष *pop.* मीस *n.* ढोंग *n.* कोंग *n.* व्याज *m. n.* कपट *n.*

MOCKING-STOCK, *n.* v. LAUGHING-STOCK. उपहासास्पद *n.* उपहासस्थान *n.*

MODAL, *a. relating to form or mode.* रूपाविषयींचा, रूपविषयक-संबंधी, प्रकाराविषयींचा, प्रकारविषयक-संबंधी.

MODE, *n.*—in metaphysics. विशेषवस्तुरूप *n.* विशेषवस्तुप्रकार *m.* विशेषद्रव्यरूप *n.* विशेषद्रव्यप्रकार *m.*

2 *manner of existing or being, form.* रूप *n.* आकार *m.* प्रकार *m.*

3 *method, way, fashion,* v. MANNER. रीति *pop.* रीत *f.* मार्ग *m.* चाल *f.* पर्याय *m.*

4 *fashionable custom or way.* सभ्यसंप्रदाय *m.* शिष्टसंप्रदाय *m.* लोकप्रचार *m.* लोकप्रघात *m.*

5—in music. See MUSIC. 6—in grammar. See MOOD.

MODEL, *n. representation of.* नमुना *or* नमोना *m.* नकशा *m.* नकाशा *m.* सांचा *m.* बेत *m.* प्रतिमा *f.* प्रतिरूप *n.* उपमा *f.*

2 *pattern, exemplar.* नमुना *or* नमोना *m.* कित्ता *m.* सांचा *m.* फर्मा *m.* मासला *m.* ठिकडें *n.* बीड *n.*

To furnish with a m. किता *m.* घालून देणें.

3 *mould.* सांचा *m.* मूस *f.* ठसा *m.*

To MODEL, *v. a. mould, shape,* v. To FORM. घडणें, वळवणें, उतरणें, बनावणें.

MODERATE, *a. temperate, observing reasonable bounds in indulgence.* नेमस्त, परिमिताचारी, अल्पभोगी, अल्पविहारी, स्वल्पभोगी, नियतवर्ती, नियतवृत्ति, आहारविहारनियमवान्, अल्पसंतोषी, अल्पसंतुष्ट, अनतिक्रमी, अतिक्रमवर्जी.

2 *restrained in passion, temper, desire, &c.* अल्पाकांक्षी, अल्पाभिलाषी, अलोभी, अलुब्ध, नियतवर्ती, नियतवृत्ति, समवृत्ति, अनतिक्रमी, अतिक्रमवर्जी.

3 *temperate, not extreme, not excessive, not violent or rigorous.* नेमस्त, नेमाचा, सुमाराचा, सुमारवट, बेताचा, ठेपेचा, कोमल *or* ळ, माफक, मध्यम, मर्यादेचा, मित, परिमित, समर्याद, सावधि, सावधिक, तोलींव, मोतादी, रजपजचा *or* रजापजाचा, हलका.

4 *of the middling degree,* v. MIDDLING. मध्यम, मध्यमप्रतीचा, मधलंड.

To MODERATE, *v. a. make temperate, qualify,* v. To TEMPER. नेमस्त-माफक-सुमाराचा-बेताचा-समधात-सुसह-&c. करणें.

2 *reduce from a state of excess or violence, repress, restrain.* हलका-नेमस्त-बेताचा-नर्म-&c. करणें, अटोपणें *or* अटपणें, अटपता धरणें, आवरणें, आवरता धरणें, शमविणें, उपशम *m.*-उपशांति *f.*-&c. करणें *g. of o.* [कावणें मंदावणें, उतरणें.

To MODERATE, *v. n. become less violent, &c.* v. To ABATE. हल-

MODERATED, *p.* v. V. A. 1. सुमाराचा केलेला, माफक केलेला, &c.

2 हलका केलेला, अटपता धरलेला, शमवलेला &c. शमित.

MODERATELY, *adv.* v. A. 1. नेमस्त, सुमारानें, सुमाराचा *decl.* बेताचा *decl.* बेतानें, सुमारवट, यावत्तावत्. [*decl.*

2 सुमाराचा *decl.* सुमारवट, माफक, साहीलाहीसा *decl.* सोसेसा

MODERATENESS, MODERATION, *n.* v. A. 1. नेमस्तपणा *m.* परिमिताचरण *n.* परिमिताचार *m.* नियतवर्त्तन *n.* नियतवृत्ति *f.* अल्पभोग *m.* आहारविहारनियम *m.* अनतिक्रम *m.* अतिक्रमवर्जन *n.*

2 अल्पाकांक्षा *f.* अलोभ *m.* समानवृत्ति *f.* समवृत्ति *f.* नियतवृत्ति *f.* अल्पसंतुष्टता *f.*

3 नेमस्तपणा *m.* माफकपणा *m.* रजपज *f.* समर्यादता *f.* सावधिकता *f.* मिति *f.* [वादसभाध्यक्ष.

MODERATOR, *n.* (at disputations). वादमध्यस्थ, वादसभापति,

MODERN, *a. not ancient, pertaining to present or recent time.* नवथर, नवा, नूतन, अलीकडचा, अलीकडील, अलीकडला, हल्लींचा, आधुनिक, अर्वाचीन, अप्राचीन, सद्यस्कालीन, इदानींतन.

MODERNS, *n.* हाल्लींचे-अलीकडचे लोक *m. pl.* सद्यस्कालीन लोक *m. pl.*

MODEST, *a. not boastful, arrogant, &c.* निगर्व *pop.* निगर्वी, निरभिमान *pop.* निरभिमानी, निरहंकार *pop.* निरहंकारी, अमानी, विनयी, सविनय, विनीत, अभिमानरहित-शून्य-&c. अनात्मश्लाघी.

To be very m. मान *f.* वर न करणें.

2 *not forward, bold, pert, &c.* लाजवट, लाजट, लाजरा, लाजाळू, गरीब, मर्यादशील, लज्जेचा, लज्जाशील, लज्जावान्, सलज्ज, सुलज्ज, त्रपावान्, त्रपायुक्त, त्रपान्वित, अनुद्धत.

3 *not loose, wanton, unchaste,&c.*—of a woman,v.CHASTE. अव्यभिचारिणी, कासोट्याची-निरीची-&c. बळकट-धड-खबरदार. —esp. of a wife सती, पतिव्रता, साध्वी. [रिमित.

4 *not excessive, &c.* v. MODERATE. मर्यादेचा, सुमाराचा, प-

MODESTLY, *adv.* v. A. 1. निगर्वानें, निरभिमानानें, निरभिमानपूर्वक, निरभिमानबुद्धीनें, विनयपूर्वक.

2 मर्यादेनें, मर्यादाधरून, मर्यादापूर्वक, लज्जापूर्वक, &c.

3 पतिव्रताधर्मानें, पातिव्रत्यानें, साधुभावानें, सतीधर्मानें, &c.

MODESTY, MODESTNESS, *n.* v. A. 1. निगर्वीपणा *m.* निरहंकारीपणा *m.* &c. अनभिमान *m.* निरभिमान *m.* अभिमानराहित्य *n.* &c. विनय *m.* विनयिता *f.*

2 लाजवटपणा *m.* लाजटपणा *m.* लाज *f.* लज्जा *f.* त्रपा *f.* मर्यादशीलता *f.* लज्जाशीलता *f.* ऱ्ही *f.* पडदा *m.* डोळ्यांत पाणी *n.* अपत्रपा *f.*

M., decency, decorousness, &c.—gener. *or* indef. लाजलज्जा *f.* लाजमर्यादा *f.*

3 पतिव्रताधर्म *m.* पातिव्रत्य *n.* साध्वीभाव *m.* सतीधर्म *m.* सतीत्व *n.* साध्वीत्व *n.*

4 See MODERATION.

MODICUM, *n. pittance.* जरा-जरासा-जराकसा-&c. *used with a noun.* अत्यल्पांश *m.*

MODIFIABLE, *a.* v. V. 1. रूप फिरवायाजोगा, &c. विकारशक्य, परिणामशक्य, परिणामांतरशक्य, रूपांतरशक्य.

MODIFICATION, *n.* v. V. 1.—*act.* फिरवणें *n.* पालटणें *n.* &c. रूपांतर करण *n.* स्वरूपांतरकरण *n.*—*state.* रूपभेद *m.* स्वरूपभेद *m.* रूपांतर *n.* स्वरूपांतर *n.* [*f.* परिणाम *m.*

I. *altered form or mode of being.* रूप *n.* विकार *m.* विकृति

MODIFIED, *p.* v. V. 1. रूप फिरवलेला, &c. विकृत, वैकृत.

2 फिरवलेला, फेरफार केलेला, &c.

To MODIFY, *v. a. change the form or shape of* रूप *n.*-स्वरूप *n.* -&c. फिरवणें-पालटणें *g. of o.* रूपांतर *n.*-स्वरूपांतर *n.*-रूपभेद *m.* -विकार *m.*-विकृति *f.*-&c. करणें *g. of o.*

2 *alter, vary,* v. To CHANGE. फिरवणें, पालटणें, फेरफार *m.*-&c. करणें *g. of o.* [लका-&c. करणें.

3 *moderate, qualify, soften.* कांहीं मऊ-कांहींनर्म-माफक-ह-

MODISH, *a. fashionable, stylish.* दरबारी, दरबारीचालीचा, शहरी, सभ्यसंप्रदायाचा, डौली, डौलाचा, छानदारडौलाचा, छानीचा.

To MODULATE, *v. a. form sound to a certain key, &c.* स्वर *m.* काढणें-घेणें-बांधणें-साधणें. [घेणें.

2 *inflect sound.* स्वरभेद *m.* करणें, खोंच *f.*-खांचखोंच *f.*-&c.

MODULATOIN, *n.* v. V. 1. स्वर काढणें *n.* &c.

2 खोंच *f.* खांचखोंच *f.* स्वरभेद *m.* कर्त्तब *n.*

MODULE. See MODEL.

MOGUL, *n.* मोगल.

Irruption, &c. of the Moguls. मोगलाण *n.*

Rule or sway of the Moguls. मोगलाई *f.*

That belongs, &c. to the Moguls. मोगली, मोगलाई.

MOHAR, MOHUR, *n.*—the coin. मोहर *f.*

MOIETY, *n.* v. HALF. अर्धूक *n.* अर्धेल *f.* निमा *m.* निमे *f.* निमाई *f.* निमसाई *f.*

To MOIL, *v. a. daub, smear, &c. with dirt.* भरणें, लेधडणें, मरदणें *or* मरदून-&c. घेणें.

To be moiled. भरणें, लिडबिडणें *or* लडबडणें.

2 v. To TIRE. शिणवणें, श्रमवणें, भागवणें.

To MOIL, *v. n. drudge,* v. To TOIL. कचाड कष्ट *m. pl.*-महारकष्ट *m. pl.* करणें, खपणें, हाडें *n. pl.* झिजवणें.

MOIST, *a. moderately wet.* ओलसर, ओलट, ओलगट, ओलवट, ओलसट, अंबटओला, आर्द्र, सार्द्र, सद्रव, चिंबट *or* चेंबट, ईषदार्द्र.

2 *that has moisture,*—a soil, &c. दमदार, दमसर, दमट, दामट, ओलवाड्डु. [&c. करणें.

To MOISTEN, *v. a.* v. A. ओलावणें, ओलवणें, ओलसर-ओलट-

2 (a culinary preparation by a dash of water, milk, &c.). अपका *m.* देणें-मारणें-टाकणें, तुसारणें, तुसार *m.*-तुसारा *m.* देणें-घालणें.

MOISTNESS, MOISTURE, *n.* v. A. 1. ओलसरपणा *m.* &c. ओलावा *m.* ओलवा *m.* ओलास्रा *m.* ओल *f. n.* आर्द्रता *f.* सार्द्रता *f.* आर्द्रभाव *m.*

2 दम *m.* दमसरपणा *m.* [लवाड्डु.

That is produced by the m. of the soil. ओलाचा, ओ-

MOLAR. See JAW-TOOTH.

MOLASSES, *n. drainings or drippings of sugar.* काकवी *f.* मळी *f.* झारा *m.* मधुधूलि *f.* शर्कराक्षार *m.*

MOLE, *n. natural spot on the body.* मस *m.* ठिकें *n.* ठीक *n.* चिथडा *m.* चिथडी *f.* वांग *m.* तिल *pop.* तीळ *m.* मत्स्य *m.* किण *m.*

A m. with hairs. लांस *n.* लांसरूं *n.* [राम. ढकशी *f.*

2 *mound, dyke.* धक्का *or* धका *m.* धमधमा *m.* बांध *m.* बंधा-

3 एक लहान प्राणी आहे.

MOLE-HILL, *n.* v. HILLOCK. वारूळ *n.* वल्मीक *m. n.*

To make a mountain of a m. पराचा कावळा करणें, पुळीचें फांपर करणें, राईचा पर्वत करणें, रजाचा गज करणें.

MOLECULE, *n. atom, minute particle of matter.* अणु *m.* परमाणु *m.* कण *m.* कणिका *f.*

MOLECULISM, *n.* अणिमा *m.* अणुत्व *n.*

To MOLEST, *v. a.* v. To TROUBLE. उपद्रव *m.*-इजा *f.*-तसदी *f.*-क्लेश *m.*-&c. देणें.

MOLESTATION, *n.* v. V. *and* TROUBLE. उपद्रव *m.* इजा *f.* तसदी *f.* दुःख *n.* नड *f.* नडाव *m.* उपसर्ग *m.* उपप्लव *m.*

MOLLIENT, *a. softening.* मऊ-&c. करणारा, मृदुकारक-कारी.

To MOLLIFY, *v. a.* lit. fig. v. To SOFTEN. मऊ-नरम-मवाळ-मृदु-&c. करणें, मऊपणा *m.*-मवाळी *f.*-मृदुत्व *n.*-&c. आणणें.

MOLLY-CODDLE, *n. one who takes over care of himself.* बाळंत *f.* [धातूचा.

MOLTEN, *a. made of melted metal.* ओतींव, सांच्याचा, ओतींव

MOMENT, *n. smallest portion of time,* v. INSTANT. पळ *n.* क्षण *m.* चिपडी *f.* पलख *m. n.* लहम *f. n.* लहज *m.* दम *m.* मात्रा *f.*

An idle or spare m. उसंत *or* उसंथ *f.* फट *f.* सवड *or* संवड *f.* उसंधि *f.* उसरत *f.* उसपत *f.*

Every m. क्षणोक्षणीं, प्रतिक्षणीं. [टिमात्रांत.

In a m., in a jiffey, &c. v.TRICE. पळमात्रांत, चुटकींत, त्रु-

2 See MOMENTUM.

3 *importance, consequence*, v. WEIGHT. भारm. भारदस्तीf. भारदारीf. मुजास or मुजास्ताf. केवा m. प्रत्यवाय m. *with neg. con.*

MOMENTANEOUS, MOMENTARY, *a. done in a moment, lasting a moment.* एका क्षणाचा, एका पळाचा, क्षणिक, क्षणस्थायी, पलस्थायी, क्षणभंगुर, उत्पन्नविनाशी, नैमिष.

MOMENTARILY, *adv. every moment.* क्षणोक्षणीं, प्रतिक्षणीं.

MOMENTOUS, *a. important*, v. WEIGHTY. भारी, वजनदार, भारदारीचा, जड, मोठा. [रीf.

MOMENTOUSNESS, *n.* V. A. *and* WEIGHT. भारदारीf. वजनदा-

MOMENTUM, *n. impetus.* चालण्याचा जोर m. वेग m. वेगमान n.

MONACHISM, *n. monastic life.* मठवास m. मठाधिष्ठितिf. वनवास m. वानप्रस्थाश्रम m. वैराग्याश्रम m.

MONAD. MONADE, *n. ultimate atom, indivisible thing.* मात्र n. तन्मात्र n. अणुमात्र n. अभेद्यवस्तु n. [स्वत्यार राजा.

MONARCH, *n. absolute sovereign*, v. DESPOT. स्वायत्तराजा, मु-
2 v. KING. राजा, पादशाहा, अधिप, अधिपति.
3 *the superior of the kind.* राज, इंद्र, both in comp.

MONARCHAL, *a.* v. REGAL. राजकीय, राजकी, पादशाही.

MONARCHIC, MONARCHICAL, *a. vested in a single ruler.* एकेराजाचे सत्तेचा, एकराजसत्ताक, एकराजाधीन, एकराजतंत्र, एकराजायत्त, एकस्वामिक.

MONARCHY, *n. government of a single ruler.* एकराजसत्ताf. एकराजशासन n. एकस्वामित्व n. एकाधिपत्य n.
2 *realm.* राज्य n.

MONASTERY, *n. house of monks, &c.* मठ m. आश्रम m.

MONASTIC, MONASTICAL, *a. relating to monks or monastic life.* मठवासाचा, मठवाससंबंधी, मठवासीसंबंधी, वानप्रस्थाश्रमाचा, वानप्रस्थाश्रमसंबंधी.

MONASTICISM. See MONACHISM.

MONDAY, *n.* सोमवार m. चंद्रवार m. इंदुवार m. इंदुवासर m.

MONETARY, *a. consisting, &c. of money.* रोखीचा, पैशाटक्याचा, पैशारुक्याचा, सोन्यानाण्याचा.

MONEY, *n.* v. RICHES. पैका m. पैसा m. दाम m. धन n. द्रव्य n. वित्त n. टका m. (in comp. as, घरटका, लग्नटका, &c.),कौडीf. (Pr. हातीं कौडीविद्या दौडी),दुडू m.—freely or loosely, पैसाअडका m. पैसाटका m. पैसारुका m. सोनेंनाणें n.—as jocosely personified, दामाजीपंत m.

A purse of m. (commonly of 1000 pieces) तोडाm.

Dearth of m. दामदुकळ m.

Examination of m. पारख f.—Price paid for it, पारखाईf. पारखणावळf.—Skill at it, पारखf.

For, with, upon, &c. ready m.—dealing. रोखारोखी, रोखीनें, नगदानगद, नगदानगदी.

Hard m. Ready m. रोकडf. रोखपैसा m. रोखऐवज m. नगद n. नगदीf. नगदपैसा m.

Love of m. धनाशाf. धनलोभ m. द्रव्यलोभ m. वित्तेषणाf.

Making m. द्रव्यार्जन n. धनार्जन n. [&c. खर्चीf.

M. taken for probable expenses; pocket m., road m.,

M. returned to be exchanged. बदला m.

M. thrown away, *useless expense.* वृथादान n.

Raising of m. fraudulently. उचका m. [पार m.

Ready m.-dealing. रोखीचा-नगदीचा-&c. उदीम m.-व्यापारी.

Ready m.-dealer. रोखीचा-&c.उदमी-व्यापारी.

To examine m. पारखणें, पारख f. करणें g. of o.

Money-makes the mare to go. दाम करील काम, धनावांचून दुनिया पंगू, द्रव्येणसर्वेवशाः.

MONEY-BAG, *n.* v. BAG. हमिणीf. [and bonds.

MONEY-BORROWER, *n.* v. DEBTOR. रिणको&रिणकोनाम in notes

MONEY-BOX, *n. till to hold money.* गल्ल्याची पेटीf. गोलक m.

MONEY-BROKER. See MONEY-DEALER.

MONEY-CHANGER, *n.* सराफ, नाणेबटी or बट्टी.

Money bag of m. बदरीf.

MONEY-CHANGING, *n.* सराफीf. सट्टा m. सट्टाबट्टा m. नाणेबटी or बट्टीf.—loosely or compreh. व्याजबट्टा m.

MONEY-DEALER, *n.* सावकार or साहुकार, धनव्यापारी.

MONEY-DEALING, *n.* सावकारीf. घेवाणदेवाण n. देणेंघेणें n. देघेf.

MONEY-LENDER, *n.* v. CREDITOR. कर्जकरी, कर्जदार;—in notes and bonds, धनको & धनकोनाम.

Premium or bonus to a m. मंडाईf. मंडावणn. मनोतीf.

Relative standing or bearing of money lender and money borrower. धनकोरिणको n.

MONEY-LESS, *a.* v. POOR. निर्धन, धनहीन, धनावेगळा, धनानिराळा, अधन, अकांचन.

MONEY-MATTER, *n.* देणे घेण्याची (or देण्या घेण्याची) गोष्टf.-प्रकरणn.-&c. खात्यापोत्याचें प्रकरणn. [ऐवजm.

MONEY'S WORTH, *n. something that will bring money.* मोलn.

MONEYED, MONIED, *a.* v. RICH. पैकेकरी, पैसेकरी, पैकेवान्, पैसेवान्, पैकेवाला, पैसेवाला, पैकेपूर, पैसेपूर, धनवान्, धनिक

The m. body or interest. सावकाराm.

MONG-CORN, *n.* v. MESLIN. खेडf. खेडकरधान्यn.

MONGER, *n. dealer in, seller of.* विक्या (as मासेविक्या fishmonger, &c.), वाला (in comp.),बाज (in comp.), व्यापारी, व्यवसायी, विक्रेता.

MONGREL, *a. of mixed breed.* संकराचा, संकरजातीचा, संकरजात, संकरज, संकरजातीय, मिश्रजातीचा, मिश्रजातीय.

MONITION, *n.* v. ADMONITION, WARNING. ताकीदf. उपदेशm.

MONITIVE. See MONITORY.

MONITOR, *n. warner, instructor, &c.* शिक्षक, उपदेशक, हितोपदेशक, मंत्री, अभिमंता.
2 (at schools). मालचाटी or चाट्या, उपशिक्षक, उपगुरु.

MONITORIAL, *a. belonging to, &c. monitors.* मालचाट्यांचा, उपशिक्षकांचा.
2 See MOMITORY.

MONITORY, *a. giving or containing admonition.* उपदेशाचा, उपदेशक, उपदेशात्मक, उपदेशरूप, उपदेशपर, उद्बोधक.

MONK, *n. a religious recluse, inhabitant of a monastery,&c.* v. MENDICANT, ASCETIC. रोमनक्याथोलिक धर्मांतील जोगी-&c.—Hindu m. मठवासी, जोगी, अरण्य, वानप्रस्थ,वैराग्याश्रमी.

To turn m. भगवेंn. करणें-घेणें, जोगm. घेणें.

MONKEY, *n.* माकड, वानर, मर्कट, कपि, टाळेंभेंकेंn. डरा, रामदूत, शाखामृग, प्लवंग.

Cry or whoop of the m. हूपf. भुभुःकारm. भुपकारm.

Depredations of monkeys. वानरखादf.

Female m. माकडी *and* माकडीणf. मकडीf. वानरी *pop.* वानरीणf. &c.

Female m. with her suckling. बेंगलण *f.*

Male m. *leader of the troop.* झुपट, झुप्या, धोण्या.

M. of a male troop. सडेझुपट, सडेझुप्या.

M.-faces. वानरविचकुल्या *or* वेंचकुल्या *f. pl.*

M.-faced. माकडतोंड्या, वानरतोंड्या, वानऱ्या.

M.-tricks. वानरचेष्टा *f.* माकडचेष्टा *f.* वानरथेर*m.n.* मर्कटचेष्टा *f.* चेष्टा *f.* [खेंसणें.

To gnash, spit, & chatter at,—a monkey. खेंकणें, खेंकाटणें,

2 *beater of a pavior, &c.* मोगरा *m.* धुमस *m.*

MONKISH, *a.* जोग्याचा, मठवाशाचा, &c. मठवासिसंबंधी, मठवासिसदृश.

MONOCHORD, *n. instrument with one string.* एकतारी वाद्य *n.* Some kinds are, तुणतुणें *n.* (player on it, तुणतुण्या), किंगरी *f.* किन्नरी *f.* चवटकें *or* चवंडकें *n.*

MONOCULAR, MONOCULOUS, *a. having one eye.* एकडोळ्या, एकाक्ष, एकनेत्र, एकलोचन, काणा.

Pauci monoculi sunt honesti. क्वचित् काणो भवेत् साधुः.

MONODY, *n. song, &c. sung by one.* एकानें गायाचें गीत *n.*

MONOGAMIST, *a. one who disallows second marriages.* एकपत्नी, एकपत्नीव्रती, एकभार्यक, सकृत्विवाही, अपुनर्विवाही, सकृत्पत्नीक. [एकभार्याव्रत *n.*

MONOGAMY, *n. marriage with one wife only.* एकपत्नीव्रत *n.*

MONOGRAM, *n.* जोडलेलीं नामांचीं आद्यअक्षरें *n. pl.*

MONOLITH, *n.* एका दगडाचा खांब *m.* एक पाषाणस्तंभ *m.*

MONOLOGUE, *n. soliloquy.* आपल्या जिवाशीं-आपल्याशीं-आपल्या पाशीं-&c. केलेलें भाषण *n.* स्वसमीप भाषण *n.*

MONOMACHY, *n.* v. DUEL. द्वंद्वयुद्ध *n.*

MONOMANIA, MONOMANY, *n. derangement with respect to a particular subject.* एकविषयविक्षेप *m.* एकविषयभ्रम *m.* एकविषयोन्माद *m.*

MONOMANIAC, *a.* v. N. एकविषयविक्षिप्त, एकविषयभ्रांत.

MONOPETALOUS, *a. having only one petal.* एकपाकळीचा, एकफकडी, एकदलक.

MONOPOLIST, MONOPOLIZER, *n.* v. V. 1. साऱ्याचें सारें घेणारा, सगळ्याचा सगळा घेणारा.

2 मक्ता घेणारा, गादी घेणारा, मक्तेवाला, गादीवाला, खोत.

I. (esp. of the revenue, customs, &c.). इजारदार, खोत.

To MONOPOLIZE, *v. a. engross a commodity.* साऱ्याचें सारें *n.* घेणें, सगळ्याचा सगळा घेणें, सारें *n.* मारणें, एकट्यानें हात *m.* मारणें.

2 *obtain the exclusive right of selling or trading.* मक्ता *m.* -गुतका *m.*-गादी *f.*-&c. घेणें *g. of o.*

MONOPOLY, *n. sole power of selling or trading.* मक्ता *m.* गादी *f.* गुतका *m.* गुत्ता *m.* हुंडवा *or* हुंडा *m.*

2 (of customs, revenue, &c.). इजारा *m.* खोती *f.* खोतकी *f.* खंडणूक *f.* [एकाक्षर, एकाच्क.

MONOSYLLABIC, *a. having only one syllable.* एक अक्षराचा,

MONOSYLLABLE, *n.* एक अक्षर *n.* एकाक्षर *n.* एकाक्षरी शब्द *m.*

MONOTHEISM, *n.* एकेश्वरवाद *m.* एकेश्वरमत *n.*

MONOTHEIST, *n.* एकेश्वरवादी, एकेश्वरमतावलंबी.

MONOTHEISTIC, *a.* एकेश्वरवादसंबंधी, एकेश्वरमतसंबंधी.

MONOTONOUS, *a. continued in the same tone.* एकेसवनेचा, एकस्वराचा, एकसुरी, एकेच सवनेवर-एकेच स्वरावर-&c. घेतलेला, एकसवन, एकस्वर.

2 *unvaried, always the same.* एकसारखा, एकचप्रकारचा, एकप्रकारी, एकसुती, एकरंगी, एकरूपी.

MONOTONOUSLY, *adv.* v. A. 2. एकसारखा *decl.*

MONOTONY, *n.* v. A. 1. *uniformity of tone, want of inflection, &c.* एकसवन *f. n.* एकस्वर *m.* सवनभेदाभाव *m.*

2 *sameness, want of variety.* एकप्रकारीपणा *m.* एकरंगीपणा*m.* &c.एकप्रकार*m.* एकव्यापार*m.* व्यापारभेदाभाव*m.* अविशेषभाव*m.*

MONSOON, *n. rainy season.* पाऊसकाळ *m.* पाऊसकाळा *m.* पावसाळा *m.* पर्जन्यकाल *m.*

Closing rains of the m. वळवाचा पाऊस *or* वळीव पाऊस*m.*

Dampness and chilliness at the beginning of the m. मृगशितळाई *f.*

Of or belonging to the m. पाऊस काळाचा, वार्षिक.

The four months of the m. चौमास *m.* चतुर्मास *m.* चातुर्मास्य *n.*

MONSTER, *n. unnatural production.* विपरीं *n.* अद्भुत *n.* अद्भुनविषय *m.* चिह्न *n.* अवचिह्न *n.* ध्यान *n.* [नाटा *m.*

2 *person or thing unnaturally large.* धूड *n.* जुंगाड *n.* स-

3 *horribly wicked person.* अवतार *m.* राक्षस *m.* रावण *m.* पापराशि *m.* पापपुरुष *m.* कर्मचंडाळ.

MONSTROSITY. See MONSTROUSNESS, MONSTER.

MONSTROUS, *a. deviating from the course of nature.* विलक्षण, अद्भुत, विजातीय *pop.* विजाती, विरूप, सृष्टिपद्धतिबाह्य, सृष्टिक्रमबाह्य.

2 *enormous, huge, vast, &c.* v. LARGE. ऐवट, जगड्वाळ, जरब, जबर, अकराळविकराळ, अकटोविकट *or* अकटविकट, सनाटा- *indecl.* सपाटा.

3 *strange, striking, atrocious, &c.* अघोर, अकटोविकट, विकट, राक्षसी, अचाट, अघटित, अवघड. [चा *decl.*

MONSTROUS, *adv.* v. EXCESSIVELY. अतिशय, फारच, पराकाष्ठे-

MONSTROUSLY, *adv.* v. A. 1. 3. अकटोविकट.

I. See EXCESSIVELY. [पता *f.*

MONSTROUSNESS, *n.* v. A. 1. वैलक्षण्य *n.* विलक्षणभाव *m.* विरू-

2 ऐवटपणा *m.* अकराळविकराळपणा *m.* &c.

3 अघोरपणा *m.* अकटोविकटपणा *m.* &c.

MONTH, *n.* मास*m.* महिना *m.* माहे *m.* (in comp. as a prefix to the names of the months; as, माहे चैत्र, माहे मोहरम, &c.). The twelve months are, चैत्र, वैशाख, ज्येष्ठ, आषाढ, श्रावण, भाद्रपद, आश्विन, कार्तिक, मार्गशीर्ष, पौष, माघ, फाल्गुन. And the twelve *Muhammadan* months are, मोहरम (محرم), सफर (صفر), रबिलावल (ربيع الأول), रबिलाखर (ربيع الآخر), जमादिलावल (جماد الاول), जमादिलाखर (جماد الآخر) रजब (رجب), शाबान (شعبان), रमजान (رمضان), श-व्वाल (شوال), जिलकाद (ذي القعدة), जिल्हेज (ذي الحجة).

A half of a lunar m. पक्ष *m.* पाख *m.*

By the m. माहेवारीनें, माहेवार.

Dark or second half of the lunar m. वद्यपक्ष *m.* कृष्णपक्ष *m.* उत्तरपक्ष *m.* काळोखपाख *m.* दुसरापाख *m.* अपरपक्ष *m.* बहुल *m.*

Intercalary m. अधिकमास *m.* अधिकमहिना *m.* धोंडमास *m.* धोंडमहिना *m.* धोंडा *m.* मलमास *m.* पुरुषोत्तममास *m.*—occurring in a year in which a क्षयमास falls, संसर्प*m.*

Last day of the lunar half-m. पक्षांत *m.* पक्षावसर *m.*
Light or first half of the lunar m. शुद्धपक्ष *m.* शुक्लपक्ष *m.* चांदणें पाख *m.* पहिला पाख *m.* पूर्वपक्ष *m.* प्रथमपक्ष *m.* सितपक्ष *m.* देवपक्ष *m.*
Lunar m. चांद्रमास *m.* पक्षद्वय *n.* पक्षयुग *n.*
Period of four months. चौमास *m.*
Solar m. सौरमास *m.* सौर *m.*
Synodical m. यांतिकमास *m.*
That serves by the m. महिनेकरी. [नेमाल.
That is engaged by the m. (not by the trip). महि-
The coming m. पेसतरमास*m.* पुढचा-पुढला महिना *m.*
The current m. चालता महिना *m.* माहे मजकूर *m.*
The past m. माहे गुदस्त.
Within the *or* a m. महिन्याचे कांठीं.

MONTHLY, *a. performed, &c. in a month.* महिन्याचा, मासिक. 2 *happening once a month or every month.* महिन्याचा, प्रतिमहिन्याचा, मासिक, प्रातिमासिक.
Half-m. आर्द्धमासिक, पाक्षिक.
M. allowance. महिनेवारी *f.* माहेवारी *f.* माहेवार *n. v.* बांध, बांधून दे, ठरिव. [सिक *n.*
M. pay or wages. दरमाहा*m.* महिना*m.* माहेवार*n.f.* मा-

MONTHLY, *adv. once a month, every month.* दरमहिन्यास, दरमहां *or* माहां, महिन्याच्या महिन्यास, प्रतिमहिन्यास, प्रतिमासीं, चांद्रातीस.

MONUMENT, *n.* v. MEMORIAL. यादगारी *or* यादगिरी *f.* अठवणूक *f.* 2 *tomb, cenotaph, memorial column.* छत्री *f.* थडें *n.* थडगें *n.* चैत्य *n.* चिताचूडक *m.*
M. over a *Muhammadan.* रोजा *m.*
M. over a *Sannyási.* समाधि *m. pop.* समाध *f.*

MONUMENTAL, *a. belonging, &c. to a monument.* छत्रीचा, थडग्याचा, थडग्यावरचा.
2 See MEMORIAL.

To MOO, *v. n.*—a cow. हंबरणें *or* हंबारणें.

MOOD, *n.*—in grammar. अर्थ *m.* is the word used by recent Maráthí Grammarians.
2—in logic. प्रकार *m.* रूप *n.* [मनःस्थिति *f.*
3 *temper or state of mind.* वृत्ति *f.* भाव *m.* मनोवस्था *f.*
Merry m. आनंदवृत्ति *f.* हास्यवृत्ति *f.*

MOODINESS, *n.* v. A. खपीमर्जी *f.* रुसवा *m.* खटेपणा *m.* रुष्टता *f.*

MOODY, *a. angry, out of humour.* खपा, खटा, रुष्ट, विक्षिप्तवृत्ति, उद्विग्न, उद्विग्नमनस्क.

MOON, *n.* चांद *m.* चंद्र *m.* चंद्रमा *m.* सोम *m.* इंदु *m.* शशी *m.* शशधर, शशांक, नक्षत्रनाथ, विधु, सुधांशु, निशाकर.
Day of the m. तिथि *pop.* तीथ *f.* See them under LUNAR. [*f.* दर्श*m.*
Day of new m. आंवस *f.* अमावास्या *f.* अमावस्या *f.* अमा
Day of new or full m. पक्षांत *m.* [मासी *f.*
Day of full m. पुनव *or* पुनींव *f.* पूर्णिमा *f.* पौर्णिमा *f.* पूर्ण-
Digit of the m. चंद्रकला *f.* इंदुरेखा *f.*
Disk of the m. चंद्रबिंब *m. n.* चंद्रमंडल *n.* इंदुमंडल *n.*
Emersion of the m. चंद्रोदय *m.* [रात्र *f.*
First night of the m. after conjunction. चांदरात *or*
Fortnight of the waxing m. v. MONTH. शुक्लपक्ष *m.* शुद्धपक्ष *m.* [वद्यपक्ष*m.*
Fortnight of the waning m. v. MONTH. कृष्णपक्ष *m.*
Full m. पूर्णचंद्र *m.*
Mansion of the m. *asterism.* नक्षत्र *n.* See them under MANSION. [चक्र *n.*
Mansions of the m.—collectively. नक्षत्रमाला *f.* नक्षत्र-
M. of the first quarter. बालचंद्र *m.*
M. in an inauspicious mansion. घातचंद्र *m.*
New m. नवचांद *m.* प्रतिपच्चंद्र *m.*
Propitiousness of the m. चंद्रबल *or* ळ *n.*
Region or sphere of the m. चंद्रमंडल *n.*
Spots upon the disk of the m. लांच्छन *n.* कलंक *m.*
That blow on the rise of the m.—flowers. चंद्रविकासी.
Wane of the m. उतरतीकळा *f.*
Waxing of the m. चढतीकळा *f.*
To be about to rise—the m. मोहरणें. [पडतें.
The moon shines brightly. चांदणें पीठ पडतें, चांदणें टिपूर

MOON-BEAM, *n.* चंद्रकिरण *m.* चंद्ररश्मि *m.*

MOON-LIGHT, MOON-SHINE, *n.* चांदणें *n.* चंद्रप्रकाश *m.* चंद्रिका *f.* चंद्रजोत *f.* चंद्रज्योति *f.* चंद्रप्रभा *f.* कौमुदी *f.*
Bright m. चांदणेंपीठ *n.* चांदणें टिपूर, चटक चांदणें *n.*
A bag of m. भ्रमाचा *or* भरमाचा भोपळा *m.*

MOON-PLANT, *n. asclepias acida or aphylla.* सोम *m.* (the juice of it सोम *m.*) सोमलता *f.* सोमवल्ली *f.*

MOON-RISE, *n.* चंद्रोदय *m.*

MOONSHINY, MOONSHINE, *a.* चांदण्याचा, चंद्रप्रकाशाचा.
A m. night. चांदणीरात *f.*

MOON-STONE, *n.* चंद्रकांत *m.* सोमकांत *m.* चंद्रमणि *m.*

MOON-STRUCK, See LUNATIC.

MOONY, *a. having a crescent for a standard.* अर्धचंद्रध्वजांकित, अर्धचंद्रध्वजविशिष्ट.

MOOR, *n.* v. HEATH. रान *n.* [चिखडभुई *f.*
2 *marshy ground.* पाणथळ रान *n.* चिखड रान*n.* चिखडजमीन*f.*

To MOOR, *v. n. confine* (a ship, &c.) *by ropes, cables, &c.* खुंटवणें, बांधून ठेवणें.

MOORAGE, *n. place for mooring.* खुंटविण्याची जागा *f.*

MOOR-LAND. See MOOR.

MOORISH. See MARSHY.

MOOSE, *n. elk.* शंबर *pop.* सांबर *m.*

To MOOT, *v. a. bring forward, touch upon,* v. To MENTION. काढणें, गोष्ट *f.*-प्रसंग *m.*-उल्लेख *m.*-&c. काढणें *g. of o.*
2 See To ARGUE.

MOOT-CASE, MOOT-POINT, *n. unsettled case, disputed or disputable point.* लढा *m.* लडथड *f.* लांझा *m.*

MOP, *n.*—for cleaning. दांडपोतेरें *n.* पोतागा ?
2 *head of hair.* केंसटी *f.*

To MOP, *v. a.* दांडपोतेऱ्यानें साफ करणें.

To MOPE, *v. n. be dull & spiritless.* उदास-उदासी-मलूल-बेदिल-विषण्ण-&c. असणें-होऊन बसणें, उदासासारखा-वाणी-परी-&c. बसणें-करणें. [णारा, &c.

MOPE, *n.* MOPER, *n.* MOPISH, *a.* उदास,उदासी,उदासवाणी बस-

MOPE-EYED, *a. short sighted, purblind.* उफराट्या बाहुल्यांचा.

MOPPET, MOPSEY, *n. a rag baby.* चिरगुटाची पुतळी *f.*

Moral, *a. relating to conduct as right or wrong, relating to virtue and vice.* वर्त्तणुकीचा, वर्त्तणुकीविषयींचा, व्यवहाराचा, पापपुण्याच्या विचाराचा, नीतीच्या विचाराचा, व्यवहारविषयक-संबंधी, सदसद्विचारविषयक-संबंधी, सदसदाचारविषयक-संबंधी, विधिनिषेधान्वित, विधिनिषेधान्वयी.

2 *capable of moral actions, under moral laws.* विधिनिषेधाधीन, विधिनिषेधाचरणी, विधिनिषेधवान्, विधिनिषेधायत्त, नीतिज्ञ.

3 *supported by reason & probability.* युक्तिसिद्ध, अनुमानसिद्ध, तर्कसिद्ध, आनुमानिक, युक्तिभाव्य.

4 v. Virtuous, Just. सदाचरणी, सदाचारी, धर्माचारी, नीतिमान्, धर्म्य, सदाचरण संपन्न, नेकीचा, नेतीचा, नीतीचा.

Moral philosophy. नीति *f.* नीतिशास्त्र *n.* व्यवहारशास्त्र *n.*

M. rectitude. सुनीति *f.*

Moral, *n. doctrine inculcated by a fable, &c.* तात्पर्य*n.* तात्पर्यार्थ *m.* भावार्थ *m.* अभिप्राय *m.* हाशील *or* हासील *n.* तात्विक *n.* गर्भ *m.* रहस्य *n.* रस *m.* खुबी *f.* खोंच *f.* नोक *f.* निर्गलितार्थ *m.* ध्वन्यर्थ *m.*

Moralist, *n. teacher of morality.* नीतीचा उपदेश करणारा, नीतिमार्ग दाखवणारा-सांगणारा-&c. नीत्युपदेशक, नीत्युपदेष्टा, नीतिविवेचक, नीतिशिक्षक, सदसद्विवेचक.

2 *mere moral person.* सदाचारमार्गी, नीतिमार्गावलंबी, केवलनीतिमार्गाश्रयी.

Morality, *n. system of moral duties, ethics.* नीति *f.* नीतिशास्त्र *n.* नीतिविद्या *f.* व्यवहारशास्त्र *n.* अर्थशास्त्र *n.* नय *m.* सद्सद्विचार *m.* कर्त्तव्याकर्त्तव्यविचार *m.* बार्हस्पत्य *n.*

2 *practice of moral duties.* धर्माचरण *n.* धर्माचार *m.* सदाचरण *n.* नीतिमार्ग *m.* धर्मानुष्ठान *n.*

3 *moral quality.* धर्मत्व *n.* धर्म्यता *f.* नीति *f.* न्याय*m.* न्याय्यता*f.* धर्मानुसारिता *f.*

To **Moralize**, *v. a. apply to a moral purpose.* हितोपदेश *m.* करणें *with* वरून *of o.* नीति *f.* काढणें *with* पासून *of o.* हितोपदेशास्पद करणें.

To **Moralize**, *v. n. make moral reflections.* नीतीचा विचार*m.*-नीतीविषयींचा तर्क *m.*-हितोपदेशाची कल्पना *f.*-हितोपदेशाचा विचार*m.*-&c. करणें-काढणें.

Morally, *adv.* v. A. 1. नीतीनें, नीतीचा विचार पाहिला असतां, नीतिशास्त्राप्रमाणें, नीतितः.

3 युक्तीनें, अनुमानानें, अनुमानाच्यामार्गानें-रितीनें-&c.

4 सदाचरणानें, धर्माचारानें, सदाचरणें करून, धर्मतः.

Morals, *n. ethics*, v. Morality, 1. नीति *f.* नीतिशास्त्र *n.* नीतिविद्या *f.* दंडनीति *f.*

Good m. सुनीति *f.*

2 *course of life in regard to good and evil*, v. Conduct. आचरण *n.* आचार *m.* बर्त्तणूक *f.* वर्त्तन *n.* वृत्त *n.* वृत्ति *f.*

Morass, *n.* v. Marsh. पाणथळ *n.* पाणथळजमीन *n.* दलदल *f.*

Morassy, *a.* v. Marshy. दलदलीचा.

Morbid, *a. diseased, disordered.* अस्वस्थ, रोगी, रोगट, विकारी, विकाराचा, विकृत, रोगसंबंधी, रुग्ण. [रुग्णावस्था *f.*

Morbidness, *n.* v. A. रोगीपणा *m.* &c. अस्वस्थता*f.* अस्वास्थ्य *n.*

Morbific, **Morbifical**, *a. causing disease.* रोग उत्पन्नकरणारा, रोगी, रोगकारक-जनक, विकार कारक-कारी, रोगप्रद.

Morbose, *a. caused by disease.* रोगापासून झालेला, रोगोत्पन्न, रोगजनित, विकारजनित.

Mordacious, *a. given to biting.* चावरा, चावका, चावखोर, डसरा, डसका, डसकर. [*m.* &c.

Mordaciousness, **Mordacity**, *n.* v. A. चावरेपणा *m.* डसरेपणा

More, *a. greater in degree, quality, amount, &c.* अधिक, ज्यास्त, ज्यादा, ज्याफा, ज्यास्ती, जाजती, जबाद, अगळा, सरस.

M. or less. अधिकउणा, उणापुरा, कमज्यास्त, कंपेश, न्यूनाधिक, न्यूनातिरेक.

Rather m. अधिक आगळा.

2 *additional.* दुसरा, अणखीएक. [विशेष

More, *adv. to a greater degree.* अधिक, ज्यास्त, ज्यादा, ज्याफा,

More and more. उत्तरोत्तर, अधिकाधिक.

2 *a second or another time*, v. Again. अणखी, अणीक, पुनः.

To be no more. गमावणें, गत होणें.

To say no more, *at the least.* किंबहुना.

Moreover, *adv. further, besides, likewise.* अणखी, अणीक, शिवाई, दुसरा *decl.* एतदतिरिक्त, तदतिरिक्त;—as used in notes, &c. दिगर, दिगरमजमून.

Moribund, *a. that is in a dying state.* मरणोन्मुख, मुमूर्षु, मुमूर्षित, मरणानें जिंकलेला.

Morigerous, *a.* v. Obedient. आज्ञांकित, आज्ञाधारक, हुकुमबंदा.

Moringa. See Morunga.

Morion, *n. helment.* शिरस्त्राण *n.*

Morn, **Morning**, *n. early part of the day.* सकाळ *f.* प्रातःकाल *or* ळ *m.* प्रभात *n.* प्रभातकाल *m.* प्रत्यूष *m. n.* प्रत्यूषकाल *m.*

At m. and evening. सकाळसंध्याकाळ, सकाळसांज, सांजसकाळ, दोहींसांज, दुवेळां, दुवेळीं, दुवक्तां.

At m., noon, and evening. तिहींसांज *or* सांजा, तिहीं त्रिकाळ, त्रिकाल *or* ळ.

First sale of goods in the m. बोहणी *or* नी *f.*

In the m. सकाळ, सकाळां, सकाळीं, प्रातः, बोहणीचे प्रहरीं *or* पहारीं.

Repast in the early m. (to stay the stomach). बाळबाटी *f.* v. झोक, कर, चढव.

The m. meal (breakfast.) प्रातर्भोजन *n.*

To morrow m. सकाळीं, सकाळ, सकाळां.

2—as opp. to *afternoon.* दिनपूर्वार्ध *n.* पूर्वाह्ण*m.* पूर्वाह्णकाल*m.*

Morning, *a.* सकाळचा, प्रातःकाळचा, प्रातःकालिक.

Morning-star, *n.* पहाटेसदिसणारा शुक्र *m.* प्रभातसूचकतारा *f.*

Morose, *a. sour, sullen, crabbed.* कुरठा, दाष्ट, द्वाष्ट, दुष्ट, द्वाष्टीक, खंक, घुणा, घुम्या, कुधण, कटुस्वभाव.

Moroseness, *n.* v. A. कुरठेपणा *m.* दाष्टपणा *m.* दाष्टिकपणा *m.* &c. कटुस्वभाव *m.*

Morris, **Morris-dance**, *n.* टिपर (*or* टिपूर) खेळ*m.* टिपूरघाई *f.*

Morris-dancer, *n.* टिपर (*or* टिपूर) खेळ्या, टिपऱ्या.

Morrow, *n. day after the present day.* उद्यांचा दिवस *m.* दुसरा दिवस.

To morrow. उद्यां, उदयीक, फजर.

To m. morning. सकाळीं, सकाळ, सकाळां, फजर.

2 See Morning.

Morsel, *n. mouthful, piece of something to be eaten.* ग्रास*pop.* घास *m.* कवल *m.*

A dainty m. सुग्रास *m.*

2 v. Bit. तुकडा *m.* तुकडी *f.* नखभर (अन्न, &c.).

MORSURE, *n. act of biting.* चावा *m. v.* घे, दंश *pop.* डास *m.* & डांसा *m.* दंशन *n.*

MORTAL, *a. subject to death.* मरणधर्मी, मृत्युधर्मी, कालधर्मी, मरणधर्मक, मृत्युधर्मक, मर्त्य, मर्त्तव्य, मरणाधीन, मृत्युधीन, कालाधीन, कालवश, अंतवंत, नाशवंत, अनित्य.

The m. state. संसार *m.*

2 *killing, destructive of life,* v. DEADLY. प्राणघेणा, जीवघेणा, प्राणघातक, प्राणघातकी, अंतकर, अंतक, मरणप्रद, मृत्युप्रद, जिवासाड.

3—crime, &c. v. CAPITAL. प्राणांतदंडाचा, मृत्युदंडार्ह.

4 *belonging to man,* v. HUMAN. मनुष्यजातीचा, मनुष्यजातीय, मानुष. [क, अतिशयित.

5 *of the highest degree,* v. EXTREME. पराकाष्ठेचा, आत्यंति-

MORTAL, *n. a being subject to death, a human being.* मनुष्य *n.* मृत्युधर्मकव्यक्ति *f.* कालधर्मकव्यक्ति *f.* मर्त्य, मृत्युपात्र *n.* मरणपात्र *n.* मृत्यूचें खाजें *n.* काळाचें खाजें *n.* काळाचा पिंड *m.*

MORTALITY, *n.* v. A. 1. मृत्युधर्म *m.* मरणधर्म *m.* मर्त्यता *f.* मृत्युवशता *f.* मरणाधीनता *f.* अनित्यता *f.*

I. *humanity, human nature.* मनुष्यत्व *n.* मानुष्य *n.*

II. *frequency of death.* मरणाची सांत *f.*-धाम *f.*-सातरें *n.*

MORTALLY, *adv.* v. A. 2. मरण येईसा *decl.* मरण होईसा *decl.* जीवजाईसा *decl.* आप्राणांत, आमरण.

5 पराकाष्ठेचा *decl.* अतिशय. [ऊलूखल *n.*

MORTAR, *n. pounding vessel.* खल *m.* उखळी *f.* हमाम *m.* वाहान *n.*

Large m. usually fixed in the ground. उखळ *n.*

Pestle and m. हमामदस्ता *m.* खलबत्ता *m.*

Prepared by rubbing in a m. खलवी, घोटींव.

Rubbing in a m. खल *m.*

Stone-m. वाईन *n.* घांटवाईन *n.*

To rub in a m. खलणें, घोटणें.

2 (esp. for levigating medicaments). गरगटा *m.* गरगटणें *n.*

3 (for grinding snuff, bháng, &c.). कुंडी *f.* कुंडा *m.* कुंडला *m.* कुंड्या *m.*

4 *cement of lime, &c.* v. LIME. कमावलेला चुना *m.* चुन्याचा गारा *m.*-रद्दा *m.* चुना *m.* सुधा *f.*

5 *bomb-gun.* गुबारा *m.* गरनाळ *f. n.* गडगोळ *f.*

MORT DE CHIEN, *n. cholera.* मोडशी *f.* तरळ *f.* तरळमेंढी *f.* कुळीक *f.* कुळका *f.* विषूचिका *or* विशूचिका *f.*

MORTGAGE, *n. dead pledge.* गहाण ठेवलेली जमीन *f.* स्थावराधि *m.* क्षेत्राधि *m.*

In m. गहाणवट, गहाणवटीस.

To MORTGAGE, *v. a. pledge.* गहाण ठेवणें, गहाणवटीस-गहाणवट-ठेवणें, आधीकरण *n.* करणें *g. of o.* [कृत.

MORTGAGED, *p.* v. V. गहाण ठेवलेला, गहाणवटीस ठेवलेला, आधी-

MORTGAGEE, *n. person to whom an estate is mortgaged.* गहाण घेणारा, आधिधारी, आधिधारक, न्यासधारी.

MORTGAGER, *n.* v. V. गहाण ठेवणारा, गहाणवटीस ठेवणारा, आधीकरणकर्त्ता.

MORTIFEROUS, *a.* v. DEADLY. प्राणघातक, प्राणांतकर, मृत्युप्रद.

MORTIFICATION, *n.* v. V. A.—*act.* सडवणें *n.* &c.—*state.* चैतन्य नाश *m.* चेतनानाश *m.* जीवित्वनाश *m.*

2 मारणें *n.* स्तंभन *n.* स्तंभ *m.*

3 दंडणें *n.* दंडन *n.* दमन *n.* संयमन *n.*

4 रगमोड *f.* छानमोड *f.* बोडणें *n.* बोडणी *f.* मानखंडन *n.* मानभंजन *n.* अभिमानखंडन *n.* मुखभंजन *n.*—*state.* पाणउतारा *m.* मानभंग *m.* फजिती *f.* मानहानि *f.* तेजोभंग *m.* बदशान *f.*

v. V. N.—*state.* चेतनानाश *m.* जीवित्वनाश *m.* मांसनाश *m.* मांसातिपाक *m.*

3 जोग *m. v.* घे, तप *n.* तपश्चर्या *f.* वैराग्य *n.*

MORTIFIED, *p.* v. V. A. 1. सडवलेला &c.

3—lust or appetite. दंडित, दमित, संयमित, वशीकृत.—person. जितेंद्रिय, विषयातीत, मोहातीत, विरक्त, वीतकाम, वीतराग, वीतस्पृह, संयतेंद्रिय, विषयपराङ्मुख. Some terms, epithets, &c. for a mortified person are, वैरागी, गोस्वामी *pop.* गोसावी, संत, प्रशांतमनुष्य, प्रशांतात्मा, त्यागी, संयमी, वैराग्यशाली, तपःशाली, वशी, देहीं असून विदेही, जितकामक्रोधादि.

To MORTIFY, *v. a. destroy the vitality of.* सडवणें, जाळणें, चैतन्यनाश *m.*-चेतनानाश *m.*-जीवित्वनाश *m.*-&c. करणें, चैतन्य *n.* नष्ट करणें. [&c. करणें *g. of. o.*

2 *destroy the active power of.* मारणें, स्तंभन *n.*-स्तंभ *m.*-

3 *subdue, reduce, restrain, &c.*—the body, a lust, &c. दंडणें, जाळणें, मारणें, जीव *m.* जाळणें-वाळवणें, दंडन *n.*-दमन *n.*-दम *m.*-&c. करणें, इंद्रियें *n. pl.* जिंकणें-वश करणें, इंद्रियदमन *n.*-इंद्रियपराजय *m.*-&c. करणें.

4 *abase, vex, depress, &c.* v. To HUMBLE. लाजवणें, पाणउतारा *m.*-रगमोड *f.*-फजिती *f.*-मानभंग *m.*-&c. करणें *g. of o.* नाक *n.*-मान *f.* खालीं करणें *or* करविणें *g. of o.* खालीं पाहायास लावणें, अधोमुख करणें, फजीत करणें.

To MORTIFY, *v. n. die, gangrene, lose vitality, &c.* मरणें, सडणें, जीवित्व *n.*-&c. जाणें *g. of s.* मांसनाश *m.*-चेतनानाश *m.*-जीवित्वनाश *m.*-&c. होणें *g. of s.*

2 *lose active power.* मरणें, स्तंभ *m.*-स्तंभन *n.* होणें *g. of s.*

3 *practise religious austerities.* जोग *m.* घेणें, वैराग्य *n.* धरणें, तप *n.*-तपश्चर्या *f.*-देहदंडन *n.*-वैराग्याचरण *n.*-&c. करणें.

MORTIFYING, *p. a.* v. V. A. 4. *and* HUMBLING. पाणउतान्याचा, मानभंजक.

MORTISE, *n. cut to receive a tenon.* कुसूचें घर *n.* भोंक *n.* दर *m. f.* खोबळा *m.* खोबण *f. m.* खोबणी *f.* विंधी *f.*

To MORTISE, *v. a. join by a mortise.* कळाशी *or* सी *f.* करणें-बसवणें.

MORTMAIN, *n. possession without power of alienation.* अदेय भोग *m.* अन्यादेय भोग *m.*

MORTUARY, *a. belonging to the burial of the dead.* मूठमातीचा, मरतिकाचा, उत्तरकार्याचा.

MORUNGA, *n.*—hyperanthera or guilandina. शेवगा *or* शेगवा *m.* शेगट *m.* शेगूळ *m.* शोभांजन *or* सौभांजन *m.* शिग्रु *m.*

MORUNGY-ROOT, *n.* शेवग्याचें-&c. मूळ *n.* शोभांजन मूल *n.* शिग्रुमूल *n.*

MOSAIC, *a.*—work, &c. चौरंगी, पांचरंगी, विचित्र जडावाचा.

MOSQUE, *n.* मसीद *or* मशीद *f.* दरगा *m.*

Sweeper of a m. मुजावर.

MOSQUITO. See MUSQUITO.

MOSS, *n.* शेवाळ *n.* शैवाल *m.* These words answer also for the green mosslike substance which grows on the surface of stagnant water.

To be covered with m. शेवाळणें.

Moss-grown, **Mossed**, **Mossy**, *a. overgrown, &c. with moss.* शेवाळलेला, शैवालविशिष्ट, शैवालयुक्त, शैवलित.

Most, *a. consisting of the greatest number.* बहुतकरून सर्व, बहुतकरून सगळा, फार, बहुत, बहुतेक.

For the m. part. फारकरून, बहुतकरून, प्रायः, प्रायशः.

Most, *adv. in the greatest degree.* बहुत, फार, अति, अतिशय, सर्वांपेक्षां अधिक.

Most, *n. greatest number or part.* बहुतेक *with a noun*, फारकरून *with a noun.* [त्तम शेरा *m.*

2 *greatest degree or quantity.* पराकाष्ठा *f.* उत्तमपक्ष *m.* उ-

At m. At the m. फार झाला (*decl.*) तर, फार केला(*decl.*) तर, पराकाष्ठा झाली तर, उत्तम पक्षाचा *decl.*

Mostly, *adv. for the greatest part, chiefly.* फारकरून, बहुतकरून, नौबांटे, नव्याण्णवबांटे, बहुधा, बहुशः, सामान्यतः.

Mote, *n. small particle.* अणु *m.* कण *m.* कणिका *f.* त्रसरेणु *m.f.*

The motes in a sunbeam. अणुरेणु *m. pl.* अणुरेणुजाल *n.*

Moth, *n.*—the insect. पतंग *m.* तसर *m.* पिंगाणें *n.*

2 (of books and cloth). कसर *f.*

Moth-eaten, *a.* कसर लागलेला, कसरखाल्लेला, कसरखाद.

Mother, *n.* आई *f.* माय *f.* मा *f.* माता *f.* अंबा *f.* जननी *f.* मातृ (in comp. as m's. family, मातृकुल, मातृगोत्र, &c.)—in respect, मातृश्री *pop.* मातोश्री *or* मातुश्री *f.* मावली *or* माउली *f.* मायमाउली *f.* [सापत्न, सावत्र.

Born of a different m. भिन्नोदर, अन्योदर, असहोदर,

Foster m. उपमाता *f.*

Half-m., step-m. सापत्नआई *f.* सावत्रआई *f.* [रें *n. pl.*

M. and father. आईबाप *m. pl.* आईबापें *n. pl.* मातापित-

Mother's house (of a married girl). माहेर *n.* माहेरघर*n.* मातृगृह *n.*—Married girl living in it. माहेरकरीण *f.* माहेरवाशीण *f.*—Living in it of do. माहेरवास *m.*

O mother earth receive me into thy bosom. दे माय धरणी ठाव. [त्यक्ता *f.*

2 *a woman having children.* लेंकुरवाळी *f.* लेकुरकरीण *f.* अप-

3 (in vinegar, &c.). दोर *m.* चिकटा *m.* [हृजिक.

Mother, *a. native.* आंगचा, जातीचा, जन्माचा, स्वाभाविक, सा-

Mother-in-law, *n.* सासू *f.* श्वश्रू *f.* मामी *f.* (e.i. wife's mother.)

Father of m. आजेसासरा *m.*

Mother of m. आजेसासू *f.*

M. of one's son or daughter. विहीण *f.*

Mother of pearl, *n.* मोतीं शिंप *f.* मुक्तास्फोट *m.* मुक्तागार*n.*

Mother-tongue, *n.* आंगची बोली *f.* जन्माची बोली *f.* जन्मभाषा *f.* जातिभाषा *f.*

Motherhood, *n.* आईपणा *m.* मातृत्व *n.*

Motherless, *a. of whom the mother is dead.* आईपोरका, मतमातृक, मृतमातृक, हीनमातृक.

Motherliness, *n.* v. A. 2. माउलपण *n.* माउलपणा *m.*

Motherly, *a. belonging to a mother.* आईचा, आईच्याविषयींचा, मातृक, मातृसंबंधी.

2 *becoming a mother, tender, parental.* आईसारखा, माउलीसारखा, मातृधर्माचा, माउलपणाचा, मातृसदृश, मातृकल्प.

M. old woman. आईबाई *f.* माउली *or* मावली *f.*

Motherly, *adv. like a mother.* आईसारखा *decl.* आईवाणी, आईपरी, आईच्यापरी.

Motion, *n.*—as opposed to rest. गति *f.* चाल *f.* गमन *n.* चलन *n.* हालणें *n.* चालणें *n.* फिरणें *n.* चार *m.*

M. of a machine. सेळ *m.* [रणें.

To set or put in m. चालीस लावणें, चालता *or* चालू क

2 *animal life and action.* चलनवलन *pop.* चळणवळण *n.* हालचाल *f.* चेष्टा *f.*

3 *gesture, &c.* v. Action. अंगविक्षेप *m.* आंगिकचेष्टा *f.*

4 *agitation, intestine action.* गडबड *f.* गलबल *f.* खडबड *f.* खळबळ *f.* गदळागदळ *f.* खवळाखवळ *f.* क्षोभ *m.* क्षुब्धता *f.*

5 *feeling or thought arising, impulse.* भाव *m.* वासना *f.* बुद्धि *f.* कल्पना *f.* मनोदय *m.* मनोवृत्ति *f.* चेव *m.*

6 *proposal made.* काढलेला अभिप्राय *m.* सुचवलेला अभिप्राय*m.* कार्यकर्तव्यसूचना *f.* कार्यसूचकभाषण *n.* कर्त्तव्योपन्यास *m.*

7—in medicine ; *stool.* ढाळ *m.* रेच *m.*

To **Motion**, *v. n. make a gesture.* खूण *f.*-इशारत *f.*-इशारा *m.* -&c. करणें.

Motionless, *a.* निश्चल *or* ळ, स्थिर, स्तब्ध, अचल, निचेष्ट, अचेष्ट, गतिहीन-शून्य, चेत. [जक.

Motive, *a. causing motion,* v. Mover. चालक, प्रवर्त्तक, प्रयो-

Motive, *n. that which incites to action.* कारण *n.* हेतु *m.* निमित्त *n.* प्रवृत्तिनिमित्त *n.* सबब *f.* प्रवर्त्तक *n.* प्रयोजक *n.* उत्तेजन *n.* प्रयोजन *n.*

Relation between the m. (or efficient) and the work (or effect proposed). प्रयोज्य प्रयोजकभाव *m.*

Motley, *a. composed of different colors.* अनेकरंगी, पंचरंगी, नानारंगी, बहुरंगी, चित्रविचित्र.

2 *composed of different kinds, &c.* v. Medley. पंचमिसळीचा, विजातीय, विजोड.

Motor Motory. See Mover.

Motto, *n. sentence or phrase*—as on a signet, prefixed to an essay, &c. किताबत *f.* मुद्रादिकावरील वाक्य *n.*-लेख *m.* मुद्रालेख *m.*

Mould, *n. concretion from damp.* बुरशी *or* सी *f.* बुरसा *m.* बुरा *m.* केनशी *f.* केमी *f.* चित्ती *f.*

A shooting or thread of m. जळमट *n.*

White m. भूर *f.* भुरी *f.*

2 *earth,* v. Soil. माती *f.*

Black m. काळी *f.* बावरी *f.* बावरीमाती *f.*

3 *matrix.* सांचा *m.* मूस *f.* ओतणी *f.*

4 *cast, figure,* v. Form. ढाळ *m.* घाट *m.* डौल *m.* मटी *f.*

Of the same m. प्रतीचा. [बुरसाविणें.

To **Mould**, *v. a. make mouldy.* बुरशी *f.*-&c. आणणें-चढवणें,

2 *fashion, make,* v. To Form. घडणें, वळवणें, काढणें, उतरणें, बनावणें, घाट *m.* घालणें, आकार *m.* देणें.

To m. to ones wishes or will. माठरणें, माठळणें.

3 v. To Knead. मळणें, तिंबणें, मर्दणें.

To **Mould**, *v. n. get mouldy.* बुरशेणें, बुरसणें, बुरसावणें, बुरसटणें, बुरटणें, उबटणें, केनसावणें, केमुसणें, बुरशी *f.*-&c. येणें-चढणें.

2—as melons, &c. *contract black m.* कोजळणें.

Moulded, *p.* v. V. A. 2. घडलेला, काढलेला, आकार दिल्हेला, &c.

3 मळलेला, मर्दित. [काढणारा, &c.

Moulder, *n.* **Moulding**, *p. a.* v. V. A. 2. घडणारा, उतरणारा,

To **Moulder**, *v. n. turn to dust, crumble away.* झुरणें, झिरणें,

झरणें, गळणें, मातीशींमिळून जाणें, मातीसमिळणें, माती *f.*-चुराडा *m.*-धूळ *f.*-&c. होणें *g. of s.*

2 *dwindle away, waste away.* घटणें, लाहनालणें, झुरणें, क्षय *m.*-&c. होणें *g. of s.*

MOULDINESS, *n.* v. A. 1. *and* MOULD. बुरशेपणा *m.* बुरसलेलेपणा *m.* &c. चेती *or* चिती *f.*

2 कुबटपणा *m.* सापटपणा *m.* &c.

I.—as appearing in fine hairs or lines. कापूस *m.*

MOULDING, *n.* v. V. A. 2.—*act.* घडणें *n.* काडणें *n.* बळबळणें *n.* &c. घडणी *f.*

3 मळणें *n.* &c. मळणी *f.* मर्दन *n.*

I.—in architecture. कंगणी *f.* कंगोरा *m.*

MOULDY, *a. overgrown with mould.* बुरशा *or* बुरसा, बुरसलेला, केमुसलेला, बुरशी चढलेला, &c. बुरशेल, बुरशेला.

To become m. v. To MOULD. केनसावणें, बुरटणें.

2—of smells. कुबट, कुबीट *or* कुईट, सापट, उबट.

To smell m. कुबटणें.

To MOULT, *v. n. shed or cast the feathers, hair, &c.* पिसें *n. pl.*-पर *m.pl.*-पंख *m.pl*-&c. झडणें *g. of s.* पर*m.*-पिसें *n. pl.*-&c. गाळणें-टाकणें-बदलणें-पालटणें-झाडणें.

MOULTING, *n.* v. V.—*act.* परझाडणी *f.* पिसेझाडणी *f.* परगळणी *f.* वार्षिकपक्षपात *m. or* पतन *n.*

To MOUNCH. See To MUNCH.

MOUND, MOUNT, *n. raised bank,* v. BANK. बांध *m.* बांधण *n.* बंधारा *m.* धमधमा *m.* धमामा *m.* धक्का *m.* ताल *f.* बरंबा *m.*

2 *eminence, &c.* v. HILL, HILLOCK. डोंगरी *f.* टेंकडी *f.* टेंकडें *n.* बिडा *m.* टेंब *m.* टेंक *f.* उंचाड *n.*

To MOUNT, *v. n. rise on high, ascend.* उडणें, वर जाणें, उंच जाणें, ऊर्ध्वगमन*n.*-उपरिगमन*n.*-&c. करणें.

2 *get on horseback, &c.* चढणें, आरूढणें, सवार *or* स्वार होणें, आरोहण*n.*-अवरोहण*n.*-&c. करणें.

3 See To AMOUNT.

To MOUNT, *v. a. lift on high,* v. To RAISE. चढवणें, उंच करणें.

2 (a horse, hill, &c.) *climb, ascend.* चढणें-चढून बसणें *with* वर *of o.* आरोह*m.*-आरोहण*n.*-&c. करणें *with* वर *of o.* आरूढ होणें.

3 *place on horseback, furnish with a steed.* चढवणें, सवार *or* स्वार करणें, बसवणें, घोडा*m.*-&c. देणें, आरूढ करणें.

4 (guard) पाहरा*m.* करणें, पाहऱ्यावर जाणें.

5 (a map, &c.) रूल पट्टी *f.* बसवणें.

6 (a gem) कोंदणांत बसवणें.

MOUNTAIN, *n. hill.* डोंगर*m.* पर्वत*m.* पहाड*m.* गिरि*m.* नग*m.* शैल*m.* अद्रि*m.* भूधर*m.* धरणीधर*m.* धरणीकीलक*m.* अचल*m.*

Crest or brow of a m. माथा*m.* शिखर*n.* घाटमाथा*m.* नगमूर्द्धा*m.*

Country at the foot of a m. तळघाट*m.*

Face of a m. आडवण*n.*

Foot of a m. तळघाट*m.*

Pass over a m. घाट*m.*

Range of mountains. घाट*m.* पर्वत*m.* कुलपर्वत*m.* कुलाद्रि *m.* कुलाचल*m.*

Ridge of a m. घाटमाथा*m.* घाटसरी *f.*

The seven great *ranges of mountains* in India are, सह्याद्रि, विंध्याद्रि, मलयाद्रि, माहेंद्राद्रि, शुक्त्यद्रि, ऋक्षाद्रि, पारियात्राद्रि.

To make a m. of a mole hill. रजाचा गज*m.* करणें, राईचा पर्वत*m.* करणें, पराचा कावळा*m.* करणें, पुळीचें फाफर*n.* करणें.

MOUNTAIN, *a. belonging, &c. to a m.* डोंगराचा, पर्वताचा, &c. डोंगरी, पर्वतीय, शैल, पर्वतसंबंधी, &c.

MOUNTAINEER, *n. highlander.* पहाडी, डोंगरी, पहाड्या, डोंगऱ्या, डोंगरकरी, पर्वतीयमनुष्य.

MOUNTAINOUS, *a. hilly.* डोंगरी, डोंगराचा, डोंगराळ, डोंगरबट, पहाडी, पर्वतीय, पर्वतमय, शैल.

2 See LARGE.

MOUNTEBANK, *n. quack, charlatan, ignorant pretender to medicine.* ढोंगी वैद्य, वाय वैद्य, बायीचा वैद्य, नाकाडोळ्याचा वैद्य, टाण्याटोण्याचा वैद्य, बाडी वैद्य, पहाडी वैद्य, अविदितागम वैद्य.

2 See PRETENDER.

MOUNTED, *p.* v. V. N. 2. चढलेला, सवार *or* स्वार, आरूढ.

v. V. A. 2. सवार केलेला-झालेला, आरूढ.

MOUNTING, *n.* v. V. N. 1.—*act.* उडणें*n.* वर जाणें*n.* आरोहण*n.* ऊर्ध्वगमन*n.* उपरिगमन*n.*

2 चढणें*n.* आरोह*m.* आरोहण*n.* अवरोहण*n.* अधिरोहण*n.*

v. V. A. 2. आरोह*m.* आरोहण*n.* अवरोहण*n.*

3 सवार करणें*n.* बसवणें*n.* &c. आरूढीकरण*n.*

I. *ornament mounted,* v. ORNAMENT. डागिना*m.*

End piece of the m. of a sword scabbard. तहनाल*n.*

To MOURN, *v. n. sorrow, grieve.* रडणें, दुःख*n.*-खेद*m.*-हायहाय *f.*-र *f.*-&c. करणें, दुःखांत-&c. असणें.

2 (for a dead person) *wear the habit of sorrow.* सुतकीवेष *m.*-अमंगलवेष*m.*-&c. धरणें-घेणें.

To MOURN, *v. a. deplore, bewail, regret,* v. To LAMENT. रडणें, दुःख*m.*-खेद*m.*-शोक*m.*-&c. करणें-बाळगणें-मानणें *g. of o.* शोचणें.

MOURNER, *n.* MOURNING, *p. a.* v. V. N. 1. रडणारा, दुःख करणारा, खेद करणारा, खिन्न, खेदी, शोकी.

2 सुतकीवेष घेणारा-घेतलेला, &c. सुतकी.

MOURNFUL, *n.*—of persons, v. SORROWFUL. खिन्न, खेदी, शोकी, दिलगीर, खेदयुक्त.

2—of events, appearances, &c. v. CALAMITOUS, LAMENTABLE. दुःखकारक, दुखप्रद, दुःखावह, खेदजनक, खेदप्रद, शोच्य.

3 *expressing sorrow, betokening grief.* खेद दाखवणारा, खेदसूचक, खेददर्शक, खेदबोधक, अशुभसूचक-दर्शक-ज्ञापक.

4—of sounds; *dolorous, piteous.* रडका, रडवा, काकळूतवाणा, काकळूतवाणी, किलवाणा *or* णी, केविलवाणा *or* णी.

MOURNFULLY, *adv.* v. A. दुःखाचें चालीनें-गतीनें, रडके चालीनें, खेदानें, दुःखानें, खेदपूर्वक, खेदसूचनापूर्वक.

MOURNFULNESS. See SORROW.

MOURNING, *n.* v. V. N. 1.—*and* SORROW. दुःख *n.* खेद *m.* शोक *m.* रड *f.* र *f.* रुदन *n.* रोदन*n.*

I. *the dress of mourners.* सुतकीपांघरूण *n.* सुतकीवेष *m.* मरतीकवेष *m.* अशुभकालीनवेष *m.* शोकसूचकवेष *m.* The Hindus express mourning by leaving off the turban, sandals, robes, &c.

MOUSE, *n.* v. RAT. उंदीर *m.* पिटकुलाउंदीर *m.* मूषक *m.* There is no word in common use for a *mouse* as distinguished from a rat.

Still as a m. चिप्प जिता की मेला.

MOUSE-TRAP, *n.* उंदिराचा *or* उंदराचा सांपळा *m.* उंदराची पिंजरी *f.*

MOUTH, *n.* तोंड *n.* मुख *n.* वदन *n.* आस्य *n.* तुंड *n.* आनन *n.* वक्त्र *n.*—contemptuously, v. FACE, MUZZLE. भोकाड *n.* भोकाडा *m.* मुसकाड *n.* मुसकूट *n.* आ *m.* तोंडाची मूस *f.*—corresponding to *mill, grinding machine, &c.* जातें *n.* धाणा *m.* जेवणी *f.* चरक *m.* चाबा *m.*

A toothless m. बोळकें *n.*

By word of m. तोंडजबानी, मुखजबानी, तोंडजबानीनें, मुखजबानीनें, तोंडातोंडीं. [बानीचा.

Conducted by word of m. तोंडचा, मुखजबानीचा, तोंडज-

Corners of the m. सृक्किणी *f. pl.*

Dryness or parchedness of the m. मुखशोष *m.*

From m. to m.—a report. कानोकानीं, कर्णोपकर्णीं lit. from ear to ear. [तोमुखीं.

In every body's m. सर्वांतोंडीं, सर्वांमुखीं, सर्वतोमुखीं, विश्व-

M. (i. e. person) requiring to be fed. खातेंतोंड *n.*

Roof of the m. टाळू *f.* टाळें *n.* [&c.) मुखरस *m.*

Slime at the corner of the m. (from much speaking,

Stopping the m. of तोंडबंदी *f.* वागुरोध *m.* वाक्स्तंभ *m.*

That lives from hand to m. उत्पन्नभक्षी.

Washing the m. (after meals &c.). मुखमार्जन *n.* मुखप्रक्षालन *n.* [*m. f.* चुळका *m.*

Water taken to rinse the m. गुळणा *m.* गुळणी *f.* चूळ

Water rising in the m. गरटई *or* गरडई *f.* गरळ *f.*

To affect the m. तोंड *n.* देणें.

To beat the m. with the back of the hand,—in sign of distress. बोंब *f.* मारणें-ठोकणें, तोंड *n.* घेणें, शंख *m.*-शिमगा *m.*-शंखाचें *n.*-शंखध्वनि *m.*-पांचजन्य *or* पांचजन्याचें *n.*-कार्त्तिक पंचक *n.*-अर्जुनवाद्य *n.* करणें.

To be down in the m. तोंड *n.*-मुखश्री *f.*-&c. उतरणें *g. of s.* पायपोसासारखें-शेणखाल्ल्यासारखें तोंड *n.* करणें *or* होणें *with g. of s.*

To be in every body's m. गाजणें.

To become sore,—the m. तोंड *n.* येणें.

To bring on a sore m. (through mercury, &c.). तोंड *n.* आणणें-घेणें. [लाळ *f.* घोटणें.

To have one's m. watering for. तोंडाला पाणी *n.* सुटणें,

To lock up the m. तोंडास खीळ *f.* घालणें.

To make mouths at, v. To MIMIC. तोंड *n.* विचकणें, बांकुल्या *or* वांकोल्या *f. pl.*-&c. दाखवणें.

To open one's m. to speak. तोंड *n.* लावणें.

To run at the m. लाळणें.

To sit with the open m. of expectation. आ वासून *or* पसरून बसणें.

To stop the m. of (by bribe). तोंड *n.* बांधणें.

To strike across the m. तोंडावर मारणें, मुसकटणें *or* मुसकुटणें, थोबाडणें.

To wag the m. at. तोंड *n.* टाकणें.

2 *aperture, orifice.* तोंड *n.* मुख *n.* द्वार *n.*

3 (of a river). मुख *n.*

To MOUTH, *v. n. speak with a loud, affected, pompous voice.* मोठ्या आवानें-डौलानें-आडंबरानें-&c. बोलणें, गळा फुगवून बोलणें, मोठ्यानें बोलणें, उचलून बोलणें.

To MOUTH, *v. a. utter pompously, affectedly, &c.* डौलानें-काशीकरी डौलानें-&c. बोलणें-सांगणें-वाचणें, गळा फुगवून बोलणें-सांगणें.

2 *grind in the mouth.* चावणें.

3 *seize with the mouth.* तोंडांत धरणें.

4 v. To MOCK. वेडावणें, वेडावणी *f.*-वेटावणी *f.*-&c. दाखवणें.

MOUTH-FRIEND, *n. a friend only in profession.* तोंडाचा मित्र, तोंडापुरता मित्र. [मुखपूरण *n.*

MOUTH-FUL, *n.* ग्रास *pop.* घास *or* घांस *m.* कवल *pop.* कवळ *m.*

Huge m. (esp. of parched grain or dry food). बोकाणा *m.* बोकणा *m.* बोकणी *f.* बोकांडा *m.*

Mere m. तोंडीं लावणें *n.*

M. of liquid taken to spit out. गुळणा *m.* गुळणी *f.*

M. of boiled rice. उंडी *f.* [ग्रास *m.*

M. put aside as an offering to avert an evil eye. दृष्टि-

MOUTH-HONOR, *n. hollow civility.* तोंडचा आदर *m.* तोंडचा सन्मान *m.* पैठणी आदर *m.*

MOUTH-PIECE, *n.* (of a wind instrument, &c.). जिव्हाळी *f.* पिंपाणी *or* पिंपारी *f.* पेपाणी *f.* पिंकाणी *f.* पेंपेरें *or* पोंपेरें *n.*

2 वांटचा-वतीचा-&c. बोलणारा.

MOUTHED, *p. and a.* v. V. A. 1. मोठ्या आवानें बोललेला, &c.

I. *furnished with a mouth.* तोंडाचा, तोंडी (in comp.), तोंडा (in comp.).

MOVABLE, *a.* v. V. *not stationary.* चालाया-चालवायाजोगा-सारखा-&c. चर, चल, जंगम, अस्थावर, चरिष्णु, गमनयोग्य, गमनार्ह, गमनशक्य.

M. and immovable. चलाचल, चराचर.

MOVABLENESS, *n.* v. A. चरभाव *m.* चलभाव *m.* गमनयोग्यता *f.* गमनशक्ति *f.*

MOVABLES, *n. goods not fixed, chattels.* उचलाऊमाल *m.* जिंदगी *f.* घरजिंदगी *f.* चीजवस्त *f.* मालमत्ता *f.* चरद्रव्य *n.* इस्ताद *m. f.* जंगममाल *m.* जंगमजिंदगी *f.*

To MOVE, *v. a. put in motion, cause to change place or posture.* चालवणें, हालवणें, चालेसा-हालेसा-&c. करणें, चालता-चालू-&c. करणें, चाल *f.*-गति *f.*-&c. देणें, स्थानांतर *n.*-गमन *n.*-&c. करविणें *g. of o.*

2 *give impulse to.* सरकावणें, सरसावणें, सारणें, ढाळणें, सरकविणें, चालता-चालू-&c. करणें, प्रवर्त्तवणें.

3 *advance, recommend, &c.* v. To PROPOSE. उद्दू *m.*-विचार *m.*-गोष्ट *f.*-&c. काढणें *g. of o.* कर्त्तव्योपन्यास *m.*-कर्त्तव्योपस्थान *n.*-कर्त्तव्योद्भावन *n.* करणें.

4 *influence, induce, lead, persuade.* वळवणें, मानवणें, ओढणें, मनावून-ओढून-&c. घेणें, बधवणें, प्रवर्त्तवणें, प्रवृत्त-उन्मुख-उद्युक्त-&c. करणें, ओढ *f.*-ओढा *m.*-&c. लागणें *in. con.*

5 *touch pathetically, excite feeling in,* v. To AFFECT. पाझरवणें, द्रवविणें, पघळवणें, पाझर *m.*-कळवळा *m.*-कळवळ *f.*-द्रव *m.*-&c. आणणें.

6 *put into commotion, excite tumult, agitate; &c.* गडबडवणें, गलबलवणें, क्षोभवणें, गलबल *f.*-गडबड *f.*-डामाडूळ *f.*- क्षोभ *m.*-व्याक्षोभ *m.*-&c. करणें.

7 *provoke, &c.* v. To ANGER. चेष्टावणें, चेखवणें.

To MOVE, *v. n. be in motion.* हालणें *or* हलणें *or* हिलणें, चालणें, फिरणें, खेळणें, चेष्टणें, चालता-चालू-गतिविशिष्ट-&c. असणें.

To m. aside, *make way, leave room.* फरकणें, फरक होणें, सरकणें.

2 *yield on impulse, &c. stir, go.* चालणें, सरणें, सरकणें, सरकावणें, सरसावणें, चालता-चालू-&c. होणें, प्रवर्त्तणें.

3 *proceed, pass, walk, go.* चालणें, जाणें, स्थलांतर *n.*-स्थानांतर *n.*-&c. करणें *or* होणें *with g. of s.*

4 *have vital action.* चलनवलन*pop.* चळणबळण *n.*-हालचाल*f.*-चेष्टा *f.*-&c. असणें, चेष्टणें. [हालवणें.

To begin to m. (stir, work, act, &c.). हातपाय *m. pl.*

5 about; *stir, turn.* फिरणें, फिरकणें, हालणें, हालणेंहिलणें, चिडमिडणें, हिचमिचणें, हिचकणें.

6 *change residence.* घर *n.*-स्थान *n.*-स्थळ*n.*-&c. बदलणें, स्थानांतर *n.*-स्थलांतर *n.*-गृहांतर *n.*-वासांतर *n.*-&c. करणें.

To move out in preparation for a journey. प्रस्थान*n.*-अंगप्रस्थान *n.* करणें.

Move, *n.*—at chess, &c. डाव *m.* खेळ *m.* खेळी *f.*

Moved, *p.* v. V. A. 1. हालवलेला, चालवलेला, &c. स्थलांतरित, स्थलांतरप्राप्त, स्थलांतरापन्न.

2 सरसावलेला, सरकावलेला, सारलेला, &c. चालता केलेला, सारित, चालित, प्रवृत्त, प्रवर्त्तित.

4 वळवलेला, मनावलेला, प्रवृत्त केलेला, प्रवण केलेला.

5 पाझरवलेला, द्रव आणलेला, &c. सद्गद, सद्गदित.

To be m. दया *f.*-&c. येणें, द्रवणें, पाझरणें.

6 गडबडवलेला, क्षुब्ध, क्षोभित.

Moveless. See Firm.

Movement, Move, *n.* v.V.N.1. 5. हालणें *n.* चालणें *n.* फिरणें*n.* खेळणें *n.* &c. चाल *f.* गति *f.* स्थानांतर *n.* स्थानभेद*m.* स्थलांतर *n.* स्थलभेद *m.*

Military movements. कवाईत *or* द *f.*

That is on the m. गमनोन्मुख, गंतुकाम, जिगमिषु, चर.

Mover, *n.* Moving, *p. a.* v. V. A. 1. हालवणारा, चालवणारा, &c. स्थानांतर करवणारा, सारक.

Secret m. अंतरसुती.

2 सरकावणारा, सारणारा, &c. चालक, सारक.

3 उहू काढणारा, &c. कर्त्तव्योपस्थापक.

5 and Pathetic. द्रव आणणारा, &c. करुणाजनक, करुणोत्पादक, करुणापर, करुण, हृदयवेधक, हृदयंगम, चित्तद्रावक, चित्ताद्रर्ईकारी. [गतिमान्, सरक, चल.

v. V. N. 1. हालणारा, चालणारा, &c. हालता, चालता, फिरता,

2 चालणारा, &c. चालता, प्रवर्त्तमान.

3 चालणारा, &c. चालता, गमनकर्त्ता, &c. चारी (in comp. as, आकाशचारी, पदचारी, &c.).

Movingly, *adv.* v. A. 5. करुणायेईसा *decl.* द्रवयेईसा *decl.* &c.

Mow, *n.* v. Rick, Stack. सुडी *f.* उडवी *f.* उडवें *n.* बुचाड *n.*

M. of *jawári* (holcus sorghum). कात्रा *m.*

To Mow, *v. a. cut.* कापणें. The Maráthás have no implement like a scythe, but cut their grass, &c. with an इळा or sickle.

2 down; *destroy in great numbers,* v. To Kill. कत्तल *f.* उडवणें, कापाकापी *f.*-काटाकाटी *f.*-&c. करणें.

To Mow-burn, *v. n. heat and ferment in the mow.* सुडी *f.*-&c. उबणें.

Much, *a. great in quantity, amount, &c.*v. Exuberant.बहुत, फार, पुष्कल *or* ळ, भारी, उदंड, मुबलक *or* ख, बहुल, प्रचुर, उत्कट, ढिगार, मुराद, नितांत.

As m. as. जेवढा, जितका correl. with तेवढा & तितका So much. [यत्प्रमाण.

How m. किती, केवढा, कितका, कितीक, कितेक, कियत्, कि-

Just so m. इतकासा.

So m. इतका, एवढा, इतपत, इयत्.

To make m.of, *esteem highly.* लाख-लक्ष मानणें. 2 *caress, treat tenderly.* अलोलकी *f.* करणें *g. of o.*

Much, *adv. in a great degree.* बहुत, फार, पुष्कल *or* ळ, भारी.

As m. as. जितपत, correl. with तितपत, तावन्मात्र, तावत्.

As m. as, *quantum tantum.* यावत्तावत्. [&c.).

How m. कितपत,कियत् (in comp. as कियत्काल, कियद्दूर,

Much, *n. a great quantity,* v. Abundance, Exuberance. पुष्कळपणा *m.* प्राचुर्य *n.* बाहुल्य *n.* उत्कर्ष *m.*

Mucilage, *n.*—of vegetables. चीक *m.* चिकचीक *f.* बलक *m.* ओलाडीक *m.*

2—of the joints and articulations. कफ *m.*

Mucilaginous, *a.* v. N. 1. *slimy, &c.* v. Viscous. चिकण, चिकट, चिकचिकीत, चिकाळ, चिकाळा, चिकाळया.

Mucilaginousness, *n.* v. A. चिकटण *f.* चिकचीक *f.*

Muck, *n. dung, &c. for manure,* v. Manure. खत *or* खात *m.n.*

Heap or mass of m. खातेरें *n.*

2 *mire, filth, mud, dirt.* रेबड *f.* चेंदा *m.* चेंद *f.* चेंदाड *f.* खस्त *n.* बेंदाड *f.* रेंदाड *f.* बेंद *f.* खताड *n.* राडा *m.* चिखल *m.* कर्दम *m.*

3 *slop, mess, &c.* घाण *f.* ढाण *n.* तन्हाण *n.* राड *f.* राडा *m.*

Muck-heap, Muck-hill, *n.* नरक *m.* [*m.* घामटा*m.*

Muck-sweat, *n. profuse sweat.* मोठा घाम *m.* घाणसुटेसा घाम

To be in a m. घामाच्या धारा *f.pl.*-घामाचा पाझर*m.* लागणें.

Muck-worm, *n.* खतकिडा *m.* शेणकिडा*m.*

Muckiness, *n.* v. A. चिडचीड *f.* चिगचीग *f.* चिबचीब *f.* राड *f.* चेंदा *m.* चेंद *f.* चेंदाड *f.* चेंदरड *f.* रेबड *f.*

Mucky, *a. covered with muck; filthy, dirty, &c.* चिडचिडीत, खस्ती, रेंदाड, चेंदीचा, चेंदाडीचा, चिखलाचा, रेंदाडीचा, &c.

Mucous, *a. slimy, &c.* v. Viscous. चिकण, चिकचिकीत.

2 *secreting a slimy substance.* कफादिमल करणारा, कफादिमलोत्पादक.

Mucus, *n. viscid fluid secreted by a membrane.* मल *m.n. pop.* मळ *m.* इंद्रियमल *m. n.* कफादिमल *m. n.*

M. of the nose. शेंबूड *m.* शेंब *or* शेम *f.*

M. of the throat. कफ *m.*

M. of the bowels. आंव *f.* आम *m.* शेंब *or* शेम *f.*

M. of the eye. बुरूस *m.*

Mud, *n.* चिखल *m.* राड *f.* राडा *m.* चेंदा *m.* रेबड *f.* रेब *f.* गाळ *m.* कर्दम *m.* पंक *m.*

Chaps in the feet from treading in m.चिखल्या *f.pl.*—To be affected with them. चिखलणें.

Mass of m. रेंप *f. m.*

Thick and clammy m. चिकटा *m.* [क्रीडा *f.* करणें.

To play in the m. चिखल *m.* खेळणें, राड *f.* खेळणें, पंक-

2 *wetted and trampled earth for mortar.* गारा *m.*

Mud-wall, *n.* मातीची भिंत *f.* कच्ची भिंत *f.*

To Mud, *To* Mudlle, *v. a. make foul or turbid.* गढुळणें, खडु-

ळणें, गढ़ळणें, गादवणें or गाढावणें, कचंबणें, कचमळणें, खवंदळणें, रंवदळणें or रंवदाळणें, रेंदावणें, उमदळणें, गढूळ-गदळ-&c. करणें, रेंदा m.-चवढव f.-रंवदळ f.-&c. करणें g. of o.

2 *fuddle.* अमलानें गढूळ करणें, निशा f.-गुंगी f. आणणें.

MUDDED, MUDDLED, p. v. V. 1. गढुळलेला, गदळलेला, &c. गढूळ, खडूळ, गदळ, डहूळ, रेंदाड, चवढव, चवढवीत, कलुशित.

2 अमलानें गढूळ, निशेनें गढूळ.

MUDDEDNESS, MUDDLEDNESS, n. v. P. 1. रंवदळ f. रंवदळा m. रंवदाळा m. चवढव f. वचमंगळ n.

MUDDINESS, n. v. A. 1. चिखल m. चिडचीड f. चिकचीक f. चिवाचीब f. चिगढाण f. चेंदा m. चेंदाड f. बेंद f. बेंदाड f. रेंदाड f. गचपच f. सपंकता f.

3 गढुळपणा m. गदळपणा m. &c. कलुषता f. कालुष्य n.

MUDDING, MUDDLING, n. v. V. 1.—*act.* गढुळणें n. गदळणें n. गादवणें n. &c. रंवदळणी f.

MUDDY, a. *having mud.* चिखलाचा, सपंक, सकर्दम, पंकिल, पंकप्रचुर, पंकमय, बेंदाड.

M. water. चिखलवणी n.

A m. road. चिखलवाट f.

M. and sticky. चिडचिडीत, चिकचिकीत, चिगचीग.

2 *readily turning to mud.* चिखलवट, बेंदाड.

3 *turbid, foul, feculent.* गढूळ, गदळ, खडूळ, डहूळ, रेंदगूड, रेंदाड, राड, बेंदाड, रेंदाळ, कलुष.

To become m. गढुळणें, खडुळणें, गादणें.

4 *soiled with mud.* चिखलानें भरलेला.

5 *dull, dim, dusky.* मजीत, मलूल.

6 *dull, heavy,* v. STUPID. जड, जडबुद्धि, स्थूलबुद्धि, मंदमति.

To MUDDY, v. a. v. To MUD. गढुळणें, गदळणें, गढूळ-&c. करणें.

2 *make heavy, dull, &c.* बुद्धि f. मंद करणें, बुद्धि f. जड करणें, बुद्धीला जाड्य n.-&c. आणणें.

MUDDY-HEADED, a. v. STUPID. जड, मठ्या.

MUFF, n. सलोम कातड्याचें केलेलें हस्तवेष्टन n.

MUFFIN, n. See CAKE.

To MUFFLE, v. a. *cover, conceal by a cloth, &c.*—the face, neck, &c. गुरगुटणें or गुरगटणें, गुरगुटून-बोखारून-घुगटून-मुसकटून-झांकून-&c. घेणें, टाफर f.-टापशी f.-&c. बांधणें, घुंगट m.-बुरखा m.-बोंथारा m.-&c.घेणें,घोंगाटn.घालणें, बुंध f.-बुंधी f.घेणें-मारणें, झांपड f.-झांपडी f. घालणें, अवगुंठन n. करणें g. of o. अवगुंठित करणें. [घालणें.

2 fig v. To CONCEAL. झांकणें, ढांपणें, आच्छादणें, पांघरूण n.

3 (drum, &c.) नाद m. मंद-गंभीर होण्याकरितां फडक्यानें-&c. बांधणें.

To MUFFLE, v. n. *speak thickly,* v. To MUTTER. घुरमुळणें, तोंडच्या तोंडांत बोलणें.

MUFFLED, p. v. V. A. 1. गुरगुटलेला, गुरगुटून घेतलेला, टाफर बांधलेला, बुरखाघेतलेला, घोंगाट घातलेला, &c.

MUFFLER, n. MUFFLING, p. a. v. V. A. 1. गुरगुटणारा, टाफर बांधणारा, बुरखा घेणारा, घोंगाट घालणारा, &c.

I. *cover for the face.* बुरखा m. घुंगटm. बुंध f. बुंधी f. बोंथारा m. बोंथारी f. टापर or टाफर f.

MUFTI, n.—of Muhammadans. मुफ्ती m.

MUG, n. *cup.* v. VESSEL. पेला m. पानपात्र n.

MUGGINESS, n. v. A. 2. ऊब f. गदमद f.

MUGGISH, MUGGY, a. v. DAMP. ओला, दामट.

2 *close and warm,*—weather. उबेचा, उबाऱ्याचा, गदमदीचा.

To be m. गदमदणें, गदगदणें, उकडणें, उबणें, उबावणें, ढाजणें, तावणें, शिजणें, all impersonal.

MUHAMMADAN. See MUSSULMAN.

MULBERRY, n.—the tree. तुती f. तूत f. शहातूत f.—the fruit. तुतें n. तूत n. शहातूत n.

MULCT, n. v. FINE. दंड m. गुन्हेगारी f.

2—as imposed on a state, country, &c. खंड m. खंडणी f.

To MULCT, v. a. *fine.* दंड m. करणें, दंड m.-गुन्हेगारी f. घेणें.

2 (a state, &c.) खंड m.-खंडणी f. घेणें.

MULE, n. *mongrel offspring of a horse and an ass.* खेंचर m. n. खेंचरी f. अश्वतर m.

Young m. शिगरू n.

MULETEER, n. *mule-driver.* खेंचरवाला, खेंचरवान, खेंचरहाक्या.

MULIEBRITY, n. *womanhood.* बायकोपणा m. स्त्रीभाव m. स्त्रीत्व n. नारीत्व n.

MULISH, a. *stubborn,* v. OBSTINATE. गाटा, गाटी, गाट्या, गाताडा, हेंकट, हेंकड, घेलट, घेलाड.

MULISHNESS, n. v. A. गाटपणा m. हेंकटपणा m. &c. घेलटचाल f.

To MULL, v. a. *heat with spices.* मसाला घालून कढवणें-ऊन करणें-&c. [m. बत्ताm.

MULLER, n. *rubbing stone, or roller.* घोटाm. कुतकाm. लाट्या

2 (for spices, drugs, &c.). वरवंटा or वरोंटाm. वाटणाm. वाटणागुंडाm.

MULLET, n. एकमासाआहे.

MULLIGRUBS. See GRIPES. [बहुत्र.

MULTANGULAR, a. *having many angles.* बहुकोण, बहुतकोनी,

MULTIFARIOUS, a. *having great variety.* बहुतप्रकारचा, बहुप्रकार, अनेकप्रकार, बहुविध, अनेकविध, नानाविध, अनेकरूप, नानारूप, बहुरूप, बहुप्रकरण, हरभांत, शतशास्र.

MULTIFID, MULTIFIGOUS, a. *having many divisions.*बहुशाख, बहुशफ.

MULTIFORM, a. *having many forms.* बहुतरूपांचा, बहुरूप, नानारूप, अनेकरूप, अनंतरूप, अनेकाकार, बहुविध, नानाविध, चित्रविचित्र.

MULTIFORMITY, n. v. A. रूपबाहुल्यn. आकारबाहुल्यn. नानारूपता f. बहुविधता f.

MULTILATERAL, a. *having many sides.* बहुतबाजूंचा, बहुपार्श्व, अनेकपार्श्व. [बहुरेख.

MULTILINERAL, a. *having many lines.* बहुतरेखांचा, बहुरेष,

MULTILOGUOUS, a. v. TALKATIVE. बहुभाष, बहुभाषी.

MULTINOMIAL, MULTINOMINAL, a. *having many names.* बहुत नावांचा, बहुनामक, बहुसंज्ञक, बहुसंज्ञी.

MULTIPAROUS, a. *producing many at a birth.* दरखेपेस बहुतविणारा, बहुप्रसव (f. प्रसवा).

MULTIPED, a. *having many feet.* बहुत पायांचा, बहुपद, बहुपाद.

MULTIPLE, n. गुणाकारm. There are tables of *mutiples of fractions* from $\frac{1}{4}$ to $3\frac{1}{2}$. These tables are called, पावकें, निमकें, पाउणकें, सवाकें, दिडकें, अडिचकें, औटकें, or, $\frac{1}{4}$, $\frac{1}{2}$, $\frac{3}{4}$, $1\frac{1}{4}$, $1\frac{1}{2}$, $2\frac{1}{2}$, $3\frac{1}{2}$.

MULTIPLIABLE, MULTIPLICABLE, a. v. V. A. 1. वाढवायाजोगा-जोगता-&c. बहुत करायास योग्य-शक्य-&c. प्रचुरीकरणशक्य.

2 गुणायाजोगा-जोगता-&c. गुण्य, गुणनशक्य.

Multiplicand, *n. number to be multiplied.* गुण्यांकm. गुण्यm.

Multiplicate, *a. conisting of many, or more than one.* अनेक, बहुत.

Multiplication, *n.* v. V. A. 1.—*act.* वाढवणेंn. बहुत करणेंn. &c. बहुलीकरणn. प्रचुरीकरणn. [अंकपूरण n.

2—*act.* गुणणेंn. गुणाकारm. गुणनn. घातm. गुणता *f.* पूरणn.

Column of the m.-table. पाडा *or* फाडाm.

Cross drawn in proving a m. कांटाm.—To prove by this cross, कांटाm. करणें. Some of the modes of *multiplication* are, कोष्टकी गुणाकार m. by a figure subdivided into squares. धावरागुणाकार the ordinary method. बैठा गुणाकार a complicated cross mode. स्थानगुणन m. according to the places *i. e.* in the common way. विभागगुणन m. by sub-multiples. of the multiplier. खंडगुणन m. by dividing the multiplier into parts and taking the sums of the products of the multiplier. स्वरूपगुणन m. by the whole multiplier at once. वज्राभ्यास or वज्रवध cross m. कपाटसंधि and कपटसिंधु the same as कोष्टकी गुणाकार. गोमूत्रिका duodecimal multiplication. In the multiplication of number by number certain particles are used (e. g. in multiplying by *one* एकीं *or* एकें (as एक एकीं एक one once is one, तीन एके तीन, &c.)—by *one and a half*, दिढें;—by *two*, दुणें, दुरकी, बे;—by *two and a half*, अडचें;—by *three*, तिरकी *or* तिरकें, त्रिक;—by *four*, चौक *or* चौकी;—by *five*, पांची, पंचें;—by six, सकें, साहीं;—by *seven*, सत, सतें *or* सत्तें *or* सत्तीं;—by *eight*, अठीं *or* अठें;—by *nine*, नवीं *or* नवें;—by *ten*, दाहीं. For the tables of the multiples of numbers from ¼ to 3½ see under Multiple. The *eleven-table* or table exhibiting the multiplication of the numbers from 11 to 20 into one another is, अकर्कीं *n. pl.* The *table of squares* is, एकोत्रीं *n. pl.*

Compound m. विविधगुणाकार *m.*

v. V. N. See Increase.

Multiplicator, Multiplier, *n. the number by which another is multiplied.* गुणकांक *m.* गुणक *m.* गुण *m.* पूरक *m.* अंकपूरक *m.*

Multiplicious, *a.* v. Manifold, Multifarious. बहुत, बहुप्रकार, शतशाखा.

Multiplicity, *n. state of being many.* बहुतपणा *m.* पुष्कळपणा *m.* अनेकत्व *n.* बहुत्व *n.* बाहुल्य *n.* (esp. in comp. as उद्योगबाहुल्य m. of occupations, विषयबाहुल्य m. of objects, &c.).

2 See Many. [चुरीकृत.

Multiplied, *p.* v. V. A. 1. वाढवलेला, बहुत केलेला, &c. प्र-

2 गुणलेला, &c. गुणित, पूरित.

To Multiply, *v. a. increase in number.* वाढवणें, बहुत-पुष्कळ-&c. करणें. [*of o.*

2—in arithmetic. गुणणें, गुणाकार *m.*-गुणन *n.*-&c. करणें *g.*

To Multiply, *v. n.* v. To Increase. वाढणें, बहुत-पुष्कळ-बहुल-&c. होणें.

Multipotent, *a. having power to do many things.* बहुकार्यशक्तिक, बहुकार्यसमर्थ, बहुशक्तिक.

Multipresence, *n. the being present in many places.* बहुविद्यमानता *f.* बहुस्थलविद्यमानता *f.* [विधवेत्ता.

Multiscious, *a. knowing many things.* बहुज्ञ, बहुविषयज्ञ, वि-

Multisonous, *a. having many sounds, or sounding much.* बहुध्वनि, नानाध्वनि, बहुनाद.

Multitude, *n. state of being many.* बहुतपणा *m.* पुष्कळपणा *m.* बहुत्व *n.* अनेकत्व *n.* बाहुल्य *n.* (esp. in comp.).

2 *a number collectively*; *collection, assemblage.* जमाव *m.* मेळा *m.* मेळावा *m.* गण *m.* समुदाय *m.* समूह *m.* समुच्चय *m.* चुंग *f.* झुंड *f.* मंडण *n.* संघ *m.* संघात *m.* वृंद *n.* कदंब *n.* व्रज *m.* सार्थ *m.* स्तोम *m.* जात *n.*

By or in multitudes. संघशः.

3 *a great number or sum,*—loosely. भरणा *m.* गाडा *m.* डोंगर *m.* पर्वत *m.* बार *m.* The word in this sense is usually rendered by the use of the adjectives बहुत, पुष्कळ, &c.

4 *the populace, mass of mankind,* v. People. दुनिया *f.* अलमदुनिया *f.* जहान *or* जहन *n.*

To flatter the m. हजारांच्या डोईस *n.* पाणी *n.* लावणें.

To follow the m. प्रवाहांत पडणें, लोकानुसरण *n.*-जनानुसरण-&c. करणें.

An individual must conform to the multitude. घरासारखा पाहुणा होतो पाहुण्यासारखें घर होत नाहीं.

Multitudinary, Multitudinous, *a.* v. Numerous. बहुत, पुष्कल *or* ळ, बहुसंघ.

2 See Manifold.

Multivagant, Multivagous, *a. that wanders much.* बहुत फिरणारा, बहुभ्रमक, बह्वाटक.

Multivious, *a. having many ways.* बहुतवाटांचा, बहुमार्ग, बहुपथ. [चन, बहुक्ष.

Multocular, *a. having many eyes.* बहुडोळ्या, बहुनेत्र, बहुलो-

Multure. See Grinding.

Mum, *interj, hush.* चप्प ! मुट्ट, मट-कन-कर-&c. निमूट.

Mum, *a.* v. Silent. मौन्य धरलेला.

To sit, &c. m. मटकन-मुट्ट-&c. बसणें.

To Mumble, *v. n. speak suppressedly, inarticulately, &c.* v. To Mutter. ओंठांत बोलणें, गुणगुणणें, गुळमुळणें, मुळमुळणें, घुरमुळणें, धुसधुसणें, धुसमुसणें, गुरमळणें.

2 *chew with the mouth closed.* ओंठ लावून चावणें-खाणें, चघळून-गुटमळून-लुबलूब *adv.* खाणें.

To Mumble, *v. a. utter with a low inarticulate voice,* v. To Mutter. ओंठांत बोलणें, तोंडांत-तोंडच्या तोंडांत-गुळमुळीत-मुळमुळीत-&c. बोलणें.

2 *mouth gently.* ओंठ लावून चावणें.

Mumbler, *n.* Mumbling, *p. a.* v. V. N. 1. गुणगुणणारा, गुळमुळणारा, &c. गुणगुण्या, गुळमुळ्या, घुरमुळ्या, गुरमळ्या.

2 ओंठ लावून चावणारा, &c.

Mumbling, *n.* v. V. N. 1. गुणगुणणें *n.* गुळमुळणें *n.* &c. गुणगूण *f.* बुडबुड *f.* मुळमूळ *f.* धुसधूस *f.* धुसमूस *f.*

v. V. A. 1. ओंठांत बोलणें *n.*

Mumblingly, *adv.* v. A. गुणगुणून, गुरमळून, ओंठांत, तोंडच्या तोंडांत, मुळमुळीत.

Mummer, *n. one who makes sport in a mask.* मुखवटा घेऊन-घालून खेळणारा, खेळी, सोंग्या, सोंगी.

MUMMERY, *n. masking, sport in masks, low diversion, &c.* मुखवट्याचा खेळ *m.* शिमग्याचा खेळ *m.* शिमग्याचा तमाशा *m.* तमाशा *m.* [क्षितशव *n.*

MUMMY, *n. preserved dead body.* मसालाभरलेलें प्रेत *n.* सुगंधर-
2—the medicine. ममई or मुंबई *f.* It was the common opinion, a few years back, of the Natives in the interior that this medicine was prepared in Bombay by hanging a living human being over a fire.

To beat to a m. v. To BEAT. ममई *f.*-मलिदा *m.*-चेंदामेंदा *m.*-चेंदूमेंदू *m.*-चेंदू *m.* करणें *g. of o.* कुट्टा *m.* काढणें-करणें *g.ofo.*

To MUMP, *v. n. nibble, bite quickly.* चपचप-चकचक-मटमट-मटकमटक-&c. खाणें-चावणें.

To MUMP, *v. n. make mouths, grin, &c.* v. To MOCK. वेंटाबण्या *f. pl.*-वेंचकुल्या *f. pl.*-&c. दाखवणें.

MUMPS, *n. swelling of the parotid glands.* गालगुंड *n.* गालगुंडी *f.* गालफुगी *f.* गालफें *n.* कानवळ *m.* कर्णमूल *n.* लालापिंडशोथ *m.*
2 *silent anger.* घुमाराग *m.* मनच्या मनांतला राग *m.* अंतःक्रोध*m.*

To have the m. मुरमुसणें, अंटरणें, अबटरणें *or* अबठरणें, मूग गिळून बसणें.

To MUNCH, *v. n. eat or chew slowly turning over in the mouth.* चघळून-घोळून-घोळवून-&c. खाणें.

To MUNCH, *v. a. eat slowly, &c.* चघळणें, चघळून खाणें.

MUNDANE, *a. earthly, terrestrial.* भूलोकाचा, मृत्युलोकाचा, इहलोकाचा, इहलोकींचा, ऐहलौकिक, ऐहिक.

MUNDATION, MUNDATORY, &c. See CLEANSING, &c.

MUNDIVAGANT, *a. wandering over the world.* पृथ्वीपर्यटक, पृथ्वीभ्रमणकर्त्ता.

MUNGCORN. See MANGCORN.

MUNGOOSE, *n. viverra ichneumon.* मुंगस *or* मुंगूस *m.* नकूल *m.*

MUNGREL. See MONGREL.

MUNICIPAL, *a. belonging to a city or corporation.* कसब्याचा, कसब्यांतला, सनदीगांवचा, सनदीगांवच्या प्रकरणांतला.
2 *belonging to a country.* मुलकी, देशी.

MUNICIPALITY, *n. division of country,* v. COUNTY. जिल्हा *m.*
2 शहरसुधारणुकीची मंडळी.

MUNIFICENCE, *n.* v. A. उदारपणा *m.* धौतालीf. धौतालपणा *m.* दानत *f.* वदान्यता *f.* औदार्य *n.*दानशौर्य *n.* प्राशस्त्य *n.* अतिदान *n.* सत्र *n.*

MUNIFICENT, *a. generous, &c.* v. LIBERAL. उदार, हाताचा मोकळा-सुटा-सढळ, धौताल, सढळ, दानशूर, दानशौंड, प्रशस्त, औदार्यशाली. [पूर्वक, &c.

MUNIFICENTLY, *adv.* v. A. उदारपणानें, सढळ हातानें, &c. औदार्य

MUNITION, *n. ammunition.* लढाईचें सामान *n.* युद्धसाहित्य *n.* युद्धसामग्री *f.* अजबाब *f.* [संबंधी.

MURAL, *a. belonging to a wall.* भिंतीचा, भिंतीविषयींचा, भिंति-
. 2 See STEEP.

MURDER, *n. unlawful or malicious killing.* खून *m.* हत्या *f.* हिंसा *f.* वध *m.* द्वेषपूर्वकमनुष्यवध *m.* कायिकहिंसा *f.*

M. will out. खून चढेलच.

To MURDER, *v. a.* v. To KILL. खून *m.*-हत्या *f.*-हिंसा *f.*-वध *m.*-&c. करणें *g. of o.* द्वेषानें प्राण *m.*-जीव *m.* घेणें, मारणें, हिंसणें.

MURDERER, *n.*v.V. *and* MURDEROUS. खून करणारा, &c. हिंसाकर्त्ता, वधकर्त्ता, हत्यारा *or* हत्यारी esp. in comp. घ्न (in comp. as पितृघ्न, मातृघ्न, &c.)

MURDEROUS, *a. that murders.* खून करणारा, खुनी, खुनेरा, हिंसाकर्त्ता-कारी-&c. वधकर्त्ता-कारी-&c. हत्यारा *or* हत्यारी (esp. in comp. as,बालहत्यारा,ब्रह्महत्यारा &c.) घ्न (in comp. as, पितृघ्न, &c.), प्राणघातक, प्राणघातकी, घातक, घातकी, घातुक, हिंसक.
2 *bloody, sanguinary, &c.* v. CRUEL. खुनी, खुनेरा, हिंसक, हिंसालु, हिंस्र, हिंसाबुद्धि, जिघांसु, हिंसाभिसंधि.

M. intent. हिंसाबुद्धि *f.*

MURK, *n. darkness and gloominess of weather.* ओंद *or* ओंध *f.* अंधारी *f.* काहूर *n.* झांपड *f.* काळंबण *n.* v. पड.

MURKY, *a.* v. N. अंधारीचा, ओंधट, झांपडीचा, काहूर आलेला.

MURMUR, MURMURING, *n.* v. V. 1. गुणगुणणें *n.* भणभणणें *n.* &c. गुणगूण *f.* भणभण *f.* खळखळ *f.*
2 कुरकुरणें *n.* कुरमुरणें *n.* कुरचुरणें *n.* &c. कुरकूर *f.* कुरबूर *f.* मुरमूर *f.* चुरमूर *f.* धुसफूस *f.* धुसमूस *f.* काणकूण *f.*

To MURMUR, *v. n. make a low noise.* गुणगुणणें, भणभणणें *or* भिणभिणणें, भणभण-खळखळ-खळकन-&c. *adv.* वाजणें-वाहणें, भणभण *f.*-खळखळ *f.*-&c. होणें-चालणें *g. of s.*
2 *grumble, complain sullenly and suppressedly.* कुरकुरणें, कुरबुरणें, कुरमुरणें, मुरमुरणें, तुरबुरणें, धुसफुसणें, धुसमुसणें, कुरकूर *f.*-कुरबूर *f.*-धुसफूस *f.*-&c. करणें, कुरकूर *f.*-&c. चालणें-होणें *g. of s.*

MURMURER, *n.* MURMURING, *p. a.* v. V. 1. गुणगुणणारा, भणभणणारा, भणभण वाजणारा, खळखळ वाजणारा, &c. खळखळीत.
2 कुरकुरणारा, कुरचुरणारा, &c. कुरकूर करणारा, &c. कुरकुऱ्या, कुरबुऱ्या, कुरमुऱ्या.

MURRAIN, *n. plague among cattle.* मरी *f.* मर *f.* धाम *f.* वादें *n.* *or* वादा *m.* मरोडा *m.*

MUSCÆ VOLITANTES, *n.* काजवे *m. pl.* तारे *m. pl.*

To have m. लकलक *adv.* करणें, लकलकणें.

MUSCLE, *n.*—in anatomy. स्नायु *m.* मांसपेशी *f.* मांसरज्जु *f.* साव *or* सांव *f.* सावर *n. f.*

Tendon of the trapezium m. मन्या *f.*
2—the fish. शिंपीतला किडा *m.* शंबूक *m.*

MUSCULAR, MUSCULOUS, *a. belonging, &c. to a muscle.* स्नायुचा, स्नायुसंबंधी.

M. action. चालन *n.*
2 *brawny, fleshy.* मांसल *pop.* मासाळ, गाठळ *or* गांठाळ, गट्ट, गोलदार, बेडकीचा.

MUSE, *n. divinity of poetry.*सरस्वती *f.* वाग्देवता *f.* काव्यदेवता *f.*
2 *deep thought,* v. MEDITATION. ध्यान *n.* चिंतन*n.* विचार*m.*

To be in a m. ध्यानांत असणें, विचारांत असणें. 2 भानावर-&c. नसणें.

To MUSE, *v. n. meditate, ponder over.* ध्यान *n.*-चिंतन *n.*-मनन *n.* करणें, विचार *m.* करणें, ध्यान *n.* लावणें.

MUSEFUL. See MEDITATIVE.

MUSEUM, *n. cabinet of curiosities.* कौतुक सांठवण्याची जागा *f.* कौतुकसंग्रहालय *n.* चमत्कारिकपदार्थसंग्रहस्थान *n.*

MUSHROOM, *n. a fungus.* छत्री *f.* अळंबें *or* अळंभें *n.* कळलें *n.* कुत्र्याचें मूत *n.* कुत्र्याचें छत्र *n.* छत्राक *n.* भुईछत्री *f.*

MUSIC, *n.*—the art or science. गाण्यावाजविण्याची विद्या *f.* सुस्वरविद्या *f.* सुस्वरशास्त्र *n.* गंधर्वविद्या *f.* गंधर्ववेद *m.* संगीतविद्या *f.* संगीतशास्त्र *n.* वादनविद्या *f.* वाद्यविद्या *f.*

Mode of m. राग *m.* रागिणी *f.*—The musical modes are personified. Some of the *male* personifications are, अडाणा, अहंग, कलंगडा, कल्याण, काफी, कामबोध, केदारा, कौशीकानडा *or* कानडा, खट, खमाज, गौडसारंग, छायानट *or* नाट, तोडी, त्रोटकी, नट, पंचम, परज, पर्या, बिलावर *or* बिलावल, भूपकल्याण, भैरव, मालवा *or* मालव, मालकोश *pop.* मालकंस, ललत, वसंत, बिभास, शंकरी *or* शंकराभरण, सारंग, सोहनी, हिंदोल *pop.* हिंडोळ. Some of the *female* are, अल्हया, आसावरी, गुनकली *or* गुणकली, गोडी, जंगला, जयजयवंती, जोगी, झिंझोटी, दीपक *or* दीपकल्याण, धनेश्वरी, पूर्वी, बरवा, भूपाळी, भैरवी, मधुमाधवी, मल्हार, मुलतानी, रामकेली *pop.* रामकली *or* कली, सुगराई, सैंधवी. Some *musical measures* are, एकताल, त्रिताल, चौताल, अह्वताल, बिलंदी, गरण. The *notes of music* are, निषाद *pop.* निसाद, ऋषभ, गांधार, षड्ज, मध्यम, पंचम, धैवत. Some of the *musical instruments* are, अमृतकुंडली, करणा, करताल, किंगरी, किन्नरी, कोंका, गोमुख, खंजिरी, घुमट, घुमरी, चवघडा, चोंटकें *or* चोंडकें, छतार, जलतरंग, झंगड, झांज, टाळ, डफ, डांक, डौर, ढोल *dim.* ढोलक & ढोलकी & ढोलकें, तबला, तंबुरा, तंबुरी, ताशा, तुणतुणें *or* नें, तुतारी, दुंडी, दिंडी, धवशा, नगारा, नौबत, पखवाज, पांवा, बीन, ब्रह्मवीणा, भोंबारा *dim.* भोंबारी, मंजिरी, मर्फा, मृदंग, रणहलगी, रुद्रविणा, वीणा *pop.* विणा, सनई, संबळ, सरोदा, सारंगी, सारमंडळ, सुरसोटा, सुर.

With shouting and sounding of m. instruments. वाजत गाजत. [वाद्यघोष *m.*

2 *playing on a musical instrument.* बाजा *m.* बजावणें *n.*

A band of m. बाजा *m.*

Entertainment of instrumental and vocal m. संगीत *n.*

Musical, *a. belonging to music.* गाण्याबाजविण्याचे विद्येचा, सुस्वरविद्येचा, सुस्वरशास्त्रसंबंधी, गंधर्वविद्यासंबंधी, वादनविद्याविषयक-संबंधी, &c.

M. instrument. वाद्य *n.*

M. glasses. जलतरंग *m.* [शिष्ट.

2 v. Harmonious, Melodious. सुश्राव्य, सुस्वर, सुस्वरवि-

3 *fond of music.* गाण्याबाजविण्याचा अळका, वाद्यप्रिय, वादनशील, नादलुब्ध, नादप्रिय, नादासक्त, वाद्यश्रवणासक्त.

Musician, *n. performer on an instrument of m.* बाजंत्री, वाद्य बाजविणारा, वादक, वादनकर्त्ता, घडसी *or* शी (a particular caste), होलार (a particular class of the máng, and mahár castes), खालू (they are Muhammadans). The न्हावी (barbers) and गुरव (Shúdra priests) are also musicians.

Band of musicians. ताफा *m.*

Head man of a band of m. खलीपा.

2 *one skilled in music.* बाजविण्याचा वस्ताद, वादनकुशल, वादनविद्यावेत्ता, गंधर्वविद्यावेत्ता.

Musk, *n.*—the scent. कस्तूरी *f.* मृगनाभि *m.* मृगमद *m.* दर्प *m.*

Bag or pod of m. नाभा *m.* नाफा *m.* नाभ *f.* अंड *m.n.*

Musk-deer, *n.* कस्तूरीमृग *m.*

Musk-melon, *n.*—the plant. खरबूज *f.* खरबुजी *f.*—the fruit. खरबूज *n.*

Musk-rat, *n.* चिचुंदरी *or* चिचोंदरी *f.*

Musket, *n.* बंदूक *or* बंदूख *f.* तुबक *f. n.* चापाची बंदूक *f.*

Fly of a m. मोहरी *f.*

Stock of a m. दस्ता *m.*

Musketeer, *n.* बंदुक्या, बंदुकवाला, बरकंदाज.

Musketeering, *n. practice of a musketeer.* बरकंदाजी *f.*

Musketoon, *n. blunderbuss.* बकमार *f.* बकमाल *f.*

Musketry, *n.* बंदुक्या *f. pl.*

Muskitto, **Musquitto**, *n.* मुरकूट *f. n.* मच्छर *m.* चांचड *n.* चांचण *n.* चिलट *n.* डांस *m. f.* मत्सर *m.* मशक *m.*—jocosely. पाहुणा *m.*

M.—curtains, मच्छरदानी *f.*

Musky, *a. having the smell of musk.* कस्तूरीच्या वासाचा, कस्तूरीगंधयुक्त, कस्तूरीवासित.

Muslin, *n.*—the cloth. मलमल *f.*

Muslin, *a.* v. N. मलमलीचा. [मुसपट्टा *m.*

Musrole, *n. nose-band of a bridle.* पुंजीपट्टा *m.* नाकाडकांडकें *n.*

Mussulman, *n.* मुसलमान.

Mussulman, *a.* v. N. मुसलमानी, महमदी.

M. rule or sway. मुसलमानी *f.*

Must, *v. n. to be necessitated &c.* पाहिजे (as तो गेलापाहिजे, त्याला गेलेंपाहिजे He must go), भाग असणें, (as मला जाणें भाग I must go), लागणें (as त्याला जावें लागतें), प्राप्त असणें (as मला जाणें प्राप्त आहे).

To **Must**, *v. n. grow mouldy and sour.* उबटणें, उबट-&c. होणें.

Mustache, *n. s.* **Mustaches**, *n. pl. hair on the upper lip.* मिशी *f.*—contemptuously, *urchin m.* मिसरूड *f. n.*-मिसरूं *n.*

Discontinuous m. खंडमिशी *f.* [गलगुच्छ *m.*

M. bunching over the cheeks. गलमूच्छ *m.* गलमुच्छी *f.*

That has full bushy m. मिशाळ, मिशाळा.

The curling extremity of a m. गलकल्ला *m.* गलमिशी *f.*

That has m. curling over the cheeks. गलमुच्छा.

To twist or stroke the m. haughtily or in anger. मिशी *f.* पाजवणें-पाजळणें, मिशीवर ताव देणें, मिशीवर हात *m.* टाकणें, मिशीला पीळ *m.* घालणें-देणें.

Mustard, *n.*—the plant. मोहरी *f.* राई *f.*—the seed. मोहरी *f.*

Some kinds are पांढरी मोहरी *f.* सिद्धार्थ *m.* white m.—काळी मोहरी *f.* राजिका *f.* black m.—शिरस *m.* सर्षप *m.* *sinapis dichotoma.* Oil extracted from it, शिरशेल *n.*

To **Muster**, *v. a. assemble, &c.* v. To Gather. मिळवणें, जमविणें, गोळा करणें.

2 (troops). हाजिरी *f.*-मोजदाद *f.*-गिणती *f.*-&c. घेणें *g. of o.*

To **Muster**, *v. n.* v. To Gather. मिळणें, जमा होणें.

Muster, **Mustering**, *n.* v. V. A. 1.—*act.* मिळवणें *n.* गोळा करणें *n.* जमाव *m.* एकीकरण *n.*

2 हाजिरी घेणें *n.* हाजिरी *f.*

To pass m. पसंत होणें-पडणें, रुजू होणें-पडणें.

I. v. Muster-roll. हाजिरीचा पट *m.*-कागद *m.*

II. *specimen*, v. Sample. मासला *m.* बानगी *f.*

Muster-master, *n.* v. V. A. 2. हाजिरी घेणारा, हाजिरनीस, टिपनीस.

Muster-roll, *n. roll or register of troops.* हाजिरीचा पट *m.* -कागद *m.* हाजिरीची याद *f.* नावनिशी *f.* इसमवारी *f.*

A name upon a m. असामी *f.*

Mustiness, *n.* v. A. उबटपणा *m.* उबटलेपणा *m.* कुबटपणा *m.* सांपटपणा *m.* &c. कुमटाई *f.*

1. *stale and sour smell.* उबटाण *f.* उबसाण *f.* कुबटाण *f.*

MUSTY, *a. mouldy, that stinks from age, &c.* उबट, कुबट *or* कुमट, कुईट, सांपट *or* सापट, सापई, मुगट, बाशेळा, बासाळ, बासट. To turn m. उबणें, उबटणें.

MUTABILITY, MUTABLENESS, *n.* v. A. 1. अस्थिरता *f.* अस्थैर्य*n.* अस्थायिता *f.* स्थैर्याभाव*m.* परिणामशीलता *f.* परिणामप्रावण्य*n.*

2 चंचळपणा*m.* चांचल्य*n.* चंचलता *f.* पाऊलबुद्धि *f.* क्षणिकबुद्धि *f.*

MUTABLE, *a. subject to change or vicissitude.* अस्थिर, अस्थायी, अनियत, चंचल *or* ळ, अनेकावस्थाक, परिणामशील, परिणामप्रवण, परिणामस्वभावक.

2 *fickle, inconstant,* v. CHANGEABLE. चंचल *or* ळ, चंचलचित्त, चंचलवृत्ति, अस्थिर, क्षणिकबुद्धि.

MUTATION. See CHANGE.

MUTE, *a. not vocal.* मुका, मोना, नादशून्य, वाक् शून्य, वाणीहीन -रहित-शून्य, निश्शब्द.

2 *not speaking,* v. SILENT. मोना, मुका, निश्शब्द.

MUTE, *n.* v. A. मुकें माणूस*n.* [नोच्चार्यव्यंजन*n.*

2—in grammar. अंतस्थानुनासिकव्यतिरिक्तव्यंजन*n.* स्वरसहि-

To MUTE, *v. n. dung,*—birds. शिटणें.

MUTE, *n. dung of birds.* शीट *f.*

MUTELY, *adv.* v. A. 2. *and* SILENTLY. चप *or* चप्प, गपचीप *or* चूप, मट्ट, मुट्ट, मटकन-कर-दिशीं, मुकाट्यां, घम.

MUTENESS, *n.* v. A. 1. मुकेपणा *m.* मोनेपणा *m.* वाकूराहित्य *n.* नादाभाव*m.* वाकूशून्यता *f.* [मौनभाव *m.*

2 *and* SILENCE. मुकेपणा*m.* मोनेपणा*m.* मौन *pop.* मौन्य*n.*

To MUTILATE, *v. a. maim, deprive of a limb or essential part.* आंग*n.* तोडणें *g. of o.* अंगछेद*m.*-अंगछेदन*n.*-&c. करणें *g. of o.* पंगु-विकल-व्यंग-विकलांग-&c. करणें.

MUTILATED, *p.* v. A. आंग तोडलेला, &c. अंगविकल, विकलांग, छिन्नांग, पंगु, व्यंग, अपांग, न्यूनांग, अंगहीन, हीनांग, खंडितविग्रह.

MUTILATION, *n.* v. V.—*act.* आंग तोडणें*n.* आंगतोडणी *f.* अंगछेद*m.* अंगछेदन*n.* विकली करण*n.* व्यंगी करण*n.*—*state.* विकलता *f.* वैकल्य*n.* अंगवैकल्य*n.* विकलभाव*m.*

M. (of a thief, &c.) right and left. डावें उजवें*n.*

MUTINEER, *n. one guilty of mutiny.* फौजेंत बंड करणारा, दंगा करणारा, बैदा करणारा. [टोंग, खलेल.

MUTINOUS, *a.* v. N. दंगेखोर, बेदेखोर, दंग्याचा, बेकैदी, शिरजोर,

MUTINY, *n. military insurrection.* फौजेंतलें बंड*n.* दंगा*m.* बेदा*m.* अधिपतीचे-अधिकाऱ्याचे-&c. आज्ञेचा त्याग*m.* शासनव्युत्थान*n.* आज्ञाव्युत्थान*n.*

To MUTINY, *v. n. rise against one's officers, &c.* दंगा*m.*-बेदा *m.*-&c. करणें, धन्यावर-&c. फिरणें-उठणें, धन्यावर-&c. उलटून-उठणें-उलटचाल *f.* करणें.

To MUTTER, *v.n. speak suppressedly or inarticulately, mumble, murmur, grumble.* बुडबुडणें *or* बुरबुरणें, मुरमुरणें, कुरकुरणें, कुरबुरणें, कुरमुरणें, चुरमुरणें, कुणकुणणें, गुणगुणणें, बुटबुटणें, फुटफुटणें, फिणफिणणें, गुरमळणें, घुरमुळणें, गुळमुळणें, मुळमुळणें, धुसधुसणें, धुसमुसणें, धुसमणें, कुरकूर *f.*-बुडबूड *f.*-मुरमूर *f.*-गुणगूण *f.*-कुणकूण *f.*-धुसमूस *f.*-&c. करणें.

2—thunder. गडगडणें, गडगड-गडगडां वाजणें.

To MUTTER, *v. a. utter with a low murmuring voice.* ओंठांत-तोंडांत-तोंडच्या तोंडांत बोलणें-म्हणणें-सांगणें, मुळमुळून-गुरमुळून-घुरमुळून-&c. बोलणें-सांगणें-&c. गुळमुळीत-मुळमुळीत-&c. बोलणें.

2 (prayers, &c. inarticulately). जप*m.* करणें, जपणें.

MUTTER, MUTTERING, *n.* v. V. N. 1. कुरकुडणें *n.* कुरकुरणें *n.* &c. &c. बुडबूड *or* बुरबूर *f.* कुरकूर *f.* मुरमूर *f.* कुरबूर *f.* चुरमूर *f.* बुटबूट *f.* फुटफूट *f.* पुटपूट *f.* फिणफीण *f.* मुळमूळ *f.* गुणगूण *f.* कुणकूण *f.* धुसधूस *f.* धुसमूस *f.* घसघस *f.*

v. V. A. 1.—*act.* ओंठांत बोलणें *n.* तोंडांत बोलणें *n.* &c.

2 जप *m.* जपणें *n.* [जाप्य*n.*

M.—compreh. *muttering and reciting devotions.* जप-

MUTTERED, *p.* v. V. A. 1. ओंठांत बोललेला, मुळमुळीत सांगितेलला, &c.

MUTTERER, *n.* MUTTERING, *p. a.* v. V. N. 1. बुडबुडणारा, कुरकुरणारा, कुरबुरणारा, &c. बुडबुड्या, कुरकुऱ्या, कुरबुऱ्या, घसघशा. v. V. A. 1. ओंठांत बोलणारा, तोंडांत बोलणारा, मुळमुळीत बोलणारा, &c.

MUTTON, *n. flesh of sheep.* मेंढराची सागुती *f.*

MUTUAL, *a. reciprocal, interchanged.* परस्पर, एकमेक, परस्परांचा, एकमेकांचा, अन्योन्य. [श्रय *m.*

M.—support, protection, dependence, &c. अन्योन्या-

That receive m. support, &c. अन्योन्याश्रित.

MUTUALITY, MUTUALNESS, *n.* v. A. परस्परता *f.* परस्परभाव *m.* अन्योन्यभाव *m.*

MUTUALLY, *adv.* v. A. परस्परां, परस्परें, एकमेकास, मिथः.

MUZZLE, *n. mouth,*—of a tube, &c. तोंड *n.*

2—of animals, and, contemptuously, of man. मुसकट *n.* मुसकड *n.* मुसकल *n.* मुसकाड *n.* मुसकूट *n.* मुसकें *n.* मुसकुरी *f.*

3 *fastening for the mouth.* मुसकें *n.* मुंगसें *n.* जाळी *f.* मुखबंधन *n.*

To MUZZLE, *v. a. bind the mouth.* तोंडाला मुसकें *n.*-&c. बांधणें-घालणें, तोंड *n.* बांधणें, मुसकणें, मुसकटणें *or* मुसकाटणें.

MUZZLED, *p.* v. V. तोंड बांधलेला, मुसकें बांधलेला, &c. बद्धमुख.

MY, *pro. a.* माझा, आपला, मम.

MYOLOGY, *n. description of the muscles.* स्नायूंचें वर्णन *n.* मांसपेशीचें वर्णन *n.*

MYOPE, *n. short sighted person.* डोळ्याजवळचा पाहणारा, वरडोळ्या, गजनेत्री, गजदृष्टि.

MYOPY, *n. shortness of sight.* डोळ्याजवळची दृष्टि *f.* गजदृष्टि *f.*

MYRIAD, *n. ten thousand.* दहाहजार, दशसहस्र, अयुत *n.*

Myriads, by myriads, &c. क्रोडों, लाखों.

MYRMIDON, *n. a rude, bullying soldier or attendant.* कुत्रा *m.* इमामदांडगा, थोंट *or* थोंठ, लंड, लद्दनिरंजन, लद्दभारती.

MYROBALAN, *n.*—emblic m. *phyllanthus emblica,*—the plant. अंबळी *or* आंवळी *f.* धोत्री *f.* आमलकी *f.*—the fruit. अंवळा *or* आंवळा *m.* आमलक *m.*—beliric m. *termenalia belerica,* —the plant. बेहडा *m.* वेहळा *m.* कलिद्रुम *m.* अक्ष *m.* अक्षक*m.* —the fruit. बेहडा *m.* वेहळा *m.*—yellow or chebulic m. *terminalia chebula,*—the plant. हरडा *or* हिरडा *m.* चेतकी *f.* हरीतकी *f.*—the fruit. हरडा *or* हिरडा *m.* हरीतकी *f.*

Chebulic m. gathered and dried when young. बाळहिरडा *m.* बालहरीतकी *f.*

Dried myrobalans. अंबळकटी *or* ठी *f.* आमलकी *f.*

The three myrobalans. (हिरडा, बेहडा & अंबळकटी) त्रिफला *or* ळा *m. f.*

Wild m. जंगली हिरडा *m.* चाम्हार हिरडा *m.* रंगारी (*or* रंगाचा) हिरडा *m.*

MYRRH, *n.*—the gum. बोल *pop.* बोळ *m.* गंधरस *m.* Some sorts are, बाळंतबोळ, रक्याबोळ *or* तांबडा बोळ, रक्तबोळ.

MYRTLE, *n.* एक झाड आहे.

MYSELF, *pro.* मी, आपण.

MYSTERIOUS, *a. obscure, hid from the understanding, &c.* गूढ, गहन, निगूढ, गूढार्थक, गूढार्थ, गुप्त, गुप्तार्थ, गुह्य, दुर्बोध, दुर्ज्ञेय, अकळ.

2 *artfully perplexed, &c.* लपेटीचा, घोटाळयाचा, गुप्तमार्गाचा, झांकल्या मार्गाचा-व्यवहाराचा.

MYSTERIOUSNESS, *n.* v. A. 1. गूढपणा *m.* गूढार्थता *f.* गूढता *f.* दुर्ज्ञेयता *f.* &c.

2 लपेट *f.* घोंटाळा *m.* गुप्त मार्ग *m.* गुप्त व्यवहार *m.* झांकला मार्ग *m.* झांकला व्यवहार *m.* [*n.* गुह्य गोष्ट *f.*

MYSTERY, *n.* v. SECRET. रहस्य *pop.* रहस्श *n.* गूढ *n.* मर्म *n.* ब्रह्म

2 See MYSTERIOUSNESS 2.

MYSTIC, MYSTICAL, *a. obscure, &c.* v. MYSTERIOUS. गूढ, गूढार्थक, गुप्तार्थक, गुह्य.

M. prayer or incantation. M. verse. मंत्र*m.* गुह्यभाषित*n.*

M. word or sound. व्याहृति *f.*

2 *involving a secret meaning,* v. EMBLEMATIC. लाक्षणिक, संकेतगर्भित, संकेताचा, गूढार्थगर्भित, गूढाभिप्रायक.

MYSTICALNESS, MYSTICISM, *n.* v. A. 1. गूढपणा *m.* गूढता *f.* गूढार्थता *f.* &c.

To MYSTIFY, *v. a. involve in mystery.* गूढ-&c. करणें-करून दाखवणें, कूट *n.*-कोडें *n.* करणें *g. of o.* लौकर न समजेसाकरणें, न उलगडेसा करणें, गूढता *f.*-&c. आणणें, घोंटाळा *m.*-&c.करणें *g. of o.*

MYTH, *n.* पुराणकथा *f.* पुरावृत्तकथा *f.*

MYTHOLOGICAL, *a. relating to mythology.* पुराणांतला, पुराणाचा, पुराणसंबंधी, पुराणोक्त, देवमालिकाख्यानसंबंधी-विषयक.

MYTHOLOGY, *n. system of fables respecting heathen gods.* पुराणें *n. pl.* पुराणोक्तितिहास *m.* देवमालिकाख्यान *n.*

N.

N. This letter is represented by न.

To NAB, *v. a. catch suddenly,* v. To SEIZE. पटकावणें, मटकावणें, पछाडणें, गांठणें, मट्टा *m.* मारणें *with* वर *of o.*

NABOB, *n. Indian viceroy.* नवाब *m.*

NADIR, *n. point opposite the zenith.* अधर *m.* अधोबिंदु *m.* अधोदिशा *f.* अधःस्वस्तिक *m.* समम्य *m.*

NAG, *n.* v. HORSE. घोडें *n.* घोडा *m.*

NAIAD, *n. water-nymph.* जलदेवता *f.* आप्सा *f. pl.*

NAIL, *n.* (of the fingers, &c.). नख *m.* *n.* नखूट *n.* कररुह *m.* —in contempt, नखरूड*n.* [*or* बुचकरा *m.*

A gripe or rude seizure with talons or nails. बुचकुरा

Dough rolled upon the n. नखला *m.*

Inflammation and gathering at the corner of a n. कोंपरी *f.* कोर *f.*

N.-mark, *scratch with a n.* नखोरा *m.*

N.-parer. नखशी *f.* नखजीन *n.* नरणी *f.* नराणी *f.* नरपातें *n.* नाचकंड *or* ण *n.* कंडारणें *n.*

Poison of the n. नखविख *n.* नखविष *n.*

The tender flesh under the n. जिव्हाळी *f.* जिभाळी *or* जिभोळी *f.* जीभ *f.*

To bite the nails. दांतांनीं नखें *n. pl.* खुडतुडणें.

To tear or break off with the n. खुडतुडणें, खुडणें.

2 See CLAW.

3 (of iron, &c.). खिळा *m.* मेख *f.* खुरसा *m.* चूक *f.* शंकु *m.*

Double pointed n. तुरई *f.* तूर *f.* बाघी *f.*

Head of a n. गूल *m.*

Large n. with a knobby head. गूलखिळा *m.*

On the n. *told down at once*—money in payment. हातावर रोख, रोखठोक.

To NAIL, *v. a. fasten with nails.* खिळा *m.*-खिळे *m. pl.* मारणें-देणें-मारून बंद करणें, खिळणें, खिळून टाकणें, खिळ्यांनीं गच्च-&c. करणें, खिळण *n.*-खिळेबंदी *f.* करणें.

NAILED, *p.* v. V. खिळे मारलेला, खिळलेला, &c. खिळींब.

NAIVE. See SIMPLE.

NAIVELY, *adv.* v. N. भोळेभावानें, भोळेपणानें, भोळाईनें.

NAIVETE, *n. simplicity, ingenuousness.* भोळाभाव *m.* भोळाभावार्थ *m.* भोळेपणा *m.* भोळाई *f.*

NAKED, *a. without clothes or covering.* नागवा, नंगा, नागा, नाकटा, नागडा, नग्गा, नग्न, निर्वस्त्र, विवस्त्र, अवस्त्र, वस्त्रहीन-शून्य-&c. विवसन, अवासा, दिगंबर, विनग्न.

Stark n. निपट नागवा, उघडाबंब, नंगधडंग, उघडानागडा, उघडावाघडा, लक्क.

To go or be stark n.—in covert, &c. phrase. नागमोडीचा पितांबर *m.*-नागवा पाटाव *m.* नेसणें.—Some terms for a fellow stark naked are, नगन नारायण, नागवा गोसावी, लंडभारती, दिगंबर, निपट निरंजन.

2 (from the waist upwards, or covered only around the loins). उघडा, उघडा बोडका, उघडे आंगाचा, खुला, खुले आंगाचा. [शुद्ध, केवल *or* ळ.

3 *bare, mere, abstract,* v. SIMPLE. नुस्ता *or* नुस्था, निखा,

4 *wanting something usual,* v. BARE. ओंका *or* वका, खुला, भुंडा *or* भुंढा, बोडका, शून्य *pop.* सुना & सुनका, रंडका.

5 *unarmed, exposed.* उघडा, हत्यारांनीं उघडा, शस्त्रावांचून नागवा.

NAKEDLY, *adv.* v. A. 1. नागवा *decl.* &c. नागव्यानें, नागव्या आंगानें, नागवा होऊन, वस्त्ररहित, &c.

2 उघड्या आंगानें, उघड्यानें, खुले आंगानें.

NAKEDNESS, *n.* v. A. 1. नागवेपणा *m.* नंगेपणा *m.* &c. नग्नता *f.* नग्नावस्था *f.* नग्नभाव *m.* वस्त्राराहित्य *n.*

2 उघडेपणा *m.* &c.

4 ओंकेपणा *m.* बोडकेपणा *m.* सुनेपणा *m.* &c.

5 उघडेपणा *m.* नागवेपणा *m.*

I. *private part.* आंग *n.* शरीर *n.* काया *f.* नागवें *n.* लाज *f.*

NAME, *n. designation, &c.* नांव*n.* नाम*n.* संज्ञा *f.* इसम *or* इसीम *n.* *f.* अभिधान *n.* अभिधेय *n.* आख्या *f.* आव्हा *f.* व्यपदेश *m.*

Boys get their names on the 12th day, Girls on the 13th day, of their age. The name given on the 12th day is called जन्मनाम. Besides the above name it is usual for Bráhman boys to have a name for common use. This is called व्यावहारिकनाम. It is called also प्रतिष्ठानाम, उपचारिकनांव, चालतेंनांव, & बाहतेंनांव. Besides the above two there is नाक्षत्रनाम or a name taken from the *Nakshatra* in which the Moon was at the boys birth. It is used at his *munj*. It is called also गुप्तनाम.

A girl receives a new name at her marriage, which becomes her सासरचेंनांव; her former name (her जन्मनांव) continuing to be her माहेरचें नांव.

Natives use familiar abbreviations of Names. Thus नारायण becomes नाना, सदाशिव becomes सदू, बळवंत becomes बाळू, रामचंद्र becomes रामा, &c. &c.

The family names (surnames) of females take a feminine form, as होळकर-होळकरीण, साठा-साठी, रास्त्या-रास्ती, &c. &c.

It is usual for a Bràhman to use his father's name between his own name and his surname, as परशुराम बल्लाळ गोडबोले.

There are numerous affixes of honor or respect attached to *proper names*. Some are collected here. Affixes to names of males generally, बाबा, बा, जी, बावा, अपा, अण्णा, दाजी, दादा, नाना, भाऊ, काका, तात्या, साहेब, (as मणोबा, विठोबा, गंगाजी, गोविंदपंत अपा, चिंतोपंत नाना, बापूसाहेब, &c.);—to names of Bràhmans, शर्म;—to names of Bràhman shroffs, नाईक (as त्रिंबक नाईक);—to names of Bràhman writers, पंत;—to names of Kshatriyas, वर्म (as कृष्णवर्मांक्षत्रिय);—to names of Maráṭhás or Shùdras, पाटील (as रावजीपाटील);—to names of merchants and tradesmen, शेट or शेठ, शेटजी;—to names of soldiers or clerks, राव or राय (as बळवंतराव);—to names of *Lingàits*, लिंग;—to names of carpenters, &c. बाड्या;—to names of barbers, महाला or ल्या or ली, माली, (as त्रिंबकमहाल्या);—to names of Mahárs, &c. नाईक or नाक (as रामनाक);—to names of Chámbhárs &c. म्हेतर (as हिरम्हेतर);—to names of *office* or *condition*, भाई (as कारकूनभाई, शिपाईभाई, भटभाई;—to names of *Madrasees*, अय्या,—to respectful names and titles generally, साहेब(as नानासाहेब, दादासाहेब, also to the designation of, as. पाटेलसाहेब, सुभेदार साहेब, &c.);—to names of females, gener. बाई, बया, ताई, दादी, नानी, माई, जिजी, काकू, दाई;—to names of Shúdra women, आऊ, अवा, अवाजी.

Addressing by n. नामग्रहण *n.* नामग्रह *m.*

Bad, unlucky, &c. n. दुर्नाम *n.*

Bearing the n. of. नांवाचा, नामधारी (in comp.).

Calling to mind the n. of (a god, &c.). नामस्मरण *n.*

Ceremony of giving the name on the twelfth day. बारसें *n.* बारसा *m.* नामकरण *n.* [कुलनाम*n.*

Family n., Surname. आडनांव*n.* उपनांव*n.* उपनाम*n.* अडक*f.*

In the n. of (in bonds, &c.) बेशमी or बेश्म.

List or roll of names. नांवनिशी *f.* इसमवारी *f.* नामावलि *pop.* नामावळी & नामावळ *f.*

N. and all particulars. नांवनिशाण *n.* [वार.

Name by n.—nomination. नांवनिशीवार, नांववार, इसम-

One's own n. स्वनाम *n.*

Recitation of the n. of (a god, &c.). नामोच्चारण *n.*

Recitation *mentally* of the n. for (a god, &c.) स्मरण *n.* स्मरणें *n.*—Rosary used at it. स्मरणी *f.*

To the n. or account of. नांवावर.

To call names. नांव *n.* ठेवणें.

To pass under the n. of. नांवाखालीं मोडणें, नांवावर विकणें.

May his name perish! नांव जळो, नांवास हळद लागो.

I cannot bear even the name of it. त्याचें मला नांव नको.

2 *character, credit*, v. REPUTATION. नांव *n.* आब्रू *f.* आब *m.* नामोश *m.*

Bad n. नांव *n.*

Good n. नांव *n.* नामोश *m.* नामुशी *f.* हुरमत *f.*

To blast or sully one's good n. नांवावर पाणी *n.* घालणें.

To destroy one's good n. नांव *n.* बुडवणें, नाद *m.* दवडणें-घालवणें.

To get a bad n. खोडणें.

To lose one's good n. नाक *n.* गमावणें, नाद *m.*-नाक *n.*-&c. जाणें *g. of s.* [गवणें.

To preserve one's good n. नांव *n.*-पागोटें *n.* संभाळणें-वा-

3 *celebrity*, v. FAME. नांव *n.* नाम *n.* नांवरूप *n.* नांवलौकीक *m.* लौकीक, नामना *f.* विख्याति *f.* प्रख्याति *f.*

To NAME, *v. a. give a name to, call, denominate.* नांव *n.*-नाम *n.*-संज्ञा *f.*-अभिधान *n.*-&c.देणें-ठेवणें-करणें, म्हणणें, बोलणें, आव्हानणें.

2 *mention by name.* नांव *n.*-&c. घेणें-काढणें-उच्चारणें *g. of o.* नामग्रहण *n.* करणें-घेणें-काढणें-उच्चारणें *g. of o.* म्हणणें, नांवसारणें, आव्हानणें, नामोच्चारण *n.* करणें *g. of o.*

To be named. अभिधेय.

NAMED, *p. & a.* v. V. 1. नांव दिल्हेला, &c. प्राप्तनाम, लब्धनाम, प्राप्ताभिधान. [ख्यात.

2 नांव घेतलेला, म्हटलेला, नांवस्वारलेला, &c. नामोच्चारित, आ-

I. *bearing the name of.* नांवाचा, &c. नामक (in comp. as, हरीपंत नामक), नामा (in comp. as, गंगावरनामा, and fem. नाम्नी as गंगानाम्नी), नामधारी, नामधारक, आख्य (in comp. as, कृष्णाख्य), संज्ञी (in comp.).

NAMELESS, *a.* निनावा, निनाव्या, अनामक, नामरहित-शून्य-&c. निर्नामिक, अनभिधान.

NAMELY, *adv. that is to say.* म्हणजे.

NAMESAKE, *n. one that bears the same name.* नांवकरी, स्वनामी, समनामधारी, नामधारी. [स्थापन *n.*

NAMING, *n.* v. V. 1.—*act.* नांव देणें *n.* &c. नामकरण *n.* नाम-

Ceremony of n. a child. बारसें *n.* नामकरण *n.*

2—*act.* नांव घेणें *n.* नामग्रहण *n.* नामनिर्देश *m.* नामोच्चारण *n.*

NAP, *n. a short sleep.* निद्रेचा-झोपेचा चुटका *m.*-झुटका*m.* झोपेची झुळूक *f. v.* ये, डुकली *f.* डुलकी *f. v.* खा, घे, वामकुक्षि *f.*

To take a n. डोळ्यांचा कड *m.*-डोळयांचें कडू *n.* मोडणें.

2 *down.* फूल *n.*

To NAP, *v. n.* v. N. 1. डुकली *f.*-&c. घेणें-खाणें.

NAPE, *n. joint of the neck behind.* मानेचा कांटा *m.*-मेंढा *m.*-कुकस *m.*-मणका *m.* ग्रीवा *f.* मन्या *f.*

NAPTHA, *n.* नक्तेल *n.* रोगणाचें तेल *n.* नफतें *n.* नफतेल *n.*

NAPKIN, *n.* v. TOWEL. पुसणें *n.* तोंडपुसणें *n.*

NAPLESS, *a. that has no down.* बिनफुलाचा.

NAPPY, *a. that has much down.* बहुतफुलाचा.

2 See FROTHY.

NARCOSIS, *n. effect of a narcotic.* माजरें *n.*

NARCOTIC, *a. causing stupor.* माजरा, लागरा, मादक, मदकारी.
2 See OPIATE, SOPORIFIC.

NAROTIC, *n. medicine which causes stupor.* मदकारी औषध *n.* गुंगीचें औषध *m.* ग्राही *m.* उपविष *n.*

NARD, *n. spikenard.* जटामांसी *f.*

NARRABLE, *a. that may be related.* सांगायाजोगा-&c. निरूपण करायास योग्य, कथ्य, कथनीय, निरूपणीय, निरूप्य.

To NARRATE, *v. a. relate,* v. To TELL. सांगणें, कथणें, निरूपणें, कथन *n.*-निरूपण *n.*-&c. करणें *g. of o.* वदणें.

NARRATED, *p.* v. V. सांगितलेला, &c. निरूपित, कथित.

NARRATION, *n.* v. V.—*act.* सांगणें *n.* &c. निरूपण *n.* कथन *n.* वर्णन *n.* वदणूक *f.*
I. *account given,* v. NARRATIVE. कथा *f.* गोष्ट *f.*

NARRATIVE, *n. relation, story, history.* कथा *f.* गोष्ट *f.* कहाणी *f.* हकिकत *f.* बखर *f.* वर्णन *n.* वाका *m.* वृत्तांत *m.*

NARRATOR, *n.* v. V. सांगणारा &c. निरूपक, कथक, निरूपणकर्त्ता, कथनकर्त्ता, &c.

NARROW, *a. not broad or wide.* अरुंद, निरुंद, लहान, बारीक, अंबळ (*dim.* अंबळसर), अविस्तीर्ण, अप्रशस्त, अविस्तृत, संकोचाचा, संकोचित, संकुचित, संकट.
2—of space, *confined.* सांकड, अवघड, अडचणीचा, कुंचड, कोचकील, संकोचाचा, अल्पावकाश, संकोचित, अप्रशस्त.
3 *of confined views and sentiments.* अप्रशस्त मनाचा, संकोचित मनाचा, एकचाली, एकमार्गी, एकमोडी, एककल्ली, अल्पदृष्टि, अप्रशस्त मनस्क.
4 *close, vigilant, strict.* बारीक, बारीक दृष्टीचा, सूक्ष्म, पक्का, कचा, छडाछडीचा. [दार, अव्ययशील.
5 *close, stingy,* v. MISERLY. कृपण, किरमाडी, किरटा, अनु-
6 *contracted, small,*—means, circumstances. अडचणीचा, तंगचाईचा, ओढगस्तीचा, तंग, अप्रशस्त, संकोचित, अल्प in comp. स्वल्प in comp.
7 *near, barely sufficient to avoid evil.* संकटाचा, मुशकिलीचा, थोडक्या अंतराचा.

To NARROW, *v. a. lessen the breadth of, contract.* अरुंद-निरुंद-लहान-बारीक-&c. करणें, संकोच *m.* करणें *g. of o.* रुंदी *f.* कमी करणें *g. of o.*

To NARROW, *v. n. become narrow.* अरुंद-संकोचित-&c. होणें, संकोचणें, संकोच *m.* होणें *g. of s.* लहानावणें, बारकावणें.

NARROW-MINDED, *a.* v. NARROW, 3. अप्रशस्तमनाचा, एकचाली, एककल्ली. [संकीर्ण.

NARROWED, *p.* v. V. A. 1. अरुंद केलेला, &c. संकोचित, संकुचित,

NARROWLY, *adv.* v. A. 1. 2. अरुंद, अरुंदपणानें, अरुंदीनें, अल्पविस्ताराचा *decl.*
4 बारकाईनें, बारीक दृष्टीनें, सूक्ष्म दृष्टीनें, पंक्तेपणानें.
7 v. HARDLY. संकटानें, मुशकिलीनें, थोडक्यांत, थोड्यांत.
This adverb and its adjective above are best rendered by adopting some other construction, as मी मरतां मरतां वांचलों I had a narrow escape from death, मी बुडतां बुडतां वांचलों I narrowly escaped drowning, &c.

NARROWNESS, *n.* v. A. 1. अरुंदपणा *m.* &c. अरुंदी *f.* निरुंदी *f.* अल्पविस्तार *m.* संकोच *m.* अप्रशस्तता *f.* अविस्तीर्णता *f.* संकुचितभाव *m.*
2 सांकडपणा *m.* &c. अडचण *f.* अल्पावकाश *m.* अप्रशस्तता *f.*
3 मनाचा अप्रशस्तपणा *m.* अप्रशस्तता *f.* अप्राशस्त्य *n.*
4 बारिकपणा *m.* बारकाई *f.* सूक्ष्मता *f.* पक्केपणा *m.*
5 कृपणपणा *m.* किरमाडीपणा *m.* कार्पण्य *n.* अनुदारत्व *n.*
6 अडचण *f.* तारंबळ *f.* तंगचाई *f.* तंगची *f.*

NASAL, *a. belonging, &c. to the nose.* नाकाचा, नाकचा, नस्य, नासिकासंबंधी. [गिणगिणीत.
2—utterance, &c. नाकांतला, गेंगाणा, गुणगुण्या, गिणगिणा, N. utterace. गुणगूण *f.* गिणगीण *f.*
3—in grmmar. अनुनासिक, सानुनासिक, सानुस्वार.
The nasal dot or character. पूज्य *n.* बिंदु *m.* बिंदलें *n.* अनुस्वार *m.* अनुनासिकचिह्न *n.*

NASAL, *n.* अनुनासिकवर्ण *m.*

NASALLY, *adv.* v. A. 2. नाकांत, नाकांतून.
That speaks n. गुणगुण्या, गिणगिण्या.
To speak n. गुणगुणणें, गुणणें, गिणगिणणें, गेंगणें.

NASCENT, *a. beginning to exist.* भूयमान.

NASTILY, *adv.* v. A. 1. घाणीनें, घाण करून, घाणेरे रीतीनें, &c.

NASTINESS, *n.* v. A. 1. घाणेरेपणा *m.* ओखटेपणा *m.* &c.
2 See OBSCENITY.
I. *slop, muck, &c.* v. MESS. घाण *f.* तन्हाण *n.* रेबड *f.*

NASTY, *a. dirty, filthy, nauseous.* घाणीचा, घाणेरडा, घाणेरा, घाणेला, मळीण, ओंगळवाणा, ओंगळ, ओखटा, मळमळीत, हिडशा, हिडीस, हेंदरा, घामट *or* घामड, कुत्सित.
2 See OBSCENE.

NATAL, *a. pertaining to birth.* जन्माचा, जन्मलेला, जन्मसंबंधी, जन्मविषयक, जन्म (in comp. as, जन्मस्थान, जन्मदिन, &c.).

NATHLESS. See NEVERTHELESS.

NATION, *n. people.* लोक *m.* खूम *m. m.* जाति *f.* विशेषदेशजनता *f.*

NATIONAL, *a. belonging, &c. to a nation.* विशेष देशांतील लोकांचा, लोकांचा, विशेषदेशजनतासंबंधी, देशाचा, राष्ट्रीय, राष्ट्रिक, दैशिक. [र्म *m.*
N. custom. देशधर्म *m.* देशाचार *m.* देशव्यवहार *m.* जनपदध-
2 *attached to one's nation.* स्वलोकाभिमानी, स्वदेशाभिमानी, स्वराष्ट्राभिमानी. [*f.* जातित्व *n.*

NATIONALITY, NATIONALNESS, *n.* v. A. 1. लोकपणा *m.* लोकता
2 स्वलोकाभिमान *m.* स्वदेशाभिमान *m.*

NATIONALLY, *adv.* v. A. 1. लोक म्हणून, जात म्हणून, लोकतः, जातितः, सगळे लोक, यावत् लोक.

NATIVE, *a. not artificial, not acquired,* v. NATURAL. जातीचा, आंगचा, मूळचा, स्वाभाविक *pop.* स्वभाविक, स्वभावसिद्ध, प्राकृत, सांसिद्धिक. [जित.
2 *conferred by birth.* जन्माचा, जन्मप्राप्त, जन्मसिद्ध, जन्मा-
3 *natal.* जन्माचा, जन्म in comp.
N. country, N. land. जन्मदेश *m.* जन्मभूमि *f.* स्वदेश *m.*
4 *indigenous, not foreign.* मुलकी *or* मुलखी, देशाचा, देशी, देशीय, देशोत्पन्न. [(in comp.).

NATIVE, *n. one born in any place.* जन्मलेला, उपजलेला, देशीय

NATIVITY, *n.* v. BIRTH. जन्म *m. n.* उपज *m.* उत्पत्ति *f.* पैदास्त *f.*
Astrological calculation of a n. जातक *n.* ताजक *n.*
Astrological record of a n. जन्मपत्र *n.* जन्मपत्री *f.* जन्मपत्रिका *f.* जन्मटिपण *n.* यादवान *n.*
Determination of the name at a n. नांवरस *f.*

Figure (of the zodiac, &c.) drawn in tracing the aspects of a n. जन्मकुंडली *f.*

Month of one's n. जन्ममास *m.*

Name given at one's n. जन्मनाम *n.* राशिनाम *pop.* रासनांव *n.* नक्षत्रनाम *n.* नांवरस *f.* नांवरसनांव *n.*

Planet of a n. जन्मनक्षत्र *n.* नाडीनक्षत्र *n.*

Sign of a n. जन्मराशि *m. f. pop.* जन्मरास *f.* जन्मलग्न *n.*

NATRON, *n. impure carbonate of soda.* सज्जाक्षार *or* सज्जीखार*m.* सर्जिखार *m.* सर्जी *f.* सर्जिका *f.* सर्जिकाक्षार *m.* कापोत *m.*

NATTINESS, *n.* v. A. चाकचोपी *f.* चापचोपी *f.* चापीचोपी *f.* ठाकसठिकसपणा *m.*

NATTY, *a. nice and spruce,* v. NEAT. चापचोप्या, ठाकठिक्या, चकपक, ठाकसठिकस *or* ठिकसठाकस.

NATURAL, *a. pertaining to nature, effected by nature, derived from nature, innate, native, &c.; not artificial, not acquired.* जातीचा, आंगचा, जन्माचा, स्वभावाचा, प्रकृतीचा, मूळचा, &c. स्वाभाविक *pop.* स्वभाविक, स्वभावसिद्ध, सहज, साहजिक, सहजात, प्रकृत, प्राकृतिक, प्रकृतिसिद्ध, सांसिद्धिक, अकृत्रिम, स्वतःसिद्ध, नैसर्गिक, औत्सर्गिक, स्वभावज, निसर्गज, प्रकृतिस्थ, अंतर्जात, अंतर्भव, भाविक.

N. friend or ally. सहजमित्र, प्राकृतमित्र.

N. enemy. सहजशत्रु, सहजारि, प्राकृतारि.

N. neutral. सहजोदासीन.

2 *regular, reasonable, following the natural course.* मार्गाचा, रीतीचा, सोईचा, पथाचा, चालीचा, रुईचा, न्यायाचा, वाजवी, यथामार्ग, यथाक्रम, यथायोग्य, यथायुक्त.

3 *not forced, not far fetched, &c.* सोईचा, मार्गाचा, सरल, सुरळीत, ऋजु *pop.* उजू, सहजचा, साहजिक, अक्लिष्ट.

4 *illegitimate,* v. BASTARD. दासीचा, अनौरस, अविधिजात, विवाह्यजात.

5—as opposed to violent, premature, &c. सुखाचा, सुघड, सुघडपणाचा, अनपघाती, यथाकाल, चालीचा, रितीचा.

N. death. आपलें मरण *n.* आपमरण *n.* सुमरण *n.*

6 *according to truth or reality.* यथातथ, यथायोग्य, यथार्थ.

N. History. स्थावरजंगमविद्या *f.* स्थावरजंगमशास्त्र *n.* जडाजडशास्त्र *n.*

N. Philosophy. पदार्थविज्ञान *n.* पदार्थमात्रशास्त्र *n.*

N. Theology. सृष्टिजन्य ईश्वरज्ञान *n.*

NATURAL, *n. idiot.* जन्माचा खुळा, जन्माचा वेडा, यथाजात, नंद*m.*

NATURALIST, *n. student of natural history, &c.* स्थावरजंगमविज्ञानी, स्थावरजंगमविचारी, स्थावरजंगमशोधी.

To NATURALIZE, *v. a. confer on the rights of a native.* देशीय मंडळींत घेणें, देशीय-&c. करणें, देशजाधिकारप्रापण *n.* करणें.

2 *make natural; make familiar, &c.* सवई *f.*-सराव *m.*-अभ्यास *m.*-खांद *m.*-&c. पडणें *in. con. with g. of o.* सवई *f.*-सराव *m.*-अभ्यास *m.*-&c. पाडणें, घसवटीखालीं-सहवासाखालीं-अभ्यासाखालीं-&c. आणणें.

3 (words, &c.) आपलासा करणें.

NATURALLY, *adv.* v. A. 1. स्वभावानें, जातीनें, गुणानें, स्वभावेंकरून, प्रकृतीनें, जन्मानें, उपजत, स्वभावतः, प्रकृतितः, जातितः, जन्मतः, गुणतः, स्वतः *pop.* स्वतां, स्वभावगतीं *or* गत्या, जात्या, प्रकृत्या, सहज.

2 मार्गानें, रीतीनें, सोइनें, &c. यथामार्ग, यथाक्रम, यथायोग्य.

3 मार्गानें, सरळपणानें,&c. सुरळीत, सहज, सहजगत्या, सहजगतीनें.

5 सुखानें, सुघडपणानें, &c.

6 यथार्थ, हुबहू *f.* यथातथ, थेट.

NATURALNESS, *n.* v. A. 1. स्वभाविकपणा *m.* स्वाभाविकत्व *n.* प्राकृतिकत्व *n.* प्राकृतत्व *n.* &c.

3 सरळपणा *m.* सुरळितपणा *m.* उजुपणा *m.* &c. सारल्य *n.*

6 यथार्थता *f.* याथातथ्य *n.*

NATURE, *n.* This supposed *goddess* or genitress of the material world, believed by Hindus to be illusory and unreal, has several names or titles in their mythology. माया *f.* आदिमाया *f.* महामाया *f.* प्रकृति *f.* शक्ति *f.* आदिशक्ति *f.* अविद्या *f.* प्रधान *n.* लिंग *n.*

The net (blind cast over the understanding and senses) of N. मायाजाल *n.*

The sleight and art of N. मायालाघव *n.*

2 *native state, constituting properties, essential qualities, &c.* स्वभाव *m.* जात *f.* जातिस्वभाव*m.* प्रकृति *f.* प्रकृतिस्वभाव*m.* प्रकृतिभाव *m.* उपजतस्वभाव *m.* धर्म *m.* स्वधर्म *m.* शील *or* शीळ *n.* धर्मत्व *n.* वस्तुस्वभाव *m.* वस्तुशक्ति *f.* भाव *m.* भावना *f.* निसर्ग *m.* निसर्गभाव *m.* रूप *n.* स्वरूप *n.* संसिद्धि *f.* सर्ग *m.* सृष्टि *f.* आत्मा *m.* वस्तु *n.* तत्व *n.* सत्व *n.*

By n. *naturally.* जातीनें, जात्या, जन्मतः, उपजत.

Blind by n. जात्यंध, जन्मांध, गर्भांध.

Not in the n. or being of. अष्टांगीं नाहीं, गांवीं नाहीं, जन्मांत नाहीं.

In the expression of *the unalterableness of an evil Nature,* and, in close correspondence with the phrases, Can the Ethiopian change his skin or the leopard his spots? Wash a sow and she'll return to her wallowing. What's bred in the bone cant be got out of the flesh. Who can wash a Blackamoor white? Crooked by nature crooked for ever. &c. are the following in Maráthi, सहा महिने नळकांड्यांत जरीं घातलें (कुत्र्याचें शेंपूट) तरीं वांकड्याचें वांकडेंच; जित्याची खोड मेल्याशिवाई जात नाहीं; सुंभ जळेल पण पीळ (*or* वळ) जळत नाहीं; हेल्याच्याकानीं किंगरी वाजवली तरीं तो आपली टोंय सोडीत नाहीं; बळचणीचें पाणी आड्याला चढत नाहीं; मुसळाचें धनु कोठें होतें! पाण्यावर गाडा आणि भुईवर नाव चालायाची नाहीं.

3 *disposition of mind, temper.* स्वभाव *m.* प्रकृति *f.* तबियत *f.*

4 *established or regular course of things.* मार्ग *m.* रीति *pop.* रीत *f.* चाल *f.* नीति *f.* न्याय *m.* पथ *m.* क्रम *m.* परिपाटी *f.* परंपरा *f.* आनुपूर्वी *f.*

5 *compass of natural existence; the mundane system,* v. WORLD, UNIVERSE. जग *n.* जगतीतल *n.* सृष्टि *f.* भूमंडल *n.* विश्व *n.* ब्रह्मसृष्टि *f.*

Course of n. सृष्टिक्रम *m.*

To attain through N. unto Nature's God. सगुणाच्या आधारानें निर्गुणास पावणें.

6 *natural affections, native feeling, &c.* स्वभाव *m.* स्वभावधर्म *m.* स्वभावगुण *m. pl.* प्रकृतिधर्म *m.* प्रकृतिगुण *m. pl.*

7 *sort, species, kind.* जाति *pop.* जात *f.* प्रकार *m.* रीति *f.*

8 *constitution, the vital qualities and energies.* शक्ति *f.* जीवित्वशक्ति *f.* प्राण *m. pl.* जीवनशक्ति *f.* ओज *n.* चलनवलनश-

कि *f.* प्राणबल *n.*

To be exhausted—n. प्राण *m. pl.* धकणें.

Offices of nature. देहधर्म *m.*

Easing or relieving n. शौच *n.* मलविसर्ग *m.* मलविसर्जन *n.* मलोत्सर्ग *m.* मलमूत्रविसर्जन *n.* दीर्घशंका *f.*

Convenience for relieving n. हगरी *f.*

General place for relieving n. हगाड *f.* हगाडी *f.* हगंदरी *f.* हगंदारी *f.* गुखाड *f.* गुखाडी *f.* गुवाड *f.*

To ease, disburden, relieve, &c. n. हगणें, देहधर्माचें *n.* करणें, परसाकडे बसणें, मैदान बसणें.

To go to ease, &c. n. परसाकडे-दिशेस-बहिर्दिशेस-बहिर्भूमीस-मैदानास-&c. जाणें.

To want (have a call) to ease n. परसाकडे *n.*-परसाकड *f.*-शौच *n.*-मैदान *n.*-&c. लागणें *in. con.* हगूट *m.* लागणें-येणें *in. con.* शौचास लागणें-दिशेस लागणें *impers.* हगुटणें.

NATURED, *a.* स्वभावाचा, प्रकृतीचा, &c. शील (in comp. as सुशील good-n. कुशील ill-n. &c.).

NAUGHT, *n.* v. NOTHING. काहींच नाहीं.

For n. फुकत, फुकतवारी.

To set at n. See To CONTEMN.

NAUGHT, *a. worthless*, v. BAD. वाईट, खराब, दुष्ट.

NAUGHTINESS, *n.* v. A. 1. वाइटपणा*m.* दुष्टाई *f.*

NAUGHTY, *a. evil, bad*, v. WICKED. वाईट, दुष्ट, पापी.

2 *worthless*, v. BAD. वाईट, खराब, दुष्ट, लुसकान *or* लुकसान.

3—as applied to children See. MISCHIEVOUS.

NAULAGE, *n. passage money.* नोर*m.* गलबताचें भाडें*n.* उतार*m.*

NAUMACHY, *n. sea-fight.* नौकायुद्ध*n.* नाविकयुद्ध*n.* नाविकयुद्धकौतुक *n.*

NAUSEA, *n. propensity to vomit*, v. QUALMISHNESS. कळमळ *f.* मळमळ *f.* मळमळी *f.* ओकारा*m.* ओकारी *f. v.* ये, शिसारी *f.* शिसकारी *f.*

Until n. *usque ad nauseam.* ओयेई तोंपर्यंत.

2 fig. *loathing*, v. DISGUST. कंटाळा*m.* वीट*m.* किळस *f. m.* चिळस *f.* चिकारा*m.* चिणका*m.* चिणकारा*m.* संत *f.* शिसकारी *f.* विकली *f.* विकळूत *f.*

To NAUSEATE, *v. a. loathe.* कंटाळणें, किळसणें, विटणें, उचाटणें, ओकणें, संतावणें, कंटाळा*m.*-वीट*m.*-किळस*f.m.*—&c. येणें *g. of o. with in. con.* [*f.*-&c. आणणें.

2 *affect with disgust.* v. To DISGUST. किळस *f. m.*-चिळस

NAUSEOUS, *a. loathsome, &c.* v. DISGUSTING. ओकारवाणा, ओखटा, ओखटवाणी, कंटाळवाणा *or* वाणी, घाणेरडा, घाणेरा, ओंगळ. [*m.* &c.

NAUSEOUSNESS, *n.* v. A. औखटेपणा*m.* घाणेरडेपणा*m.* ओंगळपणा

NAUTICAL, *a. pertaining to navigation; &c.* नाव-&c. चालविण्याचा-हांकण्याचा-&c. गलबतप्रकरणाचा, नौकाचालनविद्यासंबंधी.

N. person. दर्यावर्दी, नौकाजीवी.

NAVAL, *a. consisting of ships.* गलबतांचा, &c. नौकामय.

A. n. armament. अर्मर *or* अमार*n.*

2 *belonging, &c. to ships.* गलबतांचा &c. नाविक, नाव्य, अर्मरी *or* अर्मारी, नौकासंबंधी, नौकाविषयक.

NAVE, *n.* (of a wheel). मांदळा*m.* पिंडी *f.* तुंब*n.* तुंबा*m.* नाभि *f.m.*

Lining of a n. वसूं*n.*

2 (of a temple, &c.) देवळाचा मधला भाग*m.*

NAVEL, *n.* बेंबी *f.* बोंबी *f.* नाभि *f. m.* नाभिकमल*n.* उदरावर्त्त*m.* —of animals, and, contemptuously of man. बेंबट*n.*-contemptuously. नकपट*m.*

Coil of the umbilical cord in the pit of the n. बेंड*n.*

Enlarged n. बेंड*n.* बेंबट*n.*

Hollow or pit of the n. नाभ्यावर्त्त*m.*

Region of the n. नाभिचक्र*n.*

Region below the n. *pubic region.* खालचें*or*खाललेंपोट*n.*

Swollen n. बेंड *n.* बेंबट *n.*

That has a swollen n. बेंडा *or* बेंड्या.

NAVEL-STRING, *n.* नाल *or* नाळ *n.* गर्भनाडी *f.*

Cutting of the n. नालछेद *m.* नालछेदन *n.*

NAVIGABLE, *a. that may be passed in a ship.* गलबतजायाजोगा-सारखा-लायक-&c. नाव्य, नौकागम्य, नौकागमनार्ह, नौतार्य.

To NAVIGATE, *v. n. pass on water in ships, sail.* गलबतानें-&c. जाणें-चालणें-जाणें येणें*n.* करणें, सफर*f.*-नौकापर्यटन*n.*-नौकायात्रा *f.*-&c. करणें.

To NAVIGATE, *v. a. sail over, pass over by ship.* गलबतानें-&c. बहिवाटणें, गलबतानें-&c. चालणें-जाणें येणें*n.* करणें-सफर *f.* करणें-&c. *with* वर *of o.*

2 *direct or manage in a course.* चालवणें, नेणें, वळवणें, हांकणें.

NAVIGATION, *n.* v. V. N.—*act.* गलबतानें जाणें येणें*n.* &c. सफर *f.* नौकापर्यटन*n.* नौकायात्रा *f.* नौकागमनागमन*n.*

v. V. A. 2.—*act.* चालवणें*n.* &c. नौकानयन*n.* नौकाचालन*n.*

I.—the art. नाव-गलबत-&c. चालविण्याची विद्या*f.* नावाडको*f.* नाविकविद्या *f.* नौकाचालनविद्या *f.* नौकानयनविद्या *f.*

NAVIGATOR, *n.* v. V. N. *and* SAILOR. गलबतानें जाणारा-येणारा, &c. सफरी, समुद्रयायी, समुद्रगामी, समुद्रपर्यटक.

v. V. A. 2. गलबत चालवणारा, &c. मालीम, नावाडी, नावाड्या, नाविक, नौकानेता, नौकानयनकर्त्ता.

NAVY, *n. assemblage of ships.* गलबतें *n. pl.* तारवें *n. pl.* तरांडीं*n. pl.* नौकासमूह *m.*

2 *fleet of ships of war.* अर्मर *or* अर्मार *n.*

NAY, *adv. no.* न, नाहीं, ना.

2 *not only this.* असें केवळ नाहीं, बलकी, किंबहुना.

NEAP, NEAP-TIDE, *n. low tide.* भांग*m.* मोडजोहार*m.f.* मोडभांग*m.*

To be at the n. भांगणें.

NEAP, *a.* v. N. भांगाचा.

NEAR, *a. nigh, not distant.* जवळचा, जवळील, जवळला, नजीक *or* ख, पासचा, पासला, जवळपासचा, शेजारचा, लगत्याचा, समीप, समीपस्थ, निकटवर्त्ती, समीपवर्त्ती, उपांत, उपांतिक, सन्निकृष्ट, सन्निहित, आसन्न, प्रत्यासन्न, संसक्त, अंतिक.

2—as a road; *short, direct.* जवळचा, जवळ, नजीक *or* ख, नीट, सरल *pop.* सरळ. [पासला.

3 *closely related.* जवळचा, जवळ, जवळच्या नात्याचा, पासचा,

4 *closely concerning, affecting one's interest.* जवळचा, जवळ लागणारा, निकटसंबंधाचा, अंतरंग, अंतरंगींचा, अंतरींचा, जिव्हाळ्याचा. [अदत्त.

5 *close, stingy, &c.* v. MISERLY. चिकट, चिंबट, हाताचाजड,

6—*opposed to* off ; *of the near side.* अलीकडचा, अलीकडला, अलीकडील, जवळचा, अल्याडचा.

On the n. side. अलीकडे, अरता, अल्याड.

NEAR, *adv. at hand.* जवळ, जवळपास, जवळसर, नजीक *or* ख,

निकट, समीप, सरसा *decl.* सन्निकृष्ट, सन्निध.

2 *within a little*, v. ALMOST. जवळ, प्राय:, बहुतकरून.

NEAR, *prep.* जवळ, पाशीं *or* पासीं, नजीक *or* ख, लगत, समीप, सरसा *decl.* सन्निध, सन्निकृष्ट.

To NEAR, *v. a.* जवळ-नजीक-&c. करणें.

NEAR-SIGHTED, *a. short-sighted.* जवळच्या दृष्टीचा, उलट्याबाहुल्यांचा, उफराट्या बाहुल्यांचा, बरडोळ्या, अदूरदर्शी, गजनेत्री.

NEARLY, *adv.* v. A. 1. *and* NEAR. जवळ.

3 जवळचा *decl.* जवळच्या नात्याचा *decl.* जवळिकीचा *decl.*

4 जवळ, अतरंगीं, जिव्हाळीं.

5 चिकटपणानें, रुपणपणानें.

I. *within a little*, v. ALMOST. जवळ, प्राय:, बहुतकरून.

NEARNESS, *n.* v.A. 1. जवळपणा *m.* जवळीक *f.* समीपता *f.* सामीप्य *n.* नैकट्य *n.* सान्निध्य *n.* समीपवर्त्तित्व *n.* निकटवर्त्तित्व *n.* सन्निकृष्टता *f.* सन्निहितत्व*n.* सन्निधान *n.* सन्निकर्ष *m.* उपांत्य *n.*

2 जवळपणा *m.* &c.

3 जवळपणा *m.* जवळीक *f.* जवळचें नातें *n.* जवळचा संबंध *m.*

5 चिकटपणा *m.* किरटेपणा *m.* बारीकदृष्टी *f.* बारीकनजर *f.* कार्पण्य *n.* रुपणत्व *n.*

NEAT, *n. black cattle.* ढोरें *n. pl.* गुरें *n. pl.* गुरेंढोरें *n. pl.*

2 *an ox or cow.* ढोर *n.* गुरूं *n.*

NEAT, *a. clean and trim*,—house, clothes, &c. ठाकठीक *or* ठीकठाक, ठाकसठिकस *or* ठिकसठाकस, चकपक, चाकपाक, चक्क, चाक *or* चाख, चकचकीत, लकपक, लकलकीत, लक्क, चाकचोप *or* चापचोप, ठाकठिकीचा, चाकचोपीचा, &c.

2 *shapely, of just proportions.* आकारशुद्ध, आवशुद्ध, कांतींवकोरींव, कोरींवकांतींव, कांतींव, नीटनेटका, नेटका, निटस, गोजरा, गोजिरवाणा, सुरेख, साखसुरत, सुतरा, जंत्रीं ओतलेला, बेताबाताचा, माकुलबाणा, डौलदार, सुघटित.

3 *natty, nice, &c.*—of persons. ठाकठिक्या, चाकचोप्या, चापचोप्या, चाकचोप, ठाकसठिकस *or* ठिकसठाकस, चाकचोपीचा, चापचोपीचा.

4 See NET.

NEAT-HERD, *n.* v. COW-HERD. गुराखी, गुराख्या.

NEATLY, *adv.* v. A. 1. 3. ठाकठिकीनें, ठाकीठिकीनें, चापचोपीनें *or* चाकचोपीनें, चकपकीनें.

NEATNESS, *n.* v. A. 1. 3. ठाकठीकपणा *m.* ठाकसठिकसपणा *m.* &c. ठाकठिकी *f.* चाकचोपी *or* चापचोपी *f.* चापीचोपी *f.* चकपक *f.* ओज *f.*

2 आकारशुद्धि *f.* नेटकेपणा *m.* निटसपणा *m.* गोजरेपणा *m.* &c. निटाई *f.* सुरेखाई *f.* सुरेखी *f.* सफाई *f.* आब *m.* छब *f.* खुमास *f.* कुसरी *f.*

NEBULA, *n. film in the eye.* पटल *pop.* पडळ *n.* पडदा *m.* भूर *f.* भुरी *f.* तवंग *m.* तरंग *m.* तरंज *f.* नब *m. f.*

NEBULOUS. See CLOUDY.

NECESSARIAN, *n. one who holds the doctrine of philosophical necessity.* दैववादी, अदृष्टवादी, दैष्टिक, दैवचिंतक, दैवकर्तृवादी, दैवैकवादी. [नन्यगत्या.

NECESSARILY, *adv.* v. A. 2. अवश्य, अवश्यक, अनन्यगतीनें, अ-

3 अगत्य, अगत्यपूर्वक, अगत्यरूप, अगत्यपुरस्सर, अवश्य, अनन्यगतिक, अवश्यमेव.

4 दैववशेंकरून, दैववशात्, दैवाधीनत्तेनें. [आपेक्षा *f.*

NECESSARINESS, *n.* v. A. 1. *and.* NEED. दर्कार *f.* आकांक्षा *f.*

2 आवश्यकत्व *n.* आवश्यकता *or* अवश्यकता *f.* आवश्य *n.* आवश्यक *n.* नांतरीयकभाव *m.* नांतरीयकता *f.* अनन्यथासंभव *m.* अन्यथात्वासंभव *m.* अनन्यगतिकभाव *m.*

3 आवश्यकत्व *n.* आवश्यकता *f.* आवश्य *n.* तदेकहेतुता *f.* तदेकहेतुभाव *m.*

NECESSARY, *a. needful, requisite, urgently wanted.* जरुरीचा, फारजरुरीचा, अगत्याचा, आकांक्षित, अपेक्षित, आवश्यक, अवश्योपयोगी, गरजेचा.

Is n. पाहिजे, पाहिजेल, व्हावा, सप्रयोजन.

Was n. पाहिजे होता.

To be n. लागणें, पाहिजे असणें.

2 *that must be, that cannot be otherwise, unavoidable.* नांतरीयक, अनन्यगतिक, अनन्योपाय, अनन्यथासिद्ध, अनन्यथासाध्य, अन्यथात्वासंभवी, अनन्यथासंभव, अवश, आवश्यक, अनिवार्य.

3 *indispensable, essential.* आवश्यक, अवश्यकर्त्तव्य, अगत्याचा, नियतावश्यक, नाप्राप्त, अवश्यप्राप्त, तदेकहेतुक, सत्तैकहेतुक.

4 *acting from necessity; not free.* दैववशकारी, अदृष्टवशकारी, दैवाधीन, अदृष्टाधीन, विधिवशकारी, दैवपर. [कूप *m.*

NECESSARY, *n. privy.* शेतखाना *m.* तारत *or* तारदखाना *m.* शौच-

2 *a necessary thing.* अगत्याची गोष्ट *f.*-वस्त *f.*-&c.

Necessaries. साहित्य *n.* सामग्री *f.* सामान *n.*

N. of life. अन्नपाणी *n.* अन्नोदक *n.* अन्नवस्त्र*n.*अन्नाछादन*n.*

NECESSITARIAN. See NECESSARIAN.

To NECESSITATE, *v. a. make necessary or unavoidable.* अगत्यपणा *m.*-आवश्यकता *f.*-अवश्यकर्त्तव्यता *f.*-&c. आणणें *with* स *or* ला *of o.* जरूर-आवश्यक-अनिवार्य-&c. करणें, भाग असणें-प्राप्त असणें *in. con. with* मुळें *of agent.*

2 *oblige, constrain.* See To COMPEL.

To be necessitated. निरुपाय-अनन्यगतिक-अनन्योपाय-गत्यंतररहित-&c. असणें-होणें.

NECESSITOUS, NECESSITOUSNESS. See NEEDY, NEED.

NECESSITY, *n. state of being requisite, need.* जरुरी *f.* जरूर *n.* दर्कार *f.* गरज *f.* अगत्य *n.* प्रयोजन *n.* आकांक्षा *f.* अपेक्षा *f.*

2 *unavoidableness, the impossibleness of being otherwise,* v. NECESSARINESS. आवश्यकता *f.* आवश्यक *n.* नांतरीयकभाव *m.* अन्यथात्वासंभव *m.* अनिवार्यता *f.*

3 *fate, fatality.* दैवाधीनता *f.* अदृष्टाधीनता *f.* दैवपरत्व *n.* दैवायत्तता *f.* अदृष्ट *n.* अदृष्टकर्तृत्व *n.* [जाणें-&c.

To yield to n. or fate. काळावर दृष्ट देऊन *or* ठेवून करणें-

4 *want, indigence,* v. POVERTY. अनुपपत्ति *pop.* अनुपत *f.* कंगाली *f.* तारंबळ *f.*दारिद्र्य *n.*

N. has no law. भुकेलें गुरूं वळचण ओढतें.

NECK, *n.* मान *f.* गर्दन *f.* ग्रीवा *f.* कंधरा *f.*—with reproachful implication, or with reference to seizing, shoving, squeezing, or other such action, मानगोटी *or* गुद्दी *f.* गचांडी *f.* गरगोटी *f.* गोकटी *f.* गळचिपी *f.* बोकांडी *f.* बोकांडें *n.* कांठें *n.*

A clutch by the n. अर्धचंद्र *m.*

A thrust or shove upon the n. गळचंडी *f.* गळचोंडी *f.* गळचुटी *f.* गचांडी *or* गचोंडी *f.*

Inflammation and swelling. of the n. माण *f.* माणगें *n.* गंडमाळा *f. pl.* गलगंड *m.*

Handsome necked. सुग्रीव.
Lines of short hair on the nape of the n. मानबळे *m. pl.* मानबळ्या *f. pl.*
Long necked person. बाळेभोंक *or* बाळभोंक *n.*
N. and rump (of a beast). गचा बोचा *m.*
N. or nothing. उडी नाहीं तर बुडी.
On the n. of. पाठोपाठ, मागोमाग, पाठीवर.
To break the n. of. lit. fig. मान *f.*-डिकशी *f.* मोडणें.
To turn out n. and crop. पाळेंमुळें *n. pl.* खणून टाकणें *g. of o.*
2 (of a vessel). गळा *m.* कंठ *m.*
Up to the n.—a vessel filled, &c. गळबट *or* गळबंड, गळवणा *or* गळवणी.
NECK-CLOTH, *n.* गळेबंद *m.* कंठावरण *n.* कंठवस्त्र *n.*
NECK-LACE, *n.* माला *pop.* माळ *f.* हार *m.* कंठमाला *f.*
Large middle gem of a n. मेरु *m.* मेरुस्थान *n.*
Certain Necklaces or Neck-ornanents are, अक्षमाला, एकदाणें, कंठा, कंठी, कमालखानीहार, गरसळी *or* गरसोळी, गळसरी, गांठलें, गिजबिजलें *n.* चंद्रहार, चांपेकळी *or* चांपेकळ्यांची माळ, टिका, ठुशा *or* ठुशांचीगळसरी, तुळसीची माळ, नवरत्नहार, नक्षत्रमाळा, पुत्रवंतीची माळ, पेट्या *or* पेट्यांचा हार, पेंडें, मोहनमाळ, रुद्राक्षमाळ, सरी.
NECROLOGY, *n. register of deaths.* मरतिकांची याद *f.*
NECROMANCER, *n.* v. MAGICIAN. स्मशानमंत्रजप्या, प्रेतसिद्धिकर्त्ता.
NECROMANCY, *n. magical communication with the dead,* v. MAGIC. प्रेतसिद्धि *f.* भूतविद्या *f.* पिशाचविद्या *f.* कुविद्या *f.*
NECTAR, *n. drink of the gods.* अमृत *n.* सुधा *f.* सुधारस *m.* पीयूष *n.*
NECTAREAN, NECTAREOUS, *a.* v. N. अमृताचा, अमृतमय, अमृतप्राय, अमृततुल्य.
NECTARINE, *n.* एक फळ आहे.
NECTARY, *n.* फुलांतील मधाची जागा *f.*
NEED, *n. indigence, want,* v. POVERTY. अनुपपत्ति *pop.* अनुपत *f.* गरिबदारी *f.* गिरिबदारी *f.* चणचण *f.* तारंबळ *f.*
2 *strait, want of help, difficulty.* संकट *n.* दुःख *n.* संकष्ट *n.* अडचण *f.* कच *f.* कोडें *n.*
At the hour of n. अयतेवेळेस.
Giving or a gift in n. अर्थी दान *n.*
The hour of n. अवसान *n.*
A friend in need is a friend indeed. अयतेवेळेस मित्र नोच मित्र.
A gift in need is a gift indeed. अर्थी दान महा पुण्य.
3 *want, lack of, occasion for.* गरज *f.* दर्कार *f.* जरुरी *f.* प्रयोजन *n.* अगत्य *n.* काम *n.* कारण *n.* आकांक्षा *f.* अपेक्षा *f.* उपयोग *m.*
To supply one's n. or lack. गरज *f.* चालविणें-करणें-पुरविणें.
To NEED, *v. a. want, require.* गरज *f.*-दर्कार *f.*-प्रयोजन *n.*-अगत्य *n.*-काम *n.*-&c. असणें-लागणें *g. of o. with in. con.*
To NEED, *v. n. be necessary.* For this word as an auxiliary, पाहिजे is a good rendering, and with negation construction, नको. Ex. वाघ आला तर भ्यालें पाहिजे, शेळी आली तर भ्यायास नको.
NEEDED, *p.v.* V. A. गरज लागलेला, &c. अपेक्षित, आकांक्षित.
NEEDER, *n.* NEEDING, *p. a.* v. V. A. गरजवंत, गर्जी, गर्जू, अर्थी (in comp. as धनार्थी, &c.).
NEEDFUL, *a. requisite,* v. NECESSARY. आवश्यक, अपेक्षित, आकांक्षित.
Is needful. पाहिजे.
The "one thing needful." परमार्थ *m.*
NEEDINESS, *n.* v. A. *and* POVERTY. गरिबदारी *f.* गिरिबदारी *f.* कंगाली *f.* अनुपपत्ति *f.*
NEEDLE, *n.* सुई *f.* सू *f.* सूची *f.* सूचिका *f.*— large n. सुवा *m.*
Eye of a n. नेहें *or* नेढें *n.* नाक *n.*
Point of a n. सुईची अणी *f.* सुईचें टोंक *n.* सूच्यग्र *n.*
2 (of the compass). कांटा *m.*
NEEDLE-WORK, *n. work done by the needle.* शिवणकाम *n.* शिवणें *n.* शिवण *n.* शिवणावळ *f.*
2 *embroidery by the needle.* कशीदा *m.*
NEEDLESS, *a. not wanted, not requisite, not called for.* अकारण *pop.* अकारणी, निष्कारण *pop.* निकारणी, नस्ता, अप्रयोजक, निष्प्रयोजन, निरर्थक, व्यर्थ, अकारणक.
NEEDLESSLY, *adv.* v. A. कारणावांचून, प्रयोजनावांचून, &c. अकारण, निःकारण, निष्प्रयोजन, उगा, उगीच, व्यर्थ.
NEEDLESSNESS, *n.* v. A. अकारणीपणा *m.* निकारणीपणा *m.* &c. अकारणत्व *n.* निष्कारणत्व *n.* &c. प्रयोजनाभाव *m.* कारणाभाव *m.* प्रयोजनराहित्य *n.*
NEEDS, *adv.* v. NECESSARILY. अगत्य, अगत्यरूप, अगत्यपूर्वक, जरूर.
NEEDY, *a. necessitous, indigent,* v POOR. गरजवंत, गरजी, अनुत्पन्न, अनुपपन्न, गिरिबदार, कंगाल, भुकेकंगाल, महाग & मोताद (in comp. with a noun in the objective case,as अन्नास महाग n. of food; वस्त्रास महाग n. of clothing, &c.).
NEFARIOUS, *a. heinous, atrocious,* v. WICKED. मोठ्या पापाचा, महापातकाचा, अतिदुष्ट, अकटोविकट.
NEFARIOUSNESS, *n.* v. A. मोठेंपाप *n.* &c. अतिदुष्टता *f.*
NEGATION, *n.* v. DENIAL. नकार *or* नाकार *m.* अस्वीकार *m.*
2—in logic; *privation, exclusion.* अभाव *m.* Four kinds are mentioned, viz. प्रध्वंसाभाव *m. annihilation,* or *extinction;* प्रागभाव *antecedent non existence;* अन्योन्याभाव *reciprocal or relative negation;* अत्यंताभाव *pure or simple non-being.* Another division of अभाव is made into two classes, viz. संसर्गाभाव—*universal nejation,* and अन्योन्याभाव *relative or mutual negation.*
NEGATIVE, *a. implying denial,*—opposed to affirmative, नचा, नकाराचा, नच्याफाड्याचा, नास्तिपक्षाचा, निषेधाचा, निषेधमुखाचा, निषेधवृत्ति, अस्वीकारसूचक, निषेधसूचक.
2 *privative, implying absence,*—opposed to positive. अभावसूचक, अभावदर्शक, अभावरूप, अभावात्मक, अभावकोटींतला, अकरणरूप, अक्रियारूप, अननुष्ठानरूप, अकरणात्मक.
N. quantity,—in algebra. ऋण *n.*
3 *having the power of stopping by non-consent.* नाहीं म्हणून बंद करण्याच्या शक्तीचा, निषेधद्वारा प्रतिबंधसमर्थ.
NEGATIVE, *n. a word that denies.* नकाराचा शब्द *m.* अस्वीकारसूचकपद *n.* निषेधार्थक शब्द *m.*
2 *proposition by which something is denied.* नकाराचा पक्ष *m.*नास्तिपक्ष*m.*निषेधसूचक-अभावसूचक-&c. पक्ष*m.*-वाक्य*n.*-&c.
3 *right of preventing by non-consent.* नाहीं म्हणून बंद करण्याचीशक्ति *f.*-सत्ता *f.*-अधिकार *m.* निषेधद्वारा प्रतिबंधसामर्थ्य *n.*
To NEGATIVE, *v. a. refuse to enact, prevent by withholding consent.* नाहीं म्हणणें, नाहीं म्हणून बंद करणें-निवारणें-&c. नि-

षेधद्वाराप्रतिबंध *m.* करणें, निषेध *m.* करणें *g. of o.*

2 See To DISPROVE.

NEGATIVELY, *adv.* v. A. 1. नाहीं म्हणून, नकारानें, &c. निषेधरूपें, निषेध मुखें.

2 नास्तिपक्षानें, निषेधपक्षानें, नास्तिपक्ष धरून.

To NEGLECT, *v. a. omit from carelessness, &c. forbear to do, &c.*गफलत *f.*-हयगई *f.*-आळस*m.*-विसर*m.*-विस्मृति *f.*&c. करणें *g. of o.* or, *with* विषयीं, विसरणें, विसरून-चुकून सोडणें-ठेवणें, गफलतीनें-आळसानें-विस्मृतीनें-&c. सोडणें-टाकणें-न करणें-&c.

2 *slight, disregard,* v. To CONTEMN. उपेक्षा *f.*-अव्हेर *m.*-हयगई *f.*-अनमान *m.*- कानडोळा *m.*-आनाकानी *f.*-&c. करणें *g. of o.* उपेक्षणें, अव्हेरणें, अनमानणें, अनास्था *f.*-उदासपणा *m.*-औदासीन्य *n.*-&c. करणें-धरणें-बाळगणें *with* विषयीं *of o.*

3 *not treat carefully.* अबाळ *f.*-अवजतन *f.*-अवनिगा *or* अवनिघा *f.*-गैरनिगा *f.*-गैरजतन *f.*-अशुश्रूषा *f.*-अरक्षण *n.*-&c. करणें *g. of o.*

NEGLECT, NEGLECTING, *n.* v. V. 1. गफलत करणें *n.* आळस करणें *n.* विसरणें *n.* &c. गफलत *f.* घालघसर *f.* तफावत *f.* गुंजावीस *f.* कमतर *f.*

2 उपेक्षणें *n.* अव्हेरणें *n.* अनमानणें *n.* &c. उपेक्षा *f.* अनमान *m.* अव्हेर *m.* हयगई *f.* कानाडोळा *m.* आनाकानी *f.* हेलसांड *f.*

3 अबाळ *f.* अवजतन *f.* अवनिगा *or* घा *f.* अनिगा *or* घा *f.* गैरनिगा *f.* गैरजतन *f.* अशुश्रूषा *f.* अरक्षण *n.* अरक्षा *f.*

I. See NEGLIGENCE.

NEGLECTED, *p.* v. V. 1. गफलतीनें सोडलेला-राहिलेला, आळसानें सोडलेला-राहिलेला, विसरलेला, आलस्याकृत.

2 अव्हेरलेला, अनमानलेला, &c. उपेक्षित, अवमानित, अवगणित, अनपेक्षित, अवज्ञात.

3 अबाळ केलेला, &c. अबाळलेला, अबाळीचा, अरक्षित.

NEGLECTER, *n.* NEGLECTING, *p. a.* v. V. 1. गफलत करणारा, आळस करणारा, विसरणारा, गफलतीनें सोडणारा, &c.

2 उपेक्षा करणारा, उपेक्षणारा, अव्हेरणारा, अमानणारा, &c. उपेक्षक.

3 अबाळ करणारा, अवजतन करणारा, &c. अरक्षक, अशुश्रूषक.

NEGLECTFUL, NEGLECTIVE, NEGLIGENT, *a. heedless, inattentive, apt to forget or omit,* v. CARELESS. गफलती, गफलत्या, गाफल *or* फील, गाफली, गफलतीचा, हयगईचा, विसराळू, विसरभोळा, बेसावध, प्रमादी.

2 *treating with disregard or slight,* v. INDIFFERENT. उपेक्षाकरणारा, अव्हेर करणारा, अनमान करणारा, उपेक्षाकर्त्ता, उपेक्षक.

NEGLECTFULNESS, NEGLIGENCE, *n.* v. A. 1. *and* CARELESSNESS. गाफिलपणा *m.* विसराळूपणा *m.* गैदीपणा *m.*बेसावधपणा*m.* &c. गफलत *f.* हयगई *or* हयगय *or* हैगई *or* य *f.* आळस *m.* प्रमाद *m.*

2 उपेक्षा *f.* अव्हेर *m.* अनमान *m.* हेलसांड *f.*

I. *instance of neglect.* गफलत *f.* विसर *m.* चूक *f.* प्रमाद *m.*

NEGLECTFULLY, NEGLIGENTLY, *adv.*v. A. 1.गाफिलपणानें, &c. गफलतीनें, प्रमादानें, अलस्यानें, &c. &c. प्रमादपूर्वक, अवधानपूर्वक, प्रमादतः.

2 उपेक्षा करून-धरून, अनमान करून, हेलसांड करून, &c. उपेक्षाबुद्धीनें, उपेक्षापूर्वक, उपेक्षाबुद्ध्या.

To NEGOCIATE,*To* NEGOTIATE, *v. a. procure by mutual intercourse and agreement.* बोलणें चालणें *n.*-बोलीभाष *f.*-&c.करणें *or* करून घडवणें-घडवून आणणें-जमविणें-&c.घटना *f.*-घटवटना *f.*-जमवाजमव *f.*-घडवाघडव *f.*-&c. करणें *g. of o.*

2 (a bill of exchange,). *sell.* विकणें, चालवणें.

To NEGOCIATE, *To* NEGOTIATE, *v. n. treat with, hold intercourse with in bargaining.* बोलणेंचालणें *n.*-बोलाचाली *f.*-बोलाबोली *f.*- बोलीचाली *f.*-बोलीभाष *f.*-&c. करणें *or*, *with in. con.* होणें-चालणें *g. of s. recip.*

NEGOCIATED, *p.* v. V. A. 1. बोलणेंचालणें करून घडविलेला-&c.

NEGOCIATION, NEGOTIATION, *n.* v. V. A. 1. बोलणेंचालणें करून घडवणें *n.* &c. घटना *f.* घटवटना *f.* जमवाजमव *f.* घडवाघडव *f.*

2 विकणें *n.* चालवणें *n.*

v. V. N. बोलणेंचालणें *n.* बोलाबोली *f.* बोलाचाली *f.* बोलीचाली *f.* बोलीभाष *f.*

NEGOCIATOR, NEGOTIATOR, *n.* NEGOTIATING, *p. a.* v. V. A. 1. बोलणेंचालणें करून घडवणारा-&c. घटवटना करणारा, &c. कट, वकील, दलाल.—esp. of matrimonial alliances. घटक.

Able n. संधिविचक्षण, संधिकुशल.

2 विकणारा, चालवणारा.

v. V. N. बोलणेंचालणें करणारा, &c.

NEGRESS, *n. female negro.* हबशीण *f.* शिद्दीण *or* शिद्दीण *f.*

NEGRO, *n.* v. BLACKAMOOR. हबशी, शिद्दी *or* शिद्दी.

To NEIGH, *v. n.*— a horse. खंकाळणें, खंखाळणें, खिंकाळणें *or* खिंखाळणें, खेंकाळणें, खंकारणें, हिंसणें, हेंसणें, हिणहिणणें.

NEIGH, NEIGHING, *n.* v. V. खंकाळणें *n.* खिंकाळणें *n.* &c. खेंकाळणी *f.* खिंकाळी *f.* खेंकाळी *f.* हेषा *f.*

NEIGHBOUR, *a.* v. NEIGHBOURING. शेजारचा, पडोसचा, जवळचा.

NEIGHBOUR, *n. one who lives near.* शेजारी, पडोसी, शिंवशेजारी, शिंवधडी, शिंवधड्या, निकटवासी, प्रतिवासी, सामंत, सामंतवासी, हमशाईदार,—compreh. or indef. शेजारी पाजारी, अडोसी पडोसी, शेजारी पासारी.

A female n. शेजारीण *f.*-&c. शेजी *f.*

Love your n. as yourself. आत्मौपम्यानें जग पहावें.

NEIGHBOURHOOD, *n. state of being near,* v. NEARNESS. शेजारीपणा *m.* शेजारपणा *m.* शेजार *m.* अडोसीपडोसीपणा *m.* हमशाई *f.* निकटवर्त्तित्व *n.* सामंतत्व *n.*

The law of n. *duty of neighbours one to another.* शेजारधर्म *m.*

2 *place or places near ; vicinity.* शेजार *m.* पडोसा *m.* जवळचा प्रदेश *m.* आसपासचा देश *m.* भोंवरदेश *m.* सामंत *n.* सामंतदेश *m.* अंतिक *n.* जवार *n.f.* भोंवरगांव *m. pl.*—gener. indef. carelessly, &c. शेजारपाजार *m.*

From the n. शेजारून, आसपासून.

In the n. शेजारीं, पडोशास, पडोशीस, आसपास, जवळसर, जवळसार, अडोशींपडोशीं, जवळपास, भोंवर, आजूबाजू, आदिपश्चात्.

Village in the n. of. भोंवरगांव *m.*

3 *inhabitants of the neighbourhood.* शेजारीपाजारी *m.pl.* शेजारीपासारी *m. pl.* अडोसीपडोसी *m. pl.*

NEIGHBOURING, *a. living or being near.* शेजारचा, पडोशाचा, पडोसचा, पडोशींचा, आसपासचा *or* ला, पासचा *or* ला, जवळपासचा *or* ला, जवळचा, आसपासील, भोंवरपासचा, भोंवरचा

or भोंवारचा, अडोशी पडोशी, अडोशींपडोशींचा, शिवधड्या, शिवधड्याचा, शेजारचा पाजारचा, चहुंकडला or कडील, भोंवतालचा, सभोवरचा, सामंत, सामंतवासी, अंतिक, निकटवर्ती.

From the n. parts. इकडून तिकडून.

NEIGHBOURLINESS, *n.* v. A. शेजारधर्मास लायकी *f.* &c. सामंतव्यवहारयोग्यता *f.* घरोबा *m.* भाइचारा *m.* भाइबंदी *f.*

NEIGHBOURLY, *a. becoming a neighbour, civil, kind.* शेजारधर्माचा, शेजारधर्मास योग्य-उचित-लायक-&c. शेजारपणासारखा-लायक-&c. शेजाऱ्याचेरीतीचा, भाइचाऱ्याचा, भाइबंदीचा, सामंतव्यवहारयोग्य.

NEITHER, *pro.* कोणताही नाहीं, एकही नाहीं, हा नाहीं तो नाहीं.

NEITHER, *conj.* आणि ही नाहीं, Ex. त्यानें स्पर्श केला नाहीं आणि वासही घेतला नाहीं. He did not touch neither did he smell.

NEM CON, *unanimously.* सर्व सम्मतानें, सर्व सम्मतीनें, सर्वानुमतानें.

NEOLOGIC, NEOLOGICAL, *a. employing new words.* नूतन शब्दाश्रयी, नूतनशब्दाश्रयणकर्त्ता-कारी, नूतन शब्दसेवी.

2 *entertaining new notions or opinions.* नूतनमताश्रयी, नूतनमताश्रयणकर्त्ता-कारी.

NEOLOGIST, *n. one who introduces new words.* नूतनशब्दसेवी, नूतनशब्दाश्रयी.

NEOLOGY, *n. introduction of new words.* नूतनशब्दसेवन *n.* नूतनशब्दाश्रयण *n.*

2 *new opinions &c.* नूतनमत *n.* नवीनमत *n.* नूतनमताश्रयण *n.* नूतनमतसेवन *n.*

NEOPHYTE, *n. new disciple or learner, novice.* नवाशिष्य, नवशिका or शिका, नवशीख or शीक, नवछात्र. [आधुनिक.

NEOTERIC, *a. modern,* v. NEW. नवा, नवीन, नूतन, अर्वाचीन,

NEPENTHE, *n. drug that relieves pain.* दुःखहारक औषध *n.*

NEPHEW, *n. a man's brother's son.* पुतण्या *m.* भ्रातृपुत्र *m.* भ्रातृव्य *m.*

2 *a sister's son.*—whether of a man or woman. भाचा *m.* (भाचरूं *n. sister's child*) भगिनीपुत्र *m.* भागिनेय *m.*

Wife of a n. भाचेसून *f.* [(भाचरूं *n.*)

3 *woman's brother's son, or husband's sister's son.* भाचा *m.*

4 *husband's brother's son.* पुतण्या *m.*

NEPHRITIC, NEPHRITICAL, *a. pertaining to the kidneys.* मूत्रपिंडाचा, गुर्दाचा, मूत्रपिंडसंबंधी, मूत्रपिंडविषयक.

2 *curing diseases of the kidney.* मूत्रपिंडरोगनाशक, मूत्ररोगघ्न.

NEPOTISM, *n. affection for nephews.* पुतण्यांचा-भाचांचा पक्षपात *m.*-ममता *f.*-&c. भ्रातृव्यभागिनेयस्नेह *m.* [ओढ *f.*

2 *undue attachment to relatives.* आप्तांचा ओढा *m.* आप्तांची

NEREID, *n. sea nymph.* जलदेवी *f.*

NERVE, *n. organ of sensation and motion.* मज्जातंतु *m.* ज्ञानतंतु *m.* चेतनातंतु *m.* ज्ञानवाहिनी *f.* शीर *f.* शिरा *f.*

To strain every n. *make great efforts.* जीव *m.* देणें-टाकणें, जोर *m.* मारणें, छातीवर काम *n.* करणें, दांतींबळ *n.* धरणें, भगीरथप्रयत्न *m.* करणें, आकाशपाताळ *n.* एक करून देणें.

2 *firmness of body,* v. STRENGTH. शरीराची बळकटी *f.* जोम *m.* जोर *m.* गात्रदार्ढ्य *n.*

3 *firmness of mind,* v. FORTITUDE. धैर्य *n.* छाती *f.* धारिष्ट *n.*

To NERVE, *v. a. give strength or vigor to,* v. To STRENGTHEN. बळ *n.*-जोर *m.*-जोम *m.*-&c. देणें-आणणें, बळकट-जोरदार-&c. करणें.

NERVELESS, *a.* v. WEAK. कमजोर, निर्बळ, दुर्बळ.

NERVOUS, *a. pertaining to the nerves, affecting the nerves.* मज्जातंतूचा, मज्जातंतुसंबंधी-विषयक, मज्जातंतुस्थ, मज्जातंतुगत, ज्ञानतंतूचा, &c. [कंपशील.

2 *having the nerves affected.* मज्जातंतुविकारी, मज्जातंतुरोगी,

3 *vigorous,* v. STRONG. जोरदार, जोमदार, जोमाचा, जोराचा.

4 *pithy, vigorous,*—style, &c. दृढ, सुदृढ, कडकडीत, कटावाचा.

NERVOUSLY, *adv.* v. A. 2. मज्जातंतुविकारपूर्वक, मज्जातंतुरोगपूर्वक.

3 जोमानें, जोरानें.

NERVOUSNESS, *n.* v. A. 2. मज्जातंतुविकार *m.* मज्जातंतुरोग *m.* मज्जातंतुविकारिता *f.* मज्जातंतुविकृति *f.* कंपशीलता *f.*

3 जोम *m.* जोमदारी *f.*

4 दृढता *f.* सुदृढता *f.* [ज्ञानाभाव *m.*

NESCIENCE, *n. ignorance.* नेणतेपणा *m.* अजाणपणा *m.* अज्ञान *n.*

NESCIENT, *a. ignorant.* नेणता, अजाण, अजाणता.

NESS. The terminations which answer to *ness* are पण and पणा of Prâkrit words, and ता and त्व of Sanscrit words.

NEST, *n. abode of a bird.* कोटें *n.* खोपा *m.* घरटा *m.* घरकुंडा *m.* खोपड *f.* खोपाड *n.* नीड *m. n.* कुलाय *m.*

To feather one's n. घर *n.* भरणें, घराची भर *f.* करणें, उखळ *n.* पांढरें करणें.

2 fig.—of thieves, &c. घर *n.* अखाडा *m.* अड्डा *m.* वाडा *m.* (in comp. as चोरवाडा *m.* &c.).

To NEST, *v. n. build and occupy a nest.* कोटें *n.*-घरकुंडा *m.*-&c. करणें-करून राहणें.

NEST-EGG, *n.* घरराखण *f.*

To NESTLE, *v. n. live snug and comfortable.* सुखेंकरून-सुखानें-&c. राहणें-नांदणें-वास *m.* करणें, सुखवास *m.*-आनंदवास *m.*-&c. करणें.

To NESTLE, *v. a. cherish.* पाळणें, पालन *n.*-&c. करणें.

NESTLING, *a. that is yet in the nest.* घरकुंड्यांतील, घरकुंड्यांतला, कुलायस्थ.

NESTLING, *n. young bird in or from the nest.* घरकुंड्यांतलें पिलें *n.* कोवळें पिलें *n.*

NESTOR, *n.*—compellation for a sage old man. बृहस्पति *m.* जांबुवंत *m.*

NET, *n. twine interwoven with meshes.* जाळें *n.* जाल *n.* पाश *m.*

Casting n. पाग *m.*

Large fishing n. डोळ *f.*

Long sea-n. बावरीचें जाळें *n.*

2 (for catching birds and beasts) *snare, &c.* फास *m.* फांसा *m.* पाश *m.* वागुरा *f.* [वा *m.*

3 (to carry or hold fruit, &c.). आंखी *f.* आंखा *m.* गांज-

NET, *a. clear* ;—of receipts, quantities, profits, &c. निवळ, निका, ठाम, ठास, सहता.

N. amount. ठामबेरीज *f.* ठामरकम *f.* ठासबेरीज *f.* ठासरकम *f.* ठोकबेरीज *f.* ठोकरकम *f.* निवळ *f.*

NET-WORK, *n.* जाळीदार काम *n.* जाळीचें काम *n.* जाळी *f.*

A n. for mangos, melons, &c. गांजवा *m.* गांजा *m.*

NETHER, *a.* v. LOWER. खालचा, खालला.

NETHERMOST, *a.* v. LOWEST. सर्वांखालचा, सर्वांखालील, सर्वां-

हून खालचा, तळचा.

NETTING. See NETWORK.

NETTLE, *n.* आग्या *m.* खाजकोलती *f.* पीतपर्णी *f.*

To NETTLE, *v. a. irritate, fret, &c.* v. To ANGER. खिजवणें *or* खिजावणें, खाजवणें, चिथवणें *or* चिथावणें, संतापवणें, चिढीस-आणणें-देणें.

NETTLED, *p.* v. V. खिजवलेला, चिथवलेला, &c. संतप्त, संतापित.

NEURALGIA, NEURALGY, *n.* मज्जातंतुव्यथा *f.*

NEUROLOGY, *n. description of the nerves.* मज्जातंतुवर्णन *n.*

NEUROTIC, *a. seated in the nerves,* v. NERVOUS. मज्जातंतुस्थ, मज्जातंतुगत. [ज्जाततुच्छेद *m.*

NEUROTOMY, *n. dissection of a nerve.* मज्जातंतुच्छेदन *n.* म-

NEUTER, NEUTRAL, *a. indifferent, not engaged on either side.* दोहोंपक्षांबाहेरचा-निराळा-वेगळा, उदासीन, तिऱ्हाईत, तटस्थ, उभयपक्षभिन्न, उभयपक्षीं समान, उभयसाधारण, उभयसामान्य, सम.

2—in grammar. नपुंसक.—verb. अकर्मक.

NEUTER, NEUTRAL, *n. one that takes no part in a contest between others,* v. A. उदासीन, तिऱ्हाईत.

2 *a person of neither sex, or one impotent.* नपुंसक *n. m.* हिजडें *n.* राशी *c.* शंड *or* शंढ *or* षंड *c.* फूलमेंगा *m.*

A n. dressing as a female. सौरी *f.*

NEUTRALITY, NEUTRALNESS, *n.* v. A. 1. तिऱ्हाईतपणा *m.* तटस्थपणा *m.* औदासीन्य *n.* उदासीनता *f.* उदासीनभाव *m.* ताटस्थ्य *n.* साम्य *n.* उभयसाधारण्य *n.*

NEUTRALIZATION, NEUTRALIZING, *n.* v. V. 1.—*act.* मारणें *n.* मारण *n.* विशेषधर्मनाशन *n.* विशेषगुणनाशन *n.*

2 निर्बळ करणें *n.* &c. निर्बलीकरण *n.* वीर्यभंग *m.* वीर्यनाश *m.* वीर्यनाशन *n.* तेजोभंग *m.*

To NEUTRALIZE, *v. a. destroy the peculiar properties of; render inert.* मारणें, मारण *n.* करणें, विशेषधर्मनाश *m.*-&c. करणें *g. of o.*

2 *render weak, inefficient, &c. reduce to inactivity, &c.* निर्बल *or* ळ-निश्शक्त-निर्वीर्य-पळपळीत-वालथर-&c. करणें, वीर्यभंग *m.*-वीर्यनाश *m.*-&c. करणें *g. of o.*

NEUTRALIZED, *p.* v. V. 1. मारलेला, विशेषधर्मनष्ट, नष्टविशेषधर्म.

2 निर्बळ केलेला, निर्वीर्यकेलेला, &c. हतवीर्य, नष्टवीर्य, नष्टपराक्रम, नष्टप्राबल्य, नष्टशक्तिक.

NEUTRALIZER, *n.* NEUTRALIZING, *p. a.* मारणारा, मारक, मारणकर्त्ता, विशेषधर्मनाशक, &c.

2 निर्बळ करणारा, &c. वीर्यनाशकर्त्ता, वीर्यभंजक, &c.

NEUTRALLY, *adv.* v. A. 1. तिऱ्हाईतपणानें, तटस्थपणानें, तिऱ्हाईत-होऊन, औदासीन्यपूर्वक, &c.

NEVER, *adv. not ever.* कद्धीं नाहीं, कधीं नाहीं, न कधीं, केव्हां नाहीं, कदापि नाहीं, न कदापि ;—emphatically, कालत्रयीं नाहीं, कल्पांतरी नाहीं, कल्पांतीं नाहीं, काळांतरीं नाहीं, तिनीतळीं नाहीं, परिछिन्न *with neg. con.* For the sense as expressed by the phrases, *on the day after doomsday, on the Greek Kalends, &c.* some corresponding phrases are, कडच्या (or कडेच्या) आदितवारीं, हाट होऊन बुद्धवारीं, शेवटच्या वारीं, शेवटच्या आदित्वारीं.

N.before. कधीं नव्हता, कधीं नव्हत.

N. so. कसाही, कितीही.

That has been never or scarcely ever before. कधीं नव्हतेला. [अथापि.

NEVERTHELESS, *n. still, but, yet.* तरीं, तथापि, तत्रापि, पर, परंतु,

NEW, *a. lately made or come into being, fresh, recent, not stale.* नवा, नवीन, नूतन, ताजा, साजूक, नव, नव्य, नवसर, नवथर, अभिनव, नवोत्पन्न. Involving this sense as *enhanced* or *intended,* and as apparent under such formations, expressions, and combinations as *bran-new, spick and span new, newcoined, fresh from the forge, fresh from the hammer, just off the stocks, &c. &c.* some words are, करकरीत, नवा करकरीत, कोरा करकरीत, ताजाकरकरीत, कोरा, घणकोरा, घणाखालचा, घणांतला, नव्या ताण्याचा, नवघड, लोणकढा, सद्यस्तप्त.

Newish. नवट, नवाट *or* नवाठ.

2 *novel, not being before.* नवा, नवल, नवळका, नवखा *or* नौखा, अपूर्व, अभूतपूर्व. [इदानींतन.

3 *not ancient,* v. MODERN. नवा, नूतन, आधुनिक, अप्राचीन,

4 *different from former.* नवा, दुसरा, अन्य, परका *or* परखा, पारखा.

5 *not habituated, not practised, &c.* नवा, नवखा, नवशिका, कोरा, अजाण, असुदा, अनभ्यस्त.

6 *unused, unapplied.* कोरा, नवा, अनसूट, अनुपभुक्त, अप्रयुक्त.

7 *not familiar to.* नवा, अनोळखी, अनोळखीचा, गैरवागीचा, गैररफताचा, अपरिचयाचा, अनभ्यासाचा, अनभ्यस्त, अपरिचित.

NEW-BORN, *a.* नवा जन्मलेला, नुक्का जन्मलेला, सद्योजात.

NEW-COINED, *a.* v. NEW. घणकोरा, घणाखालचा, नवघड.

NEW-COMER, *n.* नवा आलेला, नवागत.

NEW-FANGLED, *a.* नवायोजलेला, नवेयोजणुकीचा, नवीनकल्पनेचा, कालचा, कालचा रचलेला.

NEW-FASHIONED, *a.* नवीन रीतीचा, नवेचालीचा.

NEWLY, *adv.* v. A. 1. नवा *decl.* नुक्का *decl.* निक्का *decl.* नवथर, नवसर, नव्यानें.

2 नव्यानें, &c.

NEWNESS, *n.* v. A. 1. नवेपणा *m.* ताजेपणा *m.* साजुकपणा *m.*&c. नवीनता *f.* &c. नाव्य *n.*

2 नवेपणा *m.* नवलपणा *m.* नवखेपणा *m.*&c. अपूर्वता *f.* नाव्य *n.*

NEWS, *n. tidings, accounts, intelligence.* बातमी *f.* वर्त्तमान *n.* खबर *f.* वार्त्ता *f.* वृत्तांत *m.* समाचार *m.* पेंठ *f.* संदेश *m.* वृत्त *n.* वाचिक *n.* जनवाद *m.* जनप्रवाद *m.* जनश्रुति *f.* गप *or* गप्प *f.* —compreh. *news and tidings.* खबर बखर *f.* खबरबाता *f. pl.*

Any news? Any thing new? कांहीं नवलविशेष ! कांहीं नवल अपरूप !

Bad n. दुर्वार्त्ता *f.* अनिष्टवार्त्ता *f.* अशुभवार्त्ता *f.*

Good n. सुवार्त्ता *f.* शुभवार्त्ता *f.* शुभवर्त्तमान *n.* शुभवृत्तांत *m.* इष्टवार्त्ता *f.*

NEWS-MONGER, *n. one that delights in telling news.* खबऱ्या, बात्या, बातखबात्या, गप्पी, गप्पीनाथ, गप्पीदास.

NEWS-PAPER, *n.* खबरेचा कागद *m.* वर्त्तमानपत्र *n.* समाचारपत्र *n.* वार्त्तापत्र *n.*

NEWS-WRITER, *n.* (at Courts). अखबारनवीस. [डवा *m.*

NEW-YEAR'S DAY, *n.* वर्षप्रतिपदा *f.* संवत्सरप्रतिपदा *f.* गुढीचा पा-

Pole erected before the door on n. गुढी *f.*—The erection of it. गुढी उभारणें *n.* ध्वजारोपण *n.*

NEXT, *a. nearest.* अगदी जवळचा, जवळचा, पासचा, पासला, बाजूचा, मागचा, मागला, पाठीमागचा, पाठचा, पाठीवरचा, पुढचा, पुढला, येता, अनंतर, पार्श्वस्थ.
N. time. दुसरे खेपेस, दुसरेवेळेस. [पाठीवर.

NEXT, *adv. at the time or turn nearest.* मग, नंतर, मागून,

NIB, *n. bill, beak.* चोंच *f.* टोंक *f.* टोंच *f.* चंचु *m.*
2 (of a pen, &c.), *point, tip, end.* टांक *m.* अणकुची *f.* अणी *f.* अग्र *n.*

NIBBED, *a. having a nib.* टोंकाचा, अणीदार.

To NIBBLE, *v. a. eat as rats, &c.* कुरकुटणें, कुरतुडणें, कुरकुडणें, करडणें *or* कंरडणें.

To NIBBLE, *v. n.*—as fishes, &c. कुरकुडून-कुरकुटून खाणें, तोंडन. लावणें, तोंडानें डोंचणें.
2 *find fault with, peck at,* v. To CARP. दिक्कत *f.* करणें-धरणें, तकरार *f.* घेणें-करणें, आडफांटे *m. pl.*-फांटे *m. pl.* फोडणें.

NIBBLED, *p.* v. V. A. कुरकुटलेला, कुरतुडलेला, &c.

NIBBLING, *n.* v. V. A.—*act.* कुरकुटणें *n.* कुरकुडणें *n. &c.*

NICE, *a. accurate, that judges with exactness, discerns minutely, &c.* बारीक पाहणारा, बारीकदृष्टीचा, सूक्ष्मदृष्टि, सूक्ष्मदर्शी, कुशाग्रदृष्टि, सूक्ष्मशोधक, सूत्रक, सूत्रा.
2 *delicate, minutely cautious,* v. SCRUPULOUS. ओढक, खंतखोर, दिक्कती, दिक्कतखोर, कांक्षी.
3 *fastidious, squeamish,* v. DAINTY. खोडकर, कंटाळखोर, खंतखोर, चोखनळ.
4 *dainty, sweet or pleasant to the taste,* v. DELICIOUS. गोड, रुचिक, रुचिकर *pop.* रुचकर, मिष्ट, यथारुचि.
5 *easily injured,* v. DELICATE. नाजूक, बारीक, कोमल *or* ळ, सुकुमार, सोंवळ.
6 *minutely exact;*—of things, matters, &c. v. ACCURATE. बेताबाताचा, सुताचा, सुती, बराबर, रेखला, तवताक.
7 *requiring minute care.* बारीक, नाजूक, बारीकदृष्टीचा, बारीक नजरेचा, सूक्ष्म, सूक्ष्मदृष्टीचा.
8 *affectedly particular,* v. FINICAL. ठाकठिक्या, चाकचोप्या.
9 *fine, pretty, pleasing, &c.*—freely. गोड, चांगला, सुंदर, चोख, चोखट, रुचीक, रुच्य, रुचिकर.

NICELY, *adv.* v. A. 1. 6. बारीकदृष्टीनें, सूक्ष्मदृष्टीनें, बेताबातानें, बराबर, खास.
6 चांगला *decl.* सुंदर, &c.

NICENESS, NICETY, *n.* v. A. 1. बारीकदृष्टि *f.* सूक्ष्मदृष्टि *f.* कुशाग्रदृष्टि *f.* बारीकशोध *m.* सूक्ष्मशोध *m.*
2 दिक्कतखोरपणा *m.* दिकतीपणा *m.* खंत *f.* [जकाई *f.*
3 खोडकरपणा *m.* मिजाजखोरी *f.* मिजाज *f.* नाजुकपणा *m.* ना-
4 गोडपणा *m.* गोडी *f.* खुमारी *f.* मजेदारी *f.* रुचिकपणा *m.* चव *f.* रुच्यता *f.*
7 बारिकपणा *m.* नाजुकपणा *m.* बारकाई *f.* बारकावा *m.* लाघव *n.* सूक्ष्मता *f.* सौक्ष्म्य *n.* [चोपी *f.*
8 ठाकठिकेपणा *m.* टापटीप *f.* चाकचोपी *f.* चापचोपी *f.* चापी-
9 गोडी *f.* सुंदरपणा *m.* खुमास *m.* खुमाशी *f.* खुबी *f.*
1. *delicate management, &c.* v. ADDRESS. युक्ति *pop.* जुगूत *f.* लाघव *n.*
Niceties. See DAINTIES.

NICHE, *n. recess in a wall.* कोनाडा *m.* कोनाडें *n.* कोनडा *m.* कोनडें *n.* देवळी *f.*
A secret n. चोरकोनाडा *m.*

NICK, *n. exact point of time, critical juncture.* ऐन वेळ *f* अणी *or* आणी *f.* बाणी *f.* आणीबाणीची वेळ *f.* टिपण *n.* संध *f.* संधि *m.f.* ताण *n.* गव *f.* टोणें *n.* मळणी *f.* अवसान *n.* डेवण *or* डेवणें *n.*
Just at the n. नेमका, वेळावर.
To come in the n. of time. प्रसंगास-वेळेस-समयास-&c. येणें, ताण *n.*-टोणें *n.*-संध *f.*-&c. साधणें.
2 See NOTCH.

To NICK, *v. a. hit, touch luckily.* टिपणें, टिपण साधून करणें.
2 See To NOTCH.

NICK-NAME, *n. name given in contempt, &c.* टोंगमताचें नांव *n.* हेंगमताचें नांव *n.* निंदानाम *n.* निंदासूचक नाम *n.* उपाधि *f.* उपाधिनाम *n.*

To NICKNAME, *v. a. give a name of reproach.* टेंग *or* टोंगमताचें नांव *n.* देणें, नांव *n.* ठेवणें, निंदेचें नांव *n.* ठेवणें, निंदेनें म्हणणें.

NICTATION. See WINKING.

NIDE, *n. brood.* वेन *n.* वीण *f.* [डरचना *f.*

NIDIFICATION, *n. nest-building.* घरटा करणें *n.* नीडरचन *n.* नी-

NIDUS. See NEST. [कन्या *f.*

NIECE, *a. a man's brother's daughter.* पुतणी *f.* ध्याडी *f.* भ्रातृ-
2 *a sister's daughter,*—whether of a man or a woman. भाची *f.* (neuter form भाचरूं sister's child), भगिनीकन्या *f.* भागिनेयी *f.*
Husband of this n. भाचे जांवई *m.*
3 *a woman's brother's daughter, or a husband's sister's daughter.* भाची *f.* (भाचरूं *n.*).
Husband of this n. भाचे जांवई *m.*
4 *husband's brother's daughter.* पुतणी *f.* ध्याडी *f.*

NIGGARD, *n.* v. MISER. कृपण, कौडीचुंबक, गट्ठीछोड.

NIGGARD, NIGGARDLY, *a. stingy, parsimonious,* v. MISERLY. कृपण, चिकटा, किरमाडी, किरटा, केड, हिमटा *or* ट्या, हिंचुटा, हातचा जड, बारीक पाहणारा, बारीक दृष्टीचा, व्ययशत्रु, अल्पदृष्टि.

NIGGARDLINESS, NIGGARDNESS, *n.* v. A. कृपणपणा *m.* चिकटेपणा *m.* किरटेपणा *m.* &c. कार्पण्य *n.* बारीकदृष्टि *f.* बारीक नजर *f.* [नें, कार्पण्यपूर्वक.

NIGGARDLY, *adv.* v. A. कृपणपणानें, किरटेपणानें, &c. बारीकदृष्टी-

NIGH. See NEAR.

NIGHT, *n.* रात्रि *pop.* रात्र *and* रात *f.* निशा *f.* रजनी *f.* नक्त *n.*
A dark n. काळोखी रात्र *f.*
At n., by n. रातचा *decl.* रात्रीं, रात्रीचेवेळेस, रात्रौ, रात्रीविलीं, रात्रीबेरात्रीं, नक्त. [शिदिन.
By n. and by day. रात्रंदिवस, रात्रंदीस, निशिदिनीं, नि-
Concluding part or division of the n. अपररात्र *f.* पहांटची रात्र *f.* [रात्र *f.* पूर्वरात्र *f.*
Early part of the n. अवस *or* औस *or* आवोस *f.* औसीची
First part of the n.—the evening. प्रदोष *m.*
Good night. सुखशयन, सुखनिद्रा.
In the early part of the n. आवोशीं.
Latter half of the n. उत्तर रात्र *f.*
To n. *this night.* आजरात्रीं, रात्रीं, रातचा *decl.*
That watches at night. रात्रीजागर.
The whole period or term of the n. रातवा *m.*

Watching at night. रात्रि जागरण *n.*

To set out whilst yet night. रातवा घेऊन निघणें.

To spend the n. watching by a light. दिव्यानें रात्र *f.* काढणें-लोटणें.

To spend the night sleepless. डोळ्यांनीं रात्र *f.* काढणें, डोळ्यांनीं दिवस *m.* उगविणें.

To be n.—To come on—the n. रातावणें.

The night rings (as with the sound of the cricket, &c.). रात्र ओरडती.

Night-blindness, *n.* रातांधळें *n.*

Afflicted with n. रातांधळा, रात्रांध.

Night-cap, *n.* रातची टोपी *f.* रातचा रुमाल *m.*

Night-clothes, *n.* रातचें पांघरूण *n.*

Night-fall, *n.* v. Evening. प्रदोष *m.*

Night-mare, *n. incubus.* कुस्वप्न *m. n.* स्वप्नभय *n.* स्वप्नभीति *f.* अजीर्णप्रयुक्त स्वप्न *m. n.*

Night-rain, *n.* रातवा *m.* [बोचेबुलबूल *m.*

Nightingale, *n.*—the Indian n. बुलबूल *m.* बुलबूलबोचा *m.*

Nightly, *a. happening, &c. at night.* रातचा, रात्रीचा, रात्रीचे वेळचा, रात्रिसंबंधी, रात्रिज, नैश.

2 *happening, &c. every night.* प्रतिरात्रीचा, दररात्रीचा.

Nightly, *adv. by night.* रात्रीं, रातीं, रात्रीस, रातचा *decl.* रात्रौ, नक्तं.

2 *every night.* दररात्रीस, प्रतिरात्रीस.

Night-roving, Night-wandering, *a.* निशाचर, निशाचारी, रजनीचर, नक्तचारी.

Night-shade, *n.*—the prickly. रिंगणी *f.* कांटेरिंगणी *f.* बृहती *f.* —fruit of it, रिंगणें *n.*

Nihility, *n. nothingness.* नाहींपणा *m.* अभाव *m.* नास्तित्व *n.* असत्ता *f.* असत्व *n.*

Nimble, *a. agile,* v. Active. आंगचा चपळ, आंगसूट, चपल *or* ळ, चपलांग, पायसूट. [चालक, चालूक.

Nimble-footed, *a.* पायसूट, पायांचा जलद-चपळ, हलक्या पायाचा,

Nimble-witted, *a. sharp,* v. Quick. जलद, चप्प, शीघ्रबुद्धि.

Nimbleness, *n.* v. A. आंगचपळाई *f.* चपळाई *f.* चलाकी *f.* अंगचापल्य *n.* चापल्य *n.* [अंगचापल्यपूर्वक.

Nimbly, *adv.* v. A. आंगचपळाईनें, चपळाईनें, चलाकीनें, जलदीनें,

Nincompoop, *n.* v. Fool. गाबदी, मूर्ख, गयाळ, गयाळी.

Nine, *a.* नऊ *or* नव.

Nineteen, *a.* एकुणीस, एकूणवीस, एकोणीस.

Nineteenth, *a.* एकुणिसावा.

Ninety, *a.* नव्वद;—one, एक्याण्णव;—two, ब्याण्णव;—three, त्र्याण्णव;—four, चौऱ्याण्णव;—five, पंचाण्णव;—six, शाण्णव *or* शाणणौ;—seven, सत्याण्णव;—eight, अठ्याण्णव;—nine, नव्याण्णव.

Ninny, Ninnyhammer, *n.* v. Fool. गाबदी, मूर्ख, गयाळ.

Ninth, *a.* नववा, नवम.

Ninth, *n.* नवबाहिस्सा *m.* नवमांश *m.*

To **Nip,** *v. a. bite or pinch off with the nails or teeth.* बोंखडणें *or* बोंखाडणें, बोचरणें, खुटणें, खुडणें, कुचरणें, कुरतडणें, खुडतुडणें *or* खुरतुडणें, खुडसणें, कृंतणें, निकृंतणें.

2 *blast, destroy.* मोडणें, नष्ट-हत-नाहींसा-&c. करणें.

3 See To Clip, To Cut. 4—as frost, &c. करपवणें, जाळणें.

To be nipped. करपणें, करपा *m.* पडणें.

Nip, Nipping, *n.* v. V. 1. बोंखडणें *n.* बोचरणें *n.* कृंतणें *n.* &c. कृंतन *n.* निकृंतन *n.* निकंदन *n.*

Nippers, *n. pincers.* चिमटा *m.* गाबी *f.*

To pull out with n. चिमटा *m.* घेणें-करणें.

2 (of a goldsmith) सवाणा *m.*

Nipple, *n. teat.* बोंडी *f. dim.* बोंडूक *n.* बोंडशी *f.* स्तनमुख *n.* स्तनाग्र *n.* कुचाग्र *n.* चूचुक *m. n.*

Nit, *n. egg of a louse, &c.* लीख *f.* लिक्षा *f.* उवेचें अंडें *n.* बेरड *f.*

Nitency, Nitid. See Brightness, Bright.

Nitre, *n. salt-petre.* सोरा *m* सोरमीठ *n.* सूर्यखार *m.*

Nitrate of potash. यवक्षार *pop.* यवखार *m.* [राचा.

Nitrous, *a. pertaining to nitre.* सोऱ्याचा, सोरमिठाचा, सूर्यखा-

Nitty, *n. full of nits.* लिखाळा, बहुलिक्ष, लिक्षाप्रचुर.

Nival, Niveous. See Snowy.

No, *adv.* नाहीं, न, ना, उंहुं, ऊंहुं.

To say no to every thing, to be ever no-ing. नचा फाडा *m.* वाचणें, नचापाठ *m.* असणें *in. con.* नायरी *f.*-नाबली *f.* करणें.

Though you say no, yet say no sweetly. गूळ नाहीं पण गुळाचीवाचा तरी असावी.

No, *a. none.* कोणी नाहीं, काहीं नाहीं. The sense is often involved in the use of the negative particle; as, तो सामान्य मुलगा नाहीं He is no vulgar boy.

No one. कोणी नाहीं.

Nobility, Nobleness, *n.* v. A. 1. खांदानी *f.* महाकुलीनता *f.* महाकुलता *f.* सद्वंशता *f.* अभिजाति *f.* आभिजात्य *n.*

2 श्रीमंती *f.* बहादरी *f.* अमिराची पदवी *f.* बडेलोकांची पदवी *f.*

3 मोठेपणा *m.* प्रौढी *f.* उंचपणा *m.* मोठीयोग्यता *f.* [लभ्य *n.*

4 मोठेपणा *m.* थोरपणा *m.* थोरवी *f.* उंचपणा *m.* प्राशस्त्य *n.* प्राग-

5 उमदेपणा *m.* नामीपणा *m.* &c. शानदारी *f.* छान *f.*

6 मनाचा मोठेपणा *m.* मोठेंमन *n.* उदारमन *n.* औदार्य *n.* प्राशस्त्य *n.*

I. *nobility.* बडेलोक *m. pl.* मोठेलोक *m. pl.* अमीर उमराव *m. pl.*

II. *dignity, pomp, &c. of a nobleman.* अमिरी *f.*

Noble, *a. of an ancient and high family,* v. Gentle. मोठ्या कुळांतला, मोठ्याकुळाचा, मोठ्यावंशाचा, महाकुलीन, महाकुल, अभिजात, सद्वंश, वंशविशुद्ध, सछत्र.

The n. and plebeian. हालीमवाली *m. pl.*

2 *distinguished from commoners by rank and title.* बडेलोकांतला, मोठेलोकांतला, अमीरलोकांतला, श्रीमंत, श्रीमान्, नामदार, आलिशां, बहादर *or* दूर, राजमान्य.

3 *illustrious, worthy, great.* मोठा, मोठेपणाचा, प्रौढ, प्रौढीचा, फार चांगला, अत्युत्तम, उंच, उमदा, शूर, बुजूर्ख, मोठे योग्यतेचा, मोठ्या कोटींतला.

4 *exalted, sublime.* मोठा, थोर, उंच, प्रौढ, प्रशस्त, प्रगल्भ.

5 *magnificent, splendid, &c.*—freely, v. Fine. मोठा, उमदा, नामी, भव्य, शानदार, खासा, उत्कृष्ट, अत्युत्कृष्ट, आलिजाहां.

6 *generous, liberal, ingenuous, &c.* मनाचा मोठा, उदारमनाचा, उदार, प्रशस्त, प्रशस्तमनाचा, उदारमनस्क, उदारधी, उरुसत्व.

Noble, *interj.* शाबास.

Noble, Nobleman, *n. grandee.* बडा लोक *m.* बडे लोकांतला पुरुष *m.* मोठा पुरुष *m.* अमीर *m.* उमराव *m.*

Noble-minded, *a.* मनाचा मोठा, उदार मनाचा, मोठ्यामनाचा, महात्मा, संभावितात्मा, उदारधी.

NOBLE-WOMAN, *n.* बडे लोकांतली-बडे लोकाची बायको *f.*
NOBLE, *adv.* v. A. 1. मोठ्या कुळाचा *decl.* मोठ्या वंशाचा *decl.*
5 मोठा *decl.* खासा *decl.* उत्कृष्ट, नामी.
6 मोठ्या मनानें, उदार मनानें, &c. उदारपणानें, औदार्यें करून, औदार्यपूर्वक.
NO-BODY, *n.* कोणी नाहीं, चिपुटचिंगळी *f.* नाहीं.
NOCENT, NOCUOUS See HURTFUL.
NOCTIDIAL, *a. comprising a night and a day.* एकरातदिवसाचा, अहोरात्राचा.
NOCTIVAGANT, *a.* v. NIGHT-ROVING. निशाचर.
NOCTURNAL, *a. nightly.* रातचा, रात्रीचा, रात्रिसंबंधी, रात्रिकालसंबंधी, रात्रिकालिक, नैश.
To NOD, *v. n. bend or incline with a quick motion.* तुकणें, झुलणें, झुकणें, डुलणें.
2 (in assent, approbation, beckoning, &c.) मान *f.*-डोई *f.*-हालवणें-डोलवणें, मान *f.*-डोई *f.* हालणें-डोलणें-तुकणें *g. of s.* तुकणें, खुणावणें.
3 (through drowsiness). डुकली *or* डुलकी *f.*-डोवे *m. pl.* खाणें, डुलकणें, पेंगणें, झिंबणें, संमणें, पेंगणी *f.* दणें-घेणें-खाणें-मारणें.
4 *walk noddingly.* डुलणें, झुकणें, झुकतझुकत चालणें, डुलतडुलत चालणें.
To NOD, *v. a. bend or shake with quick motion.* तुकावणें *or* तुकवणें, डोलवणें, हालवणें.
NOD, NODDING, *n.* v. V. N. 1. तुकणें *n.* झुलणें *n.* &c. झोंक *m.* झोका *m.* हेलकावा *m.*
3 डुकली *or* डुलकी *f.* v. खा, पेंगणें *n.* &c. पेंगणी *f.* लखणी *f.*
I. *sign made by a move of the head*, v. SIGN. खूण *f.* इशारत *f.* इशारा *m.* शिरस्संकेत *m.* मस्तक संकेत *m.*
NODATION, *n. act of making a knot.* गांठ देणें *n.* गांठ मारणें *n.*
NODDLE, *n.* v. HEAD. बोड *n.* बोडकें *n.* बोडकूल *n.* टाळकें *n.* नारळ *m.*
NODDY. See NINNY.
NODE, *n. swelling on the bone.* गांठ *f.* अस्थिगुल्म *m.*
2—in astronomy. उपग्रह *m.* The *ascending* node is राहु *m.* The *descending* node is केतु *m.*
NODULE, *n.* v. LUMP. खडा *m.*
NOGGIN, *n. wooden cup.* कटोरा *m.* कटोरी *f.*
NOISE, *n.* v. SOUND. नाद *m.* ध्वनि *m.* शब्द *m.* आवाज *m.* स्वन *m.*
N. in the ears. कर्णनाद *m.*
2 *loud sound*, v. CLATTER, DIN. मोठा शब्द *m.* मोठा आवाज *m.* खणका *m.* दणका *m.* दणकें *n,* दणदणाट *m.* उच्चैःस्वर *m.*
3 *outcry, clamour*, v. UPROAR. गलका *m.* गलबा *m.* कल्लोल *or* ळ *m.* कला *m.* कलकल *m. intens.* कलकलाट *m.* बोंब *f.* बोभाटा *m.* [माडणें.
To make a n. about. कळाकळा *adv.* करणें, बोंब *f.* मारणें-
4 *public talk.* गवगवा *m.* गाजावाजा *m.* वाजागाजा *m.* अगाजा *m.*
To make a n. in the world. नांव *n.*-कीर्त्ति *f.*-&c. गाजवणें, गाजणें, ढोलकें *n.*-डंका *m.*-नगारा *m.*-&c. वाजणें *g. of s.*
To NOISE, *v. a. spread by report, tell generally.* गाजवणें, उघडा करणें-पाडणें, डंका *m.*-नौबत *f.*-नगारा *m.*-ढोलकें *n.*-&c. वाजवणें *g. of o.* थाळी *f.*-दंवडी *f.*-&c. पिटणें *g. of o.* नगाऱ्यावर घालणें, उघडीक *f.*-प्रसिद्धि *f.*-बोभाटा *m.*-बभ्रा *m.*-&c. करणें *g. of o.* बाजार महशूर करणें.
To be noised abroad. गाजणें, अगाजणें, वाजणें, बोभाटणें, वाजणेंगाजणें, डंका *m.*-नौबत *f.*-नगारा *m.*-ढोलकें *n.*-&c. वाजणें *g. of s.* नगाऱ्यावर-डफऱ्यावर-&c. पडणें, उमाठ्यासयेणें, उमाठा *m.* होणें *g. of s.* रुढणें, आरूढणें, दणकणें, हाकाटणें, नगाऱ्यावर टिपरूं *n.* पडणें.
NOISED, *p.* v. V. गाजवलेला, उघडा केलेला, डंका वाजलेला, &c. बाजार महशूर, आख्यात.
NOISELESS, *a. that makes no noise.* अशब्द, निश्शब्द.
NOISELESSLY, *adv.* v. V. *and* SILENTLY शब्द न करतां.
NOISILY, *adv.* v. A. मोठा शब्द करून, दणका करून, &c. दणदण, दणकन, दणकर, &c. [*f.* महानादता *f.*
NOISINESS, *n.* v. A. 1. मोठा शब्द *m.* मोठा नाद *m.* महाध्वनिता
2 गलगलेपणा *m.* गोंगाटेपणा *m.* &c. [धूम *f.*
3 गोंगाट *m.* गलबल *f.* गलबला *m.* दणका *m.* कडाखा *m.* धाम-
4 गजबज *f.* गजबजितपणा *m.* गजगजितपणा *m.*
NOISING, *n.* v. V.—*act.* गाजवणें *n.* उघडा करणें *n.* प्रसिद्ध करणें *n.* डंका वाजवणें *n.* &c. वाजवावाजव *f.* गाजवागाजव *f.* घोंघाट *m.* कळवाकळव *f.* परिस्फोट *m.* चौघाचार *m.*
NOISOME, *a. noxious, unwholesome.* अपकारक, अपकारी, बाधक, अहितकारक-कारी-प्रद-जनक-&c. अनिष्टकारक-जनक-&c. वावडा.
2 *offensive, &c.* v. DISGUSTING. कंटाळवाणा, कंटाळवाणी, घाणेरडा, ओखटा, अघोरी.
NOISOMENESS, *n.* v. A. 1. अपकारीपणा *m.* वावडेपणा *m.* अपकारिता *f.* अपकारकत्व *n.* बाधकत्व *n.*
2 घाणेरडेपणा *m.* ओखटेपणा *m.* &c.
NOISY, *a. loud-sounding.* मोठ्या शब्दाचा, मोठ्या नादाचा, महाध्वनि, महानाद, महानादी, बृहन्नाद, महाशब्दकारी.
2 *vociferous, &c.* v. CLAMOROUS. गलगल्या, गलबल्या, गोंगाट्या.
3 *full of noise and bustle*—a place, procession, wedding, &c. गोंगाटाचा, गलबल्याचा, गलबलाटाचा, ओरडाओरडीचा, दणक्याचा, कडाख्याचा, दणदणीत, धामधुमीचा.
4 *full of noise,*—a town, &c. गजबजीचा, गजगजीत, गजबजीत, गलबलाचा.
NOLENS VOLENS. खामखा *or* खामखाव, हमखास, हटकून.
NOMAD, NOMADIC, *a. that wanders with flocks.* कळप घेऊन फिरणारा, गुरें घेऊन फिरणारा, प्रचारानुसारवासी.
NOMANCY, *n. divination by the letters of a name.* नांवावरून भाकित पाहणें *n.*
NOMBLES, *n.* हरणाचीं आंतडीं *n. pl.*
NOMENCLATOR, *n. one who gives names to things.* नांव देणारा, नामस्थापक. [घंट *m.*
NOMENCLATURE, *n. vocabulary.* शब्दकोश *m.* शब्दमाला *f.* नि-
2 *technical terms of a science, &c.* पारिभाषिकशब्द *m. pl.*
NOMINAL, *a. pertaining to a name.* नामाविषयींचा, नामसंबंधी, नामविषयक, शाब्द.
2 *existing in name only.* नामाचा *or* नांवाचा, नामधारी.
NOMINALLY, *adv.* v. A. 2. नांवानें, नांवेंकरून, नांवाचा *decl.*
To NOMINATE, *v. a.* v. To NAME. नांव *n.* घेणें-काढणें-उच्चारणें *g. of o.*
2 *give a name to*, v. To NAME. म्हणणें, बोलणें.
3 *name for an office*, v. To APPOINT. योजणें, नेमणें, योजणूक *f.*-नेमणूक *f.*-&c. करणें *g. of o.* नामजाद करणें,

NOMINATED, *p.* v. V. 3. योजलेला,नेमलेला,योजित,नामजाद *or* त.

NOMINATION, *n.* v. V. 3.—*act.* योजणें *n.* नेमणें *n.* योजणूक *f.* नेमणूक *f.*

I. *power of appointing.* नेमण्याचा अधिकार *m.* नेमण्याची सत्ता *f.* नियोजनाधिकार *m.*

NOMINATIVE, *n.*—in grammar. प्रथमा *f.* कर्त्ता *m.* कर्तृकारक *n.*

NOMINATOR, *n.* v. V. 3. योजणारा, नेमणारा, नेमणूक करणारा, &c. नियोजक.

NOMINEE, *n. person appointed by.* नेमलेला, नियोजित.

NON. This prefix is rendered by, अ, अन, नि, गैर, &c.

NON-ACCEPTANCE, *n.* अपरिग्रह *m.* अस्वीकार *m.*

NON-ACCOMPLISHMENT, *n.* असाधन *n.* असिद्धि *f.* अनुपपत्ति *f.*

NON-ACQUAINTANCE, *n.* अपरिचय *m.* अनोळख *f.*

NON-ACQUIESCENCE, *n.* अस्वीकार *m.* असम्मति *f.*

NON-ADMISSION, *n. not allowing.* अस्वीकार *m.* अनंगीकार *m.*

NON-ADVERTENCE, *n.* अलक्ष्य *n.* दुर्लक्ष्य *n.* गैरसावधपणा *m.* अविचार *m.* अनवधान *n.*

NON-AGE, *n.* v. MINORITY. बालदशा *f.* अप्राप्तव्यवहारावस्था *f.*

NON-AGED, *a.* v. MINOR. अप्राप्तवयस्क, अप्राप्तव्यवहार.

NON-AGESIMAL, *n.*—the degree. त्रिभोनलग्न *n.* वित्रिभलग्न *n.*

NON-APPEARANCE, NON-ATTENDANCE, *n.* गैरहाजिरी *f.* अविद्यमानता *f.* अदर्शन *n.*

NON-ARRIVAL, *n.* अनागमन *n.* अनागम *m.*

NON-ATTAINMENT, *n.* अप्राप्ति *f.* अलाभ *m.*

NON-ATTENTION, *n.* अनवधान *n.* अलक्ष्य *n.* दुर्लक्ष्य *n.*

NON-CHALANCE, *n.* v. INDIFFERENCE. अनास्था *f.* उदासीनता *f.*

NON-COMMISSIONED, *a.* बिनसनदी.

NON-COMPLIANCE, *n.* अस्वीकार *m.* अननुरोध *m.* [वाहक.

NON-CONDUCTOR, *n.* NON-CONDUCTING, *a.* अनेता, अप्रापक, अ-

NON-CONFORMIST, *n.* अननुरोधी,अननुसारी,अननुयायी,अननुवर्त्ती.

2 *dissenter from the established church.* देशस्थापितमताननुरोधी, देशस्थापितधर्माननुसारी, स्थापितधर्मासम्मत.

NON-CONFORMITY, *n.* अननुरोध *m.* अननुसरण *n.* अननुवर्त्तन *n.*

2 *dissent from the established church.* देशस्थापितमताननुरोध *m.* देशस्थापितधर्माननुसरण *n.* देशस्थापितधर्मासम्मति *f.*

NON-CONTACT, *n.* अस्पर्श *m.* असंसर्ग *m.*

NON-CURRENCY, *n.* गैरचलन *n.*

NON-DELIVERY, *n.* असमर्पण *n.* अप्रदान *n.* [क्षण.

NON-DESCRIPT, *a.* अवर्णित, अवर्णगत, अनिश्चितलक्षण, अकृतल-

NON-ELECT, *a.* अवृत, अवृत्त, अजातवरण.

NON-ENJOYMENT, *n.* अभोग *m.* असंभोग *m.* अनुपभोग *m.*

NON-ENTITY, *n. non-existence.* नाहींपणा *m.* नास्तित्व *n.* अभाव *m.* असत्ता *f.* असत्व *n.* असंभव *m.* अजीव *m.* अजीवनि *f.* संसर्गाभाव *m.*

2 *a non-entity.* असत्पदार्थ *m.* अलीकपदार्थ *m.* अवस्तु *n.*

NON-ESSENTIAL, *a.* अनावश्यक, कृताकृत, अनांतरीयक.

NON-EXISTENCE. See NON-ENTITY.

NON-EXISTENT, *a. not having existence.* अवर्त्तमान, अविद्यमान, अभूत, असत्, निःसत्व, असंभव, असंभूत.

NON-OBSERVANCE, *n.* अपालन *n.*

NON-OBTAINMENT, *n.* अलाभ *m.* [अद्वितीय.

NON-PAREIL, *a. peerless,* v. INCOMPARABLE. अनुपम, निरूपम,

NON-PLUS, *n. state of perplexity and puzzle.* गोंधळ *m.* घोळ *m.* गळफटा *or* गळफाटा *m.* थाक *f.* पेंचाटी *f.* पेंच *m.*

To NON-PLUS, *v. a. puzzle, put to a stand.* पेंचणें, गळफटणें *or* गळफाटणें, घोळ *m.*-गळफटा *m.*-&c. करणें *g. of o.* ग्रासणें, थक्-कुंठित-गतिहीन-निरुत्तर-&c. करणें. [णें.

To be non-plussed. खुंटणें, थकणें, कुंठित-गतिहीन-&c. हो-

NON-PLUSSED, *p.* v. V. गळफटलेला, &c. गतिहीन, कुंठित, थक्.

NON-PRACTICE, *n.* अनभ्यास *m.*

NON-PRODUCTION, *n.* अनुत्पत्ति *f.* असूति *f.*

NON-PROFICIENT, *a.* अनिपुण, अनिष्णात, अपटु.

NON-RECOVERY, *n.* असमाहार *m.*

NON-RESIDENCE, *n.* अवसति *f.* अवास *m.* अवास्तव्य *n.*

NON-RESIDENT, *a.* अवासी, अधिकारस्थलावासी, स्वस्थानावासी, ओंवडेकरी, ओवंड्याचा.

NON-RESISTANCE, *n.* अनिवारण *n.* अप्रतीकार *m.* अनिरोध *m.*

NON-RESPECT, *n.* अननुलक्ष्य *n.*

N. of persons. आपामरसाधारणवृत्ति *f.* समानवृत्ति *f.*

NON-SENSE, *n. words or language without meaning or relevance.* अचावचा-अनर्थक-निरर्थक-&c. बोलणें *n.*-भाषण *n.*-वाक्य *n.*-&c. अकडंतिकडं *n.* इधरतिधर *n.* अगडतगड *n.* अगडबगड *n.* अटरफटर *n.* सटरफटर *n.* लटरफटर *n.* अनर्थ *m.* काहींचें बाहीं *n.*

To talk n. झक *f.* मारणें.

2 *trifles, trumpery, trash, &c.* अगडतगड *n.* अगडबगड *n.* अटरफटर *n.* फांसफूंस *f.* गूळखोबरें *n.*

NON-SENSICAL, *a. unmeaning.* अनर्थक, निरर्थक, अर्थहीन-शून्य-रहित-&c. अगडबगड, अगडतगड, अचावचा, अच्चाबच्चे, अचावाचा, अन्योविन्य, अयुक्तिक, असंगत, असंबद्ध, बावकळ, बावटळ.

NON-SENSICALLY, *adv.* अर्थावांचून, अगडतगड, अगडबगड, कांहींचें बाहीं.

NON-SENSICALNESS, *n.* v. A. अनर्थकता *f.* निरर्थकता *f.* अर्थाभाव *m.* अर्थराहित्य *n.* आनर्थक्य *n.* असंगतता *f.* &c. अयुक्ति *f.*

NON-SEQUITUR, *n.* अपसिद्धांत *m.*

NON-SOLUTION, *n.* अलापन *n.* अलापनिका *f.* अव्याख्या *f.*

NON-SOLVENCY. See INSOLVENCY. [नष्टवाद.

NON-SUITED, *a.*—in law. अवसादित, अवसन्न, हीनवाद, हतवाद,

To be n. हरणें, नष्ट-हीन-&c. होणें.

NONAGON, *n.* नवकोण *m.* नवास्र *n.*

NONAGONAL, *a.* नवकोण, नवास्र.

NONE, *a. not one.* कोणी नाहीं, एकही नाहीं.

2 *not any.* काहीं नाहीं.—emphatically, *none at all*; *not even the name, shadow, smell, &c. of.* अगदी नाहीं, निस्नूक नाहीं, निश्शंक नाहीं, सुतराम् नाहीं, किमपि नाहीं, कांहींएक नाहीं, नांव नाहीं *g. of s.* नांवास देखील नाहीं, नांवानें पूज *g. of s.* नांवावर पूज पडलें *g. of s.* वार्त्ता *f.*-वास *m.*-गंध *m.*-वासवारा *m.*-छाया *f.*-लवलेश *m.*-स्पर्श *m.*-&c. नाहीं *g. of s.* सुताचा नोडा *m.* नाहीं *g. of s.* रामाचें नांव नाहीं *g. of s.* तीळभर नाहीं, काडी मात्र नाहीं, काडीभर नाहीं. See the words for *jot, iota, &c.* under BIT, and add the negative नाहीं.

NOODLE, *n. simpleton,* v. FOOL. गावदी, गयाळ.

NOOK, *n.* v. CORNER. कोपरा *m.* कोन *m.* एकवसा *m.*

N. or corner,—gener. कोनकोपरा *m.* सांधकोंद *f.* (generally used plurally सांधीकोंदी *f. pl.*).

In nooks & corners सांधोसांधीं *or* सांदोसांदीं.

NOON, NOON-DAY, NOON-TIDE, *n.* दुपार *f.* दोनप्रहर *m. pl.* दोनप्रहरची वेळ *f.* दोनप्रहर दिवस *m.* v. ये, मध्याह्न *m.* मध्याह्नकाल *m.*

About n. दुपारीं तिपारीं.

At n. दुपारां, दुपारीं, दोनप्रहरीं.

Height of n., high, flaming, &c. n. उभी दुपार *f.* खडीदुपार *f.* भणभणीत-भर-ऐन-टळटळ-टळटळीत दुपार *f.*-दोनप्रहर *m. pl.* उभेदोन प्रहर *m. pl.* खडेदोनप्रहर *m. pl.* भिन्नदुपार *f.* सुळीं द्यायाची वेळ *f.* डोकें मारायाची वेळ *f.* गळीं द्यायाची वेळ *f.*

The glowing or ardor of n. रणरण *f.*

It is high n. दुपार टळो टळो करती, दुपार रसरसती *or* रसरस करती, दुपार रणरणती *or* रणरण करती.

NOON, NOON-DAY, NOON-TIDE, *a. of or belonging to noon, meridional.* दुपारचा, दोनप्रहरचा, दुपारचे वेळचा, दोनप्रहरचे वेळचा, दोनप्रहर दिवसाचा, माध्याह्निक.

NOONING, *n. repose at noon.* दुपारची वामकुक्षि *f.*

NOOSE, *n.* फांस *m.* फांसा *m.* सरफांस *m.* सरकफांस *m.* सोडगांठ *f.* शेसरगांठ *f.* शेसरा *m.* पाश *m.*

N. for the neck. गळफांस *m.*

N. to entangle in. नागपाश *m.*

To NOOSE, *v. a. catch in a noose.* फांसणें, फांशांत-&c. धरणें.

NOR, *con.* न, ना.

NORMAL, *a. relating to rudiments, teaching rudiments.* मूलतत्वांचा, मूलविद्येचा, मूलतत्वें-मूलविद्या-विद्योपक्रम-&c. शिकवणारा.

N. school. पंतोजी तयार करण्याची शाळ *f.*

2 v. REGULAR. नियमाचा, यथाविधि, नैयमिक, विधियुक्त, वैध.

NORTH, *n.* उत्तर *f.* उत्तरा *f.* उत्तरदिशा *f.* उदीची *f.* कौबेरी *f.* सौम्या *f.*

NORTH, *a. belonging to the north, situated in the north.* उत्तरेचा, उत्तरेकडचा, उत्तरदिशेचा, उत्तर, उत्तरसंबंधी, उत्तरस्थ, उदीचीन.

NORTH-EAST, *n.* ऐशानी *pop.* ईशानी *or* ईशान्य *f.* पूर्वोत्तर *f.*

NORTH-EAST, NORTH-EASTERN, NORTH-EASTERLY, *a.* ईशानीचा, ईशानीकडचा.

NORTH-POLE, *n.* उत्तरध्रुव *m.*

NORTH-STAR, *n.* ध्रुव *m.*

NORTH-WEST, *n.* वायवी *pop.* वायव्य *f.*

NORTH-WEST, NORTH-WESTERN, NORTH-WESTERLY, *a.* वायव्येचा, वायव्येकडील, वायवीसंबंधी.

NORTH-WIND, *n.* उत्तरेकडचा-उत्तरेकडील-उत्तरेचा-&c. वारा *m.*-वायु *m.*-&c. उत्तरवायु *m.* उतराण *or* उत्तराण *f.* उनरण *f.*

NORTHERLY, NORTHERN, *a.* उत्तरेचा, उत्तरेकडचा, उत्तरसंबंधी, उदीचीन.

NORTHING, *n.* (of the sun). उत्तरायण *n.* उदगयन *n.* सौम्यायन *n.*

NORTHWARD, NORTHWARDS, *adv.* उत्तरेकडे, उत्तरत्र, उत्तरात, उत्तरतः.

NOSE, *n.* नाक *n.* नासिक *n.* नासा *f.* नासिका *f.* घ्राण *n.*—contemptuously; with the power of *snout, proboscis, nozzle.* नाकाड *n.* नाकाडा *m.* नाकोटा *m.* नाकोटें *n.* सोंड *f.*

Aquiline n., Roman n. शुकनासिका *f.* गरुडनासिका *f. pop.* गरुडनाक *n.*—that has one शुकनासिक, गरुडनासिक *pop.* गरुडनाक्या.

Bone of the n., Bridge of the n. नाकाचा दांडा *m.*-बांसा *m.* दांडारा *m.* नासावंश *m.*

Bore made in the n. for nose-ring. नाक *n.*

Catarrhal defluxion of mucus and pus from the n. पीनस *pop.* पिनास *m.*

Dry mucus of the n. मेकूड *m. n.*

Fine nosed, stright-nosed. नाकील *or* नाकेल.

Having a large & squat n. फेपाणा.

Large-nosed. नाकाड्या, डेंबऱ्या नाकाचा, उग्रनासिक.

Mucus of the n. शेंबूड *m.* नाकाचा मळ *m.* नासिकामल *n.*

Running at the n. शेंब *or* शेमी *f.* नासिकस्राव *m.* नासापरिस्राव *m.* आमपीनस *m.*

Septum of the n. नाकाचा पडदा *m.* ओंस *m.*—The fleshy root of it. गुणगुणा *or* घुणघुणा *m.* घोळणा *or* घोळाणा *m.* घोंगणा *or* घोंगाणा *m.* घोणा *m.*

Short-nosed. अप्रा *or* अप्रेनाकाचा.

String drawn through the n. of a bullock, &c. by which to guide it. नथणी *f.* [*errhine.* नस *m.*

Thing administered medicinally through the n. *an*

Tip of the n. नाकाचा शेंडा *m.* नाकाची बोंडी *f. dim.* बोंडूक *n.* नासाग्र *n.* नासिकाग्र *n.*

Tone or note drawn through the n. नकी *or* नक्की *f.*

That speaks through his n. गेंगाणा. [चपणी.

That has a snub or squat n. नकटा, नाकचिबा, फेंदरा,

To bleed at the n. नाक फुटणें.

To clear or blow the n. नाक *n.*-शेंबूड *m.* फेडणें-झाडणें-शिंकरणें, शिंकरणें. [जळणें *g. of o.*

To have one's n. offended. नाकांतले केस *m. pl.*-नाक *n.*

To have the n. bleed. घोणा *m.*-&c. फुटणें *g. of s.* नाक *n.* फुटणें.

To lead by the n. नाकीं वेसन *f.* घालणें *g. of o.*

To put one's n. out of joint, *fig.* नाक *n.* कापणें.

To rifle the n. नाक *n.* ओरबडणें.

To speak through the n. नाकांत *or* नाकानें बोलणें, गेंगणें, गुणगुणणें, गेंमणें बोलणें.

To turn up one's n. at. नाक *n.* वर करणें, नाक तोंड *n.* मुरुडणें *or* मुरडणें, नाक *n.* मोडणें, नाक *n.* झाडणें, नाकाला शिमोटा *m.* घालणें, नाकुरती *or* नाकोरती *f.* मारणें-देणें-हाणणें.

As plain as the n. upon one's face. करतलामलक, हातचें कांकण.

Follow your nose. नाकासमोर जा.

NOSE-BAG, *n.*—of a horse. तोबरा *m.* [नास्य *n.*

NOSE-BRIDLE, *n.* (of a bullock, &c.) वेसण *or* वेसग *f.* नाथ *m.*

NOSE-CUT, *a.* नकटा, छिन्ननासिक, छिन्ननास.

NOSE-GAY, *n. bunch of flowers to smell at.* फुलांचा गुच्छ *m.*-झुबका *m.* झेला *m.*

NOSE-LESS, *a.* अनासिक, निर्नासिक, विनासिक, गतनासिक, नासिकाहीन-शून्य-&c.

NOSE-RING, *n.* नथ *f.* नथणी *f.*—large. नथडा *m.*

Circle of pearls around a n. सरजा *m.*—that has it—a nosering. सरजेदार.

Pendant ring of a n. हालकडी *f.* [मिळ्या *f. pl.*

Pendants or hanging jewels of a n. हालकडी *f.* झिल-

NOSEY, *n. person with a large nose.* नाकाड्या.

NOSOLOGY, *n. science of the classification of diseases.* रोगनिदानशास्त्र *n.* रोगवर्गीकरणविद्या *f.* [दक.

NOSOPOETIC, *a. producing disease.* रोगकर, रोगजनक, रोगोत्पा-

NOSTRIL, *n.* नाकपुडी *f.* नासापुट *n.* नासारंध्र *n.*

Air breathed through a n. सूर *m.* स्वर *m.* नाकसूर *m. pl*

Cartilage which divides the nostrils. नाकाचा पडदा *m.* ओंस *m.*

Dryness of the nostrils. नासाशोष *m.*

To dilate the nostrils (as in anger). नाक *n.* फिंदारणें.

To stink in one's nostrils. घाण *f.* येणें *g. of s.*

NOSTRUM, *n. secret or quack medicine.* बुटी *f.* जडीबुटी *f.* वली *f.* गूढौषध *n.*

NOT, *adv.* नाहीं, ना, नव्हे, नये, न ;—as used with the imperative, नको in the singular, and नका in the plural. For the emphatic expression of the sense of *not* as conveyed by the phrases, *On no account whatsoever, by no means, on no consideration or ground, in no wise, or way, or sense, &c. &c.* some current phrases are, सर्वार्थी नाहीं, सर्वात्मना नाहीं, अगदी नाहीं, सहसानाहीं, अर्थाअर्थी नाहीं, कोणत्याही अर्थानें नाहीं, सर्वथा नाहीं, सर्वांशीं नाहीं, सर्वथैव नाहीं, सर्व प्रकारें नाहीं, कसाही नाहीं, परिछिन्न नाहीं, किमपि नाहीं, एकरूप नाहीं.

To be as n. *be lost, destroyed, &c.* नाहींसा होणें.

It is not, There is not. नाहीं, नास्ति.

NOTABLE, *a. remarkable, memorable.* लक्ष्यांत ठेवायाजोगा- सारखा-&c. जमेस धरायाजोगा-सारखा-&c. सांगायाजोगा-सारखा-&c. नांवघ्यायाजोगता-सारखा-&c. विशेष, जमेंतला, गणनेंतला, लक्ष्य, स्मरणीय.

2 *active, busy,* v. BUSTLING. कामी, कामसू, खटपट्या, कामठ.

A n. housewife. सुगरीण *or* सुगरण *f.*

3 *notorious,* v. NOTED. प्रसिद्ध.

NOTABLENESS, v. A. 2. कामीपणा*m.* कामसूपणा*m.* &c.

NOTABLY, *adv.* v. A. 1. लक्ष्यांत ठेवायाजोगा-*&c. decl.* जमेस धरायाजोगा-&c. *decl.* विशेष.

NOTARY, NOTARY-PUBLIC, *n. person who attests contracts, deeds, &c.* करारनामावगैरे कागदांवर सही करणारा वकील, दबीर.

NOTATION, *n. recording by figures or marks.* अंकणें*n.* अंकणी *f.* अंकन*n.* अंकन्यास*m.* परिपाटी *or* टी *f.*

NOTCH, *n. nock, nick, indentation.* सड*m.* कातरा*m.* खांच*f.* खांड *f.* खाप *f.* कच *f.*

2—as made for or worn by a rope. करकोचा*m.* करवा*m.* अरखुंडा*m.* असोटा*m.*

3—as cut to facilitate breaking. तोड *f.*

4—as cut on a tree, made in a wall, &c. for the foot. पावका*m.* पावंडा*m.* पायंडा*m.* पायटा*m.* पायठण*f.* खाप *f.n.* खोंगा*m.*

To NOTCH, *v. a.* सड*m. pl.*-कातरे*m. pl.*-खांडी *f. pl.*-खापी *f. pl.*-खापे*n. pl.*-&c. पाडणें.

NOTCHED, *p.* v. V. सड पाडलेला, कांतरे पाडलेला.

NOTE, *n. token, sign,* v. MARK. खूण *f.* निशाणी*f.* चिह्न*n.* लक्षण*n.*

2 *notice,* v. HEED. लक्ष*n.* लक्ष्य*n.* धोरण*n.* मनोयोग*m.*

3 *reputation, consequence,* v. RESPECTABILITY, WEIGHT. आब्रू *f.* आब*m.* आबदाब*m.* नांव*n.* प्रतिष्ठा *f.* भारदस्ती *f.*

4 *single sound*—in music. स्वर *m.* सूर*m.* मातृका *f.* मूर्च्छना*f.*

A high and cracked n. काकस्वर*m.*

An unmusical n. अपस्वर*m.* विस्वर*m.*

Leading or key n. वादी*m.*

Piping one n. गावा*m. v.* लाव, गा.

Running over the notes in tuning the voice or catching the key. अलाप *or* अलाफ*m.* अलापचारी *f.* तान *f.* तानकर्म *n.* तानबाजी *f.* तनाना*m.* तननं*n.* जोड*m.*

To run over the notes. अलापणें, तान *f.*-जोड*m.*-अलापचारीचाडाव*m.*-&c. घेणें.

5 *short hint, minute, memorandum, &c.* टीप *f.* टिपण*n.* टाचण*n.* याद *f.* चकती *f.*

6 *small epistle.* चिट्टी *or* चिठ्ठी*f.* चिटोरा *or* चिठोरा*m.* चिटोरें*n.* कागद*m.* पत्र*n.* शुक्का*m.*

At the instant of seeing the n. देखतचिट्ठी.

Mere n. writing. चिटनिशी *f.* चिटनिशी *f.*

7 *note of hand.* खत*n.* रोखा*m.* कर्जखत*n.* कर्जरोखा*m.* दस्त-ऐवज*m.* तमासूक*m.*

An empty n. झोकचिट्ठी *f.*

8 *annotation,* v. COMMENT. टीप *f.* टीका *f.*

To NOTE, *v. a. observe, notice, mark.* लक्ष्य*n.*-लक्ष*n.*-ध्यान*n.*-धोरण*n.*-चित्त*n.*-&c. देणें-लावणें-राखणें-धरणें *or* देऊन-लावून-&c. पाहणें-ऐकणें-&c. पाहणें, लक्षिणें, ध्यानांत-लक्ष्यांत-&c. आणणें, लक्ष्यांत-ध्यानांत-&c. येणें *in. con.*

2 *set down, make memorandum of.* टिपणें, टाचणें, मांडणें, मांडून-टिपून-&c. ठेवणें, टीप *f.*-टिपण*n.* लिहणें *g. of o.* खरडणें, टांक*m.* लावणें *g. of o.* टांकलावणी *f.* करणें *g. of o.*

NOTED, *p. and a.* v. V. 1. पाहिलेला, लक्षिलेला.

2 टिपलेला, टिपून ठेवलेला, &c.

I. *celebrated, eminent,* v. FAMOUS. प्रसिद्ध, प्रसिद्धीचा, अस्कन्याचा, नांवालौकिकाचा, महशूर, व्याख्यात, नामजाद.

NOTE-WORTHY. See NOTABLE.

NOTHING, *n. nihility,* v. NON-ENTITY. नास्तित्व*n.* अभाव*m.* [शून्यता *f.*

Doctrine of nothingness.शून्यवाद*m.*—Holder of it. शून्यवादी.

2 *not any thing,* v. NONE. काहीं नाहीं.

As if n. had happened. कांहीं नव्हतेला, Ex. रात्रीं चोरी करून दिवसास काहीं नव्हतेल्या गोष्टी सांगतो.

N. at all, *not a bit, jot, &c.* कांहींएक नाहीं, कांहींच नाहीं, तीळभर नाहीं, काडीभर नाहीं, काडी मात्र नाही, रजभर नाहीं.

3 *no importance, no use, &c.* किम्मत *f.* कथा *f.* केवा *m.* मुजाख *or* मुजाखा *m. f. all with neg. con.*

4 *no possession or fortune,* v. POVERTY. कंगाली *f.* कंगालपणा *m.* धनाभाव *m.* पैक्याचे नांवानें-द्रव्याचें नांवानें-&c. पूज *n.*-शून्य *n.*

5 *trifle, thing of no consequence.* कांहीं नाहीं, हलकी गोष्ट *f.*

A mere n. परसांतील भाजी *f.* [कट.

For n. फुकट, फुकटावारी, फुकटाफुकट, फुकटाफुकटीं, फुकटफा-

Good for n. v. USELESS. कांहीं कामाचा नाहीं, अकिंचित्कर, बत्तीस लक्षणी, फुकट्या.

To go for n. पोकळी खालीं *or* पोकळीस जाणें, सुना जाणें.

To make n. of. तृणवत्-कःपदार्थ-तुच्छ-&c. मोजणें-मानणें-समजणें.

To serve for n. पोट बांधून चाकरी *f.*-काम *n.*-&c. करणें.

NOTHING, *adv. in no degree, not at all,* v. NOT. कांहींच नाहीं, किमपि नाहीं, अगदीं नाहीं, बिलकूल नाहीं.

He is n. of a Paṇḍit. तो कांहीं पंडित नाहीं.

NOTHINGNESS. See NON-ENTITY.

To NOTICE, *v. a. observe,* v. TO NOTE, TO SEE. पाहणें, लक्ष्यां-

त-ध्यानांत-&c. येणें *in. con.* समजणें *in. con.*

2 *heed, regard, give attention to.* लक्ष *n.*-लक्ष्य *n.*-चित्त *n.*-ध्यान *n.*-धोरण *n.*-&c. देणें-लावणें-ठेवणें-राखणें-धरणें.

3 *mention, remark on.* बोलणें-&c. *with* विषयीं *of o.* नांव *n.* घेणें *g. of o.* गोष्ट *f.* काढणें *g. of o.*

4 *treat with attention.* आदरणें, आदर *m.*- सन्मान *m.*-सत्कार *m.*-आदरसत्कार *m.*-&c. करणें *g. of o.*

NOTICE, *n. observation by the eye or by other senses.* पाहणेंn. दृष्टि *f.* अवलोकन *n.* नजर *f.* अढळ *m.* इंद्रियव्यापार *m.*

To come under the n. of. अढळणें, अढळ *m.* असणें *g.ofs.*

2 *observation by the mind*, v. HEED. लक्ष्य *n.* लक्ष *n.* ध्यान *n.* धोरण *n.*

3 *intelligence, intimation.* बातमी *f.* खबर *f.* जाहिरखबर *f.* सूचना *f.* सुचें *n.* [पिट, बाज.

4 *proclamation.* दवंडी *f.* डांगोरा *m.* दांडोरा *or* ढांढोरा *m.* v. Written n. जाहीरनामा *m.* जाहिरात *f.* प्रसिद्धिपत्र *n.*

5 *attention, respectful treatment.* आदर *m.* सत्कार *m.* सन्मान *m.* संभावना *f.* आदरसत्कार *m.*

NOTICEABLE, *a worthy of notice*, v. NOTABLE. लक्ष्यांत ठेवायाजोगा-सारखा-&c.

NOTICED, *p.* v. V. 1. पाहिलेला, लक्षिलेला, &c. इंद्रियव्यापारगत.

2 लक्ष दिल्हेला, &c.

4 सन्मानित, आदृत.

NOTIFICATION, *n.* v. V. 1.—*act.* कळवणें *n.* ज्ञापन *n.* ज्ञप्ति *f.* विज्ञापन *n.* विज्ञापना *f.*

2 सुचविणें *n.* &c. सूचन *n.* सूचना *f.*

I. *paper giving notice.* जाहिरात *f.* जाहीरनामा*m.* प्रसिद्धिपत्र*n.*

NOTIFIED, *p.* v. V. 1. कळवलेला, &c. ज्ञापित, ज्ञपित, ज्ञप्त, विज्ञप्त.

2 सुचवलेला, &c. सूचित.

To NOTIFY, *v. a. make known, declare.* कळवणें, ज्ञापणें, बदणें, प्रसिद्धि *f.*-जाहिरात *f.*-ज्ञापन *n.*-विज्ञापन *n.*-&c. करणें *g. of o.* जाहीर-विदित-प्रसिद्ध-&c. करणें.

2 *give notice of*, v. To INFORM. सुचवणें, सूचन*n.*- सूचना*f.* करणें-देणें, खबर *f.*-बातमी *f.*-&c. देणें.

NOTION, *n. idea, conception, thought, view.* कल्पना *f.* भावना *f.* संभावना *f.* ग्रह *m.* शक्तिग्रह *m.* ज्ञान *n.* बुद्धि *f.* तर्क *m.* भान *n.* भास *m.* वचक *m* v. जा,हो *in. con.*

2 *sentiment, opinion.* मत *n.* मति *f.* बुद्धि *f.*

High notions and fancies. मिजाज *f.* आढ्यता *f.*

NOTIONAL, *a. existing in the mind only*, v. IMAGINARY. काल्पनिक, कल्पित, कल्पनासिद्ध.

NOTORIETY, NOTORIOUSNESS, *n.* v. A. 1. प्रसिद्धि *f.* उघडीक *f.* उघड *f.* लौकिक *m.* लोकप्रसिद्धि *f.* जगत्प्रसिद्धि *pop.* जगप्रसिद्धि*f.* रूढि *f.* प्रकाश *m.* ख्याति *f.* विख्याति *f.* परिस्फोट *m.* परिस्फुट*m.* पसारा *m.* आख्या *f.* लोकविश्रुति *f.* प्राकट्य *n.* बाजार *m.* नांवलौकिक *m.* जघन्य *n.* चतुष्टाई *f.* घोंघाट *m.* गजर *m.* गवगवा *m.* गूल *f.* वाच्यता *f.* दिवाणदर्बार *n.* धौंसा *m.* डंका *m.* v. बाज.

2—esp. in an evil sense. बोभाटा *m.* बभरा *or* बभ्रा *m.* हाक *f.* हाकाहाक *f.* हाकाटा *m.* हाकाटी *f.* हाकारा *m.* नादाळी *f.* बाजट *n.* धिंडबडा *m.* कीर्त्तवडा *m.* दवंडी *f.* v. पिट, टिमकी *f.* v. बाज, डंका *m.* धांडोरा *m.* धांडोरें *n.* कुकीर्त्ति *f.* आढ्यता *f.*

NOTORIOUS, *a. public, well known.* उघड, उघडा, प्रसिद्ध, जाहीर, जगजाहीर, जनजाहीर, महशूर, सरकार महशूर, लोकप्रसिद्ध, लोकविश्रुत, प्रकट *pop.* प्रगट, जगत्प्रसिद्ध *pop.* जगप्रसिद्ध, नांवलौकिकाचा, ख्यात, विख्यात, नावसता, बाजट. [बजें *g.of o.*

To make n. v. To NOISE. गाजवणें, डंका *m.*-&c. वाज-

To be n. *be noised abroad*, v. To NOISE. गाजणें, डफन्यावर पडणें, ढोलकें *n.*-डंका *m.*-&c. वाजणें *g. of s.* हाकाटणें, दणकणें.

2—esp. in an ill sense. जगजाहीर, जनजाहीर, जगत्प्रसिद्ध *pop.* जगप्रसिद्ध, बाजारमहशूर, दरबारमहशूर, सरकारमहशूर,बाजारनिरख, डंका वाजलेला. [बोभाटणें.

To be n. दिवा *m.* लावणें, नादावणें, गुढी *f.* उभारणें *g. of s.*

NOTORIOUSLY, *adv.* v. A. 1. उघड, प्रसिद्ध, उघडपणीं, प्रसिद्धपणीं.

2 बाजारनिरख, बाजारमहशूर, &c.

NOTWITHSTANDING, *conjunc.* तरीं, परंतु, अथापि, तथापि,तत्रापि, असें असतांही, तदपि.

NOTUS, *n. south wind.* दक्षिणवारा *m.* दक्षिणेचा वारा *m.* हेटचा वारा*m.* दक्षिणवायु *m.*

NOUGHT, *n.* v. NOTHING. कांहीं नाहीं. [च्छ मानणें.

To set at n. v. To CONTEMN. अवमानणें, अवगणणें, तु-

NOUN, *n.* नाम *n.* विशेष्य *n.* संज्ञा *f.* संकेतशब्द *m.*

Crude n. प्रातिपदिक *n.*

N. of action. कारक *n.* क्रिया *f.*

N. of agency. कर्तृवाच्य *n.*

N. animate. प्राणिवाचक *m.*

N. abstract. भाववाचक *m.*

N. collective. संघवाचक *m.*

N. communicative. अपादानवाच्य *n.*

N. denominative. क्रियावाचक *m.*

N. ending in a vowel. अजंत *m.*

N. gentile. जातिवाचक *m.*

N. inanimate. अप्राणिवाचक *m.*

N. instrumental. कारणवाच्य *n.*

N. inflected or of any case. कारक *n.*

N. of holding or having. अधिकरणवाच्य *n.*

N. passive. कर्मवाचक*m.* कर्मणिवाच्यशब्द*m.*संप्रदानवाच्य*n.*

N. simple or nominative. भाववाच्य *n.* लिंग.

N. verbal. क्रियावाचक *m.*

To NOURISH, *v. a. feed, support, cherish.* पोसणें, पोषणें, पाळणें, प्रतिपाळणें, पालन *pop.* पाळण *n.*-पोषण *n.*-पालनपोषण *n.*-प्रतिपाळ *m.*-&c. करणें *g. of o.*

NOURISHABLE, *a.* v. V. पोसायाजोगा-जोगता-&c. पोष्य, पोषणीय, पोषणार्ह. [पुष्ट, भरित.

NOURISHED, *p.* v. V. पोसलेला, &c. पोषित, पालित, प्रतिपालित,

NOURISHER, *n.* NOURISHING, *p. a.* v. V. पोसणारा, पालक, पोषक, प्रतिपालक, पालनकर्त्ता, &c. पोष्टा, भर्ता, बृंहक.

I. *fattening*, v. NUTRITIOUS. पौष्टिक.

NOURISHING, NOURISHMENT, *n.* v. V.—*act.* पोसणें *n.* पाळणें *n.* &c. पाळणूक *f.* पाळग्रहण *n.* पालन *pop.* पाळण *n.* पोषण *n.* पाळणपोषण *n.* प्रतिपाल *pop.* प्रतिपाळ *m.* प्रतिपालन *n.* परवरीस *f.* परवरशी *f.* परवस्ती *f.* आप्यायन *n.* भरण *n.* भृति *f.* बृंहण *n.*

I. *nutriment, aliment*, v. FOOD. भक्ष्य *n.* आहार *m.* जीवन*n.* प्राणन *n.*

II. *power of nourishing.* v. पौष्टिकगुण *m.* धातुपोषकत्व *n.* पौष्टिकत्व *n.* बलवर्धकत्व *n.*

Novel, *a. new, unusual.* नवा, नवखा *or* नौखा, नवल, नवळका, अपरूप, अपूर्व, अप्राचीन.

2 *strange, marvellous*, v.Strange. नवल, विलक्षण, अपरूप, अद्भुत, अलौकिक.

Novel, *n. fictitious tale.* कल्पित गोष्ट *f.* कथा *f.* उपाख्यान *n.* अख्यान *n.* कादंबरी *f.*

Novelist, *n.* कल्पित गोष्ट-&c. रचणारा-लिहणारा.

Novelty, *n.* v. A. 1. नवेपणा *m.* नवखेपणा *m.* नवलपणा *m.* &c. नवलाई *f.* अपूर्वाई *f.* अपरुवाई *f.* अपूर्वता *f.*

2 नवलपणा *m.* अलौकिकपणा *m.* विलक्षणता *f.* वैलक्षण्य *n.* पडप *n.*

I. *a novelty.* नवल *n.* नवलाई *f.* नवलपरी *f.* कौतुक *n.* बूट *m.* आश्चर्य *n.*

November, *n.* इंग्रेजी वर्षाचा अकरावा महिना *m.* कार्त्तिक-मार्गशीर्ष *m.*

Novennial, *a. done every ninth year.* नवव्या नवव्या वर्षाचा, नवव्या नवव्या वर्षानें येणारा-घडणारा-&c. नौसाली.

Novercal, *a. pertaining, like, &c. to a step-mother.* सावत्र आईचा, सावत्र आईच्या चालीचा, सावत्र आईच्यासारखा, सापत्नमातृवत्.

Novice, *n. a beginner, one new in a business.* नवा, नवशिका *or* नवशिखा, नवशिक्या, नवशीक *or* ख, नूतनाभ्यासी, नवीनाभ्यासी, नवछात्र.

Ever a n. नित्यनवा.

Novitiate, *n. state of being a novice.* नवशिकेपणा *m.* नवशिकपणा *m.* &c. नवछात्रता *f.* नवछात्रदशा *f.* नूतनाभ्यासिता *f.* नवीनाभ्यासित्व *n.*

2 *period of being a novice.* नवशिकपणाचा काळ *m.* &c. नूतनाभ्यासकाल *m.* विद्याप्रारंभकाल *m.* नवीनाभ्यासित्वकाल *m.*

Now, *adv. at the present time.* एव्हां, आतां, एव्हांशी, आतांशीं *or* शें *or* शां, हल्लीं, हालीं, हाल, सांप्रत, सांप्रतकालीं, ह्यावेळीं, ह्यावेळेस, प्रस्तुत, आजकाल, आजकालीं, वर्त्तमानकालीं, तूर्त्त, तूर्त्तकालीं, सद्यः *pop.* सद्यां, सद्यस्कालीं *pop.* सद्याकालीं, इदानीम्, प्रकृत, अथ, संप्रति, एथवां, अधुना.

From n. *henceforth.* इतःपर.

N. and then. केव्हां केव्हां, केव्हां केव्हां, कधींमधीं, कधींकधीं, कधींकालीं, कदाकालीं, मध्यें मध्यें, सटीं सामाशीं, टगळमंगळ.

Now-a-days आजकाल.

Till n. एथपर्यंत, एथवर, एथपावेतों, अद्याप, आद्यापि.

2 *just now, a little while ago.* मघां, मघाशीं *or* सीं, एव्हांशीं, आतां, आतांच, नुक्ता *decl.* निक्ता *decl.* नेटका *decl.* नवसर, नवथर.

3 *after this, things being so.* आतां, ह्यावर, असें असतां.

4—as a particle of connection. तर.

5 *at one time; at another time.* कधीं.

Now-a-days, *adv.* v. Now. आजकाल, सांप्रतकालीं, अबकाळ, अथ.

Noway, Noways, Nowise, *adv. in no manner or degree*, v. Not. कोणत्याही प्रकारानें नाहीं, कसाही नाहीं, अर्धाअर्धीं नाहीं, सर्वथा नाहीं, सर्वथैव नाहीं, किमपि नाहीं.

Nowhere, *adv.* कोठें नाहीं, कुत्रापि न, क्वापि न;—emphatically, त्रिभुवनांत नाहीं, त्रैकोक्यांत नाहीं, तिनीतालीं नाहीं.

No where else. दुसऱ्या कोठें नाहीं.

Noxous, *a. pernicious, injurious, unwholesome*, v. Hurtful. उपद्रवी, उपद्रवीक, अपकारक, अहितकारक, वाईट, दुष्ट, बाधक, बावडा. [*f.* अपकारकत्व *n.*

Noxiousness, *n.* v. A. अपकारीपणा *m.* बावडेपणा *m.* अपकारिता

Nozle, Nozzle, *n. snout*, v. Nose. सोंड *f.* तोंड *n.*—of a पत्रान्ट, &c. मुंडा *m.* [होपयुक.

Nubile, *a.* v. Marriageable. विवाहाजोगा, विवाहयोग्य, विवा-

Nubilous, *a.* v. Cloudy. मेघाकीर्ण, मघाच्छादित, मघाच्छन्न.

Nucleus, *n.* See Kernel. 2. *any body about which matter collects.* समुच्चयास्पद, संचयास्पद, अनेकसंचयी, अनेकसमुच्चयी.

Nude, Nudity. See Naked, Nakedness.

To **Nudge**, *v. a. touch hintingly.* डोचणें.

Nugatory, *a. trifling, insignificant*, v. Light. हलका, पोकळ, अनर्थक, एरशेर.

2 *ineffectual*, v. Fruitless. निरर्थक, अनर्थक, पोकळ, व्यर्थ.

Nuisance, *a. any thing which annoys*, v. Plague. उपाध *f.* उपाधि *f.* व्याध *f.* जाच *m.* पीडा *f.* खूळ *n.* संकट *n.* मड *n.*

Null, *a. void, invalid.* व्यर्थ, निरर्थक, निर्जीव, पोकळ, रद्द, बालथर.

To **Null**, *To* **Nullify**, *v. a. annul*, v. To Abolish. मोडणें, रद्द-नाहींसा-रहित-निरर्थक-&c. करणें.

Nullity, *n.* v. A. पोकळपणा *m.* निरर्थकता *f.* व्यर्थता *f.*

I. *nothingness*, v. Non-entity. अभाव *m.* नास्तित्व *n.*

Numb, *a.* **Numbed**, *p.* v.V. N. *and* Torpid. बहिरा, मुना, गुंग, मेहरलेला, सुस्त, जड, सुप्त, सुप्तत्वचू, सैरभैर, बेशुद्ध, स्तब्धचेष्ट.

N. form cold. गार.

To **Numb**, *v. a. make torpid.* बहिरा-सुस्त-सुना-जड-स्तब्धचेष्ट-&c. करणें, काकडा *m.* बळणें *g. of o.* चैतन्यस्तंभ *m.*-चैतन्यस्तंभन *n.* करणें *g. of o.* [गारटणें *or* गारठणें.

To **Numb**, *v.n. become torpid.* बहिरावणें, मेहरणें, भारावणें, गुंगणें,

To **Number**, *v. a.* v. To Count. मोजणें, गणणें, संख्या *f.* करणें *g. of o.* मोजदाद *f.*-मोजदास्त *f.* घेणें-करणें *g. of o.*

2 *affix a number to.* आंकडा *m.*-आंक *m.*-&c. घालणें, अंकपट्टी *f.* लावणें.

Number, *n.*—the species of quantity. संख्या *f.*

2 *an aggregate of units.* संख्या *f.*

Even n. समसंख्या *f.* बेकी *f.*

Odd n. विषमसंख्या *f.* एकी *f.*

Of what n. कितकावा, कितवा, कित्यावा, Ex. हा तुमचा कितकावा मुलगा आहे ?

Whole n. अभिन्न *n.*

3 *numerical amount.* संख्या *f.* गणती *f.* गणना *f.* सुमार *m.*

4 *more than one, many.* कितिएक, बहुत एक, अनेक, पुष्कळ, बहुत.

5 v. Multitude. संख्या *f.* बाहुल्य *n.* बहुत्व *n.* [णणा *f.*

6 *aggregated body or number.* संख्या *f.* गण *m.* गणती *f.* ग-

7 *figure, arithmetical sign.* अंकडा *or* आंकडा *m.* अंक *m.* आंख *m.* संख्या *f.*

Numbers, *figures, practical arithmetic.* हिशेब *or* हिशोब *m.*

Table of numbers. अंकजाल *n.* अंकपत्र *n.* सारणी *f.* (esp. in comp. as ग्रहसारणी, योग सारणी, नक्षत्रसारणी, &c.).

8—in grammar. वचन *n.*

Dual n. द्विवचन.

Plural n. अनेकवचन, बहुवचन.

Singular n. एक वचन.

9 Numbers, v. Poetry. कविता *f.* पद्यरचना *f.*

Flowing numbers. द्राक्षापाक *m.*

Numbered, *p.* v. V. मोजलेला, गणलेला, &c.

2 आंकडा घातलेला, &c. अंकी *or* अंखी.

NUMBERER, *n.* NUMBERING, *p. a.* v. V. 1 मोजणारा, गणणारा, संख्या करणारा, &c. संख्याकारक, गणनकर्त्ता &c.

N. of houses, trees, &c. in a village. टीपकर.

NUMBERING, *n.* v. V. 1.—*act.* मोजणें *n.* गणणें *n.* &c. गणती *f.* मोजदाद *f.* मोजदास्त *f.* गणन *n.* गणना *f.*

N. of houses, trees, &c. in a village. टीप *f.*

2 आंकडा घालणें *n.* &c.

NUMBERLESS, *a.* v. COUNTLESS. असंख्य, असंख्यात, अगणित.

NUMBLES, *n. entrails of a deer.* हरणाचीं आंतडीं *n. pl.*

NUMBNESS, *n.* v. A. बहिरेपणा *m.* मेहरी *f.* सुनेपणा *m.* सुस्ती *f.* गुंगी *f.* सुप्ति *f.* स्वाप *m.* बाद *m.* बांध *f.* चैतन्यस्तंभ *m.* चैतन्यस्तब्धता *f.*

To be affected with n.—a limb. मेहरणें.

NUMBERABLE, *a. that may be numbered.* मोजायाजोगा-&c. गणनीय, गण्य, गणेय, संख्येय, परिगणनीय, सुमारी.

NUMERAL, *a. relating to or consisting of numbers.* संख्येचा, सुमारी, सांख्य, संख्यात्मक, संख्याविषयक, संख्यासंबंधी, गणनात्मक.

2—in gram. संख्यावाचक. [स *m.* संख्या *f.*

NUMERAL, *n. numeral character.* अंकडा *or* आंकडा *m.* अंक *m.* आं-

NUMERALLY, *adv. according to the number, in number, &c.* संख्येनें, गणतीनें, सुमारानें, सुमारें, यथासंख्य.

NUMERARY, *n. belonging to a certain number.* अमुकसंख्येचा, अमुकसंख्य. [संख्यापरिमाण *n.*

NUMERATION, *n.*—in arithmetic. अंकांची मोडणी *f.*-मांडणी *f.*

NUMERATOR, *n.*—of a fraction. अंश *m.* लव *m.*

NUMERICAL, *a.* v. NUMERAL. संख्येचा, संख्याविषयक, संख्यासंबंधी, सांख्य.

2 *consisting of numbers or figures.* अंकांचा, आंकड्यांचा, &c. अंकी *or* अंखी, अंकात्मक, संख्यात्मक.

NUMERICALLY, *adv. with respect to numbers.* संख्येनें, गणतीनें, यथासंख्य.

2 *in figures or numbers.* अंकांनीं, आंकड्यांनीं.

NUMEROUS, *a. being many, consisting of many.* मोठे संख्येचा, मोठ्या गणतीचा, बहुत, पुष्कळ, मोठा, बहुसंख्य, महासंख्य.

NUMEROUSLY, *adv.* v. A. मोठ्या संख्येनें, संघशः, संख्यातः, घवघव *or* वां.

NUMEROUSNESS, *n.* v. A. पुष्कळपणा *m.* बहुतपणा *m.* &c. बहुसंख्यत्व *n.* महासंख्यत्व *n.*

NUMISMATIC, *a. relating to coins or medals.* नाणकसंबंधी, नाणकविषयक.

NUMISMATICS, *n. pl.* नाणकविद्या *f.*

NUMMARY, NUMMULAR, *a. relating to money.* पैक्याचा, पैशाचा, सोन्यानाण्याचा, वित्तसंबंधी.

NUMSKULL, *n.* v. FOOL. दगड *m.* धोंडा *m.* दुघडओनाम्या, बुद्धीचा ठणठणपाळ, ठो, ढ.

NUN, *n. woman devoted to seclusion and austerity,* v. ASCETIC. मठांत राहणारी विरक्तस्त्री *f.* जोगीण *f.* बैरागीण *f.* गोसावीण *f.* मठनिवासिनी *f.*

NUNCIO. See AMBASSADOR.

NUNCUPATIVE, NUNCUPATORY, *a. orally pronounced.* तोंडचा, तोंडजबानीचा, मुखजबानीचा, अलिखित.

NUNNERY, *n. house in which nuns live.* जोगणींचें घर *n.*-मठ *m.*

NUPTIAL, *a. pertaining to marriage.* लग्नाचा, विवाहाचा, वऱ्हाडाचा, वऱ्हाडी, विवाहसंबंधी, वैवाहिक, औद्वाहिक.

NUPTIALS, *n.* v. MARRIAGE. लग्न *n.* विवाह *m.* सावधान *n.*

NURSE, *n. a. woman that has the care of infants.* मुलें बाळगणारी *f.*- बाळगणारीण *f.*- संभाळणारी *f.* आया *f.* is used in the families of Europeans.

2 *a woman who suckles an infant.* दूधकरीण *f.* थानकरीण *f.* दूधपाजणारी *f.* पाजणारी *f.* दाई *f.* धात्री *f.* उपमाता *f.* अमा *f.*

3 (of a sick person). रोग्याची चाकरी करणारी स्त्री *f.* रोग्याची तनू राखणारी *f.* रोग्याची टूक संभाळणारी *f.* रुग्णपरिचारिका *f.* रुग्णसेवका *f.* पाणी देणारी *f.*

4 fig. *fosterer, cherisher, &c.* पालक, प्रतिपालक, पालनकर्त्ता-कारक-कारी-&c.

To NURSE, *v. a.* (an infant) *tend.* बाळगणें, संभाळणें, राखणें, पाळणें, संभाळ *m.*-बालगण *f.*-&c. करणें *g. of o.* [घेणें.

2 *suckle.* दूध *n.*-स्तन *n.*-थान *n.* पाजणें-देणें, पाजणें, आंगावर

3 (a sick person). रोग्याची चाकरी *f.*-सेवा *f.*-शुश्रूषा *f.*-&c. करणें. [करणें *g. of o.*

4 *foster, cherish.* पाळणें, प्रतिपाळणें, पालन *n.*-प्रतिपाल *m.*-&c.

NURSERY, *n.* (for children). मुलांची खोली *f.*-कोठडी *f.* बालगृह *n.*

2 (of young trees, &c.). रोपांची जागा *f.* रोपांचा बाग *m.*

3—a gener. *fostering place.* पालनस्थान *n.*

NURSLING, *n.* v. INFANT. तान्हेंमूल *n.*

NURTURE, *n. nourishment,* v. FOOD. भक्ष्य *n.* आहार *m.*

2 *education, instruction.* शिक्षा *f.* उपदेश *m.* शिक्षण *n.*

To NURTURE. See To NOURISH, To EDUCATE.

NUT, *n. fruit with a kernel and shell.* कंवचीचें फळ *n.* टणकसालीचें फळ *n.* सकवचफल *n.* [those words.

Note. For cashew-nut, cocoanut, &c. see under

Marking nut, *semecarpus anacardium.* बिबवा *m.*

NUT-CRACKER, *n.* अडकिता *or* त्या *m.* सरोता *m.*

NUT-MEG, *n.* जायफळ *n.* जातिफल *n.*

NUT-SHELL, *n.* कंवची *f.* [वन *n.* प्राणन *n.*

NUTRIMENT, *n. nourishment,* v. FOOD. भक्ष्य *n.* आहार *m.* जी-

2 *quality of nourishing.* पौष्टिकगुण *m.* धातुपोषकत्व *n.* पौष्टिकत्व *n.* धातुवर्द्धकत्व *n.*

NUTRIMENTAL, NUTRITIOUS, NUTRITIVE, *a. having the quality of nourishing.* पुष्टीचा, धातुपुष्ट, पौष्टिक, पुष्टिकर, पुष्टिकारक, पुष्टिजनक, धातुपोषक, बलवर्धक.

NUTRITION. See NOURISHMENT, NUTRIMENT. [चली *f.*

NUX-VOMICA, *n.*—the tree. काजरा *m.* कुचला *m.*—the seed कु-

To NUZZLE, *v. a. foster,* v. To NOURISH. पाळणें, पाळणूक *f.*-पालन *n.*-प्रतिपाल *m.*-&c. करणें. *g. of o.*

To NUZZLE, *v.n. go with the nose near the ground.* नाक भुईस लावून जाणें.

2 See To NESTLE. [निशादृष्टि.

NYCTALOPS, *n. one who sees best at night.* रातडोळ्या, रात्रदृष्टि,

2 *one who is blind at night.* रातांधळा, रात्रांध.

NYCTALOPY, *n. night-sight.* रात्रदृष्टि *f.*

2 *night-blindness.* रातांधळें *n.*

NYMPH, *n. goddess of wood or water.* जलवनदेवता *f.* जलवनदेवी *f.* यक्षिणी *f.*

2 *lass, girl, &c.* v. WOMAN. तन्वंगी *f.*

NYMPHOMANIA, *n. furor uterinus.* अतिचरणा *f.*

O.

O. This vowel is represented by ओ. Oo is represented by ऊ.

O, *interj.* रे, अरे ;—in respect, हे, हो, अहो.

OAF, *n. dolt, &c.* v. FOOL. ढ, धोंडा *m.* ठ, गावदी.

OAFISH, *a.* v. FOOLISH. गावदी, मट्ठ, मठ्या.

OAK, *n.* एक वृक्ष आहे.

OAKUM, *n. old rope untwisted.* जुने दोरीचा काथा *m.*

OAR, *n. instrument for rowing.* अवला *m.* अवलें *n.* वलें *or* वल्हें *n.* चाटू *m.* क्षेपणी *f.* नौकादंड *m.*

Blade of an o. चपणी *f.* अलात *n.*

Man that handles an o. अवलेकरी, वल्हेकरी, अवल्या.

Shaft of an o. दांडी *f.* पतिंगा *m.*

To OAR. See To ROW.

OASIS, *n. green spot in a desert.* रानांत ओलाव्याची जागा *f.* ओलवण *f.* वनमध्यगतशाद्वलस्थल *n.*

OAT, *n.* एक धान्य आहे.

OATH, *n. solemn appeal to God.* आण *f.* शपथ *f.* सोगंद *f.* सोगण *f.* सत्य *n.* क्रिया *f.*

O. in the name of some god. देवाची आण (*pop.* देवाचेण [*f.*).-शपथ *f.*

O. on a cow. गाईची आण *f.*-शपथ *f.*

O. on the leg of. पायाची आण *f.*-शपथ *f.*

O. on the throat or life of. गळ्याची आण *f.*-शपथ *f.*

O. on one's food. अन्नाची शपथ *f.* अन्नाची आण *pop.* अन्नाचाण *f.*

O. on the sacred thread. जानव्याची शपथ *f.*-आण *f.*

Oaths and protestations—compreh. or gener. आण, शपथ *f.*

Promise confirmed by an o. आणभाक *or* भाष *f.*

Upon one's o. सत्योत्तरें, सत्योत्तर.

With an o. शपथपुरस्सर, शपथपूर्वक.

To administer an o. शपथ *f.*-आण *f.*-सोगंद *f.*-&c. घालणें.

To substantiate by o. क्रिया *f.* करणें.

To take an o. शपथ *f.* करणें-वाहणें-खाणें-घेणें-देणें, आण *f.* [वाहणें.

There are various forms of making an oath or solemn appeal. Some are, बेलभंडार *m.* करणें, तुलसी *f.* उचलणें, गाईचें शेंपूट *n.* धरणें *or* बरपणें, जोंधळे *m. pl.* उचलणें, गंगाजळी *f.* घेणें, देवाचा पाय *m.* शिवणें, देवावर हात *m.* ठेवणें, देवावरचीं फुलें *n. pl.* काढणें.

OATH-BREAKING, *n.* शपथभंग *m.* क्रियाभंग *m.* क्रियानाश *m.*

To OBDUCE, *v. a. draw over.* आंढणें-ओढूनघेणें *with* वर *of* o.

OBDURACY, OBDURATENESS, *n.* v. A. 1. पापनिग्रह *m.* पापनिग्रहिता *f.* पापनिर्भर *m.* पापात्यागिता *f.* अनुतापविमुखता *f.*

OBDURATE, *a. hardened in heart, persisting in evil.* पापाग्रही, पापनिग्रही, दुराग्रही, पापात्यागी, निगरगेटा, निचाडा, अनुतापविमुख, अनुतापपराङ्मुख.

2 See OBSTINATE.

OBEDIENCE, *n. compliance with a command.* मानणें *n.* ऐकणें *n.* मान्यता *f.* आज्ञापालन *n.* आज्ञानुवर्त्तन *n.* आज्ञानुसरण *n.* आज्ञाधारण *n.* हुकुमबरदारी *f.* आज्ञाधीनता *f.* आज्ञांकितत्व *n.* &c.

OBEDIENT, *a. submissive to authority, dutiful, compliant, &c.* आज्ञेंत वागणारा, आज्ञेंत राहणारा, हुकमी, हुकुमबरदार, आज्ञापालक, आज्ञाधारक, आज्ञाधारी, आज्ञांकित, आज्ञानुयायी, आज्ञानुसारी, आज्ञानुवर्त्ती, आज्ञावाहक, आज्ञावह, आज्ञासंपादक, आज्ञानुरूप, वचनग्राही, विनयग्राही, अनुविधायी, विनयी, विनीत, वशवर्त्ती ;—intensively, and with the power of the phrases, *at the nod or beck of, under the thumb of, in the leading string of, &c.* अर्घ्यांवचनांतला, अर्घ्याबोलांतला, कह्यांतला, छापेखालचा, बगल्या, बुद्धीस लागलेला, विकलेला.

To be o. to, *be under the thumb of.* कह्यांत-बळणांत-तिर्ढ़ी-&c. असणें *with g. of* o. गांठीस असणें, बुद्धीस लागणें.

OBEDIENTLY, *adv.* v. A. आज्ञा मानून, आज्ञेंत राहून, कैदवार, कैदेनें, हुकुमानें, हुकुमबरदारीनें, यथानुज्ञ.

OBEISANCE, *n. act of reverence,*—as made by a bráhman to a bráhman. नमस्कार *m.* नमन *n.* नमस्या *f.* प्रणाम *m.* प्रणति *f.* प्रणिपात *m.* नति *f.*

—as made by a bráhman to a person of inferior caste. आशीर्वाद *m.* रामराम *m.*

—as made by Hindus of inferior castes. दंडवत *n.* रामराम *m.*

—as made to a master or employer. मुजरा *m.*

—as made by or to Muhammadans, Europeans, &c. सलाम *m.* कुरनिशात *f.* कुरनीस *f.*

—as made to an idol, superior, &c. वंदन *n.*

—as made to a teacher, guru, &c. अभिवादन *n.* अभिवंदन *n.* In making obeisance, certain words of salutation are uttered by certain orders, castes, or classes. The word used by *Kánpháte* gosáwís is, आदेश ;

—by banians, जयगोपाल.

—by chámbhárs, mahárs, &c. जोहार.

—by attendants of kings to their masters. जोहार.

—by learned or clerical bráhmans. आशीर्वाद.

—by Hindus of the middle classes generally. रामराम.

—by bairágis. जयसीताराम.

Profound o. *obeisance with all the members of the body.* शिरसाष्टांगनमस्कार *m.* साष्टांग नमस्कार *m.* साष्टांगप्रणाम *m.*

To make o. नमणें, नमस्कार *m.*-&c. करणें.

OBELISK, *n.* मनोरा *m.*

OBERRATION, *n. wandering.* पर्यटन *n.*

OBESE, *a.* v. FAT. पुष्ट, मोठा, मासाळ, मेदस्वी.

OBESENESS, OBESITY, *n.* v. A. पुष्टता *f.* पुष्टि *f.* मेदोवृद्धि *f.* मेदोरोग *m.* मेदोव्याधि *m.* भोपळयारोग *m.*

To OBEY, *v. a. submit to, be obedient to.* मानणें, ऐकणें, आज्ञेंत-कह्यांत-हुकुमांत-वचनांत-सत्तेंत-&c. वागणें-राहणें-असणें *g. of* o. आज्ञापालन *n.*-आज्ञानुवर्त्तन *n.*-&c. करणें *g. of* o. वश-आज्ञांकित-&c. असणें;—implicitly, obsequiously, &c. डोळापाहून-कलपाहून-झोकपाहून-&c. वागणें-चालणें.

2 *comply with, act according to.* मानणें, पाळणें, राखणें, बजावणें (*used with* हुकूम), पालन *n.*-&c. करणें *g. of* o.

OBEYED, *p.* v. V. मानलेला, &c. मानित.

To OBFUSCATE, OBFUSCATION. See To OBSCURE, &c.

OBIT. See OBSEQUIES.

OBITUARY, *n. list or register of the dead.* मयतयाद *f.* मयतनामा *m.* मर्तिकांची याद *f.* मृतसंख्यापत्र *n.*

2 *account of a deceased person.* मृतवर्णन *n.* मृतचरित्र *n.*

OBJECT, *n. that about which any power or faculty is employed.* विषय *m.* गोचर *m.* अर्थ *m.* इंद्रियार्थ *m.* पात्र *n.* (in comp. much elegant use is made of this word: ex. कृपापात्र o. of favor, प्रीतिपात्र o. of love, and, दानपात्र, लोभपात्र, क्रोधपात्र, मोहपात्र, क्षमापात्र, &c. &c.), भाजन *n.* (in comp. as मानभाजन, स्तुतिभाजन, निंदाभाजन, दयाभाजन, &c.).

An external o. इदंकारास्पद *n.*

Apprehension of objects. विषयीकरण *n.*

Deserving o. (of charity or favor). कृपापात्र, सुपात्र, दानपात्र.

Unworthy o. कुपात्र, अपात्र.

2 *that to which the mind is directed for attainment; purpose.* आशय*m.* अभिप्राय*m.* उद्देश्य*n.* लाग*m.* लक्ष*n.* लक्ष्य*n.* हेतु *m.* तात्पर्य *n.* निमित्त*n.* खुलासा*m.* अर्थ*m.* विषय*m.* अभिसंधि*m.* कार्यवस्तु *n.*

The four *objects of man.* (पुरुषार्थ)—of the human affections and faculties (चतुर्वर्ग) are, धर्म, अर्थ, काम, and मोक्ष.

The three objects of human desire, &c.—collectively. त्रिवर्ग *m.* त्रिगण *m.*

Accomplishment of an o. इष्टापत्ति *f.* कार्यसिद्धि *f.* चरितार्थ *m.*

Accomplishment of one's o. स्वार्थसिद्धि *f.*

Having one o. or aim. एकरोखी, एकनिष्ठ, एकताण.

Obtainment of all ones objects. सर्वसिद्धि *f.*

Private o. or end. स्वार्थ *m.* स्वसाधन *n.* स्वहित *n.*

That has accomplished his o. कृतकृत्य, कृतार्थ, आशाप्राप्त.

That has accomplished all his objects. सर्वसिध्धार्थ-&c.

To accomplish one's o. बेडा *m.* पार करणें (and to be accomplished पार होणें-जाणें-असणें), लाग *m.* साधणें *g. of s.* काठी *f.* शिखरास लागणें *g. of s.* गंगेस घोडे *m. pl.* नाहणें.

To fail or miss one's o. लाग *m.* फसणें-चुकणें *g. of s.*

Keep one object in view. एकतत्वीं जीव धरा *or* ठेवा,

3—in grammar. कर्म *n.* कर्मपद *n.*

To OBJECT, *v. a. present in opposition.* आडवा करणें.

2 fig. *offer in opposition, cast against.* दोषरूपानें पुढें करणें*or* आणणें, आडवा करणें *or* आणणें, बद्धक-प्रतिबंधक-&c. करणें, आक्षेपणें, आक्षेप *m.* करणें *g. of o,*

To OBJECT, *v. n. oppose in words or arguments, raise objections.* आडवें *n.*-दिक्कत*f.*-आक्षेप*m.*-&c. घेणें, तकरार *f.* करणें-घेणें, अडचण *f.* सांगणें, नाकबूल असणें-जाणें, असम्मत-&c. असणें, अस्वीकार *m.* करणें, अननुमोदन *n.* देणें-करणें.

OBJECTION, *n. adverse reason or argument proposed; difficulty started or made.* शंका *f.* आशंका *f.* कांक्षा *pop.* आकांक्षा *f.* कक्षा *f.* आक्षेप *m.* तकरार *f.* आडवें *n.* आड *f.* फांट *m.* कोटि *f.*

A possible o. उत्थाप्याकांक्षा *f.*

A captious, frivolous, perverse, &c. o. आडफांटा *m.* हुजत *f.* दिक्कत *f.* अधांटी *f.*

Removal of an o. समाधान *n.*

That starts objections, makes difficulties, &c. दिक्कतखोर, दिकती, वेव्हारी, सतरा फणगडे फोडणारा, कांद्या,

To raise objections and difficulties, v. To CARP. आडवें *n.* घेणें, हुजत *f.*-हुजतखोरी *f.*-&c. करणें, फणगडे *m.pl.*-फरगडे *m. pl.*-फांटे *m. pl.*-&c. फोडणें, अडचणी *f. pl.* सांगणें, बयाद *m. f.* सांगणें-लावणें, वेव्हार *m.* सांगणें-करणें, अढेवेढे *m. pl.* करणें-घेणें.

2 *opposing ground; ground of hesitation or difficulty.* बाध *m.* हरकत *f.* दिक्कत *f.* अड *f.* गुंता *m.* प्रत्यवाय *m.* प्रतिबंध*m.* बाधक *n.*

3 v. FAULT. दोष *m.*

OBJECTIONABLE, *a. liable to objections.* आकांक्षा घ्यायाजोगासारखा-&c. आक्षेप घ्यायाजोगा-&c. सदोष, सबाध, बाध्य, दूष्य, अपवाद्य, प्रतिषेधार्ह.

OBJECTIONABLENESS, *n.* v. A. दोष *m.* बाध *m.* प्रत्यवाय *m.* दिक्कत *f.* सदोषता *f.*

OBJECTIVE, *a. belonging to the object.* स्वाश्रयस्थित, स्वाधारस्थित, स्वाधारनिष्ठ, पदार्थाश्रित, पात्रसंबंधी, विषयसंबंधी.

2—in grammar. कर्मपदविषयक.

OBJURGATION, *n.* v. SCOLDING. दोष देणें *n.* बोल ठेवणें *n.*

OBJURGATORY, *a. containing censure.* दोषप्रद, दोषावह.

OBLATE, *a. flattened at the poles.* दोहों बाजूंस चपटा.

OBLATION, *n.* v. OFFERING. बलि *pop.* बळी *m. f.* देवोपायन *n.* देवोपहार *m.*

To OBLIGATE, *v. a. bind by duty or contract.* बांधणें, गुंतवणें, बांधून-गुंतवून घेणें.

OBLIGATED, *p.* v. V. बांधलेला, बांधून घेतलेला, &c.

To be o. बांधला जाणें-होणें.

OBLIGATION, *n. binding power,* (as of a promise, oath, &c.); *incumbency, necessity.* आवश्यकता *f.* कर्त्तव्यता *f.* विधेयता *f.* अवश्यकर्त्तव्यता *f.* अवश्यकार्यता *f.*

Under the o. of (a promise, oath, &c.). भरल्या बंदांत, भरल्याबंधनांत, [म *m.*

2 *act binding,* v. ENGAGEMENT. प्रतिज्ञा *f.* वायदा *m.* नियम *m.*

Religious o. व्रत *n.*

That is under a religious o. व्रती, व्रतस्थ.

Violating a religious o. व्रतलोपन *n.* व्रतलोप *m.*

3 *bound state.* बांधलेपणा *m.* गुंतलेपणा *m.* गुंता *m.* गुतागूत *f.* बद्धता *f.* जामीनगत *f.*

4 *favor or kindness obliging.* उपकार *m.* आभार *m.* एहसान *n.* कृतोपकार *m.*

To lay under an o. उपकार *m.* ठेवणें.

5 See BOND.

OBLIGATORY, *a. binding.* आवश्यक, अवश्यमाननीय, अवश्यपालनीय, अवश्यकर्त्तव्य, अवश्यमंतव्य, प्राप्त, नाप्राप्त.

To OBLIGE, *v. a.* v. To COMPEL. भाग पाडणें, भागास आणणें, ना प्राप्त करणें.

To be obliged to. भागास येणें, भाग असणें, प्राप्त असणें, भार *m.* पडणें *all with in. con.*

2 *indebt, bind by favors, &c.* v. To BIND. उपकारानें बांधणें-बांधून घेणें, उपकारबद्ध-उपकृत-मिंधा-&c. करणें.

3 *do a favor to, please.* कृपा *f.*-मेहरबानी *f.*-मेहरबानगी *f.*-मेहर *f.*-उपकार *m.*-&c. करणें *with* वर *of o.*

OBLIGED, *p.* v. V. 2. *and* BOUND. उपकारानें बांधलेला, &c. उपकारी, आभारी, ऋणी, उपकारबद्ध, उपकृत, लागला.

To be o. or indebted to. लागला जाणें *with* स *or* ला.

OBLIGING, *a. disposed to do favors*, v. KIND. उपकारी, उपकारशील, परोपकारी, कार्यकर्त्ता.

OBLIGINGLY, *adv.* v. A. मेहरबानीनें, मेहरबानगीनें, उपकारबुद्धीनें, कृपाबुद्धीनें, उपकारबुद्ध्या, कृपाबुद्ध्या.

OBLIGINGNESS, *n.* v. A. मेहरबानगी *f.* मेहरबानी *f.* उपकारबुद्धि *f.* परोपकार *m.* परोपकारिता *f.* उपकारशीलता *f.*

OBLIQUE, *a. not direct, not perpendicular.* आडवा, तिरका, तिरपा, तिरकस, आडवा तिडवा, बांकडा, वक्र, तिर्यक्.

2 fig. *by insinuation, by innuendo, &c.* उपरोधाचा, उपरोधी, उपरोधीक, वक्र.

3—in grammar. कारकविभक्तीचा, कारकविभक्तिक.

O. case. कारक *n.* कारकविभक्ति *f.*

OBLIQUELY, *adv.* v. A. 1. आडवा *decl.* तिरका *decl.* तिरकस, ओझरता *decl.* फाकरता *decl.* कालरता *decl.* कसरता *decl.* कापता *decl.* कह्राता *decl.* कातरा *decl.* तिर्यक्.

2 उपरोधानें, अन्योक्तीनें, वक्रोक्तीनें.

OBLIQUENESS, OBLIQUITY, *n.* v. A. 1. आडवेपणा *m.* तिरकेपणा *m.* बांकडेपणा *m.* &c. तिरखाई *f.* बांक *or* बाक *m.* वक्रता *f.*

I. *deviation from moral rectitude.* चळ *m.* असदाचार *m.* असदाचरण *n.* विपथगमन *n.* अपथगमन *n.*

To OBLITERATE, *v. a. blot out, erase, wear out, &c.* v. To EFFACE. पुसणें, पुसून टाकणें, बोळा *m.* फिरवणें, घसवटणें, उडवणें, बुझवणें, नाहींसा करणें, दिसेनासा करणें.

To be obliterated. घसवटणें, उडणें, झडणें, बुझणें, पुसून जाणें.

OBLITERATION, *n.* v. V.—*act.* पुसणें *n.* घसवटणें *n.* &c.

OBLIVION, *n. forgetfulness.* विसर *m.* विस्मरण *n.* विस्मृति *f.* व्यामोह *m.*

2 *forgotten state.* विसर *m.* विस्मृति *f.* विस्मरण *n.* अस्फूर्त्ति *f.*

In o. नांवनट.

That has not fallen into o.—a science. उपस्थित.

To bury in o. माती *f.* टाकणें-लोटणें *with* वर *of o.*

3 *amnesty.* अपराधांची माफी *f.* दोषविस्मरण *n.* सकलापराधमोचन *n.*

OBLIVIOUS, *a. causing oblivion.* विसर पाडणारा, विसरपाड्या, विस्मृतिकारक, विस्मृतिजनक, विस्मारक.

2 *forgetful.* विसरणारा, विसराळू, विसऱ्या.

OBLIVIOUSNESS, *n.* v. A. 2. *and* FORGETFULNESS. विसराळूपणा *m.* विस्मरण *n.* विस्मृति *f.*

OBLONG, *a. longer than broad.* लांबोडा *or* लांबुडा, लांबोळा, लांबचौडा, दीर्घचतुरस्त्र.

OBLONG, *n.*—the figure. आयत *n.* [*m.* परुषोक्ति *f.*

OBLOQUY, *n. reproach.* निंदा *f.* निंदोक्ति *f.* कुत्सा *f.* गर्हा *f.* अपवाद

OBMUTESCENCE, *n. loss of speech, silence.* मुकेपणा *m.* वाकूस्तंभ *m.* वाग्रोध *m.* गतवाक्त्व *n.*

2 *observation of silence.* मौन *pop.* मौन्य *n.* अभाषण *n.* वाङ्नियम *m.* वाङ्निश्चय *m.*

OBNOXIOUS, *a. subject, liable, exposed.* जोगा, योग्य, वश, स्वाधीन, अधीन, पात्र (in comp. as रोगपात्र, मरणपात्र, &c.), आस्पद (in comp. as रोगास्पद, &c.), अधिकारी.

To be o. to. तोंडांत-दाढेंत-&c. असणें.

2 *liable to punishment.* दंडास योग्य, दंडार्ह, दंड्य, दोषी, सदोष.

3 *offensive, displeasing, disagreeable.* नावडता, नावडा, अनावड, नावडीचा, अप्रीतीचा, अप्रीतींतला, अनिष्ट, असंतोषपात्र, असंतोषकारक-कारी. [अधीनता *f.*

OBNOXIOUSNESS, *n.* v. A. 1. जोगेपणा *m.* योग्यता *f.* वशता *f.*

2 दंडयोग्यता *f.* दंडार्हता *f.* दंड्यता *f.*

3 नावडतेपणा *m.* नावडेपणा *m.* अनिष्टता *f.*

OBSCENE, *a. offensive to chastity, &c. indecent, impure.* बीभत्स, बीभत्सरसाचा, विचकट, अचकटविचकट, चवनट, अभद्र, अमंगल *or* ळ, अवाच्य, मळीण, फुटका.

2—of persons. विचकट, अचकटविचकट, बीभत्स, तोंडाचा फटकळ-शिनळ, तोंडशिनळ, तोंडशिंदळ, काळजिभ्या, वाग्दुष्ट.

3 *filthy, &c.* v. DISGUSTING. मळीण, हिडीस, हिडशा *or* सा, हेंदरा. [चक.

4 *ill omened.* अशुभ, अभद्र, अमंगल, अभद्रसूचक, अमंगलसू-

OBSCENENESS, OBSENITY, *n.* v. A. 1. बीभत्सपणा *m.* बीभत्सभाव *m.* बीभत्सरस *m.* विचकटपणा *m.* अचकटविचकटपणा *m.*

I. v. LEWDNESS. बदफैली *f.*

II. *obscene speech.* विचकटभाषण *n.* दुर्वचन *n.* दुर्भाषण *n.* दुर्वाक्य *n.* दुरुक्ति *f.*

OBSCURATION, *n.* v. V. 1.—*act.* पुसकटणें *n.* कांतिहरण *n.* प्रकाशहरण *n.* अस्पष्टीकरण *n.*—*state.* तेजोऱ्हास *m.* तेजोक्षय *m.* तेजोक्षति *f.* तेजोहानि *f.* प्रकाशक्षय *m.* कांतिक्षय *m.* प्रभाक्षय *m.*

I.—of a planet. अस्त *m. n.*

OBSCURE, *a. dull, dim; not clear, full, or distinct.* ओंधट, अंधक, पुसका, पुसकट, पुसट, मळकट, अस्पष्ट, अव्यक्त, दुर्दर्श.

2 *occult, abstruse, not easily intelligible.* गूढ, गूढार्थ, गूढार्थक, खोल, अस्पष्ट, अव्यक्त, दुर्बोध, दुर्गम, दुर्ज्ञेय.

3 *without note, eminence, &c.* अप्रसिद्ध, अप्रसिद्धीचा, कमी प्रतिष्ठेचा, अविख्यात, आडगळचा, गल्लीकुचीचा, वाटेवरचा, अध्याचा, सांधीकोंदीचा, सांधीचा, सांधीभानेचा, सांदभाना *or* सांदमान्या, सांदकोंद्या, न्यूनप्रतिष्ठ, अल्पप्रतिष्ठ, न्यूनकीर्त्ति, अल्पकीर्त्ति.

4 *retired, remote, from observation,*—place. आडकुशीचा, आडवाटेचा, आडवळणाचा, एकेकडचा, एकोशाचा, गैरवळणाचा.

To OBSCURE, *v. a. darken; make less visible, bright, glorious, &c.* lit. fig. प्रकाश *m.*-तेज *n.*-कांति *f.*-&c. कमी करणें *g. of o.* स्पष्ट दिसेनासा करणें, पुसकटणें, पुसटणें, मळकट-अस्पष्ट-अंधक-पुसकट-&c. करणें, तेजोऱ्हास *m.*-प्रकाशक्षय *m.*-कांतिहरण *n.*-कांतिक्षय *m.*-&c. करणें *g. of o.*

2 *make less intelligible.* अवघड-कठीण-दुर्बोध-अस्पष्ट-&c. करणें, अस्पष्टता *f.*-दुर्बोधता *f.*-&c. आणणें.

OBSCURED, *p.* v. V. 1. अंधक केलेला, मळकट केलेला, &c. धुंद, हतप्रकाश, क्षीणप्रकाश, क्षीणप्रभ, मलिनप्रभ, नष्टप्रभ, हतप्रभ, क्षतप्रभ, क्षततेजा, क्षततेजस्क, क्षीणतेजस्क.

OBSCURELY, *adv.* v. A. 1. अंधक, धुंदूक धुंदूक, धुंदूकमुंदूक, धुंदूसमुंदूस, झुजूकमुंजूक.

2 अस्पष्ट, अव्यक्त, अस्पष्टतेनें, अस्पष्टरूपानें.

3 अप्रसिद्ध, अविख्यात, अप्रसिद्धीनें, &c. अप्रसिद्धिपूर्वक, &c.

4 आडकुशीस, एकोशास, एकोशीं, आडवळणीं.

OBSCURENESS, OBSCURITY, *n.* v. A. 1. ओंधटपणा *m.* पुसकेपणा *m.* &c. अंधकत्व *n.* ओंध *f.* मळभ *n.* न्यूनप्रकाश *m.* अल्पप्रकाश *m.*

2 खोलपणा *m.* गूढता *f.* गहनता *f.* अस्पष्टता *f.* दुर्बोधता *f.* दुर्ज्ञेयता *f.*

3 अप्रसिद्धि *f.* अविख्याति *f.* अल्पप्रतिष्ठा *f.* न्यूनप्रतिष्ठा *f.* अल्पकीर्त्ति *f.* कीर्त्यभाव *m.* सांदकोंदेपणा *m.* &c. सांदीकोंदीस पड-

लपणा m.

OBSECRATION. See ENTREATY.

OBSEQUIAL, *a. belonging to obsequies.* मरतिकाचा, उत्तरक्रियेचा, उत्तरकार्याचा, &c. उत्तरकार्यविषयक, उत्तरकार्यसंबंधी, &c. और्ध्वदेहिक.

OBSEQUIES, *n. funeral rites.* मरतीक *n.* क्रिया *f.* उत्तरक्रिया *f.* उत्तरकार्य *n.* उत्तरकर्म *n.* प्रेतकर्म *n.* प्रेतकार्य *n.* प्रेतक्रिया *f.* प्रेतसंस्कार *m.* कर्मांतर *n.* क्रियाकर्मांतर *n.* अंत्यकर्म *n.* अंत्यक्रिया *f.* अंत्येष्टि *f.* मृतक *n.* मृतक्रिया *f.* मृतकार्य *n.* मृतकर्म *n.* मृतसंस्कार *m.* अतीतसंस्कार *m.* और्ध्वदेहिक *n.* पारलौकिक *n.* अशुभकर्म *n.* अशुभकार्य *n.*—revilingly कारट *n.* Certain ceremonies or points included under *obsequies* are, अकरावा, अस्थिसंचयन, अस्थिसिंचन, उदकक्रिया, कपाळमोक्ष, जलांजलि, तिलांजलि *or* तिलोदकदान, तेरावा *or* तेरावें, दशाह, पालाशविधि, बारावा, मडाग्नि, मंत्राग्नि, राख सावडणें, वायसपिंड, वायसबलि, वेदिकाश्राद्ध, विषमश्राद्ध, सामासें, श्राद्ध.

Conductor or performer of o. कर्मांतऱ्या, कर्मसांगणारा, कर्म चालविणारा, दर्भ्या,—revilingly, कारटा *or* कारट्या, प्रेत्या.

Obsequial fees. कारट *n.*—One that takes them, कारट खाऊ.

Obsequial offerings. श्राद्ध *n.*

OBSEQUIOUS, *a. compliant, &c.* See OBEDIENT.

2 *meanly or servilely compliant.* आर्जवी, आर्जवू, आर्जवाचा, मनधरणीचा, खुशामती *or* दी, खुशामत्या, तोंडाकडे पाहणारा, तोंडदेख्या, तोंडासारखें बोलणारा, डोळे पाहून वागणारा, मर्जीचा कल पाहून वर्त्तणारा, जीजी म्हणणारा-करणारा, तोंडचाट्या, थुकी झेलणारा, थुकीझेल्या, तोंडपुज्या, छंदानुरोधी, वशवर्त्ती.

To be o. डोळे पाहून वागणें.

Some phrases expressing the sense *to be salvishly submissive to, to be obsequious to, to follow implicitly, to be led by the nose by, &c.* are. ओंजळीनें पाणी पिणें, मुठींत असणें, अर्धेवचनांत असणें *or* वागणें, कच्याधाग्यांत असणें, कच्छपीं असणें, तिळीं असणें *all with g. of o.*

OBSEQUIOUSLY, *adv.* v. A. 2. आर्जवानें, आर्जवकरून, खुशामतीनें, डोळे पाहून, तोंडाकडे पाहून, तोंडासारखा *decl.*

OBSEQUIOUSNESS, *n.* v. A. 2. आर्जव *m. n.* आर्जवीपणा *m.* खुशामत *or* द *f.* खिदमत *f.* गुलामगिरी *f.* उपार्जना *f.* छंदानुरोध *m.* अनुवृत्ति *f.* अनुलक्ष्य *n.*

OBSERVABLE, *a.* v. V. A. 1. पहायाजोगा-सारखा-&c. लक्ष्य द्यायाजोगा-&c. लक्ष्यांत आणायाजोगा-&c.

2 पहायाजोगा-&c. नजरेस यायाजोगा-&c. पाहण्यांत यायाजोगा, दिसायाजोगा-&c. लक्ष्य, दृश्य, दृष्टिगोचर.

OBSERVANCE, OBSERVATION, *n.* v. V. A. 1.—*act.* पाहणें *n.* निरेखणें *n.* निरीक्षण *n.* निरीक्षा *f.* अवेक्षण *n.* अवेक्षा *f.* लक्ष्य *n.* लक्ष *n.* ध्यान *n.* धोरण *n.*

2 पाहणें *n.* लक्षिणें *n.* &c. दृष्टि *f.* नजर *f.* अवलोकन *n.*

Under personal o. or experience. दृष्टेत्पत्तीस, दृष्टीच्या अमलांत, दृष्टीखालीं.

To elude the o. of. दृष्टि *f.* चुकवणें *or* चोरणें.

To fall under o. दृष्टीस पडणें, दृष्टीच्या अमलांत येणें.

To take an observation (of a heavenly body) वेध *m.* करणें.

3 पाळणें *n.* मानणें *n.* &c. पालन *pop.* पाळण *n.* पाळणूक *f.* आचरण *n.* धारण *n.* वसा *or* ओंवसा *m.* v. घे. Note. This is confined to women.

4 करणें *n.* आचरणें *n.* &c. आचरण *n.* धारण *n.* अनुष्ठान *n.*

5 पाळणें *n.* &c. पालन *pop.* पाळण *n.* पाळणूक *f.* अनुसरण *n.* अनुलक्ष्य *n.* अनुरोध *m.*

6 सेवणें *n.* सेवन *n.*

v. V. N. बोलणें *n.* &c. बोल *m.* भाषण *n.*

I. *respect paid.* सन्मान *m.* मान *m.* सत्कार *m.* आदर *m.*

II. *religious rite.* व्रत *n.* नियम *pop.* नेम *m.* विधान *n.*—among women. वसा *or* वसा *m.* Some of the *observances* of the Maráthá people are, अनंतचतुर्दशीव्रत, एकभुक्तव्रत, एकादशी, कोकिलाव्रत, कोजागर, दधिव्रत, नक्तव्रत, निशिभार्गव, पयोव्रत, प्रदोषव्रत, भुईपारणें, मधुव्रत, भीष्मपंचक, विनायकी, शर्कराव्रत, शाकाव्रत, श्रवणद्वादशी, सदावर्त्त, सोमवारव्रत. Some of the *observances peculiar to women* are, अचळविवाण, अदुःखनवमी, अधणेंनिववण, अवचितफळ, अवडनिवड, अष्टफळी *or* आठोफळी, आदित्यव्रत, ऋषिपंचमी, कहाणी, गजगौरी (*or* हस्तगौरी) व्रत, गोपद्मव्रत, गोवत्सद्वादशी, पाठोरापिठोरा, बुधाष्टमी, मंगलागौरीव्रत, महालक्ष्मीव्रत, रथसप्तमी, वटसावित्रीव्रत, शाकंभरी, शिवामूठ, शीतलागौरी, सोमवतीव्रत, हरितालिकाव्रत.

A woman under a vow to perform some o. वशेळी *f.*

Closing ceremony of an o. संपूर्ण *n.*

Female observances or vows—compreh. or gener. [वाणवसा *m.*

Imposing on one's self some o. व्रतसंग्रह *m.*

Self imposed o. व्रत *n.*

That is holding some o. व्रती, व्रतस्थ, धृतव्रत.

OBSERVANT, *a.* OBSERVER, *n.* OBSERVING, *p. a.* v. V. A. 1. पाहणारा, लक्षिणारा, निरेखणारा, निरखून पाहणारा, लक्ष्य लावणारा, ध्यानांत आणणारा, &c. &c. निरीक्षक, प्रेक्षक, नजरबाज.

2 पाहणारा, लक्षिणारा, &c.

3 पाळणारा, मानणारा, &c. पालक, पालनकर्त्ता.

4 करणारा, आचरणारा, &c. आचरण कर्त्ता.

5 *and* OBEDIENT. पाळणारा, मानणारा, आज्ञापालक, अनुसारी.

6 सेवणारा, सेवनकर्त्ता.

OBSERVATORY, *n. place for making observations on the stars, &c.* वेधशाला *f.* तारांगण *n.* नलिकाबंध *m.* नलिकाबंधस्थल *n.*

To OBSERVE, *v. a. regard, note, mark, watch.* पाहणें, लक्षिणें, निरेखणें *or* निरखणें, निरीक्षणें, निरखून-&c. पाहणें, दृष्टि *f.* घालणें *with* कडे *or* वर *of o.* लक्ष्य *n.*-लक्ष *n.*-ध्यान *n.*-चित्त *n.*-&c. देणें-लावणें-&c. *or* देऊन-लावून-&c. पाहणें-ऐकणें-&c. ध्यानांत-लक्ष्यांत-&c. आणणें.

2 *remark, note, notice, see.* पाहणें, लक्षिणें, नजरेस-दृष्टीस-&c. पडणें-येणें *in. con. with g. of s.* दृष्टीखालीं येणें *in. con. with g. of s.* पाहण्यांत-लक्ष्यांत-ध्यानांत-&c. येणें *in. con.*

3 *regard religiously, keep, celebrate, &c.* पाळणें, मानणें, राखणें, करणें, बाळगणें, आदरणें, आचरणें, साधणें, धरणें, वसणें *or* ओवसणें *or* वसवणें. Note. This word is confined to women.

To o. (rite, day, &c.) in a cold & perfunctory way. [साजरा करणें.

4 *practise ritually.* करणें, आचरणें, धरणें, अनुष्ठणें.

5 *obey, follow, keep.* पाळणें, राखणें, मानणें, ऐकणें, अनुसरणें, उपासना *f.* करणें *g. of o.*

6 (a point or rule of regimen, &c. सेवणें, सेवन *n.* करणें [*g. of o.*

To OBSERVE, *v. n. make a remark.* बोलणें, सांगणें, म्हणणें.

OBSERVED, *p.* v. V. A. 1. पाहिलेला, निरेखलेला, निरखून पाहिलेला, लक्ष्यांत आणलेला, &c.

2 पाहिलेला, लक्षिलेला, &c. देखील, अवलोकित, अवेक्षित.

3 पाळलेला, &c. पालित, आचरित.

4 केलेला, आचरलेला, &c. आचरित, अनुष्ठित.

5 पाळलेला, मानलेला, &c. पालित, अनुसृत.

6 सेवलेला, सेवित. [धातून.

OBSERVINGLY, *adv.* v. A. 1. लक्ष्य देऊन-लावून, निरखून, दृष्टि 5 अनुलक्षून, अनुरोधानें.

OBSOLETE, *a. gone out of use.* व्यवहारांतून गेलेला, मावळलेला, माजी, गैरचालू, रद्द, बाळ, अनुपस्थित, अनुपलब्ध, अव्यवहारित, लुप्त, अस्थित, नैरुक्त, कालांतरित, गतकालिक.

OBSOLETENESS, *n.* v. A. रद्दपणा *m.* &c. अनुपस्थिति *f.* अनुपलब्धि *f.* बाळ *f.* लोप *m.* लुप्तता *f.* अव्यवहारितत्व *n.* अप्रचार *m.* अस्थिति *f.*

OBSTACLE, *n. that which opposes or stands in the way; obstruction, impediment, hinderance.* अड *m. f.* अडती *f.* अडकें *n.* आडकाठी *f.* अडथळा *m.* अटकाव *m.* नड *f.* नडाव *m.* अडखुळ *f.* आडफांटा *m.* खेंव *m.* बेध *m.* बाध *m.* बंदी *f.* हरकत *f.* मोडा *m.* मोडती *f.* विघ्न *m. n.* प्रतिबंध *m.* प्रतिबंधक *n.* अंतराय *m.* व्याघात *m.* व्याक्षेप *m.* व्यवधान *n.* विघात *m.*

Removing obstacles. विघ्नसिद्धि *f.* विघातसिद्धि *f.*

OBSTETRIC, *a. relating to midwifery.* दाइपणाचा, सुविणपणाचा, गर्भमोचनसंबंधी, गर्भमोचनविषयक.

OBSTETRICS, *n. science of midwifery.* गर्भमोचनविद्या *f.*

OBSTINACY, OBSTINATENESS, *n.* v. A. 1. हेंकटपणा *m.* हट्टीपणा *m.* निक्षीपणा *m.* &c. अट *f.* अड *f.* हठ *pop.* हट *m.* हेका *m.* आग्रह *m.* दुराग्रह *m.* निग्रह *m.* खणपट *f.* खणखापट *f. v.* घे, हटवाद *m.* दुर्मद *m.*

A fit of o. खळ *m. v.* घे, अंबटा *m. v.* धर.

To take a fit of o., to be obstinate. हट्टास पेटणें, खळ *m.*-खणपट *f.*-&c. घेणें, खणपटीस बसणें-लागणें, खणपटीस येणें.

OBSTINATE, *a. stubborn, pertinacious, &c.* हट्टी, हटखोर, हट घेणारा, हेंकट *or* हेंकड, हेंकेखोर, खळ घेणारा, खळ्या, अडिवाळ, निक्षी, अटीचा, अटखोर, अटदार, अटबाज, अडखोर, अडील, अडेल, आडकर, हटेला, खणपट्या, खणकुदळ्या, दुराग्रही, आग्रही, निग्रही, खळवादी, हटवादी, गाटा *or* गाट्या, गाटी, गाताडा, घेलट, घेलाड, अगस्ताळा, जाळगा.

2—of diseases. खिळण घेतलेला, खणकुदळ्या, अटीचा, खिळणीचा, रेंगळलेला, जडावलेला, कृच्छ्रसाध्य.

OBSTINATELY, *adv.* v. A. हट घेऊन, हेंका घेऊन, आग्रह धरून, &c. आग्रहानें, हेंक्यानें, &c. दाटवळें, दाटून, हटकून, हटेंच.

OBSTIPATION. See COSTIVENESS.

OBSTREPEROUS, *a. noisy, vociferous,* v. CLAMOROUS. कलकल्या, गलबल्या, गलगल्या, बोलभांड.

OBSTREPEROUSLY, *adv.* v. A. गलबा-गलबला-&c. करून, गलबल्यानें, &c. [बल *f.* कलकल *f.*

OBSTREPEROUSNESS, *n.* v. A. *and* CLAMOUR. गलबला *m.* गल-

To OBSTRUCT, *v. a. block up.* रोधणें, अवरोधणें, कोंदणें, कोंदून टाकणें, मुंदणें *or* मुंधणें, बंद करणें, बुजवणें, बुझणें, रोध *m.*-अवरोध *m.*-निरोध *m.*-&c. करणें *g. of o.*

2 *impede, oppose, stop,* v. To HINDER. अडवणें, अटकावणें, नडणें, बाधणें, रोधणें, अवरोधणें, गतिरोध *m.*-प्रतिरोध *m.*-प्रतिबंध *m.*-अटकाव *m.*-&c. करणें *g. of o.* [रुद्ध *m.*

OBSTRUCTED, *p.* v. V. 1. रोधलेला, अवरोधलेला, कोंदलेला, &c.

2 अडवलेला, अटकावलेला, &c. रुद्ध, प्रतिबद्ध, कुंठित, अगतिक.

OBSTRUCTER, *n.* OBSTRUCTING, *p. a.* OBSTRUCTIVE, *a.* v. V. 1. रोधणारा, कोंदणारा, बुजवणारा, &c. रोधक, अवरोधक, अवरोध-&c. कर्त्ता.

2 अडवणारा, अटकावणारा, नडणारा, अटकाव करणारा, &c. बाधक, प्रतिबंधक, प्रतिरोधक, प्रतिबाधक, प्रतिबंधकर्त्ता-कारी, प्रतिरोधकर्त्ता-कारी, बद्धक, विघ्नकर-कारी-जनक-&c. हरकती, हरकतखोर.

OBSTRUCTION, *n.* v. V. 1.—*act.* रोधणें *n.* कोंदणें *n.* मुंदणें *n.* &c. रोधणूक *f.* कोंदणी *f.*—*act or state.* रोध *m.* अवरोध *m.* निरोध *m.* विष्टंभ *m.*

2—*act.* अडवणें *n.* अटकावणें *n.* रोधणें *n.* &c.—*state.* अडथळा *m.* अटक *f.* अटकाव *m.* अटकावा *m.* गुंता *or* गुना *m.* खोटी *f.* रुद्धता *f.* प्रतिबद्धता *f.*—*a. or s.* प्रतिरोध *m.* रोध *m.* प्रतिबंध *m.* हरकत *f.* अवरोध *m.*

1. *obstructing or impeding cause,* v. OBSTACLE. अड *m. f.* अटक *f.* अट *f.* नड *f.* नडाव *m.* आडफांटा *m.* आडकाठी *f.* प्रतिबंध *m.* व्यवधान *n.*

To OBTAIN, *v. a. gain, acquire, procure,* v. To GET. मिळवणें, संपादणें, पावणें, जोडणें, प्राप्त होणें *in. con.*

Desire of obtaining. लिप्सा *f.*—Desirous of o. लिप्सु.

To OBTAIN, *v. n. be in use, stand, be established, hold.* चालणें, प्रवर्त्तणें, चालू असणें, प्रवृत्ति *f.*-&c. होणें-असणें-राहणें-पडणें.

OBTAINABLE, *a.* v. V. A. मिळवायाजोगा-जोगता-सारखा, &c. प्राप्य, प्राप्तव्य, लभ्य, उपलभ्य, समासाद्य.

Easily or readily o. सुलभ, सुप्राप्य, सुसाध्य.

OBTAINED, *p.* v. V. A. मिळवलेला, संपादलेला, &c. प्राप्त, संपादित, आप्त, आपन्न, संपन्न, आसादित.

OBTAINER, *n.* OBTAINING, *p. a.* v. V. A. मिळवणारा, पावणारा, &c. संपादक, संपादनकर्त्ता-&c.

OBTAINMENT, *n.* v. V. A.—*act.* मिळवणें *n.* संपादणें *n.* पावणें *n.* &c. संपादणी *f.* संपादणूक *f.* संपादन *n.* आसादन *n.*—*state.* प्राप्ति *f.* संप्राप्ति *f.* आपत्ति *f.* (in comp.) आप्ति *f.* (in comp.).

OBTENEBRATION, *n. darkening, darkenedness.* अंधार *m.* अंधेरी *f.* तिमिर *n.*

To OBTEST, OBTESTATION. See To BEG, &c.

To OBTRUDE, *v. a. thrust in, force upon, urge on against the will.* बळें देणें-घालणें-शिरवणें-पुढें करणें-प्रविष्ट करणें, धसकणें, घुसविणें, बळेंच पदरीं बांधणें-पदरीं घालणें. [लणें.

To o. one's self. पुढच्या पुढें करणें, आपलें घोडें *n.* पुढें ढक-

To OBTRUDE, *v. n. enter, &c. uninvited.* घुसणें, घुसडणें, शिरणें, न बोलावतां येणें-जाणें, दत्त म्हणून येणें-जाणें, अनाहूतागमन *n.* करणें.

OBTRUDED, *p.* v. V. A. बळेंच घातलेला-शिरवलेला-पुढें केलेला-&c.

OBTRUDER, *n.* OBTRUDING, *p. a.* OBTRUSIVE, *a.* v. V. A. बळेंच घालणारा-शिरवणारा-पुढें करणारा-&c.

v. V. N. घुसणारा, न बोलावतां येणारा, &c. घुशा, लुबरा, लुडबुड्या, लचांड, लचाळ, लवाळ.

OBTRUDING, OBTRUSION, *n.* v. V. A.—*act.* बळेंच देणें *n.* बळेंच घालणें *n.* बळेंच पुढें करणें *n.* &c.

v. V. N. घुसणें n. शिरणें n. &c.

I. *officious meddling*, v. OFFICIOUSNESS. लुबलूब f. घुचाकारभार m. लांडाकारभार m.

OBTRUSIVENESS, n. v. A. लुबरेपणा m. लुडबुडेपणा m.

To OBTUND, v. a. *dullen, take off the edge of*, v. To BLUNT. बोथवणें, मुंडवणें, बसवणें, धार f. मोडणें g. of o. नरम करणें.

OBTUSANGULAR, a. विशाल कोणविशिष्ट, बहिर्लंब कोण.

OBTUSE, a. *not acute or pointed.* बोंथा, मुंढा, अनग्र, निरग्र, अतीक्ष्ण, बिन अणीचा, बिनकोंचीचा.

O. angle. विशाल कोण m. बहिर्लंब कोण m.

2 *dull, not sharp*, v. STUPID. ठोंसर बुद्धीचा, जड, मंद, स्थूलबुद्धि, मंदमति, मतिमंद, अतीक्ष्ण.

OBTUSENESS, n. v. A. 1. बोंथेपणा m. मुंडेपणा m. निरग्रता f.

2 जडपणा m. मंदपणा m. टोंसरबुद्धि f. स्थूलबुद्धि f. मंदमति f. जाड्य n.

To OBVIATE, v. a. *prevent, oppose, remove.* निवारणें, वारणें, टाळणें, दूर करणें, चुकवणें, घालवणें, निवारण n.-वारण n.-निवृत्ति f.-&c. करणें g. of o. [निवृत्त.

OBVIATED, p. v. V. निवारलेला, टाळलेला, &c. निवारित, वारित,

OBVIATER, n. OBVIATING, p. a. v.V. निवारणारा, टाळणारा, &c. निवारक, निवारण-&c. कर्त्ता-कारी.

OBVIOUS, a. *open, apparent, conspicuous, &c.* v. PLAIN. उघड, उघडा, स्पष्ट, व्यक्त, सुव्यक्त, जागरूक, प्रत्यक्ष, सुलक्ष्य, सुदर्श, सुज्ञेय.

OBVIOUSLY, adv. v. A. उघड, साफ, स्पष्ट, धडधडीत, निवळ, साक्षात्, प्रत्यक्ष, प्रत्यक्षतः.

OBVIOUSNESS, n. v. V. उघडपणा m. उघडेपणा m. &c. स्पष्टता f. प्रत्यक्षता f. सुलक्ष्यता f. सुज्ञेयता f. &c.

OCCASION, n. *occurrence, happening.* घटणा f. उपस्थान n.

2 *incident, event.* गोष्ट f. वृत्त n.

3 *favorable time, season, or circumstance.* v. OPPORTUNITY. प्रसंग m. समय m. अवसर m. जागा f. m. स्थान n. घात f. द्वार n.

A single o. or time. प्रसंग m. खेप f. समय m. वेळ f. वक्त m.

Upon o. प्रसंगविशेषीं.

Upon the spur of the o. प्रसंगवशात्, प्रसंगवशें.

To come of use upon o. प्रसंगास-समयास-समयीं-&c. उपयोगीं पडणें.

4 *accidental cause.* कारण n. प्रयोजन n. बीज n. हेतु m. निमित्त n. उपाधि m. उपष्टंभ m.

That seeks o. निमित्तखोर.

To seek o. निमित्तास टेंकणें.

To take or make o. निमित्त n. घेणें.

5 *incidental need.* कारण n. काम n. प्रयोजन n. जरूरी f. गरज f. दरकार f. उपयोग m.

To OCCASION, v. a. *cause casually.* प्रयोजन n.- कारण n.- निमित्त n.-&c. होणें in. con. कारणभूत-निमित्तभूत-&c. होणें in. con.

2 *cause, produce, effect.* उत्पन्न करणें, उद्भवणें, उत्पादणें, आणणें, उभारणें, उपस्थापन n.-उपस्थिति f.-&c. करणें g. of o. उपस्थित-प्रयुक्त-&c. करणें.

OCCASIONAL, a. *incidental, casual, that happens at times, not regular.* कधींमधींचा, केव्हांकेव्हांचा, केव्हांकेव्हांचा, कधींकधींचा, आगंतुक, अनित्य, कादाचित्क, विरलागत, अनियतकारणक.

2 *produced by or on some special occasion.* नैमित्तिक, प्रासंगिक, सामयिक, प्रसंगप्राप्त, प्रसंगोत्पन्न, प्रसंगागत, प्रसंगोपस्थित, प्रसंगकारणक.

OCCASIONALLY, adv. v. A. 1. कधींकधीं, कधींमधीं, केव्हांकेव्हां, केव्हांकेव्हां, कधींकाळीं, खंडळमंडळ, टंगळमंगळ.

2 प्रसंगानें, निमित्तानें, &c. प्रसंगानुसार, यथाप्रसंग, प्रसंगवशात्, प्रसंगानुरूप, प्रसंगोपात्त pop. प्रसंगोपात.

OCCASIONED, p. v. V. 2. उत्पन्न केलेला, &c. निमित्तक (in comp. as पापनिमित्तकदंड, &c.), प्रयुक्त (in comp. as पापप्रयुक्तदुःख, उपवास प्रयुक्तज्वर, &c.), प्रयोजित, उत्पादित, उत्पन्न, समुदित.

OCCASIONER, n. OCCASIONING, p. a. v. V. 2. उत्पन्न करणारा, उद्भवणारा, &c. प्रयोजक, उपस्थापक, उपस्थितिकारक.

OCCASIONING, n. v. V. 2.—*act.* उत्पन्न करणें n. उत्पादणें n. &c. उपस्थापन n. उपस्थिती f.

OCCIDENTAL. See WESTERN.

OCCIPITAL, a. *pertaining to the occiput.* मस्तकाच्या पृष्ठभागाचा, शिरःपृष्ठसंबंधी. [n. शिरःपृष्ठभाग m.

OCCIPUT, n. *back part of the head.* मस्तकाचा पृष्ठभाग, शिरःपृष्ठ

Pit or hollow of the o. पोंढो f. फोंडवळी f.

OCCULT, a. *hidden from the eye or understanding.* गुप्त, अविदित, अज्ञात, खोल, गूढ, गूढार्थक, गूढार्थ, अप्रसिद्ध, दुरवबोध.

An o. science or art. चोरविद्या f.

OCCULTATION, n.—in astronomy. समागम m.

OCCULTNESS, n. v. A. गुप्तता f. गूढता f. &c. अप्रसिद्धि f.

OCCUPANCY, OCCUPATION, n. v. V.A. 1.—*act.* धरून ठेवणें n. घेणें n. अटपणें n. &c. पहिली वहिवाट f. प्रथमभोग m.

2 वहिवाटणें n. वापरणें n. &c. वहिवाट f. भोग m. भोगवटा m.

3 घेणें n. व्यापणें n. आक्रमणें n. आक्रमण n. व्यापन n.

4 वापरणें n. राबवणें n. &c.

v. V. N. व्यापार m. अभ्यास m. कसरत f.

I. *employment, avocation, &c.* v. BUSINESS. धंदा m. उद्योग m. काम n. उद्यम m. पेशा m.

OCCUPANT, n. OCCUPIER, n. OCCUPYING, p. a. v. V. A. 1. धरून ठेवणारा, अटपणारा, पहिली वहिवाट करणारा.

2 वहिवाटणारा, वापरणारा, वहिवाट करणारा, भोगणारा, &c. भोगकर्त्ता.

3 घेणारा, व्यापणारा, आक्रमणारा, व्यापक, व्यापन कर्त्ता.

OCCUPIED, p. v. V. A. धरून ठेवलेला, अटपलेला, पहिल्यानें वहिवाटलेला.

2 वहिवाटलेला, वापरलेला.

3 व्यापलेला, आक्रमलेला, &c. आक्रांत, व्याप्त, समाक्रांत.

4 वापरलेला, राबवलेला, &c. व्यापारित.

5 रुद्ध, व्यापृत, प्रवृत्त.

To OCCUPY, v. a. *take possession.* धरून ठेवणें, घेणें, अटपणें, गुंतवणें, आपलासा करणें, आपल्या अमलांत आणणें, पहिली वहिवाट f. करणें g. of o. पहिल्यानें वहिवाटणें-वापरणें, प्रथमभोग m. करणें g. of o.

2 *possess, hold, keep.* वहिवाटणें, वापरणें, धरणें, धरून असणें, धारण n. करणें g. of o. बाळगणें, वहिवाट f.-भोग m.-&c. करणें g. of o.

3 *take up, cover, fill.* व्यापणें, वेढणें, घेणें, अटवणें, खाणें, आक्रमणें, कवळणें, कवटाळणें, गुंडाळणें, आक्रमण n. करणें g. of o.

To be occupied. भरणें.

4 *employ, busy.* वापरणें, वहिवाटणें, खपवणें, राबवणें.

5 (one's self). *be occupied, engaged, &c.* वापरणें, राबणें,

खपणें, वापरणें, रुधणें, रुद्ध-व्यापृत-&c. असणें.

To OCCUPY, *v. n. follow business.* व्यापार *m.*-व्यवहार *m.*-व्यवसाय *m.*-&c. करणें.

To OCCUR, *v. n. appear or arise unto, meet, be found.* आढळणें, मिळणें, सांपडणें, अडकळणें, अटकळणें, दृष्टीस पडणें-येणें, पाहण्यांत येणें.

2 *take place,* v. To HAPPEN. घडणें, होणें, उपस्थित होणें.

3 *suggest itself to the mind or memory.* सुचणें, स्फुरणें, आठवणें, मनांत येणें. [अढळ *m.*

OCCURRENCE, OCCURRING, *n.* v. V. 1.—*act.* आढळणें *n.* &c.

2 घडणें, उपस्थान *n.* उपस्थिति *f.* घटना *f.* नियोग *m.*

3 आठवण *f.* स्मरण *n.* स्फूर्ति *pop.* स्फूर्त *f.* स्फुरण*n.*उपस्थिति *f.*

· I. *incident, event.* गोष्ट *f.* वृत्त *n.* वृत्तांत *m.* बाका *m.* उपस्थितकार्य *m.* उदितकार्य *n.*

OCCURSION, *n. a meeting together, clash, clashing.* एकमेकांची धडक *f.* एकमेकांस लागणें *n.* संघट्टन *n.*

OCEAN, *n. sea, great sea.* समुद्र *m.* सागर *m.* महासागर *m.* अब्धि *m.* अंबुधि *m.* अंभोधि *m.* महार्णव *m.* अर्णव *m.* उदधि *m.* जलधि *m.* महोदधि *m.* अंभोनिधि *m.* सिंधु *m.* रत्नाकर *m.* नदीपति *m.* तीर्थराज *m.* The seven oceans named in the Hindu Purans are those of लवण (salt), इक्षुरस (sugar cane juice), सुरा (spirit), घृत (clarified butter), क्षीर (milk), दधि (curds and whey), शुद्धोदक (pure water). At the churning of the ocean (समुद्रमंथन) celebrated in the Purans, fourteen precious things (चौदा *or* चतुर्दशरत्न) are said to have been obtained. They are लक्ष्मी, कौस्तुभ, पारिजात, सुरा, धन्वंतरि, चंद्र, कामधेनु, ऐरावत, अप्सरा, उच्चैःश्रवा, विष, इंद्रधनुष्य, शंख, अमृत.

Bounded by the o. समुद्रवलयांकित.

Mountain used in churning the o. मंदर *or* मंदराचल*m.*

Poison produced on churning the o. हलाहल *m. n. or* हालाहल *n.*

OCEAN, OCEANIC, *a. belonging, &c. to the ocean.* समुद्राचा, महासागराचा, &c. महासागरसंबंधी.

OCHER, OCHRE, *n.*—red. काव *f.* (it is of two sorts लोखंडीकाव & सोनकाव), गेरू *f.* हुरमूज *f.*

That is of the colour of red o. भगवा, कषाय.

2—yellow. पिवळीमाती *f.* हळदिवी माती *f.*

OCHREOUS, *a.* v. N. कावेचा, कावेसारखा, भगवा, हुरमुजी.

OCTAGON, *n. figure of eight angles.* अष्टकोणाकृति *f.* अष्टकोण *m.* अष्टास्र *n.* [अष्टास्र, अष्टास्रय.

OCTAGONAL, OCTANGULAR, *a.* v. N. अष्टकोण, *pop.* अष्टकोनी,

OCTAVO, *a. of which a sheet is folded into eight leaves.* आठवरखांचा, आठवरखी, आठबंदी, अष्टपत्री.

OCTENNIAL, *a. happening every eighth year.* आठव्या आठव्या वर्षानें येणारा-घडणारा-&c. प्रत्यष्टाब्दिक. [स्थायी.

2 *lasting eight years.* आठवर्षांचा, अष्टवर्षस्थायी, वर्षाष्टक-

OCTOBER, *n.* इंग्रजी सालाचा दहावा महिना *m.* आश्विन-कार्त्तिक*m.*

OCTOGENARIAN, OCTOGENARY, *a. that is eighty years old.* ऐशींवर्षांचा, अशीतिवयस्क, अशीतिक.

OCTOPETALOUS, *a.* अष्टदल.

OCTOLATERAL, *a. having eight sides.* अष्टपैलू.

OCTUPLE, *a. eight fold.* आठपट, अष्टगुण,

OCULAR, *a. depending on the eye, &c.* डोळ्यांचा, दृष्टीचा, चक्षुनें झालेला, प्रत्यक्ष, चाक्षुष, चक्षुस्संबंधी.

O. deception. नजरभूल *f.*

O. proof. प्रत्यक्षप्रमाण *n.* चक्षुःप्रमाण *n.* दृक् प्रत्यय*m.*

OCULIST, *n. one who treats diseases of the eye.* डोळ्यांचा वैद्य *m.* नेत्रवैद्य *m.* चक्षुर्वैद्य *m.* [अयुग.

ODD, *a. not even.* विषम संख्येचा, विषम, विखम, असम, अयुग्म,

O. and even—the game. एकीबेकी *f.* नकी दुवा *m.*

2 *more than, or remaining over a specified number.* धरलेलेरकमेबाहेरचा, भररकमेबाहेरचा, बेरजेबाहेरचा, विवक्षितसंख्यातिरिक्त.

3 *singular, extraordinary,* v. STRANGE. विलक्षण, अपरूप, तऱ्हेचा, तऱ्हेदार, तऱ्हेवाईक, एकाड, एकप्रकार, तमाशाचा.

4 *not under the common head or account.* फुटकळ, फुटका, अडपझडप, किरकोळ, राहिलासाहिला, उरलासुरला, पडलाझडला.

5 *broken, not complete or entire.* फुटकर, फुटकळ, तुटका, लंगडा, व्यंग.

6 *loose, of an incomplete set, &c.* फुटकळ, तुटक, सुटा, स्फुट.

7 *that does not suit.* विजोड, विलग.

ODDITY, *n.* See ODDNESS. 2 *odd person.* एकप्रकार *m.* एकप्रकरण *n.* एकचिन्ह *n.* एकविलक्षण, एकविचित्र, एकतऱ्हेचा, कौतुक *n.* तमाशाचा. [नवल अद्भुत *n.*

3 *odd thing or matter.* नवल *n.* विलक्षण गोष्ट *f.* कौतुक *n.*

ODDLY, *adv.* v. A. 1. विषमरूपानें, वैषम्यपूर्वक.

3 विलक्षण, विचित्र, नवल वाटायासारखा *decl.* कौतुक वाटायासारखा *decl.* परवडीनें.

ODDNESS, *n.* v. A. 1. विषमता *f.* असमता *f.* वैषम्य*n.* विषमभाव*n.*

3 अपरूपपणा *m.* विलक्षणपणा *m.* वैलक्षण्य *n.* विलक्षणभाव *m.*

ODDS, *n. inequality,* v. DIFFERENCE. न्यूनाधिक *n.* न्यूनाधिकभाव *m.* विषमता *f.*

2 *advantage,* v. SUPERIORITY. वर्चस *n.* वर्चस्व *n.* उपराळा *m.*

3 odds and ends, *miscellaneous articles, sundries.* ऐलपैलवस्तू *f. pl.* अगडतगड *n.* अगडबगड *n.* सटरफटर *n.* फाटकळफुटकळ *f.* बलायबत्तर *n.*

To be at odds, *be at variance.* वांकडें *n.*-वैमनस्य *n.*-&c. असणें *g. of s. recip.*

ODE, *n.* v. POEM, SONG. गजल *m.* गेयकवन *n.*

ODIOUS, *a.* v. HATEFUL. द्वेषी, द्वेष्य, द्वेषयोग्य, द्वेषार्ह, द्वेषपात्र.

2 *causing hate,* v. INVIDIOUS.द्वेषकारक,द्वेषोत्पादक, द्वेषजनक.

ODIOUSNESS, *n.* v. A. द्वेषीपणा *m.* द्वेष्यता *f.* द्वेषार्हता *f.*

2 द्वेषकारकत्व *n.* द्वेषोत्पादकत्व *n.* &c.

ODIUM, *n.* v. HATRED. द्वेष *m.* [पात्रता *f.*

2 *invidiousness.* दोष *m.* ठपका *m.* द्वेषीपणा *m.* द्वेष्यता *f.* द्वेष-

To cast the o. of upon. डोईवर हंडी *f.*-खापर *n.* फोडणें.

To incur o. वाईटपणा *m.* आणणें, वाईटपणा *m.* येणें.

ODONTALGIC, *a.* v. N. दांतसुळाचा, दंतशूलाचा, दंतशूलसंबंधीविषयक.

ODONTALGY, *n. tooth-ache.* दंतशूल *pop.* दांतसूळ *m.*

ODORIFEROUS, ODOROUS, *a.* v. FRAGRANT. सुवासिक, सुगंधिक, सगंध, गंधवान्, गंधगुण.

ODORIFEROUSNESS, ODOROUSNESS, *n.* v. A. सुवासिकपणा *m.* सौगंध्य *n.* सौरभ्य *n.* सगंधता *f.*

ODORLESS, *a. scentless.* निर्गंध, अगंध, गंध रहित-&c.

ODOUR, *n. scent*,—gener. v. SMELL. वास *m.* गंध *m.*

Bad o. fig. *disfavour.* बदबोई *f.*

2 *sweet scent*, v. FRAGRANCE. सुवास *m.* सुगंध *m.* खुशबोई *f.*

ŒCUMENICAL, *a.* v. GENERAL. सर्वसाधारण, सर्वसंबंधी.

ŒSOPHAGUS, *n.* घसा *m.* अन्नमार्ग *m.* अन्नवाहिस्रोत *n.*

OF, *prep.* चा-ची-चें.

2—noting subjection to, connection with, &c. चा-ची-चें, कडे, संबंधीं, विषयीं, पैकीं. For the other senses of *of*, See FROM, BY, AMONG, &c.

Of him-her-it-one's &c. self. आपलेआपण, आपल्याआपण, आपोआप.

OFF, *adv. from*—noting distance. लांब, दूर.

2 *from*—with the action of separating, &c. This sense is given by the combination of two verbs, as कापून टाकणें to cut off, काढून घेणें to take off, फाडून घेणें-टाकणें to tear off, &c. &c.

3 *from*—noting departure. This sense is involved in the word जाणें, or is rendered by the combination of निघणें with जाणें *or* येणें, as तो निघून गेला he went off, हें निघून आलें आहे this has come off.

4 *from, not toward.* बाहेर, सोडून, बगळून.

Badly off; Ill off; *in bad circumstances.* अनुपपन्न, अनुपन्न.

Well off; *in good circumstances.* सुखी,घरचा सुखी,संपन्न.

Off and on. धरून सोडून, धरसोडीनें.

Off-hand, *smack, direct.* सरधोपट.

Off-hand person. रपाट्या, झपाट्या, रगड्या.

To be off, *recede from an engagement &c.* मागें होणें-सरणें-फिरणें, पाय *m.*-आंग *n.*-हात *m.* काढणें, बदलामीवर येणें.

To come off, To get off, *escape*, or *fare in the event.* निभणें, निभावणें, निभाव *m.*-निभावणी *f.*-&c. होणें *g. of s.* सुटणें.

To get off, *alight.* उतरणें.

To go off, *be discharged*,—guns, &c. उडणें, बार *m.* होणें *g. of s.*

OFF, *prep. not on.* निराळा *decl.* वेगळा *decl.* बाहेर, सोडून.

Off the ground. भुईसांड.

Off the road. एकोशास, एकोशीं, एकोस, एकीकडे.

2 *from.* वरून.

OFF, *interj.* चल, जा, निघ, दूर हो, धीस.

OFF, *a. distant, belonging to the off side.* पलीकडचा *or* ला, बाहेरचा.

OFFAL, *n. waste meat.* टाकाऊ मास *n.* अनुपयोगी मांस *n.* घेण्याजोगें नाहीं असें मास *n.*

2—gener. v. REFUSE. गाबाळ *m.n.*गाळ *m.*गाळसाळ *f.* वगळ*f.*

OFFENCE, *n. misdeed, transgression*, v. CRIME. अपराध *m.* अन्याय *m.* गुन्हा *m.* पातक *n.*

2 *displeasure conceived, huff, anger.* चीढ *f. v.* ये, चिरड *f. v.* ये, रुसवा *m.* रुसावा *m.* खोंच *f.* खीज *f.* रीस *f.* इतराजी *f.* करडी मर्जी *f.* खपीमर्जी *f.* करडीकमान *f.* गैरमर्जी *f.* गैरखुशी *f.* असंतोष *m.* अवरुपा *f.*

Easy of o. रुसका.

To take o. रुसणें, चिरडणें, चिडणें, खिजणें, मनांत सर्द होणें, चीढ *f.*-&c. येणें *in. con.*

3 *assailing*, v. ATTACK. चढ *m.* चढाई *f.* घाला *m.*

OFFENCELESS. See INNOCENT.

To OFFEND, *v. a. displease, anger, huff, &c.* रुसवणें, राग *m.*-&c. आगणें, मर्जी *f.* मोडणें-तोडणें-खपा करणें-करडी करणें-&c. *g. of o.* खपा-नाखूश-रंजीस-रुष्ट-&c. करणें, खोंचणें, रागवणें, कोपवणें, राग येईसा करणें.

2 *disgust, shock, nauseate, displease, annoy.* चिळस *m.*-कंटाळा *m.*-खंत *f.*-त्रास *m.*-&c. आणणें, कंटाळा *m.*-त्रास *m.*-&c. येणें-वाटणें *in. con. with g. of s.* वाईट वाटणें *in. con.* त्रासवणें, त्रास *m.* देणें, कंटाळवणें.

3 *break, violate, transgress.* मोडणें, तोडणें, उलंघणें, अतिक्रमणें, भंग *m.*-उल्लंघन *n.*-&c. करणें *g. of o.*

4 *cause to sin, &c.* पापांत पाडणें-पाडूं पाहणें.

To OFFEND, *v. n. transgress, be criminal.* वाईट *n.*-अपराध *m.*-अन्याय *m.*-गुन्हा *m.*-गैरवर्त्तणूक *f.*-&c. करणें, अपराधी-गुन्हेगार-अन्यायी-&c. होणें.

2 against; v. To TRANSGRESS. उलंघणें, उलंघ *m.* उलंघन *n.*-[&c. करणें *g. of o.*

OFFENDED, *p.* v. V. A. 1. रुसवलेला, &c. रंजीस, खपा, नाखूश, गैरखूश, गैरराजी, खट्टा, खट्टू, खट्टी, रुष्ट, चुरस, असंतुष्ट.

To be o. रुसणें, रागें भरणें, राग *m.*-चीढ *f.*-&c. येणें *in. con.* खिजणें, चिरडणें.

2 त्रासवलेला, कंटाळवलेला, &c. त्रस्त, त्रासित, असंतुष्ट.

OFFENDER, *n.* OFFENDING, *p. a.* v. V. N. 1. *and* CRIMINAL. अपराधी, अन्यायी, गुन्हेगार, अपराध कर्त्ता-कारी, अन्याय कर्त्ता-कारी.

OFFENSE. See OFFENCE.

OFFENSIVE, *a.* v. V. A. 1. *displeasing.* राग आणणारा, राग आणण्याचा, कोपवायाचा, &c. चिरडीचा, चिडवणीचा, खोंचणीचा, वाईट, क्रोधजनक, क्रोधोत्पादक.

2 कंटाळा आणण्याचा, त्रासवायाचा, &c. वाईट, नापसंत, नावड, अप्रिय, कंटाळवाणा, त्रासदायक-कारक, त्रासक.

I.—opposed to defensive,—war, &c. चढाईचा, चढावाचा, आगळिकीचा, अन्याक्रमक, पराक्रमक.

II.—weapon. मारक, मारू, परघातोपयोगी, परघाताई.

OFFENSIVELY, *adv.* v. A. 1. राग आणायाजोगा *decl.* राग यायाजोगा *decl.*

I. चढाईच्या वाटेनें, चढाव करून, अन्याक्रमणपूर्वक.

OFFENSIVENESS, *n.* v. A. 1. क्रोधजनकत्व*n.* क्रोधोत्पादकत्व*n.*

2 कंटाळवाणेपणा*m.* नावडपणा*m.* वाईटपणा*m.* त्रासदायकत्व *n.* त्रासकारकत्व*n.*

To OFFER, *v. a. present for acceptance.* देण्यास-द्यायाला काढणें-पुढें करणें-पुढें ठेवणें, देऊं इच्छिणें, देऊं लागणें, देण्यास प्रवृत्त होणें, द्या म्हणणें, सादर-हाजीर करणें, अर्पणें, समर्पणें, निवेदणें, अर्पण *n.*-&c. करणें *g. of o.*

2 *present as an act of worship.* देणें, वाहणें, अर्पणें, समर्पणें, निवेदणें, बलि *pop.* बळी *m.*-बळ *f.* देणें *g. of o.* अर्पण *n.*-निवेदन *n.*-उत्सर्ग *m.*-&c. करणें *g. of o.* बलिदान*n.* करणें *g. of o.*

3 (with fire). होमणें, होम*m.*-हवन *n.*-&c.करणें *g. of o.* हुत करणें.

4 *propose, exhibit, put forth.* पुढें करणें-ठेवणें, दाखवणें, सांगणें, बोलण्यांत आणणें.

5 (a price, &c.) *bid.* बोलणें, सांगणें, बोलणें*n.*-&c. करणें-लावणें *g. of o.* देऊं म्हणणें, घे म्हणणें.

6 (a reward, &c.) *agree to give.* देऊं करणें, देण्याचा करणें.

To o. violence. बळात्कार*m.*-&c. करणें.

To OFFER, *v. n. present itself, appear, arise, occur.* येणें, पुढें

होणें, दिसणें, सांपडणें, प्रसंग*m.*-उपस्थिति *f.*-उदय *m.*-&c. होणें *g. of s.* प्राप्त-उपस्थित-उदित-&c. होणें.

2 *declare willingness, or readiness.* पुढें होणें, तयार-सिद्ध-उद्युक्त-&c. होणें, सरसावणें, बोलणें-म्हणणें-सांगणें *with the present or future tense of another verb* (as he offered to go मी जाईन म्हणून बोलला, you offered to write आम्ही लिहितों म्हणून तुम्हीं म्हटलें, &c.). [करणें.

3 *make an attempt*, v. To ATTEMPT. उद्योग*m.*-प्रयत्न*m.*-&c.

OFFER, OFFERING, *n.* v. V. A. 1.—*act.* पुढें करणें*n.* पुढें ठेवणें*n.* &c. अर्पण*n.* समर्पण*n.* निवेदन*n.* [*n.*उत्सर्ग*m.*

2—*act.* देणें*n.* वाहणें*n.* &c. अर्पण*n.* समर्पण*n.* निवेदन*n.* बलिदान

3—*act.* होमणें*n.* हवन*n.*

5 बोलणें*n.* सांगणें*n.* म्हणणें*n.*

I. *price, &c. offered.* म्हटलेलें मोल*n.* म्हटलेली किम्मत *f.* &c.

II. *sacrifice, oblation.* बलि *pop.* बळी*m.* बळ *f.* बलिदान*n.* पूजा *f.* देवोपायन*n.* देवोपहार*m.*

Burnt o. होम*m.* आहुति *f.* हुत*n.* अवदान*n.* हव्य*n.*

Article fit for use as a burnt o. हव्य*n.* हवि*n.* हविष्य*n.* हविष्यान्न*n.* होमद्रव्य*n.* हविर्द्रव्य*n.* [*m. n.*

Grand and extraordinary o. महाबलि *or* ळी*m.* महानैवेद्य

O. of some eatable. नैवेद्य*m. n.* बोनें*n.* उपार*m.*

O. to all the deities. वैश्वदेव*m. n.* वैश्वदेवकर्म*n.*

O. of water, or (of rice, flowers, &c.) with water. अर्घ्य*n.*

O. dressed for the deities. हव्यपाक*m.*

Offerings (to the deities and to the manes)-compreh or gener. हव्यकव्य*n.* चरु*m.*

O. at the shrine of some Muhammadan saint. उरूस*m.*

To be presented in o. चढणें.

OFFERED, *p.* v. V. A. 1. देण्यास काढलेला, पुढें केलेला, &c. समर्पित, अर्पित, निवेदित.

2 वाहिलेला, &c. अर्पित, समर्पित, निवेदित.

3 होमलेला, हुत.

5 बोललेला, म्हटलेला, &c.

6 देऊं केलेला, &c.

OFFERER, *n.* OFFERING, *p. a.* v. V. A. 1. देण्यास काढणारा, पुढें करणारा, &c. अर्पक, समर्पक, निवेदक.

2 वाहणारा, अर्पणारा, बळी देणारा, &c. अर्पक, समर्पक, निवेदक, अर्पण-&c. कर्त्ता-कारी. [म्या, हवन्या.

3 होम करणारा, होता, हवनकर्त्ता,—contemptuously, &c. हो-

OFFICE, *n. post, charge, duty, trust, &c.* अधिकार *m.* ओहदा *or* हुद्दा *m.* असामी *f.* पदवी *f.* पद *n.* अमल *m.* अमलदारी *f.*

Public o. सरकारी असामी *f.* दिवाण असामी *f.*

Hereditary public o. वतन *n.* दरक *m.* स्थिराधिकार *m.* (as *distinguished from* personal or temporary o. चलाधिकार *m.*).

Ejection from o. उठकळ *f. v.* ये, उठकट *f.*

Fixing, &c. in o. बहाली *f.* [पदभ्रष्ट.

Fallen, &c. from o. अधिकारच्युत, अधिकारभ्रष्ट, पदच्युत,

Invested with o. अधिकार प्राप्त, प्राप्ताधिकार, अधिकारापन्न, अधिकृत, अधिकारस्थ.

Lucrative post or o. ताजारोजगार *m.* ताजीरोटी *f.* तरतारोजगार *m.* ओलारोजगार *m.*

Resignation of o. अधिकारोत्सर्ग *m.* अधिकारत्याग *m.*—Paper containing resignation. राजीनामा*m.* [पदारूढ.

That is in o. अधिकारस्थ, अधिकारारूढ, अधिकारस्थित,

2 *function, use, peculiar business.* काम *n.* अधिकार *m.* कर्म *n.* ओहदा *or* हुद्दा *m.* विषय *m.* अरुता *f.* मान *m.*

3 *act of kindness.* उपकार *m.* उपकृति *f.* उपक्रिया *f.* आभार *m.* कृतोपकार *m.*

4 *ill office.* अपकार *m.* अपकृति *f.* अपक्रिया *f.*

5 v. FORMULARY. पद्धति *f.*

6 *room, &c. for business.* कचेरी *f.* दफ्तरखाना *m.* उद्योगागार *n.* हापीस *n.* from the English.

7 See OUTHOUSE.

OFFICE-BEARER, *n.* v. OFFICER. अधिकारी, कामदार, जिम्मेदार, दिम्मतदार, अमलदार, अमली असामी.

OFFICER, *n. person appointed or authorized to discharge an office.* अधिकारी, हुद्देदार, कामगार, कामदार, अमलदार, अमली असामी, जिम्मेदार, दिम्मतदार;—of the Govt. सरकारकामदार, राजभृत्य;—esp. hereditary दरकदार, दरकी असामी, वतनदार. —Some of the *Officers* of the Native Governments are, कमावीसदार, कोठनीस, कोठीवाला, खजीनदार, खासगीवाला, चिटनीस, जमनीस, जमीननीस, जामदार, टीपनीस, टीपकर, ठाणेदार, तगाददार, तगादगीर, तजकरनीस, तपासनीस, तरजुमान, तरफदार, तलाठी, दफ्तरदार, दफ्तरनीस, दबीर, देशकुलकरणी, देशपांड्या, देशमुख, देसाई, पोतदार, पोतनीस, फडनीस, फारसनीस, बारनीस, महालकरी, मजमूदार *or* मजूमदार, मामलतदार, मुद्राधारी, वाकनीस, शिक्केनीस, शिक्केबरदार, शेखदार, सबनीस, सभासद, सरकमावीसदार, सरकानूनगो, सरदेशमुख, सरदेशपांड्या, सरसुभेदार, सुरनीस, हवालदार, हशमनवीस *or* नीस, हशमफड, नवीस, हाजीरनवीस. For explanation the reader may consult the M. and E. Dictionary.

A petty o. नायकवडी.

Change of public officers. हालीमाजी *f.* नवेंजुनें *n.*

Tax upon public officers. दरकपट्टी *f.*

OFFICIAL, *a. pertaining to an office or trust.* अधिकाराचा, असामीचा, हुद्द्याचा, &c. अधिकाराविषयींचा, आधिकारिक, अधिकारसंबंधी-विषयक, पदसंबंधी.

2 *made or communicated by virtue of authority.* सरकारी, सरकारीनात्याचा, अधिकारसंबंधाचा, अधिकाराचे नात्याचा, अधिकाऱ्याकडचा, कलमी, अधिकारप्रयुक्त.

OFFICIAL, *n. subordinate officer.* खालचा अधिकारी-कामगार-&c.

OFFICIALLY, *adv.* v.A. 2. सरकारीनात्यानें, अधिकाराच्या नात्यानें, अधिकारसंबंधानें, अधिकारपरत्वें, अधिकाराच्या योगानें.

To OFFICIATE, *v. n. discharge an office.* काम *n.*-अधिकार *m.*-असामी *f.*-&c. चालवणें-करणें-वहिवाटणें-पाहणें-&c.

2 *perform the official duties of another.* बदलीचें काम *n.*-बदलीची असामी *f.*-&c. करणें-चालवणें, वारचा *decl.*-वांटचा *decl.* काम *n.*-&c. करणें-चालवणें-&c. [रा-&c.

OFFICIATER, *n.* OFFICIATING, *p. a.* v. V. 1. काम-&c. करणा-

2 वारचा-वांटचा करणारा-चालवणारा, &c. [नांतला.

OFFICINAL, *a. used in or belonging to a shop.* दुकानचा, दुका-

OFFICIOUS, *a. obliging,* v. KIND. उपकारी, उपकारकर्त्ता, मेहरबान.

2 *busy, forward, meddlesome.* लुडबुड्या, लुबरा, लडबड्या, नाचरा, पुढच्या पुढें नाचणारा, चोंबडा, लांडाकारभारी, बुचाकार-

भारी, नस्ताकारभारी, अनधिकारचर्चक.

To be o. लुडबुडणें, पुढच्यापुढें करणें-नाचणें.

OFFICIOUSLY. *adv.* v. A. 2. लुडबुडपणानें, लुडबुड करून, &c.

OFFICIOUSNESS, *n.* v. A. 2. लुडबुडपणा *m.* लुबरेपणा *m.* &c. लडबड *or* लुडबुड *f.* लुबलूब *f.* लांडाकारभार *m.* बुचाकारभार *m.* नस्ताकारभार *m.* चोंबडकी *f.* चोंबडेचाळे *m. pl.* अनधिकारचर्चा *f.*

OFFSCOURING, *n. scrapings, &c. of dishes.* निपटी शिपटी *f.* खरवड *f.*

2 fig. *that which is vile and despised.* खरवड *f.* निपटारा *m.* गाढवाचा सदका, शाहण्याचा सदका, ओवाळून टाकलेला, जगामुलखानें सोडलेला, लोकांत ओवाळलेला, गांवादेशानें ओवाळलेला, गांवची सखूज *f.*-खट *f.*

OFFSET, *n. shoot,* v. SPROUT. मोड *m.* कोम *m.* अंकुर *m.*

OFFSPRING, *n. child or children.* संतान *n.* संतति *pop.* संतत *f.* वंश *m.* अपत्य *n.* बीज *n.* बिजवट *n.* बिल्हय *f.* फल *or* फळ *n.* प्रजा *f.* प्रजोत्पत्ति *f.* प्रसव *m.* प्रसूति *f.* सूति *f.* वेल *m.* वेलविस्तार *m.* तंतु *m.* अवलाद *f.* पोटचा गोळा *m.*

Female o. कन्यासंतान *n.* कन्यासंतति *f.* स्त्रीसंतान *n.* स्त्रीसंतति *f.* स्त्र्यपत्य *n.* धर्मसंतति *f.* धर्मसंतान *n.* allusively, covertly, &c. जायजणी *f.* जायाची *f.* जाती वस्त *f.* परधन *n.*

Male o. पुत्रसंतान *n.* पुत्रसंतति *f.* पुंसंतान *n.* पुंसंतति *f.* पुमपत्य *n.* पुत्र पौत्रादिवंश *m.*

Tender o. बालापत्य *n.*

That has o. लेंकुरवाला *commonly* लेंकुरवाळा, पोरवाला, कबेचबेवाला, संततिमान्, प्रजावान्, सप्रज, ससंतान, सापत्य.

That has male o. पुती (in comp. as, एकपुती, दुपुती, सातपुती, &c.).

That has no male o. निपुत्र, निपुत्री, निपुत्रीक.

Woman without offspring. सडीसाड *f.* सडीसांट *f.* सडीवागको *f.* [अवा उतरला.

All her offspring have lived, reached puberty. तिचा

OFT, OFTEN, OFTEN-TIMES, OFT-TIMES, *adv.* बहुतवेळ, अनेकवेळ, बहुवेळां, अनेकवेळां, बहुदां, बहुवार, अनेकवार, अनेकदां, वारंवार, वेळोवेळां, फारदां, बहुसाल.

How often ? कितीदां ? किती वेळ ?

To OGLE, *v. n. view with side glances.* डोळे *m. pl.* मोडणें-मोडून पाहणें, काण्या डोळ्यानें-कटाक्षानें-कटाक्ष दृष्टीनें-&c. पाहणें, डोळ्यानें मारणें, कटाक्षावेक्षण *n.*-अपांगदर्शन *n.*-अपांगवीक्षण *n.*-&c. करणें.

OGLE, OGLING, *n.* v. V.—*act.* डोळे मोडणें *n.* &c. कटाक्ष *m.* कटाक्षावेक्षण *n.* अपांगवीक्षण *n.* कटाक्षदर्शन *n.* अपांगदर्शन *n.* नेत्रपल्लवी *f.*

OGLIO, *n.* v. MEDLEY. गोतांबील *f.* खिचडी *f.*

OGRE, *n.* राक्षस *m.* उग्रव्यक्ति *f.*

OH, *interj.* v. INTERJECTION. आ, आये.

Oh ! Oh !(of pain). हुंहुं, उस, ओय.

Oh dear ! फेंफें, फें.

OIL, *n.* तेल *n.* तैल *n.* स्नेह *m.*

Dregs of o. बेरी *f.* [कट तेल *n.*

Dreggy or feculent o. बेरकट *or* बेरकूट *n.* बेरट *n.* बेर-

Essential o. or extract of o. अर्क *m.* अत्तर *n.* एल *n.* (in comp. as. फुलेल *n.* तिळेल *n.*-&c.).

Stink of o. तेलसाण *f.* तेलटाण *f.* तेलष्टाण *f.* तेलकटाण *f.*

Sweet o. चोखतेल *n.* [&c. बेरकटणें.

To be fouled from the dregs of o.—a lamp, vessel,

To be smeared or wetted with o. तेलकटणें.

To rub with medicated o. चोपडणें, चोपड *m. f.* करणें, चोपडा *m.* देणें-लावणें.

To OIL, *v. a.* तेल *n.* लावणें-देणें-माखणें, तेलावणें, चोपडणें, चुळबुळावणें, चोंबळणें.

To be oiled. तेलकटणें, चुळचुळणें.

OIL-CAKE, *n.* पेंड *f.* पेंडराणें *n.* खली *f.*

OIL-CLOTH, *n.* तेलकापड *n.*

OIL-MAN, *n.* तेली, तैलकार, स्नेहकार ;— in contempt, तेल्गंड.

Monday o. सोमवान्या तेली.

Saturday o. शनवान्या तेली.

Wife of o. तेलीण *f.*

OIL-MILL, *n.* तेलघाणा *m.* घाणा *m.*

Roller of an o. लाट *f.*

Site of an o. घाणवट *f.*

Wipings of an o. खोबीपोतेरें *n.*

OIL-NUT-TREE, *n. callophyllum Inophyllum.* उंडी *f.* उंडीण *f.* उंडिणी *f.*—the fruit. उंडें *n.*

OILED, *p.* v. V. तेल लावलेला, तेलावलेला, &c. तेलकट *or* तेलगट, मेणकट, चुळचुळीत. [तेलघडी *f.*

O. folds (of cotton, cloth, &c.) applied to a sore.

OILINESS, *n.* v.A. 1. तैलप्राचुर्य *n.* [*m.* तैलांश *m.*

2 तेलटपणा *m.* तेलवटपणा *m.* चिकणाई *f.* स्नेह *m.* स्नैग्ध्य *n.* स्नेहांश

3 तेलकटपणा *m.* तेलकटी *f.* बुळबुळितपणा *m.* चुळचुळितपणा *m.* ओशट *n.* बुळबूळ *f. intens.* बुळबुळाट *m.*

OILY, *a. consisting of oil.* तेलाचा, तैलमय, तैलप्रचुर.

O. or unctuous substances. मवागी *f.* मोवारी *f.* चोपड *f. n.*

2 *containing oil.* तेलट, तेलकट *or* तेलगट, तेलस, तेलसर, तेलवट, चिकण, चिकणवट.

Rather o. तेलसर, तेलस, स्नेहाळ, स्निग्ध, सतैल.

3 *oiled, greasy, &c.* तेलकट *or* तेलगट, तेलावलेला, बुळबुळीत, चुळचुळीत, ओशट, सतैल, तैलयुक्त, तैलाक्त.

4—a smell. मेणकट, तेलकट.

OINTMENT, *n. unguent.* माखण *n.* विलेपन *n.* लेपन *n.*

O. of fragrant ingredients. उटणें *n.*

2 *salve.* मलम *m. n.*

OLD. *a. aged, advanced in life.* म्हातारा, वयाचा, उतारवयाचा, उत्तरवयाचा, उतरत्यावयाचा, उतरतेपराईचा, वृद्ध, उत्तरवयस्क, वयस्क, वयातीत, वयोवृद्ध, वयःस्थ *or* वयस्थ, गतायु, गतवयस्क, वयोगत, उतार.

O. and heavy, *veternosus.* आळसभोंडारा.

O. person. पिकलें पान (a sear leaf), हातापायांचा चौरंग झालेला, गोळंकारी, नम्रमूर्ति;—in contempt, भोंडार, म्हातारडा, म्हातारखड *n.* म्हातारडूक *n.* Some terms for *an old, hale, tough, enduring fellow,* are, जुनाखोड, वृद्धकाक, काळाचा कांकडा, जुनापापी.

Too or very o. अतिवयस्क, वर्षीयान्.

Very o. and wasted. थेरडा, थेर, डोकरा, लुळाखुडा *or* लुडाखुडा, भोंडा, खटारा *or* खट्यारा, खांकर *or* खोंकर, खगार, खब्बू, खप्पड, खल्लड, जखखम्हातारा *or* जखख, भालूसारखा झालेला, जरठ *pop.* जरंड.

To grow or be getting o. and infirm. गुडघm. *pl.* टेंकूं लागणें *g. of s.* गुडघ्यावर हातm. *pl.* टेंकूं लागणें *or, with g. of s.* येऊं लागणें, पडणीस येणें, काळ्यांचे पांढरे होणें *g. of s.* मेटेंn. *pl.* बसणें *g. of s.* हातm. *pl.* टेंकणें.

2 *having been long used, decayed by time.* जुना, जुनाट, पुराणा, जीर्ण;—compreh. or indef. जुनापुराणा, जुनापाना.

Oldish, *rather old and worn.* आडजुना, जुनवट, जुनापाना.

To become o. जुनावणें.

3 *of long standing.* बहुत काळी, बहुत दिवसी, बहुत काळाचा, बहुत दिवसांचा, फार दिवसांचा, फारदिसी, जुना, जुनाट, पुराणा, पुराण, पुरातन, बहुकालिक, चिरकालिक, चिरकाळी, चिरस्थायी, चिरंतन, कदीम, कधींचा, कदाकाळांचा.

4 *not modern,* v. Ancient. जुना, जुनाट, पुराणा, प्राचीन, पूर्वकालीन, पूर्वकालिक.

5 *that has been long made ; not new or fresh.* जुना, जुन्याकाळचा, मागल्या काळचा, फार दिवस करून ठेवलेला.

6 *of a certain duration.* This sense is usually expressed by the sign of the possessive चा, as how old is he ? तो किती वर्षांचा आहे ? A year old एक वर्षाचा, &c.

7 See Former.

Of o. See Formerly.

Old age, *n.* v. Age. वृद्धावस्था *f.* वृद्धापकाळ *m.* [तो.

Old bachelor, *n.* उतारवयाचा असून ज्याचा विवाह झाला नाहीं

Old clothes, *n.* जुनेरीं *n. pl.* जुनेरें *n. pl.*

Old-fashioned, *a.* जुने चालीचा, जुने रीतीचा-ढबीचा.

Old maid, *n.* उतारवयाची असून जिचाविवाह झाला नाहीं ती.

Olden. See Old. [वृद्धत्व *n.*

Oldness, *n.* v. A. 1. *and* Age. म्हातारपण *n.* म्हातारपणा *m.*

2 जुनेपणा *m.* पुराणेपणा *m.* जीर्णत्व *n.*

3 जुनेपणा *m.* &c. बहुकालिकत्व *n.* &c.

Oleaginous, &c. See Oily, &c.

Oleander, *n.*—nerium odorum. कण्हेर *m. f.*

Oleiferous, *a.* तैलोत्पादक.

Oleraceous, *a. pertaining to pot-herbs.* शाकभाजीचा, भाजीपाल्याचा, शाकसंबंधी-विषयक.

Olfactory, *a. pertaining to the sense of smelling.* घ्राणेंद्रियाचा, घाणेंद्रियविषयक-संबंधी.

Olibanum, *n.*—the perfume. कवड्याऊद *m.* बेरोजा *m.* लोभान *m.* लोभानीऊद *m.*

Oligarchal, Oligarchical, *a.* v. N. अल्पजनाधिपत्यसंबंधी-विषयक, &c. अल्पजनस्वामिक.

Oligarchy, *n. government by a few.* अल्पजनाधिपत्य *n.* अल्पजनप्रभुत्व *n.* कतिपयाधिपत्य *n.* अल्पलोक सत्ताकराज्य प्रकार*m.*

Olio, Olla, *n.* v. Medley. गोतांबील *f.* खिचडी *f.*

Olitory, *a. belonging to pot herbs.* शाकभाजीचा, भाजीपाल्याचा, शाकसंबंधी.

Olive, *n.* एक झाड आहे. [सूचकचिन्ह *n.*

Omen, *n. prognostic.* शकुन *m.* प्रश्न *m.* शुभाशुभलक्षण *n.* भावि-

Evil o. अपशकुन *m.* दुःशकुन *m.* दुर्लक्षण *n.* दुश्चिन्ह *n.* अवचिन्ह *n.* अवलक्षण *n.*

Good o. शकुनगांठ *f.* सुचिन्ह *n.*

Interpretation of omens. शाकुनिक *n.*

Ominous word. अपशब्द *m.*

Omentum, *n. caul.* पोटाचापडदा *m.* अन्त्रवेष्टन *n.* अंत्रावरण *n.* मेदोधरा *f.*

Ominous, *a. of or belonging to omens.* शकुनाविषयींचा, शाकुन, शाकुनिक, शकुनसंबंधी-विषयक, शुभाशुभसूचक.

2 *foreboding evil.* अनिष्टसूचक, अभद्रसूचक, अमंगलसूचक, दुर्लक्षणी, अभद्र, काळदांत्या, अवचिया.

Ominousness, *n.* v. A. 1. शाकुनिकत्व *n.* शुभाशुभसूचकत्व *n.*

2 अनिष्टसूचकत्व *n.* &c. अभद्रता *f.*

Omission, *n.* v. V. 1.—*act.* सांडणें *n.* वगळणें *n.* &c. वगळणी *f.* वगळणूक *f.* वर्जन *n.* [नर *n.* ढळ *m.*

2 विसरणें *n.* &c. कमतर *f.* कसर *f.* तफावत *f.* गुंजावीस *f.* अं-

To Omit, *v. a. leave out.* सांडणें, गाळणें, टाकणें, वगळणें, अंतरणें, वर्जणें, करायाचा-&c. ठेवणें, वर्जन *n.*-&c. करणें *g. of o.*

To be omitted. गळणें, राहणें, चुकणें, ओघळणें.

2 *neglect to practise,* v. To Neglect. विसरणें, विसरून-भुलून-&c. ठेवणें, आळस *m.*-गफलत *f.*-हयगई *f.*-उपेक्षा *f.*-&c. करणें *g. of o.* अंतरणें.

Omitted, *p.* v. V. 1. गाळलेला, वगळलेला, &c. वर्जित, वर्ज, गळीत.

2 विसरलेला, &c. अंत्रिक *or* आंत्रिक, अंतरित.

Omnibus, *n.* जनरथ *m.*

Omnifarious, *a. of all kinds.* सर्वविध, सर्व प्रकारचा.

Omniferous, *a. that bears all kinds.* सर्व पिकी, सर्वफलद.

Omnigenous, *a. of all kinds.* सर्वविध, सर्वप्रकारचा.

Omnipotence, *n. unlimited power.* सर्वकार्यशक्ति *f.* अपारशक्ति *f.* अपरंपारशक्ति *f.* अपरंपारसामर्थ्य *n.*

Omnipotent, *a. having unlimited power.* सर्वशक्तिक, सर्वकार्यशक्तिक, सर्वशक्तिमान्, अपारशक्तिविशिष्ट, अपरंपारशक्तीचा, अपरंपारसामर्थ्याचा, &c.

Omnipresence, *n. presence in every placce.* व्याप्ति *f.* अभिव्याप्ति *f.* त्रैलोक्यविस्तार *m.* विश्वव्यापकत्व *n.* सर्वव्यापिता *f.*

Omnipresent, *a.* v. N. सर्वव्यापक, सर्वव्यापी, विश्वव्यापक, त्रैलोक्यविस्तार, सर्वभूतभूतांतर, जळींस्थळींकाष्टींपाषाणीं असणारा, विभु.

Omniscience, *n. knowledge of all things.* सर्वविषयज्ञान *n.* सर्वज्ञान *n.* सर्वज्ञता *f.* अपारज्ञान *n.* अपरंपारज्ञान *n.*

Omniscient, *a.* v. N. सर्वज्ञ, सर्ववेदी, सर्ववेत्ता, सर्वदर्शी, सर्वसाक्षी, त्रिकालज्ञ, त्रिकालदर्शी, त्रिकालविद्, विश्ववेदा.

Omnivagant, Omnivagous, *a. wandering every where.* सर्वग, सर्वभ्रमक.

Omnivorous, *a. that eats all things.* सर्वभक्ष, सर्वभक्षक, सर्वभोजी, सर्वाशी, स्वेच्छाहार. [बंधी.

Omphalic, *a. belonging to the navel.* नाभीचा, नाभ्य, नाभिसं-

Omphalocele, *n. rupture at the navel.* नाभिवर्द्धन *n.*

Omphalotomy, *n. dividing the navel string.* नाभिछेदन *n.* नालछेद *m.*

On, *prep.* वर, वरता *decl.* वरती *or* ती *or* तें, उपरि.

2 *at or near.* स, ला, सीं *or* शीं (all added to the noun), जवळ, पासीं *or* शीं.

3 *at the time of.* स, ला, ईं (all added to the noun, as मी सोमवारीं येईन I will come on Monday).

On or before. पर्यंत, पावेतों, as मी मंगळवारपर्यंत येईन I will come on or before Tuesday.

4 *concerning, about.* विषयीं, संबंधी, प्रकरणीं, स *or* ला (as तो कांहीं कामाला आला होता He had come on some business).

5 *in consequence of, after.* वर, नंतर, अनंतर.

On this or that account. या-त्या मुळें-स्तव-साठीं-करितां-&c.

6—with reference to the limbs. आंत, ईं, स, (added to the noun, as पायांत जोडा घालणें to put shoes on the feet, बोटांत कडी घालणें to put a ring on the finger, आंगांत आंगरखा घालणें to put an *angrakhá* on, डोकीस पागोटें बांधणें to put a turban on the head, &c.).

ON, *adv. forward, in progression.* पुढें, मोहरें.

2 *forward; in succession.* पुढें.

3 *in continuance.* पुढें. This sense is often best expressed by the combination of चालणें *or* राहणें with another verb, as बोलत चालणें to go on speaking, गात राहणें to go on singing, &c.

4 *upon* (the body, &c.). स, ला (joined to the noun) with reference to the head, as डोईस पागोटें, डोकीला रुमाल, &c. वर with reference to parts where clothes sit loosely, as आंगावर वस्त्र. The locative case (आंत, ईं, &c.) is used where articles fit closely, as आंगांत आंगरखा, पायांत जोडा, हातांत तोडा, बोटांत जोडवें.

ON, *interj.* चला.

ONCE, *adv. one time.* एकदा, एकवेळ, एकवेळां, एकवार, एकबार, एकवक्त, एकखेप, सकृत्, एक (in comp. as एकभाज once roasted, &c.).

O. for all. एकामीं *or* में, एकंदर.

O. and away. कदाकाळीं, कधीं काळीं, कधीं कधीं, कधीं नव्हत.

2 v. FORMERLY. मागें, पूर्वीं.

3 *one time, though no more.* एकदांचा *decl.* संधेवीं, संधेवींला *decl.* संदिसा *decl.*

At o. *at the same time.* एकदम, एकवेळ, एकदां, एककाळीं, एकसमयावच्छेदेंकरून, युगपत्.

At o. *at one time, at one act, one stretch, one effort, &c.* एकदां, एकदम, एकेवेळीं, एकामीं *or* में, एकादमानें, एकातडाख्यानें, एकासपाट्यानें, एकेखेपेनें, &c. खेपेनें, खेपेसरसा, तडाख्यासरसा, &c. एकतंत्र.

At o. *promptly, on the spot, outright.* तसाच, तेव्हांच, तेव्हांचे तेव्हांच, उभाउभी, खडीचोट, खडोखड, खडाखड.

At o. *together, in a body.* एकामीं *or* में, मिळून, एकमेळीं, एकसंगें, एकवट, संघशः, युगपत्.

All at o. *in one lump or quantity.* एकथोक, एकठोक, एकथोप, एकरकम, एकमेळणी, एकमेळी, घाऊक, एकंदररगट.

All at o. v. SUDDENLY. एकाएकीं, अकस्मात्.

ONCE, *n.* एक जनावर आहे.

ONE, *a. single in number.* एक.

One and a half. दीड,—consisting of one and a half दिडका, दिडता;—quantity of one and a half दिढी *f.*

The figure one (1.). एकडा *m.*

2 *single, undivided.* एक, एकच.

3 *some one, any one, indefinitely.* एखादा, एखाद, कोणीएक, [कोणताही.

4 *like, identical.* एक, सारखा, एकसारखा.

Become one with. तन्मय.

5 *single in kind, the same.* एक, एकच.

6—noting diversity. एक (as बोलणें एक आणि करणें एक It is one thing to talk and another to act, देऊं करणें एक आणि देणें एक It is one thing to promise and another to give, हें औषध एक आणि तें एक, एकसारखा गुण कसा येईल ? This is one medicine and that is a different one, how can they have the same effect ?) अणीक (as येऊं म्हणणें अणीक आणि येणें अणीक It is one thing to promise to come and another to come), भिन्न.

7—as following any. कोणी, कोणी एक.

8—as used with *another* and noting mutuality. एकमेक.

With one anther. एकमेक, एकमेकांशीं, एकमेकांत, आपसांत, आपसांमध्यें.

9—particularly or pre-eminently. एक (as a hero, a minister, &c. *without parallel*, एकवीर, एक कारभारी, &c. A scamp, liar, &c. *unique, unrivalled*, एक सोदा, एक लबाड, &c.).

Such a one. *a certain person.* अमुक, अमका, फलाणा.

All o. *one and the same thing.* एकुनएक.

Every o. *all without exception.* एकान एक, जोतो.

One by o. एकएक *or* एकेक, एक एकटा, एक एकला, प्रत्येक.

Many a o. किती एक.

O. closely after another. बराबर, बरच्यावर.

O. with another, *together, in a lump, &c.* एकंदर, एकुनएर.

Relating to one or two. एकट्यादुकट्याचा.

ONE, *n.* v. PERSON, MAN. मनुष्य *n.* माणूस *n.*

One's self. आपण.

One's own. आपला.

Of one's self. आपोआप.

2 *any one*—indef. एक, कोणी, कोणीएक.

3—the figure 1. एकडा *m.*

ONE-EYED, *a.* एकडोळ्या, एकाक्ष, एकनेत्र, एकचक्षु, काणा;—jocosely, शुक्राचार्य.

ONE-SIDED, *a.* v. PARTIAL. एकतरफी, एकतरफा, एकपक्षी.

ONENESS, *n. unity, &c.* एकपणा *m.* एकी *f.* ऐक्य *n.* ऐक्यभाव *m.* अद्वैत *n.* अभेद *m.* तादात्म्य *n.*

The doctrine of o. in philosophy (one principle in the universe). अद्वैत *n.* अद्वैतमत *n.* अद्वैतवाद *m.* अभेद *m.* अभेदमत *n.* अभेदवाद *m.* ऐक्य *n.* निर्द्वंद्व *n.*

Holder of the doctrine of o. अद्वैतवादी, अभेदवादी, निर्द्वंद्व, निर्विकल्प.

Holding the doctrine of o. अभेददृष्टि *f.* अभेदभाव *m.* अभेदबुद्धि *f.* अद्वैतदृष्टि *f.* &c.

As opposed to the above is the doctrine of *duality*, or the assertion of two principles, especially of the distinctness of God and the world. भेदमत *n.* भेदवाद *m.* द्वैत *n.* द्वैतमत *n.* द्वैतवाद *m.*—Holder of it, भेदवादी, द्वैतवादी, भेदबुद्धि, भेदप्रत्ययी;—holding it, भेददृष्टि *f.* भेदभाव *m.* भेदबुद्धि *f.* भेदप्रत्यय *m.* द्वैतदृष्टि *f.* &c.

To ONERATE. See To LOAD.

ONEROUS, *a. burdensome.* जड, भारी, कठीण, दुर्भर, दुःसह.

ONION, *n.* कांदा *m.* पलांडू *m.* कंदर्प *m.* Some significant terms for it are, सुकंद *m.* कृष्णावळ *f.* म्लेच्छ भोजन *n.*

ONION-COLORED, *a.* प्याजी.

ONLY, *a. single, sole, one alone.* एक, एकच, एकचएक, एकटा, एकला, एकाकी, केवल *or* ळ.

2 *one and no more, this and no other.* एकच (with the

pronoun हा *or* तो), एकुलता, एकुलताएक.

ONLY, *adv. simply, merely, singly.* केवळ, मात्र, शुद्ध, नुस्ता *decl.* फक्त, एकटा *decl.* च *added to the adjective.*

2 *so and no otherwise.* केवळ, च *added to the adjective.*

ONOMANCY, *n. divination by the letters of a name.* नामाक्षर-भविष्यविद्या *f.*

ONOMATOPEIA, *n.*—in grammar. अनुकरण *n.* अनुकरणशब्द *m.*

ONSET, ONSLAUGHT, *n. a rushing on, determined assault,* v. ATTACK. हल्ला *m.* चाल *f.* घेघा *or* घेगा *m.* घेघे *f.* घेघेमार *m.* घेमार *m.* एलगार *m.* एल्कोट *m.*

At the first o. पहिले धडाक्यानें, पहिले तडाख्यानें.

ONTOLOGIST, *n.* सत्वमात्र विचारी, भूतमात्र विचारी.

ONTOLOGY, *n. science of beings.* तत्वमात्रमीमांसा *f.* सत्वमात्र-विचार *m.* भूतमात्रविचार *m.*

ONWARD, ONWARDS, *adv. forward, progressively.* पुढें, मोहरें.

2 *in advance.* पुढें, पुढपुढें.

3 *somewhat further.* कांहीं पुढें, पुढें.

ONWARD, *a. advanced or advancing.* पुढें गेलेला *or* जाण्याचा, पुढें चाललेला *or* चालण्याचा.

ONYX, *n.* गोमेद *m.* शिवधातु *m.* शिलेमान *or* शिलेमणी *m.*

OOZE. *n. slime, soft mud.* गाळ *m.* रेबड *f.* रेव *f.*

2 *soft flow, trickling, exudation.* पाझर *m.* निझर *m.* निचरा *m.* द्रव *m.* पाघळ *m.* स्रवण *n.* स्रव *m.*

Concealed vent through which there is an o. मूर *f.*

3 *oozing matter,* v. SWEAT. पाघळ *m.* पाझर *m.* निचरा *m.* द्रव*m.*तेव *m.* निझरवणी *n.* उपळी *f.*

To OOZE, *v. n. percolate, exude, flow through pores.* पाझरणें, झरणें, निचरणें, निझरणें, झुरणें, ओझरणें, स्रवणें,श्रावणें, झिरपणें, चिघळणें, ओहूळणें, होळणें, ओघळणें, घळणें, ठिपकणें, क्षरणें, पाझर *m.*-ओझर *m.*-&c. होणें *g. of s.*

2 v. To SWEAT. पाघळणें, पाघळ *m.*-&c. होणें.

OOZED, *p.* v. V. 1. पाझरलेला, &c. पाझरींव, स्रुत, क्षरित.

OOZER, *n.* OOZING, *p. a.* v. V. 1. पाझरणारा, &c. क्षर, सद्रव.

OOZINESS, *n.* v. A. 1. रेबड *f.* गाळ *m.*

I.—of the ground after heavy rain. उपळ *f.* उमळ *f.*

OOZING, *n.* v. V. 1.—*act.* पाझरणें *n.* &c. पाझर *m.* निचरा *m.* स्राव *m.* श्राव *m.* झिरपा *m.* गळ *f.* गळती *f.* ओघळ *m.* ओहूळ *m.* ओहूळी *f.* ओलंगर *m.* मूर *f.* क्षरण *n.* गलन *n.* स्रवण *n.* स्रव *m.* स्यंदन *n.*

2 पाघळणें *n.* पाघळ *m.*

OOZY, *a. slimy, &c.* रेबडीचा, चिखलाचा, गाळाचा, पंकमय.

2 *sweaty, soft.* चिघळ्या, वाहूवरा, उमळा, गलगलीत, सद्रव.

To be o. उमळणें.

OPACITY, OPACOUSNESS, OPAKENESS, *n.* v. A. 1. अपारदर्शकत्व *n.* प्रकाशाभेद्यता *f.* प्रकाशप्रतिबंधकत्व *n.* किरणरोधकत्व *n.*&c.

2 न्यूनप्रभता *f.* निष्प्रभता *f.* प्रभान्यूनता *f.* अस्वच्छता *f.*

OPACOUS, OPAKE, *a. not transparent.* अपारदर्शक, प्रकाशाभेद्य, प्रकाशप्रतिबंधक, प्रकाशरोधक, किरणरोधक, दृष्टिरोधक, किरणाभेद्य, किरणप्रतिबंधक, अस्वच्छ.

2 *dark, obscure.* निष्प्रभ, न्यूनप्रभ, अस्वच्छ.

OPAL, *n.* शिवधातु *m.* क्षीरस्फटिक *m.* गोमेदसन्निभ *m.*

To OPE, *To* OPEN, *v. a. unclose, unlock.* उघडणें, उघडा-मोकळा-&c. करणें, उद्घाटन *n.*-&c. करणें *g. of o.*

To o. one's mind. पोट *n.* फोडणें, मन मोकळें करणें.

2 *expand, spread, &c.* उघडणें, पसरणें, सोडणें, उमलविणें, प्रकाश *m.*-विकाश *m.*-&c. करणें. *g. of o.* प्रकाशित-विकाशित-&c. करणें.

3 *crack, split, divide.* तडविणें, तडकविणें, उलविणें, भेगलविणें.

4 *draw out kindly.* फुलविणें, खुलावणें, प्रफुल्लित-विकसित-&c. करणें.

5 *explicate, expound,* v. To EXPLAIN. उलगडणें, उकलणें, उलगडा *m.*-फाड *m.*-परिस्फोट *m.*-उद्घाटन *n.*-&c. करणें *g. of o.* उघडा-स्पष्ट-&c. करणें.

6 *break the seal of and unfold.* फोडणें, उघडणें.

7 v. To BEGIN. उपोद्घात *m.*-उपक्रम *m.*-&c. करणें *g. of o.* उहू *m.* काढणें *g. of o.*

8 (a tumour, &c.). फाडणें, फोडणें, कापणें, चिरणें.

9 (a road, passage, &c.). पाडणें, करणें, मोकळा करणें.

To OPEN, *v. n. unclose, &c.* उघडणें, उघडा-मोकळा-&c. होणें.

2 *expand, unfold, &c.* उकलणें, उमलणें, उफलणें, विकसणें, प्रकाश *m.*-&c. होणें *g. of s.*

3 *crack, split, &c.* तडणें, तडकणें, भेगलणें, उलणें, भेग *f.*-चीर *f.*-&c. पडणें *in. con.*

4 *dilate kindly, &c.* खुलणें, फुलणें, फुल्फुलणें, उफलणें, उमलणें, उबळणें, उबळणें.

5—a seam; *come undone.* उसवणें.

6 out, abroad, widely, &c.—legs, eyes, mouth, &c. वासणें,विचकणें, पसरणें, तडाडणें.—horns, branches, &c. फांकटणें, फांकणें.

7 *lose closeness of texture.* विरणें, विरघळणें.

8—as soaked grains, &c. उमलणें, उफलणें.

9 out ; fig. *come forth, display one's talents, &c.* खुलणें.

OPEN, *a. not shut, not closed, &c.* उघडा, खुला, मोकळा.

2 *not secret or concealed, public.* उघड, उघडा, प्रसिद्ध, प्रगट, स्पष्ट, प्रसिद्धपणाचा, उघडपणाचा, प्रगटपणाचा, &c. उघडपणींचा, प्रसिद्धपणींचा, &c. राजरोशीचा, उजागरीचा.

3 *artless, sincere, ingenuous, &c.* v. FRANK. मनाचा मोकळा-निर्मळ-&c. मोकळ्या मनाचा, निर्मळमनाचा, निष्कपट, निष्प्रांजल, खणखणीत, खडखडीत, घळघळीत, घळमळीत,घळघळीन, अगूढभाव.

4 *exposed, unprotected, unsheltered*—a place. उघडा, मोकळा, उघडाबाघडा,उघडबसाऱ्याचा,उघडवासऱ्याचा, निराश्रयाचा, अनाश्रयाचा, निराश्रय, अनाश्रय, वाऱ्याचा,वाऱ्यावरचा.

In the open air, yard, street, &c. उघड्यावर, उघडबासऱ्यांत.

5 *free to all comers, admitting without restraint.* मोकळा, खुला, मोकळ्या दरवाज्याचा, मुक्तद्वाराचा, मुक्तद्वार, येत्याजात्याचा, पहिपाहुण्याचा, प्रतिबंधरहित-शून्य-&c. [अनावृत.

6 *uncovered, not having a cover,*—a vessel. उघड तोंडाचा,

7 *clear, free, unobstructed, roomy, &c.* मोकळा, खुला, कुशाद, खुलास, खुलाशाचा, ऐसपैस, पैस, ऐसपैसाचा, प्रशस्त, उदार.

8 *not crowding or close.* विरल *or* ळ, विरूळ, विसकळ, सुटा, मोकळा, तुरळ, पातळ.

9 *not settled, not closed,*—account, &c. चालू, उभा, ओढता, खरकटा. [शस्त.

10 *full, commanding, fine,*—countenance, &c. उदार, प्र-

11 *unobstructed, clear,*—river, &c. मोकळा, चालता.
12—seam, joint, &c. उसू.
13—a vowel, &c. उदात्त, विवृत.
14—the organs of speech. विवृत.
In o. day, *in broad day light.* दिवसाढवळ्या, दिवा, दिसाधडी, दिवसाउजेडीं, दिसा उजेडीं, मर दिवसास.
OPEN-HANDED, *a.* v. GENEROUS. हाताचा मोकळा-सुटा-सढळ-ढसळ-उदार-&c. उदारहस्त, मुक्तहस्त.
OPEN-HEARTED, *a.* v. FRANK. मनाचा मोकळा.
OPEN-MOUTHED, *a.* आ वासलेला, तोंड वासलेला, तोंड पसरलेला, वासलेल्या तोंडाचा.
To fall upon o. ओरडून गळां पडणें.
OPENED, *p.* v. V. A. 1. उघडलेला, मोकळा केलेला, &c. उद्घाटित.
2 उघडलेला, पसरलेला, &c. पसरट, विकासित, प्रकाशित.
5 उकललेला, &c. स्फुट, स्फुटित.
I.—an eclipse. उन्मीलित.
OPENER, *n.* OPENING, *p. a.* v. V. A. 1. उघडणारा, उघडा करणारा, &c. उद्घाटन कर्त्ता.
2 उघडणारा, पसरणारा, &c. विकाश-प्रकाश-&c.कर्त्ता.
I. See APERIENT, LAXATIVE.
OPENING, *n.* v.V. A. 1.—*act.* उघडणें *n.* &c. उद्घाटन *n.*
O. and shutting (reiteratedly, &c.). उघडझांक *f.* उघडमीट *f.*
2—*act.* उघडणें *n.* पसरणें *n.* &c.—*state.* प्रकाश *m.* विकाश*m.*
5—*act.* उलगडणें *n.* &c. उद्घाटन *n.* स्पष्टीकरण *n.*—*state.* उलगडा *m.* फाड *m.* परिस्फोट *m.* स्फोट *m.*
6—*state.* उपोद्घात *m.* उपक्रम*m.* प्रारंभ *m.* आरंभ *m.*
I. *aperture, hole, perforation, crack, mouth, &c.* भोंक *n.* रंध्र *n.* सिंड *f.* भेग *f.* भेर *f.* चीर *f.* तोंड *n.* मुख *n.* वाट *f.* द्वार*n.*
OPENLY, *adv.* v. A. 2. उघड, उघडपणीं *or* उघडपणें, &c. प्रसिद्धपणीं, प्रगटपणीं, स्पष्टपणीं, उघडमाथा, उघडवाघड, राजरोस, उजागर, उजागरीनें, बोलून चालून, साकसुरत.
O. and secretly,—telling, teaching.अंधारीं उजेडीं (सांगणें, शिकवणें). [वांचून.
3 मोकळया मनानें, मन मोकळें करून, कपट ठेवून-सोडून, कपटा-
OPENNESS, *n.* v. A. 1. उघडेपणा *m.* मोकळेपणा *m.* खुलेपणा *m.*
2 उघडपणा *m.* उघडेपणा *m.* प्रसिद्धपणा *m.* प्रगटपणा*m.* उघड *f.* उघडीक *f.* उजागरी *f.* प्रसिद्धि *f.* प्रसिद्धता *f.*
3 मनाचा मोकळेपणा *m.* खणखणितपणा *m.* &c. अकापट्य *n.* निष्कापट्य *n.* सरलभाव *m.*
4 उघडेपणा*m.*-&c. निराश्रयता *f.* अनाश्रयता *f.* आश्रयराहित्य*n.*
7 मोकळेपणा *m.* खुलेपणा *m.* &c. खुलासा *m.* प्राशस्त्य *n.*
8 विरळपणा *m.* विसकळपणा *m.* &c. वैरल्य *n.* विरलभाव *m.*
10 उदारपणा *m.* प्रशस्तपणा *m.* प्राशस्त्य *n.* [ट्य *n.*
OPERA, *n.*—the entertainment. संगीत *n.* तौर्य्यत्रिक *n.* ना-
To OPERATE, *v. n. work, perform function,* v. To ACT. चालणें, खेळणें, वर्त्तणें, कार्य *n.*-कृति *f.*-चेष्टा *f.*-खेळ *m.*-व्यापार *m.*-&c. करणें *and, in. con.* असणें *g. of s.*
2 *work causatively, produce effect,* v. To ACT. कर्त्तृत्व *n.*-कृति *f.*-&c. करणें, गुण *m.*-&c. करणें, लागू-चालू-&c. होणें-असणें *with* वर.
3—in surgery. शस्त्रवैद्याचें काम *n.*-शस्त्रक्रिया *f.*-&c. करणें, शस्त्राचा उपाय *m.*-शस्त्रोपाय *m.* करणें.

OPERATION, *n.* v. V. 1.—*act.* चालणें *n.* खेळणें*n.* &c. खेळ *m.* व्यापार *m.* चेष्टा *f.* हालचाल *f.* कृति *f.*
2 *and* ACTION. कर्त्तृत्व *n.* कृति *f.*
I.—in surgery. शस्त्रवैद्याचें काम *n.* शस्त्रक्रिया *f.* शस्त्रकृत्य *n.* शस्त्रोपाय *m.* शस्त्रोपचार *m.*
II. *act, deed, &c.* v. ACTION. काम *n.* कर्म *n.* कार्य *n.* कृत्य*n.*
OPERATIVE, *a. having or exerting agency.* कर्मकार, कर्मकारी, क्रियाकारी, क्रियाकारक, कारक.
2 *producing effect,* v. EFFICACIOUS. गुणकारक-कारी-कर्त्ता, गुणावह, कार्यसाधक, कार्यसंपादक.
Quickly o.—medicine. आशुकारी.
OPERATIVE, *n. labouring artisan, &c.* कामकरी, कारिगर, हातासालचा कारिगर. [कारक.
OPERATOR, *n.* v. V. 1. *and* AGENT. कर्त्ता, करणारा, कार्यकर्त्ता-
I.—in surgery. शस्त्रवैद्याचें काम करणारा, शस्त्रक्रियाकर्त्ता, शस्त्रोपचार कर्त्ता.
OPEROSE, *a. toilsome,* v. LABORIOUS. कष्टाचा, श्रमाचा, डोईफोड, डोईजड, कष्टसाध्य, श्रमसाध्य.
OPEROSENESS, *n.* v. A. डोईफोडपणा*m.* कष्टसाध्यता*f.* श्रमसाध्यता*f.*
OPHIDIAN, *a. pertaining, &c. to serpents.* सर्पसंबंधी, सर्पविषयक.
OPHIOPHAGOUS, *a. serpent-eating.* सर्पभक्षक, सर्पभक्ष, सर्पभोजी.
OPHTHALMIA, OPHTHALMY, *n. disease of the eye.* नेत्ररोग *m.* चक्षूरोग *m.* नेत्रामय *m.* लोचनामय *m.*
Acute o. कांटेडोळे *m. pl.*
Purulent o. शेण्ये *or* शेणे डोळे *m. pl.* मेणेडोळे *m. pl.*
Pricking of the eyes under o. खुपरी *f.* हरळ *m.* v. ये.
To have o. डोळे *m. pl.* येणें *g. of s.*
OPHTHALMIC, *a. pertaining to the eye.* डोळ्याचा, नेत्राचा, डोळ्याविषयींचा, नेत्रसंबंधी, चक्षुस्संबंधी, चाक्षुष.
OPIATE, *n. medicine that causes sleep or rest.* झोंपेचें-निजेचें-&c. औषध *n.* निद्राकारी औषध *n.* उपशमन *n.*
OPIATE, *a. soporific.* झोंप आणणारा, &c. निद्राकारी-जनक-&c. उपशमनकर्त्ता, उपशमकारी, उपशायी.
To OPINE. See To THINK.
OPINIATED, OPINIATIVE, *a. obstinate in one's own opinion.* स्वमताभिमानी, स्वमताग्रही, स्वमतवादी, मतवादी, मताभिमानी, हटवादी, खळवादी, हटखोर, दुराग्रही.
OPINIATIVENESS, OPINIATRY, *n.* v. A. स्वमताभिमान *m.* स्वमताग्रह *m.* स्वमताभिमानिता *f.* मताभिमान *m.* दुराग्रह *m.* खट्टा *m.* रग *f.* हठ *pop.* हट *n.* हटवाद *m.* [मजूत *f.*
OPINION, *n. persuasion of the mind.* मत *n.* मनसमजूत *f.* स-
A different o. विकल्प *m.* [विकल्प *m.*
Opposition or difference of o. मतभेद *m.* विप्रतिपत्ति *f.*
Opposed in o. विप्रतिपन्न.
2 *notion, judgment, mind, thought.* मत *n.* बुद्धि *f.* समज *m. f.* समजूत *f.* तर्क *m.* विचार *m.* ग्रह *m.* शक्तिग्रह *m.* भान *n.* भास *m.* कयास *m.*
Ill o. दुष्टभाव *m.*
Public o. लोकमत *n.* जनमत *n.* बहुमत *n.*
Regard to public o. लोकलज्जा *f.* जनलज्जा *f.*
3 *set of tenets, particular view.* मत *n.* कल्प *m.* पक्ष*m.*
4 *favorable judgment, esteem.* खातर *f.* खातरी *f.* योग्यताग्रह *m.* योग्यताबुद्धि *f.* योग्यतादृष्टि *f.*

OPINIONATED, OPINIONATIVE, *a.* v. OPINIATED. स्वमताभिमानी, मताभिमानी, मतवादी, दुराग्रही. [दुराग्रह *m.*

OPINIONATIVENESS, *n.* v. A. स्वमताभिमान *m.* मताभिमान *m.*

OPIUM, *n.* अफू *f.* अफीण *f.* अफीम *f.* अफेन *f.* अहिफेन *m.*—covertly or allusively, कडवी *f.* गुरुप्रसाद *m.*

Addicted to o.-eating. अफिण्या, अफिम्या, अफीमखाऊ.

To inhale the smoke of o. अफूचा चंडोल करणें.

OPOSSUM, *n.* एकजनावर आहे.

OPPIDAN, *a. of or belonging to a town.* शहरी, नगरी, नगरीय, नागर, नागरिक, पौर.

OPPONENT, *a.* v. ADVERSE, CONTRARY. उलटा, विपरीत, विमुख, विरोधी, विरुद्ध.

OPPONENT, *n. adversary,* v. ENEMY. वैरी, विरोधी, शत्रु.

2—in disputation, *opener of a dispute.* वादी, पूर्ववादी, पूर्वपक्षी, अग्रवादी.

3—gener. *opposing party.* प्रतिपक्षी, प्रतिपक्ष, प्रतिवादी, उत्तरवादी, वादी, प्रतियोगी, प्रतिरोधी, विपक्ष.

OPPORTUNE, *a. timely, well-timed,* v. SEASONABLE. समयोचित, सामयिक, प्रसंगोचित, प्राप्तकाल, प्राप्तावसर, अवसरपठित, कालसदृश.

OPPORTUNELY, *adv.* v. A. *and* SEASONABLY. प्रसंगास, वेळेस, &c. बरा *decl.* नेमका *decl.* प्रसंगोपात्त, प्रसंगानुसार, गवसार.

To come o. प्रसंगास येणें.

OPPORTUNENESS, *n.* v. A. समयौचित्य *n.* समयानुकूल्य *n.* प्रसंगौचित्य *n.* आनुकूल्य *n.* अनुकूल *n.*

OPPORTUNITY, *n. fit or convenient time.* प्रसंग *m.* अवसर *m.* वेळ *f.* समय *m.* वक्त *m.* सवड *f.* संधि *m. f.* डाव *m.* घावडाव *m.* घात *f.* अवकाश *m.* योग *m.* कालयोग *m.* पर्व *n.* तानमान *n.* फग *f.*

According to o. यथाप्रसंग, यथावसर, यथावकाश.

To rob one of one's o. घात *m. f.* घेणें.

2 *convenient means.* सोई *f.* साधन *n.* संधान *n.* योग *m.* लाग *m.*

To OPPOSE, *v. a. resist, act against.* आड-आडवा-प्रतिकूल-विरुद्ध-&c. होणें-असणें-येणें, अडवणें, रोधणें, आडवें *n.*-आडमेळें *n.* आणणें, वारणें, निवारणें, अडणूक *f.*-अडवणूक *f.*-विरोध *m.*-प्रतिरोध *m.*-प्रतिकार *m.*-&c. करणें, अडती *f.*-अड *f.*-&c. घालणें.

2 *set against, place in opposition.* विरोधी-प्रतिरोधी-&c. उभाकरणें, आड-आडवा-प्रतिकूल-&c. आणणें.

To o. one's self to another. तोंडावर तोंड *n.* देणें.

OPPOSED, *p. and a.* v. V. 1. अडवलेला, रोधलेला, &c. वारित, निवारित.

2 आडवाकेलेला, &c.

I. v. ADVERSE. विमत, विमुख, प्रतिकूल, विरुद्ध.

OPPOSER, *n.* OPPOSING, *p. a.* v. V. 1. *and* ADVERSE. आडयेणारा-आलेला, अडवणारा, वारणारा, &c. विरोध-&c. करणारा, विरोधी, प्रतिरोधी, विरोधक, प्रातिकूलिक.

OPPOSITE, *a. fronting, facing.* सम्मुख *pop.* सन्मुख, समोरचा, अभिमुख, अभिसम्मुख.

2 *hostile, repugnant,* v. ADVERSE. विरोधी, प्रतिरोधी, &c. प्रतिकूल, विरुद्ध, विपरीत.

3 *contrary,* v. REVERSE. उलटा, विपरीत.

4 *further, remote, on the other side.* पलीकडचा *or* ला, पलीकडील, पर (in comp. as परतीर the o. bank), अपर.

OPPOSITE, *n. a contrary.* विपक्ष *m.* प्रतिपक्ष *m.* प्रतिपक्षी *m.* प्रतियोगी *m.*

OPPOSITELY, *adv.* v. A. 1. समोर, समोरासमोर, समक्ष.

2 विरोधानें, विरोधभावानें, विरोधबुद्धीनें, विरोधपूर्वक.

3 उलटा *decl.* उलटून, विपर्यासपूर्वक, विपर्ययपूर्वक.

OPPOSITENESS, *n.* v. A. 1. समोरी *f.* समक्षता *f.* सम्मुखता *f.* आभिमुख्य *n.*

2 विरोध *m.* विरुद्धता *f.* विरोधभाव *m.* विरुद्धभाव *m.* प्रातिकूल्य *n.* प्रतिकूलभाव *n.*

3 विपर्यास *m.* विपर्यय *m.* वैपरीत्य *n.* विपरीतभाव *m.* प्रतियोगिता *f.* व्यत्यय *m.* व्यत्यास *m.*

OPPOSITION, *n.* v. V. 1.—*act.* आडवा येणें *n.* अडवणें *n.* अवरोधन *n.* प्रतिरोध *m.* अवरोध *m.* प्रतिकार *m.* प्रतिक्रिया *f.* वारण *n.* निवारण *n.* [टकाव *m.*

I. *impediment,* v. HINDERANCE. अडती *f.* अडथळा *m.* अ-

II. *hostile feeling.* विरुद्धभाव *m.* द्वेषभाव *m.*

III. *collective body of opposers.* विरोधिजनसमूह *m.* प्रतियोगिपक्ष *m.*

For other meanings, See OPPOSITENESS.

To OPPRESS, *v. a. treat with excessive and unjust severity.* जुलूम *m.*-जुलूमजास्ती *f.*-जबरी *f.*-&c. करणें *with* वर *of o.* पिळणें, पिळून घेणें, जाचणें, जाळणें, पिडणें, घोटणें, खलणें, चेंगरणें, चेंचणें, जळजळाट *m.*-उपद्रव *m.*-उपमर्द *m.*-&c. करणें-देणें, खल *m.* घेणें-मांडणें, घाण्यांत-चरकांत-&c. घालणें, चरकी-करवती-करवतासाळींतारकशीं धरणें, खडे *m. pl.* खाविवणें-चारणें, जळींत जाळणें, तेल *n.* काढणें, पुरेपुरेसा *decl.*-नकोनकोसा *decl.*-&c. करणें, नाकीं नऊ आणणें, त्राहित्राहि *adv.* करणें.

2 *overburden, overpower, press.* उरावर-छातीवर-&c. बसणें *g. of o.* ऊर *m.*-छाती *f.*-&c. दडपणें, *g. of o.* दडपणें, दाबणें, खालीं करणें, पाडणें, धरणीवर-भुईवर-&c. पाडणें, लंघविणें, जड पडणें *in. con.* मोडकळा *f.*-&c. आणणें, उटवणीस-&c. आणणें, जेर-&c. करणें, नाकीं नऊ आणणें.

To be oppressed. नाकीं नऊ येणें, मोडावणें, उटवणीस येणें; —through emotion. गळा *m.*-ऊर *m.*-हृदय *n.*-&c. दाटणें *g. of s.*

OPPRESSED, *p.* v. V. 1. पिळलेला, जाळलेला, &c. उपद्रुत, उपप्लुत.

2 दडपलेला, दाबलेला, जेर केलेला, धरणीवर पाडलेला, &c.

OPPRESSION, *n.* v. V. 1.—*act.* पिळणें *n.* जाचणें *n.* जाळणें *n.* &c. जाचणी *f.* जाचणूक *f.* जाळणूक *f.* काच *f.* काचणी *f.* जुलूम *m.* जुलूमज्यास्ती *f.* जुलूमदस्ती *f.* जुलूमज्यास्त *f.* ज्यास्ती *f.* जलेली *f.* जबरदस्ती *f.* जबरी *f.* जोरजबरी *f.* जळजळाट *m.* बाटाघाट *m. f.* बेदाद *f.* उपद्रव *m.* उपमर्द *m.* उपमर्दन *n.* विमर्दन *n.* पीडन *n.* प्रजापीडन *n.*

Regal o. and injustice. राजीक *n.*

To have or feel an o. of the chest. ऊर *m.* दडपणें *g. of s.* उरावर ओझें *n.*-&c. वाटणें.

OPPRESSIVE, *a.* v. V. 1. जुलमाचा, जुलूमज्यास्तीचा, जबरीचा, जबरदस्तीचा, &c. जबरदस्त, जालीम, त्रासदायक-कारक, त्रासक, उपद्रव कारक.

2 उरावर बसणारा, ऊरदडपणारा, धरणीवर पाडणारा, &c. कठीण, जालीम, जबर, भारी, सख्त.

OPPRESSIVENESS, *n.* v. A. 1. जालिमपणा *m.* जलाली *f.* त्रासदायकत्व *n.* त्रासकत्व *n.* &c.

2 कठिणपणा *m.* जालिमपणा *m.* &c.

OPPRESSOR, *n.* OPPRESSING, *p. a.* v. V. 1. जाचणारा, जाळणारा, पिळूनघेणारा, जुलूमकरणारा, &c. जालीम, जबरदस्त, उपद्रवकर्ता-

-कारी, त्रासदायक, प्रजापीडक.

OPPROBRIOUS, *a. reproachful, scurrilous.* निंदेचा, हेंटाळणीचा, हेंटाळ्याचा, कुचोद्याचा, कुटाळीचा, &c. अपवादक, निंदक, निंदात्मक, निंदार्थक, निंदारूप, निंदासूचक, गर्हात्मक.

OPPROBRIOUSLY, *adv.* v. A. निंदेनें, कुटाळीनें, निंदा करून, निंदापूर्वक, &c. [दकता *f.*

OPPROBRIOUSNESS, *n.* v. A. निंदकत्व *n.* निंदासूचकत्व *n.* अपवा-

OPPROBRIUM, *n.* v. REPROACH. निंदा *f.* अपवाद *m.* गर्हा *f.* कुत्सा *f.*

To OPPUGN, *v. a. resist*, v. To OPPOSE. आडवा येणें-होणें.

OPPUGNANCY, *n.* v. OPPOSITION. विरोध *m.* प्रातिकूल्य *n.* वैपरीत्य *n.* विरुद्धभाव *m.* प्रतियोगिता *f.*

OPTATIVE, *a. expressing desire.* इच्छासूचक-बोधक-&c. अभिलाषबोधक.

OPTIC, OPTICAL, *a. relating to sight or vision.* दृष्टीचा, नजरेचा, दृष्टिसंबंधी, दृष्टिविषयक, चाक्षुष.

2 *relating to the science of optics.* दृग्विद्येचा, दृक्शास्त्रसंबंधी, दृक्शास्त्रविषयक, दर्शनानुशासनशास्त्र संबंधी.

OPTIC, *n. organ of sight.* चक्षुरिंद्रिय *n.* दृगिंद्रिय *n.* दर्शनसाधन *n.*

OPTICIAN, *n. one skilled in optics.* दृक्शास्त्री, दृक्शास्त्रज्ञ, दृक्शास्त्रवेत्ता.

2 *maker of optical instruments.* दृष्टिसाधकयंत्र करणारा.

OPTICS, *n. science of vision.* दृग्विद्या *f.* दृष्टिविद्या *f.* दृक्शास्त्र *n.* दर्शनानुशासनशास्त्र *n.*

OPTION. See CHOICE.

OPTIONAL, *a. left to choice.* खुशीचा, इच्छेचा, विकल्पाचा, ऐच्छिक, वैकल्पिक, विकल्पित, विभाषित, काम्य. [षय *m.*

An o. matter. खुशीचासवदा *m.* विभाषाविषय *m.* विकल्पवि-

OPULENCE, OPULENCY, *n.* v. WEALTH. संपत्ति *f.* लक्ष्मी *f.* श्रीमंती *f.* मातबरी *f.* तालेवारी *f.* गजांतलक्ष्मी *f.* ऐश्वर्य *n.*

OPULENT, *a. wealthy*, v. RICH. श्रीमान् *pop.* श्रीमंत, मातबर, तालेवार, तालेवंत, संपत्तिवान्, संपत्तिमान्, संपन्न, लक्ष्मीवान्, सार्थ.

2—esp. a merchant. गडगंज, गबरू, गब्बर, श्रीमंत, श्रीकार.

OR, *conj.* कीं, किंवा, का, या, अथवा, वा, यद्वा.

2 *else.* नाहीतर, अन्यथा, इतरथा.

3—as expressing an alternative of terms or definitions of the same thing in different words. म्हणजे.

ORACLE, *n. response of a god or inspired person to a question put.* प्रश्न *m.* प्रसाद *m.* शकुन *m.*—through a voice, आकाशवाणी *f.* देववाणी *f.*

2 *the deity who gives a response.* प्रसादाचा देव *m.* प्रसादाची देवता *f.* प्रसाददेवता *f.* प्रसाद लावण्याचा-मागण्याचा देव *m.* प्रश्न -&c. मागण्याचा देव *m.*

3 *the place where a response is given.* भाकणुकीची जागा *f.* प्रसादस्थान *n.* प्रश्नस्थान *n.* शकुनस्थान *n.*

The usual mode in which Maráthás consult an oracle and seek divine direction is by sticking grains of rice, bits of betel nut, flowers, leaves, &c. on an idol. If these grains, &c. fall off to the right hand, the question has received a favorable answer; if to the left hand, an unfavorable answer.

The grains of rice, &c. stuck on an idol when it is consulted. कौल *m.* प्रसाद *m.* गुळ्या *f. pl.* विणती *f.*

To consult an o. by sticking grains of rice, &c. कौल *m.*-प्रसाद *m.*-गुळ्या *f. pl.*-&c. लावणें-मागणें.

To consult gods and oracles. देवीं धर्मीं विचारणें.

To give an answer,—an o. thus consulted. कौल *m.*-प्रसाद *m.*-&c. देणें.

To give a favorable answer,—an o. उजवी *f.* देणें,—to give an unfavorable answer, डावी *f.* देणें.

4 *a person whose opinion is to be regarded as an oracle.* ठोक्याचा माणूस, खऱ्या बत्तिशीचा माणूस, आप्तवचनी, अभियुक्तवचनी.

5 *wise or authoritative sentence.* अभियुक्तवचन *n.* अभियुक्तोक्ति *f.* आप्तवचन *n.* आप्तोक्ति *f.*

ORACULAR, ORACULOUS, *a.* v. N. *uttering oracles.* प्रसाद देण्याचा, कौल देण्याचा, प्रश्न देण्याचा, &c.

2 *like an oracle.* देववाणीतुल्य, देववाणीसदृश, &c.

ORACULARLY, ORACULOUSLY, *adv.* देववाणीनें, आकाशवाणीनें, देववाणी करून, &c.

ORAL, *a. spoken, not written.* तोंडचा, तोंडजबानीचा, मुखजबानीचा, मुखतीय, अलिखित.

O. answer. तोंडजाब *m.* [र *m.*

O. intercourse or communication. तोंडच्यातोंडीं व्यवहा-

O. statement or communication. तोंडजबानी *f.* मुखजबानी *f.*

ORALLY, *adv.* v. A. मुखजबानीनें, तोंडजबानीनें, मुखजबानी, तोंडजबानी, तोंडातोंडीं, मुखतः.

ORANGE, *n.*—the tree. नारंगी *or* नारिंगी *f.* नारिंग *f.* नारंग *m.*—the fruit, नारिंग *n.* Some kinds are, कौला, मोसंबी, रेशमीनारिंग.

Slice or division of an o. पाकळी *f.* पाकोळी *f.*

ORANGE, ORANGE-COLORED, *a.* नारंगी, नारंजी.

ORANGERY, *n. plantation of orange trees.* नारिंगाचा-नारिंगीचा-&c. बाग *m.*

ORATION, *n. set speech*, v. HARANGUE. वाक्प्रबंध *m.* प्रवचन *n.* सोपपत्तिकसालंकारभाषण *n.*

ORATOR, *n. public speaker or declaimer.* सभावक्ता, सभापंडित, सभावादी, सभाप्रवक्ता.

2 *eloquent speaker.* सुवक्ता, प्रौढवक्ता, प्रवक्ता, सभापंडित, प्रवचनकर्त्ता, प्रवचनप्रटु, वाक्पंडित.

ORATORIAL, ORATORICAL, *a. pertaining to oratory or an orator.* सभापांडित्याचा, सभावक्तृत्वाचा, सोपपत्तिकसालंकारभाषणाचा, &c. सभापांडित्यविषयक, प्रवचनसंबंधी, प्रवचनविषयक, सभापंडितविषयक-संबंधी.

ORATORIALLY, ORATORICALLY, *adv.* v. A. सभावक्तृत्वानें, सभापांडित्यानें, सभावक्तृत्वेंकरून, &c. सोपपत्तिकसालंकारभाषणाच्या प्रकारानें, सभापांडित्यपूर्वक, &c.

ORATORIO, *n. sacred drama set to music.* कीर्त्तन *n.* कथा *f.*

ORATORY, *n. art of public speaking.* सभापांडित्य *n.* सभावक्तृत्व *n.* सभाप्रवचनविद्या *f.*

2 *art of speaking well*, v. ELOQUENCE. शब्दचातुर्य *n.* वाक्चातुर्य *n.* वक्तृत्व *n.*

3 *place for prayer.* प्रार्थनागार *n.* प्रार्थनालय *n.*

ORB, *n. spherical body*, v. SPHERE. गोल *m.* गोलक *m.* मंडल *n.*

2 v. ORBIT. फेरी *f.* कक्षा *f.*

3 *circular array of troops.* चक्रव्यूह *m.*

ORBICULAR, ORBICULATE, *a. spherical*, v. ROUND. गोल, गोलाकार, वर्तुल, वर्तुलाकार.

ORBIT, *n. path of a planet.* फेरी *f.* कक्षा *f.* कक्ष *m.* ग्रहपथ *m.* ग्रहमार्ग *m.* मंडल *n.* विमंडल *n.* विक्षेपवृत्त *n.*

Apex of an o. उच्च *m.*

Apsis of an o. मंदोच्च *m.*

The greatest inclination of a planet's o. विक्षेपध्रुव *m.*

ORCHARD, *n. inclosure for fruit trees.* फळांची बाग *f.* फळझाडांचें वाडगें *n.* वाटी *f.* वाटिका *f.* वृक्षवाटिका *f.* फलवृक्षवाटिका *f.* उपवन *n.*

ORCHESTRA, *n. place for a band.* नौबतखाना *m.* नगारखाना *m.* बाजंत्र्यांचें स्थान *n.* वादित्रस्थल *n.*

2 *body of musicians.* बाजंत्र्यांचा ताफा *m.*-मेळा *m.* वादित्रसमुदाय *m.*

To ORDAIN, *v.a. establish, prescribe, institute,* v. TO APPOINT. नेमणें, लावणें, नेमून-लावून देणें, स्थापणें, स्थापना *f.*-चोदन *n.*-चोदना *f.*-&c. करणें *g. of o.* स्थापित-&c. करणें.

2 *appoint to an office.* नेमणें, योजणें, स्थापणें, नेमणूक *f.*-योजना *f.*-योजन *n.*-नियोजन *n.*-&c. करणें *g. of o.* अधिकृत-&c. करणें.

3 *invest with ministerial functions.* धर्माधिकाराची दीक्षा *f.* देणें, उपाध्येपणाच्या कामावर योजणें-नेमणें, धर्मपददीक्षित-धर्मपदनियुक्त-&c. करणें.

ORDAINED, *p.* v. V. 1. नेमलेला, स्थापलेला, &c. स्थापित, चोदित, विहित, नियमित.

2 नेमलेला, योजलेला, &c. योजित, नियोजित, नियुक्त.

3 धर्मपदनियुक्त, धर्मपददीक्षित, धर्माधिकारदीक्षित.

ORDAINER, *n.* ORDAINING, *p. a.* v. V. 1. नेमणारा, लावणारा, स्थापणारा, &c. स्थापक, स्थापनकर्ता, चोदनकर्त्ता, विधाता, विधायक, विधायी.

2 नेमणारा, योजणारा, नेमणूककरणारा, &c. योजक, नियोजक.

3 धर्माधिकाराची दीक्षा देणारा, धर्मपददीक्षित करणारा, धर्मपदनियोजक.

ORDAINING. See ORDINATION.

ORDEAL, *n. trial by fire, water, &c.* दिव्य *n.* सत्य *n.* क्रिया *f.* प्रमाण *n.* कोश *or* कोष *n. m.*

Fiery o. अग्निदिव्य *n.* तप्तदिव्य *n.* अग्निपरीक्षा *f.*

O. of the balance. तुलाकोश *m.* तुलापरीक्षा *f.*

Purification by o. कोशशुद्धि *f.*

Proved by o. शापित.

That undergoes an o. दिव्यकारी.

Undergoing an o. कोशग्रहण *n.*

To come safe out of an o. दिव्यांतून *or* दिव्यास उतरणें, दिव्य *n.* उतरणें *in. con.*

To take effect injuriously—an o. दिव्य *n.* लागणें.

To take a piece of metal out of heated oil as an o. रवा *m.* काढणें.

To undergo an o. दिव्य *n.* काढणें-घेणें-करणें, क्रिया *f.*-कोष *m. n.*-सत्य-&c. करणें.

ORDER, *n. method, regular disposition, arrangement.* क्रम *m.* अनुक्रम *m.* परिपाटी *f.* बेत *m.* व्यवस्था *f.* परिनालिका *f.* परणाळी *f.* प्रणालिका *f.* प्रणाली *f.* परंपरा *f.* पारंपर्य *n.* आनुपूर्वी *f.* आनुपूर्व्य *n.* पर्याय *m.* विल्हय *f.*

Inverted or retrogade o. व्यतिक्रम *m.* व्युत्क्रम *m.* व्यत्यय *m.* व्यत्यास *m.*

2 *established process, settled mode of operation.* क्रम *m.* मार्ग *m.* रीति *pop.* रीत *f.* परिपाठ *m.* परिपाटी *f.* पद्धति *pop.* पद्धत *f.* परिनालिका *f.* परणाळी *f.* मोड *f.* मोडणी *f.* प्रणालिका *f.* प्रणाली *f.* नियम *pop.* नेम *m.* पर्याय *m.*

Direct o. आनुलोम्य *n.*

Inverse or reverse o. प्रातिलोम्य *n.*

That is in regular and in reverse o. उलटापालटा, उफराटसुफराट, उफराटासुफराटा, उलटासुलटा, उलथापालथा, अनुलोमविलोम.

That is in o. मार्गाचा, मार्गांतला, रितीचा, &c.

3 *proper state or condition.* व्यवस्था *f.* बंदोबस्त *m.* यथावस्थिति *f.* रंग *m.* रूप *n.*

That is in good o.—affairs, articles, &c. चांगला, योग्य, स्थितीचा;—an animal, ताजा, ताजातवाना.

To be in good o. यथास्थित असणें.

To bring into regularity and o. सुर्तीपार्ती-सुर्ती-सुतास-रीतीस-&c. लावणें, वाटेवर-वाटेस-मार्गावर-मार्गास-&c. आणणें, विल्हेस लावणें.

To come into regularity and o. सुर्ती पार्ती-सुर्ती-सुतास-&c. लागणें, वाटेस-मार्गास-वाटेवर-&c. येणें, विल्हेस लागणें.

To get out of o. बिघडणें.

4 *rank, class, grade, division.* गण *m.* वर्ग *m.* वर्ण *m.* जाति *pop.* जात *f.* प्रत *f.* विल्हे *f.* विल्हा *m.* कोटी *f.*

The middle or common o. सामान्यपक्ष *m.* साधारणपक्ष *m.*

Disposing into classes or orders. विल्हेवारी *f.*

The whole o. or class. मात्र *n.* (as मनुष्यमात्र).

5 *society, body, fraternity.* गण *m.* मंडळी *f.* अखाडा *m.*

The lower orders, v. PEOPLE. तेली तांबोळी *m. pl.* कुणबी माळी *m. pl.* अडाण जात *f.*

The upper orders; *gentle folk.* खाशी पंगत *f.* खाशी मंडळी *f.* खास पंगत *f.* खासा लोक *m.*

6 *religious fraternity.* मार्ग *m.* पंथ *m.* (professor or follower of it. पंथी as नानकपंथी, कबीर पंथी, ज्ञानेश्वर पंथी, &c) आश्रम *m.* (This order is of four kinds, viz. ब्रह्मचर्य, गार्हस्थ्य, वानप्रस्थ, & सन्यास) संप्रदाय *m.* (follower of it, संप्रदायी, as स्मार्त्तसंप्रदायी, नाथसंप्रदायी, &c.).

Head of a religious o. महंत, आश्रमगुरु.

7 *precept*, v. COMMAND. आज्ञा *f.* हुकूम *m.* आदेश *m.* निदेश *m.* निर्देश *m.* नियोग *m.* फरमान *or* ना *m.*

General o. सदरहुकूम *m.* वटहुकूम *m.* सामान्यशासन *n.* साधारणाज्ञा *f.*

Made or done to o. फरमाशी *or* सी, काढींव, काढाऊ.

Under the o. of. कह्यांत.

Written o. लेखी हुकूम *m.* हुकूमनामा *m.*

8 upon ;—for money. रोखा *m.* वरात *f.* तनखा *m.*

9 *regulation*, v. RULE. कायदा *m.* दस्तक *n.*

10 *license, warrant, pass.* चिठ्ठी *f.* परवाना *m.* परवानगीचिठ्ठी *f.*

In o. to, *for the purpose, to the end.* साठीं, खब, करितां.

To take o. *take measures.* बंदोबस्त *m.*-तजवीज *f.*-&c. करणें-करून ठेवणें, तरतीब *n.* ठेवणें.

To ORDER, *v. a. arrange, put in order*, v. TO DISPOSE. रचणें, लावणें, थांगारणें, रचना *f.*-योजना *f.*-बंदोबस्त *m.*-बंदोबस्ती *f.*-व्यवस्था *f.*-&c. करणें *g. of o.* व्यवस्थित-व्यवस्थापित करणें.

2 *lead, conduct, manage, &c.* चालवणें, वागवणें, निर्वाहणें, बहिवाट *f.*-निर्वाह *m.*-&c. करणें *g. of o.*

3 *direct*, v. To COMMAND. आज्ञा *f.*-हुकूम *m.*-&c. देणें-करणें, आज्ञापणें, निदेशणें, फरमाविणें. [व्यवस्थापित.

ORDERED, *p.* v. V. 1. रचलेला, थांगारलेला, &c. रचित, योजित,

2 चालवलेला, वागवलेला, &c.

3 हुकूम केलेला, &c. आज्ञापित, निर्दिष्ट.

ORDERER, *n.* ORDERING, *p. a.* v. V. 1. रचणारा, थांगारणारा, &c. रचक, योजक, व्यवस्थापक, रचना-&c. कर्त्ता-कारी.

2 चालवणारा, वागवणारा, निर्वाह करणारा, &c.

3 हुकूम करणारा, &c. आज्ञापक.

ORDERING, *n.* v. V. 1.—*act.* रचणें *n.* &c. रचना *f.* योजना *f.* व्यवस्थापन *n.* तरतीब *n.*

2—*act.* चालवणें *n.* वागवणें *n.* &c. निर्वाह *m.* बहिवाट *f.*

3—*act.* आज्ञा करणें *n.* &c. आज्ञापन *n.* [क्रमरहित.

ORDERLESS, *a.* v. DISORDERLY. अव्यवस्थित, अक्रम, क्रमशून्य,

ORDERLINESS, *n.* v. A. 1. क्रम *m.* बेत *m.* बेतबात *m.* बंदोबस्त *m.* बंदोबस्ती *f.* व्यवस्था *f.* संजोग *m.* ठाकठिकी *f.* शिश्टाई *f.* शिश्टाइकी *f.* चाफचोपी *f.* चापचोपी *f.* व्यवस्थितपणा *m.* क्रमिकत्व *n.* यथाक्रमता *f.* सक्रमता *f.* यथानुक्रमता *f.*

2 व्यवस्थितपणा *m.* ठाकसठिकसपणा *m.* ठाकठिकी *f.* चापचोपी *f.* चाकचोपी *f.* चापीचोपी *f.* चकपक *f.* नियमशीलता *f.* क्रमानुकारिता *f.* क्रमकारिता *f.*

ORDERLY, *a. methodical, regularly,*—of things. क्रमाचा, बेताचा, बेताबाताचा, बंदोबस्ताचा, व्यवस्थेचा, नियमाचा *or* नेमाचा, संजोगाचा, संजुकता *or* संजुगता, ठीकठाक *or* ठाकठीक, साससुरत, चकपक, चापचोपीचा, &c. बेतीव, व्यवस्थित, यथाक्रम, यथानुक्रम, क्रमिक, सक्रम, क्रमशुद्ध, संप्रदायशुद्ध, अनुपूर्व, आन्वयिक, आनुलोमिक.

2—of persons. बेताचा, बेतबाती *or* त्या, बंदोबस्तीचा, नियमाचा *or* नेमाचा, नियमी *or* नेमी, नियमशील, ठाकसठिकस *or* ठिकसठाकस, टाकठिक्या, चाकचोप्या, चापचोप्या, चाकचोपीचा, व्यवस्थित, क्रमानुकारी, यथाक्रमकारी, क्रमकारी.

ORDERLY, *adv.* v. A. क्रमानें, अनुक्रमानें, अनुक्रमेंकरून, बेतानें, &c. यथाक्रम, यथानुक्रम, विल्हेवार.

ORDINAL, *a. noting order.* क्रमसूचक, क्रमदर्शक, क्रमवाचक,

ORDINAL, *n. ritual.* पद्धति *f.*

2 क्रमवाचक संख्या *f.*

ORDINANCE, *n. law, rule, decree, statute.* कायदा *m.* नियम *m.* कानू *f.* दस्तूर अमल *m.* विधि *m.* विधान *n.* चोदना *f.* शासन *n.*

2—of religion, *prescribed act or rite.* विधि *m.* अनुष्ठान *n.* संस्कार *m.* कर्म *n.* क्रिया *f.*

Succedaneous o. प्रतिविधि *m.* प्रत्याम्नाय *m.*

ORDINARILY, *adv.* v. A. 1. *and* COMMONLY. प्रायः, प्रायशः

ORDINARY, *a. customary, common, usual, &c.* नित्यचालीचा, चालीचा, रूढीचा, नित्यपाठांतला, नित्यव्यवहारांतला, मामूलशिरिस्त्याचा, व्यावहारिक *pop.* व्यवहारिक *or* रीक, प्रायिक, यथापद्धति, यथासंप्रदाय.

2 *of the common kind*, v. COMMON, MIDDLING. मध्यम, मध्यमप्रतीचा, रासवट, साधारण, सामान्य, तादृश.

In o. *in actual and constant service.* नित्याचा, नित्यांतला.

ORDINARY, *n. eating house.* भटारखाना *m.* जेवणावळीचें घर *n.* साधारणभोजनशाला *f.*

ORDINATE. See ORDERLY.

ORDINATION, ORDAINING, *n.* v. V. 1.—*act.* नेमणें *n.* स्थापणें *n.* &c. स्थापना *f.* स्थापन *n.* विधान *n.* चोदना *f.*

O. of Providence. घटितार्थ *m.* घटित *n.*

2 नेमणें *n.* नेमणूक *f.* योजना *f.* योजन *n.* नियोजन *n.* नियोग *m.*

3 धर्माधिकारदीक्षा *f.* धर्मपदनियोजन *n.* धर्मपदनियोग *m.*

ORDNANCE, *n. cannon, guns.* तोफा *f. pl.* तोफखाना *m.*

Piece of o. तोफ *f.* उल्हाटयंत्र *n.*

ORDURE, *n.* v. DUNG. हग *m.* गू *m.* विष्ठा *f.*

Heap of o. नरक *m.*

ORE, *n. unrefined metal.* असंस्कृतधातु *m.* अशोधित धातु *m.* The ore of a particular metal is often expressed by the adjective कच्चा prefixed to it, as कच्चें लोखंड, कच्चें तांबें iron ore, copper ore, &c. or by माती *or* दगड used with it in the possessive case, as सोन्याची माती *f.* लोखंडाचा दगड *m.*

2 *metal.* धातु *m. f.* [करण *n.*

ORGAN, *n. natural instrument of action.* साधन *n.* कर्मसाधन *n.*

2—of sense or perception. इंद्रिय *n.* ज्ञानेंद्रिय *n.* ज्ञानसाधन *n.* अध्यात्म *n.* These are, श्रोत्र, त्वक्, चक्षु, जिह्वा, घ्राण.

O. of action. कर्मेंद्रिय *n.* The organs of action are, वाक्, पाणि, पाद, पायु and उपस्थ.

O. of the mind or soul. अंतरिंद्रिय *n.* These are मन, बुद्धि, अहंकार, चित्त.

Organs of sense—collectively. इंद्रियग्राम *m.* इंद्रियवर्ग *m.*

3 *instrument or means of communication.* द्वार *n.* साधन *n.*

4 एक वाद्य आहे.

ORGANIC, ORGANICAL, *a. possessing organs of vitality or action.* इंद्रियवान्, इंद्रियसंपन्न, इंद्रियविशिष्ट, जीवित्वसाधनविशिष्ट, प्राणित्वसाधनसंपन्न, स्वस्वकर्मसाधनसंपन्न, करणसंपन्न, सकरण.

2 *consisting, &c. of organs.* कर्मसाधनमय, कर्मसाधनरूप, कर्मसाधनप्रचुर.

3 *produced &c. by the organs.* इंद्रियांचा, इंद्रियसंबंधी, इंद्रियजनित, इंद्रियोत्पन्न.

ORGANISM, *n. organic structure.* इंद्रियविशिष्ट रचना *f.*

ORGANIZATION, *n.* v. V. 1.—*act.* इंद्रियविशिष्ट करणें *n.* &c. इंद्रियविशिष्टकरण *n.* कर्मसाधनसंपन्नकरण *n.*

2 कामगार नेमणें *n.* कामगारांचा बंदोबस्त करणें *n.* &c.

I. *suitable disposition of parts.* इंद्रियांचा-कर्मसाधनांचा-&c. बंदोबस्त *m.*-बेतबात *m.*-व्यवस्था *f.*-&c.

To ORGANIZE, *v. a. form with organs.* इंद्रियवान्-इंद्रियसंपन्न-कर्मेंद्रियसंपन्न-कर्मसाधनसंपन्न-कर्मसाधनयुक्त-अवयवी-अवयवसंपन्न-सांग-सांगोपांग-अंगोपांगसंपन्न-&c. करणें.

2 *arrange by appointing officers, agents, &c.* कामगार नेमून-अमलदार नेमून-&c. बंदोबस्त *m.*-बंदोबस्ती *f.*-बेत *m.*-व्यवस्था *f.*-&c. करणें *g. of o.* [व्रेश *m.*

ORGASM, *n. excitement.* उकळी *f.* उकळ *m.* ऊत *m.* कढ *m.* आ-

ORGIES, *n. drunken revels.* दारूबाजीचा गोंधळ *m.* भैरवीचक्राचा गोंधळ *m.*

ORIENT, *a. rising*—the sun, &c. उदयी, उदयमान.

2 See EASTERN. 3 See BRIGHT.

ORIENT, *n.* v. EAST. पूर्व *f.*

ORIENTAL, *a.* v. EASTERN. पूर्वेचा, पूर्वदेशीय, पूर्वदेशस्थ,

ORIENTAL, *n.* पूर्वदिशेकडील राहणारा, एशियाखंडांतील राहणारा.

ORIENTALIST, *n.* एशियाखंडांतील भाषा जाणणारा.

ORIFICE, *n. mouth, aperture.* तोंड *n.* मुख *n.* दार *n.*

ORIGIN, ORIGINAL, *n. beginning, first existence, spring,* v. RISE. मूल *pop.* मूळ *n.* मूळारंभ *m.* *m.* उद्गम *pop.* उगम *and vulg.* उग्रम *m.* उपक्रम *m.* आगम *m.* उपज *m.* उत्पत्ति *f.*

2 *fountain, place of origin,* v. SOURCE. घर *n.* झरा *m.* खाण *f.* मूल *n.* बीज *n.* आदि *m.* आदिकारण *n.* हेतु *m.* उत्पत्तिस्थान *n.* आगमस्थान *n.*

3 *archetype, first copy.* मूळ *n.* मूलपत्र *n.* मूळप्रत *f.* आदर्श *m.*

4 *text,*—opposed to a translation, &c. मूल *n.* मूलग्रंथ *m.*

ORIGINAL, *a. primitive, pristine.* मूळचा, प्रथमचा, अवलचा, प्रारंभींचा, उत्पत्तिकालचा, असल, अवल, पहिल्यापासूनचा, पहिला, प्रथम, प्राथमिक, आद्य, अपूर्व, मौल, मौलिक, मूलिक.

2 *having power to originate new thoughts.* नवी योजना करणारा, अपूर्वकल्पक, अपूर्वयोजक, स्वतःकल्पक.

3 *not made before or by another.* नवेयोजनेचा, नवेरचनेचा, नवेरूनीचा, स्वतःकल्पनेचा, अपूर्व, अपूर्वकर्तृक, अपूर्वसिद्ध, अपूर्वरचित.

ORIGINALITY, ORIGINALNESS, *n.* v. A. 1. असलपणा *m.* अवलपणा *m.*

2 अपूर्वकल्पनाशक्ति *f.* अपूर्वकल्पकत्व *n.*

3 अपूर्वसिद्धता *f.* अपूर्वरचितत्व *n.*

ORIGINALLY, *adv. from the rise or origin.* मुळाहून, पहिल्यापासून, उपजत, मूळस्वभावानें, मूळस्वभावेंकरून, आदितः, जातितः, उत्पत्तितः.

2 *at first, at the origin.* पहिला *decl.* पहिल्यानें, मुळीं, आदीं, मुळारंभीं, प्रारंभीं, अवल.

ORIGINARY. See ORIGINATOR.

To ORIGINATE, *v. a. bring into existence.* काढणें, उत्पन्न-उपस्थित-&c. करणें, प्रारंभ *m.*-प्रथमोद्भव *m.*-प्रथमोत्पत्ति *f.*-प्रथमोपस्थिति *f.*-&c. करणें *g. of o.* मूळ *n.*-उपक्रम *m.*-उग्रम *m.*-&c. काढणें *g. of o.*

To ORIGINATE, *v. n. take existence, begin,* v. To RISE. होणें, उत्पन्न-उपस्थित-सुरू-चालू-प्रवृत्त-&c. होणें, उठणें, प्रारंभ *m.*-उपक्रम *m.*-उत्थान *n.*- उत्थिति *f.*-&c. होणें *g. of s.* संभवणें.

ORIGINATED, *p.* v. V. A. काढलेला, उत्पन्न केलेला, उपक्रम काढलेला, &c. उत्पन्न.

ORIGINATION, *n.* v. V. A.—*act.* काढणें *n.* &c. प्रथमोत्पादन *n.* प्रथमोद्भावन *n.*—*state.* v. BEGINNING. प्रारंभ *m.* उपक्रम *m.* उद्गम *m.* प्रथमोत्पत्ति *f.*

ORIGINATOR, *n.* ORIGINATING, *p. a.* v. V. A. काढणारा, उत्पन्न-करणारा, उपस्थित करणारा, मूळ काढणारा, मूलोत्पादक, प्रथमोत्पादक, प्रथमोद्भावक.

ORION, *n.*—the constellation. मृगशीर्ष *n.*

ORISON, *n.* v. PRAYER. प्रार्थना *f.* वाचिकप्रार्थना *f.*

ORNAMENT, *n. decoration, embellishment, additional beauty.* शोभा *f.* भूषा *f.* भूषण *n.* विभूषा *f.* विभूषण *n.* रूप *n.* रंग *m.* अलंकार *m.* मंडन *n.* आभरण *n.* नेपथ्य *n.*

2 *thing ornamenting; trinket, &c.* अलंकार *m.* भूषण *n.* वस्त *f.* डागिणा *or* ना *m.* दागिना *m.* नग *m.* नगोटें *n.* आभरण *n.*

Ornaments—compreh. *trinkets and traps.* नगनगोटा *m.* नगनगोटें *n.* नगवज *m.* लेणें *n.* जडजवाहीर *n.*

O. of dress. अलंकार *m.*

O. of language. अलंकार *m.*

O. of sense. अर्थालंकार *m.*

O. for the ankles of dancers. चाळ *m.*

O. set with jems. जडीन *n.*

Trumpery ornaments. लावट बेगड दागिने *m. pl.*-वस्ना *f. [pl.*

Verbal o. शब्दालंकार *n.*

Some of the *ornaments* of *women* are, अडकण, अनवट, कंठा, कर्णफूल, कमरपट्टा, कांकण, कांची, कांडोळें, काप, कारलें, कुडरी, कुरडुं, केतक, केवडा, खड्गपात्र, खपट, खटूं, गळसरी, गेंद, गुळखी, गोठ, गोफ, घोंसबाळी, चंद्रकोर, चंद्रहार, चांदणी, चिंचपेटी, चितंग, चितांग, चुटकी, चुडा, छंद, जवा, जुगणी, जोडवें, ठुशी, नकट, तन्मणि, तांदळीपोत, तानवड, तायतळें, तिदाणें, तोडा, तोरडी, तोळबंदी, धुशी, दडकडी, नग, नथ, नाग, पाटली, पायजिभी, पैंजण, पोत, पोल्हार, फूल, बहिरव, बांगडी, बाजूबंद, बाळी, बिजवरा, बिंदी, बिरी, बुगडी, बुलाक, भांगसळ, मंगळसूत्र, मासोळी, माळ, मुखडा, मुद, मोती, राखडी, लफा, वज्रटीक, वांकी, वाळा, विरचळी, वेळ, शिसफूल, समती, सरी, सासळी, हार. Some of the *ornaments* of *men* are, अंगठी, कंठी, कडें, कलगी, गेठा, गांटा, गौरीशंकर, चौकडा, जिगा *or* जेगा, तुरा, तोडा, दंडपेटी, पवित्रक, पोंहची, भिकबाळी, शिरपेंच.

To ORNAMENT, *v. a.* v. To ADORN. अलंकारणें, भूषवणें, शोभवणें, शोभेसा करणें, मंडन *n.*-भूषण *n.*-&c. करणें *g. of o.*

ORNAMENTAL, *a.* ORNAMENTING, *p. a.* v. V. शोभवणारा, शोभादेणारा-करणारा, शोभेचा, शोभाकर, शोभाकारक, शोभाप्रद, शोभादायक, शोभावह, भूषाकर, भूषावह, अलंकारक.

ORNAMENTED, *p.* v. V. *and* ADORNED. अलंकारलेला, शोभवलेला, &c. अलंकृत, सालंकृत, सालंकार, भूषित, मंडित, विभूषित.

ORNAMENTING, *n.* v. V.—*act.* अलंकारणें *n.* &c. मंडन *n.* भूषण *n.* अलंकरण *n.*

ORNATE. See ADORNED.

ORNITHOLOGIST, *n. one skilled in the history of birds.* पक्षिविषयकविद्यावेत्ता.

ORNITHOLOGY, *n. natural history of birds.* पक्षिविषयकविद्या *f.* पक्षिवर्णनविद्या *f.*

ORPHAN, *n. child bereaved of its parents.* पोरका *m.* (पोरकी *f.*) पोरापोरका *m.* (पोरीपोरकी *f.*).

2 *bereaved of father.* बापपोरका (की *f.*) मृतपितृक, गतपितृक.

3 *bereaved of mother.* आई पोरका (की *f.*) मृतमातृक, गतमातृक.

ORPHAN, *a. bereaved of parents.* पोरापोरका, पोरका, दोहीं आंगीं उणा, उघडा, अनाथ, मातृपितृहीन-विहीन-&c.

2 *bereaved of one parent.* आंगी उणा, एकांगीं उणा.

ORPHANAGE, ORPHANISM, *n.* v. A. 1. पोरकेपणा *m.* पोरेपोरकेपणा *m.* मातृपितृहीनता *f.*

ORPIMENT, *n.*—yellow. हरिताल *m. pop.* हरताळ *f. m.* गोदंती हरताळ *f.* ताल *m.*

Golden colored o. पञ्याहरताळ *m. f.*

Red o. रक्तधातु *m.*

ORRERY, *n. planetarium.* ग्रहगतिसूचकयंत्र *n.*

ORRIS-ROOT, *n.* वेखंड *n.* श्वेतवचा *f.* हैमवतीवचा *f.* चव्या *f.* वचा *f.*

Black o. जटिल वेखंड *n.* [बोनें *n.*

ORT, *n.* ORTS, *n. pl. fragment or piece left.* उष्टें *n.* उच्छिष्ट *n.*

ORTHODOX, *a. sound in the faith, not heretical.* खऱ्या मार्गाचा, दक्षिणमार्गाचा, सत्पथगामी, सत्पथवर्त्ती, सत्पथावलंबी, दक्षिणमार्गी, दक्षिणमार्गानुयायी, यथाशास्त्र.

ORTHODOXY, *n. sound faith.* सत्पथ *m.* सन्मार्ग *m.* दक्षिणमार्ग *m.* दक्षिणाचार *m.*

2 *consonance to right doctrine.* सत्पथानुयायिता *f.* सन्मार्गानुयायिता *f.* यथाशास्त्रता *f.*

ORTHOEPY, *n. correct pronunciation.* शुद्धोच्चार *m.* शुद्धोच्चारण *n.*

ORTHOGONAL. See RECTANGULAR.

ORTHOGRAPHIC, ORTHOGRAPHICAL, *a. relating to correct spelling.* शुद्धलिहिण्याचा, शुद्धलिहिण्याविषयींचा, शुद्धाक्षरन्यासविषयक-संबंधी, वर्णन्याससंबंधी.

ORTHOGRAPHY, *n. correct spelling.* शुद्धलिहिणें *n.* शुद्धाक्षरन्यास *m.* वर्णन्यास *m.*

OS COCCYGIS, *n.* माकडहाड *n.* मणका *m.*

To OSCILLATE, *v. n. vibrate,* v. To SWING. झोलणें, आंदुळणें, झोके *m. pl.*-झोंपे *m. pl.*-झेंपा *f. pl.*-&c. देणें-घेणें-खाणें.

OSCILLATION, *n.* v. V.—*act.* झोलणें *n.* &c. झोका *m.* झोंपा *m.* झोंप *f.* झेंप *f.* हेलकावा *m.* हेलावा *m.* आंदोलन *n.* गतागत *n.*

OSCILLATORY, *a.* OSCILLATING, *p. a.* v. V. झोलणारा, आंदुळणारा, झोके-&c. घेणारा-खाणारा-&c. दोलायमान, आंदोलायमान.

OSCITANCY, OSCITATION, *n.* v. YAWNING. जांभई *f.* जृंभण *f.* जृंभिका *f.* जृंभावात *m.*

OSCITANT, *a.* v. YAWNING. जृंभमाण, जृंभावान्.

OSIER. See WILLOW.

OSPRAY, *n. sea eagle.* कुरर *m.* कुररी *f.* पंक्तिचर *m.* उत्क्रोश *m.*

OSSEOUS, *a.* v. BONY. हाडाचा, अस्थिमय.

OSSICLE, *n. small bone.* हाडकी *f.* हडूक *n.* क्षुद्रास्थि *n.* लघ्वस्थि *n.*

OSSIFIC, *a. having power to turn into bone.* अस्थिकर-कारक-जनक-&c.

OSSIFICATION, *n. change into bone.* हाडहोणें *n.* अस्थिभवन *n.* अस्थिभाव *m.* अस्थिभूय *n.* अस्थिपरिणाम *m.*

To OSSIFY, *v. a. turn to bone.* हाड *n.*-अस्थि *n.*-&c. करणें-बनावणें *g. of o.*

To OSSIFY, *v. n. become bone.* हाड *n.*-अस्थि *n.*-&c. होणें, अस्थि परिणाम *m.*-&c. होणें *g. of s.* अस्थिभूत-&c. होणें.

OSSIVOROUS, *a. bone-eating.* हाडखाऊ, अस्थिभक्षक, अस्थिभोजी.

OSSUARY, *n. place for bones, charnel house.* हाडोळा *m.* हाडवळ *f.* अस्थ्यालय *n.* अस्थ्यागार *n.*

OSTENSIBLE, *a. apparent, declared or avowed.* दिसण्याचा, दिसण्यांतला, प्रत्यक्ष, प्रसिद्ध.

2—esp. as implying insincerity, &c. वरकरणी, वरघडीचा, वरपंकाचा, वरपंकी, बाह्यात्काराचा, बाह्यरंगाचा.

OSTENSIBLY, *adv.* v. 1. दिसण्यांत, पाहण्यांत, दिसायास, प्रत्यक्षांत. 2 वरवर, वरवरता *or* तीं, बाह्यात्कारीं.

OSTENTATION, *n. ambitious or imposing display,* v. SHOW. डौल *m.* डामडौल *m.* मिरवणूक *f.* मिरवण *f.* डबला *m.* *v.* मिरव, प्रतिष्ठा *f.* *v.* मिरव, आडंबर *n.* आव *m.* *v.* घाल, दाखव, टामटूम *or* टुमटाम *f.*

2—esp. as fraudulent, *pretension to.* दंभ *or* डंभ *m.* स्तोम *n.* पोम *m.* ढोंग *n.*

OSTENTATIOUS, *a. fond of display,* v. N. 1. आडंबराचा, आवाचा, डौलाचा, डामडौलाचा, &c. आडंबरी, अवडंबऱ्या, आव घालणारा, आवघाल्या, खटाटोपी *or* प्या.

2 ढोंगी, ढोंग्या, दंभी *or* डंभी, दांभिक.

OSTENTATIOUSLY, *adv.* v. A. 1. डौलानें, डौल दाखवून, &c. गाजून वाजून, टामटूम करून.

OSTEOCOPE, *n. pain in the bones.* हाडाचें दुःख *n.* अस्थिवेदना *f.* अस्थिशूल *m. n.*

OSTEOLOGY, *n. description of the bones.* अस्थिवर्णन *n.* अस्थिप्रकरण *n.*

OSTIARY, *n. mouth*—of a river. मुख *n.*

OSTLER. See GROOM.

OSTRICH, *n.* शहामृग *m.*

OTHER, *a. not this, different.* दुसरा, इतर, अन्य, अणीक, एक, एर, परका *or* परखा, परकी, पर (in comp. as परदेश, &c.), अपर.

2 *some else, some besides.* दुसरा, दुजा.

Other's, *belonging to another.* दुसऱ्याचा, अन्यदीय, परकीय, पर (in comp. as परधन, परस्त्री, &c.), परका.

Some (odd, stray, chance, &c.) o. एखाद दुसरा.

The others, *the rest.* दुसरे, वरकड *or* वरकट, इतर, बाकीचे, वरचील, अवांतर.

3 *not this but the contrary.* दुसरा, तो as opposed to हा [*this*, अपर.

On the o. side. पैलीकडे, पैलपार.

The o. side, bank, &c. पैलाड *f.*

4—each other. एकमेक, परस्पर.

5 *the next.* दुसरा.

Every o. day. एकदिवस आड.

The other day. कांहीं दिवसांमागें, कांहीं दिवस झाले, चार दिवस झाले.

OTHER-WHERE, *adv.* दुसऱ्या-&c. ठिकाणीं-जागीं-स्थळीं-&c. अन्यत्र, इतरत्र.

OTHERWISE, *adv. in a different manner.* दुसऱ्या रितीनें, अन्यप्रकारानें, निराळा *decl.* वेगळा *decl.* अन्यथा, अन्यत्, इतरथा.

2 *by other causes.* दुसऱ्या-अन्य-&c. कारणानें, कारणांतरें करून.

3 v. ELSE. नाहींतर, अन्यथा, एरवीं.

4 *in other respect.* एरवीं, नाहींतर, त्यावांचून, वरकड।विषयीं.

OTTAR, OTTER, *n. essential oil of flowers.* अत्तर *n.*

Phial or vessel for o. अत्तरदानी *f.*

Vender of o. अत्तार *or* अत्तारी.

OTTER, *n.* पाणमांजर *n.* जलमार्जार *m.* उद्र *m.* पानीयनकुल *m.*

OUGHT, *v. imperfect. to be necessary, &c.* पाहिजे, प्राप्त-भाग असणें, भागास येणें.

OUNCE, *n.* v. MEASURE. अर्धटांक *m.* is about an o.

OUR, *a.* आमचा, आपला, अस्मदीय.

OUR-SELVES, *pr.* आम्ही, आपण.

OURANG-OUTANG, *n.* रानमाणूस *n.*

To OUST, *v. a. eject.* v. To EXPEL. काढणें, काढून देणें-टाकणें, निखळणें, उधडणें, उखडणें, उखळणें, पाय *m.*-दुमची *f.*-तळी *f.*-&c. उचलणें *g. of o.* मेखा *f. pl.*-खुंटी *f.*-&c. उपटणें *g. of o.* खो *m. f.* घालणें, उत्थापन *n.*-उद्वासन *n.*-&c. करणें *g. of o.*

OUSTED, *p.* v. V. काढलेला, उधडलेला, खुंटी उपटलेला, &c. उद्वासित, उत्थापित.

OUSTER, *n.* OUSTING, *p. a.* v. V. काढणारा, उधडणारा, पाय उचलणारा, &c. खुंटीउपट्या.

OUT, *adv. not in, abroad.* बाहेर.

2 *in a state of extinction.* गेलेला, विझून गेलेला.

To go out. जाणें, विझणें, राम *m.* म्हणणें.

To put out. विझवणें, माल्वणें, निरोप *m.* देणें.

To flap out. पाल्वणें, पदर *m.* देणें.

3 *in exhaustion, consumption, &c.* To be out. खपणें, उडणें, संपणें, अटपणें, सरणें, दिवाळें *n.*-भदें*n.*-टाळ*m.*-थाळा*m.*-घंटा *f.*-&c. वाजणें *g. of s.* ठणठणाट *m.*-खडखडाट *m.*-&c. होणें *g. of s.* बियाण्यासनसणें.

4 *not in office, employment, &c.* निराळा (कामा-&c. निराळा), वेगळा (कामा-&c. वेगळा).

That is out of employment. रिकामा, बेकार, बेरोजगार.

5 *through, to the end.* पार, शेवट-आखेरी-&c.पर्यंत, संपेतों, साद्यंत.

6 *audibly, loudly.* मोठ्यानें, उंच्या *or* उंच गळ्यानें.

7 *publicly, openly.* प्रसिद्धपणें, उघड, उघडपणीं.

8 *in error, at fault.* To be out. फसणें, चुकणें, चकणें, थकणें.

To get safely o. of or through. पार पडणें, निभावणें, निभणें.

To out with, *rap out.* कडकावणें, धडकावणें, भडकावणें.

OUT, *interj.* धिस, हत्त.

OUT OF, *prep. from*;—noting produce, procession, &c. पासून, आंतून, पैकीं, जवळून.

2 *not in*;—noting exclusion, absence, &c. बाहेर, आंतून, वेगळा *decl.* निराळा *decl.*

3 *not within.* बाहेर.

4 *not in*;—noting deviation, exorbitance, &c. सोडून, टाकून, निराळा *decl.* वेगळा *decl.*

5 *beyond.* बाहेर, पलीकडे.

That is beyond. अतीत in comp.

6 *in destitution of through consumption, &c.* To be out —an article; *or*, to be o. of—a person. सरणें, खपणें, संपणें, उरकणें *g. of s.* (as my clarified butter is out, *or* I am out of clarified butter माझें तूप सरलें, &c.).

7 *through, from*;—noting ground, reason, cause, motive. नें (as क्रोधानें out of anger, प्रीतीनें out of love, &c.), स्तव, मुळें.

Out of hand, v. IMMEDIATELY. हातच्या हातीं.

To OUTBALANCE. See To OUTWEIGH.

To OUTBID, *v. a. bid more than.* चढ *m.* करणें-टाकणें-बोलणें, अधिक-&c. बोलणें.

To OUTBRAVE, *v. a. bear down by more daring or insolent conduct.* अधिकधीट-सवाधीट-&c. होणें-होऊन दाबणें-दडपणें-&c. शेरास सवाशेर होणें-होऊन दाबणें-दडपणें-&c. धिटाईवर-&c.धिटाई *f.* करणें *g. of o.* धृष्टत्वाधिक्य करून दडपणें.

To OUTBRAZEN, *v. a. bear down by impudence.* धिटाईनें चढ *m.* करणें, धिटाईचा चढ *m.* करणें, धिटास सवाधीट होणें.

OUTBREAK, See ERUPTION.

OUTCAST, *a. expelled from society, &c.* जातिभ्रष्ट, जातिबाह्य, जातिबहिष्कृत, बहिष्कृत, पंक्तिबाह्य, अपांक, लोकबाह्य, वाळ, वाळीत, पंक्तिदूषक.

2 *of a low, mean caste; void of decent practices.* जातिहीन, हीनजाति, हीनवर्ण, वर्णहीन, आचारहीन, आचारवर्जित.

OUTCRY, *n. cry of distress.* रड *f.* आरड *f.* बोंब *f.* बोभाटा *m.* रडारोई *f.* धाय *f. v.* फोड-मोकल-घे, आकांत *m.* आक्रोश *m.* घोर*m.*

Vehement and causeless o. अवांब *n.*

2 *clamour against.* नांवाचीबोंब *f. g. of o.* नांवानें बोंब *f. g. of o.* हाकाटा *m.* हाकारा *m.* बोभाट *m. n.* बोभाटा *m.*

General o. against. बोंबाबोंब *f.* जनापवाद *m.*

To raise an o. against. नांवें बोंब *f.* मारणें *g. of o.*

To have an o. against one. नांवाची बोंब *f.* पडणें *g. of s.*

To be a great o. for or after. बोंब *f.* पडणें-होणें-वाजणें *g. of s.*

3 *hubbub, vociferation,* v. UPROAR. गल्गल *f.* गल्बल *f.* गलबला *m.* गूल *f.* गोंगाट *m.* कोल्हाळ *m.* कल्लोळ *m.* कुलुली *f.*

4 *auction.* निलाम *or* लिलाम *or* लिलांव *m. n.*

To OUTDO, *v. a. surpass,* v. To EXCEL. मागें-पाठीमागें टाकणें-पाडणें-सांडणें, चढ *m.* करणें *with* वर *of o.* उणें *n.* आणणें, कान *n. pl.* कापणें *g. of s.*

OUT-DOOR, *a.* घराबाहेरचा, घराबाहेरला.

OUTER, *a. external,*—opposed to inner. बाहेरचा, बाहेरला, बाहेरील, बाहेरल्या बाजूचा *or* ला, बाहेरल्या कडचा *or* ला, बाहेरल्या धडचा *or* ला, बाहेरल्या आंगाचा, बहिर्भागाचा, बहिर्भागींचा, बाह्य, बहिर्भागस्थ, बहिर्भूत.

OUTER-MOST, *a.* सर्वांच्या बाहेरचा, सर्वांहून बाहेरचा, सर्वांच्या पलीकडचा, सर्वांच्या शेवटचा, कडे शेवटचा.

To OUTFACE. See To OUTBRAVE.

OUTFIT, *n. equipment for a journey, voyage, &c.* प्रवासाचें-सफरेचें-&c. सामान*n.*-साहित्य *n.*

To OUTGO, *v.a.*v. To EXCEL. मागें-पाठीमागें टाकणें-पाडणें-सांडणें, चढ*m.* करणें *with* वर *of o.*

To OUTGROW, *v. a. surpass in growth.* वाढीनें मागें पाडणें-टाकणें-सांडणें, वाढीस चढणें *with* त्याहून *of o.* वाढीचा चढ*m.* करणें *with* वर *of o.* [&c. करणें.

2 *grow too large for.* वाढून-वाढीनें लहान-अडस-दाटता-दाट-

OUTHOUSE, *n.* पडसाळ *f.* पडशाळा *f.* पडघर*n.* उपगृह*n.* मोठ्याघराजवळ चाकरलोक वगैरे राहण्याचें घर *n.*

To OUTKNAVE, *v. a. exceed in knavery.* ठकास ठक भेटणें, ठकास सवाई ठक भेटणें, ठकबाजीवर ठकबाजी *f.* करणें, ठकबाजीचा चढ *m.*-&c. करणें. [बासी.

OUTLANDISH, *a.* v. FOREIGN. परदेशचा, दूरदेशचा, परदेशीय, दूर-

2 *rude, rustic,* v. BARBAROUS. कानडा, हेंगडा *or* हेंगाडा, हेंगडूमेंगडू, रांगडा.

O. fellow. जळमाणूस*n.* रानमाणूस *n.* जलचर *m.*

O. speech or fashion. कानडें *n.*

To OUTLAST, *v. a. last longer than.* टिकण्याविषयीं-तगण्याविषयीं-&c. मागें पाडणें-टाकणें-&c. अधिकटिकणें-तगणें-&c. *with* हून-पेक्षां-&c. *of o.*

OUTLAW, *n.* OUTLAWED, *p.* v. V. *person excluded from the benefit and protection of the law.* राजरक्षणबाह्य, न्यायरक्षणबाह्य, व्यवहारबहिष्कृत, धर्मद्वारबहिष्कृत, न्यायरक्षणबहिष्कृत.

To OUTLAW, *v. a. put out of the protection of the law.* राज्यरक्षणाच्याबाहेर-न्यायरक्षणाच्याबाहेर-&c. करणें-ठेवणें, राजरक्षणबाह्य-न्यायरक्षणबहिष्कृत-&c. करणें.

OUTLAWRY, *n.* v. V. राजरक्षणबहिष्करण*n.*न्यायरक्षणबहिष्करण*n.*

OUTLAY, *n.* v. EXPENDITURE. खर्च *m.* व्यय*m.*

2 *laying out in order.* मांड *m.* मांडणूक *f.* मांडावळ *f.* मांडणी *f.* पसारा *m.*

OUTLET, *n. passage outward.* निघण्याची-बाहेर जाण्याची-&c.

वाट *f.* दार *dim.* दारे *n.* द्वार *n.* बाहेरवाट *f.* बारें *n.* निकाल *m.* मम *f.* निर्गमद्वार *n.* निर्गममार्ग *m.*

OUTLINE, *n. exterior line.* मर्यादेची-बाहेरची-&c. रेघ *f.*-रेषा *f.*

Contour or general o. रूपरेषा *f.* वळण *f. n.*

2—outlines; *first sketch of a figure or subject.* अरासडा *m.* आडामोडा *m.* बेन *m.* बेतचात *m.* कचा आकार *m.* वस्तुमात्र *n.*

To OUTLINE. See To DELINEATE.

To OUTLIVE, *v. a. survive.* मागें-पाठीमागें राहणें-वांचणें-जगणें *g. of o.* मादून मरणें, मागें-पाठीमागें मरणें *g. of o.*

OUTLYING, *a.* दूरचा, बाहेरचा, बाहेरील.

To OUTMARCH, *v. a. leave behind in marching.* चालण्यानें मागें टाकणें-घालणें, &c.

OUTMOST. See OUTERMOST.

To OUTNUMBER, *v. a. exceed in number.* गणतींत-संख्येंत-गणतीनें-&c. मागें टाकणें-पाडणें-&c. अधिक असणें *with* हून-पेक्षां-&c. *of o.*

OUTPOST, *n.* बाहेरचें ठाणें *n.*

OUTRAGE, *n. injurious violence or excess,* v. EXCESS. जुलूम *m.* जुलूमज्यास्ती *f.* बलात्कार *m.* उपमर्द *m.* गजब *m.* अनर्थ *m.* कहर *m.* आकांत *m.* अतिशय *m.* साहस *n.* भालेराई *f.* उत्पात *m.*

To OUTRAGE, *v. a. treat with violence and wrong.* जुलूम *m.*-जुलूमज्यास्ती *f.*- बलात्कार *m.*- अनर्थ *m.*- अतिशय *m.*-&c. करणें *with* वर *of o.* उपमर्द *m.* करणें *g. of o.* लथडणें *or* लथाडणें.

OUTRAGEOUS, *a. violent, exceeding reason or bounds,* v. EXCESSIVE. अनर्थाचा, कहराचा, आकांताचा, उत्पाताचा, कल्पांताचा, &c. कहरी, चंड, विकोपास गेलेला.

2 *furious, wildly raging.* तग्रबग्र, तारकाबारका *or* तारखाबारखा, कावराबावरा, राक्षसी, साहसी, कहरी.

OUTRAGEOUSLY, *adv.* v. A. 1. कहरानें, अनर्थानें, जुलमानें, &c. अनर्थ करून, कहर करून, &c.अनर्थाचा *decl.* जुलमाचा *decl. &c.*

OUTRAGEOUSNESS, *n.* v. A. 1. *and* EXCESS. गजब *m.* एकगजब *m.* कहर *m.* अनर्थ *m.* सतम *f. n.* साहस *n.* चंडत्व *n.* प्रचंडत्व *n.*

OUTRÉ. See EXTRAVAGANT.

To OUTREACH, *v. a. go beyond.* मागें टाकणें-पाडणें-घालणें-&c. माघारणें, मागसांडणें, पलीकडे जाणें *g. of o.*

2 v. To DECEIVE. फसवणें, ठकवणें, भोंदणें, मुंडणें, धुतारणें.

OUTRIDER, *n. attendant on horseback.* जिलबीचा स्वार, गाडीचा-स्वार.

OUTRIGGER, *n.* (of a canoe). उलंडी *f.*

OUTRIGHT, *adv. immediately, at once, on the spot.* खडोखड, खडोखडी, खडाखड, खडीचोट, तेव्हांचेतेव्हांच, तात्काल, तसाच, उभाउभी, रोकडा *decl.* रोखारोखी, रोखठोक, हातच्या हातीं.

2 *plainly, plump, flat, smack.* साफ, निक्षून, धड, धडधडीत, रोकडा, रोखारोखी, रोखठोक, भडकण, भडकर, भडदिशी, ठसठोंबराबाटाण्याची अक्षत.

To OUTROOT, *v. a.* v. To ROOT OUT. मुळासुद्धां उपटून टाकणें-उपटून काढणें-&c. निर्मूलन *n.*-&c. करणें *g. of o.*

To OUTRUN, *v.a. exceed in running.* धांवतां-धावण्यांत-&c.मागें-टाकणें-सांडणें-पाडणें-घालणें, अटपून मागें टाकणें, मागसांडणें, माघारणें.

2 *exceed, excel.* मागें-पाठीमागें टाकणें-सांडणें-पाडणें-&c. अतिक्रम *m.*-अतिक्रमण *n.* करणें.

OUTSET, *n. first entrance on any business,* v. BEGINNING. प्रारंभ *m.* प्रथमारंभ *m.* मुळारंभ *m.*आगम *m.*उपक्रम *m.*गणपतिपूजन *n.*

At the very o. मुळारंभीं, प्रथमदर्शनीं, सकृद्दर्शनीं, मुळींच, मूळ मुहूर्त. [त *m.*

The o. and the issue. आगमनिर्गम *m.*उपजनिपज *m.* आद्यं-

To OUTSHINE, *v. a. excel in lustre.* शोभेंत-शोभा देण्यांत-&c. मागें पाडणें-घालणें-&c. अधिकशोभा *f.* देणें, अधिक शोभणें *with* हून-पेक्षां-&c. *of o.* फिका पाडणें. [पाडणें.

To OUTSHINE, *v. n. shine out,* v. To SHINE. तपणें, किरण *m.*

2 See To EXCELL.

OUTSIDE, *n. superficies, surface, exterior.* बाहेरचें-बाहेरील-बाहेरलें-वरचें आंग *n.* बाहेरली-बाहेरची-&c. बाजू *f.* बाहेरची धड *f.* वरघाट *m.* बहिर्भाग *m.*

At, on, &c. the o. बाहेर, बाहेरल्या बाजूस-कडेस-धडीस.

2 *outer side, (of an enclosure).* बाहेरचा प्रदेश *m.* बाहेरची जागा *f.* बाहेरवार *n.* बहिःप्रदेश *m.*

At, on, &c. the o. बाहेरवारा *decl.*

3 *extreme or outer part.* कड *f.* शेवट *m.* कडे शेवट *m.*

At the o. *at the utmost.* निदानीं, निदान.

OUTSIDE, *a. belonging, &c. to the outside.* बाहेरचा, बाहेरल्या आंगाचा-बाजूचा-&c.

2 fig. *that has only outward appearance; not solid, deep, real, &c.* वरवंचाईचा, वरपंकाचा, वरघडीचा, वरकरणी, वरपंकी, वरपंगी, वरकर्मी.

OUTSKIRT, *n. border, precinct, &c.* शींव *f.* सीमा *f.* सीमाप्रदेश *m.* पल्लव *pop.* पालव *m.* दर *f.*

At the outskirts. दरेमेरेस.

OUTSTANDING, *a. not collected, unpaid.*—debts, &c. न उगवलेला, न उकळलेला, यायाचा, उगवायाचा, बेबसुली.

To OUTSTEP, *v. a. go beyond, transgress.* उल्लंघणें, मर्यादा *f.* सोडणें, उलंघ *m.*-उल्लंघन *n.*-अतिक्रम *m.*-अतिक्रमण *n.*-अतिपात *m.*-&c. करणें.

To OUTSTRIP, *v. a.* v. To EXCEL. मागें टाकणें-पाडणें-घालणें-&c. माघारणें, मागसांडणें, अंतरणें, आक्रम *m.*-आक्रमण *n.* करणें.

OUTSTRIPPED, *p.* v. V. मागें टाकलेला, &c. अंतरित.

To OUTVIE, *v. a.* v. To EXCEED. मागें टाकणें-पाडणें-सांडणें-&c. मागसांडणें, माघारणें, अतिक्रम *m.*-अतिक्रमण *n.*-&c. करणें.

OUTWARD, *a. tending out.* बाहेरचा, बाहेरल्या कडचा.

2 *external, belonging to the outer part, &c.* v. OUTER. बाहेरचा, बाहेरला, बाहेरील, बाहेरल्या आंगाचा-कडचा-बाजूचा-&c. बहिर्भागाचा, बाह्य.

The o. being or state. बहिर्भाव *m.*

3 *apparent, superficial; not deep, solid, real, &c.*वरघडीचा, वरपंकाचा, वरपंकी, वरकरणी, वरकर्मी.

4—letters, papers, &c. जावक.

OUTWARD, OUTWARDS, *adv.* v. A.1. बाहेर, बाहेरल्या कडे, बाहेरल्या देशाकडे, बाहेरल्या भागाकडे.

OUTWARD-BOUND, *a.*—ship, &c. बाहेर-&c. जाणारा-जाण्याचा.

OUTWARDLY, *adv.* v. A. 2. बाहेर, बाहेरचा *decl.* बाहेरून, बाह्यात्कारीं, दिसण्यांत, बहिरंगीं, बाह्यतः, बहिः.

O. and inwardly. सबाह्याभ्यंतर.

3 वरवर, वरवरता *or* ती.

To OUTWEIGH, *v. a. exceed in weight.* वजनांत अधिक भारी-&c. असणें *with* हून-पेक्षां-&c. *of o.*

2 fig. *exceed in importance.* हलका-कमतोल-&c. करणें, मागें पाडणें-सारणें-करणें-&c.

To Outwit, *v. a. overreach, surpass in stratagem.* उलटा *decl.* -उलटून फसवणें, पागोटें *n.* घेणें *g. of o.* तोंडाला पानें *n. pl.* पुसणें *g. of o.* दांत *m. pl.* पाडणें *g. of o.* कान *m. pl.* कापणें *g. of o.* डोकीवर हात *m.* फिरवणें *g. of o.* पाणी *n.* पाजणें.

To o. one's self. चावून चिकट करणें.

Outwork, *n.*—in fortification. बाहेरकोट *m.* [अंडाकृति.

Oval, *a. of the shape of an egg.* अंड्याच्या आकाराचा, अंडाकार,

Oval, *n.* अंडाकार *m.* अंडाकृति *f.*

Ovarian, *a.* अंडाशयसंबंधी, डिंबाशयसंबंधी.

Ovarious, *a. consisting of eggs.* अंड्यांचा, अंडमय.

Ovary, *n.*—in anatomy. अंडाशय *m.* डिंबाशय *m.* फूल *n.*

Oven, *n. baking plate.* तवा *m.*

2 *furnace, &c.* भट्टी *f.*

3 fig. *hot & close place.* उबवलें *n.* उबलें *n.* उबाऱ्याची जागा *f.*

Over, *prep. above, upon, &c.* वर, वरता *decl.* वरती, वरतीं, वरतें, उपरि.

2 *across, from side to side.* वरून.

3 *upon the whole surface.* वरून.

Over, *adv. above the top.* वर, वरून.

2 *on the opposite side.* पार, पलीकडे.

3 *more than, additionally.* शिवाय, वर, अधिक, आगळा *decl.* उवारीस, उवाऱ्यास.

O. and above. अधिक, आगळा, उफाळ.

To be o. *remain, be left.* राहणें, उरणें, शिलकेस राहणें, उवारीस-उवाऱ्यास येणें, मागें पडणें.

4 *throughout, from beginning to end.* पार, आरपार, आद्यंत, साद्यंत, अथइतिपर्यंत, सर्व, सगळा *decl.*

5 *too much, excessively.* फार, अधिक, अति, अमर्याद.

O. again, *once more, afresh,* v. Again. फिरून, मानूक्यान, दुसऱ्यानें.

O. and over again, v. Repeatedly. फिरफिरून, पुन:पुन:.

O. against, v. Opposite. समोर, सन्मुख.

O. night, *before night.* रात्रीआधीं, निजायाच्या पूर्वीं, अंवशीं, अंवशीस, पूर्वरात्रीस.

To be over, *be past, ended, consumed, &c.* होणें, संपणें, होऊन जाणें, उरकणें, उलगडणें, उलगणें, जाणें, राहणें, अटोपणें.

To give o. *cease from,* v. To Cease. पुरे-बस-&c. करणें, सोडणें.

To give o. *abandon as lost.* आशा *f.*-उमेद *f.*-वाट *f.*-वार्त्ता *f.*-&c. सोडणें *g. of o.*

Note. There are several senses in which this adverb cannot be rendered in Maráthí except in conjunction with a verb. To the verb therefore let the student refer.

To Overact, *v. a. act to excess.* अधिक करणें-&c. अतिशय *m.* करणें.

To Overawe, *v. a. restrain by awe.* दाब *m.*-दबदबा *m.*-धाक *m.* -दरारा *m.*-&c. घालणें-बसवणें, दाबणें, दबावणें, दाबादाबी *f.*-&c. करणें *g. of o.* जरब *f.* देणें-दास्तविणें. [*or* धा.

Overawed, *p.* v. V. दाब घातलेला, दाबलेला, &c. दबेल, शरमिंदा

Overawing, *n.* v. V.—*act.* दाब बसवणें *n.* दाबणें *n.* &c. दाबादाबी *f.* दाबडुबी *f.* दाबदूब *f.* जरब *f.*

Overbalance, *n. excess of weight, &c.* उपराळा *m.*

To Overbalance. See To Outweigh.

To Overbear, *v. a. bear down.* दपटणें, दाबणें, दबेसा करणें, लोटणें.

Overbearer, *n.* Overbearing, *p. a.* v. V. दाबणारा, दपटणारा, &c.

I. *disposed to bully, &c.*—of persons. दांडगा, दांड, बाडगा, खलेल, उदमस्त, उद्दाम, उर्मट, ठोंग, उद्धट, उद्धत, कोदंड, दंडेल, दंडाईत, कटमस्त *or* स्ता, धटकुला, लांठा, खणक्या, अतुरबळी, अतुलबळी, जालीम, लडबडलाटण्या *or* लाट्या.

II.—of acts, &c. दांडगेपणाचा, दांडगाईचा, उर्मटाईचा, &c.

Overbearing, *n.* v. V.—*act.* दाबणें *n.* दपटणें *n.* &c.

I. *bullying, insolent behaviour.* दांडगाई *f.* खलेली *f.* उर्मटाई *f.* उर्मटाई *f.* ठोंगाई *f.* दंडेली *f.* औद्धत्य *n.* दांडगावें *n.* दांडगावा *m.* लट्ठामिश्राई *f.* लंडाई *f.* लाठाई *f.*

Overboard, *adv.* गलबतावरून, &c. पाण्यांत.

To Overburden, *v. a. load too much.* अधिक-फार-&c. ओझें *n.* लादणें-घालणें-&c. भारी-फार-&c. लादणें, ओझ्याखालीं दबेसा करणें, भाराक्रांत-&c. करणें. [करणें.

To Overcast, *v. a. darken, cloud.* झांकणें, आच्छादणें, धुंद-&c.

Overcast, *p.* v.V. आच्छादलेला, &c. मेघाच्छादित, मेघाच्छन्न, घनारुद्ध, घनावरुद्ध.

To Overcharge, *v. a. surcharge,* v. To Overburden. अधिक ओझें *n.* घालणें, भाराक्रांत-&c. करणें. [भरणें.

2 (a gun). अधिक-फार-ज्यास्त-&c. भरणें, अधिक बार *m.*

3 (in an account, &c.). अधिकमोल *n.*-अधिककिम्मत *f.*-अधिकदर *m.*-&c. सांगणें-लिहणें-मांडणें.

To Overcloud. See To Overcast.

To Overcome, *v. a. vanquish, &c.* v. To Conquer. जिंकणें, पराजय *m.*-पराभव *m.*-&c. करणें *g. of o.* वश-जित-&c. करणें, सर करणें.

2 *reduce to distress, exhaust, &c.* जेरीस-रकमेस-डबघाईस-&c. आणणें, जेर-जेरदस्त-श्रमी-बेजार-आक्रांत-व्याकुल-&c. करणें, दमवणें, श्रमवणें.

3 *get the better of,* v. To Surmount. पार पाडणें, मोडणें, खालीं घालणें, डोकीवर-उरावर-नाकावर-&c. पाय *m.* देणें *g. of o.* पासला पाडणें. [*m.* होणें *g. of s.*

To Overcome, *v. n. be victorious.* जय *m.* पावणें-मिळवणें, जय

Overcome, *p.* v. V. A. 1. जिंकलेला, &c. पराभूत, पराजित, जित, विजित.

2 जेरीस आणलेला-आलेला, श्रमवलेला, &c. जेर, जेरदस्त, काईल, श्रमी, पराक्रांत, व्याकुल, आक्रांत (esp. in comp. as क्षुधाक्रांत, चिंताक्रांत, &c.), आतुर in comp. ग्रस्त in comp.

To be o. जेरीस-रकमेस-&c. येणें.

3 पार पाडलेला, मोडलेला, उत्तीर्ण.

Over-cunning, *a.* अतिशाहणा. [करणें.

To Overdo, *v. a. do too much.* अधिक-&c. करणें, अतिशय *m.*

2 *roast, bake, &c. too much.* फार-अधिक-&c. भाजणें-रांधणें-शिजवणें, अतिपाक *m.*-&c. करणें *g. of o.* अतिपक्व करणें.

To Overestimate. See To Overrate.

Overfatigue, *n.* अतिश्रम *m.* अतिश्रांति *f.*

To Overflow, *v. n. run over.* वरून-वरसून-उफाटून-&c. चालणें-वाहणें-सांडणें, वरसांडहोणें, उचंबळणें, उळंबळणें, उलंडणें, तासाबाहेर-&c. येणें.

To o. with tears,—the eyes. डबडबणें.

2 *abound, exuberate.* जळबंब *n.*-रेळ *f.*-रेड *f.*-रेळचेळ *f.*-शीग-लोट *m. f.*-&c. असणें *g. of s.*

To OVERFLOW, *v. a. deluge, inundate.* बुडविणें, गर्क करणें, जलमय-जलप्लुत-जलप्लावित करणें.

OVERFLOW, OVERFLOWING, *n.* v. V. N. 1. उचंबळ *f.* वरसांड *f.* उसाण *n.* उसांड *f.*

2 *and* EXUBERANCE. रेळ *f.* रेळचेळ *f.* जळबंब *n.*

OVERFLOWER, *n.* OVERFLOWING, *p. a.* v. V. N. 1. वरून सांडणारा-सांडलेला, &c. जळबंब, डबडबीत.

O. or plentiful state. जळबंब *n.*

O. with tears—the eyes. डबडबीत, डुबडुबीत.

To OVERGROW, *v. a. cover by growing over.* रुझून व्यापणें-व्यापून टाकणें-व्यापून घेणें-भरून टाकणें.

To be overgrown with. भरणें.

2 *grow beyond.* वाढणें *with* हून *or* पेक्षां *of o.* [वाढणें.

To OVERGROW, *v. n. grow to excess.* फार-अधिक-अति-&c.

OVERGROWN, *p.* v. V. A. 1. व्यापलेला, व्यापून टाकलेला, भरून टाकलेला.

v. V. N. फार वाढलेला, अधिकवाढीचा, अतिवर्द्धित.

OVERGROWTH, *n.* v. V. N. अधिकवाढ *m. f.* फारवाढ *m. f.* अतिवृद्धि *f.*

To OVERHANG, *v. a.* वरयेणें-असणें *with g. of o.*

To OVERHAUL, *v. a. turn over and examine.* चाळून-शोधून-झाडून-&c. पाहणें, झाडा *m.* घेणें *g. of o.* चाळणें, चाळाचाळ *f.*-चाळाचाळी *f.*-&c. करणें *g. of o.*

2 *examine again.* दुसऱ्यानें-फिरून-मातूक्यान-&c. पाहणें-चाळणें-झाडा *m.* घेणें, चाळणीची-&c. दुसारणी *f.* करणें.

OVERHEAD, *adv. above, aloft, &c.* डोक्यावर, डोकीवर, मस्तकावर, &c. वर, वरतीं.

To OVERHEAR, *v. a. hear what was not designed for one's hearing.* सहज-सहजांत-&c. ऐकणें, बोलणाऱ्यास न कळतां ऐकणें, ऐकूं पावणें, कानीं-कानांत-&c. पडणें *in. con. g. of s.* ऐकूं येणें *in. con.* ओझरता-निसरता-&c. ऐकणें.

To OVERHEAT, *v. a. heat to excess.* अधिक-फार-&c. तापवणें, अधिक-&c. उष्ण करणें.

Overheated state of the body or system. आंगाची-शरीराची लाही-लाहकी *f.* आंगाचा-&c. गदका *or* गतका *m.*

OVERJOY, *n. transport, &c.* v. JOY. अत्यानंद *m.* परमानंद *m.* ब्रह्मानंद *m.*

OVERJOYED, *a. transported.* परमानंदित, अतिहर्षित, महानंदयुक्त, हर्षरोमांचित.

To be o. आनंद *m.*-हर्ष *m.*-&c. ब्रह्मांडांत न मावे *g. of s.* आनंदानें-हर्षानें-&c. कोठेंच माईनासा होणें, सुपाएवढें काळीज *n.* होणें *g. of s.*

To OVERLADE. See To OVERBURDEN. [गांचा.

OVERLAND, *a.*—journey, &c. खुशकीचा, जमिनीवरचा, स्थलमा-

To OVERLAY, *v. a.* (an infant) *smother with close covering.* फार पांघरूण *n.*-अधिक पांघरूण *n.* घालून घुसमटवणें, पांघरूण घालण्याखालीं मारणें.

2 *smother, overwhelm.* दडपणें, दाबणें, दडपून-दाबून मारणें, दडपून-&c. टाकणें. [करणें.

3 *cover superficially.* मढवणें, मढणें, मढवणी *f.*-मढवणूक *f.*

4 *oppress with weight.* ओझ्याखालीं-&c. दडपणें-दाबणें, भाराक्रांत-&c. करणें.

To OVERLEAP, *v. a.* उडून पार जाणें, उडी *f.* मारून जाणें.

To OVERLOAD. See To OVERBURDEN.

OVERLONG, *a. too long.* फारलांब, अतिलांब, योग्यतेपेक्षां लांब.

To OVERLOOK, *v. a. stand higher than, afford means of looking down on.* उंच असणें *with* हून *or* पेक्षां *of o.* पारदर्शक असणें.

2 *oversee,* v. To SUPERINTEND. पाहणें, देखरेख *f.*-पाहणी *f.* -&c. करणें *g. of o.* चौकशी *f.*-&c. ठेवणें *g. of o.*

3 *pass by, pass over, excuse.* सोडणें, पोटीं घालणें, सांड *f.* करणें-देणें, गम *m.* खाणें, क्षमा *f.*-गई *f.* -मुलाजा *m.* -कानाडोळा *m.*-&c. करणें.

To be overlooked. खमणें.

4 *pass by, omit, take no notice of.* बगळणें, डावलणें, अंतरणें, गाळणें, उपेक्षणें, अव्हेर *m.*-उपेक्षा *f.*-आनाकानी *f.*-कानाडोळा *m.*-&c. करणें *g. of o.*

OVERLOOKER, *n.* OVERLOOKING, *p. a.* v. V. 2. पाहणारा, देखरेख करणारा, &c. देखरेख्या, अध्यक्ष, उपद्रष्टा.

4 बगळणारा, डावलणारा, &c. उपेक्षक, उपेक्षाकर्त्ता.

OVERLOOKING, *n.* v. V. 2.—*act.* पाहणें *n.* देखरेख *f.* चौकशी *f.*

3 सोडणें *n.* सांड *f.* सोडसांड *f.* विसरसांड *f.* गई *f.* गम *m.* v. खा, मुलाजा *m.* कानडोळा*m.* कानाडोळा*m.* मामलत *f.* मामुलती*f.*

4 उपेक्षणें *n.* &c. उपेक्षा *f.* अव्हेर *m.* सांड *f.* अनमान *m.*

OVERMUCH, *a.* v. EXCESSIVE. फार, अतिशय, अतिशयित, योग्यतेपेक्षां अधिक, अतिमर्याद, अतिमान.

OVERMUCH, *adv.* फारच, अतिशय, अति. [लांडणें.

To OVERPASS, *v. a.* v. To CROSS. पार जाणें, उतरून जाणें, ओ-

2 *omit, pass by,* v. To OVERLOOK. अंतरणें,उपेक्षणें, उपेक्षा*f*.-आनाकानी *f.*- अव्हेर *m.*-&c. करणें *g. of o.*

OVERPAST, *a. gone by, past.* गेलेला, गुजरलेला, गत.

To OVERPERSUADE, *v. a. persuade against one's inclination.* भीड घालून-बळेंच-&c. समजावणें-समजूत *f.* करणें-मनाविणें-&c.

OVERPLUS, *a.* v. SURPLUS. उफाळ, उबार, फाजील, फालतू.

OVERPLUS, *n.* v. SURPLUS. ऊर *f.* उरवण *f.* उरावा *m.* उरी *f.* शिलक *f.* सई *f.* v. ये.

To OVERPOWER, *v. a. bear down, vanquish, &c. by superior power.* जोर *m.*-बळ *n.*-पराक्रम *m.*-&c. चालवणें *or* चालवून खालीं करणें-दडपणें- दाबणें-जिंकणें, पाडणें, मारणें, लोटणें, गुंडाळणें, चीत करणें, पासला पाडणें, चालेनासा करणें *g. of o.* शेरबाजू *f.* करणें *with* वर *of o.* जेर-जेरदस्त-कुंठित-निरुपाय-वश-जित-&c. करणें.

2 *reduce to distress,* v. To OVERCOME. जेरीस-&c. आणणें, जेर-जेरदस्त-व्याकुल-&c.करणें.

OVERPOWERED, *p.* v. V. 1. पाडलेला, मोडलेला, लोटलेला, जेर, जेरदस्त केलेला, कुंठित.

2 जेरीस आणलेला, जेर, जेरदस्त, व्याकुल, आक्रांत (esp. in comp.), आकुल (in comp. as क्रोधाकुल, चिंताकुल, भयाकुल, &c.) [पाडणारा, &c.

OVERPOWERER, *n.* OVERPOWERING, *p. a.* v. V. 1. जिंकणारा,

2 जेरीस आणणारा, जेर करणारा. [जबर.

I.—esp. of smell, &c. *strong.* उद्दाम, उग्र, उगीर, उग्रट,

To OVERPRIZE, *To* OVERRATE, *v.a. value or rate too highly.*

किमतीपेक्षां-मोलापेक्षां-योग्यतेपेक्षां-&c. मानणें, अतियोग्यता *f.* -&c. मानणें *g. of o.*

To OVERREACH. See To DECEIVE.

To OVERRIDE, *v. a.* (a horse) दमेपर्यंत चालवणें, दामटणें.

OVERRIGHTEOUS, *a. superstitiously strict, &c.* अत्याचारी.

OVERRIGHTEOUSNESS, *n.* v. A. अत्याचार *m.*

OVERRIPE, *a.* फार पिकलेला, अतिपक्व, विनाशोन्मुख.

To OVERRIPEN, *v. n.* उपिकणें, अविकणें.

To OVERRULE, *v. a. control by predominant authority.* वरचा अधिकार *m.*-धनीपणा *m.*-अमल *m.*-&c. चालवणें *with* वर *of. o.* वरच्या अधिकारानें-अधिकाराच्या बळानें-&c. चालवणें-नियमित करणें.

2 *make null, &c. put aside.* वरचढपणानें-&c. उडवणें-घालवणें-मागें सारणें *or* पाडणें-रद्द करणें, लटपटिवणें.

OVERRULER, *n.* OVERRULING, *p. a.* v. V. वरचा अधिकार करणारा, वरचा अमल चालवणारा, &c.

2 उडवणारा, मागें पाडणारा, &c.

To OVERRUN, *v. a. overspread, cover over.* व्यापणें, भरणें, वेढणें, ग्रासणें, आच्छादणें, व्यापून-भरून-वेढून-&c. टाकणें-घेणें, आच्छन्न-आकीर्ण-&c. करणें. [आक्रमित करणें.

2 *rove over hastily.* आक्रमणें, स्वाऱ्या *f. pl* घालणें, आक्रांत-

3 See To OUTRUN. 4 *cover swarmingly,* v. To SWARM. व्यापून-भरून घेणें-टाकणें.

To be overrun. व्यापणें, भरणें.

OVERRUN, *p.* v. V. A. 1. व्यापलेला, व्यापून टाकलेला, &c. व्याप्त, आच्छन्न, आकीर्ण, आस्तीर्ण.

2 आक्रमलेला, आक्रांत, आक्रमित.

4 व्यापलेला, व्यापून टाकलेका, &c. [&c. व्यापन *n.*

OVERRUNNING, *n.* v. V. A. 1.—*act.* व्यापणें *n.* व्यापून घेणें *n.*

2 आक्रमणें *n.* आक्रम *m.* आक्रमण *n.* अधिक्रमण *n.*

To OVERSEE, *v. a. overlook,* v. To SUPERINTEND. पाहणें, देखरेख *f.*-चौकशी *f.*-&c. करणें-ठेवणें.

OVERSEER, *n.* v. V. *and* SUPERINTEDENT. पाहणारा, देखरेख करणारा, देखरेख्या, चौकसनीस, दरोगा, मिरधा, उपद्रष्टा.

To OVERSET. See To UPSET.

To OVERSHADE, *To* OVERSHADOW, *v. a. throw a shadow over.* सावली *f.*-छाया *f.* करणें-घालणें *with* वर *of o.* छायावृत-छायाच्छन्न-छायाच्छादित-&c. करणें.

To OVERSHOOT, *v. a. shoot beyond.* निशानाच्या-&c. पलीकडे बाण *m.* जाणें. लक्ष्यातिक्रम *m.*-लक्ष्योल्लंघन *n.*-लक्ष्यातिक्षेप *m.*-&c. करणें. [णें.

To o. one's mark, *fig. outwit one's self.* चाबूनचिकर कर-

OVERSIGHT, *n.* v. SUPERINTENDENCE. देखरेख *f.* चौकशी *f.* शोध *m.* v. ठेव. [दृष्टिदोष *m.* भोळें *n.*

2 *mistake, blunder, overlooking.* नजरचूक *f.* दृष्टीची चूक *f.*

To OVERSLEEP, *v. a.*(one's self)फाजझोप *f.*-अतिनिद्रा *f.*-&c. घेणें.

To OVERSPREAD, *v. a. cover over, occupy the whole surface of.* व्यापणें, आक्रमणें, भरणें, आच्छादणें, वेढणें, ग्रासणें, गिळणें, व्यापून-भरून-&c. घेणें-टाकणें, व्यापन *n.*-आक्रमण *n.*-आच्छादन *n.*-&c. करणें *g. of o.* आच्छन्न-आक्रांत-आकीर्ण-&c. करणें.

OVERSPREAD, *p.* v. V. व्यापलेला, आच्छादलेला, &c. आच्छादित, आच्छन्न, प्रच्छादित, प्रच्छन्न, आक्रांत, व्याप्त, समाक्रांत in comp. आकीर्ण in comp. आस्तीर्ण.

To OVERSTATE. See To EXAGGERATE.

To OVERSTEP, *v. a. go beyond,* v. To TRANSGRESS. उल्लंघणें, उल्लंघ *m.*-उल्लंघन *n.*-&c. करणें *g. of o.*

To OVERSTOCK, *v. a. supply with more than is requisite.* अधिकबेजमी *f.*-ज्यास्तबेजमी *f.*-अधिकपूर्ति *f.*-अतिपूर्त्ति *f.*-&c. करणें, भरपूर करणें.

To OVERSTRAIN, *v. n. make too great effort.* अतिप्रयत्न *m.*-अतिप्रयास *m.*-&c. करणें.

OVERT, *a. not concealed or secret,* v. OPEN. उघड, उघडपणाचा, प्रसिद्धपणाचा, प्रगटपणाचा, उघडपणींचा, राजरोशीचा.

To OVERTAKE, *v. a. come up with in pursuit.* अटपणें, अटपून घेणें, मिळवणें, मिळवून घेणें, पाठ *f.* धरणें *g. of o.*

2 *come on unawares, take by surprise.* गांठणें, सांपडवणें.

To be overtaken. सांपडणें.

To OVERTASK, *v. a. impose too heavy a task on.* अधिक काम *n.*-फार काम *n.*-&c. सांगणें, जिवा आगळें काम *n.*-जिवापरतें काम *n.* -&c. सांगणें.

To OVERTHROW, *v. a. overturn,* v. To UPSET. पाडणें, पाडून देणें, उलटणें, उपरांडणें, उलंडणें, उलटा-पालथा-&c. करणें.

2 *vanquish,* v. To DEFEAT. मारणें, मोडणें, पाडाव *m.*-पराभव *m.*-&c. करणें *g. of o.*

3 *subvert,* v. To DESTROY, To RUIN. मोडणें, मारणें, नासणें, नष्ट करणें, लयास नेणें, भंग *m.*-विघात *m.*-विध्वंस *m.*-&c. करणें *g. of o.* [उलटणें *n.* &c.

OVERTHROW, OVERTHROWING, *n.* v. V. 1.—*act.* पाडणें *n.*

2—*act.* मारणें *n.* मोडणें *n.* &c.—*state.* मोड *m.* पाडाव *m.* पराभव *m.* भंग *m.* पराजय *m.*

3—*act.* मोडणें *n.* नासणें *n.*—*state.* मोड *m.* नाश *m.* भंग *m.* विघात *m.* विध्वंस *m.*

OVERTHROWN, *p.* v. V. 1. पाडलेला, उलटलेला, &c.

2 मारलेला, मोडलेला, पाडावकेलेला, &c. पराभूत, जित, जमीनदोस्त, चीत.

3 मोडलेला, नासलेला, &c. नष्ट, भग्न.

OVERTLY, *adv.* v. A. उघड, उघडपणीं, प्रसिद्धपणीं, &c.

OVERTNESS, *n.* v. A. उघडपणा *m.* प्रसिद्धपणा *m.* प्रगटपणा *m.* प्रसिद्धि *f.* [हून-&c. *of o.*

To OVERTOP, *v. a.* वरजाणें *with g. of o.* उंच असणें *with* पेक्षां-

OVERTURE, *n. proposal.* उद्गार *m.* बोलणें *n.*

2 *prelude, &c.* पूर्वरंग *m.* उपोद्घात *m.*

To OVERTURN, *v. a.* v. To UPSET. पाडणें, उलटणें, उपरांडणें, उलटा-&c. करणें.

2 *subvert,* v. To DESTROY. मोडणें, नासणें, नष्ट करणें, भंग *m.*-विघात *m.*-&c. करणें *g. of o.*

To OVERTURN, *v. n.* v. To UPSET. उपरांडणें, उलंडणें, कलथणें.

To OVERVALUE, *v. a. rate too high.* मोलाआगळा-अधिक मोलाचा-&c. मानणें, मोलापेक्षां-किमतीपेक्षां-&c. अधिक मानणें, अतियोग्यता *f.* मानणें *g. of o.*

OVERWEENING, *a. conceited, vain.* पत्राजीचा, अभिमानाचा, अहंकाराचा, अहंपणाचा, फुशारीचा, फुशारकीचा, अहंकारप्रयुक्त.

OVERWEENINGLY, *adv.* v. A. पत्राजीनें, अभिमानानें, अभिमानपूर्वक, अहंकारपूर्वक, अहंतापूर्वक.

To OVERWEIGH. See To OUTWEIGH.

OVERWEIGHT, *n.* अधिकभार *n.* भाराधिक्य *n.*

To OVERWHELM, *v. a. crush or bear down beneath something that covers.* दडपणें, दाबणें, दडपून-दाबून-&c. टाकणें, पाडणें, पासला-पालथा-&c. पाडणें, लोळवणें,भुईस-जमिनीस-&c.मिळवणें. 2 fig. *immerse and bear down.* बुडविणें, बुडवूनटाकणें, गर्क-गडप-निमग्न-&c. करणें, ग्रासणें, घेरणें, आक्रांत-&c. करणें.

To be overwhelmed. गर्क-गडप-&c. होणें.

OVERWHELMED, *p.* v. V. 1. दडपलेला, दडपून टाकलेला.
2 बुडवलेला, गर्क केलेला-झालेला, घेरलेला, ग्रासलेला, निमग्न, मग्न, ग्रस्त, आक्रांत.

OVERWHELMER, *n.* OVERWHELMING, *p. a.* v. V. 1. दडपणारा, दडपून टाकणारा, पासला पाडणारा, &c.
2 बुडवणारा, ग्रासणारा, घेरणारा, गर्क करणारा, &c.

OVERWISE, *a.* अतिशाहणा.

To OVERWORK, *v. a. work too hard,* v. To TIRE. शक्तीपलीकडचें काम-जिवापलीकडचें काम *n.*-&c. घेणें, शक्तीपेक्षां-&c. खपविणें-राबविणें, खुंदलणें *or* खुंदळणें, घुसडणें, घुसळणें, खुरदमा *m.*-चुरा *m.*-&c. करणें, घुमा *m.* घालणें, घुसडा *m.*-भुसडा *m.*-भूस *n.*-&c. पाडणें.

OVERWORKED, OVERWORN. See EXHAUSTED.

OVERWROUGHT, *a. labored to excess.* अतिसंस्काराचा, अतिपरिष्काराचा, अतिसंस्कृत, अतिपरिष्कृत.

OVERZEALOUS, *a.* अत्यास्थिक, अत्युत्सुक, अत्युत्कंठित, अत्यासक्त.

OVIFORM, *a. oval.* अंडाकार, अंडाकृति.

OVIPAROUS, *a. producing young from eggs.* अंडज (lit. *produced from eggs*), अंडप्रसू, अंडप्रज.

An o. animal—gener. द्विज.

To OWE, *v.a. be indebted, be bound to pay.* ऋण*n.*-कर्ज*n.*-देणें*n.*-&c. लागणें-असणें. (The verb agrees with the pronoun, as I owe him 500 rupees मी त्याचे पांचशें रुपये ऋण *n.* लागतों *or* मी त्याचे पांचशें रुपये लागतों; he owes me 20 rupees तो माझे वीस रुपये देणें (or माझे वीस रुपये) लागतो, &c.), ऋणकरी-कर्जकरी-देणेकरी-&c. असणें *with g. of o.* (as मी त्याचा पांचशें रुपायांचा ऋणकरी आहें) ऋण*n.*-कर्ज *n.*-देणें *n.*-&c. बाळगणें-राखणें.
2 *be obliged for.* उपकारी-आभारी-ऋणी-&c. लागणें-असणें (as I owe my post to you. आसामीविषयीं मी तुमचा आभारी लागतों).

OWING, *a. due.* यायाचा *or* यावयाचा, द्यायाचा *or* द्यावयाचा.
2 *consequential, ascribable to.* चा sign of the possessive, (as this fever is owing to fasting हा ताप उपास केल्याचा *or* उपासाचा आहे) नें-मुळें (as this cold is owing to the rain ही थंडी पावसानें झाली), प्रयुक्त (in comp. as उपवासप्रयुक्तज्वर) मूलक (in comp. as श्रममूलक, अपथ्यमूलक).
3 *imputable to as agent.* चा, कर्तृक (as जलकर्तृक-अग्निकर्तृक), द्वारक (in comp. as वैद्यद्वारक).

OWL, *n.* घुबड *n.* उलूक *m.* घुडगें *n.* दिवांध *m.* दिवाभीत *m.*—revilingly the *foul* or *ominous thing.* ओकटें *or* ओसटें *n.*
2 *dolt, blockhead, &c.* v. FOOL. उलूका बच्चा *m.* उलू *m.*

OWN, *a. pertaining or relating to self, peculiar, proper.* आपला, आंगचा, पदरचा, खासगीचा, स्वसत्तेचा, खास, खासगत, खासगी, निज, स्वकीय, स्वीय, आत्मीय, स्वक, स्व, स्वयं (in comp.), आत्म (in comp.), स्वसत्ताक, स्वसत्तात्मक, अनन्यस्वामिक, अनन्यवर्त्ती, अनन्यसंबंधी, अनन्याधीन. Compounds are formed copiously and elegantly with several of the above, as स्वकर्म one's own duty, functions, &c. स्वछंद one's own fancy, &c. स्वकष्ट one's own toil, स्वभाव own nature, निजगूज one's own secret, आत्मबुद्धि one's own wisdom, thought, &c. स्वकीया, स्वीया one's own wife; आत्मज, स्वज own son, स्वजाति own caste, kind, &c. स्वधर्म own office, duty, &c. स्वदेश own country; स्वार्थ, आत्महित own advantage, &c. &c.

One's own. This phrase as occurring in *one's own physician, carpenter, clerk, manager, &c.&c.* is rendered by आंगचा, (as आंगचा वैद्य-सुतार-कारकून-कारभारी-&c.), स्वयं (as स्वयंदास *one's own servant*), and sometimes by घरचा *or* आपल्या घरचा (as घरचा कारिगर-&c.) [आपलाला.

Each his o. आपापला (as ते आपापलीं पुस्तकें घेऊन आले),

O. and other. आपपर, आपपरकी, आपलातुपला.

To make one's o. *to appropriate.* आत्मसात् करणें.

To OWN, *v. a. allow, admit, confess,* v. To ACKNOWLEDGE. अंगीकारणें, स्वीकारणें, पदरीं घेणें, कबूल करणें-होणें, पतकरणें, अंगीकार *m.*-स्वीकार *m.*-&c. करणें *g. of o.*
2 *acknowledge to belong to.* मानणें, माझा-आपला-मम-स्वकीय-&c. म्हणणें, स्वीकारणें, अंगीकारणें, जाणणें, ओळखणें, स्वीकार *m.*-अंगीकार *m.*-&c. करणें *g. of o.*
3 *have the rightful title to.* धनीपणा *m.*-सत्ता *f.*-स्वत्व *n.*-&c. ठेवणें-बाळगणें *or with* असणें *g. of s. with* वर *of o.* असणें *with g. of s.* (as तें पुस्तक माझें आहे), धनी-मालक-&c. असणें *g. of o.*

OWNED, *p.* v. V.1. अंगीकारलेला, स्वीकारलेला, पदरीं घेतलेला, &c. अंगीकृत, स्वीकृत.
2 मानलेला, आपला म्हटलेला, &c. अंगीकृत, स्वीकृत.
3 सत्तेंतला, स्वत्वांतला, स्वत्वविशिष्ट, सत्ताविशिष्ट (as मत्स्वत्वविशिष्ट धन), सत्ताक (as मत्सत्ताक).

OWNER, *n.* OWNING, *p. a.* v. V. 1. अंगीकारणारा, स्वीकारणारा, पदरीं घेणारा, अंगीकारकर्त्ता-कारी, स्वीकारकर्त्ता-&c.
2 मानणारा, आपला म्हणणारा, स्वीकारणारा,&c.स्वीकारकर्त्ता,&c.
3 धनीपणा ठेवणारा, धनी, पति, स्वामी, मालक *or* मालीक, खावंद, सत्ताधारी, सत्ताधीश, सत्तापुरुष.

OWNERSHIP, *n. proprietorship.* धनीपणा *m.* मालकी *f.* सत्ता *f.* स्वत्व*n.* स्वामित्व*n.* स्वाम्य*n.*

OWNING, *n.* v. V. 1.—*act.* अंगीकारणें*n.* पदरीं घेणें*n.* &c. अंगीकार*m.* स्वीकार*m.* अंगीकरण*n.* स्वीकरण*n.*
2—*act.* मानणें*n.* आपला म्हणणें*n.* &c. अंगीकार*m.* स्वीकार*m.* अंगीकरण*n.* स्वीकरण*n.*

OX, *n. castrated bull.* बैल*m.* भादा*m.* भाद्या बैल*m.*
2 *male of the bovine genus.* बैल*m.* बलीवर्द*m.* वृषभ*m.*
3 wild o. *bos gavæus or cavifrons.* गवा*m.* गवय*m.*

Horn of the w. o. गवादी*f.*

OXYGEN, *n.* प्राणवायु*m.*

OXYMEL, *n.* मधाचें पन्हें*n.* सिकंजी *or* शिकंजी *f.*

OYSTER, *n.*—the animal.कालव*n.*कालू*n.*कृमिशुक्ति *f.*—the shell, कालव*n.* कालू *f.* शिंपला*m.*

Half or single shell of an o. परडें*n.*

Pearl o. शुक्ति *f.*

P.

P. This letter is expressed by प,and when aspirated by फ.

PA, *short for papa.* बा.

PABULAR, PABULOUS. See ALIMENTAL, NUTRITIOUS.

PABULUM, *n.* v. FOOD. खाद्यन. खाद *f.* जीवनन. निक्षेप *m.*

PACE, *n. step.* पाऊलन. कदमम. पावंडम. पावंडाम. पदन्यासम. पद-

2—the pace. पाऊलन. कदमम.

3 *gait, walk.* चाल *f.* गति *f.*

Running p. धांवचाल *f.* [वेगम.

4 *speed of walk or moving.* गति *f.* गतीचें मानन. वेग *m.* गति-

To drive at a gentle p. पावंडाखालीं हाकणें-चालविणें-&c.

To move or go at a gentle p. पावंडाखालीं चालणें-जाणें.

To keep p. with. पाऊलन. बरोबर चालवणें, पाऊलन. बरोबर असणें, बरोबर चालणें.

5 (of horses) v. HORSE. चाल *f.*

To PACE, *v. n. move slowly or measuredly.* पाऊलन. टाकीत चालणें, पावलेंn. *pl.* मोजीत जाणें-चालणें, बरमाईचे चालीनें चालणें--जाणें-&c. [करणें.

To p. up and down. पसारm. करणें, टेहलणें, टेहलणी *f.*

A watch in which the watchman or sentry is to pace up & down. टेहलता पाहराm. A pacing watchman टेहलता-पाहरेकरीm.

To PACE, *v. a. measure by step.* पावलें *n.pl.* मोजणें *g. of o.* पावलेंn. *pl.* घालून मोजणें, पाऊलमोजणी *f.* करणें *g. of o.*

PACED, *a. having a particular pace.* चालीचा, गतीचा, गतिक.

PACIFIC,*a. tending to make or restore peace, mild, gentle,&c.* सामाचा, सामदामाचा *or* सामादामाचा, सामोपचाराचा, सामोपायाचा, शमतेचा, मिलाफाचा, समेटाचा, &c. सामोपचारक, सामोपायक, शमकारक-कारी-&c. विरोधभंजक-नाशक-&c.

2 *tranquil, &c.* v. CALM. शांत, शमी, शांत्यात्मक.

PACIFICATION, *n.* v. V.—*act.* शांतवणेंn. &c. समजावणेंn. &c. सांत्वन *pop.* शांतवनn. समजावशी *f.* समजावीस *f.* समजी *f.* शमनn. प्रशमनn. सांत्वनाf. संतापहरणn. क्रोधहरणn. क्रोधशांति *f.* शांति *f.* (also in comp. as रोगशांति, तृषाशांति *f.* &c.) क्षमापनn.

I. *act of making peace.* समेट करणेंn. मिलाफ करणेंn. समेटm. संधिकरणn. ऐक्यकरणn.

II. *peace made.*समेट *m.* मिलाफm. संधिm. कलहशांतिf.सल्लाm.

PACIFICATOR, *n. peace-maker.* समेट करणारा, मिलाफ करणारा, संधिकर्त्ता, विरोधभंजक-नाशक-&c. विग्रहनाशक.

PACIFICATORY, *a. tending to peace,* v. PACIFIC. सामाचा, सामोपायाचा, शमकारक, विरोधभंजक-नाशक.

PACIFIED, *p.* v. V. शांतवलेला, शांत केलेला, &c. शमित, शांत, क्रोधातीत, हृतक्रोध, हृततापन, नष्टक्रोध, नष्टताप.

PACIFIER, *n.* PACIFYING, *p. a.* v. V. शांतवणारा, समजावणारा, भ्रंडकरणारा, शमक, क्रोधहर-हर्त्ता-हारक-&c. ताप *or* संतापहर-हर्त्ता-&c. शांतिकर-कर्त्ता-कारी-&c. शमकर्त्ता-कारी, क्रोधभंजक-नाशक-&c.

To PACIFY, *v. a. appease, calm, quiet, allay.* शांतवणें *or* सांतवणें, संताव्रणें *or* संथावणें, शमवणें, समजावणें, अळवणें, शांत-थंड-&c. करणें, शांत्वन *pop.* शांतवन *n.*-समजावशी *f.*-समजूत *f.*-समजावीस *f.*-शांति *f.*-शम *m.*-उपशम *m.*-उपशमन *n.*-प्रशमन *n.*-क्षमापन *n.*-क्रोधहरण-&c. करणें *g. of o.*

PACK, *n. bundle, bale.* गठ्ठा *m.* बस्ता *m.* गांठोडें *n.* बासन *n.*

2 (of cards). गंजिफा *m.* जोड *m.*

3 (of hounds). झुंड *f.* खांड *n.* कळप *m.*

4 *gang, crew, knot,* v. BAND. गट *or* गट्ट *m.* गट्टा *m.* पेंढं*n.* चौक *m.* मुठाण *n.* मेळा *m.* नवग्रह *m.* घोळका *m.*

P. of knaves & scamps. चंडाळ चौकडी *f.*

5 *peck, heap, multitude.* ढिगर *or* ढिगार *m.* ढिगारा *m.* ढीग*m.* रास *f.* डोंगर *m.* राष्ट्र *m. n.* गोण *f.*

To PACK, *v. a. place and press together.* दडपून भरणें-लावणें, भरणें, भराभर *f.* करणें *g. of o.*

To p. closely. खचून भरणें.

2 *bind for carriage.* बांधणें, बांधून टाकणें-ठेवणें, अवळणें, अवळाअवळी *f.*-बांधाबांध *f.*-बांधाबांधी *f.* करणें *g. of o.*

3 *send hurriedly,* v. To DESPATCH. घाईनें-लगवगीनें-&c. धाडणें-पाठवणें, फेंकणें. [करणें-मिळवणें.

4 *unite in fraud.* संगनमताचा-एकतरफी-चंडाळचौकडीचा-&c.

5 off; *bundle off,* v. To DISMISS. यांटेस लावणें, लावून देणें, मेखा *f. pl.*-मेखाट्या *f. pl.*-गांठोडें *n.*-&c. खांद्यावर देणें-घालणें *or* खांदाडीस-खांदाडीं देणें-घालणें.

6 up. गुंडाळणें, अटपणें, बांधणें, बंद करणें, गांठोडें *n.* गुंडाळणें-अटपणें-बांधणें, बांधाबांध *f.* करणें *g. of o.*

To PACK, (with off,) *v. n. depart in haste.* सडकणें, झटकणें, तडक-तकट-लगबग-लगेलगे-&c. जाणें-निघून जाणें, इयां म्हणणें, वाळया *f. pl.* हाकणें.

PACK, *a. fit for or used for burdens.* ओझेल, ओझेली, कंठाळ्या.

PACK-CLOTH, *n.* बासन *n.* वेष्टन *n.*

PACK-HORSE, *n.* पाठाळ *n.* पाठवळ *n.* पडदळ्या-पडदळयाचा-पडनळ्याचा तट्टू *m.*-घोडा *m.*-&c. कंठाळ्या घोडा.

PACK-NEEDLE, *n.* दाभण *m. n.*

PACK-SACK, *n.* गोण *f.* गोणी *f.*

PACK-SADDLE, *n.* मूठ *f.* खोगीर *n.*—esp. of camels and elephants. पल्याण *n. pop.* पलाण *f.* [आंडदोरी *f.*

Back tie of a p. which passes between the hind legs.

Breech band of a p. (passing around the haunches) मागोटा *m.* मागोटी *f.* बांडगा *m.* बांडगें *n.*

Dorsal-pad of a p. सांडका *m.*

Girth of a bullock's p. पठार *f.* पताड *f.*

Stuffed roll under a p. बळी *f.*

PACK-THREAD, *n.* सुतळी *f.* सडा *m.* शणसूत्र *n.*

PACKAGE, *n. thing packed.* गठ्ठा *m.* बासन *n.*

2 *charge for packing.* बांधणावळ *f.*

PACKET,*n. small bundle or parcel.* पुडका *m.*पुडकेंn. पुडा *m. dim.* पुडी *f.*—esp. of papers तबलक *f.*

String confining a p. of papers. तबलक *f.*

2 *mail, post.* डांक *f.*

3 *post-ship.* डांकेचें गलबत *n.* [करणें*g. of o.*

To PACKET, *v. a. bind up in a packet.* पुडका *m.*-पुडकें *n.*-&c.

PACT, PACTION, *n. bargain,* v. AGREEMENT. होड *f.* बोली *f.* करार *m.* संकेत *m.*समय *m.*

PACTIONAL, PACTITIOUS, *a. belonging to a pact or bargain.* बोलीचा, संकेताचा, समयाचा, सांकेतिक, संकेतित.

PAD, *n. foot-path.* पायवाट *f.* पायरस्ता *m.*
2 *easy-horse.* नरमचालीचा घोडा *m.*
3 *foot pad.* वाटमाऱ्या, वाटपाड्या.
4 *bolster, cushion, &c.* गादी *f.* तक्या *m.*—little, circular, and flat. गिरदी *f.*
5 (for a horse). खोगीर *n.*
Front fastening or tie of a p. गोरबंद *m.*
To PAD, *v. n. travel gently.* धिमेधिमे-धिरेधिरे-हळूहळू-&c.चालणें.
PADAR, *n. coarse flour.* भरड *m.* भरडपीठ *n.*
PADDING. See STUFFING.
To PADDLE, *v. n. row, beat water.* वल्हवणें, वल्हें *n.* मारणें, दांड्यानें पाणी *n.* लोटणें.
2 *play in the water.* डुचणें, डुबकणें, पाण्यांत डबडब करणें.
3 *finger, toy with.* बोटचाळा *m. or* चाळे *m. pl.*-हातचाळा *m.* -बोटखेळ *m.*-अंगुलिव्यापार *m.*-अंगुलिचेष्टा *f.*-&c. करणें.
To PADDLE, *v. a. propel by a paddle.* हातवल्ह्यानें चालवणें-नेणें, हातानें वल्हवणें.
PADDLE, *n. short oar for a canoe.* हातवल्हें *n.*
2 *blade of an oar.* चपणी *f.*
PADDOCK, *n.* v. ENCLOSURE. वाडी *f. dim.* वाडगें *n.* वाडकुलें *n.*
2 v. FROG. बेडूक *m.* भेक *m.*
PADDY, *n.* v. RICE. भात *n.* साळ *f.*
PADLOCK, *n.* टाळें *n.* कुलूप *n.* ताला *m.* तालें *n.* तालक *n.*
Common English p. बेडकीचें कुलूप *n.*
Common Native p. नळीचें कुलूप *n.* भेंगळी कुलूप *n.*
Double p. दुकांटी कुलूप *n.*
Concealed p. पडद्याचें कुलूप *n.*
PÆAN, *n. song of triumph.* जयगान *n.* जयगीत *m. n.*
PAGAN, PAGANISH, *a. heathen, idolatrous.* मूर्त्तिपूजक, असद्धर्मी, असद्धर्मावलंबी.
PAGANISM, *n. heathenism.* मूर्त्तिपूजा *f.* असद्धर्म *m.* असद्धर्मावलंबन *n.* असद्धर्मसेवन *n.*
PAGE, *n.* (of a book &c.). पृष्ठ *n.*
2 *boy-attendant on a great person.* खवास, हुजऱ्या, पोरगा, पोऱ्या, खिदमतगार *or* दार, अंतिक, पार्श्वानुचर.
To PAGE, *v. a.* पृष्ठांचे आंकडे मांडणें.
PAGEANT, *n. show, spectacle.* तमाशा *m.* खेळ *m.*
2 *statue, &c. in show.* शोभामूर्त्ति *f.* शोभेची बाहुली *f.*
A mere p. of a person. टिक्याचाधनी, टिकोजी, टिकोबा, निमित्तधारी. [मिरवणा.
PAGEANT, *a.* v. SHOWY. थाटमाटाचा, टामटुमीचा, शोभेचा, टिक-
PAGEANTRY, *n. pomp, parade,* v. SHOW. थाटमाट *m.* टामटूम *or* टुमटाम *f.* धामधूम *or* धुमधाम *f.* डामडौल *m.* सोंग *n.* शोभा *f.*
PAGINAL, *a. consisting of pages.* पृष्ठांचा, पृष्ठांकित.
PAGOD, *n. idol.* मूर्त्ति *f.*
PAGODA, *n. idol-temple,* v. TEMPLE. देऊळ *n.*
2—the coin. होन *m.* वरहं *or* वराई *f.*
PAID, *p.* v. V. दिल्हेला, फेडलेला. [पीप *n.*
PAIL, *n. vessel for drawing or holding water.* पोहरा*m.* डोल *m.*
PAIN, *n.*—the sensation. दुःख *n.* पीडा *f.* वेदना *f.* बाधा *f.* यातना *f.* व्यथा *f.* आर्त्ति *f.*
Bodily p.—*as opp. to* mental pain. व्याधि *pop.* व्याध *f.* शरीरपीडा *f.* कृच्छ्र *n.*
Mental p.—*as opp. to* bodily pain. आधि*m.f.*मनःपीडा*f.*
Creeping or flying p. वेग *m.*
Freed from p. दुःखातीत.
Pains of death. प्राणांत वेदना *f.*
Pains and disease ; *or* pains and sorrows ;—compreh. दुखणें बाहणें *n.* [चक *f.*शिलक *f.*
Rheumatic p. in the back or loins. कण *f.* करक *f.* क-
Sharp, shooting, or lancinating p. कळ *f.* तिडीक*f.* कणक *f.* धमक *f.* चमक *f.* शिणक *f.* शिणीक*f.*सल *f.*सलक *f.*—esp. in the trunk of the body. उसण *f.* उसणब *f.* उसबण *f.* उसणावळ *f.* टिचें *n.* एलकी *f.*
Sharp or acute p. शूल *pop.* शूळ *or* सूळ *m.*
Stinging or pungent p. चुरचूर *f.*
Suffering p. दुःखभोगी. [शिणकणें.
To be effected with a sharp, shooting p.—limb, &c.
2 *disquietude, uneasiness of mind.* दुःख *n.* क्लेश *m. pl.* श्रम *m. pl.* कष्ट *m. or m. pl.* ताप *m.* संताप*m.* मनस्ताप *m.* चुरचूर *f.* आधि *f. m.* मनःपीडा *f.* मनोव्यथा *f.* आर्त्ति *f.* हळहळ *f.* हुरहूर *f.* चटपट *f.*
3—pains ; *toil, care, labor.* श्रम *m.* or *m. pl.* कष्ट *m.* or *m. pl.* मेहनत *f.* खटपट *f.* मशागत *f.* खस्ता *f. pl. v.* काढ-खा, कडाकूट *f.* खवदव *f.* उपद्व्याप *m.* प्रयास *m.* सायास *m.* आयास *m. pl.* कसोशी *f.* धावधूप *f.*
Through great pains. लोंबी झोंबीनें.
To take great p. about. श्रम *m. pl.*-कष्ट *m. pl.*-मेहनत *f.* -&c. घेणें-करणें-भोगणें, तिडका *f. pl.* खाणें-सोसणें.
4 *throe of childbirth.* वेण *f.* तिडीक *f.* प्रसूतिवेदना *f.* प्रसवव्यथा *f.* प्रसववेदना *f.* [शिक्षा *f.*
5 *punishment denounced, penalty,* v. PUNISHMENT. दंड*m.*
To PAIN, *v. a. cause pain to.* दुःख *n.*-पीडा *f.*-व्यथा *f.*- &c. करणें-देणें, पीडणें *or* पिडणें, दुखवणें *or* दुखावणें, झोंबणें. (Note. —This word does not inflect the agent) दुखवणूक *f.*-पिडणूक *f.*-पीडन *n.* करणें.
2 *distress, grieve, &c.* v. TO AFFLICT. दुःख *n.*-&c. देणें-करणें, दुखवणें *or* दुखावणें, श्रमवणें,क्लेशणें, झोंबणें, सलणें, श्रमी-दुःखी-कष्टी-&c. करणें.
To PAIN, *v. n. be painful.* दुखणें, तिडकणें.
PAINED, *p.* v. V. A. 1. दुःख दिल्हेला, पिडलेला, दुखवलेला, &c. पीडित, व्यथित, दुःखार्त्त, आर्त्त, कृच्छ्रगत.
2 दुःख दिल्हेला, &c. दुःखी, दुःखित, कष्टी, श्रमी, क्लेशी, क्लेशित, दुःखान्वित, दुःखार्त्त.
PAINFUL, *a. giving pain, causing smart.* दुःखाचा, वेदनेचा, &c. दुःखकर-कारक-प्रद, दुखद, दुःखावह, पीडाकर-कारक-जनक-&c. वेदनाकारक-जनक-&c. व्यथक.
2 *distressing, &c.* v. AFFLICTIVE. दुःखाचा, दुःखप्रद, दुःखद, दुःखकर-कारक-दायक-&c. क्लेशकारक, कष्टकर, श्रमकर, व्यथक.
3 *arduous,* v. DIFFICULT. कठिन *pop.* कठीण, श्रमाचा, कष्टाचा, दुष्कर, दुःसाध्य, कष्टसाध्य, श्रमसाध्य, कष्टैकसाध्य.
4 *laborious, pains taking,* v. DILIGENT. मेहनती, मेहनत्या, कष्टाळू, खप्या, कष्टकरी, उपद्व्यापी, श्रामक.
PAINFULLY, *adv.* v. A. 1. दुःखानें, दुःखेंकरून, वेदनेनें, &c.
2 दुःखानें, श्रमानें, कष्टानें, &c.
4 मेहनतीनें, &c, श्रमेंकरून, &c. श्रमकरून-घेऊन-भोगून, कष्ट

खाऊन-करून-भोगून, आटाआट-आटाघाट-&c. करून, रुच्छेंकरून.

PAINFULNESS, *n.* v. A. 1. दुःख *n.* दुःखकारकत्व *n.* दुःखदायकत्व *n.* पीडाकारकत्व *n.* &c.

2 दुःखदायकत्व *n.* कष्टकारकत्व *n.* क्लेशकारकत्व *n.* &c.

3 कठीणपणा *m.* कष्टसाध्यता *f.* श्रमसाध्यता *f.*

4 *and* PAIN. कष्ट *m.* श्रम *m.* मेहनत *f.*

PAINIM. See PAGAN.

PAINLESS, *a. free from pain.* निर्दुःखी, दुःखहीन-रहित-शून्य, व्यथाहीन-शून्य-&c. मुका.

2 *free from trouble.* See EASY.

PAINSTAKER, *n.* PAINSTAKING, *a. industrious, &c.* v. DILIGENT. मेहनती, मशागती, कष्टाळू, खप्या, उद्योगी, श्रामक.

To PAINT, *v. a. draw a figure of in colors.* रंगानें *or* रंगाचें चित्र *n.*-नकशा *m.*-नकाशा *m.*-&c. काढणें *g. of o.*

2 *cover with colour, paint, or figures.* रंग *m.* देणें-लावणें, रंगणें, रंगवणें, चितारणें, रंगरेजी *f.*-रंगामेजी *f.* करणें *g. of o.*

3 *depict, portray,* v. To DESCRIBE. वर्णणें, वर्णन *n.* करणें *g. of o.*

To PAINT, *v. n. rouge.* गालांवर-तोंडावर-&c. रंग *m.* लावणें.

PAINT, *n. coloring substance.* रंग *m.* रंगाचें द्रव्य *n.*

PAINTED, *p.* v. V.A. 1. रंगाचा काढलेला, रंगानें काढलेला, चित्रगत.

2 रंग दिल्हेला, रंगवलेला, रंगलेला, चितारलेला, &c. रंगी, रंगीत.

3 वर्णलेला, वर्णित.

PAINTER, *n.* PAINTING, *p. a.* v. V. A. 1. रंगाचें चित्र काढणारा, चितारी, चित्रकार, चित्रकर्मा, चित्रलेखक, लेखक, रंगाजीव.

2 रंग देणारा, रंगवणारा, &c. रंगारी, रंगरेज, रंगाजीव, रागी.

3 वर्णणारा, वर्णन कर्त्ता-कारी.

PAINTER, *n. the rope by which a boat is secured.* पाग *m.*

PAINTING, *n.* v.V.A. 1.—*act.* रंगानें काढणें *n.* रंगाचें चित्र काढणें *n.* &c. चित्रलिपि *f.* लिपि *f.*

2 रंग देणें *n.* रंगवणें *n.* &c. रंगरेजी *f.* रंजन *n.*—esp. of a house, room, &c. रंगामेजी *f.*

Cost or price of p. रंगणावळ *f.* रंगाई *f.*

3 वर्णणें *n.* वर्णन *n.* रंजन *n.* [र्म *n.* चित्रक्रिया *f.*

I. *art or business of a painter.* चितान्याचें कसब *n.* चित्रक-

II. *thing painted, a picture.* चित्र *or* रंगाचें चित्र *n.* नकशा *m.* नकाशा *m.*

PAIR, *n. two things suiting.* जोडी *f.* जोडा *m.* जोड *m.*

Of a p. जोडीचा.

2 *two, brace,* v. COUPLE. जुळी *f.* जुंबळी *f.* जुळें *n.* द्वय *n.*

3 *male and female.* जोडा *m.* जोडपें *n.* जोडें *n.* द्वंद्व *n.* मिथुन *n.*

4 *man and wife.* स्त्रीपुरुषें *n. pl.* जोडा *m.* जोडें *n.* जोडपें *n.* दंपत्य *n.* दंपती *m.n.* मेहूण *n.* [युग्मभोजन *n.*

Feasting of a married p. by Bráhmans. दंपतीभोजन *n.*

Honors paid to a married p. by Bráhmans. दंपतीपूजन *n.*

Newly married p. on their visit to the idol. वधूवरें *n. pl.* वहूवरें *n. p.* [त्रा *f.*

Procession of a newly married p. to the idol. वहूरज-

Squabbles of a married p. दंपतीकलह *m.*

To PAIR, *v. n. suit, fit.* जुडणें, जुळणें, जुळणी *f.*-जुगल *f.*-&c. होणें *g. of s.* जोडीचा-जोड्याचा-&c. असणें.

2 *be joined in pairs.* जोडा *m.*-जोडी *f.*-जोड *m.*-जूग *n.*-&c. होणें-जमणें-बनणें, जुगणें.

To PAIR, *v. a. join in suit, unite so as to pair.* जोडी *f.*- जोडा *m.*-&c. करणें *g. of o.* जुळणी *f.*-जुगल *f.*-&c. करणें, जोडणें.

2 *join in pairs or two.* जुळी *f.*-जुंबळी *f.*-जुळें *n.*-&c. करणें *g. of o.* जूळ *f.* घालणें.

PALACE, *n. royal or noble house.* राजवाडा *m.* वाडा *m.* राऊळ *n.* राजमहाल *m.* राजमंदिर *n.* हवेली *f.* राजगृह *n.* सौध *m. n.* प्रासाद *m.*

PALACE-YARD, *n.* राजांगण *n.* [खाना *m.* रंगांगण *n.*

PALÆSTRA, *n. place for wrestling.* मल्लभू *f.* मल्लभूमि *f.* तालीम-

PALANKEEN, PALANQUIN, *n.* For the swinging litter suspended from a pole in which the Native nobility and gentry ride, the words are पालखी *f.* शिबिका *f.* नरयान *n.* For the oblong box-like conveyance the words are म्याना *or* मेना *m.* though Europeans generally use पालखी for it.

Bed (pensile portion) of a p. तबकडी *f.*

Entitled to ride in a p. पालखीपदस्थ.

House for a palankeen and bearers. भोइखाना *m.*

Padding along the pole of a p. सोंडगादी *f.* [राज.

P.-bearer. भोई, हमाल, कहार, वाहक,—respectfully, भोई-

Set of p.-bearers. पहाडी *f.*

To set down or take up a p. थोपणें.

PALATABLE, *a. agreeable to the taste,* v. TASTEFUL. रुचकर, चवदार, मजेदार, स्वादु, स्वादिष्ट, मुखप्रिय.

To become p. *cease to offend the stomach.* जिरमाणीस-पचणीस-जिरणीस पडणें.

PALATAL, *a. uttered by the aid of the palate.* तालव्य.

PALATAL, PALATIAL, PALATIC, *a. belonging to the palate.* ताळूचा *or* ताळवेचा, तालुसंबंधी.

PALATE, *n. roof of the mouth.* तालु *n. pop.* ताळू *f.* काकुद *m.*

2 v. TASTE. रुचि *f.* चव *f.*

Vitiation of the p. अरुचि *f.* अरोचक *n.*

To indulge the p. जिह्वा *f.*-तोंड *n.* हातीं धरणें.

PALATIAL, *a. pertaining, &c. to a palace.* राजवाड्याचा, राजमंदिरसंबंधी.

PALAVER, *n. soft and pleasing but hollow speech.* गूळपापडी *f.* गूळखोबरें *n.* घमटगुळवणी *n.* गुळगुळथापडी *f.* लमगोष्टी *f. pl.* थंतरमंतर *n.* फोल *n.* झुलजीफुलजीच्या गोष्टी *f. pl.*

PALE, *a. white of look, wan.* पांढरा, पिकूट, पिकुटलेला, &c. उफट *or* उफीट *or* ओफट, निस्तेज, कयाहीन, नीरक्त, म्लान, विवर्ण, गतवर्ण.

Deadly p *white as a sheet, &c.* गोरामोरा.

To turn p. पिकुटणें, तोंडचें पाणी *n.* पळणें *g. of s.* काळवटणें *or* काळवंडणें.

2 *not high-colored, light.* फिका *or* फिक्का, पिकूट, उभरंग, उभरा, उणेरंगाचा, न्यूनप्रभ, न्यूनकांति.

A p. color. उभरंग *m.*

Palish. फिकट *or* फिक्कट.

PALE, *n. stick or pointed board of a paling.* गरादा *m.* गराज *f.* कथड्याचा गज *m.* गराद *f.* शंकु *m.*

2 See STAKE. 3 See ENCLOSURE.

To PALE, *v. n. turn pale.* See PALE.

To PALE, *v. a. enclose with paling.* कठडा *m.*-&c. घालणें, मेढेबंदी *f.*-मेढेकोट *m.* करणें-घालणें.

PALE-EYED, *a.* निस्तेज डोळ्यांचा, कांतिहीननेत्र, न्यूनप्रभाक्ष.
PALE-FACED, *a.* पांढरेफटकतोंडाचा, विवर्णवदन, म्लानवदन.
PALENESS, *n.* v. A. 1. पांढरेपणा *m.* पिकुटपणा *m.* उफटपणा *m.*&c. काळवटी *f.* काळवंडी *f.* नीरक्तता *f.* वैवर्ण्य *n.* मुखवैवर्ण्य *n.*
Livid p. मडेकळा *f.* [कांति *f.*
2 फिकेपणा *m.* पिकुटपणा *m.* उभरेपणा *m.* &c. न्यूनप्रभा *f.* न्यून-
PALESTRA. See PALÆSTRA.
PALESTRIAN, PALESTRIC, *a. pertaining to wrestling.* कुस्तीचा, झोंबीचा, झोंबीविषयींचा, मल्लयुद्धसंबंधी-विषयक.
PALETTE, *n. painter's board.* चितान्याचीरंगपाटी *f.* वर्णपत्र *n.*
PALFREY, *n. horse fit for ladies.* बायकांचे स्वारीचा घोडा *m.* माघारणीचा-नरमचालीचा घोडा *m.*-तट्टू *m.*-&c.
PALINDROME, *n. word or sentence which is the same read backward or forward.* मुरजबंध *m.* अनुलोमविलोमश्लोक *m.*
PALING, *n. fence formed with pales.* कठडा *m.* कठरडा *m.* कठारा *m.* कटारा *m.* कटंजन *n.* मेढेकोट *m.* मेढेबंदी *f.* लकडकोट *m.* मेढा *m.*
PALINODE. See RECANTATION.
PALISADE, PALISADO, *n.* v. PALING. कठडा *m.* मेढेकोट *m.* लकडकोट *m.* मेढेबंदी *f.*
To PALISADE, *v. a.* v. N. कठडा *m.*-&c. घालणें, मेढेबंदी *f.*-मेढेकोट *m.*-&c. करणें-घालणें.
PALL, *n. mantle of state.* शेला *m.*
2 (over a corpse). सेंडा *m.* प्रेतावरची चादर *f.*
To PALL, *v. n. grow vapid and insipid.* सपक-मळमळीत-मुळमुळीत-पळपळीत-नकोसा-&c. होणें-होऊं लागणें-वाटूं लागणें, गोडी *f.* -रुचि *f.*-&c. जाणें *g. of s.* शिसारी *f.*-वीट *m.*-उपरति *f.*-&c. येणें *g. of s.*
To PALL, *v. a. make vapid.* सपक-मळमळीत-मुळमुळीत-&c. करणें, शिसारी *f.*-वीट *m.*-कंटाळा *m.*-&c. आणणें *g. of o.* गोडी *f.*-रुचि *f.* -&c. नाहींसी करणें *g. of o.*
2 See To CLOY.
PALLADIUM, *n. that which affords protection.* राखण *f.* रक्षण *n.*
PALLET, *n. small or mean bed.* निजायाचें पटकूर *n.*-पटकर *n.*-पुदरट *n.*-तळकट *n.*
2 See PALETTE.
To PALLIATE, *v. a. excuse, cover, extenuate, &c.* निमित्त *n.*-सबब *f.*-बहाणा *m.*-&c. सांगणें *or* सांगून उडवणें-हलका करणें-हलका करून दाखवणें, पांघरूण *n.* घालणें.
2 *reduce in violence; mitigate, lessen, &c.* हलका-कमी-लघु-&c. करणें, उपशम *m.*-उपशमन *n.*-&c. करणें *g. of o.*
PALLIATION, *n.* v. V. 1.—*act.* निमित्त सांगणें *n.* सबब सांगणें *n.* &c. दोषलघूकरण *n.* दोषन्यूनत्वाधान *n.* दोषन्यूनीकरण *n.*
2 हलका करणें *n.* &c. उपशमन *n.* उपशम *m.* अल्पशमन *n.* अल्पशम *m.*
PALLIATIVE, *n. that which excuses:* दोषपरिहारक गोष्ट *f.* दोषन्यूनत्वाधायक गोष्ट *f.* दोषन्यूनतासाधक गोष्ट *f.* [*m.*-&c.
2 *that which mitigates.* उपशमक-शमक-अल्पशमक-&c. विषय
PALLID, PALLIDNESS. See PALE, PALENESS.
PALM, *n. inner part of the hand.* तळहात *m.* तळवा *m.* हस्ततल *m.* करतल *m.* पंजा *m.*
The p. hollowed to hold. पसा *m.* खोंगा *m.* खोबळा *m.* कुडचा *or* कुडता *m.* साक *f.*—esp. liquid. चूळ *m. f.* चुळका *m.*—both palms put side by side and hollowed. ओंजळ *or* ओंजळ *f. m.* अंजलि *m. f. pop.* अंजळी *f.* अंजलिपुट *n.*
That has an itchy p. *fig.* हातलावा *or* लाव्या, हाताळ.
With the palms hollowed and placed one over the other. कृतांजलि, बद्धांजलि.
2 *borassus flabelliformis, or fan-palm.* ताड *m.* ताल *m.*
Some species or varieties of the *Palm tribe* are, केकताड, भायताड, सुरमाड, भेरलामाड *or* भेरलीमाड *or* भेरळ.
For the other palms see COCOANUT and DATE.
Branch of a p. झावळी *f.* ताडकन.—Lower or base-portion of it. पिढा *or* पिढा *m.* थरपील *n.*
Branch of a p. divided longitudinally. तळकट *n.* तळकटी *f.*
Case made of matted p.-leaves. कपात *n.*
Cord-ring for the feet used in ascending a p. खाडवें *n.*
Exudation from the p. ताडी *f.*—He who extracts it. ताड्या *m.*
Female or fruit-bearing p. tree. फळताड *m.*
Fermented juice of the p.-tree. ताडी *f.*
Fruit of the p. ताडफळ *n.*—Young fruit. खासोटा *m.*
Fruit stalk or spadix of the p. whilst incased. गाभा *m.*
Gourd or earthern vessel used to receive the liquor from the p. घडी *f.* कोंड्या *m.* खुद *m.*
Head or bush of the p. गाभा *m.* पिंजरा *m.* खबळा *m.*
Leaf or spike of the p. ताडपत्र *n.*
Longitudinal division of a p. tree. चोप *f.* चोपट *n.*
Male or barren p. tree. बळताड *m.* लेंड्याताड *m.*
Notch for the foot cut in a p. tree. पायका *m.* पावका *m.* पावटा *m.* पायंडा *m.* पावंडा *m.* खाप *f.*
Pitcher fastened to the spathe of a p. to receive the exudation. घडा *m.* घडी *f.*
Rib of the leaf of the p. tree. हिरकूट *n.*
Spathe or calyx of the fruit stalk of the p. पोगी *f* —The extremity of it as cut to induce exudation, कोंत *n.*—Wounding or cutting it to induce exudation, शेव *f.* v. घाल. [रा *m.*
Spirits distilled from the exudation of the p.-tree. स-
Tall p. लकड *or* लांकड *f.*
To cut notches in a p. for climbing. खापणें.
3 See TRIUMPH.
To PALM, *v. a. conceal in the palm.* हातांत-तळहातांत-&c. लपवणें-चोरणें-चोरून ठेवणें-गप्प करणें.
2 *impose by fraud.* दगलबाजीनें-ठकबाजीनें-&c. घेवविणें-चालवणें-पदरीं घालणें-गळीं बांधणें.
PALMATED, *a. of the shape of the hand.* हाताच्या आकाराचा, हस्ताकृतीचा, हस्ताकृति, हस्ताकार.
PALMER. See PILGRIM. [पानविंचू *m.*
PALMER-WORM, *n.* सुरवंट *or* सुरवट *m.* कुसरूड *m.* कुशिरडा *m.*
PALMISTER, *n. one who deals in palmistry.* हात पाहणारा, सामुद्रिक.
PALMISTRY, *n. divining by the lines in the palm.* हात पाहण्याची विद्या *f.* हस्तसामुद्रिक *n.*
PALMY, *a. bearing or abounding with palms.* तालबहुल, तालप्रचुर, तालसंकीर्ण.

2 fig. *happy, prosperous.* सुबत्तेचा, भरभरीचा, चढते कळेचा, अमदानीचा, सुखाचा, सुखबाहुल्याचा.

PALMYRA. See PALM.

PALPABILITY, PALPABLENESS, *n.* v. A.1. स्पृश्यता *f.* स्पर्शनीयता *f.* स्पर्शगोचरता *f.* स्पर्शेंद्रियग्राह्यता *f.*

2 स्पष्टपणा *m.* उघडपणा *m.* &c. प्रत्यक्षता *f.*

3 ढोबळेपणा *m.* &c. स्थूलत्व *n.*

PALPABLE, *a. tangible.* स्पर्श करायाजोगा, स्पृश्य, स्पर्शनीय, स्पर्शगोचर, स्पर्शज्ञेय, त्वगिंद्रियज्ञेय, स्पर्शेंद्रियग्राह्य, संस्पृश्य.

2 *manifest, striking,* v. PLAIN. स्पष्ट, उघड, धडधडीत, प्रत्यक्ष.

3 *gross, coarse, easily detected.* ढोबळा, ढोबळ, ढळढळीत, टळटळीत, स्थूल.

PALPABLY, *adv.* v. A. 1. स्पर्शानें समजायाजोगा-जोगता, &c.

2 स्पष्ट, उघड, प्रत्यक्ष, प्रत्यक्षत:.

To PALPITATE, *v. n. go pit a pat.* धकधकणें *or* धगधगणें, धडकणें, धुगधुगणें, धडधडणें, धसधसणें, ऊर *m.* उडणें *g. of s.* धडकी *f.*-धगधग *f.*-&c. भरणें,—*intens.* उडून जाणें.

PALPITATION, *n.* v. V. धकधकणें *n.* &c. धकधक *or* धगधग *f.* धुगधूग *f.* धुगधुगी *f.* धकाधक *f.* धडकी *f.* धडधडी *f.* धसधस *f.* धासधूस *f.* बाकबूक *f.* स्फुरण *n.* हृत्कंप *m.*

PALSICAL, PALSIED, *a.* v. N. वारा गेलेला, पक्षघाती, पक्षवायुग्रस्त, अर्धांगवायुग्रस्त, खुडा *or* खुडे *indecl.* [खोडा *m.*

P. state of the limbs. खोडाबिडी *or* बेडी *f.* खोडामोडा *m.*

To become p. खुडावणें, आंगावरून वारा *m.*-वारें *n.* जाणें.

PALSY, *n. paralysis, loss of motion.* स्वाप *m.* सुप्ति *f.* अवष्टंभ *m.* विष्टंभ *m.* स्तंभ *m.* संस्तंभ *m.* स्पर्शाज्ञता *f.* अंगपात *m.*

2 *hemiplegia.* अर्धांग *n.* अर्धांगवायु *m.* पक्षवायु *m.* पक्षाघात *m.*

Shaking p. कंपवायु *m.* कंपवात *m.*

To get a stroke of the p. आंगावरून वारा *m.* जाणें *g.of s.*

To PALSY, &c. See To PARALYSE, &c.

To PALTER, See To FAIL.

PALTRINESS, *n.* v. A. हलकेपणा *m.* गैरीपणा *m.* एरपणा *m.* &c.

PALTRY, *a. poor, sorry, despicable, &c.* v. MEAN, WORTHLESS. हलका, गैरी, एर, एरशेर, लुकसान *or* लुसकान, नादान, नाकारा, कमतोल, किलवाणा *or* णी, तुच्छ, कृपण.

To PAMPER, *v. a. feed or gratify to the full.* यथेच्छ खावविणें, खाऊं घालून माजवणें-मातवणें, भर *f.* करणें *g. of o.* लाड *m.*-लडिवाळ *m.*-लाडकी *f.*-&c. पुरवणें-चालवणें *g. of o.* धण *f.* पुरवणें-करणें-भरणें *g. of o.* धण करून-भरूनचढवणें, पुष्ट-धष्टपुष्ट-&c. करणें.

PAMPERED, *p.* v. V. भर केलेला, माजवलेला-मातवलेला *or* माजलेला-मातलेला, &c.

A p. fellow. पोळ *m.* वसू *m.* वहुधा, बठाळया.

PAMPHLET, *n. stitched book.* वही *f.* चोपडी *f.* शिवलेली पोथी *f.*

PAMPHLETEER, *n.* चोपड्या *f. pl.*-&c. रचणारा-लिहणारा *m.*

PAN, *n. flat broad vessel,* v. POT. भांडें *n.* हांडी *f.* थाळा *m. dim.* थाळी *f.*

2 (of a gun). काना *m.* रंजकीचा पेला *m.*

Double panned. दुकानी;—Single panned. एककानी.

To flash in the p. रंजक *f.* पिणें.

3 (of the knee). गुडघ्याची वाटी *f.* [मणि *m.*

PANACEA, *n. universal medicine.* सर्वौषधीचूर्ण *n.* त्रैलोक्यचिंतामणि *m.*

PANCAKE, *n. fried cake.* ढेंबरें *n.* धिरडें *n.* वेढणी *f.*

PANCRATIC, PANCRATICAL, *a. excelling in gymnastics; athletic.* तालमी, तालिमबाज, कसरती, मल्लविद्यानिपुण, जोरदार, जोरकस.

PANDECT, *n. complete treatise on a science.* विद्यासंग्रह *m.*

2 (of laws). संहिता *f.*

PANDEMIC, *a. incident to a whole people.* सर्वलोकांचा, सकलजनव्यापक, सर्वव्यापक, सर्वसाधारण.

PANDER, *n. pimp.* कुंटण, कुटण्या, भडवा, संधानकर्त्ता.

To PANDER, *v. n.* v. N. कुंटणपणा *m.*-कुंटणगिरी *f.*-भडवेपणा *m.* -&c. करणें.

PANDERING, PANDERAGE, PANDERISM, *n.* v. V. कुंटणपणा *m.* कुंटणकी *f.* कुंटणगिरी *f.* भडवेपणा *m.*

PANDICULATION, *n. yawning and stretching.* आंगमोडा *m.* आंगपिळा *m.* आंगमोडणी *f.* आंगपिळणी *f.*

PANDIT, PUNDIT, *n.* पंडित.

PANE, *n.* (of glass). ताव *m.* तावदान *n.* भिंग *n.*

PANEGYRIC, *n. eulogium.* स्तुतिवाद *m.* प्रशंसावाद *m.* स्तुतिपाठ *m.* गुणोत्कीर्त्तन *n.* स्तोत्र *n.*

2 See PRAISE.

PANEGYRICAL, *a.* v. N. स्तुतीचा, स्तुतिप्रद, स्तुतिविषयक, स्तुतिरूप, स्तुत्यात्मक.

PANEGYRIST, *n. encomiast, eulogist.* स्तुति करणारा, स्तुतिपाठक, स्तोता, बंदी, बंदिजन.

To PANEGYRIZE. See To PRAISE.

PANEL, *n. square piece, &c. of a door.* कवाडाचा-कवाडांतला-&c. खण *m.* लांकडीतावदान *n.* चकला *m.*

2 (of a jury). पंचांचे नांवनिशीची याद *f.*

PANG, *n. sudden paroxysm of extreme pain.* तिडीक *f.* कळ *f.* वेण *f.* वेग *or* दुःखाचा वेग *m.* दुःखाची लहर *f.* चटका *m.* चरका *m.*

2 pangs; *extreme pain, agony.* वेदना *f.* यातना *f.* व्यथा *f.* शूल *m.* अतिवेदना *f.* अतिव्यथा *f.* प्राणांत यातना *f.*

PANGOLIN, *n.* खवल्यामांजर *m. n.* वज्रकीट *m.*

PANIC, *n. sudden fear,* v. FRIGHT. अपधाक *m.* धसका *m.* धस्स *n.* धडकी *f.* चर्र *n.* दचका *m.* दचक *f.* बाच *or* बाज *m.* कच्च *n.*

PANICSEED, *n. panicum Italicum.* कांगुणी *or* कांगोणी *f.* कांगू *m.*

PANIC-STRUCK, *a.* v. N. धसका बसलेला, &c. हौलदिल *or* हवालदिल.

PANNEL, *n. saddle.* खोगीर *n.*

PANNIER, *n.* v. BASKET. पेटारा *m.*

PANOPLY, *n. complete armour.* सगळें आंग राखायाचें चिलखत *n.*-बखतर *n.*-&c. सर्वांग कवच *n.*

PANORAMA, *n.* सर्वदिशा दाखविणारें चित्र *n.* सर्वदिग्दर्शक चित्र *n.*

PANSY, *n.* एक फूल आहे.

To PANT, *v. n. have the breast heave; gasp, blow, &c.* धापणें, धापलणें, धापा *f. pl.* देणें-दाटणें-टाकणें, श्वास *m.* टाकणें, लाहक्या *f. pl.*-अहाळण्या *f. pl.* देणें, धापा *f. pl.* भरणें *in. con.* हवावी *f.*-दम *m.*-दमा *m.*-धाप *f.*-&c. लागणें *in. con.* कांसळणें, उस्कारा *m.* देणें, लहालहा *adv.* करणें, झायाझ्या *f. pl.* देणें-टाकणें.

2 *beat,* v. To PALPITATE. धडकणें, धडधडणें, धडकी *f.* भरणें *in. con.*

3 *long, hanker, &c.* v. To DESIRE. नितांतणें, धोपणें, मरणें, खुरखुरणें, प्राण *m.* सोखणें *g. of s.* कंठीं प्राण *m.* धरणें, जीव *m.* टांगला असणें *g. of s.*

PANTALOONS, *n. pl. trowsers.* इजार *f.* पायजामा *m.* सुरवार *f.*

PANTHEISM, *n. the doctrine that the universe is god.* जगदी-

श्वरमत *n.* जगदीश्वरवाद *m.* बिराट्स्वरूपमत *n.* बिराट्देहमत *n.* बिराट्देहवाद *m.* अद्वैतमत *n.* अद्वैतवाद *m.* अभेदमत *n.* अभेदवाद *m.*

PANTHEIST, *n. maintainer of pantheism.* जगदीश्वरवादी, जगदीश्वरमतावलंबी, जगदीश्वरमताश्रयी, अद्वैतवादी, अभेदवादी, अद्वैतमतावलंबी.

PANTHEISTIC, PANTHEISTICAL, *a.* v. N. जगदीश्वरमताचा, जगदीश्वरमतसंबंधी-विषयक, अद्वैतमताचा, &c. अद्वैतमतविषयक-संबंधी.

PANTHEON, *n. temple for all the gods.* सर्वदेवालय *n.*

PANTHER, *n.* बिब्ळ्यावाघ *m.* बिबळा *m.* बिबळ्यावाघ *m.*

PANTILE, *n. hollow tile.* नळा *m.*

PANTING, *n.* v. V. 1. धापणें *n.* &c. धाप *f.* दम *m.* दमा *m.* हवावी *f.* श्वास *m.* ऊर्ध्व *m.*

3 See DESIRE.

PANTOMIME, *n. one that represents by imitation.* अबोल्या सोंगाडी, नुस्ता हावभाव करून बतावणी करणारा, केवलाभिनयी.

2 *representation in dumb show.* मुकेंसोंग *n.* मुग्धनाट्य *n.* मुग्धनृत्य *n.* [बंधी-विषयक.

PANTOMIME, PANTOMIMIC, *a.* v. N. मुकेंसोंगाचा, मुग्धनाट्यसं-

PANTRY, *n. room or closet for provisions.* फराळाची कोठडी *f.*-खोली *f.* सोंवळ्याची खोली *f.* खाद्यशाला *f.*

PAP, *n.* v. NIPPLE. बोंडी *f.* स्तनाग्र *n.* स्तनमुख *n.*

2 v. BREAST. स्तन *m.* कुच *m.*

3 *food for infants.* मुलांचा-मुलांसाठीं काला *m.* लापशी *or* लाफशी *f.* घाट *f.*

To feed with p. भरवणें.

4 See PULP.

PAPA, *n.* v. FATHER. बा.

PAPACY, *n.* पोपाचा अधिकार *m.*

2 *line of popes.* पोपांची परंपरा *f.*

PAPAL, *a.* पोपाचा, पोपाकडील, पोपाच्या संबंधाचा.

PAPAW, *n. papaya.* पोपय *or* या *m.*

PAPER, *a.*—the substance. कागद *m.* Some kinds are, कळकी कागद, जुन्नरी कागद, दौलताबादी कागद, बालापुरी कागद, बहादूरखानी कागद, मधघडी *or* मधघडीचा कागद.

Bundle or quantity of ten quires of p. गड्डी *or* गद्दी *f.* गादी *f.* [णें, कलमी करणें.

To commit to p. To put down on p. गांढऱ्यावर काळें कर-

2 *piece of paper.* कागद *m.* Some terms for *paper as folded in different forms* are, दुटें *n.* दुट्टा *m.* दुंडा *m.* दुंडी *f.* फर्द *m.* बंद *m.*

Blank p. कोराकागद *m.*—Blank at the back, पाठकोरा.

Small piece of p. पुरजा *m.* पारजा पुरजा *m.*

Shred, slip, or scrap of p. for writing. चिटोरा *or* चिठोरा *m.* चिठोरें *n.* चिठडी *or* चिठोडी *f.* [*n.* पत्रक *n.*

3 *written sheet or paper ; a writing.* कागद *m.* लेख *m.* पत्र

Business or official papers—compreh. लिखापढा *m.* लेखपढा *m.* लेखपत्र *n.* लिखापुसा *m.* लेखपूस *m.* लिहिणें पुसणें *n.* लिहिलें पुसलें *n.*

Bundle or packet of papers. तबलक *f.*—The string or paper confining them. तबलक *f.*

Bundle of official, &c. papers. दफ्तर *n.* रुमाल *m.*

String to tie official papers. दफ्तरणी *f.*

Waste papers. गाबाळ *m.* *n.* गबाळ *m.* *n.*

4 *deed, document, &c.* कागद *m.* लेख *m.* दस्तऐवज *m.* पत्र *n.* पत्रक *n.* खत *n.*

5 *newspaper.* खबरेचा कागद *m.* वर्तमानपत्र *n.* गाजेट *n.* from the English is common with natives who read papers.

To get into the papers. फडास येणें.

PAPER, *a. made &c. of paper.* कागदाचा, कागदी.

2 fig. *slight, slim, &c.* v. FLIMSY. कागदाचा, कागदी, जुजबी.

To PAPER, *v. a.* (wall, &c.) कागद *m.* लावणें-मढवणें.

PAPER-KITE, *n.* बावडी *f.* तुक्कल *f.* पतंग *m.* कनकावळा *m.*—Note. These words express varieties.

Jerking string (or check) of a p. जामीन *m.*

PAPER-MAKER, कागदकुटारी, कागदकुट्या.

PAPESCENT, *n. pulpy.* दळदार, मगजाचा, गिराचा, समज्ज.

PAPILLIO. See BUTTERFLY.

PAPILLARY, PAPILLOUS, *a. resembling nipples.* बोंडीसारखा, स्तनाग्रवत्, स्तनाग्रसदृश.

PAPPY, *a. soft.* बिलबिलीत, बिलबिला, पुळपुळीत, पिळपिळीत.

PAPULÆ, *n. pimples, eruption.* पुरळ *m.* फुटकुळ्या *f. pl.*

PAPULOSE, PAPULOUS, *a. full of pimples.* फोडेला, फोडाळ, फुटकुळ्यांचा, फोडांचा.

PAR, *n. state of equality.* बराबरी *f.* समता *f.* समभाव *m.*

That is at p. बराबरीचा, समकक्ष, समानकक्ष.

That is above p. अधिकोत्तर.

PARABLE, *n.* v. ALLEGORY. दृष्टांत *m.* दृष्टांतरूपकथा *f.*

PARABOLA, *n.* in conic sections. समकलछिन्न *n.* समकक्षछिन्न *n.*

PARABOLIC, PARABOLICAL, *a. expressed, &c. by a parable.* दृष्टांताचा, दृष्टांतरूप, दृष्टांतोक्त. [कार.

2 *having the form of a parabola.* समकलछिन्नाकार, बाणा-

PARABOLICALLY, *adv.* v. A. दृष्टांतानें, दृष्टांतेंकरून, दृष्टांतपूर्वक.

PARABOLIFORM. See PARABOLIC, 2. [मंडलत्यागी.

PARACENTRIC, PARACENTRICAL, *a. deviating from circularity.*

PARADE, *n. ostentation, pomp, vain display,* v. SHOW. आव *m.* थाट *m.* थाटमाट *m.* टामटूम *or* टुमटाम *f.* छांकूं *n.* ठांठूं *n.* हांहूं *n.*

To make empty p. प्रतिष्ठा *f.*-डौल *m.* मिरवणें.

To make a p. of मिरवणें.

2 See PROCESSION. 3. *military exercise, &c.* कवाईद *or* कवाईत *f.* [गा *f.*

4 *parade-ground.* कवाइतीची जागा *f.* कवाईत करण्याची जा-

To PARADE, *v. n.*—*troops.* कवाईत करण्यास जमणें-मिळणें, कवाईत *f.* होणें *g. of s.* [थटून काढणें.

2 *go about pompously.* मिरवणें, मिरवणूक *f.* काढणें, नटूम

To PARADE, *v. a.* (troops). कवाईत *f.* करवणें *g. of o.* कवाईत करण्यास मिळवणें.

2 *exhibit ostentatiously.* मिरवणें, मिरवणूक *f.* करणें-काढणें *g. of o.* डौल *m.* मारणें-दाखवणें *g. of o.*

PARADING, *n.* v. V. N. 2—*act.* मिरवणें *n.* मिरवणूक *f.* मिरवण *f.* मिरवणी *f.*

v. V. A. 2. मिरवणें *n.* मिरवणूक *f.* मिरवण *f.* मिरवणी *f.*

PARADIGM, *n.* See EXAMPLE. 2—in grammar. उदाहरणार्थ लिहिलेली धातूंचीं सर्वरूपें *n. pl.* धातुरूपमालिका *f.*

PARADISE, *n. region of supreme felicity.* आनंदलोक *m.* सुखलोक *m.* आनंदभुवन *n.* सुखधाम *n.*

Paradisiacal, **Paradisean**, *a.* v. N. आनंदलोकाचा, &c. आनंदलोकसंबंधी-विषयक.

Paradox, *n. proposition seemingly absurd yet true.* लोकविरुद्धभास *m.* असत्याभास *m.* अयुकाभास *m.* [भासरूप.

Paradoxical, *a.* v. N.—opinions. अयुकाभासात्मक, अयुका-

2—of persons. अयुकाभासवादी, अयुकाभाससेवी, अयुकाभासावलंबी.

Paragon, *n.* v. **Model**. कित्ता *m.* नमुना *m.*

2 fig. *an eminent or superior person.* मोहरा*m.* राजमोहरा*m.* धेंड *n.* प्रकरण*n.* प्रस्थान*n.* प्रस्थ*n.* चूडामणि*m.* व्यक्ति*f.* ठिकडें*n.*

Paragraph, *n. distinct part of a writing.* कलम *n.* वाक्य *n.* लेखपरिच्छेद *m.* लेखखंड *m.*

A distinct or additional p. खेरीज कमल *n.*

P. added as a postsceprit. ताजाकलम *n.*

Paragraphically, *adv.* v. N. कलमवार, कलमें करून.

Paralipomena, *n. supplementary book, &c.* शेषग्रंथ*m.*पुरवणी*f.*

Parallax, *n.*—in astronomy. शीघ्र *m.* स्थानभेद*m.* द्रष्टस्थानभेदोपाधिकदृश्यस्थानभेद *m.* लंबन *n.*

Parallel, *a.*—in geometry. एकदिङ्मुखसमांतर, एकदिग्गतसमांतर, समांतर, सरलसमांतर.

P. lines. एकदिग्गतसमांतर रेषा *f. pl.*

2 *similar, resembling*, v. **Like**. सारखा, बराबर, सम, तुल्य, समभाव, समवर्ण, साम्यबहुल.

Parallel, *n. line equidistant from another.* समांतररेषा *f.*

2 (of latitude). अक्षवृत्त *n.* अक्षांशवृत्त *n.* स्पष्टपरिधि *m.*

3 *resemblance*, v. **Likeness**. बरोबरी *f.* सारखेपणा*m.* समता *f.* तुलना *f.* समभाव *m.*

4 v. **Simile**. उपमा *f.*

5 *match, equal.* तोड *f.* जोडा *m.* तुलना *f.*

To **Parallel**, *v. a. make or keep parallel.* समांतर करणें-राखणें.

2 *compare with, liken to.* उपमा *f.*-तुलना *f.*-बरोबरी*f.*-&c.देणें -करणें-सांगणें, उपमणें, तुळणें, तोलणें.

3 *be equal to, correspond with, resemble.* सारखा-सम-बराबर -&c. असणें, बराबरी *f.*-सारखेपणा *m.*-&c. येणें *g. of s. with* सा *or* ला *of o.* तुळणें. [भाव *m.*

Parallelism, *n. state of being parallel.* समांतरता *f.* समांतर-

2 *resemblance, similarity*, v. **Likeness**. बरोबरी *f.* सारखेपणा *m.* समता *f.* साम्य *n.* समभाव *m.* तुलना *pop.* तुळणा *f.*

Parallelly, *adv.* v. A. 1. समांतर भावानें, समांतरतापूर्वक.

Parallelogram, *n.*—in geometry. समांतरबाजू चौकोन*m.* दीर्घचतुरस्र *n.* आयतचतुर्भुज *m.* समसमद्विभुज *m.*

Parallelogramical, *a.* v. N. दीर्घचतुरस्र.

Parallelopiped, *n.*—in geometry. समखात *m.*

Paralogism, **Paralogy**, *n. fallacious argument or reasoning.* आभास *m.* सिद्धांताभास *m.* अयुक्ति *f.*

Paralysis, **Paralytic**. See **Palsy**, **Palsied**.

Paralytic, *n. person affected with palsy.* वारा गेलेलें मनुष्य *n.* अर्धांगरोगी,—with the power of such words as *log, stock, inert mass, &c.* गोळा *m.* खोड *n.* मोट *f.* हातापायांचा चौरंग झालेला.

To **Paralyze**, *v. a. check or destroy the power of action.* नबळेपणा *m.*-निजोरपणा *m.*-निर्बळपणा *m.*-&c. आणणें, लटका-&c. पाडणें, चलन वलनशक्ति *f.* नाहींसी करणें *g. of o.* चलनवलनावष्टंभ *m.*-चलनवलनाष्टंभन *n.*-चेष्टास्तंभन *n.*-&c. करणें *g. of o.* अवस्तब्ध-स्तंभित-नष्टेंद्रिय-&c. करणें.

Paralyzed, *p.* v. V. लटका पाडलेला, &c. स्तब्ध, स्तब्धीकृत, जडीकृत, जडीभूत, अवस्तब्ध, स्तंभित, नष्टेंद्रिय, इंद्रियनष्ट.

Paralyzing, *n.* v. V.—*act.* नबळेपणा आणणें *n.* लटका पाडणें *n.* &c. स्तंभन *n.* चलनवलनाष्टंभ*m.* चलनवलनावष्टंभन*n.* चेष्टास्तंभन *n.* स्तब्धीकरण *n.* जडीकरण *n.*

Paramount, *a. superior to.* वरचा, वरचढ, वर्चस्वी, श्रेष्ठ.

A lord p. सर्वेश्वर, सम्राट्.

Sway or rule of a lord p. साम्राज्य *n.*

Paramour, *n. gallant, man connected with a woman in illicit love.* धगड, सोयरा, यार, दोस्त, जार, लाग्या, साग्या, उपपति, विट.

A fellow p. दरभाऊ, सवतळा *or* ताळा.

2 *mistress, concubine, &c.* राख *f.* उपस्त्री *f.* जारिणी *f.* दोस्तदारीण *f.* मैत्रीण *f.*

Paranymph, *n. brideman.* पावण, पावता.

Parapet, *n. wall or rampart breast high.* वरबंड *or* वरंड *f.* वरवंडी *or* वरंडी *f.* छातीएवढी उंच भिंत *f.* पाळ *f.* पौळ *f.* धका*m.*

Paraphernalia, *n. goods at a wife's disposal.* स्त्रीधन *n.* यौतक *n.*

2 v. **Trappings**. साज *m.*

Paraphrase, *n. translation or explanation in many words.* टीका *f.* व्याख्या *f.* विवरण *n.* टिप्पण *n.* टिप्पणी *f.* छायानुहरण *n.* सविस्तरभाषांतर *n.* सविस्तरार्थकथन *n.*

To **Paraphrase**, *v. a.* v. N. टीका *f.*-व्याख्या *f.*-विवरण *n.*-&c. करणें *g. of o.* विस्तारानें-विस्तारपूर्वक-&c. अर्थ *m.* सांगणें-भाषांतर *n.* करणें. [जातविवरण, &c.

Paraphrased, *p.* v. V. टीका केलेला, &c. व्याख्यात, विवृत,

Paraphrast, **Paraphraser**, *n.* v. V. टीका करणारा, &c. टीकाकर्त्ता, व्याख्याकर्त्ता, टीकाकार.

Paraphrastic, **Paraphrastical**, *a. not literal, not close.* टीकारूप, व्याख्यारूप, विस्ताररूप, अधिकशब्दक, मूलाधिकशब्दक.

Paraquet, **Paraquito**. See **Parrot**.

Parasite, *n.*—in botany. बांडगूळ *n.* बांधें *n.* बादांगूळ *n.* आकाशवेल *f.* आकाशवल्ली *f.* वृक्षादनी *f.* वृक्षरुहा *f.* जीवंतिका *f.* वंदा *f.*

2 *sponger, trencher fly, idle hanger on, &c.* हांजी करून-खुशामद करून-आर्जव करून-&c. पोट भरणारा, परान्नरुचि, परपाकरुचि, परान्नपुष्ट, परान्नभक्षी, परान्नभोजी, पात्रेसंमित, आर्जववृत्ति, आर्जवोपजीवी, तुकडमोड्या, पानपुज्या, वारकरी, पंक्तिपठाण, पंक्तिबारगीर, उंडीकबाल, उंडीउकळ्या, तैलंग्या, तैलंगभट्ट, ताजेघोड्याची गोमाशी. [वृक्षरुह.

Parasitic, **Parasitical**, *a.* v. N. 1. बांडगुळाचे जातीचा, &c.

2 *flattering, &c.* आर्जवी, आर्जवाचा, खुशामती, खुशामदखोर, आर्जववृत्ति, आर्जववृत्तीचा.

Parasol, *n.* स्त्रियांची लहान छत्री *f.* छत्री *f.* छत्र *n.* आतपत्र *n.*

To **Parboil**, *v. a. boil in part.* अर्धेकच्चें-अर्धेमुर्धें-अर्धबोबडें-&c. शिजवणें-रांधणें.

Parboiled, *p.* v. V. अर्धशिजवलेला *or* शिजलेला, &c. अर्धशिजा.

Parcel, *n. small bundle.* पुडकें *n.* पुडका *m.* पुडा *m. dim.* पुडी *f.* जुडी *f.*

2 *part, portion*, v. **Part**. अंश *m.* भाग *m.* विभाग *m.*

3 *quantity, mass.* राशि *m. pop.* रास *f.* ढीग *m.* ढिगार *m.*

डिगारा *m.*

4 *number, multitude,*—contemptuously, v. BAND. गट्टा *m.* मुठाण *n.* मंडळी *f.*—Note. The contempt is usually expressed by the form of the word for the persons or things composing the multitude, as न्हावगंडांची-तेलगंडांची-छुतारड्यांची-&c. मंडळी parcel of barbers-oilmen-carpenters, &c. or by such formations as पोरवडा a parcel of boys, रांडवडा a parcel of women, &c.

5 (of ground) *lot, patch.* ठिकें *n.* फाळी *f.* दळें *or* दळ्हें *n.*

To PARCEL, *v. a. divide into portions.* वांटणें, विभागणें, वांटणी *f.*-वांटप *n.*-&c. करणें *g. of o.* वांटे *m. pl.*-विभाग *m. pl.*-प्रती *f. pl.*-&c. करणें *g. of o.* भांजणें. [भांजणी *f.*

PARCELLING, *n.* v. V.—*act.* वांटणें *n.* &c. वांटणी *f.* वांटप *n.*

PARCENER, *n.* v. CO-HEIR. विभागी, भागी, अंशी, अंशक.

PARCENERY, *n. co-heirship, joint-enjoyment.* अविभक्तदायभोग *m.* साधारणरिक्थभोग *m.*

To PARCH, *v. a. burn superficially ; scorch, &c.* भाजणें, भुजणें, हुरडणें, हुरपळणें, हुरफळणें, होळपणें, भाजण *n.*-भाजप *n.*-&c. करणें *g. of o.*

To be parched (with thirst, &c.). शोखणें *or* सोखणें, प्राण *m.* सोखणें *g. of s.*

Cost of parching grain. भाजणावळ *f.*

Flour made of four or five sorts of grain parched and ground together. भाजणी *or* भाजाणी *f.*

Gram parched. फुटाणे *m. pl.*

Grain parched. भाजाणे *m. pl.*

Green pods of grain parched. हुळा *or* हुवळा *m.*

Green wheat parched. ओंब्या *f. pl.*

Matter (grain &c.) to be parched. भाजण *n.* भाजप *n.* भाजणें *n.*

Matter (grain, &c.) parched. भाजलेलें *n.*

Quantity or batch parched. भाजण *n.* भाजप *n.* भाजणें *n.* भाजा *m.* भाजींव *n.*

Rice, wheat, &c. blown out by parching. लाह्या *f. pl.*

PARCHED, *p.* v. V. भाजलेला, हुरपळलेला, *&c.* भाजका, भाजींव, भर्जित, भृष्ट.

Slightly p. भाजट, भाजकट. [*n.* भृष्टता *f.*

PARCHEDNESS, *n.* v. P. भाजलेलेपणा *m.* भाजकेपणा *m.* भर्जितत्व

P. from thirst. जलशोष *m.*

PARCHER, *n.* PARCHING, *p. a.* v. V. भाजणारा, हुरडणारा, हुरपळणारा, &c. भर्जनकर्त्ता—of corn, &c. भुजारा, भुजारी, भाजपी, भडभुंजा, भट्टीभाजणारा.

PARCHING, *n.* v. V.—*act.* भाजणें *n.* हुरपळणें *n.* हुरडणें *n.*&c. भाजण *n.* भाजप *n.* भर्जन *n.*

PARCHMENT, *n. skin prepared for writing.* चर्मपट *m.* चर्मपत्र *n.*

PARD, PARDALE. See LEOPARD.

To PARDON, *v. a. forgive, remit.* माफ करणें, क्षमा करणें, सोडणें, माफी *f.*-क्षमा *f.*-&c. करणें *g. of o.* बक्षीस *n.* करणें-देणें, अपराध *m.*-दंड *m.*-&c. सोडणें *g. of o.* अपराधमोचन *n.*-&c. करणें *g. of o.*

PARDON, PARDONING, *n.* v. V. सोडणें *n.* माफी *f.* क्षमा *f.* सुटका *f.* सूट *f.* बक्षिशी *f.* बक्षीस *n.* बहाली *f.* अपराधमोचन *n.* अपराधमुक्ति *f.* दोष मोचन *n.* दोषमुक्ति *f.*

I beg your p. मी पायां पडतों, तुझ्या पायां पडतों, मी क्षमा मागतों.

PARDONABLE, *a.*v.V. माफ करायाजोगा-सारखा-&c.क्षमा करायाजोगा-&c. सोडायाजोगा-&c.क्षमायोग्य, क्षमार्ह, क्षमोचित, उपेक्षणीय.

P. person. क्षमापात्र.

PARDONABLY, *adv.* v. A. क्षमा व्हायाजोगा *decl.* यथाक्षंतव्य.

PARDONED, *p.* v. V. माफ केलेला, क्षमा केलेला, सोडलेला, माफ, बहाल, क्षांत, मुक्तदंड, दंडमुक्त, मुक्तशासन, शासनमुक्त.

PARDONER, *n.* PARDONING, *p. a.* v. V. माफ करणारा, क्षमा करणारा, सोडणारा, &c. दंडमोचनकर्त्ता, अपराधमोचनकर्त्ता.

To PARE, *v. a. cut away, clip off.* तासणें, छाटणें, साळणें.

To p. the nails. नख *m. n.* काढणें.

2 *skin, peel.* छिलणें, सोलणें, साल *f. n.* काढणें *g. of o.*

PARED, *p.* v. V. 1. तासलेला, &c. तासींव, छाटींव, साळींव, तष्ट, त्वष्ट.

PAREGORIC, *a. mitigating or assuaging pain.* दुःखशमक, उपशमक, उपशमकारी.

PARENT, *n.* See FATHER, MOTHER.

Parents. आईबाप *m. pl.* आईबाप *m.* आईबापें *n. pl.* मायबाप *m. pl.* मातापितरें *n. pl.* पितर *n. pl.* जनकजननी *f.*

2 *source, cause.* कारण *n.* हेतु *m.* उत्पादक *n.* प्रभव *m.* जन्महेतु *m.*

PARENTAGE, *n. birth, extraction,* v. FAMILY. कुळी *f.* जन्म *m.n.* उत्पत्ति *f.* पैदास्त *f.*—compreh. जातकुळी *f.* जातकूळ *n.*

PARENTAL, *a. pertaining, &c. to parents.* आईबापांचा, मातापितृसंबंधी, पैतृक, मातापितृवत्. [तानममता *f.*

P. affection. अपत्यस्नेह *m.* पुत्रस्नेह *m.* अपत्यममता *f.* सं-

PARENTLESS, *a.* मातापितृहीन-विहीन-रहित-&c. हीनपितृक.

PARENTHESIS, *n. sentence inserted in a sentence.* कुंडलींतला ग्रंथ *m.* कुंडलींतलें वाक्य *n.* कंसांतलें वाक्य *n.* प्रक्षिप्तप्रधानवाक्य *n.*

2 *the brackets within which a sentence is included.* कुंडली *f.* कंस *m.*

PARER, *n.* PARING, *p. a.* v. V. 1. तासणारा, &c. तष्टा, त्वष्टा.

Nail-p. नराणी *or* नऱ्हाणी *f.* नाचकंड *or* नाचकन *n.* नखजीन *n.* नखशी *f.*

PARHELION, *n. mock sun.* सूर्याभास *m.* मिथ्यासूर्य *m.*

PARING, *n.* v. V. 1.—*act.* तासणें *n.* छाटणें *n.* &c. तासणी *f.* छांटणी *f.* छाटछूट *m. f.* साळणी *f.* तक्षण *n.*

2—*act.* छिलणें *n.* &c. [तासेरा *m.*

I. parings; *matter pared.* छाट *m.* छाटछूट *m. f.* ताशेरा *or*

PARISH, *n.*—the division of country. पाद्रीची-उपाध्याची पांढर *f.*-तप्पा *m.*-देश *m.* उपाध्यपणाचा-यजमानकृत्याचा-&c. देश *m.*-प्रदेश *m.* पौरोहित्यदेश *m.* पौरोहित्यभूमि *f.*

PARISH, *a.* v.N. पांढरीचा, तप्याचा, उपाध्यपणाच्या देशाचा, &c.

PARISHIONER, *n. one that belongs to a parish.* पांढरींत राहणारा, पांढरींतला, पांढरींतली-उपाध्यपणाच्या देशांतली-&c. असामी *f.*

PARITY, *n.* v. EQUALITY. बरोबरी *f.* साम्य *n.* समता *f.*

PARK, *n. enclosure for chace, recreation, &c.* रमणा *m.* कृत्रिमवन *n.* मृगयालय *n.* मृगयाभूमि *f.*

2 (of artillery). तोफखाना *m.* [गोष्टीमाता *f. pl.*

PARLANCE, *n.* v. CONVERSATION. बोलाचाली *f.* बोलाबोली *f.*

To PARLEY, *v. n.* See To CONVERSE, 2. *confer with an enemy.* युद्धामध्यें बोलाबोली *f.*-सल्याचें बोलणें *n.*-&c. करणें.

PARLEY, *n.* v. CONVERSATION. बोलाबोली *f.* बोलाचाली *f.* संभाषण *n.*

2 *conference with an enemy.* युद्धामध्यें बोलाबोली *f.*-सल्याचें बोलणें *n.* शत्रूशीं बोलाबोली *f.* संधिसंभाषण *n.* संधिप्रसंग *m.*
To ask a p. रुमाल *m.* फिरवणें. [पार्लेमेंत *n.*

PARLIAMENT, *n.* इंग्लंदांत राज्यकारभार पाहणारी एक मंडळी आहे.

PARLIAMENTARY, *a.* पार्लेमेंताचा, पार्लेमेंताच्या संबंधाचा, &c.

PARLOUR, *n.* *sitting room.* बसायाची-बैठकीची खोली *f.*-कोठडी *f.*

PAROCHIAL, *a. belonging to a parish.* पांढरीचा, पांढरसंबंधींचा, उपाध्यपणाचे देशचा.

PARODY, *n. burlesque imitation.* विनोदार्थानुकरणकविता *f.* भिन्नरसकप्रतिकविता *f.*

PAROLE, *n.* v. WORD, PROMISE. वचन *n.*
2—of a prisoner of war. पाडाव केलेले शत्रूचें वचन *n.*
3 in a camp. वर्दीचा शब्द *m.*

PAROLE, PAROL, *a.* See ORAL.

PARONOMASIA, *n.* v. PUN. श्लेष *m.*

PARONYCHIA. See WHITLOW.

PAROQUET, *n.* v. PARROT. पोपट *m.* हिरामण *m.*

PAROXYSM, *n. fit of a disease.* भर *m.* भरतें *n.* चढ *m.* पाळी *f.* फेरा *m.* सर *m.f.* उचल *f.* लहर *f.* लाहडा*m.* झटका*m.* झटकारा*m.*
P. of anger. भिरड *f.*भिरडी *f.* तेरम*m.* तैष*m.* त्वेष*m.*रागाचा-&c. भराका *m.* सर*m.f.*

PARRICIDAL, PARRICIDIOUS, *a. pertaining, &c. to parricide.* पितृवधाचा, &c. पितृवधसंबंधी, पितृवधविषयक, पितृवधात्मक, पितृवधरूप.
2 *committing parricide.* पितृघ्न, पितृहिंसक, पितृघातक.

PARRICIDE, *n. murderer of a parent.* पित्याचा-बापाचा-&c. जीव घेणारा, पितृहत्यारा, पितृघ्न, पितृहंता, पितृहा.
2 *murder of a parent.* पितृवध *m.* पितृहत्या *f.* पितृहिंसा *f.* पितृघात *m.*

PARRIED, *p.* v. V. वारलेला, टाळलेला, &c. निवारित, वारित.

PARROT, *n.* पोपट *m.* राघू *or* राघो *m.* (राघी *f.*) रांबा *m.* तोता *m.* कीर *m.* शुक *m.* Some species are, चंदनी *or* चंदन्या पोपट, टुया, धामण्या पोपट, नुरी, पहाडीपोपट, पाकचंदन, भावनगरीपोपट, रामनगरीपोपट.
Common wild p. (not having the marks of a speaking p.). करंटापोपट *m.* किरोंटा *m.*
Fruit &c. pecked by parrots. किरसाद *f.*
Speaking p. बोलका पोपट-राघो.
That has been pecked by parrots. किरसादलेला.
To train a p. पोपटाला-&c. शिकवणें-तालीम *f.* देणें.
2 fig. *person whose learning is all by rote.* घोकीव, घोक्या, घोककाम्या.

To PARRY, *v. a. ward, turn off.* चुकवणें, टाळणें, वारणें, निवारणें, वारण *n.*-निवारण *n.*-&c. करणें *g. of o.*

To PARSE, *v. a.* (in grammar). व्याकरण *n.* करणें-सांगणें, लिंगनिर्देश *m.*-पदभंजन *n.*-पदछेद *m.*-&c. करणें, साधणें.

PARSEE, *n.* पारसी.

PARSEE, *a.* पारसी लोकांचा, पारसी धर्माचा.

PARSIMONIOUS, *a. stingy, close, penurious, &c.* v. MISERLY. कृपण, हाताचा जड, किरटा, तर्पण्या, अल्पव्ययी, अव्यय, व्ययशत्रु, बद्धमुष्टि.
2 *frugal,* v. ECONOMICAL. कसरी, काटकसऱ्या, कतरबेती *or* कतरबेत्या, विचारव्ययी, अल्पव्ययी.

PARSIMONIOUSLY, *adv.* v. A. 1. कृपणपणानें, कृपणबुद्धीनें, कार्पण्यबुद्धीनें, बारीकदृष्टीनें, &c. कार्पण्यपूर्वक. [&c. पूर्वक.
2 काटकसरीनें, कतर बेतानें, अल्पव्ययानें, अल्पव्यय-स्वल्पव्यय-

PARSIMONIOUSNESS, PARSIMONY, *n.* v. A. 1. कृपणपणा *m.* किरटेपणा *m.* कार्पण्य *n.* कृपणत्व *n.* कार्पण्यबुद्धि *f.* कृपणबुद्धि *f.* कृपणभाव *m.* बारीकदृष्टि *f.* बारीकनजर *f.*
2 काटकसर *f.* कतरबेत *m.* अल्पव्यय *m.* स्वल्पव्यय *m.*

PARSING, *n.* v. V. पदभंजन *n.* पदछेद *m.* साधनिका *f.*

PARSLEY, *n. apium involucratum.* अजमोदा *m.*

PARSON, *n.* पाद्री *m.*

PART, *n. portion,* v. PIECE. भाग *m.* बिभाग *m.* अंश *m.* तुकडा*m.* शकल *n.* विभक्ति *f.*
2 *portion, division*—as not separated. भाग *m.* अंश *m.* *m.* अंग *n.* अवयव *m.*
By or in parts. अंशतः.
Composed of parts. अवयवी.
Inward p. अंतरंग *m.*
Private parts. उपस्थ *m. pl.*
For the most p. बहुतकरून, बहुधा, बहुशः.
3 *member, particular, distinct item.* अंग *n.* अवयव *m.* प्रकरण *n.* विषय *m.* [वयवीं संपूर्ण.
Complete in all parts or members. सर्वांगीं संपूर्ण, सर्वा
Minor p. प्रत्यंग *n.*
Part by p. अवयवशः. [स्सा *m.*
4 *portion allotted,* v. SHARE. भाग *m.* वांटा *m.* अंश *m.* हि-
5 *concern or share in, connection with.* अंग *n.* हात *m.* संबंध *m.* बोट *n.* सामलात *f.*
On the p. of. निसबत, निसबतीनें, मारफतीनें, अंगत्वानें, अंगत्वें, अंगून, तरफेनें, बतीं *or* बतीनें. [टेचा.
That is on the p. of. निसबतीचा, तरफेचा, वांटचा *or* वां-
6 *proportional quantity.* भाग *m.* वांटा *m.* हिस्सा *m.* अंश*m.*
7 *side, party, cause, interest.* पक्ष *m.* बाजू *f.* तरफ *f.* कड *f.*
To espouse the p. of, take the p. of. पक्ष *m.* धरणें *g. of o.* कैवार *m.* धरणें-घेणें-करणें *g. of o.* कासेस मारणें.
8 *office, duty,* v. BUSINESS. कर्म *n.* धर्म *m.* स्वकर्म *n.* स्वधर्म*m.*
To become the p. or duty of. भागास येणें.
9 (in the drama) *character.* सोंग *n.*
Maintaining a p. सोंग संपादणी *f.*
Minor or subordinate p. आडसोंग *n.*
10 parts; *talents, powers.* बुद्धि *f.* गुण *m. pl.*
11 parts; *regions, quarters.* प्रांत *m.* देश *m.* प्रदेश *m.*
For (my,&c.) p. कडून, Ex. तुम्ही पाहिजे तें करा, मजकडून मी कांहीं करणार नाहीं You may do as you please, I for my p. will do nothing.
To take in good part. गोडकरूनघेणें. [कांहीं अंश.
In part, v. PARTLY. कांहींवांटे, कांहींवांट्यांनीं, कांहीं भाग,

To PART, *v. a. distribute, divide, share.* वांटणें, वांटून देणें-घेणें, विभागणें, विभागून घेणें-देणें, वांटणी *f.*-वांटप*n.*-विभक्ति *f.*-&c. करणें *g. of o.* [*pl.*-&c. करणें *g. of o.*
2 *sever into pieces, separate.* फोडणें, खांडणें, तोडणें, तुकडे*m.*
3 *separate, disunite.* दोहोंकडे करणें,वेगळणें, फोडणें, बियोग*m.*-भेद*m.*-बिभेद*m.*-&c. करणें *g. of o.* अंतर*n.* करणें-पाडणें, वेगळा-&c. करणें.

4 *keep asunder.* बेगळा-निराळा-अलग-भिन्न-&c. ठेवणें-राखणें.

To PART, *v. n. become separate; open out, come asunder, &c.* सुटणें, तुटणें, बेगळा-निराळा-अलग-भिन्न-मोकळा-&c. होणें, उकलणें, उसळणें, वियोगm.-भेदm.-&c. होणें *g. of s.*

2 *have a share.* वांटाm.-विभागm.-हिस्साm.-अंशm.-&c. पावणें *or in. con.* मिळणें.

3 *quit each other.* दोहोंकडे होणें. [ऊन जाणें.

4 *take farewell, set out from.* निरोपm.-आज्ञा *f.*-&c. घेणें-घे-

5 with; *quit, resign.*सोडणें, सोडून देणें,देणें, जाऊं देणें, सत्वत्याग *m.*-सत्वोत्सर्गm.-सत्वनिवृत्ति *f.*-&c. करणें.

To PARTAKE, *To* PARTICIPATE, *v. n. have a share or part.* वांटा-विभागm.-हिस्साm.-वांटणी *f.*-&c. घेणें-पावणें *or in. con.* मिळणें-येणें-पावणें, भागीदार-भागेली-अंशी-&c. होणें-असणें.

To PARTAKE, *To* PARTICIPATE, *v. a. share with others.* वांटा *m.*-हिस्साm.-विभागm.-अंशm.-&c. घेणें-पावणें, सहभोगm. करणें *g. of o.*

PARTAKEN, PARTICIPATED, *p.* v. V. A. 1. सहभुक्त, अनेकभुक्त.

PARTAKER, *n.* PARTAKING, *p. a.* PARTICIPATER, *n.* PARTICIPATING, *p. a.* v. V. वांटा घेणारा, वांटा पावणारा, &c. अंशी, भागीदार, भागेली, भागीलदार, अंशग्राही, अंशभोगी, सहभागी, सहभोगी.

I. See ACCOMPLICE.

PARTAKING, PARTICIPATION, *n.* v. V.—*act.* वांटा घेणेंn. &c. सहभोगm. अंशभोगm.

PARTERRE, *n.* v. GARDEN. फूलबागm. *f.* चमन *f. n.*

PARTIAL, *a. inclined to one side more than another,*—of persons. पक्षपाती, तरफदार, एकरोंखी, असमदृष्टि, असमदर्शी, असम.

2—of judgements, &c. तरफदारीचा, पक्षपाताचा, एकतरफी, पाक्षिक.

3 *not general or total.* एकपक्षी, एकदेशी, एकांगी, एकतरफी, अपूर्ण, अव्यापी, असार्वत्रिक, खखंड, खंड (in comp. as खंडग्रास, खंडवृष्टि, खंडप्रलय, &c. p. eclipse-shower-deluge-&c.).

PARTIALITY, *n.* v. A. 1. पक्षपातm. तरफदारी *f.* असमदृष्टि *f.* असमबुद्धि *f.* न्यूनाधिकबुद्धि *f.*

I. *fondness for, inclination, &c.* v. LIKING. चहा *f.*

PARTIALLY, *adv.* v. A. 1. पक्षपातानें, पक्षपात धरून-करून, तरफदारीनें, पक्षपातपूर्वक, असमदृष्टीनें.

3 एकदेशीं, एकपक्षीं, पक्षीं, कांहीं वांटे, कांहीं हिस्से, कांहीं अंश, कांहीं वांट्यांनीं, अंशतः,खंडशः,असर्वतः.

To PARTICIPATE, &c. See To PARTAKE, &c.

PARTICIPIAL, *a.*—in grammar. सकालकृदंतरूप.

PARTICIPLE, *n.*—in grammar. सकालकृदंतm. कालबोधककृदंतm. कृदंतm.

PARTICLE, *n. atom, minute bit,* v. BIT. कणm. *dim.* कणी *f.* कणूn. कणिका *f.* लवm. लेशm. कला *f.* किणकिणी *f.* सुपारीचें खांडn. सुईच्या शेंड्यावरची माती*f.*नखभर माती*f.*सूच्यग्रमृत्तिका*f.*

Extremely minute particles. अणुरेणु *m. f. pop.* अणूरेणू *m. pl.*

2—in grammar. अव्यय *n.* अव्ययशब्द *m.*

Declinable p. अर्धाव्यय *n.*

PARTICULAR, *a. relating to singles; not general.* असाधारण, असामान्य, विशेषाविषयींचा, अमकयाविषयींचा, विशेषविषयक, अव्यापक, अव्यापी, एकदेशी, एकपक्षी.

2 *individual, one distinct.* विशेष, भिन्न, निराळा, निरनिराळा, अमुक, अमका, विशिष्ट, विवक्षित, उद्दिष्ट, पृथगात्मक, व्यक्तिक, पृथग्व्यक्तिक.

P. person. अमुक, अमका. [मान्य, विशिष्ट.

3—noting something peculiar. विशेष, असाधारण, असा-

4 *special, more than ordinary.* विशेष, अधिकोत्तर, लोकोत्तर.

It is nothing p. तादृश नव्हे, हा तितपत आहे.

5 *odd, singular, &c.* v. STRANGE. विलक्षण, विलक्षणीक, अलौकिक.

6 *attentive to particulars, minute*—of persons. कचें पाहणारा, बारीक पाहणारा, सूक्ष्मदर्शी, सूक्ष्मदृष्टि, अकटचिकट.

7 *embracing particulars,*—of statements, accounts, &c. तपसिलाचा, बयादीचा, कच्चा, सविस्तर, जिन्नसवार, तपसीलवार, बयादवार. [कलम *n.*

PARTICULAR, *n. single point.* गोष्ट *f.* बाबत *f.* प्रकरण *n.* रकम *f.*

2 See INDIVIDUAL. 3 *private interest.* स्वार्थ *m.*स्वहित *n.*

In particular. विशेष, विशेषेंकरून, विशेषतः.

PARTICULARITY, *n.* v. A. 1. असाधारणपणा *m.* असाधारणता *f.* अव्यापकत्व *n.* &c. एकदेशीपणा*m.*

2 विशेष *m.* विशेषभाव *m.* विशिष्टता *f.* भिन्नता *f.* व्यस्तता *f.*

7 *and* DETAIL. तपसील *m.* विस्तार *m.*

I. a *particularity; something peculiar.* विशेष *m.* विशेष गोष्ट *f.* विशेषात्कार *m.*

PARTICULARIZATION, *n.* v.V.—*act.*विशेषवर्णन *n.* विशेषनिर्देश*m.* अवच्छेद *m.* व्यवच्छेद *m.*

To PARTICULARIZE, *v. a. mention distinctly or in particular.* विशेषवर्णन *n.*-&c. करणें *g. of o.* तपसीलवार-&c. सांगणें-बोलणें-लिहणें, अमुक-अमका म्हणून सांगणें, अवच्छेद *m.*-व्यवच्छेद *m.*-&c. करणें *g. of o.*

PARTICULARIZED, *p.* v. V. विशेषवर्णन केलेला, &c. अमुक म्हणून सांगितलेला, विशेषित, विशिष्ट, अवच्छिन्न, व्यवच्छिन्न.

PARTICULARIZER, *n.* PARTICULARIZING, *p. a.* v. V. विशेषवर्णन करणारा, अमुक म्हणून सांगणारा, तपसीलवार बोलणारा, &c. अवच्छेदक, व्यवच्छेदक. [असामान्यतः.

PARTICULARLY, *adv.* v. A. 1. असाधारणपणानें, असाधारणतः,

4 विशेषेंकरून, विशेष, विशेषतः, विशेषात्कारें करून.

7 तपसीलवार, बितपसील, बयादवार, जिन्नसवार, सविस्तर.

PARTING, *n.* v.V.A.1.—*act.* वांटणें *n.* &c. वांटणी *f.* वांटप *n.* विभक्ति *f.*

3—*act.* बेगळा करणें *n.* &c. वियोगकरण *n.* विभेदकरण *n.*

v. V. N. सुटणें *n.* तुटणें *n.* &c. स्फुटन *n.*

3—*state.* वियोग *m.* विरह *m.* विगम *m.*

PARTING, *a. given, &c. at separation.* जातेवेळचा, प्रास्थानिक, प्रयाण (in comp. as प्रयाणालिंगन p. embrace), प्रस्थान (in comp. as प्रस्थानालिंगन).

PARTISAN, *n. pike, halberd,* v. SPEAR. भाला *m.*

2 *adherent to a party.* तरफेचा, तरफदार, पक्षाचा, बाहीदार, बगल्या, पक्षपाती, पक्षधारी, पक्षधर, सपक्ष, पार्श्वक, पार्श्विक.

PARTISANSHIP, *n.* v. N. 2. तरफदारी *f.* पक्षपात *m.* कैवार *m.* पक्षधारण *n.* पक्षावलंबन *n.* पक्षधारिता *f.*

PARTITION, *n.* See PARTING. 2 *place parted off.* खण *m.* खाना *m.* खिसा *m.* पूड *m. n.*

3 *that by which a partition is made.* पडदा *m.* पडदी *f.* चिर-

णी *f.* आडभित *f.* कूड *m.* आडकूड *m.* जमनीक *f.* व्यवधान *n.*

To PARTITION, *v. a. divide into distinct parts.* खण *m. pl.*-खाने *m. pl.*-खोली *f.*-&c. करणें *g. of o.*

2 See To SHARE. 3 off. पडदा *m.*-भित *f.*-&c. घालून वेगळा करणें, व्यवहित करणें.

PARTLY, *adv. in part, in some measure,&c.* कांहीं वांटे, कांहीं हिस्से, कांहीं अंश, कांहीं अंशांनीं, कांहीं, कांहींसा *decl.* किंचित्, थोडा *decl.* थोडाबहूत *decl.*

PARTNER, *n.* (in business, &c.). भागीदार, भागीलदार, भागी, भागेली, विभागी, पातीदार, सरकतदार, सरकती *or* त्या, वंतदार, अंशी, अंशहर, अंशहारी.

The working p. (as distinguised from the monied p.) अंगवांटेकरी *m.* [ती, संगू.

2 (at play, &c.) v. FELLOW. गडी, जोडपी, जोडीचा, सोब-

Partners,—at certain plays. संगूमंगू *m. pl.*

3 *husband or wife.* जन्माचा सोबती *m. or* जन्माची सोबतीण *f.* सुखादुःखाचा सोबती *m. or* सुखादुःखाची सोबतीण*f.*

PARTNERSHIP, *n. association, union, &c.* भागीदारी *f.* पातीदारी *f.* सरकतदारी *f.*

2 *joint interest.* भागी *f.* सरकत *f.*

Share in a p. भागी *f.* पाती *f.* सरकत *f.*

Schedule of the terms of a p. सरकतनामा *m.*

PARTRIDGE, *n.*—the francoline p. तित्तर *m.* कवडा *m.* कपिंजल *m.* तित्तर *m.* तित्तिरि *m.*—the painted p. काळातित्तर *m.*—Greek p. चकोर *m.*

PARTS. See PART.

PARTURIENT, *a. about to bring forth.* कोननिघणारा, प्रसवोन्मुख, आसन्नप्रसव, उन्मुखप्रसव.

PARTURITION, *n. bringing forth.* प्रसव *m.* प्रसूति *f.* सूति *f.*

Gentle or easy p. सुखप्रसव *m.* सुवेत *n.*

PARTY, *n. confederated body or number.* जूट *m. f.* जूग *n.* तट *m.* तड *m.* फळी *f.* प्रकरण *n.* पक्ष *m.* स्तोम *n.* मंडली *or* ळी *f.*

Division into two parties. दुफळी *f.*

2 *part, side, cause.* पक्ष *m.* तरफ *f.* बाजू *f.* कड *f.* मत *n.*

P. in the right. शुक्लपक्ष *m.* शुद्धपक्ष *m.*

The opposite p. प्रतिपक्ष *m.* [क्षकार *m.*

3 *one of two litigants.* वादी, वाद्या, असामी *f.* पक्षकर *or* प-

4 *select assembly.* बैठक *f.* चारमंडळी *f.* बोलाविलेली मंडळी *f.*

5 (of soldiers, &c.). तुकडी *f.* टोळी *f.*

6 *person particularized.* असामी *f.* मनुष्य *n.* माणूस *n.* विवक्षित मनुष्य *n.* [शी, संबंधी.

7 *person concerned or interested in.* भागीदार, विभागी, अं-

PARTY-COLORED, *a. having divers colors.* विचित्र, चित्रविचित्र, विचित्र वर्णाचा, विचित्रवर्ण, नानारंगी, विचित्ररंगाचा.

2 (a horse, &c.). अबलक *or* ख.

PARTY-MAN, *n.* v. PARTISAN. तरफदार, पक्षपाती.

PARTY-WALL, *n. wall separating one house from another.* दोनघरांची मधली भिंत *f.* मधली भिंत *f.*

PARVENU. See UPSTART.

PASQUINADE, *n.* v. SATIRE. निंदेचा पोवाडा *m.*

To PASS, *v. n.*v. To GO, To MOVE. चालणें, जाणें, गमन *n.*-गति *f.*-&c. होणें *g. of s.*

2 *be spent,*—time &c. जाणें, गुजरणें, गुदरणें, चालणें, लोटणें, उडणें, मोडणें;—pleasantly, करमणें, गमणें, सरणें,—painfully, बाईट-अबघड-दुःखाचा-&c. जाणें.

3 *gain reception, be current.* चालणें, पडणें, विकणें, चाल *f.*-चलन *f.*-चलती *f.*-&c. असणें *g. of s.* चालता-चालू होणें.

4 *be admitted or approved of.* पटणें, पसंत पडणें, उतरणें, रुजू पडणें, मान्य पडणें, नांदणें, विकणें.

5 *be regarded as.* वाटणें, भासणें, मोजला-धरला-&c. जाणें, म्हणून चालणें, गणती *f.*-गणना *f.*-संख्या *f.*-&c. असणें *g. of s.* मोडणें *with* मध्यें-खालीं-&c.

6 *occur, take place.* घडणें, होणें, वर्त्तणें.

7 away; off; over; *vanish, disappear, be lost, be spent,&c.* ओसरणें, निघणें, जाणें, चालणें, गुजरणें, गुदरणें, उलगडणें, उलगणें, टळणें, निसरणें, माहींसाहोणें, गतणें, गत होणें, परतणें, वाहवणें, वितुळणें, मागें-पाठीमागें पडणें.

To p. off well. पटणें.

8 on; *proceed.* पुढें जाणें-चालणें. [सा करणें.

To bring to p. *bring about.* घडवणें, घडवून आणणें, घडे-

To come to p. v. To HAPPEN. घडणें, पडणें, होणें.

To come to p. *be fulfilled.* पटणें, दाखल्यास-अनुभवास-प्रत्ययास-ताळयास-निदर्शनास-&c. येणें.

To let p. *let go unheeded, &c.* सांड *f.* करणें *g. of o.* सांड *f.* देणें, सोडणें (as बोलायास-जेवायास-भांडायास-&c. सोडणें *with neg. con.*).

To p. safely through (a difficulty, danger,&c.) तरणें, निभणें, तरणूक *f.*-निभाव *m.*-&c.होणें *g. of s.*

To PASS, *v. a. go beyond, by, through.* ओलांडणें, उल्लंघणें, खेटणें, पार-पलीकडे-&c. जाणें *g. of o.* पार होणें *g. of o.* मागें टाकणें-सोडणें, वाटवणें *or* वटावणें, अतिक्रमणें, क्रमणें, अंतरणें, उल्लंघ *m.*-उल्लंघन *n.*-अतिक्रमण *n.*-&c. करणें *g. of o.* अतिक्रांत-उत्तीर्ण-तीर्ण-&c. करणें.

2 (time) *spend.* घालवणें, क्रमणें, नेणें, कढलणें, गुदरवणें, कालक्षेप *m.*-कालहरण *n.*-कालक्रमण *n.*-&c. करणें,—pleasantly, करमणें, करमणूक *f.*-गमत*f.*-कालक्रमण*f.*-&c.करणें,—painfully, काढणें, कंठणें—under shifts and expedients, ढकलणें, लोटणें, कढलणें,ढकलपट्टी *f.*-चालढकल *f.*-कालगुजारा *m.*-कालगुजारी *f.*-कालगुद्राण *f.*-&c. करणें,—idly, in diversion, &c. घालवणें, कालवंचना *f.* करणें, व्यर्थकालक्षेप *m.*-&c. करणें.

3 *cause to pass or proceed.* चालवणें, चालता करणें-ठेवणें, पहोंचता करणें, धाडणें.

To pass the eye over. डोळ्याखालीं-दृष्टीखालीं-नजरेखालीं-&c. घालणें-घालून देणें.

4 *transfer,* v. To MAKE OVER. निरवणें, ओपणें, हवालणें.

5 (a law, &c.) *enact* करणें, स्थापणें, ठरवणें, रचणें, बांधणें, सिद्ध करणें.

6 (sentence). सांगणें. [टे काढणें.

7 (censure, remark, &c.). बोलणें, सांगणें, उच्चारणें, तोंडावा-

8 v. To OMIT, To NEGLECT. वगळणें, गाळणें, अंतरणें, सोडणें, डावलणें.

9 *impose fraudulently, palm.* कपटानें घेवविणें-चालवणें, चांगला भासवून *or* वाटवून घेवविणें. [सादर करणें.

10 (a bill, account, &c.) *admit.* वार-रुजू करणें, सही करणें,

11 by; over; *omit, overlook, neglect, disregard.* सोडणें, वगळणें, सांडणें, गाळणें, अंतरणें, डावलणें, उपेक्षणें, उपेक्षा *f.*-सांड

f.-&c. करणें *g. of o.*

12 by; over; *overlook, excuse, forgive, &c.* पोटीं घालणें, गई *f.* करणें *g. of o.* गम *m. f.* खाणें, माफ-क्षमा करणें, सांड *f.*-कानडोळा *m.*-कानाडोळा *m.* करणें *g. of o.* सांड *f.* देणें.

13 by; *pass near and beyond.* जवळून-वरून जाणें.

14 off. See To PALM.

15 through. See To STRAIN.

PASS, *n. passage, way,* v. ROAD. रस्ता *m.* वाट *f.*

2 *narrow passage.* खिंड *f.* गोंड *f. n.* बारी *f.* नळी *f.* नळीची वाट *f.* चिंचोळीवाट *f.*

3 (over a hill). घाट *m. dim.* घाटी *f.*

Blocking up of a p. घाटबंदी *f.*

Foot or bottom of a p. घाटपाय *m.*

Head or outlet of a p. घाटमाथा *m.*

Toll-gatherer for passes and roads. पाणसरा *m.*

4 *passport.* परवाना *m.* दस्तक *n.* रवाना *m.* राहदारीची-रस्त्याची-&c. चिट्ठी *or* चिठी *f.*-&c.

P. over the sea, a river, &c. उतारचिठी *f.*

5 *push in fencing.* हूल *f.* ढुसणी *or* ढोसणी *f.*

6 *state,* v. CONDITION. अवस्था *f.* दशा *f.* गति *pop.* गत *f.*

Note. As the implication of this word is usually that of distressful condition, see also STRAIT.

PASS-WORD, *n. watch-word.* वर्दीचाशब्द *m.*

PASSABLE, *a. that may be passed over.* जायाजोगा-जोगता-&c. गमनीय, गम्य, गमनार्ह, गमनयोग्य, सुगम.

2 *tolerable, bearable, that can be made to do.* चलाऊ, कामचलाऊ, चालायाजोगा-जोगता-सारखा, चालवून घ्यायाचा-जोगा-&c. निर्वाहाचा, चालढकलीचा, बरा, माफक, चालीवजा.

3 *capable of admission or currency.* चालायाजोगता-सारखा-&c. पटायाजोगा-जोगता-&c.

PASSABLY, *adv.* v. A.2. चालाया-चालवून घ्याया-&c. जोगा-जोगता-सारखा *decl.* बरा *decl.* [*f.* गमन *n.* चलन *n.*

PASSAGE, PASSING, *n.*v.V.N.1.—*act.* जाणें *n.* &c. चाल *f.* गति

P. to and fro on a road. राहदारी *or* रहदारी *f.*

v. V. A. 1.—*act.* ओलंडणें *n.* उल्लंघणें *n.* &c. ओलंडणी *f.* उल्लंघ *m.* उल्लंघन *n.* अतिक्रम *m.* अतिक्रमण *n.* संक्रमण *n.* संक्रम *m.* संक्रांति *f.* क्रांति *f.*

I. *way,* v. ROAD. रस्ता *m.* वाट *f.* मार्ग *m.*

II. *liberty to pass.* जाण्यायेण्याची परवानगी *f.*-मोकळीक *f.* खुलारस्ता *m.* उघडादरवाजा *m.* मुक्तद्वार *n.*

III.—as between houses ; *alley.* चिरण *f.* गल्ली *f.* बोळ *m.* शेरी *f.* चिलण *f.*

IV. *part of a book.* स्थल *n.* जागा *f.* ठिकाण *n.*

A difficult p. गूढार्थ *m.*

V. v. JOURNEY, VOYAGE. सफर *f.*

P. money. नोर *m.* भाडें *n.*

VI. (in a house) बोळ *m.*

VII. *incident, event.* वृत्त *n.* घडलेली गोष्ट *f.*

PASSED, *p.* v. V. N. 2. गेलेला, गुदरलेला, &c. गत, गुदस्त *or* गुदस्ता, माजी, भूत, अतीत, व्यतीत.

v. V. A. 1. ओलंडलेला, उल्लंघलेला, खेटलेला, &c. उल्लंघित, अतिक्रांत, संक्रांत, उत्तीर्ण, तीर्ण. [क, आंत्रीक.

8 & 11. वगळलेला, अंतरलेला, &c. अंतरित, अंतरीक *or* अंत्री-

10 बार केलेला-झालेला, &c. रुजू, बार, सादर.

P. in the past year. रुजूगुदस्त.

PASSENGER, *n. way-farer,* v. TRAVELLER. येताजाता, येणारा जाणारा, वाटसरू, वाटमार्गी, उतारकरी, उतारकरू, उतारू, उतारी, मार्गस्थ.

2 (in a vehicle). उतारू, उतारकरी, उतारकरू, उतारी.

PASSIBILITY, *n.* v. A. सुखदुःखयोग्यता *f.* सुखदुःखक्षमता *f.* सुखदुःखवेदनक्षमता *f.* सुखदुःखवेदित्व *n.* सुखदुःखसहत्व *n.*

PASSIBLE, *a. susceptible of feeling.* सुखदुःख योग्य,सुखदुःखक्षम, सुखदुःखवेदनक्षम, सुखदुःखवेदी. [बरचढ.

PASSING, *a. eminent, superior,* v. SURPASSING. श्रेष्ठ, वरिष्ठ,

PASSING, PASSINGLY, *adv.* v. EXCEEDINGLY. अत्यंत, अतिशय, अति *in comp.*

PASSION, *n.*—*as opposed to* action. सोसणें *n.* सहन *n.* सहत्व *n.* ग्रहण *n.* कर्माश्रयत्व *n.* कर्मपात्रता *f.*

2 See PASSIBILITY.

3 *mental commotion.* क्षोभ *m.* मनःक्षोभ *m.* व्याक्षोभ *m.* संताप *m.* मनस्ताप *m.* व्याकुलता *f.* मनोव्याकुलता *f.*

4 *mental feeling,* v. AFFECTION. भाव *m.* मनोधर्म *m.* मनोविकार *m.* मनोविकृति *f.* रस *m.* राग *m.*

The passions. काम क्रोधादि *m. pl.* षड्वर्ग*m.* षड्रिपु *m. pl.*

Absence of p. or desire. विराग *m.* वैराग्य*n.* विरक्ति *f.*

Of subdued passions. कामक्रोधलोभाद्यतीत, जितेंद्रिय, नियतेंद्रिय, निर्जितेंद्रिय, संयतेंद्रिय.

Subduing or restraining the passions. कामक्रोधलोभादिदमन *n.*-निग्रह *m.* इंद्रियदमन*n.* इंद्रियनिग्रह*m.* इंद्रियनियम*m.*

That has warm passions. रागी, अनुरागी.

Void of p. or desire. विरागी, विरक्त, वीतराग.

5—as one of the three properties of Humanity. रज *n. m.* रजोगुण *m.*—that has it predominant.रजोगुणी.

6 v. ANGER, RAGE. राग*m.* क्रोध*m.* कोप *m.* प्रकोप *m.* संताप*m.* रोष *m.* जळप *m.* क्रोधावेश *m.*

A fit, gust, transport, &c. of p. रागाचा झटका *m.* सर*m. f.* भिरड *f.* भिरडी *f.* भिरिरी *f.* तेख *m.* तेषम.

To fly into a p. पित्त*n.* खवळणें-चढणें *g.of s.* पायांचें पित्त मस्तकास जाणें *g. of. s.* चढवून येणें, वर येणें, विकोपास जाणें.

Passion leads to poverty. अतिराग भीक माग त्याहून राग देश त्याग.

7 *zeal, ardor, eagerness.* आस्था *f.* उत्साह *m.* आसक्ति *f.* उत्कंठा *f.* उत्सुकता *f.* औत्सुक्य *n.* अनुराग *m.* अनुरक्ति *f.* अनुरति *f.* गरळ *f.* पोटाग *f.* आग *f.*

8 *violent desire.* वेड *n.* पिसें *n.* छंद*m.* व्यसन *n.* इष्क*m.* नाद*m.*

9 See LOVE.

PASSION-FLOWER, *n.*—the tree and flower. कंगोरी *f.*

PASSIONATE, *a. irritable, fiery, &c.* रागीट, तापट, तापड, क्रोधी, कोपी, कोपट, रागिष्ट, कोपिष्ट, क्रोधिष्ट, तापिष्ट, संतापी, क्रोधशील, कोपशील, संतापशील, शीघ्रकोपी, शीघ्रक्रोधी, चिरडखोर, चिरडीखोर, चिडखोर, चिडचिड्या, चिडरा, जलद, उष्ण, पित्तवेगी, पित्तप्रकृति, पित्तस्वभाव, पितळा, पित्त प्रकृतीचा,पित्तस्वभावाचा, कोपवान्, क्रोधवान्, संतापवान्, आग्या, अतिरागा, तामस, तामसी, तामसगुणी, तमोगुणी, तमस्वी, क्रोधवश, क्रोधाधीन, अमर्षवान्, अमर्षी, अमर्षण, क्रोधन, तबरी, चंड, रौद्र. Terms expressing with particularity of aspect or allusion a *person eminently passionate or fiery*, and thus answering to *Hotspur, Hotblood, Fireball, Spitfire, Pepperbox, &c. &c.* are रुद्रावतार, जमदग्नि, अकरावारुद्र, आगजाळ्या, तुफान, रौद्र, सैतान, आगीचालोळ or कल्लोळ, आगीचापुलाव, आग्यावेताळ, आग्यागारुडि, ओलीआग, जळतीआग, ओलीमांग, अतत्यायी or अतितायी, दैत्यांशी, दैत्यपुरुष, पंचानन, साक्षात् दैत्य, साकीगोसावी, जिवंत पिशाच, खवीस, सकृद्दर्शनीं तापणारा-उसळणारा, ज्यास पाण्यांत देखील घाम येतो.

2 *eager, excited, vehement, warm.* उत्साहाचा, उत्कंठेचा, आसक्तीचा, अनुरागाचा, आवेशाचा, हौशीचा, शौकाचा, उत्कंठित, सोत्साह, आस्थिक, आस्थावान्, अनुरागी, अनुरक्त, अनुरत, सानुराग, सराग. [क्रोधपूर्वक, &c.

PASSIONATELY, *adv.* v. A. 1. रागानें, क्रोधानें, &c. क्रोधभावानें, 2 उत्साहानें, उत्कंठेनें, शौकानें, हौशीनें, &c. अनुरागपूर्वक, आसक्तिपूर्वक, अत्युत्साहपूर्वक,&c.

PASSIONATENESS, *n.* v. A. 1. रागिटपणा *m.* कोपिष्टपणा *m.* तापडपणा *m.* तापडाई *f.* क्रोधशीलता *f.* कोपशीलता *f.* क्रोधवशता *f.* क्रोधाधीनता *f.* शीघ्रकोपिता *f.* &c. पित्तप्रकृति *f.* पित्तस्वभाव *m.* तम *m. n.* तमोगुण *m.* नाकावरराग *m.*

2 अनुत्कंठा *f.* आसक्ति *f.* अनुराग *m.* अनुरक्ति *f.* अनुरति *f.* सानुरागता *f.* आवेश *m.* हौस *f.* शौक *m.*

PASSIONLESS, *a. not easily excited.* थंड, थंडा, शांत, शांतप्रकृतीचा, शांत स्वभावाचा. [&c. अननुरागी.

2 *void of passion.* विरागी, विरक्त, वीतराग, अनुरागहीन-शून्य-

PASSIVE, *a.—as opposed to* active. निर्व्यापार, निष्क्रिय, निश्चेष्ट, कर्मपात्र, कर्माधार, कर्माश्रय.

2 *unresisting.* सोसणारा, सोसून घेणारा, सहिष्णु, तितिक्षु, सहनशील, सहनकर, सहनवृत्तीचा, सहनवृत्ति, सह, सहनधर्माचा, सहनधर्मक, सहनप्रधान, अनिवारक, अप्रतीकारक.

3—in grammar. P. voice. कर्मणि आत्मनेपद *n.* कर्मणिवाच्य *n.*—reflective p. कर्मणिकर्तृवाच्य *n.* —impersonal p. भाववाच्य *n.*

PASSIVELY, *adv.* v. A. 1. निर्व्यापार, निष्क्रिय, व्यापाराभावपूर्वक. 2 सोसून, सहन करून, सहनवृत्तीनें, सहनधर्मानें, निवारण न करितां.

PASSIVENESS, PASSIVITY, *n.* v. A. 1. निर्व्यापारता *f.* निष्क्रियता *f.* कर्मपात्रता *f.* कर्माश्रयता *f.*

2 सहिष्णुता *f.* सहनशीलता *f.* &c. सहनवृत्ति *f.* सहनधर्म *m.* अनिवारकधर्म *m.* अनिवारकभाव *m.* अनिवारकता *f.*

PASSPORT, *n. written license or pass.* परवाना *m.* दस्तक *n.* रवाना *m.* राहदारीची चिठ्ठी *f.* रस्त्याची चिठ्ठी *f.*

PAST, *p.* See PASSED.

PAST, *n. past time.* गेलाकाळ *m.* गतकाल *m.* भूतकाल *m.*

2 *past occurrences.* गेल्या-झाल्या गोष्टी *f. pl.* [बर.

PAST, *prep. farther than,* v. BEYOND. पुढें, पुढां, पलीकडे, बाहेर,

2 *beyond,*—in time. पसार (in comp. as दोनपसार past-two, & तीन पसार, चारपसार, &c.).

3 *from, along, by.* जवळून, वरून, पुढून.

4 *beyond, above, out of the reach of.* बाहेर, पलीकडे.

That is p. अतीत (in comp. as उपायातीत that is p. remedy, वयातीत that is past age &c.)

PASTE, *n. composition made of flour and water, &c.* खळ *f.* चिकटा *m.* चीक *m.* चिकी *f.*

P. of iron rust &c. (applied to the ends of the drum पखवाज or मृदंग) शाई *f.* [टवणें-बसवणें.

To PASTE, *v. a. fasten with paste.* खळीनें-खळ लावून-&c. चिक-

2 *size.* खळणें, खळ *f.* लावणें-देणें.

PASTEBOARD, *n.* खळीनें अनेक कागद चिकटवून केलेला जाड कागद *m.*

P. cover (for a book) पुष्टिपत्र *n.*

PASTERN, *n.*—of a horse. नेऊर or नेवर *m.*

Ring of hair on the p. खिमावर्त *m.*

2 *leg*—in contempt. तंगडी or तांगडी *f.* डोंका *m.* टांग *f.*

PASTERN-JOINT, *n.* मणगट *n.* मूठ *f.*

PASTIL, *n. scented stick, &c. burnt for perfume.* उदकाडी *f.* उदबत्ती *f.* अगरबत्ती *f.*

PASTIME, *n. amusement, diversion, &c.* v. PLAY. खेळ *m.* क्रीडा *f.* कौतुक *n.* गमत *f.* करमणूक *f.* करमत *f.* कालक्रमण *n.* कालक्रमणा *f.* विरंगुळा *m.* इच्छाविलास *m.*

PASTOR, *n. shepherd.* मेंढक्या or मेंढका, मेंढ्या, मेंढपाळ, मेषपाळ.

2 fig. *spiritual instructor.* गुरु, धर्मोपदेशक, धर्मोपदेष्टा, आचार्य, पालक.

PASTORAL, *a.* v. N. 1. *relating, &c. to shepherds.* मेंढक्यांचा, &c. मेंढ्याविषयींचा, मेषपालसंबंधी-विषयक.

2 fig. धर्मोपदेशकाचा, धर्मोपदेशकसंबंधी-विषयक.

PASTORAL, *n.* मेषपालनादिविषयक काव्य *n.*

PASTRY, *n.* v. SWEETMEATS. मळलेल्या पिठाचीं पक्वान्नें *n. pl.*

PASTRY-COOK, *n.* हलवई, पक्वान्न्या.

PASTURAGE, *n.* See PASTURE. 2 *price paid for grazing.* चराई *f.* गुरचराई *f.* गुरचरण *f.*—on waste lands. बनचराई *f.* वण *f.*

PASTURE, *n. grazing land.* गुरचरण *f.* चरण *f.* चरगण *n.* चरींव *n.* चरवण *n.* चरवा *m.* गायरान *n.*

A p. clog. खोडा *m.*

P. and water—as affecting cattle. पाणसा *m.* पाणवसा *m.*

To feed in rich p. चरणें.

To send or put out to p. चारणीस-चारणीला-चारणीवर-&c. पाठवणें-घालणें-ठेवणें.

2 *grass for the food of cattle.* चारा *m.* चार *f.* चरण *f.* चरगण *n.* चरींव *n.* चरवण *n.* चरवा *m.*

To PASTURE, *v. a. feed on a pasture.* चारणें, चरायाला घालणें, चरणीस-वणीस-&c. घालणें, चरविणें.

To PASTURE, *v. n. graze.* चरणें.

Price paid for tending at pasture. चराई *f.* चरिंदा *m.*

PASTURE-HOBBLES, *n.* दुपकी *f.* कळवा *m.* कळावा *m.* मानखुंट *n.* मानखोडा *m.* डचकला *m.* खोडा *m.*

PASTURING, *n.* v. A.—*act.* चारणें *n.* चारणी *f.* वण or वन *f.* वणीचा व्यापार *m.*

v. V. N.—*act.* चरणें *n.* चरणी *f.*

PAT, *adv. fitly, exactly.* नेमका or नेमकाच *decl.* ठिकला *decl.* टापास टीप, टापटीप, डिकास तेल.

PAT, *a.* v. FIT. योग्य.

PAT, *n. tap, light blow.* थाप *f.* थापड *f.* थापडी *f.* थापट *f.* थापटी *f.* थपाटी *f.* चपेट *f.*

2 (of butter, &c.) *small flattish lump.* चपटी *f.* चापटी *f.* थापटी *f.* थापा *m.* वटिका *f.* वटी *f.* वडी *f.* चकती *f.* खपटी *f.*

To PAT, *v. a. tap, &c.* थापटणें or थोपटणें, थाप *f.*-&c. मारणें-देणें, ठोकणें.

To p. and coax. थापटणें, थापणें, थोपटणें. [*f*. देणें.

To p. on the back approvingly, &c. पाठीवर शाबासकी

2 *beat into shape by patting*. थापणें, चापटणें, चोपटणें, पेटणें, चोपणें, चोपणी *f*.-टापटीप *f*. करणें, चोप *m*.-पेट *m*. देणें-काढणें--घेणें-मारणें.

Instrument of masons to pat with. थापटणें *n*. थापटी *f*. थापी *f*. चोपणी *f*.—of potters. थापटणें*n*.

PATCH, *n*. *piece* (*of cloth*, &c.) *sewed or put on to mend*. ठिगळ *n*. *dim*. ठिगळी *f*. कप्पा *or* कपा *m*. कप्पी *or* कपी *f*. पट्टी *f*. —esp. of leather or wood. गाबडी *f*. गाबडें *n*. पुस्ती *f*.

2 (of land) *piece*. ठिकें *n*. जमिनीचा तुकडा *m*. दळें *or* दळ्हें *n*.

By patches. ठिकेवार.

Patch on the side of a hill cleared & burned. दळा *m*.

3—on the face. टिकली *f*. पट्टी *f*.

To PATCH, *v*. *a*. *mend by sewing on*, *&c*. *pieces*. ठिगळणें, ठिगळ *n*.-ठिगळी *f*.-&c. लावणें-देणें, ठिगळाठिगळ *f*. करणें *g*. *of o*.

2 *or*,patch up; *do up or mend hastily or clumsily*. तांगडणें, तांगडून घेणें, डागडूग *f*.-डागडुजी *or* डोजी *f*.-थंतरमंतर *n*.-&c. करणें, लाखलिप *f*. करणें *g*. *of o*. लाखलिपट करणें.

3 *or*, patch up; *make up of pieces*. तुकड्याताकड्याचा-तुकडेजोडीचा-जोडाचा-जोडगिरीचा-जोडाजोडीचा-&c. करणें.

PATCH-WORK, *n*. *work composed of pieces*. तुकड्याताकड्याचें-जोडाजोडीचें-तुकडेजोडीचें-&c. काम *n*.

A garment or cloth of p. गोदडी *f*. वाकळ *f*.

PATCHED, *p*. v. V. 1. ठिगळ लावलेला, &c. जोडींव, जोडगिरी, जोडाचा-ठिगळाठिगळांचा.

2 तांगडलेला, तांगडून घेतलेला, थंतरमंतर केलेला, &c.

3 तुकड्याताकड्याचा, तुकडे जोडीचा, जोडाचा, जोडगिरीचा, जोडाजोडीचा.

PATCHERY, *n*. *clumsy*, *bungling work*. ओबडधोबड काम *n*.

PATE, *n*. v. HEAD. डोई *f*. डोकसें *n*. टकली *f*. टकलें *n*. नारळ *m*.

PATELLA, *n*. v. KNEE-PAN. गुडघ्याची वाटी *f*.

PATENT, *a*. *open*, *apparent*, *conspicuous*, *&c*. v. PLAIN. उघड, उघडा, स्पष्ट, व्यक्त.

2 *appropriated*, *&c*. *by letters patent*. सनदी, सनदेचा.

PATENT, *n*. *writing granting a privilege*. सनद *f*. फर्मान *or* फरमाना *m*. परवाना *m*. विशेषाधिकारपत्रिका *f*. [दार.

PATENTEE, *n*. *person to whom a patent is given*. सनदी, सनद-

PATER-FAMILIAS, *n*. *person having a family*. कुटुंबी, घरवासी, कुटुंबवत्सल. [पैत्र, पित्र्य.

PATERNAL, *a*. *pertaining*, *&c*. *to a father*. पित्याचा, &c. पैतृक,

P. affection. पुत्रलोभ *m*. पुत्रममता *f*. &c.

2 *fatherly*, *like a father*. बापासारखा, पितृसम, पितृतुल्य, पितृसदृश. [डिलोपार्जित.

3 v. HEREDITARY. बापापासून आलेला, पित्रागत, पितृप्राप्त, व-

PATERNALLY, *adv*. v. A. 2. बापासारखा *decl*. पितृवत्.

PATERNITY, *n*. *fathership*. बापपणा *m*. पितृत्व *n*. पितृसंबंध *m*. पितृभाव *m*.

PATH, *n*. *way*, v. ROAD. वाट *f*. रस्ता *m*. मार्ग *m*. पथ *pop*. पंथ*m*.

By p., off p. आडवाट *f*. फुटवाट *f*. गोंवडी *or* गोंडी *f*.

Foot p. पाउलवाट *f*.एकपावलीवाट *f*.माणुसवाट *f*.बारीकवाट*f*.

Horse p. घोडेवाट *f*.

P. beaten on a muddy road. पावटी *f*. *or pl*. पावट्या.

The right p. सत्पथ *m*. सन्मार्ग *m*.

PATHLESS, *a*. बिनवाटेचा, अपथ, निष्पथ.

PATH-WAY. See PATH.

PATHETIC, PATHETICAL, *a*. *moving*, *touching*, *affecting*. द्रव आणणारा, करुणारसाचा, रसिक, रसभरित, करुणारसभरित, करुणाजनक, करुणोत्पादक, करुणामय, करुणात्मक, कारुणिक,करुण, करुणापर, द्रावक, चित्तद्रावक, वेधक, चित्तवेधक, मनोवेधक, हृदयवेधक, चित्तमोहक, मोहजनक, हृदयंगम, हृदयाविधु, मनोद्रावक, चित्ताद्रकारी. [द्रवसुटेसा *decl*.

PATHETICALLY, *adv*. v. A. द्रव यायाजोगा-जोगता-सारखा *decl*.

PATHETICALNESS, *n*. v. A. करुणा *f*. करुणरस*m*. वेधकत्व *n*. चित्तवेधकत्व *n*. द्रावकत्व*n*. चित्तद्रावकत्व *n*. [बोचू.

PATHIC, *n*. *catamite*. गांडमराऊ, गंडिया *or* गांड्या, झोजा, बोचाळू,

PATHOLOGICAL, *a*. v. N. निदानाचा, निदानविषयक-संबंधी.

PATHOLOGY, *n*. *science of the causes*, *symptoms*, *&c*. *of disease*.निदान *or* रोगनिदान*n*. निदानशास्त्र*n*. रोगनिरूपणविद्या*f*.

PATHOS, *n*. *patheticalness*. करुणारस*m*. रस *m*.

PATIENCE, *n*. *calm endurance*. सोशिकपणा *m*. कंठकपणा *m*. धीर *m*. धैर्य*n*. सोसणूक *f*. सहन*n*. सहनशक्ति *f*. सहनशीलता *f*. सहिष्णुता *f*. तितिक्षा *f*. तितिक्षा बुद्धि *f*.

2 *calm waiting*, *expecting*, *&c*. धीर *m*.धैर्य *n*.दम *m*.सबुरी *f* सबुराई *f*. सबूर *f*. धिमाई *or* धिम्माई *f*.

To have p. धिरणें, धीर *m*.-दम *m*.-&c. धरणें-खाणें-छाटणें.

3 (of injury or affront). सोशिकपणा *m*. क्षमा *f*. क्षांति *f*. गई *f*. गम *m*.

PATIENT, *a*. v. N. 1. सोशीक *or* सोसीक, सोसक, सोसाळू, कठक, धीर, धैर्यवान्, सहनशील, सहिष्णु, सह esp. in comp. तितिक्षु, तितिक्षाबुद्धि. [बुऱ्या.

2 धीर, धिराचा, धैर्याचा, दमाचा, धैर्यवान्, धिम्मा *or* धिमा, स-

3 सोसीक *or* सोशीक, सोसक, सोसाळू, सहनशील, क्षमी, क्षमावान्, क्षमापर, क्षांत, क्षमिता, क्षंता, क्षम, बहुक्षम.

PATIENT, *n*.—*as opposed to* agent. कर्मपात्र, कर्माधार, कर्माश्रय.

2 *sick person*. दुखणेकरी, रोगी, वैद्याचें कूळ*n*.वैद्याची असामी*f*.

PATIENTLY, *adv*. v.A. 1. सोसकपणानें, धिरानें, &c. धैर्य धरून,तितिक्षापूर्वक, सहनपूर्वक, &c.

2 धिरानें, धिमाईनें, &c. दम धरून, धीर धरून, धैर्य धरून,

3 गईनें, गईकरून, गम खाऊन, क्षमापूर्वक, क्षांतिपूर्वक.

PATIMAH, *n*.—the native boat. फतेमारी *f*.

PATLY. See PAT. [णबोली *f*.

PATOIS,*n*.*dialect of the lower classes*. अडाणजातीची बोली*f*.अडा-

PATRIARCH,*n*. *head or founder of a family*. मूलपुरुष,आदिपुरुष, कूटस्थ, गोत्रस्वामी, गोत्रपति, गोत्रजनक, गोत्र, वृद्धपिता, आजाबा.

2 fig. *dignified and venerable person*. गुरुजन, वृद्धजन.

PATRIARCHAL, *a*. *belonging*, *&c*. *to a patriarch*. मूलपुरुषाचा, गोत्रपतीचा, &c. मूलपुरुषसंबंधी, कूटस्थसंबंधी-विषयक.

PATRICIAN, *a*. *noble*, *not plebeian*, v. GENTLE. मोठ्या कुळांतला, मोठ्या कुळाचा, कुळवंत, कुलीन, अभिजात.

PATRICIAN, *n*. *nobleman*, v. A. कुलीन पुरुष.

PATRIMONIAL, *a*. *pertaining*, *&c*. *to a patrimony*. वतनाचा, वतनाविषयींचा, वतनी, वतनसंबंधाचा, वतनसंबंधी.

2 *inherited from ancestors*,v. HEREDITARY. वडिलांपासूनचा, वडिलोपार्जित, वडीलपरंपरागत, पितृप्राप्त, पित्रागत, पैतृक.

P. estate. वतनवाडी *f*.

PATRIMONY, *n. an inherited right or estate.* बतनn. बारसाm. बारीसm. वतनवाडी *f.* गोत्ररिक्थn. वडिलांची भाकर *f.* बापरोटी *f.* स्वतेंn.

Confiscation of a p. वृत्तिच्छेदm. वृत्तिच्छेदनn.

Sequestration of a p. वतनजप्ती *f.*

Title-deed of a p. बतनपत्रn. [देशभक्त.

PATRIOT, *n. lover, &c. of his country.* स्वदेशाभिमानी पुरुष, स्व-

PATRIOT, PATRIOTIC, *a.* v. N. स्वदेशाभिमानी, स्वदेशाभिमानाचा, स्वदेशासक्त, स्वदेशहितकारी, स्वदेशहितेच्छु.

PATRIOTISM, *n. love, &c. of one's country.* स्वदेशाभिमानm. स्वदेशभक्ति *f.* स्वदेशप्रीति *f.* स्वदेशासक्ति *f.* स्वदेशानुरागm.

PATROL, *n. walking round of a guard.* गस्त *f.* तलावाm.

2 *patrolling body.* गस्त *f.* तलावाm. रोंदn. from the English "rounds" is common. [रगस्त.

P. proceeding with music. वाजगस्त*f.*—opposed to चो-

A man of the p. गस्तकरी, रोंदवाला.

To PATROL, *v. n. walk round as a guard.* तलावाm. देणें, गस्त*f.* घालणें-करणें, जागरm.-जागल *f.* करीत फिरणें.

PATRON, *n. protector, supporter, &c.* पोशिंदा *or* पोसिंदा, पोषक, पालक, यजमान, मुरब्बी, आश्रय, आश्रयभूत, आश्रयस्थान, कैवारी, मददगार, पक्षधारी,पुरस्कारी, पुरस्कर्त्ता, हिमाइती, हिमाइत दार, ओंठगणn. ओंथंबा *m.* पांघरूण *n.* ढांसण *m.* तणावा *m.* बाजू *f.* वाली *or* वाल्ही, प्रणतवत्सल, दीनवत्सल.

2 *appreciator of merit.* जाणता, जाण, गुणग्राहक, गुणग्राही, गुणज्ञ, ग्राहक, ग्राही, गुणदर्शी, गिऱ्हाईक, भोक्ता.

PATRON-LESS, *a.* निराश्रय, निराश्रित, निराधार.

PATRONAGE, *n. support, protection afforded.* हिमाईत *or* हिमायत *f.* मददगारी *f.* पुस्तपन्हा *m.* पालन *n.* पालनपोषण *n.* आश्रय *m.* आधार *m.* बग *f.* शिफारस *f.* [त्व *n.*

2 *appreciation of merit.* गुणग्रहण *n.* गुणज्ञान *n.* गुणग्राहक-

PATRONAL, *a. pertaining, &c. to a patron.* पोशिंद्याचा, यजमानाचा, हिमाइतदाराचा,&c.हिमाइतीचा, पुस्तपन्ह्याचा, &c. पालक, पोषक, पालन संबंधी. [णारी *f.*

PATRONESS, *n. female patron.* यजमानीण *or* न *f.* पोषण कर-

To PATRONIZE, *v.a. support, countenance, &c.* हिमाइत *f.*-आश्रय *m.*-आधार *m.*-पुस्ती *f.*-&c. देणें, पुरस्कार *m.*-पुस्तपन्हा *m.*-&c. करणें *g. of o.* कैवार *m.* घेणें *g. of o.* पालन *n.*-पोषणn.-&c. करणें *g. of o.* काखेस-बगलेस मारणें, हातीं धरणें.

PATRONIZED, *p.* v. V. हिमाईत दिल्हेला, &c. शिफारसी.

PATRONYMIC, *n.* अपत्यवाचक *m.*

PATTEN, *n. wooden shoe.* खडवा *or* खडावा *f. pl.* काष्ठपादुका *f.*

To PATTER, *v. n. strike with a quick succession of small sounds*—falling rain, &c. पटपट-पटपटां-फडफड-फडाफड-सडसड-सळसळ-सटपट-&c. पडणें, सडसडणें.

2—feet in quick movement. दडदडणें, दडदड-दडदडां-&c. चालणें-धावणें. [*intens.* फडफडाटm.

PATTERING, *n.*v. V. 1.—*act.* सडसडणें *n.* फडफड पडणें *n.* &c.—2—*act.* दडदडणें *n.* &c.—*intens.* दडदडाट *m.*

PATTERINGLY, *adv.* v. V. 1. फडफड, पटपट, पटपटां, सडसड, सडसडां, सळसळ,—*intens.* फडाफड, फडाडां, सटासट, सटाटां.

2 दडदड, दडदडां, लुटलुट, लुटुलुटु.—*intens.* दडाडां.

PATTERN, *n. model, exemplar.* नमुना *m.* सांचा *m.* फर्मा *m.* मासला *m.* कित्ता *m.*

2 *specimen, sample.* प्रत *f.* नमुना *m.* मासला *m.* बानगी *f.*

3 *kind, sort.* तऱ्हा *f.* प्रत *f.* प्रकार *m.*

PAUCITY, *n. smallness of number, fewness.* थोडेपणा *m.* अल्पता *f.* संख्याल्पत्व *n.* [न्यूनता *f.*

2 *smallness of quantity.* थोडेपणा *m.* कमीपणा *m.* अल्पता *f.*

PAUNCH, *n.* v. BELLY. पोट *n.* उदर *n.*

Distended p. *pot-belly.* ढेर *f.* भेर *f.*

PAUPER, *n. person subsisting on charity.* भिकारी, भिक्षाजीवी, भिक्षोपजीवी, अन्यदत्तोपजीवी.

2—in law. नादार.

PAUPERISM, *n. state of indigence requiring support from others.* भिकारीपणा *m.* भिक्षोपजीविका *f.* भिक्षावृत्ति *f.* अन्यदत्तोपजीविका *f.* [&c. करणें.

To PAUPERIZE, *v. a. reduce to poverty.* भिकेस लावणें, भिकारी-

PAUSE, *n. temporary stop or cessation.* तूट *f.* महकुची *f.* तकूब *n.* तकुबी *f.* खंड *m.* खळ *m.* अवसान *n.* विराम *m.* व्यवधान *n.* अवसाय *m.* याम *m.*

2 *suspense, doubt.* दुग्धा *f.* द्वामुष्य *n.* भावसंधि *m.*

3 (in music, poetry, &c.). थाक *f.* अवसानn. यति *m.*

4 *intermission of labor or work.* खाडा *m.* खळ *m.* नागा *m.* संधि *m. f.* उसंधि *f.* उसंत *or* उसंथ *f.* उसरत *f.* उसपंत *f.* आंसारा *m.*

To PAUSE, *v. n. make a short stop, forbear for a time.* मध्यें राहणें-काम *n.* ठेवणें, थांबणें, खळणें, थोपणें, विसावणें *or* विसवणें, विरमणें, विसंबणें *or* विसमणें, खोळंबणें, दम *m.* खाणें-घेणें-धरणें, उसंथ *f.* घेणें-खाणें.

2 v. TO DELIBERATE, TO HESITATE. करूं न करूं करणें-पाहणें, बानबा *m. f.* करणें.

To PAVE, *v. a. floor with brick or stone.* फरसबंदी *f.*-चिरेबंदी *f.* करणें *g. of o.* फरस *m.* बांधणें-करणें, फरश्या *f. pl.* लावणें-बसवणें.

2 the way for; *facilitate the introduction of.* वाट *f.*-रस्ताm.-&c. करणें-पाडणें.

PAVED, *a.* फरसबंदी.

PAVEMENT, PAVING, PAVE-WORK, *n. floor of stones or bricks.* फरसबंदी *f.* चिरेबंदी *f.* फरस *m. dim.* फरशी *f.*

Flat p. पापडी *f.* पटंगण *or* पटांगण *n.*

PAVER, PAVIER, *n.* v. V. 1. फरसबंदी करणारा, फरस बांधणारा, &c. फरसबंद्या.

PAVILION, *n.* v. TENT. डेरा *m.*

PAW, *n. foot of a beast.* पंजा *m.* पशुपद *n.*—of a cat. डाबली *f.*

To PAW, *v. n.*—as a horse, &c. टाप *f.*-टाफर *f.* मारणें, भुई *f.*-&c. टापारणें *or* टापरणें *or* टाफरणें, टापरणें *or* टाफरणें.

To PAW, *v. a. scrape with the fore foot.* टापरणें *or* टाफरणें.

2 *handle rudely or roughly.* हात *m.*-पंजा *m.* टाकणें, हताळणें, घुसडणें, हस्तव्यापार *m.* करणें.

PAWN, *n. pledge.* गहाण *n.* बंधक *n.* निक्षेप *m.* आधि *m.*

In p. At p. गहाणवट.

2—at chess. प्यादा *m.* प्यादें *n.*

Check mate with p. प्यादी *f.* प्यादेमात *or* प्यादमात *f.*

To PAWN, *v. a. given in pledge.* गहाण ठेवणें, गहाण लावून देणें, गहाणवट ठेवणें.

PAWN-BROKER, *n.* गहाणाचा व्यापारी.

P's. ticket. गहाणखत *n.* गहाणपत्र *n.*

PAWNED, *p.* v. V. गहाण ठेवलेला, गहाणवट ठेवलेला, &c. निक्षिप्त, आधीकृत.

To PAY, *v. a.* (a debt) *liquidate, discharge.* फेडणें, देणें, वारणें, अदा करणें, वारापाणी *f. n.*-&c. करणें *g. of o.*

To p. in full, v. To CLEAR. फडशा *m.*-बेबारा *m.* करणें *g. of o.* बेबाक-फिटंफाट-फारीक-&c. करणें, उरता न ठेवणें.

To p. in part. उरता करणें.

2 *give pay to.* तलब *f.*-रोजमुरा *m.*-पगार *m.*-वेतन *n.*-&c. देणें-वांटणें, चिठ्ठा *m.* वांटणें.

3 *render, give.* देणें, करणें.

4 for ; (an article bought). किम्मत *f.*-मोल *n.*-दाम *m.*-पैका *m.*- मूल्य *n.*-&c. देणें.

5 for ; *atone by suffering.* निरपणें, निस्तरणें *or* निस्तारणें, फेडणें.

6 in ; (monies, &c. due). भरणें.

7 off ; *lit. fig.* v. To RETALIATE. फेडणें, उरता न ठेवणें.

To be paid off ; *lit. fig.* फिटणें.

PAY, *n. wages, hire, &c.* पगार *m.* पाग *m.* तलब *f.* रोजमरा *or* मुरा *m.* मजूरी *f.* चिठ्ठा *m.* तैनात *f.* मुशारा *or* मुशाहिरा *m.* वेतन *n.* देणावळ *f.* भृति *f.* भाटक *n.*

Daily p. रोज *m.* रोजी *f.*

General serving out of p. or wages. बटवडा *m.*

Monthly p. दरमाहा *m.* महिना *m.* मासिक *n.*

Yearly p. वार्षिक *n.*

P.–roll. बटवडे पत्रक *n.*

To settle the monthly p. of. दरमाहा *m.* करणें.

PAY-DAY, *n.* पगार वांटण्याचा दिवस *m.* चांदरात झाडायाचा दिवस *m.*

PAY-MASTER, *n. one who is to pay.* तलब-रोजमरा-वेतन-&c. देणारा, वेतनदाता, भृतिदाता.

2—military. पगार-चिठ्ठा-&c. वांटणारा, सबनीस.

PAYABLE, *a. due.* द्यायाचा, देय.

2 *that can be paid.* द्यायाजोगा-जोगता-सारखा-&c. फेडायाजोगा-सारखा-&c. दानयोग्य, दानोचित.

PAYING, PAYMENT, *n.* v. V. 1.—*act.* फेडणें *n.* देणें *n.* फेडणी *f.*—*state.* फेड *f.* फीट *f.* फिटाफीट *f.*

The closing and clearing p. झाडबाकी *f.*

PEA, *n.* वाटाणा *m.* कलाय *m.* सतीनक *m.*

Half of a split p. &c. डाळकण *m.* डाळिंबी *f.*

PEACE, *n.*—*as opposed to* war. तह *m.* सल्ला *m.* सलूक *or* सुलूक *or* सख *m. f.* सलूका *m.* संधि *m.* सख्य *n.* ऐक्य *n.* निर्द्वंद्व *n.* युद्धाभाव *m.* असंग्राम *m.* अविग्रह *m.*

P. and war. संधिविग्रह *m.*

Treaty or treating of p. तह *m.*

Written treaty of p. तहनामा *m.*

Welcome defeat for peace sake. हार मानली पण झगडा [तुटो.

2 *rest from commotion or agitation* ; *quiet, ease, &c.* स्वस्थपणा *m.* चैन *n.* सुख *n.* सुखसमाधान *n.* शांति *f.* समाधान *n.* स्वस्थता *f.* स्वास्थ्य *n.*

Internal p. P. of mind. अंतःसुख *pop.* अंतरसुख *n.*

In p. and safety. सलामत.

Peace be with thee. स्वस्ति.

3 *freedom from tumult, riot, &c.* स्वस्थपणा *m.* स्वस्थता *f.* स्वास्थ्य *n.* निरुपद्रवता *f.* उपद्रवाभाव *m.* उपद्रवराहित्य *n.* निष्कंटक *n.* कंटकराहित्य *n.* उपप्लवराहित्य *n.* उपप्लवाभाव *m.*

P. prevails every where. जिकडे तिकडे स्वस्थ आहे.

P. and plenty. P. and prosperity. आबादानी *f.* आबादी *f.*

4 *harmony, concord, reconciliation.* मिलाफ *m.* समेट *m.* संधि *m. f. pop.* संध *f.* अविरोध *m.* विरोधाभाव *m.* निर्द्वंद्व *n.*

5 *silence.* मुकेपणा *m.* मौन *pop.* मौन्य *n.* अभाषण *n.*

To hold one's p. उगाच राहणें, मुकेपणा *m.*-मौन *n.* धरणें, मूग *m. pl.* खाणें-गिळणें, मुगाचें *n.* करणें, मौनावणें.

Peace ! चप्प !

PEACEABLE, *a. free from war, tumult, &c.* स्वस्थ, स्वस्थपणाचा, निरुपद्रवाचा, उपद्रवाभावाचा, युद्धाभावाचा, निरुपद्रव, निष्कंटक, निरुपप्लव, निरुपसर्ग, साम्राज्याचा, उपसर्ग-उपप्लव-&c. शून्य-रहित-&c.

2 *quiet, not agitated by passion,* v. CALM. शांत, थंड, स्वस्थ.

3 *not rough or violent,* v. PACIFIC. सामाचा, सामोपचाराचा, सामोपायाचा.

4 *not quarrelsome, turbulent, &c.* गरीब, सालस, साळसूध *or* द, संथ, शांत, शमी, शांतिप्रिय, गहीन, कलहशत्रु, कलहविमुख, कलहपराङ्मुख, कलहभीरु, संधिप्रिय.

PEACEABLENESS, *n.* v. A. 1. स्वस्थपणा *m.* स्वस्थता *f.* स्वास्थ्य *n.* निरुपद्रवता *f.* निरुपप्लवता *f.* &c. युद्धाभाव *m.* उपद्रवाभाव *m.* उपप्लवाभाव *m.* &c.

2 स्वस्थपणा *m.* स्वस्थता *f.* शांति *f.* थंडाई *f.*

4 गरीबी *f.* सालसपणा *m.* &c. कलहद्वेष *m.* कलहविमुखता *f.*

PEACEABLY, *adv.* v. A. 1. स्वस्थ, स्वस्थपणानें, &c. निरुपद्रव, निरुपसर्गतः.

3 सामोपचारानें, सामोपायानें.

PEACE-BREAKER, *n.* बिघडपाड्या, संधिभेदक-भंजक-विघातक.

PEACE-MAKER, *n.* समेट करणारा, कळमिटव्या, कज्जामिटव्या, मिलाफ्या, संधिकर्त्ता.

PEACE-MAKING, *n.* समेट *m.* मिटवामिटव *f.* कळमिटवणी *f.* संधि- [करण *n.*

PEACEFUL, PEACEFULNESS. See PEACEABLE, &c.

PEACH, *n.* सप्तालू *n.*

PEACHICK, *n.* मोराचें पिलूं *n.*

PEACOCK, *n.* मोर *m.* केकी *m.* मयूर *m.* शिखंडी *m.* शिखी *m.*

Crest of a p. चूडा *f.* मयूरशिखा *f.*

Cry of a p. टाहो *m.* केका *f.* मयूरशब्द *m.*

Fan or brush of p. feathers. मोरकुंचा *m.* कुंचा *m.* मोरचल *or* चेल *m. n.*

Tail of p. मोराचा पिसारा *m.* शिखंड *m.* बर्ह *n.*—Eye in it डोळा *m.* चंद्रक *m.* मेचक *m.*

To have attained full plumage,—a p. कुचळणें.

PEAGREEN, *a.* पिस्ताई.

PEA-HEN, *n.* लांडोर *or* लांडूर *f. n.* मयूरी *f.* शिखिनी *f.*—in con- [tempt, लांडरूं *n.*

PEAK, *n.* कूट *n.* शिखर *n.* शृंग *n.* पर्वताग्र *n.* शैलाग्र *n.* अद्रिशृंग *n.*

2 (of things generally) v. POINT. कोकी *or* कोंकी *f.* कोंच *f.* कोंचकी *f.* सुळका *m. dim.* सुळकी *f.* शिखर *n.* अगरडा *m.*

3 (of grain, &c. above the level of a measure). शीग *f.*

PEAKED, *a.* v. N. 1. शृंगी, शृंगवान्, शिखरी.

2 शिखरी, कोंकीदार, कोंचकीदार, सूच्यग्र.

To PEAL, *v. n. sound loudly, &c.* दणदणणें, कडकडणें, घडघडणें, फडफडणें, कडाका *m.*-तडाका *m.*-&c. होणें-चालणें-&c. *g. of s.* —*intens.* दणाणणें, कडाडणें, घडाडणें, धडाडणें, भडाडणें.

PEAL, PEALING, *n.* v. V. दणका *m.* खणका *m.* धडाका *m.* तडाका

or खा *m.* कडाका *or* खा *m.* झडाका *m.* ठांका *m.* कडका *m.*—*intens.* दणदणाट *m.* दणाण *m.* घणघणाट *m.* कडकडाट *m.* कडाड *m.* कडाडा *m.* धडाड *m.* फडाड *m.* भडाड *m.*

By peals, pealingly, &c. कडडड, कडाकड, कडाडां, धडडड, भडडड, घडडड, कटकडां, कडाकड, कडाडां, धडाधड, धडाडां, फडाफड, फडाडां, भडाभड, भडाडां.

PEALER, *n.* PEALING, *p. a.* v. V. दणदणणारा, घडघडणारा, &c. दणदणीत, कडाकड-धडाधड-&c. वाजणारा.

PEAR, *n.* एक फळ आहे.

2 prickly pear, v. EUPHORBIA. निवडुंग*n.* *m.* निवडुंगट *m. n.* पेरकूट *n.*

Leaf of the prickly p. फडा *m.*

PEARL, *n.* मोतीं *n.* मौक्तिक *n.* मुक्ताफल *n.* मुक्ता *f.* मुक्तिका *f.*

Cluster of pearls. मुक्ताजाल *n.* [फुगेंमोतीं *n.*

Imitation p. कापुरमोतीं, कागदीमोतीं, पाऱ्याचें मोतीं, फुगा*m.*

Lack lustre p. खरडा *m.* काहलाबंदरी मोतीं.

Mother of p. मोतीशिंप *or* मोताशिंप *f.* मोताशिंपी *f.*

Suit or set of four pearls. चौकडा *m.*

To fall asunder,—strung pearls, &c. ओघळणें.

PEARL-OYSTER, *n.* मोत्याचा शिंपला *m.* शुक्ति*f.* शुक्तिका *f.* [कित.

PEARLED, *a. adorned with pearls.* मुक्तालंकृत, मुक्तिकामंडित, मुक्तां-

PEARLY, *a. abounding with pearls.* मुक्तामय, मुक्ताप्रचुर, मुक्ताबहुल.

2 *resembling pearls.* मोत्यासारखा, मुक्तावत्, मुक्तातुल्य, मुक्ताधवल, मुक्तागौर, मुक्ताशुभ्र.

PEASANT, *n. rustic,* v. COUNTRYMAN. शेतखऱ्या, नांगऱ्या, जोत्या, खेड्या, खेती, अउत्या, काळीप्रजा *f.* क्षेत्राजीव, क्षेत्री.

PEASANT, *a.* See RUSTIC.

PEASANTRY, *n. body of peasants.* रयत *f.* रयतावा*m.* शेतकरीलोक *m. pl.* कुणबीमाळी *m. pl.* क्षेत्रजनता *f.*

PEBBLE, PEBBLE STONE, *n. roundish stone.* गोटा *m.* गोटी *f.* खडा *m.* गुंडा *m.* कंकर *m.*

Black p. sacred to Vishnu. शालिग्राम *m.*

Desert tract covered with pebbles. खडेरान *n.*

Little p. सकेरा *or* सकिरा *m.*

P. sacred to Shiva. बाण *m.*—the stone (of the shape of the योनि) in the centre of which it is placed. शाळुंका *or* खा *f.*

Pebbles, small stones. खडी *f.*

PEBBLY, *a. abounding, &c. with pebbles.* गोट्यांचा, खड्यांचा.

PECCABILITY, *n.* v. A. पापाधीनता *f.* पापवशता *f.* पापक्षमता *f.* पापसंभव *m.* पापसंभावना *f.* पापसंभवधर्म *m.*

PECCABLE, *a. liable or subject to sin.* पापाधीन, पापवश, पापक्षम, संभाव्यपाप, संभावितपाप, पापसंभवधर्मा, शक्यपाप.

PECCADILLO, *n. slight fault.* चुकी *f.* चूक *f.* हलका अपराध *m.*-दोष *m.* अल्पापराध *m.* क्षुद्रापराध *m.*

PECCANCY, *n.* v. A. 2. विकार *m.* विकृति *f.* दोष *m.*

PECCANT, *a. faulty,* v. CRIMINAL. अपराधी, अन्यायी, सापराध.

2 *corrupt, morbid, vitiated.* विकृत, विकारयुक्त, दूषित, दोषयुक्त.

PECCAVI, दोषांगीकार *m.* दोषस्वीकार *m.* [घेणें.

To cry p. चीं म्हणणें, बें करणें-म्हणणें, जांपणें, दांतीं तृण *n.*

To make to cry p. चीं-बें-म्हणविणें, जांपविणें.

PECK, *n.* v. MEASURE. एक कैलीमाप आहे.

2 fig. *large number or quantity.* खंडी *f.*

To PECK, *v. a. strike with the beak.* चोंच *f.*-टोंच *f.* मारणें, चोंचावणें, टोंकरणें, टोंचळणें, बोंचलणें, कुरकुटणें, कुरकुडणें.

2 (a hole.). चोंचीनें-&c. पाडणें-करणें, टोंचून-टोंकरून-कुरकुटून -&c. पाडणें, टोंकरणें.

3 *pick up with the beak.* वेंचणें, टिपणें.

To feed by pecking grains. चरणें.

4 at; fig. *find fault with constantly.* किरकिरणें, किरकीर *f.*-पिरपीर *f.*-रिपरीप *f.*-टिरटीर *f.*-जिकीर *f.*-जिगजीग *or* जिकजीक *f.*-घासणी *f.*-घासाघीस *f.*-घासघीस *f.*-घसघस *f.*-घिसधीस *f.*-खिसखीस *f.*-कटकट *f.*-टकटक *f.*-टिकटीक *f.*-टुरटूर*f.*-&c. करणें -लावणें-मांडणें-चालवणें, वाधंग *m.* लावणें-मांडणें-सांगणें.

PECKED, *p.* v. V. 1. चोंच मारलेला, चोंचावलेला, &c.—fruit, &c. खाद. [कुरकुटणारा, &c.

PECKER, *n.* PECKING, *p. a.* v.V. 1. चोंच मारणारा, चोंचावणारा, 4 किरकीर करणारा, &c. घसघशा, घिसघिशा, किरकिरा *or* ऱ्या, पिरपिरा *or* ऱ्या, जिकिरी.

PECTINAL, *a. like, &c. a comb.* फणीचा, फणीसारखा.

PECTORAL, *a. belonging to the breast.* उराचा, छातीचा, &c. उरःसंबंधी, वक्षस्संबंधी, औरस.

PECTORAL, *n. a medicine for the chest and lungs.* कासघ्न *n.* कासशमक *n.* कफनाशक *n.*

To PECULATE, *v. n. defraud the public,* v. To EMBEZZLE. तनाखोरी *f.*-हरामखोरी *f.*-&c. करणें, शिकार *f.* मारणें-साधणें, द्रव्यावर ताव *m.* देणें, खादगी *f.* खाणें, चावणें, खाणें.

PECULATION, *n.* v. V.—*act.* तनाखोरी करणें *n.* &c. तनाखोरी *f.* हरामखोरी *f.* तजकरा *or* तसकरा *m.* आप्यायन *n.*

I. *illicit gain.* खाद *f.* खादगी *f.* हरामखोरी *f.* शिकार *f.*

PECULATOR, *n.* PECULATING, *p. a.* v. V. तनाखोरी करणारा, खादगी खाणारा, &c. हरामखोर, खादू.

PECULIAR, *a. proper, appropiate, exclusively own.* आपला, खास, खासगत, खासगी, खासगीचा, खुद, खुदनिसबतीचा, खुदजातीचा, निज & स्व *in comp.* स्वकीय, स्वीय, स्वक, स्वयं, असाधारण, असामान्य, अनन्यवर्त्ती, तन्मात्रवर्त्ती, अनन्यसंबंधी, तन्मात्राधीन, अनन्यस्वामिक, अव्यापक, अव्यापी, अव्यभिचारी *in comp.* आत्म, आत्मीय, आत्मभूत.

2 *particular, special.* विशेष, असाधारण, असामान्य.

PECULIAR, *n. exclusive property.* आपलाच माल *m.* निजधन*n.* निजस्व *n.* स्वस्व *n.* असाधारण -असामान्य-अनन्यस्वामिक- &c. धन *n.*-&c.

PECULIARITY, *n.* v. A. 1. खासपणा *m.* असाधारणता *f.* असाधारण्य *n.* अनन्यवर्त्तित्व *n.* तन्मात्रवर्त्तित्व *n.* &c.

I. *a peculiarity ; a distinguishing property.* विशेष *m.* विशेषधर्म *m.* -गुण *m.*-लक्षण *n.*-&c. स्वधर्म *m.* धर्म *m.* उपाधि *m.* धर्मत्व *n.*

To PECULIARIZE. See To APPROPRIATE.

PECULIARLY, *adv.* v.A. 1. असाधारण्यें करून, असाधारण्यानें, असाधारणतः, असाधारणरूपानें, विशेष, विशेषेंकरून, विशेषतः.

PECUNIARY, *a. relating, &c. to money.* पैक्याचा, द्रव्याचा, धनाचा, &c. पैक्याविषयींचा, &c. धनसंबंधी-विषयक.

2 *consisting of money.* पैक्याचा, धनाचा, द्रव्याचा, &c. धनरूप, द्रव्यरूप, धन & द्रव्य (in comp. as धनदंड, द्रव्यदंड, &c.).

PED. See PAD.

PEDAGOGIC, PEDAGOGICAL, *a.* v. N. पंतोजीचा, शिक्षकाचा, शिक्षकसंबंधी.

PEDAGOGUE, *n. schoolmaster.* पंतोजी, शिक्षक, अध्यापक, शिशुपाठक, बालपाठक.

2 See PEDANT. [पादविषयक.

PEDAL, *a. belonging to a foot.* पायाचा, चरणाचा, पादसंबंधी,

PEDAL, *n.* पायानें चालवायाचें किती एक वाद्यांचें साधन *n.*—of a loom, &c. पांवडा *m.* पावठणी *f.* पावठी *f.* पावसरा *or* पावसारा*m.*

PEDANEOUS, *a. going on foot.* चरणचालीचा, पादचारी, पादगामी.

PEDANT, *n. one who makes a display of learning.* विद्यामिरवणारा, पांडित्यमिरवणारा, विद्येचा डौल-आडंबर-आव-&c. घालणारा-मांडणारा-माजविणारा-&c. विद्येचा डौली, विद्येचा आडंबऱ्या, पांडित्यमिरव्या, गागाभट्ट.

Ignorant and conceited p. पंडितंमन्य, पंडितमानी.

PEDANTIC, PEDANTICAL, *a. making a show of learning,*—of things. विद्येचे डौलाचा, विद्येच्या पोमाचा, &c. पांडित्याचा, पांडित्यदर्शक, पांडित्यगर्भित, पांडित्यप्रचुर.

2—of persons, v. PEDANT. पांडित्य मिरवणारा, विद्येचा डौली, पांडित्यदर्शी, विद्यादांभिक.

PEDANTICALLY, *adv.* v. A. पांडित्य दाखवून-करून, विद्येचा आव-&c. घालून, विद्या मिरवून.

To PEDANTIZE, *v. n. play the pedant.* पांडित्य *n.* करणें-दाखवणें, विद्या *f.* मिरवणें, विद्येचें देव्हारें *n.* माजवणें.

PEDANTRY, *n. vain show of learning.* पांडित्य *n.* विद्येचा डौल *m.*-आव *m.*-खटाटोप *m.* विद्येचें आडंबर *n.*-देव्हारें *n.*-पोम *n.*-स्तोम *n.* गागाभट्टी *f.*

To PEDDLE. See To PIDDLE.

PEDESTAL, *n.*—of a pillar, &c. खांबाचा पाय *m.*-बुंधा *m.*-बुंधारा *m.* स्तंभपद *n.*

2 See STAND. [दसंबंधी-विषयक.

PEDESTRIAL, *a. pertaining to the foot.* पायाचा, चरणाचा, पा-

PEDESTRIAN, PEDESTRIOUS, *a. going on foot.* पायीं-पायानें चालणारा, चरणचालीचा, पादचालीचा, पादचारी, पादगामी.

2 *performed on foot.* चरणचालीचा, पादचालीचा, पायउतारा करायाचा-केलेला.

PEDESTRIAN, *n.* v. A. पायीं चालणारा, पादगामी, पादचारी, पदाति.

An able p. पायांचा *or* पायींचा पारवा *m.*

PEDESTRIANISM, *n. walking.* पायीं चालणें *n.* चरणचाल *f.* पादचाल *f.*

PEDICLE, *n. foot-stalk.* देंठ *m.* वृंत *n.* पुष्पबंधन *n.* प्रसवबंधन *n.*

A compound p. मंजरी *f.* तुरंबी *or* तुरमी *f.*

PEDICULAR. See LOUSY.

PEDIGREE, *n. lineage.* वंशावळ *or* ळी *f.* वंशावलि *f.* वंशपरंपरा *f.*

2 *genealogical list or account.* वंशचरित्र*n.* वंशानुचरित*n.*

PEDILUVIUM, PEDILUVY, *n. bathing the feet.* पाय धुणें*n.* पादक्षालन*n.* पादप्रक्षालन*n.*

PEDLER, *n. travelling petty merchant.* फेरीवाला, फेरेकरी, फिरता फडकरी *or* फड्या, फिरस्ता, बिछाइती, हळ्या.

PEDLERY, *n. business of a pedler.* फिरस्तेपणा*m.* हळी *f.* फेरीवाल्याचा धंदा*m.*

2 *articles of a pedler.* फेरीवाल्याचा माल*m.*-सामान*n.*-जिन्नस *m.* बिछाइतीमाल*m.*-जिन्नस*m.*

PEDOBAPTISM, *n. baptism of children.* लहानमुलांस बाप्तिस्मादेणें.

PEDOMETER, *n. instrument to measure paces.* पाउलें मोजण्याचें यंत्र*n.* पादन्यासमापकयंत्र*n.*

PEDUNCLE, *n.* मंजिरी *f.*

To PEEL, *v. a. deprive of skin, bark, rind, &c.* सोलणें, निसणें, छिलणें, साल *f. n.*-सालपट*n.*-&c. काढणें. [त्वचा *f.*

PEEL, *n. skin, rind, &c.* साल *f. n.* सालपट*n.* सालपंड*n.* छिलटा*m.*

2 *baker's instrument for turning bread.* उलथणें*n.* उचटणें *n.* उचकटणें*n.* हातखोरणें*n.* कलथा*m.*

PEELED, *p.* v. V. सोललेला, साल काढलेला, &c. सोलींव, निस्तुष, निस्तुषित, निस्त्वक्.

PEELING, *n.* v. V.—*act.* सोलणें*n.* निसणें*n.* &c. सोलणी *f.*

I *a peeling off, a detached crust, &c.* खपला*m.* खपली *f.* पापुद्रा *or* पापोद्रा*m.* पापोडा *or* पापोटा*m.* पातोडा*m.* पोपडा*m.* पदडा*m.* चकदळ*n.* खरपुडी *f.* कपचा*m.* कपची *f.* कळपा*m.* सालडें*n.* सालपट*n.* साल *f. n.*—esp. from a sore, &c. भोत*m.* कोशेटा *m.* कोशेटी *f.* फोपेटा*m.* कवंद *f.*

To PEEP, *v. n. come in sight, appear.* दिसून येणें, दिसणें, दृष्टीस-&c. पडणें, दृष्टीस-नजरेस-&c. येणें, दिसूंलागणें, बाहेर पडणें.

2 *look slily, curiously, &c.* चोरून-चोरदृष्टीनें-चोरमळ्या-डोकावून-टोकावून-सरसावून-&c. पाहणें-बघणें.

To p. over. टोकावणें *or* टोकणें.

PEEP, PEEPING, *n.* v. V.—*act.* दिसून येणें*n.* दिसणें*n.* &c.

P. of day. पहानपट *f.* पांचपट *f.*

2 चोरून पाहणें*n.* &c. चोरपाहणी *f.* [झरोका*m.*

PEEP-HOLE, PEEPING-HOLE, *n.* चोरखिडकी *f.* खिडकी *f.* जंगी *f.*

PEEPER, *n.* PEEPING, *p. a.* v. V. 1. दिसून येणारा, दिसणारा.

2 चोरून पाहणारा, चोरदृष्टीनें पाहणारा, &c.

PEER, *n. one of the same rank, equal.* बरोबरीचा-जोडीचा-तोडीचा-तोलाचा-&c. मनुष्य*m.* समपदस्थ.

2 See FELLOW. 3 See NOBLEMAN.

To PEER, *v. n. look narrowly, &c.* टोंकावणें *or* टोंकणें, टोंकावून पाहणें, बारीक दृष्टीनें पाहणें, टेहळणें *or* टेहेळणें, टेहेळूनपाहणें, हेरणें, हेरून पाहणें, निहाळून पाहणें.

2 *appear.* See To PEEP. [&c.पदवी *f.*

PEERAGE, *n. rank of a peer.* अमिराची-उमरावाची-बडेलोकांची-

2 *body of nobles.* अमिरांची-अमीरलोकांची-&c. मंडळी *f.* बडेलोक*m. pl.* अमीरलोक*m. pl.*

PEERER, *n.* PEERING, *p. a.* v. V. 1. टोंकावून पाहणारा, टेहेळून पाहणारा, &c. हेऱ्या, टेहळ्या, बानरदृष्टि.

PEERESS, *n. noble lady.* बडेलोकांच्या पदवीची स्त्री *f.*

PEERING, *n.* v. V. 1.—*act.* टोंकावणें*n.* टेहेळणें*n.* &c. टेहळणी *f.* टेहळी *f.* [र्वोत्तम, सर्वोत्कृष्ट.

PEERLESS, *a. without an equal.* अनुपम, अद्वितीय, अप्रतिम, स-

PEEVISH, *a. petulant, fretful.* खिसखिशा, किरकिऱ्या, पिरपिरा *or* ऱ्या, रिपरिप्या, किरकिरीत,कटकट्या, जितखोर, जिकिरी, जिकिरखोर, चिडखोर, चिरडखोर, चिरड्या, चिडचिड्या, चिरडीखोर, तिडतिडा *or* तिडतिड्या, तिडका, टुरटुऱ्या, कैदी, सैंन्या, काविरडा, तुसडा.

P. contention or discussion. खिसखीस *f.* [रून.

PEEVISHLY, *adv.* v. A. खिसखीस-किरकीर-पिरपीर-रिपरीप-&c. क-

PEEVISHNESS, *n.* v. A. खिसखिशेपणा *m.* पिरपिरेपणा *m.* कटकटेपणा *m.*चिरडेपणा*m.* काविरडेपणा*m.* &c. खिसखीस *f.* जिकीर *f.* किरकीर *f.* पिरपीर *f.* रिपरीप *f.* टुरटूर *f.*

Peg, *n. wooden nail, &c.* मेख *f.* खुंटा *m. dim.* खुंटी *f.* कील *m.*
Stretching out and tying to four pegs and beating. चौखुंटीमार *m.* [उतरणें.
To take down a p. To take a p. lower, v. To **Humble**.
2 (*of an instrument,*) *pin, &c.* खुंटी *f.* खीळ *f.* कील *m.*
To **Peg**, *v. a.* मेख *f.*-खुंटा *m.*-खुंटी *f.* मारणें-मारून बांधणें-&c.
Pelf, *n. money*, v. **Riches**. पैका *m.* पैसा *m.*
2 *illicit gains.* हरामाचा पैसा *m.* लुचपत *f.* शिकार *f.* लूट *f.*
Pelican, *n.* पाणकोळी *m.* [चिमखडा *m.*
Pellet, *n. small ball.* गोळी *f.* गोटी *f.* गुटिका *f. pop.* गुटका *m.*
Pellet-bow, *n.* धनुकली *or* धनकुली *f.* धनकुंची *f.* गलूल *or* गलोल *f.* गलोली *f.*
Pellet or stone for a p. गलूलखडा *m.* चिमखडा *m.*
Place for the pellet of a p. फडें *n.*
Pellicle, *n. thin skin or film.* तवंग *m.* कोशेरा *m.* कोशेटा *m.* कोशेटी *f.* करा *f.* सायरा *m.* तव *m. f.*
That has a film or p. तवंगट.
Pellitory, *n. anthemis pyrethum.* अक्कलकरा *or* कारा *or* काढ *or* काढा *or* काला *or* खार *m.*
Pellmell, *adv. confusedly, tumultuously.* गोंधळ करून, गर्दी करून, एकमेकावर पडून, घोटाळाहोऊन, गोंधळानें, घोळंकारानें, घोळक्यानें, गर्दीनें.
Pellucid, *a. clear, transparent.* स्वच्छ, निर्मल *or* ळ, प्रांजल *or* ळ, नितळ, दृष्ट्यरोधक,अदृष्टिरोधक, किरणभेद्य.
Pellucidity, **Pellucidness**, *n.* v. A. स्वच्छपणा *m.* निर्मळपणा*m.*&c. स्वच्छता, निर्मल्य*n.*दृष्ट्यरोधकता*f.*किरणभेद्यता*f.*&c.
Pelt, *n. skin*, v. **Hide**. चामडें *n.* चरसा *m.*
2 *thump*, v. **Blow**. टोला *m.* तडाका *or* खा *m.* प्रहार *m.*
To **Pelt**, *v. a. strike with something thrown.* सडकणें, सडकावणें, मारणें, फेंकून मारणें (with the name of the thing thrown prefixed, as धोंडे फेंकून मारणें to pelt with stones), मार *m.*-भडिमार *m.*-&c. करणें(with a noun prefixed, as आंब्याचामार *or* आंबेमार *m.* करणें to pelt with mangoes).
To **Pelt**, *v. n. rain hard, rattle down.* सडसडणें, सडसडून-झडझडून येणें-पडणें, सडसड-सडसडां-&c. पाऊस *m.* पडणें.
Pelt-monger, *n.* चामडेविक्या, पशुचर्मविक्रयी.
Pelter *n.* **Pelting**, *p.a.* v. V. A. सडकणारा, मारणारा, फेंकून मारणारा, मार-भडिमार करणारा.
v. V. N. सडसडणारा, सडसडून पडणारा, &c. सडसडीत, झडझडीत, सडाक्याचा, झडाक्याचा, तडाक्याचा, मुसळधार.
Pelting, *n.* v. V. A.—*act.* सडकणें *n.* मारणें *n.* &c. मार *m.* मारा *m.* भडिमार *m.*
v.V. N. सडसडणें *n.*&c. सडाका *m.* तडाका *or* खा*m.* फटकारा*m.*
Peltingly, *adv.* v. V. N. सडसड, सडसडां, सडासड, सडाडां.
Pelvic *a.* बस्तिप्रदेशाचा, बस्तिप्रदेशसंबंधी.
Pelvis, *n.*—in anatomy. खालचें पोट *n.* ओंटी *f.* बस्ति प्रदेश *m.*
Pen, *n.*—for writing. लेखनी *pop.* लेखणी *f.* लेखण *f.* कलम *n.*
Errors of the p. कलम कुचराई *f.*
2 *coop, fold, &c.* कोंडवाडा*m.* कोंडवाड *f.* कोंडी *f.* कोंडण *f.* माची *f.* वाडा *m.* (in comp. as मेंढवाडा sheep pen).
P. or fold for calves. खुडी *f.*
To **Pen**, *v. a. shut in a pen.* कोंडणें, कोंडणी *f.* करणें *g. of o.* कोंडवाड्यांत-कोंडींत-&c. घालणें.

2 *compose and commit to paper.* लिहणें, लिहून ठेवणें, कल्मीं करणें.
Penal, *a.relating, &c. to punishment.* दंडाविषयींचा, दंडप्रकरणाचा, पारपत्याविषयींचा, दंडसंबंधी-विषयक, ताडनसंबंधी-विषयक.
2 *incurring punishment.* दंडासयोग्य, दंड्य, दंडनीय, दंडार्ह.
Penalty, *n. punishment annexed to a crime.* दंड *m.* शासन *n.* शिक्षा *f.*
Pecuniary p.v. **Fine**. द्रव्यदंड *m.* गुन्हेगारी *f.* [अटक *f.*
2 *forfeit attached to an engagement.* अड *f.* अट *f.* अडनी *f.*
Penance, *n. pain or suffering imposed for sin.* प्रायश्चित्त *n.* तपस्या *f.* तपश्चर्या *f.* तप *n.*
Bodily p. देहदंडन *n.* देहदंड *m.*
General p. *p. for sins in the gross.* सर्वप्रायश्चित्त *n.*
Mortal or extreme p. देहांतप्रायश्चित्त *n.*
Penates,*n. household gods.* आराध्यदेवता *f.pl.* आराध्यदैवतें *n.pl.* आराध्यें *n.pl.*
Worship of the p. देवकार्य *n.*
Penchant, *n. liking for.* चट *f.* चटक *f.* अफेक *m.*
Pencil, *n. brush of a painter.* कलम *n.* लेखणी *f.*बोंथ *f.*बोंथी *f.*
2 *lead-pen.* शिशाची लेखणी *f.* शिशाची पेनसिल *f.* from the English.
3—for writing on a slate. दगडाची लेखणी *f.* दगडाची-दगडी पेनसिल *f.* from the English.
4 (of sun rays) अंशुजाल *n.* किरणजाल *n.* किरणसमूह *m.*
Pendant, *n. bob; hanging ornament.* झुमका *m.* झुबका *m.* तोंगल *n.* लोळी *f.* लोलक *m.* भोंकर *n.* झिलमिली *f.*
An ear ring, (of females) having a p. भोंकर बाळी *f.* झुबकबाळी *or* झुबकेबाळी *f.* तोंगलबाळी.
2 See **Flag**.
Pendent, *a. hanging.* लोंबणारा, लोंबकळणारा, लोंबता, लटकता, लोंबकळता, लोंबकळलेला, लटकलेला, लंब, लंबमान, अवलंबित, आलंबित, आलंबी, लंबित.
Pending, *a. yet undecided.* लटकलेला, भिजत-लोंबत-तरंगत-&c. पडलेला, चालू, चालता, खरकटा, अनिर्धारित, अजातनिर्धार. अजातनिश्चय, अजातनिर्णय.
Pendulous, *a. hanging*, v.**Pendent**. लोंबता, लटकता, लोंबकळता, लंब, लंबमान. [लंबत्व *n.*
Pendulousness, **Pendulosity**, *n.* v. A. लोंबतेपणा *m.*&c.
Pendulum, **Pendule**, *n.*—of a clock, &c.लोळा*m.dim.* लोळी*f.*
Penetrability, *n.* v. A. भेद्यता *f.* वेध्यता *f.* प्रवेश्यता *f.*&c.
Penetrable, *a.* v. V. A. 1. भेदाया-बेधाया-&c. चा-जोगता-जोगा-&c.भेद्य, भेदनीय, वेध्य, वेधनीय, भेदार्ह, भेदयोग्य भेदशक्य, प्रवेशनीय, प्रवेश्य.
Penetrancy, **Penetrativeness**, *n.* v. A. 1. भेदनशक्ति *f.* वेधनशक्ति *f.* भेदकत्व *n.* वेधकत्व *n.*
2 वेधकत्व *n.* विषयवेधकत्व *n.* मार्मिकत्व *n.* कुशाग्रमति *f.* कुशाग्रबुद्धि *f.* तीक्ष्णबुद्धि *f.* प्रखरबुद्धि *f.*
Penetrant, **Penetrative**, *a.* **Penetrating**, *p. a.* v. V. A. 1. भेदणारा, वेधणारा, भेद करणारा, &c. वेधक, भेदक, भेदकर्त्ता-कारी-&c.
2 अर्थभेदकरणारा, &c. वेधक, विषयवेधक, मार्मिक, कुशाग्रमति, कुशाग्रबुद्धि, तीक्ष्णबुद्धि, तीक्ष्णमति, प्रखरबुद्धि, दीर्घदृष्टि.
To **Penetrate**, *v.a. enter, pierce,&c.* भेदणें,वेधणें,बिंधणें, भेद*m.*

-बेध *m.*-&c. करणें *g. of o.* प्रवेश *m.* करणें.

2 *reach the meaning*, v. To UNDERSTAND. समजणें, अर्थभेद *m.*-मर्मभेद *m.* करणें *g. of o.* गति *f.*-अर्थगति *f.*-बोध *m.* -अर्थबोध *m.* होणें *in. con. with g. of o.*

3 (the mind). v. To AFFECT भरून आणणें.

To be penetrated. मन *n.* भरून जाणें *g. of s.*

To PENETRATE, *v. n. enter, make way.* शिरणें, शिरकणें, प्रवेशणें, रिघणें, रुतणें, रुपणें, प्रवेश *m.*-रिघाव *m.*-&c. होणें *g. of s.*

To cause to p. शिरकविणें *or* शिरकाविणें.

2 fig. अर्थभेद *m.*-मर्मभेद *m.*-&c. होणें.

PENETRATION, *n.* v. V. A.1.—*act.* भेदणें *n.* वेधणें*n.* &c. भेद *m.* वेध *m.* भेदन *n.* वेधन *n.*

2 अर्थभेद *m.* मर्मभेद *m.* अर्थबोध *m.*

I. *acuteness, shrewdness, &c.* v. SHARPNESS. कुशाग्रमति *f.* कुशाग्रबुद्धि *f.* तीक्ष्णबुद्धि *f.* सूक्ष्मबुद्धि *f.*

PENINSULA, *n. portion of land nearly surrounded by water.* द्वीपकल्प *m.*

PENINSULAR, *a. pertaining, &c. to a peninsula.* द्वीपकल्पाचा, द्वीपकल्पसंबंधी-विषयक, द्वीपकल्पस्थ, प्रायोजलवेष्टित.

PENITENCE, PENITENCY, *n.* v. A. *and* REPENTANCE. पश्चात्ताप *m.* अनुताप *m.* दुष्कृतखेद *m.* अनुतापबुद्धि *f.* पश्चात्तापबुद्धि *f.*

PENITENT, *a.* v. REPENTANT. पश्चात्तापी, अनुतापी, पश्चात्तापयुक्त, पश्चात्तापबुद्धि, अनुतापबुद्धि.

PENITENT, *n.* See the ADJECTIVE.

PENITENTIAL, *a. proceeding from or expressing penitence.* पश्चात्तापाचा, अनुतापाचा, अनुतापबुद्धीचा, पश्चात्तापबुद्धीचा, पश्चात्ताप-अनुताप सूचक-बोधक-दर्शक, अनुतापजनित, पश्चात्तापजनित.

PENITENTIARY, *n. place of penance, house of correction.* प्रायश्चित्तगृह *n.* प्रायश्चित्तशाला *f.* प्रायश्चित्तमठ *m.* कारागार *n.* कारागृह *n.* [यक-कथक-वक्ता-&c.

2 *prescriber of penance.* प्रायश्चित्त सांगणारा, प्रायश्चित्तविधा-

3 See PENITENT.

PENITENTLY, *adv.* v. A. पश्चात्ताप करून-होऊन, पश्चात्तापपूर्वक, दुष्कृतखेदपूर्वक, &c. पश्चात्तापबुद्धीनें, अनुतापबुद्धीनें.

PENKNIFE, *n.* चाकू *m.*

PENMAN, *n. a good or skilful writer.* कलमसूत्रा, कलमबहाद्दर, जलद कलमी, लेखणीचापुरा-बहाद्दर-धड.

2 See AUTHOR. [लेखकी *f.*

PENMANSHIP, *n. art of writing.* लिहिण्याचें कसब *n.* लिहणें *n.*

2 *fine writing.* चांगलें लिहणें *n.* कलमसफाई *f.* मोत्यांची ओळ *f.* मुक्ताफल *n.*

PENNANT, *n.* v. FLAG. पताक *f.* पताका *f.* फरारा *m.*

PENNATED, *a. winged.* पक्षाचा, सपक्ष, पक्षयुक्त-विशिष्ट.

PENNILESS, *a.* v. POOR. निकवड्या, निर्धन, निर्धातुक, अकांचन, निःकांचन, रंक, खलक.

P. wretch. रवळनाथाचें कूळ *n.*

PENNON, *n. pennant.* पताक *f.* पताका *f.* फरारा *m.*

PENNY, *n.* The words that most nearly express the value of a penny are, टका *or* टक्का *m.* ढब्बू *m.* पाऊण अणा *m.*

Penny in the pound. रुंडीस नवटकें *n.*

The last p. निर्वाणीचा पैसा *m.*

Steal a penny steal a pound. काडीचोर तो पाडीचोर.

2 v. MONEY. पैका *m.* टका *or* टक्का *m.*

PENNY-WISE, *a. niggardly prudent.* ल्हान गोष्टीमध्यें कसर करणारा, क्षुद्रव्ययशंकी.

P. wise and pound foolish. इळा मोडून खिळा करणारा.

PENSILE, *a. hanging*, v. PENDENT. लोंबणारा, &c. लोंबता, लटकता, लोंबकळता, लंब, लंबमान.

PENSION, *n. allowance made without requirement of service.* बैठा पगार*m.* बैठीरोटी *f.* बैठेंवेतन*n.* बैठीनेमणूक *f.* The English word is commonly used under the form of पेनसन *or* पेनसील *n.*

To PENSION, *v. a. give a pension to.* बैठापगार *m.*-बैठी नेमणूक *f.*-&c. देणें-करून देणें.

PENSIONER, *n. receiver of a pension.* बैठापगार-&c. पावणारा-भोगणारा-खाणारा-&c. बैठापगारी, पेनसनवाला, पेनसनदार.

PENSIVE, *a. sorrowfully thoughtful*,—of persons. सचिंत, चिंताक्रांत, चिंतातुर, सखेदचिंतक, सखेदध्यानस्थ, दिलगीर, उदास.

2—of poetry, &c. चिंतासूचक-बोधक. [र्वक.

PENSIVELY, *adv.* v. A. दिलगीर होऊन, उदास होऊन,सखेदचिंतापू-

PENSIVENESS, *n.* v. A. सखेदचिंता *f.* खेदमिश्रितचिंता *f.* सखेदध्यान *n.* दिलगिरी *f.* उदासपणा *m.*

PENT, *p.* v. V. 1. कोंडलेला.

PENTACHORD, *n. musical instrument with five strings.* पांचतारांचें वाद्य *n.* पंचतारा वाद्य *n.*

PENTAEDROUS, *a. having five sides.* पंचपैलू, पंचभुज.

PENTAGON, *n. figure of five sides and angles.* पंचकोण*m.*पंचास्र*n.*

PENTAGONAL, *a.*v. N. पांचकोणांचा,पंचकोण, पंचकोणाकृति,पंचास्र.

PENTANGULAR, *a. having five angles.* पंचकोण.

PENTAPETALOUS, *a. having five flower leaves.* पंचदल.

PENT HOUSE, *n. shed standing aslope from a building.* पडवी *f.* मोहटी *f.* [पसन्न.

PENULTIMATE, *a. last but one.* शेवटच्या जवळचा, उपांत्य, अंत्यो-

PENUMBRA, *n. partial shade.* अपूर्णछाया *f.*

PENURIOUS, *a. niggardly, close*, v. MISERLY. कृपण, चेंगट, किरटा, हाताचा जड, व्ययशत्रु, व्ययशंकित, अव्ययबुद्धि,कार्पण्यबुद्धि.

PENURIOUSLY, *adv.* v. A. कृपणपणानें, चेंगटपणानें, कृपणभावानें, &c. कार्पण्यपूर्वक.

PENURIOUSNESS, *n.* v. A. कृपणपण *n.* किरटेपण *n.* चेंगटपण *n.* बारीकदृष्टि *f.* बारीकनजर *f.* कृपणभाव *m.* कार्पण्य *n.* व्ययद्वेष *m.* कार्पण्यबुद्धि *f.* अव्ययबुद्धि *f.*

PENURY, *n. indigence*, v. POVERTY. अनुपपत्ति *pop.* अनुपत *f.* कंगाली *f.* दारिद्र्य *n.* दरिद्रता *f.*

PEON, *n. belted attendant.* चपरासी, पट्टेवाला, पट्टेकरी, पाइक.

2 See PAWN.

PEOPLE, *n. nation.* लोक *m.* खूम *n.* जाति *f.* विशेषदेशजनता *f.*

2 *the populace, the vulgar, the common people.* लोक *m. pl.* कुणबीमाळी *m. pl.* तेलीतांबोळी *m. pl.* साळी कोष्टी *m. pl.* धनगर कुळवाडी *m. pl.*—And with implication of *lowness and vileness*, as expressed by such words as *rabble, riffraff, tag rag and bobtail, canaille, the mob, mobility, the crowd, herd, &c.* महारपोर *m. n.* लुर्के *n.* जंगमढवळें *n.* आडजात *f.* आडाणजात *f.* गवाळलोक *m. pl.* लोकांचा गाळ *m.* लोकांचें गदळ *n.* लोकांची खरवड *f.* निपटारा *m.* कतवार *n.* बाजारबुणगें *n.* ऐगूबैगू *m. pl.* गोमाजीसोमाजी *m. pl.*

3 *community, commonalty, the general body.* लोक *m. pl.* पांढर *f.* शाई *f.* रयासत *f.* रयताबा *m.* प्रजा *f.* खलकत *f.* जन *m.n.* अठरापगड जात *f.*

Amongst the p. लोकांतीं.

By or through the p. लोकालोकीं.

Conforming to the p. लौकिकानुसरण *n.*

Courting the p. लोकरंजन *n.* जनरंजन *n.* लोकसंपादणी *f.*

Down through the p. लोकालोकीं.

Regard or deference to, fear or shame of, the p. जनलज्जा *f.* लोकलज्जा *f.* लोकलाज *f.* लोकेषणा *f.*

The whole p. आबालवृद्ध, आपामर, लहानथोर.

Popular procedure or practice, popular usage or course. लोकरीति *f.* जनरीति *f.* शाईशिरस्ता *m.* लोकशिरस्ता*m.* जनशिरस्ता *m.* लोकाचार *m.* जनाचार *m.* जनप्रवाह *m.* लोकप्रवाह *m.* लोकव्यवहार *m.* जनव्यवहार *m.* लोकनीति *f.*

Popular report or talk. जनप्रवाद *m.* लोकप्रवाद *m.* जनश्रुति *f.* जनरव *m.* जनवाद *m.* जनवार्त्ता *f.* जनवदंती *f.* लोकवाद *m.* लोकवार्त्ता *f.* प्रवाद *m.* लोकचर्चा *f.*

Vox populi vox dei. पांचांचे मुखीं परमेश्वर, जनीं जनार्दन.

4 *folks, persons, men.* लोक *m. or m. pl.* माणसें *n. pl.* जन *m. n.* जग*n.* जगती *f.* आलम *f.* आलमदुन्या *f.* जनलोक *m. pl.*

Certain p. *some.* बाजेलोक.

5 *servants, followers.* माणसें *n. pl.* लोक *m. pl.* चाकरलोक *m. pl.* चाकरमाणसें *n.pl.* गडीमाणसें *n. pl.* सेवकजन *m.* सेवकवर्ग*m.*

6 *particular class or body.* लोक *m.* जन*m.*शाई *f.* (in comp. with the designating noun prefixed, as ब्राह्मणलोक, शूद्रलोक, सेवक जन, ब्राह्मणशाई, &c.).

To PEOPLE, *v. a. stock with inhabitants.* वसवणें, वसात *or* वसाहत *f.* करणें, दिवा *m.* लावणें, दिवेलावणी *f.* करणें, वसता-वसाहतीचा-जनविशिष्ट-सजन-&c. करणें.

Lease granted to settlers in a desert place. दिवेलावणीचा कौल *m.*

To be peopled. वसणें.

PEOPLED, *p.* v. V. वसवलेला, &c.

1 *inhabited,* वसता, वसाहतीचा, जनविशिष्ट, सजन.

Well-p. *populous.* आबाद, वासित, आबादान.

PEPPER, *n.*—black p. plant. मिरी *f.* मिरवेल *f.*—the fruit. मिरीं *n. pl.* मिरें *n. pl.* काळीं मिरें *n. pl.* मरीच *n.*—Chili p. Red p. plant and fruit, मिरची *f.* लालमिरची *f.* (Some kinds are वेलमिरची, लवंगी मिरची, भोपळी मिरची, मोगली मिरची), मिरसंग *or* शेंग *f.*—Long p.—plant and fruit, पिंपळी*f.* कणा *f.*

Black p. powdered. मिरपूड *or* मिरपूट *f.* मिरकूट *n.*

Black p. pounded up with other spices. तिखट *n.*

Bruised peppers. कूट *n.*

Cluster of pepper berries. मिरगोंड *n.*

Decoction of black p. मिरकाढा *m.* मिरवणी *n.*

Red p. pounded. भुरका *m.*

To PEPPER, *v. a. sprinkle with pepper.* मिरें *n. pl.*-मिरीं *n. pl.*-&c. घालणें-टाकणें.

2 *overwhelm with shot, blows, &c.* भडिमार *m.*-वर्षाव *m.* करणें, सडकणें, झोडणें, झोड *f.* लावणें.

PEPPER-BOX, *n.* मिऱ्यांचें पात्रें *n.* मरीचपात्र *n.*

PEPPER-CORN, *n.* मिरूं *n.* मिरें *n.* मिऱ्यें *n.*

A p. covered over with flour and fried. मिरगोंड*n.* मिरयोंड *n.* मिरघाटा *m.*

Cluster of pepper corns. गोंड *n.*

PEPPERMINT, *n.*—the plant. पुदिना*m.* पुदाणा*m.*—the essence. पुदिन्याचा अर्क *m.*

PEPPERY, See PASSIONATE.

PEPTIC, *a, promoting digestion.* पाचक, अग्निवर्धक, अग्निप्रद, अग्निदीपक, दीपक.

PER, *prep. by, to, &c.*—severally. दर, प्रति, गणीक (as खिडकी गणीक, खेपे गणीक, झाडागणीक, घरागणीक).

PER ANNUM, *by the year.* दरवर्षास, प्रतिवर्षास.

PER CENT, *by the hundred.* दरशेंकडा, शेंकडा.

PER CENTAGE, *n. allowance, &c. on a hundred.* शेंकड्यास-शेंकड्यावर दस्तुरी *f.*-दलाली *f.*-&c.

The sense of this word is expressed by उत्तर *beyond, over,* taken up into composition with a numeral prefix:—as, percentage of one एकोतरा*m.*—of two दोहोतरा, and तिहोतरा, चहोतरा, पंचोतरा, &c. &c. &c. These terms, however, though sometimes they express the rate of *taxing* or of *surplusage in sales,* respect *especially* the per centage of *interest.*

PERADVENTURE, *adv. perhaps.* कदाचित् *pop.* कदाचित, कोण जाणे, न जाणे, कायजाणू, कोणास ठाऊक, पक्षीं, कथंचित्.

To PERAMBULATE, *v.a. walk through or over.*फिरणें,हद्दीहद्दीनें-सिमेसिमेनें-&c. फिरणें-जाणें, अहद्दतहद्द फिरणें-जाणें, फेरा*m.*-फेरी *f.*-गस्त *f.* घालणें, परिक्रमण*n.*-परिभ्रमण*n.*-&c. करणें.

PERAMBULATION, *n.* v. V.—*act.* फिरणें*n.* &c. गस्त *f.* फेरा*m.* फेरी *f.* परिक्रमण*n.* परिभ्रमण*n.* पर्यटन*n.*

P. of village bounds by the bárá balute. सीमांतपूजन*n.*

PERAMBULATOR, *n.* अंतर मोजण्याचें एक यंत्र आहे.

2 *carriage for a child propelled from behind.* मागून लोटण्याची मुलाचीगाडी *f.*

PERCEIVABLE, PERCEIVABLENESS. See PERCEPTIBLE, &c.

To PERCEIVE, *v. a. see, apprehend by a sense or bodily organ.* पाहणें, लक्षिणें, इंद्रियानें घेणें-जाणणें-समजणें, दिसणें *in. con.* वाटणें *in. con.* प्रत्यक्ष *n.*-इंद्रियग्रह*m.*-अनुभव *m.*-बोध*m.*-समज *m.*-ज्ञान*n.*-&c.होणें *g.of o. with in. con.* लक्ष्यांत-लक्षांत-&c. येणें *in. con.* इंद्रिय गोचर-गोचर-इंद्रियविषय-इंद्रियारूढ-&c. करणें *or, with in. con.* होणें.As the use of the verb which respects a particular sense, is more common in Maráthi the student may refer to the verbs, To SEE, To HEAR, To SMELL, &c.

2 *know, be conscious of.* जाणणें, समजणें, समज*m.*-ज्ञान *n.*-बोध*m.*-&c. होणें *g. of o. with in. con.* ठाऊक-&c. होणें-पडणें, समजणें *in. con.* ओळखणें.

PERCEIVED, *p.* v. V. 1. पाहिलेला, लक्षांत आलेला, इंद्रियानें घेतलेला, इंद्रियगोचर झालेला, &c. इंद्रियगोचर, गोचर (in comp. as कर्णगोचर, दृष्टिगोचर, &c.), इंद्रियारूढ, लक्षित.

2 जाणलेला, ठाऊक पडलेला, &c.

PERCEIVER, *n.* PERCEIVING, *p. a.* v. V. 1. पाहणारा, लक्षिणारा, इंद्रियानें घेणारा, &c. लक्षक, प्रत्यक्षी, बोद्धा, विषयग्राहक, विषयग्रहणकर्त्ता.

PERCEPTIBILITY, *n.* v. A. 1. इंद्रियानें समजायाजोगेपणा*m.* इंद्रियगोचरता *f.* गोचरता *f.* इंद्रियगम्यता *f.* वेद्यता *f.* वेदनीयता *f.*

PERCEPTIBLE, *a.* v. V. 1. पहायाजोगा-&c. इंद्रियानें घ्याया-समजाया-&c. जोगा-जोगता-&c. इंद्रियगोचर, गोचर (in comp. as कर्णगोचर, दृष्टिगोचर, &c.), इंद्रियविषय, विषय (in comp. दृष्टिविषय, &c.), गम्य (in comp. as इंद्रियगम्य, दृष्टिगम्य, &c.), ऐंद्रियक, प्रत्यक्ष, वेद्य, वेदनीय.

PERCEPTIBLY, *adv.* पहायाजोगा-&c. *decl.* इंद्रियानें समजायाजोगा-सारखा-&c. *decl.* इंद्रियग्रह व्हाया जोगा *decl.* समजेसा-कळेसा-दिसेसा-&c. *decl.*

PERCEPTION, *n.* v. V. 1.—*act.* पाहणें *n.* इंद्रियानें घेणें-समजणें-&c. &c. ग्रह *m.* इंद्रियग्रह *m.* विषयग्रह *m.* विषयग्रहण *n.* विषयीकरण *n.* प्रत्यक्ष *n.* बोध *m.* भास*m.* वेदन *n.*

2—*act.* समज *m.* ज्ञान *n.* बोध *m.*

I. *faculty or power of perceiving.* जाणीव *f.* चैतन्य *n.* विषयग्रहणशक्ति *f.* विषयग्राहकत्व *n.* विषयवेदनशक्ति *f.* इंद्रिय *n.* इंद्रियग्रहणक्षमता *f.*

II. *idea.* See NOTION.

PERCEPTIVE. See PERCIPIENT.

PERCH, *n. roost.* अड्डा *m.*

2 *measuring rod,* v. MEASURE. काठी *f.*

3 नदींतला एक मासा आहे.

To PERCH, *v. n. sit or roost.* बसणें, पांखरा सारखा बसणें.

To PERCH, *v. a. place or fix.* बसवणें.

PERCHANCE, *adv. peradventure,* v. PERHAPS. नकळे, नजाणे, कदाचित्, यदाकदाचित्, कथंचित्.

PERCIPIENCE, See PERCEPTION.

PERCIPIENT, *a. having the faculty of perception.* चेतन, सचेतन, विषयग्रहणशक्तिक, विषयग्रहणसमर्थ, विषयग्रहक्षम, विषयवेदनक्षम.

To PERCOLATE, *v. a.* v. To STRAIN. गाळणें, छानणें, शोधणें.

To PERCOLATE, *v. n. pass through small interstices.* गळणें, पाझरणें, स्त्रवणें.

PERCOLATION, *n.* v. V. A.—*act.* गाळणें *n.* गाळणी *f.*

v. V. N. पाझरणें *n.* गळणें *n.* पाझर *m.* गळणी *f.*

PERCUSSION, *n. striking of one body against another.* आपटणें *n.* आदळणें *n.* धडक *f.* प्रहार *m.* आघात *m.*

PERCUSSION CAP, *n.* बंदुकीच्या घोड्याची टोपी*f.* [त्यनाश*m.*

PERDITION, *n. ruin,* v. DESTRUCTION. नाश *m.* विनाश *m.* स-

The time of p. विनाशकाल *m.*

2 *loss of final happiness, eternal death.* अधोगति *f.* दुर्गति *f.* अधोगमन *n.* नरकवास *m.* नरकपात *m.* अधःपात *m.* अधःपतन *n.*

PERDU, *adv. in concealment.* दडीस, दडून, लिकून.

To PEREGRINATE, *v. n. travel about, live abroad.* परिभ्रमणें, प्रवास *m.*-देशाटन *n.*-परिभ्रमण *n.*-देशभ्रमण *n.*-&c. करणें, अटणें.

To p. in beggary or wretchedness. देशधडीस-देशोधडीस जाणें-लागणें-होणें.

PEREGRINATOR, *n.* PEREGRINATING, *p. a.* v. V. प्रवास करणारा, देशभ्रमण करणारा, देशाटन करणारा, प्रवासी, परदेशवासी, देशिक, विदेशस्थ.

PEREGRINATION, *n.* v. V.—*act.* परिभ्रमण *n.* देशभ्रमण *n.* देशाटन *n.* परदेश *m.* प्रवास *m.* विप्रवास *m.* विदेशवास *m.* मुशाफरी *f.*

PEREMPTORILY, *adv.* v. A. 1. निक्षून, निखालस, परिछिन्न, खरपूस, खसखसीत, धडधडीत, धड, हडसून खडसून *or* खडसून हडसून, झाडून, तुकडा तोडून.

PEREMPTORINESS, *n.* v. A. 1. खरपूसपणा *m.* निखालसपणा *m.* खसखसितपणा *m.* &c.

PEREMPTORY, *a. express, positive, flat,*—orders, measures, &c. खरपूस, निखालस, खसखसीत, स्पष्ट, साफ, चरचरीत, ठास, खरमरीत.

2 *positive, prompt, determined, impetuous, &c.*—person, &c. खरपूस, खणखणीत, खसखसीत, निखालस, खणक्या, खरमऱ्या, खरमरा, खरमरीत, जालीम, सक्तुवादी.

PERENNIAL, *a. lasting through the year.* बारमाही, बारमाहीचा, बारा महिन्यांचा, वर्षस्थायी, वर्षावधिक.

2 *unceasing,* v. CONTINUAL, PERPETUAL. नेहमीचा, नित्य, सदांचा, सतत, निरंतर.

3—in botany. दोनवर्षांहून अधिक वांचणारा-राहणारा.

PERENNIAL, *n. plant that lives more than two years.* दोनवर्षांहून अधिक वांचणारें झाड *n.* वर्षद्वयाधिकजीवी.

PERENNIALLY. See CONTINUALLY.

PERFECT, *a. consummate, complete, finished, not defective in any thing.* पुरता, पुरा, पूर्ण, संपूर्ण, परिपूर्ण, सिद्ध, तयार, सर्वसिद्ध, सांग, अन्यून, अव्यंग, अदोष, निर्दोष, सर्वोत्कृष्ट.

2 *fully informed, completely skilled, &c.* पुरा, पुरता, पूर्ण, सिद्ध, तयार, पक्का, निपुण, निष्णात, प्रवीण, पारंगत, संपन्न, अभिज्ञ, धुरीण, धुरंधर, दीक्षित, अभ्यासप्रवीण, परिपक्व, गाढा, तरबेत *or* द.

To PERFECT, *v. a. complete, finish.* पुरा-पुरता-पूर्ण-निष्पन्न-&c. करणें, पूर्ति *f.*-पूर्णता *f.*-&c. करणें *g. of o.* सिद्धीस-पूर्ततेस-पूर्णतेस-पूर्णदशेस-&c. आणणें.

2 *make proficient, adept, &c.* पुरा-पूर्ण-परिपूर्ण-प्रवीण-निपुण-तयार-सिद्ध-&c. करणें.

PERFECTIBLE, *a.* पूर्ण-संपूर्ण-निर्दोष-सर्वोत्कृष्ट-&c. करण्याजोगा-&c.

PERFECTION, PERFECTNESS, *n.* v. V. 1.—*state.* पुरेपणा*m.* &c. पूर्ति*f.* परिपूर्ति*f.* पूर्णता*f.* सिद्धि *f.* सर्वतिद्धि *f.*सर्वसिद्धता *f.* संसिद्धि *f.* सिद्धावस्था *f.* पूर्णदशा *f.* पूर्णावस्था*f.* सांगता*f.* अन्यूनता*f.* अन्यूनावस्था *f.* विपाक *m.* कमाल *n.*

2—*state.* तयारी *f.* सिद्धि *f.* सिद्धता *f.* प्रवीणता *f.* परिपक्वता *f.* नैपुण्य *n.*

I. *highest pitch of excellence.* सर्वोत्तमता *f.* सर्वोत्कृष्टता *f.* सर्वोत्कर्ष्य *n.* सर्वगुणोत्कर्ष *m.* सत्वपूर्णता *f.* सर्वसंपन्नता *f.*

II. *a perfection, an excellency, grace, &c.* गुण *m.* सद्गुण*m.*

PERFECTLY, *adv.* v. A. 1. *and* WHOLLY. पुरता, पुरा, &c. *all decl.* पुरतेपणीं, पुरेपणीं.

PERFIDIOUS, *a. treacherous,* v. FALSE. खोटा, खोटारा, खोटसाळ, बेइमान, बेइमानाचा, विश्वासघाताचा, विश्वासघातक, विश्वासघातकी, निमकहराम, कुजका, कुडा, कूड, कृत्रिमी.

PERFIDIOUSLY, *adv.* v. A. खोटाइनें, बेइमानानें, लबाडीनें, निमकहरामीनें, विश्वासघातानें, कृत्रिमभावानें, &c. विश्वासघात करून, विश्वासघातपूर्वक.

PERFIDIOUSNESS, *n.* v. A. खोटेपणा *m.* &c. खोटाई *f.* बेइमानी *f.* बेइमान *n.* निमकहरामी *f.* लबाडी *f.* फिसरत *f.* कपटभाव *m.* कृत्रिमभाव *m.* विश्वासघातबुद्धि *f.*

PERFIDY, *n. treachery, breach of faith.* विश्वासघात *m.* दगा *m.*

लबाडी *f.* निमकहरामी *f.* कृत्रिम *n.* कापट्य *n.* कैतव *n.*

To PERFORATE, *v. a. bore through*, v. To PIERCE. वेधणें, विंधणें, भोंकणें, भोंक *n.*-वेध *m.*-रंध्र *n.*-छिद्र *n.*-&c. पाडणें-करणें, वेधन *n.*-&c. करणें.

PERFORATED, *p.* v. V. वेधलेला, भोंक पाडलेला, &c. वेधित, विद्ध, छिद्रित, रंध्रित.

PERFORATOR, *n.* PERFORATING, *p. a.* v. V. वेधणारा, विंधणारा, &c. वेधक, वेधी, वेधनकर्त्ता.

PERFORATION, *n.* v. V.—*act.* वेधणें *n.* विंधणें *n.* वेध *m.* वेधन *n.*
I. *hole bored.* भोंक *n.* वेध *m.* विंध *n.* विंधी *f.* (*dim.* विंधुका *or* विंधुरका*m.* विंधू *or* विंधरूं *n.* विंधुक *or* विंधरूक *n.*).

PERFORCE, *adv. by violence*, v. COMPULSORILY. बळें, जुलमानें, बलात्कारानें, जबरीनें, &c. अळेंबळें.

To PERFORM, *v. a. achieve, do, execute*, v. To ACCOMPLISH. करणें, साधणें, संपादणें, उरकणें, उलगडणें, झेंपणें, झेंपाविणें, पेलणें, झोकणें, सर करणें, बजावणें, निर्वाहणें, सिद्ध करणें, सिद्धीस-शेवटास-&c. नेणें, आचरणें.
2 *make good, do*, v. To FULFIL. पुरा-पूर्ण-सत्य-&c. करणें.
3 (a part). See To ACT.

To PERFORM, *v. n. act a part in a play.* सोंग *n.* घेणें-आणणें-संपादणें, सोंगाची संपादणी *f.*-संपादणूक *f.* करणें. [करणें.
2 *play on an instrument.* वाद्य *n.* वाजवणें, छेड *or* छड *f.*

PERFORMABLE, *a.* v. V. A. कराया-साधाया-&c. जोगा-सारखा-&c. साध्य, संपादनीय, संपाद्य, साध्य, निर्वाह्य, आचरणीय.

PERFORMANCE, *n.* v. V. A. 1.—*act.* करणें *n.* साधणें *n.* संपादणें *n.* &c. संपादणी *f.* संपादणूक *f.* संपादन *n.* साधन *n.* निर्वाह *m.* ओज *f.*
2 अनुष्ठान *n.* आचरण *n.* आवृत्ति *f.* पुरा करणें *n.* &c.
I. *thing performed; work, act, &c.* v. ACTION. काम *n.* कर्म *n.* कृति *f.* कृत्य *n.* क्रिया *f.* करणी *f.*
II. *acting or exhibition of feats.* खेळ *m.* तमाशा *m.*

PERFORMED, *p.* v. V. A. 1. केलेला, साधलेला, संपादलेला, &c. कृत, साधित, संपादित, आचरित, अनुष्ठित, निर्वहित.

PERFORMER, *n.* PERFORMING, *p. a.* v. V. A. 1. करणारा, साधणारा, संपादणारा, &c. कर्त्ता, कार्यकर्त्ता, कारक, साधक, संपादक, निर्वाहक, नेता. [णी करणारा.
v. V. N. *and* ACTOR सोंग आणणारा-संपादणारा-&c. संपाद-
I. v. MUSICIAN. वाजंत्री, साजिंदा. [परिमल*m.*

PERFUME, *n. odour, scent, &c.* सुवास *m.* सुगंध *m.* आमोद *m.*
2 *odorous substance.* सुगंधिद्रव्य *n.* आमोदद्रव्य *n.* सुवासिकद्रव्य *n.* परिमलद्रव्य *n.* Some of the common *perfumes* are अबीर *m.* अरगजा *m.* कचरी *f. or* कचोला *m.* कस्तूरी *f.* गव्हला *m.* नखला *m.* नागरमोथा *m.* बुका *m.*
A bit or lump of p. खोड *n.*

To PERFUME, *v. a. scent.* सुवास *m.*-सुगंध *m.*-&c. लावणें-देणें, वासन *n.* करणें *g. of o.* सुवासित-वासित-आमोदित-परिमलित-&c. करणें.
To be perfumed. परिमलणें.

PERFUMED, *p.* v. V. सुवास लावलेला, सुवासितकेलेला, &c. सुवासित, वासित *or* वाशित, आमोदित, परिमलित, सुगंधित.

PERFUMER, *n. vender of perfumes.* गंधी, गंध्या, सुगंधी, अत्तार *or* अत्तारी, गंधविक्रयी.

PERFUMERY, *n. perfumes.* गंधी सामान *n.*-जिन्नस *m. pl.*

PERFUNCTORILY, *adv.* v. A. लगडतगड *or* धगड, गडबडगुंडा करून, लथडपथड करून, लथडालथड करून, &c. बरबर, लगेलगे करून, टंगळमंगळ, शाखार्थ, शाखाला.
To do p. शाखार्थ *m.* शाख *n.* करणें *g. of o.*

PERFUNCTORY, *a. slight, careless, negligent.* बरबरचा, बरकरणी, बरपंगी, लगडतगडीचा, लथडालथडीचा, लथडपथडीचा, गडबडगुंड्याचा, चालढकलीचा.

PERHAPS, *adv. peradventure, perchance.* कदाचित् *pop.* कदाचित *and, vulg.* कदाश्चित, कोणजाणे, नजाणे, कायजाणूं, कोणास कळे, कोणास ठाऊक, कथंचित्, जातुपक्षीं, आहेआहे नाहींनाहीं. The sense is often expressed by a reduplication of the verb ; as in the following examples, आला तर येईल *or* येईल तर येईल perhaps he will come, गेला तर जाईल perhaps he will go, वांचला तर वांचेल perhaps he will live.
If p. *if in remote possibility.* यथाकदाचित्, यथाकथंचित्, यदाकदाचित्.

PERIAPT. See AMULET. [श *m.*

PERICARDIUM, *n. membrane round the heart.* हृदाशय *m.* हृत्को-

PERICARP, *n. seed vessel.* बीजकोश *m.*

PERICRANIUM, *n. membrane investing the skull.* कपाळावरील आंतली त्वचा *f.* कपालावरकांतस्त्वक् *f.*

PERIERGY, *n. unnecessary work or observance.* अत्याचार *m.*

PERIGEE, PERIGEUM, *n.*—in astronomy. नीच *n.* नीचस्थान *n.*

PERIHELION, *n.* शीघ्रोच्च *m.*
The p. of a planet's orbit. चलोच्च *n.*

PERIL, *n. jeopardy, hazard*, v. DANGER. भय*n.* जोखीम *f. n.* धोका *m.* खत्रा *m.* [पाडणें.

To PERIL, *v. a.* v. To ENDANGER. भयांत-धोक्यांत-&c. घालणें-

PERILOUS, *a. hazardous*, v. DANGEROUS. भयाचा, धोक्याचा, जोखमाचा, जोखमी, सकंटक, सभय.

PERILOUSNESS, *n.* v. A. भय *n.* जोखीम *f. n.* सभयता *f.*

PERIMETER, *n.*—in geometry. सीमासूत्र *n.*

PERIOD, *n. circuit,*—of a planet, &c. फेरी *f.* फेरा *m.*
2 *round of time, revolution of years; cycle. &c.* कालमान*n.* कालपरिमाण *n.* कालचक्र *n.* चक्र *n.* कालगण *m.* वर्षगण *m.* संवत्सरचक्र *n.* अहर्गण*m.* Some of the *Periods* are, कल्प,गंड,तप (12 years), मंडल (42 days), मन्वंतर, युग, साठी (60 years).
Periods and ages have rolled away. अहर्गणाचे अहर्गण लोटले आहेत.
3 *term, length of duration.* मुद्दत *f.* वायदा *m.* टेप *f.* पल्ला *m.* वेळ *f. m.* बक्त *vulg.* बकत *m. n.* अवधि *m. f* कालमर्यादा *f.*
An unfixed, undefined, or open p. or term. खुली मुद्दत *f.* कच्ची मुद्दत *f.*
A fixed or stated p. or term. बंदी मुद्दत *f.*
For, from, according to, &c. the broken periods(part liquidation of a debt). तुटमितीनें, तुटमुद्दतीनें.
Inauspicious p. कालवेला *or* वेळा *f.* काळवेळ *f.*
4 *conclusion*, v. END. शेवट *m.* अंत *m.* अखेरी *f.*
5 *indefinite portion or stage of a continued state, or series of events.* अवस्था *f.* कालावयव *m.* कालांश *m.* कालभाग*m.*
P. of life. वय *n.* (as प्रथम वय, मध्यमवय, अंत्यवय), पराई *f.* (one of two, viz. चढती पराई, उतरतीपराई).
6 *complete sentence.* पूर्णवाक्य *n.* फांकी *f.* गाथा *f.* फक्किका

pop. फकिका *f.*

An elaborated p. गड्डालिका *f.* चूर्णिका *f.*

PERIODICAL, *a. performed, &c. in a circuit.* परिवर्त्तनात्मक, परिवर्त्तनविषयक, परिवर्त्तनसंबंधी, परिवर्त्तनविशिष्ट.

2 *regularly recurring.* नेमलेले काळाचा, कालनियमाचा *or* नेमाचा, नियतकालिक, नियमितकालिक, नित्य.

PERIODICAL, *n.* नियमित कालानें निघणारें पुस्तक *n.*-&c.

PERIODICALLY, *adv.* v. A. 2. नेमलेले काळानें, कालनियमानें.

PERIODICALNESS, PERIODICITY, *n.* v. A. 2. कालनियतत्व *n.* नियतकालिकत्व *n.*

PERIOSTEUM, *n.*—in anatomy. अस्थित्वचा *f.* अस्थित्वक् *f.*

PERIPHERY, *n.* v. CIRCUMFERENCE. घेरा *m.* वेढ *m.* परिधि *m.* वृत्तपाली *f.*

2 *circular frame (as of a drum, sieve, &c.).* गाडा *m.* गाडी *f.*

PERIPHRASE, PERIPHRASIS, *n. circuit of words,* v. CIRCUMLOCUTION. गिरकांडा *m.* बोलण्याचा फेरा *m.*-घेरा *m.*-भोंवाडा *m.*

To PERIPHRASE, *v. n. use circumlocution.* गिरकांडा-घेरा-फेरा-&c. घेऊन बोलणें, भोंवाड्यानें-&c. बोलणें.

PERIPHRASTIC, PERIPHRASTICAL, *a.* v. CIRCUMLOCUTORY. फेऱ्याचा, गिरकांड्याचा. [गिरकांड्यानें.

PERIPHRASTICALLY, *adv.* v. A. गिरकांडा-भोंवाडा-&c. घेऊन,

PERIPNEUMONY, *n. inflammation of the lungs.* फुप्फुसदाह *m.*

To PERISH, *v. n. lose life,* v. To DIE. मरणें, जिवास-प्राणास मुकणें-अंतरणें-आंचवणें, जिवानूशी-प्राणानूशी जाणें, माव *m.* सोडणें.

To p. with hunger. उपासी मरणें.

To p. with cold. थंडीनें मरणें.

2 *be destroyed, be ruined, come to nothing.* बुडणें, नाहींसा होणें, नाश *m.*-विनाश *m.*-सत्यनाश *m.*-&c. पावणें, नष्ट होणें, नाबूद-नावनष्ट-नाट-गडद-गडप-&c. होणें, नाबूद जाणें-बुडणें, नाशm.-विनाशm.-सत्यनाशm.-विघातm.-ध्वंसm.-धूळf. होणें *g. of s.* सप्पाm.-फन्नाm.-फडशाm.-&c. उडणें *g. of. s.* गळणें, गंहारणें.

Ready to p. विनाशोन्मुख.

3 *be lost eternally.* नरकास-अधोगतीस-दुर्गतीस-&c. जाणें, अधोगति *f.*-दुर्गति *f.*-अधःपात *m.*-&c. होणें *g. of s.*

PERISHABLE, *a.* v. V. 2. *liable to perish, &c.* नाशवंत, नासका, नश्वर, नाशशील, बिनाशी, नाशाधीन, नाशवश, क्षयशील, अंतवंत, क्षयिष्णु.

P. goods. नासकें केणें *n.*

I. *subject to speedy decay.* लौकर नासायाचा-जायाचा-&c. भंगुर, क्षणभंगुर, क्षणिक.

PERISTALTIC, *a. worm like.* कृमिवत्, कृमिसदृश.

P. motion. सर्पगति *f.*

PERITONEUM, *n.*—in anatomy. पोटाचा पडदा *m.* अंत्रवेष्टन *n.* उदरांतस्त्वक् *f.* वपा *f.*

PERIWIG, *n.* केशांची लहान टोपी *f.* [खुबी *f.*

PERIWINKLE, *n.*—the shell fish. घुला *m.* घूल *f.* खुबा *m. dim.*

To PERJURE, *v. a.* (one's self) *make a false oath.* खोटी शपथ *f.* वाहणें-घेणें-करणें-देणें-खाणें *or* वाहून-&c. बोलणें, शपथपूर्वक खोटी साक्ष *f.* देणें.

PERJURED, *p.* v. V. खोटी शपथ वाहिलेला-घेतलेला-&c. शपथपूर्वक खोटी साक्ष दिल्हेला, कूटसाक्षी, क्रियाभ्रष्ट, क्रियानष्ट.

PERJURY, *n. false swearing.* खोटीशपथ *f.* कूटसाक्ष्य *n.*

To PERK, *v. n. affect airs.* नटणें, अकड *f.*-नखरा *m.*-&c. करणें.

PERK, *a. affected.* मिजाजी, नखरेबाज.

PERMANENCE, PERMANENCY, *n.* v. A. शाश्वती *f.* स्थिरपणा *m.* स्थायीपणा *m.* टिकावा *m.* तगाव *m.* स्थैर्य *n.* स्थिरता *f.* स्थायित्व *n.* ध्रुवता *f.* शाश्वत *n.*

PERMANENT, *a. durable, abiding,* v. LASTING, ENDURING. टिकाऊ, टिकाव्याचा, शाश्वतीचा, जाधूचा, नेहमीचा, खडा, स्थिर, स्थायी, चिरस्थायी, चिरकालिक, नित्य, अढळ, शाश्वतिक, ध्रुव, मुकरर, करारी, काईमदाईम. [थंपूर्वक.

PERMANENTLY, *adv.* v. A. मुकरर, अढळ, जाधू, नित्य, स्थिर, स्थै-

PERMEABILITY, PERMEABLENESS, *n.* v. A. मूर *f.* भेदनयोग्यता *f.* भेदनगम्यता *f.*

PERMEABLE, *a.* v. V. भेदून जायाजोगा, भेदनगम्य.

Universally p. व्याप्य.

To PERMEATE, *v. a. penetrate and pass through.* भेदून-वेधून-मुरून-&c. जाणें-पारजाणें, व्यापणें. [पार जाणारा.

PERMEATER, *n.* PERMEATING, *p. a.* v. V. भेदून जाणारा, मुरून-

P. universally. व्यापक.

PERMEATION, *n.* v. V. भेदून जाणें *n.*

Universal p. व्याप्ति *f.* व्यापन *n.*

PERMISSIBLE, *a.* v. V. परवानगी द्यायाजोगा, परवानगी व्हावयाजोगा, परवानगीजोगा, अनुज्ञार्ह, अभ्यनुज्ञार्ह, अनुज्ञेय.

PERMISSION, *n. liberty granted.* परवानगी *f.* हुकूम *m.* आज्ञा *f.* मोकळीक *f.* रजा *f.* अभ्यनुज्ञा *f.* अनुज्ञा *f.* अनुमत *n.*

Full and free p. मुबा *or* मुभा *f.* मुक्तद्वार *n.*

With or by the p. of. रजावंतीनें *or* रजावंदीनें.

Writ of p. परवानगीचिठी *f.*

PERMISSIVE, *a.* PERMITTER, *n.* v. V. परवानगी देणारा, &c. अनुज्ञादायक, अनुज्ञाप्रद, अभ्यनुज्ञाप्रद, &c.

To PERMIT, *v. a. allow, give leave, let, &c.* परवानगी *f.*-हुकूम *m.*-आज्ञा *f.*-अनुमत *n.*-&c. देणें, देणें in combination with another verb, as जाऊं देणें to permit to go, येऊं देणें to permit to come, &c. अनुमोदन *n.* करणें-देणें, अनुमोदणें.

PERMIT, *n. written leave.* परवाना *m.* परवानगीचिट्ठी *f.* रवाना *m.* दस्तक *n.*

PERMITTANCE. See PERMISSION.

PERMITTED, *p.* v. V. परवानगी दिल्हेला, आज्ञा दिल्हेला, &c. परवानगीचा, मोकळिकीचा, &c. अनुज्ञात, अभ्यनुज्ञात, अनुमोदित, अवर्जित, अनिषिद्ध. [निमय *m.*

PERMUTATION, *n.* v. EXCHANGE. अदलाबदल *f.* बदलाबदल *f.* वि-

2—in arithmetic. अंकपाश *m.*

PERNICIOUS, *a. injurious,* v. HURTFUL. अपकारक, अपकारी, अपकारकारी-कारक, अहितकारी-कारक-&c. अपायकारक-&c. दुष्ट, वाईट. [&c. होईसा *decl.*

PERNICIOUSLY, *adv.* v. A. अपकारहोईसा *decl.* अहित-नुकसान-

PERNICIOUSNESS, *n.* v. A. अपकारीपणा *m.* अपकारकता *f.*

PERORATION, *n. closing part of an oration.* कथोपसंहार *m.* भाषणोपसंहार *m.*

PERPENDICULAR, *a. vertical, upright.* सरळउभा, नीटउभा, नीट, ऋजु, सुती, सूत्रक, सूत्रा, सूत्री, सरलोर्ध्वाधःस्थित, ऊर्ध्वाधर.

That deviates from the p. विथर. [कोणगामी.

2 *falling on or crossing at right angles.* समकोणपाती, सम-

PERPENDICULAR, *n. line falling at right angles.* लंब *m.* लंबक *m.* अवलंब *m.* अधोलंब *m.*

PERPENDICULARITY, *n.* v. A. 1. सरळउभेपणा *m.* नीट उभेपणा *m.* सरलता *f.* सारल्य *n.*

PERPENDICULARLY, *adv.* v. A. 1. सरळउभा *decl.* नीटउभा *decl.* उभा *decl.* सरळ, लंबरूपानें.

2 समकोणहोईसा *decl.* समकोणगतीनें.

To PERPETRATE, *v. a.* v. To Do. करणें. The Maráthí has no word restricted to an evil act.

PERPETUAL, *a. never ceasing or intermitting, constant, permanent.* नित्य, निरंतर, शाश्वत, शाश्वतिक, शाश्वतीचा, जाधूचा, सतत, संतत, अनंत, अखंड, अविरत, अनवरत, अनारत, अव्यवहित, नियत, चिरस्थायी, चिरकालस्थायी, नित्यस्थायी, सर्वकालस्थायी, सर्वकालीन, सार्वकालिक, खडा, नित्याचा, नेहमीचा, दाईम, काईमदाईम.

PERPETUALLY, *adv.* v. A. *and* EVER. नित्य, निरंतर, नित्यांत, सतत, संतत, सर्वकाल *or* ळ, नेहमी.

To PERPETUATE, *v. a. make perpetual, cause to endure.* शाश्वत-स्थिर-चिरस्थायी-&c. करणें, अखंडचालेसा-सततचालेसा-नित्यचालेसा-&c. करणें, निरंतरराहीसा-अखंडराहीसा-सदोदितराहीसा-&c. करणें.

PERPETUATED, *p.* v. V. शाश्वत केलेला, अखंड चालेसा केलेला, निरंतर राहीसा केलेला, &c. शाश्वतीकृत.

PERPETUATION, *n.* v. V.—*act.* शाश्वत करणें *n.* निरंतर राहीसा करणें *n.* &c. शाश्वतीकरण *n.* चिरस्थायीकरण *n.*

PERPETUITY, *n. endless duration, uninterrupted existence.* शाश्वती *f.* शाश्वत *n.* सातत्य *n.* सांतत्य *n.* स्थिरता *f.* नित्यता *f.* चिरस्थायिता *f.* चिरकालस्थायिता *f.* &c. अनवरतत्व *n.* स्थिरस्थिति *f.* अखंडस्थिति *f.* निरंतरस्थिति *f.* अक्षयस्थिति *f.* &c. दाइमी *f.*

To PERPLEX, *v. a. involve, complicate,* v. To ENTANGLE. गुंतवणें, गुरपटणें *or* गुरफटणें, गुंताडा *m.*-गुतागूत *f.*-घोंटाळा *m.*-घोळ *m.*-गुरपटा *m.*-&c. करणें *g. of o.*

2 *embarrass, puzzle, bewilder, &c.* v. To CONFOUND. गुरपटणें *or* गुरफटणें, गोंधळवणें, गडबडवणें, गोंफाटणें, गोफाट्यांत-गुरपट्यांत-पेंचांत-&c. पाडणें-घालणें, घोंटाळा *m.*-घोळ *m.*-गोंधळ *m.*-धांदल *f.*-तारांबळ *f.*-चित्तवैकल्य *n.*-&c. करणें *g. of o.*

PERPLEXED, *p.* v. V. 1. गुंतवलेला, गुरपटलेला, &c. गुंताड्याचा, गुंतागुंतीचा, घोंटाळ्याचा, &c.

To be or become p. गोंधळणें, गोंधरणें, गोंधवणें.

2 गुरपटलेला, गडबडवलेला, &c. भ्रांत, संभ्रांत, व्यस्त, विमनस्क, विमना, मूढ, संदिग्ध मनस्क.

To be or become p. गोंधळणें, घोंटाळणें.

PERPLEXER, *n.* PERPLEXING, *p. a.* v. V. 1. गुंतवणारा, गुरपटणारा, गुंताडाकरणारा, &c.

2 गडबडवणारा, गोंधळ-धांदल-घोंटाळा-&c. करणारा, गुरपट्यांत-पेंचांत-&c. पाडणारा, &c. पंचाइतीचा, विचाराचा, विवंचनेचा, &c. भ्रामक, भ्रांतिजनक-कर.

PERPLEXEDNESS, PERPLEXITY, *n.* v. A. 1. गुंतवलेलेपणा *m.* गुरपटलेलेपणा *m.* &c. गुरपटा *or* गुरफटा *m.* गोंधळ *m.* गुंताडा *m.* गुतागूत *f.* घोंटाळा *m.* घोळ *m.* घपाघोळ *or* घप्पाघोळ *m.* गोफाटा *m.*

2 गडबडवलेलेपणा *m.* &c. घोंटाळा *m.* गोंधळ *m.* धांदल *f.* तारांबळ *f.* तारातीर *f.* गलफटा *or* गलफाटा *m.* गुरपटा *or* गुरफटा *m.* घोळ *m.* पंचाइत *f.* विचार *m.* विवंचना *f.* ओढाओढ *f.* ओढाताण *f.* कुतरओढ *f.*

1. a *perplexity ; a perplexing business,* v. TROUBLE. पेंच *m.* पेंचाटी *f.* घोंटाळा *m.* पंचाईत *f.* विचारणा *f.* विचार *m.*

PERQUISITE, *n. fee, allowance beyond pay.* दस्तुरी *f.* खेरीजमिळकत *f.* खेरीजप्राप्ति *f.* बालाईयाफूत *f.* अवांतरलाभ *m.* आगंतुकलाभ *m.*

P. of hereditary village officers, &c. हक्क *m.* कर *m.*

To PERSECUTE, *v.a. pursue so as to afflict, injure, vex, annoy, harass, &c.* v. To TEASE. सतावणें, छळणें, छडणें, गांजणें, जाचणें, जाचणूक *f.*-छळणूक *f.*-छडणूक *f.*-गांजणूक *f.*-&c. करणें *g. of o.* इजा *f.*-दुःख *n.*-उपद्रव *m.*-&c. देणें-करणें, पाठीस लागणें *g.of o.* पाठ *f.*-पिच्छा *m.*-&c. घेणें *g.of o.* राशीस लागणें-बसणें *g.of o.*

2 *pester with importunity,* v. To HANG UPON. पाठीस लागणें *g. of o.* पाठ *f.* घेणें *g. of o.* बोकांडीस बसणें, राशीस लागणें-बसणें *g. of o.* दुमची *f.* पुरवणें *g. of o.*

PERSECUTION, *n.* v. V. 1.—*act.* सतावणें *n.* छडणें *n.* छळणें *n.* &c. छळणूक *f.* छडणूक *f.* गांजणूक *f.* जाचणूक *f.* छळ *m.* छलना *f.*

2 पाठीस लागणें *n.*-&c.

PERSECUTOR, *n.* PERSECUTING, *p. a.* v. V. 1. सतावणारा, छळणारा, छडणारा, &c. छळकरणारा, दुःख-इजा-उपद्रव-&c. देणारा, क्लेशद.

2 पाठीस लागणारा, पाठ घेणारा, बोकांडीस बसणारा, &c.

PERSEVERANCE, PERSISTENCE, *n.* v. V. चिटकणें *n.* चिकटूनराहणें *n.* &c. उद्योग *m.* आग्रह *m.* दीर्घप्रयत्न *m.* व्यवसाय *m.* अध्यवसाय *m.* अभिनिवेश *m.*

I.—the quality or virtue. चिकटपणा *m.* चेंगटपणा *m.* चेंगटाई *f.* दम *m.* धीर *m.* नेट *m.* स्थैर्य *n.* धारणा *f.* धृति *f.* स्थिति *pop.* स्थीत *f.* संस्था *f.*

PERSEVERANT, *a.* PERSEVERING, *p. a.* PERSISTING, *p. a.* v.V. 1. चिकटून राहणारा, आग्रही, निग्रही, आग्रहाचा, चिकट, चिकट्या, चेंगट, उद्योगी, चिवट, अकटचिकट, धीर, धिराचा, दमदार, दमाचा, नेटदार, नेटक, नेटाचा, उद्यमी, व्यवसायी, यत्नवान्, यत्नी, प्रयत्नवान्, प्रयत्नी, महोत्साह, महोद्यम, सोद्योग.

2 खणपटीस बसणारा, &c. लहांचट, लहांचड.

PERSEVERANTLY, PERSEVERINGLY, PERSISTINGLY, *adv.* v. A. चिकटपणानें, चेंगटपणानें, चेंगटाईनें, आग्रहानें, आग्रह धरून, आग्रहपूर्वक, हट्ट धरून, चिकटून, चिकटून राहून, अभिनिवेशपूर्वक.

To PERSEVERE, *To* PERSIST, *v. n. continue steadfast in.* चिकटून-लगटून-धरून-अवलंबून-&c. राहणें-चालणें, स्थिर-चिकट-&c. राहणें, दम धरून-धीर धरून-&c. राहणें-चालणें, आग्रह *m.*-&c. धरणें-धरून राहणें, टिकणें, ठरणें, टिकाव, *m.*-टिकावा *m.*-&c. होणें *g. of s.*

2 (in importunity, &c.). v. To HANG UPON. खणपटीस बसणें, खणपट *f.* धरणें-घेणें. [शचा.

PERSIAN, PERSIC, *a. of or belonging to Persia.* फारशी, इराणदेशचा.

PERSIAN, *n.*—the language. फारशीबोली *f.*-भाषा *f.*

PERSON, *n. individual, human being.* माणूस *n.* मनुष्य *n.* जण *m. f. n.* (The plural is जण *m.* जणी *f.* जणें *n.* It always requires a numeral prefixed; and to express *two, three,* or *four* दोघे, तिघे, चौघे (declined into घी *or* घ्या *f. pl.* & घें *or* घीं *n. pl.*) are required instead of दोन, तीन, चार) असामी *f.* इसम *m.* नफर *m.* व्यक्ति *f.*

2 *body, human being with respect to corporeal existence.* अंग *pop.* आंग *n.* शरीर *n.* देह *m.* अहंकारास्पद *n.*

Decoration of the p. शरीरसंस्कार. *m.* अंगसंस्कार *m.*

In p. *in propria persona.* जातीनें, जात्यां, खुदजातीनें, जाननिसबत, जातिनूशीं *or* जातीनिशी, खुदनिसबत, खासगत, खाशानिशी, खुद, आंगीं, आंगानें, बजाहां, स्वतः *pop.* स्वतां, साक्षात्, प्रत्यक्ष.

In, by, through, &c. one's own p. आपल्या आंगें, आपल्या जातीनें, जातीनें, आपण, स्वतः*pop.* स्वतां, साक्षात्.

Proving, establishing, &c. in one's own p. साक्षात्कार*m.*

To take about one's p. जवळ करणें-धरणें.

3 *one, a body, a human being.* माणूस *n.* मनुष्य *n.* गडी *m.* गृहस्थ *m.* मूर्त्ति *f.* असामी *f. m.*

4 *exterior appearance.* रूप *n.* आकार *m.* आकृति *f.*

5 *character* (in a drama). सोंग *n.* रूप *n.* वेष *m.*

6—in grammar. पुरुष *m.* The persons are,—the first p. उत्तमपुरुष *m.* प्रथमपुरुष *m.* (In *Sanskrit* grammar प्रथमपुरुष is the third person.). प्रथमा *f.* अस्मद्वाच्य *n.*—the second p. द्वितीय पुरुष *m.* मध्यम पुरुष *m.* युष्मद्वाच्य *n.*—the third p. तृतीयपुरुष *n.* उत्तर पुरुष *m.* नामवाच्य *n.*

PERSONABLE, *a. having a well formed person,* v. HANDSOME. रूपाचा, सुरूप, रूपस, रूपवान्, आकारशुद्ध, आवशुद्ध, निटस, देखणा, सुरेख.

PERSONABLENESS, *n.* v. A. सुरूपता *f.* रूपलावण्य *n.* रूपसौंदर्य *n.* आकारशुद्धि *f.* निटसपणा *m.* &c.

PERSONAGE, *n. person of eminence.* मोठें मनुष्य *n.* थोर-संभावित-&c. मनुष्य *n.* गृहस्थ *m.* श्रेष्ठजन *m.* महाजन *m.* व्यक्ति *f.* स्वारी *f.* Some terms for a superior personage are, प्रस्थ*n.* प्रस्थान *n.* वृंद *n.* [PERSON.

2 *exterior appearance.* See PERSON. 3 *character.* See

PERSONAL, *a. belonging to persons, not to things.* मनुष्यजातीचा, मनुष्यव्यक्तीचा, पौरुषेय, पुरुषवाचक.

P. pronoun. पुरुषवाचकसर्वनाम *n.*

2 *affecting a particular person, relating to an individul.* खास, खासगत, खासगी, खासगीचा, जातीचा, खुद, खुदनिसबतीचा, आपला, विशेषव्यक्तीचा, स्व in comp. निज in comp.

P. property. खासगी *f.*

3 *done, &c. in person.* आंगचा, जातीचा, स्वतांचा, खासगत, जातीनिशीचा, खाशानिशीचा, साक्षात्संबंधाचा, प्रत्यक्षसंबंधाचा, साक्षात्कृत, स्वकृत, स्वयंकृत, आंग (used in comp. as आंगमेहनत p. labour, &c.).

P. connexion. साक्षात्संबंध *m.*

4 *exterior, belonging to the outward person.* रूपाचा, आकाराचा, रूपाविषयींचा, रूपसंबंधी, रूपविषयक, दैहिक, वरचा, वरील.

5—in law. अस्थावर, जंगम.

6 *reflecting on an individual.* लावून बोलण्याचा, घालून पाडण्याचा, विशेषव्यक्त्युद्देश्य, विशेषस्पृक्, विशेषस्पर्शक.

PERSONALITY, *n.* v. INDIVIDUALITY. व्यक्ति *f.* व्यक्तिता *f.* पृथगात्मिका *f.* स्वत्व *n.*

2 *direct application or applicability to a person.* विशेषव्यक्तीवर प्रयोग *m.* विशेषव्यक्त्युद्देशिता *f.* विशेषसंस्पर्शिता *f.*

3 *a personal remark.* लावून बोलणें *n.* लावून भाषण *n.* मर्मभाषण *n.* व्यक्तिनिर्देशात्मक भाषण *n.* विशेषसंस्पर्शक भाषण *n.*

PERSONALLY, *adv.* v. A. 1. व्यक्तीनें, व्यक्तितः.

2 खुद, साक्षात्, प्रत्यक्ष, विशेष.

3 *in person,* v. PERSON. जातीनें, साक्षात्, स्वांगें.

6 लावून, घालून पाडून. [गमद्रव्य *n.*

PERSONALITY, *n. personal estate.* जंगममाल *m.* चरद्रव्य *n.* जं-

To PERSONATE, *v. a. represent by an assumed character, pretend to be.* वेष *m.*-मिष *n.*-सोंग *n.*-&c. घेणें-धरणें *g. of o.* मिषानें-वेषानें-&c. येणें *g. of o.* तोतया *m.* होणें *g. of o.* आपणास म्हणवणें *with the name of the o.* तादात्म्य *n.*-तद्रूपता *f.*-&c. घेणें-धारण करणें-ग्रहण करणें *g. of o.*

2 *act the part of.* सोंग *n.*-वेष *m.*-रूप *n.*-&c. घेणें-धरणें *g. of o.*

PERSONATOR, *n.* PERSONATING, *p. a.* v. V. 1. वेष घेणारा, &c. तोतया.

PERSONATION, *n.* v. V. 1.—*act.* वेष घेणें *n.* &c. तोतया *m.* तादात्म्य धारण *n.* तादात्म्यग्रहण *n.*

PERSONIFICATION, *n.* v. V.—*act.* आरोपगर्भितोत्प्रेक्षा *f.* चेतनधर्मोत्प्रेक्षा *f.* चेतनधर्मारोप *m.* चेतनत्वारोप *m.* मनुष्यगुणारोप *m.*

To PERSONIFY, *v. a. represent with the affections and actions of a person.* चेतन धर्मारोप *m.*-चेतनत्वारोप *m.*-&c. करणें.

PERSPECTIVE, *n. glass for viewing objects.* दुर्बीन *f.*

2—in drawing. यथास्थानदृश्यचित्रलेखन विद्या *f.* यथादर्शनचित्रलेखन *n.*

PERSPICACIOUS, *a. sharp of sight.* तीक्ष्णदृष्टि, शीघ्रदृष्टि, चपलदृष्टि, तीव्रदृष्टि, दृक्कुशल.

2 *of acute discernment,* v. SHARP. तीक्ष्णबुद्धि, कुशाग्रबुद्धि, कुशाग्रमति, मेधावी.

PERSPICACIOUSNESS, PERSPICACITY, *n.* v. A. 1. तीक्ष्णदृष्टि *f.* तीव्रदृष्टि *f.* शीघ्रदृष्टि *f.* दृष्टिपाटव *n.* दृक्कौशल *n.*

2 तीक्ष्णबुद्धि *f.* कुशाग्रबुद्धि *f.* बुद्धिकौशल *n.* तार्किक्य *n.*

PERSPICUITY, PERSPICUOUSNESS, *n.* v. A. 1. निर्मलता *f.* स्वच्छता *f.*

2 बालबोधपणा *m.* सुबोधपणा *m.* सुबोधता *f.* उत्तानार्थ *m.* सुज्ञेयता *f.* सुव्यक्तता *f.* वैशद्य *n.*

PERSPICUOUS, *a. transparent.* निर्मल, स्वच्छ, प्रांजळ.

2 *clear to the mind,* v. PLAIN. उघडा, स्पष्ट, उघड्या अर्थाचा, सुबोध, सुज्ञेय, सुव्यक्त, उत्तानार्थ, उत्तानार्थक, स्पष्टार्थक, विशद.

PERSPICUOUSLY, *adv.* v. A. 2. सुबोध, स्पष्ट, लौकर समजेसा *decl.* सुव्यक्त. [स्वेदस्राव *m.*

PERSPIRATION, *n.* v. V. N. 1.—*act.* घाम येणें *n.* घर्मस्राव *m.*

I. *perspiring matter,* v. SWEAT. घाम *m.* घर्म *m.* क्लेद *m.*

To PERSPIRE, *v. n. evacuate fluid,*—the skin, &c. घाम *m.*-&c. येणें-निघणें-सुटणें-पाझरणें *in. con.* घामावणें, घामेजणें, घामेणें, स्वेदस्राव *m.*-घर्मस्राव *m.*-&c. होणें *in. con.*

2 *be excreted by the skin*—a fluid, &c. रोमरंध्रानें-रोमगर्तांनें-&c. पाझरणें-स्रवणें-द्रवणें.

To PERSPIRE, *v. a. emit by the pores.* रोमरंध्रानें-रोमकूपानें-&c. रोमकूपद्वारा-रोमरंध्रद्वारा-&c. सोडणें-विसर्जन *n.* करणें-निष्कासन *n.* करणें, &c.

PERSPIRER, *n.* PERSPIRING, *p. a.* v. V. N. 1. घाम सुटलेला,&c. स्वेदित, स्वेदस्रावी, सघर्म.

PERSUADABLE, &c. See PERSUASIBLE, &c.

To PERSUADE, *v. a. bring to a particular opinion,* v. TO CONVINCE. समजावणें, समजूत *f.*-समजाविशी *f.*-समजावीस *f.*-सातर *f.*-सातरजमा *f.*-&c. करणें *g. of o.*

2 *influence by arguments, entreaties, advice, &c. bring*

over. मनावणें, मन *n.* मनावणें-मानविणें *g. of o.* बधवणें, बळवणें, मंथणें, समजावणें, समजूत *f.*-&c. करणें *g. of o.* ओढ *f.* लावणें, बळवून-बधवून-&c. घेणें, कान *m.* टोचणें *g. of o.*

PERSUADED, *p.* v. V. 1. *and* ASSURED. समजूत-खातर-&c. केलेला-झालेला, जातनिश्चय, जातनिर्धार.

To be p. खातर *f.*-खातरी *f.*-खातरजमा *f.*-निश्चय *m.*-भरवसा *m.*-&c. होणें-असणें *g. of s.*

2 मनावलेला, बधवलेला, बळवलेला, &c.

PERSUADING, PERSUASION, *n.* v.V.1.—*act.* समजावणें *n.* खातर करणें. *n.* &c. समजाविशी *f.* समजूत *f.* समजावीस *f.* समजी *f.* —*state.* खातर *f.* खातरजमा *f.* खातरी *f.* निशा *f.* निश्चय*m.* निधडा*m.* धडा*m.*

2—*act.* मनावणें *n.* बधवणें *n.* बळवणें *n.* &c. मनावणी *f.* बधवणूक *f.* बळवणूक *f.* बळवणी *f.*

I. *religious system or body.* मत *n.* मार्ग *m.* पंथ*m.* संप्रदाय*m.*

Of the p. of. संप्रदायी in comp.

PERSUASIBLE, *a.* v. V. 1. समजावयाजोगा-जोगता-&c. समजाविशीजोगा, समजुतीजोगा, खातर करायाजोगा-&c.

2 मनावयाजोगा-&c. बधवयाजोगा-&c.

PERSUASIVE, PERSUASORY, *n.* v. V. 1. खातरी करणारा-आणणारा, समजूत करणारा, समजूत करायाजोगा.

2 मनावणारा, बळवणारा, बधवणारा, &c. मनावून-बधवून-&c. घेण्याचा-घ्यायाजोगा-&c. वशकारक.

P. or appeasing speech. लळतीगोष्ट *f.* लळतेंबोलणें*n.*

PERT, *a. brisk, active, &c.* v. SMART. चपळा, चपल *or* ळ, चलाक *or* ख.

2 *forward, impertinent,* v. SAUCY. धीट, धिटाईचा, बाट, बाटगा, बेजबाबी, चरमरीत, चरबट, चिन्नादानी, अविनय.

To PERTAIN, *v. n.* v. To BELONG, To RELATE. असणें with चा-कडे-&c. लागणें,संबंध*m.*-&c. असणें, काम*n.*-कार्य*n.*-प्रकरण*n.* -&c. असणें.

PERTAINER, *n.* PERTAINING, *p. a.* v. V. विषयींचा, संबंधाचा, निसबतीचा, संबंधी, संबंधीक, विषयक.

PERTINACIOUS, *a. stubborn,* v. OBSTINATE. हट्टी, हटखोर, दुराग्रही, हेकट, हेकड, हेकेखोर, हटवादी, खळवादी, बातट *or* बातड.

2 *persistent, persevering,* v. RESOLUTE. धीर, धिराचा, चिकट, चिकट्या, नेटक, नेटदार, नेटाचा, नेटापाटाचा, निग्रही.

PERTINACIOUSLY, *adv.* v.A.1. हट्टानें, हट्ट धरून-घेऊन, हेंकाघेऊन, हेंक्यानें, हटेंच, हटकून, दाटबळें, दाटून.

2 नेटानें, धैर्यानें, धीर धरून, आग्रह धरून, आग्रहपूर्वक.

PERTINACIOUSNESS, PERTINACITY, *n.* v. A. 1. दुराग्रह*m.* हट *or* हट्ट*m.* अट *f.* अड *f.* हेंका*m.* [निर्भर*m.*

2 धीर*m.* दम*m.* धैर्य*n.* चिकटपणा*m.* नेट*m.* *n.* निर्बंध*m.* निग्रह*m.*

PERTINENCE, PERTINENCY, *n.* v. A. प्रासंगिकत्व*n.* प्रसंगसंगति *f.* प्रसंगानुसारिता *f.* प्रसंगयोग्यता *f.* यथायोग्यता *f.* समर्पकपणा*m.*

PERTINENT, *a. related to the subject in hand,* v. APPOSITE. प्रासंगिक,प्रसंगानुसारी,प्रसंगोचित, प्रसंगसंगत, प्रसंगोपात्त, प्रसंगप्राप्त, प्रस्तावसदृश, यथायोग्य, यथायुक्त, समर्पक.

PERTINENTLY, *adv.* v. A प्रसंगानुसार, प्रसंगसंगतीने, प्रसंगत:, यथोचित, यथायुक्त, समर्पक.

PERTLY, *adv.* v. A. 1. चपळपणानें, चलाकीनें, चापल्यपूर्वक.

2 धिटाईनें, अमर्यादेनें, बाटपणानें, बाटगेपणानें, बेजबाब, अविनयपूर्वक.

PERTNESS, *n.* v. A. 1. चपळपणा*m.* चलाकी *or* खी *f.* चापल्य*n.* चपलता *f.* [*m. pl.* अविनय*m.*

2 धिटाई *f.* अमर्यादा *f.* बाटपणा*m.* बाटगेपणा*m.* चरचट *f.* गमजा

To PERTURB, *To* PERTURBATE, *v. a disquiet, &c.* v. To DISCOMPOSE. संतापविणें, क्षोभवणें, संताप*m.*-क्षोभ*m.*-&c. करणें *g. of o.* संतप्त-क्षुब्ध-&c. करणें.

2 *disorder.* See To CONFUSE.

PERTURBATION, *n.* v. V. 1.—*state.* संताप*m.* क्षोभ*m.* व्याक्षोभ*m.* उद्वेग*m.* डामाडूळ *f.* तलखली *f.* तळमळ *f.*

PERTURBATOR, PERTURBER, *n.* v.V.1. क्षोभवणारा, संतापवणारा, क्षोभ करणारा.

PERTURBED, *p.* v. V. 1. क्षोभवलेला, क्षुब्ध केलेला, &c. क्षुब्ध, संतापित, संतप्त, क्षुभित, व्याकुल *or* ळ.

PERUKE. See WIG.

PERUSAL, *To* PERUSE. See READING, To READ.

To PERVADE, *v. a. pass through.* See To PERMEATE. 2 *pass or spread through the whole extent.* व्यापणें, व्यापून घेणें, वेढणें, वेढून घेणें, कवटाळणें, ग्रासणें, आक्रमणें, अभिव्यापणें,आक्रमण*n.*-&c. करणें *g. of o.* व्याप्त-आक्रांत-&c. करणें.

PERVADED, *p.* v. V. 2. व्यापलेला, व्यापून घेतलेला, आक्रमलेला, &c. व्याप्त, आक्रांत.

PERVADER, *n.* PERVADING, *p. a.* PERVASIVE, *a.*v.V. 2. व्यापणारा, व्यापून घेणारा, &c. व्यापक, व्यापी (esp. in comp. as. जगद्व्यापी, सर्वव्यापी, &c.), अभिव्यापक, सर्वांगीण.

PERVASIBLE, *a.* v. V. 2. व्यापून घ्यायाचा-जोगा-&c. व्याप्य.

PERVASION, *n.* v. V. 2.—*act.* व्यापणें *n.* व्यापून घेणें *n.* &c. व्याप्ति *f.* व्यापन *n.* आक्रमण *n.*

Universal p. अभिव्याप्ति *f.*

PERVERSE, *a. devious, distorted.* वांकडा, वेडावांकडा, वक्र, कुटिल.

2 *piggish, mulish, stubborn, untractable, &c.* करनकर, करनकऱ्या *or* करनकरी, अकरनकर, अकरताळा, अगस्ताळा, हेंकट, हेंकड, हेंकेखोर, हटखोर, जिद्दखोर, जिद्दी, वेडावांकडा, खेंकड, खेंकटेखोर, खळया, खळवादी, खडंगूळ, अडिवाळ, अडजात, अडफांट्या, अडगात्या, गाताडा,क्षक्कर, कुटिल *pop.* कुटीळ, कुटिलबुद्धि, कुटिलाशय, विपरीतकर्त्ता, विपरीतकारी.

PERVERSELY, *adv.* v. A. 2. हेंकटपणानें, खेंकडपणानें, अकरनकरपणानें, &c. अकरनकरीनें, हेंक्यानें, कुटिलबुद्धीनें, हटातटानें, &c. हेंका घेऊन, हटकून, हटेंच.

PERVERSENESS, PERVERSITY, *n.* v. A. 1. वांकडेपणा *m.* &c. वांक *n.* वक्रता *f.* वक्रभाव *m.* विपर्यास *m.* विपर्यय *m.* कौटिल्य *n.*

2 करनकरपणा *m.* अकरनकरपणा *m.* अकरताळेपणा *m.* हेंकडपणा *m.* आडफांटेपणा *m.* वेडेवांकडेपणा *m.* &c. अकरनकर *f.* करनकर *f.* पीळ *m.* हेंकेखोरी *f.* जिद्दखोरी *f.* कुटिलबुद्धि *f.* कौटिल्य*n.* कौत्रिसत्य *n.* दुर्मद *m.*

PERVERSION, *n.* v. V. 1.—*act.* फिरवणें *n.* उलटिवणें *n.* &c. विपरीतकरण *n.* विपर्यस्त करण *n.* अन्यथाकरण *n.* असद्विनियोग *m.*—*state.* विपर्यास *m.* विपर्यय *m.* वैपरीत्य *n.* विपरीतार्थ *m.* विपरिणाम *m.*

2—*act.* बिघडवणें *n.* &c.

To PERVERT, *v.a. turn from its purpose, use, end, &c.* फिरवणें, उलटिवणें, उलटा करणें, अन्यथा करणें, विपरीत-विपर्यस्त-&c.करणें, अनाठायीं-अस्थानीं -अमार्गी-&c. लावणें-घालणें, विपर्यास *m.*-विपर्यय *m.*-विपरीतार्थ *m.*-&c. करणें *g. of o.* असद्विनियोग

m.-&c. करणें *g. of o.*

2 *turn from the right*, v. To CORRUPT. बिघडवणें, कुमार्गांत -&c. आणणें, भ्रष्ट-&c. करणें. [आलेला मनुष्य.

PERVERT, *n. one turned from the right way.* कुमार्गांत आणलेला-

PERVERTED, *p.* v. V. 1. फिरवलेला, उलटा-विपरीत-विपर्यस्त-&c. केलेला, अनाठायीं लावलेला, &c. साचीकृत.

2 बिघडवलेला, भ्रष्ट केलेला, &c.

PERVERTER, *n.* PERVERTING, *p. a.* v. V. 1. फिरवणारा, उलटा-विपरीत-&c. करणारा, अनाठायीं लावणारा, &c.

PERVESTIGATION, *n. diligent enquiry*, v. RESEARCH. अन्वेषण *n.* गवेषण *n.*

PERVICACIOUS, PERVICACITY. See OBSTINATE, PERVERSE, &c.

PERVIOUS, *a. admitting passage, that may be penetrated.* भेद्य, भेदनीय, भेदनार्ह, भेदशक्य, प्रवेश्य, प्रवेशनीय, प्रवेशार्ह, अरोधक.

PERVIOUSNESS, *n.* v. A. भेद्यता *f.* भेदनीयता *f.* &c.

PEST, *a. plague*, v. PLAGUE. मरी *f.* मरगी *f.*

2 *hateful fellow or thing*, v. PLAGUE. व्याधि *or* व्याध *f.* पीडा *f.* उपाधि *or* उपाध *f.* कांटा *m.* कंटक *m.* काळकंटक *m.* कलांट *n.* आगधाड *f.* झट *n.* ग्रह *or* दाहवा ग्रह *m.* सेंकटें *n.* खूळ *n.* जंजाळ *m.n.* खटराग *m.*

PEST-HOUSE, *n. hospital for infectious patients.* सांक्रामिक रोगग्रस्तालय *n.* मारिग्रस्तालय *n.*

To PESTER, *v. a. annoy, harass with little vexations*, v. To TEASE. छळणें, छडणें, छळणूक *f.*-छडणूक *f.*-छळ *m.*-&c. करणें *g. of o.* दुःख *n.*-उपद्रव *m.*-इजा *f.*-तस्दी *f.* -क्लेश *m.*-&c. देणें.

2 See To ENCUMBER.

PESTERER, *n.* PESTERING, *p. a.* v. V. 1. छळणारा, छडणारा, दुःख देणारा, उपद्रव देणारा, उपद्रवी.

PESTIFEROUS, PESTILENT, PESTILENTIAL, *a. producing pestilence, &c.* मरगीचा, मरीचा, मरगीकरणारा, मार्युत्पादक, मारकोत्पादक, मारकजनक.

2 *noxious, pernicious, &c.* v. HURTFUL. अपकारक, अपकारी, अहितकारक-कारी, अनिष्टकारक-कारी.

3 *troublesome, teasing, &c.* v. MISCHIEVOUS. उपद्रव करणारा-देणारा, उपद्रवी, कुचाळ, कुटाळ, कुत्सित, दुष्ट.

PESTILENCE, *n. epidemic and mortal disease*, v. PLAGUE, मरी *f.* मरगी *f.* धाम *f.* मारक *m.* मारि *f.*

PESTLE, *n. instrument for pounding in a mortar.* दस्ता *m.* बत्ता *m.* कुतकाम. मुसल *pop.* मुसळ *n.*

Wooden p. for cleaning rice. मुसळ *n.*

P. and mortar. खलबत्ता *or* बत्ता *m.* हमामदस्ता *m.*

PET, *n. peevishness or passion.* रागाचा चिणकारा *m.*-झटका *m.* रागाची लहर *f.*-चुणूक *f.*-झुळूक *f.* ईषत्कोप *m.*

2 *darling, fondling, &c.* लाडका, देवतन. छाबडें *n.* प्रीतिपात्र *n.* प्रेमास्पद *n.* खेळवणा *m.* क्रीडामृग *m.* बगलबिल्ली *f.*

To PET, *v. a. fondle, cocker*, v. To INDULGE. लाडावणें, लाडकावणें, लाडकणें.

PETAL, *n. flower leaf.* पाकळी *f.* पाकोळी *f.* फकडी *f.* दल *or* दळ *n.*

Of one row of petals, एकमाळी—of two rows, दुमाळी,—of three rows, तिमाळी.

PETALED, PETALOUS, *a.* पाकळ्यांचा, सदल, दल in comp. (as द्विदल Bipetalous) माळी *or* माळ in comp. (as दुमाळी).

PETECHIÆ, *n. pl. spots on the skin in fever.* काळज्वराचे ठिपके *m.pl.*

PETIT. See PETTY.

PETITION, *n. request, supplication.* अर्ज *m.* अर्जी *f.* विनंती *f.* प्रार्थना *f*, दर्खास्त *or* दर्खास *f.* अभ्यर्थना *f.* [दी *f.*

2—written p. अर्जी *f.* अर्जदास्त *f.* विनंतीपत्र *n.* याद *f.* या-

To PETITION, *v. a. make a request to*, v. To BEG. अर्ज *m.*-विनंती *f.*-प्रार्थना *f.*-&c. करणें, अर्जी *f.* देणें.

PETITIONER, *n.* PETITIONING, *p. a.* v. V. अर्ज करणारा, &c. अर्जदार, अर्जीवाला. [रिणाम.

PETRESCENT, *a. becoming stone.* दगडहोणारा, आरब्धपाषाण प-

PETRIFACTION, *n.* v. V. A. 1.—*act.* दगड करणें *n.* पाषाण करणें *n.* पाषाणीकरण *n.* दृषत् करण *n.*—*state.* पाषाणपरिणाम *m.* v. V. N. दगड होणें *n.* पाषाण होणें *n.* पाषाणी भवन *n.* दृषत्भवन *n.* पाषाणपरिणाम *m.*

I. *thing petrified.* पाषाण झालेला पदार्थ *m.* कृत्रिम पाषाण *m.*

PETRIFIED, *p.* v. V. A. 1. दगड केलेला, पाषाण केलेला, &c.

2 कठोर केलेला, &c. पाषाणमय, दगडाचा, गतद्रव.

3 प्रेतवत् केलेला, &c. प्रेतवत्, काष्ठवत्, गतप्राण.

v. V. N. दगड झालेला, पाषाण झालेला, पाषाणीभूत, पाषाणपरिणामी, पाषाणस्वापन्न, प्राप्तपाषाणत्व.

To PETRIFY, *v. a. convert into stone.* दगड *m.*-पाषाण *m.*-&c. करणें, पाषाण परिणाम *m.* करणें, पाषाणपरिणाम *m.*-पाषाणत्व *n.*-&c. पावविणें-प्रापण करणें. [-&c. करणें.

2 *make callous.* कठीण-कठोर-निष्ठुर-पाषाणमय-गतद्रव-नष्टद्रव

3 *fix with fear, &c.* v. To ASTONISH, To FRIGHTEN. प्रेतवत्-काष्ठवत्-स्तब्ध-&c. करणें, थिजवणें.

To PETRIFY, *v. n. turn into stone.* दगड *m.*-पाषाण *m.*-&c. होणें, पाषाणपरिणाम *m.*-पाषाणत्व *n.*-&c. पावणें. [भूमितैल *n.*

PETROL, PETROLEUM, *n. rock oil.* मातीचें तेल *n.* शिलारस *m.*

PETRONEL, *n. horseman's pistol.* करोला *m.*

PETTICOAT, *n.*—the garment. The following words express varieties. उडदावळ *f.* उडदीलुगडें *n.* कणेरेंलुगडें *n.* खारबें *n.* गुजरी *or* कृष्णगुजरी *f.* गुलाली *f.* घागरा *m.* चंद्रकळा *f.* चौकटी लुगडें *n.* तपशिला *m.* दंडिया *m.* नखी *or* नकली नामावळ *f.* नामदारी लुगडें *n.* पडबळी लुगडें *n.* पाटाव *m. m.* (of silk) पाडगें *n.* पातळ *n.* पितांबर *m.* (of silk) फुटाणी लुगडें *n.* बळगी *f.* बांड *m.* बेली *f.* मिराणें लुगडें *n.* मुगबें *n.* राजावळ *f.* रास्ता *m.* लहंगा *m.* लुगडें *n.* शेलारी *f.* साडी *f.* सावळें *n.* सुताडा *m.* सुरखी *f.* सुशी *f.* हुंडा *m.* हलगत *f.* क्षीरोदक *m.* (of silk).

P. of a child. चिरडी *f.* परकर *or* परकोर *m.*

End or point of a p. (The two meet around the waist, and are drawn together in tightening the waistband). ओढण *n. f.* ओढील *or* ळ *f.*

Petticoat-hall, *house where are only women.* रांडवडा *m.*

Under p. फडका *m.*

To put on the p. *to become effeminate.* बांगडी भरणें.

PETTIFOGGER, *n. petty lawyer.* हलका-छोटेखानी-&c. वकील.

Pettifogging practices. जघन्यवृत्ति *f.*

PETTINESS, *n.* v. A. 1. लहानपणा *m.*

2 लहानपणा *m.* हलकेपणा *m.* लघुत्व *n.* क्षुद्रता *f.*

PETTISH, *a. fretful*, v. PEEVISH. चिरडखोर, चिरडीखोर, चिरड्या, तिडतिडा *or* तिडतिड्या, तुसडा, खिसखिशा.

PETTISHLY, *adv.* v. A. चिरडीनें, &c. चिरड येऊन, रुसून, चिडून,

चिडचिडून, रागाची लहर येऊन.

Pettishness, *n.* v. A. चिरडखोरी *f.* चिरड *f.* चीढ *f.* खिसखीस *f.* तिडतीड *f.* तिडतिडेपणा *m.* खिसखिशेपणा *m.*

Petty, *a. little*, v. Small. लहान.

2 *inconsiderable, insignificant, &c.*v. Mean. लहान, हलका, हलकेकिमतीचा, हलके योग्यतेचा, छोटेसानी, एर, एरशेर, अल्प, लघु, क्षुल्लक, क्षुद्र.

Petulance, Petulancy, *n.* v. A. 1. तिडतीड *f.* चिरडखोरी *f.* खिसखीस *f.* तिडतिडेपणा *m.* खिसखिशेपणा *m.* तिरसटपणा *m.*

Petulant, *a. pettish, fretful*, v. Peevish, Cross. चिरडखोर, चिरडीखोर, चिरड्या, खिसखिशा, तिरसट.

2 *proceeding from petulance*. चिरडखोरीचा, चिरडीचा, रागाच्याचिणकाऱ्याचा, तिरसटपणाचा.

Petulantly, *adv.* v. A. चिरडीनें, चिरड येऊन, चिडून, चिडचिडून, रागाची लहर येऊन.

Pewter, *n.* जस्त *n.* Some sorts of *pewter* are चिनीजस्त *or* रूपजस्त *n.* खर्परसूत्र *pop.* खापरसूत *n.*

P. puffed by the action of fire. फूल *n.*

Pewter, *a.* जस्ती, जस्ताचा.

Phaeton, *n.* एकेप्रकारची गाडी आहे. [गट्टा *m.*

Phalanx, *n. body of troops in close array.* घनव्यूह *m.* गट *m.*

Phallus, *n. emblematic representation of Shiwa.* लिंग *n.* पिंडी *f.* There are 12, viz. महाकालेश्वर (उजनीचा), सोमनाथ (सोरटीचा), केदारेश्वर (बद्रिकाश्रमाचा), विश्वेश्वर (काशीचा), ओंकारेश्वर (महेश्वरचा), त्र्यंबकेश्वर (त्र्यंबकचा), घृष्णेश्वर (एरुळचा), नागनाथ (अंवढ्याचा), वैजनाथ (परळीचा), भीमाशंकर (भीमाशंकरचा), मल्लिकार्जुन (श्रीशैलपर्वताचा), रामेश्वर (सेतुबंधाचा).

Phantasm, Phantasma, *n. airy appearance, fancied vision.* भास *m.* आभास *m.* छाया *f.* उचका *m.*

Phantasy. See Fancy.

Phantom, *n.* See Phantasm. 2 See Ghost.

Pharisaic, Pharisaical, *a. making a show of devotion without the spirit of it.* भक्तीच्या-&c. पोमाचा-ढोंगाचा-डौलाचा-दंभाचा, कोरडे ब्रह्मज्ञानाचा, बकध्यानाचा, &c. माजलेल्या-फैलावलेल्या देव्हाऱ्याचा, कोरडा, पोकळ, शुष्क, साधुम्मन्य.

Pharisaicalness, Pharisaism, *n. outward show of religion without the spirit*, v. Hypocrisy. भक्तीचाडौल *m.*-पोम *n.*-ढोंग *n.*-दंभ *m.*-&c. बकध्यान *n.* बोकेसन्यास *m.* कोरडें ब्रह्मज्ञान *n.* हरदासी ब्रह्मज्ञान *n.*

Pharisee, *n. one who makes a show of religion*, v. Hypocrite.- भक्तीचा दंभी-दांभिक-ढोंगी-&c.धर्मध्वजी,बकध्यानी,बोकेसन्यासी.

Pharmaceutic, Pharmaceutical, *a. pertaining to pharmacy.* औषधकृतीचा, औषधक्रियेचा, औषधकरणविद्या संबंधी-विषयक.

Pharmacopœia, *n. treatise on the preparation of medicines.* औषधें तयार करण्याच्या विषयावर ग्रंथ *m.* औषधक्रियाकल्प *m.*

Pharmacy, *n. art of preparing medicines.* औषधें तयार करण्याची विद्या *f.* औषधक्रिया *f.* औषधकृति *f.* औषधकरणविद्या *f.* अगदकरणविद्या *f.*

Pharos. See Light-house.

Pharynx, *n.* अन्नमार्गाचा वरचा भाग *m.*

Phase, Phasis, *n. appearance*—of the moon, &c. दर्शन *n.* दर्शनभेद *m.* दर्शनप्रकार *m.* दिसणें *n.*

Pheasant, *n.* एकपक्षी आहे.

Phenix, *n.*—the fabulous bird. स्वभस्मजन्मपक्षी.

2 fig. *remarkable personage*, v. Paragon. धेंड *n.* प्रस्थ *n.* प्रस्थान *n.* प्रकरण *n.*

Phenomenon, *n. any thing visible.* दृष्टीचा विषय*m.* दृष्टिविषय*m.*

2 *remarkable or unusual appearance.* चमत्कार *m.* अद्भुत *n.* उत्पात *m.*

Phial, *n. small bottle.* शिशी *f.* कुपी *f.*

Philanthropic, Philanthropical, *a. having general benevolence, loving mankind.* लोकोपकारी, जनोपकारी, परोपकारी, सर्वोपकारी, विश्वोपकारी, जगदुपकारी, परोपकारबुद्धि, लोकोपकारबुद्धि, &c. परोपकारशूर, जनप्रिय, जनवल्लभ, जनहितेच्छु, जनहितैषी, सर्वकार्यकर्त्ता, विश्वमित्र, जगन्मित्र *pop.* जगमित्र, विश्वकुटुंबी, जगद्वत्सल, जगत्सुहृत्.

2—of acts, measures, &c. परोपकाराचा, जनोपकाराचा, जनप्रीतीचा, परोपकार बुद्धीचा, &c.

Philanthropist, *n.* See the Adjective.

Philanthropy, *n. general benevolence, love of mankind.* लोकोपकारबुद्धि *f.* जनोपकारबुद्धि *f.* सर्वोपकारबुद्धि *f.* परोपकारबुद्धि *f.* परोपकार *m.* जनोपकार *m.* जनप्रीति *f.* विश्वप्रीति *f.* धर्मबुद्धि *f.* भूतदया *f.*

Philippic, *n. invective declamation.* भर्त्सनात्मक भाषण *n.* भर्त्सनारूप वाग्प्रबंध *m.*

Philologer, Philologist, *n. one versed in philolgy.* शब्दशास्त्री, शाब्दिक, शब्दशास्त्रवेत्ता, वैयाकरण.

Philological, *a. pertaining to philology.* शब्दशास्त्राचा, शब्दशास्त्रसंबंधी-विषयक.

Philology, *n. science of the construction, &c. of language.* शब्दशास्त्र *n.* शब्दशासनविद्या *f.* [नुत, जिज्ञासु.

Philomath, *n. lover of learning.* विद्याभक्त, विद्यावल्लभ, विद्या-

Philosopher, *n. one versed in philosophy, one devoted to physical or moral science, a sage.* ज्ञाननिष्ठ, ज्ञानविज्ञाननिष्ठ, ज्ञानी, ज्ञानवान्, प्रज्ञी, प्रज्ञावान्, विशेषविद्वान्, तत्वज्ञानी, तत्वज्ञ, तत्वविचारक, तत्वशोधक, तात्विक, पदार्थविज्ञानी, पदार्थपरिज्ञानी, तार्किक.

Philosopher's stone, *n.* परीस *m.* स्पर्शमणि *or* स्पर्श *m.* Answering to this word as understood in the sense of *a possession which procures for its possessor every object of his desires*, are कल्पवृक्ष *m.* कल्पतरु *m.* कल्पद्रुम *m.* कल्पलता *f.* कामधेनु *f.* चिंतामणि *m.*

Philosophic, Philosophical, *a. pertaining, &c. to philosophy.* तत्वज्ञानाचा, तत्वज्ञानाविषयींचा, ज्ञानविज्ञानाचा,&c. तत्वज्ञानविषयक-संबंधी, तात्विक.

2 *addicted, &c. to philosophy.* तत्वज्ञाननिष्ठ, तत्वविचारनिष्ठ, तत्वविचारपर, ज्ञानविज्ञाननिष्ठ.

To **Philosophize**, *v. n. search into the reasons of things.* तत्वविचार *m.*-तत्वशोध *m.*-तत्वान्वीक्षण *n.*-ज्ञानविज्ञानविचार*m.*-&c. करणें.

Philosophy, *n. science of the reasons of things.* तत्वज्ञान *n.* तत्वशास्त्र *n.* ज्ञान *n.* विज्ञान *n.* ज्ञानविज्ञान *n.*

Logical p. न्याय *m.* न्यायशास्त्र *n.*

Moral p. नीति *f.* नीतिशास्त्र *n.* [स्त्र *n.*

Natural p. or Physics. पदार्थविज्ञान *or* पदार्थविज्ञानशा-

PHILTER, *n. potion, &c. to excite love.* वश करण्याचें-मोहनीचें औषध *n.* वशीकरण औषध *n.*

PHIZ, *n.* v. FACE. श्रीमुख *n.* मुसडा *m.*

PHLEBOTOMIST, *n. one that performs phlebotomy.* शीरतोडणारा-सोडविणारा, शिरामोक्षक.

PHLEBOTOMY, *n. bleeding by opening a vein.* शीरतोडणी *f.* शिरामोक्ष *m.* शिरामोक्षण *n.* शिरावेध *m.* रक्तसांड *f.* रक्तमोक्षण *n.*

PHLEGM, *n.*—the humor, also the mucus. कफ *m.* श्लेष्मा *m.*

A gob of p. सांकरा *m.* बडका *or* बेडका *m.*

A string of p. गळसट *n.*

P. collected and impeding utterance. सांकर *m.* सांकारा *m.*

Tough, viscid p. बडस *m.*

To force up p. संकारणें.

2 fig. *coldness, apathy, &c.* थंडाई *f.* थंडी *f.* जाड्य *n.*

PHLEGMAGOGUE, *n. medicine for expelling phlegm.* कफसारक-कफनाशक-कफघ्न-&c. औषध *n.*

PHLEGMATIC, *a. relating to phlegm.* कफाचा, कफाविषयींचा, कफसंबंधी-विषयक, श्लैष्मिक.

A p. constitution or temperament. कफप्रकृति *f.*

2 *generating phlegm.* कफ करणारा, कफ कारी-कारक-जनक-&c. कफोत्पादक, श्लेष्माजनक-कारक-&c.

3 *abounding with phlegm.* कफाचा, कफमय, कफप्रचुर, कफविशिष्ट, श्लेष्मायुक्त, &c.

4 *cold, apathetic, dull, &c.* थंड, थंडा, मंद, जड, सुस्त, शीत, शीतप्रकृति, जडप्रकृति.

PHLEME, *n. instrument to bleed cattle.* पशूची शीर तोडण्याचें नस्तर *n.* पशुरक्तमोक्षणयंत्र *n.*

PHONETIC, PHONIC, *a. expressive of or relating to sound.* शाब्द, शाब्दिक, ध्वनिसंबंधी-विषयक.

PHONICS, *n. science of sounds.* ध्वनिशास्त्र *n.* ध्वनिविद्या *f.*

PHONOCAMPTIC, *a. that inflects sound.* ध्वनिपरिवर्त्तनकारी, ध्वनिपरिवर्त्तक.

PHOSPHORUS, *n.* मूलतत्वांतला एक ज्वालाग्राही पदार्थ आहे.

PHOTOGRAPHY, *n.* सूर्यकिरणांच्या योगानें चित्रें काढण्याची विद्या *f.*

PHRASE, *n. short sentence.* वाक्य *n.*

2 *particular mode of speech, idiomatic expression.* बोलण्याचा-भाषणाचा संप्रदाय *m.*-प्रकार *m.*-पर्याय *m.*

3 *phraseology,* v. STYLE. बोलण्याची-लिहण्याची-भाषणाची-&c. धाटणी *f.*-धाटी *f.*-धरती *f.*-&c.

To PHRASE, *v. a.* v. TO CALL. म्हणणें.

PHRASEOLOGY, *n. diction, manner of expression,* v. STYLE. बोलण्याची-लिहण्याची-भाषणाची-&c. धाटणी *f.* -धाटी *f.*-ठेव *f.* -धरती *f.*-&c.

PHRENETIC, PHRENTIC. See FRANTIC.

PHRENITIS, PHRENSY, *n.*—in medicine. सन्निपातज्वर *m.*

2 v. MADNESS. उन्माद *m.* मदात्यय *or* मदात्ययवायु *m.*

PHRENOLOGY, *n.* कपाललक्षणविद्या *f.* कपालसामुद्रिक *n.*

PHRENSIED, *a.* v. FRANTIC. खाबराबावरा.

PHTHISIC, *n. difficult breathing.* दमा *m.* कृच्छ्रश्वास *m.*

PHTHISICAL, *a.* v. CONSUMPTIVE. क्षयरोगी, क्षयी, क्षयरोगविशिष्ट.

PHTHISIS, *n. pulmonary consumption.* क्षय *or* क्षयरोग *m.* कफक्षय *m.* यक्ष्मा *or* यक्ष्मरोग *m.* राजयक्ष्मा *m.* रोगराज *m.* अतिरोग *m.* शोष *m.* सोस *m.*

PHYSIC, *n. art or practice of healing.* वैद्यक *n.* वैद्यकी *f.* चिकित्सा *f.* वैद्यकर्म *n.* वैद्यक्रिया *f.*

2 *medicine.* औषध *n.* औषधपाणी *n.* दवा *m. f.* भेषज *n.*

3 physics; *natural philosophy.* स्थूलपदार्थविज्ञान *n.* साकारपदार्थविज्ञान *n.* पदार्थविज्ञान *n.* स्थूलपदार्थशास्त्र *n.* सिद्धपदार्थविज्ञान *n.*

To PHYSIC, *v. a. treat with physic.* औषध *n.*-औषधपाणी *n.*-&c. देणें, औषधोपचार *m.*-औषधप्रयोग *m.*-चिकित्सा *f.*-&c. करणें.

PHYSICAL, *a. relating to nature or natural productions, or to things material as opposed to things moral, &c.* v. NATURAL. MATERIAL. स्थूलपदार्थांचा, साकारपदार्थांचा, सिद्धपदार्थांचा, &c. स्थूलपदार्थविषयींचा, &c. स्थूलपदार्थरूप, स्थूल, जड, जडज.

Physical force. आंगबळ *n.* आंगबळकटी *f.* आंगजोर *m.*

2 See MEDICINAL, MEDICAL.

PHYSICALLY. See NATURALLY.

PHYSICIAN, *n. one who practises physic.* वैद्य, चिकित्सक, तबीब, हकीम (used esp. of a Musalmán physician), भिषक्, आयुर्वेदी, अगदंकार, प्राणाचार्य. Some terms or appellatives for an *eminent or skilful physician,* corresponding with Æsculapius, Apollo, &c. are राजवैद्य, धन्वंतरी, अश्विनीकुमार, अश्विनीपुत्र, शतमारी.

Business, acts, dues, &c. of a p. वैद्यकी *f.* हकिमी *f.* हकिमाई *f.*

Fee to a p. for attendance. पायकोडणी *f.*

Medicine bag or case of a p. धन्वंतरि *m.*

P. who employs charmed water. पाणीवैद्य.

PHYSICKED, *p.* v. V. औषध दिल्हेला, &c. चिकित्सित.

PHYSIOGNOMER, PHYSIOGNOMIST, *n. one skilled in physiognomy.* तोंडावरून-मुखलक्षणावरून-&c. स्वभाव जाणणारा, मुखलक्षणवेत्ता, मुखसामुद्रिक.

PHYSIOGNOMY, *n. art of discerning the character, &c. from the features.* तोंडावरून-मुखलक्षणावरून-&c. स्वभाव जाणण्याची विद्या *f.* मुखसामुद्रिक *n.*

2 *cast of the look,* v. FACE. तोंडवळण *n.* तोंडवळा *m.*

PHYSIOLOGICAL, *a. pertaining to physiology.* प्राणिधर्मगुणविद्येचा, प्राणिधर्मगुणविद्यासंबंधी-विषयक.

PHYSIOLOGIST, *n. one versed in physiology.* प्राणिधर्मगुणविद्यावेत्ता.

PHYSIOLOGY, *n. the science of the properties and functions of living beings.* प्राणिधर्मगुणज्ञान *n.* प्राणिधर्मगुणविद्या *f.* प्राणिगुणधर्मशास्त्र *n.*

PIACULAR, PIACULOUS, *a. expiatory.* प्रायश्चित्तकारी.

PIAMATER, *n. membrane investing the brain.* मस्तिष्कावरकत्वचा *f.*

PIANO FORTE, *n.* एक वाद्य आहे.

PIAZZA, *n. a. covered way, &c.* मांडवीचा-छावणीचा रस्ता *m.*-वाट *f.*-&c. ढेलज *or* ढेलच *f.* मंडपपथ *m.*

To PICK, *v. a. gather or separate by plucking with the fingers, cutting with the nails, &c.* खुटणें, खुडणें, खुरतुडणें *or* खुडतुडणें, काढणें, खुटून-खुडून काढणें-तोडणें, कुरतणें, बोखडणें *or* बोखाडणें, वेंटणें *or* वेंटणें.

2 *clean by picking from.* निसणें, निसणें टुपणें, निवडणें.

3 *cull, select.* निवडणें, वेंचणें.

To p. one's words. वेंचे वेंचे-वेंचलें वेंचलें बोलणें, वेंचला घेणें.

4 *rob, peculate.* खाणें, हरामखोरी *f.* करणें.

5 up; *take up.* उचलणें, उचलून घेणें.

To p. up one by one. टिपणें, वेंचणें.

6 up; *find &c.* सहज-चालतां चालतां-&c. मिळवणें-संपादणें, गवसणें, गावणें, सांपडणें *these three with in. con.*

7 off; out from; *single out.* टिपणें, वेंचणें.

8 *mess, and pull about,* (food, &c.) किचवटणें, किचमंदणें, किवचणें, चिवडणें.

9 (the teeth). कोरणें.

10 (the nose). उकरणें.

11 (a lock). सळईनें-खिळयानें-&c. उघडणें.

12 v. To PECK. चोंचणें, टोंचणें.

To p. a hole in one's coat. छिद्र *n.*-&c. पाहणें, छिद्रान्वेषण *n.* करणें.

To p. a quarrel. कज्जा *m.*-&c. उकरून काढणें.

To PICK, *v. n. eat slowly.* वेंचलें वेंचलें खाणें, चाखतमाखत-चाखून खाणें. [*or* धरधरवणें.

2 up; *recover.* सावरणें, सावर *m.* घेणें, आंग*n.* धरणें, धरधरणें

PICK, *n. pickaxe.* पिकांव *n.* पिकंदर *n.*

2 See CHOICE.

PICK-AXE, *n.*—the implement. पिकांव *n.* पिकंदर *n.*

PICK-LOCK, *n. instrument for opening locks.* कुलूप उघडायाची सळई *f.*

PICK-POCKET, PICK-PURSE, *n.* खिसाकाप्या, खिसाकातऱ्या, उचक्या, उचल्या, उपट्या, भामट्या, हातचोर, भुरटेचोर.

PICK-THANK. See OFFICIOUS.

PICK-TOOTH, *n. tooth-pick.* दांतकोरणें *n.* दांतकोरणी *f.*

PICKBACK, *adv. on the back.* पाठकुळी *or* पाठकोळी *or* पाठगुळी *or* पाठुंगळी *or* पाठकुळीस-&c. *v.* घे, मार, आण, बस.

Back prepared for receiving a p. कुरघोडी *f.*

PICKED, *p. and a.* v. V. 1. खुटलेला, खुडलेला, खुडून काढलेला, &c.

2 निसलेला, निवडलेला. [णित.

3 निवडलेला, &c. वेंचका, वेंचक, वेंचला, निवड, निवडक, परिग-

6 गवसलेला, &c. गवशा.

I. *sharp,* v. POINTED. नोकदार, अणीदार.

PICKET, *n.*—of an army, &c. तलावा *m.* छबिना *m.*

2 v. STAKE. मेख *f.* खुंटा *m.* [शिक्षा *f.*

3—the punishment. मेखेवर एकपाय ठेवून उभें करण्याची

To PICKET, *v. a. fasten to a picket.* मेखलणें, मेखेस-खुंट्यास बांधणें, गोवणें, खुंट्याशीं खिळविणें.

PICKING, *n.* v. V. A. 1.—*act.* खुटणें *n.* खुडणें *n.* &c.

2 निसणें *n.* निवडणें *n.* [रिगणना *f.*

3 निवडणें *n.* निवड *f.* निवडणी *f.* निवडणूक *f.* परिगणन *n.* प-

4 खाणें *n.* हरामखोरी *f.*

P. and stealing. चोरीचकारी *f.* चोरीचपाटी *f.* चोरटेचाळे *m. pl.*

I. pickings; *indirect or extra profits or gains.* शिवाय-अवांतर-खेरीज-&c. मिळकत *f.*-प्राप्ति *f.*-&c. पोटस्थ *or* पोटस्त *n.*

Illicit pickings. खाज *f.* खाद *f.* कसर *f.* [मसाला *m.*

PICKLE, *n. pickling material.* खार *m.* खारेंपाणी *n.* खारवणी *n.*

To take the p. खारणें, खारावणें, रांपणें.

2 *thing pickled.* लोणचें *n.* आचार *m.* लवणशाक *f.* खार *m.*

3 *plight, trim, sad state,* v. MESS. गति *pop.* गत *f.* हबेलंडी *f.* गळ्हाटा *or* गव्हाठा *m.* गुडाकू *or* गुडाखू *f.* चवढव *f.* चवचव *f.*

Woeful p. फटफजिती *f.*

To PICKLE, *v. a.* v. N. लोणचें *n.*-खार *m.* घालणें-करणें *g. of o.*

PICKLE, PIGHTEL, PINGLE, *n. small enclosure.* वाडगें *n.* वाडकुलें *n.*

PICKNICK, *n.* रानजेवण *n.* वनभोजन *n.*

PICTORIAL, *a. done by a painter.* चित्रकाराचा, चित्रकारोत्पन्न, चित्रकारजनित.

2 *illustrated, &c. by pictures.* चित्राचा केलेला, चित्रांचा, सचित्र, चित्रयुक्त, चित्रलिखित.

PICTURE, *n. painting, &c.* चित्र *n.* तस्वीर *or* तस्वीर *f.* नकशा *m.* नकाशा *m.* आलेख्य *n.*

2 See RESEMBLANCE.

To PICTURE, *v. a. represent by painting, &c.* चित्र *n.*-तस्वीर *f.*-&c. काढणें-उतरणें-लिहणें *g. of o.*

PICTURESQUE, *a. pleasing like a picture.* चित्रासारखा, चित्रकाढल्यासारखा, चित्रसदृश.

2—a country; *rural, diversified with wood, water, &c.* जांगल, पर्वतवननदीमिश्रित.

To PIDDLE, *v. n. pick at table.* चाखत-चाखतमाखत-चवघेनघेन-नाकाओंठावर-&c. खाणें-जेवणें.

2 *trifle, toy, &c.* v. To DAWDLE. गमणें, विरंगुळणें, रेंगणें, रेंगळणें, चाचपणें, चापणें, उचलाठेव *f.*-घालकाढ *f.*-उचलाडेवर *f.*-&c. करणें, शेण *n.* खाणें.

3 *urine.* मुतणें.

PIDDLER, *n.* PIDDLING, *p. a.* v. V.1. चाखत माखत खाणारा, &c.

2 *and* DAWDLE. गमणारा, गमरा, गम्या, रिकामटवळा.

I. *petty, small, &c.* लहान, हलका, लहानसहान, तुटपुटा.

PIDDLING, *n.* v. V. 2.—*act.* गमणें *n.* रेंगणें *n.* &c. उचलाठेव *f.* उचलाउचल *f.* उचलाडेवर *f.* घालकाढ *f.*

PIEBALD, *a. party colored.* नानारंगी, विचित्ररंगी, कबरा, अबलक *or* ख, विचित्र.

PIECE, *n. fragment, separated part,* v. BIT. तुकडा *m. dim.* तुकडी *f.* कुटका *m.* खंड *n.* खांड *n.* खांडोळें *n.* शकल *n.*—esp. of fruits, esculent roots, cakes, &c. फोड *f.* फाड *f.* फाक *f.* कापटी *f.* चकती *f.* टवरा *m.*—as torn off from a mass by the hand or mouth. लचका *m.* लंबका *or* लबका *m.*

A p. of flesh as bitten or pinched out. लोळा *m.* *v.* घे, तोड, काढ.

Pieces,—compreh. तुकडे ताकडे *m. pl.*

Pieces, *bits, shivers, &c.* v. FRAGMENTS. चाराचुरा *m.* चकाचूर *m.*

Broken in pieces. बिशकल, शतचूर्ण.

Made of two pieces. दुतुकडा,—of three तितुकडा,—of four चौतुकडा.

P. added (to cloth, wood, &c.). जोड *m.* सांधा *m.* पट्टी *f.*

To break in pieces. फोडणें, फोडून टाकणें, तुकडे *m. pl.*-चूर *m.*-&c. करणें *g. of o.*

To fall to pieces; *fall asunder*;—wreath, rosary, &c. ओघळणें, ओहळणें, घळणें, सुटणें,—a building, machine, &c. कोसळणें, ढासळणें *or* धासळणें, विसळणें, निसळणें, रेलणें, उलगडणें.

To pull or take to pieces; *break up, undo.* उसळणें, निखळणें, विखळणें, उलगडणें, उलकटणें, उसकटणें, उसकटाउसकट *f.*-उखळाउखळ *f.*-&c. करणें *g. of o.*—a garment, couch,

&c. उत्तरणें,—fig. *expose, &c.* बिचकणें.

2 *part of a whole, member, portion.* भाग m. विभाग m. अंश m. अंग n. खंड n.

Of a p. *alike.* एकसारखा, एकप्रतीचा.

Of a p. with, *alike.* सारखा, सदृश.

Of one p. *without juncture, seam, &c.* एकसंध, एकसंधी, सदट or सधट, सलग, अखंड.

3 *a separate or distinct thing or performance.* This sense is usually best expressed by the word of which a piece is under mention, ex. gr. *a piece of* poetry कविता f. *a piece of* composition ग्रंथ m. *a piece of* work काम n. &c.

A p. of song. गाण्याची चीज f.

4 *item, article.* डाग m. डागिणा or डागिना m. नग m.

5 (of cloth) *whole web.* थान n. ताका or तागा m.

6 (of a bale of cloths) *single one.* दाणा m. सनंग n.

7 (of money) v. COIN. नाणें n. मुद्रा f.

A copper p. ताम्रमुद्रा f.—A gold p. सुवर्णमुद्रा f.—A silver p. रौप्यमुद्रा f.

8 (of ordnance.). तोफ f. भांडें n.

9 See MUSKET. [कास.

A piece, *to each.* दर असामीस or ला, दर मनुष्यास, प्रत्ये-

P. learning. *scraps of knowledge.* टाणाटोणा m.

To PIECE, *v. a.* v. To PATCH. ठिगळणें, ठिगळ n.-ठिगळी f. देणें-लावणें.

2 *enlarge by piecing.* सांधा m.-जोड m. देणें-लावणें or देऊन-&c. वाढवणें-लांबविणें.

3 v. To JOIN. जोडणें, सांधणें.

PIECED, *p.* v. V. 1. ठिगळलेला, ठिगळ दिल्हेला, &c.

2 जोड दिल्हेला, &c. जोडींव, जडींव, सांधींव, जोडगिरी, जोडगीर, जोडाचा, सांध्याचा.

3 जोडलेला, सांधलेला, सांधींव.

PIECE-LESS, *a. not made of pieces.* एकसंध, एकसंधी, सलग, अखंड, बिनजोड, सधट. [लवशः.

PIECE-MEAL, *adv. by pieces.* अंशतः, अंशशः, खंडशः, विभागशः,

2 *in pieces.* तुकडे तुकडे करून, खंडशःखंडशः.

To tear p. तुकडेतुकडे m. pl.-मणी मणी m. pl.-तीळतीळ m. pl.-तीळतीळ तुकडे m. pl. करणें, तीळतीळ तोडून टाकणें.

PIECE-WORK, *n.* उक्तें काम n. खंडकाम n.

PIED, *a. partycolored.* नानारंगी, विचित्ररंगी, चित्र, चित्रविचित्र.

PIEDNESS, *n.* v. A. चित्रविचित्रपणाm. विचित्ररंगm. रंगविचित्रता f.

PIER, *n.*—of a bridge. खांब m. पाय m. स्तंभ m.

2 *mole.* धक्का m.

To PIERCE, *v. a. puncture, perforate, bore, &c.* टोचणें, बोचणें, भोंकणें, बोचकणें, वेधणें, भेदणें, विंधणें, चुबकणें, विद्ध-&c. करणें, भोंक n.-वेध m.-रंध्र n.-&c. पाडणें-करणें, वेध m.-भेद m.-वेधन n. -&c. करणें *g. of o.*

2—with force and sound; *stab, gore, &c.* भसकणें, भसकावणें, भोसकणें or भोकसणें, भोसणें.

3 See To PENETRATE.

To PIERCE, *v. n. enter, penetrate,*—as a pointed instrument, &c. रुतणें, रुपणें, रोवणें, रोंचणें, बोचणें, रिघणें, शिरणें, शिरकणें, टुपणें.

PIERCEABLE, *a.* v. V. A. 1. वेधायाजोगा-&c. वेधनीय, वेध्य.

PIERCED, *p.* v. V. A. 1. टोंचलेला, वेधलेला, &c. वेधित, भेदित, विद्ध, सूचित.

2 भसकलेला, &c.

PIERCER, *n.* PIERCING, *p. a.* v. V. A. 1. टोचणारा, वेधणारा, &c. वेधक, वेधी, भेदक, वेधनकर्त्ता, &c. सूचक, सूची.

2 भसकणारा, &c.

v. V. N. रुतणारा, रुपणारा, &c.

I. *pinching, biting,*—cold, &c. कडक, कडकडीत, कडक्याचा, कडाख्याचा, हाडफोड, हाड फोडा, हाडें खिळणारा-फोडणारा, खर, जलाल. [डीत, कर्कश.

II. *thrilling, shrill,*—of sounds. वेधक, वेधी, कडक, कडक-

PIERCING, *n.* v. V. A. 1.—*act.* टोचणें n. वेधणें n. भेदणें n. &c. वेध m. भेद m. वेधन n. भेदन n. सूचना f. सूचन n. सूची f.

PIETISM, *n. affectation of piety.* भक्त्यभिमान m. भक्तीचें ढेंव्हा रें n.- पोम n.-&c.

PIETIST, *n. one who affects piety.* भक्तीचा अभिमानी-पोम्या.

PIETY, *n. love, &c. of God.* भक्ति f. देवभक्ति f. ईश्वरभक्ति f. परमेश्वरभक्ति f. भगवद्भक्ति f. देवपरायणबुद्धि f. धर्मपरायणबुद्धि f. भक्तिपरायणबुद्धि f. धर्मनिष्ठा f. धर्मासक्ति f. ईश्वरनिष्ठा f. ईश्वरीभावना f. धर्मत्व n. धर्मनिबंध m. धर्मशीलता f.

Eminent in p. धर्मप्रधान.

Path of p. भक्तिमार्ग m.

To set up a pretence of p. कटासन n. घालूनबसणें.

2 *love, &c. of parents.* आईबापांची भक्ति f.-सेवा f.-&c. अपत्यधर्म m. पुत्रधर्म m. मातापितृभक्ति f.

PIG, *n. swine.* डुकर c. [करणें.

Buying a p. in a poke. पाण्यांत म्हैस आणि बाहेर मोल

What can you expect from a p. but a grunt. कोळसा उगाळल्यानें काळेंच निघतें.

2 (of metal). अघड धातूचा गोळा m. खोट f.

To PIG, *v. c.* डुकरें विणें. [गाटारा, हेंकड.

PIG-HEADED, PIGGISH, *a.* v. PERVERSE. गाटा, गाटी, गाट्या,

2 v. STUPID. माठ्या, मट्ठ, मठ्या.

PIG-STYE, *n.* डुकरवाडा m. सूकरालय n.

Living in a p. *fig.* नरकवास m.

PIGEON, *a.*—the bird. खबुतर or कबुतर n. कपोत m.—Some kinds are गुलटोप, गिरेबाज, रुमाली, लक्का, लोटण.

Blue p. *columba œnas.* पारवा m.

Domestic p. गृहकपोतक m.

Keeper of pigeons (for sport, &c.). कबुतरबाज.

Milky white p. कागदी खबुतर n.

Pigeon fancier. खबुतरबाज.

A fat pigeon, *fig.* दुमतीगाय f.

PIGEON-BREAST, *n.* उराड n.

PIGEON-GRASS, *n.* कोलर्डे n.

PIGEON-HEARTED, *a.* v. FEARFUL. हरिणकाळजी.

PIGEON-HOLE, *n. cell or division.* घर n. खण m. खाना m.

PIGEON-HOUSE, PIGEON-COT, *n.* खुबडी f. खुराडें n. धाबळ or धाबळी f. खुडी f. कबुतरखाना m.

PIGMENT, *n.* v. PAINT. रंग m.

P. for the forehead or body. गंध m.

Pigments. लेणें n.

PIGMY, *n.* v. DWARF. वामन n. वामनमूर्त्ति f. बालखिल्य n.

PIGMY, PIGMEAN, *a.* v. DWARFISH. टारगा, वामनमूर्त्ति, अल्पमूर्त्ति, अल्पतनु, बुटबैंगन.

PIKE, *n.* v. SPEAR. भाला *m.* बरची *f.* शूल *n.* *pop.* शूळ *or* सूळ *m.*
2 *pitch-fork.* टोचणी *f.* खोचेरा *m.*
3 नदींतला एक मासा आहे. [शूलपाणि.

PIKE-MAN, *n.* v. SPEARMAN. बरचीवाला, भालेकरी, शूलधारी,

PIKE-STAFF, *n.* भालेकाठी *f.* शूलदंड *m.*
As plain as a p. हातचें कांकण *n.* करतलामलक *m.*

PILASTER, *n.* *square column.* चौकोनी खांब *m.* चौधारीखांब *m.* चतुष्कोणस्तंभ *m.*

PILE, *n.* *driven stake.* रोवलेला खांब *m.*-&c. खुंट *m. n.* खुंटण *n.*
2 *round mass, orderly heap,* v. HEAP. चळथ *f.* चवड *f.* डाळ *m.* डाळा *m.* ढिंग *m.* *dim.* ढिंगोरा *m.* & ढिंगोळी *f.* ढुंग *m.* *dim.* ढुंगी *f.* ढुंगा *m.* राशि *m. f.* *pop.* रास *f.* गंज *m.*
3 (as of shot, pitchers, &c.). डाळ *m.* डाळा *m.* उतरंड *f.* उतरड *f.* खंडेमेरु *m.*
4 *edifice,* v. BUILDING. वाडा *m.* इमारत *f.*
5 *pyre.* सरण *n.* चिता *f.*
6 See HAIR, NAP.
7 piles; *hemorrhoids.* मूळव्याधि *pop.* मूळव्याध *f.* अर्श *m. n.* गुदरोग *m.* गुदार्श *m.* गुदांकुर *m. pl.*
Afflicted with p. मूळव्याध्या, मूळव्याधीचा, अर्शी, अर्शोरोगी.
Bleeding p. रक्तीमूळव्याध *f.*
Blind p. वादीमूळव्याध *f.*

To PILE, *v. a.* v. To HEAP. चळथणें, डाळणें, चुणणें, रचणें, एकावर एक रचून ठेवणें, रास *f.*-&c. करणें *g. of o.*

PILED, *p.* v. V. चळथलेला, डाळलेला, रासकेलेला, &c. रचित.

PILING, *n.* v. V.—*act.* चळथणें *n.* &c. रचणूक *f.* रचना *f.*

To PILFER, *v. a.* *filch, gain by petty theft.* उपटणें, उचलणें, उचकणें, उचलून नेणें, उपटा *or* उपाटा *m.* देणें *with* वर *or* ला, ताव *m.* देणें, हात *m.* मारणें, पट्टा *m.* मारणें.

To PILFER, *v. n.* *practise petty theft.* हलकीचोरी *f.*-उचलेपणा *m.*-भुट्टेचोरी *f.*-भामटेपणा *m.*-&c. करणें.

PILFERER, *n.* PILFERING, *p. a.* v. V. A. उपटणारा, उचलणारा, &c. उपट्या, उचल्या, उचक्या, भामट्या *or* भांबट्या, भुट्टेचोर *or* भुट्टेचोर, भुरटाचोर. [&c.

PILFERING, *n.* v. V. A.—*act.* उपटणें *n.* उचलणें *n.* उपटा देणें *n.* v. V. N. उचलेपणा *m.* भामटेपणा *m.* उचकेपणा *m.* हलकीचोरी *f.* हरामखोरी *f.* भुट्टेचोरी *f.* बुरटीचोरी.

PIL-GARLIC, PILLED-GARLIC, *n.* *a forlorn wretch,* v. WRETCHED. दैवाचा भोपळा *m.* फुटक्या दैवाचा.

PILGRIM, *n.* *traveller to holy places.* यात्रेकरी, यात्रेकरू, यात्रकरू, जत्रेकरी *or* जत्रेकरू, तीर्थकरी, तीर्थकरू, फिरस्त *or* फिरस्ता, यात्रिक.
A company of pilgrims. यात्रा *pop.* जत्रा *f.*
A p.—pedler. कापडी.
Pilgrims and sojourners. उतारू पातारू.

PILGRIMAGE, *n.* *journey to a sacred place.* तीर्थ *n.* यात्रा *pop.* जत्रा *f.*—with implication of frequence. तीर्थयात्रा *f.* तीर्थाटन *n.* [*m. pl.*
Ceremony to be observed at a place of p. तीर्थविधि
Favors (flowers, holy water, ashes, &c.) granted by the idol at a p. तीर्थप्रसाद *m.*
Offerings (to the idol and Bráhmans) on return from p. मावंदें *or* मावंधें *n.*
Periodical resort to a place of p. जत्रा *f.* वारी *f.* खेटा *m.*
Performer of periodical p. वारकरी.
P. to the three holy places. (प्रयाग, काशी, & गया) तिरस्थळी *f.*
Place of p. तीर्थ *n.* क्षेत्र *n.*
The great p. (viz. to Benares). महायात्रा *f.*
To wander about on p. तीर्थें *n. pl.* फिरणें.

PILL, *n.* *little ball of medicine.* गोळी *f.* गुटिका *f.* वटिका *f.* वटी *f.*

To PILL, *v. a.* v. To PEEL. सोलणें, त्वचा *f.*-&c. काढणें *g. of o.*
2 *strip, pillage, &c.* v. To PLUNDER. लुटणें, नाडणें, नागवणें, घासणें, वासटणें, बोडणें.

To PILLAGE, *v. a.* *spoil, strip &c.* v. To PLUNDER. लुटणें, नागवणें, लुगारणें, बुचाडणें, धुवून नेणें, लूट *f.*-लूटपाट *f.*-&c. करणें *g. of o.*

PILLAGE, PILLAGING, *n.* v. V.—*act.* लुटणें *n.* लुगारणें *n.* &c. लूट *f.* लूटपाट *f.* लुटालूट *f.* लुंटन *n.*
I. *booty, spoil.* लूट *f.*

PILLAR, *n.* खांब *m.* स्तंभ *m.* स्थूणा *f.*
Erected upon two pillars,—a building. दुखांबी.
Main p. of a house. धरणखांब *m.* धारण *m.* मूलस्तंभ *m.*
Stone p. मनोरा *m.* [ची गादी *f.*

PILLION, *n.* *a woman's riding cushion.* घोड्यावर स्त्रीची बसण्या-

PILLORY, *n.* *frame on which an offender is exposed.* मानखोडा *m.* मान अडकवणें *n.*

PILLOW, *n.* *cushion for the head.* उशी *f.* उसें *n.* तक्या *m.*
Small p. गिरदी *f.*

PILLOW-CASE, *n.* उशीचा अभ्रा *m.* उशीची गवसणी *f.*

PILOT, *n.* *steerer of a ship in or out of harbour, &c.* v. STEERSMAN. पाण्यांतला वाटाडी, बंदरवाटाडी *or* वाटाड्या, नाविक, कर्णधार, समुद्रमार्गप्रदर्शक.
2 fig. v. CONDUCTOR. सारथि *or* सारथी.

PILOTAGE, *n.* *hire of a pilot.* पाण्यांतले वाटाड्याचें वेतन *n.*

PIMENTO, *n.* *myrtus pimenta.* कंकोल *or* ळ *m. n.*

PIMP, *n.* *pander, procurer.* कुंटण, भडवा.
Business of a p. कुंटणकी *f.* कुंटणपणा *m.* भडवेपणा *m.*

To PIMP, *v. n.* v. N. कुंटणकी *f.*-भडवेपणा *m.*-&c. करणें.

PIMPING, *n.* v. V.—*act.* कुंटणकी *f.* कुंटणपणा *m.*

PIMPING, *a.* *petty, little.* लहान, लहानप्रतीचा, नसकोणा, नकटा, बिटकुला, बिटका.

PIMPLE, *n.* *pustule, &c.* फुटकळी *or* फुटकुळी *f.* पुटकळी *or* पुटकुळी *f.* पुळी *f.* फोड *m.* फोडी *f.* स्फोट *m.* विस्फोट *m.*
Eruption on the face (about puberty) of little pimples. मुरूम *m.*—a single p. of this eruption. मुरूमाची पुळी *f.* मुरूम *m.*
To be covered with pimples. फुटकळणें.

PIMPLED, *a.* *having pimples.* फुटकळयांचा, पुटकळया आलेला, फुटकळलेला, सस्फोट.

PIN, *n.* टांचणी *f.* शलाका *f.*
2 *peg, bolt, &c.* खुंटा *m.* *dim.* खुंटी *f.* खीळ *f.* कील *m.* सळई *f.* शंकु *m.*—of bamboo, &c. to pin leaves. चुई *or* चांई *f.* चुइटी *f.*—as of a broach, &c. दांडा *m.*—of a कांबळा, तइस *m.*

Sharp dartings or shootings like the pricking of pins (in the belly). तडस *m. pl. v.* भर, लाग.

3 *linch pin.* चाकाची-आंसाची खीळ *f.*

4—the disease of the eye. काडी *f.* सडी *f.*

5 *trifling thing.* काडी *f.* तणकाडी *f.* कवडी *f.*

To PIN, *v. a. fasten with a pin, &c.* टांचणी *f.*-खीळ *f.* लावणें-घालणें-मारणें, टांचणें, टांचून ठेवणें, खिळणें, खिळण *f.* करणें.

PINAFORE, *n.* मुलाचें मळवस्त्र *n.*

To leave off one's p. *fig.* ओंठावरचें दूध वाळणें-जिरणें *g. of s.*

PIN-CUSHION, *n.* टांचण्या बसविण्यासाठीं केलेली गादी *f.*

PIN-MONEY, *n. allowance to a wife for petty expenses.* चोळी-बांगडीची खर्ची *f.*- नेमणूक *f.* स्त्रीची खाऊखर्ची *f.*- पानखर्ची *f.* चिरीखर्च *m.*

PINCERS, *n. instrument for griping, drawing nails, &c.* चिमटा *m.* अंबर *or* अंबूर *m. dim.* अंबरी *f.* सांडस *m. dim.* सांडशी *f.*—esp. of goldsmiths. गावी *f.* गही *f.*

To PINCH, *v. a. squeeze between the ends of the fingers.* चिमटा *m.*-चिमटी *f.*-चिमखुरा *m.*-चुटकी *f.*-&c. घेणें-काढणें, चिमट्यांत धरणें, विचकुरणें.

2 *squeeze, press between.* चिमटणें, चिंबळणें, चेंगरणें.

3 *gripe, oppress, press hard,* v. To OPPRESS. पिळणें, चेंगरणें, चेंचणें, खळणें.

4 *straiten, drive to extremity or distress,* v. To DISTRESS. अडचणींत-&c. आणणें, अडचणवणें, ताण *m.* बसणें *with* वर *of o.*

To be pinched. अडचणणें, तंगणें.

5 (the belly). पोट *n.* मारणें-बांधणें, पोटमारा *m.*-उपासमारा *m.* करणें.

6—as cold, &c. कांकडवणें, अखुडवणें, कांकडा *m.* वळवणें.

To be pinched with cold. कांकडणें, अखुडणें, कांकडा *m.* वळणें *g. of s.*

7—as clothes. दाटणें, अडस-दाट-घट्ट-&c. असणें, अडचणें.

PINCH, *n. compression with the fingers.* चिमटा *m.* चिमट *f.* चिमटी *f.* चिमखुरा *or* खोरा *m.* चिमूट *or* चिमोट *f.* चिम्रोटा *m.* चिंचकुला *m.* चिंचकुली *f.* विचकुरा *m. all with* घे.

2 (of snuff, &c.) *quantity compressed between the thumb and finger.* चिमट *f.* चुकटी *or* चुटकी *f.*

3 *distress, strait, difficulty.* अडचण *f.* चिमटा *m.* संकट *n.* संकष्ट *n. m.*

PINCH-BECK, *n.* तांबें व जस्त ह्यांपासून केलेलें एक मिश्र धातु आहे.

PINCH-FIST, PINCH-PENNY. See MISER.

PINCHED, *p.* v. V. 1. चिमटा घेतलेला, &c.

2 चिमटलेला, &c.

4 अडचणींत आणलेला, तंग.

P. by poverty. ओढग्रस्त, ओढग्रस्त, ओढिस्त, ओढीक.

PINCHING, *p. a.* v. V. 6. *and* PIERCING. कडक, कडकडीत, कडक्याचा, सर, जलाल.

PINDARIE, *n.*—the freebooter. पेंढारी.

Body of Pindaries. पेंढार *n.*

PINE, *n. pinus longifolia.* देवदारु *pop.* देवदार *m.* सरल *m.*

Exudation from the p. सरलद्रव्य *n.*

To PINE, *v. n. languish and waste away, lose flesh under distress.* v. LEAN. झुरणें, धुपणें, झिजणें, गळणें, सुखणें, मरीस लागणें-जाणें, झुरण *f.*-&c. लागणें, काष्ठ *n.* होणें, हिंग *n.* होणें.

2 *long for, whine after, &c.* v. To DESIRE. धोपणें, रुणा *m.* -खुरखुर *f.* लागणें, टाहो *m.*-घोर *m.*-खंत *f.*-टाप *f.*-रुणा *m.* घेणें *g. of o.* टुकळा *or* टोकळा *m.* धरणें-करणें, छंद *m.* घेणें-धरणें.

PINE-APPLE, *n.*—the plant. अननस *or* अननास *f.*—the fruit. अननस *or* नास *m. n.*

PINERY, *n.* अननसांचा मळा *m.*

PINGLE. See ENCLOSURE.

PINION, *n.* v. WING. पांख *m.*

2 *band for the arms.* मुसक्या बांधण्याची काढणी *f.*

To PINION, *v. a. bind or confine the wings.* पांख *m.*-&c. बांधणें.

2 *confine by binding the arms to the body.* पिचुंड्या *f. pl.*-मुसक्या *f. pl.* बांधणें, चतुर्भुज करणें, चौमेखणें, दंड *m. pl.* अवळणें-बांधणें, दंडाला काढण्या *f. pl.* लावणें.

PINK, *n.* एक फूल आहे.

2—the colour. पांढरा तांबडारंग *m.* पाटलरंग *m.*

3 *pinnacle, tip top (in excellency, &c.).* सीमा *f.* पराकाष्ठा *f.* कळस *m.* शिखर *n.*

To PINK, *v. a. pierce with small holes,* v. To PIERCE. लहान लहान भोकें *n. pl.* पाडणें.

To PINK, *v. n.* See To WINK.

PINK-EYED, *a. having small eyes.* लहान डोळ्यांचा, चिमणडोळ्या, डुचका, डुळका, गजनेत्री.

PINNACE, *n.* एके प्रकारची नाव आहे.

PINNACLE, *n.*—of a building. कळस *m.* शृंग *n.* प्रासादशृंग *n.* प्रासाद्य *n.*

2 *spire, shaft.* सुळका *m. dim.* सुळकी *f.* शिखर *n.*

3 fig. *acme, summit.* शिखर *n.* कळस *m.*

PINNED, *p.* v. V. टांचणी लावलेला, खीळ घातलेला, &c. कीलित.

PINT, *n.* v. MEASURE. In some places it is अर्धशेर, in others पावशेर.

PIONEER, *n.*—of an army. बेलदार.

PIOUS, *a. godly, religious, devout,*—persons. भक्तिमान् *or* भक्तिमंत, धर्मशील, धार्मिक, धर्मी, धर्मिष्ठ, ईश्वरमनस्क, ईश्वरपरायण, परमार्थपरायण, परमार्थी, पारमार्थिक, देवभक्तिप्रवण, देवभक्तिनिष्ठ, ईश्वरभक्तिपरायण, भजनी, भजनशील, धर्मनिबंधी.

2 *proceeding from piety.* भक्तिभावाचा, भक्तिबुद्धीचा, ईश्वरनिष्ठेचा, धर्मनिष्ठेचा, देवपरायणबुद्धीचा, भक्तिमूलक.

3 *practised under the pretence of religion.* धर्माच्या निमित्तानें केलेला.

PIOUSLY, *adv.* v. A. भक्तिबुद्धीनें, भक्तिभावानें, ईश्वरनिष्ठेनें, &c.

PIP, *n.* (of fowls). रूं *n.* ?

2 (of an apple, &c.). दाणा *m.* बीज *n.*

To PIP, *v. n. chirp.* चूंचूं *n.*-चिवचीव *f.* करणें.

PIPE, *n. tube.* नळी *f.* नाड *f.* पन्हळ *m. dim.* पन्हळी *f.* नलिका *f.*

2—the musical instrument. पंवा *or* पांवा *m. dim.* पांवरी *f.* पोंवा *m. dim.* पोंवरी *f.* पुंगी *f.* अलगुजें *n.* वंशी *f.* वंशनालिका *f.* वेणु *m.*—esp. as made of a plantain-leaf, mango-stone, &c. पेपाणी *or* पिंपाणी *f.* पिंपारी *f.* पेंपेरें *or* पोंपेरें *n.* पिंकाणी *f.*

To stop one's p. fig. *make to be silent.* पुंगी *f.* बंद करणें *g. of o.*

3 *cask.* पीप *n.*

4 *tobacco pipe.* चुट्टा *m.*

To PIPE, *v. n. play on a pipe.* पोंवा *m.*-&c. वाजवणें.

2 v. To CRY. रडणें, डोळे *m. pl.* पुसणें.

To begin to p. वाजंत्रें चालू होणें.

Pipe-clay, *n.* चिकणखडू *m. f.* खडी *f.* खडू *m. f.* शाडू *or* शेडू*m. f.* श्वेतमृत्तिका *f.*

Piper, *n.* Piping, *p. a.* v. V. 1. पोंवा-&c. वाजवणारा.

I. piping hot. गरमागरम, उन्हून *or* उनून.

Pipkin, *n.* v. Pot. मडकें *n.* लोटा *m. dim.* लोटी *f.*

Glazed p. लाखलोटें *n.* [खमंगाई *f.* चरमर *f.*

Piquancy, *n.* v. A. 1. खमखमितपणा *m.* चणचणितपणा *m.* &c.

2 चरमरितपणा *m.* &c. चरमर *f.*

Piquant, *a. highly seasoned, &c.* खमखमीत, खमंग, चणचणीत, चमचमीत, चरचरीत, चरमरीत, खारटतुरट.

2 fig. *witty, smart,* v. Sharp. चरमरीत, अणखर, खारटतुरट.

Pique, *n. slight offence taken.* चीढ *f. v.* ये, रुसवा *m.* खपीमर्जी *f.* रीस *f.* खोंच *f.*

To Pique, *v. a. offend, nettle, fret, &c.*v. To Anger. चिथवणें, चिढीस आणणें, संताप *m.* आणणें, संतापवणें, खोंचणें, खोंचरणें.

2 *stimulate, touch with some passion.* अभिमानास घालणें, आग्रहास पाडणें, हटास पेटवणें.

3 (one's self upon). अभिमान *m.*-बाणा *m.*बाळगणें *g. of o.* बिरीद *n.* बांधणें-बाळगणें *g. of o.* चंग *m.* बांधणें *g. of o.*

Piqued, *p.* v. V. 1. चिढीस आणलेला, *&c.* संतप्त.

2 अभिमानास घातलेला, &c.

Piracy, *n. robbery on the seas.* गलबतावरचा-समुद्रावरचा दरवडा *m.* गलबत लुटणें *n.* चांचेपणा *m.*

Pirate, *n. robber on the sea.* गलबतावर-&c. दरवडाघालणारा, गलबत-&c. लुटणारा, गलबत लुटारू, चांचा.

Band or body of pirates. चांच *n.*

2 लुटारू गलबत *n.* चांच्यांचें गलबत *n.*

Piratical, *a.* चांच्याचा, चांचेपणाचा, समुद्रावर दरवडाघालण्याचा.

Piscation, *n. fishing.* मासे धरणें *n.*

Piscatory, Piscine, *a. belonging to fishes.* माशांचा, मत्स्यसंबंधी, मत्स्यविषयक.

Pisces, *n.*—the zodiacal sign. मीन *m.* [मत्स्याद.

Piscivorous, *a. living on fish.* मत्स्याहारी,मत्स्यजीवी,मत्स्याशी,

Pish, *interj.*—expressing contempt, impatience, &c. फिश्श, फिश्शो, फिस, छिछी, छ, छत्, छिः,छी, धिक्, ऊंः, धत्त,इश *or* इस.

Pismire, *n.* v. Ant. मुंगी *f.*

Piss, To Piss. See Urine.

Pistachio, *n.*—the plant and the fruit. पिस्ता *m.*

Pistil, *n.*—in botany. पुष्पगर्भतंतु *m.* गर्भकेसर *m.* स्त्रीकेसर *m.*

Pistol, *n.*—the weapon. तमंचा *or* तबंचा *m.*पिस्तोल *or* पिस्तूल *n.* from the English is common.

To Pistol, *v. a.* पिस्तुलानें गोळी घालून मारणें.

Piston, *n.* (of an engine). दट्ट्या *m.* चेपणें *n.* चेपणकाठी *f.*

Pit, *n. cavity, hole, &c.* खांच *f.* खळगा *m.* खळगी *f.* खळी *f.* खाडा *m.* गडदा *m.* गार *f.* हांडा *m.* गर्त्ता *f.* अवट *m.* खांचर *n.* —*intens.* खाचाड *n.*

Pits & holes-compreh. or indef. खांचखळ *f.* खांचखळगा *m.* खांचरखळगा *m.* खांचरखुचर *n.*

2 (as in stone, wood, &c.). खोंच *f.* [*f.* खनि *f.*

3 (as of chalk, stone, clay, &c.) v. Quarry. खाण *f.* गडद

4 (of the stomach). शिंप *f.* उराची शिंप *f.*-खळगी *f.*

5 (of the small pox) देवीनें झालेली खळी *f.* देवीचावण *m.*

6 (of a theatre). नाटक घरांतील तळची जागा *f.*

To Pit, *v. a. mark with little hollows.* खळ्या *f. pl.*-खांचा *f.pl.* -&c. पाडणें.

2 *set in competition.* लढायास लावणें, बरोबरी करायास लावणें.

Pit-apat, *adv. with palpitation.* धकधक *or* धगधग, धकाधक, धधधस,मटमूट *or* माटमूट, तुरतूर *or* तुरुतुरू,दुडदूड, दडदुडा, दुडुदुडु.

To beat p. धकधकणें, धगधगणें.

Pit-fall, *n. pit for catching beasts.* चोरखळी *f.*

Pitch, *n. resin.* राळ *f.* राल *m.* यक्षधूप *m.*—used in paying ships or boats. कारी *f.*

P. darkness. गदड *n.* काळी किट्टरात्र *f.*

The coating of p. applied over the bottoms of ships, &c. शिपार *or* शिफार *f.*

2 *degree of elevation.* मान *n.* उंचीचें मान *n.* महत्वमान *n.*

Highest p. पराकाष्ठा *f.* कळस *m.* भरेंं *n.*

To such a p. एथवर, एथपावेतों.

3 (of voice). गळा*m.* स्वर *pop.* सूर*m.*

A high p. चढासूर*m.*

4 See Slope. [कटवणें.

To Pitch, *v. a. smear with pitch.* राळ *f.*-&c. लावणें-माखणें-चि-

2 *throw,* v. To Cast. झुगारणें, फेंकणें.

3 (a tent). देणें, उभारणें, उभा करणें.

4 (a tune). सूर*m.* धरणें, स्वरस्थिति *f.* करणें.

5 (the voice). लावणें.

To be pitched—the voice, an instrument, &c. लागणें.

To Pitch, *v. n. drop, light, settle.* उतरणें, बसणें, पडणें, तळ*m.*-डेरा*m.* देणें. [ठोकणें.

2 *encamp.* डेरा*m.*-तंबू-राहुटी *f.*-&c. देणें, तळ*m.* देणें, तंबू*m.*

3 *fall headlong.* डोई-डोकी-&c. कडून पडणें, डोकीच्या-डोईच्या-&c. झोकानें पडणें.

4 upon; *fix choice,* v. To Choose. पसंत करणें.

Pitched, *a.* (battle). व्यूहपूर्वक केलेला, व्यूहाचा.

Pitch-farthing, *n.*—the play. गलकोंड्या *f. pl.*

Pitch-fork, *n. fork for throwing with.* टोंचणी *f.* खोचेरा*m.*

Pitch-pipe, *n. instrument for pitching a tune.* सूर*m.*

Pitcher, *n. earthen vessel.* घडा*m.* घागर *f.* मडकें*n.* मडकी *f.* मडकूल*n.* डेरा*m.* (*dim.* डेरका*m.* डेरकी *f.*) घट*m.* कुंभ*m.* कुडु*n.* कलश*m.* खापर*n.*

Circle of straw, rope, &c. to place under a p. शिंकण*n.*

Half of a broken p. कपाल*n.* कचकल*n. m.* कचकोल*m.*

Lower portion of a broken p. खापर*n.* भदें *or* भदें*n.*

P. with a spout. कळसा*m.* करा *or* कऱ्हा*m.*

P. with the mouth, or upper half broken. कचकोल*m.* कांठमोरा*m.* [कांठमोरा*m.*

Upper half of a p. as broken off. कांठमा*m.* कांठारा*m.*

Piteous, *a. that may excite or move pity; mournful, dolorous, &c.* काकळूतवाणा *or* वाणी, केविलवाणा *or* वाणी, किलवाणा *or* वाणी, दीनवाणा *or* वाणी, दैनवाणा *or* वाणी, बापुडवाणा *or* वाणी, काकलुतीचा, &c. करुण, करुणारसोत्पादक, दीन, रडवा, रडका.

P. accents or tones. किळकिळ्या *or* कळकळ्या *f. pl. v.* दे, काकळूत *f. v.* कर, काकळूत मामलूत *f.* कींव *f.* कींव काकळूत *f.* कन्हव *f.* कारणा *f.* करुणस्वर*m. pl.* रिपरीप *f.*

2 *deserving pity; miserable, &c.* v. Wretched. दुःखाचा,

संकटाचा, दया येण्याचा, दया यायाजोगा, दया योग्य, करुणायोग्य, अनुकंप्य.

3 *compassionate*. See PITIFUL.

PITEOUSLY, *adv.* v. A. 1. काकळूत करून, कळकळ्या देऊन, दया येईसा *decl.* दीनवाणी, गयांबयां *or* गायांबायां *v.* कर, गळगळां *v.* ये.

3 दयेनें, &c. दयाबुद्धीनें, दयापूर्वक, &c.

PITEOUSNESS, *n.* v. A. 1. दीनवाणेपणा*m.* केविलवाणेपणा*m.* &c. काकळूत *f.* काकळूतपणा*m.*

2 दयायोग्यता *f.* अनुकंपायोग्यता *f.* &c. दैन*n.*

PITH, *n. soft inside of plants, &c.* गाभा*m.* भेंड*n.* गर*m.* गीर*m.* सार*m.* गर्भ*m.* विरखुंड*n.* मगज*m.* भिरकुंडें*n.* भिरकूट*n.* मज्जा *f.*

2 *quintessence, cream, sum and substance,* v. ESSENCE. सार*m.n.* सारांश*m.* तत्व*n.* तत्वार्थ*m.* सत्व*n.* तत्तामाल*m.* कस*m.*

3 *energy, spirit, fire, vigour, &c.* सत्व*n.* सार*m. n.* कस*m.* तेज*n.* जीव*m.* ऐवज*m.* बळ*n.* बळकटी *f.* मजबुती *f.*

PITHINESS, *n.* v. A. 2. तेज*n.* रस*m.* सत्व*n.* जीव*m.* बळकटी *f.* मजबुती *f.* कस*m.* सार*m. n.* [निगर्भ.

PITHLESS, *a. wanting pith.* गराबेगळा-निराळा, असार, अगर्भ,

2 *wanting energy, spirit, &c.* निस्सत्व, असार, निर्जीव, निस्तेज, फुसका, फुसकुला, पोकळ.

PITHY, *a. having, &c. pith.* गराचा, गाभ्याचा, गरभरू, कसदार, सगर्भ, सकस, सात्विक.

2 *forcible, energetic.* कसदार, जीवदार, जिवट, बळकट, बळकटीचा, मजबुतीचा, सत्वाचा, सतेज, ससत्व, रसभरित.

PITIABLE, *a. deserving pity, miserable,* v. WRETCHED. दया येण्याचा, दया यायाजोगा, दया योग्य, करुणायोग्य, अनुकंपायोग्य, अनुकंप्य, दयाविषय, दयापात्र, दयाभाजन, दयास्पद.

PITIABLENESS, *n.* v.A. दयायोग्यता *f.* करुणायोग्यता*f.* अनुकंप्यता*f.* दैन *n.*

PITIED, *p.* v. V. दया केलेला, &c. अनुकंपित.

PITIER, *n.* PITYING, *p. a.* v. V. दया करणारा, &c.

PITIFUL, *a. full of pity, compassionate.* दयेचा, &c. दयावान्*pop.* दयावंत, दयालु *or* ळू, दयाळ, दयाशील,दयाविशिष्ट, दयायुक्त, दयामय, सदय, दयान्वित, दयासंपन्न, दयापूर्ण, दयाढ्य, रुपाळ, रुपाळू, कन्हवाळू, करुण, कारुणिक, करुणाशील, सकरुण, करुणापर, करुणामय, दयारूप, दयाभूत, घृणी, घृणावान्, घृणाशील, सानुकंप, दयार्द्र, करुणार्द्र, दयार्द्रचित्त, दयार्द्रमनस्क, हृदयालु, हृदयवान्.

Some terms and phrases for a *pitiful person* are दयासागर, दयासमुद्र, दयाब्धि, दयासिंधु, दयानिधि, दयानिधान, दयाकर, करुणाकर, करुणासागर-समुद्र-निधि-&c. अनाथनाथ,अनाथबंधु, दीनदयाळ, दीननाथ, दीनबंधु, दीनवत्सल, आर्त्तसाधु, आर्त्तबंधु, आर्त्ताभिमानी, प्रणतवत्सल.

2 *pity-moving,* v. PITEOUS. काकळूतवाणा *or* वाणी, बापुडवाणा *or* वाणी, केविलवाणा.

3 *piteous, pitiable, miserable,* v. WRETCHED. दया येण्याचा, दया यायाजोगा, दयायोग्य.

4 *paltry, petty, wretched, sorry, little, insignificant, &c.* किलवाणा *or* वाणी, केविलवाणा *or* वाणी, गयाळ, हलका, फुसका, नाकारा, गैरी, क्षुद्र, क्षुल्लक, रुपण, भिकार.

PITIFULLY, *adv.* v. A. 1. दयेनें, दयाबुद्धीनें, दयादृष्टीनें, दयापूर्वक, दयापुरस्सर.

2. 3. काकळूत करून, कळकळ्या देऊन, काकळूतवाणी.

4 केविलवाणी, हलका *decl.* भिकाररितीनें.

PITIFULNESS, *n.* v. A. 1. *and* PITY. दया *f.* दयाळूपणा *m.* &c. करुणा *f.* कारुण्य *n.* अनुकंपा *f.* घृणा*f.* चित्ताची आर्द्रता*f.* चित्ताची कोमलता *f.* सकरुणता *f.*

4 हलकेपणा *m.* गयाळपणा *m.* गैरीपणा *m.* क्षुद्रता *f.* क्षुल्लकता *f.*

PITILESS, *a. without pity,* v. CRUEL. निर्दय, दयाशून्य, दयाहीन, दयारहित, &c. अदय, अकरुण, दये-करुणे-&c. बेगळा *or* निराळा, कठोर, क्रूर. [या सोडून-टाकून.

PITILESSLY, *adv.* v. A. निर्दयपणानें, निर्दय होऊन, दयेवांचून, द-

PITILESSNESS, *n.* v. A. निर्दयपणा *m.* दयाशून्यता *f.* दयाराहित्य *n.* दया हीनता *f.* कठोरपणा *m.* क्रूरता *f.* क्रौर्य *n.*

PITTANCE, *n. allowance of victuals.* मोताद *f.* चंदी *f.* शेर *m.* शिधा *m.* शेरसिधा *m.* शेरपीठ *n.*

2 *very small portion or allowance.* लहान-थोडी-हलकी-&c. मोताद *f.*-नेमणूक *f.*-&c.

Mere p. See LIVELIHOOD.

3 *small quantity.* थोडा अंश *m.* अल्पांश *m.* अत्यल्पांश *m.* जरा-जरासा-जराकसा *used with a noun.*

An idiomatical way of rendering this sense is by the use of some adjective meaning little, as अल्पविद्या a p. of learning, अल्पधन a p. of money, &c.

PITTED, *p.* v. V. खळया पाडलेला, सांचा पाडलेला.

I. (with the small pox). फोडेला, उकटलेला, देवीच्या वणाचा.

II.—a coin. उखळ्या. [परीप *f.*

PITTER PATTER, *n.* (of rain). बुटबूट *f.* पुटपूट *f.* पिटपीट *f.* रि-

2 (of feet). दुडदड *or* दुडदूड *f. intens.* दुडदुडाट *m.*

To PITTER PATTER, *v. n.*—rain. पिटपिटणें, पुटपुटणें, पुटपूट *adv.* पडणें.

PITUITARY, *a. that secretes phlegm.* कफोत्पादक.

PITUITOUS, *a. consisting of phlegm.* कफाचा, कफमय.

PITY, *n. compassion, &c.* दया *f.* करुणा *f.* करुणारस *m.* माया *f.* अनुकंपा *f.* घृणा *f.* कींव *f.* किवण *f. n.* काकळूत *f. v.* ये, कन्हवळा *m.* कळवळ *f.* कळवळा *m.* कळकळ *f.* कणव *f.* कारुण्य *n.*

To feel p. कळकळ *f.*-कळवळा *m.*-कींव *f.*-काकळूत *f.*-&c. येणें *in. con.* कळवळणें.

To appeal to p. *make piteous whinings and moanings.* करुणा *f.* भाकणें, काकळूत *f.* करणें, काकळुतीस-काकुळती येणें, दैना *f. pl.* भाकणें-सांगणें-दाखवणें, किरकणें.

To take p. on. काकळूत *f.* करणें.

2 *ground of pity, cause of grief.* दयेसकारण *n.* दयेसहेतु *m.* दुःखास कारण *n.*

To PITY, *v. a. feel compassion for.* दया *f.*-&c. करणें *with* वर *of o.* दया *f.*-काकळूत *f.*-कळकळ *f.*-कळवळा *m.*-कींव *f.*-&c. येणें *in. con. with g. of o.* कळवळणें *with* वर *of o.*

PIVOT, *n. pin on which any thing turns.* कांटा *m.*

PLACABILITY, PLACABLENESS, *n.* v. A. सांत्वनीयता *f.* सांत्वनयोग्यता *f.* सांत्वनशक्यता *f.*

PLACABLE, *a. that may be appeased.* सांत्वनीय, क्षमापनीय, सांत्वनयोग्य, सांत्वनशक्य, आराधनीय, सुखाराध्य.

PLACARD, *n. writing posted in a public place.* प्रसिद्ध ठिकाणीं चिकटवलेला जाहीरनामा *m.*

PLACE, *n. portion of space.* जागा *m. f.* ठिकाण *n.* ठिकाणा *m.* ठाय *m.* ठाव *m.* देश *m.* प्रदेश *m.* स्थान *n.* स्थल *or* ळ *n.* प्रांत *m.* थांगा *m.* निलय *n. m.*

At the p. (house, country, &c.) of. एथे *or* तेथें *with* च्या.
From all places around. जिकडून तिकडून, जिकडणें तिकडणें.
Genius of a p. स्थानमाहात्म्य *n.*
In both places. उभयत्र.
In every p. or direction. जिकडे तिकडे.
In various places or parts. जागोजाग.
In a by p. अठायीं. [कोठला.
Of what p. ? कुठचा *or* कोठचा, कुठील-कुठला *or* कोठील-
Of which p.—relatively. जेथचा *or* ला, जेथील.
Purification or clearance of a p. स्थलशुद्धि *f.*
Search of a p. on moving from it. स्थलशुद्धि *f.*
2 *place of, the proper place.* जागा *m. f.* ठिकाण *n.* ठिकाणा *m.* ठाव *m.* ठाय *m.* थांग *m.* थांगा *m.* स्थान *n.* स्थल *or* ळ *n.* देश *m.* शाला *pop.* शाळ & साळ *f.* (in comp. as होमशाला, पाकशाला, पाठशाला, नृत्यशाला, टंकसाळ, घोडसाळ, &c.), खाना *m.* (in comp. as मोदीखाना, पिलखाना, तोफखाना, &c.).
Out of its p. गैरविल्हेईस *or* गैरविल्हेस, अनाठायीं.
To be in (its or one's) proper p. आपल्या पायरीवर असणें.
To keep in its p. ठिकाणीं ठेवणें.
To leave its proper p. ठाव *m.*-पायरी *f.*-&c. सोडणें.
To put into its proper p. ठिकाणीं ठेवणें.
Every thing is good in its place. पायांचा मोजा पायांतच बरा डोकीवर चढवूं नये.
3 *room, stead.* जागा *m. f.* ठिकाण *n.* स्थान *n.* स्थल *or* ळ *n.*
In the p. or room of. जागां, जागीं, जागें, बारचा *decl.* बांटचा *decl.*
4 *post, official situation,* v. OFFICE. जागा *f.* असामी *f.* पदवी *f.* स्थल *or* ळ *n.* [स्थलच्युत.
Dismissed, &c. from p. स्थानभ्रष्ट, स्थानच्युत, स्थलभ्रष्ट,
5 *room, warrant, &c.* v. GROUND. जागा *m. f.* ठिकाण *n.* आधार *m.* आश्रय *m.*
In the first p. पहिलें *or* पहिल्यानें, मुळीं, मुदलीं.—In the second p. दुसरें, दुसऱ्यानें, &c. &c. [*neg. con*).
To give p. to, *allow the superiority of.* दाद *f.* देणें (*with*
To give place, *make room.* जागा *f.* घेणें.
To take place, v. To HAPPEN. घडणें, पडणें.
6 *province, office,* v. BUSINESS. काम *n.* अरुता *f.* अरू *f.*

To PLACE, *v. a. put, set in a particular portion of space.* ठेवणें, स्थापणें, न्यसणें, स्थापना *f.*-अधिष्ठान *n.*-न्यास *m.*-&c. करणें *g. of o.*
2 *set, fix, establish.* ठेवणें, राखणें, आधान *n.*-अधिष्ठान *n.* -न्यास *m.*-&c. करणें *g. of o.* [मणें, योजणें.
3 (in an office or situation), v. To APPOINT. ठेवणें, ने-

PLACE-MAN. See OFFICER.

PLACED, *p.* v. V. 1. ठेवलेला, &c. स्थापित, अधिष्ठित, विन्यस्त, न्यस्त, आसादित, आहित, विहित, समाहित, उपहित, निक्षिप्त, स्थानारूढ, स्थलारूढ.
2 ठेवलेला, &c. अधिष्ठित, आधेय.
3 ठेवलेला, नेमलेला, योजलेला, &c. अधिकारारूढ, पदारूढ.

PLACENTA. *n.* गर्भवेष्टन *n.*

PLACER, *n.* PLACING, *p. a.* v. V. 1. ठेवणारा, &c. स्थापक.
2 ठेवणारा, &c. आधायक, विधायी, विधाता.

PLACID, *a. gentle, quiet, serene, &c.* v. MILD. संथ, संत, शांत, मऊ, सौम्य, अक्रोध, विनीत, शांतमनस्क, सुमना, सुमनस्क.

PLACIDITY, PLACIDNESS, *n.* v. A. संथपणा *m.* मऊपणा *m.* &c. सौम्यता *f.* शांति *f.* सौमनस्य *n.* क्रोधाभाव *m.*

PLACING, *n.* v. V. 1—*act.* ठेवणें *n.* स्थापणें *n.* &c. स्थापन *n.* स्थापना *f.* अधिष्ठान *n.* न्यास *m.* विन्यास *m.* आसादन *n.* निक्षेप *m.*
2 ठेवणें *n.* &c. स्थापना *f.* आधान *n.* विधान *n.* उपधान *n.*

PLAGIARISM, *n. literary theft.* ग्रंथाची-शब्दांची-&c. चोरी *f.* कवनचौर्य *n.* काव्यचौर्य *n.* ग्रंथचौर्य *n.* शब्दचौर्य *n.* उच्छिष्टभाषण *n.* उच्छिष्टभाषण *n.*-श्लोक *m.*-वाक्य *n.*-&c.

PLAGIARIST, PLAGIARY, *n. thief in literature.* ग्रंथाचा-कवि-नेचा-&c. चोर, शब्दचोर, काव्यचोर, कवनचोर, उष्टबोल.

PLAGUE, *n. pestilence, epidemic disease,* v. EPIDEMIC. मरी *f.* मरगी *f.* धाम *f.* मारी *f.* मारक *m.*
2 *great evil or calamity,* v. CALAMITY. अरिष्ट *n.* अनर्थ *m.* अनर्थापात *m.* अरिष्टापात *m.*
3 *pest, bore, &c.* व्याध *f.* उपाध *f.* जाच *m.* आधि *m. f.* नड *f.* नडाब *m.* पीडा *f.* कांटा *m.* कंटक *m.* ग्रह *or* दाहाबा ग्रह *m.* खूळ *n.* मड *n.* धाड *f.* आगधाड *f.* जंजाळ *m.* झट *n.* पलिस्त *n.* कलांट *n.* झोंबट *n.* झोंबडें *n.* बलागत *f.* बलाय *f.* खेकटें *n.* खटराग *f.* सल *n.* शल्य *n.* सुदर्शन *n.* विवशी *f.* शनि *m.*—esp. as used of persons, लचांडी *m.* शुक्लकाष्ठ *n.* जिद्द *m.*
To be delivered from one's p. कांटा *m.* उपटण *g. of s.*

To PLAGUE, *v. a. infest with pestilence, calamity, &c.* मरगीनें-&c. पिडणें, मारीग्रस्त-मारीपीडित-मारकग्रस्त-मारकपीडित-&c. करणें.
2 *vex, harass, &c.* v. To TEASE. जाचणें, गांजणें, सतावणें, इजा *f.*-उपद्रव *m.*-दुःख *n.*-तस्दी *f.*-&c. देणें.

PLAGUER, *n.* PLAGUING, *p. a.* PLAGUY, *a.* v. V. 2. जाचणारा, गांजणारा, इजादेणारा, &c. जीवघेण्या *or* घेणा, प्राणघेण्या *or* घेणा, खचरट, खडतर, स्वष्ट, क्लिष्ट, जिकिरीचा.

PLAIN, *a. flat, level, smooth,* v. EVEN. सपाट, सारखा, समान.
2 *without ornament.* साधा, अलंकारावांचूनचा, अनलंकृत, अभूषित, अनलंकार, निरलंकार, निर्भूषण, बिननकशी.
3 *artless, simple, unaffected, not learned, not refined, &c.* साधा, भोळा, साळढाळ, साळाभोळा, साळसूद *or* सूध, उमा, बाळबद, बाळबोध, प्राकृत, प्राकृत्या.
4 *open, straight forward, unreserved, &c.* v. FRANK, BLUNT. खणखणीत, खसखसीत, कडकडीत, धोपटमार्गी, उघडेमराठीचा, परिस्फुट, उजू, सरलबुद्धीचा, सरल *or* ळ.
5 *not beautiful, not handsome; homely, &c.*—of features साधेरूपाचा, साधारणरूपाचा, रूपाचा साधारण, दहाजणासारखा, रूपमध्यम.
6 *mere, bare,* v. SIMPLE. नुस्ता, केवल *or* ळ, शुद्ध.
7 *evident, clear, apparent, manifest, &c.* उघड, उघडा, साफ, स्पष्ट, व्यक्त, अभिव्यक्त, प्रकट *pop.* प्रगट, प्रसिद्ध, प्रत्यक्ष, झळझळीत, टळटळीत, सुदृश्य.
To be p. clear, conspicuous, &c.—a stamp, उमटणें.
8 *evident to the understanding, perspicuous, &c.* v. CLEAR. उघड, उघडा, स्पष्ट, सुबोध, बालबोध, उत्तानार्थ, विशद, अगूढ, अगूढार्थक.
9 *unseasoned, &c.* नुस्ता *or* नुस्था, निकळा, निर्व्यंजन, अव्यंजन, व्यंजनव्यतिरिक्त-रहित-&c.

10 *not difficult, not embarrassing, &c.* साधा, सुरळीत, सरल or ळ, बिनसोचीचा, बिननडीचा, बिनपेंचाचा, सोईचा, सोईकर.

PLAIN, *n. level ground.* मैदान *n.* सपाटी *f.* पटंगण or पटांगण *n.* पाटा *m.* तवा *m.* तळवट *n.* माळ *m.*

PLAIN, *adv.* See PLAINLY.

PLAIN-DEALING, PLAIN-SPOKEN, *a. open, straight forward, &c.* v. FRANK, BLUNT. खसखसीत, खडसडीत, निसालस, धोपटमार्ग्या.

PLAIN-DEALING, PLAIN-SPEAKING, *n. speaking and acting without art, disguise, &c.* उघड or उघडीमराठी *f.* धोपटमार्ग *m.* सरळमार्ग *m.* उभादांडा *m.* [NESS.

PLAIN-HEARTED, PLAIN-HEARTEDNESS. See FRANK, FRANK-

PLAINLY, *adv.* v. A. 2. साधा *decl.* साधेरितीनें, शोभेवांचून, अलंकारावांचून. [कृत्रिमरहित.

3 साधा *decl.* साळाभोळा *decl.* साळसूद, बाळबद, कपटावांचून,

4 v. FRANKLY, BLUNTLY. साफ, स्पष्ट, स्वच्छ, खणखणीत, धादांत, निवळ, धडधडीत.

7 उघड, स्पष्ट, साफ, व्यक्त, धडधडीत, निवळ, टळटळीत, ढळढळीत.

8 उघड, स्पष्ट, धादांत, निवळ. [समता *f.*

PLAINNESS, *n.* v. A. 1. सपाटपणा *m.* सारखेपणा *m.* सपाटी *f.*

2 साधेपणा *m.* साधाडौल *m.* साधेंरूप *n.* अलंकारराहित्य *n.* अलंकाराभाव *m.* भूषणाभाव *m.* भूषणराहित्य *n.*

3 साधेपणा *m.* भोळेपणा *m.* साळसूदपणा *m.* साळढाळपणा *m.* &c. भोळाभाव *m.* कपटराहित्य *n.* सारल्य *n.* सरलभाव *m.*

4 खणखणितपणा *m.* खसखसितपणा *m.* &c. उघड or उघडीमराठी *f.* धोपटमार्ग *m.* उभादांडा *m.*

6 नुसतेपणा *m.* केवळपणा *m.* &c.

7 उघडपणा *m.* स्पष्टपणा *m.* &c. व्यक्ति *f.* अभिव्यक्ति *f.* प्राकट्य *n.*

8 उघडपणा *m.* बालबोधपणा *m.* &c. वैशद्य *n.* विशदता *f.* सुबोधता *f.* उत्तानार्थ *m.*

PLAINT, *n.* v. COMPLAINT. रड *f.* विल्हाळ *m.*

To make loud plaints and ululations. हाका *f. pl.* मारणें.

2—in law. फिर्याद *f.* पूर्ववाद *m.* भाषापाद *m.*

PLAINTIFF, *n.*—in Law. फिर्यादी, वादी, पूर्ववादी, अग्रवादी.

PLAINTIVE, *a. expressive of sorrow, mournful.* दुःख-खेद दाखवणारा, केविलवाणा or णी, बापुडवाणा or णी, किलवाणा or णी, काकळूतवाणा or णी, रडवा, रडका, खेदसूचक-दर्शक-बोधक-&c.

PLAIT, *n. double.* v. FOLD. चुणी *f.* पट्टी *f.* निरी *f.*

To PLAIT, *v. a.* v. N. चुणणें, चुण्या *f. pl.*-निऱ्या *f. pl.*-&c. करणें-घालणें.

2 (the hair) v. To WEAVE. विणणें, वेणी *f.* घालणें.

PLAITED, *p.* v. V. 1. चुणलेला, चुण्या घातलेला, &c.

2 विणलेला, वेणी घातलेला, विणींव.

PLAN, *n. scheme, project,* v. DESIGN. कल्पना *f.* मसलत *f.* तजवीज *f.* उड्ड *m.* अनुसंधान *n.* उपाय *m.*

2 *draught, model, &c.* बेत *m.* नमुना *m.* नकशा *m.* नकाशा *m.*

3 (of an engine, machine, *&c.*) *mode of construction, operation, &c.* कला *f.* कळ *f.* कल्पना *f.* कृप्ति *f.*

To PLAN, *v. a. scheme, devise, &c.* कल्पना *f.*-मसलत *f.*-तजवीज *f.*-&c. करणें *g. of o.* कल्पिणें, योजणें, रचणें, काढणें, बांधणें.

2 *model, &c.* बेत *m.*-नकशा *m.*-&c. करणें-काढणें *g. of o.*

To PLANCH, &c. See To PLANK, &c.

PLANE, *n.*—in geometry ; *level surface.* क्षेत्र *n.* तल *n.* पातळी *f.*

2—the tool. रंधा or रंदा *m.* रोखणी *f.*

P. for rounding edges. रंधागोल *m.* [करणें.

To PLANE, *v. a. level, smooth.* सारखावणें, सारखा-सपाट-सम-&c.

2 *smooth with a plane.* रंधणें, रोखणें, रोखणी *f.*-रंधा *m.* करणें, रंधा *m.* फिरवणें.

PLANED, *p.* v. V. 1. सारखा केलेला, &c.

2 रंधलेला, रंधा फिरवलेला, &c.

PLANET, *n.*—the celestial body. ग्रह *m.* खेचर *m.* खेट *m.*

The planets,—collectively. ग्रहगण *m.* ग्रहमंडल *n.* The Hindus reckon nine (नवग्रह) viz. सूर्य, चंद्र, मंगल, बुध, गुरु, शुक्र, शनि, राहु, केतु, or the sun, the moon, venus, mercury, mars, jupiter, saturn, and the ascending and descending node. The two last are called minor planets.

An auspicious or good p. शुभग्रह, सौम्यग्रह, सुग्रह.—Four are reckoned, viz. बुध, शुक्र, गुरु, चंद्र.

An inauspicious or bad p. कुग्रह, पापग्रह, खडतरग्रह.—Five are reckoned, viz. मंगल, सूर्य, शनि, राहु, केतु.

Ascertainment (by calculation, &c.) of the aspect of the planets. ग्रहसाधन *n.*

Calculations or tables for determining the position of the planets. ग्रहसारणी *f.* [कुंडली *f.*

Diagram representing the aspect of the planets. ग्रह-

Distance of a p. from the beginning of the sidereal zodiac. स्फुटग्रह *m.* स्पष्टग्रह *m.*

Incantations to render the planets propitious. ग्रहजप *m.*

Longitude of a p. सायनखेट *m.* सायनग्रह *m.*

Meeting of the seven planets under one sign. सप्तग्रही *f.*

Minor p. उपग्रह *m.*

Motion of the planets. ग्रहचार *m.*

Motion of a p. in its orbit. गति *f.*

Planetary conjunction. संगम *m.*

Planetary malignity. संक्रांत or संक्रांति *f.*

Planetary affliction or evil. ग्रहपीडा *f.* ग्रहबाधा *f.*

Planetary aspect and influence. ग्रहदशा *f.* ग्रहयोग *m.*

Planetary sphere. ग्रहमंडल *n.*

Presents made to Bráhmans for propitiating the planets. ग्रहदान *n.*

Propitiation of the planets. ग्रहशांति *f.* ग्रहसाधन *n.*

Propitiousness of the planets. ग्रहबल *n.* ग्रहानुकूल्य *n.*

Sacrifice in propitiation of the planets. ग्रहयज्ञ *m.* ग्रहमख *m.*

The annual parallax of the exterior planets, and the elongation of the interior. चलफल *n.* [ग्रहाविष्ट.

PLANET-STRUCK, *a. affected by a planet.* ग्रहबाधित, ग्रहपीडित,

PLANETARY, *a. belonging, &c. to the planets.* ग्रहांचा, ग्रहांविषयींचा, ग्रहविषयक, ग्रहमय, ग्रह in comp. (as ग्रहपीडा, ग्रहबाधा, &c.).

PLANING, *n.* v. V. 1.—*act.* सारखा करणें *n.* &c.

2—*act.* रंधणें *n.* &c. रोखणी *f.* रंधा or रंदा *m.* तक्षण *n.*

PLANK, *n. piece of sawed timber.* फळी *f.* तक्ता *m.* फर्दा *m.*

Ceiling or floor of planks. तक्तपोशी *f.* पाटणी *f.*

Large p. फळा *m.*

Rude or coarse p. फळें *n.*

To PLANK, *v. a. cover or lay with planks.* पाटणें, पाटणी *f.*-

तक्तपोशी *f.*-तक्तेबंदी *f.* करणें.

PLANKED, *p.* v. V. पाटलेला, तक्तपोशी केलेला, &c. पाटींव, तक्तपोशीचा, फळी (in comp. as एकफळी one p.—दुफळी two p. and तिफळी-चौफळी, &c.).

PLANKING, *n.* v. V.—*act.* पाटणें*n.* तक्तपोशीकरणें*n.* &c. पाटणी *f.* कडीपाट*m.* [रचित.

PLANNED, *p.* v. V. 1. योजलेला, काढलेला, रचलेला, &c. योजित,

PLANNER, *n.* PLANNING, *p. a.* v. V. 1. योजणारा, रचणारा, मसलत करणारा, &c. योजक, रचक.

A wise p. अनुसंधानी.

PLANNING, *n.* v.V. 1. योजणें*n.* रचणें*n.* &c. योजणूक *f.* योजना *f.* रचना *f.* तजवीज *f.* मसलत *f.* अनुसंधान*n.* संदर्भ*m.*

PLANT, *n. vegetable, &c.* औषधी *f.* वनस्पति *f.* झाड*n.* उद्भिद्*n.*

Small or young p. रोंप*n.* रोपा*m.* बिरढा*m.*

To PLANT, *v. a. put into the ground for growth.* लावणें, रोवणें, रोपणें, खुंटळणें, रुझत घालणें.

To be planted. लागणें.

2 (a tree, &c.) *set to grow.* लावणें, पुरणें.

3 (a post, &c.) *fix in the ground, &c.* रोवणें, पुरणें, रोपणें, उभारणें, नेमणें, नेमवणें, आरोपणें.

To be planted. पुरणें.

4 (a cannon, &c.) *set, direct.* रोंखणें, लावणें, नेमणें.

5 (a colony, &c.) *establish, settle.* वसवणें, बसवणें, करणें.

PLANTAIN, *n. musa paradisiaca,*—the tree. केळ*f.* रंभा*f.* कदली *f.*—the fruit, केळ*n.* केळें*n.* Some of the varieties of the plantain are, कणेरीकेळ, कन्याळ, खापराळ, गोबराळ, जिरेळ *or* जिरेली, मुठाळीकेळ *or* मुठेळीकेळ *or* मुठेळ—(the fruit of it, मुठाळेंकेळें*n.*) रसबेळ *or* रसबेळी *or* रसबेळकेळी—(the fruit of it, रसबेळें *or* रसबेळकेळें*n.*) रायकेळ *or* राजकेळ *or* राजेळ—(the fruit of it, राजकेळें *or* राजेळें*n.*) लोखंडीकेळ—(fruit of it, लोखंडीकेळें*n.*) शिंगाळीकेळ *or* शिंगेळ (fruit of it, शिंगाळेंकेळें*n.*) —Some *wild* varieties are, कवदर, कौदरी, काष्ठकदली, चवई *or* चवईण *or* चवेण *or* चवेणी, बनकेळ *or* बनेळ, रानकेळ.

Bunch of plantains, or the bunch of fruit stems. लोंगर*n.* घड*m.* फणी *f.* घडुलें*n.* केळवंड *f.* [*m.* बोंड*n.*

Calyx of the fruit stalk of a p.-tree, the spathe. कोंका

Dried p.-leaf or a piece of one. वाळवत *f.n.* सुकवत *f.n.*

Fruit stalk of the p.-tree. फणा*m.* [काल*n.*

Heart or tender core of the stock of a p.-tree. कालें*n.*

Integument or coating of the p.-tree. सोप*n.* सोपट*n.*

Instrument to cut p.-leaves. पिंपिळा*m.* पानकापें*n.*

Leaf of a p.-tree. डांग *f.* डेंग *f.*—Tip or end of leaf divided crosswise, आगोतली *or* आगोथली *f.* आगोती *f.*—Portion, *gener.* of leaf, divided crosswise. दांडाळवत *n.* —Leaf of which the end is broken off, परखंडा *m.*

Last leaf evolved by a p.-tree. आखुडवत *n.* खुंटपान *n.*

Piece torn from a side of a p.-leaf. चिरटा *m. dim.* चिरटी *f.* चिरणा *m. dim.* चिरण *f.* चिरोटी *f.* चिरणी*f.* फाळका *m. dim.* फाळकी *f.* फाळवत *n.*

P. just formed. जीर *m.*

P.-fool, *mixture of plantains and milk with sugar and spices.* शिखरण *f.* शिखरिणी *f.* [सुकीकेळ *n.*

Ripe p. peeled and dried. सुकेंकेळ *n.* सुकेळ *n.* सुकेळें *n.*

Small slip or shred of a p.-leaf. चिरी *f.*

Spadix of the p.-tree. केळफूल *n.*

Stem of a p.-tree. खांब *m.*

Stem of a p.-leaf. दांडोळा *or* नांदोळा *m.*

Spike of unexpanded leaves of a p.-tree. सुई *f.* सुयरा *m.* सुयटा *m. dim.* सुयटी *f.* (*or* सुइरा *m.* &c.)

Young p.-tree. पासंबा *m.*

Young p.-tree, as shooting from the root of its parent. केळंबा *or* केळंभा *m.* केळवा *m.* मुळंबा *m.* मुनवा *or* मोनवा *or* मोना *m.*

To shoot out its spadix—a p.-tree. पसवणें, विणें.

PLANTATION, PLANTING, *n.* v. V. 1. लावणें *n.* रोवणें*n.* &c. लावणी *f.* लागवण *f.*

2 लावणें *n.* &c.

3 रोवणें *n.* आरोपणें *n.* &c. आरोपण *n.* आरोप *m.*

I. *place planted.* वाटी *f.* बाग *m. f.* फड *m.* बन *n.* थळ *n.* लावणें *n.* उपवन *n.* कृत्रिमवन *n.* वाटिका *f.* (esp. in comp. as वृक्षवाटिका, वल्लीवाटिका, &c.)—esp. of vegetables, मळा*m.* —of cocoanut or betelnut trees, आगर *m. n.*—of sugar canes, थळ *n.* उशील *n.* Note, a provincial word.

Series of plantations. आगरमालिका *f.*

II. See COLONY. [वणीचा.

PLANTED, *p.* v. V. 1. लावलेला, रोवलेला, रुझत घातलेला, &c. ला-

3 रोवलेला, पुरलेला, नेमलेला, आरोपलेला,&c. आरोपित.

PLANTER, *n.* PLANTING, *p. a.* v. V. 1. लावणारा, रुझत घालणारा, लावणी करणारा.

3 रोवणारा, पुरणारा, &c. आरोपणकर्ता. [आगरकरी.

I. *master of a plantation.* फडकरी, बागवाला, मळेकरी,

PLASH, *n.* v. PUDDLE. डबका *m.* डबकी *f.* डबरा *m.*

PLASHY, *a. abounding with plashes,* v. MARSHY. डबक्यांचा, डबऱ्यांचा, पाणथळाचा, अनूप.

PLASTER, *n.* (of a wall). गिलावा*m.* लेप *m.*

2 *emplastrum.* मलम *m. n.* मलमपट्टी *f.* प्लास्तर *m. n.* from the English is common.—esp. of medicaments and earth to an affected limb, लेप *m.* लेपन *n.*

A rudely large p. लेपाटा *m.*

To PLASTER, *v. a.* v. N. 1. *cover with plaster.* गिलावा *m.* करणें, लेप*m.*-उपलेप*m.* देणें, लेपन*n.*-उपलेपन*n.*-&c. करणें*g. of o.*

PLASTERED, *p.* v.V. गिलावा केलेला,&c.गिलाव्याचा, लिप्त,उपलिप्त.

PLASTERER, *n.* PLASTERING, *p. a.* v. V. गिलावा करणारा, लेप देणारा, लेप-उपलेप-&c. कर्त्ता-कारक-&c. उपलेपक, प्रलेपक.

PLASTERING, *n.* v. V.—*act.* गिलावा करणें *n.* &c. लेप *m.* लेपन*n.* उपलेप *m.* उपलेपन *n.* लिपि *f.*

I. *plaster-work,* v. PLASTER. गिलावा *m.*

PLASTIC, *a. having power to give form or fashion.* घडवणारा, बळबळणारा, रूपदेणारा, आकारकरणारा, आकारकर्त्ता-कारी.

2 *capable of being molded, &c.* वळविण्याजोगा-सारखा-&c.

To PLAT, *v. a.* v. To WEAVE. विणणें, गुंफणें, वळणें, गांथणें.

PLAT, PLATTING, *n.* v. V.—*act.* विणणें*n.* गुंफणें *n.* गांथणें*n.* गांथण *or* गांठण *f.*

I. *work platted.* गांथण *or* गांठण *f.* विणकाम *n.*

II. *piece of flat, even ground,*—esp. of a garden,&c. तक्ता *m.* वाफा *m.*मळी *f.*क्यारी *f.*ताटवा *m.*वाटी *f.*वाटिका *f.*खाचान *n.*

PLATE, *n. flat piece of metal.* पत्राm. पत्रn. तकट *or* तगट n. तकटें *or* तगटें *n.*
Circular and thin p. चकती *f.*
A copper p.—on which grants, privileges, &c. are inscribed. ताम्रपट *m.*
P. of a belt. चपरास *f.*
2 *armour of plates.* पत्र्यांचें चिलखत *n.*
3 *wrought silver or gold; vessel, &c. of silver or gold.* रुपेरी सामान *n.* रुप्याचें सामान *n.* रुप्याचा संच *m.* सोन्याचें सामान *n.*
4 *vessel from which food is eaten.* बासन *n.* बसी *f.* पात्र *n.* भोजनपात्र *n.* सानक *f. n.*—of earth, परळ *or* पराळ *m. n.* तगारी *f.* सरावलें *n.* शराव *m.* रान्हें *n.*—of silver or other metal, तबक *n. dim.* तबकडी *f.* ताट *n. dim.* ताटली *f.* थाटी *f.* ताम्हण *or* ताम्हन *n.*—of leaves tacked together, पत्रावळ *f.* विस्तारी *f.* (Some varieties as to size, shape, use &c. are, ठिकोळें *or* ठिगोळें *n.* तिकटें *n.*)—of a leaf, piece of matting, or sackcloth, &c. ठावकें*n.* ठावका *m.* ठाव*m.* ठाय*m.*
A p. or dish of victuals. ठाव *m.* ठाय *m.*
Circular p. of leaves. मंडळवत *n.*
5 छापलेलें चित्र *n.*

To PLATE, *v. a. wash with silver.* रुप्याचा लेप *m.*-रुप्याचा मुलामा *m.*-&c. देणें, रुपेरीलेप *m.* देणें, मुलामा *m.* करणें-देणें-चढवणें, ओप *f.* देणें, ओपविणें.

PLATED, *p.* v. V. रुप्याचा मुलामा दिल्हेला, &c. रुपेरी, मुलामी, मुलाम्याचा, रजतान्वित.

PLATFORM, *n. plan, ichnography.* सपाटीचा-भुईचा-&c. नकशा *m.*
2 *floor of planks, &c.* मंचक *m.* मंच *m.*
3 *plan,* v. SCHEME. बेत *m.*

PLATING, *n.* v. V.—*act.* मुलामा देणें *n.* &c.
I. *wash of silver.* रुपेरीलेप*m.*मुलामा *m.* ओप *f.* रुप्याचें पाणी*n.*

PLATINUM, PLATINA, *n.* एक धातु आहे.

PLATTED, *p.* v. V. विणलेला, &c. विणींव, वळींव.

PLATTER, *n*, PLATTING, *p. a.* v. V. विणणारा, वळणारा, &c.
I. *broad and shallow dish for holding provisions.* परळ *or* पराळ *m. n. dim.* परळी *f.* सरावलें *n.* शराव *m.* जोगली *f.* खापर *m.* थाळा *m. dim.* थाळी *f.* परात *f.* Note. The above words express different sorts of platters.
Wooden p. परडें *n.*

PLAUDIT, *n. applause,* v. PRAISE. शाबासकी *f.* वाहवा *f.*

PLAUSIBILITY, *n.* v. A. 1. सत्याभास *m.* प्रमाणाभास *m.* अर्थाभास *m.* सत्यसन्निभता *f.*

PLAUSIBLE, *a. superficially pleasing, &c.* v. SPECIOUS. सामान्य लोकांस पसंत व्हायाजोगा, वरघडीचा, वरपंकाचा, देखणाऊ, दिसाऊ, लटका पर नेटका, सत्याभासाचा,सत्याभासात्मक, प्रमाणाभासात्मक, सत्यसदृश, सत्यसन्निभ, सत्यसंकाश, अविचाररमणीय, आपातरमणीय. [लाघवी.
2 *using specious arguments, &c.* तोंडावर गोड, तोंडापुरता गोड,

PLAUSIBLY, *adv.* v. A. 1. चांगला वाटायाजोगा *decl.* पसंत व्हावयाजोगा *decl.* सत्याभासपूर्वक, प्रमाणाभासपूर्वक. [क्रीडणें.

To PLAY, *v. n. sport, frolic.* खेळणें, खेळ *m.*-क्रीडा *f.*-&c. करणें,
2 *toy, trifle, act wantonly.* खेळणें, गमणें, रमणें.
3 *contend at some game.* खेळणें.
4 *perform on a musical instrument.* वाद्य *n.* वाजवणें, वाजवणें, बाजा *m.* करणें.
5 *operate, work, act, be in motion.* खेळणें, चालणें, वाहणें, खेळ *m.*-व्यापार *m.*-&c. करणें, खेळ *m.*-चेष्टा *f.*-&c. होणें *g. of s.*
6 *move irregularly, lightly, &c., wanton.* खेळणें.
7—as a demon in possession, *stir, work.* घुमणें, घुमरणें.
8 *act a part, personate a character,* v. To ACT. सोंग *n.* आणणें, सोंगसंपादणी *f.* करणें.
9 *act in any particular character.* होऊन with another verb as बायको होऊन रडणें, to weep and play the woman; मर्द होऊन मात करणें, to play the man and perform feats; बेडा होऊन झक *f.* मारणें, to play the fool & talk nonsense.

To PLAY, *v. a. put in action.* खेळवणें, चालवणें, चालता-चालू करणें.
2 (a musical instrument, &c.). वाजवणें, बजावणें, खेळणें, छडणें, वादन *n.* करणें.
3 *represent dramatically,* v. To ACT. करणें, दाखवणें, खेळवणें, संपादणें, बतावणी *f.* करणें *g. of o.*
4 *perform, act, do.* करणें, साधणें, संपादणें, मचावणें (with a bad sense—as tricks, pranks, &c.).

PLAY, *n. sport, frolic, diversion.* खेळ *m.* खेळी *f.* क्रीडा *f.* मौज *f.* कौतुक *n.* क्रीडाकौतुक *n.* तमाशा *m.* लीला *f.* विलास *m.* कुतूहल *n.* केलि *f.* क्रीडन *n.* देवन *n.* विहरण *n.* विहार *m.*
Boisterous p. v. ROMPS. धुमकूस *m.* धुमश्चक्री *f.* धुमाकूळ *m. f.* धुमाळी *f.*
Boys-p. पोरखेळ *m.*
Skilful at p. खिलाडी *or* डू.
What begins in play may end in a fray. मस्करी करितां तस्करी होती, मस्करीची कुस्करी.—Some of the *plays* amongst children are, आट्यापाट्या, अकुटेंदुकुटें, अप्पाधप्पा, इरगीमिरगी, खांबखांबोळी, खिचकुला, खुंटाफळी, गायचाळा, घारमोर, छापो, डोळेझांकणी, टिपरघाई *or* घाळी, दडकुली, ढुंबली, ढुतुतु, ढुंबर, ढुरकुंड. [*f.* चलनवलन *n.*
2 See GAMBLING. 3. *operation, action, work.* खेळ *m.* चेष्टा
4 *drama.* नाटक *n. m.*
5 *practice, action.* व्यापार *m.* व्यवहार *m.* कृति *f.* क्रिया *f.*
6 *room for free motion.* वाव *m.* अवकाश *m.* फिरक *f.* मोकळेपणा *m.* चेष्टापर्याप्तस्थल *n.* [खेळी *f.*

PLAY-DAY, *n.* खेळाचा-खेळणीचा-सुटीचा-&c. दिवस *m.* खेळणी *f.*

PLAY-FELLOW, PLAY-MATE, *n.* खेळगडी, सवंगडा, सवंगडी, खेलगडी, खेळाचा सोबती-साथी-&c. संगू.

PLAY-HOUSE, *n.* v. THEATRE. नाटकशाला *f.* नाटकगृह *n.* नाटकमंदिर *n.* नृत्यशाला *f.*

PLAY-THING, *n. toy.* खेळ *m.* खेळवणा *m.* खेळणें *n.*

PLAYED, *p.* v. V. A. 1. खेळवलेला, चालवलेला.
2 वाजवलेला, &c. वादित.
3 दाखवलेला, खेळवलेला, संपादलेला, &c.

PLAYER, *n.* PLAYING, *p. a.* v. V. N. 1. खेळणारा, खेळ-क्रीडा-&c. करणारा, क्रीडमान.
2 खेळणारा, गमणारा, गमदसडा *or* दासडा *or* दासरा.
4 *and* MUSICIAN. बाजंत्री.
8 *and* ACTOR. सोंगाडी *or* सोंगाड्या, सोंगाळ्या, सोंगी *or* सोंग्या, बहुरूपी, भांड, भवई, फडकरी, नाटकी, नटवा, नट, नर्त्तक.
An under p. अंडगडी.

Master or leader of a band of players. शाहीर.

Principal actor or manager of a company of players. सूत्रधार.

Strolling p. दास्री.

v. V. A. 1. खेळवणारा, चालवणारा, प्रवर्त्तवणारा, &c.

2 वाजवणारा, &c. वादक, वादनकर्त्ता.

PLAYFUL, PLAYSOME, *a. sportive, &c.* खेळकर, खेळण्याचे स्वभावाचा, खिलाडी, खिलाडू, कौतुकी, मौज्या, मौजाळा, ख्याली,खेळगड *or* गर, विलासी, क्रीडावान्, क्रीडापर, क्रीडापरायण,क्रीडासक्त, क्रीडाचित्त, क्रीडाबुद्धि, लीलापर, लीलापरायण, सलील.

PLAYFULLY, *adv.* v. A. खेळानें, विनोदानें, मौजेनें, &c. खेळाच्या बुद्धीनें, खेळून, क्रीडाबुद्धीनें, विनोदबुद्धीनें, परिहासबुद्धीनें.

PLAYFULNESS, PLAYSOMENESS, *n.* v. A. खेळकरपणा *m.* खेळण्याचा स्वभाव *m.* क्रीडाबुद्धि *f.* क्रीडासक्ति *f.* क्रीडापरता *f.* &c.

PLEA, *n.*—in law. उत्तरवाद *m.* उत्तरपाद *n.* उत्तर *n.*

2 *that which is alleged in support, excuse, &c.* निमित्त *n.* सबब *f.* कारण *n.*

False or bad p. दुर्निमित्त *n.* बहाणा *m.*

3 See LAWSUIT.

To PLEAD, *v. n. speak, argue, supplicate, &c. in behalf of.* पक्ष *m.* धरून बोलणें, बोलणें *with* साठीं-करितां-&c. वाद *m.* करणें-सांगणें, रदबदली *f.*-रदबदल *f.*-&c. करणें *with* साठीं -&c. *or with g. of o.* सांग सरभरा *f.* करणें.

To PLEAD, *v. a. discuss, maintain by arguments, &c.* वाद *m.*-कज्जा *m.*-तकरार *f.* करणें-सांगणें, बोलणें.

2 *allege in pleading,* v. To ADDUCE. बोलणें, सांगणें, पुढें करणें, उपन्यास *m.* करणें *g. of o.* उपन्यस्त करणें.

3 *offer in excuse.* निमित्त *n.*-सबब *f.*-कारण *n.*-&c. सांगणें-करणें-दाखवणें.

PLEADABLE, *a.* v. V. A. 1. वादांत-&c. बोलायाजोगा, &c.

2 बोलायाजोगा, &c. उपन्यास करायाजोगा, उपन्यसनीय, उपन्यास्य.

3 निमित्त सांगायाजोगा-&c.

PLEADER, *n.* PLEADING, *p. a.* v. V. N. पक्ष धरून बोलणारा, वाद सांगणारा, रदबदली करणारा.

I. v. LAWYER. वकील.

PLEADINGS, *n. pl.* वादी प्रतिवादी ह्यांची तकरार *f.*

PLEASANT, *a.* v. AGREEABLE. गोड, चांगला, सुखाचा, सुखावह, सुखद, सुखप्रद, सुखकर.

2 See CHEERFUL, MERRY.

PLEASANTLY, *adv.* v.A.1. सुख वाटेसा *decl.* सुख वाटायाजोगा*decl.* सुखेंकरून, सुखेनैव, सुखरूप, सुदामत, यथासुख.

PLEASANTNESS, *n.* v. A. 1. गोडी *f.* चांगुलपणा *m.* सुखदायकत्व *n.*

PLEASANTRY, *n. gayety, &c.* v. MERRIMENT, MIRTH. हंसाबाजी *f.* थट्टामस्करी *f.* मजाख *f.* विनोद *m.* रहस्य *n.*

2 *sprightly saying, witticism, &c.* मजाखीचें-थट्टेचें-&c. बोलणें *n.*-वाक्य *n.* विनोदोक्ति *f.* विनोदवाक्य *n.* नर्मभाषण *n.* नर्मोक्ति *f.*

To PLEASE, *v. a. delight, gratify, gladden.* सुख *n.*-आनंद *m.*-संतोष *m.*-हर्ष *m.*-&c. देणें-करणें, आनंदविणें, हर्षविणें,संतोषविणें, मन *n.*-चित्त *n.*-&c. खुश करणें *g. of o.* तोषणें, खुश-सुखी-संतुष्ट-&c. करणें, रिझवणें, रंजवणें, हर्षण *n.*-आल्हादन *n.*-रंजन *n.*-&c. करणें *g. of. o.*

2 *content,* v. To SATISFY. समाधान *n.*-संतोष *m.*-&c.करणें, तर्पिणें, तर्पण *n.*-संतर्पण *n.* करणें *g. of o.*

3 *suit, approve itself unto.* आवडणें, बरा वाटणें, *in. con.* पसंत-मान्य-&c. असणें *in. con.* पटणें *in. con.* खातरेस पटणें *g. of o.* रुचणें *in. con.* मनास-मर्जीस-खुशीस-खातरीस-&c. येणें *in. con.* पतकरणें *or* कारणें *in. con.* पुरवणें *in. con.* मानणें *in. con.* मानवणें *in. con.*

To PLEASE, *v. n. choose, list,* v. To LIKE. चाहणें *in. con.* मन *n.*-खुशी *f.*-मर्जी *f.*-&c. असणें *g. of s.* भावणें *in. con.* मनास-खुशीस-मर्जीस-&c. येणें *in. con.* गमणें *in. con.*

2—as a word of ceremony; *condescend, be pleased.* कृपा *f.* करणें (as कृपा करून तें मला द्या, please to give me that).

PLEASED, *p.* v. V. A. 1. *and joyful.* खुश केलेला, आनंदविलेला, &c. खुश, खुशी, संतुष्ट, संतोषित, आनंदित, रंजित, तोषित, तुष्ट, प्रीत, उत्साहित, उल्लसित, मोदित, मुदित, प्रमोदित, प्रमुदित, प्रसन्न, प्रसादित, प्रसन्नवृत्ति.

That is easily p. अल्पसंतुष्ट, अल्पसंतोषी.

To be p. आनंद *m.*-संतोष *m.*-&c. वाटणें *in. con.* संतोषणें, तुष्टणें,—*intens.* बाल बाल खुश होणें.

2 समाधान केलेला, &c. संतुष्ट, संतोषित, तोषित, तुष्ट, तृप्त, तर्पित.

PLEASER, *n.* PLEASING, *p. a.* v. V. A. 1. *and* AGREEABLE. सुख करणारा-देणारा, आनंदविणारा, हर्षविणारा,&c. रिझाऊ, रंजक, मनोरंजक, सुखप्रद, सुखद, सुखकर, संतोषप्रद, संतोषद, हर्षप्रद, &c. रुचिकर, रुचिर, रुच्य, सुरभि, प्रिय, मनःप्रिय, तोषक, मोदक, मनासारखा, मनोनुकूल.

PLEASING, *n.* v. V. A. 1. —*act.* सुख देणें *n.* आनंदविणें *n.* &c. तोषण *n.* हर्षण *n.* आनंदन *n.* रंजन *n.* नंदन *n.* प्रसादन *n.* प्रीणन *n.*

2 समाधान करणें *n.* तर्पण *n.* तोषण *n.*

PLEASINGNESS, *n.* v. A. रिझाऊपणा *m.* सुखदायकत्व *n.* रंजकत्व *n.* रुचिरता *f.* सौरम्य *n.*

PLEASURABLE, PLEASURABLENESS. See PLEASANT, PLEASANTNESS.

PLEASURE, *n. delight, gratification, enjoyment.* सुख *n.* आनंद *m.* संतोष *m.* हर्ष *m.* खुशी *f.* मौज *f.* खुशाली *f.* तुष्टि *f.* तोष *m.* परितोष *m.* तोख *m.* सौख्य *n.* उल्लास *m.* मोद *m.* प्रमोद *m.* विलास *m.* शर्म *n.* प्रीति *f.*—*intens.* See RAPTURE.

Carnal or sensual p. विषयसुख *n.* विषयानंद *m.* काम *m.*

True p. सद्विलास *m.*

Why make pain of a p. ज्या सोन्यानें कान तुटतो तें कशाला.

2 *choice, liking, will, inclination.* मर्जी *f.* खुशी *f.* इच्छा *f.* मनोदय *m.* मनोरथ *m.* मनोत्साह *m.* छंद *m.*

At p. कामतः, यथाकाम, अनुकाम.

3 *loose gratification, sensual enjoyment.* विषयसुख *n.* विषयभोग *m.* भोगविलास *m.* विलास *m.* ऐशआराम *m.* चैन *f.* चैनबाजी *f.* रंग *m.* ख्याली खुशाली*f.* भोगभुरका.

Goddess or genius of p. रंगदेवता *f.*

4 *cause or occasion of pleasure.* सुखकारण *n.* सुखहेतु *m.*

PLEASURE-GROUND, *n.* रमायाची जागा *f.* रमणा *m.* विलासकानन *n.* विलासवन *n.*

PLEASURE-HOUSE, *n.* विलासमंदिर *n.*

PLEASURE-HUNTER, PLEASURIST, *n. person devoted to pleasure.* भोगी, विलासी, विहारी, रंगी, रंगेला, रंगेल, चैनी, चैनबाज, गुल-

हौशी *or* हवसी, चंदनहौशी, मौज्या *or* मौजी, मौजाळा, हौशी *or* हौसी, हौशा, शोसी *or* शौकी, कौतुकी.—Some appellations and attributives, &c. are खुशालचंद, कृष्णावतार, सुखानंद, घमंड, घमंडानंद, घमंडानंदी.

PLEBEIAN, *a. vulgar*, v. LOW. गल्लीकुचीचा, सांदीकोंदीचा, कुणबाऊ, प्राकृत, हलके जातीचा, हलके कुळीचा, नीच जातीचा, अकुलीन, अकुलज.

PLEDGE, *n.* v. PAWN. गहाण *n.* आधि *m.*

In p. By way of p. गहाणवट. [हडप *n.*

2 *surety, hostage, warrant, &c.* जामीन *c.* ओल *f.* तारण *n.*

To PLEDGE, *v. a. pawn.* गहाण ठेवणें, गहाण लावून देणें, गहाणवट-गहाणवटीस ठेवणें, आधीकरण *n.* करणें.

2 *give as warrant, security, &c.* ओलीस-&c. ठेवणें, तारण*n.* -गहाण*n.*-&c. ठेवणें.

To p. one's self (to a work, &c.). सतीचें वाण*n.* घेणें.

To p. one's word. भाक *f.*-भाष *f.*-वचन*n.*-प्रतिज्ञा *f.* देणें.

PLEDGED, *p.* v. V. 1. गहाण ठेवलेला, &c. आधीकृत, निक्षिप्त.

2 ओलीस ठेवलेला, &c. [वचन, वचनबद्ध.

I. *that has pledged his word.* भाक दिल्हेला, कृतप्रतिज्ञ, दत्त-

PLEDGET, *n.*—in surgery. घडी *f.* [निक्षेप*m.*

PLEDGING, *n.* v. V. 1.—*act.* गहाण ठेवणें*n.* &c. आधीकरण*n.*

2 ओलीस ठेवणें *n.*&c.

PLEIADS, PLEIADES, *n.*—the constellation. कृत्तिका *f.* विंचू*m.* कात्या *or* काथ्या *f. pl.*

PLENARILY, PLENARY, &c. See COMPLETELY, COMPLETE, &c.

PLENILUNAR, PLENILUNARY, *a. relating, &c. to the full moon.* पूर्णचंद्राचा, पूर्णचंद्रसंबंधी-विषयक.

PLENIPOTENCE, *n. fullness of power.* पूर्णसामर्थ्य*n.* सामर्थ्यपूर्णता*f.*

PLENIPOTENT, *n. having full power.* पूर्णसमर्थ, पूर्णशक्तिमान्.

PLENIPOTENTIARY, *n. person invested with full powers.* कुलकारभारी, कुलअखत्यार, कुलकुला.

PLENIST, *n. one who maintains that space is full of matter.* पूर्णतावादी.

PLENITUDE, *n. fullness,—as opposed to* vacuity. पूर्णता *f.*

2 *fullness, completeness, exuberance, &c.* भर *m.* पूर्णता *f.* समृद्धि *f.* उत्कर्ष*m.* प्रकर्ष*m.* वैपुल्य*n.*

PLENTEOUS, PLENTIFUL, *a. copious, abundant, &c.* v. EXUBERANT. बहुत, पुष्कळ, पुरबठ्याचा, उरून पुरायाजोगा-&c. विपुल, प्रचुर, समृद्धीचा, मुबलक *or* ख, भरपूर, समतिरिक्त, समृद्ध, समीचीन.

To be overflowingly p. लोटणें.

PLENTEOUSLY, PLENTIFULLY, *adv.* v. A. पुरून उरायाजोगासारखा-&c. *decl.* पुरून उरेसा *decl.* भरपूर, बहुत, पुष्कळ.

PLENTEOUSNESS, PLENTIFULNESS, *n.* v. A. *and* PLENTY. पुष्कळपणा*m.* पुरपुराट*m.* वैपुल्य*n.* समृद्धि *f.* उत्कर्ष*m.*

PLENTY, *n. abundance,* v. EXUBERANCE. पुष्कळपणा*m.* पुरून उरायाजोगेपणा*m.* पुरवटा *or* ठा*m.* पुरपुराट*m.* विपुलता *f.* वैपुल्य*n.* उत्कर्ष*m.* प्रकर्ष*m.* समृद्धि *or* संवृद्धि*f.* रेल*f.* रेलचेल *f.* वाहतझरा*m.*

Overflowing p. लोट*m.* लोंढा*m.*

2 *state of abundance of the necessaries of life.* सुपीक*n.* सुबत्ता *f.* सुभिक्ष*n.* सुकळ *or* सुकाळ*m.* सुकाळपुरा*m.* धान्यसमृद्धि*f.*

Time of peace and p. सुबत्ताकाळ*m.*

Time of p. and cheapness. सुकळ *or* सुकाळ*m.*

PLEONASM, *n. redundancy of words.* शब्दातिशय*m.* शब्दबाहुल्य *n.* शब्दप्रकर्ष*m.* स्वार्थ*m.*

PLEONASTIC, *a.* v. N. शब्दबाहुल्याचा, शब्दातिशयाचा, &c. स्वार्थ.

PLETHORA, *n. fullness of blood or habit.* रक्तातिशय*m.* रक्ताधिक्य *n.* अतिपुष्टि *f.* रक्तपित्त*n.* पित्तरक्त*n.*

PLETHORIC, *a.* v. N. रक्तातिशयाचा, रक्ताधिक्याचा, रक्तपित्ताचा.

PLEURISY, *n. inflammation of the membrane of the chest.* उरोग्रह*m.* वक्षोग्रह*m.*

PLEURITIC, *a.* v. N. उरोग्रहरोगी.

PLIABILITY, PLIABLENESS, PLIANCY, *n.* v. A. 1. लवकेपणा*m.* लवचीकपणा*m.* मऊपणा*m.* &c. मृदुता *f.*

PLIABLE, PLIANT, *a. flexible.* लवका, लवचीक, लवखर, लवकिरा, मऊ, मृदु, सुनम्य, नमनशील.

2 fig. *soft, yielding.* वळवायास सोपा, मृदुस्वभावाचा, सुघर्ष, वश्य.

To PLIGHT. See To PLEDGE.

PLIGHT, *n.* See GAGE. 2 *state, case, &c.* v. CONDITION. अवस्था *f.* स्थिति *f.* गति *pop.* गत *f.*

3 *ill condition, miserable state, pickle, &c.* v. MESS. गति *pop.* गत *f.* चवढव *f.* चवचव *f.* घाण *f.* गुडाकू *or* खू *f.* गळहाटा *or* ठा *m.* बच्छान *f.* दैना *f.*

PLINTH, *n.*—of a wall. कंगणी *f.* कंगोरा *m.*

To PLOD, *v. n. drudge, &c.* v. TOIL. खपणें, कष्ट *m.*-श्रम *m.*-&c. करणें.

2 *travel or work with heavy diligence.* रेंरें *n.* करणें *or* करून जाणें-चालणें-शिकणें-अध्ययन *n.* करणें-&c. आयासानें-श्रमानें-कष्टानें-&c. करीत जाणें-शिकत जाणें-&c.

PLODDER, *n.* PLODDING, *p. a.* v. V. 2. रेंरें करून जाणारा-शिकणारा-&c. आयासाध्ययनी, श्रमाध्ययनी, आयासव्यासंगी, आयाससाधक, आयासगामी, पिपीलिकामार्गी.

PLODDING, *n.* v. V. 2.—*act.* रेंरें करणें *n.* श्रमाचें-कष्टाचें-&c. अध्ययन *n.* आयासाध्ययन *n.* श्रमाध्ययन *n.*

PLOT, *n.* (of ground) v. PLAT. तक्ता *m.* ठिकें *n.*

2 *scheme, plan, form.* बेत *m.* आकार *m.*

3 *conspiracy.* कूट *n.* संगनमत *n.* कंत्राण *or* कंत्राड *or* कंत्राट *n.* कट *m.* कटाव *m.* काट *m.*

4 *intrigue, complicated affair.* फंद *m.* काट *m.* कूट *n.* कारस्थान *n.* कुलंगडें *or* कुलांगडें *n.*

Plots—compreh. plots, intrigues, cabals, and combinations. फंद फितूर *m.*

5 *stratagem, device, project,* v. CONTRIVANCE. तजवीज *f.* युक्ति *f.* उपाय *m.* मसलत *f.* कल्पना *f.* मनसुबा *m.* कंत्राण *or* कंत्राड *n.* [सृष्टि *f.*

Wild or silly p. गैरमसलत *f.* गैरमनसुबा *m.* कुतर्क *m.* कु-

6 (of a play, poem, &c.). वस्तु *n.* जामीनसांखळी *f.* संविधानक *n.*

A secondary p. or incident. प्रतिमुख *n.*

To PLOT, *v. n. form a scheme, contrive a plan.* युक्ति *f.*-मसलत *f.*-तजवीज *f.*-&c. करणें.

To p. together. जुगल करणें.

2 (against). कुभांड *n.*-कुफरांड *n.*-कचाट *n.*-कंत्राण *n.*-तरकट *n.*-लचांड *n.*-&c.रचणें *with* वर *of o.* फंद *m.* करणें, अथर्वण *n.* करणें.

To PLOT, *v. a. scheme, contrive,* v. To PLAN. मसलत *f.*-तजवीज *f.*-&c. करणें *g. of o.* योजणें.

Plotter, *n.* **Plotting**, *p. a.* v. V. N. 1. *and* Ingenious. योजक, युक्त्या, लागलाव्या, कारस्थानी, काटदार.
2 कचाट-&c. रचणारा, &c.
I. *one ever engaged in plots.* कचाट्या, झेंगट्या, लचांडी, लचांडखोर, फंदी, सेळ्या, कारस्थानी.
v. V. A. योजणारा, रचणारा, &c. योजक, रचक.

Plough, *n.* नांगर *m.* अऊत *or* औत *n.* हल *m.* जोत *n.*
A bout or turn of the p. काकरी *f. v.* घे.
Band confining the share to the head of the p. वसूं *n.*
Cord to fasten the p. to the yoke. नांगरडा *m.*
Drill-p. पाभर *f.* फण *f.* कुडी *f.* तिफण *f.*
Grain box of a drill-p. चाडें *n.*
Handle of a p. रुमणी *f. or* रुमणें *n. or* रोमणी *f.* रोमणें *n.* ईषादंड *m.*—pin fastening or steadying it. कवळ *m.* कवळी *f.*
Head of a p. नांगरखुंट *m.* खडसा *m.*
Iron tip of a tooth of the Pábhar or drill-p. फारोळें *n.* फारोळा *m.* फाळोरें *n.*
Of or belonging to a p. नांगऱ्या.
Pole or shaft of a p. इसाड *n.* ईस *n.* इसकाड *n.* हळस *or* हळीस *m. f.* ईषा *f.*
Share of a p. फाळ *m.*
Share-piece or spindle of a p. खडसा *m.* नांगरखुंट *m.*
To hold, follow, drive &c. the p. जोत *n.* धरणें-चालवणें, आऊत *n.* हाकणें-धरणें.

To **Plough**, *v. n.* जमीन *f.*-&c. नांगरणें, जोत *n.*-नांगर *m.*-औत *n.* धरणें-चालवणें-हाकणें.

To **Plough**, *v. a.* नांगरणें, नांगरानें-&c. फोडणें-उकरणें, नांगरणी *f.* -&c. करणें *g. of o.* कर्षणें—for the first time, *turn up the ground.* उखळणें, उखळ *f.* करणें *g. of o.*—the second time, दुसारणें, दुहारणें, दुणणें, बेरणें.
To cross p. बेरणें.
To p. the ground before its moisture has evaporated. ओल *f. n.* धरणें.

Plough-boy, *n.* आगल्या, अऊत्या.

Plough-land, *n. land that is ploughed.* नांगरवट *or* ठ *f.* नांगरट *or* ठ *f.* नांगरड *f.*

Plough-man, *n.* नांगऱ्या, जोत्या, अऊत्या *or* औत्या, अऊतकरी, नांगरहाक्या, हलधर.

Ploughshare, *n.* फाल *or* फाळ *m.* (contempt. फाळवट *or* फाळट *n.*) जगल *f.* फल *n.* दांत *m.*
To be turned up by the p.—ground. उफाळणें.
To be rubbed or cut by the p.—bullock. फाळटणें.

Ploughed, *p.* v. V. A. नांगरलेला, &c. नांगरट *or* ठ , नांगरवट *or* ठ, कर्षित, हल्य.
P. ground. नांगरट *or* ठ *f.* नांगरवट *or* ठ *f.* नांगरड *f.*

Plougher, *n.* **Ploughing**, *p. a.* v. V. N. नांगर-जोत-&c. धरणारा-चालवणारा-हांकणारा, जोत्या, नांगऱ्या.
v. V. A. नांगरणारा, &c. नांगरणी-&c. करणारा, कर्षक.

Ploughing, *n.*v. V. N. जोत धरणें *n.* जोत चालवणें *n.* औत हाकणें *n.* &c. नांगरकी *f.* नांगरणी *f.*
v. V. A. नांगरणें *n.* &c. नांगरकी *f.* नांगरणी *f.* कर्षण *n.* कृषि *f.* संकर्षण *n.*—for the first time, उखळ *f.* उखळणी *f.*—for the second time, दुसारणें *n.* &c. दुसारणी *f.* दूण *f.* बेर *f.*
A bout of p. *one act of p. up & down.* मुरडाण *or* न *n.*
Complete p. *p. lengthwise and cross-wise.* उखळांदर *or* उखळबेर *f.*
Cross-p. बेर *f.*
To smooth a field after p. ओखरणें.

Plover, *n. edicnurus crepitans.* धाकटा तनमोर *m.*

Plow, *To* **Plow**, &c. See **Plough**, &c.

To **Pluck**, *v. a. pull with sudden force, take with a twitch,* v. To Snatch. हिसकावणें, असडणें, हिसडणें, हिमकणें, छिनावणें, उचकटणें, हिसका *m.*-असडा *m.*-झटका *m.*-&c. देणें-देऊन काढणें-देऊन घेणें, हिसक्यानें-हिसड्यानें-झटक्यानें-&c. घेणें.
2 (fruit, vegetables, &c.) v. To Crop. खुटणें, खुडणें, तोडणें, खुटणी *f.*-तोडणी *f.*-तोडा *m.* करणें *g. of o.*
3 *strip off the feathers of.* पिसें *n. pl.*-&c. उपटणें-निपसणें *g. of o.* लुंचणें, पिमुडणें, बुचाडणें *or* बुचडणें, बुचडून काढणें.
4 fig. *pill, chouse, &c.* v. To Plunder. ओंचकणें, द्रव्य *n.*-&c. असडणें-हिसडणें-उपटणें-हिसकणें-&c. लुचवणें, लुचाडणें, लुगारणें, नाडणें, बुचाडणें.
5 (up, out, &c.). उपडणें, उपटणें, उचकटणें, उपटून-&c. काढणें.
To p. up courage, &c. धैर्य *n.* धरणें.

Pluck, *n. pull, draw, &c.* असडा *m.* हिसडा *m.* हिसका *m.*
2 *mettle, heart, &c.* v. Spirit. दम *m.* जीव *m.* पाणी *n.* जीवनपाणी *n.*

Plucking, *n.* v. V. 1. हिसकावणें *n.* &c.

Plug, *n. stopper, &c.* दट्टा *or* दट्ट्या *or* दाटा *m.* दडा *m.* चोंदी *f.* बूज *m.* पाचर *f. n.* पाचेरूं *n.* बुटणें *n.* बुचटणें *n.* बुचूं *n.* गुड्डी *f.*—esp. of old clouts, straw, &c. चोंथा *m.* बोंथा *m.* बोंधी *f.* चोंबा *m.*

To **Plug**, *v. a. stop with a plug.* दट्टा *m.*-दडा *m.*-&c. घालणें-मारणें-बसवणें *or* घालून-&c. बुझणें-बुझवणें.

Plum, *n.*—the fruit. एक फळ आहे.
Dried p.s from Bukhárá. आलू *m.* आलूबोखार *m.*
2 *the sum of* 100,000 (*rupees*). लाखरुपय *m. pl.* रुपयांची लाखोली *f.*
That is worth a p. लाख्या, लक्षाधीश.
He is worth a p. ह्यानें कोटिध्वज लाविला *or* उभारिला.
3 See Raisin.

Plumage, *n. feathers of a bird.* पिसारा *m.* पिसें *n. pl.* पंखाड *n.*

Plumb. See **Plummet**. 2 See **Plump**.

To **Plumb**, *v. a. regulate by the plumb.* ओळंबा लावून-ओळंब्यानें करणें-सुधारणें- बराबर करणें-&c. ओळंबणें.
2 See To Sound.

Plumbago, *n.*—Zeylanica. चित्रक *m.* चित्रमूळ *f.*

Plumbean, **Plumbeous**, *a. leaden.* शिशाचा, सीसमय.

Plumber, *n. worker in lead.* शिशाचें काम करणारा.

Plumbery, *n. works in lead.* शिशाचें काम *n.*

Plumb-line. See **Plummet**.

Plume, *n. feather.* पीस *n.* पर *m.*
2 *ornamental feathers, &c. crest.* तुरा *m.* कलगी *f.* चूडा *f.* शिखा *f.* शेखर *m.*

To **Plume**, *v. a. adjust feathers.* पिसें *n. pl.*-पर *m. pl.*-&c. निटावणें-सुधारणें. [*g. of o.*
2 *strip of feathers,* v. To **Pluck**. पिसें *n.pl.* उपटणें-निपसणें

3 fig. pill, chouse, &c. v. To PLUCK. बुचाडणें, नाडणें, लुघवणें.

4 (one's self) pride (one's self). अकड f.-शेखी f.-आढ्यता f.-&c. बाळगणें-धरणें-मिरवणें g. of o. अभिमान m. बाळगणें-भोगणें-धरणें g. of o. बाणा m.-बीर m.-&c. बाळगणें g. of o.

PLUMIGEROUS, a. having feathers. पिसांचा, परांचा, पिसाऱ्याचा, सपक्ष, पक्षविशिष्ट.

PLUMIPED, a. that has feathers on the feet. पिसांचे पायांचा, सपक्षपाद, सपक्षचरण.

PLUMMET, n.—of masons, carpenters, &c. ओळंबा m. लंब m. लंबक m. साधन f. तोळंबा m.

To prove by the p. ओळंबणें.

2 sounding lead. बुडीद m. गळ m.

PLUMOUS. See FEATHERED.

PLUMP, a. filled out in flesh, &c. v. FAT. गबगबीत or गुबगुबीत, टमटमीत or टुमटुमीत, दुमदुमीत, दुलदुलीत, गुलगुलीत, गुडगुडीत, घबघबीत, रसरसीत, भरदार, गोंडस, ताजा, धाटामोटा, खुराकाचा, तुंद.

To get p. & sleek on good living. शेवाळणें.

To grow chubby & p.—a child. बाळसावणें, बाळसणें.

2 puffed, risen. फुगरा, फुगीर.

PLUMP, n. See CLUMP, CLUSTER.

PLUMP, adv. with a sudden & heavy fall. ढब्ब-कन-कर-&c. or धब-कन-कर-&c. डुब-कन-कर-&c. or दुब-कन-कर-&c. दप-कन-कर-&c. धप-कन-कर-&c. बुट-कन-कर-&c. सभर, घसंवकर.

2 See PLUMPLY.

To PLUMP, v. n. fall heavily and at once. धबकणें, ढब्ब-ढब्बकन-डुबकन-&c. पडणें.

To PLUMP, v. a. dilate, fill out, &c. v. To SWELL. फुगवणें, फुगरा-फुगीर करणें.

PLUMPLY, adv. fully, roundly, &c. v. BLUNTLY, POSITIVELY. साफ, निखालस, निक्षूण, परिछिन्न.

To refuse or deny p. वाटाण्याची अक्षत f. लावणें.

PLUMPNESS, n. v. A. 1. गबगबितपणा m. गुलगुलितपणा m. टुमटुमितपणा m. ताजेपणा n. &c. पुष्टि f.

The p. of infancy. बाळसें n.

2 फुगरेपणा m. फुगारा m.

PLUMY. See FEATHERED.

To PLUNDER, v. a. pillage, spoil, &c. लुटणें, झांबडणें or झांबाडणें, नागवणें,—with the implication, bearing, or power of such words as to pill, fleece, rifle, strip, shave, pluck, chouse, plume, &c. नागवणें, बोडणें, नाडणें, लुटणें, लुगारणें, लुचाडणें, लुबाडणें, बुचाडणें, बुचकणें, घासणें, घासटणें, लुंघवणें, ओरपणें, ओरफडणें or ओखडणें, धाब्यावरबसवणें, मुडणें, धुणें, धुऊन नेणें, घर n. धुणें g. of o. पोखरून खाणें, आंचकणें, द्रव्यn.-&c. असडणें-हिसडणें-उपटणें-हिसकणें-&c. g. of o. वाटोळें n. करणें g. of o. चाटून पुसून सोडणें, पिळून घेणें, शुद्धबुद्ध करणें, नागवणूक f.-मुंडन n.-मुंडि मोचन n.-&c. करणें g. of o.

PLUNDER, PLUNDERING, n. v. V.—act. लुटणें n. नागवणें n. &c. नागवण f. नागवणूक f. नाडणूक f. झांबडणी f. लुगारणी f. लुबाडणी f. लूट f. हजामत f. मुंडन n., मुंडिमोचन n. लुंटन pop. लंटण n.

Acquired by p. लुटाऊ.

General plundering. लुटालूट f.

I. spoil, booty. लूट f. [शुद्धबुद्ध.

PLUNDERED, p. v. V. लुटलेला, नागवलेला, लुगारलेला, &c. निधूत,

PLUNDERER, n. PLUNDERING, p. a. v. V. लुटणारा, नागवणारा, &c. लुटारी, लुटारू, लुगारू, लुगाऱ्या, नागवण्या, लुबाड्या.

To PLUNGE, v. a. thrust or drive into (a fluid, &c.). घालणें, बुडवणें, पाडणें, मज्जन-निमज्जन n.-&c. करणें g. of o. मज्जित-निमज्जित-&c. करणें.

2 See To THRUST.

To PLUNGE, v.n. rush into, thrust, &c. one's self into. उडी f. टाकणें-मारणें, बुडी f.-डुबकी f.-डुबी f.-&c. मारणें, सुरकांडी f.-&c. मारणें, घालून घेणें.

PLUNGE, PLUNGING, n. v. V. A. 1.—act. घालणें n. बुडवणें n. &c. मज्जन n. निमज्जन n.

v. V. N. उडी टाकणें n. उडी मारणें n. &c. बुडी f. डुबकी f. डुबी f. सुरकांडी f. मुसांडी f.

I.—of a paper kite, dip. गोता m.

PLUNGED, p. v. V. A.1. घातलेला, &c. निमज्जित.

PLURAL, a. consisting of two or more. अनेक, बहुत. [तला.

2—in grammar. अनेकवचनाचा, अनेकवचनांतला, बहुवचनां-

P. number. अनेकवचन n. बहुवचन n.

PLURALITY, n. v. A. 1. अनेकत्व n. अनैक्य n. बहुत्व n.

PLURALLY, adv. v. A. 2. अनेकवचनांत, बहुवचनांत.

PLUS, n.—the affirmative quantity. धन n. अधिक, स्व.

PLUTO, n.—the Indian P. यम m.

PLUTUS, n. the god of wealth. कुबेर m.

The nine treasures of P. नवनिधि m. pl.—these are, महापद्म, पद्म, शंख, मकर, कच्छप, मुकुंद, कुंद, नील, खर्व.

PLUVIAL, PLUVIOUS. See RAINY.

PLUVIOMETER, n. rain-gauge. वृष्टिमापनयंत्र n.

To PLY, v. a. lay on with force and repetition. लागोपाठ-लागोलाग-&c. मारणें-लावणें, लगावणें.

2 employ diligently, apply closely, keep busy. झडझड-झडाझड-&c. चालवणें-वहिवाटणें-वापरणें, दामटणें.

3 practise diligently. वहिवाटणें, चालवणें, झटून करणें, करणें.

4 urge. See To IMPORTUNE.

To PLY, v. n. work, do service, busy one's self. खपणें, काम n.-&c. करणें, झटणें.

PLY, n. plait, v. FOLD. चुणी f. निरी f.

2 See BEND. [वाऱ्याचा, वायुमय.

PNEUMATIC, PNEUMATICAL, a. consisting, &c. of air. वायूचा,

2 relating, &c. to air. वायूचा, वाऱ्याचा, वाऱ्याविषयींचा, वायुसंबंधी, वायुविषयक.

3 moved or played by air. वायूचा, वायु (in comp. as वायुयंत्र, वायुवाद्य, &c.).

PNEUMATICS, n. science of the air. वायुविद्या f. वायुशास्त्र n.

PNEUMONIC, a. belonging, &c. to the lungs. फुफुसाचा, फुप्फुससंबंधी-विषयक.

To POACH, v. a. boil slightly. कांहींसा decl.-थोडा decl.-&c.शिजवणें- रांधणें, अर्धशिजा-अर्धबोबडा-&c. करणें.

2 steal, pocket. चोरणें, चोरून नेणें, चोरून पिशवींत घालणें.

To POACH, v. n. steal game. पारध f.-शिकार f.-&c. चोरणें-चोरून नेणें.

POACHED, p. v. A. 1. कांहींसा शिजवलेला, अर्धशिजाकेलेला, &c.

2 चोरलेला, चोरून नेलेला, &c.

POACHER, *n.* v. V. N. पारध चोरून नेणारा, &c. मृगयाचोर.

POACHING, *n.* v. V. N.—*act.* पारधचोरणें *n.* &c. पारधचोरी *f.* शिकारचोरी *f.* मृगयाचौर्य *n.*

POACHINESS, *n.* v. A. बरबरितपणा *m.* &c.

POACHY, *a. wet and soft*,—land. बरबरीत, रबरबीत.

POCK, *n. pustule of small-pox, &c.* फोडी *f.* देवी *f.* (Ex. या मुलाला तीनच देवी आल्या).

2 (of the chicken pox,). कांजणी *f.*

POCK-HOLE, POCK-PIT, *n.* देवीची माव *or* माऊ *f.* देवीचा वण *m.* देवीचीखांच *f.*

POCK-PITTED, *a.* देवीचे वणांचा, बरड, उधेल, उकटलेला, फोडांच्या तोंडाचा, उधेल तोंडाचा, उकटलेल्या तोंडाचा,—jocosely. चक्रांकित, मोरचेला.

To be p. बरडणें. [*or* कपा *m.* जेब *f.*

POCKET, *n. bag inserted in a garment.* खिसा *m.* पिशवी *f.* कप्पा

A secret p. चोरखिसा *m.*

P.-picking. उचका *m.* उचकाउचक *f.*

To have to pay out of one's p., To be out of p. पदर *m.* चाळणें-भरणें-गमावणें.

2 *single compartment or division*, (as of a purse, bag, &c.). पूड *n.* कप्पा *or* कपा *m.* [घालणें.

To POCKET, *v. a. put into the pocket.* खिशांत-पिशवींत-&c.

2 *abstract furtively*, v. To STEAL. चोरणें, चोरून घेणें-नेणें, कासाटीस-काखेस मारणें, काखाटणें, काखाळणें, ताव *m.* देणें, हात *m.* मारणें, हाताळणें, लांबविणें.

3 (an affront, &c.) *put up with*, v. To BEAR. गिळणें, पिऊन-गिळून जाणें, पोटांत घालणें-ठेवणें.

To be pocketed. खमणें, जिरणें, मुरणें.

4 *receive as profit.* राशीस-संग्रहास-&c. घालणें, पिशवींत-&c. टाकणें, मागें-संग्रहीं-&c. पाडणें, राशी पुंजीस पडणें-येणें *in. con.*

POCKET-BOOK, *n.* खिशांतली वही *f.* टिपणवही *f.*

POCKET-HANDKERCHIEF, *n.* हातरुमाल *m.*

POCKET-MONEY, *n.* खाऊचा-मिठाईचा-पानसुपारीचा-&c.पैसा *m.*-&c. खर्ची *f.*

POCKINESS, *n.* v. A. उचकटलेलेपणा *m.* बरडपणा *m.*

POCKY, *a. infected with pocks.* देवीचे वणांचा, उचकटलेला, बरड.

POCULENT, *a. fit for drink.* प्यायाजोगा-जोगता-&c. पेय.

POD, *n. seedcase, &c.* शेंग *f.* शिंबी *f.*

Blind or empty p. चिंब *n.* फेल *n.* फोल *n.*

PODAGRIC. See GOUTY. [युक्त.

PODDED, *a. having its pods formed.* शेंगा आलेला-फुटलेला, शिंबी

POEM, *n. a metrical composition.* काव्य *n.* कविता *f.* कवन *n.*

POESY, *n. art or skill of writing poetry.* कविता *f.* कवित्व *pop.* कवीत *n.* कविताशक्ति *f.* काव्यविद्या *f.* काव्यलेखनकौशल्य *n.* काव्यलेखनसामर्थ्य *n.* श्लोकरचना *f.*

2 *metrical composition.* कविता *f.* काव्य *n.*

POET, *n.* कवि, पद्यरचक, काव्यकर्त्ता, शाहीर.

A ready p. शीघ्रकवि. [वि *m.*

POETASTER, *n. petty poet.* हलका कवि *m.* दळयाकवि *m.* पिट्याक-

POETIC, POETICAL, *a. pertaining, &c. to poetry.* कवितेचा, काव्याचा, कविता करण्याचा, कविताशक्तीचा, कवितासंबंधी-विषयक.

2 *expressed in poetry.* कवितेचा, कवितारूप, काव्यरूप, कवितामय, पद्यरूप, श्लोकबद्ध.

3 *possessing the beauties of poetry.* कविता रसभरित, काव्यरसभरित, रसिक. [*n.* पद्य *n.*

POETRY, *n. metrical composition, verse.* कविता *f.* काव्य *n.* कवन

Sacred p. सत्कविता *f.* सत्कवन *n.* सत्काव्य *n.*

2 *art or practice of writing verse.* कविता *f.* कवित्व *n.* कवीत *n.* कविता शक्ति *f.* कवितावद्या *f.* श्लोकरचना *f.*

The genius of p. कविताशक्ति *f.*

POIGNANCY, *n.* v. A. 1. तिखटपणा *m.* तीक्ष्णता *f.* तीव्रता *f.*

2 तिखटपणा *m.* तीक्ष्णता *f.* तीव्रता *f.* प्रखरता *f.* तिक्त *m.*

POIGNANT, *a. sharp, stimulating, &c.* v. PUNGENT. तिखट, तीक्ष्ण, तीव्र, प्रखर.

2 *pointed, keen, irritating, &c.* तिखट, तीक्ष्ण, तीव्र, खोंचणीचा, खोंचीचा, नोकदार, नोकझोंकीचा, खर, प्रखर, भेदक, मर्मभेदक.

3 *severe, deep, piercing, painful, &c.*—grief, pain, &c. तीव्र, तीक्ष्ण, भेदक, प्राणभेदक, प्राणवेधक, प्राणांतिक, छातीफोड, पराकाष्ठेचा, काळिजाला भोंक *or* घरा पाडणारा.

POINT, *n. sharp end.* टोंक *n.* बोंथी *f.* कोंच *f.* चोंच *f.* बोंच *f.* अणकुची *f.* अणी *f.* अग्र *n.* मुळका *m. dim.* मुळकी *f.*

2 *head-land.* टोंक *n.* भूशलाका *f.*

3 *sting, wit, moral, &c.* खोंच *f.* नोक *f.* खुबी *f.* मखी *f.* दृन्द *f. m.* रहस्य *n.* छद्म *n.* वर्म *n.* मर्म *n.* दंश *m.*

4 (of space or time). परमाणु *m.* संधि *m.*

5 *punctilio, nicety.* बारीक-सूक्ष्म-क्षुद्र-&c. गोष्ट *f.*

6 *critical moment*, v. CRISIS. टिपण *n.* अणी *f.*

That is on the p. of. उदित, उद्यत, उद्युक्त, कृतपुंख, उन्मुख, (in comp. as, मरणोन्मुख on the p. of death, गमनोन्मुख on the p. of going, प्रसवोन्मुख on the p. of bringing forth, &c.).

To be on the p. of. टेंकणें, टेंकावणें, गुडणें.

7—as made with a pen, &c. *spot, mark*, v. DOT. बिंदु *m. dim.* बिंदुकली *f.* & बिंदुकलें *n.*

8 *pitch, stage, degree.* पर्याय *m.* पायरी *f.*

Highest p. पराकाष्ठा *f.* कळस *m.* सीमा *f.* शिखर *n.*

Lowest p. कडेची पायरी *f.*

To such a p. एथवर, एथपर्यंत.

9 (of the compass). दिशा *f.*

An intermediate p. विदिशा *f.* [*n.* कलम *n.*

10 *particular; single subject, item.* विषय *m.* गोष्ट *f.* प्रकरण

A particular p. टूक *f.*

A sore p. वर्म *n.* मर्म *n.*

A striking p. or excellency. टूम *f.* खुबी *f.*

A weak p. नागवें *n.*

In point of. प्रकरणीं, विषयीं, मध्यें.

That has a sore or weak p. वर्मी, मर्मी.

To touch a sore p. टोंचणें, मर्मस्पर्श *m.*-मर्मभेद *m.*-&c.करणें.

11 (of view, sight, &c.) v. LIGHT. दृष्टि *f.*

If you look at it in this p. असें पाहिलें असतां.

12 *aim, object.* लक्ष्य *n.* लक्ष *n.* टिपण *n.*

13 *position, assertion, subject of discussion, &c.* गोष्ट *f.* विषय *m.* प्रसंग *m.* प्रस्ताव *m.* स्थल *n.*

That is to the p. प्रास्ताविक, प्रासंगिक.

Point-blank. नीटसमोरचा, नीट, समरेषेचा, समसूत्राचा.

14 (in punctuation). अवसानाचीखूण *f.* विरामचिह्न *n.* विश्रामचिह्न *n.* [शेवटणें.

To POINT, *v. a. sharpen to a point.* अणी *f.*-&c. करणें-काढणें,

2 *direct towards,* v. To AIM. रोंखणें, योजणें, नेमणें, लावणें, धरणें, लक्षणें,—a sword, a stick, &c. menacingly. उगारणें.

3 *punctuate.* अवसानाच्याखुणा *f.pl.*-विरामचिह्नें *n. pl.*-विश्रामचिह्नें *n. pl.* करणें-घालणें.

4 (a wall, &c.). दरजगिरी *f.* करणें, दर्जा *f. pl.* करणें.

5 out; *shew,* v. To SHEW. बोट *n.* करणें, बोट करून-बोटानें दाखवणें, निर्देश *m.*-अंगुलिनिर्देश *m.* करणें-करून दाखवणें.

To POINT, *v. n.* (with the finger, &c.). बोट *n.* करणें-दाखवणें, हात *m.* दाखवणें, अंगुलिनिर्देश *m.* करणें.

2 *have aim or direction.* रोंख-नेम *m.*-संधान *n.*-शिस्त *f.*-&c. असणें *g. of s. with* कडे *of o.*

POINTED, *p. & a.* v. V. A. 1. अणी काढलेला, शेवटलेला, &c.

2 रोंखलेला, नेमलेला, योजलेला, &c.

5 बोटानें दाखवलेला, &c. निर्दिष्ट, अंगुलिनिर्दिष्ट, निदिष्ट.

I. *having a sharp end.* टोंकाचा, अणीचा, &c. अणीदार, बोचेरा, साग्र, सूच्यग्र.

II. *epigrammatical, sharp, &c.* नोकदार, नोकीचा, खोंचीचा.

POINTER, *n.* POINTING, *p. a.* v. V. A. 5. बोटानें दाखवणारा,&c. निर्देश करणारा, &c. निर्देष्टा, निदेष्टा, निदेशी.

POINTEDLY, *adv.* v. A. II. नोकदारीनें, नोकझोकीनें.

I. *with direct reference to a subject.* विशेष लक्ष्यानें, विशेष उद्देशानें, तदेकलक्षानें, विवक्षापूर्वक.

POINTEDNESS, *n.* v. A. II. नोकदारी *f.* नोकझोक *f.*

POINTING, *n.* v. V. A. 5. बोटानें दाखवणें *n.* &c. निर्देश *m.* अंगुलिनिर्देश *m.* निदेश *m.*

POINTLESS. See BLUNT, DULL.

POISE. See WEIGHT, EQUIPOISE.

To POISE. See To WEIGH, To BALANCE.

POISON, *n.* विष *n. pop.* विख्स *or* विख *n.* जहर *n.* विखार *m.* विषार *m.* गर *n.* गरल *n.* कालकूट *m. n.* हलाहल *m. n.*

Animal p. जंगमविष *n.*—mineral or vegetable p. स्थावरविष *n.*

Application or use of p. विषप्रयोग *m.*

Charm against p. गारूड *n.* [लिक.

Poison-doctor, curer of snake-&c. bites. विषवैद्य, जांगु-

To POISON, *v. a. infect with poison.* विखारा-विखारी-विषयुक्त-&c. करणें, विखारणें, विखारवणें, विष *n.*-विखार *m.*-&c. घालणें-लावणें.

To p. the ear of. कान *m.* फुंकणें *g. of o.*

2 *injure or kill by poison, administer poison to.* विष *n.*-विख *n.*-&c. देणें-पाजणें-चारणें-&c. विषप्रयोग *m.* करणें, विखारवणें, विष *n.*-&c. देऊन-&c. मारणें-जीव *m.* घेणें.

To be poisoned. विखारणें, विषारणें, विखार *or* विषार *m.* होणें *in. con.*

3 (one's self) *take poison.* विष *n.*-&c. घेणें-खाणें-पिणें-सेवणें-&c. *or* घेऊन-&c. मरणें, विषप्रयोगकरून मरणें.

4 *taint, corrupt.* बिघडवणें, नासणें, भ्रष्ट-दुष्ट- वाईट-&c. करणें.

POISONED, *p.* v. V. 1. विखारा केलेला, विखारवलेला, विषयुक्त.

2 विष पाजलेला-चारलेला-&c. विखारलेला, विखार झालेला, &c.

4 बिघडवलेला, नासलेला, भ्रष्ट केलेला.

POISON-ROOT, *n.* बचनाग *or* कम.

POISONING, *n.* v. V. 1.—*act.* विखारा करणें *n.* विखारणें *n.* विष घालणें *n.* &c.

2 विष देणें *n.* विखारणें *n.* &c. विषप्रयोग *m.*

4 बिघडवणें *n.* &c.

POISONOUS, *a. having the qualities of poison.* विखारा, विखारी, विखाराचा, विषाचा, जहरी, विषधर्मक, विषगुणक, विषालु, गरली, विषमय. [विखार *m.*

POISONOUSNESS, *n.* v. A. विखारेपणा *m.* &c. विषालुता *f.* &c.

POITREL, *n. armour for the breast,* v. ARMOUR. उरस्त्राण *n.* वक्षस्त्राण *n.*

To POKE, *v. a. thrust, stick.* ढुसकणें, ढुसणें, ढोसणें, मोसकणें *or* भोकसणें, बोचणें, बोचकणें.

To p. the head over or forward. डोकावणें, टोकावणें, टोंकणें, ढुंकून पाहणें, टोकावणी *f.*-&c. करणें.

2 out; *search for, grope for.* चांचपून-चांचपत-&c. काढणें-पाहणें-शोधणें. [चापसणें.

To POKE, *v. n. feel about.* चांचपणें, चांचपडणें, चापणें, चांपचणें,

2 *piddle, trifle, do any thing slowly, hesitatingly, &c.* v. To DAWDLE. रेंगणें, रेंगळणें, चांचपणें, चापणें, चांचपत-चांचपडत-&c. करणें, कांचकळणें.

POKE, *n.* See THRUST. 2 See BAG.

A pig in a p. पाण्यांत म्हैस वर मोल.

3 *piddler, &c.* v. DAWDLER. रेमेडोंक्या, रड्या, रेंग्या, चांचप्या, चांपच्या, चांचपडत काम करणारा, चघळ, अगटचिगट, गोयावा.

POKER, *n.* POKING, *p. a.*v.V. N. 1. चांचपणारा, चांचपडणारा, &c.

2 See POKE, 3.

I. *instrument for stirring the fire.* खोरणें *n.* उकरणें *n.*

POKING, *n.* v. V. A. 1.—*act.* ढुसकणें *n.* ढुसणें *n.* बोचणें *n.* &c. ढुसकणी *f.* ढुसणी *f.* ढुसकी *f.*

2 चांचपून काढणें *n.* &c.

v. V. N. 1. चांचपणें *n.* चांचपडणें *n.* &c.

2 रेंगणें *n.* चापणें *n.* फेंदणें *n.* कांचकळणें *n.* &c. फेंदी *f.* चघळकाम *n.* अर्धजरतीय *n.* द्राविडप्राणायाम *m.*

POKINGLY, *adv.* v. V. N. 2. चांचपत, चांपसत, चांचपडत, रेंगत, रडतरडत, रडतखडत, फेंदत, फेंदीखालीं.

POLAR, *a. belonging, &c. to the poles of the earth.* ध्रुवाचा, ध्रुवाकडचा, ध्रुवाकडला, ध्रुवाकडील, ध्रुवसंबंधी, ध्रुवविषयक.

Polar circle. ध्रुववृत्त *n.* [ध्रुवांश *m.*

The p. distance of a heavenly body. द्युज्याचापांश *m.*

POLARITY, *n. tendency to the pole.* ध्रुवाभिसरणशीलता *f.* ध्रुवाभिमुखशीलता *f.* ध्रुवाभिसरणप्रीति *f.*

POLARY, *a. having a tendency toward the pole.* ध्रुवाभिसरणशील, ध्रुवाभिसारी, ध्रुवाभिमुखशील. [सोटा *m.*

POLE, *n. long staff.* काठी *f.* दांडा *m.* वांसा *m.* सरा *m.* सर *m.* सोट *m.*

Bearer of the p. (in processions, &c.). काठकर.

Long p. used in pushing a boat through shallow water. ताज *f. m.*—That uses it. ताज्या *m.* ताजकरी *m.*

P. with a crook to pull down pods, fruits, &c. शेकाटा *m.* शेगाडा *m.* शेकाटी *f.*

P. rounded by the lathe. गोल *m.* काटगोल *m.*

2 (of a palanquin). दांडी *f.* दंड *m.* (in. comp.).

3 (of a tent). खांब *m.*

4—the measure of length. काठी *f.* (5 cubits and 5 hand breadths). दंड*m.* (4 cubits).

5 (of the earth). ध्रुव*m.*—North p. उत्तरध्रुव*m.* उत्तराग्र*n.*—South p. दक्षिणध्रुव*m.* दक्षिणाग्र*n.*

Elevation of the p. ध्रुवोन्नति *f.*

Far as the poles asunder. आकाश पाताळचा भेद, काशीरामेश्वरचें अंतर, जमीन आसमानचा फेर.

POLE-AXE, *n.* लांबदांड्याचीफरशी *f.*-फरश *or* फरस *m.*

POLE-CAT, *n.* केशाळमांजर *n.* लोमशमार्जार *m.* पूतिशारिजा *f.*

POLE-STAR, *n.* ध्रुव *m.* ध्रुवाचा तारा *m.* मेढ *f.*

POLED, *a. that has a pole,*—a tent, &c. खांबाचा, खांबी.

Single p. एक खांबी, एकबुरजी.—Double p. दुखांबी, दुबुरजी.

POLEMIC, POLEMICAL, *a.* v. CONTROVERSIAL. वादविवादाचा, विप्रतिपत्तीचा, वादविवादात्मक. [&c. कर्त्ता.

POLEMICAL, *n. disputant.* वादविवाद करणारा, विवादी, वादविवाद-

POLEMICS, *n.* v. CONTROVERSY. वादविवाद *m.*

POLICE, *n. government of a city or town.* गांवची-शहरची-&c. बंदोबस्ती *f.* गांवचा-&c. बंदोबस्त *m.* ग्रामव्यवस्था *f.* नगरव्यवस्था *f.*

2 *internal government of a state.* देशचा-&c. बंदोबस्त *m.* देशची-&c. बंदोबस्ती *f.* देशव्यवस्था *f.* राज्यव्यवस्था *f.*

3—the body of civil officers. पोलीस *n.* from the English.

The department of p. पोलीस खातें *n.*

POLICE-MAGISTRATE, *n.* कोतवाल, फौजदार, पोलीसअमलदार.

Hall or court of a p. कोतवालचावडी *f.* फौजदाराची चावडी *f.*

Office or business of a p. कोतवाली *f.* फौजदारी *f.*

POLICE-MAN, *n.* कोतवालीचा-फौजदारीचा-पोलीसचा शिपाई.

POLICE-OFFICER, *n.* पोलीस अमलदार.

POLICE-STATION, *n.* पोलिसाचेंठाणें *n.* चौकी *f.*

POLICY, *n. art or system of government.* राज्य चालवण्याची नीति *f.*-रीति *f.*-धोरण *n.*-&c. राजनीति *f.* राजनय *m.* राज्यनयन *n.* राज्यधुरावहन *n.* राज्यनयनमार्ग *m.*

A matter of state p. राजकारण *n.*

2 *art, wisdom, &c. in the management of public affairs.* राज्य चालवण्याची चतुराई *f.* राज्य चालवण्याचे डावपेच *m. pl.*-मसलती *f. pl.* राज्यचातुर्य *n.* राज्यकौशल *n.* राज्यनयनकौशल *n.* राज्यकरणयुक्ति *f.*

3 *wisdom, skill, &c. in the conduct of affairs,*—gener. कामकरण्याची-व्यवहाराची-&c. चतुराई *f.* व्यवहारचातुर्य *n.* व्यवहारदक्षता *f.* व्यवहारदाक्ष्य *n.* व्यवहारकौशल्य *n.* व्यवहारयुक्ति *f.*

A crooked p. कुवेडें *n.* उलटेंशाहणपण *n.* गैरमसलत *f.* गैरमनसुबा *m.*

4 (in commerce). विम्याचा करारनामा *m.*

To POLISH, *v. a. make smooth and glossy by rubbing, &c.* उजळणें, नितळणें, निसळणें, उजळणी *f.*-&c. करणें *g. of o.* सफाई *f.*-चकचकी *f.*-जिल्हई *f.*-झील *f.*-&c. आणणें, उजळा *m.*-ओप *f.* देणें, घोटणें, घोटून चकचकी *f.*-&c. आणणें, मोहरा *m.* करणें -आणणें, उज्ज्वलन *n.* करणें *g. of o.*—weapons, tools, &c. शिकल *f.* करणें.

2 *refine, make elegant, &c.* सुधारणें, सजवणें, सजणें, सुधारणूक *f.*-&c. करणें *g. of o.* सभ्य-शिष्ट-सभ्यतासंपन्न-शिष्टतासंपन्न-&c. करणें, सभ्यता *f.*-शिष्टता *f.*-प्रौढि *f.*-&c. आणणें-देणें.

POLISH, *n. gloss,* lit. सफाई *f.* नितळाई *f.* जिल्हई *f.* झील *f.* उजळा*m.* ओप *f.* मोहरा *m.* चकचकी *f.* तकतकी *f.* तकाकी *f.* तजला *or* तजेला *m.* तजेली *f.* तिळतिळी *f.* लकेरी *f.*

To take p. ओप *f.* घेणें, ओप *f.* बसणें *in. con.*

2 fig. *refinement, elegance of manners, &c.* सभ्यता *f.* शिष्टता *f.* शिष्टाइकी *f.* प्रौढि *f.* सभाचातुर्य *n.* सुजनता *f.* सौजन्य *n.* शिष्टाचारसंपन्नता *f.* सभ्याचारसंपन्नता *f.*

POLISHED, *p.* v. V. 1. उजळलेला, नितळलेला, ओपदिल्हेला, &c. उज्ज्वलित, तेजित. [यसंपन्न.

2 सभ्यकेलेला, &c. सभ्य, प्रौढ, शिष्ट, शिष्टाचारसंपन्न, सभ्यसंप्रदा-

POLISHER, *n.* POLISHING, *p. a.* v. V. 1. उजळणारा, ओपदेणारा, सफाई आणणारा, &c.—esp. of weapons or tools. शिकलगर *or* गार *or* कर.

2 सभ्यकरणारा, सभ्यता आणणारा, सुधारणारा, &c.

I. *polishing instrument (for metals, &c.).* ओपसळई *f.* ओपणी *f.* नितळणा *m.* घोटा *m.* मोहरा *m.*

POLISHING, *n.* v. V. 1.—*act.* उजळणें *n.* नितळणें *n.* &c. उजळणी *f.* ओप *f.v.* दे, ओपवणी *f.* ओपसरा *m.* उज्ज्वलन *n.*—esp. of weapons or tools, शिकल *or* सिकल *f.*

2 सभ्य करणें *n.* &c.

POLITE, *a. of polished manners, refined behaviour, &c.* सभ्य, शिष्ट, शिष्टपणाचा, सभ्यतेचा, प्रौढीचा, प्रौढ, शिष्टाचारसंपन्न, सभ्यसंप्रदाय संपन्न.

2 *courteous, complaisant, &c.* v. CIVIL. गृहस्थी, सत्कारी, गौरवी, आदरशील.

POLITELY, *adv.* v. A. 1. शिष्टपणानें, सभ्यतेनें, &c. शिष्टसंप्रदायानुसार, सभ्यसंप्रदायानुसार.

2 गृहस्थपणानें, गृहस्थगिरीनें, &c. ताजीम देऊन.

POLITENESS, *n.* v. A. 1. शिष्टपणा *m.* &c. सभ्यता *f.* शिष्टता *f.* शिष्टाइकी *f.* प्रौढि *f.* शिष्टाचारसंपन्नता *f.* सभ्यसंप्रदायसंपन्नता *f.* सुजनता *f.* सौजन्य *n.* [म *f. v.* दे, घे.

2 गृहस्थपणा *m.* गृहस्थगिरी *f.* गृहस्थाई *f.* रीतरवेस *m. f.* ताजी-

Hollow p. वरकर्मी आदर *m.* पैठणी आदर *m.*

I. *polite behaviour.* शिष्टाचार *m.* शिष्टाचरण *n.* सभ्याचार *m.* सभ्याचरण *n.* सभ्यसंप्रदायानुवर्त्तन *n.*

POLITIC, *a. sagacious in government.* राजनीतिकुशल, राजनीतिज्ञ, नीतिकौशलसंपन्न, नीतिदक्ष.

2 *skilled in policy, sagacious in adapting means to an end,* v. SKILFUL, CUNNING. लागलाव्या, लाग्या, मतलबी, कवाइती, कवाईतदार, कारस्थानी.

3 *wise, well devised, adapted to secure its end.* तजविजीचा, युक्तीचा, सुयुक्तीचा, समंजसपणाचा, समंजस, सुविचाराचा, शाहणपणाचा, सुयुक्त.

4 See POLITICAL.

POLITICAL, *a. pertaining to polity.* राजकारभाराचा, राज्य चालवण्याविषयींचा, &c. राजनीतीचा, राजनीतिविद्येचा, राजनयाचा, राजनीतिसंबंधी-विषयक, राज्यकार्याचा, राज्यनयनसंबंधी-विषयक, राजकीय.

POLITICAL ECONOMY, *n. science of the management, &c. of the resources of a country.* अर्थशास्त्र *n.* राज्याची-देशाची-राष्ट्राची-&c. व्यवस्था करण्याची विद्या *f.* राज्यव्यवस्थाविद्या *f.* देशसंजोग*m.* देशकल्याणविद्या *f.* राष्ट्रपोषणविद्या *f.* राष्ट्रोपचयविद्या *f.*

2 See POLITICS. [राज्यनयनप्रकरणीं.

POLITICALLY, *adv.* v. A. राजकारभाराविषयीं, राज्यनयनाविषयीं,

POLITICIAN, *n. one skilled in politics.* राजनीतिकुशल, राजनी-

निविशारद, राजनीतिज्ञ, राजकारणी. [कवाईतदार.
2 *a man of cunning, &c.* v. POLITIC. लागलाध्या, कवाइती,
POLITICS, *n. science of government.* राजनीति *f.* राजनय *m.* राजनीतिविद्या *f.* राजनीतिशास्त्र *n.* राज्यनयनविद्या *f.* राज्यशासनविद्या *f.* राज्यधुरावहनविद्या *f.*
2 *public affairs.* राजकारभाराचें प्रकरण *n.*-खटलें *n.*-&c. राजकारभाराची गोष्ट *f.* राजप्रकरण *n.* राज्यविषय *m.* *pl.* सरकारचीं कामें *n. pl.*
POLITY, *n. form or system of government,* v. CONSTITUTION. राज्यनीतिरूप *n.* राज्यव्यवस्था *f.* राज्यनियम *m.* *pl.*
POLL, *n.* v. HEAD. डोई *f.* ढोसकें *n.*
2 *list of persons.* डोईपट्टी *f.* माणूसपट्टी *f.*
To POLL, *v. a.* (trees) v. To LOP. खडसणें, डुंसणें, बोडकावणें.
2 (the head, &c.). केश *or* केस *m. pl.* कापणें-कातरणें.
3 *fleece, spoil.* See To PLUNDER. 4 *enter on a list of names.* नांवनिशीचे यादीवर घालणें-दाखल करणें.
POLL-TAX, *n. capitation tax.* डोईपट्टी *f.*
POLLARD, *n. a. lopped tree.* डेंसण *n.* डुंसण *n.* डुंख *n.*
2 *sheep, &c. without horns.* मुंढा-बुंढा-&c. (with the noun required).
POLLED, *p.* v. V. 1. खडसलेला, डुंसलेला, &c. मुंढा, बुंठा *or* बोंठा, बोडका *or* खा.
POLLEN, *n.*—of flower. फुलांतला बुका *m.* पराग *m.* रज *n.*
To POLLUTE, *v. a. foul,* v. To DIRTY. मळवणें, मळवटणें, मळकट-मळीण-&c. करणें.
2 *taint, contaminate, &c.* v. To DEFILE. अपवित्र-भ्रष्ट-मळीण-&c. करणें, विघडवणें, भ्रष्टविणें.
3—ceremonially. विटाळणें, विटाळवणें, बाटवणें, ओंवळा करणें, भ्रष्टकरणें, बाटेसा-विटाळेसा-&c. करणें, भ्रष्टविणें.
4 *violate by illegal sexual commerce.* चोंढाळणें, भ्रष्ट-खराब-&c. करणें.
POLLUTED, *p.* v. V. 1. *and* DIRTY. मळवलेला, मळका केलेला, &c.
2 v. IMPURE. अपवित्र केलेला, अपवित्र, भ्रष्ट, निर्माल्य.
3 v. IMPURE. विटाळलेला, बाटवलेला *or* बाटलेला, बाट्या, बाटींव, बाटगा, ओंवळा.
To be p. बाटणें, विटाळणें. [करणारा.
POLLUTER, *n.* POLLUTING, *p. a.* v. V. 1. मळवणारा, मळीण
2 अपवित्र करणारा, भ्रष्ट करणारा, भ्रष्टकर.
3 विटाळणारा, बाटवणारा, ओंवळा करणारा, &c.
4 चोंढाळणारा, &c. [मळवलेलेपणा *m.*
POLLUTION, *n.* v. V. 1.—*act.* मळवणें *n.* मळवटणें *n.* &c.—*state.*
2—*act.* अपवित्र करणें *n.* &c. भ्रष्टीकरण *n.* अपवित्रीकरण *n.* —*state.* अपवित्रता *f.* भ्रष्टता *f.*
3—*state.* v. IMPURITY. विटाळ *m.* बाट *m.* बाटणूक *f.* बाटणी *f.*
General or wide spread p. बाटबडा *or* बाटोडा *m.* बाटाबाट *f.* भ्रष्टाभ्रष्ट *f.* भ्रष्टाकार *m.*
I.—in medicine; *pollutio nocturna.* स्वप्नदोष *m.* स्वप्नावस्था *f.* स्वप्नांत वीर्यपात *m.*
POLTROON, *n.* v. COWARD. नामर्द, लंडी, फटलंडी, भागूबाई *f.*
POLTROONERY, *n.* v. COWARDICE. नामर्दी *f.* भितरेपणा *m.*
POLY. This prefix is rendered by बहु, अनेक.
POLYANDRY, *n. plurality of husbands.* अनेकनवरे करण्याची चाल *f.* बहुभर्तृधारण *n.* बहुभर्तृत्व *n.*
POLYCHORD, *a.* बहुतंतु.
POLYGAMIST, *n. defender of polygamy.* बहुपत्नीवादी.
POLYGAMY, *n. plurality of wives.* अनेकबायका करण्याची चाल *f.* बहुनारी करण्याची चाल *f.* बहुभार्यता *f.* बहुपत्नीत्व *n.*
POLYGENOUS, *a. of many kinds.* बहुविध, अनेकविध.
POLYGLOT, *a. having many languages.* बहुभाष, अनेकभाष.
POLYGLOT, *n. book in many languages.* बहुभाषग्रंथ *m.*
POLYGON, *n. figure of many sides or angles.* बहुकोण *m.* बहुस्राकृति *f.* अनेकास्राकृति *f.* ऋजुभुज क्षेत्र *n.*
POLYGONAL, POLYGONOUS, *a.* v. N. बहुकोण, बहुस्र, अनेकास्र.
POLYMATHY, *n. knowledge of many arts and sciences.* बहुविद्याज्ञान *n.* बहुविद्यापरिज्ञान *n.*
POLYPETALOUS, *a.* बहुदल.
POLYSPERMOUS, *a.* बहुबीज.
POLYSYLLABIC, *a.* बह्वच्क, बह्वक्षर. [बहुदेवमत *n.*
POLYTHEISM, *n. doctrine of a plurality of gods.* अनेकदेवमत *n.*
POLYTHEIST, *n. maintainer of polytheism.* अनेकदेवमतवादी, अनेकदेवमतावलंबी.
POMEGRANATE, *n.*—the tree. डाळिंब *f.* अनार *n.m.*—the fruit, डाळिंब *n.* अनार *n. m.*
Marked as with seeds of the p.—cloth. अनारदाणी.
Of the colour, &c. of a p.—cloth. डाळिंबी.
POMFRET, *n.*—the fish. सरगुटली *f.* सरंगा *m.*
2 black p. हलवा *m.*
POMMEL, *n. round ball, &c.* v. KNOB. बोंड *n.* बोंडस *n.*
To POMMEL, *v. a.* v. To BEAT. कुदकणें, कुदवणें, खुदलणें *or* खुदळणें, खुबलणें, बडवणें, घुमसणें, कुंदी *f.*-कुट्टा *m.*-&c. काढणें *g. of o.*
POMMELLING, *n.* v. V.—*act.* कुदकणें *n.* &c. कुंदी *f.* *v.* काढ, कुट्टा *m.* *v.* काढ.
POMP, *n. splendid procession.* समारंभाची-डामडौलाची-थाटमाटाची-&c. स्वारी *f.*-यात्रा *f.*-&c. समारभयात्रा *f.*
2 *splendour, pageantry, show.* थाट *m.* थाटमाट *or* थाटमांड *m.* बडेजाव *f.* डामडौल *m.* धुमधाम *or* धामधूम *f.* टामटूम *or* टूमटाम *f.* छान *f.* शान *f.* डौल *m.* भडक *f.*
POMPELMOOSE, *n. citrus decumana,*—the fruit. चकोत्रा *m.* पपन्नस *n.* बंपारा *m.*—the tree. पपन्नस *f.*
POMPION. See PUMPKIN.
POMPOUS, *a. displaying pomp, showy, &c.* v. N. 2. *and* FINE. थाटाचा, थाटमाटाचा, डामडौलाचा, टामटुमीचा, छानीचा, &c. छानदार, शानदार, समारंभाचा.
2 *boastful, ostentatious.* बडिवाराचा, बढाईचा, बढाइकीचा, बुटटकीचा, मोठाईचा, शेखीचा.
POMPOUSLY, *adv.* v. A. 1. थाटानें, थाटमाटानें, डौलानें, डामडौलानें, &c. थाट-शान-&c. करून, नटून, थटून, नटूनथटून.
POMPOUSNESS, POMPOSITY, *n.* v. A. 1. *and* POMP. थाट *m.* थाटमाट *m.* छान *f.* छानदारी *f.* शान *f.* शानदारी *f.* डौल *m.*
2 बडिवार *m.* बढाई *f.* बढाइकी *f.* बुटटकी *f.* शेखी *f.*
POND, *n. tank, small lake.* तळें *n.* तळाव *m.* पोखर *n.* पोखरण *f.* पुष्करणी *f.* तळी *f.*
POND-WEED, *n.* हृड *f.*
To PONDER, *v. a. weigh in the mind.* विचारून-अवांकून-तोलून-घोळून-विचार करून-&c. पाहणें, मनांत पाहणें, चिंतणें, विचार *m.* -चिंतन *n.*-ऊहापोह *m.*-&c. करणें *g. of o.*

To PONDER, *v. n.* See To THINK.

PONDERABLE, *a. that may be weighed.* तोलायाजोगा-जोगता-सारखा-&c. वजन कराया जोगा-जोगता-&c. तुलायोग्य.

2 fig. *that may be pondered.* चिंत्य, चिंतनीय.

PONDERAL, *a. estimated by weight.* वजनी, वजनाचा.

PONDERED, *p.* v. V. A. अवांकून पाहिलेला, घोळून पाहिलेला, &c. चिंतित.

PONDERING, PONDERATION, *n.* v. V. A. *and* CONSIDERATION. चिंतन *n.* चिंतणी *f.* चिंतणूक *f.* विचार *m.* विचारण *n.* विचारणा *f.* ऊहापोह *m.* संभावना *f.*

PONDEROUS, PONDEROUSNESS, &c. See WEIGHTY, WEIGHT.

PONIARD, *n.* v. DAGGER. कटार *f.* खंजीर *m.* जंब्या *m.*

PONTAGE, *n. tax or duty for bridges.* पूलपट्टी *f.*

PONTIFF, *n. high priest.* उपाध्यायाचार्य, धर्माचा मुख्यअधिकारी.

PONTOON, *n.* पूल बांधण्याची नाव *f.*

PONY, *n. small horse.* तट्टू *m. n.* (*f.* तटाणी).

Strong p. बट *m.*

POODLE, *n.* कुतऱ्याची एक जात आहे.

POOH, *interj.* फू, धत्त. [सर *n.* थिल्लर *n.*

POOL, *n. reservoir of water,* v. TANK, LAKE. कुंड *n.* पल्वल *n.*

2 *hole filled with water.* डबराor डहुरा *or* डोहरा *m.* डोहण *n.* —esp. as dug in the bed or by the brink of a stream, विहिरा *m.* बुडकी *f.*—as dug to receive water, कोंडकी *f.* कोंडकें *n.*

Large p. or puddle. डबाड *n.* [*m.* ताल *n.*

P. of blood, milk, &c. spilled. थारोळें *n.* थारळें *n.* थाया

3 See PUDDLE. 4 (at dice, &c). बळ्ती *f.*

POOP, *n.*—of a ship. गलबताचा-&c. मागला भाग *m.*-पिछाडा *m.*

POOR, *a. not rich; indigent, necessitous, moneyless, &c.* गरीब, दरिद्री, कंगाल, रंक, धनावेगळा *or* निराळा, अधन, निर्धन, निर्धात, द्रव्यहीन, धनहीन, दुबळा, अकांचन, हीनद्रव्य, हीनधन, धनशून्य, द्रव्यशून्य, गिरिबदार, ओढस्त, ओढिस्त, नस्ता, बोन्या, मिसकीन, निःकांचन *or* निष्कांचन, अनर्थ, अर्थहीन, दरिद्र, दरिद्रित, दारिद्र्यग्रस्त, अल्पधन, अल्पद्रव्य, अकिंचन, दुर्बल *or* ळ, असंपन्न, हीनावस्थ, भुकेकंगाल, भुकेबंगाल, दीन, बुभुक्षित, भुकिस्त.—intens. *poor as a beggar, &c.* निपट दरिद्री, कफल्, कफल्लक, सकाण. [गरीबदुबळे.

The poor; *poor people.* गोरगरीब, दीनदुर्बल, गरीबगुरीब,

Compassionate to the p. दीनदयाळ, दीननाथ, दीनबंधु.

To be p. दांताबर मांस *n.* नसणें.

The poor must not be dainty. दरिद्र्यास खोड असूं नये.

2 *paltry, pitiful, sorry, despicable &c.* v. MEAN, WORTHLESS. दरिद्री, भिकारी, भिकार, फाटका, फुसका, गैरी, लुकसान *or* लुसकान, कुंगार, बिचारा, नादान, नाकारा, किलवाणा *or* णी, हलका, तुच्छ, रुपण.

3 *gentle, harmless, soft, spoony, spiritless, &c.* बापडा, बापुडवाणा *or* णी, बिचारा, मेण्या, मेणचट.

4 *pitiable, wretched, feeble, &c.* दरिद्री, बापडा, बापुडवाणा *or* णी, लुकसान *or* लुसकान, दुर्बल *or* ळ, दुबळा, कंगाल.

5 *not good, fit, adequate, &c.* अयोग्य, फुसका, नाकारा, निकामा, निकामी, यारदा, यारदी.

6—as a word of tenderness, *dear.* बापुडा.

7 *thin, starveling,* v. LEAN. रोड, किडकिडीत, भुकिस्त, भुकड,

8—as soil. निकस, निकशी, मानटी, उसर, धापड, हलुवट *or* हलवट, भुकिस्त, भुकड, बरड *or* भरड, बरडा, रूक्ष.

P. and sterile land. मान- *n.* बरडा *m.*

9—fare, diet, &c. रखरखीन, रूखा, रूक्ष.

P. fare. अरबचरब *n.* अरबटचरबट *n.* अकंसचकंत *n.*

POOR-ASYLUM, *n.* धर्मशाळ *f.* धर्मशाळा *f.*

POOR-SPIRITED, *a.* v. WEAK, COWARDLY. धैर्यहीन, रांड्या, मेंग्या, मेण्या, मेणचट. [&c.

POORLY, *adv.* v.A. 1. गरीबीच्या रीत-, कंगालपणानें, दरिद्रपणानें, I. *with little success, profit, eclat, &c.* फळावांचून, लाभावांचून, यशावांचून, रंगावांचून, रडतखडत, रडनरडन.

POORLY, *a. indisposed, not in health.* अस्वस्थ.

To feel p. जिवास बरें न वाटणें, समाधान*n.* नसणें.

POORNESS, *n.* v. A. 1. *and* POVERTY. गरीबी *f.* कंगाली *f.* दारिद्र्य *n.* निर्धनता *f.* धनहीनता *f.* द्रव्यहीनता *f.* &c.

2 भिकारपणा *m.* फाटकपणा *m.* गैरीपणा *m.* &c.

POP, *adv.* फटकन-कर-&c. सट-कण-कर-&c. सुर-कण-कर-&c.

Pop! pop! फटफट *or* टां, तटतट *or* टां, फटाफट, फटाटां.

To POP, *v. n. move with a quick, sudden motion.* फटकन-तटकन-तट्टकन-सटकन-&c. चालणें-येणें-जाणें-&c.

2 in; upon; *enter, &c. unexpectedly.* गांठणें, दत्त म्हणून-त्रे म्हणून-हूं म्हणून-&c. येणें, टाकलेला येणें.

3 off; v. To START. सटकणें, सडकणें, सुटकणें, झटकणें, उडणें.

To POP, *v. a. thrust, &c. with a quick, sudden motion.* झटकन-पटकन-सटकण-&c. टाकणें.

POP, *n. small, sharp sound.* खुट &c. वाजलेला आवाज *m.*

With a p. खुट-कन कर-&c. घुट-कन-कर-&c.

POP-GUN, *n.* फटकफळी *f.* नपटी *f.* नेपटी *f.*

POPE, *n.* रोमन क्याथोलिक धर्माचा मुख्य अधिकारी.

POPERY, *n.* रोमन क्याथोलिक धर्म *m.*

POPISH, *a.* रोमन क्याथोलिक धर्माचा.

POPINJAY, *n.* See PARROT, POP.

POPLAR, *n.* हिवर *m.*

POPPY, *n.* खसखसीचें झाड *n.*—seeds, खसखस *f.*—head or capsule. खसखसीचें बोंड *n.* पोस्तबोंड *n.*

P.-seed,—considered as a measure of weight, $\frac{1}{16}$ of a mustard seed. लिक्षा *f.*

POPULACE, *n. the common people,* v. PEOPLE. कुणबी माळी *m. pl.* साधारण लोक *m. pl.* सामान्य पदवीचे लोक *m. pl.*

POPULAR, *a. belonging, &c. to the common people.* सामान्य लोकांचा, साधारण लोकांचा, लोकांतला, लोकांचा, सामान्य लोकांविषयींचा, &c.

Courting p. favor. जनरंजन *n.* लोकसंपादणी *f.*

2 *prevailing among the people, general, prevalent, &c.* v. COMMON. लौकिक, लौकिकी, लोकांतला, रूढ, लोकरूढीचा, लोकसिद्ध, लोकप्रसिद्ध, बहुमत.

P. accusation. जनापवाद *m.* लोकापवाद *m.*

P. apprehension or acceptation. लोकग्रह*m.* लोकसमजून *f.*

P. story. जनकथा *f.* दंतकथा *f.* लोककथा *f.*

P. talk. जनप्रवाद *m.* जनवाद *m.* जनवार्त्ता *f.* जनश्रुति *f.* लोकवाद *m.* लोकवार्त्ता *f.*

P. usage, *general practice.* जनरीति pop. जनरीत *f.* जनव्यवहार *m.* जनशिरस्ता *m.* जनप्रवाह *m.* जनाचार *m.* लोका-

चार *m.* लौकिकाचार *m.* जनरूढी *f.* लोकशिरस्ता *m.* लोकव्यहार *m.*
3 *suitable to common people.* सामान्य लोकांच्या उपयोगाचा, सर्वांच्या उपयोगाचा, सामान्यलोकोपयोगी, सर्वलोकोपयोगी.
4 *beloved by people in general.* लोकांचे आवडीचा-प्रीतीचा-&c. लोकप्रिय, जनप्रिय, लोकग्राह्य.

To POPULARIZE, *v.a. spread among the people.* लोकांत-साधारण लोकांत-&c. चालू-प्रवृत्त-&c. करणें, लोकांला समजेल असें करणें.

POPULARITY, *n.* v. A. 4. लोकप्रीति *f.* जनप्रीति *f.* लोकानुकूल्य *n.* जनानुकूल्य *n.* जनानुराग *m.* लोकप्रियता *f.* जनप्रियता *f.* सर्वप्रियता *f.* लोकग्राह्यता *f.*
Desire of p. लोकेषणा *f.*

POPULARLY, v. A. 2. लोकांमध्यें, व्यवहारांत, लौकिकांत, लोकरूढींत, लोकरूढीनें. [&c. करणें.

To POPULATE, *v. a.* v. To PEOPLE. बसवणें, वसता-जनविशिष्ट-

To POPULATE, *v. n. propagate, breed.* प्रजोत्पादन *n.*-प्रजोत्पत्ति *f.*-प्रजावृद्धि *f.*-&c. करणें.

POPULATION, *n. whole number of people in a country, &c.* लोक *m. pl.* जन *m. pl.* प्रजा *f.* प्रजासंख्या *f.* लोकसंख्या *f.* देशजनता *f.*

POPULOUS, *a. having many inhabitants.* दाटवस्तीचा, भरवस्तीचा, आबाद, आबादान, बहुप्रज, बहुजन, प्रजाबहुल.

POPULOUSNESS, *n.* v. A. भरवस्ती *f.* आबादी *f.* आबादानी *f.* बहुप्रजता *f.* प्रजाबाहुल्य *n.* प्रजाप्राचुर्य *n.*

PORCELAIN, *n.* चिनीभांडीं *n. pl.*

PORCH, *n. vestibule.* देवडी *or* देवढी *f.* देहुडी *f.* ढेलच *or* ढेलज *f.* ओटी *f.* पडवी *f.* पडवें *n.* देहली *f.* द्वारमंडप *m. n.*
Side seat of a p. मृगासन *n.* [मंडप *n.*
P. before a temple for people to assemble in. सभा-

PORCINE, *a. relating, &c. to swine.* डुकरांचा, डुकरांविषयींचा.

PORCUPINE, *n.* साळू *f.* सायाळ *f.* साळ *f.* साळी *f.* साळजिवाद *n.* साळिंदर *or* साळिंद्र *n.* सारसई *f.* साळशीट *or* त *or* द *n.*
A quill of a p. साळपीस *n.* साळशीट *or* त *or* द *n.* साळिंदर *or* साळिंद्र *n.* सायाळ *n.*

PORE, *n.*—in anatomy. रोमकूप *m.* रोमरंध्र *n.* तनुकूप *m.* स्वेदद्वार *n.* स्वेदमार्ग *m.*
2—gener. *small spiracle, passage for fluids.* सूक्ष्मरंध्र *n.*

To PORE, *v. n. look with continued application.* डोळे *m. pl.* लावणें-ठेवणें-गाडणें *or* लावून-ठेवून-गाडून पाहणें-असणें, पाहत असणें, डोळेफोड *f.*-दृष्टिफोड *f.* करणें, हेरणें.

PORE-BLIND. See PURBLIND.

PORER, *n.* PORING, *p. a.* v. V. डोळे गाडून पाहणारा, डोळेफोड करणारा, &c. हेऱ्या. [हेर *f.*

PORING, *n.* v. V.—*act.* डोळेगाडणें *n.* &c. डोळेफोड *f.* दृष्टिफोड *f.*

PORK, *n.* डुकराचें मास *n.*

PORKER. See HOG. [रोमकूपमय.

POROUS, *a. having pores,* v. N. 1. रोमकूपयुक्त, रोमकूपविशिष्ट,
2 *that permits exudation.* पाझरणारा, पाझरता, निचरता, शिथिलावयवक, विरलावयवक, द्रावकावयवक.
A p. place. झूर *f.* मूर *f.* [र्य *n.*

POROUSNESS, POROSITY, *n.* v. A. रोमकूपवैशिष्ट्य *n.* रोमकूपप्राचु-
2 पाझरतेपणा *m.* निचरतेपणा *m.* &c. मूर *f.* झूर *f.* अवयववैरल्य *n.*

PORPOISE, PORPUS, *n.*—the fish. गादा, घड्याळ *n.* बुळका *m.*
2 fig. *flesh mountain, &c.* ढोण *n.* ढोणसकड *n.* ढब्बू *m.* अगडधूद.

PORRIDGE, *n. stir-about.* घाटा *m.*

PORRINGER, *n.* v. POT. कटोरा *m.*

PORT, *n. harbour.* बंदर *n.*
An inferior p. आडबंदर *n.*
That has made the p. बंदरसई *or* सही.
Toll paid by ships on clearing out of a p. पाग *f.*
To touch at a p. बंदर *n.* करणें.
2 *gun port.* गलबतावरील तोफेची खिडकी *f.* बारी *f.* जंगी *f.*
3 See AIR, MIEN. 4 See GATE.
5 गलबताची-&c. डावीबाजू *f.*
6 एक प्रकारचा शराब आहे.

PORT, *a. of or belonging to a port.* बंदरचा, बंदरी.

To PORT, *v. a.* (helm) डावीकडे फिरवणें.

PORT-HOLE, *n.* v. PORT. बारी *f.* जंगी *f.*

PORT-TOWN, *n.* बंदर *n.* बंदरगांव *m.* उतारपेंठ *f.*

PORTABLE, *a. that may be easily carried about.* सहज वाहाया-झेलाया-&c. जोगा, हलकूल, हलखूद, अनायासवाह्य, सुवाह्य, सहजवाह्य.

PORTABLENESS, PORTABILITY, *n.* v. A. हलखुदपणा *m.* सुवाह्यता *f.* सहजवाह्यता *f.* &c.

PORTAGE. See PORTERAGE.

PORTAL, *n.* v. GATE. दार *n.* दरवाजा *m.*

To PORTEND, *v. a. foretoken,* v. To BODE. सुचवणें, दर्शवणें, चिह्न *n.*-लक्षण *n.*-शकुन *m.*-&c. दाखवणें *g. of o.* अग्रसूचन *n.*-पूर्वसूचन *n.*-&c. करणें *g. of o.*

PORTENDED, *p.* v. V. सुचवलेला, शकुनानें दाखवलेला, &c. अग्रसूचित, पूर्वसूचित.

PORTENDER, *n.* PORTENDING, *p. a.* v. V. सुचवणारा, दर्शवणारा, &c. अग्रसूचक, पूर्वसूचक.

PORTENT, *n. omen of ill.* उत्पात *m.* दुश्चिह्न *n.* अवचिह्न *n.* अवलक्षण *n.* अपशकुन *m.* अद्भुत *n.* अरिष्ट *n.* व्यतीपात *m.* उपसर्ग *m.*
Ceremonies to avert evil indicated by portents. अद्भुतशांति *f.*

PORTENTOUS, *a. ominous of evil.* अरिष्टसूचक, अद्भुतसूचक, अभद्रसूचक, &c. अद्भुत, औत्पातिक, औपसर्गिक, विनिपातशंसी.

PORTER, *n. door-keeper.* दर्वाजकरी, दर्वान, देवडीवान, देवडीवाला, द्वारपाल *or* ळ.
2 *carrier of a burden.* हेलकरी, ओझें वाहणारा, ओझेकरी, मोट्या, हमाल, भारवाहक, भारवाही, भारवाह.
3 एक प्रकारचें पेय आहे.

PORTERAGE, *n. cost of carriage by a porter.* हेल *m. f.* हमाली *f.* ओझें वाहणावळ *f.*
2 *business, &c. of a porter.* हेलवाहणें *n.* हेल *m. f.* हेलपाटी *f.*

PORTFOLIO, *n. case to hold papers.* जुजदान *n.* जुगदान *n.* पोवसंड *n.*

PORTICO, *n. piazza, &c.* ढेलज *or* ढेलच *f.*

PORTION, *n.* v. PART. अंश *m.* खंड *m.* विभाग *m.*
2 *part assigned, allotment,* v. SHARE. अंश *m.* भाग *m.* विभाग *m.* वांटा *m.* वर्गणी *f.*
3 *part of an inheritance.* रिक्थांश *m.* रिक्थभाग *m.* द्रव्यांश *m.*
4 *wife's fortune,* v. DOWER. स्त्रीधन *n.* यौतक *n.* पारिबर्ह *n.* कन्याधन *n.*

To PORTION, *v. a.* v. To PARCEL. विभागणें, वांटणें, वांटून देणें,

भाजणें, बिभाग *m.*-&c. करणें *g. of o.*

2 (a maiden). हुंडा *m.*-&c. देणें.

Portioning, *n.* v. V. 1.—*act.* विभागणें*n.*&c. वांटणी *f.* बिभाग*m.*

Portionless, *a.* v. N. अंशहीन, निरंश.

Portliness, *n.* v. A. घवघवितपणा *m.* पुष्टिशालिता *f.* बृहत्वशालिता *f.*

Portly, *a. of large and noble appearance.* घवघवीत, पुष्टिश्री, पुष्टिशाली, स्थौल्यशाली, बृहत्वशाली, भव्यकाय, धष्टपुष्ट.

Portmanteau, *n. leathern box.* कातड्याची पेटी *f.* जामदानी *f.*

Portrait, Portraiture, *n. picture.* तस्वीर *or* तस्वीर *f.* चित्र*n.*

To Portray, *v. a.* v. To Paint. तस्वीर *f.*-चित्र *n.*-&c. काढणें *g. of o.*

2 *depict, &c.* v. To Describe. वर्णणें, वर्णन *n.*-निरूपण *n.* -&c. करणें *g. of o.*

Portrayed, *p.* v. V. काढलेला.

2 वर्णलेला, वर्णित.

Portraying, *n.* v. V. 1. काढणें *n.*

2 वर्णणें *n.* वर्णन *n.* निरूपण *n.*

Pory. See Porous.

To Pose, *v. a. puzzle, gravel.* कोंडणें, पेचणें, गुंडाळणें, निरुत्तर-काईल-&c. करणें, पछाडणें, कोलणें, ग्रासणें, दांत *m. pl.* पाडणें *g. of o.* तोंड*n.* बंद करणें *g. of o.* टांके *m. pl.* ढील करणें *g. of o.*

Posed, *p.* v. V. कोंडलेला, &c. निरुत्तर, काईल, घायाळ, कुंठित, अनुत्तर, इति कर्त्तव्यतामूढ.

To be p. खुटणें, अटकणें. [णारा.

Poser, *n.* Posing, *p. a.* v. V. कोंडणारा, कोलणारा, &c. कुंठित कर-

Posing, *n.* v. V.—*act.* कोंडणें *n.* कुंठित करणें *n.* &c. कोंडणी *f.*

Position, *n. situation.* स्थान *n.* स्थिति *pop.* स्थीत *f.* अवस्थिति *f.*

2 *attitude, posture, &c.* अंगस्थिति *f.* ठाण *n.*—in fencing, &c. हात *m.*

Saluting p. सलामीचा हात *m.*

3 *principle laid down, proposition advanced, point to be proved, &c.* पक्ष *m.* पूर्वपक्ष *m.* प्रतिज्ञा *f.* भाषा *f.* प्रमेय *n.* फक्किका *f.* प्रतिज्ञात अर्थ *m.*

4 *state, circumstances,* v. Condition. स्थिति *pop.* स्थीत *f.* अवस्था *f.* दशा *f.*

5—in arithmetic. इष्टराशि *m.* इष्टराशिक *m.*—Double p. दुहिरी इष्टराशि *m.*-इष्टराशिक *m.*

Positive, *a. not negative; real, absolute.* खरा, खरेंचा, वास्तविक, वास्तव, तथ्य, यथातथ, यथार्थ, सत्.

2 *not implied; direct, explicit, express.* साफ, स्पष्ट, निखालस, खचीत, प्रत्यक्ष, निक्षीचा, धडधडीत, चरचरीत, अगर्भित, प्रत्यक्षसिद्ध.

3 *not admitting condition or discretion; peremptory, absolute.* खसखसीत, खंबीर, खरपूस, खरमरीत, ठाम, ठास, निखालस, खचीत, चरचरीत, बिनतरीचा, नियत.

4 *imposed or settled by arbitrary appointment.* नियोगप्रयुक्त, नियोगसिद्ध, नियोगहेतु, नियोगनिमित्तक.

5 *confident, sure, &c.* v. Certain. निस्संशय, निस्संदेह, निभ्रांत, दृढनिश्चय, बद्धनिश्चय.

6 *dogmatic, over confident in assertion.* मताभिमानी, मताग्रही, उक्तनिर्वाही, प्रोक्तनिर्वाही.

7—in grammar. See Comparison.

Positively, *adv.* v. A. 1. जातीनें, &c. वास्तविक, वस्तुगत्या, वस्तुनः, यथातथ, गुणतः.

2 साफ, स्पष्ट, धडधडीत, खचीत, खास, खासखा, निखालस, आवर्जून, ठासून, उदमेखून, आक्षेपून, हटकून, तात्पुरचा, आहत्य, परिच्छिन्न, निक्षून, अवश्य, अगत्य, जरूर, खरोखर, खरोखरी, खरोखरें, अलबत्त *or* त्ता. [न्न, खास.

3 खसखसीत, खरपूस, खडमून, खरावून, हडसून, निक्षून, परिच्छि-

5 खचीत, निस्संशय, निश्चयेंकरून, निश्चयात्मक, दृढनिश्चयपूर्वक, संदेहाभावपूर्वक.

6 मताभिमानानें, मताग्रहानें, &c.

Positiveness, *n.* v. A. 1. खरेपणा *m.* वास्तविकपणा *m.* वास्तविकता *f.* तथ्यता *f.* याथातथ्य *n.* सत्य *n.* सत्व *n.* सत्ता *f.*

2 स्पष्टपणा *m.* निखालसपणा*m.* खचितपणा*m.* &c. अगर्भितत्व*n.*

3 खंबिरपणा *m.* खरपुसपणा *m.* खरमरितपणा *m.* &c. निखालसता *f.* खंबिरी *f.*

4 नियोगप्रयुक्तता *f.* नियोगहेतुता *f.* [भाव *m.*

5 निस्संशयपणा *m.* &c. दृढनिश्चयता *f.* संशयराहित्य *n.* संशया-

6 मताभिमान *m.* मताग्रह *m.*

Posse, Posse comitatus, *n. party sent to apprehend an offender.* धरणी *f.* धरणें *n.* धावणें *n.*

2 See Crowd, Rabble.

To Possess, *v. a. have, hold, own, &c.* पाशीं-जवळ-पदरीं-हातीं-गांठीस-&c. असणें *in. con. with g. of s.* असणें *in. con.* धरणें, बाळगणें, राखणें *or* धरून-बाळगून-&c. असणें, मालकी *f.*-स्वामित्व *n.*-सत्ता *f.*-&c. असणें *g. of o. with* कडे *of s.*

2 *hold in use, enjoy, &c.* v. To Occupy. वहिवाटणें, भोग *m.*-भोगवटा *m.*-वहिवाट *f.*-&c. करणें *g. of o. or* असणें *g. of o. with* कडे *of s.*

3 *seize, gain, obtain the occupation of.* धरणें, घेणें, हस्तगत-स्वाधीन-काबीज-&c. करणें-करून घेणें, अवटाळणें, कवटाळणें.

4 of *or* with ; *give possession, command, or occupancy.* सत्ता *f.*-अधिकार*m.*-&c. देणें, सत्तेबाईक-सत्ताधारी-युक्त-विशिष्ट-आविष्ट-समाविष्ट-&c. करणें.

5—as a thought, idea, passion, &c. v. To Engross. घेरणें, वेढणें, ग्रासणें, व्यापणें, व्याप्त-ग्रस्त-&c. करणें, आवेश *m.* असणें *g. of s. with in. con.*

6—as an evil spirit. भरणें, संचरणें, भूतावेश *m.*-भूतसंचार*m.*-&c. होणें *in. con.*

To get possessed. लागीरणें, भुताटणें.

Possessed, *p.* v. V. 1. बाळगलेला, धरलेला, &c. सत्ताक्रांत, स्वत्वाक्रांत, धृत.

P. of. संपन्न in comp.

2 वहिवाटलेला, &c.

3 धरलेला, हस्तगत केलेला, &c.

4 युक्त (in comp. as क्रोधयुक्त, &c.) विशिष्ट (in comp.).

5 घेरलेला, व्यापलेला, &c. युक्त, ग्रस्त, व्याप्त, आविष्ट (in comp. as रूपाविष्ट, कामाविष्ट, ईर्ष्याविष्ट, लोभाविष्ट, मदाविष्ट, मत्सराविष्ट, हर्षाविष्ट, शोकाविष्ट, &c. &c.), समाविष्ट, समन्वित.

6 पिशाचाविष्ट, भूतग्रस्त, भूताविष्ट, भूतार्त्त, भूतसंचरित, समाविष्ट, लागीर.

Possession, *n.* v. V. जवळ असणें *n.* पदरीं असणें *n.* &c. मालकी असणें *n.* &c. धारण *n.* हात *m.*

In the p. or at the disposal of. हाताखालीं, हातीं.

2 वहिवाट *f.* भोग *m.* भोगवटा *m.* भुक्ति *f.*

Prior p. पूर्वभुक्ति *f.*

5 आवेश*m.* (in comp. as रूपावेश, कामावेश, ईर्ष्यावेश, लोभावेश, मदावेश, मत्सरावेश, हर्षावेश, शोकावेश, &c. &c.), समावेश*m.* आविष्टता *f.*

6 बाधा *f.* बाहेरची बाधा *f.* बाहेर बाधा *f.* बाहेरवसा*m.* पिशाचबाधा *f.* भूतबाधा *f.* आवेश*m.* भूतावेश*m.* पिशाचावेश*m.* आवेशन*n.* भूतसंचार*m.* पिशाचसंचार*m.* भूतक्रांति *f.* पीडा *f.* उपद्रव*m.* महाभय*m.* पिशाचपीडा *f.* भूतपीडा *f.* उपसर्ग *n.* लागीर *n. f.* लागोर *f.*

Bewildered through demoniac p. बावरा.

Stirring of a demon in p. चेष्टा *f.*

The subject of demoniac p. भूताचें-पिशाचाचें-&c. झाड*n.* *or* झाड्या. [*or* वतारणें.

To be under the working of demoniac p. वाढणें, वतरणें

To be under the bewilderment of demoniac p. बावरणें.

To enter into p.—a devil. आंगास-आंगीं येणें, वतरणें *or* वतारणें.

I. *thing possessed.* माल*m.* स्व*n.*

A rightful p. हक्कमाल*m.*

Possessions. माल*m.* मालमत्ता *f.* वित्त*n.* वित्तविषय*m.*

POSSESSIVE, *a.*—in grammar. संबंधवाचक.

P. case. षष्ठी *f.* संबंध*m.*

POSSESSOR, *n.* POSSESSING, *p. a.* v. V. 1. *and* OWNER. बाळगणारा, धरणारा, धनी, स्वामी, धाता.

2 वहिवाटणारा, &c. वहिवाट करणारा, भोक्ता, उपभोक्ता.

POSSET, *n.* शराब वगैरे घालून जमवलेलें दूध*n.*

To POSSET, *v. a.* See To CURDLE. [क्यता *f.*

POSSIBILITY, *n.* v. A. 1. संभव*m.* संभावना *f.* संभूति *f.* घटनश-

2 शक्यता *f.* साध्यता *f.*

POSSIBLE, *a. that may be, may happen, &c.* व्हायाजोगा-जोगता-सारखा-&c. घडायास-व्हायास-&c. शक्य, घटनशक्य, संभावित, संभाव्य, संभावनीय, संभूत, कादाचित्क.

As much as p. यथाशक्ति.

To be p. संभवणें.

2 (to be done) v. PRACTICABLE. शक्य, करणीय, साध्य.

POSSIBLY, *adv.* v. A. 1. *and* PERHAPS. कदाचित्, कथंचित्, पक्षीं, आहे आहे नाहीं नाहीं.

POST, *n.*—for carrying letters. टप्पाल*n.* डांक *f.*

Relay to convey the p. डांक *f.* टप्पा*m.*

To travel p. मजल दरमजल-कूच दर कूच-&c. जाणें-चालणें.

2 *public office, place,* v. OFFICE. असामी *f.* अधिकार*m.* हुद्दा*m.*

3 *station of watch or duty.* ठाणें*n.* चौकी *f.* स्थान*n.*

4 *military station.* ठाणें*n.* [स्थूणा *f.*

5 *pillar, stake, &c.* खांब*m. dim.* खांबणी *f.* खांबट*n.* स्तंभ*m.*

Main p. (of poor houses) reaching from the ground to the roof. धरणखांब*m.* धारण *m. or* धारणी *f.*

Piece between a p. and its burden. पिढें*n* हस्त*m.*

P. planted or set in the ground. पुरखांब*m.*

6—as term of reproach for a stupid and silent person. मोगरा, मुका म्हसोबा, मुकीमण्वार.

To POST, *v. n. travel with speed and without stopping.* डांकोडांक-टांकोटांक-मजलदरमजल-कूचदरकूच-रातोरात-&c. जाणें-चालणें, उभेपायीं येणें-जाणें, धडकणें, धडक-धडकून जाणें-चालणें.

To POST, *v. a. station, fix.* ठेवणें, बसवणें, स्थापणें, स्थापना *f.*-&c. करणें *g. of o.*

2 *fix on a post.* खांबावर-&c. घालणें-चिकटवणें.

3 *expose, hold up to public scorn.* धिंड *f.*-धिंडवडा*m.*-वरात *f.*-&c. काढणें *g. of o.* घरास हाड*n.* बांधणें-रोवणें.

4 (in accounts). खतावणी *f.* करणें *g. of o.*

5 (a letter, &c.) टप्पालांत-&c. घालणें-टाकणें.

POST, *adv. with speed, without stopping, &c.* डांकोडांक, टांकोटांक, मजलदरमजल, कूच दरकूच, रातोरात, उभेपायीं, उभ्यापायानें.

POST-BOY, *n.* डांक्या, डांकवाला.

POST-HASTE, *adv.* See POST.

POST-HORSE, *n.* डांकेचा घोडा *m.*

POST-MAN, *n.* डांकवाला, टप्पालचा शिपाई.

Bag of p. तोबरा *m.* [री-&c.

POST-MASTER, *n.* डांकेचा-टप्पालचा कारखानदार-कारभारी-अधिका-

POST-OFFICE, *n.* डांकेचें-टप्पालचें घर *n.* टप्पाल *n.*

POST-PAID, *a.* हाशील दिल्हेला.

POSTAGE, *n.* डांकेंतल्या कागदाचें हाशील *n.*

To POST-DATE, *v. a. date after the real time.* आगाऊ तारीख*f.*-पुढली तारीख *f.*-पुढली मिति *f.*-&c. घालणें-लिहणें.

POST-DILUVIAN, *a. subsequent to the deluge.* प्रलयानंतरचा, प्रलयोत्तरकालीन.

POSTERIOR, *a. later in time.* पाठीमागचा, ऐलीकडचा, नंतरचा, पश्चात्कालीन, पश्चात्कालिक, पाश्चात्य, अपर, अवर, अपरकालिक, अवरकालिक. [अपरकालिकता *f.*

POSTERIORITY, *n.* v. A. पश्चात्कालिकता *f.* अपरता *f.* अवरता *f.*

POSTERIORS, *n. back-side.* गांड *f.* बृहती *f.* गुदप्रदेश *m.* नितंब *m.* कुले *m. pl.* बोचा *m.*

A bump with the knee upon the p. गांडगुडघा *m.* गांडगुडघी *f.* गांडगुंडा *m. v.* दे, मार, बस.

A woman with large & handsome p. नितंबिनी.

Breeches just covering the p. गांडचोळणा *m.*

POSTERITY, *n. descendants, offspring, &c. race that proceeds from a progenitor.* संतति *pop.* संतत *f.* संतान *n.*

2—*opposed to* ancestors; *succeeding generations.* पुढली परंपरा *f.* पुढले लोक *m. pl.* पुढल्या परंपरेचे लोक *m. pl.* पुत्रपौत्रादिवंशपरंपरा *f.* पुत्रपौत्रादिसंतति *f.* पुत्रपौत्राद्यन्वय *m.*

POSTERN, *n. back, small, or private door.* मागलें दार *n.* खिडकी *f.* चोरखिडकी *f.* दिंडी *f.*

POSTHUMOUS, *a. born after the death of its parent.* बाप मेल्यावर झालेला, जनकगत्युत्तरक, पितृमृत्युत्तरक, पितृमरणोत्तरज, बापमारा, आईमारा.

2 *published after the death of its author.* कर्त्ता मेल्यावर प्रसिद्ध झालेला, कर्तृगत्युत्तरक, कर्तृमृत्युत्तरक.

POSTMERIDIAN, *a. belonging, &c. to the afternoon.* दोन प्रहरानंतरचा, आपराह्णिक, अपराह्णकालिक, पराह्णकालिक.

POSTMORTEM, *a. made after death.* मरणानंतरचा, मरणोत्तरचा, मरणोत्तर.

POSTPERFORMANCE, *n.* अनुकर्ष *m.* अनुवृत्ति *f.*

To POSTPONE, *v. a. put off,* v. To DEFER. दिवसगती वर टाकणें-लोटणें, टाळा *m.* देणें, महाल मजकुरावर *or* खालींघालणें, लांबणीवर घालणें, पाठीवर टाकणें. [णीवर पडणें.

To be postponed. महालमजकुरावर *or* खालीं पडणें, लांब-

Postponed, *p.* v. V. दिवसगतीवर टाकलेला, पाठीवर टाकलेला, &c.

Postponement, *n.* v. V.—*act.* मुद्दतीवर टाकणें *n.* पाठीवर टाकणें *n.* &c.

Postscript, *n. paragraph added to a concluded letter, &c.* ताजाकलम *n. m.* पश्चात्लेख *m.*

Postulate, **Postulatum**, *n. position assumed without proof.* सिद्धवत्गृहीतपद *n.*-पक्ष *m.*-गोष्ट *f.* स्वीकृतपक्ष *m.* इष्टकल्पना *f.*

Posture, *n.* (of body). ठाण *n.* ठाणें *n.* आंगठाण *n.* ठाणमाण *n.* आसन *n.* बैठक *f.* अंगस्थिति *f.* अंगसंस्थिति *f.* अंगविन्यास *m.* शरीरस्थिति *f.* शरीरविन्यास *m.* शरीरसंस्था *f.* मुद्रा *f.* Hindu ascetics and devotees adopt a variety of *postures.* Some of them are collected here. अगोचरीमुद्रा, कुक्कुटासन, कूर्मासन, खेचरीमुद्रा, गोमुखासन, गोरक्षासन, चांचरीमुद्रा, देहुडा *or* देहुडाचरण, पद्मासन, प्रेतासन, भद्रासन, भूचरीमुद्रा, मयूरासन, वासन. Some other *postures* are, अढी, अलखटपालखट *or* अलखंडपालखंड, खुरडिंची, खुरमांडी, खोंगी *f. v.* घालून बस, गेठा *m. v.* मारून बस, घोण *f. v.* घालून बस, जेठा *m. v.* मारून बस, दंडासन *n.* मुडमुशी *f. v.* मार, मुरकुंडी *f. v.* मार, बळ, मुरमुशी *f. v.* मार, वीरासन *n.*
2 *position, state*, v. **Condition.** स्थिति *pop.* स्थीत *f.* अवस्था *f.* दशा *f.*

Posturemaster, *n.* अंगविक्षेपशिक्षक, अंगविक्षेपदेशिक, अंगविन्यास शिक्षक.

Posy, *n. motto on a ring, &c.* मुद्रेवरील लेख *m.* मुद्रालेख *m.* मुद्रास्थवाक्य *n.*
2 See **Nosegay.**

Pot, *n. vessel for domestic use,*—gener. भांडें *n.* भांड *n.* बासन *n.* पात्र *n.* हंडा *or* हांडा *m. dim.* हंडी *or* हांडी *f.*—contemptuously, हंडोल *or* हांडोल *n.*—indef. or compreh. हंडीमडकी *f.* हंडेंमडकें *n.* हंडेंभांडें *n.*
2—culinary. हंडा *or* हांडा *m.* हंडी *or* हांडी *f.* स्थाली *pop.* थाली *f.* देग *or* डेग *f.* डेगचा *m.* तपेलें *n. dim.* तपेली *f.* पातळी *f.* पातेलें *n. dim.* पातेली *f.* बहुगुणें *n.* कटाह *m.* The above words express sorts. रंधनपात्र *n.*
3—water pot. घागर *f.* घडा *m.* घट *m.* कळशी *f.* कलश *m.* कुंभ *m.* The *pots* used by the Hindus whether *earthen* or *metal* have numerous names; some of the common *metal* pots are, अमृती, अपकरा, उभातांब्या, उरोळी, ओळक, कचोळें, कढई, कटाह, कटोरा, कटोरी, कथली *or* लें, कलश, कळशी, कासंडी, कुळणी, केळी, गंगाळ, गडवा *or* गडू, गिंडी, गुंड *dim.* गुंडी, चंबू, टोप, डेग, डेगचा, तपेलें, तपेली, तबली, तवी, तसराळें, तांब्या, तुंग, तांबली, तांबलें, थाळा *m. dim.* थाळी, द्रोणी, पंचपात्र, परात, बहुगुणें *or* बगुणें, बिनगा, बुटली, लोटा, शिंपला, सुरई. Some of the *earthen* are, कटोरा, कटोरी, कऱ्हा, कलश, कळसा, कळशी, कुंडी, केळा *dim.* केळी, गाडगा, गाडगें, गाडला, गाडलें, गोळ्या, घागर, चरवट, चिटकी, टिंबी, ठिल्या, डेरा *dim.* डेरका *m.* डेरकी *f.* डेरकें *n.* तबई, तबली, तवी, दुड्या, नांद, बुटकुलें *or* बुडकुलें, मडकी, मुंच, रांझण *or* राझण, *dim.* रांजणी, सुगड.
Clumsy, misshapen p. तांदळा *m.*
Cover (*i. e.* another pot) of a cooking p. वर झांकण *n.*
Old and worn metal p. कावल *or* कावर *n.* कावलें भांडें *n.* बखल *n.* [*pl.* थाली-ठावकें.
Pots and pans,—compreh. हंडीं मडकीं *n. pl.* हंडीभांडीं *n.*
To go to p. *be dished, &c.* चुलीत जाणें, रसातळास जाणें, खटीं खापरीं लागणें-जाणें-मिळणें.

Pot-bellied, *a.* दोंदाळ, दोंदी, दोंदील, ढेऱ्या, ढेरपोट्या, दोंद्या, ढोल्या, डबरा *or* डुबरा, डेंबरा, डबरपोट्या, तुंदिल, बृहन्नाभि, बृहत्कुक्षि.
P. person or animal. ढोलार *n.* ढेर *f.* भेर *f.*

Pot-belly, *n.* दोंद *n.* ढेर *f.* ढोल *n.* ढोलार *n.* डेरा *m.* डिऱ्या *m.* पखाल *f.* भेर *f.* दुड्या *m.* डेरका *m.* डेरकी *f.* डेरकें *n.* (*or* पोटाचा डेरका *m.* &c.).

Pot-herb, *n.* शाक *m. f.*
Pot-herbs and esculent vegetables—compreh. or gener. शाकभाजी *f.* शाकपाला *m.* भाजीपाला *m.*

Pot-hook, *n.* Pot hooks & hangers, *scrawled letters.* कुत्र्या मांजराचे पाय *m. pl.*

Pot-sherd, *n.* खापरखुंटी *f.* खापर *n.*

Pot-valiant, *a.* अमलाचा-कैफाचा-निशेचा-&c. शूर.

Pot-wash, *n.* रांधवणी *n.*

Potable, *a. drinkable.* प्यायाचा-जोगा-सारखा-&c. पेय, पानार्ह, पानयोग्य.

Potableness, *n.* v. A. प्यायाजोगेपणा *m.* &c. पानार्हता *f.* पानयोग्यता *f.*

Potash, *n. impure alkali.* क्षार *pop.* खार *m.*
Nitrate of p. यवक्षार *pop.* यवखार *m.*

Potation, *n. carousal.* पानोत्सव *m.* पानसमारंभ *m.*
2 See **Draught, Drink.**

Potatoe, *n.* बटाटा *m.* आलू *m.*
Sweet p.—the plant. रताळी *f.*—the root. रताळूं *n.* रताळें *n.*

Potency, *n.* v. A. 1. पराक्रम *m.* प्रताप *m.* तेज *n.* तेजगी *f.* गुणकारिता *f.* विरी *f.* वीर *f.* वीर्य *n.* बळावळ *f.* जहाली *f.*
2 पराक्रम *m.* बल *or* बळ *n.* बलाढ्यता *f.* बलशालिता *f.*

Potent, *a. powerful, efficacious,*—medicines, drink, &c. v. **Strong.** पराक्रमी, प्रतापी, अमोघ, तेजस्वी, सतेज, गुणकारक, गुणकारी, बळकट, जाज्वल्य, जालीम, झाल, जलाल, सकस, धनत्तर.
2 *having great dominion.* पराक्रमी, बलवान्, बलाढ्य, बलशाली.

Potentate, *n.* v. **King.** नृपति, भूपाल, महीपाल, अधिपति.

Potential, *a. existing in possibility*, v. **Possible.** संभाव्य, संभवी, संभावनीय, भाविसंभाव्य, भविष्यसंभाव्य.
2—in grammar. शक्य, विधिलिङ्.

Potentiality, *n.* v. A. 1. संभाव्यता *f.* संभावनीयता *f.*

Potently. See **Powerfully.**

Pother, *n.* v. **Bustle.** गडबड *f.* गडबडी *f.* हडबड *f.* हूल *f.*

Poton, *n. medicinal draught.* पिण्याचें-प्यायाचें औषध *n.* पेयौषध *n.*

Pottage, *n.* v. **Broth.** मासाची कढी *f.*

Potter, *n.* कुंभार, कुंभकार, कुलाल *or* ळ, घटीकार.
Art or business of a p. कुंभारकी *f.*
Frame used by potters for carrying earth. मंची *f.*
Pile of pots arranged by a p. for burning. अवा *m.*
Potter's patting instrument. थापटणें *n.*
Potter's clay-pit. मातखण *or* मातखाण *f.*

Pottery, *n.*—the place. कुंभारशाळा *f.* कुंभारसाळ *f.* कुंभाराचाअखर *m.*
2 *earthen-ware.* कुंभारकाम *n.* मातीचीं भांडीं *n. pl.*

Pottle, *n.* एक कैली माप आहे.

Pouch, *n. bag, pocket.* थैली *f.* पिशवी *f.* खिसा *m.*
2 (of a monkey). गालदोडी *f.* गालफड *n.* गालफट *n.*
3 *cartridge box.* तोसदान *n.*
4 (of a bird.). पिशवी *f.*

To **Pouch.** See *To* **Pocket.**

POULT, *n. thump, &c.* v. BLOW. ढोसा *m.* ठोसा *m.* ढुस्सा *m.*

POULTERER, *n. seller of fowls.* कोंबडींविक्या, कोंबडीवाला.

POULTICE, *n. soft composition of meal, &c. to be applied medicinally.* पिकवण *n.* पिठाची पोटडी *f.*-पुरचुंडी *f.*-पोचंडी *f.* पाकजनकपिष्टप्रलेप *m.* The English word is common under the form of पोटीस *n.*

P. of simples or herbs for a sprain. उपणा *m.* पेंड *m.*

To POULTICE, *v. a.* v. N. पिकवण *n.*-पोटीस *n.*-&c. बांधणें.

POULTRY, *n. domestic fowls.* कोंबडींबिंचडीं *n. pl.* कोंबड्याबिंचड्या *f. pl.* भक्षणोपयोगी ग्राम्यपक्षी *m. pl.*

POUNCE, *n. talon.* पंजा *m.*

2—for drying writing. रेती *f.* The word means sand, which is used in India for this purpose.

To POUNCE, *v. n. spring upon.* झेंपावणें, झडपणें, झेंप *f.*-झांप *f.*-&c. मारणें, झडप *f.*-झडपडा *m.*-झड *f.*-&c. घालणें, लवसाद *f.* पडणें *g. of o.*

POUNCE-BOX, *n.* रेतदानी *f.*

POUND, *n.* v. MEASURE. एक वजनी माप आहे.

2 *inclosure for confining cattle.* चुकारू गुरांची कोंडी *f.* सरकारीकोंडवाड *m.f.*-कोंडवाडा *m.*

To POUND, *v. a.* v. N. 2. कोंडींत-कोंडवाड्यांत-&c. घालणें.

2 *beat so as to bruise,* v. To BRUISE. कुटणें, कांडणें, बडवणें, ठेंचणें.

3 (rice, &c. to husk it). कांडणें, सडणें, कुटणें, कांडण *n.*-सडण *n.*-सड *f.*-सडणी *f.*-&c. करणें *g. of o.*

To p. hardly & coarsely. धुमसणें.

Quantity to be pounded at one time. कांडण *n.* सडण *n.*

Quantity thrown at once into the mortar. घाणा *m.* घाणी *f.*

POUNDAGE, *n.* v. V. 3. *cost of pounding.* कांडणावळ *f.* सडणावळ *f.* सडाई *f.* कांडण *n.* कांडप *n.* कुटाई *f.*

2 *fee, due, &c.* दस्तुरी *f.*

POUNDED, *p.* v. A. 1. कोंडींत घातलेला, कोंडवाड्यांत घातलेला.

2 कुटलेला, कांडलेला, बडवलेला, चूर्णित, चूर्णीकृत, क्षुण्ण.

Coarsely p. or bruised,—peppers, &c. अर्धबोबडा.

3 कांडलेला, सडलेला, &c. सडीक.

Once pounded,—rice, &c. एकसडी, एकसडा.—Twice p. दुसडी, दुसडा, दुबारा, दुसड.—Thrice p. तिसडी, तिसडा.

POUNDER, *n.* POUNDING, *p. a.* v. V. 2. कुटणारा, बडवणारा, कांडणारा, &c. कुट्टनकर्त्ता, कंडनकर्त्ता.

3 कांडणारा, सडणारा, &c. कांडपी, गोल्या, गोलेवाला.

I. *thing to pound with.* बडवणें *n.*—for rice, lime, &c. मुसळ *or* मुसल *n.*—for rice, गोल्या *m.*

II.—apparatus of a beam with a head for pounding. ढंग *or* दंग *m.* ढेकी *f.* लंगर *m.*

POUNDING, *n.* v. A. 1.—*act.* कोंडींत घालणें *n.* कोंडणें *n.*

2—*act.* कुटणें *n.* कांडणें *n.* बडवणें *n.* &c. कुट्टन *n.* कंडन *n.*

3—*act.* कांडणें *n.* सडणें *n.* &c. कांडणी *f.* कांडण *n.* सडण *n.* सड *f.* सडणी *f.* कांडप *n.* कंडन *n.*

P. and grinding,—compreh. *husking and bruising.* कांडाभरडा *m.* कांडादळा *m.* दळाकांडा *m.* कांडकूट *f.* कांडण कुटण *n.*

The first p. एकसड *f.*—The second p. दुसड *f.* दुबारें *n.* —The third p. तिसड *f.* [*f.* पाडणें *g. of o.*

To POUR, *v. a. throw in a stream.* ओतणें, घालणें, सोडणें, धार

2 forth ; out ; *send forth, emit, &c. copiously.* भडभडवणें, पाऊस *m.* पाडणें *g. of o.* वृष्टि *f.*-वर्षाव *m.*-&c. करणें *g. of o.* लासोली *f.* करणें-वाहवणें *g. of o.*

3 in; भरणें, ओतणें, घालणें.

4 off; रिचवणें.

5 out; रिचवणें, ओलंडणें.

To POUR, *v. n. stream, flow,*—copiously, &c. धार *f.* लागणें *g. of s.* भडभडणें, धारेनें पडणें, भळभळ-भूळभूळ-भडभड *adv.* वाहणें-सुटणें, भडभडाट *m.* चालणें *g. of s.*

2—rain. डवडवणें, डवडव *adv.* येणें-पडणें, मुसळधार-धुवाधार-धोधाट-&c. पडणें-लागणें, ढासळणें.

3 *rush in a crowd, &c.* v. To RUSH. लोटणें, धाड *f.* पडणें, डोरणें *or* डवरणें, मुसंडा *or* मुसांडा *m.*-मुसंडी *or* मुसांडी *f.*-&c. चालणें-निघणें *g. of s.* [*g. of s.*

4 forth; *issue copiously.* पेंव *n.*-बीळ *n.*-ढुंडार *n.*-&c. फुटणें

To POUT, *v. n. thrust out the lips in sullenness; look sulky.* फुरगुटणें *or* फुरंगुटणें, फुरकटणें, ओंठ *m. pl.*-गाल *m. pl.* फुगवणें, फुगून बसणें, मुरमुसणें, फुरकट *or* फुरगूट *n.* येणें-चढणें *in. con.*

2 *shoot out,*—the lips, &c. बाहेर *adv.* येणें-असणें.

POUTER, *n.* POUTING, *p. a.* v. V. 1. फुरकटणारा, &c. फुरकटलेला, फुरकट्या.

2 बाहेर आलेला, &c.

POUTING, *n.* v. V. 1. फुरकटणें *n.* &c. फुरकट *or* फुरगूट *n.v.* चढ, ये.

POVERTY, *n. indigence, need, necessity, straitness of circumstances, &c.* दरिद्रपणा *m.* गरीबी *f.* कंगाली *f.* अनुपपत्ति *pop.* अनुपत *f.* दारिद्र्य *n.* दरिद्रदशा *f.* दरिद्रावस्था *f.* दरिद्र *n.* निर्धनता *f.* निर्द्रव्यता *f.* धनाभाव *m.* द्रव्याभाव *m.* अर्थाभाव *m.* धनहीनता *f.* &c. अल्पधनता *f.* &c. गरिबदारी *or* गिरिबदारी *f.* दैन्य *n.* ददात *or* दधात *f.* ददाती *f.* चडचड *f.* चणचण *f.* तारंबळ *f.* तंगचाई *f.* तापत्रय *n.* ओढ *f.* ओढगस्ती *f.* अडचण *f.* अडचणूक *f.* वसवस *f.* हलाकी *f.* दुबळें *n.* दुर्गति *f.* Some figures and phrases expressing *extreme poverty* are, चुलीमध्यें मांजरें व्यालीं आहेत, चुलीस अक्षत लागली आहे, घरीं शिवरात्र आहे, घरामध्यें नकार घंटा वाजती. [विगतश्रीक.

Reduced to p. नष्टधन, नष्टार्थ, गतधन, विगतधन, नष्टैश्वर्य,

To be in great p. भुईशीं आंग *n.* लागणें *g. of s.* जमिनीस पाठ *f.* लागणें *g. of s.* भुईवर पडणें-पडलेला असणें, टिकटिक *adv.* करून राहणें.

P. of language. शब्दन्यूनता *f.* [दारिद्र्यग्रस्त.

POVERTY-STRICKEN, *a.* v. POOR. गिरिबदार, ओढगस्त, ओढिस्त,

POWDER, *n. pulverized substance.* भुगा *or* भुका *m.* भुगी *or* भुकी *f.* भुकणी *f.* बुकणी *f.* बुकी *f.* बुकटी *f.* भुकटी *f.* भुकटा *m.* पीठ *n.* पूड *f.* पूट *or* पूठ *n.* चूर्ण *n.* पिष्ट *n.*—esp. of fragrant substances and used in offerings. बुका *m.* अबीर *m.*—esp. of wood sawed, worm-eaten, &c. *dust.* भुसकट *n.* भुसकूट *n.* भुसकटा *m.* भुसा *m.* भूस *n.* भुसकुरा *m.* भुंशी *f.*

To reduce to p. चुरणें.

2 *gun-powder.* दारू *f.*

3—medicinal preparation. मात्रा *f.* [चुरणें.

To POWDER, *v. a. pulverize.* भुगा *m.*-&c. करणें-पाडणें *g. of o.*

2 *sprinkle with powder.* भुग्याचें पिठाचें-धुळीचें-&c. शिंपणें *n.* -शिंपणी *f.* करणें.

3 (meat). *corn.* मीठ *n.* घालणें, मिठांत-मिठानें मळणें, खारवणें.

POWDER-FLASK, POWDER-HORN, *n.* शिंगडा *m.*

POWDER-MAGAZINE, *n.* दारूखाना *m.*

POWDER-WORK, *n.* दारूखाना *m.* [&c.

POWDERINESS, *n.* v. A. भगरा *m.* भुसभुशितपणा *m.* पिठुळपणा *m.*

POWDERY, *a. friable, crumbly.* भुसभुशीत, पिठूळ, पिठाळ, पिठा, भुगाळ.

POWER, *n. force, vigor,* v. STRENGTH. जोर *m.* शक्ति *f.* बल *pop.* बळ *n.* सामर्थ्य *n.* कुवत *f.* तकवा *m.* तवका *m.* ताकत *f.* ऐपत *f.* पराक्रम *m.* धमक *f.*

2 *ability*,—natural or moral. शक्ति *f.* बल *or* बळ *n.* सामर्थ्य *n.* खुदरत *f.* मखदूर *m. f.* हात *m.* ताकत *f.* तवांका *m.* मजाल *f.* अवांका *m.* पराक्रम *m.* अवकात *or* द *f. with neg. con.* कर्तृत्व *n.*

According to one's p. To the best of one's p. यथाशक्ति *pop.* यथानशक्ति *or* क्त्या, यथानुशक्ति *or* क्त्या, यथासामर्थ्य, बलपरत्वें *or* परत्वेंकरून, शक्तिपरत्वें *or* परत्वेंकरून, सामर्थ्यपरत्वें *or* परत्वेंकरून, शक्तितः.

In the p. or compass of आहारीं.

To have p. हात *m.* चालणें *g. of s.*

To come or fall within the p. of. अवांक्यांत-अवसानांत-अटोक्यांत-अटोपांत-अटकळींत-&c. येणें *g. of s.* [हात *m.*

3 *compass, grasp, &c.* v. REACH, CLUTCHES. आवांका *m.*

P.—of a word. शक्ति *f.* [डणें.

To fall into the p. of. गावणें, तावडीस-तावडींत-&c. सांप-

4 *command, dominion, authority.* हुकूम *m.* जोरा *m.* सत्ता *f.* अधिकार *m.* ऐश्वर्य *n.*

Day or season of p. चालताकाळ *m.* चलती *f.* जारी *f.*

Plenitude of one's p. ऐन ऐश्वर्य *n.* [प्रभाव *m.*

5 *prevalence, weight, &c.* v. INFLUENCE. चाल *f.* चलती *f.*

6 *potency, strength, good quality, &c.* v. VIRTUE. बल *or* बळ *n.* तेज *n.* तेजगी *f.* गुण *m.* गुणांश *m.* सत्व *n.* सत्वांश *m.* वीर्य *n. pop.* विरी *f.* वीर *f.*

7 (of an engine, &c.) *motive force.* बल *pop.* बळ*n.*

8 (of the mind) *faculty.* गुण*m.* शक्ति *f.*

9 *legal authority, warrant.* सत्ता *f.* अधिकार*m.* मुखत्यारी *f.* अखत्यारी *f.*

Full powers. कुलमुखत्यारी *f.* कुलअखत्यारी *f.*

10 *force, armament.* सैन्य*n.* बल *or* बळ*n.* सैन्यभार*m.* दलभार *m.* सेनाभार*m.*

11 v. POTENTATE. अधिकारी, अधिपति. [रगड *f.*

12 *abundance,* v. EXUBERANCE. महापूर *f.* लूट *f.* बळकटी *f.*

P. of attorney. मुखत्यारपत्र*n.*

POWERFUL, *a. possessing great strength,* v. STRONG. बळकट, जोराचा, बळाचा, बलवान्, सबल, प्रबल, धनत्तर.

2 *forcible to persuade, convince, &c.* बळकट, जिवट, दृढ, सुदृढ, सबल, प्रबल, बलिष्ठ, सतेज, निश्चायक.

3 *mighty, puissant, potent.* पराक्रमाचा, पराक्रमी, प्रतापी, प्रतापवान्, बळवान्, बलिष्ठ, बलाढ्य, बलशाली, प्रतापशाली.

4 *efficacious, potent, &c.* v. STRONG. बळकट, पराक्रमी, अमोघ, तेजस्वी, सतेज, गुणकारी, गुणकारक, जालीम, जाज्वल्य.

POWERLESS, *a.* v. WEAK. निर्बल *pop.* निर्बळ, अशक, निशक्त, असमर्थ, शक्तिशून्य, शक्तिहीन, &c. हीनशक्ति, हीनबल, हीनसामर्थ्य, निष्पराक्रम, अविक्रम.

POWERLESSNESS, *n.* v. A. अशक्ति *f.* असामर्थ्य *n.* अपराक्रम *m.* आबल्य*n.* शक्तिशून्यता *f.* बलाभाव*m.* &c.

POX, *n.*—small pox. देवी *f. pl.* माता *f. pl.* बाया *f. pl.* फोड्या *f. pl.* शीतला *f. pl.* फुगें*n.* आंगचें*n.* मसूरिका *f.* मसूरी *f.*

Some varieties or modes of *small pox* are, घागऱ्यादेवी, घुड्यादेवी, कांथिबऱ्यादेवी, कथल्यादेवी, नांदळ्यादेवी.

Inoculated small p. काढलेल्या *or* काढीव देवी, शिकूधाच्या देवी, कुंभाराच्या देवी *or* माता.

Small p. personified. शीतला देवी *f.* [*pl.* काढणें.

To inoculate for the small p. v. To INOCULATE. देवी *f.*

To be pitted with the small pox. उकटणें.

2—chicken-pox. कांजण्या *f. pl.* कांण्या *f. pl.*

3—cow-pox. गोस्तनशीतला *f. pl.* Note. The Maráṭhás do not distinguish between the cow-pox and small pox, but use for the former the words expressing the latter.

4—venereal. दुःख*n. v.* भर, लाग, गर्मी *f.* उपदंश*m.* वीसनर्साची बाधा *f.*

Afflicted with the p. दुःखभऱ्या, भरलेला, दुखाळू, उपदंशी.

To POZE, &c. See To POSE, &c.

PRACTICABILITY, PRACTICABLENESS, *n.* v. A. 1. करायाजोगेपणा *m.* &c. सवघडपणा *m.* शक्यता *f.* साध्यता *f.* सुसाध्यता *f.* सुगमता *f.* &c. [हैता *f.* &c.

2 जायाजोगेपणा *m.* चढायाजोगेपणा *m.* &c. गम्यता *f.* गमना-

PRACTICABLE, *a. that may be done, performed, &c.* करायाजोगा-जोगता-सारखा-&c. सवघड, सोपा, शक्य, साध्य, करणीय, करणशक्य, सुखसाध्य, सुकर, सुसाध्य, सुगम, गमनीय.

2 (a breach). जायाजोगा-सारखा, चढाया जोगा-सारखा-&c. चालता, गम्य, गमनीय, गमनार्ह.

PRACTICAL, *a. relating, &c. to action.* क्रियेचा, क्रियेविषयींचा, कृतीचा, कर्मांचा, कर्ममार्गाचा, व्यापाराविषयींचा, व्यवहाराविषयींचा.

P. joke. करून दाखविलेली थट्टा *f.*

2 *that may be applied to use.* व्यवहाराच्या उपयोगाचा, व्यवहाराच्या कामाचा, वहिवाटीच्या कामाचा-उपयोगाचा, व्यवहारोपयोगी, व्यवहारोचित, व्यवहार्य.

3 *derived from practice or experience.* अभ्यासाचा, सरावाचा, कसरतीचा, रफूताचा, अनुभवाचा, कृतीचा, कर्मज्ञानाचा, अभ्याससिद्ध, अभ्यासप्राप्त, क्रियासिद्ध, क्रियाजनित.

PRACTICALLY, *adv.* v. A. 1. क्रियेविषयीं, क्रियेसंबंधीं, कर्मसंबंधीं.

2 *in practice.* व्यवहारांत, व्यवहारप्रकरणांत.

3 *by practice.* अभ्यासानें, अभ्यासें करून, कसरतीनें, रफूतानें, सरावानें, &c. अभ्यासतः.

PRACTICE, *n. reiterated or habitual doing.* अभ्यास *m.* वहिवाट *f.* रफूत *m.* राब *m.* राबता *m.* सराव *m.* पाठ *m.* परिपाठ *m.* प्रघात *m.* कसरत *f.* इस्तमाली *f.* वृत्ति *f.* वृत्त *n.* अभ्यसन *n.* आवर्त्तन *n.*

Attainable by p. अभ्यासगम्य.

Daily or constant p. नित्यपाठ *m.* निष्ठा *f.* [अंगवण *f.*

Skill acquired by p. v. EXPERTNESS. कसरत *f.* खांद *m.*

To be in general p. or use. प्रचार *m.*-प्रघात *m.*-वहिवाट *f.* -संप्रदाय *m.*-रीति *pop.* रीत *f.*-&c. असणें *g. of s.*

2 *actual doing* ;—*as opposed to* theory. करणें *n.* आचरणें*n.* &c. क्रिया *f.* कर्म *n.* कृति *f.* व्यापार *m.* आचरण *n.* अनुष्ठान *n.* सेवन *n.*

3 *course of procedure, usage,* v. CUSTOM. चाल *f.* रीति *pop.*

रीत *f.* बहिवाट *f.* प्रघात *m.* व्यवहार *m.*
4 *exercise of a profession.* सेवन *n.* आचरण *n.* अनुष्ठान *n.*
5 *medical treatment of diseases.* चिकित्सा *f.* वैद्यक्रिया *f.* उपचार *m.* रुक्प्रतिक्रिया *f.*
6—military. शस्त्राभ्यास *m.*
Ball-p. गोळीबार *m.*
Blank-p. वायबार*m.* शुष्केष्टि *f.* [वृत्त *n.*
7 practices ; v. CONDUCT. चाल *f.* वर्त्तणूक *f.* चर्या *f.* वृत्ति *f.*
Mal-practices. असद्व्यापार *m.*

To PRACTISE, *v. a. do habitually.* परिपाठ *m.*-परिपाटी *f.*-बहिवाट *f.*-रफूत *m.*-राबता *m.*-अभ्यास *m.*-नित्यनियम *m.*-नित्यनेम *m.*-&c. ठेवणें-मांडणें-घालणें *g. of o.* नित्य-रोज-हरहमेश-&c. करणें-करीत असणें, अभ्यास *m.* करणें-राखणें *g. of o.* अभ्यासणें.
2 (a profession or art). करणें,करीत असणें, आचरणें, चालवणें, वापरणें, बहिवाटणें, सेवणें, सेवन *n.*-&c. करणें.
3 *do, perform, &c.* करणें, आचरणें, अनुष्ठणें.
4 *exercise, use in order to dexterity.* वापरणें, बहिवाटणें, घोळणें, बळवणें, राबवणें.

To PRACTISE, *v. n. perform to keep up the knowledge or habit of.* अभ्यास *m.*-सराव *m.*-रफूत *m.*-राबता *m.*-सवई *f.*-&c. ठेवणें-राखणें.
2 *exercise a profession.* धंदा *m.*-उद्योग *m.*-कसब *n.*-काम *n.*-व्यवसाय *m.*-&c. करणें-चालवणें-आचरणें.
3 *use artifices, &c.* कसब *n.*-कपट *n.*-कावा *m.*-कावादावा *m.*-कृत्रिम *n.*-गौडबंगाल *n.*-डावपेंच *m. pl.*-पेंचपाच *m. pl.*-&c. चालवणें-खेळवणें.

PRACTISED, *p. and a.* v. V. A. 1. नित्यकेलेला, &c. अभ्यस्त,
2 केलेला, आचरलेला, &c. व्यवहृत, सेवित, अनुयात.
3 केलेला, &c. आचरित, अनुष्ठित.
4 वापरलेला, बहिवाटलेला, &c.
I. *able or skilful from practice, versed, conversant, &c.* v. EXPERIENCED. अभ्यासी, अभ्यस्त, कसरती, कसबी, वापरलेला, घसवटलेला, घोळलेला, बहिवाटलेला, हात बळलेला, घटींव, कृतकर्मा, क्षुण्ण. [णें, रहाटणें.
To be p. *be versed or skilled.* घटणें, कटणें, कसणें, घसवट-

PRACTISER, *n.* PRACTISING, *p. a.* v. V. A. 1. परिपाठ ठेवणारा, बहिवाट ठेवणारा, नित्यकरणारा, अभ्यासी.
2 करणारा, आचरणारा, सेवणारा, &c. प्रवर्त्तमान, सेवी, सेवमान,

PRACTITIONER, *n. one who exercises a profession.* धंदा करणारा, धंदा चालवणारा, उद्योग करणारा, सेवी, सेवमान, वृत्तिक (in comp. as वैद्यवृत्तिक), वृत्तक (in comp.), व्यवसायी.
Medical p. v. PHYSICIAN. वैद्य, चिकित्सक.

PRAGMATIC, PRAGMATICAL, *a.* v. OFFICIOUS. लुडबुड्या, चोंबडा, लांडा कारभारी, अनधिकारचर्चक.

PRAGMATICALLY, *adv.* v. A. लुडबुडपणानें, लुडबूडकरून, लांडा कारभार करून.

PRAGMATICALNESS, *n.* v. A. लुडबुडपणा *m.* &c. लुडबूड *f.* लुबलूब *f.* लांडाकारभार *m.* अनधिकारचर्चा *f.*

PRAIRIE, PRAIRY, *n. plain covered with coarse grass.* तांबेटीचा माळ *m.* कोळंबाचा माळ *m.*

PRAISABLE. See PRAISEWORTHY.

PRAISE, PRAISING, *n.* v. V.—*act.* स्तवणें *n.* &c. स्तुति *f.* वाखाण *f.* वाखाणणी *f.* वाखाणणूक *f.* वर्णणूक *f.* नावाजणी *f.* नावाजणूक *f.* तारीफ *f.* नवाजस *or* नवाजीस *f.* शाबासकी *f.* स्तवन *n.* कीर्त्तन *n.* वर्णन *n.* वर्णना *f.* स्तव *m.* प्रशंसा *f.* श्लाघा *f.* स्तुतिवाद *m.* अर्थवाद *m.* गुणानुवाद *m.* गुणस्तुति *f.* संस्तव *m.* स्तोत्र *n.* स्तोतृत्य *n.*
I. *ground, &c. of praise.* स्तुतीस कारण *n.* स्तुतिहेतु *m.*

To PRAISE, *v. a. applaud, extol, commend, laud, &c.* स्तवणें, गाणें, वाखाणणें, प्रशंसणें, वर्णणें, कीर्त्तणें, श्लाघणें, नवाजणें, शाबासकी *f.* देणें, स्तुति *f.*-स्तव *m.*-प्रशंसा *f.*-&c. करणें *g. of o.* कीर्त्तन *n.*-वर्णन *n.*-&c. करणें *g. of o.* गुण *m. pl.* सांगणें-वर्णणें *g. of o.* गुणोत्कीर्त्तन *n.*-गुणानुवाद *m.* करणें *g. of o.*
To p. up, *cry up.* बडिवार *m.*-बढाई *f.*-&c. सांगणें *g. of o.*

PRAISED, *p.* v. V. स्तवलेला, वाखाणलेला, &c. कीर्त्तित, वर्णित, प्रशंसित, प्रशस्त, स्तुत, प्रस्तुत, संस्तुत.

PRAISER, *n.* PRAISING, *p. a.* v. V. स्तवणारा, वाखाणणारा, &c. प्रशंसक, स्तावक, स्तोता, स्तव-स्तवन-स्तुति-&c. कर्त्ता-कारक-&c.

PRAISEWORTHILY, *adv.* v. A. स्तुति मिळाया जोगा *decl.* शाबासकीमिळायाजोगा *decl.* [योग्यता *f.* &c.

PRAISEWORTHINESS, *n.* v. A. प्रशंसनीयता *f.* श्लाघ्यता *f.* स्तुति-

PRAISEWORTHY, *a. laudable, commendable, &c.* स्तुतीजोगा, शाबासकी मिळाया-करायाजोगा, शाबासकीचा, प्रशंसनीय, प्रशंस्य, स्तुत्य, स्तवनीय, स्तोतव्य, स्तुतियोग्य, श्लाघ्य, श्लाघनीय, वर्णनीय, तारीफदार.
A p. person. स्तुतिपात्र, प्रशंसापात्र, श्लाघापात्र, स्तुतिभाजन, प्रशंसाभाजन. [ड्या *f. pl.* मारणें.

To PRANCE, *v. n. bound, &c.*—a horse. नाचणें, फांदणें, उ-
2 *ride with bounding movements.* घोडा नाचवीत चालणें.

PRANCER, *n.* PRANCING, *p. a.* v. V. 1. नाचणारा, फांदणारा, &c. नाचरा.

PRANCING, *n.* v. V. 1.—*act.* नाचणें *n.* फांदणें *n.* &c.
The p. and pawing of a stallion or mettlesome horse. कलुली *or* कुलुली *f.* कुलकुली *f.*

To PRANK, *v. a. bedeck, bedizen.* v. To ADONIZE. टाकमटिका *m.*-टाकमटिकला *m.*-चट्टीपट्टी *f.*-&c. करणें.

PRANK, PRANKS, *n. trick, &c.* चाळे *m.pl.* चेष्टा *f.* कुचेष्टा *f.* कुचोदी *f.* ढंग *m. pl.* कुढंग *m. pl.* आपढंग *m. pl.* छंद *m. pl.* छंदफंद *m. pl.* छंदविछंद *m. pl.* धंगडे *m. pl.* उत्पात *m. pl.* ख्याल *m. pl.* चार *m. pl.* चोज *n.* ढगड्या *f. pl.* रगड्या *f. pl.* रंगड्या ढंगड्या *f. pl.* टिणगिण्या *f. pl. v.* मार, रंगढंग *m. pl.* माकडचेष्टा *f.* मर्कटचेष्टा *f.* टिवल्या बाव्हल्या *f. pl.* उनाडकी *f.* उनाडचाळा *m.* अनर्गळी *f.* अनावळी *f.*
To play p. उड्या *f. pl.* मारणें.

PRANKISH, *a. full of pranks.* चेष्टेखोर, चेष्टेबाज, कुचेष्टखोर, ख्याली, छंदी, छंदिष्ट, छंदखोर, छंदवाईक, खोडकर, उत्पाती, चारगट, उनाड, चाळक, शतछंदी, तंताळ.

To PRATE, *v. n. talk much and idly.* बकणें, बकबकणें, बडबडणें, बटवटणें, बतवतणें, जल्पणें, प्रलापणें, बकबक *f.*-बकवा *m.*- बडबड *f.*-बटवट *f.*-&c. करणें-लावणें-मांडणें, बाता *f. pl.* कुटणें-सबाळणें-छाटणें-मारणें-हाणणें, लाफा *f. pl.* मारणें, काथा *m.*-कथील*n.*-&c. कुटणें, फाल्या *f. pl.* करणें-मारणें-पाडणें, गाथा *f.* कुटणें, बचवच *adv.* करणें, काथाकूट *f.*-गोष्टिश्राद्ध *n.*-&c. करणें, फकांड्या *f. pl.* मारणें, लबलब *adv.* बोलणें.—intens. *run on, talk away, &c.* भडभडणें, कडकडणें, कचकावून-&c. बोलणें, भिरभिर *adv.*-भडभड *or* डां *adv.* बोलणें, बालबाल *adv.* बोलणें, लंबलंब *f.* बोलणें *g.*

of s. चराचर-बटबट-&c. बोलणें, लबनलब *adv.* बोलणें, मळभभर बोलणें, तोंडावर नक्षत्र *n.* पडणें *g. of s.* तोंड *n.* सुटणें *g. of s.*

PRATE, PRATING, *n.* v. V.—*act.* बकणें *n.* बडबडणें *n.* बकणी *f.* काथाकूट *f.* बटबट *f.* बडबड *f.* बटका *m.* बतबत *f.* जल्पना *f.* जल्प *m.* चाबटाई *f.*

I. *idle talk, chat.* बकबक *f.* बकवा *m.* बका *f. pl.* बकवाद *m.* बडबड *f.* खबरा *f. pl.* भाकडकथा *f.* गप *or* गप्प *f.* गाथा *f.* कोरड्या गाथा *f. pl.* काथाकूट *f.* कथीलकूट *f.* अकडंतिकडं *n.* चबरचबर *n.* अगडतगड *n.* अगडबगड *n.* अरबचरब *n.* अरबटचरबट *n.* बरळ *f.* बडबडाध्याय *m.* गोष्टिश्राद्ध *n.* लाफा *f. pl.* गवगव *f.* गवगवा *m.* गलगल *f.* फकांड्या *f. pl.* जल्प *m.* जल्पना *f.* वाग्जल्प *m.* वाग्जल्पना *f.* विप्रलाप *m.* भाजीपाला *m.* लुबलूब *f.*

PRATER, *n.* PRATING, *p. a.* v. V. बडबडणारा, बकबकणारा, बकबक करणारा, बाताकुटणारा, चराचर बोलणारा, &c. बडबड्या, बकबक्या, बचवच्या, गप्पी *or* गप्प्या, गप्पीदास, गप्पाष्टक्या, चावट, चावटनट, फकांडी *or* ड्या, भाट, वाचाट, वाचाल, वायचाळा, बहुचक, जल्पक, तोंडावर नक्षत्र पडलेला. There are some expressive terms and phrases agreeing with this word and answering to *prate-apace, chatter-box, bell-clapper, rattler, jaw-monger, jabberer, &c.* कथीलकुट्या, गप्पाष्टक्या, गप्पी *or* गप्प्या, गप्पीदास, बातकुट्या, बकबक्या, बकऱ्या, बडबड्या, गोष्टीखबाल्या, बाताखबाल्या, गागादीक्षित, बोलघेवडा, बोलगाडा, बटबट्या, गडबड्या, लुबरा, तुरुतुरू-तुरतूर-बालबाल-लवनलब *adv.* बोलणारा.

PRATINGLY, *adv.* v. A. बचबच, बचाबचा, बडबड करून, लबलब.

To PRATTLE, *v. n. chatter,*—children. किलबिलणें, किलकिलणें, किलबील *m. f.*-किलकील *m. f.* (*intens.* किलबिलाट *m.* & किलकिलाट *m.*) करणें, बालभाषण *n.*-बालालाप *m.*-&c. करणें.

PRATTLE, PRATTLING, *n.* v. V. मुलांचें-&c. किलबिलणें *n.*-किलकिलणें *n.* मुलांची किलबील *f.*-किलकील *f.* बोबडें बोलणें *n.* बालभाषण *n.* बालालाप *m.* बालशब्द *m.*

PRATTLER, *n.* PRATTLING, *p. a.* v. V. किलबिलणारा, &c. बोबडें बोलणारा, बालभाषी, बालालापी.

PRAWN, *n.*—the fish. कोळंबें *n.* झिंगा *m.* अभिमत्स्य *m.*

To PRAY, *v. n.*—in worship. प्रार्थना *f.*-नमाज *or* निमाज *f.*-देवप्रार्थना *f.*-देवप्रार्थन *n.*-भगवत्प्रार्थना *f.*-&c. करणें, देवाजवळ-देवाची-&c. प्रार्थना *f.* करणें.

To PRAY, *v. a. entreat, implore, &c.* v. To BEG. प्रार्थणें, प्रार्थना *f.*-विनंती *f.*-&c. करणें *g. of o.*—earnestly, &c. दाढी *f.* धरणें *g. of o.* पदर पसरून प्रार्थणें, नाकीं दुराही *f.* काढणें.

I. pray, pray. रुपाकरून.

PRAYED, *p.* v. V. A. प्रार्थिलेला, &c. प्रार्थित.

PRAYER, *n.* PRAYING, *p. a.* v. V. A. प्रार्थणारा, प्रार्थना करणारा, प्रार्थक.

PRAYER, PRAYING, *n.* v. V. N. *and* WORSHIP. देवाची-ईश्वराची-देवाजवळ-&c. प्रार्थना *f.* नमाज *or* निमाज *f.* भगवत्प्रार्थना *f.* v. V. N. प्रार्थणें *n.* प्रार्थना *f.* प्रार्थन *n.* विनति *pop.* विनंती *f.* पायधरणी *f.*

I. *request,* v. PETITION. प्रार्थना *f.* विनंती *f.* अर्ज *m.*

PRAYER-BOOK, *n.* प्रार्थनापद्धति *f.*

PRAYERFUL, *a. devotional.* भजननिष्ठ, भजनशील, भजनपरायण.

PRE. This pefix is usually rendered by पूर्व, आदि, प्राक्.

To PREACH, *v. n. discourse on religion.* धर्माचा उपदेश *m.*-धर्मोपदेश *m.*-धर्मकथन *n.*-धर्मोपदेशभाषण *n.*-&c. करणें, धर्म *m.*-पुराण *n.* सांगणें.

To PREACH, *v. a. proclaim or publish in religious discourses.* धर्म सांगणाऱ्याच्या नात्यानें सांगणें-प्रसिद्ध करणें-शिकवणें-&c. उद्घोष *m.*-घोषणा *f.*-घोष *m.*-&c. करणें *g. of o.*

PREACHER, *n.* PREACHING, *p. a.* v. V. N. धर्माचा उपदेश करणारा, धर्मोपदेशकर्त्ता, धर्मकथक, धर्मसांगणारा, पुराण सांगणारा. v. V. A. धर्म सांगणाऱ्याच्या नात्यानें सांगणारा-&c. उद्घोष-घोषणाकर्त्ता.

PREACHING, *n.* v. V. A.—*act.* धर्म सांगणाऱ्याच्या नात्यानें सांगणें *n.* &c. उद्घोष *m.* घोषणा *f.*

PREAMBLE, *n.* v. PREFACE. प्रस्तावना *f.* उपोद्घात *m.* सदर *n.*

PRECARIOUS, *a. depending on the will of another or on contingencies; uncertain, &c.* अस्वाधीन, अस्वायत्त, अन्याधीन, पराधीन, अस्थिर, अनिश्चित, अनैष्ठिक, जायजणा, स्थितिसंशयी, स्थितिशंकी.

PRECARIOUSNESS, *n.* v. A. अस्वाधीनता *f.* अन्याधीनता *f.* अस्थिरता *f.* स्थितिसंशयिता *f.* &c. अनैश्चित्य *n.*

PRECATIVE, PRECATORY, *a. suppliant.* प्रार्थक, प्रार्थनात्मक, प्रार्थनारूप.

PRECAUTION, *n. previous caution or measure.* पुढचा विचार *m.* पूर्वीचा करून ठेवलेला उपाय *m.*-बंदोबस्त *m.*-&c. पूर्वोपाय *m.* अनिष्टनिवारणोपाय *m.*

To take precautions against. बारें *n.* बांधणें-बांधून ठेवणें, द्वारबंध *m.* करणें.

PRECAUTIONARY, *a. adapted to prevent evil or to secure good.* पूर्वीच्या विचाराचा, पूर्वीच्या बंदोबस्ताचा, पूर्वोपायरूप, पूर्वोपायसाधक.

To PRECEDE, *v. a. go before in place or time.* पुढें-अगोदर-&c. असणें-चालणें-जाणें-येणें-&c. *g. of o.* पुरोगमन *n.*-&c. करणें.

2 *go before in rank or importance.* मानसन्मानाविषयीं पहिला-प्रथम-पुरस्सर-अग्रगण्य-&c. असणें.

PRECEDENCE, PRECEDENCY, PRECEDING, *n.* v. V. 1.—*act.* पुढें असणें *n.* पुढेंजाणें *n.* &c. पुरोगमन *n.* पुरोगति *f.* अग्रगमन *n.* 2—*state.* अग्रगण्यता *f.* अग्रपूजा *f.* अग्रमान *m.* अग्रपूज्यता *f.* अग्रमानार्हता *f.*

I. *superiority, superior influence.* मुख्यता *f.* प्राधान्य *n.* श्रेष्ठत्व *n.* श्रैष्ठ्य *n.*

PRECEDENT, *a.* PRECEDER, *n.* PRECEDING, *p. a.* v. V. 1. पुढें-&c. असणारा-&c. मागला, पुढला, पुढील, अगोदरचा, अगोदरील, आगला, अदला, पूर्व, पुरोगामी, पुरोगम, पुरोगति, अग्रगामी, पुरस्सर, पुरोगत, पूर्वसर, प्राकन, पलीकडचा *or* ला, पलीकडील (*or* पैलीकडचा, &c.).

The preceding and the following. पूर्वापर, पूर्वोत्तर.

PRECEDENT, *n previous similar case.* मागला दाखला *m.* मागलें उदाहरण *n.* मागला दृष्टांत *m.* पूर्वदृष्टांत *m.*

PRECEDENTED, *a. having a previous similar case.* दृष्टोदाहरण, दृष्टोदाहरणक, दृष्टसादृश्य, भूतपूर्व.

PRECENTOR, *n. leader of a choir.* मोहरक्या गाणारा, सुरक्या, अग्रगायक, अग्रगाता.

PRECEPT, *n.* v. COMMAND, RULE. विधि *m.* विधान *n.* अनुशासन *n.* कल्प *m.* सूत्र *n.*

A succedaneous p. अनुकल्प *m.*

PRECEPTIVE, PRECEPTORY, *a. containing, &c. precepts.* विधायक, विधिरूप, विधिप्रदर्शक, विधिप्रकाशक, विधिमय, सौत्र, काल्प.

PRECEPTOR, *n.* v. TEACHER. शिक्षक, गुरु, अध्यापक, उपदेशक.

2—in religion, *spiritual teacher.* गुरु, उपाध्याय, आचार्य, पाठक.

Family p. कुलगुरु, कुलोपाध्याय.

PRECESSION, *n.*—of the equinox. अयनांश *m.* विषुवायन *n.*

PRECINCT, *n.* v. BOUND. सीमा *pop.* शींव *f.* हद्द *f.*

PRECIOUS, *a. costly.* मोठे किमतीचा, बहुमोली, बहुमूल्य, महामूल्य, महार्घ.

P. stone. रत्न *n.*

2 *of great value or worth.* मोठे किमतीचा, मोठे योग्यतेचा, अमोल, अमोलिक, अमूल्य, अनर्घ *pop.* अनर्घ्य, महामूल्य, अपरूप, नादर, उत्कृष्ट, अपूर्व.

Very p. सोन्याचा, लाखलाखरुपयांचा.

The p. metals. सोनेंरुपें *n.*

3—as used of scamps, blackguards, &c. v. ARRANT. अट्टल, इरसाल, बिलंद, पक्का. [ल्यता *f.*

PRECIOUSNESS, *n.* v. A. 1. मोठी किम्मत *f.* मोठें मोल *n.* बहुमू-

2 मोठी किम्मत *f.* मोठी योग्यता *f.* अमोलिकपणा *m.* अमूल्यत्व *n.* &c. अपरुपाई *f.* अपूर्वाई *f.* [अतट *n.*

PRECIPICE, *n. steep descent of land.* कडा *m.* डगर *f.* प्रपात *m.*

Casting (a criminal, &c.) down a p. कडेलोट *m.*

Precipitation of one's self down a p. अंगपात *m.* कडेलोट *m.*

PRECIPITANCE, PRECIPITANCY, PRECIPITATION, *n.* v. A. 2. उतावळेपणा *m.* उताविळपणा *m.* हूडपणा *m.* उतावळ *f.* उतावळी *f.* घाई *f.* जलदी *f.* आगपाई *f.* आवेग *m.* धडपड *or* धडफड *f.* धडबड *f.* अविमृश्यकारिता *f.*

PRECIPITANT, PRECIPITATE, *a. rushing headlong.* मुसांडा मारणारा, अधोधावी.

2 *rashly hasty,* v. RASH, IMPETUOUS. उतावळा, उतावीळ, हूड, हुरमट, लगबग्या, धडपड्या *or* फड्या, धडबड्या, मुसांड्या, अविमृश्यकारी.

3 *adopted with haste.* उतावळेपणाचा, उतावळीचा, जलदीचा, घाईचा, धडपडीचा, कच्चेमसलतीचा. [धोमुस.

PRECIPITANTLY, PRECIPITATELY, *adv.* v. A. 1. मुसांडा मारून, अ-

2 उतावळेपणानें, उतावळीनें, हूडपणानें, घाईनें, &c. मागें पुढें पाहिल्यावांचून, पुरता विचार केल्यावांचून, घे म्हटल्या, घे म्हटल्यावर, डुर्योडुर्यो करून, सहसा.

To PRECIPITATE, *v. a. throw headlong.* डोईकडून-डोकीकडून-&c. टाकणें-फेंकणें, खालीं टाकणें-ढकलणें-ढकलून देणें, अधःक्षेप *m.*-अधःक्षेपण *n.*-&c. करणें *g. of o.*

To be precipitated. धासळणें, कोसळणें, ढकलणें.

2 *urge, press, drive, &c.* v. To HURRY. घाई *f.*-घायकूत *f.*-जलदी *f.*-उतावळी *f.*-वळावळ *f.*-&c. करणें, घायतावणें, ताधरावणें, धरधरावणें.

3—in chemistry. निवळीनें-&c. बसवणें, बसवणें, तळीं बसवणें.

To PRECIPITATE, *v. n. fall to the bottom.* निवळीनें बसणें, तळीं बसणें.

PRECIPITATED, *p.* v. V. A. 1. डोईकडून टाकलेला, &c. अधःक्षिप्त.

2 घाई केलेला, घायतावलेला, ताधरावलेला.

PRECIPITATION, *n.* v. V. A. 1.—*act.* डोईकडून टाकणें *n.* &c. अधःक्षेप *m.* अधःक्षेपण *n.*

2—*act.* घाई करणें *n.* घायतावणें *n.* &c.

3—*act.* बसवणें *n.* &c. [श्यकारिता *f.*

I. *rash haste,* v. PRECIPITANCE. उतावळी *f.* घाई *f.* अविमृ-

PRECIPITOUS, *a.* v. STEEP. कडातुटलेला, कड्याचा, उभा.

2 v. PRECIPITANT. उतावळा, उतावळीचा, उतावीळ, हुरमट.

PRECIPITOUSNESS, *n.* v. A. 1. उभी चढण *f.* उभेपणा *m.*

2 उतावळेपणा *m.* उतावळी *f.*

PRECISE, *a. not loose or vague; exact, nice, defined, &c.* ठास, ठाम, खचीत, रेखलेला, रेखाटून दिल्हेला, मेजलेला, सुताचा, सुती, सुतानें केलेला, बरोबर, बेताचा, बेताबाताचा, रजपजचा, तवताक, बंदिस्त, बंदिस्तीचा, केवल *or* केवळ, कांटेकोर, वस्तुनिर्देशात्मक, नामनिर्देशात्मक.

2 *formal, finical, nice, &c.*—of persons. बेतबात्या, टापटिप्या, टाकठिक्या, टाकसठिकस *or* ठिकसटाकस, टापटीप-&c. करणारा, आटछाटीचा.

PRECISELY, *adv.* v. A. 1. ठास, ठाम, बरोबर, खास, तंत, थेट, केवल *or* ळ, नामनिर्देशपूर्वक, वस्तुनिर्देशपूर्वक.

2 टापटिपीनें, टाकसठिकसपणानें, टाकठिकेपणानें.

PRECISENESS, PRECISION, *n.* v. V. 1. ठासपणा *m.* ठामपणा *m.* खचितपणा *m.* &c. वस्तुनिर्देश *m.* नामनिर्देश *m.*

2 टापटीप *f.* टाकठिकेपणा *m.* टाकसठिकसपणा *m.* आटछाट *f.* आटपाट *f.*

To PRECLUDE, *v. a. debar, exclude, &c.* v. To HINDER. वारणें, आड-आड्या-&c. येणें *with* स *or* ला, अडवणें, प्रतिबंध *m.*-&c. करणें, प्रतिबंधक-&c. असणें. [भोगवारित.

PRECLUDED, *p.* v. V. वारलेला, अडवलेला, &c. वारित, निवारित,

PRECLUDER, *n.* PRECLUDING, *p. a.* PRECLUSIVE, *a.* v. V. वारणारा, अडवणारा, प्रतिबंध करणारा, प्रतिबंधक.

PRECLUSION, *n.* v. V.—*act.* वारणें *n.* &c. निवारण *n.*—*state.* वारलेलेपणा *m.* बंदी *f.* रोध *m.* प्रतिबंध *m.* वारितत्व *n.* निवारितत्व *n.* भोगप्रतिबंध *m.* भोगरोध *m.*

PRECOCIOUS, *a. ripe before the time.* आगस, आगसलेला, हळवा, हव्वा, अपूर्णकालपक्क, कालपूर्वफली.

2 fig. लहान असून प्रौढबुद्धीचा, बालप्रौढ, बालपक्क.

PRECOCIOUSNESS, PRECOCITY, *n.* v. A. 1. आगसपणा *m.* हळवेपणा *m.* &c. अपूर्णकालपक्कता *f.*

2 बालप्रौढि *f.* बालपक्कता *f.*

To PRECONCEIVE, *v. a. imagine beforehand.* पूर्वी-अगोदर-पहिल्यानें-&c. कल्पिणें-मनांत आणणें *or* धरणें-समजणें-&c. पूर्वी बुद्धि *f.*-तर्क *m.*-&c. करणें, पूर्वकल्पना *f.*-पूर्वतर्क *m.*-&c. करणें *g. of o.*

PRECONCEIVED, *p.* v. V. पूर्वी कल्पिलेला, &c. पूर्वकल्पित.

PRECONCEPTION, *n.* v. V. अगोदरचा समज *m.* पूर्वकल्पना *f.* पूर्वतर्क *m.*

PRECONCERTED, *a. settled by previous agreement.* पूर्वसंकेताचा, संकेताचा, संगनमताचा, पूर्वी योजलेला, &c. सांकेतिक.

PRECURSOR, *n. forerunner, that which precedes and indicates approach.* प्राग्गामी, अग्रगामी, प्राग्भावी, पूर्वचिह्न *n.* पूर्वलक्षण *n.*

PRECURSORY, *a. indicating something to follow.* प्राग्भावी, पूर्वसूचक. [लुटारा.

PREDATORY, *a. practising, &c. rapine.* लुटीचा, लुटारू, लुटारी,

PREDECESSOR, *n. one who has preceded in an office.* मागला (as मागला अधिकारी-अमलदार-&c.), माजी (as माजी माम-

लेदार-कारकून-&c.) पूर्वाधिकारी.

Predestinarian, Predestinator, *n. holder of the doctrine of predestination.* अदृष्टवादी, अदृष्टमतावलंबी, प्रारब्धवादी, दैष्टिक, दैवचिंतक, दैष्टिकवादी.

To **Predestinate,** *To* **Predestine,** *v. a. fore-ordain, decree or appoint beforehand.* पूर्वी-अगोदर-पहिल्यानें-&c. योजणें-योजून ठेवणें-नेमणें-नेमून ठेवणें-निर्मिणें-&c. निर्मिणें, पूर्वनिरूपण *n.*-पूर्वयोजना *f.*-&c. करणें *g. of o.* कपाळीं-भाळीं-अदृष्टीं-&c. लिहणें-घालणें.

Predestinate, *a.* **Predestinated, Predestined,** *p. v.* V. पूर्वी-योजलेला, &c. निर्मित, ईश्वरनिर्मित, ललाटलिखित, पूर्वनिरूपित, पूर्वयोजित, दैष्टिक.

Predestination, *n.* v. V.—*act.* पूर्वीयोजणें *n.* &c. पूर्वयोजना *f.* पूर्वयोजन *n.* पूर्वनिरूपण *n.*

I.—the doctrine. अदृष्टवाद *m.* अदृष्टमत *n.* दैष्टिकता *f.* दैववाद *m.* प्रारब्धवाद *m.* दैष्टिकवाद *m.*

Predetermination, *n.* v. V.—*act.* पूर्वीचा ठराव *m.*

I. *previously formed purpose.* पूर्वीचा ठराव *m.*-निश्चय *m.*-&c. पूर्वनिश्चय *m.* पूर्वसंकल्प *m.*

To **Predetermine,** *v. a. settle in purpose beforehand.* पूर्वी-अगोदर-पहिल्यानें-&c.ठरवणें-निश्चित करणें-&c. पूर्वी-&c. निश्चय *m.*-संकल्प *m.*-ठराव *m.*-&c. करणें-करून ठेवणें-&c. *g. of o.*

Predetermined, *p.* **Predeterminate,** *a.* v.V. पूर्वी ठरवलेला, &c. पूर्वसंकल्पित, पूर्वनिश्चित.

Predial, *a. consisting, &c. of farms.* कुणबाव्याचा, क्षेत्रिक.

P. slave. क्षेत्रदास.

Predicability, *n.*v. A. वाच्यता *f.* कथनीयता *f.*

Predicable, *a. that may be affirmed of.* वाच्य, कथनीय, वक्तुम् शक्य, सुवच, संभवदुक्तिक.

Predicament, *n.*—in logic; *category.* पदार्थ *m.* प्रकृति *f.*

2 v. Class. जात *f.* बिल्हे *f.* बिल्हा *m.* प्रत *f.*

3 *pickle, plight,* v. Mess. दशा *f.* गति *pop.* गत *f.* घाण *f.*

To **Predicate,** *v. a. affirm of.* बोलणें, सांगणें, कथणें, विधान *n.* करणें *g. of o.*

Predicate, *n. that which is affirmed of.* वाच्य *n.* विशेषण *n.* विशेषक *m. n.* पदाभिधेय *n.* पदशक्य *n.* पदवाच्य *n.*

Relation between the p. and subject. वाच्यवाचकभाव *m.* विशेषण विशेष्यभाव *m.*

Subject of a p. विशेष्य *n.* अनुवाद्य *n.*

Predicated, *p.*v.V.सांगितलेला, कथिलेला, &c. विहित, विशेषित.

Predication, *n.*v. V.—*act.* सांगणें *n.* कथणें *n.* विधान *n.*

To **Predict,** *v. a.* v. To Fore-tell. भाकीत *n.*-भविष्य *n.*-&c. करणें-सांगणें *g. of o.* भाकणें, पूर्वी कथून-&c. ठेवणें, भविष्यकथन *n.*-भाविकथन *n.*-&c. करणें.

Predicted, *p.*v.V. भाकिलेला, भाकून ठेवलेला, पूर्वी कथून ठेवलेला, &c. भविष्यकथित.

Prediction, *n.* v. V.—*act.* भाकणें *n.* भाकणूक *f.* &c. भविष्यकथन *n.* भाविकथन *n.*

A p. of the weather. ठोका *m.* ठोकारोका *m.*

I. *matter predicted.* भविष्य *n.* भाकीत *n.* होरा *m.*

Predictor, *n.* **Predicting,** *p. a.* v. V. भाकणारा, भाकीत सांगणारा, पूर्वी कथून ठेवणारा, &c. भविष्यकथक, भाविकथक.

Predilection, *n. previous liking, prepossession.* अगोदरची-पूर्वीची-&c. प्रीति *f.*-ओढ *f.*-होस *f.*-धांव *f.*-&c. प्रवृत्ति *f.* प्रवाह *m.* छंद *m.* प्रावण्य *n.*

To **Predispose,** *v. a. incline beforehand* (the mind). अगोदर-पूर्वी-&c. वळवणें-कलवणें-कल *m.* देणें-झोक *m.* देणें-ओढणें, मन कलसा करणें *g. of o. with* कडे, प्रवण-उन्मुख-उत्सुक-&c. करणें. 2 (the body). अगोदरचा-&c. तयार-सिद्ध-योग्य-&c. करणें, पात्र-आस्पद-&c. करणें. [-&c.

Predisposed, *p.* v V. 1. पूर्वी वळवलेला-कलवलेला-कल दिल्हेला

2 अगोदरचा तयार केलेला-झालेला-&c.

Predisposed, *n.* **Predisposing,** *p. a.*v. V. 1. अगोदर वळवणारा-कल देणारा-&c. प्रवणकर्ता-कारी-&c.

2 अगोदरचा तयार करणारा, &c.

Predisposition, *n.* v. V. 1.—*state.* पूर्वीचा कल *m.* पूर्वीचा झोक *m.* पूर्वीची ओढ *f.*-&c. प्रवाह *m.* मनःप्रावण्य *n.* प्रावण्य *n.* प्रवृत्ति *f.*

2—*state.* पूर्वीची तयारी *f.*

P. to disease. रोगसुभेद्यता *f.* रोगसुग्राह्यता *f.* रोगग्राह्यदशा *f.* रोगभेद्यदशा *f.*

Predominance, Predominancy, Predomination, *n.* v. A. जोरा *m.* बळकटी *f.* प्राबल्य *n.* प्रबलता *f.* प्राधान्य *n.* प्रधानता *f.* आधिक्य *n.* वर्चस्व *n.*

Predominant, *a. prevalent over others, superior in influence, &c.* जोराचा, बळकट, प्रबल, अधिक, प्रधान.

Predominantly, *adv.* v. A. प्रबल होऊन, प्राधान्येंकरून, प्रधानतः.

To **Predominate,** *v. n. be superior in strength, influence, &c.* प्रबल-प्रधान-अधिक जोराचा-&c. असणें, प्राधान्य *n.*-प्राबल्य *n.* -&c. असणें *g. of s.* वर्चस्व *n.*-प्राबल्य *n.*-&c. पावणें.

Pre-eminence, *n.* v. A. वर्चस *n.* वर्चस्व *n.* वर्चस्वता *f.* श्रेष्ठता *f.* ज्येष्ठता *f.* श्रैष्ठ्य *n.* ज्यैष्ठ्य *n.* प्रधानता *f.* प्राधान्य *n.* मुख्यता *f.* मौख्य *n.* अग्रगण्यता *f.*

Pre-eminent, *a. surpassing in excellence, &c.* v. Chief श्रेष्ठ, मुख्य, वरचढ, वर्चस्वी, ज्येष्ठ, बिनीचा, उत्कृष्ट, प्रधान, विशेष, अग्रगण्य, ग्रामणी, पर, सर्वोत्तम, प्रधानोत्तम, सर्वोत्कृष्ट.

Pre-eminently, *adv.* v. A. मुख्यत्वेंकरून, प्राधान्येंकरून, विशेषेंकरून, प्रकर्षेंकरून, प्रधानतः.

Pre-emption, *n.right of purchasing before others.* पहिला विकत घेण्याचा अधिकार *m.*-हक्क *m.* अग्रक्रयाधिकार *m.*

To **Pre-engage,** *v. a. engage by previous agreement.* अगोदर-पूर्वी-&c. गुंतवणें-गुंतवून ठेवणें, पूर्वी-पहिल्यानें बोली करून ठेवणें, पूर्वसंकेत *m.*-पूर्वनियम *m.*-&c. करणें. [तिज्ञान.

Pre-engaged, *p.* v. V. अगोदर गुंतवलेला, &c. पूर्वसंकेतित, पूर्वप्र-

Pre-engagement, *n.*v.V. पूर्वीची बोली *f.*पूर्वीचा करार *m.*-संकेत *m.* -नियम *m.* पूर्वसंकेत *m.* पूर्वप्रतिज्ञा *f.* पूर्वनियम *m.*

To **Pre-exist,** *v. n.* पूर्वी असणें.

Pre-existence, *n. previous existence.* पूर्वभव *m.* पूर्वभूति *f.* पूर्वसत्व *n.* पूर्वजन्म *n.* पूर्वदेह *m.*

Pre-existent, *a.* पूर्वभूत, पूर्वजन्माचा.

Preface, *n. introduction, &c.* प्रस्तावना *f.* प्रस्ताबन *n.* परिभाषा *f.* सूची *f.* उपोद्घात *m.* उपन्यास *m.* प्रकरण *n.* वाङ्मुख *n.* आभाष *m.* उपक्रमोक्ति *f.* [न करणें.

To **Preface,** *v. a.* v. N. प्रस्तावना *f.*-&c. करणें-लिहणें, सप्रस्ताव-

Prefatory, *a. introductory.* प्रस्तावनेचा, उपोद्घाताचा, &c. प्रस्तावनारूप, &c. पारिभाषिक, उपक्रमोक्त.

Prefect, *n.* v. Mayor, Ruler. पुराध्यक्ष, पुराधिपति.

To PREFER, *v. a. regard more than.* अधिक-विशेष-&c. चाहणें-पसंत करणें, चाह *f.*-आवड *f.*-&c. धरणें *with* पेक्षां-हून-&c. चांगला-इष्ट-&c. जाणणें-समजणें-मानणें *with* पेक्षां-हून-&c. आवड *f.*-प्रीति *f.*-चाड *f.*-&c. अधिक लागणें *g. of o. with in. con.* परिगणन *n.* करणें *g. of o.* पूर्वी-प्रथम-अगोदर-&c. घेणें-ग्रहण *n.* करणें.

2 *exalt, promote,* v. To ADVANCE. वाढवणें, चढवणें, वाढवून-&c. असामी *f.* देणें.

3 *offer solemnly, present, propose, exhibit.* समर्पणें, अर्पणें, निवेदणें, समर्पण *n.*-निवेदन *n.*-&c. करणें, करणें.

PREFERABLE, *a.* v. V. 1. अगोदर-&c. घ्यायाजोगा, पूर्वग्राह्य, प्रथम ग्राह्य, अग्रग्राह्य, चांगला-उत्तम-&c. *with* पेक्षां-हून-&c. परिगणनीय.

PREFERABLENESS, *n.* v. A. पूर्वग्राह्यता *f.* प्रथमग्राह्यता *f.* अग्रग्राह्यता *f.* श्रेष्ठता *f.* श्रेष्ठ्य *n.* वरता *f.*

PREFERABLY, *adv.* v. A. उत्तम-श्रेष्ठ-&c. समजून-&c. वरम्.

PREFERENCE, PREFERMENT, *n.* v. V. 1.—*act.* पूर्वी घेणें *n.* &c. अधिकचाह *f.* अधिक आवड *f.*

In p. to. पूर्वी, अगोदर.

To give the p. to, v. To PREFER. अधिक चाहणें.

2—*act.* वाढवणें *n.* चढवणें *n.* पदवर्द्धन *n.*—*state.* चढती *f.* सरफराजी *f.* पदवृद्धि *f.* स्थानवृद्धि *f.*

3—*act.* समर्पणें *n.* &c. समर्पण *n.* अर्पण *n.* निवेदन *n.*

I. *superior place or office.* मोठी पदवी *f.* मोठें पद*n.* मोठे पायरीची-मोठे पदवीची-&c. असामी *f.*

PREFIGURATION, PREFIGURING, *n.* v. V. प्रतिरूपानें अगोदर दाखवणें*n.* &c. प्रतिरूपद्वारा पूर्वप्रदर्शन*n.* सादृश्यतःप्राक्प्रदर्शन*n.*

PREFIGURATIVE, *a.* v. V. प्रतिरूपानें दाखवणारा, &c. बोधक, उद्बोधक, पूर्वप्रदर्शक, लाक्षणिक.

To PREFIGURE, *To* PREFIGURATE, *v. a. show antecedently by figure or similitude.* प्रतिरूप*n.*-प्रतिरूपक*n.*-प्रतिबिंब*n.*-&c. करणें *or* करून दाखवणें *g. of o.* प्रतिरूपानें-&c. अगोदर-पूर्वी-&c. दाखवणें-दर्शवणें-सुचवणें-&c. प्रतिरूपद्वारा पूर्वप्रदर्शन*n.*-&c. करणें.

PREFIGURED, *p.* v. V. प्रतिरूपानें पूर्वी दाखवलेला, &c. प्रतिरूपद्वारा-&c. पूर्वप्रदर्शित-पूर्वसूचित-&c.

To PREFIX, *v. a. put before or at the beginning of.* वर-मागें-पूर्वी लावणें-घालणें-जोडणें.

2 *fix beforehand.* पूर्वी-अगोदर-&c. ठरवणें-नेमणें.

PREFIX, *n. particle, &c. prefixed.* उपसर्ग*m.*

PREFIXED, *p.* v. V. 1. वरलावलेला, वरघातलेला, मागेंजोडलेला, &c.

2 पूर्वी ठरवलेला, &c. पूर्वसांकेतित, पूर्वनिश्चित.

PREFIXING, *n.* v. V. 1.—*act.* वर लावणें*n.* &c.

2—*act.* पूर्वी ठरवणें*n.* &c.

PREGNANCY, *n.* v. A. गर्भारपण*n.* गरोदरपण*n.* गर्भारशीपणा*m.* &c. गर्भिणीत्व*n.* &c. सगर्भता *f.* सगर्भावस्था *f.* धृतगर्भता *f.* पोट*n.* गर्भ*m.*

Longings of p. डोहळा*m.* दोहद*n.*

Sign of p. गर्भच्छाया *f.* गर्भलक्षण*n.*

To cause the resolution of p. पोट*n.* जिरवणें.

To be resolved,—p. पोट*n.* जिरणें *g. of s.*

PREGNANT, *a. being with young.* पोटाशी *or* सी, गर्भार *or* गव्हार, गर्भारशी *or* गव्हारशी, गरोदर, सगर्भ, धृतगर्भ. Note. Such of the above words as end in ई are in the feminine form.

A p. woman. गर्भवती *f.* गर्भिणी *f.* आसन्नगर्भा *f.* उदरिणी *f.* गुर्विणी *f.* अंतर्वत्नी *f.* दोन जिवांचें माणूस*n.*

A p. woman in her last stage. पुरमाशीण *f.* पूर्णगर्भा *f.*

To be p. पोटाशी असणें-राहणें.

To PREJUDGE, *To* PREJUDICATE, *v. a. judge and determine beforehand.* पूर्वी-अगोदर-&c. *or* चौकसीचे पूर्वी-&c. ठरवणें-निश्चय*m.* करणें, चौकसी केल्यावांचून-विचार केल्यावांचून-&c. पूर्वीच निश्चय*m.*-निवाडा*m.*-&c. करून ठेवणें.

PREJUDICE, *n. opinion or sentiment formed without examination.* पोकळ-व्यर्थ-अविचाराची बुद्धि *f.*-कल्पना *f.*-भावना *f.*-भ्रांति *f.* अविचाराचें मत*n.* अविचारपूर्वक मनोधर्म*m.*-मनोदय*m.*-ग्रह*m.*-&c.

2 *bias against.* मनांत गांठ *f.* अट *f.* अढी *f.* अढी *f.* पीळ*m.* तिढा*m.* तीड *f.* बांक*m.n.* बांक*m.* बांकडें*n.* काळें*n.* काळेंबेरें*n.* अंबळा*m.*

3 *bias for.* पक्षपात*m.* तरफदारी *f.* ओढ *f.* ओढा*m.*

4 *detriment, harm, &c.* v. HURT. नुकसान*n.* खराबी *f.* धक्का*m.* अपकार*m.*

To PREJUDICE, *v. a. bias against.* अट *f.*-अढी *f.*-बांकडें*n.*-काळें*n.*-&c. मनांत आणणें *g. of o. with* विषयीं, पीळ*m.*-बांक*m.*-&c. आणणें-पाडणें.

2 *bias for.* वळवणें, कल*m.*-झोक*m.*-तोल*m.*-ओढ *f.*-&c. देणें.

3 *cause detriment to,* v. To HURT. नुकसान*n.*-नुकसानी *f.*-&c. करणें, धक्का*n.*-हिसका*m.* देणें-मारणें.

PREJUDICED, *p.* v. V. 1. अढी-पीळ-&c. आणलेला-धरलेला-आलेला, बांकडा, बांकड्यामनाचा.

2 वळवलेला, कल दिल्हेला, &c.

3 नुकसान केलेला-झालेला, &c. अपकारित.

PREJUDICIAL, *a.* v. V. 3. *and* HURTFUL. अपकारक, अपकारी, बावडा, अहित, अहितकारक. [रकत्व *n.*

PREJUDICIALNESS, *n.* v. A. अपकारीपणा *m.* बावडेपणा *m.* अपका-

PREJUDICIALLY, *adv.* v. A. नुकसान होईसा *decl.* अपकार होईसा *decl.*

PRE-KNOWLEDGE, *n. previous knowledge.* पूर्वीचें ज्ञान*n.* पूर्वज्ञान*n.*

PRELACY, *n.* मुख्य धर्माध्यक्षाची जागा *f.*-अधिकार *m.*-पदवी *f.*

PRELATE, *n.* मुख्य धर्माध्यक्ष *m.*

PRELECTION, *n.* v. LECTURE. पाठ *m.*

PRELECTOR, *n.* v. LECTURER. पाठ सांगणारा, पाठक.

PRELIBATION, *n.* v. FORETASTE. पूर्वभोग *m.* पूर्वानुभव *m.*

PRELIMINARY, *a. that precedes the main business, previous, introductory, preparatory.* उपक्रमाचा, पूर्वीचा, मुळारंभींचा, प्राथमिक, पारिभाषिक, कर्माद्य, पूर्वकर्त्तव्य, पूर्वकरणीय, अग्रकरणीय, अग्रकर्त्तव्य, उपक्रमस्थ, उमक्रमसाधक.

PRELIMINARY, *n. something previous or preparatory.* उपक्रमाचे-प्रारंभाचे-&c. पूर्वीचा विषय *m.*-गोष्ट *f.*-&c. उपक्रमपूर्वविषय *m.* पूर्वांग *n.* आद्यांग *n.* उपकरणीं *n. pl.*

P. observations. परिभाषा *f.*

PRELUDE, *n.*—in music. पूर्वरंग *m.* पूर्ववादन *n.*

2 *something introductory and indicative.* पूर्वरूप *n.* पूर्वरंग*m.* पूर्वलक्षण *n.* पूर्वसूचक *n.*

Dramatic p. प्रस्तावना *f.* प्रस्तावन *n.*

PRELUSIVE, PRELUSORY, *a. introductory and indicative.* पूर्वरूपाचा, पूर्वरंगाचा, &c. पूर्वसूचक. [लपूर्वपक्क.

PREMATURE, *a. ripe before the time.* कालाचे पूर्वीपिकलेला, का-

2 *happening, &c. before the proper time.* कालाचे पूर्वींचा,

कालाचे पूर्वीं आलेला-झालेला-घडलेला-&c. कालापकर्षाचा, अपूर्णकाल, अपूर्णकालिक, अपूर्णकालज, अपूर्णकालोत्पन्न, कालपूर्वकालिक.
3 *adopting hasty measures*, v. PRECIPITANT, उतावळा, अकालसह, अविमृश्यकारी.

PREMATURELY, *adv.* v. A. 1. 2. कालाचे पूर्वीं, कालाचे अगोदर.

PREMATURENESS, PREMATURITY, *n.* v. A. 1. कालाचे पूर्वीं पिकलेलेपणा *m.* कालपूर्वपक्वता *f.* [लोद्भव *m.*
2 कालापकर्ष *m.* अपूर्णकालिकता *f.* अपूर्णकालोत्पत्ति *f.* अपूर्णका-
3 उतावळेपणा *m.* उतावळी *f.*

To PREMEDITATE, *v. a. revolve or contrive in the mind beforehand.* मनांत पूर्वीं कल्पून ठेवणें-योजून ठेवणें, विचार *m.*-कल्पना *f.*-योजना *f.*-रचना *f.*-अनुसंधान *n.*-&c. पूर्वीं करणें *g. of o.* पूर्वकल्पना *f.*-पूर्वरचना *f.*-पूर्वयोजना *f.*-पूर्वानुसंधान *n.*-&c. करणें *g. of o.*

To PREMEDITATE, *v. n. meditate or think beforehand.* अगोदर-पूर्वीं-&c. विचार *m.*-मनन *n.*-&c. करणें.

PREMEDITATED, *p.* v. V. A. *and* INTENTIONAL. मनांत पूर्वीं योजून ठेवलेला, &c. पूर्वकल्पित, पूर्वयोजित, पूर्वरचित, बुद्धिकृत, सांकल्पिक, संकल्पकृत, पूर्वसंकल्पित.

PREMEDITATION, *n.* v. V. A.—*act.* पूर्वीं योजून ठेवणें *n.* &c. पूर्वकल्पना *f.* पूर्वयोजना *f.* पूर्वरचना *f.* पूर्वानुसंधान *n.* पूर्वसंकल्प *m.* v. V. N. पूर्वविचार *m.* पूर्वमनन *n.* पूर्वचिंतन *n.*

PREMICES, *n.* v. FIRST FRUITS. नवाळी *f.* नवान्न *n.* नवीनवाळ *f.*

PREMIER, *a. principal.* प्रधान, मुख्य.

PREMIER, *n. prime minister.* मुख्यप्रधान *m.* प्रधानमंत्री *m.* प्रधानामात्य *m.* पेशवा *m.*

PREMIERSHIP, *n. office of premier.* मुख्यप्रधानकी *f.* मुख्यप्रधानाची-प्रधानमंत्र्याची-&c. पदवी *f.*-असामी *f.*-&c.

To PREMISE, *v. a. speak or write before as introductory.* पूर्वीं-आगोदर- पहिल्यानें आरंभीं-आद्यारंभीं-&c. सांगणें-सांगून ठेवणें-लिहणें-&c. मुख्यविषयाचेपूर्वीं सांगणें-बोलणें-लिहणें-&c. प्रस्तावपूर्वकथन *n.*-प्रस्तावपूर्वसूचन *n.*-&c. करणें *g. of o.* प्राक्कथन *n.* करणें.

PREMISED, *p.* v. V.—पूर्वीं सांगितलेला, मुख्यविषयाचेपूर्वीं सांगितलेला, &c. पूर्वकथित, प्रस्तावपूर्वकथित, प्रस्तावपूर्वसूचित.

PREMISING, *n.* v. V.—*act.* पूर्वीं सांगणें *n.* &c. पूर्वकथन *n.* पूर्वसूचन *n.* प्रस्तावपूर्वकथन *n.* प्रस्तावपूर्वसूचन *n.* आरंभाद्यकथन *n.* प्राक्कथन *n.*

PREMISES, *n.*—in logic. पूर्वपक्ष *m.* प्रतिज्ञा *f.* साधन *n.* आद्यपक्ष *m.* हेत्वादिपक्ष *m.*
2—in law; *enclosure and house.* घरवाडा *m.* घरवाडी *f.* विसवाट *m. n.* घरभाट *n.*

PREMISE, *n. antecedent proposition.* पूर्वपक्ष *m.* आद्यपक्ष *m.*

PREMIUM, *n. bonus to a money lender.* मनोती *f.* मंडाई *f.* मंडावण *f.* [पारितोषिक *n.*
2 *prize, bounty, gift.* देणगी *f.* बक्षीस *n.* इनाम *m. n.* दान *n.*

To PREMONISH, *v. a. fore-warn.* पूर्वीं-&c. सांगणें-जतावणें-सुचवणें-ताकीद *f.* देणें *or* करणें, पूर्वसूचन *n*-पूर्वसूचना *f.*-&c. करणें.

PREMONISHED, *p.* v. V. पूर्वींजतावलेला &c. पूर्वसूचित.

PREMONISHER, *n.* PREMONISHING, *p. a.* PREMONITORY, *a.* v. V. पूर्वीं जतावणारा-सुचवणारा-&c. पूर्वसूचक, पूर्वसूचनकारी.

PREMONISHMENT, PREMONITION, *n.* v. V.—*act.* पूर्वीं जतावणें *n.* &c. पूर्वींची ताकीद *f.* पूर्वसूचन *n.* पूर्वसूचना *f.*

PRENOMEN, *n. name prefixed to the family name.* व्यक्तिनाम *n.* पहिलें नांव *n.*

PRENTICE. See APPRENTICE.

PRE-OCCUPANCY, PRE-OCCUPATION, *n.* v. V.—*act.* पूर्वीं धरणें *n.* &c. पूर्वींची-पहिली-&c. वहिवाट *f.* पूर्वींचा-पहिला-प्रथम-&c. भोग *m.*-भोगवटा *m.* पूर्वधारण *n.* पूर्वग्रहण *n.* पूर्वभोग *m.*

PRE-OCCUPIED, *p.* v. V. पूर्वीं धरलेला, &c. पूर्वगृहीत.

PRE-OCCUPIER, *n.* PRE-OCCUPYING, *p. a.* v. V. अगोदर धरणारा-घेणारा-&c.

To PRE-OCCUPY, *v. a. take possession before another.* अगोदर-पूर्वीं-आघाडीसाधून-आघाडीमारून-&c. धरणें-घेणें-आपला करणें-सईकरणें-स्वत्वाक्रांत करणें-&c. पूर्वीं-&c. वहिवाट *f.*-भोग *m.*-भोगवटा *m.*-&c. करणें *g. of o.* पूर्वधारण *n.*-&c. करणें *g. of o.*

To PRE-ORDAIN, *v. a. ordain beforehand.* पूर्वीं-अगोदर-&c. नेमणें-स्थापणें-योजणें *or* नेमून-&c. देणें-ठेवणें, पूर्वविधि *m.*-पूर्वविधान *m.*-पूर्वस्थापना *f.*-&c करणें *g. of o.*

PREORDAINED, *p.* v. V. पूर्वीं-अगोदर-&c.-नेमलेला-नेमून ठेवलेला, &c. पूर्वयोजित, पूर्वनियोजित. [पूर्वस्थापना *f.*

PREORDINATION, *n.* v. V. पूर्वीं नेमणें *n.* पूर्वविधान *n.* पूर्वविधि *m.*

PREPAID, *a.*—letter, & हाशील-पैसा-किंमत-&c-अगोदर दिल्हेला.

PREPARATION, *n.* v. V A. 1.—*act.* तयार करणें *n.* सिद्ध करणें *n.* &c.—*state.* तयारी *or* तैयारी *f.* सिद्धता *f.* सिद्धि *f.* लायकी *f.* तवताकपणा *m.* लेसपणा *m.* &c. बंदोबस्त *m.* बंदोबस्ती *f.*
2—*act.* तयार करणें *n.* सजवणें *n.* सजणें *n.* &c. तर्तूद *or* तर्दूद *f.* संजोग *m.* तजवीज *f.* सज्जना *f.* सज्जीकरण—*state.* तयारी *or* तैयारी *f.* सिद्धता *f.* सिद्धि *f.*
3—*act.* कमावणें *n.* ओजवणें *n.* &c. कमाविशी *f.* कमाई *f.* कमावीस *f.* मरामत *f.* मशागत *f.* संस्कार *m.*
4—*act.* करणें *n.* रचणें *n.* रचना *f.*
v. V. N. तयारी *or* तैयारी *f.* तर्तूद *or* तर्दूद *f.* तजवीज *f.*
2 तयारी *f.* कमरबंदी *f.* कमरबस्ता *m.*
I. *preparative measures.* तयारी *or* तैयारी *f.* तर्तूद *or* तर्दूद *f.* तजवीज *f.* उपाय *m.*
II. *that which has been prepared, compounded, &c.*—of food. पक्वान्न *n.* पदार्थ *m.*—of medicine, v. COMPOUND. पाक *m.* रसायन *n.* रांधा *m.*

PREPARATIVE, PREPARATORY, *a. tending, &c. to prepare, qualify, fit, &c.* तयारी-&c. करणारा-&c. तयारीच्या उपयोगाचा, तयारीच्या कामाचा, सिद्धताकारक-जनक-&c. योग्यताकारक-जनक-&c. उपक्रमसहाय, उपक्रमोपकारी, उपक्रमसाधक.

PREPARATIVE, *n. that which prepares or fits.* सिद्धताजनकविषय *m.*-कृत्य *n.*-&c.

PREPARATIVELY, *adv.* v. A. तयारीसाठीं, तयारी व्हावी म्हणून, तयारीच्या उद्देशानें, तयारीचेअर्थीं.

To PREPARE, *v. a. fit, adjust, qualify, make ready for, &c.* तयार-सिद्ध-लेस *or* लेश-योग्य *pop.* जोगता *or* जोगा-लायक-तवनाक *or* ग *or* तवतार-उपयुक्त- कार्यक्षम-क्षम (in comp.)-&c. करणें, तयारी *f.*-सिद्धता *f.*-योग्यता *f.*-&c. करणें *g. of o.* योग्यता *f.*-&c. देणें-आणणें, तयारीत आणणें, ओजविणें, सुधारणें, बंदोबस्त *m.*-बंदोबस्ती *f.*-व्यवस्था *f.*-&c. करणें *g. of o.*
2 *provide, make ready beforehand.* तयार-सिद्ध-&c. करणें-करून ठेवणें, तयारी *f.*-सिद्धता *f.*-सिद्ध *f.*-तर्तूद *f.*-संयोग *m.*-बेगमी *or* बेजमी *f.*-तजवीज *f.*-संच *m.*-साहित्य *n.*-&c. करणें-करून ठेवणें *g. of o.* सजवणें, सजणें, संजोगणें, सज्जना *f.*-&c. करणें *g. of o.*

3 *dress, work up, make ready by process.* कमावणें, ओजवणें, कमावशी *f.*-कमाई *f.*-मशागत *f.*-मेहनत *f.*-मरामत *f.*-संस्कार *m.*-&c. करणें *g. of o.*

4 v. To Make, To Form. करणें, तयार करणें, रचणें, रचना *f.* रचणूक *f.*-&c. करणें *g. of o.*

To Prepare, *v. n. take previous measures, get things ready.* तयारी *f.*-तर्तूद *f.*-तजवीज *f.*-बंदोबस्त *m.*-बंदोबस्ती *f.*-&c. करणें.

2 *make one's self ready.* तयारी *f.*-&c. करणें,तयार-&c. असणें, कमर *f.* बांधणें, कमरबंदी *f.*-कमरबस्ता *m.*-&c. करणें.

Prepared, *p.* v. V. A. 1. तयार केलेला-झालेला, सिद्ध केलेला-झालेला, तयारींत आणलेला, &c. तयार *or* तैयार, सिद्ध, लेस *or* लेश, नबताक, योग्य *pop.* जोगता, लायक, मुस्तेद.

2 तयार करून ठेवलेला, सजवलेला, सजलेला, तयार *or* तैयार, सिद्ध, सज्ज, सज्जित, सज्जीकृत, संज्य.

3 कमावलेला, ओजवलेला, &c. संस्कारित.

Preparedness, *n.* v. P. तयारी *or* तैयारी *f.* सिद्धता *f.*

Preparer, *n.* Preparing, *p. a.* v. V. A. 1. तयार करणारा, सिद्ध करणारा, तयारी करणारा, तयारींत आणणारा.

2 तयार करणारा, सजवणारा, सज्जित करणारा, &c.

3 कमावणारा, &c.

4 करणारा, रचणारा, &c.

Prepayment, *n.* अगोदर हाशील-पैसा-किंमत-&c. देणें *n.*

Prepense. See Premeditated. [राधिक्य *n.*

Preponderance, *n.* v. A. 1. अधिक वजन *n.* अधिकभार *m.* भा-

2 उपराळा *m.* प्राधान्य *n.* प्रधानता *f.*

Preponderant, *a. outweighing.* अधिक वजनाचा, अधिक भाराचा, भाराधिक्याचा, अधिकभारी. [चा.

2 fig. *superior in force, weight, &c.* प्रधान, प्रबल, प्राधान्या-

To Preponderate, *v. n. exceed in weight.* अधिकभारी-अधिकभाराचा-&c. असणें, भारी-जड-वजनदार-&c. असणें *with* पेक्षां-हून-&c.

2 fig. *exceed in force, weight, influence, &c.* प्रधान-बळकट-प्रबल-&c. असणें, उपराळा *m.*-प्राधान्य *n.*-&c. असणें *g. of s.*

Preposition, *n.*—in grammar. शब्दयोगी अव्यय *n.*

An inseparable preposition is उपसर्ग *m.* Many of the most expressive words of the language are formed with one or other of these inseparable prepositions.

Prepositional, Prepositive, *a.* v. N. उपसर्गाचा, उपसर्गसंबंधी, औपसर्गिक.

To Prepossess, *v. a.* lit. See To Pre-occupy.

2 fig. *incline or impress previously in favor of.* पूर्वी-अगोदर-पहिल्यानें-&c. वळवणें-ओढणें-चित्त *n.* ओढणें-कल *m.* देणें-चित्ताकर्षण *n.* करणें-&c.

3 *impress previously against.* See To Prejudice.

Prepossessed, *p.* v. V. 2. पूर्वी वळवलेला, &c.

Prepossessor, Prepossessing, *p. a.* v. V. 2. पूर्वीच चित्त ओढणारा, पाहण्याबरोबर चित्त ओढणारा, &c. दृष्टमात्र चित्ताकर्षक.

Prepossession, *n.* v.V. 2. *previous impression or inclination.* ओळखीचे पूर्वीची भावना *f.*-बुद्धि *f.*-कल्पना *f.*-समजूत *f.*-उमज *m.*-समज *m.*-ओढ *f.*-कल *m.* [कमाचा.

Preposterous, *a. inverted in order.* उफराट्याक्रमाचा, विपरीत

2 v. Absurd, Foolish. उलटा, विपरीत, बांकडा, अन्याय्य, अयुक्त.

Preposterously, *adv.* v. A. 1. उफराट्या क्रमानें, उलट्या क्रमानें, विपरीत क्रमानें.

2 उलटा *decl.* बांकडा *decl.* &c. अयुक्ति पूर्वक, नीतिविपर्यासपूर्वक.

Preposterousness, *n.* v. A. उफराटाक्रम *m.* उलटाक्रम *m.* विपरीतक्रम *m.*

2 उलटेपणा *m.* विपरीतपणा *m.* वैपरीत्य *n.* अयुक्ति *f.* अयुक्तता *f.*

Prepuce, *n. foreskin.* टोपी *f.* मुसी *f.* बोंडी *f.* पुढली चामडी *f.* अग्रत्वक् *f.*

Frenum of the p. शिवण *f.* सीवनी *f.* सेवन *n.*

Prerequisite, *a. previously required,* v. Necessary. अगोदर-पहिल्यानें-&c. असायाचा, पूर्वावश्यक, पूर्वापेक्षित, पूर्वाकांक्षित.

Prerequisite, *n. something previously required,* v. Necessary. अगोदर असायाचा पदार्थ *m.*-विषय *m.*-&c. पूर्वावश्यक-&c. विषय *m.*-&c. [विशेषसत्ता *f.*

Prerogative, *n. peculiar privilege.* हक्क *m.* विशेषाधिकार *m.*

Presage, *n.* v Prognostic. पूर्वलक्षण *n.* पूर्वचिह्न *n.*

To Presage, *v. a.* v. To Foreshow, To Prognosticate. पूर्वी दाखवणें-दर्शवणें, पूर्वसूचन *n.*-अग्रसूचन *n.*-&c. करणें *g. of o.* पूर्वलक्षण *n.* असणें *g. of o.* [व्यदर्शन *n.*

Prescience, *n. fore-knowledge.* पूर्वज्ञान *n.* भविष्यज्ञान *n.* भवि-

Prescient, Prescious, *a. fore knowing.* भविष्यज्ञानी, भविष्यदर्शी, पूर्वी जाणणारा.

To Prescribe, *v. a. order, direct, lay down as a rule or law.* नेमणें, नेमून देणें, बंधारण *n.* बांधून देणें, नियम *or* नेम *m.*-विधि *m.*-विधान *n.*-हुकूम *m.*-आज्ञा *f.*-&c. करणें, कायदा *m.*-धडा *m.* घालून देणें, सांगणें.

2 *direct medically.* सांगणें, देणें, उपचार *m.* सांगणें-योजणें.

To Prescribe, *v. n. direct remedies.* उपचार *m.*-औषध *n.*-औषधोपचार *m.*-&c. सांगणें-योजणें, औषध *n.* देणें.

Prescribed, *p.* v. V. A. 1. नेमून दिल्हेला, &c. नियमित, चोदित, निर्दिष्ट, निदिष्ट, आदिष्ट, विध्युक्त, वैध, विधिप्रोक्त, वाचनिक.

2 सांगितलेला, उपचाराचा सांगितलेला.

Prescriber, *n.* Prescribing, *p. a.* v. V. A. 1. नेमून देणारा, नेमकरणारा, विधि करणारा, कायदा घालून देणारा.

Prescript, *n.* v. Command. आज्ञा *f.* निर्देश *m.* आदेश *m.*

Prescription, *n.* v. V. A. 1.—*act.* नेमणें *n.* नेमून देणें *n.* &c. नियम *or* नेम *m.* चोदना *f.* विधि *m.* विधान *n.*

2—*act.* सांगणें *n.* &c. उपचाराची योजना *f.*

I. *medical recipe.* औषधाची याद *f.* औषधविधि *m.* उपचारविधि *m.* चिकित्सालेख *m.*

II. *immemorial use and enjoyment,*—as furnishing a claim or title. जुनीवहिवाट *f.* जुनीचाल *f.* प्राचीन भोगवटा *m.* अनादिपरंपरा *f.* वृद्धपरंपरा *f.* चिरकालभोग *m.*

Prescriptive, *a. consisting in or acquired by prescription.* जुनेवहिवाटीचा, प्राचीनभोगवट्याचा, जुनेचालीचा, अनादिपरंपराश्रयी, अनादिपरंपरायात, चिरकालभोगाश्रयी.

Presence, *n.*—*as opposed* to absence. हाजिरी *f.* विद्यमानता *f.* प्रत्यक्षता *f.* समक्षता *f.* आभिमुख्य *n.* समक्षासमक्ष *f.*

In the p. of. पुढें, समक्ष, विद्यमान, रूबरू *or* रूबुरू, प्रत्यक्ष, प्रत्यक्षतः, हुजूर, हुजराहुजूर.

P. as a witness, of a third person. विद्यमान *f. n.*

To suffer to be in one's p. जवळ उभा करणें, जवळ करणें-धरणें.

2 (of mind) *self-possession.* सावधपणा *m.* सावधगिरी *f.* काम *f.* भान *n.* देहभान *n.* देहशुद्धि *f.* अवसान *n.* प्रसंगावधान *n.*

3 *state before a great person.* हुजूर *n.*

4 See PRESENCE-CHAMBER. 5 See MIEN.

PRESENCE-CHAMBER, *n.* हुजूर *n.* दिवाणखाना *m.*

PRESENT, *a. not absent.* हाजीर, रुजू, विद्यमान, प्रत्यक्ष, अभिमुख, अपरोक्ष, उपस्थायी.

2 *being now in view or under consideration.* चालता, चाललेला, सांप्रतचा, विद्यमान, प्रकृत, प्रस्तुत, उपस्थित.

3 *not past or future, now existing, now being, belonging to the present time.* चालता, चालतेकाळचा, विद्यमान, हालींचा, सांप्रतचा, सांप्रतकाळचा, प्रस्तुतकाळचा, सद्यस्कालीन, सद्यस्क, वर्त्तमान, इदानींतन, आधुनिक.

The present year. सालमजकूर—the p.month माहेमजकूर.

At p. at the p. time, v. NOW. एव्हां, हालीं, सांप्रत, सांप्रतकाळीं, सद्यः *pop.* सद्या *or* सद्ध्या, तूर्त, प्रस्तुत, प्रकृत.

For the p. सांप्रतकाळाला, तूर्तकाळाला, तूर्त.

4 (tense). वर्त्तमान, विद्यमान.

5 *collected, self-possessed.* सावध, सावधान, सुचित्त, स्वस्थचित्त, स्थिरचित्त, समाहितमनस्क, समाहितमना, अवहित.

PRESENT, *n.* v. GIFT. दान *n.* देणगी *f.* बक्षीस *n.* इनाम *n.*

Complimentary p. *p. to a superior, or amongst persons of rank.* नजर *f.* नजराणा *m.* भेट *f.* फर्माश *or* फर्मास *f.* उपहार *m.* उपायन *n.* उपग्राह्य *n.*

Presents to superiors—compreh. नजरनजराणा *m.*

P. made to a great person on being introduced. भेट *f.* नजरभेट *f.*

P. (of articles of apparel, &c.) from off the person. उतार पोशाक*m.* उतार *m.*

Presents by votaries to Bráhmans, &c. बाण *n.*

To PRESENT, *v. a. introduce, &c.* हाजीर-रुजू-&c. करणें, भेटवणें, भेट *f.* करून देणें, भेटीस नेणें, पुढें करणें, गुजरावणें, गुजरणें.

2 (one's self). हाजीर-&c. होणें, दर्शनास-भेटीस-&c. येणें, दर्शन *n.*-भेट *f.*-&c. घेणें, मुजऱ्याला येणें.

3 *exhibit, offer, afford.* दाखवणें, दर्शवणें, दृष्टीस आणणें-पाडणें, प्राप्तहोणें-मिळणें-हातास येणें-पावणें-पोहंचणें *in. con. with* पासून, सांपडणें *with* आंत *or* मध्यें, प्रापण *n.* करणें.

4 *give formally.* अर्पिणें, समर्पिणें, निवेदणें, अर्पण *n.*-समर्पण*n.*-निवेदन *n.* करणें, नजर *f.*-&c. करणें *g. of o.*

5 v. To GIVE. देणें, दान *n.* करणें, ओपणें.

6 *lay before.* पुढें ठेवणें.

7 (a missile,&c.) v. To POINT. रोंखणें, नेमणें, योजणें,लावणें.

PRESENTATION, PRESENTING, *n.* v. V. 1.—*act.* रुजू करणें *n.* भेट करणें *n.*

2 हाजीर होणें *n.* &c.

Cross p. (of the fœtus). आडवें येणें *n.*

3 दाखवणें *n.* &c. दाखवणूक *f.* दर्शन *n.* प्रदर्शन *n.*

4 अर्पिणें *n.* &c. अर्पण *n.* समर्पण *n.* निवेदन *n.* वेदना *f.*

PRESENTED, *p.* v. V. 1. रुजू केलेला, भेटवलेला, &c.

3 दाखवलेला, &c. दर्शित, प्रदर्शित.

4 अर्पिलेला, &c. अर्पित, समर्पित, निवेदित.

7 रोंखलेला, नेमलेला, योजलेला, &c.

PRESENTER, *n.* PRESENTING, *p. a.* v. V. 1. रुजू करणारा, भेटकरणारा, भेटवणारा.

3 दाखवणारा, दृष्टीस आणणारा.

4 अर्पिणारा, &c. अर्पणकर्त्ता, समर्पणकर्त्ता, निवेदनकर्त्ता, अर्पक, [समर्पक.

PRESENTIMENT, *n. previous conception, impression, apprehension, &c.* भास *m.* भान *n. or* पूर्वीचा भास *m.* पूर्वीचें भान *n.* अगा *m. f.* पूर्वभावना *f.* पूर्वकल्पना *f.*

P. of evil. अनर्थभान *n.*

PRESENTLY, *adv.* v. NOW. सद्यः *pop.* सद्ध्या *or* सद्या, सांप्रत, [सांप्रतकाळीं, तूर्त.

2 *shortly, soon.* थोडके वेळानें, लौकर, थोडेवेळानंतर, मग, क्षणभरानें, अमळशानें, आतांशीं, इतक्यांत, किंचित् काळानें.

3 See IMMEDIATELY, INSTANTLY.

PRESERVABLE. *a.* v.V.1. राखायाजोगा-जोगता-&c. रक्षणीय, रक्ष्य.

PRESERVATION, PRESERVING, *n.* v. V. 1.—*act.* राखणें *n.* &c. राखण *f.* रक्षण *n.* संरक्षण *n.* बचाव *m.* संभाळ *m.* तारण *n.* त्राण *n.* सुरक्षण *n.* रक्षा *f.* परित्राण *n.* पालन *pop.* पाळण *n.* परिपालन *n.* गोपन*n.* संगोपन *n.* गुप्ति *f.* अवन *n.* उपजीवन *n.* उस्तवारी *f.* खबरदारी *f.*

2—*act.* जोगवणें *n.*&c. जतन *f.* जोपासना *f.* जोपाशीर *f.* जोपासणी *f.* जोपाशील *f.* जोपा *f.*

PRESERVATIVE, *a. having the power or quality of preserving.* रक्षक, रक्षणकर्त्ता-कारी, संरक्षणकर्त्ता-कारी-&c. तारक, त्राणकर्त्ता-कारी-&c. रक्षणसाधक.

PRESERVATIVE, *n. that which preserves.* रक्षण *n.* राखण *f.* रक्षणसाधन *n.* त्राणसाधन *n.* रक्षणोपाय *m.*

To PRESERVE, *v. a. save, defend, keep, protect.* राखणें, रक्षणें, संरक्षणें, बचावणें, संभाळणें, तारणें, वांचविणें, ठेवणें, पाळणें, रक्षण *n.*-संरक्षण *n.*-त्राण *n.*-&c. करणें *g. of o.*

2 *keep or lay by carefully.* जतनेस ठेवणें-घालणें, जतन करणें-ठेवणें-राखणें, जतन करून ठेवणें, जपून ठेवणें, जोगवणें, जोंबाळणें, जोपासणें, जोपासना *f.*-&c. करणें *g. of o.* फुलांत घालून ठेवणें *or* राखणें.

3 (fruits, &c.). मुरब्बा *m.* करणें *g. of o.* साखरेनें पाकणें-पाकवणें-रांपविणें-रावणें. [कलेलें फळ *n.*

PRESERVE. *n. conserve of fruit.* मुरब्बा *or* मुरंबा *m.* साखरेनेंपा-

P. of mangoes. गुळंचा *m.* गुळांब *m.* गुळांबा *m.*

2 *place for the shelter of game.* शिकारीचीं जनावरें-मासे-&c. राखण्याची जागा *f.*

PRESERVED, *p.* v.V.1. राखलेला, &c. रक्षित, संरक्षित, सुरक्षित, तारित, त्रात, संगोपित, गोपित, गुप्त, पालित, परिपालित.

2 जतन ठेवलेला, जतन केलेला, जोगवलेला.

3 साखरेनें पाकलेला-रांपवलेला-&c.

PRESERVER, *n.* PRESERVING, *p. a.* v. V. 1. राखणारा, तारणारा, &c. संरक्षक, रक्षक, तारक, त्राता, रक्षणकर्त्ता-कारी-&c. संरक्षणकर्त्ता-कारी-&c. पालक, गोपक, संगोपक, पालनकर्त्ता-कारी-&c. पाल & पालक (in comp. as, भूपाल, महीपाल,&c.), प (in comp. as, भूमिप, धनप, &c.).

2 जतन ठेवणारा, जतन राखणारा, जोंबाळणारा, जोपासणारा, &c.

3 साखरेनें पाकणारा, मुरब्बा करणारा, &c.

To PRESIDE, *v. n. be the head, chief, superintendent, manager, &c.* मुखरण-मुख्य-अधिकारी- अध्यक्ष-प्रधान-नायक-मुरब्बा-&c. असणें, नायकी*f.*-सरदारी *f.*-&c. करणें, देखरेख *f.*-&c. करणें, वरअसणें. [अध्यक्षता *f.*

PRESIDENCY, *n.* v. SUPERINTENDENCE. देखरेख *f.* अधिकार *m.*

2 *office of a president.* अध्यक्षाची-&c. जागा *f.*-पदवी *f.*-&c. नायकी *f.* सरदारी*f.* अध्यक्षपणा*m.* अध्यक्षता *f.* उपद्रष्टृत्व *n.*

3 *country of a president.* इलाखा*m.* खातें*n.* अमलांतला देश*m.*

PRESIDENT, *n.* PRESIDER, *n.* PRESIDING, *p. a.* v. V. मुखरण, मुख्य, अध्यक्ष, नायक, सरदार, देखरेख करणारा, उपद्रष्टा, मुरब्बी, सरचश्मा *or* सरचष्मा. [मानायक.

P. of an assembly, council, &c. सभापति, सभाध्यक्ष, स-

PRESIDENTSHIP. See PRESIDENCY.

To PRESS, *v. a. compress, squeeze, &c.* चेपणें, चेपटणें, दाबणें, चेंचटणें, चापणें, दडपणें, दडकणें, आवळणें.

A weight placed to p. down. दडपण *n.* दडपा *m.* दडकण *n.* चेपण *or* णें *n.*

To p. and squeeze to discover (the seat of pain, &c.) चांपणें, चांपाचांपी *f.* करणें.

2 *constrain, urge, drive, &c.* v. To URGE. दपटणें, दामटणें, खटाळणें, गांजणें, टाचळणें, गळग्रह*m.*-गळ*m.* घालणें, भार*m.* घालणें-करणें, निकड *f.* लावणें, आग्रह*m.* करणें, घायकूत *f. n.* करणें, ताण *m.* देणें, गळचिपी *f.* लावणें-करणें, तांतड *f.*-तांतडी *f.* लावणें-करणें, गळा *m.*-गळचिपी *f.*-&c. धरणें *g. of o.* बोकांडीस-मानेस-उरावर-छातीवर-&c. बसणें *g. of o.*

3 *enforce, inculcate urgently.* आग्रह*m.*-निकड *f.*-&c. करणें *g. of o. or* आग्रह करून-निकड करून-नेटानें-&c. सांगणें-पदरीं बांधणें, गळीं बांधणें, पाठीस लावणें.

4 *straiten, distress, &c.* अडचणींत-संकटांत-पेचांत-*&c.*आणणें-पाडणें, अडचणविणें.

To be pressed. अडचणणें, अवघडणें.

5 *bear strongly on, act on with weight or force.* भार *m.* घालणें-करणें, भार *m.*-नेट*m.*-जोर *m.*-ओझें*n.*-&c. पडणें *g. of s. with* वर *of o.*

6 *impose by importunity.* गळीं-पदरीं बांधणें, पाठीस लावणें, बळेंच गळीं पडून-आग्रहानें-&c. देणें-घेवविणें.

7 *urge, importune,* v. To HANG UPON. आग्रह *m.* करणें, गळ *m.* घालणें, गळीं पडणें, बोकांडीस-खपाटीस-मानकुटीस-गचांडीस-गळचांडीस-&c. बसणें *g. of o.* गळा *m.*-गळचिपी *f.*-नरडें*n.*-&c. धरणें-आवळणें *g. of o.* वेबंतणें, वेबंतून घेणें.

8 (into service) *impress.* वेठीस-बिगारीस धरणें, बळानें-बळेंच-बळजोरीनें-&c. धरणें-चाकरीस ठेवणें.

Pressed service. वेठ *f.* बिगार *or* बेगार *f.* धरबिगार *f.* धरवेठ *f.* विष्टि *f.*—freely or compreh. वेठ बिगार *f.*वेठबिरळा *m.*

9 v. To CROWD. दाटी *f.* करणें.

10 v. To EMBRACE. वेंगेंत धरणें, उरींपोटीं धरणें.

To PRESS, *v. n. push on, go forward.* पुढें जाणें-चालणें, रेंटून जाणें, रेंटत जाणें, चालत्यापावलीं जाणें, न विसंबतां-&c. जाणें-चालणें.

2 *throng,* v. To CROWD. दाटी *f.* करणें, दाटी करून येणें-जाणें-&c. लोटणें, खेटणें, चेप *m.*-चेपाचेप *f.*- चेपारा *m.*-&c. करणें.

3 on; upon ; &c. *bear strongly on,*—a work, &c. उरावर-छातीवर-&c. बसणें, मानेस बसणें.

To p. hard upon, *be close at one's heels.* नेटणें, भिडणें, खेटणें, दूम *m. f.*-पिच्छा *m.* पुरवणें. [जावणें, धज *f.* देणें.

To p. through or forward: *force one's way.* धजणें *or* ध-

PRESS, PRESSING, PRESSURE, *n.* v. V. A. 1.—*act.* चेपणें *n.* दाबणें *n.* &c. चेपणी *f.* चेपणूक *f.* दाबणी *f.* दाबणूक *f.* दडपणी *f.* दाचादाबी *f.* चेपाचेपी *f.*

Pressing and squeezing. चांपाचांप *or* पी *f.*

2 दपटणें *n.* दामटणें *n.* &c. ताण *m.* घायकूत *f.* निकड *f.* आग्रह *m.* गळचिपी *f.*

5 भार *m.* नेट *m.* जोर *m.* ओझें *n.* ताण *m.* दबडगा *or* घा *m.*

Press of business, cares, &c. कामाचा-&c. कचका *m.*-रगडा *m.*-रगाडा *m.*-रट्टा *m.*-रबडगा*m.*-रामरगडा*m.*-आर *f.*-राडा*m.*

7 आग्रह *m.* गळचिपी *f.*

v. V. N. 2. दाटी *f.* गर्दी *f.* खेटणी *f.* खेटाखेट *f.* खेटा *m.* खेटण *f.* दबडगा *or* घा *m.* रगडा *m.* रगाडा *m.* नेट *m.* कच *f.* चिडमोड *f.* चिडचीड *f.* चिडिकामिडी *f.* चिडीमिडी *f.* कचमा *m.* झुड *f.* झुम *f.* [जिमा *m.*

I. *throng,* v. CROWD. चेप *m.* चेपारा *m.* रगडा *m.* गट्टा *m.* हा-

II. *instrument to press*—gener. चाप *m.* चापण्याचें-दाबण्याचें-&c. यंत्र *n.*

III. *sugar press.* चरक *m.*

IV. *printing press.* छापण्याचें यंत्र *n.* छाप *m.* प्रेस *m.* is commonly used by Maráṭhás conversant with our printing offices.

V. (for clothes, &c.) कपाट *n.*

PRESSED, *p.* v. V. A. 1. चेपलेला, दाबलेला, चापलेला, &c.

2 दपटलेला, दामटलेला, ताण दिल्हेला, &c.

4 अडचणींत पाडलेला, अडचणलेला, अवघडलेला.

6 गळीं बांधलेला, पाठीस लावलेला, आग्रहानें दिल्हेला, &c.

7 गळ घातलेला, गळा धरलेला. [लेला.

8 वेठीस धरलेला, बिगारीस धरलेला, बळजोरीनें चाकरीस ठेव-

Person p. वेठ्या, वेठकरी, बिगारी *or* बेगारी, धरबिगारी, धरवेठ्या ;—keeping up of p. persons for conveyance of burdens, हाजीर बिगार *f.* हाजीरवेठ *f.*—Person kept up in readiness, हाजीरबिगारी, हाजीरवेठ्या.—Burden conveyed by p. person, बिगार *or* बेगार *f.* वेठ *f.* पेंड *m.*

PRESSER, *n.* PRESSING, *p.* v. V. A. 1. चेपणारा, दाबणारा, चापणारा, &c.

2 दपटणारा, दामटणारा, ताण देणारा, गळ घालणारा, गळचिपी लावणारा, &c. गळा धरणारा-धरलेला, बोकांडीस बसणारा-बसलेला, &c.

4 अडचणींत आणणारा-पाडणारा, &c.

5 *and* URGENT. भार घालणारा, निकडीचा, जरूरीचा, तांतडीचा, नेटाचा, नेटबाजीचा, घाईचा, उरावर बसलेला, मानेस बसलेला, बोकांडीवरचा, गळ्यावरचा.

7 आग्रह करणारा-धरणारा, खपाटीस-&c. बसणारा-बसलेला, गळा धरणारा-धरलेला, &c. [णारा.

8 वेठीस धरणारा, बिगारीस धरणारा, बळजोरीनें चाकरीस ठेव-

PRESTIGE. *n.* See CHARM. 2 *influence from past success.* छाप*f.*

PRESTO. See QUICKLY. [चा,&c.

PRESUMABLE, *a* v. V. A. प्रमाणावांचून घ्यायाचा-ग्रहणकराया-

To PRESUME, *v. a. take or suppose to be true without proof, examination, &c.* प्रमाणावांचून-चौकशीवांचून-&c.घेणें-समजणें-जाणणें-मानणें-ग्रहण करणें, कल्पिणें, कल्पना *f.*-अनुमान *n.*-तर्क *m.*-&c. करणें *g. of o.* सिद्धवत् घेणें-जाणणें-मानणें, अनुमानग्रहण *n.* करणें.

To PRESUME, *v. n. venture without leave, make bold.* अगळीक *f.*-अगळीक *f.*-अगळीत *f.*-धिटाई *f.*-धार्ष्ट्य *n.*-साहस *n.*-अति-

क्रम m. अतिक्रमण n.-निर्भिडपणा m.-&c. करणें-करून वागणें, धीट-निर्भिड-&c. असणें-असून चालणें-बोलणें-करणें-&c. अतिक्रमवर्त्तन n.-अतिक्रमाचार m.-&c.करणें.

2 *have arrogant and vainglorious notions.* अभिमानm.-अहंकार m.-अहंकृति f.-&c. धरणें-बाळगणें, आढ्यता f.-शेखी f.-तोरा m.-&c. बाळगणें-करणें-मिरवणें.

3 *indulge unreasonable confidence.* पोकळअवसान n.-पोकळ उमेद f.-रितें अवसान n.-&c. धरणें-करणें.

PRESUMER, *n.* PRESUMING, *p. a.* v. V. A. प्रमाणावांचून घेणारा, सिद्धवत् घेणारा, &c.

v. V. N. 1. अगळीक करणारा, अतिक्रम करणारा, धिटाई करणारा, आगळिक्या, धीट, धारिष्ट, निर्भीड, अतिक्रमाचारी, अतिक्रमकर्त्ता, अतिक्रमवर्त्ती, अतिवर्त्ती, अत्याचारी.

2 अभिमान धरणारा-बाळगणारा, आढ्यता बाळगणारा.

3 पोकळ अवसान धरणारा, नस्ती उमेद धरणारा, शुष्काभिमानी.

PRESUMPTION, *n.* v. V. A.—*act.* प्रमाणावांचून घेणें n. सिद्धवत् घेणें n. &c. अटकळ f. अनुमान n. तर्क m. अनुमिति f. कल्पना f. अनुमानग्रहण n.

v. V. N. 1. अगळीक f. अगळी f. अगळीत f. धिटाई f. धाष्टर्य n. अतिक्रम m. अतिक्रमण n. अतिक्रमवर्त्तन n. अतिक्रमाचार m. अतिवर्त्तन n. अत्याचार m. [मान m.

2 *and* PRIDE. अभिमान m. अहंकार m. अहंकृति f. अत्यभि-

3 शुष्काभिमान m. शुष्काहंकार m. रितें अवसान n. नस्ती उमेद f. पोकळ अवसान n. पोकळ उमेद f. अमर्यादावसान n.

I. *strong probability.* संभावना f. संभव m.

Ground for p. मुद्दा m.

PRESUMPTIVE, *a. taken by previous supposition, grounded on probability.* अटकळीचा, अनुमानाचा, तर्काचा, आनुमानिक, अनुमानाश्रयी, तर्काश्रयी, अनुमानाधार, तर्काधार, अनुमानावलंबी, तर्कावलंबी. [नाधिकारी.

Presumptive heir. संभावितस्थानाधिकारी, सप्रतिबंधस्था-

2 See PRESUMPTUOUS.

PRESUMPTUOUS, *a. over venturesome, rashly bold, &c.* अचाटबुद्धीचा, अचाटबुद्धि खेळवणारा, साहसबुद्धि, साहसिक, हाडकपाळी, सिद्धिसंभवातिवर्ती, सिद्धिसंभवातिक्रमी, सिद्धिसंभवातिचारी.

2 *arrogant, assuming,* v. PROUD. अभिमानी, अहंकारी, मगरूर, अभिमानाचा, दिमाखाचा.

3 *founded on presumption.* अभिमानाचा, अत्यभिमानाचा,शुष्काभिमानाचा, अभिमानमूलक, पोकळ उमेदीचा, पोकळ अवसानाचा, &c.

4 *wilful, done in defiance of conscience.* दाटबळाचा, दाटून-हटकून-दाटबळें-&c. केलेला.

PRESUMPTUOUSLY, *adv.* v. A. 1. अचाटबुद्धीनें, साहसबुद्धीनें, उलेढालेपणानें, &c. सिद्धिसंभवातिक्रमण करून, सिद्धिसंभवातिक्रमपूर्वक, &c. [कारपूर्वक.

2 अभिमानानें, अहंकारानें, मगरुरीनें, &c. अभिमानपूर्वक, अहं-

3 पोकळ उमेदीनें, नस्ते उमेदीनें, नस्त्या अभिमानानें, रिकाम्या अवसानानें, &c.

4 दाटबळें, हटकून, दाटून, जाणूनबुजून, बुद्धिपुरस्सर, बुद्धिपूर्वक, मुद्दाम, तात्पुरचा *decl.*

PRESUMPTUOUSNESS, *n.* v. A. 1. *and* PRESUMPTION. अचाटबुद्धि f. साहसबुद्धि f. धिटाई f. धाष्टर्य n. अतिक्रमाचारिता f. अत्याचारिता f.

2 अभिमान m. अहंकार m. मगरूरी f. अभिमानिता f. अहंकारिता f.

3 अत्यभिमान m. शुष्काभिमान m. नस्ता अभिमान m. पोकळ उमेद f. पोकळअवसान n. शुष्कावसान n.

PRESUPPOSAL, PRESUPPOSITION, *n.* v. V.—*act.* पूर्वकल्पना f. पूर्वग्रहण n. पूर्वभावना f.

To PRESUPPOSE, *v. a. suppose as previous, imply as antecedent.* पूर्वी-&c. कल्पिणें-धरणें-घेणें-&c. पूर्वकल्पना f.-पूर्वभावना f.-पूर्वग्रहण n.-&c. करणें *g. of o.* [त, पूर्वगृहीत.

PRESUPPOSED, *p.* v. V. पूर्वी कल्पिलेला, &c. पूर्वकल्पित, पूर्वभावि-

PRETENCE, *n. show of, sham, feint.* सोंग n. ढोंग n. कोंग or कोंघ n. गतक n. मिष *pop.* मीस n. पोम n. हिल्ला m. दाखवणूक f. हुलकावणी f. हूल f. छल m. अपदेश m. व्याज n.

2 *false plea, pretext.* निमित्त n. बहाणा m. मिष *pop.* मीस n. छद्म n. अपदेश m. व्याज m.

For a p. निमित्तास.

To lay hold of or take a p. निमित्त n. घेणें n.

To watch or wait for a p. निमित्तास टेंकणें.

3 *claim.* दावा m. हक्क m. सत्ता f. अधिकार m.

To PRETEND, *v. a. show hypocritically, sham, feign.* सोंग n.-कोंग n.-ढोंग n.-मीस n.-गतक n.-बहाणा m.-&c. घेणें-करणें-दाखवणें *g. of o.* हूल f.-हुलकावणी f.-दाखवणूक f. दाखवणें *g. of o.* डौल m.-आव m.-&c. करणें-घालणें-मारणें *g. of o.*

2 *allege falsely, hypocritically, &c.* निमित्त n.-बहाणा m.-मीस n.-&c. सांगणें-करणें-घेणें *g. of o.*

3 (to;) *lay claim to, profess to have.* बाणा m.-अड्डा m.-अभिमान m.-अहंकार m.-अहंपणा m.-अहंता f.-मीपणा m.-&c. बाळगणें-धरणें *g. of o.* बिरुद *pop.* बिरीद n.-चंग m.-कंकण n.-चवर n. बांधणें *g. of o.*

To PRETEND, *v. n. hold out an appearance of, make as if.* सोंग n.-ढोंग n.-&c. करणें-घेणें-दाखवणें, डौल m.-&c. दाखवणें-करणें.

2 *profess, lay a claim to.* बाणा m.-चंग m.-बिरुद *pop.* बिरीद n.-&c. बांधणें, अड्डा m.-अभिमान m.-&c. बाळगणें-धरणें.

PRETENDED, *p.* v. V. A. 1. ढोंगानें केलेला, &c. ढोंगाचा, सोंगाचा, मिसाचा, बतावणीचा, हुलकावणीचा, बनावाचा, &c. बरकरणी, बरघडीचा, बरपंकाचा, बरपंकी, बाहेरचा, बाह्यात्काराचा, लुटुफुटूचा, लुटुबुटूचा. [व्याजाचा.

2 निमित्तानें सांगितलेला, &c. निमित्ताचा, बहाण्याचा, मिसाचा,

PRETENDER, *n.* PRETENDING, *p. a.* v. V. A. 1. & V. N. 1. सोंग घेणारा, ढोंग करणारा, गतकघेणारा, &c. कोंगी, कोंग्या, ढोंगी, मिसखोर, डौलदाखवणारा.

2 निमित्त सांगणारा, बहाणा सांगणारा-करणारा, &c.

3 *and* v. N. 2. बाणा बांधणारा, चंग बांधणारा, बिरीद बांधणारा, अड्डाबाळगणारा, अभिमान बाळगणारा-धरणारा, अभिमानी, अड्डेबाज, अड्डेवाईक, बिरदी.

Empty p. to great knowledge. सोमाजी सकळकळ्या.

P. to a throne. तोतया m.

PRETENSION, *n. claim.* दावा m. इलाखा m. स्वामित्वबाद m. स्वत्ववाद m. स्वार्थवाद m.

To set up p. to (skill, ability, &c.). बिरीद n.-चंग m. -कंकण n.-&c. बांधणें *g. of o.* बाणा m.-अभिमान m.-अड्डा m. बाळगणें. [बाढविणें.

To set up grand pretensions. प्रस्थ n.-पोम n. माजविणें-

That sets up p. to. अड्डेबाज, अड्डेवाईक.

PRETERIMPERFECT, *a.*—in grammar. अपूर्णभूत.

PRETERIT, *a.*—in grammar. भूत.

PRETERMISSION, *n.* v. V. गाळणें *n.* सोडणें *n.* वगळणें *n.* &c. गाळणी *f.* गाळणूक *f.* वगळणी *f.* वगळणूक *f.* सांड *f.* [सांडणें.

To PRETERMIT, *v. a. omit,* v. To PASS. सोडणें, गाळणें, वगळणें,

PRETERMITTED, *p.* v. V. सोडलेला, गाळलेला, वगळलेला.

PRETERNATURAL, *a. unnatural, beyond nature.* स्वभावनियमाचेबाहेरचा, स्वभावनियमबाह्य, प्रकृतिनियमबाह्य, प्रकृतिक्रमबाह्य, निसर्गनियमबाह्य, निसर्गक्रमबाह्य, विलक्षण, अद्भुत.

PRETERNATURALLY, *adv.* v. A. स्वभावनियम-प्रकृतिनियम-&c. सोडून, विलक्षण, अद्भुत.

PRETERPERFECT, *a.*—in grammar. पूर्णभूत.

PRETERPLUPERFECT, *a.*—in grammar. प्राक्पूर्णभूत.

PRETEXT. See PRETENCE.

PRETTILY, *adv.* v. A. चांगला *decl.* सुंदर, शोभेसा *decl.* सुंदर-सुरेख-&c. वाटेसा *decl.*-दिसेसा *decl.*

PRETTINESS, *n.* v. A. सुंदरपणा *m.* सुरेखपणा *m.* साजरेपणा *m.* &c. सुरेखाई *f.* सुरेखी *f.* खुबसुरती *f.* खुबी *f.* छब *f.* छबी *f.* खुमास *f.* खुमारी *f.*

PRETTY, *a. handsome, neat, pleasing, &c.* सुंदर, चांगला, खुबसुरत, सुरूप, सुरेख, साजरा, सुबक, गोजरा *or* गोजिरा, गोजिरवाणा, छानदार, छबीला *or* छबेला, छबडा, नेटका, नीटनेटका, सासुरत, सुतरा, खासा, देखणा, दर्शनी, दृष्टिमरू, माकुला, माकुलवाणा, माणकुला.

Little and p. चिमकुला, चिमका, चिमणा.

PRETTY, *adv. in some degree, moderately, &c.* v. So so. बरा *decl.* बरासा *decl.* कांहींसा *decl.* सुमाराचा *decl.*

To PREVAIL, *v. n. be in force, have influence.* चालणें, चाल *f.*-चलती *f.*-चलचल *f.*-प्रवृत्ति *f.*-प्रसिद्धि *f.*-प्रचार*m.*-प्रघात*m.*-पसारा *m.*-परिपाठ*m.*-&c. असणें *g. of s.* चालू-चालता-&c. असणें, वर्त्तणें.

2 *overcome, gain superiority or advantage.* जय*m.* पावणें, जय*m.* होणें *g. of s.* जबर-शेर-प्रबल-सबल-&c. होणें-असणें, चालणें *with g. of s.* (as, आमचें चाललें &c.) प्राबल्य*n.*-प्राधान्य *n.*-वर्चस्व*n.*-&c. पावणें *and, with g. of s.* होणें-असणें, जोर*m.*-बळ*n.*-&c. चालणें *g. of s. with* वर.

3 *operate effectually, make or take effect.* लागू होणें, साधणें, सफल होणें, गुण*m.* करणें, कारागिरी *f.* करणें, कारागीर होणें, गुण*m.*-फळ*n.*-&c. होणें *g. of s. or with* पासून.

4 (with, upon, &c.) *persuade,* v. To INDUCE. मनावणें, वळवणें, बधवणें, *or* मनावून-वळवून-&c. घेणें, प्रवृत्त करणें.

PREVAILER, *n.* PREVAILING, *p. a.* PREVALENT, *a.* v.V. 1. चालता, चालू, चलतीचा, चलचलीचा, प्रचारांतला, प्रवृत्तीचा, &c. प्रसिद्ध, प्रवृत्त, वर्त्तमान. [कटीचा.

2 जयपावणारा, &c. जबर, शेर, प्रबल, सबल, प्रधान, जोराचा, बळ-

3 लागू होणारा, साधणारा, &c. लागू, गुणकारी, गुणकारक, सफल, साधक, कारागीर *or* कारिगर.

PREVALENCE, PREVAILING, *n.* v. V. 1.—*state.* चलती *f.* चाल*f.* चलचल *f.* (*intens.* चलचलाट*m.*) चालचलाव*f.* ज्यारी *f.* प्रसिद्धि *f.* प्रवृत्ति *f.* पसारा*m.* व्याप्ति*f.* प्रचार*m.* प्रघात*m.* परिपाठ*m.* पाठ*m.*

2 वर्चस्व*n.* वर्चस*n.* वर्चस्विता *f.* प्राबल्य*n.* प्रबलता *f.* प्राधान्य*n.* जोर*m.* जबरपणा*m.* शेरपणा*m.* बळ*n.* आधिक्य*n.*

3 गुणकारिता *f.* साधकता *f.* कार्यसाधकता *f.* कारागिरी *f.*

To PREVARICATE, *v. n. quibble, shuffle in speech.* होय नाहीं*n.*-इधरतिधर*n.*-अकडंतिकडं*n.* करणें, बोलणें*n.*-शब्द*m.*-वचन*n.*-&c. फिरवणें-बदलणें, दोनबोलणी*n. pl.* बोलणें, बदलून-पालटून-धरून सोडून-&c. बोलणें, दोनजिभा *f. pl.* करणें, बाबंघा *f. pl.* फोडणें-घेणें, पर्याय*m.* फोडणें-सांगणें, बदलामीवर येणें, उपेट *f.* मारणें.

PREVARICATION, *n.* v. V. बोलणें फिरवणें*n.* &c. इधरतिधर*n.* अकडंतिकडं*n.* होय नाहीं*n.* दुतोंडीं बोलणें*n.* धरसोड *f.* चलविचल *f.* वाक्छल*n.* अर्थवैकल्य*n.* हीनवाद*m.* अन्यवचन*n.*

PREVARICATING, *p. a.* PREVARICATOR, *n.* v. V. बोलणें फिरवणारा, बदलून बोलणारा, &c. दोनजिभ्या, दुतोंडी, दुबोल्या, द्विजिह्व, अन्यवादी, हीनवादी.

To PREVENT, *v. a. obstruct, stop, turn off, &c.* v. To HINDER. निवारणें, वारणें, अडवणें, रोधणें, आड येणें, बाधणें, निवारण*n.*-&c. करणें *g. of o.* मोडती *f.*-मोडा*m.*-&c. घालणें, होऊं-येऊं-&c. नदेणें.

2 *go before.* पुढें-मोहरें-&c. जाणें *g. of o.* पुरोगमन*n.*-अग्रगमन *n.*-&c.करणें *g. of o.*

3 *anticipate.* आघाडी *f.*-अवली *f.* मारणें-साधणें-ठोकणें.

PREVENTABLE, *a.* v. V. 1. वारायाजोगा-जोगता-&c. निवारायाजोगा-जोगता-&c. निवारण करायाजोगा-जोगता-&c.

PREVENTED, *p.* v. V. 1. वारलेला, निवारलेला, अडवलेला, &c निवारित, वारित.

PREVENTER, *n.* PREVENTING, *p. a.* PREVENTIVE, *a.* v. V. 1. वारणारा, निवारणारा, अडवणारा, &c. निवारक, वारक, निवारणवारण कर्त्ता-कारी, रोधक, बाधक, प्रतिबंधक.

PREVENTION, *n.* v. V. 1.—*act.* निवारणें *n.* वारणें *n.* रोधणें *n.* &c. निवारण *n.* वारण *n.* प्रतिबंध *m.* रोध *m.*

2 पुढें जाणें *n.* &c. पुरोगमन *n.* अग्रगमन *n.*

PREVENTIVE, *n. that which prevents.* वारण *n.* निवारण *n.* निवारक-&c. पदार्थ *m.*-विषय *m.*-&c.

PREVIOUS, *a. going, happening, &c. before,* v. ANTECEDENT. अगोदरचा, पूर्वींचा, आगला, पूर्व.

PREVIOUSLY, *adv.* v. A. अगोदर, पूर्वीं, पहिल्यानें, पूर्व in comp.

PREY, *n. spoil, plunder.* लूट *f.*

2 *that which is seized for food.* शिकार *f.* पारध *f.* भक्ष्य *n.*

Beast of p. पशूपजीवी-पशुभक्षक-&c. प्राणी, हिंस्र-घातुक प्राणी.

To PREY, (on) *v. a. seize and devour.* शिकार *f.*-पारध *f.* करणें, आहार *m.*-भक्ष्य *n.*-&c. असणें *g. of o.*

2 (on) *corrode, cause to waste or pine.* खाणें, जाळणें, खणणें, धुपविणें, झुरविणें, शुष्क-क्षीण-&c. करणें.

3 (on; upon). See To PLUNDER.

PRICE, *n. value set or paid.* मोल *n.* किम्मत *f.* दाम *m.* मूल्य *n.* अर्घ *m.* पैसा *m.* पैका *m.* The *price* or *cost* of a work is generally expressed by words formed with the affixes आवळ and आई, as लिहिणावळ p. of writing, दळणावळ p. of pounding, राखणावळ p. of watching, शिवणावळ & शिलाई p. of sewing, &c.

To ask a high p. महाग सांगणें. [पाड *m.* धारा *m.*

2 *current value or rate.* दर *m.* भाव *m.* धारण *f.* निरख *m.*

To rise in p. मोलावणें, दर *m.* येणें.

To raise in p. मोलाविणें.

3 *estimation, value, worth.* किम्मत *f.* मोल *n.* पाड *m. with neg. con.* योग्यता *f.*

To PRICE, *v. a. set a price on.* मोल *n.*-किम्मत *f.*-&c. बसवणें-

ठरवणें-ठेवणें, मोलाविणें.

PRICE-CURRENT, *n.* निरखाची-बाजारभावाची-&c. याद *f.*

PRICED, *p.* v. V. मोल ठरवलेला, &c. मोलाचा.
  High-p. मोठ्या मोलाचा, मोठ्या दराचा, &c.
  Low-p. हलक्या-लहान-&c. मोलाचा-किमतीचा-दराचा-&c.

PRICELESS, *a.* v. INVALUABLE. अमोलिक.
  2 See WORTHLESS.

To PRICK, *v. a. puncture,* v. To PIERCE. टोंचणें, बोंचणें, टोंचळणें, डेंचणें *or* डबंचणें, टोंचणी *f.*-बोंचणी *f.*-&c. करणें, टोंच *n.*-टोंचा *m.*-टोंची *f.* पाडणें. [रोंसणें.
  2 (the ears). उभा &c. करणें, उभारणें, टोंकारणें, थुरथुरवणें,
  3 *pain by puncture.* खुपणें, टोंचणें, सलणें.
  4 (on &c.). *goad, spur,* v. To INCITE. टोंचणें, टोंचणी *f.* देणें-लावणें, डेंचणें, डबंचणें, आर *f.* लावणें-टोंचणें, चिग्या *f. pl.* लावणें.
  5 *affect with pain, sting with remorse.* टोंचणें, खोंचणें, खोंचरणें, खुपणें, सलणें, डांचणें, खाणें, चुरचुरणें, चुरचूर *f.*-चुणचूण *f.*-&c. लागणें *in. con. & g. of s.* झोंचणें. [करणें.
  6 *designate by a mark or puncture.* टिंच *n.* देणें, खूण *f.*

PRICK, *n. instrument to puncture or prick with.* टोंचणी *f.* कांटा *m.* आर *f.* [चुबक *f.*
  2 *puncture.* टोंच *n.* टोंचा *m. dim.* टोंची *f.* बोंच *n.* टचका *m.*
  The pain or sense of a p. खुप *f. m.* खुपरी *f.*
  3 fig. *pang of remorse.* चुरचूर *f.* चुणचूण *f.* खरखर *f.* हळहळ *f.*

PRICKED, *p.* v. V. 1. टोंचलेला, टोंचलेला, डेंचलेला, &c.
  4 टोंचलेला, आर लावलेला, &c.
  5 टोंचलेला, खोंचलेला, खुपलेला, डांचलेला, चुरचूर लागलेला, &c.
  6 टिंब दिल्हेला, &c.

PRICKER, *n.* PRICKING, *p. a.* v. V. 1. टोंचणारा, बोंचणारा, &c.
  3 खुपणारा, सलणारा.
  4 टोंचणारा, डेंचणारा, टोंचणी लावणारा, &c.
  5 टोंचणारा, खोंचणारा, खुपणारा, सलणारा, &c.
  I. *instrument to prick with.* टोंचणी *f.* आर *f.* कांटा *m.*

PRICKING, *n. sensation of being pricked.* चिणचीण *f.*
  P. of the eyes in ophthalmia. खुपरी *f.*
  2 *tingling sensation of a limb asleep.* मुंगी *f.*

PRICKLY, *n. small pointed shoot.* कांटा *m.* सालीचा कांटा *m.* कंटक *m.* त्वक्कंटक *m.*

PRICKLY, *a. full of prickles.* कांटेरा, कांटेरी, सकंटक.

PRICKLY HEAT, *n.* घायमोळें *n.*

PRIDE, *n. self esteem, conceit, loftiness, haughtiness, &c.* गर्व *m.* अभिमान *m.* अहंकार *m.* अहंकृति *f.* दर्प *m.* मीपणा *m.* मगरूरी *f.* माज *m.* माजुरीपणा *m.* मस्ती *f.* मस्तवाली *f.* बदमस्ती *f.* मद *m.* उन्माद *m.* उन्मत्तता *f.* दिमाख *m.* दिमाखदारी *f.* पतरास *f.* अकड *f.* तोरा *m.* तोरेदारी *f.* तऊर *m.* मान *m.* अहम्मान *m.* अहम्मति *f.* आत्माभिमान *m.* आढ्यता *f.* दम *m.* दंभ *m.* ताटा *m.* इशीम *f.* खट्टा *m.*
  2 *generous elation, noble self-esteem.* अभिमान *m.* स्वाभिमान *m.* गुणाभिमान *m.* इशीम *f.*
  3 *sexual excitement,* v. HEAT. माज *m.* उधान *n.*

To PRIDE, *v. a.* (one's self) *take pride in, plume one's self on.* अभिमान *m.*-अकड *f.*-अड्डा *m.*-&c. बाळगणें-धरणें *g. of o.* बाणा *m.*-बीर *m.* बाळगणें *g. of o.* शेखी *f.*-आढ्यता *f.*-तोरा *m.*-प्रतिष्ठा *f.*-&c. मिरवणें-भोगणें *g. of o.*

PRIEST, *n. officiator in sacred offices.* पुजारा, पुजारी, याज्ञिक, याज्ञिक्या, याजक, उपाध्याय *pop.* उपाध्या, पुरोहित, भट, आचार्य.
  P. of Shiva. गुरव.
  Family p. पुरोहित, उपाध्याय *pop.* उपाध्या.

PRIEST-CRAFT, *n. frauds, artifices, and impositions, &c. of priests.* उपाध्याचे-भटाचे &c. खेळम. *pl.*-डावपेच *m. pl.* उपाध्याच केनव *n.* उपाध्यायकापट्य *n.* उपाध्यायछल *n.*

PRIEST-ESS, *n.* पुजारीण *f.* भक्तीण *or* भगतीण *f.* उपाध्याया *f.*

PRIEST-HOOD, *n. office, &c. of a priest.* याज्ञिकी *f.* उपाधीक *n.* उपाध्यपण *n.* पौरोहित्य *n.*
  2 *order of priests.* उपाध्येमंडळी *f.* याज्ञिकसमूह *m.* याज्ञिकगण *m.*

PRIESTLY, *a. pertaining, &c. to a priest.* याज्ञिकी, याज्ञिकाचा, पुजाऱ्याचा, &c. याज्ञिकसंबंधी-विषयक, याजकसंबंधी-विषयक.
  2 *becoming, &c. a priest.* याज्ञिकास-उपाध्यास-भटास-&c. योग्य-लायक-उचित-&c. याज्ञिकोचित, याज्ञिकार्ह.

PRIEST-RIDDEN, *a. governed by priests.* भटांनी-&c. चालवलेला, उपाध्यायांकित, उपाध्यायाधीन, उपाध्यायवश, &c. भट्टाधीन, भट्टांकित.

PRIM, *a. formal, precise, finical, &c.* टापटिप्या, टाकठिक्या, टाकसठिकस *or* ठिकसटाकस, बेतबात्या, चोखनळ. [&c.

PRIMACY, PRIMATESHIP, *n.* प्रधानोपाध्यायाची जागा *f.*-पदवी *f.*-

PRIMARILY, *adv.* v. A. 1. पहिला *decl.* प्रथम, मुळीं, प्रारंभीं, आदि, अवल.
  2 मुख्यत्वेंकरून, प्राधान्येंकरून, प्रधानतः.

PRIMARINESS, *n.* v. A. 2. मुख्यत्व *n.* प्रधानता *f.* प्राधान्य *n.*

PRIMARY, *a. first,* v. ORIGINAL. पहिला, मूळचा, प्रथमचा, प्रथम, प्राथमिक, आदि, आद्य, अवल.
  P. cause. आदिकारण *n.* आद्यबीज *n.*
  2 *first in dignity or importance,* v. CHIEF. मुख्य, प्रधान.
  3 See ELEMENTAL, RUDIMENTAL.

PRIMATE, *n. chief ecclesiastic.* प्रधानोपाध्याय, मुख्योपाध्याय.

PRIME, *a. first,* v. ORIGINAL. पहिला, मूळचा, असल.
  P. cost. मूळची किम्मत *f.* मोकार *n.*
  At p. cost. मोकार.
  2 *first in rank, &c.* v. CHIEF. पहिला, मुख्य, प्रधान, अवल.
  P. Minister, v. PREMIER. मुख्यप्रधान.
  3 *first in excellence,* v. FINE. उत्तम, पहिलेप्रतीचा, अवल, असल, असलाईचा, खासा, शेलका, इरसाल, बावनकशी, उमदा, उत्कृष्ट, सर्वोत्कृष्ट, नगद, नगदा नगदी.

PRIME, *n.* v. DAWN. पहाट *f.* प्रातःकाल *m.*
  2 *best part.* तत्तामाल *m.* उत्तमांश *m.* नगद *n.*
  3 *highest or best state, heyday, zenith, fullness, &c.* v. HEIGHT. भर *m.* बहर *or* बहार *m.* ऐन (in comp. as, ऐन जवानी *f.* p. of youth), भर (in comp. as, भरजवानी *f.*).
  To reach one's p. रसांत-पणांत-उमेदींत-उमतींत-&c. येणें.
  4 See SPRING.

To PRIME, *v. a.* (a musket) रंजक *f.* भरणें-पाजणें, काना *m.* भरणें.
  2 fig. *give a cue.* बार *m.* देणें-ठासणें-भरणें.

PRIMED, *p.* v. V. 1. रंजक भरलेला-पाजलेला, काना भरलेला.

PRIMELY, *adv.* v. A. 1. पहिला *decl.* मुळीं.
  3 उत्तम, उत्कृष्ट, खासा *decl.*

PRIMENESS, *n.* v. A. 3. *and* EXCELLENCE. अवलपणा *m.* अस-

लाई *f.* उत्कृष्टपणा *m.* इरसालपणा *m.* उत्तमता *f.* उत्कृष्टता *f.*

PRIMER, *n. first book for children.* वर्णमाळेची पोथी *f.* लेंकरांचें पहिलें पुस्तक *n.* पहिलीपोथी *f.*

PRIMEVAL, PRIMEVOUS, *a. primitive.* v. ORIGINAL. पहिला, प्रथमचा, मूळचा.

PRIMING, *n. powder in the pan of a gun.* रंजक *f.* रंजकीचीदारू *f.*
Match for firing the p. रंजकीची बिडी. [नी *f.*
Flask or horn for priming powder, रंजकदान *n.* रंजकदा-

PRIMITIVE, *a. pertaining to the beginning, first, &c.* v. ORIGINAL. पहिला, प्रथमचा, मूळचा, प्राथमिक, अवल, पहिले काळचा, आद्यकालिक, प्रथमकालिक.
2 *not derived, primary, radical,*—word, &c. मूळचा, मूलिक, मौल, अव्युत्पन्न, असाधित, सिद्ध.
3 *following the ancient practice or rule.* पहिले चालीचा, पहिले काळचे चालीचा, आद्यकालानुयायी, प्रथमकालानुयायी.

PRIMITIVELY, v. A. 1. पहिला *decl.* प्रथम, मुळीं.
3 पहिले चालीनें, पहिले चालीप्रमाणें, आद्यकालानुसार, आद्यकालानुरूप.

PRIMITIVENESS, v. A. 1. अवलपणा *m.* प्राथमिकत्व *n.* आद्यकालिकत्व *n.*
3 पहिली चाल *f.* आद्यकालानुयायिता *f.* आद्यकालानुसारिता *f.*

PRIMNESS, *n.* v. A. ठाकठिकेपणा *m.* ठाकसठिकसपणा *m.* &c. चाकचोपी *f.* चापचोपी *f.*

PRIMOGENITOR, *n. first father or forefather.* आद्यपुरुष, मूळपुरुष, आद्यजनक, आदिपिता.

PRIMOGENITURE, *n. state of being firstborn; seniority.* वडीलपणा *m.* ज्येष्ठपणा *m.* ज्येष्ठत्व *n.* ज्यैष्ठ्य *n.* अग्रजत्व *n.* आदिजत्व *n.* आदिजातत्व *n.*

PRIMORDIAL, PRIMORDIATE, *a. first in order, existing from the beginning,* v. ORIGINAL. पहिल्यापासूनचा, मूळचा, असल, अवल, आद्यकालिक, पाक्कालिक, मौलिक, मौल.

PRIMROSE, *n.* एक फूल आहे. [नृपति.

PRINCE, *n. ruler, sovereign,* v. KING. राजा, छत्रपति, भूपाल,
2 *subordinate sovereign.* मांडलिक राजा, देशपति.
3 *son of a king.* राजकुमार, राजकुवर, राजपुत्र, राजतनय, राजसुत, युवराज, नृपपुत्र, भूपपुत्र.

PRINCE-DOM. See KINGDOM.

PRINCE-LIKE, PRINCELY, *a. resembling a prince, royal, stately, dignified, &c.* राजकीय, नृपजातीय, भूपजातीय, नृपसदृश, नृपवत्, प्रतापशाली, प्रभावशाली, वैभवशाली.
2 *of the rank of princes.* राजकीय, नृपजातीचा, छत्रपतीचे कुळीचा, नृपजातीय, भूपजातीय, छत्रपतिकुलज.
3 *becoming a prince, royal, grand, magnificent.* राजास योग्य, राजयोग्य, राजार्ह, राजकीय, राजोपचाराचा, राजोपचारिक, राजोपयुक्त.

PRINCE'S METAL, *n.* कांसें *n.* कांस्य *n.* रिरी *f.* रीति *f.* [हिषी *f.*

PRINCESS, *n. female sovereign,* v. QUEEN. राणी *f.* राज्ञी *f.* म-
2 *daughter of a king.* राजकुमारी *f.* राजकुमरी *f.* राजकुंवरी *f.* राजकन्या *f.* राजसुता *f.* राजपुत्री *f.* राजपुत्रिका *f.*

PRINCIPAL, *a. highest in rank or importance,* v. CHIEF. मुख्य, प्रधान, श्रेष्ठ.

PRINCIPAL, *n.* v. CHIEF, CONDUCTOR. मुख्य, सरदार, नायक.
2 *capital sum.* मुद्दल *n.* मूळ *n.* मूलद्रव्य *n.* मूलधन *n.* ऐनरुपये *m. pl.* ऐनधन *n.*

PRINCIPALITY, *n. country of a prince.* मांडलिकराज्य *n.* मांडलिकराष्ट्र *n.*
2 See POWER, AUTHORITY.

PRINCIPALLY, *adv.* v A. मुख्यत्वेंकरून, प्राधान्येंकरून, विशेषेंकरून, बहुतकरून, मुख्यशः, प्राधान्यतः.

PRINCIPLE, *n. constituent part, element.* तत्व *n.* मूलतत्व *n.* धातु *m.* द्रव्य *n.* मूलद्रव्य *n.* कारण *n.*
2 *cause, origin.* कारण *n.* बीज *n.* मूल *n.* प्रयोजन *n.* हेतु *m.*
3 *fundamental truth, element, first point.* तत्व *n.* मूल *or* मूळ *n.* मूलतत्व *n.* बीज *n.* पग *n.* परिभाषा *f.* मूळपीठिका *f.* सूत्र *n.* मूलसूत्र *n.*
4 *rule, law, general truth, &c. of science or morals.* न्याय *m.* नियम *m.* सूत्र *n.* मूलसूत्र *n.* उत्सर्ग *m.*
5 *foundation of action, motive,* v. GROUND. मूल *or* मूळ *n.* आधार *m.* हेतु *m.* प्रमाण *n.*
6 (of human nature) *property, natural propensity, &c.* धर्म *m.* गुण *m.* स्वभाव *m.* भाव *m.*

To PRINK, *v. n. dress for show,* v. To ADONIZE. चट्टीपट्टी *f.*-टाकमटिका *m.*-टाकमटिका *m.*-टिलाटोपी *f.*-&c. करणें.

To PRINT, *v. a. impress with a mark ; stamp.* छापणें, छाप *m.*-ठसा *m.*-मुद्रा *f.*-&c. मारणें *with* वर *of o.*
2 *form by impression.* छापणें, ठसवणें, छाप *m.*-छापा *m.*-ठसा *m.*-&c. मारणें *g. of o.*

PRINT, *n. mark made by impression.* छाप *m.* छापा *m.* ठसा *m.* शिक्का *m.* मुद्रा *f.* मुद्रिका *f.*
2 *instrument for impressing a mark.* छाप *m.* ठसा *m.* शिक्का *m.* मोहर *f.* मुद्रा *f.* [*m.* अक्षरें *n. pl.*
3 *impression of types as to form, size, &c.* छाप *m.* ठसा
4 v. PICTURE. नकशा *m.* नकाशा *m.* चित्र *n.*
To be out of p. खेप *f.*-आवृत्ति *f.* सरणें-संपणें *g. of s.*

PRINTED, *p.* v. V. 1. 2. छापलेला, छाप मारलेला, &c. छापी, छापींव, छापील.

PRINTER, *n.* PRINTING, *p. a.* v. V. 1. 2. छापणारा, छाप-&c. मारणारा, छापारी *m.*

PRINTING, *n. typography.* पोथी-पुस्तक-ग्रंथ-&c. छापणें *n.*

PRINTING-INK, *n.* छापण्याची-छापण्याच्या उपयोगाची-&c. शाई *f.*

PRINTING-OFFICE, *n.* छापखाना *m.* [गद *m.*

PRINTING-PAPER, *n.* छापण्याचा-छापण्याच्या उपयोगाचा-&c. का-

PRINTING-PRESS, *n.* छाप *m.* छापण्याचें यंत्र *n.*

PRIOR, *a. going before, first,* v. ANTECEDENT. अगोदरचा, पूर्वीचा, पहिला, अगला, पूर्व, अग्र.

PRIOR, *n.* (of a convent). महंत, मठाधिपति, मठाधिकारी.

PRIORITY, *n.* v. A. अगलेपणा *m.* &c. आद्यता *f.* अग्रता *f.*
2 (in rank, &c.) *precedence.* अग्रमान्यता *f.* अग्रपूज्यता *f.* अग्रपूजा *f.* अग्रमान *m.*

PRIORY, *n.* मठ *m.*

PRISM, *n.*—the optical glass. त्रिपार्श्वकाच *m.*

PRISMATIC, *a. pertaining to a prism.* त्रिपार्श्वकाच संबंधी-विषयक.
2 *resembling a prism.* त्रिपार्श्वकाच सदृश, त्रिपार्श्वकाचाकार.
3 *separated by a prism.* त्रिपार्श्वकाच विकीर्ण.

PRISON, PRISON-HOUSE, *n.* v. JAIL. तुरुंग *m.* बंदिखाना *m.* बंदिशाळा *f.* कैदखाना *m.* कारागार *n.* कारागृह *n.*

To PRISON. See To IMPRISON.

PRISONER, *n. person in confinement.* कैदी, बंदिवान.
2 *one taken in war, captive.* पाडाव केलेला, युद्धधृत, युद्धगृहीत, युद्धदास. [मूळचा.
PRISTINE, *a. first, primitive,* v. ORIGINAL. पहिला, प्रथमचा,
PRIVACY, *n. state of retirement or secrecy.* एकांत *m.* एकांतवास *m.* विविक्तता *f.* विविक्तवास *m.* रह *m.* रहोभाव *m.* पडदा *m.* पडदपोशी *or* पडतपोशी *f.*
In p. and in public. एकांतीं लोकांतीं.
2 *place of retirement.* एकांत *m.* एकांताची जागा *f.* एकांताचें स्थळ *n.* रहःस्थान *n.* रहःस्थल *n.*
3 *concealment.* See SECRECY.
PRIVATE, *a. unconnected with others, peculiar to self,* v. PERSONAL, PECULIAR. खास, खासगत, खासगीचा, खुद, खुदनिसबतीचा, असाधारण.
P. property. खासगी *f.* खासगीचा माल *m.*-पैसा *m.*-&c.
2 *secluded, sequestered, secret.* एकांताचा, एकीकडचा, आडवळणी, आडवळणाचा, गैरराबत्याचा, नित्रस, एकांतवासाचा, विविक्त, चोर (in comp. as, चोरवाट, चोरखिडकी, &c.).
In p. एकांतीं, गुप्तपणें, पडद्यांत.
P. parts. See PRIVITY.
3 *done, &c. in private; not public, not open.* एकांतींचा, गुप्तपणाचा, गुप्त, पडद्यांतला, पडद्याचा, पडदपोशीचा.
In p. एकांतीं, पडद्यांत, गुप्तपणें.
4 *not holding public office, &c.* दरकाबेगळा-निराळा, बिनहुद्द्याचा, अनधिकारी, अधिकारानारूढ, अनधिकृत.
A p. person. सुखवस्तु *c.*
5 *not official, &c.* खासगत, खासगतनात्याचा, खासगीनात्याचा, खासगतसंबंधाचा, घरगुती, घरगुतीनात्याचा.
PRIVATE, *n. common soldier.* शिपाइ *or* सिपाई *m.* नुस्ताशिपाई *m.* प्यादा *m.* [खास, जातीनें.
PRIVATELY, *adv.* v. A. 1. *and* PERSONALLY. खुद, खुदजातीनें,
3 एकांतीं, गुप्तपणें, पडद्यांत.
5 खासगतनात्यानें, घरगुतीनात्यानें, &c.
PRIVATENESS. See PRIVACY. [राहित्य *n.*
PRIVATION, *n. negation, absence of,* v. NEGATION. अभाव *m.*
2 *deprivation or absence of what is necessary for comfort.* अन्नवस्त्राचे हाल *m. pl.* अन्नवस्त्राचा तोटा *m.* तहानभूक *f.* सुखसाधनलोप *m.*
To endure p.s. उपासतान *f.* काढणें.
PRIVATIVE, *a. causing privation.* हानिकारक.
2 *consisting in the absence of something,* v. NEGATIVE. अभावसूचक, अभावदर्शक, अभावात्मक.
PRIVATIVE, *n. that of which the essence is the absence of something.* अभाव *m.*
2—in grammar. नपद *n.* नञ्पद *n.*
PRIVILEGE, *n. particular right, benefit, exemption, &c.* हक्क *m.* अधिकार *m.* मान *m.* सत्ता *f.* असाधारणाधिकार *m.* विशेषाधिकार *m.*
To PRIVILEGE, *v. a. grant a privilege to.* हक्क *m.*-अधिकार *m.*-विशेषाधिकार *m.*-&c. देणें, हक्कदार करणें.
PRIVILEGED, *p.* v. V. हक्क दिल्हेला, &c. हक्कदार केलेला, विशेषाधिकार, विशिष्ट.
P. person. मानकरी, हक्कदार.

PRIVILY, *adv.* v. A. 3. *and* CLANDESTINELY. गुपचुप, गुपचुपीनं, चोरून, लिकाचोरीचा.
PRIVITY, *n. joint knowledge or consciousness of.* दुसऱ्याचे गोष्टीची माहिती *f.*-माहितगारी *f.*-दखलगिरी *f.*-आंतून माहिती *f.*-&c. सहज्ञान *n.* सहवेदन *n.* समवेदन *n.* समवेतृत्व *n*
2 privities; *private or secret parts.* उपस्थ *m.n.* गुह्य *n.* गुह्यांग *n.* गुप्तांग *n.* गुह्यस्थान *n.* गुह्यस्थल *n.* गुप्तेंद्रिय *n.* अंग *pop.* आंग *n.* काया *f.* शरीर *n.* नागवें *n.*
Cloth to cover the p. लंगोटा *m. dim.* लंगोटी *f. or* लंगुटा *m.* &. लंगुटी *f.* कौपीन *f. n.*
PRIVY, *a. peculiar, own, &c.* v. PRIVATE. खास, खासगत, खुद, खुदनिसबतीचा. [एकांतवासाचा,
2 *retired, secluded, &c.* v. PRIVATE. एकांताचा, एकीकडचा,
3 v. CLANDESTINE, SECRET. गुपचुपीचा, लिकाचोरीचा.
4 *participating in the knowledge of.* दुसऱ्याच्या गोष्टीचा वाकबदार-माहितगार-&c. आंतून माहितगार-&c. समज्ञानी, सहज्ञानी, समवेत्ता, सहवेत्ता.
5—council, counsellor, &c. एकांताचा, एकांत करण्याचा, सलबताचा, मसलतीचा.
PRIVY, *n. necessary.* शेतखाना *m.* पायखाना *m.* नारत *or* तारदखाना *m.* काकुसखाना *m.* शौचकूप *m.* संडास *m.*
A p. within a compound or yard. आवारखाना *m.*
PRIZE, *n. spoil, plunder.* लूट *f.* लढाईंत धरलेला माल *m.* युद्धसंपादित धन *n.* युद्धजितधन *n.* युद्धसंपादितद्रव्य *n.*
2 *reward of competition.* बक्षीस *n.* पणजय *n.* पणजितधन *n.*-द्रव्य *n.*-पदार्थ *m.*-&c. जयपरितोषिक *n.*
3 *valuable acquisition.* परीस *m.* निधि *m.* रत्न *n.*
4 (in a lottery) सांडत *f.* (as त्याच्या नांवानें सांडत आली).
To PRIZE, *v. a. estimate the price of, rate.* किम्मत *f.*-मोल *n.*-&c. करणें-ठरवणें *g. of o.*
2 *esteem highly.* मानणें, मोजणें, लेखणें, उत्कृष्ट-चांगला-उत्तम-&c. मानणें, सोन्याचा-लाखाचा-&c. समजणें- मानणें. [मल्ल.
PRIZE-FIGHTER, *n.* शर्यतीचा-पणाचा-&c. जेठी-पहिलवान-&c. पण-
PRIZE-FIGHTING, *n.* शर्यतीची-पणाची-&c. कुस्ती *f.*-&c.
PRIZE-MONEY, *n.* लुटीचा-लढाईंत धरलेल्या मालाचा-&c. वांटा *m.*
PRO-AND-CON. In this phrase *pro* may be rendered by भावकोटि *f.* विधिपक्ष *m.* विधिकोटि *f.* कर्तव्यपक्ष *m.* and *con* by अभावकोटि *f.* निषेधपक्ष *m.* निषेधकोटि *f.* अकर्तव्यपक्ष *m.*
PROBABILITY, *n.* v. A. संभावना *f.* संभव *m.*
In all p. v. PROBABLY. बहुतकरून.
PROBABLE, *a.* v. LIKELY. जोगा-जागता-सारखा-&c. (used with the verb indicated, as व्हायाजोगा-&c.), संभाव्य, संभावनीय, संभावनार्ह.
To be p. संभवणें.
PROBABLY, *adv.* v. A. बहुतकरून, फारकरून, अधिककरून, शंभरबांटे, हजारवांटे *or* शंभरवांट्यांनीं, &c. प्रायः, प्रायशः, असा संभव आहे, असेल.
PROBATE, *n.*—of a will. मृतलेखप्रमाण *n.*
PROBATION, *n.* v. TRIAL. परीक्षा *f.* पारख *f.* कसोटी *f.* कसणी *f.*
2 See PROOF.
PROBATIONER, *n. person under probation.* पारखीवर-परीक्षेवर-&c. असणारा, परीक्षा देणारा, परीक्ष्यमाण, परीक्षारूढ, उमेदवार though strictly speaking it means *aspirant* or *candidate,* is

sometimes used for *probationer.*

PROBATORY, PROBATIONAL, PROBATIONARY, *a. serving for trial.* परीक्षेचा, परीक्षेच्या उपयोगाचा.

PROBE, *n.*—of a surgeon. घाव-क्षत-&c. पाहण्याची सळई *f.* एषिणी *f.* क्षतशोधनी *f.* [णें.

To PROBE, *v. a. examine with a probe.* सळईनें-सळई घालून पाह-
2 fig. v. To EXAMINE. खणून-खोदून-खणखणून-खोदखोदून-घोळून-घोळघाळून-&c. पुसणें-पाहणें-विचारणें.

PROBITY, *n.* v. HONESTY, INTEGRITY. खरेपणा *m.* खराई *f.* इमान *n.* प्रमाणिकपणा *m.* नेत *f.* नेकी *f.* नेक *f.* सचोटी *f.*

PROBLEM, *n.*—in logic; *questionable or disputable point.* विकल्पविषय *m.* विवादविषय *m* वाद *m.* प्रश्न *m.*
2—in geometry. कृतिसापेक्षसिद्धांत *m.* कृत्य *n.* वस्तूपपाद्य *n.*

PROBLEMATICAL, *a. questionable, uncertain,* v. DOUBTFUL. संशयाचा, विकल्पाचा, वानव्याचा, संदिग्ध, अनिश्चित, सविकल्प, वैकल्पिक.

PROBLEMATICALLY, *adv.* v. A. संशयपूर्वक.

PROBOSCIS, *n. snout,*—of an elephant, &c. सोंड *f.* शुंडा *f.*

PROCEDURE, PROCEEDING, *n.* v. V. 1. चालणें *n.* &c. चाल *f.* गति *pop.* गत *f.* गमन *n.* चार *m.*
I. *step, measure taken, transaction.* काम *n.* कर्म *n.* क्रिया *f.* कृति *f.* करणी *f.* पाऊल *n.* पग *n. both with v.* टाक.
II. proceedings; *train of actions,* v. COURSE, CONDUCT. चाल *f.* वहिवाट *f.* व्यवहार *m.* आचार *m.* आचरण *n.* मोला *m.* वळण *n.* ओळ *f.* करणी *f.*
Legal p. v. PROCESS. व्यवहार *m.*
III. *manner or order of proceeding,* v. COURSE. रीति *pop.* रीत *f.* मार्ग *m.* वाट *f.* संप्रदाय *m.* ओळ *f.*
Report of p. हकिकत *f.* हक्किकतनामा *m.* रोजनामा *m.*

To PROCEED, *v. n. move on, go forward, renew or continue motion.* चालणें, पुढें जाणें-चालणें-&c. [&c. चालणें.
To p. on one's journey. आपल्या वाटेनें-मार्गानें-वाटेवर-
2 *pass from one point, stage, topic, &c. to another.* जाणें-चालणें-&c. with पासून *and* वर, क्रम *m.*-क्रमण *n.*-&c. करणें.
3 *enter on a course,* v. To BEGIN. पाऊल *n.* पुढें ठेवणें, प्रवर्त्तणें, प्रवृत्त होणें.
4 *issue or come as from a source.* निघणें, येणें, होणें, उत्पन्न-&c. होणें, उपजणें, निपजणें, उद्भवणें, प्रसवणें, उत्पत्ति *f.*-&c. होणें *with g. of s. and* पासून *of o.*
5 *act, transact, conduct, carry on measures.* करणें, चालणें, वर्त्तणें, वहिवाटणें, वापरणें, गति *f.*-युक्ति *f.*-रीति *f.*-उपाय *m.*-तजबीज *f.*-वाट *f.*-&c. करणें, पाऊल *n.*-पग *n.* टाकणें.
6 against,—at law; *take legal measures.* खटला *m.*-खटलें *n.*-वाद *m.*-&c. उभा-उपस्थित-&c. करणें.
7 *have a course, take effect, take place, &c.* होणें, चालणें, लागू-चालू-&c. होणें, चाल *f.*-वहिवाट *f.*-&c. असणें-होणें *g. of s.*
8 See To ADVANCE.

PROCEEDS, *n.*—in commerce; *value of goods sold.* उत्पन्न *n.* आलेली किम्मत *f.* आलेलें मोल *n.* विक्री *f.* विक्रीचापैसा *m.*

PROCESS, *n. moving forward, progressive course, tendency.* गति *pop* गत *f.* चाल *f.* वळण *n.* धांव *f.* प्रवृत्ति *f.*
P. of time. कालगति *f.*
2 *gradual course, progress.* गति *pop.* गत *f.* क्रम *m.* क्रमण *n.*
3 *line or order of proceeding,* v. COURSE. ओळ *f.* क्रम *m.* अनुक्रम *m.* रहाटी *f.* रीति *pop.* रीत *f.* धारा *m.* परिपाटी *f.* पद्धति *f.* कार्यक्रम *m.* इतिकर्त्तव्यता *f.* इतिक्रिया *f.*
4—in law; *legal proceedings,* v. SUIT. व्यवहार *m.* खटला *m.* खटलें *n.* व्यवहारमार्ग *m.*

PROCESSION, *n.* v. V. 1.—*act.* चालणें *n.* चाल *f.* गति *f.* गमन *n.*
4 निघणें *n.* &c.
I. *train of persons moving with state and ceremony.* सवारी *or* स्वारी *f.* यात्रा *pop.* जत्रा *f.* छबिना *m.* दिंडी *f.* मांबसाळें *n.*
Marriage p. वरात *f.*
To go or move in p. मिरवणें, मिरवण *f.*-मिरवणूक *f.* करणें.

PROCESSIONAL, PROCESSIONARY, *a. relating, &c. to a procession.* स्वारीचा, यात्रेचा, मिरवण्याचा, मिरवणुकीचा, &c. यात्रिक.

To PROCLAIM, *v. a. publish officially or authoritatively; announce, promulgate, &c* डांगोरा *m.*-दंवडी *f.*-धांडोरा *m.*-धांडोरें *n.*-&c. वाजविणें-पिटणें *g. of o.* जाहीरनामा *m.* लावणें *g. of o.* घोषण *n.*-घोषणा *f.*-घोष *m.* करणें *g. of o.*
2 *make public, declare openly,* v. To PUBLISH, जाहीर-प्रसिद्ध-उघड-&c.करणें, थाळा *m.*-थाळी *f.*-डंका *m.*-नगारा *m.*-&c. वाजविणें-पिटणें *g. of o.*

PROCLAIMED, *p.* v. V. 1. डांगोरा पिटलेला, &c. घोषित.
2 जाहीर केलेला, डंका वाजलेला, &c.

PROCLAIMER, *n.* PROCLAIMING, *p. a.* v. V. 1. डांगोरा वाजवणारा-&c. दंवडी पिटणारा &c. डांगोऱ्या, डांगोरापिट्या, दंवडीपिट्या, धांडोऱ्या, घोषक, घोषणकर्त्ता-कारी-&c.
2 जाहीर करणारा, प्रसिद्ध करणारा, डंका वाजवणारा, थाळी पिटणारा, &c.

PROCLAMATION, PROCLAIMING, *n.* v. V. 1. डांगोरा *m.* दंवडी *f.* धांडोरा *or* ढांडोरा *m.* धांडोरें *n.* घोषण *n.* घोषणा *f.* घोष *m.*
I. *paper containing a government official notice.* जाहीरनामा *m.*
To circulate a p. of prohibition. द्वाही *f.* फिरवणें.

PROCLIVITY, *n.* v. A. *and* INCLINATION. मनाची ओढ *f.* प्रावण्य *n.* प्रवृत्ति *f.*

PROCLIVOUS, *a. inclined, disposed, prone.* प्रवण, प्रवृत्त.

To PROCRASTINATE, *v. a. delay,* v. To DEFER. उशीर *m.*-विलंब *m.*-दिरिंग *m.*-&c. लावणें-करणें. वेळ *m.* लावणें, ढकलणें, लोटणें, दिवसगतीवर लोटणें-ढकलणें, उपेक्षा *f.* करणें *g. of o.* उपेक्षणें.

To PROCRASTINATE, *v. n. delay, be dilatory.* वेळ *m.* लावणें, आजउद्यां *f. n.*-आजकाल *f. n.* करणें, ढकलाढकल *f.*-ढकलपट्टी *f.*-लोटालोटी *f.*-अळमटळम *f. n.*- टाळाटाळ *f.*-&c. करणें.

PROCRASTINATION, *n.* v V.N. आजउद्यां *f. n.* आजकाल *f. n.* ढकलाढकल *f.* ढकलपट्टी *f.* लोटालोटी *f.* अळमटळम *f. n.* टाळाटाळ *f.* टाळाटाळी *f.* टालमटोला *m.* घालघसर *f.* चेंगटाई *f.*

PROCRASTINATOR, *n.* v. V. N. *and* DAWDLER. वेळ लावणारा, आजउद्यां करणारा, ढकलाढकल करणारा, वेळलाव्या, घालघसऱ्या, लोटालोट्या, चेंगट, दीर्घसूत्र.

To PROCREATE, *v. a. generate,* v. To BEGET. उत्पन्न करणें, उत्पादणें, जन्म *m. n.* देणें, जनन *n.*-प्रजनन *n.*-&c. करणें, उत्पत्ति *f.*-&c. करणें *g. of o.*

PROCREATED, *p.* v. V. उत्पन्न केलेला, &c. जनित, प्रजनित.

PROCREATING, *p. a.* PROCREANT, *a.* PROCREATOR, *n.* v. V. उत्पन्न करणारा, जन्म देणारा, उत्पादक, जनक, प्रजनक, जनिता,

प्रजनिता, जनन-प्रजननकर्त्ता.

PROCREATION, *n.* v. V.—*act.* उत्पादणें *n.* &c. जनन *n.* प्रजनन *n.* उत्पादन *n.* उत्पत्ति *f.* प्रजोत्पादन *n.* प्रजोत्पत्ति *f.*

PROCREATIVE, *a. having the power to beget.* प्रजननशक्तीचा, प्रजननशक्तिक, प्रजननशक्तियुक्त-विशिष्ट-संपन्न. [नशक्ति *f.*

PROCREATIVENESS, *n.* v. A. प्रजननशक्ति *f.* जननशक्ति *f.* उत्पाद-

PROCTOR, *n. attorney, agent.* वकील, मुखत्यार.

PROCUMBENT, *a. prone.* पालथा, उपडा, उपडी.

PROCURABLE, *a.* v. V. मिळवायाजोगा-जोगता-सारखा, प्राप्य, प्राप्तव्य, प्रापणीय, लभ्य, उपलभ्य, समासाद्य.

Easily p. सुलभ्य, सुप्राप्य, सुसाध्य.

To PROCURE, *v. a. obtain, &c.* v. TO GET, TO GAIN. मिळवणें *or* मेळवणें, संपादणें, अर्जणें, पैदाकरणें, साध्य करणें, संपादणी *f.*-संपादन *n.*-&c. करणें.

To be procured. मिळणें, लाभणें, लाधणें, लाहणें.

2 *bring about, bring on, effect.* मिळवणें *or* मेळवणें, साधणें, संपादणें,करवणें, करणें,करून घेणें, आणणें,घडवणें, घडवून आणणें.

To PROCURE, *v. n. pimp.* कुंटणकी *f.*-कुंटणपणा *m.*-भडवेपणा *m.*-&c. करणें. [प्राप्त.

PROCURED, *p.* v. V. A. 1. मिळवलेला, संपादलेला, &c. संपादित,

2 मिळवलेला, साधलेला, &c.प्रयुक्त(in comp. as पापप्रयुक्त,&c.).

PROCUREMENT, PROCURING, PROCURATION, *n.* v. V.A. 1. मिळवणें *n.* संपादणें *n.* &c. संपादणी *f.* संपादणूक *f.* संपादन *n.*

PROCURER, *n.* PROCURING, *p. a.* v.V.A.1. मिळवणारा, संपादणारा, पैदा करणारा, &c. संपादक,संपादनकर्त्ता-कारी.

2 मिळवणारा, साधणारा, संपादणारा, &c. प्रयोजक.

P. cause. प्रयोजन *n.*

v. V. N. कुंटण, भडवा, कुंटणकी-&c. करणारा, कुटण्या.

PROCURESS, *n. bawd.* कुंटीण *f.* कुंटण *f.* कुटणी.

PRODIGAL, *a. lavish, wasteful,* v. EXTRAVAGANT. उधळा, उधळ्या, उडाऊ, उडव्या, सांडरा, व्ययशील, अपरिमितव्ययी, बहुव्ययी.

PRODIGAL, *n.* See the ADJECTIVE.

PRODIGALITY, *n.* v. A. उधळेपणा *m.* उधळपट्टी *f.* उधळाउधळ *f.* उधळ *f.* उधळमाधळ *f.* उफानगिरी *f.* उडवण *f.* उडवाउडव *f.* बहुव्यय *m.* अतिव्यय *m.* व्ययबुद्धि *f.*

PRODIGALLY, *adv.* v. V. उधळेपणानें, उधळपट्टीनें,&c. उधळाउधळ-उडवाउडव-&c. करून.

PRODIGIOUS, *a. vast, huge, enormous, &c.* v. LARGE, EXCESSIVE. ऐवट, अवजड *or* अवजाड, अफाट, अवाढव्य, धक्कर, बेहद्द, बेसुमार.

2 See WONDERFUL.

PRODIGIOUSLY, *adv.* v. A. 1. अतिशय, अमर्याद, भारी, बेसुमार, पराकाष्ठेचा *decl.* अत्यंत.

2 नवल वाटायाजोगा *decl.* नवल वाटेसा *decl.*

PRODIGY, *n.* v. PORTENT. उत्पात *m.* अद्भुत *n.* [स्तोम *n.*

2 *remarkable personage.* धेंड *n.* प्रस्थान *n.* प्रस्थ *n.* प्रकरण *n.*

To PRODUCE, *v. a. offer to view, bring forward.* बाहेर काढणें, दृष्टीस पाडणें, काढून दाखवणें, दाखवणें, हाजीर-&c.करणें, दृष्टीपुढें-डोळ्यांपुढें-&c. आणणें, प्रत्यक्ष-प्रसिद्ध-उघड-&c. करणें, मैदानांत-पटांगणांत-&c. आणणें-येऊं देणें.

2 *bear, bring forth, yield, &c.*—soil, plants, &c. देणें, उपजवणें, उत्पन्न-&c.होणें *in.con. with* पासून,उत्पादणें,प्रसवणें,विणें.

3 *bring into existence, occasion, effect, &c.* v. TO CAUSE. करणें, करवणें, उत्पादणें, उत्पन्न करणें, निष्पादणें.

To be produced. उत्पन्न होणें, उपजणें, निपजणें.

4 (grain, &c.) *raise.* काढणें, उपजवणें, निपजवणें, करणें, उदीम *m.* करणें *g. of o.*

5 (in geometry) वाढवणें.

PRODUCE, *n. that which is brought forth, yielded, &c.*उत्पन्न *n.* निष्पन्न *n.* उपज *m.* निपज *m.* पैदास्त *f.* फळ *n.*

P. of a field. पीक *n.*—P. of fields as distinguished from that of garden land, जिराईत *or* जिरायत *n.*—P. of garden land, बागाईत *n.* [ठेवलेला, &c.

PRODUCED, *p.* v. V.1. बाहेर काढलेला, काढून दाखवलेला, दृष्टीपुढे

2 दिल्हेला, उत्पादलेला, उपजवलेला, &c. उत्पन्न, निष्पन्न.

3 उत्पन्न केलेला, &c. उत्पन्न, पैदा, उत्पादित, निष्पन्न, निष्पादित, जन्य, प्रयुक्त (in comp. as पापप्रयुक्त दुःख), मूलक (in comp. as पापमूलकदुःख).

PRODUCER, *n.* PRODUCING, *p. a.* v. V. 1. काढणारा, काढून दाखवणारा, दृष्टीस पाडणारा, &c.

2 देणारा, उपजवणारा, प्रसवणारा.

3 करणारा, उत्पन्न करणारा, उत्पादणारा.

4 काढणारा, उपजवणारा, &c.

I.—as opposed to a consumer; *earning or acquiring person.* जोडका, जोडता, मिळवणारा.

PRODUCIBLE, *a.* v. V. 1. काढायाजोगा-जोगता-सारखा-&c. काढून दाखवायाजोगा-जोगता-सारखा-&c.

2 करायाजोगा-जोगता-&c. उत्पन्न-निष्पन्न-&c. करायाजोगा-&c.

PRODUCT, *n.* v. PRODUCE. उत्पन्न *n.* उपज *m.* फळ *n.*

2—in arithmetic. गुणाकार *m.* फल *or* फळ *n.* घात *m.*

3 *effect, &c.* v. CONSEQUENCE. फल *or* फळ *n.* परिणाम *m.*

PRODUCTION, *n.* v. V. 1.—*act.* बाहेर काढणें *n.* काढणें *n.* काढून दाखवणें *n.* &c.

2—*act.* देणें *n.* उपजवणें *n.*&c.

3—*act.* करणें *n.* उत्पादण *n.* &c. उत्पादन *n.* निष्पादन *n.* जनन *n.* उद्भावन *n.*—*state.* पैदास्त *f.* जन्म *m. n.* उत्पत्ति *f.* निष्पत्ति *f.* उद्भव *m.* उद्भाव *m.* व्युत्पत्ति *f.* संभव *m.* संभूति *f.* भूति *f.* जनि *f.* उत्था *f.* समुद्गम *m.*

Law of reciprocal p. and reproduction. बीजांकुरन्याय *m.*

I. *thing produced,* v. PRODUCE. उत्पन्न *n.* उपज *m.* निपज *m.* फळ *n.* [दार्थ *m.*

II.—of art, intellect, &c. कृत्य *n.* कृति *f.* निर्मितवस्तु *n.*-प-

PRODUCTIVE, *a. bringing into being, producing, causing, &c.* उत्पन्न करणारा, उत्पादक, निष्पादक, उत्पत्तिकर-कारक-&c. उद्भवकर-कारक-&c.

2—of soils, &c. v. FERTILE. सुपिकाचा, पिकाऊ, पिकाळ, मातबर, बहुप्रसव, बहुफल.

3—a business, labor, &c. *lucrative,* v. GAINFUL. ओला, ओलाव्याचा, जिवट, जीवदार, गबाल, फलप्रद, फलावह, फलापधायक, अवंध्य.

4—as used of the earning or workig classes (of a society or member of a family, &c.). जोडका, जोडता, मिळवता, कमावता, कर्त्ता.

PRODUCTIVENESS, *n.* v. A. 2. पिकाऊपणा *m.* पिकाळपणा *m.* बहुप्रसवत्व *n.* बहुफलत्व *n.*

3 ओलेपणाm. ओलावाm. ओलासाm. फलदायकत्वn. &c.

PROEM, PROEMIAL. See PREFACE, PREFATORY.

PROFANATION, n. v. V. 1.—act. बाटवणेंn. भ्रष्टकरणेंn. &c. भ्रष्टीकरणn.

PROFANE, a. v. IRRELIGIOUS, IMPIOUS. देवलंड, धर्मलंड, कर्मलंड, देवलंडाईचा, देवनिंदक, धर्मनिंदक, देवद्वेषी, धर्मद्वेषी, देवनिंदात्मक.

2 not sacred; secular, &c. धर्मप्रकरणा बाहेरचा-निराळा-वेगळा, धर्मकथन-धर्मप्रकरण-&c. व्यतिरिक्त, प्रापंचिक, व्यावहारिक, लौकिक, सांसारिक.

3—ceremonially. ओवळा, ओवळ्याच्या उपयोगाचा-कामाचा.

To PROFANE, v. a. violate the sanctity of, pollute, &c. बाटवणें, विटाळणें, विटाळवणें, विटाळm. करणें-लावणें-आणणें, भ्रष्टविणें, भ्रष्ट-दूषित-&c. करणें, दूषणें, पवित्रपणाm.-&c. दवडणें g. of o.

2 treat with irreverence. हेलसांडणें, हेळणें, हेलना pop. हेळणा f.-हेलसांड f.-हेला pop. हेळा f.- अपमानm.-अनादरm.-निंदा f.-&c. करणें g. of o. अनादरबुद्धीनें-अपमानबुद्धीनें-&c. घेणें-वहिवाटणें-वापरणें.

PROFANED, p. v. V. 1. बाटवलेला, विटाळवलेला, &c. भ्रष्ट, दूषित.

2 हेलसांडलेला, &c. अपमानित, अनादृत, असत्कृत.

PROFANELY, adv. v. A. 1. देवलंडाईनें, धर्मलडाईनें, देवनिंदाबुद्धीनें, धर्मनिंदाबुद्धीनें.

PROFANENESS, PROFANITY, n. v. A. 1. देवलंडाई f. धर्मलंडाई f. कर्मलंडाई f. देवनिंदा f. धर्मनिंदा f. देवनिंदाबुद्धि f. धर्मनिंदाबुद्धि f.

PROFANER, n. PROFANING, p. a. v. V. 1. बाटवणारा, विटाळणारा, भ्रष्ट करणारा, &c.

2 हेलसांडणारा, हेळसांड करणारा, &c. अनादर-अपमान-&c. कर्त्ता, अपमानक.

To PROFESS, v. a. openly declare, avow, assert, &c. उघडपणें-&c. बोलणें-बोलून दाखवणें, आहे म्हणून बोलणें, तोंडानें कबूल करणें, अंगीकारणें, स्वीकारणें, वदणें, अंगीकारपूर्वक सांगणें, प्रसिद्धकथन n.-&c. करणें, उद्गारणें, उसमरणें, प्रतिज्ञा f. करणें g. of o.

2 (an art or business). धंदा m.-उद्योग m.-व्यवहार m.-व्यापार m.-वृत्ति f.-&c. करणें.

3 (one's self) v. To PRETEND. अड्डा m. बाळगणें g. of o. चंग m.-बाणा m.-कंकण n.-चबर n.-&c. बांधणें g. of o.

PROFESSED, p. v. V. 1. उघडपणें बोललेला, तोंडानें कबूल केलेला-झालेला, &c. स्वप्रतिज्ञात, प्रतिज्ञापुरस्सर, प्रतिज्ञापूर्वक.

PROFESSEDLY, adv. by professed or avowed intention or declaration. सांगून-पुढें करून-प्रसिद्ध करून-&c. with a noun (as आईची भेट सांगून तो या गांवास आला), प्रतिज्ञापूर्वक.

PROFESSION, n. v. V. 1.—act. वदणें n. वदणूक f. अंगीकार m. स्वीकार m. प्रसिद्धकथन n. उद्गार m.

Hollow professions. बऱ्हाडगोष्टी f. pl. लग्नगोष्टी f. pl.

To make great or flaming p. of. अधिष्ठान n. मिरवणें g. of o. अड्डा m. बाळगणें g. of o. चंग m.-कंकण n.-बाणा m.-&c. बांधणें g. of o.

That makes a great p. of. अड्डेबाज, अड्डेबाईक.

Act up to your professions. जसें सोंग तसी संपादणी, वेडीचें सोंग घेतलें म्हणजे पाटांव फाडला (or लें) पाहिजे.

I. calling, employment, &c. v. BUSINESS. उद्योग m. धंदा m. पेशा m. कसब n. व्यवहार m. वृत्ति f. वृत्त n.

Military p. शिपाईगिरी f. शिपाईबाणा m.

II. collective body of persons engaged in a calling. पेशा m.

PROFESSIONAL, a. pertaining, &c. to a calling or profession. धंद्याचा, उद्योगाचा, कसबाचा, स्वकर्माचा, &c. कसबाविषयींचा, कसबासंबंधींचा, &c. वृत्तिसंबंधी, वृत्तिविषयक.

2 engaged in a profession. रोजगारी, धंदेवाईक, व्यवहारी, उद्योगी, वृत्त्युपजीवी, वृत्तिमान् pop. वृत्तिमंत.

PROFESSIONALLY, adv. v. A. उद्योगाच्या-कसबाच्या-&c. संबंधानें-नात्यानें-&c. उद्योगानें, उद्योगपरत्वें, वृत्तिपरत्वें.

PROFESSOR, n. PROFESSING, p. a. v. V. उघडपणें बोलणारा, वदणारा, तोंडानें कबूल करणारा- होणारा.

1. public teacher. गुरु, अध्यापक, पाठक, वस्ताद.

PROFESSORIAL, a. पाठकाचा, पाठकसंबंधी-&c.

PROFFER, To PROFFER. See OFFER, To OFFER.

PROFICIENCY, PROFICIENCE, n. v. A. गति f. प्रवेश m. निवेशm. अभिनिवेश m. सन्निवेश m. नैपुण्य n. निपुणता f. व्युत्पत्ति f. संचार m. वैचक्षण्य n.

POFICIENT, a. accomplished, adept, versed, &c. v. CLEVER. पुरामाहितो, निपुण, प्रवीण, गाढा, पट्टाईत, निष्णात, पारंगत, विचक्षण, अभिज्ञ, व्युत्पन्न, निविष्ट, विशाद, सन्निविष्ट, अभिनिविष्ट.

PROFILE, n. head or face drawn in a side view. एकचश्मी एकडोळी-एकबाजूचें-&c. चित्र n.

PROFIT, n. pecuniary acquisition, v. GAIN. नफा m. किफायत f. मिळवत or मिळकत f. कमाई f. प्राप्ति f. आय m. आदाय m. उत्पन्न n. उपज m. निपज m. निष्पन्न n. गवान n. गवानी f. गाऊल n. लब्धि f. लभ्यांश m.

P. and loss. खातें पोतें n. नफा नुकसान n.

To have equal p. and loss. खातेंपोतें n. बराबर होणें g. of s. रमारम f.-रमारमी f. होणें, जमाखर्च m.-&c. बराबर होणें g. of s.

2 benefit, good, v. ADVANTAGE. लाभ m. फायदा m. किफायत f. फल or फळ n. हित n. हाशील n.

P. and loss. लाभालाभ m.

To PROFIT, v. a. promote the good of, benefit. हित n.-बरें n.-कल्याण n.-&c. करणें g. of o. उपयोगी-हितकारक-हितप्रद-हितावह-&c. होणें with in. con.

2 (one's self) improve. आपलें हित n.-आपलें कल्याण n.-&c. करणें, गुण m.-कसब n.-कौशल n.-&c. वाढवणें, गुणवृद्धि f.-कलावृद्धि f.-चातुर्य वृद्धि f.-&c. करणें-करून घेणें.

To PROFIT, v. n. make profit in trade, &c. नफा m.-लाभ m.-मिळकत f.-किफायत f.-&c. होणें-मिळणें in con.

2 make improvement, advance in excellence, &c. गुण m.-कसब n.- कौशल n.-&c. वाढणें अधिक होणें-&c. g. of s. गुणवृद्धिन n.-गुणवृद्धि f.-&c. होणें g. of s. रूपास-रंगास-तेजास-&c. चढणें.

3 be of use or advantage. लाभणें, लाधणें, लाहणें, उपयोग m.-हित n.-फायदा m.-&c. होणें-पडणें g. of s. उपयोगी-हितकारक-हितावह-&c. होणें-पडणें-&c.

PROFITABLE, a. yielding profit, lucrative, v. GAINFUL. नफ्याचा, मिळकतीचा, किफायती, नफेवार, किफायतवार, ओला, ओल्याचा, गवान.

To begin to be p. उत्पन्नास येणें.

2 beneficial, v. ADVANTAGEOUS. उपयोगी, उपयोगाचा, &c. हितकारक, हितदायक, हितावह, हितप्रद, उपकारी.

PROFITABLENESS, n. v. A. 1. नफेवारी f. किफायतवारी f. ओलावा m. ओलपणा m. ओलासा m.

2 उपयोगीपणा m. उपयोगिता f. उपकारिता f. हितकारकत्व n.

हितदायकत्व *n.* [गवसार.

PROFITABLY, *adv.* v. A. 1. नफेवार, किफायतवार, सरफेवार, 2 उपयोग व्हायाजोगा-सारखा *decl.*

PROFITING, *n.* v. V. N. 2. गुणवर्द्धन *n.* गुणवृद्धि *f.* चातुर्यवर्द्धन *n.*

PROFITLESS, *a. void of profit or advantage.* लाभांवगळा-निराळा, निर्लाभ, निष्फळ.

PROFLIGACY, PROFLIGATENESS, *n.* v. A. लुचाइ *f.* लुचेगिरी *f.* लुचेशाई *f.* सोदावें *n.* सोदेगिरी *f.* दुर्वृत्ति *f.* दुर्वृत्त *n.* दुर्वर्त्तन *n.* दुराचरण *n.* भ्रष्टाचरण *n.* बदफैली *f.*

PROFLIGATE, *a.* v. LOOSE, WICKED. लुचा, सोदा, लुचेगिरीचा, लुचेशाईचा, &c. व्यसनी, दुर्व्यसनी, दुर्वृत्त, बदफैल, दुराचारी, दुराचरणी, भ्रष्टाचारी, भ्रष्टाचरणी, निसत, निसूक, *or* ग.

PROFLIGATE, *n.* v. A. दुराचरणी, दुराचारी, व्यसनी, फंदी.

PROFLIGATELY, *adv.* v. A. बदफैलीनें, दुराचरणानें, भ्रष्टाचरणानें, &c. I. See SHAMELESSLY.

PROFOUND, *a.* v. DEEP. खोल, ओंड *or* ओंढ, सखल, गंभीर, निम्न.
2 fig. *not superficial, &c.* v. ABSTRUSE. खोल, सखोल, गूढ, निगूढ.
3 *that has penetrated deeply, &c.*—a scholar, &c. खोल गेलेला, गडून गेलेला, प्रवीण, गाढा, अभिज्ञ, निष्णात, सन्निविष्ट, अभिनिविष्ट.
4 *low, deep, great, &c.*—affection of the mind. मनापासूनचा, बेंबीच्या देंठापासूनचा, अत्यंत, फार.

PROFOUNDLY, *adv.* v. A. 2.3. खोलगडून, अभिनिवेशपूर्वक, सन्निवेशपूर्वक, अभिज्ञानपूर्वक.
4 अत्यंत, फार, मनापासून, बेंबीच्या देंठापासून.

PROFOUNDNESS, PROFUNDITY, *n.* v. A. 1. खोलपणा *m.* &c. खोली *f.*-खोलावा *m.* गांभीर्य *n.*
2 खोलपणा *m.* &c. गूढता *f.* निगूढता *f.*
3 प्रवीणता *f.* प्रावीण्य *n.* अभिज्ञता *f.* सन्निवेश *m.* अभिनिवेश *m.*

PROFUSE, *a. prodigal, wasteful,* v. EXTRAVAGANT. उडाऊ, उधळ्या, उधळपट्या, धिंग, ढस्सर.
2 *spending or bestowing freely, lavish,* v. LIBERAL. सढळ, ढसळ *or* ढसाळ, ढिसळ *or* ढिसाळ, धोताल *or* ल्या.
3 *over abounding,* v. EXUBERANT. चौकळ, चळचंळीत, चमचमीत, अमनचैन *or* अमीन चमीन. [नें, &c.

PROFUSELY, *adv.* v. A. 1. उडाऊपणानें, उधळेपणानें, उधळपट्टी-
2 सढळहातानें, मोकळ्या हातानें, उदारहस्तें, छणछण, छणाछण.
3 चंगलपट्टीनें, &c. फडाच्या मापानें, मारून (ex. मारून लाडू वाढले) रगडून, उपटून, चंगळ, लैलूट, तडक, तडका, घळघळ *or* ळां, घळघळीत, घवघव, रगड, मनस्वी.

PROFUSENESS, PROFUSION, *n.* v. A. 1. उडाऊपणा *m.* उधळेपणा *m.* &c. उधळपट्टी *f.* उफानगिरी *f.* धिंगाई *f.* ढपलशाई *f.* अवासवाखर्च *m.* अपरिमित व्यय *m.* [उदारहस्त *m.*
2 सढळपणा *m.* ढसळपणा *m.* &c. मोकळाहात *m.* सढळहात *m.*
3 रेळ *f.* रेळचेळ *f.* चंगळ *f.* चंगळपट्टी *f.* लूट *f.* लैलूट *f.* रगड *f.* रगडपट्टी *f.* महामुरी *f.*

PROG, *n. victuals sought by begging.* भिक्षेचें अन्न *n.*—as given dressed, ओलीभिक्षा *f.* माधुकरी *f.*
2 See FOOD, VICTUALS.

PROGENITOR, *n.* v. ANCESTOR. कुलपुरुष, पूर्वज.

PROGENY *n.* v. OFFSPRING. संतान *n.* संतति *f.* अपत्य *n.*

PROGNOSIS, *n.*—in medicine. चिकित्सा *f.* परिभाषा *f.*

PROGNOSTIC, *a. foreshowing, foreboding.* पूर्वसूचक, भविष्यसूचक, अग्रसूचक, उद्बोधक.

PROGNOSTIC, *n. sign of something future; fore-token.* पूर्वलक्षण *n.* पूर्वरूप *n.* पूर्वचिह्न *n.* शकुन *m.* प्रश्न *m.* छाया *f.* लक्षण *n.* चिह्न *n.*

To PROGNOSTICATE, *v. a.* v. To BODE, To FORESHOW. पूर्वी &c. दाखवणें-सुचवणें, पूर्वसूचन *n.*-भविष्यसूचन *n.*-&c. करणें, लक्षण *n.*-पूर्वलक्षण *n.*-पूर्वरूप *n.*-&c. असणें *in. con. with g. of o.*

PROGNOSTICATION, *n.* v. V.—*act.* पूर्वी सुचवणें *n.* &c. पूर्वसूचन *n.* अग्रसूचन *n.* भविष्यसूचन *n.* भाविसूचन *n.*
I. See PROGNOSTIC.

PROGNOSTICATOR, *n.* v. V. पूर्वी दाखवणारा-सुचवणारा, पूर्वसूचक, अग्रसूचक, भविष्यसूचक, भाविसूचक.

PROGRAMME, *n.* पूर्वलेख *m.*

PROGRESS, PROGRESSION, *n. procession, passage, course onward.* गति *pop.* गत *f.* गमन *n.* क्रमण *n.* क्रांति *f.* क्रम *m.* यात्रा *f.* चार *m.* संचार *m.* प्रस्थान *n.* प्रगमन *n.*
That is in p. उभा, चालता, चालू, घटमान.
2—in learning, &c. v. ADVANCE. वाढणें *n.* वाढ *m. f.* वृद्धि *f.* संवृद्धि *f.* अभ्यास *m.*
That has made great p. v. PROFICIENT. अभिज्ञ.
3—in arithmetic. चय *m.* अनुपात *m.* श्रेधी *f. or* श्रेढी *f.*
Ascending p. चढती श्रेढी *f.*—Descending p. उतरती श्रेढी.
4—in geometry. गुणोत्तर *n.* चय *m.*
Common difference in p. (a. or g.). उत्तर *n.*
First term in p. (a. or g.) आदिधन *n.* आदिपद *n.* आदिवदन *n.* [*n.* अंत्यधन *n.*
Last place or term in p. (a. or g.). गच्छ *m.* अंत्यपद
5 *journey of state, circuit.* मोठ्या माणसाची फेरी *f.* स्वारी *f.*

To PROGRESS. See To PROCEED, To ADVANCE.

PROGRESSIVE, *a. going onwards, advancing.* पुढें पुढें चालणारा, पुढेंपुढें चालण्याचा, &c. उत्तरोत्तर-अधिक अधिक वर्धमान, क्रमक.
2 *advancing, improving.* वाढतेदशेचा, चढतेकळेचा, चढते कमानीचा. [धिक, क्रमशः, क्रमतः.

PROGRESSIVELY, *adv.* v. A. 1. पुढेंपुढें चालून, उत्तरोत्तर, अधिका-
2 चढते कळेनें, चढते कमानीनें. [*f.* क्रमकता *f.*

PROGRESSIVENESS, *n.* v. A. 1. पुढेंपुढें चालणें *n.* &c. क्रमकगति
2 वाढतीदशा *f.* चढतीकळा *f.* चढती कमान *f.* वाढ *f. n.* वृद्धि *f.*

To PROHIBIT, PROHIBITION, &c. See To FORBID, &c.

PROHIBITIVE, PROHIBITORY. See INTERDICTORY.

PROJECT, *n. scheme, &c.* v. CONTRIVANCE. कल्पना *f.* तजवीज *f.* युक्ति *f.* उपाय *m.* डाव *m. v.* खेळ.
2—as wild or bold, v. SCHEME. झेंगट *n.* खेंकटें *n.* झट *n.*

To PROJECT, *v. a. cast forward,* v. To CAST. टाकणें, सोडणें, पाडणें, प्रक्षेपणें, प्रक्षेप *m.*-प्रक्षेपण *n.*-&c. करणें *g. of o.*
2 *cast in the mind,* v. To CONTRIVE. योजणें, योजना *f.*-&c. करणें *g. of o.*

To PROJECT, *v. n. shoot forward, jut.* पुढें येणें.

PROJECTILE, *a. impelling forward.* पुढें ढकलणारा, दूरवेधी.

PROJECTILE, *n.*—weapon. दूरवेधि शस्त्र *n.*

PROJECTION, *n. a jutting out.* बाहेर आलेला प्रदेश *m.* शृंग *n.* कंगोरा *m.*
Projections,—gener. कान कोपरे *m. pl.*

PROJECTOR, s. v. V. A. 2. योजणारा, योजक, कल्पक, योजनाकल्पना-&c. कर्ता-कारक-&c. [त्या, झतेल or ती.

1. (of wild or bold projects). लचांडखोर, लचांडी, झेंग-

PROLAPSE, PROLAPSUS. s. *falling down*—of an intestine, &c. भ्रंश m.

P. ani. गुदभ्रंश m. अंगपात m.—The prolapsed gut. आंग n. आगंड n. आगंड n. कुत्रा m.

P. uteri. गर्भाशयभ्रंश m. योन्यर्श n. अंगपात m.—The prolapsed member. मांड n.

To PROLAPSE. v. n. *fall down or out*. खाली पडणें. बाहेर पडणें. भ्रंश m. होणें *g. of s.*

PROLATION, s. v. DRAWLING. दीर्घोच्चारण n. द्राविडप्राणायामm.

PROLEGOMENA, s. *preliminary observations*, v. PREFACE. परिभाषा *f.* पूर्वपीठिका *f.*

PROLEGOMENARY. See INTRODUCTORY. PREFATORY.

PROLEPSIS. See ANTEDATE. 2 See ANTICIPATION.

PROLIFIC, a. *fruitful. not barren*. प्रसवशील, बहुप्रसव, बहुफल, गर्भधारणशील, अवंध्य.

2 v. PRODUCTIVE. फलोत्पादक, फलदायक, संतानोत्पादक.

PROLIX, a. *long, of minute detail*,—speaker or speech, v. TEDIOUS. बवादी, दयादखोर, दीर्घसूत्री, चावट, चावटाईचा, चावनट.

P. story. लापणिका *f.* तरडक n. चरपट n. *f.* चरपटपंजरी *f.*

PROLIXITY, PROLIXNESS. s. v. A. विस्तार m. विस्तर m. ग्रंथविस्तार or विस्तर m. वाक्यविस्तर m. दीर्घसूत्र n. v. लाब, चावटाई *f.* दीर्घसूत्रीपणा m.

PROLOGUE. s.—in the Drama. प्रस्तावन n. प्रस्तावना *f.* प्रवेशक m. नांदी *f.* पूर्वरंग m.

Speaker of a p. नांदीकर, नांदीवादी.

To PROLONG, *To* PROLONGATE. v. a. *extend in duration. lengthen*. लांबविणें, वाढवणें. दीर्घ-लांब-&c. करणें.

2 *lengthen out, protract*. लांबता धरणें. लांबणीवर-लांबीवर धरणें-घालणें-टाकणें, लांबण *f.* लावणें.

To be prolonged. लांबणीवर-लांबीवर पडणें.

3 *extend in space*, v. To LENGTHEN. लांबविणें, लांब-&c. करणें, वाढवणें.

PROLONGED. PROLONGATED, p. v. V. 1. लांबविलेला, &c.

2 लांबणीवर धरलेला-टाकलेला-&c.

3 लांबविलेला, &c.

PROLONGATION, s. v. V. 1. लांबवणें n. वाढवणें n. &c.

2 लांबणीवर धरणें n. &c.

3 लांबवणें n. वाढवणें n. &c.

PROMENADE. s. *walking for exercise or amusement*. सहल *f.* तलावा m. v. दे, मार, रपेट *f.* फेरा m. v. मार, विहार m.

2 *place for walking*. सहल करण्याची-तलावा करण्याची-हवा खाण्याची-&c. जागा *f.*-कट *f.*-&c. रमणा m.

To PROMENADE, v. n. *walk for exercise or amusement*. सहल *f.* करणें, तलावा m. देणें-मारणें. रपेट *f.*-फेरा m. मारणें.

PROMINENCE, PROMINENCY. s. v. A. 1. उंचपणा m. उमरेपणाm.

2 ठळठळितपणा m. ठळकपणा m.

3 मुख्यस्थान n. प्रधानता *f.* प्राधान्य n.

1. *prominent part*. उंचवटा m. [उमरा.

PROMINENT, a. *standing out. protuberant*. बाहेर आलेला, उंच.

2 *conspicuous, striking to the eye*. मुख्य स्थानाचा, ठळठळीत, ठळठळीत, ठळक, प्रथमदृग्विषय, प्रथमदृग्गोचर.

3 *principal, eminent*, &c. मुख्यस्थानाचा, प्रधान, मुख्य, मुखरण.

P. person. नाक n. मोहरा m.

PROMISCUOUS, a. *mingled without order, undistinguished*, क्रमविचारहीन, भेदविचारहीन, सान्निपातिक, एकवाटाचा, एकमंगटाचा, देवढाचा, अविवेक, निर्विशेष.

P. intermingling or intercourse. एकमंगल n. एकवाट m. एकमेल *f.* एकवर्ण m. गोकुल or गोकूळ n. गोतांगोत n. जंगमढवळे n. लावळे गोंधळे n.

PROMISCUOUSLY, adv. v. A. एकवाट, सकट or सगट, सकट निरट or सगट निगट, अव्हलतव्हल, क्रमविचाररहित n. अविशेषतः.

PROMISCUOUSNESS, s. v. A. क्रमविचारराहित्य n. भेदविचारराहित्य n.

PROMISE, s. वचन n. बोली *f.* माष *f.* माक *f.* माकवाहण *f.* पण m. प्रतिज्ञा *f.* करार m. कौलकरार m. वायदा m. अभिवचन n. वाचा *f.*

Amusing or beguiling with empty promises. झोंकपट्टी *f.* झुगार पट्टी *f.*

Hollow &c. promises. झोंकपट्टीचें-&c. बोलणें n. रिक्त माषण n. शब्दपांडित्य n.

Pledge for performance of a p. माक *f.*

P. upon oath. आण माक or माष *f.*

P.-observing, v. PROMISE-KEEPER. सत्यप्रतिज्ञ.

Sure. unfailing p. भीष्मप्रतिज्ञा *f.* रामप्रतिज्ञा *f.* रामवचन n. रामबाण m.

To be bound by one's word or p. माकेंत गुंतणें.

To break a p. वचन n.-&c. मोडणें, वचनभंग m.-प्रतिज्ञाभंग m.-प्रतिज्ञाउल्लंघन m.-&c. करणें.

To redeem or make good one's p. माक *f.*-माष *f.*-&c. सत्य करणें- खरा करणें, वचन n. सत्य करणें-पार पाडणें, वचनोद्धार m. करणें.

To PROMISE, v. a. *give assurance of*. वचन n.-माक *f.*-माष *f.*-&c. देणें *g. of o.* बोली *f.*-प्रतिज्ञा *f.*-पण m.-&c. करणें *g. of o.* तोंडानें देणें, वाग्दान n.-वाचादान n.-&c. करणें *g. of. o.* देऊं करणें.

To PROMISE, v. n. माक *f.*-वचन n.-&c. देणें, प्रतिज्ञा *f.*-बोली *f.*-पण m.-&c. करणें, उरास-उरावर-उराशीं हात m. लावणें, टाळी *f.* मारणें-देणें, हातावर हात m. मारणें, वाचाश m. करणें, वचनीं-वचनास-वचनांत-&c. गुंतणें, जामीन *f.*-जिम्मती *f.* हातणें *g. of s.*

2 *afford hope, give ground for expectation*. पुढें होईल अशी आशा *f.* असणें, होईल असें दिसणें.

PROMISE-BREACH. s. वचनभंग m. प्रतिज्ञाभंग m. वचनमोड *f.*

PROMISE-BREAKER. s. PROMISE-BREAKING, a. वचनमोड्या, वचनतोड्या, वचनबुडव्या, वचन घालव्या, वचनघातकी.

PROMISE-KEEPER. s. PROMISE-KEEPING, a. वचनाचा खरा, एकवचनी, सत्यवचनाचा, कराराचा, करारी, सत्यप्रतिज्ञ, वचनतान्या, उक्तनिर्वाहक.

PROMISED. p. v. V. A. वचन केलेला, &c. वचनाचा, माकेचा, &c. पणित, प्रतिज्ञात, वाचादत्त, वाग्दत्त.

PROMISER, s. v. V. A. वचन-&c. देणारा, बोली-प्रतिज्ञा-&c. करणारा. प्रतिज्ञाकारी-वादी.

PROMISING, a. *affording good ground of hope*. होनकर, होतकरू, व्हावाजोगा-सारखा, दयास यावाजोगा.

A. p. matter or thing. होनोवस्त *f.*

Promissory, *a. containing a promise.* वचनाचा, &c. वचनविशिष्ट, प्रतिज्ञाविशिष्ट, सप्रतिज्ञ.

P. note. रोखा *m.* चिट्ठी *f* दस्तऐवज *m.* कतबा *m.*

Promontory, *n.* भुईचें उंच टोंक *n.*

To **Promote**, *v. a. forward, advance, further.* चालवणें, वाढवणें, सरचरा *f.*-पुरस्कार *m.*-उपकार *m.*-उपकारिता *f.*-पुस्तपन्हा *m.*-साहाय्य *pop.* सहाय्य *n.*-&c. करणें, हिमाईत *f.*-पुस्ती *f.*-बळ *n.*-&c. देणें, सिद्ध्यनुकूलता *f.*-सिद्ध्यानुकूल्य *n.*-सिद्धिसाधन *n.* करणें.

2 *elevate, prefer,* v. To Exalt. वाढवणें, चढवणें, सर्फराजी *f.* करणें *g. of o.* पदवी *f.* वाढवणें *g. of o.* मोठें काम *n.*-मोठी पदवी *f.*-&c. देणें-सांगणें, पदवर्द्धन *n.*-पदवृद्धि *f.*-&c. करणें.

Promoted, *p.* v. V. 1. चालवलेला, वाढवलेला, &c. प्रवर्त्तित.

2 वाढवलेला, चढवलेला.

Promoter, *n.* **Promoting**, *p. a.* v. V. 1. पुरस्कार करणारा, हिमाईत देणारा, &c. पुरस्कारी, पुरस्कर्त्ता, प्रवर्त्तक, उपकारी, उपकारक, उपकर्त्ता.

2 वाढवणारा, चढवणारा, सर्फराजी करणारा.

Promotion, *n.* v. V. 1.—*act.* चालवणें *n.* &c. पुरस्कार *m.* प्रवर्त्तन *n.* संवर्द्धन *n.* वर्द्धन *n.* वृद्धि *f.* उपकार *m.* उपकारिता *f.* पुस्तपन्हा *m.* पुष्टि *f.* वाहीदारी *f.*

2—*act.* वाढवणें *n.* चढवणें *n.* &c. पदवर्द्धन *n.*—*state.* सर्फराजी [*f.* पदवृद्धि *f.*

Promotive, *a.* v. V. 1. वर्धक, संवर्द्धक, साधक, साधनी, संवर्द्धनकारक, वृद्धिकारक.

Prompt, *a. ready, apt, quick, &c. in disposition; not dilatory, &c.* कडक, कडकडीत, उड्या, तडकफडक, धडकफडक *or* भडक, तलख, तापड. फणशा, कचक्या, समक्या, समशा, सणक्या, सरमन्या, सरपून, फांकडा, शिताब.

2 *ready, quick, smart, done at once,*—of acts, speech, payment, &c. रोकडा, रोख, रोखठोक, रोखीचा, खडाखडीचा.

To **Prompt**, *v. a. help at a loss, remind.* आठवण *f.* देणें, सूचना *f.* करणें, कानांत जपणें, विस्मृतसूचन *n.*-&c. करणें.

2 *spur, set on,* v. To Incite. उचलणें, चढवणें, चढीं देणें, वीर *m.* भरणें-देणें, उटाळणी *f.* करणें, उत्तेजन *n.*-&c. करणें.

Prompter, *n.* **Prompting**, *p. a.* v. V. 1. आठवण देणारा, सूचनाकरणारा.

2 उचलणारा, चढवणारा, वीर भरणारा, &c. उत्तेजक, उत्तेजन कर्त्ता-कारी, प्रवर्त्तक, गुरु.

Prompting, *n.* v. V. 1.—*act.* आठवण देणें *n.* &c. विस्मृत सूचन *n.* विस्मृतसूचना *f.* अपस्मृतसूचन *n.*

2 उचलणें *n.* &c. उठावणी *f.* उटाळणी *f.* उचल *f.* उत्तेजन *n.* प्रेरण *n.* प्रेरणा *f.*

Promptitude, **Promptness**, *n.* v. A. 1. कडकपणा *m.* कडकडीतपणा *m.* तापडपणा *m.* &c. वेग *m.* उठाउठी *f.* शिताबी *f.* जलदी *f.* कचका *m.*

2 रोकडेपणा *m.* रोखठोकपणा *m.*

Promptly, *adv.* v. A. 1. *rapidly, smartly, &c.* कडक, कडका, तडक, तडका, धडक, धडका, कडकावून, तडकावून, तडकून, कचकावून, कचकून, तावडतोब *or* प.

2 तुरूत *or* तूर्न, खडाखड *or* डी *or* खडोखड *or* डी, रोखारोखी, रोखठोक, रोकडा *decl.*

To **Promulgate**, *To* **Promulge**, &c. See To Publish, &c.

Prone, *a. lying with the face downward.* उपडा, उपडी, पालथा, अधोमुख, अधोवदन.

2 *not erect; inclined, looking downwards.* खालतोंड्या, अधोमुख, अधोवदन, प्रणत, प्रणतमस्तक.

3 *propense, inclined.* प्रवण, तयार, सिद्ध, स्वभावाचा-कल्लाचा-झोकाचा (conjoined with the object as रहण्याच्या स्वभावाचा,&c.), शील (in comp.), स्वभाव & स्वभावी (in comp.).

Proneness, *n.* v. A. 1. उपडेपणा *m.* पालथेपणा *m.* &c. अधोमुखता *f.*

2 खालतोंडेपणा *m.* अधोमुखता *f.* प्रणतत्व *n.*

3 प्रावण्य *n.* प्रवृत्ति *f.* प्रवाह *m.* झोंक *m.* कल *m.* ओढ *f.* स्वभाव *m.* तयारी *f.* सिद्धता *f.*

Prong, *n.*—of a fork, &c. कांटा *m.* सुवा *m.* शृङ्ग *m.*

Pronominal, *a. belonging, &c. to a pronoun.* सर्वनामाचा, सर्वनामसंबंधी, सर्वनामविषयक.

Pronoun, *n.*—in grammar. सर्वनाम *n.*

The proximate p. यत्शब्द *m.*

To **Pronounce**, *v. a. utter articulately.* उच्चारणें, बोलणें, उच्चार *m.*-उल्लेख *m.*-&c. करणें.

2 *utter confidently,* v. To Affirm. सचीत सांगणें, निश्चयपूर्वक-निर्णयपूर्वक-&c. सांगणें-वदणें.

3 See To Speak, To Utter.

To **Pronounce**, *v. n.* See To Affirm. [चार्य.

Pronounceable, *a.* v. V. A. 1. उच्चारायाजोगा-जोगता-&c. उ-

Pronounced, *p.* v. V. A. 1. उच्चारलेला, उच्चारित.

2 निश्चयपूर्वक सांगितलेला, &c.

Pronouncer, *n.* **Pronouncing**, *p. a.* v. V. A. 1. उच्चारणारा, उच्चार करणारा.

2 निश्चयपूर्वक सांगणारा, &c.

Pronounciation, **Pronouncing**, *n.* v. V. A. 1.—*act.* उच्चारणें *n.* उच्चार *m.* उच्चारण *n.* उल्लेख *m.* उल्लेखन *n.* वर्णोच्चार *m.*

Distinct p. उटाळा *m.* अक्षरवटिका *f.*

2 सचीत सांगणें *n.* &c.

Proof, *n.* v. Evidence. प्रमाण *n.* दाखला *m.* गमक *n.* प्रामाण्य *n.*

Absence of p. अप्रामाण्य *n.*

According to p. प्रमाणतः.

2 *corroborating or verifying event, circumstance, thing, &c.* दाखला *m.* मुद्दा *m.*—gener. मुद्दापत्ता *m.* दाखलादुखला *m.* दाखलामुकाबला *m.*

3—in arithmetic. ताळा *m.* पडताळा *m. v.* पाह, उपपत्ति *f.*

Cross p. आडताळा *m. v.* घे, पाह.

4 v. Trial. परीक्षा *f* प्रतीति *f.*

To put to the p. परीक्षा *f.*-प्रतीति *f.*-&c. पाहणें-घेणें *g. of o.*

5 (in printing). शुद्ध करण्या करितां काढलेला छाप.बयाच्या लेखाचा खरडा *m.*

Proof, *a.* (against) *of proof, impenetrable, &c.* अभेद्य, अविकार्य, अबाध्य, खबरदार, संचीर, सुदृढ.

Proofsheet. See Proof, 5.

Proofless, *a.* v. N. 1. अप्रमाण, प्रमाणरहित-शून्य.

To **Prop**, *v. a. keep up by putting something under or against.* टेकावणें, टेकवा *or* टेकावा *m.*-धिरा *m.*-&c. देणें.

Prop, *n. that which props or sustains.* टेकण *or* टेकणें *n.* टेकवा *or* टेकावा *m* टेका *m.* धिरा *m.* धिरासा *m.* ढिगी *f.* ढिगावा *m.* डेंग *f.* डगी *f.* धट *m.* नेटावा *m.* ढासण *n* लमा *m.* तीर *m.* जामीन *m.* अवष्टंभ *m.* ओठंगण *n.* आधार *m.* मेढ्या *m.*

To PROPAGATE, *v. a. continue by successive generation or production.* उत्पत्तिपरंपरेनें-क्रमिकोत्पत्तीनें-अनुक्रमोत्पत्तीनें-प्रत्युत्पत्तीनें-&c. चालवणें-वाढवणें-&c.

2 v. To INCREASE, To SPREAD. वाढवणें, पसरणें, पेरणें, फैलावणें, प्रसार *m.*-&c. करणें *g. of o.*

3 See To GENERATE.

PROPAGATION, PROPAGATING, *n.* v. V. 1.—*act.* क्रमिकोत्पत्ति *f.* अनुक्रमोत्पत्ति *f.* प्रत्युत्पत्ति *f.*

2—*act.* पसरणें *n.* फैलावणें *n.* &c. प्रसारण *n.* प्रसार *m.* फैलावा *m.* पसारा *m.* विस्तार *m.*

To PROPEL, *v. a. drive forward.* पुढें चालवणें, धाववणें, पुढें ढकलणें.

PROPENSE, *a. inclined, disposed,* v. PRONE. प्रवण.

PROPENSION, PROPENSITY, PROPENSENESS, *n.* v. A. ओढ *f.* ओढा *m.* कल *m.* प्रवाह *m.* प्रवृत्ति *f.* प्रावण्य *n.*

1. *a* p. छंद *m.* व्यसन *n.* नाद *m.* इष्क *m.* संवई *f.* संवका *m.* चटक *f.*

Evil p. दुर्व्यसन *n.* व्यसन *n.*

Of evil propensities. दुर्व्यसनी.

PROPER, *a. appropriate, exclusively own, &c.* v. PECULIAR. खास, खासगत, खुद, आपला, निज, स्व, स्वकीय, स्वीय, स्वक, आत्म, आत्मीय, स्वयं, अव्यभिचारी, असाधारण.

2 *fit, suitable,* v. RIGHT. योग्य, यथायोग्य, उचित, उपयुक्त, उपयोगी, लायक, शिस्त, शिस्तवार, ठीक, विहित, समुचित, शुद्ध (esp. in comp. as आकारशुद्ध, आचारशुद्ध,&c.),आर्य, बरहक्क, हलाल, हिशेबी*or*हिशोबी. Note. The sense of Proper is expressed by the Sanskrit participle, as करणीय p. to be done, भक्षणीय p. to be eaten, &c. &c.

3 v. HANDSOME, NEAT. नीटनेटका, नेटका, साजरा.

4—in free phrasecol. *full, good, &c.* v. FULL. पक्का, ताठर, तब्यल, चरब.

P. noun. विशेषनाम *n.* व्यक्तिनाम *n.*

PROPERLY, *adv.* v. A. 2. योग्य, यथायोग्य, यथोचित, ठीक, बराबर, यथास्थित, न्यायतः, धर्मतः, उजू.

I. *in a strict sense.* बारीक पाहिलें असतां, बारीक विचार केला असतां, सूक्ष्म-तत्वतः-&c. पाहिलें असतां, तत्वतः, वस्तुगत्या, विचार्यमाणे.

PROPERTY, *n. quality.* गुण *m.* धर्म *m.* लक्षण *n.*

An evil p. दुर्गुण *m.*

A good p. सद्गुण *m.*

Essential p. वस्तुशक्ति *f.*

General or common p. साधारण धर्म *m.*

Latent p. (or virtue). मर्म *n.*

Native p. सहजगुण *m.* प्रकृतिगुण *m.*

Properties. गुणजात *n.*

The three properties of created things. गुणत्रय *n.* They are सत्व, रज, and तम.

2 *native quality,* v. NATURE. स्वभाव *m.* स्वधर्म *m.*

3 *right of possession.* धनीपणा *m.* मालकी *f.* स्वामित्व *n.* सत्ता *f.* स्वत्व *n.* स्वाम्य *n.*

4 *thing owned*; *possession.* माल *m.*

4 *estate, substance, wealth,* v. RICHES. माल *m.* मत्ता *f.* मालमत्ता *f.* धन *n.* द्रव्य *n.* ऐवज *m.* संपत्ति *f.* गांठोडें *n.* उबारा *m.* निधान *n.* बिसात *or* द *f.* तेगार *n.* विषय *m.* वित्तविषय *m.*

Articles of p. v. GOODS. इस्ताद *f.*

Immovable p. स्थावर माल *m.* स्थावर *n.*

Man of p. ताजें कूळ *n.* ऐपतदार *m.*

Movable p. जंगम माल *m.*

One's whole p. सर्वस्व *n.*

Public p. गणद्रव्य *n.* गणधन *n.* गणान्न *n.*

PROPHECY, *n. prediction, declaration of something future,*—the act. भाकीत सांगणें *n.* भाकणें *n.* भाकणूक *f.* भविष्यकथन *n.* भाविकथन *n.*

2 *matter predicted.* भविष्य *n.* भाकीत *n.* होईक *n.* भवितव्य *n.* भविष्यार्थ *m.* होरा *m.*

Sure p. राम बाण *m.*

3 *teaching, expounding.* प्रवचन *n.* अर्थसांगणें *n.*

To PROPHESY, *v. a. foretell, predict.* भविष्य *n.*- भाकीत *n.*-होईक *n.*-&c. सांगणें-बोलणें-करणें-करून ठेवणें *g. of o.* भाकणें, भाकणूक *f.* करणें *g. of o.* पूर्वींच-अगोदरच-&c. सांगून ठेवणें-कथून ठेवणें, भविष्य कथन *n.*-भाविकथन *n.*-&c. करणें.

To PROPHESY, *v. n. utter predictions.* भविष्य *n.*-भवितव्य *n.* -भविष्यार्थ *m.*-&c. सांगणें-बोलणें.

2 प्रवचन *n.* करणें, अर्थ *m.* सांगणें.

PROPHET, *n.* v. V. भविष्य-भाकीत-होईक-&c. सांगणारा-बोलणारा, भविष्यभाषी, भविष्यवादी, भविष्यवादक, भविष्यकथक *pop.* भविष्यकथ्या, भविष्यद्वक्ता, पेगमबर *or* पैगमबर.

2 प्रवक्ता.

PROPHETESS, *n.* v. PROPHET. भविष्य-&c. सांगणारी *f.*-बोलणारी *f.* भविष्यभाषिणी *f.* भविष्यवादिनी *f.* &c.

PROPHETIC, PROPHETICAL, *a. containing, &c. prophecy.* भविष्यसूचक, भविष्यदर्शक, भविष्यमय,भविष्यप्रचुर, भविष्यकथनप्रचुर, भविष्यकथनविषयक.

PROPHYLACTIC, *a.*—in medicine. रोग-&c. निवारक.

PROPINQUITY, *n.* v. NEARNESS. जवळपणा *m.* जवळीक *f.* नैकट्य *n.* समीपता *f.* सामीप्य *n.* सन्निधान *n.*

PROPITIABLE, *a.* v. V. 1. आराध्य, आराधनीय, आराधनशक्य.

To PROPITIATE, *v. a. make propitious.* खुलावणें, खुलिवणें, आळवणें, बळवणें, मनावणें, आराधणें, प्रसन्न-अनुकूल-अभिमुख-&c. करणें-करून घेणें, प्रसन्नता *f.*-प्रसाद *m.*-अनुकूलता *f.*-&c. करून घेणें *g. of o.* मनधरणी *f.*-मनवळवणी *f.*-&c. करणें *g. of o.*

2 *appease and render favorable,* v. To PACIFY. शांत-&c. करणें-करून घेणें, शांति *f.*-सांत्वन *n.*-&c. करणें *g. of o.*

PROPITIATED, *p.* v. V. 1. खुलावलेला, आळवलेला, &c. प्रसन्न केलेला, &c. आराधित,प्रासादित, प्रसन्न.

2 शांत केलेला, &c. शांत.

PROPITIATION, *n.* v. V. 1.—*act.* खुलावणें *n.* आराधणें *n.* आळवणें *n.* &c. मनमनावणी *f.* मनधरणी *f.* मनवळवणी *f.* मनवळणी *f.* आराधना *f.* आराधन *n.* आराधणूक *f.* प्रसादन *n.*

2 शांत करणें *n.* &c. सांत्वन *n.* सांत्वना *f.* शांति *f.*

Ceremonies in p. शांति *f.* शांतिक *n.* शांतिकपौष्टिक *n.*

Course of ceremonies in p. अनुष्ठान *n.*

I. *atonement, or atoning sacrifice.* प्रायश्चित *n.*

PROPITIATOR, *n.* PROPITIATING, *p. a.* PROPITATORY, *a.* v. V. 1. खुलावणारा, आळवणारा, आराधणारा, &c. मनधरणीचा, मनवळणीचा, &c. आराधक, प्रसन्नकारक, प्रसादाधायक.

2 शांत करणारा, &c. शांतिकर-कारक-प्रद-दायक-&c. शांतिक.

Propitious, *a.* v. Favorable. अनुकूल, धारजणा *or* धारजिणा, प्रसन्न, सुप्रसन्न, अभीष्ट, अभिमुख.

2 See Auspicious.

To become p. ;—fortune, destiny. उघडणें, उफलणें, खुलणें, उदेणें, फळफळणें.

Propitiously, *adv.* v.A. प्रसन्न-अनुकूल-&c. होऊन, प्रसन्नतेनें, &c. प्रसादपूर्वक.

Propitiousness, *n.* v. A. 1. प्रसन्नता *f.* प्रसाद *m.* अनुकूलता *f.* आनुकूल्य*n.* धारजणें *or* धारजिणें*n.*आभिमुख्य*n.* बहाली *f.*यश *n.*

Proponent, *n. one that lays down a proposition.* पूर्ववादी,अग्रवादी, पूर्वपक्षी, प्रतिज्ञावादी.

Proportion, *n. comparative relation.* परिमाण *n.* प्रमाण *n.* परस्परानुगुण्य *n.* बेत *m.* हिशेब *m.*

In p. to. प्रमाणें, जसा *with* तसा *decl.* बेतानें, हिशेबानें, अनुरूप, अनुसार, यथा prefixed.

2—in arithmetic. अनुपात *m.*

Mean p. शेरा *m.* बसतन *or* बसतान *n.*

3 *adaptation, symmetry.* संजोग *m.* बेत *m.* बेतबात *m.* जम *m.* जवा *m.* जुगल *f.* जुळणी *f.* तानमान *n.* मेळ *m.* संधान *n.* अनुसंधान *n.* अन्वय *m.*

4 v. Share. हिस्सा *m.* वांटा *m.* वर्गणी *f.*

To **Proportion**, *To* **Proportionate**, *v. a. adjust the proportion of.* प्रमाण *n.* ठेवणें *with g. of o. recip.* जम *m.*-जवा *m.*-मेळ *m.*- &c. बसवणें *with g. of o. recip.*

Proportionable, **Proportional**, **Proportionate**, *a. that is in suitable proportion or relation.* बेताचा, प्रमाणाचा, बराबरीचा, संजोगाचा, &c. समतोल, समप्रमाणक, प्रमित, परिमित, आनुषंगिक.

Proportionableness, **Proportionality**, **Proportionateness.** *n.* v. A. बराबरी *f.* समप्रमाणकता *f.* समतोलपणा *m.*

Proportionably, **Proportionally**, *adv.* v. A. प्रमाणें, प्रमाणानें, प्रमाणतः, यथाप्रमाण, त्या बेतानें, त्याबेतांप्रमाणें.

Proposal, *n. something offered for consideration, &c.*बोलणें *n.* कर्त्तव्यसूचन *n.* कर्त्तव्यसूचना *f.*

To **Propose**, *To* **Propound**, *v. a. advance, offer for consideration.* घालणें, करणें, बोलणें, म्हणणें, पुढें ठेवणें, उहू *m.*-उल्लेख *m.*-उद्गार *m.*-&c. काढणें-करणें *g. of o.* उपपादन, *n.* करणें, उपपादणें, उपोद्घात *m.*-उपक्रम *m.*-प्रस्तावना *f.*-प्रस्ताव *m.*-&c. करणें *g. of o.*

2 (to one's self) v. To Intend. मनांत योजणें.

Proposition, *n. sentence.* वाक्य *n.* फक्किका *pop.* फांकी *f.*

2—in logic ; v. Position. प्रतिज्ञा *f.* पूर्वपक्ष *m.* प्रतिज्ञात अर्थ *m.* उपपाद्य *n.* [ज्ञाहानि *f.*

Abandonment of the original p. प्रतिज्ञासंन्यास *m.* प्रति-

Completing the p. आकांक्षापूरण *n.*

Denial of a p. प्रतिज्ञाविरोध *m.*

3 See Proposal. 4—in mathematics. सिद्धांत *m.*

Proprietor, **Proprietary**, *n. owner, person having the right or title to.* सत्तेवाईक, सत्ताधारी, धनी, मालक *or* मालीक, खावंद, सत्तेदार, सत्तापुरुष, वारसेदार, वारीसदार.

Proprietorship, *n.* धनीपणा *m.* मालकी *f.* सत्ता *f.* स्वाम्य *n.* स्वामित्व *n.* वारसा *m.* वारीस *m.*

Proprietress, *n. female owner, &c.* धनीण *f.* अधिकारिणी *pop.* अधिकारीण *f.* मालकीण *f.* स्वामिनी *pop.* स्वामीण *f.* सत्ताधारिणी *f.* &c.

Propriety, *n. right of possession.* धनीपणा *m.* अधिकार *m.* सत्ता *f.* मालकी *f.* स्वामित्व *n.*

2 *fitness, justness.* योग्यता *f.* निटाई *f.* शिस्तवारी *f.* शिस्तवारपणा *m.* दुरुस्ती *f.* दुरुस्तपणा *m.* लायकी *f.* यथायोग्यता *f.* यथायुक्तता *f.* औचित्य *n.* याथार्थ्य *n.* हिशेब *m.* लाग *m.* संभव *m.* संभावना *f.*

Propulsion, *n.* v. V. पुढें चालवणें *n.* पुढें ढकलणें*n.* &c.

Prorogation, *n.* v. V. 1. मोडून लांबचे मुदतीवर नेणें *n.* &c.

To **Prorogue**, *v. a. adjourn to a distant period.* मोडून लांबचे मुदतीवर नेणें-लोटणें.

2 See To Prolong, To Defer.

Prorogued, *p.* v. V. 1. मोडून लांबचे मुदतीवर नेलेला-&c.

Prosaic, *a. pertaining, &c. to prose.* गद्यरूप, गाथारूप, गद्यात्मक, गद्यमय, छंदोहीन, छंदोरहित, अछंदस्क. [चावट,

2 *dull, tiresome, prosy.* चरपटीचा, चरपटपंजरीचा, चघळाचा,

To **Proscribe**, *v. a. put out of the protection of the law. doom to death.* माणसांतून उठवणें-काढणें *or* उठवून-काढून मृत्युपात्र मृत्युस्थान-&c. करणें, मरणाचे स्वाधीन-मरणाचे हातीं-&c. देणें.

2 *condemn and interdict.* वाईट-अयोग्य-अपात्र-दुष्ट-&c. म्हणवून-ठरवून-&c. निषेधणें.

Prose, *n.*—*opposed to* metrical composition. गाथा *f.* गद्य *n.* छंदोरहितभाषण *n.*

P. and verse. गद्यपद्य *n.*

Alternate p. and verse. चंपू *m.*

Writer of p. गाथिक.

Prose, *a.* गद्यरूप, गद्यात्मक.

To **Prose**, *v. n. be tedious in relation.* चावटाई *f.*-चर्वितचर्वण *n.*-&c. करणें, चरकट *or* चरपट *n.*-चरपटपंजरी *f.*-चरपटिका *f.*-तरढक *n.*-वासलात *f.*-लापण्णिका *f.*-&c. लावणें, चघळ बोलणें *n.* द्राविडप्राणायाम *m.*-शब्दपाल्हाळ *m.*-&c. करणें *or* लावणें.

To **Prosecute**, *v. a.* v. To Pursue. पाठीस लागणें *g. of o.* पाठ *f.*-पिच्छा *m.* घेणें-धरणें-पुरवणें *g. of o.* पिच्छ्यास बसणें-लागणें-असणें *g. of o.*

2 *carry on,* v. To Conduct. चालवणें, वाहणें, हाकणें.

To p. to a successful close. निर्वाहणें, निभावणें, निर्वाह *m.*-निभाव *m.*-निभावणी *f.*-निभावणूक *f.*-&c. करणें *g. of o.*

3 *pursue by law.* फिर्याद *f.* करणें *with* वर *of o.* खटला *m.*-वाद *m.*-&c. उभा करणें-उपस्थित करणें, व्यवहाराभिशंसन *n.*-व्यवहाराभियोग *m.*-&c. करणें.

Prosecuted, *p.* v. V. 1. पाठीस लागलेला, &c. अनुधावित.

2 चालवलेला, &c.

3 व्यवहाराभिशस्त, अभियुक्त, व्यवहाराभियुक्त.

Prosecution, **Prosecuting**, *n.* v. V. 1. पाठीस लागणें *n.* &c. पाठलाग *m.* अनुधावन *n.*

2 चालवणें *n.* &c. [*m.* अभियोग *m.*

3 फिर्याद *f.* अभिशंसन *n.* व्यवहाराभिशंसन *n.* व्यवहाराभियोग

Prosecutor, *n.* **Prosecuting**, *p. a.* v. V. 1. पाठीस लागणारा, पिच्छ्यास बसणारा-&c.

2 चालवणारा, &c.

3 फिर्यादी, मुद्दई, मुदाईम, अभिशंसन-व्यवहाराभिशंसन-अभियोग-&c. कर्त्ता-कारी-&c.

PROSELYTE, *To* PROSELYTE. See CONVERT, To CONVERT.

PROSER, *n.* PROSING, *p. a.* v. V. चावटाई-चरपट-&c. करणारा-लावणारा, चघळ, चाहटळ *or* चहाटळ, चावट, चावनट, बहुचक्र, तोंडाचा जड, बयादी, बयादखोर.

PROSING, *n.*v. V. चघळ बोलणें*n.* चावटाई *f.* चरपट *f.n.* चरपटपंजरी *f.* चरकट*m.* चरडक *or* चरढक*n.*

PROSODIAL, PROSODICAL, *a. pertaining, &c. to prosody.* छंदःशास्त्राचा, छंदःशास्त्रसंबंधी-विषयक, छांदस.

PROSODIAN, *n. one skilled in prosody.* छंदःशास्त्री, छंदःशास्त्रज्ञ, छंदःशास्त्रवेत्ता. [*f.*

PROSODY, *n. rules of versification.* छंद*m.n.* छंदःशास्त्र*n.* छंदोविद्या

PROSOPOPEIA. See PERSONIFICATION. [अमल*m.*

PROSPECT, *n. view.* दृष्टि *f.* पाहणें*n.* दृष्टिपात*m.* दृक्पात*m.* दृष्टीचा-

2 *view of things to come, expectation.* भाविदर्शन*n.* भाविघटनादर्शन*n.* मानसिकदृष्टिपात*m.* आशा *f.*

3 *apprehension of as likely to happen.* अगा *f.* घांग *f.* धोरण *n.* भास*m.* भान*n.* ध्यान*n.* रंग*m.* सुमार*m.* लाग*m.* संभावना *f.* संभव*m.* संभूति *f.*

4 *that which is presented to the eye.* दृष्टीखालचादेश*m.* दृक्पातविषय*m.* दृष्टिपतनविषय*m.* दृष्टिपातांतर्गतदेश *m.* दृक्पातांतर्गत देश*m.*

PROSPECTIVE, *a. referring to future time.* पुढल्या काळाचे धोरणाचा, भाविकालापेक्षक, भाविकालापेक्षी, भाविस्पृक्, भाविकालसापेक्ष.

PROSPECTIVELY, *adv.* v. A. पुढल्या काळाचे धोरणानें, पुढल्या काळाचेंधोरण धरून, भाविकालापेक्षेनें, भाविकालापेक्षापूर्वक.

PROSPECTIVENESS, *n.* v. A. पुढल्या काळाचें धोरण*n.* भाविकालापेक्षा *f.* भाविकालापेक्षिता *f.*

PROSPECTUS, *n. plan of a work.* कर्त्तव्यप्रसिद्धिपत्र *n.* कर्त्तव्यार्थप्रसिद्धिपत्र *n.*

To PROSPER, *v. a. render successful.* सफल-सुफल-फलद्रूप-&c. करणें, सार्थक्य *pop.* सार्थक*n.*-सिद्धि *f.*-सिद्धता *f.*-संसिद्धि *f.*-बोलबाला*m.*-समृद्धि *f.*-संवर्द्धन*n.*-संवृद्धि*f.*-&c. करणें *g. of o.* बरकत *f. n.*-यश*n.* देणें-करणें, धडीस-सिद्धीस-शेवटास-&c. नेणें-जाईसा *decl.* करणें, पार पाडणें, यश *n.* येईसा *decl.* करणें, गुणास येईसा *decl.*-जयास जाईसा *decl.*-&c. करणें.

To PROSPER, *v. n. be successful, &c.*—of persons. जिंकणें, जयी-कृतार्थ-कृतकृत्य-कृतकृतार्थ-प्राप्तार्थ-प्राप्तयश-&c. होणें-असणें, तडीस-&c. जाणें, सिद्धि-जय-&c. पावणें, पार पडणें-जाणें, यश*n.* येणें *in. con.* पिकणें *g. of s.* फते *f.* होणें *g. of s.* लाग*m.*-&c. साधणें *g. of s.* भरभर *f.*-भरभराट*m.*-कार्यसिद्धि *f.*-&c. होणें *g. of s.* तरतरणें, तरारणें, चलती *f.*-चालताकाळ *m.*-चढता काळ*m.*-&c. असणें *g. of s.*

2—of measures, &c. सिद्धीस-शेवटास-धडीस-जयास-परिणामास-&c. जाणें, साधणें, लागणें, सफल-लागू-&c. होणें, पार जाणें-पडणें, गुणास-फळास-&c. येणें, फळणें, यश*n.*-बरकत*f.* येणें *in. con.* रंगास-&c. चढणें.

3 (in business, trade, &c.). चढती कळा *f.*-चढती कमाण *f.*-चढतापाया*m.*-चढतीपायरी *f.*-&c. असणें *g. of s.* चढती *f.*-वृद्धि *f.*-&c. होणें *g. of s.* उदय*m.*-&c. होणें *g. of s.*

PROSPERER, *n.* PROSPERING, *p. a.* v. V. A. 1. सफल करणारा, सार्थक करणारा, सिद्धीसनेणारा, &c. संवर्द्धक, संवृद्धिकर्त्ता-कारक-&c. v. V. N. See PROSPEROUS.

PROSPERITY, PROSPEROUSNESS, *n.* v. A. 1. बखतवारी *f.* तालेवारी *f.* ऊर्जित *n.* उत्कर्ष *m.* भाग्य *n.* होतीदशा *f.* चढतीदशा *f.* वाढतीदशा *f.* येतापाया *m.* चढतापाया *m.* चढतीकमाण *f.* चढती पायरी *f.* वाढतापाया *m.* बोलबाला *m.* बडेजाव *m. pl.* भरभर *f.* भरभराट *m.* संपत्ति *f.* नांदी *f.* श्री *f.* श्रेय *n.* भद्र *n.* मंगल *n.* बरकत *f. n.* प्रकर्ष *m.* सद्दी *f.* संपदा *f.* सिद्धि *f.* कार्यसिद्धि *f.* अर्थसिद्धि *f.* ऋद्धि *f.* समृद्धि *f.* संवृद्धि *f.*

Flush or overflow of p. संपतीचा ऊत *m.*

High tide or heyday of p. भरदौलत *f.* ऐन दौलत *f.*

Season of p. सायाप्यायाचे दिवस *m. pl.* त्याया नेसायाचे दिवस *m. pl.* घातीचे दिवस *m. pl.* उदयकाल *m.* उदितकाल *m.* ऊर्जितकाळ *m.* सन्मुखकाळ *m.* चढताकाळ *m.* वाढताकाळ *m.* चढतीवेळ *f.* लक्ष्मीचा होरा *m.* दैवोद्घाटनसमय *m.*

4 आबादी *f.* आबादानी *f.* सुबत्ता *m.*

PROSPEROUS, *a. successful, flourishing,*—of persons. लक्ष्मीवान्, लक्ष्मीवंत, श्रीमान्, श्रीमंत, श्रीकार, तालेवार, तालेवंत, बखतवार, कृतार्थ, कृतकृत्य, कृतकृतार्थ, चरितार्थ, प्राप्तयश, पद्महस्ती, बरदहस्ती, यशस्वी, जयी, कल्याणी, सातापिता, भद्र, क्षेम, संपन्न.

2—of measures, &c. सफल, सुफल, गुणावह, सिद्धीस-&c. जायाजोगा, सफल व्हायायोगा, सुदामत-सुरळीत-&c. चाललेला.

3—trade, a trader, &c. *thriving.* उदयी, उदयास आलेला, चढतेकळेचा, चढतेपायरीचा, चढतेकमाणीचा, &c. ऊर्जितकाळाचा, भरभरीचा, वाढता, चढता, वृद्धिमान्, वर्द्धिष्णु, वर्धमान, समृद्ध.

P. or flourishing state. भरभर *f.*—*intens.* भरभराट *m.*

4—as a town, country, &c. आबाद, आबादान, आबादानीचा, आबादीचा, सुबत्त्याचा, समृद्ध.

PROSTITUTE, *n.* v. HARLOT. कसबीण *f.* बसवी *f.* वेश्या *f.* गणिका *f.* सामान्या *f.* हट्टविलासिनी *f.*

Ceremony of licensing a p. मिशी *f.*

License of a p. कसबचिठी *f.*

Trade of a p. कसब *n.*

To PROSTITUTE, *v. a. sell to lewdness* (a daughter, wife, &c.). भाडीस देणें-लावणें, भाड *f.* खाणें *g. of o.*

2 *devote to base purposes for reward.* लोभानें-धनाशेनें-पैका घेऊन-&c. वाईट कामास-नीच कामास-&c. लावणें-विकणें.

PROSTITUTION, *n.* v. V. 1.—*act.* भाडीस लावणें *n.*

I. *practice, trade, life, &c. of a prostitute.* कसब *n.* कसबिणीचा धंदा *m.*-व्यापार *m.* वेश्यावृत्ति *f.* भगवृत्ति *f.* भगव्यापार *m.* वेश्याजीविका *f.* भगजीविका *f.* वारसेवा *f.* गणसेवा *f.*

Earnings of letting out to p. भाड *f.* भाटक *n.*—that subsists on these. भाडखाऊ.

PROSTRATE, *a. lying at length.* भुईवर-&c. पडलेला, जमिनदोस्तचीत झालेला-केलेला, लंबा-लंबे झालेला, भूमिशायी.

2—as in supplication, adoration, &c. साष्टांगनमस्कार घातलेला, साष्टांगपतित, साष्टांगप्रणत, पादप्रणत, शरणपतित, पादपतित, चरणगत.

3 (in strength) v. WEAKENED. क्षीणशक्ति, शक्तिक्षीण, गतशक्ति, नष्टशक्ति, प्रशांतौजः.

To PROSTRATE, *v. a. lay flat, throw down.* पाडणें, भुईशीं-भुईसनिजवणें, लंबा करणें, जमिनदोस्त-चीत-&c. करणें, लोळवणें.

2 (one's self in reverence, &c.). पायां पडणें, दंडवत *m. n.*-साष्टांग *m.*-साष्टांगनमस्कार *m.*-साष्टांग प्रणाम *m.*-पादप्रणाम

m.-&c. करणें. [ला, &c.

PROSTRATED, *p.* v. V. 1. पाडलेला, जमिनदोस्त केलेला, लंबा केले-

2 See PROSTRATE. [*n.* &c.

PROSTRATION, *n.* v. V. 1.—*act.* पाडणें *n.* निजवणें *n.* लंबाकरणें

2 पायां पडणें *n.* &c. दंडवत *m. n.* अष्टांगपात *m.* अष्टांगपतन *n.* अष्टांगप्रणाम *m. or* साष्टांगपात *m.* &c. पादप्रणाम *m.* चरणपतन *n.* पादपतन *n.*

I. (of strength). उठवण *f.* शीण *m.* भागशीण *m.* चुरा *m.* चुराडा *m.* शक्तिपात *m.* ग्लानि *f.* बुद्दा *m.* चूर *m.*

To suffer p. of strength. उठवणीस येणें *or* उठवण *f.* घेणें.

II. (of spirits). v. DEPRESSION. अवसाद*m.* विषाद*m.* ग्लानि*f.*

PROSY, *a. prolix, dull, &c.* चरपटीचा, चरपटपंजरीचा, चावटाईचा, तरढकाचा, पाल्हाळीक.

To PROTECT, *v. a. defend, guard, keep,* v. To PRESERVE. राखणें, रक्षणें, संरक्षणें, पाठीसीं घालणें-घेणें, बचावणें, पाळणें, संभाळणें, आश्रय *m.*-&c. देणें, राखण *f.*-रक्षण *n.*-संरक्षण *n.*-बचाव *m.*-पालन *n.*-&c. करणें *g. of o.*

PROTECTED, *p.* v. V. राखलेला, रक्षिलेला, &c. रक्षित, संरक्षित, सुरक्षित, तारित, त्रात, आश्रित, परिपालित, संगोपित, गोपित, गुप्त.

PROTECTION, *n.* v. V.—*act.* राखणें *n.* &c. राखण *f.* रक्षण *n.* संरक्षण *n.* पालन *n.* परिपालन *n.* बचाव *m.* परित्राण *n.* गोपन *n.* संगोपन *n.*

To commit to the p. of. पदरीं-ओटींत-उत्संगीं-ओशंगला-&c. घालणें-देणें *g. of o.*

To seek p. of. आश्रय *m.*-दुमाला *m.* धरणें *g. of o.* पाठ *f.* निघणें *g. of o.* शरण जाणें-येणें, पोटांत डोकी *f.* घालणें *g. of o.* मांडीवर शिर *n.* ठेवणें *g. of o.*

I. *shelter or defence afforded.* आश्रय *pop.* आस्रा*m.* शरण*n.* छाया *f.* पांघरूण *n.* छत्र *n.*

II. v. PASS. दस्तक *n.* अभयपत्र *n.*

PROTECTOR, *n.* PROTECTING, *p. a.* PROTECTIVE, *a.* v. V. राखणारा, रक्षणारा, रक्षक, संरक्षक, रक्षण-संरक्षण-&c. कर्त्ता-कारी, पालक, प्रतिपालक, गोपक, शरण, भयत्राता, आश्रयदाता-दायक, आश्रयभूत, आश्रयप्रद, मायबाप, वाली *or* वाल्ही.

PROTECTRESS, *n.* राखणारी *f.* रक्षण-संरक्षण-&c. कर्त्री *pop.* कर्त्ती*f.*

PROTEGÉ, *n. one under the protection of another.* आश्रित, हिमाईतदार, हिमाइती, बगल्या, पदरचा, पोष्य, कृपापात्र.

Among the millions of (your &c.) protegées. आश्रित कोटि निविष्ट, आश्रित कोट्यंतर्गत.

To PROTEND, *v. a.* v. To STRETCH FORTH. लांब करणें.

To PROTEST, *v. n. affirm solemnly.* प्रतिज्ञेनें-प्रतिज्ञा करून-प्रतिज्ञापूर्वक-सत्योत्तरें-सत्योत्तरकरून-सत्यस्मरून-&c. बोलणें-म्हणणें, उरावर हात *m.* लावणें-लावून बोलणें.

2 against; *make a solemn declaration of opposition.* नाहींच नाहीं म्हणणें-म्हणून बोलणें, प्रतिज्ञा करून-प्रतिज्ञापूर्वक-निश्चयपूर्वक-&c. नाहीं म्हणणें-अस्वीकार *m.* करणें-निषेध *m.* करणें-अस्वीकारप्रकाश *m.* करणें.

3 (in writing.). निश्चयपूर्वक-प्रतिज्ञापूर्वक-&c. आपली असम्मति *f.* लिहून ठेवणें.

PROTEST, PROTESTATION, *n.* v. V. 1. प्रतिज्ञेनें बोलणें *n.* &c. प्रतिज्ञापूर्वकभाषण *n.*

2 प्रतिज्ञापूर्वकनिषेध *m.* प्रतिज्ञापूर्वकास्वीकार *m.* निश्चयपूर्वकासम्मति *f.* असम्मतिप्रकाश *m.*

3 असम्मतिलेख *m.* अनंगीकारलेख *m.*

PROTESTANT, *n.* रोमनक्याथोलिक मताला असम्मत खिस्ती.

PROTEUS, *n. one who assumes a shape at will.* इच्छारूपी. कामरूपी.

PROTOTYPE, *n. original pattern.* मूळ *n.* मूळरूप *n.* प्रकृति *f.*

To PROTRACT, *v. a. prolong, lengthen in time.* लांबवणें, बाढवणें, लांबण *f.* लावणें-करणें, लांबणीवर घालणें-टाकणें, लांबन धरणें, लांबलचक *f.* लावणें.

To be protracted. लांबणीवर पडणें.

2 See To DEFER. [लंबित.

PROTRACTED, *p.* v. V.1. लांबवलेला, लांबणीवर घातलेला-&c. वि-

PROTRACTER, *n.* PROTRACTING, *p. a.* v. V. 1. लांबणारा, लांबण लावणारा, लांबणीवर घालणारा, विलंबनकर्त्ता.

PROTRACTION, *n.* v. V. 1. लांबवणें *n.* &c. लांबवणी *f.* लांबण *f.* लांबलचक *f.* विलंबन *n.*

To PROTRUDE, *v. a. thrust forward or out.* पुढें-बाहेर ढकलणें-लोटणें-करणें-काढणें.

To PROTRUDE, *v. n. shoot forward, &c.* पुढें-बाहेर येणें-पडणें, फुटून बाहेर पडणें.

PROTRUDED, *p.* v. V. A. पुढें ढकललेला, &c.

v. V. N. पुढें आलेला, बाहेर आलेला, &c.

PROTRUDER, *n.* PROTRUDING, *p. a.* PROTRUSIVE, *a.* v. V. A. पुढें ढकलणारा-लोटणारा-&c.

PROTRUSION, *n.* v. V. A.—*act.* पुढें ढकलणें *n.* पुढें लोटणें *n.* &c. v. V. N. पुढें येणें *n.* बाहेर येणें *n.* &c.

PROTUBERANCE, *n.* v. A. उंचपणा *m.* फुगलेलेपणा *m.* &c.

I. *a* p. v. RISING. उंचवटा *m.* उंचाड *n.* टेंगूळ *n.*

PROTUBERANT, PROTUBEROUS, *a. swelling out, prominent.* बाहेर आलेला, उंच, फुगलेला, फुगीर.

To PROTUBERATE, *v. n.* v. To BELLY. बाहेर येणें, फुगणें, फुगा *m.*-फुगारा *m.* येणें, उंचावणें.

PROUD, *a. having pride.* गर्वी, गर्विष्ट, गर्वित, सगर्व, अभिमानी, साभिमान, मानी, मानवान्, अहंकारी, अहंकारवान्, अहम्मानी, साहंकार, मगरुरीचा, मगरूर, दिमाखाचा, दिमाखदार, दिमाखी, पिळदार, तोरेदार, चढेल, वरडोळ्या, मस्त, मस्तवाला, बदमस्त, उन्मत्त, उदगा, उदगामादगा, उदमस्त, दर्पित, माजोरा, माजोरी *or* माजुरी, समुद्धत, ऊर्ध्वदृष्टि, उन्नतशिरस्क, अविनय,—in high degree; गर्वाधीन, मदाकुल, मदाक्रांत, मदाविष्ट, प्रमत्त, दर्पध्मात. Some appellatives, allusive terms, expressive phrases. &c. for *A proud person* are, गजमस्तकारूढ, मगरमस्त, जालीम, डोळे ताठलेला, यास आकाश पाताळ एक, याच्या डोक्याला आभाळ *or* स्वर्ग &c. लागूं लागलें *or* दोन बोटें उरलें &c. याच्या आंगीं तीन मण तिखें जळलें.

To become p. Conveying this simple sense, though with varying implications, as there are numerous phraseologies in English, so are there in *Maràṭhi*; but all the phraseologies in *Maràṭhi*, which correspond to those in English in conveying the *sense*, are not, and cannot be expected to be, corresponding also in *implication and aspect.* Of such then the insertion can manifestly be no where but under the general and comprehensive word. Here accordingly are collected the phrases agreeing with *To get puffed up, lifted up.*

inflated, blinded, &c., To get high notions, a stiff neck, &c. To lose or forget one's self, To give one's self airs, To grow big, lofty, a great man, &c. To get one's head turned, &c. &c. फुलणें, माजणें, मातणें, चढणें, फुगणें, जडावणें, जडकावणें, मस्तावणें, उफाळणें, उतणणें, उताटणें, उंडारणें, शेफरणें *or* शफारणें, गजस्कंधीं बसणें, आसन *n.* जड होणें *g. of s.* मान *n.* चढणें *g. of s.* डोईनें चालूं लागणें, डोळ्यांवर धूर *m.* येणें *g. of s.* डोळे *m. pl.* उरफाटणें-फिरणें-चढणें *g. of s.* परडें *n.* चढणें *or* जड होत जाणें *g. of s.* शीड *n.* चढणें *g. of s.* अडीच कांड्यावर येणें.—*And* To be p. इशीम *f.* बाळगणें-भोगणें, आढ्यता *f.* मिरवणें-बाळगणें-ओढणें, प्रतिष्ठा *f.* बाळगणें-मिरवणें, मान *f.* कांद्यावर नसणें *g. of s.* डोईनें चालणें, स्वर्ग *m.* दोन बोटें उरणें,—*And* To make p.—as involving the general sense of *to puff up, lift up, inflate, blind, &c.* is answered by चण्याच्या झाडावर चढवणें.

P. though in rags. हालमस्त.

2 of; *pluming one's self upon.* अभिमानी, अभिमान धरणारा-धरलेला, &c. अकड बाळगणारा-&c. बाणाईत, बाण्याचा, बाणीचा, बाणीदार, अड्डेबाज, अड्डेबाईक.

P. of birth. कुलाभिमानी.

3 See Grand, Magnificent. 4—flesh. मुडदार.

Proudly, *adv.* v. A. 1. गर्वानें, मगरुरीनें, अभिमानानें, &c. गर्वपूर्वक, अभिमानपूर्वक, &c.

Provable, *a.* v. V. 1. स्थापायाजोगा-&c. सिद्ध करायाजोगा-&c. प्रमेय, प्रतिपाद्य, प्रतिपादनीय, स्थापनीय, समर्थनीय.

To Prove, *v. a. evince, demonstrate, establish.* स्थापणें, खरा-सत्य-&c. करणें-करून देणें-करून दाखवणें, शाबूत-सिद्ध-स्थापित-&c. करणें, प्रतिपादणें, प्रपादणें, पुरवणें, सप्रमाणकरणें, प्रमाण *n.* करून दाखवणें, *g. of o.* प्रपादणी *f.*-स्थापन *n.*-स्थापना *f.*-प्रतिपादन *n.*-उपपादन *n.*-उपपत्ति *f.*-समर्थन *n.*-मंडन *n.*-&c. करणें *g. of o.*

To p. upon. पदरीं घालणें, आंगीं लावणें, लागू करणें.

2 *bring to the test, try.* पारखणें, ताडणें, पाहणें, पडतळणें *or* पडताळणें, ताडून-पडताळून पाहणें, परीक्षणें, परीक्षा *f.*-परीक्षण *n.*-पारख *f.*-&c. करणें-घेणें *g. of o.* धूम *m.* पाहणें *g. of o.* पडतळा *or* पडताळा *m.*-पडोसा *m.*-&c. घेणें-पाहणें.

3 v. To Experience. चव *f.* घेणें-पाहणें *g. of o.* दाखल्यास येणें-उतरणें, साक्षात्कार *m.* करून पाहणें-करणें-घेणें *g. of o.* परीक्षणें, दाखला *m.*-अनुभव *m.*-प्रत्यय *m.*-प्रतीति *pop.* प्रचीति *or* प्रचीत *f.*-&c. घेणें-पाहणें *or with in. con.* येणें-होणें.

To Prove, *v. n. make trial.* पाहणें, परीक्षा *f.* घेणें-करणें.

2 *be found eventually, issue.* पटणें, पडणें, निघणें, होणें, उतरणें, निपजणें, येणें, ठरणें, दृष्टीस-नजरेस-&c. येणें, दिसून येणें.

To p. true. पटणें.

Proved, *p.* v. V. A. 1. स्थापलेला, खरा करून दिल्हेला, &c. सिद्ध, शाबूत *or* द, स्थापित, प्रतिपादित, उपपादित, प्रमित, उपपन्न, समर्थित, मंडित.

2 ताडलेला, ताडून पाहिलेला, &c. परीक्षित.

3 *and* Experienced. दाखल्यास आलेला, &c. साक्षात्कृत, प्रतीत.

Provedore, *n. purveyor,* v. Caterer. मोदी, वाकनीस.

Provender, *n. food for beasts.* दाणाचारा *m.* चारादाणा *m.* वैरण *f.* घासपात *m.*

Green p. चार *f.*

Prover, *n.* Proving, *p. a.* v. V. A. 1. स्थापणारा, शाबूत करणारा, &c. प्रतिपादक, प्रमाता, उपपादक, प्रतिपत्ति-उपपत्ति-&c. कर्त्ता-कारी.

Proverb, *n. saw, adage.* म्हण *f.* म्हणणी *f.* आणा *m.* आहणा *m.* न्याय *m.* लोकोक्ति *f.*

Proverbial, *a. mentioned in a proverb.* म्हणीचा, म्हणींतला, म्हणींतम्हटलेला, म्हणींत आलेला.

2 *comprised in a proverb, current as a proverb.* न्यायरूप, न्यायोक्त, न्यायप्रसिद्ध.

3 *pertaining, suitable, &c. to a proverb.* म्हणीचा.

To Provide, *v. a. procure or prepare beforehand.* पुढें-&c. करून ठेवणें, तयार *or* तैयार-सिद्ध-&c. करून ठेवणें, बेजमी *f.*-संजोग *m.*-साहित्य *n.*-तरतूद *or* तरदूद *f.*-तयारी *or* तैयारी *f.*-योजना *f.*-उपाय *m.*-तजवीज *f.*-बंदोबस्त *m.*-&c. करणें-करून ठेवणें.

2 *supply, furnish, give.* देणें, करणें, पुरवणें, साहित्य *n.*-सामग्री *f.*-&c. करणें *g. of o.* पुरवणी *f.*-पुरावा *m.*-भरती *f.*-&c. करणें *g. of o.*

3 v. To Stipulate. संकेत *m.* करणें.

To p. against. अगा *m.*-धोरण *n.*-संधान *n.*-&c. बांधणें *g. of o.*

To p. for, *put into a livelihood.* अन्नास लावणें.

To be provided for. अन्नास लागणें.

To p. for comfortably. स्वास्थ्य *n.* करणें *g. of o.*

Provided, *p.* v. V. 1. पुढें करून ठेवलेला, तयार-सिद्ध-&c. करून ठेवलेला, &c.

2 दिल्हेला, पुरवलेला, &c.

3 संकेतित, सांकेतिक.

Providence, *n. fore-thought, foresight, fore-concern.* दुरंदेशा *m.* दूरदर्शन *n.* दूरदृष्टि *f.* दीर्घदृष्टि *f.* दीर्घदर्शन *n.* पूर्वविचार *m.* दूरविचार *m.* भविष्यचिंतन *n.* भविष्यदर्शन *n.* भाविकालावलोकन *n.* आगमिष्यमाणदिनविचार *m.*

2 (of God). ईश्वरीतंत्र *n.* ईश्वरीसूत्र *n.* ईश्वरीसंधान *n.* ईश्वरानुसंधान *n.* देवानुसंधान *n.* ईश्वरीकरणी *f.*

3—as an epithet of God, v. God. अनागतविधाता.

Provident, *a. fore casting.* दुरंदेश, दीर्घदर्शी, दीर्घदृष्टि, दूरदर्शी, दूरदृष्टि, परिणामदर्शी, भविष्यदर्शी, दूरविचारी, भविष्यचिंतक, संधानी, अनुसंधानी, अनागत विधाता.

Providential, *a. effected by the providence of God.* ईश्वरीकरणीचा, ईश्वरीसूत्राचा, ईश्वरीकृतीचा.

Providentially, *adv.* v. A. ईश्वरीकरणीनें, ईश्वरीसूत्रानें.

Providently, *adv.* v. A. दूरदृष्टीनें, दीर्घदृष्टीनें, &c. दूरदृष्टिपूर्वक, दीर्घदृष्टिपूर्वक, &c.

Provider, *n.* Providing, *p. a.* v. V. 1. पुढेंकरून ठेवणारा, तयारकरून ठेवणारा, तरतूद करणारा, बेजमी करणारा, &c.

2 देणारा, पुरवणारा, &c.

Province, *n. division of a state.* सुभा *m.* प्रांत *m.* मंडळ *n.*

Government of a p. सुभेदारी *f.*

Governor of a p. सुभेदार, मंडलेश्वर, मांडलिक.

2 *proper office or sphere,* v. Business. काम *n.* प्रकरण *n.* अधिकार *m.* सातें *n.* स्वधर्म *m.* हक्क *m. n.* बकल *n.*

To fall or be in p. of. हकाटकांत येणें-असणें *g. of s.*

Provincial, *a. belonging, &c. to a province.* सुभ्याचा, प्रांताचा, प्रांतांतला, प्रांतस्थ, एकदेशी, एकप्रांती, देशिक.

2 See Rustic.

PROVISION, *n.* v. V. 1.—*act.* तयार करणें *n.* तयार करून ठेवणें *n.* &c. तरतूद *or* तरदूद *f.* तयारी *f.* तरतीब *n.*

I. *preparations, measures taken.* तरतूद *or* तरदूद *f.* तयारी *f.* तजवीज *f.* योजना *f.* बंदोबस्त *m.* उपाय *m.*

II. *stock collected, things provided.* साहित्य *n.* सामग्री *f.* बेगमी *f.* बेजमी *f.* संग्रह *m.* संचय *m.* भरती *f.* बरव *or* बरू *f.* पुरावा *m.* उपराळा *m.*

III. *victual,* v. FOOD. अन्न *n.* खाणें *n.* आहार *m.* आटापाणी *n.*
Undressed provisions. सिधा *m.* उलफा *m.* आमान्न *n.*

IV. *stipulation,* v. CONDITION. संकेत *m.*

To PROVISION, *v. a. supply with food.* अन्नाची-&c. बेजमी *f.*-&c. करणें-करून ठेवणें.

PROVISIONAL, PROVISIONARY, *a. provided for the present occasion.* चालत्या कामाचा, चालत्या गरजेचा, चालत्या प्रसंगाचा, आपाततोनियोजित, आपाततःस्थापित.

PROVISIONALLY, *adv.* v. A. चालत्या कामाला, चालत्या प्रसंगाला.

PROVISO, *n. stipulation,* v. CONDITION. संकेत *m.* शरत *f.*

PROVOCATION, *n.* v. V. 1.—*act.* चेतवणें *n.* &c. उत्तेजन *n.* उद्दीपन *n.* उद्बोधन *n.*

2—*act.* चितावणें *n.* चेष्टवणें *n.* &c. चेष्टावणी *f.* खिजवणी *f.* तळतळ *f.* चेष्टा *f.* उपराळा *m.* उत्तेजन *n.* उद्बोधन *n.* क्रोधोद्बोधन *n.* क्रोधोद्दीपन *n.* [भाषण *n.*

I. *provoking language.* चिडवणीच्या गोष्टी *f. pl.* चिडवणीचें

To PROVOKE, *v. a. arouse, stir up,* v. To EXCITE. चेतवणें, चेष्टवणें, उत्तेजन *n.*-उद्दीपन *n.*-उद्बोधन-&c. करणें *g. of o.*

2 *excite to anger,* v. To ANGER. चितावणें, चेष्टवणें, चाळवणें, चिढीस देणें, कोपविणें, तळतळावणें, तळतळ *f.* देणें, खाजवणें, खिजावणें, क्षोभवणें, (मुक्या पुढें) नाक *n.* खाजवणें, बाटेसजाणें *g. of o.*

3 (a fight, quarrel, argument, &c.). उचलून जाणें (युद्धाविषयीं, वादाविषयीं, &c.).

PROVOKED, *p.* v. V. 1. चेतवलेला, &c. उद्दीपित, उत्तेजित, उद्दीप्त, उद्बुद्ध, उद्बोधित.

2 चितावलेला, खिजावलेला, &c. कोपित, संतापित, संतप्त.

PROVOKER, *n.* PROVOKING, *p. a.* PROVOCATIVE, *a.* v. V. 1. चेतवणारा, &c. उत्तेजक, उद्दीपक, उद्बोधक, उत्तेजन-&c. कर्त्ता-कारी-&c.

2 चितावणारा, चेष्टवणारा, चिढीसदेणारा, &c. रागासआणणारा, उद्बोधक, उत्तेजक, क्रोधोद्बोधक, क्रोधोद्दीपक, क्रोधोत्तेजक.

PROVOKINGLY, *adv.* v.V. 2. चितावण्याजोगा-सारखा-&c. *decl.*

PROVOST, *n.* अधिकारी.

PROW, *n. fore part of a ship.* नाळ *f.*

2—kind of boat. पडाव *or* पडांव *m.*

PROWESS, *n. valour, gallantry, &c.* पराक्रम *m.* प्रताप *m.* पुरुषार्थ *m.* बहादरी *f.* जवानमर्दी *f.* प्रौढि *f.* वीर्य *n.* विक्रम *n.*
Personal p. बाहुवीर्य *n.*

To PROWL, *v. n. wander about for prey.* शिकारीसाठीं फिरणें, शिकारीचे-पारधीचे-&c. लागावर फिरणें, घिरट्या *f. pl.* घालणें, तलपणें *or* तळपणें, पाळतीवर फिरणें.

PROWLER, *n.* PROWLING, *p. a.* v.V. शिकारीसाठीं-शिकारीच्या लागावर-&c. फिरणारा, घिरट्या घालणारा, पाळत्या.

PROXIMATE, *a.* v. NEXT, NEAR. लगतीचा, लगत्याचा, संसक्त, उपश्लिष्ट.

P. cause, v. CAUSE. उपादानकारण *n.* उपादान *n.*

PROXIMITY, *n.* v. A. लगन *f.* लगता *m.* संसक्ति *f.* संसर्ग *m.* सन्निधान *n.* सन्निधि *f.* उपश्लेष *m.*

PROXY, *n. agency of a substitute.* प्रतिनिधित्व *n.*
By p. प्रतिनिधिद्वारा, प्रतिनिधीकडून.
2 v. SUBSTITUTE. प्रतिनिधि, वारचा, बदल्या.

PRUDE, *n. woman who affects modesty.* बाहेरची लाजाळू बायको *f.* मुरकामारणारी स्त्री *f.* मुरकेखोर स्त्री *f.* लज्जेचा आव घालणारी *f.* लाजेची सोंगाडीण *f.*

To play the p. मुरकणें, तोंड *n.* मुरकणें, मुरका *m.* मारणें.

PRUDENCE, *n.* v. CAUTION, WISDOM. समजदारी *f.* समजुतदारी *f.* समजिकपणा *m.* दुरंदेशा *m.* पगदस्ती *f.* पूर्वापरविचार *m.* परिणामदर्शन *n.* मागलापुढलाविचार *m.* सदसद्दर्शन *n.* तजवीज *f.* समीक्ष्यकारिता *f.* विमृश्यकारिता *f.*

PRUDENT, *a.* v. CAUTIOUS, WISE. समजदार, समजूतदार, समजीक, समंजस, दुरंदेश, पूर्वापरविचारी, परिणामदर्शी, दूरदर्शी, मागें पुढें पाहणारा, सदसद्दर्शी, समीक्ष्यकारी, विमृश्यकारी.

PRUDENTIAL, *a. proceeding, &c. from prudence.* समजदारीचा, पूर्वापरविचाराचा, परिणामदर्शनाचा, सविवेक, सविचार.

PRUDENTLY, PRUDENTIALLY, *adv.* v. A. समजदारीनें, समंजसपणानें, &c. परिणामदर्शनपूर्वक, सदसद्दर्शनपूर्वक, &c.

PRUDERY, *n. affected modesty, &c.* लाजेचें-लज्जेचें मीस *n.*-सोंग *n.*-ढोंग *n.*-पोम-&c. गमजे *m. pl.* नखरे *m. pl.* नखरेबाजी *f.*

PRUDISH, *a. affectedly modest,*—a female. मुरकेखोर, तोंडमुरड्या (*f.* डी), लाजेचे मिसाचा, &c. ओढून आणलेले लाजेचा, नखरेदार, नखरेबाज.

PRUDISHNESS, *n.* v. A. ओढून आणलेली लाज *f.*-लज्जा *f.*-&c. लाजेचें-&c. सोंग *n.*-ढोंग *n.*-&c. [साळणें.

To PRUNE, *v. a. lop, &c.* कलम *n.*-खसी *f.* करणें, खडसणें, छाटणें,

PRUNED, *p.* v. V. खसी केलेला, खडसलेला, &c. खसी.

PRUNING, *n.* v. V.—*act.* खसी *f.* कलम करणें *n.* छाटणी *f.* साळणी *f.*

PRUNING-HOOK, *n.* कोयता *m.*

PRURIENCE, PRURIENCY, *n.* v. ITCH, fig. खाज *f.* कंडू *f.*

PRURIENT, *a.* v. N. खाज सुटलेला, खाजाळू.

To PRY, *v. n.* into; *inspect closely, with attempt to discover something.* बारीक पाहणें, शोधणी *f.*-शोधणूक *f.*-चिकित्सा *f.*-कसोसी *f.*-हुंगाहुंगी *f.* करणें, पाळतीवर असणें, पाळत *or* ध *f.* घेणें-लावणें- काढणें, सूक्ष्मदर्शन *n.*-मर्मान्वेषण *n.*-मर्मगवेषण *n.* करणें.

2 about. टेहळणें, हेरणें, टेहळणी *f.*-टेहळटिकोरी *f.*-&c. करणें.

PRYING, *p. a.* v. V. 1. कसोसी करणारा, हुंगाहुंगी करणारा, &c. हुंग्या, हुंगाड्या , चिकित्सक, सूक्ष्मदर्शी, सूक्ष्मदृष्टि.

2 टेहळणारा, हेरणारा, हेऱ्या, टेहळ्या.

PSALM, *n.* स्तोत्र *n.* गीत *n.*

PSALMIST, *n.* स्तोत्रकार, स्तोत्रकवि.

PSALMODY, *n.* स्तोत्रगान *n.* पंचपदी *f.* *v.* कर, म्हण.

PSALTER, *n.* गीतांचें पुस्तक *n.* [ऊंः, धत्त.

PSHAW, *interj.* v. INTERJECTION. छिछि, छी, छ, छत्, छिः, धिक्,

PSEUDO. This prefix is rendered by मिथ्या, मृषा, कृत्रिम,&c.

PSYCHOLOGICAL, *a.* v. N. आत्मतत्वविद्यासंबंधी, अध्यात्मविषयक.

PSYCHOLOGY, *n. science of man's spiritual nature.* आत्मतत्त्वविद्या *f.* अध्यात्मशास्त्र *n.* अध्यात्मविद्या *f.*

PUBERTY, PUBESCENCE, *n. ripe age in the sexes.* उमेद *f.* वय *n.*

यौवन *n.* यौवनावस्था *f.* तारुण्य *n.* तारुण्यावस्था *f.* तरुणत्व *n.* प्रौढदशा *f.* जवानी *f.* भरजवानी *f. or* ज्वानी *f.* मोठेपणा *m.*

The fire & flush of youth or p. मुसमुशी *or* मुसमूस *f.*

Glowing under the ardor of p. मुसमुशीत.

Not arrived at p. अप्राप्तयौवन.

To be under the excitement of p. मुसमुसणें.

To attain p.—a male or female. अळणें, वयांत-पणांत-उमरींत-भरांत-रसांत-&c. येणें.—a female. नहाणपदास येणें.

PUBESCENT, *a. arrived at puberty.* वयांत-पणात-भरांत-रसांत-&c. आलेला, प्राप्तयौवन, वयस्क.

PUBIC, *a.* बास्तेय.

PUBLIC, *a. of or belonging to the people or community.* सर्व लोकांचा, सर्वांचा, अवघ्यांचा, सर्वसंबंधी, सर्वविषयक, सार्वजनिक, सार्वजनीन, सर्वसाधारण, सर्वसामान्य, सर्वस्वामिक, सर्वसत्ताक, देशाचा, राज्याचा, पांढरीचा, जातीचा, &c.

2 *current among all people, commonly known.* उघड, उघडा, प्रसिद्ध, जाहीर, सर्वप्रसिद्ध, लोकप्रसिद्ध, जगत्प्रसिद्ध, जनप्रसिद्ध, देशप्रसिद्ध, दरबार महशूर, जगजाहीर, जनजाहीर.

P. report, P. talk, &c. See under POPULAR, PEOPLE.

To become p. फुटणें, बाहेर पडणें, माजणें, चौघांत येणें, लौकिक *m.* होणें *g. of s.*

PUBLIC, *n. the general body of the nation, &c.* v. COMMUNITY. लोक *m. pl.* सर्व लोक *m. pl.* चौघे *m. pl.*

In p. लोकांत, लोकांतीं, चौघांत, उघड, प्रकट *pop.* प्रगट.

In p. and in private. लोकांतांत एकांतांत, एकांतीं लोकांतीं, जनींवनीं. [लोकेषणा *f.*

Regard or deference to the p. लोकलज्जा *f.* जनलज्जा *f.*

To come before the p. फडास येणें.

PUBLIC-HOUSE. See INN.

PUBLIC-MINDED, PUBLIC-SPIRITED, *a.* लोकार्थी, लोकोपकर्त्ता, जनार्थी, परार्थी, परार्थशूर.

PUBLIC-MINDEDNESS, PUBLIC-SPIRITEDNESS, *n.* v.A. लोकार्थबुद्धि *f.* जनार्थबुद्धि *f.* लोकोपकारबुद्धि *f.* जनोपकारबुद्धि *f.*

PUBLICAN, *n. inn keeper; seller of spirits, &c.* भटारी, कलाल, दारूविक्या.

2 *collector of taxes or customs.* जकातदार.

PUBLICATION, PUBLISHING, *n.* v. V. 1.—*act.* प्रसिद्ध करणें *n.* &c. आविष्करण *n.* प्रकटीकरण *n.* उद्घाटन *n.* घोषणा *f.* परिस्फोट *m.* परिस्फूट *f.* घोंघाट *m.*

3 छापून प्रसिद्ध करणें *n.* &c.

4 चालवणें *n.* [*m.*-पुस्तक *n.*-&c.

I. *published book, &c.* छापून प्रसिद्ध केलेला *or* झालेला ग्रंथ

PUBLICITY, PUBLICNESS, *n.* v. A. 1. सर्वसंबंधिता *f.* सर्वविषयकत्व *n.* सर्वसंबंध *m.*

2 उघड *f.* उघडी *f.* उजागरी *f.* प्रसिद्धि *f.* लौकिक *m.* लोकप्रसिद्धि *f.* जनप्रसिद्धि *f.* अगाजा *m.* बाजट *n.* चतुष्ठाई *f.* परिस्फोट *m.* परिस्फूट *f.* प्रख्याति *f.* प्राकट्य *n.* गजर *m.* गूल *f.*

PUBLICLY, *adv.* v. A. 1. सर्वांकडून, सर्वलोकांकडून, देशाकडून, गांवाकडून, पांढरीकडून, &c.

2 उघड, उघडवाघड, प्रसिद्ध, चौघांत, जनांत, पांचांत, लोकांत, बाजार निरख, गाजूनवाजून, हाजीरमजालस, चावडीवर, बाजारांत, चवाठ्यांत, रस्त्यांत.

I. *with open glorying or utter shamelessness.* बाजत ढोलानें, उजागरीनें, उजागर, नगारा-नौबत-डंका-&c. बाजवून-बाजवितां-बाजवीत, दवंडी-डांगोरा-&c. पिटून-पिटीत.

To PUBLISH, *v. a. make publicly known; proclaim, promulgate, announce, &c.* जाहीर-प्रसिद्ध-उघड-प्रगट-विदित-&c. करणें, सांगणें, लोकांत-चौघांत-&c. सांगणें-आणणें, प्रकटणें *or* प्रगटणें, परिस्फूट *f.*-परिस्फोट *m.*-प्रकाश *m.*-प्रसिद्धि *f.*-उघडीक *f.*-लौकिक *m.*-&c. करणें, प्रसिद्धींत-उघडिकींत-&c. आणणें, घोषणा *f.*-उद्घाटन *n.* &c. करणें *g. of o.* प्रकटीकरण *n.*-&c. करणें *g. of o.*

2—abroad, far and wide; with the power of *To blaze, to blazon, to noise abroad,* v. To NOISE. उघडा पाडणें, गाजवणें, चौघांत-पांचांत-दाहांत-शंभरांत-&c. सांगणें, षटकर्ण-षटकर्णी करणें, तोंडावाटें काढावें आणि देशांतरास दवडावें, गूल *f.*-गजर *m.*-बोभाटा *m.*-बाजार *m.*-&c. करणें *g. of o.*

3 (a book, &c.). छापून प्रसिद्ध करणें, छापून चौघांत-लोकांत-लौकिकांत-&c. आणणें. [बापरणें.

4 *put into circulation, utter (false document, &c.)* चालवणें,

PUBLISHED, *p.* v. V. 1. प्रसिद्ध केलेला, जाहीरकेलेला, &c. जाहीर, प्रकट *pop.* प्रगट, प्रकटित, आविष्कृत, प्रस्फुट, प्रस्फुटित, प्रकीर्ण, प्रथित, उद्घाटित, घोषित.

PUBLISHER, *n.* v. V. 1. प्रसिद्ध करणारा, जाहीर करणारा, &c. प्रकाश-उद्घाटन-&c. कर्त्ता-कारी-&c.

3 छापून प्रसिद्ध करणारा.

4 चालवणारा, बापरणारा.

To PUCKER, *v. a. contract or gather into folds.* मुरुडणें *or* मुरडणें, सुरकुतविणें, आक्रसवणें, सुरकुत्या *f. pl.* आणणें-पाडणें.

Puckered seam (of an *angrakhá, &c.*). चीण *m. f.*

To PUCKER, *v. n. be contracted into folds.* सुरकुतणें, मुरुडणें *or* मुरडणें, चिरमुटणें *or* चुरमुटणें, आक्रसणें *or* आक्रुसणें, अटरणें, अवटरणें, सुरकुत्या *f. pl.*-&c. पडणें-येणें.

PUCKER, PUCKERING, *n.* v. V. N. सुरकुती *f.* चिरमी *f.* चुरमुटी *f.* वळकती *f.* वळी *f.* ओंचा *m.* वळकुटी सुरकुटी *f.*

PUDDER, *To* PUDDER. See BOTHER, To BOTHER.

PUDDING-TIME, *n. nick of time.* मळणी *f.* घात *f.*

P. jack. आयतोजी, आयतगब्बू, भोजनभाऊ, भोजन्या.

PUDDLE, *n. small stand or collection of dirty water.* डबकें *n.* डपकें *n.* डबकण *n.* डपकण *n.* डबक *n.* डबका *m.* डबकी *f.* डबरा *m.* डवरा *m.* डहुरा *or* डोहरा *m.* डोभण *n.* सांचवण *n.* थिल्लर *n.* गोपद *n.*

Water collected in puddles. सांचवण *n.* थिल्लरोदक *n.*

To PUDLLE, *v. a.* See To MUDDEN. 2 *make close with clay.* चिकणमाती लावून पाणी न जाईसा करणें.

PUDENDA, *n.* v. PRIVITIES. उपस्थ *m.n.* गुह्यांग *n.*

PUERILE, *a. boyish,* v. CHILDISH. पोरकट, पोरगळ, पोरवट.

PUERILITY, *n.* v. CHILDISHNESS. पोरपणा *m.* लेंकुरपणा *m.*

PUERPERAL, *a. pertaining to childbirth.* बाळंतपणाचा, बाळंत (in comp. as बाळंतरोग) प्रसूतीचा, प्रसूति (in comp.) प्रासूतिक.

P. woman. बाळंत *f.* बाळंतीण *f.* [*f.* फुंकर *m.*

PUFF, *n. blast with the mouth.* फुंका *m.* फुंकार *m.* फुंकारा *m.* फुंक *m.*

2 (of wind) *blast, gust.* घुगी *f.* झुकी *f.* झटका *m.* झटकारा *m* झपाटा *m.* भबका *m. dim.* भबकी *f.* सोंसा *m.* सनाटा *m.* सुसाटा *m.* चपेटा *m.*

Gentle p. झुळूक *f.* लहर *f.*

In puffs. सोंसों, घोघो.

Strong p. भबका *m. dim.* भबकी *f.* भबकारा *m.*

4 *light cake.* करंजी *f.* कानवला *m.* गुळवरी *or* गुरवळी *f.*
5 *tumid commendation, &c.* फुशारकी *f.* फुशारी *f.* बढाई *f.* पोम *n.* बढाईचा-फुशारीचा-&c. लेख *m.*-वर्णन *n.*-&c.

To PUFF, *v. n. breathe hard, blow,* v. To PANT. कासळणें, हुसकारणें, सुसकारणें, हवावी *f.*-दम *m.* लागणें *in. con.* धापा *f. pl.* देणें-टाकणें, सुसकारे *m. pl.*-हुसकारे *m. pl.*-असासाउसासा *m.* टाकणें-देणें.

To p. and blow (as in fever or passion) फुंपणें.
2 *blow with the mouth.* फुंकम *f.*-फुंकर *m.*-फुंका *m.*-फुंकार *m.*-फुंकारा *m.* मारणें. [पोहरणें.
3 *swell with air.* तट्ट फुगणें, धोदरणें, तरतरणें *intens.* तरारणें,

To PUFF, *v. a.* v. To INFLATE. फुगवणें, फुगीर करणें.
2 *blow away.* फुंकून-फुंकेसरसा *decl.*-फुंकाऱ्यानें-&c. उडवणें.
3 up; *elate with pride.* फुगवणें, चढवणें, माजवणें, शेपारवणें, शीड *n.* चढवणें *g. of o.* शेंडीस फुलें *n. pl.* बांधणें, चण्याच्या झाडावर चढवणें, गजस्कंधीं-गंडस्थलीं-हत्तीवर-घोड्यावर-&c. बसवणें, फुलविणें, फुलारून घेणें.
4 *praise tumidly, &c.* चढवणें, बढाई *f.*-फुशारी *f.*-फुशारकी *f.*-&c. करणें-सांगणें *g. of o.* पोम *n.* वाढवणें-माजवणें *g. of o.* पखरड *f.* सांगणें-चोलणें *g. of o.*

PUFFED, *p.* v. V. A. 1. फुगवलेला, &c. फुगरा, फुगीर *remiss.* फुगट, गुरगुरीत, वाऱ्यानें वापसलेला.
3 फुगवलेला, शेपारवलेला, &c. तुंद.
To be p. up. उंडारणें, फुगणें, चढणें, माजणें, शेपारणें, शेफरणें, शेरडावणें, शीड *n.* चढणें *g. of s.* घोड्यावर-हत्तीवर-गजस्कंधीं-&c.बसणें, उतणणें.

PUFFEDNESS, *n.* v. P. 1. फूग *f.* फुगवटी *or* फुगोटी *f.* फुगवशी *or* फुगोशी *f.* [or ळ.

PUFFY, *a. swelled with air, &c.* वायूनें फुगलेला, वातमय, वातूल

PUG-DOG, *n.* माकडासारखें ज्याचें तोंड आहे अशी कुत्र्याची जात आहे.

PUG-FACED, *a.* माकडतोंड्या.

PUG-NOSE, *n.* फेंदरें नाक *n.*

PUGH, *interj.* फू, धत्त.

PUGILISM, PUGILIST. See BOXING, BOXER.

PUGNACIOUS, *a. disposed to fight,* v. QUARRELSOME. हातचा फटकळ, भांडरा, भांडगा, भांडखोर, युयुत्सु.

PUGNACITY, *n.* v. A. भांडरेपणा *m.* &c. युयुत्सा *f.*

PUISNE, *a.* v. INFERIOR. खालच्या पदवीचा. [विक्रम *m.*

PUISSANCE, *n. might, power.* पराक्रम *m.* बल *n.* बलाढ्यता *f.*

PUISSANT, *a. mighty, powerful.* पराक्रमी, प्रतापी, बलवान्, बलशाली, बलाढ्य, विक्रमशाली, प्रौढप्रताप.

PUKE, *To* PUKE. See VOMIT, TO VOMIT.

PULCHRITUDE. See BEAUTY.

To PULE, *v. n.* v. To WHINE. टेंटें *n.*-गेंगें *n.*-रेंरें *n.*- केंकें *n.* करणें.

To PULL, *v. a. draw.* ओढणें, ओढूनघेणें, ताणणें, आकर्षणें, खेंचणें, खेंचून घेणें, ओढ *f.*-ओढा *m.*-&c. देणें.
To p. and haul. To p. and push about (rudely, &c.). घुसळणें, घुसडणें, हिसडणें, घोळणें, घोळसणें, घोळसावणें, खुंदलणें *or* खुंदळणें, सेबाळणें, फचकावणें, ओढा ओढ *or* ढी *f.*-ओढाताण *f.*-ताणाताण *f.*-खेंचाखेंच *f.*-&c. करणें *g. of o.*
To p. (at a smoking apparatus), *take a whiff.* दम *m.* मारणें, झुटका *m.*-झुरका *m.* घेणें, झुरकणें.

To p. suddenly and smartly. हिसकणें, हिसडणें, फचकाविणें, हिसका *m.*-हिसडा *m.*-झटका *m.*-झटकारा *m.*-&c. देणें.
To p. together, *agree.* वेंट *m.* वळणें *g. of. s.*
2 *pluck, gather.* तोडणें, काढणें, खुडणें, तोडणी *f.*-तोडा *m.* करणें *g. of o.*
3 down; to pieces; *take to pieces.* उसकटणें, सोडिवणें, उखळणें, विशकल-&c. करणें, विशकलन *n.*-&c. करणें *g. of o.*
4 off, out, v. To EXTRACT. काढणें, काढून घेणें.
5 to pieces; *rend.* तुकडे तुकडे *m. pl.* करणें *g. of o.*
6 up; v. To ROOT UP. काढणें, उपटणें, उपडणें.

PULL, PULLING, *n.* v. V. 1.—*act.* ओढणें *n.* &c. ओढ *f.* ओढा *m.* संकर्षण *n.* विकर्षण *n.*
A sudden & smart p. फचका *m.*
A long p. and a strong p. and a p. all together. भरेरी *f.* v. लाव, घाल, वेंट *m.* v. वळ.
At a p. एक ओढ *or* एका ओढीनें.
P. and hauling. ओढाताण *f.* ओढाताड *f.* खेंचाखेंच *f.*
I. *strain, stress.* ओढ *f.* ओढा *m.* ओढण *f. n.* ओढप *f.* जोर *m.* नेट *m. n.* [विकर्ष.

PULLED, *p.* v. V. 1. ओढलेला, खेंचलेला, &c. आकर्षित, विकर्षित,

PULLER, *n.* PULLING, *p. a.* v. V. 1. ओढणारा, खेंचणारा, &c. आकर्षक, विकर्षक, आकर्षण-&c. कर्ता-कारी-&c.

PULLET, *n. young hen.* तरणी कोंबडी *f.*

PULLEY, *n.*—of a block. कप्प्यांतलें चाक *n.* गाडी *f.* फिरकी *f.*

PULLEY BLOCK, *n.* कप्पा *m.* कप्पी *f.* मणी *m.* मणका *m.*

PULMONARY, PULMONIC, *a. pertaining to the lungs.* फुफुसाचा, फुप्फुससंबंधी, फुप्फुसविषयक, फुप्फुसनिष्ठ.
P. consumption. कफक्षय *m.*

PULP, *n. soft part of fruit, &c.* गर *m.* गीर *m.* गीळ *m.* दळ *n.* गर्भ *m.* मगज *m.*
2 *soft mass*—gener. लगदा *m.*

PULPIT, *n.* उपदेशासन *n.* उपदेशपीठ *n.* व्यासपीठ *n.* व्यासासन *n.*

PULPOUS, PULPY, *a. having much pulp.* दळदार, भरदार, गबगबीत *or* गुबगुबीत, मासभरू, मांसल *pop.* मासाळ, गरभरू, गाभडा, गाभूळ, ठसठसीत *or* ठुसठुसीत.
To become p. and sweetish. गाभुळणें. [गळीत.
2 *soft, pappy, like pulp.* मऊ, गिलगिलीत, चिलचिलीत, गल-

PULPOUSNESS, PULPINESS, *n.* v. A. 1. गबगबितपणा *m.* मासाळपणा *m.* &c.
2 मऊपणा *m.* गिलगिलितपणा *m.*

To PULSATE. See To THROB, To PALPITATE.

PULSATION, *n. beating or throbbing of the heart, an artery, &c.* हृदयाचें-नाडीचें-&c. उडणें *n.*-स्फुरण *n.*-ठोका *m.*-आघात *m.*

PULSE, *n.* (of the blood). नाडीचें उडणें *n.*-स्फुरण *n.* नाडीचा आघात *m.*-ठोका *m.* नाडी *f.* नाड *f.*
To feel the p. नाडी *f.* पाहणें, नाडीपरीक्षा *f.* करणें.
To feel the p. *fig. sound.* मन *n.*-&c. पाहणें, सडा *m.* टाकून पाहणें.
To find one's p. (natural temper or disposition), नाडी *f.* सापडणें *in. con. and g. of o.*
To shew (suffer to be felt) one's p. नाडी *f.* दाखवणें.
2 *legumes.* कडदण *n.* काठण *or* कठाण *n.* कठाण महाण *n.* कडधान्य *n.* काष्ठधान्य *n.* द्विदल *pop.* दुडाळ *n.* काड *n.*

A germinated grain of p. चिरडी *or* ढी *f. or* डें *n.*
A grain of shelled p. सोलाणा *m.* सोला *m.*
A half of a split grain of p. दाळकण *n.*
A whole grain amongst split p. दाळगोटा *m.*
Bits and powder among split p. चुरी *f.* कळणा *m.* आउदाळ *f.*
Grain remaining unhusked amongst split p. डोळ *m.*
Green pods of p. parched. उत्रा *or* हुळा *m.*
Husked p. डोळ *m.* भरडा *m.*
Mass of dry pods of p. शिंगडी *f. or* डें *n.*
Parched p. कडकडा वाल *m.*
P. parched and ground. डाळें *n.*
P. boiled whole. घुगरी *f.*
Parched p. boiled up with salt *or* P. salted and parched. मिठपाणे *or* मिठाणे *m. pl.*
P. &c. boiled up with vegetables. वंजन *n.* वरदळ *n.*
P. ground and fried. वडा *m.* वटक *m.*
P. roughly ground. मरड *or* भरडा *m.*
P.-water. कट *n.* कटवणी *n.* कढण *n.*
Split p. दाळ *or* डाळ *f.*
Split p. imperfectly husked. डोळदाळ *f.* डोळस दाळ *f.*
Stub or stalk of p. काडसर *n.*
Water in which split p., rice bits, &c. have been boiled. तरण *or* तरवणी *n.*

PULVERABLE, PULVERIZABLE, *a. that may be reduced to powder.* चुरायाजोगा-सारखा-&c. चूर्ण-&c. करायाजोगा-सारखा-&c. कुटरा, कुटीर, चूर्णीकरणयोग्य.

PULVERIZATION, *n.* v. V. चुरणें *n.* भुगा करणें *n.* &c. चूर्णीकरण *n.*

To PULVERIZE, *To* PULVERATE, *v. a. reduce to powder.* चुरणें, भुकणी *f.*-भुगा *m.*-चूर्ण *n.*-चुराडा *m.*-&c. करणें *g. of o.*

PULVERIZED, *p.* v. V. चुरलेला, भुगा केलेला, चूर्णीकृत.

PUMP, *n.*—the hydraulic engine. बंब *m.*

To PUMP, *v. a. raise by a pump.* बंबानें काढणें-सोडणें.
2 out; *fig.* (secrets). खणणें *or* खणून काढणें, उकरून काढणें, मन *n.* पाहणें *g. of o.* आंतडीं *n. pl.* निपसणें *g. of o.*

PUMPION, PUMPKIN, *n.*—the plant. भोपळी *f.* कोव्हाळी *or* कोहळी *f.*—the fruit, भोपळा *m.* कोव्हाळा *m. or* ळें *n.* कोहळा *m. or* ळें *n.* काशीफळ *n.* कूष्मांड *n.*
Dark green p. काळी भोपळी *f.* देवडांगर *m.* (its fruit, काळा भोपळा *m.* देवडांगर *m.*).
Long white p. दुध्या *m.* दुधी भोपळी *f.* दूध भोपळी *f.* दुधीण *f.* (its fruit, दुध्या भोपळा *m.* पांढरा भोपळा *m.* मुगा भोपळा *m.*).
Young p. घटा *m.*

PUN, *n. play upon words.* श्लेष *m.* श्लेषोक्ति *f.* श्लेषालंकार *m.*

To PUNCH, *v. a. bore, &c.* टिचणीनें-&c. पाडणें, भोंकणें, घर *n.* पाडणें.
2 (with the fist, elbow, &c.). गुद्दा *m.*-&c. मारणें, ढोंसणें, ढोंगसणें, कोंपरढोंसा *m.*-कोंपरखळी *f.*-कोंपरबुक्की *f.*-&c. मारणें.
3 (clothes in washing them). पोंचारणें, चुबकणें.

PUNCH, *n.*—the instrument. टिचणी *f.* पोगर *m.*
2 v. BLOW. गुद्दा *m.* घुस्सा *m.* ढोंसा *m.* कोंपरखळी *or* खिळी *f.* कोंपरबुक्की *f.* कोंपर ढोंसा *m.* कोंपरढुस्सा *m.* गुच्छी *f.*
3 See BUFFOON. 4 एक प्रकारचें पेय आहे.

PUNCHEON. See STAMP. 2 See CASK.

PUNCHINELLO See BUFFOON.

PUNCHY, *a. short and fat.* आखुड्या आंगाचा, बाटोळ्या बांध्याचा, बाटोळ्या आंगाचा.

PUNCTILIO, *n. nice point of ceremony or behaviour.* शिष्टाचाराची-सन्मानाची-आदरोपचाराची-&c. बारीक गोष्ट *f.*

PUNCTILIOUS, *a. nice or exact in points of ceremony or behaviour.* आदरउपचाराच्या बारीक गोष्टी पाहणारा, नेमळ, नेमाळ्या, सूक्ष्मसत्कारदर्शी, सूक्ष्मोपचारदर्शी, आदरोपचारनिष्ठ, सुक्ष्मोपचार निष्ठ, बारीकपाहणारा, अल्पदृष्टि, अत्याचारी.

PUNCTILIOUSNESS, *n.* v. A. सूक्ष्मोपचारनिष्ठा *f.* सूक्ष्मोपचारदर्शन *n.* सूक्ष्मसत्कारदर्शन *n.* सूक्ष्मसत्कारदृष्टि *f.* सूक्ष्मोपचारदृष्टि *f.* बारीकदृष्टि *f.* अत्याचार *m.*

PUNCTUAL, *a. particular in the observance of time, engagements, &c.* वक्तशीर, वायदा राख्या, समयरक्षक, समयपालक, समयनिष्ठ, कालरक्षक-पालक-निष्ठ, नेमळ, नेमाळ्या, अवधिनिष्ठ, समयसेवी, नियमनिष्ठ, प्रतिज्ञानिष्ठ, संकेतनिष्ठ, वचननिष्ठ, सामयिक.
2 See EXACT. 3 See PUNCTILIOUS.

PUNCTUALITY, PUNCTUALNESS, *n.* v. A. 1. वक्तशीरपणा *m.* समयरक्षण *n.* समयपालन *n.* कालपालन *n.* समयसेवन *n.* समयसेवा *f.* समयनिष्ठा *f.* नियमनिष्ठा *f.* वचननिष्ठा *f.* संकेतनिष्ठा *f.* प्रतिज्ञानिष्ठा *f.*

PUNCTUALLY, *adv.* v. A. 1. वेळेस, वेळीं, वेळचे वेळेस, बोलल्या वेळेस, वेळ-समय-&c. साधून-राखून-&c. समयनिष्ठापूर्वक.

To PUNCTUATE, *v. a. point, mark with stops.* अवसानाच्या खुणा *f. pl.* घालणें-देणें, विरामचिह्न *n.* करणें-देणें, विरामचिह्नांकित करणें.

PUNCTUATION, *n.* v. V. अवसानाच्या खुणा देणें *n.* विरामचिह्नांकन *n.* अवसानचिह्नांकन *n.*

PUNCTURE, *To* PUNCTURE. See PRICK, To PRICK.

PUNDLE, *n. short and fat woman.* पसालपार्वती *f.* मुग्धम्मा *f.*

PUNGENCY, *n.* v. A. 1. तिखटपणा *m.* &c. तिखटाई *f.* तलखाई *f.* जहाली *f.* तीक्ष्णता *f.* तीव्रता *f.* तिक्त *m.* तैक्ष्ण्य *n.* तेज *n.* प्रखरता *f.* प्राखर्य्य *n.* चरमर *f.*

PUNGENT, *a. hot, biting, acid, stimulating, &c. lit. fig.* तिखट *intens.* तिखटडोंब, तलख, तीक्ष्ण, तीव्र, रूंबरा *remiss.* खंवरट, खबिरडा, खवट, तिक्त, खर, प्रखर, कडक, खरमरीत, चरमरीत, चरचरीत, कटु, तेजबानू, जहाल *or* झयाल, जलाल, जालीम, झणझणीत, चणचणीत, जळजळीत, भगभगीत, ठसठसीत. [कडक.
2—pain, grief, &c. v. POIGNANT. तिखट, तीक्ष्ण, तीव्र, प्रखर,

PUNINESS, *n.* v. A. लहानपणा *m.* &c. क्षुद्रता *f.*

To PUNISH, *v. a. inflict penal suffering on or for.* दंडणें, ताडणें, शासणें, शिक्षणें, दंड *m.*-दंडन *n.*-शासन *n.*-शिक्षा *f.*-शिक्षण *n.*-सजा *f.*-पारपत्य *or* पारिपत्य *n.*-&c. करणें-देणें.

PUNISHABLE, *a.* v. V. दंडायाजोगा-&c. दंडनीय, दंड्य, दंडार्ह, दंडनार्ह, ताडनीय, ताड्य, शासनीय, शास्य, शासनार्ह, शिक्षणीय, शिक्ष्य, शिक्षार्ह.

PUNISHED, *p.* v. V. दंडलेला, &c. दंडित, ताडित, शासित, शिक्षित.

PUNISHER, *n.* PUNISHING, *p. a.* v. V. दंडणारा, ताडणारा, शिक्षादेणारा, &c. शासक, शास्ता, शिक्षक.

PUNISHMENT, *n.* v. V. शिक्षा *f.* शासन *n.* ताडन *n.* दंडन *n.* दंड *m.* पारपत्य *or* पारिपत्य *n.* सजा *f.* नसीहत *f.* तंबी *f.* शिक्षण *n.*

Capital p. जीवांतदंड *m.* प्राणांतदंड *m.* वधदंड*m.* देहांतदंड*m.*
Corporal p. देहदंडन *n.* देहदंड*m.* शरीरदंड *m.*
Fear of p. दंडभीति *f.*
General and indiscriminate p. सकटसंक्रांत *f. v.* बस.
Legal or just p. सम्यक्दंडन *n.*
Severe p. त्रिवारशिक्षा *f.* त्रिवारदंड *m.*
Severity of p. दंडपारुष्य *n.* [ताडन *n.*-&c.
Undeserved p. नसता दंड*m.*-दंडन *n.*-शासन*n.*-शिक्षा *f.*-

PUNITIVE, PUNITORY, *a.* v. PENAL. दंडाविषयींचा, शिक्षेचा, ताडनसंबंधी-विषयक, दंडसंबधी-विषयक. [वादी.

PUNNER, PUNSTER, *n. one that makes use of puns.* सश्लेषवक्ता-

PUNY, *a. small and feeble,* v. SMALL, MEAN. टिन्या, लहान, क्षुद्र, चिमुरडा, चिलबाण *or* णा, नसकोणा, इवलासा.

PUP, *n.* कुतरीचें पिलूं *n.*

To PUP, *v. n.* विणें, पिलें *n. pl.* घालणें.

PUPIL, *n.* v. SCHOLAR. शिष्य, चेला, विद्यार्थी, छात्र.
For the faults of the p. punish the master. शिष्यापराधे गुरोर्दंडः.
2 (of the eye). डोळ्याचा तारा *m.* डोळ्याची बाहुली *f.* पुतळी *f.* तारा *m. f.* तारका *f.* अक्षितारा *f.* कनीनिका *f.*

PUPILAGE, *n. state of being a pupil.* शिष्यावस्था *f.* शिष्यदशा *f.* शिष्यत्व *n.*

PUPPET, *n. image, doll.* पुतळी *f.* बाहुला *m.* बाहुली *f.* बाहुलें*n.* कळसूत्राची बाहुली *f.* खांबसूत्राची बाहुली *f.* पुत्रिका *f.*
Mere p. *fig.* टिक्याचा धनी, बाहुलें *n.*
String of a p. कळसूत्र *n.* सूत्र *n.*

PUPPET-MAN, PUPPET-PLAYER, *n.* बाहुले भोरपी, कळसूत्री, खांबसूत्री, सूत्रधार, सूत्रधारी.

PUPPET-SHOW, *n.* कळसूत्राचा खेळ *m.* बाहुलेभोरीप *n.* पडदेभोरीप *n.* खांबसूत्र *n.*

PUPPY, *n.* कुतरीचें पिलूं *n.*
2 fig. *term of contempt for a man.* माणसाचा लेंक *m.* माणसाचा अवतार *m.* बच्चाजी *m.* बच्चाराम *m.*

PURA'N, *n.* पुराण *n.*
Expounder of p. पुराणीक, व्यास, पुराण सांगणारा.—Seat of do. व्यासपीठ *n.* व्यासासन *n.*—Honors paid to him. व्यासपूजा *f.*

PURA'NIC, *a.* पुराणाचा, पुराणाविषयींचा.

PURBLIND, *a. dim-sighted, short-sighted.* डोळ्याचा- दृष्टीचा- &c. मंद-अधू, उफराट्या बाहुल्यांचा, चोंधळा. [क्रेतव्य.

PURCHASEABLE, *a.* v. V. विकतघ्यायाचा-जोगा-&c. क्रय्य, क्रेय,

To PURCHASE, *v. a. buy.* विकत घेणें-आणणें-मिळवणें, खरीद करणें-घेणें,फरोकघेणें, खरिदी *f.*-क्रय *m.*-क्रीणन *n.*-&c. करणें *g.of o.*

PURCHASE, PURCHASING, *n.* v. V.—*act.* विकत घेणें *n.* &c. खरिदी *f.* खरीद *f.* क्रय *m.* क्रयण *n.* क्रीणन *n.*
I. *thing purchased.* खरिदी *f.* खरीद *f.* क्रीतवस्तु *n.* सौदा *m.*
II. *mechanical hold or power.* जोर *m.* नेटावा*m.*

PURCHASE-MONEY, *n.* v. PRICE. खरिदीचा पैसा*m.* पैका *m.* मोल*n.*

PURCHASED, *p.* v. V. विकत घेतलेला, खरीद केलेला, &c. खरीद, क्रीत, क्रयक्रीत.

PURCHASER, *n.* PURCHASING, *p. a.* v. V. विकत घेणारा, खरीद करणारा, खरीददार, गिन्हाईक *or* ग्राहीक, क्रयी, क्रेता.

PURE, *a. clear, not muddy, &c.* निर्मल *or* ळ, स्वच्छ, नीरा, चोखाळ, साफ, निवळ, विशुद्ध, पाक, शुचि, अमल, विमल.
2—ceremonially. पवित्र, पावन, पूत, पाक, सोवळा, शुचि, शुचिष्मंत, मेध्य.
Particular about being p. अकटविकट सोवळा.
3—morally ; *not guilty, &c. clear,* v. INNOCENT. शुद्ध, साफ, दिलपाक, निष्प्रांजल, प्रांजळ, कोरा, चोख, चोखाळ, निष्कलंक, अकृतपाप, अज्ञातपाप, विशुद्ध, सात्विक, साधु, अलिप्त, शुचिर्भूत, शुचिष्मंत, दुधानें धुपलेला.
P. in heart. दिलपाक.
P. even to the nails. नखाला माती लागली नाहीं.
4 *mere, simple, unmingled.* शुद्ध, केवळ, निर्भेळ, निर्दंम, निग, निरू, थेट, निखालस, नुस्ता, चोख, चोखाळ.
5—speech. शुद्ध, शिस्तवार, शिस्त, निर्दोष, साधु, अपशब्दरहित-हीन-शून्य, अपप्रयोगहीन-रहित-&c.
6—of females ; *ignorant of sexual intercourse,* v. CHASTE, CONTINENT. अज्ञातव्यवाया, अज्ञानपतिका, पुरुषास्पृष्टा. Note. These adjectives are in the feminine form.
7 *unalloyed, unadulterated.* खरा, शुद्ध, असल, चोख, चोखाळ, थेट, निर्भेळ, अदूषित, अदुष्ट.
Very p.—gold. बावनकसी.
8 *of unmixed descent.* ब्यांचा.

PURELY, *adv.* v. A. 4. निरखळ *or* निखळ, निखालस, निखळ, निवळ, एकजात.

PURENESS, PURITY, *n.* v. A. 1. निर्मळपणा *m.* स्वच्छपणा *m.* &c. निर्मलता *f.* स्वच्छता *f.* विमलता *f.* शुद्धि *f.* विशुद्धि *f.* मलराहित्य *n.* &c. सत्व *n.*
2 पवित्रता *f.* सोवळेपणा *m.* शौच *n.* सोवळें *n.*
3 चोखपणा *m.* चोखाळपणा *m.* &c. शुद्धि *f.* साफी *f.* दिलपाकी *f.* सत्य *n.* सत्व *n.* साधुत्व *n.* विशुद्धि *f.* अंतःशौच *n.* कलंकराहित्य *n.* कलंकाभाव *m.* निष्कलंकता *f.* &c.
4 निर्भेळपणा *m.* निर्दंमपणा *m.* निरेपणा *m.* चोखपणा *m.* &c.
5 शुद्धपणा *m.* शिस्तपणा *m.* &c. अपशब्दराहित्य *n.* अपप्रयोगराहित्य *n.* &c. साधुत्व *n.* [&c.
6 See CHASTITY. 7 खरेपणा *m.* असलपणा *m.* चोखपणा *m.*

PURGATION, PURGING, *n.* v. V. 1.—*act.* ढाळवणें *n.* विरेक *m.* विरेचन *n.*

PURGATIVE, *a.* PURGING, *p. a.* v. V. ढाळवणारा, &c. ढाळक, सारक, शोधक, रेचक.

PURGATIVE, *n. medicine that evacuates the bowels.* ढाळ *m.* ढाळक *n.* जुलाब *m.* रेचक *n.* रेचन *n.* रेच *m.* विरेचन *n.*
Mild and gentle p. सुखढाळ *m.*
Violent p. जेपाळाचा ढाळ *m.*

PURGATORY, *n.* भैरवयातनास्थान *n.*
Pain of p. भैरवीयातना *f.*

PURGE, *n.* v. PURGATIVE. ढाळ *m.* जुलाब *m.*
2 *stool, motion.* ढाळ *m.* जुलाब *m.* झाडा *m.* विरेक *m.* रेचन *n.* रेच *m.* विरेचन *n.*
Copious or loose p. बुळकांडी *f.* बुळकी *f.* भसरें *n.*
Gentle and easy p. सुखढाळ *m.*

To PURGE, *v. a. evacuate the bowels.* ढाळ *m.*-रेच *m.*-&c. देणें, पोट *n.*-कोठा *m.* साफ करणें *g. of o.* ढाळवणें, कोष्ठशुद्धि *f.*-मलशुद्धि *f.*-&c. करणें *g. of o.*
2 See To CLEANSE, To CLEAR.

PURGED, *p.* v. V. 1. ढाळवलेला, &c. रेचित, विरेचित, सारित.

PURGING, *n. looseness of the bowels.* हगवण *f.* हगरड *f.* परसाकडचा-शौचाचा-&c. उपद्रव *m.*

P. and vomiting. हगओक *f. n.*

P. and urining. हगमूत *f.*

To have p. पोट *n.* चालणें *g. of o.*

PURIFICATION, *n.* v. V. 1.—*act.* शोधणें *n.* निर्मळ करणें *n.* &c. शोधन *n.* शोध *m.* संशोधन *n.* विशोधन *n.* मलापकर्षण *n.* निर्मलीकरण *n.* स्वच्छीकरण *n.*—*state.* शुद्धि *f.* विशुद्धि *f.* संशुद्धि *f.* शुद्धता *f.* विशुद्धता *f.* शोधितत्व *n.* शौच *m.* शुचिता *f.*

2—*act.* पवित्र करणें *n.* &c. पवित्रीकरण *n.*—*state.* पवित्रता *f.* शुद्धि *f.* पूति *f.* पावितत्व *n.*

PURIFICATORY, *a.* PURIFIER, *n.* PURIFYING, *p. a.* v. V. 1. शोधणारा, निर्मळ करणारा, &c. शोधक, संशोधक, विशोधक, शोधन-शुद्धि-&c. कर्त्ता-कारी-&c. मलापकर्षक.

2 पवित्र करणारा, बिटाळ काढणारा, पवित्रकारक, पावन, पावक, पावी, पूति-&c. कारक-कारी-&c.

PURIFIED, *p.* v. V. 1. शोधलेला, निर्मळ केलेला, &c. शोधींव, शोधित, शुद्ध, विशुद्ध, निर्गलित.

2 पवित्र केलेला, &c. पवित्रित, पवित्रीकृत, पावित, पूत, पुनीत, पूतपाप, शुचिर्भूत, कृतशौच.

To PURIFY, *v. a. make pure or clear.* निर्मळ-स्वच्छ-साफ-&c. करणें, शोधणें, मळ *m.*-मळी *f.*-&c. काढणें-छाटणें *g. of o.* शोध *m.*-शोधन *n.*-शुद्धि *f.*-&c. करणें *g. of o.*

2—ceremonially or morally. पवित्र-शुद्ध-पाक-सोवळा-&c. करणें, बिटाळ *m.*-&c. काढणें-दूरकरणें *g. of o.* शुद्धता *f.*-पवित्रता *f.* -&c.आणणें, शुद्धि *f.*-विशुद्धि *f.*-पूति *f.*-&c. करणें.

PURITY. See PURENESS.

To PURL, *v. n.*—a brook. झुळझुळ वाहणें, सळसळणें, सळसळ *f.*-झुळझुळ *f.* करणें. [किनारी *f.*

PURL, *n. an embroidered & puckered border.* चुणीदार जरी

2 एक प्रकारचें पेय आहे. 3 See PURLING.

PURLER, *n.* PURLING, *p. a.* v. V. झुळझुळ वाहणारा, सळसळीत.

PURLIEU, *n. border.* शेव *m.* पालव *m.* लत्ता *m.* अग्रेवन *n.*

PURLING, *n.* v. V.—*act.* सळसळ *f.* झुळझुळ *f.*

PURLINGLY, *adv.* v. A. झुरझुर *or* झुरुझुरु, झुळझुळ, दुरुदुरु.

PURLINS, *n.*—in architecture. पोट मांडणी *f.* पोटसर *m.*

To PURLOIN. See To STEAL.

PURPET, *n.*—the cloth. पटू *or* पटू *m. f.*

PURPLE, *a.*—the colour. जांबळा *or* जांभळा, सावळा *or* सांबळा, बैंगणी *or* नी, अंजिरी, नाफरमानी, धूम्र, नीललोहित.

PURPLE, *n.* जांभळारंग *m.* &c.

To PURPLE, *v. a.* जांभळारंग *m.* देणें, जांभळ्या रंगाचा करणें.

PURPORT, *n.* v. MEANING. भाव *m.* खुलासा *m.* तात्पर्य *n.* हासील *n.* अभिप्राय *m.*

To PURPORT. See To MEAN, To INTEND.

PURPOSE, *n. intention,* v. DESIGN. उद्देश *m.* उद्देश्य *n.* आशय *m.* मतलब *m.* बुद्धि *f.* मानस *n.* संकल्प *m.* अर्थ *m.* निमित्त *n.* इंगित *n.*

Firm or fixed p. त्रिवार निश्चय *or* संकल्प *m.*

Of unfailing p. सत्यसंकल्प.

On p. *expressly.* मुद्दाम, मुजरत *or* द, तात्पुरचा *decl.*

Secret p. अंतरगर्भ *m.*

To no p. वृथा, व्यर्थ.

To no good p. नदेवायनधर्माय.

To what p. कशास.

To PURPOSE, *v. a.* v. To DESIGN. उद्देशणें, संकल्पणें, कल्पिणें, अवांकणें, उद्देश *m.*-संकल्प *m.*-&c. करणें-धरणें.

PURPOSED, *p.* v. V. उद्देशलेला, &c. उद्दिष्ट, मानसोद्दिष्ट, संकल्पित.

I.—a person, v. RESOLVED. कृतसंकल्प, कृतनिश्चय.

PURPOSELY, *adv.* v. DESIGNEDLY. जाणून, बुद्ध्या, जाणून बुजून.

I. *with special design,* v. EXPRESSLY. मुद्दाम, मुजरत, हटकून, दाटून, हुकमें, तात्पुरचा *decl.* उदमेखून.

PURR, PURRING, *n.* v. V. 1.—*act.* घुरणें *n.* &c. घुरघूर *f.*

2 फुरफुरणें *n.* फुरफुराट *m.*

To PURR, *v. n.*—a cat. घुरणें, घुरघुरणें, घुरघूर *f.*-&c. करणें.

2 (with the lips) *whirr.* फुरफुरणें.

PURSE, *n.* v. BAG. पिशवी *f.* हमिणी *f.* खलीता *m.*

Close p. *reserved sum.* बांधली गांठ *f.*

Draw-p. पुरवटा *or* ठा *m.*

Lightness of p. दामदुकल *m.*

Long, narrow p. (to be tied around the loins). कसणी *f.* कसा *m.* कमरकसा *m.*

Long p. (to be carried across a beast). हसबी *f.*

To pay out of one's own p. गांठचा वाहणें, पदरचा देणें.

2 *bag of money.* तोडा *m.* [णें, मिटणें.

To PURSE, *v. a. contract,* (the mouth, &c.). निमुटणें *or* निमट-

PURSE-BEARER, PURSE-KEEPER, *n.* पोतनीस, पोतदार.

PURSE-PRIDE, *n.* धनगर्व *m.* धनदर्प *m.* धनाभिमान *m.*

PURSE-PROUD, *a.* धनगर्वित, धनमस्त, धनाभिमानी, मालमस्त.

PURSER, *n.* गलबतावरचा पोतनीस. [घोळ &c.)

PURSLANE, *n. portulaca oleracea.* घोळ *f.* (and राजघोळ, रान-

PURSUANCE, *n.* v.V. 3. लाग *m.* अनुसंधान *n.*

In pursuance of, *following, conformably to,* v. ACCORDANT. प्रमाणें, अनुसार, अनुरूप, बमूजीब.

PURSUANT, *a. according to or with,* v. ACCORDANT. अनुरूप, अनुसारी, बमूजीब.

To PURSUE, *v. a. go after,* v. To FOLLOW. मागें-पाठीमागें-मागून -&c. जाणें-चालणें-&c. *g. of o.* अनुगमन *n.*-आनुयान *n.*-&c. करणें.

2 *follow with a view to overtake; chase, &c.* पाठीस लागणें *g. of o.* पाठलाग *m.* अनुधावन *n.*-&c.करणें, पाठ *f.*-पिच्छा *m.*-दूम *f.*-&c. घेणें-धरणें-पुरवणें *g. of o.* पिच्छ्यास बसणें-लागणें *g. of o.*

To p. with dire purpose. हात धुऊन पाठीस लागणें.

3 fig. *follow with a view to obtain, use measures to acquire, seek.* उद्योग *m.*-यत्न *m.*-प्रयत्न *m.*&c.चालवणें-करणें *g.of o.* अनुसंधान *n.*-लाग *m.*चालवणें *g.of o.*धोरणांत-लागांत-अनुसंधानांत-&c. असणें *g. of o.* साक्षेप *m.* करणें *g. of o.*

To p. intently and devotedly नादांत-नादीं-छंदांत-&c. असणें-लागणें-भरणें *g. of o.* नादावणें, व्यासंग *m.*-परिशीलन *n.* करणें.

4 *carry on, prosecute,* v. To CONDUCT. चालवणें, वाहणें.

5 (a course, &c.) *observe, adopt and practise,* v. To FOLLOW. करणें, आचरणें, सेवणें, धरणें.

PURSUER, *n.* PURSUING, *p. a.* v. V. 1. मागें-&c. चालणारा-&c. अनुगामी, अनुयायी, अनुगमन-&c.कर्त्ता-&c.

2 पाठीस लागणारा-लागलेला, पिच्छा धरणारा-धरलेला, &c.

PURSUIT, PURSUING, *n.* v. V. 2.—*act.* पिच्छा पुरवणें *n.* पाठ घेणें *n.* &c. पाठलाग *m.* अनुधावन *n.* पश्चाद्धावन *n.*

To desist from the p. of. पाठ *f.* सोडणें *g. of o.*

To send in p. of. दुमाल्यावर पाठवणें *g. of. o.*

3 उद्योग *m.* प्रयत्न *n.* यत्न *m.* अनुसंधान *n.* परिशीलन *n.* अनुशीलन *n.* व्यासंग *m.*

I. *course of occupation or employment.* उद्योग *m.* उद्यम *m.*

PURSUIVANT, *n.* v. MACE-BEARER. चोबदार.

PURSY, *a, short winded.* दम्या, दमटाक्या, दमभऱ्या.

PURTENANCE. See APPURTENANCE.

PURULENT, *a. mattery, consisting, &c. of pus.* पुवाचा, पूयरूप, पूयमय, पूयप्रधान.

2 *running with pus.* पुवानें भरलेला, पूयस्रावी, बरबरीत.

To PURVEY, PURVEYOR. See To CATER, CATERER.

PUS, *n. matter.* पू *m.* पूय *m.*

Bloody p. रेंद *m. f.* बर *f. n.*

Running with p. पूयस्रावी, बरबरीत.

To fill with p.—a sore. पुवळणें, पुवारणें, पुळणास येणें, उमाळ्यास येणें, पुलेणें.

To gather bloody p. रेंदावणें.

To run with purulent or sanious matter. बरबरणें *n.*

To PUSH, *v. a. shove.* ढकलणें, रेंटणें, लोटणें, सरकावणें, सारणें, सरवणें, सरसावणें, ठेलणें, धक्का *m.*-&c. देणें. [&c. करणें.

To p. about. सारासार *m.*-रेंटारेंट *f.*-रेंटाई *f.*-धकाधकी *f.*-

To p. and pommel. धकाबुकी *f.*-धकीबुकी *f.* करणें.

To p. aside, *move out of the way.* सेंटणें, सेंचणें.

To p. with the horns or head. हुंदडणें *or* हुंदाडणें.

2 *importune, urge, &c.* See To PRESS.

To PUSH, *v. n.* at ; *make a push or thrust.* ढुशी *f.*-ढुसकी *f.*-हुंडका *m.*-हुंदडा *m.* मारणें.

2 in ; *force one's self in.* घुशी *f.* मारणें, घुसडणें, घुसणें, घुसून-&c. शिरणें, रिघणें, ढुसणें, रिघाव *or* वा *m.*-रीघ *m. f.* करणें.

3 on ; *press forward.* पुढें-&c. जाणें, रगडून-रेंटून-रेंटीत-&c. जाणें.

PUSH, PUSHING, *n.* v. V. A. 1. धका *or* धक्का *or* ढका *m.* धकी *f.* रेंटा *m.* सारण *n.* अपसारण*n.* धडकी *f.*

P. and shoving. धकाधकी *f.* रेंटारेंट *f.* लोटालोट *or* टी *f.*

P. or blow with the head. हुंदका *m.* हुंदडा *m.*

PUSHED, *p.* v. V.A. 1. ढकललेला, रेंटलेला, सरकावलेला, &c. अपसारित.

PUSHER, *n.* PUSHING, *p. a.* v. V. A. ढकलणारा, रेंटणारा, &c. सारक, अपसारक.

I. *enterprising,* v. ADVENTUROUS. खटपट्या, कचाटी, कचाट्या, उलेढाल्या, उद्योगी, उद्यमी, साहसबुद्धि.

PUSILLANIMOUS, *a.*v. COWARDLY. भितरा, नामर्द, नामर्दीचा, हीनधैर्य, हीनशौर्य, हीनपराक्रम.

PUSILLANIMOUSNESS, PUSILLANIMITY, *n.* v. A. भितरेपणा *m.* नामर्दी *f.* शौर्यहीनता *f.*

PUSS, PUSSY, *n.* v. CAT. मंगी *f.* माई *f.* मांऊं *n.* म्यौ *f.* मंगोडें *n.*

The word used in calling to a cat is स्प.

PUSTULE, *n.* v. PIMPLE. पुटकळी *or* पुटकुळी *f.* पुळी *f.* करांटी *f.* फोड *m.* [ing p. मुकागुरू.

A flowing p. in measles or small pox. गुरू *m.*-an unflowing p. मुकागुरू.

Eruption into pustules. पुरळ *or* पूरळ *m.*

To be covered with pustules. पुटकळणें *or* पुटकुळणें, पुरळणें, फोडाळणें. [स्थापणें.

To PUT, *v. a. place, lay, deposit.* ठेवणें, घालणें, मांडणें, लावणें, स्थापणें.

To p. in fear, v. To FRIGHTEN. भय *n.* घालणें-दासवणें.

To p. in mind, v. To REMIND. आठवण *f.*-सई *f.*-याद *f.*-&c. देणें.

To p. in practice. See To USE, To EXERCISE.

To p. in writing. कलमी करणें, कलमबंदी *f.* करणें *g. of o.* पांढऱ्यावर काळा करणें.

To p. to death, v. To KILL. जिवें मारणें.

2 *apply.* घालणें, धरणें, लावणें.

3 (a question, &c.) v. To PROPOSE. घालणें, करणें.

4 about; (a ship or boat). हेरें *n.* घेणें.

5 away. दूर करणें, बाहेर करणें, बाद *f.* करणें *g. of o.* टाळणें, बारणें, अपसारण *n.*-दूरीकरण *n.*-&c. करणें *g. of. o.*

6 by; *lay aside.* ठेवणें.

7 forth. See To PROPOSE. 8 off; *postpone,* v. To. DEFER. उपेक्षणें, ढकलणें, झुलवणें, ढकलाढकल *f.*-ढकलपट्टी *f.*-टालमटोला *m.*-टाळा *m.*-उपेक्षा *f.*-&c. करणें.

9 off; *evade, shuffle.* झुलविणें *or* झुलाविणें, झुलकविणें *or* झुलकाविणें, ढकलणें, टाळणें, टाळा *m.*-टालमटोला-अळमटळम *n.*-ढकलपट्टी *f.*-झोला *m.*-&c. देणें, झोंकपट्टी *f.*-झुगारपट्टी *f.*-चांभार चाळवणी *f.*-&c. करणें-चालवणें, टोलाविणें, टोलावणी *f.* करणें.

To put off deceitfully & reiteratedly. झुलबाझुलब *or* वी *f.* करणें-लावणें- मांडणें.

10 off; *lay aside, divest one's self of.* ठेवणें, काढून टेवणें.

11 off; *put out to sea or from shore, &c.* हकारणें, हकालणें.

12 on *or* to; v. To INCITE. भर *m.* देणें, उत्तेजन *n.*-&c. करणें.

13 on; (clothes). वस्त्रपरिधान *n.*-परिधान *n.* करणें. Of this sense the *Marâṭhás* make numerous divisions, and for the expression of them they have numerous restricted or particularly respecting terms. The *putting on*—of the articles of the head-dress,—of the articles of the body-dress, and of these, again as *lower,* and *upper,*—of the stockings, shoes, &c. of the feet,—and of the ornaments of the limbs and members,—are viewed by them as different and distinguishable acts, and are distinguished by them in their commonest colloquy. To huddle together, therefore, in rendering this verb, घालणें, घेणें, पांघरणें, चढवणें, प्रावरणें, परिधानणें, नेसणें, भरणें, लेणें, बांधणें, टाकणें, लावणें, मारणें, and other such verbs, would necessarily be to mislead the student ignorant of the distinction, and to perplex him who, acquainted with the fact of it, might hope, through the Dictionary, to discover the nature of it. The following explication and detail therefore will be duly valued: To put on—(the turban, hat, cap, skull-cap, &c. the पागोटें, पगडी, टोपी, टोपडें, कुंचडें, बताना, गाभा, &c.) is, where it is viewed as ready-made up and as simply to be placed upon the head, घालणें; where it is, as is commonly the case of the turban, to be formed by being folded around the head, बांधणें;—(the rainy &c. hood

or cloak, the खोळ, टापशी &c.) बांधणें (& the बुंथी &c.) घेणें & मारणें;—(the coarse cloak or similar covering, the कांबळा, घोंगडी &c.) पांघरणें, प्रावरणें *or* घालणें, टाकणें;—(the shoulder-cloth, the दुपट्टा, शेला, &c.) घेणें;—(the upper garments, the आंगरखा, बंडी, आंगडें, झगलें &c.) घालणें, चढवणें;—(the bodice, the चोळी, &c.) घालणें, लेणें, चढवणें;—(the breeches, drawers, trowsers, the चोळणा, गुडघी, सुरवार, पायजामा&c.) घालणें;—(the धोतर, पंचा, गजा & the kinds of petticoat, the लुगडें, साडी, पातळ, लहंगा, परकोर &c.) नेसणें;—(the stockings, and shoes or boots) घालणें, चढवणें;—(the sandals) घालणें & बांधणें;—(trinkets & ornaments) लेणें & भरणें (e. g. बांगड्या भरल्या, गोठ भरले,);—and the paints and earths &c. to make sect-marks and beauty-spots) लेणें, लावणें, घालणें, देणें. To this we may add as a *general* intimation that To throw on, slip on, &c. is घालणें, & sometimes टाकणें & मारणें;—To throw on loosely or to cast over & fold around is पांघरणें, प्रावरणें, लेणें and *sometimes*, घेणें; To bind or fasten on is बांधणें; To put on (by pulling over the limbs or by passing the limbs through or into) is घालणें; & by girding or wrapping around, tucking in the skirt is नेसणें; To put on (trinkets and articles of ornaments) is लेणें & भरणें; To lay on or apply (pigments, unguents, collyrium, the lines and points of sectarial distinction, and the spots and dots of personal decoration) is लेणें, लावणें, घालणें, करणें, देणें, and others.

Fit to be p. on. नेसाऊ. [स्वीकारणें.

14 on; *assume.* धरणें, घेणें, लावणें, धारण करणें, अंगीकारणें,

15 out; *extend.* लांब करणें, पुढें करणें.

16 out; (a horse). v. To GALLOP. हकारणें.

17 out; v. To QUENCH. विझवणें.

18 out; v. To CONFUSE. भ्रमविणें, गांगरविणें, भांबावणें.

19 to it; *distress.* संकटांत-अडचणींत-पेंचांत-&c. पाडणें.

To be put to it. अडचणणें, पेंचांत-संकटांत-&c. असणें-पडणें-सांपडणें.

20 up; *shut up, lay aside, gather and lay by.* अटपणें, लावून ठेवणें, ठेवणें, उभवणें, उधवणें, उलगाउलग *f.*-उलगामालगी *f.*-&c. करणें. [ढ्यांत-&c. घालणें.

21 up; *pack for carriage.* गाठोडें *n.*-&c. करणें-गुंडाळणें, गाठो-

22 up; *alight, &c.* उतरणें, बिऱ्हाड *n.* करणें-लावणें-ठेवणें, प्रस्थान *n.* ठेवणें, गाठोडें *n.*-कंठाळ *f.*-&c. लावणें, वस्तीसराहणें.

23 upon. See To DECEIVE. 24 up with; *make shift with.* गरज *f.* करणें *g. of o.* [पोटांत घालणें.

25 up with; *overlook, brook,* v. To BEAR. सोसणें, साहणें,

PUT. See CLOWN. 2 See HARLOT.

PUT-OFF. See EXCUSE, EVASION.

PUTAGE, PUTANISM. See HARLOTRY.

PUTATIVE, *a. supposed, reputed.* लोकसमजुतीचा, लौकिकसमजुतीचा, जनप्रसिद्धीचा, मानलेला.

PUTREFACTION, *n. process of animal and vegetable decomposition.* कुजणें *n.* सडणें *n.*

PUTREFIED, *p.* PUTRID, *a.* v. V. सडलेला, कुजलेला, कुजका,

To PUTREFY, *v. n. rot, be decomposed.* कुजणें, सडणें.

To PUTREFY, *v. a.* कुजवणें, सडवणें, कुजेसा-सडेसा करणें.

PUTRID SORE-THROAT, *n. cynanche maligna.* घांटसर्प *m.* घांटरू *n.*

PUTRIDITY, PUTRIDNESS, *n.* v. A. सडलेलेपणा *m.* कुजलेलेपणा *m.*

Smell of p. कुजकटाण *f.* कुजटाण *f.*

PUTTING-STONE, *n. stone for trying strength.* गोटी *f.* बाळगुंडा *m.*

PUTTY, *n. glazier's paste.* लुकण *n.* लांबी *f.*

To PUZZLE, *v. a. pose, gravel, &c.* v. To CONFOUND. कोंडणें, गळफटणें *or* फाटणें, निरुत्तर-कुंठित-&c. करणें, तोंड *n.* बंद करणें *g. of o.* कांहीं सुचेनासा करणें, घोळ *m.*-घोंटाळा *m.*-&c. करणें *g. of o.* गोफाट्यांत-पेंचांत-&c. पाडणें.

PUZZLE, *n. enigma, &c.* कूट *n.* गूढ *n.* कोडें *n.* चौऱ्याशीचा फेरा *m.* करामत *f.* समस्या *f.* v. घाल, पुरव, सडकल *n.*

2 *puzzledness, perplexity,* v. CONFUSION. गळफटा *or* फाटा *m.* गिरकांडा *m.* गिरकांडी *f.* पंचाईत *f.* विवंचना *f.* विचार *m.* घोळ *m.* घोंटाळा *m.* गोंधळ *m.* भ्रम *m.*

PUZZLE-HEADED, PUZZLE-NOSE, *a.* v. DOUBTFUL. गोंधळ्या, भ्रांत्या, भ्रांतिखोर, भ्रांतिष्ट, भ्रमिष्ट, भ्रमी, भ्रांतहृदय.

PUZZLED, *p.* v. V. कोंडलेला, गळफाटलेला, &c. भ्रांत, संभ्रांत, विचारमूढ, इतिकर्त्तव्यतामूढ.

PUZZLER, *n.* PUZZLING, *p. a.* v. V. कोंडणारा, घोळ करणारा, &c. पंचाइतीचा, विचाराचा, &c.

PYEBALD, *a.* अबलक *or* ख.

PYGMY, PYGMEAN. See DWARF, DWARFISH. [रत *f.*

PYRAMID, *n.* खालीं रुंद असून वर अरुंद होत गेलेली मोठी उंच इमा-

PYRAMIDAL, PYRAMIDICAL, *a.* निमुळता *or* निमोळता, सूच्यग्र, गायदूम.

PYRE, *n. funeral pile.* सरण *or* शरण *n.* चिता *f.*

PYRITES, *n. fire-stone.* सुवर्णमुखी *f.* सुवर्णमाक्षिक *n.* बिटमाक्षिक *n.* आवर्त्त *m.*

Iron p. नीलमृत्तिका *f.*

Hepatic p. of iron. रूप्यमाक्षिक *n.* कास्यमाक्षिक *n.*

PYROTECHNIC, *a. pertaining to fire works.* दारूकामाचा, आतसबाजीचा, अग्निक्रीडासंबंधी.

PYROTECHNICS, *n. art of making fire works.* दारूकाम करण्याची विद्या *f.* अग्निक्रीडाविद्या *f.*

Q.

Q. has no representative in *Maráṭhí.* The compound letter क्व expresses its power.

QUACK, *n. cry of the duck.* बदकाचा आवाज *m.* जलकुक्कुटशब्द *m.*-नाद *m.*-&c.

2 *quack-doctor, empiric, &c.* वाडीवैद्य, नाकाडोळ्याचा वैद्य, टाणाटोणावैद्य, टाणाटोण्या, ताकपिठ्यावैद्य, जडीबुट्या, पहाडीवैद्य, ढोंगीवैद्य, वैद्यकीचापोम्या, वैद्यमानी, जाणता.

Murderous q. शतमारी, यमसहोदर, यमकिंकर.

3 *boastful pretender to skill or knowledge.* विद्येचा आव घालणारा, पोममाजविणारा, डौल्या, चिकित्सक. [रणें.

To QUACK, *v. n. utter its cry*—the duck. ओरडणें, शब्द *m.* क-

QUACK, *a.*—medicine, &c. वाडीवैद्याचा, टाणाटोण्याचा.

QUACKERY, *n. empiricism.* वैद्यकीचें पोम *n.*-ढोंग *n.*-&c. वैद्यकीचे

टाणेटोणे *m. pl.* [चिकित्सा *f.*
2 *boastful pretensions to knowledge.* पोम *n.* टाणेटोणे *m. pl.*

QUADRANGLE, *n. square or oblong space.* चौक *m.* चौकट *f.* चौसोपी *f.* चौपेट *f.*

QUADRANGULAR, *a. having four sides and four angles.* चतुष्कोण *pop.* चौकोन *or* नी, चौखुंदा, चतुरस्र *pop.* चौरस.

QUADRANT, *n. quarter of a circle.* त्रिज्या *f.* वर्तुलपाद *m.* पद *n.*
2—the instrument. तुरीययंत्र *n.* सूर्ययंत्र *n.*

QUADRATE, *To* QUADRATE. See SQUARE, To SQUARE.

QUADRATIC, *a.* v. SQUARE. चौकोणी.
A q. equation. वर्ग समीकरण *n.*

QUADRENNIAL, *a. comprising four years.* चारवर्षांचा, चातुरब्दिक, चौसाली, चौसनी.
2 *happening once in four years.* चारचार वर्षांनीं येणारा-घडणारा, चौसाली, चौसनी, चातुरब्दिक.

QUADRILATERAL, *a. having four sides.* चौपेलू, चौबाजूंचा.

QUADRILLE, *n.* नाचाचा प्रकार आहे. [चतुष्पाद.

QUADRUPED, *a. having four feet.* चौपायी, चौपायांचा, चतुष्पद,

QUADRUPED, *n.* पशु *m.* चतुष्पाद प्राणी *m.*

QUADRUPLE, *a. fourfold.* चौपट, चतुर्गुण.

To QUADRUPLE, *To* QUADRUPLICATE, *v. a. make four fold.* चौपट करणें-वाढवणें.

To QUAFF, *v. a. drink largely*, v. To DRINK. ढोसणें, घोटा *m.* लावणें, घोटणें, गटगटणें, गटगट-&c. पिणें.

QUAGGY, *a. boggy, &c.* दलदलीत, थलथलीत, बरबरीत, गलगलीत.

QUAG, QUAGMIRE, *n. bog, marsh, &c.* दलदल *f.* रुतण *f.* रुपण *f.* रेवण *f.* फसण *f.*

To QUAIL, *v. n. sink in hopes, &c.* v. To FAIL. खचणें, खचळणें, गंढारणें, मेटें *n. pl.* बसणें *g. of s.* अवसान *n.* गाळणें.

QUAIL, *n. perdix chinensis.* लावा *or* लाहूर *m.*

QUAINT, *a. having petty elegance.* चाकचोपीचा, चापचोपीचा, चाकचोप.
2 *odd, fanciful.* तन्हेदार, तन्हेवाईक, मौजेचा, विलक्षण.

QUAINTLY, *adv.* v. A.1. चापचोपीनें.
2 विलक्षणपणानें, विलक्षण.

QUAINTNESS, *n.* v. A. 1. चाकचोपी *f.* चापचोपी *f.*
2 तन्हेवाइकपणा *m.* &c.

To QUAKE, *v. n.* v. To TREMBLE. कांपणें, कांप *m.*- कांपरा *m.*- कांपरी *f.*-कांपरें *n.*-&c. सुटणें-भरणें, थरथरणें *intens.* धरारणें, पाठ *f.* कांपणें, हुडहुडणें, डगडगणें, डगमगणें.

QUAKE, QUAKING, *n.* v. V.—*act.* कांपणें *n.* कांप *m.* कांपरा *m.* कांपरी *f.* कांपरें *n.* थरथरी *f.* कंप *m.* कंपन *n.*
Excessive quaking through fear. चळकांप *m.* चळाळ *m.*

QUAKER, *n.* QUAKING, *p. a.* v. V. कांपणारा, कांप सुटलेला, &c. कांपरा, कंपमान, कंपान्वित.

QUALIFICATION, *n.* v. V. 1.—*state.* योग्यता *f.* उपयुक्तता *f.* लायकी *f.* क्षमता *f.* कार्यक्षमता *f.* गुणविशिष्टता *f.* गुणवैशिष्ट्य *n.*
I. v. LIMITATION, RESTRICTION. मर्यादा *f.* आळा *m.* आळाबांधा *m.*
II. a q. v. ACCOMPLISHMENT. गुण*m.*

QUALIFIED, *p.* v. V. 1. योग्य केलेला, &c. गुणी, लायक, उपयुक्त, क्षम, कार्यक्षम, योग्यतासंपन्न.
2 नरम—माफक-नेमस्त-&c. केलेला.

QUALIFIER, *a.* QUALIFYING, *p. a.* v. V. 1. योग्य-लायक-&c. करणारा, योग्यता-&c. देणारा.
2 नरम-माफक-&c. करणारा.

To QUALIFY, *v. a. make capable or competent.* योग्य-लायक-गुणी-गुणविशिष्ट-क्षम-&c. करणें, योग्यता *f.*-गुण *m. pl.*-लायकी *f.*-&c. देणें-आणणें.
2 *moderate, modify, soften, temper, &c.* नरमवणें, नरम-बेताचा-नेमस्त-&c. करणें.

QUALITY, *n. property.* गुण *m.* धर्म *m.* लक्षण *m.*
Bad or evil q. अवगुण *m.* दुर्गुण *m.*—Of bad q. अवगुणी, दुर्गुणी.
Essential or inherent q. अनुगतधर्म *m.* वस्तुशक्ति *f.*
Good q. सद्गुण *pop.* सुगुण *m.*
2 *character with respect to right or wrong*, v. CHARACTER. बरेवाइटपणा *m.* सदसद्भाव *m.* सत्त्वासत्त्व *n.* गुणावगुण *m.* गुणागुण *m.*
3 *high rank.* मोठी पदवी *f.* पदश्रेष्ठता *f.*
People of q. बडेलोक *m. pl.*

QUALM, *n. rising in the stomach.* उमास *m.* उमासा *m.* उमाळा *m.* उमाळी *f.* उबक *m.* [चूर *f.*
2 (of conscience). v. REMORSE. चुणचूण *f.* खरखर *f.* चुर-

QUALMISH, *a. inclined to vomit.* कळमळ आलेला, मळमळ सुटलेला, &c. वमनोन्मुख, वांत्युन्मुख.
To feel q. उमदळणें, कळमळणें, उचंबळणें,उचलणें, खबदळणें, ढबळणें, (all *impersonal*).

QUALMISHNESS, *n.* v. A. कळमळ *f.* कळकळी *f.* मळमळ *f.* मळमळी *f.* उमळ *f.* उमळावण *n.* उमास *m.* उमासा *m.* उमाळा *m.* उमाळी *f.* उमट *or* ओकारीचा उमट *m.* उमड *m.* ओकारा*m.* ओकारी *f.* शिसारी *f.* शिसकारी *f.*

QUANDARY, *n. state of doubt and perplexity.* विवंचना *f.* विचार *m.* विचारणा *f.* पंचाईत *f.*
To be in a q. अष्टाक्षरी *f. or* अष्टाक्षरीमंत्र *m.* जपणें (These eight letters are करें करूं काय करूं) मसलत *f.*-पंचाईत *f.*-विचार *m.*-&c. पडणें *in. con.*

QUANTITY, *n. magnitude, &c.* परिमाण *n.* प्रमाण *n.* मान *n.* परिमिति *f. pop.* परिमीत *f. n.*
Great q. मोठें परिमाण *n.* The sense is best rendered by using the adjectives पुष्कळ, बहुत, &c.
For this sense as expressed by such words as *peck, bushel, load, cart-load, heap, mountain,* some words or phrases are, गाडाभर, गाडेगणती, मुलूखभर, मळभभर, खंडीभर, खंडीगणती, पर्वत *m.* डोंगर *m.* ब्रह्मांड (as ब्रह्मांड कर्ज-खर्च-काम &c.). See also under EXUBERANCE.
Settled q. or allowance. मोताद *f.* रतीब *m.* चंदी *f.* वसा *m.* आहार *m.*
Small q. मात्रा *f.* मुष्टिमात्र *n.* मुष्टिपरिमाण *n.* To express "a small quantity" several words are in idiomatic use, some of which are here collected: a small quantity of curds दह्याचीकचडी,—of butter milk ताकाचाथेंब or ताकाचेंपाणी;—of clarified butter तुपाची धार, तुपाचा शितोडा, तुपाचें नख;—of oil तेलाची धार, तेलाचा टिकला;—of honey मधाचें बोट;—of butter लोण्याची कणी, लोण्याचें बोट. —The sense is often best rendered by the adjectives

थोडा, इवला, &c.
A small q. (of oil, ghee, milk, honey.). धारभर.
2—in prosody. मात्रा *f.*
3—in algebra; *a known q.* रूप *n.* व्यक्तराशि *m.*
Figurate q. क्षेत्रराषि *m.*
Infinite q. अनंतराशि *m.*
Negative q. क्षय *m.* ऋण *n.*
Unknown q. अव्यक्त *m.* अव्यक्तराशि *m.*

QUANTUM, *n. settled allowance, &c.* मोताद *f.* नेमणूक *f.* आहार *m.* रतीब *m.* [सटीप.
Quantum sufficit. जितक्यास तितका, कार्याकारण, टापा-

QUARANTINE, *n. prohibition from landing on the suspicion of disease.* रोग पाहण्याचा खुटवा *m.* रोग पाहण्याची मुदत *f.*

QUARREL, QUARRELLING, *n.* v. V. 1. मैत्रीभंग *m.* नाचक्की *f.* तुटातूट *f.* फुटाफूट *f.* बिनसाबिनस *f.* बिघाड *m.* तूट *f.*
Making up a q. निर्तुटक *n.*
Private adjustment of a q. घरसमजूत *f.*
Q. in play or fun. क्रीडाकलह *m.*
To kindle a q. फुणगी *f.* टाकणें or लावणें.
2 भांडण *n.* झगडा *m.* कज्जा *m.* बखेडा *m.* जुंज or झुंज *n.* झटपट *f.* झोंबट *n.* तंटा *m.* लढाई *f.* झमाझमी *f.* झकमक *f.* कलागत *f.* लटपट *f.* खणाजंगी *f.* नाचक्की *f.* कलह *m.*
Mutual or general q. भांडाभांड *f.* झगडाझगड *f.*
Quarrels—compreh. *quarrels and squabbles, disputes and differences.* कज्जा खोकला *m.* कज्जाकफावत *f.* कज्जाभांडण *n.* तंटा बखेडा *m.* झटझोंबट *n.*
To fall a q. बिन कदलीवर येणें.
To pick a q. दाटून-खोदून-खांदून कज्जा *m.* काढणें.
To set a q. बीर *m.* भरणें or देणें, लावालाव *f.*-लावालावी *f.* करणें, धरावर कुतरें *n.* चढवणें, खुंटी *f.* पिरगाळणें-पिळणें-पिळवटणें, मारणें.
I. *glaziers diamond.* काच कापायाची हिरकणी *f.*

To QUARREL, *v. n. fall out.* तुटणें, बिघडणें, फुटणें, बिघाड or बिघड *m.* पडणें *g. of s. recip.* तुटातूट *f.*-मैत्रीभंग*m.*-बिनसाबिनस*f.*-&c. होणें *g. of s. recip.* बिघडणें- बिनसणें *g. of s. recip.*
2 *squabble, contend, fight.* भांडणें, झगडणें, झगटणें, झुगटणें or झुगडणें, जुंजणें or झुंजणें, तंडणें, लढणें, रणें *n.pl.* पडणें, खटपटणें, भांडण *n.*-झगडा *m.*-&c. करणें, झकमक *f.*-चकमक *f.* झडणें *g. of s.*
3 *cavil, find fault,* v. To CARP. फांटा *m.* फोडणें, आडवें *n.* घेणें, कांक्षा *f.*-आक्षेप *m.* घेणें. [णारा, &c.

QUARRELLER, *n.* QUARRELLING, *p. a.* v. V. 1. बिघडणारा, तुट-
2 भांडणारा, झगडणारा, &c.

QUARRELSOME, *a. apt to fall out and break with.* तुटसाळ, तुटक, तुटरा, तुडस, तोडक, बिघड्या.
2 *given to contention, pugnacious.* भांडरा, भांडगा, भांडखोर, कज्जेखोर, कज्जेदलाल, बखेडखोर, तंटेखोर, तंटेबाज, कैपती, कैपतखोर, झगड्या, झगडाऊ, झगडाळू, खाजळा, खाजाळू, खजाळ, खटलेखोर, भंड, कलभांड, बोलभांड, कलागत्या, कलागतखोर, कलहकारी, कलहप्रिय, युयुत्सु.
Q. person. भांड, जगभांड, भांडकुदळ, वाऱ्याबरोबर भांडणारा, पाणी पिपिऊन भांडणारा, भांडणांतला वीरपीर.

QUARRELSOMENESS, *n.* v. A. 1. तुटसाळपणा *m.* तुटकपणा *m.*&c.
2 भांडरेपणा *m.* भांडगेपणा *m.* &c.

QUARRY, *n. mine, pit, &c.* खाण *f.* खाणी *f.* खनि *f.* आकर *m.*

QUART, *n.* v. MEASURE. एक कैलीमाप आहे. It is about a शेर.

QUARTAN, *n. ague that comes every fourth day.* चातुर्थिक *m.* चातुर्थक.

QUARTER, *n. fourth part.* चौथावांटा *m.*-हिस्सा *m.* पाव*m.* पाई *f.* चौथाई *f.* पावकें *n.* पाद *m.* चौन *m.* चतुर्थांश *m.* चतुर्भाग *m.* —esp. of a cake, of certain fruits, &c. चतकोर *m.f.* चतकर *m.f.*—of a rupee, पावला *m.*—of a year, तीनमहिने *m. pl.* पाववर्ष *n.* वर्षपाद *m.*
The silver coin equivalent to a q. of a rupee.पावली *f.*
Of a q. less. पाऊण (in comp. as पाऊणशेर, पाऊणहात, पाऊणभाकरी, &c. *i. e.* a sher, &c. all but a quarter). Before the numerals it becomes पाऊणे, as पाऊणेदोन, पाऊणेतीन, &c. a q. less than 2, &c. *i. e.* one and three quarters, &c.
Of a q. more. सवा (as सवामण, सवाशेर, सवादोन, सवातीन, &c. a maund and a quarter, a sher and a quarter, two and a quarter, &c.) [काष्टा *f.* ककुभ् *f.*
2 (of the heavens). दिशा *f.* दिक् *f.* घर *n.* आशा *f.* आंग *n.*
In, towards, &c. the four quarters. चौखुंट.
Regent of a q. दिक्पाल, लोकपाल.
To charm the quarters. दिशा *f. pl.* भारणें or बांधणें, दिग्बंधन *n.*-दिशाबंधन *n.* करणें.
3 (of a country, &c.). कड *f.* बाजू *f.* प्रदेश *m.*
From all quarters. चहुंकडून, जिकडूनतिकडून.
Of the quarters or regions round. चहुंकडला, चहुंकडील.
4 (of a town, &c.). वाडा *m.* महला *m.* पुरा *m.* पेंठ *f.* पट्टी *f.* पारवडा *m.*
Q. of the *mahárs.* महारवडा or वाडा *m.*
Q. of the poor. अडाणवस्ती *f.*
5 *sparing a life in battle.* जीवदान *n.* प्राणदान *n.* दया *f.*
To ask q. दांतींतृण *n.* धरणें, मी गाय आहें म्हणणें.
6 quarters; *lodgings, &c.* v. RESIDENCE. बिऱ्हाड *n.* घर *n.* वसतिस्थान *n.*
7 close quarters. बाहुयुद्ध *n.*
To come to close quarters. शरीरसंबंधावर येणें.

To QUARTER, *v. a. divide into four parts.* चारभाग *m. pl.*-चारवांटे *m. pl.*-&c. करणें *g. of o.* चौभागणें.
2 *place for lodging.* बिऱ्हाडास-रहायास-&c. ठेवणें-नेमणें, बिऱ्हाड *n.*-&c. देविणें.

To QUARTER, *v. n.* See To LODGE.

QUARTERLY, *a.* तीन तीन महिन्यांचा, तिमाही, त्रैमासिक.

QUARTERLY, *adv.* v. A. तीन तीन महिन्यांनीं.

QUARTERMASTER GENERAL, *n.* बिनीवाला.

QUARTO, *a.* चौबंदी, चारपानांचा.
Q. sheet. चौबंदी पान *n.* चौबंदी कागद *m.*

QUARTZ, *n.*—the mineral. काचमणि *m.*
Milky q. लसणा or लसण्या *m.*

To QUASH, *v. a. quell, subdue.* मोडणें, नाहींसा करणें, दाबणें.
2 *annul, make void,* v. To ABOLISH. मोडणें, रद्द करणें.

QUATERNARY, QUATERNION, *n. aggregate of four.* चतुष्टय *n.* चौकडी *f.* चतुष्क *n.* [कविता *f.*

QUATRAIN, *n. stanza of four lines.* चौचरणी श्लोक *m.* चतुष्पाद-

To QUAVER, *v. n. vibrate, &c.* v. V. To TREMBLE. कांपणें, कंप *m.* होणें *g. of s.*

2 (with the voice, or on an instrument). कंप *m.*-फिरक *f.*-फिरकी *f.*-गत *f.*-झील *f.*-शारीर *n.*-&c. घेणें.

QUAVER, QUAVERING, *n.* v. V. 1. कंपणें *n.* कंप *m.*

2 फिरक *f.* फिरकी *f.* गिरकी *f.* गिटकडी *f.* गिटकारी *f.* गत *f.* झील *f.* कंप *m.* शारीर *n.*

QUAY, *n. mole.* घाट *m.* धका *or* धक्का *m.*

QUEAN. See WENCH.

QUEASINESS, QUEASY. See QUALMISHNESS, QUALMISH.

QUEEN, *n. wife of a king.* राणी *f.* राजपत्नी *f.* महिषी *f.* राज्ञी *f.* नायका *f.*

Apartments of the q. राणबसा *m.*

Q. inaugurated and crowned. पट्टराणी *f.* पट्टमहिषी *f.* पट्टदेवी *f.* पट्टाभिषिक्त राणी *f.*

2 *woman who is sovereign of a country.* राणी *f.* राज्ञी *f.* राज्यकारिणी महिषी *f.*

3—at chess. बजीर *m.* प्रधान *m.*

QUEEN'S METAL, *n.* कांस्य *pop.* कांसें *n.* [बाईक.

QUEER, *a. odd, singular,* v. STRANGE. विलक्षण, अपरूप, तऱ्हे-

QUEERNESS, *n.* v. A. विलक्षणपणा *m.* अपरूपपणा *m.* वैलक्षण्य *n.*

To QUELL, *v. a. quash, &c.* v. To SUBDUE. मोडणें, तोडणें, दाबणें, नाहींसा करणें.

2 *quiet,* v. To COMPOSE. शांत-&c. करणें, शांति *f.*-शमन *n.*-उपशमन *n.*-&c. करणें *g. of o.* [करणें.

To QUENCH, *v. a.* (fire). विझविणें, विझण *n.* घालणें, निर्वापन *n.*

2 (a lamp). मालवणें, विझवणें, गूल *m.* करणें, निरोप *m.* देणें, पदर *m.* घालणें-देणें, शेव *f.* देणें.—by flapping. पालविणें.

3 (thirst, &c.) मोडणें, घालवणें, शमवणें, भागवणें, शांत-&c. करणें, शांति *f.*-&c. करणें *g. of o.*

QUENCHED, *p.* v. V. 1. विझवलेला, विझण घातलेला, निर्वापित.

To be q. विझणें, विझण *n.* पडणें.

2 मालवलेला, &c.

3 मोडलेला, घालवलेला, &c. शांत.

QUENCHLESS, *a. that cannot be quenched.* विझवतां यायाचा नाहीं, अनिर्वापनीय, निर्वापनाशक्य.

QUERIST, *n. inquirer.* सवाल करणारा, पुसणारा, पृच्छक, प्रष्टा.

QUERN, *n. hand-mill.* जातें *n.* घरट *m.*

QUERULOUS, QUERIMONIOUS, *a. habitually complaining.* रडगाण्या, रडकथ्या, रडका, गऱ्हाणखोर, गऱ्हाण्या, पिरपिरा, पिरपिऱ्या, रिपरिपा.

2 *expressing complaint,*—tone &c. रडका, रडगाण्याचा.

QUERULOUSNESS, QUERIMONIOUSNESS, *n.*v. A.1. रडकेपणा *m.* पिरपिरेपणा *m.* &c.

QUERY, *n.* v. QUESTION. प्रश्न *m.* सवाल *m.*

QUEST, *n.* v. SEARCH. शोध *m.* सुदावा *m.* तलाश *m.* सुगावा *m.*

QUESTION, QUESTIONING, *n.* v.V.1. पुसणें *n.* &c. प्रश्न *m.* सवाल *m.* पृच्छा *f.* पुरशीस *or* पुरसीस *f.*

String of questions. प्रश्नमाला *f.* प्रश्नावलि *f.*

To blink the q. डोळे झांकून बोलणें, लपेटीखालीं नेणें, लपेटून नेणें.

2 दिक्कत *f.* संशय *m.* शंका *f.*

To call in q. दिक्कत *f.*-&c. धरणें-घेणें *g. of o.* तकरार *f.*-वाद *m.* सांगणें-घेणें *g. of o.*

I. *dispute or subject of dispute.* वाद *m.* वादविषय *m.* विषय *m.* गोष्ट *f.* खटला *m.* खटलें *n.* साध्यार्थ *m.*

To be out of the q. बाहेर असणें.

To QUESTION, *v. a. interrogate,* v. To ASK. पुसणें, विचारणें, पुरशीस *f.*-सवाल *m.*-प्रश्न *m.*-&c. करणें-घालणें,—straitly, closely, &c. v. To EXAMINE. खोदून *or* खणून विचारणें-पुसणें, पुरसीस *f.* घालणें-करणें, खरावून विचारणें, पुसापुसी *f.*-पुस्तापास्त *or* पास्तपुस्त *f.* करणें, घोळणें-घोळघोळून घेणें.

2 v. To DOUBT, To DISPUTE. संशय *m.*-शंका *f.*-दिक्कत *f.*-&c. धरणें-घेणें *g. of o.* संशय *m.*-शंका *f.*-&c. येणें *in.con. with g. of o.*

QUESTIONABLE, *a.* v. V. 2. *and* DOUBTFUL. शंकनीय, आशंकनीय, शंकार्ह, शंकायोग्य. [बहुल.

QUESTIONARY, *a. containing questions.* प्रश्नमय, प्रश्नप्रचुर, प्रश्न-

QUESTIONER, *n.* QUESTIONING, *p. a.* v. V. 1. पुसणारा, सवाल करणारा, पृच्छक, प्रष्टा.

2 संशय धरणारा, शंका घेणारा, &c.

QUESTIONLESS. See CERTAINLY.

To QUIBBLE, *v. n. cavil, &c.* v. To CARP. आडफांटा *m.*-अढेवेढे *m. pl.* घेणें, फंगरूड *n.* फोडणें, पर्याय *m. pl.* सांगणें-फोडणें, लपेट *f.* मारणें, वाकूछल *m. n.*-वक्रोक्ति *f.* करणें.

QUIBBLE, QUIBBLING, *n.* v. V. आडफांटा *m.* अढेवेढे *m. pl.* अधांटी *f.* फंगरूड *or* फुगरूड *n.* फरगडे *or* फरगटे *m. pl.* बोलण्याची-भाषणाची लपेट *f.* वाकूछल *m. n.* वक्रोक्ति *f.*

QUIBBLER, *n.* QUIBBLING, *p. a.* v. V. आडफांटा घेणारा, &c. आडफांटे फोडणारा, अढेवेढे घेणारा, आडफांट्या, अधांट्या.

QUICK, *a.* v. LIVING. जिता, जिवंत, सजीव.

2 *speedy, swift.* जलदीचा, त्वरेचा, शीघ्र, सत्वर, वेगवान्, त्वरित, तरस्वी, क्षिप्र.

3 *active, lively, brisk,* v. SMART. जलद, चपला, शिताब, चलाक *or* ख, चटपटी *or* ट्या, झटपट्या.

4 *of ready apprehension,* v. SHARP. जलद, शीघ्रबुद्धि, चप्पू, हुशार, चणचणीत, सकृद्ग्राही, मेधावी.

5—of flesh, *as opposed to* dead, callous, proud. जिता, जिवा, जिवंत, गोडा.

6 (with child) v. PREGNANT. गर्भवती, चलितगर्भा.

QUICK, QUICKLY, *adv.* v. A. 2. लवकर, वेगीं, वेगून, जलद, जलदी, सत्वर, त्वरित, शीघ्र, वेगतः, वेगें *or* वेगीं, भडभड, क्षिप्र, लवडीसवडी, चालतांबोलतां *or* चालतबोलत असतां, थुंकीघाळून, घोड्याचे पाठीवर. For formations expressing this sense which answer to, *in a jiffey, in a trice, as soon as you can say Jack Robinson, &c.* See under TRICE.

Quick! smart's the word. झरझर, त्वरेस मोल आहे, बल्हा.

QUICK, *n. living flesh; sensible part.* जिव्हाळी *f.* वर्म *n.* वर्मस्थल *n.* वर्मस्थान *n.*

In or to the q. जिव्हाळीं, जिव्हारीं.

That touches the q. मर्मस्पृक्.

To be touched to the q. वरमणें *or* विरमणें.

To touch to the q. *lit. fig.* जिव्हाळीं लागणें, झोंबणें, डागणें, काळजीं लागणें, जिवीं लागणें, आंगीं *or* आंगास येणें, नाळीवर लागणें, लागणें, हडीं *or* हडांबर घाव *m.* घालणें, सोंचणें, सोंचरणें, वर्मभेद *m.*-मर्मभेद *m.*-&c. करणें.

QUICK-LIME, *n. burnt limestone.* चुनकळया *f. pl.* कळया *f. pl.* भाजलेले चुनखडे *m. pl.*

QUICK-SAND, *n. loose, watery sand.* नेहर *or* नेहेर *n.* रेवण *f.* रुतण *f.* रुपण *f.* रुतणीची-रुपणीची पुळण *f.*

QUICK-SCENTED, *a. of acute smell.* जलदहुंग्या, शीघ्रघ्राण.

QUICK-SET, *n. living plant set to grow.* कलम *n.* मेढा *m.* खुंट *m.*

QUICK-SIGHTED, QUICK-EYED, *a.* जलददृष्टीचा, दृष्टीचा जलद, शीघ्रदृष्टि, तीक्ष्णदृष्टि, प्रखरदृष्टि.

QUICK-SILVER, *n.* पारा *m.* पारद *m.* रस *m.*

Calcining q. मूर्च्छन *n.*

QUICK-WITTED, *a.* v. SHARP. शीघ्रबुद्धि, तीक्ष्णबुद्धि.

To QUICKEN, *v. n. become living.* जिता-जिवंत-सजीव-&c. होणें, जीव *m.* धरणें, जीवित्व *n.*-चैतन्य *n.* पावणें.

2 (a pregnant woman). गर्भचलन *n.* होणें *g. of s.* चलितगर्भा-&c. होणें.

3 *have increased motion, &c.* गति *f.* त्वरित होत जाणें *g. of s.* गतिवर्द्धन *n.*-गतिवृद्धि *f.*-&c. होणें *g. of s.*

To QUICKEN, *v. a. make alive.* जिता-जिवंत-सजीव-&c. करणें, जीव *m.* देणें.

2 v. To ACCELERATE, To HASTEN. त्वरा *f.*-&c. करणें *g. of o.* त्वरित-&c. करणें, गतिवर्द्धन *n.*-&c. करणें *g. of o.*

3 *stimulate,* v. To INCITE. उत्तेजन *n.*-उद्दीपन *n.*-&c. करणें *g. of o.*

QUICKLY. See QUICK.

QUICKNESS, *n.* v. A. 2. जलदी *f.* त्वरा *f.* शीघ्रता *f.* शैघ्र्य *n.*

3 जलदपणा *m.* जलदी *f.* चपलाई *f.* चलाकी *f.* शिताबी *f.* चटपट *f.*

4 जलदपणा *m.* हुशारी *f.* चप्पुपणा *m.* &c. शीघ्रबुद्धि *f.* मेधा *f.*

QUIESCENCE, *n.* v. REST. चलनाभाव *m.* निश्चलता *f.* नैश्चल्य *n.* निश्चलभाव *m.*

QUIESCENT, *a. not moving,* v. STILL. स्थिर, निश्चल, अचल, अचर.

2—in grammar. अनुच्चारित, लुप्तोच्चार.

Q. mark, *the mark (') denoting quiescence.* विराम *m.*

QUIET, *a. not moving,* v. STILL. स्थिर, निश्चल, अचल.

2 *still, unruffled, &c.* v. CALM. स्थिर, अक्षुब्ध, निवांत.

3 *serene, tranquil, &c.* v. CALM. थंड, थंडा, स्वस्थ, शांत.

4 *peaceable, gentle, &c.* v. MILD. गरीब, सालस, साळढाळ, निरुपद्रवीक.

5 *unmolested, undisturbed.* स्वस्थ, निर्बंध, निर्विघ्न, निर्व्याकुल, निष्कंटक, निरुपद्रव, अबाध, अप्रतिबंध, अप्रतिकारित, प्रतिबंधरहित-हीन-&c.

QUIET, *n.* v. REST. स्थिरता *f.* निश्चलता *f.* नैश्चल्य *n.* स्वस्थपणा *m.* निवांतपणा *m.* चैन *n.* स्वास्थ्य *n.* निष्कंटक *n.* उपद्रवाभाव *m.* कंटकाभाव *m.*

To QUIET, *v. a.* v. To CALM, To COMPOSE. संतावणें *or* संथावणें, शांतवणें *or* सांतवणें, शांत-स्वस्थ-&c. करणें, समजूत *f.*-शांति *f.*-&c. करणें *g. of o.*

QUIETISM, *n. dispassion, &c., contemplative religion.* शांति *f.* शम *m.* निवृत्तिमार्ग *m.* According to the *Wedánta* system there are six particular stages of the state, or six particular duties incumbent upon him who seeks it; viz. श्रद्धा, समाधान, तितिक्षा, उपरति, दम, शम.

QUIETIST, *n. one who maintains the principles of quietism.* निवृत्तिमार्गी, वेदांती, वेदांताधिकारी, वेदांतमार्गी, वेदांतसेवी.

QUIETLY, *adv.* v. A. 1. स्थिर, निश्चळ, निचळ, निवांत, चप *or* चप्प, गुपीचप *or* चूप, उगामुगा.

2. 3. 5. स्वस्थ, स्वस्थपणें, निवांत, अबाध, निरुपद्रव, निष्कंटक, उपद्रवावांचून.

I. *not hurriedly.* सावकाशीनें, सावकाश, धिमा *decl.*

QUIETNESS, *n.* v. A. 1. स्थिरता *f.* निश्चलता *f.* नैश्चल्य *n.*

2 निवांतपणा *m.* स्थिरता *f.* अक्षुब्धता *f.* अक्षोभ *m.*

3 थंडपणा *m.* थंडाई *f.* स्वस्थपणा *m.*

4 गरीबी *f.* सालसपणा *m.* &c. सालसाई *f.*

5 विघ्नाभाव *m.* कंटकाभाव *m.* उपद्रवाभाव *m.*

QUIETUDE. See QUIET.

QUILL, *n. feather.* पीस *n.* पर *m.*

To drive the q. खरडे *m. pl.* घासणें.

2 (of a porcupine). साळपीस *n.* साळेचा कांटा *m.*

3 (of weavers). कांडी *f.*

QUILL-DRIVER, *n. contemptuous term for a clerk, &c.* खरड्या, खरडघाशा, कारकुंडें *n.*

QUILT, *n. stuffed bed cover, garment, &c.* रजई *or* रजाई *f.* न्याहली *or* न्याहाली *f.* लेंप *n. m.* लेंपडी *f.* लेपडें *n.* दुलई *or* दुलाई *f.* [खळ *f.*

2 (of patchwork). गोदडी *f.* गोदडें *n.* कंथा *f.* बाकळ *or* बा-

To QUILT, *v. a. stuff with cotton &c. and stitch.* रू *m.* भरणें, रूभरून शिवणें, रूदार करणें.

QUILTED, *p.* v. V. रूभरलेला, रूदार, रूभरी, रुवाचा.

QUINARY, *a. consisting of five.* पांचांचा, पांचपांचांचा, पंचक.

QUINCE, *n. Bengal q.* श्रीफल *or* ळ *n.* बिफळ *n.*

Q.-seed. बेदाणा *or* मोगली बेदाणा *m.*

QUININE, *n.* एक औषध *n.* आहे.

QUINQUENNIAL, *a. lasting, &c. five years.* पांचपांच वर्षांचा, पांचसाली, पंचवार्षिक.

QUINSY, *n.*—the disease. घटसर्प *m.* घांटसर्प *m.*

QUINTESSENCE. See ESSENCE.

QUINTUPLE, *a. five fold.* पांचपट, पंचगुण.

QUIP, *n.* v. SARCASM. टोमणा *m.* टोला *m.*

To QUIP. See To TAUNT.

QUIRE, *n.* (of paper). दस्ता *m.*

Bundle or quantity of 10 quires. गड्डी *f.* गादी *f.*

QUIRE, &c. See CHOIR, &c.

QUIRK, *n. conceit, &c.* v. FANCY. चुटका *m.* नुतका *or* नुक्ता *m.*

2 *artful turn or evasion in speech.* बोलण्याची-भाषणाची-&c. लपेट *f.* बोलण्याचे छक्केपंजे *m. pl.* वाक्छल *m. n.* वक्रोक्ति *f.*

3 See QUIBBLE.

To QUIT, *v. a. resign,* v. To GIVE UP. सोडणें, सोडून देणें, उत्सर्ग *m.*-उत्सर्जन *n.*-&c. करणें *g. of o.*

2 *depart from, leave.* सोडणें, सोडून जाणें, सोडून देणें, टाकणें, वर्जणें, विसर्जणें, विसर्जन *n.*-त्याग *m.*-&c. करणें *g. of o.*

3 See To REQUITE. 4 See To ACQUIT.

QUIT, *a. discharged from, absolved.* मोकळा, उतराई, उत्तीर्ण, ऋणमुक्त, उपकारमुक्त.

QUITE, *adv. completely, entirely,* v. WHOLLY. केवल *or* ळ, अगदीं, निपट, निखालस, निखालस.

2 (as) *up to,* v. FULL. बरोबरीचा, तंत.

QUITS, To be q. उतराई होणें *g. of s.* बराबरी *f.* होणें *g. of s.*

recip. [वर्णे-मिळवणें.

To give q. यमकाला यमक *n.*-प्रासाला प्रास *m.* लावणें-बस-

QUITTANCE. See ACQUITTANCE.

QUIVER, *n. case for arrows.* भाता *m.* तरकश *or* स *m.* भातड *n.* भातडा *m.* शराश्रय *m.* तूण *m.* तूणीर *m.*—in contempt. भातडी *f.*

To QUIVER, *v. n.* (through cold, &c.) v. To SHIVER. कांपणें, हुडहुडणें, शिरशिरणें, खुडखुडणें, थुडथुडणें, कांप *m.*-कंप *m.* सुटणें *in. con.*

2 *shake tremulously,* v. To TREMBLE. डकडकणें, लुखलुख *adv.* हालणें, लटलटणें, लटलट *adv.* करणें.

3--the skin, &c. फुरफुरणें, स्फुरणें, स्फुरण *n.*-स्फूर्त्ति *f.*-&c. होणें *g. of s.*

4 (with impatience, to speak, strike, &c.)—the tongue, hand, foot. फुरफुरणें, फुरणें, हुळहुळणें, वळवळणें.

QUIVERER, *n.* QUIVERING, *p. a.* v. V. 1. कांपणारा, &c. कांपसुटलेला, &c. कंपमान, सकंप.

2 डकडकणारा, लटलटणारा, लटलट हालणारा.

3 फुरफुरणारा, &c. [ची खुडखुडी *f.*

QUIVERING, v. V. 1. कांपणें *n.* &c. हुडहुडी *f.* खुडखुडी *f.* थंडी-

3 स्फुरण *pop.* फुरण *n.* स्फूर्त्ति *f.* भोंवरा *m.*

4 स्फुरण *pop.* फुरण *n.* फुरफुरणें *n. intens.* फुरफुराट *m.*

QUIXOTIC. See ROMANTIC.

QUIZZ, *n.* See ODDITY. 2. थट्टा-मस्करी-विनोद-&c. करणारा.

To QUIZZ, *v. a. make fun of.* थट्टा *f.*-मस्करी *f.*-विनोद *m.*-&c. करणें *g. of o.*

QUOIT, *n. discus.* चक्र *n.*

QUONDAM, *a.* v. FORMER. पहिला, पूर्वीचा.

QUORUM, *n. such a number as is competent to transact business.* काम चालवायापुरती संख्या *f.* -मंडळी *f.* कार्यसाधकावरसंख्या *f.*

QUOTA, *n. share, part or portion assigned.* वर्गणी *f.* वर्गत *f. n.* वांटणी *f.* चंदा *m.* खापणी *f.* हिसेरसी *f.* [दामाशाई *f.*

Drawing out or determining quotas. हिसेरशी *or* सी *f.*

QUOTATION, *n.* v. V.—*act.* अवतरण *n.* उपन्यास *m.*

I. *passage quoted.* दुसऱ्याचें घेतलेलें वाक्य *n.* उपन्यस्तवाक्य *n.*-वचन *n.*-लेख *m.*-&c.

To QUOTE, *v. a. adduce a passage from an author or speaker.* दुसऱ्याचें वाक्य *n.*-लेख *m.*-&c. घेणें, उपन्यास *m.*-अवतरण *n.* करणें *g. of o.*

QUOTED, *p.* v. V. उपन्यस्त.

QUOTH, *imperfect v. said.* Q. I. मी बोललों. Q. He. तो बोलला.

QUOTIDIAN, *a.*—fever. ऐकाहिक, अन्येद्युस्क.

QUOTIENT, *n. number resulting from division.* भाग *m.* भागाकार *m.* फल *n.* लब्धि *f.* आप्त *n.* भजनफल *n.*

R.

R. is represented by र.

RABBIT, *n.* ससा *m.* शश *or* शशक *m.* Note. The Maráthás do not distinguish between the hare and the rabbit.

RABBLEMENT, RABBLE, *n.* v. PEOPLE. लुचें *n.* जंगमडबरें *n.* बाजारबुणगें *n.* कतवार *n.*

RABID, *a.* v. MAD. पिसा, पिसळलेला.

RACE, *n.* v. FAMILY, OFFSPRING. वंश *m.* वंशपरंपरा *f.* तंतु *m.* घर *n.* पुत्रपौत्रादिवंशपरंपरा *f.* बीज *n.* विल्हय *f.* विल्हाणा *m.*

Destruction of a r. वंशच्छेद *m.* वंशच्छेदन *n.*

2 (of cattle) *breed, stock.* ताणा *m.* बिजवट *n.* थळ *f.* साण *f.* जात *f.*

3 (of ginger, &c.) कांडी *f.* कुडें *n.* फडा *m. f.* फणा *m.*

4 *contest in running.* धांव *f.* दौड *or* दवड *f.*—for a prize. शर्यतीची-पैजेची-&c. दवड *f.*

5 Horse races. शर्यत *f.* (Ex. आज शर्यत होणार आहे.)

To run a r. दौड *or* दवड *f.* मारणें.

To RACE, *v. n.* v. To RUN. धावणें, दौड *or* दवड *f.* मारणें, धांव *f.* मारणें-टाकणें. [न्ढणारा घोडा *m.*

RACE-HORSE, RACER, *n.* शर्यतीचा घोडा *m.* पैजेचा घोडा *m.* शर्यत

RACK, *n. grate for hay.* गव्हाण *or* गव्हाणी *f.* वैरण *or* औयरण *f.*

2 v. TORTURE. यातना करण्याचें एक यंत्र आहे.

To put to the r. See To TORTURE.

To RACK, *v. a.* See To TORTURE.

2 v. To STRETCH. ओढणें, ताणणें.

To r. one's brains. कपाळकूट *f.*-&c. करणें.

RACKET, *n.* v. UPROAR. गलबल *f.* गलबला *m.* कुलकुलाट *m.* घोर *m.* कल्लोळ *m.*

2 (of children) See ROMPS.

RACKETY, *a.* गलबल्या, गलबल-&c. करणारा.

RACY. See STRONG, TASTEFUL.

RADIANCE, RADIANT. See BRIGHTNESS, BRIGHT. [यणें.

To RADIATE, *v. n. issue in rays.* किरणद्वारा-किरणरूपानें निघणें-

2 *issue and proceed in straight lines from a point.* केंद्रापासून नीट-सरळ-समोर-&c. निघणें-निघून चालणें.

RADICAL, *a.* v. ORIGINAL. मूळचा, मुळाविषयींचा, मुळींचा, मूलिक, मौल. [*pop.* स्वभाविक.

2 *native,* v. NATURAL. जातीचा, जन्माचा, असल, स्वाभाविक

3 *primitive, underived, &c.*—a word. मूळचा, मूलिक *m.*

RADICALLY, *adv.* v. A. 1. मुळीं, मुळींचा *or* मूळचा *decl.* आमूल.

2 जातीनें, जातीचा-&c. *decl.* स्वभावतः, जातितः.

To RADICATE. See To ROOT.

RADISH, *n.*—the plant. मुळा *m.* मूलक *m.*

Follicle of a r. मोगरी *f.* चिटकी *f.* डिंगरी *f.*

RADIUS, *n.* (of a circle). त्रिज्या *f.* व्यासार्ध *n.* व्यासार्धरेषा *f.*

2 (of the arm). कांब *f.* कांबीट *f.* हाताची *or* मणगटाची कांब *f.*

RAFFLE, *n.* v. V. सोडतीचा एक प्रकार आहे. [घालणें.

To RAFFLE, *v. n. contend for an article in a lottery.* सोडत *f.*

RAFT, *n. a float of timbers.* ताफा *m.* तर *f.* तरण *n.* तराफा *m.*

RAFTER, *n. a roof timber.* वांसा *m.* (*dim. deprec. dispar. &c.* वांसकटी *f.* वांसटी *f.* वांसोडी *f.* वांसोळी *f.*)

Corner r. कोनवासा *m.* कोना *m.*

Cross slip along ends of rafters. पाणसापुड *n.*

Cross piece receiving the ends of rafters. माढुटीचें पान *n. or* माढुटी *f.* (*or* मोहटीचें पान *or* मोहटी).

Round r. काटगोल *m.*

Stout r. or pole. तरक *m.f.*

RAG, *n. torn or torn off piece of cloth.* चिंधी *f.* चिंधूक *n.* चिंधूट *n.* चिंधडी *f.* चिरगूट *n.* चिथडा *m.* चिंथडी *f.* फडका *m.* फडकें *n.* सुडका *m.* सुडकें *n.* धुडका *m.* धुडकी *f.* बाभारा *m.* लत्ती *f.*

R. wetted to tie over a cut or sore. पाणकापड *n.* पाणपट्टी *f.*

Rags. Rags and tatters. चिंधड्या *f. pl.* बागुन्या *f.pl.* बसले *m.pl.* चिंध्यामिंध्या *f.* चिंधाचांधा *m.* चिंध्याचांध्या *f. pl.* लत्तरबाळ्या *f. pl.* लत्त्याबत्त्या *f. pl.*

To tear &c. to rags. चिंध्या *f. pl.*-बसले *m. pl.*-&c. करून टाकणें-उडवणें *g. of o.*

2—as used in contempt of an article of clothing. चिंधी *f.* चिंधीचोळा *m.* चिंधकुली *or* चिंधकोली *f.* चिंधुकली *f.* बातेरें *n.* सुडकें *n.* बोळा *m.* पुदरट *or* फुदरट *n.* पटकर *or* पटकूर *n.* बाकळ *f.*

Rags, *tattered and beggarly garments.* धुडक्या *f. pl.* धुडके *m. pl.* शतचिंध्या *f. pl.*

RAGAMUFFIN, *n. person dressed in rags.* फटकुन्या, चिंधोट्या, चिंध्यापीरं, चिंधाडभाई, गोदड्या, गोदडशाई, गोदडशहा, कलिंदरी, सुडके नेसलेला.

RAGE, *n. violent anger ; fury, passion.* क्रोध *m.* संताप *m.* क्षोभ *m.* कोप *m.* प्रकोप *m.* तळतळ *f.* तळतळाट *m.* जळप *m.* जळ *or* जाळ *m.* ताण *m.* वणवा *m.* घुसा *m.* तवक *m.* तैष *m.* तेख *m.* रोष *m.* अमर्ष *m.* क्रोधावेश *m.* कोपावेश *m.* अतिराग *m.* अतिक्रोध *m.* अतिकोप *m.*

Fit, paroxysm, transport, &c. of r. भिरका *m.* भिरका *m.* रागाचा झटका *m.*

To be livid from r. रागानें हिरवापिवळा होणें.

2 *violence, extreme exacerbation,* v. FURIOUSNESS. बेग *m.* जोर *m.* क्षोभ *m.* तडाखा *m.* धडाखा *m.*

3 *violent desire,* v. PASSION. वेड *n.* पिसें *n.* छंद *m.*

To RAGE, *v. n. be furious with anger, be violently agitated with passion.* तडफडणें, धडफडणें *or* धडबडणें, चडफडणें, जळणें, जळ्पणें, जळजळणें, तपणें, संतापणें, क्षोभणें, तमणें, तळतळणें. The *intensive* sense of this word, as conveyed by the expressive combinations *To storm and stamp, roar and bellow, rave and rant, rail and rattle at, fret and ferment, swell and fluster, chafe and fume, toss and fling, &c.* is with equal expressiveness and force conveyed by words and phrases in *Maráthi.* जळफळ *f.*-चडफड *f.* धडफड *f.*-आदळ आपट *f.*-अदळ उफळ *f.*-&c. मांडणें-करणें, डोक्याचा चेंडू *m.* करणें, डोक्याचें उखळ *n.* करणें, दांतओंठ *m. pl.* खाणें, जीव *m.* पाखडणें, मणगटें *n. pl.* तोडणें-चावणें, आंगास मीठ मोहऱ्या *f. pl.* लागणें *g. of s.* हिरवा पिवळा होणें, हातपाय *m. pl.* चोळणें-आपटणें-आदळणें, ताप तोबारा *m.* करणें, दंगा *m.* करणें, नाकपुड्या *f. pl.* पिंजारणें-फुगवणें, वादळणें, विदविदणें *or* वितवितणें, तातवणें *or* तातावणें, कडकडणें, चवतळणें *or* ताळणें, जळजळणें, जळफळणें, तळतळणें, फणफणणें, टापगणें, टाफरणें, डाफरणें, डाभरणें, चाचावणें, चिवचिवणें, फुणफुणणें, तणतणणें, तमतमणें, खुणखुणणें, धुमसणें, दांतवणें, वरदळणें, काव्हणें, डुरडुरणें. *And* To fly or rise into a rage, is rendered by, भडकणें, तापणें, पेटणें, आंगास आग *f.* लागणें-पेटणें, चढून येणें, रुद्रावतार धारण *n.* करणें, सिंहावतार *m.* धरणें *or* घेणें, तृतीय नेत्र *m. n.* उघडणें, वरदळीस येणें, लळितावर येणें, दांतीं येणें, शिखासूत्रावर येणें, कह्रातीस येणें, हातीं धोंडे *m. pl.* घेणें *or* धोंडे *m.pl.* मारूं लागणें, डोकें *n.* फिरणें *g. of s.* आंगाची होळी होणें *g. of s.* अंगुष्टाची आग *f.* मस्तकांत जाणें-चढणें *g. of s.* पायांचा जाळ मस्तकीं जाणें *g. of s.* चिरडी *f.* नेसणें, जानवें *n.* तोडायास उठणें *or* जानव्यास हात *m.* घालणें, आंगाचे तिळपापड *m. pl.* होणें *g. of s.* आंगाची लाही *f.* होणें *g. of s.* तान *m.* येणें *in. con.* इयाल होणें *with* वर *of o.* खवंदळणें, खवळणें.

To r. impotently. दांत खाऊन अवलक्षण होणें.

2 *prevail with fatal effect.* अनर्थ *m.*-कहर *m.*-गजब *m.*-प्रलय *m.*-&c. करणें-मांडणें, तडाखा *m.*-झपाटा *m.*-धूम *f.*-&c. उठवणें-चालवणें-मांडणें, तडाखा *m.*-झपाटा *m.*-&c. चालणें *g. of s.*

RAGEFUL, *a.* RAGER, *n.* RAGING, *p. a.* v. V. 1. *and* ANGRY. जळणारा, तडफडणारा, &c. संतापलेला, &c. जळजळया, तडफड्या, धडबड्या, &c. संताप्या, कोपी, क्रोधी, कहरी, अतत्यायी, संतप्त, संतापित, संतापयुक्त. Terms expressing this sense as *intended,* and as apparent under the words and combinations, *frantic, phrenzied, one mad with rage, one foaming with fury, storming with passion, bursting with anger, &c.* are; तग्रबग्र, काबराबाबरा, तारकाबारका, क्रोधांध, कोपज्वलित, कोपान्वित, कोपविक्षिप्त, क्रोधविक्षिप्त, अकराबारुद्र, रुद्रावतार, सिंहावतार, जमदग्नि.

2 अनर्थाचा, कहराचा, तडाख्याचा, झपाट्याचा, अवधंड्याचा, जबर, चंड, प्रचंड, विकोपास गेलेला.

RAGGED, *a. rent into tatters, torn.* फाटका, चिरलेला, चिरफळ्या-चिरफाळ्या-बामारे-&c. गेलेला-उडालेला-निघालेला, चिरफळ्यांचा, शतच्छिद्र.

2 *dressed in rags.* सुडके नेसलेला, चिंध्या नेसलेला, फडकें नेसलेला, चिंधोट्या, लगोऱ्या.

3 *uneven, rugged.* उखरवाखर, उखरावाखर, खरबरीत *or* खरबडीत, खाबडखुबड.

RAGGEDNESS, *n.* v. A. 1. फाटकेपणा *m.* &c.

2 चिंधोटेपणा *m.* लगोरेपणा *m.* छिन्नवस्त्रता *f.*

3 उखरवाखरपणा *m.* &c.

RAGING, *n.* v. V. 1. तडफड *f.* धडफड *or* बड *f.* चडफड *f.* डुरडूर *f.* आदळ आपट *f.* आदळ उफळ *f.* आदळ आफळ *f.* त्राण *n.*—*intens.* तडफडाट *m.* धडफडाट *m.* चडफडाट *m.* तळतळाट *m.*

RAIL, *n. bar of iron or wood used in inclosing.* गराज *f.* गराद *f.* गरादा *m.* गज *m.* फिरकी *f.*

Cross r. सर *m.* सरी *f.*

Rails. See RAILING.

2 See RAILWAY.

To RAIL, *v. a. enclose with rails.* कठडा *m.*-&c. करणें-घालणें-बांधणें-लावणें, कुडणें, कठडेबंदी *f.* करणें.

To RAIL, *v. n. speak revilingly, roar at, rattle at,* v. To ABUSE. To SCOLD. तोंड *n.* सोडणें-टाकणें, तोंडाचा तोफखाना *m.* सोडणें, दांतकिसाळी *f.* करणें, शिव्यांची तान *f.* झाडणें, फडफड *adv.* शिव्या *f. pl.* देणें, फडफडणें, कडकडणें.

RAIL-ROAD, RAIL-WAY, *n.* लोखंडीरस्ता *m.*-सडक *f.*

RAILER, *n.* RAILING, *p. a.* v. V. N. *and* ABUSIVE. तोंड सोडणारा-टाकणारा, &c. दांतकिसाळ्या, अपवादक, निर्भर्त्सक.

RAILING, *n.* v. V.A.—*act.* कठडा करणें *n.* &c. कुडण *n.* v. V. N. *and* ABUSE. दांतकिसाळी *f.* शिवीगाळ *f.* गालीगलोची *f.* दुर्भाषण *n.* अपभाषण *n.*

I. *series of rails.* कठडा *m.* कठरडा *m.* कठारा *m.* कटारा *m.* लकडकोट *m.* कटंजन *n.* कुपण *n.* कुडण *n.*

RAILINGLY, *adv.* v. A. फडफड (*intens.* फडाफड, फडाडां) तोंड सोडून, तोंड टाकून, शिवी-शिवीगाळ-&c देऊन.

RAILLERY, *n. banter,* v. RIDICULE. विनोद *m.* थट्टा *f.* मस्करी *f.*

RAIMENT, *n.* v. CLOTHES. वस्त्र *n.* चिरगूट *n.*

To RAIN, *v. n. fall from the clouds,*—water. पाऊस *m.*-पाणी -&c.पडणें, पाऊस *m.*-&c. लागणें,वर्षणें. [पडणें.

To r. briskly and passingly. शिडशिडणें, शिडशीड *adv.*

To r. heavily, in torrents, &c. स्रोखावणें, पावसाचें पोट *n.* फुटणें, पावसानें धार *f.* धरणें, झिम-धुमाधार *or* धुवाधार-झमझम *or* मां-झमाझम-सटसट *or* टां-सटासट-सटाटां-धोधोधो--&c. पाऊस पडणें.

To r. spittingly. पिरपिरणें.

To RAIN, *v. a. pour from above like rain.* पाऊस *m.*-वृष्टि *f.*-वर्षाव *m.*-&c.पाडणें-करणें *g. of. o.* वर्षणें.

RAIN, *n.* पाऊस *m.* पर्जन्य *m.* वृष्टि *f.* बरसात *f.* पाणी *n.*—indef. *or* freely. पाऊसपाणी *n.* पाणीपाऊस *m.* [वना *f.*

Beginning to rain, setting in of r. पावसाची पडती भा-

Brisk and passing r. शिडशिडी *f.*

Broken or partial r. तुटपाऊस *m.* खंडवृष्टि *f.*

Continuing r. रांप *or* रांफ *f.* रांपेचा *or* रांफेचा पाउस *m.*

Deluge of r. पलकदर्याव *m.*

Excessive r. अतिवृष्टि *f.*

Fall of r. वर्षाव *m.*

Favorable or beneficial r. सुपाऊस *m.* [मातृक.

Fertilized by r. (*opp. to* नदीमातृक *or* जलमातृक) देव-

Heavy fall of r. मोड *m. f.*

Heavy r. धडधडीत पाऊस *m.* धडकवणी *n.*मुसळधार *f.* मुसळधारपाऊस *m.* चळकधार पाऊस *m.* धारासम्पात *m.* पलकदर्याव*m.*

Light and long continuing r. झिमझीम *f. n.*

Lightly falling r. बुरबूर *f.*

Pelting r. फटकाऱ्याचा पाऊस *m.*

R. during sunshine. ऊनपाऊस *m.* नागवा पाऊस *m.*

Signs of r. पावसाचे डोहळे *m. pl.* पावसाचा रंग *m.*

Soaking r.(*as distinguished from* a pelting and passing shower, फटकाऱ्याचा पाऊस), भिजपाऊस *m.* जिरवणी *n.*जिरविणीचा पाऊस *m.*

Spitting r. पिरपिरा *or* ऱ्या पाऊस, पावसाची धुईधुई *f.* पिरपीर *f.* मुळमूळ *f.*

Spoiled by much r.—crop. पाणपिसा.

Unceasing pour of r. झिंबड *or* डी *f.* झुंबड *f.* झड *f.* झडी *f.* झोड *f.* पावसाची टक *f.*

Untimely r. अकळवणी *n.* अकालवृष्टि *f.* नासवणी *n.* अवकाळवणी *n.*

The rain has set in. पावसानें धरलें.

2 the rains ; *rainy season.* पावसाळा *m.* पाऊसकाळ *m.* पाऊसकाळा *m.* पावसाळी *f.* बरसात *f.* प्रावृट् *f.* प्रावृट्कालम. प्रावृषा*f.* वर्षा *f.* वर्षाकाल *m.* वर्षाऋतु *m.*

Height or middle of the r. ऐन पावसाळा *m.*

In the middle of the r. पडत्या पावसांत.

Moisture from first showers of the r. तान्हीबल *f.*

Throughout the r. पाऊसभर.

The *rains* have set in. पावसाचा पडता पाया लागला, पावसाची पडती भावना झाली. [शक्रधनु *n.*

RAIN-BOW, *n.* धनुष्य *or* इंद्र धनुष्य*n.* इंद्रचाप*n.* इंद्रधनु*n.* इंद्रायुध*n.*

RAINED, *p.* v. V. A. पाऊस पाडलेला &c. वर्षित.

RAININESS, *n.* v. A. पावसाळें *n.* बांचट *f.* रांप *or* रांफ *f.* वृष्टिप्राचुर्य *n.* वृष्टिबाहुल्य *n.* वर्षुकता *f.*

RAINING, *n.* v. V. N. वर्षाव *m.* वर्षण *n.* वर्ष *n.*

RAIN-WATER, *n.* पावसाचें पाणी *n.* पर्जन्योदक *n.*

R. caught. धरवणी *n.*

RAINY, *a. abounding with rain.* पावसाचा, पर्जन्याचा, झडीचा, &c. वर्षुक, वृष्टिमय, वृष्टिप्रचुर, वृष्टिबहुल.

To RAISE, *v. a. lift, heave.* उचलणें, उचलून घेणें, उठवणें, उंच करणें, उचल *f.*-उठावणी *f.*-उन्नयन *n.*-उत्थापन *n.*-उत्तोलन*n.* करणें.

To r. from the ground. भुईसांड-जमीनसांड करणें.

To r. and rest (burdens). उचला डेवर *f.* करणें.

2 *set upright.* उभा करणें, उभारणें, उभविणें, उंच करणें, उंचावणें.

3 *erect, &c.* v. To BUILD. उभा करणें,उभवणें, उभवणी *f.* करणें.

4 *elevate, promote,* v. To EXALT. चढवणें, वाढवणें, मोठेपणास आणणें, उंचावणें, न्यहाल करणें, उन्नति *f.*-&c. करणें *g of o.*

5 (in price). चढवणें, मोल *n.*-किम्मत *f.*-दर *m.*-भाव *m.*-&c. चढवणें.

6 v. To EXCITE, To INCITE. उचलणें, उठावणें, उचल *f.*-उठावणी *f.*-उत्तेजन *n.*-&c. करणें *g. of o.* उभारणें.

7 (a report, &c.) उठवणें, उडवणें, रचणें, फेंकणें, उत्थापित करणें.

8 (troops) *levy.* जमवणें, मिळवणें, जमाबंदी *f.* करणें.

9 (monies) v. To COLLECT, To LEVY. मिळवणें, जमवणें, उत्पन्न करणें.

10 (crops, cattle, &c.). निपजवणें, उपजवणें, पिकवणें, उत्पन्न करणें, काढवणें. [उगारणें.

11 (a sword, stick, hand, &c.) *lift & hold menancingly.*

12 (a siege, &c.) उठविणें, काढणें.

13 (game, by beating bushes, &c.) रान *n.* काढणें-हाकणें.

To r. one's voice. मोठ्यानें बोलणें, स्वर *m.*-&c. मोठा करणें.

To r. one's voice against, v. To EXCLAIM. हाकाटा *m.* करणें.

RAISIN, *n.* मनूक *f.* मनुका *f. pl.*—without pips. खिसमीस *or* किसमीस *f.* बेदाणा *or* ना *m.* [*m.* फण *m.*

RAKE, *n.*—the instrument. दांताळ *n.* दांताळें *or* दंताळें *n.* दांता

2 *loose fellow, libertine.* चंगी, चंगीभंगी *or* भंगीचंगी, इष्कबाज, रांडबाज, व्यसनी, बिसनी, स्त्रीव्यसनी, फंदी, सोदा, लुच्चा, शृंगारी, बळी. [&c.

To RAKE, *v. a. gather with a rake.* दांताळ्यानें-&c. गोळा करणें-

2 *clear &c. with a rake.* दांताळ्यानें नीट-साफ-&c. करणें, दांताळें *n.* फिरवणें. [करणें.

3 (together) *collect.* ओढून आणणें, जथणें, जथवणें, गोळा

4 (a ship) नाळेकडून सुकाणाकडे किंवा सुकाणाकडून नाळेकडे गोळे जातील अशा प्रकारें तोफा *f. pl.* सोडणें.

To RAKE, *v. n. be dissolute.* सोदेगिरी *f.*-&c. करणें-चालवणें, चौंढाळणें, आवगणें, चवणें *or* चेवणें.

RAKERY, RAKISHNESS, *n. dissolute practices.* सोदेगिरी *f.* सोदेशाई *f.* सोदाबें *n.* सोदेपणा *m.* सोदाई *f.* टवाळकी *or* टवाळी *f.* रांडबाजी *f.* इष्कबाजी *f.* रांडव्यसन *n.*

RAKISH, *n. dissolute,* v. LOOSE. सोदेशाई, सोदा, टवाळ, टवाळखो-

र, बटाऊ *or* बटाब, रांडव्यसनी, व्यसनी, सोदेगिरीचा.

To RALLY, *v. a.* (troops, &c.) *bring again into order.* सावरणें, सुधारणें, सुधारासुधार *f.*-धीरथावर *f.*-थावराथावर *f.*-सावरासावर *f.*-&c. करणें *g. of o.*

2 *jest, jeer,* v. To RIDICULE. मस्करी *f.*-थट्टा *f.*-खिल्या *f.pl.*-विनोद *m.*-उपहास *m.*-&c. करणें *g. of o.*

To RALLY, *v. n. recover order, &c.* सावरणें, सावर *m.* घेणें, थावरणें, सुधारणें, पहिल्या स्थितीवर-पूर्वस्थितीवर-ठिकाणावर-&c. येणें.

RAM, *n. male sheep.* मेंढा *m.* एडका *m.* मेष *m.*

Full grown r. *a tup.* टपूर *m.*

Young r. बाळिंगा *m.*

2 (the sign aries). मेष *m.*

3 See BATTERING RAM.

To RAM, *v. a. drive hard.* सचणें, ठासणें, ठोकणें, चेंदणें, मारणें, चेळणें, ठेंबरणें, ठासणी *f.*-&c. करणें *g. of o.*

2 See To STUFF.

RAM-ROD, *n.* गज *m.*

To RAMBLE, *v. n.* v. To WANDER. इकडे तिकडे-जिकडेतिकडे-&c. फिरणें, रमणें, हिंडणें, हिंडत फिरणें, फेरफटका *m.* करणें.

2 (in speech). चांचरणें, रानांत शिरणें, रान *n.* घेणें, वाहवणें.

RAMBLE, RAMBLING, *n.* v. V. 1. फेरफटका *m.* फेर *m.* सहल *f.* रपेट *f.* टेहळ टिकोरी *f.* इतस्ततःभ्रमण *n.*

To take a r. (or turn). चक्कर *n.* मारून येणें.

RAMBLER, *n.* RAMBLING, *p. a.* v. V. 1. इकडे तिकडे फिरणारा, हिंडणारा, &c. हिंडफिऱ्या, सहलबाज, ओढाळ.

2 चांचरणारा, वाहवरा.

RAMBLINGLY, *adv.* v. V. 1. रमत रमत, रमते रमते.

RAMIFICATION, *n. small branch or subdivision.* मुळी *f.* मूळखंड *n.* मुळकुंड *n.* मुळकुंडी *f.* पाळ *n.* पाळक *m.* फणगडा *m.* फुटी *m.* पागोरा *m.* उपशाखा *f.*

2 See SUBDIVISION.

To RAMIFY, *v. n.* फांटे *n. pl.*-फणगडे *m. pl.*-&c. फुटणें. [*m.*

RAMMER, *n. thing to ram with,* v. MALLET, POUNDER. मोगरा

2 See RAM-ROD.

R. of a cannon. सुंबा *m.*

RAMMISH, RAMMY. See RANK.

RAMOUS. See BRANCHY.

To RAMP. See To LEAP.

RAMPANCY, *n.* v. A. माजलेलेपणा *m.* माज *m.* मात *m.* ऊत *m.*

RAMPANT, *a.* v. LUXURIANT, EXCESSIVE. माजलेला, मातलेला, माजाचा, जबर, जबरदस्त, मर्यादातीत.

To get r. माजणें, मातणें.

2—lion. उपायीं आलेला.

RAMPART, RAMPIRE, *n. wall of a fort.* तट *m.* किल्ल्याची भिंत *f.* प्राकार *m.* सफेली *f.*

RANCID, *a. having a rank sour smell.* खंवट *remiss.* खंवचट, खंवटेल, खोमट, कुईट *or* कुबीट, वासट, वासकट, वाशेळा, वाशेरा, वासाळ, घुरट.

R. or rank smell. खंवटाण *f.* [वासटपणा *m.*

RANCIDNESS, RANCIDITY, *n.* v. A. खंवटपणा *m.* कुईटपणा *m.*

RANCOROUS, *a.* v. MALICIOUS. द्वेषी, चुरसी, खुनसी, चुरसीचा, द्रोहाचा, द्रोही, हाडवैराचा, दीर्घद्वेषी, आडगांठ्या,

RANCOUR, *n.* v. MALICE. चुरस *f.* खुनस *m. f.* कोर *f.* कोरवंदी *f.* द्रोह *m.* हाडवैर *n.* दीर्घद्वेष *m.*

RANDOM, *a. that was without settled aim or purpose.* असंधानाचा, अलक्ष्याचा, नेमाबांचूनचा, बेशिस्त, संधानरहित, भलता, बेडावांकडा. [लता.

At r. संधानावांचून, नेमावांचून, शिस्त धरल्यावांचून, &c. भ-

To begin to talk or act at r. वाऱ्यावर सरणें, रानांत शिरणें, रान *n.* घेणें.

To roam or rove at r. सैरावैरा हिंडणें-फिरणें.

RANDY, *a. that has grown riotous.* मस्त, मस्त्या, मस्ता, उन्मत्त, माजलेला.

To get r. माजणें, मातणें, उंडारणें.

To RANGE, *v. a. arrange,* v. To DISPOSE. योजणें, रचणें, योजून -&c. ठेवणें, बेतानें-&c. ठेवणें, रचना *f.*-व्यवस्था *f.*-&c. करणें *g. of o.*

2 (the coast). बाजूनें जाणें-चालणें.

To RANGE, *v. n. rove,* v. To WANDER. फिरणें, हिंडणें.

2 *have a particular direction.* कल *m.*-झोंक *m.*-&c. असणें.

3 See To RANK. [श्रेणी *f.*

RANGE, *n. rank, line,* v. ROW. ओळ *f.* रांग *f.* हार *f.* आवलि *f.*

2 (as of an arrow, ball, &c.). टप्पा *m.* पल्ला *m.* छट्टा *m.* खांच *f.* मारा *m.*

Of a long r. पल्लेदार.

3 (of a building). सोपा *m.* चाळ *f.*

4 *extent, compass,* v. REACH. पहोंच *f. m.* अटोका *m.*

5 *step of a ladder,* v. STEP. पावटा *m.*

6 *order.* See CLASS.

RANGER, *n. keeper of a forest.* अरण्यरक्षक, अध्यक्ष.

RANK, *a. high growing,* v. LUXURIANT. माजलेला, बोकडलेला, उफाड्याचा, उद्दाम.

To run r. माजणें, बोकडणें, बोकळणें, वाळेणें.

2 *strong scented, high tasted, rancid.* वासट, वासकट, वाशेळा, वाशेरा, वासाळ, खवट *remiss.* खंवचट, कुईट *or* कुबीट, घुरट, उग्र, उग्रट, उद्दाम, उग्रवासाचा, उग्रस्वादाचा.

A r. smell. घुरटाण *f.* घुरष्टाण *f.*

3 See EXCESSIVE.

RANK, *n. line,* v. ROW. ओळ *f.* रांग *f.* हार *f.* आवलि *f.*

2 *station, grade.* पायरी *f.* पदवी *f.* पद *n.* दरजा *m.* मान *m.* रुतबा *m.*

3 *high station, dignity, quality.* मोठी पदवी *f.* मोठेपणा *m.* मोठादरजा *m.* मरातब *m. f.* मरतबा *m.* उच्चपदता *f.*

4 *order,* v. CLASS. वर्ग *m.* गण *m.* विल्हे *f.* विल्हा *m.*

To RANK, *v. a. range in a particular class.* धरणें, मोजणें, गणणें, गणना *f.*-&c. करणें *g. of o.*

2 See To RANGE.

To RANK, *v. n. be ranged in a particular class.* मोडणें, गणना *f.*-&c. असणें *g. of s.*

2 (with). बराबर-समतोल-सममान-&c. असणें.

To RANKLE, *v. n. be inflamed, fester.* सलणें, खुपणें, डाचणें, जळणें, खाणें, डिवणें.

RANKNESS, *n.* v. A. 1. माज *m.* मात *m.* उफाडा *m.*

2 वासटपणा *m.* वासकटपणा *m.* खवटपणा *m.* &c. उग्रवास *m.* उग्रस्वाद *m.*

3 See Excess.

To Ransack, *v. a. search thoroughly.* ढंढुळणें *or* ढुंढाळणें, धुंडाळणें *or* धांडळणें, खळबटणें, चाळणें, चाळून-चोखळून पाहणें, धुंडाळा *m.*-चाळाचाळ *f.*-चाळाचाळी *f.*-&c. करणें *g. of o.*

2 See To Plunder. [सोडणावळ *f.*

Ransom, *n. price paid for redemption.* खंड *m.* खंडणी *f.* दंड*m.*

2 See Deliverance. [देऊन सोडवणें.

To Ransom, *v. a. redeem by paying a ransom.* खंड *m.*-&c.

2 See To Deliver.

To Rant, *v. n. rave, use extravagant and empty speech.* बरळणें, चावळणें, बडबडणें, प्रलापणें, तोंड *n.* हातीं धरणें, गटंपटं *n.*-गट्टापट्टा *m.*-लप्पंछप्पं *n.*-&c. लावणें-मांडणें-चालवणें, सतरा पंधरा गोष्टी *f. pl.* सांगणें, बाराबाविशा *f. pl.*-बाराबत्तिशा *f. pl.* लावणें.

Rant, *n. extravagant and empty speech.* अकडं तिकडं *n.* लप्पंछप्पं *n.* घटं पटं *n.* गटंगटं *n.* गट्टा पट्टा *m.* इधरतिधर *n.* खणका *m.* बरळ *f.* बडबड *f.* प्रलाप *m.* खोटी थाकी *or* थाकी *f. v.* सांग, छांछूं *n. f.* बारेमाप *n.*

Ranter, *n.* Ranting, *p. a.* v. V. बरळणारा, बडबडणारा, गटंपटं करणारा, &c. बरळ्या, बडबड्या, थाक्यासांगणारा, प्रलापी, वाहवरा.

Ranting, *n.* v. V.—*act.* बरळणें *n.* &c. खणका *m.* ठांका *m.* दणका *m. intens.* दणदणाट *m.* & दणाणा *m.*

Rantipole, *a. roving, wild, &c.* हिंडगा, उनाड, उनाडबाकुला, पारपळ *or* पारपोळ, झाडपंचाळ, यथेच्छचारी, पायांवर नक्षत्र पडलेला.

R. proceedings. उनाडचाळे *m. pl.*

Rap, *n. smart blow.* रपका *m.* रपाटा *m.* चपका *m.* तडाका *or* खा *m.* काठी *f.* थाप *f.*

With a r. चण-कन-कर-&c. थाड-कन-कर-&c. फट-कन-कर-&c.—(of a whip, cane, &c.) ताड-कन-कर-&c.

Rap, *interj.* रप, रप-कण-कर-&c. फट-कन-कर-&c.

Rap! Rap! रपरप *or* पां, तडतड *or* डां, थडथड *or* डां, चणचण *or* णां, फट फट *or* टां, फडफड *or* डां;—*intens.* रपारप, रपापां, तडातड, तडाडां, थडाथड, थडाडां, थाडथाड, चणाचण, चणाणां, फटाफट, फटाटां *or* फडाफड, फडाडां, छडाछड.

To Rap, *v. a.* v. N. ठोकणें, ठोठावणें, तडकावणें, फडफडवणें.

2 *snatch away,* v. To Seize. रपाटणें, रगडणें, हात *m.* मारणें.

3 *strike with ecstacy, &c.* तन्मय-तल्लीन-समाधिस्थ-&c. करणें, तन्मयावस्था *f.* प्राप्त करणें.

4 out; *rattle forth,* v. To Blurt. कडकावणें, तडकावणें, धसकावून बोलणें.

Rapacious, *a. given to plunder.* लुटारा, लुटारू, लुटारी, लुगान्या, लुगारू, हाताळ, हातलाव्या, गप्प करण्याच्यास्वभावाचा, अपहारी, हरणशील, अपहरणशील, अपहारबुद्धि, अपहारप्रवण.

Rapaciousness, Rapacity, *n.* v. A. लुटारेपणा*m.* हाताळपणा*m.* अपहारिता *f.* अपहारशीलता *f.* अपहारबुद्धि *f.*

I. *exercise of plunder.* लुटालूट *f.* मूठमर्दाई *f.* हातमारणी *f.*

Rape, *n. forcible carnal knowledge.* जुलमाचा-बलात्काराचा-&c. स्त्रीसंभोग *m.* जुलूम*m.* बलात्कार*m.* हठधर्षण*n.* हठसंभोग *m.*

2 v. Robbery. अपहरण *n.* अपहार *m.* [गवान्.

Rapid, *a.* v. Quick, Swift. जलद, जलदीचा, वेगाचा, शीघ्र, वे-

Rapid, *n.* नदींत शीघ्र प्रवाहाचें स्थल *n.* [ग्रता *f.*

Rapidity, Rapidness, *n.* v. A. जलदी *f.* त्वरा *f.* वेग *m.* शी-

Rapidly, *adv.* v. A. जलद, &c. जलदीनें, &c. घडघड *or* डां.

Rapier, *n.* v. Sword. खंडा *m.*

Rapine, *n.* v. Plundering. लुटपाट *f.* लुटालूट *f.* मूठमर्दाई *f.* झांबडा झांबड *f.*

2 v. Violence. जबरी *f.* जुलूम *m.*

Rapping, *n.* v. V. 1.—*act.* ठोकणें*n.* &c. तडाका *or* खा *m.* धडाथडी *f.* फडत्कार *m.*—*intens.* थडाड*m.* फडाड*m.* फडफडाट *m.*

Rapt, *p.* v. V. 3. तन्मय केलेला-झालेला, तल्लीन केलेला-झालेला.

Rapture, *n. ecstacy, transport,* v. Joy. अत्यानंद*m.* ब्रह्मानंद*m.* ब्रह्मसुख *n.* हर्षावेश *m.* बालोबाल खुशी *f.* रोमरोम सुख *n.* आल्हाद *m.* प्राल्हाद *m.* [अतितोषक.

Rapturous, *a.* v. N. अत्यानंदाचा, ब्रह्मानंदाचा, ब्रह्मसुखाचा, &c.

Rare, *a. scarce, uncommon.* विरळ *or* विरळ, विरळा *indecl.* विरळा, थोडा, थोडका, दुर्लभ, दुर्मिल *or* ळ, अलभ्य, विरलागत, क्वाचित्क.

Any r. or precious thing (as offered or presented). वानोळा *m.* वानगी *f.*

To become r. and precious. हळद *f.* लागणें *with* ला *or* स *of s.* हरताळ *f.* पडणें *g. of s.*

2 *unusually excellent,* v. Fine. नादर, तोफा, सरस, नामी, सर्वोत्कृष्ट, अनवा, अपूर्व, दाणा, सौंदर्यविरल.

3 *subtil, tenuous,* v. Thin. पातळ, सूक्ष्म.

Raree-show, *n.* फिरवून नेऊन दाखविण्याचा तमाशा *m.*

Rarefaction, *n.* v. V.—*act.* पातळ करणें*n.*-होणें*n.*-&c.—*state.* तापप्रयुक्त सूक्ष्मता *f.*

To Rarefy, *v. a. make thin.* पातळ-सूक्ष्म करणें.

To Rarefy, *v. n. become thin.* पातळ-सूक्ष्म होणें.

Rarely, *adv.* v. A. 1. विरळा, क्वचित्, कधीं नव्हत, कदाकाळीं.

Rareness, Rarity, *n.* v. A. 1. विरळपणा *m.* विरलता *f.* वैरल्य *n.* दौर्लभ्य *n.* [री *f.* अनवाई *f.*

2 सरसपणा *m.* नादरपणा *m.* अनवेपणा *m.* &c. अपूर्वाई *f.* नाद-

3 पातळपणा *m.* पातळी *f.* पातळाई *f.* सूक्ष्मता *f.* सौक्ष्म्य *n.*

I. *a rare thing.* दुर्लभ-दुर्मिल-अपूर्व-&c. पदार्थ *m.*-वस्तु*n.*-&c. अपूर्वचीज *f.* उंबराचें फूल *n.*

Rascal, Rascallion, *n.* v. Blackguard. लुच्चा, हुच्चा, सोदा, हरामी, लकारविल्ह्यांतला, काबू, काबूयार, काफर, गुलाम, गुलामजादा, काशीकर, खट.

Rascality, *n.* v. Blackguardism. लुच्चेगिरी *f.* सोदेगिरी *f.* लकारी *f.* सकारी *f.* काबूयारी *f.* थोटाई *f.* लबाडी *f.* लबाडीलचाडी *f.* लबाडी लाताडी *f.*

Rascally, *a.* v. Black-guard, Black-guardly. लुच्चा, लुच्चेशाई, सोदेशाई, थोट *or* थोठ, खटनट, लुच्चेगिरीचा, सोदेगिरीचा.

To Rase, *v. a. skim, graze.* घसटणें, घसवटणें, घावटणें, घावटळणें, चाटणें, झाजरणें, झळंबणें.

To be rased. खरचटणें.

2 See To Erase. 3 See To Raze.

Rash, *a. acting without caution or reflection, precipitate, hasty.* उतावळा, उतावीळ, अविचारी, हाडकपाळी *or* ळ्या, हूड, हुरमट, धसक्या, धडबड्या, हुरळ्या, अविमृश्यकारी, असमीक्ष्यकारी, अविचार्यकारी, अपरिणामदर्शी, अदूरदर्शी.

2—of measures, &c. अविचाराचा, उतावळीचा, उतावळेपणाचा, घाईचा, धडपडीचा, कच्चे मसलतीचा.

Rash, *n. efflorescence.* पुरळ *or* पुरूळ *m.* कोंडा *m.*

Bilious r. पित्तांची *f.*

To have a r. पुरळणें.

Rashly, *adv.* v. A. 1. उतावळीनें, उतावळेपणानें, अविचारानें, &c.

घे म्हटल्यां or म्हटल्यावर.

RASHNESS, n. v. A. 1. उतावळी f. उतावळेपणा m. घाई f. झुडपणा m. अविचार m. अविचारिता f. अविमृश्यकारिता f. विषमसाहस n. दुःसाहस n.

To RASP, *v. a. rub or grate with a file.* किसणें.

RASP, RASPER, *n. grater.* किसणी f.

RAT, *n.* उंदीर, मूषक, आखु. [टा m.

Bow-form apparatus to catch r. धनकुटा m. चापी धनकु-

A field-rat. घुरप्या उंदीर.

To smell a r. *fig.* बास m.-गंध m. येणें *in. con.* मन n. चमकणें, चमकणें.

To RAT, *v. n.* स्वपक्षसोडून परपक्ष m. स्वीकारणें.

RATAN, *n. cane.* वेत f. वेत्र n. वेतस m. वेतसी f.

2 *a* r. वेताटी f. वेत m. छडी f. वेतस m.

Strip or shred of r. वेतसरी f.

RATE, *n. price or amount fixed, price current.* धारण f. धारा m. भाव m. पाड m. निरख m. दर m.

2 *value set,* v. PRICE. मोल n. किम्मत f.

3 *standard, proportion.* दर m. भाव m. शेरा m. मान n. प्रमाण n.

At the r. of. प्रमाणें.

At this r. onwards. असें करितां.

4 v. ALLOWANCE. नेमणूक f.

5 *tax assessed.* पट्टी f.

To RATE, *v. a.* v. To VALUE, To ESTIMATE. गणणें, मोजणें, मानणें, भावणें, जोखणें, दर m.-भाव m.-&c. बसवणें-ठरवणें.

2 v. To SCOLD. खडखडवणें, खडसणें, खरकावणें, खणकावणें, घसरा m. देणें, खांकर वासा m. घालणें.

RATHER, *adv. sooner, preferably.* उत्तम, वरम्. This adverb is best rendered by some other construction, as जाण्यापेक्षां मला राहणें बरें वाटतें I would rather stay than go. मरण पुरवेल पण भीख पुरवणार नाहीं I would rather die than beg.

2 *somewhat, a little.* अमळ, अमळसा, कांहीं, कांहींसा, कांहीं बाहीं, जरा, जरासा, जराक, जराकसा, इवला, इवलासा, थोडाबहूत, थोडासा, किंचित्, ईषत्.

RATIFICATION, *n.* v. V.—*act.* बहाल करणें n. &c. सई f.

R. of a bargain. सत्यंकार m. सत्याकृति f. सत्यापन n.

To RATIFY, *v.a. approve and sanction, confirm.* बहाल-मुकरर-मंजूर-काईम &c. करणें, सई or सही करणें-म्हणणें.

RATIO, *n. proportion.* दर m. शेरा m. प्रमाण n. मान n. परिमाण n. बस्तन or बस्तान n. अंदाजा m. [ज्ञान n.

RATIOCINATION, *a.* v. REASONING. तर्कविद्या f. तर्कशास्त्र n. तर्क-

RATIOCINATIVE, *a.* v. REASONING. तर्कविद्येचा, उपपत्तीचा.

RATION, *n. fixed allowance of provisions, &c.* शेर m. शेरपीठ n. शेरशिधा m. मोताद f. आहार m. रतीब m. टोकळा m.

RATIONAL, *a. having reason, or the faculty of reasoning.* ज्ञानशक्तिक, चिच्छक्तिक, तर्कशक्तिक, तर्कज्ञ, तर्कशक्तिसंपन्न, बुद्धिजीवी, सचेतन, सचेता.

2 v. REASONABLE. युक्तिसिद्ध, युक्त, सयुक्तिक.

RATIONALE, *n. detailed account or explication of principles, &c.* उपपत्ति f.

RATIONALISM, *n.* हेतुवाद, कारणवाद.

RATIONALIST, *n.* हेतुवादी, कारणवादी. [f. तर्कशक्ति f.

RATIONALITY, RATIONALNESS, *n.* v.A.1. ज्ञानशक्ति f. चिच्छक्ति

2 युक्ति f. युक्तिसिद्धता f. सयुक्तिकता f.

RATIONALLY. SEE REASONABLY.

RATOON, *n.*—of sugar cane. खडवा or खोडवा m.

RATS BANE, *n.* सोमल वगैरे उंदीर मारायाचें विष n.

To RATTLE, *v. n. make a succession of sharp quick sounds.* फडफडणें, खडखडणें, खरखरणें, गडगडणें, घडघडणें, कडकडणें,—*intens.* खडाडणें, खरारणें, गडाडणें, घडाडणें, कडाडणें.

To r. against. खडतरणें.

To r. along. गडबडां *adv.* जाणें-चालणें, गडबडणें.

2—a dry pod, kernel, &c. खळखळणें, खुळखुळणें, खळखळ-&c. वाजणें.

3—the throat. घरघरणें, खरखरणें, खरखर f. लागणें-सुटणें.

4 *speak rapidly and noisily, &c.* v. To PRATE. कचकावून-कडकडून-चराचर-लवलव-&c. बोलणें, कडकडणें, भडभडणें, भडभड-भडभडां-&c. बोलणें, तोंड n. or तोंडाचा तोफखाना m. सुटणें *g. of s.*

To RATTLE, *v. a. cause to make a rattling sound.* खळखळवणें, खणखणवणें, खडखडवणें, खडखड-&c. बाजवणें.

RATTLE, RATTLING, *n.* v. V. N. 1.—*act.* फडफडणें n. खडखडणें n. &c. दणका m.—*intens.* फडफडाट m. फडाड m. खडखडाट m. खरखराट m. खडाड m. खरार m. गडाड m. घडाड m. गडगडाट m. घडघडाट m. कडाड m. कडकडाट m. कडाकडी f. दणदणाट m. दणाण m. भडभडाट m. भडाड m.

2 खळखळणें n. खळखळ f. *intens.* खळखळाट m. खुळखूळ f. *intens.* खुळखुळाट m.

3 घरघरणें n. खरखरणें n. घरघर f. घुरघूर f. घरघरी f. घरघरा m. घोर m. घोरांटी f.

4 डमडम f. वटवट f. बडबड f. करकर f. कळकळ f.

I. (of cannon, musketry, &c.). तडाका or खा m. धडाधडी f. फडफडाट m. फडाड m.

II. *child's rattle.* खुळखुळा m. खुळखुळणें n. घागरा m. झुणझुणा m. *dim.* झुणझुणी f. डमरू m. डहुर m. डौर m. तुडतुडणें n.

III. *staff with bits of irons attached to dangle and rattle.* खुळखुळा सोटा m. खुळखुळी काठी f. घोळ काठी or घोळदार काठी f.

RATTLE-CHOPS, RATTLER, *n.* v. PRATER. चराचर बोलणारा, बडबड्या, वटवट्या, फटमूळ.

RATTLER, *n.* RATTLING, *p. a.* v. V. N. 1. फडफडणारा, खडखडणारा, &c. खडखड-घडघड-&c. वाजणारा.

2 खळखळणारा, खुळखुळा, खळखळीत, गुडगुडा.

4 See PRATER.

RATTLE TRAPS, *n. traps, things.* इलासिला m. काण्णू बाण्णू n.

RATTLINGLY, *adv.* v. V. N. 1. फडफड or डां, खडखड or डां, गडगड or डां, घडघड or डां, पटपट,—*intens.* फडाफड, फडाडां, खडाखड, खडाडां, कडाकड, कडाडां, पटापट, पटाटां.

2 खुळखुळ or ळां, गुडगुड or डां. [डाडां.

I. (of musketry &c.). फडफड or डां—*intens.* फडाफड & फ-

To RAVAGE, *v. a. spoil, devastate, waste, &c.* नासधूस f.-नासधूळ f.-पायमल्ली f.-वळव f.-उडव f.-सफेजंगी f.-वाटोळें n.-&c. करणें *g. of o.* सप्पा n. करणें-उडवणें *g. of o.* धुवा m.-चंदन n.-गोपचंदन n.-&c. उडवणें *g.of o.* खटारणें, वैराण करणें, पाटाबरवटा m. करणें *g. of o.* उपप्लव m.-उत्पात m.-&c. करणें.

RAVAGE, *n.* v. V. *and* DEVASTATION. नासधूस f. नासधूळ f.

पायमल्ली *f.* वैराणी *f.* कंदाळी *f.* उपप्लव *m.* उत्पात *m.*

RAVAGER, *n.* RAVAGING, *p. a.* v. V. नासधूस-&c. करणारा, सप्पाकरणारा-उडवणारा, गोपचंदन उडवणारा.

To RAVE, *v. n. talk wildly, &c.* चावळणें, बरळणें, बाबचळणें *or* वाबचळणें, वायचळणें, बडबडणें, बरंगळणें, विकळणें, मोहें करून बोलणें, अवद्ध बोलणें, कांहींचेंबाहीं *adv.* बोलणें, बारा तिरपगडे *m. pl.* बोलणें, तीन तेरा गोष्टी *f. pl.* सांगणें, सतरा पंधरा गोष्टी *f. pl.* सांगणें, अवतरणें, बाचणें.

To r. and rant in anger. जळणें.

2—as in fever, &c. बरळणें, प्रलाप *m.*-जल्प*m.*-जल्पना *f.*-&c. करणें, वसणणें *or* वसणवणें *or* वसणावणें, प्रलापणें *or* प्रलपणें.

3 *be furious or raging,*—a madman. वेडानें-&c. ओरडणें, वेडानें-&c. ओरडा ओरड *f.*-बोंबलपट्टी *f.* करणें, वेडामारका-कावराबावरा-&c. असणें.

To RAVEL, *v. a.* v. To ENTANGLE. गुंतवणें, गुंता *m.*-गुतागूत *f.*-&c. करणें *g. of.*

2 See To UNRAVEL.

To RAVEL, *v. n. become entangled.* गुंतणें, गोंधणें, गोंधरणें, गोंधवणें, गुंताडा *m.*-गुतागूत *f.*-&c. होणें *g. of s.*

RAVELIN, *n.*—in fortification. बाहेर कोट *m.*

RAVEN, *n.* डोंब कावळा *m.* दग्धकाक *m.* द्रोणकाक *m.*

2 fig. v. CROAKER. काळजिभ्या.

3 See PREY. 4 See RAPACITY.

To RAVEN, *v. n.* v. To HUNGER. बखबखणें, खाखावणें, धादावणें.

To RAVEN, *v. a. devour with eagerness.* गपागप-गपापून खाणें, रपाटणें, बोकांदणें.

RAVENOUS, *a.* v. HUNGRY. खाखा सुटलेला, खाखावलेला, बखबखलेला, बखवख्या, अतिक्षुधित, क्षुधापीडित, हवळा, अधाशी.

RAVENOUSNESS, *n.* v.A. खाखा *or* खायखाय *f.* बखबख *f.* लाहो*m.* बाळभूक *f.* बराडीपणा *m.*

RAVER, *n.* RAVING, *p. a.* v. V. 3. वेडानें ओरडणारा-बोंबलपट्टी करणारा, वेडामारका, कावराबावरा.

RAVINE, *n hollow between hills.* दरा *m.* घोळ *m.* खोडा *m.*

2 *hollow worn by a torrent.* घळण *f. n.* घळय *f.* घळ *f.* नाला *m.* ओघळ *f.* ओहळ *f.*

RAVING *n.* v. V.1. बरळणें *n.* बाबचळणें *n.* बडबडणें *n.* &c. बरळ*f.* बडबड *f.* वाचणूक *f.* वाचणी *f.* प्रलाप *m.* जल्प *m.*

I.—the disorder. प्रलापवात *m.* प्रलापवायु *m.*

To RAVISH, *v. a. have carnal knowledge of by force.* रपाटणें, दपटणें, धर्षणें *or* जबरीनें &c. रपाटणें-दपटणें-धर्षणें, जुलूम*m.*-बळात्कार *m.*-&c. करणें *with* वर *of o.* जुलमानें-बळात्कारानें-&c. संभोगणें, भ्रष्ट-&c.करणें, हठसंभोग *m.*-हठधर्षण *n.* करणें.

2 *seize by force,* v. To SEIZE. बळकावणें, दस्तावणें, हात *m.* मारणें, हिरणें *or* हिरावणें.

3 *enrapture,* v. To REJOICE. फारच संतोषविणें, आनंदनिमग्न-&c. करणें.

RAVISHED, *p.* v. V. 1. जबरीनें रपाटलेला, &c. धर्षित, हठभ्रष्ट, हठधर्षित.

3 आनंदभरित, आनंदपूर्ण, आनंदनिमग्न.

RAVISHER, *n.* RAVISHING, *p. a.* v. V. 1. बळानें रपाटणारा, बळात्कार-&c. करणारा, बळत्कारानें संभोग करणारा.

3 अतितोषक, अतिसंतोषप्रद, मनोहारक.

RAVISHING, RAVISHMENT, *n.* v. V. 1. जबरीनें रपाटणें *n.* जुलूम करणें *n.* &c. धर्षण *n.*

2 बळकावणें *n.* हिरावणें *n.* &c.

R. or abduction of a woman. स्त्रीहरण *n.*

3 See JOY.

RAW, *a. undressed, uncooked.* कच्चा, हिरवा, आम, अपक्व.

2 *unseasoned, unripe in skill, &c.* v. INEXPERIENCED. कच्चा, कोवळा, अल्लड, अपेट, अर्धघाट, अधुरा, अनबुद्ध.

3 *unripe, crude, immature, &c.*—counsel, wit, &c. कच्चा. कोवळा, हिरवा (*remiss.* हिरवंडा, हिरवस, हिरवट), अपक्व, हरित.

4 *not covered with skin, bare.* कातडी निघालेला, कातडी चोळलेला, कातडीवेगळा, घासलेला, चोळवटलेला, विचर्म, विगतचर्म, चर्मरहित.

R. from a burn, &c. भाना-भोत निघालेला.

R. place or the back of a beast: *gall.* नाळ *f.*

5 *chill, damp, &c.* सरद, सरदीचा.

6 *unmixed, unadulterated,* (spirits). निरा, निर्भेळ.

RAWNESS, *n.* v. A. 1. कच्चेपणा *m.* हिरवेपणा *m.* अपक्वता *f.*

2 कच्चेपणा *m.* कोवळेपणा *m.* अल्लडपणा *m.* &c. कोवळीक *f.*

3 कच्चेपणा *m.* हिरवेपणा *m.* &c.

5 सरदपणा *m.* सरदी *f.*

6 निरेपणा *m.*

RAY, *n.*—of light. किरण *m.* कर *m.* मरीचि *m. f.* रश्मि *m.*

Pencil of rays. करजाल *n.* अंशुजाल *n.*

To RAZE, *v. a. overthrow, demolish,* v. To DESTROY. जमिनीस मिळवणें, जमीन दोस्त करणें, सपाट करणें, नाबूद करणें, उच्छेदणें.

RAZED, *p.* v. V. जमिनीस मिळवलेला, नाबूद केलेला, &c.

RAZOR, *n.* वस्तरा *or* वस्त्रा *m.* क्षुर *m.*

RAZOR CASE, *n.* (of barbers). धोकटी *or* धोंगटी *f.*

RAZOR-STRAP, *n.* पलाटणें *n.*

RE. This particle is rendered by फिरून, पुनः, उलट, परत, &c. For the words of which it forms a part in the sense of *again* (such as to *To re-appear, re-ascend, re-assemble, &c.*), let the reader turn to the verbs *appear, ascend, &c.* and prefix फिरून, पुनः, &c. and for the words of which it forms a part in the sense of *back* (as *To re-deliver, re-demand, &c.*) let the reader take the simple verb and prefix परत, माघारा, &c.

REA, *n. the four hundredth part of a rupee.* रेस *or* रेंस *m.*

To REACH, *v. a. arrive at, attain.* पावणें, पोहोंचणें, अटपणें, रुई करणें, दाखल-प्राप्त-&c. होणें.

2 *extend to so as to touch.* पुरणें, पोहोंचणें, पावणें.

3 out *or* forth; *stretch out.* लांब करणें, लांबवणें, पुढें करणें.

To REACH, *v. n. extend, stretch unto.* पोहोंचणें, पावणें, लागणें, लगटणें, ठेपणें.

2 *come to hand, be received.* पावणें, पोहोंचणें, दाखल-प्राप्त-प्रविष्ट-&c. होणें, पावती *f.*-पोंहच *f.*-पेवस्ती *f.*-&c. होणें *g. of s.*

3 See To RETCH.

REACH, *n. power of reaching, extent, range, sphere, &c.* अटोंका *m.* अवांका*m.* गति *f.* चलती *f.* पोंहच *or* पोंहोंच *f.* टप्पा *m.* छट्टा*n.* हात*m.* अवसान *n.* उडी *f.* सुमार *m.* वेन*m.* मकान *m. n.* In expressing the sense of *reach* great use is made of the preposition पर्यंत (as शिपायाचें ज्ञान रणांगणापर्यंत, भिक्षाचें ज्ञान निरापर्यंत, कारकुनाचें ज्ञान लेखणीपर्यंत, सोनाराचें

ज्ञान आगटीपर्यंत).

That is out of one's r. बेलाग.

2 See ARTIFICE.

REACHED, *p.* v. V. N. 1. पोहंचता, प्राप्त, लागू, अधिगत.

2 पावता, पोहंचता, प्राप्त, दाखल, सादर, लागू, प्रविष्ट.

To REACT, *v. n. resist action by an opposite force.* उलट *m. f.* मारणें, प्रतिकार *m.*-प्रतिक्रिया *f.*-प्रतिरुति *f.*-प्रतिघात *or* प्रत्याघात *m.*-&c. करणें.

REACTER, *n.* REACTING, *p. a.* v. V. उलट मारणारा, प्रतिकारक, प्रतिघातक *or* प्रत्याघातक, प्रतिकार-&c. कर्त्ता-कारी-&c.

REACTION, *n.* v. V. उलट *m. f.* प्रतिकारक *m.* प्रतिक्रिया *f.* प्रतिरुति *f.* प्रतिघात *m.* प्रत्याघात *m.*

To READ, *v. a. peruse.* वाचणें, पढणें, पठन *n.*-&c. करणें.

Easy to be read. सुवाच्य.

To r. mentally, to one's self, &c. मनांत वाचणें, पाहणें.

To r. off. सरधोपट-एकसारखा-&c. म्हणणें-वाचणें.

To r. out; *recite.* म्हणणें, मोठ्यानें वाचणें, पठन *n.*-&c. करणें.

To r. through. पारायण *n.* करणें *g. of o.* साद्यंत पठन *n.* करणें.

That has read through. पारायणी.

2 *discover from indications.* पाहणें, लक्षिणें, समजणें.

To READ, *v. n. be studious, practise reading.* पढणें, अध्ययन *n.* -पठन *n.*-विद्याभ्यास *m.*-&c. करणें.

READ, *p. and a.* v. V.A. 1. वाचलेला, &c. पठित, निपठित, अधीत.

I. *literary*, v. LEARNED. पढीक, साक्षर, अध्ययनी, कृताध्ययन, अभ्यस्तविद्य.

READABLE, *a.* v. V.A. 1. वाचायाजोगा-जोगता-&c. पठनीय.

READER, *n.* READING, *p. a.* v. V. A. 1. वाचणारा, &c. वाचक, पठन-अध्ययन-&c. कारी-कर्त्ता-&c. अध्ययनी.

Public r. (of the *Purāṇas, &c.*). पाठक.

READILY, *adv.* v. WILLINGLY. खुशीनें, संतोषानें, उत्साहानें, &c. बिनदिक्कत *or* बेदिक्कत.

2 v. EASILY. सहज, सहजासहजीं, अक्लेश, अक्लिष्टपणें, अकुष्टपणें, सुखरूप, सुखेनैव.

READINESS, *n.* v. A. 1. तयारी *or* तैयारी *f.* सिद्धि *f.* सिद्धता *f.* तवताकपणा *m.* लेसपणा *m.* कमरबंदी *f.* कमरबस्ता *m.*

2 तयारी *or* तैयारी *f.* सिद्धि *f.* सिद्धता *f.* परिपाक *m.*

R. of wit or understanding. तरतरी *f.*

READING, *n.* v. V. A. 1.—*act.* वाचणें *n.* &c. वाचणी *f.* पठन *n.* वाचन *n.* अध्ययन *n.* पाठ *m.*

Committing to memory upon r. पाठ*m.* (Quickness at or power of doing it, पाठशक्ति *f.*—Quick or powerful at it, पाठी—esp. in comp. as एकपाठी, दुपाठी, तिपाठी, &c. That commits upon *once, twice, thrice, &c.* reading).

Plain r. *r. without the due chant, &c.* लोलो *m.* v. घाल.

R. and writing. लिहिणें पुसणें *n.*

R. through. पारायण *n.*

Suspension of r. (esp. of the sacred books). अनध्याय*m.*

That is in r. पठ्यमान.

v. V. N. पढणें *n.* अध्ययन *n.*

I. *matter read or studied.* अध्ययन *n.*

II. *variation of copies.* पाठ *m.* पाठांतर *n.* अपरपाठ *m.*

False r. अपपाठ *m.*

READY, *a. prepared, &c. lit. fig.*—of persons. तयार *or* तैयार, सिद्ध, उभा, रुजू, मुस्तैद, तवताक, सादर, लेश *or* लेस, कमरबंद, कमर बांधलेला, तंगबार, उदित, उद्यत, उद्युक्त, उत्सुक, उन्मुख (in comp. as गमनोन्मुख, मरणोन्मुख, &c.).

2 *prepared,*—of things. तैयार *or* तयार, सिद्ध, पक्का, हाजीर, प्रस्तुत, परिपक्व, तवताक, लेश *or* लेस, मुस्तैद, सज्ज, सज्जित.

To make r. v. To PREPARE. सजवणें.

3 *convenient, opportune, near, easy, &c.* सहज गतीचा, सहज रीतीचा, अनायासाचा, अश्रमाचा, अनुकूल, सोईचा.

4—a knowledge, &c. *not rusty.* जागता, जागरूक, जागृत, हातखंडा, तयार, उपस्थित, लकलकीत, कडकडीत.

5 (of understanding, &c.) *quick, apt*, v. SHARP. सुजाण, कडक, कडकडीत, मेधावी. [चा, जलद.

6 *quick, prompt, &c.* v. SMART. रोकडा, रोखठोक, रोख, रोखी-

7 *dexterous, skilful*, v. EXPERT. तारखडा, फरडा, दक्ष, कुशल.

8 *consisting in cash.* रोकडा, रोख, रोखठोक, नक्त.

READY, READY-MONEY, *n.* रोकड *f.* नगद *n.* नगदी *f.* नगदपैसा*m.* नक्त *n.*

In the way of r. नगदानगद *or* दी, रोखारोखी.

Sale for r. नगदविकरी *f.* रोखविकरी *f.*

Trade or business conducted on the principle of r. रोखी *f.* रोखारोखी *f.*

READY-MADE, *a.* आयता, तयार, तयार करून ठेवलेला ;—an article of smith's work, घडितघाट, घडलाघाट.

READY-SPOKEN, *a.* जाबसाली, जबेतराश *or* स, जबेफराश *or* स.

READY-WITTED, *a.* हाजीरजबाबी, हाजीरजबाब, जाबसाली, तोंडच्यातोंडीं उत्तर करणारा *or* बोलणारा, समयसूचक.

REAL, *a. true, existing, actual.* खरा, खरोखरा *or* खराखुरा, सत्य, खरेंचा, वास्तविक, वास्तव, तथ्य, असल, अकपट, अकल्पित, अकृत्रिम, विद्यमान, सत्, सात्विक, यथार्थ, यथातथ, निर्मायिक, तात्विक, अन्वर्थ, अन्वर्थक, मूर्तिमंत.

2—in law. स्थावर, जंगमेतर.

R. property. स्थावर धन *n.*-माल *m.*-&c.

REALITY, *n.* v. A. 1. खरेपणा *m.* वास्तविकपणा *m.* &c. खराई *f.* सत्य *n.* सत्यता *f.* तत्व *n.* तत्वार्थ *m.* अस्तित्व *n.* सत्व *n.* अकल्पितत्व *n.* तथ्यत्व*n.* याथातथ्य*n.* वास्तविकत्व *n.* वास्तवत्व *n.* &c.

In r. v. REALLY. वास्तविक, वस्तुतः.

I. *a reality.* सत्व *n.* अस्तित्वविषय *m.* सत्वविषय *m.*

REALIZATION, *a.* v. V. 1.—*act.* कृतींत आणणें *n.* &c. साधणें *n.*

2 आत्मसंबंधांत धरणें *n.* वास्तविक मानणें *n.* &c.

3 वसूल करणें *n.* &c. उगावा *m.* उग्राणी *f.* उकळीत *n.* उगवणी *f.* उगवील *f.*

To REALIZE, *v. a. bring into act.* कृतींत-क्रियेंत-व्यवहारांत-करण्यांत-&c. आणणें, साधणें, सिद्ध करणें.

2 *bring home to one's self, consider as real, &c.* आत्मसंबंधांत धरणें, स्वसंबंधांत धरणें, खरा-सत्य-वास्तविक-&c. मानणें, जवळ-समीप-&c. मानणें.

3 (monies, profits). उत्पन्न करणें, वसूल करणें, उकळणें, उगवणें, उभा करणें, उगावा *m.*- उग्राणी *f.*-&c. करणें *g. of o.*

To be realized. उभा होणें-राहणें.

REALLY, *adv.* v. A. 1. खरा *decl.* &c. सत्य, वास्तविक, तत्वतः, वस्तुतः, वस्तुगत्या, वस्तुदृष्ट्या, यथातथ्य, यथार्थ.

REALM, *n. kingdom.* राज्य *n.* राष्ट्र *n.*

REAM, *n.*—of paper. रेजीम *n.* रीम *n.* from the English.—of 10 quires, गड्डी *f.*

To REANIMATE, *v. a. restore to life.* फिरून जीव *m.* आणणें, फिरून जिवंत करणें, जिवांत जीव *m.* घालणें, संजीवन *n.* करणें, पुनर्जीवित करणें.

REANIMATION, *n.* v. V. जिवांतजीवघालणें *n.* &c. संजीवन*n.*

To REAP, *v. a.* (corn, &c.) *cut.* कापणें, सवंगणें, कापणी *f.*-सवंगणी *f.*-&c. करणें *g. of o.* काढणें.

2 fig. *receive as fruit of an action.* भोगणें, जेवणें, खाणें, अनुभवणें, पावणें.

REAPER, *n.* REAPING, *p. a.* v. V. 1. कापणारा, सवंगणारा, कापणी-&c. करणारा, लवनकर्त्ता-कारी.

REAPING, *n.* v. V. 1.—*act.* कापणें *n.* &c. कापणी *f.* सवंगणी *f.* लाण *f.* लाणी *or* लाहणी *f.* लवन *n.*

Cost of r. कापणावळ *f.*

REAPING-HOOK, *n.* v. SICKLE. इळा *m.* कोयती *f.*

REAR, REAR-WARD, *n.* (of an army). पिछाडी *f.* हरोल *m.*

In the r. *behind, &c.* पाठीमागें, मागें, पिछाडीस.

To cast in the r. माघारणें, मागसांडणें, मागसावणें.

To REAR, *v. n.*—a horse, &c. उपायीं येणें, दुपायीं येणें, मागल्या-पायांवर उभा राहणें, उपावणें, टाळी येणें, वरता *or* वरतीं येणें.

To REAR, *v. a. bring up to maturity, raise.* लहानाचा मोठा *or* थोर करणें, लहानाचा वाढवणें, बाळगणें, वाढवणें, वयांत येई पावेतों-मोठाहोई पावेतों-&c. पाळणें-पोसणें. &c.

2 *raise, breed.* उपजवणें, निपजवणें, उत्पन्न करणें, काढवणें.

3 *erect, raise.* उभा करणें, उभारणें, उभवणें.

REAR-GUARD, *n.* पिछाडीची टोळी *f.*

REAR-MOUSE, *n.* चामचिराई *f.* [पाळींब.

REARED, *p.* v. V. A. 1. लहानाचा मोठा केलेला, वाढवलेला, &c.

2 उपजवलेला, &c. उत्पन्न.

REASON, *n. discursive power, rational faculty,* v. UNDERSTANDING. बुद्धि *f.* चिच्छक्ति *f.* तर्कशक्ति *f.* चित्त *n.* चित् *f.*

2 v. RIGHT, JUSTICE. समर्पकपणा *m.* उजूपणा *m.* रास्तपणा *m.* योग्यता *f.* यथायोग्यता *f.* यथार्थता *f.* लायकी *f.* युक्तता *f.* युक्ति *f.*

With or without r. हक्कनाहक्क, हक्कनाक, बळें, दाटबळें, दाटून.

To come to r. To listen to r. समजणें, समजूत *f.*-&c. होणें *g. of s.* [जन *n.* सबब *f.*

3 *ground, principle, cause.* कारण *n.* निमित्त *n.* हेतु *m.* प्रयो-

To REASON, *v. n. exercise the faculty of reason, deduce inferences from premises, &c.* तर्क *m.*-वितर्क *m.*-वितर्कण *n.*-ऊह *m.*-ऊहापोह *m.*-सिद्धासिद्धविचार *m.*-अर्थापत्ति *f.*-&c. करणें.

2 *debate,* v. To ARGUE. वाद *m.*-विवाद *m.*-वादविवाद *m.*-वादानुवाद *m.*-&c. करणें.

3 (with). हितवाद *m.*-बुद्धिवाद *m.* करणें, समजुतीचें बोलणें *n.*-भाषण *n.*-&c. करणें.

To REASON, *v. a. discuss,* v. To ARGUE. घाटणें, घोळणें, वाटावाट *f.*-&c. करणें *g. of o.*

REASONABLE, *a. having reason,* v. RATIONAL. तर्कशक्तिसंपन्न, तर्कशक्तिक, ज्ञानशक्तिक, सज्ञान.

2 *governed by reason, acting rationally,* v. WISE, JUST. समंजस, उत्तमचालीचा, नीतीचा.

3 *agreeable to reason,* v. JUST, RIGHT. वाजवी, योग्य, यथायोग्य, उपयुक्त, लायक, न्यायाचा, नीतीचा, मार्गाचा, तात्त्विक,

4 *not excessive, &c.* v. MODERATE. बेताचा, सुमाराचा, नेमस्त, माफक. [शक्ति *f.*

REASONABLENESS, *n.* v. A. 1. *and* REASON. ज्ञानशक्ति *f.* तर्क-

3 वाजवीपणा *m.* योग्यता *f.* यथायोग्यता *f.* उपयुक्तता *f.* मयना *or* माना *m.* लाग *m.* मान *n.* संभव *m.*संभावना *f.* संभूति *f.*

4 नेमस्तपणा *m.* माफकपणा *m.* &c.

REASONABLY, *adv.* v. A. 3. वाजवी, योग्य, &c. नीतीनें, रीतीनें, &c. नीतीचा-हिशेबाचा-&c. *decl.*

4 सुमाराचा-बेताचा-&c. *decl.*

REASONER, *n.* REASONING, *p. a.* v. V. N. 1. तर्क-वितर्क-&c. करणारा-कर्त्ता-कारी, तर्की, तर्कबाज, तार्किक, तर्कविद्येचा, अर्थापत्तीचा.

REASONING, *n.* v. V. N. 1.—*act.* तर्क करणें *n.* &c. ऊह *m.* ऊहापोह *m.* तर्क *m.* वितर्क *m.* वितर्कण *n.* तर्कविद्या *f.* तर्कशास्त्र *n.* तर्कज्ञान *n.* अर्थापत्ति *f.*

Skill in r. तार्किक्य *pop.* तार्किक *n.* तर्ककौशल्य *n.*

REASSURANCE, *n.* v. V. दिलासा *m.* दिलदिलासा *m.* दिलभरवसा *m.* आश्वासन *n.* पुनराश्वासन *n.* पुनराशा *f.* धिरा *m.*नाभिकार *m.*

To REASSURE, *v. a. restore confidence or courage to.* धीर *m.*-दिलासा *m.*-दिलदिलासा *m.*-&c. देणें-फिरून देणें-पुन्हा देणें-&c. अश्वासणें, आश्वासन *n.* देणें, पुनराश्वासन *n.* करणें, पुनराश्वासित-पुनराश्वस्त करणें. [सित, पुनराश्वस्त.

REASSURED, *p.* v. V. दिलासा दिल्हेला, &c. आश्वासित, पुनराश्वा-

REASSURER, *n.* REASSURING, *p. a.* v. V. दिलासा-दिलभरवसा-&c. देणारा-फिरून देणारा-&c. आश्वासक, आश्वासन दाता-कर्त्ता, पुनराश्वासनकर्त्ता.

REBECK, *n. fiddle.* रबक *n.* रबाब *n.*

REBEL, REBELLER, *n.* REBELLING, *p. a.* v. V. सरकारावर-राजावर-&c. उठलेला-फिरलेला, बंड, बंडवाला, बंड करणारा, राजद्रोही, स्वामिद्रोही, बैदा-&c. करणारा.

To REBEL, *v. n. revolt, rise against government.* फिरणें-उठणें *with* वर *of o.* बंड *n.*-बैदा *m.*-दंगा *m.*-&c. करणें, शासनत्याग*m.*-सत्तात्याग *m.*-&c. करणें.

REBELLION, *n.* v. V.—*act.* सरकारावर उठणें *n.* &c. बैदा *m.* बंड *n.* दंगा*m.* राजद्रोह*m.* स्वामिद्रोह*m.* शासनत्याग*m.* सत्तात्याग*m.*

REBELLIOUS, *a.* v. V. सरकारावर उठणारा-फिरणारा, &c. बंडी, बंड्या, बंडाचा, दंगेखोर, राजद्रोही.

I. *refractory, contumacious, &c.* v. PERVERSE. शिरजोर, टोंग, खलेल, आपढंगी, आपगंड.

To REBOUND, *v. n. spring back.* उलटणें, उडणें, उसळणें, हुशी *f.*-उसळी *f.*-उसाळी *f.*-टप्प *f.*-&c. खाणें, उलट *m. f.* खाणें-मारणें.

REBOUND, *v. a.* v. To REVERBERATE. उलटविणें.

REBOUND, REBOUNDING, *n.* v. V. N.—*act.* उलटणें *n.* &c. टप्पा *m.* टप्प *f.* उलट *m. f.* हुशी *f.* उसळी *f.* उसाळी *f.*

REBUFF, *n.* v. CHECK. दाब *m.* दडपण *n.*

To give a r. तोंडावर मारणें.

To meet with a r. तोंडांत खाणें.

2 v. DENIAL. निझाडा *m.*

To REBUKE, *v. a. chide, &c.* v. To REPROVE. शब्दाचामार *m.* देणें, वाग्दंड *m.*-शब्ददंड *m.*-&c. करणें.

2 v. To CHECK. दाबणें, दडपणें.

3 *repress, check, silence, &c. by reproof.* धमकावणें, दटावणें, दपटणें, दबावणें, धमकी *f.*-&c. देणें. [*m.*शब्ददंड *m.*

REBUKE, REBUKING, *n.* v. V. 1.—*act.* शब्दाचामार *m.* वाग्दंड

2 दाब *m.* दडपणी *f.*
3 धमकी *f.* दबावणी *f.*

REBUS. See RIDDLE.

To REBUT, *v. a.*—in LAW. प्रत्युत्तर *n.* देणें.
2 See To REPEL.

To RECALL, *v. a. call back.* माघारा-परत-&c. बोलावणें.
2 *revoke, annul, &c.* मोडणें, रद्द-&c. करणें.
3 (words, &c.) *retract.* फिरवणें, परतवणें, उलटवणें, उलटणें, बदलणें, परत-माघारा-&c. घेणें.
4 See To RECOLLECT.

To RECANT, *v. a.* (words, &c.) v. To RECALL. फिरवणें, बदलणें, परत-माघारा-&c. घेणें.

To RECANT, *v. n. recall words, &c., retract.* बोलणें *n.*-&c. फिरवणें-परतवणें-पालटविणें-माघारा घेणें.

RECANTATION, *n.* v. V. A. फिरवणें *n.* परत घेणें *n.* &c.
v. V. N. बोलणें फिरवणें *n.* &c.
I. *declaration contradictory of a former one.* उलट बोलणें *n.* उलटीचें बोलणें *n.*

To RECAPITULATE, *v. a. repeat the principal points of a discourse.* संक्षेपानें फिरून सांगणें, गोळाबेरीज *f.*-गोश्वारा *m.*-सारांश *m.*-&c. सांगणें-करणें.

RECAPITULATION, *n.* v. V.—*act.* संक्षेपानें फिरून सांगणें *n.* &c.
I. *summary of a preceding discourse.* मागल्या बोलण्याची गोळाबेरीज *f.* संक्षेपतः पुनःकथन *n.*

To RECEDE, *v. n. fall back.* हटणें, पाऊल *n.* माघारें काढणें-आंतघेणें, खिचणें, पाठीमागें सरणें, सोडतें घेणें, कचकणें, कचकरणें.
2 (from a promise, &c.) v. To DRAW BACK. माघार *f.*-बिचल *m. f.*-&c. खाणें, उलटी *f.*-उलट *f.*-&c. घेणें-मारणें, परतणें, फिरणें, फिसकटणें, फिसकणें, बदलाईस येणें, बिचलणें, बदलणें, पगडी *f.* फिरवणें *or* फेरपगडी *f.* करणें, पायमोडें *n.* घेणें, बदलामीवर येणें.

To RECEDE, *v. a. give back.* परतदेणें-करणें.

RECEIPT, *n.* v. V. 1.—*act.* घेणें *n.* &c.
I. *receipts*; v. INCOME. जमा *f.* आय *m.* आदाय *m.* वासलात *f.*
Back-receipts, *loans received back and cancelled.* परत जमा *f.*
Receipts and expenses. जमाखर्च *m.* आयव्यय *m.*
II. *note of acknowledgement.* पावती *f.* पोहोंच *f.* भरपाई *f.* कबज *n.* रसीद *f.*
III. (esp. of a letter, parcel, &c.). पैवस्ती *f.*
IV. *prescription, recipe.* कृतीची-करणीची-ठिकीची-ठीची-&c. याद *f.* कृतीचा-&c. लेख *m.*-विधि *m.*

To RECEIPT, *v. a.* भरपाई *f.* करून देणें.

RECEIVABLE, *a.* v. V. 1. घ्यायाजोगा-जोगता-&c. ग्राह्य, ग्रहणीय, प्रतिग्राह्य, स्वीकरणीय, आदेय, उपादेय.

To RECEIVE, *v. a.* v. To TAKE, To GET. घेणें, पावणें, आदान *n.*-उपादान *n.* करणें, स्वीकारणें, अंगीकारणें, अंगीकार *m.*-स्वीकार *m.*-ग्रहण *n.*-&c. करणें.
The arriving and being received (of monies due). पोहेंच *or* पोहोंच *f. m.*
To be received by, *come to hand.* पोहोंचणें, पावणें, मिळणें, हालास येणें.
To r. in full. भरून पावणें.
2 (a guest). v. To ENTERTAIN. संभावणें, आगतस्वागत *n.*-आदर आतिथ्य *n.*-संभावना *f.*-&c. करणें *g. of o.*
3 amongst or in; *admit.* घेणें, कबळणें, कवटाळणें.
4 See To ALLOW. 5 See To CONTAIN.

RECEIVER, *n.* RECEIVING, *p. a.* v. V. 1. घेणारा, पावणारा, &c. ग्राहक, प्रतिग्राहक, ग्रहण-आदान-&c. कर्ता, प्रापक. [हंडी *f.*
I.—in Natural philosophy. वाताकर्षक यंत्रावरचे तबकडीवरची-

RECEIVED, *p.* v. V. 1. घेतलेला, पावलेला, &c. प्राप्त, लब्ध, उपात्त.

REGENCY, RECENT, RECENTLY. See LATENESS, LATE, LATELY.

RECEPTACLE, *a. vessel, &c. which receives or contains.* पात्र *n.* आशय *m.* (esp. in comp. as, जलाशय, अन्नाशय, आमाशय, मलाशय, &c.) भाजन *n.* निधान *n.* निधि *m.* अधिकरण *n.* बारदान *n.* घर *n.* आधार *m.*

RECEPTION, RECEIVING, *n.* v. V. 1.—*act.* घेणें *n.* &c. ग्रहण *n.* प्रतिग्रहण *n.* उपादान *n.* आदान *n.* अंगीकार *m.* अंगीकरण *n.* स्वीकार *m.* स्वीकरण *n.*
2 आगतस्वागत *n.* संभावना *f.*

RECEPTIVE, *a.* घेणारा, घेण्याच्या उपयोगाचा, ग्राहक.

RECESS, RECESSION, *n.* v. V. N. 1. मागें हटणें, खिचणें *n.* पाठीमागें सरणें *n.* &c.
2 माघार *f.* बिचल *m. f.* उलटी *f.* उलट *m. f.* परतणें *n.*
I.—as in a wall, *niche.* कोनडा *or* कोनाडा *m.* कोनाडें *or* कोनाडें *n.* देवळी *f.* [हडपा *m.* दुलाब *f.*
R. with shelves and shutters, v. CUPBOARD. फडताळ *n.*
Secret r. चोरकोनाडा *m.* [नागा *m.*
II. *temporary suspension of business.* बिराम *m.* खळ *m.* खंड *m.*
III. See PRIVACY, RETIREMENT.

RECIPE. See RECEIPT.

RECIPIENT. See RECEIVER.

RECIPROCAL, *a. mutual.* परस्पर, एकमेक, परस्परांचा, एकमेकांचा, अन्योन्य, इतरेतर, इतरेतराश्रय.
2 See ALTERNATE.

RECIPROCALLY, *adv.* v. A. 1. परस्पर, परस्परां, परस्परें, मिथः.

RECIPROCALNESS, RECIPROCITY, *n.* v. A. 1. परस्परता *f.* परस्परत्व *n.* परस्परभाव *m.* अन्योन्यभाव *m.* अन्योन्यत्व *n.*

To RECIPROCATE. See To ALTERNATE, To EXCHANGE.

RECIPROCATION. See ALTERNATION, EXCHANGE.

RECITAL, RECITATION, *n.* v. V.—*act.* म्हणणें *n.* म्हणणी *f.* पठन *n.* उद्घोष *m.* अनुवाद *m.* अनुवादन.
Alternate r. (by two parties). चर्चा *f.*
2 सांगणें *n.* &c. सुनावणी *f.* कथन *n.* निरूपण *n.* वर्णन *n.*

To RECITE, *v. a. rehearse, repeat,* (a lesson, &c.). म्हणणें, म्हणणी *f.* -&c. करणें *g. of o.* अनुवादणें, अनुवाद *m.*-&c. करणें *g. of o.*
2 *relate, narrate,* v. To TELL. सांगणें, कथणें, सुनावणें, निरूपिणें, कथन *n.*-निरूपण *n.*-&c. करणें.

RECITED, *p.* v. V. 1. म्हटलेला, पठित.
2 सांगितलेला, &c. निरूपित, कथित, वर्णित.

RECITER, *n.* RECITING, *p. a.* v. V. 1. म्हणणारा, पठनकर्ता-कारी.
2 सांगणारा, &c. कथक, निरूपक.

To RECK. See To HEED.

RECKLESS, *a.* v. CARELESS, IMPETUOUS. निर्धास्त, बेपरवा, बेशक, निश्शंक, बेधडक, निर्भीड, कपाळफोड्या, साहसी, साहसिक, बांक-

डा, बांका, कहाती.

RECKLESSLY, *adv.* v. A. निर्धास्त, निर्धास्तपणें, बेपरवेपणानें,&c. दाटबळें, बेनिसबत, बेलाशक, बेचरक, बेउजूर, बेवसवसा.

RECKLESSNESS, *n.* v. A. निर्धास्तपणा *m.* बेपरवेपणा *m.* बेशकपणा *m.* साहस *n.* साहसबुद्धि *f.*

To RECKON, *v. a. number*, v. To COUNT. गणणें, मोजणें, गणती *f.*-मोजदाद *f.*-गणना *f.*-संख्या *f.*-&c. करणें *g. of o.* [धरणें.

2 *esteem, account, regard, &c.* गणणें, मोजणें, मानणें, लेखणें,

To RECKON, *v. n.* v. To THINK, To SUPPOSE. कल्पिणें, कल्पना *f.*-&c. करणें, सुमार *m.* करणें-पाहणें-बांधणें.

2 for; *be answerable.* हिशोब *m.*-मोसबा *m.*-झाडा *m.*-&c. देणें.

3 on; *lay stress or dependence on.* भरवसा *m.*-अधण *n.*-&c. ठेवणें, टेंकणें, ठेप *f.* ठेवणें.

4 with; *settle accounts with.* हिशोब *m.* घेणें-पाहणें, हिशोब*m.* देणें घेणें, खातें *n.* पाहणें-तपासणें, खात्याची रुजवात *f.* घेणें देणें.

RECKONING, *n.* v. V. A. 1.—*act.* गणणें *n.* &c. मोजणी *f.* गणती *f.* गणन *n.* गणना *f.* संख्या *f.*

2—*state.* गणना *f.* गणती *f.* हिशोब *m.* लेखा *m.* पाड *m.*

I. v. ACCOUNT. हिशोब *or* हिशेब *m.*

A strict r. झाडा *m.* झाडाझडती *f.* v. घे.

II. *state and comparison of accounts.* हिशोब घेणें देणें*n.* खात्यांची रुजवात *f.*

To RECLAIM, *v. a. call back from error or vice.* सुधारणें, उजरणें, नीट-&c. करणें, मार्गावर-वाटेवर-सुताावर-&c. आणणें.

2 See To TAME. 3 (land from the sea) काढणें, लागवडीच्या उपयोगास आणणें.

To RECLINE, *v. n.* v. To LEAN. टेकणें, ओठंगणें.

2 *lie down*, v. To LIE. निजणें, आडय *or* आडव *f.* घेणें, आडवणें *or* आडवारणें, आंग *n.* टाकणें, पासल *f.* घेणें.

To RECLINE, *v. a.* टेंकणें.

RECLUSE, *n. person who lives in seclusion.* एकलकोट, एकलकोंडा, एकांतवासी, एकांतसेवी, विविक्तसेवी, विविक्तवासी, रहोवासी, विजनवासी, कूपांतला मंडूक, आडांतला बेडूक, वन्य.

To RECOGNISE, *v. a. know again.* ओळखणें, जाणणें, पछानणें.

2 See To ACKNOWLEDGE.

RECOGNITION, RECOGNISANCE, *n.* v. V. ओळखणें *n.* &c. ओळख *f.* स्मरण *n.*

2—in law. करारनामा *m.* कबुलात *f.* मुचलका*m.*जातमुचलका*m.*

To RECOIL, *v. n. move, start, &c. back.* सरकणें, हटणें, मागें सरणें-निसटणें-निसपटणें-येणें, माघार *f.* खाणें-घेणें.

2—a gun. झाडणें, हिसकणें.

3 See To REBOUND.

RECOIL, RECOILING, *n.* v. V. 1.—*act.* सरकणें *n.* हटणें *n.* &c.

To RECOLLECT, *v. a. recall the knowledge of.* आठवणें, स्मरणें, आठवण *f.*-याद *f.*-स्मरण *n.*-सई *f.*-&c. करणें *g. of o.* स्फूर्ति *f.* होणें *g. of o.*

To be recollected. आठवणें, आठवण *f.*-याद *f.*-सई *f.*-&c. होणें *g. of s.* स्मृत-संस्मृत-स्फूर्त्त-&c. होणें.

To r. one's self. आपणारा-जीव *m.*-&c. शुद्धीवर-ठिकाणावर-&c. आणणें, धैर्य *n.* धरणें, धैर्यावलंबन *n.* करणें.

RECOLLECTION, *n.* v. V. आठवणें *n.* &c. आठवण *f.* आठवणूक *f.* स्मरण *n.* स्मृति *f.* संस्मरण *n.* संस्मृति *f.* स्मर्तृत्व*n.* स्मर*m.*पांग *f.*

Proximate cause of r. स्मृतिहेतु *m.*

To RECOMMEND, *v. a. commend to another's notice, &c. by favorable representations.* दुसऱ्याजवळ शिफारस *or* सिफारस *f.*-तारीफ *f.*-गुणवर्णन *n.*-&c. करणें *g. of o.*

2 See To COMMIT. 3 See To ADVISE.

RECOMMENDATION, *n.* v. V. 1. शिफारस *or* सिफारस *f.* तारीफ *f.* गुणवर्णन *n.* गुणव्याख्या *f.*

Letter or message of r. शिफारशीचें पत्र *n.* साहित्यपत्र *n.* भलावण *f.* भलावणपत्र *n.*

I. *that which recommends.* रुपाकारण *n.* रूपाहेतु *m.*

RECOMPENSE, *n.* v. REWARD. प्रतिदान *n.* प्रतिफल *n.*

To RECOMPENSE, *v. a.* (for sufferings, service, &c.). See To COMPENSATE, To REWARD.

2 *repay, requite, retaliate, return.* प्रतिदान *n.* देणें-करणें, फेडणें, उलट *m. f.* करणें-देणें, प्रतिकृति *f.*-प्रतिक्रिया *f.* करणें *g. of o.* प्रतिफल *n.* देणें, उपराळा *m.* करणें.

RECOMPENSED, *p.* v. V. 2. फेडलेला, &c. प्रतिफलित.

RECONCILABLE, v. V. 1. मिलाफ करण्याजोगा-सारखा, समजूत पाडाया जोगा-&c.

2 मेळ पाडाया जोगा, जम बसवाया जोगा-&c.

To RECONCILE, *v. a. bring back into friendship and union.* मिलाफ *m.*-समेट *m.*-सलूक *or* ख *m.* करणें *g. of o.* समजी *f.*-समजूत *f.*-&c. पाडणें-करणें-काढणें *g. of o. recip.* संधि *m.*-संधान *n.*-एकीकरण *n.* करणें *g. of o.* पुनःसख्य *n.*-पुनर्मैत्री *f.*-&c. करणें *g. of o.*

2 *make consistent.* ताळा *m.*-मेळ *m.*-&c. पाडणें *g. of o. recip.* जम *m.*-जुवा *m.*-&c. बसवणें *g. of o. recip.* जुळणें, मिळवणें, एकवाक्यता *f.*-&c. करणें *g.of o.* [त-राजी-&c.करणें.

3 *bring to acquiescence, &c.* संतोष *m.*&c. वाटेसा करणें, सम्म-

To be reconciled to. गोड करून घेणें, मानून घेणें.

RECONCILEMENT, RECONCILIATION, *n.* v. V. 1.—*act.* समजाविशी *f.* समजावीस *f.* समजी *f.* समजूत *f.* समेट *m.* एकीकरण *n.*—*state.* संधि *m.* संध *f.* संवित्ति *f.* पुनःसख्य *n.* पुनर्मैत्री *f.* पुनःस्नेह *m.*

2—*act.* ताळा पाडणें *n.* मिळवणें *n.* &c. मिळवणी *f.* एकीकरण *n.*—*state.* मेळ *m.* जम *m.* जवा *m.* जुळणी *f.* जमाव *m.* एकवाक्यता *f.*

RECONCILER, *n.* RECONCILING, *p. a.* v. V. 1. मिलाफ-समेट-&c. करणारा, समजूत-&c. पाडणारा, संधान कर्त्ता, संधि कर्त्ता, &c.

RECONDITE, *a.* v. ABSTRUSE. खोल, गहन, गुरुगम्य, अगम्य.

RECONNOISSANCE, *n.* v. V. टेहळणी *f.* नजर पाहणी *f.*

To RECONNOITER, *v. a.* (an enemy's camp, &c.). *survey, examine by the eye.* हेरणें, टेहळणें, हेर *f.*-टेहळणी *f.*-नजरपाहणी *f.*-&c. करणें.

To RECORD, *v. a. register, write in a book, &c.* लिहून ठेवणें, मांडून ठेवणें, दफ्तरांत घालणें-लिहणें-मांडणें, लेख्यारूढ-पटारूढ-पत्रारूढ-&c. करणें. [पट *m.* लेख्य *n.*

RECORD, *n. register, writing containing account of.* लेख *m.*

2 *book of records.* दफ्तर *n.*

RECORD-OFFICE, *n.* दफ्तरखाना *m.* दफ्तर *n.*

RECORDED, *p.* v. V. लिहून ठेवलेला, दफ्तरांत घातलेला, &c. लेख्यारूढ, पटारूढ, पत्रारूढ.

RECORDER, *n.* RECORDING, *p. a.* v. V. लिहून ठेवणारा, दफ्तरांत मांडणारा, &c. दफ्तरदार, दफ्तरनीस.

I. v. JUDGE. न्यायाधीश *m.*

To RECOUNT, *v. a. relate in detail, recite,* v. To TELL. तपसीलवार-तपसिलानें-सविस्तर-एकएक-&c. सांगणें, कथणें, निरूपिणें, कथन *n.*-चर्चा *f.*-&c. करणें *g. of o.*

RECOUNTED, *p.* v. V. तपसीलवार-सविस्तर-&c. सांगितलेला, कथित, निरूपित, चर्चित.

RECOUNTER, *n.* RECOUNTING, *p. a.* v. V. तपसीलवार-&c. सांगणारा, कथक, निरूपक, कथन-&c. कर्त्ता.

RECOURSE, *n. application to for help, &c.* आश्रयण *n.* अवलंबन *n.* आश्रयकरण *n.*

To have or make r. to. आश्रय *pop.* आसरा *m.*-आधार*m.* करणें-धरणें *g. of o.* पाठ *f.* रिघणें-निघणें *g. of o.* आश्रवणें, अवलंबणें, अवलंब *m.*-अवलंबन *n.*-आश्रवण *n.*-&c. करणें *g. of o.* शरण जाणें.

To RECOVER, *v. a. restore from sickness,* v. To CURE. बरा-निरोगी-&c. करणें, सावरणें.

2 v. To REPAIR, To RESTORE. सावरणें, सांपसारणें, उजरणें.

3 *regain.* फिरून-पुनः-&c. मिळवणें-सांपडवणें-प्राप्त करणें-&c.पुनर्लाभ *m.*-पुनःप्राप्ति *f.*-&c. करणें *g. of o.* प्रत्युद्धरण*n.*-प्रत्युद्धार*m.* करणें *g. of o.* [वणें-&c.

To be recovered. फिरून-पुनः-परत-&c. मिळणें-सांपडणें-पा-

To RECOVER, *v. n. come right again,*—gener. उजरणें, निटावणें, सुधारणें, नीट-दुरूस्त-पूर्ववत्-यथास्थित-&c. होणें, स्थितीवर-पूर्वस्थिती वर-&c. येणें.

2 (from sickness). बरा-चांगला-तवाना-निरोगी-रोगमुक्त-&c. होणें, सांवरणें, सांवर *m.* घेणें, तवानणें, आरोग्य *n.*-&c. पावणें, उजरणें, उबजरणें, उबजन्यास येणें, उभवणें, उमजणें, धाबरणें, धरधरणें *or* धरधरावणें.

To begin to r. जगण्याच्या-वांचण्याच्या पंथास लागणें, जगत्यापंथास लागणें, पाठ *f.* उचलणें, जीव *m.* धरणें, धर *m.* धरणें, उठणें.

RECOVERABLE, *a.* v.V. A. 3. फिरून मिळवायाजोगा-सारखा-&c, पुनर्लभ्य, पुनःप्राप्य.

RECOVERED, *p.* v. V. A. 1. *and* V. N. 2. बरा-&c. केलेला-झालेला-&c. नष्टरोग, नष्टामय, निवृत्तरोग, मुक्तरोग, गतरोग.

2 उजरलेला, सावरलेला.

3 फिरून मिळवलेला, पुनर्लब्ध, पुनःप्राप्त.

RECOVERY, *n.* v. V. A. 1.—*act.* बरा करणें *n.* &c. रोगमोचन *n.* रोगनिरसन *n.* रोगनिवारण *n.*—*state.* रोगमुक्तता *f.* रोगमुक्ति *f.*

2—*act.* सावरणें *n.* &c.

3 फिरून मिळवणें *n.* &c. पुनर्लाभ *m.* पुनःप्राप्ति *f.*

v. V. N. 2. बरा होणें *n.* &c. सावर *m.* उबजरा *m.*

RECREANT, *a.* See COWARD. 2 *false, &c.* क्रियाभ्रष्ट, क्रियानष्ट, भ्रष्टसंकल्प.

To RECREATE. See To REFRESH, To AMUSE.

RECREATION. See REFRESHMENT, AMUSEMENT.

RECREMENT, *n.* v. DROSS, REFUSE. मल *m. n. pop.* मळ *m.* मळी *f.* गाळ *m.* गू *m.*

RECREMENTITIOUS, *a.* v.N. मळाचा, गाळाचा, &c.

To RECRIMINATE, *v. n. return one accusation with another.* उलट आळ *m.*-फेरआळ *m. f.*-&c. घेणें-आणणें, उलटादोष *m.* लावणें-ठेवणें, प्रत्यारोप *m.*-प्रत्यभियोग *m.*-&c. करणें, उलटून-&c. दोष *m.* लावणें-ठेवणें.

RECRIMINATION, *n.* v. V. उलट-उलटा-फेर-&c. आळ *m. f.* उलटादोषारोप *m.* प्रत्यारोप *m.* प्रत्यभियोग *m.* प्रत्यपवाद *m.*

RECRIMINATOR, *n.* RECRIMINATING, *p. a.* RECRIMINATORY, *a.* v. V. उलट आळ घेणारा, उलटा दोष लावणारा, उलटून दोष ठेवणारा, &c. प्रत्यारोप-&c.कर्त्ता-कारक-&c. प्रत्यारोपक, प्रत्यभियोगी, प्रत्यपवादक.

To RECRUIT, *v. a.* v. To REPAIR. सावरणें, सांपसारणें, सुधारणें, उजरणें, फिरून आणणें, पूर्ववत् करणें, स्थितीवर आणणें.

To RECRUIT, *v. n. recover strength, spirits, &c.* उजरणें, सुधारणें, निटावणें, सावरणें, सावर *m.* घेणें, स्थितीवर येणें, पूर्ववत्-यथास्थित-&c. होणें.

2 *raise new soldiers.* नवे शिपाई *m. pl.* जमविणें, नवे शिपायांची जमाबंदी *f.*-जमाजम *f.*-&c. करणें.

RECRUIT, *n. newly enlisted soldier.* नवाशिपाई *m.*

RECTANGLE, *n.* समकोणाकृति *f.*

RECTANGULAR, *a.* समकोण, समचतुरस्र.

RECTIFIABLE, *a.* v. V. सुधारायाजोगा-सारखा-&c.

RECTIFICATION, *n.* v. V.—*act.* सुधारणें *n.* उजरणें *n.* निटावणें*n.* &c. सुधारणी *f.* सुधारणूक *f.* निटावणी *f.*

To RECTIFY, *v. a. set right, correct.* निटावणें, सुधारणें, सुधारणें, उजरणें, नीट-निटस-दुरूस्त-शुद्ध-&c. करणें, निटावणी *f.*-सुधारणूक *f.*-&c. करणें *g. of o.* शुद्धि *f.*-विशुद्धि *f.*-&c. करणें *g. of o.*

RECTILINEAL, RECTILINEAR, *a. right-lined.* सरळरेघांचा, सरलरेषामय. [ता *f.* आर्जव *n.*

RECTITUDE, *n.* v. STRAIGHTNESS. सरळपणा *m.* सारल्य *n.* सरल-

2 fig. v. HONESTY, JUSTNESS, VIRTUOUSNESS. सरळपणा*m.* सारल्य *n.* सरलभाव *m.* खरेपणा *m.* सचोटी *f.* आर्जव *n.*

Law of r. नीति *f.* [*of s.*

To deviate from the path of r. पाऊल *n.* बांकडें पडणें *g.*

Deviation from r. is deviation from peace. जें सदाचरणास बांकडें तें समाधानास बांकडें.

RECTOR, *n.* अधिकारी विशेष.

RECTUM, *n.*—the intestine. मळाचा कोठा *m.* मलाशय *m.*

The r. protruding at stool. गुळी *f. v.* उतर.

RECUMBENCE, RECUMBENCY, *n.* v. A. आडय *f. v.* घे, पासल *f.* पासलपट्टी *f. v.* घे, कुक्षिशयन *n.* कुक्षिशय्या *f.*

RECUMBENT, *a. lying down.* आडवा, आडय घेतलेला, पासल घेतलेला, पासला.

RECUMBENTLY, *adv.* v. A. आडवा होऊन, आडय-पासल-&c. घेऊन, कुशीस निजून.

To RECUR, *v. n. happen again.* फिरून-पुनः-&c. घडणें-घडून येणें-येणें-होणें-उपस्थित होणें-&c. पुनर्घटना *f.*-&c. होणें *g. of s.*

2 (to memory). आठवणें, सुचणें, स्मरणें, स्फुरणें, आठवण *f.* -स्मरण *n.*-स्फुरण *n.*-स्फूर्ति *f.*-सई *f.*-&c. होणें *g. of s.*

RECURRENCE, *a.* v. V. 1. फिरून घडणें *n.* &c. पुनर्घटना *f.* पुनरुपस्थिति *f.* पुनर्वर्त्तन *n.* पुनरागमन *n.*

R. of a fever, &c. माघार *f. v.* घे. [सई *f*

2 स्फुरणें*n.* स्मरणें*n.* &c. आठवण *f.* स्मरण *n.* स्फुरण *n.* स्फूर्त्ति *f.*

RECURRENT, *a. returning from time to time.* वारंवार-&c. येणारा-घडणारा, पुनःपुनरागामी, पुनःपुनर्वर्त्ती.

RECURVATE, RECURVOUS, *a. bent backward.* पाठीमागें-पाठीकडे-&c. वांकलेला-मुरडलेला-&c.

RECUSANT. See NONCONFORMIST.

RED, *a.* तांबडा (*remiss.* तांबूस *reddish*), लाल, रक्त, आरक्त, लोहित.
Dark r. अरुण.
Dusky r.—esp. of cattle. पोबळा.
Flaming r. Deep r. तांबडालाल, तांबडाजर्द, लालभडक, लालभबूक, लालबुंद, जर्दतांबडा, निखाररंगी.
House r. जांबा.
Pale or light r. पाटल, गोरा भुरका, श्वेतरक्त.
Yellowish r. तुशी.
RED-COAT. See SOLDIER.
RED-HOT, *a.* तापून लाल झालेला, निखाररंगी, अग्निवर्ण.
RED-LEAD, *a. minium.* शेंदूर *m.* सिंदूर *m.*
R. in little spars. कांब्या शेंदूर *m.*
RED-OCHRE, *n.* तांबडीमाती *f.* तांबडमाती *f.* लोखंडी काव *f.* गेरू *f.*
To REDDEN, *v. n. become red.* तांबडा-&c. होणें, तांबरणें.
To REDDEN, *v. a.* तांबडा-&c. करणें.
REDDISH, *a.* तांबूस, तांबडासा, तांबडसर, तांबा, ईषद्रक्त.
REDDISHNESS, *n.* v. A. तांबुसपणा *m.* &c.
REDDLE. See RED OCHRE.
To REDEEM, *v. a. ransom, &c.* खंड *m.*-खंडणी *f.*-पैका *m.*-&c. देऊन सोडवणें-मोकळा करणें-मुक्त करणें-काढणें.
2 *purchase back.* विकलेला परत विकत घेणें, परिक्रय *m.*-परिक्रयण *n.* करणें. [करणें *g. of o.*
3—in theology, v. To SAVE. तारणें, तारण*n.*-उद्धार *m.*-&c.
4 See To RESCUE.
To r. one's word, promise, pledge, &c. See To FULFIL.
REDEEMED, *p.* v. V. 1. खंड देऊन सोडवलेला, &c.
2 परत विकत घेतलेला, परिक्रीत.
3 तारलेला, तारित. [रा, &c.
REDEEMER, *n.* REDEEMING, *p. a.* v. A. 1. खंड देऊन सोडवणा-
2 विकलेला परत घेणारा, परिक्रेता, परिक्रयकर्त्ता.
3 *and* SAVIOUR. तारणारा, तारक, त्राता, उद्धारक, उद्धर्त्ता.
REDEMPTION, *n.* v. V. 1. खंड देऊन सोडवणें *n.* &c.
2 विकलेला परतघेणें*n.* परिक्रय *m.* परिक्रयण *n.*
3 तारणें*n.* तारण *n.* उद्धार *m.*
REDNESS, *n.* v. A. तांबडेपणा *m.* लालपणा *m.* &c. लाली *f.* रक्तत्व *n.* रक्तिमा *m.* लौहित्य *n.* अरुणिमा *m.*
R. of sky (at sun rise or sun set). तांब *f.*
REDOLENCE, REDOLENT. See FRAGRANCE, FRAGRANT.
To REDOUBLE, *v. a. increase by a double quantity.* दुणावणें, दुणारणें, दुपट-दुणा-&c. करणें-चालवणें-वाढवणें.
To REDOUBLE, *v. n.* दुणावणें, दुणारणें, दुणा-दुपट-&c. होणें-चालणें-वाढणें.
REDOUBT, *n. out work.* बाहेरकोट *m.* [तापसिंह.
REDOUBTABLE, *a. formidable.* भीम, प्रतापभीम, प्रतापव्याघ्र, प्र-
To REDOUND, *v. n. conduce in the consequence.* परिणामी-पर्यवसायी-पर्यवसानी असणें-होणें, परिणामीं-शेवटीं-&c. प्रयोजक-साधक-&c. असणें.
To REDRESS, *v. a.* (grievance, wrongs, &c.) *remedy, repair, &c.* दाद *f.* देणें, फिर्यादीची-अपराधाची-&c. तजवीज *f.*-उपाय*m.*-इलाज *m.* -बंदोबस्त *m.*-&c. करणें *g. of o.*
REDRESS, *n. relief of grievances.* दाद *f.* v. लाग, दे, फिर्यादीचा-अपराधाचा-&c. उपाय *m.*-बंदोबस्त*m.*-तजवीज *f.*-इलाज *m.*
To REDUCE, *v. a. lower, contract, &c.* v. To LESSEN. कमी-हलका-थोडा-न्यून-&c. करणें, उतरणें, अल्पीकरण*n.*-लघुकरण*n.* करणें *g. of o.*
2 *bring into any state.* आणणें, लावणें, मिळवणें, आपन्न (in comp.) -संपन्न (in comp.) करणें.
3 (to poverty). भिकेस-कंगालीस-दरिद्रदशेस-&c. आणणें-मिळवणें-लावणें. [करणें.
4—in arithmetic. रूप *n.* देणें, रूपांतर *n.* करणें, सवर्णन *n.*
5 *make thin, wear away,*—sickness, &c. रोड-क्षीण-शुष्क-&c. करणें, गळ्हाटणें, झिजवणें, आंग *n.* जर्जर-&c. करणें *g. of o.* कर्शन *n.* करणें *g. of o.*
To be reduced, v. LEAN. रोडणें, खंगणें, अटणें, राडवणें.
6 See To CONQUER, To SUBDUE.
7 (a dislocated limb) आपले जागेवर-&c. बसविणें-आणणें.
To r. to the ranks. शिपाईच्या पदवीवर आणणें.
REDUCED, *p.* v. V. 1. कमी-लहान-&c. केलेला, उतरलेला, अल्पीकृत, लघूकृत, ऊनीकृत. [तश्रीक, नष्टश्री.
3 भिकेस आणलेला, &c. फाटका, दुबळा, गतश्री, ,विगतश्री, विग-
4 सवर्णित. [गाचा.
5 *and* LEAN. रोड-क्षीण-कृश-&c. केलेला-झालेला, फाटक्या आं-
REDUCTION, *n.* v. V. 1. कमी करणें *n.* &c. उतरणें *n.* अल्पीकरण *n.* लघूकरण *n.* ऊनीकरण *n.*
I. The Rule in arithmetic. भांजणी *f.*
REDUNDANCE, REDUNDANCY, *n.* v.A. *and* EXUBERANCE. अधिकाई *f.* आधिक्य *n.* अपेक्षिताधिक्य *n.* अतिरेक*m.*
R. of words. शब्दबाहुल्य *n.* शब्दाधिक्य *n.*
REDUNDANT, *a.* v. EXUBERANT, *n.* अधिक, अपेक्षिताधिक, बहुल, अतिरिक्त.
To REDUPLICATE. See To DOUBLE.
REDUPLICATION, *n.* (of a word or letter). द्वित्व *n.*
Word formed by r. प्रतिशब्द *m.*
REED, *n. cane.* वेत *m.* वेत्र *n.*
Writing r. बरू *or* बोरू *m.*
Pen formed of the writing r. लेखणी *f.* लेखण *f.*
2 See PIPE.
REEDY, *n. abounding, &c. with reeds.* वेतांचा, वेतखान्.
REEF, *n.* (of a sail). शिकी *f.* [ओळ *f.*
2 (of rocks) खराबा *m.* पाण्यांतले खडक *m. pl.* खडकांची
REEK. See STEAM.
To REEK, *v. n. emit steam.* वाफ *f. or* वाफा *f. pl.*-धूर *m.* निघणें-येणें *in. con. with* पासून *of s.* वाफ *f.*-वाफा *f. pl.*-धूर *m.* सोडणें-टाकणें.
REEL, REELING, *n.* v. V. N. चाचरणें *n.* &c. भिरकंडी *f.* भेलकंड *n.* भेलकंडा *m.* भेलकंडी *f.* झोकांडी*f.* झेप *f.* भकांडा*m.* भकांडी *f.* भिरकांडा *m.* भिरकांडी *f.*
I. *frame for winding cotton.* चरक *m.*
II. एक प्रकारचा नाच आहे.
To REEL, *v. n. stagger, &c.* चाचरणें, चाचरत जाणें, चाचरी *f.* जाणें, जातां जातां चाचरी *f.* खाणें, रेलणें, डुल्लणें*or*डोलणें, झुकणें, झोकणें, भेलकंडणें, झेंपा *f. pl.*-झड्या पड्या *f. pl.* देणें-खाणें-घेणें, हेलकांडे *m. pl.*-झोके *m. pl.*-झोकांड्या *f. pl.*देणें-खाणें, *or with in. con.* जाणें, दोहीं आंगावर झुलणें-तोलणें.
To REEL, *v. a. wind upon a reel.* चरकावर गुंडाळणें.
REELER, *n.* REELING, *p. a.* v. V. N. चाचरी खाणारा, रेलणारा,

डुलणारा, &c.

To Re-enforce, *v. a.* (an army or navy). नवे-अणखी-&c. शिपाई *m. pl.*-अणखी गलबतें *n. pl.*-&c. पाठवणें-पाठवून सबल करणें, बळ *n.* वाढवणें, पुरावा *m.* पाठवणें, बलाधिक्य *n.*-सेनाधिक्य *n.* करणें.

Re-enforcement, *n. additional force sent.* मदतीस-भरतीस-&c. पाठवलेले शिपाई *m. pl.*-पाठवलेली गलबतें *n. pl.* पुराव *or* पुरावा *m.* उपराळा *m.* कुमक *f.*

Refection. See Refreshment, Repast.

Refectory, *n. place of refreshment.* फराळाची कोठडी *f.*-जागा *f.* उपहारगृह *n.* उपहारशाला *f.*

To Refer, *v. a. direct, send, dismiss, &c. to another.* सोंपणें, हवालणें, हवाला *m.* देणें, टाकणें, ठेवणें, घालणें, पुसायाला-पहायाला-&c. लावणें-धाडणें-सांगणें.

To Refer, *v. n. respect.* लागणें, लागू होणें-पडणें, संबंध *m.*-धोरण *n.*-संधान *n.* असणें *with* कडे & *g. of o.*

2 See To Allude. 3 See To Appeal.

Referee, *n.* v. Arbiter. तिऱ्हाईत.

Reference, *n.* v. V. A. 1.—*act.* सोंपणें *n.* हवालणें *n.* &c. सोंपणी *f.* हवाला *m.*

v. V. N. 1. संबंध *m.* इलाखा *m.* धोरण *n.* संधान *n.* लक्षणा *f.* अन्वय *m.* विवक्षा *f.*

In r. to. विषयीं, संबंधीं.

I.—person named as a sort of surety. ओळख *f.*

To Refine, *v. a. defecate, clear, &c.* शोधणें, मळ *m.*-मळी *f.*-&c. काढणें-छाटणें *g. of o.* साफ-शुद्ध-&c. करणें, शोधन *n.*-शोध *m.*-शुद्धि *f.*-&c. करणें *g. of o.*

2 *make elegant, &c.* v. To Polish. सुधारणें, सजवणें, सुधारणूक *f.*-&c. करणें *g. of o.* सभ्य-शिष्ट-साजरा-&c. करणें.

To Refine, *v. n. become clear.* निवळणें, मळ *m.*-मळी *f.*-&c. बसणें *g. of s.*

Refined, *p.* v. V. A. 1. शोधलेला, मळछाटलेला, &c. शोधींव, शोधित, संशोधित, संशुद्ध, विशोधित.

2 सुधारलेला, &c. सभ्य, शिष्ट, सभ्यतासंपन्न.

Refinement, *n.* v. V. A. 1.—*act.* शोधणें *n.* मळछाटणें *n.* &c. शोध *m.* शोधन *n.* संशोधन *n.* विशोधन *n.*—*state.* शुद्धि *f.* शोधितत्व *n.* संशोधितत्व *n.* निर्गलितत्व *n.*

2—*act.* सुधारणें *n.* &c. सुधारणूक *f.* सभ्यकरण *n.* शिष्टकरण *n.* &c.—*state.* सभ्यता *f.* शिष्टता *f.* सुजनता *f.* सौजन्य *n.*

I. *affected nicety.* नाजकाई *f.*

Refiner, *n.* Refining, *p. a.* v.V.A. 1. शोधणारा, मळकाढणारा-छाटणारा, &c. शोधक, संशोधक, शोधन-&c. कर्त्ता-कारी-&c.

2 सुधारणारा, सभ्यकरणारा, सभ्यता आणणारा, &c.

To Reflect, *v. a. throw back an image of.* प्रतिबिंब *n.* पाडणें *g. of o.* प्रतिबिंबित-&c. करणें.

2 (light, heat &c.) परावर्त्तन *n.* करणें *g. of o.* परावृत्त-&c. करणें, प्रतिक्षेप *m.* करणें *g. of o.*

To Reflect, *v. n.*—the mind, &c. मनन *n.*-चिंतन *n.*-अनुचिंतन *n.*-अनुचिंता *f.*-&c. करणें, चिंतणें.

2 on ; *cast censure or reproach,* v. To Blame. शब्द *m.*-बोल *m.*-ठपका *m.*-दोष *m.*-&c. ठेवणें.

Reflected, *p.* v. V. A. प्रतिबिंबित.

To be r. प्रतिबिंबणें, प्रतिबिंब *n.* होणें-पडणें-उठणें *g. of s.*

2 परावृत्त, परावर्तित, प्रतिहत, प्रतिफलित.

Reflecter, *n.* Reflecting, *p. a.* Reflective, *a.* v. V. A. प्रतिबिंब पाडणारा.

2 परावर्त्तन करणारा, परावर्त्तक, परावर्त्तन कारी-&c.

v. V. N. 1. मनन-चिंतन-अनुचिंतन-&c. करणारा-कर्त्ता-&c. गंभीर, मननशील, अनुचिंतनशील. [रणें *n.*

Reflection, *n.* v. V. A.—*act.* प्रतिबिंब पाडणें *n.* प्रतिबिंबित क-

2 प्रतिक्षेप *m.* प्रतिहति *f.* परावर्त्तन *n.*

v. N. N. 1. विचार *m.* चिंतणूक *f.* चिंतन *n.* मनन *n.* अनुचिंतन *n.* अनुचिंता *f.* अनुमनन *n.* पश्चान्मनन *n.*

I. *image, &c. reflected.* प्रतिछाया *f.*-प्रतिबिंब *n.* प्रतिरूप *n.* प्रतिभास *m.* प्रतिकृति *f.* प्रतिफल *n.*

R. of the beams of the sun or moon from the floor of a house. कवडसा *m.*

Virtuous r. उपाधि *m.* उपधान *n.* छटा *f.* छाया *f.*

Reflector, *n.* (of a lamp, &c.) किरणपरावर्त्तन होण्यासाठीं दिव्याचे मागें जी गुळगुळीत तबकडी करून लावतात ती.

Reflex. See Reflected.

Reflexibility, *n.* v. A. परावर्त्तनीयता *f.* परावर्त्तन योग्यता *f.*

Reflexible, *a. capable of being thrown back.* परावर्त्तनीय, परावर्त्तनयोग्य.

Reflux, Refluence, *n. a flowing back.* (of the ocean.). ओहट *m.* ओहटी *f.* ओहटें *n.* उलट *f.*

To Reform, *v. a. change from worse to better, amend.* सुधारणें, उजरणें, वाटेवर-मार्गावर-सुतावर-रीतीवर-ताळ्यावर-चालीवर-गतीवर-&c. आणणें, चांगले दशेप्रत परत आणणें.

2 *correct, &c.* See To Rectify.

To Reform, *v. n. return to good conduct.* सुधारणें, वाटेवर-मार्गावर-सुतावर-रीतीवर-&c. येणें.

Reform, Reformation, *n.* v. V. A.—*act.* सुधारणें *n.* वाटेवर आणणें *n.* सुधारणा *f.* सुधारणूक *f.* सुधारणी *f.*—*state.* सुधारलेलेपणा *m.*

v. V. N. सुधारणें *n.* सुधारणूक *f.*

Reformed, *p.* v. V. सुधारलेला, मार्गावर-&c. आणलेला-आलेला.

Reformer, *n.* Reforming, *p. a.* v. V. A. सुधारणारा, वाटेवर-मार्गावर-&c. आणणारा.

To Refract, *v. a.* (rays of light,) *turn from a direct course.* फिरवणें, वांकवणें, वांकडा-वक्र-&c. करणें, वक्रगति *f.* करविणें *g. of o.*

Refracted, *p.* v. V. फिरवलेला, वांकडा केलेला, वळवलेला.

Refracter, *n.* Refracting, *p. a.* v. V. फिरवणारा, वांकडा करणारा, वळवणारा, &c.

Refraction, *n.* v. V.—*act.* फिरवणें *n.* वांकडा करणें *n.* वक्रीकरण *n.* &c.—*state.* वक्रगति *f.* वक्रीभवन *n.*

Refractoriness, *n.* v. A. दांडगेपणा *m.* दांडपणा *m.* &c. दांडगाई *f.* टोंगाई *f.* खलेली *f.* शिरजोरी *f.*

Refractory, *a. self-willed, heady, wilful, stubborn, &c.* v. Perverse. दांडगा, दांड, शिरजोर, बाडगा, टोंग, औबास, खलेल, अडिबाळ, गाताडा, उरमट, आपढंगी, आपगंड, अवकळ, दुःसाध्य, विपरीतकारी.

Refragable, *a. susceptible of confutation.* खंडनीय, खंडनशक्य, खंडनार्ह. [थांबणें.

To Refrain, *v. n. forbear,* v. To Abstain. राहणें, धिरणें,

To REFRAIN, *v. a. hold back, keep from action,* v. To RESTRAIN. राहविणें, थांबविणें, अटोपणें.

REFRAIN, *n.*—of a song. See BURDEN.

REFRANGIBLE, *a. capable of being refracted.* वांकडाकरण्याजोगा-&c. वक्रकरणीय.

To REFRESH, *v. a. relieve after fatigue; recreate, &c.* ताजा-असुदा-थंड-श्रांत-विश्रांत-&c. करणें, विसांवा *m.*-विश्रांति *f.* देणें-करणें, श्रमापहार *m.*-क्लांत्यपहार *m.*-क्लांतिच्छेद *m.*-&c. करणें *g. of o.* सावरणें.

REFRESHED, *p.* v. V. ताजा-&c. केलेला, &c. श्रांत,विश्रांत, अपहृतश्रम, नष्टश्रम, गतश्रम, छिन्नक्लांति.

REFRESHER, *n.* REFRESHING, *p. a.* v. V. ताजा-थंड-&c.करणारा, विसांवा देणारा, &c. श्रमापह, श्रांत्यपह, क्लांतिहर-हारक-हारी, क्लांतिच्छित्, क्लांत्यपह.

REFRESHING, REFRESHMENT, *n.* v. V.—*act.* ताजा करणें *n.* थंडकरणें *n.* &c. श्रमापहार *m.* श्रमापहरण *n.* क्लांत्यपहार *m.* क्लांत्यपहरण*n.*क्लांतिच्छेद *m.*—*state.* विसांवा*m.*विसवटा*m.*विश्रांति*f.* I. *slight repast.* फलाहार *m.* अल्पाहार *m.* उपाहार *m.* लघुभोजन *n.* लघ्वाहार *m.*

REFRIGERANT, *a. cooling.* थंड, थंडकरणारा, दाहहर.

REFRIGERATION, *n. cooling.* दाहहरण *n.* निर्वापन *n.*

REFUGE, *n. shelter, protection.* आश्रय *m.* आस्रा *m.* शरण *n.* अवलंब *m.*

To take r. with. शरण जाणें *or* येणें, पाठ *f.* निघणें *or* रिघणें *g. of o.* पाय *m.* धरणें *g. of o.* आश्रयणें, आश्रयण *n.*-अवलंब *m.*-अवलंबन *n.*-&c. करणें *g. of o.*

2 *cause or afforder of refuge.* आश्रय *pop.* आस्रा *m.* शरण *n.* माहेर *n.* मायपोट *n.*

3 *expedient, remedy,* v. RESOURCE. उपाय *m.* इलाज *m.* तरणोपाय *m.* युक्ति *f.* गति *f.*

REFUGEE, *n. one who has fled for shelter.* शरणागत, शरणार्थी, अवलंबित, अवलंबी, शरणैषी.

Kind, &c. to refugees. शरणागतवत्सल.

REFULGENCE, REFULGENT. See BRIGHTNESS, BRIGHT.

To REFUND, *v. a. repay, pay back.* परत-&c. देणें, परत-&c. करणें.

REFUSAL, *n.* v. V. 1.—*act.* नकारणें *n.* &c. नकार *or* नाकार *m.* निषेध *m.* निराकरण *n.* निराकृति *f.* प्रत्यादेश *m.* प्रत्याख्यान *n.* नचा फाडा *m.* नची ओळ *f.* नकारघंटा *f.*

2 नको म्हणणें *n.* नकारणें *n.* &c. नकार *or* नाकार *m.* अस्वीकार *m.* अस्वीकरण *n.* अनंगीकार *m.* अनंगीकरण *n.* अग्रहण*n.* निरसन *n.* निरास *m.* निराकरण *n.* निराकृति *f.*

I. *the right of taking or refusing.* पतकरूं कीं न पतकरूं-घेऊं कीं न घेऊं-&c. हें म्हणण्याचा पहिला अधिकार.

To REFUSE, *v. a. decline to do or grant; deny.* नकारणें *or* नाकारणें, निषेधणें, नकार *or* नाकार *m.* करणें-देणें, ना-न-नाहीं-उंहूं -&c. म्हणणें-बोलणें-सांगणें, नचा फाडा *m.*-नची ओळ *f.*-&c. वाचणें, नकार घंटा *f.* वाजवणें, निषेध *m.*-निराकरण-&c. करणें *g. of o.*—flatly, smack, outright, bluntly, &c. झाडणें, निझाडा *m.* देणें, तुकडा *m.*-कुटका *m.* तोडून देणें, वाढाण्याची अक्षत *f.*लावणें-देणें.

2 *decline to accept; reject.* नको-नलगे-नाहीं-उंहूं-&c. म्हणणें-बोलणें-सांगणें, नकारणें, *or* नाकारणें, नकार *or* नाकार *m.* करणें, अस्वीकार *m.*-अनंगीकार *m.*-अग्रहण *n.*-&c करणें *g. of o.*

REFUSE, *a. left as unworthy of acceptance.* टाकवणा, टाकाऊ, बगळ, रद्दी, रद्द, निपटारा, खेर, निबड, गाळसाळ, राळसाळ, गाळवट, गाळाचा, &c.

REFUSE, *n. that which is left as useless.* गाळ *m. f.* गाळसाळ *f.* गदळ *f.* बगळ *f.* केर *m.* गबाळ *or* गाबाळ *m. n.* छाट *m.* खेर *f.* खेरभेर *f.* निबड *f.*

REFUSED, *p.* v. V. 1. नकारलेला, नाहीं म्हटलेला, निषेधलेला, &c. निषेधित, निषिद्ध.

2 नकारलेला, नको म्हटलेला, &c. रद्द, अस्वीकृत, अनंगीकृत, बर्ज, वर्जित, निरसित, निरस्त, निराकृत.

REFUSER, *n.* REFUSING, *p. a.* v. N. 1. नकारणारा, नाहीं म्हणणारा, नकार करणारा-देणारा, &c. निषेध-निराकरण कर्त्ता-कारी.

2 नकारणारा, नको म्हणणारा, &c. अस्वीकारी, अनंगीकारी, अस्वीकार-&c. कर्त्ता-कारी.

REFUTABLE, *a.* v. V. खंडायाजोगा-सारखा-&c. खंडनीय, खंडनयोग्य, खंडनशक्य, &c.

REFUTAL, REFUTATION, *n.* v. V.—*act.* खंडणें *n.* &c. मोड *m.* खंडन *n.* पक्षाघात *m.* प्रत्याख्यान *n.* निराकरण *n.* विक्षेप *m.* वितंडा *f.* बाध *m.*

R. and establishment. खंडनमंडन *n.*

To REFUTE, *v. a. confute, disprove.* खंडणें, मोडणें, काडंल-&c. करणें, मोड *m.*-खंडन*n.*-निराकरण *n.*-&c. करणें *g. of o.* खोटा करून दाखवणें.

REFUTED, *p.* v. V. खंडलेला, खंडन केलेला, &c. खंडित, प्रत्याख्यात, निराकृत, विक्षिप्त.

REFUTER, *n.* REFUTING, *p. a.* v. V. खंडणारा, खोटा करून दाखवणारा, &c. खंडन-निराकरण-&c. कर्त्ता-कारी.

To REGAIN, *v. a. get back again,* v. To RECOVER. फिरून पावणें-मिळवणें-&c. [विषयक.

REGAL, *a.* v. KINGLY, ROYAL. राजाचा, राजकीय, राजसंबंधी-

Man of the r. (or military) tribe. क्षत्रिय, राजपुत्र *pop.* रजपूत, राजन्य.

To REGALE, *v. a. entertain, gratify, treat.* सुख *n.*-संतोष *m.*-&c. देणें-करणें, खुश-संतुष्ट-&c. करणें, उत्सव *m.*-उत्साह *m.*-मेजमानी *or* मेजवानी *f.*-&c. करणें *g. of o.*

2 (one's self). See To FEAST.

REGALEMENT. See ENTERTAINMENT.

REGALIA, *n. ensigns of royalty.* राजचिह्नें*n. pl.* राजलक्षणें *n.pl.*

REGALITY. See KINGSHIP, ROYALTY.

To REGARD, *v. a. observe, note.* पाहणें, टेहळणें, दृष्टि *f*-नजर *f.*-&c. देणें-लावणें.

2 *heed, mind.* मानणें, ऐकणें, गणणें, विचारणें, पाहणें, पुसणें, बूज *f.* राखणें *g. of o.* मनास-चित्तास-मनावर-चित्तांत-लक्ष्यांत-&c. आणणें-घेणें, जमेंत घेणें, जमेस धरणें.

3 *observe religiously,* v. To KEEP. पाळणें, करणें.

4 *esteem, love, hold in respect.* चांगला-&c. मानणें-लेखणें-धरणें-मोजणें-समजणें, प्रीति *f.* करणें *g. of o.* मान्यता *f.*-मान *m.*-भीड *f.*-बूज *f.*-भार *m.* राखणें *g. of o.* मान *m.*-सन्मान *m.*-&c. करणें *g. of o.*

REGARD, REGARDING, *n,* v. V. 1. लक्ष *n.* लक्ष्य *n.* ध्यान *n.* अनुलक्ष्य *n.* अनुसंधान *n.* अपेक्षा *f.* अवेक्षा *f.* अवेक्षण *n.* प्रतीक्षा *f.*

2 मानणें *n.* ऐकणें *n.* &c. मान *m.* मान्यता *f.* गणती *f.* गणना

f. खातरी *f.* खातर *f.* चाड *f.* मदार *f.* गुमान *m.*

3 पाळणें *n.* पालन *n.*

4 रुपादृष्टि *f.* रुपाकटाक्ष *m.* नजर *f.* दृष्टि *f.* मुलाजा *m.* मान *m.* मान्यता *f.* भीड *f.* चहा *m. f.*

I. *look, aspect.* दृष्टि *f.*

Hostile or evil r. वक्रदृष्टि *f.*

Of hostile or evil r. वक्रदृष्टि.

To have hostile or evil r. वक्री होणें *with* वर *of o.*

In r. to. विषयीं.

REGARDED, *p.* v. V. 1. पाहिलेला, &c. प्रतीक्षित, अवेक्षित.

REGARDER, *n.* REGARDFUL, *a.* REGARDING, *p. a.* v. V. 1. पाहणारा, लक्ष-&c. देणारा-लावणारा, अवेक्षक, प्रतीक्षक, अवेक्षण-&c. कर्त्ता.

2 मानणारा, ऐकणारा, बूज राखणारा, मनास आणणारा, &c.

4 चांगला मानणारा, मान्यता राखणारा, भीड राखणारा, &c. भिडस्त.

REGARDING, *prep.* v. ABOUT. विषयीं.

REGARDLESS, *a.* v. CARELESS. बेपरवा, बेफिकीर, निश्चिंत, उदासीन, उदास, उपेक्षक. [उपेक्षा *f.*

REGARDLESSNESS, *n.* v. V. उदासपणा *m.* बेफिकीरपणा *m.* &c.

REGATTA, *n.* नावांची शर्यत *f.*-पैज *f.* नौकाक्रीडा *f.*

REGENCY, *n.* See RULE. 2 *vicarious government.* राजप्रतिनिधीचा अधिकार *m.*-अमल *m.*-&c.

3 *body of persons governing vicariously.* राजप्रतिनिधिमंडळी *f.* राजप्रतिनिधिसमुदाय*m.*-समाज*m.*-&c. राजप्रतिनिधि*m.pl.*

REGENERACY, REGENERATENESS, *n.* v. A. पुनर्जन्म *m. n.* पुनर्जातत्व *n.* द्विजन्मावस्था *f.* पुनर्जातावस्था *f.*

To REGENERATE, *v. a. cause to be born again.* दुसऱ्यानें जन्मविणें-जन्म *m.* देणें, पुनर्जन्म *m. n.* देणें.

REGENERATE, *a.* REGENERATED, *p.* v. V. दुसऱ्यानें जन्म पावलेला, पुनर्जात, द्विजन्मा, द्विज.

REGENERATION, *n.* v.V.—*state.* पुनर्जन्म *m. n.*

REGENT, *n.* v. RULER. अधिकारी, अधिपति.

Queen r. गादीची मालक जी राणी ती, राज्यकारिणी महिषी.

R. of a quarter. दिक्पाल *m.*

2 *one exercising vicarious royalty.* राजप्रतिनिधि.

REGICIDE, *n. killing of a king.* राजवध *m.* राजहत्या *f.* राजघात*m.* नृपघात *m.* नृपहिंसा *f.* &c.

2 *killer of a king.* राजवध-राजहत्या-&c. करणारा, राजघाती, राजहिंसक, नृपहिंसक.

REGIMEN, *n. regulation of diet.* पथ्य *n.* पथ्यापथ्यविचार *m.*

Deviation from r. अपथ्य *n.*

One under r. पथ्यकरी.

Wrong r. अपथ्य *n.* [(from the English.)

REGIMENT, *n.* (of soldiers) पलटण *or* पलटन *n. f.* रिजमींट *f.*

REGIMENTAL, *n. belonging, &c. to a regiment.* पलटणचा, पलटणांतला, पलटनी, रिजमिंटींतला, &c.

REGIMENTALS, *n. pl.* पलटनी पोशाक *m.* बाणगुम्री *f.*

REGION, *n.* v. COUNTRY. देश *m.* प्रांत *m.* मंडल *n.* चक्र *n.* राष्ट्र *n.*

The lower regions, *regions below the earth.* अधोलोक *m.* अधोभुवन *n.* [भुवन *n.*

The upper regions, *the world above.* ऊर्ध्वलोक *m.* ऊर्ध्व-

2 (of the sky) v. QUARTER. दिशा *f.* घर *n.*

3 *part of the body.* चक्र *n.* मंडल *n.* (in comp. as मस्तकमंडल, कुचमंडल, कर्णमंडल).

REGISTER, *n. written account of acts, judgments, &c., record,* v. WRITING. लेख *m.* जाबता *m.* पट *m.* लेख्य *n.*

2 *book of records or entries.* दफ्तर *n.* रजिस्तर *n.* (from the English.)

General r. दफातें *n.*

State r. बेहडा *m.* [तरनीस.

3 *registering officer.* दफ्तरांत दाखल करणारा, दफ्तरदार, दफ्

To REGISTER, *v. a. write in a book, record.* लिहून ठेवणें, दफ्तरांत लिहणें-मांडणें-दाखल करणें, लेखारूढ-&c. करणें.

2 *copy into a register.* बार करणें, नोंदणें.

REGISTERED, *p.* v.V.1. लिहून ठेवलेला, दफ्तरांत दाखल केलेला, &c. लेख्यारूढ, पटारूढ, लेखारूढ, पत्रारूढ.

2 बार केलेला, नोंदलेला. [रक्षक.

REGISTRAR, *n. keeper of the registers.* फडनीस, दफ्तरदार, पट-

REGISTRATION, REGISTERING, REGISTRY, *n.* v. V. 1.—*act.* लिहून ठेवणें *n.* दफ्तरांत घालणें *n.*-&c.

2 बार करणें *n.* नोंदणें *n.*

REGNANT. See REIGNING.

REGRESS, REGRESSION. See RETURN.

REGRET, *n. sorrow for something past, remorse, &c.* चटपट *f.* चुरचूर *f. intens.* चुरचुराट *m.* चुळचूळ *f.* चुळचुळा *m.* रुखरूख *f.* खरखर *f.* खुणखुण *f.* हुरहूर *f.* चुटका *or* चटका *m.* पस्तावा *or* प्रस्तावा *m.* खेद *m.* पश्चात्ताप *m.* मनस्ताप *m.* उद्वेग*m.* अनुताप*m.* अनुशोक *m.* अनुशोचन *n.* शोचन *n.*

2 *sorrow, grief,* v. AFFLICTION. दुःख *n.* खेद*m.*

To REGRET, *v. a. be sorry for, grieve at, repent of.* रडणें, खेद *m.*-पस्तावा *m.*-दुःख *n.*-पश्चात्ताप *m.*-&c. करणें-पावणें *g. of o.* पश्चात्ताप*m.*-पस्तावा *m.*-&c. होणें *in. con. with g. of o.*चुरचूर*f.* चटपट *f.*-खरखर *f.*-रुखरूख *f.*-हुरहूर *f.*-&c. लागणें *in. con. with g. of o.* शोचणें.

REGRETFUL. See SORROWFUL.

REGRETTED, *p.* v. V. रडलेला, खेद केलेला, &c.

REGRETTER, *n.* REGRETTING, *p. a.* v. V. *and* REPENTANT. दुःख-खेद-पस्तावा-&c. करणारा, अनुशोचित, चटपटी, अनुतापी, अनुशोचक.

REGULAR, *a. agreeable to rule.* कायदेशीर, यथाविधि, यथापद्धति, यथाशास्त्र, यथामार्ग, नैयमिक, ससूत्र, सुसूत्र, सौत्र, सविधि, विधियुक्त, विधिदृष्ट, वैध, वैधिक, मार्गानुसारी, विध्यनुसारी, संप्रदायानुसारी, संप्रदायशुद्ध, सांप्रदायिक, आचारशुद्ध, आचारिक.

2—of persons ; *observant of rule.* नियमी *pop.* नेमी, नियमाचा *pop.* नेमाचा, ठेपीचा *or* ठेपेचा, नियमशील, नियमनिष्ठ, नियमपर, नियमिष्ठ *pop.* नेमिष्ठ, नियमानुसारी, नियमानुयायी, आचारसंपन्न, आचारपूत, कायदेशीर, विधिमार्गी, विधिवर्त्ती, विध्यनुवर्त्ती, विध्यनुयायी, यथामार्गचारी.

3—of arrangements, acts, &c. नेमाचा, बेताचा, मार्गाचा, रुईचा, सुताचा, रीतीचा, &c. बराबर, सुफराटा, सुलटा, यथाक्रम, यथानुक्रम, रेखला, सुसूत्र, सुतरा, साखसुरत, हिशेबी *or* हिशोबी, साफ, निटस, पारंपरिक, अनुलोम.

REGULARITY, *n.* v. A. 1. कायदेशीरपणा *m.* यथाविधिता *f.* &c. विध्यनुसारिता *f.* &c. विध्यनुरोध *m.* सविधिता *f.* ससूत्रता *f.*

2 नियमनिष्ठा *f.* नियमशीलता *f.* नियमपरता *f.* विधिमार्गिता *f.*

विध्यनुवर्त्तित्व *n.* विध्यनुयायिता *f.* &c.

3 बेत *m.* बेतबात *m.* व्यवस्था *f.* सुफराटेपणा *m.* सुलटेपणा *m.* &c. ठेपठाप *f.* क्रम *m.* अनुक्रम *m.* यथाक्रमता *f.* आनुलोम्य *n.*

REGULARLY, *adv.* v. A. 1. 2. कायदेशीर, कायदेमाफक, कायद्याप्रमाणें, नेमी *or* नेहमी, नियमाचा *or* नेमाचा, पद्धतवार, विधिपूर्वक, विधिवत्, विध्यनुसार, विध्यनुरूप, मार्गानुसार, &c. यथाविधि, यथासूत्र, यथामार्ग,&c. सुसूत्र.

3 बेतानें, बेताबातानें, &c. बराबर, यथाअनुक्रमें, यथानुक्रमें, यथाक्रमानें, यथाक्रमें, यथाक्रम, क्रमशः, पद्धतवार, सुसूत्र.

R. and reversely. क्रमोत्क्रम.

To REGULATE, *v. a. adjust by a rule or method.* बेतानें-नेमानें-धोरणानें-&c. चालवणें-वर्त्तवणें-सुधारणें-बंदोबस्त *m.* करणें-व्यवस्था *f.* करणें-&c. *with g. of the rule.* बेताबर-धोरेणावर-ताळयावर-तालावर-&c. आणणें *with g. of rule.*

2 *subject to restriction and rules ; direct.* कायदा *m.*-नियम *m.*-बेत *m.*-&c. ठेवणें-बांधणें-लावणें-&c. परिमित-नियमित-&c.करणें, बंदोबस्त *m.*-व्यवस्था *f.*-&c. करणें *g. of o.* अनुशासणें, अनुशासन *n.* करणें *g. of o.*

REGULATED, *p.* v. V. 1. बेतानें सुधारलेला-वर्त्तवलेला, &c.

2 कायदा बांधलेला, &c. नियमित, अनुशासित, परिमित, प्रमित.

REGULATION, *n.* v.V. 1.—*act.* बेतानें चालवणें*n.* बेतावर आणणें*n.* &c. सुधारणें *n.* सुधारणूक *f.* व्यवस्थापन *n.—state.* बंदोबस्त *m.* बंदोबस्ती *f.* व्यवस्था *f.*

2—*act.* कायदाबांधणें *n.* नियम ठेवणें*n.*&c. अनुशासन *n.–state.* बंदोबस्त *m.* बंदोबस्ती *f.* व्यवस्था *f.* [कानू *f.*

I. *a* r. *a rule, canon, statute.* कायदा *m.* चक *m.* जाबता *m.*

Code of regulations. ठराबबंद *m.* कानुजाबता *m.*

REGULATOR, *n.* REGULATING, *p. a.* v. V. 1. बेतावर आणणारा, &c. सुधारणारा, बंदोबस्त करणारा.

2 कायदा बांधणारा, नियम ठेवणारा, &c. अनुशासक, अनुशास्ता.

I.—of a machine. यंत्राचीगति-यंत्राचावेग-&c. नीट ठेवणारीकळ.

REHEARSAL, *n.* v. V. 1.—*act.* म्हणणें *n.* पाठ म्हणणें *n.* &c. म्हणणी *f.* अनुवाद *m.* उल्लेख *m.* पठन *n.* [योग *n.*

2 तयारी पाहण्याचें म्हणणें *n.* भाव्यनुकरण *n.* शुष्केष्टि *f.* शुष्कप्र-

To REHEARSE, *v. a. repeat the words of another.* म्हणणें, पाठ म्हणणें, अनुवादणें, अनुवाद *m.*-पठन *n.*-&c. करणें *g. of o.*

2 *recite in private preparatory to a public representation.* तयारी पाहण्यासाठीं म्हणणें, भाव्यनुकरण *n.* करणें, शुष्केष्टि *f.*-शुष्कप्रयोग *m.* करणें *g. of o.*

3 *narrate.* See To TELL. [पठित.

REHEARSED, *p.* v. V. 1. म्हटलेला, पाठ म्हटलेला, &c. अनुवादित,

REHEARSER, *n.* REHEARSING, *p. a.* v. V. 1. म्हणणारा, पाठ म्हणणारा, &c. अनुवादक, अनुवाद-&c. कर्त्ता-कारी.

REIGLE. See GROOVE.

To REIGN, *v.n. rule, &c.* राज्य *n.*-अमल *m.*-राजाधिकार *m.*-राजसत्ता *f.*-&c. करणें, तक्तावर-गादीवर-सिंहासनावर-&c. बसणें, सिंहासनारूढ-&c. असणें.

REIGN, REIGNING, *n.* v. V.—*act.* राज्य *n.* अमल *m.* शक *m.*

I. *period of rule.* अमल *m.* राज्य *n.* कारकीर्द *f.* राजबय *m.* राजवट *f.*

II. See PREVALENCE.

REIGNER, *n.* REIGNING, *p. a.* v. V. राज्य करणारा, तक्तावर-&c. बसणारा-बसलेला, राज्यारूढ, सिंहासनारूढ, राजपदारूढ, सिंहासनाधिपति, तक्ताधिपति.

I. See PREVALENT. [परत करणें

To REIMBURSE, *v.a. refund, pay back to.* भरून देणें, देणें, भरणें,

REIN, *n. strap of a bridle.* लगामाची दोरी *f.*-वादी *f.* अनीन *f.*

A bearing r. कायदा *m.* काजगी *f.* काजा *or* कायजा *m.*

To hold a tight r. *lit. fig.* लगाम *m. f.* अवल धरणें.

To hold with a slack r. *lit. fig.* सैल दोरी *f.* देणें.

To let loose the reins. To give the reins. लगाम *m. f.* सोडणें.

REINDEER, *n.* एक जातीचा हरीण आहे.

REINS, *n. lower part of the back,* v. LOINS. कमर *f.* माजाड *n.* कटिपश्चात्भाग *m.*

2 See KIDNEY.

REINSTATE, *v. a. put again in possession.* फिरून-&c. ठेवणें-योजणें-नेमणें-&c. बहाल करणें, बहाली *f.* करणें *g.of o.* पुनःस्थापन *n.*-पुनःस्थापना *f.*-&c. करणें *g. of o.* [पित.

REINSTATED, *p.* v. V. फिरून ठेवलेला, बहाल केलेला, &c. पुनःस्था-

REINSTATEMENT, *n.* v. V. बहाल करणें *n.* बहाली *f.* पुनःस्थापन *n.* पुनःस्थापना *f.* पुनर्नियोग *m.*

To REITERATE, *v. a.* v. To REPEAT. फिरफिरून-फिरून फिरून-पुनः-वारंवार-पुनःपुनः-&c. करणें, उगाळणें, उजरणें, सरावणें.

REITERATED, *p.* v. V. फिरून केलेला, वारंवार केलेला, &c. उजरलेला, उगाळलेला, &c. त्रिवार, पौनःपुनिक, इजा बिजा तिजा.

REITERATEDLY, *adv.* v. P. फिरूनफिरून, फिरफिरून, वारंवार, पुनः पुनः.

REITERATION, *n.* v. V.—*act.* फिरफिरून करणें *n.* उगाळणें *n.* &c. उगाळणी *f.* उजरणी *f.* पुनःपुनःकरण *n.—state.* पौनःपुन्य *n.*

To REJECT, *v. a. refuse to have, not choose, return as bad, disapprove, disallow, &c.* नापसंत-नामंजूर-रद्द-अमान्य-&c. करणें, फिरवणें, टाकणें, गाळणें, बगळणें, निरसणें, घालवणें, नाखूश करणें, वर्जकरणें, गाळण *f.*-वर्जन *n.*-&c. करणें *g.of o.* अस्वीकार *m.*-अनंगीकार*m.*-&c. करणें *g. of o.*

2 *cast off, forsake,* v. To ABANDON. सोडणें, टाकणें, सोडून-टाकून जाणें-देणें, त्याग*m.*-&c. करणें.

3 *refuse to accept or grant,* v. To REFUSE. नकारणें *or* नाकारणें, नकार *or* नाकार*m.* करणें *g. of o.*—scornfully, rudely, &c. v. To CONTEMN. उडवणें, धुतकारणें, धुतकावणें, हडहडावणें, हडहड *f.* करणें, झिडकावणें, झिडकारणें, हुंडारणें, झाडणें, हात*m.* झाडणें *with* ला *or* स, नाक *n.* मुरडणें-मोडणें-उडवणें *with* ला *or* स, थुकरणें *or* थुकारणें, थुंकणें.

REJECTABLE, *a.* v.V. 1. टाकायाजोगा-&c. टाकाऊ, टाकवणा.

REJECTED, *p.* v. V. 1. नापसंत केलेला, रद्द केलेला, फिरवलेला, टाकलेला, गाळलेला, &c. नापसंत, रद्द, रद्दी, खर, वर्ज, वर्जित, निरसित, निरस्त, निराकृत.

2 सोडलेला, &c. त्यक्त.

3 नकारलेला, &c. अनंगीकृत, अस्वीकृत, निरसित, निरस्त.

REJECTER, *n.* REJECTING, *p. a.* v. V. 1. नापसंत करणारा, फिरवणारा, टाकणारा, गाळणारा, &c. गाळण-&c. करणारा, वर्जन-निरसन-&c. कर्त्ता-कारी-&c.

2 सोडणारा, &c. त्यागकर्त्ता-कारी-&c.

3 नकारणारा, नकार करणारा, &c.

REJECTION, *n.* v. V. 1.—*act.* नापसंत करणें *n.* रद्द करणें *n.* फिरवणें *n.* गाळणें *n.* &c. गाळण *f.* वर्जन *n.* निरसन *n.* निरास *m.*

निराकृति *f.* अस्वीकार *m.* अनंगीकार *m.* अग्रहण *n.* प्रत्याख्यान *n.* प्रत्यादेश *m.*

2—*act.* टाकणें *n.* &c. त्याग *m.*

3 नकारणें *n.* &c. नकार *or* नाकार *m.* नाकुली *f.* नाकमोड *f.*

To REJOICE, *v. n. be glad, experience joy.* आनंदणें, हर्षणें, खुशालणें, उल्लासणें, उल्लाळणें, मोदणें, आनंद *m.*-संतोष *m.*-&c. करणें, आनंद *m.*-संतोष *m.*-&c. पावणें, आनंद *m.*-संतोष *m.*-हर्ष *m.*-उत्साह *m.*-&c. होणें-वाटणें *in. con.* आनंदित-&c. होणें.

To REJOICE, *v. a. make glad, &c.* आनंद *m.*-हर्ष *m.*-संतोष *m.*-आल्हाद *m.*-&c.देणें-करणें, खुश-आनंदयुक्त-हर्षयुक्त -आनंदित-&c. करणें, हर्षविणें, आनंदविणें, संतोषविणें, आल्हाददणें, हर्षण *n.*-&c. करणें *g. of o.*—as enhanced, and as answering to *enrapture, enravish, &c.* आनंद मावेनासा करणें, अत्यानंद *m.* देणें-करणें, फारच संतोषविणें-हर्षविणें-&c. अतिसंतोषण *n.*-अतिहर्षण *n.*-परमानंदन *n.*-&c. करणें *g. of o.* आनंदमय-आनंदनिमग्न-आनंदभरित-&c. करणें.

REJOICED, *p.* v. V. *and* JOYFUL. हर्षविलेला, आनंदित, हर्षित, उत्साहित, उल्लसित, परितुष्ट, हृषित, हृष्ट.

REJOICER, *n.* REJOICING, *p. a.* v. V. A. आनंद देणारा- करणारा, हर्षविणारा, &c. हर्षक, नंदक, आनंदकर, आनंदद, आनंदप्रद, आल्हादक, मोदक.

v. V. N. आनंद करणारा-पावणारा, &c. हर्षमाण, मोदमान.

REJOICING, *n.* v. V. A.—*act.* हर्षविणें *n.* &c. हर्षण *n.* संतोषण *n.* आनंदन *n.* आल्हादन *n.* नंदन *n.*

v. V. N. उत्साह *m.* उत्सव *m.* उत्साव *m.*

Public r. or festivity. उत्साह *m.* उत्सव *m.* उत्साव *m.*

To REJOIN, *v. n. answer to a reply.* प्रत्युत्तर *n.*-&c. करणें.

2 See. To REPLY.

REJOINDER, *n. answer to a reply.* उलटगोष्ट *f.* उलटजबाब *m.* प्रत्युत्तर *n.* कोटि *f.* उत्तरपक्ष *m.* सदूजबाब *m.*

Reply and r. उत्तरप्रत्युत्तर *n.*

2 See REPLY.

To RELAPSE, *v. n.* (into vice or error), *fall back.* फिरून बिघडणें-बिथरणें-&c. दुराचरणाकडे-&c. उलटणें-फिरणें-परतणें, उगळणें, पहिल्यावर-पूर्वपदावर-पूर्वपदास-मूलपदावर-&c. येणें.

2 (into sickness.) माघारणें, उलटणें, माघार *f.*-उलट *m. f.* खाणें-घेणें,&c. दुखणें *n.*-रोग *m.*-&c. परतणें-दुपरतणें *or* दुपरतणीस पडणें *g. of s.* बाचटणें.

RELAPSE, *n.* RELAPSING, *n.* v. V. 1. फिरून बिघडणें *n.* &c. उलट *m. f.* उलटी *f.* परतणी *f.*

2 माघारणें *n.* &c. माघार *f.* उलट *m. f.* परतणी *f.* दुपरतणी *f.*

To RELATE, *v. a.* v. To TELL. सांगणें, कथणें, निवेदणें, निरूपिणें.

To RELATE, *v n. have relation or reference to.* लागणें, लागू होणें-पडणें, संबंध *m.*-संधान *n.*-धोरण *n.*-&c. ठेवणें-राखणें *or* असणें *with* कडे *of o.* संबंधी-विषयक-निसबतीचा-&c. असणें.

RELATED, *p. and a.* v. V. A. सांगितलेला, &c. कथित, निवेदित, निरूपित.

v. V. N. संबद्ध, ससंबंध, सान्वय, लागी, संबंधी.

Mutually r. or connected. व्यपेक्षित.

I. *connected by consanguinity; belonging to the same family, of kin by the father's side.* गोत्री, गोत्रसंबंधी,गोत्रज, एकगोत्र, सगोत्र, एकगोत्रज,सकुल्य, वंशीय, सजातीय,स्वजातीय, आत्मीय, आत्मीयसंबंधी, स्वीय, एकरक्त, एकशरीर, एकशरीरसंबंधी, एकशरीरान्वयी, एकरक्तसंबंधी, एकशरीरावयव, एकारक्ताचा, एकारक्तामांसाचा.

Note. There are some niceties respecting the सपिंड and the समानोदक for which the curious, if they please, may consult Wilson's Sanskrit Dictionary.

II.—by birth on the mother's side or by marriage. नातलग, नातेदार, नातेवाईक, आंगलग, सोयरा, पासचा, पासला, आप्त, आप्तविषयी, आप्तसंबंधी, संबंधी, लगती, लगतीचा, शरीरसंबंधाचा, शरीरसंबंधी, योनिसंबंधाचा, योनिसंबंधी, यौन.

To be r. to. लागणें (as तो तुम्हास काय लागतो ?) लेखणें (as तो मला मामा लेखतो). See also RELATION.

RELATER, *n.* RELATING, *p. a.* v. V. A. सांगणारा, &c. कथक, कथन-&c. कर्त्ता-कारी-&c.

v. V. N. लागी, संबंध ठेवणारा, संबंधाचा, संबंधी, संबंधीक.

RELATION, *n.* v. V. A.—*act.* सांगणें*n.* बयाणा *or* ना*m.* कथणें *n.* कथन *n.* निवेदन *n.* निरूपण *n.*

Faithful and exact r. वस्तुकथन *n.* वस्तुस्थितिकथन *n.*

Minute and particular r. बयाद *or* ज *m.f.* बयावल *n.*

v. V. N. संबंध *m.* अन्वय *m.* लाग *m.* लागीपणा *m.*

In r. to. संबंधीं *m.* विषयीं.

Intimate and inseparable r. समवाय*m.* समवायसंबंध *m.* नित्यसंबंध *m.*

Inseparable r. or cause(as of material with produce). [समवायिकारण *n.*

I. *proportion.* बरोबरी *f.* तुलना *f.* साम्य *n.* समता *f.*

II. *connection between, mutual respect,* v. CONNECTION. नातें *n.* संबंध *m.* भाव *m.*

Mutual r. or connection. व्यपेक्षा *f.*

III. *connection by blood, alliance of kin, consanguinity.* गोत्रसंबंध *m.*ज्ञातित्व *n.* सगोत्रत्व *n.* एकगोत्रता *f.* एकशरीरसंबंध *m.* एकरक्तसंबंध *m.* समरक्तसंबंध*m.* एकशरीरान्वय*m.* सापिंड्य*n.*

IV. (by kin on the mother's side or by marriage), v. AFFINITY. नातें *n.* आप्तपणा *m.* आप्तभाव *m.* सोयरीक *f.* पदर*m.* लगत*f.*अन्वय *m.*शरीरसंबंध *m.*—freely. नातेंगोतें*n.* नातेंपोतें *n.*

Distant r. पदरानपदर *m.*

That stands in the r. of to. लागणें- लेखणें (as तो आम्हास चुलता-मामा-&c. लागतो *or* लेखतो).

V. *person related by consanguinity,*v. KINSMAN, RELATED. भाऊबंद, बापभाऊ, गोत्रभाऊ, गोत्रबंधु, दाईज, दायाद, दायजी, गोत्रपुरुष, गोत्री.

Relations ; *kinsfolk, kindred.* भाऊबंद*m. pl.* गोत्री *m.pl.* गोत्रज *m. pl.* &c. दाईजगोत्रज *m. pl.* गोत*n.* गणगोत*n.* गोतवळा *or* गोतोळा *m.* गोतपत *or* गोतपात *n.* गोत्रसमुदाय *m.* बंधुवर्ग *m.* बंधुजन *m.*

VI. *person related by the mother's side or by marriage,* v. RELATED. नातलग, नातेदार, नातेवाईक, सोयरा, आप्त, आप्तसंबंधी, संबंधी, शरीरसंबंधी, सोयराधायरा.

Relations ; *relations and connections.* आप्तसंबंधी *m. pl.* आप्तविषयी *m. pl.* सोयरेधायरे *m. pl.* आप्तवर्ग *m.*

The terms for common relations and connections, as uncle, aunt, cousin, father-in-law, brother-in-law, &c. &c. will be found under these words in their proper places ; but as the Maráthás have names for many relations and connections for which the English have no corresponding definite terms, it is thought the student will be thankful to find here a collection of such.

व्याही one's son's or daughter's father-in-law.
विहीण do. do. mother-in-law.
साडू one's wife's sister's husband.
नणंद one's husband's sister.
दीर one's husband's brother —esp. younger one.
भावा do. —elder one.
जाऊ *or* जावू one's husband's brother's wife.
भावजई one's brother's wife.
आजेसासरा one's husband's or wife's grandfather.
आजी *or* आजेसासू wife of do.
पणजेसासरा one's husband's or wife's great-grandfather.
पणजीसासू wife of do.
चुलतसासरा do. do. paternal uncle.
चुलतसासू wife of do.
चुलतआजा one's father's paternal uncle.
चुलतआजी wife of do.
चुलतचुलता one's father's paternal first cousin, one's own first cousin one remove.
चुलतचुलती wife of do.
चुलतचुलतभाऊ one's paternal second cousin.
चुलतचुलत भावजई wife of do.
चुलतचुलत बहीण one's paternal second cousin female.
चुलतचुलतमेहुणा husband of do.
चुलतमामा one's mother's paternal first cousin, one's own first cousin one remove.
मावसनणंद one's husband's maternal cousin female.
मावसभावजई one's maternal cousin's wife.
मावसमेहुणा one's wife's maternal cousin.
मावसमेहुणी do. do. female.
आतेसासू one's husband's or wife's paternal aunt.
आतेसासरा husband of do.
चुलतमामी wife of do.
चुलतमावशी *or* माउसी one's mother's paternal first cousin.
चुलतदीर one's husband's paternal first cousin.
चुलतनणंद do. do. female.
चुलतजाऊ one's husband's paternal first cousin's wife.
चुलतचुलतजाऊ one's husband's paternal second cousin's wife.
चुलतचुलतनणंद one's husband's paternal second cousin female.
चुलतभावजई one's paternal cousin's wife.
मामेसासरा one's husband's or wife's maternal uncle.
मामेसासू wife of do.
मामेदीर one's husband's maternal first cousin.
मामेजाऊ wife of do.
मामेनणंद one's husband's maternal first cousin female.
मामेभावजई one's maternal first cousin's wife.
मामेमेहुणा one's wife's maternal first cousin.
मामेमेहुणी do. female.
मावससासू one's husband's or wife's maternal aunt.
मावससासरा husband of do.
मावसआजी one's mother's maternal aunt.
मावसआजा husband of do.
मावसदीर one's husband's maternal cousin.
मावसजाऊ wife of do.
आतेदीर one's husband's paternal cousin.
आतेजाऊ wife of do.
आतेनणंद one's husband's paternal cousin female.
आतेभावजई one's paternal cousin's wife.
आतेमेहुणा one's wife's paternal cousin.
आतेमेहुणी do. do. female.

The word सावत्र prefixed to any term of relationship, indicates that it is a "step" or "half" relationship; as सावत्रआई step mother, सावत्रमावशी step mother's sister (aunt through one's step mother), सावत्रभावजई step brother's wife, सावत्रनणंद husband's step sister. This notice will serve instead of a repetition of the terms. It must here be mentioned that though in English the words *paternal cousin and maternal cousin* are applied equally to the children respectively of one's father's and one's mother's brothers and sisters, the Maráthí has distinct names for them. The word चुलत, prefixed to any term of relationship, indicates that it is through one's father's brother, and आते through his sister. मामे indicates relationship through one's mother's brother, and मावस through her sister. The student must bear this in mind in rendering terms of relationship.

It will be seen by observing the above list that the relations and connections which are acquired through marriage are expressed by affixing in the case of relation of prior grades (*i. e.* uncles, aunts, parents, &c.) and prefixing in the case of collateral relations (as brothers, sisters, cousins and their husbands or wives) a word indicative of the new connection to the word which expresses the direct relationship. To express the former the words सासरा and सासू (father and mother in-law) are used, as आजेसासरा, आजेसासू husband's or wife's grand-father and mother. In the same way चुलतसासरा, मामेसासरा, चुलतसासू, मामेसासू, &c. &c. are formed. The acquired *collateral* relations are expressed by prefixing चुलत, आते, मामे *or* मावस (according as the relationship is through a father's brother or sister or a mother's brother or sister), to the word which renders the direct relationship; ex. चुलतदीर, चुलतनणंद, मामेमेहुणा, मामेजाऊ, &c. &c. The relations which in English are expressed by prefixing "great" (as *great* uncle, *great* aunt), are expressed in Maráthí by affixing आजा as चुलतआजा one's father's paternal uncle, *i. e.* one's own *grand-father-uncle*, or brother of one's grandfather. Paternal first cousins *one remove* are expressed by a reduplication of the word चुलता, as चुलतचुलता, and *second* cousins are rendered by affixing भाऊ and बहीण to the reduplicated चुलता, as चुलतचुलत भाऊ, चुलतचुलत बहीण, *i. e.* brother and sister through one's चुलतचुलता. The principle of viewing cousins as brothers and sisters, runs throughout. Thus a man's चुलतभाऊ or paternal first cousin (*brother* by his uncle) is a woman's चुलतदीर. His मामेभाऊ is his wife's मामेदीर; his मावसभाऊ is her मावसदीर; and so on. Thus also a woman's चुलतभाऊ (*brother* through her uncle) is her husband's चुलत मेहुणा; her आतेभाऊ is his आतेमेहुणा; and so on. See also चुलतनणंद, मावसनणंद, चुलतजावू, चुलत भावजई, and the other combinations with नणंद, जावू and भावजई, in all which the same rule holds. The terms of relationship in the line of *paternal uncle*, are more numerous than in the lines of paternal aunt or maternal uncle or aunt. Paternal aunts go into other families by marriage, and maternal uncle and aunts are still of a different family: they are therefore not so much regarded.

RELATIONSHIP. See RELATION.

RELATIVE, *a. having relation, respecting.* संबंधी, विषयक, संबंधीक, लागी, परायण.

2 *not absolute; considered as respecting something else.* सापेक्ष, अन्यसापेक्ष, अन्यापेक्षी, ससंबंधिक, ससंबंधी.

3 *implying relation.* See CORRELATIVE. 4—in grammar. तत्पदापेक्षी, तत्पदापेक्षक.

R. pronoun. संबंधी सर्वनाम *n.*

RELATIVE, *n.* v. KINSMAN, RELATION. भाऊबंद, नातेदार, नातेवाईक, संबंधी, आप्त.

RELATIVELY, *adv.* v. A. 2. अन्यापेक्षेनें, अन्यसापेक्ष, अन्यसापे[क्षतः.

To RELAX, *v. a. make less tense or tight*, lit. fig. v. To SLACKEN, To LOOSEN. सैलावणें, ढिलावणें, ढील-सैल-पोकळ-&c. करणें, खिळखिळा-खिळखिळीत करणें.

To r. one's joints. टांके *m. pl.* ढील करणें.

2 *diminish the intenseness of*, v. To REMIT. ढिला-ढील-शिथिल-&c. करणें, ढिलाई *f.*-&c. करणें-मांडणें-पाडणें *g. of o.* ढिलाईवर-&c. घेणें-धरणें.

3 *unbend, lose, relieve from close attention.* विसांवा *m.*-विश्रांति *f.*-&c. देणें, मोकळीक *f.* करणें-देणें.

4 (the bowels). अदळ-ढिला-&c. करणें, अदळपणा *m.*-ढिलेपणा *m.*-लघुकोष्ठता *f.*-&c. आणणें, कोठा*m.* सैल-ढिला-&c. करणें.

To RELAX, *v. n. remit in close attention.* ढिला-ढील-सुस्त-&c. होणें, ढिलाई *f.*-ढिलेपणा *m.*-ढिल्ली *f.*-सुस्ताई *f.*-&c. करणें-धरणें, उद्योग *m.* सैल-शिथिल-&c. करणें, उद्योगशैथिल्य *n.* करणें.

RELAXATION, *n.* v. V. A. 1. 2.—*act.* सैलावणें *n.* सैल करणें *n.* &c. शिथिलीकरण *n.*—*state.* सैलावलेलेपणा *m.* सैलपणा *m.* ढिलेपणा *m.* खिळखिळी *f.* ढिल्ली *f.* शिथिलता *f.* शैथिल्य *n.*

3 *and* AMUSEMENT, REFRESHMENT.—*state.* विसांवा *m.* विश्रांति *f.* उद्योगविश्राम *m.* उद्योगविश्रांति *f.*

4—*state.* अदळपणा *m.* ढिलेपणा *m.* लघुकोष्ठता *f.*

RELAXED, *p.* v. V. A. 1. सैलावलेला, सैल केलेला-झालेला, &c. सैल, ढील, ढिला, शिथिल, खिळखिळा, खिळखिळीत, लंपट *or* लांपट, लांपळ *or* लांफळ, शिथिलीकृत, विगलित.

4 अदळ, ढिला. [कोष्ठ.

Of r. bowels. पोटाचा अदळ, अदळ पोटाचा, लघुकोष्ठ, मृदु-

RELAXER, *n.* RELAXING, *p. a.* v. V. A. 1. सैलावणारा, सैलकरणारा, ढिलाई करणारा, &c. शैथिल्य-&c. कर्त्ता-कारक-&c. शिथिलीकरण कर्त्ता.

4 अदळ करणारा, अदळपणा आणणारा, &c.

I. *rendering languid.* टांके ढील करणारा, ग्लानि-मांद्य-&c. करणारा-आणणारा-कारक-प्रद-&c. बलशैथिल्यकारक. [ती *f.*

RELAY, *n.* (of horses, runners, &c.). डांक *f.* टप्पा *m.* डांकपा

R. stage-station. डांकचौकी *f.*

To RELEASE, *v. a. liberate, set free*, v. To FREE. सोडणें, सोडवणें, सोडवणूक *f.*-सुटका *f.*-बंदखलास *m.*-&c. करणें *g. of o.* बंदखलास-मोकळा-मुक्त-&c. करणें.

RELEASE, RELEASING, *n.* v. V.—*act.* सोडणें *n.* सोडवणें *n.* &c. सोडवण *f.* सोडवणूक *f.* सोड *f.* बंदखलास *m.* मोचन *n.* उद्धरण*n.* मोक्ष *m.*—*state.* सुटका *f.* सूट *f.* मोकळीक *f.* मुक्ति *f.*

I. *acquittance from a debt, &c.* सोडचिठ्ठी *f.* बेदावापत्र *n.* निदावापत्र *n.*

RELEASED, *p.* v. V. सोडलेला, सोडवलेला, मोकळा केलेला, &c. बंदखलास, मुक्त.

I. (from an obligation, a promise, &c.). उतराई, उत्तीर्ण.

RELEASER, *n.* RELEASING, *p. a.* v. V. सोडणारा, सोडवणारा, मोकळा करणारा, सोडवण-&c. करणारा, मुक्तकर्त्ता, मोचनकर्त्ता, मोचक.

To RELENT, *v. n. become pitiful or tender.* दया *f.*-कळवळा *m.*-कळकळ *f.*-पान्हा *m.*-&c. येणें *in. con.* द्रवणें, कळवळणें, द्रव *m.*-पाझर *m.*-&c. सुटणें *in. con.* मऊ-नरम-मृदु-&c. होणें, मऊपणा *m.*-मृदुता *f.*-मार्दव *n.*-&c. येणें *in. con.*

RELENTING, *n.* v. V. कळवळा *m.* पान्हा *m.* द्रव *m.* दयेचा पाझर *m.*

RELENTLESS, *a. pitiless*, v. CRUEL. कठोर, पाषाणहृदय, मांसहृदय, निर्द्रवहृदय. [मनानें.

RELENTLESSLY, *adv. without pity.* दयेवांचून, निर्दयपणानें, कठोर-

RELENTLESSNESS, *n.* v. A. कठोरपणा *m.* निर्दयपणा *m.* पाषाणहृदय *n.*

RELEVANCY, *n.* v. A. प्रासंगिकता *f.* प्राकरणिकत्व *n.*&c. प्रसंगौचित्य *n.* प्रस्तावौचित्य *n.*

RELEVANT, *a. applicable to the subject in hand, pertinent.* प्रासंगिक, प्राकरणिक, प्रसंगानुसारी, प्रसंगोचित, प्रस्तावसदृश, प्रास्ताविक, प्रस्तावानुसारी, प्रस्तावोचित, प्रस्तावान्वयी.

RELIABLE, *n.* v. TRUSTWORTHY. विश्वासाचा, भरवशाचा, विश्वासू.

RELIANCE, *n.* v. CONFIDENCE. विश्वास *m.* भरोसा *or* भरवसा *m.* इतबार *m.* प्रत्यय *m.* निष्ठा *f.* Some terms for a person or thing in or on which reliance is placed, are. भरवशाचीमोट *f.* भरवशाचेंकूळ *n.* भरवशाची म्हैस *f.*

RELIC, *n. that which remains after the loss or decay of the rest.* अवशेष *m.* शेष *m.* शिलक *f.* अवशिष्टांश *m.* नष्टशिष्टांश *m.*

2 relics; v. CORPSE. शव *n.*

RELICT, *n.* v. WIDOW. विधवा *f.*

RELIEF, *n. removal or alleviation of pain, grief, distress, &c.* दुःखशमन *n.* दुःखपरिहार *m.* दुःखमोचन *n.* दुःखपरिमार्जन *n.* अनिष्टपरिहार *m.* अनिष्टपरिमार्जन *n.* &c. श्रमपरिहार *m.* श्रमपरिमार्जन *n.* &c.

2 *ease or rest obtained.* आराम *m.* आरामी *f.* चैन*n.* समाधान *n.* सुख*n.* स्वस्थपणा*m.* स्वस्थता *f.* स्वास्थ्य*n.* विसांवा*m.* विसवटा *m.* विश्राम *m.* विश्रांति *f.* शांति *f.* शांतता *f.*

3 (of a sentry, &c.). बदलणें *n.* बदली *f.* पाहऱ्याचा पालट*m.*

4 *person, &c. relieving.* बदली, बदल्या.

5 See HELP. 6 See REDRESS.

That is in r.—sculpture, &c. उचलला.

To RELIEVE, *v. a. free wholly or partially from pain, grief, distress, &c.* आराम *m.*-सुख *n.*-चैन *n.*-&c. देणें-करणें, आराम *m.*-चैन *n.* पाडणें, दुःखपरिहार *m.*-दुःखपरिमार्जन *n.*-&c. करणें.

To r. one's need. गरज *f.* चालवणें *g. of o.*

2 *alleviate, mitigate, &c.* v. To EASE. शमवणें, शम *m.*-उपशम *m.*-प्रशमन *n.*-शांति *f.*-&c. करणें *g.of o.*

3 *succour*, v. To HELP. मदद *f.*-कुमक *f.*-&c. करणें-देणें,

4 (a sentinel, &c.). बदलणें, पालटणें, बदली *f.* करणें *g. of o.*

RELIEVED, *p.* v. V. 1. आराम दिल्हेला, &c. परिहृतदुःख, परिहृत श्रम, मुक्तदुःख, मुक्तश्रम, शमितदुःख, शांतदुःख, &c. प्राप्तविराम, प्राप्तविश्राम. [प्रशांत.

2 शमवलेला, हलका केलेला, &c. हलका, हलू, शमित, प्रशमित,

4 बदललेला, &c.

RELIEVER, *n.* RELIEVING, *p. a.* v. V. 1. आराम देणारा-पाडणारा- करणारा, &c. दुःखपरिहारक, दुःखपरिमार्जक-नाशक-निवारक-शमक, श्रमपरिहारक- परिमार्जक-&c. विश्रांतिप्रद-दायक-&c. समाधानप्रद-दायक-&c.

2 शमवणारा, शमक, &c. प्रशमन-&c. कर्त्ता-कारी-&c.

4 बदलणारा, पालटणारा, बदली करणारा, बदली, बदल्या.

RELIGION, *n.* v. PIETY. धर्म *m.* देवभक्ति *f.* भक्ति *f.* भक्तिभाव *m.*

Course of r. *religious offices and exercises,*—compreh. देवधर्म *m.* देवदेव *m.* देवदेवपूजा *f.*

Destruction or extinction of r. or a r. धर्मोच्छेद *m.*

Establishment of r. or a r. धर्मसंस्थापन *n.*

2 *a* r. *a faith.* धर्म *m.* मत *n.* मार्ग *m.* धर्ममार्ग *m.*

Good r. सद्धर्म *m.*

Hindu r. शेंडीधर्म *m.*

RELIGIOUS, *n.* v. PIOUS.—of persons. धार्मिक, धर्मशील, धर्मपरायण, भक्तिमान्, भक्तिमंत, भजनशील, भजनी, आचारवान्, कर्मशील, कर्मनिष्ठ, कर्मिष्ठ, कर्मठ, कर्मशूर, क्रियावान्, नियमशील, नियमनिष्ठ, नियमी, नियमपर, नियमिष्ठ *pop.* नेमिष्ठ, वशिष्ठ.

2 *of, or belonging to religion.* धर्माचा, धर्मविषयींचा, धर्मप्रकरणाचा, धर्मविषयक, धर्मसंबंधी. [&c. धर्मपरायण.

RELIGIOUSLY, *adv.* v. A. 1. भक्तिबुद्धीनें, भक्तिभावानें, देवभक्तीनें,

RELIGIOUSNESS, *n.* v. A. 1. धार्मिकपणा *m.* धर्मशीलता *f.* भजनशीलता *f.* धर्मनिष्ठा *f.* भजननिष्ठा *f.* नियमनिष्ठा *f.* कर्मनिष्ठा *f.*

To RELINQUISH, *v. a.* v. To ABANDON, To GIVE UP. सोडणें, सोडून देणें, त्याग *m.*-&c. करणें *g. of o.* विसर्जणें.

RELINQUISHMENT, *n.* v. V. सोडणें *n.* त्याग *m.* त्यजन *n.* उत्सर्ग *m.* विसर्ग *m.* विसर्जन *n.*

R. of right or title to. सत्तानिवृत्ति *f.* स्वत्वनिवृत्ति *f.*

RELISH, *n.* v. TASTE. चव *f.* गोडी *f.* रुचि *f.* अभिरुचि *f.*

2 *cast, smack, flavor, &c.* v. TASTE. छट्टा *f.* स्वाद *m.* वास *n.*

3 *something eaten with food to give a relish.* तोंडीं लावणें *n.* कोरड्यास केलेला पदार्थ *m.*

To RELISH, *v. a. give a nice taste to.* चव *f.*-स्वाद *m.*-गोडी *f.*-&c. आणणें-देणें.

2 *like the taste of.* गोडी *f.*-चव *f.*-रुचि *f.*-&c. येणें-वाटणें *g. of o. with in. con.* गोड-&c. वाटणें-लागणें *in. con.*

To RELISH, *v. n. have a pleasing taste.* चव *f.*-गोडी *f.*-रुचि *f.*-&c. वाटणें *g. of s.* गोड-&c. लागणें-वाटणें.

2 *have a flavor or taste of.* छट्टा *f.*-स्वाद *m.*-वास *m.*-गंध *m.*-ध्वनि *m.*-&c. येणें-मारणें *g. of o.*

RELUCTANCE, *n.* v. A. *and* UNWILLINGNESS. कंटाळा *m.* संकट *n.* त्रास *m.* नाखुशी *f.* विमति *f.* विमुखता *f.* [असंतोषी.

RELUCTANT, *a.* v. UNWILLING. नाराजी, नाखुश, विमत, विमुख,

RELUCTANTLY, *adv.* v. A. मोठ्या संकटानें, रुच्छूंकरून, नाखुशीनें, &c.

To RELY, *v. n.* v. To CONFIDE. भरवसा *m.*-विश्वास *m.*-&c. ठेवणें, टेंकणें, ओठंगणें, पातणें.

To REMAIN, *v. n. be left, be as residue.* उरणें, राहणें, शिल्लक-&c. असणें-राहणें, उवारीस *or* उबाऱ्यास येणें, शिल्केस असणें-गहणें, मागेंपडणें, वांचणें, पारठा पडणें, बाकी *f.*-&c. राहणें *g. of s.*

2 *continue, last,* v. To ENDURE. राहणें, टिकणें, तगणें, नांदणें, असणें. [पडणें.

3 *stay, dwell,* v. To RESIDE. राहणें, असणें, मुक्काम *m.* करणें,

REMAINDER, *n. that which is left.* ऊर *f.* उरी *f.* उरबई *f.* उबेर *f.* उबेरी *f.* बाकी *f.* शेष *m. n.* अवशेष *m.* शेषखंड *n.* राहिलेला भाग *m.*-अंश *m.*-&c.

Filling up (or supplying) the r. उरोट्याला पुरटा *m.* निपुरवट्याला पुरवटा *m.*

That is without r. अशेष.

2—in Arithmetic. बादबाकी *f.* बाकी *f.* अंतर *n.*

REMAINER, *n.* REMAINING, *p.* v. V. 1. राहणारा-राहिलेला, &c. उरता, राहता, बाकी, बाकीचा, शिल्लक, शिल्लकी, शिल्लकीचा, अवशिष्ट, शिष्ट, उर्वरित—compreh. उरलासुरला, उरसूर.

REMAINS, *n.* v. RELIC, REMAINDER. शेष *m. n.* अवशेष *m.*

2 v. CORPSE. शव *n.* प्रेत *n.*

To REMAND, *v. a. send or call back.* फिरून-परत-माघारा-&c. पाठवणें-प्रेरणें-प्रेषणें-बोलावून आणणें.

REMANENT. See REMNANT.

REMARK. See NOTICE, OBSERVATION.

To REMARK. See To NOTE, To OBSERVE.

REMARKABLE. See NOTABLE, STRANGE.

REMARKABLY, *adv.* लक्ष्यांत यावया जोगा-ठेवण्याजोगा-&c. लक्ष्यांत आल्यावांचून राहणार नाहीं असा, फारच.

REMARRIAGE, *n.* पुनर्विवाह *m.*

REMEDIABLE, *a.* v. V. परिहार करायाजोगा-&c. उपाय करायाजोगा, उपायसाध्य, उपाययोग्य, परिहार्य, उपायपरिहार्य, उपायप्रतिकार्य, प्रतिसमाधेय.

REMEDIAL, *a. affording, &c. a remedy.* उपायाचा, इलाजाचा, परिहाराचा, परिहारक, प्रतिकारक.

REMEDIED, *p.* v. V. उपाय केलेला, परिहृत.

REMEDILESS, *a. admitting no remedy.* निरुपाय, हीनोपाय, अनुपाय, उपायशून्य-हीन-&c. उपायासाध्य, गतिहीन.

REMEDY, *n. that which cures or counteracts.* उपाय *m.* उपाव *m.* इलाज *m.* उपचार *m.*

Harsh, violent, &c. r. आसुरी उपाय *m.* आसुरी चिकित्सा *f.* राक्षसीउपाय *m.* राक्षसी उपचार *m.* तामसी उपचार *m.* तामसोपचार *m.* [सौम्योपचार *m.*

Mild, &c. r. सामोपाय *m.* सामोपचार *m.* राजोपचार *m.*

Temporary r. वायदेचिट्ठी *f.* वायदेरास्ता *m.*

To REMEDY, *v. a. cure or remove.* उपाय *m.*-&c. करणें, परिहारणें, परिहार *m.*-प्रतिकार *m.*-निरसन *n.*-निरास *m.*-&c. करणें *g. of o.*

To REMEMBER, *v. a. have or retain in mind.* आठवण *f.*-स्मरण *n.*-याद *f.*-सई *f.*-&c. ठेवणें-धरणें-राखणें *g. of o.* मनांत ठेवणें, आठवण *f.*-स्मरण *n.*-&c. असणें-राहणें *g. of o. with in. con.* स्मरणें, अवधारणें.

To fail to r. नाठवणें.

2 *recall to mind.* v. To RECOLLECT. आठवणें, स्मरणें, आठवण *f.*-&c. करणें *g. of o.* [&c.

REMEMBERED, *p.* v. V. 1. आठवण ठेवलेला, आठवण राहिलेला,

2 आठवलेला, स्मरलेला, &c. स्मृत, हृद्गत.

REMEMBERER, *n.* REMEMBERING, *p. a.* v. V. आठवण ठेवणारा-राखणारा, &c. मनांत ठेवणारा, स्मृतिमान्.

2 आठवणारा, स्मरणारा, &c. स्मर्त्ता, स्मरण-&c. कर्त्ता.

REMEMBRANCE, *n. the having or retaining in mind.* आठवण *f.* आठव *m.* आठवणूक *f.* याद *f.* यादगारी *f.* सई *f.* ध्यान *n.* स्मरण *n.* स्मृति *f.* धांग *f.* (*with neg. con.*) अवधारण *n.* अवधारणा *f.* स्मर्तृत्व *n.* [&c. होणें.

To come suddenly into r. स्फुरणें, स्फुरण *n.*-स्फूर्त्ति *f.*-

2 *a memento,* v. MEMORIAL. आठवणूक *f.* यादगारी *f.*

REMEMBRANCER, *n. he or that which reminds.* आठवण-स्मरण करवणारा, स्मारक.

To REMIND, *v. a. put in mind of.* आठवण *f.*-स्मरण *n.*-&c. देणें-करणें-करवणें, स्मरवणें, सुचवणें, मनांत-आठवणींत-स्मरणांत-&c. आणणें, स्मारण, *n.*-सूचन*n.*-सूचना *f.* करणें *g. of o.*

REMINDED, *p.* v. V. आठवण दिल्हेला, &c. स्मारित.

REMINDER, *n.* REMINDING, *p. a.*v. V. आठवण देणारा, स्मरणदेणारा,&c. स्मरवणारा,स्मारक, स्मृति-स्मरण-&c.कारक-जनक-&c.

REMINISCENCE. See MEMORY, RECOLLECTION.

REMISS, *a. slack, lax, &c.* v. DILATORY. NEGLIGENT. ढिला *or* ढिल्या, ढील, ढिलाईचा, हयगईचा, शिथिल, भोंगळ, भसभोंगळ, सुस्त, सुस्त, अव्यवसायी, अव्यवसायवान्.

REMISSION, v. V. A. 1.—*act.* ढिला करणें *n.* ढिलाईवर घेणें *n.* &c.—*state.* ढिला केलेलेपणा *m.* &c. कमीपणा *m.* उतार *m.* ढिलाई *f.* सुस्ताई *f.* मंदी *f.* [*f.* मोचन*n.*

2—*act.* सोडणें *n.* माफ करणें *n.* &c. बक्षीस *n.* माफी *f.* क्षमा

3—*act.* सोडणें*n.* &c. सूट *f.* सोड *f.* माफी *f.*

I. *matter remitted.* सोड *f.* सूट *f.*

II. (of a distemper). उतार *m.* उकाल *m.*

R. and exacerbation. उतारचढ *m.* [शैथिल्यपूर्वक.

REMISSLY, *adv.* v. A. ढिलेपणानें, ढिलाईनें, &c. हयगई-&c. करून,

REMISSNESS, *n.* v. A. ढिलेपण *n.* ढिलेपणा *m.* ढिलाई *f.* ढिल्ली *f.* ढील *f.* हयगई *f.* आळस *m.* सुस्ताई *f.* सुस्ती *f.* शिथिलता *f.* शैथिल्य *n.* अव्यवसाय *m.*

To REMIT, *v.a. relax, slacken, diminish intensity of.* ढिला-ढील-शिथिल-&c. करणें, ढिलाई *f.*-सुस्ताई *f.*-&c. करणें-पाडणें-धरणें *g. of o.* ढिलाईवर-सुस्ताईवर-आळसावर-&c. घेणें-धरणें, जोर *m.*-बळ *n.*-तेजगी *f.*-&c. कमी करणें *g. of o.*

2 (a punishment or fault) *forgive, pardon.* सोडणें, माफ करणें, बक्षीस करणें, माफी *f.* करणें *g. of o.*

3 *release, waive, yield, give up.* सोडणें, माफ करणें, सूट *f.*-सोड *f.*-&c. देणें-घालणें.

4 (monies). पाठवणें, पाठवणी *f.*-पाठवणूक *f.*-&c. करणें *g. of o.*

To r. by bill. हुंडी करणें.

5 See To REFER. 6 See To REMAND.

To REMIT, *v. n. slacken, become less intense,* v. To ABATE. हलकावणें, मंदावणें, कमतावणें, उतरणें, कमी-हलका-&c. होणें, जोम *m.*-&c. कमी-&c. होणें *g. of s.*

2—fever, &c. उतार *m.*-उकाल *m.* पडणें, उतरणें.

REMITTANCE, *n.* पाठवणी *f.* पाठवलेला पैसा *m.*

REMITTENT, *a.*—fever. विषमज्वर *m.*

REMNANT, *n.* See REMAINDER. 2 (of cloth). करगूट *n.* फडकें *n.* रेजा *m.* ओल *f.* कप्पा *or* कपा *m.*

Small r. धांद *f. dim.* धांदी *f.* धांदोटी *f.*

Remnants. *pieces, scraps, odds & ends.* रेजगण *m. n.*

REMONSTRANCE, *n. expostulation.* कानउघडणी *f.* कानझाडणी *f.* तकरार *f.* आपत्ति *f.* आपत्तिभाषण *n.* आपत्तिवाद*m.* आपत्तिलेख*m.*

To REMONSTRATE, *v. n. expostulate.* कान *m. pl.* उघडणें-झाडणें, तकरार *f.* करणें-करून बोलणें, दोन गोष्टी *f. pl.* सांगणें.

REMORSE, *n. pain of conscience,* v. REGRET. पश्चात्ताप *m.* अनुताप *m.* मनस्ताप *m.* चुरचूर *f. intens.* चुरचुराट *m.* खरखर *f.* चुणचूण *f.* चुळचूळ *f.* चुळचुळा *m.* खेद *m.* खुडसणी *f.*

REMORSEFUL, *a.* v. REPENTANT, पश्चात्तापी, अनुतापी, अनुतप्त, पश्चात्तापाचा, अनुतापाचा, मनस्तप्त.

REMORSELESS, *a. pitiless,* v. CRUEL. निर्दय, पाषाणहृदय, कठोर.

REMORSELESSLY, *adv.* v. A. निर्दयपणानें, कठोरमनानें, &c.

REMORSELESSNESS, *n.* v.A. निर्दयपणा *m.* मनाचाकठोरपणा *m.*

REMOTE, *a.* v. DISTANT. दूर, दूरचा, लांब, दूरस्थित, दूरस्थ, दूरांदूरचा, असमीप, असन्निहित, विप्रकृष्ट.

REMOTENESS, *n.* v. A. दूरपणा *m.* लांबी *f.* दूरत्व *n.* दूरता *f.* दूरस्थता *f.* असन्निधान *n.* विप्रकर्ष *m.*

REMOVABLE, *a.* v. V. काढायाजोगा-&c. स्थान पालटायाजोगा-&c. स्थानांतरकरणीय. [व्यावर्त्य, निर्वाह्य.

2 दूर करायाजोगा-सारखा-&c. वारायाजोगा-&c. हार्य, परिहार्य,

3 दूर कराया जोगा, काढायाजोगा, &c.

REMOVAL, REMOVING, *n.* v. V. A. 1.—*act.* काढणें *n.* उठवणें*n.* स्थानांतर करणें *n.* &c.—*state.* स्थानपालट *m.* स्थानांतर *n.* स्थलांतर *n.* स्थानभेद *m.* स्थलभेद *m.*

2—*act.* दूर करणें *n.* हरणें *n.* &c. दूरीकरण *n.* हरण *n.* परिहार *m.* सारण *n.* निस्सारण *n.* अपसारण *n.* अवसारण *n.* उत्सारण*n.* निरसन *n.* निरास *m.* अपनयन *n.* अपवर्त्तन *n.* निर्वाह *m.*

3—*act.* काढणें *n.* दूर करणें *n.* &c. दूरीकरण *n.*उत्थापन *n.* निःकासन *or* निष्कासन *n.*

v. V. N. जागापालटणें *n.* &c. स्थानपालट *m.* स्थानांतर *n.* स्थलांतर *n.* स्थानभेद *m.* स्थलभेद*m.*

I. See DEATH.

To REMOVE, *v. a. put or move from its place, cause to change place.* काढणें, उठवणें, उचलणें, नेणें, घेऊन जाणें, जागा *f.*-स्थान *n.*-स्थळ *n.*-&c. बदलणें-पालटणें *g. of o.* स्थानांतर *n.*-स्थलांतर *n.*-&c. करणें-करविणें *g. of o.* स्थानभ्रष्ट-&c. करणें.

2 (evils, complaints, &c.). *take or put away; cure, remedy.* दूरकरणें, घालवणें, हरणें, नेणें, निरसणें, सारणें, परिहारणें, वारणें, निवारणें, वहिवाटणें, हरण *n.*-परिहार *m.*-निरसन *n.*-&c. करणें *g. of o.*

3 (from a post or office) v. To DISMISS. काढणें, दूर करणें, घालवणें.

To REMOVE, *v. n. change place, go from one place to another.* जागा *f.*-स्थान *n.*-&c. पालटणें-बदलणें, स्थानभेद *m.*- स्थलभेद *m.*-स्थानांतर *n.*-&c. होणें *g. of s.*

REMOVE, *n.* See REMOVAL. 2 *step in a gradation.* पायरी *f.*

3 (in farriery). खोलबंदी *f.*

REMOVED, *p. & a.* v. V. A. 1. काढलेला, उठवलेला, &c. स्थानांतरित, स्थलांतरित, स्थानांतरप्राप्त, स्थलांतरप्राप्त.

To be far r. दुरावणें.

2 दूर केलेला, घालवलेला, &c. दूरीकृत, अपसारित, अपसृत, निस्सारित, निरसित, निरस्त, परिहृत, परास्त, अपनीत, वारित.

3 काढलेला, दूर केलेला, &c. निःकासित *or* निष्कासित, उत्थापित.
I. See REMOTE.

REMOVER, *n.* REMOVING, *p. a.* v. V. A. 1. काढणारा, उठवणारा, &c. स्थलांतर करणारा, &c. सारक.
2 दूर करणारा, &c. उत्सारक, परिहारक, हरण-परिहार-&c. कर्त्ता-कारी, हर-हर्त्ता-हारक-हारी (in comp.), निर्वाहक.

To REMUNERATE. See To REWARD, To COMPENSATE.

REMUNERATION, *n.* v. REWARD. देणगी *f.* देणावळ *f.* पारितोषिक *n.*
2 See COMPENSATION.

RENAL, *a. belonging to the kidneys or reins.* मूत्रपिंडाचा, गुर्दाचा, मूत्रपिंड संबंधी.

RENCOUNTER, &c. See CLASH, SCUFFLE, SKIRMISH, &c.

To REND, *v. a.* v. To TEAR. फाडणें, फाडून घेणें, चिरणें, टरकावणें, टरकणें, विदारणें, उदफाळणें, विदारण *n.*-विदारणा *f.*-स्फोट *m.*-विघटन *or* विघाटन *n.*-&c. करणें *g. of o.*
To r. in two. दुफाड *f.* करणें *g. of o.*
To r. in pieces. फाड फाडून घेणें. [करणें-देणें.

To RENDER, *v. a.* v. To RETURN. परत करणें-देणें, परत-उलट-&c.
2 *give, afford, yield, &c.* देणें, करणें, प्रापण *n.* करणें.
3 *make or cause to be.* करणें, बनवणें, युक्त-विशिष्ट (in comp.) करणें.
4 v. To TRANSLATE. भाषांतर *n.*-&c. करणें *g. of o.*

RENDERING, See VERSION, TRANSLATION.

RENDEZVOUS, *n. meeting, assembling.* जमाव *m.* जमणें *n.* खेट *f.*
2—place of assembling. मिळण्याची-&c. जागा *f.* खेट *f.* टिपण *n.* पडण *n.* ठेप *f.* संकेतस्थान *n.* संकेतस्थल *n.*

To RENDEZVOUS. See To ASSEMBLE.

RENEGADE, RENEGADO, *n. apostate, &c.* स्वधर्मत्यागी, स्वपक्षत्यागी, स्वमतत्यागी, कुऱ्हाडीचा दांडा *m.*

To RENEW, *v. a. make new, renovate, restore to a former or good state.* नवा-ताजा-नवट-नव्यासारखा-&c. करणें, उजरणें, नवतरणें *or* नवतारणें, नवसरणें *or* नवसारणें, उजरणी *f.*-जीर्णोद्धार *m.*-&c. करणें *g. of o.*
2 *make or do again or afresh,* v. To REPEAT. नवा-&c. करणें, फिरून-पुनः-नव्यानें-&c. करणें-&c.

RENEWABLE, *a.* v. V. 1. नवा-&c. करायाजोगा-सारखा-&c.
2 फिरून-नव्यानें-&c. करायाजोगा-जोगता-सारखा.

RENEWAL, RENEWING, *n.* v. V. 1. नवा करणें *n.* नवसारणें *n.* &c. नवसारणी *f.* उजरणी *f.* नवीकरण *n.* जीर्णोद्धार *m.* उद्धरण *n.* उद्धार *m.*
2 नवा करणें *n.* फिरून करणें *n.* नवीकरण *n.*

RENEWED, *p.* v. V. 1. नवा केलेला, नवसारलेला, &c. नवीकृत.
2 नवा केलेला, फिरून केलेला, &c. नवीकृत, पुनःकृत.

RENNET. See RUNNET.

To RENOUNCE, *v. a. disown, disclaim, &c.* v. To DENY. आंगाबाहेर-आंगानिराळा-&c. टाकणें-करणें, नाकारणें, अनंगीकार *m.*-अस्वीकार *m.*-&c. करणें *g. of o.*
2 *relinquish, cast off, forsake, &c.* v. To GIVE UP. टाकणें, सोडणें, नांव *n.* सोडणें *g. of o.* शपथ *f.* वाहणें-घेणें- वाहून घेणें *g. of o.* तिलांजलि *m. f.* देणें, उत्सर्ग *m.*-उत्सर्जन *n.*-त्याग *m.*-&c. करणें *g. of o.*

RENOUNCED. *p.* v. V. 1. आंगाबाहेर टाकलेला, &c. अस्वीकृत, अनंगीकृत.
2 टाकलेला, सोडलेला, उत्सर्जित, त्यक्त.

RENOUNCEMENT. See RENUNCIATION.

To RENOVATE, RENOVATION. See To RENEW, RENEWAL.

RENOWN, *n.* v. FAME. कीर्त्ति *f.* नांव *n.* नाम *n.* आख्या *f.* प्रख्याति *f.* विख्याति *f.*

RENOWNED, *a.* v. FAMOUS. नामांकित, नांवाचा, कीर्त्तिमान्, नामधारी, नामदार, नामजात *or* द, जगजाहीर, जगत्प्रसिद्ध *pop.* जगप्रसिद्ध, प्रख्यात, विख्यात.

RENT, *p.* v. V. फाडलेला, चिरलेला, &c. विदीर्ण, विदारित, स्फुट, स्फुटित, विघटित *or* विघाटित.

RENT, *n. hire paid for a house.* भाडें *n.* किराया *m.* भाटक *n.*—loose or indef. भाडेंतोडें *n.*
2 (of land). धारा *m.* सोनधारा *m.* सारा *m.* वसूल *m.*
Nominal r. सलामी *f.*
R. paid in kind. बटाई *f.*
3 *slit, tear, &c.* चीर *f.* फाळा *m. v.* निघ, जा, वाभाग *m. v.* निघ, जा, वाभा *m.* वाधडा *m. v.* निघ.

To RENT, *v. a. let to* (houses, tenements). भाड्यानें-भाड्यास देणें-लावणें, भाडें घेऊन देणें, (lands) साऱ्यानें देणें-लावणें.
2 *hold from,* (houses, tenements). भाड्यानें घेणें-ठेवणें, भाडें देऊन घेणें—(lands) साऱ्यानें-&c. घेणें.

RENTAL, RENT-ROLL, *n. list or account of rents.* शिस्त *f.* तहसील *f. n.* तनखा *m.* वसुलाची-वसूलबाकीची-जमाबंदीची-&c. याद *f.* जमाबंदी *f.*

RENTER, *n.* RENTING, *p. a.* v. V. 1. भाड्यानें-भाड्यास देणारा-लावणारा,—(of lands) साऱ्यानें देणारा, &c.
2 भाड्यानें घेणारा, &c. भाडेकरी, भाडोतरी,—(of lands) साऱ्यानें घेणारा.

RENUNCIATION, *n.* v. V. 1.—*act.* आंगाबाहेर टाकणें *n.* नाकारणें *n.* नाकार *m.* अस्वीकार *m.* अनंगीकार *m.* [उत्सर्जन *n.*
2—*act.* टाकणें *n.* सोडणें *n.* &c. त्याग *m.* परित्याग *m.* उत्सर्ग *m.*
R. of the world. सर्वसंगपरित्याग *m.* See also under WORLD.

REPAID, *p.* v. V. 1. परत केलेला, फेडलेला, &c.
2 फेडलेला, &c. प्रतिदत्त.

To REPAIR, *v. a. restore to a good or sound state: mend, &c.* सुधारणें, सुधरणें *or* सुधारणें, नवतरणें *or* नवतारणें, नवसरणें *or* नवसारणें, ओजवणें, दुरूस्त-नीट-&c. करणें, सांपसारणें, थावरणें, उस्तवारी *f.*-मरामत *f.* करणें *g. of o.* जीर्णोद्धार *m.* करणें *g. of o.* For this word as understood in the enlarged or free sense of *to mend hurriedly, cursorily, superficially, &c.* and as conveying the general sense of such words and phrases as, *to do up, stitch up, patch up, to patch and piece, to doctor, to put somewhat to rights, to set into some order, &c.* some colloquialisms are, तांगडणें, ठोकून ठाकून नीट करणें, ठीकठाक करणें, डागडूग *f.*-डागडुजी *or* डागडोजी *f.*-ठाकठिकी *f.*-धंतरमंतर *n.*-तांगडातांगड *f.*-सांदासांद *f.*-मोडतोड *f.*-जोडाजोड *f.*-लासलिंप *f.*-&c. करणें *g. of o.*
2 *supply loss.* भरणें *or* भरून देणें.
3 (a measure, a fault, &c.) *retrieve.* साबरणें, साबर *m.*-सुधारणूक *f.*-&c. करणें *g. of o.* प्रतिकार *m.*-निष्कृति *f.*-&c. करणें, उपाय *m.*-तजवीज *f.*-&c. करणें *g. of o.*

To REPAIR, *v. n.* v. To RESORT. जाणें, येणें, येनजाणें, सेप *f.*

घालणें, येणेंजाणें *n.*-येरझार *f.* करणें.

REPAIR, REPAIRING, *n.* v. V. A. 1.—*act.* सुधारणें *n.* नीट करणें *n.* &c. सुधारणी *f.* सुधारणूक *f.* उस्तवारी *f.* मरामत *f.* जीर्णोद्धार *m.* उद्धरण *n.*—cursory, superficial, &c. डागडुजी *or* डागडोजी *f.* डागडूग *f.* तांगडातांगड *f.* सांदासांद *f.* मोडतोड *f.* तोडमोड *f.* मोडजोड *f.* जोडाजोड *f.* थंतरमंतर *n.* लासलिंप *f.*

To keep in r. डागडुजी *f.*-ऊर्जा *f.*-ओज *f.*-मरामत *f.*-उस्तवारी *f.* राखणें.

To look after the repairs of. मोडतोड *f.* पाहणें.

REPAIRABLE, REPARABLE, *a.* v. V. A. 1. सुधारायाजोगा-जोगता-&c. नीट करायाजोगा-सारखा-&c. उद्धरणीय, उद्धार्य.

REPAIRED, *p.* v. V. A. 1. सुधारलेला, नीट केलेला, तांगडलेला, मरामत केलेला, &c. ठीकठाक.

REPAIRER, *n.* REPAIRING, *p. a.* v. V. A. 1. सुधारणारा, नीट करणारा, तांगडणारा, उस्तवारी-&c. करणारा, जीर्णोद्धारक, जीर्णोद्धारकर्त्ता.

REPARATION. See AMENDS, COMPENSATION.

REPARTEE. *n. ready and witty reply.* नोकीचें-नोकझोकीचें उत्तर *n.* हाजीरजबाब *m.* रसिकोत्तर *n.*

REPAST, *n.* v. MEAL. जेवण *n.* जेवा *m.* [लघ्वाहार *m.*

Slight r. फराळ *m.* उपाहार *m.* अल्पाहार *m.* लघुभोजन *n.*

To REPAY, *v. a. pay back.* परत करणें-देणें, देणें, फेडणें.

2 *make return or requital.* परत-उलट-फेर-&c. देणें, फेडणें, फेड *f.* करणें *g. of o.* प्रतिफल *n.* देणें, प्रतिदान *n.* करणें.

REPAYMENT, *n.* v. V. 1. परत करणें *n.* परत देणें *n.* &c. परतदान*n.*

2 परत देणें *n.* &c. फेड *f.* प्रतिफल *n.* प्रतिदान *n.*

To REPEAL, *v. a. abrogate, annul,* v. To ABOLISH. मोडणें, रद्द-बातील-&c. करणें.

REPEAL, REPEALING, *n.* v. V.—*act.* मोडणें *n.* रद्द करणें *n.* &c. —*state.* भंग *m.* लोप *m.* उच्छेद *m.*

To REPEAT, *v. a. do again, do over again.* फिरून-पुन्हा-पुनः-दुसऱ्यानें-&c. करणें-&c. उलटणें, उलटून-परतून करणें, दुसारणें, दुहारणें, दुसारणी *f.*-दुसरी आवृत्ति *f.*-पुनरावृत्ति *f.*-&c. करणें *g. of o.*

To r. a second time, i. e. *do a third time.* तिसारणें, तिसारणी *f.* करणें *g. of o.*

2 *say again.* फिरून-पुन्हा-दुसऱ्यानें-मातक्यान-&c. बोलणें-&c. उलटून-परतून -&c. बोलणें -म्हणणें-&c. अनुवादणें, पुनरुक्ति *f.*-&c. करणें.

3 *recite, rehearse.* म्हणणें, म्हणणी *f.* करणें, अनुवादणें, पठन*n.* करणें, अनुवाद *m.* करणें.

To r. from memory. पाठ म्हणणें.

To r. frequently so as to fix in the mind; *to con.* घोकणें, घोकणी *f.* करणें.

4 v. To BLAB, To TELL. दुसऱ्याजवळ-&c. बोलणें-सांगणें, फोडणें, अनुवादणें, अनुवाद *m.* करणें *g. of o.*

REPEATED, *p.* v. V. 1. फिरून-पुन्हा-दुसऱ्यानें-&c. केलेला, दुसारलेला, &c. पुनरावर्त्तित, पुनरावृत्त, द्विरावृत्त. [द्विरुक्त.

2 फिरून-पुन्हा -दुसऱ्यानें-&c. म्हटलेला-बोललेला, &c. पुनरुक्त,

3 म्हटलेला, &c. पठित.

REPEATEDLY, *adv. again and again,* v. OFTEN. वारंवार, फिरफिरून, फिरून फिरून, मातक्यान् मातक्यान्, पुनःपुनः, बेळोबेळ, घडीघडी, घडोघडी, उठतां बसतां, आंगोघडी, इजा बिजा तिजा, असकृत्, मुहुर्मुहुः.

REPEATER, *n.* REPEATING, *p. a.* v.V. 1. फिरून-पुन्हा-दुसऱ्यानें-&c. करणारा-&c. उलटणारा, उलटून करणारा-&c. पुनरावृत्ति-द्विरावृत्तिकर्त्ता-कारी-&c.

2 फिरून-दुसऱ्यानें-&c. बोलणारा-म्हणणारा-&c. उलटून बोलणारा-&c. अनुवादक, पुनरुक्ति-&c. कर्त्ता-कारी-&c. पुनर्वक्ता.

3 म्हणणारा, &c. पठन-अनुवाद कर्त्ता-कारी-&c. अनुवादक.

4 दुसऱ्याजवळ बोलणारा, &c. अनुवादक.

I. *repeating watch.* जबाबी घड्याळ *n.*

To REPEL, *v. a. drive back.* मागें-माघारां-&c. घालणें-सारणें-लोटणें-रेंटणें-पळवणें-फिरवणें-&c. हटवणें, बारणें, माघारवणें, प्रतिसारण *n.*-बारण *n.*-निवारण *n.*-&c. करणें.

2 See To OPPOSE.

REPELLED, *p.* v. V. 1. मागें घातलेला-सारलेला-लोटलेला-&c. हटवलेला, प्रतिसारित, निवारित, प्रतिहत, पराहत, व्याहत, परास्त.

REPELLENT, *a.* REPELLER, *n.* REPELLING, *p. a.* v. V. 1. मागें घालणारा-सारणारा-लोटणारा-&c. बारण-प्रतिसारण-&c. कर्त्ता-कारी-&c. प्रतिसारक, निवारक, प्रतिघाती.

REPELLING, *n.* v. V. 1. मागें घालणें *n.* मागें सारणें *n.* &c. हटवणें *n.* &c. वारण *n.* निवारण *n.* प्रतिसारण *n.*

To REPENT, *v. n. be the subject of regret or remorse.* पस्तावणें, पस्तावा *m.*-पश्चात्ताप *m.*-अनुताप *m.*-&c. पावणें, पस्तावीं-पश्चात्तापांत-अनुतापांत-&c. पडणें, पस्तावा *m.*-पश्चात्ताप *m.*-&c. होणें *in. con.* पश्चात्ताप *m.*-&c. करणें, अनुतापणें, तोबातोबा *f. or adv.*-शिवशिव *n.* करणें-बोलणें, कानाला खडा *m.* लावणें-लावून घेणें, कान *m.* पिळून घेणें.

2 *change the mind.* मन *n.*-बुद्धि *f.*-&c. पालटणें-फिरवणें, मन *n.*-बुद्धि *f.*-&c. पालटणें-फिरणें-बदलणें *g. of s.*

To REPENT, *v. a.* पश्चात्ताप *m.*-खेद *m.*-&c. करणें *or with in. con.* होणें *with* विषयीं *of o.*

REPENTANCE, *n.* v. V. N. 1. पश्चात्ताप *pop.* पस्तावा *or* प्रस्तावा*m.* पस्तावणी *f.* अनुताप *m.* मनस्ताप *m.* दुष्कृतखेद *m.* पश्चात्तापबुद्धि *f.* अनुतापबुद्धि *f.* अनुशय *m.* अनुशोक *m.* अनुशोचन *n.* विप्रतीसार *m.*

REPENTANT, *a.* REPENTER, *n.* REPENTING, *p. a.* v.V. N.1. पश्चात्ताप पावणारा *or* पावलेला, &c. पश्चात्तापी, अनुतापी, अनुतप्त, पश्चात्तापयुक्त, पश्चात्तापान्वित, अनुशयी, दुष्कृतस्मृतिपीडित, जातखेद, जातानुशोक, पापस्मृतिपीडित, पश्चात्तापबुद्धि, अनुतापबुद्धि. [तिहृति *f.*

REPERCUSSION, *n. driving back.* उलटविणें *n.* प्रतिसारण *n.* प्र-

REPERTORY. See MAGAZINE.

To REPERUSE, *n. read over again.* दुसऱ्यानें-&c. वाचणें, पुनरावृत्ति *f.* करणें *g. of o.*

REPETITION, *n.* v. V. 1.—*act.* फिरून करणें *n.* दुसऱ्यानें करणें *n.* &c. दुसारणें *n.* दुहारणें *n.* दुसारणी *f.* दुसरी आवृत्ति *f.* पुनरावृत्ति *f.* द्विरावृत्ति *f.* पुनरावर्त्तन*n.* आवर्त्तन*n.* आवृत्ति *f.* पौनःपुन्य*n.*

2 फिरून बोलणें *n.* दुसऱ्यानें बोलणें *n.* &c. पुनरुक्ति *f.* पुनःकथन *n.* पुनर्वचन *n.* द्विरुक्ति *f.* पौनरुक्त्य *n.* अनुलाप *m.* मुहुर्भाषा *f.* अनुवाद *m.* आम्रेडित *n.* आम्रेडन *n.*

3 म्हणणें *n.* म्हणणी *f.* पठन *n.* अनुवाद *m.*

4 दुसऱ्याजवळ बोलणें *n.* &c. अनुवाद *m.*

To REPINE, *v. n. grieve at,* v. To FRET, To COMPLAIN. चुरमुरणें, चुळमुळणें, मनांत कुडणें *or* कुढणें-झुरणें-चिडचिडणें-विरपि-

रणें-धुसमुसणें, खंत *f*. धरणें-घेणें. [पिरपीर *f*.

REPINING, *n*. v. V. चुरमुरणें *n*. &c. चुरमूर *f*. चुळमूळ *f*. खंत *f*.

REPINING, *a*. *disposed to complain*. चिडचिड्या, पिरपिरा, पिरपिऱ्या, खंती.

To REPLACE, *v.a*. *put again in its place*. आपल्या जागीं-स्थळीं-स्थानावर-&c. फिरून-&c. ठेवणें, पुनराधान *n*.-पुनःस्थापन *n*.-पुनःस्थापना *f*. करणें *g*. *of o*.

2 *supply the place of by a substitute*. डागास डाग-नगास नग-वस्तूस वस्तु-&c.देऊन भरून देणें, बदला देणें.

To REPLENISH, *v*. *a*. See To FILL.

2 *fill again*. फिरून-पुन्हा-पुनः-मातृक्यान-&c. भरणें-पूर्ण करणें.

REPLETE, *a*. v. FULL. पूर्ण, परिपूर्ण, पर्याप्त.

REPLETION, *n*. v. A. पूर्णता *f*. परिपूर्णता *f*. पर्याप्ति *f*.

1. *fullness of blood*. रक्तबाहुल्य *n*. रक्तवृद्धि *f*.

REPLICATION. See ANSWER. 2 See REJOINDER.

To REPLY, *v*. *n*. v. To ANSWER. उत्तर *n*.-जबाब *or* जाब *m*.-&c. देणें-करणें.

To r. flatly, smack, &c. फडका *m*. फाडणें-फाडून देणें.

2—in Law; उत्तरालाप्रत्युत्तर *n*. देणें.

REPLY, *n*. v. ANSWER. उत्तर *n*. प्रत्युत्तर *n*. जवाब *or* जाब *m*.

Ready at r. जाबसाली. [*f*.) कोटि *f*.

2—in disputations. प्रत्युत्तर *n*. कक्षा *f*. (*corruptly* आकांक्षा

REPORT, *n*. *account returned*. वाका *m*. हकिकत *f*. कैफियत *f*. रपोट *m*. from the English word is common.

Reports or advices of emissaries at foreign courts. अखबार *pop*. अकबर *f*.

Written r. हकिकतनामा *m*. वर्त्तमानलेख *m*.

2 (of guns, &c.) *sound*, v. NOISE. बार *m*. *v*. सोड, उड, आवाज *m*. शब्द *m*.

Loud r. धडाका *m*.

3 *repute, character*, v. REPUTATION. नांव*n*. नाम *n*. कीर्त्ति *f*. लौकिक *m*. आबरू *f*.

Good r. कीर्त्ति *f*. भलाई *f*. भलीभलाई *f*. *v*. मिळ, मिळव.

Ill r. कुकीर्त्ति *f*. कीर्त्तवडा *m*.

4 *bruit, rumour, general talk*. बातमी *f*. अवई *or* आवई *f*. गप *or* गप्प *f*. भुमका *m*. भुमकी *f*. अफवा *f*. बोलवा *m*. *f*. सांगासांगी *or* सांगोसांगी *f*. हाक *f*. बका *f*. *pl*. प्रवाद *m*. वाद *m*. उपश्रुति *f*. वदंता *f*. वदंती *f*. किंवदंती *f*. वार्त्ता *f*. गाजावाजा*m*. जनवदंती *f*. जनवार्त्ता *f*. जनवाद *m*. जनरव *m*. जनश्रुति *f*. लोकप्रवाद *m*. आख्या *f*. चर्चा *f*. ध्वनि *f*. उद्घोष *m*. कानकूण *f*.

False r. v. FABRICATION. कंडी *f*. कंडाळी *f*. नीळरांप *f*. *m*.

Flying r. हूक *f*.

Idle reports. कोरड्या गाथा *f*. *pl*. झोंकली बातमी *f*. बाजार बातमी *f*. बाजार अफवा *f*. बाजार अवाई *or* अवई *f*. चवळी *f*. *v*. निघ, उठ, चिलमी खबर *or* बातमी *f*.

To spread idle reports. गपा *f*. *pl*. झोंकणें, बाता *f*. *pl*. उडवणें-फेंकणें-हाकणें.

To spread a r. बातमी*f*.फुंकणें *or* फोंकणें-पेरणें.

The r. is worse than the reality. तवई पुरवती अवई पुरवत नाहीं *or* तवईपेक्षां अवई कठीण.

5—in law; *record of a decision*. निवाडपत्र *n*.

To REPORT, *v*. *a*. *give an official account or statement of*. वाका *m*.-हकिकत *f*.-&c. सांगणें-लिहणें-पाठवणें, रपोट*m*.करणें*g*. *of o*.

2 *relate, &c*. v. To TELL. सांगणें, बोलणें, कळवणें, सुनावणें, जाहीर-&c. करणें.

To be reported, *be the subject of general talk*. वाजणें.

REPORTER, *n*. *intelligencer at foreign courts*. अखबारनवीस *or* नीस *or* अकबरनवीस *or* नीस, वार्त्तिक.

2 (of a Newspaper, &c.) वर्त्तमानपत्राचा-&c. बातमीदार, वार्त्ताहर, वार्त्तिक.

To REPOSE, *v*. *n*. *sleep, rest, lie*. निजणें, आंग *n*. टाकणें, लवंडणें, आराम *m*. करणें-घेणें, विश्रामणें, शय्या *f*.-शयन *n*.-&c. करणें.

2 *rest in confidence*, v. To CONFIDE. भरवसा *m*.-विश्वास *m*. ठेवणें, टेंकणें, ओठंगणें, पातणें.

To REPOSE, *v*. *a*. See To REST. 2 See To PLACE.

REPOSE, *n*. v. REST. आराम *m*. विश्राम *m*. विश्रांति *f*. विश्रामा *m*.

To REPOSIT, *v.a*. *lay up for safety or preservation*,v.To LAY. रक्षणास-रक्षणार्थ-संरक्षणार्थ-&c. ठेवणें, जतनेस ठेवणें-घालणें, ठेवणें, घालणें, न्यास *m*.-&c. करणें, न्यस्त करणें.

2 *lay up*, v. To STORE. सांठवणें, सांचवणें, सांठवण *f*.-&c. करणें *g*. *of o*.

REPOSITED, *p*. v. V. 1. रक्षणास ठेवलेला-घातलेला, न्यस्त.

2 सांठवलेला.

REPOSITORY, *n*. v. STORE-HOUSE. सांठवण *n*. निधि*m*. निधान *n*. (esp. in comp. as गुणनिधान, दयानिधान, पुण्यनिधान, पापनिधान).

To REPREHEND, &c. See To BLAME, To REPROVE, &c.

REPREHENSIBLE, *a*. v. BLAMABLE. दूषणीय, दूष्य, दूषणार्ह.

To REPRESENT, *v*. *a*. *show, exhibit, &c*. दाखवणें, दर्शिवणें, दर्शन *n*.-प्रदर्शन *n*.-&c. करणें *g*. *of o*.

2 v. To DESCRIBE. वर्णणें, वर्णन *n*. करणें *g*. *of o*.

3 *state respectfully*, v. To TELL. सांगणें, विज्ञापणें, अर्ज *m*. करणें, निवेदणें, निवेदन *n*.-विज्ञापना *f*.-&c. करणें.

4 (a character, &c.) v. To PERSONATE, To ACT. सोंग*n*.-वेष *m*.-&c. घेणें-धारण करणें *g*. *of o*. बनाविणें.

5 *act for vicariously,stand for*.स्थानीं-जागीं-स्थळीं-बारचा-&c. वकील-प्रतिनिधि-&c. असणें *g*. *of o*. [दर्शन *n*.

REPRESENTATION, *n*. v. V. 1.—*act*. दाखवणें *n*. &c. दर्शन *n*. प्र-

2 वर्णणें *n*. वर्णन *n*.

3 सांगणें *n*. अर्ज करणें *n*. निवेदन *n*. अर्ज *m*. विनंती *f*. विज्ञापना *f*. विज्ञप्ति *f*. आवेदन *n*. वेदना *f*. उपपादन *n*. उपन्यास *m*.

4 सोंग *n*. संपादणी *f*. बतावणी *f*.

5 वकिली *f*. प्रतिनिधित्व *n*.

I. *matter represented*. अर्ज *m*. अर्जी *f*. विज्ञापना *f*. करिणा *m*. याद *f*. यादी *f*.

II. *image, semblance, &c*. v. LIKENESS. प्रतिमा *f*. प्रतिरूप *n*. प्रतिकृति *f*. प्रतिनिधि *m*. प्रतिबिंब *n*.

III. *delineation*, v. SKETCH. नमुना *m*. नकाशा *m*.

REPRESENTATIVE, *n*. *one who stands or acts for another*. प्रतिनिधि, वकील, बारचा, बांटचा.

REPRESENTATIVELY, *adv*. *as a representative*; *in the character of another*. अंगत्वानें,अंगत्वें*or*अंगत्वें करून*g*. *of o*. होत्सातां.

REPRESENTED, *p*. v. V. 1. दाखवलेला, दर्शिवलेला, दर्शित, प्रदर्शित.

2 वर्णिलेला, वर्णित. [उपन्यस्त.

3 सांगितलेला, &c. निवेदित, विज्ञापित, विज्ञप्त, वेदित, उपपादित,

To REPRESS, *v*. *a*. v. To RESTRAIN, To SUBDUE. दाबणें, द-

थविणें, दडपणें, दाब m.-दाबादाबी f.-निग्रह m.-निग्रहण n.-&c. करणें g. of o. छुकू interj. करणें-म्हणणें.

REPRESSED, p. v. V. दाबलेला, दडपलेला, &c. पराहत, निगृहीत, जातनिग्रह.

REPRESSER, n. REPRESSING, p. a. REPRESSIVE, a. v. V. दाबणारा, दाब करणारा, &c. दाबाचा-&c. निग्रह-&c. कर्त्ता-कारी, निग्रहीता.

REPRESSION, n. v. V. दाबणें n. &c.

Sense or feeling of r. दबाव m. दबदबा m.

REPRIEVE, n. *temporary suspension of punishment.* शिक्षेची-पारिपत्याची-&c. तहकुबी f.-महकुबी f. शिक्षाविलंबन n. दंडनविलंबन n. दंडनकालांतरनयन n.

To REPRIEVE, v. a. v. N. शिक्षेची-&c. तहकुबी f.-महकुबी f. करणें, शिक्षाविलंबन n.-दंडविलंबन n. करणें.

2 See To RESPITE.

To REPRIMAND, v. a. v. To REPROVE, To SCOLD. तोंडची शिक्षा f.-शब्दमार m.-शब्दताडन n.-मुखदंडन n.-मुखदंड m.-धिग्दंड m.-वाग्दंड m.-&c. करणें, धमकी f.-&c. देणें.

REPRIMAND, n. v. REPROOF. शब्दमार m. तोंडची शिक्षा f. वाग्दंड m. धिग्दंड m. मुखदंड m. मुखदंडन n. शब्दताडन n.

REPRISAL, n. *retaliation on an enemy.* प्रत्यपकार m. प्रतिपीडन n. प्रत्यपहार m. प्रतिहरण n. बदला n. v. घे.

REPROACH, n. *contumelious language, obloquy, &c.* v. ABUSE. निंदा f. जुगुप्सा f. गर्हा f. परुषोक्ति f. परुषवचन n. कुत्सा f. अपवाद m.

2 See SHAME. 3 *object of scorn, &c.* निंदास्पद, निंदेसपात्रn.

To REPROACH, v. a. *upbraid*, v. To BLAME, To ABUSE. निंदणें n. निंदा f.-गर्हा f.-कुत्सा f.-&c. करणें g. of o. नाकांत काड्या f. pl. घालणें, दोष m.-ठपका m. आणणें-ठेवणें, तोंडीं काढणें, ओठावणें.

To r. one's self. आपल्या जिवाला खाणें-खाऊन घेणें.

REPROACHFUL, a. *scurrilous, &c.* v. ABUSIVE, OPPROBRIOUS. निंदेचा, गर्हेचा, निंदात्मक, निंदामय, निंदारूप, कुत्सात्मक, गर्हात्मक. 2 v. SHAMEFUL. लाजिरवाणा, इजतघेणा, आब्रूघेणा, निंदाप्रद, लज्जाप्रद. [र्वक, &c.

REPROACHFULLY, adv. v. A. 1. निंदेनें, &c. निंदाकरून, निंदापू-

REPROBATE, a. *abandoned, graceless*, v. SHAMELESS. देवाधर्मानें टाकलेला, मुलखानें सोडलेला, देवाधर्मानें ओवाळलेला, निसवलेला, त्यक्तधर्म, धर्मबाह्य, देवत्यक्त, माणसांतून उठलेला.

REPROBATE, n. See the words under the adjective.

To REPROBATE, v. a. *disapprove utterly*, v. To ABHOR, To REJECT. फारच नापसंत करणें-नामंजूर करणें-&c. नाकारणें, निंदणें, थुकारणें or थुकरणें, ओकारणें.

REPROBATED, p. v. V. फारच नापसंत केलेला, &c. अस्वीकृत, अनंगीकृत.

REPROBATION, n. v. V.—*act.* नापसंत करणें n. नाकारणें n. &c. अस्वीकार m. अस्वीकरण n. अनंगीकार m. अनंगीकरण n.

REPROOF, n. *reprimand, rebuke.* बोल m. शब्द m. शब्दमार m. तोंडची नसिहत f. तोंडची शिक्षा f. वाग्दंड m. मुखदंड m. धिग्दंड m. मुखदंडन n. मुखताडन n. शब्दप्रहार m.

To REPROVE, v. a. *censure*, v. To BLAME. बोलणें, बोल m. लावणें, शब्द m. लावणें-ठेवणें, ठपका m. आणणें-ठेवणें, निंदा f.-&c. करणें.

2 *chide, reprimand, &c.* v. To SCOLD. तोंडची शिक्षा f.-नसिहत f. करणें, शब्दाचा मारm.-शब्दमार m.-वाग्दंड m.-मुखदंडm.-धिग्दंड m.-&c. करणें.—continually, crabbedly, &c. as expressed by the verbs, *to nag, to peck at, to be ever finding fault, &c.* किरकिरणें, किरकीर f.-घसघस f.-घिसघीस f.-जिकीर f.-जिगजीग f.-टकटक f.-कटकट f.-&c. करणें.

REPROVER, n. REPROVING, p. a. v. V. 1. बोलणारा, बोल लावणारा, ठपका ठेवणारा, &c. बोललाव्या.

2 तोंडची शिक्षा करणारा, शब्दाचा मार करणारा, वाग्दंड-मुखदंड-धिग्दंड-&c. कर्त्ता-कारी.

REPTILE, a. सरपटत चालणारा, उरोगामी.

2 *grovelling*, v. LOW. पाजी, जघन्य.

REPTILE, n. जिवडा m. किडा m. किडूक n. किडें n. पायाखालचा जीव or पायाखालचा m.

Bite, sting, &c. of a r. पायाखालचें n.

REPUBLIC, n. *government by the people.* लोकसत्ताकराज्य n. लोककर्तृकप्रभुत्व n. लोकाधिपत्य n. साधारणजनकर्तृकराज्यn. बहुनायकी f.

REPUBLICAN, a. v. N. लोकाधिपत्याचा, बहुनायकीचा, लोककर्तृकप्रभुत्वाचा, &c. साधारणजनकर्तृकराज्यसंबंधी-विषयक, &c. लोककर्तृकप्रभुत्वसंबंधी-विषयक, &c. [&c.

REPUBLICAN, n.—a person. लोककर्तृकप्रभुत्ववादी-प्रवर्त्तक-पक्षपाती-

To REPUDIATE, v. a. v. To REJECT. नाकारणें.

2 See To DIVORCE.

REPUGNANCE, REPUGNANCY, n. v. A. 1. वांकडेपणा m. प्रातिकूल्य n. विरोध m. विरोधभाव m.

2 नाखुशी f. कंटाळा m. संकट n. त्रास m. विमति f. विमुखता f.

REPUGNANT, a. *opposite, hostile, contrary*, v. ADVERSE. वांकडा, प्रतिकूल, विरुद्ध, विपरीत.

2 *reluctant*, v. UNWILLING. नाराजी, नाखुश, विमन, विमुख.

REPULSE, n. v. V.—*act.* मागें सारणेंn. हटवणेंn. &c. हटवणूक f. हटवण f. प्रतिसारण n. प्रतिहति f. प्रतिघात m. निवारण n. वारण n.—*state.* हटविलेलेपणा m. &c. निवारितत्व n. प्रतिसारितत्व n.

To REPULSE, v. a. v. To REPEL. मागें-&c. सारणें-घालणें-लोटणें, प्रतिसारण n.-&c. करणें g. of o.

REPULSED, p. v. V. मागें सारलेला-&c. हटविलेला, &c. प्रतिहत, प्रतिसारित, पराहत.

REPULSION, n. *the property of repelling.* प्रतिसारकत्व n. प्रतिसारकगुण m. प्रतिसारकशक्ति f.

REPULSIVE, a. v. REPELLING. प्रतिसारक, निवारक. [अप्रसन्न.

2 v. FORBIDDING. अप्रीतिजनक, अभक्तिजनक, त्रासजनक,

REPUTABILITY, n. v. A. 1. आब्रू f. आब m. इजत f. बोज m. शिष्टाई f. शिष्टाइकी f. मान्यता f. मानमान्यता f.

REPUTABLE, a. *that is in good repute or esteem.* आब्रूचा, प्रतिष्ठेचा, हुरमतीचा, इजतीचा, साखीचा, सतीपतीचा, &c. आब्रूदार, हुरमतदार, हुरमती, प्रतिष्ठित, शिष्ट, भला, शहाजोग, तोलदार, डोईजड, सुरूयात, मातबर, साखबाज, सारोख, संभावित, माननीय, मान्य, आदरणीय.

2 *consistent with reputation, creditable.* आब्रूचा, प्रतिष्ठेचा, इजतीचा, &c. यशदायाजोगा-&c.कीर्तिप्रद-दायक,मानदायक-प्रद.

REPUTE, REPUTATION, n. *credit, honor, good name.* आब्रू or आबरू f. आब m. आबदाब m. हुरमत f. इजत f. भात f. साबका m. प्रतिष्ठा f. गौरव n. नांव n. नांवरूप n. नामोश m. नामो-

आरण n. यश n. साख f. साखी f. सारोसी f. भरम m. पाणी n. बक्कर m. f.

To bring into r. and estimation. नांवारूपास आणणें.

To come into r. and estimation. नांवारूपास येणें.

2 *character by report.* लौकिक m. कीर्त्ति *pop.* कीर्त्त f. प्रसिद्धि f. ख्याति f. नांव n. साचका m.

Good r. सुकीर्त्ति f. सत्कीर्त्ति f. साख f.

Ill r. कुकीर्त्ति f. दुष्कीर्त्ति f. कीर्त्तवडा m. आढ्यता f.

To REPUTE, *v. a. account, hold, regard.* धरणें, मानणें, लेखणें, मोजणें, समजणें, गणणें.

To REQUEST, *v. a.* v. To BEG. प्रार्थणें, मागणें, अर्ज m.-प्रार्थना f.-विनंती f.-&c. करणें.

REQUEST, *n. entreaty, petition.* विनंती f. अर्ज m. अर्जी f. प्रार्थना f. दर्खास्त *or* दर्खास f.

2 *thing asked.* मागणें n. मागितलेला विषय m.-गोष्ट f.-&c.

3 *state of being desired and sought after.* अपेक्षा f. आकांक्षा f. तलब f. इच्छा f. सोस m.

General r. हाकाहाक f. हाकाटा m. हकारा m.

REQUESTED, *p.* v. V. प्रार्थलेला, &c. प्रार्थित.

REQUESTER, *n.* REQUESTING, *p. a.* v. V. प्रार्थणारा, अर्ज-विनंती-&c. करणारा, प्रार्थक.

REQUIEM, *n.* मृतशांत्यर्थ गान n.

To REQUIRE, *v. a. demand, ask as of right and by authority.* सत्तेनें-हक्कानें-सत्तापूर्वक-सत्तेचा *decl.*-&c. मागणें-सांगणें, हुकूम m.-आज्ञा f. करणें-देणें.

2 *need, call for.* अपेक्षा f.-गरज f.-जरुरी f.-दरकार f.-&c. असणें *in. con. with g. of o.* लागणें *in. con.*

3 *take, use, employ or expend in.* लागणें *in. con.* घेणें, खाणें, खाऊन जाणें, घेऊन बसणें, अटवणें, मुरवणें.

REQUIREMENT, REQUISITION, *n.* v. V. 1.—*act.* सत्तेचें मागणें n. हक्काचें मागणें n. मागणें n. मागणी f.

I. *state of being needed and sought after.* अपेक्षा f. गरज f. दरकार f. जरुरी f. इच्छा f. तलब f. आकांक्षा f. अगत्य n.

REQUISITE, *a.* v. NECESSARY. जरुरीचा, अगत्याचा, आकांक्षित, अपेक्षित, आवश्यक.

To be r. लागणें, पाहिजे असणें.

REQUISITE, *n. a necessary thing.* अगत्याची-&c. गोष्ट f.-वस्तु f.-&c. आवश्यकविषय m.

Requisites. साहित्य n. सामग्री f.

REQUISITION. See REQUIREMENT.

REQUITAL, *n.* v. V. फेडणें n. उलट f. फेड f. प्रतिदान n. प्रतिफलन. प्रतिक्रिया f. प्रतिकर्म n. प्रतिकृति f.

To REQUITE, *v. a. return an equivalent, repay.* परत-उलट (in comp.) फेर (in comp.)-&c. करणें-देणें, फेडणें, फेड f.-उलट f.-परत f.-&c. करणें *g. of o.* उसनें n. फेडणें *g. of o.*—in an ill sense, v. To RETALIATE. उसनें घेणें-उगविणें, प्रतिक्रिया f.-प्रतिकर्म n.-&c. करणें—in a good sense. See To REWARD.

REQUITED, *p.* v. V. फेडलेला, &c. प्रतिफलित, प्रतिकृत.

REREWARD. See REAR GUARD.

To RESCIND, &c. See To ABROGATE, &c.

RESCRIPT. See EDICT.

To RESCUE, *v. a. save, deliver.* सोडवणें, सोडणें, उद्धरणें, तारणें, बचाव m.-उद्धार m.-उद्धरण n.-उद्धारगत f.-&c. करणें *g. of o.*

RESCUE, RESCUING, *n.* v. V.—*act.* सोडवणें n. &c. सोडवणूक f. सोडवण f. उद्धरण n. तारण n. त्राण n.—*state.* उद्धार m. उद्धारगत f. सुटका f. बचाव m.

RESCUED, *p.* v. V. सोडवलेला, उद्धृत.

RESCUER, *n.* RESCUING, *p. a.* v. V. सोडवणारा, उद्धरणारा, &c. उद्धारक, उद्धर्त्ता, तारक, त्राता, उद्धार-तारण-&c. कर्त्ता-कारी.

RESEARCH, *n. search, investigation,* v. EXAMINATION. अनुधावन n. गवेषण n. अन्वेषण n. मार्गण n. मीमांसा f. परीष्टि f.

RESEMBLANCE, *n.* v. LIKENESS. सारखेपणा m. सारखवट n. f. सारखवटा m. सादृश्य n. सदृशता f. उपमा f. उपमिति f. औपम्य n. आनुरूप्य n. छाया f.

2 *a r. thing resembling.* उपमा f. उपमिति f. प्रतिमा f. प्रतिमान n. प्रतिभास m. प्रतिरूप n. प्रतिबिंब n. प्रतिनिधि m. प्रतिकृति f. प्रतिछाया f. प्रतिमूर्त्ति f.

To RESEMBLE, *v. a. liken unto.* उपमा f.-तुलना f.-बरोबरी f.-&c. देणें-करणें-सांगणें, उपमणें, तुळणें.

2 *be like.* सारखा-सम-बराबर-&c. असणें, रीतीवर-स्थितीवर-वळणावर जाणें *g. of o.* मोडणीनें मोडणें *g. of o.* चालीनें चालणें *g. of o.*

RESEMBLING. See LIKE.

To RESENT, *v. a. take ill, be offended at.* वाईट मानणें, राग m.-क्रोध m.-&c. येणें *g. of o. with in. con.* वाईट वाटणें *in. con.* मनावर घेणें, मनांत आणणें, संतापणें.

RESENTFUL, *a.* v. MALICIOUS, SPITEFUL. कुन्हेवाईक, कुन्हेदार, अकसी, अकसखोर, कोरबंद.

RESENTMENT, *n.* v. ANGER, MALICE. राग m. संताप m. क्रोध m. द्वेष m. कुन्हा m. चुरस f.

RESERVATION, *n.* v. V. 1.—*act.* ठेवणें n. राखणें n. राखून ठेवणें n. &c.

2 ठेवणें n. राखणें n. &c.

I. *keeping in the mind, withholding from disclosure.* कपटानें मनांत ठेवणें n. अवंढा धरणें n. गुळणी धरणें n.

To speak without r. मन मोकळें करून बोलणें.

To RESERVE, *v. a. keep in store.* ठेवणें, राखणें, राखून ठेवणें, सांठवून ठेवणें, उरविणें, पुढल्या कामासाठीं-पुढल्या खर्चासाठीं-दुसऱ्या वेळेसाठीं-&c. ठेवणें.

2 *keep back.* ठेवणें, राखणें, गरज f. करणें *g. of o.* पोटांत ठेवणें, मागें पाडणें.

RESERVE, *n. stock laid up, store.* राखलेला-ठेवलेला-&c. पदार्थ m.-अंश m.-&c. उपराळा m. पुढल्या खर्चाचा-&c. सांठा m. घरास राखण f.

A reserved or spare article. कोतवाल c.

In r. उपराळ्यास, सांठ्यास.

To lay by as a r. घर n. म्हणून ठेवणें.

2 (of an army). राखून ठेवलेली फौज f.-तुकडी f.-&c. परिग्रह m. प्रतिग्रह m.

3 *restraint, backwardness of behaviour.* संकोच m. पडदा m. आडपडदा m. पडतपोशी f. लाज f. भीड f. भिडस्तपणा m.

2 See RESERVATION.

RESERVED, *a. cold, close.* संकोची, संकोचवृत्ति, आंतल्या गांठीचा, संकोचाचा, संकोचशील, भाषणविमुख, अनालापी, मनाचा खोल, खोल मनाचा, खोल, मखुस, मनचा.

RESERVEDNESS, *n.* v. A. संकोच m. संकोचशीलता f.

RESERVOIR, *n. large basin, &c.* टाकें n. खजिना *or* खजाना m.

सांठवण *n.* हौद *m.* जलाशय *m.* वापी *f.*

2 (of a jet d'eau). सजिना *or* सजाना *m.* हौद *m.*

To RESIDE, *v. n. dwell.* राहणें, वसणें, नांदणें, असणें, घर *n.*-वस्ती *f.*-वास *m.*-&c. करणें.

2 with or together. सहवास *m.* करणें.

RESIDENCE, RESIDING, *n.* v. V. 1. राहणें *n.* नांदणें *n.* नांदणूक *f.* नांदवट *f.* वास *m.* वस्ती *f.* वसित *n.* रहवास *m.* स्थीत *f.* स्थिति *f.* संस्थिति *f.* संस्था *f.* अवस्थिति *f.* निवास *m.* वासन *n.* वास्तव्य *n.* प्रतिष्ठा *f.* अधिष्ठान *n.* अधिष्ठिति *f.* स्थातव्य *n.*

Foreign r. प्रवास *m.*

Permanent r. स्थिरप्रतिष्ठा *f.* स्थावरप्रतिष्ठा *f.*

Temporary r. बिऱ्हाड *n.*

I. *place of abode, dwelling place.* वस्ती *f.* वास *m.* आवास*m.* वसति *f.* वसतिस्थान *n.* घर *n.* मकाण *or* न *n.* ठिकाण *n.* ठिकाणा *m.* अधिष्ठान *n.* अधिष्ठिति *f.* अवस्थिति *f.* निवास *m.* वसन *n.* वास्तु *m. n. pop.* वास्तू *m. f.* डेरा *m.* निलय *n.* भवन *n.* आयतन *n.* निकेतन *n.* मुकाम *m.* (only in letters and as prefixed to the name of the place ; ex. मुकाम मुंबई, मुकाम पुणें),—loosely &c. ठायठिकाणा *m.* ठावठिकाणा *m.*

Changing of r. ठायपालट *m.* ठावपालट *m.* थारेपालट *m.* स्थलांतरकरण *n.* स्थलांतर *n.*

RESIDENT, *a.* RESIDER, *n.* RESIDING, *p. a.* v. V. राहणारा, वसणारा, नांदणारा, &c. वस्ती करणारा, वास-&c. कारी-कर्त्ता-&c. अवस्थित, अधिष्ठित, स्थायी, स्थायिक, वासी, कर & करी (in comp. as पुणेकर, गांवकरी). निवासी (in comp. as मथुरानिवासी, द्वारकानिवासी,), रहिवासी (in comp. as मथुरारहिवासी,&c.), संस्थ (in comp. as भरतखंडसंस्थ, शाल्मलीद्वीपसंस्थ, जलसंस्थ), स्थ (in comp. as गर्भस्थ, &c.).

Temporary r. वस्तीकरू, वसतकरू, आगंतुक.

2 सहवासी.

RESIDENT, *n.* v. A. राहणारा, &c.

An old r. भुम्या, ठिकाणदार.

I. *public minister at a foreign court.* रसिडेंत from the English is used.

RESIDUAL, RESIDUARY, *a.* v. N. उरीचा, बाकीचा, &c. शेषसंबंधी-विषयक.

RESIDUE, *n. that which is left, remainder.* ऊर *f.* उरी *f.* उरलेला-राहिलेला-&c. अंश *m.*-भाग *m.*-&c. बाकी *f.* शेष *m. n.* अवशेष *m.* अवशिष्टांश *m.*

The r. of a substance of which the juice has been sqeezed, sucked, or chewed out. चोथा *or* चोंथा *m.*

To RESIGN, *v. a.* v. To GIVE UP. सोडणें, सोडून देणें, त्यागणें, त्याग *m.*-उत्सर्ग *m.*-उत्सर्जन *n.*-&c. करणें, पाणी देणें *or* सोडणें, कृष्णार्पण *n.* करणें.

To r. formally in writing. राजीनामा *m.*-राजीपत्र *n.*-राजी *f.* देणें-देऊन सोडणें.

To r. a title or claim. सत्तानिवृत्ति *f.*-स्वत्वनिवृत्ति *f.* करणें.

2 *yield or commit in confidence.* सोंपणें, निरवणें, हवाला करणें, अर्पणें, समर्पणें, अर्पण *n.*-समर्पण *n.*-&c. करणें.

RESIGNATION, RESIGNING, *n.* v. V. 1. सोडणें *n.* &c. उत्सर्ग *m.* उत्सर्जन *n.* त्याग *m.* परित्याग *m.*

Written r. राजीनामा *m.* राजीपत्र *n.* राजी *f.*

2 सोंपणें *n.* &c. अर्पण *n.* समर्पण *n.*

I. *submission to the will of God.* मान्यतावृत्ति *f.* संतोषवृत्ति *f.* तितिक्षा *f.* ईश्वरकृत्यसंतोषभावना *f.* ईश्वराज्ञामान्यतावृत्ति *f.*

RESIGNED, *p. and a.* v. V. 1. सोडलेला, राजीनामा देऊन सोडलेला, उत्सर्जित, त्यक्त, परित्यक्त.

2 सोंपलेला, &c. अर्पित, समर्पित.

I. *submissive to the will of God.* ईश्वराज्ञासंतुष्ट, ईश्वराज्ञामान्य, ईश्वरकृत्यसंतुष्ट, ईश्वरसंकल्पाभिमत, तितिक्षु, तितिक्षित.

RESILIENCE. See REBOUND.

RESIN, *n.*—the gum. राल *m. pop.* राळ *f.* सर्ज्जरस *m.* शालनिर्य्यास *m.* यक्षधूप *m.* दधि *n.*

RESINOUS, *a.* राळेचा, राळेच्या गुणाचा, सर्ज्जरसगुणक.

To RESIST, *v. a. act against,* v. To OPPOSE, To COUNTERACT. रेटणें, वारणें, निवारणें, विरोध *m.*-प्रतिकार *m.*-&c. करणें, अडती *f.*-&c. घालणें.

To RESIST, *v. n. not to yield, &c.* v. To HANG BACK. अडणें, अडणूक *f.*-&c. धरणें-घेणें, दाद *f.* न देणें.

RESISTANCE, RESISTING, *n.* v. V. A. अडती *f.* विरोध *m.* निरोध *m.* प्रतिरोध *m.* प्रतियोग *m.* प्रतिबंध *m.* प्रतिकार *m.* प्रतिष्टंभ *m.* प्रतियत्न *m.* प्रत्युपाय *m.*

v. V. N. अडणें *n.* अडणूक *f.* ओढ *f.* ओढण *f. n.*

RESISTER, *n.* RESISTING, *p. a.* v. V. A. विरोध-प्रतिरोध-प्रतिकार-प्रतिबंध-&c. करणारा-कर्त्ता-कारी-&c. विरोधी, प्रतियोगी.

RESISTIBLE, *a.* v. V. A. प्रतिकार-विरोध-&c. करायाजोगा- &c.

RESISTLESS, *a.* v. IRRESISTIBLE. अनिवार्य, अप्रतिकार्य, अनिरोध्य, अप्रतिबध्य, प्रतिकाराशक्य.

RESOLUBLE, *a.* v. SOLUBLE. द्राव्य, द्रावणीय, गालनीय.

RESOLUTE, *a. determined, steady,* v. FIRM. दमदार, हिय्येदार, धिराचा, धीर, अटीचा, धारिष्टवान्, नेटक, नेटदार, नेटाचा, नेटापाटाचा, सुधीर, निग्रही, आग्रही, दृढनिश्चय, स्थिरनिश्चय, वज्रसंकल्पी, दृढसंकल्प, चिकट, चिकट्या, चिवट.

RESOLUTELY, *adv.* v. A. चिकटपणानें, नेटानें, &c. नेट धरून, निग्रह-&c. करून-धरून, साक्षेपानें, साक्षेपधरून, निग्रह-&c. पूर्वक, दृढसंकल्पपूर्वक. [अट *f.*

RESOLUTENESS, *n.* v. RESOLUTION. दम*m.* धैर्य *n.* धीर*m.* नेट *m.*

RESOLUTION, *n. constancy, firmness.* दम*m.* धैर्य*n.* अट*f.* निकर*m.* निग्रह *m.* आग्रह *m.* धीर *m.* धीरता *f.* हुरूम *f.* हिय्या *m.* हिम्मत *f.* धारिष्ट *n.* धारणा *f* निर्भर *m.* निर्बंध *m.* नेट *m.*

2 *resolve, fixed purpose.* निश्चय *m.* ठराव *m.* निर्धार *m.* संकल्प *m.* कल्प *m.* करार *m.* साक्षेप *m.* कृतसंकल्प *m.* कृतनिश्चय *m.*

Firm r. वज्रसंकल्प *m.*

To keep a r. बेतावर बसणें.

3 See SOLUTION. [द्राव्य.

RESOLVABLE, *a.* v. V. A. 1. द्रव करायाजोगा-&c. द्रावणीय,

2 मूलतत्वें निराळीं करायाजोगा-&c.

3 उलगडाया जोगा.-&c.

To RESOLVE, *v. a. dissolve,* v. To MELT. द्रवविणें, द्रव *m.*-रस *m.*-&c. करणें *g. of o.*

2 *separate component parts.* मूलतत्वें *n. pl.* निराळीं-भिन्न-&c. करणें *g. of o.*

3 (doubts, difficulties, &c.) v. To SOLVE, To EXPLAIN. फेडणें, उलगडणें, उलगडा *m.*-&c. करणें *g. of o.*

To RESOLVE, *v. n.* v. TO MELT. द्रवणें, विघरणें, द्रव *m.*-रस *m.*-&c. होणें *g. of s.*

2—a fever, a tumor, &c. जिरणें, जिरणीस पडणें, मुरणें, मरणें, फांकणें, मावळणें.

3 *determine in one's mind.* निश्चय *m.*-संकल्प *m.*-&c. धरणें-करणें, हाल *f.* बांधणें, संकल्पिणें.

Resolve. See Resolution.

Resolved, *p.* v. V. N. 3.—agent. निश्चय धरलेला-केलेला, &c. कृतनिश्चय, कृतसंकल्प.

Resolvent, *n.*—in medicine. द्रावक *m.* द्रावण *n.*

Resonance, *n. resounding.* प्रतिध्वनि *m.* प्रतिध्वनन *n.* प्रतिनाद *m.* अनुनाद *m.*

Resonant, *a.* प्रतिध्वनि-प्रतिनाद-&c. करण्याचा, अनुनादी.

To Resort, *v. n. have recourse.* आश्रयणें, आश्रय *m.* करणें-धरणें *g. of o.* आश्रयण *n.*-सेवन *n.*-सेवा *f.*-&c. करणें, उपाय *m.* करणें-पाहणें, सेवणें.

2 *repair to.* जाणें, येणें, चालणें, जाणें *n.*-येणें *n.* करणें, खेप *f.* घालणें, पैरव *m. f.*-पैरवी *f.* घालणें.

To r. to often, *frequent.* पैरव *f. m.*-पैरवी *f.*-खेपा *f. pl.*-&c. घालणें, येणेंजाणें *n.*-येबाजाबा *m.*-येरझार *f.*-&c. करणें.

Resort, Resorting, *n.* v. V. 1. आश्रय धरणें *n.* आश्रयण *n.* सेवन *n.* सेवा *f.* धांव *f.*

A dernier r. निदानचा उपाय *m.*

2 जाणें *n.* येणें *n.* चालणें *n.* &c.

Oft or frequent r. पैरव *m. f.* पैरवी *f.* येणेंजाणें *n.* जाणें-येणें *n.* येबाजाबा *m.* येरझार *f.* राब *m.* राबता *m.* व्याप *m.*

I. *place frequented, haunt.* बैठक *f.* खेपा घालण्याची-फेरी-टाकण्याची-&c. जागा *f.* बसण्याचा अड्डा *m.* चवाठा *m.*

To Resound, *v. n. echo, ring, &c.*—sound, *or* heaven, &c. from sound घुमणें, घुमघुमणें, दुमदुमणें, दणदणणें, धुनकणें *or* धुनुकणें, गाजणें, घोषणें,—*intens.* दणाणणें, भडाडणें.

To Resound, *v. a.* See To Echo.

Resource, *n. expedient, shift, &c.* उपाय*m.* युक्ति *f.* इलाज *m.* तोड *f.* गति *f.* गत *f.* गत्यंतर *n.* तरणोपाय *m.* उपाव *m.* तजवीज *f.* इलम *m.* हुनर *m. f.* पल्ला *m.* कृप्ति *f.* शकल *f.* सद्गत *f.* सून *n.* ओलंगण *n.*

Last r. *dernier resource.* कडेशेवटचा-निदानचा उपाय *m.* निर्वाणींचा (उपाय *m.*-गति *f.*-वाट *f.*-&c.), चरमकोटि *f.* अगतिकगति *f.*

That has no r. अगतिक.

That has no other r. अनन्यगति *or* अनन्यगतिक.

To Respect, *v. a. relate to.* लागणें, लागू होणें-पडणें, संबंध *m.*-धोरण *n.*-&c. असणें *in. con. with g. of o.*

2 *reverence, regard.* मानणें, आदरणें, आदर *m.*-मान *m.*-सन्मान *m*-&c. करणें-राखणें *g. of o.* बूज *f.*-मीड *f.*-भार *m.*-धोरपणा *m.*-योग्यता *f.*-मान्यता *f.*-स्वरूप *n.*-&c. राखणें-ठेवणें-&c. *g. of o.*

Respect, *n. relation, regard, reference.* संबंध *m.* धोरण *n.* संधान *n.* अपेक्षा *f.* विवक्षा *f.*

With r. to. विषयीं, संबंधीं.

2 *reverence, veneration.* आदर *m.* मीड *f.* अदब *f.* सत्कार *m.* मान *m.* बहुमान *m.* सन्मान *m.* ताजीम *f.* मुरवत *f.* मर्यादा *f.* उजू *f.* अलोलकी *f.* अनुनय *m.* मान्यताबुद्धि *f.* पूज्यत्वबुद्धि *f.* योग्यताबुद्धि *f.*—freely, indef. &c. *regardful feeling, consideration, deference.* मीडभाड *or* भाडमीड *f.* मीडमुरवत *f.* उजूबुजू *f.*

R. of persons. भेददृष्टि *f.* भेदबुद्धि *f.* भेदभाव *m.* रूरयात *f.* वेगळीक *f.*

Respects. सलाम *m. pl.* रामराम *m.* मुजरा *m.*

Interchange of respects. सलामी *f.*

To pay one's respects. दर्शन *n.* घेणें, मुजरा *m.*-सलाम *m. pl.*-&c. करणें-करायाला जाणें.

To treat with r. मर्यादा *f.* राखणें *g. of o.*

3 *view, aspect, bearing point, particular.* विषय *m.* बाबत *f.* गोष्ट *f.* प्रकरण *n.*

In (this, that, &c.) r. (ह्या-त्या-&c.) विषयीं-प्रकरणीं.

Respectability, Respectableness, *n.* v. A. 1. आब्रू *or* आबरू *f.* आब *m.* आबदाब *m.* इजत *f.* हुरमत *f.* शिष्टाई *f.* शिष्टाइकी *f.* प्रतिष्ठा *f.* योग्यता *f.* मान्यता *f.* मानमान्यता *f.* भारदस्ती *f.* गौरव *n.* मातबरी *f.* मोठेपणा *m.* थोरपणा *m.* ठाकुरकी *f.*

Respectable, *a. worthy of respect and esteem.* आब्रूचा, आब्रूदार, इजतीचा, हुरमतीचा, हुरमती, हुरमतदार, मान्य, शिष्ट, प्रतिष्ठित, पेश, भला, आदरणीय, मातबर, तोलदार, डोइंजड, संभावित, माकूल, आर्य, पूजनार्ह.

2 *of moderate excellence.* बरा, बरासा, जमेस धरायाजोगा.

Respected, *p.* v. V. 2. मानलेला, आदरलेला, &c. आदृत, मानित, सन्मानित, प्रतिष्ठित.

Respecter, *n.* Respcting, *p. a.* v. V. 2. आदरणारा, &c. आदर-मान-&c. करणारा, बूज-&c. राखणारा, स्वरूप-&c. ठेवणारा.

He is a r. of no one. तो बापास बाप म्हणायाचा नाहीं.

Respectful, *a. that pays respect, or is marked, &c. by respect.* मर्यादेचा, आदराचा, भिडेचा, &c. मर्यादशीर, मर्यादशील, अदबशीर, आदरयुक्त, समर्याद, सादर, भिडस्त, भिडस्रू *or* स्रारू.

Respectfully, *adv.* v. A. मर्यादेनें, आदरानें, भिडेनें, &c. समर्याद, आदरपूर्वक, आदरपुरस्सर, सादर. [णा *m.* &c.

Respectfulness, *n.* v. A. मर्यादा *f.* मर्यादशीलता *f.* मर्यादशीरप-

Respecting, *prep.* विषयीं.

Respective, *a. relative.* सापेक्ष, ससंबंध.

2 *relating to a particular person or thing,* v. Particular, Own. आपला आपला, आपापला, ज्याचा त्याचा, खास, खासगत, खासगतीचा, खुद, स्वस्व in comp. [चा त्यानें.

Respectively, *adv.* v. A. 2. आपापल्यानें, आपापल्याकडून, ज्या-

Respiration, *To* Respire. See Breathing, To Breath.

Respiratory, *a.* श्वासोश्वासाचा, श्वासोच्छ्वाससंबंधी-विषयक.

Respite, *n. interval of rest,* v. Rest. विसांवा *m.* विराम *m.*

2 *reprieve.* शिक्षेची-दंडाची-&c. तहकुबी *f.*-महकुबी *f.*

To Respite, *v. a.* v. N. 1. विसांवा *m.* देणें-पाडणें, विराम *m.* करणें-पाडणें.

2 शिक्षेची-&c. तहकुबी *f.*-महकुबी *f.* करणें.

Resplendence, Resplendent. See Brightness, Bright.

To Respond. See To Correspond, To Answer.

Respondent, *n.*—in law or disputation. प्रतिवादी, प्रतिपक्षी, उत्तरपक्षी, समाधानपक्षी.

Party, side, cause, &c. of the r. उत्तरपक्ष *m.* प्रतिपक्ष *m.* समाधानपक्ष *m.*

Response, *n.* v. Answer. उत्तर *n.* प्रतिवाक्य *n.*

2—in disputations. समाधान *n.* प्रतिवाद *m.*

3 *oracular answer.* प्रश्न *m.* शकुन *m. n.*

4—in a litany, &c. उत्तरवाक्य *n.*

Responsibility, Responsibleness, *n.* v. A. जबाबदारी *f.* मोसबा *m.* मोसबेदारी *f.* जिम्मा *m.f.* जामिनी *f.* जामिनकी *f.*

R. for the repayment of money. उगवणी *f.*

Responsible, *a. accountable, &c.* v. Answerable. जबाबदार, मोसबेदार, जिम्मेदार.

R. for the repayment of money. उगवणीदार.

Responsive, *a. making answer.* उत्तर-&c. देणारा-करणारा.

2 v. Corresponding. जमणारा,जमाचा, उतरणारा.

Rest, *n. repose, sleep.* आराम *m.* निद्रा *f.* निद्रावस्था *f.* निद्रादशा *f.*

Time of r. निजायाची वेळ *f.*

To lie down to r. निजणें.

2 *cessation of motion or action, quiescence, quiet, stillness.* स्थिरता *f.* निश्चलता *f.* नैश्चल्य*n.* निश्चलभाव*m.* चलनाभाव *m.* व्यापाराभाव *m.* उद्योगाभाव *m.* निर्व्यापारता*f.* निर्व्यापारस्थिति *f.* व्यापारनिवृत्ति *f.* चेष्टानिवृत्ति *f.*

3 *quiet, peace, tranquillity.* सुख *n.* स्वस्थपणा *m.* स्वस्थता *f.* स्वास्थ्य *n.* चैन *n.* समाधान *n.* शांति *f.* शांतता *f.*

To feel at r. सुखास पडणें *in. con.* चैन *n.* पडणें.

4 *cessation of labor.* विसांवा *m.* विसवटा *m.* विश्रांति *f.* विश्राम *m.* विश्रामा *m.* विराम *m.*

5 (as of a lance, &c.). लाग *m.* आधार *m.* नेटावा*m.* घोडा*m.*

6—in music or poetry. यति *f.* लय *m.*

7 *that which is left*, v. Remainder. ऊर *f.* बाकी *f.* शेष *m.*

8 *the others, those not included in a proposition, &c.* बरकड *or* बरकट, दुसरे, राहिलेले, बाकीचे, अवांतर, बरचील, शेष, इतर, इतरविशेष.

To Rest, *v. n. repose, sleep.* निजणें, निद्रा *f.*-आराम *m.* करणें, झोप *f.* घेणें, आडवा होणें, शयन *n.*-शय्या *f.* करणें.

2 *cease from action or motion, be still.* स्थिर-निश्चल-निचेष्ट-&c. होणें, स्थिरावणें, स्थावरणें, थांबणें, पडणें, बसणें, राहणें, व्यापारस्तंभ *m.*-&c. होणें *g. of s.*

3 *be in peace, ease, quiet.* स्वस्थ-सुखी-शांत-&c. असणें,सुख*n.* पावणें-भोगणें, समाधान *n.* पावणें, सुख *n.*-समाधान *n.*-&c. असणें-वाटणें *in. con.* चैन *n.* पडणें *in. con.* सुखास पडणें *in. con.*

4 *cease from labor.* विसवणें *or* विसावणें, विश्रामणें, विसंबणें *or* विसमणें, बिरमणें, विसांवा *m.*-विराम *m.*-&c. पावणें-घेणें-खाणें, बसणें.

5 upon; *lie, lean, &c.* आधार *m.*-आश्रय *m.*-&c. करणें, आधार *m.*-आश्रय *m.*-टेकावा *m.*-नेटावा *m.*-&c. असणें *in. con. with g. of o.* टेंकणें. [टेंकणें, पातणें.

6 on, upon; *rely*, v. To Confide. विश्वास *m.*-&c. ठेवणें,

7 See To Remain. [करणें.

To Rest, *v. a. lay to rest.* निजवणें, स्वस्थ-&c. करणें-होईसा

2 *lay or place on.* बसबणें, ठेवणें, टेंकणें, सोपणें, आधार *m.*-आश्रय *m.*-&c. करणें.

Restful. See Quiet.

Restiff, Restive, *a. stubborn, refractory,&c.*v. Obstinate. अडेल *or* अडील, अडणारा, अडखोर, अडिवाळ, खलेल.

To be r. अडणें, खुटणें. [खय *or* खै *f.*

Restiffness, Restiveness, *n.* v. A. अडेलपणा*m.* &c. खलेली*f.*

Restitution, *n.* v. Restoration. परत देणें*n.* प्रतिदान *n.* परिदान *n.* हृतप्रतिदान *n.* हृतपरिदान *n.*

Restless, *a. sleepless.* झोपे-निजे-&c. बेगळा-निराळा, निद्राहीन-रहित-&c. अनागत निद्र, निद्रात्यक.

2 *agitated, uneasy, unquiet, &c.* शांतीबेगळा-निराळा, समाधाना बेगळा-निराळा, बेआराम, शांतिरहित-शून्य-&c. अशांत, अस्वस्थ, अस्वस्थचित्त, व्यग्र, व्यग्रचित्त, व्याकुल,विव्हल.

3 *fidgety, unquiet.* चुळबुळया, चळबळया *or* चळबळया, बळबळया, चंचल *pop.* चंचळ, तिरतिरा *or* तिरतिऱ्या, अडनड्या.

4—a sick person, &c. चळवळया *or* चळबळया, तळमळया, घालफेल्या, घालमेल्या, चडफड्या, उलाघाल्या, उलढाल्या.

To be r. चळवळणें, तळतळणें, तळमळणें, तगमगणें, चुळबुळणें.

Restlessness, *n.* v. A. 1. निद्राभाव *m.* निद्राराहित्य *n.* निद्राहीनता *f.*

2 असमाधान *n.* अस्वस्थपणा *m.* अस्वास्थ्य *n.* असुख *n.* बेआरामी *f.* शांतिराहित्य *n.* शांतिहीनता *f.* समाधानाभाव *m.* समाधानराहित्य*n.* तळतळ *f.* तळमळ *f.* हळहळ *f.*व्यग्रता *f.* व्याकुलता*f.*

3 चंचलपणा *m.* चपळपणा*m.* &c. उठबसी *or* उठबैस *f.* चळवळ*f.* चुळबूळ *f.* बळवळ *f.* बळका *m.* उठपळ *f.* लटपट *f.* उटेरेंटे *m. pl.* अडमड *f.* अडमडा *m.* चांचल्य *n.* चंचलता *f.*—*intens.* चळवळाट *m.* चुळबुळाट *m.* वळावळ *f.*

4 काहिली *f.* तळमळ *f.* तगमग *f.* चडफड *f.* चळवळ *f.* चळबळ*f.* उलघाल *f.* उलाघाल *f.* उलाढाल *f.* घालफेल *f.* घालमेल *f.* कालाभूल *or* भुली *f.*—*intens.* चडफडाट *m.* तडफडाट *m.* तळतळाट*m.*

Restorable, *a.* v. V. 1. परत द्यायाजोगा-जोगता-&c. परावर्त्त्य, परिदानशक्य, प्रतिदानशक्य, &c.

2 सुधारायाजोगा-जोगता-&c. उजरायाजोगा-&c. पूर्वस्थितीवर आणायाजोगा-&c.

Restoration, *n.* v. V. 1.—*act.* परत देणें *n.* माघारां देणें *n.* परतणें *n.* &c. परिदान *n.* प्रतिदान *n.* हृतपरिदान *n.* हृतप्रतिदान *n.* परावर्त्त *m.* परावृत्ति *f.* प्रत्यर्पण *n.*

2—*act.* सुधारणें *n.* उजरणें *n.* &c. सुधारणी *f.* सुधारणूक *f.* उचल *f.* उद्धार *m.* उद्धरण *n.* जीर्णोद्धार *m.*

3 पुनःस्थापन *n.* पुनःस्थापना *f.* पूर्वस्थितिस्थापन *n.* पूर्वस्थितिस्थापना *f.*

Restorative, *a.* v. Invigorant. बलवर्धक, तेजस्कर.

Restorative, *n.* बलवर्धक- &c. औषध *n.*

To Restore, *v. a. give back.* परत-माघारां-&c. देणें, परतणें, परतवणें, प्रतिदान *n.*-परिदान *n.*-परावर्त्त *m.*-&c. करणें *g. of o.*

2 *bring back to its former state; retrieve, recover, re-establish, &c.* सुधारणें, निटावणें, उजरणें, सावरणें, सुधारणूक *f.*-&c. करणें *g. of o.* उद्धार *m.*-जीर्णोद्धार *m.*-&c. करणें, फिरून-&c. चालवणें-करणें-स्थापणें, पूर्वस्थितीवर-पूर्वरूपास-पूर्वरंगास-पूर्वपदावर-&c. आणणें-स्थापणें, पुनःस्थापना *f.*-&c. करणें *g. of o.* जशाचा तसा-यथापूर्व-यथास्थित-&c. करणें.

3 *bring back.* परत-फिरून-माघारां-&c. आणणें.

4 See To Cure.

To Restrain, *v. a. hold in, back, from, &c. curb, check, repress.* आकळणें, आवरणें, राहविणें, थांबविणें, अटोपणें *or* आटपणें, आवरता-आटपता धरणें, सांखळणें, बंदांत-आळयांत-दाबांत-आटणींत-&c. ठेवणें-राखणें, बांधणें, अटकेंत घालणें, लगामीं धरणें-ठेवणें, आरेखणें, आळा *m.*-आळाबांधा *m.* घालणें-बांधणें, दडपणें, दाबणें, दाब *m.* देणें, आडकाठी *f.*-&c. घालणें, आकलन*n.*-आवरण *n.*-निरोध *m.*-निग्रह *m.*-नियमन *n.*-&c. करणें.

Restrainable, *a.* v. V. आकळायाजोगा-जोगता-&c. आवराया-

जोगा-&c. नियम्य, आकलनीय, आकलनार्ह, आकलनशक्य, &c. निग्रहशक्य, &c. दम्य, दमनीय, निवारणीय.

RESTRAINED, *p.* v. V. आकळलेला, आवरलेला, दाबलेला, &c. आकलित, निगृहीत, नियत, संयत, नियमित, संयमित, नियंत्रित, यंत्रित, दमित, निवारित, निरुद्ध.

RESTRAINER, *n.* RESTRAINING, *p. a.* v. V. आकळणारा, आवरणारा, आटपता धरणारा, &c. आवरक, नियंता, यंता, यंत्री, संयंता, नियामक, निरोधक, आकलन-आवरण-निरोध-नियमन-&c. कर्त्ता-कारी-कारक.

RESTRAINT, RESTRAINING, *n.* v. V.—*act.* आकळणें *n.* आवरणें *n.* आटपणें *n.* &c. आकलन *n.* आवरण *n.* आवर *m.* अडपडदप *f.* दाब *m.* निरोधन *n.* निवारण *m.* निग्रहण *n.* निबंधन *n.* नियमन *n.* संयमन *n.* संयम *m.* यमन *n.* यम*m.* यंत्रण *n.* नियंत्रण*n.* यंत्र *n.*—*state.* अटोप *m.* अटक *f.* आटणी *f.* दाब *m.* निग्रह *m.* अवरोध *m.* उपरोध *m.* निरोध *m.* आरेखा *f.* निबंध *m.* संग्रह *m.* आडकाठी *f.* आळा *m.* आळाबांधा *m.* आळेबंद *m.* मर्यादा *f.* पडदा *m.* कैद *f.* लगाम *m. f.*

To lie under r. आटणींत *or* अटकेंत पडणें-असणें.

I. (of speech, action, &c.) *feeling of repressedness.* भीड *f.* संकोच *m.* दाब *m.* दबाव *m.* पडदा *m.* आडपडदा *m.* उपरोध *m.*

To feel under r. भीड *f.* पडणें-असणें-वाटणें *in. con.* संकोच *m.* वाटणें.

II.—in law. आसेध *m.* (r. or limit of time कालासेध, r. or limitation of place स्थानासेध, r. from departure प्रवासासेध, r. from employment कर्मासेध).

III. *a* r. *a check.* दडपण *n.* आटणी *f.* आडकाठी *f.*

To RESTRICT, *v. a. restrain within certain bounds,* v. To LIMIT. मर्यादा *f.*-हद्द *f.*-इयत्ता *f.*-परिमिति *f.*-&c. करणें-ठेवणें-घालणें, आरेखणें, आरेखा *m.*-आळा *m.*-आळाबांधा *m.*-&c. करणें-घालणें. [सीम, समर्याद.

RESTRICTED, *p.* v. V. मर्यादा केलेला, आळा घातलेला, &c. स-

I.—in grammar;—a word. योगरूढ.

RESTRICTION, *n.* v. V.—*act.* मर्यादा करणें *n.* &c. मर्यादा *f.* आळा *m.* आळाबांधा *m.* इयत्ता *f.* परिमितता *f.* परिमिति *f.*

RESTRICTER, *n.* RESTRICTING, *p. a.* RESTRICTIVE, *a.* v. V. मर्यादा करणारा-&c. इयत्ता करणारा-&c. आळाबांधा घालणारा-&c.

RESTY. See RESTIFF.

To RESULT, *v. n. rise, issue, proceed.* निघणें, होणें, येणें, उत्पन्न-&c. होणें, उद्भवणें, उपजणें, निपजणें, पडणें, फळ *n.*-&c. होणें.

2—in logic. सिद्ध होणें.

3 in ; *issue in; end in.* परिणाम*m.*-शेवट*m.*-निर्गम*m.*-&c. होणें.

RESULT, *n. issue, end, effect, product, &c.* v. CONSEQUENCE. फल *or* फळ *n.* परिणाम *m.* निगम *m.* निर्गम *m.* निष्पन्न *n.* प्रयोग *m.* वासलात *or* द *f.*

2 *inference, deduction,*v. CONCLUSION. सिद्धांत*m.* निश्चितार्थ *m.* घटितार्थ *m.*

RESULTING, *p. a.* v. V. *and* CONSEQUENT. अनुयायी, अनुसारी, प्रयुक्त (in comp. as पापप्रयुक्त दुःख, उपवासप्रयुक्त ज्वर, चौर्यप्रयुक्त दंड, भयप्रयुक्तभक्ति, &c.).

RESUMABLE, *a.* v. V. 1. परत घ्यायाचा-जोगा-जोगता, प्रत्याहरणीय, प्रत्याहाराई, प्रत्याहारयोग्य.

To RESUME, *v. a. take back or again.* परत-माघारां-&c. घेणें, अपहरण *n.*-प्रत्याहार *m.*-प्रत्याहरण *n.*-&c. करणें *g. of o.*

2 *begin again.* फिरून-पुन्हा-पुनः-&c. आरंभिणें-सुरू करणें-चालवणें, पुनःप्रसंग *m.* चालवणें, प्रकृतानुसरण *n.* करणें.

RESUMED, *p.* v. V. 1. परत घेतलेला, अपहृत, प्रत्याहृत, दत्तापहृत. 2 फिरून सुरू केलेला, &c.

RESUMER, *n.* RESUMING, *p. a.* v. V. 1. परत घेणारा, &c. दत्तापहारक, दत्तापहारी, प्रत्याहारी, प्रत्याहारक, प्रत्याहार-&c. कर्त्ता-कारी-&c.

RESUMING, RESUMPTION, *n.* v. V. 1.—*act.* परत घेणें *n.* माघारां घेणें *n.* &c. प्रत्यहार *m.* प्रत्याहरण *n.* अपहरण *n.* दत्तापहार *m.* दत्तापहरण *n.* प्रत्यादान *n.*

RESURRECTION, *n. rising from the grave.* मेलेल्याचें फिरून उठणें *n.* मृतपुनरुत्थान *n.* मृतपुनरुत्थिति *f.* न्यायदिनमृतोत्थान *n.*

To RESUSCITATE, *v. a. revivify, reanimate.* फिरून-&c. जिवंतकरणें-सजीव करणें-चेतवणें, फिरून-&c. जीव *m.* आणणें, चेतवणें, जिवांत जीव *m.* घालणें-आणणें, उज्जीवन *n.*-संजीवन *n.*-प्रतिजीवन *n.*-&c. करणें *g. of o.*

RESUSCITATION, *n.* v. V.—*act.* फिरून जीव आणणें*n.* जिवांत जीव घालणें *n.* &c. उज्जीवन *n.* संजीवन *n.* प्रतिजीवन *n.*

To RETAIL, *v. a. sell in small quantities.* किरकूळ *or* किरकोळ विकणें, फुटकळ विकणें, किरकोळविक्री *f.*-फुटकळविक्री *f.*-&c. करणें *g. of o.* [सांगणें.

2 (idle tales, slander, &c.) दुसऱ्यांपाशीं-बहुतांपाशीं-&c.

RETAIL, RETAILING, *n.* v. V. 1. किरकोळविक्री *f.* फुटकळविक्री *f.* फुटकविक्री *f.* अल्पविक्रय *m.* खंडविक्रय *m.*

By r. किरकूळ *or* किरकोळ, फुटकळ.

RETAILED, *p.* v. V.1 .किरकोळ-फुटकळ विकलेला,&c. किरकोळविक्रीचा, फुटकळविक्रीचा, &c.

RETAILER, *n.* RETAIL-DEALER, *n.* v. V. 1. किरकोळविकणारा, &c. घेवारी, वाणी, फडकरी, फड्या, केवटी, केवट्या, तुटपुंज्या.

To RETAIN, *v. a. not to part with, &c. keep.* ठेवणें, धरणें, राखणें, राहविणें, राहवून-ठेवून-&c. घेणें, न सोडणें, न टाकणें, धरून-&c. असणें-बसणें, मागें पाडणें.

2 *take into pay, hire, engage.* ठेवणें, पदरीं-जवळ-&c. ठेवणें, मुशारा-वेतन-&c. देऊन ठेवणें.

RETAINER, *n.* v. V. 1. ठेवणारा, राखणारा, राहवून घेणारा, &c.

I. *adherent, dependant,*v. FOLLOWER, ATTENDANT. पदरचा माणूस, जवळचा माणूस, आश्रित, जिलीबदार, मुशारखोर, अनुजीवी.

Body of retainers. परिवार *m.*

To RETALIATE, *v. a. return like for like, repay evil for evil.* उलट-परत-&c. करणें-देणें, उलट *f.*-परत *f.*-फेड *f.*-&c. करणें *g. of o.* फेडणें, उसनें घेणें-उगविणें-फेडणें *g. of o.* ओढें *n.*-उटें *n.* काढणें -घेणें-उगविणें *g. of o.* प्रतिकृति *f.*-प्रतिक्रिया *f.*-&c. करणें*g. of o.* प्रतिफल *n.* देणें, वैरप्रतिक्रिया *f.*-&c. करणें.

RETALIATED, *p.* v. V. उलटकेलेला, &c. प्रतिकृत, प्रतिफलित.

RETALIATION, *n.* v. V.—*act.* उलट करणें *n.* उसनें फेडणें *n.* &c. उलट *f.* फेड*f.* प्रतिकृति*f.* प्रतिक्रिया*f.* प्रतिकर्म *n.* प्रतिफल*n.* प्रत्यपकार*m.* प्रतिहिंसा *f.* वैरप्रतिक्रिया *f.* वैरनिर्यातन *n.* वैरशुद्धि *f.*

RETALIATIVE, RETALIATORY, *a.* v.V. उसनें फेडण्याचा, प्रतिकृतीचा, प्रतिक्रियेचा.

To RETARD, *v. a. render slow in progress,* v. To HINDER. मंद-ढिला-हलका-&c. करणें-पाडणें, वेग *m.* उणा-कमी-&c. करणें *g. of o.* मंदता *f.*-&c. आणणें, मंदगति *f.*-&c. करणें-करविणें *g. of o.* वेगरोध *m.*-वेगविभारण *n.*-&c. करणें *g. of o.*

2 See To Delay.

Retardation, Retarding, *n.* v. V. 1.—*act.* वेगरोधm. वेगावरोध *m.* वेगविधारण *n.* वेगसंकोच *m.* गतिरोध *m.* गतिविलंबन *n.*

Retardative, *a.* वेगकमी करणारा, &c. वेगरोधक, गतिरोधक.

Retarded, *p.* v. V. वेग कमी केलेला, &c. वेगरुद्ध, वेगावरुद्ध, रुद्धवेग, अवरुद्धवेग.

Retarder, *n.* Retarding, *p. a.* v. V. 1. वेगकमी करणारा, &c. वेगरोधक, वेगावरोधक, वेगरोध-&c. कर्त्ता-कारी-&c.

To Retch, *v. n. make an effort to vomit.* ओंकारी *f.*-ओकारा*m.*-ओबक *m. f.*-ओ *f.*-डेंडारी *f.*-&c. देणें-काढणें *and in. con.* येणें, तोंडीं काढणें.

Retention, *n.* v. V. 1.—*act.* ठेवणें *n.* धरणें *n.* &c. धारण *n.*

I.—mental, v. Memory. धारणा*f.* धारणाशक्ति *f.* [दृढ.

Retentive, *a.*—memory. धारणेचा, धारणाशक्तिविशिष्ट-युक्त, धड,

Reticence, Reticent. See Silence, Silent.

Reticular, Reticulated, *a. made, &c. of net work.* जाळीदार, जाळीचा. [काम *n.* जाळें *n.*

Reticulation, *n. net-work.* जाळी *f.* जाळीचें काम *n.* जाळीदार-

Reticule, *n.* हातीं धरायाची बायकोची जाळीदार पिशवी *f.*

Retiform. See Reticular.

Retina, *n.* नेत्रदर्पण *n.*

Retinue, *n. attendants of a great person, train.* सवारी *or* स्वारी *f.* जिलीब *f.* लवाजिमा *m.* हशम *f.* डामडौल *m.* इतमाम *m.* खटला *m.* खटलें *n.* परिग्रह *m.* परिवार *m.* तंत्र *n.*

Light r. सडीसवारी *f.*

To Retire, *v. n. retreat, go back.* मागें सरणें, मागें घेणें, हटणें, काढतें-कसरतें घेणें, मागें होणें, माघार *f.* घेणें.

2 *withdraw into privacy or private life.* घरीं बसणें, रोजगार *m.*-सरकारचाकरी*f.*-&c. सोडणें, गृहसन्यास *m.* घेणें, विविक्तवृत्ति *f.* धरणें-सेवणें.

3 *withdraw, go away.* जाणें, उठून जाणें, निघून जाणें.

Retired, *p.* v. V. 1. मागें सरलेला, हटलेला, माघार घेतलेला.

2 घरीं बसलेला, रोजगार सोडलेला.

R. and contemplative life. निवृत्तिमार्ग *m.* निवृत्ति *f.*

I. *sequestered, secret.* आडवळणी, आडवळणाचा, एकांताचा, पडतपोशीचा, विविक्त, विविक्तवासाचा.

A r. spot. आडवळण *n.* एकवसा *m.* [घेणें*n.*&c.

Retirement, *n.* v. V. 1.—*act.* मागें सरणें *n.* हटणें *n.* माघार

2 घरीं बसणें *n.* रोजगार सोडणें *n.* &c. विविक्तवाससेवन *n.* विविक्तवृत्तिसेवन *n.*

I. *private life,* v. Privacy. एकांत *m.* एकांतवास *m.* पडतपोशीचावास *m.* विविक्तवृत्ति *f.*

II. *place of retirement, private abode.* एकांताचें-पडत पोशीचें-&c. स्थल *n.*-स्थान *n.*-&c.

Retiring, *a. not forward or obtrusive.* संकोची, संकोचाचा, संकोचवृत्ति, साभडा *or* साभळा, एकांतप्रिय, एकांतसेवी, विविक्तसेवी.

To Retort, *v. a.* (a censure, charge, &c.) *throw back,* v. To Return. उलटणें, परतणें, उलट-परत-&c. देणें-करणें, उलट *f.*-परतणी *f.*-&c. करणें *g. of o.* प्रतिक्षेप *m.*-प्रतिक्षेपण *n.*-&c. करणें *g. of o.*

To Retort, *v. n. return a censure, charge, &c.* उलटून बोलणें, उलटून गोष्टी *f. pl.* सांगणें, उत्तरास प्रत्युत्तर करणें, प्रत्यपवाद *m.*-&c. करणें.

Retort, *n. a censure, &c. returned.* उलटून सांगितलेली गोष्ट *f.*-&c. उलटजबाब *m.* उलटगोष्ट *f.* फेरजबाब *m.* फेरगोष्ट *f.* फेरपगडी *f.* फेरघोडी *f.* प्रत्यपवाद *n.*

2—in chemistry. वकयंत्र *n.* वक *m.*

Glass r. काचवक यंत्र *n.* [जाणें-येणें.

To Retrace, *v. a.* (one's steps, &c.) v. To Return. परत

To Retract, *v. a. recant,* v. To Recall. फिरवणें, उलटविणें, परतवणें, परत-माघारां-&c. घेणें.

To Retract, *v. n. recall one's words.* बोलणें *n.*-&c. फिरवणें-परतवणें-माघारां घेणें, माघार *f.* घेणें, उलट *f.* खाणें, उक्तास्वीकार *m.*-कथितास्वीकार *m.*-&c. करणें.

Retractation, Retraction, *n.* v. V. बोलणें फिरवणें *n.* &c. उक्तास्वीकार *m.* कथितास्वीकार *m.*

To Retreat, *v. n. retire, go back.* मागें सरणें-जाणें-&c. हटणें, फिरणें, परतणें, उलटणें, पाठमोरा होणें, मागें होणें, माघार *f.* घेणें, काढतें-कसरतें घेणें.

2 *retire to a place of safety.* आश्रय *m.*-आसरा *m.* धरणें.

Retreat, Retreating, *n.* v. V. 1. मागें जाणें *n.* मागें सरणें *n.* मागें होणें *n.*

I. *place of retirement or privacy.* एकांताचें-पडतपोशीचें-एकांतवासाचें-&c. स्थान *n.*-स्थल *n.*-घर *n.*-&c.

To Retrench, *v. a.* (allowances, expenses, &c.). छाटणें, कापणें, तोडणें, काटणें, उणा-कमी-&c. करणें.

To be retrenched. कटणें.

Retrenchment, Retrenching, *n.* v. V.—*act.* छाटणें *n.* कापणें *n.* &c. छाटणी *f.* छाटाछाट *m. f.* छाटाछूट *m. f.* काटकसर *f.*

I. *matter retrenched.* छाट *m.* काटकसर *f.*

Retribution, *n.* v. Requital, Reward. प्रतिफल *n.* प्रतिक्रिया *f.* प्रतिकर्म *n.* प्रतिकृति *f.*

Retributive, Retributory, *a. repaying, requiting.* प्रतिफलाचा, प्रतिक्रियेचा, प्रतिफलप्रद, प्रतिफलदायक.

To Retrieve, &c. See To Restore, &c.

Retrocession, *n. going back.* परत जाणें *n.* परतणें *n.* उलटणें *n.* प्रतिगमन *n.*

Retrograde, *a. going backwards.* परतणारा, उलटणारा, परत जाण्याचा, उलट जाण्याचा, प्रतिगामी, प्रतिगमनाचा, प्रतीप.

2—in astronomy. वक्र, वक्रगति, वक्रगामी.

3 *declining from a better to a worse state.* उलटा, उलट्या क्रमाचा, उतरत्या पायाचा, खचत्यापायाचा, माघारघेण्याचा, अपकर्षाचा, विपरीत गमनाचा, विपरीतगतीचा, प्रतीप.

To Retrograde, *v. n. go or move backward.* परत-माघारां-&c. जाणें-येणें, परतणें, उलटणें, मागल्या पायीं-मागल्या पाउलानें जाणें, प्रतिगमन *n.*-&c. करणें.

2—in astronomy. वक्री येणें-जाणें-असणें.

3 See To Decline, To Degenerate.

Retrogression, *n.* v. V. 1. परत जाणें*n.* परतणें*n.* उलटणें*n.* मागल्यापायीं जाणें*n.* &c. प्रतिगमन*n.* पश्चाद्गमन*n.*

2 वक्रगति *f.*

Retrogressive. See Retrograde.

Retrospect, *n. looking back, view of the past.* मागें पाहणें*n.* मागलें पाहणें*n.* मागल्याचा विचार*m.* मागलाविचार*m.* गतावलोकन *n.* गतकालावलोकन*n.* अनुदर्शन*n.* अनुदृष्टि *f.* अन्ववलोकन*n.* पश्चाद्दर्शन*n.*

RETROSPECTIVE, *a. looking back, taking a view of the past.* मागें पाहणारा-&c. मागला पाहणारा, मागला पाहण्याचा, मागल्या विचाराचा,गतावलोकन-अनुदर्शन*n.*-&c. कर्त्ता-कारी-&c.पश्चाद्दर्शी, गतकालावलोकी.

2 *having reference to what is past.* मागल्यास लागू पडणारा-पडायाचा, मागलाकाळधरणारा, गतकालापेक्षक, गतकालापेक्षी, भूतकालसापेक्ष, गतकालसापेक्ष.

To RETURN, *v. n. come back or again.* परत-माघारां-फिरून-&c. येणें-जाणें, पालटणें, जाऊन येणें, पुनरागमन*n.*-&c. करणें.

2 *turn back.* माघारणें, परतणें, फिरणें, उलटणें, उलटून येणें-जाणें, उलट*m. f.* खाणें, माघार *f.* घेणें,मुरडणें, मागल्यापायींयेणें.

3 See To ANSWER, To RETORT.

To RETURN, *v. a. send back.* परतणें, परतविणें, परत करणें-देणें-&c. माघारां-&c. पाठवणें-देणें-&c. फिरवणें, प्रतिप्रापण*n.* करणें.

2 *give back, repay, &c.* परतणें, परत-पाठीमागें-&c. देणें, बळता देणें, फेडणें, फेड *f.*-प्रतिदान*n.*-&c. करणें.

3 *give in recompense or requital.* फेडणें, उलट *f.*-फेड *f.*-&c. करणें *g. of o.* परत (in comp.)-उलट (in comp.)-फेर (in comp.) -&c. करणें-देणें (as परतमेजमानी करणें to return an entertainment, &c.), प्रतिफल*n.* देणें, प्रतिदान*n.* करणें-देणें, प्रतिकर्म *n.*-&c. करणें.

4 See To REPORT.

RETURN, RETURNING, *n.* v. V. N. 1. परत येणें*n.*परत जाणें*n.* जाउन येणें*n.* &c. पुनरागमन*n.* द्विरागमन*n.* प्रत्यागमन*n.* प्रत्यागम*m.* पुनरावृत्ति *f.* आवृत्ति *f.* परावर्त्तन*n.* परावृत्ति *f.* प्रतिगमन*n.*

Be sharp in your r. मागल्यापायीं ये, मागल्या पावलीं ये.

2 परतणें*n.* उलटणें*n.* उलटून येणें*n.* &c. उलट*m.f.* माघार *f.* फीर *f.* परावर्त्तन*n.* परावृत्ति *f.* प्रतिगमन*n.* प्रत्यावर्त्तन*n.*

v. V. A. 1. परतणें*n.* परत करणें*n.* फिरवणें*n.* &c. परतणी *f.* प्रतिप्रापण*n.*

2 परतणें*n.* परत देणें*n.* परत करणें*n.* &c. परतणी *f.* प्रतिदान*n.*

3 फेडणें*n.* फेड *f.* उलट *f.* प्रतिदान*n.* प्रतिक्रिया *f.* प्रतिकृति *f.* प्रतिकर्म*n.*

I. *a* r. *a return (present-benefit-injury-&c.).* उसनेवाण*n.* घेवाणदेवाण *or* देवाणघेवाण*n.* *Return* as used in comp. is rendered by उलट *or* उलटा (as, r.-abuse उलटी शिवी, r.-blow उलटीबुकी, r.-boat उलटी नाव, r.-cart उलट गाडी, r.-compliments उलटमान, r.-feast उलटमेजवानी, r.-present or gift उलटें दान, r.-visit उलटें दर्शन, *and* उलट अहेर, उलटें उत्तर, उलटा जाबसाल, उलटें पत्र, &c.), परत (as परतमेजमानी, &c.), फेर (as फेरजाब, &c.).

In r. for. बद्दुल, मोबदला.

R.-dinner by a bride-groom's party to the bride and her party. पडभोजन*n.* पडभोज*m.*

II. (of money, labor, &c.). प्राप्ति*f.* उत्पन्न*n.* निष्पन्न*n.* मिळकत *f.* पैदास्त *f.* उपज*m.* लाभ*m.*

III. v. REPORT. हकिकतनामा*m.*

Tabular, &c. r. तक्ता*m.*

A blank r. डोळापत्रक*n.* [गा-&c.

RETURNABLE, *a.* v. V. A. 1. परत करण्याजोगा-&c. परतदेण्याजो-

RETURNED, *p.* v. V. N. 1. परत आलेला, फिरून आलेला, माघारां आलेला, &c. पुनरागत, पुनरायात, निवृत.

2 परतलेला, उलटलेला, &c. परावृत्त, प्रत्यावृत्त.

v. V. A. 1. परतलेला, परत केलेला, माघारां पाठवलेला, &c.

2 परतलेला, परत दिल्हेला, प्रतिदत्त.

3 फेडलेला, &c. प्रतिफलित, प्रतिकृत.

RETURNER, *n.* RETURNING, *p. a.* v.V.N.1. परत येणारा, फिरून-माघारां-&c. येणारा-जाणारा, पुनरागंता.

2 परतणारा, उलटणारा, &c.

v. V. A. 1. परत करणारा, माघारां पाठवणारा, &c.

2 परत देणारा, माघारां देणारा, फेडणारा, &c. प्रतिदान कर्त्ता.

3 फेडणारा, &c. प्रतिदान कर्त्ता, प्रतिफलदाता, प्रतिक्रिया-&c. कर्त्ता-कारी-&c.

RE-UNION, *n. a second union.* पुनर्योग *m.* पुनर्मेलन *n.*

2 See ASSEMBLY. [ज्ञापवणें.

To REVEAL, *v. a.* v. To TELL. सांगणें, फोडणें, बदणें, कळवणें,

2 v. To MANIFEST. उघड-प्रगट-प्रसिद्ध-&c. करणें, प्रकाश *m.*-प्रसिद्धि *f.*-&c. करणें *g. of o.*

REVEALED, *p.* v. V. 1. सांगितलेला, बदलेला, &c. ज्ञापित, ज्ञपित, ज्ञप्त. [प्रस्फुटित.

2 उघड केलेला, प्रगट-प्रसिद्ध-&c. केलेला, आविष्कृत, प्रादुष्कृत,

To be r. आविर्भवणें.

REVEALER, *n.* REVEALING, *p. a.* v. V. 1. सांगणारा, बदणारा, फोडणारा, ज्ञापनकर्त्ता, ज्ञापक.

2 उघड करणारा, &c. प्रकाशक.

To REVEL, *v. n. feast merrily & noisily.* बहर *f. m.* मारणें-उडवणें, धणंगणें, आवगणें, सुसांगणें, पात्रा *f. pl.* नाचवणें, मोंजा *f. pl.* मारणें, दिवाळी *f.*-सण *m.*-दसरा*m.*-धुमश्चक्री *f.*-धुमाळी *f.*-&c. करणें.

REVELATION, REVEALING, *n.* v. V. 1.—*act.* सांगणें *n.* बदणें *n.* &c. बदणूक *f.* ज्ञापन *n.* [प्रकटीकरण *n.*

2 उघड करणें *n.* &c. आविष्करण *n.* प्रादुष्करण *n.* आविर्भवन*n.*

REVELLER, *n.* REVELLING, *p. a.* v. V. बहर मारणारा, दिवाळी करणारा, धुमश्चक्री करणारा, &c.

REVELLING, REVELRY, REVEL-ROUT, *n.* v. V. बहर मारणें *n.* &c. घमशान *n.* घमंडी *f.* घमंड*f.* दिवाळी *f.* बहार*f.* चमचमाट*m.* चंगळ *f.* धुमश्चक्री *f.* धुमाळी *f.* धुमड *f.* धुमाकूळ *f.* धुमाफळी *f.* धूम *f.* रंग *m.* रंगलूट *f.* ख्याली खुशाली *f.*

To REVENGE, *v. a. inflict pain for injury, &c.* सूड *m.* घेणें, दावा *m.*-द्वेष *m.*-वैर *n.*-सूड *m.*-&c. उगवणें-साधणें, उसनें*n.* घेणें-उगवणें-फेडणें *g.of o.* उटें *n.* घेणें-उगवणें-काढणें *g. of o.* वैरप्रतिक्रिया *f.*-वैरशुद्धि *f.*-वैरोद्धार *m.*-&c. करणें, प्रत्यपकार *m.*-प्रतिहिंसा *f.*-&c. करणें.

To threaten to r. मिशांवर ताव *m.* देणें.

REVENGE, *n.* v. V. सूड घेणें *n.* सूड उगवणें *n.* &c. प्रतिफल *n.* प्रतिक्रिया *f.* प्रतीकार *m.* प्रतिहिंसा *f.* वैरप्रतिक्रिया *f.* वैरशुद्धि *f.* वैरोद्धार *m.* वैरनिर्यातन *n.*

An act of r. बढें *or* बडें *n.*

To take r. सूड *m.* घेणें-उगवणें, खबर *f.* घेणें *g. of o.* बढें *or* बडें *n.* घेणें-काढणें-उगवणें.

REVENGED, *p.* v. V. प्रतिकृत.

REVENGEFUL, *a.* v. MALICIOUS. दंशी *pop.* डंसी *or* डंशी, अकसखोर, अकसी, खुनसी, कुढा, कुन्हेवाईक, कुन्हेदार. Some terms for a revengeful person are काळासाप, कृष्णसर्प,डोंब्यानाग, डोंब्यासाप, मुकी मण्यार.

REVENGEFULNESS, *n.* v. A. डंशीपणा *m.* अकसीपणा *m.* खुनसी-

पणा *m.* प्रतिहिंसाबुद्धि *f.* प्रत्यपकारबुद्धि *f.*

REVENGER, *n.* REVENGING, *p. a.* v. V. सूड घेणारा-उगवणारा, दावा उगवणारा, उसनें फेडणारा, वैर साधणारा, &c. प्रतिकारक, प्रतिकार-प्रतिहिंसा-&c. कर्त्ता-कारक-&c.

REVENUE, *n. income, &c.* जमा*f.* जमाबंदी*f.* जमावसूल*m.* वसूल*m.* महसूल*m.* हासील *n.* तहसील *f.* कमाविसी *f.* कमावीस *f.* वासलात *f.* कर*m.* अदा*m.* आय*m.* उत्पन्न*n.*—compreh. or loosely. वसूल वासूल *m.*

Arrears of r. due through a course of years. सनवाद बाकी *or* सनवात बाकी *f.*

Assignment for pay on the r. तनखा*m.* बरात *or* वरात *f.*

Balance due of the r. वसूल बाकी *f.*

Collection of the r. कमावीस *or* कमाविसी *f.* कमाविसदारी *f.* तहसील *f.* मामलत *f.* खोतकी *f.*

Collection of r. due from the ryots. तळाटी *or* ठी *f.*

Collector of r. कमावीसदार, तहसीलदार, वसूलदार, मामलेदार, खोत.

Extra r. खेरीज जमा *f.*

Fixed and regular r. ऐन जमा *f.* ऐन जमाबंदी *f.*

Full r. भरवसूल *m.*

General abstract of r. तरजमा *m.*

Grain-r. वसुली गल्ला *m.*

Gross r. भरजमा *f.* भरवसूल *m.*

Net r. वसुली खेरीज *f.*

Maximum of the r. कमाल *n.*

Of or belonging to the r. महसुली, वसुली.

One employed in collection of r. वसुली *or* वसुल्या.

Remission of r. सूट *f.* एहसान *n.*

R. and disbursements. जमाखर्च *m.*

R. from the soil. काळीचा वसूल *m.* काळीचा पैका *m.*

R.-police. सिबंदी *f.*

R.-survey. पाहणी *f.*

R.-surveyor. पाहणदार *or* पाहणीदार.

R.-survey-report. पहाणखरडा *m.*

Settlement of the r. *assessment of lands, &c.* जमाबंदी *f.*

Shares out of the r. of head-officers. बाबती *f.*

Sum in commutation of r. in kind. तसर *n.*

That has an assignment on the r. बरातदार.

That yields good r. वसुली.

That yields full r. भरवसुली.

The actual or realized r. वसुली जमा *f.*

To collect r. वसूल *m.* करणें.

Some other terms relating more or less closely to *revenue* are इनाम, इस्तावा, कच्चीवहिवाट, कमलावणें, कमाल, खेरीज जमा, खेरीज मक्ता, खोटखेरा, खोतखराबा, गांवनिसबत, चिल्हेर *or* चिल्लर, झाडपट्टी, टकबंदी, तसर, तुसारपट्टी, तोटा पट्टी, भरलावणें, मजरादास्त, सालबंदी, सौस्ता, जारी *or* जारी अम्मल, जारी चिट्ठा.

To REVERBERATE, *v. a. beat back.* परत करणें, माघारविणें, उलटविणें, प्रतिप्रक्षेप *m.*-&c. करणें *g. of o.* प्रतिध्वनन *n.*-प्रतिध्वनि*m.*-प्रतिशब्द *m.*-&c. करणें *g. of o.*

2 See To REFLECT.

To REVERBERATE, *v. n. be beaten back,*—sound &c. परत येणें, उलटून येणें, प्रतिध्वनित-&c. होणें, प्रतिध्वनि*m.*-&c. होणें *g. of s.*

2 v. To RESOUND. गाजणें.

REVERBERATION, *n.* v. V. A. परत करणें *n.* &c. प्रतिप्रक्षेप *m.* प्रतिप्रक्षेपण *n.* प्रतिध्वनन *n.*

v. V. N. 1. *reverberated sound.* प्रतिध्वनि *m.* प्रतिनाद *m.* प्रतिगर्जन *n.* प्रतिगर्जना *f.*

To REVERE, *To* REVERENCE, *v. a. venerate.* पूज्यबुद्धीनें-उपास्यबुद्धीनें-&c. मानणें, आदरणें, उपासणें, बूज *f.*-भीड *f.*-धोरपणा *m.*- आदर *m.*-मान *m.*-&c. राखणें-ठेवणें *g. of o.* भीड *f.* धरणें *g. of o.* आदर *m.*-आदरण *n.*-उपासना *f.*-पुरस्कार *m.*-&c. करणें *g. of o.* शिरसा मानणें, सत्कारणें, वंदणें.

REVERENCE, *n. respect, aweful regard.* भीड *f.* दबदबा *m.* दबाव *m.* पूजाबुद्धि *f.* श्रद्धा *f.* आदर *m.* सत्कार *m.* आदरबुद्धि *f.* उपासनाबुद्धि *f.* मान्यताबुद्धि *f.* पूज्यबुद्धि *f.* उपास्यबुद्धि *f.*

To lose one's r. for. भीड *f.* चेपणें *g. of s.*

With profound r. शिरसा.

Worthy to be regarded with profound r. शिरसा वंद्य-मान्य- धार्य-&c.

2 *act of reverence,* v. OBEISANCE. नमस्कार *m.* कुरनिशात *f.* कुरनीस *f.* सन्नति *f.*

R. with all the members of the body. शिरसाष्टांगनमस्कार *m.* शिरसाष्टांगदंडवत *n.*

Your r., your worship, &c. आपले पाय *m. pl.*, आपले चरण *m. pl.*

REVERENCED, REVERED, *p.* v. V. बूज राखलेला, आदरठेवलेला, &c. आदृत, सम्मानित, सत्कृत, सत्कारित, उपासित.

REVEREND, *a. worthy of reverence.* पूज्य, पूजनीय, पूजार्ह, उपास्य, उपासनीय, भजनीय, आदरणीय, आदर्य, आर्य्य, मान्य, माननीय, नमस्य, श्रद्धेय, बुद्रूख, माकूल.

REVERENT, *a.* REVERENTIAL, *a.* REVERER, *n.* REVERING, *p. a.* v. V. पूज्यबुद्धीनें मानणारा, बूज राखणारा, भीड ठेवणारा, आदरणारा, &c. भिडस्त *or* ळू, भिडस्त, आदर-&c. कर्त्ता-कारी, सादर, आदरयुक्त, आदरबुद्धि, उपासनाबुद्धि, आदरबुद्धीचा, पूज्यबुद्धीचा, &c. श्रद्धालु, श्रद्धधान, वंदनशील.

REVERENTIALLY, REVERENTLY, *adv.* v. A. आदरबुद्धीनें, सत्कारबुद्धीनें, &c. आदरानें, आदरकरून, शिरसा, सादर, डोईचे वाटेनें.

REVERIE, REVERY, *n. irregular musing.* भलतें ध्यान *n.* भलते कडलें ध्यान *n.* विशृंखलध्यान *n.* अप्रकृतध्यान *n.* बुद्धिविलास *m.*

REVERSAL, *n.* v. V. 3.—*act.* उलटवणें *n.* फिरवणें *n.*-&c. परावर्त्त *m.* परावृत्ति *f.*

I. *a reversed decision.* उलटमनसुबी *f.*

To REVERSE, *v. a. turn upside down.* उलटा-पालथा-&c. करणें, उफराटणें, उफराडणें.

2 *make contrary.* उलटवणें, फिरवणें, परतणें, परतविणें, पालटणें, उलटा-उलट-विपरीत &c. करणें-बोलणें-दाखवणें-&c. इकडचातिकडेतिकडचाइकडे-आदिपश्चात्-आदिमग-&c. करणें-ठेवणें-&c. परिवर्त्तन *n.*-व्यत्यय *m.*-&c. करणें *g. of o.*

3 (a sentence, decision, &c.). उलटवणें, उलटणें, फिरवणें, रद्द -&c. करणें, परावर्त्त *m.*-परावृत्ति *f.* करणें *g. of o.*

REVERSE, *a.* REVERSED, *p.* v. V. 1. पालथा, उलटा, उफराटा, उलटापालटा, उलटासुलटा, उलथापालथा, उफराट सुफराट, उफराटा सुफराटा, पालथा केलेला, उलटा केलेला.

2 उलटवलेला, फिरवलेला, &c. उलटा, उफराटा, विरुद्ध, व्यत्यासाचा, विपर्यासाचा, विपर्ययाचा, &c. विपरीत, व्यतिक्रांत, विपर्यस्त,

व्यत्यस्त, परावृत्त, विलोम, प्रतिलोम, वाम, सव्य, अपसव्य, प्रतीप, व्यस्त.

R. order. व्यतिक्रम *m.* व्युत्क्रम *m.*

REVERSE, *n. the contrary, the opposite.* उलटा, उलटापक्ष *m.* विपक्ष *m.* प्रतिपक्ष *m.* प्रतियोगी.

2 *vicissitude*, v. CHANGE. पालट *m.f.* फेर *m.* फेरफार *m.*

3 See MISFORTUNE, ADVERSITY. [वर्त्य.

REVERSIBLE, *a.* v. V. 3. उलटवायाजोगा, फिरवायाजोगा-&c. परा-

REVERSELY, *adv.* v. A. 2. उलटा *decl.* &c. व्यतिक्रमानें, आदिमग, आदिपश्चात्.

REVERSENESS, *n.* v. A. 2. उलटेपणा *m.* &c. उलटाभाव *m.* व्यत्यास *pop.* बेत्यास *m.* व्यत्यय *m.* विपर्यास *m.* विपर्यय *m.* वैपरीत्य *n.* वैलोम्य *n.* व्यतिक्रम *m.* [र *m.*

REVERSION, *n.* See RETURN. 2 *right of succession.* उत्तराधिका-

REVERSIONARY, *a. to be enjoyed in succession to another.* अन्यभोगोत्तरप्राप्य. [परतणें.

To REVERT, *v. n. come or fall back*, v. To RETURN. परत येणें,

To REVIEW, *v. a. look back on.* मागें पाहणें, पश्चाद्दर्शन *n.*-अनुदर्शन *n.*-अनुदृष्टि *f.*-अन्ववलोकन *n.*-&c. करणें.

2 *re-consider, revise, re-examine.* फिरून-पुन्हा-मातूक्यान-&c. पाहणें-विचार *m.* करणें, अनुदृष्टि *f.*-अनुदर्शन *n.*-पुनर्विचार *m.*-&c. करणें *g. of o.* [हणें-करणें.

3 *inspect, examine, &c.* पाहणें, पाहणी *f.* करणें, चौकसी *f.* पा-

4 (a book, &c.). गुणदोष *m. pl.* काढणें, गुणदोषविवेचन *n.*-गुणदोष विचार *m.*-&c. करणें *g. of o.*

REVIEW, REVIEWING, *n.* v. V. 1. मागें पाहणें *n.* पश्चाद्दर्शन *n.* अनुदर्शन *n.* अनुदृष्टि *f.* अन्ववलोकन *n.* सिंहावलोकन *n.*

2 फिरून पाहणें *n.* पुन्हापाहणें *n.* &c. अनुदर्शन *n.* अनुदृष्टि *f.* पश्चाद्दर्शन *n.* पुनर्विचार *m.* पुनर्विवेचन *n.* उलटपाहणी *f.* उलटतपासणी *f.* पुनरावृत्ति *f.* पुनर्दर्शन *n.* पुनर्दृष्टि *f.*

3 पाहणें *n.* पाहणी *f.* चौकशी *f.* [षप्रकाशन *n.*

4 गुणदोष काढणें *n.* गुणदोषविचार *m.* गुणदोष विवेचन *n.* गुणदो-

I. See CRITIQUE. [चक.

REVIEWER, *n.* v. V. 4. ग्रंथाचे गुणदोष काढणारा, ग्रंथगुणदोषविवे-

To REVILE, *v. a.* v. To ABUSE, To CONTEMN. निंदणें, भर्त्सणें, हेटाळणें, कंडणें, निंदा *f.*-कुत्सा *f.*-भर्त्सना *f.*-कुटाळी *f.*-&c. करणें *g. of o.*

REVILED, *p.* v. V. निंदलेला, &c. निंदित, कुत्सित, भर्त्सित, गर्हित.

REVILER, *n.* REVILING, *p. a.* v. V. निंदणारा, &c. भर्त्सक, निंदक, कुत्सक, कुटाळ, कुटाळखोर, निंदाखोर, निंदा-भर्त्सना-&c. कर्ता-कारी-&c.

REVILING, REVILEMENT, *n.* v. V. निंदणें *n.* &c. निंदा *f.* भर्त्सना *f.* कुत्सा *f.* हेटाळणी *f.* हेटाळी *f.* कुचबिंध्या *f. pl.* कुटाळी *f.* कुटाळकी *f.* कुचाळी *f.* कुचोद्य *n.* विकत्थन *n.* आक्रोश *m.* परुषोक्ति *f.* परुषवचन *n.* गालिप्रदान *n.* घृणा *f.*

REVILINGLY, *adv.* v. A. निंदा-&c. करून, हेडसफेडस.

REVISAL, REVISING, *n.* v. V.—*act.* फिरून पाहणें *n.* तपासणी *f.* शोध *m.* शोधन *n.* उलट तपासणी *f.* अनुदृष्टि *f.* अनुदर्शन *n.* पुनःशोध *m.* पुनःशोधन *n.* पुनरावृत्ति *f.*

To REVISE, *v. a. re-examine, look over with care for correction*, v. To REVIEW. फिरून-&c. पाहणें-तपासणें-शोधणें, शोध *m.*-शोधन *n.*-तपासणी *f.*-&c. करणें *g. of o.*

REVIVAL, *n.* v. V. N. 1. जीवधरणें *n.* &c. संजीवन *n.* उज्जीवन *n.* प्रतिजीवन *n.* पुनर्जीवन *n.* पुनःप्राणन *n.*

2 जीवधरणें *n.* सावरणें *n.* &c. पुनरुपस्थिति *f.* पुनःप्रवृत्ति *f.* पुनःसंस्थिति *f.*

To REVIVE, *v. n. return to life.* मरून उठणें-जिवंत होणें, जीव *m.* धरणें, जिवांत जीव *m.* येणें *g. of s.* संजीवन *n.*-उज्जीवन *n.*-प्रतिजीवन *n.*-&c. होणें *g. of s.*

2 *return to vigour, rise from depression, neglect, &c.* जीव *m.* धरणें, जिवांत जीव *m.* येणें *g. of s.* जीव *m.* येणें *in. con.* सावरणें, सावर *m.* घेणें, उचल *f.* खाणें, पाठ *f.* उचलणें, फिरून-&c. जागता-जागरूक-प्रवृत्त-उपस्थित-&c. होणें, पुनरुपस्थिति *f.*-पुनःसंस्थिति *f.*-&c. होणें *g. of s.*

To REVIVE, *v. a. restore to life*, v. To RESUSCITATE. फिरून-&c. जिवंत-सजीव-&c. करणें, जिवांत जीव *m.* घालणें-आणणें, संजीवन *n.*-उज्जीवन-&c. करणें *g. of o.*

2 *raise from depression, recover from neglect, &c.* जीव *m.* आणणें, जिवांत जीव *m.* आणणें-घालणें *g. of o.* उजरणें, उठावणी *f.*-उचल *f.*-&c. करणें *g. of o.* फिरून-&c. जागरूक-उपस्थित-प्रवृत्त-&c. करणें, तेजगी *f.*-जिवटपणा *m.*-&c. आणणें.

To REVIVIFICATE, *To* REVIVIFY, &c. See To REVIVE, &c.

REVOCATION, *n. repeal.* रद्द करणें *n.* फिरवणें *n.*

To REVOKE, *v. a. repeal, recall*, v. To ABROGATE. रद्द करणें, फिरवणें, रहित-&c. करणें.

To REVOLT, *v. n. renounce allegiance, fall away.* अमल *m.*-अधिकार *m.*-शासन *n.*-&c. टाकणें-सोडणें, फिरणें, फितूर *m.*-फितवा *m.* होणें *g. of s.* राजद्रोह *m.*-&c. करणें, फितणें *with* वर, फितूर-फितुरी-&c. होणें, डोईवर *m.*-&c. चढणें, अधिकारत्याग *m.*-&c. करणें.

REVOLT, *n. renunciation of allegiance.* फितूर *m.* फितवा or फितावा *m.* स्वस्वामित्याग *m.* स्वपक्षत्याग *m.* अधिकारत्याग *m.* शासनत्याग *m.*

REVOLTER, *n.* REVOLTING, *p. a.* v. V. फितणारा, फितूर, फितुरी, फुटणारा, स्वस्वामित्यागी, स्वपक्षत्यागी.

I. *shocking the feelings, exciting abhorrence.* त्रासदायक, त्रासोत्पादक, त्रासकारक-जनक-&c. त्रासक.

REVOLUTION, REVOLVING, *n.* v. V. A. 1.—*act.* फिरवणें *n.* आवर्त्तन *n.* आवर्त्त *m.*

2—*act.* घोळणें *n.* मंथणें *n.*&c. घोळ *m.* छान *f.* मंथन or मथन *n.* आलोडन *n.* मनन *n.* आवर्त्तन *n.* ऊहापोह *m.*

v. V. N. फिरणें *n.* &c. परिभ्रमण *n.* भ्रमण *n.* परिवर्त्तन *n.* परिवर्त्त *m.* विवर्त्तन *n.* विवर्त्त *m.* आवृत्ति *f.* आवर्त्तन *n.* आवर्त्त *m.* संभ्रम *m.* घूर्णन *n.*

I. (in a government or state). राज्याचा-राज्यस्थितीचा-&c. पालट *m.*-उलटापालट *m.* or उलथापालथ *m.f.* राज्यक्रांति *f.* राज्यपरिवर्त्तन *n.*

II. (of a planet). गति *f.*

III. (of the heavens). चक्रगति *f.*

REVOLUTIONARY, *a. pertaining, &c. to a revolution in government.* राज्याचे पालटाचा-उलटे पालटाचा-&c. राज्यपरिवर्त्तनसंबंधी, राज्यपरिवर्त्तनविषयक.

To REVOLVE, *v. n. roll or turn round.* फिरणें, भोंवणें, भ्रमणें, परिभ्रमणें, परतणें, परिभ्रमण *n.*-भ्रमण *n.*-&c. करणें-पावणें *and* होणें *with g. of s.* फेरी *f.*-फेरा *m.*-प्रदक्षिणा *f.*-&c. घालणें.

To REVOLVE, *v. a. make to turn round.* फिरवणें, फिरेसा-&c.

करणें, परिभ्रमण n.-&c. करविणें g. of o. आवर्त्तन n.-&c. करणें g. of o.

2 (in the mind) v. To CONSIDER. घोळणें, अरतणें परतणें, मंथणें or मथणें.

REVOLVER, n. REVOLVING, p. a. v. V. N. फिरणारा, &c. भ्रमण-पावणारा, &c. परिवर्त्ती, आवर्त्तमान, विवर्त्तमान, घूर्णित.

I.—the kind of pistol. एक प्रकारचें पुष्कळ बारांचें पिस्तूल आहे.

REVULSION, n. उलट f. पालट m. विपर्यास m.

To REWARD, v. a. *make a present to for something done.* इनाम n.-बक्षीस n.-देणगी f.-पारितोषिक n.-&c. देणें, फल or फळ n.-प्रतिफल n. देणें.

2 *repay, requite, &c.* v. To RECOMPENSE, To RETURN. परत-&c. देणें, उलट f.-प्रतिदान n.-&c. करणें. प्रतिकृति f.-&c. करणें.

REWARD, REWARDING, n. v. V.—*act.* इनाम देणें n. &c.

2 उलट f. प्रतिदान n. प्रतिकृति f. प्रतिक्रिया f. प्रतिफल n.

I. *recompense made.* इनाम n. बक्षीस n. देणगी f.पारितोषिकn.

R. is for work, reaping is to the sower, &c. दळील तो भरील, करील तो पावेल.

RHAPSODICAL, a. v. N. *and* NONSENSICAL. अबद्ध, सर्वाबद्ध, विसंगत, असंबद्ध, अन्योविन्य, अचावचा.

RHAPSODIST, n. *an unconnected speaker or writer.* अबद्धभाषी, असंबद्ध भाषण-असंबद्ध कविता-&c.कर्त्ता.

RHAPSODY, n. *unconnected speech.* अकडंतिकडं n. घटंपटंn. अबद्ध-असंबद्ध-विसंगत-&c. भाषण n.-कविता f.-वाक्य n.

RHETORIC, n. *the art of speaking.* अलंकारविद्या f. अलंकारशास्त्र n. साहित्यशास्त्र n. प्रवचनविद्या f.

RHETORICAL, a. *pertaining, &c. to rhetoric.* अलंकारविद्येचा, अलंकारशास्त्राचा, प्रवचनविद्येचा, अलंकारी, आलंकारिक, अलंकारशास्त्रसंबंधी-विषयक, अलंकाररूप, वाङ्मय.

A r. expression or figure. अलंकार m.

RHETORICIAN, n. *one versed in rhetoric.* अलंकारी, अलंकारशास्त्रज्ञ, अलंकारशास्त्रवेत्ता, प्रवचनपटु.

RHEUM, n.—the serous fluid. रोगपाणी n. पाणी n. श्लेष्मा m.

RHEUMATIC, a. *affected with rheumatism.* वातरोगी, वातग्रस्त, वायुग्रस्त, वाताहत.

2 *pertaining, &c. to rheumatism.* वाईचा, वायूचा,वातरोगाचा, वातरोगसंबंधी, वातरोगविषयक.

R. pains. वायकळा f. pl. [धनुर्वात m.

RHEUMATISM, n. वाई f. वायुm. वातm. वातरोगm. बावडेंn. धावरेंn.

Acute r. फूट f. वातरक्तn. वातगुल्मm.

Chronic r. from dyspepsia. आमवातm. आमवायुm.

R. in the joints. संधिवातm. संधिवायुm. संधिफुटणी f.

Shooting of r. शिलक or शिलीक f. v. भर, निघ, ये, वायकळा f. pl.

To be affected with r. फुटणें.

RHEUMY, a. *affected with rheum.* चिपडा, पिचका.

RHEUMY-EYED, a. चिपड्या डोळ्याचा, पिचक्या डोळ्याचा.

2—a horse. असुद्याळ.

RHINOCEROS, n. गेंडाm. खड्गm.

Horn of the r. खड्गm. n. खड्गपात्रn.

RHOMB, n.—in geometry. विषमचतुरस्रn.

RHOMBIC, a. v. N. विषमचतुरस्र.

RHUBARB, n. *rheum palmatum.* रेवसn. रेवचिनी or रेवाचिनी f.

RHYME, n. *correspondence of sounds in verses.* यमकm.n. अंत्ययमकm. n. अंत्यशब्दसमता f. [चा शब्दm.

3 *a word of sound to answer to another.* यमकm. n. यमका-

3 See POETRY.

Neither r. nor reason. ताळ नाहीं तंत नाहीं.

To RHYME, v.n. *agree in sound.* यमकm.n. होणें-पडणें g.of s.recip. मिळणें, मेळm. पडणें g. of s. recip.

2 *make verses.* कविता f.-कवित्वn.-कवनn.-&c. करणें.

RHYMER. See POET.

RHYTHM, RHYTHMUS, n. *musical measure or time.* तालm. तालबद्धता f. [बंद, तालबद्ध.

RHYTHMICAL, a. *regulated by measure or musical time.* ताल-

RIAL, n.—the coin. रयाळm. [पार्श्वास्थिn.

RIB, n.—in anatomy. फासली or फासोळी or पासोळी f.बरगडीf.

The ribs. पंजरm.

2 (of a leaf, &c.). दांडाm. दांडाराm. हिरकूटn. हीरm.

3 (of an umbrella, &c.). शलाका f.

RIBALD, a. *of obscene speech.* तोंडशिंदळ, तोंडशिनळ, तोंडफटकाळ or फटकळ, तोंडफट्याळ, तोंडाचा फटकळ-अभद्र-शिंदळ-&c. अभद्रभाषी, दुर्मुख, पचकळ.

RIBALDRY, n. *obscene language.* अभद्र-पचकळ-&c. बोलणें n.-भाषण n.-&c. दुरुक्ति f.

RIBAND, RIBBON, n. फीत f. दाल m.

RICE, n.—the grain in the husk. भात n. साळ or साळी f. धान्य n. धान n. शालि m. व्रीहि m.—as husked, तांदूल m. तंडुल m.—as boiled, भात m. ओदन m. n. भक्त m. n. बगर or ओगर m. शाल्योदन m. चरु m. There are many kinds of rice. Some are ओरगल or वरगल, कमोद, काळीसाळ, किंजळ, कुडा, कुदई, कोथिंबरी भात, कोळंबा, खिरसाळ, गजवेल, घुडा or घुड्या, घुड्यावरंगळ, घोंटवेल, घोसालवेल, चिमणसाळ, जिगरें, जिरगा, जिरवेल, जिरेसाळ, जोगें, टांकळ or टांकेसाळ, डामरगा, डोंगरें, तवसाळ, तांबकुडय, तांवसाळ, तुरवें or तुर्यं, दामगा, दोडका, नवधान्य or नवान्न, निणगा, पटण or पटणी, बोडकें भात, राजावळ.

Bits of r. boiled. कणेरा भात m.

Bits among r. after pounding. कणी कोंडाm. कणीकूटn.

Bundle or truss of r.-straw. घाड f. पेंढा m. आयंडा m. माचोंडा m. लाटा m.

Bundle of r.-chaff. भाळी.

Chaff in cleaned r. तुसळ f. n.

Chaff r. तुसळ तांदूळ m. pl. तुसळ करड f.

Clump or tuft of r.-plants. चोंडा m.

Colander for washing r. तांदुळ धुणी रोवळी f.

Division or banked up portion of a r.-field. चोंडाm.

Ear of r. कणशी f.

Ears of r. small but full. खरडा m.

Ears of r. withered. खराचिंब n. जडचिंब n.

Grain of boiled r. शितकण n. शीत m. n.

Grain of unhusked r. भातकण or कूण m. [वंठा m.

Ground for the reception of r.-plants. आरोंठा m. आर-

Ladle for serving out boiled r. मुदाळें n.

Land fit for the culture of r. भातजमीन f. भातशेत n.

Lumped mass of boiled r. डिखळ or डिखूळ n. dim. डिखळी f.

Morsel of dressed r. उंडी f.

Parched r. कुरमुरे m. pl. कुरमुऱ्या f. pl. (or चुरमुरे & चुरमुऱ्या, also मुरमुरे & मुरमुऱ्या) सुदामे m. pl.

Particle of r. झुरकणी f.

Pounder of r.—the person. गोल्या, गोलेवाला.

Powder or fine particles of r. झुर n. झुरण n.

Powder of parched r. कुटा m.

R.-bed or plot. खांचरी f. dim. खांचर n. खोंचर n.

R. boiled dry. बैठा भात m.

R.-cultivator. भातकरी m.

R.-dust. कूट n.

R.-field, r.-grounds, r.-lands. भातशेत n. भुईभाटलें n.

R.-field, field of untransplanted r. आंवण n.

R.-grounds as lying low. खलाटी or ठी f. ओंडण n.

R.-gruel. पेज f. पेजवणी n. पेजपाणी n. उतरवणी n.

R.-gruel soured. कांजी f.—boiled up with flour, chilies, &c. कांजवणी n.

R.-husk. करल n.

R. husked after parboiling. उकडा तांदूळ m.

R.-milk. खीर f. दूधपाक m. क्षीर f. क्षिप्रा f. पायस m. n. लापशी or लाफशी f.

R. once ground or pounded. करड f. करडे तांदूळ m. pl. बगड f. एकसड f.—twice pounded, दुसड f. दुसड तांदूळ m.pl. —thrice pounded, तिसड f. तिसडतांदूळ m. pl.

R. raised by irrigation. पाणसाळ f. पाणसाळीभात n.

R. which has shotten up too rapidly,forming nothing in the ear. वाभळ f.—Thus to shoot up—r. वाभळणें.

R.-plants in the seed plot. शेळ f.

R. plants left untransplanted. काड n.

R.-pounder or pestle. गोल्या m. मुसळ n.

R. pressed and flattened. पोहे m. pl. पृथुक m.

R. and split pulse mixed (boiled or unboiled). खिचडी f.

R. slightly pounded. मुसळकांडे m. pl. मुसळसडे तांदूळ m. pl. भातकांडे तांदूळ m. pl.

R.-straw. भातण or भातेण n. तण n. सरळ f. पराळ n. पेंढा m. पलाल m. n. साळवण or न n.

Shakings of r.-straw. ओंस f. काड n.

Soft & waxy—boiled r. मेणकुटला, मेणगट, मेणचट.

Softness & waxiness of overboiled r. मेणगटी f.

Sproutings or after crop of r. भादवी f.

Stale boiled r. reboiled with spices. तिखमिठा भात m.

Thrashing or treading floor of r. भातखळें n.

Transplantation of r. आवणी f. आविंज f.

Tuft of r. plants as transplanted. आवा m.

Watery—boiled r. पेजट, पेजवरा.

Wet rice grounds. तरी f.

Wild or spontaneous r. देव भात n. नीवार m.

RICH, a. *wealthy, affluent, opulent, &c.* धनवान्, धनवंत, द्रव्यवान्, दौलतदार, दौलतवान्, पैकेवान्, पैकेकरी, पैकेवाला, मातबर, संपत्तिमान्, लक्ष्मीवान्, लक्ष्मीवंत, तोंगल, धनिक, धनी, सधन, बहुधन, धनसंपन्न, धनेश्वर, धनाढ्य, धनत्तर, धनसमृद्ध, धनविपुल, धनबहुल, तळीगार, तळीरामगार, श्रीमान्, श्रीमंत, तालेवार, तालेवंत, दामोदर, संपन्न, उपपन्न, वित्तवान्, अर्थवान्, अर्थान्वित, सार्थ, आढ्य, गब्बर, गब्बू, कोषवान्.

Terms and phrases for *a person extremely rich,* and corresponding to *Crœsus, Plutus, rich as a Jew, a banker, the Lord mayor, &c. rolling in gold, wallowing in wealth, &c.* are कुबेर, जगत्शेट or जगत्शेटीचा नातू, दयाराम मुकुंदासाचा नातू, धालेधन्याचा लेंक, दामोदर, गांडभरू, पावड्यावर पैका ओढणारा or पावडें लावणारा, घडीनें पैसा मोजणारा, कोट्यधीश, लक्षाधीश, लखपति, नवकोटिनारायण, नवलाख्या, परीस, पैसेपूर, पैकेपूर, कोटिध्वज उभारलेला or लावलेला, ज्याच्या घरीं सोन्याचाच धूर निघतो, त्याच्या घरीं लक्ष्मी पाणी भरती.

R. and poor. हालीमवाली m. pl.

R. from birth. गर्भश्रीमंत.

To get r. टेंभा m. पाजळणें g. of s. उखळ m. n. पांढरा or पांढरें होणें g. of s.

2—a dish, diet, &c. रसरसीत, घवघवीत, मसालेदार, पक्वान्नाचा, मिठाईचा, तूपसाखरेचा, घृतप्लुत.

3—land, soil. पिकाचा, मातबर, पिकाळ, पिकाऊ.

4 *abounding in, having plentifully.* आढ्य (esp. in comp. as गुणाढ्य, बलाढ्य, विद्याढ्य, &c.), संपन्न (esp. in comp. as गुणसंपन्न, ज्ञानसंपन्न, &c.), मय in comp. प्रचुर in comp. बहुल in comp. समृद्ध in comp.

5 *showy, splendid, &c.* See FINE.

RICHES, n. *wealth, &c.* धन n. द्रव्य n. संपत्ति f. दौलत f. संपदा f. लक्ष्मी f. ऐवज m. गठडी f. अर्थ m. वित्त n. वित्तविषय m. मालमत्ता f. धनबाहुल्य n. धनसमृद्धि f. धनवैपुल्य n. लक्ष्मेश्वरी f.

Intoxication produced by r. श्रीमद m.

Puffed up by r. मालमस्त.

R. of unrighteousness. पापधन n.

That is blind through the intoxication of r. श्रीमदांध.

Thirst or lust of r. धनाशा f. धनलोभ m.

RICHLY, adv. v. A. 1. बहूतधनानें, बहूतपैसा देऊन, &c. धनसमृद्धिपूर्वक, &c.

4 पुरतेपणीं, पुरेपणीं, पुरा decl. पुरता decl. फार, पुष्कळ.

RICHNESS, n. v. A. 1. धनवंतपणा m. &c. दौलतदारी f. श्रीमंती f. मातबरी f. धनिकता f. सधनता f. धनबाहुल्य n. धनसमृद्धि f. धनवैपुल्य n. धनविपुलता f. धनसंपन्नता f. धनाढ्यता f. &c.

2 रसरसीतपणा m. घवघवीतपणा m. मिष्टता f.

3 मातबरी f.

RICK, n. *stack, &c.* गंज m. dim. गंजी f. ठिकी f. कुंभेरी f. उटी f.

2 (of unthreshed corn). सुडी f. पाथरा m. कातरा m. उड्वी f. उडवें n.

RICKETILY, adv. v. A. डगमग or गां, डगडग or गां, डकांव डकांव, लटपट or टां, लटलट or टां, लडबड or डां.

RICKETINESS, n. v. A. लटपटितपणा m. खिळखिळेपणा m. &c. खिळखिळी f. लडबड f.

RICKETY, a. *feeble or loose in the joints, infirm.* लटपटीत, लडबडीत or लिडबिडीत, डळमळीत, खिळखिळा, खिळखिळीत, डगमगीत, गटगटीत, ढिला, शिथिलसंधि, अदृढ.

To be r. लटपटणें, लटलटणें, लडबडणें or लिडबिडणें, लडबड-लटलट-&c. adv. करणें-हालणें, डकडकणें.

To RID, *v. a. set free, deliver, &c.* सोडवणें, मोकळा-मुक्त करणें, निराळा-वेगळा करणें (as चोरांवेगळा करणें to rid of thieves).
RID, *p.* v. V. सोडवलेला, मोकळा, मुक्त.
To get rid of. टाळणें *or* टाळून टाकणें, वाट *f.* करणें *g. of o.* बाहेर करणें, तागल बाट *f.* करणें-देणें, मोकळा-&c. होणें *with* पासून *of o.*
RIDDANCE, *n.* v. V.—*act.* सोडवणें *n.* सोडवण *f.* सोडवणूक *f.*—*state.* सुटका *f.* मुक्तता *f.* मुक्ति *f.*
RIDDLE, *n. enigma.* उखाणा *m.* आहणा *m.* गूढ *n.* डुमाणें *or* उमाणें *n.* दृष्टकूट *n.* कूटप्रश्न *m.* कूट *n.* प्रह्लिका *f.* प्रहेलिका *f.* Some kinds are बहिर्लापिका, अंतर्लापिका, सर्वतोभद्र.
Riddles; *covert, mysterious language.* अग्रशिखा *f.*
To find out a r. जिंकणें.
2 *coarse sieve.* मोठी चाळण *f.* घोळणा *m.*
To RIDDLE, *v. a. separate with a r.* घोळणें, चाळणें, घोळण *n.* करणें *g. of o.*
2 *make many holes in.* चाळण *f.* करणें *g. of o.*
To RIDE, *v. n. be carried by an animal or in a vehicle.* घोड्यावर-गाडीमध्यें-&c. बसणें *or* बसून जाणें-येणें, सवार होणें, सवारी *f.* करणें.
2 *be borne in or on a fluid.* तरणें, तरंगणें, पोहणें, फिरणें.
3 *to manage a horse.* घोड्यावर-&c. मांड *f.*-मांडी *f.*-आसन *n.* साधणें-ठेवणें, सवारकी *f.* करणें.
4 *take exercise on horseback.* घोड्यावर-घोड्यावर बसून-&c. रपेट *f.*-सहल *f.*-फेर *m.*-&c. करणें-मारणें-करून येणें-मारून येणें.
To RIDE, *v. a.* बसणें *or* बसून जाणें *or with* वर-मध्यें-&c. *of o.*
RIDE, *n. an excursion on horseback.* घोड्यावरची रपेट *f.*-सहेल *f.* फेर *m. v.* मार.
2 *a road for riding.* घोडेरस्ता *m.* घोडेवाट *f.*
RIDER, *n.* v. V. N. 1. *and* HORSEMAN. घोड्यावर-&c. बसणारा, सवार *or* स्वार, सवारी *or* स्वारी, अश्वसादी.
I. *addition to a paper, &c.* पुरवणी *f.*
RIDGE, *n.* (of the back, a mountain, &c.). कणा *m.* दांडा *m.* दंड *or* दांड *m.* रांग *f.*
2 (of a roof). पाटेस *m.*—of a thatched roof. मुगळ *m.*
R. pole. अढें *or* आढें *or* आडें *n.* अढेंपाट *m.* अडोळा *m.*
3—as raised on a plantation, to stop water. कांडोळें *n.* कांडें *n.* दंड *or* दांड *m.* बरबा *m.*
4—in a field, &c. दंड *m.*
RIDICULE, RIDICULING, *n.* v. V. हसें *n.* हशी *f.* ठट्ठा *or* थट्टा *f.* टर *or* टेर *f.* उपहास *m.* परिहास *m.* उपाळी *f.* विटंबना *f.* मस्करी *f.* रेवडी *f.* हुररेवडी *f.* हास्य *n.* प्रहास *m.* उलटीपुजा *f.*
To incur r. हसून घेणें.
To RIDICULE, *v. a. deride, jeer, &c.* हासणें, हसें *n.*-हशी *f.* करणें-मांडणें *g. of o.* उपहासणें, थट्टा *f.*-टेर *f.*-टर *f.*-उपहास *m.*-मस्करी *f.*-बचेरी *f.*-रेवडी *f.*-हुर्र *f.*-हुररेवडी *f.* करणें *g. of o.* गूळखोबरें *n.* करणें, सोंग *n.* करणें *g. of o.*
RIDICULED, *p.* v. V. उपहासलेला, उपहास केलेला, &c. उपहसित, जातोपहास, प्राप्तोपहास, कृतोपहास.
RIDICULER, *n.* RIDICULING, *p. a.* v. V. हसणारा, थट्टा करणारा, उपहास करणारा, &c. उपहासक, उपहासकर्त्ता-&c.
RIDICULOUS, *a. that may justly excite laughter.* हसायाजोगा, उपहास- थट्टा-&c. कराया जोगा-सारखा, उपहास्य, हास्योत्पादक, हास्यजनक, उपहासयोग्य, उपहासार्ह, उपहासविषय, उपहासास्पद.
RIDICULOUSNESS, *n.* v. A. उपहासयोग्यता *f.* उपहासार्हता *f.*
RIDING, *a.*—horse, &c. बसता, सवारीचा, बसायाचा, बसणीचा.
RIDING, *n.* v. V. N. 1. घोड्यावर-&c. बसणें *n.* सवारी *or* स्वारी *f.* अश्वारोहण *n.*
RIDING-HOUSE, RIDING-SCHOOL, *n.* अश्वशाला *f.* अश्वशिक्षाशाला *f.* अश्वारोहणशाला *f.*
RIDING-MASTER, *n.* अश्वशिक्षक, अश्वारोहणशिक्षक.
RIFE, RIFENESS. See PREVALENT, PREVALENCE.
To RIFLE, &c. See To PLUNDER, &c.
RIFF-RAFF, *n.* v. PEOPLE. बाजारबुणगें *n.* निपटारा *m.*
RIFLE, *n.* एक प्रकारची बंदूक आहे.
RIG, *To* RIG. See WANTON, To WANTON.
To RIG, *v. a.* v. *To* EQUIP. सजवणें, सज्ज करणें.
RIGGING, *n.* (of a ship). दोरखंडें *n. pl.*
RIGHT, *a. fit, just, proper.* नीट, ठीक, उजू, बरोबर *or* बराबर, चांगला, योग्य, उचित, वाजवी, लायक, दुरूस्त, शुद्ध, बेश, न्यायाचा, नीतीचा, मार्गाचा, सुधा, यथायोग्य, यथान्याय, यथानीति, यथामार्ग, यथायुक्त, यथोचित, युक्त, युक्तिसार, हिशोबाचा, हिशेबी *or* हिशोबी, शिस्त, शिस्तवार, लाजीम, सुतरा, सुसूत्र, सरल, ऋजू, प्रशस्त, प्रमाण, प्रामाणिक, प्रमाणभूत, न्याय्य, रास्त, समंजस, समुचित, साधु, विहित, हित, यथार्थ, याथार्थिक, समीचीन, तवताक, हलाल, रेखला.
R. and wrong. सव्यापसव्य.
To be r. and proper,—actions. कामावर पडणें, कामास [येणें.
To seem r. unto. उचितास-धर्मास-युक्तीस-&c. येणें *g. of s.*
To set to r. v. To RIGHT. नीट-बराबर-&c. करणें, बंदोबस्त *m.*-बंदोबस्ती *f.* करणें *g. of o.* निटावणें.
2 *true, correct.* खरा, बराबर *or* बरोबर, साच, साचा, सत्य, बास्तविक.
3 *not left.* उजवा, दक्षिण, अपसव्य, अबसव्य, वामेतर.
R. and left. सव्यापसव्य.—gloves, shoes, &c. *or* hands, feet, &c. नरमादी.
To the r. प्रदक्षिण.
Winding to the r.—spiral lines, &c. दक्षिणावर्त्त *or* र्त्ती.
4 *rightly fixed, placed, &c.* सुफराटा, सुलटा, उजू, खरा.
To set r. again. सुफराटणें.
5 *that is on the right hand.* उजव्याहातचा, उजव्याहाताकडचा-हाताकडला-हाताकडील.
RIGHT, *adv.* v. A. 1. *and* RIGHTLY. नीट, ठीक, दुरूस्त, बराबर *or* बरोबर, &c. यथान्याय, यथामार्ग, &c.
R. or wrong. हक्कनाहक्क, हक्कनाक.
2 खरा *decl.* बराबर, यथार्थ, बास्तविक.
I. *in a direct line.* नीट, थेट, धडक, धडका, सडक, ठिकला.
II. *in a great degree,* v. VERY. फारच, अति.
RIGHT, *n.* v. PROPRIETY, JUSTNESS. न्याय *m.* नीति *f.* न्याव *m.* उजूपणा *m.* रास्तपणा *m.* दुरुस्तपणा *m.* दुरूस्ती *f.* लायकी *f.* हिशेब *m.* लाग *m.* औचित्य *n.* न्याय्यता *f.* याथार्थ्य *n.*
Might makes r. फांसा पडेल तो डाव राजा करील तो न्याव.
R. and wrong. न्यायान्याय *m.*
2 *just claim, legal title, &c.* दावा *m.* हक्क *m.* अधिकार *m.* सत्ता *f.* इलाखा *m.* अरुता *f.* मान *m.* दस्त *m. n.* वारसा *m.*
That has r. in or over. सत्तेवाईक.
3 *right side.* उजवीबाजू *f.* उजवें आंग *n.* दक्षिणांग *n.*

4 *redress of wrong, justice.* न्याय*m.* इनसाफ*m.* दाद *f.* न्याव*m.*
5 *that which justly belongs to one.* हक्क*m.n.* हक्कमाल*m.* कानू *f.*
To RIGHT, *v. a. restore to a right position or place.* ठिकाणीं-ठिकाण्यावर-ताळ्यावर-स्थळावर-जाग्यावर-&c. आणणें, सुफराटा-&c. करणें, सुफराटणें. [&c. करणें.
2 *put to rights.* निटावणें, सुधारणें, सुधरणें *or* सुधारणें, नीट-
3 *do justice to.* दाद *f.*-न्याय *m.*-इनसाफ *m.* करणें *g. of o.*
To RIGHT, *v. n. become right.* निटावणें, सुफराटणें.
RIGHT-HAND, *n.* उजवा-&c. हात *m.*- हस्त *m.* [घालणें.
To leave on the r. (an object, on passing it). उजवा
Right hand (man) of a king, &c. उजवीबाजू *f.*
RIGHT-HANDED, *a.* उजखुरा *or* उजखोरा.
RIGHTEOUS, *a.* v. JUST, PIOUS. न्यायी, न्यायनिष्ठ, न्यायपर, नीतिमान्, धर्मपर, धार्मिक, साधु, रास्त.
RIGHTEOUSNESS, *n.* v. A. नेकी *f.* न्यायनिष्ठा *f.* न्यायासक्ति *f.* परनिष्ठता *f.* साधुत्व *n.* नीतिमत्त्व *n.* रास्तपणा *m.*
RIGHTFUL, *a. having a just claim.* दावेदार, दावेकरी, सत्तेचा, सत्तेवाईक, सत्ताधारी, अधिकारी, हक्कदार.
2 *being by right.* हक्काचा, सत्तेचा, हलालाचा, हक्कहलाल.
R. property. हक्कमाल *m.* [नीति, रास्त.
3 *consonant to justice,* v. JUST. न्यायाचा, यथान्याय, यथा-
RIGHTFULLY. See JUSTLY.
RIGHTFULNESS, *n.* v. A. 1. दावेदारी *f.*
3 रास्तपणा *m.* न्याय्यत्व *n.* यथान्यायता *f.* याथार्थ्य *n.*
RIGHTLY, *adv.* v. A. 1. नीट, उजू, बरोबर, &c. न्यायानें, नीतीनें, &c. यथास्थित, यथायोग्य, यथायुक्त, यथान्याय, यथामार्ग, यथोचित, धर्मतः,न्यायतः, सम्यक्, सुसूत्र, ठिकाठीक.
R. or wrongly. हक्कनाहक्क, हक्कनाक.
2 बरोबर *or* बराबर, दुरुस्त, खरा *decl.*
4 उजू, सुफराटा *decl.*
RIGHTNESS, *n.* v. A. 1. उजूपणा *m.* ठीकपणा *m.* दुरुस्तपणा*m.* रास्तपणा *m.* &c. बरोबरी *f.* लायकी *f.* दुरुस्ती *f.* न्याय *m.* नीति *f.* यथान्यायता *f.* न्याय्यत्व *n.* न्यायानुकूल्य *n.* यथार्थता *f.* याथार्थ्य *n.* यथामार्गता *f.* &c.
RIGID, *a.* v. STIFF. ताठ, ताठर.
2 *rigorous, inflexible,* v. SEVERE. करडा, खरमरा *or* खरमन्या, सखूत, जालीम.
3 (account, &c.) *minute, exact.* कौडीनकौडीचा, कौडीकौडीचा, काडीनकाडीचा, काडीकाडीचा, तिळानतिळाचा.
RIGIDITY, RIGIDNESS, *n.* v. A. 1. ताठपणा *m.* ताठरपणा *m.* ताठ *m.* खिळण *f.*
2 करडेपणा *m.* खरमरेपणा *m.* सखूतपणा *m.* जालीमपणा *m.* &c.
RIGIDLY, *adv.* v. A. 2. करडेपणानें, सखूतपणानें, &c. कांहीं न सोडतां, बिनसूट.
3 काडीकाडीचा *decl.* *&c.* तिळतीळ, खड्यानखडा.
RIGMAROLE, *n.* v. NONSENSE. अकडंतिकडं *n.* घटंपटं *n.* झाडेपवाडे *m. pl. v.* दे, लांबलेखा *f.* गडबडगुंडा *m.* गतक *n. v.* लाव.
RIGOUR, *n. sternness, &c.* v. SEVERITY. करडेपणा *m.* खरमरेपणा *m.* सखूतपणा *m.* कठोरपणा *m.* सख्ती *f.* कनका *m.*
2 (as of heat or cold) *intenseness.* कडका *m.* कडाखा *m.* ताठा *m.* ठणका *m.*
3 (in fever). कांटा *m. or* कांटे *m. pl.*
RIGOROUS, *a. stern, strict, rigid,* v. SEVERE. करडा, खरमरा *or* खरमन्या, सखन *or* सखूत, जालीम, कटोर, खपाट्या, उद्यनदंड, उद्यतबाहु. [डी कौडीचा.
2 (account) *exact, minute,* v. RIGID. काडीकाडीचा, कौ-
3 (cold, &c.) *intense.* कडकडीत, कडक, कडाख्याचा.
RIGOROUSLY, *adv.* v. A. 1. करडेपणानें, सखूतपणानें, &c. दया न करतां, कांहीं न सोडतां, बिनसूट.
2 काडीकाडीचा, कौडीकौडीचा, तिळतीळ, खड्यानखडा.
RIGOROUSNESS, *n.* v. A. 1. करडेपणा *m.* खरमरेपणा *m.* सखूनपणा *m.* &c.
3 कडकडीतपणा *m.* कडकपणा *m.* कठीणपणा *m.*
RILL, RILLET, *n. streamlet.* ओघळ *m.* ओहळ *m.* ओहळी *f.* ओळ *f.* ओळी *f.* मुतरी *f.* दोरा *m.* उपळी *f.* उपळ *m.* उमरट *n.* झील *f.* झुतरी *f.*
RIM, *n. border,* v. EDGE. कांठ *m.* किनारा *m.* कोर *f.* कडें *n.*
R.-broken,—a vessel. मुडा, कांठफुटका, कांठमोडा, कांठमोडका.
RIME, *n.* v. HOAR-FROST. तुषार *m.* नीहार *m.*
RIMY, *a.* तुषारमय, नीहारमय.
RIND, *n. skin, bark.* साल *f.* सालपट *n.* त्वचा *f.* चामडें *n.* चर्म *n.*
Having thick r. सालमेंडा.
RING, *n. circle.* कडें *n.* वेढा *m.* चक्कर *n.* चक्र *n.* मंडल *n.* कोंडाळें *n.* गरका *m.* मांदी *f.*
2 (of metal, &c.). कडी *f.* कडें *n.* कुंडल *n.* कटक *m. n.* कडोळें *n.* कडोळी *f.* वलय *n.* वाळा *m.* आटा *m.* हलकी *f.*
R. binding mallets, rammers, &c. मांडळ *f.* वसूं *n.*(*dim.* वसवी *f.*) विडी *f.*
Turning or moveable r. भोवरकडी *f.*
3—as an ornament for the wrist or ancle. तोडा *m.*
4 (finger or toe-ring). अंगठी *f.* वळें *n.* छल्ला *m.* वेढ *n. f.* वेढें *n.* मुदी *f.* मुद्रिका *f.*—for the fore or middle finger or middle toe. जोडवें *n.*
Gem or stone of a r. ठिकडें *n.* ठीक *n.* खडा *m.* नग *m.*
Guard r. पडसळण *n.*
Holy r. worn during religious ceremonies. पवित्र *n.* पवित्रक *n.* पवित्री *f.*
Silver r. for the toe of a child. खटवें *n.* खटूं *n.*
5 *circular discoloration.* आवर्त्त *m.* कडगुळें *n.*
6 *circle of persons, &c.* घेरा *m.* कचोळें *n.* कोंचाळें *n.* मांदी *f.*
7 (of grass, cloth, &c.). निवणें *n.* चुंबळ *or* चुंभळ *f.* आहरा *m.* आरा *m.*
8—at top playing, &c. रंगण *n.*
A hit within the r. रंगण टोला *m.*
9 (as of a bullock turning a mill). भोंवार *f.*
10 (of wire for the nose or ear). वाळी *f.*
11 *sound of a sonorous body.* झणकार *or* रा *m.* झणत्कार*m.*
To RING, *v. a.* (bells, &c.) *cause to ring or sound.* वाजवणें, घणघणावणें, खणखणावणें.
2 (a horse). चकरावर-मंडलावर धरणें, फेरणें, फेरफटका *m.*-फेर *m.* करणें *g. of o.*
To RING, *v. n. sound, &c.* वाजणें, झणझणणें, खणखणणें, घणघणणें, सणसणणें, ठणठणणें, भणभणणें, भिरभिरणें, गोंगणें, गोंगावणें,—*intens.* झणाणणें, खणाणणें, ठणाणणें, भणाणणें.
2—the ear; *tingle, vibrate.* झणझणणें, झणक्या *f. pl.*-झणझ-

ण्या *f. pl.* मारणें, भणभणणें, *intens.* भणाणणें, भिरभिरणें.

3 v. To Resound. दणदणणें *intens.* दणाणणें, घुमणें.

Ring-bolt, *n.* हलकी *f.*

Ring-leader, *n.* v. Leader. पुढाईत, मोहरपी, प्रवर्त्तकाचार्य *m.*

Ring-worm, *n.* दद्रु *m. pop.* दाद *f.* & दादड *m. n.* नायटा *m.* गजकर्ण *n.* चकंदळ *n.*

To be afflicted with r. दादडणें.

Ringing, *n.* v. V. A. 1. वाजवणें *n.* &c.

v. V. N. 1. झणझण *f.* झणझणी *f.* भिरभिरी *f.*—*intens.* झणझणाट *m.* झणाण *m.* खणखणाट *m.* खणाण *m.* घणघणाट *m.*

With a r. खण-कन-कर &c. खणखण *or* णां *intens.* खणाखण & खणाणां, घणघण *or* णां *intens.* घणाणां.

Ringlet, *n.* v. Curl. झुलूप *n.*

To Rinse, *v. a. wash* (a vessel). विसळणें *or* विसुळणें, धुणें.

2 *shake about in water, dip, &c. to cleanse.* खळबळणें, खळबळावणें, खुळखुळावणें, संगाळणें, आघाळणें, धुणें, ओंबळणें, बुचबुचावणें.

3 (the mouth after a meal) आंचवणें, गुळणा *m.* करणें.

Water for rinsing the mouth. आचमनीय *n.*

Riot, *n. wild festivity.* चमचमाट *m.* धुमाकूळ *f.* धुमश्चक्री *f.* धुमड *f.* धुमाळी *f.* धूम *f.* गोंधळ *m.* घमशान *n.*

2 *uproar*, v. Tumult. गर्दी *f.* धामधूम *f.* दंगा *m.* धुंदाई *f.* धुंदाधुंदी *f.* हंगामा *m.*

To run r. आवगणें, बाष्कळणें, बावचळणें *or* वावचळणें, बावकळणें, बायकळणें, बायचळणें, बुरंगळणें *or* गाळणें, बिफरणें, बिथरणें, माजणें, मातणें, वारा घेणें *or* पिणें, बिनसणें *or* बिनासणें, भडकणें, बेडगळणें.

To Riot, *v. n.* v. To Revel. धुमश्चक्री *f.*-धुमाळी *f.*-गोंधळ *m.*-&c. करणें, सुखांगणें, धणंगणें.

2 *raise an uproar.* गर्दी *f.*-दंगा *m.*-हंगामा *m.*-&c. करणें-उठवणें-माजवणें-मचावणें.

Riot-hall, *n.* v. Uproar. बाजारबाडा *m.* बाजार *m.*

Rioter, *n.* Rioting, *p. a.* v. V. 1. धुमश्चक्री-&c. करणारा.

2 गर्दी-दंगा-&c. करणारा-मचावणारा-&c.

Riotous, *a. belonging, &c. to noisy festivity.* बहर मारण्याचा, पात्रा नाचवण्याचा, धुमश्चक्रीचा, धुमाळीचा, घमंडीचा.

2 *tumultuous, seditious,*—assembly, proceeding, &c. गर्दीचा, दंग्याचा, हंगाम्याचा, मवाशीचा, पुंडाईचा, पुंडाव्याचा.

3—person, v. Rioter. गर्दी करणारा, दंगा करणारा, दंगेखोर, दंगेबाज. [गोंधळ-&c.करून.

Riotously, *adv.* v. A. 1. बहर मारून, पात्रा नाचवून, धुमश्चक्री-

2 गर्दीनें, दंग्यानें, &c. गर्दी-दंगा-&c. करून.

To Rip, *v. a. tear, lacerate.* चिरणें, फाडणें, फोडणें, चिरून-फाडून-&c. टाकणें, विदारणें, विदारण*n.* करणें.

2 open or up. उसवणें, उस्तरणें, उधडणें, उतफाळणें.

3 up; *hale forth, bring to light, &c.* v. To Expose. उचकटणें, विचकणें, विचकटणें, विदारण *n.*-विदारणा *f.*-उद्घाटन*n.* करणें *g. of o.*

To r. up faults. उखळबेरीज *f.*-उखाळ्या *f. pl.*-उखाळ्यापाखाळ्या *f. pl.* काढणें *g. of o.*

Rip, *n. tear &c.* See Rent.

Ripe, *a. lit. fig.* पक्का, पिकला *or* पिकलेला, पक्व, परिपक्व, पक्वदशेस आलेला, पक्वदशापन्न, जून, जुनाट, पिका.

That is r. and ready to fall or be gathered—a fruit. पाडाचा.

2 (in years &c.). पोक, पोक्ता, प्रौढ, प्रबुद्ध, उमेदवार, प्रगल्भ.

3 See Ready.

To Ripen, *v. n.* पिकणें, जुनावणें, पक्का-पक्व-&c.होणें,पचन*n.*-पक्वदशा *f.* होणें *g. of s.* पक्वदशेस येणें.

2—as mangoes, tamarinds, &c. गुळमटणें, गाभुळणें,गारसणें, गदरणें, पाडास येणें-लागणें.

3—a field of corn, &c. काळसरणें, काळवटणें.

To Ripen, *v. a.* पिकवणें, पक्वदशेस आणणें, पाक*m.*-विपाक*m.*-पक्वता *f.*-&c. करणें *g. of o.*

Ripened, *p.* v. V. N. पिकलेला.

R. in the house,—particular fruits. कोनपिका, कोनपीक.

R. on the tree. वरपिका, वरपीक.

Ripener, *n.* Ripening, *p. a.* v.V.A. पिकवणारा, पक्व करणारा, पक्वदशेस आणणारा, &c. पक्ता, पचमान.

v.V.N.1. पिकणारा, पक्वहोणारा, पक्वदशेस येणारा, &c. पच्यमान.

Ripeness, *n.* v. A. 1. पक्केपणा*m.* पिकलेपणा*m.* &c. पक्वता *f.* परिपक्वता *f.* पाक*m.* परिपाक*m.* पक्वदशा *f.* पीक*n.*

R. and readiness to be gathered. पाड*m.*

2 पोक्तपणा*m.* &c. प्रौढी *f.* उमेदवारी *f.* प्रागल्भ्य*n.*

Ripped, *p.* v. V. 1. चिरलेला, फाडलेला, &c. विदारित, विदीर्ण.

2 उसवलेला, &c.

3 उचकटलेला, &c. उद्घाटित.

Ripper, *n.* Ripping, *p. a.* v. V. 1. चिरणारा, फाडणारा, &c. विदारक, विदारणकर्त्ता-कारी-&c.

2 उसवणारा, उस्तरणारा, &c.

3 उचकटणारा, &c. विदारण-&c. कर्त्ता-कारी. [दारणा *f.*

Ripping, *n.* v. V. 1.—*act.* चिरणें*n.* फाडणें*n.* &c. विदारण*n.* वि-

2 उसवणें*n.* &c.

3 उचकटणें*n.* &c. उद्घाटन*n.* विदारण*n.* विदारणा *f.* विदारणी *f.*

Ripple, Rippling, *n.* v. V. खळखळ *f.* (*dim.* खळखळी *f. and intens.* &c. खळाळी *f.* & खळाळ*m.*) चुळचूळ *f.* [हणें-वाजणें.

To Ripple, *v. n.*—running water. खळखळणें, खळखळ-&c. वा-

To Ripple, &c. See To Hatchel, &c.

Rippler, *n.* Rippling, *p. a.* v.V. खळखळणारा, &c. खळखळीत.

Rippling, *adv. with a ripple.* खळ-कन-कर-&c. खळखळ *or* खुळखुळ.

To Rise, *v. n. become erect.* उठणें,उभा राहणें, उभवणें, उभारणें, आसन*n.* सोडणें, उभारणी *f.*-उन्थिति *f.*-&c. होणें *g. of s.*

2 (from rest) *get up.* निजून उठणें, उठणें, आंथरूण*n.* सोडणें.

To r. early. निजून लवकर उठणें.

To r. late. निजून उशिरां उठणें.

3 *move upward, ascend.* वर-वरती-वरता *decl.*-&c. जाणें-येणें-चढणें, आरोहण *n.*-&c. करणें, ऊर्ध्वगति *f.*-&c. होणें *g.of s.*

4 (in rank, fortune, &c.). चढणें, वाढणें, मोठा-&c. होणें, चढ *m.*-चढती *f.*-वृद्धि *f.*-चढती दौलत *f.*-पदवृद्धि *f.*-&c. होणें *g. of s.* परडें *or* पारडें *n.* चढणें-जड होत जाणें*g. of s.* न्यहाल होणें.

5—a heavenly body. उगवणें, चढणें, निघणें, उदय *m.*-&c. होणें *g. of s.* उदय *m.* पावणें, उदित-&c. होणें.

The mountain behind which the heavenly bodies are supposed to rise, is उदयगिरि *m.* उदयाचल *m.* उदयपर्वत *m.*

6 *swell,*—a river, &c. चढणें, फुगणें, पाणी *n.* चढणें.

7 *take beginning or existence, originate, issue, spring.* व्हाणें, लागणें, उत्पन्न-चालू-सुरू-उपस्थित-प्रवृत्त-&c. होणें, उद्भवणें, उठणें, उद्भव *m.*-उत्पत्ति *f.*-प्रारंभ *m.*-उपक्रम *m.*-&c. होणें *g. of s.* संभवणें, संभव *m.* होणें *g. of s.*

8 *be excited, kindled, &c.* येणें, होणें, सुटणें, उठणें, उत्पन्न-&c. होणें, प्रदीप्त-उद्दीप्त-&c. होणें.

9 *increase, become greater or more.* वाढणें, चढणें, बळावणें, जोरावणें, अधिक होणें, जोर *m.*-&c. अधिक होणें *g. of s.* वाढ *f.*-वृद्धि *f.*-&c. होणें *g. of s.* वृद्धि *f.*-&c. पावणें.

10 *break into rebellion or commotion.* उठणें, उठावणें, फिरणें *with* वर, उठावणी *f.*-उठावा *m.* करणें, डोईवर चढणें.

11—ground; *ascend from the plane of the horizon.* चढणें, चढ *m.*-चढण *f.*-&c. लागणें.

12 *appear, form, come, break out, &c.* उठणें, उचलणें, सुटणें, येणें, चढणें.

13 *break up,*—an assembly. उठणें, बरखास होणें.

14—a blister, &c. उतणें, उठणें, उफणणें *or* उफाणणें, उभारणें.

15—leaven, flour, bháng, &c. फुगणें, फुलणें, दरदरणें, तरतरणें, चढणें, दरदर-दरदरां फुगणें.

16—rate, price. चढणें, महागहोणें, तेजी *f.* होणें *g. of s.*—*intens.* चडचडणें, चणचणणें (*intens.* चणाणणें), कडकणें.

17 (in price)—an article. दर *m.*-भाव *m.*-धारण *f.*-मोल *n.*-&c.चढणें-वाढणें-&c. *g. of s.* चढणें.

18—the sea. लाटा *f. pl.* उठणें, क्षुब्ध-&c.होणें, उसळणें.

19 *have its source*—a river. उगम *m.* होणें *g. of s.*

Rise, Rising, *n.* v. V. 1.—*act.* उठणें *n.* उभा राहणें *n.*&c. उत्थान *n.* उत्थिति *f.* उत्था *f.* अभ्युत्थान *n.*

R. to receive a visitor. खडीताजीम *f.* अभ्युत्थान *n.* उत्थापन *n.* प्रत्युत्थान *n. all with v.* दे. घे.—Half rising in receiving, निमताजीम *f.*

2 निजून उठणें *n.* उठणें *n.*

3 वर जाणें *n.* चढणें *n.* &c. आरोहण *n.* आरोह *m.* ऊर्ध्वगमन *n.* उर्ध्वगति *f.* उद्गम *m.* उद्गमन *n.* उद्गति *f.*

4 चढणें *n.* &c. चढती *f.* चढ *m.* वृद्धि *f.* चढती दौलत *f.* चढती पराई *f.* चढती कळा *f.* चढतीपायरी *f.* चढता पाया *m.* चढती कमान *f.* चढती बाजू *f.*पदवृद्धि *f.*तेजोवृद्धि *f.* उदय*m.* अभ्युदय*m.*

5 उगवणें *n.* &c. उदय *m.* उद्गम *m.* अभ्युदय *m.*

Sun r. सूर्योदय *m.*

7 उत्पत्ति *f.* उद्भव *m.* उपज *m.* मूल *n.* मूलारंभ *m.* उद्गम *pop.* उगम *m.* आगम *m.* उपक्रम *m.* आरंभ *m.* प्रवृत्ति *f.* संभव *m.* उपस्थिति *f.* उपस्थान *n.*

R. and progress. उपजनिपज *m.*

9 चढती *f.* चढ *m.* वाढ *f.* भरती *f.*

R. and fall. चढउतार *m.*

10 उठणें *n.* &c. उठावा *m.* उठावणी *f.*

11 चढ *m.* चढण *f.* चढाव *m.*

R. and descent. चढउतार *m.*

16, 17. चढ *m.* तेजी *f.*—*intens.* चडचड *f.* चणचण *f.*

I. *a rising ground,* v. Hill. उंचवटा *m.* उंचवळा*m.* उंचाड *n.*

II. *a rising bump, tumour, &c.* उबाळू *n.* उगणूं *n.* उंचवटा*m.* उंचवळा *m.*

Risen, *p.* v.V. 1. उठलेला, उभा राहिलेला, &c. उत्थित, अभ्युत्थित.

2 उठलेला, निजून उठलेला, आंथरून सोडलेला, त्यक्ततल्प, त्यक्तशय्य.

3 वर गेलेला, वरती गेलेला, उद्गत.

5 उगवलेला, &c. उदित, उद्यत, अभ्युदित.

7 उद्भवलेला, &c. उपस्थित.

Riser, *n.* **Rising,** *p. a.* v. V. 1. उठणारा, उत्थान-&c.कर्त्ता-कारी.

2 उठणारा, निजून उठणारा, &c.

Late r.—jocosely. सूर्यवंशी.

4 चढणारा, &c. चढता, &c. चढतेदौलतीचा, चढतेकळेचा, चढत्या पायाचा, &c. चढाचा, चढणीचा, चढता, उंचवट, उंचट.

5 उगवणारा, उगवता, उदयी, उदयमान्.

I. *growing up to adult years.* चढतेउमरीचा, चढत्यावयाचा, आयुष्याच्या पहिल्या चरणांतला.

Risibility, Risibleness, *n.* v. A. 1. हसनशीलता *f.* हसनसामर्थ्य *n.* हसनशक्ति *f.*

2 हास्यजनकता *f.*

Risible, *a. having the faculty, &c. of laughing.* हासणारा, हसनशील, हसनसमर्थ.

2 v. Laughable, Ridiculous. हास्यजनक, हास्योत्पादक.

Risk, *n. hazard,* v. Danger. भय*n.* जोखीम*n.* धोका*m.* खत्रा*m.*

At all risks. जरूर.

To run a r. तवकल *f. n.* करणें. [घालणें-पाडणें.

To **Risk,** *v. a. hazard,* v. To Endanger. भयांत-धोक्यांत-&c.

2 See To Venture.

Rite, *n. formal act of religion, observance, ceremony.* क्रिया *f.* कर्म *n.* देवकार्य *n.* देवकर्म *n.* दैवकर्म *n.* दैवक्रिया *f.* संस्कार *m.* विधि *m.* विधान *n.* नियम *m.* रीति *f.* आचरण *n.* आचार *m.* शास्त्रकर्म *n.* शास्त्रोक्तकर्म *n.* अनुष्ठान *n.* व्रत *m. n.* The sixteen *Rites* (सोळा संस्कार *m. pl.*) purificatory of the human male and initiatory of him into society as a worthy member of it, commencing accordingly with the *first appearance of vitality in the conception,* and ending with *marriage,* are, पुंसवन, अनवलोभन, सीमंतोन्नयन, विष्णुबलि, जातकर्म, नामकरण, निष्क्रमण, अन्नप्राशन, चूडाकर्म, उपनयन, महानाम्नीव्रत, महाव्रत, उपनिषद्व्रत, गोदानव्रत, समावर्त्तन, विवाह. Of the numerous rites and ceremonies of the *Hindus,* those which could be reduced under or referred to particular departments, (ex. gr. *marriage, obsequies, thread-investiture, conception,*) are, under the words respectively expressing those departments, stated or named: the few following below are not so readily reducible to any great order or class. आचमन, उत्क्रांतिधेनु, उत्सर्जन, काकडआरती, गुरुपूजा, घटस्फोट, छूरिकाबंध, जलाधिवासन, तर्पण, तिथिपालन, तुला *or* तुलादान, दवणा, दशी वाहणें, धर्मोडा, धारणपारण, नक्त, नक्तभोजन, नक्तव्रत, निष्क्रमण, मूतशुद्धि. Of rites and ceremonies peculiar to *Women,* some are आवरण, ओंटी भरण, कोकिलाव्रत, गजगौरीव्रत, चैत्रांगण, चोरओंटीभरणें, निंब नेसणें. For other words, See Observance.

Course of rites. अनुष्ठान *n.*

Inauspicious r.—gener. अशुभकर्म *n.* अशुभकार्य *n.*

Rites and ceremonies,—compreh. *or* collect. आचारविचार *m.* नेमधर्म *m.*

Neglectful of rites and ordinances. आचारभ्रष्ट, आचारवर्जित, आचारहीन.

Regular in the practice of rites & ordinances. आचारपूत, आचारवान्, आचारसंपन्न, आचारशुद्ध, नियमनिष्ठ, नियमी, नियमशील, नैष्ठिक.

RITUAL, *a. pertaining, &c. to rites.* विधीचा, विधिकर्माचा, विधिक्रियेचा, विधिकर्माविषयींचा, क्रियासंबंधी, क्रियाविषयक, विधिविषयक, विधिसंबंधी, विधिरूप, विधिमय, वैध, विध्युक्त, वैधिक, विधि (in comp.). [शास्त्र *n.*

RITUAL, *n. book containing rites.* पद्धति *f.* कर्मपद्धति *f.* संस्कार-

RITUALIST, *n. one skilled in rituals.* क्रियावान्, अनुष्ठानी.

Mere r. प्रयोगपाठी.

RIVAL, *a. standing in competition.* स्पर्धी, प्रतिस्पर्धी, समतोल, सवत्या *or* सवता, सापत्नभावाचा, प्रतियोगी, एकार्थाभिलाषी, एकार्थेच्छु, एकार्थदृष्टि, एकार्थप्रवृत्त, एकार्थोद्युक्त.

RIVAL, *n.* v. A. दालीचा भाऊ, दालीबंदभाऊ, हरीप *or* फ, प्रतियोगी.

To RIVAL, *v. a. vie with, strive or contend with.* बराबरी *f.*-सरोबरी *f.* करणें *with* शीं *or g. of o.* स्पर्धणें, प्रतिस्पर्धणें, प्रतिस्पर्धा *f.* लावणें-धरणें-करणें-मांडणें *with* शीं *of o.* सर *f.*-सरी *f.* करणें-लावणें *with* शीं *of o.* तुळणें, झुंजणें, लढणें, टक्कर *f.* मारणें-खाणें *with* स *or* ला, मांडीस मांडी *f.* टेकून बसणें, तोलासतोल *m.* घेणें-देणें, टाक *m.* टाकणें, मणगटासीं मणगट *n.* घासणें, पोटरीस पोटरी *f.* घासणें, डाली *f.*-खांद *m.*-हाल *f.*-&c. बांधणें, पायास पाय *m.* देणें, भुजेस भूज *f.* देणें.

RIVALLING, *p. a.* v. V. बराबरी करणारा, सर करणारा, तुळणारा, डाली बांधणारा, &c. समतोल, बराबरीचा.

RIVALLING, RIVALRY, *n.* v. V. स्पर्धा *f.* प्रतिस्पर्धा *f.* बरकशी *or* बरकस *f.* चढाचढी *f.* हरिफी *f.* हडवंग *m.* हेवा *m.* हेवादेवा *m.* दुसग *or* दुसगाई *f.* सरी *f.* सापत्नभाव *m.* सापत्न्य *n.* खांद *m.* खांदाखांद *f.* खांदोस *m.* एकार्थाभिलाष *m.* एकार्थाकांक्षा *f.* एकार्थदृष्टि *f.* एकार्थप्रवृत्ति *f.* एकार्थशत्रुत्व *n.*

Mutual or general r. खांदाखांद *m.f.*

To RIVE, &c. See To SPLIT, &c.

RIVER, *n.* नदी *f.* नद *m.* (applied only to a r. personified as *male*, as सिंधु, शोणभद्र, शिव, ब्रह्मपुत्र, &c.) नयी *or* नही *f.* सरिता *f.* कुल्या *f.* पयस्विनी *f.* सिंधु *f.*

Bend or arm of a r. नदीवांक *m.*

Branch of a r. फांसूं *n.* [जलप्रवाह *m.*

Committing to the current of a sacred r. गंगाप्रवाह *m.*

Current of a r. नदीवेग *m.* नदीवेला *f.*

Deep part in a r. डोह *or* डोहो *m.* कोंड *f. n.* हूद *m.*

Dry spot in a r. खांडडोहो *m.* खांडवा *m.* खांडें *n.*

First-rate r. महानदी *f.*

Hole dug in the channel of a r. ब्रिहिरा *m.* शेवडी *f.*

Insulated spot in a r. ढेला *m.*

One subsisting upon offerings to a sacred r. गंगापुत्र.

Overflown by a r. नदीगरक.

Sacred r. गंगा *f.*

Spot where three rivers meet. तिसग *f.*

Swelling of a r. उसाण *n.* पूर *m.*

Watered by rivers,—a country. नदीमातृक, जलमातृक.

2 *copious flow, abundance.* पूर *m.* कुल्या *f.* (in comp. as घृतकुल्या, दधिकुल्या, &c.). [*n.* गाळा *m.*

RIVERWRECK, *n. rubbish that comes down with a fresh.* पुराड

RIVET, *n.*—the nail. दोहीं शेवटांनीं बोळबलेला खिळा *m.*

To RIVET, *v. a. fasten with a rivet.* खिळा मारून बोळवणें, बोळवलेल्या खिळ्यानें बांधणें-खिळणें-जोडणें-&c.

2 fig. *fasten firmly.* पक्की करणें, न हालेसा-&c. करणें.

3 See To CLINCH. [पन्हया *m.*

RIVULET, *n. streamlet,* v. RILL. ओढा *m.* ओहळ *m.* नाला *m.*

ROAD, *n. way, path, &c.* मार्ग *m.* रस्ता *m.* वाट *f.* पथ *pop.* पंथ *m.* अध्वा *m.*

Along both sides of the r. दुरस्ती.

Along the line of r. वाटशेक.

A long (esp. as bare and dreary) r. दंडवाट *f.* दंडक *n.*

Cart r. गाडेवाट *f.*

Downward r. अधःपथ *m.*

Extremity or meeting point of a r. नाका *m.*

Horse r. घोडेवाट *f.*

Meeting on the r. वाटभेट *f.*

Paved or made r. बांधवाट *f.* सडक *f.*

Pubilc r. हमरस्ता *m.* हमराह *m.* राजमार्ग *m.*

R.-expenses. वाटखर्च *m.* वाटखर्ची *f.*

R. making (or repairing.) रस्तेबंदी *f.*

Side of the r. आडमार्ग *m.* आडवाट *f.*

Spot on which three roads meet. तिवठा *or* तिवाठा *m.* तिठा *m.* तिठी *f.* तिंवधा *m.* त्रिक *n.*

Spot on which four roads meet. चवाठा *or* चवठा *m.*

That is off the main r. आडवळणी.

The right r. fig. सन्मार्ग *m.*

Unbeaten r. अक्षुण्ण मार्ग *m.*

To be on the r. *be coming.* वाट *f.* चालणें.

To beset or infest the r. मार्ग *m.*-वाट *f.*-&c. धरणें.

To lay or throw a r. रस्ता *m.*-वाट *f.* पाडणें, सडक *f.* बांधणें.

To pass, or cast behind, on the r. वाटविणें, वाटवणी *f.* करणें.

To set on the r. मार्गस्थ करणें, लावणें, बोळवणें.

2 (for ships). नांगरवाडा *m.*

3 *journey, travel.* वाट *f.* रस्ता *m.*

ROAD-STEAD, *n.* नांगरवाडा *m.*

To ROAM, *v. n.* v. To WANDER. रमणें, फिरणें, भटकणें, हिंडणें, भटक्या *f. pl.* मारणें-मारीत फिरणें, परिचार *m.*-विहार *m.*-विहरण *n.*-&c. करणें.—children or cattle. बावडणें.

ROAMER, *n.* ROAMING, *p. a.* v. V. रमणारा, फिरणारा, हिंडणारा, &c. परिचार-&c. कारी,—children or cattle. बावड.

ROAMING, *n.* v. V. रमणें *n.* फिरणें, हिंडणें *n.* &c. भ्रमण *n.* परिभ्रमण *n.* हिंडन *n.* परिचार *m.* विहार *m.* विहरण *n.*—of children or cattle बावडकी *f.*

R. for pleasure. रमण *n.* रमणूक *f.* विहरण *n.* विहार *m.*

ROAN, *a.*—a horse. चिताडा, मगसी.

To ROAR, *v. n.*—a beast. डरकणें, भरकणें, गुरकणें, गरजणें, डरका *m.*-डरकी *f.*-डरकाळी *f.*-&c. फोडणें-मारणें, भुरकणें *n.* फोडणें, आरोळी *f.* फोडणें-मारणें, गर्जना *f.* करणें.

2 *cry aloud from pain, &c.* v. To BAWL. ओरडणें, आरोळी *f.* फोडणें-मारणें, आक्रंदणें, आकांतणें, टाहो *m.* फोडणें, तोंड *n.* घेणें, हेल *m.* काढणें *or* हेल काढून रडणें, मोठा गळा करून रडणें, भोंक *n.*- भोंकण *n.* फोडणें, आक्रंदन *n.*-आक्रोश *m.* करणें, अकूसाबोकशी *or* उकूसाबोकशी रडणें.

3 *speak loudly, cry aloud, &c.* v. To BAWL. गागणें, गळाm.-घांटी *f.* फोडणें-फोडून बोलणें, गळा *m.* काढणें-काढून बोलणें, शिरा *f. pl.* ताणणें-ताणून बोलणें, ओरड *f.*-&c. करणें, आरोळी *f.* फोडणें-मारणें, भुरकण *n.* फोडणें.

4 *make a loud continuous noise; bellow, &c.*—the sea, wind, &c. घोगणें, घोंघावणें, सोसावणें, गरजणें, गाजणें, घोषणें, खळाळणें, खळाळ *m.*-कल्लोल or ळ *m.*-गर्जना *f.*-&c. करणें.

5—thunder, cannon, &c. गरजणें, गडाडणें, धडाडणें, दणदणणें, दणाणणें, भणभणणें, भणाणणें, दणका *m.*-दणदणाट *m.*-दणाण *m.*-&c. होणें-वाजणें *g. of s.*

6 at; *bluster and storm at to frighten, &c.* डरकणें, डरकावणें, डरावणें, दणदणणें, दणाणणें, दणगारणें, गुरकावणें, घेंगावणें or घेंघावणें, उद्गारणें, ढेंक *f. n.* फोडणें, ढेंकणें.

ROAR, ROARING, *n.* v. V. 1.—*act.* डरकणें &c. डरकण *f.* डरकणी or डरकाणी *f.* डरका *m.* डरकी *f.* डरकाळी *f.* गुरकणी *f.* गुरगुर or री *f.* गुरगुरणी *f.* गर्जन *n.* गर्जना *f.* भुरकण *n.* आरोळी *f.*

R. of a lion. सिंहनाद *m.* [रड or ओरड *f.*

2 ओरडणें *n.* आरोळी *f.* आकांत *m.* आक्रोश *m.* आक्रंदन *n.* अ-

To set up a r. रडण्याचा आकांत मांडणें.

4, 5. *loud and deep continuous sound,*—of the sea, wind, thunder, cannon, &c. कल्लोल or ळ *m.* खळाळ *m.* घोघाट *m.* घोष *m.* गर्जना *f.* गडाड *m.* धडाड *m.* भडाड *m.* भडभडाट *m.* कडकडाट *m.* दणका *m.* खणका *m.* ठांका *m.* दणदणाट *m.* दणाण *m.* दणाणा *m.* धूम *f.*

ROARER, *n.* ROARING, *p. a.* v. V. 1. डरकणारा, भुरकणारा, &c. डरक्या, भुरक्या, डरका-&c. फोडणारा.

2 ओरडणारा, आरोळी मारणारा, &c. &c. टाहोफोड्या.

4, 5. गरजणारा, गाजणारा, दणदणणारा, धडाडणारा, &c. &c. दणदणीत.

To ROAST, *v. a.* भाजणें.

2 fig. v. To TEASE, To RIDICULE. भाजणें, ठट्ठा *f.*-टेर *f.*-टर *f.*-रेवडी *f.*-हुररेवडी *f.*-&c. करणें *g. of o.*

ROAST, *n. that which has been roasted.* भाजप *n.* भाजण *n.* भाजका पदार्थ *m.*

To rule the roast. आपला उपर ठेवणें.

ROAST, *a.* ROASTED, *p.* v. V. भाजलेला, भाजका (*remiss.* भाजकट, भाजट,) भाजींव, भर्जित, भृष्ट, शूल्य.

ROASTING, *n.* v. V.—*act.* भाजणें *n.* भाजणूक *f.* भाजप *n.* भाजण *n.* भर्जन *n.*

2 भाजणूक *f.* ठट्ठा or थट्टा *f.* टेर *f.* टर *f.* रेवडी *f.* हुररेवडी *f.*

To ROB, *v. a. deprive of any thing feloniously or by violence; abstract by violence,* v. To PLUNDER, To STEAL. लुटणें, लुगारणें, लुबाडणें, झांबाडणें or झांबडणें, हिरणें or हिरावणें, छिनावणें or छिनणें, छिनावून-हिरावून नेणें-घेणें, झोंबाडणें, झोंबाडून नेणें, अपहरण *n.*-&c. करणें *g. of o.*

To r. on the high way. वाट *f.*-रस्ता *m.* मारणें *g. of o.*

ROBBED, *p.* v. V. लुटलेला, &c. लुंठित.

ROBBER, *n.* v. THIEF, PLUNDERER. चोर, लुटारू, हर, हारी, हारक, हर्त्ता, अपहारी, अपहारक, अपहर्त्ता.

Attack (upon a village, &c.) of a gang of robbers. दरवडा or दरोडा *m.* डांका *m.*

Gang r. दरोडेकरी, दरोडेखोर.

Gang of robbers. दरोडा or दरवडा *m.*

High way r. वाटमाऱ्या, वाटपाडू, वाटपाड्या. Amongst the *Hindus* there are *robbers* by allotment of nature and destiny. They constitute very numerous tribes and classes.

ROBBERY, ROBBING, *n.* v. V.—*act.* लुटणें *n.* &c. चोरी *f.* लूट *f.* लुंठन *n.* अपहरण *n.* अपहार *m.*

By r. and violence. चोरून मारून.

Gang-r. दरोडा or दरवडा *m.*

High way r. वाटमारा *m.* वाटमारी *f.*

R. and violence. चोरीमारी *f.*

ROBE, *n.*—the garment. शेला *m.* जामा *m.* झगा *m.* कचई *f.*—in contempt. शेलकट or गट *n.* शेलखंड *n.*

R. of honor presented by a king, &c. खिलात *f.*

R. and turban bestowed in honor. शेला पागोटें *n.* शिरपाव *m.*

To ROBE. See To ATTIRE, To DRESS.

ROBUST, *a. lusty, sturdy, &c.* v. STOUT, STRONG. धट्टाकट्टा, धट्टासट्टा, धडासडा, जोधा, बळकट, जोमदार, जोरदार, जोरकस.

2 See HALE. 3 *requiring strength.* बळाचा, जोराचा.

ROBUSTNESS, *n.* v. A. 1. धट्टेकट्टेपणा *m.* &c. जोम *m.* जोर *m.* बळकटी *f.*

ROCK, *n. mass of stone.* खडक *m. n.* धोंड *f.* शिला *f.* दगड *f.* खडपा *m.* अश्मा *m.*

Flat r. in the sea. कांसा *m.*

Hard as a r. शिलाघन.

Large r. खडक *f.*

Ledge of r. दांडा *m.* खडक *m.*

Projecting r. बिंडा *m.*

Pyramidal or peaked r. सुळकी *f.*

R. in the sea. कांटा *m.* खराबा *m.*

Sheet or stratum of r. कातळ *m.* खडक *m.* खडकून *n.* खडप *m.* खडपा *m.* खडकाळ *n.* खडकाळी *f.* तवा *m.*

Soft, friable r. तुशा खडक *m.*

Writing upon a r. दगडावरची रेघ *f.* चिऱ्यावरची रेघ *f.*

To cause the r. to flow. *lit. fig.* दगडास पाझर *m.* आणणें.

To ROCK, *v. n. move backward and forward,* v. To REEL, To SHAKE. डगणें, डकडकणें or डगडगणें *intens.* डकाकणें or डगागणें, डगमगणें, डुलणें or डोलणें, आंदुळणें, हांदुळणें or हांवदुळणें, आंदोलन *n.*-&c. होणें *g. of s.* लटपटणें, लटलटणें, लडबडणें, लटपट-लडबड-&c. *adv.* हलणें.

To ROCK, *v. a. move backward and forward on a fixed line.* डुलवणें, or डोलवणें, हांदुळणें or हांवदुळणें, डगवणें, डुलेसा-डोलेसा-डगेसा-&c. करणें, झोके *m. pl.*-झोपे *m. pl.*-&c. देणें.

2 (a child in a cradle). पाळण्यांत हालवणें, पाळण्यांत घालून डुलवणें-झोके देणें-&c.

ROCK-OIL, *n.* मातीचेंतेल *n.* भूमितैल *n.*

ROCK-SALT, *n.* शेंदे or शेंधेलोण *n.* सिंधुलवण *n.*

ROCKER, *n.* ROCKING, *p. a.* v. V. N. डुलणारा, डगणारा, &c. डगडगीत, डळडळीत, डळमळीत, लटपटीत, उलटकर.

I. *rocking stone.* उलटा दगड *m.*

ROCKET, *n.* बाण *m.* बाणा *m.* कळकी बाण *m.* अग्निबाण *m.* तारा *m.*

Bundle of twenty four rockets. कैची *f.*

Hole or eye of a r. बरमा *m.*

Sky r. हवई or हवाई *f.*

ROCKETEER, *n.* बाणदार, बाणाईत.

ROCKY, *a. full of rocks.* खडकाचा, कातळाचा, &c. खडकळ, खडकाळ, खडकील, खडकूत, कातळवट.

2 fig. See STONY.

ROD, *n. twig, &c.* काठी *f.* छडी *f.* शलाका *f.*

Lay on the r. and you'll bring on the scholar. छडी लागे चमचम विद्या येई घमघम.

2 (of office, &c.). छडी *f.* वेत्र *n.*

Bearer of the r. छडीदार, छडीबरदार.

3—in land measurement. काठी *f.*

4 *pole for angling.* काठी *f.*

RODOMONTADE, *a.* v. BOAST, BLUSTER. घटंपटं *n.* बुटटकी *f.* अरेरावकी *f.* अरेराबी *f.* गट्टापट्टा *m.* तराठा or तऱ्हाटा *m.* टाराटुरी or टाराटोरी *f.* डौला *m.* पादरधिटाई *f.*

ROE, *n. female deer.* हरिणी or हरणी *f.* मृगी *f.*

2 *spawn.* माशाचीं अंडीं.

ROEBUCK, *n.* एके जातीचा हरिण आहे.

ROGUE, *n. knave, cheat, dishonest person,* v. BLACKGUARD. ठक, ठग, ठकव्या, फसव्या, ठकबाज, दगाबाज, दगेखोर, धतुऱ्या, दगलबाज, लबाड, सोदा, सकारविल्हेचा, सकारविल्हा, कालभेल्या, खट, काबूयार, काशीकर, दिल्लीचा, अवरंगाबादी, गुलाम, गुलामजादा, हिलेबाज, वंचक, प्रवंचक, प्रतारक, धूर्त्त, शठ.

Pack of rogues. चांडालचौकडी *f.*

Slippery r., arch r. बाटोळा गोळा, बाटोळा गोटा.

Every r. is at length outrogued. शेराला सवा शेर भेटतोच आहे. [गुंड, गुंडा, बाट.

2 See VAGABOND. 3 *a sly, waggish, &c. person.* गुलाम,

ROGUERY, *n. knavery, cheating, dishonest practices.* ठगाई *f.* ठकाई *f.* ठकबाजी *f.* ठकविद्या *f.* ठकूविद्या *f.* दगाबाजी *f.* दगलबाजी *f.* सोदावें *n.* सोदेगिरी *f.* सोदेशाई *f.* लबाडी *f.* गुलामगिरी *f.* काबुयारी *f.* लबाडी लचाडी *f.* लबाडी लाताडी *f.* लबाडीलाताळी *f.* लकारी *f.* कालेंभेलें *n.* धतुरा or धत्तुरा *m.* v. दाखव, ठकडेपणा *m.* छटपणा *m.* धूर्त्तता *f.* धूर्त्ताई *f.* धौर्त्य *n.* धौर्त्तिका *f.*

ROGUISH, *a.* v. KNAVISH. ठकाऊ, ठकारू, ठकबरा, फसव्या, छट, लबाड, लबाडलचाड, लबाडलाताड, लबाडलाताळ, खटनट, नटखट, नटबाट, कितव, धूर्त्त, शठ, वंचक, प्रवंचक, प्रतारक.

2 See ARCH. 3 See MISCHIEVOUS.

To ROIL, *v. a. make turbid.* गढूळ-गदळ-&c. करणें, रेंदाविणें.

2 *excite resentment,* v. To OFFEND. रागास आणणें, खपा-क्षुब्ध-&c. करणें.

To ROIST, *To* ROISTER, *v. n.* v. To BLUSTER. ताल *m.* तोडणें, तम *m.* दाखवणें, तमणें, तमतमणें.

ROISTER, *n.* ROISTERER, *n.* ROISTERING, *p. a.* v. V. तालतोडणारा, तमदाखवणारा, तमणारा, &c. रगड्या, रपाट्या, ग्राम, ग्रामणी, तालतोड्या, तमतम्या, संदानट्टू, आततायी.

To ROLL, *v. a. move by turning on the surface.* लोटणें, लोटून नेणें, चक्रगतीनें नेणें, गरगरवून नेणें, घरळवणें, घुळवणें.

2 *make to revolve.* फिरवणें, लाटणें, गरगरवणें.

3 *wrap around.* गुंडाळणें, लपेटणें, वेष्टणें, वेढणें, गुंडणें.

4 *wrap round on itself.* गुंडाळणें.

5 (cakes, &c.) *form by rolling.* लाटणें.

Lump or mass of dough to be rolled out. लाटा *m.* लाटी *f.*

6 along, over, in ; (as in mud, dust, &c.). लोळवणें, लोळसावणें.

7 out. लाटणें.

8 up. गुंडाळणें, गुंडाळा *m.*-वळकटी *f.*-&c. करणें *g. of o.*

9 (the eyes). चाळवणें.

To ROLL, *v. n. move by turning round.* लोटणें, घरळणें, घुळघुळीत येणें-जाणें-फिरणें-चालणें, घुळणें, फिरणें, लुठणें, रुळणें.

2—as a ship, &c. v. To ROCK. आंदुळणें, डुलणें or डोलणें, हांदुळणें or हांबदुळणें, हेलकावणें, हेलावणें, हेलकावे *m. pl.*-झोके *m. pl.*-डोल *m.*-&c. खाणें. [मांडणें.

3 about (as in pain). वळवळणें, लोळणें, वळवळ *f.* करणें-

4 over,—time. लोटणें, उलगणें, गुजरणें, गत होणें.

5 over and over on the ground. लोळणें, लोटणें, गडबडणें, गडबडांलोळणें, गडबडगुंडा *m.*-लोटांगण *n.*-&c. करणें—esp. as in dogged resistance, &c. लोळण *f.*-लोळकंड *f.*-लोळकण *f.* घेणें-मारणें-घालणें. [*in. con.*

6—as horses, &c. in the sun. लोळी *f.* करणें, लोळी *f.* येणें

7 down or along. बरंगळणें or बरंघळणें.

ROLL, *n. thing rolled up.* वळकटी *f.* वळी *f.* वळवटी or वंटी *f.* चिंडा *m.* गुंडाळा *m.* गुंडळी *f.* or ळें *n.* गुंडाळी *f.* or ळें *n.* गुंडा *m.* गुंडी *f.*—esp. of paper or cloth, सुरळी *f.*—esp. of thread, &c. चिवट *n.* कोंपरी *f.* कडी *f.*—of the betel leaf, &c. पट्टी *f.*—of tape, rope, &c. मेंडाळें or मेंडोळें *n.* पेंडोळें *n.* गुंडें *n.* —as of dough, लाटा or लाट्या *m. dim.* लाटी *f.*

2 *register, list.* फर्द *m.* पट *m.* इसमवारी *f.* यादी *f.* तका *m.* फर्दा *m.*

3 (upon a drum). ताशेरा or तासेरा *m.* v. झाड.

4 See ROLLER.

ROLLED, *p.* v. V. A. 1. लोटलेला, लोटून नेलेला, &c. अवलुंठित.

3 गुंडाळलेला, लपेटलेला, &c.

4 गुंडाळलेला.

5 लाटलेला, लाटींव.

ROLLER, *n.* ROLLING, *p. a.* v. V. A. 1. लोटणारा, लोटून नेणारा, v. V. N. 1. लोटणारा, घरळणारा, लोलमान.

I.—for cakes, &c. लाटणी *f.* लाटणें *n.*

II.—for levelling ground. लाट *f.*

III. (as of a mortar). लाट्या *m.*—of stone. बरवंटा *m.*

IV. (of an oil-mill). लाट *f.*

V. *bandage, &c.* पट्टा *dim.* पट्टी *f.*

ROLLICKING. See FROLICSOME.

ROLLING, *n.* v. V. A. 1.—*act.* लोटणें *n.* लोटून नेणें *n.* &c. v. V. N. लोटणें *n.* लुठणें *n.* &c. लोट *m.* अवलुंठन *n.* लुंठन *n.*

2 आंदुळणें *n.* डुलणें *n.* &c. हेलकावा *m.*

5 लोळणें *n.* &c. लोळ *m.* लोळण *f.* लोळकंड *f.* लोळकण *f.* लोळण घोळण *f.* [लोटांगण *n.*

Proceeding to a temple, &c. by rolling over & over.

6 लोळी *f.*

ROLLING-PIN, *n.* लाटणी *f.* लाटणें *n.*

ROLONG, *n. granulous wheat flour.* गरा *m.*

ROMANCE, *n. wild tale, &c.* कादंबरी *f.* थोतांड *n.* थोतांडपुराण *n.* भंडपुराण *n.* माहात्म्य *n.* अभूतकथा *f.* असंभूतकथा *f.*

To ROMANCE, *v. n. tell wild tales.* कादंबरी *f.*-थोतांड *n.*-थोतांडपुराण *n.*-&c. सांगणें.

ROMANCER, *n.* ROMANCING, *p. a.* v. V. कादंबरी सांगणारा, &c. कादंबऱ्या, थोतांडी, थोतांडपुराणिक, नकल्या, बात्या, बात्यारा *or* बात्येरा.

ROMANTIC, *a. wild, fanciful, extravagant, &c.*—a person. अद्भुतप्रिय, अद्भुतमनस्क, अद्भुतवृत्ति, अशृंखलमनस्क.

2—notions, taste, &c. विलक्षण, अद्भुतरसाचा, अद्भुतरसात्मक, अद्भुतरसप्रचुर, वितर्कात्मक.

ROMP, *n. boisterous girl, hoiden.* घोडगी *f.* घोडी *f.* जानी *f.* धांगड *n.* धिंगड*n.* धांगडधिंगी *f.* खिदडणारी *f.* नाचणारी *f.* भोपळदेवता *f.* टोणगी *f.*

2 *or* romps; *rough play.* धिंगाणाधिंगाडा *m.* धिंगामस्ती *f.* खिदडा *m.* खिदडणें *n.* धांगडणें *n.* घमशान *n.* धुमशान *n.* धुमकूस *f.* धुडकूस *or* गूस *m.* धुमड *f.* धुमश्चक्री *f.* धुमाकूळ *m.* धांगडधिंगा *or* धाबडधिंगा*m.* धिबडी *f.* तातकथय्या *m.* ताथय्या*m.* थैथैय्या *m.* थैथैयाट *m.* थैकार *m.* हंगामा *m.* हमामा*m.* हुतुतू *m.* बोकंदळ *n.*

To ROMP, *v. n. play rudely and boisterously.* खिदडणें, खिदळणें, धिंगडणें, धांगडणें, धिंगाणा *m.* -घमशान *n.*-धांगडधिंगा *m.*-&c. घालणें-मांडणें-माजवणें, नाच *m.* मांडणें, उधळा *m.* घालणें, किलाण *n.* मांडणें-माजवणें, बोकळणें. [&c.

ROMPING, *n.* v. V. *and* ROMP. खिदडणें *n.* धांगडणें *n.* धिंगडणें *n.*

ROMPER, *n.* ROMPING, *p. a.* v. V. *and* ROMP. खिदडणारा, धांगडणारा, धिंगडणारा, धिंगाणा मांडणारा, &c. धांगडधिंगा. [य *f.*

RONION, *n. fat bulky woman.* पत्नालपार्वती *f.* मुग्धम्मा *f.* फातमा-

ROOD, *n. measure of five cubits and five hand breadths.* काठी *f.*

ROOF, *n. cover of a building.* छावणी *f.*—of thatch, छप्पर *n.* —of tiles, कौलार *n.*—flat r. of earth, धाबें *n.* धाबडें *n.* माळोद *or* माळवद *n.*

Aperture (for smoke, light, or air) in a r. धारें *n.* दादरा *m.* साहणें *or* साणें *n.* [घोण्या *m.*

Corner or diagonal rafter of a r. घोणवासा *m.* घोण *f.*

End piece of an oblong r. चांपेमोळ *n.*

Frame work of a r. थाट *m.* थाटबंद *m.* वांशीक *n.*

Lath-work over the rafters of a r. ओंबण *n.* साट *m.* साटी *f.*

Lower ridge or cross-piece supporting the extreme line of a r. गई *f.* गइसर *or* गइसरा *m.*

Of four slopes—a r. चौमोळी, चौपाखी.

Of two slopes—a r. दुमोळी, दुपाखी.

Slope or side of a r. पाखें *n.* पाख *n.* मोळ *n.* नीव *m.*

The r. (rafters, lathwork, &c.) as preparatory to the reception of the tiles or thatch. बरदळ *n.*

The thatch &c. of a r.—as distinguished from rafters and lathwork. शाकार *or* शेकार *m.*

2 (of the mouth). तालु *n. pop.* ताळू *f.* टाळू *f.*

To ROOF, *v. a.* छावणी *f.* घालणें-करणें, झांकणें.—with thatch, छप्पर *n.* घालणें-करणें, शेकारणें, शेकार *m.* घालणें.

ROOFED, *p.* v. V. छावणी घातलेला, छप्पर घातलेला, &c. छावणीचा, छप्पराचा.

ROOFING, *n.* v. V. छावणी *f.* शेकारणें *n.* &c. शेकारणी *f.*

ROOK. See CROW. 2—at chess. हत्ती *m.*

ROOM, *n. space.* अवकाश *m.* प्रदेश *m.* देश *m.*

Absence or want of r. अनवकाश *m.*

2 *vacant space.* अवकाश *m.* जागा *f. m.* उसार *m.* वाव *m.* सांच *m.* सांठ *m.* सांटपा *m.* आकाश *m. n.* वाड *f.* वार *m.* वारी *f.* सवड *f.* पैस *m.*

To make r. *get out of the way.* खिसणें *or* खिचणें, वाट *f.* देणें, जागा *f.* घेणें, ओसर *m.* देणें-घेणें.

To cause to make r. *move out of the way.* खेचणें, खेटणें.

Room! make r.! पैस!

3 *apartment.* कोठडी *f.* खोली *f.* ओबरा *or* ओरा *m.*

Inner r. गर्भगृह *n.* गर्भागार *n.* गर्भ *m.*

Suite of rooms. बठाण *n.*

Upper r. माडी *f.* उपरिभूमि *f.*

4 *lieu, stead.* जागा *f. m.* स्थान *n.* स्थल *or* ळ *n.* ठिकाण *n.*

In the r. of. जागां, जागीं, जागें, ऐवजीं.

That is in the r. of. बारचा, बांटचा.

5 *place, opportunity.* जागा *m. f.* वाव *m.* स्थान *n.* सवड *f.*

ROOMILY, *adv. loosely, at large.* ऐसपैस, पैस,पघळ, सपसल *or*ली.

To sit loosely and r. अढी *f.* घालून बसणें.

ROOMINESS, *n.* v. A. पैस *m.* ऐसपैसपणा *m.* अघळपघळपणा *m.* प्रशस्तपणा *m.* &c. प्राशस्त्य *n.* उपसारा *m.*

ROOMY, *a. spacious, wide, &c.* ऐसपैस, पैस, ऐसापैसाचा, अवकाशाचा, उपसाऱ्याचा, पघळ, अघळपघळ, सबाला, प्रशस्त, कुशाद, मोठा, घिसकळ, विशाल, विस्तीर्ण, विशद, सावकाश.

ROOST, *n.*—of a bird. अड्डा *m.* अड्डू *n.* धारा *m.* पाखराचें रातचें बसायाचें स्थान *n.*

To ROOST, *v. n.*—birds. अड्ड्यावर-धाऱ्यावर-&c. बसणें.

ROOT, *n. the part of a plant which enters the earth.* मूल *pop.* मूळ *n.* मुळी *f.* मुळकंड *or* खंड *n.* जडी *f.*

Deep roots. धरणमूळ *n.*

From r. to top. आमूलचूड.

Of firm r. बद्धमूल.

Ramification of a r. पाळ *n.* पाळक*n.*मुळकंड *n.* मुळकुंडी *f.*

The principal stem of the r. धरणमूळ *n.*

To the r. आमूल.

To take r. मुळावणें, जडी *f.* रुतणें *g. of s.* लागणें.

To take r. fig. *get firmly settled or fixed.* पाळें *n. pl.* घेणें, पाळेंमुळें *n. pl.* भूमींत जाणें *g. of s.* जडणें, नांगी *f.* लागणें *or* रुतणें *g. of s.*

To turn out r. and branch. पाळेंपाळें *n. pl.*-पाळेंमुळें *n.pl.* खणून टाकणें *g. of o.*

2 esculent r. मूळ *n.* कंद *m.*

Aquatic r. पाणकंद *m.*

Bulbous or tuberous r. कांदा *m.* कंद *m.*

Roots and simples of medicinal virtue. जडीबुटी *f.*

A vender of medicinal roots. मुळ्या.

3 *radical or lower portion.* बुडखा *m.* बुडूख *n.* बुंध *n.* बुंधा *m.* बुंधारा *m.*

4 *primary cause, original, spring, source.* मूळ *n.* बुंध *n.* बुंधा *m.* बीज *n.* आदि *n.* आदिकारण *n.* मूळकारण *n.* निदान *n.* घर *n.* अवधि *m.* बुडखा *m.* बुडूख *n.* कंद *m.* (in comp.)

Having for its r. or origin. मूलक (as पापमूलक दुःख pain of which sin is the root, लोभमूलक कलह contention of which covetousness is the root, &c. ad libitum.)

From the very r. मुळाहून *or* मुळाधरून.

5 *radical word.* प्रकृति *f.* शब्दयोनि *f.*
Relation of a r. to its ramifications. प्रकृतिविकृतिभाव *m.*
6 (of a number). मूल *n.*
7 (of a square or cube). पद *n.*
Cube r. घनमूल *n.*
Square r. वर्गमूल *n.*

To Root, *v. a. fix deeply.* जडवणें, बद्धमूल करणें.
2 out or up; *eradicate.* उपडणें, उपटणें, उपटून टाकणें, मुळासुद्धां उपडून काढणें, उन्मळणें, उत्पाटणें, उखडणें, उच्छेदणें, समूलोत्पाटन *n.*-उन्मूलन *n.*-उत्पाटन *n.*-&c. करणें *g. of o.*

To Root, *v. n. take root,* lit. fig. मुळें *n. pl.* धरणें, पाळें *n. pl.* घेणें, पाळेंमुळें *n. pl.* भूमींत जाणें *g. of s.* मुळावणें, बद्धमूल होणें, लागणें, जडणें, जडावणें, नांगी *f.* लागणें-रुतणें *g. of s.*
2—swine, *turn up the ground with the snout.* सोंडेनें जमीन *f.* उकरणें.

Rooted, *p.* v. V. A. 1. *and* v. N. 1. जडवलेला *or* जडलेला, &c. बद्धमूल, दृढमूल.
2 उपडलेला, उपटून टाकलेला, &c. उन्मूलित, उत्पाटित, उच्छिन्न, [उत्खात.

Rope, *n.* दोर *m. dim.* दोरी *f.* रस्सा *m. dim.* रस्सी *f.* नाडा *m.* चन्हाट *n.* सडक *f.* सडा *m.* रज्जु *f. pop.* राजू *m.* काढणी *f.* शेंडा *m.* गुण *m.* दोरक *m.*
Large thick r. दोरखंड *n.* दोरडें *n.* बाला *m.* सोल *m.* सोलखंड *n.* दोरकस *m.*
Mark worn by a r. करकोचा *m.* काचणी *f.* अखोटा *m.*
Piece of r. (or cord). दोरखंड *n.* सोलखंड *n.* तोडा *m.*
R. of a single strand. पेड *m.*
R. of grass, &c. बेंटी *or* बेंटी *f.*

Rope-dancer, *n.* v. Tumbler, Actor. नाडेबहुरूपी *or* नाडेभोरपी, नाडेकरी, कोल्हाटी, भोरपी.
Rope of r. नाडा *m.*

Rope-dancing, *n.* नाडेभोरीप *or* रूप *n.* भोरीप *n.*

Rope-ladder, *n.* दोराचीशिडी *f.*

Rope-maker, *n.* कंजारी. This is a particular caste.

Rope-shed, Rope-walk, *n.* करदोडी *or* करदोरी *f.*

Ropiness, *n.* v. A. दोर *m.* दोराळपणा *m.*

Ropy, *a. stringy.* दोराळ,
To be r. दोरावणें.

Rosary, *n. string of beads for counting prayers.* जपमाला *pop.* जपमाळ *or* ळा *f.* स्मरणी *f.* तसबी *f.* अक्षमाला *f.* माला *f. pop.* माळ *f.*
Fingers used as a r. करमाला *f.*

Rose, *n.*—the bush. गुलाब *m.* गुलाबाचें झाड *n.*—the flower. गुलाबाचें फूल *n.* गुलाब *m.*
China r.—the plant or flower. जपा *f.* जास्वंद *f.*
Conserve of roses. गुलकंद *m.* गुलाबचक्री *or* छकडी *f.*
Extract of roses. गुलाबी अत्तर *n.*
No r. without a thorn. धान्य तेथें घुशी, निधान तेथें विंशी.
Under the r. v. Secretly. गुप्तपणें.
2 *cooper's rose.* कांचकमल *n.*

Rose-apple, *n.*—the plant. जांब *m.* जंबु *f.*—the fruit. जांब *m.* जंबु *n.*—the plant or fruit. साखरजांब *m.* गुलाबीजांब *m.*

Rose-colored, *a.* गुलाबी, गुलाबीरंगाचा, गुलाबरंगी, पाटल.

Rose-water, *n.* गुलाबपाणी *n.* गुलाब *m.*
R.-vessel. गुलाबदान *n.* गुलाबदानी *f.*

Roseate, Rosy, *a. rose-colored.* गुलाबी, गुलाबरंगी, गुलाबीरंगाचा, पाटल.
2 *rosy, full of roses.* गुलाबांचा.

Rosin. See Resin.

Roster, *n. register, &c.* v. Roll. फर्द *m.* पट *m.*

To Rot, *v. n. putrify.* कुजणें, सडणें, उबळणें.
To r. and run,—melons, &c. डगळणें *or* ढगळणें, बुळकणें, उमळणें, बरबरणें, मुसळणें. [&c. करणें.

To Rot, *v. a. make putrid.* कुजवणें, सडवणें, कुजेसा-सडेसा-

Rot, *n.* (in cattle)—the disease. सडी *f.* वादा *m.* वादें *n.*

Rot-gut, *n. dilute & sour liquid.* खळा *m.* खळक *m.* खळगट *n.*

Rotary. See Rotatory.

Rotation, *n. wheeling, turning round, circular motion.* गरगरणें *n.* चक्रगति *f.* चक्रावर्त्त *m.* चक्रावर्त्तन *n.* घूर्णन *n.*
2 *succession.* पालटानें-पाळीनें-&c. येण्याचा-जाण्याचा-&c. क्रम *m.* आनुपूर्वी *f.* आनुपूर्व्य *n.* फिरती ओळ *f.* चक्र *n.* रहाटगाडगें *n.*
In r. पाळीनें, ओळीनें, क्रमानें.

Rotatorily, *adv.* v. A. 1. चक्रगतीनें, &c. चक्रवत्.

Rotatory, *a.* v. N. 1. *turning on its own axis, turning like a wheel.* चक्रगतीचा, चक्रावर्त्ताचा, &c. चक्रगति, चक्रगामी, चक्रावर्त्ती, चक्रवान्.
2 *following in succession.* पालटानें-पाळीनें-&c. येणारा-जाणारा, फिरत्या ओळीचा, रहाटगाडग्याचा.

Rote, *n. mere repetition.* घोकणें *n.* घोकणी *f.*
Mere r. learning. घोकींवविद्या *f.* पोपटपंडिती *f.* पोपटविद्या *f.*
That acts by r. घोककाम्या, घोक्या.
That knows only by r. घोक्या, घोकींव, पोपटपंडित.
That is known only by r. घोकींव, पोपटपंडितीचा, पोपटविद्येचा. [शीर्ण, विशीर्ण.

Rotten, *a. putrified.* कुजका *or* कुसका, कुसडा, सडका, सडेल,
Rottenish, *rather rotten.* कुजकट, कुजट, कुसकट.
R. and corrupt,—compreh. *or* gener. कुजकानासका.
2 fig. *perfidious, &c.* v. False. कुजका, मनाचा-हाडाचाकुजका.
3—used of ground. खस्ती.

Rottenness, *n.* v. A. 1. कुजकेपणा *m.* कुसकेपणा *m.* सडकेपणा *m.*

Rotund, Rotundity. See Round, Roundness.

Rotunda, *n. round building.* गोल-बुरजी-&c. घर *n.*-&c.

To Rouge, *v. n.* गालांवर-तोंडावर-&c. रंग *m.* लावणें.

Rough, *a. not smooth.* खरखरीत, खरबरीत *or* खडखडीत, खसखसीत, उखरबाखर, उखराबाखर, चेचड *or* चेचाड.
2 *not elegant or neat, not finished nicely; coarse, clumsy, &c.* किजबिडीत, किजबीड, किचबिडीत, किडबीड, किडबिडीत, किडबीड, भसाडा, रटाल्या *or* रटाला, रटेल, भरड, ढोबळ, ढोबळा, भोपळसुती, वेठीचा, रांठ *or* रंठ, कच्चा.
3 *not gentle, soft, courteous, or mild; rude, boisterous, &c.*—person. धसक्या, धशा *or* धश्शा, रगड्या, रपाट्या, बाडगा, धसमुसळा *or* ळ्या, धस्समसूल, घुसड्या, समाट्या, रंवदाळ्या, चोळवटणारा, अरबट, अडदांड, अडदांडगा, लाट्या, रांठ *or* रंठ, घटाल्या, लांठ, पडखर, असौम्य, असभ्य, अशिष्ट, अस्निग्ध.—action. धसाफत्तीचा, घुसडाघुसडीचा, रगडपट्टीचा, &c.
R. action or work. रगडपट्टी *f.* रगडमही *f.* झोडपट्टी *f.* ध-

साकशी *f.* घुसडाघुसड *f.*

4 *not gentle in operation; harsh, severe, &c.*—measure, remedy, &c. उग्र, उग्रोपचारी, उग्रोपचाराचा, राक्षसी, आसुरी, आसुरी उपायाचा, कठोर, निष्ठुर, दंडोपचारी, दंडोपचाराचा, परुष, परुषवृत्तीचा.

5—a workman; *coarse, clumsy.* घसक्या, घसट्या, घसकट्या, घशा, दगडघाशा, रगड्या, भसाडा, झोडकामी *or* म्या, रटाला *or* ल्या. [निस्नेह.

6 (to the taste) *austere, &c.* रूक्ष *pop.* रुखा, खट्टा, अरबट,

7 (to the touch) *prickly, &c.* चरचरीत, चरबट, चरबरीत.

8 *not polished, not wrought.* कच्चा, असंस्कारित, असंस्कृत, अपरिष्कृत. [व्याक्षुब्ध.

9—the sea, &c. *agitated.* खवळलेला, खळबळलेला, क्षुब्ध,

10 *tempestuous.* जोवी, वादळाचा, तुफानाचा.

11 a calculation, estimate, &c. अजमासाचा, अटकळीचा, स्थूलमानाचा.

To ROUGH, *v.a. with* it. गैरसोई *f.*-हाल *m. pl.*-&c. सोसणें-भोगणें, उपासतान *f.* काढणें.

To ROUGH-CAST, *To* ROUGH-DO, *To* ROUGH-HEW, *v. a. give the first shape, to form rudely, coarsely, &c.* भरडणें, भरडून ठेवणें, करड *n.* काढणें *g. of o.* खरडणें, खरडून ठेवणें, सडकणें, ओरखडणें, ओरबडणें, ओरखडून-&c. ठेवणें, आकारास आणणें-आणून ठेवणें.

ROUGH-DRAUGHT, *n. rude sketch, &c.* खरडा *m.* खरड *m.* खरडें *n.* कच्चाआकार *m.* मसुदा *m.*

To ROUGH-DRAW, *v. a. sketch roughly.* खरडणें, खरडूनठेवणें, ओरखडणें, ओरबडणें, ओरखडून-&c. ठेवणें, अंकणें, कच्चाआकार *m.*-खरडा *m.*-&c. काढणें *g. of o.* आंकणी *f.*-अंकन *n.* करणें *g. of o.*

To ROUGH-HEW, *v. a.* v. To ROUGH-CAST. सडकणें.

ROUGH-HEWN, *p.* v. V. सडकलेला, सडकीव.

ROUGH-RIDER, *n.* चाबुकसवार *or* स्वार.

Business of a r. चाबुकसवारी *or* स्वारी *f.*

ROUGH-SHOD, *a.* कांट्यांच्या नालाचा.

ROUGHLY, *adv.* v. A. 1. खरखरीत, खरबरीत, &c.

2 कच्चा *decl.*

3 दांडगेपणानें, घशाखशा, घशाफशा, धुमसाधुमसी, धुमसूनधुमसून.

4 कठोरपणानें, उग्रपणानें.

11 अजमासानें, &c. स्थूलमानानें, सरासरी.

ROUGHNESS, *n.* v. A. 1. खरखरीतपणा *m.* खडबडीतपणा *m.* &c.

2 किजबिडीतपणा *m.* भसाडेपणा *m.* ढोबळेपणा रटाळेपणा *m.* रांठपणा *m.* &c. [*f.* रांठाई *f.*

3 धसकेपणा *m.* रगडेपणा *m.* &c. रांठपणा *m.* लांठपणा *m.* लांठाई

4 उग्रपणा *m.* कठीणपणा *m.* कठोरपणा *m.* &c.

ROUND, *a. circular.* वाटोळा, वर्तुल *pop.* वर्त्तूल, वर्तुलाकार, वृत्त, वृत्ताकार, चक्राकार, चक्रवान्, मंडलाकार, वलयाकार, कंकणाकार, कुंडलाकार.

Exactly r. गरगरीत-&c. वाटोळा.

Roundish. वाटोळासा. [र, गोटोळा.

2 *spherical, globular.* वाटोळा, गोल, गोलाकार, वर्त्तुल, वर्तुलाका-

3 *cylindrical.* लंबवर्तुल, लंबवर्तुलाकार, दीर्घवर्तुल, गोलदार, गोल, बरखंट्याचे आकाराचा.

4—as a number. ठोक *or* थोक, थोकबंद, धाकक, ठोक रकमेचा.

A r. number, *number that ends with a cipher.* पुजाचा आंक *m.* शून्यांतकसंख्या *f.*

A r. sum or price. वरीव किम्मत *f.* वरंच मोल *n.*

5 See PLAIN, POSITIVE.

ROUND, *n. circle,* v. RING. कडें *n.* वेढा *m.* मंडल *n.* चक्कर *n.* चक्र *n.*

2 *circular slice.* चकती *f.* चकदळ *n.* चकदळी *f.*

3 (of a ladder) *rundle,* v. STEP. पावका *m.* पायरी *f.* सीळ *f.*

4 *revolution, circular course of action.* फेरा *m.* फेरी *f.* फेरणी *f.* चक्र *n.* रहाटगाडगें *n.* कुंभारचाक *n.* पर्याय *m.* आवृत्ति *f.* आवर्त्तन *n.*

5 *or* rounds (of a guard). फेरी *f.* गस्त *f.* [दक्षिणा *f.*

R. of beggars, idol-worshippers, &c. in a city. नगरप्र-

The rounds of Fortune or Destiny. कर्माचा-दैवाचा-नशिबाचा-&c. भोवाडा *m.*

6 *round about course,* v. CIRCUIT भोवाडा *m.* फेरी *f.*

7 (of rope) *coil.* वेढा *m.* बळसा *m.* वांगडी *f.*

ROUND, *adv. circularly.* चक्कर-गिरकांडी-गिरकांडा-&c. मारून, गरगर, गरगरां, गरागर, गरारां, गिरगीर, गिरगिरा, चक्रवत्, मंडलवत्.

To look r. मुरडून-पाठीमागें-&c. पाहणें, पाठीमागें डोकावून पाहणें.

To turn r. the head. मुरडणें, तोंड *n.* फिरवणें.

To turn or come r. fig. *to change opinion, &c.* फिरणें, पालटणें, बदलणें, वळणें.

To turn r. *revolve.* फिरणें, गरगरणें, गरगर-&c. फिरणें, भ्रमणें, भ्रमण *n.*-&c. करणें.

2 *or* all round; *on all sides,* v. AROUND. सभोंवार, सभोंवता, सभोंवताला, चहुंकडे, आसमंतात्.

3 *circuitously,* v. ABOUT. फेऱ्यानें, भोंवाड्यानें, फेरा खाऊन-घेऊन, गरका मारून. [मारणें.

To go r. फेरा *m.* खाणें-घेणें-मारणें, गरका *m.*-चक्कर *n.*-&c.

The whole year r. बारमास, बारमाही, बारामहिने.

ROUND, *prep. around, over the outside of,* v. ABOUT. वरून, वर, भोंवता, सभोंवता. [सभोंवता.

2 *on all sides of,* v. AROUND. आसपास, भोंवता, भोंवताला.

To ROUND, *v. a.* वाटोळा-गोल-गोलाकार-&c. करणें, वाटोळेपणा *m.*-&c. आणणें.

2 बळसा *m.*-&c. घालणें.

ROUNDABOUT, *a. circuitous.* फेऱ्याचा, भोंवाड्याचा, गिरकांड्याचा, घेऱ्याचा, गरक्याचा.

ROUNDABOUT, *adv. on all sides.* सभोंवता, सभोंवताला, सभोंवती, भोंवताला, सभोंवर, सभोंवार, अधींमधीं, अध्येंमध्यें, दरेभेरेस, आसमंतात्, समंततः, समंतात्, वाटला *decl.*

Relating to the region or parts r. भोंवतालचा.

2 *circuitously,* v. ABOUT. फेऱ्यानें, भोंवाड्यानें, फेराखाऊन.

To go r. फेरा *m.* खाणें-घेणें-मारणें, गरका *m.* मारणें, चक्कर *n.* मारणें.

ROUND-HOUSE, *n.* पोलीसाची चौकी *f.*

ROUNDLY, *adv. flatly, plump, peremptorily, &c.* v. POSITIVELY, BLUNTLY. साफ, धादांत, धडधडीत, निखालस, निक्षून, परिछिन्न.

2 *to the purpose, vigorously, &c.* v. SMARTLY, WELL. रगडून, कचकावून, बळकट, खूब.

ROUNDNESS, *n.* v. A. 1. वाटोळेपणा *m.* वर्तुळपणा *m.* गोल *m.* वर्तुलत्व *n.* वर्तुलाकृति *f.* वृत्ताकृति *f.* &c.

2 वाटोळेपणा *m.* गोलपणा *m.* गोल *m.* गोलाई *f.* गोलत्व *n.* वर्तु-

लत्व *n.* गोलाकृति *f.* &c.

3 गोलदारपणा *m.* लंबवर्तुलत्व *n.* &c.

ROUNDROBIN, *n.* मंडलाकार सह्यांची अर्जी *f.*

ROUNDS, *n. of a guard.* फेरी *f.* गस्त *f.*

ROUNDS-MAN, *n.* फेरेकरी, गस्तकरी.

To ROUSE, *v. a.* v. To AWAKEN. जागा-जागृत-सावध-&c. करणें, उठवणें, झोंपमोड *f.*-&c करणें *g. of o.* बोधन *n.*-प्रबोधन *n.*-&c. करणें *g. of o.* प्रबुद्ध-&c. करणें.

2 *stir up,* v. To EXCITE. जागा-&c. करणें, उठवणें, उचलणें, उचल *f.*-उठावणी *f.*-उद्बोधन *n.*-बोधन *n.*-प्रबोधन *n.*-&c. करणें *g. of o.* [*n.* धमाचौकडी *f.*

ROUT, *n. rabble, mob,* v. PEOPLE. लुळें *n.* कतवार *n.* जंगमढबळें

2 (of an army) *defeat and dispersion.* मोड *m.* सैन्यभंग*m.* दाणादाण *f.* भणाण *m.* तारांगण*n.* तारातीर *f.* तारतोडगर्दी *f.* तसनस *or* नास *f.* धुंवा *m.* धुमा *m.* धूळ *f.* पट्टाधूळ *f.* धुळपट *f.* धूळदशा *f.* धूळधमासा *m.* धुळधाणी *f.* फांकाफांक *f.* पांगापांग *f.* तिन्हडफांक *f.* तिरडाफांक *f.* बाताहृत *or* हात *f.* विल्हेवाट *f.* विल्हय *f.*

Utter r. भाऊगर्दी *f.* पाणपत *n.* (as पाणपत झालें).

To ROUT, *v. a. defeat and put to flight.* मोडणें, उधळणें, उडवणें, गादवणें *or* गादावणें, मोड *m.*-भंग *m.*-दाणादाण *f.*-तारातीर *f.*-&c. करणें *g. of o.* चार वाटा *f.pl.* करणें *g. of o.* तजावजा *adv.* करणें, धूळ *f.*-धुवा *m.*-&c उडवणें *g. of o.* पळवणें, पळेसा करणें, पळापळ *f.*-पळपट *f.*-&c. करणें *g. of o.*

ROUTE, *n.* v. ROAD. जाण्याचारस्ता *m.*- मार्ग *m.*

ROUTED, *p.* v. V. मोडलेला, पळवलेला, चार वाटा केलेला, &c. शिकस्त, भग्न.

To be r. भडकणें, भणभणणें *intens.* भणाणणें, दशदिशांपळणें, सैरावैरा *adv.* पळणें, बाराबाटा होणें-पळणें, तीनतेरा होणें, भयाभंगास जाणें.

ROUTINE, *n. round of duties.* नित्यपाठ *m.* नित्यपरिपाठ *m.* नित्यकर्म *n.* नित्यकृत्य *n.* नित्यक्रम *m.* नित्याचरण *n.* नित्याचार *m.* आन्हिक *n.* परिपाठ *m.*

Of the daily r. नित्यपाठांतला.

To fall under the daily r. नित्याखालीं पडणें.

To ROVE, *v. n.* v. To WANDER. हिंडणें, भटकणें, भटकत-हिंडत फिरणें, टेहळ टिकोरी *f.*-परिभ्रमण *m.*-परिक्रम *n.*-परिक्रमण *n.*-विहार *m.*-विहरण *n.*-&c. करणें, बतवत फिरणें, बतवत *f.* करणें.

ROVER, *n.* ROVING, *p. a.* v. V. हिंडणारा, भटकणारा, हिंडत फिरणारा, &c. हिंडफिऱ्या, परिभ्रमण-&c. कर्त्ता-कारी-&c. यथेष्टचारी, रमतेराम, भटक्या, हुप्या, भटकभैरव *or* भैरोबा—esp. as used of children. हिंडगा, वाकड, ओढाळ.—Female r. भटकभवानी*f.* Male r. भटकभैरव.

I.—the mind, &c. *discursive.* ओढाळ.

II. *ranging robber,* &c. पुंड.

ROW, *n. rank, line.* ओळ *or* बळ *f.* बळी *f.* पंक्ति *pop.* पंगत *f.* रांग *f.* फरा *m.* हार *f.* हर *f.* हरपंजर *f.* सर *f.* माला *pop.* माळ *f.* आवलि *f.* पद्धति *f.* राजि *f.* श्रेणी *f.*

In one continuous r. ओळीनें, हारीनें,&c.हारोहार, एकसरीं *or* रें, एकाक्रमानें.

In rows. हारोहार.

R. (of flowering shrubs or plants). ताटबा *m.* ताटी *f.*

2 (of houses) *alley,* &c. पासाडी *f.* आळी*f.* आळ *f.* चाळ*f.*

ROW, *n. riot, hubbub,* &c. v. TUMULT. दणका*m.* धूम *f.* गोंधळ*m.* धांदल *f.* धांगला*m.* गर्दी *f.* रोराण *n.*

To kick up a r. दणका*m.* माजणें.

To ROW, *v. a.* v. To SCOLD. खरकावणें, खडखडवणें, खडसणें, दराडणें, खरड *f.*-खरडपट्टी *f.*-&c. काढणें *g. of o.*

To ROW, *v. a.* (a boat). बलवणें *or* बलावणें *or* बल्हवणें, अवलणें बलवून-&c. नेणें, हकारणें *or* हकालणें, बलावणी *f.*-बलावा *or* बल्हावा*m.* करणें *g. of o.*वल्हें*n.* मारणें-मारून नेणें, खेबा*m.* मारणें.

ROWEL, *n.* See SETON. 2—of a spur. चक्र*n.*

ROWER, *n.* (of a boat). वल्हेकरी *or* वलेकरी, अवलेकरी, अवल्या, आवलकरी, अंब्या.

ROWLOCK, *n. part where the oar rests.* खुंटी *f.*

ROYAL, *a. belonging,* &c. *to a king; regal, kingly.* राजाचा, नृपाचा, &c. राजकीय, बादशाही, पादशाही,राजसंबंधी, राजविषयक, नृपसंबंधी-विषयक, &c.

R. attendant. राजसेवक.

R. audience chamber. राजदरबार*m. n.* हुजूर*n.*

R. city or town. राजनगरी *f.* राजधानी *f.* राजपुरी *f.* राजपीठ*n.*

R. circle or court. राजमंडल *or* ळ*n.* राजमंडळी *f.*

R. court or hall of justice. राजदरबार*m. n.* राजसभा *f.* राजकचेरी *f.*

R. court or assembly. राजदरबार*m. n.* राजसभा *f.*

R. delights and diversions. राजविलास*m.*

R. duty. राजकार्य*n.*

R. dynasty or genealogy. राजावलि *f.*

R. edict. राजाज्ञा *f.* राजशासन*n.*

R. letter or order. राजलेख*m.* राजपत्र*n.*

R. mansion. राजवाडा*m.* राजमंदिर*n.*

R. revenue. राजधन*n.* राजस्व*n.*

R. signet or seal. राजमुद्रा *f.*

R. stamp or seal impression. राजमुद्रा*f.* राजचिन्ह*n.*

R. symbol. राजलक्षण*n.* राजचिन्ह*n.*

2 *becoming a king, magnificent,* &c. राजासयोग्य, राजकीय, राजपसंत, राजयोग्य, राजोचित, राजार्ह, बादशाही, पादशाही, आलिजाहा.

ROYALIST, *n.* राजाचा पक्षधरणारा-बाळगणारा, राजाचाअभिमानी.

ROYALTY, *n. kingship.* राजत्व*n.* राज्य*n.* नृपत्व*n.* राजपद*n.* बादशाही *f.* पादशाही *f.* राजसायुज्य*n.*

Ensign of r. राजचिन्ह*n.* राजलक्षण*n.* नृपलिंग*n.*

Ensigns or emblems of r.—compreh. छत्रचामर*n.* छत्रसिंहासन*n.* शिक्केकटार *f.* शिक्का मोर्तब*n.*

To RUB, *v. a. apply friction to.* घासणें, चोळणें, घर्षणें, घासटणें *or* घसटणें, मळणें, मर्दणें,घोटणें, घर्षण*n.*-मर्दन*n.*-&c.करणें*g. of o.*

To r. roughly & injuriously. चोळवटणें, चोळटणें.

2 *clean by friction,* v. To WIPE. पुसणें.

3 (in a mortar) *levigate.* खलणें, घोटणें.

4 down, (a horse). मळणें, चोळमालीश *f.* करणें, चाकरी *f.* करणें. [*or* नी *f.*

Rough glove for rubbing down horses with. हातणी

5 in; (unguents, &c. on the body). चोळणें, मर्दणें, गजणें.

6 off, v. To ABRADE. घासणें, घासटणें *or* घासवटणें, घसवटणें, खरडणें.

7 out; *erase*, v. To EFFACE. पुसणें, पुसून टाकणें, खोडणें.

8 up. *fig.* घासणें, घर्षणें, उजळणें, उजळणी *f.*-&c. करणें, तांब *f.*-जंग*m.*-&c. काढणें *g. of o.*

9 with; v. To SMEAR. माखणें, माजणें, चोपडणें.

To RUB, *v. n. have friction with*, v. To GRAZE. घासून-घसवटून-&c. जाणें, घासणें, लागणें, संघट्टन*n.*-संघर्षण *n.*-संघर्ष*m.*-&c. होणें *g. of s. recip.*

2 through; *get on with difficulty.* रेंटून-रेंटाईनें-रेंटारेंट करून-रेंटारेंटी करून-कुच्छें करून-जेमतेम करून-जसातसा-जसेंतसें करून -&c. जाणें-चालणें-निभावणें-पार पडणें-&c.

RUB, RUBBING, *n.* v. V. A. 1.—*act.* घासणें *n.* &c. घासणी *f.* मळणी *f.* घर्षण *n.* मर्दन *n.* विमर्दन *n.*

I. *collision, brush against.* घसरा *m.* घष्टा *m.* घसीटा *m.*

Rough r. (or wipe, &c.). घसरा *m.* घसका *m.* घष्ट *m.* घसीटा *m.*

II. *that which causes obstruction, difficulty, &c.* अडचण *f.* हिसका *m.* धक्का *m.* पेच *m.* नड *f.* लचांड *n.*

RUBBAGE, *n. loss by rubbing.* घस *f.* चोळ *f.* झीज *f.* झिजणावळ *f.* घासणी.

RUBBED, *p.* v. V. A. 1. घासलेला, चोळलेला, मळलेला, &c. घासींव, घर्षित, घृष्ट, मर्दित.

6 घासलेला, &c.

To be r. खरचटणें, खरडणें.

RUBBER, *n.* RUBBING, *p. a.* v. V. A. 1. घासणारा, चोळणारा, &c. घर्षण-मर्दन-&c. कर्त्ता-कारी.

2 पुसणारा.

v. V. N. 1. घासून जाणारा, घसवटून जाणारा, &c.

I. *stone, &c. to smooth and polish,* (paper, metals). मोहरा *m.* घोटा *m.*

RUBBISH, *n. waste or worthless matter.* कचरा *m.* केर *m.* केरकस्तान *n.* केरकचरा *m.* गाळसाळ *f. m.* गाबाळगुबाळ *n.* कस्तान *n.* खस्त *f.* खळमळ *m.* खेर *f.* गदळ *n.* कतबार *n.* घाण *f.* कचमा *m.* कचरट *n.*

Mass of mud, scum, *or* r. thrown up by the sea or brought by a river. लढ *f.* लढ्या *m.*

R. and filth,—as heaped or lying. हिडीस *n.* हेंदर *f. n.* खच *f.* खस *m.*

2 (as of a fallen building or wall). मलमा *m.* खरीप *n.*

RUBBLE, *n.*—R. wall. गडगा *or* घा *m.* गडगें *or* घें *n.*

RUBICAN, *a.*—a horse. तेल्या कुमेत *or* कुमाईत.

RUBICUND, &c. See REDDISH, &c.

RUBRIC, *n.* प्रार्थनापद्धतिसूत्र *n.*

RUBY, *n.* माणिक्य *pop.* माणीक *n.* & *dim.* माणकी *f.* लाल *m.* याकूत *n.* पद्मराग *m.*

Small r. चुणी *f.* चूण *f.* माणकी *f.*

That has ruby lips. बिंबोष्ठ (*f.* बिंबोष्ठी) *lit.* like the fruit of the momordica monadelpha. विद्रुमोष्ठ *m.* (विद्रुमोष्ठी *f.*) *lit.* like coral.

RUBY-BEAD, *n.* लालडी *f.*

RUDDER, *n.* v. HELM. सुकाण *or* न *n.* सुकाणू *m.* फळें *n.*

RUDDINESS, *n.* v. A. 1. तांबूसपणा *m.* लाली *f.*

2 तुकतुकी *f.* टवटवी *f.* तजला *m.* तजेला *m.* तजेली *f.* तजीली *f.* तेजगी *f.* तकतकी *f.*

RUDDLE, *n.* तांबडीमाती *f.* तांबडमाती *f.* लोखंडीकाव *f.*

RUDDY, *a. inclined to red*, v. RED. तांबूस, लाल.

2 *healthy-looking, fresh, lively, blooming*,—the countenance, &c. तुकतुकीत, टवटवीत, तकतकीत, तुकतुकीचा, टवटवीचा.

RUDE, *a. untaught, uncivilized, barbarous.* रानटी, रानवट, जंगली, अनक्षर, अशिक्षित, अशिष्ट, अविद्य, विद्याचारहीन, विद्याचारशून्य, हेंगाडा, रांगडा, सैरट *or* सैराट, अरबूज *or* द, कणशा.

2 *rough, coarse, uncivil, violent, impudent, overbearing, &c.* दांडगा, दांड, दंडेल, बाडगा, तंडेल, खलेल, उद्दट, उद्धत, धट, उर्मट, टोंग, ठेंगा, थोट, कटमस्त *or* स्ता, दांडगमस्त, आडदांड, आडदांडगा, अरबटदांड, बंजारदांड, गैरसाळ, गैरशिष्ट, अशिष्ट, असभ्य, असभ्यवृत्ति, दौर्जन्यवृत्ति, दांडगाधिग, धटांगण, धटिंगण, धटकुला, धसमुसळा *or* ळ्या, धस्समसूळ, धांगड, रांठ, लांठ, कोदंड, उद्दाम, सोरट, धृष्ट, समुद्धत, बियान, निर्भिड, बेशक, बेमुरवत, निर्मर्याद, अमर्यादशील, मस्ता *or* मस्त्या, नष्टविनय, प्रणष्टविनय, अविनय, सडीक.

Exceedingly r. अलमदांड.

3 *coarsely executed*, v. ROUGH. धोबड, भसाडा, कच्चा, रटाला *or* ल्या, रांठ, भोंवळसुती, भोंपळसुती, धांगडा.

4 *not skilled or practised; raw, unskilful, &c.* v. AWKWARD. अनाडी, कच्चा, अकुशल, अदक्ष, अपटु.

5 *not polished or elegant*, v. ARTLESS. साधा, साधाभोळा.

RUDE-SPOKEN, RUDE-TONGUED, *a. of unskilful speech.* आडव्या जिभेचा.

RUDELY, *adv.* v. A. 1. रानटीपणानें, &c. विद्याचाराबांचून.

2 दांडपणानें, &c. दांडगाईनें, ठोंगाईनें, लांठाईनें, धट्टाईनें, &c. मर्यादेवांचून, मुरवतीबांचून, &c.

3 धोबड, कच्चा *decl.* &c. धोबडपणानें, &c.

4 साधा *decl.* साधेपणानें.

RUDENESS, *n.* v. A. 1. रानटीपणा *m.* रानवटपणा *m.* &c. अक्षरराहित्य *n.* शिक्षाराहित्य*n.* विद्याचारहीनता *f.* विद्याचारशून्यता*f.*

2 दांडगेपणा *m.* दांडपणा *m.* धट्टपणा *m.* &c. दांडगाई *f.* दंडेली*f.* तंडेली *f.* ठोंगाई *f.* खलेली *f.* उरमटाई *or* उरमठाई *f.* थोटाई *f.* धट्टाई *f.* लट्ठाई *f.* लांठाई *f.* मलई *f.* मल्लाई *f.* सोरठाई *f.* धिंगामस्ती *f.* अशिष्टता *f.* असभ्यता *f.* दौर्जन्य *n.* असभ्यवृत्ति *f.* दौर्जन्यवृत्ति *f.* औद्धत्य *n.* बैयात्य *n.* धृष्टता *f.* धार्ष्ट्य *n.* बिनयाभाव *m.* विनयराहित्य *n.* अविनय *m.* अननुनय *m.*

3 धोबडपणा *m.* भसाडेपणा *m.* रांठपणा *m* &c.

4 अनाडीपणा *m.* &c. अदक्षता *f.* अपटुता *f.* अकुशलता *f.*

5 साधेपणा *m.*

RUDIMENT, *n. first principle or element.* मूलतत्व *n.* तत्व *n.* कारण *n.* बीज *n.* सूत्र *n.* मूलसूत्र *n.*

Rudiments. मूळपीठिका *f.* मूलतत्वें *n. pl.* परिभाषा *f.* मूलन. पग *n.* आरंभ *m.* उपक्रम *m.*

RUDIMENTAL, RUDIMENTARY, *a. pertaining to or consisting in rudiments.* मूलतत्वांचा, मूलारंभाचा, &c. मूलतत्वसंबंधी, मूलतत्वविषयक, मूलतत्वरूप, मूलतत्वप्रतिपादक, प्राथमिक.

To RUE, *v. a.* v. To REGRET. रडणें, पस्तावा *m.*-पश्चात्ताप *m.*-&c. करणें *g. of o.*

RUE, *n.*—the plant. सताप *m.* सतापाचें झाड *n.* ब्राह्मी *f.*—the leaves. सतापाचा पाला *m.*

RUEFUL, *a. mournful, doleful*, v. SAD. रडका, रडवा, रडकुंडा.

R. countenance. रडती सुरत *f.* रडकेंतोंड *n.* रोतीसुरत *f.*

Knight of the r. countenance. रडता राऊत, रडत लक्ष्मी, रडतोंड्या.

RUEFULNESS, *n.* v. A. रडकेपणा *m.* रडवेपणा *m.* &c.

RUFFIAN, *n. fellow ready for any desperate crime,* v. BRUTE. कर्म चांडाळ, इमामदांडगा, कारक, सोरट, क्रूरकर्मा, मांगहृदय.

RUFFLE, RUFF, *n. plait, fold.* सुरकुती *f.* चुणी *f.* चूण *f.* चीण *f.* वळकटी *or* वळकुटी *f.* वळकुटी सुरकुटी *f.*

2 See DISCOMPOSURE.

To RUFFLE, *v. a. plait, pucker.* चुणणें, सुरकुत्या *f. pl.*-चुण्या *f. pl.*-&c. घालणें-पाडणें.

2 *rumple, crumple, injuriously disorder, &c.* चुरणें, चुरडणें, चोळवटणें, चोळटणें, चोळमळणें, कुसमाडणें *or* मडणें, गुडधावणें, गुधडणें, घुसडणें, घुरदळणें *or* घुरधळणें, घोळसणें *or* घोळसावणें, गुरधळ *f.*-गुरधळी *f.* घालणें-मांडणें, पेर *m.* घालणें, गुधड *m.*-गुधडा *m.* घालणें, धुडकूस *or* गूस *m.* घालणें, घुसडणी *f.*-घुसडा *m.*- चोळामोळा *m.*-चोळामोळ *f.*-चोळाचोळ *f.*-चोळाचोळी *f.*-घुरदळा *m.*-घुरदळें *n.*-गुधडा *m.*-&c. करणें *g. of o.* मळणी *f.* घालणें, गुठा *m*-गुठें *n.* घालणें.

3 (the mind) v. To DISCOMPOSE. अस्वस्थ-व्यग्र-व्याकुल-क्षुब्ध-&c. करणें, गढुळणें, क्षोभवणें, खवंदळणें, तळमळ *f.*-डामाडूळ *f.*-&c. करणें *g. of o.* घडी *f.* बिघडणें *g. of. o.*

RUFFLED, *p.* v. V. 1. चुणलेला, चुण्या घातलेला, &c.

2 चुरलेला, चोळवटलेला, गुधडलेला, &c.

3 अस्वस्थ-क्षुब्ध-&c. केलेला, व्यग्र, व्याकुल, उद्विग्न.

RUFFLER, *n.* RUFFLING, *p. a.* v. V. 2. चुरडणारा, चोळवटणारा, गुधडणारा, &c.

3 अस्वस्थ करणारा, क्षोभवणारा, गढुळणारा, घडीबिघडवणारा, &c.

RUG, *n.*—the coarse woollen cloth. नमदा *m.*

RUGGED, *a. uneven, rough, abrupt, &c.* खाबडखुबड, खडबडीत, चेचड, उखरबाखर, उखराबाखर, उटंगल, उंचनीच, उंचसखल.

2 See SHAGGY.

RUGGEDNESS, *n.* v. A. 1. खाबडखुबडपणा *m.* &c.

RUIN, *n. destruction of buildings.* चुराडा *m.* खिंडार *or* रें *n.* मलमा *m.* [खिंडार.

That is in ruins. मोडलेला, मोडावलेला, ओसाड, ओस,

To fall (or be fallen)into r. मोडणें, मोडावणें, मोडकळणें, मोडकळीस येणें.

2—gener. v. DESTRUCTION. नाश *m.* बिघड *or* बिघाड *m* ध्वंस *m.* विध्वंस *m.* विघात *m.* तळपट *f.* नासधूस *f. m.* नासधूळ *f.* नासाडी *f.* तसनस *m.* बिघडाबिघड *f.*

One rushing to (bent upon, &c.)r. अबदसा आठवलेला.

To seek the r. of. घरावर गोंवरी *f.* ठेवणें *or* निखारा *m.* ठेवणें *or* कांट्या *f.pl.* घालणें *g. of o.*

To wait for the r. of. हाडीं विसावणें *g. of o.*

3 (of fortune, estate, affairs, &c.). सत्यनाश *m.* खराबी *f.* घरचूड *f.* धाळावाटी *f.* वाताहत *f.* गुघाण *f.* अस्त *m.n.* रफरफ *f.* बिलाखिला *m.* परकळे *m. pl.* v. उड, वाटोळें *n.* वाटोळें लांबोळें *n.* हलाकी *or* खी *f.* लक्ष्मीभंग *m.* संपत्तिभंग *m.* संपत्तिनाश *m.* ऐश्वर्यभंग *m.* ऐश्वर्यनाश *m.*

That causes r. or great loss. बुडव्या, बुडवणा *or* ण्या.

To RUIN, *v. a. demolish, &c.* v. To DESTROY. मोडणें, मोडून टाकणें, पाडणें, बराबर करणें, धुळीस-जमिनीस मिळवणें.

2 *subvert, mar, &c.*v.To DESTROY, To SPOIL, To DEFEAT. नासणें, नासूनटाकणें, बिघडणें, बिघडवणें, बुडवणें, बिघड *m.*-नाश *m.*-नासाडी *f.*-नासधूळ *f.*-विचका *m.*-&c. करणें *g. of o.*

3 *deprive of fortune, impoverish, &c.* बुडवणें, नाश*m.*-खराबी *f.*-सत्यनाश *m.*-घरचूड *f.*-संपत्तिनाश *m.*-&c. करणें *g. of o.* भिकेस लावणें, भिकारी-कंगाल-कोल-हतश्री-नष्टश्री-&c. करणें.—In this sense there are numerous expressive colloquialisms and phrases. They convey the sense *to ruin* with intensity and liveliness, and with great variety of comparison or allusion. देसधडीस लावणें,दारास *or* घरास कांटी *f.* लावणें *g. of o.* घरावर गवत रुजवणें *g. of o.* संसाराची मात्रा *f.*-संसाराचें मातेरें *n.*-संसाराचा पाटावरवंटा *m.* करणें *g. of o.* वाटोळें *n.*-वाटोळें लांबोळें *n.* करणें *g. of o.* घर *n.* घेणें-धुणें *g. of o.* धूळ फुंकावयास लावणें, धुळीचे दिवे खायास लावणें, ठार बुडवणें, खाड्यांत उतरणें, गळा *m.*-मान *f.* कापणें *g. of o.* डोई *f.* मारणें *g. of o.* नाडणें, घरावर निखारा*m.* ठेवणें, घरावर कऊल*n.* राहूं नदेणें, राखरांगोळी *f.* करणें, बिधुळणीस पाडणें-मिळवणें-मिळवून टाकणें.

To RUINATE, RUINATION. See To RUIN, RUIN.

RUINED, *p.* v. V. 1. मोडलेला, बराबर केलेला, धुळीस मिळवलेला, &c. खिंडार. [ध्वस्त.

2 नासलेला, बिघडलेला, &c. नष्ट, नाशित, विध्वंसित, विध्वस्त,

3 बुडवलेला, &c. खराब, गतश्री, हतश्री, नष्टश्री, विगतश्रीक, क्षतवृत्ति, नष्टैश्वर्य. [बराबरकरणारा, &c.

RUINER, *n.* RUINING, *p. a.* v. V. 1. मोडणारा, मोडून टाकणारा,

2 नासणारा, नासवणारा, बिघडणारा, &c. नाशक, नाशी, विध्वंसक, ध्वंसक, विघातक.

3 बुडवणारा, भिकेसलावणारा, खराब करणारा, &c. बुडव्या, बुडवण्या, संपत्तिनाशक-भंजक-&c. लक्ष्मीभंजक-नाशक-&c.ऐश्वर्यनाशक-&c. कल्याणहर-हर्त्ता-हारक.

RUINOUS, *a.* See DESTRUCTIVE, HURTFUL.

2 *fallen to ruin, decayed.* मोडकळलेला, मोडलेला, मोडकळीस आलेला, मोडकळीचा, खराबीचा, पडका, मोडका, जीर्ण.

RULE, *n. sway, government, command, mastery.* अमल *or* अम्मल *m.* राज्य *n.* सरदारी *f.* साहेबी *f.* धनीपणा *m.* हुकमत *f.* नायकी *f.* कैद *f.* शक *m.* लगाम *m.* अधिकार *m.* सत्ता *f.* आधिपत्य *n.* स्वामित्व *n.* प्रभुत्व *n.* नियंतृत्व *n.*

Foreign r. परचक्र *n.*

Full r., full sway. भरअम्मल*m.*

Skill to r. नियंतृत्व *n.*

To bring under r. (and management). सुतींपोतीं *or* सुतीं *or* सुतास लावणें-आणणें.

2 *regulation, law, canon.* विधि *m.* कायदा *m.* कानू *f.* चक *m.* सूत्र *n.* नियम *pop.* नेम *m.* बंद *m.* बंध *m.* निर्बंध *m.* बंधारण *n.* धरबंद *or* ध *m.* विधान *n.* दस्तूर *m.* प्रयोग *m.* उत्सर्ग *m.*

Rules and regulations,—compreh. कानूजाबता *m.* कैद्‌कानू *f.*

To keep one's r. बेतावर बसणें. [देणें.

To lay down rules for. रेघ *or* रेषा *f.* काढून देणें *or* ओढून

3 *standard, measure.* परिमाण *n.* प्रमाण*n.* धडा *m.*

According to (that-this-&c.) r. (त्या-ह्या-&c.) प्रमाणें.

4 v. RULER. रेखाटणी *f.*

5 *law, principle.* न्याय *m.* नियम *m.*

According to r. यथाविधि, विधिवत्, विधिपूर्वक,

By r. नेमी *or* नेहमी, नियमाचा *or* नेमाचा,

General or common r. साधारण *n.*

R. of action. कर्मविधि *m.*

To judge (differing particulars) by one r. एका काठीनें हाकणें.

RULE OF THREE, *n.* त्रिराशिक *or* त्रैराशिक *n.*

The first term or the *supposition* is called, त्रिराशिक *n.*—the second or the *rate*, प्रमाण *n.*—the third or the *demand*, इच्छा *f.*—and the fourth or the *answer*, इच्छाफल*n.*

Double r. पंचराशिक *n.* समस्तराशिक, विविधत्रैराशिक.

R. direct. क्रमत्रैराशिक, समत्रैराशिक.

R. inverse. विलोम त्रैराशिक, व्यस्तत्रैराशिक.

To RULE, *v. a.* (paper, &c.) अंकणें, रेखटणें *or* रेखाटणें, रेखणें, रेघा *f. pl.*-&c. ओढणें.

2 *control, regulate, &c.* v. To GOVERN. अमल *m.*-अधिकार *m.*-हुकमत *f.*-सत्ता *f.*-&c. करणें-चालवणें *with* वर *of o.* हुकमांत-&c. चालवणें, अनुशासणें, आवरणें, आटोपणें, शासन *n.*-अनुशासन *n.*-नियमन *n.*-आवरण *n.*-आवर *m.*-&c. करणें *g. of o.*

To RULE, *v. n. exercise supreme authority.* अमल *m.*-राज्य *n.*-प्रभुत्व *n.*-सरदारी *f.*-&c. करणें-चालवणें, राज्य *n.*-अमल *m.*-प्रभुत्व *n.*-&c. असणें *g. of s.*

RULED, *p.* v. V. A. 1. अंकलेला, रेखाटलेला, &c.

2 हुकमांत चालवलेला, &c. नियमित, शासित, अनुशासित.

RULER, *n. instrument to draw lines.* अंकणी *f.* रेखणी *f.* रेखाटणें *n.* रेखटणी *or* रेखाटणी *f.*

2 *governor, lord.* अमल करणारा, अधिकारी, स्वामी, प्रभु, खाबंद, सरदार, ईश्वर, नियंता, नियामक, अनुशासक, अनुशास्ता, अनुशासन-नियमन-&c. कर्त्ता-कारी-&c.

That is under one r.—a country, &c. एकछत्री, एकतर्फा *or* र्फी, एकसत्ताक, एकस्वामिक, एकमुखी, एकमुठी.

That is under two rulers. दुछत्री, दुतर्फा *or* र्फी, दुमाला, उभयसत्ताक, उभयस्वामिक.

RUM, *n. spirit distilled from molasses.* गौडी *f.*

RUM, *a. queer, odd,* v. STRANGE. विलक्षण, तऱ्हेवाईक.

To RUMBLE, *v. n. make a low continued sound.* गडगडणें *or* घडघडणें, घरघरणें, गरजणें, गडगड-गडगडां वाजणें,—*intens.* गडाडणें, घरारणें.

2—the belly. गुरगुरणें, घुरघुरणें, गडगडणें, गरबरणें, घरघरणें, घुळघुळणें. These verbs are used also impersonally.

RUMBLING, *n.* v. V. 1. गडगडणें *n.* &c. घडघड *f.* घरघर *f.* गर्जना *f.* घोष *m.*—*intens.* गडाड *m.* गडगडाड *m.* घडाड *m.*

2 गुरगुरणें *n.* &c. गुरगूर *f.* घुडु *n.*

RUMINANT, *a.* RUMINATING, *p. a.* v. V. 1. रवंथणारा, रवंथ-&c. करणारा, रोमंथ कर्त्ता-कारी-&c.

To RUMINATE, *v. n. chew the cud.* रवंथणें *or* रोंवंथणें *or* रोंथणें, रवंथ *or* रोवंथ *or* रोंथ *m. n.*-रोमंथ *m.* करणें.

2 v. To MUSE. ध्यान *n.*-मनन *n.*-&c. करणें, ध्यानांत-&c. असणें.

RUMINATION, *n.* v. V. 1.—*act.* रवंथणें, रवंथ *or* रोंवथ *or* रोंथ*m.* [*n.* रोमंथ *m.*

RUMMAGE, RUMMAGING, *n.* v. V.—*act.* धुंडाळणें *n.* ढांढुळणें *n.* &c. धुंडाळणी *f.* चाळण *f.* धुंडाळा *m.* चाळाचाळ *f.* चाळाचाळी *f.* उचलाउचल *f.* उचलासांचल *f.*

To RUMMAGE, *v. a. search narrowly.* ढांढुळणें *or* ढुंढाळणें, धुंडाळणें *or* धांडळणें, हुडकणें, चाळणें, धुंडाळा *m.*-चाळाचाळ *or* ळी *f.* -उचलाउचल *or* उचलासांचल *f.*-&c. करणें *g. of o.*

To turn topsy turvy in rummaging. पालथा घालणें.

RUMMAGED, *p.* v. V. ढांढुळलेला, धुंडाळलेला, &c.

RUMMAGER, *n.* RUMMAGING, *p. a.* v. V. ढांढुळणारा, धुंडाळणारा, धुंडाळा करणारा, ढांढुळ्या, धुंडाळ्या.

RUMOR, *n. report, bruit, hearsay,* v. REPORT. कानकूण *f.* अवई *or* अवाई *f.* अफवा *f.* जनरव *m.* आख्या *f.* उपश्रुति *f.* चर्चा *f.* ध्वनि *m. f.* वार्त्ता *f.* लोकवार्त्ता *f.* जनवार्त्ता *f.*

General or popular r. भुमका *m.* भुमकी *f.*

To RUMOR, *v. a. report abroad, bruit.* गाजवणें, चौघांत-&c. सांगणें, षट्कर्णी करणें, अफवा *f.*-अवई *f.*-&c. फेंकणें-उडवणें-पसरणें -पेरणें *g. of o.*

To be rumored abroad. रुढणें, भुमकणें. [कुकडी *f.*

RUMP, *n. end of the back bone of beasts.* ढिमोरा *m.* चोक *m.*

The crag and the r. गचाबांचा *m.*

To sink in at the r.—cow, goat, &c. at calving or yeaning. खोलटणें, खोल्गटणें, अंकडे *m. pl.* मांडणें *g. of s.* शेपसळी *f.* पडणें *g. of s.*

2 See BUTTOCK.

RUMPLE, *n. irregular pucker or plait.* मुरकुती *f.*

To RUMPLE, *v. a.* v. To RUFFLE. मुरकुत्या *f. pl.* पाडणें, चुरणें, चुरडणें, घुरदळणें, गुडधावणें, गुधडणें, घुसडणें, फुसमाडणें *or* मडणें, गुधड *or* डा *m.* घालणें, गुरधळ *or* ळी *f.* घालणें-मांडणें, चाळाबोळा *m.* करणें *g. of o.*

RUMPLED, *p.* v. V. मुरकुत्यापाडलेला, चुरडलेला, घुरदळलेला, &c.

To RUN, *v. n. move swiftly.* धावणें, धांवत येणें-जाणें, दौडणें, धाव *f.* मारणें-ठोकणें, धावड *f.*-धावण *f.*-धूम *f.*-&c. मारणें, पळणें, पळत जाणें-येणें.

To begin to r. धांव *f.* घेणें.

2 *run away, flee.* पळणें, पळून जाणें, पळ *m. f.* काढणें, बारा *or* बाराचें करणें-म्हणणें, बाराचा फाडा *m.* वाचणें, बाराचे लख *m. pl.* वाचणें, पळपट *f.*-पळण *f.* होणें *g. of s.* नाटी *f.* कापणें, गच्छ *n.*-गच्छंतीचें *n.*-गच्छंती *f.*-पोबारा *m.* करणें-म्हणणें, यःपलायाचें *n.*-यःपलायन *n.*-यःपलाय*m.* करणें-म्हणणें, शेपूट*n.*-शेपटी *f.* झाडणें, झुरकणें, झा *f. or* झ्याझ्या *f.* करणें.

To r. away cowardly. शेपूट *n.* घालून पळणें.

To r. away openly, boldly, defyingly, &c. हातावर हात देऊन *or* मारून पळणें *or* जाणें, हातावर तुरी देऊन पळणें.

3 *let flow*; or, *flow, exude.* गळणें, झरणें, निझरणें, वाहणें.

4 *become liquid, dissolve, sweat, ooze.* चिघळणें, चहळणें, गळणें, रेळणें, झरणें, निझरणें, निचरणें, स्रवणें.

5 *pass, proceed*;—time, &c. चालणें, गुजरणें *or* गुदरणें.

6—a slit or bore; *be enlarged.* ओघळणें, ओहळणें.

7—a sore; *emit pus.* बरबरणें, दुभणें, वाहणें, बुळकणें, लस *f.*-&c. वाहणें-निचणें, उवरणें *or* उवारणें.

8—damp paper, ink, &c. फुटणें, चरणें.

9—a road, range of hills, &c. वाहणें, लागणें, चालणें.

10 after—madly, wildly, intently, vehemently; *be wholly taken up with.* भरीं भरणें *g. of o.* नादांत असणें, नादीं भरणें *or* लागणें, नादावणें, भरारणें, तऱ्हेस *or* तऱ्हीं भरणें, छंद *m.* धरणें-घेणें *g. of o.* छंदास लागणें *or* भरणें, हांवेस भरणें.

11 after; v. To FOLLOW, To PURSUE. पाठीस लागणें *g. of o.* अनुगमन *n.*-अनुधावन *n.*-&c. करणें *g. of o.*

12 down;—a river, &c. ओसरणें, उतरणें.

13 into; *prick.* रुतणें, रुपणें, रोवणें, रोंचणें, बोचणें, चुबकणें, भरणें, शिरणें, रिघणें, संचरणें.
14 on; *be continued.* चालणें, चालू असणें.
15 on; *talk incessantly,* v. To PRATE. बडबडणें, बटबटणें, बडबड *f.*-बटबट *f.*-&c. चालणें *g. of s.*
16 (off with a paramour)—a married woman. हात *m.* धरून जाणें *g. of o.* पाठीं or पाटीस लागून जाणें *g. of o.*—a man with a woman, काढणें, काढून नेणें.
17 out; v. EXHAUSTED. खपणें, संपणें.
18 over; v. To OVERFLOW. ओसंडणें, वरसांडणें.
19 (over the body, &c.)—ants, lice, fleas. लुबलुबणें, लुळलुळणें.
20 to; *seek refuge with.* आश्रय *m.*-आस्रा *m.*-कास *f.*-कसोटा *m.*-पाय *m. pl.* धरणें *g. of o.*
21 together;—a rope, &c. एकारणें.
22 up, *grow rapidly.* उफणणें.
23 up,—an account. चढणें, वाढणें.

To RUN, *v. a. cause to move swiftly.* धावविणें, धावडणें, दवडणें, पिटविणें, पळविणें. [ढोकसणें,
2 *pierce, stab.* भोसकणें or भोकसणें, ढुसकणें or ढोसकणें or
3 *into, &c.* v. To THRUST. खुपसणें, खोंचणें, खोंचरणें.
4 down; *chase to weariness.* ठकेपर्यंत-बसेपर्यंत-&c. पाठीस लागणें.
5 down. See To DECRY.
6 hard; v. To URGE, To HANG UPON. खणपटीस-खणकुदळीस-गळचिपीस-&c. बसणें.
7 over; *narrate, &c. hastily.* सरासरी-वरवर-उपराउपर-जलदीनें-&c. सांगणें-बोलणें-पाहणें.
8 through. See To SQUANDER.
9 up; *erect superficially.* जथणें, सरासरी बांधणें.

RUN, RUNNING, *n.* v. V. N. 1. धांवणें *n.* &c. धांव *f.* दौड *f.* धावण *f.* धावन *n.* धावड *f.* धांवाडा *m.* धूम *f.* तडक *f.*
At a r. *by one effort,* v. EFFORT. एकातडक्यानें, एकातडाक्यानें.
Confused and general r. about. धांवाधांव or वी *f.* दौडादौडी *f.* धांवती *f.*
To come down by the r. कोसळणें, ढासळणें, ढकलणें, डगळणें or डघळणें or ढगळणें, धांधावणें.
2 *and* FLIGHT. पळणें *n.* &c. पळ *m. f.* पलायन *n.*
3 & 4. गळणें *n.* &c. गळ *f.* निचरा *m.* स्रव *m.* स्रवण *n.* स्राव *m.* बुळकी *f.* बुळकांडी *f.*
I. *extent of a r.* धांव *f.* [डी *f.*
II. *extent of inclination or ability,* v. REACH. धांव *f.* उ-
III. *course for a season, continued succession of.* सातरें *n.* वरणी *f.* झड *f.* संततधार *f.*
At or in the long r. शेवटीं, परिणामीं, निदर्शनीं.
IV. *prevalence, general reception, &c.* चलती *f.* खप *m.* आकांक्षा *f.* मार *m.*

RUNABOUT, *a. rantipole, roving,*—a child, &c. ओढाळ, हिंडगा, हिंडफिऱ्या, पायांवर or पायीं भोवरा पडलेला-नक्षत्रपडलेला.

RUNAGATE, RUNAWAY, *n. fugitive.* पळका, पळ्या, पळपटा or ट्या or पळपुटा or ट्या.

RUNDLE, *n. round of a ladder,* v. STEP. पावका *m.* पायरी *f.*

RUNNER, *n.* RUNNING, *p. a.* v. V. N. 1. धावणारा, धांव मारणारा, धावता, धावरा, धावक.
2 पळणारा, पळूनजाणारा, &c. पळका, पळ्या.
3 गळणारा, वाहणारा, स्रावी & स्रावक (in comp. as मदस्रावी गज, अमृतस्रावी चंद्र, &c.).
4 गळणारा, &c. वाहवरा, सद्रव.
7 वाहणारा, &c. बरबरीत.
I. *not stagnant.* वाहता, जिता, जिवंत, जितासु.
II.—as an account. खडा, चालता, चालू.
III. *courier.* कासीद, जासूद.
IV. *shooting sprig.* पागोरा *m.*
V. *in succession.* लागोपाठ. [मिळवण *n.*

RUNNET, *n. substance used for coagulating milk.* विरजण *n.*

RUNNING, *n.* v. DISCHARGE. निचरा *m.* पू *m.*—sanious r. लस *f.*

RUNNION. See SCRUB.

RUNT, *n. a diminutive creature.* टारगा, बुटारणा, बुटका, बुटबैंगण *n.*

RUPEE, *a.* रुपया *m.* रुपा *m.* रौप्यमुद्रा *f.* मुद्रा *f.* मुद्रिका *f.* टांक *m.*—in cant phraseology corresp. to *whiteboy, shiner, &c.* छब्बा *m.* भुरका *m.* शुभ्रा *m.* तूळ *m.* राम *m.* धोरला नारायण *m.*—and for a half-r. टाली *f.* रेवती *f.*—and for a quarter r. पकार or रा *m.* पकारी —in contempt. रुपडी *f.* रुपटका *m,* रुपटकी *f.*
Rupees of various currencies. परचुरण *n.*
A half r. is अधेली *f.*—$\frac{1}{4}$ r. पावली *f.* पावला *m.*—$\frac{1}{8}$ r. चवली *f.* चवल *m. f.*—$\frac{1}{16}$ r. अणा *m.* दुबल *m. f.* दुबली *f.*—$\frac{1}{32}$ r. आधेल *m.* [चिचड.
Defaced & battered—a r. चेचका—*dim.* चेचकट, चेचट,
R.'s weight. भार (ex. रुपया भार, दोनरुपये भार, &c.).
To change a r. रुपयाची मान मोडणें, खुर्दा *m.* करणें.
To shell out the rupees. छणछण *adv.* रुपये देणें.

To RUPTURE, *v. a. burst, break.* तोडणें, फोडणें.

RUPTURE, RUPTION, *n.* v. V.—*act.* तोडणें *n.* फोडणें *n.* फोड *m.* स्फोट *m.* स्फोटन *n.* भेदन *n.* विघटन or विघाटन *n.*—*state.* फूट *f.* फोड *m.* स्फोट *m.* भेद *m.* विध्वंस *m.*
I. (of friendly intercourse) *quarrel.* तूट *f.* फूट *f.* बिघाड *m.* बिघड *m.* स्नेहभंग *m.*
To come to a r. बिघडणें *g. of o.*
II. *hernia.* अंतर्गळ *m.* अंत्रवृद्धि *f.*
III. *ruptured gut.* पोटळा or पोटाळा *m.*

RUPTURED, *a. having hernia.* अंतर्गळाचा, अंतर्गळ झालेला, अंत्रवृद्धिरोगी.

RURAL, *a. belonging, &c. to the country,—as opposed to a* city. खेड्यापाड्यांतला, खेड्यापाड्याचा, बाहेरगांवचा, शहराबाहेरचा, जांगल, ग्राम्य, वन्य, अनागर, अनागरिक.
2 v. AGRICULTURAL. शेतकामाचा, शेतपोताचा.

RUSE. See ARTIFICE, TRICK.

RUSH, *n.*—the plant. लव्हा *m.* लव्हाळा *m.*
2 *any thing proverbially trifling or worthless.* काडी *f.* कसपट *n.* तृण *n.* कवडी *f.*

RUSH, RUSHING, *n.* v. V. 1. धावण्याचा-चालण्याचा-&c. झपाटा *m.*-रपाटा *m.*-तडखा *m.*-सपाटा *m.*-&c. झपाट्यानें-&c. जाणें *n.*-&c.
Emulative r. अहंपूर्विका *f.*
R. and scramble. झड *f. v.* घाल, पड.

To RUSH, *v. n. move or drive forwards with vehemence and haste.* झपाट्यानें-रपाट्यानें-सपाट्यानें-&c. जाणें-चालणें-&c. झपाटा*m.*-रपाटा*m.*-सपाटा*m.*-तडाखा*m.*-&c. मारणें, झपाटून-रगडून-&c. चालणें-&c.

2 at, on, upon, &c. v. To ATTACK. मार *m.* मारणें-देणें, आंगावर तुटून पडणें, आदळणें, झटणें, घसरणें, डुरळणें, डुर्योंडुर्यो करणें.

3 in, &c. दपटून-&c. शिरणें-शिरकणें-रिघणें, घुसणें, घुशी *f.* मारणें.

4 through, into, forward, &c. headlong. मुसंडा *or* मुसांडा *m.*-मुसंडी *or* मुसांडी *f.*-डुकरमुसांडी *f.*-मुसकांडी *f.*-सुरकांडी *or* सुळकांडी *f.*-&c. मारणें-देणें *or, with g. of s.* चालणें-निघणें, तरमुंडी *or* तुरमुंडी *f.* देणें, ढुसणें *or* ढोसणें, धसणें, धसून जाणें, लोटणें, धाड *f.* पडणें *g. of s.* डौरणें *or* डवरणें.

RUSHY, *a. made, &c. of rushes.* लव्ह्याचा, लव्हाळ्याचा.

RUST, *n.*—gener. मोरचा *m.* मल *n. pop.* मळ *m.* किट्ट *n.*

2 (of iron). तांब *f.* जंग *m.* तांबरा *m.*

R. mould, or other feculence. रंजगंज *m.*—To contract it. रंजणें गंजणें.

3 (of copper). कलंक *m.*

To RUST, *v. n. contract rust.* तांबणें, जंगणें, तांबरणें, जंग *m.*-मोरचा *m.*-&c. चढणें *with* वर, मळ *m.* बसणें.

To RUST, *v. a. make rusty.* तांब *f.*-&c. आणणें, जंग *m.*-&c. चढवणें, तांबवणें, जंगवणें.

RUSTED, See RUSTY.

RUSTIC, *a. of or belonging to the country,—as opposed to* the city, v. RURAL. खेडेगांवचा, खेड्यापाड्याचा, बाहेरगांवचा.

2 *unpolished, boorish, plain, coarse, &c. suited to the country.* गांवरानी, खेडेगांवचा, खेडेगांवी, गांवठी, गांवढळ, गांवठ्या, रानवट, रानकट, रानगट, खेडोळ *or* खेडवळ, खेडुला, खेडाळू, खेडाळ *or* खेडवाळ, गांवढी, आडरानी, ग्राम्य, ग्राम्यक, कुणबाऊ *or* कुणबाव्याचा, शेतपोतचा, शेतसंबंधी.

RUSTIC, *n. clown, swain, hind,* v. COUNTRYMAN. शेतखण्या, खेड्या, खेडेगांवचा, गांवढ्या, आडगळचा, गंवार, गांवढळ.

To RUSTICATE, *v. a. banish into the country.* खेडेगांवांत राहायास लावून देणें.

RUSTICITY, *n.* v. A. 2. गांवढेपणा *m.* गंवारपणा *m.* खेडवाळपणा *m.* &c. ग्राम्यत्व *n.*

RUSTINESS, *n.* v. A. 1. जंगलेलेपणा *m.* जंगेपणा *m.* &c. तांब *f.* जंग *m.*

2 मळिणपणा *m.* मालिन्य *n.* अनुपस्थिति *f.*

To RUSTLE, *v. n. make a quick succession of small sounds.* खडबडणें, खुडबुडणें, खडखडणें, खरखरणें, खसखसणें, खुसखुसणें, खसबसणें, खुसबुसणें, सुडबुडणें, सरसर *or* रां *adv.* करणें-जाणें, सरसरणें *intens.* सरारणें, चरचरणें.

2—as stiff cloth, &c. फडफडणें, फडकणें, कडकणें.

RUSTLER, *n.* RUSTLING, *p. a.* v. V. 1. खडखडणारा, खडबडणारा, &c. कडबडीत, करकरीत.

RUSTLING, *n.* v. V. 1. खडबडणें *n.* &c. खडबड *or* खुडबूड *f.* खसखस *f.* खुसखुस *f.* खसबस *f.* खुसबूस *f.* खडखड *f.* सुडबूड *f.* —*intens.* खडबडाट *m.* खसखसाट *m.* खसबसाट *m.* खडखडाट*m.* सुडबुराट *m.*

RUSTLINGLY, *adv.* v. V. 1. खडखड, खरखर *or* रां, खसबस, खसखसां, चरचर *or* रां, सरसर *or* रां,—*intens.* चराचर, चरारां, खसाखस *or* सां, खसासां, सरासर, सरारां.

2 फडफड *or* डां *intens.* फडाफड, फडाडां.

RUSTY, *a. affected by rust.* तांबलेला, जंगलेला, तांब चढलेला, जंग चढलेला, तांबेचा, जंगाचा, &c. जंगी, जंग्या, जंगट, जंगेल, तांबनेल.

2 fig. *impaired by disuse, inaction, &c.* मलिन *pop.* मळीण, मजीत, अनुपस्थित.

RUT, *n.*—in animals, *desire of the male.* माज *m.* उधान *n.* भर *m.*—of elephants, camels, &c. मस्ती *f.*—of mares, she asses, &c. हात्याण *n.*

To be in r. माज *m.* करणें, माजास-&c. येणें.

2 (of a cart wheel). गराडी *f.* चाकारी *f.* चाकोरें *n.*

RUTHLESS, &c. See PITILESS, &c.

RUTTISH, See LUSTFUL.

RYE *n.* एक धान्य आहे.

RYOT. See SUBJECT, TENANT.

S.

S. in its initial and naturally sibilant sound, is represented by स. For it in its sound of z (as in rose, muse, &c.), the Maráṭhí has no representative. Sh. is represented by श.

SABBATH, *n.* विश्रांति वार *m.* विश्रामवार *m.*

SABLE. See BLACK.

SABRE, *n.* v. SWORD. बांकडी तरवार *f.* तेगा *m.* वक्रखड्ग *m.*

To SABRE, *v. a.* v. To KILL. तरवारीनें-&c. कापणें-तोडणें-कत्तल *f.* करणें *g. of o.*

SACCHARINE, *a. pertaining, &c. to sugar.* साखरेचा, शर्करेचा, शर्करासंबंधी-विषयक, शर्कराधर्मक, शर्करागुणक.

SACERDOTAL, *a. pertaining, &c. to priests or the priesthood.* याजकाचा, यज्ञकर्माचा, याज्ञिक्याचा, याजकसंबंधी-विषयक, याज्ञिक्यसंबंधी-विषयक.

SACHEL, *n. bag to hold paper, &c.* जुजदान *or* जुगदान *n.*

SACK, *n. large bag.* पातें *n.* थैला *m.* कोथळा *m.* तरटी *f.* बोंदरी *f.*

Double, s. (for beasts). कंठाळ *f.* गोणी *f.* गोण *f.* गोणा *m.* पडशा *f.* हसची *f.*

Double s. (for men). दुमोट *f.* दुमोटली *f.* दुमोटलें *n.*—in jocose &c. phrasecol. दुमात्रकानाकी *f.*

Large s. for holding grain. भोत *m.*

Saddle- s. पडशी *f.*

2 See PLUNDER.

To SACK, *v.a. pillage,* v. To PLUNDER. लुटणें, लुचाडणें, झांबाडणें, लुटालूट *f.*-लुबडालुबड *f.*-झाडझपट *f.*-&c. करणें.

SACK-CLOTH, SACKING, *n.* ताट *n.* तरट *or* तरंट *n.* गोणताट *n.* गोणपट *or* पाट *m. n.* गोणी *f.*

Of (made of, &c.) s. तरटी.

Old, worn s. ताटक *n.*

Sack made of s. तरटी *f.* बोंदरी *f.*

SACRAMENT, *n. solemn religious ceremony.* संस्कार *m.* There are sixteen among the Hindus, which see under RITE.

2 *the Lord's supper.* प्रभुभोजन *n.*

SACRAMENTAL, *a.* संस्काराचा, संस्कारसंबंधी, संस्कारविषयक, सं-

स्कार प्रयुक्त, संस्काररूप.

SACRED, *a. not secular or common; pertaining to God or his worship and service.* देवाचा, ईश्वराचा, ईश्वरी, ईश्वरसंबंधी, देवसंबंधी, देवाविषयींचा, देवासंबंधींचा, देवाकडचा, परमार्थाविषयींचा, पवित्र, असंसारिक, अप्रापंचिक, प्रपंचेतर.

2 *used for religious purposes.* देवभक्तीचा, ईश्वरभक्तीचा, देवभजनाचा, ईश्वरभजनाचा, ईश्वरभजनोपयोगी, देवभजनार्थक, पवित्र, पवित्रकर्मोपयोगी, पवित्रकर्मार्थक.

S. place or spot, v. HOLY. क्षेत्र *n.*

3 *inviolable, &c. as if appropriated to a deity.* देवास वाहिल्यासारखा, वाहिलेला, शिवस्वासारखा, शिवस्वतुल्य, शिवस्वसदृश, अनुल्लंघनीय, अलंघनीय, अलंघ्य, अभेद्य, सशपथ, कृतशपथ, निषेधपात्र. [गोमांस *n.*

S. thing, *thing not to be touched.* शिवस्व *n.* ब्रम्हस्व *n.*

4 v. VENERABLE. अभियुक्त.

SACREDNESS, *n.* v. A. 1. देवसंबंधिता *f.* ईश्वरसंबंधिता *f.* ईश्वरीसंबंध *m.* अप्रापंचिकत्व *n.* &c. पवित्रता *f.*

3 अनुल्लंघनीयता *f.* &c.

SACRIFICABLE, *a. that may be offered in sacrifice.* यज्ञाच्या उपयोगाचा, मेधाच्या उपयोगाचा, &c. मेध्य, यज्ञिय, याज्य, यजनीय, यजनयोग्य, हौम्य. [माचा.

SACRIFICAL, SACRIFIC, *a. employed in sacrifice.* यज्ञाच्या का-

To SACRIFICE, *v. a. immolate as an offering.* यज्ञ *m.*-मेध *m.*-होम *m.*-&c. करणें *g. of o.* बलि *pop.* बळी *m.* करणें-देणें *g. of o.* बलिदान *n.* करणें *g. of o.* आहुति *f.* देणें *g. of o.*

To s. one's self (to the service of). प्राण *m.* वाहणें.

2 *give up for the sake of.* देणें *with* साठीं-बदल-&c.

SACRIFICE, SACRIFICING, *n.* v. V. यज्ञ *m.* याग *m.* यजन *n.* याजन *n.* मेध *m.* मख *m.* सत्र *n.* क्रतु *m.* होम *m.* हवन *n.* धृति *f.* अध्वर *m.* चयन *m.* बलि *pop.* बळी *m.* बलिदान *n.* बलिप्रदान *n.* ज्योतिष्टोम *m.* नारायणबलि *m.*

Beast fit to be offered in s. यज्ञपशु *m.*

Fire for s. होमाग्नि *m.*

Human s. नरमेध *m.* नरयज्ञ *m.* नरबलि *m.*

Officiating at a s. याजन *n.*

Officiating priest at a s. याजक, याज्ञिक, होता.

Person instituting a s. and defraying its charges. यजमान *m.*

Pit for s. यज्ञकुंड *n.*

Post at a s. यूप *m.*

Pit for the fire of a s. होमकुंड *m.* हवनी *f.* हविश्री *f.*

Place of s. यज्ञशाला *f.* [रा *m.*

S. of a sheep before treading out corn. डाहोरा *or* डब-

Sacrifices,—compreh. *or* gener. यज्ञयाग *m.*

Shed for s. यज्ञमंडप *m.*

Supplementary s. अवभृथ *m.* दीक्षांत *m.* यज्ञांत *m.*

Terrace or plat for s. वेदी *or* वेदि *f.* स्थंडिल *n.*

To fall a s. fig. बळी पडणें *with g. of o.* बळी जाणें.

SACRIFICER, *n.* SACRIFICANT, *n.* &c. v. V. 1. यज्ञ-&c. करणारा-कर्ता, यजमान, याज्ञिक, याजक.

SACRIFICIAL, *a. belonging, &c. to sacrifice.* यज्ञाचा, यागाचा, &c. &c. यज्ञिय, यज्ञसंबंधी, यज्ञविषयक, &c.ऐष्टिक.

S. ceremonies. याज्ञिक्य *n.*

S. grass, *poa cynosuroides.* दर्भ *m.* कुश *m. n.*—a seat formed of it कुशासन *n.* दर्भासन *n.*

S. thread. यज्ञोपवीत *n.* See under THREAD.

SACRILEGE, *n. robbery of sacred things.* धर्मादायाची चोरी *f.* देवस्वापहार *m.* देवस्वापहरण *n.* देवस्वचौर्य *n.*

SACRILEGIOUS, *a.* v. N. देवस्वापहाराचा, देवस्वापहारसंबंधी, देवस्वापहारविषयक, देवस्वापहारी, देवस्वापहारक, देवस्वापहारकर्त्ता.

SAD, *a. affected with grief, sorrowful,* v. LOW, DISPIRITED. उदास, उदासी, उदासीन, खिन्न, खेदयुक्त, दिलगीर, दुश्चित्त, विषण्ण, विमनस्क *or* विमना.

2 *having the external appearance of sorrow, rueful, doleful, &c.* रडका, रडवा, रडकुंडा, उतरल्या तोंडाचा, उतरलेला, काळ्यातोंडाचा, म्लान, म्लानवदन, म्लानमुख.

3 v. CALAMITOUS, AFFLICTIVE. दुःखाचा, अनिष्टाचा, दुःखद, दुःखप्रद, दुःखावह.

4 *sorry, bad, &c.* v. WORTHLESS. केविलवाणा *or* णी, किलवाणा *or* णी, नादान, एर.

5 See SERIOUS.

To SADDEN, *v. a. make sorrowful.* खिन्न-उदास-&c. करणें.

SADDLE, *n.*—the European. जीन *m. n.*—the native or country. खोगीर *m. n.*

Frame of a s. खोड *n.*

That is without a s. or cloth—a horse. उपलाणा *or* णी. —to ride without a s. or cloth. उपलाणां बसणें.

Fore-tie of a s. गोर *or* घोर बंद *or* गळबंद *m.*

Leather sewn on a s. to sustain the abrasion of the girth. घशेट *f. n.* घशेटा *m.* घशेटें *n.* घसीट *f. n.* घसिटा *m.*

S. composed of folds of cloth. चारजामा *m.*

S. having two sides. छापी खोगीर *m. n.*

Side of a s. छाप *m. f.*

Sitting cloth over a s. गाशा *m.*

Strips (of broad cloth, &c.) appended to a s. सडकी *f. pl.*

Thigh-pad of a s. मांडगादी *f.* फराकी *f.*

Ties connecting the sides of a s. अलगुजीं *n. pl.*

To SADDLE, *v. a. put a saddle on.* खोगीर *or* जीन *m.* घालणें-ठेवणें-भिडवणें-बांधणें-कसणें-अवळणें, जीनबंदी *f.* करणें.

2 *fix a burden on.* ओझें *n.*-&c. घालणें *with* वर *of o.*

SADDLE-BACKED, *a.* जीनपाठीचा, जीनपाठी.

SADDLE-BAG, *n.* दुरें *n.* पडशी *f.*

SADDLE-BOW, *n.* खोड *n.*

SADDLE-CLOTH, *n.* under the s. घामोळें *n.*—over the s. गाशा *m.*

SADDE-GIRTH, *n.* तंग *m.*

Strap or leather end of a s. हयासा *m.*

SADDLE-MAKER, SADDLER, *n.* जिनगर, जीन-खोगीर करणारा.

SADDLE-MAKING, *n.* जिनगरी *f.*

SADDLE-FRAME, *n.* खोड *n.*

SADDLERY, *n.* जिनगरानें केलेलें सामान *n.*

2 जिनगराचा धंदा *m.* जिनगरी *f.*

SADLY, *adv.* v. A. 1. उदासपणानें, दिलगिरीनें, उदासपणें, &c.

I. *in a great degree, so as to cause sorrow.* फार, भारी, दुःख वाटायाजोगा *decl.*

SADNESS, *n.* v. A. 1. उदासपणा *m.* &c. दिलगिरी *f.* औदासीन्य *n.* विषाद *m.*

2 रडकेपणा *m.* रडतोंडेपणा *m.* &c. रडकीमुद्रा *f.* म्लानमुखता *f.* मुखम्लानता *f.* मुखमालिन्य *n.*

SAFE, *a. free from danger.* निजोखमी, निर्भय, निष्कंटक, निरुपद्रव, निर्विघ्न, बिनधोक, भयातीत, अकुतोभय *vulg.* अकतोभय, विपत्यतीत, अपकारातीत.

2 *free from hurt or damage.* सुरक्षित, धड, शाबूत, कुशल *or* ळ, अक्षत, अचळ, अचळवी, अजातापकार, अजातनाश.

3 *conferring safety.* निर्भय, भयाभावाचा, भयहीन, भयरहित, निजोखमी, अकुतोभय *vulg.* अकतोभय.

SAFE, *n.*—for provisions. ओलकंबली पाटी *f.* कुरपण *n.* पिंजरा*m.* भाळी *f.*

SAFE-CONDUCT, *n. pass.* अभयपत्र *n.* कौल *m.*

SAFE-GUARD, *n.* See DEFENCE, PROTECTION.

2 *pass.* अभयपत्र *n.* कौल *m.*

SAFELY, *adv.* v. A. 1. भयावांचून, निर्भयानें, निर्भय, खुशाल, सुखरूप, कुशल *or* ळ, स्वस्तिक्षेम.

2 सलामत, सुदामत, धक्कालागल्यावांचून, धक्काबसल्यावांचून, अचळ, अचानक, अक्षतमरिष्ट.

SAFETY, SAFENESS, *n.* v.A.1. निजोखमीपणा *m.* &c. निर्भयत्व*n.* निष्कंटकत्व *n.* निरुपद्रवता *f.* &c. निर्भय *n.* भयाभाव *m.* भयहीनता *f.* भयशून्यता *f.*

2 धडपणा *m.* शाबुतपणा *m.* अचळपणा *m.* सुरक्षितपणा *m.* &c. कुशलता *f.* सुरक्षितत्व *n.* अक्षतत्व *n.*

I. *shelter, cover, protection, &c.* आश्रय *m.*

SAFFLOWER, *n. carthamus,*—the plant. कुसुंबकरडई *or* कुसुंबकरडी *f.* करडई *f.* कुसुंभ *m.* —seed of it. करडई *f.*—chaff of it. करडकूट *n.* करडगूळ *n.*—oil expressed from the seed. करडेल *n.*

Dried flowers of s. कुसुंब *or* कुसुंबा *m.*

Dye prepared from the dried flowers of s.कुसुंब*or*बा*m.*

First tint obtained from s. जेठा *m.*

Of or belonging to s. कौसुंभ.

SAFFRON, *n.*—*crocus sativus.* कुंकुम *n.* केशर *n.* जाफरा *m.*

S.-wash. केशरी *f.*

SAFFRON, SAFFRONY, SAFFRON-COLORED, *a. having the colour of saffron.* केशरी, केशरी रंगाचा, जाफरमाना.

SAFFRON-BASTARD. See SAFFLOWER.

To **SAG.** See To SWAG.

SAGACIOUS, SAGACITY. See SHARP, SHARPNESS.

SAGE, *n.* See PHILOSOPHER. 2. v. SAINT. ईश्वरीपुरुष, महापुरुष, मुनि, मौनी, मुमुक्षु, यति *or* यती, गुरुजन,—As implying *one having divine or spiritual knowledge.* सिद्ध, सिद्धपुरुष, ब्रह्मज्ञ, ब्रह्मज्ञानी, ब्रह्मवेत्ता, ब्रह्मवेदी, आत्मज्ञ, आत्मतत्वज्ञ, आत्मयाजी, ज्ञानी, परमार्थवित्, परमहंस, ज्ञानचक्षु, ज्ञानदृष्टि, ज्ञातात्मा, दास.

3—the plant, *salvia Bengalensis.* कापुरकचरा*m.*कापुरकचरी*f.*

SAGE, *a.* v. WISE. शाहणा, शाहणपणाचा, चतुर.

SAGELY, *adv.* v. A. शाहणपणानें, चातुर्यानें.

SAGENESS, शाहणपणा *m.* शाहणपण *n.* चातुर्य *n.*

SAGITTAL, *a. like, &c. an arrow.* तीराचा, बाणाचा, तीरासारखा, बाणासारखा.

SAGITTARIUS, *n.*—the zodiacal sign. धनु *n.* धन *m.*

SAGO, *n.* सागू *m.* सागूचे तांदूळ *m. pl.*

Grain or granule of s. सागूदाणा *n.* सागू *m.*

SAID, *p.* v. V. म्हटलेला, &c. उक्त, प्रोक्त, भाषित, उदित, आख्यात, व्याख्यात, अभिहित, भणित.

SAIL, *n.* शीड *n.* अवजार *or* ओजार *n.*

Jib-s. फोगी *f.*

Lower end of the sail-yard. घोंस *or* घोंस *m.*

S. furled on its yard. वात *f.*

Sheet of a s. दमान *n.*

With full or swelling sails. भरघोसानें *or* भरल्याघोसानें.

To set s. *put out to sea.* गलबत-&c. हकारणें.

To set the s. शीड *n.* हकारणें, शीड *n.* उभारणें.

To shift the s. (in changing tacks). माचण *f.* घेणे.

To strike s. शीड *n.* उतरणें. [महल *f.*

2 See SHIP. 3 *an excursion in a vessel.* नावेंत-&c. वमन

To **SAIL**, *v. n. be impelled by the action of wind on sails.* शिडावर-शिडानें जाणें.

2 *pass or proceed by water.* गलबतानें-गलबतावर-गलबतावरून -&c. जाणें, पाण्यांतून जाणें, समुद्रानें-जलमार्गानें-&c. जाणें.

3 *set sail, begin a voyage.* गलबत *n.*-&c. हकारणें-काढणें-उठवणें.

4 हवेंतून चालणें-जाणें.

SAIL-CLOTH, *n.* चिवटा *m.* पडम *n.*

SAIL-YARD, *n.* शीडकाठी *f.*

The lower end of the s. *the tack on board.* घोंस *m.*

SAILOR, *n. mariner, seaman.* सफरी, गलबती माणूस, जहाजकरी, जहाजवाला, गलबतवाला, दर्यावरदी, समुद्रयायी, समुद्रग, नाविक.

Native s. सलाशी *or* सी, लशकर *or* लषकर.

Wages of a s. for a trip or voyage. सफर *f.*

SAINT, *n. holy personage,* v. SAGE. ऋषि, साधु, संत, ईश्वरीपुरुष, महापुरुष, संत, मुनि, मौनी, बली, नियतेंद्रिय, निर्जितेंद्रित, पूतात्मा, मुमुक्षु, परपरुष, अवलिया, विधिनिषेधातीत.

Patron-s. इष्टदेवता *f.* इष्टदेवत *n.*

Saints and good men—compreh. संतसज्जन *m. pl.*

Series or succession of saints. संतपरंपरा *f.*संतमालिका*f.*

The seven saints. सप्तर्षि *pop.* सप्त ऋषि *m. pl.*

Way or walk of saints. संतमार्ग *m.*

SAINT-LIKE, SAINTLY, *a. like or becoming &c.a saint.* साधूचा, संताचा, &c. संती, संताचे चालीचा-रीतीचा-&c. साधूसारखा, साधुवत्, साधुसदृश.

SAINTLINESS, *n.* v. A. संतपणा *m.* संतीचाल *f.* साधुत्व *n.* साधुसादृश्य*n.*

To assume s. कानांत तुळसी *f.* घालणें.

SAKE, *n. purpose &c.* कारण *n.* हेतु *m.*

For one's own s. आत्मार्थ.

For the s. of. साठीं, करितां, खब, निमित्त, खातर, बदल खातर, नांवावर, अर्थी, अर्थ (in comp.).

SALACIOUS, SALACIOUSNESS. See LUSTFUL, LUST.

SAL-AMMONIAC, *n.* नवसागर *or* नौसागर *m.*

SALARY, *n.* v. ALLOWANCE, WAGES. वर्षाचा पगार *m.*-&c. साल *n.* वेतन *n.* नेमणूक *f.* वार्षिक *n.*

SALE, *n.* v. V. A. विकरा *m.* विकरी *or* विक्री *f.* विक्रय *m.* क्रय *m.* विक्रयण *n.* कीणन *n.* पणन *n.*

Bill of s. सरखत *n.*

Deed of s. फरोक्त खत *n.*
Profits or amount of s. विकरी *f.*
Rescission of s. विक्रयानुशय *m.* [*or* नी *f.*
The first sale after the dawning of the day. बोहणी
That is for s. विकाऊ, विकणाऊ.
v. V. N. *vent, going off.* खप *m.* विकरी *or* विक्री *f.*

SALEABLE, *a.* v. V. विकायाजोगा-सारखा-&c. क्रेय, विक्रेय, क्रेय्य, क्रेतव्य, पण्य.

SALEP, *n.* सालंमिश्री *or* सालमिश्री *f.*

SALESMAN, *n. one who finds a sale for the goods of another.* दलाल *m.*

SALIENT, *a. projecting.* बाहेरआलेला.

SALINE, SALINOUS, *a.* v. SALT. खारा, मिठाचा, लावण, लावणिक.

SALINENESS, *n.* v. A. खारेपणा *m.* &c. लोणा *m.*

SALIVA, *n.* v. SPITTLE. थुका *m.* थुकी *f.* लाला *pop.* लाळ *f.* मुखरस *m.*

SALIVAL, SALIVARY, SALIVOUS, *a.* v. N. थुक्याचा, &c. लालासंबंधी, लालाविषयक, लालोत्पादक, लालावाहक.

To SALIVATE, *v. a. cause secretion of saliva.* तोंड *n.* आणणें, तोंड *n.* देणें.
To be salivated. तोंड *n.* येणें *in. con.* [खेज.

SALLOW, *a. of a pale, yellowish colour.* पिकूट, पिकुटलेला, नि-
S. hue (of the countenance or body). पिकटी *f.*
To get or turn s. पिकणें, पिकुटणें.

SALLOWNESS, *n.* v. A. पिकुटपणा *m.* काळवटी *f.* काळवंडी *f.* काळवण *f.* कालिमा *m. f.* पिकटी *f.*

SALLY, *n. issue of troops from a fort to attack besiegers.* छापा घालण्यासाठीं बाहेर पडणें *n.* [*f.* चुटका *m.*
2 (of humor, wit, frolic, &c.). मौज *f.* लहर *f.* बहर *m.*
3 (of auger or ardor). उसळी *f. v.* खा, झटका *m.* झटकास *m.* वेग *m.* आवेश *m.*

To SALLY, *v. n. issue from a fort &c. to attack besiegers.* छप्पा-छापा-&c. घालण्यासाठीं बाहेर पडणें.

SALLY-PORT, *n.* खिडकी *f.*

SALMON, *n.* एक जातीचा मासा आहे.

SALOON, *n. spacious hall, &c.* सदर *f.* दलान *or* दालन *n.* रंगमहाल *m.* आरसेमहाल *m.*

SALT, *n.* मीठ *n.* लवण *n.* क्षार *pop.* खार *m.* निमक *m.*
Black s. *Bitnoben.* काळेंमीठ *n.* बिडलवण *n.* बीड *n.* गंधबीड *n.* कृष्णलवण *n.* रोचक *n.* क्षार *m.* पाक्य *n.*
Culinary or common s. एरमीठ *n.*
Landing place for s. मीठबंदर *n.*
Mineral or a metallic s. उपरस *m.* रस *m.*
Mineral s. Rock s. Factitious s.—in contrad. from sea salt. खारेंमीठ *n.*
Rock s. शेंधेलोण *n.* सिंधुलवण *n.* सैंधव *n.* सौवर्चल *n.*
S. extracted from saline earth, dung, &c. सांबरमीठ-सावरमीठ-सांवरीमीठ *n.* मेंगळमीठ *or* मेंगेंमीठ *n.*
Sochal s. संचळ *n.* संचळखार *m.* सौचरलोण *n.* पादेलोण *n.*
Wanting in s. अळणी, अळणट.
To become or be impregnated with s. खारावणें.
2 (in speech) *pungency, sharpness.* मीठमिरची *f.* तिखटमीठ *n.*

SALT, *a.* खारा, खारट, लवण, लवणमय, लावण, लावणिक, क्षार, क्षारयुक्त, क्षारधर्मक, क्षारविशिष्ट, लवणाक्त.
S. ground (lying along inlets and creeks). खाजण *n.* खार *f.* खारस्थळ *n.*
Cultivator of s. ground. खारीक.
S. water. खारवणी *n.* खारोणी *n.*
2 *produced on s. marshes ; living in s. water, &c.* खारा, खारींतला.

To SALT, *v. a. season or impregnate with salt.* मीठ *n.*-खार *m.*-&c. घालणें, खारट-&c. करणें, मिठविणें.

SALT-CELLAR, *n.* निमकदान *n.* निमकदानी *f.*

SALT-LESS, *a.* v. INSIPID. अळणी.

SALT-MINE, *n.* मिठाचीखाण *f.* लवणखानि *n.* लवणाकर *m.*

SALT-PAN, SALT-PIT, *n.* कोंढी *f.* मिठागर *m. n.*

SALT-PETRE, *n.* सोरमीठ *n.* सोरा *m.* सूर्यखार *m.* सुऱ्याखार *m.* सुराखार *m.* यवक्षार *m.*
Purified s. कलमी सोरा *m.*

SALT-WORK, SALTERN, *n. tract of s. pits along shore.* मिठागर *or* आगर *m. n.* [लवणाक्त.

SALTED, *p.* v. V. मीठ घातलेला, &c. लावण, लावणिक, क्षारयुक्त,
Over s. खारट, सखार.
Under s. मंदाळणी, अळणट.
Unsalted. अळणी. [करी.

SALTER, SALT-MAKER, *n.* गावडा *or* मिठगावडा, मिठागरी, मिठ-

SALTNESS, *n.* v. A. खारेपणा *m.* खारटपणा *m.* खार *m.* खारटाई *f.* लावण्य *n.* क्षार *m.* क्षारता *f.* क्षारयुक्तता *f.* &c.
S. or saline matter in a soil. लोण *f.* लोणा *m.*

SALTY, *a. somewhat salt.* खारटतुरट.

SALUBRIOUS, *a. favorable to health, promoting health,*—(climate, water, air, &c.) शरीरास चांगला, पथ्य, पथ्यकर, पथ्याचा, सुखाचा, सात्म्याचा, आरोग्यजनक-दायक-प्रद, निरोगी, निरामय, आरोग्यवर्धक, शरीरसंपत्तिकारक-प्रद-&c. शरीरहितावह, शरीरहितकारी, शरीरगुणकारी, &c. सात्विक, पौष्टिक, पुष्टिप्रद-कर-दायक.

SALUBRIOUSNESS, SALUBRITY, *n.* v. A. निरोगीपणा *m.* &c. शरीरहितकारिता *f.* आरोग्यजनकत्व *n.* &c. [ता *f.* &c.

SALUTARINESS, *n.* v. A. 1. शरीरहितकारिता *f.* शरीरगुणकारि-
2 हितकारिता *f.* &c.

SALUTARY, *a. favorable to health* v. WHOLESOME, SALUBRIOUS. पथ्य, पथ्यकर, पथ्याचा, शरीरहितकर-कारी-कारक-प्रद-दायक-&c.
2 v. BENEFICIAL. हितकर, हितावह, हितप्रद, श्रेयोवर्द्धक.

SALUTATION, *n.* v. V. *and* OBEISANCE. सलाम करणें *n.*-सांगणें *n.* &c. नमस्कार *m.* कुरनिशात *f.* कुरनीस *f.* अभिवादन *n.* अभिवंदन *n.* कुशलप्रश्न *m.* क्षेमप्रश्न *m.*
Some forms or particular terms of *salutation* are, जयसीताराम बावाजी, जोहार, नमस्कार, नमोनारायण, रामराम, शरणार्थ, सलाम.
Mutual s. रामरामी *f.* सलामी *f.*
S. (by and to Musalmáns &c.) सलाम.
S. (by and to *Gujaráthís*). जयगोपाळ.
S. (by and to *Bairágís, &c.*). जय सीताराम.

To SALUTE, *v. a. greet, hail, address expressions of kind wishes to, make obeisance to, &c.* सलाम *m.*-रामराम *m.*-न-

मस्कार m.-आशीर्वादm.-दंडवत m. n.-कुशलप्रश्नm.-&c. करणें-सांगणें, अभिवादन n.-अभिवंदन n. करणें.

2 See To Kiss.

SALUTE. See SALUTATION. 2 See KISS.

S. in proclamation of victory. जयघोष m.

S. with guns. सलामीच्या तोफा f. pl. सलामीची सरबत्ती f.

SALUTER, n. SALUTING, p. a. v. V. 1. सलाम-नमस्कार-&c. करणारा-सांगणारा,अभिवादक,अभिवादन-अभिवंदन कर्त्ता-कारी-&c.

SALVABILITY, n. v. A. तारणपावायासयोग्यता f.-शक्यता f. तारणयोग्यता f. तारणशक्यता f.

SALVABLE, a. *that may be saved.* तारायाजोगा-सारखा-&c. तारण पावायास योग्य, तारणयोग्य, तारणशक्य.

SALVATION, n. v. PRESERVATION. तारणn. रक्षणn. संरक्षणn. बचाव m. त्राण n.

2—in theology. तारणn. उद्धारm. उद्धारगति pop. उद्धारगत f. त्राण n. पापमुक्ति f. पापमुक्तता f. ऊर्ध्वगति f.

Ark of s. निर्वाणीचा तारू m.

Means of s. तरणोपाय m.

Way of s. through worship. भक्तिमार्ग m.

Way of s. through works. कर्ममार्ग m.

SALVE, n. *composition to be applied to sores.* मलम m. n. माठवण n. लेप m. प्रलेप m. [अडणी f.

SALVER, n. *plate, waiter.* तबक n. *dim.* तबकडी f. पितळी f.

SALVO, n. *reservation.* खिडकी f. चोरखिडकी f. छिद्र n. खिसा m. पकड f. सोडवण f.

To make a s. निसरगांठ f. देऊन ठेवणें, खिसा m. राखणें, पकड f.-&c. ठेवणें.

SAME, a. *not different or other, identical.* तोच,हाच, एकही, अनन्य, अभिन्न, तन्मय, तदात्मक, तद्रूप,एकरूप.

One and the s. एकूनएक.

2 *similar, &c.* v. LIKE. सारखा, एकसारखा, सम, समान.

That is all the s. as. दाखल. [पूर्वोक्त.

3 *that was mentioned before.* मशारनिल्हा, सदरहू, मजकूर,

SAMENESS, n. v. A. 1. ऐक्य n. ऐक्यभाव m. अनन्यभाव m. अभिन्नभाव m. अनन्यता f. अभिन्नता f. तादात्म्य n. तादूप्य n. तद्रूपता f. एकरूपता f.

2 सारखेपणा m. &c. समभाव m. साम्य n. समता f.

SAMPHIRE, n.—the herb. मर्यादवेल f. हदवेल f.

SAMPLE, n. *specimen.* मासला m. बानगी f. नमुना m. प्रत f. दाखवणूक f.

SANABLE, &c. See CURABLE, &c.

SANATIVE, SANATORY, n. *tending to heal.* रोग बराकरणारा, रोग दूरकरणारा, रोग दूर करण्याचा, रोगनिवारक, रोगघ्न, रोगनाशक, आरोग्यजनक-कारक-प्रद. [n.

SANATIVENESS, n.v.A. रोगनिवारकत्वn.रोगघ्नता f. आरोग्यजनकत्व

SANCTIFICATION, n. v. V.—*act.* पवित्र करणें n. &c. पापहरण n. पापनाशन n. पापनाश m. पापध्वंस m. कल्मषहरण n. पवित्रीकरण n.—*state.* पवित्रता f. अंतःशौच n. अंतःशुद्धि f. नष्टपापता f. धूतपापता f. विगतकल्मषता f.

SANCTIFIED, p. v. V. पवित्र केलेला, &c.पवित्रित, नष्टपाप, हृतपाप, धूतपाप, धूतकल्मष, विगतकल्मष, वीतकल्मष.

I. *affectedly holy.* पवित्रतेच्या डौलाचा-पोमाचा-&c.

SANCTIFIER, n. SANCTIFYING, p. a. v. V. पवित्र करणारा, &c. पापनाशक, पापघ्न, पापहर-हर्त्ता-हारक-हारी.

To SANCTIFY, v. a. *make pure and holy.* पवित्र-स्वच्छ-शुद्ध-&c. करणें, पापहरण n.-पापनाश m.-पापध्वंस m.-&c. करणें g. *of* o. अंतःशौच n.-अंतःशुद्धि f.-&c. करणें g. *of* o. पापहीन-निष्पाप-&c. करणें, पवित्रीकरण n.-&c. करणें g. *of* o.

SANCTIMONIOUS, a. *that makes a great profession or shew of sanctity,* —of persons. भक्तीचा-पवित्रतेचा-शुद्धीचा-&c. देव्हाऱ्या-आडंबऱ्या-पोम्या-ढोंग्या-ढोंगी-डौली-&c. बकध्यानी, बोकसन्यासी, भगली *or* ल्या, ढोंगी, ढोंग्या, अतिधार्मिक, अत्याचारी, दंभी, डंभी, दांभिक, कुहक.

2 —of things. भक्तीच्या-पवित्रतेच्या-&c. डौलाचा-पोमाचा-&c. बकध्यानाचा, बोकेसन्यासाचा.

SANCTIMONIOUSNESS, SANCTIMONY, n. v. A. भक्तीचें-पुण्याचें-पवित्रतेचें-शुद्धीचें-आचाराचें-&c. आडंबर n-ढोंग n.-पोम n.-स्तोम n.-देव्हारें n.-&c. भक्तीचा डौल m.-&c. दंभ m. डंभ m. भगल f. बकध्यान n. बोकेसन्यास m. ढोंग n. भक्तिमुद्रा f. अतिभक्तीची मुद्रा f. कुहना f. कुहकवृत्ति f.

SANCTION, n. *authority, warrant.* प्रमाण n. आश्रय m. आश्रा *or* आस्रा m. आधार m. गमक n.

To SANCTION, v. a. *ratify, confirm.* पसंत-कबूल-मान्य-मुकरर-मंजूर-बहाल-काईम-&c. करणें, सई *or* सही करणें-म्हणणें.

2 *warrant.* आश्रय m.-आधार m.-&c. देणें, आश्रय m.-आधार-&c. असणें g. *of* s. *with* स *or* ला *of* o. आश्रयभूत-आधारभूत-&c. असणें.

SANCTITY, SANCTITUDE, n. v. HOLINESS. पवित्रता f. साधुता f. अंतःशौच n. अंतःशुद्धि f.

SANCTUARY, n. *inner part of a temple.* गाभाराm. गर्भारा m. गर्भागार n. गर्भगृह n.

2 *sacred place, temple, &c.* v. TEMPLE. पवित्रजागा f. पवित्रालय n. शुद्धालय n. शुद्धागार n.

3 *place of refuge, asylum.* आश्रयस्थान n. आश्रयस्थल n. अकुतोभयस्थान n. निर्भयस्थान n.

SAND, n. वाळू f. रेती f. वालुका f. सिकता f. पुळण f. पुलिनn.

Fine s. रेल f. रेव f.

Heap of s. रेंवठा m.

S. (or pounce) box. वाळूदाणी *or* नी f. रेतदानी f.

SAND-BANK, n.—in water. भाट f. भाटी f. लागm.

SAND-BOARD, n. धूळपाटी f. पाटी f.

Letters drawn upon a s. by children in learning to write. धुळाक्षरn.

Letters traced (as the copy) on a s. धडाm.

To dust a s. पाटी f. उधळणें.

SAND-FLY, n. *midge.* केंबरूंn. केंबरेंn. घुंगुरटें *or* डेंn.

SAND-GLASS, n. वाळूचें यंत्रn. वालुकायंत्रn.

SANDAL, n.—the kind of shoe. चपळ f. चेपली f. चपली f. वहाण f. पायतणn. चरणदासी f.—worn by women, चेपावलेंn.

Heel-tie of a s. खोटवादm.

Pair of sandals. जुंतेंn. [हणी.

That is without sandals (or shoes). अनवाणी, अनवा

SANDAL, n.—the tree or wood. चंदनn. श्रीखंडn. मलयागर *or* मैलागरm. मलयागरुn.

Black s.-wood. कृष्णागरु *pop.* कृष्णागरm. [चंदनेलn.

Ottar or extract of s. wood. चंदनी अत्तरn. चंदनीतेलn.

Red s.-wood. रक्तचंदनn. कुचंदनn. रंजनn. तिलपर्णीf. कुंकुमागरुn. *pop.* कुंकुमागरm.

Unctuous preparation of s.-wood. चंदन *n.*

SANDARACH, *n.*—the resin. चंद्रस *or* चंद्रुसm.

SANDERS, *n.* Red s. wood tree. सुरंजी *f.*—the wood. सुरंजm.

SANDS, *n. sandy plain or tract.* वालवंट *or* टn. *f.* पुलिनn. *pop.* पुळण *f. n.* रेंवडाm. रेताड *f.* मरुm. मरुस्थलn.

SANDY, *a. of or belonging to sand.* रेतीचा, वाळूचा *or* वाळवेचा, वालुकामय.

2 *abounding with or having sand.* रेतीचा, वाळूचा *or* वाळवेचा, वाळवट, वाळसर, रेंवट, रेंवटील, रेंवसाळ *or* रेंवसळ, पुळणवट, वालुकाप्रचुर, वालुकाविशिष्ट.

S. beach, &c. v. SANDS. वाळवंटn. *f.*

SANE, *a. not disordered in mind.* सावध, शुद्धीचा, शुद्ध, चांगला, प्रकृतिस्थ, अविक्षिप्त.

2 See HEALTHY.

SANGUIFEROUS, *a. conveying blood.* रक्तवाहक, रक्तवाही.

SANGUIFICATION, *n. production of blood.* रक्तोत्पादनn. रक्तोत्पत्ति *f.* रक्तनिर्मिति *f.* रक्तवर्द्धनn.

SANGUINARINESS, *n.* v. A. 1. बहुत रक्तपातm. रक्तपातबाहुल्यn. रक्तपातवैपुल्यn.

2 खुनीपणाm. हिंसकत्वn. हिंस्रता *f.* जिघांसा *f.*

SANGUINARY, *a. attended with much bloodshed.* बहुत रक्तपाताचा, रक्तपूराचा, रक्तस्रावी, रक्तपातबाहुल्याचा, रक्तपातबहुल, धडेंनाचण्याचा, धडेंनाचलेला, कबंधनाचण्याचा.

2 *bloody-minded,* v. CRUEL. खुनी, हिंसक, हिंसालु, हिंस्र, रक्तप्रिय, जिघांसु.

SANGUINE, *a. of a red colour.* रक्ताच्या वर्णाचा, रक्तवर्ण, आरक्त.

2 See PLETHORIC. 3—of temperament; *ardent, warm, &c.* v. EARNEST. आस्थेवाईक, आस्थावान्, आस्थिक.

4 v. CONFIDENT. उमेदवार, मोठ्या उमेदीचा, मोठ्या अवसानाचा, अवसानी, भाविलाभासंशयी.

SANGUINENESS, *n.* v. A. 1. रक्तवर्णm. रक्तवर्णता *f.*

3 आस्था *f.* उत्कंठा *f.*

4 मोठी उमेद *f.* मोठें अवसानn.

SANGUINEOUS, *a. constituting, &c. blood.* रक्ताचा, रक्तमय, रक्तरूप, रक्तप्रयोजक, रक्तहेतुक.

2 *full of blood,* v. PLETHORIC. रक्तातिशयाचा, रक्तबहुल.

SANIES, *n. serous matter.* रगतपू m. लस *f.* रंध *f.* पूयरक्त n. पूयशोणित *n.*

SANIOUS, *a. serous.* रगतपूचा *or* पुवाचा, लसीचा, &c. पूयरक्तवत्.

SANITARY, *a.* आरोग्यरक्षणाचा, रोगनिवारणाचा.

2 *excreting serous matter.* लसीचा, लसेल, पूयरक्तस्रावी, पूयशोणितस्रावी.

SANITY, *n.* v. A. 1. शुद्धि *f.* सावधपणा *m.* सुद्धबुद्ध *f.* शुद्धीवरची [स्थिति *f.*

SAP, *n. juice of plants.* रस *m.* सार *m.* द्रव *m.* पाणी *n.* मज्जा *f.* निर्यास *m.*

2 See MINE.

To SAP, *v. a. undermine, subvert the foundation of.* पायाखोदून पाडणें *g. of o.* पाया *m.* बिघडवणें-उमळवणें-ढासळणें *or* बिघडवून-&c. पाडणें-नष्ट करणें.

SAPANWOOD, *n.* रक्तचंदन *n.* पतंग *m.*

SAPID, *a.* v. TASTEFUL. चवदार, स्वादु, स्वादिष्ट.

SAPIDITY, SAPIDNESS, *n.* v. A. चव *f.* स्वाद *m.* रुचि *f.*

SAPIENCE, SAPIENT. See WISDOM, WISE.

SAPLESS, *a.* असार, निस्सार, निस्सत्व, नीरस, विरस;—intens. *utterly dry and stiff.* तरडा *or* जून, जून तरडा.

SAPLING, *n. young tree or plant.* रोप *n.* रोपा *m.* रोपटा *m.* रोपडा *m.* माडा *m.*

SAPOR. See TASTE.

SAPONACIOUS, SAPONARY. See SOAPY.

SAPPER. See MINER.

SAPPHIRE, *n.*—the gem. नील *m.* नीलकांत *m.* नीलाश्मा *m.* इंद्रनील *m.* शनिm.

SAPPHIRINE, *a. made &c. of sapphire.* नीलाचा, नीलमय.

SAPPINESS, *n.* v. A. 1. ओलेपणा *m.* दमटपणा *m.* रसाळपणा *m.* &c. ओलावा *m.* दम *m.*

SAPPY, *a. juicy, succulent.* ओला, दमट, दमसर, रसभरू, रसभरित, सरस, रसरसीत, रसमय, रसप्रचुर, सकस, जलमय.

To be s. रसरसणें.

2—in intellect, &c. See WEAK.

SARCASM, *n. taunt, satirical remark.* टोमणा *m. or* णें *n.* टोला *m.* ठोसरा *m.* ठोसा *m.* तुक्का *m. v.* टाक, मार, टेपरा *m.*टेपर*m. n.* टेपण *n.* फुसकुली*f v.* सोड, छद्म *n.* छद्मी भाषण *n.* वर्मीभाषण *n.* व्यंजन *n.* व्यंग्य*n.* व्यंग्योक्ति *f.* वक्रोक्ति *f.* चुटका *m.* आक्षेप *m.* अवक्षेप *m.*

SARCASTIC, SARCASTICAL, *a.* v. N. टोमण्याचा, टोल्याचा, &c. तिखट, छद्मी, वर्मी, उपरोधाचा, उपरोधी, उपरोधीक, औपरोधिक, साक्षेप, सावक्षेप.

SARCASTICALLY, *adv.* v. A. टोमणा-टोला-&c. देऊन-मारून, उपरोधानें, छद्मपूर्वक, आक्षेपपूर्वक, &c.

SARCOMA, *n.* v. WEN. अवाळू *n.* वाळूक *n.* मांसवृद्धि *f.*

SARCOPHAGOUS, *a. flesh eating.* मांसभक्षक, मांसभोजी, मांसाशी.

SARCOPHAGUS, *n. stone coffin.* प्रेत ठेवण्याची दगडाची पेटी *f.* प्रस्तरमयशवपेटिका *f.*

SARDINE, SARDIUS, *n.* आरक्तक *m.* ?

SARDONIC, *n.* (laugh) पिशाच स्मित *n.*

SARDONYX, *n.* गोमेद *m.* गोमेदक *m.*

SARSAPARILLA, SARSA, *n.* गंधवल्कल *n.* उत्कट *n.*

SASH, *n. ornamental girding for the loins.* कमरबंद *m.*कांच्याm.

SATAN, *n.* v. DEVIL. सैतान.

SATANIC, SATANICAL, *a.* v. DEVILISH. सैतानाचा.

SATCHEL, *n. bag for books or papers.* जुजदान *or* जुगदान *n.*

2 See BAG.

To SATE, *To* SATIATE, *v. a. glut, cloy, overfill.* उपट *f.*-टेर *f.* -टेक *f.*-निशा *f.*-&c. करणें-पाडणें *g. of o.* धालेपणा *m.*-अतितृप्ति *f.*-परितृप्ति *f.*-मनशामोड *f.*-अभर *f.*-&c. करणें *g. of o.* धालेला-परितृप्त-अतितृप्त-&c. करणें, ओकारी *f.*-वीट *m.*-&c. आणणें, तोंड *n.* फिरवणें *g. of o.* विटवणें, मिठी *f.* बसवणें, पुरेपुरेंनकोनकोसें करणें. [*g. of o.*

To s. one's self with. अभरवण *f. n.*-उपट *f.*-उमट *f.* घेणें.

SATED, SATIATED, *p.* v. V. धालेला केलेला, टेर पाडलेला, अभर केलेला, &c. धालेला, परितृप्त, अतितृप्त, पूर्णकाम, परिपूर्णकाम, पर्याप्तकाम, अलंबुद्धि.

SATEDNESS, SATIETY, *n.* v. P. धालेपणा *m.* अभर *f.* टेर *f.* टेक *f.* मनशामोड *f.* निशा *f.* परिपूर्ति *f.* परितृप्ति *f.* अतितृप्ति *f.* पर्याप्ति

f. आतृप्ति *f.* अलंबुद्धि *f.* अलंप्रतीति *f.* अलंप्रत्यय *m.* उपट *f.* उपरति *f.* तर्पण *n.*

SATELLITE, *n.*—in astronomy. उपग्रह *m.*

Satellites, *fig. courtiers, attendants, &c.* द्वारदेवता *f.* आवरणदेवता *f.*

Bribing or propitiating of s. द्वारपूजा *f.*

SATER, SATIATING, *p. a.* &c. v. V. उपट करणारा, टेर पाडणारा, मनशामोड करणारा, &c. परितृप्ति-अतितृप्ति-&c. कर्त्ता-कारक-&c.

SATIN, *n.*—the silk. अतलस *n.*

SATIN-WOOD, *n.*—the tree. हेद *m. f.* हेदू *or* हेद्दू *m.*

SATIRE, *n. a discourse or poem containing sarcastic censures.* निंदेचा पोवाडा *m.* निंदोपाख्यान *n.* निंदाख्यान *n.* दुराचरणोपहासक कविता *f.*-भाषण *n.* औपरोधिककविता *f.*-भाषण *n.*-&c. चुटका *m.*

SATIRICAL, *a.* v. N.—language, &c. निंदेचा, उपहासाचा, दुराचरणोपहासक, मर्मी, छद्मी, निंदात्मक, निंदागर्भित, निंदार्थक, औपरोधिक, साक्षेप, दोषापवादक.

2—a person. निंदा करणारा, निंदक, निंदाभाषी, मर्मभाषी, छद्मभाषी, निंदावादी.

SATIRIST. See SATIRICAL, 2.

To SATIRIZE, *v. a.* निंदा *f.*-निंदाख्यान *n.*-&c. करणें *g. of o.*

SATISFACTION, *n.* v. V. 1.—*act.* पुरवणें *n.* &c. पुरव *f.* मनशामोड *f.* पूरण *n.* तर्पण *n.* संतर्पण *n.* परितोषण *n.* इच्छानिवृत्ति *f.* आप्यायन *n.*—*state.* पूर्त्ति *f.* पर्याप्ति *f.* परिपूर्त्ति *f.* दिलखुशी *f.* खुशी *f.* समाधान *n.* संतोष *m.* मनशामोड *f.* तृप्ति *f.* इच्छातृप्ति *f.* इच्छापूर्त्ति *f.* इच्छानिवृत्ति *f.* इच्छाशांति *f.*

2—*act.* खातर करणें *n.* &c. संदेहभंजन *n.* संदेहहरण *n.* संदेहनिवृत्ति *f.* संशयनिवृत्ति *f.*—*state.* खातर *f.* खातरी *f.* खातरजमा *f.* निशा *f.*

3 See PAYMENT.

I. See AMENDS, COMPENSATION.

SATISFACTORY, *a. that gives satisfaction, yields content, relieves the mind, &c.* समाधान करणारा, खातर करणारा, खातरेसारखा, खातरपसंत, मनासारखा, मनाजोगा, इच्छेसारखा, इच्छेजोगता-जोगा, खातरेचा, &c. मनोयोग्य, संदेहभंजक, संशयनिवर्त्तक.

SATISFIABLE, *a.* v. V. 1. पुरवायाजोगा-सारखा-&c. आतृप्य, तृप्तकरायाजोगा-&c. संतर्प्य, संतर्पणीय, संतर्पणशक्य.

SATISFIED, *p.* v. V. 1. *and* CONTENTED. पुरवलेला, फेडलेला, &c. तृप्त, पर्याप्त, पूरित, तर्पित, संतर्पित, संतृप्त, परितुष्ट, पूर्णकाम, आप्यायित, समाधानी, खुश, खुशी.

To be s. पोट *n.* भरणें *g. of s.* पुरणें *n. or* पुरी *f.* पडणें *g. of s.* धण *f.* पुरणें *g. of s.* जीव *m.* खालीं पडणें *g. of s.*

2 खातर केलेला, &c. निवृत्तसंशय, निवृत्तसंदेह, नष्टसंदेह, गतसंदेह, निवृत्तशंक.

3 See CLEARED.

To be s. खातर *f.*- खातरी *f.*-&c. होणें-असणें *g. of s.*

SATISFIER, *n.* SATISFYING, *p. a.* v. V.1. पुरवणारा, फेडणारा, इच्छापुरवणारा, &c. पूरक, तर्पक, संतर्पक, संतर्पण-&c.कर्त्ता-कारक.

I.—an article of food. पुरवटेसार, पुरवणीचा.

To SATISFY, *v. a. gratify want or desire, content, fill, please.* पुरवणें, पुरणें, फेडणें, इच्छा *f.*-आशा *f.*-मनोरथ *m.*-धण *or* धणी *f.*-&c. पुरवणें-फेडणें-&c. समाधान *n.* करणें *g. of o.* पोट *n.* भरणें *g. of o.* पुरी *f.* पाडणें *g. of o.* संतर्पणें, तर्पणें, संतर्पण *n.*-तर्पण *n.*-तृप्ति *f.*-मनशामोड *f.*-&c. करणें *g. of o.* पूर्ण-तृप्त-परितृप्त-संतृप्त-&c. करणें.

2 *free from doubt, cause the mind to rest in confidence,* v. To CONVINCE. खातर *f.*-खातरी *f.*-खातरजमा *f.*-&c. करणें *g. of o.* खातरीस आणणें, समजावणें, संशय *m.* फेडणें *g. of o.* संदेहभंजन *n.*-शंकानिवृत्ति *f.*-&c. करणें *g. of o.*

3 See To PAY, To CLEAR.

SATIVE, *a. produced in a field or garden.* क्षेत्रज, उद्यानज.

To SATURATE, *v. a. entirely impregnate with.* पुरा-पूर्ण- &c. करणें, रोमरोम-कणानकण-&c. भरणें-भिजवणें-युक्तकरणें, व्याप्तकरणें, उपळवणें, उमळवणें, उपळ होईसा *decl.* करणें.

SATURATED, *p.* v. V. रोमरोम भरलेला, अतिपूर्ण. [पूरण *n.*

SATURATION, *n.* v. V. रोमरोम-&c. भरणें *n.*- भिजवणें *n.* अति-

SATURDAY, *n.* शनिवार *pop.* शनवार *m.* मंदवार *m.* मंदवासर *m.*

SATURN, *n.*—the planet. शनि *m.* शनैश्चर *m.* मंद *m.* सौर *m.*

SATURNALIA, *n.*—the Hindu. होळी *f.* शिमगा *m.*

SATURNIAN, *a. belonging to the golden age.* सत्ययुगाचा, सत्ययुगांतला, सत्ययुगसंबंधी-विषयक.

SATURNINE, *a. dull, phlegmatic.* मंद, जड, थंड, जडप्रकृति.

SATYR, *n.* कल्पितवनदेवताविशेष.

SAUCE, *n. something eaten with food to give a relish.* तोंडीं लावणें *n.* ओलवण *n.* भिजवण *n.* कालवण *n.* कोशिंबीर *f.* बोळूं *n.* कोरड्याचें *n.*

To serve for s. कोरड्यास.

The common *Sauces or Seasonings* are, अडगई, अळण, करंबट *or* करमट, करमणें, कोचकई *or* काई, गरगट, गोज, चटणी, झुणका, पंचामृत, मेथकूट, रसा, रायतें, वरण, वेसवार.

2 See IMPUDENCE.

SAUCE-BOX. See SAUCY.

SAUCE-PAN, *n.* v. POT. हांडी *f.* मुठीची हांडी *f.* मुठीचें तपेलें *n.*

SAUCER, *n.* वाटी *f.* टवळें *n.*—large. वाटगा *m.*

Wooden s. or bowl. पडगा *or* घा *m.* पडगें *or* घें *n.*

SAUCILY, *adv.* v. A. धिटाईनें, धीटपणानें, &c. दांडगा-&c. होऊन.

To speak s. टाकून बोलणें.

SAUCINESS, *n.* v. A. धिटाई *f.* धीटपणा *m.* दांडगेपणा *m.* वाटपणा *m.* दुरुत्तर *n.* दुरुक्ति *f.* अविनय *m.* गमजे *m. pl.* वैयात्य *n.*

SAUCY, *a. pert, impudent.*—of persons. धीट, बेजबाबी, दांडगा, दांड, उद्धट, बाडगा, वाट, वाटगा, टाकून बोलणारा, तोंड टाकणारा, तोंडटाक्या, ठेंगा, चरमरीत, अविनय, दुरुत्तऱ्या.

2—of speech, behaviour, &c. धीटपणाचा, धिटाईचा, दांडगेपणाचा, &c. उद्धट.

To SAUNTER, *v. n.* v. To WANDER. रमणें, रमतरमत-रमतेरमते-&c. फिरणें, गमणें, रिकामा फिरणें, रमणूक *f.*-&c. करणें, वलवत-फिरणें. [णूक *f.*

SAUNTER, SAUNTERING, *n.* v. V. रमणें *n.* रमतरमतफिरणें *n.* रम-

SAUNTERER, *n.* SAUNTERING, *p. a.* v.V. रमणारा, रमतरमतफिरणारा, &c. गम्या, गमदसडा *or* दासडा *or* दासरा, रमतेराम, हिंडफिऱ्या.

SAUNTERINGLY, *adv.* v. V. रमतरमत, रमतेरमते, गमतगमत.

SAVAGE, *a. barbarous, wild, uncivilized.* रानटी, रानवट, रानी, रान्या, रानांतला, जंगली, अशिक्षित, असभ्य, विद्याचारहीन-शून्य-रहित.

2 *brutal*, v. CRUEL. क्रूर, निर्दय, उग्र, कजाख, खंक, खंकाळ or ळ्या, करडा, खपती, रांठ, परुष, दैत्यांशी.

SAVAGE, *n. uncivilized person*, v. BARBARIAN. रानटी-&c. माणूस, किरात, बर्बर, भिल्ल.

2 *cruel, &c. person*, v. BRUTE. राक्षस, मांग, मांगहृदयाचा माणूस, खाटीक. [नें, कौर्यपूर्वक.

SAVAGELY, *adv.* v. A. 2. निर्दयपणानें, क्रूरपणानें, &c. मांगहृदया-

SAVAGENESS, *n.* v.A.1. रानटीपणा*m.* रानबटपणा *m.* &c. शिक्षाराहित्य *n.* विद्याचारहीनता *f.* विद्याचारशून्यता *f.* विद्याचाराभाव*m.*

2 निर्दयपणा *m.* क्रूरपणा *m.* &c. क्रूरता *f.* उग्रता *f.* क्रौर्य *n.* निर्दयता *f.* पारुष्य *n.*

SAVANT, *n. learned person, connoisseur, virtuoso, &c.* गुणग्राहक, पंडित, बिद्वान्, विद्यासंपन्न, चिकित्सक.

To SAVE, *v. a. protect from danger*, v. To PRESERVE. तारणें, बचावणें, बचाव*m.*-तारण *n.*-रक्षण *n.*-संरक्षण *n.*-&c. करणें *g. of o.*

Save me ! त्राहि त्राहि.

To s. appearances. फड *m.* मारणें-राखणें-संभाळणें.

2—in theology. तारणें, उद्धरणें, तारण *n.*-उद्धार *m.*-&c. करणें *g. of o.* पापापासून-नरकापासून-&c. तारणें-राखणें.

3 *hinder from being lost or spent.* वांचविणें, उरवणें, सावरणें, राखणें, संभाळणें.

4 *reserve, lay by.* ठेवणें, राखणें, गांठीस-पदरीं बांधणें, मागेंपाठीमागें-शिलकेस-पदरीं-&c. पाडणें, पिशवींत-संग्रहीं टाकणें, उरवणें, पारठा पाडणें.

5 *take or use opportunely, so as not to lose.* संभाळणें, साधणें, गांठणें, टिपण*n.*-ताण*n.*-&c. संभाळणें-साधणें *g. of o.*

6 *hinder from occurring.* निवारणें, वारणें, प्रसंग*m.* टाळणें-वारणें *g. of o.*

SAVE, SAVING. See EXCEPT.

SAVED, *p.* v. V. 1. तारलेला, बचावलेला, तारित, रक्षित, संरक्षित.

2 तारलेला, उद्धरलेला, तारित, उद्धृत, त्रात.

To be s. तरणें, उद्धार *m.*-सद्गति *f.*-उद्धारगति *f.*-&c. होणें *g. of s.* उद्धारगती जाणें, उद्धारगतीस-&c. जाणें.

3 वांचवलेला, उरवलेला, &c.

4 ठेवलेला, गांठीस बांधलेला, मागें पाडलेला, &c.

SAVER, *n.* SAVING, *p. a.* v. V. 1. तारणारा, बचावणारा, तारक, त्राता, संरक्षक, संरक्षण-&c. कर्त्ता-कारी.

2 *and* SAVIOUR. तारणारा, उद्धरणारा, &c. तारक, उद्धारक, उद्धर्त्ता, उद्धार-&c. कर्त्ता.

I. *sparing, frugal*, v. ECONOMICAL. काटकसऱ्या, काटकसरीचा, अबेच, अल्पव्ययी.

II. *that secures salvation.* उद्धारसाधक, उद्धारगतिसाधक, उद्धारप्रद, उद्धारपरिणामी.

SAVINGNESS. See ECONOMY.

SAVINGS, *n. money saved and laid by.* काटकसर *f.* छाटछूट *f.* सुलवर *f.* उरवलेला-काटकसरीचा-उरवणीचा-&c. पैसा*m.*

SAVIOUR, *n. Redeemer.* तारणारा, तारक, त्राता, उद्धारक, उद्धर्त्ता, तारणकर्त्ता, उद्धारकर्त्ता, उद्धारगतीस लावणारा-नेणारा.

SAVOUR, *n.* v. TASTE. स्वाद*m.* छटा *f.* बोय *f.*

2 See SMELL.

To SAVOUR, *v. n. have a taste or tincture of; partake of the quality of.* बास*m.*-छटा *f.*-गंध*m.*-बोय *f.*-झुणूक *f.*-धुनक or धनूक *f.*-&c. मारणें *with in. con.* चुणूक *f.*-झुणूक *f.*-बास*m.*-&c. दाखवणें. [मारी *f.* सौरस्य *n.*

SAVOURINESS, *n.* v. A. गोडी *f.* मजेदारी *f.* चव *f.* चवदारी *f.* खु-

SAVOURING, *p. a.* v. V. *that savours of.* बासाचा, घाणीचा.

SAVOURY, *a.* v. TASTEFUL. मजेदार, खुमारीचा, चणचणीत, स्वादिष्ट, मिष्ट, खमंग, खमखमीत, सुरस.

S. food. मिष्टान्न*n.*

SAW, *n.* करवत*m. dim.* करवती *f.* अरकस*m.* करपत्र*n.*

Double s. अढ्या करवत or अडवा करवत*m.* आडें or आढेंन*n.*

2 *saying, maxim.* म्हण*f.* म्हणणी*f.* आहणा*m.* अणा*m.* न्याय*m.*

Old s. वडिलांचा आहणा*m.*

To SAW, *v. a. cut with a saw.* करवतणें, कारवणें, अरकसणें, चिरणें, करवतानें कापणें-चिरणें.

SAW-DUST, *n. dust of wood from sawing.* भुसा*m.* भुसकुरा*m.* भुसकूट*n.* भुसकटा*m.* भुसकट*n.*

SAW-FISH, *n.* पोक*m. n.* बिचरें*n.*

SAWYER, *n. one who saws.* करवतणारा, करवत्या, अरकसी, अराकस, चिरकाम्या, चिरक्या.

S.'s work. चिरकाम*n.* [ढणें, उक्त करणें.

To SAY, *v. a. speak, utter.* बोलणें, म्हणणें, काढणें, तोंडावाटे का-

2 (a lesson, &c.) *re-hearse.* म्हणणें.

To s. off. सरधोपट *adv.* म्हणणें.

3 *pronounce without singing.* म्हणणें, साधा *decl.*-नुसता *decl.* -स्वराशिवाय-&c. म्हणणें.

SAY, SAYING, *n. something said,* बोलणें *n.* म्हणणें *n.* गोष्ट *f.* बोल *m.* म्हणगत *f. n.* वचन *n.* उक्ति *f.* भाषण *n.* भाषित *n.* भणित *n.* आख्यान *n.*

True s. राम वचन *n.*

To say one's s. बोल *m.* बोलणें.

I. *saw, adage.* म्हण *f.* म्हणणी *f.* आहणा*m.* अणा*m.* वाक्य *n.*

SCAB, *n. incrustation.* खपला *m. dim.* खपली *f.* खवल or ळ *n. dim.* खवली *f.* खवला *m.* कपचा *m.* कोशेटा *m. dim.* कोशेटी *f.* कोशेरा *m.* खरपुडी *f.* भोत *m.* पापुद्रा *m.* पातोडा *m.* पाणोडा or टा *m.* पोपडा *m.* खवंद *n.* or कवंद *f.* खवंदल *n.* टप्पल *n.*

2 (of cattle), *itch.* खवडे*m. pl.* कथला*m.* कथली *f.*—A scale of it. खवडा *m.*

3 *low dirty wretch*, v. SCRUB, BLACK-GUARD. गांवचा खवडा *m.* गांवाची खरवड *f.* गांवची खरूज *f.* कधली व्याध or धि *f.* घाण *f.* खेटर खाऊ. [*m.* असिकोष*m.*

SCABBARD, *n. sheath for a sword.* मेण or म्यान *n.* कोश or ष

End-piece of the mounting of a s. तहनाल or तैनाल*m.*

Tie of a s. to the hilt. सल or सळ *m.*

To put into the s. मेण करणें. [कवंद्या.

SCABBY, SCABBED, *a.* v. N. खवळ्या, खवड्या, खवडेल, खवंद्या,

S. fellow. See SCAB.

SCAFFOLD, SCAFFOLDING, *n. stage, erection.* माचोळा *m. dim.* माचोळी *f.* माळा *m.* मंचक *m.* मंच *m.* तारांगण *n.*

Portable or movable s. तकरांवा *m.*

2 (of a building). माळा *m.* परांची *f.* पहाड*m.* पाड*m.* गोवें*n.*

3 (for the execution of a criminal) अपराध्यास देहांत शिक्षा देण्याकरितां केलेली माचोळी *f.*

To SCAFFOLD, *v. a.* माचोळा *m.*-माळा *m.*-&c. बांधणें.

To SCALD, *v. a. burn with hot liquid.* ऊन पाण्यानें-&c. भाजणें, भाजणें.

To s. one's fingers. पोळणें, आंच *f.*-चटका *m.* बसणें *in. con.*

2 *heat over a fire.* कढवणें, तापवणें.

SCALD, *n. injury or burn from hot liquid.* ऊन पाण्याचा-&c. चटका *m.*-चट्टा *m.*-चरका *m.*

2 *scurf on the head.* दारुणा *or* दारणा *m.*

SCALD-HEAD, *n.*—the disease. उंदरी *f.* चाई *f.* खवडे *m. pl.* कातर *f.*

SCALDED, *p.* v. V. 1. भाजलेला, भाजका, भाजीव.

To be s. पोळणें.

SCALDER, *n.* SCALDING, *p. a.* v. V. 1. भाजणारा.

S. hot. उन्हून *or* उनून, जळजळीत, जळफळीत, अग्निवर्ण.

SCALE, *n.* (of a balance). परडें *n.* पारडें *n.*

Scales, v. BALANCE. तराजू *f.* तागडी *f.* [संग *m.*

Thing put into a light s. to produce equilibrium. पासंग *m.*

2 (of a fish, &c.). खपट *n.* खवल *or* खवळ *n. dim.* खवली *f.* खवला *m.* [कवंद *f.*

3 *thin lamina.* पापुद्रा *m.* पातोडा *m.* पापोडा *or* टा *m.* उखरखली *f.* कवंद *f.*

4—in music, v. GAMUT. ग्राम *m.*

5 *regular gradation, a series rising by steps or degrees.* श्रेढी *f.* चढता *or* उतरता क्रम *m.* चढती *or* उतरती परिपाटी *f.*-पायरी *f.*

On a small s. जुजबी.

That is on a small or manageable s. अटपता, अटोपसार, संपुष्टांतला, सुटसुटीत, संजुकता *or* संजुगता.

To reduce to a small or manageable s. संपुष्टांत आणणें.

6 See LADDER.

To SCALE, *v. a. escalade.* शिड्या लावून चढणें, धरून धरून-पाय ठेवून ठेवून-&c. चढणें.

2 *strip of scales.* खवले *m. pl.*-&c. काढणें *g. of o.*

To SCALE, *v. n. peel off.* पापुद्रा *m.*-खपला *m.*-&c. निघणें *g. of s.*

SCALENE, *a.* (triangle.) विषमत्रिभुज.

SCALL. See SCALD-HEAD.

To SCALLOP. See To INDENT.

SCALP, *n. skin of the top of the head.* माथ्याची कातडी *f.*

To SCALP, *v. a. take off the scalp.* माथ्याची कातडी *f.* काढणें.

SCALY, SCALED, *a. having scales.* खवल्या, खवल्यांचा.

SCAMMONY, *n.* महमुदी *f.*

SCAMP, *n.* v. BLACKGUARD. सोदा, गुलामजादा, काबूयार, गुणाचें गुणपात्र *n.* हालीहरामी, बजात, बारखंडा, बारमल, छट.

A thorough s. निपट निरंजन.

To turn s. बारगळणें.

To SCAMPER, *v. n.* v. To RUN, To DECAMP. पळणें, पळ *m.* काढणें, ह्या *f.* करणें-म्हणणें, घोडा *m.* हाकणें, पोबारा *m.* म्हणणें, गच्छंती *f.* करणें.

To SCAN, *v. a. scrutinize, investigate,* v. To EXAMINE. शोधणें, छानणें, छडा *m.* काढणें-घेणें-पाहणें *g. of o.* शोध *m.*-छान *f.* -&c. करणें *g. of o.*

2 (verse). छंदाच्या मात्रा *f. pl.*-छंदाचे गण *m. pl.* मोजणें-गणणें, छंदोमात्रागणन *n.*-गणाक्षरगणन *n.* करणें.

SCANDAL, *n. calumny, &c.* v. SLANDER. चुगली *f.* चहाडी *f.* चर्चा *f.* अपवाद *m.* [*f.* कलंक *m.*

2 *cause of reproach,* v. DISGRACE, SHAME. लाज *f.* शरम *f.* कलंक *m.*

To SCANDALIZE, *v. a.* v. To ASPERSE. काजळी *f.* लावणें, नुकान *n.* घेणें *g. of o.* चुगली *f.*-&c. खाणें *g. of o.* लिंपण *n.*-कलंक *m.* लावणें.

2 *displease, shock, &c.* v. To OFFEND. कंटाळा *m.*-त्रास *m.*-&c. आणणें, त्रास *m.* देणें, त्रासवणें, कंटाळवणें, त्रस्त-&c. करणें.

SCANDALOUS, *a.* v. OFFENSIVE. कंटाळा आणण्याचा, त्रास द्यायाचा, त्रासदायक-कारक-प्रद. [घृणा, अपयशस्कर.

2 *that brings infamy,* v. DISGRACEFUL. लाजिरवाणा, आबू-घृणा, अपयशस्कर.

3 v. SLANDEROUS. चुगलीचा, तुफानाचा, चहाडीचा.

SCANDALOUSLY, *adv.* v. A. 1. कंटाळा आणायाजोगा-&c. कंटाळा-त्रास-&c. व्हायाजोगा-&c.

2 आब्रूजाईसा *decl.* लाजबाटेसा *decl.* &c.

SCANDALOUSNESS, *n.* v. A. 1. कंटाळवाणेपणा *m.* &c. त्रासदायकत्व *n.* त्रासकारकत्व *n.*

2 लाजिरवाणेपणा *m.* &c.

SCANT, *To* SCANT. See SCANTY, To STINT.

SCANTILY, *adv.* v. A. थोडाथोडा *decl.* अपुरता *decl.* &c. कोनाईनें, &c. अपुरतेपणीं, &c. हात राखून, कुंचमूकुचमू, चुटुचुटू, झिटीमिटी, चुटपूट.

SCANTINESS, SCANTNESS, *n.* v. A. 1. थोडेपणा *m.* कोतेपणा *m.* अपुरतेपणा *m.* उणेपणा *m.* &c. कोताई *f.* तंगचाई *f.* चडचड *f.*

2 किरटेपणा *m.* कृपणपणा *m.*

SCANTLING, *n. dimensions of timber.* गर्भी *f.*

2 *small quantity.* नख *m. n.* नखभर-रजभर-तीळभर.—*used with a noun.* मासला *m.*

SCANTY, *a. deficient, little.* थोडा, थोडका, उणा, अपुरता, अपुरा, चुटपुटता, चुटपुटीत, चुटपुरता, चुटपूट, कोता, थेंटा *or* ठेंटा, झिटीमिटी, लांडा, अप्रशस्त. [टा, कृपण.

2 *parsimonious, niggardly,* v. MISERLY. हाताचा जड, किरटा, कृपण.

SCAPULA. See SHOULDER-BLADE.

SCAR, *n. mark of a burn, wound, &c.* दाग *or* डाग *m.* चट्टा *m.* वण *m. n.* किण *n.* माऊ *or* माव *f.* ढाण *n.* क्षतचिह्न *n.*

To SCAR, *v. a.* डाग *m.*-चट्टा *m.*-&c. पाडणें, क्षतचिन्हानें युक्त करणें.

SCARAMOUCH. See BUFFOON.

SCARCE, *a. not plentiful, not copious.* थोडा, थोडका, कोता, कमी, कमती, अल्प, स्वल्प, तोट्याचा, तोट्या रोठ्याचा, चणचणीचा, चडचडीचा, महागाईचा, अबहुल, अप्रचुर.

To become s. तेल *n.* लागणें *in. con.*

2 *few in number and scattered,* v. RARE. विरळ, विरळा, दुर्मील, दुर्लभ, दुष्प्राप, दुष्प्राप्य.

To make one's self s. तोंड *n.* काळें करणें, काळें करणें.

SCARCE, SCARCELY, *adv. barely, almost not,* v. HARDLY. जरूर, विरळा, क्वचित्, बहुत करून नाहीं, कारकरून नाहीं.

2 *with difficulty, &c.* v. HARDLY. कष्टें-श्रमें-&c. करून, जुलमानें, जुलमावर.

SCARCITY, *n.* v. A. 1. *and* DEFICIENCY. थोडेपणा *m.* कोतेपणा *m.* कमतीपणा *m.* &c. तंगचाई *f.* चडचड *f.* चणचण *f.* दुष्काल *pop.* दुकळ *or* दुकाळ *m.* आटंकाळ *m.* अल्पता *f.* स्वल्पता *f.* उणीव *f.* तोटा *m.* हाक *f.* हकाटा *m.* ताण *m. n.*

S. occasioned by drought. सुकादुकाळ.

2 विरळपणा *m.* विरलता *f.* वैरल्य *n.* दुर्मीळपणा *m.* दौर्लभ्य *n.* दुर्लभता *f.* दुष्प्राप्यता *f.*

To SCARE, *v. a.* v. To FRIGHTEN. दचकवणें, बचकवणें, बुजवणें, दचका *m.*-&c. बसवणें, पळोपळोसें करणें.

To be scared. पळोपळोसें होणें, भांबावणें, *or* भांभावणें, धा-

दूगणें, घांगरणें, घांगावणें.

SCARE-CROW, *n. any thing set up to frighten.* बुजकणें *n.* बुजगवणें *n.* बुजगावणें *n.* बुजवणें *n.* तोडगा *m.* भुलावा *m.* भयप्रदर्शन *n.* See also BUGBEAR.

To SCARF, *v. a. throw loosely on.* प्रावरणें, आंगावर घेणें.

SCARF, *n. loose cloth worn over the shoulders.* शेला *m.* अंगवस्त्र *n.* उपवस्त्र *n.* उपरणा *m.* ओढणी *f.* उत्तरी *f.* उत्तरीय *n.*

SCARF-SKIN, *n. outer-skin.* बाहेरली कातडी *f.* बाह्यत्वक् *f.*

SCARIFICATION, *n.* v. V. फांसण्या पाडणें *n.* &c.

I.—the incision. फांसणी *f.* [फांसणी *f.*

SCARIFICATOR, SCARIFIER, *n. instrument for scarification.*

To SCARIFY, *v. a. make incisions in the skin.* फांसण्या *f.* पाडणें-टाकणें-मारणें-घालणें.

2 *to scratch the surface soil.* खरवडणें.

SCARLET, *a.* v. RED. लाल, शेंदऱ्या रंगाचा.

SCARLET FEVER *n.* उदर्द *m. n.*

To SCATH, *v. a. damage* v. To HURT. नुकसान *n.*-नुकसानी *f.* -&c. करणें *g. of o.*

SCATHLESS, *a. uninjured.* नुकसानी- &c. वेगळा, अविक्षत, अक्षत, अक्षित, अनपचित, अजातापकार.

To SCATTER, *v. a. throw loosely about.* पसरणें, विखरणें *or* विखुरणें, पसरणें, पिसरणें *or* पिखुरणें, विकिरणें, पसवळणें, अंथरणें, पेरणें, विखरून-&c. टाकणें, विकिरण *n.*-प्रसरण *n.*-&c. करणें *g. of o.*

2 *dissipate*, v. To DISPERSE. उडवणें, उधळणें, फांकवणें, जिकडेतिकडे करणें, विसकळणें, फांकाफांक *f.*-उडवाउडव *f.*-चारवाटा *f.pl.*-&c. करणें *g. of o.*

3 *set thinly.* पातळ-विरळ-&c. लावणें-घालणें.

To SCATTER, *v. n.* v. To DISPERSE. फांकणें, पांगणें, जिकडे तिकडे जाणें-होणें, फांकाफांक *f.*-&c. होणें *g. of s.*

SCATTERED, *p.* v. V. A. 1. पसरलेला, विखरलेला &c. विकीर्ण, प्रसृत, प्रसारित, प्रकीर्ण.

2 उडवलेला, उधळलेला, जिकडे तिकडे केलेला, &c. परागंदा, विसकळीत, विक्षिप्त, खंडित, असंहत, बहुधागत.

3 पातळ लावलेला, &c. फुटकर, विरळ, विसकळ. [*m.*

SCATTEREDNESS, *n.* v. P. 1. पसरडा *m.* पसळ *f.* पसवळण *f.* विखरा.

2 फांकाफांक *f.* पांगापांग *f.* विसकळ *f.*

SCATTERER, *n.* SCATTERING, *p. a.* v. V. A. 1. पसरणारा, विखरणारा, &c. पसऱ्या, विखऱ्या, विकिरण-&c. कर्त्ता-कारी.

2 उडवणारा, जिकडे तिकडे करणारा, &c. उद्धूलन-&c. कर्त्ता-कारी.

SCATTERING, *n.* v. V. A. 1.—*act.* विखरणें *n.* पसरणें *n.* &c. विखरणी *f.* प्रसर *m.* प्रसार *m.* प्रसरण *n.* प्रसारण *n.* विकिरण *n.* विकिर *m.* अभिसरण *n.* अभिसार *m.*

2 उडवणें *n.* &c. उडवाउडव *f.* दाणादाण *f.* पांगापांग *f.* विसकळ *f.* उधळण *f.* उधळणी *f.* उद्धूलन *n.* विक्षेप *m.*

3 पातळ लावणें *n.* &c. पातळलावणी *f.* विरळलावणी *f.*

SCAVENGER, *n. cleaner of a street,* v. SWEEPER. झाड्या, झाडू, हलालखोर.

SCAVENGRY, *n.* झाडूचें काम *n.* हलालखोरी *f.*

SCENE, *n. division of an act of a play.* प्रवेश *m.* पात्रप्रवेश *m.*

2 *place represented.* भूमि *f.* स्थल *n.*

3 *curtain or hanging of the theatre.* पडदा *m.*

Place behind the scenes. नेपथ्य *n.*

4 *the place where anything is represented.* भूमि *f.* अखाडा *m.* फड *m.* स्थळ *n.*

5 *assemblage of objects displayed at one view.* दृष्टीखालचा पसारा *m.*-खटला *m.*-दुकान *n.*-&c. दृक्पातविषय *m.*

SCENERY, *n. the appearance of a place with respect to natural objects.* देशाची मांडणी *f.*-रचना *f.* जलतृणवृक्षादिसंस्था *f.*-रचना *f.*-परंपरा *f.* देश्य दृष्टिपातविषय रचना *f.*-परंपरा *f.*

SCENIC. See DRAMATIC.

SCENT, *n.* v. SMELL. वास *m.* गंध *m.*

That has s. or smell. सगंध, गंधयुक्त.

To get s. of. वास *m.* काढणें *g. of o.* वास *m.*-सुवास *m.*-&c. लागणें *in. con. with g. of s.*

To SCENT, *v. a. perfume.* वास *m.*-सुवास *m.*-&c. लावणें-देणें, वासयुक्त-सुवासित-&c. करणें, वासन *n.*-&c. करणें *g. of o.*

2 See To SMELL.

SCENTLESS, *a. inodorous.* निर्गंध, अगंध, गंधरहित-&c.

SCENTED, *p.* v. V. 1. वास लावलेला, &c. वासित, भावित.

SCEPTIC, SCEPTICISM. See INFIDEL, INFIDELITY.

SCEPTICAL, *a.* v. DOUBTFUL. संशयात्मा, संदिग्धमति, संदिग्धमानस, संशयापन्नमानस. [राजवेत्र *n.*

SCEPTRE, *n. the ensign of royalty borne in the hand.* राजदंड *m.*

2 *regal power or office.* छत्रसिंहासन *n.*

SCEPTERED, *a. bearing a sceptre.* राजदंडधारी.

SCHEDULE, *n.* v. LIST, INVENTORY. फर्द *m.* फेरिस्त *n.*

SCHEMATIST, *n.* v. SCHEMER. बेत्या.

SCHEME, *n. system, plan.* बेत *m.* तजवीज *f.* मसलत *f.* कल्पना *f.* अनुसंधान *n.* ग्रंथ *m.* नकशा *m.* सांचा *m.* मूस *f.* (as कामाची मूस).

2 *project, &c.* v. CONTRIVANCE. उपाय *m.* कल्पना *f.* बुद्धि *f.* हिकमत *f.* इलाज *m.* कारवाद *m.* डाव *m. v.* खेळ.

Wily s. कंत्राण *n.* कंत्राट *n.* कारस्थान *n.*

3—as in trade, &c. *speculation, project, bold adventure, wild or brisk or smart enterprise, &c.* कचाट *n.* लचंड *or* लचांड *n.* खेंकटें *n.* कट्टी मसलत *f.* चबढब *or* चबडब *f.* चगडग *f.* उलाघाल *f.* उलेंढालें *n.* झेंगट *n.*

Wild or foolish s. गैरमसलत *f.* कुडें *n.* कुडेंपावडें *n.* कुडेबेडें *n.* कुलंगडें *n.* वितर्क *m.*

To SCHEME, *v. a.* v. To CONTRIVE. कल्पिणें, काढणें, योजणें, चिंतणें, चिंतन *n.*-&c. करणें *g. of o.*

To SCHEME, *v. n. form a plan, contrive.* युक्ति *f.*-तोड *f.* तजवीज *f.*-&c. करणें-काढणें.

2—as in trade, &c. v. N. 3. कचाटें *n. pl.*-लचांडें *n. pl.*-&c. करणें-उठवणें, उलेंढालें *n.*-ढवंढाळ *f.* -घालमेल *f.*-कडाकूट *f.*- &c. करणें.

SCHEMER, *n.* SCHEMING, *p. a.* SCHEMEFUL, *a.* v. V. N. 1. *and* N. 2. युक्ति-तोड-&c. करणारा-काढणारा, उपायी, युक्त्या, युक्तिमान्, युक्तिवान्, काटदार, मसलतबाज, मसलतदार, मसलती, हिकमती *or* त्या, मनसुबदार, अनुसंधानी, संधानी, लागलाव्या, लाग्यालाग्या, कारस्थानी, साधनी, हरदमख्याली.

v. V. N. 2.—*and* N. 3. कचाटें करणारा-उठवणारा-&c. कचाट्या, लचांडखोर, लचांडी, उलेढाल्या, खेंकटेंखोर, झेंगट्या, ढवंढाळी *or* ळ्या, चबढब्या, चगडग्या, रुटपट्या, खटलेखोर, झटाळ *or* झट्याळ *or* ळी, झटेल *or* ली.

SCHISM, *n. division or separation in religion.* फूट *f.* नट *m.* मार्गभेद *m.* मतभेद *m.* धर्मभेद.

SCHISMATIC, SCHISMATICAL, *a.* v.N. धर्मांतल्याफुटीचा, &c. मार्गभेदक, मतभेदक, मार्गभेदविषयक-संबंधी, धर्मभेदक.

SCHOLAR, *n. learner.* शिकणारा, पढणारा, विद्येचा अभ्यास करणारा, शिकणाऊ, शिकाऊ, शाळेंतलें मूल *n.* विद्यार्थी, शिष्य, विद्याभ्यासी, अक्षरमुख.

Evening recitation of scholars. परोचा *or* परोता *or* प्रवचा*m.* परवड *f.*

Head-s. पट्टशिष्य.

2 *man of letters.* विद्वान्, पंडित, पंडितजन, भट्ट, पढीक, विद्वज्जन, तांत्रिक, विबुध, सुधी, दर्शक, विद्यानिधान.

SCHOLAR-SHIP, *n.* v. LEARNING. विद्या *f.* पांडित्य *n.* विद्यासंपत्ति *f.* विद्वत्ता *f.*

2 *maintenance for a scholar.* विद्यार्थ्याची नेमणूक *f.*-पगार*m.*

SCHOLASTIC, *a. belonging, &c. to a school.* शाळेचा, पाठशाळेचा, पाठशालासंबंधी-विषयक, शालासंबंधी-विषयक.

2 See PEDANTIC.

SCHOLIAST, SCHOLIUM. See COMMENTATOR, COMMENTARY.

SCHOOL, *n. place of instruction.* शाला *pop.* साळ *or* शाळ *f.* पाठशाला *or* ळा *f.* विद्यालय *n.* विद्यागृह *n.* अध्ययनागार *n.* शिक्षागृह *n.* शिक्षालय *n.*

2 *body of scholars.* शाला *pop.* साळ *or* शाळ *f.* पाठशाला *f.* विद्यार्थिसमूह *m.* शिष्यसमूह *m.*

3 *system of doctrine, &c.* शाला *pop.* साळ *f.* शिक्षासंप्रदाय*m.* शालासंप्रदाय *m.*

Difference of s. शाखाभेद *m.*

Of a bad s. गैरसाळ.

Of a good s. शालाशुद्ध.

4 *body of philosophers.* शिष्यशाखा *f.* शिष्यसंप्रदाय *m.*

To SCHOOL. See TO TEACH, TO TUTOR.

SCHOOL-BOY, *n.* शाळेंत शिकणारा-जाणारा-&c. मुलगा *m.*

SCHOOL-FELLOW, *n.* शाळेचा सोबती, शालाबंधु *m.* सहाध्यायी, गुरुबंधु.

SCHOOL-HOUSE, *n.* शाळेचें घर *n.* शालागृह *n.* शाळा *f.* साळ *f.*

SCHOOL-MASTER, *n.* v. TEACHER. पंतोजी, शालाशिक्षक, शालानायक, मुल्ला *or* मुलना (amongst Muhammadans). Some respectful terms of compellation for a *schoolmaster* are तात्या, पंतसाहेब.

Rapping-board of a s. थापटी *f.*

Whip of a s. बखानी *f.*

SCHOOL-MISTRESS, *n.* पंतोजीण *f.* शाळेची नायकीण *f.* शालानायिका *f.*

SCHOOL-ROOM, *n.* साळेची खोली *f.*-कोठडी *f.*-&c. साळ *or* शाळ *f.*

SCHOOLING, *n.* v. TEACHING. शिकवणें *n.* अध्यापन *n.*

2 *compensation for instruction.* शिकवणावळ *f.* शिक्षावेतन*n.*

SCHOONER, *n.* दुकाठी गलबत *n.*

SCIATIC, SCIATICAL, *a. affecting the hip.* श्रोणिसंबंधी-विषयक.

SCIATICA, *n.* श्रोणिवेदना *f.* श्रोणिशिरावेदना *f.*

SCIENCE, *n.* v. KNOWLEDGE. विद्या *f.* विज्ञान *n.* शास्त्र *n.*

Profane s. उपविद्या *f.*

Study of s. and literature. विद्याभ्यास *m.*

Versed in s. विद्यावान् *pop.* विद्यावंत, विद्वान्.

2 *a* s. विद्या *f.* शास्त्र *n.*

SCIENTIFIC, SCIENTIFICAL, *a. according to the rules of science.* विद्यासूत्रानुसारी, विद्यासूत्रानुयायी, विद्याक्रमानुसारी, विद्याक्रमानुयायी.

2 *versed in science.* पढीक, पढलेला, विद्वान्, विद्यावान्, शास्त्रज्ञ, विद्याक्रमवेत्ता.

3 *belonging to science.* शास्त्रीय.

SCIMITAR, *n.* v. SWORD. तेगा *m.* गुप्ती *f.*

To SCINTILLATE. See TO SPARKLE.

SCIOLISM, SCIOLIST. See SMATTERING. SMATTERER.

SCION. See CION.

SCIRRHOUS, *a. hard, knotty.* गांठीचा, ग्रंथिमान्.

SCIRRHUS, *n. indurated gland.* मांसग्रंथि *m.*

Flat s. of the spleen or liver. खापरी *f.*

SCISSIBLE. SCISSILE, *a. that may be cut or divided.* छेद्य, छेदनीय, भेद्य, भेदनीय, खंडनीय.

SCISSION, *n.* कापणें *n.* छेदन *n.* भेदन *n.*

SCISSORS, *n.* कातर *f.* कातरी *f.* कैंची *f.* कर्त्तरी *f.*

To SCOFF, *v. n. mock, jeer at, &c.* v. TO RIDICULE. उपहास *m.*-निंदा *f.*-टेर *or* टर *f.*-हुर्र *f.*-छिथू *f.*-&c. करणें *g. of o.* केंडणें, हडहड *f.* करणें.

SCOFF, SCOFFING, *n.* v. V. उपहास *m.* निंदा *f.* निंदोक्ति *f.* निंदावचन *n.* उपहासोक्ति *f.*

SCOFFER, *n.* SCOFFING, *p. a.* v. V. उपहास करणारा-कर्त्ता-&c. टेरकरणारा, छिथू करणारा, &c. निंदक, निंदाखोर.

S. at religion. देवलंड, धर्मलंड.

SCOFFINGLY, *adv.* v. A. उपहासानें, उपहास-निंदा-&c. करून.

To SCOLD, *v. a. chide or reprove vehemently and rudely.* Expressive of this sense and answering to *To rate, row, wig, blow up, set down, give it to, pitch it into, &c. &c.* there are many lively words and formations. खडसणें, खडसावणें, खडकावणें, खमकावणें, खणकावणें, झाडणें, घांसणें, खरडणें, खडखडवणें, खडकाविणें, खुडसणें, धमकावणें, दटावणें, दपटणें, दामटणें, दडवडावणें, फडफडवणें, तडकावणें, दणकावणें, दणगारणें, शिंगाटणें, गोपाटणें, झिंजारणें, हेटाळणें, मुंडणें, भादरणें, तासणें, खरड *f.*-खरवड *f.*-खरडपट्टी *f.*-खडस *f.*-खडसपट्टी *f.*-खरडी *f.*-उधळपट्टी *f.*-&c. काढणें *g. of o.* हजामत *f.*-भादरणी *f.*-उलटी हजामत *f.*-उलटी सुलटी हजामत *f.*-मुंडन *n.*-मुंडीमोचन *n.*-भादरपट्टी *f.*-&c. करणें *g. of o.* ताव *m.*-सोनताव *m.* देणें, दम *m.* देणें, तराटा *or* तऱ्हाटा *m.* देणें, दट्टा *m.* देणें, खाकरबासा *or* बसा *m.* घालणें, दपटशहा *or* दपटशा *m.*-दपाटा *m.*-दराटा *m.*-दचडगा *or* घा *m.*-दगारा *m.*-घसरा *m.*-&c. देणें, डोईचे केश नाहींतसे करणें, पूजा *f.* करणें-घालणें *g. of o.* कांशा *f. pl.* काढणें-भरडणें *g. of o.* झाल जाणें, अंतडीं *n. pl.* उघडणें-फाडणें-बाहेर काढणें-गळ्यांत घालणें *g. of o.* अबले *m. pl.* उघडणें *g. of o.* खरका *m.* देणें, खांकरबसा *m.* काढणें-करणें-घालणें *g. of o.* टोपशी *f.*-टोपसा *m.* उडविणें *g. of o.*

To SCOLD, *v. n. speak chidingly and clamorously.* कचकाघून-खडसून-खडखडून-खडसूनहडसून-खरपूस-&c. बोलणें *f.* घसघस *f.*-कटकट *f.*-कलकल *f.*-किलकोल *f.*-जिगजीग *f.*-जिकीर *f.*-पिरपीर *f.*-&c. करणें.

SCOLD, *n. woman given to scolding, shrew.* घसघशी *f.* कर्कशा *f.* केगया *f.* केगामती *f.* कैकेयी *f.* कडाशीण *f.* कैदाशीण *f.* ताटका *f.* अवदसा *f.* रूत्या *f.* असाळी *f.* महामाया *f.* केकसामावशी *f.* पूतना *f.* पूतनामावशी *f.* गजघंटा *or* गजघांट *f.* जगनाड *f.*

SCOLDER, *n.* SCOLDING, *p. a.* v. V. A. खडसणारा, खमकावणारा,

खरड काढणारा, हजामत करणारा, &c. &c.

v. V.N.खडखडून बोलणारा,&c.घसघशा,कटकट्या, जिकिऱ्या,जिकिरखोर, जिकिरी, पिरपिऱ्या, रिपरिप्या, खिसखिशा, दांतकसाळी.

SCOLDING, *n.* v.V. A.—*act.* खडसणें*n.* दपटणें *n.* धमकावणें *n.*&c. घांसणी *f.* दटावणी *f.* धमकावणी *f.* हेटाळणी *f.* हेटाळी *f.* दपाटा *m.* मुंडण *n.* मुंडीमोचन *n.* बोडंती *f.* भिरडी *f.* भलीपूजा *f.* See also the numerous nouns given under To SCOLD with their appropriate verbs.

v. V. N. खडसून बोलणें *n.* &c. घसघस *f.* खिसखीस *f.* जिकीर *f.* जिगजीग *f.* पिरपीर *f.* रिपरीप *f.* दांतकसाळ *f.* श्वानवैखरी *f.*

SCONCE, *n. hanging or projecting lamp-place.* दिवठण *or* ठाण *n.*

2 See HEAD. [कोरणें *n.*

SCOOP, *n. scooping instrument.* खवणी *f.* खवला *m.* कोरणी *f.*

2 See LADLE.

To SCOOP, *v. a. make hollow, excavate.* कोरणें, उकरणें, पोखरणें, खवणें, खवणणें, खबणें, कोरणी *f.*-खवणी*f.* करणें *g. of o.*

2 See To LADLE.

SCOOPED, *p.* v. V.1. कोरलेला, खवलेला, &c. कोरींव, उकरींव.

SCOOPINGS, *n. matter scooped out.* पोखर *m.* पोखारा *m.*

SCOPE, *n. aim, intention, drift,* v. MEANING. अभिप्राय *m.* गम *m.* खुलासा *m.* गोशेरा *or* गोश्वारा *or* गोष्वारा *m.* धारेण *n.*

2 *space, room.* जागा *f. m.* अवकाश *m.* मोकळेपणा *m.*

SCORBUTIC, *a.* नाविकरक्तपित्ताचा, नाविकरक्तपित्तसंबंधी, नाविकरक्तपित्तरोगी.

To SCORCH, *v. a. burn superficially, &c.* भाजणें, हुरडणें, हुरपणें,हुरपळणें *or* हुरफळणें, होळपणें, भाजणूक *f.*-&c. करणें *g. of o.*

To SCORCH, *v. n. be burnt on the surface.* पोळणें, भाजणें, हुरडणें, हुरपळणें *or* हुरफळणें, होळपणें, जळगणें, जळणें.

SCORCHED, *p.*v.V.A. भाजलेला, हुरपळलेला, &c. पोळींव, भाजींव, भाजका, जळका, भर्जित, भृष्ट.

To be s. पोळणें, जळगणें, अहळणें *or* अहाळणें.

SCORCHER, *n.* SCORCHING, *p. a.* v. V. A. भाजणारा, हुरडणारा, हुरपळणारा, &c. भर्जनकर्त्ता-कारी-&c.

SCORCHING, *n.* v. V. A.—*act.* भाजणें *n.* &c. भाजणूक *f.* भाजण *n.* भाजप *n.* भर्जन *n.* संतापन.

SCORE, *n. twenty.* विसा *f.* विशी *f.* खंडी *f.*—of particular things, as of pieces of cloth, of bracelets, &c. कोडी *f.*

By the s.—selling, buying. कोडबादीनें.

By scores, *by or in great numbers.* खंडी बारी.

A s. of children. खंडीभर लेंकरें *n. pl.*

2 *account.* खातें *n.*

Running up a s. उकाडा *m.* रतीब *or* रातीब *m.*

3 *account, reason, sake, &c.* कारण *n.* हेतु *m.* सबब *f.*

On the s. of. बाबत, सबब.

4 See LINE. 5 See NOTCH.

To SCORE, *v. a. mark with lines.* रेखटणें, रेखाटणें, रेखणें.

2 *set down as a debt.* मांडणें, बोट *n.* ओढणें-लावणें-घालणें *g. of o.*

3 out ; *cancel.* खोडणें.

SCORIA, *n. dross, recrement.* किट्टण *n.* कीट *n.* रीति *f.*

To SCORN, *v. a.* v. To CONTEMN. तिरस्कारणें, तिटकारणें, तुच्छ करणें-मानणें, उडवणें, उडवणी *f.* करणें *g. of o.* धिक्कारणें, धिक्कार *m.* करणें *g. of o.* धुनकारणें, छिधू *f.*-तिटकारा *m.*- तिरस्कार *m.* करणें *g. of o.* तोंडावर थुकणें, नाक *n.* झाडणें.

SCORN, *n.* v. CONTEMPT. तिरस्कार *m.* तिटकारा *m.*

2 *object of scorn.* तिरस्कारास्पद *n.* तिरस्कारपात्र *n.*

SCORNER, *n.* SCORNING, *p. a.* v. V. तिरस्कारणारा, तिटकारणारा, तुच्छ करणारा, &c. तिरस्कर्त्ता, तिरस्कारी, धिक्कार-तिरस्कार-&c. कर्त्ता-कारी.

SCORNFUL, *a.* v. CONTEMPTUOUS. तिरस्काराचा, तिटकाऱ्याचा, उडवणीचा,तिरस्कारी, निंदक, निंदाखोर, निंदात्मक, अवहेलनात्मक.

S. speech. उणें उत्तर *n.* उणें भाषण *n.*

SCORNFULLY, *adv.* v. A. तिटकाऱ्यानें, &c. तिरस्कार-&c. करून, तिरस्कारपूर्वक, तिरस्कारबुद्धीनें.

SCORPIO, SCORPION, *n.* विंचू *m. enhanc.* विंचडा *m.* वृश्चिक *m.*

Female s. विंचवी *or* विंचवीण *f.* विंचीण *f.*

Hole or nest of s. विंचवांचें पेंव *n.*

Large and black s. इंगळी *f.*

Stroke or dart of the sting of a s. फटकारा *m.* फणका *m.* फणकारा *n.*

Smart of a s. sting. फणफण *f.* धुणफुण *f.*

Tail or sting of a s. नांगा *m.* नांगडा *or* नांगाडा *or* नांगोडा *m. dim.* नांगी & नांगडी *f.* कांटा *m.*

To dart his sting—a s. फणकाविणें.

2 (of the zodiac). वृश्चिक.

SCOT, *n. portion of money assessed.* वर्गणी *f.* वर्गत *f.* पट्टी *f.*

SCOT-FREE, *a. free from payment or mulct.* दंडावेगळा-निराळा, मोकळा, सुटा.

2 *unhurt.* See SAFE.

To SCOTCH, *v. a.* (a wheel). ऊट *f.*-उटाळें *n.*-उटाळा *m.* लावणें (चाकास), उटा *m.* देणें, ढकली *f.* लावणें.

2 *cut with shallow incisions.* फांसण्या *f. pl.* टाकणें-मारणें.

SCOTCH, *n. shallow incision.* फांसणी *f.*

SCOUNDREL, *n.* v. BLACKGUARD. लुच्चा, बजात, बदजात, हरामी, हरामजादा, शठ, मात्रागमनी, खट, खटनट.

SCOUNDRELISM, *n.* v. BLACKGUARDISM. लकारी *f.* लुच्चेगिरी *f.*

To SCOUR, *v. a. scrub, rub.* घासणें, घासटणें, उटणें, चोळणें, रगडणें, उजळा*m.* देणें.

Scouring stuff. घासणी *f.* उजळा*m.*

2 (the bowels,&c.) v. To PURGE. धुणें, धुणी *f.* करणें *g. of o.* धुपविणें, धुवा धार *f.*-निरानिपटा*m.* करणें *g. of o.* खळमळ*m. f.* काढणें *g. of o.*

3 *pass swiftly over.* झपाट्यानें-तुडवून जाणें *with* वरून *of o.*

SCOURED, *p.* v. V. 1. घासलेला, उटलेला, &c. उटींव.

SCOURGE, *n.* v. WHIP. चाबूक*m.* कोरडा*m.*

To SCOURGE, *v. a.* v. To WHIP, To PUNISH. चाबूक*m.*-कोरडा *m.* मारणें-लावणें-लगावणें, फटके*m. pl.* मारणें.

SCOUT, *n. one sent out to observe the enemy.* हेर, बातमीदार, चार, गुप्तदूत, डोळा*m.* टेहळ्या.

To SCOUT, *v. n.* हेरणें, हेरणी *f.* करणें.

To SCOUT, *v. a. reject scornfully,* v. To CONTEMN. हडहडावणें, हिडसणें, हिडसावणें *or* हेडसावणें, खुडसाविणें, हडहड *adv.* करणें, हुर्यो हुर्यो *adv.* करणें, धिसपिटावणें, केंडणें, उडवणें, हुंदडणें, *or* हुंडारणें, उडवणी *f.* करणें *g. of o.* निस्कारणें, छटकट *or* छिटफिट *f.* करणें-लावणें, छिधू *f.* करणें.

To SCOWL, *v. n. look angry, severe, &c.* डोळे*m. pl.* उगारणें-

काडणें-पिंजारणें-वटारणें *or* उगारून-&c. पाहणें-दृष्टि *f.* घालणें-लावणें, भंवयांस गांठी *f. pl.* घालणें,भवया *f. pl.* चढविणें, कटाक्ष *m.*-बद्धकटाक्ष*m.*-&c. करणें.

SCOWL, SCOWLING, *n.* v. V. डोळे उगारणें*n.* डोळेकाडणें*n.* &c. कटाक्ष*m.* बद्धकटाक्ष*m.* क्रोधमुद्रा *f.* कोपमुद्रा *f.*

SCOWLER, *n.* SCOWLING, *p. a.* v. V. डोळे उगारून पाहणारा, &c. डोळे काडलेला-वटारलेला-&c. क्रोधमुद्रेचा.

To SCRABBLE. See To SCRAMBLE. 2 See To SCRIBBLE.

SCRAGGY. See LEAN. 2 See RUGGED.

To SCRAMBLE, *v. n. climb up by seizing objects with the hand, &c.* मेटे खुंट्यांनीं चढणें, हातपाय*m.* टेकून चढणें, ओळंबत आंळबत चढणें, वळघ *f.* घेणें, वळघून जाणें.

2 *catch at eagerly so as to get it before others.* झोंबाझोंबी *f.*-झटापटी *f.*-लोटालोटी *f.*-घेमार*m.*-घेघेमार*m.*-झोड *f.*-&c. करणें *and with g. of s.* होणें-चालणें, मिठी *f.* घालणें.

To be scrambled for. झूम *f.*-मिठ्या *f. pl.*-उड्या *f. pl.*-चुंब *f.*-&c. पडणें *with* वर *of o.*

SCRAP, *n. piece, fragment,* v. BIT. तुकडा*m.* खंड*n.* कुटका*m.*

Scraps, fragments, dirty dishes, &c. remaining of a meal. खरकटावळ *f.* खरकटवळ *f.* खरकटवड *f.* लेपवळ *f.* उष्टावळ *f.* खरकटवाडा*m.*

2 (of paper or writing). चिटोरा *or* ठोरा*m.* चिटोरें*n.* पुरजा *m.* चकती *f.*

SCRAP-BOOK, *n.* गवाळग्रंथ*m.* [बाडी.

SCRAP-SCHOLAR, *n.* v. SMATTERER. खंडपंडित, खंडीं खंडीं पंडित,

SCRAP-SCHOLARSHIP, *n.* v. SMATTERING. खंडितपांडित्य*n.*

To SCRAPE, *v. a. rub the surface with a sharp instrument.* खरडणें, खरवडणें, छिलणें, तासणें, वरून तासणें-छिलणें, तळसणें.

2 *shave roughly.* खरडणें, तासणें, भादरणें.

3 together; *amass, accumulate.* जथणें, जथवणें, जमावणें, जमा करणें, गोळा करणें, खळबटणें, जथा जथ*f.*-जथापत *f.*-जथबाजथव *f.*-जमाजम *f.*-&c. करणें *g. of o.*

4 up; out. उकरणें. [णें, निरडणें.

5 up, off. (esp. with the hand or fingers). निपटणें,निरप-

6 (upon a scraper or grater). किसणें.

SCRAPE, *n. strait, hobble,* v. TROUBLE. लचांड*n.* कचाट*n.* ओकटें*n.* कुळंगडें*n.* *v.* घे *or* करून घे, खेंकटें*n.* उपाध *f.* आधि*f.* चक्र*n.* काबीज*n.* गडखळ *n.*

To get into a s. धोंडयासालीं हात*m.* सांपडणें *g. of s.*

SCRAPER, *n.* SCRAPING, *p. a.* v. V. 1. खरडणारा, खरवडणारा, वरून छिलणारा, &c.

I. (for the feet). वज्री *f.*

II. (for the tongue). पात *f.*

III. (of fruits or vegetables). किसणी *f.* खवला *m.* खवणी *dim.* हातखवणी *f.* मुरळी *f.*

IV. *vile barber, fiddler, &c.* खरडघाशा, खरड्या, खुंटाळ्या, गवतकाप्या, घासकटाऊ.

SCRAPINGS, *n. matter scraped or grated.* कीस *m.*

2—as from a culinary utensil. खरवड *f.* खरडा *m.*

3 (of a dish of food). निपूटशिपूट *f. n.* निपटीशिपटी *f.* निपटाशिपटा *m.* निरपण *n.*

To SCRATCH, *v. a. lacerate or tear the surface.* ओरखडणें, ओरबडणें, ओरफडणें, ओरपणें, घावटणें, घावटळणें, ओरखडा *m.*-ओरबडा *m.* काढणें, खाकोरणें.

2 *tear with the nails.* बोचकरणें *or* बोचकडणें, चुचकरणें *or* चुचकुरणें, बिचकुरणें, बिचकुरा *m.*-बुचकरा *m.*-&c. घेणें.

3 (to allay an itching). खाजवणें, कांडवणें, कांडुळणें *or* कांडोळणें.

Violent fit of scratching. खरका *m. v.* लाव.

4 (the ground, &c.) *dig lightly.* दुखवणें, खिचवडणें, ओरखडणें, ओरफडणें *or* ओरबडणें, ओरपणें.

5 over; *cover with strokes and flourishes,* v. To SCRAWL. बिरखडणें, ओरखडणें, बिरखड्या *or* बिरखुड्या *f. pl.*-खिरचिड्या *f. pl.* काढणें.

6 out; v. To ERASE. खरडणें, खरडून काढणें, तळसणें, खोडणें.

7 up; out;—rats, &c. उकरणें.

SCRATCH, *n. laceration with a nail.* नखोरा *m.* बोचकरा *or* बोचकुरा *m.* बुचकरा *or* चुचकुरा *m.* वांकोरा *m.* ओरखडा *m.* खाकाश *m.* चिमोरा *m.* नखव्रण *m.* नखलखा *m.* नखविलेख *m.* नखपद *n.* नखांक *m.* नखचिह्न *n.*

2 *mark through scratching.* चर *m.* चरा *m.* अरासडा*m.* ओरखडा *or* ओरखाडा *m.* ओरबडा *or* ओरबाडा *m.*

3 *rudely drawn face or figure.* बिरखडी *or* बिरखुडी *f.*

SCRATCHED, *p.* v. V. 1. ओरखडलेला, &c.

To be s. खरडणें.

7 उकरलेला, उकरींव.

Heap of earth scratched. उकर *m.* उकरी *f.*

To SCRAWL, *v. a. write roughly, hastily, inelegantly, illegibly, &c.* खरडणें, ओरखडणें, बिरखडणें, भरकटणें, भरकडणें, भरभरावणें, खरडून-भरकटून-&c. लिहणें, भरभरां *adv.* लिहणें.

2 over; *cover with strokes, scratches, flourishes, &c.* चितरणें *or* चितारणें, चितरावणें, ओरखडणें, बिरखडणें, खिरचिड्या *f. pl.*-बिरखड्या *or* बिरखुड्या *f. pl.*-रेघोट्या *f. pl.*-&c. काढणें-ओढणें.

SCRAWL, *n. a hurriedly written or illegible writing.* ओरखडा *or* ओरखाडा *m.* खरड *f.* खरडें *n.* खरडा *m.* चिजबीज *f.* गिचमीड *f.* बिरखडी *or* बिरखुडी *f.* खोडाखोड *f.* राजचिह्न *n.*

SCRAWLED, *p.* v.V. 1. खरडलेला, खरडून लिहलेला, &c. किजबिडीत, किचबीड, किडबिडीत, किडबीड, किचमीड, किचबट *or* पट, चिडबीड, गिचमीड, चिटपट, चितड *or* चिताड, चिताडगुनाड, चिधड, चीत, चिरबट.

2 चितरलेला, बिरखडलेला, खिरबिड्याओढलेला-काढलेला, &c.

SCRAWLER, *n.* SCRAWLING, *p. a.* v. V. 1. खरडणारा, बिरखडणारा, &c. खरडघाशा, खरड्या.

SCRAWLINGLY, *adv.* v. A. खशाफशा *or* बशा, खिचबीड, &c.

To SCREAM, *v.n. cry out with a shrill voice.* किंकळणें, किराळणें, किंचळणें, किंकाळी *f.*-किंक *f.*-धाय *f.*-हेल *m.*-&c. मोकलणें-फोडणें-घेणें, हेल *m.* काढणें.

2—as cranes, &c. कचकचणें *intens.* कचाचणें.

3—an elephant. चिरकणें, चिरचिरणें.

SCREAM, SCREAMING, *n.* v. V. 1. किंक *f.* किंकळी *or* किंकाळी *f.* किराळी *f.* धाय *f.*

S. and squalling. धायमाय *f. v.* मोकल, फोड.

2 कचकच *f.* (*intens.* कचाच*m.* कचकचाट*m.* कचाकच*f.*).

To SCREECH, SCREECH. See To SCREAM, SCREAM.

SCREEN, *n. thing that shelters or protects.* पडदा *m.* आडपड-

दा *m.* आडकूट *or* आडकूड *n.* अंतर्धान *n.* तिरोधान *n.* व्यवधान *n.* छाया *f.*

2 *coarse sieve.* मोठ्या भोकांची चाळण *f.*

To SCREEN, *v. a. shelter or protect by concealing.* आड येणें, आड येऊन रक्षणें-बचावणें- झांकणें-&c. आस्रा *m.* देणें-घालणें, पांघरूण *n.* घालणें, झांकण *n.* घालणें, तिरोधान*n.*-&c. करणें.

SCREENED, *p.* v. V. पडद्यानें झांकलेला-&c. अंतर्हित, तिरोहित, व्यवधान रक्षित.

SCREENER, *n.* SCREENING, *p. a.* v. V. आड़ येणारा, आड येऊन रक्षणारा, &c. अंतर्धायक.

SCREW, *n.* मळसूत्र *n.* पेच *m.*

Female s. नवरी *f.* मादी *f.*

Male s. नर *m.* नवरा *m.* फिरकी *f.*

2 See MISER.

To SCREW, *v. a. fasten with a screw.* मळसूत्रानें बसवणें.

2 *move by a screw.* मळसूत्रानें फिरवणें. [णें.

3 v. To TWIST, To SQUEEZE. पिळणें, पिळवटणें, पिळून काढ-

SCREW-PLATE, *n.* नरपट्टी *f.*

SCREW TREE, *n. helicteres isora.* धामण *m.* धामणी *f.*

SCREWED, *p.* v. V. 1. मळसूत्रानें बसवलेला, मळसूत्री.

2 मळसूत्रानें फिरवलेला.

3 पिळलेला, &c.

SCRIBBLE, *To* SCRIBBLE. See SCRAWL, To SCRAWL.

SCRIBBLER. See WRITER.

SCRIBE, *n. writer.* लिहणारा, लेखक.

SCRIP, *n.* v. BAG. पिशवी *f.* जुजदान *n.*

2 *piece of paper containing a writing.* पुरजा *m.* चिट्ठी *f.* शुक्का *m.* हातचिठ्ठी *f.*

SCRIPTURAL, *a. according to the scriptures.* यथाशास्त्र, शास्त्रसिद्ध, शास्त्रीय, श्रुतिसिद्ध, यथाश्रुति, शास्त्रोक्त, वेदोक्त, वेदोदित, वैदिक, शास्त्रानुसारी, शास्त्रानुयायी.

2 *contained in the scriptures.* शास्त्राचा, शास्त्रांतला.

SCRIPTURALLY, *adv.* v. A. 1. शास्त्राप्रमाणें, &c. यथाशास्त्र, शास्त्रवत्, शास्त्रतः, शास्त्रदृष्ट्या.

SCRIPTURE, *n. sacred writing, holy writ.* शास्त्र *n.* श्रुत *n.* धर्मपुस्तक *n.* धर्मग्रंथ *m.* The *scriptures* or sacred writings of the Hindus are comprised in the *Vedas*, the *Shástras*, the *Puránas*, and their subordinate writings. The *Vedas* are four, viz. ऋग्वेद, यजुर्वेद, सामवेद, & अथर्ववेद्. Subordinate to the *Vedas* are six *Vedángas* (वेदांग) viz. शिक्षा, कल्प, व्याकरण, छंद, ज्योतिष, & निरुक्त. The theological portions of the *Vedas* are termed Upanishad (उपनिषद्) or collectively, *Vedánt*(वेदांत), which term is also the name of a philosophical system founded on the *Vedas*, teaching the unreality of all things but the Deity. A follower of this system is वेदांती. There are four *Minor Vedas* (उपवेद), viz. आयुर्वेद, धनुर्वेद, गांधर्ववेद, शस्त्रशास्त्र.

The *Shástras* are six, viz. न्याय, मीमांसा, योग, सांख्य, धर्म, and वेदांत. This last is called also उत्तर मीमांसा; मीमांसा is a twofold system, viz. पूर्वमीमांसा or मीमांसा simply, which relates to the ritual part of religion, and उत्तरमीमांसा or वेदांत which treats of the spiritual worship of the Deity or soul of the universe.

The *Purânas* are eighteen in number, viz. ब्रह्मपुराण, पद्मपुराण, ब्रह्मांडपुराण, अग्निपुराण, विष्णुपुराण, गरुडपुराण, ब्रह्मवैवर्त्तपुराण, शिवपुराण, लिंगपुराण, नारदपुराण, स्कंदपुराण, मार्कंडेय पुराण, भविष्य पुराण, मत्स्यपुराण, वराहपुराण, कूर्मपुराण, वामनपुराण, and भागवत. There are also eighteen *Upapuránas* or inferior *Purânas.*

Course of study of s. ब्रह्माधिगमन *n.*

Instruction in the s. ब्रह्मोपदेश *n.*

Mighty in the s., versed in the s. शास्त्रज्ञ, शास्त्रसंपन्न, शास्त्रदर्शी, शास्त्रविद्, शास्त्राभिज्ञ, ब्रह्मज्ञ, ब्रह्मवेत्ता, वैदिक.

Of or belonging to the *Vedas.* श्रौत.

Reading of s. ब्रह्मघोष *m.*

Sacred law (of *Manu*)&c. स्मृति *f.*—Of or belonging to it. स्मार्त्त.—Follower of it. स्मार्त्त.

Sanctity through the study of s. ब्रह्मवर्चस *n.*

Savour or excellency of s. ब्रह्मरस *m.*

Study of s. ब्रह्माभ्यास *m.*

Versedness in (or knowledge of) s. शास्त्रव्युत्पत्ति *f.* ब्रह्मज्ञान *n.* ब्रह्मवेद *m.*

SCRIVENER, *n. writer of contracts.* करारनाम्याचा लेखक.

2 See USURER. [अपची *f.*

SCROFULA, *n.*— the disease. गंडमाला *f.* कंठमाला *f.* गलगंड *m.*

SCROFULOUS, *a.* गंडमालेचा, गंडमालारोगी.

SCROLL, *n.* v. ROLL. पट *m.*

SCROTUM, *n.* अंडकोश *m.* कोश *or* ष *m.* वृषण *m. n.* अंडाशय *m.*

Enlargement of the s. कोषवृद्धि *f.* अंगवृद्धि *f.* अंडवृद्धि *f.* वृद्धि *f.*

Septum of the s. महाबीज्य *n.*

To SCRUB, *v. a. rub hard.* घासणें, घसटणें, उटणें, चोळटणें, चोळवटणें, रगडणें, रगडून-जोरानें-बळानें-&c. घासणें.

SCRUB, *n. low, mean, shabby, disreputable fellow.* The terms and phrases conveying this sense, and answering to *scab, scurvy dog, &c.* are numerous and expressive. सुडका *m.* सुडकें *n.* पायपोसखाऊ, सेटरखाऊ, पैजारखाऊ, खासडेखाऊ, टुब्बभाई *m.* टुब्बामाणूस *m.* गांवाची खरवड *f.* कथलीव्याध *or* व्याधि *f.* बाजारी, बाजार भरणा *m.* शिटाऊ, दासरी *or* दास्री, फजीतखोर, दम्यी, गाढवाचासदका *or* सत्का *m.* शाहण्याचा सदका *or* सत्का *m.* पाटींतलें मांस *n.* फटलंडी *f.* चांडाल मूर्त्ति *f.* घाण *f.* कहीबाला.

2 *worn out broom.* खुंट *m. n.* खुंटारा *m.* खराटा *m.*

3 *rough rub.* घसरा *m.* घष्टा *m.* घसका *m.*

4 *low boscage.* बनजर *n.*

Land overspread with s. बनजररान*n.* बनजर जमीन *f.*

SCRUBBED, *p.* v. V. घासलेला, उटलेला, चोळवटलेला, &c. उटींव.

I. See SCRUBBY.

SCRUBBY, *a. sorry, mean,* v. LOW. शिटाऊ, भटाऊ, हटाऊ, बाजारी, टुब्बा, तिदवळ, भिकारी, गद्दल, किलवाणा *or* णी, पाजी, निपटारा, गांवादेशानें ओवाळलेला. [कल्प *m.*

SCRUPLE, *n.* v. DOUBT. शंका *f.* आशंका *f.* किंतू *m.* दिक्कत *f.* वि-

2—the weight. एक वजनी माप आहे.

To SCRUPLE, *v. n.* v. To DOUBT, To HESITATE. ओढून धरणें, आंढतें घेणें, ओढणें, आशंकणें, शंकणें, कासकूस *f.*-नानू *f.*-&c.

करणें, विकल्प *m.*-किंतू *m.*-&c. मनांत आणणें-धरणें, आशंका *f.* धरणें-करणें.

SCRUPLER, *n.* SCRUPLING, *p. a.* SCRUPULOUS, *a.* v. V. ओढून धरणारा, ओढणारा, कासकूस करणारा, मनांत किंतू आणणारा, &c. भ्रांत्या, भ्रांतिखोर, भ्रांतिष्ट, आंढक, दिक्कती, दिक्कतखोर, संतखोर, संशयी, संशयखोर, भ्रांतहृदय, शंकाशील, संदिग्धमति, कांक्षी, शंकित, सशंक, साशंक, आशंकित, आशंक्यकारी, अत्याचारी.

SCRUPLING, *n.* v. V.—*act.* ओढून धरणें *n.* आशंका धरणें*n.*ओढ *f.* कासकूस *f.* नानू *f.* &c.

SCRUPULOSITY, SCRUPULOUSNESS, *n.* v. A. दिक्कतीपणा *m.* दिक्कतखोरी *f.* संशयीपणा *m.* किंतू-विकल्प आणण्याचा स्वभाव *m.* अत्याचार *m.*

SCRUTINEER. See SCRUTINIZER.

To SCRUTINIZE, *v. a. search closely*, v. To EXAMINE. चौकसणें, तपासणें, शोधणें, चौकशी *f.*-&c. करणें *g. of o.* छडणूक *f.*-छडाछड *f.*-&c. काढणें-लावणें *g. of o.*

2 *inspect, survey narrowly*, v. To EXAMINE. निरेखणें, निहाळणें, निरीक्षणें, कसोशी *f.*-निरीक्षण *n.*-निरीक्षा *f.*-&c. करणें *g. of o.*

SCRUTINIZER, *n.* SCRUTINIZING, *p. a.* v. V. 1. चौकसणारा, तपासणारा, छडाकाढणारा-लावणारा, &c. विचक्षण, चिकित्सक, सूक्ष्मदर्शी.

2 निरेखणारा, &c. निरीक्षण-&c. कर्त्ता-कारी.

SCRUTINIZING, SCRUTINY, *n.* v. V. 1.—*act.* चौकसणें *n.* &c. चौकसी *f.* तपास *m.* शोध *m.* छडणूक *f.* छडा *m.* छडाछड *f.* तिसड *f.* विचक्षणा *f.* चिकित्सा *f.*

2 निरेखणें *n.* निहाळणें *n.* हेर *f.* हेरणी *f.* टेहळणी *f.* कसोशी *f.* निरीक्षण *n.* निरीक्षा *f.*

To SCUD, *v. n. drive along with precipitation,*—a ship, &c. सुसाट्यानें-झपाट्यानें-झडाझड-झडाडां-झ्यांझ्यां-&c. चालणें-जाणें.

2 See To SCAMPER.

To SCUDDLE, *v. n. run with precipitation.* लगबग-लगेलगे-दड़दड-दडदडां-तुरतूर-तुरुतुरु *adv.* धांवणें-चालणें.

SCUFFLE, *n. confused and personal struggle.* धकाधकी *f.* झोंबाझोंबी *f.* सैंचासैंची *or* खेंचाखेंची *f.* झटापटी *f.* हातझोंबी *f.* झोटधरणी *f.* केशाकेशी *f.* तुडवातुडव *f.* मारामारी *f.* हातपिटी *f.* हातघाई *f.* घसराघसर *f.* शरीर संबंध *m.*

To SCUFFLE, *v. n.* v. N. धकाधकी *f.*-झोंबाझोंबी *f.*-&c. करणें, धकाधकी *f.*-झोंबाझोंबी *f.*-हातझोंबी *f.*-&c. चालणें*g. of s. recip.*

To SCULK, *v. n. lie close, lie hid,* v. To HIDE, To LURK. लपणें, छपणें, दडणें, दडा *m.* मारणें-मारून बसणें.

2 (from duty, work, &c.). काम*n.*-चाकरी *f.*-&c. चुकविणें, कामचुकाऊपणा*m.*-चुकारपणा*m.*-कामचुकावणी *f.*-&c.करणें.

SCULKER, *n.* SCULKING, *p. a.* v. V. 1. लपणारा, छपणारा, दडा मारून बसणारा, &c.

2 काम-चाकरी-&c. चुकविणारा, चुकावू, चुकारी *or* रू, कामचुकावू *or* व्या, कामचुकार *or* रू, कामचोर, चुकारतट्टू.

SCULKING, *n.* v. V. 2. कामचुकविणें *n.* चाकरी चुकविणें *n.* कामाची-&c. चुकवणी *f.*

SCULKINGLY. *adv.* v. A. 1. लपून छपून.

SCULL, *n. brain-pan.* करोटी *f.* करंटी *f.* तरंटी *f.* नरटी *f.* नरोटी *f.* मस्तकाची कवंची *f.* कवंटी *f.* कपाल *pop.* कपाळ *n.*

Necklace of sculls. कपालमाला *f.* रुंडमाला *f.*

2 *short oar.* लहानवल्हें *n.*

SCULL-CAP, *n.* टोपी *f.*

SCULLIERY, *n. place where dishes, pots, &c. are kept.* भांड्याची खोली *f.* भांडागार *n.* भांडगृह*n.* [डेघाशा.

SCULLION, *n. servant who cleans pots and pans.* खटपट्या, भां-

SCULPTOR, *n.* v. CARVER. खोदकाम्या, नकासगीर, मूर्त्तिकार.

SCULPTURE, *n.* v. CARVING. खोदकाम *n.* नकासकाम*n.* नकशा*m.*

To SCULPTURE, *v. a.* v. To CARVE, To ENGRAVE. कोरणें, खोदणें, किरवणें, नकासणें.

SCULPTURED, *p.* v. V. कोरलेला, खोदलेला, &c. कोरींव, खोदींव, नकशींव, नकशी, नकशीदार.

SCUM, *n. dirt or froth which rises to the top of liquor.* मळी *f.* तवंग *m.* फेंस *m.* करा *f.* साई *f.*

2 fig. (*of the people*). निपटारा *m.* खरवड *f.* गाळ *m.*

S. of the earth. S. of the village, &c. पृथ्वीची खरवड *f.* गांवाची खरवड *f.* [काढणें-छाटणें.

To SCUM, *v. a. take off the scum*, v. To SKIM. मळी *f.*-&c.

SCUMMER, SCUMMINGS. See SKIMMER, SKIMMINGS.

SCURF, *n. mealy crust on the skin.* कोंडा *m.* भुसा *m.* खरें *n.*

Clammy s. चिकटा *m.*

Roll of s. मळवटी *f.* मळी *f.*

SCURFY, *a.* v. N. कोंडेला, कोंड्याचा, खरब्याचा.

SCURRILOUS, *a. foul-mouthed,* v. ABUSIVE. तोंडाचा फटकळ, फटकळ, तोंडाचा शिनळ, काव्ळदांत्या, काळजिभ्या, शिवरा, वाग्दुष्ट.

2 *containing low abuse,* v. ABUSIVE. शिवरा, शिवीगाळीचा, गाळीशिवीचा, गाळ्यारा, गालीगलोचीचा, पचकळ, बेहाल.

SCURRILOUSLY, *adv.* v. A. शिवीगाळीनें, गाळीगलोचीनें, फटकळतोंडानें, फटकळ, अभद्रतोंडानें.

SCURRILOUSNESS, SCURRILITY, *n.* v. A. पचकळपणा *m.* फटकळपणा *m.* शिवरेपणा *m.* अभद्रपणा *m.* फटकळतोंड*n.* अभद्रतोंड*n.*

I. *low, abusive, indecent language.* दुर्भाषण *n.* दुरुक्ति *f.* दुर्वचन *n.* दुर्वाच्य *n.* अपभाषण *n.* वाक्पारुष्य *n.*

SCURVILY, *adv. with coarse and vulgar incivility.* घाण-राळदशा-&c. करून.

SCURVY, *n.*—the disease. नाविकरक्तपित्त *m. n.*

SCURVY, *a.* नाविकरक्तपित्ताचा, नाविकरक्तपित्त रोगी.

2 v. SCRUBBY. शिटाऊ, लिदवळ, गदळ, किलवाणा *or* र्णा.

SCUTTLE, *n. basket.* शिपतर *n.* शिबुटलें *n.*

2 *hole made in a ship.* गलबतांत-&c. केलेलें भोंक *m.*

To SCUTTLE, *v. a. sink by making holes.* भोंकें *n. pl.*-&c. पाडून बुडविणें.

To SCUTTLE, *v. n.* See To SCUDDLE.

SCYBALA, *n. lumps of hardened fæces.* खडे *m pl.* कुपित्थ *n.*

SCYTHE, *n.* मोठ्याविळ्यासारखें कापणीचें एक अऊत आहे.

SEA, *n.* v. OCEAN. समुद्र *m.* सागर *m.* दर्या *or* दरिया *m.* दर्याव*m.* सिंधु *m.*

Ablution in the s. समुद्रस्नान *n.*

Out to s. *off from the land.* नाट.

Overwhelmed by the s. दर्या गरक *or* दरिया गरक.

The four seas. चतुस्समुद्र, समुद्रचतुष्टय *n.*

The seven seas. सप्तसमुद्र *m.* सप्तसागर *m.*

To send across the s. *to transport.* काळेपाण्यावर पाठवणें.

SEA-BOAT, *n.* जोळी तारूं *n.* जोळीगलबत *n.*

SEA-BREEZE, *n.* समुद्रावरचा-दर्यावरचा-&c. वारा *m.*

SEA-COAST, *n.* समुद्रकांठ *m.* समुद्रकिनारा *m.* समुद्रतीर *n.* दर्या (*or* दरिया) किनारा *m.* समुद्रतट *n.*

SEA-ENCIRCLED, SEA-GIRT, *a.* समुद्रवलयांकित, समुद्रवेष्टित.

SEA-FARER, *n.* SEA-FARING, *a.* दर्यावरदी, सफरी, गलबती, जहाजा वरचा, गलबतावरचा, समुद्रग, नौकाजीवी, सामुद्र, समुद्रयाची, नाविक,—respectfully, बेंडा.

SEA-FISH, *n.* समुद्रांतला-खारेपाण्यांतला-&c. मासा *m.*

SEA-MAN, *n.* v. SAILOR. खलासी, लशकर *or* लषकर.

Fair weather s. तडीचा पोहणारा.

SEA-MANSHIP, *n.* गलबत चालविण्याची विद्या *f.*-कुशलता *f.*-&c.

SEA-PORT, *n. harbour.* बंदर *n.*

2 *port-town.* बंदर *n.* बंदरी गांव *m.* बंदरगांव *m.*

SEA-SHORE, SEA-SIDE, *n.* बंदर *n.* बंदरकांठ *m.* बंदरकांठा *m.* बंदरकिनारा *m.* समुद्रकिनारा *m.* समुद्रकांठा *m.* दर्याकिनारा *m.* बेला *pop.* बेळा *f.* समुद्रांत *m.*

Road by the s. बंदरवाट *f.*

SEA-SICK, *a.* गलबतलागलेला, समुद्रलागलेला, &c.

To be s. गलबत *n.*-समुद्र *m.*-&c. लागणें.

SEA-SNAIL, *n.* खुबा *m. dim.* खुबी *f.*

SEA-TIGHT, SEA-WORTHY, *a.* जौळी *or* जवळी.

SEAL, *n. stamp, &c.* मोहर *f.* शिक्का *m.* मुद्रा *f.* मुद्रिका *f.*

Great s. of a state. मोर्तब *n.* शिक्का *m.*—Officer bearing it. शिक्केवरदार, मुद्राधारी *or* राजमुद्राधारी.—Officer that affixes it. शिक्केनीस.

2 *impression.* मोहर *f.* शिक्का *m.*

3 समुद्रांतलें एक जनावर आहे. [*f.* लावणें.

To SEAL, *v. a.* v. N. मोहर *f.* करणें, शिक्का *m.* करणें-मारणें, लाख

SEALED, *p.* v. V. मोहर केलेला, मोहरबंद, मुद्रांकित, मुद्रित, समुद्र.

A s. letter. लाखोटा *m.*

SEALING-WAX, *n.* लाख *f.*

SEAM, *n. suture of two edges.* शिवण *f.* दूण *f.* सीवन *n.* सांध *f.* सांधा *m.* संधि *m. f.* जोड *m.*

Raised s. लोड *f.*

Raised strip along a s. दंड *m.*—having it. दंडारा *or* ळा.

To open at the s. (*act.* or *neut.*). उधडणें, उसवणें.

2—as between planks, layers of a wall, &c. दरज *f.*

Filling up the seams. दरजगिरी *f.*

3 See SCAR.

SEAMLESS, *a.* बिनशिवणीचा, संधिरहित.

SEAMSTRESS, *n.* शिवणकरीण *f.* शिवणारीण *f.* शिवणकामकरीण *f.*

SEAR, *n. burn made by searing.* चरका *m.* चटका *m.*

SEAR, *a. dried, withered.* वाळका, वाळलेला, वाळकुंडा.

To SEAR, *v. a. burn, scorch, cauterize.* भाजणें, डुरडणें, डागणें, चरका *m.* देणें, भाजून बहिरा-सुना-&c. करणें.

2 v. To WITHER. वाळवणें, सुकवणें.

To SEARCH, *v. a. look over or through to find something; explore, &c.* धुंडणें, शोधणें, पाहणें, शोध *m.*-&c. करणें, देखणें, डुडकणें,—closely, carefully, strictly. झाडा *m.*-झाडाझडती *f.*-झडती *f.*-झाडाझटका *m.*-&c. करणें-घेणें *g. of o.*—narrowly, thoroughly, v. To RANSACK. धुंडाळणें *or* धांडाळणें, खळवटणें, चाळणें, धुंडाळा *m.*-&c. करणें *g. of o.*

2 for; *seek, look for.* शोधणें, पाहणें, धुंडणें, डुडकणें, तलाश *m.*-शोध *m.*-शोधणूक *f.*-&c. करणें *g. of o.* शोध *m.*-सुदाबा *m.*-&c. लावणें-काढणें *g. of o.* अन्वेषणें.

3 out; v. To TRACE. उमंगणें *or* उमगणें, काढणें, शोध *m.* काढणें-लावणें *g. of o.* [*of o.*

4 (person, baggage, &c.). झाडा *m.*-झडती *f.*-तलाशी *f.* घेणें *g.*

SEARCH, SEARCHING, *n.* v. V. 1. धुंडणें *n.* शोधणें *n.* &c. शोध *m.* शोधणूक *f.* झाडा *m.* झडती *f.* झाडाझटका *m.* झाडाझडती *f.* धुंडाळा *m.*

2 शोधणें *n.* धुंडणें *n.* &c. शोध *m.* शोधणूक *f.* तलाश *m.* तपास *m.* सुदाबा *m.* सुगावा *m.* अन्वेषण *n.* अवेक्षण *n.*

4 झाडा *m.* झडती *f.* तलाशी *f.*

SEARCHED, *p.* v. V. 1. शोधलेला, धुंडलेला, &c.

SEARCHER, *n.* SEARCHING, *p. a.* v. V. 1. शोधणारा, पाहणारा, धुंडाळणारा, शोधकरणारा, &c. शोधक.

2 धुंडणारा, शोधणारा, शोधकाढणारा, &c. शोधक.

3 उमगणारा, काढणारा, उमग्या.

4 झाडेकरी. [इंचा, सूक्ष्म.

I. *close, strict, minute,*—examination, &c. बारीक, बारका-

SEARED, *p.* v. V. 1. भाजलेला, &c. भाजका, भाजींव.

2 वाळवलेला, वाळलेला, सुका.

SEASON, *n. division of the year.* ऋतु *m.*—The Hindus divide the year into six *seasons*, viz. वसंत, ग्रीष्म, वर्षा, शरत्, हेमंत, शिशिर, consisting of two months each, and commencing with the two months चैत्र & वैशाख.

Cold s. हिंवाळा *m.* हेमंत *m.* हिमकाल *m.*

Hot s. उन्हाळा *m.* ग्रीष्म *pop.* गीम *or* गिमाळा *m.* खराणेदिवस *m. pl.*—grain raised in the hot s. by irrigation. गिमवा *m.* गिमवस *f.*—ground prepared for it. गिमवस *f.*

Heat of the hot s. उन्हाळी *f.*

Rainy s. पावसाळा *m.* पाऊसकाळ *m.* पाऊसकाळा *m.* वर्षाऋतु *or* वर्षर्तु *m.* वर्षाकाल *m.* वर्षा *f.*

Revolution of the seasons. ऋतुपर्य्याय *m.*

The seasons. ऋतुगण *m.* ऋतुवर्ग *m.* षड्तु *m. pl.*

2 *fit time.* घात *f.* अवसर *m.* (esp. in comp. as भोजनावसर, स्नानावसर), सराई *f.* हंगाम *m.* सुगी *f.* ताण *or* टाण *or* टाणें *n.* समय *m.* दिवस *m. pl.* मोसम *or* मुसूम *f.* काल *or* काळ *m.* वेळ *f.* वेळा *f.* लाग *m.* प्रसंग *m.* पर्व *n.* पर्वणी *f.* प्रस्ताव *m.* पडण *n.* टच *n.* कार्यकाल *m.*

An inopportune s. आडघात *f.*

Close or last days of the s. सरतापालव *m.*

Height or heart of the s. ऐनहंगाम *m.* ऐनआमदानी *f.*

In s. and out of s. अवसरीं अनवसरीं, वेळ अवेळ.

Nectareous s. *genial time for.* अमृतवेळ.

Out of s. अनवसरीं.

3 *auspicious or fit hour, moment, &c.* मुहूर्त *m.*

4 See TIME.

For a s. *for a while,* कांहीं वेळपर्यंत, कांहीं काळपावेतों, कांहीं वेळ, कांहीं दिवस.

Inauspicious s. घातवेळ *f.* घोरवेळ *f.*

To SEASON, *v. a. give relish to, make palatable or pleasant.* मसाला *m.* घालणें-लावणें, मीठमिरची *f.* घालणें-लावणें, मसालेदार-स्वादिष्ट-खमंग-&c. करणें.

2 (a new earthen vessel, wood, &c.). वळसावणें, निरडणें, निरढवणें *or* निरढावणें, असविणें, रांवळणें, रांपवणें, पुरढणें *or* पु-

रढावणें, निर्भिद-पक्का-&c. करणें, परसविणें.

To be seasoned. रांचणें, रांपणें, निर्भिद होणें, मुरणें, पुरढणें, *or* पुरढावणें.

3 (in wickedness.). निरडणें *or* निरढणें, पुरढणें *or* पुरढावणें.

4 See To TEMPER.

SEASONABLE, *a. opportune, timely, &c.* वेळेवरचा, प्रसंगाबरचा, &c. प्रसंगाचा, प्रसंगींचा, वेळींचा, &c. गरजेवरचा, घडत्यासपडता, वक्तशीर, समयोचित, प्रसंगोचित, कालोचित, समयोपयोगी, समयोपयुक्त, कालानुरूप, समयानुरूप, प्रसंगानुरूप, कालानुकूल, उचितकालिक, कालप्राप्त, समयप्राप्त, प्रसंगप्राप्त, अवसरप्राप्त, प्राप्तकाल, प्राप्तावसर, कालिक, सामयिक, अवसरपठित, कालसदृश, प्रसंगसदृश, प्रस्तावसदृश.

2 *produced in season.* आर्त्तव, कालोद्भव, ऋतूद्भव, ऋतुजात.

SEASONABLENESS, *n.* v. A. 1. समयानुरूप्य *n.* समयानुकूल्य *n.* समयौचित्य*n.* कालौचित्य *n.* कालोचितत्व *n.* कालानुकूल्य *n.* कालानुकूलता *f.* कालानुरूप्य *n.* कालसादृश्य *n.* प्रसंगौचित्य *n.* कालप्राप्तता *f.* &c. कालधर्म *m.*

SEASONABLY, *adv.* v. A. 1. वेळेस, समयास, प्रसंगास, वक्तास, &c. यथाकालीं, यथाकाल, सुकालीं, वक्तशीर, बरा *decl.* नेमका *decl.* समयानुसार, प्रसंगानुसार, कालानुसार, प्रसंगोपात्त, योगतः.

SEASONED, *p.* v. V. 1. मसाला घातलेला, मसालेदार केलेला,&c.

High s. मसालेदार, खमखमीत, खमंग, चणचणीत, चमचमीत, चरमरीत, चरचरीत.

2 बळसावलेला, निरडलेला, निरढवलेला, &c.

SEASONING, *n. sauce, stuffing, &c.* मसाला *m.* तिळकूट *n.* तिरकूट *n.* सांभार *m.* [मिसळण *f.*

Pungent herbs & spices formed into a s. मिसळणें *n.*

SEAT, *n. thing or place to sit on.* बैठक *f.* बसक *f.* बसकर *m. f. n.* आसन *n.*

Chief s. (at assemblies &c. &c.). अग्रासन *n.*

Easy s. सुखासन *n.*

S. of earth or bricks. ओटा *m.*

Swinging s. चौपाळा *m.* चौफळा *m.*

2 *thing spread to sit on.* आंथरूण *n.* बिछाईत *f.* बैठक *f.* बसक *f.* बसकर *n. f. m.* बसकार *m.* पथारी *f.* बसणें *n.* आस्तरण *n.*

3 *place of abiding, inherence, &c.* स्थान *n.* अधिष्ठान *n.* आशय *m.* (esp. in comp. as पित्ताशय, रक्ताशय, गर्भाशय, अहंकाराशय, &c.), आयतन *n.* (in comp. as भोगायतन, मूलायतन, रोगायतन), आस्पद *n.* (in comp. as दुःखास्पद, सुखास्पद, हर्षास्पद, शोकास्पद, आनंदास्पद, भयास्पद, लोभास्पद, मोहास्पद, ममतास्पद), अधिकरण *n.* अधिष्ठिति *f.* वसति *f.* घर *n.* धाम *n.* आगर *m. n.*

S. of all happiness and honor. सकलसुखसंपत्तिवसति *f.*

4 (esp. on horseback). आसन *n.* मांड *f.* बैठक *f.*

To get or form a s. मांड *f.*-आसन *n.* जमणें-बसणें *g. of s.*

To SEAT, *v. a. cause to be seated.* बसवणें, बसायास-बसायाला देणें, उपविष्ट-आसनस्थित करणें.

2 v. To INSTAL. स्थापणें, बसवणें,पदारूढ करणें, निवेश*m.*-प्रतिष्ठापन*n.*-प्रतिष्ठा*f.*-&c. करणें *g. of o.* निविष्ट-&c. करणें.

3 (one's self) *settle, fix.* बसणें, धारणें, निवेश *m.*-&c. करणें, निविष्ट-निवेशित-निष्ठ-&c. होणें.

Fixedly or doggedly seating one's self on the ground. बसक *f.*-बसकट *f.* v. घे, मार.

SEATED, *p.* v. V. 1. बसवलेला, &c. उपविष्ट, आसनस्थित, आसनोपविष्ट, आसनारूढ, निविष्ट, निवेशित.

2 स्थापलेला, &c. पदारूढ.

3 बसलेला, &c. निविष्ट, निष्ठ (in comp. as घटनिष्ठ, देहनिष्ठ, मनोनिष्ठ),स्थ (in comp.).

SEATER, *n.* SEATING, *p. a.* v. V. 1. बसवणारा, उपविष्ट-&c. कर्त्ता.

2 स्थापणारा, &c. निवेश-प्रतिष्ठापन-&c. कर्त्ता-कारी-&c.

SECANT, *n.* छेदन रेषा *f.*

To SECEDE, *v. n. withdraw from association.* फुटणें, वेगळा-&c. होणें, बाहेर होणें-पडणें, संगत *f.*-सोबत *f.*-&c. सोडणें-टाकणें, फळी *f.* फोडणें, विभक्तहोणें, फटकून राहणें.

SECEDER, *n.* SECEDING, *p. a.* v. V. फुटणारा, फुटलेला, वेगळा होणारा-झालेला, संगतसोडणारा-सोडलेला, &c. विभक्त झालेला.

To SECERN. See To SECRETE.

SECESSION, *n.* v. V. फुटणें *n.* फूट *f.* विभक्त होणें *n.*

To SECLUDE, *v. a. separate, keep apart (from society, &c.).* वेगळा-निराळा-लोकानिराळा-&c. करणें-ठेवणें-राहविणें, पडद्यांत वसवणें-राहविणें, एकांतीं राहविणें-बसवणें, विविक्त-&c. करणें, पृथक्स्थित करणें, एकांतवास *m.*-विविक्तवास *m.* करवणें *g. of o.*

2 (one's self). एकांतीं राहणें-बसणें, एकांतवास *m.*-विविक्तवास *m.* सेवणें-करणें, सभावर्जन *n.* करणें.

3 See To EXCLUDE.

SECLUDED, *p.* v. V. 1. वेगळा राहविलेला, &c.

I. See RETIRED. [विविक्तवृत्ति *f.*

SECLUSION, *v.* v. V. 2.—*state.* एकांतवास *m.* विविक्तवास *m.* वि-

SECOND, *a.* दुसरा, द्वितीय, दुजा. [सूरभरणी *f.*

Playing or singing s. *joining in.* जुगल *f.* सूरभरणा *m.*

S. to none. अद्वितीय, अनुत्तर.

S.-rate. मध्यमप्रत *f.*

SECOND, *n. supporter, backer,* v. HELPER. पाठराखणारा, पाठराख्या, पाठिंबा, बाहिदार, बाजू *f.* सारथी, संभाळणारा, कांवसा *or* कौंशा.

A s. at vocal or instrumental music. साथकरी *m.* सुरत्या, सूरकरी, सूरदेणारा, सुऱ्या.

2 (of time). विकला *f.* ($\frac{1}{60}$ of a kalá). विपल *n.* ($\frac{1}{60}$ of a pala). सेकंद *m.* (the English word.).

To SECOND, *v. a. back, support,* v. To HELP. पाठ *f.* देणें, पाठ *f.* राखणें *g. of o.* बाहिदारी *f.*-उपराळा *m.* करणें, बाजू *f.* राखणें-संभाळणें *g. of o.* शेव *m.* घालणें.

To s. a singer. शेव *m.* देणें-पोहोंचविणें.

SECOND-HAND, *a. not new.* उष्टा, आडजुना, अन्यपूर्व, अन्योपभुक्त, अन्यभुक्त, उच्छिष्ट.

2 *not original, heard from another.* मधला, दुसऱ्याचा, दुसऱ्याच्या तोंडचा ऐकलेला, स्वतःचा-&c. नव्हे, अन्योक्त, अन्यरुत.

SECOND-RATE, *a. of the second quality, &c.* दुसरे-मध्यम प्रतीचा-किमतीचा-योग्यतेचा-दराचा-&c. [प्रति *f.*

SECOND-SIGHT, *n. supernatural sight.* दिव्यचक्षु *m. n.* दिव्यदृ-

That is endowed with s. दिव्यचक्षु, दिव्यदृष्टि.

SECONDARILY, *adv.* v. A. 2. गौणभावानें, गौणतः, अनुषंगतः.

SECONDARINESS, *n.* v.A.1. गौणता *f.* अप्रधानता *f.* &c. गौणभाव*m.*

SECONDARY, *a. not of the first intention, not primary.* गौण, अप्रधान, अमुख्य, गुणभूत.

S. object or end. गौणकल्प *m.*

2 *not of the first order or rate.* दुसरे-मध्यम-खालच्या-&c. प्रतीचा-दराचा-किमतीचा-योग्यतेचा-&c.

SECONDLY, *adv.* v. A. दुसरा *decl.* दुसऱ्यानें.

SECRECY, SECRETNESS, *n.* v. A. 1. गुप्तपणा *m.* &c. गुप्तता *f.* गुह्यता *f.* गुप्तभाव *m.* अन्याज्ञातता *f.*

I. *seclusion.* एकांतवास *m.* विविक्तवास *m.*

II. *forbearance of disclosure; silence.* मौनn. अभाषण *n.* अनुद्गार *m.* अनुद्घाटन *n.* गुह्यगोपन *n.* रहस्यगोपन *n.*

Profound s. घनसंवृत्ति *f.*

SECRET, *a. hidden, concealed, not known to others.* गुप्त, गुह्य, गौप्य *pop.* गोप्य, रहस्य, गुप्तपणाचा, गुप्तभावाचा, रहस्याचा, गुप्तपणींचा, अन्याज्ञात, अंतस्थ, चोरटा, चोरीचा (as चोरीची शिनळकी, चोरीचें श्रवणn.-मनन *n.*-&c.) चोर (in comp. as चोरखण s. cell or drawer, चोरखिसा s. pocket, also चोरअंक, चोरकोनाडा, चोरखिडकी, चोरगल्ली, चोरगस्त, चोरगांठ, चोरघडी, चोरघर, चोरबातमी, चोरवाट, &c. &c.)

2 *retired, private,*— a place. आडवळणी, आडवळणाचा, एकांताचा, पडतपोशीचा, विविक्त, विविक्तवासाचा.

3 *close, incommunicative, keeping secrets.* गुजराख्या, खोल, तोंडाचा खबरदार-बळकट-घट्ट, गुह्यभाषी, गुह्याकथक, गुह्यानिवेदी.

4 *occult, not apparent, &c.* v. OBSCURE. गुप्त, गूढ, अस्पष्ट.

5 *not proper to be seen.* गुह्य.

SECRET, *n. thing kept concealed.* गूज *n.* गुजगोष्ट *f.* रहस्य *pop.* रहश्य *n.* गुप्तगोष्ट *f.* गुह्यगोष्ट *f.* हितगूज *n.* गुह्यविषय *m.* भेद *m.* मर्म *n.*

Disclosure of secrets. अंतर्भेद *m.*

Diving into the s. of. मर्मभेद *m.* मर्मान्वेषण *n.*—person that dives, मर्मभेदी, मर्मान्वेषी.

Knower of the secrets of. अंतर्भेदी, भेदी, भेद्या, मर्मज्ञ, मर्मी, मार्मिक, दरदी.

One's own s. निजगूज *n.*

2 (as of a piece of mechanism, &c.) *key, trick, &c.* v. ART. मर्म *n.* कालगूत *n.* किल्ली *or* गुरुकिल्ली *f.*

3 secrets; *private parts,* v. PRIVITY. गुह्यांग *n.*

SECRETARY, *n. official-writer, &c.* दबीर, चिटनवीस *or* चिटनीस.

The English word is frequently used as सेक्रेटरी, sometimes सकटतार.

Persian s. मुनशी.

2 See MINISTER, OFFICER.

To SECRETE, *v.a. conceal,* v. To HIDE. लपवणें, झांकणें, चोरणें.

2—in the animal economy. वेगळा-&c. करणें, काढणें, उत्पन्न करणें. [निर्माणकरण *n.*

SECRETION, *n.* v. V. 2. वेगळाकरणें *n.* काढणें *n.* &c. पृथक्करण *n.*

I. *the matter secreted.* रक्तापासून वेगळा केलेला पदार्थm.मळm.

SECRETLY, *adv.* v. A. 1. गुप्तपणीं, गुप्त, लिकून चोरून, लपून छपून, झांकून, चोरगस्तीनें.

SECRETORY, *a. performing the office of secretion.* वेगळा करण्याचे कामाचा-उपयोगाचा, &c. उत्पादक.

SECT, *n.*—in religion. मत *n.* संप्रदाय *m.* पक्ष *m.* पथ *pop.* पंथm मार्ग *m.* पंथा *m.* शाखा *f.* एकदेशिमार्ग *m.*गण *m.*

SECTARIAN, SECTARY, *n. one of a sect.* शाखामार्गी, शाखामार्गानुयायी, शाखानुयायी, शाखावलंबी, शाखाधारी, शाखाश्रयी, भिन्नमार्गानुयायी, एकदेशिमार्गानुयायी, एकदेशिमार्गावलंबी-सेवी-&c.

SECTARIAN, *a.* शाखामार्गाचा, एकदेशिमार्गाचा, एकदेशिमार्गाविषयींचा, स्फुटमार्गावलंबी-सेवी-आश्रयी-&c.

SECTION, *n.* v. DIVISION. छेदन *n.* भेदन *n.* परिछेद *m.*

2—in geometry. मार्ग *m.*

3 (of a book). अध्याय *m.* पर्वn. वर्गm. कांडm. *n.* खंडm. *n.* स्कंध *m.* भाग *m.* शाखा *f.* प्रकरण *n.* परिछेद *m.* विछेद *m.*

SECTIONAL, *a.* भागाचा, खंडाचा.

SECTOR, *n.* विछेदक *m.* वृत्तांश *m.*

SECULAR, *a. relating, &c. to this present world; not spiritual,* —matters. यालोकचा, इहलोकचा, ऐहिक, इहलोकाविषयींचा,इहलोकविषयक-संबंधी, लौकिक, लोकव्यवहाराचा, जनव्यवहाराचा, व्यवहाराचा, प्रपंचाविषयींचा, संसाराविषयींचा, व्यावहारिक, संसारीक, प्रपंची, प्रापंचिक, ग्राम्य, प्रवृत्त, प्रपंचसापेक्ष.

The science or law of s. or social walk. व्यवहारशास्त्रn.

2—person; v. LAY. व्यवहारी, संसारी, प्रपंची, खटलेबाईक.

SECULARIST,*n. one who maintains the worth of things sensible.* दृष्टार्थवादी *n.*

SECULARITY, SECULARNESS, *n. worldliness of spirit.* ऐहिक दृष्टि *f.* ऐहिकबुद्धि *f.* ऐहिकप्राबण्य *n.* ऐहिकासक्ति *f.* प्रपंचासक्ति *f.* संसारासक्ति *f.* प्रपंचबुद्धि *f.* प्रपंचदृष्टि *f.*

2 *the system of things sensible.* दृष्टार्थशास्त्र *n.* दृष्टार्थवाद *m.*

SECUNDINES,*n.*v. AFTERBIRTH. वार *f.*खोळ *f.*गर्भवेष्टनn.गर्भाशयm.

SECURE, *a. free from apprehension of danger, assured, sure,* v. CONFIDENT. निर्भय, निश्चिंत, निश्शंक, अशंक, भयशंकारहित, निरातंक.

2 *free from danger, safe.* निर्भय, निजोखमी, भयातीत, निष्कंटक, निर्विघ्न, निरुपद्रव, अकुतोमय *vulg.* अकुतोभय, असंभाव्योपद्रव, असंभाव्यभय, असंभाव्यापकार, उपद्रवसंभवातीत, &c.

To SECURE, *v. a. make safe, guard from danger.* निर्भय-निजोखमी-&c. करणें, भयानिराळा-भयावेगळा-भयातीत-&c. करणें, निर्भयपणा *m.* करणें *g. of o.* निर्भयपणा *m.* आणणें, बंदोबस्त *m.*-बंदोबस्ती *f.*-रक्षण *n.*-&c. करणें *g. of o.* भयनिवृत्ति *f.*-भयनिरास *m.*-&c. करणें *g. of o.* सुरक्षित-&c. करणें.

2 *make certain.* खचीत-मुकरर-निश्चित-पक्का-निभ्रांत-&c. करणें -करून घेणें, खचिती *f.*-निश्चिती *f.*-निश्चय *m.*-&c. करणें-करून घेणें *g. of o.* [निश्चित.

SECURELY, *adv.* v. A. 1. निर्भयपणें, भयावांचून, भयरहित, निर्भय,

2 *and* SAFELY. निर्भय, खुशाल, सलामत, सुदामत.

SECURITY, *n.* v. A. 1. निर्भयपणा *m.* निश्शंकपणा *m.* निश्चितपणा *m.* &c. शंकाराहित्य *n.* शंकाशून्यता *f.* आतंकराहित्य *n.*

2 निर्भयपणा *m.* निजोखमीपणा *m.* निष्कंटकपणा *m.* &c. निर्भयता *f.* भयाभाव *m.* भयराहित्य *n.* अकुतोभयता *f.* निर्विघ्नता *f.* निष्कंटक *n.* निर्भय *n.*

I. *pledge given, surety.* जामिनी *f.* तारणn. हामी *f.* निशा *f.*

S.—bond. जामीनकतबा *or* कदबा *m.* जामीनखत *n.*

II. *surety;*—of porsons. जामीन, जामीनदार, दर्म्यान, हामीदार, प्रतिनिधि *m.* प्रतिभू *m.*

Chain or round of securities. जामीनसांखळी *f.*

III. (for goods or money). मालजामीन,—as disting. from हाजीरजामीन S. for the appearance of the person. For this, also दर्शनप्रतिभू *m.*

SEDAN, *n. portable chair.* नालकी *f.*

SEDATE, *a. staid, steady, composed.* स्थिर, भरकुंब *or* भरखम्म, गं

भीर, शांत, स्थिरबुद्धि. [स्थैर्यपूर्वक.

SEDATELY, *adv.* v. A. स्थिरपणें, भरखुमीनें, &c. गांभीर्यपूर्वक,

SEDATENESS, *n.* v. A. स्थिरपणा *m.* गंभीरपणा *m.* भरकुंबपणा *m.* भरखुमी *f.* गांभीर्य *n.* गंभीरता *f.* स्थिरता *f.* स्थैर्य *n.* स्थिरबुद्धि *f.*

SEDATIVE, *n.*—in medicine. शमन *n.* उपशमन *n.* थमन *n.* ग्राही *m.*

SEDATIVE, *a.* v. COMPOSING. शमनकर्त्ता-कारी-&c. उपशमनकर्त्ता-&c. संतापहर-&c. [राहित्य *n.*

SEDENTARINESS, *n.* v. A. 2. बैठेपणा *m.* &c. चलनाभाव *m.* चलन-

SEDENTARY, *accustomed to sit much.* बसकामी, बसकाम्या, बैठकामी, बैठकाम्या.

2 *requiring sitting, passed in sitting.* बैठकीचा, बसकीचा, बैठा, बसलेठिकाणचा, जागचा, गादीचा, बसलेबैठकीचा, चलनाभावाचा, चलनरहित.

SEDGE, *n.* एक वनस्पति आहे.

SEDIMENT, *n.* v. DREGS. गाळ *m.* गदळ *n.* सांका *m.* सांसारा *m.*

SEDIMENTARY, *a.* गाळाचा, गदळाचा.

SEDITION, *n. factious or rebellious commotion.* बंड *n.* बंडावा *m.* दंगा *m.* बैदा *m.*

Plot or scheme of s. फंद *m.*

SEDITIOUS, *a. factious, turbulent.* बंडी, बंड्या, बंडाचा, बंडाव्याचा, बंडेफरोशी, दंग्याचा, दंगेखोर, बडखोर, फंदी, फंदफितुराचा.

S. practices. बंडाई *f.* बंडावा *m.*

S. risings and plots,—compreh. फंदफितूर *m.* फितूरफांदा *m.* फंदफुरई *f.*

To SEDUCE, *v. a. entice from the path of rectitude.* फुसलावणें, भुलवणें, फुसलावून-भुलवून-भुलताप देऊन-भुलवण घालून-&c. बहकिवणें-बिथरवणें-बिचलवणें-बिघडवणें-सन्मार्गच्युत-सन्मार्गभ्रष्ट-&c. करणें, पाऊल *n.* वांकडें पाडणें-पाडविणें *g. of o.* पाय *m.* वांकडा पाडणें-पाडविणें *g. of o.* आडवाटेस-आडमार्गास-गैरमार्गानें-&c. लावणें, फितवणें *or* फितावणें, फितुरणें, फोडणें, फितवा *m.* करणें *g. of o.* फिसकाविणें.

2 (a female). फुसलावून-&c. आंगाखालीं घालणें, वशकरून-बधवून-&c. उपभोगणें-भ्रष्ट करणें-सतीत्वनाश *m.* करणें.

To s. and elope with. काढणें-काढून नेणें.

SEDUCED, *p.* v. V. 1. फुसलावून बहकवलेला-बिथरवलेला-बिघडवलेला-&c. फितवलेला, आडमार्गास लावलेला, &c.

2 बधवून भ्रष्ट केलेला, &c.

SEDUCER, *n.* SEDUCING, *p. a.* SEDUCTIVE, *a.* V. 1. फुसलावणारा, भुलवणारा, भुलताप देणारा, फुसलावून बहकवणारा-बिथरवणारा-&c. फितवणारा, फितुरणारा, आडमार्गास लावणारा, &c. भुलविण्याचा, भुलताप देण्याचा.

2 बधवून भ्रष्ट करणारा, बधवून उपभोगणारा, &c.

SEDUCTION, *n.* v. V. 1.—*act.* फुसलावणें *n.* भुलवणें *n.* फुसलावून नेणें *n.*-बहकविणें *n.*-&c.

2 बधवून उपभोगणें *n.* कापट्यपूर्वकसतीत्वनाश *m.* स्त्रीसंग्रहण *n.*

SEDULITY, SEDULOUSNESS, *n.* v. A. उद्योगीपणा *m.* उद्योग *m.* उद्यम *m.* साक्षेप *m.* व्यासंग *m.* परिश्रम *m.* व्यवसाय *m.* अध्यवसाय *m.* उद्योगशीलता *f.* आसक्ति *f.* संसक्ति *f.*

SEDULOUS, *a. assiduous,* v. DILIGENT. उद्योगी, उद्योगासक्त, उद्यमी, साक्षेपी, व्यासंगी, परिश्रमी, आसक्त, संसक्त, अभ्यासी, व्यवसायी.

SEDULOUSLY, *adv.* v. A. ताण देऊन, श्रम घेऊन, व्यासंगपूर्वक, परिश्रमपूर्वक, आसक्तिपूर्वक.

To SEE, *v. a. perceive by the eye.* पाहणें, देखणें, लक्षिणें, अवलोकणें, विलोकणें, बघणें *or* बगणें, प्रेक्षणें, दर्शन *n.*-दृष्टि *f.*-अवलोक *m.*-अवलोकन *n.*-&c. करणें, दिसणें *in. con.* दृष्टीस-&c. पडणें *in. con.* ईक्षण *n.*-दर्श *m.*-संदर्शन *n.*-प्रेक्षण *n.*-प्रेक्षा *f.*-वीक्षण *n.*-&c. करणें. [णें, जाणणें.

2 *discover, descry, perceive.* लक्षिणें, पाहणें, ताडणें, समज-

3 off ; *conduct on the way.* घालवणें, बोळवणें, बोळवणी *f.* करणें *g. of o.*

To SEE, *v. n. have the power of sight.* पाहणें, दृष्टि *f.*- डोळे *m. pl.* &c. असणें *in. con.* दिसणें *impers.* डोळस-&c. असणें.

2 *direct the sight,* v. To LOOK. पाहणें, बगणें *or* बघणें, दृष्टि *f.* घालणें-लावणें.

3 into, through ; *discern, penetrate, &c.* वेधणें, लक्षिणें, जाणणें, वर्म *n.*-मर्म *n.*-&c. जाणणें, भेदणें, भेद *m.*-&c. करणें.

4 *examine, enquire.* पाहणें, बगणें *or* बघणें, शोध *m.*-चोकशी *f.*- विचार *m.*-&c. करणें.

5 *beware, take care.* जपणें, संभाळणें.

SEED, *n.* बीं *n.* बीज *n.*

Raised from s. बिजाळू. [रोव *m.* रहू *m.*

S. springing or just sprung. रुजवण *n.* रोहटी *f.* रोहू *m.*

2 *a* s. बी *f.* बीज *n.*

3 (of stone fruits). अठळी *f.* अटी *f.* अठोळी *f.*

4 *stock, source.* बीज *n.* बिजवट *n.*

5 v. OFFSPRING. बीज *n.* बिजवट *n.* बिजवड *n.*

Failure or extinction of s. बींबूड *f.* निर्वंश *m.*

6 *portion reserved for seed to be sown.* बियाणें *or* बेणें *n.* बिंब्यांचा *or* बियांचा दाणा *m.* बिरवण *or* बींबिरवण *f.*

Mixed sowing s. बेवड *f.*

S. roots, slips, &c. reserved for sowing and setting,—compreh. बीं बियाणें *n.* बीं बिंवळा *m.* बींबेणें *or* बीं ब्याणें *n.* बीं भरण *n.*

7 (animal) *sperm, seminal fluid.* धातु *m. f.* धात *f.* रेत *n.* वीर्य *n.* शुक्र *n.* बीज *n.* बिजवट *n.* इंद्रिय *n.*

To SEED, *v.n. grow to maturity so as to produce seed.* पूर्णदशेस येऊन बीं *n.* येणें-भरणें. [लोढणें, वटणें.

To SEED, *v. a.* See To Sow. 2 (cotton) *extract the seed.*

Cost of seeding cotton. लोढाई *f.*

SEED-LING, *n.* v. PLANT. रोप *n.*

SEED-PLOT, *n.* आंवण *n.* आंवणाची जागा *f.* रोपांचा वाफा *m.*

SEED-TIME, *n.* पेरण्याची घात *f.* पेरण्याचा समय *m.*

SEEDLESS, *a.* निर्बीज, निष्फल.

2 *wanting its stone or nut,*—fruit. पोलकट.

SEEDY, *a. exhausted, looking poorly.* म्लान.

SEEING, *n.* v. SIGHT. दृष्टि *f.*

SEEING, SEEING THAT, v. SINCE. जेव्हां, ज्यापक्षीं.

To SEEK, *v. a. look for,* v. To SEARCH. शोधणें, पाहणें, अन्वेषणें.

Long sought for. चिरचेष्टित. [रणें *g. of o.*

2 *solicit, ask,* v. To BEG. मागणें, अर्थणें, याचना *f.*-&c. क-

To SEEK, *v. n. make search.* पाहणें, शोध *m.*-तलाश *m.*-&c. करणें, शोधांत-&c. असणें.

SEEKER, *n.* SEEKING, *p. a.* v. V. A. 1. शोधणारा, शोध करणारा, तलाश करणारा, अन्वेषी, अन्वेष्टा.

2 मागणारा, अर्थी (esp. in comp. as विद्यार्थी, धनार्थी, &c.).

To SEEM, *v. a. appear.* दिसणें, भासणें, वाटणें, गमणें.
2 *as opp. to* be in reality. दिसणें, बाहेरून-वरून-&c. दिसणें, रंग *m.*-डौल *m.*-घाट *m.*-धोरण *n.*-&c. असणें *in. con.*

SEEMER, *n.* SEEMING, *p. a.* v. V. 1. दिसणारा, भासणारा, &c.
2 बाहेरून दिसणारा, बाहेरच्या डौलाचा.

SEEMING, *n. appearance, semblance.* आकार *m.* रूप *n.* स्वरूप *n.* डौल *m.* भास *m.* [रीं, जणू.

SEEMINGLY, *adv. in appearance.* दिसण्यांत, बाहेरून, बाह्यात्का-

SEEMLINESS, *n.* v. A. रूपलावण्य *n.* लवलक्षण *n.* आव *m.*
2 लायकी *f.* योग्यता *f.* औचित्य *n.* [य, दृष्टिभरू.

SEEMLY, *a. comely, &c.* v. BEAUTIFUL. देखणा, देखाऊ, दर्शनी-
2 *becoming,* v. FIT. योग्य, उचित, लायक, शिस्त, शिस्तवार.

SEEN, *p.* v. V. A. 1. पाहिलेला, &c. देखींव, दृष्ट, लक्षित, दर्शित, अवलोकित, ईक्षित, प्रेक्षित, वीक्षित.

SEER, *n.* SEEING, *p. a.* v. V. A. 1. पाहणारा, &c. देखता.
v. V. N. पाहणारा, डोळस, दर्शी (in comp. as दूरदर्शी, दोषदर्शी, दीर्घदर्शी, गुणदर्शी, छिद्रदर्शी, &c. &c.), द्रष्टा, चक्षुष्मान्.
I. v. PROPHET, SAGE. भविष्य पाहणारा, भविष्यदर्शी, दूरदर्शी, सिद्ध, सिद्धपुरुष.

SEE-SAW, *n. vibratory or reciprocating motion.* झुलाझुली *f.* झोकाझोकी *f.* ओढाओढी *f.*

To SEETHE, *v. a.* v. To BOIL. शिजवणें, रांधणें, उकडणें.

To SEETHE, *v. n. be in seething.* शिजणें, उकडणें.

SEETHED, *p.* v. V. A. शिजवलेला, उकडलेला, &c.

SEETHER, *n.* v. V. A. शिजवणारा, उकडणारा, &c.
I. See POT, BOILER.

SEGAR, *n. cigar.* चुट्टा *m.* विडी *f.*

SEGMENT, *n.*—of a circle. धनुष्य *n.* वर्त्तुलखंड *m.*

SEGREGARIOUS, *a. that keeps by itself.* एकचर, एकचारी.

To SEGREGATE, &c. See To SEPARATE, &c.

SEIGNIOR, See LORD.

SEINE, *n. fishing net.* पाग *m.* डोळ *m.* मळई *f.*

SEIZABLE, *a.* v. V. धराया-&c. जोगा-सारखा-&c. धार्य.

To SEIZE, *v. a. catch, clutch, grasp, lay hold of.* धरणें, हातांत-मुठींत-पंजांत-&c. धरणें, पकडणें, झोंबणें, झोंबाडणें, मटकावणें, पछाडणें, मट्टा *m.*-झोंबाडा *m.* मारणें-घालणें *with* वर *of o.*
2 *take by violence, &c.* जबरदस्तीनें-&c. घेणें-धरणें, बळकटून-धरणें, बळकावणें, दस्त करणें, काबीज करणें, हरणें, हिरणें, हिरावणें, हिरावून घेणें, हिसकावणें, छिनावणें, गुंडाळणें, हिसकावून-हिसडून-हिसकून घेणें, रगडणें, रपाटणें, दपटणें, अवळणें, गवसणी *f.* घालणें, गवाळ्यांत घालणें *or* टाकणें.
3 *invade suddenly, take hold of, overpower,*—a fever, &c. घेरणें, पछाडणें, ग्रासणें, आक्रमणें, ग्रस्त करणें.
4—in law; *sequestrate.* जप्त करणें.
5 upon; *fall on and grasp.* झोंबाडणें, झोंबाडा *m.* घालणें-मारणें, पटकावणें, मटकावणें.

SEIZED, *p.* v. V. 1. धरलेला, पकडलेला, धृत, हृत.
2 जबरदस्तीनें घेतलेला, बळकावलेला, &c. काबीज.
3 घेरलेला, &c. ग्रस्त, आक्रांत.
4 जप्त केलेला, जप्त.

SEIZER, *n.* SEIZING, *p. a.* v. V. 1. धरणारा, हातांत-&c. धरणारा, पकडणारा, &c. धर्त्ता.
2 जबरदस्तीनें-&c. घेणारा, बळकावणारा, हिरावून घेणारा, दपटणारा, &c. दपट्या, हारी, हारक, हर, हर्त्ता, हरक, अपहर्त्ता, अपहारक. [हण *n.* ग्रह *m.*

SEIZING, SEIZURE, *n.* v. V. 1.—*act.* धरणें *n.* पकडणें *n.* &c. ग्र-
2—*act.* बळकावणें *n.* हिसकावणें *n.* दपटणें *n.* &c. हरण *n.* हार *m.* अपहरण *n.* अपहार *m.* मूठमर्दाई *f.*
3—*act.* घेरणें *n.* पछाडणें *n.* &c.
4—*act.* जप्त करणें *n.* जप्ती *f.*

SELDOM, *adv. not often, not frequently; rarely.* क्कचित्, विरळा.

To SELECT, *v. a.* v. To CHOOSE. निवडणें, निवडून घेणें, काढणें, छानणें, वरणें, परिगणन *n.*-परिगणना *f.* करणें *g. of o.*

SELECT, *a.* v. CHOICE. निवडक, निवडींव, वेंचला.

SELECTION, *n.* v. V.—*act.* निवडणें *n.* छानणें *n.* वरणें *n.*
I. *a* s. (from a book, &c.). वेंचा *m.*

SELF, *a.* or *pro. very,* v. SAME. तोच, हाच.
2—as conjoined with a pronoun reciprocally. अपण *or* आपण,—as conjoined with a pronoun for emphasis अपण *or* आपण, च.
Myself, ourselves, himself, yourself, &c. *i. e. by one's self, in person, in propriá personá,* v. PERSON. अपण *or* आपण, जातीनें, खुद, आपहस्तें, आपहस्तकीं, स्वहस्तें, जिवानूशी, साक्षात्, स्वरूपतः.
Amongst (our-your-their) selves. आपसांत, आपसामध्यें, आपआपल्यांत, एकमेक, एकमेकांत, एकमेकाशीं.
As or like one's s. आत्मवत्.
By (my-him-their, &c.) self or selves; *alone.* एकटा, एकला, एकएकटा, एकएकला, *all decl.*
Of (its-him-their, &c.) self *or* selves, *of own accord,* v. SPONTANEOUSLY. स्वतः *pop.* स्वतां, स्वयें, आपोआप, आपण होऊन.
Equality with one's s. आत्मौपम्य *n.* [हंमति *f.*
Sense or apprehension of s. अहंकार *m.* अहंभाव *m.* अ-
Sparer of one's s. आंगराख्या, आंगचोर, आंगनुकानू *or* रू, आंगचुकार.
Upon one's own s. *upon one's own means or responsibility.* आंगावर. [सी *f.* करणें.
To act like one's s. आपल्यासारखें-आपलेसें करणें, आपली-
To be beside one's s. देहावर-शुद्धीवर-स्थितीवर-&c. नसणें.
To cast off from one's s. (care, concern, blame, &c.). आंगानिराळा-वेगळा-बाहेर टाकणें.
To come to one's s. देहावर-शुद्धीवर-&c. येणें.
To enrich one's s. घर *n.* भरणें.
To lay by or put by for one's s. आंगाखालीं घालणें.
To spare one's s. आंग *n.* राखणें-चोरणें.
3 *own self, own soul.* आत्मा *m.* स्व *m.*
Self, in composition, is rendered by आत्म, स्व, स्वतः, स्वयं, as will be seen by the words that follow in order.

SELF-ABUSE, *n.* आत्मनिंदा *f.* आत्मगर्हा *f.* आत्मकुत्सा *f.*

SELF-ACCOMPLISHED, *a.* स्वतःसिद्ध.

SELF-ACQUIRED, *a.* स्वोपार्जित, स्वार्जित.

SELF-ACTUATING, *a.* स्वयंवह.

SELF-ADVANTAGE, *n.* आत्महित *n.* आत्मसिद्धि *f.* आत्मोदय *m.* आत्मविवृद्धि *f.*

SELF-AFFAIRS, *n.* स्वकार्य *n.* स्वकर्म *n.*

SELF-AGGRANDIZEMENT, *n.* स्वमहत्त्ववृद्धि *f.*

SELF-APPLAUSE, *n.* आत्मस्तुति *f.* आत्मश्लाघा *f.* [त्मभूत.

SELF-BEGOTTEN, SELF-BORN, *a.* आत्मजनित, स्वोत्पन्न, स्वज, आ-

SELF-BEGUILED, *a.* स्ववंचित, स्वप्रतारित.

SELF-COLLECTEDNESS, *n.* फाम *f.* स्वस्थता *f.* देहभान *n.*

SELF-CONCEIT, *n.* v. CONCEIT. मीपणा *m.* अभिमान *m.* स्वाभिमान *m.* अहम्मान *m.* अहम्मति *f.* आत्माभिमान *m.* अहमहमिका *f.*

SELF-CONCEITED, *a.* v. CONCEITED. अभिमानी, अहम्मानी, स्वाभिमान *pop.* स्वाभिमानी, आत्माभिमानी.

SELF-CONFIDENCE, *n.* v. CONFIDENCE. अवसान *n.* हमतम *m. f.* स्वमतनिष्ठा *f.* स्वबुद्धिनिष्ठा *f.*

SELF-CONFIDENT, *a.* v. CONFIDENT. आपमसलतीचा, स्वमतनिष्ठ, स्वबुद्धिनिष्ठ.

SELF-CONSECRATION, *n.* आत्मार्पण *n.*

SELF-CONTROL, *n.* संयम *m.* आत्मसंयम *m.* आत्मनियम *m.* आत्मवश *m.* आत्मनिग्रह *m.*

Possessing *s.* जितमनस्क.

SELF-CREATED, *a.* स्वयंकृत, स्वज, स्वोत्पन्न. [णा *f.*

SELF-DECEIT, SELF-DECEPTION, *n.* आत्मवंचना *f.* आत्मप्रतार-

SELF-DECEIVED, *a.* आत्मवंचित, स्ववंचित, आत्मप्रतारित, स्वप्रतारित. [रक.

SELF-DECEIVER, *n.* SELF-DECEIVING, *a.* आत्मवंचक, आत्मप्रता-

SELF-DEFENCE, *n.* आत्मरक्षण *n.* आत्मतारण *n.* स्वत्राण *n.*

SELF-DENIAL, *n.* संयम *m.* आत्मनियम *m.* आत्मनिरोध *m.*

SELF-DENYING, *a.* आत्मनियामक, आत्मनिरोधी.

SELF-DEPENDENCE, *n.* आत्माश्रय *m.* आत्माधार *m.*

SEEF-DEPENDENT, SELF-DEPENDING, *a.* आत्माश्रय, आत्माश्रयी.

SELF-DESTRUCTION, *n.* आत्मघात *m.* आत्महत्या *f.* आत्महनन *n.* आत्मनाश *m.* स्वनाश *m.*

SELF-DEVISED, *a.* स्वयोजित, आत्मयोजित, स्वकल्पित.

SELF-DEVOTED, *a.* आत्मार्पित, आत्मनिवेदित.

SELF-DEVOTEMENT, SELF-DEVOTION, *n.* आत्मार्पण *n.* आत्मनिवेदन *n.*

SELF-EDUCATED, *a.* आत्मशिक्षित, स्वाध्यापित.

SELF-ENJOYMENT, *n.* आत्मसुख *n.* स्वात्मसुख *n.*

SELF-ESTEEM, *n.* v. CONCEIT. अहम्मान *m.* अहम्मति *f.*

SELF-EVIDENT, *a.* स्वतःसिद्ध, स्वतःप्रमाण, स्वतःस्पष्ट.

SELF-EXAMINATION, *n.* आत्मपृच्छा *f.* आत्मविचारण *n.* आत्मविभावन *n.* आत्मपरीक्षण *n.* &c.

SELF-EXECUTED, *a.* आत्मकृत, स्वकृत.

SELF-EXISTENCE, *n.* स्वतःसिद्धि *f.* स्वत्व *n.* स्वयंजातत्व *n.*

SELF-EXISTENT, *a.* स्वयंभू, आत्मभू, स्वतःसिद्ध, निजमूर्ति, अकृत्रिम.

SELF-GAINED, SELF-GOT, *a.* स्वार्जित, आत्मार्जित, स्वोपार्जित, स्वसंपादित.

SELF-GIVEN, *a.* स्वयंदत्त, आत्मदत्त, दत्तात्मा.

SELF-GOVERNMENT, *n.* आत्मशासन *n.* आत्मनियमन *n.* आत्मवश *m.*

SELF-IGNORANCE, *n.* आत्माज्ञान *n.* स्वाविद्या *f.* स्वावेदन *n.*

SELF-IGNORANT, *a.* आत्माज्ञानी. [स्वै *f.*

SELF-IMPORTANCE, *n.* v. CONCEIT. मान *m.* मीपण *n.* मीपणा *m.*

SELF-INTEREST, *n.* स्वार्थ *m.* स्वहित *n.* आत्महित *n.*

SELF-INTERESTED, *a.* स्वार्थी, स्वार्थनिष्ठ, स्वार्थबुद्धि, स्वार्थपर, स्वार्थपरायण.

SELF-INVITED, *a.* आत्माहूत, आत्मनिमंत्रित.

SELF-KNOWER, *n.* SELF-KNOWING, *a.* आत्मज्ञ, आत्मज्ञानी, आत्मतत्वज्ञ, आत्मदर्शी.

SELF-KNOWLEDGE, *n.* आत्मज्ञान *n.* आत्मविद्या *f.* आत्मबोध *m.* निजबोध *m.* आत्मपरिचय *m.* आत्मवेदन *n.* स्वात्मानुभव *m.*

SELF-LOVE, *n.* अहंकार *m.* अहंभाव *m.* अहंमति *f.* अहंममता *f.*

SELF-MOVED, SELF-MOVING, *a.* स्वयंवह, स्वैरी.

SELF-MURDER, *n.* आत्मघात *m.* आत्महत्या *f.* आत्मवध *m.* आत्महिंसा *f.* [त्यागी.

SELF-MURDERER, *n.* आत्मघाती, आत्मघातक, आत्महत्यारा, आत्म-

SELF-OPINIONED, SELF-OPINIONATED, *a.* v. CONCEITED. स्वाभिमानी, स्वमताभिमानी.

SELF-POSSESSED, *a.* आत्मवान्, जितमनस्क, धृतात्मा, मनस्वी.

SELF-POSSESSION, *n.* देहभान *n.* देहशुद्धि *f.* फाम *f.* सावधगिरी *f.* प्रसंगावधान *n.*

SELF-PRAISE, *n.* आत्मस्तुति *f.* आत्मश्लाघा *f.* आत्मप्रशंसा *f.*

SELF-PRESERVATION, *n.* आत्मरक्षण *n.* स्वरक्षण *n.* स्वत्राण *n.*

SELF-RESPECT, *n.* स्वाभिमान *m.* आत्ममान *m.*

SELF-RESPECTING, *a.* आत्ममानी.

SELF-RESTRAINED, *a.* आत्मसंयत, आत्मनियंत्रित, आत्मनिरुद्ध.

SELF-RESTRAINT, *a.* आत्मसंयम *m.* आत्मनिग्रह *m.* आत्मसंयमन *n.* दम *m.*

SELF-RIGHTEOUS, *a.* साधुम्मन्य.

SELF-SAME, *a.* v. SAME. तोच, हाच, अनन्य.

SELF-SEARCHER, *n.* आत्मदर्शी. [र्थपर.

SELF-SEEKER, *n.* SELF-SEEKING, *a.*v. SELFISH. स्वार्थनिष्ठ, स्वा-

SELF-SEEKING, *n.* v. SELFISHNESS. स्वार्थदृष्टि *f.* स्वार्थनिष्ठा *f.* स्वहितेच्छा *f.*

SELF-SUBDUED, *a.*v. MORTIFIED. जितात्मा, जितेंद्रिय, जितषड्वर्ग.

SELF-SUFFICIENCY, *n.* v. CONCEIT. स्वाभिमान *m.* स्वास्थ्य *n.* स्वस्थता *f.* [निष्ठ.

SELF-SUFFICIENT, *a.* v. CONCEITED. स्वाभिमानी, स्वस्थ, स्व-

SELF-WILLED, *a.* v. OBSTINATE, WILFUL. स्वच्छंद, स्वच्छंदी, स्वेच्छ, स्वेच्छाचारी, स्वरुचि, सैरट *or* सैराट, स्वैरी, स्वैरगति, स्वतंत्र, आपगंड, अडण, आपढंगी.

SELF-WILLEDNESS, *n.* v. A. आपढंग *m.* स्वच्छंदीपणा *m.* स्वाच्छंद्य *m.* स्वातंत्र्य *n.* स्वैरगति *f.*

SELFISH, *a. regarding only one's own interest.* आपलेंच हित पाहणारा, स्वार्थी, आपस्वार्थी, आपलपोट्या, आपलपोटाऱ्या, आपगरजी, मतलबी, गरजसाधू, आत्मसंतोषी, आपमतलबी, लाभदृष्टि, लाभलोभी, स्वार्थदृष्टि, स्वार्थपर, स्वार्थपरायण, स्वलाभदृष्टि, स्वलाभपर, स्वहितदृष्टि, स्वहितपर, स्वहितपरायण, स्वार्थनिष्ठ, आत्मंभरि, आत्मग्राही.

2—of actions, &c. स्वार्थबुद्धीचा, स्वार्थदृष्टीचा, स्वलाभदृष्टीचा, &c. काम्य. [र्थबुद्धीनें, &c.

SELFISHLY, *adv.* v. A. आपलेंच हित पाहून, &c. स्वार्थदृष्टीनें, स्वा-

SELFISHNESS, *n.*v.A. स्वार्थीपणा *m.* आपस्वार्थीपणा *m.* आपलपोटेपणा *m.* &c. स्वार्थदृष्टि *f.* स्वार्थबुद्धि *f.* स्वार्थनिष्ठा *f.* स्वलाभदृष्टि *f.* स्वहितदृष्टि *f.* &c.

To SELL, *v. a. part with for a price.* विकणें, विकनदेणें, विकता *decl.* देणें, पैसा *m.*-&c. घेऊन देणें, मोलानें देणें, ओपणें, फरोक्त करणें, विक्रय *m.*-&c. करणें *g. of o.*

To SELL, *v.n. be sold, be disposed of for a price.* विकणें, खपणें, जाणें, मोलानें-&c. जाणें, खप *m.*-&c. होणें *g. of s.*

To s. off smartly. लाही f. उडणें g. of s.

SELLER, n. SELLING, p. a. v. V. A. विकणारा, विकत देणारा, मोलानें देणारा, &c. विक्या in comp. विक्रेता, विक्रय-&c. कर्त्ता -कारी-&c. [बखप्रांत m.

SELVAGE, SELVEDGE, n. the edge of cloth. अंचळ f.m. दशा f.pl.

SEMBLANCE, n. v. LIKENESS. सारखेपणा m. सादृश्य n. आभास m. भास n.

2 appearance, form, &c. v. LIKENESS. रूप n. डौल m.

SEMEN, n. v. SEED. रेत n. वीर्य n.

To emit s.—man or beast. खरणें.

SEMI. This word is rendered in composition by अर्ध, निम, &c. as will be seen from the words that follow.

SEMI-ANIMATE, a. अर्ध्याजिवाचा, अर्धमेला, मृतप्राय, मृतकल्प, निप्राण.

SEMI-BREVE, n. दीर्घस्वर m.

SEMI-CIRCLE, n. अर्धवृत्त n. अर्धवर्तुळ n. वृत्तार्ध n. अर्धवृत्त n.

SEMI-CIRCULAR, a. अर्धवृत्ताकृति, वृत्तार्धाकृति.

SEMI-CYLINDRICAL, a. निमगोल.

SEMI-DIAMETER, n. अर्धव्यास m.

SEMI-LUNAR, a. अर्धचंद्राकार, अर्धचंद्राकृति.

SEMI-METAL, n. उपधातु m.

SEMI-TONE, n. मूर्च्छना f.

SEMI-VOWEL, n. अर्धस्वर m. [पयक, बैजिक.

SEMINAL, a. relating, &c. to seed. बीजाचा, बीजसंबंधी, बीजवि-

S. fluid, v. SEED. धातु m.f. वीर्य n.

SEMINARY, n. seed-plot. आंबण n. आंबणीची जागा f. रोपन्नाका m.

2 school, &c. पाठशाळा f. विद्यालय n.

SEMPITERNAL. See ETERNAL.

SENATE, n. legislative assembly. राज्यकाभाराची सभा f. राजमंत्रसभा f. राज्यसभा f. वृद्धसंघ m. वृद्धसभा f.

2 कारभार पाहणारी सभा f.

SENATOR, n. member of a senate. राज्यसभासद, राजमंत्रसभासद.

SENATORIAL, a. सभासदसंबंधी-विषयक.

To SEND, v.a. cause to go or pass. पाठवणें, धाडणें, पाठवून-धाडून देणें, प्रेरणें, प्रेषणें, प्रेरण n.-प्रेषण n.-&c. करणें g. of o. [लाबणें.

2 away; off; v. To DISMISS. लाबणें, घालवणें, वाटे or वाटेस

3 away (a visitor &c.) v. To DISMISS. निरोप m. देणें, पाठवणी f.-बिदाई f.-पाठवणूक f.-रवानगी f.-&c. करणें, विदा करणें.

Gift on sending away. पाठवणी f. पाठवणूक f. रवानगी f. बिदाई f. बिदागी f. बिदाइकी f.

4 for; request by message to come or be brought. बोलावणें, बोलवायास पाठवणें, बोलावूं पाठवणें, आणवणें, मागवणें.

5 See To CAST. 6 See To GIVE, To INFLICT.

SENDER, n. SENDING, p. a. v.V. 1. पाठवणारा, धाडणारा, &c. प्रेरक, प्रेषक, प्रेरिता, प्रेरयिता, प्रेरण-&c. कर्त्ता-कारी-&c.

SENDING, n. v. V. 1.—act. पाठवणें n. धाडणें n. &c. प्रेरण n. प्रेरणा f. प्रेषण n. प्रस्थापन n.

SENILE, a. belonging, &c. to old age. म्हतारपणाचा, म्हतारपणाविषयींचा, वृद्धावस्थेचा, वृद्धावस्थासंबंधी, वार्द्धक्यसंबंधी-विषयक.

SENILITY, n. old age, v. AGE. वृद्धावस्था f. वार्द्धक्य n.

SENIOR, n. one older, v. ELDER. वडील, वयानें वडील, वरिष्ठ.

2 elderly person. पुरखा, गुरुजन.

SENIOR, a. See ELDER. 2. superior or older in office, &c. वरचा, पदवीचा मोठा, पायरीचामोठा, वडील, ज्येष्ठ, मोठा, पहिल्या नेमणुकीचा, आगोदरच्या नेमणुकीचा, कालानें वडील, कालज्येष्ठ, अधिकारज्येष्ठ.

—as distinguished from junior (खुर्द). बुझुर्ग.

SENIORITY, n. v. A. 2. वरचेपणा m. वडिलाई f. ज्येष्ठत्व n. ज्येष्ठ्य n. कालज्येष्ठ्य n. अधिकारज्येष्ठ्य n.

Relation of s. and juniority. लाहनवी थोरवी f.

SENNA-PLANT, n. सोनामुकी or खी f.

Blunt-leaved variety of s. आयरण or ऐरण f.

SENNIGHT, n. v. WEEK. आठवडा m.

On Monday, Tuesday, &c. s.पुढल्या सोमवारीं·मंगळवारीं-&c.On next Monday,&c. is expressed by या सोमवारीं,&c.

SENSATION, n. perception by means of the senses. इंद्रियज्ञान n. इंद्रियग्रह m. इंद्रियबोध m. कलना f. वेदना f.

2 state of excited feeling. संभ्रम m. आवेश m.

SENSE, n. principle or organ of percipience. इंद्रिय n. इंद्रियबुद्धि f. इंद्रियज्ञान n. अध्यात्म n.—The five senses are, त्वगिंद्रिय, चक्षुरिंद्रिय, श्रोत्रेंद्रिय, रसनेंद्रिय, घ्राणेंद्रिय; they are called, ज्ञानेंद्रिय. The five organs or members of action are, वागिंद्रिय, हस्तेंद्रिय, पादेंद्रिय, गुदेंद्रिय, उपस्थेंद्रिय; they are called, कर्मेंद्रिय. To these ten the Mind मन is sometimes added. [राम.

Dead to the objects of s. जितेंद्रिय, स्वायत्तेंद्रिय, आत्मा-

Disorder of the senses. इंद्रियवैकल्य.

Evident to s. प्रत्यक्षसिद्ध.

Evidently to s. प्रत्यक्ष, प्रत्यक्षतः.

The five senses (or organs of s.)—collect. पंचेंद्रिय n. pl. इंद्रियग्राम m. इंद्रियवर्ग m. इंद्रियगण m.

Object of s. इंद्रियविषय m. इंद्रियगोचर m. विषयगोचर m. इंद्रियार्थ m. इंद्रियबोधन n. गोचर m. The objects of s. शब्दादिविषय m. pl.

Opposition of s. इंद्रियविप्रतिपत्ति f.

Perceptible by the senses. इंद्रियगोचर, इंद्रियग्राह्य.

Perceptible by two senses. द्वींद्रियग्राह्य.

Pleasure of s. or sensual pleasure. विषयसुख n. इंद्रियसुख n. काम m.

Restored to one's senses. लब्धचेता, लब्धचेष्ट, लब्धसंज्ञ.

Sharpness or soundness of the senses. इंद्रियपाटव n.

Subduing or restraining the senses. इंद्रियदमन n. इंद्रियनिग्रह m. इंद्रियनियम m. करणनियम m.

Walker by s. विषयी.

Wanting a s. निरिंद्रिय. [असणें.

To be in one's senses or right mind. शुद्धीवर-देहावर-&c.

To come to one's senses lit. fig. शुद्धीवर-देहावर-ध्यानावर-स्थितीवर-&c. येणें, संज्ञा f. होणें g. of s.

To lose one's senses. पिसळणें or पिसाळणें, पिसाटणें, बेइगळणें, बेडाळणें, ब्रेडावणें, चळणें, वेड n.-&c. लागणें.

2 apprehension by s., perception, sensation. इंद्रियज्ञान n. इंद्रियबुद्धि f. इंद्रियग्रह m. इंद्रियबोध m.

3 apprehension by the intellect. ज्ञान n. समज m. f. उमज m. बोध m. ग्रह m.

4 understanding, judgment. बुद्धि f. ज्ञान n. समज m. उमज m. अक्कल f. बकूब m.

5 reasonable meaning. अर्थ m. जीव m. ऐवज m. हाशील or

हासील *n.* युक्ति *f.* युक्तता *f.*

6 *signification*, v. MEANING. अर्थ *n.*

According to the s. अर्थतः.

Apprehension of the verbal or literal s. शाब्दबोध*m.*

Tenor or strain of the s. अर्थानुसंधान *n.*

SENSELESS, *a. impercipient.* विषयग्रहणाशक्त, विषयग्रहणाक्षम, इंद्रियविषयाग्राही, इंद्रियार्थाग्राही, अचेतन.

2 *foolish, unwise, &c.*—of persons. बुद्धी बेगळा *or* निराळा, ज्ञानाबेगळा *or* निराळा, बुद्धिहीन-रहित-&c. मतिहीन-&c. असमंजस, निर्बुद्ध.

3 *unreasonable, foolish &c.*—of actions, &c. वेडेपणाचा, मूर्खपणाचा, बेकुबीचा, अज्ञानाचा, &c. असमंजस, अयुक्त, अयुक्तिक, अयुक्तिसिद्ध.

4 *inconscious.* गैरसावध, निपचेत, निपचीप, चेत, गुंग, धुंद, नष्टेंद्रिय, नष्टचेतन, नष्टचेष्ट.

5 *unmeaning*, v. NONSENSICAL. निरर्थक, अनर्थक.

SENSELESSNESS, *n.* v. A. 2. बुद्धीबेगळेपणा*m.* ज्ञानाबेगळेपणा*m.* असमंजसपणा*m.* &c. बुद्धिहीनता *f.* बुद्धिराहित्य*n.*

3 असमंजसपणा*m.* &c. मूर्खपण*n.* वेडेपण*n.* &c. अयुक्तता *f.* अयुक्ति *f.* अयुक्तिकत्व*n.* युक्तिविरुद्धता *f.*

SENSIBILITY, SENSIBLENESS, *n.* v. A. 1. शुद्धि *f.* देहशुद्धि *f.* भान*n.* देहभान*n.* सावधगिरी *f.* सावधपणा*m.* चैतन्य*n.* चेतना *f.* फाम *f.* होष*m.* संज्ञा *f.* ससंज्ञता *f.* प्रबोध*m.* संज्ञावैशिष्ट्य*n.*

2 विषयग्रहणक्षमता *f.* विषयग्रहणशक्ति *f.* जाणतेपणा*m.* इंद्रियशक्ति *f.* कलना *f.*

3 इंद्रियगोचरता *f.* इंद्रियगम्यता *f.* इंद्रियभेद्यता *f.* इंद्रियज्ञेयता *f.*

4 जाणतेपणा*m.* वाकबदारी *f.* माहितगारी *f.*

6 जाणपणा*m.* जाणतेपणा*m.* दरद *f.* दरदीपणा*m.* अभिज्ञता *f.*

8 बुद्धि *f.* अक्कल *f.* शहाणपण*n.* समज*m. f.* समंजसपणा*m.* समजदारी *f.* सुज्ञता *f.* प्राज्ञा *f.*

9 समंजसपणा*m.* समर्पकपणा*m.* सुयुक्तता *f.* सयुक्तिकत्व*n.*

SENSIBLE, *a. possessing one's senses, conscious.* सावध, हुशार, सुचित्त, देहभानी, सचेतन, सचेता, चेतन, चेतनावान्, संज्ञावान्, संज्ञाविशिष्ट, ससंज्ञ, चैतन्यविशिष्ट, चेतयमाम.

To be s. देहावर-शुद्धीवर-देहभानावर-&c. असणें.

2 *sentient, percipient, capable of receiving impression.* जाणता, विषयग्रहणक्षम, विषयग्रहणशक्त, इंद्रियविषयग्राही.

3 *perceptible by a sense.* समजायाजोगा, इंद्रियगोचर, इंद्रियगम्य, इंद्रियग्राह्य, इंद्रियज्ञेय, इंद्रियवेद्य, इंद्रियारूढ,इंद्रियविषय, ऐंद्रियक, वैषयिक, प्रत्यक्षसिद्ध, व्यक्त.

4 *perceiving or having perception of, conscious.* जाणता, वाकबदार, माहितगार, जातबोध, प्राप्तबोध, लब्धबोध, जातज्ञान, प्राप्तज्ञान, लब्धज्ञान. [जूक.

5 *quickly sensible of pain.* दुखरा, गोडा, कोंवळा, कोमल, ना-

6 *of quick feeling.* जाण, जाणता, जाणणारा, दरदी, अभिज्ञ (esp. in comp. as गुणाभिज्ञ, उपकाराभिज्ञ, &c.), ज्ञ(in comp. as उपकारज्ञ,&c.), सहृदय, ग्राहक (in comp. as गुणग्राहक, &c.), शीघ्रग्राहक.

7—of flesh, not *callous, proud, &c.* गोडा.

8—of persons; *judicious, reasonable*, v. WISE. समजदार, समजूतदार, समजीक, समंजस, सुजाण, सुज्ञ, ज्ञानी, बुद्धिमान्, अक्कलवान् *or* वंत, अक्कलबाज, धीमान्, मतिमान्, सुबुद्ध, सुधी, प्राज्ञ, सुमेधा, उचितज्ञ, ज्ञानशाली.

9—of speech, &c. *consonant with reason.* शहाणपणाचा, बुद्धीचा, समंजसपणाचा,&c.समंजस, समर्पक, युक्त, सुयुक्त, सयुक्तिक.

SENSIBLY, *adv.* v. A. 3. समजायाजोगा-सारखा-&c. *decl.* कळाया-ध्यानांत यावा-&c. जोगा-सारखा-&c.

9 समंजसपणानें, शहाणपणानें, &c. शहाण्यासारखा, शहाण्यापरी, शहाण्यावाणी, चांगला *decl. or* चांगलें, समर्पक, सयुक्तिक, सुज्ञतापूर्वक.

SENSITIVE, *a. having sense or feeling, capable of receiving impressions, sentient.* विषयग्रहणक्षम, विषयग्रहणशक्त, चेतन, सचेतन, इंद्रियज्ञानविशिष्ट, इंद्रियशक्तिक.

2 *having feelings easily excited; tender*, v. PITIFUL, KIND. कोंवळ्यामनाचा, सहृदय, हृदयवान्, कोमलहृदय, कोमलांतःकरण, करुणार्द्र.

3 *pertaining to the senses or sensation.* इंद्रियज्ञानाचा, इंद्रियबुद्धीचा, इंद्रियज्ञानसंबंधी-विषयक.

SENSITIVE-PLANT, *n.* लाजरी *f.* लाजाळू *n.* लज्जालु *m.*

To shrink from touch—the s. लाजणें.

SENSORIUM, *n. seat of sense and perception.* चेतनाशय *m.* चैतन्यास्पद *n.*

SENSUAL, *a. consisting in sense, pertaining to the senses, &c.* विषयाचा, इंद्रियविषयाचा, इंद्रियाचा, विषयसंबंधी, वैषयिक.

S. pleasure. विषयसुख *n.*

2 *devoted to sense, voluptuous, carnal.* विषयी, विषयपरायण, विषयरत, विषयाधीन, विषयोन्मुख, विषयासक्त, विषयवश, विषयाभिमुख, विषयग्रस्त, विषयाविष्ट, विषयलंपट, विषयतत्पर, विषयलीन, विषयलुब्ध, विषयैकतान, विषयतल्लीन, विषयसुखलुब्ध-लंपट-तत्पर-&c. इंद्रियवश, इंद्रियसुखासक्त, &c. रजोगुणी, राजस, आशाबद्ध, आशापाशनिबद्ध.

SENSUALIST, *n. sensual person*, v. A. विषयी, गुलहौसी, हवसी *or* हौसी, चंदनहौसी, भोका, केलीनागर.

SENSUALITY, SENSUALNESS, *n.* v. A. 2. विषयीपणा *m.*&c. विषयदृष्टि *f.* विषयबुद्धि *f.* विषयासक्ति *f.* विषयसुखासक्ति *f.* इंद्रियसुखासक्ति *f.* विषयोपसेवा *f.* विषयव्यासंग *m.* विषयाधीनता *f.* विषयवशता *f.* विषयलांपट्य *n.* विषयतत्परता *f.* &c.

SENSUOUS, *a.* विषयाचा, विषयसंबंधी, वैषयिक.

SENT, *p.*v.V. 1. पाठवलेला, धाडलेला, &c. प्रेषित, प्रेरित, प्रस्थापित.

SENTENCE, *n.*—in law; *judgment pronounced, award of punishment.* शिक्षेचा-&c. हुकूम *m.* दंडाज्ञा *f.* दंडकथन *n.* दंडनियोग *m.* निर्णय *m.* निर्णयपाद *m.*

2 *determination or decision respecting*, v. OPINION. मत *n.* तजवीज *f.* निश्चय *m.*

3 *paragraph, period.* वाक्य *n.* गाथा *f.* फक्किका *pop.* फाकी *f.* फाकरूट *n.* चूर्णिका *f.*

Construction of sentences. वाक्यरचना *f.* वाक्ययोजना *f.*

Law or rule of constructing sentences. वाक्यपद्धति *f.*

To SENTENCE, *v. a. pass or pronounce judgment on.* शिक्षेचा-&c. हुकूम *m.* करणें-सांगणें.

SENTENTIOUS, *a. abounding with axioms and maxims; short and pithy.* म्हणींचा, न्यायप्रचुर, न्यायबहुल, सूत्रसदृश, सूत्रप्राय.

2 *that uses short and pithy sentences.* म्हणींचा बोलका, सूत्रप्रायभाषी, सूत्रप्रायवक्ता.

SENTENTIOUSLY, *adv.* v. A. न्यायबाहुल्यपूर्वक.

SENTENTIOUSNESS, *n.* v. A. 1. न्यायबाहुल्य *n.* न्यायसादृश्य *n.*

सूत्रसादृश्य *n.*

SENTIENCE, *n.* v. A. चेतनपणा *m.* चैतन्य *n.* चेतना *f.* चिच्छक्ति *f.*

SENTIENT, *a. having the quality of perception.* चेतन, सचेतन, चैतन्ययुक्त, चैतन्यविशिष्ट, चेतयमान, विषयग्रहणशक्तिक, विषयग्रहणक्षम, इंद्रियज्ञानविशिष्ट, इंद्रियशक्तिक, चिच्छक्तिसंपन्न.

SENTIMENT, *n. thought, opinion.* कल्पना *f.* तर्क *m.* तजवीज *f.* मनसमजूत *f.* मनांतली-जिवांतली-जिवाची-&c. समजूत *f.*-गोष्ट *f.* मत *n.* अभिप्राय *m.*

2 *sense contained in words, meaning.* अभिप्राय *m.* अर्थ *m.* आशय *m.* कल्पना *f.*

3 *passion, feeling.* भाव *m.* रस *m.* (These are nine. शृंगार *or* रति, उत्साह *or* हास्य, कारुण्य, रौद्र *or* क्रोध, विस्मय *or* अद्भुत, भय, बीभत्स, शांत, & वात्सल्य; or शृंगार, हास्य, करुणा, रौद्र, वीर, भयानक, बीभत्स, अद्भुत, & वात्सल्य,), मनोधर्म *m.* मनोवृत्ति *f.*

Mingled s. or emotion. भावसंकर *m.*

Moral s. संत *f.*

Vacillating state of mind between different sentiments. भावसंधि *m.*

SENTIMENTAL, *a. abounding with sentiment or feeling.* भाविक, रसिक, रसभरित, रसात्मक, रसमय, सरस.

2 *affecting feeling or sensibility.* रसाचा ढोली-ढोंगी-दांभिक-&c. रसानुकारी, भावानुकारी.

SENTIMENTALIST, *n.* See A. 2.

SENTIMENTALITY, *n. affectation of fine feeling.* रसाचें ढोंग *n.*-पोम *n.*-स्तोम *n.*-&c. रसानुकारिता *f.* भावानुकारिता *f.*

SENTINEL, SENTRY, *n. person set to keep watch.* पहारेकरी *or* पाहरेकरी, चौकीदार.

Disposition of sentinels. पाहरेबंदी *f.* [वर्त्य.

SEPARABLE, *a.* v. V. A. भेदायाजोगा-सारखा-&c. भेद्य, व्या-

To SEPARATE, *v. n. part, be disunited, withdraw from each other.* तुटणें, वेगळा-&c. होणें, सुटणें, फाटणें, तूट *f.*-वियोग *m.*-भेद *m.*-&c. होणें *g. of s.* दुरावणें.

To SEPARATE, *v. a. disunite, sever, part.* भेदणें, तोडणें, वेगळणें, सोडणें, वेगळा-निराळा-भिन्न-वियुक्त-विभक्त-&c. करणें, फूट *f.*-तूट *f.*-भेद *m.*-वियोग *m.*-&c. करणें *g. of o.* संबंध *m.*-&c. तोडणें-मोडणें *g. of o.*

SEPARATE, *a. distinct, not connected.* वेगळा, निराळा, न्यारा, सुटा, स्फुट, जुदा, अलग, वायला (vulgar), सवता (vulgar), भिन्न, मोकळा, निरालस, व्यतिरिक्त, अलाहिदा, वहिला, पृथक्, असंबद्ध, असंलग्न, असंसृष्ट, व्यस्त.

SEPARATED, *p.* v. V. A. भेदलेला, वेगळा केलेला, &c. तुटका, तुटक, विभिन्न, परिछिन्न, विच्छिन्न, अवच्छिन्न, निर्मुक्त, विभक्त, वियुक्त, वियोजित, विगत, पृथक्कृत, द्वैधीकृत, व्यावृत्त.

I.—esp. of persons. विरही, अंतरित.

SEPARATELY, *adv.* v. A. अलग, अलगत, अलाहिदा, वेगळा *decl.* निराळा *decl.* पृथक्, वेगळावेगळा *decl.* वेगवेगळाला *decl.* निरनिराळा *decl.*

SEPARATENESS, *n.* v. A. वेगळेपणा *m.* निराळेपणा *m.* जुदेपणा *m.* न्यारेपणा *m.* &c.

SEPARATER, *n.* SEPARATING, *p. a.* v. V. A. भेदणारा, भेदकरणारा, वेगळा करणारा, &c. भेदक, भेद-भेदन-&c. कर्ता-कारी-&c. विच्छेदक, परिछेदक, अवच्छेदक, व्यावर्त्तक.

SEPARATION, *n.* v. V. A.—*act.* भेदणें *n.* &c. फोड *f.* भेद *m.* भेदन *n.* विभेद *m.* पृथक्करण *n.* द्वैधीकरण *n.* वियोग *m.* विप्रयोग *m.* वियोजन *n.* विच्छेद *m.* परिछेद *m.* अवच्छेद *m.* विश्लेष *m.* असंधान *n.*—*state.* वेगळीक *f.* तूट *f.* फूट *f.* भेद *m.* वियोग *m.* विप्रयोग *m.* विभक्तभाव *m.* पार्थक्य *n.* फाट *m.* फाटफूट *f.* तुटातुटी *or* तुटातूट *f.* व्यतिरेक *m.* व्यावृत्ति *f.* [विश्लेष *m.*

I.—esp. of lovers or friends. विघड *m.* विरह *m.* वियोग *m.*

Fever or anguish of s. विरहज्वर *m.* विरह *m.*

Fire of s. विरहानल *m.* वियोगानल *m.* विरहाग्नि *m.*

Violent and painful s. तोडातोड *or* डी *f.* [हिणी *f.*

Woman suffering s. (from husband or lover). विर-

SEPOY. See SOLDIER. [शास्त्र.

SEPTANGULAR, *a. having seven angles.* सातकोना, सप्तकोण, स-

SEPTEMBER, *n.* इंग्रेजी सालाचा नववा महिना *m.* भाद्रपद-आश्विन *m.*

SEPTENARY, *a. consisting of seven.* सातांचा, सप्तसंख्याक.

SEPTENNIAL, *a. lasting seven years, or occurring once in seven years.* सातसातवर्षांचा, सातवर्षा, सप्ताब्दिक.

SEPTIC, SEPTICAL, *a. that promotes putrefaction.* कुजवणारा, सडवणारा, विगलनकारी. [पार्श्वक.

SEPTILATERAL, *a. having seven sides.* सातपयलू, सप्तास्त्र, सप्त-

SEPTUPLE, *a. sevenfold.* सातपट.

SEPULCHRAL, *a. belonging, &c. to a sepulchre.* थडग्याचा, समाधिसंबंधी-विषयक.

SEPULCHRE, *n.* v. GRAVE, TOMB. थडगें *n.* समाधि *m. f.* कबर *f.* शवमंदिर *n.* प्रेतमंदिर *n.*

SEPULTURE, *n.* v. BURIAL. मूठमाती *f.*

SEQUEL, *n. that which follows, succeeding part.* उत्तरभाग *m.* उत्तरार्ध *n.* शेषभाग *m.*

2 *event*, v. CONSEQUENCE. परिणाम *m.* शेवट *m.*

SEQUENCE. See SUCCESSION.

SEQUENT. See FOLLOWING, SUCCEEDING.

To SEQUESTER, *To* SEQUESTRATE, *v. a.*—in law. जप्त करणें, कोळ *or* कोल *n.* धरून ठेवणें.

2 See To SECLUDE. [जप्त.

SEQESTERED, *p. and a.* v. V. 1. जप्त केलेला, कोल धरून ठेवलेला,

I. *retired, out of the way,* v. RETIRED. आडवळणी, आडवळणाचा, विविक्त.

S. spot. आडवळण *n.* [*n.*

SEQUESTRATION, *n.* v. V.—*act.* जप्तकरणें *n.* &c. जप्ती *f.* कबज

I. *thing sequestered.* कबज *n.* कोळ *or* कोल *n.* जप्तीचा माल *m.*

SER, SHER, *n.*—the Indian measure. शेर *m.*

That holds a s. शेरका.

That weighs a s. शेरका.

SERAGLIO, *n. apartments of the women, harem.* जनानखाना *m.* महाल *m.* रंगमहाल *m.* खासमहाल *or* खाशेमहाल *m.* अंतःपुर *n.* स्त्र्यगार *n.* अवरोध *m.* अवरोधन *n.* शुद्धांत *m.*

Royal s. राणवसा *or* राणिवसा *m.*

SERE. See SEAR.

SERENADE, *n.* घराबाहेर रात्रीस केलेलें संगीत *n.*

SERENE, *a. placid, peaceful, tranquil,* v. CALM, MILD. संथ, शांत, चित्तप्रसन्न, शांतमनस्क, शांतचित्त, सुमना, सुमनस्क, अनुद्विग्न, अनुद्वेग.

2—sky, &c. v. CLEAR. निवळ, स्वच्छ, प्रसन्न, प्रांजल, संथ.

SERENELY, *adv.* v. A. 1. संथपणानें, शांतचित्तानें, &c.

SERENENESS, SERENITY, *n.* A. 1. शांति *f.* चित्तप्रसन्नता *f.* मनःशांति *f.* चित्तशांति *f.* सौमनस्य*n.* अनुद्वेग*m.*

2 निवळपणा*m.* स्वच्छता *f.* प्रसन्नता *f.* &c.

SERF, *n.* v. SLAVE. शेतकीच्या कामास लावलेला दास, क्षेत्रदास*m.*

SERGE, *n.* एक प्रकारचें कापड आहे.

SERGEANT, *n.*—the petty military officer. हवालदार.

SERIAL, *a.* क्रमाचा, क्रमिक.

SERIATIM, क्रमानें, अनुक्रमानें, यथाक्रम.

SERIES, *n. a. continued succession, regular order, concatenation, line.* शेज*n. f.* सांखळी *f.* माला *pop.* माळ *f.* मालिका *f. pop.* माळका *f.* देवड *f.* शृंखला *f.* आवलि *f.* श्रेणी *f.* परंपरा *f.* हार *f.*

Infinite s.—in arithmetic. अनंत श्रेणी *f.* 2—in algebra &c. वही *f.*

Sum of the s.—in arithmetic. सर्वधन *n.* गणित*n.*

The first term of a s.—in arithmetic. वदन *n.*

3 *regular sequence or consecution,* v. SUCCESSION. क्रम*m.* परंपरा *f.* आनुपूर्वी *f.* अनुपूर्व्य*n.* शिलशिला *or* ल्हा*m.*

SERIOUS, *a. habitually grave, solemn.* गंभीर, सखोल, भरकूम *or* खूम, गंभीरमनाचा, गंभीरस्वभाव, गंभीरमनस्क, गंभीरवृत्ति, अविनोदी.

2 *that is in earnest, not jesting or in jest.* थट्टेवेगळा *or* निराळा, खरेपणाचा, बिनथट्टेचा, वास्तविक, सद्रूप, विनोदरहित.

3 *important, &c.* v. WEIGHTY. मोठा, भारी, भारदस्तीचा.

4 See RELIGIOUS.

SERIOUSLY, *adv.* v. A. 1. गंभीरपणानें, गंभीरमनानें.

2 खऱ्यानें, खरा *decl.* नहासतां, थट्टेवांचून.

SERIOUSNESS, *n.* v. A. 1. गंभीरपणा*m.* भरकूमपणा*m.* &c. भरकुमी *f.* गांभीर्य*n.* गंभीरता *f.* गंभीरस्वभाव*m.* गंभीरमन*n.*

2 खरेपणा*m.* वास्तविकपणा*m.* विनोदाभाव*m.*

3 मोठेपणा*m.* भारीपणा*m.* भारदस्ती *f.* भारदारी *f.*

SERMON, *n. religious discourse.* धर्मोपदेश*m.* धर्मकथन*n.*

SEROUS, *a. thin and watery.* रक्ताच्या पाण्यासारखा.

SERPENT, *n. snake.* सर्प *pop.* साप*m.* किरडूं*n.* किडें*n.* जिवाणूं*n.* जिवडा*m.* उरग*m.* उरःसर*m.* चक्षुःश्रवा*m.* नाग*m.* व्याळ*m.*

Double headed s. *amphisbæna.* मालुंड*m. n.*

SERPENTINE, *a. of or belonging to a serpent.* सर्पाचा, सापाचा, सापाविषयींचा, &c. सर्पसंबंधी-विषयक, सार्प, औरग.

2 *winding, sinuous.* नागमोडी, नागमोडीचा, सर्पगतिवत्, सर्पगति, सर्पगत्यात्मक.

S. motion. वळवळ *f.* [सळ्या.

SERPIGINOUS, *a. affected with serpigo.* इसपकरी, इसप्या *or* इ-

SERPIGO, *n.*—the disease. इसप *or* इसब*m.* [तरकुतर.

SERRATE, SERRATED, *a. notched like a saw.* करवतीकांठी, का-

SERUM, *n. the thin part of the blood.* रक्ताचा पातळ अंश *m.* रक्तांतलें पाणी *n.* रक्तद्रव *m.* चर्मसार *m.*

2 See WHEY.

SERVANT, *n.*—correlative of master ; *attendant, &c.* चाकर, सेवक, चाकरमानी *or* न्या, सेवेकरी, नौकर, दास, किंकर, मुशारखोर, शागिर्दपेशा, भृत्य, भृतक, पार्श्विक, परिचारक, परिजन, अनुचर, प्रेष्य, वेतनोपजीवी, वेतनजीवी, भृतिजीवी, सेवोपजीवी, सेवाजीवी.

Body s. खिदमतगार *or* दार, पार्श्वानुचर.

By or through servants. चाकराचाकरीं *adv.* चाकरानफरीं.

Relation between s. and master. सेव्यसेवकभाव *m.*

Second or inferior s. पडचाकर.

S. for low or petty work. नफर *n.*

Servants,—compreh. चाकरनफर *m.pl.* चाकरचुकर *m.pl.* चाकर माणसें *n. pl.* चाकरपेशा *m.* दासवर्ग *m.* सेवकवर्ग *m.*

S. of servants. दासानुदास. [पोटभरू.

S. who receives no wages but only food. पोटबंदा *m.*

Table or waiting s. वाढणारा, वाढपी, वाढप्या, परिवेष्टा.

That is one's own s. स्वयंदास, एकलपायी.

Your humble s. आपल्या पायांचा सेवक, व्याप्यकोटिप्रविष्ट, व्याप्यकोट्यंतर्गत.

SERVANT-MAID, *n. female servant,* चाकरीण *f.* सेवकी *f. pop.* सेवकीण *f.* सैरंध्री *f.* परिचारिका *f.* प्रेष्या.

To SERVE, *v. a. work for, attend upon, &c.* सेवणें, चाकरी *f.*-सेवा *f.*-&c. करणें *g. of o.* चाकरी *f.* काढणें *g. of o.* बरदाम्न *f.* करणें *g. of o.* समाचार *m.* घेणें *g. of o.* अनुवर्त्तणें.

2 *supply, answer, satisfy, &c.* पुरणें, पुरवणें, निभाव *m.*-निर्वाह *m.*-पूर्त्ति *f.*- पर्याप्ति *f.*-&c. करणें *g. of o.* पूर्ण-पुरता-&c. करणें, बस-पुरा-&c. होणें-पडणें.

3 v. To TREAT. वागवणें, बहिवाटणें, वर्त्तवणें. [*g. of o.*

4 v. To WORSHIP. उपासणें, उपासना *f.*-सेवा *f.*-&c. करणें

5 for ; *stand instead of.* काम *n.*-उपयोग*m.*-&c. करणें *g. of o.* कामास-उपयोगास-&c. पडणें *g. of o.* दाखल असणें.

6 out ; *deal out, distribute.* वांटणें, वांटून देणें, वांटणी *f.*-वांटावांट *f.*-&c. करणें *g. of o.*

7 up ; (meat). वाढणें, घालणें.

Food taken to be served round. वाढण *n.* वाढप *n.*—vessel holding it, वाढणी *f.*

To SERVE, *v. n. be a servant, be in servitude.* चाकरी *f.*-&c. करणें, चाकरी *f.*-&c. असणें *in. con.* चाकर-&c. असणें.

2 *accomplish or produce the end,* v. To ANSWER. चालणें, जमणें, नांदणें. [-&c. होणें-पडणें.

3 *be useful, conduce, &c.* कामास-उपयोगास पडणें, उपयोगी

SERVED, *p.* v. V. A. 1. सेवलेला, &c. सेवित.

2 पुरलेला, पुरवलेला, &c.

4 उपासलेला, आराधित, उपासित.

SERVER, *n.* SERVING. *p. a.* v. V. A. 1. सेवणारा, चाकरीकरणारा, &c. अनुवर्त्ती, सेवमान, सेवी & सेवक (esp. in comp.).

2 पुरणारा, पुरवणारा, निर्वाहकरणारा, &c. निर्वाहक.

4 उपासणारा, &c. आराधक, उपासक.

7 वाढणारा, वाढपी *or* वाढप्या, परिवेष्टा.

SERVICE, SERVING, *n.* v. V. A. 1. चाकरी *f.* सेवा *f.* खिदमत *f.* सेवन *n.* शुश्रूषा *f.* अनुवृत्ति *f.* उपचारकरण *n.* उपचारकर्म *n.* परिचरण *n.* परिचर्या *f.*

Close (unintermitting) s. खडीचाकरी *f.*

S. exacted (by a Government or person in power), without remuneration. वेठ *f.* बिगार *or* वेगार *f.* विष्टि *f.*

The duties, obligations, &c. of s. सेवाधर्म *m.*

To do active s. घोड्यापुढें धावणें.

4 आराधना *f.* आराधन *n.* आराधणूक *f.* उपासना *f.*

6 वांटणें *n.* वांटप *n.* वांटावांट *f.*
7 वाढणें *n.* वाढण *n.* वाढप *n.* परिवेषण *n.*
I. *serving state.* चाकरपेशा *m.* चाकरीचा पेशा *m.* चाकरी *f.* सेवकदशा *f.* सेवादशा *f.* कैंकर्य *n.* भृत्यत्व *n.* रोजगार *m.*
Free s. *s. during pleasure* खुलीचाकरी *f.*
Home s. बैठी चाकरी *f.* बैठा रोजगार *m.*
That is in s. रोजगारी, रोजगारशीर.
That is out of s. बेरोजगार, रिकामा.
II.—military. शिपाईपेशा *m.* शिपाईगिरी *f.* सैनिकवृत्ति *f.*
Actual s. लढाईचा-युद्धाचा-&c. प्रसंग *m.*
Grant (of villages &c.) for s. सरंजाम *m.*
Grant for personal s. जातसरंजाम *m.*
III. *advantage,* v. USE. उपयोग *m.* काम *n.*
IV. *course of rites.* अनुष्ठान *n.*
Conductor of a s. अनुष्ठानी, अनुष्ठाता.
V. *acts or points of a worship.* पूजोपचार *m.pl.* उपचार *m.pl.*

SERVICEABLE, *a. beneficial,* v. ADVANTAGEOUS, USEFUL. कामाचा, उपयोगाचा, उपयोगी, उपयुक्त, उपकारी, कारणी, कारणीक.
2 *fit or good for service.* कामाचा, उपयोगी, कामास पडायाजोगा, चालायाजोगा-सारखा, ऐवजदार, ऐवजशीर, बळकट, नेटापाटाचा, कार्यक्षम, व्यवहार्य. [योगिता *f.*

SERVICEABLENESS, *n.* v. A. 1. उपयोग *m.* उपयोगीपणा *m.* उप-
2 उपयोगीपणा *m.* कामासपडायाजोगेपणा *m.* कार्यक्षमता *f.*

SERVILE, *a. of or belonging to slavery or slaves.* गुलामगिरीचा, गुलामाचा, दास्याचा, दासाचा, दास्यसंबंधी-विषयक.
2 *meanly submissive, cringing, &c.* v. OBSEQUIOUS. आर्जवाचा, आर्जवी, गुलाम गिरीचा, खिदमतीचा, खुशामतीचा, थुंकी झेलणारा, छंदानुरोधाचा, छंदानुरोधी, छंदानुवृत्तीचा.

SERVILELY, *adv.* v. A. 2. आर्जवानें, छंदानुरोधानें, &c.

SERVILENESS, SERVILITY, *n.* v. A. 2. आर्जवीपणा *m.* आर्जव *n.* गुलामगिरी *f.* खिदमत *f.* खुशामद *f.* पायांचीसेवा *f.* चरणसेवा *f.* छंदानुरोध *m.* छंदानुवृत्ति *f.*
I. See SERVITUDE.

SERVITUDE, *n. state of a slave.* गुलामगिरी *f.* दास्य *n.* दासत्व *n.* अन्याधीनता *f.* पराधीनता *f.* परवशता *f.*
2 See SERVICE.

SESAME, *n.* तिल *pop.* तीळ *m.*
Black s. काळेतीळ *m. pl.*
White s. होरा *or* हवरा *m.* हवरी *f.*—Some other kinds of s. are. तिळयी, तिळी, भादवातीळ, मळा *m.*
S. oil. तिळेल *n.* तिलतैल *n.* तिलस्नेह *m.* तिलरस *m.*
S. pounded mixed with sugar. कोंद *f.*
S. seed. तिल *pop.* तीळ *m.*
S.-water. तिलोदक *n.*
Scented s.-oil. फुलेल *n.* [*f.* सभा *f.*

SESSION, *n. sitting or meeting of an assembly or court.* बैठक
Full s. भरमजलस *or* मजालस *f.*
2 *space or term of the meeting of a court.* बैठक *f.* सभा *f.* सभाकाल *m.* सभाकार्यकाल *m.*
3 SEE SITTING.

To SET, *v. a. place, put, lay.* ठेवणें, मांडणें, घालणें, स्थापणें, मांडणी *f.*-मांडणूक *f.*-विधान *n.*-स्थापन *n.*-स्थापना *f.*-&c. करणें *g. of o.*
To s. free. To s. at liberty, v. To FREE. सोडणें, मोकळा करणें-सोडणें.
To s. in order, v. To DISPOSE. योजणें, रचणें, व्यवस्था *f.*-&c. करणें *g. of o.*
To s. on fire, v. To KINDLE. आग *f.* लावणें.
2 *plant.* लावणें, रोपणें, आरोपणें, रोंवणें, आरोप *m.*-आरोपण *n.* करणें, *g. of o.*
3 *fix, appoint, settle.* नेमणें, ठरावणें, नेम *m.*-ठराव *m.*-निश्चय *m.*-&c. करणें *g. of o.* [चणें, खांचरणें.
4 *fix in the ground.* रोवणें, पुरणें, नेमणें, नेमवणें, लावणें, खो-
5 *fix in metal.* जडणें, जडविणें, खचणें, जडण *f.*-जडाव *m.*-जडप *n.*-कोंदण *n.*-&c. करणें *g. of o.*
Gold used in setting. कोंदण *n.*
Price or cost of setting. जडण *n.* जडणावळ *f.* जडाई *f.*
Skill in setting. जडणावळ *f.*
6 *whet.* लावणें (and *neut.* लागणें), धार *f.* लावणें-काढणें.
7 (a lesson, problem, sum, &c.). घालणें, देणें.
8 (a mus. instr.) *tune.* लावणें (and *neut.* लागणें).
9 (a limb, &c.). बसवणें, सांधणें, जोडणें, जमवणें.
10 about; at. लावणें, घालणें, जुंपणें, योजणें.
11 against; v. To OPPOSE. विरोधी-&c. उभा करणें, आडवा आणणें. [*of o.*
To s. one's self against. खांद *m.* बांधणें-करणें *with* शीं
12 apart. See To SEPARATE.
13 aside; *omit, &c.* एकीकडे ठेवणें, ठेवणें, वर्जकरणें, गाळणें.
14 aside. See To REJECT, To ANNUL.
15 down; *place on the ground, &c.* खालीं ठेवणें, ठेवणें, उतरणें, डेवरणें, डेवर *f.*-न्यास *m.*-&c.करणें.
16 down; *put in writing.* लिहून ठेवणें, मांडून ठेवणें, मांडणें, टांक *m.* मारणें.
17 forth. See To PUBLISH, To SHOW.
18 off; (a train of bullocks, carts, &c.). हकारणें, हकालणें.
19 off; *shew to advantage.* शोभवणें, शोभा *f.* देणें-आणणें, साजरा करणें, छत भरणें, सुशोभित-&c. करणें, शोभेसा करणें, ओप *f.* देणें.
20 off; (a horse) *put out.* फेंकणें.
21 on; *incite action.* छू करणें *or* म्हणणें, लावणें, उचलणें, चेहरावणें, भर *m.* घालणें-देणें, वीर भरणें, उठावणी *f.*-&c. करणें.
22 over; *appoint to be inspector, ruler, &c.* अधिकारी-अध्यक्ष-&c. करणें-नेमणें.
23 up; *erect.* उभारणें, उभवणें, स्थापणें, लावणें, उभारणी *f.*-स्थापना *f.*-उत्थापन *n.*-&c. करणें *g. of o.*
To s. up and pull down. घडामोड *f.*-घडमोड *f.* करणें.
24 up; on foot; agoing; in motion; &c. चालू-चालता-&c. करणें, उभारणें, प्रवर्त्तणें, मांडणें, घालणें, स्थापणें, प्रवर्त्तन *n.*-स्थापन *n.*-स्थापना *f.*-प्रतिष्ठापन *n.*-प्रतिष्ठा *f.*-उत्थापन *n.*-संस्थापन *n.*-&c. करणें *g. of o.*

To SET, *v. n.*—a heavenly body. मावळणें, अस्तास जाणें, बुडणें, अस्त *m. n.*-अस्तमय *m.*-अस्तमयन *n.*-अस्तावलंबन *n.*-&c. होणें *g. of o.*
Mountain behind which heavenly bodies set. अस्ताचल *m.* अस्तगिरि *m.*
2 *have a certain direction or motion.* वळण *n.*-ओघ *m.*-वहा-

णी *f.*-झोंक *m.*-प्रवाह *m.*-रोख *m.*-&c. लागणें-जाणें *g. of s.*

3 at; upon; *fall upon, assail,* v. To ATTACK. हल्ला *m.*-घेघेमार *m.*-घेघे *f.*-घेगा *m.*-हंगामा *m.*-कोल्हेहूक *f.*-लांडगेतोड *or* लांडगतोड *f.*-&c. करणें, आंगावर येणें-पडणें-तुटून पडणें *with g. of o.* झडझडणें.

4 in; *take place for continuance,*—rain, cold, &c. लागणें, धरणें, बसणें, चेकळणें, चेहरणें, मांडवमेड *f.* रोवणें.

5 off;—horse, &c. सुटणें, निघणें.

6 out; *go on one's way.* निघणें, निघून जाणें, चलणें, चालणें, मार्ग *m.*-वाट *f.*-&c. धरणें, वाट चालूं लागणें, वाटेस लागणें, चालीस लागणें, निघवा *m.*-निर्याण *n.*-&c. होणें *g. of s.* चालता-मार्गस्थ-रवाना-&c. होणें, प्रस्थान *n.* करणें.

Preparation for setting out. निघावा *m.*

7 to; at; *apply one's self sedulously & studiously to,* v. To ATTACK. पडणें, तुटूनपडणें, उठावणें, जुडणें, बसणें, बिलगणें, घसरणें, झडझडणें, (*intens.* झडाडणें), मिसळणें, गणm. नमणें *or* नेमणें, उठावणी *f.*-उठावा *m.*-चाल *f.*-घेघे *f.*-घेघेमार *m.*-खणती *f.* खणकुदळ *f.*-&c. घेणें, घर्षण *n.* करणें, ताण *m.* घेणें-देणें, लगट *m. f.* करणें,—headlong, with full swing, &c. चेकळणें, नेटावणें, सुटणें, चेहरणें, झटणें, पैजेचा विडा *m.* उचलणें.

8 up for; v. To PRETEND. अड्डा *m.* बाळगणें, चंग *m.* बांधणें.

That sets up for. अड्डेबाज, अड्डेबाईक.

SET, *n. number of things, &c. suited to each other.* जोड *m.* प्रत *f.* सांचा *m.* वर्ग *m.* गंज *m.* डाव *m.*

2 *number of persons,* v. BAND. जमात *f.* थवा *m.* झुंड *f.*

3 (of musicians, dancing girls, &c.). जोडी *f.* ताफा *m.* फड *m.* चक्री *f.* मेळ *m.* [ठाण *n.*

4 (of rogues, idlers, &c.) v. BAND. चौकट *f.* चौक *m.* मु-

5 *young plant for growth.* कलम *n.* रोप *n.*

SET, *p. and a.* v. V. A. 1. ठेवलेला, मांडलेला, &c. स्थापित.

2 लावलेला, रोपलेला, रोंवलेला, &c. आरोपित.

5 जडलेला, &c. जडीत, खचित (in comp. as, रत्नखचित, मणिखचित, मौक्तिकखचित, &c.).

Imbedded or set jewels. जडावजोहार *m. pl.* जडावाचेडागिने *m. pl.* जडीतजोहार *n.*

6 लावलेला, धार लावलेला, &c.

v. V. N. 1. मावळलेला, अस्तासगेलेला, &c. अस्त, अस्तमित, अस्तगत, अस्तंगत, निर्वाण.

7 *and* INTENT, DILIGENT. जुडलेला, &c. एकनिष्ठ, आसक्त, आसक्तमनस्क, अभिमुख, उन्मुख.

I. *regular, prescribed, &c.* नियमाचा *or* नेमाचा, बेताचा, निश्चयाचा, नियमित, निश्चित.

II. *fixed in opinion,* v. FIRM. नेटाचा, निर्धाराचा, निर्धारी, दृढनिश्चय, स्थिरनिश्चय.

III. up; *well-erect.* सडक (also सडक *s. f. a set up person*).

To be s.—the eyes in death. थिजणें.

SETACEOUS. See BRISTLY.

SETON, *n.*—in surgery. पोंत *or* पोंथ *m.* वात *f.*

SETTEE, *n. bench.* बांक *m.* मंचक *m.* मंच *m.*

SETTER, *n.* SETTING, *p. a.* v. V. A. 1. ठेवणारा, मांडणारा, स्थापणारा, &c. विधायक, विधायी, विधाता, स्थापक, स्थापन-&c. कर्ता-कारी-&c.

2 लावणारा, रोवणारा, &c.

5 जडणारा, &c. जड्या.

v. V. N. 1. मावळणारा, बुडणारा, मावळता, बुडता, अस्तावलंबी.

SETTING, *n.* v. V. A. 1.—*act.* ठेवणें *n.* मांडणें *n.* स्थापणें *n.* &c. मांडणी *f.* मांडणूक *f.* मांडणावळ *f.* मांडावळ *f.* मांड *m.* स्थापन *n.* स्थापना *f.* विधान *n.* आधान *n.*

2 लावणें *n.* &c. आरोप *m.* आरोपण *n.*

3 नेमणें *n.* नेमकरणें *n.* &c.

4 रोवणें *n.* पुरणें *n.* &c.

5 जडणें *n.* &c. जडण *f.* जडप *n.* जडाव *m.* कोंदणें *n.*

6 लावणें *n.* धार लावणें *n.*

v. V. N. 1. मावळणें *n.* &c. अस्त *m. n.* अस्तमय *m.* अस्तमयन *n.* अस्तावलंबन *n.*

To SETTLE, *v. a. place at rest, &c.* स्थिरावणें, थारावणें *or* थिरावणें, स्थिर-स्वस्थ-&c. करणें, बसवणें, स्थिरस्थावर *n.*-थिरथावर *n.*-स्थिरता *f.*-स्थिरस्थिति *f.*-स्थिरासन *n.*-&c. करणें *g. of o.*

2 *fix in life.* जोडणें, गोवणें, जडवणें, गोवून-जडवून देणें, धान्यास-ठिकाणी-थाऱ्यास-सोईस-देठीं-थायीं-&c. लावणें, सोई *f.*-जन्माची सोई *f.*-संस्था *f.*-&c. करणें *g. of o.* प्रतिष्ठा *f.* करणें *g. of o.* प्रतिष्ठित करणें.

3 *establish, appoint, &c.* v. To FIX. स्थापणें, नेमणें, बांधणें, नेमून-बांधून देणें, ठराव *m.*-नियम *pop.* नेम *m.* करणें *g. of o.* स्थापना *f.* करणें *g. of o.*

4 *decide, fix, determine, &c.* ठरावणें, ठरविणें, फैसल्ला *m.*-निवड *f.*-निवाडा *m.*-निश्चय *m.*-निर्णय *m.*-निर्धार *m.*-निधारण *n.*-अवधारण *n.*-&c. करणें *g. of o.* निर्णीत-निर्धारित-निश्चित-&c. करणें, अवधारणें, निधारणें.

To be settled. ठरणें.

5 (a pension, allowance, &c.). नेमणूक *f.* करणें-करून देणें.

6 *quiet, still,* v. To COMPOSE. संतावणें *or* संथावणें, बसवणें, निववणें, शांत-स्वस्थ-&c. करणें, स्थिरावणें, स्थिरस्थावर *n.*-थिरथावर *n.* करणें *g. of o.*

7 (a debt, accounts, &c.) v. To CLEAR OFF, To LIQUIDATE. चुकवणें, तोडणें, फेडणें, चुकता करणें, फारक *or* फारीक-रफेदफे-&c. करणें, फैसल्ला *m.*-रफेदफे *f.*-चुकवती *f.*-&c. करणें *g. of o.*

To s. considerately, &c. कावड ताबड *f.*-तोडजोड *f.*-तोडमोड *f.* करणें *g. of o.*

To be settled. चुकणें, फिटणें.

8 (a dispute) *adjust.* तोडणें, समेटणें, चुकवणें, मिटविणें, संपविणें, तोडीवर घेणें आणणें, तटका *m.* तोडणें, तोड *f.*-समेट *m.*-&c. करणें *g. of o.*

To be settled. चुकणें, मिटणें, तुटणें.

9 *cause to subside or fall to the bottom.* बसवणें, खालीं बसवणें, स्थिरावणें.

10 See To COLONIZE.

To SETTLE, *v. n. subside, sink.* बसणें, खालीं बसणें-पडणें, ठरणें, स्थिरावणें, थारावणें, ठरणें.

2 *deposit sediment, clear.* निवळणें, नितळणें, गाळ *m.*-मळ *m.*-&c. बसणें *g. of s.*

3 *establish a domestic state.* घर *n.*-घरदार *n.*-घरसंसार *m.*-संसार *m.*-&c. करणें-करूं लागणें, बायको *f.* करणें, सोईस-थान्यास-देठीं-&c. लागणें.

4 *establish a residence.* स्थिरावणें, थारणें *or* थारावणें, थिरावणें, थावरणें, तळ *m.* घालून बसणें, थारा *m.*-थांगा *m.*-&c. ध-

रणें, थान्यास-थांग्यास-&c. लागणें-राहणें.

5 *become fixed, stationary, permanent, &c. after fluctuation.* बसणें, स्थिरावणें, थारणें *or* थारावणें, थिरावणें, स्थिर-&c. होणें, स्थिरता *f.*-स्थिरस्थावर *n.*-थिरथावर *n.*-&c. होणें, स्थिरासन *n.* होणें *g. of s.*

Resting or settling place, lit. fig. थार *m.* थारा *m.*

To s. in a particular quarter,—the wind. धरणें (as दक्षिण *f.*-उत्तर *f.*-पश्चिम *f.*-&c. धरणें).

6 *become still, quiet, &c.* v. To CALM. बसणें, स्थावरणें, स्थिरता *f.*-स्थिरस्थावर *n.*-थिरथावर *n.*-&c. होणें *g. of s.*

7 (into compactness and firmness). जमणें, अटणें, घटणें, आळणें, अवळणें, दृढावणें, अटींव-घटींव-&c. होणें.

8 (in an office, a disease, a habit) *become confirmed, &c.* जडणें, घटणें, दृढावणें, जडावणें, बद्धमूल-दृढमूल-दृढासन-&c. होणें.

To be comfortably settled in an office, &c. बसम. बसणें *g. of s.* मांड *m.* मांडणं *g. of s.* बस्तान *n.* बसणें *g. of s.*

SETTLED, *p.* v. V. A. 1. स्थिरावलेला, स्थिर केलेला, &c. थिर, स्थिरस्थावराचा, स्थिरीकृत. [श्चित, निश्चयाचा.

3 *and* FIXED. नेमलेला, स्थापलेला, &c. नियमित, नेमाचा, नि-

4 ठरावलेला, निर्णय केलेला-झालेला, फैसला केलेला-झालेला, &c. निर्णीत, निर्धारित, अवधारित, निश्चित.

6 स्थिरावलेला, शांतकेलेला, &c. स्थिर, शांत, स्वस्थ.

7 चुकवलेला, तोडलेला, रफेदफे केलेला-झालेला, &c.

8 तोडलेला, समेटलेला, समेटकेलेला-झालेला, &c.

SETTLEMENT, SETTLING, *n.* v. V. A. 1.—*act.* स्थिरावणें *n.* थारावणें *n.* &c. स्थिरीकरण *n.*—*state.* स्थिरस्थावर *n.* थिरथावर *n.* स्थिरता *f.* स्थैर्य *n.* स्थिरावस्था *f.* स्थिरस्थिति *f.*

2—*act.* थान्यासलावणें *n.* थांग्यासलावणें *n.* देठीं लावणें *n.* &c. प्रतिष्ठा *f.*

3—*act.* नेमणें *n.* बांधणें *n.* स्थापणें *n.* &c. स्थापन *n.* अवस्थापन *n.* स्थापना *f.* अवस्थापना *f.* व्यवस्थापन *n.* ठराव *m.* नियम *pop.* नेम *m.*

4—*act.* ठरावणें *n.* &c. ठरावणी *f.* ठरावणूक *f.* निर्धारण *n.* निर्णयन *n.* अवधारण *n.*—*state.* निर्धार *m.* ठराव *m.* निवाडा *m.* निवड *f.* फैसला *m.* फैसल *m. f.* निश्चय *m.* निर्णय *m.* नीर *m.*

7—*act.* चुकवणें *n.* तोडणें *n.* फेडणें *n.* &c. फेडणी *f.*—*state.* चुकोती *or* चुकवती *f.* चुकती *f.* तोड *f.* फैसल *m. f.* फैसला *m.* रफेदफे *f.*

Considerste, &c. s. कावड तावड *f.* तोडमोड *f.* तोडजोड *f.*

8—*act.* चुकवणें *n.* तोडणें *n.* समेटणें *n.* &c.—*state.* समेट *m.* तोड *f.* चुकवती *or* चुकोती *f.* मसलाशी *or* सी *f.* फैसल *m. f.* फैसला *m.* निर्तुटक *n.*

v. V. N. 1. बसणें *n.* थिरावणें *n.* &c.

2 निवळणें *n.* नितळणें *n.* गाळबसणें *n.* &c.

The clear liquid of any mixture which remains after s. निवळ *f.* निवळण *n.* निवळी *f.*

4 स्थिरावणें *n.* थारणें *n.* थारावणें *n.* &c.

I. See JOINTURE.

SETTLER, *n.* SETTLING, *p. a.* v. V. A. 1. स्थिरावणारा, थारावणारा, स्थिर करणारा, &c. [कारी.

3 नेमणारा, नेमून देणारा, निश्चय करणारा, नियमन-&c. कर्त्ता-

4 ठरावणारा, निर्णय-निश्चय-&c. करणारा-कर्त्ता-&c.

6 स्थिरावणारा, स्थिरस्थावर करणारा, &c. शांतिकर्त्ता-कारी.

7 चुकवणारा, फेडणारा, तोडणारा, &c.

8 चुकवणारा, समेटणारा, समेटकरणारा, &c.

v. V. N. 4. स्थिरावणारा, थळघालूनबसणारा-बसलेला, थाराधरणारा-धरलेला, थान्यास राहणारा-राहिलेला, &c.

Old s. भुम्या.

SEVEN, *a.* सात, सप्त.

Aggregate of s. सातकें *n.* साथकी *f.* सप्तक *n.*

By excess of s. *seven times, sevenfold.* सातसवाई, सातसवाईनें. [त्रा.

Born after seven months gestation. सातवळा *or* साता-

Period of s. days. सातें *n.*

SEVENFOLD, *a.* सातपट, सप्तगुण, सप्तगुणित, सातसवाईचा.

SEVENFOLD, *adv.* सातपट, सातसवाई, सातसवाईनें, सप्तगुण.

SEVENTEEN, *a.* सतरा *or* सत्रा, सप्तदश.

SEVENTEENTH, *a.* सतरावा *or* सत्रावा.

SEVENTH, *a.* सातवा.

SEVENTIETH, *a.* सत्तरावा.

SEVENTY, *a.* सत्तर, सप्तति,—one एके *or* एका *or* एक्याहत्तर *or* हात्तर,—two बा *or* ब्याहत्तर *or* हात्तर,—three ञ्या *or* त्रेहत्तर *or* हात्तर,—four चौरे *or* चौऱ्याहत्तर *or* हात्तर,—five पंच्या *or* पंचेहत्तर *or* हात्तर,—six शाहत्तर *or* हात्तर,—seven सत्या *or* सत्तेहत्तर *or* हात्तर,—eight अठ्या *or* अठेहत्तर *or* हात्तर,—nine एकुणैशीं *or* एकुणऐशीं.

To SEVER, *v. a. part by violence.* खांडणें, तोडणें, फोडणें, छेदणें, विदारणें, फांदडणें *or* फांदाडणें, विच्छेद *m.*-&c. करणें.

2 *part from,* v. To SEPARATE. वेगळा-निराळा-जुदा-पृथक्-&c. करणें, फोड *f.*-भेद *m.*-&c. करणें *g. of o.*

SEVERAL, *a. divers, sundry,* v. MANY. कितीएक *or* कित्येक, कांहींएक, कोणीएक, अनेक.

2 *individual, distinct, single,* v. PARTICULAR, SEPARATE. वेगळा, वेगवेगळा, निराळा, निरनिराळा, व्यस्त, पृथगात्मक, पृथग्व्यक्तिक.

3 *appropriate, &c.* v. PECULIAR. आपला, आपापला.

SEVERALLY, *adv.* v. A. 2. निराळा *decl.* निरनिराळा *decl.* वेगवेगळा *decl.* प्रत्येक, एकएक, पृथक् पृथक्, असामीवार, आंगोगडी *or* आंगागवडी, आंगागणीक, व्यक्तितः, व्यक्तिशः.

Jointly and s. जथीमथीनें.

SEVERALITY, *n.* v. A. 2. निराळेपणा *m.* निरनिराळेपणा *m.* वेगवेगळेपणा *m.* पृथक्त्व *n.* व्यस्तता *f.* व्यक्तिता *f.* पार्थक्य *n.*

SEVERANCE. SEE SEPARATION.

SEVERE, *a.*—of persons; *strict, rigorous, apt to punish, &c.* कडवा, करडा, सख्त, कडक, खरमरा *or* ऱ्या, कदरखोर, कैदखोर, कैदी, कठोर, कठीण, तिखट, प्रखर, कहरी, निष्ठुर, तरवारीच्या धारेवर वागवणारा, करवतीवर वागवणारा, उग्रदंड, उग्रशासन, भैरवशासन, दंडनशील, दंडबुद्धि, उद्यतदंड, उद्यतबाहु.

2—of punishment, measures, &c. जड, जबर, अवघड, कडक, कडक्याचा, कनक्याचा, जालीम, सख्त, तिखट, प्रखर, तीव्र, निर्वाण, उग्र, कहरी, कहराचा, दुःसह, कष्टसाह्य.

3—cold or heat; *intense, exceeding.* कडकडीत, कडक, कडाक्याचा, दुःसह, अतिशय, फार, पराकाष्ठेचा.

4—a sickness; *violent, &c.* मोठा, अवघड, कठीण, दुःसाध्य, जिवावरचा, भारी, जबर, जबरा.

SEVERED. SEE PARTED, SEPARATED.

SEVERITY, *n.* v. A.1. कडवेपणा *m.* करडेपणा *m.* सखूतपणा *m.* कडकपणा *m.* &c. सख्ती *f.* नैष्ठुर्य *n.*

2 जडपणा *m.* जबरपणा *m.* अवघडपणा *m.* &c. सख्ती *f.* तिखटाई *f.* कडका *m.* कवका *m.* तीव्रता *f.* उग्रता *f.* दुःसहता *f.* कष्टसाह्यता *f.*

3 कडका *m.* कडाखा *m.* ठणका *m.* दुःसहता *f.*

4 मोठेपणा *m.* भारीपणा *m.* जबरपणा*m.* &c. दुःसाध्यता *f.*

I. *excessive punishment.* अतिदंड*m.*अतिदंडन*n.* दंडनाधिक्य*n.*

To SEW, *v. a. fasten with a needle and thread.* शिवणें, शिवून देणें, दोरा *m.* घालणें,—compreh. *sew, stitch, tack, &c.* शिवणें टुपणें *or* टिपणें.

SEWER, *n. drain, &c.* नहर *m.*नाला *m.* गंधानाला *m.*

SEWING, *n.* v. V. शिवणें *n.* शिवणावळ *f.* सीवन *n.* सेवन *n.* स्यूति *or* सूति *f.*

Cost or charge for s. शिवणावळ *f.* शिलाई *f.*

S.-work. शिवणकाम *n.*

SEX, *n. gender.* लिंग *n.* लिंगभेद *m.* जाति *pop.* जात *f.* स्त्रीपुरुषभेद *m.* स्त्रीपुरुषव्यक्तिभेद *m.* स्त्रीपुरुषत्वविषयकभेद *m.*

The male s. पुरुषजाति *f.* पुंजाति *f.* नरजाति *f.*

The female s. स्त्रीजाति *f.* बायकांची जात *f.*

SEXAGENARIAN, *a. aged sixty years.* साठवर्षांच्या वयाचा,साठ्या.

To be getting s. साठळणें.

SEXANGULAR, *a. having six angles.* षट्कोण.

SEXENNIAL, *a. happening once in six years, or lasting six years.* साहासाहावर्षांचा, साहासाली, षडब्दिक.

SEXTANT, *n. sixth part of a circle.* वृत्तषष्ठांश *m.*

2—the instrument. एक यंत्र विशेष आहे, सूर्ययंत्र *n.*

SEXTUPLE. See SIXFOLD.

SEXUAL, *a. pertaining to sex.* लिंगाचा, लिंगाविषयींचा, स्त्रीपुरुषभेदाचा, स्त्रीपुरुषचिन्हाचा, स्त्रीपुरुषधर्माचा, स्त्रीपुरुषधर्मसंबंधी, स्त्रीपुरुषभेदविषयक, स्त्रीपुरुषभेददर्शक, स्त्रीपुरुषत्वविषयक-संबंधी, मैथुनसंबंधी.

S. intercourse. See COPULATION.

SHABBINESS, *n.* v. A. 1. जुनापुदरटपणा *m.* मजितपणा *m.* &c.

2 किलबाणेपणा *m.* गदळपणा *m.* हुचेपणा *m.*

SHABBY, *a.*—clothes ; *worn, torn, soiled, &c.* जुनापुदरट, जुना पुराणा, जुनापाना, जुनाफाटका, मजीत, बातीचा, पोतेऱ्याचा.

2 *mean, low, despicable.* किलबाणा *or* णी, गदळ, भिकार, भिकारी, भिकारचालीचा, भिकारलक्षणाचा, भिकारचाळ्याचा, रुपणपणाचा, दर्भ्या, हुचा, लिदवळ, भटाऊ, येरिव्ळवाणा, पाजी, जघन्यवृत्ति.

To SHACKLE, *v. a. fetter &c.* lit. fig. v. To BIND, To CLOG. बांधणें, बांधून घेणें, तांगडणें, गळा *m.* बांधणें-गोवणें *g. of o.* पाय *m.pl.* बांधून घेणें-गोवणें *g. of o.* पायांत खोडा *m.* देणें.

SHACKLE, *n.* v. FETTER, CLOG. बिडी *or* बेडी *f.* पायबंद *m.* गळग्रह *m.* बंध *m.* बंद *m.* बंधन *n.*

SHADDOCK, *n. citrus decumana.* चकोतरा *or* चकोत्रा *m.*

SHADE, *n. darkness or obscurity caused by interception of light.* सावली *f.* छाया *f.* बसवा *m.* बावळें *n.* आतपाभाव *m.* अनातप *m.*

S. (of certain things) viewed as evil. ओशत *or* द *f.* ओसद *f.* कवडसा *m.*

2 *degree or gradation (of light or colours).* कस *m.* कांकण *n.* अंश *m.*

3 v. SCREEN. पडदा *m.*

4 *spirit*, v. GHOST. अपछाया *f.*

5 See SHADOW.

To SHADE, *v. a. screen from light or heat.* सावली *f.*- आडोसा *m.*-छाया *f.*-&c. करणें-पाडणें, उष्णनिवारण *n.*-उष्णप्रतिबंध *m.*-&c. करणें.

SHADINESS, *n.* v. A. 1. सावली *f.* सावट *n. f.* छायायुक्तता *f.* छायावैशिष्ट्य *n.* छायाबाहुल्य *n.*

2 नित्य सावली *f.* सावट *f. n.* आतपराहित्य *n.*

SHADOW, *n. shade representing the form of the body which causes it.* छाया *f.* पडछाया *f.* सावली *f.* पडसावली *f.* प्रतिछाया *f.* प्रतिबिंब *n.*

Middle or mean s. मध्यछाया *f.*

Relation of a s. with its substance. बिंबप्रतिबिंबभाव *m.*

S. cast by the gnomon of a dial. शंकुछाया *f.* प्रभा *f.*

S. of the earth. भूभा *f.*

That casts a s. छायाकर, छायामय.

2 *imperfect representation.* छाया *f.*

3 v. SHELTER. आश्रय *pop.* आस्रा *m.*

To SHADOW. See To SHADE. 2 See To ADUMBRATE.

SHADOWY, *a. not bright, &c.* v. DIM. उणेतेजाचा, कमीतेजाचा, मंदतेजस्क, न्यूनप्रभ, न्यूनकांति, न्यूनतेजस्क.

2 *unsubstantial, unreal.* छायेचा, छायारूप, छायात्मक, छायाकृति, अवास्तविक.

SHADY, *a. abounding with shade.* सावलीचा, छायेचा, सावटाचा *or* सावटीचा, छायामय, छायाबहुल, छायाविशिष्ट, छायावृत, छायाच्छन्न, छायाच्छादित.

2 *ever covered from the sun.* नित्यछायेचा, सावलीचा,सावटी, सावटीचा *or* सावटाचा, आतपरहित, आतपशून्य-हीन-&c.

SHAFT, *n. spire.* दांडा *m.* शंकु *m.*

2 (of a carriage). दांडी *f.* धूर *f.* धुरी *f.*

Extremity of a s. or pole. धूर *f.*

Middle s. (if there be three). डोमल *m. n.* डामाळें *n.*

S.-bullock, &c. *thiller.* धुरकरी *or* धुरेकरी, धुरेचाबैल-&c.

S.-man, *driver.* धूरकरी.

S.-pin. धूरखीळ *f.*

Tie connecting the s. with the yoke. धुरेकट*m.* धूरएटक*n.*

3 v. ARROW. बाण *m.*

4 v. HANDLE. मूठ *f.* धरूं *n.* परज *m.* दांडा *m.* दांडी *f.*

SHAG, *n. rough, coarse, or woolly hair.* भींस *f.* जाडलोकर *f.* केंसटी *f.* केसुरडी *f*

SHAGGY, *a.* v. N. भिसीचा, केंसटीचा, &c. भिसाळ, झिपऱ्या.

I. v. RUGGED. खरबरीत.

To SHAKE, *v. a. put into a vibrating motion, agitate, &c.* हालवणें, हिलवणें, हिलकावणें, हादरणें, हांदुळणें *or* हांवदुळणें, डुलवणें, डोल्वणें, घोळणें, घुसळणें, खुंदलणें *or* खुंदळणें, आंदोलन *n.*-हांदळ हिंदळ *f.*-&c. करणें, कांपवणें.

2 (a cloth, &c.). झटकणें, झटकावणें, झाडणें, झटका *m.*-झटकारा *m.*-&c.देणें,—briskly, smartly, &c. झडझडीत झाडणें, झडझडून झाडणें, हिसडणें.

3 *give concussion.* ढकलणें, हिसडणें, हिसकणें, आंचकणें, ध-

क्का m.-हिसडा m.-हिसका m.-&c. देणें.

4 (liquids in a vessel). डचमळणें.

5 fig. (confidence, courage, &c.). धक्का m.-हिसका m.-आंचका m.-&c. देणें-बसवणें-मारणें, घसरा m. देणें, घसरेसा-ढळेसा -&c. करणें. [गच्चा करणें.

6 off; *get rid of.* घालवणें, टाकणें, सोडणें, दवडणें, दूरकरणें, बे-

To SHAKE, *v. n. be agitated with vibratory motion.* हालणें, हिन्लणें, हादरणें, डुलणें, डोलणें, आंदुळणें *or* आंदोळणें, झोके *m. pl.* -&c. खाणें.

2—liquids in a vessel, v. To FLOP. डचमळणें, डळमळणें.

3 (as with laughter). झुलणें.

4—tremulously, v. To TOTTER, To TREMBLE. कांपणें, लटलट *adv.*-लुखुलुखु *adv.*-&c. हालणें-करणें, डकडकणें *or* डगडगणें, डगमगणें, डगणें, हदहदणें, दलदल *adv.* हालणें करणें, दलदलणें.

5 (from cold). See To SHIVER.

SHAKE, SHAKING, *n.* v. V. A. 1.—*act.* हालवणें *n.* हादरणें *n.* हांदुळणें *n.* &c. घोळ *m.* आंदोलन *n.*—reiteratedly, &c. हालवाहालव *f.* हिलवा हिलव *f.* हांदळ हिंदळ *f.* डोलबाडोलब *f.*

2 झटकणें *n.* झटका *m.* झटकारा *m.*

3 ढकलणें *n.* &c. धक्का *m.* हिसडा *m.* हिसका *m.* हबका *m.*

5 धक्का *m.* हिसका *m.*

v. V. N. 1. हालणें *n.* डुलणें *n.* आंदुळणें *n.* &c. आंदोलन *n.*

4 See TREMBLING. 5 See QUIVERING.

I.—in music. कंप *m.* गिरकी *f.* गिटकडी *f.* गिटकारी *f.* खटका *m.* झील *f.* सरांटा *m. v.* घे, बाजव.

Shakes and quavers;—revilingly. अडेवडे *m. pl. v.* घे.

In a s. v. TRICE. झटक मारून, लवलाही *or* हें, लवडीसवडी, झटक्यापटक्यांत, झटझट *or* टां.

To be off in a s. सटकणें *or* सडकणें *or* सुटकणें, झटकणें.

SHAKEN, *p.* v. V. A. 1. हालवलेला, डोलवलेला, हांदुळलेला, &c. घोळींव, आंदोलित.

SHAKER *n.* SHAKING, *p. a.* v. V. A. 1. हालवणारा, हांदुळणारा, आंदोलन कर्त्ता-कारी.

2 झटकरणारा, झटका देणारा, &c.

v. V. N. 1. हालणारा, डुलणारा, आंदुळणारा, &c.

4 कांपणारा, डकडकणारा, &c. डळमळीत, कंपित, विलोल.

SHAKY, *a. unstable, &c.* v. RICKETY. डळमळीत, लटपटीत.

SHALLOW, *a. having little depth.* उथळ *or* उत्थळ, उत्तान, गाध. —of rice-ground. उखर, कुरवंडा.

2 fig; *superficial, &c.* बुद्धीचा-मनाचा-विवेचा-&c. उथळ, उथळबुद्धीचा-मनाचा-विवेचा, वरवरबुद्धीचा-मनाचा-विवेचा, उपरटप्पी, उपरटप्याचा, बरकर्मी, अल्पज्ञ, अल्पविद्य, अल्पबुद्धि, अल्पमति, थिलर.

SHALLOW, *n. shoal, sand-bank, &c.* भाट *f. n.* भाटी *f.* लाग *m.*

SHALLOW-BRAINED, SHALLOW-PATED, SHALLOW-WITTED, *a.* v. SHALLOW. उथळबुद्धीचा, वरवरबुद्धीचा, अल्पज्ञ.

SHALLOWNESS, *n.* v. A. 1. उथळपणा *m.* &c.

2 उथळबुद्धि *f.* उथळविद्या *f.* वरवरबुद्धि *f.* वरवरविद्या *f.* अल्पबुद्धि *f.* अल्पमति *f.* अल्पबुद्धिता *f.*

To SHAM, *v. a. feign, pretend.* मीस *n.*-सोंग *n.*-गतक *n.*-&c. घेणें-करणें *g. of o.* बतावणी *f.*-&c. करणें *g. of o.*

SHAM, *n. pretence, trick.* कोंग *n.* कोंघ *n.* निमित्त *n.* छल *m.* बहाणा *m.* हिला *m.* ढोंग *n.* सोंग *n.* मिष *pop.* मीस *n.* गतक *n.* मकर *n.* खटाटोप *m.* फट *f.*

SHAM, *a. feigned, fictitious.* सोंगाचा, ढोंगाचा, मिसाचा, गतकाचा, बहाण्याचा, &c. बतावणीचा, कपटाचा, ओढून आणलेला, ओढून चंद्रबळाचा, कृत्रिम.

To SHAMBLE, *v. n walk awkwardly & unsteadily.* फेंगडत चालणें, गुल्पत चालणें. [जार *m.* सूना *f.*

SHAMBLES, *n. flesh-market.* सागुतीचा बाजार *m.* खाटकाचा बा-

SHAME, *n. the sensation or feeling of conscious guilt, &c.* लाज *f.* लज्जा *f.* शरम *f.* संकोच *m.* मुखसंकोच *m.* अपत्रपा *f.* ओशाळी *f.* ओशाळगत *f.* ओशाळीक *f.* मिंधेपणा *m.*

2 *sense of shame,* v. MODESTY. लाज *f.* लज्जा *f.* शरम *f.* खंत *f.* दरद *m.* व्रीडा *f.*

To cast off s. पडदा *m.* उडवणें.

To take s. to one's self. लाजणें, शरमणें, ओशाळणें, लाज *f.* वाटणें *in. con.*

To throw off all sense of s. नाक *n.* तोडून कडोस्रीस खोवणें, नाक *n.* कापून हातांत घेणें, नाक *n.* मुठींत धरणें, पागोटें बगलेस मारणें, ढोंगचें-ढोंगणाचें-कंबरचें-&c. सोडून डोकीस गुंडाळणें.

3 *shamedness, reproach,* v. DISGRACE. अपमान *m.* अप्रतिष्ठा *f.* मानभंग *m.* पाणउतारा *m.* तोंडास काळोखी *f.* कालिमा *m. pop.* कालिमा *f.*

To put to s. See To SHAME.

4 *cause or reason of shame.* लाजेस-लज्जेस-&c. कारण *n.*-हेतु *m.* लज्जाहेतु *m.* लज्जाकारण *n.* लज्जास्पद *n.*

To glory in one's s. ढोंगचें सोडून डोकीस गुंडाळणें.

To SHAME, *v. a. make ashamed, abash, &c.* लाजवणें, लाजावणें, शरमिवणें, चपापवणें, ओशाळवणें, संकोच *or* मुखसंकोच *m.* करणें *g. of o.* खालीं पहायास लावणें, तोंड *m.*-मान *f.* खालीं करणें *g. of o.* ओशाळा-मिंधा-सलज्ज-लज्जित-&c. करणें, पाण्यापेक्षां-पातळ करणें.

2 See To DISGRACE.

To SHAME, *v. n. be ashamed.* लाजणें, शरमणें, ओशाळणें.

SHAME-FACED, *a.* v. BASHFUL. लाजाळू, लाजरा, लाजट, संकोची.

SHAME-FACEDLY, *adv.* v. A. लाजिरवाणा *or* णें, लाजरेपणानें, संकोचानें, &c.

SHAME-FACEDNESS, *n.* v. A. लाजरेपणा *m.* &c. संकोच *m.* लाज *f.* लज्जा *f.* भीड *f.*

SHAMEFUL, *a. that brings shame, ignominious, &c.* v. DISGRACEFUL. लाजेचा, लज्जेचा, लाजिरवाणा, लाजलावण्या *or* लाव्या, अपयशस्कर, आब्रूघेणा, इजतखाऊ, इजतघेणा, लज्जाप्रद, लज्जावह, निंदाप्रद, लज्जाकर.

2 *raising shame in another,* v. INDECENT. लाजिरवाणा, लाजेचा, लज्जेचा, शरमेचा, लज्जावह, लज्जाप्रद, अशिष्ट, अचकट विचकट, कुत्सित.

SHAMEFULLY, *adv.* v. A. 1. लाज सोडून, आब्रू सोडून-दवडून, लाजिरवाणी, लाज आणण्याजोगा *decl.*

2 आब्रू घेऊन, अपयशकरून, बेआब्रूनें, बेहुरमतीनें, &c.

SHAMELESS, *a. wanting shame or modesty; callous, hardened, abandoned, &c.* निलाजरा, निर्लज्ज, बेशरम, बेहया, लज्जाहीन-रहित-शून्य-&c. त्रपाहीन-&c. निसत, निसवलेला, निसूक *or* ग, निदरदी, बेदरदी, कोडगा, अवीट, ओशाळ, निगर्गटा, निचाडा, उजागीर, सुरखुरू, लाज टाकलेला, मुसळ नेसलेला-पांघरलेला, खुंभनेसलेला, निस्मंगळ, विलज्ज, त्यक्तलज्ज, मुक्तलज्ज, हतलज्ज, निरप-

त्रप, घायकटर or कटार, घायखेंटर, लतकुटार, लतकोडगा, देवाधर्मानें टाकलेला, देवाधर्मानें ओवाळलेला, माणसांतून उठलेला.

2 *indicating want of shame, done without shame.* निलाजरेपणाचा, बेशरमेचा, निलाजरा, निर्लज्जतेचा, लज्जाराहित्याचा, &c.

SHAMELESSLY, *adv.* v. A. निलाजरेपणानें, बेशरमपणानें, निर्लज्जतेनें, &c. लाज-लज्जा-&c. सोडून-टाकून-&c. उजागरीनें, लज्जाराहित्यपूर्वक, &c. मुसळनेसून, सुंभनेसून, नाकमुठींत धरून, &c.

SHAMELESSNESS, *n.* v. A. 1. निलाजरेपणा *m.* बेशरमपणा *m.* कोडगेपणा *m.* निदरदीपणा *m.* निचाडेपणा *m.* &c. लज्जाराहित्य *n.* लज्जाहीनता *f.* &c. त्यक्तलज्जता *f.* मुक्तलज्जता *f.* &c.

SHAMMER, *n.* SHAMMING, *p. a.* v. V. गतक घेणारा, ढोंग करणारा, निमित्तखोर, मिसखोर, ढोंगी, गतक्या, गतकाळ्या, सोंग लाव्या, सोंगी or ग्या, सोंगाडी or ड्या or ळ्या, कोंगी or ग्या.

To SHAMPOO, *v. a. rub and percuss, knead and work* (the body, &c.). मुटकणें, मुटकळणें, मळणें, रगडणें, मुटका *m.* मारणें देणें, चुरणें, संवाहन *n.* करणें.

SHANK, *n. bone of the leg, tibia.* नडगी *f.* नडघा *m.* नळकुटी or नळगुटी *f.* नळगुडी *f.* नळा *m.* नळी *f.*

2 *leg*—in contempt. तंगड or तगडी *f.* डोंका or डोका *m.*

To SHAPE, *v. a. form, model, fashion.* घडणें, बळवणें, काढणें, उतरणें, बनावणें, डौल *m.*-आकार *m.*-&c. करणें-देणें.

SHAPE, *n.* v. FORM. आकार *m.* आकृति *f.* रूप *n.* घडण *f.* डौल *m.*

SHAPED, *a. having the shape of.* आकाराचा, रूपाचा, डौलाचा, &c. आकार, आकृति, रूप (all three in comp.).

SHAPELESS, *a. destitute of regular form, &c.* बेडौल, बेढब, अरूप, अमूर्त्त, रूपहीन-रहित-शून्य, आकारहीन-शून्य-&c.

SHAPELESSNESS, *n.* v. A. बेडौलपणा *m.* बेढबपणा *m.* अमूर्त्ति *f.* रूपराहित्य *n.* आकारराहित्य *n.*

SHAPELINESS, *n.* v. A. आकारशुद्धि *f.* रूपशुद्धि *f.* वळणशुद्धपणा *m.* आवशुद्धपणा *m.* रूपसपणा *m.* &c. रूपलावण्य *n.*

SHAPELY, *a. well formed, symmetrical.* आकारशुद्ध, रूपशुद्ध, आवशुद्ध, वळणशुद्ध, अवयवशुद्ध, बांधशुद्ध, आकारवान्, रूपवान्, वळणदार, डौलदार, रूपस, नेटका, नीटनेटका, बेताबाताचा, जंत्रींओतलेला, सुभट, सुढाळ.

SHARD, *n. piece of an earthen vessel.* खापरखुंटी *f.* खापरी *f.* मडक्याचें बखल *n.* चिपोळी *f.* करप *f.* खापर *n.* कपरा *m. dim.* कपरी *f.* भेंदें or भेंदेंन. [*n.* कचकलम.

Shards, *heap of shards, bits of glass, &c.* कचकोल *m.*

To SHARE, *v. a. distribute,* v. To DIVIDE. वांटणें, वांटून देणें, वांटणी *f.* करणें-करून देणें, भाजणें.

2 *partake with another.* वांटून घेणें-देणें, विभागून घेणें-देणें, अविभक्तभोग *m.*-सहोपभोग *m.* करणें *g. of o.*

To SHARE, *v. n. participate, have part.* वांटा *m.*-&c. घेणें-पावणें, वांटा *m.*-&c. मिळणें *in. con.*

SHARE, *n. part, portion.* वांटा or वाटा *m.* भाग *m.* विभाग *m.* वांटणी *f.* अंश *m.* हिस्सा *m.* तक्सीम *f.* [समभागी.

Equal s. समभाग *m.*—That has an e. s. समभाग *pop.*

2 (of a mercantile, &c. concern). पाती or पांती *f.* पाथी *f.* भागी *f.* वंत *m.* हिसा *m.* [ल्या).

Half s. अर्धेल *f.* (and, person holding it, अर्धेली or

3 (of a property divided). अंश *m.* भाग *m.* भागाळी *f.* वंत *m.*

Calculating the shares. हिसेरसी *f.*

Schedule of shares. वांटणी पत्र *n.*

4 (of a plough). फाल or ळ *m.*

SHARE-HOLDER, *n.* SHARE-HOLDING, *a.* वांटेकरी, वांटेदार, वांटेलदार, वांटेली, पातीदार or पांतीदार, भागी, भागीदार, भागीलदार, तक्सीमदार, विभागदार, विभागी, हिस्सेदार, वंतदार.

SHARED, *p.* v. V. A. 1. वांटलेला, वांटून दिलेला, विभागित.

2 वांटून घेतलेला, &c. सहोपभुक्त.

SHARER, *n.* SHARING, *p. a.* v. V. A. 1. वांटणारा, वांटून देणारा, विभागणारा, &c.

2 *and* V. N. भागीदार, भागीलदार, भागेली, अंशी, हिस्सेदार, तक्सीमदार, भागहर, अंशहर, अंशहारी.

SHARK, *n.* तंतु *m.* नक्रराज *m.* ग्राह *m.*

SHARP, *a. keen edged, not blunt.* तिखटधारेचा, तिखट, तीक्ष्ण, तीव्र, पाणीदार, पाण्याचा, तीक्ष्णधार, शितधार, तेजवान्, वाहता, धांवता, कडक, जलाल.

2 *having a fine point.* तिखट अणीचा, तिखटटोंकाचा, बोचेरा, तीक्ष्णाग्र, शिताग्र, तीक्ष्ण, सूच्यग्र.

3 *acute of mind, quick, ready, smart, apt, &c.* उमजीक, जलद, तिखट, तीक्ष्ण, चरमरीत, चणचणीत, चुणचुणीत, चणच, शाहणा, हुशार, बहादूर or हुर, बाट, बाटगा, बाजिंदा, बिचवा or बिचका, पटु, चौरस, डोळस, खडाण, कडकडीत, कुशाग्रबुद्धि, कुशाग्रमति, तीक्ष्णबुद्धि, तीव्रबुद्धि, प्रखरबुद्धि, &c. सुजाण, तर्कबाज, तर्की, तार्किक, धूर्त्त, जिवट, तासडा, कागडा, चिमखडा, चरचीक, पंजाबी, चंच, चंचिवाग or चंचुवाग, चुणूकदार, चुणूकबाज, मेधावी, प्राज्ञ, सुधी. [शीघ्रग्राही.

4—a sense; *acute, quick.* जलद, तिखट, तीक्ष्ण, तीव्र, सूक्ष्म,

5—of sounds. कर्कश, उदात्त.

6 *acid, &c.* v. SOUR. अंबट, तुरट.

7—of language; *harsh, biting, severe, &c.* तिखट, तीक्ष्ण, कठोर, कटु, खंबट, वेधक, मर्मभेदक, दंशी.

8—pain, &c. *afflictive, severe, pungent.* तिखट, तीक्ष्ण, तीव्र, प्रखर, कडक, खर, जबर, जालीम, जलाल. [हाडफोडा.

9—of cold, &c. कडक, कडक्याचा, खर, तिखट, तीक्ष्ण, तीव्र,

10—of sayings, &c. *witty, smart.* नोकदार, खारट तुरट, चरमरीत, चरचरीत, अणखर, रसिक, सूक्ष्म.

11 *prompt, quick, &c.* v. SMART. जलद, झटपट्या.

SHARP-EDGED, *a.* v. SHARP. तिखटधारेचा, तीक्ष्णधार, शितधार.

SHARP-POINTED, *a.* v. POINTED, SHARP. तिखट अणीचा, तिखट टोंकाचा, तीक्ष्णाग्र.

SHARP-SET. See RAVENOUS, HUNGRY.

SHARP-SIGHTED, *a.* नजरबाज, तिखटडोळ्यांचा, तिखटडोळ्या, तीव्रदृष्टि, तीक्ष्णदृष्टि, काकदृष्टि, डोळस.

2 fig. *acute, &c.* v. SHARP. तीव्रदृष्टि, सूक्ष्मदर्शी, सूक्ष्मदृष्टि, कुशाग्रमति, डोळस. [दृष्टि *f.*

SHARP-SIGHTEDNESS, *n.* v. A. 1. तीव्रदृष्टि *f.* तीक्ष्णदृष्टि *f.* काक-

SHARP-WITTED, *n.* v. SHARP. तीक्ष्णबुद्धि, कुशाग्रबुद्धि, कुशाग्रमति, शीघ्रबुद्धि.

SHARP-WITTEDNESS, *a.* v. A. *and* ACUMEN. तीक्ष्णबुद्धि *f.* कुशाग्रबुद्धि *f.* शीघ्रबुद्धि *f.*

To SHARPEN, *v. n. make sharp,* v. A. 1. 2. धार *f.* करणें-आणणें-काढणें, पाणी *n.* देणें, लावणें (and, *neut.* लागणें), धार *f.* लावणें, तेज *n.* करणें-आणणें, तिखट-तीक्ष्ण-&c. करणें.

SHARPENED, *p.* v. V. धार केलेला-लावलेला, &c. तेजित, निशित.

SHARPER, *n. cheat, rogue, &c.* v. BLACKGUARD. उचल्या, उप-

ट्या, पांढरा परीस, अवरंगाबादी, मारवाडी, सोदा, छट, धूर्त.

SHARPLY. See SMARTLY.

SHARPNESS, *n.* v. A. 1. तिखटपणा *m.* &c. तीक्ष्णता *f.* तैक्ष्ण्य *n.* &c. पाणी *n.* तेज *n.* तिखटधार *f.* चरचर *f.*
2 तिखट अणी *f.* तिखटटोंक *n.* तीक्ष्णाग्रत्व *n.*
3 चरमरितपणा *m.* शहाणपणा *m.* जलदपणा *m.* तिखटपणा *m.* &c. हुशारी *f.* चतुराई *f.* तिखटाई *f.* जीव *m.* तार्किक्य *n.* पाटव *n.* कुशाग्रबुद्धि *f.* कुशाग्रमति *f.* तैक्ष्ण्य *n.* मेधा *f.* प्रज्ञा *f.*
4 जलदपणा *m.* तिखटपणा *m.* &c. तीक्ष्णता *f.* तैक्ष्ण्य *n.*
6 अंबटपणा *m.* तुरटपणा *m.* [क्ष्ण्य *n.*
7 तिखटपणा *m.* खंबटपणा *m.* कठोरपणा *m.* &c. तीक्ष्णता *f.* तै-
8 तिखटपणा *m.* &c. तीक्ष्णता *f.* तीव्रता *f.* तैक्ष्ण्य *n.* ठणका *m.*
9 कडका *m.* कडकाई *f.* कडकपणा *m.* तिखटपणा *m.* &c. ठणका *m.* तीक्ष्णता *f.* &c.
10 कचका *m.* कडका *m.* तडाखा *m.* धडाखा *m.*

SHASTER, SHÁSTRA. See SCRIPTURE.

To SHATTER, *v.a. break into many pieces, shiver.* खंडें खंडें *n. pl. or* खंडविखंड *n.* करून टाकणें, तुकडेतुकडे *m. pl.*-शंभरतुकडे *m. pl.*-कचकोल *n.*-कचकल *m.*-खुर्दा *m.*-चकनाचूर *m.*-चकाचूर *m.*-चुराडा*m.*-&c. करणें *g. of o.* विघडणें, विध्वंसणें, खंडन *n.*-विघात *m.*-विध्वंसन*n.*-विच्छेद *m.*-&c. करणें *g.of o.* छिन्नभिन्न-चकनाचूर -चकाचूर-शतचूर्ण-&c. करणें.
2 fig. *disorder, derange, impair, &c.* v. To DESTROY, To RUIN. मोडणें, नाश *m.*-धूळ *f.*-घाण *f.*-माती *f.*-चकनाचूर *m.*-चकाचूर *m.*-विघात *m.*-विध्वंस *m.*-&c. करणें *g. of o.*

SHATTER-BRAINED. See CRAZY.

SHATTERED, *p.* v. V. 1. तुकडेतुकडे केलेला, चकनाचूरकेलेला, &c. चकनाचूर, चकाचूर, शतचूर्ण, शतशकल, विशकल, खंडित, छिन्नभिन्न, विच्छिन्न, विघटित, विघाटित, विध्वंसित, विध्वस्त, विभग्न.

SHATTERER, *n.* SHATTERING, *p. a.* तुकडेतुकडे करणारा, चकनाचूर करणारा, &c. विघातक, विघाती, विच्छेदक, विच्छेद-विध्वंस-&c. कर्त्ता-कारी-कारक.
2 मोडणारा, नाश-धूळ-&c. करणारा.

SHATTERING, *n.* v. V. 1.—*act.* तुकडेतुकडे करणें*n.* विघडणें*n.* विध्वंसणें*n.* &c. खंडन*n.* विघात*m.* विच्छेद*m.* विघटन*n.* विघाटन*n.* विध्वंसन*n.* विध्वंस*m.*

SHATTERS, *n. pl.* तुकडेतुकडे*m. pl.* खंडेंखंडें*n. pl.*
To break into s. See To SHATTER.

To SHAVE, *v. a. cut or pare off with a razor.* हजामत *f.*-वपन *n.*-क्षौर*n.*-&c.करणें *g.of o.*—(the head) डोई *f.*करणें, मुंडणें, मुंडावणें, मुंडन *or pop.* मुंडण*n.*-क्षौरन*.*-कापणोरणी *f.*-भद्राकरण*n.*-श्मश्रु *f.*-&c. करणें;—(beard, whiskers), दाढी *f.* करणें, दाढी *f.*-मिशा *f. pl.* उतरणें;—in contempt, भादरणें, बोडणें, बोडणी *f.*-&c. करणें.—the head of a woman. केश*m. pl.* काढणें *g.of o.*
To s. cleanly. झील *f.* चढवणें.
2 v. To PARE. तासणें, तक्षण*n.*-&c. करणें *g. of o.*
3 *pill, fleece,* v. To PLUNDER. मुंडणें, बोडणें, लुबाडणें, बोडणी *f.*-मुंडन*n.*-&c. करणें *g. of o.*

SHAVELING, *n. a person shaved.* मुंडी, मुंड्या, मुंडलेला.

SHAVEN, SHAVED, *p.* v. V. 1. हजामतकेलेला, मुंडलेला, &c. मुंडित, वापित.
3 बोडलेला, मुंडलेला, &c.

SHAVER, *n.* SHAVING, *p. a.* v. V. 1. हजामत करणारा, मुंडणारा, वपन-मुंडन-क्षौर-&c. कर्त्ता-कारी.
I. v. BOY. बोड्या.

SHAVING, *n. thin slice or chip,* v. CHIP. चैली *f.* ढपला*m. dim.* ढपली *f.* ढलपा*m. dim.* ढलपी *f.* कुळपटा *or* कुळपुटा*m.* खळप*n.*
Shavings. सालपा*m.*

SHAWL, *n.*—the garment. शाल *f.* पासोडी *f.* ओढणी *f.*
Colored s. of children. फडकी *f.*
Double s. शालजोडी *f.* दुशाला *f.*
S. with flowers and figures worked. शालनामा*m.*

SHE, *pr.* ती, ही, एरी.
2 See FEMALE.

SHEAF, *n. bundle of stalks of grain.* पेंढी *f.* पुला*m. dim.* पुली *f.* कबळी *f.* पेंडका*m. dim.* पेंडकी *f.*
Binding in sheaves. बांधणी *f.* बांधील *f.* वेंटाळणी *f.*
Gathering together of sheaves. खळवटणी *f.*
Sheaves or bundles (of जोंधळा, सजगुरा, wheat, &c.) with the ear. गूड *or* ढन.

To SHEAR, *v. a. cut or clip with scissors, &c.* कातरणें, कापटणें, कापडणें, भादरणें, मुंडणें, कातरणी *f.*-&c. करणें *g. of o.*

SHEARED, *p.* v.V. कातरलेला, भादरलेला, &c. [कारी-&c.

SHEARER, *n.* SHEARING, *p. a.* v. V. कातरणारा, &c. कर्त्तन-कर्त्ता-

SHEARING, *n.* v. V.—*act.* कातरणें*n.* &c. कातरण *f.* कातरणी *f.* कापणी *f.* कापडणें *n.* भादरणी *f.* कर्त्तन*n.* मुंडन*n.*

SHEARLING, *n.* पहिल्या कातरणीचें मेंढरूं*n.*

SHEARS, *n. shearing instrument.* कातर *f.* कर्त्तरी *f.*
S. of thatchers. नारकस*n.* [म्यान*n.*

SHEATH, *n. scabbard, case, &c.* कोष *or* श*m.* गिलेफ*m.* मेण *or*
Having a s. कोशस्थ.

To SHEATH, *v. a. put into a scabbard.* मेणांत-कोषांत-&c. घालणें, म्यान करणें.
2 *protect by an outward covering.* वेष्टणें, मढविणें, वेष्टन*n.* करणें-घालणें-देणें, वेष्टित-&c. करणें.

To SHED, *v. a. spill.* पाडणें, सांडणें, वाहविणें, पात *m.*-सांड *f.*-&c. करणें *g. of o.*
To s. by agitating a vessel. उचंडळणें.
2 *drop, cast.* गाळणें, टाकणें, सांडणें, झाडणें.
To be shed. झडणें, गळणें.
To s. tears. आंसवें *n. pl.*-अश्रु *m. pl.*-ठिंग्या *f. pl.*-टिपें *n. pl.*-बिंदु *m.pl.*-थेंब *m.pl.*-&c.गाळणें-पाडणें-टाकणें-काढणें-ढाळणें.

SHED, *p.* v. V. 1. पाडलेला, सांडलेला, &c.
2 गाळलेला, &c. गलित, विगलित.

SHED, *n. temporary erection,* v. HUT. पडसाळ *f.* पडवी *f.* बेडें *n.* छप्पर*n. dim.* छप्परी *f.* मांडुकली *f.*आवसा*m.* निवारा *m.*काबण*n.*
Cow s. बेडें *n.*
Festive s. or erection. मांडव *m.* मंडप *m.*
Forked post of festive s. मांडवमेड *f.*
Long s. सोपा *m.*
Open and rude s. खागर *m.*
S. for cattle during the heat of the day. खानवटा*or*ठा*m.*

SHEEN. See BRIGHT.

SHEEP, *n.* मेंढा (ढा *m.* ढी *f.* ढरूं & ढें *n.*) मेष*m.* (मेषी *f.*)
To offer (in sacrifice) a string of s. मेंढरांची दावण *f.* देणें.

SHEEP-COT, SHEEP-FOLD, *n. pen,* v. FOLD. मेंढवाडा *m.* मेषालय *n.* मेषशाला *f.*

SHEEP-FACED, SHEEPISH, *a. overmodest, meanly diffident,* v. BASHFUL. मेशा *or* मेशी, गायनोंड्या, गोमुख्या, मेंगा *or* मेंग्या, मेलतोंड्या, मेमलतोंड्या, लाजकोंबडा, लाजरा, गरंगील.

SHEEP-WALK, *n. place where sheep are fed.* मेंढरान *n.*

SHEEP'S-EYE, *n.* नेत्रकटाक्ष *m.*

SHEEPISHNESS, *n.* v. A. मेशेपणा *m.* गायतोंडेपणा *m.* लाजरेपणा *m.* &c. लज्जाधिक्य *n.* अतिलज्जा *f.*

SHEER, *a. mere, pure, unmingled.* केवल *or* ळ, शुद्ध, निखालस.

SHEER, *adv.* v. CLEAN. साफ, शुद्ध.

To SHEER OFF. See To DECAMP.

SHEET, *n.*—of a bed. चादर *f.*

S. gathered up at the corners. झोळणा *m.* झोळी *f.*

2 (of paper). ताव *m.* पान *n.* दुटें *n.* दुट्टा *m.* दुंडा *m.*

Half-sheet. पान *n.*—revilingly, पानट *n.* पानरट *n.*

S. doubled into four leaves. चौबंदीपान ;—into two leaves, दुबंदी पान.

S. doubled breadth wise. बंद *m.*

3 (of metal &c.). पत्र *n.* पत्रा *m.* तकट *or* टें *n.*

4 (as of fire, water, &c.). झोत *m.* लोळ *m.* गल्लल *m.*

5—the nautical term. बांसरूं *n.* दमान *n.*

SHEET-ANCHOR, *n.* थोरला-मोठा-&c नांगर *m.*-लंगर*m.*

2 fig. निदानचा आस्रा *m.*

SHELF, *n.* तका *m.* फळी *f.* घडवंचीची फळी *f.*

Shelves, *case or stand.* घडवंची *f.* चालतें फडताळ *n.* मजल्यांची-फळ्यांची घडवंची *f.* कपाट *n.*

2 *sand-bank, shoal.* भाट *f. n.* भाटी *f.* [*n.m.*

SHELL, *n.* (of an egg, a nut, &c.). कंवटी *f.* कंवची *f.* कवच

Cocoa-nut s. करटी *f.* करोटी *f.* नरटी *f.* नरोटी *f.*

2 (of an animal). घर *n.* कंबची *f.* कबच *m. n.*

Conch s. शंख *m. n.* शंबूक *m.* शंखनख *m.*

Oyster s. शिंपला *m.* शिंपा *m.* कालव *n.*—Half of one. शिंप *f.* सिंपी *or* शिंपी *f.* शुक्ति *f.*

S. of the cypræa moneta, *cowrie.* कवडी *f.*

3 (of the seeds of plants) v. HUSK. टरफल *n.*

4 (as of a house) v. FRAME. सांगाडा *m.* सटारा *m.*

5 (of a tent) कलंदरा *or* कलंद्रा *m.*

6 *bomb.* कुलपी गोळा *m.* [&c. काढणें.

To SHELL, *v. a. take out of the shell.* सोलणें, फोलणें, शेंगांतून-

2 *assault with bombs.* कुलपी गोळ्यांचा भडमार*m.* करणें, कुलपी गोळे *m. pl.* टाकणें.

SHELLED, *p.* v. V. 1. सोललेला, फोललेला, सोलींव.

A s. vetch, bean, or pea. सोला *m.* सोलाणा *m.*

SHELTER, *n. that which covers or defends from annoyance; cover, harbour, asylum.* आश्रय *m.* आस्रा *m.* छाया *f.* दडण *f.* लपण *f.* थारा *m.* थार *m.* अडकूट *or* ड *n.* समाश्रय *m.* संश्रय *m.* शरण *n.* छत्र *n.*

S. from wind, &c. निवारा *m.*

Situate in the s. of. आडचा, आडील.

That is under s. निवा-याचा.

Under s. आडमोहरी.

2 *state of being covered and defended.* आश्रय *m.* आस्रा *m.* आडोसा *or* अडोसा *m.* निवारा *m.* साबट *f.*

In s. निवाऱ्यास, आडोशास.

To take s. आश्रय *m.*-आस्रा *m.*-&c. धरणें-करणें.

To SHELTER, *v. a. give cover or shelter to.* आश्रय *m.*-आस्रा *m.* -&c. देणें, पाखर *f.* घालणें. [धरणें-करणें.

2 (one's self) *betake to cover.* आश्रय *m.*-आस्रा *m.*-&c.

SHELTERED, *p.* v. V. 1. आश्रय दिल्हेला, आश्रय केलेला, आडचा, आडील, आश्रित, समाश्रित, साश्रय, संश्रित.

SHELTERER, *n.* SHELTERING, *p. a.* v. V. 1. आश्रय-&c. देणारा, आश्रयदाता.

SHELTERLESS, *a.* अनाश्रय, निराश्रय, हीनाश्रय, आश्रयरहित.

SHELVING, *a. inclining, sloping.* उतरता, उतरवट, ढळता *or* ढाळता.

SHEPHERD, *n.* मेंढका *or* क्या, मेंढेराख्या, मेषपाल, मेषपालक.

SHEPHERDESS, *n.* मेंढकी *f.* मेंढेराखी *f.* मेंढरें राखणारी *f.* मेषपालका *f.*

SHERBET, *n.*—the drink. शरबत *or* सरबत *n.* पानक *pop.* पन्हें *n.*

SHERD. See SHARD.

SHERIFF, *n.*—of a court of justice. नाजर *or* नाजीर.

SHERIFFSHIP, *n.* नाजरी *f.* नजारत *f.*

SHEW, *To* SHEW. See SHOW, To SHOW.

To SHIE, *v. a.* v. To THROW. फेंकणें.

SHIELD, *n.* ढाल *f.* फलक *m. n.*

Armed with a s. ढालाईत, फलकपाणि.

2 fig. *cover, protection.* रक्षण *n.* राखण *f.* पांघरूण *n.*

To SHIELD, *v. a. cover, defend,* v. To PROTECT. राखणें, रक्षिणें, रक्षण *n.*-संरक्षण *n.*-&c. करणें *g. of s.*

To SHIFT, *v. n. change place, direction, &c.* स्थान *n.*-स्थळ *n.*-दिशा *f.*-रोख *m.*-&c. पालटणें-फिरवणें-बदलणें, दिशेचा-रोखाचा-&c. पालट *m.*-&c. करणें *and* होणें *with g. of s.*

2 *change clothes.* पांघरुणें *n. pl.*-वस्त्र *n.*-नेसतें *n.*-नेसणें*n.*-&c. बदलणें-पालटणें-फिरवणें, वस्त्रांतर *n.* करणें.

3 *manage to subsist.* निर्वाह *m.* करणें, जोगवणें, कालगुजारा *m.* -कालगुजारी *f.*-कालगुजराण *f.*-गुजर *m.*-गुजराण *f.*-गुजारा *m.*-चालढकल *f.*-दिननिर्वाह *m.*-रोजगुजारा *m.*-अगतिकगति *f.*-&c. करणें.

4 with; *manage with.* गरज *f.* करणें, चालतें घेणें, चालीवर घेणें, चाल *f.*-चालढकल *f.*-जोगवण *f.*-जोगवणी *f.*-ढकलगुजर *f.*-ढकलगुजारा *m.*-ढकलगुजराण *f.*-ढकलपट्टी *f.*-ढकलाढकल *f.*-&c. करणें.

To SHIFT, *v. a.* v. To CHANGE. पालटणें, बदलणें, परतणें, पालट *m.*-&c. करणें *g. of o.* घडमोड *or* घडामोड *f.*-&c. करणें *g. of o.*

2 *change from one place, &c. to another.* स्थान *n.*-स्थळ *n.*-जागा *m. f.*-&c. पालटणें-बदलणें-&c. *g. of o.* स्थानांतर *n.*-&c. करणें *g. of o.* [ढकलणें.

3 off; *cast off from one's self (on another).* कोलणें, लोटणें,

SHIFT, *n. expedient, remedy,* v. RESOURCE. उपाय *m.* युक्ति *f.* तोड *f.* हिकमत *f.* गति *pop.* गत *f.*

2 *evasion, trick, subterfuge.* सबड *f.* सोडवण *f.* खिडकी *f.* कुलंगडें *n.* खेंकटें *n.*

3 *chemise.* बायकोचें कमीज *or* खमीस *n.*

SHILLY-SHALLY, *To* SHILLY-SHALLY. See HESITATION, To HESITATE.

SHIN, *n. fore part of the leg.* नडगी *f.* नळी *f.* [प्रभा *f.*

SHINE, *n. splendor, lustre,* v. BRIGHTNESS. रोशनाई *f.* कांति *f.*

2 *shining weather,* v. SUN-SHINE. ऊन *n.* निवर *n.*

To SHINE, *v. n. give out light.* तपणें, किरण *m. pl.* पाडणें, उजेड *m.*-प्रकाश *m.*-&c. पाडणें-करणें, प्रकाशणें.
Faint & tremulous shining (as of an expiring lamp) लिकलिकी *or* लुकलुकी *f.*
To s. tremulously, *to flicker.* लिकलिकणें *or* लुकलुकणें.
To s. out suddenly. गोंडा *m.* फोडणें.
2 *sparkle, glitter, gleam.* चकचकणें, तकतकणें, झकझकणें, चमकणें, चकमकणें, झगमगणें, झमकणें, लकलकणें, झळकणें, झळझळणें, झिगझिगणें, लुकलुकणें, तळपणें, झळक *f.*-&c. मारणें, तकतकलकलक *or* लुकलुक *or* लिकलिक *adv.* करणें.—brightly, glaringly, intensely, v. To GLARE. झकाकणें, झगागणें, तकाकणें, चकाकणें, झळाळणें, लकाकणें.
3 *be glossy.* तिळतिळणें, तुळतुळणें, लुसलुसणें, टवटवणें, तकतकणें, टकटकणें, तकतकी *f.*-तजेला *m.*-&c. मारणें, तकतकीत-लुसलुसीत-&c. असणें.
4 *be eminent or conspicuous.* शोभणें, तपणें, चमकावणें, तेज *n.*-शोभा *f.*-&c. होणें *g. of s.*
To s. out. उगवणें, खुलणें.
5 *be splendid, gorgeous, flashy, fine.* चमकावणें, विराजणें, राजणें, विलसणें.
SHINGLE. See PLANK. 2 See GRAVEL.
SHINING, *p. a.* v. V. 1. तपणारा, &c. प्रकाशक, प्रकाशमान, द्युतिकर, विद्योतमान.
2 *and* BRIGHT, BRILLIANT. प्रकाशवंत, तेजस्वी, लकलकीत, चकचकीत, प्रकाशमान, दीप्तिमान्, शोभमान, विद्योतमान, देदीप्यमान *pop.* देदीप्यमान, द्युतिमान्, सोज्वल, सोज्वलित.
4 तेजस्वी, शाली (in comp. as पुण्यशाली, तपःशाली, विद्याशाली, भाग्यशाली, वैराग्यशाली.)
5 विलसित, विराजमान, विराजित.
SHINY, *a.* See BRIGHT. 2 See SUNSHINY.
SHIP, This termination denoting *state* or *office* is rendered by पण, पणा, ता, त्व, &c.
SHIP, *n.* v. VESSEL. तारूं *n.* जहाज *or* झाज *n.* तरांडें *n.* गलबत *n.* जलयान *n.*—generally *or* laxly. तारूं तरांडें *n.*
Bottom of a s. or boat. पठार *n.*
Imported on a s. तारवटी.
Side of s. or boat. बोंडद् *n.*
Toll paid by a s. on clearing out. पाग *f.* [-&c.
2 (of burden). काबाडी गलबत *n.* जिन्नसी गलबत *n.*-तारूं *n.*
3 (of war). लढाऊ गलबत *n.* &c. अर्मर *or* अर्मार *n.*
To SHIP, *v. a. put or receive into a ship.* गलबतावर-&c. भरणें-चढवणें-लादणें-घेणें-&c. [vessel. तांडेल *m.*
SHIP-MASTER, *n. captain.* नाखवा, *or* नाखोदा *m.*—of a small
SHIP-MATE, *n.* गलबतावरचा-&c. सोबती-साथी-&c.
SHIP-WRECK, *n.* तारूंफूट *f.* तारूंमोड *f.* नौकाभंग *m.* नौकानाश *m.*
SHIP-WRECKED, *a.* फुटल्या तारवावरचा, नष्टनौकेंतला, नष्टनौकासंबंधी.
SHIPPING, *n. ships in general.* तारवें *n. pl.* गलबतें *n. pl.* &c.
To SHIRK, *v. n. evade duty.* काम *n.*-चाकरी *f.*-&c. चुकवणें, आंग *n.* काढणें-चोरणें, काढतें घेणें.
SHIRKER, *n.* SHIRKING, *p. a.* v. V. काम चुकवणारा, कामचुकार *or* रू, कामचुकावू *or* व्या, कामचोर, चुकावू, चुकारी *or* रू, चुकारतट्टू, आंगचुकाऊ, आंगचोर, आंगचुकार, आंगकाढू, निमित्तखोर.
SHIRT, *n.*—the garment. कमीज *or* खमीस *n.* आंतला आंगरखा *m.*
2—for children. पेहरण *n.* आंगडें *n.*
To SHIVER, *v. a. break into small pieces,* v. To SHATTER. खंडें-खंडें *n. pl.*-खंडविखंड *n.*-&c. करून टाकणें, विध्वंसणें, छिन्नभिन्न-चकनाचूर *or* चकाचूर-शतचूर्ण-&c. करणें, विध्वंसन *n.*-&c. करणें *g. of o.*
To SHIVER, *v. n. quake, tremble, shake, &c. from cold, ague, fear, &c.* कांपणें, हुडहुडणें, शिरशिरणें, खुडखुडणें, थडथडून-थडाडून *adv.* हींव *n.* येणें-वाजणें *in. con.* कासकुशा *f. pl.* घेणें-देणें, हींव *n.*-कांप *m.*-कांपरा *m.*-कांपरी *f.*-कांपरें *n.*-हुडहुडी *f.*-शिसारी *f.*-&c. सुटणें-भरणें *in. con.* कांटा *m.* भरणें, थंडी *f.* कुडकुड वाजणें *in. con.*
2 *be affected with a nervous thrilling.* शिसारी *f.* येणें *in. con.*
3 (esp. under demoniac possession). वाफेर *n.* भरणें-येणें *in. con.*
SHIVER, *a.* v. FRAGMENT. खंड *n.* छिन्न *n.* [चूर *m.*
Shivers, *pieces, bits.* चूर *m.* चुराडा *m.* चकनाचूर *m.* चका-
2 shivers; *shaking fit,* v. SHIVERING. खुडखुडी *f.* हुडहुडी *f.* शिसारी *f.*
SHIVERED, *p.* v. V. A. खंडें खंडें केलेला, चकाचूर केलेला, कडाचूर केलेला &c. चकनाचूर, चकाचूर, छिन्नभिन्न, शतचूर्ण, शतशकल, विशकल.
SHIVERER, *n.* SHIVERING, *p. a.* v. V. N. 1. कांपणारा, &c. कांप-हींव-हुडहुडी-&c. भरलेला-सुटलेला, कंपायमान.
SHIVERING, *n.* v. V. N. 1. कांप *m.* कांपरा *m.* कांपरी *f.* कांपरें *n.* खुडखुडी *f.* हुडहुडी *f.* हुडहूड *f.* कुडकुडा *m.* कुडकुडी *or* थंडीची कुडकुडी *f.* शिसारी *f.* शिरशिरी *f.*
SHOAL, *n. shallow.* भाट *f.* भाटी *f.* लाग *m.* खांडडोह *or* डोहो *m.* खांडवा *m.* खांडें *n.*
2 *multitude, throng.* झुंड *f.* घोळ *m.* घोळका *m.* थवा *m.*
SHOCK, *n. concussion; violent shake or jolt.* धका *or* धक्का *m. or* ढका *m.* गचका *m.* गचकी *f.* गचांदा *or* गचांदा *m.* आंचका *m.* हिसका *m.* धडक *f.* धडका *m.* हबका *m.*
2 *impression of terror, disgust, &c.* धका *or* धक्का *m.* आंच *f.* आंचका *m.* दचक *f.* दचका *m.* डचक *f.* डचका *m.* धक्क *n.* धडकी *f.* धपका *or* धबका *m.* धस *m.* धसका *m.* धस्स *n.* धासरा *or* धोसरा *m.* घसरा *m.* घसोटा *m.* कचका *m.* लक्क *n.*
3 *pile of sheaves.* सुडी *f.* गंज *m.* गंजी *f.*
To SHOCK, *v. a. shake suddenly,* v. To JOLT. धक्का *m.* देणें-मारणें-लावणें, आंचकणें, हबकणें.
To be shocked. डचकणें *or* दचकणें, गचकणें, आंचका *m.*-गचका *m.*-हिसका *m.*-हबका *m.*-&c. बसणें *in. con.* धक्का *m.*-धडक *f.*-धडका *m.*-&c. लागणें-बसणें *in. con.*
2 *strike with horror and disgust,* v. To OFFEND. धक्का *m.* देणें-मारणें, धसका *m.*-धडकी *f.*-&c. बसवणें, त्रासणें, त्रास *m.* देणें-आणणें.
To be shocked. धडकणें, धपका *or* धबका *m.*-धडक *f.*-&c. भरणें *in. con.* आंच *f.*-आंचका *m.*-दचका *m.*-धस *or* धसका *m.*-धडकी *f.*-धक्का *m.*-&c. बसणें *in. con.* लक्क होणें.
3 *pile sheaves of corn.* सुडी *f.*-गंज *m.*-&c. रचणें, खळवटणें, खळवटणी *f.* करणें *g. of o.*
SHOCKING, *p. a.* v. V. A. 2. धडकी बसवणारा, &c. अकटोविकट, घोर, अघोर, त्रासकारक, त्रासद.
SHOE, *n.* जोडा *m.* जुती *f.* मोचा *m.* पायपोश *or* स *m.* पैजार *f.* पा-

दुका *f.* चरणसंपुष्ट *m.* पादत्राण *n.* पादरक्षा *f.*—revilingly, as *old, torn, &c.* or with reference to striking with it. खेटर *m. n.* खासडा *m.* मोचा *m.*

Coarse and clumsy shoes. जासुदी जोडा *m.*

Wooden shoes. खडवा *or* खडावा *f. pl.* पादुका *f.*

Worn and worthless pair of shoes. दरबारी जोडा *m.*

The wearer best knows where the s. pinches. अळवाची खाज अळवास ठाऊक.

2 *horse-shoe.* नाल *m.*

To SHOE, *v. a.* (a horse, &c.). नालबंदी *f.* करणें *g. of o.* नाल *m. pl.* बांधणें *dat. of o.*

To s. all four feet. चौबंदी *f.* करणें.

To change the shoes. खोलबंदी *f.* करणें.

SHOE-FLOWER, *n.*—the plant. जास्वंद *f.* जास्वन *f.* जासुमी *f.* जपा *f.*—the flower. जास्वंद *or* जास्वन *f. n.* जपा *f.* [कार.

SHOE-MAKER, *n.* मोची, मोचेकरी, चांभार *or* चाम्हार, चर्मक, चर्म-

To SHOOT, *v. a.* (as from a gun or bow). सोडणें, मारणें, उडवणें, काढणें, विसर्जन *n.*-प्रक्षेप *m.*-&c. करणें *g. of o.*

2 *strike with something shot.* मारणें (with the word expressive of the missile, as बाण *m.* मारणें to shoot with an arrow, गोळी *f.* मारणें to shoot with a ball), बंदुकीनें-बाणानें-गोळीनें-&c. मारणें.

3 (a bolt, &c.) *propel.* सरसावणें, सारणें, पुढें करणें.

4 (a gulf, &c.) *pass through with swiftness.* झडकन-वेगानें-त्वरेनें-&c. पारजाणें-पारकरणें.

5 (leaves, branches, &c.) *put forth.* बाहेर काढणें.

6 off; v. To DISCHARGE. सोडणें, डागणें.

To SHOOT, *v. n. discharge a gun, arrow, &c.* बंदूक *f.* मारणें-सोडणें, बाण *m.* मारणें-सोडणें.

2 v. To SPROUT. अंकुरणें, फुटणें, रुजणें *or* रुझणें.

3 *burst the ground.* जमीन *f.* सोडणें, उगवणें, रुजणें *or* रुझणें.

4 *move with velocity.* वेगानें-त्वरेनें-झडकन-&c.-बाणासारखा-&c. जाणें-चालणें.

5—of boils, aches, &c. *throb, feel a shooting pain.* ठुणठुणणें, टचटचणें, शिणकणें, धमकणें, तिडीक *f.* उठणें-येणें, उसण *f.* भरणें-निघणें, धमक *f.* घेणें-उठणें-निघणें, पिंजणें, पिंजापिंजणें, धुसधुसणें.

6 forward, out; *project.* पुढें येणें.

7 up; *advance in height,* v. To GROW. उफाटणें, उचलणें, उचंगणें, सरसावणें, सरळणें, उसळणें.—sugar cane. कांडारणें.

8 (into ears—corn) *shoot the hose.* निसवणें, घशाबाहेर पडणें (पीक, कणसें, &c.) [रीf.

SHOOT, *n.* v. SPROUT. अंकुर *m.* कोंब *or* कोम *m.* मोड *m.* आंक-

Shoots from reaped corn —through rain. करा *m.*

2 (from a branch) *young branch.* फणगडा *m.* फांटा *m.* पागोरा *m.*

3 *seed shot up.* रुजवण *or* रुझवण *n.* [द्भिद.

SHOOTING, *p. a.* v. V. N. 2. फुटणारा, रुजणारा, &c. उद्भिज, उ-

SHOOTING, *n.* v. V. N. 1. बंदूक मारणें *n.* बंदूक सोडणें *n.* बाण मारणें *n.*

2 फुटणें *n.* &c. उद्भेद *m.*

5 *shooting pain.* ठुणठुणी *f.* (*intens.* ठुणठुणाट *m.*) तिडीक *f.* धमक *f.* चमक *f.* ठसक *f.* ठणका *m.* शिलक *f.* शिणक *or* शिणीक *f.* सणका *m.* कणक *f.* कचक *f.* करक *f.* उसण *f.* सन्न *f.* सलक *f.* हूक *f.* धुमधुस *f.*

Charmed ring fixed to cure s. सल्कडें *n.*

8 निसवणें *n.* निसवणी *f.* निसवील *f.* [कयशाला *f.*

SHOP, *n. house or room for the sale of articles.* दुकान *n.* वि-

2 *work shop.* दुकान *n.* कारखाना *m.*

To set up s. दुकान *n.* घालणें-मांडणें-स्थापणें.

To shut up s. *retire from business.* दुकान *n.* मोडणें.

To shut up the shops (as under some uproar). हरताळ *f.* पाडणें (बाजारांत).

To SHOP, *v. n. visit a shop or shops to purchase goods.* जिन्नस विकत घेण्या करितां दुकानांत जाणें, बाजार *m.* करणें.

SHOP-BOOK, *n.* दुकानाची-दुकानांतली वही *f.*

SHOP-KEEPER, *n.* दुकानदार, बकाल.

Shopkeepers & traders-compreh. वाणी बकाल *m. pl.*

The body of shopkeepers. बकाल *n.*

SHOP-KEEPING, *n.* दुकानदारी *f.* बकाली *f.* उदीम *m.* [मटका.

SHOP-LIFTER, *n. one who steals in a shop.* उचल्या, उपट्या, भा-

SHOP-LIFTING, *n. stealing in a shop.* उचलणें *n.* उपटणें *n.* उपट मारणें *n.* उचलेपणा *m.* भामटेपणा *m.*

SHOP-MAN, *n.* दुकानांतला चाकर-&c.

SHORE, *n. coast.* कांठ *m.* तड *or* थड *f.* तीर *n.* किनारा *m.* तट *m. n.* समुद्रकांठा *m.* कांठा *m.* कांठारा *m.*

Furrow or channel worn into a s. ओंहोर *or* ओहर *m.*

To get to s. (with any business) *fig.* तड *f. or* शेवट *m.* घेणें.

2 v. PROP. टेंका *m.* घुसी *f.* तीर *m.*

To SHORE. See To PROP.

SHORELESS. See INFINITE.

SHORN, *p.* v. V. To SHEAR. कातरलेला, भादरलेला, केस कापलेला, &c. मुंडित, छिन्नकेश.

SHORT, *a. not having great length or extension.* लहान, थोडा, अल्प, स्वल्प, लघु, क्षुद्र, लहान पल्ल्याचा, थोडेलांबणीचा.

2 *not of long duration.* थोड्या काळाचा-मुहूर्तीचा-&c. अल्पकालिक, स्वल्पकालिक, अल्पस्थायी, अचिरस्थायी, दोनदिवसांचा, थोड्या दिवसांचा.

3 *of deficient length, of short size.* अखुड, तोकडा, अपुरता, अपुरा *vulg.* अप्रा, टिचका, तिटा *or* थिटा, थेंटा *or* ठेंटा, कोना, टारगा, लांडा, टांचा, बुटुकणा, बुटका, उणाअप्रा.

4 *inadequate, insufficient, scanty.* उणा, कमी, कम, थोडा, थोडका, कोता, अपुरा, अपुरता, न्यून, अप्रशस्त.

5 *deficient in, not adequately supplied with.* उणा, कमी, न्यून, &c. *all with g. of o.* अल्प (in comp. as अल्पबुद्धि s. of wit, अल्पधन s. of money, &c.). [*g. of o.*

To be s. of. तोटा *m.*-कमताई *f.*-नपूर *f.*-&c. असणें *with.*

6 (of stature) v. LITTLE. लहान, ठेंगणा, मटगा, ससल, ह्रस्व, नीच, बुटुकणा, बुटारणा, बुटुंगणा *or* बुटुंगा, बुट्टा, जामण *or* जामन.

S. and comely. ठेंगणारेंगणा.

S. and stout. गुटुंगा, गट्ट, गबदू, गबदूल, पठडा *or* पठाडा, गिट्टा *or* गिड्डा, ठुळा, कुलंगा, गड्डू.

Shorter. धाकटा *or* ला.

Shortish. ससलबट.

7—as breathing. दम्याचा, धाप्या, उतावळा.

8 *brief.* संक्षेपाचा, संक्षिप्त, अल्पविस्ताराचा, अविस्ताराचा, विस्ताराभावाचा, अल्पशब्दक.

In s. एकूण *or* न, एवंच.

9—a vowel. ऱ्हस्व, लघु.

10 *brittle, friable.* तुटरा, तुटीर.

To come short, *be deficient in duty,* v. To FAIL. चुकणें, नाट *adv.* जाणें-येणें.

To cut short, *abridge,* v. To LESSEN. कमी-&c. करणें.—to cut a matter s. तटका तोडणें, तटका तोडून टाकणें *or* देणें.

To fall short, *become scanty,* v. To FAIL. खुटणें, कमी पडणें.

To fall short, *fail in duty,* v. To FAIL. चुकणें, अंतर *n.*-कसर *f.*-&c. पडणें-होणें-करणें.

To fall short, *be less.* कमी-&c. पडणें.

To stop short, *stop at once.* एकाएकीं-अकस्मात्-तसाच-&c. उभा राहणें-थोपणें.

To stop short, *stop without reaching the point.* मध्यें-मधच्यामध्यें खुटणें-थोपणें-राहणें.

To turn round short. त्यापावलीं *or* पायीं-चालत्यापावलीं *or* पायीं फिरणें-परतणें.

SHORT-COMING, *n.* v. FAULT. तफावत *f.* अंतर *n.* तजावूज *n.*

SHORT-COURAGED, *a.* अल्पधैर्य, आरंभशूर.

SHORT-HAND, *n.* संक्षिप्त अक्षरांनीं लिहण्याची रीत *f.*

SHORT-LIVED, *a.* अल्पायु, अल्पायुषी, आठवडेवाईक *or* आठवडेपाईक, अल्पकालिक, अचिरस्थायी.

SHORT-SIGHTED, *a. lit.* जवळच्या दृष्टीचा, उफराट्या बाहुल्यांचा, उलट्या बाहुल्यांचा, गजनेत्री.

2 *fig.* अदूरदर्शी, अदूरदृष्टि, अल्पदृष्टि, निकटदर्शी.

SHORT-SIGHTEDNESS, SHORT-SIGHT, *n.* v. A. 1. जवळची दृष्टि *f.* उलटीबाहुली *f.* &c.

2 अल्पदृष्टि *f.* अदूरदृष्टि *f.*

SHORT-SIZED, *a.* v. SHORT. लहान, टारगा.

SHORT-WINDED, *a. asthmatic.* धापाळू, धाप्या, दमेकरी, दम्या.

To SHORTEN, *v. a. make short,*—in time or space. लहान-थोडा-&c. करणें, कमी-&c. करणें.

2 *draw up, in, &c.* v. To CONTRACT. अखुडणें *or* अखडणें, अवटरणें, तांभिक करणें.

SHORTLY, *adv.* v. A. 7. थोडक्यांत, अल्पविस्तारानें.

I. *in a little time, soon.* लौकर, थोडक्या वेळानें, थोडक्या काळानें, थोडक्यांत, थोड्यांत, अचिरात्.

SHORTNESS, *n.* v. A. 1. लहानपणा *m.* थोडेपणा *m.* अल्पता *f.* अल्पत्व *n.*

2 थोडा काळ *m.* थोडीमुद्दत *f.* काळाचा-&c. थोडेपणा *m.*

3 अखुडपणा *m.* तोकडेपणा *m.* अपुरेपणा *m.* &c.

4 उणेपणा *m.* कमीपणा *m.* &c. न्यूनता *f.*

6 लहानपणा *m.* ठेंगणेपणा *m.*

8 विस्ताराभाव *m.* अल्पविस्तार *m.*

SHOT, *n. ball or bullet.* गोळा *m. dim.* गोळी *f.*

2 *small shot.* छर्रा *m.*

3 *reach of flight* ;—as bow-shot, cannon-shot, musket-shot, ear-shot, &c. टप्पा *m.* पल्ला *m.*

4 See MARKSMAN.

SHOT, *p.* v. V. 1. सोडलेला, मारलेला, &c.

2 बंदुकीनें-&c. मारलेला.

SHOULDER, *n.* खांदा *m.* स्कंध *m.*—contemptuously or loosely. खांदाड *n.*—with reference to carrying. खांद *m.*

Blow or shove with the s. बकांदा *m.* बखंडी *or* बखांदी *f.* ढुंदडा *m.* ढुंडका *m.* [*m.*

Top or upper part of the s. बावखंड *n.* बावखड *n.* बाव्हळा

To lend a s. बाही *f.* देणें, खांद *m.* देणें. [*f.* देणें.

To put the s. to. *apply sedulously.* धजणें *or* धजावणें, धज

2 (of a horse, &c.). फरा *m.* खांद *m.*

Gall or sore between the shoulders. खुबेनाल *f.*

3 *neck or shoulders,*—with reference to carriage. खांदाडी *f.* खांदा *m.* खांद *m.*

Changing the s. खांदेपालट *m.*

S.-carrier, *one who carries on shoulders.* खांद्या, खांदकरी.

S.-load. खांदाडी *f.* खांदाडीभर *m.*

Upon the shoulders of. *fig.* आंगावर, गळ्यावर, गळ्यांत, माथ्यावर, डोईवर.

To rest (a head-load) awhile upon the s. खांदलणें *or* खांदळणें.

To ride or sit a straddle upon the s. of. खांदाडीस बसणें.

To take upon one's own shoulders, fig. डोईवर-आंगावर-&c. घेणें.

To SHOULDER, *v. a. take on the shoulder.* खांद्यावर-&c. घेणें, खांदाडीं-खांदाडीस घालणें, खांदाडणें. [बखांदणें.

2 *strike with the shoulder.* बकांदा *m.*-&c. मारणें, बखंदणें *or*

SHOULDER-BELT, *n.* पडदळें *or* पडदाळें *n.* पडदळ *n.*

SHOULDER-BLADE, *n.* फरा *m.* बकाट *n.* असफलक *n.* कपाल *n.*

SHOULDER-JOINT, *n.* खवा *m.* खवाट *n.* खवाटा *m.* खुबा *m.* भुजबट *n. m.* भुजवटा *m.*

SHOUT, *n. loud cry.* आरोळी *f.* अरडा *m.* कुई *f.* पुकारा *m.* घेगा *m.* घेघे *f.* कल्लोळ *m.* महाघोष *m.* महानाद *m.* महाध्वनि *m.* सिंहनाद *m.*

2 (of joy or triumph). जयशब्द *m.* जयघोष *m.* जयध्वनि *m.* जयकार *m.* जयजयकार *m.* जयजय *m.* एकगजर *or* गजर *m.* शाबासकी *f.*

To SHOUT, *v. n. utter a loud cry,* v. N. 1. *and* To BAWL. ओरडणें, पुकारणें, ललकारणें, आरोळी *f.*-&c. मारणें, ललकारणी *f.*-ललकारी *f.* करणें, पुकारा *m.*-&c. करणें.

2 जयशब्द *m.*-जयघोष *m.*-&c. करणें.

To SHOVE, *v. a.* v. To PUSH. ढकलणें, रेंटणें, लाटणें.

SHOVE, SHOVING, *n.* v. PUSH. ढका *m.* रेंटा *m.*

A rude s. in passing by. घसरा *m.* घष्टा *m.*

Shoving and pushing. ढकलाढकली *f.* रेंटाई *f.* रेंटारेंटी *f.* रेंटारेंट *f.*

SHOVEL, *n.* एक अऊत आहे.

To SHOW, *v. a. exhibit, &c. present to the view of, make to see.* दाखवणें, दावणें, नजरेस-दृष्टीस पाडणें, पाहवणें, बघवणें, निरखवणें, &c. प्रदर्शवणें, दर्शवणें, दर्शन *n.*-प्रदर्शन *n.* (esp. in comp. as गुणप्रदर्शन, भयप्रदर्शन, दैन्यप्रदर्शन, दिक्प्रदर्शन, &c.) -&c. करणें.

To s. off one's self, *cut a figure.* आंग *n.* दाखवणें, राजणें, विराजणें, विलसणें, छान *f.* मारणें, फड *m.* मारणें-संपादणें, धटकारणें.

2 *indicate, point out, make known.* दाखवणें, दर्शवणें, प्रदर्शवणें, सुचवणें, बोधवणें, ज्ञापवणें, दर्शन *n.*-प्रदर्शन *n.*-ज्ञापन *n.*-बोधन *n.*-&c. करणें. [करणें.
3 See To INFORM. 4 (favor, kindness, &c.) *confer, &c.*
5 forth. See To MANIFEST. 6 in; into. See To CONDUCT.
7 (with the recip. pronoun) v. To APPEAR. दृष्टीस पडणें-येणें, पाहण्यांत येणें.

To SHOW, *v. n. look, &c.* v. To APPEAR. दिसणें.

SHOW, *n. spectacle.* तमाशा *m.* खेळ *m.*

2 *ostentatious display or parade; imposing demonstration.* आव *m.* आवारा *m.* आडंबर *pop.* अवडंबर *n.* जगडंबर *n.* थाट *m.* थाटमाट *m.* टामटूम *or* टूमटाम *f.* घटाव *m.* कटाव *m.* खटाटोप *m.* डौल *m.* डामडौल *m.* डबला *m. v.* मिरव, मिरवणूक *f.* मिरवण *f.* झांझू *n.* ठांठू *n.* हांहू *n.*

3 *semblance, seeming, look.* आकार *m.* रूप *n.* स्वरूप *n.* घाट *m.* डौल *m.* आभास *m.* भास *m.* [विणें.

To make a s. of. आकार *m.*-&c. दाखविणें *g. of o.* दाख-

4 *mere seeming, mere appearance.* दाखवणूक *f.* सोंग *n.* पोम *n.* स्तोम *n.* दंभ *m.* ढोंगधतुरा *m.* नस्ताडौल *m.* पोकळडौल*m.*

In mere outward s. वरवर, वरवरता *adv. decl.* वरवरतीं.

To go through the s. of, *pretend to do.* वरवर करणें.

SHOW-MAN, *n.* तमाशगीर, खेळकरी.

SHOWER, *n.* v. V. 1. दाखवणारा, &c. दर्शक, प्रदर्शक, दर्शन-प्रदर्शन कर्त्ता-कारी-&c.

2 दाखवणारा, दर्शिवणारा, &c. दर्शक, प्रदर्शक, ज्ञापक, सूचक, बोधक, दर्शन *n.*-ज्ञापन*n.*-&c. कर्त्ता-कारी-&c.

SHOWER, *n. temporary fall of rain.* सर *f.* सरवा *m.* पाहळ *f.* पाहळी *f.* वर्षाव *m.* वृष्टि *f.*—in contempt as *a mere sprinkling, &c.* सरकट *n.* सरवट *n.* हजार पांचशें पाऊस *m.* [*m.*

Droppings from a tree after a s. ओथिळा *or* ओथिवळा

April or spring s. गौरीचे डोहळे *m. pl.* चैत्रींशिपणें *n.*

Dashing s. सलक *or* स्व *f.*

Heavy s. दगडसर *f.* सळका *m.* चळक *f.*

In heavy showers. चळकधार.

Scanty and passing s. शिडशिडी *f.*

Sunshine s. ऊनपाऊस *m.* नागवापाऊस *m.*

2 fig. *profuse fall or effusion; copious distribution, &c.* वृष्टि *f.* वर्षाव *m.* पाऊस *m.*

To SHOWER, *v. a. pour down,* lit. fig. v. To RAIN. पाऊस *m.*-वृष्टि *f.*-&c. पाडणें *g. of o.* वर्षणें, सडकणें.

SHOWER-BATH, *n.* डोईवरून-&c. आंघोळ *f.* शिरस्नान *n.*

SHOWERY, *a. abounding with showers.* सरींचा, उघडझांपीचा, राहूनराहून पावसाचा.

SHOWINESS, *n.* v. A. भळभळाट *m.* टूम *f.* छान *f. v.* मार, भडक *f. v.* मार, ठळकपणा *m.* घवघवितपणा *m.* [प्रदर्शन *n.*

SHOWING, *n.* v. V. 1.—*act.* दाखवणें *n.* दावणें *n.* &c. दर्शन *n.*

2 दाखवणें *n.* दर्शिवणें *n.* &c. दर्शन *n.* प्रदर्शन *n.* सूचन *n.* सूचना *f.* बोधन *n.* ज्ञापन *n.* बोध *m.*

SHOWN, *p. v.* V. A. 1. दाखवलेला, &c. दर्शित, प्रदर्शित.

2 दाखवलेला, दर्शिवलेला, &c. दर्शित, प्रदर्शित, सूचित, बोधित, ज्ञापित, ज्ञपित, ज्ञप्त.

SHOWY, *a. splendid, gaudy,* v. FINE. देखणाऊ, देखाऊ, दर्शनी, छानीचा, छानदार, भडकेचा, ठळक, टिकमिरवणा, टूमदार, ढबदार, घवघवीत, चौस, शोभवणा.

SHRED, *n. long narrow piece cut off; strip, slip, &c.* चिंधी *f.* चिरगूट *n.* चिरटी *f.* चिरांटी *f.* चिंधडी *f.* चिंधूक *n. dim.* चिंधुकली *f.* चिंधूट *n. dim.* चिंधोटी *f.* धुडका *m.* धुडकी *f.* बाभारा *m.* शेड *f.* धांद *f.* धांत *f.* धांतळी *f.* धांदी *f.* धांदोटी *f.* चिरकाळी *f.* चिरफळी *or* चिरफाळी *f.* फाळा *m.* परकळा *m.* पिंजुळी *or* पिंजोळी *f.* भिरकंडा *or* भिरकांडा *m.* [*v.* काढ, निघ.

A s. or strip of bark, rind, or skin torn off. धोरडा*m.*

Ornamental s. (of paper, cloth, fringe, &c.) झिलमिली*f.*

Shreds. चिंधड्या *f. pl.* छाट *m.* छाटछूट *m.*

Shreds and tatters (as of a garment). लकतऱ्या *f.pl.* वागुऱ्या *or* वागोऱ्या *f. pl.*

To rend into shreds. भिरकंडे *m.pl.* उडविणें *g. of o.*

To SHRED, *v. a. cut into shreds.* चिंध्या *f. pl.*-चिरफळ्या *f. pl.* &c. करणें-काढणें *g. of o.* [शीण *f.* केदाशीण *f.*

SHREW, *n.* v. SCOLD. अकाबाई *f.* कर्कशा *f.* केकसा मावशी *f.* कडा-

SHREWD, *a. sly, arch, &c.* v. CUNNING, KNOWING. शाहणा, हुशार, चतुर, चौकस, चौकसदार, चंचिबाग *or* ज, चंचुबाग, चंच, धूर्त्त, कागडा, गुंडा, गुंड, धोरणी, तारकी पारखी, विचक्षण, चाणक्ष.

2 *proceeding from cunning or sagacity.* शाहणपणाचा, चातुर्याचा, चतुराईचा, &c. दीर्घदृष्टीचा.

SHREWDNESS, *n.* v. A. शाहणपणा *m.* शाहणपण *n.* कागडेपणा *m.* &c. चतुराई *f.* चातुर्य *n.* हुशारी *f.* धूर्त्ताई *f.* धूर्त्तावा *m.* धूर्त्तता *f.*

SHREWISH, SHREWISHNESS. See PEEVISH, PEEVISHNESS.

To SHRIEK, *v. n.* v. To SCREAM. किंकळणें, किराळणें, किंकळी *f.*-किंक *f.*-&c. फोडणें-मोकळणें.

SHRIEK, *n.* v. SCREAM. किंकळी *or* किंकाळी *f.* किंक *f.* किराळी *f.*

SHRIKE, *n.*—crested s. टीव *f.*

2 rufous-backed s. लटोरा *m.*

SHRILL, *a. sharp, acute, piercing.* किर्र, किन्हेरा, बारीक, बारीकस्वराचा, कर्कश, किरकिऱ्या, कडक, कर्णवेधक.

SHRILLNESS, *n.* v. A. किन्हेरेपणा *m.* &c. गळी *f.* बारकाई *f.* बारीक स्वर *m.* कार्कश्य *n.*

SHRIMP, *n.*—the shell fish. झिंगा *m. dim.* झिंगी *f.* झिंगरू *n.* चिंगाटी *f.* कोळंबी *f.*

2 *puny, &c. meagre man, &c.* v. STARVELING. झुडतर.

SHRINE, *n. case for an idol, &c.* देव्हारा *m.* जीवरखी *f.*

To SHRINK, *v. n. contract, &c.* अखुडणें, अटणें, अवळणें, घटणें, दाटणें, ओढणें, अवटरणें, अटरणें, चिरमुटणें, संकोचणें, आक्रसणें *or* आकुसणें, आकुंचन *n.*-&c. होणें *g. of. s.* वांठणें, वांठरणें.

2 from; back; &c. v. To FLINCH, To DRAW-BACK. कचकचणें, कचणें, कचकरणें, कच *f.* खाणें, माघार *f.*-&c. घेणें, मागें सरणें-पाहणें-होणें.

3 *be abashed.* चपापणें, संकोच *m.* वाटणें *in. con.*

To SHRINK, *v. a.* आक्रसेसा-&c. करणें, संकोच *m.* करणें *g. of o.*

SHRINKAGE, SHRINKING, *n.* v. V. N. 1. अखुडणें *n.* &c. संकोच *m.* आकुंचन *n.*

2 कचकचणें *n.* &c. कच खाणें*n.* &c.

To SHRIVEL, *v. n. contract or be drawn into wrinkles.* चिरमुटणें *or* चुरमुटणें, अखुडणें, अंवळणें, संकोचणें, अवटरणें, अटरणें, चिरम्या *f. pl.*-सुरकुत्या *f. pl.*-वळ्या *f. pl.*-&c. पडणें *in. con.*

To SHRIVEL, *v. a. contract or draw into wrinkles.* अखुडणें, चिरमुटवणें, अटरवणें, चिरम्या *f. pl.*-सुरकुत्या *f. pl.*-&c. पाडणें.

SHRIVELLED, *p.* v. V. 1. चिरम्या पाडलेला-पडलेला, &c. चिंबका, चिंबट, चेंबट, चिंबा, वाळका.
I.—features, as from age. खप्पड, खखड. [सराफडा.

SHROFF, *n. money changer*. सराफ, नाणेवटीoरट्टी.—in contempt.
A line or row of shroffs seated. सराफफाटा *m.* सराफा*m.*
Business of a s. सराफी *f.*
Seat or stand of a s. पेढी *f.*

SHROUD, *n. winding sheet.* कफण *n.* खेंडा *m.* प्रेतवस्त्र *n.*
2 See SHELTER.

To SHROUD. See To SHELTER. 2 See To HIDE.

SHRUB, *n.* v. PLANT, TREE. झाड *n.* झुडूप *or* झुडप *n.* औषधी *f.* क्षुद्रवृक्ष *m.* गुल्म *m.*
Dense and spreading s. झांकर *n.*

SHRUBBERY, *n.* झाडी *f.*

To SHRUG, *v. n. raise the shoulders in token of dissatisfaction, &c.* खांदे *m. pl.*-बाव्हळे *m. pl.*-बावडें *n. pl.* उचलणें-चढवणें-हालवणें-मुरडणें *or* उचलून-&c. नाकारणें, नाक *n.* मोडणें-मुरडणें-उडवणें, कान *m. pl.* झाडणें, कानावर हात *m.* ठेवणें, कानांत बोट *n.* घालणें, अंगुस्ती *f.* देणें. Note. Some of the above phrases mean to turn up the nose, put the hand on, or a finger in, the ear, &c. which actions are with Maráthás equivalent to our shrug.

SHRUG, *n.* v. V. खांदे मुरडणें *n.* &c. खांदमोड *f.*

SHRUNKEN, *p.* v. V. 1. अखुडलेला, अटलेला, चिंबका, चिंबा, चिंबट, चेंबट, संकीर्ण.

To SHUDDER, *v.n. shake with fear or aversion,* v.To TREMBLE. आंग *n.* कांपणें-थरथरणें-थरारणें *g. of s.* शिसारी *f.* येणें *in. con.* टिरी *or* टिऱ्या *f. pl.*-पाठ *f.* कांपणें *g. of s.* कांटा *m.* उभा राहणें, रोमांच *m.* होणें, रोमांच *m. pl.* उभे राहणें, अंगुस्ती *f.* येणें-वाटणें *in. con.* रसकसणें, रसकस *f.* येणें-वाटणें *in. con.*

SHUDDER, SHUDDERING, *n.* v. V. आंग कांपणें *n.* &c. शिसारी *f.* लटपट *f.* अंगुस्ती *f.* रसकस *f.*

To SHUFFLE, *v. a. huddle together,* v. To CONFOUND. गोंधळणें, गडबडवणें, ढवळणें, गोबडणें, गफलतणें, गोंधळ *m.*-गफलत *f.*-गलत *f.*-घालमेल *f.*-&c. करणें *g. of o.* [करणें.
2 (cards). घोळणें, घोळ *m.*-घोळंकार *m.* करणें *g. of o.* गलत *f.*
3 off; *push off.* लोटणें, ढकलून-लोटून देणें, टालमटोला *m.*-टाका *m.*-झोकाझोक *f.*-झुगारपट्टी *f.* देणें, ढाळ *m.* देणें, टोलणें.
4 up; *make or form in haste and confusion,* v. To SLUBBER. ढकलणें, गडबडविणें, लाटणें, गोफाटणें, गडबड्गुंडा *m.*-ढकल *f.*-चालढकल *f.*-लगडतगड *f.*-&c. करणें.

To SHUFFLE, *v. n. play mean tricks.* अकडंतिकडं *n.*-इधरतिधर*n.* घटंपटं *n.*-गट्टंपट्टं *n.*-गट्टेपट्टे *m. pl.*-गड्डेपड्डे *m. pl.*-हुंगेतंगें *n.*-हिंगेतिंगें *n.*-अळमटळम *n. f.*-लप्पंछप्पं *n.*-कावडदावड *f.*-छक्केपंजे *m. pl.*-चकरमकर *f.*-झुलवाझुलव *f.*-टालमटोला *m.*-&c. लावणें-मांडणें-चालवणें-करणें. [त-&c. चालणें.
2—in gait or walk. गुलपणें *or* गुलफणें, लटपट-लटपटत- गुलप-

SHUFFLE, SHUFFLING, *n.* v. V. A.—*act.* गोंधळणें *n.* ढवळणें*n.* &c.
v. V. N. 1. अकडंतिकडं *n.* इधरतिधर *n.* गट्टंपट्टं *n.* *and the other nouns under the verb.*
2 गुलपणें *n.* गुलपत चालणें *n.*

SHUFFLER, *n.* SHUFFLING, *p. a.* v. V. A. 1. गोंधळणारा, ढवळणारा, गफलतणारा, घालमेल करणारा, &c. गफलती *or* त्या.
2 घोळणारा, घोळ-&c. करणारा.
3 लोटणारा, ढकलणारा, टाळा देणारा, &c. उडाऊ, छप्पी, झोकाझोकीचा, झुगारपट्टीचा, टालमटोल्या.
v. V. N. 1. अकडंतिकडं-इधरतिधर-&c. करणारा-चालवणारा.
2 गुलपणारा, गुलपत चालणारा, &c.

To SHUN, *v. a. eschew, &c.* v. To AVOID. वर्जणें, वर्जकरणें, वगळणें, टाकणें, सोडणें, दूर *adv.* सोडणें-टाकणें, जवळ-&c. न जाणें, दूर-&c. राहणें *with* पासून *of o.* सावलीस-वाऱ्यास उभा न राहणें *or* न राहूं देणें.
2 v. To ESCAPE. चुकवणें, टाळणें.

SHUNNED, *p.* v. V. 1. वर्जलेला, वर्ज केलेला, दूर सोडलेला, &c. वर्जित, वर्जीकृत.
2 चुकवलेला, &c.

To SHUT, *v. a. close, &c.* बंद करणें, लावणें, झांकणें, ढांपणें, मिटणें, मिटवणें;—door, window shutter, &c. फळणें;—esp. the gates of a fort or village. महामूर करणें.
2 in. See To CONFINE, To SURROUND. 3 out; See To EXCLUDE. [दून टाकणें.
4 up; *block up, in, &c.* v. To OBSTRUCT. रोधणें, कोंदणें, कों-
5 up; v. To CONFINE, To IMPRISON. कोंडणें, कोंडून ठेवणें.
6 up ; *conclude, put by, &c.* अटपणें, ठेवणें, बंद करणें, गुंडाळणें, पुरा *decl.* करणें, बस करणें, समारोप *m.* करणें *g. of o.*
7 up ; (*a house, &c.*) *close the entrances to.* दारें *n. pl.* लावणें-बंद करणें-फळणें, दारफळणी *f.*-दारबंदी *f.*-दारलावणी *f.*-&c. करणें.
Shut up ! *be silent.* म्यामकर.

To SHUT, *v. n. close.* लागणें, मिटणें, बंद होणें, झांकणें, ढांपणें ;—door, shutter, &c. फळणें ;—flowers, पाकुळणें, मावळणें (in the evening), संकोच *m.* होणें *g. of s.*

SHUT, *p.* v. V. 1. बंद केलेला, लावलेला, मिटलेला, झांकलेला, &c.

SHUTTER, *n.* v. COVER. ढांपा*m.* ढांपण *n.* झडपा *m.* झडप *f. n.*
Sliding shutters (as of a shop). फडताळ *or* फडताव *n.*
Shop-room, &c. having sliding shutters. फडताळ *or* फडताळ *n.*
To shut to the shutters. फळणें.

SHUTTLE, *n.*—the weaver's instrument. धोटें*n.* बिरकांडी *f.* सूत्रयंत्र *n.* नाडिचीर *n.*
2 *shuttle cock.* चेंडू *m.*
Battle-dore and shuttle cock. चेंडूफळी *f.*

SHY, *a. fearful of near approach or familiarity, timid, coy, &c.* जवळ येण्याचा भितरा, सलगीचा भितरा, मुरका, लाजाळू, बुजट, बुजरा, बुजीर, भितरा, बिचका *or* बिचक्या, आगमनभीरु, सभाभीरु, भाषणविमुख.

To SHY, *v. n.* shrink back,—a horse. बुजणें, बिचकणें.

SHY-COCK, *n.* लाज कोंबडा *m.*

SHYNESS, *n.* v. A. जवळ येण्याचें भय *n.* सलगीचें भय *n.* लाजाळूपणा *m.* &c. सभाभीति *f.* सभाकंप *m.* उपरोध *m.*

SIBILANT, *a.*—a letter. ऊष्मा.

SICK, *a. diseased, disordered, ailing, &c.* दुखणाईत, दुखणारू, दुखणेकरी, अस्वस्थ, असमाधानी, आजारी, बिकारी, रोगी, रोगट, गदी, मांदा, काहिला, रोगान्वित, रोगग्रस्त, रोगातुर, रोगार्त्त, व्याधिग्रस्त, व्याधित, रुग्ण, सामय.
To fall s. दुखण्यास पडणें.

2—at stomach. ओकारी आलेला, वांति आलेला, वांति झालेला.
To be s. To feel s. ओकारी *f.*-वांति *f.*-&c. येणें *in. con.* कळमळणें *or* पोटांत कळमळणें *v. imp.* [त्रस्त.

3 v. DISGUSTED. कंटाळा आलेला, वीट आलेला, दिक्क, खपा,
To be s. of. ओकारी *f.*-कंटाळा *m.*-वीट *m.*-&c. येणें *in. con. with g. of o.* विटणें.

To SICKEN, *v. a. make sick.* दुखणेकरी-आजारी-&c. करणें, दुखण्यास पाडणें, दुखणें *n.*-&c. आणणें. [आणणें.

2 *make squeamish.* कळमळवणें, कळमळ *f.*-मळमळ *f.*-&c.

3 v. To DISGUST. ओकारी *f.*-कंटाळा *m.*-&c. आणणें, त्रस्त करणें.

To SICKEN, *v. n. fall sick.* दुखणें *n.* -&c. येणें-लागणें, दुखणें *n.* घेणें, दुखणेकरी-&c. होणें, दुखण्यास-दुखण्यांत पडणें.

2 *get qualmish, &c.* ओकारी *f.*-कळमळ *f.*-&c. येणें.

3 *grow disgusted.* कंटाळा *m.*-ओकारी *f.*-वीट *m.*-तिटकारा *m.*-&c. येणें *in. con.* उचाटणें, विटणें, मन *n.* विटणें *g. of s.*

4 See To LANGUISH, To DROOP.

SICKENED, *p.* v. V. A. 2. कळमळवलेला, &c.

3 कंटाळवलेला &c. विटका, त्रस्त, विरक्त.

SICKENER, *n.* SICKENING, *p. a.* v. V. A. 1. दुखणें आणणारा, दुखण्यास पाडणारा, &c. व्याधिकर.

2 कळमळ आणणारा, &c.

3 ओकारी आणणारा, कंटाळा आणणारा, &c.

v. V. N. 1. दुखणेकरी होणारा, दुखण्यास पडणारा, &c.

SICKLE, *n.*—the instrument. इळा *m.* कोयती *f.* कोयतें*n.* पायळी *f.* खराळी *f.* कोंगळी *f.* लवित्र *n.*

Denticulated s. दांतइळा*m.* दांतरेकोयती *f.*

SICKLINESS, *n.* v. V. 1. रोगीपणा *m.* &c. रुग्णता *f.*

2 रोगीपणा *m.* रोगिष्टपणा *m.* रोगाळेपणा *m.* &c.

3 रोगीपणा *m.* असात्म्य *n.* असात्म्यता *f.*

SICKLY, *a. unwell,* v. SICK. रोगी, दुखणेकरी, रोगट, रुग्ण.

To be s. रोगटणें.

2 *of weak health.* रोगी, रोग्या, रोगिष्ट,रोगेला, रोगाला,रोगाड्या, दुखाळू, किळशा, किळोशी, सदारोगी, रोगाधीन.

S. from nature or birth.जन्माचा रोगी, जन्मरोगी, पिंडरोगी.

S. person. रोगमल्ल, अठरा गुणांचा खंडोबा.

3 *insalubrious,* v. UNHEALTHY. रोगी, रोगाचा, रोगप्रचुर, रोगबहुल.

SICKLY-LOOKING, *a.* कयाहीन, उफट *or* ओफट *or* उफिट, पिकुटलेला, निस्तेज, रुग्णबदन.

SICKNESS, *n. ill state of health.* रोग *m.* रोगीपणा *m.* विकार *m.* विकृति *f.* असमाधान *n.* अस्वास्थ्य *n.* शरीरास्वास्थ्य *n.* आमय *m.* रुग्णावस्था *f.* रुग्णदशा *f.* रोगव्याप्ति *f.* रोगग्रस्तता *f.*

To feign s. दुखणें *n.* घेणें.

2—at stomach ; *nausea, qualmishness.* कळमळ *f.* मळमळ *f.* मळमळी *f.* ओकारी *f.* [व्याध *f.*

3 *a* s. v. DISORDER. रोग *m.* दुखणें *n.* आजार *m.* व्याधि *pop.*

SIDE, *n.* (of animals). बाजू *f.* कूस *f.* आंग *n.* कुक्षि *m. f.* पार्श्व *m.* पार्श्वभाग *m.* अर्धांग *n.* पक्ष *m.* कडण *f.* कडसणी *f.* बख *m. f.* बरगडी *f.* कक्ष *m.*

Pain in the s. पार्श्वशूल *m.* कुक्षिशूल *m.*

Hollow of a s. (esp. from fasting.) वासल *f.*

To lie on one a s. कानवडणें, कानवडा निजणें-पडणें-होणें.

2 *part or place on a side.* बाजू *f.* हात *m.* आंग *n.* तरफ *f.* बगल *f.* बगल *n.*

Farther or that s. पार *m.* पैलाड *f.*

From all sides. चहुंकडून.

From s. to s. आरपार.

From this s. अलीकडून *or* ऐलीकडून.

Hither or *this* s. ऐलाड *f.* ऐलतीर *n.*ऐलकांठ *m.*

Of this s. अलीकडचा *or* ऐलीकडचा *or* ला, अलीकडील *or* ऐलीकडील, ऐला.

On this s. अरता.

On, of, from, &c. *that* s. पलीकडेस *or* पैलीकडेस, परता, पड्याल, पलाड, तवार, पार, पलीकडचा *or* पैलीकडचा, पलीकडील *or* पैलीकडील, पलीकडून *or* पैलीकडून, पैलपार, पैला.

On all sides, v. AROUND. चहुंकडे, चहुंदिशांस, चहुंफेरीं, आजूबाजू, आजूबाजूस.

On both sides. दुबाजू, दुतर्फा, दुशिकडे, उभयतः, उभयत्र, ऐलपैल, अरतापरता.

On one s. एकीकडे *or* कडेस.

On one s. out of the direct road. आडबाजूस,आडकुशीस, एकोशास, एकोशीं, एकांस. [अवार.

On this s. ऐलीकडे *or* स, ऐल, अरता, अड्याल, अलाड,

On this and that s., अरतापरता, ऐलपैल.

That is on one s. आडमोरा. [*f.* धड *f.*

3 *face, part distinguished.* बाजू *f.* आंग *n.* पयलू *or* पैलू *m.*

Fair s. दर्शनी आंग *n.*

From s. to s. आरपार.

4 *verge,* v. EDGE. किनारा *m.* कांठ*m.* बाजू *f.* कुपट *n.*

5 *party, cause, &c.* पक्ष *m.* तड *f.* फळी *f.* बाजू *f.* तरफ *f.* शेलें *n.* तड *n. m.*

Minor or inferior s. गौणपक्ष *m.*

Negative s. नाहींपक्ष *m.*

Of the same s. सपक्ष.

Opposite s. प्रतिपक्ष *m.* [-धरणें *g. of o.*

To take the s. of. पक्ष *m.*-&c. धरणें *g. of o.* कड *f.* ओढणें

SIDE, *a. lateral.* बाजूचा, कडचा.

2 *indirect, devious.* आडबाजूचा, आडकुशीचा, आडवाटेचा, आडव्याहाताचा.

To SIDE, *v. n. lean to a side or party.* पक्ष *m.* धरणें, पक्षपात *m.* करणें, कैवार *m.* घेणें-धरणें.

SIDE, *a.* v. LATERAL. बाजूचा, बाजूकडचा, कडचा.

SIDE-LONG, *a.* v. LATERAL, OBLIQUE. बाजूकडचा, पार्श्विक, अनुपार्श्व, पार्श्वस्थ. [आडवें.

SIDE-LONG, *adv. laterally.* बाजूकडे, बाजूनें, बाजूवर, आडवा *decl.*

2 *on the side.* बाजूवर, कुशीवर, आडवा *decl.*

SIDE-LOOK, *n.* कटाक्ष *m.* नेत्रकटाक्ष *m.* अपांगदृष्टि *f.*

SIDE-SADDLE, *n.* बायको बसायाचा जीन *m.* जनानी जीन *m.*

SIDE-WAYS, SIDE-WISE, *adv. laterally.* बाजूकडे, बाजूनें, बाजूवर,आडवा *decl.*

SIDER, *n.* SIDING, *p. a.* v. V. पक्षधरणारा, कैवार घेणारा, &c. पक्षी, पक्षपाती, पक्षधर, पक्षोद्ग्राही.

SIDERAL, SIDEREAL, *a. of or belonging, &c. to stars.* तारांचा, ताराविषयक, तारासंबंधी, नक्षत्रविषयक, नक्षत्रसंबंधी.

2 See STARRY.

To SIDLE, *v. n. move side foremost.* बाजूनें-कसरता-&c. चालणें-जाणें, कसरत जाणें.

SIDLINGLY, *adv.* v. V. कसरता, कहाता, काकरता.

SIEGE, *n. investing a place by an army.* फौजेचा गराडा *m.*-वेढा *m.* -&c. सैन्यवेष्टन *n.*

To lay s. गराडा *m.*-&c. घालणें.

To raise s. गराडा *m.*-&c. उठविणें.

SIESTA, *n. short sleep (after eating, &c.)* v. To LIE DOWN. निद्रेचा चुटका *m.*

To take a s. वामकुक्षि *m. f.* करणें.

SIEVE, *n. utensil for sifting.* गाळणें *n.* चाळण *f.* चाळणी *f.*

2—for washing vegetables, rice, &c. v. COLANDER. रोवळा *m. dim.* रोवळी *f.*

To SIFT, *v. a. separate by a sieve, &c.* गाळणें, चाळणें, छानणें, झारणें, चाळण *f.*-चाळाचाळ *or* ळी *f.*-&c. करणें *g. of o.*

Dirt separated by sifting. गाळा *m.*

Matter to be sifted. गाळण *n.* चाळण *n.*

Price or cost of sifting. गाळणावळ *f.* चाळणावळ *f.*

2 (grain, &c. in a fan). घोळणें, वेंचणें, आसुडणें, पाखडणें, फटकणें, खिरणें, घोळण *n.*-&c. करणें *g. of o.*

I have sifted him. म्यां त्याचें खिरणें *n.* केलें.

3 fig. *investigate minutely, &c.* v. To EXAMINE. चाळणें, छानणें, घोळणें, चौकसणें, कसणें, मंथणें *or* मथणें, खोदखोदून विचारणें *or* पुसणें, खोलून खोलून विचारणें, आखुड पाखुड *f.*-छान *f.*-घोळ *m.*-कसोशी *f.*-मंथन *or* मथन *n.*-घर्षण *n.*-चौकशी *f.*-शुद्धि *f.*-&c. करणें *g. of o.*

4 (cards in hand). चाळणें.

SIFTED, *p.* v. V. 1. गाळलेला, चाळलेला &c. गाळींव, चाळणीचा.

2 घोळलेला, आसुडलेला, पाखडलेला, &c. पाखडींव.

3 चाळलेला, छानलेला, घोळलेला, &c. मंथित *or* मथित.

SIFTER, *n.* SIFTING, *p. a.* v. V. 1. गाळणारा, चाळणारा, चाळण करणारा, &c.

2 घोळणारा, आसुडणारा, पाखडणारा, &c.

3 चाळणारा, छाणणारा, &c.मंथन-&c. कर्त्ता-कारी-&c.

SIFTING, *n.* v. V. 1.—*act.* गाळणें *n.* चाळणें *n.* &c. चाळण*f.* चाळाचाळ*f.* चाळाचाळी *f.* छान *f.* छानाछान *f.*

2 घोळणें *n.* आसुडणें *n.* पाखडणें*n.* &c. घोळण *n.* पाखडणी*f.* पाखडण *n.* [चपाखड *f.*

S. and shaking in a fan—compreh. आसूड पाखड *f.* वें-

Price of s. पाखडणावळ *f.* पाखडाई *f.*

Fan or basket for s. सूप *n.*

3 चाळणें, छानणें *n.* घोळणें *n.* &c. घोळ *m.* छान *f.* छानाछान*f.* चौकशी *f.* मंथन *or* मथन *n,* घर्षण *n.*

To SIGH, *v. n. breathe deeply as in grief, &c.* उसासा *m.*-उच्छ्वास *m.*-दुःखाचा उसासा *m.*-&c. टाकणें-देणें, सुसकारणें, उसमरणें.

SIGH, *n. deep breathing.* उसासा*m.* उच्छ्वास*m.* दुःखाचा उच्छ्वास*m.* सुसकार *or* सुसकारा *m.* उसमरा *m.* सुसासा *m.*

Heavy s. हुसकारा *m. v.* टाक, सोड.

SIGHER, *n.* SIGHING, *p. a.* v. V. उसासा-&c. टाकणारा-देणारा.

SIGHT, *n.*—the sense. दृष्टि *f.* डोळे *m. pl.* नेत्र *m. pl.* चक्षुरिंद्रिय *n.* द्रष्टृत्व *n.*

Before one's s. दृष्टिदेखत *or* तां, डोळेदेखत, प्रत्यक्ष.

Charming and bewitching of the s. दृष्टिबंध *m.* दृष्टिबंधन *n.* नजरबंदी *f.*

Deception of s.—as effected by conjurors, &c. देखतभुली *f.* देखतभूल *f.*

Error of the sight, i. e. *inadvertent mistake.* नजरचूक *f.*

Error of s. i. e. *ocular illusion.* नजरभूल *f.*

Evidently to the s. of. साक्षात्, प्रत्यक्ष.

In the s. (or presence) of. देखत *or* तां, नजरेहुजूर.

Object of s. चक्षुर्विषय *m.* दृग्विषय *m.*

Of sharp or good s. प्रेक्षावान् *pop.* प्रेक्षावंत.

2—organ, v. EYE. डोळा *m.* नेत्र *n. m.* चक्षुरिंद्रिय *n.*

3 *perception, vision, view.* पाहणें *n.* दृष्टि *f.* दर्शन *n.* नजर *f.* दर्श *m.* अवलोकन *n.* ईक्षण *n.* लक्षण *n.* दिठी *f.* दीठ *f.*

At s.—in commerce. पत्रदर्शनीं.

At the very first s. सकृद्दर्शनीं.

First s. of. अपूर्वदर्शन *n.*

Knowledge (of a person) by s. तोंडओळख *f.*

To be in s. *be visible.* दिसणें, दिसून येणें, दृष्टीस पडणें.

To be in s. of, *be visible from.* दृष्टीच्या टप्प्यांत-दृष्टीच्या अटोक्यांत-दृष्टीच्या अमलांत-&c. असणें.

To be unable to bear the s. of (through envy, &c.). देखूं न सकणें *impers.* डोळे *m. pl.* फुटणें *g. of s.*

To give a s. of. देखवा *or* देखावा *m.* दाखवणें *g. of o.*

4 (of a gun, &c.). माशी *f.* मासकी *f.* मखी *f.*

5 *spectacle.* पाहण्याचा पदार्थ *m.* दृष्टिविषय *m.* दृष्टीचा खटला *m.*—esp. as novel or remarkable. कौतुक *n.* मौज *f.* तमाशा *m.*

Seeker of sights & shows. तमाशगीर.

SIGHTLESS, *a.* v. BLIND. नेत्रहीन, आंधळा, अचक्षु.

SIGHTLINESS, *n.* v. A. देखणेपणा *m.* देखणाऊपणा *m.* डोळेफोडपणा *m.* &c.

SIGHTLY, *a. pleasing to the eye, seemly, &c.* v. BEAUTIFUL. देखणा, देखणाऊ, दिसाऊ, दृष्टिभरू, डोळेफोड, दर्शनी, दर्शनीय, सुदर्शन.

SIGN, *n. symbol, indication, &c.* v. MARK. निशाणी *or* नी *f.* चिन्ह *n.* खूण *f.* लक्षण *n.* सूचक *n.*

Auspicious or good s. सुचिन्ह *n.*

Inauspicious or bad s. अपचिन्ह*n.* अवलक्षण*n.* कुलक्षण*n.*

Secret s. अंतरखूण *f.* चोरखूण *f.*

Signs of rain. पावसाचे डोहळे *m. pl.*

To shew signs. तोंड *n.* पडणें *in. con.*

2 *prodigy, portent.* उत्पात *m.* अद्भुत *n.* चमत्कार *m.*

3 (of the zodiac). राशि *m.*

4 *indicative nod or action; signal.* खूण *f.* इशारत *f.* इशारा *m.* संकेत *m.* इंगित *n.* संज्ञा *f.*

5 See SIGNATURE.

S. manual, v. SIGNATURE. स्वदस्तूर *n.* हस्ताक्षर *n.*

To SIGN, *v. a. affix one's name or mark to.* सही *f.* करणें-घालणें, दस्तूर *n.*-&c. घालणें-लावणें, दस्तखत *n.* करणें.

SIGNAL, *n.* v. SIGN. चिन्ह *n.* इशारत *f.* इशारा *m.*

SIGNAL, *a. distinguished from what is ordinary,* v. REMARKABLE. विशेष, विलक्षण, विचित्र, नामी, मोठा.

To SIGNALIZE, *v. a. render distinguished.* गाजवणें, मिरवणें,

प्रसिद्ध-&c. करणें.

2 (one's self). नाम *n.*-कीर्त्ति *f.*-&c. मिळवणें-संपादणें.

SIGNATURE, *n. sign manual; name subscribed.* सही *or* सई *f.* दस्तखत *n.* दस्तऐवज *m.* स्वदस्तूर*n.* दस्तूरखुद*n.*हस्ताक्षर*n.*स्वाक्षर*n.*

S. of the Amanuensis. बिकलम *n.* दस्तूर *n.* हस्ताक्षर *n.*

To affix one's s. v. To SIGN. सही *f.* करणें, पांढऱ्यावर कालें करणें.

SIGNET, *n.* v. SEAL. मुद्रा *f.* मुद्रिका *f.*

SIGNIFICANCE, *n.* v. MEANING. अर्थ *m.* अभिप्राय *m.* हार्द *pop.* हरद *or* हरिद्र *or* हार्द *n.*

2 *importance,* v. WEIGHT. भार *m.* भारदस्ती *f.* मुजास *f.* मुजास्ता *m.* बिशाद *or* त *with neg. con. or implic.*

SIGNIFICANT, SIGNIFICATIVE, *a. having meaning.* अर्थाचा, अर्थवान्, अर्थान्वित, आर्थिक, अर्थयुक्त, सार्थ, सार्थक, अर्थबोधक, अर्थसूचक, शक.

2 *indicative, declarative, expressive.* सूचक, संज्ञीक, अन्वर्थ, अन्वर्थक, संकेतगर्भित, सांकेतिक, हेतुगर्भ, दर्शक, प्रदर्शक, दर्शी (in comp.), लाक्षणिक, उद्बोधक.

SIGNIFICATION, *n.* v. MEANING. अर्थ *m.* अभिप्राय *m.*

Etymological s. अवयवार्थ *m.*

SIGNIFIED, *p.* v. V. 1. खूण केलेला, खुणेनें सुचवलेला, &c. संज्ञासूचित, संज्ञाज्ञापित.

To SIGNIFY, *v. a. make known by signs.* खूण *f.*-इशारत *f.*-&c. करणें *g. of o.* खुणेनें-&c. समजावणें-सुचवणें-.

2 *make known, communicate, &c.*v.To TELL, To INFORM. जाणवणें, कळवणें, सुचवणें, समजावणें, सूचना *f.*-&c. करणें *g. of o.* विदित-माहीत-&c. करणें.

3 *have a certain sense.* v. To MEAN. अर्थ *m.*-&c. असणें *g. of o. with in. con* अर्थ *m.*-&c. धरणें-दाखवणें.

4 *matter, import, have consequence.* भार *m.*-भारदस्ती *f.*-मुजास *f.*-मुजास्ता *m.*-बिशात *f.*-&c.-असणें *g. of o. with in. con.*

SILENCE, *n. forbearance of speech.* मौन *pop.* मौन्य *n.* गुपचुपी *f.* अभाषण *n.* अनालाप *m.* भाषणाभाव *m.* तूष्णीम्भाव *m.*

Dogged s. मुखस्तंभ *m.* वाक्स्तंभ *m.* मुखरोग *m.*

S. of offence or huff. अबोला *m.*

Vow (or rule) of s. वाङ्नियम *m.* मौनव्रत *m. n.*

To keep dogged or sulky s. बोद्यावतार *m.* धरणें *or* घेणें, दांतकिरकिटी *f.* देऊन बसणें, मुखस्तंभ *m.* होणें *g. of s.*

To keep s. *restrain one's speech.* गुळणी *f.* धरणें, मूग *m. pl.* खाणें-गिळणें *or* मुगांचें करणें, मौनावणें.

2 See STILLNESS.

SILENCE, *interj.* चुप *or* चप *or* चप्प !

To SILENCE, *v. a. stop the speaking of.* तोंड *n.*-बोलणें *n*-&c. बंद करणें *g. of o.* उगा-मुका-&c. करणें, चुप करणें, उगा राहवणें, तोंड *n.* मिटणें-सिटवणें, तोंडमिटणी *f.* करणें *g. of o.* कैंपरी *f.*-पुंगी *f.* बंद करणें *g. of o.* दाढ *f.* बांधणें *g. of o.* वाग्बंधन *n.*-वाग्रोध *m.*-&c. करणें *g. of o.* निरुत्तर-&c. करणें.

SILENT, *a. not speaking, mute.* मुका, उगा, मौन *pop.* मौना & मौनी, शब्दावेगळा-निराळा, अभाषी, अनालापी, तूष्णीम्भूत.

One doggedly and sulkily s. मुखरोगी, मुकामैंद.

2 *having no noise,* v. STILL. सामसुमेचा, निःशब्द.

SILENTLY, *adv.* v. A. 1. उगां, उगी, गपचीप *or* गुपचूप, चिप्प, चुप्प, निमूट, मुकाट्यां, मुकाट्यांनी *or* नें, मट्ट, मुट्ट, मटकन-कर-&c. तूष्णीम्, घम *or* घुम.

2 सामसूम.

SILK, *n.* रेशीम *n.*

Refuse s. गुदड *m.*

Roll of s. फाळा *m.*—as wound off the wheel. असार.

S.-cord. कंकरी *f.*

Spun s. काकरी *f.*

Spun s. yet raw or unboiled. कोरट *f.*

Stick of s. कळी *f.* (Four कळी form one धोक, two धोक one शेरिया).

Twisted s. मखतूल *m.*

Washed s. नखी *f.*

2 *stuff made of silk.* रेशिमाचें कापड *n.* रेशमीकापड *n.* नरमिना *m.* दुकूल *n.* पट्ट *m.* पट्टकूल *n.*—Certain *stuffs* are, एरंडें, कद, कलिंदरा, किनखाब, कोशेरें, खजूरछडी, गुलबदन, घोडेघाटी, चिकटा, चिवली, चेताबंदरेशीम, तसरांब, ताफता, पाटांऊ *or* ब, पांबरी *or* पामरी, पितांबर *or* पीतांबर, मशरू, मुगवा *or* मुगा, मुखज्जर.

SILK, *a.* रेशिमाचा, रेशमी, कौशेय.

SILK-COTTON-TREE, *n.* शेवरी *f.* सांवर *f.* सांवरी *f.*

SILK-REEL, *n.* आसारी *f.*

SILK-WEAVER, *n.* खतरी.

SILK-WORM, *n.* रेशिमाचाकिडा *m.* कोसला *m.* कोळिसरा *m.* कोशकार *m.* तनुकीट *m.*

Cord or cocoon of a s. कोसला *m.* कोळिसरा *m.*

SILKEN, *a. made &c. of silk.* रेशिमाचा, रेशमी, कौशेय.

SILKY, *a. silken.* रेशिमाचा, रेशमी, कौशेय.

2 v. SOFT. रेशमी, मऊ, मृदु.

SILL, *n.* (of a door or window) v. THRESHOLD. चौकटीची खालची बाजू *f.* शिला *f.*

SILLILY, *adv.* v. V. 1. भोळेपणानें, खुळसरपणानें, बावळेपणानें.

SILLINESS, *n.* v. A. 1. खुळकटपणा *m.* खुळसरपणा *m.* भोळेपणा *m.* बावळेपणा *m.* वावसें *n.*

SILLY, *a. weak in intellect, simple, &c.* v. FOOLISH. खुळकट, खुळसट, खुळसर, वेडसर, पचकळ, वावसा, अचरट, भोळा, भाळाभोळा, बावळा, गयाळ, गयाळी, गैरी *or* गैरा, गलतान, बेकूब, लेंचापेंचा *or* लेंचीपेंची, हीनबुद्धि, मंदबुद्धि, गरंगील.

To become s. वावसळणें.

2—action, conduct, &c. वेडेपणाचा, खुळकटपणाचा, भोळेपणाचा, &c. वेडा, वेडसर, वेडावांकडा, वावगा, पोकळ, पचकळ, फुसका, फुसकुला.

SILT, *n. deposit of mud, &c.* मळई *f.*

SILVAN, *a. pertaining, &c. to woods or groves.* बनाचा, बनासंबंधीचा, वन्य, वनस्थ, वनाश्रय, वनाश्रयी, वनेचर, आरण्यक, वान.

SILVER, *a. made of silver.* रुप्याचा, चांदीचा, रौप्य, राजत.

2 *white like silver.* रुप्याचा, रौप्यवर्ण, रौप्यसदृश.

3—tones, &c. रुप्याच्यानादासारखा खणखणीत.

SILVER, *n.*— the metal. रौप्य *pop.* रुपें *n.* रूप्य *n.* रजत *n.*

Pure s. चांदी *f.*

Plated, or washed with s. रुपेरी.

2 *coin made of silver.* रुप्याचीं नाणीं *n. pl.* रुपये *m. pl.*

To SILVER, *v. a. cover with a coating of silver.* रुप्याचेंपाणी *n.* देणें, रुप्याचा मुलामा *m.* देणें-करणें.

SILVERLING, *n. silver coin.* रुप्याचें नाणें *n.* रौप्यमुद्रा *f.*

SILVERSMITH, *n.* v. GOLDSMITH. रौप्यकार.

SILVERY, *a. white like silver.* रुप्याचा, रौप्यवर्ण, रौप्यसदृश.

SIMILAR, *a.* v. LIKE. सारखा, बराबर, तुल्य, सम, समान, सदृश.

SIMILARITY, *n.* v. A. *and* LIKENESS. सारखेपणा *m.* सारखवटा *m.* सारखवट *n. f.* बरावरी *f.* सादृश्य *n.* तुल्यता *f.* समता *f.* साम्य *n.* औपम्य *n.*

SIMILARLY, *adv. in like manner.* तसाच *decl.* त्याचप्रमाणें, त्यासारखा *decl.* तद्वत्. [त्प्रेक्षा *f.*

SIMILE, *n.* v. ILLUSTRATION. दाखला *m.* दृष्टांत *m.* उपमा *f.* उ-

SIMILITUDE, *n.* v. LIKENESS. सारखेपणा *m.* सादृश्य *n.* तुल्यता *f.* समता *f.* साम्य *n.* औपम्य *n.*

2 *form, appearance,* v. LIKENESS. आकार *m.* रूप *n.*

3 See SIMILE. [सणसणणें, वाजणें.

To SIMMER, *v. n. boil with gentle hissing.* चरचरणें, चटचटणें,

SIMMERING, *n.* चरचरणें *n.* सणसणणें *n.* &c. सणसण *f.*

To SIMPER, *v. n. smile in a silly manner,* v. To SMILE. गालांत-गालावर हासणें. [निःशब्दहास्य *n.*

SIMPER, SIMPERING, *n.* v. V. गालांत हासणें *n.* &c. अनर्थक नि-

SIMPERER, *n.* SIMPERING, *p. a.* v. V. गालांत हासणारा, अनर्थकनिःशब्दहास्यकर्त्ता.

SIMPLE, *a. not compound; uncombined with anything.* शुद्ध, निर्मळ, निखालस, केवल *or* केवळ, निर्दम, निरवयव.

2 *plain, artless, guileless.* भोळा (*remiss.* भोळसर, भोळवट *simplish*), मनाचा भोळा, भावार्थी, भोळा भावार्थी, सालस, सावळा *or* सांवडा, भाचडा, साबडा भावडा, साधा, उमा, अजाणता, निवळ, बाळबोध *or* बाळबद, ऋजू *pop.* उजू, साळसूद *or* ध, साळढाळ, साळाभोळा, भाळाभोळा, निष्कपट, अकपट, निष्कृत्रिम, अकृत्रिम, शुद्धमति, निष्प्रपंच, अमायी, अमायिक, अमाय.

3 *not subtil, abstruse, involved, &c.* v. EASY, PLAIN. बाळबोध *or* बाळबद, सरल *or* सरळ, सुरळीत, साधा, उजू, साळाभोळा.

4 *mere, bare.* शुद्ध, केवल *or* केवळ, नुस्ता *or* निस्ता, साधा.

SIMPLE, *n. herb, &c.* बुटी *f.* वनस्पति *f.* औषधि *f.*

Simples,—compreh. झाडपाला *m.* जडीबुटी *f.*

SIMPLE-MINDED, *a.* v. SIMPLE. भोळा, मनाचा भोळा, भोळाभावार्थी, मनाचा कोवळा.

SIMPLE-MINDEDNESS, *n.* v. A. भोळेपणा *m.* मनाचा भोळेपणा *m.* भोळाभाव *m.* भोळाभावार्थ *m.*

SIMPLETON, *n.* v. FOOL. भोळानाथ *m.* भोळाशंकर *m.* भोळासांब *m.* सांब *m.* शंभु *m.*

SIMPLICITY, SIMPLENESS, *n.* v. A. 1. शुद्धपणा *m.* निखालसपणा *m.* निर्मळपणा *m.* &c. अमिश्रभाव *m.* केवलत्व *n.*

2 भोळेपणा *m.* मनाचा भोळेपणा *m.* साबळेपणा *m.* साधेपणा *m.* साळसूदपणा *m.* &c. भोळाभाव *m.* सालसाई *f.* सालशी *f.* साळसुदकी *f.* भावार्थ *m.* अकपट *n.* अमाया *f.* कपटाभाव *m.* कपटराहित्य *n.* अकापट्य *n.* निष्कापट्य *n.* अनन्यभाव *m.* भोळीव *f.*

Good luck to s. May s. prosper ! भोळाभाव सिद्धीस जाव.

3 बाळबोधपणा *m.* सरळपणा *m.* सुरळितपणा *m.* &c. सारल्य *n.* सरलता *f.* [त-&c. करणें.

To SIMPLIFY, *v. a. make plain or easy.* सोपा-साधा-सरळ-सुरळी-

SIMPLY, *adv.* v. A. 1. निखळ *or* निखळ, निखालस, निसळ, निस्तूक, निरंक.

4 एरवीं, सहज, सहजासाळीं, सहजगतीनें, सहजगत्या, सहजरीतीनें, सहजरीत्या, स्वाभाविक *pop.* सभावीक, फक्त, साहजिक.

To SIMULATE, *v. a. assume the appearance of,* v. To FEIGN, To PRETEND. डौल *m.* घालणें-धरणें *g. of o.* सोंग *n.*-गतक *n.*-रूप *n.*-&c. घेणें *g. of o.* [बरपंकाचा.

SIMULATED, *p.* v. V. डौल घातलेला, &c. बरकरणी, बरघडीचा,

SIMULATION, *n.* v. V. डौल घालणें *n.* सोंग घेणें *n.* &c. अपदेश *m.* व्याज *m.*

SIMULTANEITY, SIMULTANEOUSNESS, *n.* v. V. एककालिकता *f.* समकालिकता *f.* कालैक्य *n.* एककालता *f.* एकसमयता *f.* यौगपद्य *n.* युगपद्भाव *m.*

SIMULTANEOUS, *a. existing or happening at the same time.* एकेवेळचा, एकेकाळचा, एककालिक, एककालीन, एकसमय, समकालिक, कालैक्यविशिष्ट.

SIMULTANEOUSLY, *adv.* v. A. एकेवेळेस, एकेसमयास, खेपेसरसा, खेपेनें, एकसमयावच्छेदेंकरून, युगपत्.

SIN, *n.* पाप *n.* पातक *n.* दोष *m.* अघ *n.* शमल *n.* अशुभ *n.* कल्मष *n.* किल्मिष *n.* दुरित *n.* कलुष *n.*

S. is sweet in the beginning, but bitter in the end. पातक आगमीं गोड निर्गमीं कडू.

Sold under s. Slave of s. पापाधीन, पापवश.

Whose s. is put away. निर्धूतपाप, धूतपाप, धूतकल्मष.

2 *a s. a bad action,* v. CRIME. कुकर्म *n.* पापकर्म *n.* अकर्म *n.* दुष्कर्म *n.* पाप *n.* पातक *n.* दुष्कृत *n.* दुष्कृति *f.* Sins of the first order are five(पंच महापातकें *n. pl.*) viz. ब्रह्महत्या (killing a Bráhman), सुवर्णस्तेय (stealing gold), सुरापान (drinking spirits), गुरुतल्पगमन (adultery with the wife of a spiritual teacher), and तत्संसर्ग (association with a person guilty of any of the above).

Awful s. अघोरपातक *n.* अघोरपाप *n.*

Freed from s. पापमुक्त. [क *n.* अनुपातक *n.*

Heinous or flagrant s. महापातक *n.* महापाप *n.* अतिपात-

Secret sins. प्रच्छन्नपातकें *n. pl.* गुप्तपातकें *n. pl.*

To SIN, *v. n.* पाप *n.*-पातक *n.*-पापकर्म *n.*-दुष्कृत *n.*-&c. करणें.

SIN-DESTROYING, *a.* पापनाशी, पापनाशक, पापघ्न.

SINCE, *prep. or adv. after, from the time that.* पासून, पाठीवरून, धरून, अलीकडे *or* ऐलीकडे, अलीकडून *or* ऐलीकडून, अनंतर, नंतर.

2 *ago, past, before this.* मागें, झाला, गेला, (as एकमहिना झाला a month since, दोन दिवस झाले).

SINCE, *conj. because that, seeing that.* जेव्हां, ज्यापक्षीं *pop.* ज्यापेक्षां, ज्याअर्थी, ज्यासाठीं.

SINCERE, *a. unfeigning, guileless,* v. HONEST, SIMPLE. खरा, निष्कपट, अकपट, निष्कृत्रिम, अकृत्रिम, सात्विक, प्रांजल, अमायी, अमायिक, अमाय, निष्प्रपंच, मनाचा मोकळा, ऋजु *pop.* उजू, भावार्थी, सत्यव्रत, हृद्य.

2 *unfeigned, real, heartfelt, &c.* v. TRUE. खरा, खराखुरा, वास्तविक, अकृत्रिम, निष्कपट, पोटांतला, मनापासूनचा, जिव्हाळ्याचा, नाभिकमळापासूनचा, जिवाभावाचा, आस्थेचा, अंतर्यामीचा, अंतर्यामी, आंतड्याच्यापिळाचा, बेंबीच्या देंठाचा.

SINCERELY, *adv.* v. A. निष्कपटपणानें, कपटावांचून, कपटसोडून, &c. मनापासून, मनोभावें *or* मनोभावेंकरून, जिवाभावानें, पोटांतून, अंतर्यामापासून, बेंबीच्या देंठापासून, नाभिकमळापासून, मनःपूर्वक, जीवादारभ्य.

SINCERITY, SINCERENESS, v. A. 1. खरेपणा *m.* निष्कपटपणा *m.*

निष्कृत्रिमपणा *m.* &c. निष्कापट्य *n.* अकापट्य *n.* &c. भावार्थ *m.* अकपट *n.* आर्जव *n.* ऋजुभाव *m.* सरलभाव *m.* अनन्यभाव *m.*
2 खरेपणा *m.* वास्तविकपणा *m.* निष्कपटपणा *m.* &c. सत्यता *f.* निष्कृत्रिमता *f.* &c.

SINCIPUT, *n. fore part of the head.* टोकी *f.* टवळी *f.* कपाल *pop.* कपाळ *n.* तालु *pop.* टाळू *f.* कंवटी *f.* मस्तकाग्रभाग *m.*

SINE, *n.*—in geometry. ज्या *f.*
S. of an arc. भुजज्या *f.*
Versed s. इषु *m. f.*

SINECURE, *n. office with pay without work.* बैठारोजगार *m.* बैठीअसामी *f.* बैठीचाकरी *f.* बैठेंवेतन *n.*
Stipend of a s. बैठापगार *m.*

SINEW, *n. tendon.* नस *m.* स्नायु *n.m.* रग *f.* स्नायुश्वेतांश *m.* स्नाव *m.*
2 sinews ; *strength.* बल *or* बळ *n.* मुख्यसाधन *n.*

SINEWY, *a. consisting of a sinew.* स्नायूचा, स्नायुमय.
2 See STRONG.

SINFUL, *a. tainted with sin,* v. WICKED. पापी, पापिष्ठ, पातकी, पापकर्त्ता, पापकर्मा *pop.* पापकर्मी, पापकर, पापात्मक, पापपरायण, दुरित.
2 *containing sin, contrary to right,* v. WICKED. पापाचा, दुष्कर्माचा, अधर्माचा, &c. प्रत्यवायी.

SINFULLY, *adv.* v. A. पापानें, पापकरून, पापबुद्धीनें.

SINFULNESS, *n.* v. A. *and* SIN. पापीपणा *m.* पापिष्ठपणा *m.* &c. पापबुद्धि *f.*
2 वाईट *n.* दुष्टपणा *m.* वाईटपणा *m.* प्रत्यवाय *m.*

To SING, *v. a. utter with musical modulations.* गाणें, गाऊन म्हणणें, स्वरावर-चालीवर-&c. म्हणणें-वाचणें. [र्त्तणें.
2 fig. v. To PRAISE. गाणें, वर्णणें *pop.* वाणणें, वाखाणणें, की-

To SING, *v. n.* गाणें, गाणें *n.*-गायन *n.*-गान *n.*-तनरी *f.*-तननं *n.* करणें,—in a hoarse or cracked voice, रेंकणें,—badly ; *to screech, squall, scream, &c.* गद्धेमल्हार *m.*-कुत्तेमल्हार *m.*-दळूबाईदळू *n.*-चकरतान *f.*-रंडागीत *n.* करणें, तारे तुटतान असें गाणें.
To s. like an old cow. रेंकणें.
To s. out. गळ्यावर मारणें.
To s. second with. स्वर *m.* देणें, सूर *m.* धरणें.
2—a bee, top, &c. गुंगणें, गोंगणें, गोंगावणें, चुचावणें, भिरभिरणें, रुणरुणणें, चूं *adv.* -घूं *adv.* करणें, सणका *m.* (*intens.* सणसणाट *m.* सणाणा *m.*) करणें.
3—in boiling. सणसणणें *intens.* सणाणणें, चरचरणें, चटचटणें.

SING-SONG, *n. bad singing.* v. To SING. गद्धेमल्हार *m.*

To SINGE, *v. a. burn superficially, scorch.* बाहेरून-वरवर-&c. जाळणें, भाजणें, डुरडणें, डुरपळणें, डुरफळणें, होळपणें.

SINGED, *p.* v. V. बाहेरून जाळलेला, भाजलेला, जळका, भाजका, पोळींव, माजींव.
To be singed. पोळणें, जळगणें, शेकावणें, डुरडणें, डुरपळणें, डुरफळणें, होळपणें, अग्निस्पर्श *m.* होणें *in. con.*

SINGER, *n.* SINGING, *p. a.* v. V. N. 1. गाणारा, गाणेवाला, गवई *or* गवयी, गायक, गायनी, कवाल, उद्गाना.—in contempt, दळ्या.
Public s. गवय्या *m.*
S. in second. सूरकरी.
Sweet s. गोडगळ्याचा.
3 सणसणणारा, &c. सणसणीत.

SINGLE, *a. not double.* एकेरा, एकेरी, एकपदरी.
2 *sole, alone, one.* एक, एकटा, एकला, एकुलता, एकुलताएक, एकएकटा, एकएकला, एकाकी, एकवुरा, एकवडा, असंग, निस्संग, असहाय.
A person quite solitary or s. एकटा *or* एकला टिकोजी.
3 *individual,* See PARTICULAR.
4 *unmarried,* v. BACHELOR, SPINSTER. अवरठा, अविवाहित (-ता *f.*). अनूढ (-ढा *f.*).
5 *unembarrassed with family or wife.* सडा, सडासांटा *or* सडेसांट *or* सडासोट, निस्संग.
6 *uncompounded,* v. SIMPLE. शुद्ध, निर्भेल. [काढणें.

To SINGLE, *v. a. select.* निवडणें, निवडून घेणें, ओळखून निवडणें-

SINGLE-EYED, *a. one eyed.* एकाक्ष.
2 *having one object or aim.* एकरोंखी, एकलक्षी.

SINGLE-COMBAT, SINGLE-FIGHT, *n.* द्वंद्वयुद्ध *n.*

SINGLE-HANDED, *a. without assistance.* एकटा, एकाकी, असहाय, स्वबाहुसहाय, दोस्सहाय.

SINGLE-HEARTED, SINGLE-MINDED, *a.* v. SIMPLE. एकनिष्ठ, एकचित्त, एकरोंखी, एकाकार, अनन्यवृत्ति, एकानुसंधानी.

SINGLE-HEARTEDNESS, SINGLE-MINDEDNESS, *n.* v. A. एकनिष्ठा *f.* अनन्यभाव *m.* अनन्यनिष्ठा *f.* अनन्यवृत्ति *f.*

SINGLE-SIDED, *a.*—chintzes, silks, &c. एकांगी, एकरोंखी.

SINGLE-STICK, *n.*—the play. दांडपट्टा *m.* दांडपट्ट्याचा खेळ *m.* द्विदंडि *adv.* युद्ध *n.*-खेळ *m.*-खेळणें *n.* द्विदंडिप्रहरण *n.* द्विमुसलिप्रहरण *n.*

SINGLENESS, *n.* v. A. 1. एकेरेपणा *m.* एकेरीपणा *m.* &c.
2 एकटेपणा *m.* एकलेपणा *m.* एकाकीपणा *m.*
4 *and* CELIBACY. अवरठेपणा *m.* अविवाहितत्व *n.* अनूढता *f.*

SINGLY, *adv.* v. A. 1. एकेरा *decl.* एकपदरी. [असहाय.
2 एकटा *decl.* एकला *decl.* &c. मदतीवांचून, सहायावांचून, &c.
3 *and* SEVERALLY, एकएक, आंगोगडी.

SINGULAR, *a. sole,* v. SINGLE. एक, एकटा, एकाकी.
2 *existing by itself, unexampled, &c.* अद्वितीय, असदृश, अप्रमित, अनुपम, अपूर्व, एकमात्र, अनन्यसाधारण.
3 *particular, not customary, common, &c.* v. STRANGE. विलक्षण, एकप्रकार, एकप्रकारचा, एकतऱ्हेचा, एकाड, नवल, निराळा, तऱ्हेचा, तऱ्हेदार, तऱ्हेवाईक, असाधारण, अनन्यसाधारण, विजातीय, विशेष, लोकबाह्य, लोकोत्तर, स्वप्रत्यय.
4—in grammar. एकवचन *n.*
Language (address or mention) in the s. number. एकेरा शब्द *m.*

SINGULARITY, *n.* v. A. 1. एकटेपणा *m.* &c [रणता *f.*
2 अद्वितीयता *f.* असदृशता *f.* अप्रमितता *f.* &c. अनन्यसाधा-
3 विलक्षणपणा *m.* एकाडपणा *m.* निराळेपणा *m.* असाधारणता *f.* &c.

SINGULARLY, *adv.* v. A. 3. विलक्षण, &c. विशेषेंकरून, विशेषतः.

SINISTER, *a.* See LEFT. 2 *evil, dishonest, crooked, &c.* वांकडा, कपटाचा, कापट्याचा, वक्र, असरल, अनृजु.
3 *inauspicious.* अशुभ, अभद्र, अमंगल. [मवर्त्ती.

SINISTRAL, SINISTROUS, *a. being on the left.* वामस्थ, वा-

To SINK, *v. n.* (in water, &c.). बुडणें, डुबणें, बसणें, खालीं बसणें, निमज्जन *n.*-&c. होणें *g. of s.*
2 (as into mud, &c.). रुतणें, रुपणें, आंत जाणें, गडणें.
3 *soak into.* जिरणें, जिरून जाणें, मुरणें, मुरून जाणें, भिनणें,

भिनरणें or भिनारणें.

4 *lose prominence or height, fall in.* बसणें, सचणें, रेवणें, निचावणें, दबणें, बिसवणें.

5—the eyes, &c. *become deep.* खोल जाणें, आंत जाणें, खोलगटणें, खोलटणें, पोंडळणें. [उपतिष्ठणें.

6 (into the mind). ठसणें, बिंबणें, भिनणें, मरणें, बितणें,

7 *decrease, deteriorate,* v. To DECLINE. उतरणें, गळणें, खालावणें, घसरणें, अवतार *m.* होणें-संपणें *g. of s.* परडें *n.* उतरणें-बसणें *g. of s.*

8—spirits, &c. v. To FAIL. सचणें, गळणें, थकणें, बसणें.

9—money, &c. *go, be lost.* बुडणें, थकणें, डुलणें, निजणें, फसणें, जिरणें, मुरणें, मरणें.

To SINK, *v. a. cause to sink.* बुडवणें, डुबवणें. [करणें.

2 (money, &c.) *lose, dissipate.* बुडवणें, फसवणें, गरक-&c.

3 (a well, &c.) खणणें.

SINK, *n. drain, sewer.* नाला *m.* मोरी *f.*

SINLESS, *a.* पापानिराळा-वेगळा, निष्पाप, अपाप, पापहीन-रहित-&c. निष्कल्मष.

SINLESSNESS, *n.* v. A. निष्पापता *f.* पापराहित्य *n.* पापशून्यता *f.* पापाभाव *m.* [कर्मी.

SINNER, *n.* v. SINFUL. पापीमनुष्य *pop.* पापी माणूस, कुकर्मी, अ-

Some terms for *an atrocious sinner* are, पापमूर्त्ति, पापराशि, पापात्मा, पापस्वरूप, पापनिधि, पापपुरुष.

SINUOUS, *a.* v. WINDING. बांकाचा, नागमोडी.

SINUS, *n. fistulous sore.* नाडी *f.* नाडीव्रण *n.* गति *f.*

To SIP, *v. a. drink in small quantities by the lips.* ओंठांनीं-थोडाथोडा *decl.*-अल्पअल्प-&c. पिणें, चाखतचाखत पिणें, घोंट *m.* -भुरका *m.* घेणें *g. of o.* ईषत्पान *n.* करणें *g. of o.*

Sipping of water before or after meals, &c. आपोशन *n.* आचमन *n.*

2 (with a flurruping noise) ओरपणें.

SIP, SIPPING, *n.* v. V.—*act.* ओंठांनीं पिणें *n.* थोडाथोडा पिणें *n.* &c. ईषत्पान *n.*

2 *small draught taken with the lips.* घोंट *m.* भुरका *m.* झुरका *m.*

SIR, *n.*—the word of respect. जी, महाराज, साहेब, खुदावंत.

SIRE, *n.*—the word of address to a king. महाराज *or* महाराजा.

2 v. FATHER. बाप *m.* जनक *m.*

SIREN, *n. an enticing woman,* v. BEAUTY. मोहणारी स्त्री, मोहिनी *f.* चाळकभवानी *f.*

SIRIUS, *n. dog-star.* लुब्धक *m.* व्याध *m.*

SIRNAME. See SURNAME.

SIRRAH,—the contemptuous term of address. अरे, रे, बेट्या, मसण्या, माणसाच्या लेंका, माणसाच्या कांद्या.

SIRUP, *n. sweet-juice of fruits, &c.* शिरा *m.* पाक *m.* पंक *m.*

To prepare with s. पांकणें.

SISTER, *n.* बहीण *f.* भगिनी *f.* स्वसा *f.*

Elder s. अग्रजा *f.*

S.'s daughter. स्वस्त्रीया *or* स्वस्त्रेया *f.* [श्याल *m.*

S.'s husband. मेहुणा *m.* साला *m.* शालक *m.* श्यालक *m.*

S.'s son. स्वस्त्रीय *or* स्वस्त्रेय *m.*

Younger s. अवरजा *f.*

SISTER-IN-LAW, *n. wife's sister.* मेहुणी *f.* जायाभगिनी *f.*

2 *husband's sister.* नणंद *f.* वनसें *or* वेनसें *n. pl. or* वनसा *f. pl.* नणदुली *or* नणदोली *f.*

3 *brother's wife.* भावजई *f.* भ्रातृजाया *f.*

SISTERHOOD, *n. state, office, &c. of a sister.* बहीणपण *n.* बहीणपणा *m.* भगिनीत्व *n.*

2 *community of women.* स्त्रीमंडळी *f.* स्त्रीसमाज *m.* स्त्रीगण *m.*

SISTERLY, *a.* बहिणीचा, बहिणीलायक, बहिणीसारखा, भगिनीयोग्य.

To SIT, *v. n.* बसणें, बैठक *f.*-बसक *f.* मारणें-घेणें, उपवेश *m.*-उपवेशन *n.*-&c. करणें, उपविष्ट-आसित-&c. होणें.—in cant phraseol. बूड *m. n.* टेंकणें.

Leisure or opportunity to sit. बसकल *f. n.*

To s. down in despair. बसकण *f.* मारणें-घेणें.

To s. loosely and roomily. गोठण *f. n.* घालून बसणें, तरंगण *f.* मारून बसणें.

To s. moaning and fretting. चुरमुरत बसणें, चुरमुरे *m. pl.* खातबसणें-देतबसणें.

2 *lie, rest, press upon.* बसणें.

3 *be idle or unemployed.* बसणें.

4 *incubate,* v. To BROOD. बसणें, पाखर *f.* घालणें.

5—an assembly, &c. बसणें, बैठक *f.*-बसणी *f.*-&c. होणें-असणें *g. of s.*

6 down. बसणें, खालीं बसणें.

7 up; *rise from a recumbent posture.* उठून बसणें.

8 up; *not to go to bed.* बसणें, जागणें, जागत बसणें, जागरण *n.* करणें.

SITE, *n. local position,* v. PLACE. स्थान *n.* स्थल *n.* ठाण *n.* पद *n.*

Purification of a s. for buildings, sacrifice, &c. तळझाडा *m.* स्थलशुद्धि *f.*

S. of a ruined house. घरटा *m.* घरटण *n.* घरटणा *m.*

SITTER, *n.* SITTING, *p. a.* v. V. 1. बसणारा, बसलेला, &c. आसीन, उपविष्ट. [न *n.*

SITTING, *n.* v. V. 1. बसणें *n.* बैठक *f.* बसक *f.* उपवेश *m.* उपवेस-

5 बसणें *n.* बैठक *f.* बसणी *f.*

At one s. एकाबसणीं, एका बसणीस, एका बैठकीस.

SITUATE, SITUATED, *a. placed with respect to any other object.* बसवलेला, बसलेला, स्थित, अवस्थित, स्थानस्थित, स्थानापन्न.

2 *being in any state with regard to men or things.* अवस्थेचा, &c. अवस्थापन्न, अवस्थाप्राप्त, अवस्थ in comp.

To be s. अवस्था *f.*-&c. असणें *g. of s.*

SITUATION, *n. local respect,* v. PLACE. जागा *f.* स्थान *n.* स्थिति *pop.* स्थीत *f.* अवस्थान *n.* अवस्थिति *f.* पद *n.*

2 *state,* v. CONDITION. अवस्था *f.* दशा *f.* [स्थळ *n.*

3 *place, appointment,* v. POST. जागा *f.* असामी *f.* स्थल *or*

SIX, *a.* सहा, षट् in comp. षड् in comp. [टूक.

Aggregate of s. छकडी *f.* छक्का *m.* सकडा *m.* सक *m. n.* ष-

Sixes and sevens. तेराबारा. (literally thirteen & twelve).

2 (on a dice &c.) सक *or* सख *m.*

SIX-FINGERED, *a.* सहाबोट्या, षडंगुल.

SIX-FOLD, *a.* सहापट, षड्गुण, षट्क.

SIX-FOOTED, *a.* सहापायांचा, सहापायी, षट्पद.

SIX-SIDED, *a.* सहापैलू, षडानन.

SIX-TOED, *a.* सहाबोट्या, षडंगुल.

SIXTEEN, *a.* सोळा, षोडश.

Aggregate or body of s. सोळकी *f.*

Consisting of s. (*payli*, maunds, candies, &c.). सोळुला.

SIXTEENTH, *a.* सोळावा.

SIXTH, *a.* सहावा.

SIXTIETH, *a.* साठावा.

SIXTY, *a.* साठ, षष्टि.—one, एकसष्ट, एकसट;—two, बासष्ट, बासट,—three, त्रेसष्ट, त्रेसट *or* तिरेसट;—four, चौसष्ट, चौसट;—five, पांसष्ट, पांसट;—six, सहासष्ट, सहासट;—seven, सतसष्ट, सतसट;—eight, अडसष्ट,अडसट;—nine, एकुणहत्तर,एकुणसत्तर.

Age of s. साठी *f.*

Aggregate of s. साठी *f.*

SIZE, *n. bulk, magnitude.* आकारमान *n.* आकृतिमान *n.* महत्त्वमान *n.* परिमाण *n.* मान *n.* आकार *m.* आकृति *f.* लांबीरुंदी *f.*

Disparity or ineqality of s.लाहनवीथोरवी*f.*लाहनीथोरी*f.*

2 *glue, paste.* चिकटवण *n.* डकवण *n.* चिकटा*m.*सरस*m.* खळ *f.*

To SIZE, *v. a. arrange according to size.* लाहानमोठेपणा *m.*-लाहनवीथोरवी *f.*-&c. पाहून रचणें-योजणें-मांडणें-&c.

2 *glue, paste.* चिकटवणें, खळणें.

SIZED, *a. having a particular magnitude.* आकाराचा, आकृतीचा.

SIZY. See VISCOUS. [परी *f.* मुठा *m.*

SKAIN, SKEIN, *n. hank (of thread, &c.).* कुकडें *n.* पाष्ट *n.* कोंS. doubled up. मुठ्ठा *m.*

SKELETON, *n. connected bones of an animal without the flesh.* हाडांचा पिंजरा *m.* पंजर *m.* अस्थिपंजर *m.* हाडगात *n.* सांपळा*m.*

Reduced to a s. त्वगस्थिमात्रशेष.

To become or be a mere s. सांपळा*m.* बळणें-राहणें *g. of s.*

2 fig. *compages, case,* v. FRAME. सांगाडा *m.* सांकाटा *m.* खटारा *m.*

To SKETCH, *v. a. trace the outline of,* v. To DELINEATE. अंकणें, उतरणें, काढणें, बेत*m.*-नकाशा*m.*-&c. काढणें-करणें*g.of o.*

SKETCH, SKETCHING, *n.* v.V.—*act.*अंकणें*n.*&c.अंकणी*f.*अंकन*n.*

I. *outline, general delineation.* नकशा *m.* नकाशा *m.* चित्र *n.* बेत *m.* बेतबात *m.*

Rough s. अराखडा *m.* मसुदा *m.* खाका *m.*

SKEWER, *n. wooden or iron pin.* सळई *f.* शलाका *f.*

SKIFF, *n. small boat,* v. VESSEL. लहानहोडी *f.* डिंगी *f.*

SKILFUL, SKILLED, *a.* v. CLEVER, KNOWING. कुशल, कसबी, हुशार, चतुर, सुगर, सुघड, सराईत, हुनरी, हिकमती *or* त्या, तरबेत *or* द, कलावंत, करामती, बिचक्षण, खबरदार, जाणसळ *or* जाणसाळ, कौशल्यशाली, प्रवीण, निपुण, कृतकर्मा, परिज्ञाता, अभिज्ञ. [*or* जाणसाळणें.

To be s. through conversancy or practice. जाणसळणें

SKILFULLY, *adv.* v. A. कुशलपणानें, चातुर्यानें, कौशल्यानें, सुगराईनें, युक्तीनें, &c. युक्तिवता, युक्त्या, कौशल्यपूर्वक.

SKILFULNESS, SKILLEDNESS, *n.* v. A. कुशलपणा *m.* चतुरपणा*m.* सुगरपणा *m.* &c. चातुर्य *n.* सुगराई *f.* जाणसळ *or* जाणसाळ *f.* दक्षता *f.* वैचक्षण्य *n.* नैपुण्य *n.* प्रवीणता *f.* प्रावीण्य *n.*

SKILL, *n. familiar knowledge with dexterity.* युक्ति *f.* युगूत *f.* हिकमत *f.* कला *or* कळा *f.* कळाकुशलता *f.* कलाकौशल्य *n.* कसरत *f.* चातुर्य *n.* कौशल *n.* कौशल्य *n.* कसबदारी *f.* कसब *n.* कारिगिरी *f.* कुसरी *f.* कर्त्तब *n.* कर्त्तबदारी *f.* बस्तादगिरी *f.* बस्तादी*f.* हुनर *m.f.* कडासणी *f.* छाप *m.* छापी *f.*

SKILLET, *n. vessel with a handle for heating in.* थावर *m.*

To SKIM, *v. a. clear off from the surface.* झान्यानें-&c. काढणें, छाटणें, झाडणें, काढणें, छाटून काढणें, छाटणी *f.*-&c. करणें*g. of o.*

2 *take off the scum from.* मळई *f.*-मळी *f.*-साय *f.*-&c. काढणें-छाटणें *g. of o.*

A basket or bowl for skimming sugarcane juice, &c. झारांवा *m.* झारें *n.*

3 *pass near the surface, glide along the surface of.* सरपटणें, सरपटत-सरसून-&c. जाणें *with* वरून *of o.*

To SKIM, *v. n. glide along.* सरपटणें, सरकटणें, सरपटत-सरकटत जाणें-चालणें, सरसून *prep.* जाणें-चालणें, धारबा धरून जाणें-चालणें, सुळकण-सुळदिशी-&c. जाणें-चालणें.

2 over; *read or attend to superficially.* सरासरी-वरवर-उपराउपर-&c. पाहणें, चालतांचालतां-अवझडतां-येरझडतां-&c. पाहणें.

SKIMMER, *n. utensil to skim with.* झारा *m.* शिबें *n.*

SKIM-MILK, *n.* साय काढलेलें दूध *n.*

SKIMMINGLY, *adv.* v. V. N. 1. सरपट्यां, भुईसरपट *or* टां.

2 वरवर, वरवरतां *or* तीं, सरासरी, उपराउपर.

SKIMMINGS, *n. matter skimmed.* साय *f.*

SKIN, *n. the natural covering of animals.* कातडी *f.* त्वचा *f.* चामडें *n.* चामडी *f.* चमडी *f.* चर्म *n.*—as enveloping the body, सालटी *f.* सालटें *n.* कातडी *f.* साल *f.*—as rubbed or peeled off. साल *f. n.* सालटी *or* डी *f.*

A hanging strip of s. सातडें *n.*

Insensibility of s. *tactus imminutus.* सुनबहिरी *f.* बहिरीव्यथा *f.* त्वक्शून्यवात *m.*

True s. अंतरसाल *f.* बसा *f.*

To save one's s. *to save one's bacon.* धड *or* धडे गांडीनें निघणें-सुटणें-पार पडणें-&c.

2 *pelt,* v. HIDE. कातडें *or* कातडें*n.* चरसा *m.*आधोड *f.*सातडें*n.*

3 v. HUSK. सालपट *n.* टरफल *n.* छिलका*m.* छिलटा *m.*

4 (as of kernels, certain fruits, &c.). कोरोटा *m.* कोशेरा *m.*

To SKIN, *v. a. flay.* कातडें *n.*-त्वचा *f.*-साल *f.*-&c. काढणें *g. of o.* सोलणें, छिलणें.

To SKIN, *v. n.*—a wound. कातडी *f.* धरणें.

SKIN-DEEP, *a.* v. SUPERFICIAL. वरवरचा, वरकमी.

SKIN-FLINT, *n.* v. MISER. कवडीचुंबक, मखीचूस.

SKINNED, *p.*v. V. कातडें काढलेला, सोललेला, &c. सोलींव, निस्त्वच.

SKINNY, *a.* v. LEAN. सडपातळ, सडसडीत, चर्ममात्रावशेष.

To SKIP, *v. n. leap, spring, &c.* टिपण *n.* टाकणें, ठिकणें, कुदणें, उडतउडत *adv.* जाणें-चालणें, प्लुति *f.*-प्लुतगति *f.*-&c. करणें.

2 *caper about,* v. To FRISK. उडणें, नाचणें, नाचणें उडणें, नाचूंउडूं लागणें, खिदडणें, खिदळणें, उडी *f.* मारणें, खिदड्डा *m.* घालणें, बागडणें.

3 over; v. To OMIT. बगळणें, गाळणें.

To SKIP, *v. a. pass over, miss, omit.* सोडणें, अंतरणें, बगळणें, गाळणें, उल्लंघणें.

SKIP, SKIPPING, *n.* v. V. N. 1. टिकणें *n.* कुदणें *n.* &c. प्लुति *f.* प्लुतगति *f.* प्लुतगमन *n.* मंडूकप्लुति *f.* मंडूकगति *f.*

2 उडणें *n.* उडी मारणें *n.* &c. उडी *f.*

S. of a flat stone &c. skimming water. काकर *f.*

SKIP-JACK, *a.* उडाणटप्पू, पायसूट.

SKIPPED, *p.*v. V. A. बगळलेला, अंतरलेला, &c. अंतरित.

SKIPPER, *n.* SKIPPING, *p. a.*v. N. 1. टिपण टाकणारा, उडतउडत-

जाणारा, &c. प्लुतगामी.
2 उडणारा, नाचणारा, उड्या मारणारा, &c. [खवा*m.*
I. *captain of a merchant vessel.* जिन्नसी गलबताचा-&c. ना-

To **Skirmish**, *v. n. fight slightly at a distance, or in small parties.* फटका फटकी *f.*-झडपाझडपी *f.*-नोकानोक *f.*-नोकानोकी-ची लढाई *f.*-&c. चालणें *g. of o.* दुरून लढाई *f.* करणें.

Skirmish, Skirmishing, *n.* v. V. फटकाफटकी *f.* झडपाझडपी *f.* ठांठू *n. f.* चकमक *f.* नोकानोक *f.* नोकानोकीची लढाई *f.* दूरची लढाई *f.* गोळागोळी *f.* सेनामुखयुद्ध *n.*

Skirt, *n.* (of a garment) *lower and loose part.* घेर *m.* घोळ *m.* झोल *m.* झोला *m.* पदर *m.* पल्लव *pop.* पालव *m.* फेर *m.* पागोरा *m.* सोगा *m.*
To wave the s. (in order to summon). पदर *m.* टाकणें, शेव *m.* घालणें, पालव *m.* टाकणें-घालणें.
To beckon by waving a s. पालविणें, पालवणी *f.* करणें.
2 v. Edge. कांठ *m.* किनारा *m.* शेव *m.* प्रांतभाग *m.*
3 (esp. of a turban or sash). शेमला *or* समला *m.*
4 *or* skirts; *precincts*, v. Border. सीमा *f. pop.* शींव *f.* शेव *m.* पालव *m.* दर *f.* शिरा *or* शेरा *m.*

To **Skirt**, *v. a. form a border to, run along the edges.* बाजू *f.*-सीमा *f.*-&c. धरणें, बाजू *f.*-सीमा *f.*-शींव *f.*-&c. असणें *in. con.*

Skirted, *a. that has a skirt or border.* घेरदार, घोळदार.

Skittish, *a. shy*, *&c.* बुजट *or* बुझट, बुजरा, बुजीर, बिचका *or* बिचक्या.
2 v. Frisky. नाचरा, कुलुल्या.

Skittishness, *n.* v. A. 1. बुजटपणा*m.* बुजरेपणा*m.* &c.
2 नाचरेपणा*m.* कुलुली *f.* मस्ती *f.*

Skreen, Skulk, Skull. See Screen, &c.

Sky, *n. aerial region, &c.* v. Heaven. अभाळ*or* आभाळ*n.* आकाश *m.n.* आस्मान*n.* निराळ*n.* गगन*n.* अंतरिक्ष*n.* अंतराळ*n.* अभ्र *n.* नभ*n.* अंबर*n.* व्योम*n.*
Mackerel s. कसर *f.* [तांबट *f.*
Redness of s. at sunrise and sunset. तांब *f.* तांबोटी *f.*
The s. is overcast. अभाळ आलें.

Sky-colored, *a.* आस्मानी, आस्मानीरंगाचा, आकाशवर्ण.

Sky-kissing, Sky-kissed, *a.* गगनचुंबित, गगनचुंबी, नभचुंबित *or* चुंबी, गगनासीं भांडणारा.

Sky-lark, *n.* कुकुटकुभा *or* कुकुडकुंभा*m.* कुकुडकोंबा*m.* कुक्कुडकुंभा*m.* कुंबेकुकूड*m.* कुंभारकुकूड*m.* भरद्वाज*m.*

Sky-larking. See To Frolic.

Sky-light, *n. window in the top of a house.* धारें*n.* झारें*n.* सोणें *or* साणें*n.* गवाक्ष*m. n.*

Sky-rocket, *n.*—the fire work. हवई *or* हवाई *f.* बाण*m.*
Bundle of twenty four sky rockets. कैची *f.*

Slab, *n. plank or table of stone.* शिला *pop.* शीळ *f.* चीप *f.*
S. for grinding condiments, &c. पाटा*m.* शिलापट*m.*

Slabber, *n. saliva drivelling from the mouth.* लाळ *f.*

To **Slabber**, *v. n. drivel, &c.* लाळ *f.*-मुखरस*m.* गळणें-पाघळणें *g. of s.* लाळ *f.* गाळणें-टाकणें, लाळणें.

Slabberer, *n.* **Slabbering**, *p. a.* v. V. लाळ गाळणारा, &c. लाळ्या, लाळगाळ्या, लाळतोंड्या.

Slack, *a. not tense, &c.* v. Loose. ढिला, ढील, ढिलता, सैल (*remiss.* सलींव *slackish*), शिथिल, पोकळ, अलबेला, उसू, अरळतरळ, बुळका.
A s. rein, *lit. fig.* सैलदोरी *f.*
S. from the twist having run back. उवळ *or* उवीळ.
2 *rickety, not fast.* खिळखिळा, खिळखिळीत, उसू, गटगटीत, लंपट *or* लांपट, लांपळ *or* लांफळ.
3 *remiss, &c.* ढिला, ढील, सुस्त, शिथिल, गबाळी *or* ळ्या, गेंदी, गेंबती, गेबल्या, गैनी, गैरात, मळमळीत, अरळतरळ, अलबलीत-गलबतीत, अलगरजी *or* जू, थिल्लट.
4 *loose jointed.* ढिल्या, लुंगा, शिथिलसंधि.
5 See Slow.

To **Slack**, *To* **Slacken**, *v. a. make less tense, &c.* ढिला-ढील-सैल-पोकळ-&c. करणें, ढिलावणें, सैलाविणें.
2 v. To Remit. ढिला-शिथिल-&c. करणें, ढिलाई *f.*-&c. करणें-धरणें *g. of o.* ढिलाईवर-&c. धरणें, जोर*m.*-वेग*m.*-&c. कमीकरणें *g. of o.*
3 See To Slake.

To **Slacken**, *v. n. become less tense, &c.* ढिला-ढील-सैल-शिथिल-&c. होणें-होत जाणें, सैलावणें.
2 *become remiss, &c.* ढिला-ढील-सुस्त-&c. होणें-होत जाणें, धिलाई *f.*-सुस्ताई *f.*-&c.धरणें,आळसणें, आळसावणें,सुस्तावणें,मंदावणें

Slackly, *adv.* v. A. 1. ढिला *decl.* ढील, सैल, ढिलाहोईसा *decl.*
3 ढिलेपणानें, ढिलाईनें, सुस्ताईनें, आळसानें, &c. आळस करून, अलगरजी, अलगरजीनें.

Slackness, *n.* v. A. 1. ढिलेपणा*m.* ढीलपणा*m.* सैलपणा*m.* &c. ढिलाई *f.* शैथिल्य*n.*
2 खिळखिळेपणा*m.* &c. खिळखिळी *f.*
3 ढीलपणा*m.* सुस्तपणा*m.* &c. ढिलाई *f.* ढिली *f.* ढील*f.* आळस*m.* सुस्ताई *f.* मंदाई *f.* मंदावा*m.* मंदी *f.* कस्त*n. v.* घे, आळाटाळी *f.* थिल्लटाई *f.*

Slain, *p.* v. V. मारलेला, जिवें मारलेला.

To **Slake**, *v. a.* (lime). पाणी*n.* घालणें,भिजवणें,विरवणें,उमलवणें.
2 See To Quench.

To **Slake**, *v. n.*—lime. उमलणें.

To **Slam**, *v. a. shut with force and noise.* धडकन-धडदिशी-धडकून-बाजवून-आदळून-आपटून-मोठ्यानें-जोरानें-&c. लावणें-बंद करणें.

To **Slander**, *v. a. malign, traduce, defame, &c.* v. To Asperse. तुफान *n.*-तोहमत *or* तोबत *f.*-आळ *f. m.*-&c. घालणें-आणणें, तुफान *n.* करणें *with* वर *of o.* चहाडी *or* चाहडी *f.* करणें- सांगणें *g. of o.* चुगली *f.*-चुगल *f.* खाणें-करणें *g. of o.* कुभांड *n.*-&c. रचणें-घालणें-&c. कूट *f.* खाणें *g. of. o.* कोरडी किटाळ *f.* घालणें-उठवणें, अपवाद *m.*-अभिशंसन *n.*-अभिशाप *m.*-&c. करणें.

Slander, *n. false or malicious report to the injury of another.* बलांट *or* बालंट *n.* तुफान *n.* तोहमत *or* तोबत *f.* आळ *m. f.* चहाडी *or* चाहडी *f.* चुगली *f.* धोतांड *or* धोथाड *n.* बगलांट *or* ठ *n.* बलांड *n.* बलांडा *m.* कुफराण *n.* अदावत *f.* कूट *f.* नालिस्त *or* स्ती *f.* पैशुन्य *n.* तकराळ *f.* तुनिया *f.* अपवाद *m.* अभिशाप *m.* असूया *f.* निमित्त *n.* पेलकट *n.* कैवाड *n.*—in cant phraseol. चकारी *f.*

Slandered, *p.* v. V. आळ घेतलेला-घातलेला-आलेला, &c. अभिशस्त, अभिशप्त, अभिशापित, अपवादित.

Slanderer, *n.* **Slandering**, *p. a.* v. V. तुफान घेणारा, &c.

चुगलखोर, चुगलीखोर, चुगल, बालंटखोर, बालंटी *or* ट्या, तुफानखोर, तुफानी, चहाड, चहाडखोर, कुभांडी, कुभांडखोर, कुधांडी, चहाडखुचका, धोतांडी, बगलांटी *or* टी, कवटाल्या *or* ळ्या, कैवाडी, कुटाळखोर, कुटाळ *or* कुचाळ & कुचाळखोर, अदावती *or* त्या, अपवादक, अभिशंसक, अभिशंसी, अभिशंसनकर्त्ता,—in cant phraseol. चकारबिल्हा.

SLANDEROUS, *a.* See SLANDERER. 2 *containing slander, calumnious.* तुफानाचा, चुगलीचा, चहाडीचा, &c. तुफानी, कुभांडी, कुधांडी, अपवादक, अपवादात्मक, अभिशंसक.

SLANDEROUSLY, *adv.* v. A. तुफान घेऊन-करून-&c. चहाडी करून-सांगून, आळ घेऊन, बालंट रचून, &c.

SLANG, *n. low, vulgar language.* आडबोली *f.* अडाणी बोली *f.*

SLANT, SLANTING, *To* SLANT, &c. See SLOPE, SLOPING, &c.

SLAP, *n. blow with the open hand.* चपराक *or* चपडाक *f.* चपाटी *f.* चापट *or* चापटी *f.* चपेटा *m.* चपेट *f.* थपाटी *f.* थाप *f.* थापडी *f.* थापट *f. dim* थापटी *f.* थबडाक *f.* थबकड *f.* धपका *or* धबका *m.* धप्पा *m.* धपाटा*m.* धमाटा *m.* धब्बल *f.* धप्पल *f.* छकड *f.* चडक *f.* चडकण *or* चडकाण *f.* चडकणी *or* चडकाणी *f.* चटकणी *f.* बादडा *m.* चापटपोळी *f. v.* मार, आस्फोट *m.* टपला *m.*

One subject to slaps & cuffs. थापडखाईक, थप्पडखाऊ, थप्पडखाईक, थोबाडखाईक, थोपटखाईक, थोपडखाईक.

To threaten a s. थापट *f.* उगारणें.

SLAP, *adv. with a sudden & smart blow.* स्प-कण-कर-&c. रपरप *or* पां (*intens.* रपारप, रपापां).

SLAP, SLAPDASH, *adv. with vehemence, promptness, and heedlessness of action,* v. IMPETUOUSLY, SMACK. झपाट्यानें, तडाक्यानें, सपाट्यानें, &c. मार, मारे, घसकन-कर-दिशी-&c. फटकन-कर-दिशी-&c. साफ.

To SLAP, *v. a. strike with the open hand or something flat.* चपराकणें, भडकावणें, फडकावणें, चपराक *f.*-चपेट *f.*-&c. मारणें-देणें, थबकणें, धपकावणें *or* धबकावणें, धमाटणें, चकचकावणें, चडबणें, चाखबणें, चमकावणें, वेतवणें, टिकाविणें, रंगवणें, धप्पेबाजी *f.*-&c. करणें.

To s. the face. थोबाडणें.

SLAPPING, *a.* See LARGE.

To SLASH, *v. a. cut violently & at random.* धसकावणें, धसधसळपाळप-सपासप-&c. तोडणें-काटणें-&c. धपकावणें *or* धबकावणें, खापलणें, सचाटणें, खसाटणें, धसाधशी *f.*-सपासपी *f.*-कचकच *f. intens.* कचकचाट *m.*-&c करणें.

SLASH, *n. long cut or wound.* तरवारीची-&c. चीर *f.* वार *m.* फाळा *m. v.* निघ.

SLASHINGLY, *adv.* v. V. धसधस *or* सां, कचकच *or* चां,—*intens.* कचाकच, धसाधस, छटाछट, छडाछड, छपाळप.

SLATE, *n.* एक जातीचा मऊ दगड आहे, त्याच्या चिपा सहज होतात. 2 *thin slab of stone.* चीप *f. dim.* चिपोळी *f.*

3—for writing on. दगडाची *or* दगडी पाटी *f.* स्लेट *f.*is commonly used in schools, &c.

SLATTERN, *n.* v. SLUT. आडव्या सुडक्याची बायको *f.* जोगम्मा *f.*

To dress as a s. उभें *n.* नेसणें घेणें-लावणें.

To SLAUGHTER, *v. a.* v. To KILL. काटणें, कत्तल *f.*-कट्टा *m.*-काटा काटी *f.*-कदन *n.*-सूदन *n.*-&c. करणें *g. of o.* संहारणें.

2—a butcher. मारणें, कापणें.

SLAUGHTER, *n.* v. V. काटणें *n.* कत्तल *f.* कट्टा *m.* काटाकाटी *f.* कदन *n.* सूदन *n.* सूना *f.* निकृंतन *pop.* निकंदन *n.* संहार *m.*

2 मारणें *n.* कापणें *n.*

SLAVE, *n. person wholly under the power of another.* दास, बंदा *or* बांदा, गुलाम, भक्तदास.

Dealer in s.-girls. कन्यापाल.

Domestic s. गृहदास. [रांड *f.*

Female s. बटीक *f.* दासी *f.* बांदी *f.* लवंडी *f.* कुणबीण *f.*

Home-born s. खानाजाद.

Male child of a female s. of the state. मुलगा *m.*

Offspring of a female s. बटीकपोर *c.* कडू *c.* कडवा *m.* गुलाम *m.* बंदा *or* बांदा *m.* बांदीचा, गर्भदास *m.* गर्भदासी *f.*

I am your s., your humble servant, &c. मी तुम्हा-आपला-&c. दासानुदास आहें, मी तुम्ही-आपली-&c. पायधूळ आहें.

2 fig. *one who slaves for another.* भाडेकरी *g. of s.*

To SLAVE, *v. n.* v. To LABOR. महारकष्ट *m. pl.*-कबाडकष्ट*m.pl.*-&c. करणें, हाडांचीं काडें *n. pl.* करणें, कटणें, मरीं मरणें, गुलामगिरी *f.* करणें, कच्च्या घड्यानें पाणी *n.* भरणें.

SLAVE-TRADE, *n.* गुलामांचा-&c. व्यापार *m.*

SLAVER, *To* SLAVER. See SLABBER, To SLABBER.

SLAVERY, *n. bondage, servitude,* बंदेपणा *m.* गुलामपणा *m.* गुलामगिरी *f.* दासत्व *n.* दास्य *n.* दासावस्था *f.* दासदशा *f.*

2 *drudgery,* v. LABOR. कबाडकष्ट *m. pl.* महारकष्ट *m. pl.*

SLAVISH, SLAVISHNESS. See SERVILE, SERVILITY.

To SLAY, *v. a.* v. To KILL. मारणें, जिवेंमारणें, जीव *m.*-प्राण *m.* घेणें *g. of o.* वध *m.*-&c. करणें *g. of o.*

SLAYER, *n.* SLAYING, *p. a.* v. V. मारणारा, &c.

SLEDGE, *n.*—the hammer. घन *or* घण *m.*—the wielder of it. घणकरी *m.*

2 *a carriage without wheels.* बिन चाकांची गाडी *f.* काढवान *n.*

SLEEK, *a.* See SMOOTH. 2 *plump, filled out, &c.* गोंडस, गुलगुलीत, गुबगुबीत, गुडगुडीत, ताजा, खुराकाचा.

SLEEKNESS, *n.* v. A. 2. गोंडसपणा *m.* गुलगुलितपणा *m.* गुबगुबितपणा *m.* &c.

To SLEEP, *v. n.* निजणें, झोंप *f.*-नीज *f.*-निद्रा *f.* घेणें *or in. con.* येणें-लागणें, शयन *n.*- शय्या *f.*-स्वपन *n.*-स्वप्न *m.* *n.*-सुप्ति *f.*-&c. करणें.

To desire to s. लोळी *f.* येणें *in. con.*

To go to s. fig. *sink into heedlessness.* डोळे *m. pl.*झांकणें.

To s. at ease (i. e. in rich realization of comfort and security). डरडरावून निजणें, ताणून निजणें, गुरगुम निजणें, सावकाश निजणें.

2 *not to be noticed or agitated,* v. To REST. पडणें, राहणें.

SLEEP, *n.* झोंप *f.* निद्रा *pop.* नीज *f.*शयन *n.* सुप्ति *f.* सुप्त *n.* स्वाप *m.* सर्वेंद्रियाव्यापार *m.*

A good s. कडक झोंप *f.* तबलझोंप *f.*

Breaking or interruption of s. झोंपमोड *f.* नीजमोड *or* नीदमोड *f.* निद्राभंग *m.*

Dead s. अघोर निद्रा *f.* आसुरी निद्रा *f.* गाढमूढनिद्रा *f.*

Fatal or unlucky s. काळझोंप *f.*

Morning s. or snooze. साखरझोंप *f.* गुलाबी झोंप *f.*

Overcome with s. निद्राकुल, निद्राग्रस्त, निद्राक्रांत.

Sound s. Fast s. सुषुप्ति *f.*

That is in a sound s. सुषुप्त.

Waking or light s. जागतीझोंप *f.* जागतीनिद्रा *f.*

To talk in s. ओसणणें, ओसणावणें *or* ओष्णावणें, ओष्णेणें.

SLEEP-WALKER, &c. See SOMNAMBULIST, &c.

SLEEPER, SLEEPING, *p. a.* v. V. झोंप घेणारा, झोंप आलेला-लागलेला-&c. निद्रित, निद्रिस्त, निद्रायमान, सुप्त.

I. *occupied with sleep.* झोंप घेण्याचा, निजण्याचा.

SLEEPINESS, *n.* v. A. निजाळूपणा *m.* निद्राळूपणा *m.* &c. निद्रालुता *f.*

2 झोंप *f.* झोंपेची गुंगी *f.*-तार *f.*-झाक *f.*-रवरवी *f.* सुरसुरी *f.* सुस्ती *f.* तंद्री *f.* तंद्रा *f.* निद्रेच्छा *f.*

SLEEPLESS, *a. without sleep.* झोंपे वेगळा-निराळा, निद्राहीन-रहित-&c. अनागतनिद्र, निद्रात्यक्त. [नता *f.*

SLEEPLESSNESS, *n.* v. A. निद्राभाव *m.* निद्राराहित्य *n.* निद्राहीनता *f.*

SLEEPY, *a. habitually disposed to sleep.* निजाळू, झोंपाळू, निद्रालु *or* ळू, झोंप्या, गुंग्या, निद्राशील, शयालु, स्वप्नशील, तंद्रालु.

2 *overcome by sleepiness.* लोढी आलेला, गुंगी आलेला, गुंगलेला, झोंपेची तार आलेला, निद्रातुर, निद्रान्वित, निद्राकुल, निद्राक्रांत, निद्राग्रस्त, तंद्रालु.

SLEEPY-HEAD, *n.* v. SLUGGARD. कुंभकर्ण *m.* घोरड *n.*

SLEEPY-HEADED, *a.* See SLEEPY.

SLEET, *n. fall of hail & rain.* गारांचापाऊस *m.* तुषारवृष्टि *f.*

SLEEVE, *n. covering for the arm.* बाही *f.* अस्तनी *f.* हातपा *m.*

To laugh in one's s. गालांत हासणें, ओंठांत हासणें, पदर लावून हासणें.

SLEIGHT, *n.* (of hand) v. JUGGLERY. हातचलाकी *f.* हातचलाकीचा खेळ *n.* हस्तलाघव *n.* कुसृति *f.*

SLENDER, *a. thin, slim, &c.* पातळ, पातळांगी *or* ग्या, सडकपातळ, सडपातळ, चिवळ, रुंगाळा, किरकूळ *or* किरकोळ, किचकट *or* किचकाट, अंबळ, शाहांगी *or* ग्या, काठांग्या, कडकांगी, एकांगी, एकेरी आंगाचा, बारीक, कृश, कृशांग, तनु, सूक्ष्म, काटकुळा *or* काटकोळा.

2 *small, inconsiderable, weak, feeble, &c.* थोडा, हलका, अल्प, निर्बल, लघु, क्षुद्र.

3 v. INADEQUATE, SCANTY. थोडा, अपुरता, चुटपुरता.

SLENDER-WAISTED, *a.* बारीक माजाचा, बारीक कमरेचा, सिंहकटि, मृगकटि, क्षीणमध्य.

SLENDERNESS, *n.* v. A. 1. पातळपणा *m.* सडकपातळपणा *m.* बारिकपणा *m.* &c. पातळाई *f.* पातळी *f.* बारकाई *f.* बारकावा *m.* कृशता *f.* कार्श्य *n.* सूक्ष्मता *f.* सौक्ष्म्य *n.*

2 थोडेपणा *m.* हलकेपणा *m.* अल्पता *f.* &c.

To SLEW, *v. a.* v. To SLUE. कलथणें.

To SLICE, *v. a. cut into slices.* फांकी *or* फांका *f. pl.*-&c. करणें *g. of o.* फांकणें, कापणें.

SLICE, *n. thin broad piece.* फांक *dim.* फांकळी *f.* फाड *f.* शकल *n.* छकल *n.* चकळ *n.*

2 *piece sliced off.* टिवळी *or* टवळी *f.* टोंचा *m.* टवकी *f.* टोंका *m.* टोंकी *f.* टवरा *m.* भेत *f. n. dim.* भेतूक *n.* डपला *m. dim.* डपली *f.* धपला *m. dim.* धपली *f.* धलपा *m. dim.* धलपी *f.*

A circular s. चकती *f.* चकदळ *n.* चकदळी *f.*

3 (esp. of fruits). काप *or* खाप *f.* फोड *f.* कापटी *f.* कातळा *m.* पाकळी *f.* शेड *f.*

To SLIDE, *v. n. move smoothly along,* v. To SLIP, To GLIDE. घसरणें, सुळकणें, सरपटणें, घरळणें, निसरणें, खरकणें *or* खुरकणें, सरपटत-सरपट्यां *adv.* जाणें-चालणें-&c. संसर्प *m.*-रिंगण *n.*-&c. करणें.

2—on ice. थिजलेल्या पाण्यावर-&c. घसरत जाणें.

To SLIDE, *v. a. with* in. खुपसणें, खुपसून घालणें.

SLIDE, *n. place to slide on.* घसरड *f.* घसरडें *n.* घसरण *f.*

SLIGHT, *a. small, thin, &c.* v. SLENDER. पातळ, बारीक, किरकूळ *or* किरकोळ, कागदी, सूक्ष्म.

2 *not strong, not cogent, not forcible,* v. LIGHT, FLIMSY. हलका, लहान, बारीक, पोकळ, फुसकुला, कमतणूक, कमजोर, जुजबी, कागदी, अलबेला.

3 *little, faint, feeble.* हलका, बारीक, सूक्ष्म, पातळ, कळत न कळत *or* कळे न कळे इतका, कळे न कळेसा, जाणे न जाणेसा.

To SLIGHT, *v. a. neglect, disregard,* v. To CONTEMN, To NEGLECT. तुच्छ मानणें-करणें, उपेक्षणें, अव्हेरणें, तिरस्कारणें, अनादरणें, हेळणें, डावलणें, उबगणें, उंडारणें, गाळण *f.*-उपेक्षा *f.*-हेलसांड *f.*-हेलना *f.*-हेला *f.*-अवज्ञा *f.*-थेर *n.*-&c. करणें *g. of o.*

SLIGHT, SLIGHTING, *n.* v. V. उपेक्षणें *m.* अव्हेरणें *n.* &c. अनादर *m.* अव्हेर *m.* हेलना *f.* हेला *f.* हेलसांड *f.* उपेक्षा *f.* अवज्ञा *f.* कानाडोळा *m.* आनाकानी *f.* अवगणना *f.* अवगणन *n.*

To treat with exceeding s. पोतेडें *n.* करून टाकणें.

SLIGHTED, *p.* v. V. अव्हेरलेला, &c. उपेक्षित, अवमानित, अवगणित, अवज्ञात.

SLIGHTER, *n.* SLIGHTING, *p. a.* v. V. अव्हेरणारा, उपेक्षा करणारा, &c. उपेक्षक, अवगणन-&c. कर्त्ता-कारी-&c.

SLIGHTINGLY, *adv.* v. A. उपेक्षा करून-धरून, हेलसांड करून, उपेक्षाबुद्धीनें, उपेक्षापूर्वक.

SLIGHTLY, *adv.* v. A. 3. जरासा *decl.* जराकसा *decl.* थोडा *decl.* कळेनकळेसा *decl.* &c.

SLIGHTNESS, *n.* v. A. 1. पातळपणा *m.* बारिकपणा *m.* सूक्ष्मता *f.* सौक्ष्म्य *n.* &c. पातळाई *f.* पातळी *f.* [लहानवी *f.*

2 हलकेपणा *m.* बारिकपणा *m.* पोकळपणा *m.* लहानपणा *m.* &c.

3 हलकेपणा *m.* बारिकपणा *m.* &c.

SLIM, *a.* v. SLENDER. पातळ, पातळांगी *or* ग्या, सडपातळ, सडकपातळ, बारीक, चिवळ, एकेरी आंगाचा, किरकूळ *or* किरकोळ, शाहांगी *or* ग्या, एकांगी, कृशांग, काटकुळा.

SLIME, *n. mire, &c.* गाल *m.* रेबड *f.*

2 (of plants, &c.). चीक *m.* गलगल *m.*

3 (of animals). बार *f.* लाळ *f.* बील *m.* बळस *m.*

SLIMNESS, *n.* v. A. पातळपणा *m.* सडपातळपणा *m.* &c. पातळाई *f.* पातळी *f.* [मळा.

SLIMY, *a.* v. N. चिकाळ *or* ळा *or* ळ्या, गलगलीत, बिळबिळीत, उपाल *m.*

SLING, *n.*—the weapon. गोफण *f.*

Stone of a s. गोफणगुंडा *m.* गोफणगोटा *m.* भिंडी *f.* भिंडीपाल *m.*

Strap of a s. फडें *n.* [शिक्य *n.*

2—as for a vessel, &c. शिंकें *or* शिकें *n.* दांतळी *or* दांताळी *f.*

Basket confined within a s. शिंकरणी *or* शिंकारणी *f.*

Cord around a vessel for the s. शिकाळी *f.*—Vessel so furnished शिकाळी *f.*

3—for a weight or load. नवघण *or* नौघण *f. n.* झोळी *f.*

S. for four carriers. चवाळें *n.*

4—for a basket, &c. डंगी *f.* डाली *f.* शिकरणी *or* शिकारणी *f.*

5 *pole with slings.* बहंगी *or* बंगी *f.* कावड *f.* भारयष्टि *f.*

6 (with a wooden bottom). शिकारी *f.*

7 (for an arm, &c.). गळंगती *f.* ओळकंबें *n.*

8 *juice of sugarcane not duly inspissated.* काकवी *f.* काकी *f.*

To SLING, *v. a. cast by a sling.* गोफणणें, गोफणीनें फेंकणें-मारणें, भिरकांडणें, भिरकाविणें.

2 (a pitcher, a basket, &c.). शिकारणें, शिकाळणें.

To SLINK, *v. n. steal away, slip off.* गुपचूप &c. निघून जाणें, काढतें-कसरतें-निघतें-सरतें-सरकतें-निसरतें-&c. घेणें, निसटणें, सटकणें, झुरणें, गुंगणें, मुठींत नाक धरून जाणें, मेंगाबणें, दृष्टि चुकवून-नजर चुकवून जाणें.

2 *miscarry,*—of beasts. गाभुटणें *or* गाभुडणें, गाभसांडणें, गाभ *m.* पडणें *g. of s.* गाभ *m.* टाकणें-सांडणें.

To SLIP, *v. n. slide, &c.* निसरणें, निसटणें, निखून जाणें, निसपटणें, घसरणें, सरकटणें, सरकणें, सरणें, सरसावणें, सरपटणें, झुळकणें, ढळणें, च्यवणें,—with a noise. सरकणें *or* खुरकणें.

To s.—the tongue. जिव्हा *f.* बांकडी पडणें.

2 *fall into fault, err.* चुकणें, भुलणें, घसरणें, चळणें, च्यवणें, चूक *f.*-चळ *m.*-&c. होणें.

3 aside; off; *move out of place.* निसटणें, निसपटणें, निखून जाणें, कचणें, कचकणें, कसरणें.

4 away; off; *give the slip, decamp.* चोरून-गुपचूप निघून जाणें, झुकणें, झुकाटणें, झुरणें, झटकणें, झुरकणें, पोबारा *m.* करणें, काढतें-कसरतें-निघतें-&c. घेणें, इया *f.* म्हणणें *or* करणें, सुंझ्या *f.* करणें, ताटी *f.* कापणें, निसटणें, सटकणें, सटालणें, बाळ्या *f. pl.* हांकणें, पलायंतीचें करणें, झुकाटी *f.*-झुकांडी *f.*-झोकांडी *f.*-झुकापुरी *f.*-झुगारा *m.*-&c. देणें, हातावर तुरी देऊन पळणें, गुंगारा *m.*-देणें, बंचणें.

To s. out of a promise or engagement. सटकणें, सटाली *f.*-सटल *or* ळी *f.* खाणें. [टाली *or* ल्या.

That slips out of a promise, &c. सटली *or* सटल्या, स-

5 into; *enter by oversight.* पडणें, शिरणें, घुसणें.

To SLIP, *v. a. cause to slide.* सारणें, सरकावणें, सरविणें.

2 v. To LOSE. हरवणें, घालवणें.

3 *let loose.* सोडणें, मोकळा करणें-सोडणें, दांवें *n.* सोडणें.

4 in; into; *convey secretly.* चोरून-गुपचूप-हळू-&c. घालणें-टाकणें-शिरवणें- खुपसणें.

5 on; *put on hastily, loosely, &c.* आंगांत अडकवणें.

SLIP, SLIPPING, *n.* v. V. N. 1. निसरणें *n.* निसटणें, घसरणें *n.* &c. घसरणी *f.* चळ *m.* ढळ *m.* च्यवन *n.* च्युति *f.*

To give the s. v. To SLIP AWAY. झुकणें, झुकाटी *f.*-झुगारा *m.*-&c. देणें.

2 *and* FAULT. चूक *f.* दोष *m.* (in comp. as हस्तदोष, &c.) ढळ *m.* चळ *m.* च्युति *f.* स्खलन *n.* गुंजाबीस *f.* संचार *m.*

I. *twig, &c. set to grow.* कलम *n.* लागवण *n.*

II. (of cloth, &c.) *long narrow piece.* पट्टी *f.* धांदोटी *f.* धांद *f.* चिंधोटी *f.* चिरफळी *f.* चिरी *f.* ओल *f.* फडका*m.* फडकें*n.* फाळ *m.* फाळा *m.* फळी *f.* परकळा *m.*

III. (of bamboo, &c.). कांब *f.* कांबीट *n. f.* कांबट *n. f.* कांबटी *f.* चिपोटा *m.* काडी *f.* कांडी *f.* पिंजूळी *or* पिंज़ोळी *f.* पिंजट *n.* बेळ *n.* शेड *f.* सरी *f.*

IV. (of metal). कांब *f.*

V. (of land). पट्टी *f.* चिरटी *f.* चिरोटी *f.* दांडा *m.* पट्टा *m.* पाटी *f.* फाळकी *f.* फाळी *f.*

VI. (of leather or gut). तंतु *m.* तांतू *m.*

SLIP-KNOT, *n.* v. KNOT. सरकगांठ *f.* निसरगांठ *f.* शेंसरगांठ *f.* सुटगांठ *f.* झुरगांठ *f.* सरकफांस *m.*

SLIPPED, *p.* v. V. N. 1. निसरलेला, निसटलेला, घसरलेला, च्युत (esp. in comp. as स्थानच्युत, बंधच्युत, पदच्युत, अधिकारच्युत, &c.), स्खलित.

SLIPPER, *n.* v. SHOE. पायपोश *or* स *m.* पैजार *f.*—revilingly. मोचा *m.* खेटर *n.* खांसडा *m.* [पायपोसगिरी *f.*

Beating with a s. खेटरमार *m.* खांसडेमार *m.* मोचमार *m.*

S.-fight. खांसडेमार *m.* खेटरमार *m.* खेटरासेटरी *f.* पायपोसापायपोशी *f.* मोचामोची *f.* जुनेपैजार *f.* [*con.* चमणें.

To get beaten with a s. मोचे *m. pl.* खाणें *or with in.*

SLIPPERINESS, *n.* v. A. 1. निसरडेपणा *m.* घसरडेपणा *m.* सरकटेपणा *m.* &c. घसरडें *n.* सरकटें *n.* निसरड *f.* निसरण *f.* निसरडें *n.* चळ *m.* स्नेह *m.* स्नैग्ध्य *n.*

2 चंचळपणा *m.* चंचलता *f.* चांचल्य *n.*

SLIPPERY, *a. not affording firm footing.* घसरडा, घसरट, घसरबट, घसरता, निसरडा, निसरट, निसरता, सरकटा, गुळगुळीत, बुळबुळीत.

S. place. घसरड *f.* घसरण *f.* घसरडें*n.* निसरण *f.* निसरणी *f.*

2 fig.—of women, v. WANTON. चंचल *pop.* चंचळ.

3 See UNCERTAIN. [निशीं.

SLIP-SHOD, *adv. with shoes worn as slippers.* पाइलेल्या जोड्यां-

SLIP-SLOP, *n.* v. SLOP. गरगट *n.* ढपळवणी *n.*

To SLIT, *v. a. cut lengthwise, make a long fissure in, &c.* v. To SPLIT. चिरणें, उभा *decl.* कापणें-कातरणें-फाडणें-&c. चीर *f.*-फाळा *m.*-&c. काढणें *g. of o.*

2 (bamboos, reeds, &c.). पिंजणें, पिंजणी *f.* करणें.

To SLIT, *v. n. tear lengthwise,* v. To SPLIT. पिचणें, पिंजणें, पेंचणें, तडणें.

SLIT, *n. long cut or fissure.* चीर *f.* फाळा *m. v.* निघ, जा, उभीभेग *f.*-भेर *f.*-भेळ *f.*-&c. तडा *m. v.* जा, तीड *f.*

SLIT, *p.* v. V. A. 1. चिरलेला, &c. चिरींव.

2 पिंजलेला, पिंजका.

v. V. N. पिचलेला, &c. पिचका, पिंजका.

SLOAT, *n.*—of a cart, &c. करळी *f.* खुडगा*m.*

To SLOBBER, *v. n.* v. To SLABBER. लाळ *f.* गाळणें, लाळ *f.*-मुखरस*m.* गळणें-पाझरणें *g. of s.*

SLOOP, *n.* एककाठी गलबत*n.*-&c.

SLOP, *a. vile liquor,*—gener. गरगट*n.* घमंडगुळवणी*n.* शंखवणी*n.* खळगट*n.* ढपळवणी*n.*

2 *mess, muddiness, &c.* घाण *f.* ढाण *f.* तन्हाण *f.* रेंद *f.* कर्दम*m.*

SLOPE, *n. declivity, slant.* उतरड *f.* उतरण *f.* उतरवण *f.* उतार*m.* ढाळ*m.* घसरड *f.* बरंगळ *or* बरंघळ *f.* प्रावण्य*n.* [चौमोळी.

That has four slopes,—a house, &c. चौढाळ, चौपाखी,

Of great s.—a roof, &c. खर, पाणढाळ.

Of moderate s.—a roof, &c. माठ, शीतळ, बसका.

Path along the summit of a s. दंड*m.* कणा*m.*

S. to carry off water. पाणढाळ*m.* पाणलोट*m.* पाणसळ *f.*

A s. of a hill. पाखर *f.*

2 *steep bank.* डगर *f.* दरड *f.* धस*m.* धसरड *f.*

SLOPE, SLOPEWISE, SLOPINGLY, *adv.* v. ASLANT. उतरता *decl.* उतरवट, ढळता *decl.* घसरता *decl.* तिरपा *decl.* ओझरता *decl.* कसरता *decl.*

To SLOPE, *v. a. form with a slope.* उतरता-ढळता-घसरता-&c. करणें, ढाळ*m.*-&c. देणें.

To SLOPE, *v. n.* *be declivous or inclined.* उतरता-ढळता-&c.-असणें, उतरणें, ढाळm. असणें *in. con.* [प्रवण.

SLOPING, *p. a.* v. V. N. उतरता, उतरवट, ढाळसर, ढाळदार, ढाळू, Smoothly s. नेपाळ.

SLOPPINESS, *n.* v. A. 1. चिडचिडितपणाm. रबरबितपणाm. &c. रेबडf. राडf. चेंदf. चेंदरडf. चेंदाडf. चिडचीडf. चिबचीबf. रेंदf. रेंदगडn.

SLOPPY, *a.*—as ground, *wet, plashy, miry.* चिडचिडीत, रबरबीत, थलथलीत, बरबरीत, चिबचिबीत, रेबडीचा, चेंदाडीचा, &c. To be s. चिबचिबणें.

2 *wishywashy, watery.* उमळा, सरबरीत, बचबचीत.

SLOPS, *n. pl. ready made clothes.* आयतीं वस्त्रेंn. *pl.*

SLOTH, *n.* v. LAZINESS. आळसm. सुस्ती f. सुस्तपणाm. आलस्यn. उद्योगद्वेषm. [आळसाचा.

SLOTHFUL, *a.* v. LAZY. आळसी *remiss.* आळसट, सुस्त, सुस्तीचा,

SLOTHFULLY, *adv.* v. A. *and* LAZILY. आळसानें, आळस करून, आलस्यपूर्वक. [m. सुस्तपणाm.

SLOTHFULNESS, *n.* v. A. *and* LAZINESS. आळसीपणाm. आळस

SLOUCH, *n.* v.V. मुंडी खालीं घालून जाण्याची चालf. अनाडी चालf.

To SLOUCH, *v. n. walk with a depressed body, &c.* तोंड खालीं करून-मुंडी खालीं घालून-मान खालीं करून-चपापून-&c. चालणें.

SLOUGH, *n. miry place.* राडf. दलदलf. बांबरn. चिखलाची रुतण f.-रुपण f.-फसण f.

2 (of a serpent). मेंगf. कंचुकm. कांतf.

3 (from a wound). जळमटn. क्षतगलितमांसn.

To SLOUGH, *v. n.*—a serpent. मेंगावणें, मेंगf.-कांतf.-&c. टाकणें.

2—a wound. जळमटेंn. *pl.* निघणें *g. of s.*

SLOVEN, *n.* v. SLOVENLY. नेभळ भट, माभळ भट, भोंगळ भट, गोबरा गणेश, लटूबगाड्या.

SLOVENLINESS, *n.* v. A. 1. नेभळेपणाm. गेंदीपणाm. गैंनीपणाm. &c. पांघरुणाची-वस्त्रप्रावरणाची-&c. अव्यवस्था f.-हयगई f.-&c. गड्याळकी f. गड्याळी f.

2 गबाळीपणाm. गहाळपणाm. गेंदीपणाm. &c.

SLOVENLY, *a. negligent of dress or neatness.* भोंगळ, नेमळा, मलिन *pop.* मळीण, गेंदी, गैबती, गैबत्या, गैबी, गबाळी *or* ळ्या, भांभळ *or* ळ्या, ऐदी, गैरात, गहाळ, बोंदरा, हालबोंदरा, गड्याळ *or* ळी, गयाळ *or* ळी.

2 *not neat, not orderly,*—dress, work,&c. गबाळी *or* ळ्या, गलत्या, भांमळ *or* ळ्या, ऐदी, गेंदी, भोंगळ, भसभोंगळ, गहाळ, गयाळ *or* ळी, अलबेला, बाबसा, हयगईचा, अलबलीत गलबलीत, बुलका, बुळा, फळकट, प्रामादिक.

SLOVENLY, *adv.* v. A. नेभळेपणानें, गेंदीपणानें, &c. अफरातफरा.

SLOW, *a. not swift, not rapid, &c.* धिमा *or* धिम्मा, मंद, मंदगति, मंदगतीचा, मंदचालीचा, लिंगशा, अद्रुत.

S. fire. मंदाग f. मंदाग्नि m.—By a s. fire. मंदागीं.

2 *not prompt,* v. DULL, SLUGGISH. मंद, जड, सुस्त, सुस्ता, मदड *or* मदाड, मदट, मठ्ठ, थंड, थंडा, चघळ, अगटचिगट, घृतबुद्धि, स्थूलबुद्धि, मंदमति, मंदबुद्धि, स्तिमित.

3 *not precipitate or rash.* धिमा *or* धिम्मा, धीर, विमृश्यकारी, समीक्ष्यकारी.

4—time; in music. विलंबित.

SLOW-BACK, SLOW-COACH, *n.* v. DAWDLER. रेंगा, रेंग्या.

SLOW-GOING, SLOW-PACED, *a.* मंदचालीचा, मंदगतीचा, मंदगति, मंदगामी.

SLOWLY, *adv.* v. A. 1. मंदगतीनें, मंदचालीनें, मंदीनें, &c. शनैःशनैः, सावकाश, हलका *decl.* हळू.

SLOWLY,! *interj.* धिरा, धिरेधिरे, धिरे, धिराधिरे, रिघेरिघे.

SLOWNESS, *n.* v. A. 1. धिमेपणा m. मंदपणा m. &c. मंदाई f. मंदावा m. मंदी f. लिंगस्ताई *or* लिंगस्थाई f. मांद्य n. मंदगति f. मंदचाल f.

2 मंदपणा m. जडपणा m. सुस्तपणा m. &c. सुस्ताई f. सुस्ती f. ढिल्ली f. घृतबुद्धि f. स्थूलबुद्धि f. मंदबुद्धि f. बुद्धिमांद्य n. &c.

3 सावकाशी f. धीरपणाm. धिमाई *or* धिम्माई f. विमृश्यकारिता f.

To SLUBBER, *v. a. hurry over, perform carelessly, hurriedly, and roughly.* ढकलणें, दपटणें, लाटणें, लोटणें, लगटणें, लगेतगे करून करणें, टंगळमंगळ करणें, घसटणें, रगडणें, चरकटणें, फरकटणें, भरकटणें, ओढणें, ओढून टाकणें, गडबडवणें, गडबडगुंडा m. करणें *or* करून अटपणें *g.of o.* गडबडघोंटाळ्याचा *decl.* करणें, निर्दाळणें, बिगार *or* बेगार f.-वेठ f. करणें *or* काढणें, वेठीचें करणें, करड f. n. काढणें, बिगार f.-वेठ f.- उळग n. वारणें-निस्तारणें, ओरबडून टाकणें, गुंफाटणें, गोफाटणें, सरासरी *adv.*-बरवर *adv.* करणें, शास्त्रार्थ m. करणें *g. of o.* ढकल f.-चालढकल f.-घालघुसड f.-&c. करणें *g. of o.* लाटा m. फिरविणें *with* वर *of o.*

Work or business slubbered over. बिगार *or* बेगार f. बिगारकाम n.

SLUBBERER, *n.* SLUBBERING, *p a.* v. V. ढकलणारा, लोटणारा, बिगार काढणारा, वेठ करणारा, वरवर करणारा, &c. &c. ढकल्या, ढकलचंद, ढकलआपा, कामलाट्या, लाट्या, घसट्या, घसक्या, चरकट्या, फरकट्या, भरकट्या, गफलती *or* त्या, अलगर्जी.

SLUBBERING, *n.* v. V.—*act.* ढकलणें n. दपटणें n. लाटणें n. बिगार काढणें n. &c. &c. ढकल f. चालढकल f. घालघुसर f. लगडतगड *or* धगड f. लथडपथड f. लथडसथड f. लथडालथड f. टंगळ मंगळ n. रगडमल्ली f. चुकवाचुकव f. निर्दळण *or* निर्दाळण n. निर्दळणी *or* निर्दाळणी f.

SLUBBERINGLY, *adv.* v. A. लगेतगे करून, लगडतगड, लथड पथड, लथडसथड, टंगळमंगळ, गडबडगुंडा करून, बिगार काढून, वेठ काढून, &c. सपसप *or* पां.

SLUDGE. See MIRE, MUD.

To SLUE, *v. a. turn on its axis.* चकरणें, कलथणें, फिरवणें.

SLUG. See SNAIL.

SLUGGARD, *n.* The terms and phrases expressing the sense of this word, viz. *A slow, heavy, and indolent person,* and answering to *slug, sloth, drowsy head, sleepy head, lazy bones, bed presser, &c.* are collected here. आळशांचा मायबाप, शताळशी, अचळोजी, अचळोबा, अजगर, आर, रीस, ऐदी, शनि, पेंदपोह्या, ढोणसकड, थापा, मोघळा, म्हसोबा, म्हशा, रेड्या, उठवळ, हल्या, पिकल्या झाडाखालीं उपासी मरणारा. *See also the adjective.*

SLUGGISH, *a. inert, inactive, heavy.* सुस्त, सुस्ता, जड, आंगजड, मंद, मंदट, ढिला, मैंद, मठ्ठ, मठ्ठ्या *or* मठ्या, पड्या, घैंशा, घैंस, बठ्ठ, लिंगशा, अनुद्योगी, रेंद, दुश्वर *intens.* सुदुश्वर, स्तिमित.

SLUGGISHNESS, *n.* v. A. सुस्तपणाm. जडपणाm. सुस्ताई f. सुस्ती f. मंदाई f. मंदावा m. जाड्य n. मांद्य n. तंद्रा f. लिंगस्ताई *or* लिंगस्थाई f. स्तिमिताई f.

SLUICE, *n. flood-gate.* उघडी f. सांडवा m. सांड f.

To SLUMBER, *v. n. sleep lightly.* हलकी झोंप f.-&c. घेणें.

2 See To SLEEP.

SLUMBER, *n. light sleep.* हलकी झोंप *f.*-नीज *f.* लघुनिद्रा *f.* कुनरझोंप *f.* श्वाननिद्रा *f.*

2 See SLEEP.

SLUMBEROUS. See SOPORIFEROUS.

To SLUR, *v. a. sully, soil.* बट्टा *m.*-काळें *n.*-काळोखी *f.*-कलंक *m.*-&c. आणणें-लावणें, दाग *or* डाग *m.*-काजळी *f.* लावणें, डागणें, खोडणें, दूषणें, सकलंक-&c. करणें.

2 *do rapidly and roughly, &c.* v. To SLUBBER. करड *f. n.* काढणें, गुंफाटणें, गोफाटणें.

3 *pass lightly over, conceal.* उडतउडत-उडताउडता छपावून-&c. सांगणें, छपावणें, लपूनछपून-बरवर-राखून राखून-&c. सांगणें.

SLUR, *n. stigma, mark of reproach,* v. STAIN. काळें *n.* काजळी *f.* काळवटी *f.* काळवण *f.* डाग *or* दाग *m.* कलंक *m.* काळोखी *f.* काहूर *n.* कालिमा *m. f.* मस *f.* दूषण *n.* दोष *m.* खोड *f.*

To cast a s. upon. खोड *f.*-बाट *m.*-&c. ठेवणें.

SLUSH, *n. soft dirt, filth, &c.* खळमळ *m.* रस्त *n.*

SLUSHY, *a.* v. N. गळगलीत *or* गिलगिलीत, खळमळाचा.

SLUT, *n. slovenly & dirty woman.* आडव्या सुडक्याची बायको *f.*-स्त्री *f.*-&c. जोगम्मा *f.* अवझा *f.* माभळभटीण *f.* सांडरू *n.* डुकर *f.* रीस *n.* भोंगळ भटीण *f.* नेभळी-हिडशी-&c. बायको *f.*-स्त्री *f.*-&c. भोंगळी *f.* बाबाची माशी *f.*

2—the word of contempt for a woman, See WOMAN.

SLUTTISH. See SLOVENLY.

SLY, *a.* v. CUNNING. कावेदार, मतलबी, कसबाती, धूर्त्त, बाट, बाटगा, लिकीर, छद्मी, नजरचोर, दृष्टिचोर, दृष्टिचुकव्या, गुंड.

2—of things. कावेदारीचा, नजर चोरीचा, बाटपणाचा, &c.

SLYLY, *adv.* v. A. धूर्त्तपणानें, बाटपणानें, &c. दृष्टि चुकवून, दृष्टि चोरून, चोरून, लिकून चोरून, लपूनछपून.

SLYNESS, *n.* v. A. कावेदारी *f.* धूर्त्तपणा *m.* बाटपणा *m.* नजरचोरी *f.* लपंडाव*m.* लपंडाई *f.*

To SMACK, *v.n. have a taste of,* v. To TASTE. छटा *f.*-स्वाद *m.*-चुणूक *f.*-धुनक *f.*-वास*m.*-गंध*m.*-ध्वनि*m.*-&c. येणें-मारणें *g. of o.*

2—with the lips. मिटकी *f.*-मिटका*m.* मारणें.

To SMACK, *v. a.* (the face, &c.) v. To SLAP. चपराक *f.* मारणें-&c. चपराकणें, रंगवणें.

Smacking & cuffing. टपलेबाजी *f.*

2 *kiss with a smack.* मिटकी मारून मुका *m.* घेणें, मिटक्यांचा मुका*m.* घेणें.

3 (a whip) *crack.* कडकावणें, कडकडवणें, तडतडवणें.

SMACK, *adv. with a sudden and smart blow; with a smack, crack &c.* सपकुन-कर-&c. रपरप *or* पां (*intens.* रपारप, रपापां) फटकन-कर-&c. फटफट *or* टां (*intens.* फटाफट, फटाटां,) चटकन-कर-&c. ताड-कन-कर-&c. *or* धाड-कन-&c.

2 *with vehemence and heedlessness of action.* झपाट्यानें, तडाक्यानें, &c. सपाटा-झपाटा-&c. मारून, मार, मारे, मारून, धसकन-कर-&c. फटकन- कर-&c.

3 *promptly, smartly, at once.* तसाच, तेव्हांच, लागलाच, पटकण, सरधोपट, सधट.

4 *smack and smooth, smartly and cleanly.* साफ, घट, झाडून, हडसून खडसून, शुद्धबुद्ध.

SMACK, *n. savour, tincture,* v. TASTE. छटा *f.* बोय *f.* वास *m.* लजत *f.* लकेरी *f.* असार *m.*

2 (of a whip) *crack.* कडाका *m.* फटकारा *m.*

3 of the lips. मिटकी *f.* मिटका *m.*

4 *sounding kiss.* मिटक्यांचा मुका *m.* सशब्दचुंबन *n.*

6 v. SLAP. चपराक *or* चपडाक *f.* चपाटी *f.* चापट *f.* चापटी *f.* थप्पल *f.* धप्पा *m.* रपका *m.* रपाटा *m.* चडक *f.* चडकण *f.* चडकणी *f.* छकड *f.* बादडा *m.* आस्फोट *m.* टपला *m.*

7 एक प्रकारचें गलबत आहे.

SMALL, *a. not large.* लहान, लघु, क्षुद्र, क्षुल्लक, ननु, कनिष्ठ.

S.—compreh. *s. and short, &c.* लहानसहान.

S. and compact. अटोपसार, टेंगणाठुसका, टेंगणारेंगणा.

S. and great. लहानथोर, लहानमोठा.

Smaller. धाकटा *or* धाकला.

Smallest. अल्पिष्ठ.

Smallish. लहानसर.

2 *little in amount or degree.* थोडा, थोडका, हलका, अल्प, स्वल्प, इवला, इवलासा, इवलिसा *or* उल्सिा.

3 the voice; *feeble, single.* बारीक, एकेरा *or* एकेरी.

SMALL, *n.*—of the back. चौक *m.* बगड *n.* बगडा *m.*

SMALL-HOOFED, *a.* लहानखुरी. [गचें *n.*

SMALL-POX, *n.* v. POX. देवी. *f. pl* माता *f. pl.* शीतला *f. pl.* आं-

Inoculated s. कुंभाराच्या देवी *f. pl.*-माता *f. pl.*

S. with epileptic fits. फेपऱ्यादेवी *f. pl.* [लहान.

SMALL-SIZED, *a.* आकाराचा-&c. लहान, अल्पमूर्त्ति,लहानाळ, लहु-

SMALLNESS, *n.* v. A. 1. लहानपणा*m.* लहानवी *f.* लघुता *f.* लघुत्व *n.* &c.

2 थोडकेपणा *m.* थोडेपणा *m.* हलकेपणा *m.* &c.

SMARAGDINE, *a. of emerald colour.* जंबुरद्दी.

SMART, SMARTING, *n. quick, pungent pain.* दुःख *n.* वेदना *f.* चुणचूण *f.* चुणूक *f.* चुणका *m.* चुरचूर *f.* छुणछुणी *f.* तिडीक *f.* चिणचीण *f.* फणफण *f.* शूल *pop.* शूळ *or* सूळ *m.* सल *f.* सलक *f.*—*intens.* चुणचुणाट *m.* चुरचुराट *m.* छुणछुणाट *m.* चिणचिणाट *m.* फणफणाट *m.*

SMART, *a. sharp, painful.* तिखट, तीक्ष्ण, तीव्र.

2—of persons; *brisk, quick, active, vigorous, prompt, &c.* चपल *or* ळ, चपळा, चलाक *or* ख, उड्या, कडकडीत, चटपटी *or* ट्या, झटपट्या, हुशार, जलद, झपाट्या, फणशा, कचक्या, खबरदार, फांकडा, तडकसार, खमक्या,खमशा, खरपूस,कट्टा, खडाण, अटोपी, साटोप, शिताब, शितरपाड, लगधगी *or* ग्या.

3 *lively, quick, apt, intelligent, &c.* v. SHARP. चप्पू, चंच, चंचिबाग, चंचुबाग, चंचिबाज, चरचीक, चणचणीत, चुणचुणीत, ताखडा.

4 *quick, energetic, vigorous, sharp, &c.*—blow, action, measure, &c. झपाट्याचा, कडाक्याचा, तडाख्याचा, धडाक्याचा, ठसक्याचा, &c. झटापटीचा, लटापटीचा, कडकडीत, कडक, नडकफडक, ठसठशीत.

5 *spruce, &c.* v. NEAT, FINE. चकपक, चकचकीत, चकू, लकपक, लक्कू, लकलकीत, चाक *or* ख, चाकचोप, चाकपाक, चापचोप, ठाकसठिकस *or* ठिकसठाकस, चापचोपीचा, चाकचोपीचा, छानीचा, छानदार.

6 *witty, acute.* नोकदार, नोकीचा, खुबीचा, बांका, मार्मिक.

A s. lively saying. फरडूक *or* फुरडूक *n.*

One ready with s. sayings and repartees. फरडुक्या.

SMART, *interj. sharp!* बल्हा, त्वरेस मोल.

To SMART, *v. n. feel a sharp, pungent pain.* दुसणें, चुणचुणणें, छुणछुणणें, चणचणणें, चिणचिणणें, चुरचुरणें, तिडकणें, सलणें, खुपणें, दुःख *n.*-वेदना *f.*-चुणचूण *f.*-चुरचूर *f.*-&c. लागणें-होणें *in. con.* तिडीक *f.*-सल *f.* मारणें.—*intens.* चणाणणें.

2 for; *bear the penalty or evil consequence of a thing, be punished.* दुःख *n.* भोगणें, तोंडांत खाणें, निस्तरणें *or* निस्तारणें.

To cause to s. for. भोवणें, जाणवणें.

SMARTLY, *adv.* v. A. 2. 4. चलाकीनें, झटपटीनें, झपाट्यानें, कडक्यानें, धडाक्यानें, &c. कडकडून, कडकावून, कचकावून, करकचून, तडकून, तडकावून, रगडून, तकट, तकटून, सपाटून, ससाटून, घसकन-कर-दिशी-&c. धडकून, झडझडून, करकचून, तडक *or* तडका, धडक *or* धडका, धडधड *or* धडधडा, कडक *or* कडका, मारून, बळकट, बळकटून, झपझप, झपझपां, झपाझप, झपापां, भरभर, भरभरां, भराभर, भरारां, झरझर, झरझरां, झराझर, झरारां, झडझड, झडझडां, झडाझड, झडाडां, फडफड, फडफडां, फडाफड, फडाडां, चपचप, चपचपां, चपाचप, चपापां, पटकापटकी, पटपट, पटपटां, पटापट, पटाटां, खडाखड, खडाखडी *or* खडोखड & खडोखडी, ताबडतोब *or* प, झपकन-कर-दिशी-&c. मटकन-कर-दिशी-&c घसकन-दिनी-दिशी- &c. फटकन-कर-दिशी-&c. झटकन-कर-दिशी-&c. सरकन-कर-दिशी-&c. भरकन-कर-दिशी-&c. चपकन-करदिशी-&c. पटकन-कर-दिशी, तूरूत, तूर्त, तुर्तचेतूर्त-तुर्तातुर्ती-तुर्तातूर्त, तडकातडकीं *or* तडकाफडकीं, तडाफडी, हातोहात, हतोपात, हातचेहातीं, उठाउठी, उभाउभी, उभ्यांउभ्यां, उभ्यांउभ्यांनी, धूम, लवलाहें *or* लवलाही. See also TRICE.

To be off s. सडकणें. [छानमारून.

5 चकपक, चकचकीत, &c. चापचोपीनें, चाकचोपीनें, चापूनचोपून,

SMARTNESS, *n.* v. A. 1. तिखटपणा *m.* तीक्ष्णता *f.* तीव्रता *f.* तैक्ष्ण्य *n.*

2 चपळपणा *m.* &c. &c. चपळाई *f.* चलाकी *f. or* खी *f.* झटपट *f.* चटपट *f.* चकपक *f.* हुशारी *f.* जलदी *f.* त्वरा *f.* सफाई *f.* आंगसफाई *f.* चपलता *f.* चापल्य *n.* शितरपाडी *f.* शिताबी *f.* तडका *m.* लगधग *f.*

3 चप्पूपणा *m.* चणचणितपणा *m.* तासडेपणा *m.* &c.

4 झपाटा *m.* कडाखा *m.* तडाखा *m.* धडाका *m.* सपाटा *m.* भिराका *m.* रगडा *m.* रगाडा *m.* धूम *f.* मार *m.* धोशा *m.* खरका *m.* तडका *m.*

5 चकपकपणा *m.* लकपकपणा *m.* &c. चाकचोपी *f.* चापचोपी *f.* चापीचोपी *f.* छान *f.* छानदारी *f.* डामडौल *m.* कटाव *m.* धजाव *m.* धज *f.*

6 नोकदारी *f.* नोक *f.* खुबी *f.* मार्मिकता *f.* [शतचूर्ण *n.*

SMASH, *n. smashed or shattered mass.* चकनाचूर *or* चकाचूर *m.*

2 *smashed &c. state.* चुराडा *m.* चूर *m.* वैशकल्य *n.* रफरफ *f.*

To SMASH, *v.a. break in pieces, dash to pieces.* ठार *adv.* फोडणें-मोडणें-&c. चकनाचूर *m.*-चकाचूर *m.*-चूर *m.* करणें-करून टाकणें *g. of o.* विघडणें, विघाट *m.*-विघटन *or* विघाटन *n.*-&c. करणें *g. of o.*

2 fig. v.To DEFEAT. हुसकटणें, हुसकणें, लथडणें *or* लथाडणें.

SMASHED, *p.*v.V.1. ठार फोडलेला, चकनाचूर केलेला, &c. चकनाचूर, चकाचूर, शतचूर्ण, विघटित *or* विघाटित.

To be s. भंगास जाणें.

SMATTERER, *n. one who has a slight superficial knowledge.* पुस्तकावरून ओढलेला, ओरसडलेला, खंडींखंडींपंडित, कोवळाव्युत्पन्न, अर्धचाट *or* चाटगा (बोलणारा, लिहिणारा, &c.), अर्धकच्चा, पंडिताभास, टाणाटोण्या *or* टोण्याटाणा, बाडी *or* बाड्या (वैद्य, जोशी, &c.) अल्पविद्य, किंचिज्ज्ञ, मंत्रमुख, ताकपिठ्या, साक्षर.

SMATTER, SMATTERING, *n. slight superficial knowledge.* कच्चेंज्ञान *n.* पुस्तकावरून ओढलेलें ज्ञान *n.* ओरसडलेलें ज्ञान *n.* ओरखडलेली माहिती *f.* बाडेंज्ञान *n.* टाणेटोणे *or* टोणेटोणे *m. pl.* ऐकभट्टिचेंज्ञान *n.* किंचित् ज्ञान *n.* खंडपांडित्य *n.*

To acquire a s. of. बरखडणें *or* ओरखडणें

To give a s. of. वरून ओढून टाकणें-ताणणें.

To SMEAR, *v. a. overspread with any thing unctuous.* लिंपणें, लेपणें, माखणें, चुळबुळावणें, चोपडणें, लेथडणें, लेपटणें, लेपडणें, लिडबिडणें *or* लडबडणें, भरणें, भरावणें, बोंबणें, माथणें, माखण *n.*-लिंपण *f. n.*-लेप *n.*-लेपन *n.*-उपलेप *m.*-&c. करणें *g. of o.*

To be smeared with grease or oil. चुळबुळणें.

To s. with dung or dirt. गोबाडणें.

2 (as unctuous substance) *rub over, spread over a surface.* लिंपणें, माखणें, लेपणें, लेथडणें, लेपटणें, लेपडणें, माथणें, चोपडणें, लावणें, माखण *n. f.*-लेपन *n.*-लेप *m.*-&c. करणें.

3 (an idol) with oil, redlead, &c. माजणें *or* मांजणें, माजण *or* मांजण *n.* करणें. [र्चन *n.* करणें.

4 (sandal wood, ashes, &c. on the body.) चार्चिणें, च-

SMEARED, *p.* v. V. लिंपलेला, लेपलेला, माखलेला, &c. चुळबुळीत, लिडबिडीत *or* लडबडीत, लिप्त, अवलिप्त, उपलिप्त, विलेपित.

To be s. गिरबडणें, लिडबिडणें *or* लडबडणें.

SMEAREDNESS, *n.* v. P. लिंपलेलेपणा *m.* &c. निर्लेप *m.* उपलेप *m.* लिंपण *f. n.*

SMEARER, *n.* SMEARING, *p. a.* v. V. लिंपणारा, माखणारा, लेपणारा, &c. लेपक, उपलेपक, अवलेपक, लेपन-&c. कर्त्ता-कारी-&c.

SMEARING, *n.* v. V.—*act.* लिंपणें *n.* माखणें *n.* लेपणें *n.* माथणें *n.* &c. लेथडणी *f.* माखण *n.* लिंपण *n. f.* लेप *m.* लेपन *n.* उपलेप *m.* उपलेपन *n.* अवलेप *m.* विलेपन *n.* विलेप *m.* लिपि *f.*

To SMELL, *v. a. perceive by the nose.* हुंगणें, सुंगणें, हुंगून-सुंगून घेणें, वास *m.* घेणें *g. of o.* नाक *n.* लावणें, नाकाशीं नेणें, घ्राणन *n.*-आघ्राण *n.*-&c. करणें *g. of o.* नाकानें-नाकावाटे घेणें-ग्रहण करणें.

2 out; *discover.* हुंगणें, हुंगून काढणें, वासानें काढणें.

To SMELL, *v. n. have or emit an odour.* वास *m.* असणें *in. con.* वास *m.*-&c. येणें *g. of s.*—strongly and diffusively. घमघमणें, दमदमणें, दणदणणें, घमघम *adv. or* दमदम *adv.* वास *m.* सुटणें *g. of s.*—strongly and grossly. दरवळणें.

2 *have a bad smell,* v. To STINK. वास *m.* मारणें, घाण *f.*-वास *m.* येणें-मारणें *g. of s. also with in. con.*

SMELL, *n.*—the power or sense. घ्राणेंद्रिय *n.* घ्राण *n.* घ्राणशक्ति *f.* गंधग्रहणशक्ति *f.*

2—the perception. घ्राण *n.* आघ्राण *n.* अवघ्राण *n.* गंधग्रहण *n.*

3 *scent, odour.* वास *m.* गंध *m.*

S. of a fry. तळसाण *f.*

S. of burned food. करपटाण *f.*

S. of an extinguished lamp. दिपुष्टाण *or* दिपोष्टाण *f.*

S. of a thing burned, scorched, parched. भाष्टाण *f.*

S. of dampness. हिंवसाण *f.* हिवळसाण *f.* ओलष्टाण *f.*

S. of herbage, green wood, &c. हिरवटाण *f.* हिरवसाण *f.*

S. of mouldiness. उबटाण *f.* उबसाण *f.*

S. of new earthen vessels, new cloth, &c. कोरटाण *f.* कोरष्टाण *f.* कोरसाण *f.*

S. of oiled things, or oil. तेलसाण *f.* तेलटाण *f.* तेलक-

टाण *f.* तेलष्टाण *f.*

S. of rancidity or rankness. खवटाण *f.* घुरटाण *f.* घुरष्टा- [ण *f.*

S. of rancid तूप (clarified butter). तुपटाण *f.* तुपसाण *f.* तुपष्टाण *f.*

S. of ripe fruits or ripeness. पिकटाण *f.*

S. of rottenness. कुजकटाण *f.* कुजटाण *f.* कुष्टाण *f.*

S. of smoke. धुरटाण *f.* धुरकटाण *f.*

S. of sourness. आंबटाण *f.* आंबसाण *f.* आंबष्टाण *f.*

S. of strong effluvia. ओरटाण *f.* ओरष्टाण *f.*

Strong s. उग्रटाण *f.* उग्रष्टाण *f.* दर्प *m.* दरवळ *m.*

Strong and diffusive and sweet s. परिमल *or* ळ *m.* आमोद *m.* घमघमाट *m.* दमदमाट *m.* दणदणाट *m.*

To be diffused widely & strongly—offensive smells. दरवळणें.

4 *ill smell*, v. STINK. घाण *f.*

5 *good smell*, v. FRAGRANCE. सुवास *m.* सुगंध *m.* [नी.

SMELL-FEAST, *n.* v. PARASITE. परान्नरुचि, परपाकरुचि, अनुसंधा-

SMELLED, *p.* v. V. A. 1. हुंगलेला, &c. घ्रात, आघ्रात, अवघ्रात.

SMELLER, *n.* SMELLING, *p. a.* v. V. A. 1. हुंगणारा, वास घेणारा, &c. घ्राण-आघ्राण-&c. कर्त्ता-कारी-&c.

2 हुंगणारा, हुंगून काढणारा, &c. हुंग्या, हुंगाड्या.

v. V. N. 1. गंधाचा, वासाचा, &c. वासयुक्त, गंधवान्, गंधयुक्त, सगंध, गंधगुण, गंधधर्मक.

To SMELT, *v. a.* (ore) *melt.* रस *m.* करणें *g. of o.* रस करून गाळणें, अटणें.

SMELTER, *n.* v. V. रस करून गाळणारा, धावड *is the name of a caste whose occupation is smelting.*

To SMILE, *v.n. contract the features so as to express pleasure.* मंद हासणें, मंदहास्य *n.*-स्मित*n.*-&c. करणें, गालांत-गालावर-गालीं गालीं-&c. हसणें, हास्यवदन*n.*-हास्यमुख *pop.* हसतमुख *n.*-&c. करणें.

2 *be propitious.* फुलणें, खुलणें, प्रसन्नहोणें, कृपादृष्टि *f.* ठेवणें-करणें *and in. con.* असणें.

SMILE, SMILING, *n.* v. V. 1. मंदहसणें*n.* गालांतलें हसणें*n.* गालावरहसणें*n.* &c. मंदहास्य *n.* ईषद्धास *m.* स्मित *n.* विहसन *n.* विहसित *n.*

2 कृपादृष्टि *f.* कृपाकटाक्ष *m.* कृपावलोकन *n.*

SMILER, *n.* SMILING, *p. a.* v. V. मंदहसणारा, गालावर-गालांत-&c. हसणारा, &c. स्मित, सस्मित, प्रसन्नमुख, प्रफुल्ल.

A s. countenance. हास्यमुद्रा *f.* हास्यमुख *n.* हास्यवदन*n.* हसतमुख *n.*

Of a s. countenance. हसतमुख (vulg. हस्तमुख) हास्यमुख, हास्यवदन, स्मेरमुख.

To SMIRCH, *v. a. cloud, soil.* भरणें, काळसर-मजीत-&c. करणें.

SMIRK, *n. affected, silly, &c. smile.* कपटाचें-थट्टेचें-वेडेपणाचें-&c. हसणें *n.*-हास्य*n.* अपहसित*n.* जिह्महसित*n.* जिह्महास्य*n.* मानभावी हसणें *n.*

To SMIRK, *v. n.* v. N. कपटाचें-वेडेपणाचें-&c. हसणें करणें.

To SMITE, *v. a.* v. To STRIKE. मारणें, प्रहार *m.*-&c. करणें.

2 *slay*, v. To KILL. जिवें मारणें, मारून टाकणें.

3 *affect with passion.* मोहणें, मोहित-लुब्ध-रत-आसक्त-निरत-&c. करणें.

SMITER, *n.* SMITING, *p. a.* v. V 1. मारणारा, &c.

2 जिवें मारणारा.

SMITH, *n. forger with a hammer.* घडकामी, घडकाम्या, ठोककामा, ठोककाम्या. [लोहाण्डा *m.*

2 *blacksmith.* लोहकार *pop.* लोहार*m.* घिसाडी *m.*-in contempt.

Business of a s. लोहारकी *f.*

SMITH-CRAFT, *n.* घडकाम*n.* ठोककाम *n.*

SMITH-WORK, *n.* घडकाम *n.* ठोककाम *n.* [घडीत*n.*

Price or rate of s. घडणावळ *f.* घडण *f.* घडाई *f.* घडावण*n.*

SMITHERY, *n. shop of a blacksmith.* लोहारसाळ *f.* लोहाराचें दुकान *n.*

2 *smith-work.* घडकाम *n.*

SMITHY, *n. shop of a blacksmith.* लोहारसाळ*f.* लोहाराचें दुकान*n.*

SMITTEN, *p.* v. V. 1. मारलेला, &c.

2 जिवें मारलेला, &c.

3 *and* ENAMOURED. मोहलेला, मोहित, लुब्ध, रत (in comp.) वेडा, आसक्त, निरत.

To be s. भुलणें, रंजणें, रिझणें, भाळणें, रंगणें. [समीस*n.*

SMOCK, *n. a woman's under garment.* बायकोचें-&c. कमीज *or*

SMOKE, *n. exhalation from a burning substance.* धूर *m.* धूम्र*m.* धूम *m.* धुकट *m.* [धूमावलि *f.*

Cloud or volume of s. धुराडी *f.* धुराटी*f.* धुरंदळ *n.* पटल*n.*

To end in s. v. To DEFEAT. फिसकणें, फसकटणें, फसकणें, फिसकटणें, बोंचलणें, वितुळणें.

To be soiled or affected by s. धुरकटणें.

To SMOKE, *v. a. affect by smoke.* धुरावणें, धूर *m.*-धुरी *f.* देणें, धुकटावणें, धुरकटावणें, धुरकट-&c. करणें.

2 (tobacco, a pipe, &c.). पिणें, ओढणें.

3 *smell, find out.* हुंगणें, हुंगून काढणें, वासानें काढणें.

4 (timbers, &c. to harden them). आगिवळा*m.* देणें.

To SMOKE, *v. n. emit smoke,*—green wood, &c. धुमसणें, धुमणें, धुपणें. [पिणें-ओढणें.

2 *use tobacco in a pipe, &c.* हुक्का *m.*-झरझरी *f.*-विडी *f.*-&c.

SMOKE-COLORED, *a.* धुराच्या रंगाचा, धूम्रवर्ण.

To SMOKE-DRY, *v. a.* धुरावर वाळवणें.

SMOKE-LESS, *a.* विनधुराचा, निर्धूम, निर्धूम्र, विधूम.

SMOKE-VENT, *n.* धुराडें *or* णें *or* धारें *n.* दादरा *m.* साहणें *or* साणें*n.* धाराणें *n.* धुरोळें *n.*

SMOKED, *p.*v.V. A. 1. धुरावलेला, धुरकट केलेला,&c. धुरकट, धुरट.

To be s. धुरकटणें, धुरटणें, धुरावणें, धुकटावणें, धूर*m.* लागणें *in. con.* [&c. धुमरा.

SMOKER, *n.* SMOKING, *p. a.* v. V. N. 1. धुमसणारा, धुमणारा,

2 हुक्का-विडी-&c. पिणारा-ओढणारा, गुडगुड्या, हुक्केबाज, चिलमी *or* म्या. [*n.* धूमपान*n.*

SMOKING, *n.* v. V.N. 2. हुक्का ओढणें *n.* हुक्कापिणें*n.* &c. धूम्रपान

Smoking apparatus. हुक्का*m.* गुडगुडी *f.* गुरगुडी *f.* झरझरी*f.*

Note. These words denote different kinds.

SMOKY, *a. of or belonging, &c. to s.* धुराचा, धुमाचा, धुरकटाचा, धूम्रमय, धूममय.

S. smell or taste. धुरकटाण *f.* धुरटाण *f.*

Smoked or s. water. धुरवणी *n.*

2 *emitting s.* धुमरा, धुरकट.

3 *tarnished with s.* धूरलागलेला, धुरकटलेला, धुरटलेला.

SMOOTH, *a. not rough.* गुळगुळीत *or* गुलगुलीत, साफ, मऊ, मृदु,

मुलाईम, नितळ, तुळतुळीत, सफाईदार, चिक्कण, मसृण.
S. and polished. सुळसुळीत.
2 *equal*, *level*, v. EVEN. सारखा, बराबर, न्यहार, सपाट, सपाटीचा, नेपाळ, सम.
3 *flowing*, *fluent*, *easy*, *even*. सुरळीत, सरळ, धाराबाहिक, धाराबाही, अनुस्यूत.
4 *soft*, *soothing*, *bland*, *glib*, *&c.* मऊ, मृदु, लाघवी, गोडबोल्या, गुळगुळथापडीचा, सांत्ववादाचा, मधुरभाषी, लाडीगोडीचा, गोडीगुलाबीचा, सुबाळीमबाळीचा.
5 *softly flowing*, v. CALM. संथ, संथचाललेला, स्थिर, स्थिरचाललेला, निवळ.

To SMOOTH, *v. a. make soft*, *&c.*; *remove roughness*, v. To POLISH. गुळगुळीत-मऊ-साफ-&c.; करणें,—esp. by rubbing, नितळणें, घोंटणें.
2 *make even*, *&c.* सारखा-बराबर-सपाट-सम-&c. करणें, न्यहारणें, सारखावणें, नेपाळणें, नेपाळणी *f.* करणें. [&c. करणें.
3 *make easy*. सोपा-सुरळीत-सोईचा-&c. करणें, सुरळीतचालेसा-
4—as in fondling, *stroke*. गोंजारणें *or* गोंजरणें, कुरवाळणें, चोंबाळणें, अंजारणें *or* अंजारणें गोंजारणें.

SMOOTH-FACED, *a. mild looking*. गोमुख्या.
A s. villain. मिसकीनमात्रागमनी, मिसकीनमारवाडी.

SMOOTH-TONGUED, *a.* गोडबोल्या.

SMOOTHLY, *adv.* v. A. 3. *and* FLOWINGLY. सुरळीत, सरळ, घमघम *or* मां (*intens.* घमाघम) सुदामत.
4 मऊपणानें, &c. लाडीगोडीनें, गोडीगुलाबीनें, गोडगोडबोलून.

SMOOTHNESS, *n.* v. A. 1. गुळगुळितपणा*m.* तुळतुळितपणा*m.* &c. नितळाई *f.* साफी *f.* सफाई *f.* सफाईदारी *f.* मृदुता *f.*
2 सारखेपणा*m.* &c. सपाटी *f.* समता *f.* साम्य*n.*
3 सुरळितपणा*m.* सरळपणा*m.*
4 *and* BLANDISHMENT. मऊपणा*m.* लाघव *n.* लाडीगोडी *f.* गोडीगुलाबी *f.* मधुरभाषिता *f.*
5 संथपणा*m.* स्थिरपणा*m.*

To SMOTHER, *v. a. suffocate*. दमकोंडून-श्वासकोंडून-&c. मारणें, गुदमारणें, घुसमटवणें, गुदमारून-घुसमटवून मारणें, कोंडमार*m.*-कोंडमारा*m.*-श्वासावरोध*m.*-&c. करणें.
2 v. To SUPPRESS. दाबणें, दडपणें, चेपाचेप *f.*-&c. करणें.

To SMOTHER, *v. n. be suffocated*. गुदमरणें, घुसमटणें, गोफाटणें.
2 See To SMOULDER.

SMOTHERED, *p.* v. V. 1. दम कोंडून मारलेला, गुदमारलेला, &c.
2 दाबलेला, दडपलेला.

To SMOULDER, *v. n. burn and smoke without flame*. धुमसणें, धुमणें, धुपणें, कुरमणें, अंतर्दाह*m.* होणें *g. of s.*

SMOULDERING, *p. a.* SMOULDRY, *a.* v. V. धुमणारा, धुमसणारा, &c. धुमसता, &c.

SMUG, &c. See SPRUCE, &c.

To SMUGGLE, *v.a. import or export clandestinely and without payment of duty*. जकात-&c. चुकवून *or* टाळून आणणें-नेणें, जकात दिल्हावांचून-जकातचोरीनें-&c. आणणें-नेणें.
2 *convey clandestinely*. चोरून-लपून छपून-&c. नेणें-आणणें.

SMUGGLED, *p.* v. V. 1. जकातदिल्हावांचून आणलेला, &c. जकातचोरीचा.

SMUGGLER, *n.* SMUGGLING, *p. a.* v. V. 1. जकात दिल्हावांचून आणणारा, जकातचोरी-&c. करणारा.

SMUGGLING, *n.* v. V. 1. जकात दिल्हावांचून आणणें *n.*-&c. जकातचोरी *f.* नाके चोरी *f.*

SMUT, *n. the dirt of soot*, *lampblack*, *&c.* मस *f.* मशेरी *f.* मषी *f.*
2 (of corn). काजळी *f.* अंगारा *m.*—of जोंधळा. काहणी *f.*
3 *obscene language*. विचकट-अचकटविचकट-बीभत्स-&c. बोलणें *n.*-भाषण *n.*-&c. दुर्वचन *n.* दुर्भाषण *n.*

To SMUT, *To* SMUTCH, *v. a. blacken with soot*, *&c.* मस *f.*-&c. लावणें, काळा करणें, काळें *n.* लावणें.

To SMUT, *v. n. gather smut*. मस *f.* जमणें, मशिरणें, मसकटणें.

SMUTTINESS. See SMUT.

SMUTTY, *a.* v. N. 1. मसीचा, &c. मस लागलेला, मसकट, मसकटलेला, मशिरलेला.
2 काजळीचा, काजळी लागलेला, अंगारा लागलेला.
3 *and* OBSCENE. विचकट, अचकटविचकट, बीभत्स, तोंडचाशिनळ, तोंडशिनळ, चवनट.

SNACK. See SHARE.

SNAFFLE, *n.* साधा-सुतळी *or* सुतळयालगाम *m. f.*

SNAG, *n. jag*, *&c.* धस *m.* खणपूस *n.* कांटा *m.* खुंट*m. n.* खोचाटा*m.* खोंच *f.* सुळका *m.* सुळकी *f.* हीर *m.*अखोटा *m.* शल्य *n.*
2 See TOOTH. [शंबूक*m.* पाळूक *n.*

SNAIL, *n.*—the animal. गोगलगाय *f.* पिकूळ *n. dim.* पिकळी *f.*
2 fig. *slow coach*, *&c.* v. DAWDLE. मुंगीच्या पायाचा, मुंगीच्या पायानें चालणारा.

SNAKE, *n.* साप *m.* सर्प *m.* किडें *n.* उरग *m.* उरःसर *m.* भुजंग *m.* विखार *m.* अहि *m.* कुंडली *m.* कंचुकी *m.* व्याल *m.* भोगी *m.*—in covert or cant phraseology, पांढरा *m.* पायाखालचें *n.* पायाखायलें*n.* Of venomous *Snakes* the most common are आगीमण्यार *f.* आग्याघणस *m.* आग्यें फुरसें *n.* कवड्याघणस *m.* कवड्यासर्प *or* साप *m.* कांडार *or* कांदार *m. f.* कांबळया *m.* कुसडाघणस *m.* घणस *m.* चाकण *f.* जोगी *m.* डुरडुरा *m.* डोंब्यानाग *or* डोंब्यासर्प *m.* तक्षक *m.* दुतोंडें *n.* धामण्या *m.* नाग *m.* नांदिटा *or* नानेटा *m.* *or* टी *or* ठी *f.* फुरसें *n.* मणेर *or* मण्यार *f.* मण्यासाप *m.* महांडूळ *or* मांडूळ *or* मालुंड *n.*
The exuvies or slough of a s. मेंग *f.*
Fork for poking out snakes. वाभेरें *n.*
Hooded s. फणी.
Lines under the throat of snakes. लहरी *f. pl.*
Young s. पोंगा *m.* पोंवा *m.*

SNAKE-CHARMER, SNAKE-DOCTOR, *n.* गारुडी *or* गारोडी, मंत्रवादी, मंत्री, सर्पमंत्री, विषवैद्य, जांगुलिक, मदारी.

SNAKE-GOURD, *n.* परवर *f.*—the fruit. परवर *n.*

SNAKE-HOLE, *n.* सांपलें *n.*

SNAKE-LILY, *n.* सापकंद *m.* सापकांदा *m.*

SNAKE-STONE, *n.* सर्पमणि *m.*नागमणि *m.*

SNAKY, *a. pertaining*, *&c. to snakes*. सापाचा, सर्पाचा, सापाविषयींचा, सार्प.
2 *infested with snakes*, (road, &c.) पायाखायला.

To SNAP, *v. a. break at once*, *break short*. कटकन-कटकर-कटदिशी-पटकन-पटकर-पटदिशी-फटकन-फटकर-तटकन-&c. मोडणें-तोडणें.
2 (the fingers). चुटकी *f.*-चटकी *f.*-टिचकी *f.* मारणें-वाजवणें.
3 See To BITE. 4 up; See To SNATCH. 5—a whip. See To CRACK.

To SNAP, *v. n. break short.* कटकन-कटकर-&c. मोडणें-तुटणें, उतटणें *or* उताटणें, तटतटणें *or* तडतडणें—*intens.* तटाटणें.

Ready to s.—thread. तुटरा, तुटीर.

2 at; *try to seize and bite.* तोंड *n.* टाकणें, डसायाला-चावायाला-&c. करणें.

3 at; fig. *turn upon, speak angrily to, &c.* खेंकणें, खेंकावणें, खेंसणें, खिसणें, खिंकावणें, तिडतिडणें, टणटणणें, टणटण उडणें-बोलणें, कातवणें *or* कातावणें, बसबसणें, बसकणें, बसकन-&c. आंगावर येणें, तुटून आंगावर येणें-जाणें, दांतरी *f.* करणें.

SNAP, *n.* (with the fingers). चुटकी *f.* चटकी *f.* चिटकी *f.* टिचकी *f.* चुकटी *f.*

SNAPPISH, *a.* v. CROSS. खिसखिशा, तिडतिडा, तिडका, चिरडखोर, चिरडीखोर, चिडखोर, चिडचिड्या, चिडचिडा, चिडरा, खेंकड, खेन्या, हिरवट, हिरवा, तुटरा, तुडतुड्या, तडतड्या, काविरडा, जिद्‌खोर.

2—a dog. तोंडटाकण्याच्या-डसण्याच्या-&c. स्वभावाचा, डसरा, चावरा. [*or* णां.

SNAPPISHLY, *adv.* v. A. बसकन-कर-&c. बसबस *or* सां, टणटण

SNAPPISHNESS, *n.* v. A. 1. चिरड *f.* तिडतीड *f.* चिरडेपणा *m.* चिरडखोरी *f.* चिडचिडेपणा *m.* तिडतिडेपणा *m.* &c.

SNARE, *n. instrument for catching animals,* lit. fig. फांस *m.* फांसा *m.* पाश *m.* (esp. in comp. and with great neatness and power, as प्रपंचपाश, भवपाश, स्नेहपाश, मोहपाश, &c.), जाल*n.*(esp. in comp. as प्रपंच जाल, भवजाल, मोहजाल, &c.), पाशबंध *m.* वावर *f.* वागुरा *f.* फांसकी *f.* गचका *m.* पेंच *m.*

One who catches animals by a s. or net. फांसेपारधी *m.*

To SNARE, *v. a. entrap,* lit. fig. फाशांत-&c. धरणें-आणणें-पाडणें-सांपडवणें, फशींदेणें-पाडणें, पाशबद्ध-जालबद्ध करणें.

SNARED, *p.v.*V.फाशांत धरलेला-सांपडवलेला-&c. पाशबद्ध, जालबद्ध.

To SNARL, *v.n.* v. To GROWL. गुरकणें, गुरगुरणें *or* घुरघुरणें, गुरगुरावणें *or* घुरघुरावणें.

SNARL, SNARLING, *n.* v. V.—*act.* गुरगुरणें *n.* &c. गुरगूर *or* घुरघूर *f. intens.* गुरगुराट *or* घुरघुराट *m.* श्वानवैखरी *f.*

I. *knot on a rope.* अढी *f.*

SNARLER, *n.* SNARLING, *p. a.* v. V. गुरगुरणारा, &c. गुरगूर-&c. करणारा, गुरगुऱ्या, गुरक्या.

To SNATCH, *v. a. seize hastily.* हिसकणें, हिसकावणें, हिसकून घेणें, छिनावणें, असडणें, हिसडणें, झोंबाडणें, हबकणें, झोंबाडा *m.*-&c. घालणें-मारणें, झडप *f.*-झडपडा*m.* घालणें, हिसडा*m.*-असडा*m.*-झटका *m.*-&c. देणें-देऊनघेणें, हिसक्यानें-हिसकादेऊन-&c. धरणें-पकडणें.

2 up; *seize rudely, pounce upon, &c.* उचकणें, उचलणें, पटकावणें, मटकावणें, बोचकरणें, हात *m.* मारणें, रगडणें, रपाटणें, दपटणें, दपटगिरी *f.*-दपटनिशी *f.*-हबकाहबक *f.*-&c. करणें.

To s. up and pocket, *seize furtively.* उपटणें, बगलाविणें, काखाटणें, काखाविणें.

To SNATCH, *v. n. make attempt to seize suddenly, catch at.* झोंबणें, झोंबाडा *m.*-क्षेप *f.*-झाप *f.*-झडप *f.*-झडपडा *m.*-&c. घालणें, हिसका *m.*-&c. मारणें.

SNATCH, SNATCHING, *n.* v. V. A. 1.—*act.* हिसकणें *n.* असडणें *n.* झोंबाडणें *n.* &c. झोंबाडा *m.* हिसडा *m.* असडा *m.* झडप *f.* झडपडा *m.*

2 पटकावणें *n.* मटकावणें *n.* हात मारणें *n.* &c. दपटगिरी *f.* दपटनिशी *f.* हबकाहबक *f.*

I. *a broken or interrupted portion.* चुटका*m.*

S. of sunshine. उन्हाचा चुटका *m.* तिरीप *f.*

S. of a song. तुक *n.*

To SNEAK, *v. n. cringe, behave with servility,* v. To FAWN. थुंका *m.*-थुंकी *f.* झेलणें, थुंकीला ओणवणें, नाक*n.* घासणें, जीजी *f.* करणें, हांजी *f.* करणें-म्हणणें.

2 off; v. To SLINK. गुपचूप-&c. निघून जाणें, कसरतें-काढतें-निघतें-&c. घेणें, मुठींत नाक धरून जाणें, मेंगावणें.

SNEAK, *n.* SNEAKER, *n.* SNEAKING, *p. a.* v. V. 1. *and* OBSEQUIOUS. थुंकीझेलणारा, जीजी करणारा, हांजी म्हणणारा, आर्जवी, आर्जवाचा.

2 गुपचूप निघून जाणारा, कसरतें-&c. घेणारा, मुठींत नाक धरून जाणारा, दृष्टिचोर, नजरचोर, नजरचुकाव.

To SNEER, *v. n. show contempt by looks, &c.* नाक *n.* वर करणें-झाडणें-मोडणें, नाकाला झिमोटा *m.* घालणें, नाक झाडणी *f.*-&c. करणें.

2 *show contempt by expressions.* लावून-खोचून-बोचून-टोचून-&c. बोलणें, उपरोध*m.*-आक्षेप *m.* करणें, टोमणा *m.*-टोला *m.*-टोसरा *m.*-तुक्का *m.*-&c. मारणें-टाकणें. [नाकमोडणी *f.*

SNEER, SNEERING, *n.* v. V. 1. नाकझाडणें *n.* &c. नाकझाडणी *f.*

2 *and* SARCASM. लावून बोलणें *n.* &c. उपरोध *m.* आक्षेप *m.*

SNEERER, *n.* SNEERING, *p. a.* v. V. 1. नाक वर करणारा, नाक झाडणारा-मोडणारा.

2 *and* SARCASTIC. लावून बोलणारा, खोंचून बोलणारा, &c.

SNEERINGLY, *adv.* v. A. 1. नाक वर करून, नाक झाडून, &c.

2 उपरोधानें, लावून, खोंचून, टोमणा-&c. मारून.

To SNEEZE, *v. n. emit air violently through the nose.* शिंकणें *or* सिंकणें, शिंक *or* सिंक *f.* जाणें-येणें.

The exclamation upon a person's sneezing is शतंजीव.

SNEEZE, SNEEZING, *n.* v. V.—*act.* शिंकणें *n.* शिंक *or* शिंक *or* सिंक *f.* शिंकणी *f.* छिक्का *f.* क्षुत् *f.*

To SNIFF, *v. n. draw air through the nose.* सुंगणें, सूं *n.*-सूंसूं *n.* करणें, नाकानें- नाकावाटे श्वास *m.* घेणें.

To s. deeply at (snuff, &c.). झुरकणें, झुरका *m.* घेणें.

To SNIP, *v. a. cut off with scissors.* कातरून घेणें, कातरणें, कातरणी *f.* करणें.

SNIPE, *n.* पाणलव्हा *or* लावा *m.*

To SNIPE, *v. a. pick off.* टिपणें, टिपून घेणें-काढणें.

SNIPSNAP, *n.* v. SQUABBLE. कचाकच *f.* चकमक *f.*

SNIVEL, *n.* v. SNOT. शेंबूड *m.* जळमट *n.*

To SNIVEL, *v. n. run at the nose.* नाक *n.* वाहणें *g. of s.* बरबरणें, नाकांतून शेंबूड *m.* वाहणें-गळणें, नासिकास्राव *m.*-&c. होणें *g. of s.*

2—as children; *cry whimperingly.* धुसमुसणें, नुसमुसणें, धुसमणें, कुसमुसणें, रडूनशेंबूड *m.* गाळणें.

SNIVELLER, *n.* SNIVELLING, *p. a.* v. V. 1. नाक वाहिलेला, &c. बरबरीत, शेंबडा, शेंबड्या, शेंबडेरा.

2 मुसमुसणारा, धुसमुसणारा, &c.

SNOB, *n.* SNOBBISH, *a.* सभ्यंमन्य.

SNOOD, *n. hair-braid.* अगूळ *f. m. n.* रफटा*m.*

SNOOZE, See NAP. [लावणें.

To SNORE, *v. n. breathe harshly in sleep.* घोरणें, घुरघूर *f.* करणें-

SNORER, *n.* SNORING, *p. a.* v. V. घोरणारा, &c.

To SNORT, *v. n.*—as a horse, &c. *blow through the nose.* खेंसणें, खेंकणें, फुरफुरणें *intens.* फुरारणें, नाकपुड्या *f. pl.* पिंजारणें, फुर्र *adv.* करणें, फुरफूर *f.*-फुरफुराट *m.*-&c. करणें, फुंपणें.

SNORTER, *n.* SNORTING, *p. a.* v. V. खेंसणारा, फुरफुरणारा, &c.

SNORTING, *n.* v. V.—*act.* खेंसणें *n.* फुरफुरणें *n.* &c. फुरफुरणी *f.* फुरफूर *f. intens.* फुरफुराट *m.*

SNOT, *n. mucus of the nose,*—as running or moist. शेंबूड *m.* शेंब *or* शेम *f.* नाकाचा मळ *m.* नासिकामल *n.*

Lump of s. शिंकरा *m.* बडका *or* बेडका *m.*

String of s. जळमट *n.* लोळी *f.*

2—as hard or dry. मेकूड *n.*

SNOTTY, *a. foul with snot.* शेंबडा, शेंबड्या, शेंबूड भरलेला, बरबरीत, नाक बरबरलेला.

SNOTTY-NOSED, *a.* शेंबडा *or* ड्या, शेंबडेरा.

SNOUT, *n.* v. NOSE. सोंड *f.*

That has a trunk or s. सोंड्या.

SNOW, *n. frozen vapour.* बर्फ *n.* तुषार *m.* हिम *n.*

SNOWY, *a. abounding, &c. with snow.* बर्फाचा, हिम्य, तुषारमय, तुषारप्रचुर, हिममय, हिमप्रचुर. [राभ.

2 *white like snow,* v. WHITE. पांढरा फटफटीत, हिमाभ, कर्पू-

To SNUB, *v. a.* v. To SCOLD. धमकावणें, दबकावणें, दबावणें, दाबणें, दटावणें, दडबडावणें, दरडावणें, दामटणें, धडकावणें, छुकू *adv.* करणें-म्हणणें.

SNUB-NOSED, *a.* नकटा, नाकचिंबा, चपणी, फेंदरा, बसकटनाक्या, ज्याचा नाशिक परगणा ओसाड आहे, ज्याचें नाशिक त्रिंबकास गेलें.

SNUFF, *n.*(of a torch, a wick, &c.). गूल *m.* काजळी *f.* कोजळी *f.* कोळशी *f.* कोळी *m.* चिंचळा *m.* शेंबूड *m.*

Stink of a s. दिपुष्टाण *f.* [जळणें.

To be coverd with s. or *cabbage,*—a lighted wick. को-

2 *powdered tobacco.* तपकीर *or* ल *or* तपखीर *or* ल *f. n.* नास *f.* नस्य *n.* नासिकाचूर्ण *n.*

Pungent s. मासुकमारी *or* रें तपकीर *f. n.*

To take s. तपकीर *f. n.* ओढणें.

To SNUFF, *v. n.*—a wick, &c. कोजळणें.

2 at; *turn up the nose at.* नाक *n.* झाडणें-मोडणें-वर करणें-बर नेणें-मुरडणें.

3 See To SNIFF, To SNORT.

To SNUFF, *v. a.* (a wick, &c.). काजळी *f.*-कोजळी *f.*-&c. कातरणें-काढणें-झाडणें *g. of o.* [बरोबर घेणें.

2 *draw in with the breath, inhale.* घेणें, ओढून घेणें, श्वासा

3 v. To SMELL. हुंगणें, हुंगून घेणें, वास *m.* घेणें *g. of o.*

SNUFF-BOX, *n.* तपकिरीची-तपकिराची डबी *f.*

SNUFF-COLORED, *a.* तपकिरी, तपकीररंगी.

SNUFF-SELLER, *n.* तपकिऱ्या *or* ल्या, तपकीरविक्या, तपकीरवाला.

SNUFF-TAKER, SNUFFER, *n.* तपकिऱ्या *or* ल्या.

SNUFFERS, *n.* दिव्याची-कोजळीची-&c. कातर *f.*

To SNUFFLE, *v. n. speak through the nose.* नाकांत बोलणें, गुणगुणणें, खुणखुणणें, गुंगणें, गेंगणें, गुणगुण-गेंगत-गुंगत-&c. बोलणें. [ण्या, गेंगाणा.

SNUFFLER, *n.* SNUFFLING, *p. a.* v. V. नाकांत बोलणारा, गुणगु-

SNUFFY, *a. soiled, &c. with snuff.* तपकिरीनें बरबटलेला-भरलेला, तपकीरमय.

To SNUG, *v. n. lie close, cuddle.* चिकटून-लगटून-&c. निजणें, कुशींत शिरणें-शिरून निजणें, सरसा *decl.* निजणें.

SNUG, *a.*—of places, &c. *neat, &c.* सुटसुटीत, खुटखुटीत, अटपता, अटकर, सोईचा, सुबक, धालाधाकटा.

2—of persons; *lying close.* चिकटलेला, लगटलेला.

To lie s. चिकटून-लगटून निजणें, सरसा *decl.* निजणें.

To SNUGGLE, *v. n. lie close for warmth.* गुरगुटून निजणें, घुरघूस *f.* मारणें-मारून निजणें.

SO, *adv. in this manner.* असा, ह्या प्रमाणें, एवम्.

And so forth. इत्यादि.

So, so be it. तथा, तथास्तु, अस्तु.

So so. *moderately.* असातसा, जसातसा, जसतसा, सुमारमाफक, सुमाराचा, माफक, तादृश, तितपत, तावन्मात्र, यथातथा, यावत्तावत्, चालीवजा, छोटेखानी.

2—as correlatively with *as.* तसा, त्याप्रमाणें, तथा.

3 *to such a degree.* इतका, एवढा, एथ *or* इथपर्यंत-पावेतों-वर.

4 *for this reason.* ह्या-त्यामुळें-साठीं-स्तव-&c. म्हणून, असें असतां, तर, मग. [करणें *g. of o.*

To SOAK, *v. a. steep, &c.* भिजवणें, भिजत-भिजूं घालणें, भीज *f.*

2 *wet through,* v. To DRENCH. चिंब-&c. भिजवणें-करणें, उपळवणें. [&c. करणें *g. of o.*

3 v. To ABSORB. शोषणें, शोषून घेणें, पिणें, शोष *m.*-शोषण *n.*-

To SOAK, *v. n. lie steeped.* भिजत पडणें.

2 *enter into pores, be absorbed.* मुरणें, जिरणें, भिनणें, मुरून-&c. जाणें, सोसणें *or* शोषणें, सोखून-&c. जाणें.

SOAKED, *p.* v. V. A. 1. भिजूं घातलेला, भिजवलेला, &c.

2 चिंब भिजवलेला-भिजलेला-केलेला.

To be s. चिंब-&c. भिजणें, उपळणें. [ळणारा, &c.

SOAKER, *n.* SOAKING, *p. a.* v. V. A. 1. भिजवणारा, भिजत घा-

2 चिंब-&c. भिजवणारा-करणारा, &c. [भिजपाऊस *m.*

Soaking rain(i.e. rain that will soak into the ground).

SOAP, *n.* साबू *or* साबूण *m.*

To SOAP, *v. a.* साबूण *m.* लावणें. [रिंगें *n.*

SOAP BERRY-TREE, *n.* रिठा *m.* रिंठी *f.* रिंगी *f.*—the fruit. रिठें *n.*

SOAP-BOILER, *n. soap-maker.* साबूण करणारा, साबूणगर.

SOAP-SUDS, *n.* साबुणाचें पाणी *n.* [लेला.

SOAPY, *a. smeared with soap.* साबूण लावलेला, साबुणानें बरबट-

2 *like soap, having the quality of soap.* साबुणासारखा, साबुणाच्या धर्माचा.

To SOAR, *v. n. fly aloft.* उडणें, उंचजाणें, उंचावणें, उड्डान *n.*-ऊर्ध्वगमन *n.*-नभोगति *f.*-उत्क्रमण *n.*-&c. करणें.

2 fig. *tower in thought, &c.* उंचविषय *m.*-उत्तमविषय *m.*-प्रौढविषय *m.*-&c. धरणें-घेणें.

3 See To ASPIRE.

4—the voice. चढणें.

SOARER, *n.* SOARING, *p. a.* v. V. 1. उडणारा, &c. ऊर्ध्वगामी, आकाशगामी, आकाशचारी, उड्डीयमान, समुच्चर.

SOARING, *n.* v. V. 1.—*act.* उडण *n.* उड्डान *n.* ऊर्ध्वगमन *n.* ऊर्ध्वगति *f.* आकाशगमन *n.* नभोगति *f.* नभोगमन *n.* उत्क्रमण *n.*

To SOB, *v. n. sigh convulsively in crying.* स्फुंदणें, स्फुंदस्फुंदणें, फुंदणें, मुसमुसणें, धुसमुसणें, धुसमणें, कुसमुसणें, ठिणकणें, उसंबणें *or* ओसंबणें, उस्मरणें, उस्मरे *m. pl.*-हुंडके *or* हुंडूक *m. pl.* -&c. टाकणें *or* येणें *with in. con.* फांप्या *f. pl.* मारणें.

SOB, SOBBING, *n.* v. V. फुंदणें *n.* मुसमुसणें *n.* ठिणकणें *n.* &c.

फुद *m.* फुंदणी *f.* हुंडका *m.* हुंडूक *m.* फाप्या *f. pl.* स्फुंदन *n.*

SOBBINGLY, *adv.* v. V. फुंदफुंदु, फुंदस्फुंदु, हामसाहामसी.

SOBER, *a. temperate in drink.* बेताचा-बेतानें पिणारा, मितप्राशी-पानी-&c. परिमितप्राशी-पानी-&c. पानसंयमी.

2 *not drunk.* सावध, बिन अमली, अमल न चढलेला, कैफाबेगळा-निराळा-&c. अनागतमद, अमत्त, निर्मद.

3 *calm, cool, serious.* स्थिर, धीर, थंड, थंडा, स्थिरमनस्क, स्थिरबुद्धि, विनीत, अमत्त, विचारी, विचारवान्, विचारशील, विचारबुद्धि, विमृश्यकारी, नियतवर्त्ती, नियतवृत्ति.

To SOBER, *v. n. become sober.* निवळणें, अमल *m.*-कैफ *m.*-&c. उतरणें-जाणें *g. of s.* शुद्धीवर-ध्यानावर-भानावर-&c. येणें.

To SOBER, *v. a. make sober, cure of intoxication.* निवळवणें, अमल *m.*-कैफ *m.*-&c. उतरणें *g. of o.* शुद्धीवर-भानावर-&c. आणणें.

SOBER-MINDED, *a.* v. SOBER, 3. स्थिर, स्थिरमनस्क, विचारवान्.

SOBER-MINDEDNESS, *n.* v. A. स्थिरता *f.* स्थैर्य *n.* विचारशीलता *f.*

SOBERLY, *adv.* v. A. 1. 2. अमलावांचून, कैफावांचून, अमल न येईसा *decl.* &c. बेतानें, सुमारपाहून.

3 थंडपणानें, थंडाईनें, विचारानें, &c. विचारपूर्वक, स्थैर्यपूर्वक.

SOBERNESS, SOBRIETY, *n.* v. A. 1. बेताचें पिणें *n.* मितप्राशन *n.* परिमितप्राशन *n.* मितपान *n.* पानसंयम *m.* पानसंयमन *n.*

2 सावधपणा *m.* बिनअमलीपणा *m.* कैफाबेगळेपणा *m.* अमत्तता *f.* मद्याभाव *m.*

3 थंडपणा *m.* &c. स्थिरता *f.* स्थैर्य *n.* विचारशीलता *f.* नियतवर्त्तन *n.* नियतवृत्ति *f.*

SOCIABLE, *a. inclined to company, disposed to associate with others.* सोबतीचा-संगतीचा-&c. आवडता, मिळताऊ, मिलाफी, सख्यभावाचा, भलमाणसाईचा, जनसंगासक्त, जनसंगप्रिय, रहाळसाळ *or* सहाळ, संलापप्रिय, सोबतीवेल्हाळ, सोबतीचा अळकुवाभुकेला, स्नेहबुद्धि.

2 See FAMILIAR, AFFABLE.

SOCIABLENESS, SOCIABILITY, *n.* v. A. 1. मिळताऊपणा *m.* मिलाफीपणा *m.* भलमाणसाई *f.* सख्यभाव *m.* स्नेहबुद्धि *f.* जनसंगासक्ति *f.* जनसंगप्रीति *f.* संलापासक्ति *f.*

SOCIAL, *a. of or belonging to society.* सोबतीचा, संगतीचा, &c. संगतिधर्मांचा, संगतिधर्माविषयींचा, सहवासाविषयींचा, सहभावाचा, संगतिभावाचा, सहवाससंबंधी-विषयक, सांगतिक, सांसर्गिक.

2 v. SOCIABLE. सोबतीचा-&c. आवडता, अनेकचर, समूहचर.

It is good to be s. दिल्हें घेतलें गोड.

SOCIETY, *n. communion, consociation,* v. COMPANY. सोबत *f.* संग *m.* संगति *f.* समागम *m.* साह्य *n.* सहभाव *m.* साहित्य *n.* लोकयात्रा *f.* पंक्ति *pop.* पंगत *f.*

2 *a* s. v. COMMUNITY, COMPANY. मंडळी *f.* पंक्ति *pop.* पंगत *f.*

SOCK, *n.*—for the foot. पायाचा मोजा *m.*

SOCKET, *n. receptacle.* घर *n.* पात्र *n.* कामाठी *f.* उथळा *m. dim.* उथळी *f.* उथळें *or* उथाळें *n.* खुरसी *f.* ठेपसा *m.*—for a post. तोळंबा *m.*

Stone forming a s. for the foot of a post. तळखडा *m.*

SOD, *n. turf, sward.* गवताची जमीन *f.* तृणावृतभूमि *f.*

2 *a* s. गवताची हुंडी *f.* पेंड *m.*

SODA, *n. natron, alkali.* सौवर्चल *n.* कापोत *m.* रुचक *n.*

Sub-carbonate of s. पापडखार *m.*

Impure carbonate of s. सज्जाखार *or* सज्जीखार *m.* सर्जिखार *m.* सजिकाक्षार *m.* सर्जी *f.* वज्रक्षार *m.*

To SODER. See To SOLDER.

SODOMITE, *n. one guilty of sodomy,* v. CATAMITE, PATHIC. बचेबाज, गुदमैथुनकर्त्ता.

SODOMY, *n.* गुदमैथुन *n.* पुंमैथुन *n.* बचेबाजी *f.*

SOFA, *n.* कोच *m.* (from the English "couch").

SOFT, *a. not hard.* मऊ (*remiss.* मऊसर *softish*), मृदु, नरम, मृदुस्पर्श, मुलाईम, मवाळ, गुलगुलीत, मऊसूत, मृदुल.

2 *friable, crumbling.* फुसफुसीत, फुसका, फुसकुला, विसविसीत.

3—esp. of articles of food ; *not crisp.* दबदबीत, मिचमिचीत, मेचट.

4 *lax, flaccid, wanting firmness or stiffness.* मिसमिसीत, लिबलिबीत, बिळबिळीत, बिलबिलीत, बिलबिला, विदविदा, लेंचापेंचा.

5 *weak and easy, imbecile,* v. WEAK, SIMPLE. मनाचा कोंवळा-नरम, नरम, भोळा, डाळपिट्या, पिठ्या, मेण्या, मेणाचा, रेशमी, मळमळीत. [करुणाई.

6 *gentle, &c.* v. MILD. मऊ, नरम, मृदु, सौम्य, गोडा, हलका, S. and balmy,—air, breeze, &c. मंदसुगंध.

7— of voice or sound. मऊ, मृदु, मंजूल *pop.* मंजूळ, मंजूळवाणा, मधुर, हलका.

To speak s. and fair. मऊमऊ बोलणें.

8—water; *not mixed with salts.* गोडवा *or* गोडा.

SOFT, *interj.* हळू, सावकाश, धिरे, धिरेधिरे, धिराधिरे.

To SOFTEN, *v. n. make less hard,* lit. मऊ-नरम-मवाळ-मृदु-&c. करणें, मऊपणा *m.*-नरमपणा *m.*-मवाळी *f.*-मृदुत्व *n.*-&c. आणणें.

2 *mollify, qualify, &c.* v. To MODERATE. नरमवणें *or* नरमावणें, मऊ-नरम-बेताचा-हलका-&c. करणें, मऊपणा *m.*-नरमपणा *m.*-&c. आणणें.

3 *make pitiful, tender, compassionate.* मऊ-नरम-सद्रव-सदय-साई-करुणाई-&c. करणें, मऊपणा *m.*-नरमपणा *m.*-&c. आणणें, द्रववणें, पाघळवणें, पाझरवणें.

To SOFTEN, *v. n. become less hard,* lit. मऊ-नरम-मृदु-&c. होणें-होतजाणें, मऊपणा*m.*-मवाळी *f.*-मृदुत्व*n.*-&c. येणें *in. con.*

2 fig. *become less harsh, less severe, less obdurate, &c.* मऊ-नरम-साई-&c. होणें, नरमणें, नरमावणें, द्रवणें, पाझरणें, &c. द्रव*m.*-ओलावा *m.*-&c. येणें *in. con.*

SOFTLY, *adv.* v. A. 6. *and* GENTLY. हलक्यानें, हळू, हळुकर, सावकाश, अलगपीत, रिघेरिघे.

7 हलक्यानें, हळू, &c. मंजूळवाणीनें.

SOFTNESS, *n.* v. A. 1. मऊपणा *m.* नरमपणा *m.* &c. नरमाई *f.* मवाई *f.* मवाळी *f.* मृदुता *f.* मार्दव *n.*

2 फुसफुसीतपणा *m.* फुसकेपणा *m.* &c.

3 दबदबीतपणा *m.* मिचमिचीतपणा *m.* &c.

4 मिसमिसीतपणा *m.* लिबलिबीतपणा *m.* &c. [बर रडें *n.*

5 मनाचा कोंवळेपणा *m.*-नरमपणा *m.* मनाची नरमाई *f.* नाका-

6 मऊपणा*m.* &c. मृदुत्व *n.* मार्दव *n.*

Blandness or s. (of speech, disposition, or deportment.) लोहनाळी मोहनाळी *f.*

7 मऊपणा *m.* मंजूळपणा *m.* &c. मधुरता *f.* माधुर्य *n.*

To SOIL, *v. n. get dirty or tarnished.* मळकटणें, मळगावणें *or* मळघावणें, मळणें, विटणें, मलीन-मळकट-&c. होणें.

To SOIL, *v. a. tarnish, slur, &c.* v. To STAIN. मळवणें, मळगा-

वर्णे or मळघावणें, बिटवणें, मळकट-&c. करणें.

SOIL, *n. earth.* माती *f.* काळी *f.* भुई *f.* जमीन *f.*

Black s. काळीमाती *f.*

Classification of soils. प्रतबंदी *f.*

Classification of soils in a revenue survey. तरमबंदी *f.* —the classifier. तरम *m.*

Meagre and poor s. बरड जमीन *f.* थुंक्यानें भिजती चांदण्यानें वाळती (जमीन &c.).

Red s. तांबड *f.* तांबळ *n. f.* तांबडी माती *f.*

Roll of the several classes of soils. प्रतवारी *f.*

S. of first sort. अवल;—of second, दूम;—of third, शीम.

Wet s. पाणथळ *n.* पाणसळ *n.*

White s. पांढर *f.* पांढरमाती *f.*

To lose its fertility—soil. बरकत *f.* सोडणें.

2 See MANURE. 3 See STAIN.

SOILED, *p.* v. V. मळगावलेला, &c. मजीत, बिटकर, विटका, मळीण, मळका, लिप्त, अवलिप्त.

To SOJOURN, *v. n. reside for a time.* चारदिवस-कांहींकाळ-उसना *decl.*-कांहीं काळचा *decl.*-उचला *decl.*-उचललेला-&c. राहणें, उसनें राहणें *n.*-प्रवास *m.*-&c. करणें.

SOJOURN, SOJOURNING, *n.* v. V.—*act.* चारदिवस राहणें *n.* कांहींकाळचें राहणें *n.* उसनें राहणें *n.* उचलें राहणें *n.* प्रवास *m.* देशांतरवास *m.*

SOJOURNER, *n.* SOJOURNING, *p. a.* v. V. चारदिवस राहणारा, कांहींकाळ राहणारा, &c. उसनाराहणारा, उपरी, वसतकरू, वस्तीकरू, उतारी, उचल्या, उपलाणू, उचलटप्पू, उडलटप्पू, आगंतुक, फिरस्त or स्ता, प्रवासी, खुंटावरला कावळा.

To SOLACE, SOLACE, &c. See To COMFORT, COMFORT, &c.

SOLANUM, *n.*—s. macrorhizon. डोरली *f.*—its fruit. डोरलें.—s. jacquini. डोरली रिंगणी *f.*—s. insanum. डोरली वांगी *f.*—its fruit. डोरलें वांगें *n.*

SOLAR, *a. of or belonging to the sun.* सूर्याचा, सूर्यसंबंधी, सूर्यविषयक, सौर.

S. disk. प्रतिसूर्य *m.*

S. dynasty. सूर्यवंश *m.*

2—of time. सावन, सौर. [विक्रीत.

SOLD, *p.* v. V. A. 1. विकलेला, विकतदिल्हेला, &c. फरोक्त, क्रीत,

To SOLDER, *v. a. unite with metallic cement.* झाळणें, कस्तर or कस्तूर *m. n.* करणें, कस्तरणें, कस्तूरी करणें, डांक *m.* लावणें, झाळणी *f.* करणें, डांकणें, डांखळणें. [संध *m.*

SOLDER, *n. metallic cement.* कस्तर or कस्तूर *m.n.* डांक *m.* खार-

Cake or strip of s. डांकपट्टी *f.* डांकपाती *f.*

Instrument with which s. is applied. कस्तूरगोल *m.*

To alloy (gold, &c.) with s. डांखळणें.

SOLDERED, *p.* v. V. झाळलेला, डांक लावलेला, &c. डांकलग, डांकील, डांकीव.

To be s. डांखळणें.

SOLDIER, *n. man in military service.* शिपाई or सिपाई, शिपाईगिरी करणारा, सैनिक, शस्त्रधर, शस्त्रधारी, शस्त्रोपजीवी, युद्धोपजीवी;—gener. or compreh. शिपाईप्यादा, शिपाईराणा;—contemptuously, शिपायडा *m.* शिपायडें *n.*

The profession or practice of a s. शिपाईगिरी *f.*

2—emphatically, v. WARRIOR. योद्धा.

SOLDIERING, *n. practice, &c. of a soldier.* शिपाईगिरी *f.* शिपाईपेशा *m.* लशकरगिरी *f.*

SOLDIER-LIKE, SOLDIERLY, *n.* शिपाईगिरीचा, शिपाई पेशाचा, शिपायास लायक-&c.

SOLDIERSHIP, *n. character, &c. of a soldier.* शिपाईगिरी *f.*

SOLDIERY, *n. body of soldiers, soldiers collectively.* शिपाई *m. pl.* शिपाईलोक *m. pl.*

Irregular s. शिबंदी or सिबंदी *f.*

SOLE. *n.* (of a foot). तळवा *m.* तळपाय *m.* पादतल *n.* चरणतल *n.*

From the s. of the foot to the crown of the head. आनखशिख, आपादतलमस्तक, आपादमस्तक.

2 (of a shoe). तळ *m.* टाचें *n.*

3—the fish. लेफ or लेप *n. m.*

SOLE, *a. alone,* v. SINGLE. एकला, एकटा, एकाकी, एकचएक, केवळ or ळ, शुद्ध. [अशुद्धप्रयोग *m.*

SOLECISM, *n. impropriety in language.* अप्रयोग *m.* अपप्रयोग *m.*

SOLELY, *adv.* v. A. एकला *decl.* एकटा *decl.* &c. केवळ, च.

SOLEMN, *a. marked with pomp and sanctity; belonging to religion, attended with religious rites, &c.* समारंभाचा, देवकार्याचा, देवाधर्माच्या खटल्याचा, देवाधर्माच्या प्रकरणांतला, समारंभयुक्त, समारंभसहित, देवकार्ययुक्त, देवकार्यसहित.

2 *adapted to impress awe or affect with seriousness.* इभ्रतीचा, जरबीचा, धाकवसायाचा, गंभीरपणाचा, गंभीर, गुरु.

3 *sober, serious, &c.* v. GRAVE. गंभीर, भरकूम, दीर्घ.

SOLEMNITY, SOLEMNESS, *n.*v.A. 2. गंभीरपणा *m.* इभ्रत *f.* जरब *f.*

3 गंभीरपणा *m.* गांभीर्य *n.* गुरुत्व *n.* गौरव *n.* गंभीरवृत्ति *f.*

I. *religious ceremony.* देवकार्य *n.* देवकृत्य *n.* समारंभ *m.* उत्साह *m.* उत्सव *m.*

To SOLEMNIZE, *v. a. perform with ceremonies, celebrate.* समारंभानें-&c. करणें, समारंभ *m.*-&c. करणें *g. of o.* यथाविधि-यथाशास्त्र &c. करणें. [&c. आणणें.

2 *make serious and grave.* गंभीर-&c. करणें, गंभीरपणा *m.*-

SOLEMNLY, *adv.* v. A. 1. समारंभानें, &c. समारंभपूर्वक, देवकार्यासहित, यथाविधि.

3 गंभीरपणानें, गंभीरमनानें, &c.

I. *with solemn asseveration and invocation.* सत्योत्तरें, सत्योत्तर, सत्यस्मरून, ईश्वरस्मरून. [करणें.

To SOL-FA, *v. n. pronounce the notes of the gamut.* सरिगम *f.*

To SOLICIT, *v. n. entreat, implore,* v.To BEG. विनवणें, विनंती *f.* अर्ज *m.*-&c. करणें, मिनत *f.*-मिनती *f.*-&c. करणें.

2 *seek by petition,* v.To BEG. मागणें, याचणें, विनंती *f.*-याचना *f.*-&c. करणें *g. of o.* मिनतीनें-मिनतवार-&c. मागणें.

SOLICITATION, *n.* v. V. 1.—*act.* विनवणें *n.* विनवणी *f.* याचना *f.* प्रार्थना *f.* मिनत *f.* मिनती *f.* मिनतवारी *f.*

SOLICITOR, *n.*v. V. विनवणारा, विनंती-&c. करणारा, याचक.

I. *lawyer.* वकील.

SOLICITOUS, *a.* v. ANXIOUS, CAREFUL. चिंतेचा, काळजीचा, चिंतायुक्त, चिंताक्रांत, चिंताग्रस्त.

2 *greatly desirous,* v. EARNEST. उत्सुक, उत्कंठित, सोत्कंठ.

SOLICITOUSLY. See ANXIOUSLY, EARNESTLY.

SOLICITUDE, *n.* v. ANXIETY, CARE. चिंता *f.* काळजी *f.* घोर *m.*

2 v. EARNESTNESS. उत्कंठा *f.* कळकळ *f.* तिडीक *f.* उदमेख *m.*

SOLID, *a. not liquid or fluid.* घट्ट, घन, अद्रव, अप्रवाही, जड.

2 *not hollow* भरींव, सगर्भ, गर्भपूर्ण.

3 *hard, compact,* v. FIRM, SUBSTANTIAL. बळकट, खंबीर, घट्ट, ऐवजदार, ऐवजशीर, घन, घनसर, संगीन, कणखर, पोक or पोका, मोठाधाटा.

4 *sound, valid, just, &c.* v. SUBSTANTIAL. दृढ, बळकट, जिवदार, ऐवजदार, साबूत.

SOLID, *n. cubical body.* घन *m.*

Contents of a s. घनफल *n.*

To SOLIDIFY, *v. a.* घट्ट-घन- &c. करणें.

SOLIDITY, SOLIDNESS, *n.* v. A. 1. घट्टपणा *m.* घनता *f.* अद्रवता *f.* अप्रवाहिता *f.*

2 भरींवपणा *m.* गर्भपूर्णता *f.* [काठिन्य *n.*

3 बळकटपणा *m.* खंबिरपणा *m.* घट्टपणा *m.* &c. खंबिरी *f.* घट्टाई *f.*

4 दृढपणा *m.* बळकटपणा *m.* &c. जीव *m.* ऐवज *m.*

SOLIDUNGULOUS, *a. not cloven in the hoofs.* एकशफ, एकखुर.

SOLILOQUY, *n. a talking to one's self.* आपल्याशीं बोलणें *n.*-भाषण *n.* आत्मगतभाषण *n.* आत्मभाषण *n.*

SOLITARINESS, *n.* v. A. 1. सोबती वेगळेपणा *m.* संगराहित्य *n.* संसर्गाभाव *m.* जनसंसर्गाभाव *m.* असंगता *f.* एकांतवृत्ति *f.* विविक्तवृत्ति *f.*

2 उदासपणा *m.* भणभणितपणा *m.*

SOLITARY, SOLITAIRE, *n.* v. RECLUSE. एकला राहणारा, एकांतवासी, वनवासी, एकटा टिकोजी.

SOLITARY, *a. living alone.* एकला-&c. राहणारा, सोबती वेगळा-निराळा, बिनसोबती, बिनसोबतीचा, असंग, असहाय, असंसर्ग, विविक्तसेवी, एकांतसेवी, विजनस्थ, निर्जनस्थ, जनसंसर्गहीन-रहित-&c.

To be or feel s. रानांत-आडरानांत-वनांत-&c. पडणें-पडल्यासारखा असणें, उदासवाटणें *in. con.*

2—of places, &c. *lone, not frequented.* गैरराबत्याचा, गैरबळणाचा, उदास, गुह्य, विविक्त, विजन, निर्जन, भणभणीत, भयाण.

3 *single, sole.* एकच, एकटा, एकला, एकाकी.

SOLITUDE, *n. lonely state.* सोबतीवेगळेपणा *m.* सोबतीनिराळेपणा *m.* विविक्तवृत्ति *f.* एकांतवृत्ति *f.* असंगता *f.* जनसंसर्गराहित्य *n.* एकांतवासित्व *n.*

2—of places; *lonesomeness.* उदासपणा *m.* भणभणीतपणा *m.* भणभणाट *m.* भणाण *m.*

3 *lonely place.* रान *n.* आडरान *n.* अरण्य *n.* विविक्तस्थल *n.*

SOLMIZATION, *n. repetition of the notes of the gamut.* सरिगम *f.*

SOLO, *n. song or tune by one.* एकानें करायाचें गाणें *n.*-वाजवणें *n.* एकाकी गाणें *n.*-वाजवणें *n.*

SOLOMON. See WISEACRE.

SOLSTICE, *n.*—in astronomy. अयनान्त *m.* अयन *n.*

The summer s. उत्तरायणान्त *m.*

The winter s. दक्षिणायणान्त *m.*

SOLSTITIAL, *a.* v. N. अयनांतसंबंधी, अयनांतविषयक, अयनांतकालिक.

SOLUBLE, *a.* v. V. A. 2. द्रव करायाजोगा-जोगता-&c. द्राव्य, द्रावणीय, द्रावणार्ह, द्रावणशक्य.

v. V. N. द्रवव्हायाजोगा-&c. गलनीय, द्रवार्ह.

SOLUBLENESS, SOLUBILITY, *n.* v. A. 1. द्रवकरायाजोगेपणा *m.* &c. द्राव्यता *f.* द्रावणीयता *f.* द्रावणशक्यता *f.*

2 द्रवव्हायाजोगेपणा *m.* &c. गलनीयता *f.*

SOLUTION, *n.* v. V. 1. *and* EXPLANATION,—*act.* फेडणें *n.* &c. लापन *n.* लापनिका *f.*—*state.* उलगडा *m.* फोड *m.*

2—*act.* द्रवविणें *n.* द्रवकरणें *n.* द्रावण *n.*

I. *chemical union.* द्रवमूलकसारूप्यसंयोग *m.*

II. *that which contains matter dissolved.* पाणी *n.* वणी *n.* (in comp. as मिठवणी, &c.).

To SOLVE, *v. a.* (a problem, riddle, &c.) *resolve, unfold, &c.* v. To. EXPLAIN. फेडणें, उलगडणें, उलगडा *m.*-लापन *n.*-लापनिका *f.*-&c. करणें *g. of o.* उलटणें.

2 *dissolve,* v. To MELT. द्रवविणें, द्रव *m.*-&c. करणें *g. of o.*

To SOLVE, *v. n. be dissolved,* v. To MELT. द्रव *m.*-रस *m.*-&c. होणें *g. of s.*

SOLVENCY, *n.* v. A. 2. कर्ज फेडण्याची लायकी *f.* ऋणशोधनक्षमता *f.* ऋणाधिकधनता *f.* &c.

SOLVENT, *a. dissolvent.* द्रवकरणारा, द्रावक, द्रवकारक, स्रावक.

2 *able to pay.* कर्ज फेडण्याच्या लायकीचा, दार (used chiefly in opposition to नादार insolvent), ऋणशोधनक्षम, ऋणाधिकधन, ऋणाधिकधनसंपन्न.

SOLVENT, *n. menstruum.* द्रावकरस *m.*

SOLVER, *n.* v. V. A. 1. फेडणारा, उलगडा करणारा, &c.

SOMBRE, *a.* See GLOOMY. 2—a complexion. काळसावळा.

SOME, *a. more or less.* कांहीं, कांहींतरी, अल्पस्वल्प.

2 *more or fewer.* कोणी, कितीएक, केक, कांहीं, कांहींएक, कांहींक, कांहींकांहीं, अनेक.

3 *a small quantity or number.* कांहीं, थोडा, थोडका, कांहींसा, थोडासा, इवला, इवलासा.

4 *certain persons.* कोणी *m. pl.* कितीएक, कितीक, किती, कितेक, कांहीं, कांहीं कांहीं, कश्चन or कश्चित्.

S., certain, parlicular. अमका, अमकातमका, फलाणा.

5—noting a person or thing not known or not specified. कोणी, कोणीतरी, एखाद, एखादा.

S. besides. एखादा, or एखाद्दुसरा.

SOME BODY, SOME ONE, *n.* कोणएक, कोणीतरी, कोणसा, अमुकतमूक or अमकातमका, यःकश्चन, यःकश्चित्, कश्चन, कश्चित्, देवदत्त;—loosely, *some fellow or other,* अलबत्या गलबत्या, अलता भलता, फलाणा बिस्ताना.

SOME HOW, *adv. by hook or crook.* जसातसा, जसेंतसें करून, यथातथा, जेमतेम.

S. or other. कांहीं करून, कसेंही करून.

SOMERSAULT, SOMERSET, *n. leap with heels over head.* कोल्हांठ or ट or गोलांठ or ट *n.* किराण *n.* उपरछडी *f.*

SOMETHING, *n. some matter, some event.* कांहीं.

S. or other. कांहींतरी, अमुकतमूक, कांहींसा.

2 *some, a little,* v. SOMEWHAT. कांहीं, किंचित्, यत्किंचित्, अल्पस्वल्प.

SOMETIME, *adv. at some time future.* केव्हांतरी, कधींतरी, कोणेवेळेस, एखादेवेळेस, केव्हांनकेव्हां. [क्वोकाळ भविष्यति).

It will be s. or other. काले काले भविष्यति (or, pop. का-

2 sometimes; *occasionally.* केव्हां केव्हां, कधीं कधीं, केव्हां बेव्हां, कधींमधीं, कधींबधीं, वेळेनसार.

SOMEWHAT, *adv. in some degree.* कांहीं, कांहींसा *decl.* कांहीं बाहीं, कांहीं तरी, थोडा *decl.* थोडासा *decl.* जरा, जरासा *decl.* ज-

राक, जराकसा *decl.* इवला *decl.* इवलासा *decl.* किंचित्, यत्किंचित्, थोडाबहुत.

SOMEWHERE, *adv.* कोणे-कोणत्याजागीं-स्थळीं-&c. कुत्रापि, कुत्रचित्, क्वापि, क्वचित्.

S. or other. एखाद्याजागीं-स्थळीं-&c. कोठेंतरी,कोठें, कोठें कोठें, बाहेरभितर, कोठेंमोठें, यत्रकुत्रचित्, यत्रकुत्रापि.

SOMNAMBULISM, *n. walking in sleep.* झोंपेंत फिरणें *n.*-चालणें *n.* -&c. झोंपेंतलें फिरणें *n.*-&c. निद्राभ्रमण *n.* निद्राचार *m.*

SOMNAMBULIST, *n. one who walks in sleep.* झोंपेंत फिरणारा-चालणारा-&c. निद्राचारी, निद्राभ्रमणकर्त्ता-कारी-&c.

SOMNIFEROUS, SOMNIFIC, *a. causing sleep.* झोंपेचा, झोंप-&c. आणणारा, निद्राकर-कारक-कारी-जनक-प्रापक-&c. सुप्तिकर-कारक-&c.

SOMNILOQUIST, *n. one who talks in sleep.* ओसणणारा, झोंपेंत बोलणारा, निद्राभाषी, निद्रालापी.

SOMNILOQUISM, *n. talking in sleep.* ओसणणें *n.* झोंपेंत बोलणें*n.* झोंपेंतलें बोलणें *n.* निद्रालाप *m.* निद्राभाषण *n.*

To SOMNILOQUIZE, *v.n. talk in sleep.* ओसणणें, झोंपेंत-&c. बोलणें, निद्राभाषण *n.*-निद्रालाप *m.* करणें,—wildly or incoherently, बरळणें, चावळणें.

SOMNOLENCY, SOMNOLENT. See SLEEPINESS, SLEEPY.

SON, *n.* लेक *or* लेंक *m.* मुलगा *m.* पुत्र *m.* पूत *m.* पुत्रक *m.* चिरंजीव *m.* आत्मज *m.* अंगज *m.* आंडोर *or* ल *m.* नंदन *m.* तनुज *m.* तनय *m.* सूनु *m.* सुत *m.*

Duty of a s. पुत्रधर्म *m.*

Dutiful and affectionate s. सुपुत्र *m.* सत्पुत्र *m.*

From s. to s.—patrimony, &c. descending. पोरापोरीं, लेंकरालेंकरीं.

Having sons or a s. पुत्री, पुत्रवान् *pop.* पुत्रवंत, सपुत्र.

Joy or rejoicing on the birth of a s. पुत्रोत्सव *m.* पुत्रोत्साह *m.* पुत्रानंद *m.*

Sorrow at the death of a s. पुत्रशोक*m.*

S. of—as expressed by *Fitz, Ap, Ben, O', &c.* बिन (in comp. and prefixed, as कृष्ण भट्ट बिन राम भट्ट), वलद (prefixed and used esp. in notes and of *Muhammadans*). In the case of Bráhmans the father's name is usually put next to the individual's name and before the surname, as रघुनाथ रामचंद्र पर्वते i. e. Raghunáth (son of) Rámachandra Parwate.

S. of an unmarried girl. कन्या पुत्र *m.*

SON-IN-LAW, *n.* जावई *or* जावाई *m.* जामात *m.*

Sister of one's s. जावईण *f.*

SONG, *n. singing, modulated voice.* गाणें *n.* गायन *n.* गान *n.* गायकी *f.* गीत *n.* विगीत *n.* गीति *f.* गांधर्व *n.*

S. and sport. रागरंग *m.*

S. with music संगीत *n.*

Sweet s. गोड गळा *m.*

2 *a* s. *a ballad, &c.* गीत *n.* Some modes or kinds are, कवीत, कलगी, कवाल *or* कवाली, खंदारी बाणी, ख्याल, चौताल, झांजू, टप्पा, ठुंबरी, तराणा *or* तिल्लाणा, तुरा, दीपचंदी, ध्रुपद, पक्का ख्याल, प्रबंध, रास, लावणी.

Holy or spiritual s. सद्गीत *n.*

Introductory stanza of a s. ध्रुपद *n.* ध्रुव *m.*

3 See POETRY, POESY.

SONGSTER, *n.* See SINGER. 2 *a bird that sings.* गाणारें पाखरूं*n.* गायक पक्षी *m.*

SONGSTRESS, *n. female singer.* गाणारी *f.* गाणारीण *f.*

SONIFEROUS, *a. producing sound.* शब्द-ध्वनि-नाद-&c. कर-कारक -जनक-&c. [पुत्रहीन-रहित-&c.

SONLESS, *a.* निपुत्र, निपुत्री, अपुत्र, अपुत्रक, अपुत्री, निपुत्रीक,

SONNET, *n. short poem.* लघुकविता *f.* चीज *f.*

SONORIFIC. See SONIFEROUS.

SONOROUS, *a. that emits sound when struck.* नादाचा, वाजणारा, वाजता, वाजट, नादी, सनाद, मुखर, शब्दकार.

2 *clear sounding, full, &c.* आवाजदार, घोस, उद्दाम, खणखणीत, ठणठणीत, झार, डोर, पहाड, कान भरायाजोगा-जोगता-&c. मेघगंभीर.

SONOROUSLY, *adv.* v.A. 2. खणखणीत, ठणठणीत, &c. कानभरायाजोगा-जोगता-*decl.* [सनादता*f.*

SONOROUSNESS, *n.* v. A. 1. वाजतेपणा *m.* नादीपणा *m.* नादिता *f.* 2 खणखणितपणा *m.* ठणठणितपणा *m.* &c.

SONSHIP, *n. state, character, &c. of a son.* पुत्रपणा *m.* &c. पुत्रत्व *n.* पुत्रभाव *m.*

SOON, *adv. in a short time.* लवकर, थोडक्या वेळानें, थोडक्याकाळानें, अल्पकालानें, थोडक्यांत, थोड्यांत, इतक्यांत, अविलंबेंकरून, अचिरात्.

As s. as, v. IMMEDIATELY. जंव *or* जों.

Sooner or later. आगें मागें, मागेंपुढें, आदिपश्चात्, आदि मग.

No sooner said than done. उचलली जीभ आणि लावली टाळ्यास.

2 v. EARLY. लवकर, सकळबेळीं.

3 *readily,* v. WILLINGLY. खुशीनें, संतोषानें, &c. Note. There is no Maráṭhí word that expresses this word in the phrase, *would as soon.* The phrase must be rendered by a periphrasis ; ex. I would as soon go as stay, जसा खुशीनें राहीन तसा खुशीनें जाईन *or*मला जाणें राहणें एकच (*or* सारखेंच) आहे.

SOOT, *n. the dirt of smoke.* घरोसा *or* घेरोसा *m.* मषी *pop.* मस *f.* मशेरी *f.* धुरकट *n.* धुरट *n.* घस *f.*

Filament of s. जळमट *n.*

Filaments of s., straws, &c. केरडोक *n.* घरू *m.* घरोसा *m.*

To SOOTHE, *v. a.* v. To COAX. अळवणें, मठारणें, थापटणें, लुलुपुतु *n.*-&c. करणें *g. of o.* पाठ *f.* गोंजारणें *g. of o.* पाठीवर-पाठीवरून हात *m.* फिरवणें *g. of o.* उरीं पोटीं धरणें, कुरवाळणें.

2 *assuage, mollify, mitigate,* v. To EASE. शांतवणें *or* सांतवणें, सांत्वन *pop.* सांतवन *or* सांतवीण *n.*-उपशम *m.*-&c. करणें *g. of o.*

3 *appease,* v. To PACIFY. शांतवणें *or* सांतवणें, शांत-&c. करणें, शांति *f.*-समाधान *n.*-समजूत *f.*-&c. करणें *g. of o.*

SOOTHER, *n.* SOOTHING, *p. a.* v. V. 1. आळवणारा, थापटणारा, &c. लुलुपुतूचा, लाडी गोडीचा, लडिवाळ.

2 शांतवणारा, &c. सांत्वनकर्त्ता-कारी, उपशमक.

3 शांतवणारा, शांतकरणारा, &c. शांतिकर्त्ता-कारक-&c. क्रोध-ताप-&c. हर-हारी-&c.

SOOTHING, *n.* v. 1.—*act.* आळवणें*n.* थापटणें *n.* &c. लुलुपुतू*n.* 2 शांतवणें *n.* &c. सांत्वन *pop.* सांत्वण *or* शांतवन*n.* सांत्वीण *n.*

उपशम *m.* प्रशम *m.* प्रशमन *n.*

3 शांतवणें *n.* शांतकरणें *n.* &c. समजावशी *f.* समजावीस *f.* क्रोधहरण *n.* तापहरण *n.*

SOOTHINGLY, *adv.* v. V. 1. लुलुपुतू करून, पाठीवरहातफिरवून, उरींपोटीं धरून, &c. [TELL, &c.

To SOOTHSAY, SOOTHSAYER, &c. See To DIVINE, To FORE-

SOOTY, *a. covered, &c. with soot.* घरोसाबसलेला-जमलेला-&c. धुरकटलेला, काळा.

SOP, *n. any thing dipped and softened in liquor.* भिजततुकडा *m.* भिजवलेली भाकर *f.*-&c.

2 See BRIBE.

SOPHISM, SOPHISTRY, *n. specious but fallacious argument, fallacious reasoning.* आभास *m.* सिद्धांताभास *m.* प्रतिभास *m.* सत्याभास *m.* वाक्छल *n.*

SOPHIST, *n. fallacious reasoner.* आभासवादी, सिद्धांताभासवादी.

2 *sceptical philosopher.* चार्वाक. [भासात्मक.

SOPHISTIC, SOPHISTICAL, *a.* v. FALLACIOUS. आभासाचा, आ-

SOPORIFEROUS, SOPORIFIC, *a. causing sleep.* झोप आणणारा, निद्राकारक-कारी-जनक. [प्राशनीय.

SORBILE, *a. that may be drunk.* प्यायाजोगा-सारखा-&c. पेय,

SORCERER, *n.* v. MAGICIAN, CONJURER. जादूगीर, इलमी, बीरमंत्री, चेटकाळ्या, चेटकी, चेटक्या. [ळीण *f.*

SORCERESS, *n. female sorcerer.* जादूगरीण *f.* चेटकाळी *f.* कंवटा-

SORCERY, *n.* v. MAGIC. जादू *f.* जादूगिरी *f.* चेटक *n.* बीरविद्या *f.* कुविद्या *f.*

SORDES, *n. excrementitious matter.* मलम. *n. pop.* मळम. किट्टन.

S. of the head. चिकटी *f.*

S. of the skin. चिकटा *m.*

SORDID, *a. mean, base, vile.* नीच, हुब्बा, हलका, निपटारा, लिद्वळ, अधम, पाजी, पामर, जघन्य, जघन्यवृत्ति.

2 v. COVETOUS, MISERLY. रूपण, कद्रू, किरटा, किरमाडी, किलवाणा *or* णी.

SORDIDNESS, *n.* v. A. 1. नीचपणा *m.* हुब्बेपणा *m.* निपटारेपणा *m.* &c. अधमत्व *n.* पामरत्व *n.* जघन्यवृत्ति *f.* पामरवृत्ति *f.* अधमवृत्ति *f.*

2 रूपणपणा *m.* किरटेपणा *m.* &c. कार्पण्य *n.*

SORE, *n. wound, tender place, &c.* क्षत *n.* खत *n.* खट *n.* व्रण *m.* खवंद *or* खऊंद *n.* खवंदळ *n.* दुःख *n.* दुखापत *f.* दुखरू *n.* चट्टा *m.*

Maggoty s. किवण *n.*

S. on the back of a beast. नाळ *f.*

Spreading s. फांपर *n.*

Ulcerous s. घाड *f.* भग *n.*

To apply salt to a s. दुःखावर डाग *m.* देणें *or* फासण्या *f. pl.* घालणें, घायावर घाय *m.* घालणें.

To clean a s. व्रणशोधन *n.* करणें.

2 fig. *s. place.* मर्मस्थान *n.* मर्मस्थल *n.* मर्म *n.* वर्म *n.* कुस्पृष्ट *n.*

Prober of a s. मर्मान्वेषी, मर्मभेदक.

To probe a s. मर्मान्वेषण *n.*-मर्मभेद *m.*-&c. करणें.

To rip up an old s. खपली *f.* काढणें, मर्मोद्घाटन *n.*-&c. करणें.

SORE, *a. that has been hurt, and is tender and susceptible of pain.* दुखापत झालेला, दुखारलेला, दुखापतीचा, दुखरा, दुखता, दुखणारा, घायाळ, हुळहुळा, स्पर्शासह.

2 (mentally). मनांत दुखबलला, वरमलेला, मर्मभेददुःखित, मर्मभेददुःखी.

3 *grievous, severe,* v. AFFLICTIVE. भारी, कठीण, जबर, जरब, जालीम, जिवावरचा, क्लेशद, क्लेशप्रद.

4 (the eyes) *inflamed.* खरावलेला, खुपरा.

To have s. eyes. डोळे *m. pl.* येणें *in. con.*

SORE, SORELY, *adv.* v. A. 3. फारच, अतिशय. [णा *m.*

SORENESS, *n.* v. A. 1. दुःख *n.* दुखापत *f.* दुखरेपणा *m.* हुळहुळेप-

2 वरमलेलेपणा *m.* मर्मभेददुःख *n.*

3 भारीपणा *m.* कठीण पणा *m.* जबरपणा *m.* &c.

SORREL, *a.* v. BAY. तेल्याचोर. [लाम्ल *n.*

SORREL, *n.*—the plant. चुक्रिका *f. pop.* चुका *m.* शतवेधी *m.* द-

SORRILY, *adv.* v. A. 3. केविलवाणा, भिकार, निरुष्ट, कवडीच्या किमतीचा *decl.* &c. [रपणा *m.* &c.

SORRINESS, *n.* v. A. 3. केविलवाणेपणा *m.* नाकारेपणा *m.* भिका-

To SORROW, *v. n. grieve, be sad, &c.* दुःख *n.*-खेद *m.*-शोक *m.*-&c. करणें, दुःख *n.*-खेद *m.*-श्रम *m. pl.*-कष्ट *m. pl.*-&c. वाटणें *in. con.* दुःखी-श्रमी-खिन्न-&c. असणें, दुखारणें, रडणें.

SORROW, *n. grief,* v. AFFLICTION. दुःख *n.* खेद *m.* दिलगिरी *f.* शोक *m.* हुरहूर *f.* मनस्ताप *m.*

Freed from all s. and suffering. आधिव्याधिनिर्मुक्त.

This is but the beginning of sorrows. नखांला आग लागली, अझून सारें आंग जळायाचें आहे.

SORROWFUL, *a.* v. AFFLICTED. दुःखी, दिलगीर, खिन्न, खेदयुक्त, उदास, उदासी, श्रमी, कष्टी, शोकयुक्त, शोकात्मक.

2—the voice, accents, &c. v. PITEOUS. काकळूत वाणा *or* णी, किलवाणा *or* णी.

3—countenance, &c. v. SAD. रडका, रडवा.

4 *producing sorrow, exciting grief, &c.* v. CALAMITOUS, AFFLICTIVE. दुःखाचा, दुःखप्रद, दुःखदायक, दुःखावह, शोकप्रद, शोकजनक.

SORROWFULNESS. See SORROW.

SORRY, *a. grieved for, pained at,* v. AFFLICTED. दुःखी, खिन्न, खेदयुक्त, अपसोशी.

To be s. दुःख *n.*-&c. वाटणें *in. con.* दुखारणें, रडणें.

2—for one's own conduct, v. REPENTANT. पश्चात्तापी.

To be s. पश्चात्ताप *m.*-पस्तावा *m.*-&c. होणें वाटणें *in. con.*

3 *poor, paltry, &c.* v. MEAN, WORTHLESS. किलवाणा *or* णी, केविलवाणा *or* णी, चिलवाणा *or* णी, लुकसान, लेंचापेंचा, नादान, नाकार, भिकार, दमडीच्या मोलाचा, दमडीच्या किमतीचा, कवडीच्या किमतीचा.

SORT, *n.* v. KIND. जाति *f.* जात *f.* प्रकार *m.* विध *m.* (in comp.).

Of first s. अवल. Of second s. दूम. Of third s. शीम.

Of all sorts or kinds. हरजिनशी *or* सी, हरभांत, चतुर्विध.

Of many sorts and fashions. परीप्रकारचा.

To be or feel out of sorts. अवघड-असकड होणें *or* वाटणें *impers. and in. con.* चुकलें चुकलेंसें-चुकल्यासारखें वाटणें *impers. and in. con.* आंग *n.*-जीव *m.*-&c. वांगवांग करणें.

2 *manner, fashion,* v. WAY. प्रकार *m.* रीति *pop.* रीत *f.* तऱ्हा *f.*

To SORT, *v. a.* v. To CLASSIFY. छाटणें, प्रत *f.*-प्रती *f. pl.* लावणें *g. of o.* प्रतवार लावणें, छाट *m.* करणें *g. of o.* वगांवर्गी *f.* करणें, उत्तममध्यमकनिष्ठपर्याय *m. pl.* करणें *g. of o.*

2 *select, cull, pick out,* v. To CHOOSE. निवडणें, वेंचणें.

To SORT, *v. n.* See To CONSORT, To SUIT.

SORTIE. See SALLY.

To Sot, *v. n. tipple to stupidity.* झिंगणें, दारूबाजी *f.*-निशाखोरी *f.*-छाकटेपणा *m.*-&c. करणें.

Sot, *n.* Sottish, *a. habitual drunkard.* झिंग्या, झिंगीखोर *remiss* झिंगट, निशाबाज, निशाखोर, अमली, कैफी, मस्ता *or* मस्त्या, दारूबाज, पोस्ती, छाकटा, पानव्यसनी, मद्यपी, मद्यासक्त.

2 See Stupid.

Sottishness, *n.* v. A. 1. दारूबाजी *f.* निशाबाजी *f.* निशाखोरी *f.* कैफीपणा *m.* &c. मद्यासक्ति *f.*

Soul, *n. immaterial essence, viewed as an emanation from the Deity ; the rational soul.* परमात्मा *m.* आत्मा *m.* शिवात्मा *m.* सच्चिदंश *m.* चित्कला *f.* चिदाभास *m.* त्वंपदार्थ *m.* अंतर्याम *n.* अंतर्यामी *m.*

S. of the universe. ब्रह्म *n.* परमात्मा *m.*

2 *vivifying or animal soul, the vital principle or spirit.* जीवात्मा *m.* प्राणात्मा *m.* आत्मा *m.* जीव *m.* प्राण *m.* आत्माराम *m.* क्षेत्रज्ञ *m.* चैतन्य *n.* चैतन्यकारण *n.* जीवनकला *f.* पुरुष *m.*

Living s. जिता जीव *m.*

Oneness of s. or sentiment. ऐक्यभाव *m.* तादात्म्य *n.*

Seated or inherent in the s. आत्मनिष्ट.

Union of s. and body. चित्‌जडसंयोग *m.*

With one's whole s. जिवाभावानें *or* जिवेंभावें, जिवाभ्यास, जिवाभ्यासानें, जिवापाडीं, जीवादारभ्य. [*m.* देणें.

To love (a friend, &c.) as one's own s. जिवास जीव

To work with all one's s. and strength. जीव खाऊन काम *n.* करणें.

3 *self, the abstract individual.* आत्मा *m.* स्व *m. n.*

4 *essence, quintessence.* तत्वांश *m.* सार *m.* सारांश *m.* सत्वांश *m.* जिव्हाळा *m.* तन्मात्र *n.* [च्या *m.*

5 *fire, salt, life, &c.* v. Spirit. जीव *m.* तेज *n.* धमक *f.* हि-

6 *human being.* See Person.

Sound, *a. not diseased, &c.* v. Healthy, Hale. रोगानिराळा-वेगळा, दुखण्या निराळा-वेगळा, निरोगी, अरोगी, अरोग, धडाखडा, धडधोप, धडधोपट, खडस, खडसा, अरुग्ण, चंगा.

2 *not hurt, not wounded, &c.* धड, अव्रण, अक्षत, क्षतरहित, क्षतहीन, अभंग, अव्यंग, अभिन्न, अजातव्रण, अजातक्षत.

3 v. Orthodox. सन्यामार्गाचा, सत्पथवर्त्ती, सत्पथावलंबी.

4 *unhurt, unimpaired, firm, in good condition.* धड, धडका, धडसा, धडधाकट *or* ड, धडधोप *or* धडधोपट, धडसा खडसा, साबूत *or* द *or* साबीत, अव्यंग, सुरक्षित, जिवट, खबरदार, बळकट, मजबूत.

5 (arguments, reasoning, &c.) *solid, valid, just.* बरोबर, न्यायाचा, नीतीचा, मार्गाचा, &c. समर्पक, सयुक्तिक, बळकट, शाबूत *or* साबूत, शाबीत *or* साबीत, असंडनीय, अपरिहार्य, वज्रप्रमाण. [गुरघूस.

6—of sleep. गाढ, निबिड, दृढ, बळकट, गहद *or* गरद, गरक,

7—of beating, &c. जबर, बळकट, पलाखती *or* पलाखतीचा, कडक, फरमाशी, गाढ.

8 *without flaw or blemish.* साफ, सलम, निखोड, निखोडी, निर्दोष, निकोप, निकोपी.

Sound, *n. noise.* नाद *m.* आवाज *m.* ध्वनि *m.* शब्द *m.* वाद *m.* रव *m.* स्वन *m.* स्वनि *m.* स्वर *m.* निस्वन *m.* क्वण *m.*

Auspicious, &c. s. जयध्वनि *m.* [घोष *m.*

Deep or hollow s. घुमटा *m.* गंभीरनाद *m.* ध्वनि *m.* शब्द *m.*

Faint or lingering s. धुनक *or* धुनूक *f.*

Loud thundering s. धडाड *m.* धडधडाट *m.*

Of a good s. आवाजदार.

Prolonged or continuing s. नाद *m.* धून *f.*

2 *strait.* सामुद्रधुनी *f.*

To Sound, *v. a. cause to make a noise.* वाजवणें, बजावणें, नादावणें, नाद *m.*-शब्द *m.*-&c. काढणें *g. of o.* वादन *n.*-ध्वनन *n.*-शब्दन *n.*-&c. करणें *g. of o.*

2 *search with a plummet, &c.* गळानें-गळ टाकून पाहणें-मोजणें, तळ *m.* पाहणें, तळपाहणी *f.*-&c. करणें *g. of o.*

3 v. To Pump. युक्तीनें-हळू-&c. पुसून पाहणें, मन *n.* पाहणें.

4 v. To Publish. गाजवणें.

To Sound, *v. n. make a noise.* वाजणें, बोलणें, गाजणें, शब्द *m.*-नाद *m.*-&c. करणें-देणें, नाद *m.*-शब्द *m.*-ध्वनन *n.*-क्वणन *n.*-&c. होणें *g. of s.*

To sound cracked. नादावणें.

To s. dead, flat, hollow. भद्भदणें, खबखबणें.

To s. deep and hollow. घुमणें, घुमघुमणें.

2—an instr. of music. वाजणें, बोलणें.

3 *use the line and lead to search the depth of water.* गळानें-गळ टाकून-&c. तळ *m.* पाहणें-पाणी *n.* पाहणें-पाणी *n.* मोजणें-तळपाहणी *f.* करणें.

Sound, *adv.* See Soundly.

Sounded, *p.* v. V. A. 1. वाजवलेला, &c. वादित, ध्वनित, नादित, शब्दित, स्वरित, स्वनित, क्वणित.

2 गळानें पाहिलेला, &c.

Sounder, *n.* Sounding, *p. a.* v. V. A. 1. वाजवणारा, &c. वादक, वादन-&c. कर्त्ता-कारी-&c.

v. V. N. 1. *and* Sonorous. वाजणारा, वाजता, नाद करणारा, &c. नादाचा, नादी, सनाद, शब्दकार, शब्दायमान, मुखर.

That sounds hollow or flat. खबखबीत.

I. (of wild hogs). साइर *f.*

Soundly, *adv.* v. A. 5. बरोबर, न्यायानें, नीतीनें, मार्गानें, &c. यथान्याय, यथायोग्य.

6 गाढ, गडद *or* गरद.

7 रगडून, कचकावून, कडकावून, धडकावून, बळकट, सडकून, जबर.

Soundness, *n.* v. A. 1. रोगानिराळेपणा *m.* &c. निरोगीपणा *m.* धडधोपटपणा *m.* &c. रोगाभाव *m.* रोगराहित्य *n.* निरोगिता *f.* &c.

2 धडपणा *m.* व्रणाभाव *m.* क्षताभाव *m.* क्षतराहित्य *n.*

3 See Orthodoxy. 4 धडपणा *m.* धडसेपणा *m.* साबुतपणा *m.* &c. धड *n.* खबरदारी *f.* बळकटी *f.* मजबुती *f.* साबुती *f.* जीव *m.*

5 समर्पकपणा *m.* सयुक्तिकपणा *m.* साबुतपणा *m.* &c. जीव *m.* साबुती *f.* बळकटी *f.* ऐवज *m.* असंडनीयता *f.*

6 गाढपणा *m.* निबिडपणा *m.* गडदपणा *m.* &c.

8 निकोपपणा *m.* निखोडपणा *m.* दोषराहित्य *n.*

Soup, *n.* v. Broth. सागुतीचा रसा *m.*

Sour, *a. acid, tart.* अंबट *or* आंबट, आंबटा, खट्टा, खट्या, अम्ल, अम्लरस,—remissively, *sourish,* आंबटसर, आंबटसा, आंबूस; —enhancingly, *very sour,* आंबटढाण, आंबटडसाण, आंबटटस, आंबटवाणा, वज्रअंबट,—an eructation, &c. करपट, करपा.

Of a sour kind,—a fruit, &c. आंबट्या.

S. and tough,—food. अंबटचिंबट.

Sweety s. आमगूळ.

To become s. आंबणें.

2 *harsh of temper; crabbed, morose, &c.* v. CROSS. खट्याळ, दाष्ट, द्राष्ट, दाष्टीक, तुसडा, कैदी, कैदखोर, कुरटा, कुधाण *or* न, कर्कश.

3 *expressing discontent, &c.*—face, &c. शेणखाल्ल्यासारखा, खापरासारखा, खापरलेला, हिमट, हिमटा, हिमटतोंड्या, कुडुकबाणा *or* णी.

To make a s. face. आंबट तोंड *n.*-हिमटतोंड *n.* करणें.

To SOUR, *v. a. make acid.* आंबट-आंबटा-&c. करणें, आंबवणें, आंबटपणा *m.*-&c. आणणें. [अंबवण *n.*

Matter thrown into (flour, tobacco, &c.) to s. it.

To s. by exposure to the air. अंबवणें, अंबत घालणें-ठेवणें -टाकणें, &c.

2 *make cross.* खट्याळ-दाष्ट-तुसडा-खट्टा-खट्टू-&c. करणें.

To SOUR, *v. n. turn acid.* आंबणें, आंबट-खट्टा-&c. होणें.

To s. through exposure to the air. आंबणें.

2—the teeth or palate. अंबटावणें, आंबणें.

SOUR-LOOKING, *a.* v. SOUR. हिमटतोंड्या, रोंगा.

SOURCE, *n. spring, fountain, origin.* उगम *m.* उद्गम *m.* खाण *f.* खाणी *f.* झरा *or* झिरा *m.* जिव्हाळा *m.* घर *n.* उपज *m.* उत्पत्ति *f.* उत्पत्तिस्थान *n.* बीज *n.* मूळ *n.* मूलायतन *n.* योनि *f.* आदि *m.* अवधि *m. f.*

SOURED, *p.* v. V. A. 1. आंबट केलेला, आंबवलेला, &c.

2 खट्याळ केलेला, &c. खट्टी, खट्टा, खट्टू.

SOURNESS, *n.* v. A. 1. आंबटपणा *m.* आंबटेपणा *m.* खट्टेपणा *m.* आंबटाई *f.* खट्टाई *f.* खटास *f.* अम्लता *f.* अम्लभाव *m.*

2 खट्याळपणा *m.* दाष्टपणा *m.* तुसडेपणा *m.* कर्कशपणा *m.* &c. करडीमरजी *f.*

To SOUSE, *v. n.*—a bird of prey. झडप *f.*-झड *f.*-झाप *f.*-झेप *f.*-&c. घालणें-मारणें.

To SOUSE, *v. a. immerse suddenly,* v. To PLUNGE. दुबकन-कर-डुबकन-कर-&c. बुडवणें.

SOUSE, *adv. plump.* दुब-कन-कर-&c. धप-कन-कर-&c.

SOUTH, *a. belonging, &c. to the south.* दक्षिणेचा, दक्षिणेकडचा, दक्षिणेकडील, दक्षिणदिशेचा, दक्षिण.

SOUTH, *n.* दक्षिण *f.* दक्षिणा *f.* दक्षिणदिशा *f.* याम्या *f.*

Lying north and s. दक्षिणोत्तर.

Pointing to or facing the s. दक्षिणाग्र, दक्षिणाभिमुख, राक्षसमुखी.

Towards the s. राक्षसमोहरी.

To be s.-scorched.—fruit trees, &c. दक्षिणणें, दक्षिण *f.* बाधणें *in. con.* [आग्नेय) *f.*

SOUTH-EAST, *n.* दक्षिणपूर्वा *f.* अग्नि*m.* आग्नेयी (*or corruptly,*

SOUTH-EASTERN, SOUTH-EASTERLY, *a.* आग्नेयीचा, दक्षिणपूर्वेचा.

S. wind. चिल्या *m.*

SOUTH-WARD, *adv.* दक्षिणेकडे, दक्षिणदिशेकडे, दक्षिणात्.

SOUTH-WEST, *n.* निर्ऋति *f.* नैर्ऋती *f.*

SOUTH-WEST, SOUTH-WESTERN, SOUTH-WESTERLY, *a.* नैर्ऋतीचा.

SOUTHERLY, SOUTHERN, *a. belonging, &c. to the south.* दक्षिणेचा, दक्षिण, दक्षिणी, दक्षिणदिशेचा, दक्षिणाभिमुख, सव्य, दाक्षिण, दाक्षिणात्य.

SOUTHERN-WOOD, *n. artemisia.* दमनक *pop.* दवणा*m.*

SOUTHING, *n.* (of the sun). दक्षिणायन*n.* याम्यायन*n.*

SOUVENIR, *n.* v. MEMORIAL. ओळख *f.* यादगारी *f.*

SOVEREIGN, *a. supreme,* v. CHIEF. मुख्य, प्रधान, श्रेष्ठ, कर्तुमकर्तुमन्यथाकर्तुंसमर्थ. [सर्वाधिकारी.

SOVEREIGN, *n.* v. KING. राजा, महाराज, सत्ताधीश, सत्तापुरुष,

S. paramount. सम्राट्.

2 सोन्याचें एक नाणें आहे.

SOVEREIGNTY, *n. supreme authority, supremacy.* मुख्य-श्रेष्ठ-प्रधान-&c. अधिकार*m.*-सत्ता *f.*-&c. सर्वाधिकार*m.* आधिराज्य*n.*

S. paramount. साम्राज्य*n.*

SOW, *n. female pig.* डुकरी *or* डुकरीण *f.* सूकरी *f.*

To SOW, *v. n. scatter seed for growth.* बीं*n.*-&c. पेरणें-टाकणें-फोकणें-&c. पेरणी *f.*-बींपेरणी *f.*-पेरा*m.*-&c. करणें.

To SOW, *v. a.* (seed, *or,* a field). पेरणें, वपणें *or* उपणें, पहिरणें, रोंबणें, रोपणें, पेरा*m.*-वपन*n.*-वाप*m.*-बीजारोप*m.*-बीजारोपण*n.*-&c. करणें, रुजतघालणें.

Sowing,—compreh. *s. and setting, weeding, &c.* लावणी टुपणी *f.* लावणी वेणणी *f.*

To s. by dropping seed into holes. टोंबणें, टुपणें.

To s. by scattering. फोकणें, वाकणें.

To s. (rice &c.) with the hand. मूठ पेरणें *or* टाकणें.

As you s. so shall you reap. रांधावें तसें जेवावें, करावें तसें पावावें, यथा अनुष्ठान तथासिद्धि, श्रमानुसार लाभ.

To reap you must s. दळील तो भरील.

2 (discord, dissension, &c.) *spread.* पेरणें, फैलावणें.

SOWER, *n.* SOWING, *p. a.* v. V. A. 1. पेरणारा, वपणारा, &c. बीजारोपक, बीजारोपणकर्त्ता, वप्ता.

SOWING, *n.* v. V. A. 1. पेरणें*n.* वपणें*n.*&c. पेरणी *f.* पेरा*m.* वपणी *f.* वपन*n.* वाप*m.* बीजारोप*m.* बीजारोपण*n.*

Fit state (of the ground) for s. वाफ *f.* वापसा*m.*

Omission of the usual s. नापेर*n. f.* नापेरा*m.* नापेरी *f.*

SOWINS, *n. sour gruel.* कांजी *f.*

SOWN, *n.* v. V. A. 1. पेरलेला, वपलेला, &c. पेरींव, वापित.

S. by the hand. फोकींव. [पेरींव.

S.—*as opposed to* wild; *sown or set.* पेरणीचा, लावणीचा,

SPACE, *n. abstract extension.* आकाश*n.* देश*m.* शून्य*n.*

Empty s. पोकळी *f.* शून्य*n.*

Included s. अभ्यंतर*n.*

Infinite s. (—*as opposed to* finite s. घटाकाश*n.* मठाकाश*n.*) महाकाश*m.*

Spreading through all s. दिग्व्यापी, अभिव्याप्त.

2 *place,* v. ROOM. अवकाश *m.* आकाश *m. n.* जागा *f.* उसार *m.* सवड *f.* अंतर *n.*

3 *a s. a spot,* v. PLACE. जागा *m. f.*

Open or clear s. *a void spot.* बसळ *f.*

4 *a s. an extent of space,* v. DISTANCE. पल्ला *m.* लांबण *f.*

5 *quantity of time,* v. PERIOD. मुद्दत *f.* अवधि *m.* कालमर्यादा *f.*

SPACIOUS, *a.* v. ROOMY. ऐसपैस, पैस, पघळ, अघळपघळ.

2 *extensive.* पसरट, रुंद, लांबरुंद, मोठ्याविस्ताराचा, कुशाद, प्रशस्त, विस्तीर्ण, विस्तृत, साळमाळ, विशाल *or* ळ, विशद.

SPACIOUSNESS, *n.* v. A. 1. ऐसपैसपणा*m.* पैसपणा *m.* पघळपणा*m.*

2 पसरटपणा *m.* प्रशस्तपणा *m.* &c. विस्तार*m.* प्रशस्तता *f.* प्राशस्त्य*n.* विशालत्व *n.* वैशद्य *n.*

SPADE, *n.* खणपटें *n.* खनित्र *n.* खननास्त्र *n.*

SPADIX, *n.*—S. of a plantain tree. केळफूल *n.* केळचोंड *n.*

SPAN, *n.* (of the thumb and little finger). वीत *f.* वितस्ति *f.*
2 (of the thumb and fore-finger). टिंच *or* टीच *f.* प्रादेश *m.*
3 (of timber) *girth.* गर्भी *f.*

To SPAN, *v. a. measure by the span.* वितीनें मोजणें, वितींत धरणें.

SPANCEL, *n. cord to confine a cow's legs.* चाहटा *m.* भाला *m.*

SPANGLE, *n. bit of metal or any thing sparkling used as an ornament.* चमकी *f.* कांचोटी *f.* टिकली *f.* भिंगटिकली *f.* कांचटिकली *f.*

To SPANGLE, *v. a. set with spangles.* चमक्या *f. pl.*-टिकल्या *f. pl.* -&c. लावणें-जडवणें.

SPANGLED, *p.* v. V. चमक्या लावलेला-जडवलेला, &c. चमक्यांचा, टिकल्यांचा, &c.

SPANIEL, *n.* कुत्र्याची एक जात आहे.

To SPANK, *v. a.* See To SLAP.

To SPANK, *v. n.* (along) *tear along,* v. IMPETUOUSLY. धडकधडका-धडकून-&c. चालणें-जाणें, धसकावणें, सडकावणें.

SPANKER, *n. a tall, strapping, striding fellow,* v. LARGE. ढेंगाळ, ढेंगाळ्या, धिपाड *or* धिप्पाड.

SPANKING, *a. whacking, &c.* v. LARGE. रपाटा, झपाटा, बताणा, बताडा.

SPANKINGLY, *adv.* v. V. *and* IMPETUOUSLY. धडक *or* का, धडकून, झपाट्यानें.

SPAN NEW. See NEW.

SPAR, *n. round or squared piece of timber.* सोट *m.* सोटा *m.* सर *m.* कडी *f.* खांड *n.* दीर्घ काष्ठ *n.* तुळई *f.*
2—the mineral, calcareous s. सुफेदसुरमा *m.*

To SPAR, *v. n. fight prelusively.* हाताफळी *f.*-हाताहाती *f.*-हातपिटी *f.*-&c. चालणें *g. of s. recip.*
2 See To WRANGLE.

To SPARE, *v. a. use frugally, apply scantily.* राखून-हात सावरून-हात आवरून-हात आखडून-हात राखून-&c. खर्चणें-खर्च *m.* करणें, गरज करणें, काटकसर *f.*-तंगचाई *f.*-कुचराई *f.*-&c. करणें, काटकसरीनें-&c. खर्च *m.* करणें, बाण *f.*-तोटा *m.*-कमताई *f.*-&c. करणें *g. of o.* काटकसरीचा-तंगचाईचा-&c. खर्च *m.* करणें, चोरणें (as आंग *n.*-हात *m.*-पाय *m.*-कसब *n.*-&c. चोरणें).
To s. one's self. *save one's strength.* आंग *n.* चोरणें-राखणें, जीव *m.* राखणें, पाठ *f.* चोरणें-काढणें.
2 *part with without inconvenience.* खोळंबा-खोटी-&c. न पडेसा *decl.*-न होईसा *decl.* देणें, देऊं पावणें, सुखानें-सोईनें-&c. देणें.
Enough and to spare. उरून पुरायाजोगा.
3 *omit, forbear to inflict, or impose.* सोडणें, माफ करणें, बक्षीस करणें, माफी *f.*-क्षमा *f.*-&c. करणें, बांचविणें.

SPARE, *a.* v. SURPLUS. उबार, उफाळ, फालतू, अत्रप *or* ब, ठेवणीचा, शिलकीचा, अदकाब, अदकाबाचा.
S. item (of clothing, &c.). कांतबाल.
S. time, v. LEISURE. फुरसत *f.* रिकामी वेळ *f.*
2 *meagre,* v. LEAN. रोडंगा, पातळपोट्या, बाळकुंडा, कमतनूक, शाहांगी *or* ग्या, कृश, कृशांग.
3 v. SCANTY. थोडा, अपुरा, चुटपूट, अल्प.

SPARENESS, *n.* v. A. 2. रोडंगेपणा *m.* &c. कृशता *f.* कृशांगता *f.* अंगकार्श्य *n.*

SPARER, *n.* SPARING, *p. a.* v. V. 1. *and* ECONOMICAL. हात राखून खर्चणारा, काटकसरीचा खर्च करणारा, &c. काटकसऱ्या, कतरचेल्या, काटकसरीचा, अल्पव्ययी, व्ययशंकित.

SPARINGLY, *adv.* v. A. *and* SCANTILY. हात राखून-आंवरून-&c. काटकसरीनें, तंगचाईनें.

SPARK, *n.* (of fire). ठिणगी *or* थिणगी *f.* थिगळी *f.* ठेणा *m.* स्फुलिंग *pop.* फुलिंग *m.* अग्निकण *m.* कीट *f.* किटण *n.* तिडकी *f.* कांजळी *f.* फूल *n.*
2 *gay fellow, &c.* v. BUCK. नट, नटवा, छेला, छालछबीला.
3 See LOVER. 4 *small portion,* v. PARTICLE, BIT. कण *m.* कणिका *f.* किणकिणी *f.* लेश *m.* अंश *m.*

SPARKISH. See BUCKISH.

SPARKLE, *n.* See SPARK. 2. *luminous thing.* तेजःकण *pop.* तेजकण *m.* चमकी *f.* कांचोटी *f.*

To SPARKLE, *v. n. emit sparks.* ठिणग्या *f. pl.*-&c. काढणें-झाडणें-टाकणें, ठिणग्या *f. pl.* निघणें *g. of s.*
2 *glitter,* v. To SHINE. झकझकणें, झगझगणें, लकलकणें *or* लुकलुकणें *or* लिकलिकणें, तकतक-लकलक-लक्क *adv.* करणें, चमकणें, झळकणें, झळक *f.*-&c. मारणें, लकलकी *or* लिकलिकी *f.* होणें *g. of s.* स्फुरणें, स्फुरण *n.* होणें *g. of s.*

SPARKLER, *n.* SPARKLING, *p. a.* v. V. 2. लकलकणारा, लकलक करणारा, &c. झकझकीत, झगझगीत, लकलकीत *or* लुकलुकीत, लक्क, तकतकीत, जोतदार, जोतीवंत, पाणीदार.

SPARKLINGNESS. See BRILLIANCE.

SPARRING, *n.* v. V. हातपिटी *f.* हाताहाती *f.* झकमक *f.*

SPARROW, *n.*—the cock. चिमणा *m.*—the hen, चिमणी *f.* चिडी *f.*
Flock of sparrows. ताफा *m.*

SPARROW-HAWK, *n.* ससाण्यांतला भेद आहे.

SPARSE, SPARSENESS. See THIN, THINNESS.

SPASM, *n. contraction of the muscles.* पेटका *m.* पेटकी *f.* पेडगा *m.* पेंडका *m.* वळ *f.* पीळ *m.* बेडकी *f.* बरवंट *m.* बरवंटा *m.* मिंडकी *f.* वेग *m.* रेंगडी *f.* संकोच *m.* ग्रह *m.* लहर *f.* गोळा *m.* अंगग्रह *m.*
S. of the legs. करळी *or* कराळी *f.* कराळ्या *f. pl. v.* चढ.

SPASMODIC, *a.* v. N. पेटक्यांचा, &c. पेटके येण्याचा.

SPATHE, *n.*—S. of a plantain tree. कोंका *m.*

To SPATTER, *v. a.* v. To SPRINKLE. छांटे *m. pl.* उडवणें, भरविणें.

SPAVIN, *n.* (on a horse's leg). वारूळ *n.* पाषाणा *m.*

To SPAWL, See To SPEW.

SPAWN, *n. eggs of fish.* माशांचीं अंडीं *n. pl.*

To SPAWN, *v. n.* अंडीं *n. pl.* घालणें-टाकणें.

To SPEAK, *v. n. utter words or speech.* बोलणें, वदणें, जीभ *f.*-जिभली *f.*-वाणी *f.* वदणें *g. of s.* तोंड *n.*-जीभ *f.*-ओंठ *m. pl.* हालवणें, तोंड *n.*-जीभ *f.*-&c. हालणें *g. of s.* जल्पणें, भाषण *n.*-कथन *n.*-उक्ति *f.*-वदणूक *f.*-वाग्व्यापार *m.*-शब्दव्यापार *m.*-&c. करणें.
To begin to s. वाणी *f.*-वाचा *f.*-शब्द *m.* फुटणें *in. con.*
To cease to s. with. अबोला *m.* धरणें *with* सीं *of o.*
To s. loudly, v. To BAWL. गागणें, गळीं लागणें.
To s. one's fill. तोंड भरून बोलणें.
To s. quickly. चुरचूर-झरझर *or* रां-भरभर *or* रां-&c. बोलणें.
2 *for or against, dispute,* v. To ARGUE. बोलणें, भांडणें, वाद *m.* करणें.

3 of; v. To MENTION. बोलणें, उल्लेख m.-उहू m.-&c. काढणें-करणें g. of o.

To SPEAK, *v. a. pronounce, utter.* बोलणें, म्हणणें, उच्चारणें, तोंडाबाटे काढणें, उच्चार m.-&c. करणें.

SPEAKER, *n.* SPEAKING, *p. a.* v. V. N. 1. बोलणारा, &c. बोलता, बोलका, वक्ता, वादी, भाषी (in comp. as मितभाषी, अल्पभाषी, बहुभाषी, मधुरभाषी, सत्यभाषी, अनृतभाषी, &c.).

The intention or aim of the s. विवक्षा *f.* विवक्षित *n.*

Smart and able s. बांका बोलणारा.

I. *president of certain assemblies.* सभाध्यक्ष.

SPEAR, *n. lance, &c.* भाला *m.* बरची *f.* बल्लम or बह्लम *m.* इटाm. शूल *m. n.*

Iron s. सांग *f.* शक्ति *f.*

S. with a string to recover it. सैती *f.*

To SPEAR, *v. a.* भाला *m.*-सांग *f.*-&c. मारणें, भाल्यानें-&c. भोसकणें-टोचणें-&c.

SPEAR-HEAD, *n.* फळ *n.* भाल *f.* [शूलपाणि.

SPEAR-MAN, *n.* भालेकरी, इटेकरी, बरचीवाला, सांगवाला, भालाईत,

SPEAR-STAFF, *n.* भालकाठी *f.*

SPECIAL, *a. belonging to a species.* जातीचा, जातिसंबंधी-विषयक, जातीय, जातिवाचक. [अव्यापी.

2 v. PARTICULAR. विशेष, असाधारण, असामान्य, अव्यापक,

S. rule. विशेषविधि *m.*

S. text. विशेषवचन *n.*

That is provided for (enjoined or forbidden) by s. mention. प्रतिपदोक्त. [कोत्तर.

3 *more than ordinary, &c.* विशेष, लोकोत्तर, अधिक, अधि-

4 *designed for a particular purpose.* मुद्दाम-मुजरत-तात्पुरचा-&c. केलेला, मुद्दामचा, मुजरतचा, तात्पुरचा, &c. तदहेतुक, तदुद्दिष्ट, तन्निमित्तक.

5 *limited to a certain class of subjects.* विशेष विषयांचा.

SPECIALITY, SPECIALTY, *n.* v. A. 1. जातिसंबंधिता *f.* जातीयता *f.* &c. जातित्व *n.*

2 विशेषता *f.* असाधारणत्व *n.* &c. विशेष *m.* असाधारण *n.* असामान्य *n.* वैशेष्य *n.* विशेषात्कार *m.*

I. *a* s. विशेष *m.*

SPECIALLY, *adv.* v. A. 2. विशेषेंकरून, विशेष, विशेषतः, असाधारणतः, विशेषात्कारें करून.

4 *and* EXPRESSLY. मुद्दाम, तात्पुरचा, मुजरत or द.

SPECIE, *n. gold or silver coin.* सोननाणें *n.* नगदी ऐवज *m.*

SPECIES, *n. sort, class, kind.* जात *f.* जाति *f.* प्रकार *m.*

The s.—collect. जातिपक्ष *m.*

SPECIFIC, SPECIFICAL, *a. constituting a species, and distinguishing it from others.* विशेषजातीचा, विशेषजातीविषयींचा, विशेषजातीय, विशेषजातिविषयक, विशेषजातिसंबंधी, विशेष, असाधारण, असामान्य.

S. constitution or character. जातिस्वभाव *m.* साधारण*n.* साधारण्य *n.* सामान्य *n.*

2 (a medicine). हुकमी, अवश्य गुणकरणारा, करारी, अचूक, अचूकसंधानी.

A s. medicine. रामबाण *m.*

SPECIFICALLY, *adv.* v. A. जातीनें, जातीचा *decl.* स्वभावानें, जातितः, स्वभावतः, निसर्गतः.

SPECIFICALNESS, v. A. विशेषजाति *f.* विशेषजातिता *f.* असाधारणता *f.* असामान्यता *f.* विशेषजातिसंबंधिता *f.* विशेष *m.* जातित्व *n.*

SPECIFICATION, *n.* v. V.—*act.* विशेषनिर्देश *m.* भेदन *n.* अभिधान *n.* अवच्छेद *m.* व्यवच्छेद *m.* उद्देशन *n.* उपदेश *m.*

Without s. उभागत.

SPECIFIED, *p.* v. V. अमुक म्हणून सांगितलेला, &c. विशेषित, भेदित, अवच्छिन्न, व्यवच्छिन्न, उद्दिष्ट, निर्दिष्ट, उपदिष्ट.

SPECIFIER, *n.* SPECIFYING. *p. a.* v. V. अमुक-अमका म्हणून सांगणारा, &c. उद्देशक, निर्देशक, अवच्छेदक, व्यवच्छेदक, भेदक, अभिधायक, उद्देशन-&c. कर्त्ता-कारी.

To SPECIFY, *To* SPECIFICATE, *v. a. mention in particular.* तपसीलवार-&c. बोलणें-लिहणें-&c. विशेषवर्णन *n.*-&c. करणें *g. of o.* अमुक-अमका म्हणून सांगणें, भेदन *n.*-अभिधान *n.*-उद्देशन *n.*-&c. करणें *g. of o.*

SPECIMEN, *n. sample.* मासला *m.* नमुना *m.* वानगी *f.* वाण *n. m.* दासवणूक *f.* v. दासवणें.

SPECIOUS, *a. showy,* v. FINE. देखणा, देखणाऊ, दर्शनी.

2 *superficially fair or correct; plausible, &c.* देखणाऊ, दिसाऊ, वरघडीचा, वरपंकाचा, वरपंकी, वरकांती or वरकांतीचा, लटकापर नेटका, सत्याभासाचा, प्रमाणाभासाचा, सत्याभासात्मक, प्रमाणाभासात्मक, सत्यसदृश, सत्यसंनिभ, सत्यसंकाश, आपातरमणीय, अविचाररमणीय, अविचारसुंदर.

3 *using specious arguments, &c.* तोंडावर गोड, तोंडा पुरता गोड, लाघवी.

SPECIOUSLY, *adv.* v. A. 2. देखणाऊपणानें, &c. सत्याभासपूर्वक, प्रमाणाभासपूर्वक.

SPECIOUSNESS, *n.* A. 2. देखणाऊपणा *m.* दिसाऊपणा *m.* &c. सत्याभास *m.* प्रमाणाभास *m.* सत्यसन्निभता *f.* आपातरमणीयता *f.*

SPECK, *n. spot, mark, stain, discoloration.* ठिकें *n.* ठिपका *m.* ठीक *n.* चिथडा *m.* दाग or डाग *m.* लासें *n.* चिह्न *n.* कवडी *f.*

S. (of mud, blood, &c.) splashed, spurted, &c. against. शितोडा *m.* छिटा *m.*

2 (in the eye). फूल *n.* पुष्प *n.* तिलपुष्प *n.*

3 *minute thing,* v. PARTICLE. कण *m.* कणिका *f.* सूक्ष्म *m.*

SPECKLE, *n. spot, &c.* v. SPECK. ठिकें *n.* चिथडा *m.*

SPECKLED, SPECKED, *a. variegated with spots.* ठिपक्यांचा, ठिकांचा, बुंदक्यांचा, ठिपकेदार, चित्र, विचित्र, चित्रविचित्र.

SPECKLEDNESS, *n.* v. A. ठिपकेदारपणा *m.* चित्रविचित्रपणा *m.*

SPECTACLE, *n. something extraordinary exhibited.* खेळ *m.* तमाशा *m.* कौतुक *n.* चमत्कार *m.* मौज *f.*

2 *any thing seen, a sight,* v. SCENE. पाहण्याचा पदार्थ *m.* दृष्टिविषय *m.*

3 spectacles. अयनक or ऐनक *n.f.* ऐनाm. उपनेत्र*n.* चश्माm. चाळसी *f.* चाळीसपत्र *n.* आरसी or शी *f.* [तमाशगीर.

SPECTATOR, *n. looker, beholder.* पाहणारा, मौज-&c. पाहणारा,

SPECTRE, *n.* v. GHOST. भूत *n.* छाया *f.* समंध *m.*

2 *meagre person, &c.* v. STARVELING. गिन्हाm. गिन्हाबळ *f.* दिपाचा कवडा *m.*

SPECULAR, *a. having the qualities of a mirror.* आरशाच्याधर्माचा or गुणाचा, दर्पणधर्मक, दर्पणगुणक, आदर्शधर्मक.

To SPECULATE, *v. n.*—in commerce. v. *To* SCHEME. उलेंढालें *n.*-लेंकेंडें *n.*-&c. करणें, उलेंढालयाचा-उलाघालीचा-&c. व्यापार *m.*-उदीम *m.* करणें.

2 *meditate, contemplate, &c.* कल्पना *f.*-तर्क *m.*-वितर्क *m.pl.*-&c. करणें *or with g. of s.* चालणें, तर्करचना *f.*-वितर्करचना *f.*-&c. करणें, वितर्कणें.

SPECULATION, *n.* v. SCHEME. कचाट *n.* सेंकटें *n.* उलेंढालें *n.* ढबंढाळ *n.* उलगाघाल *f.* उलाघाल *f.*

2 *mental view, &c.* कल्पना *f.* तर्क *m.* वितर्क *m.* मनाचा-बुद्धीचा-&c. तरंग *m.*-खेळ *m.* चालना *f.* [ध्यानी.

SPECULATIVE, *a.* v. CONTEMPLATIVE. मननशील, ध्यानशील,

2 *theoretical, not practical.* मानसिक, मनोमय, काल्पनिक, व्यवहारागम्य, अव्यावहारिक.

SPECULATOR, *n.* SPECULATING, *p. a.* v. V. 1. *and* SCHEMER. कचाट्या, सेंकटेसोर, उलेंढाल्या, ढबंढाळी *or* ळ्या, उचक्या, चळवळ्या.

SPECULUM. See MIRROR.

SPEECH, *n.*—the faculty. वाणी *f.* वाचा *f.* वाक् *f.* उक्ति *f.* वैखरी *f.* सरस्वती *f.* भारती *f.* शब्दजाल *n.* वाक्य *n.*

Cleverness, or skilfulness of s. वाक्चातुर्य *n.* वाक्कौशल्य *n.* वाक्पाटव *n.*

Volubility or glibness of s. वाक्चापल्य *n.*

To acquire s. वाचा *f.* फुटणें *in. con.*

To lose s. *become speechless.* गळा *m.* धरणें *g. of s.*

According to Hindu philosophy Speech has four stages from the first stirring of the air or breath to articulate utterance. They are: the first stage, परा *f.* —the first stirring of the breath: the second, पश्यंती *f.* —the faint whispering at the breast: the third, मध्यमा *f*: the fourth, वैखरी or articulate utterance.

2 *speaking.* बोलणें *n.* भाषण *n.* जावसाल *m.* उक्ति *f.* वाग्व्यापार *m.* शब्दव्यापार *m.* वाद *m.* जाप *m.* निर्देश *m.*

Control of s. वाङ्निरोध *m.* वाङ्नियमन *n.* वाग्दंड *m.*

Liberty of s. तोंडसुटका *f.* तोंडमोकळीक *f.* वाङ्मुक्ति *f.* वाग्प्रतिबंध *m.*

Low, faint, or feeble s. मिणमिण *f.*—to speak with such. मिणमिणणें.

Slow of s. जिव्हेचाजड.

Softness and sweetness of s. गौल्यता *f.* वाक्माधुर्य *n.*

Stopping one's s. वाग्बंधन *n.* [&c.

To control one's s. तोंड *n.*-जीभ *f.*-&c. अटोपणें-संभाळणें-

To have no consistency in one's s. बोलांत बोल *m.* नसणें *g. of s.*

3 *words, language*; or, *matter spoken.* बोलणें *n.* म्हणणें *n.* बोल *m.* भाषण *n.* म्हणगत *n.* जावसाल *m.* वचन *n.* वाक्य *n.* उक्ति *f.* गोष्ट *f.*

Beguiling or cajoling s. गूळखोबरें *n.* गूळपापडी *f.*

Artful involution or ambiguity of s. लपेट *f.*

Definite s. नेमोत्तर *n.*

Disguised or covert s. व्याजोक्ति *f.*

Elegance of s. शब्दलालित्य *n.*

Mere s. वाङ्मात्र *n.*

Of measured s. मितभाषी.

Opening of s. वाङ्मुख *n.*

Unlucky or ill-omened s. दुर्वाच्य *n.* अवाच्य *n.* दुर्भाषण *n.* दुर्वचन *n.* दुरुक्ति *f.*

To catch one in his s. पर्गी-पगदर्स्ती धरणें—To be caught. पर्गी-पगदर्स्ती सांपडणें.

4 *a s.* v. LANGUAGE. बोली *f.* भाषा *f.*

5 *set speech, oration.* See HARANGUE.

Part of s.—in grammar. शब्द *m.*

There are some occult or covert schemes *of speech*, as चिकारी, फुलकारी, &c. as there are schemes also of occult *writing*. See under CIPHER.

SPEECHLESS, *a. destitute of speech.* मुका, मोना, मूक, अवाक्, अमू, वाचाहीन, वाचारहित, वाग्रहित.

2 *mute, silent, deprived of speech.* कुंठित, निरुत्तर, अनुत्तर, बोलवेनासा झालेला, कुंठितवाक्, स्तंभितवाक्.

SPEED, *n.* v. SWIFTNESS. वेग *m.* त्वरा *f.* जव *m.*

At full s. भरदवड *or* भरदौड, भरधांव, भरधूम, भरचाल.

2 *expedition, despatch,* v. SMARTNESS. जलद्पणा *m.* जलदी *f.* त्वरा *f.* झटपट *f.* चटपट *f.*

To SPEED. See To HASTEN, To PROSPER.

SPEEDILY, *adv.* v. A. *and* QUICKLY. जलदी, लौकर, जलदीनें.

SPEEDY, *a.* v. SWIFT. त्वरित, त्वरितगामी, त्वरितगति, शीघ्रगामी, शीघ्रगति, वेगवान्.

2 *expeditious, not dilatory,* v. SMART. जलदीचा, त्वरेचा, झटपटीचा, चटपटीचा, त्वरित.

SPELL, *n.* v. CHARM. मंत्र *m. v.* घाल, मार, टाक, भार *m.* मारणी *f. v.* घाल, टाक, कुबेडें *n.* कंबटल *or* ल्य *n.* कंचटाळ *n.*

S.-book. मंत्रशास्त्र *n.*

S.-man. मंत्रवादी, मंत्री.

2 *turn of work, relief.* पाळी *f.* पालट *m.* वारी *f.*

3 *a setting to, about.* दम *m.* पाळी *f.* उठावणी *f.*

SPELL-BOUND, *a.* भारलेला, मंत्रित.

To SPELL, *v. n.* शब्दाचीं अक्षरें *n. pl.* जोडणें-सांगणें, अक्षरांची जोडणी *f.*-वर्णयोजना *f.*-वर्णरचना *f.*-&c. करणें.

To SPELL, *v. a.* See To CHARM.

2 See V. N.

SPELLING, *n.* अक्षरांची जोडणी *f.* वर्णरचना *f.* वर्णयोजना *f.* वर्णन्यास *m.*

Variation of s. पाठ *m.* पाठांतर *n.*

SPELTER, *n. coarse kind of pewter.* जस्त *n.*

SPENCER, *n.*—the short coat. चोळा *m.* बंडी *f.*

To SPEND, *v. a. consume,* v. To EXHAUST. खर्चणें, उडवणें, संपवणें, खपवणें, फडशा *m.*-फन्ना *m.*-&c. करणें-उडवणें *g. of o.*

To s. and be spent in. जीव पासडून *or* अटून-आंग मोडून-&c. करणें-खपणें-&c.

2 *expend.* खर्चणें, वेचणें, खर्च *m.*-खर्चवेच *m.*-व्यय *m.*-व्ययीकरण *n.*-&c. करणें *g. of o.*—lavishly, freely, &c. v. To SQUANDER. छमकावणें.

3 *waste, wear out, exhaust,* v. To TIRE. भागवणें, शिणवणें, बेजार-बेदम-&c. करणें.

4 (time). v. To PASS. काढणें, घालवणें, नेणें.

SPENDER, *n.* SPENDING, *p. a.* v. V. 1. खर्चणारा, खर्च करणारा, फडशा करणारा, &c.

2 खर्चणारा, वेचणारा, खर्च करणारा, &c. व्ययी, व्ययकर्ता-कारी.

SPENDTHRIFT, *n.* v. SQUANDERER. उडाऊ, सांडरा, दिवाळखोर.

SPENDING, *n.* v. V. 1.—*act.* खर्चणें *n.* सारणें *n.* खपवणें *n.* &c.

खर्च *m.*

2—*act.* खर्चणें *n.* वेचणें *n.* खर्च *m.* वेच *m.* खर्चवेच *m.* वेचखर्च *m.* व्यय *m.* व्ययीकरण *n.*

3—*act.* भागवणें *n.* &c.

4—*act.* काढणें *n.* घालवणें *n.* &c. [&c.

SPENT, *p.* v. V. 1. खर्चलेला, खर्च केलेला, फडशा केलेला, खपवलेला, To be spent. खपणें, सरणें, संपणें.

2 खर्चलेला, वेचलेला, &c. व्ययित, व्ययीकृत. [क्लांत.

3 शिणवलेला, &c. वेजार, वेदम, दिक्क, चकनाचूर *or* चकाचूर, To be s. v. EXHAUSTED. दमणें, शिणणें, वेंगणें, थकणें. To be s.—a ball &c. निवणें.

4 काढलेला, घालवलेला, &c.

SPERABLE, *a. that may be hoped.* अपेक्षणीय, अपेक्ष्य.

SPERM, *n. animal seed,* v. SEED. धात *f.* वीर्य *n.* शुक *n.*

2 See SPAWN.

SPERMATIC, *a. belonging &c. to sperm.* धातीचा, शुकाचा, वीर्याचा, &c. शुकविषयक, शुकसंबंधी, वीर्यविषयक-संबंधी.

2 *producing sperm.* शुककर, वीर्यकर, शुकल.

SPERMATOCELE, *n.* भेलगा *m.* भेरगा *m.* [टाकणें.

To SPEW, *v. a. eject from the stomach,* v. To VOMIT. ओकून

To SPEW, *v. n. eject the contents of the stomach,* v. To VOMIT. ओकणें, वमणें, वमन *n.*-वांति *f.*-&c. करणें *or with in. con.* होणें.

SPHERE, *n. orb, globe.* गोल *m.* गोलक *m.* मंडल *n.* वर्तुल *n.* The Armillary s. खगोल *m.*

2 *circuit of action, &c., province.* प्रकरण *n.* इलाखा *m.* अमल *m.* कामाचा टप्पा *m.* अटोका *m.* बकल *n.*

3 See RANK.

SPHERICAL, *a.* v. GLOBULAR, ROUND. गोल, गोलाकार, वर्तुल, वर्तुलाकार, गोटोळा.

SPHERICALNESS, SPHERICITY, *n.* v. A. *and* ROUNDNESS. गोलत्व *n.* वर्तुलत्व, गोलाकृति *f.* [गोलाध्याय *m.*

SPHERICS, *n. doctrine of the sphere.* गोलशास्त्र *n.* गोलविद्या *f.*

SPHEROIDAL, *a. approaching to spherical.* गोलकल्प, गोलप्राय, गोलसदृश,—oblate, चपटागोल—prolate, लांबोडा *or* डा, लांबटगोल, अंडाकार.

SPHERULE, *n. small spherical body.* लहानगोल *m.* लघुगोल *m.* लघुवर्तुल *n.* [मसाल्याची वस्त *f.*

SPICE, *n. aromatic production.* व्यंजन *n.* मसाल्याचा जिन्नस *m.* Hot s. गरम मसाला *m.*

2 fig. *small quantity, smack, tincture, &c.* v. TASTE. चुणूक *f.* धुमक *f.* वास *m.*

To SPICE, *v. a. season with spice.* मसाला *m.*-व्यंजन *n.* घालणें-घालून तिखट-चवचवीत-खमंग-&c. करणें.

SPICE-BOX, *n.* चौकुडा *m.* अटवंदण *n.*

SPICE-GRASS, *n. andropogon schœnanthus.* गांजणीचें गवत *n.*

SPICERY, *n. spices.* मसाला *m.* जिन्नसजिन्नस *n.*

SPICINESS, *n.* v. A. 2. मसालेदारपणा *m.*

SPICK and SPAN, *a.* v. NEW. कोराकरकरीत.

SPICY, *a. of or belonging to spices.* मसाल्याचा, जिन्नसजिन्नसांचा, जिन्नसाजिन्नसाचा.

2 v. PIQUANT. मसालेदार, मसाल्याचा, खमखमीत.

SPIDER, *n.*—the animal. कातीण *f.* कोळी *m.* मकडण *f.* लुतेरा *m.* कोटी *m.* कोशकार *m.* अष्टपाद *m.* ऊर्णनाभि *m.* लूता *f.* माशांचा वाघ *m.* Earthen nest of the s. called कोढी *or* कोशा, कोश *m.*—Fine threads woven by it. कोलशीट *n.* कोळशेटें *n.* कोळिष्टक *n.*

SPIGOT. See PEG, PLUG.

SPIKE, *n.* (of corn) v. EAR. कणीस *n.*

2 (as of a top, goad, &c.). आर *f.* अरी *f.*

3 v. NAIL. खिळा *m.* खीळ *f.* सळई *f.* शूळ *pop.* शूळ *or* सूळ *m.* शंकु *m.* शलाका *f.* शल्य *n.*

To SPIKE, *v. a.* (cannon, &c.) खिळा *m.*-&c. मारणें-ठोकणें.

SPIKENARD, *n.*—Indian. जटामांसी *pop.* जटामावसी *f.*

SPILE, SPILL, *n.* See PEG.

To SPILL, *v. a. suffer to fall or run off a vessel.* सांडणें, सांडवणें, गाळणें, गळवणें, ढोळणें, ढोळवणें, सांडून-&c. देणें.

2—through turning over. लवंडणें, लवंडवणें, उलंडणें, सांडलवंड *f.* करणें.

3—through shaking. हिसळणें, उचंबळणें, उचंबळणें.

4 *cause to flow out, shed.* सांडणें, पाडणें, वाहवणें, पात *m.*-&c. करणें *g. of o.*

To SPILL, *v. n. be shed.* सांडणें.

2—through turning over. लवंडणें.

3—through shaking. हिसळणें, उचंबळणें.

SPILLING, *n.* v. V. A. 1.—*act.* सांडणें *n.* &c.

4 पाडणें *n.* &c. पात *m.*

To SPIN, *v. a. form threads, &c.* कांतणें, सूत *n.* काढणें-कांतणें *g. of o.* कर्त्तन *n.*-&c. करणें.

2 (a top, &c.) फिरवणें, चकावर धरणें.

3 out; *protract, &c.* लांबला धरणें, लांबण *f.*-लांबलचक *f.*-लांबलेला *m.* लांबवणें, लांबणीवर टाकणें.

To SPIN, *v. n. work at drawing and twisting threads.* सूत *n.* कांतणें-काढणें.

2—a top &c. भोवणें, फिरणें.

SPINAL, *a. belonging &c. to the spine.* कण्याचा, पाठीच्या दांड्याचा, पृष्ठवंशसंबंधी, पृष्ठवंशविषयक, पृष्ठवंशस्थ.

SPINDLE, *n. pin of a spinning wheel.* चाते *n.* चाती *f.* तकु *f.* नकुटी *f.* सूत्रतकुटी *f.*

Spindles, *legs.* ढोंका *or* ढोका *m.* टांग *f.*

SPINDLE-SHANKED, *a.* लांबटांग्या.

SPINE, *n. backbone.* कणा *m.* पाठीचा दांडा *m.* पृष्ठवंश *m.* Apex of the s. मानेचा कळस *m.*- कांटा *m.* Lower extremity of the s. कमरेचाकांटा *m.* पेकडहाड *n.* रिकचु *f.* त्रिकास्थि *f.*

2 See SHIN. 3 See THORN.

SPINNER, *n.* SPINNING, *p. a.* v. V. A. 1. *and* v. N. 1. कांतणारा, सूत कांतणारा-काढणारा.

SPINNING, *n.* v. V. 1. सूत कांतणें *n.* सूत काढणें *n.*

SPINNING-WHEEL, *n.* चरकी *f.*

SPINSTER, *n. unmarried woman.* अवरढी *f.* निवरा *f.* अवरा *f.* अनूढा *f.* अविवाहिता *f.* अपरिणीता *f.* अविवाहित-&c. स्त्री *f.*-बायको *f.*

SPIRACLE, *n. air-hole.* उच्छ्वास *pop.* उसास *m.* उसासा *m.* जन्तोच्छ्वास *m.* वायुमार्ग *m.* वायुपथ *m.*

SPIRAL, *a. winding and rising like a screw.* नागमोडी, नागमोडीचा, मळसूत्राच्या आकाराचा, वांकीच्या आकाराचा.

S. lines. S. course. नागमोड *f.* [कारानें.

SPIRALLY, *adv.* v. A. मळसूत्रासारखा *decl.* नागमोडीच्या आ-

SPIRE, *n. winding line, &c.* नागमोड *f.*

2 (of flame). आगशी *f.* आगिवरा *m.* आगिवळी *f.* अग्निशिखा *f.* शिखा *f.*

3 *pinnacle, pyramid, shaft.* सुळका *m. dim.* सुळकी *f.* दांडा *m.* शंकु *m.* शिखर *n.* सुळक्याचें शिखर *n.*

SPIRIT, *n.* v. BREATH, AIR. आत्मा *m.*

2 *soul, &c.* See SOUL. 3 v. GHOST. भूत *n.* पिशाच *n.* प्रेत *n.* छाया *f.* अपछाया *f.*

The Supreme S. v. GOD. परमात्मा *m.*

4 *habitude of mind, temper.* स्वभाव *m.* प्रकृति *f.* मनाची भावना *f.* प्रकृतिभाव *m.* तबियत *f.*

Conquest of one's own s. मनोजय *m.*

Proudness of s. जळ *m.* तवर *n.*

To restrain or keep in one's s. दम *m.* कोंडणें.

5 *turn of mind, occasional state.* बुद्धि *f.* भाव *m.* मन *n.* वृत्ति *f.*

Good spirits. हर्षवृत्ति *f.*

Low spirits. विषाद *m.*

That is in good spirits. रंगलेला, हर्षित, हर्षवृत्ति, हृष्टचित्त, खुशाल, स्वस्थ.

That is in low spirits, v. LOW. दिलगीर, खिन्न, उदास, विषादी.

6 *life, ardor, mettle, alacrity, fire, &c.* दम *m.* धमक *f.* पाणी *n.* जिवनपाणी *n.* हिय्या *m.* हिम्मत *f.* रग *f.* रगदारी *f.* धूम *f.* तेज *n.* तेजगी *f.* जीव *m.* जिवटपणा *m.* जिवसपणा *m.* धिया *m.* उत्साह *m.* प्रोत्साह *m.* उत्सुकता *f.* अवसान *n.* धीर *m.* धैर्य *n.* त्राण *m. n.* हवस or हौस *f.* हांव *f.* आव *m.* रस *m.* रंग *m.*

7 *essential portion.* अर्क *m.* सत्व *n.* सत्वांश *m.* तत्व *n.* तत्वांश *m.* सार *m. n.* सारांश *m.* दम *m.* रस *m.*

8 *strong, pungent liquor,*—esp. that obtained by distillation. भट्टीची दारू *f.* दारू *f.* मद्य *n.* सुरा *f.* सरा *m.* वारुणी *f.* झिंगी *f.* मदिरा *f.* आसव *m.*—in cant phraseol. corresponding with *mountain dew, sublime beverage, &c.* are आकाशपाणी *n.* ऊर्ध्वपान *n.* The three kinds of spirit are गौडी *f.* माधवी *f.* and पैष्टी *f.* (spirit distilled from sugar, from honey, and from meal.)

Distiller or vender of s. कलाल, काळण.

Drinking of s. सुरापान *n.* मद्यपान *n.*

Spirituous exudation or extract,—gener. आसव *m.*

9 *life, virtue, &c.* v. GOODNESS. रस *m.* रहस्य *n.* सार *m. n.* कस *m.* जीव *m.* तेज *n.* सत्व *n.* बारें *n.* [तात्पर्य *n.*

10 *real meaning, scope, &c.* अर्थ *m.* भावार्थ *m.* आशय *m.*

To SPIRIT. See To ANIMATE.

SPIRITED, *a.* v. N. 6. तेजाचा, दमाचा, अवसानाचा, हिमतीचा, &c. जीवदार, पाणीदार, दमदार, रगदार, हिय्येदार, जिवट, रगेल, रग्या, हिम्मती, हिम्मतदार, अवसानदार, अवसानी, तेजस्वी, तेजवान्, सतेज, मानी, उडया, प्रोत्साही, सोत्साह.

I.—in composition, noting turn of mind. स्वभावाचा, प्रकृतीचा, बुद्धीचा, &c. स्वभाव (in comp. as उग्रस्वभाव, &c.), प्रकृति (in comp. as सौम्यप्रकृति, &c.).

SPIRITEDNESS. See SPIRIT.

SPIRITLESS, *a.* v. DISPIRITED. उदास, उदासी, निरुत्साह.

2 *without energy, vigor, fire, courage, &c.* v. WEAK. मेणचट, मेण्या, पेंगळा, निर्वीर्य.

To be s. or listless. पेंगणें, पेंगळणें.

3 *vapid, flat, jejune, dry, &c.* फिका or फिक्का, निस्सत्व, अळणी, बाकस or बाकूस, बेकस, पचपचीत, मचमचीत, मळमळीत or मुळमुळीत, मिटमिटीत, पळपळीत, निरस, बिरस, निस्सार, निस्तेज, बाळधर.

SPIRITUAL, *a. immaterial.* अमूर्त, अमूर्तिमान्, निराकार, अमात्रवत्, चिद्रूप, सद्रूप, आत्मस्वरूप, आत्मिक, आध्यात्मिक, नित्यमुक्त.

2 *not lay, temporal, secular, &c.* धर्मप्रकरणाचा, धर्मकृत्याचा, धर्मप्रकरणाविषयींचा, धर्मसंबंधाचा, देवाधर्माच्यासंबंधाचा, धर्मप्रकरणसंबंधी.

3 *not carnal, gross, sensual, &c.* परमार्थाचा, परमार्थाविषयींचा, परमार्थसंबंधी-विषयक, पारमार्थिक, ज्ञानमार्गाचा, निवृत्तिमार्गाचा, निवृत्तिमार्गसंबंधी-विषयक, ज्ञानमार्ग संबंधी-विषयक.

4 See SPIRITUALLY-MINDED.

SPIRITUALISM, *n. the profession or following of spiritual things.* ज्ञानमार्ग *m.* ज्ञानाभ्यास *m.* निवृत्तिमार्ग *m.*

SPIRITUALIST, *n.* ज्ञानमार्गी, ज्ञानाभ्यासी, निवृत्तिमार्गी, ब्रह्मवादी.

SPIRITUALITY, *n.* v. A. 1. अमूर्ति *f.* निराकारता *f.* अमात्रवत्त्व *n.* आत्मस्वरूपता *f.* चिद्रूपता *f.*

3 परमार्थसंबंधिता *f.* पारमार्थिकता *f.* निवृत्तिमार्गसंबंधिता *f.*

4 See SPIRITUALLY-MINDEDNESS.

To SPIRITUALIZE, *v. a. make spiritual.* परमार्थाकडे ओढणें-लावणें, परमार्थनिष्ठ-परमार्थासक्त-&c. करणें.

SPIRITUALLY-MINDED, *a. having the affections raised above sensual objects.* परमार्थी, पारमार्थिक, परमार्थनिष्ठ, परमार्थबुद्धि, परमार्थासक्त, परमार्थपरायण-तत्पर-&c.

SPIRITUALLY-MINDEDNESS, *n.* v. A. परमार्थीपणा *m.* परमार्थबुद्धि *f.* परमार्थनिष्ठा *f.* परमार्थासक्ति *f.*

SPIRITUALLY-WISE, *a.* ज्ञानवान्, ज्ञानपर, आत्मज्ञानी.

SPIRITUOUS, *a. consisting of or containing spirit, ardent, highly intoxicating.* भट्टीचा, यंत्राचा, यंत्रसंधानाचा, फार अमली, शीघ्रमादक, विशेषमादकगुणविशिष्ट-युक्त, जलाल, जालीम, तीव्र.

SPIRY. See SPIRAL.

SPIT, *n.* v. SPITTLE. पिंक *f.* लाळ *f.* उगळ *f.*

2 (of iron, &c.). शूल *pop.* शूळ or सूळ *m.* सुळा *m.*

To SPIT, *v. a. put upon a spit.* सुळावर-&c. घालणें, गोवणें, ग्रंथणें, शूल्य करणें.

2 *eject from the mouth.* थुंकणें, थुंकरणें, थुंकून टाकणें, उगळणें.

Matter spit out. उगळ *f.*

To SPIT, *v. n. void spittle.* थुंकणें, थुंका *m.*-थुंकी *f.* टाकणें-थुंकणें.

2 v. To SPUTTER. चटचटणें, चरचरणें, तटतटणें or तडतडणें, चिवचिवणें,—*intens.* चराडणें, तटाटणें, फुरारणें.

3—rain; v. To DRIZZLE. सिंतोडणें, थुईथुई *adv.*-&c. येणें.

4—a cat, angry dog, &c. फिसकारणें, फिसकणें, फुसफुसणें, फूत्कारणें, खिसणें.

SPIT-BOX, SPITTING-POT, SPIT-TOON, *n.* पिंकदाणी *f.* पतद्ग्रह *m.* चर्वितपात्र *n.* [काळ.

SPIT-FIRE, *n.* v. PASSIONATE. आग्यावेताळ, खवीस, काळाचा

SPITE, *n.* v. MALICE. अकस *m. f.* खुनस *m. f.* कपट *n.* डाव *m.*

दावा m. अदावत f. कोर f. कोरबंदी f. चुरस f. डंश m. द्वेष m. खंदोस m. द्रोह m. कसर or कुसूर m.

A s. against. हट m.

Great s. वज्रद्रोह m.

In s. of; *maugre, notwithstanding*. हटकून, हटेंच, दाटवळें, दाटून, नमानतां, नऐकतां.

To do a thing in s. of. नाकावर निंबू घासून-नाकास चुना लावून-नाकावर पाय देऊन-&c. करणें.

To SPITE, *v. a. treat maliciously, thwart.* अकसानें-चुरसीनें-&c.मनोभंग m.-उत्साहभंग m.-&c. करणें g. of o. अकसानें-खुनसानें-चुरसीनें-&c. दिक्क-जिक्क-&c. करणें or त्रास m.-कंटाळा m.-&c. देणें.

SPITEFUL, *a.* v. N. *and* MALICIOUS. अकसखोर, अकसी, दावेदार, दावेकरी, आडगांठ्या, कपटी, खुनशा, खुनसी, चुरसी, डंशी, द्रोही, द्रोहबुद्धि.

SPITEFULLY, *adv.* v. A. अकसानें, अकसधरून, चुरसीनें, खुनसानें, खुनसधरून, &c. द्रोहपूर्वक, द्रोहबुद्धीनें.

SPITEFULNESS, *n.* v. A. अकसीपणा m. खुनसीपणा m. &c.

SPITTING, *n.* (of rain). पिरपोर f. मुळमूळ f. पावसाची थुईथुई f.-थिवथिव f. चुरचूर f. [डरसा m.

2 (of a cat, &c.). फुसकारा m. फुसफूस f. फुस्स n. फूत्कार m.

SPITTLE, *n. saliva.* थुंका m. थुंकी f. पिंक or पीक f. n. थूक f. n. पिकी f. लाला pop. लाळ f.—in cant phraseol. मुसरस m.

Fasting s. पारोसाथुंका m.

S.—as gulped or swallowed. अंवढा m.

To swallow one's s. अंवढा m. गिळणें-जाणें-उतरणें *in. con.*

To SPLASH, *v. a. spatter with water, &c.* छाटे m. *pl.*-शितोडे m. *pl.*-&c. उडवणें-उडवून भरविणें, भरविणें.

To SPLASH, *v. n. rise or fly up.* हिसळणें or हिंसळणें or हेसळणें, हिंदकळणें, उसळणें, उफाळणें, उफाळा m. निघणें-येणें g. of s.

SPLEEN, *n.*—the organ. पाणथरी f. प्लीहा pop. पिहा or प्याहा m. गुल्म m. तिळी f.

2 *disease of the s.* पाणथरी f. कौलू f. प्लीहा pop. प्याहा or पिहा m. उदरग्रंथि m. प्लीहागुल्म m.

3 See ANGER, SPITE. 4 See MELANCHOLY.

SPLENDID, *a.* v. BRILLIANT, BRIGHT. शोभमान, शोभिवंत, कांतिमान्, तेजोमय, तेजवान् pop. तेजवंत, तेजस्वी.

2 *magnificent, grand, &c.* v. FINE. शोभिवंत, भव्य, उमदा, थाटमाटाचा, छानीचा, आलिज्याहां, शोभमान pop. शोभायमान, विराजमान, विराजित, विलसित.

To be s. विराजणें, विलसणें. [decl.-&c.

SPLENDIDLY, *adv.* v. A. 2. फारशोभेसा *decl.* शोभाहांईसा-येईसा

SPLENDOUR, *n.* v. BRILLIANCY, BRIGHTNESS. रोशनाई f. शोभा f. कांति f. छवि f. तेज n.

2 *magnificence, &c.* शोभा f. छान f. छानदारी f. थाटमाट m. थाटमांड m. शिकल f. नकाशा m.

SPLENETIC, *a. fretful, &c.* v. PEEVISH. चिडचिड्या, चिरडीखोर, किरकिन्या, निडतिड्या. [धी-विषयक.

SPLENIC, *a. belonging to the spleen.* पाणथरीचा, &c. प्लीहासंबं-

To SPLICE, *v. a. join without a knot.* गांठदिल्यावांचून जोडणें-सांधणें-मिळवणें, चारणें.

SPLICE, *n.* गांठदिल्यावांचून जोड m. f.

SPLINT, SPLINTER, *n. spill, shiver,* v. CHIP. ढलपा m. ढलपी f. किपळी f. कपचा m. कपची f.

2—as entered into the flesh. खोंचा m. सरांटा m. शल्य pop. सल n. खणपूस n. धस n. हार m.

3—in surgery. भावी f. सांपळी f.

To SPLINTER. See To SPLIT.

To SPLIT, *v. a. cleave, rive.* चिरणें, फोडणें, फाडणें, छेदणें, भेदणें, फांदडणें, विदारणें, विदारण n.-विदारणा f.-&c. करणें g. of o.

To s. the sides (from laughter). कडण्या f.-बरगड्या f. *pl.* दुखततों हासणें.

To SPLIT, *v. n. open, part.* चिरणें, फाटणें, फुटणें, उलणें, उकलणें, भेगलणें, तडकणें, तडावणें, तिरळणें, पिचणें, भेतळणें, चीर f.-तडा m.-भेग f.-तडक f.-&c. जाणें *in. con.*

SPLIT, *p.* v. V. A. चिरलेला, &c. चिरीव, फोडीव, विदीर्ण, विदारित. v. V. N. चिरलेला, फाटलेला, तडक गेलेला, &c. फुटीर.—esp. of reeds, sticks, &c. पिचका, पिंजका *remiss.* पिंजट.

SPLIT, *n.* v. CRACK. चीर m. f. फूट f. भेग f. तडा m.

SPLITTER, *n.* SPLITTING, *p. a.* v. V. A. 1. चिरणारा, फोडणारा, &c. भेदक, छेदक, विदारक, भेदन-&c. कर्त्ता-कारी.

SPLITTING, *n.* v. V. A.—*act.* चिरणें n. फाडणें n. भेदणें n. &c. विदारणी f. भेद m. भेदन n. छेद m. छेदन n. विदारण n. विदारणा f.

SPLUTTER, *n.* v. BUSTLE. गडबड f. हडबड f.

To SPLUTTER. See To SPUTTER.

To SPOIL, *v. a.* v. To PLUNDER. लुटणें, लुगारणें, लुबाडणें, झांबाडणें, नाडणें, नागवणें, धुणें, खटारणें.

2 *corrupt, injure.* नासणें, विनासणें or बिनसणें, नासवणें, बिघडणें or बिघडणें, बिघडवणें, बिघाडणें, खराब-बाईट-&c. करणें, नाश m.-&c. करणें g. of o.

3 (children, &c.) v. To INDULGE. लाडकावणें, लाडावणें, लालन n. करणें g. of o.

To be spoiled. लाडणें.

To SPOIL, *v. n. grow corrupt, &c.* नासणें, विनासणें or बिनसणें, बिघडणें, बिघडणें, खराब-बाईट-&c. होणें, सडणें, कुजणें, नाश m.-&c. होणें g. of s.

2 (fruits, &c.) through heat and moisture. उबणें, उबटणें, उबारणें, उबाळणें, उमळणें, विडुळणें.

To s. and break,—milk, curds, buttermilk. बितकळणें.

SPOIL, *n. booty, plunder.* लूट f.

2 *slough of a serpent.* कात f. मेंग f.

SPOILED, SPOILT, *p.* v. V. A. 1. लुटलेला, लुबाडलेला, &c.

2 नासलेला, बिघडलेला, खराब केलेला, &c. नासका, नाशित, दूषित, नष्ट.

3 लाडकावलेला, लाडावलेला, लालित.

v. V. N. नासलेला, बिघडलेला, &c. खराब, नासका.

SPOILER, *n.* SPOILING, *p. a.* v. V. A. 1. लुटणारा, लुगारणारा.

2 नासणारा, नासवणारा, खराबकरणारा, &c. नाशक, नाशी, नाश-&c. कर्त्ता-कारी-&c.

3 लाडकावणारा, लाडावणारा, लालनकर्त्ता-&c.

SPOKE, *n.* (of a wheel). आर f. अर m. आरा m. रवा m.

Beam or piece of wood fit to be made into spokes. खेकड n.

SPOKEN, *p.* v. V. A. म्हटलेला, &c. उक्त, भाषित, जल्पित, उदित, कथित, ओक्त (in comp.).

Eloquently or well s. सुभाषित.

SPOKESMAN, *n.* बोलणारा, बोलण्याचा मोहरक्या-मोहरपी-&c.

To SPOLIATE, &c. See To SPOIL, &c.

SPONDEE, *n.* गग *m.* गर्वाक्षरद्वय *n.* कर्ण *m.*

SPONGE, *n.* स्पंज *or* इस्पंज*m.* from the English word is common.

SPONGE-CAKE, *n.* फेणी *f.*

To SPONGE, *v. a.* स्पंजानें पुसणें- साफ करणें.

To SPONGE, *v. n. suck out of* (*a dinner, &c.*). तुंबडी *f.* लावणें, डोई *f.* टेंकणें, परान्न *n.*-आगंतुकी *f.*-&c. करणें.

SPONGER, *n.* v. V. N. *and* PARASITE. उंडीबकाल, उंडीउकल्या, वारकरी, जेव्या, परपाकरुचि, परान्नरुचि, परान्नोत्सुक, परान्नपुष्ट, पराड्या, तेलंगभट, ढुंग्या, आगंतुक.

SPONSAL. See NUPTIAL.

SPONSOR, *n. surety*, v. SECURITY. जामीन.

2 धर्मपिता *m.* धर्ममाता *f.*

SPONSORSHIP, *n.* जामीनकी *f.* जामीनगत *f.*

SPONTANEITY, SPONTANEOUSNESS, *n.* v. A. स्वसंतोष *m.* आपखुशी *f.* दिलखुशी *f.* यदृच्छा *f.*

SPONTANEOUS, *a. voluntary, proceeding from own will, accord, impulse, &c.* स्वसंतोषाचा, आत्मसंतोषाचा, आपखुषीचा, दिलखुशीचा, स्वयंभू, स्वयंजात, स्वयंकृत, स्वतःसिद्ध, कामहेतुक, स्वाभाविक *pop.* स्वभाविक, यदृच्छामूलक.

SPONTANEOUSLY, *adv.* v. A. आपखुशीनें, आपसुखानें *or* सुखें *or* सुख, आपल्याआपण, आपणहोऊन, आपआप, आपआपसांत, आपोआप, अपाप, आपैसा *or* सें, आपाआप, आपशांच *or* आपशेंच, स्वयें, स्वयं, स्वाभाविक *pop.* स्वभाविक, एरवीं.

SPOOL, *n.*—of a weaver. गणा *m.* कांडी *f.* सूतकाडी *f.* रिकोडी *f.*

SPOON, *n.*—the utensil. चमचा *m.* चमच *m.* चमस *m.* पळी *f.* दर्वी *f.*

SPOON-MEAT, *n.* पळी वाढें-&c. अन्न *n.*-खाणें *n.*-भक्ष्य *n.*

SPORT, *n.* v. PLAY. खेळ *m.* क्रीडा *f.* क्रीडन *n.* ख्यालीखुशाली *f.* खेळी *f.* खेळीमेळी *f.* कौतुक *n.* लीला *pop.* लिळा *f.* इच्छाविलास *m.* केलि *f.* तमाशा *m.* मौज *f.* मजा *f.* मस्करी *f.* विनोद *m.* कुतूहल *n.* रमण *n.* रमणूक *f.* विलास *m.* हेला *f.* विहरण *m.* विहार *m.* ऐशआराम *m.*

In s. खेळानें, खेळें-विनोदें-मस्करी-&c. करून, खेळकुडीनें.

Maker of s. at the *shimgá, &c.* खेळी, खेळ्या.

Place fitted up for sports & pastimes. रंगभूमि *f.* रंगमंडप *m.* रंगशाला *f.* रंगांगण *n.*

2 *mockery.* उपहास *m.* थट्टा *or* ठट्टा *f.* मस्करी *f.*

To make s. of. सोंग *n.* करणें *g. of o.*

3 *object of sport,* v. BUTT. खेळवणा *m.*

4 *diversion of the field.* शिकार *f.* पारध *f.* मृगया *f.*

To SPORT, *v. n. frolic, &c.* v. To PLAY. खेळणें, क्रीडणें, खेळ*m.*-&c. करणें, विहरणें, रमणें, रतणें.

2 See To JEST.

SPORTSMAN, *n.* पारधी, शिकारबाज.

Cords of s.'s saddle, by which the game is tied up. शिकारबंद *m. pl.*

SPORTER, *n.* SPORTIVE, SPORTFUL, *a.* v. V. *and* PLAYFUL. खेळणारा, &c. खेळकर, खिलाडी, खिलाडू, मौजी, मौजाळा, कौतुकी, विहारी, केलिपर, बिलासवान्, क्रीडावान्, सलील.

SPORTIVELY, SPORTFULLY, *adv.* v. A. *and* PLAYFULLY. खेळानें, &c. खेळाच्याबुद्धीनें, मौजेनें, क्रीडाबुद्धीनें.

SPORTIVENESS, SPORTFULNESS, *n.* v. A. खेळकरपणा *m.* खेळण्याचास्वभाव *m.* क्रीडाबुद्धि *f.* लीलाबुद्धि *f.* विलासबुद्धि *f.*

SPOT, *n. blot, &c.* v. STAIN. दाग *or* डाग *m.* कलंक *m.* लांच्छन *n.* ठिपका *m.* खोड *f.*

2 *dot, speck,* v. MARK. चिन्ह *n.* चिथडा *m.* चिथडी *f.* ठिपका *m.* बुंदका *m.* बुंदकी *f.*

3 (on the body) *discoloration.* लासें *n.* ठिकें *n.* ठीक *n.*

A circular s. or patch. चकंदळ *m. n.* चकंदळा*m.* चकदा*m.* चकदळ *n.*

4 (as upon the body of a tiger, &c.). बिबट *n.* ठिपका*m.*

5 (as of rottenness, on fruits, &c.). लासें*n.*डाण*n.* डागें*n.*

6 v. PLACE. जागा *m. f.* स्थल *or* ळ *n.* स्थान *n.* तळ *m.* धळ *n.* प्रदेश *m.* प्रांत *m.* क्षेत्र *n.*

A retired unfrequented s. आडवळण *n.*

Upon the s. जागचे जागीं, खडीचोट, खडाखड, खडोखड *or* डी, रोखारोखी, रोख, रोकठोक, उभेउभ्यां, उभेउभ्यांनीं, उभ्यांउभ्यां, उभ्यांधाई.

To kill on the s. *kill outright.* ठार मारणें.

7 (of a thing lost and sought). ठिकाण *n.* ठिकाणा *m.* ठाव *m.* थांग *m. v.* लाग, लाव.

To SPOT, *v. a. mark with spots.* डाग *m. pl.*-ठिपके *m. pl.*-बुंदके *m. pl*-&c. पाडणें-घालणें.

2 *stain,* v. To SLUR. बट्टा *m.*-कलंक *m.*-&c. आणणें-लावणें, डागणें, सकलंक-&c. करणें.

SPOTLESS, *a.* v. N. 1. *and* PURE. ऐबा-बट्टया-&c. निराळा-वेगळा, बिनबट्टा, बिनऐब, निष्कलंक, निर्दोष, चोखनळ, कलंकरहित, कलंकहीन, दोषरहित-हीन-&c.निर्मल.

SPOTLESSNESS, *n.* v. A. ऐबानिराळेपणा *m.* &c. निष्कलंकता *f.* कलंकराहित्य *n.* दोषराहित्य *n.*

SPOTTED, *p.* SPOTTY, *a.* v. V. 1. डागपाडलेला, &c. ठिपकेपाडलेला, &c. ठिपक्यांचा, ठिक्यांचा, &c. बुंदकेदार, चिन्हित, चित्र, चित्रविचित्र, डागील.

I.—as the body of a tiger. बिबटा.

S. with black and white.—cattle, &c. पारा.

II.—fruits &c. from rottenness. लाशा.

To become s. डागळणें, डांसळणें.

SPOUSAL. See CONJUGAL, NUPTIAL.

SPOUSALS. See MARRIAGE.

SPOUSE, *n.* v. HUSBAND, WIFE. दादला*m.* बायको *f.* पति*m.*स्त्री*f.*

To choose a s. परणणें *or* प्रणणें.

SPOUT, *n. projecting mouth, nosel, &c.* तोटी *f.* झारी *f.*

Little hole made by way of a s. नाचकें*n.*

2 *pipe, &c. for water.* नळी *f.* पन्हळ *m.*

3 See WATERSPOUT.

To SPOUT, *v.a. throw or pour out as from a spout.* सोडणें,फेंकणें, उभड्डा*m.*-चिरकांडी *f.*-&c. उडवणें, फवारा*m.* टाकणें-सोडणें.

2 See To MOUTH.

To SPOUT, *v. n. issue as from a spout,* v. To GUSH. भळभळ-&c. सुटणें-वाहणें, उभट *m.*-उभडा *m.*-चिरकांडी *f.*-तुंबाडा *m.*-&c. सुटणें-निघणें *g. of s.*

2 See To MOUTH. [सणाव्रळ *f.*

SPRAIN, *n. excessive strain.* लचक *f.* कचक *f.* करक *f.* उसण *f.* उ-

To SPRAIN, *v. a. overstrain.* कन्हारणें, विद्गुडणें, लचकवणें, लवंगवणें, कचवणें, लचक *f.*-करक *f.*-&c. भरवणें.

To be sprained. लचकणें, लचक*f.*-कचक*f.*-करक *f.*-चमक*f.*-भरणें *in. con.* कचकणें, कचावणें, लवंगणें, पेंचणें, कन्हारणें, तिरपणें *or* तिरपावणें.

To SPRAWL, *v. n. lie with the limbs spread out.* हातपाय *m. pl.* पसरून निजणें-पडणें, सपाट-लंबा-सोटसा-सपसल *adv.* पडणें-निजणें.

To lay sprawling. लोळवणें.

2 See To FLOUNDER.

SPRAWLING, *p.* v. V. 1. सफसल-&c. पडलेला.

SPRAY, *n.* See SPRIG. 2 (of the sea, of rain, &c.) तुषार *pop.* तुसार *or* रा*m.* झड *f.* हेंस *f.* वसाडा *m. or* वावझड *f.* वाबझडी *f.* ओसाडा *m. or* ओसाडे *m. pl.*

Cold s. हिंवस *f.*

Drop or particle of s. as sprinkled, spurted, &c. शितोडा *m.* शिंट *f.* शिंटा *m.*

Fence against s. before a door or window. झड *f.*

S. driven by the wind. वावझड *f.*

To SPREAD, *v. a.* (a carpet, mat, &c.). अंथरणें, बिछावणें, घालणें, टाकणें, आस्तरणें, पसरणें, रुंदावणें, आस्तरण *n.*-&c. करणें *g. of o.*

Any thing to s. (*as* carpeting, matting, bedding, covering cloth, &c.). बिछाईत *f.* अंथरूण *n.* अंथरी *f.* आस्तरण *n.*

2 *expand, extend, diffuse.* फैलावणें, पसरणें, पसरवणें, विस्तारणें, विस्तार *m.*-फैलाव *m.*-प्रसार *m.*-प्रसारण*n.*-&c. करणें *g. of o.*

3 *disperse, scatter over a large surface.* पसरणें, पसरवणें, विखरणें, पांगवणें, बिसकळणें.

4 See To SMEAR. 5 (a report, &c.) v. To PUBLISH. पसरणें, पेरणें, गाजवणें, प्रसार *m.*-प्रसारण *n*-&c. करणें *g. of o.*

To SPREAD, *v. n. expand, extend.* पसरणें, प्रसरणें, माजणें, वाढणें, पसारा *m.*-फैलाव *m.*-प्रसर *m.*-प्रसरण *n.*-&c. होणें *g. of s.*

2—as an ulcer or sore. चरणें, पचुरणें *or* पचरणें, चर*m.* घेणें.

3—branches, horns, &c. फांकटणें, फांकणें.

4—a report, &c. पसरणें, लांबणें, माजणें, गाजणें.

5—as odours. भडकणें.

SPREAD, SPREADING, *n.* v. V. A. 1.—*act.* अंथरणें *n.* &c. आस्तरण *n.* प्रसारण *n.*

2—*act.* फैलावणें*n.* पसरणें*n.* &c. फैलावणी *f.* प्रसारण*n.*—*state.* फैलाव *m.* फैलावा *m.* पसारा *m.* विस्तार *m.* प्रसार *m.*

3—*act.* पसरणें *n.* विखरणें *n.* &c.

5—*act.* पसरणें *n.* पेरणें *n.* प्रसारण *n.*—*state.* प्रसार *m.*

v. V. N. पसरणें *n.* &c. फैलाव*m.* फैलावा *m.* पसारा *m.* प्रसर*m.* प्रसरण *n.* विस्तर *m.* विस्तृति *f.* पैसाव *m.* प्रपंच *m.* विसर *m.*

SPREAD, *p.* v. V. A. 1. अंथरलेला, पसरलेला, &c. आस्तीर्ण, आस्तृत, प्रसारित, वितत. [स्तृत, प्रसृत.

2 फैलावलेला, विस्तारलेला, पसरलेला,&c.विस्तारित, विस्तीर्ण,वि-

v. V. N. 1. पसरलेला, &c. पसरट, प्रसृत, विस्तीर्ण,विस्तृत, विसृत, विकीर्ण, प्रकीर्ण, प्रवृद्ध, सविकाश.

3 फांकटलेला, &c. फांकट.

SPREADER, *n.* SPREADING, *p. a.* v. V. A. 1. अंथरणारा, पसरणारा, &c. आस्तरणकर्त्ता-कारी.

2 फैलावणारा, पसरणारा, विस्तार-&c.करणारा.

3 पसरणारा, विखरणारा, &c.

v. V. N. 1. पसरणारा, माजणारा, वाढणारा.

SPREE. See FROLIC, FUN.

SPRIG, *n. shoot or twig.* टाहळा *or* डाहळा *m.* (or टहाळा *or* डहाळा). *dim.* टाहळी & डाहळी *f.* ढाळा *m.* ढाळी *f.* डघळा *m.* डघळी *f.* डांगळी *f.* फांदोरी *f.* उपशाखा *f.*

SPRIGHTLINESS, SPRIGHTFULNESS, *n.* v. A. उल्हासीपणा *m.*&c. आनंदवृत्ति *f.* उल्हासवृत्ति *f.*

SPRIGHTLY, SPRIGHTFUL, *a. lively, &c.* v. MERRY. आनंदी, उल्हासी, आल्हादी, उल्हासवृत्ति, आनंदवृत्ति.

To SPRING, *v. n.* (out of the ground). रुजणें *or* रूझणें, फुटणें, जमीन *f.* सोडणें, उगवणें, उदय *m.*-&c. होणें *g. of s.*

To s.—seed sown. वाफणें.

2 *proceed or issue from,* v. To PROCEED. उपजणें, निपजणें, उद्भवणें, उत्पन्न होणें, निघणें, उपज*m.*-उगम*m.*-उद्भव*m.*-&c. होणें *g. of s.*

3 v. To LEAP. उडणें, कुदणें, उडी*f.* घालणें-मारणें-टाकणें, किलाण *n.* मारणें-टाकणें-साधणें, टिपण *n.* टाकणें, फलंग *f.* मारणें.

4 *fly elastically, start,* v. To START. उसळणें.

5 up or out, suddenly. उडणें, उसळणें, उसळी*f.* खाणें-मारणें, निसटणें, निसपटणें.

6 upon or at; as to catch. झडपणें, झडप *f.*-झांप *f.*-झेंप *f.*-झडपडा *m.*-&c. घालणें.

To s. forwards. झेंप *f.* मारणें-टाकणें, झेंपावणें.

To SPRING, *v. a.* (a mine) *cause to explode.* उडवणें.

2 (a leak). फूट *f.* घेणें, झरा *m.* लागणें *in. con.*

SPRING,*n. vernal season.* वसंत *m.* वसंतऋतु *m.* पुष्पसमय*m.* पुष्पमास *m.* मधु *m.*

Budding and blooming of s. चैत्रपालवी *f.* चैत्रपल्लव *m.n.*

2 fig. *prime, &c.* v. HEIGHT. बहर *or* बहार *m.*

3 *elastic body.* कमाण *or* न *f.* कला *f.* दाबखीळ *f.*

4 *elastic force or power,* lit. fig. See ELASTICITY, SPIRIT.

5 *sally, bounce, bound,* v. LEAP. उडी *f.* फलंग *f.* किलाण *n.* टिपण *n.* उसळी *f.*

6 (upon or at; as to catch). झेंप *f.*झडप *f.* झांप *f.* झडपडा*m.*

7 *fountain.* झरा *or* झिरा *m. dim.* झरी *f.* जिव्हाळा *m.* निर्झर*m.*

Hot s. उन्हाळें *n.* उन्हेरें *n.*

Living s. वाहत *or* वाहता झरा *m.*

S. water. झरवणी *or* झिरवणी *n.*

Subterranean channel or vein of a s. जलनाडी *f.*

8 *origin, &c.* v. SOURCE. खाण *f.* खाणी *f.* जिव्हाळा *m.* झरा *or* झिरा *m.*

9 *beginning, origination,* v. RISE. मूळ *n.* उपज *m.* उद्गम *pop.* उगम *and, vulg.* उग्रम *m.*

SPRING-TIDE, *n.* v. TIDE. उधान *n.* उसाण *n.*

To be at the s. or at the springs,—the ocean. उधानणें.

SPRINGE. See SNARE.

SPRINGINESS, SPRINGY. See ELASTICITY, ELASTIC.

SPRINGING, *n.* v. V. 1. रुजणें *n.* फुटणें *n.* &c. उदय *m.* उद्भेद *m.* उपस्थान *n.*

To SPRINKLE, *v. n.* v. To DRIZZLE. शिंतोडणें *or* सिंतोडणें.

To SPRINKLE, *v. a. scatter in small drops or particles*; also, *to besprinkle.* शिंपणें, शिंपडणें, सिंचणें, छिडकणें *or* शिडकणें, शिडकाव *m.* देणें, प्रोक्षणें, छाटणें, छिडकाव *m.*-सिंचन *n.*-सेक *m.*-प्रोक्षण *n.*-&c. करणें.

2 (cowdung-wash, &c.) सडा *m.* घालणें-देणें.

To s. and smear,—compreh. सडासारवण *n.*-सडासम्मार्जन *n.*-&c. करणें. [प्रोक्षित.

SPRINKLED, *p.* v. V. A. शिंपलेला, सिंचलेला, &c. सिंचित, सिक्त,

SPRINKLER, *n.* SPRINKLING, *p. a.* v. V. A. शिंपणारा, सिंचणारा, &c. सेक्ता, सेचक, प्रोक्षक, प्रोक्षण-&c. कर्त्ता-कारी.

SPRINKLING, *n.* v. V.—*act.* शिंपणें *n.* सिंचणें *n.* &c. शिंपणी *f.* छिडकाव *m.* शिडकाव *m.* सिंचन*n.* सेचन*n.* सेक*m.* अभिषेचन *n.* प्रोक्षण *n.* मार्जन *n.* [छाटे *m. pl.*

I. *quantity sprinkled.* शिडकाव *or* छिडकाव *m.* शितोडा *m.*

II. *drizzling, drizzle, light rain.* शितोडा *or* सितोडा *m.* तुषारपात *m.* सवतबणी माधवणी *n.*

Drop of a s. शिट *f.* शिटा *m.*

SPRITE. See SPIRIT, GHOST.

To SPROUT, *v. n. germinate.* अंकुरणें, फुटणें, मोडावणें, पालवणें, रुजणें *or* रुझणें, अंकुर *m.*-मोड *m.*-कोंब *m.*-&c. येणें *in. con.*

SPROUT, *n. shoot of a plant.* अंकुर *m.* कोंब *or* कोम *m.* कोंबरा *m. dim.* कोंबरी *f.* पोंगा *m.*अगारी *f.* मोग *or* मोख*m.* प्ररोह *m.*

After-sprouts, *sprouts from a stump or root.* खुंटभाजी *f.* निपालवाची भाजी *f.*—of leguminous plants,&c. पांगशी*f.*

Tobacco after-sprouts. पांगशीची तमाखू *f.*

Sproutings. पल्लव *m. pop.* पालव *m. or* वी *f.* पालवण *n.*

2 *scarcely evolved shoot.* आंकरी *f.* डिरा *m. dim.* डिरी *f.* डीर *m.* बोंखरी *f.* बोंखी *f.* डिकशी *or* डिगशी *f.* [रित.

SPROUTED, *p.a.*v.V. अंकुरलेला, फुटलेला, अंकुर आलेला, &c. अंकु-

SPROUTING, *p. a.*v.V. अंकुरणारा, &c. उद्भिज्ज, उद्भिद्.

SPROUTING, SPROUTAGE, *n.* v. V.—*act.* अंकुरणें *n.* फुटणें *n.* &c. मोड*m.* पल्लव*m. pop.* पालव*m. or* वी *f.*कोंबरा*m.* फूट *f.* मुगारा*m.*

SPRUCE, *a. smart,* v. NEAT, FINE. चाकचोप, चाक, चकपक, चकचकीत, चक्क, लकपक, लकलकीत, लक्क, सास्रसुरत.

SPRUCELY, *adv.* v. A. चकपक, &c. चाकचोपीनें, चापचोपीनें, &c. चापून चोपून.

SPRUCENESS, *n.* v. A. चकपकपणा *m.* लकपकपणा *m.* &c. चापचोपी *f.* चाकचोपी *f.* टूम *f.* कटाव *m.*

SPRUNG, *p.* v. V. 1. रुजलेला, फुटलेला, &c. रुजट, दुपानी, रूढ (in comp.) उद्भिज्ज, उद्भिद्.

2 उपजलेला, निपजलेला, &c. उद्भूत.

SPUD, *n.*—the implement. इळत *f.*

SPUME, SPUMOUS. See FROTH, FROTHY.

SPUNGE, &c. See SPONGE, &c.

SPUNK, *n. rotten wood.* पू *m.* पूड *f.*

2 *pluck,* v. SPIRIT. दम *m.* धमक *f.*

SPUR, *n.* कांटा *m.* आर *f.* मंबरेज *m.*

2 (of a cock). नांगी *f.* नखी *f.* [*m.* पागोरा *m.*

3 See INCITEMENT. 4 (of a mountain) कानळ *m.* फांटा

To SPUR, *v. a. prick with a spur.* कांटा *m.*-आर *f.* टोंचणें, कांटा *m.* मारणें, कांट्यानें टोंचणें.

2 See To INCITE.

SPURIOUS, *a. counterfeit, not genuine,* v. FALSE. खोटा, खोटसाळ, मिथ्या, नकली, केलेला.

2 See BASTARD, ILLEGITIMATE.

SPURIOUSNESS, *n.* v. A. 1. खोटेपणा *m.* खोटसाळपणा *m.* नकलीपणा *m.* खोटाई *f.* [प्रहार*m.* करणें.

To SPURN, *v. a.* v. To KICK. लात *f.* मारणें, पादप्रहार *m.*-लत्ता-

2 *refuse with scorn,* v. To CONTEMN, To REJECT. लथडणें *or* लथाडणें, झाडणें, लातवणें *or* लाताळणें, लात *f.* मारणें, तिरस्कारणें, तिटकारणें, धिक्कारणें, धुतकारणें, धिक्कार *m.*-तिरस्कार *m.*-&c. करणें *g. of o.*

SPURN, SPURNING, *n.* v. V. 2.—*act.* लथडणें *n.* झाडणें *n.* &c. लथडणी *or* लथाडणी *f.* धिक्कार *m.* तिरस्कार *m.* तिटकार *m.* तिटकारा *m.* तिटकारणी *f.* लातपैजार *f* छिथू *f.*

SPURNED, *p.* v. V. 2. लथडलेला, झाडलेला, &c. तिरस्कृत, धिक्कृत.

SPURNER, *n.* SPURNING, *p. a.* v. V. 2. लथडणारा, झाडणारा, धिक्कारणारा, &c. धिक्कार-तिरस्कार कर्त्ता-कारी.

SPURRED, *a. wearing spurs.* कांटे लावलेला.

To SPURT, *v. a. throw or force out in a stream.* चिरकांडी *f.*-पिचकळी *f.*-चिपळी *f.*-&c. सोडणें-टाकणें-उडवणें.

To SPURT, *v. n. gush out in a stream.* चिरकांडी *f.*-पिचकळी*f.*-चिपळी *f.*-&c. सुटणें-निघणें*g. of s.* उसळणें, उफाळणें, उफाळा*m.* निघणें-येणें *g. of s.*

SPURT, *n. sudden gush or quick stream.* चिपळी *f.* चिरकांडी *f.* चिरकी *f.* पिचकळी *f.* पिचोळी *f.* पिचकारी *f.* चळकांडा *m.* उभड *m.* उभडा *m.* उफाळा *m.* दुरदुरी *f.*

2 v. EFFORT. दम *m.*

To SPURTLE, *v. a.* v. To SPRINKLE. शितोडे *m.pl.* उडवणें.

To SPUTTER, *v. n. speak spittingly.* थूथूकरीत-थुकाउडवीत-थुंकत थुंकत-थुंक्याचे शितोडे उडवीत-&c. बोलणें, बोलण्यांत-बोलण्याबरोबर-&c. थुंकणें-थुंका *m.* उडवणें.

2 *fly out in particles.* चटचटणें, चरचरणें, फुरफुरणें, तटतटणें, तडतडणें *or* तिडतिडणें, चिवचिवणें,—*intens.* चराडणें, फुरारणें, तटाटणें.

SPUTTER, SPUTTERING, *n.* v. V. 1.—*act.* थुंकत बोलणें *n.* &c.

2 चटचटणें *n.* तटतटणें *n.* तिडतीड *f.* चिवचीव *f.*—*intens.* तडतडाट *m.* फुरफुराट *m.* [णारा,&c.

SPUTTERER, *n.* SPUTTERING , *p. a.* v. V. 1. थूथू करीत बोल-

2 चटचटणारा, तटतटणारा, &c. तिडतिडा, तिडका.

SPUTTERINGLY, *adv.* v. V. 1. थूथूकरून, थुंक्याचे शितोडे उडवून, &c.

2 चटचट *or* टां, चरचर *or* रां, चुरचूर *or* रां, तडतड *or* डां,—*intens.* चराचर, चरारां.

SPY, *n. secret emissary.* बातमीदार, हेर, गुप्तदूत, चार, गूढचार, गूढचारी, गूढपुरुष, मंत्रगूढ, पाळती *or* थी.

To SPY, *v. a. gain sight of, descry,* v. To SEE. पाहणें, लक्षिणें, दृष्टीनें वेधणें, हेरणें, हेरून काढणें, हेर *f.* करणें.

2 out ; *explore,* v. To EXAMINE. हेरणें, टेहळणें, निरेखणें, हेर *f.*-हेरणी *f.* करणें.

SPY-GLASS, *n.* दुरबीन *f.*

SQUAB, *a. fat and short, squat, &c.* v. DUMPY. आडव्या बांध्याचा, गुटुंगा, गिड्डा *or* गिट्टा, बाटोळ्या आंगाचा, कुलुंगा, ठुला, चपताड *or* डा, चापट.

SQUAB, *n. stuffed cushion.* गदेला *m.* रुजामा *m.* रुगदां *m.*

2 *dumpy and fat woman.* गिरदी *f.* मुग्धम्मा *f.* गोबरी बायको*f.*

To SQUABBLE, *v. n. contend clamorously or peevishly,* v. To

WRANGLE, To QUARREL. कळवंडणें,खटपटणें, भांडणें,कटकट f.-खटपट f.-कलागत f.-तंटा m.-चखेडा m.-भांडण n.-&c. करणें, कचक f. झडणें-उडणें g. of s. झांज f. झडणें g. of. s. तोंड n. करणें, धुसफुसणें.

SQUABBLE, SQUABBLING, n. v. V. and QUARREL. कलागत f. कटकट f. धडाधडी f. कडकडी f. घासाघास or घीस f. घसमस f. तडकाफडकी f. खणकादणका m. खडका m. खडकाधडका m. चकमक f. कलकल m. किलकील m. किलकिलाट m. किलबील m. किलबिलाट m. कच f. कचक f. कचाकच f. कचकच f. खळखळ f. झमाझमी f. फटकाफटकी f. कलागत f. बाचाबाच f. कडकडणें n. कलह m. करकर f. रसकस f. धसफस f. धुसफूस f. धुसमूस f. धसाफसी f. झोटधरणी f. कट्टाकज्जा m. कट्टंभांडण n. झांज f. महारकचका m. कळवंडा कळवंडी f. हर्षामर्ष or र्षा m.

SQUABBLER, n. SQUABBLING, p. a. v. V. कळवंडणारा, भांडणारा, भांडण करणारा, &c. कलागती, कळकळ्या.

SQUABBY. See SQUAB.

SQUAD, n. party learning military exercise. नवशिकी जमात f.
That belongs to the awkward s. गवतकाप्यांचा.

SQUALID, a. foul, filthy, v. DISGUSTNG. हिडीस, ओंगळ, मुरदाड or मुडदार, कुत्सित, ओखटा, हेंदरा, बुरसा, कलाहीन.

SQUALIDITY, SQUALIDNESS, n. v. A. हिडिसपणा m. ओंगळपणा m. बुरसेपणा m. &c.

To SQUALL, v. n. v. To CRY, To SCREAM. केंकणें, केंकावणें, टाहो m. फोडणें, किंकाळी f. फोडणें.

SQUALL, n. cry, scream. टाहो m. किंक f. किंकाळी f.
2 (of wind) sudden gust. वाऱ्याचा झटका m.-झटकारा m.-झपाटा m.-&c. घुगी f. जौळ n. बावटळ f. झुंजाट f.
Squalls,—compreh. वारेवावधान n. वारेवावटळ f.
S. with rain. झंझावात m. झंझानिल m.

SQUALLY, a. abounding with squalls. जौळी, वारेवावधानाचा, वारेवावटळीचा.

To SQUANDER, v. a. spend prodigally, lavish. उडवणें, उधळणें, घालवणें, दवडणें, खेळ m. करणें g. of o. गमावणें, विधुळणीस पाडणें-मिळवणें or मिळवून टाकणें, तीनवाटा f. pl.-चारवाटा f. pl. करणें g. of o. फांफू n. f. करणें (द्रव्याचें-धान्याचें-&c.) विल्हेस लावणें, फुंकणें or फुंकून टाकणें (दौलत, द्रव्य, &c.), चणेफुटाणे m. pl.-कारेवारे m. pl. करणें g. of o. अपव्यय m.-अवासवा खर्च m. करणें g. of o. धुडके m. pl.-परकळे m. pl. उडविणें g. of o. विधवाट f.-विल्हेवाट f.-विल्हय f.-वाताहात f.-उडवाउडव f.-उधळ f.-उधळमाधळ f.-उधळपट्टी f.-उधळमाणकी f.-उफानगिरी f.-ताडाफांटा m.-तिन्हडफांटा m.-बजावाट f.-निसांठा m.-धिंगाई f.-&c. करणें g. of o.

SQUANDERED, p. v. V. उडवलेला, दवडलेला, घालवलेला, &c.
To be s. भयाभंगास जाणें, बाराबाटा f. pl. होणें g. of s. परकळे m. pl.-धुडके m. pl. उडणें g. of s. बारा वाटां पळणें.

SQUANDERER, n. SQUANDERING, p.a.v.V. and EXTRAVAGANT. उडवणारा, उधळणारा, दवडणारा, &c. उडाऊ, उधळ्या, सांडरा, दिवाळखोर.

SQUANDERING, n. v. V.—act. उडवणें n. उधळणें n. दवडणें n. &c. अतिव्यय m. अपव्यय m. उधळपट्टी f. उधळमाधळ f. उफानगिरी f. बजावाट f. उद्धूलन n.

SQUARE, a.—in geometry. समचतुष्कोण, समचतुरस्र, चौकोण, चौकोणी.
2 v. JUST, RIGHT. बरोबर, नीट, न्यायाचा, खरा, रास्त, मार्गाचा.
To make s. यमकाला यमक n.-प्रासाला प्रास m. लावणें-बसवणें-मिळवणें.

SQUARE, n. square figure. समचतुष्कोण m. चौकोण m.
Sides of a s. चतुस्सीमा f.
2 area of four sides. चौक m. चौपट f.
S. in front of a house. माणीक चौक m.
3 (of workmen.). गुणा m. काटकोना or काटकोन्या m.
The acute angled s. of the stone mason. खतवड n. खतवडी f. खनोड n. f. खतोडा m.
4 (of troops)—solid. कोट m.
5—in geometry or arithmetic. वर्ग m. द्विघात m. कृति f.
6—as in tables of figures, cell. कोष्टक m. n. घर n. पग m. n.
7—as on cloth, &c. चौकडी f.
Squares of a chequered cloth. खाटलें बाजलें n.

To SQUARE, v. a. (a piece of timber, &c.). चौपाटणें, चौपाट करणें.
2—in geometry or arithmetic. वर्ग m.-द्विघात m. करणें, समगुणन n. करणें.
3 v. To ADJUST, To REGULATE. सुधारणें.
To s. accounts. खातें n. बरावर करणें-बेबाक करणें-पूज करणें.

To SQUARE, v. n. v. To AGREE, To SUIT. मिळणें, जमणें.
2 assume an attitude for fighting. बकरकुदीवर येणें.

SQUARE-ROOT, n. वर्गमूल n. द्विघातमूल n.

SQUARED, p. v. V. A. 1. चौपाटलेला, &c. चौरस, चौपट.
2 वर्गकेलेला, &c. वर्गित.

To SQUASH, v. a. crush, v. To SQUEEZE. चेंदणें, चेंदरणें, मन्दुणें, मसंदळणें, रपाटा m.-लोंधा m.-चेंदा m.-चेंदामेंदा m.-&c. करणें g. of o.

SQUASH, n. rotting and running stuff. ढगळ f. रेबडी f. शेणखळा m. शेणप m. शेणसडा m. शेण n. थिरबिटी f. बिरबिटी f. रपटा m. लगदा m. मेंदू m. लोंधा m.
2 shock of soft bodies. ढबका m. भदका m. रपका m.

SQUASHINESS, n. v. A. गलगलीतपणा m. डुळडुळीतपणा m. उमळेपणा m. &c. थलथल f. बिलबिली f.

SQUASHY, a. watery and soft. गलगलीत or गिलगिलीत, डुळडुळीत, उमळा, थलथलीत, बरबरीत, बिलबिलीत, बिलबिला, लुगलुगीत, लोंधा, लोंधट, बिदबिदा.
Soft & s. बिदबिदा.
To be or become s.—melon, &c. बरबरणें, थलथलणें, बिदबिदणें.

To SQUAT, v. n. sit on the hams, &c. उकड-उकुडवा बसणें, आरून n. जोडणें.
To s. down suddenly and violently. थबकट adv. बसणें, थबकण f.-थपकील f. मारणें.

SQUAT, a. sitting on the hams. उकडवा or उकिडवा or उकुडवा.
2 short and thick, v. DUMPY. चपटा, चपडा, चेपट, चपताड or डा, चपतळ or ळा or चपताळा, चिपतळ or ळा or चिपताळा, चापट, बतखल or बदखल, थबकट or टा, बसकट, बसका, बसकीचा.
S. or dumpy person. बुकणा हत्ती m. बुकणा m.
3—the nose. चपणी, शिमरा, फेंदरा, बसकट, बसकल.

SQUAT-NOSED, a. चपणी, शिमरा, बसकटनाक्या.

To SQUEAK, To SQUEAL, v. n. make a shrill noise. किंकळणें or किंकाळणें, किचळणें, किंकळी f. फोडणें, चुचावणें, चींचीं n.-चूं n.-चूंचूं n.-फुईफुई f.-&c. करणें.

SQUEAK, SQUEAL, *n.* v. V. किंक *f.* किंकळी *f.* चींचीं *n.* चूं *n.* चूंचूं *n.* कुई *f.* चुचा *f.*

SQUEAKER, *n.* SQUEAKING, SQUEALING, *p. a.* v. V. किंकळणारा, चींचीं *n.*-चूंचूं-&c. करणारा.

SQUEAMISH, *a. queasy, keckish.* मळमळ आलेला-सुटलेला, कळमळ आलेला, बमनोन्मुख, वांत्युन्मुख.

2 *fastidious,* v. DAINTY. चाखनळ, चोखारी, कंटाळखोर, संतखोर, खोडकर, खोडाळ *or* खोड्याळ, सोंगळ, तिटकारी.

SQUEAMISHNESS, *n.* v. A. 1. *and* QUALMISHNESS. मळमळ *f.* कळमळ *f.* [खोड्याळी *f.*

2 चोखनळपणा *m.* खोडकरपणा *m.* खोड्याळपणा *m.* &c. खोड *f.*

To SQUEEZE, *v. a. jam, press, compress, &c.* चेपणें, चापणें, चेंबटणें, दाबणें, चिमटणें *or* चिंबटणें, चिंबळणें, चिंवळणें, अंवळणें, चिरंगटणें, चेंगरणें, चिरडणें.

To be squeezed. चेपणें, चिपणें, चिमटणें.

To s. flat. चापटी *f.*-दामटी *f.*-पोळी *f.* करून टाकणें *g. of o.*

2 *crush, knead, press roughly and injuriously.* कुसकरणें, कुसमाडणें, कुसमरणें, कोळणें, चिवडणें, चेंदणें, चेंदरणें, मसंदणें, मसंदळणें, मर्दणें. [*g. of o.*

3 fig. v. To OPPRESS. पिळणें, जाळणें, पिडणें, तेल *n.* काढणें

4 out; *press or force out.* पिळणें, पिळून घेणें.

To SQUEEZE, *v. n. urge one's way, pass by pressing.* रेंटणें, रेंटून जाणें, रेटाई *f.*-&c. करणें.

SQUEEZE, SQUEEZING, *n.* v. V. A. 1.—*act.* चेपणें *n.* चापणें *n.* अवळणें *n.* &c. चेपणी *f.*

2 कुसकरणें *n.* &c.

SQUEEZED, *p.* v. V. A. 1. चेपलेला, चेंबटलेला, &c.

2 कुसकरलेला, चेंदरलेला, &c. [रा, &c.

SQUEEZER, *n.* SQUEEZING, *p. a.* v. V. A. 1. चेपणारा, चेंबटणा-

2 कुसकरणारा, चेंदरणारा, &c. [का *m.* हातनळा *m.*

SQUIB, *n.* (of powder). फटकडी *f.* फटाकडी *f.* फटाकडा *m.* फटा-

2 *a sarcastic writing,* v. SATIRE. निंदेचा पोवाडा *m.*

To SQUINT, *v. n. see obliquely.* तिरवा *decl.*-तिरका *decl.*-&c. *or* तिरवें-तिरकें-&c. पाहणें, तिरवी दृष्टि *f.*-&c. असणें *g. of s.*

SQUINT, *a.* SQUINTER, *n.* SQUINTING, *p. a.* SQUINT-EYED, *a.* v. V. तिरवा पाहणारा, &c. तिरवा *remiss.* तिरवट, तिरळा, तिरका *remiss.* तिरकट, तिरपा, तिरपतकाना, कैरा, चकणा, चकाणा, काणा, तिरवे दृष्टीचा, वक्रदृष्टि, तिरकमशेट. [दृष्टि *f.*

SQUINTING, SQUINT, *n.* v. V. तिरवें पाहणें *n.* तिरकी दृष्टि *f.* वक्र-

SQUIRE, *n. attendant on a warrior.* खासबरदार.

2—the title. साहेब, राव. The English word is very common under the form of इस्कायर.

SQUIRREL, *n.*—the animal. खडी *f.* खार *f.* चानी *f.* खड्डूळ *f.*

To SQUIRT, *v. a. eject in a quick stream.* चिरकांडी *f.*-चिपनळी *f.*-चिपळी *f.*-&c.सोडणें-मारणें-उडवणें *g. of o.*

SQUIRT, *n. syringe.* चिरकांडी *f.* पिचकारी *f.* पिचोळी *f.* चिपनळी *f.* चिपळी *f.* [ळी *f.* दुरदुरी *f.*

2 *stream,* v. SPURT. चिरकांडी *f.* चिपळी *f.* पिचकारी *f.* पिचो-

To STAB, *v. a. pierce with a pointed weapon.* बोचणें, बोचकणें, भोकसणें *or* भोसकणें *or* भोसणें, भसकणें, भसकावणें, ढुसणें *or* ढोसणें, ढुसकणें, ढुसकी *f.*-ढुसी *f.* मारणें.

STAB, STABBING, *n.* v. V. बोचणें *n.* बोचकणें *n.* &c. ढुसकी *f.* ढुसी *or* ढुस्सी *f.* ढुसणी *f.* भसकणी *f.*

I. *wound from a sharp pointed weapon.* भोसका *m.* भोकसा *m.*

STABBED, *p.* v. V. बोचलेला, बोचकलेला, &c.

STABBER, *n.* STABBING, *p. a.* v. V. बोचणारा, भोकसणारा, &c.

STABILITY, STABLENESS, *n.* v. A. 1. मजबुतपणा *m.* बळकटपणा *m.*&c. मजबुती *f.* बळकटी *f.* संबिरी *f.* दृढता *f.* दार्ढ्य *n.* द्रढिमा *m.*

2 टिकाऊपणा *m.* &c. स्थिरता *f.* स्थैर्य *n.* स्थायित्व *n.*

STABLE, *a. steadfast, firmly fixed,* v. FIRM, FIXED. मजबूत, बळकट, साबूत, दृढ, संबीर, सम्माल, कुब्बल, काईम, काईमदाईम, अढळ, अचल, ध्रुव.

2 *durable,* v. ENDURING. टिकाऊ, स्थिर, स्थायी, ध्रुव, अढळ.

STABLE, STABLING, *n.* पागा *f.* तबेला *m.* घोडशाळा *f.* घोडसाळ *f.* अश्वशाला *f.* अश्वगोष्ठ *m.* मंदुरा *f.*

Augean s. दगडाचें पेंव *n.* हत्तीचें मडें *n.*

Hole in a s. for horse's urine. मुतारी *f.* मुतरी *f.* मुताट *f.*

Stable for a stud. घोडवळ *f.*

STABLE-BOY, STABLE-MAN, *n.* v. GROOM. मोतद्दार, पोरगा *m.*

S. of the mahár caste. महारपोरगा *m.*

To STABLISH. See To ESTABLISH.

STACK, *n. pile of grain, hay, &c.* गंज *m. f. dim.* गंजी *f.* उडवी *f.* उडवें *n.* कुंभेरी *f.* ठिकी *f.* डिंग *m. dim.* डिंगोरा *m.* डिंगोळी *f.* डुंग *m. dim.* डुंगी *f.* डुंगा *m.* [*f.*

Circular s. of sheaves (of wheat, barley, rice). मंडळी

Stand or frame for a s. माच *m.* माचोळी *f.* माळोंचा *m.*

Straw &c. strewed *or* spot prepared for s. तळवें *n.*

2 (of corn with the ears). सुडी *f.* बुचाड *n.* पाथरा *m.*

3 (of *karbá* or grass). वळई *or* वळही *f.* [डाळणें.

To STACK, *v. a. make into a pile.* गंज *m. f.*-&c. रचणें-करणें,

STACK-YARD, *n.* गंजीखाना *m.*

STADDLE, *n. frame of a stack.* माचोळी *f.* माच *m.* माळोंचा *m.*

STAFF, *a walking stick, &c.* काठी *f.* टेंकण काठी *f.* दांडा *m.* अवलंबयष्टि *f.*

2 *stick, as a weapon,* v. CUDGEL. सोंटा *or* सोटा *m.* सोडगा *m.* दांडगें *n.* दंड *m.*

Armed with or carrying a s. दंडी, दंडवान्, दंडपाणि.

3 (as of a spear, a flag, &c.). काठी *f.* दांडा *m.*

4 (as an ensign of authority,) *mace, &c.* छडी *f.* काठी *f.* वेत्र *n.*

5 *establishment of assistant officers.* कामदारांची-अधिकाऱ्यांची-&c. मंडळी *f.*

STAFF-BEARER, *n.* v. MACE-BEARER. छडीबरदार, वेत्रधर, वेत्रधारी, दंडवान्, दंडी.

STAG, *n. male deer.* काळवीट *m.* हरिण *m.* [माळोंचा *m.*

STAGE, *n. raised floor, platform, &c.* मंच *m.* मंचक *m.* माळा *m.*

Movable s. (for dancing girls, &c.) तक्तरांवा *m.*

2 (of the theatre). रंग *m.* रंगभूमि *f.* भूमिका *f.*

Speaking (as with persons) outside or off the s. आकाशभाषण *n.* आकाशभाषित *n.*

3 See THEATRE, DRAMA. [*m.* पेणें *n.*

4 (of a journey). मजल *f.* टप्पा *m.* मकाण *or* न *n.* मुकाम

By full stages—travelling. भरमजल.

Full s. भरमजल *f.*

Last s. (or state) fig. चरमावस्था *f.*

S. after s. मजल दरमजल.

5 *place at which a relay is posted.* डाकचौकी *f.* टप्पा *m.*

6 *step of a process.* मजल *f.* पर्याय *m.* मुकाम *m.* ठेप *f.*
Concluding s. सरतापालव *m.*

STAGE-COACH, *n.* डाकेची-टप्प्यांची-&c. गाडी *f.*

STAGE-PLAY, *n.* See DRAMA.
2 *mock-fight, blank menace, empty fury, &c.* v. PRETENCE. सोंग *n.* दाखवणूक *f.* झुलकावणी *f.* अजायुद्ध *n.*

STAGE-PLAYER, *n.* v. ACTOR. सोंगाडी, नाटकी.

STAGER, *n.* v. EXPERIENCED. बाराबंदर फिरलेला, गरमनरम पाहिलेला, केला भोगलेला.

To STAGGER, *v. n.* v. To REEL. चांचरणें, चांचरी *or* चांचरीत *adv.* जाणें, झुकतझुकत-डुलतडुलत-ढकलत ढकलत-&c. चालणें, झुकणें, लुडकणें, लुडगी *f.*-लुडग्या *f. pl.*-झड्यापड्या *f. pl.* खाणें.
2 *be in doubt, waver,* v. To HESITATE. कांकरणें, आशंकणें, गणबणणें, गणमणणें, अवांकणें, डगणें, डळमळणें.

To STAGGER, *v. a. cause to reel.* झोके *m. pl.*-झोकांड्या *f. pl.*-लुडग्या *f. pl.*-&c. खावविणें-खायास लावणें, झुगवणें.
2 *cause to doubt, make to hesitate.* मागें पुढें पाहायास लावणें, विचारकरायास लावणें, डगवणें, कांकरविणें, मनांत शंका *f.* आणणें *g. of o.* कांकू *f.*-नानू *f.*-&c. करायास लावणें, आशंकित-साशंक-&c. करणें.

STAGGERS, *n.* मिरगी *f.*

STAGNANCY, *n.* v. A. 1. कोंडलेलेपणा *m.* &c. गतिराहित्य *n.* गत्यभाव *m.*
2 मंदी *f.* मंदाई *f.* मंदावा *m.*

STAGNANT, *a. not flowing, not running in a stream.* कोंडलेला, सांठलेला, बांधलेला, मेलेला, गतिरहित, स्थिर.
S. water. सांठवणी *n.*
The green matter of s. water. नीळ *f.*
2 (business, trade, &c.) *not brisk.* मंद, मंदीचा, मंदाईचा.

To STAGNATE, *v. n. cease to flow.* गति *f.*-&c. अडणें-खुटणें-बंद होणें-नाहींसा होणें-&c. *g. of s.* उभा राहणें, मरणें.
2 *become dull,*—trade, &c. मंद-&c. होणें, मंदावणें, मंदी *f.*-&c. होणें *g. of s.*

STAGNATION. See STAGNANCY.

STAID, *a. steady, grave,* v. SOBER. धीर, स्थिर, स्थिरबुद्धि, भरकुंब, भरकूम *or* खुम, गंभीर, धिमा *or* धिम्मा.

STAIDNESS, *n.* v. A. भरकुंबपणा *m.* गंभीरपणा *m.* &c. भरकुमी *f.* गांभीर्य *n.* स्थिरता *f.* धीरता *f.* स्थिरबुद्धि *f.*

STAIN, *n. tinge, dye.* रंग *m.*
2 *spot, discoloration.* दाग *or* डाग *m.* चिह्न *n.* ठिकें *n.* ठीक *n.* ठिपका *m.* कलंक *m.* लांच्छन *n.* वर्णविकार *m.* वर्णविकृति *f.* वैवर्ण्य *n.*
3 fig. *sully, slur, blot.* डाग *m.* कलंक *m.* लांच्छन *n.* बट्टा *m.* ठपका *m.* कालिमा *m. f.* काळवटी *f.* काळवण *f.* काळें *n.* काळोखी *f.* मस *f* बाट *m.* खोड *f.*

To STAIN, *v. a. tinge, dye.* रंग *m.* देणें, रंगवणें.
2 *discolor, spot.* भरणें, भरविणें, डाग *m.* पाडणें, डागील-&c. करणें, विवर्ण करणें, वैवर्ण्य *n.*-वर्णविकार *m.*-&c. करणें *g. of o.*
3 *blot, sully, soil, slur.* डागणें, डाग *m.* देणें-लावणें, कलंक *m.* लावणें, काळें *n.*-&c. लावणें-आणणें, बट्टा *m.*-बाट *m.*-&c. ठेवणें, सकलंक-&c. करणें, दूषणें.

STAINED, *p.* v. V. 1. रंगदिल्हेला.
2 भरलेला, डागपाडलेला, &c. डागील, कलंकित, लांच्छित, वर्णविकृत.
3 डागलेला, डागदिल्हेला, &c. डांकलग, डागील, कलंकित, कलंकी, कलंकमय, लांच्छित, लिप्त, लिप्माळा, बट्टेखोर.

STAINER, *n.* STAINING, *p. a.* v. V. 1. रंगणारा, रंगदेणारा.
2 भरणारा, डागपाडणारा, डागीलकरणारा, &c.
3 डागणारा, डागदेणारा, कलंकलावणारा, &c.

STAINLESS, *a.* v. PURE. बिनडागाचा, डागा-ऐबा-&c. निराळा-वेगळा, बिनऐब, निष्कलंक, कलंकरहित, कलंकहीन, निर्दोष, दोषरहित.

STAIR, *n. step for ascending.* पायरी *f.* सोपान *n.* पावठणी *or* पावठाणी *f.*
3 *landing place, quay.* घाट *m.* पाणवठा *m.*
Officer presiding over a s. घाटपांड्या.
2 stairs; *flight of steps.* जिना *m.* सोपान *n.* सिडी *or* ढी *f.* or शिडी *or* ढी *f.*
Back-s. आडजिना *m.*
Down s. खालीं, खालच्या घरांत-खोलींत-मजल्यांत-&c.
Up s. माडीवर, वरच्या खोलींत-मजल्यावर-&c.

STAIR-CASE, *n.* सिडी *or* ढी *f.* शिडी *or* ढी, जिना *m.* सोपान *n.*
Shutter over a s. दादर *m.* हडपा *m.* दादरा *m.*

STAKE, *n. stick fixed or set in the ground.* खुंटा *m.* खुंट *m.* खुंटण *n.* डांभ *m.* डांभा *m.* मेख *f.* ठेंचा *m.* कील *m.* शंकु *m.*
Bifurcated s. मेढ *f.* (*dim.* मेढी *f.* मेढकी *f.* मेढकें *n.*) मेडका *m.*
To fasten to a s. (a horse, bullock, &c.). डांभणें, मेखलणें.
2 (for impaling criminals). शूल *pop.* सूळ *m.*
3 (of a fence). मेढा *m.*
4 *thing staked or wagered.* पण *m.* पैज *f.* होड *f.* जोखीम *n. f.* पणाचा-पैजेचा-शर्यतीचा-&c. विषय *m.* बळती *f.* नीवी *f.* आक्षिक *n.* आक्षिकपण *m.*—at dice playing or gambling. गाडें *n.*
To be at stake. पण *m.*-पैज *f.*-&c. असणें *g. of s.* वर असणें *with g. of s.* (as प्राणावरची गोष्ट my life is at s. अब्रूवरचा प्रसंग my honor is at s.).

To STAKE, *v. a. set* (a fence) *with stakes.* मेढावणें, मेढे *m. pl.* मारणें-पुरणें.
2 *wager, bet.* पण *m.*-पैज *f.*-होड *f.*-शर्यत *f.*-&c. मांडणें-घालणें-ठेवणें-पाडणें-करणें *g. of o.* पैजेबर-&c. मांडणें.

STALE, *a. vapid from having been kept,* v. FLAT. शिळा, वासा *remiss.* वासट, कुइंट, पारोसा, पर्युषित.—compreh. *s. and cold and dry, &c.* शिळापाका.
S. victuals. शिळवड *f.* शिळवरें *n.* शिळावट *f.* शिळावळ *f.*
To get s. शिळटणें, पारुषणें.
2 fig. *trite, &c.* उष्टा, उच्छिष्ट, लोकोच्छिष्ट, रांडापोराच्या तोंडचा.
S. joke, device, thought. उच्छिष्टकल्पना *f.*

To STALE, *v. n. urine.* मुतणें, इराकत *f.*-पाणी *n.* करणें.

STALENESS, *n.* v. A. 1. शिळेपणा *m.* वासेपणा *m.*
2 उष्टेपणा *m.* &c.

To STALK, *v. n. walk statelily.* उताणा *decl.* चालणें, छाती काढून-उराबर-डौलानें-&c. चालणें, ठमकणें *or* ठमकत चालणें, चमकणें *or* चमकून-चमकत चालणें, झमकणें, मिरवणें, ढेंगा *f. pl.* टाकीत चालणें.
2 *walk behind a cover.* अडून चालणें, लपून चालणें.

STALK, STALKING, *n.* v. V. 1. ठमकणें *n.* &c. ठमका *m.* मिरवणूक *f.* गजगति *f.* हंसगति *f.* अकड *f.* तोरा *m.*

STALK, *n. stem of a plant.* देंट *or* डेंठ *m.* डेख *m.* तांट *n. dim.* तांटूक *n.* &c. तांटोळा *m.* काठी *f.* करचड *n.* नाडी *f.*

A s. of immature or uneared corn. बाइम.

Dry (and trampled) stalks (of kaḍbá &c.). चिपाड *or* टn. चिपडn.

Stalks of leguminous plants. काड *n.*

STALKER, *n.* STALKING, *p. a.* v.V. 1. उताणा *decl.* चालणारा, छातीकाढून चालणारा, ठमकत चालणारा, &c. गजगति, हंसगति, हंसगामी.

STALL, *n. crib, &c.* ठाणn. ठाणेंn. गोथवड *f.*

Confinement (of a beast) to his s. ठाणबंदी *f.*

2 (of venders). बसक *f.* बैठक *f.* दुकानn.

To STALL, *v. a.* ठाणांत-&c. बांधणें.

STALLAGE, *n. rent paid for a stall.* बसक *f.* बसकी *f.*

STALL-FED, *a.* ठाणबंद *or* ठाणेबंद.

STALLED, *a. ever kept in the stall.* ठाणबंद *or* ठाणेबंद.

STALLION, *n. stone-horse.* वळू *or* वळूघोडाm. सुरूघोडा *m.* बेण्याचा घोडा *m.* [कुलुली *f.*

Excitement of a s. (towards the mare). कुलकुली *f.*

STAMEN, *n.*—in botany. केसरm. पुंकेसर *m.*

2 stamina; *that which constitutes the principal strength.* बलसाधन *n.* बलहेतु *m.* सारांग *n.* सारसाधन *n.*

To STAMMER, *v. n. stutter.* तोतरें बोलणें, गुलफणें, कांचकळणें, लागणें, लागत बोलणें, बोलण्यांत अडणें-अडकळणें-&c. जीभ *f.* लागणें *g. of s.* अडकळत-&c. बोलणें.

STAMMER, STAMMERING, *n.* v. V.—*act.* तोतरें बोलणें *n.* बोलण्यांत अडणें *n.* &c. अततता *f.*

STAMMERER, *n.* STAMMERING, *p. a.* v. V. तोतरें बोलणारा, &c. तोतरा, फांपरा *or* फांपा, स्खलद्गी.

To STAMP, *v. a.* (the ground &c). आपटणें, आदळणें, तळपायानें-पायानें ठोकणें-मारणें, पादाघात *m.* करणें.

2 *impress with some mark.* छापणें, बेटणें, शिक्का *m.*-छापm.-ठसा *m.*-मुद्रा *f.*-&c. मारणें *with* वर *of o.*

3 *form by impression.* छापणें, ठसवणें, छापm.-छापाm.-ठसा *m.* मारणें *g. of o.*

4 (coin). शिक्का *m.* मारणें-पाडणें, पाडणें.

To STAMP, *v. n.* v. To RAGE. भुई *f.*-&c. आपटणें-आदळणें, पाय *m. pl.* आपटणें, चडफडणें, धडफड्या *f. pl.* देणें-खाणें.

2 upon; v. To TRAMPLE. पायानें-पायाखालीं-&c. तुडवणें.

STAMP, *n. instrument of stamping.* छापm. ठसाm. शिक्का *m.* मोहर *f.* मुद्रा *f.* मुद्रिका *f.*

Goldsmith's s. बेटणें *n.* बेटणी *f.* बेटमोरा *m.*

2 *impression made.* छाप *m.* छापा *m.* शिक्का *m.* ठसा *m.* मुद्रा *f.* मुद्रिका *f.*

3 *character fixed; cast, make, &c.* v. FORM. रूप *n.* आकार *m.* घात *m.* जात *f.* प्रत *f.* मासला *m.* मुद्रा *f.* ठेव *f.* ठेवण *f.* दम्ती *f.*

Of the right s. हाडाचा खरा-चांगला-भला-&c.

4 *paper or mark affixed to letters, receipts, &c.* स्टांपm. (from the English) टिकिट *f.* (the English word ticket.)

STAMPED, *p.* v. V. A. 2. छापलेला, छापमारलेला, &c. बेटींव, छापी, छापींव, छापील, मुद्रित, मुद्रांकित, समुद्र.

3. छापलेला, ठसवलेला.

To be s. ठसणें.

STAMPER, *n.* STAMPING, *p. a.* v. V. A. 1. आपटणारा, तळपायानें ठोकणारा-मारणारा, &c.

2, 3. छापणारा, छाप-&c. मारणारा, छापारी, छापेकरी.

STAMPING, *n.* v. V. A. 1. आपटणें *n.* आदळणें *n.* तळपायानें मारणें *n.* &c.

2, 3 छापणें *n.* छापमारणें *n.* &c.

v. V. N. भुई आपटणें *n.* पायआपटणें *n.*

Furious storming & s. धडफड *or* धडबड *f. intens.* धडफडाट *or* धडबडाट *m.*

To STANCH, *v. a.* (blood) *stop the flow of.* राहविणें, थांबविणें, बंद करणें, वाहणें*n.*-&c. राहविणें-&c. *g. of o.*

To STANCH, *v. n. cease to flow.* राहणें, बंद होणें, वाहणें *n.*-प्रवाह *m.*-&c. राहणें-बंद होणें *g. of s.*

STANCH, *a.* v. CONSTANT, FIRM. धीर, सत्वधीर, सुधीर, करारी, टेंकीचा, टेंकदार, धक्क.

STANCHION, *n. small post.* खांबणी *f.* खांबोटी *f.* मोरवा *m.* कांभेरा *or* कांबिरा *m.*

STANCHNESS, *n.* v. A. धीरपणा *m.* &c. धीरता *f.* धैर्य*n.* स्थैर्य *n.* स्थिति *pop.* स्थीत *f.* [भारणें.

To STAND, *v. n. be erect, &c.* उभा-खडा असणें-होणें-राहणें, उ-

To s. in expectation. तिष्ठणें, तिष्ठतराहणें-असणें-बसणें.

2 *stop, halt.* उभा राहणें-ठाकणें, ठेपणें, ठरणें, ठैरणें, थोपणें, थांबणें, विरमणें, स्थिरावणें.

3 *be stationary; lie, cease.* पडणें, राहणें, स्तब्धणें, खोळंबणें, तकूब-&c. होणें-राहणें, खुंटणें, तटस्थ होणें-राहणें.

4 *continue, abide,* v. To ENDURE. राहणें, टिकणें, ठरणें, तगणें, स्थिर-&c. राहणें.

5 *to be in any state.* असणें, होणें, पडणें.

6 by; *be near, be present.* जवळ-&c. असणें.

7 by; *not to desert.* धरून-चिकटून-&c. राहणें. [हणें.

8 fast; *remain stationary.* राहणें, तळm.धरणें-धरून असणें-रा-

9 for; *be a candidate.* उभाराहणें, उमेदवार असणें.

10 for; *be in the place of, represent.* दाखवणें, दर्शविणें, ठिकाणीं असणें.

11 off; *keep at a distance.* दूर-&c. राहणें.

12 out; *project, be prominent.* बाहेर येणें, उमटणें *or* उमठणें.

13 out; v. To PERSIST. चिकटून-&c. राहणें.

14 over; *lie over.* खुंटीस अडकणें *or* लागणें, खडा राहणें-होणें, उभारत राहणें.

15 to; *abide by, adhere to.* चिकटून-धरून-घेऊन-अंबटाळून-&c. असणें-बसणें-राहणें.

16 up; *rise from sitting.* उठून उभाराहणें, उभाराहणें, उभारणें.

17 up for; *come forward to help.* उभाराहणें, पक्ष *m.*-कैवार *m.* धरणें.

18 with; *be consistent,* v. To AGREE. मिळणें, जमणें.

To STAND, *v. a.* v. To BEAR. सोसणें, साहणें. [खाडा *m.*

STAND, *n.* v. STATION. ठाणें *n.* ठिकाण *n.* स्थान *n.* अड्डा *m.* अ-

2 *stop, halt.* तटस्थपणा *m.* गतिस्तंभ *m.* गतिरोध *m.* गतिभ्रंश *m.* स्थिरगति *f.* ताटस्थ्य *n.*

Brought to a s. स्तंभित, स्तब्ध.

That is at a s. गतिहीन, तटस्थ, विरत.

To bring, put, &c. to a s. उभा करणें, खडकावणें, थबकविणें, स्तंभन *n.*-गतिभ्रंश *m.*-गतिरोध *m.*-&c. करणें.

To come to a s. or s. still. खुंटणें, थडकणें, थकणें, थबक-

णें, उभा होणें, गतिहीन होणें, खडकणें, खुडकणें, तरंगणें, घोडें n. थकणें g. of s.

3 (as for water pots, casks, &c.). घडोंची f. घोडा m.

4 (for a lamp, dish, &c.). ठाणवई or ठाणवी f.

5 (for swivels, native palanquins, &c.). शिपाई m.

6 (as of glass &c. vessels) *bottom-part.* बसक f. बैठक f. पेंदी or पेंधी f.

7 *frame, supporting case,*—gener. घोडाm. घोडी f. बसक f. बैठक f. बसकण n. पात्र n. चौकी f. माचोळी f. खुरशी f.

S. with three legs, *tripod.* तिवई f. तिपाई f.

STANDARD, n. *ensign,* v. FLAG. निशाण n. पताक f. बाहुटा m.

2 *rule, measure.* परिमाण n. प्रमाण n. धडा m. अवधि m. f. इयत्ता f. दुर्ते n.

STANDARD-BEARER, n. निशाणदार, निशाणबरदार, पताकी, ध्वजवान्.

STANDER, n. STANDING, p. a. v. V.N. 1. उभा राहणारा-राहिलेला, &c. उभा, खडा, स्थित, स्थ (in comp. as मार्गस्थ, &c.), स्थाता (in comp.). [राहून.

Standing, *in a standing posture.* उभ्यानें, उभ्यांनीं, उभा-

3 पडणारा-पडलेला, राहणारा-राहिलेला, &c. तटस्थ.

4 *and* ENDURING. टिकणारा, ठरणारा, &c. टिकाऊ.

I. *not in oblivion or desuetude,* v. EXTANT. चालता, उभा, उपस्थित, जागता, प्रसिद्ध, उपलभ्यमान, स्थित, अवस्थित.

II.—corn, &c. उभा.

III. See FIXED, CONTINUAL. IV. See STAGNANT.

STANDING, n. v. V. N. 1. उभा राहणें n. &c.

4 टिकणें n. ठरणें n. &c. टिकाव m. टिकावा m. स्थिति pop. स्थीत f. अवस्थिति f.

Of long s. बहुत दिवसांचा, केढोळचा, केव्हांचा, चिरकाली, चिरकालिक, चिरस्थायी, कदीम, चिरंतन.

I. *place to stand in.* उभाराहण्याची जागा f.

II. v. RANK. पदवी f.

STANDISH, n. *case for pen and ink.* कलमदान n.

STAND-STILL, n. v. STAND, 2. गतिरोध m. गतिस्तंभ m.

STANZA, n.—in poetry. श्लोक m. ग्रंथ m. कडवें n.

STAPHYLOMA, n.—the disease of the eye. वडस m.

STAPLE, a. (in commerce) *chief.* उदिमाचा मुख्य, विशेष उदिमाचा, वाणिज्यप्रधान.

STAPLE, n. *mart, emporium.* पेंठ f. उतारपेंठ f. गंज m.

2 *loop of iron, &c.* कोयंडा m.

3 (of wool, &c.). सूत n. [न्नस m.

4 *principal commodity.* उदिमाचा मुख्य जिन्नस m. पोकाजि-

STAR, n. तारा m. f. चांदणी f. तारका f. नक्षत्र n. भ n. उडु n. ऋक्ष n.

Falling s. उल्का f. तारा m. f.

Falling of a s. तारापात m. उल्कापात m.

Propitiousness of the stars. ताराबल n.

S. under which one was born. जन्मनक्षत्रn.

To shoot—stars. तारे m. pl. तुटणें.

The stars. भगण m. तारामंडल n. नक्षत्रमंडल n. नक्षत्रगण m. उडुगण m.

2 *asterisk.* चौफुली f.

3 (as on cloth, &c.). चौफुली f.

4 (as on the forehead of a bullock, &c.). चांदें n. चंद्र m.

That has a s. on the forehead. चंद्री, चांद्र, चांद्र्या, चांद्या.

STAR-BOARD, n. उजवें बोइद n.

STAR-GAZER, See ASTROLOGER.

STAR-LIGHT, n. ताऱ्यांचा उजेड m. नक्षत्रप्रकाश m.

STAR-SHOOT, n. तारापात m. उल्कापान m.

STARCH, n. *substance used to stiffen cloth.* खळ f. कल्प or फ or कलेप m. पेज f. चीक m. आहार m.

STARCH, a. *formal, precise, &c.* v. STIFF. भरकुंचीच्या डौलाचा-सोंगाचा-&c. भारदारीच्या डौलाचा-&c. ताठ्याचा, आढ्यतेचा, अनम्र, अमृदु, गंभीरमानी.

To STARCH, v. a. v. N. खळणें, खळ f.-कल्प m.-&c. लावणें-घालणें.

STARCHED, p. *and* a. v. V. खळ लावलेला, &c. कल्पदार.

I. See STARCH.

STARCHNESS, STARCHEDNESS, n. v. A. भरकुंचीचा डौल m. भारदारीचा डौल m. ताठाm. आढ्यता f.

To STARE, v. n. *look fixedly, gaze.* टक f. लावणें-लावून पाहणें, टौंकारणें or टौंकारून पाहणें, डोळे वासून-पसरून-&c. पाहणें, टकटक-टकमक-&c. पाहणें, टकणें, डोळे m. pl. बटारणें.

STARE, n. *fixed look.* टक f. v. लाव, लाग, अनिमेषदृष्टि f. अनिमेषावलोकन n.

STARER, n. STARING, p. a. v.V. टक लावणारा, टक लावून पाहणारा, डोळे वासून पाहणारा, &c. अनिमेषदृष्टि, अनिमेषावलोकी.

STARINGLY, *adv.* v.V. टक लावून, डोळे वासून, &c. टकटक or कां, टकमक or कां, टकाकां.

STARK, a. *pure, mere, thorough.* शुद्ध, केवल or ळ, निखालस, थेट.

2 See STIFF.

STARK, *adv. entirely, utterly,* v. WHOLLY. अगदी, केवळ, शुद्ध, निखळ, निखालस, निपट.

STARLING, n.—the bird. मैना m. शाळुंकी or खी f. शारिका f.

STARRY, a. *of or belonging to stars.* ताऱ्यांचा, &c. नाक्षत्र, आर्क्ष.

2 *abounding &c. with stars.* नक्षत्रमय, तारामय, नक्षत्रप्रचुर-बहुल, नक्षत्राकीर्ण, नक्षत्रव्याप्त.

S. firmament, v. HEAVEN. भचक्र n. नक्षत्रमंडल n. खगोल m. उडुगण m.

S. host. भगण m. नक्षत्रगण m. उडुगण m. [मारणें.

To START, v. n. *have a twitching, &c.* चमकणें, चमक f. भरणें-

2 *startle, shrink back.* डचकणें or दचकणें, बुजणें, विचकणें, चमकणें, भडकणें, निरबुजणें, डचकून-&c. उठणें.

3 *commence a journey,* v. To SET OUT. निघणें, चलणें, चालू-चालता-रवाना-&c. होणें, वाट चालूं लागणें, वाट f.-मार्ग m.-&c. धरणें, निघावा m.-निर्याण n.-प्रस्थान-&c. होणें g. of s. गमनोन्मुख-जिगमिषु-&c. होणें.

To get the s. of. आघाडी f. साधणें.

4 *spring or fly out of place.* सरकणें, निसटणें, निसपटणें, निसून जाणें, निसटून जाणें.

5 off; *set off suddenly.* झटकणें or झुटकणें, झडाडणें, झरकणें, झुकणें, झुकाटणें, सडकणें or सटकणें or सुटकणें, फटकणें, तकटून पळणें.

6 up; *rise eagerly or suddenly.* उठावणें, उसळणें, एकाएकी-आवेशानें-टपकन-&c. उठणें, डचकून-चमकून-&c. उठणें.

To START, v.a. *startle.* डचकविणें or दचकविणें, बिचकावणें, चमकविणें, बुजवणें.

2 (hare, bird, &c.) *cause to flee or fly*. उठवणें, भडकवणें.

3 *put into motion, cause to set off*. वाटेस-वाटे-&c. लावणें, चालता-चालू-रवाना-&c. करणें, हाकारणें.

4 *bring into view or notice ; propose*. घेणें, फोडणें, काढणें, पुढें आणणें.

START, STARTING, *n*. v. V. N. 1. चमकणें *n*. चमक *f*.

3 निघणें *n*. निघावा *m*. चलणें *n*. गमनारंभ *m*. गमनोपक्रम *m*.

I. *sudden fit or sally*, (of fancy, &c.). हुक्की *f*. लहर *f*. उकळी *f*.

By fits and starts. लहरीनें, हुक्कीनें, लहरीबरोबर, हुक्की बरोबर, खंडळमंडळ, अडातुडी.

STARTED, *p*. v. V. A. 1. इचकवलेला, बिचकावलेला, बुजवलेला.

2 उठवलेला, &c.

To STARTLE, *v. n. draw back*, v. To START. इचकणें *or* दचकणें, बुजणें, इचका *m*.-&c. बसणें.

To STARTLE, *v. a. impress with sudden fear*. इचकविणें *or* दचकविणें, बिचकाविणें, चमकविणें, बुजवणें, धक्का *m*. देणें-बसवणें, इचका *m*.-धडक *f*.-धडकी *f*.-&c. बसवणें.

STARTLE, *n. sudden fright*. धक्का *m*. इचका *m*. धडक *f*. धडकी *f*.

STARTLED, *p*. v. V. A. इचकवलेला, चमकवलेला, बुजवलेला, &c.

STARTLER, *n*. STARTLING, *p.a*. v. V.A. इचकवणारा, चमकवणारा, धक्का-इचका-&c. बसवणारा.

STARVATION, *n*. v. V. N. 1.—*state*. उपासमर *f*. उपास *m*. अन्नान्नगत *f*.

v. V. A. 1.—*act*. उपासी मारणें *n*. उपासमार *m*. उपासमारा *m*.

To STARVE, *v. n. perish with hunger*. उपासी मरणें, उपासानें-भुकेनें-क्षुधेनें-&c. मरणें, भुकेंमरणें, उपासमर *f*. होणें *g. of s*. आळवण *n*. निघणें-होणें *g. of s*.

2 *perish with cold*. थंडीनें-हिंवानें *or* हिंवें-&c. मरणें.

To STARVE, *v. a. kill or distress with hunger*. उपासी मारणें, भुकें-भुकेनें-&c. मारणें, उपासमार *m*.-उपासमारा *m*.-पोटमारा *m*. करणें *g. of o*. उपासी-&c. ठेवणें-राखणें, आळवण*n*. काढणें-घालणें *g. of o*. अन्नपाण्याची बंदी *f*. करणें.

2 *kill with cold*. थंडीनें-हिंवानें-&c. मारणें.

STARVED, *p*. v. V. A. 1. उपासी मारलेला, &c. उपासी.

v. V. N. 1. *and* STARVING. उपासी मेलेला, उपासी.

STARVELING, *a. thin from hunger*, v. LEAN. मरकाड्या, मरतुकडा *or* तुंडगा, मऱ्या, रोड्या, लकड्या.

STARVELING, *n. one thin through want of nutriment*. In expression of this sense there are numerous terms and appellatives. इंद्रमेंडे *or* मढें *n*. मरतमेंडे *or* मढें *n*. मरतुकडें *n*. करपटसड्या, गिन्हा *m*. गिन्हावळ *f*. पांढरपाल *f*. कांखा *m*. हाडांचा पिंजरा *m*. काष्ठ *n*. पाप्यांचें पितर *n*. झुडतर*n*. जरत्कारू, मृत्युगोदान *n*. सांपळा *m*. हत्या *f*. दिपाचा कवडा *m*. See also under LEAN.

STARVER, *n*. STARVING, *p. a*. v. V. N. 1. उपासी मरणारा, &c. उपासकाढू, उपासी, भुकेबंगाल, अन्नास महाग, अन्नास मोताद, अन्नार्थी, अन्नरहित.

STATE, *n*. v. CONDITION. स्थिति *pop*. स्थीत *f*. अवस्था *f*. गति *f*. दशा *f*.

Present s. अहवाल *or* हवाल *m. f*.

2 *grandeur, show, &c*. v. POMP. थाट *m*. थाटमाट *m*. थाटमाड *m*. डौल *m*. डामडौल *m*. टामटूम *f*. अमिरी *f*.

S.-carriage. रथ *m*.

3 *ruling power or body*, v. GOVERNMENT. सरकार *m*. हुजूर *n*.

The eight offices of a s. अष्टाधिकार *m. pl*.

Pillar of the s. दौलतीचा खांब *m*.

Secret of s. राजगुह्य *n*.

S.-affairs. राजकार्य *n*.

S.-counsel. राजकारण *n*. राजकारस्थान *n*.

S.-maxim or rule. राजधर्म *m*.

4 *body of people, united under a government*. राज्य *n*. राष्ट्र *n*. प्रजागण*m*.

STATE, *a. of or belonging to the government*. सरकारी, सरकारचा, सरकारसंबंधाचा, सरकारच्या संबंधाचा, सरकारी प्रकरणाचा, खालसा, खास.

2 *belonging to or requiring pomp*. थाटाचा, थाटमाटाचा, डामडौलाचा, &c.

To STATE, *v. a. set down, express particularly in writing*. कलमवार-कलमबंदीनें-&c. लिहणें-मांडणें, कलमबंदी *f*. करणें *g. of o*. मजकूर *m*.-हकिकत *f*.-वाका *m*.-वृत्तांत *m*.-&c. लिहणें-लिहून ठेवणें.

2 *express orally, narrate, &c*. v. To TELL. सांगणें, बोलणें, मजकूर *m*.-वर्तमान *n*.-हकिकत *f*.-बयाना *m*.-वृत्तांत *m*.-&c. सांगणें-कळवणें, निवेदणें, निवेदन *n*.-&c. करणें *g. of o*. निवेदित -&c. करणें.

STATE-ROOM, *n*. दिवाणखाना *m*.

STATED, *p. & a*. v. V. 2. सांगितलेला, &c. निवेदित, वेदित, कथित, उपपादित, उपन्यस्त.

I. *settled*, v. FIXED. नेमलेला, नियमाचा *or* नेमाचा, बंदा, नियमित, नियत.

STATEDLY, *adv*. v. A. नियमानें *or* नेमानें, नेमाचा *decl*. नेहमी *or* नेहेमी.

STATELINESS, *n*. v. A. मोठेपणाचा डौल *m*. डौल *m*. डामडौल *m*. डौलदारी *f*. गौरव *n. m*. प्रौढि *f*.

STATELY, *a. dignified, lofty, &c*. v. GRAND, MAJESTIC. डौलाचा, डौलदारीचा, प्रौढ.

STATEMENT, STATING, *n*. v. V. 1.—*act*. कलमवारलिहणें *n*. &c. कलमबंदी *f*.

2—*act*. सांगणें *n*. मजकूर सांगणें *n*. &c. निवेदन *n*. कथन *n*. उपपादन *n*. उपन्यास *m*. वेदना *f*.

I. *representation made*, v. ACCOUNT. हकिकत *f*. मजकूर *m*. करिणा *m*. बयाणा *or* ना *m*. वाका *m*.

II. (as of costs, profits, &c.). v. ESTIMATE. आकार *m*.

STATER, *n*. v. V. 1. कलमवार लिहणारा, मजकूर लिहणारा, &c. निवेदक, कथक, उपपादक, निवेदन-&c. कर्त्ता.

2 सांगणारा, मजकूर सांगणारा, &c.

STATESMAN, *n. one versed in the art of government*. राजकार्यधुरंधर, राजधर्मवित्, राजनीतिज्ञ, राजकर्मप्रवीण, राजनीतिकुशल, राजनीतिविशारद, राजकारणी.

2 *one employed in public affairs*. राज्यकारभारांतलीअसामी, राज्यकारभारी, राजपुरुष, राजभृत्य, राजमंत्री.

STATION, *n. place, post, stand*. जागा *m. f*. स्थान*n*. स्थल *or* ळ *n*. ठाणें *n*. ठाण *n*. ठिकाण *n*. अवस्थान *n*. अवस्थिति *f*.

2 (of bearers, &c.). अड्डा *m*. अखाडा *m*.

3 *post assigned*, v. OFFICE. जागा *f*. असामी *f*. अमल *m*. अधिकार *m*.

4 *rank, condition of life*. पदवी *f*. पद *n*. दरजा *m*.

High s. मरातब *m. f*.

5 (on a railway). ठाणें *n*. स्टेशन *n*.

To STATION, *v. a. appoint to the occupation of a place; place, set*. ठेवणें, बसवणें, उभा-&c. करणें, ठिकाण्यावर-ठाण्यावर-&c.

नेमणें-योजणें-नेमणूक *f.*-&c. करणें.

STATION-MASTER, *n.* ठाणेदार, स्टेशनमास्तर.

STATIONARY, *a. not moving, fixed.* चालण्यानिराळा-वेगळा, निश्चल *or* ळ, स्थावर, स्थिर, अचर, अचल, बैठा in comp.

2 *not advancing.* निवाढ्या, वाढीवेगळा-निराळा, अवर्द्धमान.

STATIONED, *p.* v. V. ठेवलेला, ठाण्यावर-&c. नेमलेला.

STATIONER, *n. seller of paper, &c.* कागदवगैरे विकणारा, कागद-विक्या, लेखनसामग्रीविक्रेता.

STATIONERY, *n. paper, ink, &c.* कागदवगैरे लिहिण्याचें सामान *n.* -साहित्य *n.* लेखनसामग्री *f.*

STATISTIC, STATISTICAL, *a. relating to statistics.* देशस्थिति-रीतिसंबंधी-विषयक.

STATISTICS, *n. domestic economy, social condition, &c. of a people or country.* देशावस्था *f.* देशस्थितिरीतिप्रकरण *n.*

STATUARY, *n. image-carving.* मूर्त्ति खोदणें *n.* &c. पुतळघडणी *f.* मूर्त्तिकरण *n.*

2 *image-carver.* मूर्त्ति-पुतळा-&c. खोदणारा-घडणारा, मूर्त्तिकार.

STATUE, *n. image.* मूर्त्ति *f.* पुतळा *m.* (*and* पुतळी *f.*) बाहुला *m.* (बाहुली *f. and* बाहुलें *n.*) प्रतिछाया *f.* प्रतिमा *f.*

STATURE, *n. natural height of the body.* शरीराची-देहाची-&c. उंची *f.* शरीराचीकाठी *f.* शरीरोच्चता *f.* भुई *f.*

Of graceful s. लांबलचक.

To be of short or low s. भुई *f.* ठेंगणी असणें *g. of s.* काठी *f.* खुजी-ठेंगणी-&c. असणें *g. of s.*

To be of tall or high s. भुई *f.* उफाड्याची असणें *g. of s.* काठी *f.* उंच असणें *g. of s.*

STATUTE, *n. rule, regulation,* v. LAW. कायदा *m.* जाबता *m.* कानू *f.* दस्तूर *m.* दस्तूर अम्मल *m.* नियम*m.* विधान *n.*

STATUTORY, STATUTABLE, *a. enacted by statute.* कायद्याचा, कायद्यानें स्थापलेला, नियमस्थापित, विधिस्थापित.

STAVE, *n.* (of wood). फळी *f.*

2 (of a song, &c.). कडवें *n.* [पाडणें.

To STAVE, *v. a.* (a cask, &c.) फोडणें, तोंड *n.* उघडणें, भोंक *n.*

2 off; See To DELAY, To WARD.

To STAY, *v. n. remain, continue.* राहणें, ठरणें, टिकणें, तगणें, थारावणें, थारणें, बसणें, थिरावणें.

2 *stop, stand.* राहणें, उभाराहणें, थांबणें, ठरणें, थारणें, थारा-वणें, थिरावणें, स्थिरावणें.

3 *dwell, abide,* v. To RESIDE. राहणें, नांदणें, वास *m.*-&c. करणें, असणें, ठिकाण *n.*-मकाण *or* न *n.*-&c. असणें *g. of s.*

4 for; *wait for.* राहणें, खोळंबणें, खोळंबून राहणें बसणें, थां-बणें, थिरणें, वाट *f.*-&c. पाहणें, खोळंबा *m.*-&c. करणें.

To STAY, *v. a. stop, repress, &c.* राहविणें, स्थिरावणें, थारवणें, थांबवणें, थोपवणें, अटपवणें, आवरणें, आकळणें.

2 *hinder from proceeding, make to stay,* v. To STOP, To DETAIN. राहविणें, स्थिरावणें, थिरावणें, थारावणें, ठेवून घेणें, खो-ळंबा *m.*-खोटी *f.*-&c. करणें *g. of o.*

3 *hold up,* v. To SUPPORT, To PROP. थोपवणें, धिरा*m.*-&c. देणें, थोप *f.* संभाळणें-करणें *g. of o.*

STAY, STAYING, *n.* v. V. N. 1.—*state.* राहणें*n.* ठरणें*n.* &c. स्थिति *pop.* स्थीत *f.* ठराव*m.* ठरणूक *f.* थारा*m.* थारावणी *f.* टिकाव*m.* टिकावा*m.* तगाव*m.* अवस्थिति *f.* अवस्थान*n.* अधिष्ठान *n.* संस्था *f.* संस्थिति *f.* वृत्ति *f.*

2 राहणें*n.* थांबणें*n.* ठरणें*n.* &c. थारावणी *f.*

3 *and* RESIDENCE. राहणें*n.* नांदणें*n.* नांदणूक *f.* नांदवट *f.* रहि-वास*m.* वास्तव्य*n.* स्थातव्य *n.*

Temporary s. मुकाम*m.*

4 राहणें*n.* थांबणें*n.* खोळंबणें*n.* &c. खोळंबा*m.* खोटी *f.*

I. *rope &c. to steady.* ओढा*m.* तणावा*m.*

II. v. PROP, SUPPORT. धिरा*m.* ओठंगण*n.* तणावा *m.* अवष्टंभ *m.* मेढ्या*m.* [*g. of o.*

To knock away, take away, &c. the s. of. थोप*f.* बुडवणें

STAYER, *n.* STAYING, *p. a.* v. V. N. 1. राहणारा, ठरणारा, &c. अवस्थायी, अवस्थित, स्थित, संस्थित, स्थायी and स्थायिक (in comp.), स्थाता (in comp.), संस्थ (in comp.).

STAYS, *n.* v. BODICE. कांचोळी *f.*

STEAD, *n. room, place.* जागा *f.m.* स्थान*n.* ठिकाण*n.* स्थल *or* ळ*n.*

In the s. of. जागीं, ऐवजीं, बदल.

That is in the s. of. बारचा, वांटचा, होता, होत्साता, होतला.

To stand in s. *be of use.* कामास-कामीं-उपयोगास-उपयोगीं -&c. येणें-पडणें. [अचल.

STEADFAST, STEADY, *a. fast, fixed.* निश्चल *or* ळ, स्थिर, अचर,

2 *resolute, constant,* v. FIRM. धिराचा, निश्चयाचा, स्थिर, चिकट, स्थिरचित्त, स्थिरमनस्क, स्थिरात्मा, स्थिरचेता, खंबीर, स्तब्ध, अचपल.

3 *not fluctuating, not deviating; uniform, regular.* एकसार-खा चालणारा-वाहणारा, &c. स्थिर, समगति, अस्खलित.

4 *of uniform conduct; sober, quiet, &c.* एकधोरणी, एकसुती, एकतंत्री, साळसूद *or* ध, एकचालीचा, एकरीतीचा, चालीचा, स्थिर-बुद्धीचा, स्थिरवृत्तीचा, स्थिरबुद्धि, स्थिरवृत्ति, अचंचलवृत्ति, अचं-चलबुद्धि, अव्यभिचारवृत्ति.

STEADFASTLY, STEADILY, *adv.* v. A. 2. धिरानें, निश्चयानें, स्थिरमनानें, स्थिरचित्तानें, &c.

3 एकसारखा *decl.* समगतीनें.

4 एकधोरणधरून, स्थिरबुद्धीनें, &c.

I.—carrying, moving, &c. अचळ, अचळवी, अचानक.

STEADFASTNESS, STEADINESS, *n.* v. A. 1. निश्चळपणा*m.* निश्च-लता *f.* अचलता *f.* स्थिरता *f.* स्थैर्य*n.*

2 चिकटपणा*m.* चिकटाई *f.* नेट*m.* निग्रह*m.* स्थिरता *f.* स्थैर्य*n.* स्थिति *f.* अचापल्य*n.* अचांचल्य*n.*

3 एकसारखेपणा*m.* समगति *f.*

4 एकधोरणीपणा*m.* एकसुतीपणा*m.* साळसूदपणा*m.* &c. स्थिरबु-द्धि *f.* स्थिरवृत्ति *f.*

To STEADY, *v. a. make or keep firm.* स्थिर-&c. करणें, स्थिराव-णें, स्थिरपणा*m.*-स्थिरता *f.*-&c. आणणें.

To STEAL, *v. a. carry away feloniously.* चोरी *f.*-&c. करणें *g. of o.* चोरीनें-चौर्यानें-स्तेयकर्मानें-&c. नेणें, चोरीकरून नेणें-घेणें, चोरणें, चोरून नेणें-घेणें. For this word as expressing the sense of *To pilfer, filch, purloin, &c.* are, उपटणें, उचलणें, उचकणें, लांबविणें, उपटून-&c. नेणें, आडव्याहातानें घेणें, उपटा*m.* करणें *g. of o.* उपटा *or* उपाटा*m.*-ताव*m.*-&c. देणें *with* ला *or* स *or with* वर *of o.* हात *m.*-पट्टा *m.*-डल्ला *m.*-&c. मारणें *with* वर *of o.*

To STEAL, *v. n. practise theft.* चोरी *f.*-चौर्य*n.*-चौर्यकर्म*n.*-तस्करी *f.*-स्तेय*n.*-स्तेयकर्म*n.*-&c. करणें.

2 *come or go silently, &c.* चोरपायीं-चोरपायानें-चोरपावलानें-

मुकाट्यां-चोरून-लपून-गुपचुप-&c. यणें-जाणें.

STEALER, *n.* STEALING, *p. a.* v. V. A. & V. N. 1. चोरून नेणारा, चोरी करणारा, &c. चोर, तस्कर, स्तेयी.

Heart s. चित्तचोर, चित्तचोरटा.

v. V. N. 2. चोरपायीं-चोरपायानें येणारा-जाणारा.

STEALINGLY, *n. adv.* v. V. N. 2. चोरपायीं, चोरपायानें, चोरपावलानें, चोरगस्तीनें, गुपचिप *or* चुप.

STEALTH, STEALING, *n.* v. V. A.—*act.* चोरून नेणें *n.* चोरणें *n.* &c. चोरी *f.* चौर्य *n.* मूषण *n.*

Picking and stealing. चोरीचकारी *f.* चोरीचपाटी *f.*

I. *clandestine act.* चोरी *f.* लिकाचोरी *f.* छपवणी *or* छपावणी *f.*

By s. चोरीनें, चोरून, चोरगस्तीनें, लिकून चोरून, लपूनछपून *or* लपत छपत, चोरीछपी, चोरून मारून.

STEALTHILY, *adv. by stealth,* v. STEALTH. चोरीनें, चोरून, अलगपीत.

STEALTHY, *a. done by stealth.* चोरीचा, लिकाचोरीचा, चोरपायाचा, चोरपावल्याचा, चोरगस्तीचा.

STEAM, *n. vapour.* बाफ *f.* ऊब *f.* ओप *f.* घाम *m.* स्वेद *m.* बाष्प *m.*

Of which the s. is escaped,—article cooked. बाफसांडा.

To STEAM, *v. a. expose to steam.* बाफारा *m.* देणें-घेणें, दम *m.* देणें, बाफलणें.

To STEAM, *v. n. send off visible vapour.* बाफ *f.*-&c. टाकणें-सोडणें, बाफ *f.*-&c. सुटणें-येणें *in. con.* बाफ *f.*-&c. निघणें *g. of s.*

To make to s. (by setting on or before the fire). बाफ *f.* देणें.

STEAM-BOAT, *n.* बाफेचें गलबत *n.*-जहाज *n.*-&c. आगबोट *f.*

STEAM-ENGINE, *n.* बाफेचें यंत्र *n.*

STEAMED, *p.* v. V. A. बाफारा दिल्हेला, &c. स्वेदित.

STEAMER, *n.* STEAMING, *p. a,* STEAMY, *a.* v. V.N. बाफसुटलेला-आलेला, सबाष्प. [बापसणें.

To become steamy, and thus fit for seed—the ground.

I. *steam vessel.* आगबोट *f.* (from आग fire and बोट the native form of *boat*) has become familiar. बाफेचें गलबत *n.*-&c.

STEATITE, *n. soapstone.* माल्रू *f.* खडी *f.*

STEED, *n.* v. HORSE. घोडा *m.* वारू *m.* तुरंग *m.* तुरंगम *m.*

STEEL, *n.* तिखें *n.* पोलाद *n.* मिलाब *n.* सारलोह *m.*

2 fig. v. WEAPON. हत्यार *n.* शस्त्र *n.* [लादी.

STEEL, STEELY, *a. made, &c. of steel.* तिख्याचा, पोलादाचा, पो-

To STEEL, *v. a. make hard or obdurate.* कठीण-निर्दय-पाषाणाचा-&c. करणें, न द्रवेसा करणें.

STEEL-YARD, *n.* तुलई *f.* तूळ *m.*

STEEP, *n. ascent,* v. HILL. डगर *f.* कडा *m.* घसरड *f.* घाटी *f.* घरळ *f.* बरंगळ *f.* सूळ *m.* उभासूळ *m.* उभीचढण *f.*

STEEP, *a. ascending or descending with great inclination, precipitous.* मोठ्याचढाचा, उभ्याचढाचा, उभ्या चढावाचा, उभेचढणीचा, उभ्यासुळाचा, अवघडचढाचा, कडातुटलेला, कड्याचा, डगरीचा, उभा, खर, घस, दुरारोह.

To STEEP, *v. a. macerate,* v. To SOAK. भिजत-भिजूं घालणें, भिजवणें, भीज *f.* करणें *g. of o.*

STEEPLE, *n. spire.* सुळका *m. dim.* सुळकी *f.* सुळक्याचें शिखर *n.*

STEEPNESS, *n.* v. A. उभेपणा *m.* सुळकेपणा *m.* उभाचढ *m.* उभासूळ *m.*

STEER, *n. young ox.* खोंड *m.* पाडा *m.* गोऱ्हा *m.* आडबैल *m.*

To STEER, *v. a. guide by the helm.* सुकाणूनें-सुकाणानें-&c. चालवणें.

2 See To GUIDE. [वणें-फिरवणें.

To STEER, *v. n. direct the helm.* सुकाणू *n.*-सुकाण *n.*-&c. चाल-

2 fig. *pursue a course or way.* रस्ता *m.*-वाट *f.*-मार्ग *m.* धरणें, उपाय *m.*-तजवीज *f.*-&c. करणें.

STEERER, STEERS-MAN, *n.* v. V. *and* HELMS-MAN. सुकाणदार, सुकाण्या.

STELLAR, STELLARY, *a.* v. STARRY. ताऱ्याचा, नक्षत्रांचा, नक्षत्रसंबंधी, नाक्षत्र, आर्क्ष.

STEM, *n. main body of a tree or plant,* v. TRUNK. कांड *n.* कांडें *n.* खोड *n.*

Long and straight s. तरांडा *m.*

2 v. STALK. ताट *n.* देंठ *m.* देंठी *f.*

Naked s. कांसा *m.* डांक *n.* [स *m.* वृंत *n.*

3 *peduncle or pedicle of a fruit or flower.* देंठ *m.* डेंठ *m.* डें-

To STEM, *v. a.* (a current, &c.) *make progress against.* समोर-संमुख-&c. जाणें *with* वर *of o.* उभा-समोर-&c. तोडीत जाणें, ओघावर-स्रोतावर-&c. जाणें-चढणें.

2 *resist, check, &c.* v. To STOP. रोधणें, रोध *m.*-गतिरोध *m.*-प्रतिष्टंभ *m.*-&c. करणें *g. of o.* [डाण *f.*

STENCH, *n.* v. STINK. घाण *f.* दुर्घाण *f.* दुर्गंध *m.* ओरडाण *or* वर-

STENOGRAPHY, *n. short handwriting.* संक्षिप्त अक्षरांनीं लिहण्याची रीति *f.*-विद्या *f.* संक्षिप्ताक्षरलिपि *f.* संक्षिप्ताक्षरलेखनविद्या *f.*

To STEP, *v. n. place the foot on the ground in moving.* पाय *m.*-पाऊल *n.*-पाउलें *n. pl.* ठेवणें-टाकणें-टाकीत चालणें, पदनिक्षेप *m.*-पदविक्षेप *m.*-पदन्यास *m.*-&c. करणें.

To s. unequally. पाय *m. pl.* खालवर पडणें *g. of s.*

2 *walk a little distance.* चारपाउलें-चारपावलें-चार कदम-&c. चालणें-चालून जाणें-चालून येणें, येणें, जाणें.

3 back. हटणें, पाठीमागें-&c. सरणें-सरकणें-&c.

4 forth *or* out; *come forth.* पुढें येणें-होणें, सरकणें, सरकावणें, सरळणें.

5 out; *take large steps.* पाऊल *n.*-पाय *m.*-&c. उचलणें, लांब पाऊल *n.* करणें-टाकणें, भरकदम-भरपाउलांनीं-&c. चालणें.

STEP, *n. placing of the foot in moving, pace.* पाऊल *n.* पावला *m.* कदम *m.* पावंडा *m.* पदन्यास *m.* पदविक्षेप *m.* पदप्रक्षेप *m.* पदनिक्षेप *m.* पदक्रम *m.* पदपात *m.* चरणपात *m.*

At every s. पावलोपावलीं, पदोपदीं, प्रतिपद.

Silent and stealing s. चोरपाऊल *n.*

Step by s. पदशः. [पाऊल *n.*

2 (in dancing, fencing, &c.) *cast of the foot.* पावटा *m.*

3 *space measured by a step.* पाऊल *n.* पावला *m.* कदम *m.* ढांग *f.* ढेंग *f.*

4 *hold for the foot; stair, round of a ladder, &c.* पायरी *f.* पायका *m.* पावका *m.* पावटा *or* पायटा *m.* पायंडा *m.* पावंडा *m.* पायंडी *f.* पाउठणी *or* पावठणी *f.* सोपान *n.*—as notched on a tree, down a well, &c. पावठी *f.* पांवडा *m.* पावठाणा *m.*

Flight of steps. जिना *m.* शिडी *or* सिडी *f.* सोपान *n.*

5 *gradation, stage, degree.* पायरी *f.* पर्याय *m.*

First s. or stage. प्रथम चरण *n.*

Step by s. क्रमाक्रमानें, क्रमशः, पदशः. [बीज *f.*

6 *proceeding, action,* v. MEASURE. उपाय *m.* लाग *m.* तज-

7 *a short distance.* चार पावलांची वाट् *f.* चार पावलांचें अंतर *n.*

STEP-BROTHER, *n.* *step-mother's son.* सावत्रभाऊ *m.* सापत्नबंधु *m.* वैमात्र *m.* वैमात्रेय *m.*

STEP-CHILD, *n.* *child acquired with a wife or husband.* पहिल्या घरचें-अदल्या घरचें मूल *n.*-लेकरूं *n.*-&c.—jocosely, अड्ता, ओढ्या.

STEP-FATHER, *n.* *father acquired by one's mother's second marriage.* दुसरा बाप *m.* पाटाचा बाप *m.*—loosely, सावत्रबाप *m.*

STEP-MOTHER, *n.* *mother acquired by one's father's second marriage.* सावत्रआई *f.* सापत्नमाता *f.* विमाता *f.*

STEP-SISTER, *n.* *step mother's daughter.* सावत्रबहीण *f.* सापत्नबहीण. [णी *f.*

STEP-STONE, STEPPING-STONE, *n.* v. STEP. पाउठणी *or* पावठ-

STEPPE, *n.* गवताचा माळ *m.*-माळजमीन *f.*

STERILE, STERILITY. See BARREN, BARRENNESS.

STERLING, *a.*—coin. पोतेचालीचा, पोतेचाल, पोतेचलनी, मालखरा, हाडाचा खरा-चांगला-&c.

2 v. GENUINE. हाडचा खरा, हाडाचा खरा-चांगला-भला-&c.

STERN, *a.* (of countenance). निष्ठुरमुद्रेचा, मुद्रेचा निष्ठुर, निष्ठुरवदन, उग्रमुद्र.

2 (of manners or temper). कडवा, करडा, निष्ठुर, खरमरा *or* ऱ्या, कणक्या, हीनमाय, हीनदय, मायाहीन, दयाहीन, निर्मम, जलाल, प्रखर, सख्त.

STERN, *n.* (of a ship). बराम *n.*

STERN-POST, *n.* बरा *f.*

STERNNESS, *n.* v. A. 1. मुद्रेचा निष्ठुरपणा *m.* निष्ठुरमुद्रा *f.* उग्रमुद्रा *f.* [दयाहीनता *f.*

2 कडवेपणा *m.* करडेपणा, &c. निष्ठुरता *f.* नैष्ठुर्य *n.* मायाहीनता *f.*

STERNUM, *n.* *breast bone.* उराचें हाड *n.* उरदांडा *m.* उरोस्थि *n.*

STEW, *n.*—the dish. मवागीचा-मंद आगीचा-&c. पाक *m.*

2 v. CONFUSION, FRIGHT. त्रेधा *f.* तिरपीट *f.* तारातीर *f.*

3 See BROTHEL.

To STEW, *v. a.* *boil gently and slowly.* मवागीनें-मंदागीनें-&c. शिजवणें रांधवणें-&c.

STEWARD, *n.* *manager of a household, &c.* घरकारणी, कारभारी, दिवाण, दिवाणजी, मोदी, अर्थाधिकारी, संपादक.

STEWARDSHIP, *n.* *office, &c. of a steward.* कारभारीपणा *m.* कारभाऱ्याचें काम *n.*-&c. दिवाणगिरी *f.* अर्थाधिकार *m.*

To STICK, *v. a.* *make to adhere.* चिकटवणें *or* चिकटावणें, लगटवणें *or* लगटावणें, लगटणें, डकवणें *or* डगवणें, डसवणें.

2 (a pointed instrument, &c.) v. To THRUST. ढुसकणें *or* ढोसकणें, ढुसणें *or* ढोसणें, खुपसणें, खोवणें, टुपणें.

3 (with a pointed instrument) v. To STAB. ढुसकणें *or* ढोसकणें, ढुसणें *or* ढोसणें.

4 *fasten, or cause to remain, by piercing.* खोवून-खोचून-टुपून-&c. ठेवणें, घालणें, चढवणें.

5 (out) *cause to be prominent.* बाहेर-पुढें करणें-काढणें, लांबकरणें, कोपर *m.* काढणें.

To STICK, *v. n.* *adhere.* चिकटणें, लगटणें *or* लिगटणें, लागणें, डकणें, डगणें, डसणें, धरणें, विलगणें, लगटून-&c. राहणें.

2 *stop, be arrested, stand still,* lit. fig. अटकणें, अडकणें, अडणें, खुंटणें, थकणें, फसणें.

3 *scruple, demur,* v. To HESITATE. आशंकणें, शंकणें, कासकूस *f.*-नानू *f.*-&c. करणें.

4 out; *be prominent.* बाहेर-बर येणें-निघणें.

STICK, *n.*—gener. काठी *f.* छडी *f.* लाकूड *n.* लकडी *f.* दंड *m.* यष्टि *f.* यष्टिका *f.* पालवा *m.*

Bit of s. chopped off. गंडरी *or* गंडोरी *f.*

Green s. ओलटा *m.* ओरपटा *m.* ओलपटणें *n.* ओल्हांटणें *n.* ओल्हांटा *m.*

Green sticks (as for fuel). ओलट *or* ओलवट *f.*

Heavy blow with a s. held in both hands. धोपाटी *f.* धोंप *f.*

Long piece of s. *pole, &c.* दांडा *m.* काठी *f.*

Short, thickish s. कुडपण *n.* कुडपणें *n.* कोंडका *m.* कोंढकें *n.* ढोडांका *m.* बढ्या *m.* लटिंगा *m.* लटोरा *m.* लठ्ठ *m.* सर *m.*

Smooth and roundish s. टिकोरा *m.* टिकोरें *n.*

2 *short and little piece of wood.* काडी *f.* कुटकी *f.* काटूक *n.* काडूक *n.* तांटूक *n.* कुडी *f.* काटकुटी *f.* फांटें *n.* शिरकुटी *f.* शिरपुटी *f.*

Light and dry sticks and chips. भुरकाड्या *f. pl.* काबळकाटी *f.* [रा *m.* केरकचरा *m.*

Sticks and straws. काटक्याकुटक्या *f. pl.* कस्पान *n.* कच-

3 (of an umbrella, fan, &c.) दांडी *f.*

4 (for beating on tabors, &c.). टिपरी *f.* टिपरूं *n.* टिपरें *n.*

5 *stab,* v. THRUST. ढुसी *f.* ढुसकी *f.*

STICKINESS, *n.* v. A. चिकटपणा *m.* चिकणपणा *m.* चिकचिकितपणा *m.* चिकटण *f.* चिकटाई *f.* चिकचीक *f.* किचकीच *f.*

To STICKLE, *v. n.* *contend for persistingly,* v. To INSIST. आग्रह *m.*-अट *f.*-अडती *f.*-हट *m.*-&c. धरणें-धरून असणें, ओढणें, ओढून धरणें, ओढतें *n.* घेणें, भांडणें, वाद *m.*-तकरार *f.*-&c. करणें, अडणें.

STICKLER, *n.* STICKLING, *p. a.* v. V. आग्रह धरणारा, अट धरणारा, ओढून धरणारा, वाद करणारा, ओढक, अगत्यवादी, अगत्याचा, तकरारी.

STICKLING, *n.* v. V.—*act.* आग्रह धरणें *n.* अट धरणें *n.* &c. आग्रह *m.* अगत्यवाद *m.* ओढ *f.* खारासीर *f.* तकरार *f.* वाद *m.* आक्षेप *m.*

STICKY, *a.* *adhesive, viscous, glutinous, &c.* चिकट, चिकण, चिकटाऊ, डकाऊ, चिकचिकीत, चिडचिडीत, गिजगिजीत, चिकाचा, डिकाचा, चिकाळ *or* ळा *or* ळ्या.

S. or clammy matter. चिकटा *m.* चिकचीक *f.*

To be s. चिकचिकणें.

STIFF, *a.* *not flexible or pliant; rigid, &c.* ताठ, ताठर.

2 (through dryness) v. HARD. खडक *or* कडक, खडखडीत, निबर *intens.* निबरढोण. [कळलेला.

3—as a limb, &c. खुडा, खुडे *ind.* खुडकलेला, ताठरलेला, ताट-

To be s. खुडकणें, ताठरणें, ताटकळणें, तांठणें.

4—of style, &c. अप्रशस्त.

5 *formal, starched, constrained, &c. in manner.* खळबळितपणा वेगळा-निराळा, घळबळितपणा वेगळा-निराळा, हळबळेपणा निराळा, लवण भंजनानिराळा, आदराचेआळ्यतेचा, आदराचा डौली, भरकुंबीच्याडौलाचा.

6 See OBSTINATE. 7 (a gale, &c.) जोराचा.

STIFF-HEARTED, STIFF-NECKED. See OBSTINATE.

To STIFFEN, *v. a.* *make less pliant.* ताठ-ताठर-&c. करणें.

2 *inspissate,* v. To THICKEN. घट्ट-&c. करणें.

To STIFFEN, *v. n. become less flexibe.* ताठणें, ताठरणें, ताठर-&c. होणें-होत जाणें.

2 *become dry and hard.* खडकणें, खडक-&c. होणें-होत जाणें.

3—a limb, &c. ताठणें, ताटकळणें, ठांठुरणें, दंडावणें, दांडावणें, खुडा-&c. होणें-होत जाणें.

STIFFNESS, *n.* v. A. 1. ताठपणा *m.* ताठरपणा *m.* ताठ *m.* ताठा *m.*

2 खडकपणा *m.* खडखडितपणा *m.* निबरपणा *m.*

3 खुडेपणा *m.* खुडकलेलेपणा *m.* &c. मोडम *m. f. v.* ये, ताटकळा *m.* ताटकळी *f.*

4 अप्रशस्तपणा *m.* अप्राशस्त्य *n.* अप्रशस्तता *f.*

5 लवणभंजना निरालेपणा *m.* ताठा *m.* आदराचा-&c. डौल *m.*

To STIFLE, *v. a.*v. To SUFFOCATE, To CHOKE. दम *m.*-श्वास *m.* -&c. कोंडणें-कोंडून मारणें, कोंडमार *m.*-कोंडमारा *m.* करणें *g. of o.*

2 fig. *smother,* &c. v. To SUPPRESS. दाबणें, गिळणें, पिणें.

STIGMA, *n. mark of infamy,* v. STAIN. डाग *m.* कलंक *m.* काळवटी *f.* काळवण *f.* काळें *n.* लांच्छन *n.* नांव *n.* नाम *m.* टपका *m.*

To STIGMATIZE, *v.a. set a mark of infamy on; brand.* डाग *m.*-कलंक *m.*-लांच्छन *n.*-&c. लावणें, टपका *m.* ठेवणें, नांव *n.*-नाम *n.* ठेवणें, दाढीस कांदे *m. pl.* बांधणें, निंब *m.* लावणें-ठेवणें-देणें.

STILE, *n.* (for crossing a fence, &c.) आंगर *n.* फांकटा *n.* बेंळें *n.*

2 (of a dial). शंकु *m.*

STILETTO, *n.* v. DAGGER. जंब्या *m.*

To STILL, *v. a. stop the noise of,* v. To SILENCE. चुप-उगा-&c. करणें, बोलणें *n.*-शब्द *m.*-ध्वनि *m.*-&c. बंद करणें, उगा-&c. राहविणें.

2 *stop the motion of,* v. To STOP. स्थिरावणें, स्थिर-निश्चल-&c. करणें, थीरथावर *n.*-&c. करणें *g. of o.*

3 *calm, quiet, &c.* v. To COMPOSE. संतावणें *or* संथावणें, शमविणें, शांत-थंडा-&c. करणें, शमन *n.*-शांति *f.*-&c. करणें *g. of o.*

STILL, *a. having no noise, undisturbed by noise, silent.* निवांत, निश्शब्द, निरव, सामसुमीचा, गलबलीवांचूनचा.

2 *not windy,* v. CALM. निर्वात.

3—a place; *quiet, undisturbed.* निवांत, निरुपद्रव, निष्कंटक.

4 *motionless.* स्थिर, निश्चल, अचल.

STILL, *adv. till now.* अजून *or* अझून, आजपर्यंत, आजपावेतों, आजवर, अद्याप, अद्यापि, अद्ययावत् *pop.* अद्यावत्.

2 *nevertheless.* तरी, तथापि, तत्रापि, तदपि, एतावता.

3 *in increasng degree.* अणखी.

4 *silently.* उगा *decl.* उगामुगा *decl.* गुपचीप *or* चूप, गप्प, चिप्प, चप *or* चप्प, चुप्प, घम, निमूट, मट *or* मट्ट *or* मुट्ट, सुमसाम *or* सामसूम, तूष्णीम्.

5 *without moving, quietly.* निश्चल *pop.* निश्चळ *and* निचळ, निवांत, अचळ, हालल्यावांचून, देवासारखा *decl.* उगा *decl.* जिता कीं मेला *decl.*

STILL, *n. alembic.* भबकारा *m.* अधोयंत्र *n.* दारू-अर्क-&c. काढण्याचें यंत्र *n.*

STILL-BORN, *a.* पोटांत मेलेला, पोटमेला, मरून निघालेला, मृतजात.

STILLNESS, *n.* v. A. 1. सामसूम *or* सुमसाम *f. n.* निवांतपणा *m.* शब्दाभाव *m.* निःशब्दता *f.*

2 निर्वातपणा *m.* निवांतपणा *m.* वाताभाव *m.*

3 निवांतपणा *m.* उपद्रवराहित्य *n.* &c.

STILT, *n.*—for walking. घोडा *m.* घोडेकाठी *f.*

STIMULANT, *a.*—in medicine. चेतना आणणारा, चेतनावर्द्धक, चेतनाप्रद, चेतनोत्तेजक, उद्बोधक in comp. दीपक in comp. इंद्रियबोधन.

STIMULANT, *n.* चेतनावर्द्धक औषध *n.*-&c.

To STIMULATE, *v. a. rouse to action,* v. To EXCITE. चेतवणें, उत्तेजन *n.*-उद्दीपन *n.*-दीपन *n.*-&c. करणें *g. of o.*

2—in medicine. चेतना *f.* आणणें-वाढवणें, चेतनावर्द्धन *n.*-चेतनावृद्धि *f.*-&c. करणें *g. of o.*

STIMULATED, *p.* v. V. 1. चेतवलेला, &c. उत्तेजित, उद्दीपित, दीपित, तेजित, प्रोत्साहित.

STIMULATER, *n.* STIMULATING, *p. a.* v. V. 1. चेतवणारा, उत्तेजक, उद्दीपक, दीपक, उत्तेजन-&c. कर्ता-कारी-&c. प्रोत्साहक.

2 See STIMULANT.

STIMULATION, *n.* v. V. 1.—*act.* चेतवणें *n.* उत्तेजन *n.* उद्दीपन *n.* दीपन *n.* प्रोत्साहन *n.*

2 चेतनावर्द्धन *n.* चेतनावृद्धि *f.*

STIMULUS, *n. something that rouses to action.* उत्तेजन *n.* उद्दीपन *n.*

To STING, *v. a. pierce with a sting.* डंखणें, डसणें, चावणें, नांगी *f.*-&c. मारणें, दंश *pop.* डंश *or* डंख *m.* करणें-मारणें, दंशन *n.* करणें —fiercely and eagerly, as musquitoes, gnats, &c. चणचण-चणचणा-&c. तोडणें. See under To BITE.

2—as conscience, &c. खुपणें, चुरचूर *m. f.*-खवखव *f.*-&c. लागणें *in. con.*

3—as speech, v. To BITE. झोंबणें, झळंबणें, चुरचुरणें, खाणें.

4—as peppers, &c. मिरमिरणें, खवखवणें, खवणें, खाजणें.

5—a scorpion. फणकावणें, ठणकावणें, झणकार *or* रा *m.* मारणें.

STING, *n.* (of animals). नांगी *f.* कांटा *m.* नांगा *m.* नांगाडा *m.* नांगडा *m.* आंकडा *m.* [दंशन *n.*

2 *the thrust of a sting into the flesh.* डंख *m.* डंश *m.* दंश *m.*

The burning from a scorpion's s. फणका *m.* फणकारा *m.* फणफण *f. intens.* फणफणाट *m.* झणका *m. intens.* झणझणाट *m.*

3 fig. *point, wit.* दंश *m.* नोक *f.* मखी *f.* खोंच *f.* मर्म *n.* रहस्य *n.* खुबी *f.* छप्प *n.*

STINGER, *n.* STINGING, *p. a.* v. V. 1. डसणारा, डंखणारा, दंशकरणारा, &c. दंशक, दंश-दंशन कर्त्ता-कारी.

3 झोंबणारा, &c. मर्मी, मार्मिक.

4 खाजणारा, &c. खाजरा, खरमरीत.

STINGILY, *adv.* v. A. कृपणपणानें, किरटेपणानें, &c. कृपणबुद्धीनें, कृपणदृष्टीनें, कार्पण्यपूर्वक.

STINGINESS, *n.* v. A. कृपणपणा *m.* किरटेपणा *m.* &c. कार्पण्य *n.* कृपणत्व *n.*

STINGY, *a. close, niggardly,* v. MISERLY. कृपण, केड, केवटा, किरटा, हिमटा, हातचा जड, अवेच, कद्रू.

To STINK, *v. n. emit a bad smell.* घाण *f.*-वास *m.*-&c. येणें-मारणें *g. of s.* वास *m.* मारणें, घाणवणें, घाणणें, वासटणें, वासट-&c. असणें.

STINK, *n. bad smell.* घाण *f.* दुर्गंध *m.* दुर्गंधी *f.* गंधी *f.* कुवास *m.* बदबोई *or* य *f.* पूतिवात *m.* पूतिगंध *m.*

Intense or exceeding s. दुर्घाण *f.* अत्यघाण *f.* उग्रघाण *f.* दरवळ *m.* ओरढाण *or* वरढाण *f.* दर्प *m.* दर्पटाण *or* दर्पष्टाण *f.*

STINKARD, STINKPOT, *n. dirty, stinking fellow.* घाण *f.* घाण्या, हगरा, खुदरापादरा.

STINKER, *n.* STINKING, *p. a.* v. V. घाण आलेला, वास मारणारा, &c. घाणेरडा, घाणेरा, घाणेल *or* ला, घाणट, वासट, वासेळा *or* वाशेळा, वासाळ, वाशेरा, वासकट, वासका, दुर्गंधी.

To STINT, *v. a. limit, restrict.* मोतादीवर-परिमिताबर-प्रमाणावर-&c. राखणें-ठेवणें, मोतादीचा-मेजला *or* मोजला-मोजलेला-&c. देणें, मोताद *f.*-मर्यादा *f.*-&c. करणें-ठेवणें, आळा *m.*-आळाबांधा *m.*-&c. करून देणें-घालणें.

2 (the belly). पोट *n.* बांधणें-मारणें, उपास *m.* पाडणें-घालणें, पोटमारा *m.*-उपासमार *m.*-उपासमारा *m.*-&c. करणें, फांकि *m. pl.* पाडणें.

STINT, *n. limitation, restriction.* मोताद *f.* इयत्ता *f.* आळा *m.* आळाबांधा *m.* मर्यादा *f.* मोजमाप *n.*

2 *quantity assigned or allowed,* v. ALLOWANCE. मोताद *f.*

STINTED, *p.* v. V. 1. मोतादीवर राखलेला, मेजलादिल्हेला, आळा-घातलेला, &c.

2 पोट बांधलेला, &c.

STINTER, *n.* STINTING, *p. a.* v. V. 1. मोतादीवर राखणारा, मेजलादेणारा, मर्यादा ठेवणारा, &c.

2 पोट बांधणारा, &c. [&c.

STINTING, *n.* v. V. 1.—*act.* मोतादीवर राखणें *n.* मेजला देणें *n.*

2 पोट बांधणें *n.* &c. उपासमार *m.* उपासमारा *m.*

STIPEND, *n. settled compensation for service,* v. PAY, WAGES. नेमणूक *f.* तैनात *f.* वेतन *n.* मुशारा *or* मुशाहिरा *m.* पगार *m.*

STIPENDIARY, *n. one who receives a stipend.* वेतनी, वेतन्या, तैनाती, तैनात्या, मुशारखोर, मुशाऱ्या, पगारी, वेतनग्राही.

Roll of stipendiaries. तैनातजाबता *m.*

To STIPULATE, *v.n. make agreement or covenant,* v. To AGREE. बोली *f.*-करार *m.*-ठराव *m.*-संकेत *m.*-पण *m.*-&c. करणें.

STIPULATED, *p.* v. V. बोली केलेला, &c. बोलीचा, संकेतित, पणित, प्रतिज्ञात, सामयिक.

STIPULATER, *n.* STIPULATING, *p. a.* v. V. बोली-&c. करणारा, संकेत-&c. कर्त्ता-कारी-&c.

STIPULATION, *n.* v. V.—*act.* बोली करणें *n.* ठराव करणें *n.* &c.

I. *agreement made,* v. AGREEMENT. बोली *f.* वायदा *m.* करार *m.* संकेत *m.*

To STIR, *v. a.* v. To MOVE, हालवणें, चालवणें, सारणें, सरवणें.

2 about or up;—as to mix or separate. कालवणें, ढवळणें, घाटणें, घोळणें, कचंबणें *or* कचमणें, आलोडणें *or* आलोढणें.

Instrument (stick, spoon, &c.) of stirring about. घाटणा *m.* घाटणें *n.* ढवळणा *m.*

Matter (grain, &c.) to be stirred about. घाटण *n.*

Stick with a cloth at the end to s. grain in parching. घोळणा *m.* घोळणें *n.*

3 up; *instigate,* v. To EXCITE, To INCITE. चेतवणें, चेष्टवणें, खाजवणें, उत्तेजन *n.*-&c. करणें *g. of o.*

To STIR, *v. n.*v. To MOVE. हलणें *or* हालणें, सरकणें, सरणें, हटणें, चालणें, हलचाल *f.* करणें, चिडमिडणें, चिडमीड *adv.* करणें, हिचमिचणें *neg. con.* ढिम *f.* करणें-खाणें *neg.con.* फिरकणें.

2 *be in motion, be acting.* चालणें, खेळणें, चालता-&c. असणें-होणें. [*f.* हडबड *f.*

STIR, *n.* v. BUSTLE, TUMULT. गडबड *f.* हूल *f.* हलचाल *f.* धामधूम

STIR-ABOUT, *n.*—the dish. घाट *f.* घाटलें *n.* घाटा *m.* घाटण *n.*

STIRRED, *p.* v. V. A. 1. हालवलेला, चालवलेला.

2 कालवलेला, ढवळलेला, &c. आलोडित.

3 चेतवलेला, चेष्टवलेला, &c. उत्तेजित. [&c.

STIRRER, *n.* STIRRING, *p. a.* v. V.A. 1. हालवणारा, चालवणारा,

2 कालवणारा, ढवळणारा, &c.

3 चेतवणारा, &c. उत्तेजन-&c. कर्त्ता-कारी-&c.

v. V. N. 1. हालणारा, सरकणारा, &c.

2 चालणारा, खेळणारा, &c. चालता, चालू, चेष्टित.

STIRRING, *n.* v. V. A. 1.—*act.* हालवणें *n.* &c.

2 कालवणें *n.* ढवळणें *n.* घाटणें *n.* घाटण *n.* &c. आलोडन *n.*

Hurried or violent s. about. घाटाघाट *f.*

3 चेतवणें *n.* &c. उत्तेजन *n.* चेष्टा *f.*

v. V. N. 1. हालणें *n.* सरकणें *n.*&c. हलचाल *f.* चलनवलन *pop.* चळणवळण *n.* हालडोल *f.*

STIRRUP, *n. iron ring for a rider's foot.* रिकीब *f.* रिकीबी *or* रिकेबी *f.* (*or* रिकाब & रिकाबी).

STIRRUP-LEATHER, *n.* रिकीबदाल *or* रिकाबदाल *m.f.* रिकीबवादी *f.*

To STITCH, *v. a. sew slightly,* v. To SEW. टाचणें, टाचा *or* टाका *m.* मारणें, हिलगणें.

STITCH, *n. pass of the needle.* टाका *m.* टाचा *m.*

Double s. टीपदोरा *m.* [दोरा *m.*

Running s. उभादोरा *m.* धावनादोरा *m.* धावदोरा *m.* धावरा

2 *sharp pain in the side, &c.* हूक *f.* कचक *f.* उसण *f.* पार्श्वशूल *m.*

STOCCADE, STOCKADE, *n. barrier made with stakes.* मेढेकोट *m.* लकडकोट *m.* [खोड *n.* खोट *m.*

STOCK, *n. main body of a tree, &c.* v. TRUNK. कांड *n.* कांडें *n.*

A s. with grafts or scions. इसाड *n.* इसाडा *m.*

2 *stub, &c.* v. STUMP. खुंट *m. n.* खुंटामा *m.* खरांटा *m.*थुंठण *n.*

3 v. HAFT, HANDLE. दांडा *m.* बुंध *n.* बुंधा *m.*

4 (of a musket). दस्ता *m.* कुंदा *m.*

5 *house, race,* v. FAMILY. घराणा *m.* घराणें *n.* वंश *m.* खानदान *m.* आदि *m.*

6 *capital, principal, fund.* पुंजी *f.* गांठोडें *n.*भांडवल *or* भांडोल *n.* मुद्दल *n.* बिसात *or* द *f.* गठडें *n.* गड्डा *m.* ऐपत *f.* जड *f.* मूल *n.* मूलद्रव्य *n.* मूलधन *n.* धनमूल *n.*माया *f.* नीवी *f.* केवा*m.*

Private s. घरभांडवल *n.* गांठचा *or* पदरचा पैसा *m.*

Scanty or small s. तुटपुंजी *f.*

Trader upon private s. घरभांडवली.

To break in or live upon one's s. पदर*m.* खचणें-खाणें-मोडणें, पदरमोड *f.* करणें.

7 *store, mass laid up.* बेगमी *or* बेजमी *f.* केवा *m.* जोड *f.* साटपा *m.* संचय *m.* संजोग*m.*भांडवल *or* भांडोल*n.* उपराळा*m.* बरव*f.*

Common s. गणद्रव्य *n.* गणान्न *n.*

To go to the s. राशीपुंजीस येणें.

8 stocks;—for the legs. खोडा *m.*

9 *wealth in cattle.* गोधन*n.* चर्मधन*n.* पशुसंपत्ति *f.* जीवधन*n.* गुरें ढोरें *n. pl.*

10 *breed.* ताणा *m.* बिजवट *n.* [णीचा.

Of a good s.—a horned beast. धळीचा *or* धडीचा, सा-

11 सरकारास कर्जी दिलेला पैसा *m.*

To STOCK. See To STORE.

To STOCKADE, *v. n.* मेढेकोट *m.*-लकडकोट *m.* करणें.

STOCKING. *n.* पायाचा मोजा*m.* पादत्राण *n.* पादरक्षा *f.*

STOCK-STILL, *adv.* गपचीप *or* चूप, गप्पचीप *or* चूप, काष्ठवत्.

To sit s. देवासारखा-धोंड्यासारखा-चित्रासारखा-नंदीसारखा-&c. बसणें.

STOIC, STOICAL, *a. that affects freedom from passion, and indifference to pain or pleasure.* निर्मम, उदास, उदासी, उदासीन, कामक्रोधाद्यनधीन, सुखदुःखाद्यनधीन, इंद्रियासंगी, इंद्रियानधीन, कामावसायी.

STOICALNESS, STOICISM, *n. freedom from passion, indifference to pain or pleasure.* शमm. इंद्रियशमm. इंद्रियासंगm. कामावसाय m. कामावसायिताf. औदास्य n. औदासीन्य n. कामक्रोधाद्यनधीनताf. सुखदुःखाद्यनधीनताf.

STOLE. See ROBE.

STOLEN, *p.* v. V. A. चोरून नेलेला, &c. चोरींव, चोरीचा.

STOLID, STOLIDITY. See STUPID, STUPIDITY.

STOMACH, *n.*—in anatomy. कोठा m. कोष्ठn. पोटn. जठरn. अंतर्जठर n. अन्नकोश m. अन्नाशय m. पक्वाशय m. आमाशय m.

Clearing or clearedness of s. and bowels. कोष्ठशुद्धिf.

Pit of the s. मणिपूर n.

Weight in the s. (as of food). दबका m.

With or upon an empty s. रिकाम्या पोटीं, अनशवे or अनशिळे or अनशे पोटीं.

To stay on the s. जिरमाणीं-जिरमाणीस-जिरणीं पडणें.

A full s. loathes the honeycomb. भरले पोटा उंचर कडू. [दर्प m.

2 *swelling, &c.* v. PRIDE. जळ m. खुमखुम f. ताठा m. रग f.

To bring down the proud s. of. रेंचm. मोडणें or उतरणें.

3 See APPETITE.

To STOMACH, *v. a. swallow indignantly,* fig. v. To BEAR. पोटीं घालणें, गिळणें, पिणें, पिऊन जाणें, जिरवणें.

To be stomached. जिरणें, खमणें, पचणें.

STOMACHIC, *a. of or belonging to the stomach.* कोठ्याचा, कोठ्याकडचा, &c. अन्नकोशसंबंधी-विषयक, &c. जाठर.

2 *strengthening the stomach,* v. TONIC. रोचक, रुचक, अग्निवर्द्धक, अग्न्युत्तेजक, पाचक.

STOMACHIC, *n.*—the medicine. रोचकm. रोचकौषध n. दीपनn.

STONE, *n.* दगडm. धोंडा m. पाषाण m. शिला or ळा f. खडाm. पत्थर m. अश्माm. प्रस्तर m. पर्वतफल n.

Black s. or rock. काळेथरदगडm. काळेथरधोंडा m.

Building of hewn s. चिरेबंदी f.

Efflorescence (through moisture) from s. दगडफूल n.

Hewn and shaped s. चिरा m.

Huge s. or mass of s. धोंड f. दगड f. रेप f.

Large, flat, smooth s. to wash clothes on, to sit on in ablutions, to bruise pepper, &c. on. पाथर f. *dim.* पाथरी f.

Philosopher's s. परीस m.

Pile of stones. खिळा m.

Precious s. रत्न n. मणि or मणी m.

Rocking s. *stone so set as easily to turn over.* उलटादगड m. उलटकर दगड m.

Round, rolling s. गडगडाधोंडाm. गुंडाm.

Smooth, roundish s. गोटाm. गोटी f.

S. for grinding knives, &c. *whetstone.* सहाणf. निशाणा m. निष्णाm.

S. for grinding condiments, &c. शिळ f. शिला or ळा f. शिळापट्टm. पाटाm. सहाण f.

S. smoothed on one side. तोड f. फाड f.

S.-vessel. S.-trough, &c. दगडी f. दगडतळी f.

Striking of the foot against a s. ठेच or ठेंच f. v. लाग.

Thin and flat piece of s. चीप f. *dim.* चिपोळीf. फरशी f.

To leave no s. unturned. दगडावर दगड or धोंड्यावर धोंडा-&c. घालून करणें, चहुंकडे दगडm. टाकून पाहणें.

To melt a s. दगडास पाझरm. आणणें.

2 *concretion in the kidney or bladder.* मुतखडाm. अश्मरीf. सिकताf.

3 (of fruits). अठळी f. आंठीळ f. अठोळी f. अठी f. गोळाm. अष्ठि f.—of the mango. कोय f. बांठ f. बांठाm. *dim.* बांठी f.

4 v. TESTICLE. अंड n. *pop.* आंडm. कोय f.

STONE, *a.* See STONY. 2 *having testicles.* अंडील or अंडेल.

STONE, *adv. stark, utterly, &c.* v. WHOLLY. निपट, निखालस.

To STONE, *v. a. pelt with stones.* धोंडेm. *pl.*-दगडm. *pl.* मारणें, धोंडेमारm.-दगडमारm. करणें, पाषाणप्रक्षेपm.-&c. करणें.

2(fruit) *free from stones.* अटळ्या f. *pl.*-&c. काढणें.

STONE-BLIND, *a.* निपट आंधळा.

STONE-CUTTER, STONE-BREAKER, STONE-SPLITTER, STONE-WORKER, *n.* धोंडफोड्या, पाथरफोड, पाथरफोड्या, पाथरवट, पाथरट, टंकारी, सुंमेकरी, अश्मदारक.

Chisel of a s. टंकm. टांकी f.

Splitting implement of a s. सुतकी f. सुंबा or सुंभाm. ढोंकण f. n.

STONE-CUTTING, STONE-BREAKING, &c. *n.* दगडफोडणेंn. दगडफोडणी f. पाथरवटकामn. अश्मदारणn.

STONE-DIGGER, *n.* बेलदार.

STONE-FRUIT, *n.* अठळीचें-&c. फळn.

STONE-HEARTED, *a.* v. CRUEL. पाषाणहृदय.

STONE-HORSE, *n. stallion.* वळूm. सुरूm. अंडील or अंडेल घोडाm.

STONE-PECKER, *n.*—the bird. पाथरफोडm. पाथरवट or पाथरटm.

STONE-PIT, STONE-QUARRY, *n.* दगडखाण or णी f. चिरेखाण f.

STONE'S-CAST, STONE'S-THROW, *n.* हातधोंडा m. हातगुंडा m. धोंड्याचा-&c. टप्पाm.

STONE-TROUGH, *n.* दगडी f.

STONE-WORK, *n.* चिरेबंदीf. फरसबंदीf. चिरेबंदीचें-फरसबंदीचेंकामn.

STONINESS, *n.* v. A. 2. धोंडाळपणाm. दगडाळपणाm. &c.

STONY, *a. made of stone.* दगडाचा, &c. दगडी, पाषाणी, पाषाणमय, अश्ममय, अश्मर, आश्म, आश्मन, प्रस्तरमय.

2 *abounding with stones.* धोंडाळ, धोंडगळ, दगडाळ, खडकळ, खडकील, खडकूत, खडाळ, दगडमय, पाषाणमय, पाषाणप्रचुर.

S. and sterile,—land. खरडबरड.

3 *resembling stone,* lit. fig. पाषाणवत्, पाषाण (in comp.).

STOOL, *n. seat without a back.* पाटm. चौकी f. पिढेंn. पीठn. मोडाm. चवई f. तिवई f. These words express varieties.

Small s. पिढलेंn. बाजवटn.

Square s. चौरंगm.

S. with handle. दांडेपाटm.

S. from which to winnow corn. बावडी f.

Between two stools one falls to the ground. दोहोंघरचा पाहुणा (or दुसगीचा पाहुणा) उपासी मरे.

2—in medicine; *motion,* v. PURGE. ढाळm. झाडाm.

Loose s. v. PURGE. बुळकांडीf. बुळकीf. भसरेंn. रेचनn. रेचm.

Scanty & sudden s. पिळकी *f.*

To have a sudden & scanty s. पिळकणें, पुरकणें, चिरकणें, चिरपणें, चिरपिटणें, चिरपुटणें.

To have sudden & loose stools. बुळकणें.

To STOOP, *v. n. bend.* लवणें, ओणवणें *or* वणवणें, वणावणें, नमणें, झुकणें, ओणवा-&c. होणें, कोंक *n.*-पोंक *n.*-&c. वळणें *g. of s.*

To s. in one's walk. ओणव्यानें चालणें.

2 *submit,* v. To YIELD. वांकणें, लवणें, नमणें, दबणें, वश-&c. होणें, हार जाणें, हार *f.* घेणें.

3 *descend from dignity, &c.* v. To CONDESCEND. नम्रता*f.*-लीनता *f.*-विनय *m.*-&c. धरणें-धरून वागणें.

4—a bird. झेंपावणें, झडपणें, झडप *f.*-झेंप *f.*-झपेट *f.*-झपाटा *m.*-झड *f.*-&c. घालणें.

STOOP, STOOPING, *n.* v. V. 1. लवणें *n.* ओणवणें *n.* &c.

4 झडप *f.* झेंप *f.* झांप *f.* झपेट *f.* झपाटा *m.* झड *f.*

STOOPER, *n.* STOOPING, *p. a.* v. V. 1. लवणारा, ओणवणारा,&c. ओणवा *or* वणवा, नतांग.

Stooping posture. ओणव *f.*

2 वांकणारा, लवणारा, वश होणारा, &c.

3 नम्रता धरणारा, &c.

To STOP, *v. a. make to stand or be still.* उभा करणें, थांबवणें, थोपवणें, राहविणें, खडकावणें, स्थिरावणें, थिरावणें, खोळंबवणें, उभविणें, थोकणें, रोकणें, गतिस्तंभ *m.*-गतिभंग *m.*-गतिरोध *m.*-&c. करणें *g. of o.*

2 *arrest in progress, hinder, impede, prevent.* अटकावणें, अटकवणें, अडथळणें, अडकवणें, अडवणें, खुंटवणें, रोकणें, अवरोधणें, रोधणें, अटकाव *m.*-अडथळा *m.*-अवरोध *m.*-गतिरोध *m.*-प्रतिबंध *m.*-&c. करणें *g. of o.* गळचिपी *f.* धरणें *or* आवळणें, गळचंडी *f.* धरणें, गळचुटी *f.* धरणें, मोडती *f.*-मोडा *m.*-&c. घालणें, मेखलणें, मेख*f.* मारणें, पाचर *f.* मारणें (कामांत *or* कार्यांत,&c.).

3 (a road, &c.) *render impassable.* बंद करणें, मारणें, पाडणें, रोधणें, अवरोधणें, रोध *m.*-अवरोध *m.*-&c. करणें *g. of o.*

4 (an aperture, &c.) *fill or close up.* बंद करणें, बुजणें *or* बुझणें, बुझवणें, मुंदणें *or* मुंधणें, कोंदणें.

5 v. To SUSPEND. तकूब-महकूब-&c. करणें, तकुबी *f.*-महकुबी *f.*-&c. करणें *g. of o.*

To STOP, *v. n. stand still, pause, &c.* उभा होणें-राहणें-ठाकणें, थांबणें, थडकणें, थोकणें, थोपणें, खेटणें, खोळंबणें, विसवणें *or* विसावणें, उपरमणें, विरमणें, राहणें, पडणें, बंद होणें-पडणें, चालणें *n.*-&c. बंद होणें *g. of s.* स्तब्धणें, स्थिरावणें, खडकणें, खळणें.

To s. a little. अवकाश *m.* धरणें, उशीर *m.* धरणें.

To s. at through striking against. ठेपणें, ठेपलणें, ठेप *f.* बसणें *in. con.*

2 *desist, leave off, give over, &c.* v. To CEASE. राहणें, पुरेबस *adv.* करणें, थांबणें, सोडणें, अटपणें, हात *m.* काढणें-अटोपणें.

3 at; *alight, stay.* राहणें, उतरणें, बिऱ्हाड *n.* करणें.

4 for; *tarry or wait for.* खोळंबणें, स्थिरणें, थिरणें, थांबणें, वाट *f.* पाहणें, तटणें.

STOP, STOPPING, STOPPAGE, *n.* v. V.N. 1.—*state.* उभा होणें*n.* उभा राहणें *n.* &c. उपरति *f.* उपरम *m.* गतिभ्रंश *m.* गतिस्तंभ *m.* अवसान *n.* थोप *f.* उपराम *m.* विराम *m.* विरति *f.* निवृत्ति *f.* खळब *m.* खळ *m.* मुकाम *m.* ठेप *f.* अचाल *f.*

With stops and pauses. राहूनराहून.

Without s. or pausing. चढ्या घोड्यानिशीं.

4—*state.* खोळंबा *m.* खोटी *f.*

v. V. A. 1.—*act.* उभा करणें *n.* थांबवणें *n.* &c. गतिस्तंभन *n.* स्तंभन *n.*—*a. or s.* गतिभंग *m.* गतिस्तंभ *m.* स्तंभ *m.* गतिरोध *m.* गत्यवरोध *m.*

2—*act.* अटकावणें *n.* अडथळणें *n.* अवरोधणें *n.* अडवणूक *f.* —*a. or s.* अवरोध *m.* प्रतिबंध *m.* प्रतिष्टंभ *m.* अवष्टंभ *m.* विष्टंभ *m.* व्याघात *m.* वेगाघात *m.*—*state.* मोडती *f.* मोडा *m.* अटकाव *or* वा *m.* अटक *f.* अडथळा *m.* बंदी *f.* कुंठीभाव *m.* खोटी *f.* गुंता *or* गुना *m.*

4—*act.* बंद करणें *n.* बुझणें *n.* &c.

I. *cessation, end.* अवसान *n.* संस्था *f.*

II.—in music, &c. *rest* यति *f.* अवसान *n.* विराम*m.* थाक *f.*

III.—in punctuation. अवसानाची खूण *f.* विरामचिन्ह *n.* विश्रामचिन्ह *n.* अवसानचिन्ह*n.*

IV. *stopping cause, an obstruction, &c.* v. HINDERANCE. मोडती *f.* मोडा *m.* अडकण *n.* अडकवण *n.*

To put a s. to, v. To STOP. बंद करणें, बंदी *f.*-प्रतिबंध*m.*-&c. करणें *g. of. o.*

STOPPED, *p.* v. V.A. 1. उभा केलेला, थांबवलेला, &c. निवृत्त, स्तब्ध, स्तंभित, नष्टगति, स्तब्धगति, रुद्धगति.

2 अटकावलेला, अडवलेला, &c. खोटी, कुंठित, स्तंभित, स्तब्ध, नष्टगति, रुद्धगति, अवरुद्ध, बंद.

To be s. बंद होणें-पडणें, कुंठणें, खुडकणें, खळणें, अटकणें, अडकणें, थबकणें, ठेपणें, मेख *f.* बसणें *in. con.*

3 बंद केलेला, &c. बंद, रुद्ध, अवरुद्ध.

4 बंद केलेला, बुझवलेला, &c. बंद, रुद्ध.

To be s. बुजणें *or* बुझणें, चोंदणें.

5 तकूब केलेला, &c. तकूब, महकूब.

STOPPER, *n.* STOPPING, *p. a.*v. V. A.1. उभा करणारा, थांबवणारा, थोपवणारा, &c. गतिरोधक, गतिस्तंभक, गतिभंजक, गतिरोध-&c. कर्त्ता-कारी-&c.

2 अटकावणारा, अडथळणारा, अडवणारा, अवरोधणारा, &c. अवरोधक, रोधक, प्रतिरोधक,प्रतिबंधक,अवरोध-&c. कर्त्ता-कारी-&c.

I. See STOPPLE.

STOPPLE, *n. that which stops or closes the mouth of a vessel, &c.* v. PLUG. दट्टा *m.* चोंदी *f.* बूज *m.* बुचू *or* बुजू *m.* बूच *m.* बुटणें *n.* गुडदी *f.* बोकणा *or* ना *m.*

STORAX, *n. styrax officinale.* शिलाकुसुम *n.* शिलापुष्प *n.* शिलारस *or* शिलोद्भव *m.*

STORE, *n. stock, hoard.* सांठ *m.* सांठा *m.* सांठपा *m.* संग्रह *m.* संचय *m.* केवा *m.* डबुलकें *or* गें *n.* डबुलें *or* डचोळें *n.* बेगमी *or* बेजमी *f.* भरणा *m.* भांडवल *or* भांडोल *n.* दास्तान *n.*

Hidden s. ठेव *f.* ठेवा *m.* ठेवणें *n.*—compreh. indef. &c. ठेवारेवा *m.* ठेवरेव *f.*

In s. सांठ्यास, संग्रहास, संग्रहीं, गांठीं, पदरीं.

2 *plentiful state,* v. ABUNDANCE, EXUBERANCE. चेळ *f.* ठेल *f.* समृद्धि *f.* बरू *or* बरव *f.*

3 v. STORE-HOUSE. वखार *f.* सांठवण *n.*

4 stores. सामान *n.* साहित्य *n.* सामग्री *f.*

To STORE, *v. a. fill, furnish, stock.* पुरवणें, संजोग *m.*-भरणा*m.* -सांठा *m.*-संग्रह *m.*-बेजमी *f.*-&c. करणें-करून ठेवणें, संपन्न-विशिष्ट-&c. करणें.

2 *lay up, hoard.* सांठवणें, सांचवणें, सांठवण *n.*-सांठवणी *f.*-संचय *m.*-संग्रह *m.*-&c. करणें *g. of o.* जोडणें, जोड *f.* मिळवणें-संपादणें-जोडणें *g. of o.*

3 *reposit in a store-house.* कोठींत-वखारींत-&c. ठेवणें.

STORE-HOUSE, STORE-ROOM, *n.* कोठा *m.* कोठी *f.* कोठार *n.* कोठारी *f.* जिन्नसखाना *m.* वखार *f.* सांठवण *n.* दास्तान *n.*

STORE-HOUSE-KEEPER, *n.* कोठनीस, वखारदार, वखारी, दास्तानदार, कोष्ठपाल.

STORED, *p.* v. V. 1. बेजमी केलेला, &c. संपन्न, विशिष्ट.

2 सांठवलेला, &c. संचित, संगृहीत.

3 कोठींत ठेवलेला, &c. कोशभूत.

STORER, *n.* STORING, *p. a.* v. V. 1. संजोग करणारा, बेजमी करणारा, &c.

2 सांठवणारा, संग्रह करणारा, &c.

3 कोठींत ठेवणारा, &c.

STORK. See CRANE.

STORM, *n.* *tempest.* वादळ *n. m.* वावदळ *n.* तुफान *n.* अंधी *f.* अवात *m.* जवळ *n.* वात्या *f.* वातूल *m.* चंडवात *m.* अतिवात *m.*—esp. with rain, वाऱ्याचा पाऊस *m.* झंझावात *m.* झंझानिल *m.* वाऱ्यापावसाची गर्दी *f.*

Roar and rattle of a s. वाजणेंगाजणें *n.*

To be s.-struck,—tree, &c. वादळणें.

2 *assault upon a fort,* v. ATTACK. हल्ला *m.* किल्ल्याबर छापा *m.*

3 See TUMULT. [घेणें.

To STORM, *v. a.* (a fort.). हल्ला *m.* करणें *with* वर *of o.* हल्लाकरून

To STORM, *v. n.* *bellow in anger,* v. To RAGE. कडकडणें, कडकणें, कडकावणें, जळफळणें, वादळणें, धडफडणें, खवतळणें *or* ताळणें, आदळआपट *f.* करणें, दणकावणें, दणदणणें, फुफावणें, दराडणें, वरदळणें.

STORMINESS, *n.* v. A. जौळीपणा *m.* &c. उमाड *f.* अतिवातवैशिष्ट्य *n.* प्रचंडवातवैशिष्ट्य *n.* वृष्टिवातवैशिष्ट्य *n.*

STORMY, *a.* *tempestuous.* वादळाचा, तुफानाचा, वारेवावधानाचा, वारेवावटळीचा, जवळी *or* जौळी, अतिवातविशिष्ट, अतिवातमय, अतिवातात्मक, वृष्टिवातात्मक.

STORY, *n.* *floor, stage.* ताल *or* ताळ *m.* मजला *m.* खण *m.*

The *first story* is, भूमिखण *m.* भूमिखणी *f.* पहिला *or* खालचा मजला *m.*—the *second,* दुसरा *or* मधला मजला *m.*—the *third,* उपरमाडी *f.* उपरखणी *f.*—and *an upper story,* gener. माडी *f.* माळी *f.* मजला *m.*

Of one s. एकमजला *or* ली,—of two, दुमजला *or* ली,—of three, तिमजला *or* ली, तिताली,—of four, चौमजला *or* ली, चौताली, चौखणी.

Of fourteen stories high, i. e. very high. चौदाताल *or* ळ.

That has stories. मजला, मजली (in comp. as एकमजला *or* ली, दुमजला *or* ली).

2 v. HISTORY. कथा *f.* किताबत *f.* वृत्तांत *m.*

Remaining only in s. कथाशेष.

3 *tale, narrative, fable.* कथा *f.* गोष्ट *f.* नकल *f.* कहाणी *f.* गोष्टमात *f.* कथानक *n.* आख्यान *n.* आख्यायिका *f.* उपाख्यान *n.* कथाप्रबंध *m.* गतक *n.*

Idle s. बात *f.* गप *f.* लोककथा *f.* दंतकथा *f.*

Long-winded s. भंडपुराण *n.* भारत *n.* रामायण *n.* लांबलेखाम. चऱ्हाट *n.* चरपटपंजरी *f.* चरकट *or* पट *n.* चर्पटिका *f.* बयाणा *or* ना *m.* तपसील *m.* ग्रंथ *m.* लापणिका *f.* गड्डालिका *f.* दीर्घसूत्र *n.* गतक *n.* तरडक *or* चरडक *n.* कोळ्याचें सूत *n.* हनमंताचें शेंपूट *n.* गाणें *n.*

To make a cock and bull s. सात पांच करणें.

To tell a long s. about. वासलात *f.* लावणें, गीत *n.* गाणें.

To tell idle stories. बाता *f. pl.* कुटणें-छाटणें-खबाळणें-मारणें-हाणणें.

4—as in excuse or explanation. तपसील *m.* बयाणा *or* ना *m.* बयाद *m.* बाबत *f.* v. सांग, लाव.

5 See FALSEHOOD, LIE.

STORY-TELLER, *n.* कथेकरी, वातखबात्या, बात्या, बात्यारा, गप्पी.

STOUT, *a.* *of large and strong make; robust, sturdy, lusty, strapping, &c.* मोठा *or* मोटा, धाटामोटा, मोटाधाटा, धट्टाकट्टा *or* खट्टा, कट्टा पट्टा, पठ्ठ्या, पठडा, घटमूट, घनकट *or* गट, दणगट, दांडधमकट, धमकट, गडदू *or* धू, कुप्पा, जाडगा, जाडा, जाड, ताठ, ताठर, तरणाबांड, जमदाडा *or* दाढा, धडाखडा, टणक, टणका, जोमदार, जोधा, जबर, बळकट, धब्बल, धबदूल, धोक, भक्कम, ऐवट, धक्कड, हडस, कलबूत, धष्ट, धष्टपुष्ट, मुसळा *or* ळ्या, रांकट, कटमस्त, घस्मर, जोरकस, लठ्ठ, लठ्ठा *or* लठ्ठ्या, लट्टू, लडदू *or* धू, लठुंगा, लोंठा *or* लोंठ्या, गलेलठ्ठ, वठ्ठ्या, गबदूल, गटुना *or* णा, दंडारणा, गचेंडा, अतुरबळी, अतुलबळी, दलदपट, बृहच्छरीर, बृहदंग. Some terms for *a stout, sturdy, strapping fellow,* bearing the implication of illiterateness, impudence, and overbearingness, and thus equivalent with *sturdy boor, burly brute, coal-heaver, &c. &c.* are लठ्ठाश्रम, लठ्ठेश्वर, लठ्ठभारती, लठ्ठनिरंजन, लठ्ठासिश्र, पोळ, कटमस्त, धटांगण, धटिंगण, दांडगेश्वर, मुसळकंद.

Rather s. जाडगेला, जाडसर, जाडेला.

2—of things; *strong, thick, &c.* बळकट, मजबूत, घटमूट, धोक, ऐवट, कणखर, सणसर, सणसणीत, कंडारणा, दंडारणा, भक्कम, धडवती, धणकट *or* गट, दणगट, दडस, दडदडीत, ढोसर, धटडा धोंगडा.

3 See BOLD.

STOUTNESS, *n.* v. A. 1. मोठेपणा *m.* मोटे धाटेपणा *m.* कट्टेपणा *m.* घटमूटपणा *m.* &c. जोम *m. n.* अंगबृहत्त्व *n.* शरीरबृहत्त्व *n.* अंगस्थौल्य *n.*

2 बळकटपणा *m.* मजबुतपणा *m.* कणखरपणा *m.* &c. बळकटी *f.* मजबुती *f.*

STOVE, *n.*—for cooking. चूल *f.*—contemptuously, चुलखंड *n.*

Hob of a s. अवेल *m. n.* वैल *m. n.*

Partition of the hob of a s. बहाल *n.*

Raised mass for stoves. चुलदान *n.*

2 *hole dug in the ground to hold fire.* थारोळें *n.* थाळी *f.* थाळ *f.*

3 *earthen enclosure for fire.* भट्टी *f.*

To STOW, *v. a.* *place or pack in proper place and order.* तजविजीनें-सोईनें-बंदोबस्तानें-&c. भरणें-ठेवणें-घालणें, जेथलातेथला *decl.*-&c. भरणें-ठेवणें-&c.

STOWAGE, STOWING, *n.* v. V.—*act.* तजविजीनें-&c. भरणें *n.* &c.

I. *room for stowing.* माल भरायाला जागा *f. m.*-सांठ *m.*-&c.

STOWED, *p.* v. V. सोईनें-&c. भरलेला, जेथलातेथला भरलेला, &c.

STOWER, *n.* STOWING, *p. a.* v. V. सोईनें-&c. भरणारा, जेथलातेथला भरणारा, &c.

STRABISM. See SQUINT.

To STRADDLE, *v. n.* *stand or walk with the legs apart.* टांगा *f. pl.*-पाय *m. pl.* फांकटणें-फांकणें-&c. फांकून चालणें, टांगा-&c.

फांकत चालणें, फेंगडा *decl.* चालणें, फांकटून उभा राहणें.

STRADDLER, *n.* STRADDLING, *p. a.* v. V. टांगा फांकलेला, टांगा फांकत चालणारा.

To STRAGGLE, *v. n. wander from the direct course or main body.* पांगून-फुटून-भटकून-इकडेतिकडे-रानोमाळ-&c. फिरणें-चालणें-होणें.

STRAGGLER, *n.* STRAGGLING, *p. a.*v.V. पांगून-फुटून-&c. चालणारा-चाललेला, फुटलेला, फुटकर, असंहत. [लेला.

I. *standing by itself.* सुटा, तुटक, अलग, फुटकर, फुटकळ, तुट-

STRAGGLINGLY, *adv.* v. V. फुटून, पांगून, भटकून, रानोमाळ.

STRAIGHT, *a. not crooked.* नीट, सरल or ळ, ऋजु *pop.* उजू, सुती, सूत्रक, सूत्रा, सूत्री, सम, धोपट, सरधोपट, धुदाट, शिधोट, सडक, दोरी सूत, धट or धट्ट, सरलयाची, अवक्र.

2 *fair, &c.* v. JUST. नीट, उजू, बरोबर, मार्गाचा, निटस.

STRAIGHT, STRAIGHTWAY, *adv. forthwith,* v. IMMEDIATELY. तसाच, तेव्हांच, लागलाच.

2 *directly, not turning aside.* थेट, नीट, तडक, धडक, अचानक, धट or ट्ट. [दाट.

STRAIGHT-FORWARD, *a.*—a road, &c. धोपट, सरधोपट, सडक, धु-

2 *open, plain, &c.* v. BLUNT. सरल or ळ, धोपटमार्ग्या, खणखणीत, खडखडीत, खसखसीत, सरधोपट, सडक, रहारास्त, सरलयाची.

S. speech or demeanour. उघडीमराठी *f.* ठसक्याचें भाषण *n.* ठसठसीत व्यवहार *m.* ठसक्याचा व्यवहार *m.* सडाकारभार *m.* उभा दांडा *m.* उभामार्ग *m.*

To STRAIGHTEN, *v. a. make straight.* नीट-सरळ-उजू-&c. करणें, वांकडेपणा *m.* मोडणें, ऋजुकरण *n.*-सरलीकरण *n.* करणें.

2 See To STRAITEN.

To STRAIGHTEN, *v. n. become straight.* निटावणें, नीट-सरल-उजू-&c. होणें-होतजाणें.

STRAIGHTNESS, *n.* v. A. 1. नीटपणा *m.* सरळपणा *m.* उजूपणा*m.* &c. निटाई *f.* निटावा *m.* निटोपा *m.* सारल्य *n.* सरलता *f.* ऋजुत्व *n* आर्जव *n.*

2 नीटपणा *m.* उजूपणा *m.* &c. निटोपा *m.* निटावा *m.*

To STRAIN, *v. a. squeeze through, filter.* गाळणें, गाळून काढणें, शोधणें *pop.* सोधणें, शोधून काढणें, चाळणें, खिरणें, छाननें, चाळण *f.*-गालन *n.*-&c. करणें *g. of o.* बेळणें.

Matter to be strained. गाळण *m.*

Strainings, *dirt separated.* गाळा *n.*

2 *injure by stretching,* v. To SPRAIN. कन्हारणें, विदगुडणें, लचक *f.*-&c. भरवणें, लचकविणें.

3 *draw tense, intend.* ताणणें, तणावा *m.*-ताण *m.* देणें-बसवणें, तणतणवणें, तणतणीत-&c. करणें.

4 *force beyond propriety.* ओढणें, ओढून-ओढूनताणून-खेचून-ताणूनखेचून-बळानें-&c. आणणें, बळ *n.*-&c. करणें.

To STRAIN, *v. n. run through, filter.* गळणें, पाझरणें, स्त्ररणें.

2 *make violent efforts,* v. To STRIVE. नेटणें, कुंथणें, नेट *m.* करणें, उरफोड or उरस्फोट *m. f.*-त्राण *n.*-&c. करणें, कष्ट *m.*-श्रम *m.*-&c. घेणें-करणें. [*f.*करक *f.* चमक *f.*

STRAIN, *n. injury from over exertion; sprain.* लचक *f.* कचक

2 *hereditary disposition or quality.* वसलात or द *f.*

3 *course or tendency,* v. TENOR. वळण *n.* वळवटा *m.* अन्वय *m.* अर्थान्वय *m.* [नेट *m.* जोर *m.*

4 *pull, tension, stress.* ओढ *f.* ओढा *m.* v. बस, पड, ताण*m.*

That will bear press and s. नेटदार, नेटापटाचा.

5 (as of abusing, beating, declaiming, &c.) *continuing effort.* तान *f.* v. घे, झाड, ताण *m.*

6 See SONG, SOUND. [त, शोधीव.

STRAINED, *p.* v. V. A. 1. गाळलेला, शोधलेला, &c. गाळीव, गालि-

S. through a cloth. वस्त्रगाळ, वस्त्रगाळीव.

2 कन्हारलेला, लचक-&c. भरवलेला or भरलेला, &c.

3 ताणलेला, ताणदिल्हेला, &c. टमटमीत or टुमटुमीत.

4 ओढून आणलेला, &c. बळेंचा, बळेंबळेंचा or बळयांबळयांचा, क्लिष्ट.

STRAINER, *n.* STRAINING, *p. a.* v. V. 1. गाळणारा, शोधणारा, गाळून काढणारा, &c. गालनकर्त्ता-कारी-&c.

I. *sieve, colander, &c.* गाळणें or गाळाणें *n.* चाळण *f.* चाळणी *f.* रोवळा *m. dim.* रोवळी *f.* वेळणी *f.*—of cloth, शोधणें or सोधणें *n.*साफी *f.* —of bamboo. शिपतर *n.* शिवाळी *f.* शिवाळें *n.* शिवुटलें*n.* शिवें *n.*

STRAINING, *n.* v. V. A. 1.—*act.* गाळणें *n.* शोधणें or सोधणें *n.* चाळणें *n.* &c.

2 कन्हारणें *n.* &c.

3 ताणणें *n.* ताणदेणें *n.* &c.

4 ओढणें *n.* ओढून आणणें *n.*

v. V. N. 2. कुंथणें *n.* नेटकरणें *n.* बळ करणें *n.* &c.

STRAIT, *a.* v. NARROW. अरुंद, सांकड, अप्रशस्त, अवघड, खोंचकील, खोंचाड, संकट.

2 *rigorous, &c.* v. SEVERE, STRICT. सख्त or सक्त, जालीम.

3—garment, &c. v. TIGHT. तंग, सांकड, दाट, दाटका, दाटला.

STRAIT, *n. narrow pass, &c.* v. PASS. खिंड *f.* नळी *f.* नळीचीवाट *f.* खाडी *f.* सामुद्रधुनी *f.*

2 *distress, difficulty, &c.* v. TROUBLE. संकट *n.* अडचण *f.* संकष्ट *n.* कच *f.* कचाट *n.* कोंडें *n.* सांकडें *n.* सेंकटें *n.*

To be in straits. अवघडणें, अडचणणें. [करणें.

To reduce to straits. ताण *m.* देणें, कोंडमार or कोंडमारा*m.*

3 v. DILEMMA. चिमटा *m.* कातर *f.* कचाटी *f.*बिडती *f.*पेंचाटी *f.*

STRAIT HANDED, *a.* v. MISERLY. हाताचा जड-चिकट, चिकट.

STRAIT-LACED. See STIFF, STRICT.

To STRAITEN, *v. a. reduce to straits.* संकटांत-अडचणींत-&c. आणणें-पाडणें-घालणें, अडचणवणें.

2 See To NARROW, To CONTRACT.

STRAITENED, *p.* v. V. 1. संकटांत आणलेला-&c. अडचणवलेला, &c. ओढग्रस्त or ओढगस्त, ओढिस्त, ओढीक, कृच्छ्रगत, तंग.

To be s. अडचणणें, अवघडणें, तंगणें.

STRAITENEDNESS, *n.* v. P. अडचण *f.* अडचणूक *f.* तंगचाई *f.* तारंबळ *f.* ओढगस्ती *f.* तान *m.* उपरोध *m.*

STRAITLY. See NARROWLY, STRICTLY. [संकोच *m.*

STRAITNESS, *n.* v. A. 1. अरुंदपणा *m.* सांकडपणा *m.* अडचण *f.*

2 सख्तपणा *m.* जालिमपणा *m.*

3 तंगपणा *m.* सांकडपणा *m.* दाटपणा *m.*

I. (of purse, of affairs). v. CIRCUMSTANCES, POVERTY. तंगचाई or तंगची *f.* ओढ *f.* ओढगस्ती *f.* गिरिबदारी *f.* चडचड *f.* चणचण *f.* ददात *f.*

STRAKE, *n. iron band of a wheel.* धांव *f.*

STRAMONIUM, STRAMONY. See THORN-APPLE.

STRAND, *n. beach,* v. SHORE. कांठ *m.* कांठा *m.* तीर *n.* तट *n.*

2 *twist of a rope.* पदर *m.* पेड़ *or* पेढ *m.* बेंठ *m.*

To STRAND, *v. a. run on the sea-shore.* कांठावर-कांठ्यावर-&c. चढवणें-आदळणें.

STRANDED, *p.* v. V. कांठावर चढवलेला, &c.

STRANGE, *a. of another country, &c.* v. FOREIGN. विदेशी, परदेशी, विदेशचा, परदेशचा.

2 *of another family, alien.* परका *or* खा, पारखा, बिराणा, बाहेरचा *or* ला, बाहेरील, अन्य (in comp), पर (in comp), परकी, परावा, परगोत्री, परकुलाचा, परगोत्राचा, भिन्नगोत्री, बहिरंग.

3 *novel, marvellous, &c.* v. WONDERFUL. विलक्षण, विलक्षणीक, नवल, विचित्र, चमत्कारिक, अजब, अनोठा.

4 *odd, irregular, unusual.* एकप्रकार, एकप्रकारचा, एकतऱ्हेचा, तऱ्हेचा, तऱ्हेदार, तऱ्हेवाईक, विजाती, विजातीय, विजात, विलक्षण, परीचा, लोकबाह्य, अवघड.

S. fellow, *queer, rum, &c. fellow.* चिह्न *n.*

5 *uncommon, unusual, extraordinary, &c.* बिलक्षण, बिलक्षणीक, विशेष, नवलविशेष, अचाट, अपूर्व, अधिकोत्तर, लोकाधिक, लोकबाह्य, अलौकिक, अनूप, अपरूप *or* व.

6 *unknown, or new to.* नवा, अनोळखी, अनोळखीचा, पारखा, परका *or* खा, परावा, पर, गैरवागीचा, गैररफताचा, अपरिचयाचा, अगोचर, अपरिचित.

7 *odd, uncomfortable, &c. in feelings.* उदास. [*in. con.*

To feel s. अवघड-असकड-&c. होणें *or* वाटणें *impers.* &

STRANGELY. See WONDERFULLY.

STRANGENESS, *n.* v. A. 1. परदेशीपणा *m.* विदेशीपणा *m.* विदेशिता *f.* परदेशिता *f.* [त्व *n.* &c.

2 परकेपणा *m.* पारखेपणा *m.* बिराणेपणा *m.* परखाई *f.* परगोत्रि-

3 विलक्षणपणा *m.* नवलपणा *m.* &c. वैलक्षण्य *n.*

4 एकप्रकारपणा *m.* &c. विजातिता *f.* विजातीयता *f.*

5 बिलक्षणपणा *m.* नवलपणा *m.* अचाटपणा *m.* अलौकिकपणा*m.* वैलक्षण्य *n.* लोकबाह्यता *f.*

6 नवेपणा *m.* परकेपणा *m.* अनोळखीपणा *m.* &c. गैरवाग *f.* गैररफता *m.* अपरिचय *m.*

I. See ALIENATION, COLDNESS.

STRANGER, *n. foreigner.* परदेशी, विदेशी, उपरी.

2 *one not of the family,* v. STRANGE. बाहेरचें माणूस *n.*-मनुष्य *n.*-&c. परपुरुष *m.* लोकांतला, लोक.

S. woman. परस्त्री *f.* परकामिनी *f.* [द्वैत, उदासीन.

3 *unknown person.* बाहेरचा, अनोळखी, अनोळखीचा, तिऱ्हा-

4 *one unknowing,* v. INEXPERIENCED. गैरवाकबदार, गैरमाहीत, अजाण, अपरिचित, अनभिज्ञ, अनभ्यस्त.

5 *accidental guest or visitor.* पाहुणा*m.* (पाहुणी *f.*) अतिथि, अभ्यागत, आगंतुक.

To STRANGLE, *v. a. destroy life by stopping respiration, choke,* v. To SUFFOCATE. गळफांस*m.* देणें *or* देऊन-घालून-&c. मारणें, गळफांसानें मारणें, गळा*m.* दाबणें-दाबून मारणें.

2 See To SUPPRESS.

STRANGLING, STRANGULATION, *n.* v. V. 1. गळफांसदेणें*n.* गळफांस देऊन मारणें*n.* गळादाबणें*n.* कोंडमारा*m.* श्वासरोध*m.*

STRANGURY, *n. painful discharge of urine.* मूत्रकृच्छ्र*n.* मूत्ररोध *m.* मूत्रावरोध*m.* अश्मरी *f.* [पट्टी *f.*

STRAP, *n. slip of leather, &c.* वादी *f.* चामोटा*m.* वरत्रा *f.* चर्म-

2 (for sharpening knives, &c.). थापटणें*n.* पलाटणें*n.*

To STRAP, *v. a.* v. To BEAT. वादीमार*m.* देणें-करणें.

2 *fasten with a s.* वादीनें-&c. बांधणें.

3 *sharpen on a s.* पलाटण्यावर घासून धार *f.* आणणें.

STRAPPING, *a.* v. STOUT, LARGE. दांडगा, गलेलठ्ठ, गबदूल, धिपाड, घणघाव, खमाट्या. [कसब*n.*

STRATAGEM, *n.* v. ARTIFICE. उपाय*m.* व्यूह*m.* उहूम. कृति *f.*

Stratagems. कवाईत *or* द *f.* शकटभेद*m.*

STRATEGIC, STRATEGICAL, *a.*v.N. व्यूहरचनाविद्यासंबंधी-विषयक.

STRATEGY, *n. science of arranging for battle.* व्यूहरचनाविद्या*f.* सैन्यरचनाविद्या *f.*

STRATH, *n.* थड *f.* (as भीमथड, &c.).

To STRATIFY, *v a.* थर*m.* करणें-बसवणें.

STRATUM, *n. bed, layer.* थर*m.* पड़दा*m.* मजला*m.* माण *f.*

STRATUS, *n. form of clouds.* खर *f.*

STRAW, *n.* (of wheat). काड *f.*—(of rice). तणन भातण *or* भातेण*n. or* भात्याण & भात्येण*n.* पेंढा*m.* परा*ळn.* साळवण*n.* तणस*f.* —(of legumes).काड*n.*—(of the grain नाचणी).नाचणकाड *n.*

Bits and ends of s. तणस *f.* गूत *f.*

Jack of s. नाकतोडा *or* ड्या, गवताचा ऊंट*m.*

That is not worth a s. तृणप्राय, तृणवत्.

To mind or value as a s. कसपटाप्रमाणें मोजणें.

I dont care a s. खेंटर तुटो *or* जळो.

2 *light matter, a trifle.* काडी *f.* तणसडी *or* सुडी *f.*

3 *a minute particle.* काडी *f.* कसपट*n.* केर*n.*

Straws, chips, shreds, &c. केर*m.* कचरा*m.* केरकचरा*m.* केरकस्तान*n.* केरकसपट*n.*

To STRAW. See To STREW.

STRAW-BERRY, *n.* एकफळ आहे.

To STRAY, *v. n. rove, roam, &c.* v. To WANDER. भटकणें, भटक्या *f. pl.* मारणें-मारीतफिरणें.

2 *rove deviously,* lit. fig. चुकणें, रस्ता *m.*-वाट *f.*-&c. चुकणें-चुकून जाणें, बहकणें *or* भकणें, चुकून-बहकून जाणें, गहाळणें, रस्ता*m.*-&c. सोडणें-सोडून जाणें, रान *n.* घेणें, चुकारी *f.* भरणें, भ्रमणें, भ्रमूनजाणें, भ्रम *m.*-भ्रमण*n.*-&c. करणें.

STRAY, *a. that has strayed.* चुकर, चुकार, चुकूर, चुकलामाकला *or* बाकला, बहकलेला, गहाळलेला, &c. गहाळ, सांड, दिग्भ्रमी, दिग्भ्रांत.

STRAY, *n. stray animal.* चुकार गुरूं *n.*

STRAYER, *n.* STRAYING, *p. a.* v. V. 1. भटकणारा, भटक्यामारणारा, &c. [घेणारा.

2 चुकणारा, रस्ताचुकणारा, भकणारा, रस्तासोडून जाणारा, रान-

I. *given to straying,*—bullock, &c. ओढाळ.

STRAYING, *n.* v. V. 1.—*act.* भटकणें*n.* &c.

2 चुकणें *n.* भकणें *n.* चुकून जाणें *n.* भ्रमणें *n.* &c. बहकणी *f.* भ्रम *m.* भ्रमण *n.* दिग्भ्रम *m.* दिग्भ्रमण *n.* भ्रांति *f.*

STREAK, *n. stripe, line.* रेघ *f.* रेगटी *or* रेघोटी *f.* रेखा *or* रेषा *f.* पट्टी *f.* लकीर *f.* [दोराबणें.

S. in wood, stone,&c.दोरा *m.* शीर *f.*—To have streaks.

S. on certain snakes, &c. फांकी *f.*

White vertical s. (upon the forehead of a dog, horse, &c.,) नाम *n.*

To STREAK, *v. a.* रेघा *f. pl.*-पट्ट्या *f. pl.*-&c. काढणें, रेषाविचित्र-रेखा विचित्र-&c. करणें.

STREAKED, *p.* v. V. रेघा काढलेला, &c. पट्टापट्टीचा, रेषाविचित्र, रेखा विचित्र, रेखांकित, रेषांकित.

I.—esp. of cattle. बाह्ळा *or* बाळा, बांडा.

Black-s. upon a white ground. काळाबाळा *or* बाह्ळा.

White-s. vertically upon the forehead. नाम्या.

STREAM, *n. running water,* v. RIVER, RIVULET, &c. वाहता झरा *m.* वाहतीधार *f.* ओढा *m.* ओघ *m.* वाहवणी *n.* वहाळ *m.* विन्हा *m.*

Separated and minor s. (in the bed of a river.) तास*m.*

S. turned into fields. ओहण *n.*

2 *current, course, flow,* lit. fig. ओघ *m.* धार *f.* प्रवाह*m.* वाहणी *f.* वाहण *or* वहाण *f.* वाहवण *f.* बाहवट *f.* वाहवटळ *f.* ओत*m.* ओळ *f.* ओटा*m.* ओढ *f.* प्रवृत्ति *f.* संसृति *f.* स्त्रोत*n.* वृष्टि *f.*

Against the s. प्रतिस्त्रोतः.

That drifts with a s. प्रवाहपतित.

To drift with the s. प्रवाहांत पडणें, लोंढ्यासरसा वाहून जाणें.

To float with the s. वारा वाहील तसें करणें.

The s. is rapid. पाणी केस तोडतें.

3 (as of rain, or from a vessel) *line descending or running.* धार *f.* धारवणी *n.* पन्हळी *f.* रेळा *m.* पागोळी *f.* पावळी *f.*

Continuous or unintermitting s. संततधार *f.*

To STREAM, *v. n. move in a continuous current,* v. To FLOW. वाहणें, प्रवाह *m.*-&c. चालणें *g. of s.*

2 *emit a stream, pour out abundantly.* फळफळणें, चिघळणें, धार *f.*-ओघळ *m.*- पाट *m.*- मुसांडा *m.*-&c. लागणें-वाहणें-सुटणें-निघणें *g. of s.* भडभड-भळभळ-&c. सुटणें-निघणें, चळाळणें.

3—of sweat; *flow profusely.* डवडवणें, डवडव *or* डगडगां *adv.* येणें-सुटणें-वाहणें.

To s. with tears,—the eyes. डबडबणें, भरणें.

STREAMER, *n. pennon, &c.* v. FLAG. बावटा *m.* फरारा *m.*

STREAMINGLY, *adv.* v. V. 2. घळघळ *or* ळा, फळफळ *or* ळां, भळभळ *or* ळां, भुळभूळ *or* ळां, अनुधार—*intens.* फळाफळ, फळाळां.

3 डगडग *or* गां, डगमग *or* गां, डबडब.

STREAMLET, *n. small stream.* ओघळ *m.* ओहळ *m.* ओहळी *f.* (*or* ओळ & ओळी) वाहळी *f.* जुतरी *or* झुतरी *f.* मुतरी *f.*

STREET, *n. road in a town, &c.* गावांतील-गांवांतला-&c. रस्ता *m.* -मार्ग *m.*-&c. बीद *or* बीध *f.* [LANE.

Main or principal s. राजगोंड *f. n.* राजबीध *f.* See also

STREET-WALKER, *n. prostitute,* v. HARLOT. बाजारबसवी *f.* हट्टविलासिनी *f.*

STRENGTH, *n. force, power, vigor.* बल *or* ळ *n.* जोर *m.* शक्ति *f.* सामर्थ्य *n.* कुवत *f.* आंगवण *f.* जोम *m.* बळकटी *f.* मजबुती *f.* बळावळ *f.* तवका *m.* तकवा *m.* ताकत *f.* पराक्रम *m.* ऊर्ज *n.* पौरुष *n.* प्राबल्य *n.* तेज *n.* धमक *f.* [पलीकडचा.

Beyond one's s. to bear. जिवापरता, शक्तीबाहेरचा, शक्ती-

Bodily s. v. BODILY. कमरेचा जोर *m.*

Decline of s. बळमोड *m.* बलक्षय *m.* बलऱ्हास *m.*

Loss of s. बलहानि *f.*

Prostration of s. उठवण *f.* *v.* घे (*or* उठवणीस येणें). बुड्ढा*m.*

That is under prostration of s. उठवणकर.

To gather s. बळ *n.* धरणें, बळ *n.* बांधणें, जोत *f.* धरणें.

To put out one's s. बळ *n.* करणें.

To spend one's s. हाडाचा मणी आणि रक्ताचें पाणी करणें, आंगाचें पाणी *or* पाणीपाणी *n.* करणें, जीव*m.* आटणें.

To try one's s. with. मणगटासी मणगट *n.* घासणें, मांडीस मांडी *f.* टेंकून बसणें.

2 *firmness, hardness, toughness, &c.* v. GOODNESS. जीव *m.* जोर *m.* बळकटी *f.* मजबुती *f.* कस *m.* इर *f.* ऐवज *m.* त्राण *n.* खचरदारी *f.*

3 (of liquors, &c.) *potency.* वीर्य *n.* विरी *or* वीर *f.* सामर्थ्य *n.* शक्ति *f.* दम *m.* तेज *n.* तेजगी *f.* बळाबळ *f.* जहाली *f.*

To STRENGTHEN, *v. a. make strong or stronger.* बळकट-मजबूत-सबल-बलवान्-&c. करणें, बळ *n.*-शक्ति *f.*-जोर *m.*-बळकटी *f.*-&c. देणें, बळ *n.*-शक्ति *f.* &c. वाढवणें *g. of o.* बलवृद्धि *f.*-बलवर्द्धन *n.*- &c. करणें *g. of o.*

2 *establish, corroborate, &c.* v. To CONFIRM. बळकट-दृढ-साबीत-निश्चित-&c. करणें, बळकटी *f.*-&c. देणें-आणणें, पुष्टि *f.* देणें.

3 v. To ANIMATE, To ENCOURAGE. धीर *m.*-धैर्य *n.*-&c. देणें, जीव *m.* आणणें.

To STRENGTHEN, *v. n. grow strong or stronger.* बळ *n.* धरणें, जोरावणें, बळकावणें, बळावणें, दृढावणें, बळकट-जोराचा- सबळ-&c. होणें-होतजाणें.

STRENGTHENED, *p.* v. V. A. 1. बळकट केलेला, बळदिल्हेला, &c. प्रबलीकृत, सबलीकृत, बलवर्द्धित.

STRENGTHENER, *n.* STRENGTHENING, *p. a.* v. V. A. 1. बळकट करणारा, बळदेणारा, &c. बलवर्द्धक, बलवर्द्धन-बलवृद्धि कर्ता-कारी-&c. बलवर्द्धन, बलवर्द्धी.

2 बळकट करणारा, बळकटी देणारा-आणणारा, &c. पुष्टिकारक.

STRENGTHENING, *n.* v. V. A. 1.—*act.* बळकट-&c. करणें *n.* बळ देणें *n.* &c. बलवर्द्धन *n.* बलवृद्धि *f.* सबलीकरण *n.* प्रबलीकरण *n.*

STRENUOUS, *a. vehemently active and zealous,* v. DILIGENT, EARNEST. उद्योगी, उद्यमी, परिश्रमी, उत्सुक, प्रयत्नवान्, महोत्साह, महोद्यम.

STRENUOUSLY, *adv.* v. A. परिश्रमानें, &c. नेटदेऊन, आंगमोडून, बळकरून, उत्साहपूर्वक, यत्नतः, प्रयत्नतः.

STRENUOUSNESS, *n.* v. A. उद्योगीपणा *m.* परिश्रम *m.* उद्यम *m.* उत्सुकता *f.* उत्साह *m.*

STRESS, *n. force, strain, pressure.* ओढ *f.* ओढा *m.* ओढण *f.* नेट *m.* ताण *m.* जोर *m.* बळ *n.* [ओढा *m.* ओढ *f.*

2 *stretch, strainedness.* ताण *m.* तणावा *m.* ताणलेलेपणा *m.*

STRETCH, *n.* v. EFFORT. यत्न *m.* प्रयत्न *m.* ताण *m.* नेट *m.* भलेरी *f.* *v.* लाव, घाल.

At one s. or effort. एक ओढ, एके ओढीनें, एका तडाक्यानें, एके तिडकीनें, एकदम, एकवेळीं, चढ्याघोड्यानिशीं.

2 *long run.* तावण *f.* *v.* पड, ताण *m. f.*

3 See REACH.

To STRETCH, *v. a. extend, expand,* v. To SPREAD. पसरणें, विस्तारणें, पसारा *m.*-&c. करणें *g. of o.*

2 *extend, reach out.* लांब-दीर्घ करणें, लांबविणें.

To s. one's limbs. हातपाय *m. pl.* ताणणें—through laziness or under fatigue, आंगमोडा *m.*-आंगपिळा *m.*-आंगवळा *m.*-&c.देणें.

3 *make tense,* v. To INTEND. ताणणें, ताण *m.*- तणावा *m.* देणें, ताठ-&c. करणें.

4 *strain, force,* fig. ओढणें, ओढून-ओढूनताणून-खेंचून-&c. आणणें, बळ *n.*-&c.करणें.

To STRETCH, *v. n. extend, reach out.* पसरणें, पहोंचणें, जाणें, पावणें, लागणें, ठेपणें.

2 *open out on wear.* सुटणें, पघळणें, सैल-शिथिल-&c. होणें.

3 *lie along, run, trend.* वाहणें, वाहणी *f.*- &c. असणें *g. of s.*

STRETCHED, *p.* v. V. A. 1. पसरलेला, विस्तारलेला, &c. वितत, प्रसृत.

2 लांब केलेला, &c.

3 ताणलेला, ताणदिल्हेला, ताठकेलेला, &c.

4 ओढलेला, ओढूनताणून आणलेला, &c.

STRETCHER, *n.* STRETCHING, *p. a.* v. V. A. 1. पसरणारा, विस्तारणारा, &c.

3 ताणणारा, ताणदेणारा, ताठकरणारा, &c.

4 ओढणारा, ओढूनताणून आणणारा, &c.

To STREW, *v. a. spread by scattering,* v. To SCATTER. विखरणें, पसरणें, अंथरणें, पखरणें, विखरून-&c. टाकणें.

2 *cover by being scattered over.* अंथरणें, भरणें, विखरून-&c. भरणें-आच्छादणें.

STRICKEN. See STRUCK.

STRICKLE, *n. instrument for levelling grain with the measure.* शीग मारण्याचें लाटणें *n.* शीगमारें लाकूड *n.*

Smoothed with a s. सपाट.

S.-struck—a measure. शिगलोटा.

STRICT, *a. exact, closely careful,* v. ACCURATE, PRECISE. सुती, सूत्री, रेखला, बांधलेला, कडकडीत, खरा, खास, ठास, खचीत.

2 *rigorous, &c.* v. SEVERE. खमशा, खरमरा *or* ऱ्या, कणक्या, कदरखोर, कदरवाला, निर्वाण, सख्त, कडक, कडकडीत, निक्षी, निक्षीचा.

3 See TIGHT.

STRICTLY, *adv.* v. A. 1. खास, खचीत, खरा *decl.*

2 खमशेपणानें, सख्तपणानें, कांहीं न सोडतां, दया न करतां.

I.—enjoining, charging, &c. v. PEREMPTORILY. बजावून, हडसून, तटकारून.

STRICTNESS, *n.* A. 1. सुतीपणा *m.* सूत्रीपणा *m.* &c.

2 खमशेपणा *m.* खरमरेपणा *m.* &c. निक्षी *f.*

STRICTURE, *n.* v. CONTRACTION, WRINKLE. गांठ *f.* चर्मतरंग*m.*

2 *critical remark,* v. CRITICISM. गुणदोषव्याख्या *f.*

STRIDE, *n. long step.* ढांग *f.* ढेंग *f.* डग *f.* टांग *f.*

That takes long strides. ढांगळ *or* ढांगाळ, ढेंगळ *or* ढेंगाळ.

To STRIDE, *v. n. walk with long steps.* ढेंगा *f. pl.*-&c. टाकणें-टाकीत चालणें, ढेंगलणें.

STRIFE, *n. emulation,* v. RIVALRY. प्रतिस्पर्धा *f.* स्पर्धा *f.*

2 v. CONTENTION. झोंबी *f.* झटापटी *or* झटापट *f.* जुंज *or* झुंज *n.* द्वंद्व *pop.* दंद *n.* कलि *m. pop.* कळ *f.* लटपट *f.* झगडा *m.* भांडण *n.* हडबंग *m.* तकरार *f.*

To STRIKE, *v. a. hit, knock, &c.* हणणें *or* हाणणें, मारणें, प्रहारणें, ताडणें, ठोकणें, पिटणें, प्रहार *m.*-हनन *n.*-घात*m.*-व्याघात *m.*-&c. करणें.

2 *throw smartly and lightly.* मारणें, टाकणें, फेंकणें.

3 (a sail, flag, tent, &c.) *lower, take down.* उतरणें, खालीं करणें, पाडणें.

4 *cause to sound.* पिटणें, ठोकणें, वाजवणें.

5 (with surprise, wonder, &c.) v. To ASTONISH. चकित-चक्र-&c. करणें, चौकडी *f.* भुलविणें *g. of o.*

6 *affect in some particular manner ; seem to.* वाटणें, दिसणें, भासणें *all with in. con.*

7 See To COIN. 8 *level with a strickle.* शीग *m.* मारणें.

9 against *or* upon. आदळणें, आपटणें, आफळणें.

10 off ; v. To EFFACE. छकणें *or* छेकणें, फांटा *m.* देणें, छेका *m.* मारणें.

11 off ; *impress, print.* छापणें.

12 off ; *separate by a sudden blow.* तोडून-कापून-&c. टाकणें.

13 out ; v. To EFFACE. खोडणें, काढणें, काढून टाकणें.

14 out ; *invent,* v. To CONTRIVE. काढणें,युक्ति*f.*काढणें*g.of o.*

15 up ; *begin to play, &c.* वाजवूं लागणें.

To strike a bargain. हातावर हात*m.* मारणें-देणें, टाळी *f.*-मारणें.

To STRIKE, *v. n. hit, touch, light upon.* लागणें, धक्का*m.*-धडक*f.*-धडक *f.* लागणें-बसणें *g. of s.*

2 *sound.* वाजणें.

3 *submit,* See To YIELD. 4 against ; आदळणें, आपटणें.

5 off ; *diverge.* फांकणें, फांकटणें, फुटणें.

6 out ; a swimmer. झाप *or* झेंप *f.* टाकणें-मारणें, झेंपावणें.

STRIKE, *n.* See STRICKLE.

STRIKER, *n.* STRIKING, *p. a.* v. V. A. 1. मारणारा, हणणारा, ठोकणारा, &c. हंता, हनन-&c. कर्त्ता-कारी.

5 *and* ASTONISHING. चकित करणारा, चक्र करणारा, चौकडी भुलविणारा, &c. चमत्कारिक, चमत्कारी, विस्मापक.

I. *obvious, glaring, evident.* टळटळीत, ठळठळीत, ढळढळीत, झळझळीत, धडधडीत, स्पष्ट.

STRIKING, *n.* v. V. A. 1.—*act.* हणणें *n.* मारणें *n.* ठोकणें *n.* &c. प्रहार *m.* हनन *n.* घात *m.* आघात *m.* व्याघात *m.*

v. V. N. 1. लागणें *n.* धक्का *m.* धडक *f.* धडक *f.* ठोकर *f.*

S. of the foot against. ठोकर *f. v.* खा, लाग, ठेंच *f.*

STRING, *n. slender cord, twine, &c.* दोरी *f.* सुतळी *f.* चऱ्हाट*n.* रस्सी *f.* तंतु *m.* तंत्र *n.* रज्जु *f. m.* सडा *m.* तंत *f.* दोरक *m.* गुण *m.* सूत्र *pop.* सूत *n.*

A s. of twisted silk. कंकरी *f.*

S. of a puppet, doll, &c. कळासूत्र *n.* सूत्र *n.* [तंत्र*n.*

2 (of a musical instrument). तार *f.* तंतु *m.* तंत *f.* तांत *f.*

3 *drawing cord,* v. TIE. बंद*m.*बंध*m.* बंधन *n.* कसणी *f.*कसा*m.*

4 (as of drawers, petticoats, &c.). नाडा *m.* नाडी *f.*

5 (of a bow).v. BOWSTRING. चिल्ला*m.*ज्या *f.* गुण*m.*प्रत्यंचा*f.*

6 *concatenation, line, &c.* v. SERIES. सर *f.* माला *pop.* माळ *f.* हार *f.* सांगड *f.* जाल *n.* (in. comp. as, शब्दजाल, &c.).

7 (of pearls, flowers, &c.) *file.* लड *f.* लडी *f.* सर *m.* हार *m.* माला *pop.* माळ *f.*

8 *thread of a rope or twist.* पदर *m.* पेड *or* पेढ *m.* वेंठ *m.*

9 *fastening cord or string,* v. TIE. बंद *m.*

10 See FIBRE.

To STRING, *v. a. file on a string.* ओवणें, गोवणें, गुंफणें, ग्रंथणें, पटविणें, ग्रंथ *m.*-ग्रंथन *n.*-संदर्भ *m.*-रचना *f.*-सूत्रण *n.*-&c. करणें *g. of o.*

2 *furnish with strings.* तारा *f. pl.*-तांती *or* ताता *f. pl.*-&c. लावणें-चढवणें, तंतुयुक्त-तंतुविशिष्ट-&c. करणें.

3 *make tense.* ताणणें, तणतणावणें, तणतणीत-ताठ-&c. करणें.

4 (a bow) गुण *m*.-&c.चढविणें. [तुविशिष्ट.

STRINGED, *a. having strings.* तारांचा, &c. तंत्री, तांत्र, तंतुयुक्त, तं-

Single-s.—mus. instr. एकतारी.

Two-s.—rope or cord. दुपेडी, दुबळ, दुपदरी.

STRINGENT. See STRICT.

STRINGINESS, *n.*v.A.2. दोराळपणा*m.* दोर *m.* तारा *f. pl.* रेषा *f.pl.*

STRINGY, *a. filamentous, fibrous.* तारेचा, &c. तंतुमय, सूत्रमय.

2 *ropy, viscid.* दोर झालेला, दोराळ, तारा झालेला.

To be s. दोरावणें.

STRIP, *n. narrow piece.* पट्टी *f.* चिंधी *f.* चिरोटी *f.* चिंधूक *n. dim.* चिंधुकली *f.* चिंधूट *n. dim.* चिंधोटी *f.* शेड *f.* फाळा *m. dim.* फाळी *f.*

A colored s. along a cloth. धारी *f.*

To STRIP, *v. a. deprive of covering, make naked, denude, &c.* नागवा-उघडा-विवस्त्र-वस्त्रहीन-&c. करणें, वस्त्र *n.*-वस्त्रें *n. pl.*-वेष्टन *n.*-&c. काढणें-उतरणें *g. of o.* नग्नीकरण *n.* करणें—jocosely, नागमोडीचें पाटाव *n.* देणें-नेसवणें.

2 *divest, make destitute of*, v. To DEPRIVE, To BEREAVE. नागवणें, नागवा करणें-पाडणें, वेगळा-निराळा-रहित-&c. करणें,घेणें -काढणें-काढून घेणें *with* पासून *of o.* नष्ट (in comp.)-&c. करणें.

3 *tear or pull off.* काढणें, उतरणें, उस्तरणें, उधडणें,—roughly, &c. ओरपणें, ओरबडणें *or* ओरबाडणें, भिकुटणें, बुचाडणें, बुचकणें.

4 *spoil, fleece*, v. To PLUNDER. नागवणें, बुचाडणें, बुचकणें, धुणें, ओरबडणें *or* ओरबाडणें, खाकटणें, निरानिपटा *m.* करणें *g. of o.* नागवण *f.*-नागवणूक *f.*-&c. घालणें-पाडणें, धोरडा *m.* काढणें *g. of o.*

5 *press out the last milk.* चिटणें, चिटून काढणें.

To STRIPE, *v. a. lash*, v. To BEAT. फटके *m. pl.* मारणें.

2 *form stripes.* पट्ट्या *f. pl.*-&c. काढणें, पट्ट्या-&c. काढून विचित्र करणें.

STRIPE, *n. line of different colour from the ground.* पट्टा *m.* पट्टी *f.* रेघ *f.* रेखा *f.* रेषा *f.* काडी *f.* खत *n.* लकीर *f.*

Stripes direct and transverse. पट्टापट्टी *f.* [रा *m.*

2 *stroke of a lash, &c.* v. LASH, STROKE. फटका *m.* फटका-

3 *mark of a lash, weal.* वळ *m.*

STRIPED, *a. formed with stripes, or having stripes.* पट्टापट्टीचा, पट्टाईत, पट्टे काढलेला, पट्ट्या काढलेला.

Gold or yellow s. सोनसळा.

Single-s. एकखती—Double s. दुखती.

S. in the form of daggers, waving. कटारीदार, कटारी.

2 *having raised seams.* दंडी, दंडारा, दंडाळा.

STRIPLING, *n. one just passing from boyhood to manhood ; lad.* बाप्या, आडबाप्या, बाप्यामाणूस, पोरगा, पोऱ्या, पोंगडा, आडगेखमा, गोखमा, आडमुलगा, बारवर्षा, सोळवर्षा, गोह्रो, ताकोलाबाप्या, आडमानई *or* आडमानय, मानई, किशोर, बाल.

STRIPPED, *p.* v.V.1. नागवा केलेला, वस्त्रहीन केलेला, &c. नग्नीकृत.

2 नागवलेला, नागवा-रहित-&c. केलेला, &c.

3 काढलेला, उतरलेला, &c.

4 नागवलेला, बुचाडलेला, &c. निर्धूत, शुद्धबुद्ध.

STRIPPER, *n.* STRIPPING, *p. a.* v. V. 1. नागवा-&c. करणारा, वस्त्र-वेष्टन-&c. काढणारा.

2 नागवणारा, नागवा-रहित-&c. करणारा.

3 काढणारा, उतरणारा, &c.

4 नागवणारा, बुचाडणारा, &c.

To STRIVE, *v. n. contend, &c.* v. To QUARREL. झगटणें *or* झगडणें, जुंजणें *or* झुंजणें, घासणें, तंडणें, भांडण *n.*-झगडा *m.*-विरोध *m.*-&c. करणें.

2 *make great efforts, use great exertions.* झटणें, कष्टणें, उद्योग *m.*-यत्न *m.*-प्रयत्न *m.*-आयास *m.*-प्रयास *m.*-&c. करणें, मेहनत *f.*-श्रम *m.*-कष्ट *m.*-&c. घेणें-करणें, झटून-&c. उद्योग *m.* करणें.—Conveying this sense, and corresponding with the phrases, *To agonize, to energize, to strain every nerve, to work with might and main, &c.* some words and phrases are, कुंथणें, नेटणें, बळ *n.* करणें, अगाध बळ *n.* वाहणें, अलेंबलें *adv.* झटणें, जोर *m.* मारणें, ऊर *m.* फोडणें, दांतींचक्र *n.* धरणें, अनर्थ *m.* मांडणें-करणें, भगीरथप्रयत्न-सातसायास *m. pl.* करणें, जुलूम *m.* करणें, वेणा *f. pl.*-तिडका *f. pl.* देणें, जीव *m.* देणें, जीव *m.* टाकणें, जीव *m.* अर्धा करणें, दंड *m. pl.* पेलणें, एकगजब *m.* मांडणें, घोरंकार *m.* करणें, उरफोड *or* उरस्फोड *f. m.*-कडाकूट *f.*-लोंबीझोंबी *f.*-वाटाघाट *f.*-अट्टाहास *m.*-&c. करणें. See also under To LABOR.

3 *vie with*, v. To EMULATE, To RIVAL. बरोबरी *f.*-सरोबरी *f.* करणें, सर *f.*-सरी *f.* करणें-लावणें.

STRIVER, *n.* STRIVING, *p. a.* v. V. 1. झगटणारा, झुंजणारा, &c.

2 झटणारा, झटून उद्योग करणारा, यत्नवान्, यत्नी, प्रयत्नवान्, प्रयत्नी. [र *m.* व्याघात *m.*

STROKE, *n. knock, &c.* ठोक *m.* ठोका*m.* टोला *m.* आघात *m.* प्रहा-

A s. of the hand (upon a tabor, &c.) छाप *f.*

2—with a stick, cane, &c. v. BLOW, THUMP, SLAP. फटका *m.* झटका *m.* फटकारा *m.*झटकारा *m.* धपका *or* धबका *m.* धसका *m.* धप्पा *m.* चपका *m.* घसका *m.* चटणी *f.* कुतका *m.* कुचका *m.* चपेट *f.* चोट *f.* [*m.*रामरट्टा *m.*

Sounding s. कडाखा *m.* तडाका *or* खा *m.* कचका *m.* दणका

Two-handed s. उपट *f.*

To strike with a back s. आडव्या हातानें मारणें.

3 (of calamity, affliction, &c.) *blow.* धका *or* ढका *m.* धक्का *m.* गचका *m.* घसरा *m.* घाला *m.* चट्टा *m.* चपेट *f.* गजब *m.* चोट *f.* ठोकर *f.* धोका *m.* झोका *m.* छकड *f.* ठेंच *f.* ठेम *f.* लाग*m.* तोहमत *f.*

4 (of deceit, knavery, &c.). छकड *f.* झोका *m.*

5 *touch, masterly effort.* फटकारा *m.* हात *m.* कसब *n.* वस्तादी *f.* छाप *f.* छापी *f.* [भाळणें

To put the finishing s. to. आखेरी *f.* मारणें-साधणें-सं-

6 *line drawn.* खत *n.* रेघ *f.* रेषा *f.* रेखा *f.*

Devious s. or line in writing. फरकटा *m.* फरकडा *m.* फरगटा *m.* फरगडा *m.* फरगाडा *m.* [मात्रा *f.*

The strokes and points of writing, compreh. काना-

7 *touch of the pen.* टांक *m.*

8 (of a swimmer) *striking out.* झाप *f.* झेंप*f.* छाप *f.* थाप*f.*

To STROKE, *v. a. rub gently, smooth.* हात *m.* फिरवणें, नेपाळणें, चापचोपी *f.*-चापीचोपी *f.* मांडणें.

2—by way of endearment, v. To FONDLE. कुरवाळणें, गोजरणें *or* गोजारणें, अंजारणें, पाठीवरून-&c. हात *m.* फिरवणें.

To STROLL, *v. n. ramble, rove*, v. To. WANDER. रमणें, इकडेतिकडे- रमतेरमते फिरणें, हिंडणें, उनाडणें, फेरफटका *m.*-सहल *f.*

-&c. करणें.

STROLL, STROLLING, *n.* v. V. रमणें *n.* &c. फेरफटका *m.* फेर *m.* सैर *f.* सहल *f.* रपेट *f.* सहलबाजी *f.* इतस्ततोभ्रमण *n.* विहरण *n.* विहार *m.*

To take a s. चक्कर *n.* मारून येणें.

STROLLER, *n.* STROLLING, *p. a.* v. V. रमणारा, हिंडणारा, &c. हिंडफिऱ्या, फेरेकरी, सहलबाज, यथेष्टचारी.

STROLLINGLY, *adv.* v. V. रमतरमत, रमतेरमते.

STRONG, *a. having force or strength; robust, vigorous, &c.* बलवान्, बलवंत, बळकट, बळाचा, बली, बलिष्ठ, बलाढ्य, बलशाली, सबल, प्रबल, बलसंपन्न, जोरदार, जोराचा, जोरवान्, जोरावर, जोरकस, जोमदार, जोमाचा, कुवतीचा, ताकतीचा, समर्थ, सामर्थ्यवान्, शक्तिमान्, शक्तिमंत, शक्त, जबरदस्त, जबर, पराक्रमी, प्रतापी, दलदपट.

To wax s. बळावणें, जोरावणें.

2—of things, buildings, &c. *firm, solid, substantial, &c.* खंबीर, खम्माल, मजबूत, बळकट, कणखर, सणसर, सणसणीत, धमकट, धडधोप *or* धडधोपट, दृढ, सुदृढ, जोरदार, कुब्बल, धक्क, घट्ट, मखखम, टोलेजंग, संगीन, भक्कम, ऐवजदार, ऐवजशीर, हडस, खबरदार, जिवट, दलदपट.

3—wind, tide, &c. *rapid, &c.* जोराचा, झपाट्याचा, सपाट्याचा, तडाख्याचा.

4—smell, scent. उग्र, उगीर, उग्रट.

5—cloth, thread, &c. *of firm texture.* वाणका, घनवट, धनगट, चिकण, सघन, जिवट, सणसर, सणसणीत, धडधोटा, धडधोपट, धडवती, धडवतीचा.

6—medicine, &c. *potent, efficacious, piquant, &c.* बळकट, पराक्रमी, प्रतापी, अमोघ, सतेज, तेजस्वी, गुणाचा, गुणवान्, गुणकारी, गुणकारक, कसाचा, सकस, जाज्वल्य, जालीम, बाघमाऱ्या, जलाल, झाल, ठोक्याचा, धनत्तर, वज्रप्राय.

STRONG-BUILT, STRONG-KNIT, STRONG-MADE, *a.* v. COMPACT. धमकट, काकट *or* काकड, सणसर, सणसणीत, दृढसंधि, वज्रसंधि, वळींव, राकट.

STRONG-HOLD. See FORT.

STRONG-SMELLING, *a.* v. RANK. उग्र, उग्रट, उगीर, उग्रगंध, बहुगंध.

2 *of strong and diffusive odor.* घमघमीत *or* मघमघीत, दमदमीत, दणदणीत.

STROP, *n. leather for sharpening.* पलाटणें *n.* थापटणें *n.*

STRUCK, *p.* v. V. 1. हणलेला *or* हटलेला, मारलेला, &c. हत (*also* in comp. forming valuable words endlessly, as हतश्री, हतदैव, हतभाग्य, हतचैतन्य, हतैश्वर्य, हतवीर्य, &c. of whom the fortune, life, glory, &c. is struck or blasted), आहत, उपहत, प्रतिहत, अभिहत, व्याहत.

S. (or stricken) in years. वयोवृद्ध, वयातीत.

STRUCTURE, *n. edifice, building.* इमारत *f.* इमला *m.* बंदिस्त *f.*

2 *form, make,* v. BUILD. बांधणी *f.* बांधा *m.* बंदिस्त *f.* बंदिस्ती *f.* बनावट *f.*

A particular form or structure of a sentence or proposition. प्रयोग *m.*

To STRUGGLE, *v. n. make violent efforts with contortions of the body.* धडपडणें *or* धडफडणें, धडवडणें, तडफडणें, हातपाय *m. pl.* झाडणें-आदळणें-आपटणें, तडफड *f.*-तडफडातडफड *f.*-धडपड *or* धडफड *f.*-धडबड *f.*-&c. करणें-मांडणें, आपटाआपट *f.*-आदळआपट *f.* करणें-मांडणें.

2 *use great effort,* v. To LABOR, To STRIVE. बळ *n.* करणें, जीव देऊन-जीव तोडून-जीव मरून-&c. काम *n.* करणें.

3 with; v. To WRESTLE, To STRIVE. झोंबी *f.*-झोंबाझोंबी *f.* -&c. करणें. [*f. pl.*-&c. खाणें.

4 (with difficulties, distress, &c.) गचकळणें, गचकळया

STRUGGLE, STRUGGLING, *n.* v. V. 1. धडपडणें *n.* हातपाय झाडणें *n.* तडफड *f. intens.* तडफडाट *m.* धडपड *or* धडफड *f.* धडबड *f.* आपटाआपट *f.* आदळआपट *f.*

2 *and* EFFORT. उरफोड *f.* आटाघाट *f.* आटाआट *f.* प्रयास *m.*

3 झोंबी *f.* झोंबाझोंबी *f.*

4 गचकळणें *n.* गचकळ्या *f. pl.* गटकळ्या *f. pl.* गटांगळ्या *f. pl.*

STRUMA, STRUMOUS. See SCROFULA, SCROFULOUS.

STRUMPET, *n. prostitute,* v. HARLOT. कसबीण *f.* मालजादी *f.* बाजारबसवी *f.* बाजारीण *f.* उष्टीपत्रावळ *f.* बटीक *f.* जन्मसवाशीण *f.*

Abandoned s. फटरांड *f.* [चारिणी *f.* सोदी *f.*

2 *lewd woman, whore,* v. HARLOT. शिनळबायको *f.* व्यभि-

STRUNG, *p.* v. V. गोवलेला, गुंफलेला, &c. गुंफित, ग्रंथित, सूत्रित, रचित.

To STRUT, *v. n. walk with affected dignity.* नटणें, थटणें, नखरा *m.* करणें, थटून-नटून- नटूनथटून चालणें, मिरवणें, झुमकणें, अकडणें, ठमकणें, ठमक्यानें-नखऱ्यानें-अकडीनें-डौलानें-पत्राजीनें-&c. चालणें, ठमकत-मिरवत-अकडत &c. चलणें, तोल लावूनचालणें, उताणा चालणें, ऊरकाढून-उराड काढून-उराबर-&c. चालणें, लटकत चालणें,—as used esp. of women, चमकणें *or* छमकणें, चमकून चालणें, वरमाईचे चालीनें चालणें.

STRUT, STRUTTING, *n.* v. V.—*act.* नटणें *n.* थटणें *n.* ठमकणें *n.* मिरवणें *n.* &c. अकड *f.* ठमका *m.* नखरा *m.* टूम *f.* पत्राज *or* पत्रास *f.*

STRUTTER, *n.* STRUTTING, *p. a.* v. V. नटणारा, नटून चालणारा, ठमकत चालणरा, अकडबाज.

STRUTTINGLY, *adv.* v. V. नटून, थटून, नटून थटून, मिरवून.

STUB, *n. small stump, piece of stubble, &c.* धस *m.* धसकट *n.* धसाडा *m.* धसाडी *f.* खुंटी *f.* सड *m.* ठोंच *m.* सुळा *m.* सुळका *m. dim.* सुळकी *f.* कांसा *m.* डेंसण *n.* डेंसा *m.* शल्य *n.*

2 See STUMP.

To STUB, *v. a.* v. To GRUB. खुरपणें, खुरपून काढणें, खरडणें.

STUBBED. See STUBBY.

STUBBINESS, *n.* v. A. गट्टपणा *m.* गट्टूपणा *m.* &c. आडवें आंग *n.* बाटोळें आंग *n.* आडवा बांधा *m.*

STUBBLE, *n. stump of wheat, &c., stalks left in the ground.* सड *m.* धसकट *n.* *or* धसकटें *n. pl.* धसाडा *m.* धसाडी *f.* *or* धसाड्या *f. pl.* कडसूर *n.*

STUBBORN, *a.* v. OBSTINATE, PERVERSE. आडकर, अटकर, अडेल, अडील, दुराग्रही, आग्रही, गाटा *or* गाटी, गाठ्या, गाताडा, खळ्या, खळधेणा, खलेल, झक्कड, वातट *or* ड.

STUBBORNLY, *adv.* v. A. अडेलपणानें, &c. दुराग्रहानें, दुराग्रह धरून, दुराग्रहपूर्वक.

STUBBORNNESS, *n.* v. A. आडकरपणा *m.* अडेलपणा *m.* गाटेपणा *m.* &c. दुराग्रह *m.* आग्रह *m.* दुर्मद *m.* दांडकमत *n.* ठेंगमत *n.*

STUBBY, *a. short and thick.* आडव्या आंगाचा, आडव्या बांध्याचा, बाटोळया आंगाचा, ठुसका, ठुणगा, गठ्ठ, गट्टू *or* गड्डू, गिंडा, गिड्डा, घूंट, चेंडू.

STUCCO, *n. plaster of lime.* चुन्याचा गिलावा *m.* संदला *m.*

STUD, *n. ornamental nail.* चमकी *f.*

2 *embossed nail.* गुलमेख *f.*

3 (of a shirt, &c.) गुंडी *f.*

4 (of horses). पागा *f.* घोडवळ *f.*

To STUD, *v. a. adorn with studs.* चमक्या *f. pl.*-गुलमेखा *f. pl.* जडणें-जडवणें, जडीत-खचित करणें.

STUDDED, *p.* v. V. गुलमेखा जडवलेला, &c. जडीत, खचित (in comp. as रत्नखचित, मणिखचित, मौक्तिकखचित, &c.).

STUDENT, *n. one engaged in study,* v. SCHOLAR. शिकणारा, विद्यार्थी, विद्याभ्यासी, शिष्य, अक्षरगुरु.

STUDIED, *p. and a.* v. V. 1. अधीत, शिक्षित, अभ्यासित, अभ्यस्त.

3 पूर्वीयोजून ठेवलेला, &c. पूर्वरचित, पूर्वयोजित, पूर्वसंकल्पित, पूर्वकल्पित. [ताध्ययन.

1. *versed in learning, read,* v. LEARNED. पढीक, साक्षर, रु-

STUDIOUS, *a. given to study, devoted to learning.* विद्येचा-अध्ययनाचा-पढण्याचा-&c. आस्थेवाईक-छंदी-&c. अध्ययनी, अध्ययनशील-परायण-पर-आसक्त-तत्पर-&c. अभ्यासी, विद्याभ्यासी, विद्यापरायण, व्यासंगी, विद्याव्यासंगी, विद्येच्छु, विद्याव्यसनी, अध्ययनाभिमुख, जिज्ञासु.

2 *diligent, solicitous, sedulous.* अभ्यासी, व्यासंगी, साक्षेपी, उद्योगी, व्यवसायी, अध्यवसायी, उद्यमी, आसक्त, संसक्त, तत्पर.

STUDIOUSLY, *adv.* v. A. 1. विद्येचे आस्थेनें, विद्याव्यासंगानें, अध्ययनासक्तीनें, &c. अध्ययनासक्तिपूर्वक.

2 व्यासंगानें, साक्षेपानें, साक्षेपेंकरून, आसक्तीनें, &c. आसक्तिपूर्वक, व्यासंगपूर्वक, &c.

STUDIOUSNESS, *n.* v. A. 1. विद्येची-अध्ययनाची- पढण्याची-&c. पोटाग *f.*-आस्था *f.*-&c. विद्याव्यासंग *m.* अध्ययनासक्ति *f.* अध्ययनशीलता *f.* अध्ययनतत्परता *f.* &c. जिज्ञासा *f.* अध्ययनाभिमुख्य *n.*

2 उद्योगीपणा *m.* उद्योग *m.* व्यासंग *m.* साक्षेप *m.* उद्यम *m.* व्यवसाय *m.* अध्यवसाय *m.* आसक्ति *f.* संसक्ति *f.*

STUDY, *n. application of the mind to books, &c.* अभ्यास *m.* विद्याभ्यास *m.* पढणें *n.* शिकणें *n.* अध्ययन *n.* विद्याध्ययन *n.* व्यासंग *m.* विद्याव्यासंग *m.* शिक्षा *f.* विद्यानुपालन *n.* आवर्तन *n.*

Close s. संतताध्ययन *n.* संतताभ्यास *m.* परिशीलन *n.* अनुशीलन *n.*

Discursive, desultory s. शास्त्राचंक्रमण *or* चंक्रमण *n.*

2 *consideration, contrivance.* विचार *m.* चिंतन *n.* ध्यान *n.* मनन *n.* लक्ष *n.* कल्पना *f.* घोळ *m.*

Deep s. ध्यास *m.* अनुध्यास *m.* [नविषय *m.*

3 *subject of study.* शिकण्याचाविषय *m.* अध्ययन *n.* अध्यय-

4 *room of study.* पढण्याची-अध्ययनाची-&c. खोली *f.* अध्ययनागार *n.* ज्ञानमठ *m.*

To STUDY, *v. a. apply the mind to, read in order to learn.* शिकणें, अभ्यास *m.*-अध्ययन *n.*-&c. करणें *g. of o.*

2 *ponder, &c.* v. To CONSIDER. विचार *m.*-मनन *n.*-ध्यान *n.*-&c. करणें *g. of o.* घोळणें, कुटणें.

3 *arrange by previous thought,* v. To PREMEDITATE. विचार *m.*-तजवीज *f.*- योजना *f.*- रचना *f.*-&c. पूर्वी करणें-करून ठेवणें *g. of o.*

To STUDY, *v. n. apply the mind to books and learning.* शिकणें, पढणें, विद्याभ्यास *m.*-विद्याध्ययन *n.*-विद्याव्यासंग *m.*-&c. करणें.

2 v. To MEDITATE. मनन *n.*-चिंतन *n.*-&c. करणें.

3 *endeavour diligently,* v. To STRIVE. झटणें, उद्योग *m.*-&c. करणें.

STUFF, *n. matter, material.* उपादान *n.* प्रकृति *f.* वस्तु *n.* द्रव्य *n.* परिणामिवस्तु *n.* परिणामिद्रव्य *n.* सामान *n.*

2 See CLOTH. 3 *furniture, goods.* चीजवस्त *f.* जिंदगी *f.* बखपात्र *n.* सामान *n.* सटलें *n.* इख्तिखा *m.* इस्ताद *m.* मालमत्ता *f.*

4 *rubbish, &c.* v. TRASH, NONSENSE. काण्णूबाण्णू *or* कायणूबायणू *n.* फांसफूस *f.* गूळसांयरें *n.* अटरफटर *n.* घाण *f.*

To STUFF, *v. a. cram, fill full.* चिकार-गच्च-दाट-रगडून-खचून-दपटून-कोंदून-ठासून-ठेचून-तकटून-दडपून-चांदून-ढसासून-&c. भरणें.

2 *force in, drive in, cram.* कोंदणें, कोंदाटणें, चांदणें, चांदडणें, चोंदाटणें, चांदाडणें, खचणें, ठासणें, खोसणें, ठेसणें, ठोंबरणें, तकटणें, चिणणें, चिरळणें, खचून-&c. भरणें.

3 (the nose, &c.) *block up, obstruct.* कोंदणें, बंदकरणें, बुजणें *or* बुझणें.

To STUFF, *v. n. feed gluttonously.* कचकावून-करकचून-उपटून-तकटून-बल्कट *adv.*-&c. खाणें *or* जेवणें, उपटजेवणें, उपट *f.* घेणें, बट्याचें *n.* करणें, बोकांदे *m. pl.* भरभरून खाणें, भगर्भा जेवण *n.* करणें, पुरा *m.* पाडणें-उरकणें, आंयईनोंपर्यंत खाणें, सागळ *f.* भरणें, कोंदणें, ढेंपणें, दपटणें (as आज त्यानें खूब दपटलें).

STUFFED, *p.* v. V. A. 1. चिकार-दाट-&c. भरलेला.

2 खचलेला, ठासलेला, &c.

3 कोंदलेला, बुजलेला, बंदकेलेला, कुंद.

To be s. कादणें, कोंदाटणें, चोंदणें. [मसाला *m.*

STUFFING, *n. relishing ingredients.* पुरण *n.* सारण *n.* बाखर *m.*

2 *matter to fill.* भरण *n.* भराव *m.*

S. to fill up a hole, &c. चोंदा *m.*

To STUMBLE, *v. n. trip.* अडखळणें *or* अडखुळणें, अडकळणें, ठेंचळणें, ठेंसळणें, ठोकर *f.*-ठेंच *f.*-&c. खाणें *or in. con.* लागणें, स्खलित होणें, स्खलन *n.* होणें *g. of s.*

2 on; *fall on, light on by chance.* अवचट-अवचित-अवचितां-अकल्पित-&c. सांपडणें-मिळणें-भेटणें, *all with in. con.*

To STUMBLE, *v. a. cause to trip.* अडखळवणें, ठेंचळवणें, ठोकर *f.*-ठेंच *f.*-&c. देणें खायास लावणें.

2 *perplex, puzzle, &c.* v. To CONFOUND. गोंफाटणें, गोंधळवणें, गोंफाट्यांत-&c. पाडणें-घालणें, घोटाळा *m.*-घोळ *m.*-चित्तवैकल्य *n.*-&c. करणें *g. of o.*

STUMBLE, STUMBLING, *n.* v. V. N. 1. अडखळणें *n.* ठेंचळणें *n.* ठेंच *or* ठेंस *f.* ठोकर *f.* अडखळणी *f.* स्खलन *n.*

STUMBLER, *n.* STUMBLING, *p. a.* v. V. N. 1. अडखळणारा, ठेंचळणारा, ठोकर खाणारा, &c. अडखळ्या, ठेंचळ्या, ठोकरखाऊ.

STUMBLING-BLOCK, STUMBLING-STONE, STUMBLING-PLACE, *n.* अडखळण *f.* अडखुळा *m.* अडखूळ *n.*

STUMP, *n.* (of a tree or plant) *part remaining in the earth.* खुंट *m.* खुंटा *m. dim.* खुंटी *f.* खुंटण *n.* खुंटामा *m.* खुंटारा *m.* खांड *n.* झीट *n.* झीड *n.* धोण *n.*

Sharp s. सुळा *m.* सुळका *m.*

2 (esp. of a limb or worn article). बुंठण *or* बोंठण *n.* ठुंठण *or* टोंठण *n.* थोंट *n.* थोंटण *n.* बोंटूक *m.* थोटूक *or* थोठूक *n.* झीण *f.* खणूट *n.*

Reduced to a s. बुंठा *or* बोंठा, थोंटा *or* ठोंटा.

To STUMP, *v. n. walk thumpingly.* दणदणणें, दणदण-दणकन-&c. चालणें-पाय *m. pl.* वाजवणें, पाय आपटून चालणें.

STUMPINGLY, *adv.* v. V. दणकन-कर-&c. दणदण.

STUMPY, *a. short and thick,* v. STUBBY. गिड्डा, गट्ट, घूंट.
2 *short, reduced to a stump.* थोंटा, बुंठा, लांडा.

To STUN, *v. a. make senseless by a blow.* ठोक्यानें-प्रहारानें-&c. बेसावध-बेहोष-अचेतन-&c. करणें, आघातमूर्च्छित-&c. करणें.
2 *make dizzy by noise, overpower one's hearing, deafen.* बहिरा-&c. करणें, कान *m. pl.* फोडणें-बसवणें *g. of o.* कानठळीं *or* ळें *n. pl.*-कानठळ्या *f. pl.*-&c. बसवणें *g. of o.* आवाजानें-दणक्यानें-&c. बेसावध-&c. करणें. [*g. of s.*
To be stunned. कानठळीं *or* ळें *n. pl. or* ळ्या *f. pl.* बसणें

STUNG, *p.* v. V. डसलेला, &c. दंशित, दष्ट.

STUNNED, *p.* v. V. 1. ठोक्यानें बेसावध केलेला-झालेला, आघातमूर्च्छित, प्रहारमूर्च्छित.
2 कान फोडलेला, कानठळीं बसवलेला *or* बसलेला.

STUNNER, *n.* STUNNING, *p. a.* v. V. 1 ठोक्यानें बेसावध करणारा, आघातमूर्च्छितकर्त्ता, आघातमूर्च्छाकर्त्ता-कारी.
2 कान फोडणारा, कानठळीं बसवणारा, &c.
Stunning noise. कान्हेर *m.*

To STUNT, *v. a. hinder from growth.* खुरटवणें, खिरवटणें, वाढ *f.* खुंटवणें-मोडणें *g. of o.*

STUNT, *a.* STUNTED, *p.* v. V. खुरटवलेला, &c. खुजट, खुजा, खुरंट, खिरटा, बुरट *or* बुरटा, लुडमा.
To be or become s. खुरटणें, खुरगटणें, खिरटणें, खुरडणें, बुरटणें, मिरमुटणें.

STUNTEDNESS, *n.* खुजटपणा *m.* &c.

To STUPE. See To FOMENT.

STUPEFACTION, *n. stupid or torpid state,* v. STUPOR. धुंदी *f.* गुंगी *f.* भूल *f.* माजरें *n.* मोह *m.* बेसावधपणा *m.* बेहोषपणा *m.* जडिमा *m.* स्तंभ *m.* व्यामोह *m.* तामस *m.*

STUPEFACTIVE, *a.* STUPEFIER, *n.* STUPEFYING, *p. a.* v. V. धुंदी आणणारा, गुंगी आणणारा, गुंग-&c. करणारा, मोहकारक, मोहजनक, मोहक, स्तंभक, इंद्रियस्तंभक.

STUPEFIED, *p.* v. V. धुंद केलेला, गुंग केलेला, &c. गुंग, धुंद, उल्लू, स्तंभित, स्तंभितेंद्रिय, जडीकृत, जडीभूत, तारवटलेला *or* तारकटलेला.
To be or become s. गुंगणें, गुंग-&c. होणें.

To STUPEFY, *v. a. make stupid, dull, senseless, &c.* गुंग-धुंद-&c. करणें, गुंगवणें, गुंगी *f.*-धुंदी *f.*-&c. आणणें, स्तंभ *m.*-स्तंभन *n.*-इंद्रियस्तंभ *m.*-&c. करणें *g. of o.*

STUPENDOUS, *a.* v. WONDERFUL, LARGE. चकभूल पाडणारा, अद्भुत, आश्चर्यकारक, विस्मयकारक-जनक. [ता *f.* &c.

STUPENDOUSNESS, *n.* v. A. अद्भुतपणा *m.* अद्भुतता *f.* विस्मयकारक-

STUPID, *a. dull, doltish, heavy of understanding.* जड, मंद, बुद्धीचा जड-मंद-&c. जडबुद्धि, जडमति, मंदबुद्धि, मंदमति, बुद्धिमंद, मतिमंद, अचतुर, घृतबुद्धि, जेनबुद्धि, अप्रबुद्ध, असमंजस, मूढ, मूढमति, मैंद, मूर्ख, आडमूठ, आडमुठ्या, घेलट, घेलाड, स्थूल *or* ळ, स्थूलधी, स्थूलबुद्धि, दुर्मेधा, दुर्बुद्ध, निर्बुद्ध, निर्बुद्धि, ठोसर, माठ्या, मठ्ठ, मठ्या, शामाठ्या, दगड्या, मुग्ध, आर्ष *or* आरुश, अज्ञान, ज्ञानदुर्बल, बुद्धिहीन-रहित-&c. गयाळ, गयाळी, गुंगी *or* गुंग्या, गैदी, गैरात, गैबती *or* त्या, गैबी, गाफल *or* गाफील *or* गाफली, बेकूब *or* बेवकूब, हीनचातुर्य, दुघड ओनाम्या.
2—as under sleep, intoxication, &c. गुंग, धुंद, सुस्त, जड,

STUPIDITY, STUPIDNESS, *n.* v. A. 1. बुद्धीचा जडपणा *m.*-मंदपणा *m.* &c. जडपणा *m.* जडबुद्धि *f.* मंदबुद्धि *f.* मंदमति *f.* जडमति *f.* घृतबुद्धि *f.* जेनबुद्धि *f.* मौढ्य *n.* मूर्खता *f.* मौर्ख्य *n.* स्थौल्य *n.* जाड्य *n.* जडिमा *m.* बेकुबी *or* बेवकुबी *f.* अज्ञान *n.*
2 गुंगपणा *m.* जडपणा *m.* सुस्तपणा *m.* &c. गुंगी *f.* धुंदी *f.* सुस्ती *f.*

STUPOR, *n. torpor, stupefaction, suppression of sense.* धुंदी *f.* गुंगी *f.* झांक *f.* झांप *f.* झांपण *f.* झांपड *f.* माजरें *n.* भूल *f.* बेहोषपणा *m.* बेसावधपणा *m.* बेशुद्धि *f.* बेशुद्धपणा *m.* मोह *m.* व्यामोह *m.* स्तंभ *m.* इंद्रियस्तंभ *m.* इंद्रियस्वाप *m.*

STURDINESS, *n.* v. V. A. शरीराचा बळकटपणा *m.* धट्टेकट्टेपणा *m.* गड्डूपणा *m.* &c. रांकटाई *m.*

STURDY, *a. robust, lusty, &c.* v. STOUT, STRONG. धटमूट, धट्टाकट्टा *or* सट्टा, धडासडा, धटांगण *or* धटिंगण, गडदू, गबदूल, दांडगा, ताठर, कुप्पा, कळकुंबा, कट्टा, रांकट, मुसळ्या *or* ळ्या, धमकट.

To STUTTER, STUTTERER. See To STAMMER, STAMMERER.

STY, *n.* (for hogs). डुकरखाना *m.* डुकरवाडा *m.*
2 *humor in the eyelid.* रांजणवाडी *f.* आंजिणी *f.* आंजरली *f.* आंदुळणी *f.*

To STYE, *v. a.* डुकरखान्यांत-डुकरवाड्यांत कोंडणें.

STYGIAN. See INFERNAL, HELLISH.

STYLE, *n. particular manner, air, mode, &c.* बाणी *f.* भंगी *f.* धाटी *f.* धाटणी *f.* धरती *f.* धरणी *f.* धाकी *or* ठाकी *f.* लटक *f.* ठेव *f.* ठेवण *f.* भांत *f.* मोड *f.* कडी *f.* पर्याय *m.* पर *f.* छटा *f.* घटाव *m.* डौल *m.* ढब *f.* दस्ती *f.* वृत्ति *f.*
2 *particular manner of writing or speaking.* शब्दरचनेची-बोलण्याची-कवितेची-&c. बाणी *f.*-धरती *f.*-सरणी *f.*-डौल *m.*-&c.
3 *fashion of procedure,* v. COURSE. रीति *pop.* रीत *f.* चाल *f.* मोळा *m.* धारा *m.* पद्धति *f.*
4 (of a dial, &c.). शंकु *m.*
5 *pointed iron, graver, &c.* सळई *f.* शलाका *f.*
6 (of a flower). बांड *m.* पोगाडा *m.*
7 v. TITLE. किताब *m.* प्रतिष्ठानाम *n.*
8 *dashing way, &c.* श्रीमंतीडौल *m.*

To STYLE, *v. a.* v. To CALL, To NAME. म्हणणें, किताब *m.* देणें.

STYLISH, *a. dashing,* v. FINE. छानीचा, छानदार, मासलेदार, मासलेवाईक, श्रीमंतीडौलाचा, विलसित, विराजमान, विराजित.

STYPTIC, *a. that stops hemorrhage or bleeding.* रक्त बंद करणारा, रक्तावरोधी, रक्तनिरोधक.

STYPTIC, *n.* रक्तबंद करणारें औषध *n.*

STYRAX, See STORAX.

SUASIVE, &c. See PERSUASIVE, &c.

SUAVITY, *n. softness, &c.* (*of manners or speech*). गोडबोलेपणा *m.* गोडीगुलाबी *f.* गोडबोली *f.* मधुरता *f.* माधुर्य *n.* [ईषदम्ल.

SUBACID, *a. moderately acid.* आमगूळ, आंबटगोड, मधुराम्ल,

SUBALTERN, *n.* हाताखालचा अमलदार *m.*-कामगार *m.*

SUBALTERN, *a.* हाताखालचा, खालचा.

SUBAQUATIC, SUB-AQUEOUS, *a.* पाण्याखालचा.

SUB-DEPARTMENT, *n.* पोटचें प्रकरण *n.* उपांग *n.* उपप्रकरण *n.*

To SUB-DIVIDE, *v. a. part into smaller divisions.* वांटणीची-वांटणी *f.*-&c. करणें, अंशांश *m.*-प्रतिभाग *m.*-पोटचाभाग *m.*-&c. करणें *g. of o.*

SUBDIVISION, *n. subdivided portion.* अंशांश *m.* पोटचाभाग *m.* वांट्याचा वांटा *m.* प्रत्यंग *n.* प्रतिभाग *m.* प्रभाग *m.* शाखा *f.*

To SUBDUCE, *To* SUBDUCT. See To WITHDRAW, To SUBTRACT.

To SUBDUE, *v. a. bring into subjection, reduce under dominion, vanquish, &c.* जिंकणें, वश-स्वाधीन-&c. करणें-करून घेणें, जित-पराजित-पराक्रांत-&c. करणें, वठणीस-जरीस-&c. आणणें, हुकमांत-अमलांत-ताब्यांत-&c. आणणें, दमविणें, दमन*n.*-दम*m.*-निग्रह*m.*-&c. करणें *g.of o.* हस्तगत-सर-&c.करणें.—as intended, and answering to *to crush, to overwhelm, to overpower, &c.* भुईस-जमिनीस-धुळीस मिळवणें, जमिनदोस्त-चीत-पादाक्रांत-&c. करणें, लोळवणें, लोळसावणें, मारून चुना*m.* करणें *g. of o.* मारून पीठ*n.* करणें *g. of o.* धूळ *f.* करणें *g. of o.* खाणें.

SUBDUED, *p. and a.* v. V. जिंकलेला, वशकेलेला, वठणीस आणलेला, &c. जेर, वश, वशंगत, वशीभूत, वशीकृत, पराक्रांत, दमित, दांत, अभिहत, काचीज.

To be s. वठणीस येणें.

I. *of subdued affections and passions,* v. MORTIFIED. जितेंद्रिय, वशी, वशात्मा, शांत, शमी, प्रशांत, मनस्वी, विनीत.

SUBDUER, *n.* SUBDUING, *p. a.* v. V. जिंकणारा, वशकरणारा, वठणीस आणणारा, &c. दमक, दमी, दमन-&c. कर्त्ता-कारी.

SUBDUING, SUBDUAL, *n.* v.V.—*act.* जिंकणें*n.* वठणीस आणणें*n.* जेरीस आणणें*n.* &c. वशीकरण*n.* भंग*m.* भंजन *n.* दमन*n.* (used freely and elegantly in comp. as, इंद्रियदमन, रोगदमन, क्रोधदमन, कामदमन, दुष्टदमन, शत्रुदमन, &c.), दम*m.* दंडन*n.* दंड*m.* निग्रह*m.* निग्रहण*n.*

SUBJACENT, *a. situated below.* खालचा, अधःस्थ, अधःस्थित, अधर, अधोवर्त्ती.

To SUBJECT, *v. a. put under or within the power of.* खालीं आणणें, अमलांत-&c. आणणें, वश-अधीन-स्वाधीन-&c. करणें.

2 *subjugate,* v. To SUBDUE. जिंकणें, वश-&c. करणें.

3 *expose, make liable.* वश-स्वाधीन-अधीन-योग्य-जोगा-&c. करणें, पात्र-आस्पद-&c. करणें, दाढेंत-तोंडांत आणणें.

SUBJECT, *a. under the rule of.* खालचा, खालला, खालील, हुकमांतला, ताबेदार, वश्य, वश, हुकमी, हुकूमबंदा, हुकमती, अधीन, आज्ञांकित, विवश, सत्तेचा, सत्ताक्रांत *or* सत्वाक्रांत in comp. आयत्त, परस्वाधीन, पराधीन, परवश, परतंत्र, परछंद, परायण.

2 *exposed, liable, obnoxious.* वश, स्वाधीन, अधीन, (in comp. as रोगाधीन) योग्य, जोगा, अर्ह (in comp.).

SUBJECT, *n. one that owes allegiance to.* रयत *f.* प्रजा *f.*

Subjects—collect. or compreh. रयत *f.* प्रजा *f.* रयतावा *m.* रयतानी *f.* रयतलोक *m. pl.* लोक *m.*

2 *that in which any thing adheres or exists.* अधिकरण *n.* स्थान *n.*अधिष्ठान*n.* आधार *m.* आश्रय *m.* आशय *m.* व्याप्य *m.*

S. of an inference. व्याप्य *n.*

3 (of any operation or act). आश्रय *m.* अधिष्ठान *n.* अधिकरण *n.* पात्र *n.*

4 *topic, theme.* प्रकरण *n.* विषय *m.* गोष्ट *f.* बिंब *n.* वृत्तांत *m.* मजकूर *m.* मजमून *m. n.* प्रस्ताव *m.* प्रसंग *m.* प्रसक्ति *f.* वाग्विषय *m.* प्रतिपाद्य *n.* स्थल *n.*

5—in grammar, (of a verb). कर्त्ता.

SUBJECT MATTER, *n.* v. SUBJECT. विषय *m.* प्रस्ताव *m.*

SUBJECTED, *p.* v. V. 1. खालीं आणलेला, अमलांत आणलेला, &c.

2 जिंकलेला, वश केलेला, &c. जेर, वश, वशंगत, वशीकृत, वशीभूत, पराक्रांत, काबीज.

3 वश केलेला, &c.

SUBJECTION, *n.* v. V. 1.—*act.* खालीं आणणें *n.* अमलांत आणणें *n.* &c.

2—*act.* जिंकणें *n.* वशकरणें *n.* वशीकरण *n.* वशीक्रिया *f.*—*state.* ताबेदारी *f.* अंकितपणा *m.* हुकुमबरदारी *f.* अधीनता *f.* वशता *f.* परतंत्रता *f.* पारतंत्र्य*n.*पराधीनता *f.* आज्ञांकितत्व*n.*आज्ञाधीनता *f.*

In s. or subordinacy unto. ताब्यांत.

To acknowledge s. दांतीं-तोंडीं तृण *n.* धरणें.

To reduce to s. वठणीस आणणें.

3—*state.* जोगेपणा *m.* योग्यता *f.* वशता *f.* अधीनता *f.* तंत्र *n.*

SUBJECTIVE, *a. relating to the subject not to the object.* अधिष्ठाननिष्ठ, अधिकरणनिष्ठ, अधिकरणसंबंधी.

SUBJECTIVITY, *n.* v. A. अधिष्ठाननिष्ठता *f.* &c. अधिकरणसंबंधिता *f.*

To SUBJOIN, *v. a. add at the end, add after,* v. To ADD. खालीं घालणें-जोडणें-लिहिणें-&c. दुसऱ्यास लावणें.

To SUBJUGATE, &c. See To SUBDUE, &c.

SUBJUNCTIVE, *n.*—in grammar. संशयार्थ*m.*

To SUBLET, *v. a.* आपण भाड्यानें घेतलेला (वाडा वगैरे) दुसऱ्यास भाड्यानें देणें.

SUBLIMATE, *n.*—white. रसकर्पूर *pop.* रसकापूर *m.*

SUBLIME, *a.* See HIGH. 2 *lofty, elevated, &c.* fig. उंच, प्रौढ, प्रशस्त, प्रगल्भ, अत्युत्कृष्ट.

SUBLIMENESS, SUBLIMITY, *n.* v. A. 2. उंचपणा *m.* प्रौढपणा *m.* &c. प्रौढि *f.* प्रौढता *f.* प्रशस्तता *f.* प्रगल्भता *f.* प्राशस्त्य *n.* प्रागल्भ्य *n.*

SUBLUNARY, *a. mundane,* v. EARTHLY. भूलोकचा, ऐहलौकिक, ऐहिक.

SUBMARINE, *a.* समुद्रांतला, समुद्रतळचा, समुद्रतलस्थ.

To SUBMERGE, *v. a.* v. To PLUNGE. बुडवणें, मज्जन *n.*-निमज्जन *n.* करणें *g. of o.* मज्जित-&c. करणें.

2 See To INUNDATE.

SUBMERGED, SUBMERSED, *p.*v.V.1. बुडवलेला, मज्जित, निमज्जित, मग्न, निमग्न.

SUBMERGING, SUBMERSION, *n.* v. V. 1.—*act.* बुडवणें *n.* मज्जन *n.* निमज्जन*n.*

SUBMISSION, *n.* v. V. 1. दबणें *n.* वशहोणें *n.* हारघेणें *n.*शरणजाणें *n.* &c. अधीनतास्वीकार *m.* वशत्वस्वीकार*m.* पारतंत्र्यस्वीकार*m.*

2 *and* OBEDIENCE. वशअसणें *n.* &c. हुकुमबरदारी *f.* आज्ञापालन *n.* आज्ञासेवन*n.* अधीनता *f.* अंकितत्व *n.* आज्ञांकितत्व*n.*

I. See RESIGNATION.

SUBMISSIVE, *a.* v. OBEDIENT, HUMBLE, OBSEQUIOUS. आज्ञेंत राहणारा, हुकमी, हुकुमबंदा, आज्ञानुवर्त्ती, वशवर्त्ती, दीन, विनत, विनयी, सविनय, वशतास्वीकारी,अधीनतास्वीकारी,वशंवद.

SUBMISSIVELY, *adv.* v. A. *and* V. N. 1. वशहोऊन, हारघेऊन, शरणयेऊन, &c. कैदवार, दीनपणानें, दैन्यपूर्वक, अधीनतास्वीकारपूर्वक.

SUBMISSIVENESS, *n.* v. A. हुकमीपणा *m.* दीनपणा *m.* आज्ञानुवर्त्तित्व *n.* वशवर्त्तित्व *n.* विनति *f.*

To SUBMIT, *v. a.* (with the recip. pronoun) v. To OBEY. आज्ञेंत-हुकुमांत-सत्तेंत-&c. राहणें-असणें-वागणें, आज्ञापालन*n.*-आज्ञानुवर्त्तन *n.*-&c. करणें, वश-आज्ञांकित-&c. असणें.

2 v. To REFER. सोपणें, ठेवणें, घालणें.

To SUBMIT, *v. n. give up resistance, yield to another.* दबणें, दबकणें, वश-&c. होणें, भांडायास-लढायास-बादकरायास-&c. सोडणें, हार *f.* घेणें-पतकरणें-मानणें, हारी-हार-अजित *pop.* यजीत-शरण-&c. जाणें, हात *m. pl.* टेंकणें-जोडणें, बें *n.*-ची *n.*-जी *n.* म्हणणें-करणें, दांतीं-तोंडीं-&c. तृण *n.* धरणें-घेणें, अधीनता *f.*-

&c. पतकरणें, अधीनतास्वीकार *m.*-&c. करणें, शरणागत-&c.होणें.
2 *be subject, be submissive.* आज्ञेंत-हुकुमांत-वचनांत-कह्यांत-&c. राहणें-वागणें-असणें, आज्ञापालन *n.*-आज्ञानुसरण *n.*-हुकुमबरदारी *f.*-&c.करणें, वश-अधीन-आज्ञांकित-आज्ञाधीन-हुकुमबंदा-&c. होणें-असणें.

SUBORDINACY, *n.* v. A. 1. *and* SUBJECTION. ताबेदारी *f.* हुकमीपणा *m.* &c. अधीनता *f.* वशता *f.* आज्ञांकितत्व *n.*

SUBORDINATE, *a. under the control of.* v. SUBJECT. ताबेदार, हुकमती, हुकमी, हुकुमबंदा, आज्ञांकित, बगल्या.
2 *inferior in rank, authority, &c.* v. INFERIOR. खालचा, खालच्यापायरीचा-पदवीचा-&c.
3 *of less importance, secondary.* गौण, अप्रधान, अमुख्य.

SUBORDINATION, *n.* v. A. 1. *and* SUBJECTION. ताबेदारी *f.* अधीनता *f.* वशता *f.*
2 खालची पायरी *f.* खालची पदवी *f.*
3 गौणता *f.* अप्रधानता *f.* अप्राधान्य *n.*
Principle or law of s. गौणमुख्यन्याय *m.*

To SUBORN, *v. a.* (a witness, &c.) *bribe to take a false oath.* पैसादेऊन-लांच देऊन-&c. बधवणें-बनाऊ करणें-खोटें बोलवणें.

SUBORNATION, *n.* v. V.—*act.* पैसादेऊन बधवणें *n.* कूटसाक्ष्यसाधन *n.*

SUBPŒNA, *n.* जोरतलब *f.* तलब *f.*

To SUBSCRIBE, *v. a. avouch, attest, &c. by writing one's name beneath.* सही *f.*-हस्ताक्षर *n.* करणें-घालणें, दस्तूर *n.*-दस्तखत *n.* करणें, नांव *n.* लिहिणें-घालणें, सही करून-&c. कबूल करणें-मान्य करणें, स्वनामांकित करणें.
2 (a sum of money). पट्टींत-पट्टीवर-पट्टीचा *decl.*-बर्गणीच्यायादीवर-&c. लिहिणें-घालणें-मांडणें.

To SUBSCRIBE, *v. n. assent* v. To AGREE. कबूल-मान्य-सम्मत-&c. होणें-असणें.
2 *agree to give money.* पट्टी *f.*-टीप *f.* करणें. [सहीचा.

SUBSCRIBED, *p.* v. V. A. 1. सहीकेलेला, हस्ताक्षरघातलेला, &c.
2 पट्टींत लिहिलेला, &c.

SUBSCRIBER, *n.* SUBSCRIBING, *p. a.* v. V. A. 1. सहीकरणारा, हस्ताक्षर घालणारा, &c.
2 पट्टींत-पट्टीवर-&c. लिहिणारा-घालणारा, बर्गणीदार. [*n.* &c.

SUBSCRIPTION, *n.* v. V. A. 1.—*act.* सहीकरणें *n.* हस्ताक्षरघालणें
I. *name, &c. underwritten,* v. SIGNATURE. खालीं लिहिलेलें नाव *n.* सही *f.* दस्तखत *n.* हस्ताक्षर *n.* [टीप *f.* चंदा *m.*
II. *sum subscribed.* पट्टी *f.* पट्टीचा पैसा *m.* बर्गणी *f.* बर्गत *f.*

SUBSCRIPTION-LIST, *n.* पट्टी *f.* टिपेची-पट्टीची याद *f.*

SUBSEQUENCE, *n.* v. A. अनुयान *n.* अनुगमन *n.* अनुयायिता *f.* पश्चाद्यान *n.*

SUBSEQUENT, *a. following, coming or being after.* मागून झालेला, नंतरचा, मागूनचा, पाठीमागचा, मागचा, मागला, पाठचा, पुढचा, पुढला, पश्चात्कालिक, पश्चात्कालीन, पाश्चात्य.

SUBSEQUENTLY, *adv.* v. A. *and.* AFTERWARDS. मागून, मागाहून, मग, नंतर, पाठीवरून, उत्तरत्र.

To SUBSERVE, *v. a. serve instrumentally, promote the end of.* कामास-उपयोगास-&c. पडणें *g. of o.* सहकारिता *f.*-उपयोगिता *f.*-&c. करणें *and, with in. con.* होणें-पडणें *g. of s.* कामाचा-उपयोगी-सहकारी-&c. होणें-पडणें, अनुवर्त्तणें, अनुवर्त्तन *n.*-अनुवृत्ति *f.*-आज्ञानुवर्त्तन *n.* करणें.

SUBSERVIENCE, SUBSERVIENCY, *n.* v. A. उपयोग *m.* उपकार *m.* सहकार *m.* उपयोगिता *f.* उपकारिता *f.* उपयुक्तता *f.* सहकारिता *f.* अनुवर्त्तन *n.* अनुवृत्ति *f.* तंत्र *n.*

SUBSERVIENT, *a.* SUBSERVING, *p. a.* v. V. उपयोगाचा, &c. उपयोगी, उपयुक्त, उपकारक, उपकारी, सहकारी, उपकार-सहकार-&c. कर्त्ता-कारी-&c. [अंशांश *m.*

SUB-SHARE, *n.* वांट्याचा वांटा *m.* &c. पोटचा विभाग *m.*-वांटा *m.*

SUB-SHARER, *n.* पोटचा बिभागी वांटेकरी, अंशांशी, प्रतिभागाधिकारी.

To SUBSIDE, *v. n. fall to the bottom,* v. To SETTLE. बसणें, खालीं जाणें-बसणें, थिरावणें.
2 *become quiet, calm, still, &c.* v. To DECREASE, To ABATE. बसणें, पडणें, उतरणें, थिरावणें, कमतावणें, खालावणें, शांत-&c. होणें, उतार *m.* उपशम *m.*-उपशमन *n.*-&c. होणें *g. of s.*
3 *be reduced,*—a swelling. ओसरणें, उतरणें, अमुजणें, ओझरणें, मावळणें, वरमणें, उसवणें, जिरणें, ओसार *m.*-ओसारा *m.*-&c. होणें *g. of s.*

SUBSIDENCE, SUBSIDENCY, SUBSIDING, *n.* v. V. 1. बसणें *n.* थिरावणें *n.* अधःपतन *n.*
2 बसणें *n.* पडणें *n.* &c. उतार *m.* उपशम *m.* उपशमन *n.*
3 ओसरणें *n.* उतरणें *n.* &c. ओसार *m.* ओसारा *m.*

SUBSIDIARY, *a. aiding, assisting,* v. HELPING. कुमकेचा, उपकर्त्ता, उपकारी, उपकारक, सहकारी.

SUBSIDY, *n. aid in money.* पैशाची-&c. कुमक *f.* पैक्याचा-&c. पुरावा *m.* धनरूपसाहाय्य *n.*

To SUBSIST, *v. n.* v. To BE. असणें.
2 *be maintained,* v. To LIVE. निर्वाह *m.*-गुजारा *m.*-पोटगुजारा *m.*-पोटाचें *n.*-&c. चालणें *g. of s.* पोट *n.* चालवणें-भरणें, पोट *n.* भरणें *g. of s.*
3 See To INHERE.

To SUBSIST, *v. a. maintain, support, feed.* पोषणें *or* पोसणें. पाळणें, संभाळणें, बाळगणें, वाहणें, चालवणें *with* चें *of o.* पालन *n.*-पोषण *n.*-उदरपोषण *n*-उदरनिर्वाह *m.*-पाल्यग्रहण *n.*-&c. करणें *g. of o.* खर्च *m.*-पोटाचें *n.*-निर्वाह *m.*-योगक्षेम *m.*-&c. चालवणें *g. of o.*

SUBSISTED, *p.* v. V. A. पोसलेला, पाळलेला, &c. पालित, पोषित.

SUBSISTENCE, *n.* v. V N. 1. *and* EXISTENCE. आहेपणा *m.* अस्तित्व *n.* सत्व *n.* स्थिति *f.*
2—*state,* v. LIVING. गुजारा *m.* पोटगुजारा *m.* गुजराण *f.* वर्त्तणूक *f.* उदरनिर्वाह *m.* प्रपंचनिर्वाह *m.* उदरपोषण *n.* उपजीवन *n.*
I. *means of subsisting,* v. LIVELIHOOD. उपजीविका *f.* उपजीवन *n.* उपजीव्य *n.* जीविका *f.* आटापाणी *n.* तुकडा *m.* वृत्त्युपाय *m.* उपकरण *n.* [सत्ववान्.

SUBSISTENT, *a.* v. EXISTENT. असणारा, अस्तित्वविशिष्ट, वर्त्तमान,

SUBSTANCE, *n. real being,* v. REALITY. तत्व *n.* तत्वार्थ *m.*
2 *a real being,* v. THING. पदार्थ *m.* द्रव्य *n.* वस्तु *n. pop.* वस्तू *f.* वस्त *f.* अर्थ *m.* सत्व *n.*
Substances. द्रव्यजात *n.*
3 *material, matter.* दळ *n.* द्रव्य *n.* वस्तु *n.* मूर्त्तवस्तु *n.* मूर्त्तद्रव्य *n.* मूर्त्ति *f.* घन *m.*
4 *essential or material part,* v. ESSENCE. सारांश *m.* सार *m.* *n.* गर्भ *m.* तत्वार्थ *m.*
5 *estate, wealth,* v. PROPERTY, RICHES. ऐवज *m.* ऐपत *f.* संपत्ति *f.* धन *n.* उबारा *m.* गठडी *f.* गठडें *n.* गड्डा *m.* डब्बा *m.*

केवा m. बुटी f. अर्थ m. मात्रा f. दुडू m. माया f.

One's whole s. सर्वस्व n.

SUBSTANTIABLE, a. v. V. प्रतिपादायाजोगा- सारखा-&c. प्रतिपाद्य, समर्थनीय, प्रमेय.

SUBSTANTIAL, a. *having substance, actually existing,* v. REAL, TRUE. मूर्त्तिमंत, वस्तुसत्, वास्तविक, वास्तव, वस्तुसत्ताक, वस्त्वात्मक.

2 *having much substance; solid, stout, thick, &c.* ऐवजदार, ऐवजशीर, दळदार, सकस, कसदार, दडदडीत, दडस, दाट, धमकट, घन, घणसर, सारवान्, घस्मर, घट्ट, घटमूट, मोटाधाटा, मखूसम, भक्कम, बळकट, सष्टम, ठोसर, ठोक, ठोकळ, ठळक, कुब्बल, धक्क, खंबीर, खम्माल, पोक्त, पोक्ता, ऐबट, संगीन, टपकळ.

3—of honors, &c ; *not hollow or fallacious.* कसदार, सारवान्, ओला.

4 *wealthy, responsible,* v. RICH. असता, टमटमीत or टुमटुमीत, दुमदुमीत, गबरू, गब्बर, तोंगल, जिवट, जीवदार, चिकण or चिक्कण, ठळक, खबरदार, ऐवजदार, ऐपतदार, केवेदार, बुटीवाला, सार्थ, गडगंज.

A s. man. पागोट्याचा धनी, ज्याचें जड पारडें n. साव, असतेकरी, ताजेंकूळ n. तरतेंकूळ n.

5 See MATERIAL. [अर्थतः.

SUBSTANTIALLY, *adv.* v. A. 1. *and* REALLY. तत्वतः, वस्तुतः,

SUBSTANTIALNESS, SUBSTANTIALITY, n. v. A. 1. वास्तवत्व n. वास्तविकत्व n. सत्व n. सत्ता f. वस्तुसत्ता f.

2 ठोसरपणा m. घणसरपणा m. भक्कमपणा m. &c. बट्टाई f. खंबिरी f. बळकटी f.

3 ओलेपणा m. कस m. सार m. n. साद्रता f.

4 टमटमितपणा m. गबरूपणा m. गब्बरपणा m. &c. ऐवजदारी f. ऐपतदारी f.

To SUBSTANTIATE, v. a. *evince, establish,* v. To PROVE. प्रतिपादणें, पुरवणें. पुरवून देणें, खरा-सत्य-&c. करणें-करून देणें, पुरवणी f.- पुरावा m.-प्रतिपादन n.-समर्थन n.-&c. करणें g. of o.

SUBSTANTIATED, p. v. V. प्रतिपादलेला, पुरवून दिल्हेला, खरा करून दिल्हेला, प्रतिपादित, समर्थित, शाबूत or द.

SUBSTANTIATER, n. SUBSTANTIATING, p. a. v. V. प्रतिपादणारा, पुरवून देणारा, खरा करून देणारा, &c. प्रतिपादक, प्रतिपादन-समर्थन-&c. कर्त्ता-कारी-कारक.

SUBSTANTIATION, n. v. V.—*act.* प्रतिपादणें n. पुरवून देणें n. &c. पुरवणी f. पुरावा m. पुराव m. प्रतिपादन n. समर्थन n. प्रपादन n.

SUBSTANTIVE, n.—in gram. v. NOUN. विशेष्य n. द्रव्यवाचकm.

To SUBSTITUTE, v. a. *put in the place of another.* बदल-बदला-मोबदला-ऐवजीं-जागीं-स्थानीं-&c. देणें ठेवणें, बारचा *decl.*-बांटचा *decl.*-बदली-बदल्या-&c. देणें-ठेवणें, प्रतिनिधित्वें करून ठेवणें.

SUBSTITUTE, n.—of persons. बदली, बदल्या (*fem.* बदली), इसममुखत्यारा, बारचा, बांटचा, होस्साता, हातेला, होता, प्रतिनिधि, अनुकल्प.

2—of things. गौणकल्प m. अनुकल्प m. प्रतिनिधि m.

SUBSTITUTION, n. v. V. ऐवजींठेवणें n. बदलठेवणें n. मोबदलाठेवणें n. &c.

S. of letters. आदेश m.

SUBSTITUTIONAL, STUBSTITUTIONARY, a. *pertaining, &c. to substitution.* बदलीचा, मोबदला ठेवण्याचा.

2 *succedaneous.* गौण, गौणभूत, आनुकल्पिक.

SUBSTRATUM, n. खालचा-तळचा-&c. थर m.-तह m.

2—in metaphysics; *basis,* v. SUBJECT. अधिकरण n. आधार m.

SUBTERFUGE, n. *shift, salvo, creep hole,* v. EVASION. खिडकी f. फट f. सोडवण f. हिला m. हिलाहरकत f. छिद्र n.

SUBTERRANEAN, SUBTERRANEOUS, a. *lying under ground.* जमिनींतला, जमिनींतील, भुईंतला, भुईंतील, जमिनींखालचा, भुईंखालचा.

S. cavity. भुयार or भुंयार n.

S. passage. तळवाट f. सुरंग or सुरुंग m.

SUBTILE, a. *rare, tenuous.* बारीक, पातळ, सूक्ष्म

2 *fine, nice, delicate, exquisite, &c.* नाजूक, बारीक, सूक्ष्म, तलम, लाघवी.

3 *refined, abstract, &c.* बारीक, सूक्ष्म.

4 *fine-searching, acute,* v. SHARP. सूक्ष्मशोधी, सूक्ष्मबुद्धि, सूक्ष्मद्रष्टा, सूक्ष्मदर्शी.

SUBTILITY, SUBTILNESS, n. v. A. 1. बारिकपणा m. &c. बारकाई f. बारकावा m. पातळाई f. पातळी f. सूक्ष्मता f. सौक्ष्म्य n.

2 बारिकपणा m. नाजकाई f. बारकाई f. बारकावा m. सूक्ष्मता f. सौक्ष्म्य n. लाघव n.

3 बारिकपणा m. सूक्ष्मता f. सौक्ष्म्य n.

I.—in an argument, &c. मर्म n.

SUBTLE, SUBTLENESS. See CUNNING, &c.

To SUBTRACT, v. a. *take from.* काढणें, काटणें, घेणें.

2—in arithmetic. बाद करणें-घालणें, बादणें, ऋण n. करणें, अंतर n. करणें, बजा करणें-पाडणें.

SUBTRACTED, p. V. 1. काढलेला, घेतलेला, &c.

2 बाद केलेला, &c. बजा, व्यवकलित.

SUBTRACTER, n. SUBTRACTING, p. a. v. V. 1. काढणारा, घेणारा, &c.

2 बाद करणारा, बजा करणारा, &c. शोधन-व्यवकलन-&c. कर्त्ता-कारी-&c.

SUBTRACTION, n. v. V. 1.—*act.* काढणें n. घेणें n. &c.

2 बजा करणें n. बाद करणें n. &c. बजाबाकी f. बादबाकी f. व्यवकलन n. शोधन n. विवर n.

Compound s. विविधबजाबाकी f.

The remainder after a s. बादबाकी f. बजाबाकी f.

SUBTRAHEND, n. *the sum to be subtracted.* बादकरावाचा अंक m. आंकडा m. &c. शोधक m. ऋण n.

SUBURB, SUBURBS, n. *parts outside the walls of a city.* शाखानगर n. उपनगर n. शाखापुर n. नगरोपांत m.

SUBURBAN, SUBURBIAL, a. v. N. उपनगराचा, शाखानगराचा, &c. उपनगरस्थ, शाखानगरस्थ.

SUBVERSION, n. v. V.—*act.* मोडणें n. पाडणें n. &c. ध्वंसन n. विध्वंसन n.—*state.* ध्वंस m. विध्वंस m. नाश m.

To SUBVERT, v. a. *overthrow, overturn,* v. To DESTROY, To RUIN. पाडणें, मोडणें, पाडून-मोडून देणें-टाकणें, लयास नेणें, नष्ट-&c. करणें.

SUBVERTED, p. v. V. मोडलेला, &c. ध्वंसित, विध्वंसित, ध्वस्त.

SUBVERTER, n. SUBVERTING, p. a. SUBVERSIVE, a. v. V. मोडणारा, मोडून टाकणारा, ध्वंस-ध्वंसन-&c. कर्त्ता-कारी-&c.

SUCCEDANEOUS, a. *substitutionary.* गौण, गुणभूत, आनुकल्पिक.

S. measure or mode. पर्याय m.

SUCCEDANEUM, n. v. SUBSTITUTE. गौणकल्प m. अनुकल्प m.

To SUCCEED, v. n. *follow in order.* मागें-पाठीमागें-मागून-पाठीमागून-पाठीवर-&c. येणें-जाणें-चालणें, क्रमानें-अनुक्रमानें-पर्या-

यानें-परिपाटीनें-&c. येणें होणें, पुढें-नंतर-&c. येणें.
2 *come into the place of that which has preceded.* जागां-जागीं-ठिकाणीं-स्थानीं-&c. येणें, जाग्यावर-कामावर-पदावर-&c.येणें.
3—of persons; *attain success*, v. To Prosper. जिंकणें, जिंतणें, जय *m.*-यश *n.* पावणें-मिळवणें, निभणें, निभावणें, धडीस *or* तडीस-शेवटास-&c. जाणें, पार जाणें-पडणें, तडावणें, जय*m.*-यश*n.* येणें *in. con.* फत्ते *f.* होणें *g. of s.* लाग*m.* साधणें *g. of s.*
4—of measures; *terminate as desired*, v. To Prosper.लागणें, लागू होणें, साधणें, फळणें, जयास जाणें, शेवटास-धडीस *or* धडीस जाणें, पार *adv.*जाणें-पडणें, गुणास येणें.

To Succeed, *v. a. take the place of.* जागां-जागीं-ठिकाणीं-स्थानीं-स्थानावर-जाग्यावर-कामावर-पदावर-अधिकारावर-&c.येणें*g.of o.*
2 See To Follow. 3 See To Prosper.

Succeeder, *n.* Succeeding, *p. a.* Successor, *n.* v. V. N.
1. मागें-पाठीमागें-मागून-क्रमानें-अनुक्रमानें-&c. येणारा-जाणारा-आलेला-&c. पाठचा, पाठीमागचा, मागचा,पाठीवरचा,क्रमानुयायी.
2 *and* V. A. 1. जागीं-कामावर-&c. येणारा-आलेला.

Success, *n.*—esp. of persons, v. Prosperousness. सद्धी *f.* सिद्धि *f.* निभाव *m.* यश *n.* बरकत *f.*
2 *happy issue, &c.* यश *n.* जय *m.* निर्गत *f.* निभाव *m.* बरकत *f.* सिद्धि *f.* अर्थसिद्धि *f.* फलसिद्धि *f.* कार्यसिद्धि *f.*
Instrument or means of s. फलसाधन *n.*
3 *termination* (good *or* ill), *result.* परिणाम *m.* शेवट *m.* निर्गम *m.* निगम *m.* पर्यवसान *n.*

Successful, *a.*—of persons, v. Prosperous. श्रीमान्, जयी, चरितार्थ, कृतार्थ, कृतकृतार्थ, कृतकृत्य, प्राप्तयश, प्राप्तार्थ, प्राप्ताश, आशाप्राप्त, अर्थसिद्ध, पद्महस्त *pop.* पद्महस्ती.
2—of actions, affairs, &c. लागू, शेवटास-सिद्धीस-&c. जाणारा-गेलेला, सफल, सुफल, सिद्ध, गुणावह.

Successfulness. See Success.

Succession, *n. a following of things in order, consecution.* परंपरा *f.* क्रम *m.* अनुक्रम *m.* आनुपूर्वी *f.* अन्वय *m.* अनुयान *n.* आनुपूर्व्य *n.* पारंपर्य *n.* शिलशिला *or* ला *m.* परवड *f.* देवड *f.* अनुवृत्ति *f.* अनुवर्त्तन *n.* अनुषंग *m.* लाघाळ *f.*
In close and quick s. पाठोपाठ, लागोपाठ, मागोमाग, लगोलग, हारोहार, बरावर, तारोतार, लगत.
Natural s. or order. समन्वय *m.*
2 *line, &c. of persons or things following in close succession,* v. Series. परंपरा *f* हार *f.* आवलि *f.* माळ *f.* माळका *f.*
3 *lineage,* v. Line, Family. वंश *m.* वंशपरंपरा *f.* वंशावलि *f.* अन्वय *m.* [अधिकारपर्याय *m.*
4 *power or right of succeeding to another.* उत्तराधिकार *m.*

Successional, *a.* परंपरेचा, पारंपरिक.

Successive, *a. following in uninterrupted course, consecutive.* अनुक्रमानें-&c. येणारा-आलेला, अनुक्रमाचा, पाठोपाठचा, लागोपाठचा, मागोपाठचा, &c. यथाक्रम, यथानुक्रम, क्रमानुयायी, क्रमागत, क्रमायात, परंपरागत, परंपरायात, पारंपरिक, परंपर,अनुपूर्व, आनुक्रमिक, आन्वयिक.
S. naturally. समन्वित.

Successively, *adv.* v. A. एकामागेंएक, एकापाठीमागेंएक, अनुक्रमानें, परंपरेनें, हारोहार, लगत, बराबर, अनुक्रमतः, अनुक्रमशः, अनुपूर्वशः. [अफल.

Successless, *a.* v. Unsuccessful. निष्फल, निरर्थक, विफल,

Successor. See Succeeder.

Succinct, *a. compressed, concise,* v. Brief. संक्षेपाचा, संक्षिप्त, थोडक्यांत आणलेला, अल्पविस्ताराचा, संकलित, मितविस्तारक, अल्पविस्तारक.

Succinctly *adv.* v. A. संक्षेपानें, संक्षेपेंकरून, थोडक्यांत.

Succinctness, *n.* v. A. संक्षिप्तता *f.* अल्पविस्तार*m.* मितविस्तार*m.*

Succory, *n. endive.* कासनी *f.*

Succour, *To* Succour. See Help, To Help.

Succulence, *n.* v. A. रसाळपणा*m.* रसभरितपणा*m.* सरसता *f.* रसबाहुल्य*n.*

Succulent, *a. juicy, sappy.* रसाळ, रसभरू, रसभरित, सरस, रसवान्, सद्रव, रसरसीत *or* शीत, सकस, कसदार, ओला, रसमय, रसबहुल, रसप्रचुर, जलमय.
Young and s. काकडा.
To be s. रसरसणें.

To Succumb, *v. n.* v. To Yield, To Submit. वांकणें, डगणें, दबणें, दबकणें, मेटें*n. pl.* टेंकणें *g. of s.* बें*n.* करणें-म्हणणें.

Such, *a. of this kind.* असा, असला, त्या जातीचा-प्रकाराचा-&c. असल्या जातीचा-&c. ईदृश, ह्यासारखा.
2 *of that kind.* तसा, तसला, तसल्या जातीचा-प्रकाराचा-&c. त्या जातीचा-प्रकाराचा-&c. त्यासारखा, तादृश.
3—in specifying a person or place of a certain kind. अमका, अमुक, फलाणा.
S. as. सारखा.

Such-like. See Such.

To Suck, *v. a. draw in with the mouth.* चुंफणें, चोखणें *or* चुंखणें, चुंफून-चोखून-&c. घेणें, चुंबणें, तोंडानें ओढणें, चुंफा*m.* घेणें *g. of o.* चोष*m.*-चोषण*n.*-&c. करणें *g. of o.*
A child's coral or sucking stick. चुंफणी *f.* चोखणी *f.*
2 (the breast or teat, the dam, &c.). ओढणें, तोंडानें ओढणें, स्तनपान*n.* करणें *g. of o.* दूध*n.* पिणें *g. of o.* लुंचणें.
3 up; v. To Absorb. शोषणें *pop.* शोखणें, शोषून घेणें, शोषण *n.*-शोष*m.*-&c. करणें *g. of o.*

To Suck, *v. n. draw the breast.* स्तनपान*n.* करणें, स्तन*n.*-थान*n.* पिणें, लुंचणें. [दूध*n.*

Suck, *n. milk from the breast.* थानचें-आंगचें-आंगावरचें-&c.

Sucked, *p.* v. V. A. 1. चुंफलेला, चोखलेला, &c. चोषित.
3 शोषलेला, &c. शोषित.

Sucker, *n.* Sucking, *p. a.* v. V. 1. चुंफणारा, चोखणारा, चोषक, चोषणकर्त्ता-कारक-कारी, &c.
2 *and* V. N. स्तनपान करणारा, दूधपिणारा, दुधपिता, तान्हा, तान्हवट, थानचा, आंगावरचा, थानवा, थानपिता.
3 शोषणारा, &c. शोषक, शोषणकर्त्ता-कारी-&c.
I. See Shoot.

To Suckle, *v. a. nurse at the breast.* स्तन*n.*-थान *n.*-अमा *m.*-&c. देणें-पाजणें, स्तनपान*n.* देणें, थानचें-आंगचें-&c. दूध*n.* देणें-पाजणें.
To conceive whilst suckling. ताना गाभास जाणें, तान गाभणें.
To waste through suckling. चिटणीस पडणें.

Suckling, *a.* तान्हा, तान्हवट, पिणीचा, थानचा, आंगावरचा, थानवा, दुधपिता.
Sickening of a s. through renewed conception of its

mother. परव्हाm. आयनेरेंn.—*And* To sicken, &c. आयनेरणें *or* अनारणें, अवधणणें.

SUCTION, SUCKING, *n.* v. V. A. 1.—*act.* चुंफणेंn. चोखणेंn. तोंडानें ओढणेंn. &c. चुंफाm. चोषm. चोषणn.

SUDDEN, *a. happening without previous notice, unexpected.* एकाएकींचा, अकस्मातूचा, एकाएकीं-&c. आलेला, आकस्मिक, अकल्पित.

On a s. अकस्मात्.

SUDDENLY, *adv.* v. A. एकाएकीं, अवचित, अवचितां, अवचट, अवस्तूक, अवस्तां, अकल्पित, अकस्मात्, अचानक, अलगपीत, एकसरा *decl.*

SUDDENNESS, *n.* v. A. अचानकपणा *m.* अवस्तुकपणा *m.* आकस्मिकत्व *n.* अकल्पितत्व *n.* [स्पादक.

SUDORIFIC, *a. causing sweat.* घाम आणणारा, स्वेदजनक, स्वेदो-

SUDORIFIC, *n. medicine to cause sweat.* घाम आणण्याचें औषध *n.* स्वेदन *n.* स्वेदोत्पादक औषध *n.* [णवणी *n.*

SUDS, *n. water impregnated with soap.* साबणाचें पाणी *n.* साब-

To SUE, *v. a. prosecute by law.* फिर्याद *f.* करणें *with* वर *of o.* खटला *m.*-वाद *m.*-व्यवहार *m.*-&c. करणें-उभा करणें.

To SUE, *v. n. petition,* v. To BEG. अर्ज *m.*-विनंती *f.*-प्रार्थना *f.*-&c. करणें.

SUET, *n. fat about the kidneys.* गुर्दावरील चरबी *f.* वपा *f.*

To SUFFER, *v. a. undergo, endure, feel, be the subject of.* सोसणें, साहणें, भोगणें, कंठणें, काढणें, अनुभवणें, पावणें, अनुभव *m.*-&c. होणें *g. of o. with in. con.*

2 *not to sink under; bear, support, sustain, endure.* सोसणें, साहणें, सोसून-साहून-&c. घेणें, पुरवणें *in. con.* सहन *n.*-सोसणूक *f.*-&c. करणें *g. of o.*

3 *allow, not forbid,* v. To PERMIT. परवानगी *f.*-&c. देणें, देणें in combination with another verb, as जाऊं देणें, येऊं देणें, &c. अडथळा *m.*-आडकाठी *f.*-&c. न करणें, नको न म्हणणें, निषेधाभाव *m.* असणें *g. of s.*

4 *be acted upon, be affected by.* खाणें, सोसणें, बसणें *in. con.* लागणें *in. con.* होणें *in. con.*

To s. loss. तोटा *m.*-नुकसान *n.*-&c. बसणें *in. con.*

To SUFFER, *v. n. undergo pain.* दुःख *n.*-श्रम *m.*-क्लेश *m.*-शरीरभोग *m.*-भोग *m.*-&c. भोगणें-अनुभवणें, दुःख *n.*-&c. असणें *in. con.* दुःखी-&c. असणें, कंठणें, दुःख *n.* कंठणें, दुःखात-&c. असणें.

To s. for one's folly. तोंडांत खाणें.

2 *sustain injury.* नुकसान *n.*-नुकसानी *f.*-खराबी *f.*-&c. होणें *g. of s.* धक्का *m.*-नुकसान *n.*-&c. बसणें *in. con.*—a limb or member, दुखवणें *or* दुखावणें.

SUFFERABLE, *a.* v. V. A. 2. सोसाया-सहाया-&c. जोगा-सारखा-&c. सहनीय, सह्य.

Easily s. सुसह, सुवह.

SUFFERANCE, SUFFERING, *n.* v. V. A. 1. सोसणें *n.* कंठणें *n.* अनुभवणें *n.* &c. अनुभव *m.* भोग *m.*

2 *and* PATIENCE. सोसणें *n.* &c. सोसणूक *f.* सहन *n.* सहावन. क्षमा *f.* क्षांति *f.* [बंध *m.*

3 परवानगी *f.* कानडोळा *m.* निषेधाभाव *m.* अनिषेध *m.* अप्रति-

v. V. N. 1. दुःख भोगणें *n.* दुःख कंठणें *n.* &c.

I. v. PAIN, MISERY. दुःख *n.* व्यथा *f.* श्रम *m.* क्लेश *m.* भोग *m.* शरीरभोग *m.*

SUFFERED, *p.* v. V. A. 1. सोसलेला, भोगलेला, अनुभवलेला, &c. भुक्त, उपभुक्त, अनुभूत.

2 साहलेला, &c. सहित.

3 दिल्हेला in combination with another verb, अनिषिद्ध, अप्रतिबद्ध, निषेधाभावाचा.

SUFFERER, *n.* SUFFERING, *p. a.* v. V. A. 1. सोसणारा, भोगणारा, &c. भोक्ता, भोगी. [अ., दुस्सह.]

2 सोसणारा, साहणारा, &c. सहनकर्त्ता-कारी-&c. सह (in comp.

3 देणारा in combination with another verb, कानडोळा करणारा, अनिषेधक.

v. V. N. 1. *and* AFFLICTED. दुःखी, दुःखित, कष्टी, श्रमी, दुःख भोगी, दुःखभोक्ता.

To SUFFICE, *v. n. be sufficient.* पुरणें, पुरवणें, पुरी *f.* पडणें *g. of s.* पुरवटा *or* ठा *m.*-पुरव *f.*-&c. येणें *g. of s.* पुरा-&c. होणें, संजोगणें.

To make to s. पुरवणें, पुरवून पुरवून करणें.

To SUFFICE, *v. a.* See To SATISFY.

SUFFICIENCY, *n. supply equal to the want.* पुरवटा *or* ठा *m.* पुरव *f.* पर्याप्ति *f.* संजोगणी *f.* पुरी *f.*

Ample s. v. PLENTY, EXUBERANCE. पुरपुराट *m.*

2 See COMPETENCY.

SUFFICIENT, *a. enough, equal to the want.* पुरता, पुरा, पुरेसा, सपुरता, पुरायाजोगा, पर्याप्त, पाहिजेतितका, जितक्यास तितका, कार्याकारण.

Amply s. v. EXUBERANT. पुष्कळ, विपुल.

Barely s. चुटपुटीत, चुटपुरता *or* चुटपुटता *or* चुटपूट.

2 See COMPETENT.

SUFFICIENTLY, *adv.* v. A. 1. पुरे, बस, पुरता *decl.* पुरा *decl.* पुराव्याजोगा *decl.* पाहिजेतितका *decl.*

To SUFFOCATE, *v. a. choke, stifle.* दमm.-श्वास *m.*-श्वासोश्वासm.-&c. कोंडणें-कोंडून मारणें, गळा *m.*-नरडी *f.*-&c. दाबून मारणें, कोंडमार *m.*-कोंडमारा *m.*-श्वासावरोध *m.*-श्वासरोध *m.*-&c. करणें-करून मारणें. [दुश्वास, रुद्धप्राण.

SUFFOCATED, *p.* v. V. दम कोंडलेला, दम कोंडून मारलेला, &c. रु-

SUFFOCATER, *n.* SUFFOCATING, *p. a.* SUFFOCATIVE, *a.* v. V. दमकोंडणारा, दमकोंडूनमारणारा, श्वासकोंडणारा, &c. श्वासरोधक, श्वासावरोधक.

SUFFOCATION, *n.* v. V.—*act.* दमकोंडणें *n.* दमकोंडून मारणें *n.* श्वासकोंडणें *n.*&c. कोंडमारm. कोंडमाराm. श्वासरोधm. श्वासावरोध *m.* श्वासप्रतिरोध *m.* श्वासप्रतिबंध *m.*

SUFFRAGE. See VOTE.

To SUFFUSE, *v. a.* v. To OVERSPREAD. व्यापणें, भरणें, भरवणें, व्यापून-भरून घेणें.

SUFFUSED, *p.* v. V. व्यापलेला, भरलेला, व्याप्त. [*f.*

SUFFUSION, *n.* v. V.—*act.* व्यापणें *n.* भरणें *n.* &c.—*state.* व्याप्ति

SUGAR, *n.* साखर *or* साकर *f.* शर्करा *f.* Some kinds of *sugar* are खांड, गुळी, चिनी, दाणा, दुबोटा, नाबदसाखर, फुलगोटा, बुरासाखर, मुगदुमी *or* मुगदमी साखर, रायपुरी साखर.

Coarse s. *sugar-cane-juice inspissated.* गूळ *m.* गुड *m.*

Coarse s. and water. गूळपाणी *n.* गुळवणी *n.*

Drippings from newly prepared s. काकवी *f.*

Fond of s. साखऱ्या, गोड्या.

Lump s. खडी साखर *f.* खडे साखर *f.*

Pat or ball of coarse s. भेली *f.*
Soft s. पिठीसाखर *f.* पेटीची साखर *f.*
S.-boiler. गुळव्या *m.*
S. cleaned by washing. धुवा *or* धुवासाखर *f.*
S. or syrup boiled to consistency. चिकी *f.*
S. prepared for confectionaries. चाचणी *f.* पाक *m.* पंक *m.*
S.-water boiled and thickened with flour. राब *f.*
Stone in soft s. गुळदगड *m.* गुळधोंडा *m.*
Wooden scraper of s. फणा *m.*

To SUGAR, *v. a. sprinkle, &c. with sugar, sweeten.* साखर *f.* घालणें, गोड-मिष्ट-शर्करान्वित-शर्करायुक्त-&c. करणें.

SUGAR-CANDY, *n.* खडीसाखर *f.* खडेसाखर *f.* मिश्री *or* मिसरी *f.* नाबद *f.* नाबद साखर *f.*

SUGAR-CANE, *n.* ऊंस *m.* इक्षु *m.* इक्षुकांड *n.* मधुयष्टि *f.* मधुतृण *n.* गुडतृण *n.* गुडदंड *m.* Some kinds of *sugar-cane* are, कातळाऊंस, भोंशा ऊस *or* भोंस, पुंडा *or* पोंडा.
Boiler for the juice of s. कायील *or* काईल *or* काहील *f.*
A cane of s. ऊंस *m.* उंसाचेंतांट *n.* इक्षुदंड *m.*
Head or crop of s. वाढ *or* वाढें *n.*
Hole in which boiled s. juice is inspissated. ढेंपाळी *f.* ढेपाळें *n.* खोंचा *m.* बऱ्हा *m.* वाफा *m.*
Inspissation of the juice of s. मळण *n.*
Joint or small piece of s. as exposed for sale. नाबद *f.* नाबदा *m.* [घण *n.*
Juice of s. as set in the boiler to be inspissated. अ-
Juice of s. boiled to the consistence of honey, *sling.* काकवी *f.* कांकी *f.*
Mass of inspissated s. juice. ढेप *or* गुळाची ढेप *f.*
Mass of squeezed and dry s. चिपाड *or* ट *or* चिपड *n.*
Middle portion of a s. मधकांडें *n.*
Morsel of s. *small bit* (*a joint, &c.*). गंडरी *or* गंडोरी *f.* करवा *m.* कांडी *f.* कांडें *n.*
Pressed s. घाणा *m.*
Squeezed or chewed s. चोंथा *m.* चुंमळ *f.*
S. juice inspissated. चिकी *f.* राब *f.*
S.-plantation. उशील *n.* थळ *n.* [s. उसरान *n.*
S.-plantation cleared; *or* place prepared for planting
S.-planter. थळबाईक.
S. springing from the stock, after cutting of first growth ; *also* the stock left to reshoot. खडवा *or* खोडवा *m.*

SUGAR-COLORED, *a.* साखररंगी, गुळरंगी.

SUGAR-MILL, *n.* चरक *m.* गुऱ्हाळ *n.* घाणा *m.* इक्षुयंत्र *n.* रगाडा *m.*
Beam of a s. मुसल *or* मुसळ *n.*—Beam of it to which bullocks are yoked. आडें *n.* ढोंक *n.*
Hand s. हातचरक *m.* हातरगाडा *m.*
Lower transverse beam of a s. काठवट *n.*
Middle or larger beam of a s. नवरा *m.*
Side-beam of a s. नवरी *f.*

SUGAR-WORK, *n.* गुऱ्हाळ *n.* गुऱ्हाळघर *n.* [शर्करायुक्त.

SUGARED, *p.* v. V. साखर घातलेला, &c. साखरेचा, शर्करान्वित,
S. water. गुळवणी *n.*

SUGARY, *a. sweet.* गोड, मिष्ट, साखरेचा, शर्करान्वित, शर्करायुक्त.
2 *fond of sugar.* साखऱ्या, गोड्या.

To SUGGEST, *v. a. offer to the mind,* v. To HINT. सुचवणें, काढणें, सूचना *f.*-सूचन *n.* करणें *g. of o.* [*g. of s.*
To s. itself, to be suggested. सुचणें, उपस्थिति *f.* होणें

SUGGESTED, *p.* v. V. सुचवलेला, सूचित.

SUGGESTER, *n.* SUGGESTING *p. a.* v. V. सुचवणारा, सूचक, सूचना-सूचनकर्ता-कारी-&c.

SUGGESTION, *n.* v. V.—*act.* सुचवणें *n.* सूचना *f.* सूचन *n.*
I. *matter suggested.* सूचना *f.* बुद्धिवाद *m.* v. सांग, सुचविलेलीगोष्ट *f.*

SUICIDAL, *a.* v. N. आत्मघाताचा, &c. आत्मघातक, आत्मघाती.

SUICIDE, *n. self-murder.* आत्मघात *m.* आत्महत्या *f.* आत्मवध *m.*
To commit s. जीव *m.* देणें.
2 *self-murderer.* आत्मघाती, आत्मघातक *or* की, आपघाती, आत्महत्यारा, आत्मत्यागी.

SUI GENERIS, *of its own kind, singular.* आपरूपी, एकतऱ्हेचा, एक प्रकार, एक प्रकाराचा, तऱ्हेचा, तऱ्हेदार, तऱ्हेवाईक, स्वप्रत्य.

SUIT, *n.* v. SET. जोड *m.* रंग *m.*
2 (of clothes). जोड *m.*
3 v. PETITION. अर्ज *m.*
4—in law, v. CAUSE. खटला *m.* मुकदमा *m.* वाद *m.* दावा *m.*
5 (of cards). बाजू *f.* बाजी *f.* रंग *m.* रुपें *n.*
Ascending cards of a s. चढती बाजू *f.*
Descending cards of a s. उतरती बाजू *f.*
6 *train,* v. RETINUE. परिवार *m.* स्वारी *f.* बरोबरची मंडळी *f.* जिलीब *f.* इतमाम *m.* खटला *m.* खटलें *n.* अनुचरवर्ग *m.* पोष्यवर्ग *m.* परिजनमंडळी *f.*
To take into one's s. जवळधरणें-ठेवणें.

To SUIT, *v. n. accord, &c.* v. To AGREE. मिळणें, मिळणींत असणें, बसणें, जमणें, जुगणें, जुळणें, जुडणें, लागणें, उतरणें, जम *m.*-जवा *m.*-&c. बसणें *g. of s. recip.*

To SUIT, *v. a. fit, make proper,* v. To ADAPT. मिळवणें, योग्य-माफक-&c. करणें, जमवणें, मेळ *m.*-जम *m.*-जवा *m.*-जुगल *f.* बसवणें *g. of s. recip.*
2 *fit,* v. To BECOME. शोभणें, साजणें, घटणें.
3 *approve itself unto,* v. To PLEASE. पटणें *in. con.* पसंत-मान्य-&c. असणें *in. con.* उरकणें *in. con.* चाहणें *in. con.*

SUITABLE, *a. fitting, becoming, &c.* v. FIT, RIGHT. योग्य, जोगता *or* जोगा (in comp.), यथायोग्य, यथायुक्त, उपयोगी, उपयुक्त, युक्त, सुयुक्त, युक्तिसार, यथोचित, उचित, विहित, लायक, घटित, आर्य, अनुरूप.

SUITABLENESS, *n.* v. A. योग्यता *f.* यथायोग्यता *f.* उपयुक्तता *f.* लायकी *f.* उपयोग *m.* युक्ति *f.* औचित्य *n.* संभावना *f.* सोईसुमार *m.*

SUITABLY, *adv.* v. A. योग्य, यथायोग्य, यथायुक्त, लायक, योग्यतेनें, योगत:.

SUITE, *n. train,* v. SUIT. स्वारी *f.* जिलीब *f.* इतमाम *m.*

SUITOR, *n. suer,* v. PETITIONER. अर्ज करणारा, अर्जदार.
2 *wooer.* मागणी करणारा-घालणारा, मागणीवाला, पाणिग्रहार्थी.

To SULK, *v. n. pout, be sullen.* गाल *m. pl.* फुगवणें, फूं *adv.* होणें, हट्टासपेटणें, मनांत कुढणें *or* कुढणें, फुरगुटणें *or* फुरंगुटणें, फुरकटणें, अबठरणें, मुरमुसणें, दुर्मुखणें, खुंटणें *or* खुंटून बसणें.

SULKINESS, SULLENNESS, *n.* v. A. 1. कुरठेपणा *m.* घुणेपणा *m.* &c.
2 कुडुकपणा *m.* &c. खळ *f.* अबंठा *m.*

SULKS, SULLENS, *n. sulky state.* खळ *f.* फुरगूट *or* फुरकटn. *m.* अवंठा *m.* बोसm.

To take the s. v. To SULK. हट्टास पेटणें, खळ *f.* घेणें, खुंटणें *or* खुंटून बसणें, अवंठा *m.* धरणें, अवंठरणें, अंठरणें, फुरगूट *or* फुरकट *n. m.* चढणें-येणें *in. con.*

SULKY, SULLEN, *a. gloomily close, morose.* कुचर, कुरठा, घुणा *or* ण्या, घुमा *or* घुम्या, मेणघुणा *or* घुण्या, मधघुण्या, स्वक.

2 *affected with ill humour, & of cross look.* दुर्मुसला, दुर्मुख, कुडूक, कुडुकवाणी, हट्टास पेटलेला, खळ घेतलेला, अवंठा धरलेला, फुरकटलेला.

SULLIED, *p.* v. V. 1. मळगावलेला, मळवलेला, विटवलेला, &c. विटका, मजीत, वाणढाळ, दूषित. [बलित.

2 डागलेला, डागदिल्हेला, कलंक लावलेला, कलंकित, सकलंक, अ-

SULLIER, *n.* SULLYING, *p. a.* v. V. 1. मळगावणारा, मळवणारा, विटका करणारा, दूषक.

2 डाग लावणारा, कलंक लावणारा, &c.

To SULLY, *v. a. soil, tarnish, dirt.* मळगावणें *or* मळघावणें, मळवणें, मळकटवणें, विटवणें, डागणें, डाग *m.* देणें-लावणें, दूषणें, मळकट-विटका-मजीन-डागील-&c. करणें.

2 fig. *soil, slur, blot, &c.* v. To STAIN. डाग *m.* देणें-लावणें, कलंक *m.* लावणें.

SULLY, *n. stain, blot, &c.* v. SLUR. कलंक *m.* डाग *m. v.* लाग, बट्टा *m.* कालिमा *m.* काळोखी *f.*

SULPHUR, *n. brimstone.* गंधक *m.* धातुवैरी *m.*

Crystallized s. अवळयागंधक *m.* अवळसरा *m.*

SULPHUREOUS, SULPHUROUS, SULPHURY, *a.* गंधकाचा, गंधकमय, गंधकयुक्त, गंधकान्वित, गंधकधर्मक.

SULTAN, *n.* सुलतान *m.*

SULTRINESS, *n.* v. A. ऊब *f.* उबारा *m.* उधाण *or* न *n.* उकाडा *m.* उबाळा *m.* गदमद *f.* गतका *or* गदका *m.*

S. (of Autumn) during the ripening of the crops. कणऊब *f.* [मदण्याचा.

SULTRY, *a. closely hot.* उबाऱ्याचा, उकाड्याचा, उबाळ्याचा, गद-

To be s. उबणें, उबावणें, उकडणें, गदगदणें, गदमणें, गदमदणें, गदादणें, डाजणें, तावणें, (or ऊन*n.* तावणें) शिजणें. All these verbs are *impersonal.*

SUM, *n. aggregate, total.* एकंदरआकार *m.* एकंदरबेरीज *f.* एकुणजमा *f.* एकुणात *f.* जमा *f.* जुमला *m.* एकंदरी *f.* गोळाबेरीज *or* गोळीबेरीज *f.* सुमार *m.* बेरीज *f.* गणन *n.* मुबलक *or* ख *n. m.*

2 *substance, amount.* एकुणात *f.* हांसील*n.* सारांश*m.* तात्पर्य *n.* इत्यर्थ*m.* इदमित्थ*n.* तत्वार्थ*m.* गर्भ*m.* भाग*m.* निष्कर्ष*m.* नीस*m.*

S. and substance. गोळाबेरीज *or* गोळीबेरीज *f.* तात्पर्यार्थ *m.* इत्यर्थ *m.* तत्वार्थ *m.* निर्गलितार्थ *m.* अखिलार्थ *m.* भाग *m.*

3 (of money). रकम *f.*

4 *figures set for an arithmetical operation.* राशि *m. f.* हिशेब *or* हिशोब *m.* The name of *the Rule* in which *a sum* is set, is used in this sense, as त्याला एक भागाकार घाला, त्यानें एक गुणाकार केला, &c.

To SUM, *v. a. cast up, add together.* मिळवणें, एकंदर-एकवट-एकत्र *adv.* करणें, बेरीज *f.* करणें-घेणें *g. of o.* जमा *f.* करणें *g. of o.* ठासणें.

The summing up & forming of a grand total of several amounts. तेरीज *n. f.*

2 up ; *wind up.* अटोप *m.* करून सांगणें *g. of o.* सांगितल्याची गोळाबेरीज *f.* करणें, उपसंहार *m.*-उकापसंहार *m.*-अवहार *m.*-&c. करणें.

SUMMARILY, *adv.* v. A. संक्षेपानें, संक्षेपेंकरून, संक्षपतः.

SUMMARY, *n.* v. ABRIDGEMENT. संक्षेप *m.* सारांश *m.* सारसंग्रह*m.* संक्षिप्तग्रंथ *m.*

SUMMARY, *a. concise, compendious,* v. BRIEF. संक्षेपाचा, सांक्षेपिक, संक्षिप्त, सामासिक.

2—proceeding, &c. अटपना, अटपसार, अटपत्यारितीचा, संक्षिप्तरीतीचा, तांत्रिक.

SUMMATION, *n.* v. V. 1. एकंदर करणें *n.* &c.

SUMMED, *p.* v. V. 1. मिळवलेला, एकंदर केलेला, बेरीज केलेला, &c. राशिगत.

2 अटोप करून सांगितलेला, &c. उपसंहृत. [काल *m.*

SUMMER, *n.* v. SEASON. उन्हाळा *m.* उन्हाळी *f.* ग्रीष्म *m.* ग्रीष्म-

Heat or height of s. ऐन उन्हाळा *m.*

SUMMER-HOUSE, SUMMER-SHED, *n.* उन्हाळसावली *f.* बाराद्वारी *f.* धारागृह *n.* बंगला *m.*

S. built in a creek, &c. समुद्रगृह *n.*

Water s. जलमंदिर *n.*

SUMMER-SAULT, SUMMERSET, *n. leap in which the heels are thrown over the head.* कोल्हांटी *f.* कोल्हांट *or* गोल्हांट *or* ठ *or* घोलांट *n.* घोलांटी *f. v.* मार, टाक, दे, उपरछडी *f.*

SUMMIT, *n.* v. TOP. शिखर *n.* उपरिभाग *m.* कळस *m.* चूडा *f.*

2 *highest point or degree,* v. HEIGHT. कळस *m.* सीमा *f.*

To SUMMON, *v. a. call with authority, cite.* सत्तेनें-&c. बोलावणें, सत्तेचें-&c. बोलावणें *n.* करणें, बोलावून आणणें, बोलावूं पाठवणें, सरकारच्याहुकमानें बोलावणें, तलब *f.* करणें, बोलावणें *or* बोलवणें, आवाहणें, आव्हानणें, आकारणें, आकारण *n.*-&c. करणें *g. of o.* [धरणें.

To s. up courage, resolution, &c. धैर्य *n.*-धीर *m.*-&c.

SUMMONED, *p.* v. V. सत्तेनें बोलावलेला, सरकारच्या हुकमानें बोलावलेला, बोलावूंपाठवलेला, आवाहित, आकारित, आहूत.

SUMMONER, *n.* SUMMONING, *p. a.* v. V. सत्तेनें बोलावणारा, सत्तेचें बोलावणें करणारा, बोलावणारा, &c. आव्हान-आकारण-&c. कर्त्ता-कारी.

SUMMONS, *n. call by authority.* सत्तेचें बोलावणें*n.* सरकारी बोलावणें *n.* तलब *f.* आवाहन *n.* आव्हान *n.* आकारण *n.* The English word is commonly used, as समन्स *or* सम्मान *n.*

S. of the Divinity into an image, &c. आवाहन *n.*

S. with power to compel attendance. जोरतलब *f.*

Vexatious and tiresome s. चलबुलाई *f.*

SUMMUM BONUM, *n. chief good.* परमार्थ *m.* [ळ्यातट्टू.

SUMPTER, SUMPTER-HORSE, *n. baggage horse.* पडदळयातट्टू, कंठा-

SUMPTUARY, *a. regulating expense.* व्ययनियमाचा, व्ययनियमविषयक-संबंधी.

SUMPTUOUS, *a. costly, expensive.* मोठ्या खर्चाचा, मोठ्या मोलाचा, बहुमोलाचा, उंच, बहुमोली, बहुमूल्य, महामूल्य.

2 *splendid, grand, &c.* v. FINE. उमदा, भडक, झळक, भळभळीत. [तिव्ययपूर्वक.

SUMPTUOUSLY, *adv.* v. A. 1. मोठाखर्चकरून, मोठ्या खर्चानें, अ-

SUMPTUOUSNESS, *n.* v. A. 1. मोठा खर्च *m.* मोठें मोल *n.* बहुमूल्यता *f.*

2 भडक *f.* झलक *f.* भळभळितपणा *m.*

SUN, *n.* सूर्य *m.* उगवतामावळता *m.* आदित्य *m.* रवि *m.* भास्कर *m.* भानु *m.* दिवस *m.* दिनकर *m.* मित्र *m.* गभस्ति *m.* तरणि *m.* अर्क *m.* पतंग *m.* प्रभाकर *m.* चंडकिरण *m.* चंडांशु *m.* सहस्रकिरण *m.* तेजःपुंज *m.* ग्रहराज *m.* जगत्साक्षी *m.* कर्मसाक्षी *m.*—as personified, नारायण *or* सूर्य नारायण *m.*

Belonging or relating to the s. सौर.

Disk of the s. सूर्यबिंब *n.* सूर्यमंडल *n.* रविमंडल *n.*

Early morning s. बालसूर्य *m.* बालार्क *m.* बालमित्र *m.* बालातप *m.*

Figure of the s. (as drawn for worship &c.) सूर्ययंत्र *n.*

Half yearly passage of the s. अयन *n.* The Northing is उत्तरायण *n.* The Southing दक्षिणायन *n.*

Mansion of the s. सूर्यनक्षत्र *n.* महानक्षत्र *n.*

Meridian s. तरुणसूर्य *m.*

Region of the s. *solar sphere.* सूर्यमंडल *n.* सूर्यलोक *m.*

Stroke of the s. लपेट *f.*

Under the s. अभाळाखालीं, अभाळातळीं.

To swelter or burn under a hot s. तळपणें, तळतळणें, तळतळ *f.* होणें, तळावणें.

A rush light to the s. सूर्यापुढें काडवात, सूर्यापुढें काजवा.

Clear as the s. at noonday. करतलामलक, करतलामल.

2 v. SUNSHINE. ऊन, ऊन्ह *n.*

Heating or drying in the s. सूर्यपुट *or* ठ *n.*

Heated or dried in the s. सूर्यपुटी.

To get warm (a liquor) in the s. झळणें—to heat in the s. झळवणें.

Water heated in the s. उन्हवणी *n.* झळवणी *n.*

To put in the s. to warm. उन्हत ठेवणें.

To SUN, *v. a.* उनांत ठेवणें-घालणें, उन्हत ठेवणें, सूर्यपुट *n.* देणें.

SUN-BEAM, *n.* सूर्यकिरण *m.* सूर्यमयूख *m.* सूर्यरश्मि *m.* सूर्यकर *m.* मयूख *m.*

To quiver in water—sun beams, &c. झळंबणें *or* झळमणें.

SUN-BLINK, *n. gleam of sunshine in rainy weather.* दिमवा *m.* तिरीप *f.*

SUN-BURNT, *a.* उनानें काळवटलेला-काळवंडलेला.

SUN-DIAL, *n.* छायायंत्र *n.* शंकुयंत्र *n.* प्रतोद *m.*

SUN-DRIED, *a.* उनानें वाळलेला, आतपशुष्क.

SUN-FLOWER, *n.*—the plant. सूर्याचें झाड *n.* सूर्यकमल *m.* सूर्यकमळी *f.*—the flower, सूर्यफूल *n.* सूर्यकमल *n.*

SUN-RISING, SUN-RISE, *n.* v. DAWN, MORNING. सूर्योदय *m.*

At s. दिवसाबरोबर.

SUN-SET, *n.* v. EVENING. सूर्यास्त *n. m.* अस्त *m.*

Before s. दिवसाउजेडीं, दिवसासकट, दिवसापूर्वीं, दिवसाबरोबर, दिवसासकळ, दिवसाघडीं. [बेळ *f.*

The period (inauspicious) just before s. बिणची

SUN-SHINE, *n.* ऊन *or* ऊन्ह *n.* निबर *or* निभर *n.* आतप *m.* धूप *f.* किरण *m.* घर्म *m.*

Days of s. *fig.* सुबत्ताकाळ *m.* घातीचेदिवस *m. pl.*

Gleam of s. तिरीप *f.* तिरीम *f.* तुरूप *f.*

Mild s. in rainy weather. ताप *or* ताव *f.*

Mild and tender s. (of the morning or evening.) तिरीप *f.* तिरीम *f.* तुरूप *f.*

SUN-SHINY, *a.* v. N. उनाचा, उन्हाचा, निबराचा, आतपप्राचुर्याचा, आतपप्रचुर.

SUN-STONE, SUN-GEM, *n.* सूर्यकांत *m.* सूर्यमणि *m.* रविकांत *m.*

SUN-STROKE, *n. coup de soleil.* उन्हाचा चटका *m.* झळ *f.* झळई *f.* लपेट *f.* तिरमी *f.*

SUN-WORSHIP, *n.* सूर्योपासना *f.* सूर्यभक्ति *f.*

SUN-WORSHIPPER, *n.* सूर्योपासक, सूर्यभक्त.

SUNDAY, *n.* आदित्यवार *pop.* आदितवार *or* आयतवार *m.* रविवार *m.* रविवासर *m.* भानुवार *m.* भानुवासर *m.*

To SUNDER. See To PART, To DIVIDE.

SUNDER, *n.* in sunder. दोनतुकडे.

SUNDRY, *a. diverse, several.* अनेक, नाना, अनेकप्रकारचे, नानाविध, पृथग्विध, विविध.

Sundries, *collection of various things.* सटरफटर *n.* लटरफटर *n.* अटरफटर *n.* गटरफटर *n.* सटरपटर *n.* अलबतगलबत *n.* अगडतगड *n.* अगडबगड *n.* अडगूणबडगूण *n.* काण्णूचाण्णू *or* कायणूबायणू *n.* जराबाजरा *m.* सारसुसर *f.* इत्याखिला *m.* परचुरण *n.* ऐलपैलवस्तू *f.* फलानबिस्तान *n.*

SUNG, *p.* v. V. A. 1. गायलेला, गाऊन म्हटलेला, &c. गीत.

2 गायलेला, वर्णलेला, वाखाणलेला, वर्णित, कीर्तित.

SUNK, SUNKEN, *p.* v. V. N. 1. बुडालेला, मग्न, निमग्न, गरक.

2 बुडालेला, &c. बुडीत.

SUNNINESS, *n.* v. A. 2. उतापपणा *m.* &c. तापाटी *f.* आतपप्राचुर्य *n.* आतपबाहुल्य *n.* [कडील.

SUNNY, *a. of or belonging to the sun.* सूर्याचा, सूर्याकडला, सूर्या-

2 *open to the sun.* उनाचा *or* उन्हाचा, निबराचा, उताप *or* उत्ताप, निबराष्ट *or* निबराष्ट्र, निराट, आतपप्रचुर, आतपबहुल.

S. spot, *open place.* उताप *or* उत्ताप *n.* निबराष्ट *or* निबराष्ट्र *n.*

To SUP, *v. a.* v. To SIP. ओंठांनीं पिणें, घोंट *m.*-&c. घेणें *g. of o.*

2—with a flurruping noise. ओरपणें, भुरकणें, भुरका *m.*-झुरका *m.* घेणें.

To SUP, *v. n. eat the evening meal.* रातचें-रात्रीचें जेवण *n.* करणें, रातचा *decl.* जेवणें.

SUP, SUPPING, *n.* v. V. A. 1. ओंठांनीं पिणें *n.* [रका *m.*

I. *small draught taken with the lips.* घोंट *m.* भुरका *m.* झु-

SUPER. This prefix is rendered by अधिक, अति, अतिशय, विशेष, &c. as will be seen from the words that follow below.

To SUPERABOUND, *v. n. be very abundant* v. To ABOUND. बहुत-पुष्कळ-&c. असणें, अधिकाई *f.*-ऊरपूर *f.*-वैपुल्य *n.*-&c. असणें *g. of s.*

SUPERABUNDANCE, *n.* v. EXUBERANCE. पुष्कळपणा *m.* अधिकाई *f.* अतिशय *m.* वैपुल्य *n.* प्राचुर्य *n.* आधिक्य *n.* ऊरपूर *f.* महामुरी *f.* महापूर *f.* [यित.

SUPERABUNDANT, *a.* v. EXUBERANT. अधिक, अतिशय, अतिश-

To SUPERADD, *v. a.* v. To ADD. जोडणें-घालणें-&c. *with* वरशिवाई-अधिक-&c.

SUPERANNUATED, *a. disqualified by old age, too old for office.* म्हातारपणानें-म्हातारपणचा-&c. थकलेला, अतिवयस्क, वयातीत, वार्धक्याक्षम, वार्धक्याशक्त.

To be s. साठळणें.

SUPERANNUATION, *n. the state of being too old for work.* साठी *f.* अतिवयस्कता *f.* वार्धक्याक्षमता *f.*

SUPERB, *a. magnificent, &c.* v. FINE. छानीचा, छानदार, राजसी, भडक, झळक, उमदा, भव्य, नामी, आलिजाही.

SUPERBLY, *adv.* v. A. उमदेपणानें, छानीनें, &c. भडक मारून, झळक मारून. [करणारा, कारणी.

SUPERCARGO, *n.* जिन्नसीगलबताची-कबाडीगलबताची-&c. देखरेख-

SUPERCILIOUS, *a. haughty* v. PROUD. मस्तवाल, दिमाखदार, तोरेदार, दिमाखाचा, मिजाजखोर, पीळदार, माजुरी, माजलेला, उन्मत्त, मानी, वरडोळ्या, ऊर्ध्वदृष्टि.

SUPERCILIOUSNESS, *n.* v. A. दिमाख *m.* तोरा *m.* आढ्यता *f.* माज *m.* बदमस्ती *f.* पीळ *m.*

SUPEREMINENCE, *n.* v. A. वर्चस्व *n.* वर्चस्वता *f.*

SUPEREMINENT, *a. surpassing in excellence,* v. SUPERIOR. वर्चस्वी, वरचढ, सर्वश्रेष्ठ.

SUPEREROGATION, *n. performance of more than duty requires.* अत्याचार *m.* अतिरिक्ताचरण *n.* अतिरिक्ताचार *m.* अतिरिक्तकारिता *f.* विध्यतिरेक *m.* विध्याधिक्य *n.*

SUPEREROGATORY, *a. beyond what duty requires.* अत्याचाराचा, अतिरिक्ताचरणाचा, विध्यतिरिक्त, नियमातिरिक्त, कर्त्तव्यातिरिक्त.

SUPEREXCELLENCE, *n.* श्रेष्ठत्व *n.* श्रेष्ठ्य, *n.* उत्कृष्टता *f.* अत्युत्तमता *f.* वर्चस्वता.

SUPEREXCELLENT, *a. very excellent.* उत्कृष्ट, उत्तम, उत्तमोत्तम, श्रेष्ठ, सर्वश्रेष्ठ, वरीयान्, सर्वोत्कृष्ट, वर्चस्वी, सर्वोत्तम, अत्युत्तम, श्रेयान्.

SUPERFICIAL, *a. of or belonging to the superficies.* वरचा, वरला, बाहेरल्या आंगाचा, बाहेरील, बाहेरील *or* वरील भागाचा, बाह्य, बहिर्लग्न, बहिःसंलग्न, अनिम्न.

2 *shallow, exterior, slight, &c.* वरवरचा, वरकरणी, वरकरणीचा, वरघडीचा, वरपंकाचा, वरपंकी, वरकर्मी, वरवचाईचा, उपरटप्पी *or* उपरटप्प्याचा, बिजमायली *or* इजमायली.

S. view. बाह्यदृष्टि *f.* [उपरटप्प्याचा.

3—in learning, &c. v. SMATTERER. ओरखडलेला, उपरटप्पी,

SUPERFICIALLY, *adv.* v. A. 1. वरून, बाहेरून, बाहेरच्या आंगाबरून, वरल्या आंगाबरून, बाहेर, वर, बाह्यात्कारी.

2 वरवर, वरकरणी, वरकरणीनें, वरचेवर, वरभुजारत, उपराउपर, तरासरी, यथाकथंचित्, बाह्यात्कारी, आपाततः.

SUPERFICIALNESS, *n.* v. A. 1. *and* SHALLOWNESS. उत्तानता *f.* अनिम्नता *f.*

2 वरवरपणा *m.* वरपंकीपणा *m.* &c.

3 See SMATTERING.

SUPERFICIES, *n.* v. SURFACE. वरलें *or* बाहेरलें आंग *n.* तल *n.* *m.* तलपर्यंत *m.* धरातल *n.*

SUPERFINE, *a.* फार बारीक, फार तलम, अतिसूक्ष्म.

2 *excellent, &c.* अत्युत्तम, अत्युत्कृष्ट, परमोत्कृष्ट.

SUPERFLUITY, *n. superabundance.* अधिकाई *f.* अतिरेक *m.* आधिक्य *n.* आतिरेक्य *n.* प्रयोजनातिरेक *m.* प्रयोजनातिरिक्तता *f.*

2 *superfluous things.* गरजेबाहेरची वस्तु *f.*-गोष्ट *f.*-&c.

SUPERFLUOUS, *a. more than is wanted.* अधिक, ज्यास्त, गरजेबाहेरचा, गरजेवांचूनचा, अतिरिक्त, प्रयोजनातिरिक्त, विवक्षातिरिक्त, अवश्यकातिरिक्त. [ता *f.*

SUPERFLUOUSNESS, *n.* v. A. प्रयोजनातिरिक्तता *f.* विवक्षातिरिक्त-

SUPERHUMAN, *a.* मनुष्याच्या पलीकडचा, अतिमानुष, अमानुष, अमानुष्य, अमानव, अपौरुष, मनुष्यागम्य, अतिमर्त्य.

SUPERINCUMBENT, *a.* वरपडलेला, उपरिस्थ, उपर्युपविष्ट.

To SUPERINDUCE, *v. a.* v. To INDUCE. आणणें, ओढून आणणें *with* वर.

To SUPERINTEND, *v. a. oversee, overlook, direct with authority.* पाहणें, देखरेख *f.*-पाहणी *f.*-चौकशी *f.*-&c.करणें-ठेवणें-राखणें *g. of o.* चालवणें, अध्यक्षता *f.*-&c. करणें *g. of o.*

SUPRINTENDENCE, *n.* v. V. देखरेख *f.* चौकशी *f.* पाहणी *f.* दरलगिरी *f.* अध्यक्षता *f.*

SUPERINTENDER, *n.* SUPERINTENDENT, *n.* SUPERINTENDING, *p. a.* v. V. पाहणारा, देखरेख करणारा, चौकसनीस, चौकशी ठेवणारा, &c. दरोगा *or* दारोगा, कारखानदार, कारभारी, नायक, दिम्मतदार, अध्यक्ष, वरचश्मा, मिरधा.

SUPERIOR, *a.* v. UPPER, वरचा, वरला, उपरिस्थ, ऊर्ध्व, ऊर्ध्वस्थ.

2 *higher in rank, office, dignity, &c.* वरच्या अधिकाराचा, वरचे पदवीचा, वरचे पायरीचा, &c. मोठा, वरचा, मुख्य, प्रधान, वडील, श्रेष्ठ, वरिष्ठ.

3 *greater in excellence, goodness, value, &c.* v. BETTER. उंचा, उंची, आगळा, श्रेष्ठ, सरस, अधिक, वर्चस्वी, वरचढ, वरिष्ठ, जबरदस्त. [यत्त.

4 *beyond the power or influence of.* अनधीन, अवश, अना-

SUPERIOR, *n. one more elevated in rank, office, &c.* वडील, श्रेष्ठ, ज्येष्ठ.

2 (of a monastery, &c.). महंत, आश्रमगुरु.

SUPERIORITY, *n.* v. A. 2. वरचा अधिकार *m.* वरची पदवी *f.* &c. वरचेपणा *m.* मुख्यता *f.* श्रेष्ठत्व *n.* श्रेष्ठ्य *n.* ज्येष्ठत्व*n.* ज्येष्ठ्य *n.*

According to s. प्रधानतः.

3 उंचेपणा *m.* &c. अगळेपणा *m.* &c. विशेष *m.* प्राधान्य *n.* वर्चस *or* वर्चस्व *n.* वर्चस्वता *f.* वरचढपणा *m.* आधिक्य *n.* प्राबल्य*n* श्रेष्ठत्व *n.* श्रैष्ठ्य *n.* ज्येष्ठत्व *n.* जैष्ठ्य*n.* सरसाई *f.*

4 अनधीनता *f.* अवशता *f.*

I. *upper hand of, advantage over.* उपरदवडा *m.* उपर *m.* उपराळा *m.* वरचढपणा *m.* वर्चस *or* वर्चस्व*n.* वर्चस्वता *f.* वरिष्ठता *f.* दसक *m.* शक *m.* मात्रा *f.* दस्त *m.* *v.* चढ, सरशी *or* सरश्रीयाज़ *f.* सरसाई *f.* श्रेष्ठ्य*n.*

To display one's s. आपला वरचढपणा *m.* मिरवणें.

SUPERLATIVE, *a.*— in grammar, v. COMPARISON. अतिशयार्थवाचक, परमावधिवाचक.

2 *of the highest degree, immeasurable, vast, &c.* v. EXCESSIVE. पराकाष्ठेचा, आत्यंतिक, परम (in comp.), परमावधीचा, निस्सीम, पक्का, श्रेष्ठ, सर्वश्रेष्ठ, सर्वोत्कृष्ट, अटोकाट, वरीयान्, पर in comp.

SUPERLATIVELY, *adv.* v. A. 2. सर्वोपरी, अतोनात *or* स्त.

SUPERLATIVENESS, *n.* v. A. 2. पराकाष्ठा *f.* श्रेष्ठत्व *n.* श्रेष्ठ्य *n.*

SUPERNAL, *a.* v. UPPER, वरचा, उपरिस्थ, ऊर्ध्वस्थ.

2 See HEAVENLY.

SUPERNATURAL, *a.* v. MIRACULOUS, SUPERHUMAN. देवकृतीचा, अमानुषशक्तीचा, अमानुषकर्मांचा, अलौकिक, अद्भुत, मानवासाध्य.

SUPERNUMERARY, *a. that is above the number.* नेमणुकीबाहेरचा, वरचा, ज्यास्त, अधिक, उबार, नियमातिरिक्त. [हिणें

To SUPERSCRIBE, *v. a. write on the top or surface.* वर लि-

SUPERSCRIPTION, *n. writing on the top or outside.* वरचा लेख *m.* वरला लेख *m.*

To SUPERSEDE, *v. a. set aside, render void,* मार्जा-गहू-&c.

करणें, पाठीमागें टाकणें-पाडणें, डोक्यावर-&c. बसणें *g. of o.*

2 *displace by the appointment of another.* दुसरा पाठवून-दुसरा नेमून-&c. घालवणें-बरतरफ करणें-काढणें-&c.

SUPERSEDED, *p.* v. V. 1. रद्दकेलेला, &c. माजी, रद्द.

SUPERSTITION, *n. overscrupulousness or exactness, &c. in religion; absurd or extravagant belief or practice.* अत्याचार*m.* अतिभक्ति *f.* अतिरिक्ताचार *m.* अविधिनिष्ठा *f.*-श्रद्धा *f.*-भक्ति *f.*-&c. अनुक्त-अशास्त्रीय-तामसी-&c. भक्ति *f.*-निष्ठा *f.*-श्रद्धा *f.* भक्तिवेड*n.*

2 *false religion.* अन्यथामार्ग*m.* अन्यथाधर्म*m.*

3 *credulity with respect to supernatural agency, omens, &c.* शकुनभोळेपणा*m.* शकुनपिशाचादिनिष्ठा *f.*-श्रद्धा *f.*-भक्ति *f.*-&c. शकुनादिविश्वास*m.*

SUPERSTITIOUS, *a. overscrupulous, rigid, &c. in religion.* अत्याचारी, अतिरिक्ताचारी, अविध्याचारी, अविधिनिष्ठावान्, अविधिश्रद्धावान्, &c. अविधिभक्त, भक्तीचा वेडा.

2 *proceeding from superstition.* अविधिनिष्ठेचा, अविधिश्रद्धेचा, &c. अविधिश्रद्धा-&c. मूलक-प्रयुक्त-&c.

3 *credulous regarding omens, &c.* शकुनपिशाचादिनिष्ठावान्-भक्तिमान्-श्रद्धावान्-&c. शकुनादिविश्वासी, भाविकभोळा, शकुनभोळा, प्रश्नभोळा.

SUPERSTRUCTURE, *n. building raised on a foundation.* पायावरची पायावरली-&c. इमारत *f.*-&c.

To SUPERVENE, *v. n. come upon additionally.* अणखी येणें, येणें *with* वर, नवा येणें, वाढून येणें.

2 See To HAPPEN.

SUPERVENIENT, *a.* SUPERVENING, *p. a.* v. V. 1. अणखी-नवा येणारा-आलेला. [&c. करणें.

To SUPERVISE, *v. a.* v. To SUPERINTEND. पाहणें, देखरेख *f.*-

SUPERVISION, SUPERVISAL, *n.*v.V. पाहणें*n.* देखरेख *f.* चौकशी*f.*

SUPERVISING, *p. a.* SUPERVISOR, *n.* v. V. *and* SUPERINTENDENT. पाहणारा, देखरेखकरणारा, अध्यक्ष.

SUPINE, *a. having the face upward.* उत्तान *pop.* उताणा, उताणापाताणा, उलथा, पाठीकडून पडलेला-निजलेला, ऊर्ध्वमुख.

2 v. LAZY, CARELESS. सुस्त, निरुद्योगी, ढिला.

SUPINELY, *adv.* v. A. 1. उताणा, उताणा होऊन, &c.

2 सुस्त होऊन, सुस्तीनें, ढिलेपणानें, &c.

SUPINENESS, *n.* v. A. 1. उताणेपणा*m.* उलथेपणा*m.* &c.

2 सुस्तपणा*m.* ढिलेपणा*m.* सुस्ती *f.*

SUPPER, *n. evening meal.* रातचें *or* रात्रीचें जेवण*n.*-भोजन*n.*-खाणें*n.*-&c. नक्तभोजन*n.* [डणें.

To SUPPLANT, *v. a. trip up, &c.* ठोकर *f.*-ठेंस *f.*-&c. मारून पा-

2 fig. *displace by stratagem.* युक्तीनें-&c. शिरावर-डोईवर पाय *m.* देणें *g. of o.* युक्तीनें-&c. डोईवर बसणें-जागा*m. f.*-काम *n.*-&c. हिसकणें-हिसकून घेणें.

3 v. To OVERTHROW, पाडणें, पाडाव*m.* करणें.

SUPPLANTER, *n.* SUPPLANTING, *p. a.* v. V. 2. युक्तीनें जागा हिसकून घेणारा, &c.

SUPPLE, *a. pliant, flexible.* लवचीक, लवका, लवसर, लवकिरा, नरम, नमनशील.

S. and slender person. फोकाटी *f.*

2 *cringing, submissive,* v. OBSEQUIOUS. आर्जवी, तोंडदेख्या, छंदानुरोधी, वशवर्ती.

To SUPPLE, *v. a.* v. A. 1. लवचीक-नरम-&c. करणें, लवचिकपणा *m.*-&c. आणणें.

SUPPLEMENT, *n. supply, completion,*—act. पुरवणी *f.* पुरवणूक *f.*

To fall to the s. of. पुरोठ्यास पडणें.

2 *matter or thing supplying.* पुरवणीचा-भरतीचा-&c. पदार्थ*m.*-विषय*m.*-वस्तु*n.*-&c. भरती *f.* भरण*n.*

3 *supplementary sheet or portion, appendix.* पुरवणी बंद *m.* पुरवणी *f.* पुरवणूक *f.* परिशिष्ट*n.*

SUPPLEMENTAL, SUPPLEMENTARY, SUPPLETORY, *a. added to supply what is wanting.* पुरवणीचा, भरीचा, भरतीचा, भरघालण्याचा, न्यूनतापूरक.

S. sheet. पुरवणीबंद *m.*

SUPPLENESS, *n.* v. A. 1. लवचिकपणा *m.* लवकेपणा*m.* नरमपणा*m.*

SUPPLIANT, *a.* SUPPLICANT, *a.* SUPPLICATOR, *n.* v. V. 1. प्रार्थना-विनंती-&c. करणारा, मिनतीनें-&c. मागणारा, प्रार्थक, प्रार्थना-विनति-&c. कर्त्ता-कारी, दीन, दीनवाणा *or* णी, दैनवाणा *or* दैन्यवाणा, बद्धांजलि.

S. for protection. शरणागत, शरणार्थी.

To SUPPLICATE, *v. a. petition earnestly, humbly, &c.* v. To BEG. प्रार्थना *f.*-विनंती *f.*-&c. करणें *g. of o.* प्रार्थणें, विनवणें, पाय *m.pl.* धरणें, मिनत *f.*-मिनतमाना *m.*-मिनतवारी *f.*-मिनती *f.*-&c. करणें *g. of o.*

To s. abjectly or earnestly. पदर*m.* पसरणें.

2 *entreat for, ask for by petition.* मिनतीनें मिनतवारीनें-&c. मागणें, विनंती *f.*-प्रार्थना *f.*-&c. करणें *g. of o.* याचणें, प्रार्थणें.

SUPPLICATED, *p.* v.V.1. प्रार्थिलेला, विनवलेला, प्रार्थित, अनुनीत.

2 मिनतीनें मागितलेला, मागितलेला, &c. याचित, प्रार्थित.

SUPPLICATION, *n.* v. V. 1.—प्रार्थणें *n.* विनवणें *n.* &c. प्रार्थना *f.* विनंती *f.* विनवणी *f.* मिनत *f.* मिनतमाना *m.* मिनतवारी *f.* मिनती *f.* उपार्जना *f.* अनुनय *m.* विनति *f.* उरफोड *m. f.*

To make piteous s. दैन *n.*-दैना *f. pl.* भाकणें-सांगणें.

SUPPLIED, *p.* v. V. 1. पुरवलेला, दिल्हेला, &c.

2 पुरवलेला, संपन्न (in comp.), विशिष्ट (in comp.).

SUPPLIER, *n.* SUPPLYING, *p. a.* v. V.1. पुरवणारा, पुरावा करणारा, भरती करणारा, देणारा, &c.

To SUPPLY, *v. a. furnish, provide, give what is wanted.* पोहंचवणें, पुरवणें, देणें, पुरवणी *f.*-पुरवणूक *f.*-पुराव *m.*-पुरावा *m.*-भर *f.*-भरती *f.*-संजोग *m.*-&c. करणें *g. of o.* बजमी *f.*-साहित्य *n.*, सामग्री *f.*-&c. करणें *g. of o.* प्रापण *n.*-उपधान *n.* करणें.

2 with; *furnish to.* पुरवणें, संपन्न-विशिष्ट-&c. करणें.

3 (a vacancy) *fill.* भरणें, भरती *f.* करणें *g. of o.*

4 (the place of) *serve instead of.* काम *n.* करणें *g. of o.* जागा *m. f.*-स्थान *n.*-&c. राखणें *g. of o.*

SUPPLY, *n.* SUPPLYING, *n.* v. V. 1. पुरवणें *n.* &c. पुरवणी *f.* पुरवणूक *f.* पुराव *m.* पुरावा *m.* प्रापण *n.* उपधान *n.*

I. *matter supplied.* भरती *f.* भरणा *m.* बेजमी *or* बेगमी *f.* साहित्य *n.* [मदानी *f.*खेप *f.*

Periodical or set s. (of grain, merchandise, &c.). अ-

Supplies, *loaded train, &c. coming.* भरताड *f.*

SUPPORT, SUPPORTANCE, SUPPORTING, *n.* v.V.1.—*act.*धरणें *n.* संभाळणें*n.* वाहणें *n.*&c. संभाळ *m.* धारण*n.* अवष्टंभ *m.* अवष्टंभन *n.* उपष्टंभ *m.* उपष्टंभन *n.* संभार *m.*

2—*act.* सोसणें *n.* साहणें *n.* &c. सोसणूक *f.* सहन *n.*

3—*act.* चालवणें *n.* संभाळणें *n.* संभाळ *m.* निर्वाह *m.*
4 पाळणें *n.* पोसणें *n.*&c. संभाळ*m.* पोषण*n.* पालन*n.* उदरपोषण*n.* पोषणपालन*n.*पालनपोषण*n.*उदरनिर्वाह*m.* पाळग्रहण*n.* प्रतिपालन*n.*
5 संभाळणें *n.* आश्वासणें *n.* दम देणे *n.* &c. आश्वासन *n.*
7 पाठदेणें *n.* पाठराखणें*n.*पुरावा*m.*पाठपुरावा*m.*पुस्ती *f.* पुस्तपना*m.*
I. *means of up bearing.* आधार *m.* आश्रय *pop.* आस्रा *m.* अवष्टंभ *m.* उपष्टंभ *m.*
II. *a* s. v. PROP. धिरा *m.* ओठंगण *n.* ओठंबा *m.*
Upright s. of a transverse beam. सुळा *m.* सुळका *m.*
III. *a* s. fig. *a warrant, a sanction.* आधार *m.* गमक *n.* लाग *m.* देठ *m.* प्रमाण *n.* ओठंगण *n.*
IV. *means of subsistence,* v. LIVELIHOOD. उपजीविका *f.* उपजीवन *n.* जिनगी *f.* जिनगाणी *or* नी *f.*
V. *that which maintains life ; sustenance, &c.* जीवन *n.* प्राणन *n.* उपजीवन *n.* उपजीविका *f.*

To SUPPORT, *v. a. bear up, uphold, sustain.* धरणें, धारण *n.* करणें, आधार *m.*-आस्रा *m.*- &c. देणें, वाहणें, वागवणें, संभाळणें, पडूं न देणें, अवष्टंभ *m.*-उपष्टंभ *m.*-संभार *m.*-वहन *n.*- &c. करणें *g. of o.* आश्रयभूत-आधारभूत-&c. असणें *in. con.*
2 *bear, endure, tolerate, &c.* सोसणें, सोसून घेणें, साहणें, साहून घेणें, पुरवणें *in. con.* सोसणूक*f.*-सहन *n.*-&c.करणें *g.of o.*
3 *maintain, carry on, sustain.* चालवणें, चालता-चालू-सुरू-&c. ठेवणें, संभाळणें, संभाळ *m.* करणें. *g. of o.*
4 *maintain, supply with the means of living,* v. To SUBSIST. पाळणें, पोसणें, संभाळणें, बाळगणें, बाहणें, पोषण *n.*-पालन *n.*-संभाळ *m.*- पाळग्रहण *n.*-&c. करणें *g. of o.*
5 (courage, spirits, &c.) *keep from sinking,* v. To ENCOURAGE, To CONSOLE. संभाळणें, संभाळ *m.* करणें, दम *m.*-धैर्य *n.*-अवसान *n.*-धीर *m.*-&c. देणें, आश्वासणें, आश्वासन *n.* करणें.
6 *bear the expense of,* v. To MAINTAIN. खर्च *m.* चालवणें-भागवणें *g. of o.* खर्चाचा निर्वाह *m.* करणें *g. of o.*
7 *aid, assist, back, &c.* v. To HELP. पाठ *f.*- पाठबळ *n.* देणें, पाठ *f.* राखणें *g. of o.* पुस्ती *f.*-पुस्तपना*m.*-पुरावा *m.*-पाठपुरावा*m.* &c. करणें *g. of o.*
8 (arguments, statements, &c.) *substantiate, make good, &c.* v. To MAINTAIN. संभाळणें, संभाळ *m.* करणें *g. of o.* पुरवून देणें, राखणें, पुरवणी *f.*-निर्वाह *m.*-पुष्टी *f.*-पुष्टिकरण *n.*-&c. करणें *g. of o.*

SUPPORTABLE, *a.* v. V. 1. धरायाजोगा-&c. धारण करायाजोगा-&c. धार्य. [comp.
2 सोसायाजोगा-सारखा-&c. सहन करायाजोगा-&c. सह in

SUPPORTED, *p.* v. V. 1. धरलेला, धारण केलेला, आधार दिल्हेला, &c. आधारस्थित, आश्रित, आधृत, उपष्टब्ध, अवष्टब्ध.
2 सोसलेला, सोसून घेतलेला, &c.
3 चालवलेला, चालता ठेवलेला, संभाळलेला, &c.
4 पाळलेला, पोसलेला, पालित, पोषित, प्रतिपालित, अवलंबित.
5 संभाळलेला, दम दिल्हेला, &c. आश्वासित.
7 पाठ राखलेला, &c.

SUPPORTER, *n.* SUPPORTING, *p. a.* v. V. 1. धरणारा, आधार देणारा, धारण करणारा, &c. अवष्टंभक, उपष्टंभक, धर (in comp. as, महीधर, गंगाधर), अवष्टंभ-&c. कर्त्ता-कारी-&c. [कारी.
2 सोसणारा, साहणारा, सोसून घेणारा, &c. सोसक, सहन कर्त्ता-
3 चालवणारा, चालता ठेवणारा, &c.
4 पाळणारा, पोसणारा, &c. अन्नदाता, पाळणवाला, पालक, पोषक, पालनपोषण-&c. कर्त्ता-कारी-&c. [कारी-&c.
5 संभाळणारा, दम देणारा, &c. आश्वासक, आश्वासन कर्त्ता-
7 *and* BACKER. पाठ देणारा, पाठ राखणारा, &c. पाठराख्या, पाठिंबा, सारथी.
8 संभाळणारा, पुरवून देणारा, &c. पुष्टिकारक.

SUPPORTLESS, *a.* v. UNPROTECTED. निराश्रित, निराधार.

SUPPOSABLE, *a.* v. V. 1. कल्पायाजोगा, &c. तर्कगम्य, बुद्धिगम्य, भावनीय, विभावनीय, कल्प्य, कल्पनीय.

To SUPPOSE, *v. a. assume, conceive to be, lay down or believe without proof.* कल्पिणें, मनांत धरणें-रचणें-योजणें, कल्पना *f.*-भावना *f.*-बुद्धि *f.*-अटकळ *f.*-तर्क *m.*-&c. करणें *g. of o. also, with in. con.* होणें, ग्रह *m.* धरणें-करणें, प्रमाणावांचून-प्रमाण न पाहतां-&c. धरणें-घेणें-मानणें-समजणें, आहार्यारोप *m.*-&c. करणें.
2 *imagine, fancy,* v. To THINK. कल्पिणें, कल्पना *f.*-भावना *f.*-विभावना *f.*-&c. करणें *g. of o.* दिलांत-मनांत-चित्तांत-&c. आणणें, दिलांत-मनांत-चित्तांत-&c. येणें *in. con.*
3 *presuppose, require to be.* आहेसा दाखवणें, निश्चय *m.*-&c. दाखवणें, दर्शविणें, अस्तित्वदर्शन *n.*-अस्तित्वप्रदर्शन *n.*-&c.करणें.

SUPPOSED, *p.* v. V. 1. कल्पिलेला, मनांत धरलेला, ग्रह धरलेला, प्रमाणावांचून मानलेला, &c. भावित, विभावित, कल्पित, आहार्य, इष्ट, सिद्धवत्.
2 कल्पिलेला, दिलांत आणलेला, &c.

SUPPOSER, *n.* SUPPOSING, *p. a.* v. V. 1. कल्पिणारा, मनांत योजणारा, कल्पना-भावना-बुद्धि *f.*-&c. करणारा, प्रमाणावांचून धरणारा-मानणारा-&c. आहार्यारोपकर्त्ता-कारक-&c.

SUPPOSITION, *n. matter supposed.* कल्पना *f.* भावना *f.* अवांका *m.* अटकळ *f.* ग्रह *m.* तर्क *m.* बुद्धि *f.* प्रमाणावांचून घेतलेला पक्ष *m.* इष्टपक्ष *m.* इष्टमत *n.* [काल्पनिक.

SUPPOSITIONAL, *a.* v. HYPOTHETICAL. कल्पनेचा, अटकळीचा,

SUPPOSITITIOUS, *n. put by trick for another ; not genuine.* कपटाचा, कपटानें ठेवलेला-घातलेला, कृत्रिम, खुपसलेला, बनाऊ.

To SUPPRESS, *v. a. overpower and crush, put down, destroy, &c.* मोडणें, दडपणें, नाहींसा करणें, मोड *m.*-भंग*m.*-विध्वंस *m.*-&c. करणें *g. of o.*
2 (a fact, a matter, &c.) *conceal, retain.* दडपणें, दाबणें, दाबा*m.* देणें, झांकणें, ढांकणें, ढांपणें, छपावणें, चोरणें, दाबादाबी*f.*-चेपाचेप *f.*-चोरी *f.* करणें *g. of o.*
3 (an emotion, &c.) *stifle, restrain.* गिळणें, पिणें, खाणें, दाबणें, पोटांत घालणें.

SUPPRESSED, *p.* v. V. 1. मोडलेला, दडपलेला, नाहींसा केलेला, &c.
2 दडपलेला, दाबलेला, झांकलेला, चोरलेला, &c.
3 गिळलेला, दाबलेला, &c.

SUPPRESSION, *n.* v. V. 1.—*act.* मोडणें *n.* दडपणें *n.* &c. भंग *m.* ध्वंस *m.* विध्वंस *m.*
2 दडपणें *n.* दाबणें *n.* झांकणें *n.* चोरणें *n.* &c. छपावणी *f.* दाबादाबी *f.* चेपाचेप *f.* चोरी *f.*
3 गिळणें *n.* दाबणें *n.* &c.
I. (as of urine, the seminal fluid, &c; *or* of any function or faculty). स्तंभ *m.* स्तंभन *n.* अवष्टंभ *m.* अवरोध *m.*

SUPPRESSOR, *n.* SUPPRESSING, *p. a.* v. V. 1. मोडणारा, दडपणा-

रा, &c. भंग-विध्वंस-&c. कर्त्ता-कारी-&c.
2 दडपणारा, दाबणारा, झांकणारा, चोरणारा, &c.
3 गिळणारा, खाणारा, &c.

To SUPPURATE, *v. n. generate pus.* पिकणें, पुवळणें, पुवारणें, पुळणास येणें, पू *m.* येणें *in. con.*
To cause to s. पिकविणें, उचविणें.

SUPPURATION, *n.* v. V. पिकणें *n.* &c. पुवळणी *f.* पुवारणी *f.* पाक *m.*
Burning or glow of s. गदका *or* गतका *m. v.* ये.

SUPPURATIVE, *n. a medicine that promotes suppuration.* पिकवण *n.* पुलन *or* पुळण *n.*

SUPPURATIVE, *a. that promotes suppuration.* पिकवणारा, पूयजनक-कारक, पाचक.

SUPREMACY, *n.* v. A. 1. मुख्यता *f.* मौख्य *n.* प्रधानता *f.* प्राधान्य *n.* श्रेष्ठत्व *n.* श्रैष्ठ्य *n.* ऐश्वर्य *n.* मुख्य अधिकार *m.* वरचा अधिकार *m.* ईशिता *f.* ईशित्व *n.*

SUPREME, *a. highest in authority*, v. CHIEF. सर्वांहून मोठा, सर्वांवरचा, मुख्य, प्रधान, श्रेष्ठ, वरचा अधिकारी, ईश्वर.
S. Court. पादशाही अदालत *f.* सदरअदालत *f.*
2 *of the highest degree.* परम, परम मर्यादेचा, परमावधीचा, पराकाष्ठेचा.

SUPREMELY, *adv.* v. A. 2. परम, पराकाष्ठेचा, अति.

To SURCHARGE. See To OVERBURDEN, To OVERLOAD.

SURCINGLE, *n.*—for a saddle, &c. बालातंगी *f.* तंगी *f.* पेटी *f.*

SURD, *n.*—in algebra. करणीगतराशि *m.*-संख्या *f.* करणी *f.*

SURE, *a. fixed, unfallacious, &c.* v. CERTAIN. आवश्यक, खचीत, निश्चयाचा, निर्धाराचा, निश्चित, निश्चयात्मक, स्थिर, खसूस, तहकीक.
2 *confident, undoubting*, v. CERTAIN. निभ्रांत, निस्संशय, निस्संदेह, निभ्रांतचित्त.
3 *not liable to failure, of certain action.* अचूक.
4 v. SAFE, SECURE. निर्भय.
To be sure. See SURELY.
To be sure,—as noting admission. तर, बरीक, बरें, सबोत्तम.

SURE-AIMING, *a.* अचूकसंधानी.

SURE, SURELY, *adv.* v. A. 1. *and* CERTAINLY. खचीत, निश्चयें करून, निश्चयात्मक, निखालस, खसूस.

SURENESS, *n.* v. A. 1. खचितपणा *m.* खचिती *f.* खसूसपणा *m.* &c. निभ्रांत *f.*
2 निभ्रांतपणा *m.* निभ्रांत *f.* निश्चय *m.* निर्धार *m.*

SURETISHIP, *n. state of being security.* जामिनकी *f.* जामिनगत *f.*

SURETY. See SECURITY, 2. See CERTAINTY.

SURF, *n.*—of the sea. लाटांची खळबळी *f. intens.* खळबळाट *m.* खळाळी *f. intens.* खळाळ *m.*
Mound or mole to break the s. ढकशी *f.*

SURFACE, *n. exterior part, superficies.* वरचा-बाहेरचा-वरला-&c. भाग *m.* वरचें-वरलें-&c. आंग *n.* पाठ *f.* पृष्ठ *n.* पृष्ठभाग *m.* उपरिभाग *m.* तळ *m.* दृश्यअंग *n.* दर्शनांग *n.* तल *m. n.* तलपर्यंत *m.*
Smooth s. सपाटी *f.*
On the s. वर.

To SURFEIT, *v. a. make sick from overeating, glut, &c.* फार खावबून ओकारी *f.* आणणें, ओयेईतों-ओकारी येईतों-ओकारी येईपर्यंत-&c. खावविणें-जेवायाला घालणें, ओकारी *f.*-ओ *m.* आणणें, उपट *f.*-टेर *f.*-टेक *f.*-&c. करणें-पाडणें, अभर *f.*-भर *f.* करणें, कुळकावणें, गरळया *f. pl.* आणणें.

To SURFEIT, *v. n. eat till sickness is produced.* ओकारी-ओ-&c. येईतों-येईपर्यंत खाणें, खाऊन-खाखाखाऊन-&c. ओकारी *f.* आणणें, अभरवण *f.*-उपट *f.* घेणें.

SURFEIT, *n. glutted state.* उपट *f.* अभर *f.* टेर *f.* टेक *f.*

SURGE, *n. large wave, billow.* मोठी लाट *f.* लोट *m.* कल्लोळ *m.* गह्मा *m.* दांडी *f.*

SURGEON, *n. one who practises surgery.* शस्त्राचा वैद्य, शस्त्रवैद्य, अस्त्रचिकित्सक, असुरीवैद्य, तर्बीब.
Veterinary s. शालोतरी, अश्ववैद्य.

SURGERY, *n. art of curing by manual operations, &c.* शस्त्रवैद्यकी *f.* आसुरी *f.* शस्त्रवैद्याचें काम *n.* शस्त्रवैद्याची विद्या *f.* शस्त्रवैद्यक *n.* अस्त्रचिकित्सा *f.* शस्त्रवैद्यकर्म *n.* शस्त्रवैद्यविद्या *f.*

SURGICAL, *a. pertaining to surgeons or surgery.* शस्त्रवैद्याचा, शस्त्रवैद्यानें केलेला-करायाचा, शस्त्रवैद्यकीचा, अस्त्रचिकित्सासंबंधी-विषयक.

SURLILY, *adv.* v. A. द्वाष्टपणानें, दुष्टपणानें, द्वाष्टपणें, &c. द्वाष्ट होऊन, &c.

SURLINESS, *n.* v. A. दाष्टपणा *m.* दुष्टपणा *m.* खट्याळपणा *m.* &c.

SURLY, *a. morose, crabbed, &c.* v. CROSS. दाष्ट *or* द्वाष्ट, दुष्ट, खट्याळ, खाष्टी, खंक.

To SURMISE, *v. a. imagine, apprehend*, v. To SUPPOSE, To THINK. कल्पिणें, कल्पना *f.*-भावना *f.*-बुद्धि *f.*-अटकळ *f.*-तर्क *m.*-&c. करणें *g. of o. or, with in. con.* होणें.
2 *imagine evil*, v. To SUSPECT. संशय *m.*-शंका *f.*-वहीम *m.*-अंदेशा *m.* येणें *in. con, and g. of o.* वसवसा *m.* जाणें *in. con.* बचक *m.*-बाचवा *m.*-&c. जाणें-पडणें *in. con.*

SURMISAL, SURMISE, SURMISING, *n.* v. V. 1. *imagination, apprehension.* कल्पना *f.* भावना *f.* तर्क *m.* बुद्धि *f.* अवांका *m.* अटकळ *f.* ग्रह *m.* वहमा *or* वहीम *m.*
2 *imagination of evil*, v. SUSPICION. भ्रम *pop.* भरम *m.* गुमान *m.* वसवसा *m.* वहमा *or* वहीम *m.* अंदेशा *m.* शंका *f.* बाचवा *m.* बचक *m.* खत्रा *m.* आकांक्षा *f.*

To SURMOUNT, *v. a.* (difficulties, obstacles, &c.) *overcome, get the better of.* पार पाडणें, मोडणें, टाळणें, निवारणें, रेटणें, निर्दाळणें, पासला पाडणें, तळीं घालणें, खालीं घालणें, डोकीवर-उरावर-नाकावर-&c. पाय *m.* देणें, परिहार *m.*-निवारण *n.*-&c. करणें *g. of o.*
2 See To SURPASS.

SURMOUNTABLE, *a.* v. V. 1. पार पाडायाजोगा, निवारायाजोगा, &c. साध्य, निवार्य.

SURMOUNTING, *n.* v. 1.—*act.* पार पाडणें *n.* मोडणें *n.* टाळणें *n.* &c. निवारण *n.* परिहार *m.*

SURNAME, *n. family name.* आडनांव *n.* उपनाम *n.* उपनांव *n.* अडक *f.* कुलनाम *n.*
Bearing the s. of. उपनामक (in comp.).

To SURNAME, *v. a.* v. N. आडनांव *n.*-उपनांव *n.*-&c. देणें.

SURNAMED, *p.* v. V. आडनांव दिल्हेला, आडनांवाचा, उपनामाचा, उपनामक.

To SURPASS, *v. a. exceed, go beyond*, v. To EXCEL. मागें टाकणें-पाडणें-सांडणें, अंतरणें, जिंकणें, पागोटें *n.*-पगडी *f.* घेणें *g. of o.* अवली *f.* साधणें, चढ *m.*-तोड *f.*-&c. करणें *with* वर *of o.* सरस-श्रेष्ठ-अधिक-&c. असणें *with* पेक्षां-&c. *of o.* कान *m. pl.* कापणें *g. of o.* कळस *m.* करणें, आक्रमणें, आक्रमण *n.*-&c. करणें,

कडीf. चालवणें *with* वर *of o.*

SURPASSABLE, *a.* v. V. मागें टाकायाजोगा-सारखा-&c. जिंकाया. जोगा-&c. अतिक्रमणीय, अतिक्रम्य, आक्रमणीय.

SURPASSED, *p.* v. V. मागें टाकलेला, जिंकलेला, कान कापलेला, &c. अंतरित, जित, आक्रांत, उत्क्रांत.

SURPASSER, *n.* SURPASSING, *p. a.* v. V. मागें टाकणारा-सांडणारा, जिंकणारा, पागोटें घेणारा, अगळा, सरस, वरचढ, वर्चस्वी, श्रेष्ठ, लोकोत्तर, वरिष्ठ, अतिचर.

I. *very, exceeding,* v. EXCESSIVE. परम, पराकाष्ठेचा, विशेष, आत्यंतिक, अटोकाट, उद्भट.

SURPASSING, *n.* v. V.—*act.* जिंकणें *n.* मागें टाकणें *n.* &c. चढम. अतिक्रम *m.* अतिक्रमण *n.* आक्रम *m.* आक्रमण *n.* उत्क्रम *m.* उत्क्रमण *n.* अतिचार *m.*

SURPLICE, *n.* पाद्रीचा पांढरा झगा.

SURPLUS, *a. overplus, that is in excess.* फाजील, फालतू, वर राहिलेला, वरचा, अधिक, उबार, उफाळ, अव्रप *or* व, अदकाव, अदकावाचा.

SURPLUS, *n. excess beyond what is wanted.* ऊर *f.* उराबा *m.* उरव *f.* उरवण *f.* उरी *f.* उरवटा *m.* शिलक *f.* सई *f. v.* ये, उपराळा *m.* उफाळ *m.*

SURPLUSAGE, *n.*—of grain, &c. वरताळा *m.*

Practice of borrowing grain &c. upon condition of s. वाढीदिढी *f.*

S. (of grain, &c.) upon a loan. वाढ *f.* वाढी *f.*

SURPRISE, SURPRISAL, *n.* v. V. 1.—*act.* एकाएकीं गांठणेंn. &c.

2—the sentiment, v. WONDER. विस्मय *m.* आश्चर्य *n.* चित्र *n.* अद्भुतरस *m.*

To SURPRISE, *v. a. take at unawares.* अचानक-अकस्मात्-एकाएकीं-अवचट-&c. गांठणें-घेणें-धरणें-घेरणें-&c. एकाएकीं-&c. भेटणें-भिडणें-&c. एकाएकीं-&c. पडणें *with* वर *of o.*

2 v. To ASTONISH. चकवणें, चकित-दंग-चकभूल-&c.करणें, चोजवणें, चौकडी *f.* भुलवणें *g. of o.* विस्मापन *n.* करणें *g. of o.*

SURPRISED, *p.* v. V. 1. एकाएकीं गांठलेला, &c.

2 *and* ASTONISHED. चकवलेला, &c. चकित, चक्क, दंग, विस्मित, विस्मयापन्न, विस्मयान्वित.

To be s. आश्चर्यn.-नवलn.-&c. वाटणें *in. con.*

SURPRISER, *n.* SURPRISING, *p. a.*v.V.1. एकाएकीं गांठणारा, &c.

2 *and* WONDERFUL. चकवणारा, चक्क करणारा, चौकडी भुलवणारा, &c. चमत्कारिक, चमत्कारी, विस्मयकारक-जनक, आश्चर्यकारक, विस्मापक. [गा-सारखा-&c.

SURPRISINGLY, *adv.* v. A, 2. आश्चर्य-नवल-मोज-&c. वाटायाजो-

To SURRENDER, *v.a.* v. To GIVE up, To YIELD. सोडणें, सोडून देणें, हातीं देणें, स्वाधीन करणें, हवालीं करणें, मदीं घालणें, अन्यसत्ताक-परसत्ताक-&c. करणें.

To SURRENDER, *v. n.* See To YIELD, To SUBMIT.

SURRENDER, *n.* v. V.A.—*act.* सोडणेंn. &c. त्यागm. परित्यागm. अन्यसत्ताक करणn.

SURREPTITIOUS, *a. false, spurious, &c.* खोटा, खोटसाळ, कपटाचा, खुपसलेला, शिरवलेला.

2 See CLANDESTINE.

To SURROUND, *v. a. encompass, environ, inclose on all sides.* वेढणें, घेरणें, वेष्टणें, आवरणें, घेराm.-वेढाm.-गराडाm. &c. घालणें, गोटm. घालणें-देणें, गरकाm. मारणें, भावरm.-आवरणn.-वेष्टनn.-&c. करणें *g. of o.* वेष्टित-&c. करणें.

SURROUNDED, *p.* v. V. वेढलेला, घेरलेला, &c. वेष्टित, परिवेष्टित, आवृत्त, वलयित, संवीत, संवलित.

SURROUNDER, *n.* SURROUNDING, *p. a.* v. V. वेढणारा, घेरणारा, वेष्टक, आवरक, वेष्टनकर्ता-कारक-&c.

I. *adjacent, lying round about,* v. NEIGHBOURING. चहुंकडला *or* चा, चहुंकडील, भोंवनालचा, सभोंवरचा, भोंवरपासचा, भोंवरचा.

SURROUNDING, *n.* v. V.—*act.* वेढणेंn. घेरणेंn. वेष्टणेंn. &c. आवर *m.* आवरणn. वेष्टनn. परिवेषणn.

SURTOUT, *n.* वरून घालायाचा अंगरखाm.-&c.

SURVEILLANCE, *n. watch, restraint by sight.* नजरबंदी *f.* नजरकैद *f.* दृष्टिबंधनn. दृष्टीची कैद *f.*

To place under s. नजरेखालीं ठेवणें-चालणें.

To SURVEY, *v. a. inspect, view with attention,* v. To See, To EXAMINE. पाहणें, टेहळणें, हेरणें, निरखणें, निहाळणें *or* न्याहाळणें, निरीक्षणें, निरखून-&c. पाहणें, पाहणी *f.*-अवलोकनn.-निरीक्षणn. &c. करणें *g. of o.*

2 *examine with reference to condition, value, &c.* पाहणें, पाहणी *f.* करणें, तगटणें.

3 *measure land, &c.* पैमाशी *f.* करणें, जमीन *f.*-&c. मोजणें, भूमापनn.-&c. करणें.

SURVEY, SURVEYING, *n.* v. V. 1. पाहणेंn. हेरणेंn. निरखणेंn. &c. टेहळणी *f.* टेहळी *f.* हेर *f.* हेरणी *f.* निहाळणी *or* न्याहाळणी *f.* बिनासी *f.* अवलोकनn. निरीक्षणn. निरीक्षा *f.*

2 पाहणेंn. पाहणी *f.* तगटn. तगटणी *f.*

S. by the eye. नजरपाहणी *f.*

3 पैमाशी *f.* जमिन मोजणी *f.* भूमापनn. The English word is commonly used under the form of सर्वे.

SURVEYOR, *n.* (of land, &c.). पैमाशी करणारा, जमीन मोजणारा, भूमापक, भूमापनकर्ता.

SURVIVAL, SURVIVING, *n.* v. V. वांचणेंn. जगणेंn. मागें राहणेंn.

To SURVIVE, *v. a. outlive.* मागें-पाठीमागें राहणें-वांचणें-जगणें *g. of o.* मारून-खाऊन मरणें-वांचणें, मागें-पाठीमागें मरणें *g. of o.*

To SURVIVE, *v. n. live after or still.* जगणें, वांचणें, टिकणें, मागें राहणें-उरणें.

SURVIVING, *p. a.* SURVIVOR, *n.* v. V. N. जगणारा-जगलेला, वांचणारा-वांचलेला, मागें राहणारा-राहिलेला-&c. अन्योन्तरजीवी, अन्यमरणोत्तरजीवी.

SUSCEPTIBILITY, *n.* v. A. 1. घ्यायाजोगेपणा *m.* ग्राहकत्व *n.* ग्रहणक्षमता *f.* ग्रहणशक्ति *f.* वेदनक्षमता *f.* वेदनग्राहकत्व *n.* वेदनपात्रता *f.* ग्रहणपात्रता *f.*

2 गोडेपणा *m.* दुखरेपणा *m.* &c.

3 रागिता *f.* अनुरागिता *f.* &c.

SUSCEPTIBLE, *a. capable of admitting or receiving impression, change, or affection.* घ्यायाजोगा-जोगता-सारखा, ग्राहक, ग्राही, ग्रहणक्षम, ग्रहणशक्त, वेदनक्षम, वेदनार्ह, वेदनग्राहक, वेदनसंगी, वेदनज्ञ, वेदनपात्र, ग्रहणपात्र. [कोमल, नाजूक.

2 (as of disease or injury) *tender.* गोडा, दुखरा, कोंवळा,

3 *of warm passions.* रागी, अनुरागी, शीघ्रमनोविकारी.

To SUSPECT, *v. a. imagine to be criminal.* वहीम *or* वहमा *m.*-अंदेशा *m.*-&c. धरणें *g. of o.* भ्रम *m.*-वहीम *m.*-अंदेशा *m.*-शंका *f.*-&c. येणें *in. con. with g. of o.* वसवसा *m.* जाणें *in. con.*

with g. of o. अविश्वास *m.* असणें-वाटणें *in. con. and g. of o.* वचक *m.*-वावचा *m.*-&c. जाणें-पडणें *in. con. with g. of o.* डोळ *n.* पडणें-येणें *in. con.*

2 *hold to be doubtful or uncertain, mistrust*, v. To DOUBT, शंका *f.*-आशंका *f.*-संशय *m.*-&c. धरणें-करणें *g. of o.* भ्रांति *f.*-संशय *m.*-अविश्वास *m.*-&c. येणें-असणें, *in. con. with g. of o.* शंकणें, आशंकणें.

3 *imagine, apprehend, surmise*, v. To THINK, To SUPPOSE. कल्पना *f.*-तर्क *m.*-भावना *f.*-बुद्धि *f.*-अटकळ *f.*-&c. करणें *or, with in. con.* असणें *g. of o.* वहीम *or* वहमा *m.* धरणें *or, with in. con.* येणें *g. of o.* हुंगणें.

SUSPECTED, *p.* v. V. 1. वहीमआलेला, अंदेशाआलेला, &c. वहिमाचा, भ्रमाचा, &c. शंकितदोष, शंकितापराध, अविश्वस्त.

2 संशय आलेला, शंकलेला, &c. शंकित, आशंकित, अविश्वस्त.

SUSPECTFUL. See SUSPICIOUS.

To SUSPEND, *v. a.* v. To HANG. टांगणें, लटकावणें, लोंबत ठेवणें.

2 *make to depend on.* ठेवणें, अडकवणें, गुंतवणें, ठेपवणें, ठेपीवरठेवणें.

3 *make to stop, rest, or pause.* राहता-उभा-&c. करणें, तकूब करणें-ठेवणें, महकूब करणें, चार दिवस-कांहीं वेळपर्यंत-&c. बंद करणें-थांबवणें-खोळंबवणें-राहविणें.

4 *keep undetermined, unsettled, &c.* लोंबवणें, हिलगणें, हिलगडणें, तरंगत-उभारत-अभोगत-मोहगम-अनिर्धारित-अनिश्चित-&c. ठेवणें.

5 (from an office or employment). तूर्त काम करण्याची बंदी *f.* करणें, अमानत ठेवणें-करणें. The English word is commonly used under the form of सस्पिंड करणें.

SUSPENDED, *p.* v. V. 1. टांगलेला, लटकावलेला.

To be s. लटकणें, लोंबणें, लंबित असणें.

2 ठेवलेला, अडकवलेला, &c.

3 तकूब केलेला, राहता-&c. केलेला, &c. महकूब, तकूब, तटस्थ.

To be s. थांबणें, राहता-उभा-तकूब-महकूब-&c. होणें, खोळंबणें.

4 लोंबवलेला, तरंगत-उभारत-&c. ठेवलेला.

5 अमानत ठेवलेला केलेला, सस्पिंड.

SUSPENSE, *n. unresolvedness, indecision, indetermination*, v. UNCERTAINTY. अनिश्चय *m.* अनिर्धार *m.* दुग्धा *f.* विकल्प *m.* भावसंधि *m.* कृताकृत *n.*

To be in s. तरंगणें.

To keep in s. ताणणें, अंबत ठेवणें, अंबवणें, गळचिपी *f.* धरणें, गोंकटी *f.* धरणें, तरंगविणें, तरंगायास लावणें.

SUSPENSION, *n.* v. V. 1—*act.* टांगणें *n.* लटकावणें *n.* &c.

2—*act.* ठेवणें *n.* अडकवणें *n.*

3—*act.* तकूब करणें *n.* महकूब करणें *n.* &c.—*state.* महकुबी *f.* तकूब *n.* तकुबी *f.* चार दिवसांला बंदी *f.* खळ *m.* खाडा *m.* ताटस्थ्य *n.*

4—*act.* लोंबवणें *n.* हिलगणें *n.* उभारत ठेवणें *n.* &c.

5—*act.* अमानत करणें *n.* सस्पिंड करणें *n.* &c.—*state.* अमानती *f.* अमानतपणा *m.*

SUSPICION, *n.* v. V. 1. *imagination of evil, thought of as criminal.* भ्रम *pop.* भरम *m.* वहीम *or* वहमा *m.* अंदेशा *m.* गुमान *m.* शंका *f.* आशंका *f.* आकांक्षा *f.* संशय *m.* कुभाव *m.* कुडाभाव *m.* दुष्टभाव *m.* कुतर्क *m.* दिक्कत *f.* विषमभाव *m.* विकल्प *m.* डोळन. खत्रा *m.* चिकित्सा *f. pop.* चिकशा *or* स्या *f.* वसवसा *m.* वचक *m.* वावचा *m.* वाशा *m.* कुडें *n.* काळेंढवळें *n.* काळें भेरें *n.*

Working of s. मळमळ *f.*

2 *mistrust*, v. DOUBT. संशय *m.* शंका *f.* भ्रांति *f.* अविश्वास *m.* अप्रत्यय *m.*

3 *apprehension, surmise, thought.* कल्पना *f.* भावना *f.* वहमा *or* वहीम *m.* भ्रम *m.* गुमान *m.* तर्क *m.* संभावना *f.*

SUSPICIOUS, *a.* SUSPECTER, *n.* SUSPECTFUL, *a.* &c. v. V. I. 2. *entertaining suspicion*, v. DOUBTFUL. शंकित, आशंकित, संशयापन्न, सशंक, साशंक, जातशंक, प्राप्तशंक.

I. *inclined to suspicion or mistrust.* संशयी, संशयखोर, संशयालु, संदेही, खतखोर, कुधण, संशयप्रकृतिक, संशयबुद्धि, संशयशील, कुतर्कशील, कुतर्कस्वभाव, कुतर्क्या, शंकाशील, शंकी, संदेहशील, अविश्वासी *or* सू *or* सूक, वहिमखोर.

II. *warranting suspicion, suspicable.* संशय आणणारा, वहीम आणणारा, &c. वहिमाचा, संशयाचा, &c. शंकोत्पादक, संशयजनक, शंकाजनक, संशयावह, संशयाधायक, संदेहजनक, संशयास्पद.

SUSPICIOUSNESS, *n.* v. A. I. संशयीपणा *m.* संशयखोरपणा *m.* खतखोरपणा *m.* कुधणकी *f.* संशयालुता *f.* संशयप्रकृति *f.* संशयबुद्धि *f.* संशयवृत्ति *f.* शंकाप्रकृति *f.* &c.

II. संशय आणण्याची योग्यता *f.* संशयजनकत्व *n.* शंकाजनकत्व *n.* संदेहजनकत्व *n.* &c.

To SUSTAIN. See To SUPPORT. 2 See To SUFFER.

SUSTENANCE, *n.* v. SUBSISTENCE, FOOD. अन्न *n.* भक्ष्य *n.* आहार *m.* उपजीवन *n.* उपजीविका *f.*

SUSTENTATION. See SUPPORT, MAINTENANCE.

SUTLER, *n. camp follower who sells provisions.* लशकरी-लशकरांतला-फौजेबरोबर चालणारा-&c. वाणी-दुकानदार-&c. सेनाचर.

SUTTEE, *a. widow who burns with the corpse of her husband.* सती *f.* [चाळा *m.*

SUTURE, *n.* v. SEAM, JOINT. शिवण *f.* संधि *m. f.* कळासी *f.*

2 (of the cranium). कपालसंधि *m.* चाल *f.* सेवन *n.*

SWAB, *n.*—the mop. बोळा *m.* हिराची केरसुणी *f.*

To SWAB, *v. a.* बोळ्यानें साफकरणें-पुसणें-&c.

To SWADDLE, *v. a. swathe.* गुंडाळणें, वेष्टणें, लपेटणें.

SWADDLING-BAND, SWADDLING-CLOTH, *n.* बाळंतिणीचें मूल गुंडाळायाचें वस्त्र *n.* बाळंतें *n.* बाळवतें *n.*

To SWAG, *v. n. belly*, v. To BAG. झोलणें, झोल *m.* येणें *in. con.*

To SWAGGER, *v. n. walk in a blustering way*, v. To STRUT. झटकाऱ्यानें-झटके देऊन-झिटकावीत-तमानें-डौलानें-पत्राजानें *or* पत्राजीनें-ठमक्यानें-उरावर-&c. चालणें, अकडणें.

2 v. To BLUSTER, To BOAST. तमतमणें, तमणें, तम *m.* गाजें-दाखवणें, ताल *m.* तोडणें, मोठाल्या गोष्टी *f. pl.* सांगणें, डवला *or* डौला *m.*-तोरा *m.* मिरवणें.

SWAGGER, SWAGGERING, *n.* v. V. 1. पत्राज *or* स *f. m.* अकड *f.* अकडबाजी *f.* ठमका *m.* टूम *f.*

2 तम *m.* लटपटपंची *f.* डवला *or* डौला *m.* वल्गना *f.*

SWAGGERER, *n.* SWAGGERING, *p. a.* v. V. 1. तमानें-झटकाऱ्यानें-डौलानें-&c. चालणारा, ढेंगोजी, जुर्रावावरा, पत्राजी *or* सी, अकडबाज.

2 तमतमणारा, ताल तोडणारा, &c. तमतम्या, तालतोड्या, मोठाल्या गोष्टी सांगणारा, डवलामिरवणारा, तिसमारखान, फिदालखोर.

SWAGGING, SWAGGY. See BAGGING.

SWAIN, *n.* v. COUNTRYMAN. शेतांतला जवान-बाप्या, शेतखप्या.

2 v. LOVER. नायक, प्रिय.

Faithless s. कितव, धूर्त.

To SWALE. See To SWEAL.

To SWALLOW, *v. a. take into the stomach by the throat.* गिळणें, गिळून घेणें, ग्रासणें, पोटांत घेणें, गळयाखालीं-घशाखालीं उतरणें-उतरून घेणें, घोंटणें, ग्रासm.-ग्रसन *n.*-निगरण *n.*-&c. करणें *g. of o.* [घालणें.

2 (anger, &c.) *endure quietly.* गिळणें, खाणें, पिणें, पोटीं

3 *receive without consideration, believe implicitly.* अविचारानें सत्य मानणें-खरा मानणें, न छानतां-कयास न करतां-&c. घेणें.

4 *engulph, consume,* v. To ABSORB. खाणें *or* खाऊन टाकणें, जिरवणें, मुरवणें, गडप-गडद्-गडगप *or* गडलगप *adv.* करणें.

5 up; *engage wholly, engross.* ग्रासणें, वेढणें, गरक-गडप-&c. करणें.

6 (words, letters &c. in speaking). खाणें.

SWALLOW, *n.* v. THROAT. गळा *m.* अन्नमार्ग*m.*

2—the bird. पाकोळी *f.*

SWALLOW-WORT, *n. asclepias gigantea.* अर्क *m.* मंदार *m.*

Gigantic s. रुइटी *f.* रुई *f.* [गीर्ण.

SWALLOWED, *p.* v. V. 1. गिळलेला, &c. ग्रस्त, ग्रसित, गिलित, नि-

To be s. गळयाखालीं-घशाखालीं उतरणें-उतरून जाणें, पोटांत जाणें.

2 गिळलेला, पोटीं घातलेला, &c.

3 अविचारानें घेतलेला, &c.

4 खाऊन टाकलेला, जिरवलेला, गडप केलेला, &c.

5 ग्रासलेला, गडपकेलेला, &c.—esp. as *intended,* and as implying *seized and subdued by, destroyed or lost in, overwhelmed, overpowered, overcome, &c.* ग्रस्त (esp. in comp. as चिंताग्रस्त, दारिद्र्यग्रस्त, भूतग्रस्त, क्रोधग्रस्त, कामग्रस्त, लोभग्रस्त, मोहग्रस्त, मदग्रस्त, विषयग्रस्त, कालग्रस्त, रागग्रस्त, संकटग्रस्त, शत्रुग्रस्त).

SWALLOWER, *n.* SWALLOWING, *p. a.* v. V. 1. गिळणारा, पोटांतघेणारा, ग्रास करणारा, &c. ग्रासक, ग्रसन-निगरण-&c.कर्त्ता-कारी.

SWALLOWING, *n.* v. V. 1.—*act.* गिळणें *n.* ग्रासणें *n.* &c. ग्रास *m.* गिलन *n.* ग्रसन *n.* निगरण *n.* गिरण *n.*

2 गिळणें *n.* खाणें *n.* पिणें *n.* &c.

3 अविचारानें घेणें *n.* अविचारग्रहण *n.* अविचारांगीकार *m.*

4 खाणें *n.* जिरवणें *n.* गडप करणें *n.* &c.

5 ग्रासणें *n.* वेढणें *n.* गडप करणें *n.* &c.

6 खाणें *n.* [झिलाण*n.*

SWAMP, *n. wet, soft ground,* v. MARSH. दलदल *f.* पाणथळ *n.*

SWAMPY, *a.*v.N.*and* MARSHY. दलदलीत, दलदलीचा, पाणथळाचा.

SWAN, *n.* राजहंस *m.* हंस *m.*

To SWAP, *v. a. barter,* v. To EXCHANGE. हेवडदेवड *f.*-मोबदला *m.*-साटेंलोटें *n.*-&c. करणें *g. of o.*

SWAPE, *n.*—of a well, &c. ओकती *f.*

SWARD, *n. turf, sod, grassy surface of land.* गवताचा भुईतळ*m.* गवताची जमीन *f.*-भुई *f.* सतृणभूमिपृष्ठ *n.* सतृणभूमितल *n.*

SWARM, *n.* (of flies, bees, &c.). घोंगट *or* घोंगाट *or* घोंगाण *n.* लोळ *m.* साईर *f.* भणका *m.* जहन *n.*—of honey bees. मोहळ *n.* पडळी *f.*

2 v. MULTITUDE, CROWD. चुंग *f.* चुबका *m.* चुंबा *m.* भणका *m.* जहन *n.* रह *m.* राष्ट्र *n.*

To SWARM, *v. n.*—bees, flies, &c. *fly about and buzz.* घोंघावणें *or* घोंगावणें, घोणाटणें.

2 *throng and move busily.*—maggots, lice, fleas, &c. लुमलसणें, लसलस *f.* करणें, बुचबुचणें, बुदबुदणें, सुळसुळणें, लुबलुबणें, ऊत *m.*-धाम *f.*-बुचबूच *f.*-(*intens.* बुचबुचाट *m.*-लसलमाट *m.* -सुळसुळाट *m.*)-&c. असणें *g. of s.* जोंबणें, लसलशीत असणें.

3 *be thronged, be crowded with living beings.* गजगजणें, गजबजणें, पेंव *n.* फुटणें-उघडणें *g. of s.* आबादानी *f.* असणें *g. of s.* गडगंज-गजबजीत- गजगजीत असणें. [बुचणें.

To s. with (lice, bugs, &c.)—a bed, bedstead, &c. बुच-

SWARTHINESS, *n.* v. A. काळसरपणा*m.* काळबटपणा *m.* कृष्णवर्ण*m.*

SWARTHY, *a. of a dark complexion.* काळसर, काळबट, काळामा, कृष्ण, कृष्णवर्ण. [लोंधट.

SWASH, SWASHY, *a. soft, squashy, &c.* बरबरीत, पचपचीत, लोंधा,

SWATH, *n. line cut by a mower.* पांत *f.* पाथरा *m.*

2 See BANDAGE.

To SWATHE, *v. a. bind or wrap.* गुंडाळणें, वेष्टणें, लपेटणें.

To SWAY, *v. a.* See To WIELD. 2 *bias, influence.* वळवणें, मनावणें, ओढणें, झोक *m.*-कल *m.*-तोल *m.*-&c. देणें, ओढ *f.*-ओढा *m.* लागणें *g. of agent with in. con.*

3 See To GOVERN, To RULE.

To SWAY, *v. n. be drawn to one side by weight, incline.* तोलणें, तोल *m.*-&c. असणें *g. of s.*

2 *have weight or influence.* कल *m.*-तोल *m.*-ओढ *f.*-ओढा *m.* -&c. असणें *g. of s.* भार *m.*-जोर *m.*-&c. पडणें *g. of s.*

SWAY. See INFLUENCE. 2 See RULE.

To SWEAL, *v. n. burn fiercely, blaze away.* ढळढळणें, ढणढणणें, ढळढळ *or* ळां-ढणढण *or* णां-&c. जळणें.

2 *melt and waste away.* पाझरणें, गळत जळणें.

SWEALING, *p. a.* v. V. 1. ढणढणीत, ढळढळीत.

2 गळत जळणारा.

SWEALINGLY, *adv.* v. V. 1. ढळढळ *or* ळां (*intens.* ढळाढळ, ढळाळां) ढणढण *or* णां.

To SWEAR, *v. n. make oath.* शपथ *f. m.*-आण *f.*-&c. घेणें-वाहणें-करणें-देणें, क्रिया *f.*-दिव्य *n.* करणें, शपथ-&c. घेऊन-वाहून-&c. बोलणें-सांगणें-&c. Some of the forms of *Swearing* are, देवावरचें फूल *n.* काढणें, देवावरचा बेल *m.* काढणें, बेलभंडार*m.* काढणें *or* उचलणें, देवावरचीं तुळसीफुलें *n. pl.* उचलणें, गंगा *f.* उचलणें, देवावर-गंगेवर-&c. हात*m.* ठेवणें, बेचाळीस स्मरून बोलणें.

To be enough to s. by. शाखास असणें, शाखाचा-शाखापुरता असणें.

2 *obtest the Deity profanely.* उगीच-उगीचच्याउगीच-एरवीं-निरर्थक-&c. शपथ *f. m.* वाहणें-घेणें-वाहून बोलणें.

To SWEAR, *v. a. put on oath.* शपथ *f. m.*-आण *f.*-&c. घालणें-घवविणें-&c. शपथ *f. m.*-&c. घेणें. [रा-&c.

SWEARER, *n.* SWEARING, *p. a.* v. V. N. 1. शपथ घेणारा-वाहणा-

2 उगीच शपथ वाहणारा.

SWEARING, *n.* v. V. N. 1. शपथ वाहणें *n.* &c. [स्वेदोदक*n.*

SWEAT, *n.* घाम *m.* घर्म *m.* स्वेद*m.* क्लेद *m.* तनुरस *m.* स्वेदजल *n.*

Bathed in s. In a muck of s. घामाघूम.

Engendered by s. &c. स्वेदज.

Heavy s. S. of toil, &c. घामटा *m.* v. निघ, काढ.

Muck of s. गतका *or* गदका *m.*

Piece (as in a shoe, under a saddle, in the arm-pits, &c.) to absorb s. घामोळें *n.*

Stink of s. घामसाण *f.* घामश्याण *f.* घामटाण *f.*

S. of the brow. निढळचा घाम *m.*

2 *ooze, exudation, running.* चेहृळ *m.* चिहाळ *m.* चिल्हाट *m.* तेव *m.* तेह *m.* पाघळ *m.* पाझर *m.* निचरा *m.* झिरपा *m.* शेंदव *m.*

To SWEAT, *v. n. perspire.* घाम *m.*-&c. येणें-सुटणें *in. con.* घामावणें, घामेजणें, घामेणें, सितसितणें, गतका *or* गदका *m.* येणें *in. con.*—in streams or copiously; *be in a muck of sweat.* डवडवणें, डगडगणें *intens.* डगागणें, दरदरणें *intens.* दरारणें, डवडव-डगडगां-दरदर *or* रां-दरारां-दरारून *adv.* घाम *m.* येणें-सुटणें, घामाघूम होणें, वाहणें, आंग*n.* घामानें उपळणें.

2 *ooze away, run.* तेवणें, तेहणें, निचरणें, निझरणें, झिरपणें, रेळणें, चेहळणें, झिरपा *m.*-पाझर *m.*-&c. होणें-सुटणें-चालणें *g. of s.*

3 See To TOIL.

To SWEAT, *v. a. make to sweat.* घाम *m.*-&c. आणणें, स्वेदन *n.*

2 *work hard,* v. To WORK. घामटा *m.* काढणें *g. of o.* पादडणें, पादवणें, पाद्डा *m.* घालणें-काढणें.

SWEATED, *p.* v. V. A. 1. घाम आणलेला, स्वेदित.

SWEATER, *n.* SWEATING, *p. a.* v. V. N. 1. घाम आलेला, गतका आलेला, घामावलेला, &c. घामट *or* ड, घामेल *or* ला, स्वेदित, घर्मस्रावी, स्वेदस्रावी.

2 तेवणारा, तेवलेला, &c. तेवट, तेहट. [करणें *g. of o.* [दोत्पादक. v. V. A. 1. घाम आणणारा, स्वेदक, स्वेदनकर्त्ता-कारक-&c. स्वे-

SWEATINESS, *n.* v. A. 1. घामटपणा *m.* घामेलपणा*m.* [का*m.*

2 डगडगितपणा *m.* &c. चिगचीग *f.* चिडचीड *f.* गतका *or* गद-

SWEATY, *a. moist with sweat.* घामाचा, घामट *or* ड, घामेल *or*ला.

2 *streaming with, bathed in, &c. sweat.* उमेराघामेरा, घामाघूम, डगडगीत, डवडवीत, घर्माप्लुत, स्वेदाप्लुत.

3 *oozy, running.* तेवाचा, पाझराचा, &c. चिपळ्या.

To SWEEP, *v. a. clean by a broom, &c.* झाडणें, झाडणी *f.* करणें *g. of o.* केर *m.*-केरकचरा *m.*-&c. काढणें, सम्मार्जन *n.*-&c. करणें.

To s. and shake, dust and wipe, cowdung-smear, &c. —compreh. झाडझूड *f.*-झाडझपट *f.*-झाडफेड *f.*-झाडलोट *f.*-झाडसारव *f. or* झाडसारवण *n.*-&c. करणें.

2 *clear by whisking a cloth over.* झटकणें, झटकाविणें.

3 away; *carry along or off by force.* झाहवणें, लोटणें, ढकलणें, लोटून नेणें.

4 away; *carry off or destroy in multitudes.* सप्पा *m.* उडवणें-बळवणें *g. of o.* झाडूननेणें, सपाटा *m.*-झपाटा *m.*-&c.उडवणें.

To SWEEP, *v. n. pass along with force, &c.* सपाट्यानें-झपाट्यानें-&c. जाणें-चालणें.

SWEEP, *n.* (as of a skirt, flap, or weapon) *compass of sweep.* झटका *m.* झटकारा *m.* झोंक *m.* झपाटा *m.* फेर *m.* मंडळ *n.*

2 *compass, range,* v. REACH. अटोका *m.* अवांका *m.* पोहोंच *m. f.*

3 *large oar.* पतिंगा *m.*

SWEEPER, *n.* SWEEPING, *p. a.* v. V. A. 1. झाडणारा, &c. v. V. N. झपाट्यानें चालणारा, &c. झपाट्याचा, सपाट्याचा.

I. *scavenger, jakes cleaner.* झाडूकरी, झाड्या, झाडू, भंगी, हलालखोर, म्हेतर (fem. म्हेतराणी). [गदळ *n. m.*

SWEEPINGS, *n.* v. RUBBISH. गाळ *m.* गाळसाळ *m. n.* गबाळ *m.n.*

SWEET, *a. not sour.* गोड, मिठा, गुळचट *or* गुळचीट, मिष्ट, मधु, मधुर, स्वादु.

Slightly or deficiently s. निगोड.

Sweetish. गोडसर, मिठासा, गोडसा, गुळमट, गुळसर, गुळचट, गोडील, गोडूळ.

Sweety-sour. मधुराम्ल.

2 *pleasing to a sense,* gener. v. AGREEABLE. गोड, चांगला, मधु, मधुर, मिष्ट, सुखावह, सुखप्रद, सुखद.

3 *not salt.* गोड, गोडा, मिठा.

4 *not stinking or stale,* v. FRESH, GOOD. चांगला, गोड, मिठा, प्याया-खाया-घ्याया-&c. जोगा-सारखा-&c. अवीट, मिष्ट.

5—of oil. गोडा, मिठा.

SWEET, *n. something pleasant.* सुख *n.*

2—a term of endearment. मिठा (as रेमाझ्यामिठ्या, अगे माझे मिठे, &c.).

SWEET-FLAG, *n. acorus calamus.* वेखंड *n.*

SWEET-HEART, *n.* v. LOVER, प्रिय (प्रिया *f.*) नायक (नायका *f.*). दिलभर *m.*

SWEET-MEAT, *n.* मिठाई *f.* खाऊ *m.* Some of the common *sweetmeats* are, इलाची दाणा, ओरा, कोंद, खपटी, खाजी, खापटी, गुडधान, गुळपापडी, गोडलापशी, गोडसांडणें, चिकी, चुट्याचुरमा, जिलबी *or* जिलिबी, तिळकोंद, तिळवा *or* तिळवा लाडू, लड्डू, *pop.* लाडू.

Sweetmeats, fruits, &c. presented on occasions. शेरणी *f.* वायन *pop.* वाण *n.* खिरापत *f.*

SWEET-MOUTHED, SWEET-SPOKEN, SWEET-TONGUED, *a.* गोड बोल्या, गोड्या, मिठा, मधुरभाषी, प्रियम्वद.

SWEET POTATOE, *n.*—the plant. रताळी *f.*—the root. रताळूं *n.* रताळें *n.*

SWEET-SCENTED, SWEET-SMELLING, *a.* v. FRAGRANT. सुवासाचा, सुगंधाचा, सुवासिक, सुगंधक, सुगंधि. [सौरभ्य *n.*

SWEET-SCENTEDNESS, *n.* v. A. *and* FRAGRANCE. सौगंध्य *n.*

SWEET-TOOTHED, *a. fond of sweets.* गोड्या, साखऱ्या, गोडघांशा, गोडखाऊ.

To SWEETEN, *v. a.* गोड-मिठा-मिष्ट-&c. करणें, गोडपणा *m.*-गोडी *f.* -&c. आणणें, मिष्टीकरण *n.* करणें, गोडाविणें.

To SWEETEN, *v. n.* गोड-मिठा-मिष्ट-&c. होणें-होतजाणें, मिठास *f.*-गोडी *f.*-&c. येणें *in. con.* गोडावणें, गोडिळणें *or* गोडळणें, गुळमटणें, गुरंभळणें.

SWEETENED, *p.* v. V. A. गोड केलेला, मिठा केलेला, &c. मिष्टीकृत.

SWEETENER, *n.* SWEETENING, *p. a.* v. V. A. गोड करणारा, गोडी आणणारा, &c. मिष्टीकरण कर्त्ता-&c.

SWEETLY. See AGREEABLY.

SWEETNESS, *n.* v. A. 1. गोडपणा *m.* मिठेपणा *m.* &c. गोडी *f.* मिठास *f.* मिष्टता *f.* मधुराई *f.* माधुर्य *n.* मधुरता *f.* मधुरिमा *m.*

2 गोडपणा *m.* गोडी *f.* मधुराई *f.* माधुर्य*n.* मधुरता *f.*

To SWELL, *v. a. enlarge the size of, cause to dilate.* फुगवणें, फुगारा *m.*-फूग *f.*-फुगवटा *m.*-&c. आणणें. [आणणें.

2 (a stream, &c.). फुगवणें, चढवणें, तुंबवणें, फुगारा *m.*-&c.

3 (with pride, &c.). v. To PUFF. फुगवणें, चढवणें, माजवणें, फुलवणें.

4 *enlarge, aggregate, &c.* फुगवणें, वाढवणें, मोठा *decl.* करणें.

To SWELL, *v. n. dilate, grow larger.* सुजणें, धोदरणें, फुलणें,

फुगणें, टापुसणें or टापसणें or टोपसणें, सुंबटणें, सुमारणें, सूज *f.*-धोदरा *m.*-&c. येणें *in. con.*

To s. exceedingly. ताडमाड *adv.* सुजणें-फुलणें-फुगणें-&c. आरपार-आरबार *adv.* सुजणें.

2 (with conceit or pride). *be puffed.* फुगणें, फुलणें, चढणें, ताठणें, फुरगुटणें or फुरकुटणें, फुगटणें, माजणें, टुमीनें चालणें-जाणें-वागणें.

3 (with anger). फुगणें, फुलणें, फुरगुटणें or फुरकुटणें, फुगटणें, तमणें or तमतमणें, जळका*m.* येणें *in. con.* जळजळ *f.* सुटणें *in. con.*

4 (with grief, vexation, &c.). उमास or उमासा*m.*-उमासे or उसासे *m. pl.*-&c. येणें *in. con.* हुंडूक*m. pl.* येणें *in. con.* उसासणें.

5—billows; *rise, heave.* खळबळणें, उचलणें, उठणें, उसळणें, खळबळी *f.*-&c. असणें *g. of s.*

6—a river, a stream. फुगणें, तुंबणें, चढणें, फूग *f.*-फुगा*m.* धरणें, फुगारा*m.*-फूग *f.*-&c. येणें *in. con.*

7 *be enlarged, aggravated, exaggerated, &c.* वाढणें, मोठा-&c. होणें, फुगणें, जोरावणें, बळावणें, बळकावणें, हात पाय*m. pl.* पसरणें-फुटणें-लागणें. [होणें.

8—as a sound; *grow full, deep, &c.* जमणें, उद्दाम असणें-

9 *rise, puff up,*—lime, earth, corn, &c. on wetting it. तरतरणें, फुलणें. *intens.* तरारणें.

10—a fragrance or odour; *prevail strongly and diffusively.* घमघमणें, वठणें, घमघमाट*m.*-&c. होणें-असणें *g. of s.*

SWELL, SWELLING, *n.* v.N. 1. *and* TUMOUR. सुजणें*n.* &c. सूज *f.* धोदरा*m.* धोदर *f.* फुगारा*m.* शोथ*m.* शोफ*m.* शोफा *f.* टापसा*m.* टोपशी *f.* सुमार*m.* आध्मान*n.*

White s. पूयालस*m.*

To go down—a s. असुजणें or बसुजणें.

4 हुंडका*m.* उमास or उमासा *m.* उसासा*m.* उबाळा*m.*

5 खळबळी *f. intens.* खळबळाट*m.* खळखळाट*m.* सळाळ*m.* चळबळाट*m.*

I. (of a river, &c.) *accumulated water.* फुगा*m.* फुगारा*m.* फुगवणी*n.* फूग *f.*

II. *an inflated person.* पत्राजी or सी.

To SWELTER, *v. n. be oppressed by heat.* उबणें, उबगणें, उबाबणें, डगडगणें *intens.* डगागणें, गदगदणें *intens.* गदादणें, गदमणें, गदमदणें, खितखितणें, उकडणें. All these verbs are *impers.* आंगाचा गतका or गदका*m.*-आंगाची लाहकी *f.* होणें *g. of s.* उबारणें.

SWELTERY. See SULTRY.

To SWERVE, *v. n. turn aside,* v. To DEVIATE. चळणें, ढळणें, भकणें, भकणी *f.*-चळ*m.*-व्यभिचार*m.*-&c. होणें *g. of s.*

SWIFT, *a. fleet, rapid, &c.* धावरा, पळका, जलद, जलदीचा, त्वरित, क्षिप्र, सत्वर, चालक, चालूक, वेगवान्, अतिवेगी, जंघाल *pop.* जंघाळ, शीघ्र, शीघ्रगामी, शीघ्रगति, तरस्वी, द्रुतगति, उदीर्णवेग, लघुगामी, क्षिप्रगति, जवी, जववान्, त्वरान्वित.

SWIFT-FOOTED, SWIFT-HEELED, *a.* पायसूट, पायाचा-पायचा जलद.

SWIFTLY, *adv.* v. A. *and* QUICKLY. जलदीनें, त्वरेनें, जलदी, जलद, लौकर, वेगें, शीघ्र गतीनें, &c. शीघ्र, सत्वर.

SWIFTNESS, *n.* v. A. धावरेपणा*m.* &c. जलदी *f.* त्वरा *f.* शीघ्रता *f.* शैघ्र्य*n.* वेग*m.* जव*m.* शीघ्रगति *f.* त्वरितगति *f.* क्षिप्रगति *f.* &c.

To SWIG, *To* SWILL, *v. n. drink largely and greedily.* ढोसणें, घोटणें, शोषणें, झोकणें, गटगटणें, ढसढस-ढसाढस-गटगट-गटागट-गळगळ-&c. पिणें, दारू *f.*-&c. ढासणें, घोट*n.* or घोटा*m.* लावणें, अतिपान*n.* करणें, पीपी-पीपिऊन पिणें, सेंचून-रगडून-दपटून-&c. पिणें.

SWIG, SWILL, *n. large draught.* मोठा घोट*m.* मोठा घुटका*m.*

SWILLER, SWILL-BOWL, *n.* v. V. ढोसणारा, घोटणारा, घोटें लावणारा, दारू ढासणारा, पी पी पिणारा, सेंचून पिणारा.

To SWIM, *v. n.* v. To FLOAT. तरणें, तिरणें, तरंगणें.

2 *move along in the water.* पोहणें, पोहून जाणें, पेंवणें, पोहणी *f.*-पेंवणी *f.* करणें-मारणें.

3 *be dizzy.* भोंवणें, फिरणें, तिरमिरणें, कोंडाळणें, गिरगिरणें.

4 *flow in, revel in, &c.* पोहणें.

To SWIM, *v. a. pass by swimming.* पोहणें, तरणें, पोहून जाणें, पोहणीनें जाणें.

2 (cattle, &c.) *cause to pass by swimming.* पोहवणें, पोहवून नेणें, पोहायास-पोहणीस-&c. घालणें.

SWIM, SWIMMING, *n.* v. V. N. 1. तरणें *n.* तिरणें *n.* &c.

2 पोहणें *n.* &c. पोहणी *f.* पेंवणी *f.*

At a s. एका पोहणीनें.

3 घेरी *f.* तिरमिरी *f.* भोंवंड *f.* भोंवळ *f.* भोंड *f.*

SWIMMER, *n.* SWIMMING, *p. a.* v. V. N. तरणारा, तरता, &c.

2 पोहणारा, पोहता. [हेल *f.*

S's. corks or float. सांगड *m. f.* वाहिला*m.* वाहील or वा-

S. without corks or float. आडसांगडी.

The rising & springing forwards of a s. झेंप *f.* v. घाल, मार, टाक.

SWIMMINGLY, *adv. briskly,* v. FLOWINGLY. कडक, कडका, तडक, तडका, धडक, धडका, धडकून.

To SWINDLE, *v. a. practise fraud on another to get his property.* उचकेपणा *m.*-उपटेपणा *m.*- उचका *m.*-उपटा उपटी *f.*-&c. करणें, उचकणें.

To SWINDLE, *v. n. cheat, defraud by artifice,* v. To DECEIVE. धुतारणें, प्रतारणें, मुंडवण *f.* घालणें.

SWINDLER, *n.* SWINDLING, *p. a.* v. V. N. उपट्या, उचक्या, उचल्या, खग्राशा or स्या.

SWINDLING, *n.* v. V. N. उचकेपणा *m.* उपटेपणा *m.* उचलेपणा *m.* उचका *m.* उचकाउचक *f.* उपटाउपट *f.* उपटाउपटी *f.*

SWINE, *n. pig.* डुकर *m. f. n.*

To SWING, *v. a. cause to oscillate.* आंदुळणें or हांदुळणें or हांवदुळणें, झेपा *f. pl.* काढणें-घालणें, झोपे *m. pl.* घालणें, झोके *m. pl.* देणें-घालणें, झुलवणें or झोलवणें, हिलवणें, आंदोलन *n.*&c. करणें *g. of o.*

2 *wave, move to and fro, whirl, &c.* हालवणें, फिरवणें, सेलवणें, भोंवडणें, पेलणें.

To SWING, *v. n. wave to and fro, oscillate.* आंदुळणें or हांदुळणें or हांवदुळणें, झुलणें or झोलणें, लोंबकळणें, झेपा *f. pl.* घेणें-देणें-खाणें, झोंपे *m. pl.*-झोके *m. pl.* घेणें-खाणें, ओळकंब *m. pl.* घेणें-मारणें, ओळकंबणें, ओधंबा *m.* घेणें, लोंबकळा *m.* घेणें.

SWING, *n. oscillation.* झेंप *f.* झोंपा *m.* झोका *m.* झोंप *f.* हेलकावा*m.* हेलावा*m.* ओळकंबा or कुंबा*m.* आंदोलन*n.* झुलणी *f.* लोंबकळा *m.*

2 (as of a weapon, &c.) *sway, sweep.* झटका*m.* झपाटा *m.* झटकारा *m.* झोक *m.*

3 *swinging line, seat, bed, cradle, table, &c.* हिंदुळा *or* हिंदोळा *m.* झोंपाळा *m.* चोपाळा *m.* चौफळा *m.* झुलणा *m.* झुला *m.* झुलवा*m.* झोळकुंबा *m.* आंदोल *m.* हिंदोल *m.* दोला *m.*

Rope to draw and swing a s. झेंपसा*m.* झिंपुटा*m.* झेपुटा*m.*

Strap, cord, &c. of a s. बरात *f.* बारती *f.*

S. with a board. फळें *n.*

Swinging basket &c. in which to pass over precipices. झुला *m.* [*m.*

4 (*or* swinging boxes) —erected at fairs &c. रहाटपाळणा

5 *apparatus with hook, &c. to swing devotees.* बगाड *n.*

S.fixed on cart. गाडेबगाड *n.*

6 *violent impetus, career, bent, &c.* वेग *m.* ओघ *m.* भर *m.* दम *m.* तडाखा *m.* झपाटा *m.*

With full s. साक्षेपें.

To give full s. to. हातीं धरणें, मोकळा सोडणें.

To SWINGE. See To BEAT.

SWINGE-BUCKLER, *n.* v. BULLY, HECTOR. धारराव *m.*

SWINGER, *n.* SWINGING, *p. a.* v. V. A. 1. आंदुळणारा, झोके घालणारा-देणारा, डुलवणारा, &c.

v. V. N. आंदुळणारा, झुलणारा, झोके घेणारा-खाणारा, &c. दोलायमान.

SWINGING, *a.* v. LARGE. रट, लठ्ठ, लठारणा.

SWINISH, *a. like a swine.* डुकरासारखा, डुकराचेचालीचा, सौकर, सूकरसदृश, सूकरबुद्धि, सूकरवृत्ति.

SWITCH, *n. flexible twig or rod.* छडी *f.* कमची *f.* चमकी *f.* फोक *m. dim.* फोकाटी *f.* शिपटी *or* शिमटी *f.* शिरटी *f.* शिरकुटी *f.* शिरपुटी *f.*

To SWITCH, *v. a. beat with a switch.* फोकलणें, फोकाटणें, शिपटणें, शिरटावणें, शिरपुटणें, शिरडावणें, चमकावणें.

SWIVEL, *n.*—the cannon. जेजाल *f.* फिरती-फिरकीची जेजाल *f.*-तोफ *f.* दुन्हाटी *f.*

2 *moveable ring.* भोवरकडी *f.* फिरकी *f.*

SWOLLEN, *p.* v. V. N. 1. सुजलेला, फुगलेला, धोदरलेला, सुजरा, सुजीर, फुगीर, फुगरा, धोदर, गुरगुरीत, शोथयुक्त, शोफयुक्त.

Slightly s. सुजट, सुजीर, सुजमीर.

SWOLLENNESS, *n.* v. P. सूज *f.* सुजलेपणा *m.* फुगिरपणा *m.* बापसा *m.* फुगवशी *or* फुगोशी *f.* फुगवटा *m.* फूग *f.* फुगारा *m.* धोदरी *f.* धोदरा *m. intens.* धोदराट*m.*

SWOON, *n. fainting fit, syncope.* मूर्च्छा *f.* कलम *m.* मूर्च्छना *f.* कश्मल *n.* घायतळ *f.* v. ये, मोह *m.* मुरसंड *or* मुरसंडी *f.* v. ये.

Return of consciousness after a s. संज्ञा *f.*

To SWOON, *v. n. sink into a fainting fit.* मूर्च्छा *f.*-कलम *m.*-घायतळ *f.* येणें *in. con.* मूर्च्छा *f.*-मूर्च्छना *f.*-&c. होणें, मूर्च्छापन्न-&c. होणें.

SWOONED, *p.* v. V. मूर्च्छा आलेला, कलम आलेला, &c. मूर्च्छित, मुर्च्छागत, मूर्च्छापन्न, गतचेतन.

SWOOP, *n. fall or stoop of a bird of prey.* झड *f.* झपाटा *m.* झडप *f.* झेंप *f.* झांप *f.* झपेट *f.*

To make a s. झड-*f.* झडप *f.*-&c. मारणें-घालणें.

To SWOP. See To SWAP.

SWORD, *n.* तरवार *f.* खड्ग *m.* समशेर *f.* धार *f.* असि *m.*—in contempt. phraseol. बागट *n.* घासकटाऊ *m.* कचकट *n. f.* Certain sorts of *swords* are, करांचली *f.* खंडा *m.* सांडा *m.* जमदड *or* जमदाड *f.* तेगा *m.* धोप *f.* निमचा *m.* पट्टा *m.* सडक *f.* सुरई *or* य *f.*

Belt of a s. पडदळें *n.* दाली *f.*

Blade of a s. पान *n.* पातें *n.* असिपत्र *n.*

Death in battle by the edge of the s. धारातीर्थ *n.*

Flashing of swords. असिलता *f.*

Frog or hold of a s. खजिना *m.*

Handle of a s. मूठ *f.*

Hilt of a s. परज *m.*

Point of a s. पुतळी *f.*

String or chain fastened to the hilt of a s. मेखला *f.*

To draw the s. सळ *m.* सोडणें.

To sheath the s. तरवार *f.* म्यान करणें.

SWORDS-MAN, *n.* धारकरी, धारराव.

SWORD-STICK, *n.* गुप्ती *f.*

SWORN, *p.* v. V. A. शपथ घातलेला-घेतलेला-खाललेला, शापित, कृतशपथ.

I.—friend, friendship, enemy, enmity, &c. शपथेचा.

SWUNG, *p.* v. V. A. 1. आंदुळलेला, झेप घातलेला, &c. आंदोलित.

SYCOPHANCY, SYCOPHANTRY, *n. servility, mean flattery,* v. OBSEQUIOUSNESS. आर्जव *n.* खुशामत *f.* छंदानुरोध *m.* छंदानुवृत्ति *f.*

SYCOPHANT, *n. a mean flatterer,* v. OBSEQUIOUS. आर्जवी, खुशामती, खुशामत्या, थुंकाझेल्या, थुकीझेलणारा, होयीस होय उठवणारा, टाळीसटाळी देणारा, छंदानुरोधी.

SYLLABIC, SYLLABICAL, *a.* अक्षराचा, अक्षरसंबंधी, अक्षरविषयक.

SYLLABLE, *n. a. letter or letters uttered at a single effort.* अक्षर *n.*

SYLLABUB, *n.*—the frothy compound. फेणी *f.*

SYLLABUS. See ABSTRACT.

SYLLOGISM, *n.*—in logic. न्याय *m.* अवयवी *m.* अवयवघटितवाक्य *n.* अवयवोपेतवाक्य*n.* According to the Nyáya system a syllogism has five members, which are as follows: 1. प्रतिज्ञा, 2 हेतु, 3 उदाहरण, 4 उपनय, 5 निगमन. The following is an illustration. He is a rogue, प्रतिज्ञा. Because he is one eyed, हेतु. Every one eyed man is a rogue, उदाहरण. He is a one-eyed man, उपनय. Therefore he is a rogue, निगमन. Nulli monoculi sunt honesti. The usual illustration of the Pandits is this, पर्वतोवन्हिमानिति प्रतिज्ञा ॥ धूमवत्त्वादिति हेतुः ॥ योयो धूमवान् सःसःवन्हिमान् इत्युदाहरणं ॥ तथाचायमित्युपनयः ॥ तस्मात्तथेति निगमन ॥ इतिपंचावयवोपेतं वाक्यं ॥ A syllogism according to the Mimánsa system has only the three last members.

SYLLOGISTIC, SYLLOGISTICAL, *a.* v. N. अवयवघटितवाक्यसंबंधी-विषयक-रूप-&c.

SYLPH, *n. fig. a delicate slender woman.* तन्वंगी *f.* लघ्वी *f.* परी *f.* [ब्रनचारी.

SYLVAN, *a. woody, &c.* वनचा, वन्य, वनसंबंधी, वनविषयक, वान,

SYMBOL, *n.* v. SIGN, MARK, EMBLEM. चिन्ह *n.* खूण *f.* निशाणी *or* नी *f.* संज्ञा *f.* व्यंजन *n.* व्यंजक *n.*

SYMBOLICAL, *a.* v. N. संकेताचा, संज्ञीक, लाक्षणिक, सांकेतिक, संकेतात्मक, उद्बोधक.

Symmetrical, *a. well-made*, v. Shapely. आकारशुद्ध, आवशुद्ध, बळणशुद्ध, वळणदार, बांधेशुद्ध, सुभट, सासुरत.

Symmetry, *n.* (of form or make). आकारशुद्धि *f.* आंगसंजोग *m.* अवयवसंजोग *m.* वळणशुद्धपणा*m.* आवशुद्धपणा *m.* &c.

Sympathetic, *a. having common feeling with another.* दुसऱ्याचें दुःखसुख जाणणारा, दुसऱ्याच्या दुःखानें दुःखी, दुसऱ्याच्या सुखानें सुखी, अन्यदुःखसुखमानी, परदुःखसुखमानी, परदुःखदुःखी, अन्यदुःखदुःखी, परसुखसुखी, अन्यसुखसुखी, कन्हवाळू.

S. joy. अनुमोदन *n.*

To **Sympathize**, *v. n. have a common feeling.* दुसऱ्याचें दुःखसुख *n.* जाणणें, दुसऱ्याच्यादुःखानें दुःखी होणें-सुखानें सुखी होणें, कन्हवळणें *or* कणवळणें, कन्हवळा *or* कन्हवाळा *m.* येणें.

Sympathizer, *n.* **Sympathizing**, *p. a.* v. V. *and* Sympathetic. दुसऱ्याचें दुःखसुख जाणणारा, कन्हवाळू, समदुःख, समदुःखी, सहदुःखी.

Sympathy, *n. fellow feeling, correspondent feeling with another.* अन्यदुःखदुःख *n.* परदुःखदुःख *n.* अन्यदुःखदुःखिता *f.* परदुःखदुःखिता *f.* समदुःखिता *f.* सहदुःखिता *f.* कन्हवळा *or* कन्हवाळा *m.* अन्योन्यदुःखसुखवेत्तृत्व *n.*

2 *agreement of affections, conformity of temperament.* प्रकृतीचा-स्वभावाचा-&c. सारखेपणा *m.* आनुगुण्य *n.* स्वभावानुगुण्य *n.* स्वभावसाम्य *n.* प्रकृतिसाम्य *n.* साधर्म्य *n.* आनुरूप्य *n.*

Symphonious, *a.* v. Harmonious. स्वरमेळाचा, स्वरैक्याचा, समस्वर. [*n.* तानमान *n.*

Symphony, *n.* v. Harmony. स्वरमेळ*m.* स्वरांचामेळ*m.* स्वरैक्य*n.*

Symptom, *n. indication, token, &c.* खूण *f.* लक्षण *n.* निशाणी *or* नी *f.* चिन्ह *n.* छाया *f.* सूचक *n.* रूपक *n.* व्यंजन *n.* लिंग *n.* पूर्वरूप *n.*

Symptoms,—in medicine. रोगलक्षण *n.*

Symptomatic, *a.* v. N. *indicative, &c.* दर्शक, प्रदर्शक, सूचक, उद्बोधक, बोधक, all used in comp.

Synagogue, *n.* यहुदी लोकांची भजन सभा *f.*

2 यहुदीलोकांचें भजनालय *n.* सभास्थान *n.*

Synchronism, *n. simultaneousness.* गांठ *f.* योग *m.* समकालिकता *f.* एककालिकता *f.* कालैक्य *n.* युगपद्भाव *m.* यौगपद्य *n.*

To **Synchronize**, *v. n. be simultaneous.* एककाळ *m.*-एकसमय *m.*-&c. असणें-होणें *g. of s. recip.* कालैक्य *n.*-एककालिकता *f.* -&c. असणें-होणें *g. of s.* समकालिक-एककालिक-&c. असणें.

Synchronous, Synchronal, Synchronical, *a.* v. Simultaneous. एकेकाळचा, एककालिक, समकालिक.

Syncope, *n. swoon.* मूर्च्छा *f.* घायतळ*f.* प्रलय*m.* नष्टचेष्टना*f.* तंद्रा*f.*

2—in grammar. मध्याक्षरलोप *m.*

Synecdoche, *n.*—in rhetoric. उपलक्षण *n.*

Synod, *n.* v. Assembly. सभा *f.* मजालस *f.*

Synonime, *n. a word of the same meaning.* उपशब्द *m.* पर्याय *m.* अपरपर्याय *m.*

Synonymous, *a. having the same meaning.* एकाअर्थाचा, एकार्थक, समानार्थक, तुल्यार्थक, सहार्थ.

Synopsis, *n. brief general view*, v. Abridgement, Abstract. गोशेरा *or* गोष्वारा *m.* मरजुमा *m.* सारग्रंथ *m.*

Syntactical, *a. pertaining, &c. to syntax.* वाक्यरचनेचा, वाक्ययोजनेचा, &c. पदयोजनविषयक, पदयोजनसंबंधी.

Syntax, *n.* वाक्यरचना *f.* वाक्ययोजना *f.* वाक्यपद्धति *f.* वाक्यविन्यास *m.* पदरचना *f.* पदयोजना *f.* पदविन्यास*m.* पदान्वय *m.* अन्वययोजना *f.* शब्दयोजना *f.* &c. [लन *n.*

Synthesis, *n.* v. Combination. संयोजन *n.* एकीकरण *n.* मी-

Synthetical, *a.* संयोगाचा, संयोगात्मक, संयोगरूप.

Syphilis, *n.* v. Lues venerea. उपदंश *m.*

Syringe, *n. squirt.* पिचकारी *f.* चिरकांडी *f.* चिपनळी *f.* चिपळी *f.*

To **Syringe**, *v. a. inject by a syringe.* पिचकारी *f.*-चिरकांडी *f.*-&c. मारणें.

2 *cleanse by a syringe.* पिचकारीनें-&c. धुणें-साफ करणें.

Syrup, See Sirup.

System, *n. plan, &c.* v. Scheme. बेत*m.* अनुसंधान *n.*

2 *method*, v. Order. क्रम *m.* अनुक्रम *m.* परिपाटी *f.*

3 *animal composition.* देहप्रकृति*f.* शरीरप्रकृति*f.* शरीर*n.* आंग*n.*

To enter into the s. आंगीं-शरीरीं-&c. भिनणें, काळजीं-लागणें.

Systematical, *a.* v. Orderly, Regular. क्रमाचा, बेताचा, बेतींव, बेताबाताचा, व्यवस्थित.

To **Systematize**, *To* **Systemize**, *v. a. reduce to system.* v. To Methodize. क्रम *m.*-अनुक्रम *m.*-अनुसंधान *n.* बांधणें.

Systole, *n.*—in anatomy. हृत्पिंडसंकोच *m.*

T.

T. This letter as a very soft *dental* is represented by त, and as aspirated, by थ ; as a hard *palatal*, by ट, and as aspirated, by ठ.

Tabasheer, *n. manna of the bamboo*, v. Bamboo. त्वक्क्षीरा *f.* *pop.* तवकीर *or* खीर *or* तवकील *or* खील *n.*

Tabby, *a. brindled.* बांडा, कसरा.

Tabernacle. See Tent. 2 See Temple.

To **Tabernacle**, *v. n.* v. To Dwell. राहणें.

Tabies, *n.* v. Consumption. झडी *or* झड *f.* सडी *f.* किरी *f.*

Table, *n.* मेज *n.* चवरंग *m.*

T.-expenses. भोजनखर्च *m.* [*g. o.* *s.*

To lose one's seat at a (great man's) t. पत्रावळ*f.* उडणें

2 *company at table.* भोजनमंडळी *f.* पंक्ति *f.*

3 (as of marble, &c.) *flat mass.* पाटी *f.* पत्र *n.* पत्रा *m.* पत्रिका *f.* पट्ट *m.*

4 (as of a hill, &c.) *level surface.* सपाटी *f.* समस्थल *pop.* समथळ *n.* समानक्षेत्र *n.* समक्षेत्र *n.* समानदेश *m.* समभूमि *f.* समानभूमि *f.*

5 (of numbers or figures). अंकजाल *n.* सारणी *f.* कोष्टक *n.*

6 *index, syllabus, synopsis, &c.* पत्रक*n.* तक्ता *m.* बोटखत *n.*

T. of contents. अनुक्रमणिका*f.* सूची*f.* सूचिका*f.* सूचीपत्र*n.*

To **Table**, *v. a.* तक्ता *m.*-पत्रक *n.*-&c. करणें *g. of o.*

Table-cloth, *n.* मेजाची चादर *f.* मेजाचें आंथरूण *n.*

Table-land, *n. elevated flat land.* डोंगरसपाटी *f.* सपाटी *f.* पठार *n.* पठारा *m.* माची *f.* समस्थल *pop.* समथळ*n.* सडा *m.* पर्वतभूमिका *f.*

Tablet, *n. something flat to write on.* पाटी *f.* पत्र *n.* पत्रिका *f.* पट्ट *m.* (esp. in comp. as ताम्रपट्ट, स्वर्णपट्ट).

To **Taboo**, *v. a. forbid the use of.* द्वाही *or* दुराही *f.*-अनेगा *f.*

घालणें, उपभोगासेध *m.*-भोगासेध *m.*-&c. करणें.

TABOR, TABORET, *n.* v. DRUM, TAMBORINE. मृदंग *m.* पखवाज *m.* डोर *m.* खंजिरी *f.*

That head of a t. (पखवाज) which is beaten. बाजतापुडा *m.* बाजतेंपूड *n.*

TABULAR, *a. set down in tables.* तक्त्याचा, पत्रकाचा, तक्ताकाढलेला, तक्त्याच्या आकाराचा.

TACIT, *a.* v. IMPLIED. अर्थसिद्ध, ध्वनित, फलित, गर्भित, गतार्थ, अनिषेधाधार, अनिषेधाश्रय, अनिषेधरूप.

TACITLY, *adv.* v. A. निषेधाभावानें, तूष्णीम्भावानें, निषेधकेला नाहीं म्हणून, उगाच राहण्यानें, अर्थात.

TACITURN, *a. habitually silent.* अबोल, अबोलका, अबोलणा, अबोल्या, अल्पभाषी, अल्पवादी, मौनी, अनालाप, अनालापी, अनालापशील, अनालापवृत्ति, कथाविरक्त, भाषणविरक्त, आलापविमुख.

T. person.—in contempt. phraseol. मुकाम्हसोबा *m.* मुकीमण्यार *f.* मोगरा *m.*

TACITURNITY, *n.* v. A. अबोलपणा *m.* अबोलणेपणा *m.* &c. मौन *pop.* मौन्य *n.* अनालापिता *f.* अनालापबुद्धि *f.* अनालापवृत्ति *f.* कथाविरक्ति *f.*

To TACK, *v. a. stitch together*; *append to.* हिलगणें, जडणें, टांके *or* टांचे *m. pl.* मारणें-मारून जोडणें.

2 (a ship or vessel). आयें *or* हेरें *or* हेऱ्यें *n.* घेणें, वाळियेणें.

TACK *n. small nail.* चूक *f.* गुलमेख *f.*

TACKED, *p.* v. V. 1. हिलगलेला, &c. जडींव.

TACKLE, TACKLING, *n. ropes of a ship, &c.* दोरखंडें *n. pl.* दोरदोरखंड *n.* दोऱ्या बिऱ्या *f. pl.*

2 v. GEAR, HARNESS. वेठण *n.* तेगार *m.* सामान *n.* सरंजाम*m.*

TACT, *n. peculiar skill, &c.* v. SKILL. युक्ति *f.* कळा *f.* कसब *n.* लाघव *n.* छाप *m.* छापी *f.*

TACTIC, TACTICAL, *a. relating to tactics.* कवाइतीचा, व्यूहरचनासंबंधी-विषयक, सैन्यविन्याससंबंधी-विषयक.

TACTICIAN, *n. one versed in tactics.* कवाइती *or* दी, व्यूहरचनकुशल, व्यूहरचनाभिज्ञ, सैन्यविन्यासी.

TACTICS, *n. the science of military arrangement and manœuvres.* कवाइत *or* द *f.* व्यूहरचनाविद्या *f.* व्यूहरचना *f.* सैन्यविन्यास *m.* सैन्यरचना *f.*

TACTILE, *a.* v. TANGIBILE. स्पर्शकरायाजोगा-सारखा-&c. स्पर्शनीय, स्पर्श्य, स्पृश्य. [मूलक.

TACTUAL, *a. pertaining, &c. to touch.* स्पर्शाचा, स्पर्शरूप, स्पर्श-

TADPOLE, *n. young frog.* बेडकीचें पोर *n.* बेडकीचा गोळा *m.* बेटकुळी *f.* बेडकुळी *f.*

TAFFETA, *n.*—the silk. ताफता *or* तापता *m.*

TAG, RAG, AND BOBTAIL, v. PEOPLE. महारपोर *m. n.* ऐगूबैगू *m. pl.* सोमाजी गोमाजी *m. pl.*

TAIL, *n.*—the part of an animal. शेपूट *or* शेंपूट *n.* शेप *or* शेंप *f.* (*dim.* शेपटी *or* शेंपटी *or* डी *f.* शेंपुडी *f. and, enhanc.* शेपटा *or* शेंपटा *or* डा *m.*). पुच्छ *n. m.* दूम *f.* लंगूल *or* लांगूल *n.*

A whisk with the t. (of a horse, &c.) फटकडी *f.* फटाका*m. v.* मार.

To bristle up the t. शेपूट *n.* फिंदारणें.

To follow hard at the t. of (bullock, &c .) *drive on and pursue violently.* शेपटणें, शेपट *n.* काढणें *g. of o.*

To hang at the t. of. *dance attendance upon.* कच्छपींकच्छपास-कासेस-&c. लागणें *g. of o.* कास *f.* धरणें *g. of o.* दुमची *f.* पुरवणें *g. of o.*

To turn t. शेपूट *n.* घालणें, पाठ *f.* दाखवणें-देणें, मुठींत नाक*n.* धरून जाणें, मेंगावणें.

To twist the t. (of a bullock) to urge on. शेपाळणें.

2 (of a comet) शेंडी *f.*

3 See END, EXTREMITY.

TAIL-CUT, TAIL-CROPPED, *a.* लांडा, लंडपुच्छ, छिन्नपुच्छ.

TAIL-LESS, *a.* निशेपट्या, शेपटावेगळा-निराळा, अपुच्छ, पुच्छहीनरहित-&c.

TAILED, *a. having a tail.* शेपुटकरी, शेपटाचा, शेपट्या, शेपुटवाला, दुमदार, सपुच्छ, पुच्छवान्, पुच्छविशिष्ट.

TAILOR, *n.* सिंपी *or* शिंपी *m.* दरजी *m.* सूचीकर्मकारी, सौचिक,—in contempt, सिंपुरडा *m.* The common name assumed by the tribe or body of *Tailors* is, नामदेव.

TAILOR-BIRD, *n.* सुगरण *f.*

Nest of the t. सुगरणीचें कोटें *n.*

To TAINT, *v. a.* v. To INFECT. रोग *m.*-दोष *m.*-विटाळ *m.*-&c. देणें-लावणें, रोगयुक्त-दोषयुक्त-&c. करणें.

2 v. To CORRUPT. बिघडवणें, दूषणें, घाणवणें, नासवणें, वाईट-खराब-दुष्ट-दूषित-&c. करणें.

3 *slur, sully, &c.* v. To STAIN. कलंक *m.*-काजळी *f.* लावणें, सकलंक-दूषित-&c. करणें, दूषणें.

To TAINT, *v.n. get bad—meat, &c.*लागणें, वास*m.* सुटणें *in. con.*

TAINT, *n. infection, corruption, soil.* दोष *m.* घाण *f.* विटाळ *m.* बाधा *m.* वास *m.*

2 v. STAIN. काळें *n.* काळवटी *f.* दोष *m.* दूषण *n.* कलंक *m.*

TAINTED, *p,* v. V. A. 1. रोग दिल्हेला-घेतलेला,दोष दिल्हेला-लावलेला-लागलेला, विटाळ लावलेला-लागलेला.

2 बिघडवलेला, नासवलेला, &c. दूषित.

3 कलंक लावलेला, &c. सकलंक, दूषित.

I.—as meat. लागरा *remiss.* लागट, लागलेला, वासट, वाशेळा, वासाळ, दुर्गंधयुक्त.

To TAKE, *v. a. accept, receive.* घेणें, स्वीकारणें, अंगीकारणें, ग्रहण *n.*-ग्रह *m.*-आदान *n.*-उपादान *n.*-स्वीकार *m.*-दत्तस्वीकार. *m.*-&c. करणें.

To take he understands, but *to give* he has never learned. घघाची विद्या त्याला येती पण ददाची विद्या त्याच्या गांवीं नाहीं.

2 v. To SEIZE. घेणें, धरणें.

3 *captivate,* v. To CHARM. मोहणें, मोहून वश करणें, मोह *m.*-&c. घालणें, मोहित-&c. करणें.

4 *get into one's power, ensnare, &c.* v. To CATCH. धरणें.

5 *apprehend,* v. To UNDERSTAND. घेणें, समजणें उमजणें *esp. in. con.*

To t. to be. शक्तिग्रह *m.* असणें-होणें *g. of o. and in. con.*

6 *receive, feel or be affected by.* धरणें, पावणें, मानणें, लागणें *in. con.* वाटणें *in. con.* मनावर घेणें.

7—in the general sense, (a beating, an airing, the air, heat, cold, wet, a jolt, shock, nodding, &c.) *receive, suffer, sustain, experience, be the subject of.* खाणें, घेणें, मारणें.

To t. well, (kindly, sweetly, &c.). गोड करून घेणें.

8—in the numerous variations of the sense as appearing in the phrases To take (breath, leave, farewell, revenge, a course or way). घेणें.
9 *hire, rent.* भाड्यानें घेणें. [घेणें *in. con.*
10 (*a disease, &c*). घेणें, जडणें *in. con.* लागणें *in. con.*
11 *require.* घेणें, खपवणें, अटवणें, खाणें, लागणें *in. con.*
12 (a likeness, &c.). काढणें, उतरणें, लिहणें.
13 away ; *remove.* नेणें, घेऊन जाणें, काढणें, अपनयन *n.*-उन्नयन *n.*-अवग्रह *m.*-&c. करणें.
14 away ; v. To SEIZE. हरणें, हरवणें *or* हारवणें, हिरणें, हिरावणें, हिसकावून घेणें, हरण *n.*-हार *m.*-अपहरण *n.*-अपहार *m.*-&c. करणें.
15 down ; *pull down or to pieces.* उतरणें, काढणें, उलगडणें, उसकटणें, उसकटणी *f.* करणें *g. of s.* उत्तरणें. [वणें.
16 down ; *write.* लिहून ठेवणें, कलमी करणें, मांडून-टाचून ठे-
17 in. See To COMPREHEND.
18 in; v. To CHEAT. फसवणें. [उत्तरणें.
19 off ; *divest, denude, &c.* v. To STRIP. काढणें, उतरणें,
20 off; v. To IMITATE. नकल *f.* करणें-उतरणें *g. of o.* थाकी *f.* उतरणें-साधणें-आणणें *g. of o.* उतरणें, सोंग *n.* करणें *g. of o.*
21 out ; forth ; from ; off; &c. काढणें, काढून घेणें.
22 up ; v. To LIFT. उचलणें, उचलून घेणें.
23 up ; (a defiance, an affront, &c.). झेलणें, मनावर घेणें *or* धरणें.
24 up ; (a song, tune, &c.) झेलणें, धरणें.
25 up ; (a course, a practice, &c.). धरणें, आदरणें, पतकरणें, स्वीकारणें, अंगीकारणें, आरंभिणें.
26 up ; v. To UNDERTAKE. उचलणें, पतकरणें, हातीं धरणें, अटपणें, आदरणें.
27 up ; *engross, consume, &c.* v. To OCCUPY, To ABSORB. घेणें, खाणें, ग्रासणें, वेढणें, अटणें, अटवणें, गुंतवणें.
28 up ; *borrow.* उचलणें, उचलून घेणें.
To t. care. To t. heed. जपणें, संभाळणें.
To t. effect. लागणें, लागू होणें, गुणास येणें.
To t. in hand, v. To UNDERTAKE. हातीं धरणें.
To t. place, v. To HAPPEN. घडणें, घडून येणें, होणें.
To t. part. See To SHARE.
To t. leave. निरोप *m.*-आज्ञा *f.*-हुकूम *m.*-&c. घेणें.

To TAKE, *v. n. gain reception, suit,* v. To PLEASE. चालणें, पटणें, उतरणें, मानणें, मान्य-पसंत-&c. होणें, खपणें.
2 *have effect.* लागणें, लागू होणें, गुणास येणें, वीं *n.* रुजणें *g. of s.* फळणें.
3 after ; v. To RESEMBLE. वळणावर जाणें *g. of o.* मोडणीनें मोडणें *g. of o.* चालीनें चालणें *g. of o.*
4 to ; v. To ADDICT. पडकणें, सवकणें *or* सोकणें, सोकावणें, लांचावणें, स्वर *m. pl.* वाहणें *or* भजणें *g. of s.* मन *n.* बसणें *or* लागणें *g. of s.* चकसणें, चटावणें.
5 towards ; *feel an impulse (to go to).* पाय *m.pl.* वाहणें-घेणें-वळणें *g. of s.*
6 with ; v. To PLEASE. मनास *or* मरजीस उतरणें *g. of o.*
7 place ; v. To HAPPEN. घडणें, घडून येणें.

TAKEN, *p.* v. V. A. 1. घेतलेला, &c. गृहीत, ग्रहणकेलेला, उपात्त.
2 घेतलेला, धरलेला.
3 मोहून वश केलेला, &c. मोहित, वश.
9 भाड्यानें घेतलेला.
13 नेलेला, &c. अपनीत, नीत.
14 हरलेला, &c. अपहृत, हृत.

TAKER, *n.* TAKING, *p. a.* v. V. A. 1. घेणारा, &c. ग्रहण-आदान-&c. कर्त्ता, ग्राहक, ग्राही, धारक, धारी (in comp. as रूपधारी, अवतारधारी).
2 घेणारा, धरणारा, &c.
3 मोहणारा, मोहून वश करणारा, मोह घालणारा, मोहक.
13 नेणारा, &c. अपनयन-उन्नयन-&c.कर्त्ता. [कर्त्ता.
14 हरणारा &c. हर, हर्त्ता, हारी, हारक, हरक, हरण-अपहरण-&c.

TAKING, *n.* v. V. A. 1.—*act.* घेणें *n.* &c. स्वीकार *m.* स्वीकरण *n.* अंगीकार *m.* अंगीकरण *n.* दत्तस्वीकार *m.* &c. ग्रहण *n.* ग्रह *m.* आदान *n.* उपादान *n.* संग्रह *m.*
2 घेणें *n.* धरणें *n.*
4 धरणें *n.* [*n.*
13 नेणें *n.* &c. अपनय*m.* अपनयन*n.* उन्नयन*n.* अवग्रह*m.* अवग्रहण
14 हरणें*n.* &c. हरण*n.* अपहरण*n.* हार*m.* अपहार*m.*
I. v. AGITATION, CONFUSION. तळतळ *f.* डामाडूळ *f.* त्रेधा *f.* तिरपीट *f.*

TALC, *n.*—the mineral. अभ्रक*m. n.* मेघजाल*n.*
Calx of t. अभ्रकभस्म*n.*
Yellow t. पिवळा अभ्रक*m.*

TALE, *n. narrative, fable, &c.* v. STORY. गोष्ट *f.* कथा *f.* नकल *f.* कहाणी *f.* गोष्टमात *f.* कथानक*n.* आख्यान*n.* उपाख्यान*n.* गतक*n.*
T. of olden times. गतगोष्ट *f.* गतकथा *f.*
To be as a t. नकल *f.* होणें *g. of s.* कथाशेष होणें.
To tell tales of. कुवाडेपोवाडे*m. pl.* करणें-सांगणें *g. of o.*
2 *reckoning,* v. ACCOUNT. गणती *f.* हिशेब *or* हिशोब*m.* सलई *f.*
With full t. फडाचे मापानें, भरमापानें.

TALE-BEARER, *n.* TALE-BEARING, *a.* v. INCENDIARY. चुगलखोर *or* चुगलीखोर, चुगल, चहाड, चहाडखोर, दुलावा *or* व्या, लुतरा, पिशुन.

TALE-BEARING, *n. malicious or officious information.* सांगासांगी *or* [illegible]गोसांगी *f.* चहाडी *f.* चुगल *f.* चुगली *f.* चुगलखोरी *f.* उसपाभर *f.* उठाठेव *f.* लावालाव *f.* लावालावी *f.* दोषानुवाद*m.* पैशुन्य*n.*

TALENT, *n. faculty, endowment.* गुण*m.*
2 talents; v. UNDERSTANDING. बुद्धि *f.* अक्कल *f.* प्रज्ञा *f.* बुद्धिवैभव*n.* बुद्धिकौशल*n.*

TALENTED, *a.* v. CLEVER, WISE. बुद्धिमान्, प्राज्ञ, मेधावी, बुद्धिवैभवशाली.

TALISMAN, *n.* v. AMULET, CHARM. ताईत*m.* कवच*n. m.* यंत्र*n.*

To TALK, *v. n.* v. To CONVERSE. बोलणें, गोष्टी *f. pl.* सांगणें, जाबसाल*m.*-संभाषण*n.*-भाषण*n.*-संवाद*m.*-संकथन*n.*-&c. करणें.
2 v. To SPEAK. बोलणें, भाषण*n.*-कथन*n.*-उक्ति *f.*-&c. करणें.
To t. to one's self. आपल्याशीं-आपल्या जिवाशीं बोलणें.
To t. big. उचलून बोलणें, उचलून गोष्टी *f. pl.* सांगणें, उड्या *f. pl.* मारणें, तालताल बोलणें, तमाच्या गोष्टी *f. pl.* सांगणें.
To t. idly, v. To PRATE. बकणें, बडबड *f.* करणें.
To t. in sleep. ओरणणें, ओसणवणें, ओसंडणें.

TALK, *n.* v. CONVERSATION. गोष्टीबाता *or* माता *f. pl.* बोला-

बोली *f.* संभाषण*n.* संवाद*m.*

2 *rumour*, v. REPORT. गप *or* गप्प *f.* सांगासांगी *or* सांगोसांगी *f.* बोलवा*m.f.* हाक *f.* वाद*m.* चर्चा *f.* आख्या *f.*

3 *speech, saying.* बोलणें*n.* बोल*m.* म्हणणें*n.* भाषण*n.* उक्ति *f.* वाद*m.*

Fine t. शब्दपांडित्य*n.*

Idle t.mere t.भाकडकथा*f.* वृथाकथा*f.* गाथा*f.or*कोरड्या गाथा*f.pl.* वात*f.*फकांडी*f.or*फकांड्या *f.pl.*रिकभाषण*n.*भाषणमात्र*n.* रिकामें बोलणें*n.* पोकळ बोलणें*n.* चटक्याचे मांडव*m. pl.*

Light t. Small t. लघुभाषण*n.*

TALKATIVE, *a. loquacious*, v. PRATER. फार बोलणारा, बोलका, बोलगडा *or* गाडा, तोंडाचा मोकळा, चावट, बोलघेवडा, फकांडी *or* ड्या, वाचाल *or* ळ, बहुभाषी, बहुभाष, मुखर, बाचरा *remiss.* बाचरट, वाग्मी, जल्पक, कथाप्रसंग, वावदूक.

TALKATIVENESS, *n.* v. A. बोलकेपणा*m.* वाचाळपणा*m.* चावटपणा *m.* चावटाई *f.* बहुभाषिता *f.* वाचालता *f.* &c.

TALKER, *n.* TALKING, *p. a.* v.V. 1. बोलणारा, &c. संभाषण-&c. कर्त्ता, संभाषी, संलापी.

2 बोलणारा &c. बोलता, भाषण-&c. कर्त्ता, वक्ता, वादी.

Fine t. v. ELOQUENT. सांगसुगरण, बोलून चांगला, बोलून बृहस्पति.

Mere t. *that can only talk well.* तोंडचा (as तोंडचा कारकून, तोंडचा शिपाई, &c.), सांग सुगरण.

TALL, *a. high in stature.* उंच (*remiss.* उंचवट *or* उंचट *tallish*). काठीचा-हाडाचा उंच, उंचकाठीचा, उंचहाडाचा, उंचाड, उंचेला, उच्च, उन्नत. Some terms and phrases for *An exceedingly and disproportionately tall person*, corresponding with *Gaffer bamboo, May pole, lath, walking mopstick, &c.*are कळंकीनारायण, लंबाण भाऊ, लंबाड्या, लंबाटा, लंबचडी *f.* धिपाड *or* धिप्पाड, लंबचड, शेलांटी, ढंक, ढंकाळ *or* ढांगळ *or* डंगाळा, धांडळ *or* धांडाळ, लकड, लकड्या, तुळवट, कनकाड्या, फिरकाड्या.

T. for its age. उभाड, उभाडांग, उभाड्याचा, उभाटा.

T. and stout. धिंग, धिंगड *or* धिंगाड.

T. and thin. लंबाडा *or* ड्या.

Very t. ताडभर उंच *or* तीन ताड उंच.

To grow t. उंचावणें.

TALLNESS, *n.* v. A. उंचपणा *m.* उंची *f.* उच्चत्व *n.* उन्नतत्व *n.*

TALLOW, *n.* v. FAT. चरबी *f.* मेषवपा *f.* गोवपा *f.*

TALLOW-CANDLE, *n.* चरबीची बत्ती *f.*

TALLOW-CHANDLER. *n.* चरबीच्या बत्त्या करून विकणारा.

TALLY, *n. thing suiting to.* उतारा *m.* उतार *m.* ताळा *m.* जवाब *or* जाब *m.* जोड *f.*

To TALLY, *v. n. answer, agree, correspond.* मिळणें, मिळणींत असणें, उतरणें, जमणें, जुळणें, जुडणें, बसणें, सांधा *m.* बसणें *g. of s.* जम *m.*-जवा *m.*-जुगल *f.*-जडप *n.*-उतारा *m.*-&c. पडणें-बसणें *g. of s.* ताळा माळा *m.*-ताळ *m.*-घटाव *m.*-&c. होणें *g. of s.* बस्तन *or* बस्तान *n.* बसणें-जमणें-मिळणें.

TALON, *n.* v. CLAW. पंजा *m.* नख *n. m.*

TAMARIND, *n.*—the tree. चिंच *f.* आंबली *f.* अम्ली *f.* अम्लिका *f.*—in cant phraseol. वांकडीम्हैस *or*वांकीम्हैस *f.*—the fruit, चिंच *f.* आंबली *f.* अम्ली *f.* चिंचेचेंफळ *n.*—the pod, काकडा *m.*—the seed, चिंचोका *m.*

Seed-division of pod of t. बोटूक *n.*

Short and straight pod of t. बोटूक—*as disting. from* long & crooked pod, कोंगाळें *n.*

T.-seed. चिंचोका *m.*

T. water. चिंचवणी *n.*

Tax on tamarinds. चिंचतसर *n.*

TAMBORINE, *n.*—the kind of drum. डफ *m.* (*dim.* डफडी *or* री *f.* डफडें *or* रें *n.*) हलकी *f.* खंजिरी *f.*

Hurried or animated striking of tamborines. डफघाई *f.*

T.-beating and singing. डफगाणें *n.*

TAMBORINE-PLAYER, *n.* डफ्या, डफड्या, डफकरी.

TAME, *a. not wild.* घरचा, घरसोंकील, पोसलेला, पोशींब, पाळींव, पाळलेला,बाळगलेला, माणसाळा, माणसळलेला, *or* माणसाळलेला, माणसाच्या सवईचा, सवेचा, माणसाचा सोकील, गृह्य, गांवचा, ग्राम्य, गरीब, वश्य, दमित, अहिंस्र.

2 *vapid, flat*, v. SPIRITLESS. पचपचीत, मचमचीत, पळपळीत, निस्तेज.

3 *spiritless, unresisting*, v. WEAK. लेंचापेंचा, मेंगा, मेषा, नामर्द, पराक्रमहीन.

To TAME, *v. a. make domestic.* माणसळवणें *or* माणसाळवणें, माणसाळा-माणसाच्या सवईचा-गरीब-मेंढीसा-&c. करणें, मेंढीगाय-मेणगोळी-&c. करणें, मऊ आणणें, क्रूरतानाश *m.*-क्रूरताभंग *m.*-&c. करणें *g. of o.*

2 v. To SUBDUE. वश-&c.करणें, बठणीस आणणें,मऊ आणणें, कढ *m.* जिरवणें *g. of o.* वशीकरण *n.*-दम *m.*-दमन *n.*-&c. करणें *g. of. o.*

TAMEABLE, *n.* v. V. 1. माणसळवायाजोगा-सारखा-&c. माणसाळा करायाजोगा-&c.

2 वश करायाजोगा-&c. बठणीस आणायाचा-जोगा-&c. वश्य, सुदम, दमनीय, दम्य.

TAMED, *p.* v. V. 1. माणसाळवलेला, माणसाळा केलेला, &c.

2 वशकेलेला, बठणीस आणलेला, &c. मऊ आणलेला-आलेला, वश, वशंगत, वशीकृत, वशीभूत, दमित, दांत.

TAMELY, *adv.* v. A. 3. लेंचेपेंचेपणानें, मेंगेपणानें, नामर्दपणानें, पराक्रमहीनतेनें, &c.

TAMENESS, *n.* v. A. 1. माणसाळेपणा *m.* गरीबपणा *m.* घरसोंकीलपणा *m.* &c. वश्यता *f.* गरीबी *f.* अहिंस्रता *f.*

2 पचपचितपणा *m.* मचमचितपणा *m.* &c.

3 लेंचेपेंचेपणा *m.* मेंगेपणा *m.* नामर्दपणा *m.* &c. नामर्दी *f.* पराक्रमहीनता *f.* पराक्रमाभाव *m.*

TAMER, *n.* TAMING, *p. a.* v. V. 1. माणसळवणारा, माणसाळाकरणारा, गरीबकरणारा, &c.

2 वशकरणारा, बठणीसआणणारा, दमक, दमी.

To TAMPER, *v. n.* See To MEDDLE. 2 *practise secretly.* वळवण्याकरितां-फितवण्याकरितां-&c. संधान*n.*-उद्योग*m.*-&c. चालवणें.

To TAN, *v. a.* (leather). कमावणें, रांपवणें, रांपत घालणें, तयार करणें.

2 (the skin, &c.) *make brown.* काळा करणें , काळेपणा *m.*-कालिमा *f.*-&c. आणणें, काळंवडणें, काळंवडवणें.

To TAN, *v.n.*—the complexion. काळसरणें, काळवटणें, काळंवडणें, कोळपणें.

TAN-PIT, *n.* रावणी *f.* चांभाराची कुंडी *f.*

TANG, *n. smack, &c.* v. TASTE. छटा *f.* वास *m.*

Tangent, *n.*—in geometry. स्पर्शरेषा *f.* संपातरेषा *f.* संपातरेखा *f.*
To fly off at a t. ओसरता जाणें.

Tangibility, *n.* v. A. स्पर्शायाचीयोग्यता *f.*-अर्हता *f.*-&c. स्पर्शनीयता *f.* स्पर्श्यता *f.* स्पृशता *f.* &c. स्पर्श *m.*

Tangible, *a. perceptible by the touch.* स्पर्शायाचा-जोगा-&c. स्पर्शनीय, स्पर्श्य, स्पृश्य, संपृश्य, स्पर्शयोग्य, स्पर्शार्ह, स्पर्शवेद्य.

To **Tangle**, *v. a. involve, entangle, complicate, &c.* गोवणें, गुतवणें, गळफटणें *or* गळफाटणें, गोंधळणें, गोंधवणें, गोंधरणें, गुरपटणें *or* गुरफटणें *or* गुरफाटणें, गूत *f.*-गुतागूत *f.*-गांठी *f. pl.*-गळफटा *or* गळफाटा *m.*-गुंडाळा *m.*-गुरपटा *m.*-गोंदागोंद *f.*-गुताडें *n.*-&c. करणें *g. of o.*

2 *ensnare, &c.* See To Entangle.

To **Tangle**, *v. n. be entangled.* गुतणें, गोंधळणें, गोंधवणें, गोंधरणें, गूत *f.*-गुतागूत *f.*-गळफटा *m.*-&c. होणें *g. of o.*

Tangle, *n. knot or complication of threads, &c.* गूत *f.* गुतागूत *f.* अट *f.* अटी *f.* गुंडाळा *m.* पीळ *m.* पेंडें *n.* अढा *m.* घांठ *f. or* गांठी *f. pl.* मेढा*m.*गळफटा *or* गळफाटा*m.* गुंताडा *m.* गुरपटा *m.* फांसडा *m.* लढ *f.* लढा*m.*

Tangled, *p.* v. V. A. 1. गुतवलेला, गळफटलेला, &c.

Tank, *n. lake, large reservoir.* तळें *n.* तलाव *or* तळाव *m.* सरोवर *n.* तटाक *n.* तटाग *n.* जलाशय *m.* जलाधार *m.* तडाग*n.* कासार*m.*
2 v. Cistern. टांकें *n.* टांकी *f.*

Tanned, *p.* v. V. A. 1. रांपवलेला, कमावलेला, &c.
2 *and* V. N. काळसरलेला, &c.

Tannedness, *n.* v. P. 2. काळवटी *f.* काळवंडी *f.* काळवण *f.* कालिमा *m. pop.* कालिमा *f.*

Tanner, *n.* v. V. A. 1. कातडें रांपवणारा-कमावणारा, &c. ढोहार *or* ढोर, चांभार *or* चाम्हार, चर्मक*n.* चर्मकार.
T.'s steeping vat or vessel. चर्मकाचें कुंड *n.* चर्मकुंड *n.*

Tantalization, *n.*v.V.—*act.* चाळवणें *n.* &c. चाळवणी *f.* चाळवण *f.* चाळवणूक *f.* झुलवणी *f.*

To **Tantalize**, *v. a. tease with fallacious hopes.* चाळवणें, चाळवणी दाखवणें, धूप *m.* दाखवणें, आशेस लावणें, झुलवणें, झुलवणी *f.* दाखवणें, चाळवण *f.*-चाळवणूक *f.*-&c. करणें.

Tantalized, *p.* v. V. चाळवलेला, चाळवणी दाखवलेला, &c.

Tantalizer, *n.* **Tantalizing**, *p. a.* v. V. चाळवणारा, आशेसलावणारा-लावण्याचा, चाळवणी दाखवणारा-दाखवण्याचा, &c.

Tantamount, *a.* v. Equal, Equivalent. बरोबर, सम, समतोल, समभाव.

To **Tap**, *v.a. strike with a gentle blow.* थापटणें *or* थोपटणें, थाप *f.*-थापटी *f.*-&c. मारणें-देणें, ठोठावणें, ठोकणें.
2 *broach, pierce.* भोंक *n.*-तोंड *n.* पाडणें.

Tap, *n. pat, gentle blow.* थाप *f.* थापट *f.* थापटी *f.* थापड *f.* थापडी *f.* टचका *m.*
2 (of the hand, upon a tabor, &c.). छाप *f.* हात *m.* थाप *f.*

Tape, *n.*—fine, narrow. फीत *f.* (from the Portuguese).—coarse, broad, नवार *f.*
To lace with broad t. नवारणें.
2 (of drawers, &c.) नाड *f.* नाडी *f.* नाडा *m.*

Tape-worm, *n.* लांब जंत *m.* उदरावेष्ट *m.* नाडीजंतु *m.*

Taper, *n. small wax candle.* बारीक मेणबत्ती *f.*

Taper, **Tapering**, *a. that narrows towards the point.* निमुळता *or* निमोळता, गायदूम, चिंचोळ *or* चिंचोळा, सूच्यग्र,शुंडाकृति.

To **Taper**, *v. n. become gradually smaller towards the point.* बारकावणें, चिंचोळा-निमुळता-&c. असणें-होणें-जाणें.

Tapestry, *n. cloth woven with figures.* बुटीदार *or* बुटेदार कापड *n.*-भिंतीचे पडदे *m. pl.* मुसज्जर *m.*

Tap-root, *n.* धरणमूळ *n.*

Tar, *n.*—the resinous substance. डामर *n.* सरलद्रव *m.* सरलरस *m.* सर्जरस *m.*
2 See Sailor.

To **Tar**, *v. a.* डामर *n.* लावणें.

Tardy. See Slow, Dilatory.

Tare, *n.*—in commerce. बारदान *n.* आभंड *n.*

Target, *n.* v. Shield. ढाल *f.*
2 *mark*, v. Butt. निशाण *n.* लक्ष्य *n.*
T.-practice. चांदमारी *f.*

Tariff, *v. n. cartel of commerce.* जकातीचा-&c. निरखनामा *m.*

To **Tarnish**, *v. n. become dull, lose lustre.* बिटणें, मळणें, मजीत-बिटका-&c. होणें-होत जाणें.

To **Tarnish**, *v. a.* v. To Sully. बिटवणें, मळवणें, डागणें, मजीतमळकट-बिटका-&c. करणें. [लावणें.
2 fig; v. To Stain. डाग *m.*-बट्टा *m.* आणणें-लावणें, कलंक *m.*

Tarnished, *p.* v. V. N. बिटलेला, डागलेला, &c. बिटका, बिटकर, वाणढाळ, मजीत, मळकट, सकलंक.

To **Tarry**, *v. n. continue, &c.* v. To Stay. राहणें, थारणें, ठरणें.
2 See To Delay, To Dawdle. 3 for ; *wait for*, v. To Stay. राहणें, खोळंबणें, खोळंबून राहणें.

Tart, &c. See Sour, Sharp, &c.

Tartar, *n. concretion on the teeth.* दांतांवरचें सायटें*n.* दंतमल*m.*

Tartarus, *n.* v. Hell. यमलोक *m.* नरक *m.*

Task, *n. work imposed by authority.* नेमून दिल्हेलें-घालून दिल्हेलें-माथीं मारलेलें-&c. काम *n.* धडा *m.* कामाची नेमणूक *f.*-मोताद *f.* [काम *n.*
2 See Business. 3 *burdensome employment.* जिकिरीचें
To take to t. v. To Blame, To Scold. शब्द *m.* ठेवणें.

To **Task**, *v. a. impose a task.* काम *n.* नेमून-घालून-&c. देणें, काम *n.* माथीं मारणें, धडा *m.* घालणें.

Task-master, *n.* काम नेमून देणारा-घालून देणारा, काम माथीं मारणारा, धडा घालणारा, हत्तीचा अंकुश, गळग्रह, शनि.

Tassel, *n. ornamental bunch of silk, &c.* गोंडा *m.* झुबका *m.* झुमका *m.* फुन्ना *m.*

Tasselled, *a.* v. N. झुबकेदार, झुमकेदार, फुन्नेदार.

To **Taste**, *v. a. perceive by the palate.* स्वाद *m.*-रस *m.*-&c. जाणणें-समजणें-&c. स्वादज्ञान *n.*-स्वादबोधन *n.*-&c. करणें *and, with in. con.* होणें.
2 *try by the palate.* चाखणें, आस्वादणें, चव *f.* घेणें-पाहणें *g. of o.* चाचणी *f.* पाहणें *g. of o.* आस्वाद *m.*-स्वाद *m.* घेणें *g. of o.* चाचणूक *f.*-आस्वादन *n.*-स्वादन *n.*-स्वाद*m.*-रसना *f.* करणें *g.of o.*
3 *have perception of, feel.* चाखणें, भोगणें, अनुभवणें, अनुभव*m.* घेणें *g.of o.* अनुभव *m.*-&c. येणें-होणें *g.of o. with in.con.* चव *f.* घेणें-पाहणें *g. of o.* अनुभवास-प्रत्ययास-&c. येणें *in. con.* वाटणें *in. con.* समजणें *in. con.*

To **Taste**, *v. n. seem to the taste.* लागणें, वाटणें, स्वाद *m.*-&c. असणें *in. con.*
To t. well. रुचणें, गोड लागणें-वाटणें-होणें.

2 of; *smack, have a flavour of.* स्वाद *m.*-छटा *f.*-वास *m.*-गंध *m.*-ध्वनि *m.*-चुणूक *f.*-धुनक *f.*-लकीर *f.*-&c. येणें-मारणें *g. of o.*

TASTE, *n.*—the sensation. स्वाद *m.* आस्वाद *m.* स्वादज्ञान *n.* रसज्ञान *n.* स्वादबोध *m.* रसबोध *m.*

2—the sense. रुचि *f.* रसनेंद्रिय *n.* जिभेची-तोंडाची गोडी *f.*-चव *f.* तोंड *n.* रसना *f.*

Restoration of lost t. तोंड पालट *m.*

To blunt the t. जीभ *f.*-जिह्वा *f.* विटाळणें, तोंड *n.* बाईट करणें.

To lose one's t. तोंड *n.* बाईट होणें *g. of s.* तोंड *n.* फिरणें *g. of s.* तोंडाची गोडी *f.*-चव *f.* जाणें *g. of s.*

3—as in substances. चव *f.* गोडी *f.* रुचि *pop.* रूच *f.* स्वाद *m.* आस्वाद *m.* मजा *f.* मजेदारी *f.* लजत *f.* रस *m.* उपदंश *m.*

The six tastes (*viz.* sweet, sour, salt, pungent, astringent, bitter). षड्रस *m. pl.*

4 *relish, sensual or intellectual.* चव *f.* गोडी *f.* रुचि *pop.* रूच *f.* अभिरुचि *f.* इष्क *m.* गोडवी *f.*

According to one's t. यथारुचि.

Loss of t. अरुचि *f.* अरोचक *n.*

To suit the t. रुचणें, मानणें, रुचीस उतरणें *g. of s.*

5 *nice perception.* रस *m.* रसज्ञान *n.* रसबोध *m.* मर्मज्ञान *n.* रसिकता *f.* रसज्ञता *f.*

Devoid of t. अरसिक, अरसज्ञ, अमर्मज्ञ.

Having t. रसिक, रसज्ञ, मर्मज्ञ.

Spurious or false t. रसाभास *m.*

6 *fondness for, liking.* चट *f.* चटक *f.* चटका *m.* चवणा *or* चौणा *m.* लजत *f.* हौस *f.*

To get a t. for. चटावणें, चकसणें.

7 *smack, smatch, tincture, &c.* स्वाद *m.* छटा *f.* वास *m.* गंध *m.* ध्वनि *m.* लकीर *f.* लकेरी *f.* छाया *f.* लजत *f.* धुनक *f.* चुणूक *f.*

8 *small quantity given as a specimen.* मासला *m.* बानगी *f.*

TASTED, *p. and a.* v. V. A. 1. रसनेंद्रियानें- जिभेनें-&c. जाणलेला, स्वादित, आस्वादित, ज्ञातरस, गृहीतरस.

2 चाखलेला, &c. चव घेतलेला, आस्वादित.

3 चाखलेला, &c. [स्वादविशिष्ट.

I. *having a particular taste.* स्वादाचा, चवीचा, &c. स्वादयुक्त,

TASTEFUL, TASTY, *a. having a nice relish, savory.* चवदार, रुचिकर, रुचीक, मजेदार, गोड, मिष्ट, रसिक, रसवान्, चणचणीत, खमंग, चरमरीत, खारट तुरट, चविष्ट, रुच्य, रोचक, सुस्वास्वाद, खुमारीदार, सुरस, सरस, स्वादिष्ट, स्वादु, मुखप्रिय, षड्रस.

To become t. तोंडीं लागणें.

2 *evidencing taste.* मौजेचा, खुबीदार, छबदार, मजेचा, मजेदार, रसिक, सुबक, रसज्ञतादर्शक.

TASTEFULNESS, TASTINESS, *n.* v. A. 1. चव *f.* चवदारी *f.* रुचि *f.* गोडी *f.* मजेदारी *f.* रस *m.* चणचणितपणा *m.* चरमरितपणा *m.* मिष्टता *f.* सौरस्य *n.* रुच्यता *f.* रोचकत्व *n.* स्वादिष्टत्व *n.* स्वादुत्व *n.* मुखप्रियता *f.*

2 मजेदारी *f.* खुबी *f.* छब *f.* छबदारी *f.*

TASTELESS, *a. vapid, without relish,* v. INSIPID. बेचव, निचव, बेमजा, बेस्वाद, फिका *or* फिक्का, विरस, मिटमिटीत, गळगळीत, सपक, पचकळ, अरस, नीरस, अस्वादु, स्वादरहित-विरहित-हीन-विहीन, रुचिहीन-रहित-&c.

TASTELESSNESS, *n.* v. A. बेचवपणा *m.* &c. स्वादराहित्य *n.* रसहीनता *f.* स्वादहीनता *f.* &c. अस्वादुत्व *n.* आरस्य *n.* आलवण्य *n.*

TATTER, *n.* v. RAG. सुडका *m.* सुडकें *n.* बाभारा *m.* फटकर *n.* लत्ती *f.*

TATTERDEMALION, *n.* v. RAGAMUFFIN. फटकुऱ्या, चिंधोट्या,—a female. चिंध्यादेवी.

TATTERED, *a. torn, &c.* v. RAGGED. फाटका, बाभारे गेलेला.

To TATTLE, *v. n. talk idly,* v. To PRATE. बकणें, बकबकणें, बाता *f. pl.* कुटणें-छाटणें, गप्पा *f. pl.* छाटणें-हांकणें-मारणें.

2 *tell secrets,* v. To BLAB. तोंडाळणें, मुखरस *m.* पाघळणें *g. of s.* चुगली *f.*-चहाडी *f.* सांगणें, कानगी *f.* करणें.

TATTLE, *n.* v. PRATE. गोष्टीबाता *or* माता *f. pl.* सांगासांगी *or* सांगोसांगी *f.* सांगावांगी *f.* लघाळकी *f.* लचाडकी *or* लचाळकी *f.*

TATTLER, *n.* TATTLING, *p. a.* v. V. 1. बकणारा, &c. बकबक्या, बडबड्या, लघाळ, लचाड *or* लचाळ, लहाबर *or* लहांबर.

2 तोंडाळणारा, &c. कानाचा हलका, अल्पकर्ण *or* अल्पकर्णी, जिभेचा हलका-ढिला-&c. चहाड, चहाडखोर, लुतरा, लमेचाटू, लहांबर, चोंबडा, सूचक. [गोंधणें.

To TATTOO, *v. a.* (the body) *puncture and stain.* गोंदणें *or*

TATTOO, *n. mark made by tattooing.* गोंधलें *n.*

TAUGHT, *p.* v. V. शिकवलेला, &c. शिक्षित, बोधित, उपदेशी, उपदिष्ट, विज्ञापित, अध्यापित, विज्ञप्त, ज्ञापित, ज्ञपित, ज्ञप्त.

To TAUNT, *v. a. twit, upbraid, reproach sarcastically.* बोंचणें, टोंचणें, शब्दानें टोंचणें, ओंठावणें, नाकांत काड्या *f. pl.* घालणें, लावून-बोंचून-टोंचून-खोंचून-घालूनपाडून-&c. बोलणें, टापरणें, टाप *f.*-टापरा *m.*-&c. मारणें, ठोठावणें, तोंडीं काढणें, ठोंबरा *m.*-ठोमणा *m.*-&c. मारणें-देणें, उपरोध *m.*-आक्षेप *m.* करणें, टेपलणें, टेपरा *m.*-टेपर *n.*-&c. मारणें, कुचनिंदा *f.*-कुचनिंदी *f.* करणें *g. of o.*

TAUNT, TAUNTING, *n.* v. V. *and* SARCASM. बोंचणें *n.*-&c. बोंचणी *f.* आक्षेप *m.* चुटका *m.* उपरोध *m.*

TAUNTER, *n.* TAUNTING, *p. a.* v. V. लावून बोलणारा, टोंचून बोलणारा, &c. उपरोधाचा, उपरोधी, उपरोधीक, अहाड्या पहाड्याचा.

TAUNTINGLY, *adv.* v. A. लावून, खोंचून, बोंचून, घालूनपाडून, शब्दानें टोंचून, &c. उपरोधानें, अहाडून पहाडून.

TAURUS, *n.*—the zodiacal sign. वृषभ *m.*

TAUTOLOGICAL, TAUTOLOGOUS, *a. repeating the same thing.* पुनरुक्तिचा, द्विरुक्तीचा, द्विरुक्तिरूप.

TAUTOLOGIST, *n.* तेंचतेंच फिरून बोलणारा, पुनरुक्ति-&c. करणारा, पुनरुक्ती-&c. कर्त्ता-कारी-&c.

TAUTOLOGY, *n. saying the same thing again,* v. REPETITION. पुनरुक्ति *f.* द्विरुक्ति *f.* अनुवाद *m.* अनुलाप *m.* आम्रेडन *n.*

TAVERN, *n. liquorshop, drum shop.* कलालाचें दुकान *n.* दारूचें दुकान *n.* गिडंगी *f.* पिठा *m.* मद्यशाला *f.* पानगोष्ठिका *f.* मदिरागृह *n.* गंजा *f.* गंजिका *f.*

TAVERN-KEEPER, *n.* कलाल, दारूविकणारा, दारूविक्या.

TAW, *n. large marble.* टप *m.* चट *m.* बट *m.*

T. ring. कोंड *m.*

TAWDRINESS, *n.* v. A. देखणाऊपणा *m.* &c. हलकी शोभा *f.* मुलामी शोभा *f.* बेगडी शोभा *f.* &c.

TAWDRY, *a. meanly showy, fine without taste.* हलके शोभेचा, देखणाऊ, देखाऊ, दिसाऊ, ढबीचा, पोशाकी *or* गी, अहेरी, अहेराऊ, बेगडी शोभेचा, कल्हेगिरीचा, कल्हईचा, मुलामी शोभेचा, बजाजी.

TAWNINESS, *n.* v. A. पिंगटपणा *m.* &c. पिवळट *f.* पिवळोखी *f.*

TAWNY, *a.*—the colour. पिंगट, पिंगळा, पिंगा, कपिल *pop.* कपिला.

TAX, *n. sum or rate of money assessed by government, impost.* दिवाणदेणें *n.* दिवाणधारा *m.* सरकारदेणें *n.* सरकारधारा *m.* सरकारबंत *m.* पट्टी *or* सरकारपट्टी *f.* सारा *m.* दस्त *m.* कर *m.* शुल्क *m. n.* राजस्व *n.*

Closing or clearing division of a t. झाडपट्टी *f.* झाडबाकी *f.*
Exempt from t. दस्तिवाद, गैरदस्त *or* स्ती, पाळ, अकर.
Half t. निमसारा *m.*
House t. उंबरसारा *m.* घरपट्टी *f.*
Land t. फाळा *m.* सारा *m.*
Person paying it. सारेकरी *m.*
Proportion of t. खापणी *f.* हिस्सेरसी *f.*
Remitted t. *or* Sub-t. एहसान *n.*
Settled or regular t. ऐनदस्त *m.—as disting. from* Extra t. सवाई *f.* बरताळा *m.*
T. in cash or money. नकबाब *or* नकीबाब *f.*
T. levied upon the earing of the crop. तुसारपट्टी *f.*
T. on festal occasions, joy-t. संतोषपट्टी *f.*
T. on exports and imports. जकात *f.*
T. on wells. विहिरहुंडा *m.*
T. on marriage of widows. पाटदाम *m.*
T. on shopkeepers and artisans. मोहतरफा *m.*
T. upon fields and enclosures. सारा *m.*
T. to defray contingent charges. सादिलबारपट्टी *f.*
T. to supply a defalcation. तोटापट्टी *f.*
T. upon lowest classes. अडाणपट्टी *f.*
To assign or apportion a t. हिस्सेरसी *f.* करणें-बसवणें, फाळा *m.* फाडणें, खापणी *f.* करणें, खापणें, फाळणी *f.* करणें, पट्टी *f.* फाडणें-फाळणें-तासणें. [बणें.

To TAX, *v. a. impose a tax on.* पट्टी *f.*-दस्त *m.*-कर *m.*-&c. बस-
2 See To CHARGE, To ACCUSE.

TAX-FREE, *a.* पाळ, दस्तिबाद, गैरदस्त *or* स्ती, अकर.

TAX-GATHERER, *n.* वसुलदार, वसुल्या, तहसिलदार, जकातदार.

TAX-ROLL, *n.* पट्टी *f.* शिस्त *f.* [स्थान.

TAXABLE, *a. liable to assessment.* दस्ती, वसुली, सान्याचा, शुल्क-

TAXATION, *n.* v. V. पट्टी बसवणें *n.* कर बसवणें *n.* &c. जमाबंदी *f.* करादिस्थापना *f.* राजस्वस्थापना *f.* [कर.

TAXED, *p.* v. V. दस्तबसवलेला, *&c.* दस्ताचा, कराचा, &c. दस्ती, स-
Half-t. निमदस्ती.
Sub-t. धारेएहसानी.
T. in cash. नगदी.
T. in kind. ऐनजिन्नसी.

TAXER, *n.* TAXING, *p. a.* v. V. दस्त-&c. बसवणारा.

TEA, *n.* चहा *m.* 2 (the infusion) चहाचा काढा *m.* चहा *m.*

TEA-POT, *n.* चहादान *n.* चहादानी *f.*

To TEACH, *v. a. instruct, inform; communicate the knowledge of.* बुझवणें *or* बुझावणें, शिकवणें, पढवणें, सांगणें, उपदेशणें, शिक्षणें, बोधवणें, उपदेश *m.*-शिक्षण *n.*-शिक्षा *f.*-अध्यापन *n.*-ज्ञापन *n.*-विज्ञापन *n.*-विज्ञापना *f.*-बोध *m.*-बोधन *n.*- अवबोध *m.*-&c. करणें.
Aptness to t. बोधकशक्ति *f.*
To t. one's elders or betters. शेंडीस गांठी *f. pl.* देणें.
2—in an ill sense. शिकवणें, शिकवणी *f.* करणें *g. of o.* गुण- *m.* शिकवणें.

TEACHABLE, *a.* v.V.—of matters. शिकवायाचा-जोगा-&c. सांगायाचा-जोगा-&c. शिक्षणीय, शिक्ष्य, शिक्षितव्य, अध्यापनार्ह, विज्ञापनोपयुक्त.—of persons, v. DOCILE, OBEDIENT. सुशिक्ष्य, सुशिक्षणीय, सुबोध, सुशिष्य.

TEACHABLENESS, *n.* v. A. सुशिक्ष्यता *f.* &c.

TEACHER, *n.* TEACHING. *p. a.* v. V. 1. शिकवणारा, &c. शिक्षक, उपदेशक, उपदेष्टा, उपदेशी, विज्ञापक, बोधक, अवबोधक, अध्यापक, उपदेश-शिक्षा-अध्यापन-&c. कर्त्ता-कारक-&c.
Acquired from a t.—an art, &c. वस्तादी.
Spiritual t. गुरु, आचार्य.
T. of any of the arts or accomplishments. वस्ताद.
Business or craft of a t. वस्तादगिरी *f.* वस्तादपणा *m.*

TEACHING, *n.* v. V. 1. शिकवणें *n.* &c. शिक्षा *f.* शिक्षण *n.* See the other nouns under the Verb.

TEAK, *n.*—the tree. सागवान *m.* साग *m.* साया *m.* साय *m.* सायला *m.* सायवान *m.*—the wood, सागवान *m.* साग *m.* साया *m.* साय *m.* सायला *m.* सायवान *m.* [वानी.
Of or belonging to t. सागवानी, सागली, सायली, साय-
Plantation or forest of t. सागवान *n.*

TEAL, *n.*—the bird. पाणकोंबडा (डा *m.* डी *f.* डें *n.*) पाणकुकडा *m.* (डा *m.* डी *f.* डें *n.*). [*m.f.*

TEAM, *n. horses or oxen harnessed for drawing.* जोत *n.* सांगड

TEAPOY, *n. table or stand with three legs.* तिपायी *f.* तिवई *f.*

TEAR, *n.* असू *or* आसूं *n. m.* अश्रु *n. m.* नेत्रोदक *n.* नेत्राम्बु *n.* नेत्रज *n.* बाष्प *m. n.*
Flood or torrent of tears. अश्रुधारा *f.* पागोळी *f.*
Flowing or trickling of tears. अश्रुपात *m.* अश्रुस्राव *m.*
T.-drop. अश्रुबिंदु *m.* टीप *n.*
T. of affection. प्रेमाश्रु *m. n.*
Waste tears. अरण्यरोदन *n.*
To burst into tears. रडें *n.* कोसळणें.
To melt into tears. असवें *n. pl.* उगळणें.
To shed tears. आंसवें *n. pl. or* आसूं *m. pl.* ढाळणें-गाळणें.
To stream,—tears. डोळे *m. pl.* or डोळ्यांतून पाणी *n.* ढाळणें.
To wipe the mourner's tears. रडत्याचे आसूं *m. pl.* पुसणें, डोळे *m. pl.* पुसणें *g. of o.* [करणें.
To wipe away the tears from every eye. सर्वदुःखक्षय *m.*

To TEAR, *v. a. rend.* फाडणें, फाडूनटाकणें, चिरणें, तोडणें, तोडूनटाकणें, फाळणें, विदारणें, दारण *n.*-विदारण *n.*-&c. करणें *g. of o.* —soundingly, टर-कन-कर &c. (*intens.* टरटर *or* गं-टराटर-टरारां) *adv.* फाडणें-चिरणें-तोडणें, चरकणें, टरकणें, टरकावणें.
To t. in or to pieces. फाडफाडूनटाकणें-घेणें, तुकडे *m. pl.* करणें *g. of o.* उद्फाळणें, विशकलन *n.*-&c. करणें *g. of o.*
To t. and pull asunder, about, &c. विसकटणें, विसकटा विसकट *f.* करणें.
To claw and t. लुचणें, लुचलुचणें.
To t. and pull asunder. विचकटणें.
2 *laniate, lacerate,* v. To SCRATCH. बुचकरणें *or* बुचकुरणें, बोचकरणें *or* बोचकडणें.
3 (the hair) *pull with violence.* तोडणें, ओढणें, ओढाताण *f.*-ओढातोड *f.* करणें *g. of o.*
4 up; off; away; &c. roughly. उचकटणें, उलकटणें, उसकटणें, उपटणें, उखळणें, खाकटणें, उघडणें, उतफाळणें.

To TEAR, *v. n. rend.* फाटणें, चिरणें, फाळा *m.* निघणें-जाणें *g. of s.*

—soundingly. टर-कन-कर-&c. (intens. टरटर *or* रां-टरारां-टराटर,) *adv.* फाटणें-चिरणें, धसकणें.

2 *fume, rave,* v. To RAGE. तडफडणें, धडफडणें.

3 along; through; &c. v. IMPETUOUSLY. धडकावणें, धसकावणें, धसणें, धडकावून-धसकावून-&c.जाणें-चालणें.

TEAR, *n.* v. RENT. चीर *f.* फाळा *m.* [डबडबीत.

TEAR-FUL, *a. full of tears,* v. WEEPING. भरलेला, डबडबलेला,

TEARER, *n.* TEARING, *p. a.* v. V. A. 1. फाडणारा-&c. दारण-विदारण-&c. कर्त्ता-कारी-&c.विदारक.

TEARING, *n.* v. V. A. 1.—*act.* फाडणें *n.* चिरणें *n.* तोडणें *n.* &c. फाडणी *f.* तोडणी *f.* विदारणी *f.* दारण *n.* विदारण *n.*

To TEASE, *v. a.* (wool, &c.) v. To CARD. पिंजणें, पिंजारणें, तोडणें.

2 *torment, vex, annoy, harass, &c.* गांजणें, छळणें, छडणें, जाचणें, चाळवणें, त्रासणें, जाळणें, खाजवणें, सतावणें, श्रमवणें, कंकातणें, कांताविणें, तळतळाविणें, गांजणूक *f.*-जाचणूक *f.*-जाचणी *f.*-छळणूक *f.*-छळ *m.*-छडणूक *f.*-जाळणूक *f.*-चाळवण *f.*-चाळवणूक *f.*-छलना *f.*-भाजणूक *f.*-काचणी *f.*-कुचाळी *f.*-कुचेष्टा *f.*-कुचविंध्या *f. pl.*-खवडब *f.*-खंबडाळी *f.*-&c. करणें *g. of o.* जाच *m.*-काच *f.* देणें. This word *To tease* expresses the sense of numerous lively and common words, phrases, and combinations, such as *to plague, to pester, to bother,* and, with some *enhancement* or *intension, to badger, to worry, to harass, to persecute, to tire one's life out, to tease to death, to consume one's vitals, to vex one's very soul, &c. &c.* There are formations in *Maráṭhí* equally lively and common, and equally colloquial or free. Here therefore they are collected. जाळणें, डाचणें, चितावणें, तळणें, तळतळावणें, भाजणें, तोडणें, भंडावणें, घोळणें, घाटणें, अटणें, अहाटणें, खलखलावणें, रडवणें, धुरावर धरणें, ह्यायास आणणें, छळीं छळणें *or* छळछळणें, प्राण *or* जीव *m.* खाणें-घेणें, जिवाचा घोट *m.* घेणें, जीव *m.* तोडणें, जळींत जाळणें, आंतडीं *n. pl.* निपसणें, हाडें *n. pl.* मोडणें-घुसळणें-खिळखिळीत करणें *g. of o.* खोड *f.* काढणें *or* करणें *g. of o.* अरड *f.* काढणें-घेणें *g.of o.* नखीं नस *n.* देणें *g.of o.* जिवाला अरडीं दरडीं *or* अगडींदगडीं *n. pl.* घालणें-पाडणें, कांट्या *f. pl.* घासणें *with* सीं *of o.* कुतर ओढ *f.*-लांडगतोड *f.* करणें, काचणींत धरणें, काचणी *f.* लावणें, उपमर्द *m.* करणें *g. of o.* वाटूनघाटून (पिणें, प्राण खाणें, &c.) खडे *m. pl.* खावणें, फोडून खाणें, बाटाघाट *m. f.*-अटाआट *m.*-अटाघाट *m. f.*-अटाटी *f.*-अटापिटा *m.*-अटापीट *f.*-खाजवाखाजव *f.*-&c. करणें *g. of o.* प्रकार *m. pl.*-तन्हा *f.*-परवडी *f. pl.* करणें *g. of o.* तळतळ *f.* देणें, तडकशीं तोडणें.

TEASED, *p.* v. V. 1. पिंजलेला, &c.

2 गांजलेला, &c.

TEASER, *n.* TEASING, *p. a.* v. V. 1. पिंजणारा, &c.

2 गांजणारा, &c. गांजणूक-&c. करणारा, खवडवी, छलक, त्रासक, त्रास देणारा, छलनकर्त्ता, श्रमकर्त्ता.

I. teasing; *vexing, &c.* v. TIRESOME. कुचर, किचर, किचरट, किचकट, खचरट, खट, खडतर, खिस्लीचा, जाचंद, जाचंदा.

TEASING, *n.* v. V.—*act.* पिंजणें *n.* &c.

2 गांजणें *n.* See the nouns given under the Verb.

TEAT, *n. dug of a beast.* आंचूळ *or* आंचळ *m.* आसड *m.* सड *m.* थना *m.* दोभ *m.* स्तन *m.*

Blind t. खुंट *m.* [खुंट *m.*

Clot which forms during milking on the t. खिंट *f.*

Of two teats. दुसडी.

2 See NIPPLE.

TECHNICAL, *a. belonging to a particular art or profession.* विशेषविद्येच्याविषयींचा, विशेषकलेच्याविषयींचा, विशेषविद्यासंबंधी, विशेष कलासंबंधी, लाक्षणिक, सांकेतिक, पारिभाषिक.

TECHNICALITY, *n.* v. A. विशेषविद्यासंबंधिता *f.* विशेषकलासंबंधिता *f.* लाक्षणिकत्व *n.* सांकेतिकत्व *n.*

I. *a* t. परिभाषा *f.*

To TED, *v. a.* (hay, &c.) *spread.* पिंजारणें.

TEDDER, &c. See TETHER, &c.

TEDIOUS, *a. wearisome, irksome, tiresome, &c. from continuance or prolixity,* v. TIRESOME. कंटाळा यायाजोगा-त्रास यायाजोगा-&c. लांब-लांबलेला, लांबणीचा, कंटाळयाचा, कंटाळवाणा, सरतांसरेनासा, चेंगट, चेंगटाईचा, दीर्घसूत्री.

2 *long, prolix, tiresome in relation.* बयादी, बयादखोर, चावट, चावटाईचा, चावनट, चघळ, चाहटळ, तरढकाचा, लांबलचक, द्राविडप्राणायामाचा, दीर्घसूत्री, पाल्हाळीक, चरपट्या, चन्हाट्या, चरकट्या.

TEDIOUSNESS, *n.* v. A. 1. कंटाळा यायाजोगा-&c. लांबपणा *m.*-लांबी *f.*-&c. चेंगटपणा *m.* चेंगटाई *f.*

2 चावटपणा *m.* &c. चावटाई *f.* दीर्घसूत्र *n. v.* लाब.

TEDIUM. See WEARISOMENESS. [*of s.*

To TEEM, *v. n. bring forth young.* विणें, प्रसव *m.*-&c. होणें *g.*

2 *be full, pregnant, replete, &c.* v. To ABOUND. प्रचुर-मय-&c. असणें in comp. ऊत *m.*- महापुरी *f.*-&c. असणें *g.of s.*

TEEMER, *n.* TEEMING, *p. a.* v. V. 1. विणारा.

2 आढ्य, प्रचुर, मय, पूर्ण, परिपूर्ण, भरित, आकुल, all in comp.

To TEETH, *v. n. breed teeth.* दांत *m. pl.* येणें-फुटणें-उगवणें *in. con. or, with g. of s.* दांतांचा उद्गम *m.*-&c. होणें.

TEETHING, *n.* v. V. दांत येणें *n.* &c. दंतस्फोट *m.* दंतोद्भव *m.* दंतोद्भेद *m.* दंतजनन *n.* दंतोत्पत्ति *f.* [कवच *m. n.*

TEGUMENT, *n.* v. INTEGUMENT, COVER. आवरण *n.* वेष्टन *n.*

TELEGRAPH, *n.* बातमी *f.*-&c. पाठविण्याचें यंत्र *n.*

2 (electro-magnetic). तारायंत्र *n.*

To TELEGRAPH, *v. a.* तारायंत्रांतून बातमी *f.* पाठविणें-पोहोंचविणें.

TELEGRAM, *n.* तारायंत्रांतून पाठविलेली-आलेली बातमी *f.*

TELEGRAPHY, *n.* तारायंत्रांतून बातमी पाठविण्याची विद्या *f.*

TELESCOPE, *n. spy glass.* दुर्बीन *f.*

TELESCOPIC, TELESCOPICAL, *a.* दुर्बिनीचा, दुर्बिनीच्या विषयींचा.

2 (star, &c.) दुर्बिनींतून दिसणारा.

To TELL, *v. a. relate, narrate, communicate, make known,* v. To INFORM. सांगणें, बोलणें, उच्चारणें, कळवणें, ऐकवणें, सुनावणें, जाहीर-श्रुत-&c. करणें, निरूपिणें, ज्ञापवणें, निवेदणें, कथणें, बदणें, तोंडाबाहेर-ओंठाबाहेर काढणें, सांगणी *f.*-सांगी *f.*-सांग *m.*-&c. सांगणें, कथन *n.*-बदणूक *f.*-निवेदन *n.*-निरूपण *n.*-&c. करणें.

To t. far and wide. सांगासांगी *f.* करणें *g. of o.*

To t. heavily in the end. अवघड-कठीण-जड-&c. सांगणें, जाणवणें.

To t. in two words. दुटप्पी *adv.* सांगणें.

To t. to do, *bid.* सांगणें.

2 v. To COUNT. मोजणें, गणणें.

To TELL, *v. n. take effect.* लागणें, लागू होणें, सफल-कृतकार्य-कार्यसाधक-&c. होणें. [कूट *f.* खाणें.

2 of ; *inform against.* चुगल *f.* खाणें-करणें, चहाडी *f.* करणें,

TELL-TALE, *n.* v. TALE-BEARER. चुगल, चुगलखोर *or* चुगलीखोर, कानलाग्या, सूचक.

TELLER, *n.* TELLING, *p. a.* v. V. A. 1. सांगणारा, &c. निरूपक, निरूपणकर्त्ता, निवेदनकर्त्ता, कथक.

TEMERARIOUS, TEMERITY. See RASH, RASHNESS.

To TEMPER, *v. a. qualify by mixture, &c.* मिसळून-मिसळ करून-&c. नेमाचा-सुमाराचा-बेताचा-माफक-नेमस्त-नरम-नरमगरम-समधात-समगुण-यथास्थित-यथायोग्य-&c. करणें.

To t. hot water, by pouring in cold. विसणणें *or* विसाणणें, विसावणें.—Cold water poured into hot to t. it. विसण *or* विसाण *n.* विसावण *n.*

2 See To MIX. 3 See To SOFTEN.

4 (metals). पाणी *n.* देणें.

TEMPER, *n. due quality effected by mixture.* मिसळीचा नेमस्तपणा *m.*-&c. चांगली-&c. मिसळ *f.* सुमिश्रितभाव *m.*

2 v. DISPOSITION. प्रकृति *f.* मर्जी *f.* शील *n.* शिलाणें *n.* कदर *f.* खसलत *or* खसालत *f.*

3 v. TEMPERAMENT. प्रकृति *f.* देहस्वभाव *m.* देहप्रकृति *f.*

4 *calmness, moderation.* शांतपणा *m.* शांति *f.* शांतता *f.* संयम *m.* क्रोधाभाव *m.* रोषाभाव *m.*

5 (of metals). पाणी *n.*

To try the t. of. सत्व *n.* घेणें *g. of o.*

6 See IRRITABILITY, PASSION.

TEMPERAMENT, *n. constitution,* (of mind or body). प्रकृति *f.* स्वभाव *m.* देहप्रकृति *f.* देहस्वभाव *m.* अंगस्वभाव *m.* जन्मस्वभाव *m.* तबियत *f.* मिजाज *f.* आत्मा *m.*

Bilious or choleric t. पित्तप्रकृति *f.*

Evil t. असद्भाव *m.*

Of equable t. समधात.

TEMPERANCE, TEMPERATENESS, *n.* v. A. 1. नेमस्तपणा *m.* परिमिताचरण *n.* संयम *m.* नियम *m.* यम *m.* नियंतृत्व *n.* नियतवर्त्तन *n.* नियतवृत्ति *f.*

2 नेमाचें-मोतादीचें-&c. खाणें *n.* मितभोजन *n.* मिताशन *n.* अल्पभोजन *n.* अल्पाशन *n.* अल्पाहार *m.* नियतभोजन *n.* नियताशन *n.*

3 नेमाचें-मोतादीचें-&c. पिणें *n.* मितपान *n.* परिमितपान *n.* नियतपान *n.* मात्रापान *n.* &c.

TEMPERATE, *a.*—of persons ; *moderate, sober, restrained,* v. ABSTEMIOUS, MODERATE. नेमस्त, परिमिताचारी, संयमी, नियमी, नियंता, यमवान्, नियतवर्त्ती, नियतवृत्ति, नियतभोक्ता, किंचित्सेवी.

2 *as opp. to* gluttonous, &c. नेमस्त, नेमाचा-नेमानें-मोतादीनें-&c. खाणारा-&c.. मितभक्षी, मितभोजी, मिताशी, मिताहारी, नियताहारी, यताहरी, नियतभोजी, अल्पभक्षी, अल्पभोजी, अल्पाशी, अल्पाहारी, अल्पाहार, पथ्यभक्षी, पथ्यभोजी, लघ्वाहार, लघ्वाहारी, स्वल्पाहार, स्वल्पाहारी.

3 *as opp. to* drunkard. नेमानें-नेमाचा-मोतादीनें-&c. पिणारा, मितपानी, परिमितपानी, मात्रापायी, अतिपानवर्जी.

4—of qualities ; *not excessive in degree,* v. MODERATE. मोतादी, नेमाचा, सुमाराचा, परिमित, मित, समर्याद, सावधि, सावधिक, रजपजचा.

5 *not marked with passion.* रागावेगळा-निराळा-&c. शांतीचा, थंडपणाचा, थंडाईचा, &c.

TEMPERATELY, *adv.* v. A. 1. 2. 3. नेमानें, नेमस्तपणानें, मोतादीनें, &c. परिमिताचारपूर्वक, नियतवर्त्तनपूर्वक, किंचित्भोगपूर्वक, किंचित्सेवनपूर्वक.

5 क्रोधावांचून, रागावांचून, शांतीनें, थंडपणानें, थंडाईनें, &c.

TEMPERATURE, *n. state with regard to heat or cold.* ऊनथंडीचा भाव *m.* ऊनथंडीचें प्रमाण *n.* उष्णतेची इयत्ता *f.* उष्णमान *n.* उष्णप्रमाण *n.*

Moderate t. सरदगरमी *f.*

TEMPERED, *p. and a.* v. V. 1. मिसळून नेमाचा केलेला, &c.

Well-t.—mortar, &c. कमाऊ, कमावलेला, मरामतीचा.

4 पाणी दिल्हेला, पाणीदार.

I. *disposed, of a particular temper.* स्वभावाचा, प्रकृतीचा, &c. शील (in comp. as सुशील, दुःशील, कोपशील, &c.).

TEMPEST, TEMPESTUOUS, &c. See STORM, STORMY.

TEMPLE, *n. building dedicated to a deity ; place of worship.* देवळ *or* देऊळ *n.* राऊळ *n.* देवमंदिर *n.* देवालय *n.* महालय *n.* भजनालय *n.* ठाकुरद्वार *n.* प्रासाद *m.*

Ceremony of scouring a t. and idol (after a जत्रा&c.), पखालणी *f.* पखाल पूजा *f.*

Clear space of a t. before the idol. सभामंडप *m.*

Consecration of a t. प्रतिष्ठा *f.* प्रासादप्रतिष्ठा *f.*

Court or enclosure of a t. देउळवाडा *m.*

Endowments or property of a t. देवस्व *n.*

Evening light placed in a t. सांजवात *f.*

Lamp-pillar in front of a t. दीपमाला (*pop.* दिपमाळ) *f.* त्रिपुर *m.* टिपूर *m.*

Lighting up in the eveniug of lamps of a t. दीपवन *or* वात *f.*

Made road to a t. देवघाट *m.*

Officiating priest of a t. पुजारा *or* री, भोपी *or* प्या,—of a t. of Shiva. गुरव.

Offspring of a prostitute of a t. देवळी *m.*

Open t. मंडप *m.* मांडव *m.* [भोवती *f.*

Passage around the adytum of a t. (for प्रदक्षिणा &c.)

Prostitute of a t. देवांगना *f.* भावीण *f.*—of a t. of *Khandobá.* मुरळी *f.*

Raised plat in the court of a t. (for sacrifices, sacred vessels, &c.) वेदि *or* वेदी *f.*

Sanctuary or adytum of a t गाभारा *m.* गर्भारा *m.* गर्भ *m.* गर्भगृह *n.* गर्भागार *n.*

Servant or ministering person of a t. सेवेकरी *m.* (*and* female s. सेवेकरीण).

T. dedicated to *Shiva.* शिवालय *n.* शिवमंदिर *n.*

T. of the breast. हृदयमंदिर *n.*

Temples and figures excavated (out of hills and rocks). पांडवकृत्य *n.* पांडवांचें लेणें *n.* [पोवळी) *f.*

Wall enclosing the court of a t. पोवळ *or* पोळ (*dim.*

Worship of deities at the entrance of a t. द्वारपूजा *f.*

2 (of the head). आंख *m.* कानपट्टी *f.*

Continued throbbing of the temples टक *f.* *v.* लाग.
Hair of the t. braided (of women). कानवेणी *f.*
To induce defluxion from the t. आंख *m.* मोडणें.
To throb—the temples. टकटकणें, टकटक *adv.* करणें.

TEMPORAL, *a. of or belonging to time.* काळाचा, काळाविषयींचा, कालविषयक, कालसंबंधी, कालिक, कालीन, कालीय.
2 v. SECULAR, WORLDLY. आतांचा, ह्या जन्माचा, ह्यालोकचा, ह्या लोकाविषयींचा, चालत्याकाळाचा, सांप्रतकाळचा, संसाराविषयींचा, प्रपंचाविषयींचा, ऐहिक, ऐहलौकिक. [नपटीचा.
3 *of or belonging to the temple of the head.* आंखाचा, का-

TEMPORARILY, *adv.* v. A. दोनदिवस, चारदिवस, आठचारदिवस, आठपंधरादिवस, &c. हंगामी.

TEMPORARINESS, *n.* v. A. अनित्यपणा *m.* अचिरस्थायिता *f.* अस्थायिता *f.* अनित्यता *f.* अशाश्वतत्व *n.* चंचलत्व *n.* चांचल्य*n.* क्षणिकता *f.* In expression of the idea of *temporariness* or *transiency*, and in close correspondence with the English phrases and figures, *A writing upon the sea shore, path of a ship in the waters, track of a bird in the air, morning cloud, &c.* are the following phrases and figures in Maráthi. काजव्याचा उजेड *m.* कमलिनीवरचा बिंदु *m.* पाण्यावरचा बुडबुडा *m.* पाण्यावरची रेघ *or* रेषा *f.* अळबावरचें पाणी *n.* धुळीवरलें सारवण *n.* दुपारची सावली *f.* मेघाची सावली *f.* अभाळाची सावली *f.* शिराळाची सावली *f.* अभ्रछाया*f.* खुंट्यावरला कावळा *m.* तृणाचें जळण*n.* तृणाचा शेक *m.* शाळूसोबती *m.* तेरड्याचा रंग *m.* शिराळशेटाचें राज्य *n.* औटघटीचें राज्य *n.* हरेंवारें देव्हारें (फार दिवस राहत नाहीं *or* दोन दिवसांचें), बाळकाचा हरा आणि ताकाचा डेरा (फार दिवस राहत नाहीं) पुष्कर पत्र तोय तरल,हांहां म्हणतां येऊन जाणारा.

TEMPORARY, *a. lasting only a limited time.* दोन दिवसांचा, चार दिवसांचा, महिनापंधरा दिवसांचा, थोड्या काळाचा, आठवडे पाईक *or* वाईक, येताजाता, आलागेला, उडलटप्पू, चालीबजा, हंगामी, अचिर, अचिरस्थायी, अचिरकालस्थायी, अचिरकालिक, अल्पकालिक, स्वल्पकालिक, अस्थायी, अनित्य, अशाश्वत, चंचल *or* ळ, चल, क्षणिक, क्षणभंगुर, उत्पन्न विनाशी, उत्पन्न बिनष्ट, शाळू (used with several nouns, as शाळूसोबत, शाळूसोबती, &c.), हळवा, हळवट, हळा.

To TEMPORIZE, *v. n. comply with the times.* काळ *m.*-रंग *m.*-समय *m.*-&c. पाहणें-पाहून वागणें-पाहून चालणें, बारा बाजेल तसी पाठ *f.* ओढणें-देणें, बारा वाहेल तसें करणें, दुरोखीपणा *m.* करणें, दोहों डगरीवर हात *m.* ठेवणें, समयानुसरण *n.*-समयानुरोध *m.*-समयानुवर्त्तन *n.*-&c. करणें.
2 See To PROCRASTINATE.

TEMPORIZER, *n.* TEMPORIZING, *p. a.* v. V. 1. काळ पाहून चालणारा, रंग पाहून चालणारा, बारा बाजेल तसी पाठ ओढणारा, बारावाहील तसें करणारा, दुरोखी, दोहोंडगरीवर हात ठेवणारा, समयानुसारी, समयानुवर्त्ती, कालानुवर्त्ती, कालानुसारी, कालानुरोधी, कालवशानुचारी, कालानुग.

To TEMPT, *v. a. entice or solicit to evil,* v. To ALLURE. मोहणें, मोह *m.*-मोहनी *f.* घालणें, भुलवणें, लोभवणें, भुरळ *f.*-भुरळें *n.*-&c. घालणें, उत्तेजन *n.*-प्रलोभन *n.*-&c. करणें.
2 v. To PROVE, To TRY. पारखणें, परीक्षणें, पाहणें, परीक्षा *f.* घेणें-करणें-पाहणें *g. of o.* [-करून पाहणें.
3 *essay, attempt,* v. To TRY. उद्योग *m.*-उपाय *m.*-&c. करणें
4 See To INCITE.

TEMPTATION, *n.* v. V. 1. मोहणें *n.* मोह घालणें*n.* &c. मोह*m.* मोहनी *f.* मोहन*n.* भुरळ *f.* भूल *f.*
2 पारखणें*n.* पाहणें*n.* &c. परीक्षा *f.* पारख *f.*

TEMPTED, *p.* v. V. 1. मोहलेला, मोह घातलेला, &c. मोहित.
2 पारखलेला, &c. परीक्षित.

TEMPTER, *n.* TEMPTING, *p. a.* v. V. 1. मोहणारा, मोह घालणारा, लोभवणारा, मोहनकर्त्ता-कारी, मोहक.
2 पारखणारा, परीक्षणारा, &c. परीक्षाकर्त्ता-&c. परीक्षक.

TEN, *a.* दहा, दश.
Aggregate of t. दशक *pop.* दसक *m.*
Aggregate of t. men, esp. of soldiers. दाहिजा*m.*
Place of tens—in numeration. दहमू*n.*
T. of a suit of cards. दहलू *or* ल्या*m.*
The ten carried or borrowed. दशक *pop.* दसक*n.*

TENABLE, *a. that can be held or defended,*—fortress, &c. राखाया-संभाळाया-&c. जोगा-सारखा-&c. रक्षणार्ह, रक्षणशक्य, रक्षणीय.
2 *that may be supported, made good, &c.* v. MAINTAINABLE. स्थापायाजोगा-सारखा-&c. स्थापनीय, प्रतिपादनीय, प्रतिपाद्य, समर्थनीय.

TENACIOUS, *a. inclined to hold fast, sticky,* चिकट, चिकट्या, चिकटणारा, लगटणारा, लगटून राहणारा, चिकटून राहणारा.
2—of memory; *retentive.* धारणेचा, धारणाशक्तिविशिष्ट-युक्त-संपन्न. [बळकट.
Of t. memory. आठवणीचा-स्मृतीचा-स्मरणाचा-&c. धड-
3 *persistent in a course, purpose, &c.* v. PERSEVERING, FIRM. चिकट *or* ट्या, चामट, चिंवट, आग्रही, निग्रही, दृढसंकल्प, दृढनिश्चय, निश्चयाचा, कराराचा, करारी.

TENACITY, TENACIOUSNESS, *n.* v. A. 1. चिकटपणा*m.* चिकटेपणा *m.* चिकटाई *f.* ग्रह*m.*
2 धारणा *f.* धारणाशक्ति *f.*
3 चिकटपणा*m.* &c. अभिनिवेश*m.* आग्रह*m.* निग्रह*m.*

TENANCY, TENANTRY, *n. a holding or possession of lands or tenements.* भोग*m.* भोगवटा*m.* अधिकार*m.* स्वत्व*n.*

TENANT, *n. person holding land, &c. under another.* असामी *f.* कूळ*n.* उपरी, उपलाणू, धारेकरी, सारेकरी, रयत *f.*
Tenants—collect. *tenantry.* रयतावा*m.* रयत *f.* रयतानी*f.*
2 (of a building). भाडेकरी, भाडोतरी *or* त्री.

To TENANT, *v. a.* साऱ्यानें-भाड्यानें राखणें-घेणें.

TENANTRY, *n. body of tenants.* रयतावा*m.* रयत *f.*

To TEND, *v. a. attend, watch, keep, &c.* राखणें, पाहणें, जोपासणें, जोपावणें, जोंबाळणें, निगा *f.*-निगाबानी *f.*-बरदास्त *f.*-बेहबुदि *f.* -&c. करणें-राखणें *g. of s.* खबर *f.*-समाचार*m.*-&c. घेणें *g. of o.* राखण *f.*-जोपाशीर *or* ल *f.*-जोपासना *f.*-&c. करणें *g. of o.*
2 (sheep or cattle). v. To KEEP. राखणें, वळणें, पाळणें, चारणें.

To TEND, *v. n. move or lean towards.* कलणें, झुकणें, लवणें, वळणें, तोलणें, झोक*m.*-कल*m.*-&c. जाणें *g. of s.* रोंख*m.*-लक्ष्य*n.*-धोरण*n.*-&c. असणें *g. of s.*
2 *contribute,* v. To HELP. सहाय-सहकारी-&c. असणें.

TENDENCE, TENDENCY, *n. drift, direction or course towards an object.* कल*m.* झोक*m.* तोल*m.* मोड *f.* मोडणी *f.* ओढ *f.* ओढा*m.* वळण*n.* प्रवाह*m.* प्रावण्य*n.* प्रवृत्ति *f.* संधान*n.* लक्ष्य*n.*

कटाक्षm. रोंखm.

TENDER, *a. soft, young, not firm, &c.* कोवळा (*remiss.* कोवळसर *tenderish*). कोमल *pop.* ळ, हिरवा, हलुवट *or* हळवट, कच्चा, सकवार, सोंगळ, सोमळ, सुकुमार, नरम, मृदु, नाजूक, मुलाईम.

2 *sensible of pain or injury; easily pained.* कोवळा, नरम, हलुवट *or* हलुवट, दुखरा, लौकर दुःख लागायाजोगा, कोमल *pop.*ळ.

3 *compassionate, considerate,* v. PITIFUL, KIND. कोमलचित्त, कोमळ, आर्द्र, सहार्द, सहृदय, हृदयवान्, हृदयालु, कोमलहृदय, कोमलांतःकरण, नवनीतहृदय, मायाळू, कारुणिक, कृपाळ *or* ळू, कृपावान्, कृपावंत.

4 See PATHETIC. 5 See CAREFUL.

A t. point. वर्म *n.* To be touched in a t. point. वरमणें.

TENDER, *To* TENDER. See OFFER. To OFFER.

TENDER-HEARTED, *a.* v. PITIFUL, KIND. मनाचा कोवळा, सहार्द, सुहृदय, सहृदय, हृदयवान्, हृदयालु.

TENDERNESS, *n.* v. A. 1. कोवळेपणा *m.* कोमलपणा *m.* हिरवेपणा *m.* &c. कोवळीक *f.* नाजकाई *f.* नरमाई *f.* कोमलता *f.* मृदुता *f.* &c. सौकुमार्य *n.* कौमल्य *n.* मार्दव *n.*

2 कोवळेपणा *m.* नरमपणा *m.* हळवटपणा *m.* दुखरेपणा *m.* &c.

3 कोमळपणा *m.* &c. चित्ताची कोमलता *f.* चित्ताची आर्द्रता *f.* करुणा *f.* माया *f.* अनुकंपा *f.* कोमलांतःकरण*n.* कृपा *f.* कारुण्य*n.*

T. compassion &c.—compreh. मायाममता *f.*

TENDINOUS, *a. sinewy.* शिराल *pop.* शिराळ, शिरामय.

TENDON, *n.*—in anatomy. शिरा *pop.* शीर *f.* संधिबंधन *n.* रग *f.*

Tendon Achillis. घोडशीर *f.* दवणशीर *f.* ढोणशीर *f.* घोंडशीर *f.* [तंतु *m.*

TENDRIL, *n. clasper of a vine, &c.* ताणा *m.* अगारी *f.* पागोरा *m.*

Tendrils. तुरये *or* तुरे *m. pl.*

TENEMENT, *n.* v. HOUSE, RESIDENCE. घर *n.* मकाण *or* न *m.n.* धाम *n.* सदन *n.*

2—in law. वतन *n.* मिरास *f.*

Patrimonial lands and tenements. वतनवाडी *f.*

TENESMUS, *n.*—in medicine. क्षणोक्षणीं हगण्याची ओढ *f.* हगण्याचा-परसाकडचा नेट *m.* हगवणीची मुळमूळ *f.* निथम *f.*

TENET, *n. opinion held.* मत *n.*

TENON, *n.*—in carpentry. कुसूं *n.* कूस *n.* [वाथा *m.*

2 (of a door, a window-shutter, &c.). वाता *or* वात्या *or*

Slip of wood to receive a t. वातेरपट्टी *f.* वातेरफळी *f.* वातेर *or* वातेरें *n.*

TENOR, TENOUR, *n. continued currency, whole course or strain,* v. COURSE. धारा *m.* मोळा *m.* ओघ *m.* तंत्र *n.* अनुसंधान *n.* बळण *n.* ओळ *f.* वळवटा *m.* वळवट *m.*

2 *tendency of speech, drift, purport, &c.* v. MEANING. ओढ *f.* ओढा *m.* रोंख *m.* ओघ *m.* धोरण *n.* प्रवाह *m.* भाव *m.* अभिप्राय *m.* खुलासा *m.* अन्वय *m.* भावार्थ *m.*

3—in music or chanting. मध्यसवन *n.* द्वितीयसवन *n.*

TENSE, *n.*—in grammar. काल *m.*

Imperfect t. अद्यतनभूत *m.* अद्यतन भूतकाल *m.*

Indefinite t. अनद्यतनकाल *m.*

Preterite t. अतीतकाल *m.* परोक्षभूतकाल *m.*

TENSE, *a. stretched.* v. TIGHT. ताठ, ताठर, ताणलेला.

TENSENESS, TENSION, *n.* v. A. *and* TIGHTNESS. ताठपणा *m.* ताणलेलेपणा *m.* &c. ताठा *m.* ताण *m.* ओढा *m.* तणावा *m.*

TENT, *n.* डेरा*m.* तबू*m.* शिबिर*n.* पटगृह*n.* Some particular kinds of *tent* are, राबटी *or* राहुटी, बेचोबा *or* पिचबा, पाल.

Cap of leather attached to the ends of a wall, &c. of a t. कट *m.*

Cap of a t.-pole. बादरस *f.* बादरख *f.*

Fly of a double t. बाहेरलें पुड *n.* वरलें टप *n.*

Porch of a t. तयारी *or* तैयारी *f.*

Rope of a t. तणावा *m.* तनाव *f.* तनयी *f.* ओढण *n. f.*

Shell of a double t. आंतलें पुड *n.* आंतलें टप *n.*

Wall of a t. कनात *or* थ *f.*

2 *roll of lint, &c.* बत्ती *f.* वर्त्ति *or* वर्त्ती *f.*

To TENT. See To PROBE.

TENTED, *a. covered with tents.* डेरे दिल्हेला, तंबू दिल्हेला, डेऱ्याचा, &c. शिबिराच्छन्न, शिबिरावृत. [अंकडी *f.*

TENTER, TENTER-HOOK, *n. hook for stretching on.* ताणण्याची

To be on the t-hooks. गळीं लागणें, ओढाताण *f.* असणें *g.of s.*

To keep on t.-hooks. ताणणें, ओढाताण *f.* करणें *g. of o.* ओढून धरणें.

TENTH, *a.* दहावा *or* दाहवा, दशम. [दहक *m.*

TENTH, *n. tenth part.* दहावा वांटा *m.*-हिस्सा *m.*-&c. दशमांश *m.*

To TENUATE, *v. a. make thin.* पातळ-बारीक-&c. करणें.

TENUITY, *n.* v. A.पातळपणा *m.* बारिकपणा *m.* &c. बारकाई *f.* बारकावा *m.* सूक्ष्मता *f.*

TENUOUS, *a.* v. THIN. पातळ, बारीक, सूक्ष्म.

TENURE, *n. manner of holding lands, tenements, &c.* सत्ताप्रकार *m.* स्वत्वप्रकार *m.* स्वत्वविशेष *m.*

Deed of t. सनद *f.* पत्र *n.* पट्टा *m.*

TEPID, *a.* v. LUKE-WARM. कोमट *or* कोंबट, उबट, सोमाळा, मंदोष्ण, ईषदुष्ण, कोष्ण, अनुष्णाशीत.

TEPIDNESS, TEPIDITY, *n.* v. A. कोमटपणा *m.* सोमाळेपणा *m.* &c. कोमटाई *f.* कोष्णता *f.* मंदोष्णता *f.* &c.

TERGIVERSATION, *n.* v. EVASION. अकडंतिकडं *n.* इधरतिधर *n.* घटंपटं *n.* पेचपाच *m.* हीना *f. n.*

TERM, *n. limit,* v. BOUND. मर्यादा *f.* सीमा *pop.* सीव *f.*

2 v. WORD. NAME. नाम *n.* संज्ञा *f.* अभिधान *n.*

3 *limited time,* v. PERIOD. मुदत *or* मुद्दत *f.* वायदा *m.* टेप *f.* पल्ला *m.* अवधि *m.f.* अहर्गण *m.*

Stated or appointed t. बंदीमुदत *f.*

Undetermined t. कच्चीमुदत *or* खुल्लीमुदत *f.*

4 terms ; *quality of intercourse.* बोलण्याचालण्याचा भाव *m.*

Good t. रहसाळी *f.* रहस्य *n.* सुलूक *or* ख *m.* बनाव *m.* संवित्ति *f.*

Ill t. वांक *n.* वांकडें *n.* बांक *m.* बिनुट *n.* *v.* पड.

Non-speaking t. अबोला *m.* *v.* धर.

Person on ill t. with. वांकडा.

5 terms ; *conditions.* संकेत *m.* प्रतिज्ञा *f.* अट *f.* अड *f.*

Lowest t. or price. निदान *n.*

To come to terms. See To AGREE. [मोडणें.

To state one's ultimate t. शेवटच्या बांधण्यास पाणी *n.*

6 See SESSION. 7 (of a syllogism.). अवयव*m.*

8 (of a progression) पद*n.*

First t. आदिपद*n.*

Last t. अंत्यपद*n.*

To TERM, *v. a.* v. TO CALL. बोलणें, म्हणणें, नाम *n.*-संज्ञा *f.*-अभिधान *n.*-&c. देणें-ठेवणें.

TERMAGANT, *n.* v. SCOLD, SHREW. केगया *f.* केगामती *f.* कैकेयी *f.* केकसा *f.* केकसामावसी *f.* कलहांतरिता *f.* घाघोण *f.* खेदडीबायको *f.* केदाशीण *f.*

TERMES, *n. white ant.* वाळवी *f.* उदई *or* उधई *f.*

To TERMINATE, *v. a. limit,* v. To BOUND. सीमा *f.*-मर्यादा *f.*-हद्द *f.*-&c. ठेवणें-बांधणें-घालणें. [*g. of o.*

2 v. To END. संपवणें, समाप्त-&c. करणें, समाप्ति *f.*-&c. करणें

To TERMINATE, *v. n.* v. To END. संपणें, उरकणें, समाप्त-&c. होणें, शेवट *m.*-समाप्ति *f.*-&c. होणें *g. of s.* [संस्था *f.*

TERMINATION, *n.* v. END. अंत *m.* शेवट *m.* अवधि *m.* अवसान *n.*

2— in grammar. अंत *m.* अंत्यवर्ण *m.*

TERMINUS, *n. terminating point.* अवधि *m. f.*

2 (of a railway). शेवटलें स्टेशन *n.*

TERRACE, *n. raised bank or mound of earth, &c.* धमधमा *m.* धमामा *m.* ताल *f.* ओटा *m.*—square, चौथरा *m.*

T. in front of a door. देवडी *or* देडुडी *f.* देहली *f.*

2—on the top of a house; *flat roof of earth.* माळवद *n.* धाबें *n.*—of *chunam.* गच्ची *f.* अगाशी *f.* अट्टालिका *pop.* अटाली *or* ळी *f.* सफेली *f.*

TERRAQUEOUS, *a. consisting of land and water.* खुशकीचा आणि पाण्याचा, जलस्थलमय, जलस्थलात्मक.

TERRENE. See EARTHEN. 2 See EARTHLY.

TERREOUS, *a.* v. EARTHEN. मातीचा, मृत्तिकामय.

TERRESTRIAL, TERRENE, *a.* v. EARTHEN. मातीचा, मृत्तिकामय, पार्थिव.

2 *belonging to this earth* v. EARTHLY. भूलोकचा, भूलोकींचा, भूलोकसंबंधी, ऐहलौकिक, भौम, भूलोकस्थ.

T. globe. भूगोल *m.*

3—of animals. भूचर, स्थलचर.

TERRIBLE, TERRIFIC, *a.* v. FEARFUL. घोर, अघोर, भयानक, भयंकर, भयावह, दारुण, कराल, रौद्र, क्रूर, विकट.

2 *severe, oppressive, violent, excessive.* मोठा, जबर, जबरा, जबरदस्त, भारी, जोराचा, अनर्थाचा, पराकाष्ठेचा.

TERRIBLENESS, *n.* v. A. 1. घोरपणा *m.* अघोरपणा *m.* &c. भयानकता *f.* भयंकरता *f.* &c.

2 मोठेपणा *m.* जबरपणा *m.* &c.

TERRIBLY, *adv.* v. A. 1. भयघाटायाजोगा-सारखा *decl.* भयबाटेसा *decl.* भयसुटेसा *decl.*

2 भारी, फार, अतिशय, अनर्थ, अनर्थ मांडून.

To TERRIFY, *v. a.* v. To FRIGHTEN. भिवविणें, भय *n.* बसवणें-भरवणें, पांचावर धारण *f.* बसवणें *g. of o.* पांचाची धारण *f.* बसवणें *with* वर *of o.* त्रेधा *f.* करणें *g. of o.*

TERRITORIAL, *a. belonging, &c. to territory.* अमलांतल्या देशाविषयींचा, मुलकी, राष्ट्रीय, राष्ट्रसंबंधी-विषयक.

TERRITORY, *n. land within one's jurisdiction,* v. KINGDOM, COUNTRY. अमलांतला देश *m.*-मुलूक *m.* राज्य *n.* राष्ट्र *n.* देश *m.*

TERROR, *n.* v. FRIGHT, FEAR. भय *n.* धास्ती *f.* अपधाक *m.* भीति *f.* त्रास *m.* वित्रास *m.* गात्रभंग *m.* त्रेधा *f.* घोरभय *n.*

Shock of t. or fear. वचक *m. v.* घे, बस.

2 *cause of fear.* भय *n.* भयहेतु *m.* भयकारण *n.*

The king of terrors. See DEATH.

TERSE, *a. neat and clear.* सफईचा *or* सफाईचा, साफ, नेटका, नीट नेटका.

TERSENESS, *n.* v. A. सफई *or* सफाई *f.* साफपणा *m.* नेटकेपणा *m.*

TERTIAN, *n.*—the fever. तिजांतराताप *m.* तिजारें *n.* त्र्याहिकज्वर *m.*

TESSELLATED, *a. checkered, formed in little squares.* खिडकीदार, जाळीदार, चौकड्यांचा, चौकट्यांचा.

TEST, *n.* v. TRIAL. पारख *f.* परीक्षा *f.* कसोटी *f.*

2 *means of trial.* कसोटी *f.* परीक्षासाधन *n.*

To TEST, *v. a.* v. To TRY. पारखणें, पाहणें, पडताळणें *or* पडताळणें, पडताळून पाहणें, परीक्षणें, पडताळा *m.* पाहणें *or* ताडून पाहणें, पडोसा *m.* पाहणें *g. of o.* कसोटी *f.*-कस *m.* पाहणें *g. of o.* कसोटीस लावणें.

Skill in testing. पारख *f.*

TESTACEOUS, *a. having a hard shell.* शिंपल्याचा, शंखनिवासी, शंखविशिष्ट.

TESTAMENT, *n.* v. WILL. मृत्युलेख *m.* मृत्युपत्र *n.* मृतलेख *m.* मृतपत्र *n.* मरणपत्र *n.*

TESTAMENTARY, *a. belonging, &c. to a testament.* मृत्युलेखाविषयींचा, मृतलेखसंबंधी-विषयक, मृतपत्रसंबंधी-विषयक.

2 *given by testament.* मृत्युलेखांत दिल्हेला, मृतलेखदत्त.

TESTATE, *a.* मृत्युलेख केलेला, &c.

TESTATOR, *n. maker of a testament.* मृत्युलेखकरणारा, मृत्युलेखाचा धनी, मृतलेखकर्ता.

TESTER, *n.* पलंगाचें-पलंगावरचें छप्पर *n.*

TESTICLE, *n.*—the seminal organ. अंड *n. pop.* अंड *or* आंड *m.* (*dim.* अंडकुली *f. or* लें *n.* अंडकूल *n.* अंडुकली *f. or* लें *n.*) मुष्क *m.* कोश *or* कोष *m.* बी *f.* कोय *f.*

Testicles and scrotum. अंडकोश *m.* अंडकुली *f. or* लें *n.* अंडकूल *n.* अंडुकली *f. or* लें *n.* वृषण *m.* अंडद्वय *n.* अंडयुग्म *n.* मुष्कद्वय *n.* [वृद्धि *f.*

Enlargement of a t. (or scrotum). कोशवृद्धि *f.* अंड-

Having testicles. अंडील.

Swelled t. बुरांड *m.* बृहदंड *n.*

Swelling of t. अंडशोफ *m.*

To TESTIFY, *v. n. bear witness, give evidence.* साक्ष *f.*-साक्षी *f.*-ग्वाही *f.*-शाहिदी *f.*-&c. भरणें-देणें.

2 See To AFFIRM, To CERTIFY.

To TESTIFY, *v. a. affirm in evidence, witness to.* साक्ष *f.*-साक्षी-*f.*-&c. भरणें-देणें *g. of o.*

2 See To DECLARE, To PUBLISH.

TESTIMONIAL, *n. writing or certificate in favour of.* खातरीचा कागद *m.*-लेख *m.*-&c. पत्र *n.* (in comp. as शुद्धिपत्र, अजितपत्र, अग्रपत्र, &c.), सरटिफिकेट *n.* from the English *certificate* is common.

TESTIMONY, *n.* v. EVIDENCE. साक्ष *f.* ग्वाही *f.* जबानी *f.*—as one of the kinds of *evidence.* शब्द *m.*

Oral t. तोंडजबानी *f.* मुखजबानी *f.*

TESTINESS, *n.* v. A. खिसखिशेपणा *m.* तिडतिडेपणा *m.* तुसडेपणा *m.* &c. खिसखीस *f.* खलेली *f.*

TESTY, *a.* v. CROSS, PEEVISH. खिसखिशा, तिडतिडा, तुसडा, कैदी, खलेल, खडतर.

TETANUS, *n.* धनुर्वात *m.*

TETE A TETE. तोंडास तोंड, तोंडातोंडीं, तोंडचे तोंडीं.

Tether, *n. rope by which a beast is tied for grazing.* चारण्या-ची-चारणीची सडक *f.*-सोल *f.*-दोरी *f.* चारणीचें चन्हाट *n.*

To give a long t. सैल दोरी *f.* देणें.

To **Tether**, *v. a. tie up with a tether.* चरायासाठीं दोरीलावून *or* देऊन बांधणें.

Tetotum, *n.*—the plaything. कोईळ *f.* कोयाळ *f.* कोकाटी *f.* भिंगरी *or* भिंगोरी *f.* भ्रमरी *f.*

Tetrad, *n. aggregate of four.* चौकडी *f.* चतुष्क *n.* चतुष्टय *n.*

Tetragonal, *a. having four angles.* चौकोणा, चतुष्कोण.

Tetrapetalous, *a. having four petals.* चौपाखी, चौपाकळी.

Tetrarch. See **Chief, King.**

Tetter, *n.*—the disease. चकंदळ *n.* दाद *f.*

Text, *n. subject of a comment.* मूलग्रंथ *m.* पांक्तग्रंथ *m.* प्रतीक *n.* मूल *or* ळ *n.*

2 *sentence of Scripture.* विधि *m.* वचन *n.* वाक्य *n.*

Textual, Textuary, *a. contained in the text.* वचनांतला, वचनांतील, वाचनिक.

Texture, *n. web.* विणलेलें कापड *n.*-वस्त्र *n.* विणप *n.*

Opening in a t. सरा *m.* सरी *f.*

To have or get openings in t. सरकटणें.

2 *manner or quality of weaving.* विणकर *f.* वीण *f.* विणणें *n.* विणाई *f.* सूत *n.* खुमास *f.* वाणाताणा *or* ताणावाणा *m.* पोत *m. n.* सूतपोत *m. n.* खेटणी *f.* बनावट *f.*

Of coarse t. जाडसुती, भरडसुती.

Of fine t. तलमसुती.

Of flimsy t. वालीप *or* फ.

Of good t. सपोत.

Of loose or open t. बरळ, विरल *or* ळ, विरूळ, पातळ, झिरझिरा, झिरझिरीत *or* झरझरीत, पिळपिळीत, बरगळ, थिल्हट.

Of strong t. घनवट, धनगट.

To be of open or loose t. बरगळणें.

3 *act of weaving.* विणणें *n.* [क्षया.)

Than, *adv.* पेक्षां, हून, अपेक्षया (in comp. as तदपेक्षया, मदपे-

To **Thank**, *v. a. express gratitude to.* आभारीपणा *m.*-उपकारीपणा *m.*-&c. दाखवणें-दर्शवणें, आभार *m.*-उपकार *m.*-&c. मानणें-स्वीकारणें-&c. कृतज्ञताप्रकाश *m.*-कृतज्ञताकथन *n.*-&c. करणें.

Thank, Thanks, *n. expression of gratitude.* उपकाराचें-&c. वाखाणणें *n.*-वाखाणणी *f.* उपकारस्वीकार *m.* उपकाराभिवाद *m.* उपकारस्तुति *f.* कृतज्ञताकथन *n.* कृतज्ञतादर्शन *n.* कृतज्ञताप्रकाश *m.*

Thankful, *a. grateful.* उपकारी, आभारी, उपकार वाखाणणारा, उपकार वाखाणण्याचा, उपकारज्ञ, कृतज्ञ, कृतज्ञतादर्शक-कथक-प्रकाशक, उपकाराभिवादक.

Thankfully, *adv.* v.A. उपकारी-&c. होऊन, उपकार जाणुन-मानून-&c. कृतज्ञतापूर्वक, &c.

Thankfulness, *n.* v. A. उपकारीपणा *m.* आभारीपणा *m.* उपकारज्ञता *f.* कृतज्ञता *f.*

Thankless, *a.* See **Ungrateful.** 2. *not bringing thanks.* अनुपकाराचा, उपकाराभिवादशून्य.

Thank-worthy. See **Praise-worthy.**

That, *pron.* तो, (तो, ती, तें).

That like. तसला. [परांतीक.

Upon or after t. तदनंतर, तदुत्तर, तदुपरि, तदुपरांत, तदु-

2 *which, who;*—relat. to the antec. जो, (जो, जी, जें).

That, *conj.* कीं, जे. जेका.

Thatch, *n. straw, &c. covering a house.* छप्पर *n.* शाकार *or* शकार *m.* शाकारणी *f.* केंबळा *m.* केंबळी *f.* केंबळ *n.* कोलवा *m.*

Bottom or lower edge of a t. वळचण *f.*

Bundle of old t. ढोबळा *m.*

Frame of t. थाट *m.*

Layer of grass in t. पोवा *m.*

· Matter for t. (grass, &c.). कुईट *n.* शिवण *f.*

Old and rotten t. केंबळ *n.* कोलवा *m.*

To **Thatch**, *v. a.* v.N. शाकारणें *or* शेकारणें, शिवणें, घर *n.* नेमबणे, छप्परबंदी *f.*-&c. करणें, गवन *n.*-कोलवा *m.*-शाकार *m.*-&c. घालणे.

Cost of thatching. शिवणावळ *f.*

Thatched, *p.* v. V. शाकारलेला, &c. गवताचा, घासाचा, &c. गवती, तणवी, कुयटारू, छप्परी, केंबळ्याचा, कोलव्याचा, केंबळी.

Thatcher, *n.* **Thatching**, *p. a.*v.V. शेकारणारा, &c. छप्परबंद, शिवणकर.

Needle of t. पोवा *m.*

Stick of t. to toss up grass. ढिरा *m.*

Thatching, *n.* v. V. शाकारणें *n.* &c. शाकारणी *f.* घरशाकारणी *f.* घरशिवणी *f.*

To **Thaw.** See **To Melt.**

Thaw, *n. melting of snow, ice, &c.* बर्फाचा-थिजलेल्यापाण्याचा-&c. पाघळ *m.*-पाझर *m.* हिमद्रव *m.*

The. The Student is referred to Grammarians for information respecting the use of the article in Maráthí.

Theatre, *n. play house.* नाटकाचेंघर *n.* नाट्यशाला *f.* नाटकशाला *f.* नाटकगृह *n.* नृत्यशाला *f.*

Tiring room of a t. नेपथ्य *n.*

2 *stage, arena,* lit. fig. भूमि *f.* भूमिका *f.* अखाडा *m.* फड *m.* रंगांगण *pop.* रंगण *n.* रंगभूमि *f.* रंग *m.*

Theatric, Theatrical, *a. pertaining, &c. to a theatre or to performers.* नाटकाचा, नाट्याचा, सोंगाड्यांचा, नाट्यशालेचा, &c. नाटकी, सोंगसंपादणीचा, नाटकीय, नाट्यशालासंबंधी-विषयक, नाटक संबंधी-विषयक.

Theft, *n. stealing.* चोरी *f.* तस्करी *f.* चौर्य *n.* चौर्यकर्म *n.* तास्कर्य *n.* स्तेय *n.* स्तेन *n.*

2 *thing stolen.* चोरीचा माल *m.*-डाग *m.*-डागिणा *m.*

Their, *pron.* त्यांचा, ह्यांचा *or* यांचा.

Theism, *n.—opposed to* Atheism. आस्तिक्य *n.* आस्तिक्यमत *n.* आस्तिक्यवाद *m.* ईश्वरवाद *m.* ईश्वरमत *n.* [वादी.

Theist, *n.—opposed to* Atheist. आस्तिक,आस्तिक्यवादी, ईश्वर-

Theistic, Theistical, *a. belonging, &c. to theism.* आस्तिक्याचा, आस्तिक्यमताचा, &c. आस्तिक्यमतसंबंधी-विषयक.

Theme, *n. topic, &c.* v. **Subject.** प्रकरण *n.* विषय *m.* बिंब *n.*

2 *short dissertation.* लहानसा ग्रंथ *m.* निबंध *m.* अल्पप्रबंध *m.*

Then, *adv. at that time.* तेव्हां, त्यावेळेस, त्यासमयीं, तर्धी, तत्काळ, तेधवां, तदा, तंव *or* तों.

Till t. तोंपर्यंत, तोंपावेतों, तोंवर.

2 *afterwards.* मग, त्यावर, नंतर, त्यानंतर, तदनंतर, तदुत्तर, तदुपरि, तदुपरांत, तदुपरांतीक, उपर.

3 *in that case.* तर, तरी, मग, म्हणजे *or* म्हणजेल, एकूण *or* न

T. indeed. T.—emphatic. तरच, तरींच.

Now and then, v. Now. कधीं मधीं.

THENCE, *adv. from that place.* तेथून, तेथपासून, त्या स्थळाहून-पासून, &c. तिकडून.
2 *from that time.* तेव्हांपासून, त्यावेळे-काळा-समया-&c. पासून.
3 See THEREFORE.

THENCEFORTH, THENCEFORWARD, *adv. from that time onward.* तेव्हांपासून, तेव्हांपासून पुढें, त्यापासून, त्यापासून पुढें, ततःप्रभृति, ततआरभ्य, तत्कालावधि.

THEOCRACY, *n. government immediately by God.* ईश्वरकर्तृक-राज्य *n.* ईश्वरकर्तृकशासन *n.*

THEOGONY, *n.*—in mythology. देवोत्पत्ति *f.* देवसर्ग *m.*

THEOLOGIAN, *n. person versed in theology.* परमार्थज्ञानी-वेत्ता, ब्रह्मज्ञानी, ब्रह्मविद्यावेत्ता, वेदांती, आध्यात्मी, मुल्ला (amongst Muhammadans).

THEOLOGICAL, *a. pertaining, &c. to theology.* देवज्ञानाचा, परमार्थज्ञानाचा, परमार्थप्रकरणाचा, वेदांताचा, &c. वेदांताविषयींचा, &c. परमार्थविद्याविषयक-संबंधी, अध्यात्मज्ञानसंबंधी-विषयक.

THEOLOGY, *n. science of God and divine things; divinity.* देवज्ञान *n.* परमार्थज्ञान *n.* परमार्थविद्या *f.* तत्वज्ञान *n.* तत्वविद्या *f.* अध्यात्मज्ञान *n.* अध्यात्मविद्या *f.* परमार्थप्रकरण *n.*—Hindu. ब्रह्मज्ञान *n.* ब्रह्मविद्या *f.* वेदांत *m.* ब्रह्मज्ञानप्रकरण *n.*

THEOREM, *n. proposition to be proved.* प्रमेय *n.* प्रमेयोपपाद्य *n.* सिद्धांत *m.*

THEORETICAL, *a. speculative, not practical.* कल्पनेचा, &c. मानसिक, काल्पनिक, मनोमय, अनुमानसिद्ध, अनुमानमूलक, व्यवहारागम्य, अव्यावहारिक.

THEORIST, THEORIZER, *n.* v. V. कल्पना-&c. करणारा-काढणारा-&c. उपपत्ति लावणारा.

To THEORIZE, *v. n. form a theory, speculate.* कल्पना *f.*-तर्क *m.* -वितर्क *m. pl.*-युक्ति *f.*-&c. करणें-काढणें-रचणें-बांधणें, तर्करचना *f.*-वितर्करचना *f.*-&c. करणें, वितर्कणें, उपपत्ति *f.* लावणें.

THEORY, *n. speculation, scheme, &c.* कल्पना *f.* तर्क *m.* वितर्क *m. pl.* मानससृष्टि *f.* मनःकल्पना *f.* अनुमान *n.*
2 *exposition of principles.* उपपत्ति *f.* युक्ति *f.* शास्त्र *n.* शास्त्रार्थ *m.* बीजनिर्देश *m.* इतिकर्तव्यताव्याख्या *f.*

THEOSOPHICAL, *a.* v. N. तत्वज्ञानी, ब्रह्मज्ञानी.

THEOSOPHY, *n. knowledge of God,* v. THEOLOGY. देवज्ञान *n.* तत्वज्ञान *n.* ब्रह्मज्ञान *n.*

THERAPEUTIC, *a. curative.* उपायप्रकरणाचा, उपायप्रकरणांतला, रोगनिवारक-प्रतिकारक-परिहारक.

THERAPEUTICS, *n.* औषधोपायप्रकरण *n.* औषधोपचारप्रकरण *n.* रोगशमनविद्या *f.*

THERE, *adv. in that place.* तेथें *or* तिथें, तिकडे, त्याठिकाणीं-स्थळीं-स्थानीं-&c. तत्र.

Here and there, v. HERE. इकडे तिकडे, जिकडे तिकडे, जागोजाग, जागजागीं, ठिकाणठिकाणीं.

There, when prefixed to prepositions (as there-after, there-at, there-by, there-from, there-in, there-upon, &c. &c.) and forming with them compound words, has the signification of *that* or *this,* and may be rendered accordingly; as *there-by* त्याकडून, *there-on* त्यावर, &c. Two or three of these compounds are inserted in their order, for the rest this notice will suffice.

THEREABOUT, THEREABOUTS, *near that place.* आंगेंमागें, अरता परता *decl.* आदिपश्चात्.
2 *nearly that number or quantity,* v. ABOUT. त्यासुमारास.

THEREFORE, *adv. for that or this reason.* म्हणून, त्या-यामुळें-स्तव-साठीं-&c. त्यास, यावरून, तस्मात्, अथ, सबब, त्याअर्थी (correl. with ज्याअर्थी), अर्थात्, त्यापेक्षां, पक्षीं, अतएव, अतः, अतःकारणात्.

THEREOF, *a. belonging to that place.* तेथचा *or* ला, तेथील, तिकडचा *or* ला, तिकडील, तत्रत्य, तत्स्थानिक, तत्स्थानीय.

THERMAL, *a.* v. WARM, HOT. उष्ण.
T. spring. उन्हाळें *n.* उन्हेरें *n.*

THERMOMETER, *n. instrument for measuring heat.* ऊनमोजायाचें यंत्र *n.* शीतोष्णमापकयंत्र *n.*

THESIS, *n.* v. POSITION. पक्ष *m.* पूर्वपक्ष *m.* प्रतिज्ञा *f.*

THEY, *pro.* See HE. 2—used indefinitely. लोक *m.* जन *m.* माणसें *n. pl.*

THICK, *a. not thin.* जाडा, जाड, जाडगा, दाट, मोठा *or* मोटा, घन *pop.* घण, स्थूल *pop.* ढ, घस्मर, मोठाधाटा.
Thickish. घनसर *or* घणसर, जाडसर.
2—in geometry. घन.
3 *not dilute, &c.* घट्ट, दाट, जाडा, जाड, गाढा, घन *pop.* घण, खर, सघन.
4 *turbid,* v. MUDDY. गढूळ, ढढूळ, गदळ, राड.
5 *crowding together, close.* दाट, दाटीचा, घन *pop.* घण, गच्च, सघन, अविरल.
6 *closely set with.* दाट, घन.
7—of darkness. दाट, घोर, गाढ, गडद, घन, घनघोर *or* घनाघोर, घोरांदर, निबिड, सांद्र.
8—the voice. कुंद, दाटलेला, दाटल्यासारखा, घोघरा.
9—foliage, a wood, &c. दाट, गच्च, निबिड, गर्दबाज *or* गर्दाबाज, गडद, घण, गाढ, सघन, सांद्र, घोर, घनघोर, किर्र, बुरंट.
10 v. COARSE. जाड, लठ्ठ, लठ्ठया, रटाला, धसकट.
11 *intimate,* v. FAMILIAR. दाट, दाटीचा, घळीमेळीचा.

THICK, *n.* v. HEIGHT. भर (in comp. as a prefix, as भरलढाई the thick of the fight, &c.) ऐन (in comp. as a prefix), जोर *m.* जोरगत *f.* उधान *n.*

THICK, THICKLY, *adv.* v. A. 5. 6. दाट, दाटपणें, गच्च, घण.
I. *to a great depth,*—any thing spread. दाट, दाटपणें, घण, घट्ट.
II *in quick succession.* लागोपाठ, पाठोपाठ, मागोमाग, लगोलग, देवडीनें, टिपरघाईनें.

To THICKEN, *v. a.* (milk or liquids). दाट-घट्ट-&c. करणें, अळवणें, अळणें, अटवणें, थिजवणें, जमवणें.
Material (flour, earth, &c.) used to t. मिळण *n.* मिळवण *n.*

To THICKEN, *v. n.*—milk or other liquid. अटणें, अळणें, गोठणें, दाटणें, जमणें, थिजणें, बोळणें, दाट-घट्ट-&c. होणें, सांखणें, सांखळणें, सांगुळणें.
2 *crowd together, close.* जमणें, दाटणें, दाटी *f.*-&c. होणें *g. of s.*
3—darkness. दाटणें.
4—the voice. दाटणें.
5 *become animated,*—a fight, &c. तडाखा *m.*-कडाखा *m.*-&c. होऊं लागणें, तडाख्यावर-कडाख्यावर-घाईवर-टिपर घाईवर-&c. येणें.

THICKENED, *p.* v. V. A. 1. घट्टकेलेला, &c. अटींव, घनीकृत.

THICKENING, *n. material used to thicken a liquid.* मिळण *n.* मिळवण *n.*

THICKET, *n. thick collection of shrubs, &c.* झाडी *f.* झाडोरा *m.*

जाळी *f.* जाळ *f.* गचाड *or* गिचाड *n.* झुडप *or* झुडूप *n.* झुंगाड *n.*

Brushwood t. बुरंट (*or* बुरट, बुरांट, बुरुंट, बुरटें) *n.*

THICK-HEADED. See STUPID.

THICKNESS, *n.* v. A. 1. जाडपणा *m.* &c. जाडी *f.* पिंड *m.* घनता *f.* स्थौल्य *n.* स्थूलता *f.*

2 घनता *f.* वेध *m.*

3 घट्टपणा *m.* दाटपणा *m.* &c. घट्टाई *f.* दाटण *f.* घल *m.*

4 गदळपणा *m.* &c.

5 *and* CROWDEDNESS. दाटपणा *m.* &c. दाटी *f.*

6 दाटपणा *m.* दाटी *f.* घनत्व *n.* स्थौल्य *n.* स्थूलता *f.*

7 दाटपणा *m.* गाढपणा *m.* निबिडपणा *m.* &c.

8 कुंदपणा *m.* घोगरेपणा *m.* दाटलेलेपणा *m.*

9 दाटी *f.* दाटपणा *m.* &c. गचाड *or* गिचाड *n.* नैबिड्य *n.*

THICKSET, *a.* v. COMPACT. अटींव, अटस, घट्ट, धमकट, चुबकडा.

THIEF, *n.* *one who commits theft.* चोर, चोरी-&c. करणारा, चोरटा, तस्कर, स्तेन, स्तेयी, परद्रव्यहरक, चौर्यकर्त्ता.—as expressing *one given to petty theft, a pilferer, picker and stealer, &c.* भुरटे *or* भुरट्टेचोर, उचल्या, उपल्या, उचक्या, भामट्या *or* भांबट्या.

Terms or phrases involving the sense of *an arrant thief, an adept at thievery, &c.* are स्वानचोर, स्वानोरीचोर, देखतचोर, डोळ्यांतला काजळ चोरणारा *or* नेणारा, अंजनहारी.

Thieves—compreh. *thieves and rogues.* चोरचिरटा *or* चिलटा *or* चिलट *m.*

An attack by a gang of thieves. चोरधाड *f.*

A nest or haunt of thieves. चोरवाडा *m.* चोरहट्टी*or*हाटी*f.*

The air, look, cast of a t. चोर लक्षण *n.*

Set a t. to catch a t. चोराचीं पावलें चोर ओळखतो.

To behead a string of thieves. चोरांचीदावण देणें.

To THIEVE, *v. n.* *practice theft.* चोरी *f.*-तस्करी *f.*-चोरचाळे *m. pl.*-चोरटे चाळे *m. pl.*-चौर्य *n.*-चौर्यकर्म *n.*-&c. करणें.

THIEVERY, *n.* *practice of theft.* चोरी *f.* तस्करी *f.* चोरटा धंदा *m.* चोरचाळे *m. pl.* चोरटेचाळे *m. pl.* चोरटी विद्या *f.* तस्करविद्या *f.* निशाचरी *f.*

THIEVISH, *a.* *given to stealing.* चोरटा, चोरीकरण्याचे स्वभावाचा, हाताळ, हातलावा *or* व्या, उचल्या, भामट्या, चौर्यशील, चौर्यबुद्धि, चौर्यासक्त, चौर्यलंपट-प्रवण, हातावर नक्षत्र पडलेला-&c.

T. practices, v. THIEVERY. चोरचाळे *m. pl.*

THIEVISHNESS, *n.* v. A. चोरटेपणा *m.* चोरी करण्याचा स्वभाव *m.* उचलेपणा*m.* भामटेपणा*m.* चौर्यशीलता *f.*चौर्यासक्ति *f.*चौर्यबुद्धि *f.*

THIGH, *n.*—the part of the body. जांघ *or* जांग *f.* मांडी *f.* जंघा *f.*—contemptuously. जांगड *or* जांघड *n.*

Blade of the t.-bone. फरा *m.*

Fore part of the t. अग्रजंघा *f.*

T.-joint. कमरेचा खवाटा *m.*

THILL, *n.* *shaft of a cart, &c.* गाडीची-&c. दांडी *f.*-धूर *f.*

The t.-yoke. शेलें *n.*

THILL-HORSE, THILLER, *n.* *horse &c. between the thills; last horse of a team.* धूरकरी, धुरेचा घोडा *m.*-बैल *m.*

THIMBLE, *n.* *metal cap for the finger.* अंगुस्तान*n.*बोटन*n.*टोपण*n.*

THIN, *a.* *not thick.* पातळ, बारीक.

2 *rare, subtil, &c.* पातळ, बारीक, सूक्ष्म.

3—of liquids; *dilute, &c.* v. WASHY. पातळ, फिळफिळीत, बरत्ररीत, सरसरीत, असट.

4 v. SLENDER, LEAN. बारीक, पातळ, पातळांगी, रुगाळा, ततारा, तनु, कमतनूक, क्षीण, कृश, कृशांग.

5 *not close, not crowding, &c.* पातळ, विरळ *or* ळ *or* विरळ, विसकळ, मोकळा, तुरळ.

6 *of loose texture.* पातळ, बरळ, परगळ, विरल, *or* ळ *or* विरळ, झिरझिरा, झिरझिरीत *or* झरझरीत, विरविरीत, पिळपिळीत.

THIN, THINLY, *adv.* v. A. 1. पातळ, बारीक.

5, 6. पातळ, विरळ, विसकळ, तुरळक, तुरळतुरळ.

To THIN, *v. a.* *make thin, attenuate, &c.* पातळ-बारीक-सूक्ष्म-&c. करणें, पातळपणा *m.*-&c. आणणें, पातळपणा *m.*-पातळी *f.*-&c. करणें *g. of o.*

2 *make less crowded.* पातळ-विरळ-विसकळ-&c. करणें, पातळाई *f.*-पातळी *f.*-&c. करणें *g. of o.* तुरळणें.

THIN-SKINNED, *a.* कागदी.

THIN-VISAGED, *a.* गालचिंबा.

THINE, *a.* तुझा, त्वदीय, तव, तवक.

THING, *n.* *substance.* वस्तु *n.* (*pop.* वस्तू *f. and, vulg.* बस्त *f.*) पदार्थ *m.* चीज *f.* जिन्नस*m. f.* द्रव्य *n.* अर्थ *m.* विषय *m.*भूत *n.*

Fine t. चीज *f. n.*

Shapeless or clumsy t. तांदळा *m.*

That is neither one t. nor the other. दुधड.

Things, *goods, chattels, traps, &c.* v. GOOD. सामान *n.* चीजवस्त *f.* वस्त्रपात्र *n.*

2 *matter, business, &c.* v. AFFAIR. गोष्ट *f.* विषय *m.* पदार्थ*m.*

3—in contempt, &c. चीज *f. n.*पदार्थ *m.*

Poor t. बापडा, बिचारा, बापडाबिचारा.

4 *a portion, something.* कांहीं.

THINGUMBOB, *n.* दगड्या धोंड्या *m.*

To THINK, *v. n.* *have ideas in the mind, exercise the mind.* चिंतणें, चिंतन *n.*-चिंता *f.*-चिंतणूक *f.*-चेतव्य*n.*-मानसव्यापार *m.* -मनोव्यापार *m.*-&c. करणें.

To t. highly of one's self. ओढून आणणें *m.*

2 *opine, hold as an opinion.* समजणें, वाटणें *in. con.* भासणें *in. con.* भावना *f.*-बुद्धि *f.*-तर्क *m.*-ग्रह *m.*-मत *n.*-समज *m.*-समजूत *f.*-निश्चय *m.*-&c. असणें *g. of s.*

3 *suppose, fancy, imagine.* समजणें, कल्पिणें, वाटणें *in. con.* कल्पना *f.*-भावना *f.*-तर्क *m.*-&c. करणें *and, with in. con.* होणें-येणें, मनांत-&c. आणणें-धरणें, मनांत-दिलांत-&c. येणें, मनदेवता *f.*-मनपिंगळा *m.*-मनपिंगळी *f.* लवणें-धावणें.

One would think. जणू.

4 v. To INTEND. मनांत-दिलांत-&c. येणें-असणें *g.of s.* चिंतणें.

5 *muse, meditate, consider.* चिंतणें, पाहणें, विचार *m.* करणें-पाहणें, मनन*n.*-चिंतन*n.*-ध्यान*n.*-&c. करणें, विचारांत-&c. असणें.

To t. about. मनास आणणें, मनावर घेणें.

To t. constantly upon. स्मरणी *f.* घेणें *g. of o.*

To t. over, *ponder what has been said to one.* चिंतणी *f.*-चिंतनिका *f.* करणें. [*in. con.*

6 of; v. To RECOLLECT. आठवण *f.*-स्मरण *n.* करणें, अठवणें

7 on; upon; *excogitate.* मनन करून-&c. काढणें-योजणें-रचणें, कल्पिणें.

To THINK, *v. a.* *imagine, conceive.* कल्पिणें, कल्पना*f.*-&c. करणें *g. of o.* मनांत-दिलांत-&c. आणणें-धरणें.

2 *consider, regard, believe, reckon.* मानणें, धरणें, लेखणें, मोजणें, भावणें.

THINKER, *n.* THINKING, *p. a.* v. V. N. 1. चिंतणारा, चिंतक, चिंतन-&c. कर्त्ता-कारी.

THINNESS, *n.* v. A. 1. पातळपणा *m.* &c. पातळी *f.* पातळाई *f.* बारकाई *f.* बारकावा *m.*

2 पातळपणा *m.* &c. पातळी *f.* पातळाई *f.* बारकाई *f.* बारकावा *m.* सूक्ष्मता *f.* सौक्ष्म्य *n.*

3 पातळपणा *m.* &c. पातळी *f.* पातळाई *f.*

4 पातळपणा *m.* पातळी *f.* पातळाई *f.* बारकाई *f.* बारकावा *m.* कृशता *f.* कार्श्य *n.* तानव *n.* [ळी *f.*

5 पातळपणा *m.* विसकळपणा *m.* विरळपणा *m.* &c. पातळाई *f.* पात-

6 पातळपणा *m.* बरळपणा *m.* &c. पातळी *f.* पातळाई *f.*

THIRD, *a.*—the ordinal. तिसरा, तृतीय, तिजा.

The t. doing or going over (of a work) तिसड *f.*

To make the subject of a t. operation. तिसारणें *or* तिसरणें, तिसारणी *or* तिसरणी *f.* करणें.

THIRD, *n. third part.* तिसरा वांटा *m.*-हिस्सा *m.*-अंश *m.*-&c. तिजाई *f.* तिसराव *m.* तृतीयांश *m.*

THIRDLY, *adv. in the third place.* तिसऱ्यानें, तृतीयतः.

THIRST, *n. desire to drink.* तहान *or* तान *f.* प्यास *m. f.* पिपासा *f.* पानेच्छा *f.* तृषा *f.* तृष्णा *f.*

Excessive t. शोष *pop.* सोस *m.* पाणसोस *or* पाणशोष *m.* जलशोष *m.* शोषकत्व *n.*

Morbid & excessive t. रसरस *f.* रसरसाट *m.*

Slakening of t. तहानमोड *f.*

To quench t. तहान *f.* घालवणें.

2 fig. *vehement longing,* v. DESIRE, ITCH. तहान *f.* तृषा *f.* तृष्णा *f.* प्यास *m. f.* सोस *m.* हव्यास *m.* खुमखुम *f.* खुरखुर *f.*

T. of wealth. धनाशा *f.*

To THIRST, *v. n.* v. N. 1. तहान *f.*-&c. लागणें *in. con.* तृषणें, तान्हणें *or* तान्हावणें, तरसणें.

2 fig. *hanker, long,* v. To DESIRE. सोस *m.*-हव्यास *m.*-&c. लागणें *in. con.* तृषणें, प्राण *m.* सोसणें *g. of s.*

THIRSTER, *n.* THIRSTING, *p. a.* THIRSTY, *a.* v. V. 1. तहान लागलेला, तहानेला *or* तान्हेला, तान्हाळू, तृषावान्, तृषित, तृषान्वित, तृषायुक्त, तर्षित, सतृट्, पिपासु,—in high degree, तृषाकुल, तृषातुर, तृषाविष्ट, तृषाग्रस्त, तृषाक्रांत, तृषार्त्त, तृषांध, तृषाविव्हल, तृषाधीन. [सतृष.

2 *and* DESIROUS. सोशी *or* सोसी, हव्याशी *or* सी, तृषित,

THIRTEEN, *a.* तेरा, त्रयोदश.

THIRTEENTH, *a.* तेरावा.

THIRTIETH, *a.* तिसावा.

THIRTY, *a.* तीस, त्रिंशत्,—one एकतीस,—two बत्तीस,—three तेहतीस,—four चौतीस *or* चवतीस,—five पसतीस,—six छत्तीस,—seven सततीस, सदतीस,—eight अठतीस, अडतीस,—nine एकूणचाळीस.

The age of t. तिशी *f.*

THIS, *a.* हा (हा, ही, हें.).

This, that, and the other. काण्णू बाण्णू *n.*

THISTLE, *n.*—the plant. उंटकटारा *m. or* री *f.* कांटेसुवक *m.* These are the *echinops echinatus.* or Globe Thistle. विलायती धोतरा *or* कांटे धोतरा *m.* which is very common in the Deccan, is something like the thistle.

THITHER, THITHERWARD, *adv.* तिकडे.

Hither and t. इकडेतिकडे. [चर्मपट्टी *f.*

THONG, *n. leather strop.* वादी *f.* चामोटा *m.* सल *m.* वरत्रा *f.*

THORACIC, *a. belonging to the thorax or chest.* छातीचा, उराचा, उरांतला, वक्षस्थलसंबंधी, वक्षस्थलस्थ.

THORAL, *a. belonging to a bed or sleeping couch.* खाटेचा, शय्येचा, तल्पसंबंधी.

THORAX, *n. inward part of the breast,* v. CHEST. छाती *f.* उर *n. pop.* ऊर *m.* वक्षःस्थल *n.* [वृक्ष *m.*

THORN, *n. tree or shrub armed with thorns.* कांटेझाड *n.* कंटक-

Wood of thorns. कांटवन *n.* कांटेवन *n.*

2 *thorny bush or branch.* कांटी *f.* कांटेरें *n.*

Load or bundle of t.-loppings. झांप *m.* फांस *m.* फेंसाटी *f.* पेलें *n.*

3 *prickle.* कांटा *m.* कंटक *m.*

A bed of thorns, *lit. fig.* कांट्यांचें अंथरूण *n.* इंगळ्यांचें अंथरूण *n.* (bed of scorpions), इंगळांचें अंथरूण (bed of live coals).

To pierce or run in—a t. चुबकणें. [रीं पडणें.

To be pierced with the thorns of many cares. शरपंज-

4 fig. *trouble, pest, &c.* कंटक *pop.* कांटा *m.* शल्य *pop.* सल *n.*

THORN-APPLE, *n.*—*datura.* धत्तूर *pop.* धुतरा *or* धोतरा *m.* कनक *m.* Some species are, काळा धोतरा *or* कृष्ण धत्तूर, पांढरा धोतरा, बिलोरी धोतरा, कांटेधोतरा.

Oil extracted from the t. धुतरेल *or* धोतरेल *n.*

THORNLESS, *a.* कांट्यानिराळा-वेगळा, बिनकांट्याचा, निष्कंटक, कंटकरहित.

THORNY, *a. full of thorns, armed with thorns, &c.* कांट्यांचा, कांटेरा *or* री, कंटकी, सकंटक, कांटेकुट्याचा, कांटेसराट्याचा.

2 fig. *vexatious, perplexing.* जाचाचा, त्रासाचा, जाचणीचा, यातनेचा, जिकिरीचा, सकंटक, सशल्य, कंटकप्रचुर, कंटकबहुल.

THOROUGH, *a.* v. COMPLETE, PERFECT. पुरा, पूर्ण, पक्का, पारंगत.

2 *passing through.* आरपार जाणारा-गेलेला, साद्यंत.

THOROUGH-FARE, *n. road or passage quite through.* पाररस्ता *m.* आरपार जाण्याचा रस्ता *m.* राहदारीचा रस्ता *m.*

2 *much visited house.* येणारजाणाराचें-आल्यागेल्याचें-&c. घर *n.* उतारचावडी *f.* चावडीचें घर *n.* धर्मसाळ *f.*

THOROUGHLY, *adv.* v. A. 1. *and* WHOLLY. पुरेपणीं, पक्केपणीं, पुरतेपणीं, पुरता *decl.* &c. अगदीं, अज्जी, अजीबात *or* द, खड्यानखडा, तळसून-तळासून.

To do t. उरता *f.* ठेवणें *with neg. con.*

THOROUGH-PACED, THOROUGH-SPED. See ARRANT.

THOU, *pro.* तूं, त्वं.

To THOU, *To* THOU AND THEE, *v. n. use contemptuous or familiar language, speak in the second person.* तूं मीं *adv.*-अरे-तुरे *adv.*- तुंबरी तुंबरी *f.*-हंबेतुंबे *n. f.*- तुमरी तुमरी *f.*-तेरीमेरी *f.*-अबेदबे *f.*-अहंत्वंबंच *n.*-हंत्वंबंच *n.*-&c. करणें, अरेजारे बोलणें-म्हणणें. [यउतारां *adv.* येणें.

To begin to t. and t. एक पदरीवर येणें, एकेरीवर येणें, पा-

THOUGH, *conj.* v. ALTHOUGH. जरी.

As t. जणू, जणूकाय.

THOUGHT, *p.* v. V. A. 1. कल्पिलेला, मनांत आणलेला, &c. चि-

तित, कल्पित, भावित, ध्यात.

THOUGHT, *n. operation of the mind, act of thinking.* चिंतन *n.* चिंता *f.* मनन *n.* विचार *m.* मनोव्यापार *m.* अंतःकरणव्यापार *m.* मनश्चेष्टा *f.* अंतःकरणचेष्टा *f.* चित्तव्यापार *m.* चित्तचेष्टा *f.*

In t. word and deed. काया वाचा मनेंकरून.

Lost in t. ध्यानस्थ, स्तब्ध.

Passing or beyond t. अचिंत्य.

Speed or rapidity of t. मनोवेग *m.* मनोगति *f.*

To be in one's thoughts. ध्यानींमनीं-मनींमानसीं-&c. असणें- नसणें.

2 *that which is formed in the mind; idea, conception, fancy, &c.* कल्पना *f.* तर्क *m.* भावना *f.* भान *n.* भास *m.* यहम. बचक *m.* v. जा, हो *in. con.*

Farfetched or forced t. क्लिष्ट कल्पना *f.*

Mad, wild, wicked, &c. t. कुकल्पना *f.* कुतर्क *m.*

3 *that which is entertained in the mind; purpose, sentiment, &c.* v. MIND. DESIGN. मनांतली गोष्ट *f.* मनांतला विचार *m.* &c. मनोगत *n.* मनोदय *m.* मनोभाव *m.* हृद्गत *n.* मनोवृत्ति *f.* चित्तवृत्ति *f.*

4 thoughts; *mind as directed or applied to a subject,* v. MIND. मन *n.* चित्त *n.* ध्यान *n.* लक्ष्य *n.*

5 v. CARE, CONCERN. काळजी *f.* चिंता *f.*

THOUGHTFUL, *a. thinking, reflecting, &c.* v. CONSIDERATE. विचारशील, विचारवान् *pop.* विचारवंत, विचारी, विचारदर्शी, सविचार, मननशील, गंभीर.

2 *meditative, contemplative.* ध्यानी, ध्यानस्थ, ध्याननिष्ठ, ध्यानशील, मननशील.

3 v. CAREFUL, ATTENTIVE. दरदी, सचिंत, चिंतावान्, चिंतायुक्त, चिंतापर,

THOUGHTFULNESS, *n.* v. A. 1. विचारीपणा *m.* विचारशीलता *f.* सविचारता *f.*

2 ध्यानीपणा *m.* ध्यानशीलता *f.* मननशीलता *f.* ध्याननिष्ठा *f.*

3 दरदीपणा *m.* काळजी *f.* चिंता *f.*

THOUGHTLESS, *a.* v. CARELESS, INCONSIDERATE. अविचारी, अविचारशील, निकाळजी, निश्चिंत, बेदरदी, हीनविचार, हीनविवेक.

THOUGHTLESSNESS, *n.* v. A. अविचारीपणा *m.* निकाळजीपणा *m.* निश्चिंतपणा *m.* बेदरदीपणा *m.* &c. विचारहीनता *f.* विचाराराहित्य *n.*

THOUSAND, *a.* हजार, सहस्र, दाहाशें, दशशत.

2—indef. *great number.* लाख, लक्ष.

By thousands. हजारों, सहस्रशः, सहस्रावधि.

One of a t. *a man superlatively good.* लाखाचा मनुष्य.

THOUSANDTH, *a.* हजारावा, सहस्रावा.

THOWL, *n. fulcrum of an oar.* चुलत *or* चुळत *n.* चुलेत *n.*

THRALLDOM. See SLAVERY.

To **THRASH**, &c. See To THRESH, &c.

THREAD, *n. small twist, filament.* दोरा *m.* धागा *m.* सूत *n.* सूत्र *n.* तंतु *m.* (*pop.* तंत *f.*) तांत *f.* तांतू *m.* तार *f.* दोरक *m.*

Gold or silver t. कलाबतू *m.* जरतार *f.*

Quantity of t. wound over the palm. पुंजा *m.*

Thick-twisted t. खजुरी दोरा *m.*

Work with gold t. जरदोजी *f.* [or जरबाफूत.

Worked with gold or silver t. जरी, जरतारी, जरबाब

Worker in gold t. जरदोज.

Woven with double threads. दुतार, दुतारी.

2 fig. *connection of subject.* दोरा *m.* सूत *n.* तार *f.* अनुसंधान *n.* संधान *n.* पौर्वापर्य *n.* अन्वय *m.* अर्थान्वय *m.* अर्थसंदर्भ *m.* कथासंदर्भ *m.*

3 *sacred or sacrificial cord of the Hindu.* जानवें *n.* उपवीत *n.* यज्ञोपवीत *n.* सूत्र *n.* सावित्री सूत्र *n.* ब्रह्मसूत्र *n.* The thread or cord is worn over the left shoulder and under the right: that of the *Bráhman* is of cotton, *Munja or Kusha* grass; of the *Kshetriya,* of flax; of the *Vaishya,* of wool. The youths should be invested respectively from 8 to 16, from 11 to 22, from 12 to 24 years of age. Before the shoulder-thread is put on, the youth must be invested with the sacred girdle. Certain ceremonies pertaining to this *sacred thread* are, अष्टवर्ग, उत्सर्जन & उपाकरण & उपाकर्म, चासोळा, पळसुला, व्रतभिक्षा.

Bráhman fit to be invested with the sacred t. मुंज्या.

Bráhman invested with the sacred t. मुंज्या, बटु, ब्रह्मचारी, उपनीत.

Girdle or twisted thread made of three strings of *Munja* grass worn round the loins by a young Bráhman, मुंज *f.* मौंजी *f.* मेखला *pop.* मेखळा *f.* It is put on at the investiture with the shoulder-cord but previously to it, and must be taken off before marriage.—Bráhman wearing it, मुंज्या,—Ceremony of loosening it, सोडमुंज *f.* समावर्तन *n.*

Investiture with t. See THREAD-INVESTITURE.

Knot of sacred t. ब्रह्मगांठ *f.*

Renewal of sacred t. श्रावणी *f.*

Sacred t. as worn by children. बालोपवीत *n.*

Set of threads (5) to make the sacred t. जोडा *m.*

4 See FILAMENT, 5 *spiral part of a screw, &c.* वेढा *m.*

To **THREAD**, *v. a. pass a thread through, string.* गोवणें, ओंवणें, गुंफणें, ग्रंथणें, ओंवण *f* -ग्रंथ *m.*-ग्रंथन *n.*-&c. करणें *g. of o.*

2 (a needle). ओंवणें, ओवून देणें, दोर *m.*-&c. घालणें.

THREAD-BARE, *a. having the nap worn off.* जर्जर, झिरझिरा, झिरझिरीत *or* झरझरीत, झिलट, विरविरीत, फूल झडलेला, विरलेला, फुटीर.

T. cloth. माशांचें जाळें *n.* भूर्जपत्र *n.*

To become t. and thin. विरणें, विरघळणें, विरलणें, उतरणें.

THREAD-INVESTITURE, *n.* v. THREAD, 3. मुंज *f.* मुंजी *f.* मौंजी *f.* मौंजीबंधन *n.* उपनयन *n.* बटूकरण *n.* व्रतबंध *m.*

Altar or seat at a t. बहुलें *n.*

Begging and the alms obtained by a Bráhman under t. भिक्षान्न *pop.* भिकाळ *f.* व्रतभिक्षा *f.*

Bráhman &c. of whom the t. has been omitted. व्रात्य.

Ceremony of eating with his mother of the subject of a t. मातृभोजन *n.*

Cloth or garment worn at t. बटुवस्त्र *n.* कबाय *f.*

Entertainment given to the subject of a t. बटुभोजन *n.*

THREADED, *p.* v. V. 1. गोवलेला, ओंवलेला, &c. गुंफित, ग्रंथित,

To THREAT, *To* THREATEN, *v. a. denounce future evil to, declare purpose of punishing.* भय *n.*-धाक *m.*-&c. दाखवणें *g. of o.* भय *n.*-धाक *m.*-&c. घालणें *g. of o.* अनिष्टसूचन *n.*-भयसूचन *n.*-दंडसूचन *n.*-भयप्रदर्शन *n.*-दंडप्रदर्शन *n.*-&c. करणें.
2 *attempt to terrify,* v. To MENACE, To INTIMIDATE. भय *n.* दाखवणें-घालणें, भेडावणें *n.*-भेडसावणें *n.*-भेडसावणी *f.*-&c. दाखवणें, भेडसावणें, भेडावणें.
3 *exhibit the appearance of something evil approaching.* रंग *m.*-डौल *m.*-घाट *m.*-पूर्वरूप *n.*-&c. दाखवणें, रंग *m.*-डौल *m.*-&c. असणें *g. of o.*

THREAT, THREATENING, *n.* v. V. 1. भय दाखवणें *n.* &c. दंडसूचन *n.* अनिष्टसूचन *n.* भयसूचन *n.* भयप्रदर्शन *n.* दंडसंकल्पप्रदर्शन *n.*
2 भेडावणें *n.* भेडसावणें *n.* &c. भेडसावणी *f.* भेडावणी *f.* धमकी *f.* भयप्रदर्शन *n.* भबकी *f.*
3—as of rain, &c. रंग *m.* मांड *m.* घाट *m.* पूर्वरूप *n.* डौल *m.*

THREATENER, *n.* THREATENING, *p. a.* v.V. 1.2. भयदाखवणारा, भयघालणारा, &c. भयप्रदर्शक, भयसूचक, भयप्रदर्शन कर्त्ता-कारी-&c.

THREE, *a.* तीन, तिघे (used only of living creatures), ति (in comp. as T.-storied तिमजला, T.-cornered तिकोनी, & तिणखी, तिघई, तिघडी, तिजोरी, &c.), त्रि (in comp. as त्रिलोक, त्रिभुवन, त्रिपद, त्रिगण, त्रिकोण, त्रिदंड, &c.)
Aggregate of t. v. TRIO. त्रिकूट *n.* त्रय *n.* त्रयी *f.* त्रिक् *n.* त्रितय *n.*
By threes,—clustering, strung, &c. तिघड.
Composed of threes. तिघड.
Of t. kinds or sorts. त्रिविध.
T. persons or individuals. त्रिवर्ग *m.*
T. and a half. अऊट *or* औट.—Multiple of t. and a half. अउटकें *or* औटकें *n.*

THREE-FOLD, *a.* त्रिगुण, तिप्पट, तिहेरा *or* री, तिहिरी.

THREE-JOINTED, *a.* तिपेरी, त्रिपर्व.

THREE-LOOPED, *a.* तिफांसी,

THREE-SIDED, *a.* तिबाजू.

THREE-STRINGED, *a.* तिसुती.

THRENODY, *n. song of lamentation.* मरशा *m.*

To THRESH, *v. a. separate from the husk by beating.* पिटणें, झोडणें, झोडपणें, बडवणें, मळणें, मळणी *f.* करणें-काढणें-घालणें, झोड *f.* काढणें-मारणें *g. of o.* बडवा करणें,—by treading it under the feet of bullocks, मळणें, मळणी *f.* काढणें-करणें-घालणें.
Threshing operations—compreh. चोळणीमळणी *f.*
2 *drub,* v. To BEAT. झोडणें, झोडपणें, धोपटणें, पिटणें, कुटणें, कुदकणें, कुबलणें.

THRESHED, *p.* v.V. 1. झोडलेला, बडवलेला, &c. झोडींव, बडव्याचा, —by the treading of oxen, मळलेला, मळणीचा, खळ्याचा.
2 झोडलेला, पिटलेला, कुटलेला.

THRESHER, *n.* THRESHING, *p. a.* v. V. 1. झोडणारा, मळणारा, बडवणारा, &c. मळणकर.
Corn given to hired threshers. जेवणी *f.*

THRESHING, *n.* v. V. 1. झोडणें *n.* बडवणें *n.* मळणें *n.* झोड *f.* झोडणी *f.* मळणी *f.*

THRESHING-FEAST, *n.* डहुरा *or* डोहुरा *m.* रासपूजा *f.*

THRESHING-FLOOR, *n.* खळें *n.*
Bráhman that gleans or begs at a t. खळभट.
General enclosure of the threshing-floors of a village. खळवाडी *f.* खळेवाडी *f.*
Post of a t. तिवडा *m.* खळ्याचीमेढ *f.*
The ring of bundles encompassing a t. तराळी *f.*
Team of oxen at a t. to tread out the corn. पात *f.* पाती *f.*
That has been trodden out or threshed at a t. खळ्याचा. [घालणें.
To lay the t. *place corn on it to be trodden out.* पेर *m.*

THRESHOLD, *n. door-sill, ground under the door, entrance.* दारवटा *or* ठा *m.* देवडी *or* ढी *or* देहुडी *f.* उंबरा *or* उमरा *m.* उंबरठा *m.* उमरठा *m.* देहली *f.* शिला *f.*
Stumble at the t. *fig.* प्रथमग्रास मक्षिकापात:.
To mount the t. उमरा *m.* चढणें.
To wear the t. of. उमऱ्याची साल *f.* काढणें, उमऱ्याला माती *f.* राहूंनदेणें, दाराची माती *f.* नाहींसी करणें.
2 fig. *outset,* v. BEGINNING. मुळारंभ *m.* उपक्रम *m.*

THRICE, *adv.* तीनवेळ *or* वार, तीनवेळां, तीनदां, त्रिवार.

THRIFT, THRIFTINESS, *n.* v. A. 1. *and* ECONOMY. कतरबेत *m.* काटकसर *f.* घरजुगूत *f.* घरजोगावणी *f.*

THRIFTLESS. See EXTRAVAGANT.

THRIFTY, *a. frugal,* v. ECONOMICAL. कतरबेती *or* त्या, काटकसऱ्या, घरजोगावणीचा, अल्पव्ययी, संसारीक.
2 See PROSPEROUS.

To THRILL, *v. n.* (in the ear—a sharp sound). घणघणणें, खणखणणें, झणझणणें, भिरभिरणें, कान *m.* बेधणें, किर्र *adv.* करणें.
2—the body or a member ; *feel a tingling sensation.* शिवशिवणें, शिवळणें, शिसारी *f.* शिरशिरी *f.* येणें-भरणें *in. con.* स्फुरणें. [वणें *g. of s.*
3 *pass with a tingling sensation.* शिसारी *f.* येणें-भरणें-धा-

To THRILL, *v. a.* See To PENETRATE, To PIERCE.

THRILL, THRILLING, *n.* v. V. N. 2. शिसारी *f.* शिरशिरी *f.* स्फुरण *n.* स्फूर्त्ति *f.*

THRILLING, *p. a.* v.V.N.1. कानास बेधणारा, बेधक, किर्र, घणघणीत, खणखणीत, कर्कश.

To THRIVE, &c. See To FLOURISH, To PROSPER.

THROAT, *n. fore part of the neck.* घांटी *f.* घांट *f.* घसा *m.* गळा *m.* कंठ *m.* हलक *f.* नटोरी *or* टटोरी *f.* गळसूत्र *m.*
Ablution from the t. downwards. कंठस्नान *n.*
Dryness of the t. कोरड *f.* *v.* पड, कंठशोष *m.*
In the t. गळां.
Inflammation of the t. गलचुटी *f.*
Ornament for the t. कंठभूषण *n.* कंठाभरण *n.*
Putrid sore t. घटसर्प *pop.* घांटसर्प *m.*
Seated in the t. *or* Come into the t. कंठगत.
Throat-band or yoke collar. जुंपणी *f.* जुंबाली *f.*
Ulcers in the t. गंडमाला *f.*
Up to the t. कंठमर्याद, आकंठ.
To cut one's t. कंठस्नान *n.* घालणें.
To force down the t. of. *fig.* गळां बांधणें.
To have the t. stopped up. गळ्याचा लासोटा *m.* होणें *g.*

of o. गळा *m.* लाखटणें *g. of s.*

To make one's t. hoarse (as in reproving, exhorting, &c.). कंठशोष *m.* करून घेणें.

To THROB, *v. n. beat quickly, pulsate violently, shoot, &c.* उडणें, ठुणठुणणें, टणटण *or* ठुणठुण *adv.* उडणें, टचटचणें, टचटच *adv.* वाजणें, ठणठणणें, ठणकणें, ठणकावणें, ठसठसणें *intens.* ठसासणें, ठुसठुसणें, धुसधुसणें, धमकणें, ठसठस *f.*-&c. करणें, *and, with g. of s.* चालणें, पिंजणें, पिंजपिंजणें.

2 See To PALPITATE.

THROB, THROBBING, *n.* v. V. 1. ठणकणें *n.* &c. ठणका *m.* ठणक *f.* ठसठस *or* ठुसठूस *f.* ठणठण *f.* धुसधूस *f.*

THROBBER, *n.* THROBBING, *p. a.* v. V. 1. टचटच उडणारा, ठणकणारा, &c.

THROE, *v. pain, travail.* तिडीक *f.* वेण *f.* प्रसववेदना *f.* गर्भवेदना *f.*

To heave a t. तिडीक *f.* देणें, असडा *m.* देणें.

2 *convulsive quiver.* असडा *m. v.* दे, ये, लहर *f.*

THRONE, *n. royal seat.* राजाची गादी *f.* गादी *f.* राजगादी *f.* सिंहासन *n.* राजासन *n.* तक *n.* नृपासन *n.* भद्रासन *n.* राजशय्या *f.*

Vacancy of the t. अनायक *n.* अराजक *n.*

To THRONE. See To ENTHRONE.

THRONG, *To* THRONG, &c. See CROWD, To CROWD, &c.

THROTTLE, *n.* v. THROAT. घांटी *f.* घांट *f.* गळा*m.*

To THROTTLE, *v. a. seize by the throat so as stop the breath.* गळचिपी *f.* धरणें, गळचोंडी *f.* धरणें, गळा*m.*-नरडी *f.*-नरडें*n.*-&c. अवळणें-दाबणें-चेपणें *or* दाबून-&c. मारणें, गलग्रह*m.* करणें, गळचेपी *f.* करणें.

THROUGH, *prep. from end to end of.* आरपार.

2—noting passage or channel. आंतून, मधून, वाटे. The sense is usually expressed by the inflection of the noun as या दारानें, t. this door, &c.

2 *by agency or means of.* करून *or* कडून, करवीं *or* वें, वारीं, द्वारा, द्वारानें, मारफतीनें.

THROUGH, *adv. from one end to the other.* पार, आरपार, साद्यंत.

T. and t. आरपार.

2 *from beginning to end.* पहिल्यापासून-प्रारंभापासून-आदीपासून-&c. शेवटापर्यंत *or* शेवटपर्यंत-समाप्तीपर्यंत, अथपासूनइतिपर्यंत.

3 *to the ultimate purpose, to the end.* शेवटास, सिद्धीस, परिणामास, तडीस, कडेस.

To carry t. To go t. with, &c. v. To ACCOMPLISH. शेवटास-&c. नेणें.

To go t. *undergo,* v. To SUFFER. सोसणें, काढणें.

THROUGHOUT, *prep.* or *adv.*—of time. पर्यंत (in comp. as मासपर्यंत, वर्षपर्यंत, युगपर्यंत, &c.), शेवटपर्यंत, पहिल्यापासून-प्रारंभापासून-&c. शेवटापर्यंत, अथपासूनइतिपर्यंत, भर (in comp. as दिवसभर, महिनाभर).

2—of space. इथूनतिथून, अहदतहद, साद्यंत, भर (in comp. as गांवभर, देशभर, पृथ्वीभर, &c.).

To THROW, *v. a.* v. To CAST. झोकणें, झुगारणें, टाकणें, फेंकणें, घालणें, निक्षेपणें, न्यसणें.

To t. one's self (into a pond, well, the fire, &c.). घालून घेणें. [पच्छाडणें.

2 *overturn in wrestling.* पाडणें, चीत-जमीनदोस्त-&c. करणें,

3 about; *scatter diffusely.* उधळणें, चहूंकडे फेंकणें-उडवणें, पसरंसा टाकणें, अधळणी *f.*-उद्धलन*n.* करणें.

4 away; *lose by neglect or folly, spend uselessly, &c.* घालवणें, दवडणें, उडवणें, उधळणें, गमावणें, हरवणें *or* हारवणें, साडणें.

5 by; *lay aside as useless, &c.* एकीकडे टाकणें, मोडीस टाकणें.

6 down; *overthrow, &c.* पाडणें, पाडून टाकणें.

7 off; (clothes, &c.). काढणें, काढून टाकणें, उतरणें, उतरून टाकणें, आंगाबाहेर-निराळा-&c. करणें.

8 off; *remove, expel, &c.* निरसणें, दूर करणें, टाकणें, निरसन*n.*-निरासन*n.*-निराकरण*n.*-&c. करणें *g. of o.*

9 off and upon. कोलणें, टाकणें, ढकलणें, ढोलणें, टोलावणें.

10 out (insinuations, hints, &c.). सुचवणें, दर्शवणें, सूचना *f.*-&c. करणें, आंतून फेंकणें.

11 up; *lit.* वर-ऊर्ध्वदिशेकडे-&c. टाकणें-फेंकणें, उत्क्षेपणें, उत्क्षेप *m.*-उत्क्षेपण*n.*-&c. करणें.

12 up. See To VOMIT. 13 upon. टाकणें, घालणें.

14 upon (a body of troops, &c. upon the enemy.) लोटणें.

THROW, THROWING, *n.* v. V. 1. झोकणें*n.* टाकणें*n.* &c. प्रक्षेपण*n.* क्षेप*m.* प्रक्षेप*m.* निक्षेप*m.*

I. (of dice). डाव*m. v.* टाक.

II. *distance which a missile may be thrown.* टप्पा*m.* पल्ला*m.*

Stone-t. हातधोंडा*m.* हातगुंडा*m.*

THROWER, *n.* THROWING, *p. a.* v. V. 1. झोकणारा, टाकणारा, फेंकणारा, &c. फेंक्या, झोक्या, क्षेपक, प्रक्षेपक, क्षेपण-प्रक्षेपण-&c. कर्त्ता-कारी-&c.

2 पाडणारा, जमीनदोस्त-&c. करणारा.

THROWN, *p.* v. V. 1. झोकलेला, फेंकलेला, टाकलेला, &c. क्षिप्त, प्रक्षिप्त, निक्षिप्त, विक्षिप्त, न्यस्त.

2 पाडलेला, &c. चीत, जमीनदोस्त.

6 पाडलेला, &c. पाडींव.

8 निरसलेला, &c. निरसित, निरस्त, निराकृत.

THRUM, *n. ends of weavers threads.* कातरण *n.* उलबण *n.* दशा *f. pl.* अंचलया *f. pl.* अंचळ *m. pl.*

The twisted t. वरवड *f.* [&c. वाजवणें.

To THRUM, *v. a. play coursely.* तारा *f. pl.* तोडणें, अनाडीपणानें-

THRUSH, *n. turdus salica.* सारिका *or* सारी *f.* शलाका *f.* मदनसारिका *f.*

2—the disease of the mouth. खडे *m. pl.*

To THRUST, *v. a. drive, shove,* v. To PUSH. ढकलणें, रेटणें, ठेलणें.

2 in; *push into or between.* खुपसणें, खोंचणें, खोंचरणें, खोवणें, खोसणें, धसकणें, घालणें, घालवणें, शिरकणें, शिरकावणें, भसकणें, भसकावणें, भोकसणें *or* भोसकणें *or* भोसणें, ढुसकणें, ढुसणें *or* ढोसणें, घुसडणें, संचारणें.

3 through; v. To STAB. ढुसकणें, ढुसणें *or* ढोसणें, ढुसकी *f.*-ढुसी *or* ढुस्सी *f.*-&c. मारणें.

To thrust one's self in. घुसडणें, घुसणें.

To THRUST, *v. n. make a thrust.* ढुशी *f.*-ढुसकी *f.*-&c. मारणें.

THRUST, THRUSTING, *n.* v. V. A. 1. ढकलणें, रेटणें *n.* &c. धक्का *m.* धडकी *f.*

2 खुपसणें *n.* खोंचणें *n.* &c. खुपसणी *f.* खोंचणी *f.* खोसणी *f.* ढुसणी *f.* ढुसकणी *f.* &c.

3 ढुसकणें *n.* ढुसणें *n.* &c. ढुसकणी *f.* ढुसणी *f.* ढुशी *or* ढुसी *or* ढुस्सी *f.* ढुसकी *f.*—esp. with a spear. खासडा*m.*

A soft sounding t. or blow. गबका *m.*

THRUST, *p. a.* v. V. A. 1. ढकललेला, रेंटलेला, लोटलेला, &c.
2 खुपसलेला, खोंचलेला, ढुसकलेला, &c.
3 ढुसकलेला, ढुसलेला, ढुसकी मारलेला, &c.

THRUSTER, *n.* THRUSTING, *p. a.* v. V. A. 1. ढकलणारा, रेंटणारा, लोटणारा.
2 खुपसणारा, खोंचणारा, ढुसकणारा, &c.
3 ढुसकणारा, ढुसणारा, ढुसकी-&c. मारणारा.

THUMB, *n.*—of the hand. अंगठा *m.* अंगुष्ठ *m.*
That is under the t. of. छापाखालचा.
To have under one's t. बोटावर नाचवणें.
To be under the t. of. मुठींत असणें.

To THUMB, *v. a. soil with the fingers.* अंगठ्याचा डाग *m.* पाडणें, अंगुल्यंकित करणें.

THUMB-KIN, THUMB-SCREW. चाप *m.*

THUMP, *n. heavy blow,* v. BLOW. धमका *or* धुमका *m.* धबका *m.* धपाटा *m.* कुतका *or* कुदका *m.* घुसा *or* घुस्सा *m.* ढोसा *m.*
2 *blow against, a striking against.* धडक *f.* धडका *m.* धडक *f.* धडका *m.*

THUMP, *adv.*—falling, &c. धबकन-कण-कर-दिशी-&c. धपकन-कर-दिशी-&c. भुद *or* भदकन-कर-&c.

To THUMP, *v. n. fall or strike with a dull heavy blow.* धबकन-धपकन-&c. पडणें-लागणें-आपटणें.

To THUMP, *v. a.* v. To BEAT. बुकलणें, बुचलणें, कुचलणें, कुबलणें, कुमलणें, बकालणें, बुदकणें, कुदकणें, कुमकणें, कुदवणें, गुबकणें, धमकणें *or* धुमकणें.
2 *knock or strike against, bump.* धडक *f.*-धडका *m.*-धडक *f.*-धडका *m.*-टक्कर-&c. मारणें.

To THUMP, *v. n.* See To BUMP.

THUMPER, *n. huge thing,* v. LARGE. रपाटा*m.* रपाटखान*m.* ढेर *f.*

THUMPING, *a. swinging, whacking, &c.* v. LARGE. रटाला, लठारणा, बताडा, बताणा, ठसठशीत *or* सीत.

To THUNDER, *v. n. to sound*—an explosion of electricity. गरजणें, गाजणें, गर्जना *f.*-&c. करणें *or with g. of s.* होणें, आभाळ *n.*-मेघ *m.*-&c. गडगडणें-गरजणें-घडघडणें-&c.
To t. and lighten. वीज *f.* कडकडणें, वाजणेंगाजणें.
2 *make a loud noise,* v. To ROAR. गडगडणें, गडाडणें, गडगड-गडगडां-कडाकड-&c. वाजणें, दणका *m.*-&c. होणें-वाजणें *g. of s.*

To THUNDER, *v.a. publish or emit with noise and terror.* दणकावून-धडकावून-खणखणावून-&c. बोलणें-उच्चारणें.

THUNDER,*n. the sound which follows lightning.* गर्जना*f.* गाजणें *n.* मेघनाद *m.* मेघशब्द *m.* मेघध्वनि *m.* घनशब्द *m.* घनरव *m.* घनस्वन *m.*
Loud crash of t. and lightning. विजेचा कडकडाट *m.*-कडाखा *m.*-&c. मेघाचा गडगडाट *m.*
2 *loud continuous sound,* v. ROAR. गर्जना *f.* गडाड *m.* मडाड *m.* धडाड *m.*

THUNDER-BOLT, *n.* वीज *f.* वज्र *m. n.* कुलिश *m. n.*
Falling of a t. वज्रपात *m.*
Resistless as the t. वज्रप्राय.

THUNDER-CLOUD, *n.* विजेचें अभ्र *n.* विजेचा मेघ *m.* [सर *f.*

THUNDER-STORM, *n.* विजेचा पाऊस *m.* गाजता पाऊस *m.* गाजती

THUNDER-STRUCK, *a.* v. ASTONISHED. चकित, थक्क, वज्राहत, वज्रप्रहत. [*pop.* बृहस्पतवार *m.*

THURSDAY, *n.*—the day of the week. गुरुवार *m.* बृहस्पतिवार

THUS, *adv. in this or that way.* असा *decl.* तसा *decl.* एवम्, ह्या-त्याप्रमाणें, ह्या-त्यारीतीनें, ह्या-त्याप्रकारें-प्रकारानें.
T. far, t. much, &c. एथवर, एथपर्यंत, एथपावेतों, एवढा.

THWACK, &c. See WHACK.

To THWART, *v. a. cross, oppose, &c.* v. To HINDER, To OBSTRUCT. अडथळणें, आडवा येणें, मोडा *m.* घालणें, हरकत *f.* करणें, मन *n.* मोडणें *g. of o.*
2 *cross.* आडवा *decl.* जाणें.

THWART, *a. transverse.* आडवा.

THY, *pron. a.* तुझा.

THYSELF, *pron.* तूं आपण, तूंच, आपण.

TIARA, *n.* v .CREST, CROWN. मुगूट *m.* शिरताज *m.* ललाटपट्ट *n.*

TIBIA, *n. large bone of the leg.* नडगें *n.* नडगी *f.* नडघा *m.* नळकुटी *or* नळगुटी *or* डी *f.* नळा *m.* नळी *f.*

TIBIAL, *a.* v. N. नडग्याचा, नडगीचा, &c.

TICK, *n. score, credit, trust.* उचापत *f.* उधार *m.*
One living upon t. उचापतखाऊ.
One selling upon t. उचापत्या.
Things given or taken on t. उचापत *f.*
2 *louse of dogs, &c.* गोचडी *or* गोचिडी *or* गोचिड *f.* गोचीड *m.* घागरा *or* घागऱ्यागोचीड *m.* सुळा *m.* चामीगोचीड *or* चांभाऱ्यागोचीड *m.* कोळक *f.*

To TICK, *v. n.*—a watch, &c. टणटण-किटकिट-कुटकुट-&c. वाजणें, खिटखिटणें.

TICKET, *n. written token.* चिठी *or* चिठ्ठी *f.* चकती *f.*
2 *label.* चिठी *or* चिठ्ठी *f.* चकती *f.* [बीजक *n.*
3—as appended to shew number and price. अंकपटी *f.*
4—as in a lottery, &c. टीप *f.* टिकट *n.* from the English is in common use. [चिकटवणें.

To TICKET, *v. a.* v. N. चिठी *f.*-चिठ्या *f. pl.*-&c. मारणें-लावणें-

TICKETED, *p.* v. V. चिठी लावलेला, &c. चिठ्ठीचा.

To TICKLE, *v. a. cause a thrilling sensation by the touch.* गुदगुली *f.*-गुदगुदी *f.*-गुदगूद *f.*-कुचकुली *f.*-काचकली *f.*-कातकुली *f.*-गुदगूल *f.*-&c. करणें, गुदगुदावणें. [खाजणें.
2 (the tongue, mouth, &c.)—certain articles of food.
3 fig. See To PLEASE.

To TICKLE, *v. n. feel titillation.* गुदगुली *f.*-&c. होणें.

TICKLER, *n.* TICKLING, *p. a.* v. V. A. 1. गुदगुली-गुदगुल्या-&c. करणारा.
2 खाजणारा, खाजरा.

TICKLISH, *a. easily tickled.* गुदगुल्या, गुदगुद्या, गुदगुदीचा, गुदगुलीलौकर येण्याचा.
2 fig. *unsettled,* v.TOTTERING. डळमळीत, लटपटीत, डळमळीचा, लटपटीचा, घालमेलीचा, चलबिचलीचा.

TICKLISHNESS, *n.* v. A. 1. गुदगुलेपणा *m.* &c. गुदगुली लौकर येण्याचा स्वभाव *m.*
2 जळमळ *f.* चलबिचल *f.* लटपट *f.* घालमेल *f.*

TIDAL, *a. pertaining to tides.* भरती ओहटीचा.

TIDBIT, *n. delicate piece.* गोडघास *m.* सुग्रास *m.* [उतार *m.*

TIDE, *n.* (of the sea). भरतीओहटी *f.* समुद्रांतल्या पाण्याचा चढ-
Bore or swell of the t. घोडा *m.*

High t. *time of high water.* समा *m.* सवारी *f.*

Neap t. भांग *m.*

Spring-t. उधान *n.* उसाण *n.*

T. at the equinoxes. उधान *n.* उसाण *n.*

2 See COURSE, CURRENT.

TIDINESS, *n.* v. A. चाकपणा *m.* चाकपाकपणा *m.* &c. चाकचोपी *f.* चापचोपी *f.* चापीचोपी *f.* चकपक *f.* [रम.

TIDINGS, *n.* v. NEWS. खबर *f.* बातमी *f.* वार्त्ता *f.* पत्ता *m.* समाचा-

TIDY, *a. natty, trim, &c.* v. NEAT. चाक *or* चाख, चाकचोप *or* चापचोप, चकपक *or* चाकपाक, चकचकीत, चक्र, खासखुरत, सुबक, ठीकठाक *or* ठाकठीक, चापचोपीचा, चाकचोपीचा.

To TIE, *v. a. bind, fasten, confine with a band, &c.* बांधणें, बांधून ठेवणें-टाकणें, तांगडणें, बांधणी *f.*-बांध *m.*-बंधन *n.*-निबंधन *n.*-निबंध *m.*-&c. करणें.

To t. with a knot. गांठणें, गांठ देऊन बांधणें, गांठ *f.* मारणें.

2—tightly; *bind forcibly or closely,* v. To TIGHTEN. अवळणें, कसणें, करकचणें, कचकावणें *or* खचकावणें, तकटणें, तंगडणें *or* करकचून-कचकावून-तकटून-तंगडून-&c. बांधणें-अवळणें-ओढणें, करकटून-कडसून-चौखारून-जखडून-जबकून-अवळून-ओढून-अकसून-जेथून-&c. बांधणें, जबकणें, जबखारणें.

3 down; up; *confine, hinder from action,* v. To RESTRAIN. बांधणें, बांधून ठेवणें, तांगडणें, तांगडून ठेवणें, गळा *m.* बांधणें-गोवणें *g. of o.* पाय *m. pl.*-हातपाय *m. pl.* बांधणें-बांधून-घेणें-गुंतवून घेणें.

4 up; unto; to; at; *fasten, bind.* बांधणें, बांधून ठेवणें-टाकणें, जखडणें, जखडून बांधणें, जबकणें, जबकून बांधणें, तांगडणें, तांगडून टाकणें, सांगडणें, गोवणें, गोवून घेणें, जबखारणें. [ळा*m.*

TIE, *n. fastening, binding, lit. fig.* बंद *m.* बंध *m.* बंधन *n.* आ-

2 fig. v. CONNEXION. गांठ *f.* ग्रंथि *m.* नातें *n.* लग *f.* लगा *m.* लगाबांधा *m.* धागादोरा *m.*

3 *fastening cord or string.* बंद *m.* बंध *m.* बंधन *n.* कसणी *f.* कसा *m.* कस्तान *n.* आळा *m.*

4 (as of necklaces, bracelets, &c.). पडसूत्र *n.* पडदोरा *m.*

TIED, *p.* v. V. 1. बांधलेला, तांगडलेला, बद्ध, &c.

TIER, *n.* v. ROW. ओळ *f.* रांग *f.* मजला *m.*

Of two tiers. दुमजला *or* ली,—of three. तिमजला *or* ली,—of four. चौमजला *or* ली.

TIFF. See HUFF.

TIFFIN, *n.* v. LUNCHEON. फराळ *m.* उपहार *m.*

TIFFOON, *n. sudden gale.* तुफान *n.* जौळ *n.*

TIGER, *n.* वाघ *m.* व्याघ्र *m.* शार्दूल *m.*—in contempt or endearment, वाघट *n.* वाघरूं *n.*—respectfully, वाघोबा *m.*—allusively, नकटा *m.*

Box used as a trap to catch a t. पेटा *m.*

Lair or covert of a t. वाघाची जाळी *f.* वाघचीळ *n.*

Ravages or infestation of tigers. वाघावें *or* वाघवें *n.*

Tiger's claw. वाघनख *n.*

TIGER-SKIN, *n.* वाघाचें कातडें *n.* व्याघ्रचर्म *n.*

Bag of t. (used to hold turmeric-powder, &c.). वाघी *f.* वाघ्या *m.*

Imitation t. (as body cloth for a horse, &c.). वाघी *f.*

T. worn as clothing. व्याघ्रांबर *n.*

TIGHT, *a. drawn intensely,* v. TIGHT-DRAWN. तंग, ताठ, ताठर.

2—as a garment; *pinching.* दाट, तंग, तंगदार, अटस, अवळ, घट्ट, सांकड, दाटका, दाटता, अडच *or* अडच, नाठ.

To feel t. *sit pinchingly.* दाटणें.

3 *close, firm, not open.* घट्ट, गच्च, अवळ (*remiss* अवळसर *tightish*), अडच *or* अडच.

4 *close-set, well-knit, &c.* अटस, घट्ट, अटपना, अटकर, अटोपसार, अटोपशुद्ध, सुटसुटीत, खुटखुटीत, सुबक.

TIGHT-DRAWN, *a. strained or stretched intensely.* तंग, नाठ, ताठर, तटतटीत, तणतणीत, ताणलेला, ताणदिल्हेला, टमटमीत *or* टुमटुमीत, दुमदुमीत.

To TIGHTEN, *v. a. draw tighter.* अवळणें, अवळून बांधणें, ताणणें, ताणून धरणें-बांधणें, कसणें, ओढून धरणें, अवटरणें, खचणें, चढवणें, सन्निबंधन *n.* करणें, जबकणें, जखडणें, जखडून बांधणें, जेठणें, जेठून बांधणें, करकचणें, करकचून आवळणें-बांधणें-ओढणें, खचकावणें *or* कचकावणें, तकटणें, तकटून बांधणें, तंगडणें, तंगडून आवळणें-&c. तंगाडणें, अकसणें, अकसून बांधणें-आवळणें-&c. भिडवणें (esp. in. काच्या भिडवणें & खोगीर *or* जीन भिडवणें), चौखारून बांधणें-अवळणें-ओढणें.

2 *make more close.* अवळ-गच्च-&c. करणें-बसवणें.

To TIGHTEN, *v. n. become tighter.* ताठणें, नराठणें *or* नऱ्हाटणें, तंग-&c. होणें-होत जाणें, दाटणें, अवळणें, तणणें, तणतणणें, तटतटणें *or* तडतडणें *intens.* तटाटणें, आंटरणें, आंठुरणें, उतटणें *or* उताटणें, तर्र *adv.* होणें-फुगणें, तट *adv.* फुगणें, तण *adv.* करणें.

TIGHTLY, TIGHT, *adv.* v. A. 1. तंग, ताठ, ताणून, ओढून, कसून, कडस, &c.

2 दाट, तंग, अटस.

3 घट्ट, गच्च, अडच *or* च, आइसर, अटस.

I.—as expressing vehemence, fulness of action, &c. v. SMARTLY. तकट, तकटून, बळकट, बळकटून, कडकडून, कडकावून, कचकावून, कचकून, करकचून, खपाटून, करकरून, मारून.

TIGHTNESS, *n.* v. A. 1. ताठपणा *m.* ताठरपणा *m.* &c. ताठा *m.* ताठ *m.* ताण *m.* तणावा *m.*

2 दाटपणा *m.* तंगपणा *m.* अवळपणा *m.* &c. घट्टाई *f.*

3 घट्टपणा *m.* गच्चपणा *m.* अवळपणा *m.* &c.

4 अटसपणा *m.* घट्टपणा *m.* &c.

TIGRESS, *n. female tiger.* वाघीण *f.* व्याघ्री *f.*

TILE, *n.*—for a roof, &c. कौल *or* कवूल *n.* खापर *n.*

Aggregate of ten tiles. जुट्टा *m.*

Corner t. *or* ridge t. कोना *m.* घोण्या *m.* ढापा *m.*

Flat t. खपरेल *n.* धापा *m.*

Flat t. with raised edges. पन्हळी कौल *n.* थापी कौल *n.*

Semi-cylindrical t. नळा *m.*

To TILE, *v. a. cover with tiles.* कवलें *n. pl.* घालणें-चढवणें-लावणें-शाकारणें, कौलार-&c. करणें. [परेली.

TILED, *p.* v. V. कवलेंघातलेला, &c. कौलार, कौलारू, खपरेल, ख-

A t. building. खपरेल *n.* कौलार *n.*

TILER, *n.* v. V. कवलें घालणारा-चढवणारा-&c. खपरबंद.

TILING, *n. tiled roof.* कौलार *n.* खपरेल *n.*

2 *tiles.* कवलें *n. pl.* कौल *or* कवूल *n.*

TILL, *n. tiller, drawer.* घर *n.* खण *m.* खाना *m.*

2 *money-box.* गोलक *n.*

TILL, *prep.* or *adv.* v. UNTIL. जों, जोंपर्यंत, तोंपर्यंत-पावेतों, पर्यंत, पावेतों.

From and till (one date to another). इत्तकबील तागाईत.

T. now. एव्हांपर्यंत, याकाळापर्यंत, ह्याकाळपर्यंत-पावेतों, हावेळपावेतों-पर्यंत, आतांपर्यंत-पावेतों. [तंव, तंवपर्यंत.

T. then. तेव्हांपर्यंत, तोकाळपर्यंत-पावेतों, तोवेळपर्यंत-पावेतों,

To TILL, *v. a.* v. TO CULTIVATE. राबणें, नांगरणें दुणणें, राबणूक *f.*-&c. करणें.

TILLAGE, *n.* v. V. *and* AGRICULTURE. राबणें *n.* &c. राबणूक *f.* राबणी *f.* नांगरणीदुणणी *f.* लावणीदुपणी *f.* शेती *f.* लागवड *f.* लागलागवड *f.* लागलावण *f.* वाहील *or* वाहेल *f.* कृषिकर्म *n.* कर्षण *n.*

Land under t. लागण *f.*—That is in t. वाहीत, वाहोल.

The being under t. लागण *f.*

The original bringer of land under t. लागणदार.

TILLED, *p.* v. V. राबलेला, नांगरलेलादुणलेला, &c. वहीत, कृष्ट, कर्षित.

TILLER, *n.* TILLING, *p. a.* v. V. *and* AGRICULTURIST. राबणारा, नांगरणारा, दुणणारा, &c. कर्षक.

TILLER, *n.* (of a rudder). बाजा *m.* बार्वे *n.* सुकाणाची दांडी *f.*

2 See TILL.

TILT, *n. cloth covering for a cart, boat, &c.* पडदा *m.* भुरकी *f.* चांदवा *m.* चांदणी *f.* छत *n.* [*f.*

2—the military exercise. भालाइती *f.* भालेकरोली *or* करबली

At full t. भरधांव, भरधूम, धूमठोकीत.

3 See THRUST. 4 See HAMMER.

To TILT, *v. a.* (a cask, &c.) *incline.* कलथणें, कलंडणें, कलथाकलंडा-&c. करणें.

2 See To HAMMER. [गणें.

To TILT, *v. n. fall on one side.* कलथणें, कलंडणें, एकारणें, एकां-

2 *ride and thrust with lances.* भालाइती *f.*-भालेकरोली *f.* करणें.

TIMBER, *n. wood fit for building, &c.* v. WOOD, TREE. इमारतीचें लांकूड *n.* इमारतीलांकूड *n.* सुतारकामाचें-सुतारकामी लांकूड *n.*

A pile of timbers, as prepared for building. औट *m.*

A t.-carrier. A t.-hauler. वाहतूक *m.*

Small squared piece of t. गजी *f.*

Squared piece of t. तुळई *f.* तुळवट *n.*

That is common (not teak)-t. बिजायली, रायबळ.

2 (of a house) *wood work.* लांकूडn. लांकडेंn. *pl.* लांकडीकामn.

TIMBREL. See TABOR, TAMBORINE.

TIME, *n. duration*; or, as personified, TIME. काल *or* ळ *m.* समय *m.* वेला *f. pop.* वेळ *f. m.* काळसर्प *m.* दिवस *m. pl* उच्चदेवता *f.*

By the hand (through the influence, &c.) of T. कालपरत्वें *or* परत्वेंकरून, कालवशात् *or* वशें. [*n.*

Doings (the marvellous achievements) of T. कालचरित्र

In the course of t. In t. कालगत्या, काळेंकरून, कालगतीनें, कालपरंपरेनें. [*f.*

Instrument for measuring t. कालसाधन*n.* घटीयंत्र*n.* घडी

Lapse or course of t. Revolutions of t. कालगति *f.* कालचक्र *n.* काळरहाटी *f.* [लमान *n.*

Measurement or ascertainment of t. कालसाधन*n.* का-

Spirit of the t. काळधात *f.* कालधर्म *m.* कालमहिमा *m.*

Sway or power or virtue of t. काळधात *f.* कालधर्म *m.* कालमाहात्म्य*n.* कालमहिमा*m.* कालदशा *f.* कालसत्ता *f.* वर्षधात *f.*

To kill, spend, &c. t. v. To PASS. काळ *m.*-काळाचे दिवस *m. pl.* काढणें-लोटणें-ढकलणें, कालपराभव *m.*-&c. करणें.

To spend t. rightly. सत्कालक्षेप *m.*-&c. करणें.

To pass pleasantly—t. करमणें.

2 *portion of duration, space of time.* वेळ *m. f.* काळ *m.* समय *m.* मुद्दत *f.* वायदा*m.* वक्त *or* वखूत *m.* पल्ला*m.* ठेप *f.* अवधि *m. f.* कालमर्यादा *f.*

At the present t. सद्य: *pop.* सद्यां, सद्ध्यां.

For or during a long t. वाढवेळ *or* वाढोळ, वाढवेळां, वाटकोळ.

For such (for so long) a t. तितकाकाळ-वेळ, तावत्काल.

Former t. पूर्वकाल *m.*

From t. immemorial. काळोकाळ *or* काळ:काळ.

Given or specific t. निमित्तकाल *m.*

In former t. v. FORMERLY. पूर्वी, मागल्या काळीं.

Nick of t. ऐनवेळ *f.*

Of former t. v. FORMER. पूर्वीचा, पूर्वील, मागल्याकाळचा.

Of t. immemorial, of olden t. कदाकाळांचा *or* कदाकाळींच्या, काळोकाळचा, केव्हांचा, कधींचा.

To come in the nick of t. प्रसंगास येणें.

Some t. back, *awhile ago.* मघां, मघांशीं.

The three times (the past, present, and future). कालत्रय *n.*—In the three t. त्रिकाल *or* ळ *n.*—Of or belonging to the three t. त्रैकालिक.

Throughout or durimg a t. सर्वकाल *or* ळ.

T. past. गतकाल *or* ळ *m.*

Times are changed. दिवस मागें पाहतात.

Up to that t. तितपर्यंत, तितपावेतों, तावत्काल.

To take one's t. about. सावकाशीवर घेणें, वार *m.* लावणें.

3 v. SEASON. प्रसंग *m.* घात *f.* टच *n.* डाव *m.* मन्वंतर *n.* मनु *m.* लाभवेळा *f.* [गुदर.

An adverse t. *calamitous occasion.* प्रसंग *m. v.* पड, ये,

In good t. सकळ, सकळवेळीं, वेळेवारीं.

That is in good t. वेळेवारचा.

Unseasonable t. अवेळ *f.* आडवेळ *f.* अकाल *m.* अनवसर *m.* गेरहंगाम *m.*

To consider time and season. वेळअवेळ *f. or* अवेळसवेळ *f.* पाहणें, काळवेळ *f. or* काळप्रसंग *m.* पाहणें.

To hit the favourable or fit t. काळ *m.* साधणें.

4 *particular time.* वेळ *m. f.* वेळा *f.* समय *m.* वक्त *or* वखूत *m. n.* पडण *f.* समयविशेष *m.* प्रसंगविशेष *m.*

About this t. एव्हां एव्हां.

According to the t. समयानुसार, वेळेनसार.

At some t. or other. कधींतरी, कदाचित्.

At the three times (of the day). तिवेळां, तिवेळीं.

At times, sometimes, &c. कधींकधीं, कधींबधीं, कधींमधीं, केव्हांकेव्हां, केव्हांबेव्हां.

Auspicious t. सुवेळ *f.* सन्मुख काल *m.*

Dark and troublous t. कलिकाल *m.*

Favorableness of t. कालानुकूल्य *n.*

Hard times. कडूकाळ *m.*

Inauspicious or unlucky t. काळवेळा *or* ळा *f.* दुश्वेळा *f.* नाशवेळ *f.* विमुखकाल *m.*

5 *a* t. *one* t. with reference to repetition. बेळ *f.* & बेळा *f.* (with a numeral &c. prefix, as एकवेळ, दोनवेळ, बहुवेळ) वेळां (used *adv.* with a numeral &c. prefix, as Once एकवेळां, Twice दोनवेळां Often times बहुवेळां) दा *or* दां (in comp. with a numeral &c. prefix, as एकदां, दोनदां, बहुदां, अनेकदां, कितीदां &c.) बार (in comp. as एकबार, द्विबार, त्रिबार, बहुवार, अनेकवार, *or* दोनवार, तीनवार, &c.) खेप *f.* बारी *f.* पाऊठ *f.* [कधींकाळीं.

At some few and distant times. कदांकाळीं *or* कदानकाळीं,

From t. to t. वेळोवेळां.

Oft times. बहुतवेळ, अनेकवार, वारंवार.

6 v. LEISURE. वेळ *f.* फुरसत *f.*

To have t. फावणें *impers.*

7 *this world, the present life.* इहलोक *m.* इहलोकवास *m.* ह्याजन्म *m.* इहजन्म *n. m.*

8 *time yet wanting, time until.* उशीर *m.* अवकाश *m.*

9—in music. ताल *or* ळ *m.* गति *pop.* गत *f.*

Beating t. ताल *or* ळ *m.* टाळ *m.*

Equal t. in music, dancing, &c. लय *m.*

In t. and tune. तालसुरीं.

Mean or common t. मध्य *n.* घन *n.*

Quick t. द्रुत *n.* ओघ *m.*

Slow t. ठाय *f.* विलंबितवृत्ति *f.* तत्व *n.*

That is out of t. बेताल *or* ळ.

To beat t. with a song, &c. ताल *m.* धरणें.

10—in grammar. काल *m.*

To TIME, *v. a. adapt to the time, perform at the proper season.* वेळीं-वेळेस-वेळावर-प्रसंगास-काळपाहून-काळाप्रमाणें-यथाकाल-कालानुसार-&c. करणें, काळ*m.*-समय*m.*-वेळ *m.*-काळअकाळ *m.*-वेळअवेळ *m. f.*-&c. पाहणें. [धरणें-&c.

2 *regulate as to time.* काळ *m.*-वेळ *m.*-&c. सांगणें-नेमणें-बां-

TIME-KEEPER, TIME-PIECE, *n. watch, clock, &c.* घड्याळ *n.* कालयंत्र *n.* कालमान *n.* घटीयंत्र *n.*

TIME-SERVER, *n.* TIME-SERVING, *a.*v. TEMPORIZER. काळपाहून चालणारा-वर्त्तणारा, रंग पाहून चालणारा, दुरोखी, कालानुसारी, समयानुसारी.

TIME-SERVING, *n. obsequious compliance with the humour of the times.* काळपाहून चालणें *n.* रंग पाहून चालणें *n.* समयानुसरण *n.* समयानुरोध *m.* समयानुवर्त्तन *n.*

TIMELINESS, *n.* v. A. वक्तशीरपणा *m.* समयोचित्य *n.* कालिकत्व*n.*

TIMELY, *a.* v. SEASONABLE. वेळेवरचा, वेळींचा, समयोचित, वक्तशीर, कालिक, कालीन. [वेळेस, समयास.

TIMELY, TIMEOUSLY, *adv.* v. A. *and* SEASONABLY. वेळेवारीं,

TIMID, TIMOROUS, *a.* v. FEARFUL. भितरा, भ्याड, भयशील, भीरु, बुजरा, बुजीर, बुजट, असाहसिक, कातर, दीनचेतन.

TIMIDLY, TIMOROUSLY, *adv.* v. A. भितरेपणानें, &c. साहसाभावपूर्वक.

TIMIDITY, TIMIDNESS, TIMOROUSNESS, *n.* v. A. भितरेपणा*m.* भ्याडपणा *m.* बुजरेपणा *m.* &c. भयशीलता *f.* भीरुता *f.* असाहस *n.* साहसाभाव *m.* कातर्य *n.*

TIN, *n.*—the metal. कथील *n.* कल्हई *f.* वंग *n.* रंग *n.* त्रपु *n.*

Calx of t. वंगभस्म *n.*

Tin-plate covered over with some coloring substance. बेगड *f. n.*

2 *wash of tin given to culinary utensils.* कल्हई *f.*

TIN, *a. made, &c. of tin.* कथली, कथलाचा.

To TIN, *v. a.* कल्हई *f.* करणें-लावणें-काढणें.

TIN-FOIL, *n.* कथलाचा वरख *m.*

TINCAL, *n. brute borax.* टांकणखार *m.*

TINCTURE, *n. slight taste, color, or quality superadded.* छटा *m. f.* वास *m.* गंध *m.* स्वाद*m.* धुनक *f.* चुणूक*f.* लजत *f.* लकीर*f.* लकेरी *f.* रंग *m.* ध्वनि *m.* नोक *f.*

2 v. EXTRACT. अर्क *m.* निष्कर्ष *m.*

To TINCTURE, *v. a.* v. To TINGE. छटा *f.*-धुनक *f.*-चुणूक *f.*-लजत *f.*-लकेरी *f.*-लकीर *f.*-&c. आणणें.

TINCTURED, *p.* v. V. छटा आणलेला, &c. छटेचा, लकेरीचा, छायेचा, &c. all in comp.

TINDAL, *n.*—of a boat, of lascars, &c. तांडेल.

TINDER, *n.*—for kindling a light. पेटवण *n.* चेतवण *n.* कप *or* कफ *m.* गूल *m. f.*

TINDER-BOX, *n.* चकमक *f.* चकमकीची पेटी *f.* चकमकीचें तोसदान*n.*

TINGE, *n.*v. TINCTURE. छटा*m. f.* धुनक *f.* चुणूक *f.* लजत *f.* छाया *f.*

To TINGE, *v. a. imbue, &c. with something foreign.* छटा *f.m.*-लजत *f.*-धुनक *f.*-चुणूक *f.*-लकेरी *f.*-लकीर *f.*-&c. आणणें-देणें-दाखवणें, युक्त-&c. करणें.

TINGED, *p.* v. V. छटा आणलेला, छटेचा, छायेचा, स्वादाचा, लकेरीचा, &c. छटा-&c. मारणारा.

To be t. with. छटा *f. m.*-धुनक *f.*-छाया *f.*-&c. मारणें *in. con. with g. of o.*

To TINGLE, *v. n.*—the ears, hand, &c. भणभणणें *intens.* भणाणणें, झणझणणें *intens.* झणाणणें, सणसणणें, भिरभिरणें, झणझणी *f.*-भिरभिरी *f.*-&c. येणें *in.con.*

To make to t. भणभणवणें.

2—limbs &c. as after a sting or burn. चुरचुरणें, फुणफुणणें, चुणचुणणें, सळकणें, फणफण *f.*-चुरचूर *f.*-चुणचूण *f.*-सळका*m.*-&c. सुटणें *in. con.*

3—a limb asleep. विरविरणें, रवरवणें, मुंग्या *f. pl.* येणें-चढणें *in. con.* विरवीर *f.*-रवरव *f.*-&c. येणें-सुटणें *in. con.*

4 *have a dull, creeping sensation.* सुरसुरणें, सुळसुळणें.

TINGLING, *n.* v. V. 1.—the sensation. झणझण *f.* झणझणी *f.* भणभण *f.* सणसण *f.* भिरभिरी *f.*—*intens.* झणझणाट*m.* झणाण*m.* सणसणाट*m.*

2 चुरचूर *f. intens.* चुरचुराट*m.* चुणचूण *f. intens.* चुणचुणाट*m.* फणफण*or*फुणफूण*f. intens.* फणफणाट *or* फुणफुणाट*m.* सळका*m.*

3 रवरव *f.* रवरवी *f.* विरवीर *f.* विरविरी *f.* मुंग्या *f.pl.* झुळझुळ*f.*

4 सुरसूर *or* सुरसुरी *f.* सुरमी *f.* सुळसूळ *f. intens.* सुळसुळाट*m.*

TINGLING, *p. a.* v. V. 1. भणभणणारा, &c. भणभणलेला, &c. भिरभिरी आलेला, &c.

2 फणफणणारा, &c. फणफणलेला, &c. फणफणसुटलेला, &c.

3 मुंग्या आलेला, विरवीर आलेला, &c.

TINKER, *n. mender of pots and pans.* जुनीं भांडीं नीट करणारा, मोडीचा तांबट.

To TINKLE, *v. n. make quick, sharp sounds, clink, jingle.*

किणकिणणें, खिणखिणणें, छणछणणें, खणखणणें, घणघणणें, किणकिण-खिणखिण-खणखण-छणछण-छुमछुम-&c. वाजणें.

2—toe ornaments, &c. रुणझुणणें, छणछणणें, *intens.* छणाणणें, झुणझुणणें, झुणझुणवाजणें, रुणझूण *f.*-&c. होणें-वाजणें *g. of s.* झुमझुमवाजणें.

TINKLE, TINKLING, *n.* v. V. 1. किणकिणणें*n.* खिणखिणणें*n.* &c. किणकीण *f.* खिणखीण *f.* छणछण *f.* खणखण *f.* घणघण *f.* —*intens.* खणखणाट*m.* घणघणाट*m.* छणछणाट*m.*

2 रुणझूण *f.* झमझम *f.* छमाछमी *f.*—*intens.* छणछणाट*m.* छमछमाट*m.*

TINKLE, *n.* TINKLING, *p. a.* v. V. 1. किणकिणणारा, खिणखिणणारा, &c. किणकिण वाजणारा, &c.

I. *tinkling ornament.* किंकिणी *f.*

TINKLINGLY, *adv.* v. V. 1. किणकिण *or* णां, खिणखिण *or* णां, घणघण *or* णां, छणछण *or* णां, झुणझुण *or* णां.

TINNER, TIN-MAN, *n.* v. V. कल्हई करणारा-लावणारा-काढणारा, कल्हईगर *or* कर, कल्हईवाला.

TINNING, *n.* v. V.—*act.* कल्हई करणें*n.* &c. कल्हई *f.*

TINSEL, *n. that which causes false lustre.* खोटा कलाबतू*m.* तुई *or* तोई *f.* डांकपट्टी *f.*

2 fig. बेगडी वस्त *f.* बेगडी डागिणा*m.*

TINSEL, *a. tawdry.* कल्हईचा, बेगडी, तुईचा, डांकपट्टीचा.

TINT, *n.* v. COLOR. रंग*m.* वर्ण*m.*

2 See TINCTURE.

To TINT. See To TINGE, To COLOR.

TINY, *a. small and neat,* v. LITTLE. चिमणा, चिमणसा, चिमका, चिमकुला, चिणकुला, चुटकुला *or* चिटकुला, बुचकुला, पिटकुला *or* पिटकोला *or* पिटुकला, माकुला *or* माणकुला, माटकुला, चिणारा, चिनाटी, चिनुर्ला.

TIP, *n.* v. POINT, END. अणी *f.* अणकुची *f.* टोंक*n.* बोंडी *f. dim.* बोंडूक*n.* शेंडा*m.* अग्र*n.* अघरडा *or* अगरडा*m.*

To TIP, *v. a. strike lightly.* टिचणें, टिपणें, टिचकन-टिचकर-&c. [मारणें.

2 *cover the tip or end.* अणीवर-टोंकावर-शेंड्यावर-अग्रावर-&c. लावणें-घालणें-चढवणें.

To t. the wink. डोळा *m.* घालणें.

To TIP OVER, *v. n.* लुडकणें *or* लुडगणें.

TIPCAT, *n.*—the game. इटीदांडू *or* इटूदांडू *m.*—Bat, दांडू—Hole dug, कोईल *f.* कोली *f.*—Stick used in playing, इटी *f.*

TIPPED, *p.* v. V. 2. अणीवर-शेंड्यावर-&c. लावलेला (*with the noun required,* as अणीवर सोनें लावलेली काठी *f.*), शेंड्याचा-शिखराचा-&c. (*with the noun required,* as बर्फाच्या शिखराचा डोंगर, &c.)

To TIPPLE, *v. n. drink habitually.* पिणें, दारूबाजी *f.*-निशाबाजी *f.*-झिंगेपणा *m.*-छाकटेपणा *m.*-पानाचा तडाखा *m.*-&c. करणें-मांडणें, पानव्यसन *n.* करणें.

TIPPLER, *n.* TIPPLING, *p. a.* v. V. *and* SOT. झिंगा *or* ग्या, दारूबाज, निशाबाज, छाकटा, पानव्यसनी.

TIPPLING, *n.* v. V.—*act.* दारूबाजी *f.* निशाबाजी*f.* निशाखोरी *f.* झिंगेपणा *m.* छाकटेपणा *m.* पानाचा तडाखा *m.* पानव्यसन *n.*

TIPPLING-HOUSE. See TAVERN.

TIPSY, *a.* v. DRUNK. झिंगलेला, मस्त.

TIPTOE, *n.* पायाच्या बोटाचा शेंडा *m.*

To stand on t. खुंटबावली *f.* करणें, खुंटबावलीवर उभा राहणें.

TIPTOP, *n. very highest part.* शेंड्याचाशेंडा *m.* शेवटचाशेवट *m.* अग्राचेंअग्र *n.*

T. of a tree. तिटाळी *f.*

2 fig. v. HEIGHT. कळस *m.* सीमा *f.* पराकाष्ठा *f.*

TIRADE, *n. strain* (*of abuse, declamation &c.*) शिव्याची-निंदेची-बोलण्याची-&c. तान *f.* v. घे, झाड, ताण *m.*

TIRE, *n. iron band of a wheel.* धांव *f.* धो *f.*

2 See TIARA. 3 See ATTIRE.

To TIRE, *v. a. make weary, fatigue.* श्रमवणें, भागवणें, शिणवणें, थकवणें, दमवणें, टणकवणें, बेंगवणें, कंकातणें, टणक *m.*-शीण *m.*-भागवटा *m.*-थकलेपणा *m.*-&c. आणणें-देणें, श्रमी- कष्टी-&c. करणें—as enhanced, and as answering to, *to jade, exhaust, knock up, &c.* हाडें *n. pl.* घुसळणें, खोमलणें, घुसळणें, पादवणें, मरगळीस-मरळीस-हायास-मट्ट्यास-&c. आणणें, चकाचूर-बेजार-बेदम-&c. करणें, टांके *m. pl.* ढिले करणें *g. of o.* चुरा *m.*-चुराडा *m.*-आटाआट *f.*- आटापिटा *m.*- आटापीट *f.*-खुरदमा *m.*-&c. करणें *g. of o.* नाकीं नऊ आणणें, भूस *n.*-भुसकट *n.*-बूर *m.*-&c. पाडणें *g. of o.* मरोमरोसा-&c. करणें.

To TIRE, *v. n. become weary, be fatigued.* थकणें, श्रमणें, दमणें, शिणणें, भागणें, कष्टणें, कदरणें, श्रम *m.*-शीण *m.*-भागवटा *m.*-&c. येणें *in. con.*—intens. out; utterly; *be worn out, be exhausted, knocked up, &c.* v. EXHAUSTED. बेंगणें *or* बेंघणें, डेंगणें, रेंगणें, काचणें, काचावणें, सुश्रांतणें.

2 v. To LOATHE. मन *n.* उठणें *g. of s.* कंटाळा *m.*-किळस *m. f.*-&c. येणें *in. con.* तागादणें, उबगणें, कंटाळणें.

TIRED, *p.* v. V. A. *and* EXHAUSTED. श्रमवलेला, भागवलेला, दमवलेला.

v. V. N. 1. *and* EXHAUSTED. दमलेला, थकलेला, शिणलेला, श्रमलेला, &c. काहीर, श्रमी, श्रांत, सुश्रांत, परिश्रांत.

2 मन उठलेला, कंटाळा आलेला, &c. बेजार, बेदम, जिक्क, जिगजीग, दिक्क, त्रस्त.

TIREDNESS, *n.* v. P. 1. *and* FATIGUE. दमलेलेपणा *pop.* दमलेपणा *m.* शिणलेलेपणा *pop.* शिणलेपणा *m.* भागवटा *m.* शीण *m.* श्रांति *f.* परिश्रांति *f.*

TIRESOME, *a. wearisome, exhausting the strength.* दमवणारा, श्रमवणारा, शिणवणारा, &c. श्रमाचा, भागवट्याचा, कष्टाचा, &c. भागवटा आणणारा, &c. श्रांतिकर-कारक-जनक-प्रद-&c. श्रमकर-कारक-जनक-&c. आयासजनक, कष्टप्रद-जनक-&c.

2 *teasing, vexatious, exhausting the patience.* कंटाळा आणण्याजोगा-सारखा, बेजार-जिक्क-दिक्क-&c. करणारा, कंटाळा-&c. आणणारा, किचर, किचरट, किचकट, किजट, कुचर, खचरट, खडतर, खष्ट, खिस्तीचा, ज्किीर, जिकिरीचा, जीवघेणा *or* ण्या, प्राणघेणा *or* ण्या, त्रासक, क्लिष्ट, त्रासदायक, त्रासजनक, त्रासकारी, त्रासप्रद, त्रासकर.

TIRESOMENESS, *n.* v. N. दमवणारेपणा *m.* &c. श्रम *m.* कष्ट *m.* श्रांतिकारकत्व *n.* श्रांतिजनकत्व *n.* श्रमकारकत्व *n.*

2 खचरटपणा *m.* किचरपणा *m.* कुचरपणा *m.* जीवघेणेपणा *m.* &c. त्रासकत्व *n.* त्रासदायकत्व *n.*

TIRING-ROOM, *n.*—of a theatre. नेपथ्य *n.*

TISSUE, *n.* v. BROCADE. जर *m. f.* जरीकापड *n.* तमामी *f.*

2 (of falsehoods, &c.) ग्रंथ *m.* जाळें *n.* सुताडें *n.* रचना *f.*

TIT, *n. small-horse.* तट्टू *m. n.*

2 See WOMAN.

TIT FOR TAT. टापासटीप, अदल्यास बदल, सदलबदल, फिटासफीट.
TITAN, *n.*—in mythology. दैत्य, दानव, राक्षस.
TITBIT. See TIDBIT. [पट्टी *f.*
TITHE, *n. tenth part.* दहावा हिस्सा *m.*-वांटा *m.* दहक *m.* दहक-
To TITHE, *v. a.* दहावा हिस्सा *m.*-&c. घेणें-देणें.
To TITILLATE, TITILLATION. See To TICKLE, &c. [व *n.*
TITLE, *n. heading.* सदर *n.* प्रकरणाचें-आसनाचें-स्नात्याचें-&c.नां-
2 *inscription bearing the name of.* नांवाची चिट्ठी *f.* नांवाचा लेख *m.* सरनामा *m.* नामलेख *m.* नामपत्रक *n.* शिरोनाम *n.*
3 *appellation of honor.* प्रतिष्ठानाम *n.* किताब *m.* किताबत *f.* अलकाब *m.* मरातब *m.f.*
4 v. NAME. नांव *n.* नाम *n.* उपाधि *m.f.* आख्या *f.*
5 *claim* v. RIGHT. दावा *m.* हक्क *m.* अधिकार *m.* इलाखा *m.*
TITLE-DEED, *n.* कबाला *or* कवाला *m.* आगम *m.*
T. granted by the emperor of Hindustán. महजर *m.* महजरनामा *m.*
TITLE-PAGE, *n.* ग्रंथाच्या नांवाचें पृष्ठ *n.* ग्रंथनामपृष्ठ *n.* मुखपत्र *n.*
To TITTER, *v. n.* v. To GIGGLE. खिदखिद-खिसखिस-&c. हसणें.
TITTERING, *n.* v. V. बारीक हसणें *n.* बारीक हसें *n.*
TITTLE, *n. whit, jot,* v. BIT. लेश *m.* बिंदु *m.* अणु *m.* रजःकण*m.*
TITTLE-TATTLE, *n. idle talk,* v. PRATE. बकबक *f.* बकवाद *m.* गप्प *f.*
TITULAR, *a. existing in name only.* नांवाचा, नामाचा, नामधारी.
To *prep.* or *adv.*—as the sign of the dative case; noting accession, &c. स, ला, जवळ, पाशीं, कारणें, कडे (as ज्याचें त्याजकडे दे) प्रत, शीं, लागीं.
2—as *opposed* to from; noting motion toward, nearness to. कडे, जवळ, प्रत, स, ला.
3—according to, noting adaption, &c. सारखा *decl.* जोगा *or* जोगता *decl.* प्रमाणें.
4—noting extent, degree, &c. तों, तोंवर, पावेतों, पर्यंत, सर (as मरेसर *To* death.).
5—noting extension, &c. साठीं, करितां, स, ला.
6—noting comparison. पेक्षां, हून.
7—noting appertainment. चा, कडे (as शिपायानें तरवार मारावी पण यश धन्याकडे).
8—as a sign of a verb, noting object, consequence, &c. स, ला, आयास, आयाला, करितां, साठीं.
Note. Many of the meanings of "to" are inherent in the inflections of a Maráthí noun, as hand *to* hand हातास हात, face *to* face तोंडास तोंड, *to* the number of सुमारें, sweet *to* the taste, जिभेस गोड, &c. &c.
As to. विषयीं, संबंधीं, बाबत.
To and fro. इकडे तिकडे, मारेमार, मारेमारे.
To a man. See ALL.
To one's face. तोंडावर, रूबरू, समक्ष.
TOAD, *n.* चामडें डेरक *n.* चामरडेल *f. n.*
TOAD-EATER, TOADY. See FLATTERER, PARASITE.
TOAD-STOOL, *n. mushroom.* कुत्र्याचें मूत *n.* कुत्र्याचें छत्र *n.* अळंबें *or* में *n.* घोड्याचें मूत *n.* [जप *n.* करणें.
To TOAST, *v. a. dry and scorch.* भाजणें, भुजणें, भाजण *n.*-भा-
2 *drink to the health of.* अमक्याचें नांव घेऊन त्याचें आरोग्य असो असें म्हणून कांहीं पिणें.
TOAST, *n.* भाजलेलीरोटी *f.*
TOASTED, *p.* v. V. भाजलेला, भाजका, भाजीव.
TOBACCO, *n.*—the plant. तंबाखू *or* तमाखू *m. f.*—in covert or cant phraseol. पत्रिका *f.* गुरुप्रसाद *m.*
Preparation of t. (with sugar &c.) for smoking. गुडाकू *or* खू *f.*
T. leaf (green). पत्ता *m.*
T. prepared for chewing. जरदा *m.*
T. roll (to be smoked). चुट्टा *m.*
T. roll (to be chewed). विडी *f.* [*f.*
T. rolled up in a leaf to be smoked. विडी*dim.* विडफुली
TOBACCO-PIPE, *n.* चुट्टा *m.*
TOBACCONIST, *n. dealer in tobacco.* तंबाखूविक्या, तंबाखूवाला.
TOCSIN. See ALARM-BELL.
TO-DAY, *adv.* आज, आजच्या दिवसीं-दिवसास.
To TODDLE, *walk with short steps,*—a child. लुटुलुटु-आखूड पावलांनीं-&c. चालणें.
TODDY, *n.*—the liquor, (of the Cocoanut). माडी *f.* नारिकेरासव *m.*—(of the Date). सिंधी *f.*—(of the Palmyra).ताडी*f.*
T.-tippler. माडपीर.
Vessel to receive the t. कुंडा *m.*
Toddy-extracter, Toddy-man, &c. ताड्या. [गुलि *f.*
TOE, *n.* पायाची अंगुळी *or* अंगळी *or* अंगोळी *f.* पायाचें बोट*n.* पदां-
Great t. पायाचा अंगठा *or* अंगोठा *m.* पदांगुष्ठ *m.*
Little t. पायाची अंगठी *f.* करंगळी *f.* करंगुळी *f.*
Six-toed. सांगळ्या.
Space between the toes. गेचक *n.* गेचकळ *n.*
TOE-RING, *n.* जोडवें *n.* अंगटी *f.*
TOGETHER, *adv. in company, concert, combination.* मिळून, एकवट, बराबर *or* बरोबर, एकत्र, युगपत्, एकंदर, एकतंत्र.
All t. *all in a body or at once.* एकमेळणी, एकमेळीं, एकामीं *or* में, तंत्रानें.
2 *in one heap, sum, mass, &c.* एकवट, एकत्र, एकंदर.
To tie, fasten, &c. t. एकेठिकाणीं-&c. बांधणें [कत्र.
3 *in the same place.* एकेठिकाणीं-स्थळीं-जागीं-स्थानीं-&c. ए-
4 *at the same time.* बराबर, एकेवेळेस, एकदम, एकतंत्र.
T. with, v. WITH. संगें *or* संगीं, संगतीं *or* तें, बराबर *or* बरोबर, समागमें, सहवर्त्तमान, सुद्धां.
TOGGEL, *n. peg or nail tapering towards both ends.* तूर *f.* सुरसा *m.* तुरई *f.* वाघी *f.*
To TOIL, *v. n. labor hard.* खपणें, कटणें, मशागत *f.*-कसालत *f.*-कसाला *m.*-श्रम *m.*-कष्ट *m.*-मेहनत *f.*-&c. करणें-घेणें, आयास*m.*-परिश्रम *m.*-अट्टहास *m.*-&c. करणें, दंड *m.* काढणें, वणवण *f.* करणें, खडणें, तांगडणें. This sense is expressed by numerous striking phrases, bearing of course varying implication, and thus agreeing with, *To fag, druge, moil, slave, work one's self to death, &c. &c.* कवाडकष्ट *m. pl.*-महार कष्ट *m. pl.*-कुत्तेघशी *f.* करणें, हाडें *n. pl.* झिजवणें, हाडांचीं काडें *n. pl.*-हाडांचे मणी *m. pl.* करणें, रक्ताचें पाणी *n.* करणें, जीव *m.* अटणें -पांखडणें, जीव *m.* अर्धा करणें, आंगाचें पाणी *n.* करणें, अंतडीं *n. pl.* गळ्यास येणें *g. of o.* अदवणें, अदव *m.* सोसणें-पावणें, अटाअट *m. f.*-अटाघाट *f.*-वाटाघाट *f.*-अटापिटा *m.*-अटापीट *f.*-अटापिटी *f.*-&c. करणें.

TOIL, TOILING, *n.* v. V. *and* LABOR. मेहनत *f.* श्रम *m. or m. pl.* कष्ट *m. or m. pl.* परिश्रम *m.* खप *m.* मशागत *f.* कसालत *f.* कसाला *m.* कबाडकष्ट *m. pl.* महारकष्ट *m. pl.* कुत्तेघशी *f.* आयास *m.* सायास *m.* प्रयास *m.* अट्टाहास *m.* अटाआट *m.* अटाघाट *f.* अटापिटा *m.* अटापिटी *f.* अटापीट *f.* बाटाघाट *f.* कडाकूट *f.* कपाळकूट *f.* माथाकूट *f.* कपाळफोड *f.* माथेफोड *f.* डोईफोड *f.* उरस्फोड *f.* उपद्व्याप *m.* खटपट *f.* दगदग *f.* खवदव *f.* धकाधक *f.* यातायात *f.* वणवण *f.* खस्ता *f. pl.*

Great toil and little work. सारीरात्र जागणें शेंगावांगीं [रांधणें.

Toil and trouble, fuss and pother. झट्टेपट्टे *or* झटेपटे*m. pl.* *v.* घे, खा, उलेंढालें *n.*

2 See SNARE.

TOILET, *n. dressing table.* वस्त्रें नेसण्याचा-घालण्याचा-लेण्याचा-पेहरण्याचा-&c. चवरंग *m.*

The business of the t.—of men. टिळाटोपी *f.* टिळेपट्टे*m. pl.* टिळेमिळे *m. pl.* चट्टेपट्टे *m. pl.*—of women, चट्टीपट्टी *f.* टाकमटिका *m.* टाकमटिकला *m.* टाकमटिळा*m.* टाकमटीक*m.* टिकलीमिकली *f.* वेणीफणी *f.* काजळकुंकूं *n.* टिकलेभांगले *m. pl.* चांगभांग *m.* भांगटिळा *m.* भांगपट्टी *f.* चिरीपट्टी *f.* चोळीबांगडी *f.*

TOILSOME, *a.* v. LABORIOUS. कष्टाचा, श्रमाचा, महारकष्टाचा, कष्टसाध्य, श्रमसाध्य. [ध्यता *f.*

TOILSOMENESS, *n.* v. A. कष्ट *m.* श्रम *m.* कष्टसाध्यता *f.* श्रमसा-

TOKEN, *sign, evidence,* v. MARK. खूण *f.* चिन्ह *n.* लक्षण *n.* साक्षा *f.* दाखला*m.* व्यंजन *n.* संकेत*m.* अभिज्ञान *n.* छाया *f.*

2 v. MEMORIAL. ओळख *f.* ओळखण *f.* यादगारी *f.*

TOLA, *n.*—the Indian weight. तोळा *m.*

TOLD, *p.* v. V. सांगितलेला, &c. निरूपित, कथित, विदित, उक्त, ज्ञापित, ज्ञपित, ज्ञप्त.

To TOLE, *v. a. draw on by a bait,* v. To ALLURE. आशा *f.*-लोभ*m.*-&c.-दाखवून आणणें-दाखवून नेणें.

TOLERABLE, *a. supportable, &c.* सोसाया-साहाया-&c. जोगा-सारखा-&c. सहनीय, सह्य.

2 *moderately good,* v. MIDDLING, PASSABLE. बरा, बराबाईट, माफक, चालीवजा, कामचलाऊ, चालायाजोगा-सारखा.

TOLERABLENESS, *n.* v. A. 1. सोसायाजोगेपणा *m.* &c. सहनीयता *f.* सह्यता *f.* &c.

TOLERABLY, *adv.* v. A. 2. बरा, बराच, चालायाजोगा *decl.* &c.

TOLERANT, *a.* TOLERATER, *n.* TOLERATING, *p. a.* v. V. परवानगी देणारा, नको न म्हणणारा, अडथळा न करणारा, &c. अनिषेध-&c. कर्त्ता-कारी.

To TOLERATE, *v. a. not forbid; allow, suffer,* v. To PERMIT. परवानगी *f.*-मोकळीक *f.*-&c. देणें, देणें—used with another verb as जाऊं देणें, करूं देणें, &c. नको न म्हणणें, अडथळा *m.*-आडकाठी *f.*-मनाई *f.*-&c. न करणें, अनिषेध*m.*-&c.असणें *g. of o.*

TOLERATED, *p.* v. V. परवानगी दिल्हेला, &c. अनिषिद्ध, अप्रतिबद्ध.

TOLERATION, TOLERANCE, *n.* v. V.—*act.* परवानगी देणें *n.*&c. अनिषेध *m.* अप्रतिबंध *m.*

TOLL, *n.* v. TAX. कर *m.* जकात *f.* रहदारी *f.* सायर *n.*

2 *portion exacted for permission of the rest.* हक्क *m.* दस्तुरी *f.* फसकी *f.* शेव *f.* बाब *f.* कानू *f.* [लंबितनाद*m.*

3 (of a bell). सावकाशीचा नाद *m.* राहून राहून नाद*m.* वि-

To TOLL, *v. n.*—a bell. राहून राहून-दमादमानें-&c. वाजणें.

To TOLL, *v. a.* (a bell). राहून राहून-दमादमानें-&c. वाजवणें.

TOLL-BOOTH, TOLL-HOUSE, TOLSEY, *n. place of receipt of toll.* नाका *m.* नाकें *n.* सायर*n.*

TOLL-GATHERER, *n.* नाकेदार, जकातदार, जकात्या. [गी *f.*

TOMATO, *n. solanum lycopersicum.* विलायती वांगी *f.* तांबडी वां-

TOMB, *n. grave.* मेल्या माणसाची-प्रेताची-&c. गार *f.*-खांच *f.*-&c. प्रेताचा खाडा *m.* प्रेतकुंड *n.* शवगर्त्ता *f.*

2 *erection over a grave.* धडगें*n.* थडें*n.* छत्री *f.* कबर *f.* माठें*n.*

T. of a Sanyásí. समाधि*m. f.* समाधिगृह*n.*

TOMBOY, *n.* v. ROMP. घोडी *f.* घोडगी *f.* भोंपळदेवता *f.*

TOMB-STONE, *n.* See TOMB, 2.

TOMORROW, *adv.* उद्यां, उदईक.

TOMTOM, *n.*—the Indian drum, v. DRUM. टिमकी *f.*

TON, *n. fashion, mode.* सभ्यसंप्रदाय*m.* शिष्टसंप्रदाय*m.*

TONE, *n. note, accent, &c.* v. SOUND. स्वर*m.* नाद*m.* ध्वनि*m.* आवाज*m.* सबन *f. n.*

A musical or good t. सुस्वर*m.*

Of a good t. सुस्वर.

2 *affected or peculiar sound in reading, &c.* स्वर*m.*

3—in music; *seventh part* of the scale. मूर्च्छना *f.*

Half or quarter t. स्वरांश*m.*

Quarter t. श्रुति *f.*

4—in medicine. बरेपणा*m.* सुभावना *f.* सद्भावना *f.*

TONED, *a.* स्वराचा, स्वरयुक्त.

Full-t. घोस.

Ill-t. बदसूर, कुस्वर.

Well-t. सुस्वर, आवाजदार.

TONGS, *n.* (of goldsmiths, braziers, &c.). गावी *or* घावी *f.* सांडस*m. dim.* सांडशी *f.* चिमटा*m.*-निखारा*m.*-&c. धरण्याचा चिमटा*m.*

TONGUE, *n.*—the member. जिह्वा *pop.* जिव्हा *and* जीभ *f.* (*dim.* जिभली *f.*) रसना *f.* रसनेंद्रिय*n.*

Fur of the t. जिह्वामल*m.*

Of abusive or obscene t. तोंडाचा फटकळ-फटकूळ-शिनळ.

Paralysis of the t. जिव्हास्तंभवात*m.*

On the tip of the t. तोंडापुढें, तोंडासमोर, मुखीं, जिव्हाग्रीं.

Pustules on the t. &c. from heat. खरे*m. pl.*

Ready at the t. *known by heart.* मुखपाठ, मुखोद्गत.

Root of the t. जिव्हेचा कांदा*m.* जिह्वामूल*n.*

Slip of the t. *lapsus linguæ.* जिव्हादोष*m.* वाग्दोष*m.*

To have a slip of the t. जिव्हा वांकडी पडणें *g. of s.*

That is on the tip of the t. जिह्वारूढ.

Tip of the t. जिह्वाग्र*n.* कंठाग्र*n.*

To bite the t. (from rage or vexation) जिव्हा *f.* खाणें.

To bridle the t. तोंड*n.* अटोपणें-आवरणें-संभाळणें-बंदाबरराखणें. [*n.* दाबणें.

To hold the t. तोंडास खीळ *f.* घालणें, गुळणी *f.* धरणें, तोंड

"Hold your t." (shut up.) म्यान करा.

2 (of serpents, cats, birds, &c.). जिभली *f.*

3 (of flame or fire). आगिबळा*m.* आगिवळी *f.* आगीचीजीभ *f.*

4 (of a bell). लोळा*m. dim.* लोळी *f.*

5 (of a balance). कांटा*m.*

6 See SPEECH, 7 a *speech,* v. LANGUAGE. बोली *f.* भाषा *f.*

Mother t. जन्मभाषा *f.*
Vulgar t. लोकभाषा *f.*
8 (of land) भूशलाका *f.*

TONGUE-LESS, *a.* जिभेवेगळा-&c. निजिभ्या, अजिह्व.

TONGUE-SCRAPER, *n.* जिभी *f.* जिभळी *f.* पाटली *f.* [जिह्व.

TONGUE-TIED, *a.* lit. fig. बांधलेल्या जिभेचा, तोंडबांधलेला, बद्ध-

TONGUE-TIEDNESS, *n.* v. A. बांधलेली जीभ *f.* मुखस्तंभ *m.*

TONGUED, *a.* जिभेचा, जिव्हेचा, जिह्व.
Double t., forky t. द्विरसन.
Ready t. हाजीरं जबाबी *or* हाजीर जबाब.

TONIC, *a.*—in medicine. रुचक, रोचक, क्षुधाकर, तेजस्कर, अभिवर्द्धक, दीपक.

TONIC, *n.*—a medicine. दीपन *n.*

TO NIGHT, *adv.* आजरात्रीस, यारात्रीस.

TONNAGE, *n. burden of a ship.* दास्तान *n.*

TONSIL, *n.* दिव्यकळा *f. pl* अमृतकळा *f. pl.*
Enlargement of the tonsils. अधिमांसक *m.*

TONSURE, *n. shaving the head.* डोईकरणें *n.* &c. केशकाढणें *n.*
First t. of a child. जावळ *n.* चौल *m.*
The tuft or lock left at t. शेंडी *f.* शिखा *f.*

TOO, *adv. over much,* v. EXCESSIVELY. फार, फारच, अत्यंत. अति, अतीव.
2 *also.* ही, पण, देखील *or* देखीद, अणखी, बी.

TOOL, *n. instrument of manual operation.* विसंड *n.* शस्त्र *n.* अकत *n.* हत्यार *n.* साधन *n.*
Box or set of tools. गंज *m.*
Hinder or handle end of a t. बारंग *m.*
2 fig. *instrument of another's evil will; hireling, cat's paw, &c.* हातगुंडा *m.* हातससाणा *m.* ससाणा *m.* कुत्रा *m.*
A mere t. घोककाम्या, घोक्या.

TOOTH, *n.* दांत *m.* दंत *m.* द्विज *m.* दशन *n.*
Bed or socket of the teeth. हिरडी *f.* [दंतकाष्ठ *n.*
Fibrous &c. stick for cleaning the teeth. दांतवण *n.*
Gap in the teeth. दांतखिंड *f.* दांतरखिंड *f.* खांड *f. dim.* खांडोरें *n.* बोथरखिंड *f.* बोंथरखंडें *n.*
Having a sour t. अंबट्या.
Having teeth or t. projecting over the lip. दांतरा *or* न्या, दांताळ, दंताळ *or* ळ्या, दंतुर.
Irregular, uneven—tooth or tooth-row. खेबडा.
Maggots bred in carious teeth. खिरटे *m. pl.*
Newly cut t. (or t. coming in old age.) दांतरी *f.* दांतुरडी *f.*
Row of teeth. कवळी *or* दांतकवळी *f.* दंतावलि *f.* [का *f.*
Tartar of the teeth. बुरसी *f.* बुरसा *m.* दंतशर्करा *f.* पुष्पि-
Teeth,—collect. दांताळी *f.* बत्तिसी *f.*—in contempt, &c. दांताड *n.* दांताडी *f.* दांतुरडी *f. v.* पाड, फोड, मार, दे, हालव, विचक, &c. &c.
That is in one's teeth. तोंडचा.
To the teeth of. तोंडावर.
Wisdom-t. अक्कलदाढ *f.*
To break off with the teeth. खुडतुडणें.
To brush or clean the teeth. दांत *m. pl.* घासणें, दंतशुद्धि *f.*-दंतधावन *n.*-दंतशोधन *n.*-&c. करणें.
To chatter,—the teeth. दांत *m. pl.* वाजणें.
To grind or gnash the teeth. दांत *m. pl.* खाणें-चावणें.
To knock out the teeth. बत्तिसी *f.* हालवणें-पाडणें-&c.
To pick the teeth. दांत *m. pl.* खांचरणें.
To shew the teeth. दांत *m. pl.* काढणें-दाखवणें, बत्तिसी *f.* दाखवणें-काढणें.
To succeed or do in the teeth of. नाकावर पाय *m.* देणें, नाकास चुना *m.* लावणें, नाकावर निंबू *n.* घासणें.
To throw in one's teeth. *to reproach.* ओंठावणें. [रणें.
To wear one's teeth to stumps. दांतांच्या फण्या *f. pl.* क-
To be set on edge—the teeth. शिणशिणणें. [फण *m.*
2 (of a comb, rake, saw, wheel, &c.). दांत *m.* दांना *m.*
3 See PRONG. 4 See TASTE.

TOOTH-ACHE, *n.* दांतमूळ *m.* दंतशूल *m.* दंतपीडा *f.* दंतवेदना *f.*

TOOTH-BRUSH, *n.* दांतवण *n.* दंतकाष्ठ *n.*

TOOTH-LESS, *a. wanting or deprived of teeth.* दांतांविगळा-निराळा, दांतपडका *or* गा, बोंथरा, बोंचरडा, बोंथरखंड *or* डा *or* डी, दंतहीन-रहित-&c. अदंत, निर्दशन, गतदंत.

TOOTH-PICK, *n.* दांतकोरणें *n.* वंशशलाका *f.*

TOOTH-POWDER, *n. dentifrice.* दारशिणा *m.* दांतवण *n.*

TOOTHED, *a.* दांतांचा, दंती.
Iron-t. अयोदत्.

TOOTHSOME, *a.* v. TASTEFUL. गोड, चवदार, रुचिकर.

TOOTHSOMENESS, *n.* v. A. गोडी *f.* चवदारी *f.* रुचि *f.*

TOP, *n. highest part, upper end, summit, &c.* वरचा भाग *m.* वरला भाग *m.* शेंडा *m.* माथा *m.* मस्तक *m. n.* शेवट *m.* अग्र *n.* अग्रभाग *m.* शिखर *n.* उपरिभाग *m.* चूडा *f.* शिखा *f.*
T. and bottom. शेंडाबुडखा *m.* शेंडाबुंधा *m.*
From t. to bottom, from t. to toe. शिखनखपर्यंत *or* नखशिखपर्यंत, नखशिरांत, आपादमस्तक, आनखशिख.
2 *lid,* v. COVER. टोपण *n.* झांकण *n.* सरपोस *m.*
3 *upper side,* v. SURFACE. वरला भाग *m.* बाहेरला भाग *m.* उपरिभाग *m.* उपरिभूमि *f.*
4 *highest place, highest rank.* वरची जागा *f.*-पायरी *f.*-पदवी *f.*-&c. मुख्यस्थान *n.* आद्यस्थान *n.*
5 *utmost degree,* v. HEIGHT. कळस *m.* सीमा *f.* पराकाष्ठा *f.* शेवट *m.* [ढिकशी *f.*
6 (of a plant) *head, crop, &c.* बोंखा *m.* ढिरा *m.* ढिरी *f.*
7—spinning top. भोवरा *or* भौरा *m.* चिंगाटी *f.*
Blow in the ring (at top-playing). रंगणटोला *m.*
Dead throw of a t. धापट *f.*
Hole or dint struck on a t. घुमा *m.*
String of a t. भोवरजाळी *f.* जाळी *f.*
Sleeping (swift spinning) of a t. निधा *f. v.* धर.
8—humming t. जंगीभोवरा *m.* भिंगारा *m.*
9—as used in comp. वरचा, वरला, उपरिस्थ.

To TOP, *v. n. rise above or aloft.* वर-उंच-&c. असणें *with* पेक्षां-&c.

To TOP, *v.a.* See To TIP. 2 See To SURPASS. 3 See To CROP.

TOP HEAVY, *a.* वरचाभारी-वजनदार, वरभारी, माराधिकशिरस्क, ऊर्ध्वगुरु. [*m.* सोंपा *m.*

TOP-KNOT, *n.* तुरा *m.* जुंबडा *m.* शेंडी *f.* शिखा *f.* शिखड *n.* बुचडा

TOPMOST, *a.* अगदी वरचा-वरला, शेंड्याच्याशेंड्याचा.

TOPAZ, *n.*—the gem. पुष्पराग *pop.* पुष्कराज *m.* पीताश्म *m.* पीतस्फटिक *m.*

To TOPE, *v. n. drink hard.* शोषणें *or* सोसणें, झोकणें, झिंगणें.

TOPER, *n.* v. V.—*and* SOT. झिंग्या, झिंगीखोर, छाकटा, निशाबाज.

TOPIC, *n. general head,* v. SUBJECT. विषय *m.* प्रकरण *n.* प्रसंग *m.* स्थल *n.*

TOPIC, TOPICAL, *a. of or belonging to a general head.* प्रकरणाचा, प्रकरणाविषयींचा, &c. प्राकरणिक.

2 *pertaining to a particular place, local.* एकदेशी, एकदेशीय, विशेषस्थानाचा, &c. एकस्थानिक, विशेषस्थानिक, तत्स्थानिक, स्थानिक & स्थानीय (in comp.).

TOPOGRAPHY, *n. description of a particular place.* विशेषस्थानवर्णन *n.* विशेषस्थलवर्णन *n.*

To TOPPLE, *v. n. tumble, fall forward.* पुढें-पुढल्याकडे-तोंडाकडून-&c. पडणें, लुडकणें.

TOPSYTURVY, *adv. with the top downward.* उलटापालटा, उलटपालट, उलटापालट, उलटासुलटा, उलटसुलट, उफराटसुफराट, उफराटासुफराटा, उलथापालथ, उलथापालथा, खालवर.

TORCH, *n. link, flambeau, &c.* मशाल *f.* दिवटा *m.* दिवटी *f.* पोत *m.* टेंभा *m.* काकडा *m.* उजेडी *f.*

Handle of a t. विडी *f.*

T. of wisps, or of sprigs and twigs, &c. चुडी *f.* चूड *f.*

T. carried in an iron bowl. हिलाल *m.*—bearer of it, हिलाल्या.

To light the t. of discord. बत्ती *f.* लावणें.

TORCH-BEARER, *n.* मशालची *or* जी, दिवट्या, रोशननाईक.

Oil flask of t. बुधली *f.*

To TORMENT, *v. a. put to extreme pain or anguish, torture.* पराकाष्ठेचें दुःख *n.*-फारच दुःख *n.*-यातना *f.*-अतियातना *f.*-अतिवेदना *f.*-तीव्रवेदना *f.*-&c. करणें-देणें-भोगवणें, फार पिडणें.

2 *vex, worry, harass, &c.* v. To TEASE. गांजणें, जाचणें, छळणें, खलखलावणें, गांजणूक *f.*-छळणूक *f.*-&c. करणें, काचणी *f.*-काच *f.* लावणें, खडे *m. pl.* चारणें, नळीं नख *n.* देणें, धुरावर धरणें.

TORMENT, *n. extreme pain or anguish.* फार मोठें दुःख *n.* पराकाष्ठेचें दुःख *n.* परमदुःख *n.* यातना *f.* तीव्रवेदना *f.* अतिवेदना *f.* अतिपीडा *f.* अतिव्यथा *f.* अतियातना *f.* यमयातना *f.* दारुणयातना *f.* रोमरोम वेदना *f.*

TORMENTED, *p.* v. V. 1. फारच दुःख दिलेला, &c. अतिपीडित, परमपीडित, अतिव्यथित, दुःखदग्ध, दुःखार्त्त.

2 गांजलेला, जाचलेला, &c.

TORMENTOR *or* TORMENTER, *n.* TORMENTING, *p. a.* v. V. 1. फारच दुःख देणारा, अतिवेदना-&c. करणारा-&c.

2 गांजणारा, छळणारा, &c. [विदारित, विदीर्ण.

TORN, *p.* v. V. 1. फाडलेला, चिरलेला, &c. फाटका, चिरींव, दारित, 2 बुचकरलेला, &c. नखभिन्न.

TORNADO, *n. tempest.* तुफान *n.*

TORPID, *a. that has lost power of motion and feeling, numb.* बहिरा, सुना, गुंगा, सुस्त, मेहरलेला, सुम, जड, बधिर, शून्य, निपचेत, निचेत, निचेतन, जडीकृत, जडीभूत, अचेतन, सुमसक्कू, सैरभैर, बेशुद्ध, स्तब्धचेष्ट.

TORPOR, TORPIDITY, TORPIDNESS, TORPITUDE, *n.* v. A. बहिरेपणा *m.* सुनेपणा *m.* &c. सुस्ती *f.* गुंगी *f.* मेहरी *f.* सुप्ति *f.* मांद्य *n.* जाड्य *n.* जडता *f.* जडिमा *m.* स्वाप *m.* इंद्रियस्वाप *m.* तंद्रा *f.* चैतन्यस्तंभ *m.* चैतन्यस्तब्धता *f.* चैतन्यनाश *m.*

TORRENT, *n. violent or rapid stream.* मुसुंडा *or* मुसांडा *m.* झोत *m.* पूर *m.* लोंढा *m.* लोट *m.* निर्झर *m.* धारवणी *n.* वृष्टि *f.*

To rain in torrents, v. To RAIN. झिम *adv.*-धुमाधार *adv.*-&c. पाऊस पडणें.

TORRID, *a. parched with heat.* फारउनाचा-उष्णतेचा-&c. वणव्याचा, ग्रीष्मदग्ध, उष्णदग्ध.

T. zone. उष्णकटिबंध *m.*

TORT, *n.* v. WRONG, INJURY. नुकसान *n.* नुकसानी *f.*

TORTOISE, *n.* कासव *m.* कच्छप *m.* कच्छ *m.* कूर्म *m.*

TORTOISE-SHELL, *n.* कचकडा *m.* कासवाचा खवला *m.* कासवाच्या पाठीचें हाड *n.*

TORTUOUS. See TWISTED, WINDING.

To TORTURE, *v. a. put to the rack, &c.* v. To TORMENT. शरीरास फार दुःख *n.* देणें, यातना *f.*-&c. करणें-देणें, हाल *m. pl.* करणें;—The following words express *modes of torturing,* जामगी *f.* लावणें, कानास चाप *m.* लावणें, राखेचा तोबरा *m.* देणें, उराकर-डोईवर-&c. धोंडा *m.* देणें, तव्यावर उभा करणें, करवतावर धरणें-ओढणें, मिरच्यांची धुरी *f.* देणें, पोत *m.*-सांडस *m.*-टिपऱ्या *f. pl.* लावणें, उखळांत- चरकांत घालणें, खडे *m. pl.* चारणें-खाकिबणें, नळीं नख *n.* देणें.

TORTURE, *n. extreme pain,* v. TORMENT. फार मोठें दुःख *n.* यातना *f.* तीव्रवेदना *f.*

To TOSS, *v. a. throw, &c.,* v. To CAST. फेंकणें, घालणें.

2 (the head, &c.) *throw up with a sudden motion.* कोलणें, वर-वरती-&c. मारणें-करणें.

3 *throw with the horns.* शिंगटणें *or* शिंगाटणें, शिंगानें फेंकणें-हुंडारणें, शिंगावर घेणें-उचलणें-चढवणें, शिंगानें कोलणें, शिंगाळणें.

4 about; *tumble over rudely.* उलकटणें, उसकटणें, उचलाउचल *or* उचलासांचल *f.* करणें, उस्तरणें, उलटापालट *or* उलथापालथ *f.*-उडवाउडव *f.*-उराकटाउसकट *f.*-घालमेल *f.*-&c. करणें.

To TOSS, *v. n. fling about.* तळमळणें, तडफडणें, चडफडणें, चुळबुळणें, मडबडां *adv.* लोटणें, तळमळ *f.*-तडफड *f.*-अदळउफळ *f.*-&c. करणें.

To lie tossing and heaving. तिडका देत बसणें, तिडक देत बसणें.

2 (in passion) v. To RAGE, To FUME. धडफडणें, तडफडणें.

To toss up. (for the lead in play, &c.) छापतराजू *f.* खेळणें, उन्हाळीपावसाळी *f.* करणें.

TOSS, TOSSING, *n.* v. V. A. 1.—*act.* फेंकणें *n.* &c.

2 कोलणें *n.* &c. कोलणी *f.*

3 शिंगटणें *n.* &c.

4 उलकटणें *n.* &c. उसकटणी *f.* उडवाउडव *f.* उसकटाउसकट *f.* उलथापालथ *f.* घालमेल *f.*

v. V. N. 1. तडफडणें *n.* तळमळणें *n.* &c. तळमळ *f.* तडफड *f.* चुळबूळ *f.* चडफड *f.* चडफडणी *f.* अदळउफळ *f.* अदळउपट *f.* अदळधोप *f.* अद्ळधोपट *f.*—*intens.* तळमळाट *m.* तडफडाट *m.* चडफडाट *m.*

2 धडफडणें *n.* तडफडणें *n.* &c.

TOTAL, *a.* v. ALL. सर्व, सगळा, समग्र, अवघा.

2 v. COMPLETE. पूर्ण, पुरा.

TOTAL, TOTALITY, *n. whole amount,* v. SUM. बेरीज *f.* जुमला *m.* जमा *f.* एकंदर आकार *m.* राशि *f.* साकल्य *n.* सामग्र्य *n.*

Grand t. मखलाशी *or* सी *f.* गोळा बेरीज *f.* टोक-ठाम-ठास

बेरीज *f.* तेरीज *n.f.*

TOTALLY, *adv.* v. WHOLLY. अगदी, बिलकूल, तमाम.

To TOTTER, *v. n. shake so as to threaten a fall.* डगणें, डकडकणें *or* डगडगणें, डगमगणें, डळमळणें, डुलणें *or* डोलणें, लटलटणें, लटपटणें, पडायासारखा-जोगा-&c. हालणें, डग *m.* खाणें, लटलट-लुखुलुखु-लडबड *or* लडबडां *adv.* हालणें-&c. लटलट *f.*-लडबड *f.* करणें, पाय *m. pl.* लटलटणें-लटपटणें *g. of s.* चलबिचल *f.* होणें *g. of s.* आसन *n.* डळमळणें *g. of s.*—*intens.* डगागणें *or* डकाकणें.

TOTTERING, *p. a.* v. V. डगणारा, डगमगणारा, &c. डगडगीत, डळडळीत, डळमळीत, लटपटीत, उलटकर, पतनीय.

TOTTERINGLY, *adv.* v. V. डगमग *or* गां, डकडक *or* कां, डळमळ *or* ळां, लटपट *or* टां, लटलट *or* टां, लडबड.

To TOUCH, *v. a. come in contact with.* स्पर्श *m.* करणें *g. of o.* लागणें *in. con.* स्पर्श *m.*-&c. होणें *in. con. with g. of s.* स्पर्शणें.

2 *bring into contact with one's self; handle, meddle with, &c.* स्पर्श *m.*-&c. करणें *g. of o.* स्पर्शणें, हात *m.* लावणें-घालणें, हातांत घेणें, शिवणें, घडणें, आकडणें, अफळणें.—Note. The four last words have generally, but not necessarily, an implication of communicating or receiving pollution. आतळणें, स्पर्शन *n.*-संस्पर्शन *n.*-&c. करणें *g. of o.*—mutually, शिवाशिव *f.*-स्पर्शास्पर्श *m.*-&c. करणें. [गास येणें.

3 *act upon*, v. To AFFECT. लागणें, लागू होणें, आंगीं *or* आं-

4 *move, melt*, v. To AFFECT. बेधणें, सद्गदित करणें, वळवळा *m.*-&c. आणणें. [वाजविणें.

5 See To CONCERN. 6 (an instrument) *play on.* छडणें.

7 up; v. To FINISH, To REPAIR. ओजवणें, सुधरणें *or* सुधारणें, निटावणें, उस्तवारी *f.* करणें.

To TOUCH, *v.n. come into or be in contact.* लागणें, मिळणें, भिडणें, घडणें, लागू होणें, संसक्ति *f.*-संसर्ग *m.*-&c. असणें-होणें *g. of s. recip.*

2 at;—a ship, &c. बरवा *m.*-बंदर *n.* करणें.

3 upon; v. To MENTION. गोष्ट *f.*-उहू *m.*-&c. काढणें *g. of o.*

TOUCH, *n.*—the sense. स्पर्श *m.* स्पर्शेंद्रिय *n.* त्वगिंद्रिय *n.* स्पार्शन *n.*

To judge by the t. हस्तपरीक्षा *f.* करणें.

2—the perception. स्पर्श *m.* स्पर्शबोध *m.* स्पर्शज्ञान *n.* त्वगुज्ञान *n.*

3—the act. स्पर्श *m.* स्पर्शन *n.* स्पार्शन *n.* स्पर्शव्यापार *m.*

4 See CONTACT. 5 See TEST.

6 *a small quantity intermixed.* धुनूक *f.* छटा *f.* स्पर्श *m.*

TOUCH-HOLE, *n.*—of a fire arm, &c. काना *m.* कान *m.* कोरप *n.*

TOUCH-STONE, *n. stone for examining metals.* कसोटी *or* कसबटी *f.* कस *m.* कषपाषाण *m.* निष्कर्ष *m.*

A framed t. of gold. बरकल *or* बरखल *m. f. n.*

Quality determined by the t. कस *m.*

TOUCH-WOOD, *n. decayed wood, spunk.* चेतवण *n.* पू *m.* पूड *f.*

TOUCHED, *p.v.*V.A. 1. 2. स्पर्श केलेला, &c. स्पर्शित, स्पृष्ट, संस्पृष्ट.

4 बेधलेला, कळवळा आणलेला, &c. सद्गदित, सद्गद.

To be t. कळवळणें, कळवळा *m.*-&c. येणें *in. con.* द्रवणें.

I. *slightly impaired or corrupted.* लागट, लागर, लागलेला.

TOUCHER, *n.* TOUCHING, *p. a.* v. V. A.1. 2. स्पर्श करणारा, स्पर्शणारा, &c. स्पर्शक, स्पर्शन-&c. कर्ता-कारी.

3 See CONCERNING, RELATING.

4 *and* PATHETIC. बेधणारा, कळवळा आणणारा, &c. बेधक, हृदय बेधक, हृदयाबिद्, करुणापर.

v. V. N. 1. लागणारा-लागलेला, संसक्त, संलग्न, संसर्गी, संसृष्ट.

TOUCHINESS, *n.* v. A. चिरडखोरपणा *m.* चिडचिडेपणा *m.* रुसकेपणा *m.*-&c. चिरडखोरी *f.* चिरड *f.* चीड *f.* शीघ्रकोपिता *f.*

TOUCHY, *a. irritable*, v. PEEVISH. चिरडखोर, चिरडीखोर, चिडचिड्या, काविरडा, रुसका, रुशा, हिरवट, खडतर, शीघ्रकोपी.

TOUGH, *a. not brittle, &c.* वातट *or* ड, चिवट, चामट, चावट, लोंचट *or* ड, चिकट *or* ण *or* चिक्कट *or* ण, निबर. [बरट.

2—as wood, grass, &c. v. HARD. चिबट *or* चेंबट, निबर, नि-

3 v. HARDY, HALE. चिकट *or* ण *or* चिक्कट *or* ण, कणखर, कडवा, टणक, टणका.

4 *tenacious, inflexible, &c.* चिवट, चामट, चिकट *or* ण *or* चिक्कट *or* ण, चिकट्या, लोंचट *or* ड.

To TOUGHEN, *v. a. make tough.* वातट-चिवट-चिकट-&c. करणें, चिकटपणा *m.*-&c. आणणें.

To TOUGHEN, *v. n. become tough.* वातडणें, वातट *or* ड-चिवट-&c. होणें-होत जाणें.

2—fruits, vegetables, &c. जारटणें, जुनावणें, पिकणें.

TOUGHNESS, *n.* v. A. 1. वातडपणा *m.* चिवटपणा *m.* चामटपणा *m.* चिकटपणा *m.* &c. चिकटाई *f.*

2 चिवटपणा *m.* निबरपणा *m.*

3 चिकटपणा *m.* टणकपणा *m.* &c. टणकाई *f.*

4 चिवटपणा *m.* चिकटपणा *m.* &c. चिकटाई *f.*

TOUR, *n. a journey in a circuit.* फेरा *m.* फेरी *f.* पर्यटन *n.* प्रदक्षिणा *f.* परिभ्रमण *n.*

2 *turn of duty, &c.* पाळी *f.* बारी *f.*

TOURIST, *n.* पर्यटन करणारा *m.*

TOURNAMENT, *n. tilt.* भालेकरवली *or* करोली *f.* [*n.*

TOW, *n. coarse part of hemp or flax.* तागाचें-सणाचें-&c. बुरकूल

To TOW, *v. a. drag by a rope through water.* दोरी *f.*-&c. लावून ओढणें.

TOWAGE, *n.* v. V.—the act. दोरीलाबून ओढणें *n.*

TOWARD, TOWARDS, *prep. in the direction of.* कडे.

2 *with direction to, with respect to.* विषयीं, वर, कडे.

TOWARD, TOWARDLY, TOWARDNESS. See SHARP, SHARPNESS.

TOWEL, *n. cloth for wiping the body.* रुमाल *m.* हातरुमाल *m.* आंगपुसणें *n.* आंगपुसणी *f.* करवस्त्र *n.* गात्रमार्जनी *f.* अंगमार्जनी *f.*

TOWER, *n. elevated building.* वाड्यावरला बंगला *m.*-महाल *m.*-इमला *m.* अस्मानी-आस्मानगिरी बंगला *m.*-महाल *m.* गोपुर *n. m.* मेघडंबरी *f.*

2 See FORT.

To TOWER, *v. n. rise high.* उंच-वर होणें-जाणें.

TOWN, *n. city.* शहर *n.* गांव *m. n.* नगर *n. dim.* नगरी *f.* पुर *pop.* पूर *n. and dim.* पुरी *f.* पत्तन *n.*

Manufacturing or trading t. पेंठ *f.*

Minor t. आडपेंठ *f.*

The old t. *the portion first settled.* कसबा *m.*

Poor, mean, &c. t. काणपिंठ *f.*

Walls of a t. शहरपन्हा *m.*

TOWN-FOLK, *n.* नगरांतील-गांवांतील-&c. लोक *m. pl.*-माणसें *n. pl.* नगरजन *m. pl.* [कचेरी *f.*

TOWN-HOUSE, TOWN-HALL, *n.* सरकारवाडा *m.* सरकारचावडी *f.*

TOWNS-MAN, *n.* गांवकरी.
TOY, *n. play-thing.* खेळणें *n.* खेळवणा *m.* क्रीडामृग *m.*
2 See TRIFLE.
To TOY, *v. n.* v. To TRIFLE. खेळणें, गमणें.
2 *dally amorously.* रमणें, विलास *m.*-कामक्रीडा *f.*-कामलीला *f.*-कामचेष्टा *f.*-इष्कबाजी *f.*-&c. करणें.
TRACE, *n. footsteps, track,* lit. fig. v. FOOTSTEP. पत्ता *m.* माग *m.* छडा *m.* सुवारा *m.* अरासडा *m.* मूस *m.*
T.—compreh. *track or vestige.* मागमूस *m.* मूसमारग *m.* आगमाग *m.*
T.—compreh. *news or tidings of.* पत्तादोरा *m.* थांगदोरा *m.* थांगपत्ता *m.* पत्तामुद्दा *m.* [मोडणें.
To obliterate all traces and impressions. मागमूस *m.*
2 *harness.* ओढ *f.* ओढण *f.* गळसूत्रें *n. pl.*
To TRACE, *v. a. follow by the tracks of.* उमगणें *or* उमंगणें, माग *m.* लावणें-काढणें, ठाव *m.*-ठिकाणा *m.*-ठाव ठिकाणा *m.*-थांग *m.*-&c. लावणें-पाडणें, थिकाणीं-थांगास-&c. लावणें-पाडणें, पत्ता *m.*-छडा *m.*-&c. लावणें, देठीं-डेंखीं लावणें, काढणें, शोध *m.* काढणें-लावणें, पाठलाग *m.* करणें. [गणें *g. of s.*
To be traced. पत्ता *m.*-माग *m.*-ठिकाणा*m.*-छडा *m.*-&c. ला-
2 (outlines) v. To MARK OUT. अंकणें, बेतणें, काढणें.
3 (letters of a copy in learning to write). घोटाळणें, गिरवणें. [उमग्या.
TRACER, *n.* TRACING, *p. a.* v. V. 1. माग काढणारा, मागाड्या,
TRACHEA, *n.* v. WINDPIPE. श्वासमार्ग *m.* नरडें *n.* नरडी *f.*
TRACK, *n. vestige,* v. TRACE. माग *m.* छडा *m.*
2 v. WAY, ROAD. वाट *f.* रस्ता *m.* मार्ग *m.*
Devious t. रानवाट *f.*
3 *beaten path,* fig. फरपट *f.*
4 (of a thing dragged, of a snake, &c.). ओढ *f.* फरकंड *f.* फरकंडा *m.* फरपट *f. v.* जा.
To TRACK, *v. a.* See To TRACE. 2 *drag along.* फरपटणें, फरकंडणें, फरपटीन-फरकंडीत नेणें, फरपटून-फरकंडून-फरपट्यां *adv.* ओढणें-ओढून नेणें.
3 See To TOW.
TRACKLESS, *a.* वाटेवेगळा-निराळा, बिनपावली.
TRACK-ROPE, *n.* ओढण *f.* ओढ *f.* पाग *m.*
TRACT, *n. region, quantity of land or water.* देश *m.* प्रदेश *m.* तळ *m.* मैदान *n.* पल्ला *m.* रान *n.*
2 *small pamphlet on religion.* धर्माच्या विषयाची चोपडी *f.*
TRACTABILITY, TRACTABLENESS, *n.* v. A. हुकमीपणा *m.* हुकुमबरदारी *f.* बिनयीपणा *m.* सविनयता *f.* विनय *m.* वश्यता *f.*
TRACTABLE, *a.* v. DOCILE, OBEDIENT. हुकमी, हुकुमबरदार, हुकमांत-कह्यांत-&c. राहणारा-वागणारा, विनयी, विनयस्थ, विनीत, सुधर्ष, वश्य.
To render t. वठणीस आणणें.
TRACTILE, TRACTILITY. See DUCTILE, DUCTILITY.
TRADE, TRADING, *n. traffic, commerce.* उदीम *m.* व्यापार *pop.* बेपार *m.* व्यवहार *pop.* बेवहार *m.* सौदागरी *f.* बकाली *f.* सौदा घेणें-देणें *n.* घेवदेव *m.* घेवादेवा *m. or* वी *f.* (*or* देणेंघेणें *n.* &c.) देघे *f.* देवालेवा *m.* लेणदेण *f.* लेवदेव *f.* लेवादेवा*m.* सट्टा *m.* सौदासूत *n. m.* व्यवसाय *pop.* बेवसाय *or* बेवसाव *m.* वाणिज्य*n.* वणिक्कर्म *n.* वणिक्पथ *m.* क्रयविक्रय *m.* घडमोड *f.* घडामोड *f.* उलटापालट *f.* उलथापालट *f.* वणिग्भाव *m.* सत्यानृत *n.*
T. upon a nominal capital. घेवपत धंदा-व्यापार-उद्दीम *m.*
2 *profession, occupation,* v. BUSINESS. धंदा *m.* पेशा *m.* कसब *n.* हुनर *m.* व्यवहार *m.*
Headman of a t. चौधरी.
Jack of all trades. हरकसबी, हरहुनरी, हरकामी *or* म्या.
To TRADE, *v. n.* उदीम *m.*-बेपार *m.*-व्यापार *m.*-सौदागरी *f.*-क्रयविक्रय *m.*-&c. करणें.
TRADER, *n* TRADING, *p. a.* v. V. उदीम करणारा, &c. उदमी, व्यापारी *pop.* बेपारी, महाजन, सौदागर, व्यवहारी *pop.* बेवहारी, सावकार, व्यवसायी, व्यावसायक, उद्योगी, क्रयविक्रयिक, वणिक्.
Some compellations for a t. are, शेट *or* शेठ, शेटजी.
Business-trips of traders (abroad, over the country, about the town, &c.). बणज *f.*
Petty t. तुटपुंज्या, तुटपुंजीवाला, मोडकावाणी.
Traders,—compreh. *traders and dealers, trades folk.* वाणी उदमी *m. pl.* वाणीबकाल*m. pl.* बकाल *n.* शेटसावकार*m. pl.*
Traders and trading business,-compreh. सावसावकार*m.*
2 *trading vessel.* जिन्नसी गलबत *n.* जिन्नसी तारूं *n.* बारकस *n.* काबाडी गलबत *n.*
TRADESMAN, *n.* v. SHOP-KEEPER. व्यापारी, व्यवहारी, दुकानदार.
TRADITION, *n. oral communication from age to age.* लोककथा *f.* दंतकथा *f.* पूर्वीपासून चालत आलेली गोष्ट *f.*-&c. इतिहास *m.* पिढिजाद् कथा *f.* ओघ *m.* आख्यायिका *f.* ऐतिह्य *n.* इतिह *ind.* पारपर्य *n.* पारंपर्योपदेश *m.* परंपरागतकथा *f.* गुरुक्रम *m.*
2 *traditional custom or usage.* ओढण *n. f.* ओढावण *f.* ओढावणें *n.* [देणें *n.* विधान *n.*
3 *giving into the hands of another,* v. DELIVERY. हातीं-
TRADITIONAL, TRADITIONARY, *a.* v. N. पूर्वीपासून चालत आलेला, ओघाचा, ओघानें आलेला, परंपरागत, परंपरीण, परंपरायात, ओघप्राप्त, परंपराप्राप्त, कर्णोपकर्णीचा, क्रमागत, क्रमायात, क्रमप्राप्त.
T. & authoritative doctrine. संप्रदाय *m.*
TRADITIONALLY, *adv.* v. A. पूर्वीच्या ओघानें, परंपरेनें, पारंपर्यानें, डोईनडोई, पिढीजाद, पिढीनपिढी, लोकालोकीं, कर्णोपकर्णीं.
To TRADUCE, *v. a.* v. To ASPERSE. तुफान *n.* घेणें *with* वर *of o.* चहाडी *f.*-चुगली *f.*-चुगल *f.* खाणें-सांगणें-करणें *g. of o.* तोहमत *f.* घेणें-घालणें, आळ *m. f.* घालणें-घेणें, अभिशंसन *n.*-अभिशाप *m.*-अपवाद *m.* करणें *g. of o.*
TRADUCED, *p.* v. V. तुफान घेतलेला-आलेला, &c. अभिशस्त, अभिशप्त, अपवादित.
TRADUCER, *n.* TRADUCING, *p. a.* v. V. *and* ASPERSER. तुफान घेणारा, चहाडी सांगणारा, आळ घालणारा, &c. तुफान्या, ब्रह्राडखोर, चुगलखोर, चुगल्या, अभिशंसी, अपवादक.
TRADUCING. *n.* v. V. *and* ASPERSION. विकथन *n.*
TRAFFIC, *n.* v. TRADE. उदीम *m.* व्यापार *pop.* बेपार *m.* घेणेंदेणें *n.* घेवदेव *f.* क्रयविक्रय *m.*
To TRAFFIC. See To TRADE.
TRAGEDIAN, *n. a writer of tragedy.* दुःखपरिणामकनाटककवी.
2 *an acter of tragedy.* दुःखपरिणामक नाटकाची बतावणी करणारा, करुणारसाभिनयकारी.
TRAGEDY, *n. a drama that has a fatal issue.* दुःखाच्या परिणामाचें नाटक *n.* दुःखपरिणामक नाटक *n.* करुणारसप्रधान नाटक *n.*
2 See CALAMITY.

Tragic, Tragical, *a. belonging, &c. to tragedy,* v. N. दुःख परिणामकनाटकाचा, दुःखपरिणामकनाटकसंबंधी-विषयक.

2 v. Calamitous. दुष्परिणामी, दुरंत, अस्वंत.

To **Trail,** *v. a. draw along,* v. To Track. फरपटणें, फरफंडणें, फरपटीत नेणें, ओढणें. [जाणें.

To **Trail,** *v. n. move along on the ground.* फरपटणें, फरपटत

Trail, *n. thing drawn along.* ओढ *f.*

2 *mark left.* फरपट *f.* फरकंड *f.* फरकंडा *m.* ओढ *f.* सरपट *f.*

3 *scent left.* वासाचा-गंधाचा-&c. माग *m.*

Trailingly, *adv.* v. V. फरपटत्यां, लढ्त लोंबत.

To **Train,** *v. a. teach and form by practice,* v. To Educate, To Discipline. शिकवणें, शिक्षा *f.* देणें, शिक्षित-सुशिक्षित करणें, काढणें, कमावणें, पेटवणें, उगळणें, वठणीं-वठणीस-वळणीं-वळणीस-&c. आणणें, वळण *n.* लावणें, वळणांत ठेवणें, अनुनय *m.*-&c. करणें.

2 (a horse, &c.) v. To Discipline. तालीम *f.* देणें.

Post or stake at which to t. (bullock, &c.) जांत *n.*

3 See To Draw, To Allure.

Train, *n.* (of a gown &c.). गोशा *m.* सोगा *m.* दावण *or* न *f.* झोल *m.* झोला *m.* घोळ *m.*

A long t. or trail. लगता लोळ *m.*

2 *consecution, line,* v. Series. शेज *n. f.* माला *pop.* माळ *f.* देवड *f.* हार *f.* श्रेणी *f.* लगताळ *f. m.* [ग, तार *f.*

T. of reasoning, discourse, &c. लाघाळ *f. v.* लाव, ला-

3 *line of process,* v. Order. क्रम *m.* अनुक्रम *m.* अनुसंधान *n.* शिलशिला *m.* लागटा *m.* [*g. of s.*

To be put in t.—a work, &c. शेज *n. f.* लागणें *or* पडणें

To lay a t. लाग *m.* लावणें.

To lay in t. जथणें, शेज *n. f.*-&c. लावणें *g. of o.* अनुसंधान *n.* करणें-बांधणें-रचणें *g. of o.*

4 v. Retinue. जिलीब *f.* सवारी *or* स्वारी *f.* लहंबर *or* लंबर *n.* खटला *m.* खटलें *n.*

A long t. लगतालोळ *m.*

That has his t. with him. सपरिवार.

5 *body (of men or animals) moving in order.* माळका *f.* तांडा *m.* रव *f.* रवण *f.* रस्त *f.* हरपंजर *f.* कतार *f.* कतारा *m.* साईर *f.*

6 *line of powder.* दारूची ओळ *f.* रंजकीची ओळ *f.*

7 (of gunpowder, grain, &c. spilled). लागावळ *f.*

8 *line of artillery.* तोफा *f. pl.* तोफखाना *m.*

9 (on a railway) गाड्यांची माळका *f.* [विनीत.

Trained, *p.* v. V. 1. शिकवलेला, &c. शिक्षित, शिष्ट, अनुनीत,

2 तालीम दिल्हेला, तालमी.

Trainer, *n.* **Training,** *p. a.* v. V. 1. शिकवणारा, शिक्षादेणारा, शिक्षित करणारा, वठणीस आणणारा, &c.

Training, *n.* v. V. 1.—*act.* शिकवणें *n.* पेटवणें *n.* काढणें *n.* वठणीस आणणें *n.* &c. पेटवणी *f.* शिक्षा *f.* अनुनय *m.* अनुनयन *n.*

Trait, *n.* (of character) v. Mark. लक्षण *n.* चिन्ह *n.* खोड *f.*

Bad t. कुलक्षण *n.* दुर्लक्षण *n.*

Good t. सुलक्षण *n.*

Traitor, *n. one guilty of treason.* राजाशीं फितलेला-फितुरी झालेला-&c. माणूस, राजद्रोही, देशद्रोही, राजशत्रु.

2—gener. *a betrayer of his trust.* विश्वासघातकी-घाती, अस्तनींतलीआग *f.* कुऱ्हाडीचा दांडा *m.*

Traitorous. See Treasonable, Treacherous.

Trammel, *To* **Trammel.** See Net, Clog, To Clog.

To **Tramp,** *v. n. trudge, travel, &c. wearisomely.* पाय *m. pl.* फासटणें-झिजवणें-मोडावणें, फासटणी *f.*-फासटाफासट *f.*-पायपिटी *f.*-धांवाधांव *f.*-येजा *f.*-&c. करणें.

To **Tramp,** *v. a.* See To Tread.

To **Trample,** *v. a. tread under foot, tread down.* तुडवणें, मर्दणें, रौंदळणें *or* रंवदळणें, खुंदलणें *or* खुंदळणें, खुंदणें, खुदडणें, चोंदळणें, मळणी *f.* घालणें *g. of o.* गुडघावणें, दवडणें, बरदळ *f.*-गुधडा *m.*-गुडधा *m.*-रौंदळ *f.*-रौंदळा *m.*-गुरधळ *or* ळी *f.* करणें-घालणें-मांडणें, तुडवणी *f.*-उपमर्द *m.*-मर्दन *n.*-&c. करणें *g. of o.*

Trample, Trampling, *n.* v. V. तुडवणें *n.* मर्दणें *n.* &c. तुडवणी *f.* पायतुडवणी *f.* रौंदळा *or* रंवदळा *m.* रौंदळ *or* रंवदळ *f.* उपमर्द *m.* उपमर्दन *n.* मर्दन *n.* अवमर्द *m.* अवमर्दन *n.* सम्मर्द *m.* सम्मर्दन *n.*

Trampled, *p.* v. V. तुडवलेला, रौंदळलेला, &c. मर्दित, उपमर्दित, अवमर्दित, सम्मर्दित, क्षुण्ण.

Trampler, *n.* **Trampling,** *p. a.* v. V. तुडवणारा, मळणी घालणारा, रौंदळणारा, &c. मर्दन-उपमर्दन-&c. कर्त्ता-कारी-&c.

Trance, *n. ecstacy, rapt state.* देहातीतवृत्ति *f.* तन्मयावस्था *f.* समाधि *m. f.* देहानुसंधानरहितलोकांतरचित्तवृत्ति *f.*

Tranquil, *a.* v. Calm, Composed. स्वस्थ, शांत, स्थिर, अक्षुब्ध.

To **Tranquilize,** *v. a.* v. To Compose. संतावणें *or* संथावणें, शांत-स्थिर-&c. करणें, शांति *f.*-उपशम *m.*-शम *m.*-उपशमन *n.*-&c. करणें *g. of o.*

Tranquillity, Tranquilness, *n.* v. A. स्वस्थपणा *m.* शांतपणा *m.* स्थिरपणा *m.* शांति *f.* शम *m.* क्षोभराहित्य *n.* अक्षुब्धता *f.*

To **Transact,** *v. a. do, perform, &c.* v. To Conduct, To Manage. करणें, चालवणें, आचरणें, वहिवाटणें, अनुष्ठणें, वहिवाट *f.*-आचरण *n.*-&c. करणें.

Transacted, *p.* v. V. केलेला, वहिवाटलेला, &c. वर्त्तित, अनुष्ठित.

Transaction, *n.* v. V.—*act.* करणें *n.* &c. वहिवाट *f.* आचरण *n.* निर्वाह *m.* अनुष्ठान *n.*

I. *that which has been done,* v. Action, Affair. काम *n.* कार्य *n.* गोष्ट *f.* मुकदमा *m.*

To **Transcend.** See To Exceed, To Excel. [perior.

Transcendent, Transcendental. See Surpassing, Su-

To **Transcribe, Transcript,** &c. See To Copy, Copy, &c.

To **Transfer,** *v. a. convey from one place or person to another.* एकेजाग्यापासून दुसऱ्या जाग्यास नेणें-काढून नेणें, स्थलांतर *n.*-स्थानांतर *n.*-&c. करणें *g. of o.*

2 *make over, convey.* (दुसऱ्यास) देणें-सोंपणें-सोंपून देणें-स्वाधीन करणें, हवालणें, अध्यास *m.*-&c. करणें *g. of o.* स्वत्वनिवृत्ति करून-स्वत्वनिवृत्तिपूर्वक देणें, परहस्तदत्त-अध्यस्त-&c. करणें.

Transfer, Transference, *n.* v. V. 1. काढूननेणें *n.* &c. स्थलांतर *n.* स्थानांतर *n.*

2 दुसऱ्यासदेणें *n.* &c. परहस्तदान *n.*

Transferred, *p.* v. V. 1. काढून नेलेला, स्थलांतर केलेला, &c. अध्यस्त, संक्रांत.

2 (दुसऱ्यास) दिल्हेला, &c. परहस्तदत्त.

Transferrer, *n.* **Transferring,** *p. a.* v. V. 1. काढून नेणारा,

स्थलांतर करणारा, &c.
2 दुसऱ्यास देणारा, &c.

TRANSFIGURATION, *To* TRANSFIGURE, &c. See To TRANSFORM, &c.

To TRANSFIX, *v. a. pierce through.* आरपार-पार भोसकणें-बेधणें-टोंचणें-&c.

To TRANSFORM, *v. a. change the form, &c. of.* रूप*n.*-स्वरूप*n.*-आकार*m.*-&c. फिरवणें-पालटणें *g. of o.* रूपांतर*n.*-रूपभेद*m.*-&c. करणें *g. of o.*

TRANSFORMABLE, *a.* v. V. रूपांतरकरण्याजोगा-&c. विकार्य.

TRANSFORMATION, *n.* v. V. रूपांतर*n.* रूपभेद*m.* परिणाम*m.* परिणामांतर*n.* विकार*m.* विकृति *f.* रूपविकार*m.* रूपविकृति *f.*

TRANSFORMED, *p.* v. V. रूपफिरवलेला, रूपांतरकेलेला, &c. रूपविकृत, विकृत, वेकृत, विकृतरूप, विकृताकार, परिणत.

TRANSFORMER, *n.* TRANSFORMING, *p. a.* v. V. रूपफिरवणारा, रूपांतर करणारा, &c. रूपांतर-&c. कर्त्ता-कारी-&c.

To TRANSFUSE, *v. a. pour from one into another.* एकांतून-एकांतला *decl.* काढून दुसऱ्यांत ओतणें-घालणें, पात्रांतर*n.* करणें *g. of o.*

To TRANSGRESS, *v. a. overpass* (a limit, rule, &c.) lit. fig. उल्लंघणें, लंघणें, ओलांडणें, अतिक्रमणें, तोडणें, मोडणें, भंगणें, उल्लंघ*m.*-उल्लंघन*n.*-अतिक्रमण*n.*-व्यतिक्रम*m.*-&c. करणें *g. of o.*

To TRANSGRESS, *v.n. offend by violating a law,* v. To OFFEND. आज्ञा *f.*-हुकूम*m.*-&c. उल्लंघणें-मोडणें-तोडणें, अपराध*m.*-अन्याय *m.*-&c. करणें, आज्ञाभंग*m.* करणें.

TRANSGRESSED, *p.* v. V. A. उल्लंघलेला, ओलांडलेला, &c. उल्लंघित, लंघित, अतिक्रांत, व्यतिक्रांत, उत्क्रांत.

TRANSGRESSION, *n.*v.V. A.—*act.* उल्लंघणें*n.* लंघणें*n.* ओलांडणें*n.* &c. उल्लंघ*m.* उल्लंघन*n.* लंघन*n.* रेखालंघन*n.* भंग*m.* अतिक्रम*m.* अतिक्रमण*n.* व्यतिक्रम*m.* उत्क्रम*m.* अमर्यादा *f.*
v. V. N. *and* CRIME, SIN. आज्ञाभंग*m.* आज्ञोल्लंघ*m.* आज्ञोल्लंघन*n.* अपराध*m.* अन्याय*m.* अमर्यादा *f.*

TRANSGRESSOR, *n.* TRANSGRESSING, *p. a.* v. V. A. उल्लंघणारा, ओलांडणारा, उल्लंघकरणारा, &c. उल्लंघन-अतिक्रमण-&c. कर्त्ता-कारी-&c.
v. V. N. *and* CRIMINAL, SINNER. आज्ञा तोडणारा, &c. आज्ञोल्लंघी, आज्ञोल्लंघक, अपराधी, अन्यायी.

TRANSIENT, *a.* v. TEMPORARY. थोडावेळ राहणारा, अस्थायी, क्षणिक, अशाश्वत, भंगुर, चंचल, प्राघूर्णिक.

TRANSIENTNESS, TRANSIENCY, *n.* v. A. अस्थायिता *f.* चंचलता *f.* चांचल्य *n.*

TRANSIT, *n. passing over or across.* आरपारजाणें*n.* अहदतहदगमन *n.*-गति *f.* संक्रम *m.* संक्रमण *n.* संक्रांति *f.* अतिक्रम *m.* अतिक्रमण *n.*

TRANSIT-DUTY, *n.* राहदारी *f.* राहदारी जकात *f.*

TRANSITION, *n. passage from one state, condition, place, &c. to another,* v. CHANGE. संक्रम *m.* संक्रमण *n.* संक्रांति *f.* स्थित्यंतर *n.* अवस्थांतर *n.* स्थानांतर *n.* स्थलांतर *n.*

TRANSITIVE, *a.*—in grammar. सकर्मक.

TRANSITORINESS, *n.* v. A. अस्थायित्व *n.* क्षणिकत्व *n.* चांचल्य*n.*

TRANSITORY, *a.* v. TEMPORARY. अस्थायी, अचिरस्थायी, क्षणिक, क्षणभंगुर, चंचल *or* ळ, चल.

To TRANSLATE, *v. a. remove from one place to another,* v. To REMOVE. एक्या जाग्यापासून काढून दुसऱ्या जाग्यास नेणें, थारेपालट *m.*-स्थलांतर*n.*-स्थानांतर*n.*-&c. करणें.
2 *take bodily to Heaven.* सकुडी *adv.* नेणें-चढवून घेणें, (and, *passively.* जाणें-चढणें).
3 *render into another language.* आणणें, उतरणें, करणें, भाषांतर *n.*-तरजुमा *m.*-&c. करणें *g. of o.*

TRANSLATED, *p.* v. V. 1. थारेपालट केलेला, स्थानांतर केलेला, &c.
2 सकुडी नेलेला, &c. सशरीरमुक्त, सतनुक.
3 उतरलेला, दुसऱ्या भाषेत आणलेला.

TRANSLATION, *n.* v. V. 1. स्थानपालट*m.* स्थानांतर *n.* स्थलांतर*n.*
3 तरजुमा*m.* उतारा*m.* उतार*m.* भाषांतर*n.* अवतरण*n.* अवतार*m.*
A free or loose t. *an imitation.* छायानुहरण *n.*

TRANSLATOR, *n.* v. V. 3. उतरणारा, भाषांतर करणारा, &c.

TRANSLUCENT, &c. See TRANSPARENT, &c.

TRANSMARINE, *a.* समुद्रापलीकडला-पलीकडचा.

To TRANSMIGRATE, *v. n.* See To MIGRATE. 2 *pass from one body into another.* दुसऱ्या जन्मांत-अन्यजन्मांत-जन्मांतरांत-&c. जाणें, जन्मांतर *n.*-पुनर्जन्म *m. n.*-&c. पावणें-घेणें.

TRANSMIGRATION, *n.* v. V. 2. जन्मांतरांत जाणें *n.* &c. जन्मांतर *n.* पुनर्जन्म *m. n.* जन्ममरण *n.* योनिभ्रमण *n.*

TRANSMISSION, TRANSMITTAL, *n.* v. V. 1. पाठवणें *n.* धाडणें *n.* चालवणें *n.*

To TRANSMIT, *v. a.* v. To SEND. पाठवणें, धाडणें, पोहंचवणें, चालवणें, सादर करणें, परंपरागत करणें.
2 *suffer to pass through.* जाण्याची वाट *f.*-जाण्याचामार्ग *m.* देणें, पार जाऊं देणें.

TRANSMUTATION, *n.* v. V. परिणामांतर *n.* द्रव्यांतर *n.* परिणामभेद *m.* जात्यंतर *n.*

To TRANSMUTE, *v. a. change from one substace or nature into another,* v. To CHANGE. निराळेंद्रव्य *n.*-द्रव्यांतर *n.*-&c. करणें *g. of o.* जाति *f.*-&c. फिरवणें *g. of o.*

TRANSPARENCY, TRANSPARENTNESS, *n.* v. A. 1. प्रकाशभेद्यता *f.* किरणभेद्यता *f.* प्रकाशारोधकता *f.* &c.

TRANSPARENT, *a. that transmits light, not opake.* उजेडास वाटदेणारा, प्रकाशभेद्य, किरणभेद्य, प्रकाशारोधक, प्रकाशाप्रतिबंधक, दृष्ट्यरोधक.
2 See CLEAR.

To TRANSPIERCE, *v. a. transfix.* आरपार-&c. वेधणें-भोसकणें-&c.

To TRANSPIRE, *v. n. become public.* फुटणें, बाहेरपडणें, उमगणें, उमटणें, उमठणें, चौघांत-चौघचारांत-चहाट्यास-चावडीवर-प्रसिद्धीस-&c. येणें, प्रसिद्ध-प्रगट-उघड-&c. होणें.
2 *pass off through the pores.* रोमरंध्रांतून निघणें-बाहेरपडणें.

To TRANSPLANT, *v. a. remove and plant in another place.* दुसऱ्या भुईंत लावणें, लावणी *f.*-आंवणी *f.*-&c. करणें.

TRANSPLANTATION, *n.* v. V. लावणी *f.* रोपलावणी *f.* आंवणी *f.*
A bed of rice plants, &c. raised for t. तरवा *m.*

TRANSPLANTED, *p.* v. V. दुसऱ्या भुईंत लावलेला, लावणी केलेला, &c.

To TRANSPORT, *v. a. convey,* v. To CARRY. नेणें, वाहणें.
2 (criminals;) v. To BANISH. काळ्या पाण्यावर पाठवणें-धाडणें-नेणें.
3 *enrapture, enravish,* v. To REJOICE. फारचसंतोषविणें, फारचहर्षविणें, आल्हादणें, बालबालखुश-परमानंदित-&c. करणें.
4 *hurry or carry away by violence of passion.* भान *n.*-देहभान *n.*-शुद्धि *f.*-स्मृति *f.*-&c. उडवणें-नाहींसा *decl.* करणें-घा-

लवणें *g. of o.* देव *m. pl.* देव्हाऱ्यांत नाहींतसे करणें *g. of o.*

TRANSPORT, *n. rapture,* v. JOY. फारच मोठा आनंद *m.* अत्यानंद *m.* परमानंद *m.* ब्रह्मानंद *m.* आल्हाद *m.* आल्हादन *n.* उल्हाळा *or* उल्हाळा *m.*

2 *vessel of carriage, &c.* उताऱ्यांचें-उतारूंचें-सामान नेण्याचें-&c. गलबत *n.*-&c.

TRANSPORTATION, *n.* v. V. I.—*act.* नेणें *n.* वाहणें *n.*

2 *and* BANISHMENT. काळ्या पाण्यावर पाठवणें *n.*

TRANSPORTED, *p.* v. V. 1. नेलेला, &c.

2 काळ्यापाण्यावर पाठवलेला.

3 फारच संतोषवलेला, &c. बालबालखुश, हर्षरोमांचित, रोमहर्षित.

To be t. आनंद *m.*-हर्ष *m.*-&c. ब्रह्मांडांत न मावणें *g. of s.* आनंद*m.*-&c. कोठें माईनासा होणें *g.of s.* उल्हाळणें *or* उल्हाळणें.

4 देहभान उडवलेला, &c. नष्टभान.

TRANSPORTING, *p. a.* v. V. 3. फारच हर्षवणारा, &c. परमानंदप्रद-दायक-कारक-&c. बालबाल खुश करणारा.

To TRANSPOSE, *v.a. put each in the place of the other.* जाग्याची-स्थानाची-&c. अदलाबदल *f.*-उलटापालट *f.*-&c. करणें *g.of o.* स्थानविनिमय *m.*-&c. करणें *g. of o.*

TRANSPOSED, *p.* v. V. जाग्याची उलटपालट केलेला, &c.

TRANSPOSITION, TRANSPOSAL, *n.* v. V. जाग्याची-स्थळाची-&c. अदलाबदल *f.*-उलटापालट *f.*-&c. स्थानविनिमय *m.* स्थलविनिमय *m.* स्थानपरिवर्त्त *m.* [रिणामांतर *n.*

TRANSUBSTANTIATION, *n. change of substance.* द्रव्यांतर *n.* प-

TRANSVERSAL, TRANSVERSE, *a. lying across.* आडवा, तिर्यक्.

TRANSVERSALLY, *adv.* v. A. आडवा *decl.* तिर्यक्.

TRAP, *n.* v. SNARE. सांपळा *m.*

2 fig. *stratagem or device for deceiving,* v. MACHINATION. डाव *m.* पेच *m.* कचाट *or* किचाट *n.* गचका *m.*

To catch one in his own t. ज्याच्या टांगड्या *f. pl.* त्याच्याच गळ्यांत घालणें, ज्याचें बोट *n.* त्याच्याच डोळ्यांत घालणें, ज्याचे दांत *m. pl.* त्याच्याच घशांत घालणें.

3—the play. इटीदांडू *or* इटूदांडू *m.* गोलदांडा *m.*

4—the rock or stone. कार *f. m.* काळादगड *m.* काळेभिंबरी *f.* काळबंधरी *f.*

To TRAP. See To INSNARE.

TRAP-DOOR, *n.* चोरदार *n.* चोरदरवाजा *m.*

TRAP-STICK, *n.* दांडू *m.* दांडा *m.*

To TRAPAN. See To INSNARE.

TRAPES. See SLUT.

TRAPEZIUM, *n.*—in geometry. विषमचतुरस्र *n.* विषमचतुर्भुज *n.*

TRAPEZOID, *n.* समलंबचतुर्भुज *m.*

TRAPPINGS, *n.* v. FINERY. मिरवणुकीचा-गोंधळ्याचा-नटव्याचा-कळवांतिणीचा-नवऱ्याचा-&c. पोशाक *m.*-साजु *m.* गोपाळवर्खें *n. pl.*

TRAPS, *n.* v. THINGS. चीजवस्त *f.* सामान *n.* सारसुसर *f.* इलाखिला *m.*

Travelling t. v. BAGGAGE. खाटखटलें *n.* खाटखडबड *f.* बाड़बिशात *or* द *f.*

TRASH, *n. worthless matter, rubbish, stuff, trumpery.* ऐलपैल *or* फैल *f.* ऐलपैलवस्तू *f. pl.* गटरफटर *n.* फांसफूस *f.* फूस *f.* कतवार *n.* काण्णूवाण्णू *or* कायणूवायणू *m.* खेर *f.* खेरमेर *n.* अगडबगड *n.* अगडतगड *n.* अटरफटर *n.* बगळ *f.* बगळसगळ *f.* कचराकुचरा *m.*

2 v. NONSENSE. अगडतगड *n.* अगडबगड *n.* अटरफटर *n.*

3 *improper food, green fruit, &c.* हिरवेदोडे *m. pl.* हिरवेकाकडे *m. pl.* हिरवेंकाचें-हिरवेंचिरवें-हिरवेंदुरदें-आंबटचिंबट-भलतेंसलतें-&c. फळ *n.*-खाणें *n.*-&c.

TRASHY. See WORTHLESS.

TRAVAIL, See LABOR.

To TRAVAIL, *v. n.v.* To LABOR. वेणटणें *or* वेणाटणें, वेणवणें.

To TRAVEL, *v. n. journey, pass, go, &c.* चालणें, वाट *f.*-मार्ग *m.*-रस्ता *m.*-&c. चालणें-क्रमणें, मुशाफरी *f.*-मार्गक्रमण *n.*-मार्गगमन *n.*-&c. करणें.

2 *go to a distant country, visit a foreign place.* देशांतर *n.*-प्रवास *m.*-देशाटन *n.*-देशपर्यटन *n.*-देशभ्रमण *n.*-&c. करणें, प्रवासास-देशांतरीं-मुलखावर-&c. जाणें, फिरणें, देशोदेश-देशविदेश फिरणें, अटणें.

To TRAVEL, *v. a. pass over, journey over, traverse.* फिरणें (this verb agrees with the agent), क्रमणें, लेटणें, कंठणें, पायाखालीं घालणें, तुडवणें, भोग *m.* करणें *g. of o.*

TRAVEL, TRAVELLING, *n.* v. V. N. 1. चालणें *n.* मुशाफरी *or* मुसाफरी *f.* मार्गक्रमण *n.* मार्गगमन *n.* मार्गोल्लंघन *n.* मार्गातिक्रमण *n.* यात्रा *f.*

2 *and* travels. देशांतर करणें *n.* फिरणें *n.* &c. देशांतर *n.* देशपर्यटन *n.* देशाटन *n.* देशभ्रमण *n.* प्रवास *m.* प्रवासगमन *n.* अटन *n.* पर्यटन *n.*

v. V. A. क्रमणें *n.* &c. क्रमण *n.* संक्रमण *n.* संक्रम *m.*

TRAVELLER, *n.* TRAVELLING, *p. a.* v. V. N. मार्ग चालणारा, वाटचालणारा, वाटसरू, वाटमार्गी, मुशाफर *or* मुसाफर, मार्गस्थ, पथिक, पांथस्थ, पांथ, यायी, सारणिक, उतारू.

Building for the accommodation of travellers. धर्मशाला *pop.* धर्मसाळ *f.*

2 देशांतर करणारा-केलेला, प्रवास करणारा-केलेला, &c. फिरस्त *or* स्ता, प्रवासी, देशिक.

Traveller's tale. मुशाफरीगप *f.* भंडपुराण *n.* नीळरांप *f. m.* The current sayings or phrases in reproof and rejection of the extravagant accounts of *Travellers,* or of gross and unblushing lies in general, are, सातहात तवसें नव हात बीं, सांगासांगी वडाला वांगी, सात हात लांकूड नव हात ढलपी, नीळ नासली *or* रांपली *or* निळीचा रंग नासला, त्वां लंका पाहिली तर काय झालें म्यां पडलंका पाहिली.

I. *belonging, &c. to travelling.* मुशाफरीचा, वाटेचा, मार्गाचा, वाट चालण्याचा, वाट चालण्याविषयींचा, वाटसंबंधी, मुशाफरी, मार्गसंबंधी, सारणिक.

T. expenses. वाटखर्च *m.* वाटेचाखर्च *m.*—compreh. उतारपातार *m.*

To TRAVERSE, *v. a. travel over,* v. To TRAVEL. फिरणें agrees with the agent, क्रमणें, लेटणें, कंठणें, पायाखालीं घालणें, तुडवणें.

TRAVERSE, *a. lying across.* आडवा.

To TRAVESTY. See To BURLESQUE.

TRAY, *n. salver, waiter, &c.* परात *f.* तबक *n. dim.* तबकडी *f.* पाटें *n.* ताट *n.* खांजा *m.* थाटली *f.*

2—at cards. तिक्का *m.* तिव्वा *m.*

3 See TROUGH.

TREACHEROUS, *a.* v. FALSE, PERFIDIOUS. फितुरी, फितुरखोर, दगाबाज, दगलबाज, विश्वासघातक, विश्वासघातकी, विश्वासघाता-

चा, कुजका, घालू, घाल्या, घालवा, फसव्या, कुडा.

TREACHEROUSLY, *adv.* v. A. फितुरी-&c. होऊन, विश्वासघात करून, &c. विश्वासघातपूर्वक, दगलबाजीनें, गळाकापून.

TREACHEROUSNESS, TREACHERY, *n.* v. A. फितुरपणा *m.* दगा *m.* दगल *f.* दगलबाजी *f.* विश्वासघात *m.* बेइमानी *f.* फितुरी *f.* फितूर *m.* फितुरीपणा *m.*

TREACLE, *n.* v. MOLASSES. काकवी *f.* बेरी *f.* मळी *f.*

To TREAD, *v. n. set the foot, walk, go.* पाय *m.* ठेवणें-देणें, पदन्यास *m.*-पदपात *m.*-चरणपात *m.*-&c. करणें *or with g. of s.* होणें-असणें.

To TREAD, *v. a. step or walk on.* पाय *m.* ठेवणें-देणें *or* ठेवून-देऊन जाणें *with* वर *of o.* पदन्यास *m.*-पदविक्षेप *m.*-&c. करणें *with* वर *of o.*

2 *beat or press with the feet.* मळणें, पायानें-पाय देऊन दाबणें-दडपणें-&c. तुडवणें, घोळणें, चोळणें, दळवटणें, मळणी *f.*-&c. करणें *g. of o.* चोळ *f.* पाडणें.

3 See To TRAMPLE. 4 out (corn, &c.); *press out with feet.* मळणें, मळणी *f.* करणें *g. of o.*

TREAD. See STEP.

TREAD-MILL, *n.* गिरणी *f.*

TREADINGFLOOR. See THRESHING-FLOOR.

TREASON, *n. violation of allegiance.* सरकाराशींदुशमनी *f.* राजद्रोह *m.* राजविरोध *m.* राजापकार*m.* राजप्रातिकूल्य *n.* फितूर*m.*

TREASONABLE, TREASONOUS, *a.*v.N. सरकाराशींदुशमनीचा, सरकाराशींदुशमनी करणारा, राजद्रोहाचा, राजद्रोहकर्त्ता-कारी, &c. राजद्रोहविषयक-संबंधी.

T. plots and practices. फंदफितूर *m.* फितूर फांदा*m.*

TREASURE, *n. riches hoarded,* v. HOARD. निधि *m.* निधान *n.* डल्ला *m.* पैक्याचा भरणा *m.* पैक्याची जोड *f.* सांठवलेला-&c. पैका *m.*-पैसा *m.*-धन *n.*-&c. द्रव्यसंचय *m.* धनसंचय *m.* धनसंग्रह *m.* संचितधन *n.*-&c. धनराशि *m.* निक्षेप *m.*

The nine treasures of कुबेर or Pluto. नवनिधि *or* नवनिधान*n.* These are named, महापद्म,पद्म, शंख, मकर, कच्छप, मुकुंद, कुंद, नील, खर्व.

2 *object much prized.* निधान *n.* निधि *m.* नीध *f.* गुणाचीरास *f.* गुणराशि *m.* रत्न *n.* हिरा *m.* मोतीं *n.* दाणा *m.* परीस *m.*

3 *public money.* खजाना *m.* खजीना *m.* जामदारखाना *m.* पोतें *n.* भांडार *m. n.*

To TREASURE. See To HOARD.

TREASURER, *n. officer in charge of treasure or a treasury.* खजीनदार, भंडारी, भांडारी, जामदार, जामदारखानेवाला, कोशाध्यक्ष, कोशनायक, कोष्टपाल, कोशाधिकारी, भांडागारी, भांडागारिक, धनाध्यक्ष, धनाधिकारी, धनाधिप, अर्थाधिकारी.

TREASURERSHIP, *n. office of treasurer.* खजीनदारी *f.* जामदारी *f.* कोशाधिकार *m.* धनाधिकार *m.* अर्थाधिकार *m.*

TREASURY, *n. place for keeping treasure.* भांडार *n.* भंडार *n.* भांडारखाना *m.* जामदारखाना *m.* खजाना *m.* खजीना *m.* भांडागार *n.* तोशेखाना *m.* कोश*m.* कोष्ट*m.* कोष्ठक *m.n.* वित्तशाला *f.*

Advances out of the public t. तगाई *f.*

Bill of payments into the t. सरखत *n.*

Full & overflowing t. भंडारभरपूर *n.*

Paying (of the revenue) into the t. रसदभरणा *m.*

Payments into the t. रसद *f.*

To TREAT, *v. a. use, handle, deal with, behave towards.* वागणें, वर्त्तणें, चाळणें, वागणूक *f.*-वर्त्तणूक *f.*-वहिवाट *f.*-&c. करणें; (Note, all the preceding words require शीं *of o.* Ex. तुम्हाशीं तो कसा वागला ?) करणें *with* चें *of o.* चालवणें *g. of o.* वागवणें, वर्त्तवणें, वहिवाटणें, वहिवाटवणें, वापरणें;—carefully, heedfully, जोपासणें, जोगवणें, जोंबाळणें, जोपाशीर *or* ल *f.*-जोपासना *f.*-बरदास्त *f.*-संभाळ *m.* करणें *g. of o.*—gently, tenderly, delicately, तळहाताचे फोडासारिखें वागवणें -बाळगणें-&c.जिवाचा ताईतसा मानून वागवणें:—considerately, leniently, संभाळून-वागवून घेणें;—honorably, respectfully, सन्मान *m.*-आदर *m.*-आदर सत्कार *m.*-शिष्टसंभावना *f.*-&c. करणें *g. of o.*—roughly and injuriously, कुदलणें, खुंदलणें, गुधडणें, घुसडणें, घोळणें, चुरंगटणें, चुरगळणें *or* चुरगाळणें, हेबाळणें, झाजरणें, गुधडा *m.* घालणें *g. of o.* पेर *m.* घालणें, रगडपट्टी *f.*-रगडमल्ली *f.*-घोळण *n.*-हेबाळणी *f.*-&c. करणें *g. of o.* रवखंदळ *f. n.* करणें *g. of o.*

2 *entertain without expense to the guest.* खर्च न पडूं देतां खाऊं घालणें-मेजवानी *f.* करणें, पदर *m.* घालणें-मोडणें-खर्च *m.* करणें *with* करितां-साठीं-&c. *of o.*

3 (a disease, &c.). उपाय *m.*-उपचार *m.*-चिकित्सा *f.*-&c. करणें *g. of o.*

To TREAT, *v. n. negociate terms of accommodation.* तहाचें-सल्ह्याचें-समेटाचें-&c. बोलणें *n.* करणें-चालवणें.

2 of ; *handle in writing or speaking.* विषय *m.*-प्रसंग *m.*-प्रकरण *n.*-&c. चालवणें-सांगणें-दाखवणें, विषय *m.*-प्रसंग *m.*-&c. असणें *with* मध्यें-आंत-&c.

TREAT, *n.*v. ENTERTAINMENT, FEAST. मेजमानी *or* मेजवानी *f.*

TREATISE, *n. tract, book, &c.* शास्त्र *n.* आगम *m.* प्रबंध *m.* निबंध *m.* ग्रंथ *m.* पुस्तक *n.*

Sacred t. आगम *m.* शास्त्र *n.*

TREATMENT, *n.* v. V. 1. वागवणें *n.* वापरणें *n.* &c. वागवणूक *f.* वहिवाट *f.* This transitive word is most idiomatically rendered by the intransitive word "behaviour towards;" for words expressing which, See CONDUCT.

3 उपाय करणें *n.* &c. उपचार *m.* चिकित्सा *f.* कार्यचिकित्सा *f.* क्रिया *f.* रोगप्रतिक्रिया *f.*

TREATY, *n. compact between two powers,* v. AGREEMENT. बोली *f.* समय *m.* नियम *m.*

T. of peace. तह *m.*

Written t. of peace. तहनामा *m.* सल्लानामा *m.*

TREBLE, *a. threefold.* तिपदरी, तिहिरी, तिहेरा, तिप्पट.

2 *thrice told.* तिप्पट, तिगुणा, त्रिगुण.

3—in music. किनरा *or* किन्हेरा.

TREBLE, *n.*—in music or singing. किनरी *f.* टीप *f.* टिपेचा सूर*m.* गळी*f.*उच्चसवन *f. n.*तृतीयसवन*n.*—in reading, प्रातःसवन *f. n.*

2 *treble quantity.* तिप्पट *f.*

To TREBLE, *v. a. make thrice as much.* तिप्पट-&c. करणें.

To TREBLE, *v. n. become thrice as much.* तिप्पट-&c. होणें.

TREE, *n.* झाड *n.* वृक्ष *m.* पेड *n.* तरु *m.* रूख *m.* द्रुम *m.* शाखी *m.* वनस्पति *m.*

From t. to t. झाडोझाड.

Hole or hollow in a t. कोटर *n. m.*

Holy or sacred tree. देववृक्ष *m.* देवतरु *m.*

Old and decaying t. ढांक *n.* ढांकळ *f.* झींट *n.*

Shade of trees (viewed as injurious to vegetation) ओस *n.* ओसंग *m.* ओशेटा *m.* आसवा *m.*

Skilful in climbing t. रुखाडी *or* ड्या, रुख्या.

T. having a hole. ढोलार.

T. as taken up for transplantation. पेड *n.*

Trees and bushes,—compreh. झाडझुडूप *n.* झाडझुडपी *f.* झाडझुड *n.* झाडझाडोरा *m.* झाडपेड *n.* झाडमाड *m.*

T. planted by the hand of. हातझाड *n.*

A corrupt t. cannot yield good fruit. आडांत पाणी खारट पोऱ्यांत कोठून गोड येईल.

TREFOIL, *n.* त्रिपर्ण *m. n.*

TRELLIS, TRELLISWORK, *n.* जाळी *f.* जाळें *n.* जाळीदार काम *n.* गवाक्षजाल *n.*

To TREMBLE, *v. n. shake tremulously, totter, vibrate, &c.* कांपणें,लटलट-लुखुलुखु-डगमग *or* गां-डगडग *or* गां-&c. हालणें-कांपणें-डुलणें-डोलणें, लटलटणें, डगमगणें, डकडकणें *or* डगडगणें, डळमळणें, डगणें, हदरणें, हदहदणें, दलदल-थलथल-&c. हालणें, स्फुरणें, कंप *m.*-लटलट *f.*-&c. होणें *g. of s.* लटलट *f.* करणें.

2 *shake from fear, cold, &c.; quake, quiver, shiver, shudder, &c.* कांपणें, थरथरणें, थरकणें, हुडहुडणें, शिरशिरणें, थरथर-थरकन-थरकर-&c. कांपणें-भिणें, कंप*m.*-कांप *m.*-कांपरा*m.*-कांपरी*f.*-कांपरें*n.*-थरथरी*f.*-हुडहुडी*f.*-खुडखुडी *f.*-&c.सुटणें-भरणें*in. con.* पाठ *f.* कांपणें *g. of s.* खुडखुडणें—*intens.* थरारणें, चळचळ-चळचळां-चळाचळ *adv.* कांपणें, थरारून कांप *m.* येणें-सुटणें *in. con.*

TREMBLER, *n.* TREMBLING, *p. a.* v. V. 1. कांपणारा, लटलट हालणारा, &c. लटलटीत, मळमळीत, डळमळीत, डळडळीत *or* डिळडिळीत, डगडगीत, चंचल *or* ळ, तरल, सकंप, कंपित, कंपायमान, कंपमान, कंपान्वित, विकंपित, ललित.

2 कांपणारा, थरथरणारा, कांपभरलेला, कांपरीसुटलेला, &c. सकंप, कंपित, कंपमान *pop.* कंपायमान, कंपान्वित, विकंपित.

T. *that is ever trembling and quaking.* कांपरा.

TREMBLING, *n.* v. V. 1. कांपणें *n.* डगणें *n.* डगडगणें *n.* &c. कंप *m.* लटलट *f.* डळमळ *f.* दलदल *f.* स्फुरण *n.* स्फूर्त्ति *f.*

2 कांपणें *n.* थरकणें *n.* हुडहुडणें *n.* &c. कंप *m.* कांप *m.* कांपरा *m.* कांपरी *f.* कांपरें *n.* थरथर *f.* थरथरी *f.* थरकणी *f.* हुडहुडी *f.* खुडखुडी *f.* शिसारी *f.* कंपन *n.*—*intens.* थरारी *f.* थरथराट *m.* थरकांप *m.* चळकांप *m.* चळाळ *m.*

TREMBLINGLY, *adv.* v. V. 2. कांपून, थरथरून, कांपरा भरून, &c. थरथर, थरकन, थरकर, &c.

TREMENDOUS, *a.* v. FEARFUL. भयंकर, भयानक, दारुण.

2 *violent, excessive.* मोठा, जोराचा, जबर, जबरा, जबरदस्त, प्रचंड, अनर्थाचा, पराकाष्ठेचा.

TREMOR, *n.* v. TREMBLING. कांपरी *f.* कांपरें *n.* चळकांप *m.* थरकांप *m.* चळाळ*m.* लटपट *f.* थरथरी *f. intens.* थरारी *f.* थरथर *f. intens.* थरथराट *m.* शिसारी *f.* गात्रभंग *m.* अंगकंप *m.*

That is all of a t. थरकांप झालेला.

T. with horripilation. शाहरे *m. pl.* शाहरें *n. v.* ये.

TREMULOUS, *a.* v. TREMBLING. कांपरा, डळडळीत *or* डिळडिळीत, डळमळीत, तरल, सकंप.

TREMULOUSNESS, *n.* v. A. कांपरेपणा *m.* डळडळीतपणा *m.* &c. डळमळ *f.* दलदल *f.* तारल्य *n.* तरलता *f.* सकंपता *f.*

To TRENCH. See To ENCROACH.

To TRENCH, *v. a.* (land). खंदक *m.*-&c. खणणें-पाडणें.

TRENCH, *n. ditch, furrow.* खंदक *m.* हरळ *m.* चर *m. dim.* चरी *f.* टरळी *f.* खाई *f.*

T. to carry of water. कावळा *m.* हरळ *m.* हरळा *m.*

Trenches, *intrenchment.* खंदकमोरचा *m.*

TRENCHER, *n. wooden plate.* लाकडाचें बासन *n.*-भांड *n.* पात्र *n.* काठवट *f.* मांड *f.*

TRENCHER-FLY, TRENCHER-MATE, *n.* v. PARASITE. भोजनभाऊ, भोजनऱ्या, उंडीचकाल, पात्रसंमित.

To TREND, *v. n. tend.* वाहणें, वळणें.

To TREPAN. See To INSNARE.

TREPIDATION, *n.* v. TREMBLING. कांपरा *m.* कांपरी *f.* कांपरें *n.* शिसारी *f.* चळकांप *m.* थरकांप *m.* शहारे *m. pl. v.* ये, शहारे *n. v.* ये, गात्रभंग *m.* [*g. of s.*

To be in great t. जीव *or* प्राण *m.* कांपणें-थरथरणें-कालवणें

To TRESPASS, *v. n. pass bounds, exceed propriety, violate rules, &c.* v. To OFFEND. हुकूम *m.*-आज्ञा *f.*-&c. तोडणें-तोडून जाणें *or* येणें *or* फिरणें-&c. हुकुमावांचून जाणें-येणें-&c. अगळी *f.*-अगळीक *f.*-आज्ञोलंघ *m.*-सीमोलंघन *n.*-&c. करणें, अन्याय *m.*-अपराध *m.*-&c. करणें.

TRESPASS, TRESPASSING, *n.* v. V. *and* CRIME. हुकुमावांचून जाणें *n.* &c. आज्ञाभंग *m.* आज्ञोलंघ *m.* आज्ञोलंघन *n.* सीमोलंघ *m.* सीमोलंघन *n.* सीमातिक्रमण *n.* अतिक्रमण *n.* अगळी *f.* अगळीक *f.* अगळीन *f.* अमर्यादा *f.* अपराध *m.*

TRESS, *n. knot or curl of hair.* केशाचाझुबका *m.*-गुच्छ *m.* बट *f.* झुलूप *n.*

Dishevelled or loose t. झिपटी *f.* झिपरी *f.* झिंगी *f.* झिंजी *f.* झिंटी *f.* झिंझोटी *f.* बाबर झोंटी *f. pl.* बाबरी *f.*

TRET, *n. allowance in dealing.* कडता *m.* कांटा *m.*

TREVET, *n. stool, &c. of three legs.* तिवई *f.* तिकटी *f.* तिव्हा *m.*

TRIAD, *n. trio.* त्रिकूट *n.* त्रिक *n.* त्रय *n.*

2 (of the Hindùs). त्रिमूर्त्ति *f.*

TRIAL, *n. testing, proving, experiment.* परीक्षा *f.* पारख *f.* अजमाव *m.* कसोटी *or* कसवटी *f.* परीक्षण *n.*

2 *judicial examination.* न्याय होण्याची-इनसाफ होण्याची-&c. चोकसी *f.*-तपासणी *f.*-&c. न्याय *m.* इनसाफ *m.* चोकसी *f.* पंचाईत *f.* व्यवहारदर्शन *n.* धर्मविवेचन *n.* [ताडणी *f.*

3 *essay, attempt.* करून पाहणें *n.* अजमाव *m.* अजमावणी *f.*

4 v. EXPERIENCE. अनुभव *m.*

5 See AFFLICTION, CALAMITY.

TRIANGLE, *n.* त्रिकोण *m.* त्रिकोणाकृति *f.* त्रिभुज *m.*

Acute-angled t. अंतर्लंब *m.*

Base of a t. भुज *m.*

Equilateral t. समत्रिभुज *m.*

Isosceles t. द्विसमत्रिभुज *m.*

Right-angled t. समकोण त्रिकोण *m.* जात्यत्रिभुज *m.*

Scalene t. विषमत्रिभुज *m.*

Segment of the base of a t. अबाधा *f.* अवधा *f.*

Vertical arm of a t. कोटि *f.*

2 *triangular area.* कातर *f.* चिमटा *m.* त्रिकोणक्षेत्र *n.*

3 *triangular construction of three sticks.* तिकटी *f.* तिकटें *n.* कैंची *f.*

TRIANGULAR, *a.* तिकोनी, त्रिकोण, त्रिकोणाकृति.

TRIBE, *n.* v. CAST. जाति *pop.* जात *f.* कुल *pop.* कूळ *n.* खूम *m.* गण *m.* वर्ग *m.* वर्ण *m.* जथा *m.*

A whole t. or family. जथावळ *f.*

By tribes or families. जथेबार.

TRIBULATION, *n.* v. AFFLICTION, TROUBLE. दुःख *n.* क्लेश *m.* विपत्ति *f.* आपत्ति *f.* संकट *n.*

TRIBUNAL, *n. court of justice,* v. COURT. न्यायसभा *f.* धर्मशाला *f.* धर्माधिकरण *n.* [सन *n.*

2 *seat of a judge.* न्यायाधिशाची गादी *f.* न्यायासन *n.* धर्मा-

TRIBUTARY, *n.* v. A. 1. खंडणीदार, खंडणी देणारा, सामंत *m.*

TRIBUTARY, *a. that pays tribute.* खंडणी देणारा, कर देणारा, करभार देणारा, &c. खंडणीदार, करद.

2 *paid in tribute.* खंडणीचा, कररूप. [करभार *m.*

TRIBUTE, *n. tax paid by a prince or nation.* खंडणी *f.* कर *m.*

TRICE, *n. short time,* v. INSTANT. पळ *n.* त्रुटि *f.*

In a t. *in a jiffey, shake, &c.* पळमात्रांत, एकाचुटकींत, त्रुटींत, त्रुटिमात्रांत, इतक्यांत, इतक्यामध्यें, उठाउठी, उभाउभी, उभ्यांउभ्यां,उभ्यांउभ्यानी, खडाखड *or* डी, खडीचोट, खडोखड *or* डी,चुट-कन-कर-&c. *or* चट-&c. चटपट, चप-कन-कर, &c. झटपट, झट-कन-कर, &c. झटझट *or* टां, झड-कन-कर-&c. झडझड *or* डां, झणझण *or* णां, झपकन-कर-&c. झपझप *or* पां, झर-कन-कर-&c. झरझर *or* रां, टपकन-कर-&c. टपटप *or* पां, तड्‌ट, तडकातडकी, तडकाफडकी, लक-कण-कर-&c. हातचेहातीं, हांहांम्हणतां *or* म्हणे तों, चटाचट, झटाझट, झटाटां, झडाझड, झडाडां, झपाझप, झपापां, झराझर, झरारां, पानास चुना लावी तों, पापणीस पापणी लावी तों, पात्यासपातें लावलें नाहीं तों.

To vanish in a t. सटकणें *or* सडकणें *or* सुटकणें.

TRICK, *n. stratagem to deceive, a sly fraud,* v. ARTIFICE. फसवण्याची-&c. युक्ति *f.*-हिकमत *f.*-&c. छक्कड *f. v.* दे, फट *f.* फटवण *f.* फसवणी *f.* फसवणूक *f.* कुलंगडें *n.*

Tricks, *wiles and artifices.* चकरमकर *f.* कतरभेद *m. pl.* शकटभेद *m. pl.* छक्केपंजे *m. pl.* चक्रफक्र *m. pl.* गारूड *n.* डावघाव *m. pl.*

2 *a vicious habit, a vice.* दुर्गुण *n.* अवगुण *m.* लकब *f.* टेव *f.* व्यसन *n.* दुर्लक्षण *n.* लत *f.*

Beggarly or mean t. भिकारचाळा *m.*

3 *odd or strange habit or manner.* खोड *f.* चटक *f.* सवई *f.* लटक *f.* चवणा *or* चौणा *m.* चाळा *m.* चाळ *f.* लजत *f.* लकब *f.* आदत *f.*

Tricks,—compreh. खतखोड *f.*

4 *antick, frolic, &c.* v. PRANK. खेळकुडी *f.* माकडचेष्टा *f.* माकडचाळे *m. pl.* छंद *m.* छंदफंद *m. pl.* छंदविछंद *m. pl.* पोरचेष्टा *f.* पोरचाळे *m. pl.* टिवल्याबावल्या *f. pl.*

Juggling tricks of a conjurer, &c. गारूड *n.*

5 *the artifice, mystery. secret, &c. of.* v. ART. कला *pop.* कळ *f.* युक्ति *pop.* युगूत *f.* कालगूत *n.* टूक *f.* गुरुकिल्ली *f.* कल्पना *f.*

To TRICK, *v. a.* v. TO CHEAT, TO DECEIVE. फसवणें, घुलकावणें, गोफाटणें, मुंडवण *f.* घालणें, गोता *m.* चारणें-देणें, वंचणें, वंचन *n.* -वंचना *f.* करणें.

2 *deck, bedizen, &c.* सजवणें, सजणें, नटवणें, शृंगारणें,बनविणें, साजरा-&c. करणें, शोभवणें, चट्टीपट्टी *f.*-शानशोकी *f.*-टिलाटोपी *f.*-&c. करणें *g. of o.*

To be tricked out. केळवणें, ठाकणें, नटणें, बनणें.

TRICKERY. See DECEIT, ARTIFICE.

To TRICKLE, *v. n. flow in a small gentle stream.* ओघळणें, ओहळणें, बारीक धारेनें गळणें-वाहणें, पाझरणें, ओझरणें, झुळझुळणें, झुळझुळ *adv.* वाहणें, ओघळ *m.*-ओहळ *m.*-गळती *f.* होणें-लागणें-चालणें *g. of s.* गळती *f.* धरणें, झरणें, चिघळणें, टिपकणें, वाहवणें, श्रावणें, स्रवणें, क्षरणें, झिरपणें. [क्षर.

TRICKLING, *p. a.* v. V. बारीक धारेनें गळणारा, ओहळणारा, &c.

T. water. झुळवणी *n.*

TRICKLING, *n.* v. V. बारीकधार *f.* ओघळ *m. f.* ओहळ *m. dim.* ओहळी *f.* पाझर *m.* ओझर *m.* गळ *f.* गळती *f.* श्राव *m.* स्राव *m.* स्रव *m.* स्रवण *n.* निझर *m.* द्रव *m.* क्षरण *n.* ओलंगर *m.* स्यंदन *n.*

TRIDENT, *n.* त्रिशूल *m. n.* त्रिशिख *m. n.* त्रिशीर्षक *m.* पिनाक *m.*

TRIDUAN, *a. lasting three days.* तीन दिवसांचा, तीनदिवशी, त्रिदिनात्मक, त्र्याहिक.

2 *happening every third day.* तिसऱ्या तिसऱ्या दिवसानें घडणारा-येणारा, द्व्यहांतरित.

TRIED, *p.* v. V. A. 1. ताडलेला, पारखलेला, &c. परीक्षित.

2 *and* EXPERIENCED. अनुभवलेला, अनुभव घेतलेला, आनुभविक *pop.* अनुभवीक, साक्षात्कृत.

3 तपासलेला, चौकसलेला, चौकशीकेलेला, &c.

4 हातीं घेतलेला, उद्योग करून पाहिलेला, &c.

5 पाहिलेला, कसलेला, कसूनपाहिलेला, ताडून-पडताळून-&c. पाहिलेला, &c.

I. *that has passed ordeal; proved, &c.*—a person. ताबून सुलाखून घेतलेला-पाहिलेला, कसोटीस उतरलेला.

TRIENNIAL, *a. lasting three years.* तीन वर्षांचा, तिसाली, तिवर्षी *or* तीनवर्षी, त्र्याब्दिक, त्रिवर्षात्मक, वर्षत्रयात्मक.

2 *happening every three years.* तीन तीन वर्षांनीं येणारा-होणारा-&c. तिसाली, तिवर्षी, त्रैवार्षिक, त्र्याब्दिक.

TRIENNIALLY, *adv. of or for three successive years.* तिसाला *or* लीं.

TRIER, *n.* TRYING, *p. a.* v. V. A. 1. ताडणारा, पारखणारा, परीक्षा करणारा, &c.

2 अनुभवणारा, अनुभव घेणारा, &c.

3 तपासणारा, चौकशी करणारा, &c.

4 हातीं घेणारा, उद्योग करून पाहणारा, &c.

5 पाहणारा, कसणारा, कसून पाहणारा, ताडून पाहणारा, &c.

I. *perplexing, difficult, adapted to try.* कचाटीचा, पेंचाटीचा, संकटाचा, कठीण.

To TRIFLE, *v. n. act with levity, &c.* खेळणें, खेळ *m.*-&c. करणें, गमणें, झक *f.* मारणें, गोष्टी *f. pl.* सांगणें, रिकामाकारभार *m.*-रिकामचेष्टा *f.*-&c. करणें, माशा *f. pl.* मारणें-मारीत बसणें, शेण *n.* खाणें, कुल्ले *m. pl.* खाजवणें-खाजवीत बसणें, विरंगुळणें.

TRIFLE, *n. simple or easy matter.* हलकी-लहान-&c. गोष्ट *f.* अल्प गोष्ट *f.* अल्पविषय *m.* तणसरी *f.* सुताचा तोडा *m.* आपल्या परसांतली भाजी *f.* नजरेचा खेळ *m.*

A trifle, *in a small degree,* v. LITTLE. अमळ,कांहींसा *decl.*

TRIFLER, *n.* TRIFLING, *p. a.* v. V. खेळणारा, गमणारा, झकमारणारा, माशामारणारा, &c. खेलगड्या, गमदसडा *or* दासडा *or* दासरा, रिकामटवळा, रिकामाकारभारी, छचोर.

TRIFLING, *a. trivial.* हलका, लहान, एर, एरशेर, एरळ, सैरीशैरी, जमेंतला न खरचांतला, अल्प, स्वल्प,अल्पप्रभाव, उपेक्षणीय, अगण्य, अगणेय, अगणनीय, जुजबी, क्षुल्लक, क्षुद्र.

TRIFLING, *n.* v. V. खेळणें*n.* &c. खेळ*m.* रिकामचेष्टा *f.* रिकामाकारभार*m.* रिकामचाळे*m. pl.* रिकामटबल्लेपणा*m.*

TRIFOLIATE, *a. having three leaves.* तिपानी, त्रिपर्ण, त्रिदल.

TRIFORM, *a. having a triple form.* त्रिविध. [तिसांदी.

TRIFURCATED, *a. having three branches.* तिफांटी, तिफांट्यांचा,

TRIFURCATION, *n.* तिफांटा*m.*

TRIGAMIST, *n. man that has married thrice.* तिजवर.

TRIGGER, *n.* (of a gun). कळ *f.* सरिफी *f.* [यक-संबंधी.

TRIGONOMETRICAL, *a.* v. N. त्रिकोणमितीचा, त्रिकोणमितिविष-

TRIGONOMETRY, *n.* त्रिकोणमिती *f.* त्रिकोणमापनविद्या *f.*

TRILATERAL, *a. having three sides.* तीन बाजूंचा, त्रिभुज, त्रिभुजात्मक.

TRILITERAL, *a.* तीन अक्षरांचा, त्र्यक्षरक.

TRILL, *n.* (of the voice) v. SHAKE. सरांटा*m. v.* घे, वाजव.

To TRILL, *v. a. utter with shakes.* आळवणें, कंप*m.*-सरांटा*m.* घेणें-वाजवणें *or* घेऊन गाणें *or* म्हणणें.

2 See To TRICKLE. [*or* निघणें.

To TRILL, *v. n.*—the voice &c. कंप*m.*-सरांटे*m. pl.* घेऊन उठणें

TRILLING, *p. a.* v. V. N. कंप घेऊन उठणारा, &c. सरांट्यांचा.

TRILLION, *n.*—in arithmetic. प्रयुतघन*m.*

Hundred t. अक्षौहिणी *f.*

TRIM, *a.* v. NEAT. ठाकठोक, ठीकठाक, ठिकसठाकस, ठाकसठिकस, चकपक, लकपक, चाकचोप, निटस, नेटका, सुरेख.

TRIM, *n. pickle, predicament,* v. CONDITION, MESS. गत *f.* गल्हाटा *or* गळहाठा*m.* गुडाकू *or* खू *f.* वाळवण *f.* राळवण *f.*

Good t. मरामत *f. v.* राख, कर.

To keep in good t. मरामत *f.* राखणें.

To put into good t. मरामत *f.* करणें, सुधारणें.

To TRIM, *v. a. put in due order, set to rights, make neat, dress, &c.* v. To ADJUST. ओजवणें, सुधारणें, निटावणें, दुरूस्त-नीट-सुरेख-चाकचोप-चकपक-&c. करणें, सुधारणूक *f.*-&c. करणें *g. of o.* [करणें.

2 (a boat, &c.). सारख्यावजनाचा करणें, समभार-समतोल-&c.

3 (a lamp). ताजा-जिवा-जिवंत-&c. करणें.

4 See To SCOLD. 5 v. To LOP. साळणें, साळणी *f.* करणें.

To TRIM, *v. n. fluctuate between parties,* v. To TEMPORIZE. काळ पाहून-रंग पाहून-&c. चालणें-वागणें-वर्त्तणें.

TRIMLY, *adv.* v. A. चापूनचोपून.

TRIMMER, *n.* TRIMMING, *p. a.* v. V. N. *and* TEMPORIZER. रंगपाहून चालणारा, दुरोखी, दोहों डगरीवर (*or* दरडीवर) हात ठेवणारा, &c. [-नुई *f.*-&c.

TRIMMING, *n.* (to a dress, &c.). वस्त्रास लावलेला दाल*m.*-फीत *f.*

TRIMNESS, *n.* v. A. ठाकठिकपणा *m.* चकपकपणा*m.* &c. चाकचोपी *or* चापचोपी *f.* चापीचोपी *f.* खुबी *f.* खुमास*m.* कतरबेत*m.*

TRINAL, TRINE. See THREEFOLD.

TRINITARIAN, *n. a worshipper, &c. of the Trinity.* व्यक्तित्रयात्मकदेवताश्रयी, व्यक्तित्रयात्मकदेवोपासक, &c.

TRINITY, *n.*—in theology. व्यक्तित्रयात्मकदेवता *f.*-देव*m.* व्यक्तित्रयैकत्व *n.*

TRINKET, *n. jewel, &c.* नग *m.* नगोटें *n.* डागिणा *or* ना *or* दागिना *m.* गहना *or* गह्निना *m.* वस्त *f.* जवाहीर *n.*

Mass of old, battered, and broken trinkets. रेजगण*m.* परचुरण *n.*

Petty or minor trinkets—compreh. फिडूकमिडूक *n.* लिसडीं मिसडीं *n. pl.*

Trinkets,—compreh. वस्तभाव *f.* वस्तवानी *f.* डागडागिणे *m. pl.* नगनगोटा *m.* नगनगोटें *n.* गहना *or* गह्निना *m.* गह्निनागाठा *m.* बाळीचुगडी *f.* जडावाचे दागिने *m. pl.*

TRINOCULOUS, *a.* त्रिनयन, त्रिलोचन.

TRINOMIAL, *a.*—in mathematics. त्रिपद, त्रियुक्पद.

TRIO, *n. confederacy of three.* त्रिकूट *pop.* तिरकूट *n.* त्रय *n.* त्रयी *f.* त्रिकू *n.* त्रितय *n.*

TRIOBOLAR, *a.*v. WORTHLESS. दीड दमडीचा, दीड कवडीचा.

To TRIP, *v. a. cause to fall by striking the feet from under.* उलथून पाडणें, ठोकर मारून-ठेसमारून-&c. पाडणें, पाय सारून-लोटून- सरकवून-&c. पाडणें.

To TRIP, *n. stumble.* अडखळणें *or* अडखुळणें, अडकळणें, ठेंचळणें, ठेंसळणें, ठोकर *f.*-ठेंच *f.* खाणें *or, with in. con.* लागणें, स्खलन*n.*-&c. होणें *g. of s.* [णें *g. of s.*

2—in speech. अडखळणें *or* अडखुळणें, लागणें, स्खलन *n.* हो-

3 *slip, fail,* v. To ERR. चुकणें, चूक *f.* करणें, घसरणें.

4 *walk lightly.* ठिकणें, छमकणें, ठिकत छमकत चालणें.

TRIP, TRIPPING, *n.* v. V. N. 1. अडखळणें *n.* &c. ठोकर *f.* ठेंच *f.* स्खलन *n.*

2 अडखळणें *n.* &c. स्खलन *n.*

3 चूक *f.* चुकी *f.* गुंजाबीस *f.* तफावत *f.*

I. *journey to and from.* खेप *f.*फेरी *f.* फेरा*m.* येरझार*f.* खेटा*m.* जाणें येणें *n.* जावायेवा *m.* पाऊठ *f.*

By the t. उक्ता.

Empty t. हेलपटा *m.* घिरटी *or* घरटी *f.* येजा *f.* जाये *f.* येरजार *f.* फेरा *m.* फिरका *m.* फिरकंडा *m.* गिरीघोंटी *f.* हिसका*m.* गोता *m.* खेटे *m. pl.* खेटापाटा *m.* झोंका *m.* यात्रा *f.*

That makes frequent trips. खेप्या, खेटेघाल्या, खेट्या.

To make empty trip or trips. बाट*f.* बावरणें, गिरीघोंटी*f.*-घिरटी *f.*-&c. घालणें-करणें, हिसका *m.*-हेलपटा *or* हेलपाटा *m.*-गोता *m.*-&c. खाणें-घेणें *or, with in. con.* बसणें, झोंका*m.* खाणें, तिरस्थळी *f.* करणें. [भाग,त्रिखंड.

TRIPARTITE, *a.* See TRIPLE. 2 *divided into three parts.* त्रि-

TRIPE. See ENTRAIL.

TRIPETALOUS, *a.* त्रिदल.

TRIPHTHONG, *n.* त्र्यचूक*n.*

TRIPLE, TRIPLICATE, *a. threefold, treble.* तिपदरी, तिप्पट, तिहिरी, तिहेरा, त्रिगुण.

2 *of three strings.* तिपेडी *or* डी, तिसुती. [त्रिपद *n.*

TRIPOD, TRIPOS, *n. stool with three feet.* तिवई *f.* तिपायी *f.*

TRIPPER, *n.* TRIPPING, *p. a.* v. V. N. 1. अडखळणारा, ठोकरखाणारा, ठेंचखाणारा, स्खलित.

3 चुकणारा, घसरणारा, &c.

4 ठिकणारा, ठिकतचालणारा, &c. पायसूट, पायाचा चपळ.

TRIST, THRISTFUL. See SAD. [शरी, त्र्यच्क.

TRISYLLABIC, TRISYLLABICAL, *a.* तीन अक्षरांचा, त्र्यक्षर, त्र्य-

TRISYLLABLE, *n.* त्र्यक्षरीशब्द *m.*

TRITE, *a.* v. STALE. उष्टा, जुना, उच्छिष्ट, लोकोच्छिष्ट.

TRITENESS, *n.* v. A. उष्टेपणा*m.* जुनेपणा *m.* उच्छिष्टत्व *n.*

TRITHEISM, *n. doctrine of three gods.* देवत्रयवाद *m.* देवत्रयमत *n.* देवत्रयपक्ष *m.*

Tritheist, *n. holder of tritheism.* देवत्रयवादी, देवत्रयमतावलंबी.

Triturable, *a.* v.V. वाटायाजोगा-सारखा-&c. उगाळायाजोगा-&c.

To **Triturate**, *v. n. grind to a fine powder,* v.To **Levigate**. वाटणें, उगाळणें, संघर्षm.-संघर्षणn.-&c. करणें *g. of o.*

Trituration, *n.* v. V. वाटणें *n.* &c. वाटण *n.* उगाळणी *f.* संघर्ष *m.* संघर्षण *n.*

Triumph, *n. pomp of a victory.* जयाचाथाट *m.* जयाची मिरवणूक *f.* जयोत्सव *m.* जयसमारंभ *m.* जययात्रा *f.* विजययात्रा *f.*

2 *victorious state,* or, *victory.* जय *m.* विजय *m.*

3 *joy for success, exultation.* जयानंद *m.* जयोल्लास *m.* जयहर्ष *m.* जयगर्व *m.*

To **Triumph**, *v. n. celebrate a victory.* जयोत्सव*m.*-जयसमारंभ *m.*-&c. करणें.

2 *obtain victory.* जय*m.*-विजय *m.* पावणें-मिळवणें, विजयी-&c. होणें, जय*m.*-फत्ते *f.*-&c. होणें *g. of s.* जयास-यशालाभास-&c. जाणें.

3 *exult.* जयजय *m.*-जयजयकार *m.*-जयानंद*m.*-जयोल्लास*m.*-&c. करणें, काखा *f. pl.* वाजवणें, कुल्ले *m. pl.* थोपटणें, टिरी *f. pl.* थोपटणें-थापटणें-पिटणें-वाजवणें, टाळ्या *f. pl.* वाजवणें-पिटणें, नाचणें, नागवा नाचणें.

Triumphal, *a.* v. N. 1. जयोत्सवाचा, जयसमारंभाचा, &c. जयोत्सवसंबंधी-विषयक, जयसंबंधी, जयविषयक, जय & विजय (used in comp. as जयस्तंभ, &c.).

Triumphant, *a.* **Triumpher**, *n.* **Triumphing**, *p. a.* v. V. 1. जयोत्सवकरणारा, &c. जयोत्सवाचा.

2 जयपावणारा-पावलेला, &c. जयवान् *pop.* जयवंत, विजयमान, जयी, विजयी, प्राप्तजय, लब्धजय, जयशाली, जिष्णु, जेता, जेत्र.

3 जयजयकरणारा, जयानंदकरणारा, &c. जयानंदाचा, &c. जयानंदी, जयहर्षी.

Triumphantly, *adv.* v. A. 1. जयोत्सवानें, जयाच्याथाटानें-थाटमाटानें, &c. जयोत्सव करीत, जयोत्सवपूर्वक, वाजतढोलानें, वाजतगाजत, गाज्यावाज्यानें. [पूर्वक.

2 जयपावून, जयमिळवून, जयमिळवीत, जयी-&c. होऊन, जय-

3 जयजयकरून, जयजयकारकरून, जयानंदकरून, &c. काखावाजवून, कुल्लेथोपटून, &c. [*n.*त्रय *n.*

Triumvirate, *n. coalition of three.* त्रिकूट *pop.* तिरकूट*n.* त्रिकू

Triune, *a. three in one.* त्र्यात्मकएक.

Trivet. See **Trevet.**

Trivial, *a.* v. **Trifling.** हलका, लहान, जमेस धरायास अयोग्य, जमेंतला न खर्चांतला, अगण्य, क्षुल्लक, क्षुद्र.

Triviality, Trivialness, *n.* v. A. हलकेपणा *m.* लहानपणा *m.* &c. क्षुल्लकत्व *n.* क्षुद्रता *f.*

Trochee, *n.*—in verse. गल *m.* गलपद *n.* [दाहत.

Trodden, *p.* v. V. 2. तुडवलेला, पायानें मळलेला, पादमर्दित, पा-

Well t.—mortar, &c. कमाऊ.

To appear well t.—a road. पायवटणें.

To **Troll.** See To **Roll.**

Trollop, *n.* v. **Gadabout.** नगरभवानी *f.* गांवभवानी *f.*

2 See **Slut.**

Tromp. See **Trumpet.**

Troop, *n. multitude, collection, company,* v. **Band.** मंडळी *f.* जमात *f.* जमाव *m.* चुंग *f.* गण *m.* समुदाय *m.* जुंबाड *n.*

2 (of cavalry). रिसाला *m.* पतक *m. n.*

Command of a t. रिसालदारी *f.*

Commander of a t. रिसालदार, पतक्या.

Own or private t. खासपतक *m. n.*

3 troops; *forces,* v. **Army.** सेनाभार *m.* दलभार *m.*

4 (of monkeys). साईर *f.*

5 (of pilgrims, emigrants, beggars, &c.). पेावा *or* पोहा *m.* काफला *m.* तांडा *m.* झुंड *f.*

Trooper, *n. horse soldier.* घोडेस्वार, घोडेराऊत, सवार, राऊत.

T. who is mounted by the chief or state that employs him. बारगीर.

T. who provides his own horse. शिलेदार.

Trope, *n* v. **Figure, Metaphor.** रूपक *n.*

Trophy, *n. memorial of victory.* जयाची निशाणी *f.*-खूण *f.* जयचिह्न *n.* जयस्मारक *n.*

Tropic, *n. line which bounds the sun's declination from the equator.* दक्षिणोत्तरायणसीमा *f.* अयनसीमा *f.* अयनांत *m.* अयनवृत्त *n.* क्रांतिसीमा *f.*

T. of cancer. कर्कवृत्त *n.*

T. of capricorn. मकरवृत्त *n.*

Tropics. क्रांतिवलय *n.* क्रांतिवृत्त *n.* क्रांतिमंडल *n.*

Tropical, *a. of or belonging to the tropics.* क्रांतिवलयाचा, क्रांतिवृत्ताचा, &c. क्रांतिवृत्तसंबंधी-विषयक, दक्षिणोत्तरायणसीमांतर्गत, क्रांतिवलयांतर्गत.

2 *of or belonging to tropes,* v. **Figurative, Metaphorical.** लाक्षणिक, सरूपक.

To **Trot**, *v. n.*—an animal. दुडकेचालीनें चालणें, दुडकी चालणें, दुदद्दुड-दुडूदुडू-तुरतूर-तुरुतुरू-&c. चालणें, दडदडणें.

2 fig. *get away, take one's self off.* घोडा *m.* हांकणें.

Trot, *n.*—the pace. दुडकी *f.* दुडकीचाल *f.* खुदकी *f.*

A quick and long t. देवडचाल *f.*

Troth. See **Truth, Faith.**

Trottingly, *adv.* v. V. दुडुक दुडुक *or* दुड्डुक दुड्डुक, तुरतूर *or* तुरुतुरु, दुडदुड, दुडुदुडु.

To **Trouble**, *v. a. annoy, disturb, distress,* v. To **Tease**, To **Discompose.** पिडणें, पिडवणें, क्लेशणें, दुःख *n.*-कष्ट *m. pl.*-श्रम *m. or m. pl.* क्लेश *m. or m. pl.*-उपद्रव *m.*-इजा *f.*-तस्दी *f.*-&c. देणें-करणें, भंडावणें, त्रास *m.* देणें, कंकातणें, हैराणी *f.*-हैराणगत *f.*-&c. करणें *g. of o.* उपद्व्याप *m.* देणें, श्रमी-कष्टी-हैराण-&c. करणें. In the modification of this sense as thus expressible, *To be the object of constant or great sorrow, solicitude, study, concern, &c.* and as more or less apparent in the phrases and combinations, *To engross painfully the thoughts, To haunt or hang upon the mind, To be a dead weight upon the breast, To prey or lie upon the spirits, To weigh down, pull down, &c. the soul, To oppress, burden, press heavily, sorely, &c.* corresponding colloquialisms are, उरावर-मनावर-&c. बसणें, काळजी *f.*-घोर *m.*-चिंता *f.*-&c. लावणें, काळजी *f.*-घोर *m.*-चिंता *f.*-&c. लागणें-बाटणें *g. of s. with in. con.* घांळणें, घोळांत पाडणें-घालणें, डाचणें *or* डाजणें, धोंड *f.* येणें, हाडांला खिळून असणें.

2 (one's self). श्रम *m. pl.* घेणें.

Trouble, *n. affliction, distress, difficulty, &c.* दुःख *n.* पीडा *f.* इजा *f.* श्रम*m. or m. pl.* क्लेश*m. or m. pl.* कष्ट*m. pl.* संकट*n.*

संताप *m.* ताप *m.* विपत्ति *f.* आपदा *f.* आपत्ति *f.* बिपदा *f.* हैराणी *f.* हैराणगत *f.* तळमळ *f.* अडचण *f.* पेच *m.* दैना *f.* दुर्दशा *f.* कष्टावस्था *f.* कष्टदशा *f.* हैराणदशा *f.* हाल *m. pl.* कासाविसी *f.* हळहळ *f.*

A time of t. दुःख काल *m.* कलिकाल *m.*

To be in t. आपदावणें.

To fall into deep t. पेंवांत पडणें.

2 a *trouble, a perplexity, strait, hobble, scrape, &c.* दुःख *n.* संकट *n.* संकष्ट *n.* कातर *f.* पेच *m.* पेचाटी *f.* कचाट *or* किचाट *n.* कच *f.* लचांड *or* लचेंड *n.* ओकटें *n.* सेंकटें *n.* कोंडें *n.* कफास्त *or* कफालत *f. m.* झेंगट *n.* लफडा *m.* कुलंगडें *n.* घोरपड *f.* गडसळ *n.* गड *f.* गडीज *n.* काबीज *n.* चक्र *n.* गंडांत *m.* गंडांतर *n.* संक्रांत *f.* बाजू *f.* समय *m. v.* ये, उपाधि *or* उपाध *f.* व्याधि *or* व्याध *f.* फेरा *m.* तष्ट *n.* जंजाळ *m. n.* झोंबट *n.* झोंबड *n.* झट *n.* भारूड *n.* लिगाड *n.* See also CALAMITY.

Load of troubles and cares. दुःखाचा पर्वत *m.*

Troubles and perplexities,—compreh. *or* indiff. जड अवघड *n.*

Troubles and scrapes,—compreh. *or* indiff. झटझोंबट*n.*

To give t. *prove difficult or troublesome.* जोर *m.* करणें-लावणें, जोरास येणें.

Some terms for *a trouble brought upon one's self* are, विकत खोकला, विकतश्राद्ध, विकतकज्जा, विकतकळ, सुकालफडा*m.*

3 *annoyance molestation, disturbance, &c.* दुःख *n.* पीडा *f.* उपद्रव*m.* इजा *f.* तस्दी *f.* त्रास*m.* नड *f.* नडाव*m.* छळणूक *f.* छल *or* छळ *m.* छडणूक *f.* गांजणूक *f.* जाचणूक *f.* उपसर्ग*m.* उपप्लव*m.*

4 *pains, care, toil, labor, &c.* श्रम *m.* कष्ट *m.* मेहनत *f.* खटपट *f.* खबदव *f.* मशागत *f.* उपद्व्याप *m.*—viewed as *vexatious* or *tiresome ; fuss, bother, ado.* दगदग *f.* खटखट *f.* पितरखस्ता *f. pl.* खस्ता *f. pl.* कडाकूट *f.* यातायात *f.* उठाठेव *f.* उलेंढालें *n.* छट्टेपट्टे *or* झटेपटे *m. pl.* अटअट *f.* अटाअट *f.* अटाघाट*m. f.* अटाटी *f.* अटापिटा *m.* अटापीट *f.*

Acquired by one's own t. स्वकष्टसंपादित, स्वकष्टार्जित.

TROUBLED, *p.* v. V. पिडलेला, दुःख दिल्हेला, &c. दुःखी, दुःखित, क्लेशी, श्रमी, कष्टी, पीडित, हैराण, संतापित, संतप्त, तापित, आर्त्त (esp. in comp. as क्षुधार्त्त, तृषार्त्त, भयार्त्त, शोकार्त्त, कामार्त्त, रोगार्त्त, चिंतार्त्त, &c.).

TROUBLER,*n.* TROUBLING, *p. a.* v. V. पिडणारा, दुःख देणारा, उपद्रव देणारा, तस्दी देणारा, &c. श्रमकारक, कष्टकारक, संकटकारक, &c. बद्धक, श्रमावह, श्रमप्रद, कष्टावह, &c.

I. *troublesome fellow,* v. PLAGUE. व्याध *f.* कलांट *n.*

TROUBLESOME, *a. vexatious, annoying, &c.* उपद्रवाचा, इजेचा, तस्दीचा, जाचाचा, &c. जाचक, जाचदेणारा, उपद्रव देणारा-करणारा, इजा देणारा-करणारा, त्रासदेणारा, उपद्रवी, उपद्रवीक, छळणारा, &c. दुःखावह, क्लेशावह, कष्टावह, श्रमावह, श्रमकारक, &c. सकंटक.

2 *wearisome, tedious,* v. TIRESOME. चिकीर, किचीर *or* किचर, कुचर, खचरट, खष्ट, खडतर, क्लिष्ट, खिस्तीचा, जिकिरीचा, जाचंद, जाचंदा.

3—of persons ; *teasing, wearying, &c.* v. IMPORTUNATE. खणपटीस-खपाटीस-मानेस-बोकांडीस-&c. बसणारा, खणपट्या, खणकुदळ्या, खपाट्या, जिकिऱ्या, जाचक, मेखाट्या, प्राणखाऊ, प्राणघणा.

TROUBLOUS, *a. full of affliction or trouble,*—time, &c. दुःखाचा, कष्टाचा, संकटाचा, क्लेशाचा, &c. खडतर, नष्ट, खष्ट.

TROUGH, *n.*—wooden, &c. द्रोण *m. pop.* डोण *m. or* दोण *f. n. dim.* डोणी *f. and, enhanc.* डोणगें *or* दोणगें *m.* कोटंचा *m. dim.* कोटंची *f.*

T. made by hollowing a palm-tree. भरल *or* ळ *m.*

2—for watering cattle. हाळ *m.* टांकी *f.* द्रोण *m. pop.* द्रोणा *or* दोण *m.*

To TROUNCE. See To BEAT.

TROUT, *n.* एक मासा आहे.

TROWEL, *n.*—of masons. कर्णी *pop.* करणी *f.* थापी *f.*

TROWSERS, *n.* सुरवार *f.* इजार *f.* पायजामा *m.*

Large or loose t. तुमान *f.* तुंबा *m.*

Leg of t. पायजा *m.*

TRUANT, *a. wandering, vagabond.* उनाड, उनाडकीचा, ओढाळ, हिंडगा, हिंडफिऱ्या, उंडगा, उंडगळ, रांबाड.

To play t. उनाडणें.

To TRUANT, *v. n. be idling and absent from employment.* उनाडणें, उनाडकी *f.* करणें, हिंडणवारे *m. pl.* करणें, and, *inversely,* लागणें. [रांबाडकी *f.*

TRUANTRY, *n.* v. V. उनाडकी *f.* उनाडचाळे *n. pl.* हिंडणवारे *m. pl.*

TRUBTAIL, *n.* v. SQUAB. गिरदी *f.*

TRUCE, *n. temporary cessation of hostilities.* मुद्दतीचा-ठेपीचा-चारदिवसांचा-&c. तह *m.*-सल्ला *m.* सावधिकसंधि *m.* अवहार*m.*

To wave a flag or cloth in indication of a t. रुमाल*m.* फिरवणें-उडवणें.

2 See INTERMISSION.

TRUCK, *To* TRUCK. See BARTER, To BARTER.

TRUCK, *n. a. small wooden wheel not bound with iron.* बिन धांवेचें लाकडीचाक *n.*

2 *a low carriage for goods.* सामानाची गाडी *f.*

To TRUCKLE, *v. n. crouch, bend obsequiously,* v. To YIELD, To FAWN. नाक *n.* गुंडाळणें-घासणें, दांतीं तृण *n.* धरणें, पदर *m.* पसरणें, नाकदुराही *f.* काढणें, जीजी *f.*-हांजी *f.* करणें, छंदानुरोध *m.*-इच्छानुरोध *m.*-छंदानुवर्त्तन *n.*-&c. करणें.

TRUCULENT, &c. See SAVAGE, &c.

To TRUDGE, *v. n. tramp, travel wearisomely.* पाय *m. pl.* फांसटणें-झिजवणें-मोडावणें, वणवण *f.*-पायपिटी *f.*-पायघशी *f.*-फांसटणी *f.*-फांसटाफांसट *f.*-येजा *f.*-जाये *f.*-यातायात *f.*-&c. करणें,वणवण *adv.*-बताबता *adv.* फिरणें. [णे-घणें.

To t. backwards & forwards. v. TRIP. हेलपटे*m. pl.* खा-

TRUDGING, *n.* v. V. पायफांसटणें *n.* &c. पायपिटी *f.* पायपीट *f.* पायघशी *f.* फांसटणी *f.* फांसटाफासट *f.* येजा *f* जाये *f.*

TRUE, *a. not false or pretended, not counterfeit, actual, existing,* v. REAL. खरा, सत्य, साच, साचा, असल, वास्तविक, वास्तव, तथ्य, यथातथ, यथार्थ, अकपट, अन्वर्थ, अन्वर्थक.

T. and false. सदसत्.

T. and good. T. and sound, &c. खराखुरा.

2 *agreeable with nature or fact.* खरा, सत्य, साच, साचा, रास्त, तात्त्विक, यथातथ, तथ्य, यथार्थ, ऋत, समीचीन.

To turn out t. पटणें.

3 *true-speaking.* खरा, खरें बोलणारा, सत्यवक्ता, सत्यभाषी, सत्यवचनी, सत्यवचन, सत्यवचा, सत्यवादी.

4 *observant of truth, keeping faith, &c.* v. HONEST, SINCERE. खरा, साचा, सत्य, प्रामाणिक *pop.* प्रमाणिक, इमानी, इमानदार, इमानाचा, कराराचा, करारी, सत्यशील, सत्यप्रिय, सत्यव्रत, सत्यसंध, सत्यप्रतिज्ञ, परमार्थी, सात्विक, सत्वशील, सत्ववृत्ति, सतंजय.

5 *conformable to a rule or pattern.* असलबरहुकूम काढलेला-उतरलेला, यथाप्रतकाढलेला, यथामूल, यथाप्रत, व्यभिचाररहित-शून्य. [निका.

6—a weight, measure, &c. रास्त, खरा, नकी *or* निकी *or*

TRUE-BORN, TRUE-BRED. See GENUINE.

TRUE-HEARTED. See SINCERE.

TRUENESS. See TRUTH.

TRUISM, *n. self evident truth.* स्वतःसिद्ध-स्वतःप्रमाणक-प्रमाणानपेक्ष-&c. गोष्ट *f.*-वाक्य *n.*-वचन *n.*-&c.

TRULL, *n.* v. HARLOT. उपीपत्रावळ *f.* माळजादी *f.*

TRULY, *adv.* v. A. 1. खराच *decl.* खरेंच, खऱ्यानें, वास्तविक, वास्तविकपणानें, वास्तविकपणें, खरोखर, खचीत, भावार्थ, सत्य, तत्वतः, यथातथ, यथार्थ, वस्तुतः, वस्तुगत्या, वस्तुदृष्ट्या.

2 खराच *decl.* खरेंच, सत्य, रास्ती, खास, बरोबर, तत्वतः, यथातथ, यथार्थ, सम्यक्, यथाभूत.

4 *and* SINCERELY. खराच *decl.* मनापासून.

5. 6. See ACCURATELY, EXACTLY.

I.—as a slight expletive. बरीक, सई *or* सही.

TRUMPERY, See TRASH.

TRUMPET, TRUMP, *n.* v. HORN. करणा *m.* तुतारी *f.*

To TRUMPET, *v. a.* v. To PUBLISH. करणा *m.*-तुतारी *f.*-नगारा *m.* -&c. वाजवणें *g. of o.*

2 *sing the praises of.* चडिवार *m.*-बडाई *f.*-पडप *n.*-मोठाई *f.*-थोरवी *f.*-मोठेपणा *m.*-स्फीति *f.*-&c. सांगणें-बोलणें *g. of o.*

TRUMPET-FLOWER, *n. Bignonia suaveolens.* गजरगोटी *f.* गजरी *f.* सागरगोटी *f.* [टा *m.*

Seed of the t. गजरगोटा *m.* गजरा *m.* गजगा *m.* सागरगो-

TRUMPETER, *n. sounder of a trumpet.* करणेकरी, तुताऱ्या, करणा-&c. वाजवणारा.

TRUNCHEON, *n.* v. CUDGEL. सोटा *m.* सोडगा *m.* दांडकें *n.* गदा *f.*

To TRUNDLE, *v. n. roll as a bowl,* v. To ROLL. घुळणें, घुळघुळीत-घुळत येणें-जाणें, घरळणें. [करणें.

To TRUNDLE, *v. a.* v. To ROLL. घुळवणें, घरळवणें, घुळत जाईसा-

TRUNK, *n.* (of a tree) *stem.* कांड *n.* कांडें *n.* खोड *n.* काठी *f.* पेड *f.* स्कंध *m.* प्रकांड *m. n.*

Naked or bare t. खोड *n.* स्थाणु *m.*

2 (of the body). शरीराचें कांड *n.* धड *n.*

Headless t. धड *n.* कबंध *n. m.*

3 *main body.* पोट *n.* मुख्यभाग *m.*

4 *chest,* v. Box. पेटी *f.* संदूक *f.*

5 *proboscis.* सोंड *f.* शुंडा *f.* शुंडादंड *m.* हस्त *m.*

That has a t. सोंड्या.

TRUNNION, *n.*—of a cannon, &c. कानपा *m.*

TRUSS, *n.* (as of hay, &c.) *loose bundle,* v. BUNDLE. गठ्ठा *m.* भिंडा *m.* जोंबडा *m.*—of rice straw. लाटा *or* लाठा *m.*

Large and loose t. मोधळा *m.*

2 (for hernia). दाब *m.* पट्टा *m.*

To TRUSS, *v. a. pack closely.* खचून-दडपून-&c. भरणें.

TRUST, *n. reliance,* v. CONFIDENCE. विश्वास *m.* भरवसा *or* भरोसा *m.* इतबार *m.* निष्ठा *f.* प्रत्यय *m.* प्रामाण्यग्रह *m.*

Breach of t. विश्वासघात *m.*

Object of t. विश्वासस्थान *n.* विश्वासभूमि *f.* विश्वासपात्र *n.* विश्वासभाजन *n.* विश्वासास्पद *n.* विश्वासलक्ष्य *n.* विश्वासाधिकरण *n.* [नात *f.* हवाला *m.*

2 *trusted or confidential charge.* जिम्मा *m.* दिम्मत *f.* तै-

3 *confident opinion,* v. CONFIDENCE. विश्वास *m.* भरवसा *or* भरोसा *m* खातरी *f.* निधडा *m.* निशा *f.* निश्चय *m.*

4 *tick, credit.* उचापत *f.* उधार *m.*

On t. उधार, हातावर, आंगावर, जातीवर.

To buy upon t. उधार *adv.*-&c. घेणें-आणणें-नेणें-&c.

To sell upon t. उधार *adv.* देणें, आंगावर-हातावर-जातीवर-&c. देणें.

To TRUST, *v. a. place confidence in,* v. To CONFIDE. विश्वासणें, विश्वास *m.*-भरवसा *m.*-&c. ठेवणें *with* वर *of o.* पात्यवणें *or* पातणें.

2 *commit with confidence,* v. To COMMIT. विश्वासणें, पात्यवणें *or* पातणें ओपणें, सोंपणें, हवालणें, विश्वासानें ठेवणें-देणें-&c.

3 *sell to upon credit.* माल *m.*-&c. उधार-उधारानें-उचापतीनें-&c. देणें-विकणें.

4 *venture confidently, regard without fear, &c.* पात्यवणें *or* पातणें, विश्वासणें, विसंबणें.

To TRUST, *v. n. be confident of.* विश्वास *m.*-भरवसा *m.*-आशा *f.*-&c. ठेवणें-धरणें, विश्वास-भरवसा *m.*-खातरी *f.*-निधडा *m.*-&c. असणें *g. of s.*

2 in; to; *rely on,* v. To CONFIDE. विश्वास *m.*-भरवसा *m.*-&c. ठेवणें-धरणें. [विश्वस्त.

TRUSTED, *p.* v. V. A. 1. विश्वासलेला, &c. प्रत्ययित, विश्वसित,

2 विश्वासलेला, पात्यवलेला, विश्वासानें ठेवलेला, सोंपलेला, ओपलेला.

TRUSTEE, *n. person intrusted.* जिम्मेदार, दिम्मतदार, निसबतदार.

TRUSTER, *n.* TRUSTING, *p. a.* v. V. A. 1. & v. N. 2. विश्वासठेवणारा-धरणारा, भाविक, भावूक, श्रद्धधान, प्रत्ययी, विश्वस्त.

2 विश्वासानें देणारा-ठेवणारा, ओपणारा, सोंपणारा, &c.

3 उधार-उधारानें-उचापतीनें-&c. देणारा, &c.

TRUSTINESS, TRUSTWORTHINESS, *n.* v. A. विश्वासीपणा *m.* &c. विश्वास योग्यता *f.* विश्वासार्हता *f.*

TRUSTY, TRUSTWORTHY, *a.* v. CONFIDENTIAL. खातरीचा, खातरजमेचा, विश्वासी, विश्वासू, विश्वासूक, विश्वासाचा, भरवशाचा, श्रद्धार्ह, इतबारी, विश्वासार्ह, विश्वासयोग्य, विश्वासपात्र.

TRUTH, TRUENESS, *n.* v. A. 1. खराई *f.* खरेपणा *m.* वास्तविकपणा *m.* वास्तवत्व *n.* सत्यत्व *n.* सत्यता *f.* तथ्यता *f.* यथार्थता *f.*-&c. सत्य *n.* तत्व *n.* तत्वार्थ *m.* तथ्य *n.* परमार्थ *m.* याथार्थ्य *n.* याथातथ्य *n.* सत्व *n.* सत्ता *f.*

Investigation of t. मीमांसा *f.*

That knows t. तत्ववित्.

2 खराई *f.* खरेपणा *m.* साचपणा *m.* &c. सत्यता *f.* तात्विकता *f.* यथार्थता *f.* यथातथता *f.* तथ्यता *f.* याथातथ्य *n.* याथार्थ्य *n.*

3 खरेपणा *m.* सत्यभाषिता *f.* सत्यवादिता *f.* सत्यवक्तृत्व *n.*

4 खरेपणा *m.* प्रमाणिकपणा *m.* इमानीपणा *m.* &c. सत्यता *f.* प्रामाणिकत्व *n.* सत्यशीलता *f.* सत्वशीलता *f.* &c. सत्यवृत्ति *f.* सत्व *n.* अकपट *n.*

6 खरेपणा *m.* रास्तपणा *m.* निकेपणा *m.* &c. खराई *f.*

I. *true state of facts or things.* खरीगोष्ट *f.* खरामजकूर *m.*-बाका *m.*-&c. सत्यवृत्त *n.* सत्यवृत्तांत *m.*

Way of coming to the s. आधारासपंथ *m.*

In truth, of a truth. See INDEED, TRULY.

TRUTH-FUL, TRUTH-FULNESS. See TRUE, TRUENESS.

To TRY, *v. a. examine, apply experimentally.* ताडणें, पारखणें, परीक्षणें, चौकसणें, परीक्षा *f.*-अनुभव *m.*-&c. पाहणें *g. of o.* अजमावणें, अजमावून पाहणें, अजमाव *m.* करणें *g. of o.*

2 *have knowledge by experience of,* v. To EXPERIENCE. अनुभवणें, अनुभव *m.*-प्रतीति *pop.* प्रचीति *and* प्रचीत *f.*-परीक्षा *f.*-&c. घेणें *g. of o.* सेवणें, सेवन *n.* करणें *g. of o.* साक्षात्कार*m.* करणें-करून पाहणें-घेणें *g. of o.*

3 *examine as a judge, investigate,* v. To EXAMINE. तपासणें, चौकसणें, तपास *m.*-तपासणी *f.*-चौकशी *f.*-शोध *m.*-&c. करणें-पाहणें.

4 *essay, attempt.* हातीं घेणें, उद्योग *m.*-उपाय *m.*-&c. करणें-चालवणें *or* करून-&c. पाहणें, अजमावणें.

5 *prove, bring to the test.* पाहणें, कसणें-कसूनपाहणें, ताडणें-ताडून पाहणें, पारखणें, परीक्षणें, पडतळणें *or* पडताळणें, ताळा *m.*-पडताळा *m.* पाहणें-ताडूनपाहणें *g. of o.* परीक्षा *f.*-पारख *f.*-&c. पाहणें-करणें *g. of o.* धूम *m.* पाहणें *g. of o.* कस *m.*-कसोटी *f.* पाहणें *g. of o.* पडोसा*m.* पाहणें *g. of o.*

6 (the eyes, &c.) v. To STRAIN. ताटकळवणें, ताटकळा *m.* -ताटकळी *f* आणणें.

7 on ;—a garment. घालून-नेसून-&c. पाहणें.

To TRY, *v. n. make endeavor,* v. To ATTEMPT. करून पाहणें-बघणें, अजमावणें, यत्न *m.*-प्रयत्न *m.*-उद्योग *m.*-&c. करणें-करून पाहणें, झटणें, गळा *m.* टाकून पाहणें, फांसा टाकून पाहणें.

TUB, *n. open wooden vessel.* पीप *n.* टीप*n.* लाकडी गंगाळ *n.*

TUBE, *n. pipe.* नळा *m.* (*dim.* नळी *f.* नळकट *or* कूट *n.* नळकंडें *or* नळकांडें *n.* नळकांडी *f.*). पन्हळ *m. dim.* पन्हळी *f.* नाडी *f.* नाड *f.* नलिका *f.* नाल *n.*

2 (of the body) *tubular vessel,* gener. नाडी *f.* नाड *f.* नाल *n.* धमनी *f.* शीर *f.*

TUBERCLE, *n. pimple, tumour.* फोड *m.* गांठ *f.* ग्रंथि *m.* गुल्म *m.*

TUBEROSE, *n.* गुलछब्बू *or* ब्बू *m.* निशिगंध *m.*

TUBEROUS, *a.* v. KNOBBY. गांठाळ, ग्रंथिल.

2 *having a tufted head.* गोंडी, गोंडेरा, गोंडेरी, गोंड्याचा.

TUBULAR, TUBULOUS, *a. having the form of a tube.* नळीच्या आकाराचा, नलिकाकार, नलिकाकृति.

TUCK, *n. end to be tucked in.* खोंचा *m.* खोंचण *f.* ओंचा *m.* काच्या *m.* कच्छ *m.*

2 (in a garment) *fold.* दुमड *f.* मुडपा *m.* मुडप *f.*

To TUCK, *v. a.* in ; up ; *gather up, gather and fold under.* वर सांवरणें, वरखोंवणें, सांवरून खोंवणें, दुमडून खोंवणें, खोंचे *m. pl.*-ओंचे *m. pl.* खोंवणें, मुरडणें, मुरडून खोंवणें. [सणें.

2 in ; *insert between.* खुपसणें, खोंचणें, खोंचरणें, खोंवणें, खो-

3 in ; *cram food.* तकटणें, तकटून भरणें.

TUESDAY, *n.* मंगळवार *m.* भौमवार *m.*

TUFT, *n. knob, knot, bunch, cluster, &c.* बुचका *m.* चुबका *m.* झुबका *m.* झुमका *m.* पुंजका *m.* गोंडा *m.* गुच्छ *m.* जुंबाड *n.* जुंबाडा *n.* जुंबाडें *n.* स्तबक *m.* पेंद *n.* तुरा *m.* पल्लव *pop.* पालव *m.* घोंस *m. n.*

2 *tufted head of certain flowers, &c.* गेंद *m.* गोंडा *m.*

4 (of trees) *plump, clump.* v. KNOT. झुबका *m.* बेट *n.*

4 *plume, &c.* v. CREST. तुरा *m.* चूडा *f.* शिखा *f.* अवतंस *m.*

TUFTED, *a.* v. N. 1. 2. गोंडेरा *or* री, गोंडी (as गोंडीजाम्बन, गोंडी तगर, गोंडीमखमल), झुबकेदार, झुमकेदार, चूडावान्.

To TUG, *v. a. pull with effort,* v. To PULL. श्रमानें-बळानें-बळ देऊन-बळकरून-&c. ओढणें, ओढ *f.* देणें, रग *f.* लावणें-देणें.

TUG, *n.* See PULL. 2. मोठें गलबत ओढणारी लहान आगबोट *f.*

TUITION, *n.* v. INSTRUCTION. उपदेश *m.* शिक्षा *f.* शिक्षण *n.*

To TUMBLE, *v. n.* v. To FALL. पडणें. [टपोर *f.* करणें.

2 about ; v. To ROLL, To TOSS. लोळणें, गडबडां लोळणें, लो-

3 in *or* down ; *fall en masse, or violently.* कोसळणें, ढासळणें *or* धासळणें, धोधावणें, ढकलणें, ढगणें *or* ढघळणें *or* ढगळणें, बरंगळणें *or* बरंघळणें.

4 *perform bodily feats.* कोल्हांटी खेळ *m.*-कोल्हाट्यांचा खेळ *m.*-भोरीप *n.*-&c. करणें.

To t. over. लुडकणें *or* लुडगणें.

To t. up. धडफडून उठणें.

To TUMBLE, *v. a. throw down.* पाडणें, ढकलून-लोटून-&c. पाडणें.

2 *disorder, rumple, &c.* v. To RUFFLE. गुधडणें, घुरदळणें, गुडधावणें, गुधडा *m.* घालणें.

3 *disarrange, disorder, jumble, &c.* v. To CONFOUND. ढवळणें, गोंधळणें, गोंधळवणें, घोंटाळा *m.*-गोंधळ *m.*-उलटापालट *f.*-&c. करणें *g. of o.* उलटापालट-अस्ताव्यस्त-&c. करणें.

TUMBLE. See FALL.

TUMBLER, *n. mountebank, &c.* कोल्हांटी, कैकाडी, डोंबारी, बहुरूपी *or* भोरूपी *or* भोरपी, नट, नटवा, नर्त्तक, गोपाळ.

Female t. कोल्हांटीण *f.* सोनचिडी *or* सोनचेंड, सोनचेडी.

2—the pigeon. गिरेबाज *m.* लोटण *m.*

3 *drinking glass.* कांचेचापेला *m.* कांचेची पंचपात्री *f.*

TUMBREL, *n.* v. CART. छकडा *m.* लढा *m.* रणगाडा *m.*

TUMEFACTION, *To* TUMEFY. See SWELLING, To SWELL.

TUMID, *a.* v. SWOLLEN. सुजलेला, फुगलेला. [डौली.

2 *fig.*—of style. फुगवटीचा, फुगवशीचा, ढबीचा, आबाचा,

TUMIDNESS, *n.* v. A. 1. सुजलेलेपणा *m.* &c. फुगवटी *f.* फुगवशी *f.*

2 फुगवटी *f.* फुगवशी *f.* ढब *f.* डौलीपणा *m.*

TUMOUR, *n. morbid swelling or excrescence,* v. BUMP. गलंड*or* गलांड *n.* गांठ *f.* खांडूक*n.* उठाणू*n.* गंड *n.* बंड*n.* गरस *f.* उबाळू*n.*

A t. in the groin, behind the ear, &c. *bubo.* बरम बाळा.

Indolent and sympathetic t. अवधणा *m.* वाधणा *m.* अवधान *n.* [ठरू *or* सुंदरें *n.*

Suppurating t. gener. केसतूड *m.* फिसकें *n.* उठाणूं *n.* मु-

T. in ano. आरई *f.* आर *f.*

To form again—a burst t. इंबारणें, इंचारा *m.* धरणें.

TUMP, *n.* v. HILLOCK. उटंगर *m. n.* उटंगळ *n.*

Abounding in tumps or mounds. उटंगर, उटंगळ.

Rugged with tumps or mounds,—ground. उटंबर.

TUMULT, *n. wild confusion, violent commotion, clamorous agitation, &c. of a multitude ; row, riot, disturbance, &c.* गडबड *f.* हडबड *f.* हडबडी *f.* गलबल *f.* दंगा *m.* दंगाधोपा *m.* हंगामा *m.* दंगल *f.* धांदल *f.* धांगला *m.* खलबल *f.* कुल्कट *f.* हालहूल *f.* हूलचाल *f.* हुलड *or* हुल्लड *f.* हूल *f.* खुळ *n.* बंडाळ *f.* बंडा-

ळी *f.* गर्दी *f.* दणका *m.* गोंधळ *m.* बहदा *or* बेहेदा *m.* बेदा *m.* गेर *f. m.* धूम *f.* धामधूम *f.* धुमधाम *f.* धुंदाई *f.* अंधाधुंदी *f.* धुंदावें *n.* धुंदाधुंदा *f.* धुमाकूळ *m.* धुमाळी *f.* धुमाफळी *f.* खळबळा *m.* माशावळण *n.* बचमंगळ *n.* भालराई *f.* ब्रह्मघोळ *m.* अफरातफर *f.* रोराण *n.*—Expressing a state of *wild confusion, disorder and tumult,* there are several phrases, as कोणी कोणाचा गुरु न कोणी कोणाचा चेला, कोणाचा पायपोस कोणच्या पायांत नाहीं, कोणाचें पागोटें कोणाच्या डोसक्यास नाहीं, आंधळ्यानें दळावें कुतऱ्यानें पीठ खावें, धनीना गोसावी, बेबंद राज्य झोटिंग पादशाह.

To be in a t.—a country, &c. गलबलणें, गडबडणें, खळबळणें, हलणें *or* हालणें, हलकलणें.

2 See AGITATION.

TUMULTUOUS, TUMULTUARY, *a. conducted with tumult,* v. DISORDERLY. गडबडीचा, अंधाधुंदीचा, धांदलीचा, धुंधाईचा, दंग्याचा, बंडाळीचा, &c. अंधाधुंद *or* ध, बेबंद, अव्यवस्थित, अव्यवस्थ.

2 See AGITATED.

TUMULTUOUSNESS, *n.* v.A. 1. *and* TUMULT. गडबड *f.* अंधाधुंदी *f.* गर्दी *f.* अफरातफर *f.* बचगळ *f.*

TUN, *n.* मोठें पीप*n.*

TUNABLE. See HARMONIOUS.

TUNE, *n. combination of notes.* तान *f.* चाल *f.* गति *f.* स्वर*m.* सूर*m.* धाई *f.* रागिणी *f.* रागभेद*m.* रागस्वरूप*n.* लहरा*m.*

T. and time. तानमान*n.*

To tell the t. upon hearing a string sounded. सुतानें स्वर्गास जाणें.

2 *rightly sounding state.* स्वरांचा मेळ*m.*-जम*m.*-मिलाफ*m.*-&c. मेळ*m.* स्वरैक्य*n.*

That is out of t. अपस्वर, अपसूर, अपसुऱ्या.

3 *note.* See SOUND.

4 *proper humor, fit temper, &c.* वृत्ति *f.* भाव*m.*

To be in t. for. स्वर*m. pl.* भजणें *or* वाहणें *g. of s.*

To TUNE, *v. a. put into tune.* लावणें, स्वर*m. pl.* मिळवणें-जमवणें *g. of o.* स्वरांचा मेळ*m.*-जम*m.*-&c. करणें *g. of o.*

TUNEFUL, *a.* v. HARMONIOUS, MELODIOUS. सुस्वर, सुस्वर विशिष्ट.

TUNIC, TUNICLE. See INTEGUMENT.

TUNNEL, *n.* See FUNNEL. 2 *subterraneous passage.* सुरुंगाचा रस्ता*m.* सुरंगाची वाट *f.* तळवाट *f.* विवरमार्ग*m.*

TUP, *n. full grown ram.* टपूर*m.*

TURBAN, *n.*—the head dress. पागोटें*n.* पगडी *f.* मुंडासें*n.*

Some forms of the *Turban* are, अलम*m.* फिडकीदार पागोटें, पैजारपगडी *or* पैजारीपागोटें, फेंटा, मंदील.

Aigrette of jewels in a t. शिरपेंच*m.*

The Eighteen Turbans; the Asiatic or Turban-wearing nations. अठरा पगडी *f.* अठरा पगडजात *f.* See HAT.

Encircling and prominent band of a t. कंगणी *f.* चक्री *f.*

Half of a t. rent longitudinally; or t. woven of a half breadth. बत्ती *f.*

Sewn and fixed t. (as of children). पगडी *f.*

Skirt or end of t. शेमला *or* समला*m.*

Skull-cap or cloth worn under a t. टोपी *f.* गाभा*m.* बताना*m.*

Small t. embroidered with gold. मंदील*m. n.*

T. &c. bestowed by a great man as a mark of favor. शिरपाव*m.*

Van or fore part of a t. बिनी *f.* this is immediately over the forehead; चोच *f.* this is above the projecting and encircling band.—That has a बिनी. बिनीदार.

To present with a t. पागोटें बांधणें.

To toss or cock the t. with an air. पगडी *f.* फेंकणें.

TURBAN-BINDER, *n.* पगडबंद*m.*—his business, charges, &c. पगडबंदी *f.*

TURBID, *a.* v. MUDDY. गढूल, गदळ, चबदबीत, खडूळ, डहूळ, राड, कलुष.

TURBIDNESS, *n.* v. A. गढुलपणा*m.* गदळपणा*m.* &c. कलुषता *f.*

TURBULENCE, TURBULENCY, *n.*v.A.1. बंडखोरी *f.* दंगेबाजी *f.* खलेली *f.* टोंगाई *f.* दंडेली *f.* दांडगाई *f.* मवासी *or* शी *f.* पुंडाई *f.* उद्दामपणा*m.* उर्मटपणा*m.*

TURBULENT, *a. disposed to tumult or violence.* बंडी, बंडखोर, बंड्या, दंगेखोर, दंगेबाज, खलेल, टोंग, ठोंग, धामधुम्या, धुमाळ्या, पुंड, मवास, मवासी, शिरजोर, धांदल्या, हुरदंगा, उद्दाम, उर्मट *or* ठ, दांडगा, दंडेल.

2 See AGITATED.

TURF, *n. grassy surface of land,* v. SWARD. गवताचा भुईतळ*m.* गवताची जमीन *f.*

A clod or lump of t. पेंड*m.*गवताची ढुंडी *f.*गवताचा गड्डा*m.*

Spade used in turning up t. पेंडस *m.n.*

TURGID, TURGIDITY. See TUMID, TUMIDNESS.

TURKEY, *n.* विलायती कोंबडा *m.* (डी *f.* डें *n.*).

TURKOIS, *n.*—the mineral. पेरुजा *or* पेरोजा*m.* पेरोज *m.* वैदूर्य*n.*

TURMERIC, *n.*—the plant. हळद *f.* हरिद्रा *f.*—the root. हळद *f.* हरिद्रा *f.*—Certain kinds of *Turmeric* are, आंबेहळद, गांठीहळद, दारूहळद, लोखंडीहळद.

Clove of t. हळकुंड *or* हळखुंड *n.*

Leathern bag for t.-powder. भंडारी *f.*

Of or belonging to t. हळदीचा, हरिद्र.

T.—as scraped and coloured (in preparation for कुंकू). रवा *or* रावा *m.*

T. (curcuma zanthorrizon) boiled in goat's milk. रसांजन *n.*

T.—colored. हळदिवा *or* हळदुवा.

T.—powder (esp. as used in offerings). भंडार *m.*

TURMOIL, *n. disquietude,* v. DISCOMPOSURE. तळमळ *f.* संताप *m.* ताप *m.* घालमेल *f.*

3 *harassing labor,* v. TROUBLE. खवदव *f.* खटपट *f.* दगदग *f.*

To TURN, *v. a. move circularly.* फिरवणें, भोवडणें, लोटणें, फिरेसा *decl.* करणें, परिभ्रमण *n.*-&c. करविणें *g. of o.* आवर्त्तन *n.*-&c. करणें *g. of o.*

2 *shift sides.* उलथणें, परतणें, उलटणें, पालटणें, पालट्न-&c. टाकणें, उलथा *m.*-उलथी *f.* देणें.

3 *change the direction of.* फिरवणें, वळणें, वळवणें, मुरडणें, तोंड *n.*-रोंख *m.*-&c. फिरवणें-वळवणें *g. of o.* कल *m.*-कलावा *m.* देणें.

4 *bring inside out.* उलटणें, उलथणें, उलटा-उफराटा-&c.करणें.

5 *form on a lathe.* कातणें *or* कांतणें.

6 *alter, vary,* v. To CHANGE. फिरवणें, पालटणें, फेरफार *m.*-&c. करणें *g. of o.*

7 *make acid.* गोडी *f.*-&c. फिरवणें *g. of o.* आंबटावणें, अंबवणें, आंबटपणा *m.*-&c. आणणें, विकृत-&c. करणें.

8 (the stomach). उमदळवणें, मळमळवणें, मळमळ *f.*-कळमळ *f.*-&c. आणणें-येईसें करणें.

9 (the head) *make giddy.* फिरवणें, घेरी *f.*-&c. आणणें.

10 (the head, the brain) *make mad.* फिरवणें, वारें *n.* शिरवणें, वेड *n.* भरवणें.

11 (in the mind) *revolve*, v. To CONSIDER. घोळणें, मथणें.

12 v. To DISSUADE. फिरवणें, परतवणें, मन *n.*-बुद्धि *f.*-&c. फिरवणें *g. of o.*

13 v. To TRANSLATE. उतरणें.

14 about *or* over. उलथणें, उलटणें, उफराटणें, उफराडणें, उलंडणें, पालटणें *or* पालथणें, फेरणें, कलथी *f.* देणें, उलटापालट *or* उलटपालट *or* उलथापालथ *f.* करणें, उलटी *or* उलथी *f.* देणें, लोटांगण *n.* देणें.

To t. (a cake on the baking pan.) उकटणें.

15 away, v. To DISMISS. घालवणें, हकालणें, काढणें, दूर करणें, उधडणें, भोवडणें.

16 away ; aside ; v. To AVERT. निवारणें, वारणें, टाळणें, फिरवणें.

17 back. वारणें, निवारणें, मुरुडणें *or* मुरडणें, फिरवणें, वारण *n.*-निवारण *n.*-परावर्त्त*m.*-परावर्त्तन *n.*-&c.करणें.

18 down ; in ; v. To FOLD. दुमटणें *or* दुमडणें, दुमतवणें.

19 off ; v. To DIVERT. फिरवणें, वळवणें, वळण*n.* देणें, उडवणें.

To t. off from what is right. बिथरणें.

20 off ; v. To DISMISS. घालवणें, वाटेस लावणें, दूर-&c.करणें.

21 off (a question, &c.) v. To EVADE. टाळणें, चुकवणें, वारण *n.*-निवारण *n.*-&c. करणें *g. of o.* टाळाटाळीखालीं-लपेटीखालीं-&c. नेणें, लपेटून नेणें.

22 out ; v. To OUST, To DISMISS. काढून देणें, दवडणें, निखळणें, उधडणें, विडा *m.* देणें, मेखा *f. pl.* उपटणें-खांद्यावर घालणें *or* देणें, खुंटी*f.* उपटणें, दुमची *f.* उचलणें *g. of o.* निष्कासन*or*निःकाशन *or* निःकासन *n.*-उच्चाटन *n.*-उद्वासन *n.*-उद्वर्त्तन *n.*-&c. करणें *g. of o.*

23 over ; v. 14 उलथणें, उलटणें.

24 to ; into ; v. To METAMORPHOSE, To CHANGE. करणें (with the*g. of o.* and some adjective or noun,as काळ्याचा पांढरा करणें to t. black to white, गाढवाचा घोडा करणें to t. a jackass into a horse, &c.), जात *f.*-&c. फिरवणें, द्रव्यांतर *n.*-&c. करणें *g. of o.*

To t. the back, v. To FLEE. पाठ *f.* देणें.

To t. to account. कामास-उपयोगास-&c. लावणें.

To TURN, *v. n. move round.* भोंवणें, फिरणें, भ्रमणें, भ्रमण *n.*-भ्रम *m.*-आवर्त्त *m.*-आवर्त्तन *n.*-&c. असणें-होणें *g. of s.*

2 *change direction, alter posture or position.* फिरणें, मुरडणें, तोंड *n.*-रोंख *m.*-&c. फिरवणें, वळणें, उलटणें, हालणें, परतणें, वांकणें.

To t. and twist about (as in yawning). वळेपिळे *or* अळेपिळे *m. pl.*-अळोंके पिळोंके *m. pl.*-अळ्यापिळ्या *f. pl.*-अळंगेंविळंगें *n.*-&c. देणें or *inversely*, येणें.

To t. and toss about (from sickness.). चळवळणें,चडफडणें, धडपडणें *or* फडणें *or* बडणें, लोटणें, चडफड *f.*-धडफड *or* धडबड *f.* (*intens.* धडफडाट *or* धडबडाट *m.*)-घालफेल *f.*-घालमेल *f.*-उलघाल *f.*-उलाघाल *f.*-उलाढाल *f.*-&c. करणें.

3 *change in mind, conduct, &c.*फिरणें, हालणें, बदलणें, ढळणें, चळणें, निवर्त्तणें, मन *n.*-बुद्धि *f.*-&c. फिरणें-पालटणें-&c. *g. of s.*

To t. for the worse. बिथरणें, बिनसणें *or* बिनासणें.

To t. and become favorable. वळणें.

4 *alter, vary, &c.* v. To CHANGE. फिरणें, बदलणें, फेर *m.*-फेरफार *m.*-&c. होणें *g. of s.*

5 *be transformed, become by change.* होणें (as काळ्याचा पांढरा होतो black turns to white), जात *f.*-&c. फिरणें *g. of s.* द्रव्यांतर *n.* होणें *g. of s.*

6 *become sour.* अंबणें, अंबट-&c. होणें.

7 (the head, the brain) *become giddy.* कपाळ *n.*-डोसकें*n.*-&c. फिरणें-भोंवणें, घेरी *f.*-चक्कर *n.*-&c. येणें, निरभिरणें, भांवणें *in. con.*

8 *depend on for decision.* टेंकणें, अडकणें, नेट *m.*-&c. असणें *with* वर *of o.* राहणें-असणें *with* वर *of o.*

9 against ; *become adverse.* फिरणें, उलटणें, उलथणें, उलटढाल *f.*- उलटीढाल *f.* देणें, प्रतिकूल-&c. होणें.

10 away. पाठ *f.* देणें-वळणें. [मारणें.

To t. away from, coyly. मुरकणें, तोंड *n.* मुरकणें, मुरका *m.*

11 from. पाठ *f.* वळणें-देणें.

12 in ; *bend inward.* आंत जाणें.

13 off ;—road, &c. फिरणें, फुटणें, वळणें. [वटणें.

14 out ; *prove to be.* निघणें, पडणें, उतरणें, निपजणें, येणें, नि-

To t. out well. उजवणें.

15 out ; *bend outward.* बाहेर येणें.

16 over. उलटणें, उलटा-&c. होणें.

17 round *or* back. मुरडणें *or* मुरुडणें, फिरणें, तोंड *n.* फिरवणें. मुंडारणें.

18 up ; *come to light.* उमगणें *or* उमंगणें, उमटणें *or* उमठणे, निघणें, उमग *m.*-उमट *m.*-&c. होणें *g. of s.* उपटणें.

19 upon ; *turn short upon snappishly.* टणटणा *adv.* उडणें, टणटणणें, वसवसणें, वस-कन-कर-&c. *adv.* बोलणें-आंगावर येणें-&c. उपटणें, उसळणें. [कामीं पडणें.

To t. to account. कामास-उपयोगास पडणें-येणें, उपयोगीं-

TURN, TURNING, *n* (around any thing). अढी *f.* अढा *m.* आटा *m.* विळखा *m.* वेढा *m.* पेच *m.* फेरा *m.* वळसा *m.*

To take a t. अढी *f.* घेणें, विळखा *m.* घालणें.

2 (of a road, river, &c.). फेर *m.* फेरा *m.* मोड *f.* वळण *n.* वांकण *n.* वांक *m.* कुंज *m.*

To make a t. वळणें.

3 *walk to and fro.* फेर *m.* फेरा *m.* फेरी *f.* फेरफटका *m.* पलाटन *n.* पलांटी*f.* वळसा*m.* पसार *m.* रपेट *f.* टेहलणी *f.* टेहली *f.*

To take a t. चक्कर *m.* मारून येणें, पलांटी *f.* मारणें, पसार *m.* करणें, रपेट *f.* करणें-करून येणें, टेहलणें *or* टेहेलणें, टेहलणी *f.* करणें. [*m. f.* भेद *m.*

4 *variation, alteration,* v. CHANGE. फेर*m.* फेरफार *m.* पालट

5 *recurring season, alternation, &c.* पाळी *f.* पालट *m. f.* खेप *f.* वारी *f.* वेळ *f.* पाऊल *f.*

A laboring man taking t. with others. पाळेकर *m.*--woman. पाळेकरीण *f.*

By turns. आळीपाळीनें, चाळीपाळीनें, फेरपाळीनें, चाळून पाळून, घोळून घोळून, आरगोपारगी, पारगीवारगीनें, पाळीवाळीनें, हेरीफेरीनें, हेरफेरानें, क्रमानें, पर्यायानें, परवडीनें.

6 *change from original intention, course, &c.* फेर *m.* पालट

m. f. भेद *m.* प्रकारांतर *n.* निराळें *n.* निराळीतऱ्हा *f.* निराळा प्रकार *m.* [ल *m.*
7 *shape, cast*, v. FORM. वळण *n.* मोड *f.* मरोड *f.* झोक *m.* डौ-
8 (of mind). मनाचा-&c. कल *m.*-झोक*m.*-तोल*m.*-डौल*m.*-&c. वळण *n.* धोरण *n.*

A good t. उपकार *m.* परोपकार *m.*

An ill t. वाईट *n.*

TURN-COAT. See RENEGADE, TIME-SERVER.

TURN-CROSS, *n.* राहाटपाळणा *m.*

Box of a t. (at fairs, &c.). पाळणा*m.*

TURN-SCREW, *n.* चावी *f.* कुऱ्हाडा *m.*

TURN-SOL, *n.* सूर्याचें फूल *n.* सूर्यकमल *n.*

TURN-STILE, *n.* बेळें *n.*

TURNED, *p.* v. V. A. 1. फिरवलेला, मोंवडलेला, &c.
2 उलथलेला, परतलेला, उलथादिल्हेला, &c.
3 फिरवलेला, वळवलेला, कलदिल्हेला, &c.
4 उलटलेला, उलटा केलेला, &c.
5 कांतलेला, कांतींव, चरखी.
7 आंबटावलेला, अंबवलेला.
16 वारलेला, परावृत्त, वारित, निवारित.
21 काढून दिल्हेला, उधडलेला, &c. निःकासित *or* निष्कासित.
v. V. N. 6. अंबलेला, अंबटझालेला, &c. निरुत.

To be turned—a period or stage of life. उलटणें (Ex. त्यास चाळशी उलटली. He is turned 40).

TURNER, *n.* v. V. A. 5. कांतणारा, कांतारी.

T.'s wheel or lathe. चरख *m.* नारंद *m.*

I. (as of cakes, &c. upon the baking pan). उलथणें *n.* उलथा *m.* कलथा*m.* कालथा*m.* काविलथा *m.* खुरपी *f.* उचटणें *n.* हातलोरणें *n.*

TURNIP, *n.* शलगम *m.*

TURPENTINE, *n. resinous substance from the pine, &c.* सरल देवदाराचा चीक *m.* सरलद्रव *m.* श्रीपिष्ट *m.* वृकधूप *m.* दधि *n.* The English word is used in the form of टरपनतेल *n.* तरपिटन *n.*

TURPITUDE. See BASENESS, WICKEDNESS. [रोगृह *n.*

TURRET, *n. little tower*, v. TOWER. मनोरा *m.* प्रासादशृंग *n.* शि-

TURTLE, *n. tortoise.* कासव *n.* कूर्म *m.* कच्छप *m.* कच्छ *m.*

TURTLE, TURTLE-DOVE, *n.* v. PIGEON. खबुतर *n.*

Ringed t. होला *m.*

TUSH, *interj.* v. INTERJECTION. छिः, छिछी, छी, छत्.

TUSK, *n. long pointed tooth of a beast.* सुळा *m.* सुळका *m.* दंष्ट्रा *f.* विषाण *n.*

TUSKED, *a. furnished with tusks.* सुळ्याचा, दंती, दंष्ट्री.

TUSSLE, *n. personal conflict.* ओढाओढी *f.* ओढाताणी *f.* झोंबी *f.* झोंबाझोंबी *f.* झोटधरणी *f.* धक्काधक्की *f.* धमाधमी *f.*

TUT, *interj.* v. PISH. धत्त, हत्त, छत्त, फें, छिछी, हुडुत्त.

TUTELAR, TUTELARY, *a. guardian, protecting.* राखणारा, रक्षणकारी, रक्षाकारी, रक्षिता. [*n.*

T. deity of a family. आराध्य*n.* आराध्यदेवता *f.* आराध्यदैवत

TUTENAG, *n.*—the metallic compound. जस्त*n.*

TUTOR, *n.* v. TEACHER. शिकवणारा, शिक्षक.

To TUTOR, *v. a.* v. To TEACH. शिकवणें.
2 *prompt to evil, drill, prime*, v. To INCITE. कान*m. pl.* फुंकणें-भरणें *g. of o.* बीर*m.* भरणें-देणें.

TWADDLE, TWATTLE, *n. insignificant discourse*, v. PRATE. भाकडकथा *f.* जल्प*m.* जल्पना *f.* वाग्जल्प*m.*

To TWADDLE, *To* TWATTLE, *v. n.* v. To PRATE. बडबडणें.

TWAIN. See TWO.

To TWANG, *v. n. sound with a quick sharp noise.* घणघणणें, झणझणणें, झणझणवाजणें कोकावणें, गोंगणें, गोंगावणें, चुचावणें, चोचावणें, झणत्कारणें, टणत्कारणें, रुणरुणणें,—*intens.* घणाणणें, झणाणणें, सणाणणें.

TWANG, *n. sharp quick sound.* झणकार*m.* झणकारा*m.* सणका*m.* चूं*n.* ठणत्कार*m.* टणत्कार*m.* टंकार*m.* झणत्कार*m.*—*intens.* घणघणाट*m.* घणाण*m.* सणसणाट*m.* सणाण*m.*

With a t. खण-कन-कर-&c. खणखण *or* णां, झण-कण-कर-&c. चुण-कर-&c. झण-कण-कर-&c. कुण्ण,—*intens.* खणाणां, खणाखण, घणाणा, झणाणा, झणाझण.

2 *nasal sound.* गुंगणी *f.* गेंगाणें बोलणें*n.* नाकांतला उच्चार*m.*

That has a t. गुणगुणीत *or* गिणगिणीत, गुणगुण्या.

3 See TASTE.

To TWEAK, *v. a. twitch.* चिमटून ओढणें, चिमटीनें ओढणें.

TWEEZERS, *n. small pincers.* चिमटा*m.*

TWELFTH, *a.* बारावा, द्वादश.

TWELVE, *a.* बारा, द्वादश.

TWELVE-MONTH, *n.* v. YEAR. बारामहिने*m. pl.* वर्ष*n.*

For, during, &c. the t. बारामहिने, बारमास, बारमाही, बारमहा.

Of or belonging to a t. बारमाही.

TWENTIETH, *a.* विसावा.

TWENTY, *a.* वीस, विंशति,—one एकवीस,—two बावीस *or* बेवीस,—three तेवीस,—four चव्वीस, चोवीस,—five पंचवीस,—six सव्वीस,—seven सत्तावीस,—eight अठ्ठावीस,—nine एकुणतीस.

Age of t. विशी *f.*

Aggregate of t. विशी *f.*

TWICE, *adv. two times.* दोनवेळ, दोनदा, दोनवक्त, दोनवेळां, दुबार *or* रां, द्विवार,—in multiplying, दुणें.

2 *doubly.* दुपट, द्विगुणित.

To TWIFALLOW, *v. a. plough a second time.* दुसारणें, दुणणें, दुसरणी *f.*-दुणणी *f.*-दुसरी आवृत्ति *f.*-&c. करणें.

TWIG, *n. small shoot or branch.* डाहळी *f.* डाहळा *m.* शिरकुटी *f* शिरपुटी *f.* शिपटी *f.* फोक *m.* फोकाटी *f.* उपशाखा *f.* अग्रशाखा *f.*

To beat with a t. फोकाटणें, फोकलणें.

TWILIGHT, *n.* (of evening) v. EVENING. गोधूल *or* ळ *f.* गोरज*n.* सांज *f.* तिनसांज *or* तिनिसांज *f.* तिनसांजा *or* तिनीसांजा *f. pl.* मांजर झांक *f.* संध्या *f.* संध्याकाल *m.* संधिप्रकाश *m.* माकडऊन*n.*

At or during t. तिनसांजां *or* तिनीसांजां.

Height of t. भरतिनीसांजां *f. pl.* करकरीततिनीसांजां *f. pl.* कातरवेळ *f.*

Imperfect t. फुटकीतिनीसांज *f.* [धिप्रकाश *m.*

2 (of morning) v. DAWN. धुंदुक *n.* पूर्वसंध्या *f.* संध्या *f.* सं-

TWIN, *a.* जावळा, जुवळा, जुळा, यम, यमल.

Twins. जुवळ *n.* जुळें *n.* जूळ *f.*

T.—(boys-girls-children). अवळेजावळे*m. pl.* अवळ्याजावळ्या *f. pl.* अवळींजावळीं *n. pl.*

T.—pair, *boy and girl born together.* जोडपें *n.*

2—fruits, &c. *couple*. जुळा.

To TWINE, *v. a. twist*. पिळणें, वळणें, पीळ *m.* घालणें-भरणें.

2 See To GIRD, To WRAP.

To TWINE, *v. n. convolve itself*. वेष्टून-वेढून-&c. जाणें.

TWINE, *n. string*. सुतळी *f.* सडा *m.* शणसूत्र *n.*

2 See TWIST.

To TWINGE, *v. n. have a sharp sudden shooting pain*. शिलक *f.* -चमक *f.* मारणें, कचक *f.*-करक *f.* भरणें.

TWINGE, *n. sudden sharp shooting pain*. शिलक *f.* चमक *f.* कचक *f.* करक *f.*

2 (of conscience) v. REGRET. चुरचूर *f.* चटका *m.* चरका *m.*

To TWINKLE, *v. n. shine tremulously*, v. To SPARKLE. चमकणें, स्फुरणें, स्फुरण *n.* होणें *g. of s.* लिकलिकणें.

2—the eye. लवणें, पलक *m. n.* मारणें, निमेषोन्मेष *m.*-&c. होणें *g. of s.*

TWINKLE, TWINKLING, *n.* v. V. 1. स्फुरण *n.*

2 निमिष *or* निमेष *m.* उन्मेष *m.* निमिषोन्मेष *or* निमेषोन्मेष *m.* उन्मीलन *n.* [निमेष *m.*

I. *instant*, v. MOMENT. पलक *m. n.* चिपडी *f.* निमिष *or*

To TWIRL, *v. a. turn round with rapidity*, v. To WHIRL. गरगर-गरगरां-गिरगिशी-&c. फिरवणें, गरगरवणें.

To TWIRL, *v. n. revolve with rapidity*, v. To WHIRL. गरगरणें, घिरटी *or* घरटी *f.* घालणें, गिरटी *f.*-गिरटें *n.*-गिरकी *f.*-गिरकांडा *m.*-&c. देणें-मारणें-घेणें.

TWIRL, TWIRLING, v. V. N. गरगरणें *n.* &c. घिरटी *or* घरटी *f.* गिरटी *f.* गिरकी *f.* गिरकांडा *m.* गिरकांडी *f.* फेरा *m.* फेरी *f.*

To TWIST, *v. a. form by convolution*. वळणें.

2 *contort, wring, &c.* v. To WRENCH. पिळणें, पिळवटणें, पिळगुटणें, पेचणें, मुरगळणें *or* मुरगाळणें, मुरडणें, पिळे *m. pl.* देणें, वांकडा-&c. करणें.

A twisting stick. पिळकवणें *n.* पिळें *n.*

To t. or turn in rough or rude manner. वेंटणें *or* वेंटणें *or* वेंटाळणें.

3 v. To WIND. गुंडाळणें, लपेटणें, वेष्टणें, वेंटाळणें.

4 (a meaning, &c.) *wrest, pervert*. वळवणें, ओढणें, ओढून घेणें.

To TWIST, *v. n. be convolved*. वळणें, वळत जाणें-चालणें.

TWIST, *n. convolution, twisted state*. पीळ *m.* वळ *m.* पिरंगाळा *m.* पेच *or* पेंच *m.* मुरगाळा *m.* मुरड *or* मरोड *f.* पिळण *f.* पिळा *m.*

2 *twisted string, &c.* v. STRING. सडा *m.* वेंट *or* वेंठ *m.*

Triple t. तिसुती *f.*

3 *cloth, &c. twisted and wrung*. पिळा *m.*

4 *string of a cord*. पेड *m.* पदर *m.* वेंठ *m.* वळ *m.*

5 (of grass, yarn, tobacco, &c.). वेंट *or* वेंठ *m.* वेंटी *f.* वेंटणें *n.* वेंटली *f.*

6 *contortion, writhe*. पिरंगाळा *m.* पेच *m.* तीट *m. f.*

7 (as of the bowels). वेंट *or* वेंठ *m.* v. फिर, वळ.

TWISTED, *p.* v. V. A. 1. वळलेला, वळींव, वळसर.

Lose t. उवळ *or* उंवळ *or* उंवीळ, पिळपिळीत.

Strongly t. पिळदार, पिळवट.

2 पिळलेला, मुरगाळलेला, &c.

TWISTEDNESS, *n.* v. P. 2. पीळ *m.* पिरंगाळा *m.* मुरगाळा *m.*

To TWIT, *v. a. upbraid, &c.* v. To TAUNT. ओढावणें, टेपलणें, नाकांत काड्या *f. pl.* घालणें, उपराध *m.*-आक्षेप *m.* करणें, टोमणा-&c. मारणें-देणें.

To TWITCH, *v. a. pull with a sudden jerk*, v. JERK. हिसकणें, हिसडणें *or* हसडणें, हिसका *m.*-&c. देणें.

To TWITCH, *v.n.*—the eye lids. लवणें, स्फुरणें, फुरफुरणें (*intens.* फुरारणें) फरफरणें, कचकणें, स्फुरण *n.*-&c. होणें *g. of s.*

TWITCH, *n. quick pull*. हिसका *m.* हिसडा *m.* असडा *m.* आंचका *m.* कचका *m.* [*pop.* स्फूर्त *f.*

2 (of the fibres). स्फुरण *pop.* फुरण *n.* फुरफुराट *m.* स्फूर्ति

3 (for a horse's lip or ear). पुजमाल *m.* ओंठाळी *f.*

To TWITTER, *v. n.*—birds. चिवचिवणें, किलकिलणें, किलबिलणें, कचकचणें, चिवचीव *f.*-चूंचूं *n.*-&c. करणें-मांडणें,—noisily or in number, कचाचणें.

TWITTER, TWITTERING, *n.* v. V. *and* CHATTER. चिवचीव *f.* कलकल *m.* किलकील *f. m.* किलबील *f. m.* चूंचूं *n.*—*intens.* चिवचिवाट *m.* कुलकुलाट *m.* किल्लाण *m.*

TWO, *a.* दोन, बे, दु (in comp. as दुकसची, दुकाठी, दुसंड) द्वि (in comp. as द्विपद, द्विस्तन, &c.).—of human beings. दोघ (fem. घी *or* घ्या. neuter. घें *or* घीं.)

In t. दोनतुकडे, दुधड, द्विधा.

That is in twos or pairs. जोडगिरी *or* जोडगीर.

The t. दोन्ही.

T. and a half. अडीच.

TWO-EDGED, *a.* दुधारी, दुधार.

TWO-FOLD, *a. of two sorts*. दोनप्रकारचा, दोनतऱ्हेचा, द्वैध.

2 v. DOUBLE. दुपट, द्विगुणित.

TWO-HANDED, *a.* दोनहातांचा, द्विहस्त, द्विहस्तक.

TWO-HANDLED, *a.* दुदांडी.

TWO-HEADED, *n.* दोनमस्तकांचा, द्विमूर्द्ध, द्विमस्तक.

TWO-TONGUED, *a.* दोनजिभ्या, द्विजिह्व.

TYMPAN, TYMPANUM, *n. drum of the ear*. कानाचा पडदा *m.*

TYMPANITES, TYMPANY, *n.*—the disease. कांसव्या रोग *m.* गुल्मोदर *n.* गुल्मवात *m.* गुल्म *m.* अलसक *m.*

To get t. पोटामध्यें गुबारा *m.* धरणें, पोट *n.* तडस भरणें.

TYPE, *n. emblem, sign*, v. MARK. खूण *f.* निशाणी *f.* चिन्ह *n.* लक्षण *n.*

2 *a figure of something to come*. प्रतिरूप *n.* प्रतिरूपक *n.* प्रतिबिंब *n.* दर्शक चिन्ह *n.*

3 *printing letter*. छाप *m.* ठसा *m.*

4—in medicine. भावना *f.* स्वरूप *n.*

TYPHUS FEVER, *n.* काळज्वर *m.*

TYPICAL, *a.* v. N. 1. 2. लाक्षणिक, संज्ञीक, सांकेतिक, अन्यप्रतिरूपक, अन्यप्रतिबिंबक, बोधक, उद्बोधक, अन्यदर्शक.

TYPIFIED, *p.* v. V. प्रतिरूपकानें दाखवलेला, &c. बोधित.

To TYPIFY, *v. a.* v. To PREFIGURE. प्रतिरूप *n.*-प्रतिरूपक *n.*-&c. करून दाखवणें *g. of o.* प्रतिरूपकानें-&c. दाखवणें-सुचवणें-बोधवणें.

TYPOGRAPHY. See PRINTING.

TYRANNIC, TYRANNICAL, TYRANNOUS, *a. unjustly severe, oppressive*. जुलमी, जुलूम-जुलुमजास्ती-&c. करणारा, जुलमाचा, जबरदस्तीचा, जुलुमजास्तीचा, जबरदस्त, जालीम, जोरावर, गजबी, कहरी, जळजळाटी, जळजळाट्या, प्रजोपद्रवी, प्रजोपप्लवी, प्रजापीडक, अनीतिशास्ता. [जापीडक हत्या *f.*

TYRANNICIDE, *n.*—the act. जुलम्याचा खून *m.*-वध *m.*-&c. प्र-

2—the agent. जुलम्याचा खून करणारा, &c. प्रजापीडकहंता.

To TYRANNIZE, *v. n. act the tyrant.* जुलूम *m.*-जुलुमदस्ती *f.*-जुलुम जास्ती *f.*-&c. करणें-मांडणें, आदळ *m.* लावणें, बेदाद *f.*-कुशासन *n.*-अनीतिशासन *n.*-&c. करणें.

To t. exceedingly. ओलें जाळणें.

TYRANNY, *n. absolute monarchy.* स्वतंत्रराज्य *n.* अनिर्बंधराज्य *n.*

2 *imperious domination, unjust rule.* जुलमानें-&c. राज्य *n.* जुलमाचें-जुलुमजास्तीचें-&c. राज्य *n.* राजीक *n.* राजक्रांति *f.* राजद्रोह *m.* राजोपप्लव *m.* बेदाद *f.* जुलुमपादशाही *f.* कुशासन *n.* अनीतिशासन *n.* अन्यायशासन *n.* प्रजापीडन *n.* प्रजोपद्रव *m.* प्रजोपप्लव *m.*

3 *oppression*, gener. जुलुम *m.* जुलुमदस्ती *f.* जुलुमजास्त *f.* जुलुमजास्ती *f.* जबरी *f.* जबरदस्ती *f.* जोर *m.* जोरावरी *f.* जोराबा *m.* जोरा *m.* तोशीस *f.* कहर *m.* गजब *m.* जलेल *f.* जळजळ *f. intens.* जळजळाट *m.*

TYRANT, *n. absolute monarch.* मुखत्यारराजा *m.* स्वतंत्रराजा *m.*

2 *despotic and cruel ruler,* v. A. जुलमानें-&c. राज्यकरणारा, जुलुमजास्तीचें-&c. राज्यकरणारा, जुलमी-&c. राजा *m.*-&c. प्रजापीडक.

3 *oppressor, cruel master, &c.* जुलूम-जुलुमजास्ती-जुलुमदस्ती-&c. करणारा, आगधाड *f.*

TYRO, *n. beginner in learning.* नवशिका *or* खा, नवशिक्या, नवशीक *or* ख, शिकणाऊ, शिकाऊ, नूतनअभ्यासी, किंचिज्ज्ञ, छात्र *m.*

U.

U. This letter is represented by अ, but by it is conveyed only its sound as in *run, sun, rub, &c.* Its sound as in *union, uniform, &c.* must be represented by यु; and its sounds in *bull, pull, full,* and in *ruse, truth, &c.* by उ and ऊ.

UBIQUITARY, UBIQUITOUS, *a. existing every where.* सर्वठिकाणीं असणारा, सार्वत्रिक, सर्वव्यापक, विश्वव्यापक, दिग्व्यापी, सर्वत्रस्थ, विभु.

UBIQUITY, *n. existence every where.* विश्वव्याप्ति *f.* व्याप्ति *f.* दिग्व्याप्ति *f.* विश्वव्यापकत्व *n.* अभिव्याप्ति *f.*

UDDER, *n. milk bag of beasts.* ऑटी *f.* कास *f.* अडें *n.* अडाण *or* अडण *n.*

Side or half of an u. पास्वर *f.* पास्वें *n.*

To get a distended u. कास *f.* घालणें, अणखुरणें.

UGLINESS, *n.* v. A. बदसुरत *f.* बदसुरती *f.* बदसुरतपणा *m.* विद्रूपपणा *m.* बिद्रेपणा *m.* कुरूपता *f.* विरूपता *f.* वैरूप्य *n.* मुद्राहीनता *f.* बीभत्साकृति *f.* कुत्सिताकृति *f.*

UGLY, *n. not handsome.* बदसुरत, सेंबडा, कुरूप, दुर्मुख, विरूप *pop.* बिद्रूप, बिद्रा, बिपारा, रूपहीन, हीनरूप, मुद्राहीन, हीनमुद्र, विकृतांग, बीभत्साकृति, कुत्सिताकृति, ओबडधोबड.

Excessively u. or deformed. अष्टवक्र *pop.* अष्टावक्र, बडजा.

ULCER, *n. running sore.* व्रण *vulg.* वरण *m.* क्षत *n. pop.* खटन. *f.* खबंद *or* खऊंद *n.f.* खंबदल *n.* घाड *f.* पुळी *f.* फांपर *n.* बारूळ *n.* भग *n.* सपूयक्षत *n.*

Ulcerous hole,—gener. भगेंद्र *n.*

Virulent u. जाळपुळी *f.* पूतिव्रण *m.*

Wide-spreading u. चाळणपुळी *f.*

To ULCERATE, *v. n. become ulcerous.* व्रण *m.*-क्षत *n.*-&c. पडणें, पचुरणें *or* पचरणें, व्रणित-व्रणी होणें.

ULCERATION, *n.* v. V. पचुरणें *n.* व्रणीहोणें *n.*

ULCERED, ULCEROUS, *a. affected with ulcers.* व्रणपडलेला, &c. पचुरलेला *or* पचरलेला, व्रणित, व्रणी, सक्षत, सव्रण, खवंद्या, खबंदेला, वरणी.

ULTERIOR, *a. further.* पुढीलचा, पुढचा, नंतरचा, पलीकडचा, पलीकडील, उत्तर in comp. [तिम, चरम.

ULTIMATE, *a.*v. LAST, FURTHEST. शेवटला, शेवटचा, शेवटील, अं-

ULTIMATELY, *adv.* v. A. शेवटीं, सरतेशेवटीं, अंतीं, परिणामीं.

ULTIMATUM, *n. final proposition, term, &c.* निदानचा-निदानींचा-निर्वाणचा-&c. शब्द *m.*-बोल *m.*-भाषण *n.*-&c. सरशेवट *m.*

ULTRA. See EXCESSIVE.

ULTRAMARINE, *a. being beyond the sea.* समुद्रापलीकडचा.

ULTRAMONTANE, *a. being beyond the mountain.* डोंगरापलीकडचा. [फोड.

ULULATION, *n. howling, outcry.* धाय *f.* धायमाय *f.* v. मोकल,

UMBILICAL, *a. belonging to the navel.* नाभीचा, नाभिसंबंधी, नाभ्य. [भिनाला *f.*

U. cord. नाल *pop.* नाळ *n.* गर्भनाडी *f.* नाभिनाडी *f.* ना-

U. cord as swollen (or protruded.) बोंगा *m.*

U. region. नाभिचक्र *n.* नाभिमंडल *n.*

UMBRAGE, *n.* v. OFFENCE. रुसवा *m.* गैरमर्जी *f.* असंतोष *m.*

To take u. at. वाईट मानणें, वाईट घेणें.

2 See SHADE.

UMBRAGEOUS, *a.* v. SHADY. सावलीचा, छायेचा, छायामय.

UMBRELLA, *n.*—the skreen from the sun or rain. छत्री *f.* छत्र *n.* आतपत्र *n.* आतपवारण *n.*

Radius of an u. खडा *m.*

Stick of an u. दांडी *f.*

The u. of royalty or state. छत्र *n.*

U. borne over Rajas, &c. in their processions. अबदागीर *n. dim.* अबदागिरी *f.*—bearer of t. अबदागिऱ्या.

UMPH, *interj.* अं:.

UMPIRE, *n.* v. ARBITER. तिऱ्हाईत, मध्यस्थ, अमीन, लवाद.

UN. With this negative or privative particle correspond अ and अन् (as in अशक्त, असमर्थ, अनुपयुक्त, अनुपयोग, &c.), उ (as in उसवणें, उचकटणें, उबळणें, उगळणें, उस्तरणें, &c.), गैर (as in गैरखुशी, गैरवाजवी, गैरशिस्त, &c.), बे (as in बेशिस्त, बेइलाज, बेइमान, &c.), निर् (as in निरुपयोग, निर्घात, &c.), ना (as in नालायक, नाखुश, नापसंत, &c.), वि (as in विजोड, विलग, &c.). Dr. Johnson has observed of it, that, as it is placed almost at will before adjectives, &c. all instances of its occurrence cannot be inserted. Of अ we make the same observation; and as the public animadversion upon the Doctor is rather on account of the *multitude* than on account of the *paucity* of his insertions, we have been careful to insert only the most approved of the formations with अ. Of those English words, to which sometimes *un* and sometimes *in* is prefixed, such as are not found here, should be looked for under *In.*

Unable, *a.* अशक्त, असमर्थ, अक्षम.

Unacceptable, *a.* पसंतव्हायास अयोग्य, नापसंतीचा, नापसंत, नामंजूर, अमान्य, अग्राह्य, अग्रहणीय, अस्वीकार्य, अनादेय, ग्रहणायोग्य, ग्रहणानर्ह.

Unaccepted, *a.* नापसंत, नामंजूर, अगृहीत, अस्वीकृत, अनंगीकृत.

Unaccommodated, *a. not fitted*, v. **Unsuited**. अनुपयोगी, अनुपयुक्त.

Unaccompanied, *a.* v. **Single**. सोबती वेगळा-निराळा, एकाकी, असंग, असंगत, असहाय.

Unaccomplishable, *a.* साधायास-&c. अयोग्य-अशक्य, असाधनीय, असाध्य, दुःसाध्य.

Unaccomplished, *a. incomplete.* असाधित, असंपन्न, अनिष्पन्न, अकृत, असिद्ध, अनुपपन्न, अनधिगत.

Unaccountable, *a.* v. **Inexplicable**. अव्याख्येय, अव्याख्यातव्य, अविवरणीय. [नमोसबी, पृच्छानधीन.

2 *not responsible.* मोसब्याबाहेरचा, मोसब्यावेगळा-निराळा, बि-

Unaccustomed, *a. not habituated.* बिनसवईचा *or* सवेचा, बिनराबत्याचा, गैरराबत्याचा, बिनखांदाचा, बिनघसवटीचा, &c. अनभ्यासी, अनभ्यस्त, अकृताभ्यास.

Unacknowledged, *a.* अस्वीकृत, अनंगीकृत, अजातस्वीकार.

Unacquaintance, *n.* v. **Ignorance**. गैरमाहिती *f.* गैरवाकबदारी *f.* अज्ञान *n.* अपरिचय *m.* [कबदार.

Unacquainted, *a.* v. **Ignorant**. गैरमाहीत, गैरमाहितगार, गैरवा-

Unacquiescent, *a.* अमान्य, नाकबूल, नाराजी, असम्मत.

Unacquired, *a.* अप्राप्त, अलब्ध, असंपादित, अनर्जित.

Unactionable, *a.* अव्यवहार्य्य, व्यवहारायोग्य, व्यवहारानास्पद, व्यवहाराविषय.

Unadapted, *a.* अयोग्य, अनुपयोगी, अनुपयुक्त, नालायक.

Unadorable, *a.* अपूज्य, अपूजनीय, अनाराध्य, अनाराधनीय, अनर्च्य, अनर्चनीय.

Unadorned, *a.* v. **Plain**. अलंकारावेगळा-निराळा, अनलंकृत, अभूषित, अलंकारहीन-रहित-शून्य.

Unadult, *a.* अप्राप्तयौवन, अप्रौढ.

Unadulterated, *a.* v. **Pure**. निरा, अमिश्रित, अदूषित, निर्मल.

Unadvised, &c. See **Rash**.

Unaffected, *a. unacted upon.* जशाचातसा, अलग, अपूट, अनामत, अविकृत, निर्विकार, अजातगुण, अप्राप्तगुण.

2 *unfeigned*, v. **Real**, **Sincere**. खरा, अकृत्रिम, अनाकृष्ट.

3 *free from affectation*, v. **Simple**. बिन अकडीचा, बिननखऱ्याचा, बिनकुऱ्र्याचा, &c. साळसूद *or* ध.

4 *unmoved, untouched in the heart.* गाहिंवर न आलेला, &c. अद्रुत, अजातद्रव.

Unaffectionate, *a.* ममतेवेगळा *or* निराळा, मोहावेगळा *or* निराळा, &c. निर्मोह, निर्माय, हीनमाया.

Unagitated, *a.* v. **Calm**. अक्षुब्ध, अक्षोभ.

Unaided, *a.* बिनमदतीचा, बिनकुमकीचा, &c. असहाय, निसहाय.

Unalienable, *a.* अन्यादेय, परादेय, स्थावर.

Unallowable, **Unallowed**, *a.* v. **Forbidden**. अकार्य, अकर्तव्य, निषेधविषय, वर्जविषय.

Unalloyed, *a.* निर्दम, बिनभिसळीचा, खरा, चोख, निरा.

Unalterable, *a.* v. **Immutable**. फिरवायासअयोग्य-अशक्य, फेरफारानिराळा-वेगळा, फेरफाराबाहेरचा, अनन्यथाकरणीय, अपरिवर्त्तनीय, परिवर्त्तनाशक्य, अविकार्य.

Unambiguous, *a.* v. **Clear**. असंदिग्ध, असंशयित, अद्व्यर्थ.

Unanimated, *a. inanimate.* निर्जीव, अप्राण, अजीव, अचेतन, अजातचेतन.

2 v. **Spiritless**. निर्जीव, निस्तेज, बिरस, अळणी.

Unanimity, *n.* v. **Agreement**. ऐकमत्य *n.* ऐक्य *n.* एकमन *n.* एकी *f.* एका *m.* चित्तैक्य *n.* मतैक्य *n.* एकचित्तता *f.* सप *m.* समा *m.* [मन, समभाव.

Unanimous, *a. of one mind*, v. **Agreed**. एकचित्त, एकदिल, एक-

2 *formed by unanimity.* सर्वसम्मतीचा, सर्वांच्यामताचा, सर्वैक्याचा, सर्वसम्मत.

Unannealed, *a. not tempered by fire.* निताव.

Unanswerable, *a.* v. **Irrefragable**. निरुत्तर, अनुत्तर, बिनजबाब, दुरुत्तर, दुरुद्धर, अखंडनीय.

Unanxious, *a.* निकाळजी *or* निष्काळजी, निघोर *or* री, निर्घोर, बिनघोर, अघोर, निश्चिंत, बेफिकीर, बिनधोक, निरुत्सुक.

Unanxiously, *adv.* v. A. काळजीवांचून, &c. अक्लेश, सुस्त, बिनघोर, बिनधोक.

Unapparent, *a.* अस्पष्ट, अव्यक्त, अप्रकट.

Unappeasable, *a.* v. **Implacable**. शांत करावास अयोग्य-अशक्य-&c. असमजुती *or* त्या, अप्रसाद्य, अशाम्य, असांत्वनीय, असमाधेय.

Unappeased, *a.* अशांत, अप्राप्तसमाधान, अजातसमाधान.

Unappointed, *a.* अनुक्त, अनियुक्त, अनियोजित, अनादिष्ट.

Unapprehensive, *a. not suspecting, fearing, &c.* निघोर, निघोरी, अशंक, अविशंक, शंकाहीन, शंकारहित, अविशंकित.

Unapprehensiveness, *n.* v. A. अविशंका *f.* शंकाराहित्य *n.* शंकाहीनता *f.*

Unapprised, *a.* असूचित, असंदिष्ट.

Unapproachable, *a.* जवळ जाण्याचा अयोग्य-अशक्य-&c. अगम्य, अगमनीय, अनागम्य, अगंतव्य, अनभिगम्य, अनुपसार्य, दुर्गम.

Unapproved, *a.* अमान्य, नापसंत, अनभिमत, अननुमोदित.

Unapt, *a. unfit*, v. **Unsuited**. अनुपयोगी, अनुपयुक्त.

2 *not propense, disposed, &c.* बिनकलाचा-झोकाचा-&c. अप्रवण, असिद्ध.

3 *unready, dull*, v. **Stupid**. बुद्धीचा जड-मंद-&c. मंदमति, मंदबुद्धि, अचतुर, असकृद्ग्राही.

Unarmed, *a.* बिनहत्यार, अशस्त्र, शस्त्रहीन-रहित-&c. निःशस्त्र, अस्त्रहीन, अनायुध, निरायुध.

Unarrived, *a.* अनागत.

Unartificial, *a.* v. **Natural**. अकृत्रिम.

Unascertainable, *a.* अनिर्णेय, अनिर्धार्य, अनिश्चेय, अवेद्य.

Unascertained, *a.* अनिर्णीत, अनिश्चित, अनिर्धारित.

Unasked, *a.* बिनमागणीचा, बिनपुसल्याचा, अयाचित, अप्रार्थित, अनर्थित, अभिक्षित.

Unaspirated, *a.* अल्पप्राण.

Unassailable, *a.* घाला घालायास अयोग्य-अशक्य-&c. बेलग, अनाक्रमणीय, अनाक्रम्य, आक्रमणाशक्य.

Unassayed, *a.* नितांव.

Unassisted, *a.* बिनमदतीचा, बिनकुमकीचा, &c. असहाय.

Unassociated, *a.* असंग, असंगत, असहित.

Unassuming, *a.* बिनआढ्यतेचा, बिनदिमाखाचा, अनभिमानी, निरभिमानी, मर्यादशील, साळढाळ, साळसूद *or* धं.

UNATTACHED, *a.* असंगत, असंबद्ध.

UNATTAINABLE, *a.* असाध्य, अनासाध्य, अगम्य, अनागम्य, अप्राप्य, अलभ्य, दुःसाध्य, दुर्गम, दुर्धर.

UNATTAINED, *a.* अप्राप्त, अलब्ध, अनापन्न, अनधिगत.

UNATTENDED, *a.* v. SINGLE. गड्यामाणसानिराळा-वेगळा, चाकरानफरानिराळा-वेगळा, अननुचर, अनुचरहीन-रहित-&c.

UNATTESTED, *a.* बिनसाक्षी, बिनसाक्षीचा, असाक्ष, असाक्षिक.

UNAUTHENTIC, *a.* प्रमाणावांचूनचा, अप्रमाण, अप्रामाणिक.

UNAUTHORITATIVE, *a.* बिनप्रमाणाचा, अप्रमाण, अप्रामाणिक, प्रमाणरहित, निष्प्रमाण, अनाप्त, अनार्ष.

UNAUTHORITATIVENESS, *n.* v. A. प्रमाणाभाव*m.* प्रमाणराहित्य*n.* अप्रमाणता *f.*

UNAUTHORIZED, *a.* विधीवांचूनचा, बिनहुकमाचा, गैरहुकमी, अविधि, विधिहीन, बिगरसनदी, गैरसनदी, हुकमाबाहेरचा.

UNAVAILING, *a.* v. INEFFECTUAL, FRUITLESS. निरर्थक, निष्फल, अपार्थक. [निवारणाशक्य.

UNAVOIDABLE, *a.* चुकवायास अयोग्य-अशक्य, अनिवार्य, अनिवार,

UNAWARE, UNAWARES, *adv. unexpectedly,* v. SUDDENLY. एकाएकी, अकस्मात्, अवचट, अवचित *or* तां.

To UNBAR, *v. a.* अगळ *f.*-&c. काढणें *g. of o.*

UNBATHED, *a.* बिनआंघोळीचा, अस्नात, अकृतस्नान.

UNBEARABLE, *a.* सहायास अयोग्य-अशक्य-&c. असहनीय, असह्य.

UNBEATEN, *a.*—path, &c. बिनमळलेला, बिनमळणीचा, अमर्दित.

UNBECOMING, *a.* v. INDECOROUS. अयोग्य, अनुचित, नालायक, बेशिस्त, गैरशिस्त, विशोभित.

UNBEGOTTEN, *a.* अजनित.

UNBELIEF, *n.* अविश्वास*m.* अश्रद्धा *f.* अभक्ति *f.* अनास्तिक्य*n.*

UNBELIEVER, *n.* UNBELIEVING, *a.* अविश्वासी *or* सू *or* सूक, अप्रत्ययी, अश्रद्ध, अश्रद्दधान, अश्रद्धावान्, अभक्तिमान, अभक्त, अभाविक, नास्तिक, अनास्तिक.

To UNBEND, *v. a.* (a bow, &c.). उतरणें, दोरी *f.*-&c. सोडणें *g. of o.* असज्ज करणें.

2 See To RELAX.

UNBENDING, See FIRM, OBSTINATE.

UNBIASSED, *a.* v. IMPARTIAL. निष्पक्षपात, निष्पक्षपाताचा, उदासीन, उभयपक्षीं समान, उभयसाधारण. [निमंत्रित.

UNBID, UNBIDDEN, *a.* नबोलावलेला, अनामंत्रित, अनाहूत, अ-

To UNBIND, *v. a.* v. To LOOSE. बंधन *n.*-बांध *m.*-&c. सोडणें *g. of o.* सोडणें, बंधमुक्त-बंधनमुक्त-मुक्तबंधन-&c. करणें.

UNBLAMABLE, *a.* v. INNOCENT. निर्दोष, अवाच्य, अनिंद्य, अदूष्य.

UNBLEACHED, *a.* बिनओपवलेला, बिनओपणीचा.

UNBLEMISHED, *a.* बिनऐब, अखोड, निखोड, बिनखोड, बिनगोमी, बिनडागी, निर्दोष, निर्दुष्ट, निकोप, निष्कलंक, अहत.

UNBLESSED, *a.* आशीर्वाद न दिल्हेला, अमंत्रक, निराशी, अनाशिष, निराशिष. [प्रफुल्लित.

UNBLOWN, *a.* न उमललेला, &c. अस्फुट, अविकसित, अप्रफुल्ल, अ-

UNBLUSHING, *a.* v. SHAMELESS. निलाजरा, निर्लज्ज.

UNBOILED, *a.* बिनशिजलेला, &c. अशिजा.

2—used of milk, oil, butter, &c. *unheated.* बिनतापलेला, &c. अकढा, अकढी. [छिद्रित.

UNBORED, *a.*—ear, pearl, &c. बिनटोचलेला, अविंध, अविध, अ-

UNBORN, *a.* न जन्मलेला, अजात, अजातजन्मा, अप्राप्तजन्मा, अज, अनागत.

To UNBOSOM, *v. a. tell in confidence.* पोटाबाहेर-तोंडाबाहेर-&c. काढणें, पोटानिराळा करणें, पोटफोड *f.* करणें *g. of o.* मनमोकळें करून सांगणें.

UNBOUND, *a.* न बांधलेला, &c. मोकळा, अबद्ध, अबंधन,अजातबंध.

UNBOUNDED, *a.* v. INFINITE. अपार, अमर्याद, निर्मर्याद, निरवधि, निरसीम.

UNBOUNTEOUS, UNBOUNTIFUL, *a.* अदाता, अदानशील, दातृत्वहीन, हीनदातृत्व, अवदान्य.

UNBRIDLED, *a.* v. LICENTIOUS. बिनलगामी, अनर्गल, बेकैद, उच्छृंखल *pop.* उत्संकळ *or* खळ.

UNBROKEN, *a.* बिनतुटलेला, &c. अभंग, असंडित, असंड, अतूट.

2—a horse,&c. अप्रेट, अल्हड. [हीन.

UNBROTHERLY, *a.* बिनभाईचाऱ्याचा, बिनभाऊबंदकीचा, बंधुभाव-

UNBRUISED, *a.* बिनकुटलेला, &c. अक्षुण्ण.

UNBURIED, *a.* बिनपुरलेला, बिनगाडलेला, बिनमूठमातीचा.

UNBURNT, *a.* बिनजाळलेला, अदग्ध, अजातदाह.

2—brick, &c. बिनभाजलेला, &c. कच्चा, अभर्जित.

To UNBURDEN, *v. a.* ओझ्या-&c. निराळा-वेगळा करणें, भारमोचन-&c. करणें *g. of o.* भारमुक्त-मुक्तभार-&c. करणें.

UNCAGED, *a.* पिंजऱ्यांतून सोडलेला, &c. उत्पिंजर.

UNCALLED, *a.* न बोलावलेला, &c. अहूत, अनाहूत, अनामंत्रित, अनिमंत्रित.

2 for; v. NEEDLESS. बिनकारणी, कारणावांचूनचा.

UNCANDID, *a.* मनाचा अप्रांजल-कपटी, अप्रांजल.

UNCANONICAL, *a.* अशास्त्र.

UNCAUSED, *a.* अकर्तृक, अकारण, निष्कारण.

UNCEASING, *a.* v. CONTINUAL. निरंतर, असंड, सतत, अस्थायी.

UNCEASINGLY, *adv.* v. CONTINUALLY, EVER. निरंतर, नित्य.

UNCEREMONIOUS, *a.* बिनमुरवतीचा, बिनभिडेचा, बेउजूरचा.

UNCEREMONIOUSLY, *adv.* बेचरक, बेजरब, बेउजूर, बेमुरवत.

UNCERTAIN, *a. not certainly known,* v. DOUBTFUL. बिनखचितीचा, बिनभरवशाचा, भ्रांतिवृत, संशयित, अनिश्चित, अनियत, अनिर्णीत, अनिर्धारित, अनिश्चयात्मक, अस्थिर.

2 *not confident, not sure,* v. DOUBTFUL. संशयी, संदिग्ध, अनिश्चयी, अजातनिर्धार, अजातनिश्चय.

UNCERTAINTY, *n.* v. A. 1. भ्रांतिवटपणा *m.* अनिश्चितपणा *m.* संशयितपणा *m.* &c. वानवा *f.* अत्र *n.* तथा *f.* अनिश्चय *m.* अनिश्चिती *f.* अनिर्धारितत्व *n.* अनिर्धार *m.* अनिर्णय*m.* विकल्प*m.* अनवस्था *f.* अनवस्थिति *f.* [दुभरवसा *m.*

2 *and* DOUBT. संशय *m.* संदेह *m.* दुग्धा *f.* संदिग्धता *f.* भ्रांति *f.*

UNCHANGEABLE, UNCHANGING, *a.* फेरफारा बाहेरचा,फेरफारा निराळा-वेगळा, अविकारी, अविकार, अविकार्य, निर्विकार, विकारातीत, निर्विकल्प, अविक्रिय, अव्यय. [सा, अपूट.

UNCHANGED, *a.* नफिरवलेला, &c. निर्विकार, अविकृत, जशाचा त-

2—a coin. बंदा. [ष्टि, मर्मान्वेषी.

UNCHARITABLE, *a.* v. CENSORIOUS. दोषदृष्टि, दोषदर्शी, अकृपादृ-

UNCHARITABLENESS, *n.* v. A. दोषदृष्टि *f.*

UNCHASTE, *a.* v. INCONTINENT, LOOSE. जारकर्मी, व्यभिचारी, शिनळ, जार.

U. wife. असती *f.* असाध्वी *f.* कुलटा *f.* अपतिव्रता *f.*

UNCHECKED, *a.* न आवरलेला, &c. अनर्गल *or* ळ, अनावृत.

UNCIRCUMCISED, *a.* बिनसुंती, बिनसुंत्या. [धान.

UNCIRCUMSPECT, *a.* v. CARELESS. गैरसावध, असावध, असाव-

Uncivil, *a.* v. **Rude.** अशिष्ट, असभ्य, अविनय, बेमुरवत, अमर्यादशील.

Uncivilized, *a.* v. **Barbarous.** रानटी, जंगली, अशिक्षित, निराचार, अनाचारी, विद्याचारहीन.

Unclaimed, *a. without a claimant.* बेवारीस, बेवारशी, बेवारशीक, निवारीस, निवारशी, निवारशीक, अस्वामिक, अस्वामी.

Uncle, *n. father's brother.* चुलता *m.* काका *m.* पितृव्य *m.* पितृभ्राता *m.*

Wife of paternal u. चुलती *f.* [*m.* मातृभ्राता *m.*

2 *mother's brother.* मामा *m.* मावळा *m.* मातुल *pop.* मातूल

Daughter of maternal u. मेहुणी *f.*

Wife of maternal u. मामी *f.*

3 *husband of maternal aunt.* मावसा *m.*

Unclean, Uncleanly, *a.* v. **Dirty.** मळका, मळीण, समल.

2—ceremonially; *defiled*, v. **Impure.** अपवित्र, विटाळाचा, अशुचि, नापाक. [अपूत, नापाक.

3 *unchaste, unholy*, v. **Impure, Lustful.** मळीण, अपवित्र,

Uncleanness, Uncleanliness, *n.* v. A. 1. मळकेपणा *m.* मळिणपणा *m.* समलता *f.*

2 अपवित्रता *f.* विटाळ *m.* नापाकी *f.* अशुचित्व *n.*

3 मळिणपणा *m.* नापाकी *f.*

Uncleansed, *a.* साफ न केलेला, अधावित, अशोधित, अपावित.

Unclothed, *a.* पांघरुणा वेगळा-निराळा, अवस्त्र, विवस्त्र, विवसन.

Unclouded, Uncloudy, *a.* v. **Clear.** ढगावेगळा-निराळा, निरभ्र, निर्मेघ.

Uncloying, *a.* अवीट.

Uncogged, *a.* निर्दांती.

Uncomely, *a. unbecoming.* अयोग्य, अनुचित.

2 See **Ungraceful.**

Uncomfortable, *a.*—person. असुखी, अस्वस्थ, असुस्थ.

To feel u. अवघड वाटणें *in. con.*

2—place, &c. गैरसोईचा, गैरलागी.

Uncomfortableness, *n.* v. A. 1. असुखीपणा *m.* अस्वस्थपणा *m.* असुख *n.* अस्वास्थ्य *n.*

2 गैरसोई *f.* गैरलाग *m.*

Uncommanded, *a.* बिनहुकुमाचा, &c. अवैध, अनादिष्ट, अनाज्ञप्त, अनाज्ञात, अविहित, अनुक्त. [अनधिकृत.

Uncommissioned, *a.* गैरसनदी, बेसनदी, अनियुक्त, अनियोजित,

Uncommon, *a.* v. **Rare, Scarce.** विरळ, विरळा, क्वाचित्क, अपरूप, अनोंठा.

2 *unusual*, v. **Strange.** अप्रसिद्ध, अलौकिक, विलक्षण, विशेष, लोकाबाहेरचा. [शय.

Uncommonly, *adv.* v. A. 2. *and* **Very.** फारच, विलक्षण, अति-

Uncommonness, *n.* v. A. 1. विरळपणा *m.* &c. अपूर्वाई *f.* अपरूबाई *f.*

2 अलौकिकपणा *m.* विलक्षणपणा *m.*

Uncompleted, *a.* अपुरता, अपुरा, असमाप्त, अपूर्ण.

Uncompounded, *a.* v. **Simple.** बिनमिसळीचा, असंकीर्ण, अमिश्रित, केवलशुद्ध, निरवयव.

Unconcern, *n.* v. **Carelessness.** अनास्था *f.* निकाळजी *f.* बेदरदीपणा *m.* अनुत्साह *m.* अनमान*m.* औदासीन्य*n.* अनादरबुद्धि *f.*

Unconcerned, *a.* v. **Careless, Indifferent.** निकाळजी *or* निष्काळजी, अनास्थ, बेदरदी, बेपरवा, निर्दर्दी, बिनआस्थेचा, बिनपोटागीचा, बिनकळकळीचा, उदास, उदासी, उदासीन, आग्रहवेगळा-निराळा, अनपेक्ष. [अप्रतिबंध.

Unconditional, *a.* v. **Absolute.** बिनअटीचा, बिनअडीचा,

Unconfiding, *a.* अप्रत्ययी. [ऐसपैस.

Unconfined, *a. spacious*, v. **Roomy.** खुला, खुलास, खुलाशाचा,

Uncongenial, *a.* बिनसात्म्याचा, अननुगुण, अननुकूल, प्रतिकूल.

Unconnected, *a. not coherent*, v. **Inconsistent.** असंबद्ध, निरन्वय, असंगत, बिसंगत, असलग्न, अनन्वित, अबद्ध, बिसंधित.

Unconnectedness, *n.* v. A. असंबंध *m.* असंगति *f.* अनन्वय *m.* असंदर्भ *m.*

Unconquerable, *a.* जिंकायास अशक्य-&c. अजेय, अजय्य, अजेतव्य, अजिंक, अनाधृष्य.

Unconquered, *a.* अजित, अपराजित, अजय.

Unconscionable. See **Unreasonable.** [धुंद.

Unconscious, *a.* v. **Insensible.** अचेतन, निचेतन, निश्चेतन,

2 v. **Ignorant.** अजाण, अजाणता, गैरमाहितगार.

Unconsciousness, *n.* v. A. 1. अचैतन्य *n.* चैतन्याभाव *m.* इंद्रियस्वाप *m.* धुंदी *f.*

2 अजाणपणा *m.* अजाणतेपण *n.* गैरमाहिती *f.*

Unconsecrated, *a.* अमंत्रक, अनभिमंत्रित, अप्रतिष्ठित, असंस्कृत, अजातसंस्कार. [चार.

Unconsidered, *a.* अविचारित, अतार्कित, अविभावित, अजातवि-

Unconsigned, *a.* न हवाललेला, &c. असमर्पित, अर्पित.

Unconstrained, *a.* v. **Free, Voluntary.** मोकळा, अबंध, निर्बंध, बिनजबरीचा, बिनबळाचा.

Unconstraint, *n.* v. **Freedom.** मोकळेपणा *m.* बेअटकाव *m.* बंधनाभाव *m.* अनिर्बंध *m.* अप्रतिबंध *m.* अनिरोध *m.*

Uncontaminated, *a.* सोवळा, अदूषित, अभ्रष्ट, अबाट, निर्लिप्त, अलिप्त.

Uncontested, *a.*—an estate, &c. अप्रतिरव. [अनिवार्य.

Uncontrollable, *a.* v. **Irrestrainable.** अनावर, अनिवार,

Uncontrolled, *a.* बिन अटकावाचा, बेकैद, निरवग्रह, निरंकुश, निर्गल, अनर्गल, अप्रतिबंध.

Unconversant, *a.* गैरवाकबदार, गैरमाहितगार, अनभिज्ञ, अनभ्यस्त, अप्रवीण, अनिपुण. [पाक.

Uncooked, *n.* अनशिजा, कच्चा, हिरवा, अपक्व, अपाचित. अजात-

Uncorrected, *a. unrevised.* न शोधलेला, &c. अशोधित.

Uncounted, *a.* न गणलेला, बिनमोजलेला, &c. अगणित, असंख्यात.

Uncounterfeit, *a.* v. **Genuine, Real.** अकृत्रिम. अकपट.

Uncourteous, *a.* v. **Rude.** बिनमाणुसकीचा, बिनगृहस्थीचा, &c. बेमुरवती, बेमुरवत, अविनय, अननुनय.

Uncourtliness, *n.* v. A. रानटीपणा *m.* असभ्यता *f.* अशिष्टता *f.*

Uncourtly, *a.* v. **Rude.** बिनदरबारी, रानटी, असभ्य, अशिष्ट.

Uncouth, *a.* v. **Awkward, Strange.** अडाणी, अनाडी, हेंगाडा, अवघड, विलक्षण, अपरूप.

Uncouthness, *n.* v. A. अडाणीपणा *m.* विलक्षणपणा *m.* &c.

To **Uncover**, *v. a.* उघडणें, झांकण *n.*-ढांकण *n.*-&c. काढणें-उपटणें *g. of o.* [नावृत.

Uncovered, *p.* v. V. उघडलेला, झांकण काढलेला, &c. उघडा, अ-

Uncreated, *a.* अनुत्पन्न, असृष्ट, अनिर्माण, अनिर्मित, अकृत्रिम, नित्य.

Unction. See **Anointedness. To Anoint.**

Unctuous, *a. oily. greasy.* चिक्कण *or* चिकण, स्नेही, स्निग्ध, स-

स्नेह, चोपड, चोपडा, चिकण चोपडा. [मवाळी *f.*

U. substance,—gener. चोपड *f. n.* मवागी *f.* मवारी *f.*

Softened by some u. substance. मवाळ.

2—earth or soil. चिक्कण *or* चिकण, चिकणवट.

UNCTUOUSNESS, *n.* v. A. 1. चिक्कणपणा *m.*-&c. चिकणाई *f.* ओशट *n.* स्नेहिता *f.* स्निग्धता *f.* [र्दीचा.

UNCULTIVATED, *a.* बिनलागवडीचा, नाकीर्द, पडीत, पडसर, नाकी-

2 See BARBAROUS.

UNCULTIVATEDNESS, *n.* v. A. 1. नाकीर्द *f.*

UNCURBED, *a.* v. UNRESTRAINED. बेकैद, अनावर, अनर्गळ *or* ळ, निरर्गल, निरंकुश.

To UNCURSE, *v. a.* उच्छाप *pop.* उःशाप *m.* देणें-करणें.

UNDAUNTED, *a.* v. BOLD. निधडा, निर्भय, अदांत, गाढा, अज्ञातभय.

UNDECAYED, *a.* अक्षय, अजीर्ण, अक्षित, अशीर्ण, अविशीर्ण, अजातक्षय.

UNDECAYING, *a.* अविनाशी, अनश्वर, अक्षय, अजर, निर्जर, अक्षर, अबीट, विज्वर, निरव्यय, निरपाय.

To UNDECEIVE, *v. a.* भ्रम *m.*-भ्रांति *f.*-&c. उडवणें-दूरकरणें-काढणें-घालवणें-&c. *g. of o.* निर्भ्रांत-निर्भ्रम-&c. करणें, कान *m. pl.*-डोळे *m. pl.* उघडणें *g. of o.*

UNDECIDABLE, *a.* अनिर्णेय, अनिधार्य, निर्धारायोग्य, निर्धाराशक्य.

UNDECIDED, *a. not settled.* बिननिवाड्याचा, &c. अनिर्णीत, अनिर्धारित, अभोगत.

2 *that has not formed his resolution.* निश्चय न केलेला, अकृतसंकल्प, अकृतनिश्चय.

3 See IRRESOLUTE.

UNDECIDEDNESS, *n.* v. A. 1. बानवा *f. m.* अनिश्चय *m.* अनिर्धार *m.* अनिर्णय *m.*

UNDEFILED, *a.* v. PURE. निर्मल, अदूषित, अभ्रष्ट, निर्दूषित, अलिप्त.

UNDEFINABLE, *a. that cannot be described.* लक्षण करायास अयोग्य-अशक्य-&c. अलक्ष्य, अलक्षणीय, अनिर्वचनीय, अनिर्वाच्य, निर्वचनाशक्य, निर्वचनातीत.

UNDEFINED, *a.* v. INDETERMINATE. अलक्षण, निर्लक्षण, अलक्षित, अकृतलक्षण, अकृतनिर्वचन, मोघम *or* मोहगम.

UNDELIVERED, *a.* बिनदिल्हेला, बिनओपलेला, असमर्पित, अनार्पित, अजात समर्पण, अनिवेदित. [दित.

UNDEMONSTRATED, *a.* अनुपपन्न, असिद्ध, असिद्धांतित, अप्रतिपा-

UNDENIABLE, *a.* v. INDISPUTABLE. नाहीं म्हणता यायाचा नाहीं, नाहीं न म्हणाया जोगा, अबाधित, निराकरणानर्ह, निराकरणायोग्य, अनिषेधनीय.

UNDENTICULATED, *a.* बिनदांताचा, निर्दांती, अदांती.

UNDER, *prep. beneath, below, &c.* खालीं, खालता, खालतीं, खालतें, खालें.

2 *in, as included in, as disposed of under.* वारीं (ex. खेळण्यावारीं, हासण्यावारीं, बोलण्यावारीं, मस्करीवारीं, बिनोदावारीं, प्रसादावारीं in play, in laughter, &c.), खालीं (as कामाखालीं, खेळाखालीं, कष्टाखालीं in, at, or under work, play, labor).

3 *in subjection to.* खालीं, हुकमांत, अमलांत, ताब्यांत, तसलमातींत, &c. हाताखालीं, स्वाधीन.

3 *less than &c.* खालीं, कमी-&c. *with* पेक्षां *of o.*

5 *with the cover or pretext of.* निमित्तानें, मिषानें.

6 (misfortune, pain, &c.) *in.* आंत, मध्यें.

7 *in the time of.* आंत, मध्यें, समयीं, वेळेस, *all with g. of s.*

U. the cover or protection of. आड, आडून.

UNDER, *a. nether, inferior,* v. LOWER. खालचा, खालील, खालला, अधःस्थ.

2 *subordinate.* आड (in comp. as आडगडी, आडबंदर, &c.), खालचा, हाताखालचा, उप (in comp. *as,* उपशिक्षक, उपगुरु,&c.).

UNDER-DONE, UNDER-DRESSED, *a.*—an article of cookery, &c. हिरवंडा, हिरवस, हिरवा, कच्चा, अपक्क.

To be u. आफळणें.

UNDER-FOOT, *adv.* पायाखालीं.

To UNDER-GO, *v. a. endure, bear, &c.* v. To SUFFER. सोसणें, भोगणें, कंठणें, काढणें.

To u. a change. परिणाम *m.* होणें *g. of s.* परिणाम *m.* पावणें.

UNDER-GROUND, *adv.* भुईंत, भूमींत, भुईआड, भुयारांत.

UNDER-GROUND, *a.* तळघरचा, भुयाराचा, भुईंतला, भूमिगत.

UNDER-HAND, *adv. clandestinely.* लिकून चोरून, लिकाचोरीनें, लपतछपत, लपूनछपून.

UNDER-HAND, *a.* v. CLANDESTINE. अडआडीचा, लपंडाईचा, लपंडावाचा, पडद्याचा, पडद्यांतला, जनानखान्याचा.

U. work. लपंडाव *m.* लपंडाई *f. v.* खेळ, कर, काळेंभेलें *n.*

UNDER-LABORER, *n.* आडगडी, आडखप्या.

To UNDER-LINE, *v. a.* खालीं रेघ *f.*-&c. काढणें-ओढणें.

UNDER-LING, *n. inferior agent.* आडगडी, आडखप्या, बगल्या, हस्तक, हाताखालचा-लहान-&c. कामदार.

To UNDER-MINE, *v. a. sap.* सुरंग *m.* करणें-पाडणें, पाया खोदून-पाया खणून-&c. पाडणें *g. of o.* पाया *m.* उमळवणें-डासळणें *g. of o.* खणणें, धोंड *m. pl.* खणून काढणें *g. of o.*

2 See To EXCAVATE.

UNDER-MOST, *a.* सर्वांच्या खालचा-खालला-&c. सर्वाधःस्थ.

UNDER-NEATH. See UNDER, BELOW.

To UNDER-PRIZE, *To* UNDER-RATE, *v. a.* उणे किमतींत-हलके-किमतींत-&c. आणणें-धरणें-लावणें, उणे किमतीचा-&c. मानणें-समजणें.

To UNDERSIGN, &c. See To SUBSCRIBE.

UNDERSIZED, *a.* आकाराचा-&c. लहान.

To UNDER-STAND, *v. a. apprehend, comprehend, &c.* समजणें, उमजणें, जाणणें, घेणें, धरणें, आकळणें, बुझणें, बोधणें, समजणें-उमजणें-कळणें *all with in. con.* समजून-&c. घेणें, समज *m. f.*-&c. पडणें *in. con. and g. of o.* ग्रहण *n.* करणें *g. of o.* उमज *m.*-समज *m.*-बोध *m.*-प्रबोध *m.*-ज्ञान *n.*-ग्रह *m.* होणें *in. con. and g. of o.* ध्यानांत-लक्ष्यांत-&c. येणें *in. con. and g. of o.* समज *m.*-&c. घेणें *g. of o.* तरकणें.

To make to u. समजावणें, बुझवणें *or* बुझावणें, बोधवणें.

2 *become informed of.* See To LEARN.

UNDER-STANDING, *p. a.* v. V. *and* WISE. समजणारा, जाणणारा, &c. जाणता, जाण, समजदार, समजूतदार, समजीक, ज्ञाता, प्रज्ञात.

UNDERSTANDING, *n.* v. V. 1.—*act.* समजणें *n.* घेणें *n.* &c. समज *m. f.* उमज *m.* बोध *m.* ग्रह *m.* ग्रहण *n.* प्रबोध *m.* ज्ञान *n.* आकलन *n.*

I. *intellectual powers.* बुद्धि *f.* उमज *m.* समज *m. f.* समजूत *f.* ज्ञान *n.* ज्ञानचक्षु *n.* ज्ञानदृष्टि *f.* अकल *f.* मति *f.* धी *f.* मेधा *f.* प्रज्ञा *f.* आकलनशक्ति *f.* चेतना *f.* ज्ञप्ति *f.* ध्यान *n.*

Eye of the u. ज्ञानचक्षु *n.* ज्ञानदृष्टि *f.*

Object of u. बुद्धिविषय *m.*
Of feeble u. बुद्धीचा हलबट.
Slow of u. मतिमंद, मंदमति.
Ah! extinguish not the lamp of the u. अंतरींचा ज्ञानदिवा मालवूं नकोरे.

II. *pleasant terms of intercourse, amicable relation of minds.* बनाव *m.* पाकी *f.* रहस्य *n.* रहसाळी *f.* स्नेहभाव *m.* गोडीगुलाबी *f.* तिळागुणी *n.* सुलूक *or* ख *m.f.* सोहलत *or* सौलत *f.* सौरस्य *n.* संवित्ति *f.* [पाड, काढ.

Right u. (with, towards). समजी *f.* समजूत *f. v.* कर,
To bring to a right u. समजावणें, समजाविशी *f.*-समजावीस *f.*-समजूत *f.*-समजी *f.* करणें *g. of o. recip.*
To bring to a mutual u. समजूत *f.* पाडणें.
To come to a right u. समजणें, जुगणें, घडी *f.* बसणें *g. of o. and s.*

Under-stood, *p.* v. V. 1. समजलेला, उमजलेला, &c. ज्ञानारूढ, ज्ञानस्पृक्, बुद्ध्यारूढ, आकलित, ज्ञात, विज्ञात, बुद्ध, मत, अवगत, वित्त. [लब्ध, गतार्थ.
I. *involved*, v. Implied. अर्थांमध्यें येऊन गेलेला, गर्भित, उप-

Under-strapper. See Under-ling.

To **Under-take**, *v. a. take in hand, engage to do.* उचलणें, हातीं धरणें-घेणें, पतकरणें *or* पतकारणें, अंगीकारणें, स्वीकारणें, आंगावर-माथ्यावर-डोईवर घेणें, पाठीसीं घेणें, कासेस-बगलेस मारणें, आदरणें, कबूल करणें, अटपणें, विडा *m.* उचलणें *g. of o.* पतकर *or* पतकार *m.*-अंगीकार *m.*-स्वीकार *m.*-अंगीकरण *n.*-स्वीकरण *n.*-&c. करणें *g. of o.* [स्वीकृत.

Under-taken, *p.* v. V. उचललेला, पतकरलेला, &c. अंगीकृत,

Under-taker, *n.* **Undertaking**, *p. a.* v. V. उचलणारा, पतकरणारा, हातीं धरणारा, &c. अंगीकार-स्वीकार कर्त्ता-कारी.

Under-taking, *n. matter undertaken.* काम *n.* कार्य *n.* कर्त्तव्य *n.* धंदा *m.* [साहसकर्म *n.*
Bold or hazardous u. v. Enterprise. जिवावरचें काम *n.*
Great, arduous, &c. u. हत्तींचें मडें *n.*

Under-tenant, *n.* भाडेकऱ्याचा भाडेकरी, पोटभाडेकरी.

To **Under-value**, *v. a.* See To Underrate. 2 *despise*, v. To Contemn. हलका-तुच्छ-&c. मानणें.

Under-wood, *n.* झुडपें *n. pl.* झाडी *f.*

Under-workman, हाताखालचा कामकरणारा, आडखप्या.

Under-writer, *n. insurer.* विमेदार, विमेकरी.

Underived, *a.* v. Natural. सांसिद्धिक, स्वतःसिद्ध, निसर्गसिद्ध.

Undescribable, *a.* अनिर्वाच्य, अवाच्य, वर्णनाशक्य, वर्णनातीत, कथनाशक्य, निरूपणाशक्य, वर्णनागोचर.

Undescribed, *a.* अवर्णित, अनिरूपित, अकथित.

Undeserved, *a.* बिनलायकीचा, गैरवाजिबी, नाहक्काचा, गुणावांचूनचा, अगुणसंपादित, अकर्मसंपादित.

Undeservedly, *adv.* नाहक्क, नालायक.

Undeserving, *a.* v. Unworthy. बिनयोग्यतेचा, बिनलायकीचा, अयोग्य, अनर्ह, नालायक, अपात्र.

Undesigned, *a.* बिनइराद्याचा, बिनमनसुब्याचा, उद्देशाबाहेरचा, संकल्पा-मनसुब्या-&c. निराळा-बाहेरचा, असंकल्पित, अनुद्दिष्ट, अनभिप्रेत, अबुद्धिपूर्वक, अबुद्धिकृत, असंकल्पकृत, असांकल्पिक, अविवक्षित.

Undesignedly, *adv.* v. A. बिनमनसुब्यानें, &c. उद्देशावांचून, संकल्पावांचून-विना, अबुद्धिपूर्वक, अबुद्धिपुरस्सर.

Undesigning, *n. artless,* v. Simple, Sincere. निष्कपट, अकपट, अधूर्त, निष्प्रपंच, निष्कृत्रिम, अमायी.

Undesirable, *a.* इच्छा करायास अयोग्य, अस्पृह्य, अस्पृहणीय, अनपेक्षणीय, अनपेक्ष्य, अनिष्ट, अन्याकांक्ष्य, अनाकांक्षणीय, &c. अनिच्छाविषय, अलोभविषय.

Undesired, *a.* नइच्छलेला, &c. अनिच्छित, अनाकांक्षित, अनपेक्षित, &c. अनिष्ट, अनभीष्ट.

Undesirous, *a.* इच्छेवेगळा-निराळा, निराश, निरिच्छ, अनाकांक्ष, निराकांक्ष, निरपेक्ष, निर्वासन, निस्पृह, अस्पृह, अनपेक्ष.

Undestroyed, *a.* अनष्ट, अविनष्ट, अध्वंसित, अध्वस्त.

Undeterminable, *a.* अनिर्णेय, अनिर्धार्य, अनिश्चेय, निर्णयाशक्य, निर्धाराशक्य.

Undetermined, *a. not settled,* v. Indeterminate. बिनठरावलेला, &c. अनिर्णीत, अनिर्धारित, अनिश्चित, अनिर्णय.
2 *that has not made a determination.* अकृतसंकल्प, अकृतनिश्चय.

Undeterminedness, *n.* v. A. 1. अनिर्णय *m.* अनिर्धार *m.* अनिश्चय *m.* अनियम *m.*

Undeviating, **Undevious**, *a.* बिनविचलीचा, अव्यभिचारी, व्यभिचाररहित-शून्य-&c. अस्खलित, अनपथगामी, अनपथवर्त्ती, अविपथगामी.

Undevout, *a.* v. Indevout. भक्तिहीन-रहित, अभक्तिमान्.

Undigested, *a.*—food, &c. अजीर्ण, विदग्ध, अपक्व, अपचित, अजातपाक, आम, कच्चा.
U. food. आमांश *m.*
2 *not arranged, &c.* बिनयोजलेला, बिनरचलेला, &c. कच्चा, अजातव्यवस्थ, अकृतव्यवस्थ. [वेगळा.

Undignified, *a.* अप्रौढ, अप्रशस्त, अप्रौढीचा, मोठेपणानिराळा-

Undiminished, *a.* कमी न झालेला, &c. अक्षित, अजातऱ्हास, अन्यूनीभूत. [मालूम.

Undiscernible, *a.* v. Imperceptible. अलक्ष्य, दुर्लक्ष्य, बे-

Undiscerning, **Undiscriminating**, *a.* निर्विवेक, अविवेकी, अविवेचक, अविचार, विचाररहित-शून्य, विवेकरहित-शून्य, निर्विशेष, हीनविचार, हीनविवेक.

Undisciplined, *a.* बिनशिकवलेला, बिनकवाइनी, बिनतालमी, अशिक्षित, गैरसाल, अशासित, अशिष्ट, अपेट.

Undiscoverable, *a.* v. Imperceptible. अलक्ष्य, दुर्लक्ष्य, बेमालूम. [विविक्त.

Undiscriminated, *a.* अविवेचित, अविचारित, अनुपलक्षित, अ-

Undiseased, *a.* रोगानिराळा-वेगळा, नीरोग *pop.* निरोग, अनामय, रोगरहित-&c. अव्रण, निकोप, अप्राप्तरोग, अजातामय.

Undisguised, *a.* v. Open. उघडा, उघडवाघड, बिनपडद्याचा, उघडपणाचा, अकपट, निष्कपट, निष्कृत्रिम, सडीक, कपटरहित-&c.

Undisputed, *a.* बिनतकरारीचा, तकरारीवांचूनचा, निर्विवाद, अवादग्रस्त, अविप्रतिपन्न.

Undissembling, *a.* v. Sincere. निष्कपट, अकपट.

Undistinguishable, *a. that connot be discriminated.* अलक्ष्य, अलक्षणीय, अविवेचनीय, अविभावनीय, अविभाव्य, अविज्ञेय. [वित, अविविक्त.

Undistinguished, *a. not discriminated.* अविवेचित, अविभा-
2 *not eminent.* बिननामनेचा, बिननामोशीचा, बिनअस्कऱ्याचा, &c. नामोशीनिराळा-वेगळा, अप्रसिद्ध, अलब्धकीर्त्ति, अलब्ध-

प्रतिष्ठ, अलब्धयश.

UNDISTURBED, *a. free from molestation.* निरुपद्रव, उपद्रवहीन-रहित-शून्य, निष्कंटक, अजातोपद्रव.

2 *free from perturbation.* अव्यग्र, अव्याकुल, निराकुल, अनुद्विग्न, अक्षुब्ध.

UNDIVIDED, *a.* v. WHOLE. नविभागलेला, बिनवांटलेला, अविभक्त, अविभाजित, अविभागित, अखंडित, अखंड, सबंध, अछिन्न, अविच्छिन्न, अभेद.

To UNDO, *v. a. unravel, untie, take to pieces, &c.* उखळणें, उकलणें, उलगडणें, निसळणें, विसळणें, फेडणें, सोडणें, उलगडा *m.*-उकल *or* उकाल *m.*-उकलणी *f.*-&c. करणें *g. of o.* उखळणी *f.*-उसळाउसळ *f.*-विसळाविसळ *f.*-&c. करणें *g. of o.* फेडणी *f.*-&c. करणें *g. of o.*

2 *annul, make void, reverse.* नाहींसा करणें, नझाल्यासारखा *decl.*-नकेल्यासारखा *decl.*-नकेलासा *decl.*-अकृतप्राय-&c. करणें, फिरवणें, उलटवणें, मोडणें, पूर्वावस्थेवर आणणें, पूर्ववत्करणें, परिवर्त्तन *n.*-परावृत्ति *f.*-&c. करणें *g. of o.*

3 See To DESTROY, To RUIN. [उकळींव.

UNDONE, *p. & a.* v. V. 1. उखळलेला, उकललेला, उलगडलेला, &c. To come u.—a garment, &c. सुटणें, फिटणें.

I. *unperformed.* नकेलेला, अकृत, असंपादित, असाधित, अनाचरित.

UNDOUBTED, *a.* v. CERTAIN. निस्संशय, निस्संशयाचा, निस्संदिग्ध, असंदिग्ध, अशंकित.

UNDOUBTEDLY, *adv.* v. A. *and* CERTAINLY. निस्संशय, अवश्य.

UNDOUBTFUL, UNDOUBTING, *a.* v. CERTAIN. निस्संशय, शंकाहीन-रहित-शून्य-&c. निर्भ्रांत *or* निभ्रांत, असंदिग्ध.

To UNDRESS, *v. a.* वस्त्र *n.*-पांघरूण *n.*-&c. काढणें-उतरणें, वस्त्रानिराळा *or* वेगळा-विवस्त्र-विवसन-&c. करणें.

UNDRESSED, *p. & a.* v. V. *and* NAKED. वस्त्रउतरलेला, विवस्त्र, त्यक्तवस्त्र, उत्तीर्णवस्त्र, विवसन.

I. *uncooked.* कच्चा, हिरवा, अपक्व *pop.* अपाका, आम, कोरडा (as कोरडीभिक्षा, कोरडासिधा). [कोरान्न *n.*

U. rice, pulse, &c. as given to mendicants. आमान्न *n.*

UNDUE, *a. improper,* v. WRONG. अयोग्य, नालायक, गैरवाजवी, बेशिस्त, गैरशिस्त.

2 *inordinate,* v. EXCESSIVE. अमर्याद, बेसुमार.

To UNDULATE, *v. n. wave, vibrate.* हेलावणें, हेलकावणें, हेलकावे *m. pl.*-हेलावे *m. pl.* खाणें-घेणें, उतारचढ *m.*-चढउतार *m.*-&c. करणें *and, with in. con.* असणें *g. of s.* [तानत *n.*

UNDULATION, *n.* v. V. हेलकावा *m.* हेलावा *m.* उतारचढ *m.* उक-

UNDULATORY, *a.* UNDULATING, *p. a.* v. V. उतारचढाचा, उतरताचढता, चढताउतरता, उंचनीच, डोंगरवट, नागमोडी, नागमोडीचा.

U. line on cloth. लहर *f.*

UNDULY, *adv.* v. A. 1. गैरवाजवी, नालायक.

2 *and* EXCESSIVELY. बेसुमार, अमर्याद.

UNDUTEOUS, UNDUTIFUL, *a.* v. DISOBEDIENT. बेहुकमी, असेवातत्पर, स्वधर्मविमुख, स्वधर्मोपेक्षी, स्वधर्माभक्त.

UNDUTIFULNESS, *n.* v. A. बेहुकमीपणा *m.* स्वधर्माभक्ति *f.* सेवाधर्माभक्ति *f.* सेवाधर्मानासक्ति *f.* [निर्जर.

UNDYING, *a.* v. IMMORTAL, IMPERISHABLE. अमर, अनश्वर,

UNEASINESS, *n.* v. A. अस्वस्थपणा *m.* &c. अस्वस्थता *f.* अस्वास्थ्य *n.* असमाधान *n.* असुख *n.* अशांति *f.*

UNEASY, *a.* v. RESTLESS, CAREFUL. अस्वस्थ, असमाधानी, असुखी, बेआराम, बेचैनी, हीनसुख. [अभोज्य.

UNEATABEE, *a.* खायास अयोग्य-&c. अभक्ष्य, अभक्षणीय, अखाद्य,

UNEATEN, *a.* नखाल्लेला, अभुक्त, अनशित, अखादित.

UNEDUCATED, *a.* v. ILLITERATE. बिनपढलेला, अशिक्षित, अकृताध्ययन, अनधीत, अपढीक.

UNEFFECTED, *a.* असंपन्न, असिद्ध, असाधित, असंपादित.

UNELASTIC, *a.* स्थितिस्थापकत्वरहित, मिसमिसीत, विसविसीत, लिबलिबीत.

UNEMBODIED, *a.* v. INCORPOREAL. अदेह, अशरीर, अमूर्त्त.

UNEMBODIEDNESS, *n.* v. A. अदेहत्व *n.* अमूर्त्ति *f.*

UNEMPLOYED, *a.* रिकामा, खाली, निरुद्योग, निरुद्योगी, निकामा, निकामी, निष्कर्मा, निर्व्यापार, निरुद्यम, कामावेगळा *or* निराळा, धंद्यानिराळा-वेगळा, बेकार, बेरोजगार, मोकळा, सुटा, घरीं बसलेला, बैठा.

UNEMPLOYEDNESS, *n.* v. A. रिकामपणा *m.* रिकामकी *f.* रिकामणूक *f.* निरुद्योगिता *f.* अनुद्योग *m.* उद्योगाभाव *m.* उद्योगराहित्य *n.*

UNENCLOSED, *a.* बिनकुपणाचा, बिनवईचा, &c. अनावृत.

UNENDURING, *a.* v. TEMPORARY. अशाश्वत, अस्थायी, अस्थिर, अनित्य.

UNENERGETIC, *a.* अनुत्साही, निरुत्साही, निरुत्साह, अनुत्साह, तेजोहीन, निस्तेज, शिथिल, विरस. [स्वयोग.

UNENGAGED, *a.* v. UNEMPLOYED. रिकामा, खाली, मोकळा, नि-

UNENJOINED, *a.* गैरसांगीचा, अविहित, अचोदित, अनाज्ञापित, अनादिष्ट. [तभोग.

UNENJOYED, *a.* नभोगलेला, बिनभोगाचा, अभुक्त, अनुपभुक्त, अजा-

UNENTIRE, *a.* अपूर्ण, असंपूर्ण, असमग्र, न्यूनांग, विकलांग, अंगविकल, अंगहीन, व्यंग, असांग.

UNENVIOUS, *a.* मत्सरा वेगळा *or* निराळा, निर्मत्सर, अमत्सर, विमत्सर, अनीर्ष्य, मत्सरहीन-रहित-&c.

UNEQUAL, *a. not level,* v. UNEVEN. उंचनीच, उखरवाखर *or* उखरावाखर *or* उखिर वाखीर, असम, असमान, उटंगळ.

2 *not equal,* gener. असमान, असम, अतुल्य, विषम, असमंजस, अधिकउणा, कमज्यास्त, न्यूनाधिकभावाचा.

3 *incompetent, inadequate,* v. UNFIT, INSUFFICIENT. अक्षम, कार्याक्षम, असमर्थ, नालायक.

UNEQUALLED, *a. unparalleled.* बिनतुळणेचा, बिनतोलाचा, अनुपम, निरुपम, अप्रतिम, विषम, असम, अतुल, अतुल्य, अद्वितीय, अपूर्व.

UNEQUALLEDNESS, *n.* v. A. अनुपमता *f.* आनुपम्य *n.* अतुल्यता *f.* असमता *f.* अप्रतिमत्व *n.* &c.

UNEQUALLY, *adv.* v. A. 1. उंचखाल, उखरवाखर, &c.

2 अधिकउणेपणानें, न्यूनाधिकभावानें, असमतेनें, अधिकउणा *decl.* कमज्यास्त, असम, विषम.

UNEQUIVOCAL, *a.* v. CLEAR. स्पष्ट, सुस्पष्ट, सुव्यक्त, अद्व्यर्थ, अद्व्यामुष्यायण, अश्लिष्ट.

UNERRING, *a.* बिनभ्रांतीचा, अचूक, अचूकसंधानी, अभ्रांत.

UNERRINGLY, *adv.* v. A. अचूक. [तिक.

UNESSENTIAL, *a.* बिनजरुरीचा, अनावश्यक, अनांतरीयक, अनाग-

UNESTABLISHED, *a. unproved.* बिनस्थापलेला, असिद्ध, अस्थापित, अनुपपन्न.

UNEVEN, *a. not level.* उंचसखल, उंचनीच, उखरवाखर *or* उखरावाखर *or* उखिरवाखीर, खालवर, सखरनिखर, उटंगळ, खाबडखुबड,

असमान, असम, विषम, उन्नतानत.
2 v. UNEQUAL. असम, असदृश, अतुल्य.
UNEVENLY, *adv.* v. A. 1. उंचसाल, उसरवासर, उंचनीच, &c.
UNEVENNESS, *n.* v. A. 1. उंचससलपणा *m.* उंचनीचपणा *m.* उ-सरवासरपणा*m.* &c. असाम्य *n.* असमता *f.* वैषम्य *n.* उच्चनीच-भाव *m.* उच्चावचभाव *m.*
UNEXAMINED, *a.* अपरीक्षित. [तीय.
UNEXAMPLED, *a. unprecedented.* अनुपम, निरुपम, अपूर्व, अद्वि-
UNEXCEEDED, *a.* अनतिक्रांत, अनतिक्रमित.
UNEXCEPTIONABLE, *a.* विनदिकृतीचा, विनतकरारीचा, &c. नि-र्दोष, अवाच्य, अदूष्य, अबाध, अबाधित, निर्बाध, निराबाध, निर्बाधित, &c. [अनुद्बुद्ध, अनुत्तेजित.
UNEXCITED, *a.* नचेष्टवलेला, &c. अचेष्टित, अप्रबुद्ध, अप्रबोधित,
UNEXECUTED, *a.* अकृत, अनिष्पन्न, असंपन्न, असाधित, असंसिद्ध.
UNEXERCISED, *a.* v. UNPRACTISED. अनभ्यासी, अनभ्यस्त.
UNEXISTENT, *a.* UNEXISTING, *a.* अवर्त्तमान, अविद्यमान, असिद्ध, असत्तावान्, असत्ववान्.
UNEXPECTED, *a.* v. SUDDEN. अलक्षित, अनपेक्षित, अतर्कित, अकल्पित, आकस्मिक, अचित्तकलित, अगेवांचूनचा, विनधोरणी.
UNEXPECTEDLY, *adv.* v. A. अवचट, अकल्पित, अचानक, अचंबी-त, अवचित *or* ता, एकाएकीं, धोरणाशिवाय, अगेवांचून, अवचु-कून, अकस्मात्.
UNEXPENDED, *a.* नसर्चलेला, विनसर्चलेला, अव्यय, अजातव्यय.
UNEXPERIENCED, *a.*v. UNKNOWN. न अनुभवलेला,&c. अननुभूत, अपरिचित, अपरीक्षित, अप्रतीत, अदृष्ट.
2 See INEXPERIENCED.
UNEXPLORED, *a.* शोध न केलेला, अज्ञात.
UNFADING, *a.* v. LASTING. न विटणारा, अवीट, अक्षय.
UNFAILING, *a.* v. LASTING. अढळ, अच्युत, अनश्वर, अक्षय *pop.* अक्षयी, अक्षर, अवीट, अलोट.
UNFAIR, *a.*—person. सोट्याव्यवहाराचा, सोट्याचालीचा, बेइमा-नी, अप्रामाणिक, असरल.
2—practice, &c. गैरबाजवी, अबाजवी, गैररितीचा, गैरमार्गाचा, अन्यायाचा, नारास्त, गैररास्त, असरल, अनृजु.
UNFAIRNESS, *n.* v. A. 1. व्यवहारांतलासोटेपणा *m.*-&c. सोटाव्य-वहार *m.* सोटीचाल *f.* &c. अप्रामाणिकत्व *n.*
2 गैरबाजवीपणा *m.* गैररास्तपणा *m.* गैररास्ती *f.* असारल्य *n.* असरलता *f.* &c.
UNFAITHFUL, *a.* v. FALSE. सोटा, सोटसाळ, बेइमान, बेइमानी, निमकहराम, अप्रामाणिक.
U. to a vow or oath. त्यक्तशपथ, त्यक्तशपथाचार.
UNFAITHFULNESS, *n.* v. A. सोटेपणा *m.* &c. सोटाई *f.* बेइमानी *f.* निमकहरामी *f.*
UNFALTERING. See UNHESITATING.
UNFASHIONABLE, *a.* लोकचाली वेगळा-निराळा, लोकांवेगळा-निरा-ळा, जनरूढीचे बाहेरचा, लोकबाह्य, लोकविरुद्ध, लोकविलक्षण, असभ्य, सभ्यसंप्रदायविरुद्ध, शिष्टसंप्रदायविरुद्ध, अप्रसिद्ध.
To UNFASTEN, *v. a.* v. To LOOSE, To OPEN. उघडणें, सोडणें.
UNFATHERED, *a.* निबाप्या, अपितृक.
UNFATHOMABLE, *a. lit.* तळ न लागण्याचा, अगाध, दुरंत, अपरं-पार, अतलस्पर्शी, पाताळयंत्री.
2 *fig.* v. INCOMPREHENSIBLE. बुद्धीस अगम्य, नर्कास अग-म्य, अकळ, निगूढ, गहन.

UNFAVORABLE, *a. not propitious.* अप्रसन्न, अननुकूल, अनिष्ट, अभद्र, अशुभ, अमंगल *or* ळ, विषम.
UNFAVORABLENESS, *n.* v. A. अमंगळपणा *m.* अभद्रपणा *m.* &c. अप्रसन्नता *f.* अननुकूलता *f.* &c. अनानुकूल्य *n.* वैषम्य *n.*
UNFEATHERED, *a.* v. CALLOW. पर न फुटलेला, बेपर, अजातपक्ष.
UNFEELING, *a. pitiless,* v. CRUEL. निर्दय, दयाहीन, दयेवेगळा-निराळा, निदरदी, अकरुण. [विक.
UNFEIGNED, *a.* v. REAL. सरा, अकृत्रिम, निष्कपट, अकपट, वास्त-
UNFETTERED, *a.* v. FREE. मोकळा, विशृंखल, अनर्गल, विपाश, बंधनरहित-शून्य, लोढण्यावेगळा-निराळा.
UNFIGURATIVE, *a.* अरूपक, अलाक्षणिक, अनौपचारिक.
UNFILLED, *a.* न भरलेला, विनभरलेला, अपूर्ण, अपरिपूर्ण.
UNFINISHED, *a.* अपुरा, अपुरता, अधुरा, असिद्ध, असमाप्त, अनि-ष्पन्न, अपूर्ण, कच्चा.
UNFIT, *a. improper,* v. WRONG. गैरबाजवी, गैरशिस्त, अयोग्य, अनुचित, अयथार्थ.
2 *unqualified, incompetent,* v. UNSUITABLE. अनुपयोगी, अयोग्य, अनुपयुक्त, अयुक्त, निरुपयुक्त, अक्षम, नालायक.
To UNFIT, *v. a.* अयोग्य-नालायक-अक्षम-&c.करणें, अयोग्यता *f.*-नालायकी *f.*-&c. आणणें.
UNFITNESS, *n.* v. A. 1. गैरबाजवीपणा *m.* गैरशिस्तपणा *m.* अयो-ग्यता *f.* आनुचित्य*n.* [अक्षमता *f.*
2 अनुपयोगीपणा*m.* नालायकी *f.* अनुपयोगिता *f.* अनुपयुक्तता *f.*
UNFIXED, *a. unsettled.* अस्थिर, अध्रुव, अस्थायी, अनवस्थित.
UNFLEDGED, *a.* v. CALLOW. पर न फुटलेला, बेपर, अजातपक्ष.
UNFLINCHING, *a.* v. FIRM. न घसरणारा, न कचणारा, धिराचा, सुधीर.
To UNFOLD, *v. a. open out, expand.* उलगडणें, उघडणें, उकल-णें, पसरणें, उलगडा *m.*-&c. करणें *g. of o.*
2 *reveal,* v. To DECLARE, To TELL. कळवणें, दासवणें, प्रग-ट-प्रसिद्ध-&c. करणें, प्रकाश *m.*-&c. करणें *g. of o.*
UNFORBEARING, *a.* v. UNFORGIVING. असोशीक, अक्षांत, अक्षम.
UNFORBIDDEN, *a.* विन मनाईचा, अनिषिद्ध, अप्रतिषिद्ध, अप्रति-षेधित, अवर्जित, अनिवारित, अजातनिषेध.
UNFORCED, See NATURAL, EASY.
UNFORDABLE, *a.* विनपायउताराचा, पादानुत्तार्य, पोहणी, दुर्लंघ्य.
UNFORGIVING, *a.* असोशीक, असोसक, दयेवेगळा-निराळा, अक्षम, अक्षांत, अक्षमावान्, अज्ञातक्षम, दीर्घद्वेषी.
UNFORGIVINGNESS, *n.* अक्षमा *f.*
UNFORTUNATE, *a.*—of persons. दुर्भाग्य, अभाग्य, हीनभाग्य, भा-ग्यहीन, मंदभाग्य, हतभाग्य, दुर्भागी, अभागी, हतदैव, दैवहीन, दुर्दैव, निर्दैव, हीनदैव, अपयशी *vulg.* अपेशी, उणेदैवाचा, दुर्दैवाचा, करंटा, कंबख्त, कपाळफुटका, कर्मफुटका, दैवफुटका, कपाळक-रंटा, करंट्याकपाळाचा, सापरतोंड्या, पांढऱ्यापायाचा, प्रारब्धफुट-का, फुटक्या कपाळाचा-दैवाचा-नशिबाचा-&c. दुर्भग, दग्धहस्ती, दैवोपहत, अकृतार्थ, अश्रीमान्, भद्द्या.
2—measures, affairs, &c. दुर्भाग्याचा, दुर्दैवाचा, अपयशाचा, हतदैवाचा, अनिष्टाचा, अरिष्टाचा, अनर्थाचा, आपत्तीचा, असफ-ल, अगुणावह, अपरिणामशाली. [दैववशात्.
UNFORTUNATELY, *adv.* v. A. दुर्दैवानें, दुर्दैवेंकरून, दुर्योगानें, दु-
UNFORTUNATENESS, *n.* v. A. 1. दैवाचा-&c. करंटेपणा *m.* करंटेप-णा *m.* &c. दुर्भाग्यता *f.* हतभाग्यता *f.* &c. कंबख्ती *f.* भाग्यही-नता *f.* दौर्भाग्य *n.* दुर्भाग्य *n.* अपयश *vulg.* अपेश *n.*

UNFOUNDED, *a.* मुळावेगळा-निराळा, मुळाबांचूनचा, बिनठिकाण्याचा, आधाराबांचूनचा, अमूलक, निर्मूल *or* ळ, निर्बीज, निराधार, निराश्रय, अवास्तव, अवास्तविक.

UNFREQUENTED, *a.* गैरवळणाचा, आडवळणाचा, आडवळणी, बिनवहिवाटीचा, गैरराबत्याचा, अक्षुण्ण.

U. place. आडवळण *n.*

UNFREQUENTEDNESS, *n.* v. A. गैरवळण *n.* आडवळण *n.* गैरराबता *m.* आडवळणीपणा *m.* [ह्याभाव *m.*

UNFRIENDLINESS, *n.* v. A. 1. अमित्रता *f.* अमित्रभाव *m.* स्ने-

2 अनानुकूल्य *n.* अननुकूलता *f.*

UNFRIENDLY, *a.* स्नेहभावावेगळा-निराळा, गैरमैत्रीचा, अमित्र, अस्नेही, असख, अनिष्ट, दुर्हृद, असुहृत्, अहितेच्छु.

2—of events, &c. v. UNFAVORABLE. अनिष्ट, अननुकूल, विषम.

UNFRUITFUL, *a.* निष्फल *or* ळ, अफल, फलहीन-रहित-शून्य, अफलद, अफलप्रद.

UNFRUITFULNESS, *n.* v. A. निष्फलता *f.* अफलता *f.* फलराहित्य *n.* फलहीनता *f.* [अपरिपूर्ण.

UNFULFILLED, *a.* पुरा न झालेला, पुरा व्हावयाचा, अपुरता, अपूर्ण,

To UNFURL, *v. a. loose and unfold.* सोडणें, मोकळा &c. करणें.

UNFURNISHED, *a.* v. EMPTY. सरंजामावेगळा-निराळा, रिकामा, रिकामका, रिता, रिक्त, असज्ज.

UNGAINLY, *a.* v. AWKWARD, CLUMSY. अनाडी, अडाणी, बेढब.

UNGENEROUS, *a.* अनुदार, अप्रशस्तमनस्क, लघुमनस्क, अल्पमनस्क, लघुचेता. [अपथ्य.

UNGENIAL, *a.* असात्म्याचा, अननुकूल, अननुगुण, प्रकृतिप्रतिकूल,

UNGENTEEL, UNGENTLEMANLY, *a.* अशिष्ट, असभ्य, गैरशिस्त, अशिष्ट संप्रदायी, अशिष्टाचारी, शिष्टाचारवर्जित, शिष्टसंप्रदायविरुद्ध, असभ्यवृत्ति, अशिष्टवृत्ति, दौर्जन्यवृत्ति, दौर्जन्यवृत्तीचा.

To UNGIRD, *v. a.* कमर *f.*-कमरबंद *m.* सोडणें.

UNGODLINESS, *n.* v. A. अधर्मीपणा *m.* अधार्मिकपणा *m.* अधर्म *m.* ईश्वराभक्ति *f.* ईश्वरानिष्ठा *f.* धर्मद्वेष *m.* देवनिंदा *f.* परमार्थद्वेष *m.*

UNGODLY, *a.* v. IRRELIGIOUS. अधर्मी, अधार्मिक, ईश्वराभक्त, ईश्वरानिष्ठ, अपारमार्थिक, परमार्थविमुख.

UNGOVERNABLE, *a.* v. IRRESTRAINABLE. अनिवार, अवावर, अनिवार्य, अशासनीय, अशास्य, दुःशासन, दुर्नियह.

UNGOVERNED, *a. unbridled.* बेलगामी, अवश, अदमित, अदांत, अशासित.

UNGRACEFUL, *a.* v. AWKWARD, CLUMSY. बेढब, बेडौल, विशोभित, ओबडधोबड.

UNGRACEFULNESS, *n.* v. A. बेढबपणा *m.* बेडौलपणा *m.* ओबडधोबडपणा *m.* विशोभितपणा *m.* शोभाराहित्य *n.*

UNGRACIOUS, *a.* v. UNKIND. अकृपालु, अकृप, निरुपकारी, अनुपकारी, अननुग्राही, अननुग्राहक.

UNGRAMMATICAL, *a.* व्याकरणास वांकडा, व्याकरणविरुद्ध, व्याकरणविपरीत, शब्दशास्त्रविरुद्ध.

UNGRATEFUL, *a. not feeling thankful.* अनुपकारी, निरुपकारी, निमकहराम, अजाण, कृतघ्न, उपकारानभिज्ञ, अकृतज्ञ, कृतनाशक, अप्रत्युपकारी, क्रियानष्ट, क्रियाभ्रष्ट. [रंजक.

2 v. UNPLEASANT. नावडता, असुखावह, असुखद, अरम्य, अ-

UNGRATEFULNESS, *n.* v. A. 1. *and* INGRATITUDE. अनुपकारीपणा *m.* अकृतज्ञता *f.* निमकहरामी *f.*

2 नावडतेपणा *m.* अरम्यता *f.* &c.

UNGUARDED, *a.* न रक्षिलेला, राखणीवेगळा-निराळा, अरक्षित.

2 See CARELESS. [पन *n.*

UNGUENT, *n. ointment.* उटी *f.* उटणें *n.* मारवण *n.* स्नेह *m.* विले-

Unguents. चोपडण *n.*

UNHACKNEYED, *a.* गैरराबलेला, कोरा, गोडा, असुदा, असडा, अपेट, नवथर, अनभ्यस्त, अक्षुण्ण. [मेध्य.

UNHALLOWED, *a.* v. IMPURE. अपवित्र, अमंगल *or* ळ, नापाक, अ-

UNHANDSOME, *a.* v. UGLY. कुरूप, बदसुरत, असुंदर.

2 *illiberal.* अनुदार, अप्रशस्त.

UNHANDY, *a.* v. AWKWARD. आडमूठ, आडमुठ्या, नाकसबी, अपटु.

UNHAPPINESS, *n.* v. A. 1. दुःख *n.* दुःखीपणा *m.* अकल्याण *n.* असुख *n.* अक्षेम *m. n.* अकुशल *n.* अभद्र *n.* असौख्य *n.* अशर्म *n.*

UNHAPPY, *a.* v. WRETCHED. दुःखी, असुखी, अकुशल, अकुशली, दुःखसंपन्न, दुःखापन्न.

2 See UNFORTUNATE, CALAMITOUS.

UNHARDENED, *a.* v. UNHACKNEYED. गोडा.

UNHARMED, *a.* v. UNHURT. बेनुकसान, बेनुकसानीचा, अक्षत.

UNHARMONIOUS, *a.* v. DISCORDANT. बेसूर, बदसूर, विस्वर.

UNHAZARDOUS, *a.* बिनजोखमाचा, निजोखमी, जोखमानिराळा-वेगळा.

UNHEALTHFUL. See UNHEALTHY, UNWHOLESOME.

UNHEALTHINESS, *n.* v. A. 1. सदारोगीपणा *m.* &c.

2 रोगीपणा *m.* बाधकपणा *m.* रोगजनकत्व *n.*

UNHEALTHY, *a. habitually indisposed,* v. SICKLY. सदारोगी, रोगेला, रोगिष्ठ.

2 *unfavorable to health, insalubrious.* रोगी, रोगाचा, रोगलावा, रोगआणणारा, असात्म्याचा, असात्म्य, बाधक, रोगकारक-जनक-प्रद-&c. अस्वास्थ्यकारक-जनक-&c. असमाधानकारक-जनक-&c.

3 *abounding with disease.* रोगी, रोगाचा, रोगप्रचुर, रोगबहुल.

UNHEARD, *a.* नऐकलेला, बिन ऐकलेला, अश्रुत, अकर्णस्पृष्ट.

U. of and unthought of, *utterly unknown.* कानीं मनीं नाहीं. [वाचा, अतप्त.

UNHEATED, *a.*—metals, &c. निताव, निताबी, बिनताबी, बिनता-

2—oil, butter, honey, milk, &c. अकढा, निकढा, बिनकढाचा, निरसा.

UNHEEDED, *a.* v. DISREGARDED. अनपेक्षित, उपेक्षित, अवमानित.

UNHEEDING, *a.* v. CARELESS. असावध, अनपेक्ष.

UNHESITATING, *a.* v. CONFIDENT, PROMPT. निःशंक, निधड, निधडा, बेशक.

UNHESITATINGLY, *adv.* v. A. निस्संशय, निर्भ्रांत *or* निभ्रांत, बिनदिक्कत *or* बेदिक्कत, बेवसवसा, बेलाशक, बेधडक, निधडक, बेजरब, बेचरक, बेनिसबत. [चा.

UNHEWN, *a.* अघडा, निघडा, बिनघडलेला, बिनटांकीचा, बिनसुतकी-

UNHINDERED, *a.* बिनअटकावाचा, बिनहरकतीचा, अविघ्न, अवारित, अप्रतिबंध.

To UNHINGE, *v. a.* बिजागरीं *n. pl.*-सांधे *m. pl.*-टांके *m. pl.*-&c. उखळणें-काढणें-विसंधित-&c. करणें-ढिलेकरणें-&c. *g. of o.*

UNHINGED, *p.* v. V. बिजागरींउखळलेला, &c. विसंधित.

To be u. *fig. feel prostrated.* घळघळणें, टांके *m. pl.* ढिले होणें *g. of s.* गळणें. [ता *f.* अशुद्धि *f.*

UNHOLINESS, *n.* v. A. अपवित्रपणा *m.* &c. अपवित्रता *f.* अपूत-

UNHOLY, *a. impure,* v. WICKED. अपवित्र, अपूत, अशुद्ध, अशुचि, अमंगल *or* ळ, मलिन *pop.* मळीण.

UNHONORED, *a.* v. CONTEMNED. अमानित, अवमानित.

To UNHORSE, *v. a. throw from a horse.* घोड्याखालीं करणें-आणणें, घोड्यावरून पाडणें-काढणें, घोड्याबेगळा-निराळा करणें.

To UNHOUSE, *v. a. drive from the house.* घरपारखा करणें, घरानिराळा-वेगळा करणें, घरांतून काढणें, निरालय-&c. करणें.

UNHURT, *a.* बेनुकसान, बेनुकसानीचा, बिनधक्का, अहत, अनाहत, अक्षत, अजातापकार, अप्राप्तापकार.

UNHURTFUL, *a.* v. INNOCENT. अविकारी, अबाधक, अनपकारी.

UNHUSKED, *a.*—rice, &c. असडा, असडी, अनिस्त्वक्, अनिस्त्वच, अनिस्तुष.

2—cocoanut, betelnut, &c. असोला.

UNICORN, *n. rhinoceros.* गेंडा *m.* एकशृंग *m.*

UNIDIOMATICAL, *a.* बोलण्याच्या रीतीबेगळा-निराळा, भाषणसंप्रदायविरुद्ध, अप्रशस्त.

UNIFORM, *a. of one appearance, character, &c.* एकेरूपाचा-जातीचा-तऱ्हेचा-डौलाचा-रंगाचा-प्रकाराचा-&c. सारखा, एकासारखा एक, एकसारखा, एकरूप, समरूप, सरूप, तद्रूप, एकाकार, एकाकृति, एकप्रकार, समवर्ण, बराबर, बराबरचा, एकफरमा, एकेप्रतिमेचा.

2 *of one tenor, equable.* एकसारखा, सारखा, बराबर, समान, सम, समसमान, अविशेष, अन्यूनाधिक, संगत, समस्थ.

UNIFORMITY, *n.* v. A. 1. एकसारखेपणा *m.* &c. एकथाट *m.* एकरूपता *f.* समरूपता *f.* समरूप्य *n.* सारूप्य *n.* तादूप्य *n.*

2 एकसारखेपणा *m.* &c. बराबरी *f.* समता *f.* समानता *f.* साम्य *n.* समभाव *m.* अविशेष *m.*

UNIFORMLY, *adv.* v. A. 2. सारखा *decl.* एकसारखा *decl.* एकसाहां, एकसुती, एकसोय, एकरूप, एकचरीतीनें.

UNIMAGINABLE, *a.* कल्पनेबाहेरचा, अकल्प्य, अकल्पनीय, अचिंत्य, अतर्क्य, कल्पनातीत.

UNIMAGINED, *a.* अकल्पित, अचिंतित, अतर्कित.

UNIMPAIRED, *a.* बेनुकसान, बेनुकसानाचा, अक्षत, अहत, अनुपहत, अशीर्ण, अक्षुण्ण, साबूत *or* साबीत, शाबूत *or* द, अजातापकार, अप्राप्तापकार.

UNIMPASSIONED, *a.* अराग, अरागी, अननुरागी, रागहीन-शून्य.

UNIMPEACHABLE, *a.* अदूष्य, अदूषणीय, अनिंद्य, दूषणानर्ह, दोषानारोप्य, अनारोप्यदोष.

UNIMPEACHED, *a.* अदूषित, अनिंदित, अनारोपितदोष, अनपवादित.

UNIMPORTANT, *a.* v. LIGHT, TRIFLING. बिनभाराचा, बिनवजनाचा, &c. हलका, लहान, लघु.

UNINFECTED, *a.* रोग न लागलेला, रोगानाक्रांत, रोगासंक्रमित, रोगासंसृष्ट, रोगालिप्त, अलिप्त. [त, अतप्त, असंतप्त.

UNINFLAMED, *a.* अनुद्दीप्त, अप्रदीप्त, अदीपित, अतापित, असंतापि-

UNINFLAMMABLE, *a.* पेट न घेणारा, न चेतणारा, अज्वालाग्राही, अज्वलनशील, अज्वलनधर्मक, अदाह्य.

UNINFORMED, *a.* v. IGNORANT. अज्ञान, अप्रबोधित, अप्रबुद्ध, असूचित, अज्ञापित, अनुपदिष्ट.

UNINGENIOUS, *a.* v. STUPID. युक्तिशून्य, युक्तिहीन, अयुक्तिसंपन्न.

UNINGENUOUS, *a.* अप्रांजल, अप्रशस्त, असरल, सकपट, अनृजु, कुटिल.

UNINHABITABLE, *a.* रहायास अयोग्य, वासानर्ह, वासायोग्य, अवास्य, अवसनीय, अवसितव्य.

UNINHABITED, *a.* उजाड, निर्जन, निर्मनुष्य, निर्मानुष, पुरुषवर्जित, विजन, अप्रज, निष्प्रज, प्रजाहीन, वसतिहीन, बिननांदता, बिनवसता, बेचिराख *or* ग.

UNINITIATED, *a.* बिनमुंडलेला, असंस्कारित, असंस्कृत, संस्काररहित-हीन-विरहित-वर्जित, अजातसंस्कार, अदीक्षित, अजातदीक्ष, अनुपदिष्ट, अव्रत.

UNINJURED, *a.* v. UNHURT. बेनुकसान, अक्षत, अजातापकार.

UNINSTRUCTED, *a.* v. IGNORANT. अशिक्षित, अशिक्ष, अनध्यापित, अजातशिक्ष, अनुपदिष्ट.

UNINTELLIGENCE, *n.* अज्ञान *n.* अबुद्धि *f.* अमेधा *f.* अचेतन्य *n.*

UNINTELLIGENT, *a.* v. IRRATIONAL. अज्ञान, ज्ञानशक्तिहीन, चिच्छक्तिरहित, अज्ञानपात्र, अचेतन.

2 v. STUPID. बुद्धीचा जड-मंद-&c. जडबुद्धि, जेनबुद्धि, अज्ञान.

UNINTELLIGIBLE, *a.* समजायास-ध्यानांत यायास-&c. अशक्य-कठीण-&c. बुद्धीस-&c. अगम्य-अग्राह्य, बोधागम्य, दुर्लक्ष, दुर्ज्ञेय, अकळ, बुद्ध्यगम्य, अज्ञेय, बुद्ध्यग्राह्य.

UNINTENDED, UNINTENTIONAL, *a.* v. UNDESIGNED. बिनइरादाचा, अबुद्धिकृत, असंकल्पकृत, अनभिप्रेत, असांकल्पिक.

UNINTERESTED, *a. having no concern.* निराळा, बेगळा, बेहलाख्याचा, असंबंधी, असंबंध, अनंशी, अविभागी, संबंधरहित.

2 *not having the passions engaged.* अनास्थ, बेदरदी, बेपरवा, उदास, उदासीन, आस्थेबेगळा-निराळा.

UNINTERESTEDNESS, *n.* v. A. 1. निराळेपणा *m.* &c. संबंधराहित्य *n.* संबंधाभाव *m.* असंबंधिता *f.*

2 बेदरदीपणा *m.* उदासपणा *m.* अनुत्साह *m.* अनुत्सुकता *f.* अनास्था *f.* औदासीन्य *n.*

UNINTERESTING, *a.* न रिझवणारा, बिनरिझाऊ, अरंजक, अमनोरंजक, अचित्तवेधक, अहृदयंगम.

UNINTERMITTED, UNINTERMITTING, *a.* v. CONTINUAL. निरंतर, बिनखळाचा, अविराम, अखंड, अखंडित, अविरत, अव्यवहित.

UNINTERMITTEDNESS, *n.* v. A. अखंडपणा *m.* नैरंतर्य *n.* निरंतरता *f.* खंडराहित्य *n.* विरामराहित्य *n.*

UNINTERMITTINGLY, *adv.* v. A. निरंतर, सतत, संतत, अखंड, अखंडीं, एकसारखा *decl.* एकसाहां, एकटक, अनुधार, अविच्छिन्न.

UNINTERRUPTED, *a.* अतूट, अखंड, अखंडित, निरंतर, अनंतर, अभग्न, अव्यवहित, अव्याहत, अविच्छिन्न, अस्खलित, अविरत, अविराम.

UNINTERRUPTEDNESS, *n.* v. A. अतुटपणा *m.* अखंडपणा *m.* नैरंतर्य *n.* निरंतरता *f.* खंडराहित्य *n.*

UNINVENTED, *a.* अकल्पित, अयोजित.

UNINVENTIVE, *a.* युक्तिशून्य, युक्तिरहित, अयुक्तिसंपन्न, अकल्पक, कल्पनाशक्तिशून्य.

UNINVITED, *a.* न बोलाबलेला, बिनबोलाबलेला, अनिमंत्रित, अनामंत्रित, अनाहूत, अहूत.

UNION, *n. act of uniting,* See JOINING, 2. *unitedness,* v. JUNCTION. जोड *m.* योग *m.* संयोग *m.* संधि *m. f.* संबंध *m.* समायोग *m.* संयुक्तता *f.* संग *m.* संगत *f.* संगति *f.* सायुज्य *n.*

3 *concord,* v. AGREEMENT. एकी *f.* एकोपा *or* वा *m.* ऐक्य *n.* मैथुन *n.*

UNIPAROUS, *a. producing one at a birth.* एकप्रसू.

UNIQUE, *a. single in its kind,* v. SINGULAR. एकमात्र, अनन्यसाधारण.

UNISON, *n.*—in music. नादैक्य *n.* स्वरैक्य *n.* स्वरमेल *m.* एकतान *m.* एकताल *m.* स्वरांचाबनाव *m.* घटाव *m.*

That is in strict u. सायसंगीत.

2 See AGREEMENT.

UNIT, *n.* एक *m.* एकांक *m.*

To UNITE, *v. a. make into one*, v. To JOIN. एक करणें, जोडणें, मिळवणें, साधणें, एकीकरण *n.*-संयोग *m.*-&c. करणें *g. of o.* संयुक्त-&c. करणें.

2 *make to agree.* एकपणा *m.*-ऐक्य *n.*-एकोपा *m.*-मेळ *m.*-&c. करणें *g. of o.* एक करणें, एकचित्त-एकदिल-एकमन-&c. करणें.

To UNITE, *v. n. become one, join.* मिळणें, एक होणें, संयोग *m.*-&c. होणें *g. of s.*

2 *concur*, v. To AGREE. मिळणें, एक-एकदिल-एकचित्त-सम्मत-&c. होणें, सम्मति *f.*-अनुमति *f.*-&c. देणें or, *with g. of s.* होणें.

UNITED, *p.* v. V. A. 1. जोडलेला, मिळवलेला, एककेलेला, युक्त, संयुक्त, संयोजित, संयोगित, संयुत. [&c.

2 एककेलेला, एकचित्त, एकमत, एकदिल, एकामनाचा-विचाराचा-

UNITEDLY, *adv.* v. CONJOINTLY. मिळून, मिळणीनें, योगतः.

UNITY, *n.* v. ONENESS. एकपणा *m.* ऐक्य *n.* एकत्व *n.* एकी *f.* अद्वैत *n.* अभेद *m.*

2 *concord*, v. AGREEMENT. एकी *f.* ऐक्य *n.* मिलाफ *m.* मेळ *m.* निर्द्वंद्व *n.* एकदिल *n.* एकचित्त *n.*

UNIVERSAL, *a.*—of place. सर्वठिकाणचा, सर्वठिकाणींचा, सार्वत्रिक, सर्वव्यापी, सर्वव्यापक, विश्वव्यापी, सर्वगत.

2—of persons or beings. सर्वांचा, सर्वांविषयींचा, सर्वसंबंधी, सर्वविषयक, सर्वसाधारण, सर्वमय, सर्वीय, सार्व, सर्वजनीन, सार्वजनीन, सार्वजनिक, सार्वलौकिक, विश्वमय, विश्वजनीय, विश्वजनीन.

UNIVERSALITY, *n.* v. A. 1. सर्वव्यापिता *f.* विश्वव्यापिता *f.* सर्वव्यापकत्व *n.* सार्वत्रिकत्व *n.*

2 सर्वसंबंधिता *f.* सर्वसाधारण्य *n.* सर्वीयता *f.*

UNIVERSALLY, *adv.* v. A. 1. सर्वांठिकाणीं, सर्वांस्थळीं, सर्वत्र, सर्वतः, विश्वतः.

2 सर्वांस, सर्वांनीं, सर्वांसंबंधीं, सर्वांविषयीं, विश्वतः, सर्वशः, आबालवृद्ध, अवच्छेदकावच्छेदेंकरून.

UNIVERSE, *n. the whole creation.* ब्रह्मांड *n.* ब्रह्मगोल *m.* जग *n.* जगत्समग्र *n.* जगत्सर्व *n.* जगत्कृत्स्न *n.* जगत् *n.* जगती *f.* विश्व *n.* सृष्टि *f.* भूतसृष्टि *f.* ब्रह्मकटाह *m.* ब्रह्मसृष्टि *f.* प्रत्यक्षसृष्टि *f.* त्रिभुवन *n.* त्रिलोकी *f.* त्रैलोक्य *n.* अंडकटाह *m.* विराट्देह *m.*

Soul of the u. जगदात्मा *m.* विश्वात्मा *m.* लोकात्मा *m.* परमात्मा *m.* ब्रह्म *n.* सूक्ष्म *n.*

The doctrine of the non-existence of the u. शून्यवाद *m.*—One that maintains it. शून्यवादी.

UNIVERSITY, *n. assemblage of colleges.* पाठशाला *f.* अनेकविद्यालयगण *m.* शालामंडल *n.* शालासमाज *m.* The English word transliterated is commonly used.

UNJUST, *a.*—of agents. अन्यायी, बेइनसाफी, अधर्मी, अधार्मिक, अन्यायाचा, अनीतीचा, &c. अन्यायमार्गी, नीतिहीन-शून्य-&c. हीननीति, अनीतिमान्, अप्रामाणिक, अन्यायाचारी, अन्यायकर्मी, अन्यायनिष्ठ, अन्यायशील, अनय, अन्यायानुसारी, अन्यायानुवर्ती, अन्यथाचारी.

2—of actions. अन्यायाचा, अनीतीचा, अधर्माचा, बेइनसाफाचा, बेइनसाफी, अन्याय्य, गैरवाजवी, अवाजवी, अयथान्याय, अयथार्थ, असमंजस, अयथानीति, नीतिविरुद्ध, अयाथार्थिक.

UNJUSTLY, *adv.* v. A. अन्यायानें, अन्यायेंकरून, अनीतीनें, बेदादीनें, अधर्मानें, बेइनसाफानें, गैरइनसाफानें, &c. अन्यायतः, नाहक, गैरवाजवी, अगननगन.

UNKIND, *a.* कृपेवेगळा-निराळा, ममतेवेगळा-निराळा, गैरममतेचा, दयेवेगळा-निराळा, कृपाहीन-शून्य, अकृपालु, अकृप, अस्निग्ध, अस्नेह, स्नेहरहित-हीन, अप्रिय, निर्मम, अनुपकारी, अननुग्राहक, उपकारविमुख, उपकारविमत, उपकारशत्रु.

UNKINDLINESS, *n.* v. A. अमंगलपणा *m.* अमंगलत्व *n.* अशुभत्व *n.*

UNKINDLY, *a.* v. UNFAVORABLE. अशुभ, अमंगल or ळ.

UNKINDLY, *adv.* v. A. विषम, कृपेवांचून, दयेवांचून, ममतेवांचून, गैरममतेनें.

UNKINDNESS, *n.* v. A. अकृपा *f.* अवकृपा *f.* गैरममता *f.* गैरलोभ *m.* अप्रीति *f.* अदया *f.* अस्नेह *m.* निर्ममत्व *n.* अनुपकार *m.*

UNKNOWING, *a.* v. IGNORANT. अजाणता, नेणता, अज्ञान, अज्ञ, अप्रबुद्ध, अनभिज्ञ, अप्रवीण.

UNKNOWINGLY, *adv.* v. A. नकळत, नजाणतां, नसमजतां.

UNKNOWN, *a.* अनोळखी, अनोळखीचा, गैरमाहितीचा, अज्ञात, अविदित, अपरिचित.

2 *unheard of, unseen, &c.* न देखलेला न पाहिलेला, पाहिला न देखला, देखला ना ऐकला, अश्रुत *pop.* अनश्रुत, अदृष्ट, अगोचर, अप्रसिद्ध, अदृष्टश्रुत, अनधिगत.

3—in algebra. अव्यक्त.

U. to, *without communication.* न कळतां, न समजतां, सांगितल्यावांचून, कळवल्यावांचून, जाणवल्यावांचून, कानावरघातल्यावांचून, &c. न सांगतां, न कळवतां, कानावर न घालतां, &c.

To UNLADE, *v. a.* ओझें *n.*-&c. उतरणें-काढणें, खाली-रिकामा-&c. करणें.

UNLAWFUL, *a.* सरकारीकायद्या बाहेरचा, गैरकायद्याचा, राजनियमविरुद्ध, राजाज्ञाविरुद्ध, विधिविरुद्ध, स्मृतिविरुद्ध, धर्मशास्त्रविरुद्ध, शास्त्रविरुद्ध, अस्मार्त, अशास्त्र, हराम, धर्मभ्रष्ट, उच्छास्त्र, अयथाशास्त्र.

UNLAWFULLY, *adv.* v. A. सरकारी कायदे मोडून-तोडून-सोडून-&c. शास्त्र तोडून-मोडून-&c.

UNLAWFULNESS, *n.* v. A. विधिविरुद्धता *f.* विधिविरोध *m.* शास्त्रविरुद्धता *f.* &c. अशास्त्रता *f.*

UNLEARNED, UNLETTERED, *a.* बिन पढलेला, अपढीक, अनक्षर, निरक्षर, अव्युत्पन्न, अविद्वान, विद्यारहित, हीनविद्य, अकृताध्ययन, अनधीत, अपंडित, व्यक्षर, अज्ञान, अज्ञानी, अज्ञ, प्राकृत,

Some terms for *an unlettered and rude person* are शंख *m.* शंखध्मा *m.* शंखोबा *m.* शंख्या *m.*

UNLEAVENED, *a.* बिनखमिरी, बिनफुगवलेला, बेखमीर.

UNLESS, *con.* This conjunction may be idiomatically rendered in several ways. Ex. तुम्ही आल्यावांचून-तुम्ही आल्यासेरीज-&c. मी जाणार नाहीं I will not go unless you come, पाऊस न आला तर-पाऊस पडत नसला तर-&c. मी उद्यां येईन I will come to morrow unless it should be raining.

UNLICENSED, *a.* बिनसनदी.

UNLIKE, *a.* सारखपाच्या निराळा-वेगळा, असमान, असम, असदृश, अतुल्य, विजातीय, विगुण, भिन्न, विलक्षण.

UNLIKELIHOOD, UNLIKELINESS, *n.* v. A. न व्हायाजोगेपणा *m.* असंभव *m.* असंभावना *f.* असंभूति *f.* असंगति *f.* असंगतत्व *n.*

UNLIKELY, *a.* v. IMPROBABLE. न व्हायाजोगा-जोगता-सारखा, बिनव्हायाजोगा-&c. असंभव, असंभाव्य, दुःसंभाव्य, असंगत.

UNLIKENESS, *a.* v. A. असमता *f.* असाम्य *n.* असादृश्य *n.* अतुल्यता *f.*

UNLIMITED, *a.* v. INFINITE. मोतादीवांचूनचा, मोतादी वेगळा-निराळा, अपार, असीम, अमर्याद, निरवधि. [-&c. करणें.

To UNLOAD, *v. a.* ओझें *n.*-&c. उतरणें-काढणें *g. of o.* खाली-रिता

To UNLOCK, *v. a.* कुलूप *n.* उघडणें-काढणें *g. of o.*

UNLOOKED FOR, *a. unexpected.* अनपेक्षित, अलक्षित, अतर्कित, बिनधोरणी, अगेवांचूनचा.

UNLOVELINESS, *n.* v. A. असौंदर्य *n.* अलावण्य*n.* असौष्ठव *n.* &c.

UNLOVELY, *a.* असुंदर, अरम्य, अमनोहर, अप्रियंकर, असुष्ठु.

UNLUCKILY, *adv.* v. A. दुर्दैवानें, दुर्दैवेंकरून, दुर्योगानें.

UNLUCKY, *a. not successful,* v. UNFORTUNATE. निर्भाग्य, दुर्भाग्य, कंबख्त, दग्धहस्त, दग्धहस्ती, दर्भ्या, अभद्र.

2 *not resulting in success,* v. UNFORTUNATE. दुर्भाग्याचा, दुर्दैवाचा, अपयशाचा.

3 v. INAUSPICIOUS. अभद्र, अशुभ, अमंगल *or* ळ, दग्ध.

To UNMAKE, *v. a.* v. To DESTROY. नाहींसा करणें, रद्द करणें.

To UNMAN, *v. a. deprive of the qualities of a man.* माणसानिराळा-वेगळा करणें, माणसांतून उठवणें.

2 v. To DISPIRIT. पराक्रमभंग *m.*-पौरुषभंग *m.*-वीर्यभंग*m.*-धैर्यभंग *m.*-&c. करणें *g. of o.* पराक्रमहीन-हीनपराक्रम-&c. करणें.

3 *deprive of men.* मनुष्यें *n. pl.* काढणें-कमीकरणें.

UNMANAGEABLE, *n.* v. IRRESTRAINABLE. अनिवार, अनिवार्य, अनिर्वाह्य, असाध्य, दुरुपचार, दुर्धर्ष.

UNMANIFESTED, *a.* अप्रकट *pop.* अप्रगट, अप्रसिद्ध, अप्रकाशित.

UNMANLIKE, UNMANLY, *a.* v. EFFEMINATE, COWARDLY. पुरुषास अयोग्य, पुरुषानर्ह, पुरुषधर्मास अयोग्य.

UNMANNERLINESS, *n.* v. A. गैरशिस्तपणा *m.* &c. गैरमाणुसकी *f.* अशिष्टता *f.* असभ्यता *f.*

UNMANNERLY, UNMANNERED, *a.* v. RUDE. अशिष्ट, असभ्य, गैरशिस्त, गैरमाणुसकीचा, असभ्यवृत्ति.

UNMANURED, *a.* निखती, निखाती.

UNMARKED, *a. having no mark.* बिनखुणेचा, निर्लक्षण, निश्चिह्न.

2 *unobserved.* अलक्षित, अनवलोकित, अनवेक्षित.

UNMARRIED, *a.* बिनलग्नाचा, अवरठा, सडा, निंबा, अविवाहित, अनुद्वाहित, निरूढ, अनूढ, अकृतविवाह, अजातविवाह, अपरिणीत.

To UNMASK. See To EXPOSE. [अद्वितीय.

UNMATCHED, *a.* बिनजोड्याचा, बिनतोडीचा, बिजोड, अप्रतिम,

UNMATURED, *a.* कच्चा, हिरवा, अपक्क, हरित.

UNMEANING, *a.* अनर्थक, निरर्थक, अर्थानिराळा-वेगळा, अयथार्थ, पोकळ, रिकामा, रिकामका, अर्थरहित-शून्य-&c. रिता, उपरटप्पी, उपरटप्प्याचा, बायकरणी, बायकरणीचा, बायकळ, बायफट.

UNMEANINGNESS, *n.* v. A. अनर्थकपणा *m.* निरर्थकपणा *m.* &c. आनर्थक्य *n.* अर्थराहित्य *n.* &c. [मित.

UNMEASURED, *a.* बिनमोजलेला, अपरिमित, अमित, अमोज, अप्र-

UNMEDITATED, *a.* अचिंतित, अपूर्वचिंतित, अपूर्वमनन.

UNMERCIFUL, *a.*v. CRUEL. निर्दय, दयेवेगळा-निराळा, दयाहीन-शून्य-&c. अकरुण, निष्करुण, अघृण.

UNMERCIFULLY, *adv.* v. A. निर्दयपणानें, दयेवांचून, दयासोडून.

UNMERCIFULNESS, *n.* v. A. निर्दयपणा *m.* &c. दयाहीनता *f.* दयाराहित्य *n.* दयाशून्यता *f.* &c.

UNMERITED. See UNDESERVED. [रोपित.

UNMETAPHORICAL, *a.* अलाक्षणिक, अनौपचारिक, अरूपक, अना-

UNMINDFUL, *a. inattentive,* v. CARELESS. अनवधान, अनवधानी, असावधान, गाफील, प्रमादी. [निरपेक्ष.

2 *unconcerned,* v. CARELESS. निकाळजी, बेदरदी, बेफिकीर,

UNMINDFULNESS, *n.* v. A. 1. गाफिलपणा *m.* अनवधानता *f.* अनवधान *n.* प्रमाद *m.*

2 निकाळजीपणा *m.* बेदरदीपणा *m.*

UNMINGLED, UNMIXED, *a.* बिनमिसळ, बिनमिसळीचा, निर्भेळ, केवल *or* ळ, अमिश्रित, असंकीर्ण, असमृष्ट.

2—grain. निसेड. [पद्रव.

UNMOLESTED, *a.* निरुपद्रव, निष्कंटक, उपद्रवरहित, अनु[illegible], अजातो-

UNMOVED, *a. remaining fixed,* v. FIRM. न हालवलेला, &c. अस्थलांतरप्राप्त, अस्थानांतरप्राप्त, अस्थलांतरित, स्थिर.

2 *unaffected.* न द्रवलेला, &c. असद्रद.

3 *unchanged in purpose* न वळवलेला, न वळलेला, न मानवलेला.

UNMUSICAL, *a.* अपसुऱ्या, अपस्वर, विस्वर, स्वरशून्य, रस *pop.*रसा.

UNMUTILATED, *a.* अव्यंग, सांग.

UNNAMED, *n.* नांव न घेतलेला, अगृहीतनामा, अनुच्चारितनामा, अनामनिर्दिष्ट, अनाख्यात.

UNNATURAL, *a. contrary to natural feelings and affections.* मनुष्यधर्माबाहेरचा-वेगळा-निराळा, मनुष्यधर्मविरुद्ध-प्रतिकूल-&c. स्वधर्मविरुद्ध, स्वभावविरुद्ध, स्वजातिविरुद्ध, अयथामार्ग, अयथाधर्म, गैरमार्गाचा, गैररितीचा.

2 *contrary to the laws of nature, out of the course of nature.* सृष्टीच्या क्रमाच्याबाहेरचा, सृष्टिपद्धतिबाह्य-विरुद्ध, सृष्टिक्रमबाह्य-विरुद्ध, विलक्षण, गैरमार्गाचा, अमार्गाचा, गैररितीचा.

UNNECESSARILY, *adv.* v. A. कारणावांचून, गरजेवांचून, अगत्यावांचून, विनाकारण, जरुरीशिवाय, उगाच, उगीच, उगेच.

UNNECESSARINESS, *n.* v. A. अकारणीपणा*m.* नस्तेपणा *m.* निष्कारणत्व *n.* कारणराहित्य *n.* कारणाभाव *m.*

UNNECESSARY, *a.* v. NEEDLESS. बिनजरूरीचा, बिनाकारणाचा, अगत्यावांचूनचा, &c. अकारण *pop.* अकारणी, नस्ता, निष्कारण, अप्रयोजक, निष्प्रयोजन, अनवश्यक.

UNNEIGHBOURLY, *a.* शेजारधर्मासवांकडा, शेजारधर्मानिराळा.

To UNNERVE, *v. a. deprive of strength.* बळ *n.*-जोर *m.*-&c. मोडणें-नाहींसाकरणें *g. of o.* निर्बळ-अबळ-बलहीन-&c. करणें.

UNNUMBERED, *a.* v. INNUMERABLE. अगणित, असंख्यात.

UNOBJECTIONABLE, *a.* v. UNIMPEACHABLE. अदूष्य, अदूषणीय, निर्बाध, अबाधित, निर्वाच्य.

UNOBSERVED, *a.* न पाहिलेला, अलक्षित, अनवलोकित, अनिरीक्षित.

UNOBSTRUCTED, *a.* बिनअटकावाचा, बिनहरकतीचा, न रोधलेला, निर्विघ्न, अविघ्न, निरर्गल, अप्रतिबंध, निष्प्रतिबंध, अबाधित, अबाध, अप्रतिबंधित, अप्रतिबद्ध, अकुंठित, अरुद्ध, अनवरुद्ध, अरोधित, अप्रतिरुद्ध.

UNOBTAINABLE, *a.* मिळवायास अशक्य-&c. अप्राप्य, अलभ्य, असाध्य, दुर्लभ, दुर्मील, अनागम्य.

UNOBTAINED, *a.* न मिळवलेला, अप्राप्त, अलब्ध, असंपादित, असंपन्न, अनापन्न, अनाप्त.

UNOCCUPIED, *a.* v. UNEMPLOYED. रिकामा, रिकामका, रिता, खाली, निष्कर्म, निरुद्योग. [रपराधी.

UNOFFENDING, *a.*v. INNOCENT, INOFFENSIVE. अनपराधी, नि-

UNOPENED, *a.*—bales or packages. न उघडलेला, बिनउघडलेला, सबंध.

UNOPPOSED, *a.* v. UNOBSTRUCTED. न रोधलेला, &c. अप्रतिबंध, निष्प्रतिबंध, अप्रतिबंधित, अवारित, अनिवारित.

UNORGANIZED, *a.* v. INORGANIC. निरवयव. [तव्यवस्थ.

2 *not yet arranged.* बंदोबस्त न झालेला, अजातव्यवस्थ, अकृ-

UNORNAMENTED, *a.* v. PLAIN. अलंकारावेगळा-निराळा, अनलंकृत, अभूषित, अमंडित.

UNOSTENTATIOUS, *a.* बिनडौलाचा, बिनआवाचा.
UNORTHODOX. See HETERODOX.
UNOWNED, *a.* निवारशी, निवारशीक, निवारीश, अस्वामी, अस्वामिक.
To UNPACK, *v.a. open and take out.* सोडणें, काढणें, उपसूनकाढणें.
UNPALATABLE, *a. untasteful,* v. TASTELESS. बेचव, बेमजा, अस्वादु, अरुचिकर.
2 v. DISAGREEABLE. नावडता, नावड, अरुच्य, अरुचिर.
UNPARALLELED, *a.* v. UNEQUALLED. अतुल, अतुल्य, अप्रतिम, अनुपम, निरुपम, अपूर्व, निर्तुला.
UNPARDONABLE, *a.* माफकरायास अयोग्य-अशक्य-&c. गैरमुलाज्याचा, क्षमानर्ह, क्षमानुचित.
UNPARDONED, *a.* बिनसोडलेला, बिनमाफीचा, अदंडमुक, अमुक्तशासन.
UNPARTICULARIZED, *a.* अविवक्षित, अविशेषित, अनवच्छिन्न, अव्यवच्छिन्न.
UNPASSED, *a.*—a bill, &c. गैररुजू, गैरमंजूर, नामंजूर.
UNPAUSING, *a.* v. CONTINUAL. अविराम, निरंतर.
UNPEOPLED. See UNINHABITED.
UNPERCEIVABLE, *a.* v. IMPERCEPTIBLE. अगोचर, इंद्रियागोचर, अलक्ष्य, दुर्लक्ष्य.
UNPERCEIVED, *a.* न पाहिलेला, लक्षांत न आलेला, &c. अलक्षित.
UNPERFORMED, *a.* न केलेला, &c. अकृत, असाधित, असंपादित, अनिर्वहित.
UNPERSUADABLE, *a.* असमजुती *or* त्या, असमजुतीचा, दुराकलनीय.
UNPERTURBED, *a.* न क्षोभवलेला, अक्षुब्ध, निरुद्विग्न, अनुद्विग्न.
UNPHILOSOPHIC, UNPHILOSOPHICAL, *a.* पदार्थज्ञानशास्त्रविरुद्ध, तत्वज्ञानशास्त्रविरुद्ध, अयुक्तीचा, अयुक्तिक, अयुक्तिसिद्ध, तर्कशास्त्रासिद्ध.
UNPIECED, *a. not made up of pieces.* एकसंध, एकसंधी, अखंड, असलग.
To UNPIN, *v. a.* टांचणी *f.*-&c. काढणें *g.of o.*
UNPLEASANT, *a.* v. DISAGREEABLE. नावडता, नावडा, नावडीचा, अपसंत, अप्रीतीचा, अप्रिय, विषम, अहल, अहल्य.
UNPLOUGHED, *a.* न नांगरलेला, बिननांगरलेला, बिननांगरी, अकृष्ट.
UNPOETIC, UNPOETICAL, *a.* कविताशास्त्रविरुद्ध, कविताशास्त्रासिद्ध, छंदःशास्त्राननुयायी, कवितारस शून्य-रहित-&c.
UNPOISONOUS, *a.* बिनविखाचा, निर्विष, अविष, गोडा.
UNPOLISHED, *a. unelaborated.* अपरिष्कृत, असंस्कृत, साधा.
2 *impolite,* v. RUDE. असभ्य, अशिष्ट, गैरसाळ.
UNPOLLUTED, *a.* अदूषित, अभ्रष्ट, निर्दूषित, निर्मळ.
UNPOPULAR, *a.* लोकांचा नावडता-नावडा, लोकांचे नावडीचा, लोकांचे नापसंतीचा, &c. लोकाप्रिय, जनाप्रिय, अलौकिक, लोकाग्राह्य.
UNPOPULARITY, *n.* v. A. लोकांचा नावडतेपणा *m.* &c. लोकाप्रियता *f.* जनाप्रियता *f.* लोकाग्राह्यता *f.*
UNPOUNDED,—rice, &c. असडा, असडी.
UNPRACTISED, *a.*—of persons. गैरवापरलेला, गैरवहिवाटलेला, अनभ्यासी, अनभ्यस्त, कोरा, नवखा, नवा, गैरसाळ.
UNPRECEDENTED, *a.* अपूर्व, अजातपूर्व, अज्ञातपूर्व.
UNPREJUDICED, *a.* v. IMPARTIAL. बिनगांठीचा, बिनअढीचा, बिनअटीचा, निर्ग्रंथ, बिनपिळाचा.
UNPREMEDITATED, *a.* अचिंतित, अकल्पित, अपूर्वकल्पित, अपूर्वचिंतित.
UNPREPARED, *a.* बिनतयारीचा, तयारीवांचूनचा, नामुस्तद *or* मुस्तेद, असिद्ध.
UNPRESCRIBED, *a.* विधीवेगळा-निराळा, अविहित, अनुक्त, अविध्युक्त, अवैध, अचोदित, अविधिप्रोक्त.
UNPRETENDING, *a.* v. HUMBLE. बिनबिरदी, बिनबाण्याचा.
UNPREVENTABLE, *a.* अनिवार्य, अनिवार.
UNPREVENTED, *a.* न वारलेला, अनिवारित, अवारित.
UNPRINCIPLED, *a.* v. WICKED. दुराचारी, दुराचरणी, दुर्वृत्त, बदफैल, सदसदविचारी, सदसद्विचाररहित-शून्य, सदसदुपेक्षी, सदसदनपेक्षी.
UNPRODUCTIVE, *a.*—of soil. नापीक, निपिकी, बिनपिकी.
2 v. EMPTY, FRUITLESS. कोरडा, निरर्थक, निष्फल, अजनक, फलाजनक, लाभाजनक.
UNPROFITABLE, *a.* बिननफ्याचा, बिनहाशिलाचा, बिनफायद्याचा, बिनकिफायतीचा, &c. कोरडा, अनर्थक, निरर्थक, विफल, लाभाजनक, फलाजनक.
UNPROFITABLENESS, *n.* v. A. कोरडेपणा *m.* निरर्थकपणा *m.* आनर्थक्य *n.* फलराहित्य *n.* फलशून्यता *f.* वैफल्य *n.* वैयर्थ्य *n.*
UNPROFITABLY, *adv.* v. A. फळावांचून, हाशिलावांचून, &c. व्यर्थ, फुकट, नाघाणी *or* नी.
UNPROHIBITED, *a.*v. UNFORBIDDEN. न निषेधलेला, गैरमनाईचा, अनिषिद्ध.
UNPROPITIABLE, *a.* v. INEXORABLE. दुराराध्य, दुर्वश.
UNPROPITIOUS, *a.* v. INAUSPICIOUS. अशुभ, अमंगल *or* ळ, अप्रसन्न, अननुकूल, अनिष्ट, विषम, विपरीत, दग्धहस्त.
UNPROPITIOUSNESS, *n.* v. A. अमंगळपण *n.* अशुभ *n.* अननुकूलता *f.* अशुभता *f.* वैषम्य *n.* अनिष्टता *f.*
UNPROPORTIONATE, UNPROPORTIONED, *a.* v. DISPROPORTIONATE. बिनप्रमाणाचा, अप्रमाणाचा, असमतोल, असमप्रमाणक.
UNPROSPEROUS, *a.* v. UNFORTUNATE. दुर्भाग्य, दुर्भागी, अभागी, हतभाग्य, अभद्र, अकृतार्थ, अकृतकृत्य, अयशस्वी, अकल्याणी, दग्धहस्त, अश्रीमान्.
UNPROSPEROUSNESS, *n.* v. A. दुर्भागीपणा *m.* अभागीपणा *m.* &c. दुर्भाग्यता *f.* अकृतार्थता *f.* कार्यासिद्धि *f.* अर्थासिद्धि *f.* अश्रेय *n.* अकल्याण *n.*
UNPROTECTED, *a.* बिनआश्रयाचा, आश्रयावेगळा-निराळा, बिनसाबलीचा, अनाश्रय, निराश्रय, निराश्रित, अनाश्रित, अनाथ, उघडा, निजोर, अनावृत.
UNPROVED, *a. not established.* बिनशाबूत, नाशाबूत, बिनलागू, असिद्ध, अप्रामाणिक *pop.* अप्रमाणिक, अनुपपन्न, अप्रतिपादित, अनुपपादित, असमर्थित.
2 *untested.* न ताडलेला, बिनताडलेला, अपरीक्षित.
UNPROVOKED, *a.* बिनचिडवणीचा, बिनखवंडाळीचा, बिनआगळिकीचा, बिनकुरापतीचा.
UNPUBLISHED, *a.* उघड न केलेला, अप्रसिद्ध, अप्रकट *pop.* अप्रगट.
UNPUNISHABLE, *a.* दंडकरायास अयोग्य-अशक्य, अदंड्य, अदंडनीय, दंडनानर्ह, दंडनायोग्य, अताड्य, अताडनीय, अशास्य, &c.
UNPUNISHED, *a.* न दंडलेला, अदंडित, अताडित, अशासित, अदंड.
UNQUALIFIED, *a.* v. UNSUITABLE. अयोग्य, नालायक, अनुपयुक्त, अक्षम, अगुणसंपन्न, अयोग्यतासंपन्न.
2 *not restricted by exceptions.* मर्यादारहित, प्रतिबंधरहित, निरवधिक, बिनकसरीचा, बिनतरीचा, बिनतकरारीचा, अनाक्षेप.
UNQUENCHABLE, *a.* न विझवायाचा, &c. अशमनीय, अप्रशमनीय, निर्वापनाशक्य, निर्वापनानर्ह, अनिर्वापिनीय.
UNQUENCHED, *a.* न विझवलेला, अशमित, अनिर्वापित.
UNQUESTIONABLE, *a.* v. CERTAIN. निस्संशयाचा, निस्संशय, निस्संदिग्ध.
UNQUIET, *a.* शांती वेगळा-निराळा, अस्वस्थ, अशांत, शांतिहीन-शू-

न्य-रहित, हीनशांति, बिनचैनीचा.

Unquietness, *n.* v. A. अस्वस्थपणा *m.* अशांतपणा *m.* अशांति *f.* शांतिराहित्य *n.* &c.

To **Unravel**, *a. disentangle, free from complication.* उकलणें, उगवणें, उलगडणें, उलगडा *m.*-उकल *m.*-उगवणी *f.*-फाड *m.*-&c. करणें *g. of o.* गुंता *m.*-&c. काढणें-सोडवणें *g. of o.*

Unravelled, *p.* v. V. उकललेला, उलगडलेला, &c. उकलींव.
To get u. उलगडणें.

Unreadiness, *n.* v. A. 1. नातयारी *f.* बिनतयारी *f.* असिद्धि *f.*

Unready, *a. not prepared.* नातयार, बिनतयारीचा, असिद्ध, नामुस्ताद *or* मुस्तेद.
2 *not prompt, not quick, &c.* नातयार, असिद्ध, अधुरा.
3—learning, &c. मलिन *pop.* मळीण, मजीत, अनुपस्थित.

Unreal, *a.* v. **Illusory**. खोटा, खोटसाळ, अतात्त्विक, अवास्तविक, अवास्तव, अतथ्य, वितथ, अनृत, असत्, असत्य, अविद्यमान, अमूर्त्तिमान्, आभासात्मक, कृत्रिम, अयथार्थ, अप्रसिद्ध.

Unreality, *n.* v. A. खोटेपणा *m.* अवास्तविकपणा *m.* &c. अवास्तवत्व *n.* अतात्त्विकत्व *n.* अतथ्यता *f.* अविद्यमानता *f.* असत्ता *f.*

Unreasonable, *a.* गैरवाजबी, अवाजबी, गैरमार्गाचा, गैररितीचा, गैरहिशेबाचा, अयोग्य, असमंजस, अवास्तविक, अवास्तव, असंबद्ध, असंगत, अयुक्तिक,अयुक्तिसिद्ध, अयुक्तीचा, अन्यायी, अनीतीचा, अवघड.
2 See **Excessive**.

Unreasonableness, *n.* v. A. 1. गैरवाजवीपणा *m.* असमंजसपणा *m.* &c. अयोग्यता *f.* असंबद्धता *f.* असंगतत्व *n.* असामंजस्य *n.* अयुक्ति *f.* अमार्ग *m.* अनीति *f.* युक्तिविरुद्धता *f.*

Unreasonably, *adv.* v. A. 1. गैरवाजबी, गैरमार्गानें, गैररितीनें, गैरहिशेबानें, असमंजसपणानें, अन्यायानें.

Unreceived, *a.* अप्राप्त, अलब्ध, अनुपात्त.

Unrecompensed, *a.* अप्रतिफलित, अप्राप्तफल. [खित.

Unrecorded, *a.* न लिहून ठेवलेला, अपटारूढ, अलेख्यारूढ, अलि-

Unrefined, *a. not purified.* न शोधलेला, अशोधित, अविशोधित.
2 See **Rude**, **Barbarous**. [असमंजस.

Unreflecting, *a.* v. **Inconsiderate**. अविचारी, अविचारशील,

Unrefreshed, *a.* ताजा न केलेला, अश्रांत, अनष्टश्रम, अगतश्रम, अच्छिन्नक्लांति.

Unrefuted, *a.* न खंडलेला, अखंडित, अप्रत्याख्यात, अनिराकृत.

Unregarded, *a.* v. **Disregarded**. उपेक्षित, अनपेक्षित, अवमानित. [र्जातत्व *n.*

Unregeneracy, *a.* मूळची पापदशा *f.* मूळची पापस्थिति *f.* अपुन-

Unregenerate, *a. not renewed in heart.* मूळच्या पापदशेचा, मूळच्या पापस्थितीचा, अपुनर्जात, अपरिवृत्तमनस्क.

Unregistered, *a.* न लिहून ठेवलेला, बिननोंदलेला, अपटारूढ, अलेख्यारूढ.

Unrelenting, *a.* v. **Cruel**. बिनकळवळ्याचा, कठीण, कठोर,कडबा, अवीट, पाषाणहृदय, अयोहृदय, निर्द्दयहृदय.

Unremembered, *a.* आठवण नठेवलेला, अस्मृत.

Unremitting, *a.* एकसारखा चालणारा-चाललेला, ढिला न होणारा-न झालेला, बिनढिलाईचा, एकनेटाचा, संततसमान.

Unremittingly, *adv.* v. A. एकटक,एकसारखा,एकसाह्या,एकसोष.

Unrepealed, *a.* रद्द न केलेला, अलुप्त, अजाततलोप.

Unreserved, *a.* v. **Frank**, **Open**. असंकोची, असंकोचशील, खुलबलीत.
2 *without any thing kept back.* निःशेष, निरलाप, पुरा, पूर्ण, निर्विकल्प, अनन्यभावाचा, बिनदिक्कतीचा.

Unreservedly, *adv.* v.A.1. संकोचाबांचून, संकोचरहित,मोकळ्यामनानें, मनमोकळेंकरून, निःसंकोच.
2 निस्तूक, निस्तोष, निश्शेष, पुरतेपणीं, अनन्यभावानें.

Unresisting, *a.* अनिवारक, अनिवारणकर्त्ता, अप्रतिकारकर्त्ता.

Unresolved, *a. undetermined.* अकृतनिश्चय, अकृतसंकल्प.

Unrespected, *a.* अनादृत, अमानित, अनादरयुक्त.

Unrestrained, *a. uncurbed, uncontrolled.* बेबंद, बेकैद, बेलगाम, अनावर, अनावृत, अनियत, अनिवारित, उच्छृंखल *pop.* उत्संकळ *or* खळ, अनर्गल *or* ळ, निरर्गल, निरंकुश, अबकळ, अयंत्रित, निर्यंत्रित, अनियंत्रित, अनाड, अबद्ध, विशृंखल.
2 *unreserved, free, easy, familiar, &c.* बिनसंकोचाचा, संकोचाबांचूनचा,असंकोचाचा, खुलाशाचा, संकोचरहित, खुलबलीत.

Unrevealed, *a.* प्रसिद्धनकेलेला, अप्रसिद्ध, अप्रकट *pop.* अप्रगट, अनाविष्कृत.

Unrevised, *a.* शोध न केलेला, बिनशोधलेला, अशोधित.

Unrewarded, *a.* प्रतिफळ नदिल्हेला, अप्रतिफलित.

Unrighteous, *a.*—of persons. अधर्मी, अधर्मिष्ट, अधर्मनिष्ठ, अधार्मिक, अधर्मचारी, पापाचारी, अन्यायी, अनीतिमान्.
2—of acts, &c. अधर्माचा, अन्यायाचा, अन्याय्य, अयथान्याय, अयथार्थ.

Unrighteousness, *n.* अधर्म *m.* अनीति *f.* अन्याय *m.* अधर्माचार *m.* अन्यायाचार *m.* अधर्माचरण *n.* &c. [कृदशापत्र.

Unripe, *a.* बिनपिकलेला, कच्चा, हिरवा, अपक्क, आम, हरित, अप-

Unripeness, *n.* v. A. कच्चेपणा *m.* हिरवेपणा *m.* &c. अपक्कता *f.*

Unrivalled, *a.* v. **Unequalled**. बिनसरीचा, अनुपम, निरुपम, अतुल, अतुल्य, अप्रतिम.

Unrivalledness, *n.* v. A. अनुपमता *f.* निरुपमता *f.* आनुपम्य *n.*

To **Unroll**, *v. a.* गुंडाळी *f.* उकलणें *g. of o.* सोडणें.

To **Unroof**, *v. a.* छप्पर *n.*-छावणी *f.*-&c. काढणें, उत्तरणें, उतरणें, उलगडणें, पाणझरण *n.* काढणें *g. of o.*

Unruffled, *a.* v. **Calm**. स्थिर, संत, असुब्ध.

Unruliness, *n.* v. A. शिरजोरपणा *m.* बेहुकमीपणा *m.*

Unruly, *a.* v. **Insubordinate**, **Licentious**. शिरजोर, बेहुकमी, बेलगामी, बेकैद, अशिष्ट, दुःशासन.

Unsafe, *a.* भयाचा, जोखमाचा, सभय, अनिर्भय, अनिष्कंटक.

Unsafeness, **Unsafety**, *n.* v. A. भय *n.* जोखीम *n.* सभयता *f.*

Unsaid, *a.* नसांगितलेला, अकथित, अनुक्त, अभाषित.

Unsaleable, *a.* विकायास अयोग्य-अनुपयोगी-नालायक,अविक्रेय, अपण्य.

Unsalted, *a.* अळणी, अलवण, अलवणी.

Unsanctified. See **Unholy**.

Unsatisfactory, *a.* गैरखातरीचा, बिनखातरीचा, बिनपसंतीचा, अनिश्चायक, अनिर्णायक.

Unsatisfiable, *a.* v. **Insatiable**. अनोक्षणीय, अतर्पणीय, अतर्प्य, असंतर्प्य, अनातृप्य.

Unsatisfied, *a.* न पुरलेला-धालेला, बिनपुरलेला, &c. अतृप्त, अतर्पित, असंतर्पित, असंतृप्त. [बटधाचा.

Unsatisfying, *a.*—an article of food. निपुरबटधाचा, बिनपुर-

Unsavoriness, *n.* v. A.1. बेचवपणा *m.* निचवपणा *m.* स्वादराहित्य *n.*

Unsavory, *a.* v. **Insipid**. बेचव, बेमजा, अस्वादु, अस्वादिष्ट.
2 See **Disagreeable**.

To UNSAY. See To RETRACT.

To UNSCREW, *v. a.* मळसूत्र *n.* काढणें *g. of o.* उसवळणें.

UNSCRIPTURAL, *a.* अशास्त्र, शास्त्रविरुद्ध, अयथाशास्त्र, उच्छास्त्र, अशास्त्रीय, अशास्त्रसिद्ध, अशास्त्रोक्त, अवेदोक्त, &c.

UNSCRUPULOUS, *a.* बेशक, बिनदिक्कतीचा, बिनदिक्कती, निश्शंक, अशंक, शंकाहीन-रहित, अज्ञातशंक.

To UNSEAM, *v. a. open the seams.* उसवणें, उधडणें, उस्तरणें.

UNSEARCHABLE, *a. inscrutable*, v. INCOMPREHENSIBLE. अकळ, अतर्क्य, दुर्ज्ञेय, दुर्लक्ष्य.

UNSEASONABLE, *a.* अवेळेचा, अकाळाचा, बेवक्ताचा, अवकाळा *or* ळ्या, अवेळ्या, अकाळ्या, अकाल, आकालिक, अकालीन, अप्राप्तकाल, अप्राप्तकालिक, असामयिक, समयानुचित, असमयोचित, प्रसंगानुचित, अयथाकाल, अनवसर, अप्रसंग, असमय, अकालप्राप्त, अप्रसंगप्राप्त, &c. अप्राप्तप्रसंग, अप्राप्तकाल, &c. अनवसरपठित, अकालसदृश, असमयानुरूप.

U. time. अवेळ *f.* अवकाळ *m.*

UNSEASONABLENESS, *n.* v. A. बेवक्ती *f.* असमय *m.* अनवसर *m.* असमयानुरूप्य *n.* असमयौचित्य *n.* अप्रसंगौचित्य *n.* अकालसादृश्य *n.* अकालप्राप्तता *f.* &c.

UNSEASONABLY, *adv.* v. A. अवेळीं, अकाळीं, अवकाळीं, अयथाकाल, अप्रसंगानुसार, अकालानुसार, अप्रसंगोपात्त.

UNSEASONED, *a.*—wood, &c. नवळसावलेला, बिनवळसावलेला.

2—food, &c. बिनमसाल्याचा.

UNSEEMLY, *a.* अयोग्य, नालायक, नालाजीम, गैरशिस्त.

UNSEEN, *a.* नदेखलेला, अलोकित, अनवलोकित, अदृष्ट.

2 See INVISIBLE. [अकाम्य.

UNSELFISH, *a.* अस्वार्थी, अस्वार्थदृष्टि, अस्वार्थतत्पर, अलाभदृष्टि,

UNSENT, *a.* बिनधाडलेला, अप्रेरित, अप्रेषित.

UNSEPARATED, *a.* नभेदलेला, अविछिन्न, अनवच्छिन्न, अपरिछिन्न.

UNSERVICEABLE, *a.* निरुपयोगी, अनुपयोगी, कामांतून गेलेला, नाकारा, अनुपयुक्त, निरुपयुक्त, कार्याक्षम.

UNSERVICEABLENESS, *n.* v. A. निरुपयोगीपणा *m.* अनुपयोगीपणा *m.* नाकारेपणा *m.*

UNSETTLED, *a. undecided.* फैसला न झालेला, बिननिवाड्याचा, बिनठरावलेला, अनिर्णीत, अनिश्चित, अनिर्धारित, अनवधारित.

2 *unfixed, unarranged, &c.* बिनबंदोबस्ताचा, अव्यवस्थेचा, अव्यवस्थित, अनियमित, अनियत, अजातव्यवस्थ, अकृतव्यवस्थ.

3 *variable, changeable.* चंचल *or* ळ, अस्थिर, अधीर.

UNSETTLEDNESS, *n.* v. A. 1. ह्लिगड *f.* अनिश्चय *m.* अनिर्णय *m.* अनिर्धार *m.* अनियम *m.*

2 बिनबंदोबस्ती *f.* अव्यवस्था *f.*

3 चंचळपणा *m.* अस्थिरपणा *m.* अस्थिरता *f.* [खल.

UNSHACKLED, *a,* v. FREE. बिनबेडीचा, बंदाबेगळा-निराळा, बिशृं-

UNSHAKEN, *a.* न हालवलेला, अचलित, अक्षोभ, अस्खलित.

2 See FIRM.

To UNSHEATH, *v. a.* म्यानांतून काढणें, म्यानानिराळा-वेगळा करणें, उसपणें *or* उपसणें, सळ *m.* सोडणें *g. of o.*

UNSHELLED, *a.* न सोललेला, बिनसोललेला, असोला, निसोला.

UNSHELTERED, *a.* बिनआश्रयाचा, अनाश्रय, निराश्रय, निराश्रित, उघडा. [वाणी, अनवाहणी.

UNSHOD, *a. having no shoes.* बिनजोड्याचा, बिनपायतण, अन-

UNSIGHTLY, *a.* v. UGLY. अदेखणा, बेढब, विशोभित, नेत्रत्रासक.

UNSKILFUL, UNSKILLED, *a.* v. AWKWARD. नाकसबी, आडकसबी, अनाडी, अकुशल, अदक्ष, अपटु, अचतुर, हीनकौशल्य, अदक्षिण, अकारु, अनिष्णात, अनिपुण, कौशल्यहीन-रहित-शून्य.

UNSKILFULNESS, *n.* v. A. नाकसबीपणा *m.* अनाडीपणा *m.* &c. अकौशल *n.* अदक्षता *f.* &c. कौशल्यहीनता *f.*

UNSLOPING, *a.* निढाळ, बिनढाळ, बिनढाळाचा.

UNSMEARED, *a.* विनमाखलेला, निर्लिप्त, अलिप्त, अजातलेप.

UNSOCIABLE, UNSOCIAL, *a.* माणुसघाण्या, माणुसगंधारा, माणुसगंध्या, एकलकोंडा, एकलकोंट, एकलटिका, एकाड.

UNSOLD, *a.* बिनविकलेला, बिनखपाचा, अविक्रीत.

UNSOLDERED, *a.* निडांकी, बिनडांकी, बिनडांकाचा.

UNSOLICITED, *a.* बिनमागितलेला, अप्रार्थित, अयाचित.

UNSOLICITOUS, *a.* v. UNANXIOUS. निकाळजी, बेदरदी, अनास्थ, निश्चिंत.

UNSOPHISTICATED, *a.* अमिश्रित, अदूषित, असल, चोख.

UNSOUGHT, *a. not searched for.* बिनशोधलेला-धुंडलेला-हुडकलेला-&c. अनन्वेषित, अमार्गित.

2 See UNSOLICITED.

UNSOUND, *a. defective, impaired, infirm, not in good condition*, v. FAULTY, FLIMSY, WORTHLESS. खोडीचा, ऐबाचा, खोडकर, ऐबदार, सदोष, लेचापेचा, लुकसान *or* नुकसान, नादान, फुसका.

2—of members or faculties, and of persons or animals; *wanting in tone, power, &c.* अधू, अक्षम *pop.* अखम.

3 fig. *hollow, insincere, &c.* v. EMPTY, FALSE. कुजका, पोकळ, रिकामा, रिकामका, रिता.

4 See HETERODOX. 5 (of arguments, reasoning, &c.) *not valid, just, &c.* असमंजस, असमर्पक, अयुक्तिक, अयुक्तिसिद्ध, युक्तिविरुद्ध, अनर्थक. [षता *f.*

UNSOUNDNESS, *n.* v. A. 1. खोडकरपणा *m.* &c. ऐबदारी *f.* सदो-

2 अधूपणा *m.* अखमपणा *m.* अक्षमता *f.*

3 कुजकेपणा *m.* पोकळपणा *m.* रिकामेपणा *m.* &c.

5 असमर्पकपणा *m.* असमंजसपणा *m.* अयुक्तिकत्व *n.* अयुक्ति *f.*

UNSPEAKBLE, *a. ineffable.* अवाच्य, अवचनीय, अनिर्वचनीय, अनिर्वाच्य, अकथ्य, अकथनीय, वचनागोचर, कथनागोचर, शब्दागोचर, वर्णनातीत, शब्दातीत, वर्णनाविषय, शब्दाविषय.

UNSPECIFIED, *a.* अविशेषित, अव्यवच्छिन्न, अनुद्दिष्ट, अनिर्दिष्ट, अविवक्षित.

UNSPOTTED, *a.* बिनडाग, बिनऐब, कलंकहीन, निष्कलंक.

UNSTABLE, UNSTEADFAST, *a. not fixed*, v. RICKETY. अस्थिर, अध्रुव.

2 fig. *fickle, inconstant*, v. CHANGEABLE, IRRESOLUTE. अस्थिर, अधीर, क्षणिकचित्त, क्षणिकबुद्धि, अस्थिरचित्त, अस्थिरमनस्क. [ध्रुवता *f.*

UNSTABLENESS, UNSTEADFASTNESS, *n.* v. A. अस्थिरता *f.* अ-

2 अधीरपणा *m.* अस्थिरता *f.* अस्थिरबुद्धि *f.* अनिष्ठा *f.* अस्थैर्य *n.*

UNSTEADINESS, *n.* v. A. 1. चंचळपणा *m.* अस्थिरता *f.* अधैर्य *n.*

2 अस्थैर्य *n.* चांचल्य *n.* चलबिचल *f.*

UNSTEADY, *a.* v. IRRESOLUTE. चंचळ, अस्थिर, अधीर, अधैर्य.

2 *mutable, variable*, v. CHANGEABLE. चंचळ, अस्थिर, चलबिचल. [-उतरणें.

To UNSTRING, *v. a.* (a harp, &c.) तारा *f. pl.*-&c. काढणें-सोडणें

2 *relax*, v. To LOOSEN. सैलावणें, ढील-&c. करणें.

3 *take from a string.* सरांतून-&c. काढणें.

UNSTUDIED, *a. unpremeditated.* अकल्पित, अपूर्वकल्पित.

UNSTUDIOUS, *a.* अनभ्यासी, अभ्यासंगी, अनध्ययनी, अनध्ययनशील.

UNSUBDUED, *a.* अजिंकलेला, अजित, अवश, अवशीभूत, अवशीकृत, अदांत, अदमित.

2—the passions or flesh; *or* attributively. अशांत, अप्रशांत, अजितेंद्रिय, अवशात्मा.

UNSUBJECTED, *a.* v. UNSUBDUED. अजित, अवश.

UNSUBSTANTIAL, *a. slight, flimsy, &c.* निर्जीव, पोकळ, फुसकुला, फुसका, निःसत्व, निःसार, असार, रिकामा, रिकामका, रिता.

2 v. UNREAL. अवास्तविक, अवास्तव, अमूर्तिमान्, वायुसम.

UNSUCCESSFUL, *a.*—of persons. अकृतकृत्य, अकृतार्थ, अजयी, अप्राप्तार्थ, अप्राप्तयश, अश्रीमान्, अनर्थसिद्ध, अनभीष्टसिद्ध, अनिष्टसिद्ध. [क, अगुणावह.

2—of measures, &c. असफल, निष्फल, अफल, अकार्यसंपाद-

UNSUCCESSFULLY, *adv.* v. A. कार्य केल्यावांचून, जय न मिळवतां, सिद्धीस गेल्यावांचून.

UNSUITABLE, **UNSUITED**, *a. unfit, not adapted.* अयोग्य, अनुपयोगी, निरुपयोगी, नालायक, अयुक्त, अनुपयुक्त, निरुपयुक्त, निरुपयोग, अनुचित; बिलग.

2 *incongruous*, v. INCONSISTENT. अनुपयोगी, अनुपयुक्त, विजोड, विलग, असंगत, अनन्वित.

UNSUITABLENESS, *n.* v. A. 1. अनुपयोगीपणा *m.* निरुपयोगीपणा *m.* नालायकी *f.* अयोग्यता *f.* अनुपयुक्तता *f.* अनुपयोगिता *f.* अनौचित्य *n.*

2 विजोडपणा *m.* असंगति *f.* अनन्वय *m.*

UNSULLIED, *a.* बिनडाग, निष्कलंक, कलंकरहित-हीन-&c. निर्दूषित, निर्दोष, निर्मल, स्वच्छ.

UNSUPPORTED, *a. not upheld.* आधारावांचूनचा, बिनआधारी, बिनआधाराचा, निराधार, अनवलंब, अनालंब.

2 *not assisted.* बिनपाठबळाचा, बिनपाठपुराव्याचा.

UNSURPASSED, *a.* अनतिक्रांत, अनतिक्रमित, अक्रांत, अनुत्क्रांत, अनुत्तर, अपूर्व. [अपरिवेष्टित.

UNSURROUNDED, *a.* न वेढलेला, बिनवेढलेला, आनावृत, अवेष्टित,

UNSUSPECTED, *a.* बिनसंशयाचा, अशंकित, अनाशंकित, असंदिग्ध.

UNSUSPECTING, *a.* v. SIMPLE. भोळा, साळाभोळा.

UNSUSPICIOUS, *a.* बिनभरमी, बिनभरमाचा, बिनगुमानाचा, बेवहमी, असंशयी, अकुतर्की, अशंकी, अशंकाशील, असंशयशील.

UNSWEPT, *a.* बिन झाडलेला, असम्मार्जित.

UNSYSTEMATICAL, *a.* बिनबेताचा, बिनबंदोबस्ताचा, बेबंद.

UNTAINTED, *a. not putrescent.* बिनलागलेला, बिनलागरा, बिनघाणीचा, बिनगंधीचा, अगंधयुक्त.

2 v. UNSULLIED. अदूषित, निष्कलंक.

UNTAMEABLE, *a.* अदम्य, अदमनीय, अवश्य, दुर्दम, दमनाशक्य.

UNTAMED, *a.* वठणीस न आणलेला, अवश, अदांत, अदमित.

UNTARNISHED, *a.* बिनविटलेला, बिनडागलेला, अजातकलंक.

UNTASTED, *a.* बिनचाखलेला, अनास्वादित.

UNTAUGHT, *a.* v. ILLITERATE. अशिक्षित, अशिष्ट.

UNTEACHABLE, *a. indocile.* दुःशिष्य, दुःशिक्षणीय, दुर्बोध.

UNTENABLE, *a.*—a post, fortress, &c. राखावयास अयोग्य-अशक्य-&c. अरक्षणीय, अरक्ष्य, रक्षणानर्ह, रक्षणाशक्य.

2—doctrine, &c. अस्थापनीय, अप्रतिपाद्य, अप्रतिपादनीय, असमर्थनीय.

UNTENANTED, *a.* v. EMPTY. रिकामा, खाली.

UNTHANKFUL, **UNTHANKFULNESS**. See UNGRATEFUL, INGRATITUDE.

UNTHINKING, *a.* v. INCONSIDERATE. अविचारी, अविवेकी.

UNTHINKINGLY, *adv.* v. A. अविचारानें, विचार केल्यावांचून, विचार न करितां, उगा, उगाच, उगीच, उगेच, अकल्पित, अचिंतित.

UNTHORNY, *a.* बिनकांट्याचा, अकंटक, निष्कंटक, कंटकरहित-&c.

UNTHRIVING. See UNPROSPEROUS.

UNTIDINESS, *n.* v. A. बिनचापचोपी *f.* गबाळीपणा *m.*

UNTIDY, *a.* v. SLOVENLY. बिनचापचोपीचा, बिनचापचोप्या, चापचोपी वेगळा-निराळा, गबाळी *or* ळ्या.

To **UNTIE**, *v. a. loosen, unbind.* सोडणें, मोकळा-&c. करणें, फेडणें, मोचन *n.*-&c. करणें *g. of o.*

UNTIED, *p.* v. A. सोडलेला, फेडलेला, &c.

UNTIL, *prep.*—of time. जंव *or* जों *or* जौं, जोंवर, जोंपर्यंत, (*or* जंवपर्यंत, &c.) जोंपावेतों, पर्यंत, पावेतों, तों, तंव, तोंपर्यंत, तोंपावेतों, तितपर्यंत, तितपावेतों, मर्याद (in comp. as वर्षमर्याद) तावत् (in comp. as तावत्काल), तावत्पर्यंत, अंत (in comp. as मरणांत), अवधि (in comp. as वर्षावधि).

2—of dates or time; *up to.* तागाईत.

From (a certain date) till (a certain date). इस्तकबील तागाईत (as इस्तकबीलमार्च तागाईत मे from March till May).

UNTILLED, *a. uncultivated.* बिनलागवडीचा, बिनलावणीचा, नाकीर्द, पडीत, पडसर, अकृष्ट.

UNTIMELY, *a.* v. UNSEASONABLE. आवकाळा *or* ळ्या, अकाल, अकालिक, आकालिक, अकालीन, अकालज, असामयिक.

UNTINNED, *a.*—culinary utensil. निकल्हा *or* ल्ही.

UNTIRING. See INDEFATIGABLE.

UNTO, *prep.*—of place or time. पावेतों, पर्यंत, तितपावेतों, तितपर्यंत, यावत्, तावत्, मर्याद (in comp.), अंत (in comp. as समुद्रांत, तलांत), अवधि (in comp.), आ (in comp.)

2 See To.

UNTOLD, *a.* न सांगितलेला, अकथित, अनुक्त, असंदिष्ट. [शित.

UNTOUCHED, *a.* न स्पर्शलेला, बिन शिवलेला, &c. अस्पृष्ट, अस्प-

2 *remaining unaffected by use.* भमानत *or* अनामत, अनकूट, अपूट, अचळ, अचानक, कोरा.

UNTOWARD, **UNTRACTABLE**, *a.* v. PERVERSE, INSUBORDINATE. अकरनकर, करनकर, करनकऱ्या, बेडावांकडा, विजात, आडजात, अडफांट्या, शिरजोर, बेहुकमी. [*m.* &c.

UNTRACTABLENESS, *n.* v. A. अकर नकरपणा *m.* कर नकरपणा

UNTRAINED, *a.* बिनशिकवलेला, बिनतालमीचा, अशिक्षित, अशिष्ट, अपट, अल्लड.

UNTRIED, *a.* न करून पाहिलेला, अपरीक्षित.

UNTRODDEN, *a.* न तुडवलेला, न मळलेला, अपादमर्दित, अपादाहत.

UNTRUE, *a.* v. FALSE. असत्य, असत्, अतथ्य, वितथ, अयथातथ, अतात्त्विक, अयथार्थ, अनृत, मिथ्या, निःसत्य, गैरारास्त, गैरवास्तवीक. [गैरवास्तवीक, गैरारास्त.

UNTRULY, *adv.* v. A. असत्य, मिथ्या, अनृत, अयथातथ, अन्यथा,

UNTRUSTING, *a.* अविश्वासी *or* सू *or* सूक, अप्रत्ययी, अश्रद्धधान.

UNTRUSTY, **UNTRUSTWORTHY**, *a.* गैरविश्वासाचा, गैरविश्वासी *or* सू *or* सूक, अविश्वासनीय, अविश्वासी *or* सू *or* सूक, बिनभरवशाचा, बिनखातरीचा, अप्रामाणिक *pop.* अप्रमाणिक, अश्रद्धेय.

UNTRUTH, *n.* v. FALSEHOOD. असत्य *n.* अनृत *n.* अतथ्य *n.* असत्ता *f.* कूट *n.*

UNTUNABLE, UNTUNEFUL, *a.* बेसूर, बदसूर, बिस्वर.

UNTUTORED. See UNTAUGHT.

To UNTWINE, *To* UNTWIST, *v. a.* उकलणें, उलगडणें, उलगडा *m.* -उलट *m. f.* करणें *g. of o.*

To UNTWINE, *To* UNTWIST, *v. n.* उबळणें.

UNTWINED, UNTWISTED, *p.* v. V. उकललेला, &c. उकलींव, उबळ *or* उंबळ *or* उंवीळ.

UNUNCTUOUS, *a.* बिनचिकणाईचा, निस्स्नेह, अस्निग्ध, अचिक्कण, स्नेहरहित, रुक्ष *pop.* रुखा. [ह *m.* रौक्ष्य *n.*

UNUNCTUOUSNESS, *n.* v. A. बिनचिकणाई *f.* अस्निग्धता *f.* अस्ने-

UNUSED, *a. that has not been brought into use.* बिनवापरलेला, बिनवहिवाटलेला, कोरा, अनसूट, अपूट, अभुक्त, अक्षुण्ण.

2 See UNACCUSTOMED.

UNUSUAL, *a.* लोकरूढीनिराळा-वेगळा, लोकचाली निराळा-वेगळा, जनरीतीनिराळा-वेगळा, चाली-रिती &c. वेगळा-निराळा, बिनरिवाजाचा, बिनरहाचा, शिरस्त्याबाहेरचा, गैरवहिवाटीचा, अमार्गाचा, असांप्रदायिक, अव्यावहारिक.

UNUSUALNESS, *n.* v. A. लोकरूढीनिराळेपणा *m.* &c. बिनरिवाज *m.* गैरवहिवाट *f.* अमार्ग *m.* असांप्रदायिकत्व *n.*

UNUTTERABLE, *a.* v. INEXPRESSIBLE. अवाच्य, अकथनीय.

UNVANQUISHED, *a.* अजित, अदांत, अदमित. [हित.

UNVARIED, *a.* फेरफारा निराळा वेगळा, बिनपालटाचा, न्यूनाधिक्यर-

UNVARYING, *a. uniform.* एकसारखा, एकसाहां, एकसुती, एकसोय, एकरूप.

To UNVEIL, *v. a.* बुरका *or* खा *m.*-बोखारा *m.*-&c. उघडणें-काढणें.

UNVENOMOUS, *a.* निर्विष, अविष, गोडा.

UNVERSED, *a.* बिनरावलेला, बिनघसवटलेला, बिनवापरलेला, अनभ्यासी, अनभ्यस्त, अकृतकर्मा, अपरिचित, गैरवाकब, गैरमाहीत, अनभिज्ञ, अप्रवीण, अनिष्णात, अनिपुण.

UNVITIATED, *a.* अदूषित, अभ्रष्ट.

UNVOUCHED, *a.* बिनदाखल्याचा, बिनसडीचा, आगमरहित.

UNWALLED, *a.* बिनकुसवाचा *or* बिनकुसाचा, बिनपन्ह्याचा, अप्राकार, प्राकाररहित.

UNWARILY, *adv.* v. A. गैरसावधपणानें, असावधपणानें, &c. असावधानपूर्वक, प्रमादपूर्वक, प्रमादतः.

UNWARINESS, *n.* v. A. गैरसावधपणा *m.* असावधपणा *m.* असावधान *n.* अनवधान *n.* प्रमाद *m.*

UNWARLIKE, *a. not given to war.* बिनलढाऊ,निर्वीर्य, हीनपराक्रम, निष्पराक्रम, हीनशौर्य, रणविमुख.

UNWARRANTABLE, *a.* v. WRONG. बिनहुकमाचा, बिनपरवानगीचा, अधिकारावांचूनचा, सत्तेवांचूनचा, आधारावांचूनचा, बिनप्रमाणाचा, गैरवाजवी, गैरशिस्त, अयोग्य, अविहित.

UNWARRANTED, *a. unlicensed.* गैरसनदी, बिनसनदी.

2 See UNWARRANTABLE.

UNWARY, *a. incautious.* v. CARELESS. असावध, गैरसावध, गैरहुशार, असावधान, अनवधान, अप्रमादी.

UNWASHED, *a.* न धुतलेला, बिनधुतलेला,अप्रक्षालित,अधौत.—rice &c. अधोपी, अधुपा.

UNWASTING, *a.* अतूट, अक्षय.

UNWATERED, *a. undiluted with water.* निपाणी, बिनपाण्याचा.

UNWAVERING, *a.* v. FIRM, CONSTANT. बिनधरसोडीचा, निश्चंचल, अचंचल, चांचल्यरहित.

UNWEANED, *a.* आंगावरचा, आंगावरला, बिनतोडलेला.

UNWEARIED, *a.* न दमलेला, &c. अश्रांत, अश्रमित.

2 See INDEFATIGABLE.

UNWELCOME, *a.* आगतस्वागत न केलेला, आगतस्वागत न पावलेला, अस्वागतपात्र, अस्वागतयुक्त, अस्वागतसंपन्न.

2 See DISAGREEABLE.

UNWELL, *a.* v. ILL, SICK. अस्वस्थ *pop.* असुस्थ, असमाधानी, असुखी, काहिला, मांदा.

To be u. बरें न वाटणें *in. con.*

UNWHOLESOME, *a.* अपथ्य, बावडा, अपथ्याचा, बाधक, प्रतिबाधक, अपथ्य कारक, रोग आणणारा, रोगी, रोगकारक-जनक, अस्वास्थ्यकारक-जनक, विषम, विरुद्ध.

UNWHOLESOMENESS, *n.* v. A. बावडेपणा *m.* बाधकपणा *m.* रोगीपणा *m.* रोगजनकत्व *n.* &c. अपथ्य *n.* असात्म्य *n.*

UNWIELDINESS, *n.* v. A. औजडपणा *m.* बोजडपणा *m.*

UNWIELDY, *a. that is moved, &c. with difficulty.* बिनअटोपाचा, बिनअटोपसार, औजड, औजाड, बोजड, झांबड, मोधळा, ढबल, ढबलशाई, म्हशा.

UNWILLING, *a. loath, reluctant.* नाकबूल, गैरखुश, गैरखुशी, नाखुश, नाराजी, गैरराजी, बेदिल, कष्टी, श्रमी, दुःखी, गैरमान्य, असंतोषी, असंतुष्ट, विमनस्क, विमत, विमुख, पराङ्मुख.

UNWILLINGLY, *adv.* v. A. गैरखुशीनें, गैरराजीनें, असंतोषानें, संकटानें, कष्टानें, श्रमानें, जुलमानें, जुलमावर, नाराजी-&c.होऊन.

UNWILLINGNESS, *n.* v. A. गैरखुशी *f.* नाखुशी *f.* गैरराजी *f.* बेदिलपणा *m.* कष्टीपणा *m.* &c. असंतोष *m.* कंटाळा *m.* संकट *n.* श्रम *m.* कष्ट *m.* विमति *f.* विमुखता *f.*

To UNWIND, *v. a.* उकलणें, उलगडणें, सोडणें, वेढे *m. pl.*-वळसे *m. pl.*-&c. काढणें-सोडणें *g. of o.* उलट *f.* करणें *g. of o.*

To UNWIND, *v. n.* उबळणें.

UNWISE, *a.*—of persons, v. FOOLISH, IMPRUDENT. वेडा, अज्ञान, निर्बुद्ध, हीनबुद्धि, बुद्धिहीन, असमंजस, असुज्ञ, अविद्य, अविद्वान्.

2—of measures, acts, &c. वेडा, वेडेपणाचा, मूर्खपणाचा, बेकुबीचा, अज्ञानाचा, अविचाराचा, बिनशहाणपणाचा,बिनअकलेचा.

UNWISHED, *a.* न इच्छलेला, अनिष्ट, अनभीष्ट, अनिच्छित, अनाकांक्षित. [क, निस्साक्षिक.

UNWITNESSED, *a.* बिनसाक्षीचा, साक्षीवांचूनचा, असाक्ष, असाक्षि-

UNWITTING. See IGNORANT.

UNWITTINGLY, *adv. ignorantly, unconsciously.* अजाणून, अजाणतां, नजाणतां, नेणतां, नेणतपणीं, नकळत, कळत न कळत.

UNWONTED. See UNUSUAL.

UNWOODED, *a.* बिनझाडाचा, अवृक्ष, निर्वृक्ष.

UNWORKMANLIKE, *a.* v. AWKWARD. नाकसबी.

UNWORTHINESS, *n.* v. A. 1. अयोग्यता *f.* नालायकी *f.* बिनलायकी *f.* गुणाभाव *m.* गुणराहित्य *n.* योग्यताराहित्य *n.* अपात्रता *f.*

2 अयोग्यता *f.* नालायकी *f.* अनौचित्य *n.*

UNWORTHY, *a. undeserving, wanting merit,* v. UNSUITABLE. अयोग्य, नालायक, बिनलायकीचा, अनधिकारी, अगुणी, निर्गुणी, नालागी, अनुपयुक्त, गुणहीन, गुणरहित, अपात्र, अनर्ह in comp. अनार्ह्य, योग्यताहीन-रहित-&c.

2 *unbecoming, unsuitable.* अयोग्य, नालायक, अनुचित, विशोभित.

UNWOUND, *p.* v. V. A. उकललेला, वेढे काढलेला, &c. उकलींव.

UNWOUNDED, *a.* बिनजखमी, बिनघावाचा, बिनवाराचा, घावाबेग-

ळा-निराळा, &c. अक्षत, अनाहत.

UNWRITTEN, *a.* v. ORAL. बिनलिहिलेला, बिनलेखाचा, बिनलिखा, बिनकलमी.

UNYIELDING, *a.* v. FIRM. चिक्कट.

To UNYOKE, *v. a.* जोकड *n.*-&c. सोडणें *g. of o.* जोकडापासून-&c. सोडणें.

UNZEALOUS, *a.* v. INDIFFERENT, CARELESS. बिनआस्थेचा, बिनपोटागीचा, बिनकळकळीचा, आस्थेवेगळा-निराळा, अनास्थ, अनुष्ण.

UP, *adv. aloft, on high.* वर, वरता, वरती *or* तीं *or* तें, ऊर्ध्व.

U. and down. उंचसाल, सालवर, वरसाल.

U. and down. इकडेतिकडे.

2 *out of bed.* उठलेला, निजून उठलेला.

3 *in a state of approaching.* कडे, जवळ.

4 *up the coast.* वर, उपर, वरता, वरती, वरतें.

5 to ; *to the whole amount.* भर (in comp. as शेरभर, तोळाभर, कोसभर, हातभर, घटकाभर).

6 to ; v. UNTIL. वर (as आजवर, उद्यांवर, &c.), पर्यंत.

7 to ; *to the degree of.* वर, (as पायलीवर) पर्यंत.

This adverb is much used to modify verbs. The student will in many cases find it under the verb which it modifies. Where he does not thus find it, he must look to a synonyme.

To UPBRAID, *v. a. reproach,* v. To BLAME, To ABUSE. निंदणें, निंदा *f.*-&c. करणें *g. of o.* तोंडीं काढणें, ओंठावणें, नाकांत काड्या *f. pl.* घालणें, टोला *m.*-टोमणा *m.*-&c. मारणें-देणें.

UPHILL, *a.* v. DIFFICULT. छातीफोड,दगडफोड,गडघेणा,डोंगरघेणा.

To UPHOLD. See To SUPPORT.

UPHOLSTERER, *n.* खुर्च्या पलंग वगैरे सामान पुरवणारा.

UPHOLSTERY, *n.* खुर्च्या पलंग वगैरे सामान *n.*

UPLAND, *n.* माळजमीन *f* पठार *f.*

UPON, *prep.* वर, वरता, वरती *or* तीं *or* तें, उंचीं, उपरि.

2 *in consequence of, on occasion of, on, after.* वर, वरून.

3 *relating to, about, concerning.* वर, विषयीं, संबंधीं,प्रकरणीं, स *or*ला (as मी काहीं कामाला आलों आहें I have come upon some business).

UPPER, *a. higher in place.* वरचा, वरला, वरील, उपर (in comp. as उपरमाडी), उपरिस्थ, ऊर्ध्वस्थित, ऊर्ध्वस्थ, वैला, उपरितन.

2 *higher in dignity, &c.* v. SUPERIOR. वरचा, वरला, मुख्य, प्रधान.

UPPER-HAND, *n.* v. SUPERIORITY. उपरदवडा *m.* उपर *m.*

To get the u. of. आपलादशक*m.*चढवणें, जबर-शेर-&c.होणें.

To have the u. मात्रा *f.* वर असणें *g. of s.*

That has the u. of. शिरजोर.

UPPERMOST, *a.* सर्वांच्यावरचा-वरला-&c. सर्वोपरिस्थ.

2 See SUPERIOR.

UPRIGHT, *a. erect.* उभा, सताड, तरतरीत *or* तरतरीत उभा, सडक.

Bolt u. उभासोट.

2 v. JUST, HONEST. नेकीचा, न्यायी, सरल *pop.* सरळ, सरळमार्गी, न्यायनिष्ठ, ऋजु *pop.* उजू, परनिष्ठ, रहारास्त. [&c.

UPRIGHTLY, *adv.* v. A. 2. नेकीनें, नेतीनें, न्यायानें, सरळपणानें,

UPRIGHTNESS, *n.* v. A. 1. उभेपणा*m.*सडकपणा *m.* तरतरितपणा*m.*

2 सरळपणा *m.* प्रमाणिकपणा *m.* न्यायीपणा *m.* &c नेकी *f.* नेत *f.* सचवटी *or* सचोटी *f.* न्यायनिष्ठा *f.* सरलता *f.* सारल्य *n.* अपैशुन *n.*

UPROAR, *n. clamour, outcry, hubbub, racket, noisy disturbance, &c.* गलगल *f.* गलबल *f.* गलका *m.* गलगा *m.* गलबला *m.* गलगला *m.* गबगब *f.* गबगबा *m.* गडबड *f.* गरदी *f.* गूल *f. m.* गूलगलबा *m.* हूल *f.* हाकहूल *f.* हाल्हूल *f.* हूलचाल *f.* कहा *m.* कोलाहल *m.* कोल्हाळ *m.* कल्लोळ *m.* कुलूली *f.* बोंब *f.* बोंबाबोंब *f.* रोराण *n.* हुलड *or* हुल्लड *f.* बेदा *or* बेहेदा *m.* हगामा *m.* घोळ *m.* ब्रह्मघोळ *m.* घोर *m.* हाकाटा *m. dim.* हाकाटी *f.* खणका *m.* दंगा *m.* ठांका *m.* गजाल *f.* जनरव *m.*—*intens.* गलबलाट *m.* कलकलाट *m.* गलगलाट *m.* कुलकुलाट *m.* गोंगाट *m.* कोकाट *m.*महागगजाल*f.*

To make an outrageous uproar. घर *n.* डोईवर घेणें, धिंगडणें, गरदी*f.* करणें. Some terms and phrases for *A place of uproar,* corresponding with *Bear-garden, Riot-hall, Racket-court, Babel, Bedlam, &c. &c.* are बलबलपुरी *f.* लमघर *n.* बाजार *m.* बाजारवाडा *m.* बाजारघर *n.*

UPROARIOUS, *a. clamorous.* गलगल्या, गलबल्या, गोंगाट्या, कलकलाट्या.

2 *full of noise.* See NOISY.

To UPROOT, v. *a.* मुळासुद्धां उपटणें.

To UPSET, *v. a. overturn.* उलटवणें, उलटणें, उलंडणें, उपरंडणें, उफराटणें, उफरांडणें, उलटा-उफराटा-&c. करणें, कलंडणें, कलथणें, लवंडणें, पाडणें, पासला पाडणें, कलथी *f.* देणें.

To UPSET, *v. n.* उलटणें, उलंडणें, लवंडणें, उपरंडणें, उफराटणें, उफरांडणें, कलथणें, उल्हावणें, उल्हाव*adv.*लागणें-जाणें,पासला पडणें.

UPSHOT, See RESULT, CONSEQUENCE. [अधोमुख.

UPSIDE-DOWN, *a.* उलटा, पालथा, उपडा, उपडी, उफराटा, सालवर,

2—with implication of disorder or derangement, v. TOPSYTURVY. उलटापालट *or* उलथापालथा, उलटपालट, उलटासुलटा, उफराटासुफराटा.

UPSIDE-UP, *a.* उलथा, उत्तान *pop.* उताणा, सुफराटा.

UPSTART, *n. one suddenly raised from low life.* नवाबाबू *m.* नवाश्रीमंत, अधव्याचा, अध्व्यावरचा, आजकालचा.

UPWARD, UPWARDS, *adv. toward a higher place.* वर, वरती, वरलेकडे, आकाशाकडे, ऊर्ध्व esp. in comp.

2 *more than.* वर, पुढें, अगळा in comp. अधिक.

URBAN, *a. belonging, &c. to a city.* शहरी, नगरी, शहरचा, नागर, नगरीय, नागरीय, नागरिक, पौर.

URBANE, *a. courteous,* v. CIVIL. बोलूनचालूनचांगला-भला, गृहस्थगिरीचा, माणुसकीचा.

URBANITY, *n.* v. A. *and* CIVILITY. माणुसकी *f.* गृहस्थगिरी *f.* गृहस्थपणा *m.* सौजन्य *n.* शिष्टता *f.*

URCHIN, *n.* v. CHILD. पोरटा *m.* हडीबाग *m.* ठेंगू *m.*

URETER, *n.*—in anatomy. नळी *f.* मूत्रनलिका *f.*

URETHRA, *n.*—in anatomy. मुताची वाट *f.* मूत्रमार्ग *m.* मुताटणें*n.* मूत्रद्वार *n.* मूत्रपथ *m.*

To URGE, *v. a. press, push, goad.* निकड *f.* लावणें-करणें, नेट *m.* देणें, ताण *m.* देणें, ओढ *f.* देण, टुमणी *f.* देणें, डोंचणें, डबचळणें, आर *f.* लावणें, ताधराबणें, तांतडबणें, खटावणें, टाचवणें, दपटणें, दामटणें, पिटवणें, घायताबणें, आग्रह *m.* करणें, गांजणें, तड *f.*-तांतड *f.*-तांतडी *f.* लावणें-करणें, उटाबणी *f.*-घाई *f.*-चुळचूळ *f.*-घायकूत *f.*-&c. करणें, गळ *m.*-गळग्रह *m.* घालणें, चिथावणें, तगादा *m.* करणें-लावणें.

2 *press importunately,* v. To HANG UPON. गळीं पडणें *or*

लागणें, गळग्रह *m.* घालणें, गळचिपीस-&c. बसणें, खपाटीस-&c. बसणें *or* लागणें, झुटहूट *f.*-झुलहूल *f.*-&c. लावणें.

3 on or upon. लोटणें.

URGENCY, *n.* v. A. 1. निकड *f.* जरुरी *f.* तांतड *f.* तांतडी *f.* अडचण *f.* नेट *m.* ताण *m.* गरज *f.* लावतोड *f.*

URGENT, *a. pressing with necessity.* निकडीचा, जरुरीचा, तगाद्याचा, तांतडीचा, घाईचा, त्वरेचा, नेटाचा, नेटबाजीचा, आग्रहाचा.

2 See URGING.

URGENTLY, *adv.* v. A. निकडीनें, तांतडीनें.

2 See IMPORTUNATELY.

URGER, *n.* URGING, *p. a.* v. A. 1. दपटणारा, दामटणारा, घायतावणारा, पिटवणारा, निकड लावणारा, आर लावणारा, &c. घायकुत्या, झुलझुल्या, खपाट्या.

2 *and* IMPORTUNATE. गळीं पडणारा, गळचिपीस बसणारा, आग्रह करणारा, &c. आग्रही.

URINAL, *n.* मुतायाचें तस्त *n.*-गाडगें *n.*-भांडें *n.*

URINARY, URINOUS, *a. belonging, &c. to urine.* मुताचा, मूत्राचा, मूत्रविषयक-संबंधी.

URINE, *n.*—the animal fluid. मूत्र *pop.* मूत *n.* इराकत *or* खत *f.* लघ्वी *f.* पिसाब *m.* मुतवणी *n.* लघुशंका *f.*

Discharge of u. मूत्रोत्सर्ग *m.*

Milky u. मूत्रशुक्र *n.*

Passing of blood in u. रक्तप्रमेह *m.* (*pop.* रक्तपरमें *n.*).

Passing mucous u. लालामेह *m.*

Person morbidly affected in u. प्रमेही, प्रमेहित.

Scalding of u. मूत्रदाह *m.*

Smelling &c. of u. मुतट, मुतेरा.

Suppression of u. मूत्राघात *m.* मूत्ररोध *m.* मूत्रावरोध *m.* मूत्रस्तंभ *m.* मूत्रस्तंभन *n.* मूत्रनिरोध *m.*

Urinary affection,—gener. मूत्रदोष *m.* मूत्रकृच्छ्र *n.* मेह *or* प्रमेह *m.* (There are twenty one varieties). मेहनशूल *m.* मूत्रघात*m.*

Urinary calculus. मुतखडा *m.*

White or furfuraceous sediment in u. खर *f.* खराई *f.*

To URINE, *v. n.* मुतणें, इराकत *or* खत *f.*-लघ्वी *f.*-लघुशंका *f.*-मूत्रोत्सर्ग *m.*-मूत्रविसर्जन *n.*-मेहन *n.*-&c. करणें,—copiously, चळचळां *or* चळाचळ *or* चुळचुळ *adv.* मुतणें, फळफळ *or* ळां *or* फळाफळ *adv.* मुतणें, फळफळणें, फसफस *or* सां *or* फसाफस *adv.* मुतणें, फसफसणें.

Pain in urining. मेहनशूल *m.*

That urines constantly. मुतरा, मुतीर.

To want to u. मुतायास लागणें *in. con.* [मूत्रचिकित्सा *f.*

URN, *n.* v. POT. चंबू *m.*

UROCRISIA, UROSCOPIA, *n. inspection of urine.* मूत्रपरीक्षा *f.*

URSA MAJOR, *n.*—the constellation. सप्तऋषि *or* सप्तर्षि *m. pl.*

USAGE, *n.* v. TREATMENT. वर्त्तणूक *f.* वागणूक *f.* व्यापार *m.*

2 *practice,* v. CUSTOM. वहिवाट *f.* धारा *m.* धारापेंडोळा *m.* धारेपेंडोळें *n.* रिवाज *m.* व्यवहार *m.* मामूलवहिवाट *f.* शेरा *m.* आचार *m.* आचरण *n.*

3 (of words) *usus.* रूढी *f.* वृत्ति *f.*

USE, *n.* v. V. A. 1.—*act.* वहिवाटणें *n.* वापरणें *n.* &c. वहिवाट *f.* व्यापार *pop.* वापर *m.* [&c. असणें.

To be in u. कामांत-व्यापारांत-वापरांत-वहिवाटींत-कामावर-

To be not in u. वहिवाटीवेगळा *or* निराळा-रिकामा-&c. असणें.

To be in constant or much u. घसवटणें.

To bring into u. घसवटीस *or* घसवटी खालीं घालणें-आणणें-लावणें. [ळणें.

To come into u. घसवटीस-घसवटीखालीं-&c. पडणें-येणें, रु-

To make u. of. v. To USE. कामावर लावणें.

2—*act.* v. PRACTICE. अभ्यास *m.* वहिवाट *f.* सराव *m.*

Skill or ease through u. खांद *m.* सराव*m.* कसरत *f.*

To grow or go out of u. पडीं पडणें.

To be in general u. वहिवाट *f.*-चाल *f.*-रीति *f.*-संप्रदाय *m.*-प्रघात *m.*-प्रचार *m.*-&c. असणें *g. of s.*

I. v. USEFULNESS. काम *n.* उपयोग *m.*

To come of u. कामावर-कामास पडणें-येणें.

II. *occasion for,* v. NEED. काम *n.* प्रयोजन *n.* उपयोग *m.* गरज *f.* दरकार *f.*

To USE, *v. a. employ, apply to a purpose.* कामास-कामावर-कामीं-&c. आणणें-लावणें-घालणें, व्यापारणें *pop.* वापरणें, व्यवहारणें, वहिवाटणें, वागवणें, वहिवाट *f.*-व्यापार *m.*-&c. करणें *g. of o.* उपयोग *m.* घेणें-करणें *g. of o.* Note. This word will often be best rendered by a verb which indicates the particular mode of use, as to use bad words *i. e. to speak* them ; to use clothes, *i. e.* to *wear* them; to use water for drink, *i. e.* to *drink* water.

2 *do or observe customarily,* v. To PRACTISE. अभ्यास *m.* करणें-राखणें-बाळगणें *g. of o.* वहिवाट *f.*-&c. ठेवणें *g. of o.* अभ्यासणें.

3 *habituate,* v. To ACCUSTOM. अभ्यास *m.*-&c. करवणें-पाडणें-लावणें, वहिवाटणें, रांबवणें, घसवटीखालीं-&c. आणणें.

4 v. To TREAT. वागणें, वर्त्तणें, वागणूक *f.*-वर्त्तणूक *f.*-चाल *f.*-&c. करणें Note. *The above words are intransitive and require* शीं-प्रत-वर-&c. *of o.* वापरणें.

5 v. To ENJOY. भोग *m.*-उपभोग *m.*-भोगवटा *m.*-संभोग *m.*-&c. करणें-घेणें *g. of o.* तसलमात *f.* करणें, उपभोगणें, भोगणें.

6 *bring under wear and tear, bring into use.* वापरणें, घोळणें, राबवणें, वहिवाटीस-वहिवाटींत-वहिवाटीखालीं-घसवटीस-घसवटीखालीं-&c. घालणें-लावणें- आणणें.

7—esp. in dietetics, *take, try.* घेणें, सेवणें, सेवन *n.*-उपसेवन *n.*-सेवा *f.*-&c. करणें. *g. of o.*

8 *employ upon, consume by employment.* खर्च *m.*-&c. करणें *g. of o.* खर्चणें, खलास करणें, सारणें, खपवणें, संपवणें, अटोपणें, अटपवणें, लावणें.

To USE, *v. n. be wont or accustomed.* वहिवाट *f.*-चाल *f.*-रीति *pop.* रीत *f.*-संप्रदाय *m.*-सवई *f.*-&c. असणें *g. of s.* This word is very idiomatically rendered by the habitual perfect tense either of a single verb or of the verb असणें combined with another verb, as जेव्हां काम पडे तेव्हां तो जाई *or* जात असे. [व्यवहृत, व्यापृत.

USED, *p.* v. V. A. 1. कामास लावलेला, वापरलेला, वहिवाटलेला,

3 वहिवाटलेला, वापरलेला, रहाटलेला, रुळलेला, राबलेला, अभ्यस्त.

To be u. to. अभ्यास *m.*-वहिवाट *f.*-सराव *m.*-खांद *m.*-सवई *f.*-&c. पडणें-असणें-लागणें *in. con.* रांपणें, राबणें, रुळणें, रहाळणें, रहाटणें, संवकणें.

4 वापरलेला, वागवलेला.
5 भोगलेला, &c. उपभुक्त, भुक्त.
6 बहिवाटींत आणलेला, घसवटलेला, &c.
7 घेतलेला, सेवलेला, सेविन, उपसेवित.
8 खर्चलेला, &c. खलास, समाप्त.
To be u. होणें, खलास होणें, संपणें, अटपणें, सरणें.

USEFUL, *a.* v. ADVANTAGEOUS. कामाचा, उपयोगाचा, कार्याचा, हिताचा, उपयोगी, उपयुक्त, उपकारी, उपकारक, कामी, कारणी, कारणीक.
To become u. कामावर-कामास-उपयोगी-उपयोगास-&c. येणें-[पडणें.

USEFULNESS, *n.* v. A. *and* ADVANTAGE. उपयोग*m.* उपयोगीपणा *m.* कामीपणा*m.* काम*n.* उपयुक्तता*f.* उपयोगिता*f.*

USELESS, *a.* अनुपयोगी, निरुपयोग, निरुपयोगी, उपयोगानिराळा-वेगळा, कामानिराळा-वेगळा, निकामी, निष्कारण, अकारण, अकारणी, निष्कारणी, उपयोगहीन-रहित-&c. अनुपयुक्त, अप्रयोजक, अन्यथासिद्ध, अकामी, नाकारा, नठारा, निरर्थक, टाकवणा, गयाळ.
To become u. कामांतून जाणें.

USELESSNESS, *n.* v. A. अनुपयोगीपणा*m.* निरुपयोगीपणा*m.* &c. अनुपयोग*m.* निरुपयोग*m.* अनुपयोगिता*f.* निरुपयोगिता*f.* उपयोगराहित्य*n.* उपयोगहीनता*f.* आनर्थक्य*n.* उपयोगाभाव*m.*

USHER, *n.* *introducer, &c.* परवानगीबरदार, नकीब, अर्जबेगी, छडीबरदार, छडीदार, भालदार, प्रवेशक.
2 *under teacher.* पंतोजीचा हस्तक-हस्तक्या, उपशिक्षक, उपगुरु.

To USHER. See To INTRODUCE.

USUAL, *a.*v. CUSTOMARY, COMMON. चालीचा, रीतीचा, रिवाजाचा, रहाटीचा, बहिवाटीचा, शिरस्त्याचा, प्रचाराचा, &c. व्यावहारिक *pop.* व्यवहारीक, यथापद्धति, यथासंप्रदाय, यथारीति, प्रायिक.

USUALLY, *adv.* v. A. बहुधा, बहुतकरून, बहुशः, प्रायः.

USUALNESS, *n.* v. A. व्यवहारिकपणा*m.* चाल*f.* रीत*f.* रिवाज*m.* रहाटी*f.* प्रचार*m.* प्रायिकता*f.*

USUFRUCT, *n.* *temporary use and enjoyment.* भोग*m.* भोगवटा *m.* उपभोग*m.* फलभोग*m.* भुक्ति*f.*
To have the u. of. भोगणें.

USUFRUCTUARY, *n.* *person who has the usufruct.* भोग-उपभोग-भोगवटा-फलभोग-&c. करणारा-घेणारा-&c. भुक्तिकरणारा.

USURER, *n.* *lender of money on usury.* व्याजखाऊ, व्याजखोर, सूदखाऊ, वृद्धिजीवी, वार्द्धुषिक, वृद्ध्याजीव.
Grinding u. खिस्ती, आठबडकरी *or* आठबडेकरी.

USURIOUS, *a.* *belonging to usury, comprehending usury.* व्याजी, व्याजू, व्याजाचा, सवृद्धिक.
2 See USURER.

To USURP, *v. a.* *seize and hold without right.* बळकावणें, बळकावून घेणें, दपटणें, दपटून-रगडून-&c. घेणें, बलाक्रांत करणें.
2 (the throne). राज्य*n.*-गादी*f.*-&c. बळकावणें-दपटणें-&c. राज्यापहार*m.*-&c. करणें *g. of o.*

USURPATION, *n.* v. V. 1. बळकावणें*n.* दपटणें*n.* &c.
2 राज्यबळकावणें*n.* &c. राज्यापहार*m.* राज्यापहरण*n.*

USURPER, *n.* USURPING, *p. a.*v. V. बळकावणारा, दपटणारा, &c.
2 राज्यबळकावणारा, &c. राज्यापहारी, राज्यापहार*m.*-&c. कर्ता-कारी-&c.

USURY, *n.* v. INTEREST. व्याज*n.* वार्धुष्य*n.*
Grinding u. खिस्तीचें व्याज*n.*
2 *practice of taking interest.* व्याजखोरी*f.* वृद्धिजीविका*f.*

USUS, *n.* v. USE. रूढी*f.* वृत्ति*f.*

UTENSIL, *n.* *vessel,* v. POT. भांडें*n.*
Culinary u. पाकपात्र*n.* पाकभांड*n.*
Culinary utensils compreh. or indef. *pots and pans.* हांडीभांडीं *n. pl.* हंडींमडकीं *n. pl.* हंड्यामडक्या *f. pl.*
Utensils (of hard ware) as fit to be broken up. तोडमोड *or* मोडतोड*f.* मोड*f.*
2 See INSTRUMENT, TOOL.

UTERINE, *a.* *of or belonging to the womb.* गर्भाशयाचा, गर्भकोशाचा, गर्भाचा, गार्भ, यौन.
U. tympany. गर्भवायु *m.*
2 *of the same womb.* सहोदर, एकोदर, सोदर, समानोदर, एकयोनि, समयोनिसंभव, सहज.

UTERUS, *n.* v. WOMB. गर्भकोश *m.* गर्भाशय *m.*

UTILITY, *n.* v. USEFULNESS. उपयोग *m.* उपयोगिता *f.*

UTMOST, UTTERMOST, *n.* *highest degree,* v. HEIGHT, EXTREME. पराकाष्ठा*f.* परममर्यादा*f.* बेहद्द*f.* सीमा*f.* हद्द*f.* निदान *n.*
At the u. निदानीं, कृतावस्था.
2 *extreme part of,* v. EXTREMITY. शेवट *m.* सरशेवट *m.*

UTMOST, UTTERMOST, *a.* *at or of the extremity,* v. EXTREME. शेवटचा, कडेशेवटचा, सरतेशेवटचा.
2 *of the highest degree,* v. EXCESSIVE. पराकाष्ठेचा, परममर्यादेचा, परमावधीचा, आत्यंतिक, अतिशयित, अतिमात्र.

UTTER, *a.* v. COMPLETE, PERFECT. पुरता, पूर्ण, परिपूर्ण.

To UTTER, *v. a.* *express, pronounce,* v. To SPEAK. उच्चारणें, बोलणें, म्हणणें, उद्गारणें, उच्चार *m.*-उद्गार *m.*-&c. करणें *g. of o.*
2 *divulge, declare,* v. To TELL, To PUBLISH. उच्चारणें, बोलणें, सांगणें, बदणें, तोंडावाटे काढणें, ओंठाबाहेर काढणें.
3 *put or send into circulation.* चालवणें, वापरणें.

UTTERABLE, *a.* v. V. 1. उच्चारायाजोगा-सारखा-&c. उच्चारणीय, उच्चार्य, बचनीय, वाच्य.
2 बोलाया-सांगाया-&c. जोगा-सारखा.

UTTERANCE, *n.* v. V. 1. *and* SPEECH.—*act.* उच्चारणें*n.* उच्चार*m.* उच्चारण *n.* उद्गार *m.* उल्लेख *m.* Of the phenomena of *Utterance* two divisions are made, viz. *Internal acts or movements,* आभ्यंतर प्रयत्न; and *External acts.&c.* बाह्यप्रयत्न. And four stages are supposed, viz. *The first stirring of the breath,* परा *f.* *The faint whispering at the breast,* पश्यंती *f.* *The access to the organs of speech,* मध्यमा *f.* and *Articulate utterance,* वैखरी *f.* An act or movement of the air (breath) towards the production of *Utterance* is termed प्रयत्न *m.* Simple or unaspirated *Utterance* is अल्पप्राण *m.* Full, forcible, or aspirated *Utterance* is महाप्राण *m.*
Difficult of u. दुर्वच.

UTTERED, *p.* v. N. 1. उच्चारलेला, उच्चारित, वादित, जिव्हारूढ.
To be u. clearly and distinctly. उटावणें.
2 सांगितलेला, बोललेला, बदलेला, तोंडावाटे काढलेला, &c.
To be u. वाणीवाटे निघणें.

UTTERER, *n.* UTTERING, *p. a.* v. V. 1. उच्चारणारा, &c. उच्चार-[&c. कर्ता-कारी.
2 बोलणारा, सांगणारा, तोंडावाटे काढणारा, &c.
3 चालवणारा, वापरणारा.

UTTERLY, *adv.* v. A. *and* WHOLLY. निस्तूक, निस्तोष, निपट,

निखालस, अगदीं.

UVULA, *n.*—in anatomy. पडजीभ *f.* प्रतिजिह्वा *f.* उपजिह्वा *f.* अधोजिह्विका *f.* तालुजिह्वा *f.* लोळा *m.* गलशुंडिका *f.* घंटिका *f.*

UXORIOUS, *a. that is doatingly fond of his wife.* बायकोचा बेडा-अळका-&c. बाईलवेडा, बाईलबुद्ध्या, स्त्रीवेल्हाळ, बायकोवेल्हाळ, स्त्रीबुद्धि, स्त्रीलंपट, स्त्रैण, भार्यासक्त, जायासक्त, भार्यालंपट, &c.

UXORIOUSNESS, v. A. बायकोचें वेड *n.* बाईलवेडेपणा *m.* भार्यासक्ति *f.* जायासक्ति *f.* &c.

V.

V. This letter has no other representative in Maráthì than व which is common to it and W.

VACANCY, *n.* v. A. 1. रिकामेपणा *m.* शून्यता *f.*

2 रिकामेपणा *m.* खालीपणा *m.* &c.—of a throne. अस्वामिकत्व *n.* अनायकत्व *n.* अराजकत्व *n.*

3 रिकामेपणा *m.* रिकामपणा *m.* &c. फुरसत *f.* अवकाश *m.*

4 अविचारीपणा *m* विचारलक्षणराहित्य *n.*-शून्यता *f.*-&c.

I. *void space.* शून्य *n.*

II. *place or office unoccupied.* रिकामी-&c. जागा *f.*-असामी *f.*

VACANT, *a. void,* v. EMPTY. रिकामा, शून्य.

2—an office or post; *unoccupied.* खाली, रिकामा, रिकामका, रिता, मोकळा,—esp. a throne. अराजक, अस्वामिक, अनायक.

3 *unoccupied with business.* रिकामा, रिकामका, फुरसतीचा, अवकाशाचा, फावतीचा, रिकामपणाचा.

4 *indicating want of thought.* अविचाराचा, विचाराभावाचा, विचारलक्षणशून्य-हीन-&c.

To VACATE, *v. a. quit possession of, make vacant.* रिकामा-रिता-खाली-&c. करणें-करून देणें, सोडणें, सोडून जाणें, टाकणें, टाकून जाणें.

2 See To ABROGATE.

VACATION, *n. freedom from occupation,* v. LEISURE. अवकाश *m.* रिकामपणा *m.* रिकामणूक *f.* रिकामकी *f.*

2 *recess of courts, &c.* खेळणी *f.* खेळी *f.* सुटी *f.*

VACCARY, *n. cow-house.* गोठा *m.* गायवाडा *m.* गोष्ठ *n.* गोस्थान *n.* गोशाला *f.*

2 *cow-pasture.* गायरान *n.*

To VACCINATE, *v. a.* v. To INOCULATE. देवी *f. pl.* काढणें, फोड्या *f. pl.* काढणें. The Maráthás do not distinguish between the cowpox and the small pox.

VACCINE, *a. belonging, &c. to cows.* गाईचा, गाईविषयींचा, गव्य, गोसंबंधी, गोविषयक.

To VACILLATE. See To WAVER. 2 See To HESITATE.

VACILLATION, *n.* v. V. 2 *and* HESITANCY. धरसोड *f.* धरसांड *f.*

VACUIST, *n. one who holds the doctrine of a vacuum.* शून्यवादी.

VACUITY, *n.* v. EMPTINESS. रिकामपणा *m.* शून्यता *f.*

2 *space unfilled.* रिकामीजागा *f.* पोकळी *f.* भोंगळी *f.*

VACUOUS. See EMPTY.

VACUUM, *n. space unoccupied by matter.* शून्य *n.*

VAGABOND, VAGRANT, *a. wandering, that has no settled home.* हिंडफिऱ्या, ढुण्या, भटक्या, भटकभैरव, परागंदा, जाता-पळता, उडाणटप्पू, अलाणटप्पू, घरनादाराचा, बिन घरादाराचा, बिन ठिकाणाचा, अशुद्धवासक.

V. and rakish, टवरी.

To play the v. उनाडणें, हिंडणवारे *m. pl.* करणें, and, *inversely,* लागणें.

VAGABONDRY, VAGABONDIZING, VAGRANCY, *n. wandering, state and life of a vagabond.* उनाडकी *f.* हिंडणवारे *m. pl.* भटकेपणा *m.* हिंडफिरीवृत्ति *f.*

Dissolute v. टवरकी *f.* टवरचाल *f.*

VAGARY, *n. wild freak, &c.* लहर *f.* तरंग *m.* हुक्की *f.* वेड *n.*

VAGUE, *a. indefinite,* v. INDETERMINATE. मोघम *or* मोहगम, पळपळीत *or* पुळपुळीत, पुळपुळा, अरळतरळ, संजाइती, संजाईत, संजाइतपणाचा, अलबेला, अभोगत, सवडीचा.

VAGUELY, *adv.* v. A. मोघम *or* मोहगम, पळपळीत, अळमटळम, अरळतरळ, संजाइतपणाचा *decl.* अभोगती, सवड टेवून.

VAGUENESS, *n.* v. A. मोघमपणा *m.* पळपळितपणा *m.* संजाइतपणा *m.* &c. अन्न *n.* अळमटळम *n. f.*

VAIL, &c. See VEIL, &c.

VAIN, *a. unavailing,* v. FRUITLESS, INEFFECTUAL. व्यर्थ, वृथा, पोकळ, कोरडा, भाकड, वांझा, वावंडा, वावगा, वाव, निरर्थक, लटका, असार, मोघ.

Born in v. वृथोत्पन्न.

In v. व्यर्थ, वृथा, मुधा.

2 *unreal, shadowy, &c.* v. EMPTY. रिकामा, रिकामका, रिता, रिक्त, पोकळ, निरर्थक.

3 *ostentatious, vainglorious, &c.* v. CONCEITED, PROUD. गुमानी, दिमाखी, पतरासी, अभिमानी, अहंकारी, डौल्या, डामडौल्या, फुशारखोर, बढाईखोर, अवडंबऱ्या, आडंबरी, दर्शनीयमानी, अभिमानाचा, &c.

VAIN-GLORIOUS, *a.* v. CONCEITED, PROUD. गुमानी, दिमाखी, दिमाखाचा, बुटटकीचा, बुटटक्या, बुटटकीमिरव्या.

VAIN-GLORY, *n.* v. CONCEIT, PRIDE. अभिमान *m.* गुमान *m.* फुशारकी *f.* बुटटकी *f.* तोरा *m.* शेखी *f.* पत्राज *f.*

To exhibit or manifest v. फुशारकी *f.* मिरवणें-मांडणें-करणें, बुटटकी *f.* मिरवणें-करणें.

VAINLY, *adv.* v. A. 1. व्यर्थ, उगा, वांत्र *or* वात्रा *or* वायां, वृथा, नाघाणी *or* नी.

2 उगा, उगीच, उगीचचेउगीच, एरवी, पोकळ.

3 अभिमानानें, गुमानानें, बुटटकीनें, शेखीनें, &c.

VAINNESS, VANITY, *n.* v. A. 1. पोकळपणा *m.* कोरडेपणा *m.* &c. व्यर्थता *f.* वैयर्थ्य *n.* निरर्थकता *f.*

2 रिकामेपणा *m.* रितेपणा *m.* पोकळपणा *m.* &c. निरर्थकता *f.*

Big swelling words of v. अनागोंदी बोलणें *n.*-भाषण *n.*-&c. चटक्याचे मांडव *m. pl. v.* घाल.

4 *and* CONCEIT. अभिमान *m.* गुमान *m.* दिमाख *m.* फुशारी *f.* फुशारकी *f.* फुशारखोरी *f.* बढाई *f.* बुटटकी *f.* शेखी *f.*

VALE. See VALLEY. [स्तिवचन *n.*

VALEDICTION, *n. farewell.* जातेवेळचा आशीर्वाद *m.* प्रास्थानिकस्व-

VALEDICTORY, *a.* v. N. जातेवेळच्या आशीर्वादाचा, प्रास्थानिकाशीर्वादात्मक.

VALET, *n. servant who attends on one's person.* खवास, खिदमतगार *or* दार, हुजऱ्या, अंतिक.

VALETUDINARY, VALETUDINARIAN, *n.* v. SICKLY, INVALID.

जन्मरोगी, सदारोगी, पिंडरोगी, कुरणेकरी, दुखाळू, किळसा, किळोशी, किडक्या, अधमकिडा.

Valiant, *a. brave*, v. Bold. जवानमर्द, मर्दाना, पराक्रमी, वीर्यवान्,गाढा, दाढा, शौर्यशाली, पराक्रमशाली, विक्रमशाली.

Valiantly, *adv.* v. A. मर्दाईनें, बहादुरकीनें, पराक्रमानें, पराक्रमेंकरून, &c. विक्रमपूर्वक, &c. विक्रमतः.

Valid, *a. sound, cogent, just, &c.* बळकट, जोराचा, प्रबल, दृढ, सबल, वज्रप्रमाणक.

2 *good in law, having legal force.* व्यवहाराचा, उपयोगी, व्यवहारोपयोगी, व्यवहारसमर्थ, व्यवहारसाधक.

Validity, *n.* v. A. 1. बळकटपणा*m* बळकटी*f.* प्राबल्य*n.* प्रबलता*f.* 2 व्यवहाराचा उपयोगीपणा *m.* व्यवहारोपयोगिता *f.* व्यवहारसामर्थ्य *n.* &c.

Valley, *n. hollow between hills.* दरा *m. f. dim.* दरी *f.* खोरा *m.* खोरी *f.* खोरें *n.* खोंडा *m.* आड *f.*

2 *plain bordering on a river.* थडी *f.* थड *f.* Used in composition with the name of the river, as गंगथडी the valley of the Godavery, भिमथडी, निरथडी, &c. the valley of the Bheema, Nira, &c.

Valorous. See Valiant.

Valour, *n.* v. Boldness. जवानमर्दी *f.* मर्दाई *f.* शर्तमर्दी *f.* बहादुरकी *f.* शौर्य *n.* पराक्रम *m.* विक्रम *m.*

Acquired by v. शौर्योपार्जित.

Valuable, *a.* v. Precious, Worthy. किमतीचा, मोलाचा,मोठेकिमतीचा, मोठ्यामोलाचा, मोठेयोग्यतेचा, महामूल्य, जड.

Valuation, *n.* v. V. 1. किम्मतठरवणें *n.* मोलठरवणें *n.*

Value, *n. worth, price.* किम्मत *f.* मोल *n.*

2 *estimation, importance, excellence.* किम्मत *f.* योग्यता *f.* हिशेब *or* हिशोब *m.* पाड *m.* केवा *m.* रया *f.* लेखा *m.* मान *n.m.* बिशात *f.* The six last words are used chiefly *with a neg. con. or implic.*

To **Value**, *v. a. rate at a price, appraise.* किम्मत *f.*-मोल *n.*-&c. लावणें-ठरवणें-करणें.

2 *rate highly, hold in estimation, make great account of.* गणणें, मेजणें *or* मोजणें, लेखणें, मानणें, चांगला-उत्तम-&c. समजणें-जाणणें-धरणें, विचारणें, पुसणें. [डे ठेवणें.

To v. exceedingly. सातांपड्यांच्या-सातांकाळजांच्या पलीक-

To be valued by. गणना *f.* असणें *g. of s.with* जवळ *of o.*

Valueless. See Worthless.

Valve, *n. folding door.* दुतलफी-दुझडपी-&c. द्वार *n.*

2 *lid or cover to open in one direction and close in another.* कळीचदार *n.* जिव्हाळी *f.*

To **Vamp**, *v. a piece with something new.* नवाजुना करणें.

Van, *n. front of an army.* अघाडी *f.* बिनी *f.* फौजेचा-&c. मोहरा *m.* फौजेचें-&c. तोंड *n.*

General or officer of the v. बिनीवाला.

V. and rear. अघाडी पिछाडी *f.*

To stand (and fight) in the v. तोंडीं लागणें.

Van-guard, *n.* बिनी *f.*

Vane, *n.* वायूची गति दाखविणारा पदार्थ *m.*

To **Vanish**, *v. a. pass from sight, be lost, &c.* v. To Disappear. नाहींसा-नदिसेसा-दिसेनासा-अदृश्य-&c. होणें, उडणें, सडकणें, गप्प-गयब-&c. होणें, अंतर्धान *n.*-तिरोधान *n.* पावणें.

Vanished, *p.* v. V. नाहींसा झालेला, &c. अंतर्हित, तिरोहित.

Vanity. See Vainness.

To **Vanquish.** See To Conquer.

Vantage, Vantage-ground. See Superiority.

Vapid, *a. dead, spiritless*, v. Flat. फिका *or* फिक्का, बेकम, बाकम *or* बाकूस, पाणचट, पचपचीत, पचकळ, पचरट, मळमळीत *or* मुळमुळीत, उमळा, उंबळा, निरस, विड्ळ.

Vapidness, Vapidity, *n.* v. A. फिकेपणा *m.* बेफसपणा *m.* पाणचटपणा *m.* &c.

Vaporous, Vapory, *a. full &c. of vapours.* बाफेचा, बाष्पमय, बाष्पप्रचुर, बाष्परूप.

Vapour, *n. steam, fume.* बाफ *f.* बाष्प *n.* स्वेद *m.*

2 See Mist.

Vapours. See Melancholy.

To **Vapour**, *v. n.* v. To Boast, To Bluster. तमतमणें, तमणें, तम *m.* गाणें, तमाच्यागोष्टी *f. pl.* सांगणें, बल्गना *f.* करणें.

Variable, *a.* v. Changeable. फेरफाराचा, चंचल *or* ळ, अस्थिर.

Variableness, *n.* v. A. चंचळपणा *m.* चांचल्य *n.* अस्थिरता *f.*

Variance, *n. dissimilarity*, v. Difference. अंतर *n.* भेद *m.* तफावत *f.* तकराळ *f.* वैजात्य *n.* द्वैध *n.* द्वैविध्य *n.*

2 *discord*, v. Disagreement. वांकडें *n.* नपड *f.* बेघनाव *m.* वैमनस्य *n.* विपट *n.* विनुष्ट *n.*

Variation, *n.* v. Change. फेर *m.* भेद *m.* पालट *m.*

2 See Difference. 3—in grammar. विभक्ति *f.* रूपांतर *n.*

To **Variegate**, *v. a. diversify in external appearance.* विचित्र-चित्रविचित्र-नानारंगी-बहुरंगी-&c.करणें.

Variegated, *p.* v. V. विचित्र, चित्र, चित्रविचित्र, चित्रगत, बहुरंगी, कबरा, कर्बूर, शबल, कसरा, सारंग.

Variegation, *n. diversity of colors.* विचित्रपणा*m.* बहुरंगीपणा*m.* विचित्रता *f.* वैचित्र्य *n.* रंगानैक्य *n.*

Variety, Variousness, v. A. 1. चित्रविचित्रपणा*m.* नानाविधपणा*m.* &c. विविधता *f.* विचित्रता *f.* &c.

2 विचित्रपणा*m.* &c. विचित्रता *f.* चित्र*n.*

I. (as of a species or kind). भेद*m.*

II. *many and different kinds.* This sense is best rendered by the use of some adjective for *various* with the noun required; ex. a variety of turbans नानातऱ्हेचीं पागोटीं, a great v. of fruits बहुतप्रकारचीं फळें, &c.

Various, *a. manifold, multiform, divers, sundry.* चित्रविचित्र, विचित्र, परीप्रकारचा, परोपरीचा, तऱ्हेतऱ्हेचा, परीपरीचा, भांतीभांतीचा, अनेक, अनेकतऱ्हेचा, अनेकप्रकारचा, अनेकजातीचा, नानातऱ्हेचा, नानाप्रकारचा, नानाजातीचा, नानाविध, बहुविध, अनेकविध, नानाजातीय, विविध, चतुर्विध, पृथग्विध, बहुप्रकार, विजातीय, जिन्नसवार, ऐलपैल, नाना.

2 v. Variegated. विचित्र, चित्रविचित्र.

Variously, *adv.* v. A. 1. *in various ways.* अनेकतऱ्हेनें-रीतीनें-प्रकारानें-&c. *or* तऱ्हांनीं-रीतींनीं-&c. परोपरी, परीप्रकारें, नानाप्रकारें, बहुप्रकारें, भांतीभांती *or* भांतोभांती, नानाविध,बहुविध, अनेकविध, अनेकधा.

Varlet. See Blackguard.

Varnish, *n.*—the glossy liquid used by painters and others. रोगण*n.* लुकण *or* लुकूण*n.* लुकडन.

Coating of v. रोगण*n.* लुकण*n.*

2 fig. *cover, gloss,* v. EMBELLISHMENT. लावा*m.* अर्थवाद*m.* टीका*f.* [रणें.

To VARNISH, *v. a.* v. N. 1. रोगण*n.*-&c. लावणें-देणें-चढवणें-क-
2 *and* To EMBELLISH. बनावणें, तिखटमीठ*n.* लावून सांगणें, लावालावी*f.* करणें.

VARNISHED, *p.* v. V. 1. रोगण लावलेला, &c. रोगणी.

To VARY, *v. a.* v. To CHANGE. फिरवणें, पालटणें, फेरफार*m.* करणें, रूपभेद*m.*-रूपांतर*n.*-&c. करणें *g. of o.*

To VARY, *v. n.* v. To CHANGE. फिरणें, पालटणें, फेरफार*m.*-&c. होणें *g. of s.*

2 *be dissimilar,* v. To DIFFER. भेद*m.*-फेर*m.*-फेरफार*m.*-&c. असणें *g. of s. recip.* भिन्न-&c. असणें.

2 *depart from, deviate.* अंतर*n.*-फरक*m.*-&c. पाडणें, अंतर*n.*-फरक*m.*-&c. असणें *g. of s.* न्यूनाधिक्य*n.* असणें *g. of s.*

VASCULAR, *a. consisting, &c. of vessels.* नाड्यांचा, नाडीमय, नाडीविशिष्ट.

VASE, *n.* POT. चंबू*m.* माठ*m.*

VASSAL, *n. feudatory.* जाहागीरदार, मोकासदार, मांडलिक.

2 *dependent, subject.* रयत *f.* प्रजा *f.* ताबेदार, कूळ*n.*

3 See SLAVE.

VASSALAGE, *n. state of dependence.* रयतपणा*m.* रयतावा*m.* ताबेदारी *f.* अधीनता *f.* वशता *f.*

VAST, *a. huge, immense,* v. LARGE. फारमोठा, कुब्बल, ऐवट, औजड, गरिष्ठ, अवाढव्य, अफाट, विषकट.

VASTLY, *adv.* v. VERY. फारच, अतिशय.

VASTNESS, *n.* v. V. कुब्बलपणा*m.* ऐवटपणा*m.* औजडपणा*m.*&c.

VAT, *n.* मोठें पीप*n.*

VATICINATION. See PROPHECY.

VAULT, *n. continued arch.* वाढवलेली कमाण*f.* घुमट*m.* मेघडंबरी *f.* डेरा *m.* कटाह *m.*

2 *cellar.* भुयार *n.* तळघर *n.*

3 *repository for the dead.* शवालय *n.* शवागार *n.*

4 See LEAP.

To VAULT. See To LEAP. See To ARCH.

To VAUNT, *v. n. brag,* v. To BOAST. फुशारी *f.*-शेखी *f.* मिरवणें, शेखीच्या-तमाच्या-&c. गोष्टी *f. pl.* सांगणें, वल्गना *f.* करणें.

To VAUNT, *v. a. brag of,* v. To BOAST. बढाई *f.*-मोठाई *f.*-पडप *n.*-प्रतिष्ठा *f.*-&c. सांगणें-मिरवणें *g. of o.*

VAUNT, VAUNTER. See BOAST, BOASTER.

VAUNT-MURE, *n.* पडभिंत *f.* धूळकोट *m.*

VEAL, *n.* वांसराची सागुती *f.* गोवत्समांस *n.*

VEDA. See SCRIPTURE.

To VEER, *v. n. change direction.* फिरवणें, वळणें, तोंड *n.* फिरवणें, दिशा *f.* पालटणें.

To v. about. कोंडाळणें, घोंटाळणें, गोंधळणें.

VEGETABLE, *n.* v. PLANT. औषधी *f.* वनस्पति *f.*

2—esculent. भाजी *f.* तरकारी *f.* शाक *f. n.*

Apparatus for slicing vegetables, &c. मांजरी *f.*

Fruit-v. *v. bearing esculent fruit.* फळभाजी *f.* फळशाक*f.*

Leaf-v. *v. of esculent leaf.* पालेभाजी *f.* पत्रशाक *f. n*

Vegetables—compreh. or laxly. भाजीपाला *m.* शाकपाला*m.* शाकभाजी *f.*

V. (plants, leaves, roots, fruits, &c.) dressed. भाजी*f.*

V. dressed up with flour. पिठरडी भाजी *f.*

V. dried. पळवा *m.*

V. sliced and dried. उसरी *f.* काचरी *f.*

V.—hotch potch. सर्वशाक *f.*

V.—slitter or slicer. इळी *f.*

Wild esculent v. रानभाजी *f.*

VEGETABLE, *a. belonging, &c. to plants.* वनस्पतीचा, औषधीचा, वनस्पतिसंबंधी-विषयक, वनस्पतिसंभव.

To VEGETATE, *v.n. germinate, grow as plants,* v. To SPROUT. मोड *m.*-अंकुर *m.*-कोम *m.*-&c. येणें-फुटणें *in. con.* फुटणें, अंकुरणें, मुळापानाची वाढ *f.* होणें *g. of s.* मुळापानाची वाढ *f.* धरणें.

VEGETATION, *n.* v. V. मोडफुटणें *n.* &c. मुळापानाची वाढ *f.*

I. *plants in general.* गवतझाड *n.* हिरवळ *f.* तृणजात *n.* मूलजात *n.* तृणादिजाति *f.* झाडझुडपें *n. pl.* झाडझाडोरे *m. pl.*

Luxurious or wild v. रान *n.* जंगल *n.*

Overrun with wild v. जंगलगर्क.

VEHEMENCE, *n.* v. A. 1. जोर *m.* बळ *n.* झपाटा *m.* तडाखा *m.* कडाका *or* खा *m.*

2 *mental violence, ardor, fervor.* आवेश *m.* तलखली *f.* तलखी *f.* कडकपणा *m.* खमशेपणा *m.* कडकी *f.*

VEHEMENT, *a. very forcible,* v. VIOLENT. जोराचा, झपाट्याचा, तडाक्याचा, &c. जाज्वल्य, प्रचंड, चंड, जबर, जबरदस्त.

2 *ardent, fervent, eager, &c.* v. IMPETUOUS. तलख, खमक्या, खमशा, खंदा, कडक, तलखल्या, आवेशी, उष्ण.

VEHEMENTLY, *adv.* v. A. 1. जोरानें, झपाट्यानें, तडाख्यानें, &c. कडकडून, कडकावून, कचकावून, कचकून.

2 तलखीनें, तलखलीनें, कडकपणानें, आवेशानें, &c. आवेशपूर्वक.

VEHICLE, *n. instrument or means of conveyance,* v. CARRIAGE. वहन *n.* वाहन *n.* यान *n.*

Horse-v. अश्वयान *n.*

Man-v. नरयान *n.*

2—in medicine. अनुपान *n.*

3 See MEDIUM.

VEHICULAR, *a. belonging, &c. to a vehicle.* वाहनाचा, &c. वाहनसंबंधी, वाहनविषयक.

VEIL, *n.* v. CURTAIN. आडपडदा *m.*

2 *cover for the face.* बुरका *or* खा *m.* बोखारा *m.* घुंगट *n.* टाकर *f.* ओढणी *f.*

3 *cover, cloak,* v. DISGUISE. पडदा *m.* आडपडदा *m.* तिरोधान *n.* व्याज *m.*

To VEIL, *v. a.* (the face). बुरखा *m.*-घुंगट *n.*-&c. घालणें-घेणें-ओढून घेणें, टाफर *f.* घालणें-घेणें.

VEIN, *n.*—in anatomy. शिरा *pop.* शीर *f.* नस *m. f.* नाड *f.* नाडी *f.* इडा *f.* धमनी *f.* रक्तवाहिनी *f.*

That has varicose or dilated veins. शिराळ.

2 (of a leaf, a fruit, &c.). शिरा *pop.* शीर *f.*

3 *variegating line,* v. STREAK. दोरा *m.* शिरा *pop.* शीर *f.*

4 *temper, mood.* वृत्ति *f.* भाव *m.* [शिष्ट.

VEINED, VEINY, *a. having veins.* शिराल *pop.* शिराळ, शिराविFull-v. शिराळ.

To VELLICATE, VELLICATION. See To TWITCH, TWITCH.

VELOCITY, *n.* v. SWIFTNESS. वेग *m.* जव *m.*

VELVET, *n.*—the silk stuff. मखमल *or* मखमाल *f.*

VELVET, *a.* मखमली, मखमलींचा.

VENAL, *a. mercenary.* लांचखाऊ, लांचखोर, लालचखोर, लालची, लांचखोरीचा, लांचलुचपतीचा, लांचलुचीचा, लिद्बळ.

2 *of or belonging to a vein.* शिरेचा, शिरेंतला, शिरासंबंधी-विषयक. [लांचलूच *f.*

VENALITY, *n.* v. A. 1. लांचखोरी *f.* लालचखोरी *f.* लांचलुचपत *f.*

VENARY, VENATIC, *a. relating to hunting.* शिकारी, शिकारीचा, शिकारीविषयींचा, पारधीचा.

To VEND, *v. a.* v. To SELL. विकणें, विक्रय *m.*-&c. करणें *g. of o.*

VENDER, *n.* v. V. विकणारा, विक्या in comp. विक्रेता.

VENDIBLE, *a.* v. V. विकाया जोगा-&c. पण्य, विक्रेय.

To VENEER, *v. a. inlay thin leaves of wood.* फर्दजोडणी *f.* करणें.

VENERABLE, *a.* v. V. पूज्यबुद्धीनें मानायासारखा-&c. आर्य, आदरणीय, अर्घ्य, पूजनार्ह, पूजार्ह, पूजनीय, पूज्य, नमस्य, उपास्य, अर्च्य, अर्चनीय, मान्य, माननीय, श्रद्धेय, गुरु, बुद्रुख, अभियुक्त.

VENERABLENESS, VENERABILITY, *n.* v. A. मान्यता *f.* पूज्यता *f.* आर्यता *f.* &c. थोरवी *f.* गरिमा *m.*

To VENERATE, *v. a.* v. To REVERE. पूज्यबुद्धीनें-&c. मानणें, आदरणें, उपासणें, बूज *f.*-आदर *m.*-मान *m.*-&c. राखणें-ठेवणें *g. of o.* आदर *m.*-&c. करणें *g. of o.*

VENERATION, *n.* v. REVERENCE. पूजाबुद्धि *f.* आदरबुद्धि *f.* उपासनाबुद्धि *f.* मान्यताबुद्धि *f.* श्रद्धा *f.*

VENEREAL, *a. pertaining, &c. to sexual intercourse.* संभोगाचा, रतीचा, मैथुनाचा, &c. मैथुनसंबंधी-विषयक, रतिसंबंधी-विषयक.

2—disease. उपदंशाचा, गरमीचा, बीसनखीचा.

V. disease, v. LUES VENEREA. उपदंश *m.* गरमी *f.* दुःस *n.*

V. ulcer. भग *n.*

VENERY, *n.* v. HUNTING. शिकार *f.* मृगया *f.*

2 *sexual enjoyment,* v. COPULATION. संभोग *m.* रति *f.* रतिक्रीडा *f.* रतिसुख *n.*

Provocative to v. वाजीकरण *n.*

VENESECTION, *n.* v. PHLEBOTOMY. शीरतोडणी *f.* शिरामोक्ष *m.*

To perform v. शीर *f.*-शिरा *f.* काढणें-घेणें-सोडवणें.

VENETIANS, *n.*—the windows. झिलमिळ्या *f. pl.*

VENGEANCE, *n. revenge. retribution.* प्रतिफल *n.* प्रतिक्रिया *f.* प्रतीकार *m.* प्रतिहिंसा *f.* वैरबुद्धि *f.* वैरोद्धार *m.* निर्यातन *n.* कुसर *or* कुसूर *m.*

To take v. v. To REVENGE. सूड *m.* उगवणें-घेणें, कुसर *or* कुसूर *m.* काढणें-उगवणें-घेणें.

I'll have v. नरडीचा घोट घेईन, नरडीचें रक्त पिईन, नरडी फोडीन, पाणी पाजीन (तुला, त्याला, &c.).

With a vengeance. This phrase is well rendered by अनर्थ *m.*-एकगजब *m.*-&c. मांडणें, शर्त *f.*-धूम *f.* पराकाष्ठा *f.*-&c. करणें; Ex. त्यानें मारण्याचा अनर्थ मांडला He beat with a v. [खुनसी, कुचर.

VENGEFUL, *a. revengeful,* v. MALICIOUS. अकसखोर, अकसी,

VENIAL, *a.* v. PARDONABLE. क्षमा करायाजोगा-सारखा-&c. उपेक्षणीय, क्षमार्ह, लघु, उप in comp. [मृगमांस *n.*

VENISON, *n. flesh of the deer.* हरणाची सागुती *f.* हरणाचें मास *n*

VENOM, *n.* v. POISON. विष *n.* विखार *pop.* विखार *m.* जहर *n.* गरल *n. pop.* गरळ *n. f.* हलाहल *or* हालाहल *n.* कालकूट *n.*

2 See MALICE. [गरळी, विषालु.

VENOMOUS, *a.* v. POISONOUS. विखारा, विखाराचा, गरली *pop.*

VENOMOUSNESS, *n.* v. A. 1. विखारपणा *m.* विषार *pop.* विखार *m.* विषालुता *f.*

VENOUS, *a. contained, &c. in a vein.* शिरेचा, शिरेंतला.

VENT, *n. aperture, passage, spiracle,* v. OPENING. द्वार *n.* द्वार *n.* दरवाजा *m.* उच्छ्वास *m.* वाट *f.*

To give v. to. See To VENT.

2—esp. for water. उघडी *f.* दार *n.* दारें *n.* निकाल *m.*

3 v. SALE. खप *m.*

To VENT, *v. a. let out, pour forth, &c.* सोडणें, मोकळा-&c. करणें, काढणें, रस्ता *m.* करणें, वाटे लावणें.

To VENTILATE, *v. a. expose to the free passage of the air.* वारा *m.* सोडणें-घेणें-देणें, वाऱ्याचा संचार होईसा करणें.

2 v. To WINNOW. वारावणें, वाऱ्यास देणें.

3 v. To DISCUSS. वाटाघाट *f.*-घाटाघाट *f.* करणें *g. of s.*

VENTILATION, *n.* v. V. 1. वारा घेणें *n.* &c. वारा देणें *n.* &c.

VENTILATOR, *n.* वाऱ्याचा संचार करविण्याचें यंत्र *n.*-साधन *n.*

VENTRAL, *a. belonging to the belly.* पोटाचा, पोटांतला, औदरिक, उदरस्थ, कौक्ष.

VENTRICLE, *n.* रक्ताशयांतला खोलगा *m.*

VENTRILOQUISM, *n. the art of speaking as from a distance.* गारुडवाणी *f.* ऐंद्रजालिकवाणी *f.* वाणीगारुड *n.*

VENTURE, *n.* v. HAZARD, DANGER. जोखीम *n.* खत्रा *m.*

2 *hazardous business.* जोखीम *n.* जोखमाचें काम *n.*-&c.

At a v. तबकलताल्यानें.

To VENTURE, *v. n. run the hazard.* जोखीम *n.* पतकरणें-उचलणें-स्वीकारणें-आंगावर घेणें *or* आणणें, पदरीं बांधणें, तबकल *f.* करणें.

2 v. To DARE. धमक *f.*-हिम्मत *f.*-&c. असणें *in. con.*

To VENTURE, *v. a. expose to hazard.* जोखमांत-भयांत-खत्र्यांत-&c. घालणें-पाडणें-ठेवणें, नसीबावर-दैवावर-अदृष्टावर-&c. टाकणें-हवालणें-सोंपणें, अदृष्टाधीन-दैवाधीन-&c. ठेवणें.

VENTURESOME, VENTUROUS, *a.* v. ADVENTUROUS, BOLD. साहसी, साहसिक, साहसबुद्धि.

VENUS, *n.*—in mythology. रति. She is the wife of कामदेव the Hindu Cupid.

Hottentot v. पसाळपार्वती *f.*

2—the planet. शुक्र *m.* कवि *m.* [निख.

VERACIOUS, *a.* v. TRUE. खरा, सत्य, सत्यभाषी, सत्यवचनी, पर-

VERACITY, *n.* v. A. *and* TRUTH. खरेपणा *m.* खराई *f.* सत्य *n.* इमान *n.* प्रामाण्य *n.*

VERANDA, *n.*—the kind of portico. ओसरी *f.* पडवी *f.* पडसार *f.* पडओसरी *f.* पडशाला *f.* पडाळी *f.* ओटी *f.*

VERB *n.* क्रियापद *n.*

Active v. सकर्मक क्रियापद.

Neuter v. अकर्मक क्रियापद.

Passive v. कर्मणि क्रियापद.

Causal v. प्रेरण क्रिया *f.*

Form of a v. क्रियारूप *n.* धातुरूप *n.* आख्यात *n.*

Root of a v. धातु *m.*

Subject of a v. क्रियाश्रय *m.*

Table of verbs. धातुपाठ *m.*

VERBAL, *a. expressed by words,* v. ORAL. शब्दाचा, वचनाचा, शब्दद्वारक, वाचक, वाचिक, वाचनिक.

2 *of or belonging to words.* शब्दाचा, शब्दाविषयींचा, शब्दसं-

बंधी, शब्दविषयक, शाब्द, शाब्दिक.

3 *literal*. शब्दाशब्दाचा, समपद, पदानुपदिक, शब्दरूप.

4—in gram. धातुसाधित. [रा, शब्दतः.

VERBALLY, *adv.* v. A. 1. शब्दानें, वचनानें, वाक्यानें, &c. शब्दद्वा-

VERBATIM, *adv. word for word.* शब्दाशब्द, शब्दानशब्द, शब्दशः, अक्षरशः.

VERBOSE, *a. prolix, &c.* v. TEDIOUS. शब्दविस्ताराचा, शब्दपाल्हाळाचा, शब्दाधिक्याचा, अतिशयोक्तीचा, पाल्हाळीक, अतिशयोक्तिविशिष्ट.

VERBOSITY, VERBIAGE, *n.* v. A. शब्दविस्तार *m.* शब्दपाल्हाळ *m.* अतिशयोक्ति *f.* बहुभाषिता *f.*

VERDANT, *n. covered with green grass or plants.* हिरवळीचा, निळवटीचा, सबजीचा.

VERDICT, *n.* (as of a jury) v. DECISION. फैसला *m.* तजवीज *f.* निवाडा *m.* निर्णयपाद *m.*

VERDIGRIS, *n. rust of copper or brass.* कळंक or कळंक *m.* जंगल *m.* जंगला *m.* जंगाल *m.*

Affected by v.—food, a pot, &c. कळंकट.

To be affected by v.—a substance cooked, a vessel, &c. कळंकणें, कळंकटणें, कणकणें.

VERDURE, *n. greenness of vegetation.* निळवट *f.* हिरवळ *f.* हिरवट *f.* सबजी *f.* ओलवत *f.*

VERGE, *n. rod of authority.* छडी *f.* दंड *m.*

2 *brink, border,* v. EDGE. कांठ *m.* किनारा *m.* कड *f.* मर्यादा *f.*

To VERGE, *v. n. tend, incline, approach.* झुकणें, कलणें, झोक *m.* -रोख *m.*-&c. असणें *g. of s.* घरांत असणें *g. of o.* (Ex. तो सत्तरच्या घरास आला आहे *or* घरांत आहे he is verging on 70).

VERGER, *n.* v. MACE-BEARER. छडीबरदार, दंडी.

VERIFICATION, *n.* v. V.—*act.* खरा करणें *n.* &c. सत्यंकार *m.* सत्यंकृति *f.* सत्यंकरण *n.* सत्यापन *n.*

VERIFIED, *p.* v. V. खरा करून दिल्हेला, &c. प्रतीत, ध्रुव.

To VERIFY, *v.a. prove to be true,establish, &c.*v.To CONFIRM, To PROVE. खरा-सत्य-शाबूत-&c. करून देणें, सत्यंकार *m.*-सत्यंकरण *n.*-&c. करणें *g. of o.* प्रतीति (*pop.* प्रचीति *or* प्रचीत) *f.* -प्रत्यय *m.*-&c. आणून देणें *g. of o.*

To be verified. प्रचीतीस-प्रतीतीस- प्रत्ययास-&c. येणें.

VERILY, *adv. really, truly.* सत्य, खराच, खरें, खरोखर, वास्तवीक, खचीत, अवश्य, भावार्थ, कीर, सई *or* सही.

VERITABLE, VERITY. See TRUE, TRUTH.

VERJUICE, *n.* आंबट फळांपासून काढलेला सिरका *m.*

VERMICELLI, *n.*—in cookery. शेवई *f.* (*or* शेवया *f. pl.*) कुरडई *f.* कुरवडी *f.* बळवट *n.*

Fragment of v. शेवखंड *n.*

V.—made upon a board. पाटशेवई *f.*

V.—made with the hand. हातशेवई *f.*

Vessel for taking out v. शेवगा *m.* [सदृश.

VERMICULAR, *a. like, &c. a worm.* कृमीसारखा, कृमिवत्, कृमि-

V. motion. तृणजलूकागति *f.*

VERMIFORM, *a.* कृमिरूप. [*n.* कृमिघ्न *n.* कृमिहरन.

VERMIFUGE, *n. medicine to expel worms.* जंत पाडायाचें औषध

To administer a v. जंतावर-जंताचें द्यावें.

VERMILION, *n.*—factitious. हिंगुळ *pop.* हिंगूळ *m.* हिंगुळूक *m.* शिंगरूप *or* ब *m.* दरद *m.*

VERMILION, *a.* v. A. हिंगुळी, हिंगुळाचा.

VERMIN, *n. small destructive animals or insects.* किडमुंगी *or* किडामुंगी *f.* किडेगिडे *or* बिडे *or* कुडे *m. pl.* कीड *f.* विंचूकांटा *m.* किडापतंग *m.* जीवजिवडा *m.* जीवजिवाणूं *n.* जीवजंतु *m.*

VERNACULAR, *a.* v. NATIVE. देशी, मुलखी.

V. language. देशभाषा *f.*

VERNAL, *a. belonging, &c. to spring.* वसंती, वसंतऋतूचा, वासंत.

VERSATILE, *a. variable, unsteady,* v. CHANGEABLE. चंचल *or* ळ, अस्थिर.

2 *that can turn with ease from one subject to another.* अष्टावधानी, अष्टावध, दशावधानी, चपलबुद्धि, चपलमति, अनेकबुद्धि.

VERSATILITY, *n.* v. A. चंचळपणा *m.* चांचल्य *n.* अस्थिरता *f.*

2 अष्टावधपणा *m.* &c. चपलबुद्धि *f.* बुद्धिचापल्य *n.*

VERSE, *n. metrical line.* चरण *m.* पद *m. n.*

2 *metrical composition,* v. POETRY. कविता *f.* कवन *n.* पद्य *n.*—measured by time, जाति *f.*— syllabic, वृत्त *n.*

Blank v. मुक्तप्रास *m.*

Prose and v. गद्यपद्य *n.*

3 (of a poem, song, &c.), श्लोक *m.* कडवें *n.* ओवी *f.*

4 *short division of a prose composition.* ओवी *f.* has been introduced into Maráthi by translators.

VERSED, *a. skilled, &c.* v. EXPERIENCED. अभ्यासी,अभ्यस्त, निविष्ट, निपुण, निष्णात, परिज्ञाता, अभिज्ञ, विचक्षण, कृतकर्मा, कुशल, खबरदार, कसबी, वाकबगार.

To be v. कसणें, घटणें, घसवटणें, निभणें, कटणें.

VERSEDNESS, *n.* v. A. अभ्यास *m.* आलोड्य *n. pop.* आलोढ्य *n.* घसवट *f.* वाकबगारी *f.* नैपुण्य *n.* निवेश *m.* परिज्ञान *n.* वासना *f.*

VERSIFICATION, *n.* v. V. N. *and* POESY. पदरचना *f.* श्लोकरचना *f.* पद्योजना *f.* काव्यरचना *f.* काव्यकरण *n.*

To VERSIFY, *v. n. make verses.* पदरचना *f.*-पद्योजना *f.*-श्लोकरचना *f.*-&c. करणें.

To VERSIFY, *v. a. turn into verse.* पद्यांत-श्लोकांत-&c. उतरणें, श्लोक *m. pl.*-कविता *f.*-&c. बांधणें-करणें *g. of o.* श्लोकांनीं-&c. उतरणें.

VERSION, *n.* v. TRANSLATION. भाषांतर *n.* [तर *n.* पाठभेद *m.*

2 fig. *variation of statement.* ग्रंथ *m.* पाठ *m.* ग्रंथांतर *n.* पाठां-

This is his v. तो हा ग्रंथ सांगतो.

VERTEBRAL, *a. pertaining, &c. to the joints of the spine.* मणक्यांचा, मणक्यांविषयींचा, पृष्ठवंशग्रंथिसंबंधी-विषयक.

VERTEBRE, *n. a joint of the spine.* मणका *m.* पृष्ठवंशग्रंथि *m.* वलय *n.*

VERTEX, *n.* v. TOP. शिर *n.* माथा *m.*

2 v. ZENITH. ऊर्ध्वदिशा *f.* ऊर्ध्व *m.* [समध्यस्थ.

VERTICAL, *a. that is in the zenith.* माथ्यावरचा, डोक्यावरचा,

A v. circle. दृग्वृत्त *n.* दृग्वलय *n.* दृष्टिमंडल *n.*

The prime v. समवृत्त *n.* सममंडल *n.* [समनर *m.*

Sine of the sun's altitude at the prime v. समशंकु *m.*

2 *perpendicular.* ऊर्ध्वाधर.

VERTICALLY, *adv. right down.* शेव.

Vertically & horizontally. ओतप्रोत.

VERTIGO, *n. dizziness.* v. GIDDINESS. घेरी *f.* भोवळ *f.* भोवंड *f.* गिरकी *f.* गिरगिरी *f.* मिरगी *f.* झीट *f.* तव *or* तवर *f.*

Very, *a. true*, v. Real. खराच, सत्य, वास्तविक, इत्थंभूत.

2 *mere, pure, unmingled.* केवल or ळ, शुद्ध *pop.* सुद्धा, नुस्था or स्ता or निस्था.

2 *same*,—emphat. तोच, हाच.

Very, *adv. in a great degree.* बहुत, फार, अति, अतीव, अतिशय, अत्यंत, मोठा (Ex. मोठा बळकट, &c.), भारी, पुष्कळ, लय, पराकाष्ठेचा *decl.* पराकाष्ठा, परम, सु (in comp. as, सुदूर, सुदुर्लभ, सुदुश्चर, सुदुःसह).

Vesicle, *n. pustule, bladder.* फोडm. पुळी *f.* पुटकळी or कुळी *f.*

Vesicular, Vesiculous, *a.* v. N. फोडाचा, पुटकुळयांचा.

Vesper, See Evening. [संध्या *f.*

Vespers, *n. evening service.* सांजचें भजनn. सायंभजनn. सायं-

Vespertine, *a. belonging, &c. to the evening.* सांजचा, संध्याकाळचा, सांध्य, सायंकालिक, सायंतन.

Vessel, *n. utensil for holding, receptacle,*—gener. भांडेंn. पात्रn. ठावकेंn. ठावलेंn. ठामणेंn. भाजनn. भांडn.

2 (of an animal body). नाडी *f.* वाहिनी *f.*

3 *ship or boat.* तारूंn. गलबतn. जहाजn. नाव *f.* नौका *f.* नौ *f.* तरणी *f.*तरणn. वाऱ्याचें घोडेंn.जलयानn.पुवm. Some descriptions of *vessels* are गुराब *f.* डंगी *f.* डाव m. डोंगाm. डोणी *f.* पगारm. पडावm. पालm. पागm. फतेमारी *f.* बगलाm. बजरा m. बतेलाm. बरकीण *f.* बल्यांवn. मचवाm. महागिरी *f.* मुमडाm. वाघी *f.*शिवाड *f.* सुबाळाm.सोंवळाm. or सोवळाm. होडी *f.* (*dim.* होडकी *f.* or होडकें or गेंn.).

Frame (as of bamboos) raising the sides of a v. पताइ *f.*

Passenger in a v. उतारी, उतारू, नौयायी.

Pole used in pushing a v. over shoals. ताज *f.*—man using it, ताजकरी.

Thatch over a v. खुडी *f.*

To prop up a v. (on shore). डेंकी *f.* देणें.

4 *jar, pitcher, &c.* v. Pot. भांडेंn. घटm. भांडn. घटी *f.* चंबूm. सुईर *f.* कुजाm. [भांडींn. *pl.*

Battered and worn metal vessels. नाळीक n. नाळीक

Broken v. फुटकरn.

Cost of forging metal vessels. बेठ *f.*

Hole worn in a metal v. नाळकेंn.

Squat or dumpy v.—gener. बुटकुलाm.

Vessels & pots—compreh. भांडीं कुंडींn. *pl.*

Wooden v. (as a dish or bowl). माढण or माढाणn. माणगेंn.

5—drinking vessel. तांब्याm. प्याला or पेलाm. पानपात्रn. उपपात्रn. चंबूm. सुरा *f.* चषकm. n. Some kinds are, अमृती *f.* अपकरा or आबखराm. कटोराm. जगन्नाथी *f.*जांब or जामm. तांबली *f.* or लेंn. पंचपात्री *f.* पितळी *f.* फुलपात्रn. रामपात्रn. वाटी *f.* *enhanc.* वाटगाm. सतेलn. संपुष्टm.

Copper drinking v.—compreh. तांब्यातांबली *f.* तांब्यातांबोटी *f.*

Vest, *n. outer garment, robe.* जामाm. झगाm.

2 *waistcoat.* कांचवाm. बंडी *f.*

To Vest. See To Invest.

Vestibule, *n.* v. Porch. देवडी or ढी or देहुडी *f.* ओटी *f.* ढेलज or ज *f.* देहली *f.*

Vestige, *n.* v. Trace. मागm. छडाm. पदांकm. पदचिह्नn.

Vestment, Vesture, *n.* v. Clothing, Clothes. पांघरुणn. वस्त्रn. प्रावरणn.

2 *habit*, v. Dress. वेषm. पेहरावm.

Vetch, *n.* कुळीत or थm. हुलगाm. हुलगी *f.*

Veteran, *a. long exercised, long practised*, v. Experienced. फार वापरलेला-वहिवाटलेला-&c. व्यवहारवृद्ध.

Veteran, *n.* फार दिवसांचा शिपाईm. जुना-वापरलेला-&c. शिपाईm.

Veterinary, *a. belonging, &c. to the treatment of the diseases of cattle.* जनावरांच्या वैद्यकीचा, पशुचिकित्सेचा, पशुचिकित्सासंबंधी-विषयक.

V. art or practice. जनावरांची वैद्यकी *f.* पशुचिकित्सा *f.*

V. surgeon. शालोत्री m. [नुमोदन n.

Veto, *n. prohibition.* सत्तेची मनाई *f.* निषेध m. प्रतिषेध m. अन-

To Vex, *v. a. irritate, provoke, disturb in mind*, v. To Anger. चेतवणें, खाजवणें, कांतावणें, खोड *f.*-खोडी *f.* काढणें-करणें, चाळवणें, सलसलावणें, संतापवणें, खपा-रुष्ट-&c. करणें, रुसवणें, मरजी *f.* मोडणें *g. of o.*

2 *plague, annoy, torment, &c.* v. To Trouble, To Tease. जाचणें, गांजणें, सतावणें, त्रासवणें, कांतावणें, उपद्रवm.-दुःखn.-तस्दी *f.*-इजा *f.*-&c. देणें, त्रास m. देणें, श्रमी-कष्टी-दिक्क-बेजार-&c. करणें.

Vexation, *n.* v. V. 1.—*act.* चेतवणें n. खाजवणें n. संतापवणें n. &c.—*state.* चिरड *f.* चीढ *f.* रुसवा m. रुष्टता *f.* रुष्टभाव m. खपीमरजी *f.* गैरमरजी *f.* इतराजी *f.* नाखुशी *f.* संताप m.

2 जाचणें n. गांजणें n. &c. त्रास m. श्रम m. इजा *f.* उपद्रव m. दुःख n. तस्दी *f.*

Vexatious, *a.* Vexer, *n.* Vexing, *p. a.* v. V. 1. चेतवणारा, संतापवणारा, खपा करणारा, खोड काढणारा, &c. खिजवणीचा, संतापक.

2 *and* Tiresome. जाचणारा, गांजणारा, त्रास देणारा, उपद्रव देणारा, &c. किचर, कुचर, किचरट, किचकट, खचरट, खडतड, खष्ट, क्लिष्ट, चिकीर, जीवघेणा or ण्या, त्रासदायक. [संकटें n.

A v. business or matter. लफडा m. लफडें n. लचांड n.

Vexatiousness, *n.* v. A. 1. चेतवणारेपणा m. &c. संतापकत्व n.

2 जाचणारेपणा m. खचरटपणा m. खडतरपणा m. त्रासदायकत्वn.

Vexed, *p.* v. V. 1. चेतवलेला, संतापवलेला, &c. खट्टी, खट्टा, खट्ट, खपा, खिन्न, रंजीस, नाखुश, खिशाणा, फिर्र, रुष्ट.

2 जाचलेला, गांजलेला, &c. श्रमी, कष्टी, दिक्क, बेजार, त्रस्त.

To be or become v. त्रासणें, श्रमणें, चिरडणें.

Vial, *n. small bottle.* शिशी *f.*कुपी *f.* [पक्वान्नn.

Viand, *n. meat dressed*, v. Food, Dish. खाणें n. पदार्थ m.

Delicate viands. मिष्टान्न n. स्वादन्न n.

Viatic, *a. pertaining, &c. to a way or a journey.* वाटेविषयींचा, मार्गाविषयींचा, सारणिक.

Viaticum, *n. provisions for a journey.* सिदोरी or शिदोरी *f.* भूकलाडू m. तानलाडू m. पाथेय n. फराळाचें n.तोशाm.सम्बलm.n.

To Vibrate, *v. n. quiver, &c.* v. To Tremble. कांपणें, लटलट-&c. हालणें, लटलटणें, डळमळणें, स्फुरणें, धमकणें, शिवशिवणें, शिवळणें, स्फुरण n.-&c. होणें *g. of s.*

2 *oscillate*, v. To Swing. झोलणें, आंदुळणें, झोके m. *pl.* खाणें.

Vibrating, *p. a.* Vibrative, *a.* Vibratory, *a.* v. V. 1. कांपणारा, लटलट हालणारा, &c. स्फूर्त.

2 झोलणारा, आंदुळणारा, &c. दोलायमान, आंदोलायमान.

VIBRATION, *n.* v. V. 1. कांपणें *n.* लटलटणें *n.* &c. स्फुरण *n.* स्फूर्त्ति *pop.* स्फूर्त *f.*

2 झोलणें *n.* आंदुळणें *n.* &c. झोका *m.* झोला *m.* आंदोलन *n.*

VICAR, *n.* v. SUBSTITUTE, DEPUTY. प्रतिनिधि, बारचा-बांटचा-&c. करणारा, नायब.

VICARIAL, VICARIOUS, *a. filling the place of another.* दुसऱ्याच्या बारचा-बांटचा-होत्साता, प्रतिनिधिस्वरूप, प्रतिनिधिरूप.

VICARIOUSLY, *adv.* v. A. दुसऱ्याच्या बारचा *decl.*-बांटचा *decl.*-&c. अंगत्वानें *or* अंगत्वें *or* अंगत्वेंकरून. [अनय *m.*

VICE, *n. moral evil.* अधर्म *m.* अनीति *f.* अन्याय *m.* अमार्ग *m.*

2 *depravity,* v. WICKEDNESS. दुराचरण *n.* अधर्माचरण *n.* पापाचरण *n.*

3 *a* v. *an habitual fault.* दुर्गुण *m.* अवगुण *m.* दुर्लक्षण *n.* खोड *f.* अयब *or* ऐब *m.* टेव *f.* लकब *f.* व्यसन *n.* छंद *m.* फंद *m.*

To take the v. out of, *thresh soundly.* गुण *m.* काढणें.

4 *iron press.* शेगडा *m.*

Hand v. हातशेगडा *m.*

5—in compos. See DEPUTY.

VICEGERENCY, *n. office, &c. of a vicegerent.* प्रतिनिधीपणा *m.* प्रतिनिधित्व *n.* प्रातिनिध्य *n.*

VICEGERENT, *n. vicar,* v. SUBSTITUTE, DEPUTY. प्रतिनिधि, बारचा-बांटचा-&c. करणारा, नायब.

VICENARY, *a. belonging, &c. to twenty.* विसांचा, विंशतिक.

VICEPRESIDENT, *n.* उपाध्यक्ष.

VICEROY, *n. substitute of a king.* राजप्रतिनिधि.

VICEROYALTY, *n.* राजप्रतिनिधीपणा *m.* राजप्रतिनिधित्व *n.*

VICINITY, *n.* v. NEARNESS. जवळपणा *m.* नैकट्य *n.* निकटवर्त्तित्व *n.*

2 *places near,* v. NEIGHBOURHOOD. शेजारचा देश *m.*-प्रदेश *m.* पडोसा *m.*

In the v. of. शेजारीं, पडोसीस, अडोशींपडोशीं, शेजारास, जवळपास, जवळसर.

VICIOUS, *a. corrupt, depraved,* v. WICKED. बाईट, बाईटचालीचा, दुष्ट, दुराचारी, हरामी.

2 *having vices, faults, tricks.* खोडकर, खोडाळ, खोडील, खोड्या, खोड्याळ, खोड्यारा, दुर्गुणी, अवगुणी, दुर्लक्षणी, व्यसनी, व्यसनीक, खट्याळ, नाटाळ *or* नाठळ *or* नाठाळ, अयबी *or* ऐबी, अयबदार *or* ऐबदार,—esp. of cattle, खडण, खडगळ,—esp. of horses, खंक, खाडू, खेंदडा.

To become v. नाटाळणें *or* नाठाळणें. [दुष्टता *f.*

VICIOUSNESS, *n.* v. A. 1. बाईटपणा *m.* दुष्टपणा *m.* असदाचरण *n.*

2 खोडकरपणा *m.* खोडाळपणा *m.* &c. नाटाळी *or* नाठाळी *f.* नाटाळकी *f.*

VICISSITUDE, *n.* v. SUCCESSION, ALTERNATION. अनुक्रम *m.* आनुपूर्वी *f.* अनुवृत्ति *f.*

2 v. CHANGE. फेर *m.* फेरफार *m.* पालट *f.* पालट *m.*

Vicissitudes (as of life, fortune, &c.). उलटापालट *or* उलथापालट *f.* रहाटगाडगें *n.* रहाटी *f.*

VICTIM, *n. animal slain or to be slain in sacrifice.* बळीचा पशु *m.* यज्ञपशु *m.* बलि *pop.* बळी *m.* [जेत्र.

VICTOR, *n. conqueror,* v. A. जयी, जिंकणारा, प्राप्तजय, जेता,

VICTORIOUS, *a.* v. TRIUMPHANT. जयवान् *pop.* जयवंत, जयी, विजयी, जयकर्त्ता.

2 *productive of victory.* जयावह, जयप्रद.

VICTORY, *n. winning, conquest, defeat of an enemy.* जय *m.* फते *f.* जित *f.* जीत *f.* जयश्री *f.*

Drum of v. जयदुंदुभि *m.* जयवाद्य *n.*

Flag of v. जयपताका *m.*

Flush or glow of v. जयश्री *f.*

March to v. जयप्रस्थान *n.*

Proclamation of v. जयघोष *m.* जयदुंदुभि *m.*

Record of v.—furnished by the defeated party. जयपत्र *n.* जितपत्र *n.* [हल *m.*

Shout of v. जयशब्द *m.* जयध्वनि *m.* जयरव *m.* जयकोला-

To get the v. लढाई *f.* जिंकणें.

VICTUAL, VICTUALS, *n. food.* अन्न *n.* खाणें *n.* भक्ष्य *n.* भोजन *n.* भक्षण *n.* अशन *n.* खाद *f.* आहार *m.*—compreh. खाणेंपिणें *n.* अन्नपाणी *n.* अन्नोदक *n.*

Broken v. उष्टीपाष्टीं *or* माष्टीं *n. pl.*

Distribution (to mendicants, &c.) of v. सत्र *n.* धर्मपोई *f.*

Dressed v. शिजलेलें अन्न *n.* सिद्धान्न *n.* पक्कान्न *n.*

Undressed v. सिधा *or* शिधा *m.* उलफा *m.* आमान्न *n.*

To VICTUAL, *v. a. stock with provisions.* अन्नाची-&c. बेजमी *f.* करणें-करून ठेवणें, गल्ला *m.* भरणें.

VICTUALLER, *n.* v. V. अन्नाची बेजमी करून ठेवणारा.

I. *keeper of an eating house.* भट्यारी *or* भटारी, भटारखान्याचा धनी.

VIDELICET, *adv. namely.* म्हणजे.

To VIE, *v. n.* v. To EMULATE, To RIVAL. बरोबरी *f.*-&c. करणें, तोलास तोल *m.* घेणें, सर *f.*-सरी *f.*-&c. लावणें, तुळणें, देखोदेखी *f.*-देखोवेखी *f.* करणें.

To VIEW, *v. a. inspect, survey, &c.* v. To SEE, EXAMINE. पाहणें, लक्षिणें, अवलोकणें, विलोकणें, टेहळणें, निरखणें, निरीक्षणें, वीक्षणें, अवलोकन *n.*- आलोकन *n.*-&c. करणें *g. of o.*

2 *survey intellectually,* v. To CONSIDER. पाहणें, विचार *m.*-आलोडन *n.*-&c. करणें *g. of o.*

3 *hold, regard,* v. To CONSIDER. धरणें, लेखणें, भावणें.

VIEW, VIEWING, *n.* v. V. 1.—*act.* पाहणें *n.* अवलोकणें *n.* &c. अवलोकन *n.* आलोकन *n.* आलोचन *n.* विलोकन *n.* दर्शन *n.* वीक्षण *n.*

2 पाहणें *n.* विचार *m.* आलोडन *n.*

I. *sight, reach of the eye.* दृष्टीचा-&c. अमल *n.*-टप्पा *m.*-&c. दृष्टि *f.* दृष्टिपात *m.* दृक्पात *m.*

II. v. PROSPECT. दृष्टीखालचा देश *m.* [द्धि *f.*

III. *intention,* v. DESIGN. उद्देश *m.* आशय *m.* मतलब *m.* बु-

IV. v. OPINION. मत *n.* मन *n.* समज *m.* समजूत *f.*

V.—as taken of a subject. कल्प *m.* पक्ष *m.*

In one point of v. *under one form of the case.* एकपक्षीं.

VIGIL, *n.* v. WATCH. जागरण *n.*

V. through the night. अलोचन जागरण *n.*

VIGILANCE, VIGILANCY, *n.* v. A. जागर *m.* जागरण *n.* उजागरा *m.* अनिद्रा *f.* अस्वाप *m.* निद्राभाव *m.* प्रबोध *m.*

2 जागतेपणा *m.* सावधपणा *m.* &c. सावधगिरी *f.* हुशारी *f.* सावधानता *f.*

VIGILANT, *a. wakeful, watchful.* जागरा, जागरूक, जागरणशील.

2 *watchful, wary.* जागा, जागता, जागृत, सावध, सावधान, हुशार, पगदस्त.

Vigilantly, *adv.* v. A. 2. सावधपणानें, सावधगिरीनें, हुशारीनें, &c. जपून, सावधानपूर्वक.

Vigor, Vigorousness, *n. physical force*, v. Strength. बल *pop.* बळ*n.* जोम *m.* कुवत *f.* बळावळ *f.*

2 *energy, power, active strength.* धमक *f.* धमकी *f.* वीर्य *n. pop.* ईर *f.* ऐवज *m.* तेज *n.* दम *m.* रस *m.* उत्साह *m.* औत्सुक्य*n.*

Vigorous, *a.* v. N. 1. *and* Strong. बळकट, बलवान्, सबल, जोमदार.

2 v. Energetic, Smart. उत्साही, उत्साहवान्, सोत्साह, उत्साहाचा, जिवट, तेजवान्, झपाट्या, कचक्या, कडकडीत, झपाट्याचा.

Vigorously, v. A. 1. बळानें, जोरानें, बळकरून.

2 *and* Smart. बळकट, बळकटून, कडक, झपाट्यानें, कडाक्यानें, उत्साहानें, उत्साहपूर्वक.

Vile, *a.*—of persons ; *base, mean, hateful.* बाईट, खट, खटनट, खल, द्वाड, द्वाडवाणा *or* णी, खडतर, खचरट, खंवचट, दुष्ट, हुष्ट, खराब, नष्ट, नष्टोळा, नाटाळ *or* नाठळ *or* नाठाळा, कुत्सित, कुटिल *pop.* कुटील, दुर्जन, अधम, पाजी, नीच, जघन्य, कुचाळ, कुटाळ, गदळ, कुधान *or* ण, हिडशा *or* सा, हिडीस, हेंदरा, घाणेरडा, मुरदाड *or* मुडदार, चंडाल *or* ळ *or* चांडाल *or* ळ, विजात, विजवटा, बजात, द्वेष्य.

2—of things; *execrable*, v. Worthless, Bad, Tiresome. बाईट, खराब, ओंगळ, घाणेरडा, ओखटा, गदळ, खकान, मुरदाड *or* मुडदार, कुत्सित, खचरट, खडतर, किचर, किचरट.

Vileness, *n.* v. A. 1. बाईटपणा *m.* दुष्टपणा *m.* खटपणा *m.* &c. नष्टाई *f.* नाटाळी *or* नाठाळी *f.* कौटिल्य *n.* कौत्सित्य *n.* दौर्जन्य*n.* दौष्ट्य *n.*

2 बाईटपणा *m.* ओंगळपणा *m.* ओखटेपणा *m.* &c.

Vilified, *p.* v. V. 1. अपवादित, अभिशप्त, विकत्थित, अपकृष्ट.

2 निंदलेला, हेटाळलेला, &c. निंदित, भर्त्सित.

To **Vilify**, *v. a. defame, traduce*, v. To Asperse. बदनामी *f.* करणें *g. of o.* कलंक *m.*-बट्टा *m.*-&c. लावणें, विकत्थन *n.*-अपकरणें *g. of o.* अपकर्ष *m.* करणें *g.ofo.* बाद *m.*-अभिशाप *m.*-&c. करणें *g. of o.* अपकर्ष *m.* करणें *g.ofo.*

2 *revile, vituperate*, v. To Abuse. निंदणें, हेटाळणें, भर्त्सणें, कैंडणें, कुटाळी *f.*-कुटाळकी *f.*-कुचाळी *f.*-कुचोद्य *n.*-हेटाळणी *f.*-निंदा *f.*-भर्त्सना *f.*-मानखंडना *f.*-मानहानि *f.*-&c. करणें *g. of o.*

Villa, *n. country house, &c.* बागेंतला वाडा *m.* बंगला *m.*

Village, *n. assemblage of houses less than a town.* गांव *m. n.* ग्राम *m.* मौजा *m.*

Annual propitiation of v.-*bhutas* by oblations.गांवसई *f.*

Close or dense v. भरगांव *m. n.*

Cluster of contiguous villages. पंचक्रोशी *f.*

Cluster of huts connected with a v. कोंड *m.* बाडा *m.* वाडी *f.* बाठार *m.*

Corn assigned for subsistence of a v.- officer. बलुतें *n.*

Corn &c. given on festivals to the twelve v.-officers. सणवई *f.* v. घाल, दे.

Cultivator holding land in one village while residing in another. पायकस्ता *m.* ओवंडेकरी*m.* ओवंडेकरू *m.* बाधेकरी*m.*

Current in the villages or country,—coin. गांवचलणी *or* नी, गांवचलन.

Division or distinct portion of a v. पट्टी *f.* वाडी *f.* आड *f.* वाडा *m.* बाठार *m.*

Gate of a v. बेस *f.*—Keeper of it. बेसकर *or* करी *m.*

The Eight offices or posts of a v. अष्टाधिकार *m.*

Hereditary v.-office and land-proprietary. मिरास *m.* म्हेतरकी *f.*

Hereditary v.-officer. मिरासदार, मिरासी, म्हेतर.

In the vicinity of a v. गांवखुरीस, गांवदरीस.

Isolated (unincluded) v. फुटगांव *m. n.*

Petty and mean v. आडगांव *m. n.* खेडेगांव *m.* कुग्राम *m.* अडाणवस्ती *f.*

Present made by v.-officers to a visitor. भेटवकरा *m.* [भेटवकरें*n.*

Quarter or ward of a v. वाडी *f.*

Quarter or ward of a v. occupied by the *Mahár* caste. महारवडा *or* वाडा*m.*

Rights of v.-officers. मानपान *m. pl.*

Agricultural v. खेडेगांव *n.*

Straggling v. फुटगांव *m. n.*

Sub-or appended v. बाहेरगांव *m. n.*

The Twelve hereditary v. officers. बारा बलुतीं *or* ते *or* बारा बलुतेदार. They are सुतार, लोहार, महार, मांग, चांभार, कुंभार, न्हावी, परीट, पोतदार, जोशी, मुल्ला, गुरव. The other or remaining v. officers, *comprehensively* are termed बारा अलुते. [*m.pl.*

The Twelve v.-officers,—lightly *or* freely. नारू कारू [गांवढें *n.*

V. in the vicinity of. भोवरगांव *m. n.*

Villages and hamlets, compreh. खेडें गांव *m. n.* गांव

V.-account-keeper. कुळकरणी, ग्रामलेखक.—Office or business of do. कुळकरण *n.*—Papers kept by him, कुळघडणी *f.* घडणी *f.*

V.-astronomer, almanack-monger, &c. ग्रामजोशी.

The office or business of the v.-a. जोसकी *f.* जोसपणा*n.* जोसपण *n.*

V.–boundary-stone. शिवधोंडा *m.*

V.–business. गांवकी *f.*

V.–champion or spokesman. गांवगुंड.

V.-chief or headman. पाटील (his office पाटिलकी *f.* पाटिली *f.*) ग्रामेश, ग्रामनायक, ग्रामणी, ग्रामाध्यक्ष, ग्रामाधिपति.

V.-dispute or discussion. ग्रामण्य*n.* [ग्रामकृत्या *f.*

V.-divinity. गांवदेवी *f.* गांवदेवता *f.* ग्रामदेवता *f.* ग्रामदैवत*n.*

V.-expenses. गांवखर्च *m.* ग्रामखर्च *m.*

V.-ground assigned for carcasses and bones. हडकी *f.*

V.-hereditary officers—compreh. *and* loosely. बारा अलुते आणि बारा बलुते *m. pl.*

V. in precipitous flight. गुढार *n.* गुढें *n.* गुळें *n.*

V.-lands. शिवार *m. n.* शेतवड *f.* शेताड *f.*

V.-meeting (general). गांवकी *f.*

V. of the founder of a race, *parent* v. मूळगांव*m. n.*

V.-officer. ग्रामाधिकारी.

V.-officers,—loosely. पाटील पटवारी *m. pl.*

V. on a hill or amidst hills. डोंगर गांव *m. n.*

V.-oracle-stone. उचला *m.* रुंढ *m.*

V.-people—as assembled or as considered collectively. गांव *m. n.* पांढर *f.* समाकूळ पांढर *f.* पांढरकूळ *n.* पांढरगण *n.* समस्तदाहीजण *m. pl.*

V.-priest. ग्रामयाजक, ग्रामोपाध्याय.

V.-rites and observances; V.-manners and customs. ग्रामधर्म m. ग्रामाचारm.

V.-site. गांवठण or ठाण n. गांवथळ n.

V.-Solomon. गांवगुंड.

V.-viper. V.-informant, incendiary, &c. गांवकुठारm. ग्रामकुठार m. ग्रामकंटक n.

V.-wall or fence. गांवकुसूं n.

VILLAGE, *a. of or belonging to a village, village-born.* गांवचा, खेडेगांवचा, खेड्याचा, मौज्याचा, ग्राम्य.

2 *produced, made, &c. in a village or country place,* v. RUSTIC. गांवचा, गांवठी or ठू, गांवगिरी, गांवरानी, ग्रामीय, खेडोळ or खेडवळ.

VILLAGER, *n.* गांवकरी, गांवकर, गांववाला, गांवचा माणूस, ग्रामस्थ, ग्रामवासी, ग्रामचारी.

VILLAIN, *n. scoundrel, rascal, &c.* v. BLACKGUARD. लबाड, लुच्चा, सोदा, हरामी, हरामजादा, शठ, खट, बजात, लंड, फटलंड, मातृगमनी. [ट, खल, शठ.

VILLAINOUS, *a.* v. N. *and* BLACKGUARDLY, VILE. खट, खटन-

VILLAINY, *n.* v. WICKEDNESS, BLACKGUARDRY. लबाडी *f.* लुच्चेगिरी *f.* लकारी *f.* सोदेगिरी *f.* सकारी *f.* लंडाई *f.* थोंटाई *f.* खटपणा *m.* शठपणा *m.* &c.

VINCIBLE, *a.* v. CONQUERABLE. जिंकायाजोगा-जोगता-सारखा-&c. जेतव्य, जेय, जैय्य.

VINCIBLENESS, VINCIBILITY, *n.* v. A. जेतव्यत्व *n.* जेयत्व *n.*

To VINDICATE, *v. a. assert, support, &c.* v. To MAINTAIN, To PROVE. संभाळणें, स्थापणें, खरा-&c. करूनदेणें, पुरवणें, पुरवून देणें, पटवून देणें, पुरवणी *f.*-&c. करणें *g. of o.*

2 *clear and uphold,* v. To JUSTIFY. दोष *m.* उडवणें *g. of o.* दोषावेगळा-खरा-चांगला-&c. करून दाखवणें. [लेला, &c.

VINDICATED, *p.* v. V. 1. संभाळलेला, पुरवलेला, खराकरून दाखव-

2 दोषावेगळा केलेला, &c. मुक्तदोष, परिहृतदोष, निवृत्तदोष.

VINDICATION, *n.* v. V. 1. संभाळणें *n.* स्थापणें *n.* &c. पुरवणी *f.* स्थापन *n.* प्रतिपादन *n.*

2 दोषाची उडवणी *f.* दोषमोचन *n.* दोषनिवारण *n.* दोषनिरसन*n.*

VINDICATIVE, *a.* VINDICATOR, *n.* VINDICATORY, *a.* v. V. 1. संभाळणारा, स्थापणारा, पुरवून देणारा.

2 दोषउडवणारा, दोषमोचक, दोषनिवारक.

VINDICTIVE, VINDICTIVENESS. See REVENGEFUL, &c.

VINE, *n.*—the plant. द्राक्ष *f.* द्राक्षी *f.* द्राक्षा *f.* द्राक्षाची वेल *f.*

2 v. CREEPER. वेल *f. m.* ताणा *m.*

VINE-YARD, *n.* द्राक्षांचा मळा *m.* द्राक्षांची (or चा) बाग *f. m.* द्राक्षावटिका *f.* [शुक्त *n.*

VINEGAR, *n. acid liquor obtained from wine, &c.* सिरका *m.*

VINOUS, *a. pertaining, &c. to wine.* द्राक्षांच्या दारूचा, द्राक्षामद्याचा, द्राक्षामद्यधर्मक, द्राक्षामद्यगुणक.

VINTAGE, *n. produce or crop of vines.* द्राक्षांचें पीक *n.* द्राक्षांचा लाग *m.* द्राक्षांचीं फळें *n. pl.*

2 *time of grapes.* द्राक्षांची वेळ *f.* द्राक्षांचा समय *m.*-हंगाम *m.* द्राक्षांची सराई *f.*-सुगी *f.*

VINTNER, *n. seller of wine.* द्राक्षांचा रस-द्राक्षारस-द्राक्षामद्य-&c. विकणारा, द्राक्षामद्य-द्राक्षारस विक्रेता.

VIOL. See VIOLIN.

VIOLABLE, *a.* v. V. 1. मोडाया-तोडाया-&c. जोगा-सारखा-&c. उल्लंघनीय.

To VIOLATE, *v. a. infringe, infract,* v. To TRANSGRESS. मोडणें, तोडणें, भंगणें, भंग *m.*-&c. करणें *g. of o.*

2 v. To RAVISH. बळात्कारानें-जुलमानें-&c. उपभोगणें, बळात्कार *m.*-&c. करणें *with* वर *of o.* भ्रष्ट-&c. करणें, हठधर्षण *n.*-&c. करणें *g. of o.*

3 See To HURT, To INJURE.

VIOLATED, *p.* v. V. 1. मोडलेला, तोडलेला, भंग केलेला.

2 भ्रष्ट केलेला, हठधृष्ट, बलोपभुक्त. [उल्लंघ *m.*

VIOLATION, *n.* v. V. 1. मोडणें *n.* तोडणें *n.* &c. भंग *m.* भंजन *n.*

2 बळात्कार *m.* जुलूम *m.* बळात्कारानें उपभोग *m.* हठधर्षण *n.*

V. of a virgin. कन्यादूषण *n.*

VIOLATING, *p. a.* VIOLATOR, *n.* v.V. 1. तोडणारा, मोडणारा, भंजक, भंगकर्त्ता-कारी.

2 भ्रष्ट करणारा, जुलमानें उपभोगणारा, &c. हठधर्षक.

V. of a virgin. कन्यादूषक.

VIOLENCE, *n. force of action or motion,* v. EXCESS. जोर *m.* वेग *m.* नेट *m.* ठणका *m.* उग्रम *m.* सतम *f. n.* झपाटा *m.* तडाखा *m.* धडाखा *m.*

2 *compulsion, unjust force,* v. OUTRAGE, TYRANNY. जुलूम *m.* जुलूमज्यास्ती *f.* जबरी *f.* जबरदस्ती *f.* बळात्कार *m.* बळजोरी *f.* जोरावरी *f.*

Personal v. *assault.* दंडपारुष्य *n.*

3 *vehemence, ardor, &c.* v. IMPETUOSITY. जोर *m.* जुलूम *m.* आवेश *m.* कडकपणा *m.* कडकी *f.*

4 v. RUDENESS. दांडगाई *f.* मलई *f.* खलेली *f.* लांठाई *f.*

5 *rough and violent treatment.* रगडपट्टी *f.* रगडमल्ली *f.* धरबांध *m.* घुसडाघुसड *f.*

To treat with v. See To TREAT.

VIOLENT, *a. forcible, acting with force.* जोराचा, झपाट्याचा, तडाख्याचा, वेगाचा, &c. जबर, जरब, जालीम, कडक, प्रचंड, चंड.

2 *outrageous, oppressive, tyrannical, &c.*—person, &c. जुलमाचा, जबरीचा, जबरदस्तीचा, &c. जालीम, जबरदस्त, कहरी.

3 *outrageous, furious, vehement, &c.* v. EXCESSIVE. कहराचा, अनर्थाचा, गजबाचा, जबर.

4 *vehement, ardent, &c.* v. IMPETUOUS, FIERCE. जबर, जरब, आवेशी, प्रचंड, चंड, असुरी, कपाळ फोड्या. [कोदंड.

5 *rough, overbearing,* v. RUDE. दांड, दांडगा, खलेल, लांठ,

6 (sickness, pain, &c.) v. SEVERE. जोराचा, जबर, कठीण.

V. sickness or malady. वाखा*m.* [दुर्मरणाचा.

7—death, end, &c. *not natural.* अपघाताचा, अपमृत्यूचा,

VIOLENTLY, *adv.* v. A. 1. जोरानें, झपाट्यानें, तडाख्यानें, &c. कचकावून or खचकावून, खसाटून, बशरत, हटातू.

2 आक्रांतानें, कहरानें, &c. जुलमानें, जबरीनें,&c.

3 अनर्थाचा *decl.* आक्रांतानें, कहरानें, &c. अनर्थ *m.*-आक्रांत *m.*-कहर *m.*-एकगजब *m. used with* मांडणें *and* करणें, as तिनें रडून अनर्थ केला or रडण्याचा अनर्थ मांडला, she cried violently, &c.

VIOLIN, *n.* v. FIDDLE. रबक *n.* रबाब *n.* सारंगी *f.*

VIOLINIST, *n.* सारंग्या *m.*

VIPER, See SNAKE.

VIRAGO, *n. masculine woman.* शिपाईबायको *f.* पुरुषस्वभावाची-

पुरुषचालीची-&c. बायको *f.* स्त्री *f.* फांमिंदी *f.*

2 v. Scold, Shrew. कृत्या, कर्कशा, बाघीण *f.*

Virgin, *n. a woman who has not known man*, v. Maid. कुमारी *pop.* कुंवार *f.* कन्या *f.* नवोढा *f.* कुमारिका *f.* गौरी *f.* अक्षता *f.* अक्षतयोनि *f.* अविद्धयोनि *f.* अनन्यपूर्वा *f.* पुरुषास्पृष्टा *f.* Note. The common *Prakrit* words used to render *virgin* and *virginity* express primarily the unmarried female and state.

Defiling of a v. कन्यादूषण *n.*

Defiler of a v. कन्यादूषक.

Virgin, Virginal, *a.* See Maiden, Maidenly.

2 *untouched, unused, fresh, &c.* बिन वापरलेला, कोरा, अपूट, अनसूट, अभुक्त.

Virginity, *n. maidenhead.* कुंवारपणा *m.* कुमारित्व *n.* कन्यात्व *n.* अज्ञातपुरुषदशा *f.* अक्षतयोनित्व *n.* चिरा *m.* The last word is restricted in use to professed courtezans.

Virgo, *n.*—the zodiacal sign. कन्या *f.*

Virile, *a.* v. Manly, Masculine. पुरुषाचा, पुरुषाविषयींचा, पुरुषसंबंधी-विषयक, पौरुष, पौरुषेय.

Virility, *n.* v. Manhood. पुरुषपणा *m.* पौरुष *n.*

2 *power of procreation.* पुरुषपणा *m.* पुरुषत्व *n.* घोवकी *f.* घोवपणा *m.* ओज *n.* पौरुष *n.* पुंस्त्व *n.* जननशक्ति *f.* पुरुषशक्ति *f.* पुंशक्ति *f.* चेतना *f.*

Virtual, *a. that is in effect though not in fact.* कार्यदृष्टीचा, गुणदृष्टीचा, फलदृष्टीचा, गुणाच्याधोरणाचा, कामाचा, गुणाचा, गुणसिद्ध. The sense of the word may be rendered by the use of सारखा-दाखल-सदृश, and other words that mean *like, the same as, &c.* Ex. ती भ्रष्ट झाली म्हणून तिचें वास्तविक मरण जरी झालें नाहीं तरी मेल्यादाखल मरण झालें.

Virtually, *adv.* v. A. कार्यदृष्टीनें, गुणदृष्टीनें, गुणतः.

Virtue, *n. moral goodness, practice of moral duties, &c.* नेकी *f.* नेत *f.* नेक *f.* नीति *f.* नेकीचें-&c. आचरण *n.* पुण्य *n.* पुण्याचरण *n.* पुण्याचार *m.* धर्म *m.* धर्माचरण *n.* धर्माचार *m.* सदाचरण *n.* सदाचार *m.* साधुत्व *n.* साधुवृत्ति *f.* सुकृत *n.* सुकृताचरण *n.* सत्याचरण *n.* श्रेय *n.* तप *n.* भलाई *f.* भलाईकी *f.* कल्याणाचरण *n.*

Majesty and mightiness of v. पुण्यप्रताप *m.*

Path of v. धर्ममार्ग *m.* पुण्यमार्ग *m.* सन्मार्ग *m.*

V. cannot be known but through adversity. हिऱ्याची परीक्षा घणावांचून होत नाहीं.

2 *a* v. *moral excellence.* गुण *m.* सुगुण *m.* सद्गुण *m.* सुलक्षण *n.*

Virtues and vices of. गुणागुण *m. pl.* गुणदोष *m. pl.*

3 *medicinal quality.* गुण *m.*

Latent v. मर्म *n.*

4 *excellence, spirit, good quality.*—gener. गुण *m.* गुणांश *m.* सत्व *n.* तेज *n.* रस *m.* रया *f.* कस *m.* दम *m.* वीर्य *n. pop.* ईर *or* विरी *f.* अर्थ *m.* बारें *n.* रहस्य *n.* बळावळ *f.* प्रताप *m.*

By v. of. परत्वें *or* परत्वें करून (in comp. as अधिकारपरत्वें, जातीपरत्वें, तपपरत्वें).

That keeps its v. सत्वशील, सत्वधीर.

Virtuoso, *n.* चिकित्सक.

Virtuous, *a.* v. N.1. 2. *morally good.* नेक, नेकीचा, सदाचरणी, सत्याचरणी, सदाचरणाचा, पुण्यवान्, पुण्यवंत, पुण्यशील, पुण्यात्मक, पुण्यकर्मा, पुण्यपरायण, पुण्याचा, पुण्यमार्गी, पुण्यमार्गाचा, सत्वशील, सत्वसंपन्न, सत्वस्थ, धर्मशील, धर्माचरणी, धर्मी, धार्मिष्ट, धर्मचारी, धर्मज्ञ, धर्मवान्, धार्मिक, साधु, साधुवृत्त, साधुवृत्ति, साध्वाचार, भला, सुकर्मा, सुकर्मी, सुकृती, सुकृत, कल्याणाचार, कल्याणधर्मा. Some terms for *A virtuous or excellent person* are, पुण्यपुरुष, पुण्यप्राणी, पुण्यात्मा, पुण्यपात्र, सज्जन, धर्मात्मा, धर्मावतार, गुणनिधान, गुणनिधि, (See also the compounds with गुण under Clever) तेजःपुंज.

V. man. सज्जन *m.*

V. woman or wife. सती *f.* साध्वी *f.* सुचरित्रा *f.*

2 See Medicinal. 3 See Chaste.

Virtuousness, *n.* v. A. *and* Virtue. नेकी *f.* पुण्याई *f.* सद्भाव *m.* भलाई *f.* भलीभलाई *f.* भलीभलाईकी *f.*

Virulence, Virulency, *n.* v. A. 1. जहाली *f.* जल्लाली *f.* कडकपणा *m.* &c. तलखी *f.* तलखाई *f.*

2 संवचटपणा *m.* डंशीपणा *m.* डंश *m.* डंस *m.*

Virulent, *a. active in doing mischief,*—poison, &c. जल्लाद, जहाल *or* ज्याल, जालीम, कडक, तलख, आग्या, जहरी, कहरी, कहराचा, प्रखर, तीक्ष्ण.

2 fig. v. Acrimonious, Malignant. सवंचट, डंशी, डंशीक.

Visage, *n.* v. Face. मुख *n.* मुखवटा *m.* चेहरा *m.* चेगमोरा *m.* रूप *n.*

Viscera, *n. internal organs of the body.* पोटांतले अवयव *m. pl.* पोटांतलीं अंगें *n. pl.*

2 See Bowels.

Viscid, Viscous, *a. glutinous, &c.* v. Sticky. चिकट *or* चिकूट, चिकाळ *or* ळा *or* ळ्या, घन, चिकचिकीत, गिजगिजीत.

Viscidity, Viscosity, Viscousness, *n.* v. A. चिकटपणा *m.* चिकचिकितपणा *m.* &c. चिकटण *f.* चिकटाई *f.* चिकचीक *f.* (*intens.* चिकचिकाट *m.*) किचकीच *f.* लाढा *m.*

Visibility, Visibleness, *n.* v. A. 1. पहायाचीयोग्यता *f.* &c. दृश्यता *f.* लोकनीयता *f.* दृष्टिगोचरता *f.* दृग्विषयता *f.* &c.

2 उघडपणा *m.* उघडेपणा *m.* &c.

Visible, *a. perceivable by the eye.* पहायासारखा-जोगा-जोगता-&c. दृष्टीनयेण्यासारखा-जोगा-&c. दृश्य, द्रष्टव्य, लोकनीय, दर्शनीय, दृग्गोचर, दृष्टिगोचर, दृष्टिविषय, दृग्विषय, दृष्टिगम्य, दृग्गम्य, चाक्षुष, वीक्ष्य. [त्यक्षसिद्ध.

2 *apparent, conspicuous, open.* उघड, उघडा, दर्शनी, प्रगट, प्र-

That has become v. बेणा *a. ind.* बेणी.

To become v. बेणावणें. [चा, दृश्यमान.

3 *that is in sight.* दिसता, दिसणारा, दिसून आलेला, नजरेपुढ-

Visibly, *adv.* v. A. 1. 2. प्रत्यक्ष, समक्ष, दिसेसा *decl.* दिसता *decl.* डोळ्यांदेखत, उघड, उघडपणें, &c. पश्यतः. [ह्रिय *n.*

Vision, *n. faculty of seeing*, v. Sight. दृष्टि *f.* नजर *f.* चक्षुरि-

2 *act of seeing*, v. Sight. पाहणें *n.* दृष्टि *f.* नजर *f.*

The line of v. दृक्सूत्र *n.* दृष्टिपथ *m.*

3 *supernatural dream, &c.* दृष्टावा *m.* दृष्टांत *m.* दर्शन *n.* उचका *m.* साक्षात्कार *m.* [*m.* छाया *f.*

4 *spectre, phantom, apparition.* उचका *m.* भास *m.* आभास

Visionary, *a.* v. Imaginary. मनचा, मनःकल्पित, मानसिक, मानससृष्टीचा, मनोराज्याचा, अवास्तविक, स्वप्नाकार.

2—a person. उचकेखोर, उचक्या, मनमान्या, लहरी, मनोविहारी.

To **Visit**, *v. a. go to see.* भेटीला-दर्शनास-&c. जाणें-येणें *g. of o.* भेट *f.*-&c. घेणें *g. of o.* [स जाणें.

2 *go to survey, &c. with authority.* पहायास-पाहणी कराया-

VISIT, VISITATION, *n.* v. V. 1. *and* INTERVIEW. भेटीकरितां जाणें *n.*-येणें *n.* दर्शनयात्रा *f.*
Indecently long v. *visitation.* ठाणें *n. v.* दे.
2 पाहुणी करायास जाणें *n.*- येणें *n.* पाहुणी *f.*

VISITOR, VISITANT, *n.* v. V.1. *and* GUEST. भेटीस-भेटीकरितां-&c. येणारा- आलेला, पाहुणा *m.* (पाहुणी *f.*).
Attentions to a v. v. CIVILITY. पाटपाणी *n. v.* दे.
Rising up to receive or dismiss a v. पुरीताजीम *f.* खडी ताजीम *f.*
Receiving or dismissing a v. without rising, but making an inclination to rise. निमताजीम *f.*
2 पाहुणी करणारा, पाहुणीकरायास येणारा-जाणारा, चौकसनीस.

VISOR, *n. vizard.* मुखटोप *m.* मुखवटा *m.*

VISTA. See AVENUE.

VISUAL, VISIVE, *a. pertaining, &c. to sight.* दृष्टीचा, नजरेचा, डोळ्याचा, &c. चाक्षुष, दृष्टिसंबंधी, दृष्टिविषयक, चक्षुरिंद्रियसंबंधी- विषयक.

VITAL, *a. of or belonging to life.* जिवाचा, प्राणाचा, प्राणाविषयींचा, जीवनाचा, जीवनसंबंधी, जीवसंबंधी-विषयक, प्राणसंबंधी-विषयक, जैव.
V. thread. आयुष्याचीदोरी *f.*
2 *necessary to life.* प्राणरक्षक, जीवनसाधक, जीवनकर, प्राणकर, जीवनरक्षक, जीवनोपयोगी, प्राण in comp., जीव in comp.
V. air. प्राणवायु *m.*
3 *being the seat of life, mortal.* प्राण राहण्याचा, जिव्हाळीचा.
In a v. part. जिव्हाळीं *or* जिव्हारीं.
Piercing a v. spot or part. मर्मभेद *m.* प्राणस्थानभेद *m.*
V. spot or part. जिव्हाळी *f.* मर्म *n.* मर्मस्थान *n.* मर्मस्थल *n.* प्राणस्थान *n.* वर्म *n.*
4 See ESSENTIAL.

VITALITY, *n. vital energy or power,* v. LIFE. जीव *m.* जीवशक्ति *f.* प्राणशक्ति *f.* जीवनशक्ति *f.* चेतना *f.* ओजन *n.*

VITALS, *n. parts essential to life.* जिव्हाळीचीं *or* जिव्हाराचीं स्थानें *n. pl.* जिव्हाळ्या *f. pl.* मर्मस्थानें *n. pl.*

To VITIATE, *v. a.* v. To CORRUPT, To SPOIL. बिघडणें, वाईट-खराब-भ्रष्ट-&c. करणें, दूषण *n.*-&c. करणें *g. of o.*
2 *destroy the validity of.* बातल-निरर्थक-पोकळ-व्यर्थ-रहित-&c.करणें, बातलपण *m.*-पोकळपणा *m.*-&c. आणणें.

VITIATED, *p.* v. V. 1. बिघडलेला, &c. वाईट, खराब, भ्रष्ट, दूषित, विगुण.
2 बातल केलेला, निरर्थक केलेला, &c.

VITIATION, *n.* v. V. 1. बिघडणें *n.* &c. दूषण *n.*
2 बातल करणें *n.* &c.

VITIOUS. See VICIOUS.

VITREOUS, *a.* v. GLASSY. काचेचा, काचमय, काचवत्.

To VITRIFY, *v. a. turn into glass.* काच *m.*-काचपरिणाम *m.* करणें.

To VITRIFY, *v. n. become glass.* काच *m.* होणें.

VITRIOL, *n.*—blue. मोरचूत *or* द *m. n.* ताम्रगर्भ *m.* तुत्थ *n.* मयूरक *n.* नीलांजन *n.*—green. हिराकस *m.* हिराकशी *f.* कासीस *n.* मलीमस *n.* विषद *n.* धातुशेखर *m.*—white. सफेत मोरचूत *m. n.*

VITRIOLIC, VITRIOLOUS, *a.* v. N. मोरचुताचा, मोरचुती.

To VITUPERATE, VITUPERATION, See To ABUSE, ABUSE.

VITUPERATIVE. See ABUSIVE.

VIVACIOUS, *a. lively, sprightly,* v. MERRY. उल्लासी, आनंदी, खुशदिल, आल्हादी, उल्लासवृत्ति.
2 *long lived.* दीर्घायु.
3 *tenacious of life, vigorous,* v. LIVELY. जिवट, जिवस.

VIVACIOUSNESS, VIVACITY, *n.* v. A. 1. उल्लासीपणा *m.* &c. उल्लासवृत्ति *f.* आनंदवृत्ति *f.* तेज *n.*

VIVA VOCE. तोंडच्या तोंडीं, तोंडातोंडीं, मुखजबानी, मुखजबानीनें.

VIVID, *a. of colours, &c.* v. BRIGHT, CLEAR. ठळक, ठळठळीत, गहिरा *or* गेहरा, भडक, भचूक, उजळ, लकलकीत *or* लखलखीत.
2 *lively, strong, not dull, &c.*—imagination, recollection, &c. लकलकीत *or* लखलखीत, चकचकीत, खणखणीत, कडकडीत, जिवट, जिवस.

VIVIDNESS, *n.* v. A. 1. ठळकपणा *m.* गहिरेपणा *m.* &c.
2 लकलकितपणा *m.* कडकडितपणा *m.* &c.

VIVIFIC, *a. life giving.* जीवंत करणारा, जीव-&c. देणारा, जीवप्रद.

VIVIFIED, *p.* v. V. जीवंतकेलेला, सजीवकेलेला, &c. जीवित.

To VIVIFY, *v. a.*v. To ANIMATE. जीव *m.*-&c. देणें-घालणें, सजीव-&c. करणें, चेतवणें.

VIVIPAROUS, *a. that brings forth its young alive.* जरायुज (lit. born from the womb), सचेतनप्रसु, सचेतनप्रज.

VIXEN, *n.* v. SCOLD. जिवंतअवदसा *f.* कर्कशा *f.* कलहांतरिता *f.* कृत्या *f.* कैदाशीण *f.* जगनाड *f.* जगभांड *f.* शूर्पणखा *f.* सटवाई *or* सटी *f.* वाघीण *f.*

VIZ. *adv. namely.* म्हणजे.

VIZARD, *n. mask for the face.* मुखटोप *m.* मुखवटा *m.*

VIZIER, *n.*—the minister. वजीर.

VIZIERSHIP, *n.* वजिरी *f.* वजिरात *f.*

VOCABLE, *n.* v. WORD. शब्द *m.* वाचक *m.*

VOCABULARY, *n. lexicon.* कोश *m.* शब्दकोश *m.* शब्दजाल *n.* शब्दसंग्रह *m.*

VOCAL, *a. having voice or speech.* वाग्युक्त, वाणीयुक्त, वाणीविशिष्ट, सवाक्.
2 *uttered by the voice.* वाचेचा, वाणीचा, वाचिक, वाग्जात, वाचाजात, वाणीजात.

VOCALLY, *adv. with the voice; in words.* आवाजानें, वाणीनें, वाचेनें, भाषणानें, शब्दद्वारा.

VOCATION, *n. employment, calling,* v. BUSINESS. काम *n.* धंदा *m.* उद्योग *m.* वृत्ति *f.*

VOCATIVE, *n.*—in grammar. संबोधन *n.*

To VOCIFERATE, *v. n. cry out with vehemence,* v. To BAWL, To CLAMOUR. पुकार *m.*-गोंगाट *m.*-कळकळ *f.* करणें, गागणें, कळाकळा *adv.* करणें.

VOCIFERATION, *n.* v. V. *and* CLAMOUR, UPROAR. गलका *m.* गलबा *m.* गलबल *f.* गलबला *m.* गवगव *f.* गवगवा *m.* खलबल *f.* कुलुली *f.* कोलाहल *m.* खणका *m.* कलभा *m.* एकगजर *m.* ओरडाओरड *f.* कळकळ *f.* गरगशा *m.* कळकळ्या.

VOCIFEROUS, *a.* v. CLAMOROUS, NOISY. ओरड्या, गोंगाट्या,

VOGUE, *n. practice, usage,* v. CUSTOM. वहिवाट *f.* प्रचार *m.* प्रघात *m.*
To be in v. वागणें.

VOICE, *n. sound of the mouth.* आवाज *m.* शब्द *m.* स्वर *m.* कंठ *m.* कंठरव *m.* ध्वनि *m.* कंठध्वनि *m.*
Broken or hoarse v. बसला गळा *m.* फुटका गळा *m.*
Change of v. (through sickness, &c.). स्वरभेद *m.* ध्व-

निर्विकार *m.*
Effeminate, unmanly v. रांडगळा *m.*
Of broken or cracked v. भग्नस्वर, स्वरभग्न.
Tender or soft v. बाळ गळा *m.*
To lose one's v. घसा *m.* *or* गळा *m.* चेपणें-बसणें *g. of s.*
2—in singing; *throat.* गळा *m.* आवाज *m.* कंठ *m.* हलक *f.*
Command of v. कर्त्तबदारी *f.*
Command of v. in singing or reading. सवन *f. n.*
Modulations or inflections of v. कर्त्तब *n.*
Of good v. गळेबाज, आवाजदार. [गळी.
Of a v. capable of ascending high into the treble.
Sweet or fine v. गोडगळा *m.*
Sweetness of v. कंठमाधुर्य *n.*
Treble or shrill v. रांडगळा *m.* गळी *f.*
To pitch the v. to agree with. सूर *m.* धरणें.
To get a cracked v. कंठ *m.* फुटणें *g. of s.*
3 faculty of speech, v. SPEECH. वाचा *f.*
4—in gram. वाच्य *n.*
Active v. कर्तृवाच्य *n.* परस्मैपद *n.*
Middle v. आत्मनेपद *n.*
Passive v. कर्मणिवाच्य *n.* भाववाच्य *n.*
5 See VOTE.

VOID, *a. unoccupied, vacant,* v. EMPTY. रिकामा, रिता, खाली.
2 *vain, null, without binding force.* बातल, पोकळ, निरर्थक.
To make v. See To VIOLATE, To TRANSGRESS.
3 *devoid, destitute,* v. WANTING. निराळा, वेगळा, रहित, हीन, शून्य, all in comp.

VOID, *n. vacuum.* शून्य *n.* पोकळी *f.*

To VOID, *v. a. emit as excrement,* v. To EVACUATE. टाकणें, उत्सर्ग *m.*-&c. करणें *g. of o.*
2 See To LEAVE. 3 See To NULLIFY.

VOLATILE, *a. that passes quickly into the aeriform state.* उडून जाणारा, उडून जाण्याचा, वायुपरिणामी, वायुपरिणामशील.
2—of quicksilver. जिता.
3 *fickle, airy,* v. CHANGEABLE, THOUGHTLESS. चंचल *or* ळ, चपल *or* ळ, चंचलस्वभावाचा, चिचोर *or* छिछोर, चंचलप्रकृति, चपलप्रकृति, प्रकृतितरल, तरलप्रकृति.

VOLATILITY, *n.* v. A. 1. उडूनजाण्याचा गुण *m.*-धर्म *m.* वायुपरिणामिता *f.* &c.
2 जितेपणा *m.*
3 चंचळपणा *m.* चपळपणा *m.* चिचोरी *or* छिछोरी *f.* चांचल्य *n.* चापल्य *n.* चंचल प्रकृति *f.* चपल प्रकृति *f.*

VOLCANIC, *a. belonging, &c. to volcanoes.* ज्वालामुखीचा, ज्वालामुखीसंबंधी-विषयक, ज्वालामुखीपासून झालेला.

VOLCANO, *n. burning mountain.* ज्वालामुखी *f.* अद्रिवन्हि *m.*

VOLITION, *n.* See WILL. 2 *a* v. *an act of will.* संकल्प *m.*

VOLITIVE, *a. having the power to will.* संकल्पशक्तिक, संकल्पशक्तियुक्त.

VOLLEY, *n. flight of shot; discharge of many small arms at once.* शलक *or* शिलक *f. v.* झाड, उडव, तासरा *or* ताशेरा *m. v.* झाड, पाऊस *m.* वृष्टि *f.* in comp. पलिता *or* दा *m. v.* झाड, सरबत्ती *f.*
2 fig. (as of curses, oaths, &c.). लाखोली *f.* वृष्टि *f.*

VOLUBILITY, *n.* v. A. 1. चपळपणा *m.* चपळाई *f.* लुवलुवपणा *m.*
2 जिभेची चपळाई *f.* तोंडचा जलदपणा *m.* &c. जबेफराशी *f.* वाक्चापल्य *n.*

VOLUBLE, *a.*—of the tongue or speech, v. FLUENT. चपळ, लुबलुब हालणारा, लुचलुचा, धारावाही, धारावाहिक.
2—of a speaker, v. GLIB. तोंडचा-जिभेचा-&c. खबरदार-जलद-चपळ, जबेफरास, जाबसाली, चपलवाक्, चपलजिह्व, बोलतांना टाळूस टिपळू लागूं देत नाहीं असा.

VOLUBLY, *adv.* v. A. तोंडच्या-जिभेच्या-&c. चपळाईनें, वाक्चापल्यानें, वाक्चापल्यपूर्वक, चुरचुर, चरचर, लुवलुव, गरगर,—esp. with implic. of railing, फटफट, फटफटां, फडफड, फडफडां.

VOLUME, *n.* v. BOOK. पुस्तक *n.*
2 (of a serpent) v. COIL. वेंटाळा *m.* वेंटाळें *n.* भेंडोळें *n.*
3 (of smoke). लोट *m.* गोल *m.*
4 (of water). लोंढा *m.* लोट*m.* झोत*m.*
5 (of fire). गोल *m.* झोत *m.* लोळ *m.*

VOLUMINOUS, *a. of much matter.* ग्रंथविस्ताराचा, विस्तारमय, विस्तारबहुल, विस्तारप्रचुर.
2 *consisting of many volumes.* बहुत पुस्तकांचा, बहुतग्रंथांचा, &c. पुस्तकबहुल.

VOLUMINOUSNESS, *n.* v. A. 1. ग्रंथविस्तार *m.* विस्तारबाहुल्य *n.*
2 पुस्तकबाहुल्य *n.*

VOLUNTARILY, *adv.* v. A. 2. बुद्धीनें, बुद्ध्या, बुद्धिपूर्वक, संकल्पपूर्वक, आत्मसंतोषानें *or* अत्मतापें *or* आत्मसंतोषेंकरून, आपखुशीनें, आपसुखानें *or* सुखें *or* आपसुखें, सुखासुखीं, इच्छापूर्वक, इच्छापुरस्सर, सुखसंतोषानें *or* सुखसंतोषें.

VOLUNTARY, *a. free of action,* v. FREE. स्वतंत्र, स्वेच्छाधीन, स्ववश, स्वेच्छाचारी, कामचार.
2 *willed, purposed, done by design,* v. INTENTIONAL. संकल्पाचा, इराद्याचा, संकल्पपूर्वक, संकल्पपुरस्सर, संकल्पकृत, बुद्धिकृत.
3 *proceeding from choice or free will,* v. SPONTANEOUS. आपखुशीचा, खुशीचा, स्वसंतोषाचा, आत्मसंतोषाचा, दिलखुशीचा, इच्छापूर्वक, इच्छापुरस्सर, ऐच्छिक.
4 *subject to the will.* इच्छाधीन, ऐच्छिक, इच्छावश.

VOLUNTEER, *n. a person who enters into a service of his own choice.* आपल्या इच्छेनें-आपल्या खुशीनें चाकरी करणारा, आपण होऊन चाकरी करणारा.

To VOLUNTEER, *v. n. offer to do any thing without solicitation.* आपण होऊन पुढें होणें-बोलणें-करणें-&c. धजणें, धज *f.* देणें.

To VOLUNTEER, *v. a. offer or bestow without solicitation. &c.* आपण होऊन देणें-करणें-देऊं करणें-&c.

VOLUPTUARY, *n.* v. PLEASURIST. विषयी, खुशालचंद, गुलहंसी *or* हवसी *or* हौसी *or* शी, सुखानंद, चंदनहौशी, हौशा *or* हौसी *or* शी, विलासी, भोगी, भोक्ता.

VOLUPTUOUS, *a.* v. LUXURIOUS, SENSUAL. विषयी, विलासी, विहारी, शोकी *or* शौकी, विषयाचा, विषयसुखाचा, विषयासक्तीचा.

VOLUPTUOUSNESS, *n.* v. A. विषयीपणा *m.* विलासीपणा *m.* &c. विषयोपसेवा *f.* विषयासक्ति *f.* [काजरा *m.*

VOMIC-NUT, *n. strychnos, nux vomica.*—the plant. कुचला *m.*

To VOMIT, *v. a. throw up from the stomach.* ओकणें, ओकून टाकणें, मागें पाडणें-टाकणें, तोंडीं काढणें, वमणें, उलटी *f.*- वमन *n.*-&c. होणें *g. of o. with in. con.*

VOMIT, *v. n. eject by the mouth the contents of the stomach.* ओकणें, तोंडीं काढणें, वमणें, उगळणें, उलटी *f.*-वमन *n.*-वांति *f.*-&c. होणें *in. con.*

Excessive vomiting *or* general v. ओकाबोक *f.*

Given to vomiting. ओकरा.

Straining at vomiting *or* noise made at straining. ओकारा *m.* ओकारी *f.*

To v. violently. भडभडणें, खणखणून ओकणें.

VOMIT, *n. matter vomited.* ओक *f.* वांत *f.* वांति *f.*

2 *emetic medicine.* उलट *f.* उलटी *f.* वांति *f.* उलटीचें-वांतीचें-&c. औषध *n.*

V. given to a person who has taken poison. उखाळ *or* उकळ *m.* उकाळा *m.* [उद्गीर्ण.

VOMITED, *p.* v. V. A. ओकलेला, ओकून टाकलेला, वांत, वमित,

To be v. निघणें (Ex. याला निघालें *or* अन्न &c. निघालें).

VOMITER, *n.* VOMITING, *p. a.* v. V. ओकणारा, वमणारा, उलटी करणारा, &c.

VOMITING, *n.* v. V. N. ओकणें *n.* वमणें *n.* &c. ओ *f.* उलटी *f.* उलट *f.* वमन *n.* वांति *pop.* वांत *f.* वमी *f.* उखाळ *m.* छर्दी *f.* उद्गार *m.* उद्गिरण *n.*

VOMITIVE, VOMITORY, *a. procuring vomiting.* उलटीचा, वांतीचा, &c. वांतिकारक, वमनकारक, वामक.

VORACIOUS, *a.* v. GLUTTONOUS. खाणारा *or* री, खादाड, अधासा, अधासी, घस्मर, कुक्षिंभरि, वृकोदर, अशनलोलुप, वखवख्या, बराडी, बराडलेला.

VORACIOUSNESS, VORACITY, *n.* v. A. खाणेरेपणा *m.* खादाडपणा *m.* &c. वखवख *f.* खाखा *f.* खायखाय *f. v.* सुट.

VORTEX, *n. eddy, whirlpool.* भोंवरा *m.* आवर्त्त *m.* चक्र *n.* चक्कर *n.*

VORTICAL, *a. whirling.* भोंवऱ्यासारखा, गरगरफिरणारा.

VOTARIST, VOTARY, *n. one engaged as by vow or promise to; devotee, follower.* परायण in comp. आसक्त in comp. भक्त *pop.* भगत, उपासक, सेवक, दास, गुलाम, बंदा, व्रतस्थ, व्रती.

VOTE, *n. suffrage.* सम्मति *f.* सम्मतोक्ति *f.* सम्मतप्रकाश *m.*

To VOTE, *v. a. choose by suffrage.* सम्मतीनें-सम्मति देऊन-सम्मतिपूर्वक-&c. योजणें-नेमणें-ठरवणें.

2 *give by vote.* सर्व सम्मतीनें-&c. देणें-देवविणें.

To VOTE, *v. n. express one's mind.* सम्मति *f.* देणें, सम्मतिप्रकाश *m.* करणें.

VOTER, *n.* v. V. N. सम्मति देणारा.

VOTIVE, *a. given, &c. by vow.* नवसाचा, नवशीक, नवानवसाचा.

To VOUCH, *v. n. bear witness, give attestation in support or proof.* साक्ष *f.* देणें, खातरी *f.*-निशा *f.*-&c. करणें-देणें, दाखला *m.*-सड *f.*-&c. देणें.

VOUCHER, *n. document or paper which vouches.* दाखला *m.* आगम *m.* सडी *f.* सड *f.* दस्तऐवज *m.* जाबता *m.* खातरीचा-निशेचा-&c. लेख *m.* प्रमाणलेख *m.* प्रमाणपत्र *n.*

To VOUCHSAFE, *v.a. condescend to grant.* कृपाकरून-मेहरबानी-करून-मेहरबान होऊन-कृपाळू होऊन-&c. देणें-दान करणें.

To VOUCHSAFE, *v. n.* v. To DEIGN. कृपा *f.*-मेहरबानी *f.*-&c. करणें.

VOW, *n. solemn promise made to God.* नवस *m.* मानता *f.* मानणूक *f.* आंगवण *f.* मानसिक *n.* संकल्प *m.*

Faithful to a v. of religious observances. संशितव्रत.

Making a v. of some religious observance. व्रतसंग्रह *m.*

V. imposing on one's self some religious observance. व्रत *n.* संकल्प *m.* संयम *m.*

That is under or engaged by a v. of religious observance. व्रतबद्ध, संकल्पबद्ध, धृतव्रत.

That has violated a v. of religious observance. क्षतव्रत.

To fulfil a v. नवस *m.* फेडणें-पुरवणें, (*and* to be fulfilled नवस *m.* पुरणें-फिटणें). [क *f.*

2 *solemn promise.* आणभाष *f.* आणभाक *f.* शपथ *f.* इमानभाक *f.*

To VOW, *v. a. consecrate, &c. by vow.* नवसणें, नवसानें देणें.

To VOW, *v. n. make a vow.* नवस *m.*-मानता *f.*-&c. करणें, मानणें.

VOWED, *p.* v. V. A. नवसलेला, नवसानें दिल्हेला.

VOWEL, *n. letter which can be uttered by itself.* स्वर *m.* मातृका *f.* अच् *m.* अच्वर्ण *m.* अजक्षर *n.*

Coalition of vowels. अच्संधि *m.*

Short v. मात्रा *f.* [जलयात्रा *f.* घोंस *m.*

VOYAGE, *n. journey by water.* सफर *f.* समुद्रयान *n.* जलयान *n.*

VOYAGER, *n. one who journies by water.* सफरी, समुद्रयायी, खेटेकरी, जलयात्रिक.

VULCAN, *n.*—in Hindu mythology. विश्वकर्मा, देवशिल्पी.

VULGAR, *a. of or belonging to common or low people,* v. COMMON, LOW. अडाणजातीचा, इतरजातीचा, हलक्याजातीचा, गांवढळ, कुणबाऊ, गल्लीकुचीचा, सांदीकोंदीचा, अडाणवस्तीचा.

2 *mean, coarse, unrefined, &c.* v. LOW. कुणबाऊ, कुणबाऊ-कुणबी-&c. चालीचा-वजेचा-मोळयाचा-बळणाचा-रितीचा-&c. राकट, अनाडी, गल्लीकुचीचा, पाजी, असभ्य, अशिष्ट, प्राकृत, जघन्य, असभ्यवृत्ति, असभ्यवृत्तीचा, अशिष्टाचाराचा.

3—the tongue or speech ; *popular, colloquial, vernacular.* देशी, ग्राम्य, प्राकृत.

VULGAR, *n.* v. PEOPLE. नीचलोक *m. pl.* अडाणजात *f.* तेलीतांबोळी *m. pl.* कुणबीमाळी *m. pl.* साळीकोष्टी *m. pl.*

VULGARISM, *n. vulgar expression,* v. BARBARISM. अडाणीबोली *f.* अपशब्द *m.*

VULGARITY, VULGARNESS, *n. coarseness, &c. of manners or language.* कुणबाऊ चाल *f.* कुणबाऊ रीत *f.* अडाणजातीची चाल *f.*-रीत *f.*-&c. अनाडीपणा *m.* असभ्यता *f.* अशिष्टता *f.* अशिष्टाचार *m.* अशिष्टाचरण *n.* असभ्यवृत्ति *f.* &c.

VULNERABILITY, *n.* v. A. भेद्यता *f.* भेदनीयता *f.*

VULNERABLE, *a. susceptible of wounds.* घाव लागावाजोगा-जोगता-सारखा-&c. भेद्य, भेदनीय.

V. point, v. SORE. मागवें *n.* मर्मस्थान *n.* मर्मस्थल *n.* मर्म *n.* वर्म *n.* छिद्र *n.*

VULTURE, *n.*—the bird. गीद *or* ध *n.* गिधड *or* गिधाड *n.* गिधाडा *m.* गृध्र *m.* गरुड *m.* गरुडबायलें *n.*

W.

W. This letter is represented in Maráṭhí by व.

To WABBLE, *v. n. move from side to side,*—a top, &c. डुलणें, डुलत फिरणें.

WAD, *n.* (of a gun, &c.). जामीन *m.*

2 (of cloth under a load on the head). चुंबळ *or* चुंभळ *f.*

f. आहरा *or* आरा *m.*

WADDING, *n. stuff for wads.* चोंदा *m.*

2 (for stuffing garments). पुरणाचें-पुरणीचें-&c. चिरगूट *n.*

To WADDLE, *v. n. move from side to side in walking.* डुलणें *or* डोलणें, झुकणें, झोकणें, झेंपा *f. pl.* देणें-खाणें, डुलत-झुकत-झेंपाखात-&c. चालणें, भेलकंडणें, भेलकांडी *f.*-भेलकंड *n. or* कंडा *m. or* कंडी *f.*-&c. जाणें *in. con.*

WADDLE, WADDLING, *n.* v. V. डुलणें *n.* झुकणें *n.* &c. डुलत जाण्याची-&c. चाल *f.* बदकाची चाल *f.* डुलतीचाल *f.* हंसगति *f.*

WADDLER, *n.* WADDLING, *p. a.* v. V. डुलणारा, डुलत चालणारा, &c.

To WADE, *v. n. walk through water, &c.* पायउताराने जाणें, पाण्यांतून पायीं जाणें, पाणी लोटत-पाणीतोडीत-&c. जाणें.

2 *pass with difficulty.* श्रमानें-कष्टानें-बळानें-कुच्छ्रेंकरून-जुलमानें-पायओढत-&c. जाणें-चालणें. [पापडी *f.*

WAFER, *n. thin cake.* चांदकी *f.* चांदुकली *f.* टिकली *f.* पापड *m.*

2—for letters. चिकटण्याची-लाखाची-&c. वडी *f.*-टिकली *f.* वेफर *or* वैफर *n.* from the English is commonly used by those who speak of this article.

To WAFER, *v. a.* वेफर *n.* लावणें-लावून बंदकरणें.

To WAFT, *v. a. bear through air or water.* तरंगवत-तरंगवून-वाहवत-उडवीत-उडवून-&c. नेणें.

WAFT, *v. n.* v. To FLOAT. तरंगणें, तरणें, वाहतजाणें-येणें.

To WAG. JESTER. मस्कऱ्या, ठट्टेबाज, तमाशाचा माणूस.

To WAGE, *v.* ... *f.* पण *m.* हा... करणें, मांडणें.

2 See To W...

... has won the w. जितपण.

To WAGER, *v. a. bet.* पैज *f.*-पण *m.*-शर्यत *f.*-&c. करणें-मारणें, ...ड *f.* बांधणें-घालणें.

To be ready to w. पण *m.* भोगणें.

WAGES, *n. hire, reward for service or labour.* दरमाहा *m.* पगार *m.* पाग *m.* मुशारा *or* मुशाहरा *m.* मजुरी *f.* मजुरीचा पैसा *m.* रोजमुरा *m.* मेहनत *f.* तलब *f.* वेतन *n.* भृत्या *f.* भृति *f.* भाटक *n.*

Daily w. रोज *m.* दिवस *m.* रोजी *f.*

WAGGISH, *a.* v. FROLICKSOME, PRANKISH. मौजाळा, मौज्या, ठट्ठेखोर, ख्याली, विनोदी, विनोदाचा, ख्याली खुशालीचा.

WAGGISHNESS, WAGGERY, *n.* v. A. *and* PRANK. ख्यालीखुशाली *f.* ठट्टेखोरी *f.* ठट्टेबाजी *f.* कौतुक *n.* चोज *n.* चार *m. pl.*

To WAGGLE. See To WADDLE. 2 See To MOVE.

WAGGON, *n.* v. CART. चौचाकी-चारचाकांचा गाडा *m.* Note. Four wheeled vehicles for transporting goods are not in common use by Maráthás.

WAGGONER, *n.* गाडा हांकणारा, गाडेकरी.

WAGTAIL, *n.*—the bird. खंजन *m.* खंजरीट *m.* सदानर्त्त *m.*

—Indian w. परटीण *f.*

WAIF, *n. goods found of which the owner is unknown.* सांडन. बेवारशीक माल *m.*

To WAIL, *v. n. weep aloud,* v. To LAMENT, To CRY. हेल काढून रडणें, गळा काढून रडणें, ओरडणें, आकांतणें, आक्रंदणें, बोंबलणें, विलपणें *or* विलापणें, धायमाय *f.* मोकलणें-फोडणें, आकांत *m.*-आक्रंदन *n.*-आक्रोश *m.*-विलाप *m.*-&c. करणें.

WAIL, WAILING, *n.* v. V. आकांतणें *n.* &c. आकांत *m.* आक्रंदन *n.* आक्रोश *m.* विलाप *m.* विप्रलाप *m.* व्याकोश *m.* [हाकाट *m.*

General or great w. रडारड *f.* रडारोई *f.* ओरडाओरड *f.* हा-

WAIN. See CART.

WAINSCOT, *n. lining of boards to a wall.* भिंतीला नक्षीची-मढवणी *f.* भिंतीचीतकेवंडी *f.*

WAIST, *n.*—in anatomy. कमर *f.* मध्य *m.* माज *m.* कटि *f.* कटिदेश *m.* कास *f.*—revilingly. माजाड *n.*

Money bag worn round the w. कमरकस *m.*

2 (of a mountain, vessel, &c.). पोट *n.* कमरगा *m.*

WAIST-BAND, *n. upper part of breeches, &c.* नेफा *m.*

2 See GIRDLE.

WAIST-COAT, *n.*—the garment. काचबा *m.* बंडी *f.*

To WAIT, *v. n. stay in expectation.* खोळंबणें. खोळंबून राहणें-बसणें, वाट *f.*-मार्ग *m.*-&c. पाहणें, वाट पाहत बसणें-राहणें, मार्गप्रतिक्षा *f.*-प्रतीक्षा *f.* करणें, तटणें, टपणें, थांबणें, अबगणें, तुंबणें.

To make to w. To keep waiting. नाक *n.* धरणें *g. of o.*

2 *stay, tarry.* थांबणें, खोळंबणें, थिरणें, राहणें, दम *m.* खाणें-धरणें, अवकाश *m.* धरणें, उशीर *m.* धरणें, सबुराई *f.*-सबुरी *f.*-सबूर *f.*-&c. करणें.

After waiting awhile. राहून.

To w. awhile. अवकाश *m.* धरणें, दम *m.* धरणें.

3 upon; *attend upon,* v. To SERVE. चाकरी *f.* करणें-काढणें *g. of o.* खस्ता *f. pl.* काढणें-खाणें *g. of o.* बरदास्त *f.* करणें *g. of o.* समाचार *m.* घेणें *g. of o.*

WAIT. See AMBUSH.

To lie in wait. लपून-दडून-&c. बसणें, टपणें.

WAITER, *n.* WAITING, *p. a.* v. V. 1. खोळंबणारा-खोळंबलेला, ...उपाहणारा, &c. मार्गप्रतीक्षक, तटस्थ.

&c. हुजऱ्या, ...धिरणारा, दमधरणारा, &c.

I. v. SALVER. अडणी). ...करी करणारा-काढणारा, बरदास्त करणारा,

WAITINGWOMAN, *n.* सैरंध्री *f.*

To WAIVE. See To WAVE.

To WAKE, *To* WAKEN, *v. n. not to sleep,* v. To WA... जागणें, जागा-&c. राहणें, जागरण *n.*-&c. करणें.

2 *cease from sleep.* जागा-जागृत-&c. होणें, उठणें, डोळे *m. pl.* उघडणें *g. of s.* झोप *f.*-&c. जाणें *g. of s.*

To WAKE, *To* WAKEN, *v. a. rouse from sleep.* v. To AWAKE. जागा-&c. करणें, उठवणें.

WAKE, *n. religious vigils.* जागरण *n.* v. कर, घाल.

2 (of a ship, &c.). सांखळी *f.*

WAKEFUL, *a. indisposed to sleep.* जागरा, जागरूक, जागरणशील, निद्राविमुख.

2 See WATCHFUL.

WAKEFULNESS, *n.* v. A. 1. जागरेपणा *m.* जागरूकपणा *m.* जागरण *n.* जागर *m.* उजागरा *m.* जागृति *f.* जागरणशीलता *f.* निद्राविमुखता *f.* प्रबोध *m.*

WAKING, *n. awake state.* जागेपणा *m.* जागर *m.* जागरण *n.* जागळ *f.* जाग्रदवस्था *f.* जागृति *f.*

WAKING, *a. belonging to waking state.* जागेपणाचा, जागरणाचा, जाग्रदवस्थेचा, जागृतिसंबंधी.

To WALK, *v. n. move or go on the feet.* चालणें, पायानें-पायीं-पायचाल-&c. चालणें, चालतजाणें.

Able to w. and talk ;—a child. चालता बोलता, चालका बोलका.

To w. backwards and forwards. पसार *m.* करणें.

To w. with a stately gait. ठमकणें, ठमकत चालणें.

2 *not to run; move slowly on the feet.* चालीनें-साध्याचालीनें -न धांवतां-&c. चालणें.

3 about; as for an airing, &c. पायांनीं फिरणें, पायांनीं फिरायालाजाणें, पाय *m. pl.* मोकळे करणें, सैर *f.*-सहल *f.* करणें, रपेट *f.* करणें-मारणें, फेरा *m.*-फेरफटका *m.* करणें, फैल *f.* करणें, तलावा *m.* करणें-मारणें-देणें, टेहलणें *or* टेहेलणें, परिक्रम *m.*-परिक्रमण *n.*-&c. करणें, विहरण *n.*-विहार *m.* करणें, विहरणें.

4 off ; v. To DECAMP. पवबारा *m.*-झ्यां *f.*-चलसू *f.*-&c. करणें.

5 off with ; *take furtively.* उपटणें, उपटा *or* उपाटा *m.* देणें, पळविणें.

6 v. To BEHAVE. चालणें, वर्त्तणें.

To WALK, *v. a. pass through or upon.* चालणें, फिरणें, येणें, जाणें *all with* वर, मध्नें, &c. पदगत करणें.

2 *lead, drive, ride, &c. with a slow pace.* चालीनें-हलक्याचालीनें-कदमानें-&c. चालवणें-नेणें-हांकणें-&c.

3 about ; (horse, &c.). फेरणें, फेर फटका*m.*-फेर*m.*-&c.करणें, टेहलणें *or* टेहेलणें.

WALK, WALKING, *n.* v. V. N. 1.—the act or pace. पायानें चालणें *n.* पायींचालणें *n.* पायचाल *f.* पादचाल *f.* चरणचाल *f.* पादचार *m.*

2 चालीचीचाल *f.* साधीचाल *f.*पाऊल चाल *f.*पावंड *or* पांडचाल*f.*

3 फिरणें *n.* सहल *f.* सैर *f.* रपेट *f.* फेरा *m.* फेरफटका *m.* फेर *m.* तलावा *m.* टेहलणी *f.* टेहली *f.* परिक्रम *m.* परिक्रमण *n.*

W. of a hundred paces after a meal (to promote digestion). शतपावली *f.* शतपदी *f.*

6 *and* CONDUCT. चाल *f.* वर्त्तणूक *f.*

I. *manner of walking.* चाल *f.* पाऊल *n.* चालण्याची रीत *f.*

II. *space or ground for walking.* रपेट-सहल-&c. करण्याची वाट *f.* पायांनीं फिरण्याचा रस्ता *m.*-&c. शतपावलीचीवाट *f.* शतपावलीचा रस्ता *m.*

WALKER, *n.* WALKING, *p. a.* v. V.N. 1. पायानें-पायीं-&c.चालणारा, पादचारी.

2 चालीनें-साधे चालीनें-&c. चालणारा.

WALKING-STICK, *n.* काठी *f.* हातांत धरण्याची-रपेटीची-&c. काठी *f.*

WALL, *n.* भिंत *f.* दिवार *or* ल *f.* भित्ति *f.*

Gable w. चांदई *f.*

Hollow in a w. (to contain grain). बळद *n.* मसुरा *m.*

Niche or recess in a w. कोनाडा *m.* कोनाडें *n.* देवळी *f.*

Thin w. (as of one brick). चिरणी *f.* पडदी *f.* शिती *f.*

W. enclosing the court of a temple. पौळ *or* पोव्ळ *f.* पोवळी *f.*

2 (of a village, &c.) *enclosing wall.* कुसूं*n.* कूस *n.* गांवकुसूं*n.* कोट *m.* तट *m.* अरब्बा *m.* फांद *f.* पन्हा *m.* (as शहरपन्हा, गांवपन्हा) प्राकार*m.* प्राचीर *n.*

3 (of lath and plaster). शिंद *or* शिंध *f.*

4 (of slight sticks, plastered over). कूड *m.*

To make a w. कुडणें, कुडण *n.* करणें.

5 (of stones loosely thrown up) *dry wall.* गडगा *or* घा*m.* कोरडीभिंत *f.* पोळ *f.* दगडपोळ *f.*

6 (of a tent). कनात *f.*

To WALL, *v. a.* भिंत *f.*-&c. बांधणें.

Walled up, *closed up with masonry.* बंदिस्त.

WALL-EYE, *n.* कैरा *or* खैरा डोळा *m.*

WALL-EYED, *a.* कैरा *or* खैरा, कैऱ्या डोळ्याचा.

WALL-PLATE, *n.* इंद्रकट *n.* इंद्रवट *n.* इंद्राठी *f.*

WALLET, *n.* (of travellers,). भाता *m.* धोकटी *or* धोगटी *f.* हडपी *f.* पडशी *f.*

2 (of beggars). झोळी *f.* झोळणा *m.* चौपदरी *f.*

To WALLOP. See To BOIL, To BUBBLE.

To WALLOW, *v. n. tumble and roll.* लोळणें, लोळणें, लोळगोळ *f.* करणें.

2 fig. पोहणें, गरक-&c. असणें.

WALNUT, *n.*—the tree. अखरोट *or* ड *or* अकरोट *or* ड*m.* अक्षोट*m.*—the nut, अखरोट *or* ड, अकरोट *or* ड *m. n.* अक्षोट*m.*

WALRUS, *n.* समुद्रांतलें एक जनावर आहे.

To WAMBLE, *v. n. be qualmish.* उमदळणें, कळमळणें *both impers.*

WAN, *a. of a sickly hue, pale.* उफट *or* उफीट *or* ओफट, फिका *or* फिक्का, फिकट, वाणढाळ, वाणमाऱ्या, विकळा, निस्तेज, म्लान, मलूल.

To look w.—countenance. उफटणें.

To turn w. काळवटणें, काळवंडणें, काळसरणें, जारटणें.

WAND, *n.* v. TWIG. फोकाटी *f.* कमची *f.* छडी *f.*

2 *charming rod.* कांडी *f.*

To wave his w.—a conjuror. कांडी *f.* फिरवणें-फिरगाळणें.

3 *staff of authority.* छडी *f.* काठी *f.* वेत्र *n.*

To WANDER, *v. n. roam, rove, ramble.* हिंडणें, हिंडत फिरणें, भ्रमणें, परिभ्रमणें, भटकणें, भटकतफिरणें, भटक्या *f. pl.*-भणक्या *f. pl.* मारणें-मारीत फिरणें, इकडे तिकडे-जिकडे तिकडे-सैरावैरा-भणभण-&c. फिरणें, पर्यटन *pop.* पलाटन *n.*-हिंडन *n.*-भ्रमण *n.*-परिभ्रमण *n.*-&c. करणें.

2 *go astray,* v. To DEVIATE, To ERR. चुकणें, चुकूनजाणें, बहकणें *or* भकणें, वाट *f.* सोडणें-सोडूनजाणें, भ्रमणें, भटकणें, गहाळणें, घसरणें, व्यभिचार *m.*-&c. करणें, व्यभिचार *m.*-भ्रांति *f.*-&c. होणें *g. of s.*

3 (in speech). तरंगणें, तरलणें *or* तरळणें, वाहवणें, चांचरणें, रानांत शिरणें, रान *n.* धरणें-घेणें.

4—mind, eyes, &c. तरलणें *or* तरळणें, भ्रमणें, देहावर नसणें, चित्तविभ्रम*m.*-बुद्धिविभ्रम *m.*-भ्रांति *f.*-&c. असणें *g. of s.*

WANDERER, *n.* WANDERING, *p. a.* v. V. 1. हिंडणारा, हिंडत फिरणारा, भटकत फिरणारा, &c. हिंडफिऱ्या, भटक्या, हिंडग्या, फिरस्त *or* स्ता, ओढाळ, रांबाड, भ्रमी, भ्रमणीक, चरिष्णु, पर्यटनी, भ्रमण-पर्यटन-&c. कर्त्ता-कारी-&c.

Distressed w. परागंदा.

W. in tracts unknown. दिग्भ्रांत.

2 चुकणारा, चुकून जाणारा-गेलेला, भकणारा-भकलेला,&c. चुकला माकला*or*वाकला, चुकार, चुकर, चुकूर, भ्रमी, भ्रमणीक,भ्रमणशील.

3 वाहवणारा-वाहवलेला, रानांतशिरणारा-शिरलेला, &c. वाहवरा, अचरट पचरट.

4 तरळणारा-तरळलेला, भ्रमणारा, &c. बेशुद्ध, बेसावध, भ्रमिष्ट, भ्रांत.

WANDERING, *n.* v. V. 1. हिंडणें *n.* हिंडतफिरणें *n.* भटकणें *n.* &c. पर्यटन *pop.* पलाटन *n.* हिंडन *n.* परिभ्रमण *n.* भ्रमण*n.* भ्रम *m.* परिचार*m.* विहार *m.*

W. over the earth. दिग्भ्रम *m.* दिग्भ्रमण *n.*

2 चुकणें *n.* चुकूनजाणें *n.* भटकणें *n.* भकणें *n.* &c. भ्रांति *f.* व्यभिचार *m.* विपथगमन *n.* अपथगमन *n.* विचलन *n.* विगति *f.*

4 तरलणें *n.* भ्रमणें *n.* &c. भ्रम *n.* भ्रांति *f.* चित्तभ्रम *m.* चित्तविभ्रम *m* बुद्धिविभ्रम *m.*

To WANE, *v. n.*—the moon, *decrease.* लहान-उणा-क्षीण-&c. होणें-होतजाणें, कलाक्षय *m.*-क्षय *m.*-ऱ्हास *m.*-&c. होणें *g. of s.*

2 v. To DECLINE. उतरणें, उतरतापाया *m.*-जातापाया *m.*-उतरतीदशा *f.*-&c. होणें-लागणें. *g. of s.* [जोऱ्हास *m.*

WANE, *n.* v. V. 1. लहान होणें *n.* &c. कलाक्षय *m.* अवकळा *f.* ते-

2 अवकळा *f.* उतार *m.* उतरतापाय *m.* जातापाया *m.* उतरतीदशा *f.* उतरती कमाण *or* न *f.* क्षय *m.* अपक्षय *m.* क्षिति *f.* तेजोऱ्हास *m.* सरता पालव *m.*

WANED, *p.* v. V. 1. लहान झालेला, &c. कलाक्षीण, क्षीणकल.

2 उतरलेला, &c. अपक्षीण, प्राप्तक्षय, जातक्षय, जातऱ्हास.

WANNESS, *n.* v. A. उफटपणा *m.* &c. काळवटी *f.* काळवंडी *f.* काळवण *f.* मडेकळा *f.* कालिमा *m. pop.* काळिमा *f.*

To WANT, *v.a. be without.* नसणें *with in. con. and* जवळ-पाशीं-&c. निराळा-वेगळा-विरहित-&c. असणें with the noun expressing the object, as तो बुद्धीवेगळा आहे he wants wisdom, अभाव *m.*-&c. असणें *g. of o.* वास *m.* नसणें *in. con. with g. of o.*

To w. utterly. गांवीं-अष्टांगीं नसणें *in. con. with g. of o.*

2 *have need of.* गरज *f.*-दरकार *f.*-अगत्य *n.*-प्रयोजन *n.*-काम *n.* आकांक्षा *f.*-अपेक्षा *f.*-&c. असणें-लागणें *in. con. with g. of o.* अपेक्षणें, आकांक्षणें.

What do you want? तुम्हास काय पाहिजे?

3 *wish,* v. To DESIRE. इच्छिणें, इच्छा *f.*-आकांक्षा *f.*-अपेक्षा *f.*- &c. असणें *in. con. with g. of o.*

4 *be deficient or fall short.* उणा-कमी-&c. असणें-पडणें, कमती *f.*-वाण *f.*-उणीव *f.*-उणेपणा *m.*-तोटा *m.*-&c. असणें-पडणें *in. con. with g. of o.*

To WANT, *v. n. be deficient, fall short.* उणा-कमी-&c. पडणें.

WANT, *n. absence, negation, state of not being.* नसणें *n.* नाहींपणा *m.* अभाव *m.* राहित्य *n.* शून्याकार *m.* नास्तिपक्ष *m.* ठणठणपाळ *m.* ठणठणाट *m.*

To be a w. of. शून्य *n.*-पूज *n.* असणें *with* नांवानें, Ex. विद्येच्यानांवानेंपूज, there is an utter want of learning.

2 *insufficiency, defect, lack, &c.* v. DEFICIENCY. उणवाई *f.* उणीव *f.* उणेपणा *m.* कमताई *f.* कमतणूक *f.* वाण *f.* तोटा *m.* न्यूनता *f.*

3 *occasion for, lack of,* v. NEED. गरज *f.* दरकार *f.* अगत्य *n.* प्रयोजन *n.* आकांक्षा *f.* अपेक्षा *f.* व्यपेक्षा *f.*

4 *indigence, penury, &c.* v. POVERTY. अनुपपत्ति *pop.* अनुपत *and* अनुपत्ति *f.* कंगाली *f.* चणचण *f.* चडचड *f.* तंगचाई *f.* तारंबळ *f.* खर्चाची अडचण *f.* धनाभाव *m.* द्रव्याभाव *m.*

That is above w. निर्द्दात *or* धात.

Wants; *necessities.* पांग *m. pl.*

WANTING, *a. absent, deficient, short.* उणा, कमी, न्यून, गैरहाजीर, अविद्यमान.

To be utterly w. औषधाला-शाह्याला-शपथेला-&c. नसणें.

2 *that is destitute of or deficient in.* उणा, कमी, न्यून, कोता, all used with both the possessive and the ablative case, as तो बुद्धीचा उणा आहे, हा पैशानें कमी आहे, निराळा-बेगळा-शून्य-हीन-विहीन-रहित-विरहित-व्यतिरिक्त-रिक्त, all in comp.

WANTON, *a. lascivious, lewd,* v. LUSTFUL. कामी, कामुक, इष्की, कामबुद्धीचा, कामदृष्टीचा, कामबुद्धि, कामदृष्टि,—esp. of a female. चंचल, चपल, चाळ, ललित.

2 *profligate, dissolute, &c.* v. LOOSE, LICENTIOUS. सोदा, लुचा, ढंगी, बेढंगी, व्यसनी, टवाळ, टवाळखोर, खोटचाल, इष्की, बाजिंदा.

3 *frolicsome, sportive, &c.* v. PLAYFUL, PRANKISH. कौतुकी, ख्याली, छंदी, चाळक, विलासी, सलील, ललित.

4 *unrestrained, regardless of rule, law, mode, &c.* v. IRREGULAR, LICENTIOUS. बेकैद, बेकैदी, ऐच्छिक, स्वच्छ, स्वैरगति, बाष्कळ, मनस्वी, लाडका.

W. procedure. लाडका व्यवहार *m.*

WANTON, *n. lewd woman,* v. HARLOT. चाळक बायको *f.* चाळकभवानी *f.* नाचरी *f.* नाचण *f.* नाचणघुगरी *f.* चवढवी *f.* टेबखोरखी *f.* चपला *f.* व्यभिचारिणी *f.* विलासिनी *f.* ललिता *f.* ललना *f.* स्वैरिणी *f.* रागिणी *f.* प्रमदा *f.*

To WANTON, *v. n. play lasciviously.* इष्कबाजी *f.*-विलास *m.*-विषयविलास *m.*-कामविलास *m.*-कामचेष्टा *f.*-विषयक्रीडा *f.*-रमण *n.*-रमणूक *f.*-&c. करणें, रमणें, रतणें, खेळणें, गमणें.

2 v. To REVEL. लहरा *f. pl.*-मौजा *f. pl.*-उड्या *f. pl.*-&c. मारणें, बुरंगळणें *or* बुरंगाळणें, सुसांगणें.

3—as banners, &c. खेळणें. [कामबुद्ध्या.

WANTONLY, *adv.* v. A. 1. कामबुद्धीनें, काममावानें, कामदृष्टीनें,

2 सोदेगिरीनें, लुचेगिरीनें, &c.

3 कौतुकानें, खेळाकरितां-साठीं-&c. खेळानें, लीलेनें, क्रीडेनें.

4 *and* LICENTIOUSLY. बेकैदपणानें, मनस्वी, मनास येईल तसें, यथेच्छ, यथेष्ट, यथेप्सित.

WANTONNESS, *n.* v. A. 1. कामीपणा *m.* कामुकपणा *m.* कामबुद्धि *f.* कामभाव *m.* कामदृष्टि *f.* [खोरी *f.*

2 सोदेगिरी *f.* लुचेगिरी *f.* बेढंगीपणा *m.* &c. टवाळी *f.* टवाळ-

3 कौतुक *n.* विलास *m.* क्रीडा *f.* लीला *f.*

4 बेकैदपणा *m.* &c. बेकैद *f.* बेकैदी *f.* स्वैरगति *f.* कामचार *m.* स्वेच्छागति *f.* स्वैरिता *f.*

WAR, *n. contention of states.* लढाई *f.* युद्ध *n.* रण *m.n.* संग्राम *m.*

The four schemes of prevailing or means of success in *War* are, साम, दाम, दंड, भेद (See M. & E. Dict.).

W. of stratagems. कृत्रिमयुद्ध *n.*

To WAR, *v. n. make or carry on war.* लढाई *f.*-युद्ध *n.*-&c. करणें-चालवणें-मांडणें.

WAR-CHARIOT, *n.* रथ *m.*

WAR-DRUM, *n.* रणभेरी *f.* अभयडिंडिम *n.*

WAR-HORSE, *n. charger.* बारू *m.*

To WARBLE, *v.a. sing, &c. with modulations.* आळवणें, छडणें, फिरकी *f.*-झील *f.*-उपज *f.*-शारीर *n.*-कंप *m.*-सांचखोंच *f.*-&c. घेणें-घेऊन गाणें &c. लकेरी *f.* मारणें.

To WARBLE, *v. n.* See To SING, To QUAVER.

To WARD, *v. a. fend off.* वारणें, निवारणें, रेटणें, वारण *n.*-निवारण *n.*-टाळा *m.*-&c. करणें *g. of o.* [बठार *n.*

WARD, *n. district of a town.* वाडा *m.* पुरा *m.* महला *m.* पेठ *f.*

2 *custody,* v. CONFINEMENT. कैद *f.* परज *m.*

To put in w. पहान्यांत-चौकींत-&c. ठेवणें.

3 *person under a guardian.* दिम्मती, दिम्मतींतला.

4 *ward* in comp. is rendered by कडे (*as* Homeward घराकडे, गांवाकडे, स्वदेशाकडे, &c. Hitherward इकडे, Thitherward तिकडे).

5 See WATCH, GUARD.

WARDED, *p.* v. V. वारलेला, &c. वारित, निवारित.

WARDEN, *n. keeper, guardian, &c.* दिम्मतदार, रखवालदार, अधिकारी, अध्यक्ष.

WARDER, *n.* WARDING, *p. a.* v. V. वारणारा, &c. निवारक, निवारणकर्त्ता-कारी-&c.

I. *keeper &c.* See WARDEN.

WARDROBE, *n. room where clothes, jewels, &c. are kept.* पोशाकखाना *n.* जामदारखाना *m.* तोशेखाना *m.*

Keeper of the w. and jewelry. जामदार.

2 *large box for keeping clothes.* पांघरुणाचें कपाट *n.*

3 *wearing apparel*—gener. पांघुरणें *n. pl.* वस्त्र *n.*

WARE, *a.* See WARY.

WARE, WARES, *n.* v. COMMODITY. माल *m.* सौदा *or* सवदा *m.*

China Ware. चिनई भांडीं *n. pl.*

Hard Ware. लोखंडी सामान *n.*

Potter's Ware. कुंभाराचीं भांडीं *n. pl.* कुंभारकाम *n.*

WARE-HOUSE, *n.* वखार *f.* जिन्नसखाना *m.* कोठा *m.* कोठी *f.*

WARE-HOUSE-KEEPER, *n.* वखारदार, वखारी, वखारवाला.

WARFARE, *n. military operations, war.* लढाई *f.* युद्ध *n.* लढाईबिढाई *f.* युद्धबिद्ध *n.* संग्रामबिंग्राम *m.*

WARILY, *adv.* v. A. सावधपणानें, सावधगिरीनें, सावधहोऊन, मागेंपुढें पाहून. [हुशारी *f.*

WARINESS, *n.* v. A. *and* CAUTION. सावधपणा *m.* सावधगिरी *f.*

WARLIKE, *a. fit, disposed, &c. for war.* लढाऊ, लढवई *or* वाई, जुंजार *or* झुंजार, लढता, रणवीर, रणगंभीर, रणधीर, रणशूर, रणासक्त, रणोत्सुक, रणप्रिय, वीरश्रीचा.

2 *belonging, &c. to war,* v. MARTIAL, लढाईचा, &c. युद्धाविषयींचा, युद्धविषयक, सामरिक.

WARLOCK, *n. wizard,* v. CONJURER. इलमबाज, इलमी, पाहण्या.

WARM, *a. having heat, not cold.* ऊन, उष्ण, गरम.

2 (of temperament) *fiery, hot,* v. PASSIONATE. रागी, रागीट, उष्ण, गरम, तापड, गरममिजाजेचा, उष्णप्रकृति.

3 *made warm, heated.* गरमकेलेला, तापलेला, ऊन केलेला, &c. ऊन, उष्ण, गरम, तप्त. [ष्ण, शीतोष्ण.

Warmish. कोंबट *or* कोमट, सोमट, सोमळ, सोमाळा, मंदो-

4 *enthusiastic, zealous, ardent,* v. PASSIONATE, EARNEST. उष्ण, गरम, उत्साहाचा, उत्साही, उत्साहवान्, सोत्साह, सानुराग, कडक, जहाल *or* ज्याल.

5 *smart, vehement, violent,*—fight, work, &c. कडक, कडक्याचा, तडक्याचा, झपाट्याचा, तडाख्याचा, कडाख्याचा.

To WARM, *v. a. communicate heat to.* ऊन-उष्ण-गरम-&c. करणें, तापवणें, उष्णता *f.* आणणें.

To w. before a fire, &c. ऊब *f.* देणें, शेक*m.* देणें.

To w. one's self before a fire, &c. शेकणें, शेक*m.* घेणें, शेकाटणें, शेकाटा*m.* घेणें.

2 *make zealous, ardent, &c.* उत्साह*m.*-आस्था *f.*-&c. आणणें-उत्पन्न करणें, उत्साही-आस्थेवाईक-सोत्साह-&c. करणें, आसक्त करणें, रमवणें.

To WARM, *v. n. become heated.* ऊन-गरम-&c. होणें, तापणें.

To put to w. उन्हत ठेवणें.

2 fig. *rise into ardor, become animated, expand.* उत्साह*m.*-आवेश*m.*-चेव*m.*-&c. येणें *in. con.* उत्सुक-उत्साही-&c. होणें, कढी *f.* उमलणें *g. of s.*

WARM-HEARTED, *a.* v. AFFECTIONATE, LOVING. ममतालु *or* ळू, स्नेहाळू, मायाळू, प्रेमवंत, प्रेमळ. [लेला, &c.

WARMED, *p.* v. A. 1. गरम केलेला, तापवलेला, ऊबदिल्हेला, शेक-

2 उत्साह आणलेला, उत्साही केलेला, &c.

WARMER, *n.* WARMING, *p. a.* v. V. 1. गरम करणारा, तापवणारा, ऊब देणारा, &c.

2 उत्साह आणणारा, उत्साही करणारा, &c.

WARMLY, *adv.* v. A. 4. उत्साहानें, आस्थेनें, उत्कंठेनें, &c. सात्तेपें, सात्तेपेंकरून.

5 कडकपणानें, कडक्यानें, तडक्यानें, झपाट्यानें, &c.

WARMNESS, WARMTH, *n.* v. A. 1. ऊनपणा*m.* उष्णता *f.* ऊष्मा*m.* गरमी *f.* [गरमप्रकृति *f.*

2 रागीटपणा*m.* तापडपणा*m.* &c. उष्णता *f.* गरममिजाज *f.*

3 ऊनपणा*m.* गरमपणा*m.* गरमी *f.* उष्णता *f.* तापलेलेपणा*m.*

4 उत्साह*m.* आस्था *f.* उत्सुकता *f.* गरमी *f.* उष्णता *f.*

5 कडका*m.* तडका *m.* कडकपणा *m.* झपाटा *m.* तडाखा *m.*

I. *gentle heat.* कोमटपणा *or* कोंबटपणा *m.* सोमटपणा*m.* मंदोष्ण *n.*

To WARN, *v.a. caution against.* पूर्वी-&c. जाणवणें-सुचवणें-सावध-&c. करणें, बोधवणें, सूचना *f.*-&c. करणें.

2 *admonish of a thing to be done.* बजावणें, ताकीद *f.* करणें-देणें, जगावणें, जतावणें *or* जथावणें, सांगणें, सांगून-बोलूनठेवणें,—strictly, particularly, &c. बजावून-हडसून-खराबून-&c. सांगणें-ताकीद *f.* करणें, &c.

3 *apprize previously,* v. To INFORM. सुचवणें, सूचना *f.* करणें *g. of o.* खबर *f.* देणें *g. of o.* बोधवणें, बोधित-सूचित-&c. करणें.

WARNED, *p.* v. V. 1. पूर्वी जाणवलेला-सुचवलेला-सावधकेलला, &c. सूचित, बोधित.

2 बजावलेला, जगावलेला, जतावलेला, &c.

3 सुचवलेला, &c. सूचित, बोधित. [&c.

WARNER, *n.* WARNING, *p. a.* पूर्वी जाणवणारा, सावध करणारा,

2 बजावणारा, जगावणारा, जतावणारा, सांगणारा, ताकीद करणारा, &c.

3 सुचवणारा, खबरदेणारा, सूचनाकरणारा, &c.

WARNING, *n. caution, admonition.* ताकीद *f.* सांगी *f.* बजावणें *n.* जतावणें*n.* पूर्वबोध*m.* पूर्वबोधन*n.* सूचना *f.* सूचन*n.*

To take w. from. दाखला*m.* घेणें *g. of o.*

To take w. *become compunctious, cautious, &c.* कानाला खडा*m.* लावूनघेणें, कान*m. pl.* पिळून घेणें, कान*m. pl.* होणें *in. con.* अक्कल *f.*-अद्दल *f.* घडणें *in. con.*

To be constantly giving w. कानीं कपाळीं रडणें.

2 *previous notice.* सूचना *f.* ताकीद *f.* सुचें *n.* वरदी *f.* from the English *word.*

To WARP, *v. n.*—wood, leather, &c. *be twisted,* तिडणें, बांकणें, बागणें, बांकणें, बांक *m.*-बांक *m.*—&c. येणें *in. con.* वांकडणें, वांकडा—&c. होणें.

2 fig. *swerve*, v. To DEVIATE. बहकणें, आडवाटेंत जाणें, वाट *f.* सोडणें, पाऊल *n.* वांकडें पडणें *g. of s.*

To WARP, *v. a. draw up or aside, contract, &c.* वांकवणें, तिडवणें, वागवणें, वांकडा-&c. करणें.

2 fig. *turn aside from the true direction, pervert.* वांकवणें, वागवणें, बहकवणें, वांकडा करणें, पाऊल *n.* वांकडें करणें *g. of o.*

WARP, *n. the threads that run lengthwise.* ताणा *m.* उभेंसूत *n.* ऊभीवीण *f.* उभवण *n.* उभवीण *f.*

The threads composing w. बशारणें *n.*

To stretch (lay) the w. साल *f.* घालणें.

WARPED, *p.* v. V. 1. तिडका, तिडतिडा, तिडा, वागीव, वागट.

W. in various directions and degrees. वांकडकोका, वांकडमुसका, वांकडातिडका, वांकडातिकडा, वांकडादेढुडा.

To be w. by the wind. वारसंडणें.

WARPEDNESS, *n.* v. P. तीड *f.* वांक *m.*

To WARRANT, *v. a.* v. To AUTHORIZE. अखत्यार *m.*-अधिकार *m.*-सत्ता *f.*-हुकूम *m.*-&c. देणें, अखत्यारी-मुखत्यार करणें.

2 *support by authority or proof*, v. To SANCTION. आधार *m.*-आश्रय *m.*-&c. देणें, आधार *m.*-आश्रय *m.*-&c. असणें *in. con. with g. of s.* [&c. करणें.

3 *give assurance of the goodness, &c. of.* खातरी *f.*-निशा *f.*-

WARRANT, *n. support, sanction, authority.* आधार *m.* आश्रय *pop.* आसरा *m.* प्रमाण *n.* गमक *n.* मान *n.* शेरा *m.*

2 *writ, commission, &c.* परवाना*m.* सनद *f.* हुकूमनामा *m.* अखत्यारनामा *m.* मुखत्यारनामा *m.* अधिकारपत्र *n.* शासनपत्र *n.*

3 *authority to seize.* वारंट *n.* from the English is used.

WARRANTABLE, *a. allowable, justifiable, proper*, v. RIGHT, LAWFUL. मान्य, योग्य, वाजवी, उचित, न्याय्य, न्यायाधार, साधार, साश्रय.

WARRANTABLENESS, *n.* v. A. वाजवीपणा *m.* योग्यता *f.* न्याय्यता *f.* औचित्य *n.* मान्यता *f.* मयना *or* माना *m.* मान *n.*

WARRANTABLY. See ALLOWABLY, LAWFULLY. [त्यार.

WARRANTED, *p.* v. V. 1. अखत्यार दिल्हेला, &c. अखत्यारी, मुख-

2 आधार दिल्हेला, &c. साधार, साश्रय.

3 खातरी केलेला, &c. खातरीचा, निशेचा.

WARRANTER, *n.* WARRANTING, *p. a.* v. V. 3. खातरी करणारा, निशाकरणारा.

WARRANTY, *n. security or assurance given of soundness, &c.* बिनऐबाची-बिनखोडीची-&c. खातरी *f.*-निशा *f.*

WARRIOR, *n.* See SOLDIER. 2.—emphatically, v. HERO. धारकरी, वीर, युद्धवीर, गाजीमर्द, गाजी, शूर, भट, योद्धा, लढवय्या.

Cry or shout of warriors. योधसंराव *m.*

Independent w. एकांगवीर, एकांड्या.

W.-or war-dance; *dance performed by warriors after a victory, &c.* वीरजयंतिका *or* जयंति *f.*

W.- posture. वीरासन *n.*

WART, *n.*—the excrescence on the hands, &c. चामखीळ *m. f.* चामखोड *m.* चामकोड *m.* चर्मकील *m.*

WARY, *a.* v. CAUTIOUS. सावध, हुशार, दुरंदेश, मागेंपुढें पाहणारा.

To be w. मागें पुढें पाहणें, आगापिछा *m.* पाहणें, पाउल*n.* जपून टाकणें *or* ठेवणें.

WASE, *n. ring of grass under a pitcher, &c.* चुंबळ *or* चुंभळ *f.* आहरा *or* आहारा *m.*

To WASH, *v. a. cleanse in or by water.* धुणें, धुऊन टाकणें-घेणें, पाण्यानें साफ करणें, प्रक्षाळणें, क्षाळणें, प्रक्षालन *n.*-क्षालन *n.*-&c. करणें *g. of o.*

Cost of washing. धुणावळ *f.* धुलाई *f.*

To w. slightly. ओंचळणें, चुचचुचाविणें.

Water in which any thing has been washed. धुवणी *n.*

To w. the mouth and hands after eating. आंचवणें.

To knead and squeeze in washing. चुचकणें.

2 out; v. To RINSE. विसळणें *or* विसुळणें, संगाळणें.

To WASH, *v. n. perform ablution.* आंग *n.* धुणें, स्नान *n.* करणें restricted to Bráhmans, आंघोळ *f.* करणें, न्हाणें *or* नाहणें.

WASH, *n. linen to be washed.* धुणीं *n. pl.* धुवायाचीं वस्त्रें *n. pl.*

Piece for the w. धुणें *n.*

2 *washing of clothes.* धुणें *n.* वस्त्रक्षालन *n.*

At or to the w. परटीस *v.* हो, घाल, दे, टाक.

From the w. परटीहून.

Piece fresh from the w. परीटघडी *f.* परीटधुणें *n.*

That has come from the w. परीटधुणा, परटी.

3 (of gold, silver, &c.) पाणी *n.* मुलामा *m.* धूर *m.* ओप *f.* कल्हई *f.* झाक *f.*

4 *thin, meagre, sloppy food. &c.* Answering to this word and to such words as *Wishwash, slop, slipslop, dishwater, &c.* there are numerous words equally expressive. विरविटी *f.* थिरथिटी *f.* पेजवणी *n.* फजिता*m.* गंजवणी*n.* धमंडगुळवणी *n.* ढपलवणी *n.* फळकवणी *n.* झुळकवणी *n.* डिचकें *n.* गरगट *n.* डुळकवणी *n.* कळकळवणी *n.* शंखवणी *n.*

Sour w.—as applied to dishes and sauces when too dilute and sour. खळगट *n.* खळा *m.* खळक *m.*

5 (for cattle, pigs, &c.). खरकटवणी *n.* ओखटवणी *n.* ओखटवण *f. n.* मिळवण *or* मेळवण *n.* लेपवणी *n.*

6 *water in which rice, &c. has been washed.* पाणी *n.* धुवण *or* धूण *n.*

7 (of coloring substances, of pulse, &c.). काट *m. n.* काढवणी *n.* कढण *n.*

8 (of earth and cowdung, &c.). गारा *m.* रद्दा *m.*

9 *materials to wash or smear over.* लेप *m.* लेंपन *n.*

10 *alluvion.* मळी *f.* खळमळ *m.* होर *f.* साय *f.* मळई *f.* मळकी *f.*

WASHED, *p.* v. V. A. धुतलेला, प्रक्षालित, क्षालित, धौत.

I.—cloth &c. *not new and unwashed.* धुवट.

W.-cloth. धुतवस्त्र *n.*

II. (with gold or silver). मुलामी, मुलाम्याचा, सोन्याच्या-रुप्याच्या-&c. पाण्याचा.

WASHERMAN, *n.* परीट, धोबी, मडवळ, बरठा, रजक.

W.'s stone. शीळ *f.* शिळा *f.* परीटशीळ *f.*

W.'s ward. परीटवाडा *m.*

W.'s washing place. परीटधुणी *f.* परीटघाट *m.*

WASHERWOMAN, *n.* परटीण *f.* धोबीण *f.* मडवळीण *f.* बरठीण *f.* रजकी *f.*

WASHY, *a. watery, weak, wishy washy.* पाणचट, पचपचीत, फळफळीत *or* फिळफिळीत, फिका *or* फिक्का, फिकट, गळगळीत *or* गिळगिळीत, कळकळीत *or* किळकिळीत *or* खळखळीत, असट, पाणवळ, विरविरीत, मचमचीत, मळमळीत *or* मुळमुळीत, दुळदुळीत, रवरवीत, लिबलिबीत *or* लबलबीत, कबकबीत *or* कचकचीत,

वाह्वरा, उमळा *or* उंबळा.

WASP, *n.*—vespa. गांधीलमाशी *f.* गांधील *f.* गांधीण *f.*

2—vespa solitaria. कुंभारीण *f.* भ्रमरकीट *m.* भ्रमरी *f.*

WASPISH, *a. petulant, snappish,* v. PEEVISH, CROSS. चिरडखोर, चिरडीखोर, खिसखिशा, तिडतिडा.

WASPISHNESS, *n.*v.A. चिरडखोरी *f.* चिरड *f.* तिडतीड *f.* तिडतिडेपणा *m.* &c.

WASTAGE, *n. loss by leakage, &c.* घस *f.* घट *f.* घटती *f.* तूट *f.*

To WASTE, *v. a. diminish gradually.* झरवणें, घटवणें, क्षरवणें, क्षय *m.*-ऱ्हास *m.*-क्षिति *f.*-&c. करणें *g. of o.* क्षीण करणें.

2 *consume wantonly, expend or apply uselessly &c.* v. To SQUANDER. घालवणें, उडवणें, उधळणें, दवडणें, फुकट-उगाच-एरवीं-अनाठायीं-&c. खर्चणें-खर्च *m.* करणें *g. of o.* हरवणें *or* हारवणें, गटकावणें, गट-&c.करणें, फुकटखर्च *m.*-व्यर्थखर्च *m.*-अनुपयोगी खर्च *m.*-&c. करणें *g. of o.* फांकूं *m. f.* करणें (द्रव्याचें, धान्याचें, &c.), फुंकणें (दौलत, द्रव्य &c.), पोकळी खालीं टाकणें, पोकळीस देणें, वाऱ्यावर टाकणें, बारापाणी *n.*-केरबारा *m.* करून टाकणें *g. of o.* केरावाऱ्यांत-केरावाऱ्यानिशीं देणें-टाकणें.

3 *desolate, spoil,* v. To DEVASTATE, To RAVAGE. नासधूस *f.*-वैराणी *f.*-पाटावरवंटा *m.*-&c.करणें *g. of o.* वैराण-उजाड-&c. करणें.

4 (time) *spend in idleness, &c.* झुलवणें, रिकामा *decl.* घालवणें, कालक्षेप *m.*-कालहरण *n.*-&c.करणें.

To WASTE, *v. n. dwindle away.* घटणें, अटणें, क्षिणणें,क्षरणें, क्षय *m.*-&c. पावणें, सांडवणें, क्षीण-&c. होणें, क्षय *m.*-ऱ्हास *m.*-&c. होणें *g. of s.*

2 *emaciate, macerate, lose flesh,* v. LEAN. आंग *n.* टाकणें-सोडणें-सांडणें, चोपणें, चोपटणें, चुंचणें, ढकलणें, पचणें, क्षिणणें, खंगणें, लंगणें *or* लंघणें, गळणें, सांडवणें, गंढाळणें, झडणें, झरणें, झुरणें, झुरणीस पडणें, झुरणी *f.* लागणें *in. con .* झुकणें, घसरणें, अटणें, रोडणें, रोडावणें, कडसणें, कडसणीस लागणें,झिजणें, झिरकणें, झिरणीस लागणें, रोड-कृश-&c. होणें-होतचालणें,कढी *f.* पातळ होणें *g. of s.* काष्ठ *n.* होणें, आंगाचेंपाणी *n.* होणें *g. of s.* पोटाचा कपोता *m.* वळणें *g. of s.* शरीराची ढगळ *f.* होणें *g. of s.*

A wasting disease. झडी *f.*

WASTE, *a.* WASTED, *p.* v. V. A. 1. झरवलेला, घटवलेला, &c. क्षीण, अपचित.

2 घालवलेला, दवडलेला, एरवीं खर्चलेला, पोकळीखालीं टाकलेला.

3 *and* DESOLATE. उजाड केलेला, &c. उजाड, वैराण.

To lay w. v. To RAVAGE. उजाड-&c. करणें, वैराणी *f.*-पाटावरवंटा *m.*-&c. करणें *g. of o.*

4 रिकामा घालवलेला, &c.

v. V. N. 1. घटलेला, क्षरलेला, &c. झडका, तुटार, गलित, क्षीण, अवक्षीण, क्षित, कोरंच. [पडकर.

I.—land; *lying uncultivated.* ओस, जंगली, खराब, पडसर,

II. *worthless, used for mean purposes, &c.* v. REFUSE. टाकवणा, रद्दी, निरुपयोगी, गाळाचा, गाळसाळ.

WASTE, *n. diminution, decrease, consumption.* खर्च *m.* क्षय *m.* अवक्षय *m.* क्षिति *f.* ऱ्हास *m.* क्षरण *n.* अपचय *m.*

2 *useless expenditure, worthless application.* अनुपयोगी-व्यर्थ-निष्कारणी-&c. खर्च *m.* अपव्यय *m.*

W. of time. कालक्षेप *m.* कालहरण *n.*

3 *wastage, loss.* घट *f.* घस *f.* झीज *f.* झिजणावळ *f.* घटती *f.* तूट *f.*

4 *desolate or desert ground.* जंगल *n.* रान *n.* रानवा *m.* सराया *m.* वन *n.*

WASTE-BOOK, *n. day book.* खरडा *m.* खरडें *n.* कच्चाखरडा *m.* खर्डेबंद *m.* कीर्द *or* रोजकीर्द *f.* एकवेरजी वही *f.*-चोपडी *f.*-हिशेब *m.*-&c.

WASTEFUL, *a. wantonly, &c.,-consumptive,* v. EXTRAVAGANT. उधळा, उधळ्या, सांडरा, उधळपट्टीचा, उफानगिरीचा,ढपलशाईचा.

W. person. उधळपांड्या, उधळखोर, उधळमाणक्या.

W. woman. उधळभवानी.

WASTEFULNESS, *n.* v. A. *and* EXTRAVAGANCE. उधळेपणा *m.* सांडरेपणा *m.* उधळपट्टी *f.* ढपलशाई *f.*

WASTER, *n.* WASTING, *p. a.* v. V. A. क्षीण करणारा, झरवणारा, क्षय करणारा, &c. [कणारा, &c.

2 घालवणारा, दवडणारा, फुकट खर्च करणारा, पोकळी खालीं टा-

3 नासधूस करणारा, वैराण करणारा.

v. V. N. 1. क्षीण होणारा, क्षय पावणारा, घटणारा, &c. क्षयी, क्षयगामी, क्षयिष्णु, क्षर.

2 आंग टाकणारा, &c. झड्या, सड्या.

WATCH, *n. vigilance for keeping,* v. GUARD. चौकी *f.* चौकीदारी *f.* पहारा *or* पाहरा *m.* चौकी पाहरा *m.* जागल *f.*

2 *guard, body posted.* चौकी *f.* पहारा *or* पाहरा *m.*

3 *person watching,* v. WATCHMAN. चौकीदार, जागल्या.

4 *eighth part of the day.* प्रहर *pop.* पहार *m.* याम *m.*

Second w. *noon.* दोन प्रहर *m.*

5 *pocket clock.* घड्याळ *n.*

Hand of a w. कांटा *m.* [पाहणें.

To be on the w. *to be on the look out for.* टपणें, वाट *f.*

To WATCH, *v. n. not to sleep, to wake.* जागणें, जागा-&c. राहणें-असणें, झोंपेवांचून-&c. राहणें, जागर *m.*-जागरण *n.*-&c.करणें *and* होणें *with in. con.*

2 *keep guard.* चौकी *f.*-चौकीदारी *f.*-चौकी पाहरा *m.*-पाहरा *m.*-जागल *f.*-&c. करणें.

3 *sit in expectation of.* वाट *f.* पाहणें-पाहत बसणें, टपणें, तटणें.

4 *be vigilant, attentive, &c.* जपणें, जागणें, जागा-सावध-&c. असणें-राहणें.

To WATCH, *v. a. guard, look after,* v. To KEEP, To TEND. राखणें, राखण *f.*-रक्षण *n.*-&c. करणें *g. of o.* चौकी *f.* करणें *g. of o.*

2 *observe, regard closely.* डोळा *m.*-नजर *f.*-दृष्टि *f.*-&c. ठेवणें *with* वर *of o.* चौकशी *f.*-शोध *m.*-&c. ठेवणें *g. of o.* पाळत *f.* ठेवणें-राखणें *g. of o.*

WATCH-HOUSE, *n.* चौकी *f.*

WATCH-MAKER, *n.* घड्याळें करणारा, घड्याळें नीट करणारा.

WATCH-WORD, *n. word given to sentinels, &c.* बरदीचा-खुणेचा-शब्द *m.* [जागल्या.

WATCHER, WATCHMAN, *n.* चौकी करणारा, चौकीदार, पहारेकरी,

Cost of employing a w. जागल *f.*

WATCHFUL, *a. waking.* जागा, जागता, जागरूक, जागरणशील.

2 *vigilant, wary.* सावध, जागा, जागता, जागरणशील, जागृत, हुशार, पगदस्त, सावधान, सावचित्त, सुचित्त.

To be w. जागणें, जपणें.

WATCHFULNESS, *n.* v. A. 1. जागेपणा *m.* जागतेपणा *m.* &c.

2 सावधपणा *m.* जागतेपणा *m.* हुशारपणा *m.* &c. हुशारी *f.* सावधगिरी *f.*

WATER, *n.* पाणी *n.* जल *pop.* जळ *n.* उदक *n.* आप *n.f.* नीर *n.* अंबु *n.* तोय *n.* जीवन *n.* पानीय *n.* पय *n.* सलिल *n.*—as used in comp. with nouns (ex. sugar-w. tamarind-w. &c.) वणी *n.* (ex. गुळवणी, चिंचवणी, मिठवणी, &c.).

Acidulated or soured w. अंबटवणी *n.*

Acidulated w. (comprehending tamarind-w., mango-w., lemonade, and all sherbets). पन्हें *n.* पानक*n.*

Basin for w. (as around a tree, on the top of a heap of lime &c.). अळें *n.* अळी *f.*

Boiling hot w. कढतवणी *n.*

Booth, &c. at which w. is afforded to travellers. पाणसाळ *f.* पोई *or* पाणपोई *f.* जलछत्र *n.* पन्हेरी *f.* प्रपा *f.*

By w. जलमार्गानें, तरीनें.

Channel (esp. through a house-wall) to carry off [w. नाहणी *f.*

Clear and pure w. शंखवणी *n.*

Cold w. poured into hot w. (to reduce its temperature). विसण *or* विसाण *n.* विसावण *n.* विळवण *n.* विळचण *n.*

Diversion on or in the w. (as boat-racing, bathing-gambols, &c.). जलक्रीडा *f.*

Drawn (well) w. काढवणी *n.* शेंदींव पाणी *n.*

Form of w., (as hail, snow, ice, &c.) जलाचा विकार *m.* जलपरिणाम *m.*

Foul w., muddled, &c. w. नासकवणी *n.* ओखटवणी *n.* नरकवणी *n.* रेंदवणी *n.*

Frame for carrying (upon beasts) pitchers of w. माकण *f.* (beast bearing it माकण्या, driver of the beast माकण्या) लगड *f.*

Holy-w. foot w., पादोदक *n.* पायवणी *n.* चरणतीर्थ*n.*

In w. and on land. जळीं स्थळीं.

Large hole dug for w., विहिरा*m.*

Running or quick w., spring w. जितवणी *n.* झरवणी *or* झिरवणी *n.* वाहतवणी *n.*.

Salt w. खारोणी *or* खारवणी *n.*

Salted w. मिठवणी *n.*

Smoked w. धुरवणी *n.*

Sugared w. गुळवणी *n.*

Warmed and medicated w. पालवणी *n.* चोरपाणी *n.* क- [डूपाणी *n.*

W. boiled or set to boil. अधण *n.* अधवणी *n.*

W. collected (in a pond, tank, cistern,puddle &c.). सांचवणी *n.* सांठवणी *n.*

W.-diviner, one who can direct where to dig for water. पानाडी *or* ड्या *or* पाणाडी *or* ड्या.

W. drained off from boiled articles of food. वेळवणी*n.*

W. heated in sunbeams. झळवणी *n.*

W. in which rice &c. has been washed. धुवण *n.* धूण*n.*

W. in which split pulse, &c. has been boiled. तरण *n.* तरवणी *n.*

W. poured into milk whilst boiling. धारवणी *n.*

W. that has been used; stale w. उष्टवणी*n.* रात्राचें पाणी*n.*

Way by w.—*as opp. to* Way by land. जलमार्ग *m.* तरी *f.*

To get into deep w. *enter on mysterious subjects.* खोल पाण्यांत शिरणें.

To reduce the temperature of hot w. by pouring in cold w. विसावणें, विसाविणें.

To throw cold water upon, *fig.* विबवा *m.* घालणें (कामावर &c.) नांगडा *m.* मारणें (कामामध्यें &c.).

2 (of a diamond, &c.). पाणी *n.*

3 v. URINE. मूत*n.*

To make w. v. To URINE. मुतणें.

Making w. विराकत *or* विरासत*f.* लघ्वी*f.*

4 waters; *liquor amnii.* मोट *f.* पाणमोट *f.* पाणमोटली *f.* पाणमोटलें *n.* मुतट *f.* Note. These words express the sack or receptacle. [*m.*-&c. सुटणें

To WATER, *v. n.*—the mouth; *slaver.* पाणी *n.*-लाळ *f.*-पाझर

2—the eyes. पाणी *n.* येणें *in. con.* पाण्यानें भरणें-डबडबणें.

To WATER, *v. a. supply with water.* पाणी *n.* देणें-पुरवणें-घालणें, पाण्याची पुरवणी *f.*-बेजमी *f.*-&c. करणें,—(cattle, &c.) पाणी *n.* देणें-पाजणें-दासवणें.

To take to water. पाण्यावर नेणें.

WATER-ANIMAL, *n.* पाण्यांतला जीव *m.* जलचर, जलजंतु *m.*

WATER-BAG. See WATER-SKIN.

WATER-CARRIER, *n.* पाणक्या, पाणभऱ्या.

2 (in a skin under the arm). बगलभिस्ती.

WATER-CHANNEL, *n.* परवा *m.* सारण *f.* सारणी *f.*

2 (in a garden, &c. between rows). तसरी *f.* सरी *f.*

Built up w. सांडवा *m.*

Straws, sticks, rubbish, &c. blocking up a w. साका*m.* [सांकूळ *n.*

WATER-CLOSET, *n.*v. PRIVY. पायखाना *m.*

WATER-COOLER, *n.*—the vessel. सुरई *or* य *f.*

WATER-COURSE, *n.* (as through a plantation or field). पाट *m.* पाटवण *n.* सारणी *f.* जलमार्ग *m.* पाटकुली *f.* माग *m.* दंड *m.* प्रणालिका *f.* प्रणाला *f.*

Ever-running w. ओलापाट *m.* ओलादंड *m.*

Pit dug to receive the water of a w. रतनबाब *f.*

Raised w. दंड *m.*

Water conveyed by a w. पाटवणी *n.* सांडवणी *n.*

WATER-DEITY, *n.* जलदेवता *f.* मावली *or* माउली *f.* (used pl. or मावल्या).

WATER-FALL, *n. cascade, cataract.* धोदा *or* धोधा *m.* धोधाणी *f.* धोत *m.* धबधबा *m. dim.* धबधबी *f.* ओंझर*m.* चादर *f.* मुसांडा*m.*

WATER-FOWL, *n.* पाणकोंबडें *n.* (पाणकोंबडा*m.* पाणकोंबडी *f.*) जलकुक्कुट *n.*

WATER-GALL, *n. hollow worn by a torrent.* घळ *f.*

WATER-GATE, *n. sluice.* सांडवा *m.* सांड *f.*

WATER-GRUEL, *n.* पेज *f.* उतरवणी *n.*

WATER-HEN, *n.* पाणकोंबडी *f.* जलकुक्कुटी *f.*

WATER-LILLY, *n.* पाण्यांतलें कमळ *n.* जलकमल *n.*

Stalk of the w. नाल *or* ळ *m. n.*

WATER-MAN, *n.* पाणीवाला, पाणी आणणारा-भरणारा, भिस्ती, पाणक्या,—in villages कोळी,—among Bráhmans पाणक्या, ब्राह्मणजन,—that uses a *pakhál,* पखाल्या.

WATER-MARK, *n.* भरतीचे मर्यादेची खूण *f.*

WATER-MELON, *n.*—the plant. तरबूज *f.* कलिंगड *f.* कलिंगडी *f.* कलिंगण *f.*— the fruit. तरबूज *n.* कलिंगड *n.* कलिंगडें *n.*

WATER-MILL, *n.* पाणचक्की *f.* पाणराहाट*m.* [विहिरा*m.*

WATER-PIT, *n. pit dug for water (in the bed of a river, &c.)*

Water-place, Watering-place, *n. place for washing, filling water, &c.* पाणवठा *or* पाणवटा *or* पाणोटा *or* ठा *m.* पाणघाट *m.*

Water-pot, Watering-pot, *n.* झारी *f.* हजारी *f.*

Water-proof, *a. impervious to water.* निगळता, जलाभेद्य.

Water-skin, *n.*—double w. carried on a beast. पखाल *f.*
Half or a side of a w. आसें *n.*
2—single w. or bag, as carried from, or supported by, a pole बादला *m.*
3—small w. as carried under the arm. मशक *or* मसक *f.*
Carrier of a w. भिस्ती.
Spout or vent of w.—gener. मुंढा *m.*

Water-snake, *n.* पाण्यांतला साप *m.* पाणसाप *m.* Some kinds are, पाणघोणस *m.* पाणसरडें *n.* पाणदिवड *m.* बयाळा *m. or* ळें *n.* विरोळा *n.*

Water-tight, *a. that does not leak.* निमूर, निगळ, निगळता.

Water-vehicle *n.* जलयान *n.*

Water-vessel, *n.* v. Pitcher. थागर *f.* घडा *m.*
Raised place to receive w. पाणबड *f.* पाणेरा *m.* पाणेरें *n.*

Water-wheel, *n. wheel over wells : the Persian wheel.* रहाट *m.* रहाटगाडगें *n.* घटीयंत्र *n.*
Bar or cross piece of a w. खापेकड *f.* आडी *f.*
Beam of a w. कणेकड *n.*
Beam or piece for the cogs of a w. दांतिकड *n.*
Beam of a hand-w. कणा *m.*
Bullock-w. बैलरहाट *m.*
Cogged wheel of a w. तुंब *n.*
Cross piece confining a w. पाणसरडें *n.*
Empty string of pitchers at a w. रिताड *f.*
Foot-w. पायरहाट *m.* राहटी *f.*
Hand-w. हातरहाट *m.*
Handle or turning pin of a w. हात्या *m.*
Loaded string of pitchers at a w. भरताड *f.*
Masonry supporting the beam of a w. हातणी *f.*
Member receiving the axle of the beam. रूख *m.*
Member receiving the fore-axle of the beam of a w. तोरणें *n.*
Member supporting the first trough of a w. आडनळ *m.*
Pitcher of a w. मोघा *m.* मोरवा *m.* लोटा *m.* गाडगें *n.*
Plantation irrigated by means of a w. रहाटागर *n.*
Pointed stake supporting a cogged-w. सुळकुंबा *or* खुंबा *m.* सुळखांब *m.*
Post planted in a well for the support of a w. खैरी *f.*
Rope lengthening or shortening the string of pitchers of a w. आखुडवण *n.*
Rope on which the pitchers of a w. are strung. माळ *f.*
Socket of the axle of the beam of a w. घागरें *n.* भोंवरी *f.*
String fastening each pitcher of a w. शिकरी *f.*
String of pitchers of a w. घडमाळ *f.*
Trough receiving water from the pitchers of a w. कोळंबें *or* भें *n.* कोटंभें *n.* [आडपन्हळी *f.*
Trough receiving water from the first trough of a w.
Water raised by a w. रहाटवणी *n.*
W. with spokes. चुडेरहाट *m.* [बेरहाट *m.*
W. with cogged wheel at each end of the beam. तुं-
To work a w. लाटणें.

Water-work, *n.* जलयंत्र *n.*

Watered, *p.* v. V. A. 1. पाणी दिल्हेला-पुरबलेला-&c.
Ill-w.—compreh. निपाणी, निर्जल. [सजल.
Well-w.—country, &c. जलप्राय, जलप्रचुर, जलबिपुल,
W. by rivers, &c. नदीमातृक, जलमातृक.
W. by rain. देवमातृक.

Wateriness, *n.* v. A. 4. पाणचटपणा *m.* बिरबिरीतपणा *m.* &c.

Watery, *a. of or belonging to water.* पाण्याचा, उदकाचा, &c. उदकसंबंधी, जलसंबंधी. [रूप.
2 *consisting of water.* पाण्याचा, जलाचा, &c. जलमय, जल-
3 *abounding with water, marshy,* v. Wet. पाणथळाचा, जलप्रचुर, जलसंपन्न, जलसमृद्ध, जलाढ्य.
4 *thin, tasteless, weak, spiritless,* v. Washy. बिरबिरीत, पाणचट, पाणबळ, पाण्यासारखा पातळ, कबकबीत *or* कबकबीत, किळकिळीत, गळगळीत *or* गिळगिळीत, उमळा *or* उंबळा.
To get w. (through excessive watering)—fruits, sugarcane, &c. पाणारणें.

Wattle, *n.* (of a cock). कल्ला *m.*
2 *hurdle.* ताटी *f.* गांठण *or* गांथण *f.*
Wall of wattle and dab. कूड *m.*

To **Wattle,** *v. a. interweave.* वळणें, गांठणें *or* गांथणें, बिणणें.

Wave, *n.*—of the sea. लाट *f.* लहर *f.* लहरी *f.* मौज *f.* मौजा *m.* तरंग *m.* जलतरंग *m.* हेलकावा *m.* हेलावा *m.* वीचि *f.* ऊर्मि *m. f.*
Dash or blow of a w. थाप *f.* [दांडी *f.*
Line of waves which burst upon the shore. समुद्राची
To be buffeted by waves,—a vessel. हेलकावणें, हेलावणें.

To **Wave,** *v. n. play loosely, float, &c.*—banners, &c. झुलकणें, हेलावणें, हालणें, फडकणें, फडफडणें, खेळणें. [*g. of s.*
2—a line, &c. नागमोड-नागमोडीचा असणें, नागमोड *f.* असणें
A waving line. लहर *f.*

To **Wave,** *v. a.* (a weapon, &c.) *flourish,* v. To Brandish. परजणें, फिरवणें, केळवणें, खेळवणें, बावडणें.
2 (lamps, &c. around the head of an idol, guru, &c.). ओवाळणें, ओवाळून ठेवणें, उतरणें, आरती *f.* करणें.
Matter waved. सांडणें *n.* [वाळणी *f.*
Money thrown into the platter used in waving. ओ-
Platter containing a lamp with lighted wicks to be waved. आरती *f.* औक्षवण *n.*
3 over or around (fan, brush, &c.) वारणें, ढाळणें.
4 *direct by waving,* v. To Beckon. खुणावणें, पालवणें.
5 or waive; *put aside for the present.* सोडणें, ठेवणें, माफ करणें.
6 off; (flies, &c.). वारणें.

To **Waver,** *v. n. play to and fro.* लहर *f.*-लहरा *f. pl.* मारणें, हेलावणें, हेलकावणें, डोलणें, हेलकावे *m. pl.*-&c. घेणें.
2 *fluctuate,* v. To Hesitate. आशंकणें, कांकरणें, घोटाळणें, गुटमळणें, गुरमळणें, गुपटणें, कांकू *f.*-नानू *f.*-&c. करणें, बेंघणें.

Waverer, *n.* **Wavering,** *p. a.* v. V. 1. हेलावणारा, डोलणारा, हेलकावा खाणारा, &c.
2 कांकरणारा, कांकू-&c. करणारा, फुटक्या मनाचा, दोलायमान,

Waving, *n.* v. V. A. 1. परजणें *n.* फिरवणें *n.* &c.
 2 ओवाळणें *n.* उतरणें *n.* &c. ओवाळणी *f.* उतारा *m.* आरती *f.* पंचारती *f.* कुरवंडी *f.* अक्षवण *or* अक्षुवण *n.* The phrase used by women whilst waving lamps is, इडापिडा जावो बळीचें राज्य होवो.
 W. of lamps—compreh. आरती कुरवंडी *f.*
 W. of a lamp. with incense. धुपारती *f.*
 3 वारणें *n.* ढाळणें *n.* ढाळणी *f.*
Wavy, *a. rising in waves, undulating.* लहरा मारणारा, नागमोड, नागमोडी, नागमोडीचा.
To **Wawl**, *v. n.* v. To Cry. सेंकाटणें.
Wax, *n.* (of bees). मेण *n.* मधूच्छिष्ट *n.* मधुज*n.* सिक्थक *n.*
 2—for sealing letters, &c. लाख *f.*
 3 *dirt of the ear.* कानाचा-कानांतला मळ *m.* कर्णमल *m.*
To **Wax**, *v. n.* the moon; *increase in size.* कळाकळा वाढणें, कळा *f. pl.* वाढणें *g. of s.* कलावृद्धि *f.*-&c. पावणें *and with g. of s.* होणें.
 2 *become.* होणें, होत जाणें-चालणें.
Wax-candle, *n.* मेणबत्ती *f.* मेणबात *f.*
Wax-cloth, *n.* मेणकापड *n.*
Wax-work, *n.* मेणाचे पुतळे *m. pl.* मेणाच्या पुतळ्या *f. pl.*
Waxen, *a. made, &c. of wax.* मेणाचा.
Waxy, *a. soft, &c. like wax.* मेणगट, मेणासारखा.
Way, *n. road, path.* वाट *f.* मार्ग*m.* रस्ता *m.* पथ *pop.* पंथ *m.* अध्वा *m.* सरणि *or* णी *f.* वर्त्म *n.*
 Athwart one's w. *across one's path.* आडमोरा, आडवा.
 Chance interview with on the w. वाटभेट *f.*
 In the w. before, *interjacently.* आड, आडऊड.
 Out of the w. *aside, &c.* आडबाजूस, आडकुशीस, आडबळणास, आडवळणीं, गैरसुनीं, गैरलगामीं.
 Out of the w. *not to be found.* गलत, गहाळ.—To be out of the w. हरपणें.
 Out of harm's w. नित्रस.
 Right w. *fig.* सन्मार्ग *m.* [प्रस्थान *n.*
 The w. of all the earth, v. Death. महापथ *m.* महा-
 W. by land. खुशकी *f.*
 W. by water. जलमार्ग *m.* तरी *f.*
 That has lost his w. दिग्भ्रमी, दिग्भ्रांत.
 Wrong w. *fig.* कुमार्ग *m.* विमार्ग *m.* विपथ *m.*
 To be on one's w. *to be coming.* वाट *f.* चालणें.
 To bring on the w. बोळवणें, बोळवणी *f.*-बोळवण *f.* करणें *g. of o.*
 To come across one's w. आडवा येणें.
 To fall in the w. of. अडळणें, अडळ *m.* असणें-घडणें-होणें *g. of s.* गावणें, मिळणें.
 To feel one's w. *act cautiously.* फुंकून-पाहून-&c. पाय*m.* टाकणें *or* ठेवणें.
 To get into the right w. वाटेवर येणें, वाटमार्गी लागणें.
 To go one's w. To go on one's w. निघून जाणें, चालता होणें, चालणें, आपल्यावाटेनें जाणें. [जाणें.
 To go the wrong w. (in eating or drinking) उशीत *adv.*
 To lead the w. *be foremost in the attack, &c.* तोंड*n.* देणें.
 To move out of the w. सिसणें *or* सिचणें, फरकणें, सरकणें, फरक होणें.
 To obstruct the w. वाट *f.* धरणें.
 To resume one's w. *go on again after stoppage.* वाटवणे.
 To set in the right w. वाटमार्गी लावणें.
 2 *space, line of ground,* v. Distance. वाट *f.* v. चाल-चालून येणें, पल्ला*m.* लांबण *f.* टप्पा*m.* छट्टा*m.* मजल *f.*
 That goes a great w. fig. पुरवटेसार. [मार्ग*m.*
 3 *direction or line of motion,* v. Course. वाट *f.* रस्ता*m.*
 Every w. *in all directions.* बाराबाटा, बहुंकडे, सर्वतः.
 In three ways. त्रिधा *or* त्रेधा.
 This w. इकडे.
 That way. तिकडे.
 To point out the w. lit. fig. वाट *f.*-दिशा *f.* दाखवणें, दिक्प्रदर्शन*n.* करणें.
 4 *advance, progression,* v. Progress. गति *f.*
 To be under w.—a ship. चालू-चालता-&c. होणें.
 To make w. चालणें. [करणें.
 To make w. *through, in.* रिघाव *or* वा*m.*-रीग *or* रीघ *f.*
 5 *room made, room yielded.* वाट *f.* रस्ता*m.*
 To give w. ओसर*m.* देणें, रस्ता*m.*-वाट *f.*-&c. देणें-सोडणें, फरकणें, सरकणें.
 6 *method, mode,* v. Manner. वाट *f.* मार्ग*m.* चाल *f.* तऱ्हा *f.* रीति *pop.* रीत *f.* पर्याय*m.* प्रकार*m.* पंथ *vulg.* पंथा *or* पांथा*m.* शैली *f.* पाटी *f.*
 After another w. वेगळ्या वाटेनें.
 In all ways and respects. सर्वस्वीं, सर्वस्वें, सर्वथैव, सर्वात्मना, सर्वशः, सुतराम्.
 In both ways. उभयथा.
 In various ways, in many ways. अनेकधा, बहुधा, नानाविध, परिप्रकारें, परोपरी.
 7 *manner of practice, plan of procedure,* v. Course. वाट *f.* मार्ग*m.* रीति *pop.* रीत *f.* रवेस *f. m.* रीतरवेस *f. m.* मोळा*m.* रहा *f.* सरणि *or* सरणी *f.* वृत्ति *f.*
 In the right w. यथामार्ग.
 The *or* a Right w. सन्मार्ग*m.*
 Ways, *manners.* चालचर्या *f.* रीतभात *f.*
 8 *right method.* पद्धति *f.* परिपाठ*m.* पाठ*m.* प्रघात*m.*
 9 *course of faith and practice.* मार्ग*m.* पंथ*m.*
 10 *ill habit,* v. Trick. खोड *f.* चाळा*m.*
 By the way. बरेंच स्मरण झालें.
 In the family way, v. Pregnant. पोटाशी (*f.*) गरोदर.
 Milky way, v. Galaxy. आकाशगंगा *f.*
Way-farer, *n.* **Wayfaring**, *a.* v. Traveller. वाटसरू, मार्गस्थ, पांथ *pop.* पांथस्थ, पाथिक *pop.* पांथिक.
To **Waylay**, *v. a. wait for and attack on the road.* वाट *f.*-&c. मारणें-पाडणें *g. of o.*
Way-mark, *n.* वाटखुण *f.*
Wayward, *a. froward,* v. Perverse, Wilful. करनकर, अकरताळा, गाताडा, स्वच्छंदी, आपगंड, आपढंगी. [ढंग*m.*
Waywardness, *n.* v. A. करनकरपणा*m.* स्वच्छंदीपणा*m.* &c. आप-
We, *pron.* आम्ही, आपण.
Weak, *a. feeble, infirm.* दुर्बल *or* ळ, निर्बल *or* ळ, निबळ, दुबळा, निश्शक, अशक, शक्तिहीन, शक्तिशून्य-रहित-&c. कमजोर, नि-

जोर, कमकुवत, कमतणूक, नबळा, अबल, लुकसान *or* लुसकान, स्वल्पबल, अल्पबल, अल्पशक्तिक, बलन्यून, न्यूनबल.

Of infirm make & thus w. लेबाडा *or* ड्या.

2 *feeble of mind or judgment, silly, soft, imbecile, &c.* v. FOOLISH, SIMPLE. मनाचा *or* बुद्धीचा हळवट-नरम-हलका, कम अक्कल, गैरी, ऐरीगैरी, गयाळ, गयाळी, गलतान, बेकूब, गरंगील, मळमळीत, निर्जीव, अकर्त्ता, नाकर्त्ता, नबळा, अक्षम. Terms, phrases, sayings, and various formations conveying the sense of *A weak, imbecile, spiritless person,* and answering to *Spooney, Baby, Doodle, Feeble-mind, Weakling, Woman, Silly creature, &c.* are लेंचीपेंची *or* लेंचापेंचा माणूस, शेणामेणाचा माणूस, रेमेडोक्या *or* रेमें, मेलतोंड्या, डाळपिठ्या, पिठ्या, मेंगें, मेंगा *or* ग्या, मेण्या, अंबील भुरक्या, रंडापति, रंडुला, गोयाबा, भागूबाई, हालबेंद्रा, मृत्युगोदान, लंडी, मेमुलगाडा, मेमल तोंड्या, मेषपात्र, मेषा, पोंशा, पोंशट, पोंशडा.

3—of sound. किरकोळ, हलका, किरटा.

4 *not potent, strong, &c.* v. WATERY, WASHY. फिका *or* फिक्का, पातळ, कळकळीत *or* सळसळीत, मळमळीत, कवकवीत, निकशी, निकस.

5 *not cogent or forcible,*—argument, &c. निर्बल *or* ळ, निर्जीव, पोकळ, फुसकुला, निरर्थक, दुर्बल *or* ळ.

WEAK-SIDE, *n.* मर्मस्थान *n.* मर्मस्थल *n.* मर्म *n.* नागवें *n.*

Prober of one's w. मर्मभेदी, मर्मान्वेषी.

To probe one's w. मर्मभेद *m.*-मर्मान्वेषण *n.*-&c. करणें.

To WEAKEN, *v. a. lessen the strength of, enfeeble.* दुर्बळ-कमजोर-अशक्त-&c. करणें, शक्ति *f.*-बळ *n.*-जोर *m.*-&c. उणा करणें-कमीकरणें-नेणें *g. of o.* शक्तिक्षय *m.*-शक्तिऱ्हास *m.*-शक्तिभंग *m.*-&c. करणें *g. of o*

WEAKENED, *p.* v. V. दुर्बळ केलेला, कमजोर केलेला, &c. क्षीणशक्ति *or* शक्तिक्षीण, हतवीर्य, हतौजा.

WEAKENER, *n.* WEAKENING, *p. a.* v. V. दुर्बळ करणारा, कमजोर करणारा, &c. शक्तिक्षय कर-कारी, शक्तिऱ्हास कर-कारी.

WEAKLY, *a.* v. WEAK, SICKLY. अशक्त, निर्बळ, निश्शक्त, कमजोर.

WEAKNESS, *n.* v. A. 1. दुर्बळपणा *m.* निर्बळपणा *m.* कमजोरपणा *m.* &c. अशक्तता *f.* अशक्ति *f.* शक्तिहीनता *f.* शक्तिशून्यता *f.* शक्तिराहित्य *n.* कमजोरी *f.* कमकुवत *f.* आबल्य *n.* दौर्बल्य *n.* बलन्यूनता *f.* [दता *f.* तारें *n.*

2 बुद्धीचा हलकेपणा *m.* गैरीपणा *m.* गयाळपणा *m.* &c. बुद्धिमं-

4 फिकेपणा *m.* पातळपणा *m.* मळमळीतपणा *m.* निकसपणा *m.*

5 निर्जीवपणा *m.* पोकळपणा *m.* &c. [ळक *n.* क्षुद्र *n.*

I. a w. *a foible, a failing,* v. FAULT. उणें *n.* हीन *n.* क्षु-

WEAL, *n.* v. WELFARE. बरें *n.* कल्याण *n.* क्षेम *pop.* खेम *n.* शुभ *n.*

Wishing the w. of. शुभचिंतन *n.*

2 *mark of a stripe.* वळ *m. f.*

WEALTH, *n.* v. RICHES. धन *n.* द्रव्य *n.* दौलत *f.* वित्त *n.* वित्तविषय *m.* संपत्ति *f.* ऐवज *m.* गठडी *f.* अर्थ *m.* धनसमृद्धि *f.* संपदा *f.*

W. in cattle. चर्मधन *n.*

W. in grain. धान्यधन *n.* धान्यार्थ *m.* [लावणें.

To roll in w. पावड्यावर पैका *m.* ओढणें, पैक्याला पावडें *n.*

WEALTHINESS, *n.* v. A. धनवंतपणा *m.* दौलतदारी *f.* श्रीमंती *f.* धनिकता *f.* सधनता *f.*

WEALTHY, *a.* v. RICH. धनवान् *pop.* धनवंत, द्रव्यवान्, दौलतदार, गब्बर, गब्रू, श्रीमंत, सधन, संपत्तिमान् *pop.* संपत्तिवान्.

To WEAN, *v. a. detach finally from the breast.* आंगावरचा तोडणें, आंगावरून तोडणें, दूध *n.*-थान *n.* तोडणें *g. of o.* आंगाथाना-आई-&c.-निराळा-वेगळा करणें, थान *n.*-दूध *n.* सोडविणें *g. of o.* थानमोड *f.* स्तनमोचन *n.* करणें.

2 (from the world,). मन *n.* उठवणें-उडवणें *g. of o.* विरक्त-उदास-&c. करणें, वैराग्य *n.*-&c. आणणें.

WEANED, *p.* v. V. 1. आंगावरून तोडलेला, दूध तोडलेला, थाना वेगळा केलेला, &c. थानतुटा, पाडसा, पारठा, स्तनमुक्त.

2 मन उठवलेला, &c. उठवलेल्या *or* उठलेल्या-उडाल्या मनाचा, विरक्त.

WEANEDNESS, *n.* v. P. 2. विरक्ति *f.* वैराग्य *n.* मनसुटका *f.* कर्मसमाधि *m.* प्रत्याहार *m.* इंद्रियासंग *m.*

WEANEL, WEANLING, *n. young weaned animal.* थान तुटें-दूधतुटें मूल *n.*-वासरूं *n.*-&c.

WEAPON, *n. instrument of offense.* शस्त्र *n.* हत्यार *or* हतेर *n.* आयुध *n.* अस्त्र *n.*

Charmed w. अस्त्र *n.*

To WEAR, *v. a. waste away, consume by attrition, &c.* झिजवणें, झरवणें, काचवणें, खाणें, वदळ *or* वरदळ *f.* करणें *g. of o.*

2 *carry on or about the body,* v. To PUT on. घालणें, बांधणें, आंगावर घेणें, परिधान *n.* करणें *g. of o.* नेसणें.

3 *bring under use,* v. To USE. घोळणें, वहिवाटणें, वापरणें.

4 *put on, assume.* धरणें, धारण *n.* करणें.

5 (a ship or vessel). हेरें *n.* घेणें, वाळियेणें.

6 away *or* out ; *spend tediously,* v. To PASS. काढणें, घालवणें, लोटणें, रेंटणें, ढकलणें.

7 out ; *render unserviceable by use.* वापरून-वहिवाटून-घोळून-कामासाळीं-&c. जुना-जीर्ण-जर्जर-&c. करणें, भोगजीर्ण-&c. करणें. [करणें.

8 out ; *harass, worry,* v. To TEASE. बेजार-दिक्क-श्रमी-&c.

To WEAR, *v. n. waste away.* झिजणें, झरणें, घांसणें, घसवटणें, घांसून घसवटून जाणें, कांचणें, वदळ *or* वरदळ *f.* होणें-लागणें *in. con.*—esp. the edge of a weapon, माठणें.

2 v. To LAST. टिकणें, तगणें, राहणें.

To w. well. जंग *m.* देणें.

3 off ; v. To PASS away. जिरणें, जाणें, गुदरणें, वहिवाटणें.

4 out ; *become unserviceable through use.* वापरल्यामुळें-&c. जुना-जीर्ण-जर्जर-&c. होणें.

WEAR, *n. waste through use.* चोळ *f.* झीज *f.* झिजणावळ *f.* घोळ *f.* वरदळ *or* वदळ *f.* चोळघोळ. [वरदळ *f.*

W. and tear. चोळ *f.* चोळाचोळ *f.* चोळमोळ *f.* वदळ *or*

2 v. USE. वहिवाट *f.* वापर *m.*

That has been in w. नेशीव.

WEARABLE, *a.* v. V. A. 2. घालाया-बांधाया-आंगावर घ्याया-&c, सारखा-जोगा-&c. परिधानीय, परिधेय, परिधानयोग्य, नेसाऊ.

WEARER, *n.* WEARING, *p. a.* v. V. A. 1. झिजवणारा, &c.

2 घालणारा, बांधणारा, आंगावर घेणारा, परिधानकर्त्ता-कारी.

WEARIED, *p.* v. V. श्रमी, श्रांत, क्लांत, जातश्रम, आयासी.

WEARINESS, *n.* v. A. 1. *and* FATIGUE. दमलेपणा *m.* श्रम *m.* कष्ट *m.* शीण *m.* श्रांति *f.* क्लांति *f.* आयास *m.*

2 कंटाळा *m.* त्रास *m.* उचाट *m.*-उच्छाद *m.* उबग *m.*

WEARING, *a. that is worn,*—apparel. आंगावर घ्यायाचा-जोगा-सारखा-&c. घालायाजोगा-सारखा, परिधानोपयोगी.

WEARISOME, *a. causing weariness,* v. TIRESOME. श्रमवणारा, &c. शीणआणणारा, &c. श्रमाचा, श्रांतिकर-कारक-जनक.

2 *attended with fatigue.* श्रमाचा, शिणाचा, कष्टाचा, &c.

WEARISOMENESS, *n.* v. A. 1. श्रम *m.* कष्ट *m.* श्रांतिकारकत्व *n.* श्रांतिजनकत्व *n.*

WEARY, *a. tired,* v. FATIGUED, EXHAUSTED. दमलेला, शिणलेला, क्लांत, श्रांत, म्लान.

2 *impatient of the continuance of.* कंटाळा आलेला, बेजार, बेदम, जिकू, जिकजिकू *or* जिगजिग, दिकू, त्रस्त, जातत्रास.

3 *causing weariness,* v. TIRESOME. श्रमाचा, कष्टाचा, आयासाचा.

To WEARY, *v.a. fatigue,* v. To TIRE. श्रमवणें, दमवणें, शिणवणें, टणक *m.*-शीण *m.*-भागवटा *m.*-&c. आणणें, श्रमी-श्रांत-&c. करणें.

2 *render impatient.* कंटाळवणें, कंटाळा *m.*-त्रास *m.*-उबजळा *m.*-&c. आणणें-देणें, श्रमी-कष्टी-बेदम-जिकू-दिकू-&c. करणें.

To WEARY, *v. n.* v. To TIRE. श्रमणें, कष्टणें, कंकातणें.

2 of; *tire of,* v. To LOATHE. कंटाळणें, त्रासणें, कंटाळा *m.*-उबग *m.*-किळस *m. f.*-त्रास *m.*-ओकारा *m.*-ओकारी *f.*-&c. येणें *in. con.* उच्छाद *m.*-उचाट *m.* घेणें-खाणें, उबजळा *m.* लागणें, उबगणें, उबजळणें, उचाटणें, किटणें, तगादणें.

WEATHER, *n. state of the air as respects heat, cold, &c.* हवा *f.* This word is often best rendered by the noun which expresses the state of the air to be indicated, as ऊन *warm weather,* थंडी *cold weather,* धुकें *hazy weather,* or by a noun expressing *a season,* as उन्हाळा warm weather, हिंवाळा *or* थंडीचे दिवस cold weather, &c. &c.

Fine w. सुदिन *m.*

The fine w. *the clear and cloudless days.* निखरणीचे दिवस *m. pl.*

Mild coldness of w. गुलाबी थंडी *f.*

Raininess of w. काळंबण *f. n. v.* पड.

Rawness and coldness of w. शिळट *or* टी *f v.* पड, लाग, खारी *f.* खार *f. v.* सुट, बामल *f.* घंगाळ*n.*

To WEATHER, *v. a.* (a danger, &c.) *pass with difficulty.* टाळणें, निभणें-निभावणें-पारपडणें *with* आंतून *of o.*

WEATHER-BEATEN, *a.* उनापावसाचा मारलेला-झोडलेला, ऊनपाऊस सोसलेला.

WEATHER-COCK, *n.* वाऱ्याचा रोंख दाखविणारें साधन *n.*

WEATHER-SIDE, *n.* घोस *m.*

WEATHER-WISE, *a.* हवेचा जाणता.

To WEAVE, *v. a. form by texture.* विणणें, काढणें, वळणें, वीण *f.*-वेणी *f.*-&c. करणें.

Price or cost of weaving. विणणावळ *f.* विणाई *f.*

WEAVER, *n.* v. V. विणणारा, &c. विणकरी *m.* कोष्टी, तंतुवाय.

W.'s. beam. तुरी *f.* तुरई *f.* तूर *f.*

W.'s brush. कुंची *f.*

W. in cotton or silk. साळी,—cloth woven by him. साळवट *or* टी, साळाऊ.

W. in wool. धनगर, सणगर.

WEAVER-BIRD, *n.* डुडा *m.*

WEAVING, *n.* v. V.—*act.* विणणें *n,* &c. विणणी *f.* वीण *f.* वेणी *f.*

WEB, *n. texture of threads, thing woven.* वीण *f.* विणलेलीवस्त *f.* सनंग *n.* थान *n.* ताका *m.*

An end or unwoven thread of a w. दशी *f.*—contempt. दसडी *f.* दसोडी *f.*

A thick or coarse end. दसाड *n.*

Square or division of a w. खण *m.*

Unwoven threads of a w. where divisions are to be made. चाळ *f.*

W. woven in separable squares. सणाळें *n.* सडाळें *n.* सणंग *n.*

2 (of the eye). कवडा *m.* पटल *pop.* पडळ *n.* पडदा *m.*

3 (of a spider). जाळें *n.* कोरडक *n.*—of the spider called कोळी. कोळष्टक *n.* कोळशीट *n.* कोळशेंट*n.* कोळिष्टक *n.*

WEB-FOOTED, *a.* ज्याच्या पायांचीं नखें कातड्यानें जोडलेलीं असतात तो.

To WED, *v. a.* v. To MARRY. विवाहणें, वरणें, पाणिग्रहण *n.* करणें.

To WED, *v. n.* v. To MARRY. वऱ्हाडणें, लग्न *n.* होणें *g. of s.*

WEDDED, *p.* v. V. *and* MARRIED. विवाहित, ऊढ, परिणीत.

I. *closely attached.* आसक्त, रत, लंपट.

WEDDING, *a. of or belonging to a wedding.* वऱ्हाडी, लग्नाचा, लग्नप्रकरणांतला.

WEDDING, *n. marriage ceremony, festivity,* v. MARRIAGE. लग्न *n.* वऱ्हाड *n.* शादी *f.* लग्नकार्य *n.* विवाहोत्सव *m.* लग्नसमारंभ *m.*

Clothes or cloths suitable at weddings. लग्नधर (*pop.* लगीन धर), लग्नाऊ वस्त्रें *n. pl. or* कापड *n.*

House in which a w. is celebrated. वऱ्हाडघर*n.* लगीनघर *n.*

Merry w. दणक्याचें लग्न *n.*

WEDGE, *n.*—the mechanical power. सेट *f.* पाचर *or* पाचार *f. n.* कावर *f. n.* पाचेरू *n.* लबाडी *f.*

2 (of metal). लगड *f.* ईट *f.*

To WEDGE, *v. a.* v. N. पाचर *f. n.* मारणें.

To be wedged in. fig. पाचर *f. n.* होणें.

WEDLOCK, *n.* v. MARRIAGE. विवाह *m.* विवाहितावस्था *f.* विवाहसंबंध *m.* विवाहबंधन *n.*

WEDNESDAY, *n.* बुधवार *m.* बुधवासर *m.* सौम्यवार *m.* सौम्यवासर *m.*

WEE. See LITTLE.

WEED, *n. useless plant.* उनाड झाड *n.* बावीर *n.* तृण *pop.* तण *n.* रान *n.*

Overrun with weeds. जंगल गरक.

State of being overrun with weeds. ऐचण*n.* ऐतण *n.* गचपण *n.* उबाला *m.* उबाल *n.*

Weeds growing in a field of corn. नडणी *f.* निदन *n.*

Ill weeds grow apace. कडव्या झाडास बहु वाज.

To WEED, *v. a. rid of weeds.* बेणणें, खुरपणें.

2 (field of corn). भांगलणें, कोळपणें, बसरणें, बेणणें, निदणें, नडणें, निदण *n.*-गवत *n.*-&c. काढणें, विरपणें.

3 *free from offensive things.* निवडणें, शोधणें, चाळणी *f.*-&c. करणें *g. of o.*

WEEDING, *a.* v. V. 1—*act.* बेणणें *n.* &c. बेणणी *f.*

2 बेणणें*n.* कोळपणें*n.* &c. निदणी *f.* नडणी *f.* निदण*n.* विरपणी *f.*

WEED-HOOK, *n.* इळा *m.* दाबली *f.*

WEEDY, *a. abounding with weeds.* जंगलगरक, रानमाजलेला-भरलेला, ऐचणलेला.

WEEK, *n. period of seven days.* आठवडा*m.* सप्ताह*m.* बारसमक*n.*

वार *m.* This word is not used of *one* week.
Day of the w. वार *m.* esp. in comp.
Inauspicious day of the w. घातवार *m.*

WEEKLY, *a. coming, happening, &c. once a week.* आठवड्याचा, प्रति आठवड्याचा, सातसातदिवसांचा, वारसप्तकाचा.

WEEKLY, *adv.* v. A. दरआठवड्यास, प्रतिआठवड्यास, सात सात दिवसांस, आठवड्याच्या आठवड्यास.

To WEEP, *v n.* v. To CRY. रडणें, डोळ्यांपासून-डोळ्यांतून पाणीn. काढणें, घळघळ *or* ळा *adv.* रडणें, आंसवें *n.pl.*-अश्रु *m. pl.* -बिंदू *m. pl.*-&c. पाडणें-गाळणें- काढणें-ढाळणें-टाकणें, रोदन *or* रुदन *n.*-&c.करणें,—in jocose phras. गाईपाण्यावर आणणें.

WEEPER, *n.* WEEPING, *p. a.* v. V. रडणारा, डोळ्यांपासून पाणी काढणारा, आंसवें पाडणारा, &c. रोदन-रुदन कर्त्ता.
I.—the countenance, eyes, &c. *or,* attributively. रडवा, रडका, रडकुंडा, भरलेला, डबडबलेला, डबडबीत.

WEEVIL, *n.*—the insect. टोंका *or* टोका *m.*

WEFT, *n.* See WOOF. 2 v. WEB. वीण *f.* विणलेली वस्त *f.*
3 v. WAIF. सांड *n.* बेवारशीक माल *m.*

To WEIGH, *v. a. ascertain the weight of.* जोखणें, तोलणें, वजन *n.* करणें-पाहणें *g. of o.* तुळणें, तुकणें, जोख *n.*-तोल *m.*-तुलना *f.*-तुला *f.*-&c. करणें *g. of o.* [होणें*g. of s.*
2 *be equivalent to in weight.* भरणें *or* वजन भरणें, वजन *n.*
3 (anchor) v. To RAISE. उचलणें.
4 (in the mind) *ponder,* v. To CONSIDER. तोलणें, तुकणें, तोलून पाहणें, घोळणें, घोळून पाहणें, अवांकून पाहणें, विचार*m.*-&c. करणें *g. of o.*
5 down ; *oppress with weight, depress.* दडपणें, दाबणें, भाराक्रांत-&c. करणें.

To WEIGH, *v. n. have weight.* वजन *n.* असणें *g. of s.* वजन *n.* भरणें, भारी-&c. असणें.
2 fig. *be considered as important.* वजनदार-भारदार-भारदारीचा-&c. वाटणें, वजन *n.*-&c. असणें-पडणें *g. of s.*
3 *bear heavily, press hard.* ओझें *n.*-भार*m.*-&c. असणें *g. of s.* उरावर-छातीवर-&c. बसणें.

WEIGHED, *p.* v.V. A. 1. जोखलेला, तोललेला, वजन केलेला, &c. जोखी, जोखींव, तोलींव.
4 तोललेला, घोळलेला, घोळून पाहिलेला, &c.

WEIGHER, *n.* WEIGHING, *p. a.* v. V.A.1. जोखणारा, तोलणारा, वजन करणारा, &c.
2 वजन भरणारा.
4 तोलून पाहणारा, घोळून पाहणारा, &c.

WEIGHING, *n.* v. V. 1. तोलणें *n.* जोखणें *n.* वजन करणें *n.* &c. तोल *m.* तुलना *f.* तुला *f.*

WEIGHT, *n. quantity determined by balance.* भार *m.* वजन *n.* तोल *m.* तुला *f.* उन्मान *n.* मिति *f.* गौरव *n.* जाड्य *n.* गरिमा*m.*
Man's w. (as in gold, jewels, &c.) तुलापुरुष *m.*
Of deficient w. lit. fig. कमतोल.
Of full w. वजनपूर.
Of w. *not of capacity,*—measure. जोखी, वजनी.
That is sold by w. वजनी.
Up to the w. of. भारोभार, भारंभार.
2 *a w. mass to weigh with.* वजन *n.* जोख *n.* जोखमाप *n.* तोल *n.* उन्मान *n.*

The common *Weights* of the Jeweller or Goldsmith are, गुंज *f* त्रसरेणु माष (*pop.* मासा) *m.* रती*m.* लिक्षा*m.* वाल *m. f.* विश्वा *f.* सर्षप *m.* सुवर्ण *m. n.*
3 *ponderous mass.* ओझें *n.* भार *m.*
4 *pressing load,* lit. fig. v. BURDEN. भार *m.* ओझें *n.* धोंड *f.* शीळ *f.* दडपण *n.*
5 *importance, dignity, consequence, consideration, influence, authority.* भार *m.* वजन *n.* तोल *m.* भारदारी *f* भारदस्ती *f.* वजनदारी *f.* गुरुत्व *n.* गौरव *m. n.* मोठेपणा *m.* बकर *f. n.* बोज*m.* आब *m.* आबदाब *m.* जडपणा *m.* कदर *f.* चाल *f.* चलती *f.* चलचल *f.*
6 *moment, consequence, &c.* भार *m.* बिसात *f.* मुजास्त *or* स्ता *f.* केवा *m.* कथा *f.* भारीपणा *m.* प्रत्यवाय *m.*
7—as placed upon a body to keep it down. दडपण *n.* दडपा *m.* दडकण *n.* दाबण *n.* चेपण *or* णें *n.* भार *m.*

WEIGHTY, *a. heavy.* भारी, जड, वजनदार, वजनशीर, भाराचा, वजनाचा, &c. गुरु, अवजड *or* जाड *or* ओजड *or* जाड, जबर, गरिष्ठ.
2 *influential.* तोलदार, वजनदार, वजनशीर, भारदस्त, भारदस्तीचा, भारदार, जड, जबरदस्त, पेश, चलतीचा, भारणशुद्ध.
3 *momentous, important.* भारी, जड, वजनाचा, मोठा, वजनदार, भारदार, अलघु, अक्षुद्र.

WEIR, *n.* पायगीर *m.* बोकशी *f.*

To WELCOME, *v. a. salute* (a new comer) *with kindness.* आगत *n.*-आगतस्वागत *n.* करणें *g. of o.* बरे आलां म्हणून बोलणें.

WELCOME, *a.*—a guest, &c. स्वागताचा. [&c.
2 *grateful,* v. AGREEABLE. सुखप्रद, सुखद, आनंदकारक- प्रद-
You are welcome. आपण बरे आलां, आपण चांगले आलां.

WELCOME, *n. kind reception of a guest,* v. HOSPITALITY, CIVILITY. आगतस्वागत *n.* स्वागत *n.*

To WELD, *v. a. unite when heated.* उमलणें.

WELFARE, *n. happiness, prosperity.* बरें *n.* कल्याण *n.* क्षेम *pop.* खेम *n.* खैर *f.* खैरियत *f.* (occurs in letters) धड *n.* सुख *n.* कुशल *or* ळ *n.* क्षेमकुशल *n.* कौशल्य *n.* कुशलता *f.* मंगल *or* ळ *n.* मांगल्य *n.* अभीष्ट *n.* अभीप्सित *n.* शुभ *n.* भद्र *n.* श्रेय *n.* स्वस्ति *n.* सुस्थिति *f.* प्रसाद *m.* [ली भलाई *f.*
Accounts of w. *tidings of health and proceedings.* भ-
To pray for the w. of. बरें *n.* मागणें *g. of o.*
To wish one's w. अभीष्टचिंतन *n.*-&c. करणें.
2 (of a country or state). आबादी *f.* आबादानी *f.* सुबार्त्ता *f.*

WELL, *a. in health,* v. HEALTHY. बरा, चांगला, स्वस्थ, निरामय, सुस्थ, हुशार, नीरोग *pop.* निरोग *or* निरोगी, शरीरसंपत्तिमान्.
Pretty w. बरासा, ताकोला बरा.
2—as comprehending circumstances ; *well and happy,* v. COMFORTABLE. सुखी, खुशाल, कुशल *or* ळ, सुखरूप, क्षेम.
3 *advantageous, happy, fortunate, &c.* चांगला, बरा, बऱ्याचा, हिताचा, सुखाचा, हितावह, सुखावह.

WELL, *n.*—common round w. without steps. कुवा*m.* आड*m.* कूप*m.*—rough dug, not built up with masonry. आडांव *or* आढांव*n.* आडखोल*n.*—(of masonry), गजबाव *f.*—large w. with or without steps, विहीर *f.* बावडी *f.* बाव *or* वी *f.* बारव *f.* वापी *f.* वापिका *f.* भाम *f.*
Assessment of wells. विहीरकुंडा *m.*

Basket, bucket, &c. used in clearing out a w. बाव उपसणें *or* उसपणें*n.*

Blind w. Dry w.W. filled up with rubbish. आडखोल*n.* बावखोल*n.* अंधकूप*m.* शुष्ककूप*m.*

Clearing or cleaning out of a w.बावउसपणी *or* बावउपसणी *f.*

Dryness of a w. ठणठणपाळ*m.* ठणठणाट*m.*

Line in a w. from which the masonry commences. धर*m.* ठेवण *f.*

Pavement (or chunam-work) around a w. तळी *f.*

W. with water. पाण्याचा आड*m.* जलकूप*m.*

Well-room, *n.*—of a ship, &c. गमतड *or* गमताड*f.* गमतडी *f.*

Well, *interj.* भला.

Well, *adv. not ill or wickedly; justly, rightly.* चांगला *decl.* बरा *decl.* नीट, बराबर *or* बरोबर, ठीक, चांगल्यारीतीनें, चांगल्यामार्गानें,&c.*or* रीतीनें, मार्गानें, &c. न्यायानें, न्यायतः,धर्मतः.

2 *with due skill or art, properly, correctly, &c.* चांगला *decl.* बरा *decl.* बराबर *or* बरोबर, नीट, ठीक, दुरूस्त, योग्य, यथायोग्य.

3 *completely, fully, perfectly, &c.* पुरतेपणीं, पुरेपणीं, पुरता *decl.* पुरा *compl.*

4 v. Abundantly, Sufficiently. पुरा *decl.* बहुत, पुष्कळ.

5 *favorably, with praise.* चांगला *decl.* बरा *decl.*स्तुति करून, &c. वाखाणून, &c.

6 *conveniently.* सोईनें, सोईखालीं, सोईवार, सोईसार, सोईवारपणानें.

7 *thoroughly, to the purpose, properly,to a good degree,&c.* v. Smartly. खूब, चांगला *decl.* मारून, रगडून.

8—as a term of concession, an expletive, &c. बरें.

As w. as, *also, even.* ही.

Well off, well to do, *that has a competence*, v. Competence. घरचासुखी, तळींगार, खाऊन पिऊन सुखी.

Well-advised, **Well-counselled**, *a.* सुमंत्रित.

Well-arranged, *a.* सुघटित, सुयंत्र, सुरचित.

Well-balanced, *a.* समतोल.

Well-behaved, **Well-bred**, **Well-mannered**, *a. polite, courteous.* सदाचरणी, आचारशुद्ध, सदाचार,सदाचारसंपन्न, मर्यादशील *or* ळ, मर्यादशीर, शिष्टाचाराचा, शिष्ट, शिष्टाचारसंपन्न, सद्वृत्त, सभ्य, सभ्याचाराचा, सभ्याचारसंपन्न, सुचरित, सुसर, सुनीत, सुविनीत.

Well-being, *n.* v. Welfare. कल्याण*n.* कुशल *or* ळ*n.* क्षेम *pop.* खेम*n.* शुभ*n.* सुस्थिति *f.*

Well-born, *a.* v. Gentle. कुलीन, कुळवंत, कुलज, असल, असील, आर्य, अभिजात, सुजात.

Well-bred, **Well-educated**, **Well-disciplined**, **Well-trained**, *a.* सुशिक्षित, शिष्ट, शालाशुद्ध, सुशासित, सुनीत, सुविनीत.

Well-contrived, **Well-devised**, *a.* सुघटित, सुरचित, सुयुक्त.

Well-digested, *a.* lit. सुजीर्ण.

2 fig. पक्क्याविचाराचा, ऊहापोहसिद्ध.

Well-disposed, *a. rightly disposed.* सुशील, शमशील.

2 *kindly disposed.* सुमन, सुमना*or*सुमनस्क,हितबुद्धि, हितकाम.

Well-doer, *n.* v. Virtuous. सुकर्मी, सुकर्मा, सुकृत,सुकृती.

Well-done, *interj.* भलें, वाह, वाहवाह, वाहरे, शाबास, साशी, ऐशी, बेश.

Well-dressed, *a.* नेटक्या पांघरुणाचा, सुवेषी, प्रनिष्ठित वस्त्राचा.

Well-examined, **Well-tried**, *a.* सुपरीक्षित.

Well-favored, *a.* v. Handsome, Beautiful. स्वरूपवान्, सुभावणा, नेटका, देखणा, डोळेफोड.

Well-flavored, *a.* v. Tasty. चवदार, सुरस.

Well-formed, *a.* v. Handsome. आकारशुद्ध, आवशुद्ध, बळणशुद्ध, बळणदार, घाटशुद्ध, बांधेशुद्ध, सुपिंड, सुघटित, जंत्रीं ओतलेला.

Well-informed, *a.* सुजाण, सुज्ञ, बहुज्ञ, ज्ञाता, बहुश्रुत, स्थूललक्ष्य.

Well-knit, *a.* सुसंहत, निःसंधि.

Well-known, *a. fully known.* पुरतेपणीं-चांगला *decl.*-&c. समजलेला, सुज्ञात, सुवेदित.

2 v. Notorious. जगजाहीर, जगत्प्रसिद्ध *p p.* जगप्रसिद्ध.

Well-looking, *a.* v. Handsome. सुभावणा.

W. but weak. सुरतेचा भला कमरेचा ढिला.

Well-made, *a.* v. Well-formed. आकारशुद्ध, सुघटित.

Well-meaning, **Well-intentioned**, *a.* सदभिप्राय, सदाशय, सद्धेतु.

Well-pleased, *a.* v. Glad. सुप्रसन्न.

Well-preserved, **Well-kept**, *a.* चांगला राखलेला, सुरक्षित.

Well-proportioned, **Well-shaped**, *a.* v. Well-formed. आकारशुद्ध, आवशुद्ध, बांधेशुद्ध.

Well-provided, **Well-stocked**, **Well-supplied**, &c. *a.* चांगल्या बेजमीचा, भरपूर बेजमीचा, गडगंज.

Well-regulated, **Well-ruled**, *a.* सुयंत्रित, सुयंत्र, सुशासित.

Well-said, *a.* चांगला *decl.* म्हटलेला, सूक्त, सुकथित.

Well-set, **Well-made**, **Well-compacted**, **Well-knit**, &c. *a.* v. Compact. बांधेशुद्ध, बळींव, सुसंहत.

Well-situated, *a.* चांगला *decl.* बसलेला, सुसंस्थित, सुस्थानस्थित.

Well-spent, *a.* चांगला *decl.* खर्चलेला, सद्व्ययित.

Well-spoken, *a. speaking well*, v. Eloquent. तोंडचा नीटसुगर, सुभाषित.

2 *well said.* सूक्त.

Well-taught, **Well-trained**, *a.* सुशिक्षित, शालाशुद्ध.

Well-timed, *a.* v. Seasonable. वेळेवरचा.

Well-turned, *a.* बळणदार, वळणशुद्ध.

Well-watered, *a.*—country, &c. जलमय.

Well-weighed, **Well-considered**, *a.* सुविचारित, सुचिंतित.

Well-wisher, *n.* कल्याणचिंतक, शुभचिंतक, अभीष्टचिंतक, श्रेयोर्थी, सुखैषी, हितैषी, सुमनस्क *or* सुमना.

Welt, *n. edging of cloth.* धडी *f.* कांठ *m.*

To **Welter**, *v. n. roll, wallow.* लोटणें, लोळणें.

Wem, **Wemme**, *n.* v. Scar. वण *m. n.*

Wen, *n. encysted tumor.* वाळूक *n.* अवाळूं *n.* गळगंड *n.*

That has a w. अवाळ्या, वाळक्या, गळगंड्या.

Wench, *n.*—woman in contempt, v. Woman. बायलूं *n.* रांड*f.*

2 *strumpet*, v. Harlot. रांड *f.* बटीक *f.*

To **Wench**, *v. n. fornicate.* रांडबाजी *f.*-रंडीबाजी *f.*-रांडव्यसन *n.*करणें.

Wencher, *n. lecher.* रांड्या, रांडगा, रंडीबाज *or* रांडबाज, रांडव्यसनी, रांडछंदी, छिनाल, बटक्या, दासीवल्लभ, दासीपति.

Wenchery, **Wenching**, *n. frequenting women of ill fame.* रंडीबाजी *f.* रांडबाजी *f.* रांडछंद *m.* रांडव्यसन *n.*

To **Wend**, See To Go.

WEST, *n.*—the region of the sky. पश्चिम *f.* मावळत *f.* पश्चिमदिशा *f.* वारुणी *f.* प्रतीची *f.*

WEST, WESTERLY, WESTERN, *a. of, belonging, &c. to the west.* पश्चिम, पश्चिमदिशेचा, पश्चिमेचा, पश्चिमेकडला, पश्चिमेकडचा, प्रतीचीन. [माभिमुख.

2 *facing the west.* पश्चिमेकडच्या तोंडाचा, पश्चिमेकडचा, पश्चि-

WEST, WESTWARD, WESTWARDLY, *adv. toward the west.* पश्चिमेकडे, पश्चिमदिशेकडे, पश्चिमेस, पश्चात्, वर.

WET, *n. water, humidity, moisture.* पाणी *n.* ओल *f. n.* ओलावा *m.* ओलासा *m.* [लाग.

2 *rain or rainy weather.* पाणी *n.* पाऊस *m.* शिळट *f. v.* पड,

WET, *a. having water on the surface.* ओला, भिजका *remiss.* भिजकट, भिजलेला, आर्द्र, सार्द्र, स्तिमित, क्लिन्न.

Dripping w. चिंब, चिम्म, चिप्प, चिबचिबीत *or* चुबचुबीत, चीब *or* प, तिंब, ओला चिंब, ओलातिंब, ओलाकचकचीत.

To be dripping w. चिबचिबणें *or* चुबचुबणें, तिंबणें.

To get w. *be wetted.* भिजणें, भिजणूक *f.* असणें *g. of s.*

2 v. RAINY. पावसाचा, पर्जन्याचा, वृष्टिमय.

3—of land, v. MARSHY. चिखड, पाणथळाचा, जलाढ्य.

To WET, *v. a. make wet.* भिजवणें, ओला-&c. करणें, तिंबणें, भिजवणूक *f.*-&c. करणें *g. of o.* [ता *f.*

WET-NURSE, *n.* v. NURSE. दाई *f.* अम्मा *f.* धानकरीण *f.* उपमा-

WETHER, *n. castrated ram.* खशीकेलेला मेंढा *m.*

WETNESS, *n.* v. A. ओलेपणा *m.* भिजकेपणा *m.* &c. ओल *n. f.* ओलावा *m.* ओलासरा *m.* आर्द्रता *f.* सार्द्रता *f.* स्तैमित्य*n.* क्लेद*m.*

WETTED, *p.* v. V. भिजवलेला, ओला-&c. केलेला, भिजका *remiss.* भिजकट, आप्लुत.

WHACK, *interj.* धाड-कन-कर-&c. फाड-कन-कर-&c. चट-कन-कर.

To WHACK, *v. a.* v. To BEAT. कडकावणें, सडकणें, धमकणें.

WHACK, *n.* v. BLOW. चडक *f.* चडकण *f.* चडकणी *f.* रपाटा *m.* रट्टा *m.* कचका *m.*

WHACKER, WHACKING. See LARGE.

WHALE, *n.* देवमासा *m.* तिमि *m.* राघव *m.* व्हेलमासा *m.*

WHANG, *n. leather thong.* वादी *f.*

WHAP, *interj.* धप-कन-कर-&c. *or* धब-कन-कर-&c. दप-कन-कर-&c. भुद् (*or* भद्)-कन-कर-&c.

WHAP, *n.* v. BLOW. रपाटा *m.* रट्टा *m.* रामरट्टा *m.*

WHAPPER, *n.* v. LARGE. रपाटा *m.* रट्टा *m.* रपाटखान *m.*

WHAPPING, *a.* v. LARGE. रट्ट, रटाला, रपाटा. [घाट *m.*

WHARF, *n. bank or mound for landing goods.* धका *or* धक्का *m.*

WHAT, *pron. that which.* जो (जी, जें,) काय, जो काय.

2—interrog. काय, कोण, कोणता, किं (*or* किम्).

3—as an interjection. काय.

4 *to how great degree.* काय.

WHATEVER, WHATSOEVER, *pron. any thing that may be.* जो जो, जी जी , जें जें, जें कांहीं, जो काय, काय जो.

WHATLIKE, *a.* कसचा *or* ला, कसा, कसाकसा, कसकसचा *or* ला, कसकसा.

WHEAT, *n.* गहूं *m.* गोधूम *m.* सुमन *m.* Certain kinds of *wheat* are कवडागहूं, काठ्यागहूं, खपला *or* खपल्या गहूं, जोड गहूं, दाऊदखानी गहूं, पोटा *or* पोट्यागहूं, बक्षीगहूं, बोंडगहूं.

Green w. parched. ओंबी *f.*

Suitable for w.—soil. गव्हाळा *or* गव्हळा.

W.-colored *or* spotted with spots of w. गव्हळा *or* गव्हाळया.

W.-grounds. गव्हाळ *or* ळी *f.*

W. ground coarsely and boiled. दुली *f.* सोजी *f.*

To separate the w. from the chaff. *fig.* क्षीरनीरविभाग *m.* करणें.

WHEATEN, *a. made, &c. of wheat.* गव्हांचा, गोधूमाचा, गव्हांचाकेलेला, कणकेचा, गोधूमात्मक.

W. flour. कणीक *f.*

Fine w. flour. कणकेचागरा *m.* मैदा *m.* सोजी *f.* सपीठ *n.*

Granulous w. flour. रवा *m.* सोजी *f.*

To WHEEDLE, *v. a.* v. To CAJOLE, To COAX. फुसलाविणें, घुलावणें *or* घोळावणें, मटारणें, वरधावणें.

WHEEDLER, *n.* WHEEDLING, *p. a.* v. V. फुसलावणारा, &c. फुसलाव्या, घुलाव्या.

WHEEDLING, *n.* v. V. फुसलावणें *n.* &c. फुसलावणी *f.* घुलावणी *or* घुलकावणी *f.* घोळावणी *f.* ललपतु *or* लुलुपतु *n. f.*

WHEEL, *n.* चाक *n.* चक्र *n.*

Circumference of a w. नेमि *f.*

Stone, &c. put under a. w. to prevent its rolling on. अट *f.* उटी *f.* उटाळें *n.*

2 (as of a machine or engine). रहाट *or* राहाट *m.*

3—for spinning. कांतायाचा रहाट *m.*

To WHEEL, *v. n.*—a line of men, &c. *turn, move round.* पात *f.*-पातीची पात *f.* फिरणें, चक्कर *n.* मारणें, फेरा *m.* घालणें.

2 v. To REVOLVE. फिरणें, भोंवणें.

To WHEEL, *v. a.* फिरवणें.

2 (round)—a carriage. चकारी *f.* घेणें.

WHEEL-BARROW, *n.* एकचाकी गाडी *f.*

WHEEL-CLOG, WHEEL-STOPPER,*n.* ऊट *f.* उटाळें *n.* अट *f.*

WHEEL-WRIGHT,*n.*v. CARPENTER. चाक करणारा, गाडी करणारा.

WHEELED, *a. having wheels.* चाकाचा, चाकी in comp. चक्रवान्.

To WHEEZE, *v. n. breathe hard with a sound.* घरघर *or* घुरघुर *f.* करणें, गळा *m.*-घसा *m.*-&c. घरघरणें *or* घुरघुरणें-वाजणें *g. of s.* सूंसूं *n. f.* करणें, कफश्वास *m.* करणें- सोडणें.

WHELK, *n.* v. BUMP. उटंगळ *n.*

To WHELM. See To OVERWHELM.

WHELP, *n. young of beasts.* पिलूं *n.* बच्चा *m.* पेटा *m.*

2 *young man,* in contempt. बच्चाजी, बच्चाराम.

To WHELP, *v. n.* विणें, पिलूं *n.*-&c. विणें.

WHEN, *adv. at the time that.* जेव्हां, ज्यावेळेस, ज्यावेळीं, जधीं. The above words are correlative with तेव्हां, त्यावेळेस, त्यावेळीं, तधीं. If जेव्हां be used तेव्हां must follow, but in idiomatic phrases the जेव्हां is often omitted ; ex. जेव्हां तुम्ही जेवून उठलां तेव्हां मी एथें बसलों होतों *or* तुम्ही जेवून उठलां तेव्हां मी एथें बसलों होतों.

Since w. तेव्हांपासून, त्यापासून, त्याउपरांत.

2 *at what time ?* केव्हां, कधीं, कदा, केधवां, कधी, कोणत्या वेळेस-वेळीं-&c.

About w. ? केव्हांसा.

Of w. ? कधींचा. [परांतीक.

3 *after the time that,* v. AFTERWARDS. नंतर, वर,उपरांत, उ-

WHENCE, *adv.*—interrog. कोठून, कोणीकडून, कोणत्या स्थळाहून-

पासून-&c. ? कुतः.
2—indef. जेथून or जिथून, जिकडून, जिकडणें.

WHENEVER, WHENSOEVER, *adv. at whatever time.* केव्हांजरी, कधींजरी, केव्हां used with तरी, केव्हांही, जेव्हांकधीं.

WHERE, *adv. at which place.* जेथें or जिथें, ज्या ठिकाणीं-स्थळीं-जागीं-जाग्यावर-&c. [-&c.
2 *at what place?* कोठें or कुठें, कोणत्या ठिकाणीं-स्थळीं-जागीं
Of w.? कोठचा or ला, कोठील (or कुठचा or ला or कुठील).
To w. and whence a person. कोठावणें or कुठावणें.

WHEREABOUTS, *adv. near what place.* कोठेंसा or कुठेंसा, कोठसा or कुठसा.

WHEREAS, *adv. it being so that, seeing that.* जेव्हां, ज्याअर्थीं, ज्यापेक्षां, ज्यापक्षीं, ज्याकरितां, ज्यास्तव. These are all used with their correlatives तेव्हां, त्याअर्थीं, त्यापेक्षां, त्यापक्षीं, त्याकरितां, त्यास्तव, as ज्याअर्थीं रामाजीपंत पळून गेला आहे त्याअर्थीं त्याच्या पाठीमागें धांवणें पाठविलें पाहिजे. In idiomatic phrases the जेव्हां, ज्याअर्थीं, &c. are usually omitted, as गोमाजी पळून गेला आहे त्यापेक्षां गडी पाठविला पाहिजे, &c. असें असतां, यदर्थं.
2—noting opposition; *on the contrary, when in fact.* खरें म्हटलें असतां, खरें विचारलें असतां, तत्वतः, वस्तुतः.

WHEREAT, *adv. at what.* ज्याजवर, त्याजवर, ज्याला or ज्यास, त्याला or त्यास.

WHEREBY, *adv. by which.* जेणें करून, ज्याकरून, ज्यानें.
2 *by what?* कशानें, कोणत्यानें, कशावरून.

WHEREFORE, *adv. for which reason.* ज्या कारणाला, ज्याकारणानें, ज्या कारणासाठीं-स्तव-मुळें, ज्याकरितां, ज्यास्तव-साठीं-&c. ज्यापक्षीं *pop.* ज्यापेक्षां, यदर्थं.
2 *for what reason?* कां, कशाला, कशास, कोणत्या कारणानें, कोणत्या कारणासाठीं-स्तव-&c. कासया, कायसबब.
3 *for that or this reason.* या-त्याकारणानें, या-त्या कारणासाठीं-स्तव-मुळें-&c. या-त्यासाठीं-स्तव-&c. अतएव.

WHEREIN, *adv. in which.* ज्यामध्यें, ज्यांत, ज्याविषयीं.
2 *in what?* कोणत्यांत, कोणत्यामध्यें, कोणत्याविषयीं.

WHEREOF, *adv. of which.* ज्याचा, ज्याविषयींचा, ज्याविषयीं.
2 *of what?* कशाचा. [जिथील.
3 *of which place.* जिकडचा or ला, जिकडील, जिथचा or ला,

WHERESOEVER, WHEREVER, *adv. in what place soever.* जेथें जेथें or जिथें जिथें, ज्या ज्या जागीं-ठिकाणीं-स्थळीं-&c. कोठेंही, भलकोठें, कोठेंतरी, जेथें तरी, ज्या कोणत्या ठिकाणीं, जेथें कोठें or कुठें, कुत्रापि, यत्रकुत्रापि, यत्रयत्र.

WHEREUPON, *adv. on which.* ज्यावर.
2 *on this.* या-त्यावर-नंतर-&c. मग, तेव्हां.

WHERRY, *n. canoe, boat,* v. VESSEL. तर *f.* डिंगी or डोंगी *f.*

To WHET, *v. a. rub to sharpen.* पाजणें, पाजवणें, पाजळणें, लावणें, शेवटणें, शिळेवर-निपूण्यावर-&c. धरणें, उत्तेजन *n.*-&c. करणें *g. of o.* [रणें *g. of o.*
2 *stimulate,* v. EXCITE. उठवणें, उचलणें, उत्तेजन *n.*-&c. क-

WHET-STONE, *n. sharpening stone.* निशाना or निष्णा or निसणा *m.* शीळ *f.* शाण *m. pop.* सहाण *f.*

WHETHER, *adv. which of two alternatives.* The Maráthí has no corresponding word for this. The "or" which necessarily follows it, gives all the meaning. Ex. Resolve *whether* you will go *or* not, जाल कीं रहाल याचा निश्चय करा.—As a particle distinguishing several points it may be expressed by काय & म्हणा; as I have every article you can want, whether wheat or barley or butter, गहूं काय, जव काय, तूप काय, जो जिनस पाहिजे तो आम्हाजवळ आहे. ब्राम्हण म्हणा, शूद्र म्हणा, अतिशूद्र म्हणा, जो येईल त्याला मी जेवूं घालीन, I will feed every one who comes, whether Bráhman, Shúdra, or Pariah.
W. or no; *nolens volens, at any rate.* खामखा, झक मारीत, झकत, एर्वीतेर्वी, आपोआप.

WHETHER, *pron.* कोणता. [जित.

WHETTED, *p.* v. V. पाजलेला, लावलेला, &c. निशित, तेजित, उत्ते-
To be w. लागणें.
2 उठवलेला, तेजित, उत्तेजित.

WHETTER, *n.* WHETTING, *p. a.* v. V. 1. पाजणारा, लावणारा, शिळेवर धरणारा, उत्तेजन-&c. कर्त्ता-कारी-&c.
2 उठवणारा, &c. उत्तेजन-&c. कर्त्ता-कारी-&c.

WHETTING, *n.* v V. 1.—*act.* पाजणें *n.* पाजवणें *n.* पाजळणें *n.* &c. पाजणी *f.* उत्तेजन *n.*
2 उठवणें *n.* &c. उठवणी *f.* उचल *f.* उत्तेजन *n.* उद्दीपन *n.*

WHEY, *n. serum of milk.* दह्यांतलें पाणी*n.* दह्याची निवळी *f.* मस्तु *n.*

WHICH, *pron.*—relat. जो, किं.
2—demons. कोणता.
3—interr. कोणता, कोणचा, कैंचा, कंचा.

WHICHEVER, WHICHSOEVER, *pron.* जो कोणता, जो, जोजो.

WHIFF, *n.* (in smoking) *a sudden expulsion of air from the mouth.* दम *m.* v. सोड, झुरका *m.* v. सोड.

WHIFFLER, *n. insignificant person.* हलका-एरशेर-अगण्य-&c. मनुष्य, अलबत्यागलबत्या.

WHIFFLING, *a.* v. INCONSTANT, SHUFFLING. धरसोड्या, हिंगतिंगे लावणारा, हिंगेतिंग्या.

WHILE, WHILST, *adv. during the time that.* इतक्यांत, त्यावेळेस, यावेळेस, तेव्हां. The sense of this word is well rendered without an adverb, as काल मी निजलों असतां चोर आला the thief came while I was lying down yesterday.
2 *as long as.* जंव or जों, जोंपर्यंत, जोंवर, तोंपर्यंत, तोंवर.

WHILE, *n. space of time,* v. TIME. वेळ *m.* काळ *m.*
A w. For a w. कांहींवेळ, कांहींकाळ, कांहींवेळपर्यंत, &c. अमळसा.
All this w. ह्यावेळ पर्यंत, एवढा वेळ, एढोळ. [ना मधीं.
Between whiles. मध्येंमध्यें, अधामधीं or अध्यें मध्यें, अधी-
A long w. फारवेळ, बहुतवेळ, बाढवेळ or बाढोळ, एवढावेळ or एढोळ, वेळभर, केढोळ, बहुकाल, बाटकोळ.
A little w. A short w. थोडा-थोडका-&c. वेळ, अचिरकाळ.
In a little w. अचिरें करून, अचिरात्.
What a w. केढोळ.
A w. ago. मघां, मघाशीं. [सणें-नसणें.
Worth while. उपयोग *m.*-लाभ *m.*-फळ *n.*-हाशील *m. n.* अ-

To WHILE, *v. a.* (time) *make to pass pleasantly.* करमणें, सुखानें जाईसा करणें, सुखानें घालवणें-क्रमणें, कालक्रमण *n.*-कालक्रमणा *f.* करणें.

WHIM, WHIMSEY, *n. freak, fancy.* लहर *f.* तरंग *m.* मौज *f.* चाळ *f.* डुक्की *f.* वेड *n.* कुतर्क *m.* विकल्प *m.* वारें *n.*

To WHIMPER, *v. n.* v. To WHINE. पिरगणें, कुसमुसणें, फूसफूस *f.* लावणें-करणें, फुसफुसणें.

WHIMSICAL, *a.* v. FANCIFUL. छंदखोर, छंदी, छंदिष्ट, छांदिष्ट, तन्हेवाज, मनमोज्या, लहरी, लहरीदार, लहरीबहरी, मिजाजखोर, डुकीदार, ख्याली, चिकित्सखोर, छांदसवृत्ति, आडकांट्या, मनस्वी.

WHIMSICALNESS, *n.* v.A. छंदिष्टपणा *m.* &c. छंदखोरी *f.* मिजाजखोरी *f.* मनालौल्य *n.*

To WHINE, *v. n. cry plaintively or childishly.* मिणमिणणें, गिणगिणणें, विणवणें, कणवणणें, मिडकणें, कोंकलणें, पिरंगणें, किरकणें, ठिणकणें, किरकिरणें, पिटपिटणें, पिरपिरणें, गेंगें *n.*-टेंटें *n.*-बेंबें *n.*-&c. करणें, करुणा *f.* भाकणें, कन्हेरी *f.* गाणें, रड *f.* गाणें-सांगणें, रडूंरडूं-गयांबयां-अयांबयां *adv.* करणें, इवळणें, वल्हळणें *or* विल्हाळणें.

WHINE, WHINING, *n.* v. V. मिणमिणणें *n.* गिणगिणणें *n.* किरकिरणें*n.* &c. पिटपीट *f.* पिरपीर*f.* किरकीर *f.* रिपरीप *f.* मिणमीण *f.* गिणगीण *f.* बिणबणी *f.* कणवण *f.* कळकळ्या *f. pl.* किळकिळी *f.* किंव *or* कींव *f.* मुळमूळ *f.* कारणा *f.* रड *f.* रडगाणें *n.* गाणें *n.*

WHINER, *n.* WHINING, *p. a.* v. V. मिणमिणणारा, गिणगिणणारा, &c. पिटपिट्या, पिरपिरा *or* ऱ्या, किरकिरा *or* ऱ्या, मिणमिण्या, पिरंगा, विल्हळ्या, रडका, रडवा, रड्या, रडतोंड्या, रडतलक्ष्मी, बापुडवाणा *or* णी.

WHININGLY, *adv.* v. A. मुळमूळ, गायाबायां *or* गयाबयां, गळगळां.

To WHINNY. See To NEIGH.

To WHIP, *v.a. strike with a whip.* चाबूक *m.*-कोरडा *m.*-&c. मारणें-लावणें-लगावणें-चमकावणें, चाबुकानें &c. मारणें.

2 from; into; out; round; up. To render *whip* in combination with adverbs, take an appropriate adverb from the collection under SMARTLY and prefix it to a verb expressing the action to be rendered. Ex. to whip up *i. e.* to take up smartly, झपदिशी उचलणें; to whip from, *i. e.* to take away suddenly, झटकन काढणें, &c. &c. The *intransitive* sense of the word, to whip up, to whip away, &c. *i. e.* to move up or away *smartly*, is to be rendered in the same way.

WHIP, *n.*—the instrument for chastising. चाबूक *m.*

Cartman's or ploughman's w. असूड *m.* चाव्हऱ्या *m.* चाव्हऱ्याभसूड *m.*

Lash of a w. कांकडा *m.*

Long leather w. कोरडा *m.* [चरम.

WHIP-HAND, *n. upper hand*, v. SUPERIORITY. उपरदबडा *m.* उ-

WHIP-LASH, *n.* कांकडा *m.* [फिरकरवत *m.*

WHIP-SAW, *n. saw worked by two men.* अडें *n.* अड्या करवत*m.*

WHIPPER, *n.* WHIPPING, *p. a.* v. V. 1. चाबूक मारणारा-लावणारा-&c. चाबुकानें मारणारा.

WHIPPER-SNAPPER, WHIPSTER, *n. puny insignificant fellow.* नसरूड *f.* नसकांणा *m.* नसरड *f.*

WHIPPING, *n.* v. V.—*act.* चाबूक मारणें *n.* &c. चाबूकमार *m.* चाबुकाचा मार *m.* कोरडेमार *m.* कोरड्याचा मार *m.* कोरडेबाजी*f.*

To WHIRL, *v. a. turn round rapidly, twirl.* गरगर-गरगरां-गरागर-गरारां-&c. फिरवणें-भोंवविणें-&c. गरगरवणें, गिरटी *f.*-गिरकी *f.*-&c. देणें.

To WHIRL, *v. n. move round rapidly.* भोंवडणें, भोंवणें, गरगरणें *intens.* गरारणें, फिरणें, गरगर-गरगरां-&c. फिरणें, गिरकांडा *m.*-गिरकांडी *f.*-गिरकी *f.*-गिरटी *or* घिरटी *f.*-&c. मारणें-देणें-घेणें, घिरटी *or* घरटी *f.* घालणें, भ्रमणें.

2—as wind or water; *eddy.* घोंटाळणें, गोंधळणें, कोंडाळणें.

WHIRL, WHIRLING, *n.* v. V.N. 1. गरगरणें *n.* &c. गिरकांडा *m.* गिरकांडी *f.* गिरकी *f.* गिरटी *or* घिरटी *or* घरटी *f.* भोंवरी *f.* भांवरा *m.* भरकांडा *or* भिरकांडा *m.* भिराका *m.* फेरी *f.* घोंटाळा *m.* वेढा*m.* भ्रम*m.* भ्रमण*n.* विभ्रम *m.* संभ्रम *m.* भ्रांति *f.* चक्रावर्त्त *m.*

W. round (in child's play.) ओंवळ्या भोंवळ्या *f. pl.* भिंगारा *m. or* गाडेभिंगारे *m. pl.* गाडेभिंगो-या *f. pl.* गाड्याभिंगोऱ्या *f. pl.* गिरीघोंटी *f.*

With a w. or twirl. गररर, गिर-कन-कर-&c.

2 fig. (of business or engagements). भरकांडा *m.* भिरका *m.* घोंटाळा *m.* गरगरा *m.*

To be in a w. कोंडाळणें.

WHIRL-POOL, *n. eddy, vortex.* भोंवरा *m.* चक्कर *n.* चक्र*n.* आवर्त्त *m.* भ्रम *m.* जलभ्रम *m.*

WHIRL-WIND, *n.* वावटळ *or* टूळ *f.* वायटळ *or* टूळ *f.* वाहटळ*or*टूळ *f.* वायधूळ *f.* चक्रवात *m.* आवर्त्त *m.* वातावर्त्त *m.* [त्त, भ्रांत.

WHIRLED, *p.* v. V. A. गरगर फिरवलेला, गरगरवलेला, &c. आवृ-

WHIRLER, *n.*—of a spinning wheel. चात *m.f. n.* चाती *f.*

WHIRLIGIG, *n.*—the plaything. फिरकी *f.* किंकरें *n.* किरकिरें *or* खिरखिरें *n.* गिरगिरें *or* घिरघिरें *n.* भिरभिरें *n.* भोंवरा *m.*

WHIRR, *n. noise of stone,&c. passing through the air.* भिरिरी *f.*

W. of a spinning top or whirligig. टर *f.*

With a w. भिरिरी, भुरकन-कर-&c. भिरभीर.

To WHIRR, *v. n. fly with noise.* भरभर *or* रां *adv.* उडणें-उठणें-&c. भरारणें. [भिरभीर, भिरिरी.

WHIRR, *adv. with a whirr.* भर कण-कन-&c. भुरकन-कर-&c.

WHISK, *n. quick jerk, &c.* झटका *m.* झटक *f.* झटकारा *m.* झणकार *or* झणकारा *m.* झपाटा *m.* फटकारा *m.* भिराका *or* भराका*m.*

To WHISK, *v. a. sweep or brush by whisking.* झटकणें, झटकावणें.

2 *move with a quick jerk.* झटकणें, झटकावणें, फटकारणें, झटका *m.*-झटकारा *m.* देणें-मारणें.

To WHISK, *v.n. move nimbly.* झटके *m. pl.* मारणें-देणें-मारीत चालणें- देत चालणें, झटकत चालणें.

WHISKER, *n.* (of the face). कल्ला *m.* गलमुछ *m.* गल्लश्मश्रु *n.*

2 *flapper, fan, &c.* झडपण *n.* [कल्ल्याचा.

WHISKERED, *a. furnished with whiskers.* कल्लेदार, कल्लेवाला,

WHISKY, *n.* एक प्रकारचें मद्य आहे.

To WHISPER, *v. n. speak with a low sibilant voice.* कुचकुचणें, फुसफुसणें, फसफसणें, कुजबुजणें, गुजगुजणें, गुणकुणणें, पुटपुटणें *or* फुटफुटणें, फुसफूस *f.*-कुजबूज *f.*-&c. करणें-मांडणें-लावणें, गुजुगुजू-कुजबुजू कुचकुचू-&c. बोलणें, कानगोष्ट *f.* चालणें *g. of s.*

To WHISPER, *v. a. utter in a low sibilant voice.* फुसफूस-&c. करून सांगणें, गुजुगुजू-कुचुकुचू-&c. सांगणें,कानांत सांगणें-बोलणें, कानांत जपणें.

To w. about; *tell in people's ears.* कानगी *f.* करणें.

WHISPER, WHISPERING, *n.* v. V. N. फुसफुसणें *n.* &c. फुसफूस *f.* कुजबूज *f.* गुजगूज *f.* कुचकूच *f.* पुचपूच *f.* पुटपूट *or* फुटफूट *f.* कुणकूण *f.*

Great or general w. खसबसाट *m.*

Whispers, *suppressed talk, low rumours.* कुचकूच *f.* कुजबूज *f.* पुचपूच *f.* कानकूण *f.* गुणगूण *f.*

WHISPERED, *p.* v. V. A. कानांत सांगितलेला, फुसफूस करून सांगितलेला, &c.

WHISPERER, *n.* **WHISPERING**, *p. a.* v. V. N. फुसफुसणारा, कुजबुजणारा, &c. फुसफूस-&c. करणारा, गुजुगुजू-&c. बोलणारा, फुस, कुशा, गुजगुज्या.

I. v. TALE-BEARER. INCENDIARY. कर्णेजप.

WHISPERINGLY, *adv.* ससबस or सां, गुजुगुज्, कुजुबुज्, कुचुकुचु, उपांशु.

WHIST, *interj.* चप or चप्प or चुप.

WHIST, *n.* गंजिफांचा एक खेळ आहे.

To **WHISTLE**, *v. n.* (with the mouth). शिवळणें, शिळ or शिवळ *f.*-शेळ or शीळ *f.* घालणें-वाजवणें, शिटी *f.* वाजवणें-वाजणें.

2—a bullet, arrow, &c. चुचावणें, चूं *adv.* करणें-वाजणें, सणसण-सणकर-सणदिशी-&c. वाजणें, सणसणणें *intens.* सणाणणें.

3—wind. सूंसूं-सणसण-भणभण *adv.* वाहणें, सणसणणें.

WHISTLE, **WHISTLING**, *n.* v. V. 1.—*act.* शिवळणें *n.* शीळ वाजवणें *n.* शीळ *f.* शिट्टीक *f.*

2 चुचावणें *n.* चूं *f.* सणसण *f.* सणसणाट *m.* सणाण *m.*

3 भणभण *f.* सणसण *f.* सणसणाट *m* सणाण *m.*

I. *instrument of whistling.* चिमणी *f.* शिळई *f.* शिळी *f.* पिंपाणी or पेपाणी *f.* पिंपारी *f.* पेपेरें or पोंपेरें *n.*

WHISTLER, *n.* **WHISTLING**, *p. a.* v. V. 1. शिवळणारा, शीळ वाजवणारा, &c.

WHIT, *n.* v. BIT. लेश *m.* लवलेश *m.* कण *m.* रजःकण *m.* अणु *m.*

WHITE, *n. white colour, whiteness.* पांढरा रंग *m.* सफेत रंग *m.* सफेती *f.*

2 (of eggs). पांढरा बील *m.*-बलक *m.*

3 (of the eye). कौडी *f.* पांढरें बुबूळ *n.*

WHITE, *a.* पांढरा, (*remiss.* पांढरवट, पांडुरका *whitish*) ढवळा, सफेत, धवा, शुभ्र, शुक्ल, श्वेत, धवल *pop.* धवळ, सित, गौर.

Dusky w. कवरा, कंदी, भुरका, भुरकट, धूसर.

Of a glistening w. पांडुरका or गा.

W. as snow. W. as crystal. Lily w. W. and clear, &c. पांढरा फटफटीत, पांढरासफेत or द, पांढराफटक or फटीक or फट्ट, पांढरा फेक, पांढरा स्वच्छ.

Yellowish w. पांडु, पांडुर.

To set down in black and white, *to put in writing.* पांढऱ्याचा काळा करणें or पांढऱ्यावर काळें करणें.

2 See PALE.

WHITE-ANT, *n. termes.* वाळवी *f.* उदई or उधई *f.* वाळंबा *m.*

WHITE-LEAD, *n.* सफेता *m.* [परी *f.*

WHITE-SWELLING, *n. swelling of the knee joint.* गुडघी *f.* ढों-

WHITE-WASH, *n. composition of lime and water.* सफेती *f.*

To **WHITE-WASH**, *v. a.* सफेती or दी *f.* करणें.

To **WHITE**, *To* **WHITEN**, *v. a. make white.* पांढरा-सफेत-&c. करणें, सफेती *f.* करणें-देणें-आणणें. [होणें.

To **WHITE**, *To* **WHITEN**, *v. n. become white.* पांढरा-सफेत-&c.

WHITENESS, *n.* v. A. 1. पांढरेपणा *m.* सफेतपणा *m.* ढवळेपणा *m.* सफेती or दी *f.* शुभ्रता *f.* शुक्लता *f.* श्वेतता *f.* &c. श्वैत्य *n.* धावल्य *n.* शौक्ल्य *n.*

Glistering w. पांडुरकी *f.*

WHITES, *n. fluor albus.* पांढरवणी *n.* धुपणी *f.* पांढरीधुपणी *f.* होळणी *f.* श्वेत प्रदर *m.* प्रदर *pop.* पदर*m.* असूक *n.* उपळ *m.*

WHITHER, *adv. to what place?* कोणीकडे, कोणत्या स्थळाकडे, &c. कोठें is as commonly used for कोणीकडे, as in English where is for whither.

2 *to which place.* जिकडे. [कडे पाहिजे.

WHITHERSOEVER, *adv. to whatever place.* जिकडे, भलतेकोठें, जि-

WHITLOW, *n. swelling near the nail.* नखरू *n.* नखसु *f.* नखरूड *n.* नखशी *f.* नखसूय *f.* नखमूळ *n.* नखुरडा *m.* नखुरडें *n.* नखम्पच *m.*

WHITTLE, *n. clasp knife.* मोडमुरा *m. dim.* मोडमुरी *f.*

To **WHITTLE**. *v. a.* सोलणें, छिलणें.

To **WHIZ**, *v. n. make a hissing or humming noise in flying through the air.* गोंगणें, गोंगावणें, सणसणणें *intens.* सणाणणें, सणकणें, सुरसुरणें, सूं-चुण्ण-चुणकर-&c. बाजणें-करीतजाणें.

WHIZ, **WHIZZING**, *n.* v. V. गोंगणें *n.* सणसणणें *n.* &c. सणसण *f.* चूं *n. f.* सणका*m. intens.* सणसणाट*m. and* सणाण *m.*

With a w. चुण-कर-कन-&c. चुण्ण, चुर-कन-कर-&c. चुर्र, झण-कण-कर &c. सण-कण-कर-&c. *intens.* सणसण or णां, सणासण, सणाणा, सणाण.

WHO, *pron.*—relat. जो, कि.

2—interr. कोण, कवण. [भलता कोणी.

WHOEVER, *pro. any person whatever.* जोकोणी, जो, हरकोणी,

WHOLE, *a. all, the whole mass or multitude,* v. ALL. सारा, आख्खा, आघा, सर्व, अवघा, सगळा, समग्र, समस्त, सकल *pop.* सकळ, भर in comp. अशेष, कृत्स्न, साद्यंत.

2 *complete, entire, perfect, undivided.* सगळा, आख्खा, सर्व, समग्र, समस्त, सकल *pop.* सकळ, सबंध, पुरा, पूर्ण, संपूर्ण, अखंड, अभंग, अभग्न, अफोड, साद्यंत.

3—rupee or other piece; *not changed into smaller coin.* बांधा or बंदा, सबंध.

4 *sound, unimpaired, well.* धड, धडका, धडसा, चांगला, बरा, धडधाकट or ड, धडधोप or धडधोपट, सलम, साबीत or साबून, बळकट, खबरदार, सदट or सधट. [मेचा.

5—used of number; *round.* घाऊक, ठोक or थोक, ठोक रक-

6—of relations; *opp. to* half, &c. सख्खा, सगा.

WHOLE, *n. the entire thing.* साकल्य *n.* कात्स्न्र्य *n.* कार्त्स्न्य *n.* समुदाय *m.* This word is best rendered by the use of the adjective as माझी सगळी मालमत्ता the whole of my property.

On the w. *all things considered.* मिळून, एकूण or न, सगळें-अवघें-&c. पाहतां.

WHOLENESS, *n.* v. A. 1. सगळेपणा *m.* &c. साकल्य *n.* सामग्र्य *n.*

2 सगळेपणा*m.* सबंधपणा*m.*&c. अखंडता*f.* अभगता *f.* संपूर्णता *f.* &c.

WHOLESALE, *n.—as opp. to* retail. ठोकविक्री *f.* घाऊकविक्री *f.*

By w. एकठोक, एकथोक, उधड, उधडा, उक्ता, घाऊक.

WHOLESALE, *a.* v. N. ठोक or थोक, घाऊक, ठोकविक्रीचा, घाऊकविक्रीचा, ठोकळ, उक्त्याचा.

WHOLESOME, *a that tends to promote health,* v. SALUBRIOUS. पथ्यकर, पथ्य, पथ्याचा, सात्म्याचा, सत्वस्थ, सात्विक, शरीरहितकर-कारक-प्रद-&c.

2 *conducive to happiness,* v. BENEFICIAL. हिताचा, हितकर, हितावह, हितकारक, हित, उपयुक्त.

WHOLESOMENESS, *n.* v. A. 1. पथ्यपणा *m.* चांगलेपणा *m.* पथ्यकरता *f.* शरीरहितकारकता *f.*

2 हितकारकता *f.* उपयोग *m.* उपयुक्तता *f.*

WHOLLY, *adv. totally.* निःशेष, निस्तूक, झाडून, निश्टंक, अशेषतः, तमाम, दरोबस्त, सर्वशः, सर्वतः, साकल्यें करून, यावत्, यच्चयावत्, अवच्छेदकावच्छेदें करून.

2 *altogether, utterly, entirely, perfectly, thoroughly.* अगर्दी, पुरतेपणीं, निस्तूक, निश्टंक, धड, तदंत, निपट, बिलकुल, निसळ,निसल, निखालस, चट, साफ, पस्त, सुतराम्, सर्वांशीं, सर्वात्मना, सर्वभावें, अक्लेश, अवल आखर, यच्चयावत्, अक्कलखाद.—with the emphasis and power of the intensitives, *stark, staring* (naked, mad), *stone* (blind, deaf), *dead* (drunk), *downright, regular, proper, out and out* (ass, knave, villain, &c.). अगर्दी, झळझळीत, धड, साफ, निस्तूक, निपट.

WHOOP, *interj.* हूप.

WHOOP, *n. shout of monkeys.* हूप *f.* भुपकार *m.* भुभुःकार *m.*

2 See SHOUT.

To WHOOP. See To SHOUT.

WHOP. See WHAP.

WHORE, *n. unchaste woman, strumpet, &c.* v. HARLOT. शिनळ बायको *f.*-स्त्री *f.* छिनाल *f.* स्वैरिणी *f.* स्वैरवृत्ता *f.* स्वैरगामिनी *f.*

Airs or arts of a w. छिनालनखरा *m.*

Son of a w. रांडलेंक *m. n.* रांडपोर *m.* रांडेय, रंडापुत्र *m.*

Whore's gallant. सोयरा *m.* [बाजारबसवी *f.*

2 *prostitute, courtezan,* v. HARLOT. रंडी *f.* रांड *f.* बसवी *f.*

To set up her trade,—a w. पाल *n.* घालणें-मांडणें.

To WHORE, *v.n. practice lewdness.* शिंदळकी *f.*-शिनळकी *f.*-छिनाली *f.*-&c. करणें-मांडणें, बाहेरख्याल *m.*-बदकर्म *n.*-बदफैली *f.*-&c. करणें.

WHORE-MASTER, WHORE-MONGER, *n.* v. LECHER, WENCHER. रांडबाज, रंडीबाज, छिनाल, शिनळपुरुष, बाहेरख्याली.

WHORE-SON, *n.* v. BASTARD. रांडलेंक *m. n.* रांडपोर *m.* रांडेचा, शिनळीचा, धगडीचा, जारज, रांडेय, त्रेपन्नमंगळीचा.

WHORE-DOM, *n. lewdness, unlawful intercourse.* छिनाली *f.* छिनालकी *f.* शिनळकी *f.* शिंदळकी *f.* छिनाला *m.* बाहेरख्याल *m.* बदकर्म *n.* बदअमल *m.* बदफैली *f.* जारकर्म *n.* व्यभिचार *m.* पौंश्चल्य *n.*

WHORISH, *a.* v. LUSTFUL. शिनल, शिंदळ, जारकर्मी, बाहेरख्याली, बदफैल, शिंदळकीचा, शिनळीचा, छिनालीचा.

W. affectation and airs. शिंदळनखरा *m.*

W. practice or tricks. शिंदळचार *m. pl.* शिंदळचाळे *m. pl.* शिंदळठेव *m. pl.* छिनाळचाळे *m. pl.*

WHORISHNESS, *n.* v. A. शिंदळकी *f.* शिनळकी *f.* छिनाली *f.*

WHOSE, *pron.*—relative. ज्याचा (ज्याचा, जिचा, ज्याचा *m. f. n.*) यदीय, यद् (in comp. as, यत्कथा, यत्कृत, यद्वंश, यच्चित, यन्नाम).

2—interrog. कोणाचा.

WHOSOEVER, *pron.* जोकोणी, जो, हरकोणी, भलताकोणी.

WHY, *adv. for what reason ?* कां, कशाला, कशासाठीं-मुळें-करितां-कारणें-स्तव, कायम्हणून, कांबरें, कांकां, कसकसा, किमर्थ, किन्निमित्त, कासया.

2 *for which reason.* ज्यास्तव-साठीं-मुळें-करितां-&c.

WICK, *n.* (of a light). वात *f.* काकडा *m.* बत्ती *f.* टेणा *m.* वर्त्ति *or* वर्त्ती *f.*

Shred or rag fit for a w. वातेरें *n.* [काडवात *f.*

W. to be kindled and waved (around an idol, &c.).

WICKED, *a. evil, sinful, &c.*—of persons. दुष्ट, वाईट, पापी, पापिष्ट, पातकी, दुर्जन, कुजन, शठ, पिशुन, कुकर्मी, अकर्मी, दुष्कर्मी, अधर्मी, अधार्मिक, दुष्टमानस, दुर्गुणी, हरामी, दुराचरणी, दुराचारी, पापाचारी, असदाचारी, अनाचारी, कर्मदुष्ट, दुष्कर, पापकर्मी, पापकर, पापकर्त्ता, कुचर, कुमार्गवर्त्ती, दुर्वृत्त, दुरित, पापपरायण, कुबुद्धि, कुमति, पापबुद्धि, पापमति, पापचेता, दुश्चरित्र, असाधु, तामस. Some allusive or significant terms and phrases for *an extremely wicked person,* answering to *sin personified, monster of iniquity, child of the devil, son of belial, &c.* are, पापात्मा *or* पापात्मक (पुरुष, स्त्री, &c.) पापस्वरूप, पापमूर्त्ति, पापपुरुष, पापाचापुतळा, पापराशि, पापनिधान, पापनिधि, क्रूरकर्मा, भीमकर्मा, घोरकर्मा, कर्मचंडाल, अधमात्मा.

Friendship or favor of the w. खलप्रीति *f.*

The w. do not thrive or prosper. बाघाचा बाढा बाढत नाहीं.

2—of acts, &c. पापाचा, पातकाचा, दुष्कर्माचा, अधर्माचा, पापबुद्धीचा, पापमतीचा, &c. पापिष्ट, दुष्ट, वाईट, प्रत्यवायी. [ष्ट्या.

WICKEDLY, *adv.* v. A. 1. पापबुद्धीनें, पापमतीनें, पापबुद्ध्या, पापदु-

WICKEDNESS, *n.* v. A. 1. दुष्टपणा *m.* वाईटपणा *m.* पापीपणा *m.* पापिष्टपणा *m.* दुष्टाई *f.* दुर्बुद्धि *f.* दुष्टबुद्धि *f.* पापबुद्धि *f.* पापमति *f.* दुर्मति *f.* कुबुद्धि *f.* कुमति *f.* कुभाव *m.* दौर्मनस्य *n.* दौष्ट्य *n.* दौर्जन्य *n.* दौरात्म्य *n.* शाठ्य *n.* पैशुन्य *n.* कुसृति *f.*

2 दुष्टपणा *m.* वाईटपणा *m.* वाईट *n.* प्रत्यवाय *m.*

I. *evil practices.* वाईटकाम *n.* पाप *n.* पातक *n.* दुष्कर्म *n.* कुकर्म *n.* दुराचरण *n.* पापाचरण *n.* पापाचार *m.* दुराचार *m.* असदाचरण *n.* असदाचार *m.* अनाचार *m.* अनाचरण *n.* दुष्कृत *n.* दुष्कृति *f.* कुचर्य *f.*

WICKER, *a. made of twigs or osiers.* डाहाळ्यांचा, कोंकाचा, वाळंजाचा, शेरणीचा.

WICKET, *n. small gate.* खिडकी *f.* बेसकट *f.* कवाडी *f.* दिंड *f.* दिंडी *f.*

WIDE, *a. broad,* v. EXTENSIVE. रुंद (remiss. रुंदट *or* ड *widish*). रुंदेला, रुंदीचा, विस्ताराचा, पसरट, चौडा, प्रशस्त.

Very w. रुंदाट *or* ड, रुंदाळ.

2 See DISTANT.

WIDE, WIDELY, *adv.* v. A. 1. रुंद, विस्ताराचा *decl.* विस्तारानें.

2 लांब. [आणणें.

To WIDEN, *v. a.* रुंदावणें, रुंद-&c. करणें, रुंदावा *m.*-रुंदपणा *m.*-&c.

To WIDEN, *v.n.* रुंदावणें, रुंद-&c. होणें, रुंदावा *m.*-&c. येणें *in.con.*

WIDENESS, *n.* v. A. रुंदपणा *m.* &c. रुंदी *f.* रुंदावा *m.* विस्तार *m.*

WIDOW, *n. woman who has lost her husband.* रांड *f.* रंडकी *f.* विधवा *f.* रांडव *f.* गतभर्तृका *f.* बोडकी *f.*—in tenderness or pity. रंडकीमुंडकी *f.* रांडमुंड *f.* रांडोळी *f.* रांडमामी *f.*—in contempt. रंडकी *or* रांडकी *f.* रांड *f.* रांडखांड *f.* रांडमुंड *f.* रांडरूं *or* रांडरूं *n.* राडूं *n.* बोडकूल *n.* खुंटाळी *f.* तासोपंत *m. or* पंतीण *f.* रंडा *f. n.* सांदींतलें मडकें *n.* अडव्यासुडक्याची रांड *f.*—in covert or cant phraseol. विठ्ठलसवाशीण *or* विठ्ठलसवाष्ण *f.*

Man married to a w. पाटकरी.

Marriage with a w. म्हावेर *m.* पाट *m.*

Self-immolation of a w. upon the pyre of her husband. सतीजाणें *n.* आग रिघणें *n.* अग्निप्रवेश *m.* सहगमन *n.* सहमरण *n.* अनुगमन *n.* अन्वारोहण *n.*—in cant or covert phraseol. अग्निकाष्ठ भक्षण *n.*—pit prepared for do. खाई *f.*

Shorn w. बोडकी *f.* म्हातारी *f.* [धर्मशीळ *f.*

Stone by which a w. ascends the pyre. धर्मशिला *pop.*

W. before puberty. बालरंडा *f.* बालविधवा *f.*
W. that burns with the body of her husband. सती *f.*
W. in weeds. बोडकी *f.*
W. remarried. पाटकरीण *f.* पुनर्भू *f.*
W.'s dole, *bad singing.* रंडागीत *n.*
W.'s jointure. रांडरोटा *m.*
W.'s mite. सुदामपोहे *m. pl.*
Unshorn w. केंसकरीण *f.* सकेशा *f.*
To perform ablution in preparation for mounting the pyre. सरोवर नाहणें.
Some terms of mention or address for a widow are, अयाल *or* ळ, गंगाभागीरथी. [करणें.

To WIDOW, *v. a. deprive of a husband.* रांडावणें, विधवा *f.*-&c.
To be widowed. रांडावणें, घरीं-माघारां-परत-&c. येणें, डोकीवर-नाकावर-तोंडावर पदर *m.* येणें, रांडपाटा *m. or* वांटा *m.* येणें.

WIDOWER, *n. man whose wife has died.* रंडका *or* रांडका, बोडका *or* खा, विधुर, मृतपत्नीक, मृतभार्य.

WIDOWHOOD, *n.* रांडपणा *m.* बोडकीपणा *m.* रंडकेपणा *m.* छत्रभंग *m.* वैधव्य *n.* वैधव्यदशा *f.* रंडावस्था *f.*

WIDTH, *n. breadth.* रुंदी *f.* रुंदावा *m.* रुंदपणा *m.* व्यास *m.*

To WIELD, *v. a. use or handle with full power, manage.* वापरणें, वागवणें, चालवणें, वर्त्तवणें, पेलणें, तोलणें, क्षेपणें, झोकणें, फिरवणें, खेळणें, वहिवाटणें.

WIELDED, *p.* v. V. वापरलेला, वागवलेला, &c.

WIELDER, *n.* WIELDING, *p. a.* v. V. वापरणारा, वागवणारा, चालवणारा, &c.

WIELDING, *n.* v. V.—*act.* वापरणें *n.* वागवणें *n.* क्षेपणें *n.* &c.

WIELDY, *a.* v. V. *and* MANAGEABLE. वापरायास चांगला, वापरायाजोगा-&c.

WIFE, *n.* बायको *f.* लग्नाची बायको-स्त्री *f.* कबिला *f.* बाईल *f.* कुटुंब *n.* भार्या *f.* पत्नी *f.* दारा *f.* जाया *f.* गृहिणी *f.* वल्लभा *f.* दयिता *f.* भाजा *f.* द्वितीया *f.* महिला *f.* रमणी *f.* क्षेत्र *n.* कलत्र *n.* खटला *m.* अर्धांग *n.* वामांग *n.*
Chaste and faithful w. पतिव्रता *f.* सती *f.*
Forsaken w. सांड *f.*
Having a w. v. MARRIED. सकुटुंब, सपत्नीक, सभार्य.
House of one's w.'s father. सासुरवाडी *f.* सासुरवड *f.*
Mutual jealousy and envy of rival wives. सवतमत्सर *m.* सापत्नभाव *m.*
Old w's. fable. बाबावाक्यं *n.*
One's own w. स्वकीया *f.* स्वीया *f.*
One's own son by one's own w. औरस *m.*
Perquisites or property of a w. स्त्रीधन *n.* शुल्क *n.*
Rival w. सवत *f.* सपत्नी *f.*
Rival wives—*wives* collect. *of one man.* सवतवळा *f.*
Taking a w. दारकर्म *n.* दारक्रिया *f.* दारोपसंग्रह *m.* दारसंग्रह *m.* परिणय *m.* परिणयन *n.*
That is without a w. अपत्नीक.
The happy and joyous state of wifehood. सौभाग्य *n.*
Unfaithful w. अपतिव्रता, असती, असाधुवृत्ता.
W. and children. रांडपोर *n.* [लम.
W.'s brother. मेहुणा*m.* साला*m.* शालक*m.* श्यालक *or* श्या-
W. of husbands brother. जाऊ *or* जावू *f.*
W.'s mother. सासू *f.*—as a term of address. मामी *f.*
W.'s sister. मेहुणी *f.* साली *f.* श्याली *f.*
W.'s sister's husband. साडभाऊ *m.* साडू*m.* [दारा *f.*
W. of another. परकीया *f.* परस्त्री *f.* परवधू *f.* परनारी *f.* पर-
W. run off to another man. घरघुसी *f.* परनिघी *f.*
W. whose husband is abroad. प्रोषितभर्तृका *f.*
Wives of brothers. जावका *f. pl.*
In writing the name of a wife or widow the word कोम is used before the name of her husband, as साळूबाई कोम रामजीपंत Sálú Bái wife of Rámji Pant, also जावजे *f.* [केशाचा टोप *m.*

WIG, *n. covering for the head made of hair.* केशांची टोपी *f.*
2 See REPROOF, SCOLDING.

To WIG, *v. a.* v. TO SCOLD. उलटी हजामत *f.*-मुंडण *n.*-बोडणी *f.*-बोडंती *f.*-तासणी *f.*-&c. करणें *g. of o.*

WIGHT, *n. person,* v. WRETCH. काळतोंड्या, काळमुख्या, खापरतोंड *or* खापरतोंड्या, अकाबाईचें बाळ *n.* अपयशी.

WILD, *a. of or belonging to a wilderness.* रानाचा, अरण्याचा, &c. रानांतला, जंगली, आरण्य, आरण्यक, वन्य, वान.
2 *not tame.* जंगली, रानांतला, रान (in comp. as रानडुकर, रानमांजर.) रानकट, रानगट, वन्य, वन (in comp. as वनशूकर, वनगौ).
3 *growing spontaneously.* रानट, रानटी, रानवट, जंगली, रानांतला, रानांतील, जंगलांतला, जंगली, वन्य, उनाड, रान (in comp. as रानकेळ, रानउडीद) वन (in comp. as वनवृक्ष, वनपुष्प, वनफल).
4 *uninhabited,* v. DESERT. जंगली, रानट, रखरखीत, रुक्ष, रूक्ष, वैराण *or* न.
5 *rude, uncivilized,* v. SAVAGE. जंगली, रानटी, रानवट, वनचर, वनेचर, जांगल.
6—of acts, conduct, &c. *irregular, disorderly, &c.* v. LICENTIOUS. बेकैद, बेकैदा, अनर्गळ, बेताल, बेबंद, अंधाधुंद *or* ध, अंधाधुंदीचा, वेडावांकडा.
7 *loose, unrestrained, uncurbed, unruly,* v. LICENTIOUS. बेकैद, अनर्गळ, उनाड, वावगा, उनाडबाछुला, बाष्कळ, बारगळ, बारगा, बारबंडा, वायचळ, उच्छृंखल (*pop.* उतं[illegible] *or* खळ) बहवस, स्वैरी, स्वैरगति.
To run w. उधळणें, सुटणें, रान *n.* घेणें, वाऱ्यावर सरणें, बारा *m.* घेणें-पिणें, बारगळणें, आरबळणें, बाष्कळणें, बाचरणें, बायकळणें, विकळणें, चवणें *or* चेवणें, निसवणें, बिथरणें, बिफरणें, गुण *m. pl.* सोडणें-विसरणें, आरबण्यांतून जाणें, अवनार *m.* धरणें-घेणें, अवतारणें, आवगणणें, अवदसा *f.* अठवणें *in. con.* सैरावैरा-&c. होणें.
8 *unreasonable, &c.* v. ABSURD, INCONSISTENT. वेडावांकडा, वेडाविपारा, भलताभलता, भलभलता, भलतासलता, अद्वातद्वा, अयुक्तिक, युक्तिशून्य, विचूक.
9 (through fright or rage). कावरा बावरा, तारका बारका, बावरा, तग्रवम. [जायली.
10—of the inferior timbers ; *jungle.* जंगली, रायवळ, बि-
11—of certain fruits. रायवळ.

WILD, WILDERNESS, *n. uninhabited and uncultivated tract, desert.* रान *n.* जंगल *n.* वन *n.* अरण्य *n.* रानवा *m.* आडरान *n.* माळरान *n.* तळवट *n.* खराबा *m.* मरुदेश *m.*

Howling w. भणभणीत रान *n.* ऐराण *n.*

Vast and frightful w. अटव्यरान *n.* अटव्यअरण्य *n.* अघोर अरण्य *n.*

WILD-BEAST, *n.* रानांतलें जनावर *n.* सावज *n.* वनपशु *m.*

WILD-GOOSE-CHASE, *n. pursuit of any thing unlikely to be got.* सुवर्णमृगाचाशोध *m.* हेममृगस्यपृष्ठानुगमन *n.* हेममृगानुधावन *n.* मृगतृष्णा *f.*

WILD-ROSE, *n.* रानगुलाब *n.*

WILDLY, *adv.* v. A. 3. *and* SPONTANEOUSLY. आपोआप, पेरल्यावांचून, रानांत, उनाड.

6. 7. बेकैद, बेबंद, बेकैदीनें, बेडावांकडा *decl.* रानघेऊन.

8 वेडावांकडा *decl.* भलता *decl.* भलभलता *decl.* वावंद्या सांगून, अद्वातद्वा *or* यद्वातद्वा.

9 काबराबाबरा *decl.* तारकाबारका *decl.* &c.

I. *loosely, stragglingly.* रानोमाळ.

WILDNESS, *n.* v. A. 4. जंगलीपणा *m.* रानटपणा *m.* रखरखितपणा *m.* &c. रौक्ष्य *n.*

5 रानटीपणा *m.* रानवटपणा *m.* जंगलीपणा *m.* [धाधुंदी *f.*

6 बेकैदपणा *m.* बेबंदपणा *m.* वेडेवांकडेपणा *m.* अंधाधुंदपणा *m.* अं-

7 बेकैदपणा *m.* अनर्गळपणा *m.* उनाडपणा *m.* बारगळपणा *m.* &c. उनाडकी *f.* बेकैद *f.*

8 वेडेबांकडेपणा *m.* &c. अयुक्तिकत्व *n.*

9 काबरेबाबरेपणा *m.* तारकेबारकेपणा *m.* &c.

WILE, *n. guile,* v. ART, CUNNING. कपट *n.* कावा *m.* कावित्र *n.*

2 v. ARTIFICE. शकल *f.* डाव *m.* [र *f.*

Wiles; *artifices.* छकडभेद *m. pl.* छक्केपंजे *m. pl.* चकरमक-

WILFUL, *a. stubborn, contumacious,* v. OBSTINATE, PERVERSE. खळया, अटखोर, टोंग, अडिबाळ, आपगंड, आपढंगी, अडगाल्या, गाल्या, गाताडा, गळदट, घेलट, अगस्ताळा, अकरताळा.

2 *self-willed, uncurbed, &c.* स्वच्छंद *pop.* स्वछंदी, छंदी, छंदिष्ट, उनाड, छांदिष्ट, छांदस, छांदसवृत्ति, स्वेच्छ, स्वतंत्र, स्वैरगामी, स्वैराचार, स्वैर, स्वैरगति, स्वैरवृत्त, स्वैरी, अनर्गल *or* ळ, स्वेच्छाचार, स्वेछाचारी, स्वेच्छाविहारी, स्वरुचि, स्वेच्छागामी, यथाकामी, यथेच्छ, सैरट, यथेष्टचार, यथेष्टाचारी, कामचारी, मनस्वी, बहुवस.

W. child (or person). तिताल.

3 *done or suffered by design,* v. INTENTIONAL. संकल्पाचा, संकल्पानेंकेलेला, बुद्धिपूर्वक, बुद्धिकृत, संकल्पकृत, सांकल्पिक.

WILFULLY, *adv.* v. A. 1. खळ-हट-अट-&c. धरून, हटकून, हटेंच, दाटबळें, दाटून.

2 मनासयेईल्तसा *decl.* स्वच्छंद, स्वच्छंदानें, यथेच्छ, यथेष्ट, यथेप्सित, मनसोक, अनुकामः.

3 बुद्ध्या, संकल्प करून, बुद्धिपूर्वक, संकल्पपूर्वकं, तात्पुरचा.

WILFULNESS, *n.* v. A. 1. अट *f.* हट *m.* टोंगाई *f.* जळ *m.* अडिबाळपणा *m.* अगस्ताळेपणा *m.* &c.

2 स्वछंदीपणा *m.* छंदिष्टपणा *m.* &c. उनाडकी *f.* छंद *m.* यथेष्टाचार *m.* स्वेच्छाचार *m.* स्वाच्छंद्य *n.* स्वेच्छागमन *n.* स्वेच्छाविहार *m.*

WILINESS, *n.* v. A. कावा *m.* कावादावा *m.* कावित्र *n.* कुलंगडें *n.* बिंदाण *or* न *n.* बिंदाणी *f.* [यशक्ति *f.*

WILL, *n. velleity.* मर्जी *f.* खुशी *f.* इच्छा *f.* संकल्पशक्ति *f.* निश्च-

2 *pleasure, choice, liking, disposedness of mind,* v. MIND. मजा *f.* खुशी *f.* इच्छा *f.* संकल्प *m.* मनोदय *m* मनोरथ *m.* मनोगति *f.* मनोत्साह *m.* छंद *m.*

At w. मनसोक, यथाकाम, अनुकामः.

Free to follow one's w. स्वेच्छ, स्वतंत्रेच्छ, स्वतंत्र.

Good w. मर्जी *f.* खुशमर्जी *f.* कृपा *f.*

Ill w. v. ENMITY, MALICE. दुष्टावा *m.* दुष्टभाव *m.*

Of one's own w. and pleasure. सुखसंतोषानें *or* सुखसंतोषें, स्वसंतोषानें *or* स्वसंतोषें, सुखासंतोषानें, सुखासमाधानानें.

That follows his own w. स्वेच्छाचारी, स्वेच्छाविहारी.

The doctrine of freedom of the w. प्रयत्नवाद *m.* पौरुषवाद *m.*—Maintainer of it. पौरुषवादी, प्रयत्नवादी.

3 *testament.* मृतलेख *m.* मृतपत्र *n.* मृत्युलेख *m.* मृत्युपत्र *n.*

Will with a wisp, *ignis fatuus.* भुतकोलीत *n.* भुतचुडी *f.* पिशाचदीपिका *f.*

To WILL, *v. a. determine on by an exercise of will.* संकल्प *m.*-निश्चय *m.*-ठराव *m.*-&c. करणें *g. of o.* संकल्पिणें.

2 *wish,* v. To DESIRE. इच्छिणें, इच्छा *f.*-&c. असणें *in. con. with g. of o.*

3 *desire, direct.* आज्ञा *f.*-हूकूम *m.*-&c. करणें-देणें, सांगणें.

4 *dispose of by testament.* मृतपत्रानें-मतपत्रांत-&c. बंदोबस्त *m.*-व्यवस्था *f.*-&c. करणें *g.of o.* मृत्युपत्रानें-&c. देणें-दान *n.* करणें.

To WILL, *v. n. make a volition.* संकल्प *m.*-निश्चय *m.*-&c. करणें, संकल्पिणें.

Do as you w. मनास येईल-मनमानेल-&c. तसें कर.

WILLED, *p.* v. V. A. 1. संकल्प केलेला, &c. संकल्पित, सांकल्पिक.

WILLING, *a. not averse; consenting, ready, disposed.* कबूल, खुशी, राजी, खुशरजावंत, मान्य, अनुमत, सम्मत, तयार *or* तैयार, हाजीर, सिद्ध, उत्सुक.

2 *received of choice or without reluctance.* खुशीचा, दिलखुशीचा, खुशरजावंतीचा, सम्मतीचा, &c. &c. इच्छेसारखा, इष्ट.

WILLINGLY, *adv.* v. A. खुशीनें, संतोषानें, दिलखुशीनें, आत्मसंतोषानें *or* आत्मसंतोषें, आपखुशीनें, आपसुखानें, आपसुखें, राजी-&c. होऊन, संतोषपूर्वक, प्रसन्न अंतःकरणें करून.

Right w. *with free consent of will.* सुखासंतोषानें *or* सुखसंतोषें.

WILLINGNESS, *n.* v. A. 1. खुशी *f.* दिलखुशी *f.* संतोष *m.* खुशरजावंती *f.* अनुमति *f.* सम्मति *f.* तयारी *f* हौस *f.* उत्साह *m.*

WILLOW, *n.*—the tree. वाळुंज *m. f.* वाळुंजीचें झाड *n.*

WILLY NILLY, *adv.* खामखा, अळें बळें, झकमारीत, झकत.

WILY, *a.* v. ARTFUL, CUNNING. काविबाज, कावेदार, कावेखोर, कपटी, कसबाती, छद्मी.

WIMBLE, *n.*—for boring holes. बरमा *m.*

To WIN, *v. a. gain by conquest, &c.* जिंकणें, जिंतणें, जिंकून-&c. घेणें-मिळवणें, सई करणें, हस्तगत करणें, जित *or* जीत *f.* करणें *g. of o.*

2 *gain by play.* जिंकणें, जिंतणें, जित *or* जीत *f.* करणें *g.of o.*

3 *gain, obtain,* v. To GET. मिळवणें, संपादणें, जोडणें, प्राप्त करणें.

4 *gain over.* मिळवणें, मिळवून घेणें, मनावणें, मन *n.* मनावणें *g. of o.* आपलासा करून घेणें. [पावणें.

To WIN, *v. n. be victorious.* जिंकणें, डाव *m.* जिंकणें, जय *m.*

To WINCE, *To* WINCH, *v. n. shrink from pain or a blow,* v. To FLINCH. आंग *n.*-&c. चोरणें-काढणें-हालणें-चोरून घेणें-काढून घेणें-&c. माघार *f.* घेणें.

WINCH, *n.* See HANDLE.

WIND, *n. air in motion.* बारा *m.* वायु *m.* पवन *m.* बाव *m.* हवा *f.* वात *m.* प्रभंजन *m.* समिर *or* समीर *m.* अनिल *m.* मारुत *m.*—as considered as fair or foul, &c. तारेंबारें *n.*

Dried in the w. वारे हळक.

Free as the w. बावबंदी.

A high w. उभावारा *m.* बावधाण *n.* बावधूळ *f.*

In the w. *in a draft, &c.* वारेघशीं, वाऱ्यावशीं, वाऱ्यासोई.

East wind. उगवताबारा *m.* पूर्ववारा *m.* मतलई *f.*

Northerly w. उत्तराण *f.* उत्तराबारा *m.* उत्तरवारा *m.* उपरवारा [*m.*

North-easterly w. सातरस *m.*

North-westerly w. उपरबाहेरचा वारा *m.*

Southerly w. दक्षिणवारा *m.* दक्षिण *corr.* डाखीण *f.*

South-easterly w. आग्नेय *f.* चिल्या *m.*

South-westerly w. हेटबाहेरचा वारा *m.*

Swift as the w. वायुगति, वायुवेगसम.

Westerly w. मावळत *f.* मावळण *f.* पश्चिमवारा *m.* मावळता [वारा *m.*

Whirl or blast of w. and dust. वायधूळ *or* बावधूळ *f.*

To dry in the w. बारवणें *or* वाराबणें.

To get a stroke of the w. बारें *n.* जाणें *in. con. with* वर.

To get w.—a report. फुटणें, फूट *f.* होणें *g. of s.*

To give to the *winds* v. To MISPLACE. वाऱ्यावर टाकणें, वारापाणी *n.* करून टाकणें *g. of o.* केरवारा *m.* करून टाकणें *g. of o.* केरावाऱ्यांत *or* केरावाऱ्या निशीं देणें-टाकणें. [करणें.

To mark *how* and act *as* the w. blows. वारा बाहील तसें

To wail to the winds. अरण्यरोदन *n.* करणें.

Trim your sails to the w. वारा वाजेल तशी पाठ ओढवावी.

2 *air.* वायु *m.* वारा *m.* वात *m.* आत्मा *m.* समिर *or* समीर *m.* अनिल *m.* स्पर्श *m.* स्पर्शन *m.* श्वसन *m.*

W. in the head, *craziness.* वायचळ *m.*

To break w. v. To FART. पादणें, पाद *m.* सोडणें.

To get w. in the head, *become crazy.* वायकळणें *or* बावकळणें, वायचळणें.

3 v. FLATULENCE. वायु *m.* वायगोळा *m.* वायगमन *n.* उंड *m.*

4 See BREATH.

WIND-BOUND, *a. prevented from sailing by a contrary wind.* वाऱ्यानें खुटलेला-थबकलेला-&c. वातरुद्ध, वातप्रतिबद्ध, &c.

WIND-EGG, *n.* वांझ अंडें *n.*

WIND-FALL, *n. fruit shaken down by wind.* पड *f.* पडीचें फळ *n.*

2 fig. *unexpected acquisition.* घबकें *n.* घबाड *n.* घबूक *n.* घोबें *or* गोबें *n.* टाळक *n.* कड्याळें *n.* आगंतुकलाभ *m.* अलभ्यलाभ *m.*

WIND-GAGE, *n.* वाऱ्याचा वेग व भार मोजण्याचें यंत्र *n.*

WIND-INSTRUMENT, *n.* वायुवाद्य *n.* वाजंत्र *n.* वाजंत्रें *n.*

The end or sounding piece of wind-instruments. धुतेंर [*n.*

Performer upon a w.-i. वाजंत्री *m.*

WIND-MILL, *n.* पवनचक्की *f.*

WIND-PIPE, *n. trachea,* v. THROAT. नळी *f.* नरडें *n.* तटोरी *or* टटोरी *f.* श्वासमार्ग *m.*

WIND-WARD, *adv.* वाऱ्याकडे, वाऱ्यासमोर, वाऱ्याच्या तोंडाकडे.

To beat to w. हेन्येंवाऱ्यें *n.* करणें.

WIND-WARD, *a.* वाऱ्याकडचा, वाऱ्याकडील, वाऱ्याच्या तोंडाकडला.

To **WIND**, *v. n. proceed in flexures.* वळत-वांकत-वळणांनीं-वांकांनीं-नागमोडीनें-फेऱ्यांनीं-&c. जाणें-चालणें, वळवळणें, वांकें *n. pl.* घेतजाणें-खातजाणें, वांकणें, सरपटत चालणें.

2 *twine.* वेष्टून-वेढून जाणें.

3 *bend, crook.* वांकणें, मोडणें, फिरणें, वांक *m. n.*-वळण *n.*-&c. घेणें-खाणें, वांक *m. n.*-वळण *n.*-&c. होणें *g. of s.*

To **WIND**, *v. a. turn around.* वेढणें, वेष्टणें, वेटाळणें, गुंडाळणें, गुंडणें, अळपणें, वेढा *m.* देणें-घालणें, वेष्टन *n.*-&c. करणें.

2 *cause to turn* v. To TURN. फिरवणें.

3 *follow by scent.* वास घेऊन-हुंगून-&c. पाठीस लागणें.

4 v. To BLOW. फुंकणें.

5 up; *bring to close or small compass* गुंडाळणें, अटपणें, अटोपता घेणें, आवरणें, सांपमारणें, गाठोडें *n.* आटणें-गुंडाळणें-बांधणें, विल्हाड *n.* अटोपणें *or* अटपणें, अटोप *m.*-उलगामालगी *f.*-उलगाउलग *f.*-उपसंहार *m.*-उद्यापन *n.*-&c. करणें.

6 up; (a watch, &c.). किल्ली *f.* देणें, किल्ली *f.* फिरवणें *g. of o.*

7 off; See To UNWIND.

WINDINESS, *n.* v. A. 4 *and* FLATULENCE. वातुळपणा *m.* वायु *m.* वायुरोग *m.*

5 बावडेपणा *m.* वातुळपणा *m.* वायुकरता *f.*

WINDING, *n. turn, bend, flexure.* वांकण *n.* वांक *m. n.* वळण *n.* फेर *m.* फेरा *m.* मोड *f.* मुरड *f.* वळमा *m.*

WINDING, *p. a.* v. V. N. 1. वळत चालणारा-चाललेला, वांकंघेत चालणारा-चाललेला, &c. वांकाचा, वांकणाचा, वळतीचा, नागमोडीचा, वांकडा.

WINDINGSHEET, *n.*—of a corpse. सेंडा *m.* प्रेतवस्त्र *n.* कफन *n.*

WINDLAS, *n.*—the machine for raising weights. डेकरी *f.* हात *m.*

WINDOW, *n. opening for light.* खिडकी *f.*—*dim.* झरोका *m.*—of glass. तावदानी खिडकी *f.*

WINDOW-SHUTTER, *n.* झडप *f.*

WINDY, *a. of or belonging to wind.* वाऱ्याचा, वायूचा, वाऱ्याविषयींचा, &c. वायुविषयक-संबंधी, वातीय.

2 *consisting of wind.* वाऱ्याचा, वायूचा, &c. वायुमय, वातमय.

3 *tempestuous,* v. STORMY. तुफानाचा, वारेवावधानाचा, वारेवावटळीचा.

4—state of body, v. FLATULENT. वातूल *or* ळ, वातप्रधान.

5 *tending to generate wind,* v. FLATULENT. बावडा, वातूल *or* ळ, वायुकर.

WINE, *n.*—unfermented juice of the grape. द्राक्षारस *pop.* द्राक्षरस *m.*—as fermented, द्राक्षांची दारू *f.* द्राक्षांचें मद्य *n.* &c. द्राक्षामद्य *n.* द्राक्षासव *m.* द्राक्षासुरा *f.* पक्वरस *m.*

WINE-BIBBER, *n.* v. DRUNKARD. मद्यपी.

WINE-MERCHANT, *n.* द्राक्षांची दारू-&c. विकणारा, द्राक्षामद्य-&c. [विकेता.

WING, *n. the limb of a fowl, one by which it flies.* पंख *m.* पक्ष *m.* पाख *m.*—in contempt. पंखाड *n.* पंखडी *f.*

On the w. *about to move.* चर, गमनोन्मुख.

To run under the w. of. *fig.* पाठ *f.* निघणें-रिघणें *g. of o.* पोटांत डोकी *f.* घालणें. [घालणें.

To shelter (its young) under its w.—a bird. पाखर *f.*

To take under one's w. काखेसमारणें, पाखर *f.* घालणें, पाठीसीं घालणें, हातीं धरणें.

2 (of an army, &c.) *flank.* फौजेची-&c. बाजू *f.* सेनापक्ष *m.* सैन्यपक्ष *m.* पार्श्वस्थदळ *n.*

3 (of a house). घराची बाजू *f.* अलंग *f.* सोपा *m.* गृहपक्ष *m.* गृहपार्श्वभाग *m.*

To WING, *v. a. wound in the wing.* पंख *m.*-पक्ष *m.*-&c. मारणें-टिपणें-मोडणें-&c.

WINGED, *p. a.* v. पंख मारलेला, &c. हतपक्ष.

I. *having wings.* पक्षवान्, सपक्ष, जातपक्ष.

To WINK, *v. n. close and open the eyelids.* डोळे *m. pl.* मिचकवणें *or* मिचकावणें, डोळ्यांची-&c. उघडझांक *f.*-उघडमीट *f.*-&c. करणें.

To w. at, *leer, ogle, &c.* डोळे *m. pl.* मोडणें.

2 *hint, &c.* डोळा *m.* घालणें, दृष्टि *f.* घालणें, डोळा *m.* मोडणें, डोळेमोड *m. f.*-&c. करणें.

3 at; *connive.* डोळे *m. pl.* झांकणें, डोळयांवरकातडें *n.* ओढणें, डोळ्यांवर पापणी *f.* ओढणें, डोळेझांक *f.*-डोळेमीट *f.*-कानडोळा *or* कानाडोळा *m.*-कानागाडा *m.*-&c. करणें. [त्रपल्लवी *f.*

WINK, *n. sign made by the eye.* डोळेमोड *f. m.* नेत्रसंकेत *m.* ने-

Not to sleep a w. डोळा न लागणें- न मिटणें-&c. *g. of s.* डोळयासडोळा *m.*-पात्यासपातें *n.*-पापणीस पापणी *f.*-&c. न लागणें *g. of s.*

WINKER, *n.* WINKING, *p. a.* v. V. 1. डोळे मिचकवणारा, डोळ्यांची उघडझांक करणारा, डोळेमिचक्या.

2 डोळा घालणारा-मोडणारा, &c.

3 डोळे झांकणारा, कानाडोळा-&c. करणारा.

WINNER, *n.* WINNING, *p. a.* v. V. A. 1. जिंकणारा, जिंतणारा, जिंकून घेणारा, &c.

4 मिळवून घेणारा, मनावून घेणारा, &c. मनमिळाऊ, मनमेळ, मिळाऊ, मिळताऊ.

To WINNOW, *v. a.* (grain, &c.) *separate chaff from grain by wind,*—by shaking in a fan. आंसडणें *or* आंसुडणें, पाखडणें, झडपणें, हडपणें, हडसणें *or* अडसणें, घोळणें, फटकणें, घोलण *n.*-&c. करणें,—by letting fall from a height in the wind, वारावणें, वाऱ्यास देणें, वारसंडणें, धार देणें, हडसणें, उभरणें *or* उफरणें, उफरा *m.* करणें, उपणणें *or* उफणणें,—by taking up handfulls and dropping them, कळ्हांटणें,—by whisking a fan over, सूप *n.* देणें.

2 *sift, investigate.* See To EXAMINE. [पाखडींव.

WINNOWED, *p.* v. V. 1. आसुडलेला,पाखडलेला, वारावलेला, &c.

WINNOWER, *n.* WINNOWING, *p. a.* v. V. 1. आसडणारा, पाखडणारा, &c.

Grain w. उपणें *n.*

WINNOWING, *n.* v. V. 1—*act.* आसुडणें *n.* पाखडणें *n.* झडपणें *n.* वारावणें *n.* घोळणें *n.* उपणणें *n.* उपणणी *f.* पाखडणी *f.* पाखडण *n.*

The mingled corn and chaff after the third w. बरळें *or* बरुळें *or* बरोळें *n.*

WINNOWING-FAN, WINNOWING-BASKET, *n.* सूप. *dim.* सुपली *f.* उपणपाटी *or* उपणवाटी *f.* शूर्प *n.*

WINNOWING-STAND, WINNOWING-STOOL, *n.* तिव्हा *m.* वावडी *f.*

WINTER, *n.*—the cold season, comprising 4 months. हिंवाळा *m.* थंडीचेदिवस *m. pl.* हिमऋतु *m.* हिमागम *m.* हिमकाल *m.* शीततुं *pop.* शीतऋतु *m.* शीतकाल *pop.* ळ *m.* शिशिर *or* शिशिरऋतु *m.* (this word comprises 2 months).

Depth of w. ऐनहिंवाळा *m.*

To WINTER, *v. n. spend the winter.* हिंवाळा *m.*-शीतकाळ *m.*-&c. घालवणें-काढणें-सारणें-लोटणें-&c.

WINTERY, *a.* v.N. हिंवाळ्याचा, थंडीच्या दिवसांचा, &c. हिमऋतुसंबंधी, हिमकालसंबंधी, हैम, हैमन.

W. weather. हिमदुर्दिन *n.* [फ करणें.

To WIPE, *v. a. clean by rubbing with a cloth.* पुसणें, पुसून सा-

To w. dry (the body after bathing, &c.). पुसणें, कोरडा करणें.

2 off *or* away; lit. fig. पुसून टाकणें, निरपणें.

3 out; *obliterate.* पुसणें *or* पुसून टाकणें.

WIPE, *n.* v. V. 1. पुसणें *n.*

Rough w. or rub. घसरा *m.* घसका *m.* घष्टा *m.*

I. See BLOW, SARCASM.

WIPED, *p.* v. V. 1. पुसलेला, &c.

WIPER, *n.* WIPING, *p. a.* v. V. 1. पुसणारा, पुसून साफ करणारा.

I. *clout, rag, straw, &c. used to wipe with.* पुसणें *n.* (esp. in comp. as *mouth-w.* तोंडपुसणें, *nose-w.* नाकपुसणें, *foot-w.* पायपुसणें.) चोंधा *m.* बोंधी *f.* [लाका *f.*

WIRE, *n. metal thread.* तार *f.* तांत *or* तांथ *f.* तंत्री *f.* सरी *f.* श-

Fine-drawn silver w. कसब *m.*

Gold or silver w. बादला *m.*—Made with it. बादली.

Semicylindrical or semitubular w. of gold or silver. बाया *m.*—The instrument of goldsmiths for making it. बायाची अवटी *f.*

Made of w.—vessel, ring, &c. तारकशी, तारकस.

2 (of a musical instr.). तंतु *m.* (*pop.* तंत *f.*) तांत *f.* तार *f.* तंत्र *n.*

3 (of a puppet, &c.) सूत्र *n.*

WIRE-DRAWER, *n.*—the instr. जंत्र *or* जंतर *n.* जंतरपट्टी *f.*

WIRE-DRAWING, *n.* तारकशी *f.*

WIRY, *a. made, &c. of wire; like wire.* तारेचा, तांतीचा, &c. तंतुमय, तंतुप्राय.

WISDOM, *a. the faculty or power of judging and acting rightly; sense, understanding.* शहाणपण *or* शाहणपण *n.* शहाणपणा *or* शाहणपणा *m.* बुद्धि *f.* अक्कल *f.* ज्ञान *n.* मति *f.* चातुर्य *n.* समज *m. f.* उमज *m.* बकूब *m.* धी *f.* मेधा *f.* प्रज्ञा *f.* विवेक *m.* ज्ञानदृष्टि *f.* ज्ञानचक्षु *m.* सुज्ञपणा *m.* सुज्ञता *f.* प्राज्ञता *f.* विज्ञता *f.*

False w. उलटेंशहाणपण *n.*

W.-tooth. अक्कलदाढ *f.*

WISE, *a. that has wisdom; that can judge correctly.* शहाणा *or* शहाणा शाहाणा, बुद्धिमान् *pop.* बुद्धिमंत *or* बुद्धिवंत, जाणता, जाण, चतुर, समंजस, समजूतदार, समजदार, समजीक, ज्ञानी, ज्ञानवान्, सुजाण, सुज्ञ, प्राज्ञ, ज्ञाता, विज्ञ, ज्ञानचक्षु, ज्ञानदृष्टि, सदसद्दर्शी, विवेकी, विवेकाढ्य, सविवेक, उचितज्ञ, चौरस, मतिमान्, धीमान्, मेधावी, सुमेधा, सन्मति, विदुर, बुध,—in high degree, सुबुद्धि,सुधी,सुबुद्ध, सुमेधा, ज्ञानबुद्धि, ज्ञानशाली, प्रगल्भ, प्रबुद्ध, प्रज्ञात, प्राज्ञ, बृहस्पति, बुद्धीचा सागर.

Too w. by half. दीडशाहणा, दीडचतुर, अतिशाहणा.

For the w. a word, for a fool a cudgel. शाहण्यास शब्द, मूर्खास टोणपा.

2 *dictated, &c. by wisdom; judicious, &c.* शाहणपणाचा, बुद्धीचा, ज्ञानाचा, समजुतीचा, समंजसपणाचा, विवेकाचा, &c. समंजस, समर्पक, सुयुक्त, सविवेक, विवेकयुक्त, बुद्धिविशिष्ट, बुद्धिप्रयुक्त, बुद्धिमूलक, बुद्धिजात.

WISE, See MANNER, WAY.

Wiseacre, Wiseling, *n. one who pretends to be wise.* अकलेचा संदक, दीडचतुर, दीडशाहणा, चतुरसाबाजी, सामाजी सकळ कळ्या, गाजरपारखी or ख्या, लाल बुझक्कड or लालभुज:कड, चिकित्सक.

Wisely, *adv.* v. A. 1. शाहणपणानें, बुद्धीनें, अक्कलेनें, विवेकानें, &c. शाहण्यासारखा *decl.* शाहणा-&c. होऊन, शाहणपण-&c. खर्चून, विवेकपूर्वक, प्रज्ञापूर्वक.

To **Wish,** *v. a.* v. To Desire. इच्छिणें, चिंतणें, वांच्छिणें, इच्छा *f.*-&c. धरणें-करणें *g. of o.* इच्छा *f.*-आकांक्षा *f.*-वांच्छा *f.*-&c. असणें *in. con. with g. of o.*

Wish, *n.* v. Desire. इच्छा *f.* वांच्छा *f.* आकांक्षा *f.* कांक्षा *f.* कामना *f.* मनःकामना *f.* मनेच्छा *f.* मनीषा *pop.* मनशा or मनसा *f.* मनईप्सित *vulg.* मनेप्सित *n.*

Wished, *p.* v. V. इच्छित, आकांक्षित, कांक्षित, वांच्छित, ईप्सित, इष्ट, ईहित, ऐच्छिक.

Wisher, *n.* **Wishing,** *p. a.* v. V. इच्छिणारा, चिंतणारा, इच्छाधरणारा-करणारा, इच्छु (in comp. as कल्याणेच्छु, &c.),आकांक्षी (in comp. as धनाकांक्षी, &c.).

Wishful, *a.* v. Desirous. इच्छावान्, इच्छान्वित, आकांक्षी, इच्छादृष्टीचा, सकामदृष्टि, सकामदृष्टीचा.

To look w. टोकणें.

Wishfully, Wistfully, *adv.* v. A. *and* Longingly. टुकटुक or कां, टक लावून, टकमक or कां, *intens.* टकाकां, सकामदृष्टीनें, इच्छादृष्टीनें, इच्छादृष्टिपूर्वक.

Wishwash, *n.* v. Wash. गरगट *n.* डुळकवणी *n.* ढपळवणी *n.* फळकवणी *n.* पेजवणी *n.*

Wishy-washy, *a.* v. Washy. खळखळीत, डुळडुळीत, मुळमुळीत, [गळगळीत.

Wisp, *n. small bundle of straw, &c.* गुंडाळा *m.* गुंडाळी *f.* गुंडाळें *n.* वेटणें or वेंटणें *n.* वेटाळी *f.* वेटाळी or वेंटाळी *f.*—to put on the head under a load, चुंबळ or चुंभळ *f.*—for scouring or wiping a vessel, चोंथा *m.* घासणी *f.*—*dim.* चोंथडी *f.*

To scour or wipe with a w. चोंथलणें.

Wistful. See Thoughtful.

Wit, *n. quickness of fancy, &c.* तिखट-चणचणीत-तीक्ष्ण-पसारशीघ्र-&c. बुद्धि *f.* चतुराई *f.* चप्पूपणा *m.* चातुर्य *n.* हुशारी *f.* चणचणीतपणा *m.* बुद्धिकौशल *n.* बुद्धिकौशल्य *n.* बुद्धिपाटव *n.* बुद्धितीक्ष्णता *f.* बुद्धितैक्ष्ण्य *n.*

2 *point or humour of.* खुबी *f.* रहस्य *n.* खोंच *f.* नोक *f.* मखी *f.* दरद *f.* वर्म *n.* मर्म *n.* [अक्कल *f.*

3 *sense, understanding,* v. Wisdom. बुद्धि *f.* शाहणपण *n.*

To be at one's w.'s end. मंत्रतंत्र *m. pl.*-उपाय *m. pl.*-हरणें *g. of s.*

4 *a w. a man of fancy, genius, &c.* रसिक बोलणारा, बुद्धिकुशल मनुष्य, नर्मभाषी.

5 wits; *mental faculties, soundness of mind.* सावधपणा *m.* हुशारी *f.* भान *n.* देहभान *n.* होष *m.* फाम *f.* अवसान *n.*

That has lost his wits. नष्टबुद्धि, नष्टेंद्रिय.

With one's wits about one. अकलहुशारीनें,सावध,देहावर, देहभानावर.

To be frightened out of one's wits, v. Fright. पांचांवर धारण *f.* बसणें *g. of s.* भुलीचें झाड *n.* भेटणें *in. con.* हातापायाचे ढीग *m. pl.* होणें *g. of s.* गर्भगळीत or गर्भगीळ होणें, गतप्राण होणें.

To have one's wits a wool gathering. To lose one's wits v. To be confused. रान भरी होण, हांबभरी होणं, बावरणें, पावरणें, गडबडणें.

To wit, *that is to say.* म्हणजे.

Witch, *n. sorceress.* कुसळण or कुसळीण *f.* चेटकीण *f.* चेटकाई *f.* डंखीण or डांखीण *f.* टाणेटोणेकरीण *f.* टाणेटोणी *f.* कवटाळी *f.* चेडाघालणारी *f.* सयारीण *f.* कुसरी *f.* कुसरीण *f.*

2 *enchanting woman,* v. Beauty. चटकचांदणी *f.*

Witch-craft, Witchery, *n.* v. Magic. चेटक *n.* टाणेटोणा or टोणेटाणे *m. pl.* जादूटोणा *m.* माव *f.* सयार *m.*

With, *prep.*—noting cause, means, instrument, &c. करून, कडून, योगानें, वारीं. The sense is usually expressed by the use of the तृतीया or instrumental case, as तरवारीनें with a sword, तापानें with fever, &c.

2 *under, under the control, charge, &c. of; in the hands of.* कडे (ex. त्याजकडे शंभर शिपाई आहेत, याजकडे पागा आहे, त्याजकडे माझे पंचवीस रुपये आहेत, &c.), जवळ, पासीं, हातीं.

3 *on the side of.* बाजूवर, पक्षावर, पाठीवर, पाठीशीं.

4 *in the society or company of.* संगतीं or तें, संगीं or गें, संगातें, सहित, समागमें, बरोबर or बराबर, सहवर्त्तमान, समेत, समवेत, सवें.

5—noting appendage; *together or along with.* सुद्धां, सकट, सहवर्त्तमान, निशीं.

6—noting possession or connection. The best mode of rendering this sense is by the use of the तृतीया case, as रागानें with anger, प्रीतीनें with love, &c. स (in comp. as सकाम, सक्रोध, सगुण, सदोष, साकार, सादर—prefixed to *Sanskrit* nouns with great neatness and with all amplitude. It is prefixed, though not neatly and not largely, to *Maráthi* words).

To express *a person with.* वाला (वाली *f.*) and करी (करीण *f.*) are much used. Ex. टोपीवाला a man with a hat, दूधवाली a woman with milk, पैसेवाला, पैकेकरी a man with money, बंदुकवाला a man with a gun, &c. &c.

7—noting competition, opposition, connection, &c. सीं or शीं (as मजसीं भांडतोस काय doest thou quarrel with me? त्याशीं बोल speak with him), बरोबर or बराबर (as माझेबरोबर बोलतो, &c.).

8 *amongst.* आंत, मध्यें.

Withal, *adv. likewise.* ही, देखील or द, पण, अणखी, सुद्धां.

To **With-draw,** *v. a. take back or away.* परत-माघारां-&c. घेणें, काढणें, नेणें, घेऊन जाणें, अपनयन *n.* करणें *g. of o.*

To **With-draw,** *v. n. retire, leave a company or place.* जाणें, निघणें, उठून जाणें, निघूनजाणें.

2 v. To Draw back. आंग *n.* काढणें or काढून घेणें, पाय *m.* काढणें, पाऊल *n.* माघारें काढणें, हातउगावा *m.* करणें, काढतें-निघतें-&c. घेणें, फटकणें.

With-drawal, With-drawing, With-drawment, *n.* v. V. A.—*act.* परतघेणें *n.* माघारांघेणें *n.*&c.

v. V. N. 1. जाणें *n.* उठून जाणें *n.* &c.

2 आंगकाढणें *n.* पायकाढणें *n.* &c. हातउगावा *m.*

With-drawer, *n.* **With-drawing,** *p. a.* v. V. A. परत घेणारा, माघारां घेणारा, &c.

v. V. N. 1. उठून जागारा, निघून जाणारा, &c.
2 आंग काढणारा, पाय काढणारा, &c. [अपनीत.
WITHDRAWN, *p.* v. V. A. परत घेतलेला, माघारा घेतलेला, &c.
WITHE, WITH, *n.* v. TWIG. डाहळी *f.* डाहळा *m.*
2 *band made of twigs* डाहळ्यांचा-&c. वेंठ *m.*
To WITHER, *v. n. fade. become sapless and dry.* कोमणें, कोमेजणें, कोमावणें, कोमेणें, कोमाइणें, वाळणें, सुकणें *or* सुखणें, सुकटणें *or* सुखटणें, मरणें, करपणें, वावणें, वाकुटणें, झेंबणें, झेमणें, कोळ होणें, सुकवण *or* सुखवण *f.*-वाळवण *f.*-सुकवशी *or* सुखवशी *f.* होणें *g. of. s.* रंग *m.*-टवटवी *f.*-&c. जाणें *g. of s.*
To WITHER, *v. a. cause to fade or become dry.* कोमवणें, कोमेजवणें, सुकवणें, वाळवणें, &c. सुकवण *or* सुखवण *f.*- &c. करणें *g. of o.*
WITHERED, *p.* v. V. N. कोमलेला, कोमेजलेला, सुखलेला, वाळलेला, &c. सुखट, सुकट्या, वावका, शुष्क, गतरस, शुष्कांग.
WITHEREDNESS, *n.* v. P. कोमलेलेपणा*m.* वाळलेलेपणा*m.* &c. सुकवण *or* सुखवण *f.* सुकवशी *or* सुखवशी *f.* वाळवण *f.*
WITHERS, *n.* (of a horse). खांदा*m.* खांद्यांचा सांधा*m.* स्कंध*m.* स्कंधदेश*m.*
To WITH-HOLD, *v. a. keep back, not to grant,* v. To RETAIN, To REFUSE. राखणें, ठेवणें, न देणें, दाबणें.
2 *hold back,* v. To RESTRAIN. दाबणें, आटपणें, आटपता धरणें, लगामीं धरणें. [ठेवणारा, &c.
WITH-HOLDER, *n.* WITH-HOLDING, *p. a.* v. V. 1. राखणारा,
2 दाबणारा, आटपणारा, &c.
WITH-HOLDING, *n.* v. V. 1.—*act.* राखणें*n.* ठेवणें*n.* &c.
2 दाबणें*n.* आटपणें*n.* &c. प्रत्याहार*m.*
WITHIN, *prep.* v. IN. आंत, मध्यें, भितर, आंतल्याआंत.
From w. आंतून.
W. and without. अंतर्बाह्य, पाठपोट.
WITHOUT, *prep. not with, in a state of destitution.* वांचून, बगर *or* बिगर, बिन (in comp. as बिन बट्टा, बिन अपराध, बिनसुलास, &c. also with verbs, as घेतल्या बिन, दिल्हा-बिन) वीण *or* विना (in comp. as बिनाकारण, &c.) वेगळ, वेगळा *decl.* निराळा *decl.* शिवाय, खेरीज, सोडून, व्यतिरिक्त, विरहित. [all in comp.
That is w. वेगळा, निराळा, विरहित, रहित, विहीन, हीन,
2 *not within; on the outside of.* बाहेर, बाहेरल्या बाजूसकडेस-धडीस, बाहेरबारा *decl.*
From w. बाहेरून.
To WITHSTAND, *v. a.* v. To OPPOSE, To HINDER. आडवा येणें-होणें, रोधणें, अडवणें, बाधणें, बाधक होणें, रोध*m.*-प्रतिरोध *m.*-विरोध*m.*-&c. करणें *g. of o.*
WITHSTANDER, *n.* WITHSTANDING, *p.* v. V. आडवायेणारा, रोधणारा, &c. रोधक, प्रतिरोधक.
WITLESS, *a.* v. FOOLISH. निर्बुद्ध, मतिहीन, बुद्धिहीन, हीनबुद्धि, हीनमति, ज्ञानशून्य. [साक्ष्य*n.*
WITNESS, *n. testimony.* साक्ष *f.* साक्षी *f.* शाहिदी *f.* ग्वाही *f.*
2 *one who gives testimony,* v. EVIDENCE. साक्षी, साक्षीदार, ग्वाहीदार, ग्वाही, शाहिदी, शाहिदीदार. [ससाक्षी.
That has witnesses or evidence. ससाक्ष, ससाक्षिक,
3 *one who sees, one personally present.* साक्षी, साक्ष, पाहणारा, जातीनें पाहणारा, प्रत्यक्ष पाहणारा, &c.प्रत्यक्षदर्शी, प्रत्यक्षी,
With a witness, *to a great degree.* बळकट, रगडून, खूब, अतिशय, भारी.
To WITNESS, *v. a. see by personal presence.* पाहणें, प्रत्यक्ष-साक्षात्-आंगीं-जातीनें-जातीनिशीं-खुद्द-समक्ष-&c. पाहणें-देखणें, अढळांत-पाहण्यांत-दृष्टोत्पत्तीस-अनुभवास-&c. येणें *in. con.* प्रत्यक्षदर्शन*n.*-प्रत्यक्ष*n.* करणें *g. of o.*
2 *give evidence of, testify.* साक्ष *f.*-साक्षी *f.*-ग्वाही *f.*-&c. भरणें-देणें *g. of o.* [वर *of o.*
3 (a bond, &c.). साक्ष *f.*-साक्षी *f.*-ग्वाही *f.*-&c. घालणें *with*
To WITNESS, *v. n. bear testimony, give evidence.* साक्ष *f.*-साक्षी *f.*-&c. भरणें-देणें. [&c.देखींव.
WITNESSED, *p.* v. V. A. 1. प्रत्यक्ष पाहिलेला, साक्षात् पाहिलेला,
WITTICISM, *n. witty sentence or phrase.* नोकीचें-खुबीचें-रहस्याचें-नर्माचें-&c. वाक्य*n.*-बोलणें*n.*-&c. चुटका*m.* नर्मभाषण*n.* नर्मोक्ति *f.*
WITTILY, *adv. with wit.* रहस्यानें, रसानें, रसिकपणानें, बुद्धिकौशल्य पूर्वक, &c.
WITTINGLY, *adv.* v. KNOWINGLY. जाणून, जाणूनबुजून, समजूनउमजून, अकलहुशारीनें, बुद्धिपूर्वक, बुद्धया.
WITTY, *a.*—of persons. टट्टेखोर, ठट्टेबाज, विनोदवृत्ति, नकली, नकल्या, रसाळ, रसिक, नमभाषी, नर्मवक्ता.
2—of sayings, &c. रसाळ, रसिक, रसभरित, रहस्याचा, खुबीचा, नोकीचा, चुटक्याचा, मर्माचा, खारटतुरट, तिखट, सरस.
WIZARD, *n.* v. MAGICIAN. चेटकी, चेटकाळ्या, इलमी, इलमबाज.
WO, WOE, *n. sorrow,* v. AFFLICTION. दुःख *n.* खेद*m.* शोक *m.*
2 v. CALAMITY. दुःख *n.* अनर्थ *m.* अरिष्ट *n.*
WOE-BE-GONE. See AFFLICTED, SAD.
WOEFUL, *a. sorrowful,* v. AFFLICTED. दुःखी, श्रमी, कष्टी, दुःखान्वित, क्लेशापन्न.
2 v. CALAMITOUS. दुःखाचा, अनर्थाचा, विपत्तीचा.
3 *wretched, paltry,* v. WORTHLESS. नाकारा, फुसका.
WOEFULNESS. See CALAMITY, MISERY.
WOLF, *n.*—male. लांडगा *m.* वृक *m.*—female. लांडगी *f.*
The depredations, activity, & prowling of wolves. लांडगावें *n.*
The biting & tearing of wolves. लांडगे तोड *f.* लांडग तोड *or* लांडगतोड *f.*
W. in sheep's clothing, v. HYPOCRITE. गायतोंड्या, गोमुख व्याघ्र, भगलभावार्थी, मिसकीन मात्रागमनी, सात्विकचांडाल.
To have a w. in one's belly. पोटांत ब्रह्मराक्षस असणें.
WOMAN, *n. female of the human race.* बायको *f.* स्त्री *f.* बायको माणूस *n.* अंगना *f.* नारी *pop.* नार *f.* नरी *f.* अबला *f.* कामिनी *f.* महिला *f.* योषित् *f.* योषा *f.* प्रकृति *f.* वधू *f.* ललना *f.* ललिता *f.* रमणी *f.* रामा *f.* वनिता *f.* मानवी *f.* मानवती *f.* मानिनी *f* मानुषी *f.* The Hindus make four divisions of *Womankind,* viz. पद्मिनी *pop.* पद्मीण, चित्रिणी (also हरिणी), शंखिनी *pop.* शंखीण, हस्तिणी *pop.* हस्तीण.—Some fabulous races are, नागकन्या *or* नागिनी *pop.* नागीण, गंधर्वकन्या, यक्षिणी *pop.* यक्षीण. Some terms of praise for *Woman,* as *beautiful* and *lovely,* are, कमला *f.* कांता *f.* वरांगना *f.* प्रमदा *f.* रमणी *f.* रामा *f.* सुंदरी *f.* उत्तमा *f.* शालिनी *f.* नितंबिनी *f.* चटकचांदणी *f.* छदकडी *f.* परी *f.* बोरांतली कीड *f.* ठमकठाणकी *f.* ठिकडें *n.* स्त्रीरत्न *n.* See also under BEAUTY.

Some terms for *a little* and *lovely woman* are, फटकडी *f.* फटकफळी *f.*—for a *passionate* and *fiery woman*, कोपना *f.* भामा *f.* भामिनी *f.* बजास—for a *virtuous* and *chaste woman* or wife, पतिव्रता *f.* सती *f.* साध्वी *f.* सुचरित्रा *f.* वरवर्णिनी *f.* पतिम्वरा *f.* कुलांगना *f.* कुलवधू *f.* कुलस्त्री *f.* कुलपालिका.—for a *fat* and *bloated woman*, फातमाय *f.* फत्तेलशकर *n.* ढमाली *f.* ढब्बू *m.*—for a *glib-tongued, chatty* and *pretty woman*, बोलपुतळी *f.* बोलमाणकी *f.* Some contemptuous terms for a woman answering to *hussy, wench, jade slut*, &c. are, रांड *f.* बायरूं *n.* रांडरूं *n.* सांडरूं *n.* डुकर *n.* घरडुकर *n.* रीस *n.* Some terms of *endearment* or *courtesy*, answering to *good woman, dame, &c.* are, आऊ *f.* अवा *f.* अवाजी *f.* बाई *f.* Some terms for *a young woman*, who has reached or is reaching puberty, are तरुणी *f.* बाला *f.* मुग्धा *f.* मध्यमा *f.* नवयौवना *f.* युवती *f.* पदरकरीण *f.*—for a *woman of mature age*, प्रौढा *f.* प्रगल्भा—for a *tall, lanky woman*, दीपमाळ *f.* शेलांटी *f.* ढंकाळ पार्वती *f.*

A marriageable w. नवरी *f.* वधू *f.*

An infirm & aged w. जरंडी *or* जरडी *f.*

An old w. म्हातारी *f.* वृद्धा *f.*—fig. पाऊण म्हातारी *f.* आयाबाया *f.* N. B. In the Konkan म्हातारी is an aged *widow.*

A young w. युवती *f.*

A clever w. सरस्वती *f.*

A kept w. v. MISTRESS. राख *f.* रक्षा *f.*

A married and unwidowed w. सुवासिनी *pop.* सवाशीण *or* सीन *or* सवाष्ण *f.* सौभाग्यवती *f.* अविधवा *f.* अहेव *f.* अहेवसुवाष्ण *f.* सभर्तृका *f.* सनाथा *f.* सधवा *f.* जीवत्पति *f.*

A respectable w. गरत *f.*

Doings and goings of woman. स्त्रीचरित्र *n.*

Old woman's (remedy, counsel, wisdom, &c.). बायाबापडीचा उपाय *m.*-विचार *m.*-मसलत *f.*-बोलणें *n.*-बुद्धि *f.*-&c.&c.

Old women, gener. आयाबाया *f. pl.*

Son of an unmarried woman. कानीन, कन्यापुत्र.

That quarrels with all—a w. जगदाळ, जगनाड *f.*

The women and children (of a household, &c.). बायकामुलें *n. pl.* रांडापोरें *n. pl.*

Vice or fault in woman. नारीदूषण *n.*

Woman's man. For this formation, and for the similar formations, *cotquean, smock-dangler, lady's man, gossiper, miss, sardanapalus, &c. &c.* some equivalent formations are, बाइलनाद्या, रांड्या, बाइक्या, बाइल्या, बाईलवेडा, स्त्रीसंगी, स्त्रीलंपट, रांड्याराघोबा, रांड्याराबजी.

2 *female attendant.* v. MAID. चाकरीण *f.* सेवकी *pop.* सेवकीण *f.* सैरंध्री *f.* परिचारिका *f.*

3—in comp. वाली *f.* करीण *f.* as दूधवाली milk-woman.

WOMAN-HATER, *n.* बाईलघाण्या, स्त्रीघाण्या, स्त्रीद्वेषी.

WOMAN-HOOD, *n.* बायकोपणा *m.* स्त्रीपणा *m.* स्त्रीधर्म *m.* स्त्रीगुण *m. pl.* स्त्रीत्व *n.* स्त्रैण *n.*

WOMAN-KIND, *n.* बायकांची जात *f.* स्त्रीजाति *f.* बायका *f. pl.*

WOMAN-RULED, *a.* स्त्रीजित, स्त्रीबुद्धि, स्त्र्यंकित.

WOMANISH, *a. feminine.* बायकोचा, स्त्रीचा *or* स्त्रियेचा, स्त्रीजातीचा, स्त्रीधर्माचा, स्त्रीसंबंधी, स्त्रैण.

2 *effeminate.* बाइक्या, बाइल्या, रांड्या, नामर्द, जनानी, चुलभानवशा, बायाबापडीचा.

Of w. understanding. स्त्रीबुद्धि.

WOMANLY, *a. becoming woman.* बायकोस योग्य-लायक, स्त्रीधर्माचा, स्त्र्युचित, स्त्र्यनुसार.

WOMB, *n. uterus.* पोट *n.* कूस *f.* गर्भाशय *m.* गर्भकोश *m.* गर्भस्थान *n.* कोष *m.* गर्भ *m.* कुसवा *m.*—in contempt, &c. नरक कुंड *n.* For the purification, impregnation, &c. of the *Womb*, for the purification of the fœtus, for the facilitation of delivery, and for the preservation, from malign influences, of the puerperal woman, some of the numerous ceremonies observed are, अनवलोभन *n.* अष्टमांगल्य *pop.* आठांगळें *n.* ओटी भरण *n.* गर्भाधान *n.* पुंसवन *n.* फलशोभन *n.* सीमंतोन्नयन *n.* स्थापन *n.*

A bearing w. वाहती कूस *f.*

Ceremonies and rites for the purification of the w.—compreh. क्षेत्रसंस्कार *m.*

To drop the w. गाभसांडणें, गाभ *m.* सांडणें-टाकणें, गाभटणें *or* गाभडणें *or* गाभुटणें *or* गाभुडणें, गोळा *m.* टाकणें.

WON, *p.* v.V. A. 1. जिंकलेला, जिंकून घेतलेला, &c.जित, निर्जित.

To WONDER, *v. n. be affected by surprise.* चमत्कार *m.*-आश्चर्य *n.*-नवल *n.*-अद्भुत *n.*-अचंबा *m.*-&c. करणें-मानणें or, *inversely*, वाटणें, चमत्कारणें, तोंडांत बोट *n.* घालणें.

WONDER, *n.*—the emotion. आश्चर्य *n.* अचंबा *m.* विस्मय *m.* चित्र *n.* अद्भुतरस *m.* अचाबा *m.*

2 *a w. a wonderful thing, a marvel.* चमत्कार *m.* आश्चर्य *n.* अचंबा *m.* नवल *n.* नवलविशेष *m.* नवल अद्भुत *n.* अद्भुत *n.* कौतुक *n.* चोज *n.* अघटित *n.* अघटितघटना *f.* करामत *f.* नवलाई *f.* नवलपरी *f.* नवाई *f.*—as a term or designation for a person of *surprising* abilities, or of *marvellous* exploits, and as agreeing in the general sense with *sun, star, luminary, constellation, paragon, one of the wonders of the world, &c. &c.* some renderings are, अपरसूर्य *m.* तारा *m.* तेजःपुंज *m.* घेंड *n.* मोहरा *m.* राजमोहरा *m.* प्रकरण *n.* प्रस्थान *n.* प्रस्थ *n.* विभूति *f.* ठिकडें *n.* अवतार *m.* अवतारी, अवतार घेतलेला, फरडा.

To do wonders. Corresponding to this phrase in its comprehensive sense, and especially with ironical implication, are several words and phrases. They involve in their particular variations the general power of the English phrases, *To do mighty things, to achieve prodigies, to make a noise in the world, to set the Thames on fire, &c.* दिग्विजय *m.* करणें, अनर्थ *m.* करणें, उदव *m* करणें लावणें, मात *f.*-शर्त *f*-शर्तमर्दी *f.*-&c. करणें, शक *n.*-कीर्ति *f.*-धूम *m.*-धौंसा-&c. गाजवणें, गंगेस घोडे *m. pl.* नाहणें, शतक्रतु *m.* करणें, ध्वज *m.*-झेंडा *m.* लावणें, दिवा *m.* लावणें, उजेड *m.* पाडणें-लावणें करणें, धन *f.* लावणें-पाडणें, निधार *f. or* निधारत्ती *f. pl.* लावणें-पाडणें, पाणी *n.* जाळणें, दगडास पान्हा *m.*-पाझर *m.*-&c. आणणें, ज्योतिष्टोम *m.*-सोमयाग *m.*-&c. करणें, शिलासेतु *pop.* शिळाश्वेत *m.* बांधणें.

A wonder lasts (but) nine days. नव्याचे नव दिवस.

WONDER-STRUCK, *a.* छक्क *or* चक्क, चकभूल, थक्क, सचकित, चकित, तारकावारका, दंग, विस्मयापन्न, चमत्कृत.

To be w. तोंडांत बोट *n.* घालणें.

WONDER-WORKING, *a.* चित्रकर्मा.

WONDERFUL, WONDEROUS, *a. that excites surprise.* चमत्कारिक, आश्चर्याचा, नवलाचा, चमत्काराचा, विस्मयाचा, कौतुकाचा, &c. नवल, मौज-कौतुक-नवल-&c. वाटायाजोगा-सारखा-&c. आश्चर्यकारक-जनक-&c. आश्चर्यावह, विस्मयकारक-जनक-&c. विस्मयावह, अद्भुत, अद्भुत रसोत्पादक, विस्मापक. As there are numerous English words used to convey the general sense *wonder-exciting*, and used without great strictness, so likewise are there in *Maráthi*. Corresponding then with *strange, surprising, astonishing, amazing, admirable, marvellous, stupendous, prodigious, &c.* the following *Maráthi* words and phrases are collected here. अजब, अनबा, अणीकसा, अनोठा, अचाट, अपरूप, अपूर्व, नादर, विचित्र, चित्रविचित्र, भारी.

Very w. महद्भुत.

WONDERFULLY, WONDEROUSLY, *adv.* v. A. चमत्कार-नवल-मौज-&c. वाटेसा *decl.*-वाटायाजोगा *decl.*-सारखा *decl.*-&c.

WONDERFULNESS, *n.* v. A. नवलपणा *m.* नवलाई *f.* अपूर्वाई *f.* अपरूपाई *f.*

To WONT, *To be* wont, v. To USE. सवई *f.* असणें.

WONTED, *a.* v. CUSTOMARY. शिरस्त्याचा, रिवाजाचा, चालीचा, मामूलचालीचा, &c.

To WOO, *v. a. court, solicit in love.* लग्नाच्या हेतूनें-विवाहबुद्धीनें-&c. आर्जव *n.* करणें-उपासना *f.* करणें-भजनीं लागणें-धूप*m.* घालणें-प्रीति *f.* -प्रेम *n.*-मोह *m.*-ममता *f.*-&c. लावणें-लावण्याचा उद्योग *m.* करणें.

WOOD, *n.* लांकूड *n.* काष्ठ *n.* लकडी *f.*

Bundle or load of w. लांकुडभारा *m.*

Dust or powder of worm-eaten w. घरू *m.* किरकिसा *m.*

Fragrant w. गंधकाष्ठ *n.*

Green w. आर्द्रकाष्ठ *n.*

Heart or core of w. नार *m.*

Hewer of w. तबलदार *or* तबीलदार.

Jungle or common w. (i. e. not teak, &c.). रावबळविजायली लांकूड.

Light and flimsy w. भेंड *n.*

2 *forest.* वन *n.* बन *n.* जंगल *n.* राई *f.* अरण्य *n.* रहाटी *f.* रान *n.* कांतार *n.* कानन *n.* विपिन *n.* गहन *n.* दाब *m.* अटवी *f.* वृक्षजाल *n.*

Rambling in woods. वनक्रीडा *f.*

Skirts of a w. बनांत *m.* अग्रेवन *n.*

WOOD-APPLE, *n.*—the tree. कवंठी *f.* कवंठ *f.* कपित्थ *m.*—the fruit. कवंठ *n.* कपित्थ *n.*

WOOD-CUT, *n.* लांकडावर कोरलेलें चित्र *n.*

WOOD-CUTTER, *n.* लांकुडतोड्या, रानतोड्या, लकडकसाई.

WOOD-DRINK, *n.* लांकडाचा काढा *m.* काष्ठकषाय *m.*

WOODED, *a.* झाडांचा, झाडांनीं युक्त, वृक्षमय, वृक्षप्रचुर,

WOODEN, *a. made, &c. of wood.* लांकडाचा, &c. लांकडी, काष्ठमय, दारव, दारुमय.

WOOD-HOUSE, *n. place where wood is kept.* सर्पणाची-लांकुडफाट्याची-&c. खोली *f.* लांकुडखाना *m.* लकडखाना *m.*

WOOD-LAND, *n. land on which trees grow.* शिंवार *or* शिवार*m.* *n.* रानजमीन *f.*

WOOD-LARK, *n.* the pyramid-crested w. चंडोल *m.*

WOOD-MAN, *n. forester.* रानकरी, रान्या.

WOOD-MONGER, *n. wood seller.* लकडवाला, लांकुडविक्या.

WOOD-NYMPH, *n.* वनदेवी *f.* वनदेवता *f.*

WOOD-PECKER, *n.*—the bird. सुतार *m.* काष्ठकुट्ट *m.*

WOOD-PIGEON, *n.* रानपारवा *m.*

WOOD-SORREL, *n.* चुका *m.*—yellow. आंबोती *f.*

WOOD-WORK, *n.* (of a house) लांकडी काम *n.* लांकडें *n. pl.*

WOODINESS, *n.* v. A. 2. झाडी *f.* झाडोरा *m.* वृक्षबाहुल्य *n.* वृक्षप्राचुर्य *n.*

3 जरड *f.* [काष्ठमय.

WOODY, *a. of or belonging to wood.* लांकडाचा, काष्ठाचा, लांकडी,

2 *abounding with wood.* जंगली, झाडीचा, झाडगळ, वृक्षमय, वृक्षप्रचुर, वृक्षबहुल, वृक्षाकीर्ण.

3 *fibrous, stringy.* जरगुडी, जरेडल. [&c.

WOOER, *n.* WOOING, *p. a.* v. V. लग्नाच्या हेतूनें आर्जव करणारा,

WOOF, *n. threads that cross the warp.* बाणा *m.* बाणा *m.* पूरण *n.* आडवट *n.* आडवण *n.* आडवीण *f.*

To close the w. खेटणी *f.* करणें.

2 See TEXTURE.

WOOL, *n. soft hair of sheep.* लोंकर *or* लोकर *f.* लव *or* लंव *f.* ऊर्णा *f.* मेषलोम *n.*

Great cry and little w. गजश्रद्धा *f.*

2 *woollen cloth.* पश्मीना *m.* ऊर्णा *f.*

WOOL-COMBER, *n.* लोंकर पिंजणारा *m.* पिंजारी *m.*

WOOLLEN, *a. consisting, &c. of wool.* लोंकरी *or* लोकरी, लोंकरीचा, लंवेचा, पशमी, और्ण, और्णक, ऊर्णामय, लोमश.

WOOLLEN, *n. woollen garment.* पश्मीना *m.* बनातीचें वस्त्र *n.* लोंकरीवस्त्र *n.*

WOOLLEN-CLOTH, *n.* बनात *f.* लोंकरी कापड *n.*

WOOLLY, *a. consisting, &c. of wool,* v. WOOLLEN. लोंकरीचा, लोंकरी, लोमश.

2 *resembling wool.* लोंकरीसारखा, ऊर्णासदृश, ऊर्णावत्.

WORD, *n. a single component part of speech.* शब्द*m.* पद*n.* वाचक *n.* द्रव्य *n.*

Acceptation of a w. शब्दानुशासन *n.*

At, in, &c. every w. पदोपदीं.

Force or power of a w. शब्दशक्ति *f.*

Low, vulgar, or filthy w. अपशब्द *m.* अवाक्षर *n.*

Primitive or simple w. अठोकपरब्रह्म *or* अठोपरब्रह्म *n.*

Radical form of a w. प्रकृति *f.*

Sense or meaning of a w. शब्दार्थ *m.*

2 *discourse, talk, language.* बोलणें *n.* भाषण *n.* गोष्ट *f.* बोल *m.* उक्ति *f.* जाप *m.* [वाक्य *n.* दुरुक्ति *f.*

Ill words, bad words. अपभाषण *n.* दुर्भाषण*n.* दुर्वचन*n.* दु-

Of few words. अल्पभाषी, मितभाषी, अल्पवादी.

War of words. वाग्युद्ध *n.* वाक्संग्राम *m.* शब्दयुद्ध *n.*

Waste of words. वाग्व्यय *m.*

W. in season. प्राप्तकालवचन *n.*

W. of mouth. तोंडजबानी *f.* मुखजबानी *f.* तोंडचें बोलणें *n.*

3 *a* word ; *a syllable, a sound, an utterance,*—with neg. implic. चकारशब्द*m.* चिट*n.* ब्र*n.* चांचूं*n.* हुंचूं*n.* अक्षर*n.* कूं*n.*

4 v. PROMISE, AFFIRMATION. वचन *n.* भाक *f.*

Of one w. As good as one's w. &c. एकवचनी, कराराचा.

To falsify one's w. बदलामी *f.* करणें, बदलामीवर येणें, विसंवाद *m.* करणें.

To make good one's w. बोललेला बोल *m.* सिद्धीस नेणें, उक्तनिर्वाह *m.*-प्रतिज्ञाप्रतिपालन *n.*-&c. करणें.

5 *signal, token, order,* v. COMMAND, INTIMATION. वर्दी *f.* from the English word is in common use. सूचना *f.* सुचें *n.*

6 *tidings, accounts,* v. NEWS. बातमी *f.* वर्त्तमान *n.* खबर *f.* समाचार *m.* संदेश *m.* वाचिक *n.*

7 words; *sharp or high language,* v. ALTERCATION, WRANGLING. धसधस *f.* धस्ताफशी *f.* कटकट *f.* लटपट *f.* कलकल *f.* हंवेतुंवे *f.* हंचत्वंच *n.* तिरघी मिरघी *f. v.* ये *with* वर, कटुभाषण *n.* निर्बाणशब्द *m.*

A good word. See PRAISE.

In a word, *in brief.* एकूण *or* न.

To WORD, *v. a. express in words.* बोलणें, बोलून दाखवणें, म्हणणें, लिहिणें, लिहून दाखवणें, कलमी करणें, शब्दद्वारा काढणें, शब्दरचना *f.*-शब्दयोजना *f.* करणें.

WORDINESS, *n.* v. A. शब्दविस्तार *m.* शब्दपाल्हाळ *m.* शब्दाधिक्य *n.* शब्दबाहुल्य *n.*

WORDING, *n.* v. V. शब्दरचना *f.* शब्दयोजना *f.* वाक्यरचना *f.* वाक्यरचनेची शैली *f.*

WORDY, *a. using many words, containing many words, verbose.* शब्दविस्ताराचा, शब्दपाल्हाळाचा, शब्दाधिक्याचा, पाल्हाळीक, बहुशब्दक, शब्दबहुल.

To WORK, *v. a. form by labor, manufacture, make.* करणें, घडणें, बनावणें, तयार-सिद्ध-&c. करणें, परिणाम *m.* करणें.

2 *produce, effect, bring about.* करणें, करवणें, घडवणें, घडवून-बनवून-&c. आणणें, कारणभूत-&c. असणें *in. con.*

3 *play, manage under its proper action.* व्यापारणें *pop.* वापरणें, वहिवाटणें, वागवणें, चालवणें, खेळवणें.

4 *make to work, put to labor.* कामास-कामांत-कामीं-कामावर-कामाखालीं-&c. घालणें-लावणें, काम *n.* घेणें-करून घेणें *with* पासून *of o.* खपवणें, राबवणें, कामावणें, वापरणें.

To w. hard. घुसळणें, हाडें *n. pl.* घुसळणें, कुदळणें *or* कुदलणें *or* खुदळणें, घुसडणें, घोळणें, घोळसावणें, कुदविणें, ताणणें, ताण *m.* देणें, घुमा *m.* घालणें, हेबाळणें, जंत्रीं धरणें, टांके *m. pl.* ढील करणें, तावडणें, पादडणें, पादवणें, पादडा *m.* काढणें-घालणें, आंबडणें.

5 See To EMBROIDER. 6 See To SOLVE. 7 out;—in arithmetic वर्त्तवणें, करणें, बरावर्द *f.* करणें *g. of o.*

8 up; v. To EXCITE. चेतवणें, खाजवणें, खवंदळणें, खवंडाळी *f.* करणें *g. of o.*

9 up; *dress, beat up, knead, compound.* कमावणें, ढवळणें, मशागत *f.* करणें *g. of o.*

To work oneself into the favor of. पोटांत शिरणें.

To WORK, *v. n. labor, toil.* खपणें, काम *n.* करणें, राबणें, मेहनत *f.* करणें-घेणें.

(You, he, &c.) can work (for a livelihood). (तुझ्या) खळ्हातास केंस आले नाहींत. [पोटभरी.

He that works shall eat. राबेल तो चाबेल, खटपट करी तो

2 *be in action or motion,* v. To ACT. चालणें, खेळणें, वाहणें,

8 *ferment.* करणें (as मला मळमळ करती, भोवळ करती, उन्हाळे करतान) घुमणें, लसलसणें, लसलस *adv.* करणें, फसफसणें, चिबचिबणें, खतखतणें, उतणें.

To w. and heave (in the stomach). v. To HEAVE. कळमळणें, उमळणें, *impers.*

4 on; in; *operate, &c.* v. To ACT. चालणें, चालू होणें, लागणें, लागू होणें.

To w. upon, *persuade craftily.* मंथणें.

5 *act internally;*—physic, &c. खळबळणें, खळखळणें, पोटांत कालवणें, गडबडणें.

6 fig. *brew.* धुमसणें, पिकणें.

WORK, *n. employment, occupation, something to do,* v. BUSINESS. काम *n.* कार्य *n.* उद्योग *m.* धंदा *m.* व्यापार *m.* काज *n.* कर्म *n.* कामगत *f.* कामगिरी *f.* कर्त्तव्य *n.*—compreh. *work and business,* कामकाज *n.* कामधंदा *m.* कामकारभार *m.*

A w. of difficulty or labor. श्रमकर्म *n.*

A tough w. or job. खटकर्म *n.*

A petty w. एकट्या दुकट्याचें काम *n.* [काम *n.*

Boring w. *business or operation of boring holes.* विंध-

Coarse or common w. झोडकाम *n.*

Fit for coarse or common w. झोडकामी *or* म्या.

Fine w. *w. of delicacy.* कुसरीचें काम *n.*

Odd or occasional w. लव *f.* लवई *f.* लवीचें काम *n.*

Servant of all w. हरकामी *or* म्या, हरकसबी.

2 *exertion of strength, toil,* v. LABOR. मेहनत *f.* श्रम *m.* कष्ट *m.* मशागत *f.* खप *m.*

W. without wages or remuneration. वेठ *f.* बिगार *or* बेगार *f.* विष्टि *f.*—compreh. वेठबिगार *f.* वेठबिरळा *m.*—person pressed to do such work, वेठ्या, बिगारी *or* बेगारी, वेठकरी.

To pay one for w. मेहनत *f.*-मशागत *f.* देणें-चुकवणें.

3 *that which is made or done.* काम *n.* कार्य *n.* कर्म *n.* करणी *f.* करणें *n.* कर्त्य *n.* क्रिया *f.* कृति *f.*

Destructive or injurious w., sad piece of w. अनर्थ *m.*

4 *awkward performance, bungle.* आवडधोवडकाम *n.* अडाणकाम *n.* अडवंगकाम *n.* आडमुठेंकाम *n.*

5 *composition, book.* ग्रंथ *m.* पुस्तक *n.*

6 v. EMBROIDERY. कशीदा *m.* बुटी *f.* नकशा *m.* नकशी *f.*

Pictorial or figured w. किरवण *f.*—to adorn with it किरविणें. [नुखान *n.*

7 *religious act, external performance.* कर्म *n.* क्रिया *f.* अ-

A good w. सत्कर्म *n.* सुकर्म *n.* धर्मकार्य *n.* धर्मकृत्य *n.* सत्क्रिया *f* पुण्यकर्म *n.* पुण्य *n.*

A man rich in good works. पुण्यपुरुष.

Abandonment of works and rites. कर्मत्याग *m.*

An evil or bad w. दुष्कर्म *n.* दुष्कृत *n.* अशुभकर्म *or* कार्य *n.*

Exact in the discharge of religious works. कर्मठ, कर्मशील, कर्मनिष्ठ, कर्मिष्ठ.

Neglectful of works. कर्मभ्रष्ट, कर्महीन,

Reward of good works. पुण्यफल *n.*

Rich in good works. कृतपुण्यपुंज.

Way of salvation by works. कर्ममार्ग *m.*—one who seeks salvation by it, कर्ममार्गी.

Worship or service by works. कर्मोपासना *f.*

8 works; *fortifications.* तटबंदी *f.*

WORK-FELLOW, *n.* कामभाऊ, कर्मबंधु.

WORK-FOLK, WORK-PEOPLE, *n.* v. LABORER. कामकरी *m. pl.* कामकरीमाणसें *n. pl.* [कामकरी.

WORK-MAN, *n. artificer, &c.* कारिगर or कारिगार or कारागीर,

Awkward, unskilful w. नाकसबी, गवतकाप्या.

Rough, coarse w. धसकया, धसकधया, धसकट्या, धसकनंदन, दगडघाशा.

Bad workmen find fault with their tools. नाचतां येईना म्हणून आंगण वांकडें, रांधतां येईना ओलीं लांकडें.

WORK-MAN-LIKE, WORK-MANLY, *a.*—performance, &c. कसबाचा, कसबदारीचा, कसबयाच्या हातचा, वस्तादीचा, कारागिरीचा, वस्तादगिरीचा.

WORK-MANSHIP, *n. skill of the worker.* घडण *f.* घडवण *f.* घडणावळ *f.* घडणी *f.* घडकाम *n.* कारिगिरी *f.* घटना *f.* कसब *n.* कसबदारी *f.*

2 *form, fashion, &c. of an article wrought.* घडण *f.* घडणी *f.* घडवण *f.* घडणावळ *f.* घटना *f.*

3 *thing worked.* घडण *f.* करणी *f.* कृति *f.* घटना *f.*

WORK-SHOP, WORK-YARD, &c. *n.* शाला *pop.* साळ *f.* कारखाना *m.* दुकान *n.* शिल्पशाला *f.*

WORK-WOMAN, *n.* कामकरीण *f.* शिवणकाम करणारी बायको *f.*

WORKED, *p.* v. V. A. 1. केलेला, बनावलेला, घडलेला, &c.

3 वापरलेला, वहिवाटलेला, चालवलेला, &c.

4 कामास लावलेला, खपवलेला, राबवलेला, वापरलेला.

8 चेष्टवलेला, खाजवलेला, &c.

9 कमावलेला, ढवळलेला, &c.

WORKER, *n.* WORKING, *p. a.* v. V. A. 1. करणारा, घडणारा, &c.

2 करणारा, करवणारा, घडवणारा, &c.

3 चालवणारा, वापरणारा, खेळवणारा, &c.

4 कामासलावणारा, खपवणारा, राबवणारा, &c.

v. V. N. 1. खपणारा, राबणारा, &c. खप्या (in comp. as शेत खप्या, &c.).

2 चालणारा, खेळणारा, &c. चालता, चालू.

3 घुमणारा, लसलसणारा, फसफसणारा, &c. लसलशीत or सीत.

WORKING, *n.* v. V. A. 1.—*act.* करणें *n.* घडणें *n.* &c.

2 करणें *n.* करवणें *n.* घडवणें *n.* &c.

3 वापरण *n.* चालवणें *n.* खेळवणें *n.* &c.

4 कामास लावणें *n.* वापरणें *n.* खपवणें *n.* &c.

7 बर्नवण *n.* &c. बराबर्द *f.*

8 चेष्टवणें *n.* खाजवणें *n.* &c. खाजवाखाजव *f.*

9 कमावणें *n.* &c. कमाई *f.* मशागत *f.* मरामत *f.*

v. V. N. 1. खपणें *n.* राबणें *n.* &c. खप *m.* मशागत *f.* काम *n.*

2 चालणें *n.* खेळणें *n.* &c. हालचाल *f.* चलनवलन *n.* खेळ *n.* व्यापार *m.*

3 घुमणें *n.* लसलसणें *n.* &c.

4 चालणें *n.* &c. व्यापार *m.*

I. (in the stomach) *working and heaving.* उमास *m.* उमासा *m.* उमाळा *m.* उमाळी *f.* उमाडा *m.*

WORKING-CLOTHES, *n. opp. to* holiday clothes, &c. खर्ची पांघरुण *n. pl.* खर्ची वस्त्रें *n. pl.* धडवती or धडोती *f.*

WORKING-MAN, *n.* मशागती, कामकरी. [दिकूचक्र *n.*

WORLD, *n.* v. UNIVERSE. जगत् *pop.* जग *n.* ब्रह्मांड *n.* ब्रह्मगोल *m.*

Creator of the w. जगत्स्रष्टा.

Destruction of the w. जगत्क्षय *m.* जगदंत *m.* जगद्विनाश *n.*

Material w.—viewed as illusory and unreal. मायाचक्र *n.*

Soul of the w. *universal spirit.* ब्रह्म *n.* जगदात्मा *m.* लोकात्मा *m.* विश्वात्मा *m.*

To the w.'s end. आकल्प.

2 *a* w. *a particular portion of the universe.* भुवन *n.* लोक *m.*

Of or belonging to the other w. पारलौकिक, पारत्रिक, आमुष्मिक.

Of or belonging to this w. ऐहलौकिक, ऐहिक.

The other or next w. परलोक *m.* परत्र *n.* परत्रगति *f.*

This w. हा लोक *m.* इहलोक *m.*

The three worlds. स्वर्गमृत्युपाताल *n.* त्रिभुवन *n.* त्रैलोक्य *n.* जगत्त्रय *n.* लोकत्रय *n.* भुवनत्रय *n.* तिनीताळ *m.*

3 *terrestrial globe,* v. EARTH. जग *n.* भूलोक *m.* पृथ्वी *f.* जहान दुनिया or दुनया *m.*

That has seen the w. बारा बंदरचें पाणी प्यालेला.

To have the wide w. before one. बारावाटा *f. pl.* मोकळ्या असणें *in. con.* दहादिशा *f. pl.* मोकळ्या असणें *in. con.*

4 *mundane existence, mortal state.* इहलोक *m.* इहलोकवास *m.* भूलोकची-&c. वस्ती *f.* संसार *m.* संसृति *f.* भव *m.* भूलोकवास *m.* जगन्निवास *m.* संसरण *n.*

5 *secular or public life,* v. LIFE. संसार *m.* प्रपंच *m.* संसारमार्ग *m.* लौकिक *m.* प्रवृत्तिमार्ग *m.* प्रपंचमार्ग *m.* प्रवृत्ति *f.* सत्यानृत *n.* लोकयात्रा *f.* संसारयात्रा *f.*

In the w. and in retirement. जनींवनीं, लोकांतएकांत.

To go or come down in the w. खालावणें.

To make a noise in the w.—ironically. निधाई *f.* लावणें-पाडणें निधारती *f. pl.* लावणें-पाडणें.

6—as considered as a scene or system of business and pleasures. भव *m.* भवबंध *m.* भवचक्र *n.* भवसागर *m.* भवजाल *n.* मोहजाल *n.* मोहपाश *m.* मोहास्पद *n.* मायाजाल *n.* मायाचक्र *n.* मायोत्थसंसार *m.* विषयजाल *n.* विषयपाश *m.* आशापाश *m.* संसारचक्र *n.* संसारावर्त्त *m.* दुःखसागर *m.* [सन्यास *m.*

Abandonment of worldly affections and possessions.

Dead to the w. Weaned &c. from the w. Renouncer of the w. जीवन्मुक्त, विरक्त, विरत, अवधूत, निर्मम, सन्यासी, सन्यस्त.

Deadness to the w. Indifference to the w. Weanedness from the w. विषयवैराग्य *n.* वैराग्य *n.* विषयविरक्ति *f.* विरक्ति *f.* विरति *f.* वैरक्त्य *n.* निर्वेद *m.*—as produced for a short time by the sight or thought of death, &c. श्मशानवैराग्य *n.*

Death-bed renunciation of the w. आतुरसंन्यास *m.v.* घे.

Sick of the w. भवरोगी, भवार्त्त, भवत्रस्त.

Snares of the w. *fascination or fetters of illusory objects.* मोहजाल *n.* मोहपाश *m.* मायाजाल *n.* संसाराचा जंजाळ *m.*

That has worldly ties and engagements. खटलेवाईक.

To carry on the w. *provide for the daily wants.* काळनिर्वाह *m.*-प्रपंचनिर्वाह *m.*-काळक्षेप *m.*-काळहरण *n.*-&c. करणें.

To keep one's self unspotted from the w. अलिप्त राहणें, उंचटांच *f.* करून वागणें.

To renounce or abandon the w. सन्यास *m.*-जोग *m.*

घेणें, पागोटें n. टाकणं, सर्वसंगपरित्याग m.-&c. करणें, वैराग्यमाला f. घेणें, वैराग्यमालेंत पडणें.

7 *mankind, all human beings.* जगn. लोक m. pl. जनलोकm. pl. आलम f. आलमदुनया f. दुनया or दुनिया f. जगती f. जन m. अठराखुम n. अठरा पगड जात f.

Adorable by the w. जगद्वंद्य.

In the mouth of the whole w. विश्वतोमुखी.

Life of the w. जगज्जीवन n.

Light of the w. जगद्गुरु m.

Salvation of the w. जगदुद्धार m.

Saviour of the w. जगदुद्धार m. [तें आपण करावें.

We should do as the w. around does. पांच करतील

8 *manners of men, practice of life.* लोकरीति f. जनरीति f. जनशिरस्ता m. जनसंप्रदाय m. लोकसंप्रदाय m. लोकमार्गm. लोकव्यवहार m. जनमार्ग m. जनपद्धति f. लोकपद्धति f.जनप्रघातm. लोकप्रघात m. लोकप्रचार m. जनप्रचार m.

Conformed to the w. प्रवाहपतित.

W. turned upside down. उफराटी or उलटी दुनिया f.

To turn the w. upside down—fig. and ironically. दिग्विजय m. करणें. [पडला.

The w. is turned upside down. वेड पिकलें, वेडाचा पाऊस

9 *a great multitude or quantity.* डोंगर m. पर्वत m. गाडाm. सागर m. समुद्र m.

Worldliness, n. v. A. 2. संसाराकडची दृष्टि f. प्रपंचाकडची दृष्टि f. प्रपंचीदृष्टि f.-बुद्धि f. प्रपंचासक्ति f. प्रपंचरति f. प्रपंचनिष्ठा f. प्रपंचदृष्टि f. प्रपंचबुद्धि f. इहलोकदृष्टि f. इहलोकनिष्ठा f.

Worldling, n. v. Worldly, Sensual. विषयी, प्रपंचासक्त-प्रपंचरत-प्रपंचदृष्टि-&c. मनुष्य.

Worldly, a. *of or belonging to this world; temporal, &c.* v. Secular. संसार in comp. प्रपंच in comp. संसाराचा, प्रपंचाचा, इहलोकचा, संसारमार्गाचा, &c. संसारी, संसारीक, प्रपंचाविषयींचा, लौकिक, लोकव्यवहाराचा, प्रपंची, प्रापंचिक, सांसारिक, प्रवृत्त, ऐहिक, ग्राम्य.

W. affairs, w. business. संसारm. प्रपंचm. सत्यानृतn.

W. bonds, w. fetters, v. World. आशापाशm. भवपाशm.

2 *devoted to this world, earthly, carnal, &c.* v. Sensual. प्रपंची, प्रपंचदृष्टि, प्रपंचबुद्धि, प्रपंचासक्त, प्रपचरत, विषयी, विषयाधीन, बहिर्मुख, ऐहिकदृष्टि, ऐहिकसुखपरायण, ऐहिकसुखलंपट, इहलोकनिष्ट, इहलोकासक्त, इहलोकदृष्टि, संसारैकलक्ष, संसारैकनिष्ठ.

Worldly-minded. See Worldly.

Worldly-wise, a. संसाराविषयीं-&c. शाहणा, संसारीक, संसारदक्ष, संसारज्ञानी, व्यवहारज्ञानी

Worldly-wisdom, n. संसारज्ञानn. व्यवहारज्ञानn. संसारिकज्ञानn.

Worm, n.—the animal. किडाm. किडूकn. किडकून. किडकालें n. कृमिm. क्रिमि *vulg.* किर्म or किरीमm. कीटm. कीटकm.

Affected with worms. कृमी.

Common earth w. काडूm. गांडवळ or गांडूळm. दानवाm. दानवेंn. वाणीm. दवणाm. शिडद्m.

Intestinal round w. *Teres.* जंतm.

Thread-like w. found in rivers, &c. तंतु *pop.* तंतूm.

Working of worms (in the bowels). जंतांचे वेटm.pl.v.फिर.

W. with two heads or mouths. दुतोंडेंn. मांडूळm.

Worms, *maggots, moths, &c.*—gener. कीड f. किडमुंगीf.

Worms, &c. compreh. किडामोकाडाm.

Worms, or flatulence occasioned by worms. जंत or जंताचाउपद्रवm. जंतविकारm. जंतवाताळेंn. कृमिरोगm. कृमिm. कृमिवाताळें or किर्मवाताळेंn.

To have w. at the root,—riches, fame, &c. कीड f. लागणें (संपदेस-&c.), वाळवी f. लागणें (दौलतीस-&c.), भिरड or भेरडm. लागणें *in. con.*

Worm-eaten, a. किडका, किडवळ, किडसाद, किडेला, किडकोला. लागरा *dim.* लागट, लागलेला, लागीर, किडेचा, किडलागलेला.

To be w. किडवळणें, किडणें, वरडणें.

Worm-wood, n. कडूदवणाm.

Wormy, a. v. N. किड्याचा, &c. कृमिमय, कीटमय, कृमिप्रचुर, कीटप्रचुर. [सुजीर्ण.

Worn, p. v. V. A.1. झिजलेला,&c.जर्जर, जरठ,जर्जरित, जीर्ण,

W. and wasted. जर्जर.

To be w. fig. काचणें, काचावणें.

2 आंगावर घेतलेला, परिधान केलेला, &c. नेसींव.

3 वहिवाटलेला, घोळलेला.

7 उपभोगानें जुना केलेला, भोगजीर्ण, भोगजर्जर, भोगातीत.

Worried, p. v. V. 1. तोडतोडून खाल्लेला-घेतलेला, &c.

2 छळलेला, गांजलेला, &c. उपद्रुत.

Worrier, n. **Worrying,** p. a. v. V. 1. तोडतोडून खाणार. लवकेघेणारा, &c.

2 घायकुत्या.

To **Worry,** v. a. *tear and mangle.* तोडतोडून-फाडफाडून-&c. खाणें-घेणें, तोडातोड f.-फाडाफाड f.-&c. करणें-मांडणें g. of o. लवके m. pl.-लचके m. pl.-&c. घेणें-तोडणें-काढणें g. of o. कुतरओढ f.-कुतरतोड f.-लांडगेतोड f. करणें g. of o.

2 *harass, torment,* v. To Tease. छळणें, गांजणें, जाचणें, कुतरओढ f.-लांडगतोडf. करणें g. of o. कांट्याf. pl. घासणें *with* सीं of o.

To w. to death. जिवाला अरडींदरडीं or अगडींदगडीं घालणें.

Worse, *adv.* v. A. 1. अधिक वाईट चालीनें-रीतीनें-&c. अधिक विशेष-ज्यास्त-&c. वाईट.

Worse, a. *more bad or evil.* अधिक-विशेष-&c. वाईट, दुस्तर.

2 *more sick.* अधिक-&c. रोगी-&c.

Worship, n. *religious homage, adoration.* पूजाf.पूजनn. भजनn. भक्ति f. अचन n. अर्चना f. अर्चा f. देवपूजा f. देवतार्चन n. देवभक्ति f. आराधना f. आराधनn. उपासना f. वंदनn. नमस्या f. नमस्कार m. नमन n. सन्मान m. सन्मानन n. पुरस्कार m.—compreh. *or* gener. अर्चनपूजन n.

Full, complete w. सांगपूजा f.

Mental w. मानसपूजा f.

Object of w. उपास्य.

Stated w.—compreh. स्नानसंध्या f.

Vessels and other necessaries of w. देवपूजा f. उपकरणीं n. pl. पूजोपचार m. pl. देवतार्चन n.

W. among Muhammadans. नमाज f.

W. at the three periods. संध्या f. [र्त्तनभक्ति f.

W. by chanting praises, reciting names, &c. of. की-

W. from fear. भयभक्ति *pop.* भयें भक्ति f.

W. from love, faith, &c. भावभक्ति *pop.* भावेंभक्ति f.

2—the title of honor. हजरत, खुदावंद or त, खुदावंत, नि-

यामंत, मेहरबान साहेब.

Your w. आपण, आपलेपाय *m. pl.* स्वाम.

Your worship's. आपला.

To WORSHIP, *v. a. adore.* पुजणें, भजणें, अर्चणें, उपासणें, आराधणें, वंदणें, सेवणें, पूजन *n.*—पूजा *f.*-भजन *n.*-भक्ति *f.*-आराधना *f.*-अर्चना *f.*-अर्चन *n.*-उपासना *f.*-&c. करणें *g. of o.*

2 *venerate, &c.* v. To REVERENCE, To HONOR. आदरणें, गौरवणें, मान *n.*-सन्मान *m.*-&c. करणें *g. of o.*

WORSHIPFUL, *a. worthy of worship,* v. ADORABLE. पूजनीय, पूज्य, आराधनीय, आराध्य, अर्घ्य, नमस्य.

WORSHIPPED, *p.* v. V. पुजलेला, भजलेला, &c. पूजित, आराधित, उपासित, वंदित, भक्त, अर्चित, अर्चित, नमसित, नमस्यित, सम्मानित.

2 आदरलेला, &c. सम्मानित, सन्मानित.

WORSHIPPER, *n.* WORSHIPPING, *p. a.* v. V. 1. पुजणारा, भजणारा, &c. पूजा-भजन-&c. करणारा, आराधी, पूजक, पूजन-&c. कर्त्ता-कारी-&c. उपासक, भजक, आराधक, अर्चक, भक्त *pop.* भगत, भजनिक.

2 आदरणारा, सत्कार-सन्मान-&c. करणारा-कर्त्ता.

WORST, *a. most evil or bad.* सर्वांपेक्षां-सर्वांहून वाईट-दुष्ट-&c. कनिष्ठ.

WORST, *n. most severe or aggravated state,* v. EXTREMITY, HEIGHT. वाइटपणाचा-दुःखाचा-&c. कळस *m.*-पराकाष्ठा *f.*-&c. निर्वाण *n.* निदानचीबाजू *f.*

At the w. निदानी.

To get the w. of. हरणें.

To WORST, *v. a.* v. To DEFEAT. जिंकणें, पराजित-&c. करणें.

To be worsted. हरणें, हारजाणें, तोंडांत खाणें.

WORSTED, *n.*—the yarn. लोंकरीचें-ऊर्णेचें सूत *n.*

WORSTED, *a.* v. N. लोंकरीच्या सुताचा, लोंकरी.

WORTH, *n. value.* किम्मत *f.* मोल *n.* योग्यता *f.*

2 *excellence, desert, worthiness of regard* v. GOODNESS, VIRTUE. योग्यता *f.* चांगुलपणा *m.* लायकी *f.* गुण *m.* मान *n.* मान्यता *f.* मानमान्यता *f.* [ग्यतेचा.

WORTH, *a. equal in value or price to.* किमतीचा, मोलाचा, यो-

2 *deserving of.* योग्य *pop.* जोगा & जोगता.

3 v. HAVING, OWNING. धनी, स्वामी, ऐपतीचा, ऐपतवाला.

To be w. ऐपत *f.* असणें *in. con.*

WORTHILY. See PROPERLY, RIGHTLY.

WORTHINESS, *n.* v. A. 1. भलेपणा *m.* चांगुलपणा *m. f.* भलाई *f.* योग्यता *f.* भलीभलाई *f.* भलायकी *f.*

2 योग्यता *f.* लायकी *f.*

WORTHLESS, *a.*—of persons or things, v. BAD, USELESS. बिनकिमतीचा, नालायक, अयोग्य, एर, सेर, गदळ, गयाळ, गैरी, फुकटा *or* ट्या, नाकारा, निपटारा, हेंटा, सकान, गुणावेगळा-निराळा, गुणहीन-रहित-&c. अगुणी *or* अगुण्या, निर्गुण *pop.* निर्गुणी, दांडदमडीचा, दमडीच्याकिमतीचा, दमडीच्यामोलाचा, कवडीचा, कवडीमाल, टाकाऊ, टाकवणा, यारदा, यारदी, मुरदाड *or* मुडदार, योग्यताहीन-रहित-&c. तृणवत्, तृणप्राय,—compreh. *or* gener. एरशेर, ऐरीगैरी, सैरीशैरी, खटनट, खुदरापादरा.

A w. thing. अटक्याचें घोडें *n.*

WORTHLESSNESS, *n.* v. A. नालायकी *f.* गदळपणा *m.* गयाळपणा *m.* निपटारेपणा *m.* नाकारेपणा *m.* &c. असौष्ठव *n.*

WORTHY, *a. having worth, virtue, excellence, &c.* v. GOOD, VIRTUOUS. चांगला, नेकीचा, भला, योग्य, योग्यतेचा, उत्तम, गुणी, गुणवान् *pop.* गुणवंत, गुणसंपन्न, मातबर.

2 *deserving.* योग्य, जोगता *or* जोगा (used in construction with a verb, as मारायाजोगता, पहायाजोगता, खायाजोगा, घ्यायाजोगा, &c.) लायक, अर्ह in comp. उचित in comp.

WORTHY, *n. a worthy person.* सज्जन *m.* गुणपात्र *n.* गुणभाजन *n.* मानभाजन *n.* पूजाभाजन *n.* मानपात्र *n.* पूजापात्र *n.* प्रस्थान *n.* प्रस्थ *n.*

WOUND, *p.* v. V.A. 1. वेढलेला, वेष्टलेला, गुंडाळलेला, &c. वेष्टित.

5 अटोपलेला, गुंडाळलेला, &c. उपसंहृत, उद्यापित.

WOUND, *n. hurt from a weapon, &c.* घाव *or* घाय *m.* जखम *f.* क्षत *pop.* खत *n.* वार *m.* चोट *f.* घावटा *m.* व्रण *n.* अस्त्राघात *m.* शस्त्राघात *m.*—made by a pointed and piercing instrument, खोंक *f.* खोंच *f.*

Plaster of a w. जखमपट्टी *f.*

To throw salt upon a w.v.SORE. घायावर घाय *m.* घालणें.

To WOUND, *v. a.* v. N. घाव *m.*-जखम *f.*-वार *m.*-&c. करणें-लावणें पाडणें, घाव *m.*-वार *m.* मारणें, जखमी-घायाळ-&c. करणें.

To cut at, &c. to w. घाव *m.*-वार *m.* टाकणें.

WOUNDED, *p.* v. V. घाव केलेला, &c. जखमी, घायाळ *or* घायळ, क्षत, अस्त्राहत.

Mortally w. भिन्नमर्मा. [रणारा.

WOUNDER, *n.* WOUNDING, *p. a.* v. V. घाव करणारा, जखमक-

WOVEN, *p.* v. V. विणलेला, बळलेला, &c. विणींव, तंत्री, वळींव.

WRAITH, *n.* छायापुरुष *m.*

WRANGLE, *n. brawl, clamorous contention,* v. SQUABBLE. कटकट *f.* कलागत *f.* खणकादणका *m.* खणाजंगी *f.* धडकाधडकी *f.* तडकाफडकी *f.* खडका *m.* खडकाधडका *m.* बाचणूक *f.* बाचणी *f.* अरकसबरकस *f.* अरकशीबरकशी *f.* See also the nouns under the verb.

To WRANGLE, *v. n. squabble.* किलकिलणें, किलबिलणें, बाचणें, खटपटणें, रसकसणें, अतिवाद *m.*-वाग्युद्ध *n.*-हुंबेतुंबे *f.*-हमरीतुमरी *f.*-कटकट *f.*-खटपट *f.*-खटखट *f.*-खवखळ *f.*-खळकेखळके *m. pl.*-खडबड *f.*-हटतट *m.*-खटनट *f.*-कच *f.*-कचकच *f.*-कचाकच *f.*-कलागत *f.*-किलकिल *f.*-कलकल *m.*-करकर *f.*-किलबिल *f.*-घसमस *f.*-वाक्पारुष्य *n.*-हर्षामर्ष *or* षा *m.*- विप्रलाप *m.*-&c. करणें, & चालणें-होणें *with g of s. recip.* धसफस *f.*-धसाफसी *f.*-धुसफूस *f.*-धुसमूस *f.*-रसकस *f.*-खडका *m.*-खडकाधडका *m.*-धडकाधडकी *f.*-तडकाफडकी *f.* उडणें-झडणें-चालणें-होणें *g. of s. recip.* तोंडासतोंड *n.* देणें, तोंड *n.* करणें,—vehemently, vociferously, कचाच *m.*-किलकिलाट *m.*-किलबिलाट *m.*-कलकलाट *m.* -&c. करणें-मांडणें.

WRANGLER, *n.* WRANGLING, *p. a.* v. V. कटकट-कचकच-खटपट -&c. करणारा, कटकट्या, खटखट्या, कलागत्या.

To WRAP, *v. a. roll or fold together.* गुंडाळणें, लपेटणें, गुंडाळून-लपेटून ठेवणें, घडी *f.* करणें-करून ठेवणें.

2 *cover with something rolled around.* वेष्टणें, गुंडाळणें, आवरणें, लपेटणें, लपेटून-&c. ठेवणें, वेष्टन *n.*-&c. करणें.

3 around ; *wind around or over.* गुंडाळणें, वेढणें, वेढणें, लपेटणें, अळपणें, बांधणें, गुंडाळून-वेष्टून-&c. बांधणें, वेष्टन *n.*-&c. करणें.

To w. around (the waist). वेढून घेणें.

To w. round closely. गुरगुटून बांधणें-घेणें.

Wrapped, *p.* v. V. 1. गुंडाळलेला, लपेटलेला, &c.
2 वेष्टलेला, गुंडाळलेला, &c. वेष्टित.
3 गुंडाळलेला, वेष्टलेला, लपेटलेला, &c. वेष्टित.

Wrapper, *n.* **Wrapping**, *p. a.* V. 1. गुंडाळणारा, लपेटणारा, &c.
2 वेष्टणारा, गुंडाळणारा, &c. वेष्टक.
3 गुंडाळणारा, लपेटणारा, गुंडाळून बांधणारा, &c.
I. *cloth, &c. that wraps.* वेष्टन *n.* बारदान *n.* बासन *n.* आळा *m.* रुमाल *m.* बासन *n.* बासनीवस्त्र *n.*-कापड *n.*
That is used as, or is fit for, a w. बासनी.

Wrath, *n.* v. Anger. राग *m.* कोप *m.* क्रोध *m.* रोष *m.*

Wrathful. See Angry.

To **Wreak**, *v. a.* (vengeance). द्वेष*m.*-वैर *m.*-सूड*m.*-&c. उगवणें.

Wreath, *n. thing curled or twisted.* वेंट or वेंठ*m.* नागमोडी *f.*
2 (of flowers, &c.) v. Garland. माला *pop.* माळ *f.* हार *m.* गजरा *m.* सर *m.* घोंसा *m.*
To fall in pieces,—a w. ओघळणें.
To slip off from a w. or string. ओघळणें.

To **Wreath**, *v. a. convolve, &c.* वळणें.
2 *encircle with a garland.* माळ *f.*-&c. बांधणें-लपेटणें-गुंडाळणें, मालावेष्टित-&c. करणें.

Wreck, *n.* (of a ship) *naufrage.* नावफूट *f.* तारूंफूट *f.* तारूंमोड *f.* नौकाभंग *m.*
2 *thing wrecked.* फुटलेलें तारूं *n.*-गलबत *n.*-&c. नष्ट नौका *f.*

To **Wreck**, *v. a.* (a vessel). फोडणें, भंग*m.*-नाश *m.*-&c. करणें.

Wrecked, *p.* v. V.—a vessel. फोडलेला, शिकस्त,—a person, भिन्ननौक.

To **Wrench**, *v. a. wrest, twist violently.* मुरगळणें or मुरगाळणें, पिरंगळणें or पिरंगाळणें, पिळंगुटणें, पिळवटणें, पिवळणें, पिळणें, पेंचणें, पिरंगळणी or पिरगाळणी *f.* करणें.
2 v. To Sprain. लचकवणें, लचक *f.*-&c. भरवणें.
3 from. मुरगाळून-पिळवटून-पिळून-&c. घेणें-खेंचणें.
4 off; out; open. उचटणें, उचकटणें.
To w. and tear violently. उचकटाउचकट *f.* करणें *g. of o.*

Wrench, *n. violent twist or pull.* मुरगाळा *m.* पिरंगाळा *m.* मुरडा *m.* पिळण *f.* पेंच *m.*

To **Wrest**, *v. a. twist or pull from by force.* मुरगाळून-पिळवटून-पिळून-&c. घेणें-खेंचणें, बळात्कारानें-&c. घेणें.
2 *twist from the natural meaning.* ओढणें, ओढून ताणून आणणें-घेणें, खेंचणें, खेंचून घेणें, वळवणें.

Wrest. See Twist.

Wrested, *p.* v. V. 1. मुरगाळून घेतलेला, पिळवटून घेतलेला, &c.
2 ओढलेला, ओढून घेतलेला, &c.

Wrester, *n.* **Wresting**, *p. a.* v. V. 1. मुरगाळून घेणारा, &c.
2 ओढणारा, &c.

To **Wrestle**, *v. n.* कुस्ती *f.*-मल्लयुद्ध *n.*-बाहुयुद्ध *n.*-&c. करणें, झोंबी *f.*-हातझोंबी *f.* घेणें-करणें.
2 See To Contend.

Wrestler, *n.* **Wrestling**, *p. a.* v. V. 1. कुस्ती करणारा, जेठी, कुस्तीबाज, कुस्तीवाला, मल्ल, पहिलवान.
Turnings and windings of a w. Tricks and feints of a w. डावपेंच *m. pl.* पाचपेंच *m. pl.*

Wrestling, *n.* v. V. कुस्ती *f.* झोंबी *f.* हातझोंबी *f.* झोंबणी *f.* मल्लयुद्ध *n.* मल्लक्रीडा *f.* बाहुयुद्ध *n.*

Wretch, *n. miserable person.* In the sense of *A penniless, friendless, and miserable,* or *a luckless, and luck-blasting fellow,* and with the power of *the sport of fortune, fortune's foot-ball, ill starred wight, forlorn creature, &c.* there are the following terms and phrases. दैवाचा भोपळा *m.* भाग्याचा भोपळा *m.* भिकार भोपळा *m.* अकाबाईचा बंधु *m.*-भाऊ *m.*-वडील भाऊ *m.* अकाबाईचें कूळ *n.* अकाबाईचें बाळ *n.* फुटक्या दैवाचा, फुटक्या कपाळाचा, कपाळ फुटका, अष्टकपाळ्या, हाड कपाळ्या, भद्र्या कपाळाचा, भद्र्या, सव्वनाथाचें कूळ *n.* शंख्या, बळभद्रा or भद्र्या, हतभाग्य, हतदैव, हतश्री, जळतोंड्या, काळतोंड्या, काळमुख्या, बोंबलभिक्या, पांढरेपायाचा, खुरंटपायाचा, अपयशी, फत्तेलशकर, कमबख्त, हलाक or ख, जगतूशेट, घरनादार आणि देवळीं बिन्हाड, सैशा, जन्मकरंटा, कपाळकरंटा, करंटा, खापरतोंड्या, दलभंजन, रंक, खरखरमुंडा, भणंग, पालथा जन्मला, उताणा पडलेला, धालेधन्याचालेंक, बिचारा, लाचार, दग्धहस्त, दग्धहस्ती, निखोरडा, शुद्ध स्फटिक, शुद्धबुद्ध.
2 *worthless, sordid, &c. creature.* v. Blackguard, Scrub, Wicked. हुचभाई, हुच्चमाणूस, लिदवळ, पाजी, लुच्चा, हरामी, चंडाल, चंडालमूर्त्ति, कर्म चांडाल, दुरात्मा, अधर्मात्मा, दुकारविल्हा (from दुष्ट), नराधम.

Wretched, *a. miserable, unhappy.* दुःखी, कष्टी, क्लेशी, दुःखांत पडलेला, अतिदुःखी, फार असुखी, अकुशल, दुःखसंपन्न, दुःखापन्न, दुर्दशापन्न, आपद्ग्रस्त, विपद्ग्रस्त, आपत्प्राप्त, विपत्प्राप्त, आपत्तिग्रस्त, दुरवस्थ, दुःखयुक्त, दुःखान्वित, दुःखाक्रांत, दुःखग्रस्त, दुःखव्याप्त, दुःखाप्लुत, आपन्न, विपन्न.
A w. creature or being. दुःखाचा प्राणी *m.*
2 *pitiable, pitiful, paltry,*—of persons, v. Poor. दरिद्री, बापडा, बापुडबाणा, बिचारा, भिकारी, दैन, हुच्चा, पाजी, अधम, कृपण.
3 *sorry, poor, paltry,*—of things, v. Worthless, Bad. दरिद्री, भिकारी, भिकार, फाटका, फुसका, गैरी, नादान, लुकसान or लुसकान, मुरदाड or मुडदार, यारदा, यारदी.
4 v. Calamitous, Afflictive. दुःखाचा, विपत्तीचा, अकल्याणाचा, हालअपेष्टेचा.

Wretchedness, *n.* v. A. 1. दुःख *n.* दुःखीपणा *m.* कष्ट *m. pl.* क्लेश *m. pl.* श्रम *m.* अकल्याण *n.* असुख *n.* हलाकी or खी *f.* हाल or हाल *m. pl.* हालहवाल *m. pl.* बुरेहाल *m. pl.* हालअपेष्टा *f.* दुर्दशा *f.* दुरवस्था *f.* दुःखावस्था *f.* लाचारी *f.* जेरदस्ती *f.* देसधूळ *f.* कंगाली *f.* दैन *n.* दैना *f.* आपत्ति *f.* विपत्ति *f.* आपदा *f.* हबेलंडी *f.* हलबंड्या *f. pl.* उठवण *f.* विपत्त्य *m. pl.*
To be in utter w. डोई वरून पाणी *n.* जाणें *g. of s.* दयादयां *adv.*-भयांभयां *adv.* होणें.
To lie in utter w. तळाबर बसणें or राहणें, हाका *f. pl.* मारणें, रक्षरक्ष *interj.* होणें, उताणा पडणें, उठवण *f.* घेणें, उठवणीस येणें.
To wander about in utter w. दयांदयां *adv.*-भयांभयां *adv.* करीत फिरणें or जाणें.
2 दरिद्रीपणा *m.* बापडेपणा *m.* भिकारीपणा *m.* &c.
3 दरिद्रीपणा *m.* भिकारपणा *m.* फुसकेपणा *m.* नादानपणा*m.*&c.

To **Wriggle**, *v. n. move the body to and fro with short motions.* वळवळणें, वळवळ *f.* करणें, बिळबिळणें, अळापिळा or वळापिळा *m.*-अळेपिळे *m. pl.*-अळगापिळघा *f. pl.*-&c. घेणें-देणें, लवलवणें.

WRIGGLER, *n.* WRIGGLING, *p. a.* v. V. वळवळणारा, वळवळकरणारा, अळेपिळेघेणारा-देणारा-&c.

WRIGGLING, *n.* v. V. वळवळणें *n.* अळेपिळेघेणें *n.* &c. वळवळ *f.* वळवळी *f.* वळका *m.*

To WRING, *v. a. twist or turn violently.* मुरगळणें *or* मुरगाळणें, पिरंगळणें *or* पिरंगाळणें, पिळंगुटणें, पिळवटणें, पिबळणें, पिळणें, पीळ *m.*-पिळा *m.*-&c. घालणें-देणें.

2 from ; *extort, squeeze from.* पिळणें, पिळून घेणें.

3 off ; *force off by contortion.* मुरगाळून-पिळवटून-&c.तोडणें.

4 out ; *force out by contortion.* पिळणें, पिळून-पिळवटून-&c. काढणें.

WRINGER, *n.* WRINGING, *p. a.* v. V. 1. मुरगळणारा *or* मुरगाळणारा, पिरंगळणारा, पिळवटणारा, &c.

2 पिळणारा, पिळूनघेणारा.

3 मुरगाळून-&c. तोडणारा.

4 पिळणारा, पिळून-&c. काढणारा.

Wringing wet, *dripping wet.* थबथबीत.

To WRINKLE, *v. n. shrink into furrows and ridges.* सुरकुतणें, सुरकुत्या *f. pl.*-वळया *f. pl.*-चिरम्या *f. pl.*-&c. पडणें *in. con.* चिरमुटणें.

To WRINKLE, *v. a. contract into furrows and ridges.* सुरकुतवणें, सुरकुत्या *f. pl.*-&c. पाडणें.

WRINKLE, *n. corrugation, &c.* सुरकुती *f.* चिरमी *f.* अढी *f.* अठी *f.* गांठ *f.* वळी *f.* चर्मतरंग *m.* [वळयांचा.

WRINKLED, *p.*v.V. N. सुरकुतलेला, सुरकुत्या-चिरम्या-&c. पडलेला,

WRIST, *n. joint of the hand and arm.* मणगट *n.* पोहंची *f.* मणिबंध *m.* [सोड.

Lock or gripe of the w. चिकाटी *or* चिकोटी *f.* *v.* धर,

WRIT, *n. legal instrument.* सनद *f.* परवाना *m.*

2 See SCRIPTURE.

To WRITE, *v. a. form by a pen, &c.* लिहिणें, काढणें.

2 *express by means of letters.* लिहिणें, लिखणें, लेखणें, कलमी करणें, लिखन *n.*-लेखन *n.* करणें *g. of o.*

To w. down. लिहणें, लिहून ठेवणें, मांडणें, मांडून ठेवणें, टिपणें, टिपून ठेवणें, पत्रारूढ करणें.

To w. off rapidly. फरकटणें.

To w. out under distinct heads. कलमबंदी *f.*करणें *g. of o.*

To w. roughly. खरडणें.

Cost or price for writing. लिहिणावळ *f.*

3 v. To COMPOSE. लिहिणें, करणें, रचणें, कवणें.

To WRITE, *v. n. perform the act of writing.* लिहिणें, लिखणें.—with implication of *toilsomeness and fagging.* खरडीं *n. pl.* घासणें, मानमोड *f.*-मांडीमोड *f.* करणें.

To leave intervals in writing. छेद पाडून लिहिणें.

2 *do the work of a clerk.* लिहिणें, लिहिणें *n.* लिहिणें, लेखकी *f.*-लिहण्याचें काम *n.*-&c. करणें.

3 *write and send a letter.* कागद *m.*-पत्र *n.*-&c. लिहिणें-लिहून पाठवणें-पाठवणें.

WRITER, *n.* v. V. N. 1. लिहिणारा, &c. लेखक, लिपिकर, लिपिकार. Terms signifying *A good writer*, and agreeing with *Penman, Calographer, &c.* are कलमसुत्रा, कलमबहादुर, लेखणीचाबहाद्दुर, लिहिणारा फरडा-बाका-&c. लेखणीचा धड, लेखणीस चंग बांधणारा, चित्रगुप्त, अक्षरचण, अक्षरचुंचु. Terms signifying *A bad writer*, and agreeing with *Penster, Scrawler, Scratcher, Quill-butcher,* are कलमकसाई, खरडघाशा, खरड्या, गबत काप्या *or* गबत्या.

Posture of a w. मांडी *f.* *v.* साध.

To set up for a fine w. लेखणीस चंग *m.* बांधणें.

I. *clerk, &c.* लिहिणारा, कारकून, लेखक, अक्षरजीवक.

Business of a w. लेखकी *f.*

II. *author, &c.* कवि, ग्रंथकार, ग्रंथकर्त्ता.

WRITERSHIP, *n.* v. N. 1. कारकुनी *f.* कारकुनीपेशा *m.* लेखकी *f.*

To WRITHE, *v. n. twist and turn about the body.* वळणें, वळवळणें, कळवळणें, वळवळ *f.* करणें, आंगपिळा *m.*-बळापिळा *m.*-अळेपिळे *m.pl.*-अळोकेपिळोके *m. pl.*-&c. घेणें-देणें *or, in. con.* येणें.

To WRITHE, *v. a.* See To TWIST.

WRITHER, *n.* WRITHING, *p. a.* v. V. वळवळणारा, वळवळकरणारा, अळेपिळे-&c. घेणारा-देणारा.

WRITHING, *n.* v. V. वळवळणें *n.* &c. वळवळ *f.* वळवळी *f.* वळवळा *m.* आंगपिळा *m.* आंगवळा *m.* बळापिळा *m.* अळेपिळे *m. pl.* अळयापिळ्या *f. pl.* अळोकेपिळोके *m. pl.* अळंगेंविळंगें *n.*

WRITING, *n. act of forming letters, &c.* लिहिणें *n.* लिहिण्याचें काम *n.* लिहिण्याची विद्या *f.* लिखणें *n.* लिखन *n.* लेखन *n.* लिपि *f.* लेखनविद्या *f.*

Fine or skilful w. कलमसफाई *f.* खुशखत *n.*

Hasty or bad writing. खरडनिशी *f.* कुत्र्याचेपाय मांजराचे पाय *m. pl.* [ज्ञा *f.*

Implements or materials of w. लेखनसामग्री *f.* लिपिस-

Regular and uniform w. एकटांकी लिहिणें *n.* एकटांकी अक्षर *n.* [धणें.

To set up pretensions to good w. लेखणीस चंग *m.* बां-

2 *written letters or characters, &c.* लिहिणें *n.* लेख *m.* अक्षरें *n. pl.* लिपि *f.* अक्षररचना *f.*

By or in w. लेखपुर्शी.

3 *written paper or thing.* लेख *m.* लिखित *n.* लिहिणें *n.* लिखा *m.* लिहिलें *n.* पत्रक *n.* लिखन *n.*—compreh. *or* gener. लेखपत्र *n.* लिखापढा *or* लेखपढा *m.* लिहिणें पुसणें *or* लिहिलें पुसलें *n.* लेखपूस *f.* लिखापुसा *m.* [*m. pl.*

Cancelled or waste writings. रद्दी *f.* रद्दी *or* रद्द कागद

4 *paper or document of obligation, legal instrument,* v. DEED, BOND. लेख *m.* पत्र *n.* कागद *m.* कागदपत्र *n.* लेखपत्र *n.* खत *n.* दस्तऐवज *m.* पत्रक *n.* सनद *f.*

WRITING-BOARD, *n.* पाटी *f.*

Steatite or earth to rub over a w. खडी *f.* खडू *m. f.* माळू *f.* शेडू *or* शाडू *f.*—a ball of it, माला *m. or* मालें *n.*

WRITING-MASTER, *n.* हातवळण्याचा-हातवळयाचा गुरु-शिकवणारा-&c. लेखनशिक्षक.

WRITTEN, *p.* v. V. A. लिहिलेला, लिखित, लेखित.

W. on both sides. पाठपोट लिहिलेला.

I. *as opposed to* expressed in figures. अक्षरी.

II.—*as opposed to* oral. लिहिलेला, लिखित, कलमी, लेखाचा.

WRONG, WRONGLY, *adv.* v. A. 1. 2. अन्यायानें, अनीतीनें, अधर्मानें, अमार्गानें, &c. गैरवाजबी, गैरशिस्त, अन्यायतः, वाईट, बांकडा *decl.* अन्यथा, नारास्त, अयथान्याय, अयथायोग्य, अयथायुक्त, अयथार्थ.

3. 4 चुकून, चूककरून, भ्रमानें, भ्रांतीनें, &c. अशुद्ध, अन्यथा,

गैरवाजवी, गैरशिस्त, खोटा *decl.* नादुरूस्त, नारास्त, अनाठायीं.
6 उलटा, उफराटा, उफरटा, उरफाटा, &c. *all decl.*

WRONG, *n. injustice, injury.* अपराध *m.* अन्याय *m.* बाईट *n.* जुलूम *m.* अपकार *m.* अपकृति *f.* अनिष्ट *n.* अरिष्ट *n.* अहित *n.* नुकसान *n.* नुकसानी *f.*
2 *not truth or right,* v. ERROR. भ्रम *m.* भ्रांति *f.* अविद्या *f.* असद्ग्रह *m.* अयाथार्थ्य *n.* अयाथातथ्य *n.*

WRONG, *a.*—of persons ; *acting improperly,* v. UNJUST. अन्यथा चारी, अन्यायाचारी, अधर्मचारी, अमार्गगामी, असत्पक्षचारी.
2—of actions, purposes, &c.; *unjust, improper, &c.* अन्यायाचा, अनीतीचा, अधर्माचा, अमार्गाचा, गैरचालीचा, गैररितीचा, &c. हराम, गैरवाजवी, अवाजवी, गैरशिस्त, अयोग्य, बाईट, वांकडा, सदाचरणास-न्यायास-&c. वांकडा, वावगा, नारास्त, नादुरूस्त, अनुचित, अकर्त्तव्य, अन्याय्य, प्रत्यवायी, नीतिविरुद्ध, न्यायविरुद्ध, सदोष, अशुद्ध, अयथान्याय, अयथार्थ, अयथामार्ग, असत् in comp. असाधु, अयथायुक्त, अयुक्त, अयथोचित.
3—of persons ; *erring.* चुकणारा, चुकलेला, भ्रमपडलेला, भ्रांत, भ्रमी, भ्रमयुक्त, भ्रांतियुक्त, जातभ्रम, प्राप्तभ्रम.
To be w. भ्रम *m.*-भ्रांति *f.* पडणें-होणें *in. con.* चुकणें, भुलणें.
4—of things, works, &c. *erroneous, incorrect, inaccurate.* चुकलेला, चुकीचा, भ्रांतीचा, भ्रमाचा, &c. अशुद्ध, गैरवास्तवीक, अवास्तविक, गैरवाजवी, गैररास्त, नादुरूस्त, दोषी, सदोष, अयथार्थ, अप्रमाणात्मक, खोटा.
5 *not physically right,* v. REVERSE, INVERSE. उलटा, उफराटा, उफारटा, उरफाटा, विपरीत.

To WRONG, *v. a. treat with injustice, &c.* v. To INJURE. अपराध*m.*-अन्याय*m.*-बाईट*n.*-&c. करणें *g. of o.* जुलूम*m.*-&c. करणें *with* वर *of o.*

WRONG-HEADED, WRONG-HEADEDNESS. See PERVERSE, PERVERSENESS.

WRONGED, *p.* v. V. अपराध केलेला, &c. आधर्षित, अपकृत, प्राप्तापकार, जातापकार.

WRONGER, *n.* WRONGING, *p. a.* WRONG-DOER, *n.* v. V. अपराध करणारा, अपकार करणारा, बाईट करणारा, &c. अन्यायकारी, परापकारी.

WRONGFUL, *a. unjust,* v. WRONG. अन्यायाचा, अनीतीचा, अधर्माचा, परापकाराचा.

WRONGFULLY, *adv.* v. A. *and* WRONG. अन्यायानें, अनीतीनें, अधर्मानें, नाहक, हक्कनाहक, हक्कनाक, अगननगन *or* अघननघन.

WRONGLY. See WRONG.

WRONGNESS, *n.* v. A. 2. अन्याय*m.* अनीति *f.* बाईट*n.* बाईटपणा *m.* वांकडेपणा*m.* गैरवाजवीपणा*m.* &c.

WROTH, *a.* v. ANGRY. क्रुद्ध, संतप्त, कोपज्वलित.

WROUGHT, *p. performed, done.* केलेला, कृत.
2 *worked, elaborated.* घडलेला, घडींव, संस्कारित, संस्कृत, कृप्त.
3 *stirred, worked up,* v. EXCITED. चेतवलेला, चेष्टवलेला, उत्तेजित.

WRUNG, *p.* v. V. 1. मुरगाळलेला, पिळवटलेला, &c.
Water of w. cloths, &c. पिळवणी*n.* [विकृत.

WRY, *a. distorted, twisted.* बांकडा, तिरपलेला, पीळ दिल्हेला, वक्र,

WRY-MOUTHED, *a.* वक्रमुख, वक्रतुंड.

WRYNESS, *n.* v. A. वांकडेपणा*m.* तिरपलेलेपणा*m.* वक्रता *f.*

X.

X. This letter initially has the same sound as *z* ; medially and finally it has the power of *ks,* and is represented by क्स. No Saxon or pure English word begins with it.

XANTIPPE, *n.* v. SCOLD, SHREW. कैकेयी *f.* ताटका *f.* महामाया *f.*

Y.

Y. This letter in its initial use is represented by य; in its medial and final uses by इ *or* ई.

YACHT, *n.* v. VESSEL. एकप्रकारची नाव आहे.

YAM, *n.*—the plant. कोनफळ *f.* हेंडाळू *m.* गोराडू *m. n.* पेंडाळू*m. n.* वाराही *f.*—the root, कोनफळ*n.* कोन*n.* पेंडूळ*m. n.* हेंडाळू*m.* गोराडू*m. n.* वाराहीकंद*m.* पेंडाळू*m. n.* सुकंद*m.*
Elephants foot y. सुरण*m.* मुसळेकोनफळ*n.*

YARD, *n. court, enclosure round a house, &c.* अंगण *or* अंगन*n.* वाडा*m. dim.* वाडगें*n.* वाडकुलें*n.* अवार*n.* अवाड*n.* परस *or* परसू *or* परूस*n.* परडें*n.* विसवाट*n.* खळ *or* खें*n.*
2—the measure. वार*m.* यार्द*m.* from the English is getting into use.
3 (of a ship). परवाण *or* परमान*n.* काठी *f.*

YARN, *n. woollen thread.* लोंकरीचें सूत*n.* ऊर्णासूत्र*n.*
2 *single string of a cord.* पेड*m.*
Long y. *a long-winded story.* चऱ्हाट*n.* चरपटपंजरी *f.* चरकट *or* चरपट*n.* परवड *f.* पान्हेरा *or* व्हाम*m.* दीर्घसूत्र*n.* कोळ्याचें सूत*n.*
To spin a y. परिणाळिका *f.* लावणें.

YAWL, *n.* v. VESSEL. डिंगी *f.* होडकें *n.*

To YAWN, *v. n. gape, oscitate.* जांभई *f. or* जांभ्या *f. pl.*-जांभळी *f.*-जांभळ्या *f. pl.* देणें-घेणें *or, with in.con.* येणें, जृंभणें, तोंड*n.* वासणें, तोंड*n.* विचकणें.
2 *open widely.* वासणें, विचकणें, आ *m.*-तोंड*n.* वासणें-पसरणें *or* वासून-पसरून असणें *g. of s.* हसणें *or* हासणें *or* हांसणें.

YAWN, YAWNING, *n.* v. V. 1. जांभई *f.* जांभळी *f.* जृंभा *f.*

YAWNER, *n.* YAWNING, *p. a.* v. V. 1. जांभई देणारा-दिल्हेला, &c. तोंड वासणारा-वासलेला, &c.

YE, *pron.* तुम्ही.

YEA, *adv.* v. YES. होय.
Y. and nay (procedure or speech). अर्धजरतीय.
Y. and nay (sort of person or thing). शेणामेणाचा.

To YEAN, *v. n. bring forth young.* विणें.

YEANLING. See LAMB.

YEAR, *n.*—the period of time. वर्ष *n.* साल *n.* संवत्सर *m.* वत्सर *m.* संवत् *or* संवद् *m.*
Advanced in years. वयस्क, वयोवृद्ध, वयातीत, वयोगत.
Beginning of the y. अवलसाल *n.*
By years—reckoning, &c. वर्षोंगणती.
Close of the y. आखेर साल *n.*
Coming y. पेस्तरसाल *n.* पेस्तर वर्ष *n.* सालआयंदा *m.*
Declining years. उतरतीपराई *f.* उतारवय*n.* उत्तरवय*n.* वा-

र्धक्यn. वार्धक्यावस्था f.—That is of declining years. उत्तरवयस्क.

Events or fortunes of the y.—as predetermined astrologically. वर्षफल n.

First y. of a cycle, an era, &c. अवलसाल n.

For years, *through or till many years.* वर्षो वर्ष, वर्षानवर्ष, सालोसाल.

Fourth y. ago. चौगस्त.—In or during it. चौगस्तां.

In the year of an era. सन. As, in the year 1847 सन १८४७.

Last y. of a cycle, an era, &c. आखेरसाल n.

New y.'s day. वर्षप्रतिपदा f. संवत्सर प्रतिपदा f.—Pole erected on New y.'s day. गुढी f. इंद्रध्वज m.

Once or twice a y. *occasionally.* सठीं सामाशीं.

Past or last y. गतवर्षn. गतसालn. सालगुदस्त n. गेलेलें साल n.-वर्ष n. In or during the past y. गुदस्तां, सालगुदस्तां, गेल्यासालीं, गतसालीं, &c.

Person hired or engaged by the y. वर्ष संड्या *pop.* वरीसंड्या.

Present or current y. सालमजकूर n. चालतेंसाल n.-वर्षn. In or during the present or current y. This y. अंवदा *or* औंदा *or* यंदा, यंदाच्यावर्षी-सालीं.

Relating to two years. दुसाला *or* ली.

Second y. ago. *year before last.* तिगस्त n. अदलेंवर्ष n. अदलेंसाल n. पलीकडलेंसालn.-वर्षn. In or during the second y. ago. तिगस्तां, अदल्यावर्षी, &c.

Sidereal y. आर्क्ष वर्ष n.

Stricken in years, *aged.* वयोवृद्ध, वयातीत, वयोगत.

Throughout a y. उभ्यावर्षांत, सरसाल, वर्षभर.

Throughout the y. बारमास, बारमहां, बारमांही, बारमहिने, उन्हाळ पावसाळ.

Two years old—a beast, &c. दुसा, दुवर्षा.—Three years old, तिसा, तिवर्षा.—Four years old, चौसा, चौवर्षा.

Unto the y's end. आवर्षांत.

Within *the* or *a* y. वर्षाचे कांठीं.

Whole and present (or any particularized) y. उभेंवर्ष n. उभेंसाल n. सरसाल n.—During, through, for, in, &c. the whole y. सरसाल.—Of or belonging to a whole y. सरसाली *or* ला.

Y. after y. सालदरसाल.

Y. before a particular y. अदलेंवर्ष n. अदलेंसाल n.

Y. of (in rotation). वर्षल f.—Holder for the y.—of a property held in rotation. वर्षलकरी, सालकरी.

YEARLY, *a. happening, coming, &c. every year.* वर्षाचा, प्रतिवर्षाचा, वर्षावर्षाचा, सालदरसालचा, दरसालचा, दरवर्षीचा, प्रतिवर्षीचा, सालाबाद, सालाबादी, वार्षिक, प्रतिवार्षिक, सांवत्सरिक, प्रतिसांवत्सरिक, सांवत्सर, आब्दिक.

2 *lasting a year.* एकवर्ष टिकणारा-&c. एकसाली, वर्षायु, वर्षस्थायी, वर्षजीवी.

3 *comprehending a year.* वर्षाचा, वार्षिक, आब्दिक, सांवत्सरिक, सांवत्सर, वर्षप्रमाणाचा, वर्षमानाचा.

YEARLY, *adv. every year.* दरवर्षास, दरवर्षी, प्रतिवर्षास, प्रतिवर्षी, दरसाल, सालोसाल, वर्षोवर्ष, वर्षानवर्ष, सालबसाल, सालदरसाल, प्रतिवर्ष, प्रतिवत्सरीं, सालीना.

2 *by the year.* वर्षास, वर्षाचा *decl.* सालीना.

To YEARN, *v. n. to feel the workings of tender affection and longing.* बेंबीचा देंठ m. पिळून येणें *or* दुखूं लागणें *g. of s.* बेंबीच्या देंठा पासून कळवळ f.-माया f.-&c. येणें *in. con.* जीव m. तुटणें *g. of s.* कळवळणें, पाकुळणें, अंतडीं *n. pl.* तुटणें-पिळणें *g. of s.* अंतड्यांला पीळ m. पडणें-बसणें *g. of s.* पोटांत कळकळणें, पोटांत पीळm. पडणें *in. con. with g. of s.* ओढ f.-&c. बसणें-लागणें, (Ex. कांगे बाई रोड तर गांवाची ओढ), काळीजn. पिळून येणें, काळिजाला पीळm. पडणें*in. con. with g. of s.* पोटांत तडतड तोडणें, पोटांत चावणें.

YEARNING, *n.* v. V. कळवळ f. कळवळा m. कन्हवळा m. कळकळ f. ओढ f. ओढा m. पीळ m. पाकुळकी f.

Maternal y. पोटजाळm. पोटाग f. अंतड्याकातड्याची माया f.

Y. of affection. प्रेमपान्हा m.

YEAST, YEST, *n. the froth of beer or other liquor in fermentation.* सुरामंड m. मद्यमंड m. कारोत्तम m. कारोत्तर m. यवमंड m. ताडी f. (Toddy, or the fermented juice from the tád tree) is commonly used in this country.

To YELL, *v. n. make a sharp and hideous cry or scream.* केंकणें, केंकटणें, केंकावणें, किराळणें, किराळी *or* किरोळी f. देणें-मारणें, केंकाटणें, कोंकणें, कोंकलणें.

YELL, YELLING, *n.* v. V. केंकणें n. &c. किराळी *or* किरोळी f. किंकाळी f. ख्यांवख्यांव f. श्वानबैसरी f.

YELLOW, *a.* पिवळा (remiss. पिवळट *yellowish,* and for yellowishness. पिवळट f. पिवळोसी f.) हळद्या, हळदिवा *or* हळदुवा (like turmeric) बसंती, पीत, हरिद्राभ, केशरी *and* केशरी रंगाचा (like saffron).—*intens.* bright, glaring, &c. y. पिवळा धमक, पिवळा चटक, पिवळा रसरसीत, धमधमीत *or* धवधवीत पिवळा.

Deep or dark y. पिवळा जर्द.

YELLOWNESS, *n.* v. A. पिवळेपणा m. &c. पिवळकी f. पीतरंग m. पीतवर्ण m. हरिद्रावर्ण m.

To YELP. See To BARK, To YELL.

YEOMAN, *n. farmer, respectable common man.* शेतकरी गृहस्थ, खातापिता कुणबी-गृहस्थ-&c.

To YERK, *v. n.*—of horses, &c. v. To LASH OUT. दुलाच्या f. *pl.*-&c. झाडणें.

YES, *adv.* होय, हो, हां, आ, हूं, होयकार, होकार.

Yesser, *one who always assents.* होयबा, होसहो म्हणणारा, हांजी करणारा *or* म्हणणारा.

Yes Sir! Yes your Worship. हांजी.

To say yes yes to every thing. होसहो म्हणणें.

YESTER, *a. last, last past.* गेला *or* गेलेला, मागला, कालचा, ह्यस्तन, ह्यस्त्य.

[दिवसm.

YESTERDAY, *n.* काल n. कालचा दिवस m. गेला-गेलेला-गत-&c.

Day before y. परवांचा दिवस.

On the day before y. परवां.

Man of y. अधव्याचा.

YESTERDAY, *adv.* काल, रोजगुदस्त, गेल्यादिवशीं, गतदिनीं-दिवशीं.

YESTERNIGHT, *n.* कालची-गेलेली-मागली-&c. रात f.-रात्र f.

YESTERNIGHT, *adv.* कालरात्रीस, कालच्या रात्रीस, गेल्या-मागल्या -&c. रात्रीस.

YET, *conj. notwithstanding, nevertheless.* तरी, तथापि, तत्रापि,

परंतु, पण, पर, अथापि, असें असतांही, तदपि, एताबता.

YET, *adv. over and above, beside.* अझून, अणखी.

2 *still, the state remaining the same.* तेव्हां, तेव्हांदेखील, असतांही.

3 *up to this time,* v. HITHERTO. अझून, अद्यापि *pop.* अद्याप, हाकाळतों, हा-ही-वेळतों, हीवेळ पर्यंत-पावेतों, आतां पर्यंत-पावेतों.

4 *still, in a new degree.* अझून, अणखी, अद्यापि *pop.* अद्याप, यावरही.

To YIELD, *v. a.*—land, funds, &c. *give in return, produce.* देणें, करणें, उत्पन्न करणें, होणें-उत्पन्न होणें *in. con. with* पासून *of s.* उपजवणें, निपजवणें, उपज*m.*-निपज*m.*-प्राप्ति *f.*-उत्पन्न*n.*-&c. होणें *in. con. with* पासून *of s.*

2 *produce, afford, give,*—gener. देणें, प्रापण*n.* करणें, मिळणें -प्राप्त होणें-पावणें-पहोंचणें-उत्पन्न होणें-पदरीं *or* पदरास-हातीं *or* हातास लागणें all *in. con. with* पासून *of s.* [करणें.

3 *allow, concede,* v. To ADMIT. मानणें, मान्य-कबूल-&c.

4 *cede, surrender, resign, &c.* v. To GIVE UP. देणें, सोडणें, सोडून देणें, स्वाधीन करणें, हवालीं-हवालां करणें.

YIELD, *n.* See PRODUCE.

To YIELD, *v. n. knock under, give in, &c.* v. To SUBMIT. दबणें, दबकणें, हात*m. pl.*-मेटें*n. pl.* टेंकणें, बें*n.* म्हणणें.

2 See To GIVE. [*of s.* झालेला.

YIELDED, *p.* v. V. A. 1. दिल्हेला, उत्पन्न केलेला *or with* पासून

2 दिल्हेला, मिळालेला-प्राप्त झालेला-&c. *with* पासून *of s.*

3 मान्य केलेला, कबूल केलेला, &c.

4 दिल्हेला, सोडलेला, &c.

YIELDING, *a. inclined to give way, soft, complying,* v. WEAK. नकारशून्य, नचा फाडा शिकलेला नाहीं, डाळपिठ्या.

YOKE, *n.*—for the necks of oxen. जूं *n.* जुकड *or* जोकड *or* जोखड *or* जुखड *n.* जुंबाड *n.* युग *n.*

A double y. जाडी *f.*

Peg or pin of a y. जोबणी *f.* धुराणी *f.*

Portion of the y. which sits upon the neck. शेळें*n.*

To bring under the y. *fig.* जंत्रांतून ओढणें.

To keep under the y. *fig.* करवतासालीं धरणें.

To shrink from the y.—bullock. खांद*m.* चोरणें.

2 (of oxen) *couple yoked,* v. COUPLE, PAIR. जोत*n.* जोडी*f.*

Front y. आगली *f.*—driver of it. आगल्या.

3 *bond, link,* v. CONNECTION. गांठ *f.* ग्रंथिम.

To YOKE, *v. a. put a yoke on.* जुंपणें, जोडणें, जूं*n.*-जोकड*n.*-&c. घालणें-ठेवणें, जुंपण *f.*-जुंपणी *f.* करणें.

2 *join two together, couple.* जोडणें, जोडी *f.* करणें-बांधणें-घालणें. [जंगडीचा.

YOKE-FELLOW, YOKE-MATE, *n.* जोताचा, सांगडीचा, जोडीचा,

YOKE-TIE, *n.* जुंपण*n.* जुंपणी *f.*

YOLK, *n. yellow part of an egg.* पिवळा बील*m.*

YON, YONDER, *a. being at a distance within view.* तिकडचा, तो, पलीकडचा *or* ला, पलीकडील (*or* पैलिकडचा &c.) परता.

YONDER, *adv. at a distance within view.* तिकडे, पलीकडे *or* पैलिकडे, उत्तरत्र, परता.

YORE, *adv. long.* चिर.

Days or time of y. गतकाळ*m.* [पूर्वकालिक.

Of days of y. कद्रा काळांचा *or* काळींचा, प्राचीन कालचा,

YOU, *pron.* तुम्ही.

2 *any one.* कोणी *or* कोण्ही.

YOUNG, *a. being in the first part of life, not old.* नुका-&c.जन्मलेला, लहान बयाचा-उमरीचा, थोडे-थोडके-&c. उमरीचा, कोबळे उमरीचा, पहिलेपराईचा, तरणा, तरुण, जवान, बाल, बालदशेचा, तारुण्यावस्थेचा, अल्पायु, अल्पवया, अल्पवयस्क, लहान, कोवळा.

Y. and vigorous. जवानकट्टा, जवानपट्टा, जवानमर्द, जानजवान, तरणाताठा, तरणाबांड, नबातरणा, नबातरणाफोक, जोमदार.

Y. and ardent. नवे उमेदीचा.

Younger. धाकटा *or* ला, कनिष्ठ, अनुज, अनुजन्मा, अनुजात.

YOUNG, *n. young one* (of an animal, gener). पिलूं *n.* पिला *m.* पिलवा *m.* पील *n.* जाबपें *or* जोपें *n.* बच्चा *m.* बचडा *m.* (डा, डी, डें *m. f. n.*) बक *m.* करभ *m.* पृथुक *m.* शावक *m.* शिशु *m.* बत्स *m.* [वर्षी *n. pl.*

2 *young offspring of.* वीण *f.* वेत *n.* पिलीं *or* पिलें *n. pl.* जा-

To be with y. See PREGNANT.

YOUNGLING. See YOUNG.

YOUNGSTER, YOUNKER, YOUNGLING, *n.* v. STRIPLING. बारवर्षा, सोळवर्षा. In this sense and with contemptuous implication, corresponding with *beardless brat, thing just fledged, one just unpinned from his mother's apron, &c.* नवेकाळिजाचा, देंठचा तुटलेला, कोवळे बुद्धीचा, नवेरकाचा, नवे नजरेचा, नवे उमेदीचा, बच्चाजी, बच्चाराम. And some phrases used in repressing the forwardness and pertness of *youngsters* are, तुझ्या तोंडचा जार अझून वाळला नाहीं, तुझ्या सठीच्या म्या घुगऱ्या खाल्ह्या आहेत, तुझ्या बारशास मी जेवलों आहें, तुझा ओंठ पिळला तर दूध निघेल *or* ओंठावर अझून दूध दिसतें *or* वाळलें नाहीं, तुझ्या तोंडाची घाण गेली नाहीं, तुझें बाळकडूं जिरलें नाहीं.

Youngsters; *little ones,* v. CHILDREN. पोरेंबाळें *n. pl.*

YOUR, YOUR'S, *pron.* तुमचा.

YOURSELF, *pron.* तुम्हीच, आपण.

YOUTH, *n. early part of life.* तरणेपणा*m.* तरुणपणा *m.* जवानी*f.* पहिलीपराई *f.* तारुण्य *n.* तारुण्यदशा *f.* तारुण्यावस्था *f.* नवती *f.* यौवन *n.* यौवनावस्था *f.* तारुण्यकाल *pop.* तरुणकाळ *m.* पूर्ववय *n.* प्रथमवय *n.* नवीनवय *n.* कौमार *n.* शैशव *n.* पौगंड *n.* यौवनकाल *m.* काळेकेश *m. pl.*

Fire and flush, force and vigour, &c. of y. जवानी *f.* नवतीचाभर *m.* नवतीचीलहरबहर *f.* तारुण्याचा ऊत *m.* तारुण्यबल *n.* जोम *m.* उधान *n.* नवतीचापूर *m.* मुसमुशी *f.* जवानी दिवानी *f.*

Flower of y. Spring or Prime of y. Freshness of y. नवाळी *f.* नवती *f.* नबनवती *or* नव नवतीकोवळीक *f.*

Heyday or meridian of y. भर जवानी *f.* भरमवती *f.* ऐन जवानी *f.* [णाबांड, रसरसीत.

Person in the flower, prime, &c. of y. नबातरणा, तर-

Pride of y. यौवनदर्प *m.*

Study (*i. e.* studying or the subject of study) from y. बाळपाठ *m.* बालाभ्यास *m.*

To be glowing under the fire of y. उधानणें, मुसमुसणें, रसरसणें, लसलसणें, लसलस *adv.* करणें.

2 a y. *a young man.* जवान *m.* बाप्या *m.* आडबाप्या *m.* युव॰ *m.* पोंगडा *m.* किशोर *m.*

Handsome y. गबरू.

3 *young persons*—collect. तरुणमाणसें *n. pl.* तरुणजन*m. pl.* पहिलेपराईचीं माणसें *n. pl.* तरुणमंडळी *f.* तरुणजनता *f.*

YOUTHFUL, *a.* v. YOUNG. तरणा, तरुण, तरुणावस्थेचा.

2 *of or belonging to youth.* तरुणपणाचा, तारुण्यावस्थेचा, तारुण्यदशेचा, नवतीचा, पूर्ववयाचा, &c. पूर्ववयस्कालिक.

YOUTHFULNESS, *n.* v. A. 1. तरणेपणा *m.* तरुणपणा *m.* &c. तारुण्यधर्म *m.*

YULE, *n.* नाताळ *n.* नाताळचासण *m.*

Z.

Z. This letter has no exact representative in the Maráthí alphabet. The nearest to it in sound is झ.

ZANY, *n.* v. BUFFOON. हुंडीबाग.

ZARNICH, *n. sulphuret of arsenic.* मनसील*n.*

ZEAL, *n. eager desire, passionate ardor in pursuit,* v. PASSION. EARNESTNESS. आस्था *f.* पोटाग *f.* आग *f.* कळकळ *f.* उत्कंठा *f.* अनुराग *m.* अनुरक्ति *f.* अनुरति *f.*

ZEALOT, *n. one who is over zealous.* आस्थेचा वेडा, भरीं भरलेला, पिसा (धर्माचा-विद्येचा-&c.), अत्यासक्त, अत्यनुरक्त, अत्यनुरत, अत्युत्कंठ.

ZEALOTRY, *n. over zeal.* अतिआस्था *f.* अत्यास्था *f.* अत्यासक्ति *f.* अत्यनुराग *m.* अत्यनुरक्ति *f.* वेड *n.* पिसें *n.* (धर्माचें-&c.).

ZEALOUS, *a.* v. PASSIONATE, EARNEST. आस्थेचा, पोटागीचा, आस्थिक, आस्थेकरी, आस्थेवाईक, उत्सुक, उत्कंठित, तीक्ष्ण, अनुरक्त, अनुरत.

ZEALOUSLY, *adv.* v. A. आस्थेनें, पोटागीनें, उत्कंठेनें, &c. आस्थापूर्वक, आस्थापुरस्सर.

ZEALOUSNESS. See ZEAL.

ZEDOARY, *n. curcuma zerumbet.* सठी *f.* कर्चूर *pop.* कचरा *or* कचोरा *m.*

Turmeric colored z. आंबेहळद *f.* वनहरिद्रा *f.*

ZENANA, *n.* जनानखाना *m.*

ZENITH, *n. vertical point in the heavens.* खमध्य *m.* खस्वस्तिक *n.* शिरोबिंदु *m.* ऊर्ध्व *m.* ऊर्ध्वस्वस्तिक *n.* मध्यलग्न *n.*

Pointing to z. and nadir ;—a line. ऊर्ध्वाधर.

Zenith-distance. नत *n.* नतांश *m.* नतभाग *m.*

Sine of the zenith-distance. दृग्ज्या *f.*

2 fig. v. HEIGHT. बहर *or* बहार *m.* भस्भर *f.*

ZEPHYR, *n. soft, mild breeze.* झुळूक *f.* मंदवायु *m.*

Balmy zephyrs. मंदसुगंधवायु *m.* सुखस्पर्शवायु *m.*

ZERO, *n. cipher, nothing.* शून्य *n.*

ZEST, *n. relish.* चव *f.* गोडी *f.* स्वाद *m.* रुचि *f.*

ZIGZAG, *n.* (of lighthing). असिलता *f.* विद्युल्लता *f.*

2 (of a road up a hill). सडवें *n.*

ZIGZAG, *a.* नागमोडीचा, नागमोडी.

ZINC, *n.*—the metal. जस्त *n.*

Sulphate of z. सफेत मोरचूत *m.*

Impure carbonate of z. कलखापरी *f.*

ZODIAC, *n.*—in astronomy. राशिचक्र *n.* राशिमंडल *n.* भचक्र *n.* भमंडल *n.* भागन *n.* The twelve signs, (भगण *m.* लग्नकुंडली *f.* राशिकुंडली *f.*) are मेष (aries), वृषभ (taurus), मिथुन (gemini), कर्क (cancer), सिंह (leo), कन्या (virgo), तुला *pop.* तूळ (libra), वृश्चिक (scorpio), धनु *pop.* धन (sagittarius), मकर (capricornus), कुंभ (aquarius), मीन (pisces) ; there are two divisions (गोल) viz. उत्तरगोल consisting of the signs from मेष (aries) to कन्या (virgo), and दक्षिणगोल consisting of the signs from तुला (libra) to मीन (pisces).

Circuit (of the sun, &c.) through the z. भागन *n.* भगण *m.*

Passage of the sun or a planet through a sign of the z. राशिभोग *m.*

Passage of the sun through a sign of the z. रविसंक्रमण *n.* सूर्यसंक्रमण *n.* सूर्यसंक्रांति *f.* रविसंक्रांति *f.*

Passage (of the sun or a planet) from one sign of the z. into another. संक्रांति *f.*

Rising of a sign of the z. लग्न *n.*

Rising sign of the z. उदयलग्न *n.*

Setting sign of the z. अस्तलग्न *n.*

Sign of the z. राशि *m. pop.* रास *f.* भ *n.*

String or ring of the signs of the z. लग्नकुंडली *f.*

Sun's entrance, moment of, into a sign of the z. लग्न *n.*

ZODIACAL, *a. belonging, &c. to the zodiac.* राशिचक्राचा, भचक्राचा, &c. राशिचक्रसंबंधी, भचक्रसंबंधी.

ZONE, *n.* v. GIRDLE. कमरपट्टा *m.* कांची *f.* कटिबंधन *n.* कटिमेखला *f.*

2 (of the Earth). भूमेखला *f.* भूवलय *m. n.* भूकटिबंध *m.*

Torrid z. मध्यदेश *m.* क्रांतिवलय *m. n.*

ZOOGRAPHER, *n. one who describes animals.* पशूंचें वर्णनकरणारा.

ZOOGRAPHY, *n. description of animals.* पशूंचें वर्णन *n.* पश्वादिवर्णन *n.* पश्वादिविवरण *n.*

ZOOLOGY, *n. science of animals.* जीवांचीविद्या *f.* जीवांचें शास्त्र *n.* जीवमात्रविद्या *f.* पश्वादिविद्या *f.* पश्वादिशास्त्र *n.*

ZOOTOMY, *n. dissection of beasts.* पश्वादिशवव्यवच्छेदन *n.*

FINIS.

To LAUGH, *v. n.* हसणें *or* हासणें, हास्य *n.*-हास *m.*-हसन *n.* करणें, —violently, &c. हासून जीव *m.* टाकणें, पोट धरून हासणें, अट्टहास *m.* करणें,—lightly, gigglingly, &c. खिद खिद-खस खस-खिस खिस-खुसकन-खुसकर-&c. हासणें, खिदखिदणें, खसखस *f.* पिकणें *g. of s.*

To l. gaily & lightly. गुल्कणें, गुल्कन हासणें, मुलकणें, मुलकन-&c. हासणें. [हासणें.

To l. till one's sides split. पोट दुखे तों हासणें, कळ उठे तों

To l. in one's sleeve. मनच्या मनीं-तोंडच्या तोंडीं-गालांत-आंतच्या आंत-&c. हासणें.

To l. on one side of the face. एकागालावर हासणें.

To feel disposed to l. हासें *n.*-हासूं *n.* येणें *in. con.*

To l. at; To l. to scorn. See To RIDICULE.

LAUGH, LAUGHING, *n.* v. V.—*act.* हासणें *n.* हास *m.* हसन *n.* परिहास *m.*

A free and easy l. गुल्की *f.*

L. and joking. हंसाबाजी *f.*

Wild l. and giggling. खिसाणा *m.*

LAUGHABLE, *a.* v. V. हासाया-चा-जोगता-जोगा, हासें याया-चा-जोगता-&c. हास्यजनक, हास्योत्पादक, परिहास्य.

LAUGHER, *n.* LAUGHING, *p.a.*V. हासणारा, हास्य-हास-हसन कर्त्ता. I. *given to laughing.* हासरा, हशा, हासाळू, हास्यप्रिय, हास्यमुख, हास्यवदन.

LAUGHINGLY, *adv.* हासून, हसतहसत, हसतांहसतां, हास्य-&c.करून.

LAUGHING-STOCK, *n.* v. BUTT. हासूं *n.* खेळवणा *m.* हास्यास्पद*n.* विनोदास्पद *n.* उपहासास्पद *n.*

A quiet, enduring l. पाठवळ *or* पाठाळ *n.*

LAUGHTER, *n.* हासें *n.* हासूं *n. v.* ये, हास्य *n.* प्रहास *m.*

Loud & boisterous l. गदारोळाचें हासणें *n.*

Rapid and light l. खुखु *f.*

Wild and violent l. अट्टहास *m.*

To convulse with l. लोटपोट *f.* करणें *g. of o.* [ढकलणें.

To LAUNCH, *v. a.* (a vessel). लोटणें, ढकलणें, गोदींतून लोटणें-

To LAUNCH, *v. n.* *plunge out, forth,* fig. भडकणें, धडकणें, सुटणें, सुटणें used with the present participle of another verb.

To l. into vice. निसवणें. [रजकी *f.*

LAUNDER, LAUNDRESS, *n. washerwoman.* परटीण *f.* धोबीण *f.*

LAUNDERER, *n. washerman.* परीट *m.* धोबी *m.* रजक *m.*

LAUNDRY, *n. room where clothes are washed.* परटाची खोली*f.* धुवटाची खोली *f.*

LAUREL, *n.* एकझाड आहे.

LAVA, *n. melted matter from a volcano.* ज्वालामुखीचा पाझर *m.* ज्वालामुखीनिर्गतद्रव *m.*

LAVATION. See WASHING. [न *n.*

LAVATORY, *n. place for washing.* धुण्याची जागा *f.* प्रक्षालनस्था-

2 See LOTION. [*g. of o.*

To LAVE, *v. a.* v. To WASH. धुणें, क्षालन *n.*-प्रक्षालन *n.* करणें

To LAVE, *v. n.* See To BATHE.

LAVEMENT. See CLYSTER.

LAVENDER, *n.* एक सुवासिक वनस्पति आहे.

LAVENDER-WATER, *n.* एक सुवासिक पाणी आहे.

LAVER, *n. washing basin.* तस्त *n.* गंगाळ *n.* प्रक्षालनपात्र *n.*

LAVISH, *a. prodigal, wasteful,* v. EXTRAVAGANT. उडाऊ, उधळ्या, उधळपट्ट्या, खर्चीक, धिंग, अतिव्ययी.

2 *spending or bestowing freely, profuse,* v. LIBERAL. सढळ, ढसळ *or* ढसाळ, ढिसळ *or* ढिसाळ, हाताचा ढसळ, खर्चीक.

3 *copious, profuse, lavished,* v. EXUBERANT. घळघळीत, चळचळीत, अघळपघळ, उधळपट्टीचा.

To LAVISH, *v. a. expend or give profusely,* v. To SQUANDER. उधळणें, उडवणें, दवडणें, खेळ *m.* करणें *g. of o.* मनस्वी-अवासवा-अवाचेसवा-&c. खर्च *m.* करणें, गट करणें, गटकावणें.

LAVISHLY, *adv.* v. A. 1. उडाऊपणानें, &c. उधळपट्टीनें, अतिव्ययकरून, अवासवा, अवाचेसवा.

2 सढळ हातानें, उदारहस्तें, स्थूलहस्तें, छणछण, छणाछण, खणाखण.

3 तडक *or* तडका, रगड, यथेच्छ, मनस्वी.

LAVISHNESS, *n.* v. A. 1. उडाऊपणा *m.* उधळेपणा *m.* उधळपट्टी *f.* दिवाळखोरी *f.* अवासवा खर्च *m.* धिंगाई *f.*

2 सढळपणा *m.* ढसळपणा *m.* धिंगाई *f.*

3 घळघळितपणा *m.* लोट *m.* रेळ *f.* चंगळपट्टी *f.*

LAW, *n. rule of action.* नेम *m.* नियम *m.* निर्बंध *m.* बंधारण *n.* शेरा *m.* सूत्र *n.* विधि *m.* विधिनिषेधनियम *m.* विधिनिषेधनिर्बंध *m.* कर्त्तव्याकर्त्तव्यनिर्बंध *m.* कार्याकार्यनिर्बंध.

2 *statute, edict, canon, decree, &c.* कायदा *m.* जाबता *m.* कानू *f.* शेरा *m.* विधि *m.* विधान *n.* निर्बंध*m.* नियम *m.* शासन*n.* अनुशासन *n.* सूत्र *n.* उक्तवाक्य *n.*

Administration of the laws. धर्माधिकरण *n.*

Code of laws. धर्मशास्त्र *n.* धर्मसंहिता *f.* व्यवहारविधि *m.*

L. of the Medes, and Persians, fig. राम बाण *m.*

Laws and rules, *statutes,*—compreh. कानूजाबता *m.*

4 *judicial process.* व्यवहार *m.* व्यवहारमार्ग *m.*

Court of l. अदालत *f.* न्यायसभा *f.* धर्मसभा *f.*

L. matter; *matter cognizable by law.* व्यवहारविषय *m.* व्यवहारपद *n.*

To go to l. खटला *m.*-सरकारदरबार *m. n.*-&c. करणें.

3 *the rules, precepts, code, &c. by which judicature is to be regulated, jurisprudence.* व्यवहार विधि *m.*व्यवहारशास्त्र *n.* धर्म *m.* धर्मशास्त्र *n.* धर्मविधि *m.* स्मृति *f.*

A work on l. स्मृतिशास्त्र *n.*

Criminal l. दंडविधि *m.* दंडनीति *f.*

Knowledge of l. धर्मज्ञान *n.*

Learned in the l. धर्मज्ञ.

Written declaration of the l. व्यवस्था *f.*

5 *conformity to law, right.* धर्म *m.* न्याय *m.* नीति *f.*

6 *principle, rule, axiom, &c. of science, art, nature, &c.* न्याय *m.* नियम *m.* उत्सर्ग *m.* स्वभावनिर्बंध *m.*

7—in theology; *the law of works.* कर्ममार्ग *m.* प्रवृत्तिमार्ग *m.*—esp. considered as a yoke or bondage. कर्मबंध *m.* (ex. जो पहुडला स्वानंदसागरीं कर्मबंधीं न पडे तो).

LAWFUL, *a. that is conformable to law.* See LEGAL.

2 *not forbidden, not wrong, &c.* v. RIGHT. निर्बाध, निर्दोष, अप्रत्यवायाचा, अनिषेधाचा, अनिषिद्ध, अवर्जित, अप्रतिबंध, निष्प्रत्यवाय, योग्य, यथायोग्य, बिनठपक्याचा, युक्तिसार.

3 *constituted by law, rightful.* हक्काचा, हलालाचा, सत्तेचा, न्यायाचा, नीतीचा, धर्माचा, सत्याचा.

LAWFULLY, *adv.* v. A. 1. See LEGALLY.